KEY TO WORLD MAP PAGES

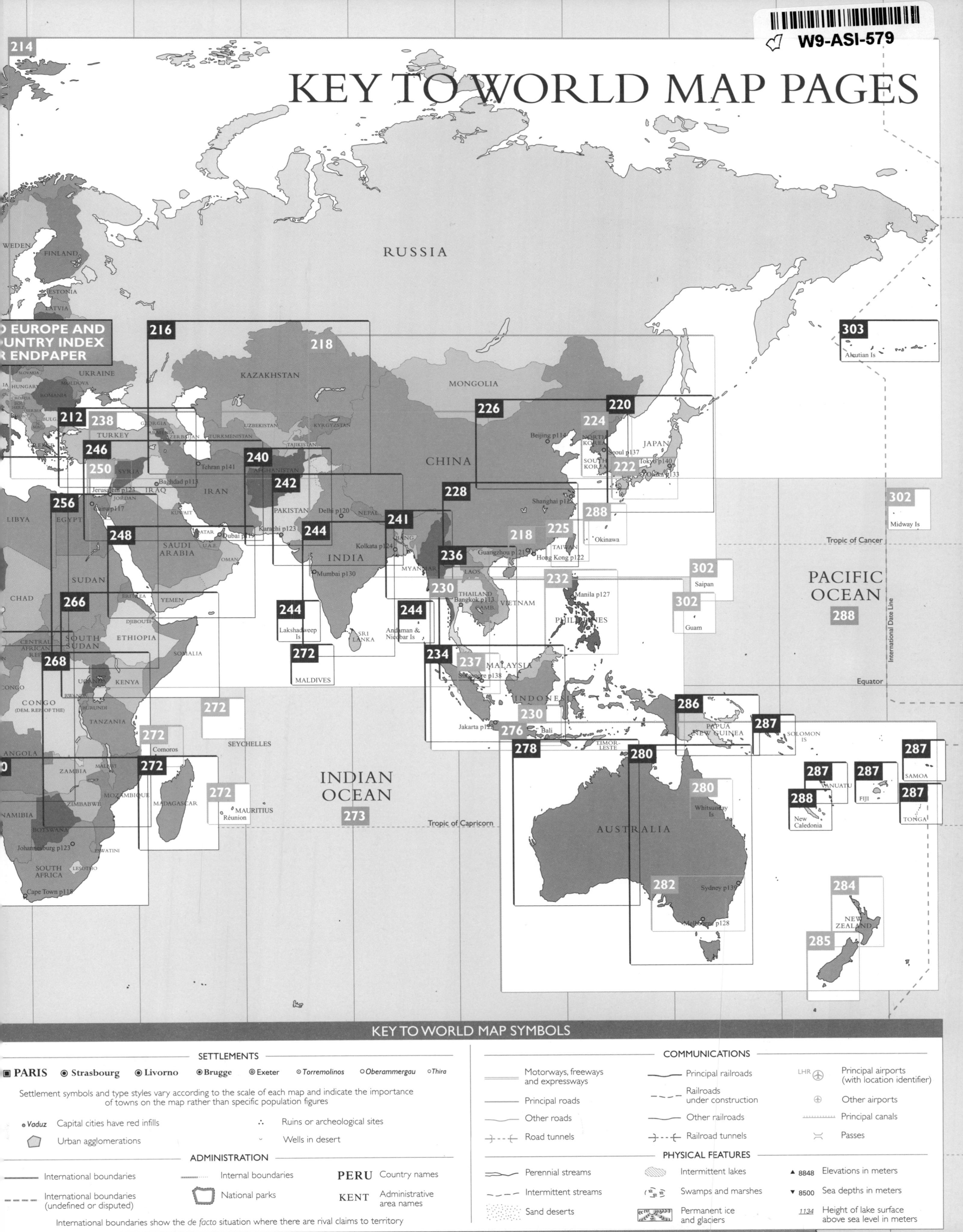

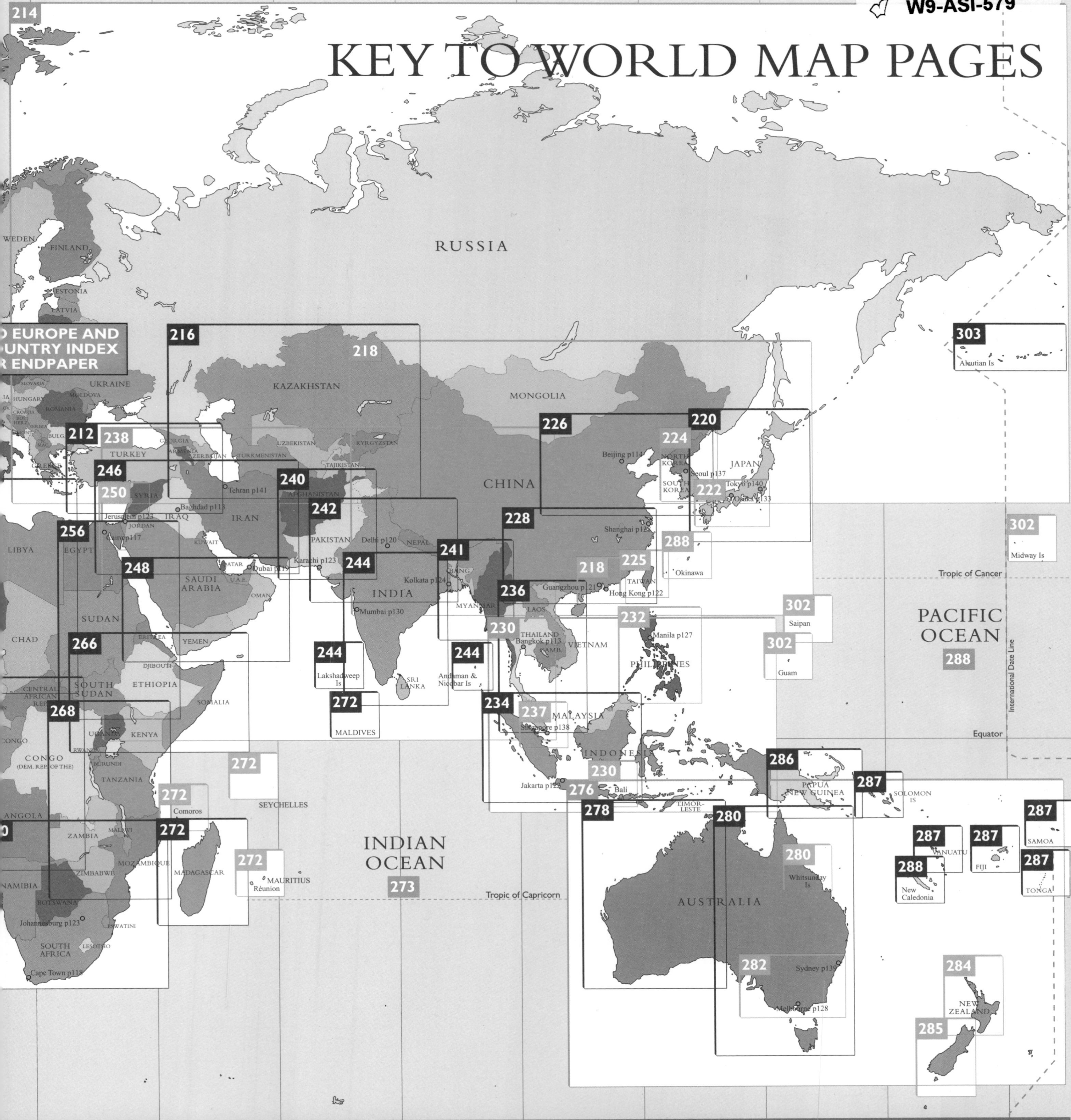

KEY TO WORLD MAP SYMBOLS

SETTLEMENTS

■ PARIS ◉ Strasbourg ◉ Livorno ◉ Brugge ◎ Exeter ⊙ *Torremolinos* ○ *Oberammergau* ○ *Thira*

Settlement symbols and type styles vary according to the scale of each map and indicate the importance of towns on the map rather than specific population figures

- *Vaduz* — Capital cities have red infills
- Ruins or archeological sites
- Urban agglomerations
- Wells in desert

ADMINISTRATION

- International boundaries
- Internal boundaries
- PERU — Country names
- International boundaries (undefined or disputed)
- National parks
- KENT — Administrative area names

International boundaries show the *de facto* situation where there are rival claims to territory

COMMUNICATIONS

- Motorways, freeways and expressways
- Principal railroads
- LHR — Principal airports (with location identifier)
- Railroads under construction
- Principal roads
- Other airports
- Other roads
- Other railroads
- Principal canals
- Road tunnels
- Railroad tunnels
- Passes

PHYSICAL FEATURES

- Perennial streams
- Intermittent lakes
- ▲ 8848 — Elevations in meters
- Intermittent streams
- Swamps and marshes
- ▼ 8500 — Sea depths in meters
- Sand deserts
- Permanent ice and glaciers
- 1134 — Height of lake surface above sea level in meters

OXFORD ATLAS OF THE WORLD

TWENTY-EIGHTH EDITION

Gazetteer of Nations
Text Keith Lye/Philip's

Photographic Acknowledgements
Alamy /*Aerial Archives* 102, /*AlamyCelebrity* 82, /*Archive Pics* 10, /*Jon Arnold Images Ltd* 93, /*B.A.E. Inc.* 79, /*Mark Conlin* 85 (bottom), /*Ashley Cooper pics* 86, /*Cultura RM* 87 (bottom), /*David R. Frazier Photolibrary, Inc.* 98, /*Michael Honegger* 12 (top), /*Bernd von Jutrczenka/dpa/Alamy Live News* 13, /*Søren Lund Hviid* 101, /*Reuters* 8–9, /*Azim Khan Ronnie* 12 (bottom), /*Kevin Schafer* 85 (top), /*Top Photo/Sipa USA* 105, /*Xinhua* 107;
Corbis /*Jay Dickman* 109 (top), /*Liba Taylor* 104, /*David Turnley* 109 (bottom);
© Crown copyright 2007. Published by the Met Office, UK 80;
Dreamstime.com /*Maxim Blinkov* 87 (top), *Tsvibrav* 87 (middle right);
Galaxy Picture Library /*Robin Scagell* 73;
Getty Images /*Alexis Huguet/AFP* 94, /*Hannele Lahti* 85 (center);
Garrett Nagle 89 (top and bottom);
iStock /*Ian Dyball* 87 (middle center);
NASA /ESA, HFF team (STScl) 68, /GSFC 81 (bottom);
NSIDC courtesy J. Maslanik and M. Tschudi, University of Colorado 81 (top);
NPA Satellite Mapping, CGG Services (UK) Ltd 14–33, 66-67, 110–111, 144–145, 156–157, 208–209, 252–253, 274–275, 290–291, 324–325;
Science Photo Library /*Sputnik* 97;
Shutterstock /*Rich Carey* 87 (top left, top right, middle left).

Editorial Acknowledgements
© OpenStreetMap contributors (openstreetmap.org); Migration 8-13: United Nations Refugee Agency (UNHCR); Plastic Pollution 86-87: OurWorldInData.org (Andrady, A., … & Law, K. L. (2015); Eriksen, M. et al. (2014); Eiksen, M. et al. (2014); Jambeck, J. R., Geyer, R., Wilcox, C., Siegler, T. R., Perryman, M.; Lebreton, L., Egger, M., & Slat, B. (2019); Hannah Ritchie and Max Roser (2018)); United Nations Environment Programme; World Bank; World Wide Fund for Nature.

Star Charts (page 69)
Wil Tirion

Cartography by Philip's

World Cities
OS Map data
Page 121, Edinburgh, and page 125, London:
This product includes mapping data licensed from Ordnance Survey® with the permission of the Controller of Her Majesty's Stationery Office. © Crown copyright 2020. All rights reserved. Licence number 100011710.

www.philips-maps.co.uk

Philip's, a division of Octopus Publishing Group Limited
(www.octopusbooks.co.uk)
Carmelite House, 50 Victoria Embankment, London EC4Y 0DZ
An Hachette UK Company (www.hachette.co.uk)

Published in North America by
Oxford University Press USA
198 Madison Avenue
New York, NY 10016

www.oup.com/us

OXFORD UNIVERSITY PRESS Oxford is a registered trademark of Oxford University Press

Library of Congress Cataloging-in-Publication Data available

ISBN 978-0-19-757752-3

Printing (last digit): 9 8 7 6 5 4 3 2 1

Printed in Malaysia

FSC MIX Paper from responsible sources FSC® C008047

FOREWORD

An authoritative and serious reference work, the Oxford *Atlas of the World* is one of the finest atlases available anywhere in the world. The atlas incorporates computer-derived maps that have been produced using the very latest in digital cartographic techniques. Country names are shown in conventional English form and are those that are in common usage. They are the forms used by publications such as *Newsweek* and *The Washington Post*, and by the BBC and the British Foreign Office. Alternative country names appear in parentheses on the maps where space permits – for example, Myanmar (Burma) – and are cross-referenced in the index, for example, Ivory Coast = Côte d'Ivoire.

How to use the Atlas

The atlas is divided into a number of sections which are explained below.

World Statistics and "Migration"

World statistics on topics such as area and population for every country in the world. Also included in this section is a listing of the world's largest cities by population, arranged in country alphabetical order. This section is followed by the highly topical "*Migration*" feature, which examines some of the major issues involved in the movement of people – either forced or voluntary, temporary or permanent.

Images of Earth

A beautifully illustrated satellite imagery section showing 17 of the world's major cities and regions in the Americas, Europe, Africa, Asia, and Australasia.

Gazetteer of Nations

A comprehensive A–Z reference providing concise profiles of every country's geography, climate, history, politics, and economy, together with ready-reference tables, and illustrated with flags and locator maps.

World Geography

A richly informative section comprising 42 pages of maps, charts, graphs, and diagrams that explain key themes about the world in which we live. The topics covered include the Solar System, climate, the natural world, population, energy, and trade. Explanatory text on each spread describes the patterns shown by the data.

World Cities

A detailed selection of maps for 70 urban areas around the world. These are useful for planning trips abroad as well as for comparative studies of cities worldwide.

World Maps

An outstanding collection of 179 pages of distinctive Philip's cartography. The highly acclaimed physical world maps combine relief shading with layer-colored contours to give a striking visual picture of the Earth's surface. Roads, railroads, canals, and airports are accurately depicted on the maps, and towns and cities are clearly marked. More information on the key features employed in the construction and presentation of the maps is given on the facing page.

Geographical Glossary and Index

The 86,000-name index to the world maps includes geographical features as well as towns and cities, with both latitude/longitude and letter/figure grid references. Preceding the index is a list of geographical terms from various foreign languages that may be found in the place names on the maps and also in the index, together with their meanings.

Specialist Geography Consultants

The editors are grateful to the following for their contributions to the '*World Geography*' section in this atlas:

Dr Dibyesh Anand
John Burden
Peter Grego
Keith Lye
Garrett Nagle
Ross Reynolds
Robin Scagell
John Woodruff

The editors would also like to thank **Richard Chiles** and the staff at **CGG Satellite Mapping, CGG Services (UK) Ltd, Edenbridge, Kent, UK** (www.cgg.com/satellite) for sourcing and processing the satellite imagery that appears in the atlas.

USER GUIDE

The reference maps which form the main body of this atlas have been prepared in accordance with the highest standards of international cartography to provide an accurate and detailed representation of the Earth. The scales and projections used have been carefully chosen to give balanced coverage of the world, while emphasizing the most densely populated and economically significant regions. A hallmark of Philip's mapping is the use of hill shading and relief coloring to create a graphic impression of landforms: this makes the maps exceptionally easy to read. However, knowledge of the key features employed in the construction and presentation of the maps will enable the reader to derive the fullest benefit from the atlas.

Map Sequence

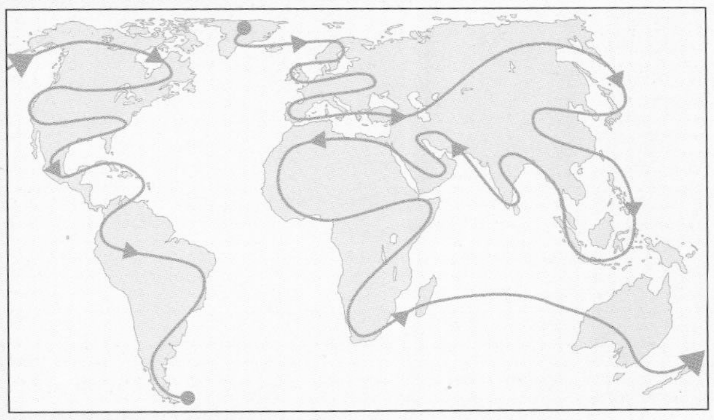

The atlas covers the Earth continent by continent: first Europe; then its land neighbor Asia (mapped north before south, in a clockwise sequence), then Africa, Australia and Oceania, North America, and South America. This is the classic arrangement adopted by most cartographers since the 16th century. For each continent, there are maps at a variety of scales. First, physical relief and political maps of the whole continent; then a series of larger-scale maps of the regions within the continent, each followed, where required, by still larger-scale maps of the most important or densely populated areas. The governing principle is that by turning the pages of the atlas, the reader moves steadily from north to south through each continent, with each map overlapping its neighbors.

Map Presentation

With very few exceptions (for example, for the Arctic and Antarctica), the maps are drawn with north at the top, regardless of whether they are presented upright or sideways on the page. In the borders will be found the map title; a locator diagram showing the area covered; continuation arrows showing the page numbers for maps of adjacent areas; the scale; the projection used; the degrees of latitude and longitude; and the letters and figures used in the index for locating place names and geographical features. Physical relief maps also have a height reference panel identifying the colors used for each layer of contouring.

Map Symbols

Each map contains a vast amount of detail which can only be conveyed clearly and accurately by the use of symbols. Points and circles of varying sizes locate and identify the relative importance of towns and cities; different styles of type are employed for administrative, geographical, and regional place names to aid identification. A variety of pictorial symbols denote landforms such as glaciers, marshes, and coral reefs, and man-made structures including roads, railroads, airports, and canals. International borders are shown by red lines. Where neighboring countries are in dispute, for example in parts of the Middle East, the maps show the *de facto* boundary between nations, regardless of the legal or historical situation.

The symbols are explained on the front endpapers of the atlas.

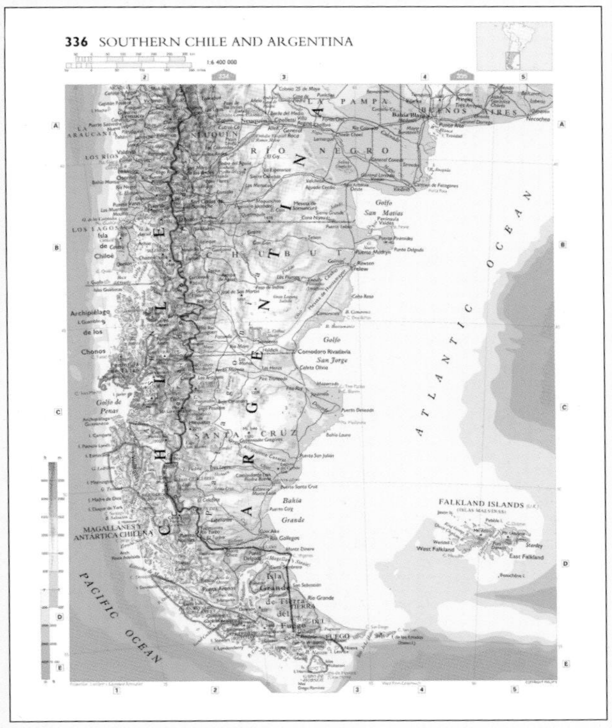

Map Scales

1:16 000 000
1 inch = 252 statute miles

The scale of each map is given in the numerical form known as the "representative fraction." The first figure is always one, signifying one unit of distance on the map; the second figure, usually in millions, is the number by which the map unit must be multiplied to give the equivalent distance on the Earth's surface. Calculations can easily be made in centimeters and kilometers, by dividing the Earth units figure by 100 000 (i.e. deleting the last five 0s). Thus 1:1 000 000 means 1 cm = 10 km. The calculation for inches and miles is more laborious, but 1 000 000 divided by 63 360 (the number of inches in a mile) shows that 1:1 000 000 means approximately 1 inch = 16 miles. The table below provides distance equivalents for scales down to 1:50 000 000.

LARGE SCALE		
1:1 000 000	1 cm = 10 km	1 inch = 16 miles
1:2 500 000	1 cm = 25 km	1 inch = 39.5 miles
1:5 000 000	1 cm = 50 km	1 inch = 79 miles
1:6 000 000	1 cm = 60 km	1 inch = 95 miles
1:8 000 000	1 cm = 80 km	1 inch = 126 miles
1:10 000 000	1 cm = 100 km	1 inch = 158 miles
1:15 000 000	1 cm = 150 km	1 inch = 237 miles
1:20 000 000	1 cm = 200 km	1 inch = 316 miles
1:50 000 000	1 cm = 500 km	1 inch = 790 miles
SMALL SCALE		

Measuring Distances

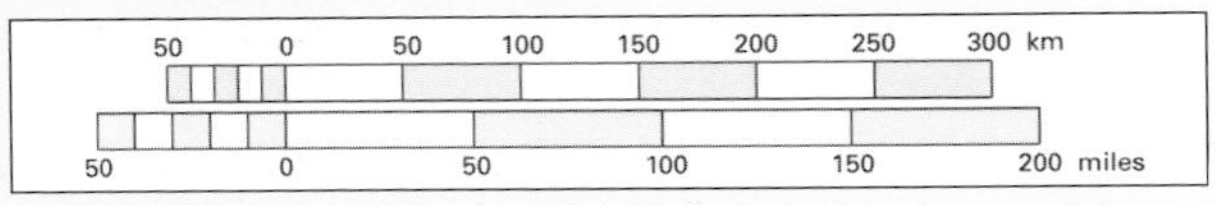

Although each map is accompanied by a scale bar, distances cannot always be measured with confidence because of the distortions involved in portraying the curved surface of the Earth on a flat page. As a general rule, the larger the map scale, the more accurate and reliable will be the distance measured. On small-scale maps such as those of the world and of entire continents, measurement may only be accurate along the "standard parallels," or central axes, and should not be attempted without considering the map projection.

Map Projections

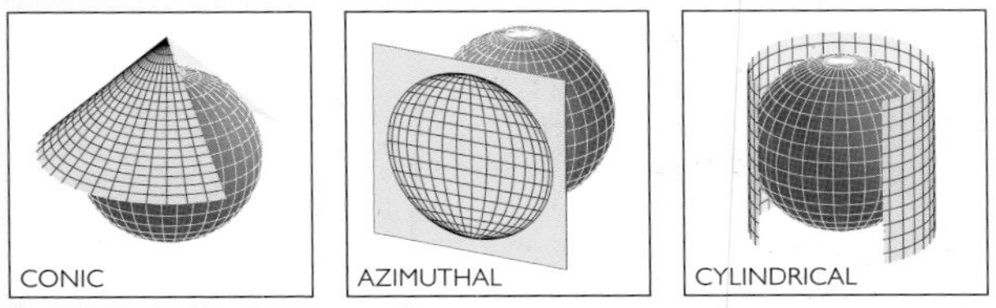

Unlike a globe, no flat map can give a true scale representation of the world in terms of area, shape, and position of every region. Each of the numerous systems that have been devised for projecting the curved surface of the Earth on to a flat page involves the sacrifice of accuracy in one or more of these elements. The variations in shape and position of land masses such as Alaska, Greenland, and Australia, for example, can be quite dramatic when different projections are compared.

For this atlas, the guiding principle has been to select projections that involve the least distortion of size and distance. The projection used for each map is noted in the border. Most fall into one of three categories – conic, azimuthal, or cylindrical – whose basic concepts are shown above. Each involves plotting the forms of the Earth's surface on a grid of latitude and longitude lines, which may be shown as parallels, curves, or radiating spokes.

Latitude and Longitude

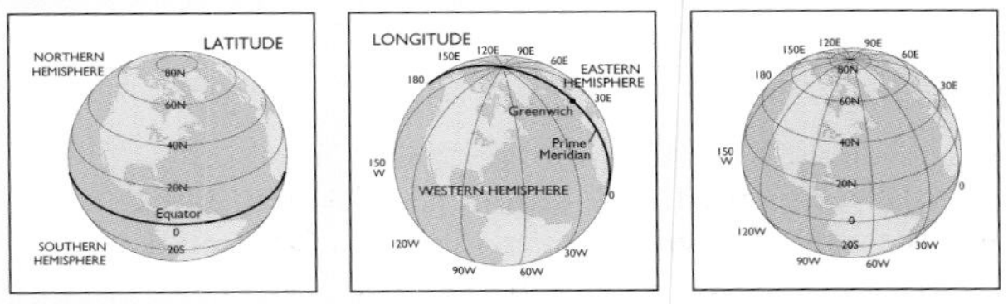

Accurate positioning of individual points on the Earth's surface is made possible by reference to the geometrical system of latitude and longitude. Latitude *parallels* are drawn west–east around the Earth and numbered by degrees north and south of the Equator, which is designated 0° of latitude. Longitude *meridians* are drawn north–south and numbered by degrees east and west of the *prime meridian*, 0° of longitude, which passes through Greenwich in England. By referring to these coordinates and their subdivisions of minutes (1/60th of a degree) and seconds (1/60th of a minute), any place on Earth can be located to within a few hundred meters. Latitude and longitude are indicated by blue lines on the maps; they are straight or curved according to the projection employed. Reference to these lines is the easiest way of determining the relative positions of places on different maps, and for plotting compass directions.

Name Forms

For ease of reference, both English and local name forms appear in the atlas. Oceans, seas, and countries are shown in English throughout the atlas; country names may be abbreviated to their commonly accepted form (for example, Germany, not The Federal Republic of Germany). Conventional English forms are also used for place names on the smaller-scale maps of the continents. However, local name forms are used on all large-scale and regional maps, with the English form given in brackets only for important cities – the large-scale map of Russia and Northern Asia thus shows Moskva (Moscow). For countries which do not use a Roman script, place names have been transcribed according to the systems adopted by the British and US Geographic Names Authorities. For China, the Pin Yin system has been used, with some more widely known forms appearing in brackets, as with Beijing (Peking). Both English and local names appear in the index, the English form being cross-referenced to the local form.

CONTENTS

World Statistics

Countries 6
Cities 7

Special Feature

Migration 8–13

Images of Earth

Helsinki, Finland 16
Brussels, Belgium 17
Lisbon, Portugal 18
Dead Sea, Israel/Jordan 19
Baghdad, Iraq 20
Karachi, Pakistan 21
Guangzhou, China 22
Shanghai, China 23
Mount Fuji, Japan 24
Manila, Philippines 25
Tenerife, Canary Islands 26
Kampala, Uganda 27
Perth, Australia 28
Toronto, Canada 29
Orlando, USA 30
La Paz, Bolivia 31

Gazetteer of Nations

An A–Z Gazetteer of Countries 34–65

World Geography

The Universe 68–69
The Solar System 70–71
Seasons, Time and Motion 72–73
Geology of the Earth 74–75
The Atmosphere 76–77
Climate 78–79
Climate Change and Global Warming 80–81
Water and Vegetation 82–83
Oceans and Seas 84–85
Plastic Pollution 86–87
Biodiversity and the Natural World 88–89
Population 90–91
Cities 92–93
Conflict and Cooperation 94–95
Energy 96–97
Minerals 98–99
Employment, Trade, and Industry 100–101
Tourism and Travel 102–103
Health 104–105
Wealth 106–107
Standards of Living 108–109

World Cities

Amsterdam 112
Athens 112
Atlanta 113
Baghdad 113
Bangkok 113
Barcelona 114
Beijing 114
Berlin 115
Boston 116
Brussels 116
Budapest 117
Buenos Aires 117
Cairo 117
Cape Town 118
Copenhagen 118
Chicago 119
Dubai 119
Dallas-Fort Worth 120
Delhi 120
Edinburgh 121
Guangzhou 121
Helsinki 121
Hong Kong 122
Istanbul 122
Jakarta 122
Jerusalem 123
Johannesburg 123
Karachi 123
Kolkata 124
Lagos 124
Las Vegas 124
Lima 124
London 125
Lisbon 126
Los Angeles 126
Madrid 127
Manila 127
Melbourne 128
Mexico City 128
Milan 128
Miami 129
Moscow 129
Montréal 130
Mumbai 130
Munich 131
New Orleans 131
New York 132
Orlando 133
Osaka 133
Oslo 133
Paris 134
Prague 135
Rio de Janeiro 135
Rome 136
San Francisco 136
St Petersburg 137
Santiago 137
São Paulo 137
Seoul 137
Shanghai 138
Singapore 138
Stockholm 139
Sydney 139
Tokyo 140
Tehran 141
Toronto 141
Venice 142
Vienna 142
Warsaw 143
Washington 143

World Maps

The World

Map Symbols Front Endpaper
The World: Physical 146–147
1:76 000 000
The World: Political 148–149
1:76 000 000
Arctic Ocean 150
1:28 000 000
Antarctica 151
1:28 000 000
Atlantic Ocean 152
1:41 000 000
Islands of the Atlantic 153
Bermuda 1:400 000
New Providence Island 1:400 000
Madeira 1:800 000
Azores 1:1 600 000
Canary Islands 1:1 600 000
Falkland Islands 1:6 400 000
Ascension Island 1:400 000
St Helena 1:400 000
Cape Verde Islands 1:8 000 000
Greenland 154
1:10 000 000
Iceland 155
1:2 000 000

Europe

Europe: Physical 158
1:16 000 000
Europe: Political 159
1:16 000 000
Scandinavia 160–161
1:4 800 000
Iceland 1:4 800 000
Færoe islands 1:4 800 000
Denmark and Southern Sweden 162–163
1:2 000 000
Southern Norway 164
1:2 000 000
British Isles 165
1:4 000 000
Ireland 166
1:1 600 000
Scotland 167
1:1 600 000
England and Wales 168–169
1:1 600 000
Netherlands, Belgium and Luxembourg 170
1:2 000 000
France 171
1:4 000 000
Northern France 172–173
1:2 000 000
Southern France 174–175
1:2 000 000
Central Europe 176–177
1:4 000 000
Germany and Switzerland 178–179
1:2 000 000
Austria, Czechia and Slovakia 180–181
1:2 000 000
Hungary, Romania and the Lower Danube 182–183
1:2 000 000
Poland and the Southern Baltic 184–185
1:2 000 000
Eastern Europe 186–187
1:8 000 000
Baltic States, Belarus and Ukraine 188–189
1:4 000 000
The Volga Basin and the Caucasus 190–191
1:4 000 000
Southern Europe 192–193
1:8 000 000
Western Spain and Portugal 194–195
1:2 000 000
Eastern Spain 196–197
1:2 000 000
Northern Italy, Slovenia and Croatia 198–199
1:2 000 000
Southern Italy 200–201
1:2 000 000
The Balkans 202–203
1:2 000 000
Southern Greece and Western Turkey 204–205
1:2 000 000
Mediterranean Islands 206–207
Ibiza, Majorca, Minorca 1:800 000
Malta 1:400 000
Corfu 1:800 000
Rhodes 1:800 000
Levkas, Zante, Cephalonia 1:800 000
Crete 1:1 000 000
Cyprus 1:1 000 000

Asia

Asia: Physical 210
1:40 000 000
Asia: Political 211
1:40 000 000
Turkey and Transcaucasia 212–213
1:4 000 000
Russia and Northern Asia 214–215
1:16 000 000

CONTENTS

Kazakhstan and Central Asia 216–217
1:8 000 000

China and the Far East 218–219
1:12 000 000
Hong Kong, Macau and Shenzhen 1:800 000

Japan 220–221
1:4 000 000
Ryukyu Islands 1:4 000 000

Southern Japan 222–223
1:2 000 000

Korea 224
1:3 100 000
Jeju-do 1:3 100 000

Taiwan 225
1:1 400 000
Chinmen 1:1 400 000
Matsu 1:1 400 000

Northern China and Korea 226–227
1:4 800 000

Southern China and Taiwan 228–229
1:4 800 000
Hainan 1:4 800 000

South-east Asia 230–231
1:10 000 000
Java and Madura 1:6 000 000
Bali 1:1 600 000

Philippines 232–233
1:3 200 000

Western Indonesia and Malaysia 234–235
1:5 600 000

Mainland South-east Asia 236–237
1:4 800 000
Ko Phuket 1:800 000
Ko Samui 1:800 000
Pinang 1:800 000
Singapore 1:800 000

Southern Asia and the Middle East 238–239
1:14 000 000

Afghanistan and Pakistan 240
1:5 600 000

Bangladesh, North-east India and Myanmar 241
1:4 800 000

Northern India, Pakistan and Nepal 242–243
1:4 800 000
Jammu and Kashmir 1:4 800 000

Southern India and Sri Lanka 244–245
1:4 800 000
Lakshadweep Islands 1:4 800 000
Andaman and Nicobar Islands 1:4 800 000

The Middle East 246–247
1:5 600 000

Southern Arabian Peninsula 248–249
1:5 600 000
Emirates of the U.A.E. 1:5 600 000

Eastern Mediterranean 250–251
1:2 000 000

Africa

Africa: Physical 254
1:33 600 000

Africa: Political 255
1:33 600 000

The Nile Valley 256–257
1:6 400 000
The Nile Delta 1:3 200 000

Central North Africa 258–259
1:6 400 000

North-west Africa 260–261
1:6 400 000

West Africa 262–263
1:6 400 000

Central Africa 264–265
1:6 400 000
São Tomé and Príncipe 1:6 400 000

Ethiopia and the Horn of Africa 266–267
1:6 400 000

East Africa 268–269
1:6 400 000

Southern Africa 270–271
1:6 400 000

Madagascar 272
1:6 400 000
Comoros 1:2 000 000
Mayotte 1:800 000
Seychelles 1:2 000 000
Réunion 1:800 000
Mauritius 1:800 000
Maldives 1:6 400 000

Indian Ocean 273
1:40 000 000

Australia and Oceania

Australia and Oceania: Physical and Political 276–277
1:16 000 000

Western Australia 278–279
1:6 400 000

Eastern Australia 280–281
1:6 400 000
Whitsunday Group 1:2 000 000
Tasmania 1:6 400 000
Torres Strait 1:6 400 000

South-eastern Australia 282–283
1:3 200 000

New Zealand – North Island 284
1:2 800 000

New Zealand – South Island 285
1:2 800 000
Chatham Islands 1:2 800 000

Papua New Guinea 286
1:5 200 000

Islands of the South-west Pacific 287
Fiji 1:4 000 000
Vanuatu 1:4 000 000
Solomon Islands 1:4 000 000
Tonga 1:4 000 000
Yap 1:830 000
Chuuk 1:830 000
Samoan Islands 1:4 000 000

Pacific Ocean 288–289
1:43 200 000
Okinawa 1:1 550 000
Iwo-Jima 1:200 000
Palau 1:1 550 000
New Caledonia 1:5 750 000
Tahiti 1:1 150 000
French Polynesia 1:26 000 000
Niue 1:830 000
Rarotonga 1:415 000

North America

North America: Physical 292
1:28 000 000

North America: Political 293
1:28 000 000

Canada 294–295
1:12 000 000
Northern Canada 1:12 000 000

Western Canada 296–297
1:5 600 000

Eastern Canada 298–299
1:5 600 000

United States 300–301
1:12 000 000
Alaska 1:12 000 000
Hawai'i 1:12 000 000

Hawai'i and the U.S. Pacific Islands 302
1:2 500 000
Hawaiian Islands 1:21 000 000
O'ahu 1:500 000
Northern Marianas 1:17 500 000
Wake Island 1:200 000
Midway Islands 1:200 000
Guam 1:800 000
Saipan and Tinian 1:800 000
Tutuila 1:640 000
Manu'a Islands 1:640 000

Alaska 303
1:8 000 000

United States – West 304–305
1:5 360 000

Central and Southern California and Western Washington 306–307
1:2 000 000

United States – Midwest and North-east 308–309
1:5 360 000

Chicago and the Midwest 310–311
1:2 000 000

North-eastern United States 312–313
1:2 000 000

United States – South 314–315
1:5 360 000

South-eastern United States 316–317
1:2 000 000

Mexico 318–319
1:6 400 000

Central America and the West Indies 320–321
1:6 400 000
Puerto Rico and the Virgin Islands 1:1 600 000
Jamaica 1:1 600 000
Panama Canal 1:800 000

Lesser Antilles 322–323
Northern Leewards 1:600 000
Antigua and Barbuda 1:600 000
St Kitts and Nevis 1:600 000
Guadeloupe 1:600 000
ABC Islands 1:600 000
Martinique 1:600 000
Dominica 1:600 000
St Lucia 1:600 000
St Vincent and the Grenadines 1:600 000
Montserrat 1:600 000
Grenada 1:600 000
Barbados 1:600 000
Trinidad and Tobago 1:600 000

South America

South America: Physical 326
1:28 000 000

South America: Political 327
1:28 000 000

South America – North-west 328–329
1:6 400 000
Margarita 1:600 000

South America – West 330–331
1:6 400 000
Galapagos Islands 1:3 200 000
Easter Island 1:400 000
Robinson Crusoe Island 1:400 000

Eastern Brazil 332–333
1:6 400 000

Central South America 334–335
1:6 400 000

Southern Chile and Argentina 336
1:6 400 000

Geographical Glossary 337–338

Index to World Maps 339–448

WORLD STATISTICS: COUNTRIES

This alphabetical list includes the principal countries and territories of the world. If a territory is not completely independent, the country it is associated with is named. The area figures give the total area of land, inland water, and ice. The population figures are 2021 estimates where available. The annual income is the Gross Domestic Product per capita (PPP) in US dollars; the figures are the latest available.

Country/Territory	Area km² Thousands	Area miles² Thousands	Population Thousands	Capital	Annual Income US $
Afghanistan	652	252	37,466	Kabul	2,100
Albania	28.7	11.1	3,088	Tirana	14,000
Algeria	2,382	920	43,577	Algiers	11,500
American Samoa (US)	0.20	0.08	46	Pago Pago	11,200
Andorra	0.47	0.18	86	Andorra La Vella	49,900
Angola	1,247	481	33,643	Luanda	6,700
Anguilla (UK)	0.10	0.04	18	The Valley	12,200
Antigua & Barbuda	0.44	0.17	99	St John's	26,400
Argentina	2,780	1,074	45,865	Buenos Aires	22,100
Armenia	29.8	11.5	3,012	Yerevan	13,700
Aruba (Netherlands)	0.19	0.07	121	Oranjestad	37,500
Australia	7,741	2,989	25,810	Canberra	62,800
Austria	83.9	32.4	8,885	Vienna	56,200
Azerbaijan	86.6	33.4	10,282	Baku	14,400
Azores (Portugal)	2.2	0.86	246	Ponta Delgada	15,200
Bahamas, The	13.9	5.4	353	Nassau	37,100
Bahrain	0.69	0.27	1,527	Manama	45,000
Bangladesh	144	55.6	164,099	Dhaka	4,800
Barbados	0.43	0.17	302	Bridgetown	18,600
Belarus	208	80.2	9,442	Minsk	19,200
Belgium	30.5	11.8	11,779	Brussels	47,500
Belize	23.0	8.9	406	Belmopan	7,000
Benin	113	43.5	13,302	Porto-Novo	3,300
Bermuda (UK)	0.05	0.02	72	Hamilton	99,400
Bhutan	47.0	18.1	857	Thimphu	11,800
Bolivia	1,099	424	11,759	La Paz/Sucre	8,700
Bosnia-Herzegovina	51.2	19.8	3,825	Sarajevo	14,900
Botswana	582	225	2,351	Gaborone	17,800
Brazil	8,514	3,287	213,445	Brasília	11,100
Brunei	5.8	2.2	471	Bandar Seri Begawan	62,100
Bulgaria	111	42.8	6,919	Sofia	23,200
Burkina Faso	274	106	21,383	Ouagadougou	2,200
Burundi	27.8	10.7	12,241	Bujumbura	800
Cabo Verde	4.0	1.6	589	Praia	7,200
Cambodia	181	69.9	17,304	Phnom Penh	4,400
Cameroon	475	184	28,524	Yaoundé	3,600
Canada	9,971	3,850	37,943	Ottawa	49,000
Canary Is. (Spain)	7.2	2.8	2,105	Las Palmas/Santa Cruz	19,900
Cayman Is. (UK)	0.26	0.10	63	George Town	71,500
Central African Republic	623	241	5,358	Bangui	900
Chad	1,284	496	17,414	Ndjaména	1,600
Chile	757	292	18,308	Santiago	15,100
China	9,597	3,705	1,397,898	Beijing	16,100
Colombia	1,139	440	50,356	Bogotá	14,700
Comoros	2.2	0.86	864	Moroni	1,400
Congo	342	132	5,417	Brazzaville	3,700
Congo (Dem. Rep. of the)	2,345	905	105,045	Kinshasa	1,100
Cook Is. (NZ)	0.24	0.09	8	Avarua	16,700
Costa Rica	51.1	19.7	5,151	San José	19,600
Côte d'Ivoire (Ivory Coast)	322	125	28,088	Yamoussoukro	5,200
Croatia	56.5	21.8	4,209	Zagreb	28,600
Cuba	111	42.8	11,032	Havana	12,300
Curaçao (Netherlands)	0.44	0.17	152	Willemstad	24,500
Cyprus	9.3	3.6	1,282	Nicosia	23,900
Czechia	78.9	30.5	10,703	Prague	40,900
Denmark	43.1	16.6	5,895	Copenhagen	57,800
Djibouti	23.2	9.0	938	Djibouti	5,500
Dominica	0.75	0.29	75	Roseau	11,900
Dominican Republic	48.5	18.7	10,597	Santo Domingo	18,400
Ecuador	284	109	17,093	Quito	11,400
Egypt	1,001	387	106,437	Cairo	11,800
El Salvador	21.0	8.1	6,528	San Salvador	8,800
Equatorial Guinea	28.1	10.8	857	Malabo	18,600
Eritrea	118	45.4	6,147	Asmara	1,600
Estonia	45.1	17.4	1,220	Tallinn	36,900
Eswatini (Swaziland)	17.4	6.7	1,113	Mbabane	8,600
Ethiopia	1,104	426	110,871	Addis Ababa	2,200
Falkland Is. (UK)	12.2	4.7	3	Stanley	70,800
Faroe Is. (Denmark)	1.4	0.54	52	Tórshavn	40,000
Fiji	18.3	7.1	940	Suva	13,700
Finland	338	131	5,587	Helsinki	49,400
France	552	213	68,084	Paris	46,200
French Guiana (France)	90.0	34.7	250	Cayenne	8,300
French Polynesia (France)	4.0	1.5	297	Papeete	17,000
Gabon	268	103	2,285	Libreville	15,000
Gambia, The	11.3	4.4	2,221	Banjul	2,200
Georgia	69.7	26.9	4,934	Tbilisi	15,000
Germany	357	138	79,903	Berlin	50,800
Ghana	239	92.1	32,373	Accra	5,400
Gibraltar (UK)	0.006	0.002	30	Gibraltar Town	61,700
Greece	132	50.9	10,570	Athens	29,800
Greenland (Denmark)	2,176	840	58	Nuuk	41,800
Grenada	0.34	0.13	114	St George's	17,000
Guadeloupe (France)	1.7	0.66	402	Basse-Terre	7,900
Guam (US)	0.55	0.21	169	Agana	35,600
Guatemala	109	42.0	17,423	Guatemala City	8,600
Guinea	246	94.9	12,878	Conakry	2,600
Guinea-Bissau	36.1	13.9	1,976	Bissau	2,000
Guyana	215	83.0	788	Georgetown	13,100
Haiti	27.8	10.7	11,198	Port-au-Prince	2,900
Honduras	112	43.3	9,346	Tegucigalpa	5,700
Hungary	93.0	35.9	9,728	Budapest	32,900
Iceland	103	39.8	354	Reykjavik	55,900
India	3,287	1,269	1,339,331	New Delhi	6,700
Indonesia	1,905	735	275,122	Jakarta	11,800
Iran	1,648	636	85,889	Tehran	12,400
Iraq	438	169	39,650	Baghdad	10,900
Ireland	70.3	27.1	5,225	Dublin	81,300
Israel	20.6	8.0	8,787	Jerusalem	40,100
Italy	301	116	62,390	Rome	42,500
Jamaica	11.0	4.2	2,817	Kingston	9,800
Japan	378	146	124,687	Tokyo	41,400
Jordan	89.3	34.5	10,910	Amman	10,100
Kazakhstan	2,725	1,052	19,246	Nur-Sultan	11,800
Kenya	580	224	54,685	Nairobi	4,300
Kiribati	0.73	0.28	113	Tarawa	2,300
Korea, North	121	46.5	25,831	Pyŏngyang	1,700
Korea, South	99.3	38.3	51,715	Seoul	42,800
Kosovo	10.9	4.2	1,935	Pristina	11,400
Kuwait	17.8	6.9	3,032	Kuwait City	49,900
Kyrgyzstan	200	77.2	6,019	Bishkek	5,300
Laos	237	91.4	7,574	Vientiane	7,800
Latvia	64.6	24.9	1,863	Riga	30,900
Lebanon	10.4	4.0	5,261	Beirut	14,600
Lesotho	30.4	11.7	2,178	Maseru	2,700
Liberia	111	43.0	5,214	Monrovia	1,400
Libya	1,760	679	7,017	Tripoli	15,200
Liechtenstein	0.16	0.06	39	Vaduz	139,100
Lithuania	65.2	25.2	2,712	Vilnius	37,200
Luxembourg	2.6	1.0	640	Luxembourg	114,500
Macedonia, North	25.7	9.9	2,128	Skopje	16,500
Madagascar	587	227	27,534	Antananarivo	1,600
Madeira (Portugal)	0.78	0.30	289	Funchal	25,800
Malawi	118	45.7	20,309	Lilongwe	1,100
Malaysia	330	127	33,519	Kuala Lumpur/Putrajaya	28,400
Maldives	0.30	0.12	391	Malé	19,500
Mali	1,240	479	20,138	Bamako	2,300
Malta	0.32	0.12	461	Valletta	37,300
Marshall Is.	0.18	0.07	79	Majuro	3,900
Martinique (France)	1.1	0.43	386	Fort-de-France	14,400
Mauritania	1,026	396	4,079	Nouakchott	5,200
Mauritius	2.0	0.79	1,386	Port Louis	22,900
Mayotte (France)	0.37	0.14	213	Mamoudzou	4,900
Mexico	1,958	756	130,207	Mexico City	19,800
Micronesia, Fed. States of	0.70	0.27	102	Palikir	3,500
Moldova	33.9	13.1	3,324	Kishinev	13,000
Monaco	0.002	0.0008	31	Monaco	115,700
Mongolia	1,567	605	3,199	Ulan Bator	12,300
Montenegro	14.0	5.4	607	Podgorica	21,500
Montserrat (UK)	0.10	0.39	5	Brades	34,000
Morocco	447	172	36,562	Rabat	7,500
Mozambique	802	309	30,888	Maputo	1,300
Myanmar (Burma)	677	261	57,069	Yangôn/Naypyidaw	5,100
Namibia	824	318	2,678	Windhoek	9,600
Nauru	0.02	0.008	10	Yaren	11,600
Nepal	147	56.8	30,425	Katmandu	3,400
Netherlands	41.5	16.0	17,337	Amsterdam/The Hague	56,900
New Caledonia (France)	18.6	7.2	294	Nouméa	31,100
New Zealand	271	104	4,991	Wellington	42,900
Nicaragua	130	50.2	6,244	Managua	5,400
Niger	1,267	489	23,606	Niamey	1,200
Nigeria	924	357	219,464	Abuja	5,100
Northern Mariana Is. (US)	0.46	0.18	52	Saipan	24,500
Norway	324	125	5,510	Oslo	63,600
Oman	310	119	3,695	Muscat	27,300
Pakistan	796	307	238,181	Islamabad	4,700
Palau	0.46	0.18	22	Melekeok	17,600
Panama	75.5	29.2	3,929	Panamá	31,500
Papua New Guinea	463	179	7,400	Port Moresby	4,400
Paraguay	407	157	7,273	Asunción	12,700
Peru	1,285	496	32,201	Lima	12,800
Philippines	300	116	110,818	Manila	8,900
Poland	323	125	38,186	Warsaw	33,200
Portugal	88.8	34.3	10,264	Lisbon	34,900
Puerto Rico (US)	8.9	3.4	3,143	San Juan	34,500
Qatar	11.0	4.2	2,480	Doha	62,000
Réunion (France)	2.5	0.97	846	St-Denis	6,200
Romania	238	92.0	21,230	Bucharest	29,900
Russia	17,075	6,593	142,321	Moscow	27,000
Rwanda	26.3	10.2	12,943	Kigali	2,200
St Kitts & Nevis	0.26	0.10	54	Basseterre	26,400
St Lucia	0.54	0.21	167	Castries	14,400
St Vincent & Grenadines	0.39	0.15	101	Kingstown	12,500
Samoa	2.8	1.1	205	Apia	5,700
San Marino	0.06	0.02	34	San Marino	59,000
São Tomé & Príncipe	0.96	0.37	214	São Tomé	4,000
Saudi Arabia	2,150	830	34,784	Riyadh	47,000
Senegal	197	76.0	16,082	Dakar	3,400
Serbia	77.5	29.9	6,974	Belgrade	18,200
Seychelles	0.46	0.18	96	Victoria	29,200
Sierra Leone	71.7	27.7	6,807	Freetown	1,700
Singapore	0.68	0.26	5,866	Singapore City	97,300
Slovakia	49.0	18.9	5,436	Bratislava	32,700
Slovenia	20.3	7.8	2,102	Ljubljana	39,100
Solomon Is.	28.9	11.2	691	Honiara	2,700
Somalia	638	246	12,095	Mogadishu	400
South Africa	1,221	471	56,979	Cape Town/Pretoria	12,500
Spain	498	192	47,261	Madrid	40,900
Sri Lanka	65.6	25.3	23,044	Colombo	13,100
Sudan	1,886	728	46,751	Khartoum	4,000
Sudan, South	620	239	10,984	Juba	1,600
Suriname	163	63.0	615	Paramaribo	16,500
Sweden	450	174	10,262	Stockholm	53,200
Switzerland	41.3	15.9	8,454	Bern	81,500
Syria	185	71.5	20,384	Damascus	2,900
Taiwan	36.0	13.9	23,572	Taipei	24,500
Tajikistan	143	55.3	8,991	Dushanbe	3,400
Tanzania	945	365	62,093	Dodoma	2,700
Thailand	513	198	69,481	Bangkok	18,500
Timor-Leste (East Timor)	14.9	5.7	1,414	Dili	3,600
Togo	56.8	21.9	8,283	Lomé	1,600
Tonga	0.65	0.25	106	Nuku'alofa	6,400
Trinidad & Tobago	5.1	2.0	1,221	Port of Spain	15,200
Tunisia	164	63.2	11,811	Tunis	10,800
Turkey	775	299	82,482	Ankara	28,400
Turkmenistan	488	188	5,580	Ashkhabad	14,800
Turks & Caicos Is. (UK)	0.43	0.17	57	Cockburn Town	29,300
Tuvalu	0.03	0.01	11	Fongafale	4,300
Uganda	241	93.1	44,712	Kampala	2,200
Ukraine	604	233	43,746	Kiev	12,800
United Arab Emirates	83.6	32.3	9,857	Abu Dhabi	67,100
United Kingdom	242	93.4	66,052	London	46,700
United States of America	9,629	3,718	334,998	Washington, DC	62,500
Uruguay	175	67.6	3,398	Montevideo	21,600
Uzbekistan	447	173	30,843	Tashkent	7,000
Vanuatu	12.2	4.7	303	Port-Vila	3,200
Vatican City	0.0004	0.0002	1	Vatican City	-
Venezuela	912	352	29,069	Caracas	7,700
Vietnam	332	128	102,790	Hanoi	8,000
Virgin Is. (UK)	0.15	0.06	38	Road Town	42,300
Virgin Is. (US)	0.35	0.13	106	Charlotte Amalie	37,000
Yemen	528	204	30,399	Sana'	2,500
Zambia	753	291	19,078	Lusaka	3,500
Zimbabwe	391	151	14,830	Harare	2,800

This list shows the principal cities with more than 1,000,000 inhabitants. The figures are taken from the most recent census or estimate available and as far as possible are the population of the metropolitan area or urban agglomeration. The list includes Metropolitan Statistical Areas from the United States Census Bureau. All the figures are in thousands. Local name forms have been used for the smaller cities (for example, Antwerpen).

AFGHANISTAN	
Kabul	4,222
ALGERIA	
Algiers	2,768
ANGOLA	
Luanda	8,330
ARGENTINA	
Buenos Aires	15,154
Córdoba	1,572
Rosario	1,532
Mendoza	1,173
ARMENIA	
Yerevan	1,086
AUSTRALIA	
Melbourne	4,968
Sydney	4,926
Brisbane	2,406
Perth	2,042
Adelaide	1,336
AUSTRIA	
Vienna	1,930
AZERBAIJAN	
Baku	2,341
BANGLADESH	
Dhaka	21,006
Chittagong	5,020
BELARUS	
Minsk	2,028
BENIN	
Abomey-Calavi	1,056
BELGIUM	
Brussels	2,081
Antwerpen	1,042
BOLIVIA	
La Paz	1,858
Santa Cruz	1,713
Cochabamba	1,304
BRAZIL	
São Paulo	22,043
Rio de Janeiro	13,458
Belo Horizonte	6,084
Brasília	4,646
Pôrto Alegre	4,137
Recife	4,127
Fortaleza	4,073
Salvador	3,839
Curitiba	3,679
Campinas	3,301
Goiânia	2,690
Belém	2,334
Manaus	2,261
Vitória	2,076
Baixada Santista	1,892
São Luís	1,486
Natal	1,457
João Pessoa	1,378
Maceió	1,323
Joinville	1,303
Florianópolis	1,239
Teresina	1,021
Aracaju	1,009
BULGARIA	
Sofia	1,281
BURKINA FASO	
Ouagadougou	2,780
BURUNDI	
Bujumbura	1,013
CAMBODIA	
Phnom Penh	2,078
CAMEROON	
Yaoundé	3,992
Douala	3,663
CANADA	
Toronto	6,197
Montréal	4,221
Vancouver	2,581
Calgary	1,547
Edmonton	1,461
Ottawa	1,393
CHAD	
Ndjamena	1,423
CHILE	
Santiago	6,767
CHINA	
Shanghai	27,058
Beijing	20,463
Chongqing	15,872
Tianjin	13,589
Guangzhou, Guangdong	13,302
Shenzhen	12,357
Chengdu	9,136
Nanjing, Jiangsu	8,847
Wuhan	8,365
Xi'an, Shaanxi	8,001
Hangzhou	7,642
Hong Kong	7,548
Dongguan, Guangdong	7,408
Foshan	7,327
Shenyang	7,220
Suzhou, Jiangsu	7,070
Harbin	6,387
Qingdao	5,620
Dalian	5,618
Jinan, Shandong	5,360
Zhengzhou	5,323
Changsha	4,578
Kunming	4,443
Changchun	4,426
Ürümqi	4,369
Shantou	4,327
Hefei	4,242
Ningbo	4,116
Shijiazhuang	4,114
Taiyuan, Shanxi	3,891
Nanning	3,860
Xiamen	3,720
Fuzhou, Fujian	3,686
Changzhou, Jiangsu	3,625
Wenzhou	3,624
Nanchang	3,598
Tangshan	3,426
Guiyang	3,317
Wuxi, Jiangsu	3,256
Lanzhou	3,081
Zhongshan	2,914
Handan	2,727
Huai'an	2,655
Weifang	2,654
Zibo	2,640
Shaoxing	2,540
Yantai	2,527
Huizhou	2,525
Luoyang	2,387
Nantong	2,276
Baotou	2,190
Liuzhou	2,165
Hohhot	2,163
Xuzhou	2,146
Yangzhou	1,993
Baoding	1,976
Linyi	1,937
Taizhou, Zhejiang	1,935
Putian	1,907
Haikou	1,889
Wuhu	1,870
Yancheng	1,864
Daqing	1,859
Lianyungang	1,820
Zhuhai	1,759
Datong	1,745
Quanzhou	1,694
Jaingmen	1,687
Xiangyang	1,658
Anshan	1,629
Cixi	1,609
Jilin	1,603
Yinchuan	1,579
Qiqihar	1,560
Yichang	1,548
Xining	1,539
Qinhuangdao	1,535
Hengyang	1,527
Jining, Shandong	1,494
Anyang	1,460
Suqian	1,440
Huainan	1,438
Zhangjiakou	1,435
Chaozhou	1,428
Taizhou, Jiangsu	1,348
Tai'an	1,339
Yiwu	1,334
Weihai	1,304
Zhanjiang	1,287
Fushun	1,285
Ganzhou	1,285
Zunyi	1,281
Dongying	1,276
Mianyang	1,276
Kaifeng	1,274
Rizhao	1,271
Jiaxing	1,260
Nanchong	1,258
Shiyan	1,241
Yingkou	1,214
Maoming	1,205
Liuan	1,196
Tengzhou	1,190
Zhuzhou	1,187
Zhenjiang	1,174
Suzhou	1,170
Liuyang	1,169
Ruian	1,169
Baoji	1,165
Chifeng	1,165
Pingdingshan	1,160
Puning	1,160
Benxi	1,157
Jieyang	1,147
Jinzhou	1,145
Nanyang	1,143
Xiangtan	1,143
Huaibei	1,142
Guilin	1,134
Jinhua	1,122
Zaozhuang	1,088
Binzhou	1,084
Xinxiang	1,081
Liupanshui	1,077
Pizhou	1,063
Yueqing	1,061
Panjin	1,053
Luohe	1,040
Jingzhou	1,038
Wenling	1,037
Fuyang	1,036
Shangrao	1,029
Zhaoqing	1,024
Ma'anshan	1,019
Yueyang	1,010
COLOMBIA	
Bogotá	10,978
Medellín	4,000
Cali	2,782
Barranquilla	2,273
Bucaramanga	1,331
Cartagena	1,063
CONGO	
Brazzaville	2,388
Pointe-Noire	1,214
CONGO (DEM. REP. OF THE)	
Kinshasa	14,342
Mbuji-Mayi	2,525
Lubumbashi	2,478
Kananga	1,458
Kisangani	1,261
Bukavu	1,078
COSTA RICA	
San José	1,400
CÔTE D'IVOIRE (IVORY COAST)	
Abidjan	5,203
CUBA	
Havana	2,140
CZECHIA	
Prague	1,306
DENMARK	
Copenhagen	1,346
DOMINICAN REPUBLIC	
Santo Domingo	3,318
ECUADOR	
Guayaquil	2,994
Quito	1,874
EGYPT	
Cairo	20,901
Alexandria	5,281
EL SALVADOR	
San Salvador	1,106
ETHIOPIA	
Addis Ababa	4,794
FINLAND	
Helsinki	1,305
FRANCE	
Paris	11,017
Lyon	1,719
Marseilles	1,608
Lille	1,063
Toulouse	1,024
GEORGIA	
Tbilisi	1 078
GERMANY	
Berlin	3,562
Hamburg	1,790
Munich	1,538
Cologne	1,119
GHANA	
Kumasi	3,348
Accra	2,514
GREECE	
Athens	3,153
GUATEMALA	
Guatemala City	2,935
GUINEA	
Conakry	1,938
HAITI	
Port-au-Prince	2,774
HONDURAS	
Tegucigalpa	1,444
HUNGARY	
Budapest	1,768
INDIA	
Delhi	30,291
Mumbai	20,411
Kolkata	14,850
Bengaluru	12,327
Chennai	10,971
Hyderabad	10,004
Ahmedabad	8,059
Surat	7,185
Pune	6,629
Jaipur	3,909
Lucknow	3,677
Calicut	3,555
Malappuram	3,391
Kanpur	3,124
Kochi	3,082
Thrissur	3,068
Indore	3,017
Nagpur	2,893
Coimbatore	2,787
Thiruvananthapuram	2,585
Patna	2,436
Bhopal	2,390
Agra	2,210
Vadodara	2,190
Vishakhapatnam	2,175
Kannur	2,167
Nashik	2,066
Vijayawada	2,040
Rajkot	1,878
Ludhiana	1,857
Kollam	1,852
Madurai	1,734
Meerut	1,696
Varanasi	1,665
Raipur	1,642
Jamshedpur	1,599
Srinagar	1,586
Aurangabad	1,558
Tiruppur	1,496
Jodhpur	1,472
Jabalpur	1,450
Ranchi	1,439
Asansol	1,431
Allahabad	1,394
Kota	1,387
Gwalior	1,378
Amritsar	1,377
Dhanbad	1,331
Bareilly	1,255
Aligarh	1,211
Mysore	1,210
Bhilainagar-Durg	1,208
Moradabad	1,197
Tiruchchirapalli	1,165
Bhubaneswar	1,163
Chandigarh	1,148
Guwahati	1,117
Hubli-Dharwad	1,117
Salem	1,102
Jalandhar	1,054
Saharanpur	1,054
Solapur	1,031
Siliguri	1,020
INDONESIA	
Jakarta	10,770
Bekasi	3,394
Surabaya	2,944
Depok	2,727
Bandung	2,580
Tangerang	2,339
Medan	2,338
Semarang	1,866
Palembang	1,723
Makassar	1,584
Batam	1,546
Pekanbaru	1,205
Bogor	1,160
Bandar Lampung	1,092
Tasikmalaya	1,056
Samarinda	1,010
IRAN	
Tehran	9,135
Mashhad	3,208
Esfahan	2,132
Shiraz	1,651
Tabriz	1,611
Karaj	1,580
Qom	1,288
Ahvaz	1,244
Kermanshah	1,026
IRAQ	
Baghdad	7,144
Mosul	1,630
Basra	1,352
Kirkuk	1,013
IRELAND	
Dublin	1,228
ISRAEL	
Tel Aviv-Yafo	4,181
Haifa	1,147
ITALY	
Rome	4,257
Milan	3,140
Naples	2,187
Turin	1,792
JAPAN	
Tokyo–Yokohama	37,393
Osaka–Kobe	19,165
Nagoya	9,552
Fukuoka–Kitakyushu	5,529
Shizuoka–Hamamatsu	2,922
Sapporo	2,670
Sendai	2,327
Hiroshima	2,083
Kyoto	1,470
JORDAN	
Amman	2,148
KAZAKHSTAN	
Almaty	1,896
Nur-Sultan	1,166
Shimkent	1,058
KENYA	
Nairobi	4,735
Mombasa	1,296
KOREA, NORTH	
Pyŏngyang	3,084
KOREA, SOUTH	
Seoul	9,963
Busan	3,465
Incheon	2,801
Daegu	2,199
Daejeon	1,566
Gwangju	1,522
Suwon	1,311
Yongin	1,083
Goyang	1,069
Changwon	1,056
KUWAIT	
Kuwait City	3,115
KYRGYZSTAN	
Bishkek	1,038
LEBANON	
Beirut	2,424
LIBERIA	
Monrovia	1,517
LIBYA	
Tripoli	1,165
MADAGASCAR	
Antananarivo	3,369
MALAWI	
Lilongwe	1,122
MALAYSIA	
Kuala Lumpur	7,997
Johor Bahru	1,024
MALI	
Bamako	2,618
MAURITANIA	
Nouakchott	1,315
MEXICO	
Mexico City	21,782
Guadalajara	5,179
Monterrey	4,874
Puebla	3,195
Toluca	2,467
Tijuana	2,140
León	1,825
La Laguna	1,615
Ciudad Juárez	1,519
Torreón	1,498
Querétaro	1,339
San Luis Potosí	1,217
Mérida	1,161
Mexicali	1,121
Aguascalientes	1,106
Cuernavaca	1,075
Chihuahua	1,055
Tampico	1,001
MONGOLIA	
Ulan Bator	1,584
MOROCCO	
Casablanca	3,752
Rabat	1,885
Fès	1,224
Tangier	1,198
Marrakesh	1,003
MOZAMBIQUE	
Matola	1,706
Maputo	1,110
MYANMAR (BURMA)	
Rangoon	5,332
Mandalay	1,438
NEPAL	
Katmandu	1,424
NETHERLANDS	
Amsterdam	1,149
Rotterdam	1,010
NEW ZEALAND	
Auckland	1,607
NICARAGUA	
Managua	1,064
NIGER	
Niamey	1,292
NIGERIA	
Lagos	14,368
Kano	3,999
Ibadan	3,552
Abuja	3,278
Port Harcourt	3,020
Benin City	1,727
Onitsha	1,415
Uyo	1,136
Kaduna	1,113
Aba	1,081
Nnewi	1,051
NORWAY	
Oslo	1,041
OMAN	
Muscat	1,550
PAKISTAN	
Karachi	16,094
Lahore	12,642
Faisalabad	3,462
Rawalpindi	2,237
Gujranwala	2,229
Peshawar	2,203
Multan	2,015
Hyderabad	1,850
Islamabad	1,129
Quetta	1,100
PANAMA	
Panamá	1,860
PARAGUAY	
Asunción	3,337
PERU	
Lima	10,719
PHILIPPINES	
Manila	13,923
Davao	1,825
POLAND	
Warsaw	1,783
PORTUGAL	
Lisbon	2,957
Porto	1,313
PUERTO RICO	
San Juan	2,448
ROMANIA	
Bucharest	1,803
RUSSIA	
Moscow	12,538
St Petersburg	5,468
Novosibirsk	1,664
Yekaterinburg	1,504
Kazan	1,272
Nizhniy Novgorod	1,258
Chelyabinsk	1,228
Omsk	1,182
Samara	1,163
Krasnoyarsk	1,137
Rostov	1,136
Ufa	1,136
Perm	1,071
Voronezh	1,068
Volgograd	1,005
RWANDA	
Kigali	1,132
SAUDI ARABIA	
Riyadh	7,231
Jedda	4,610
Mecca	2,042
Medina	1,489
Dammam	1,253
SENEGAL	
Dakar	3,140
SERBIA	
Belgrade	1,398
SIERRA LEONE	
Freetown	1,202
SINGAPORE	
Singapore City	5,935
SOMALIA	
Mogadishu	2,282
SOUTH AFRICA	
Johannesburg	5,783
Cape Town	4,618
Ekurhuleni	3,894
Durban	3,158
Pretoria	2,566
Port Elizabeth	1,254
SPAIN	
Madrid	6,618
Barcelona	5,586
SUDAN	
Khartoum	5,829
SWEDEN	
Stockholm	1,633
SWITZERLAND	
Zürich	1,395
SYRIA	
Damascus	2,392
Aleppo	1,917
Homs	1,336
TAIWAN	
Xinbei	4,398
Taipei	2,721
Taoyuan	2,245
Kaohsiung	1,538
T'aichung	1,321
TANZANIA	
Dar es Salaam	6,702
Mwanza	1,120
THAILAND	
Bangkok	10,539
Chon Buri	1,399
Samut Prakan	1,307
Chiang Mai	1,167
TOGO	
Lomé	1,828
TUNISIA	
Tunis	2,365
TURKEY	
Istanbul	15,190
Ankara	5,118
Izmir	2,993
Bursa	1,986
Adana	1,771
Gaziantep	1,704
Konya	1,328
Antalya	1,254
Diyarbakir	1,039
Mersin	1,016
UGANDA	
Kampala	3,298
UKRAINE	
Kiev	2,988
Kharkov	1,429
Odessa	1,009
UNITED ARAB EMIRATES	
Dubai	2,878
Sharjah	1,685
Abu Dhabi	1,483
UNITED KINGDOM	
London	9,304
Manchester	2,730
Birmingham	2,607
Glasgow	1,673
UNITED STATES OF AMERICA	
New York	18,804
Los Angeles	12,447
Chicago	8,865
Houston	6,371
Dallas–Fort Worth	6,301
Miami	6,122
Atlanta	5,803
Philadelphia	5,717
Washington, DC	5,322
Phoenix–Mesa	4,511
Boston	4,309
Detroit	3,548
Seattle	3,433
San Francisco	3,314
San Diego	3,251
Minneapolis–St Paul	2,926
Tampa–St Petersburg	2,877
Denver	2,827
Las Vegas	2,699
Riverside-San Bernardino	2,469
Baltimore	2,325
San Antonio	2,320
St Louis	2,213
Portland	2,151
Sacramento	2,123
Charlotte	2,054
Austin	2,053
Orlando	1,964
Indianapolis	1,807
San Jose	1,791
Cleveland	1,763
Cincinnati	1,746
Pittsburgh	1,704
Kansas City	1,686
Columbus	1,644
Virginia Beach–Norfolk	1,477
Raleigh	1,444
Milwaukee	1,439
Jacksonville	1,280
Nashville	1,249
Providence	1,200
Salt Lake City	1,169
Memphis	1,150
Richmond	1,105
Louisville	1,089
URUGUAY	
Montevideo	1,752
UZBEKISTAN	
Tashkent	2,517
VENEZUELA	
Caracas	2,939
Maracaibo	2,258
Valencia	1,910
Barquisimeto	1,214
Maracay	1,203
VIETNAM	
Ho Chi Minh City	8,602
Hanoi	4,678
Can Tho	1,618
Haiphong	1,300
Da Nang	1,125
Bien Hoa	1,013
YEMEN	
Sana'	2,973
ZAMBIA	
Lusaka	2,774
ZIMBABWE	
Harare	1,530

MIGRATION

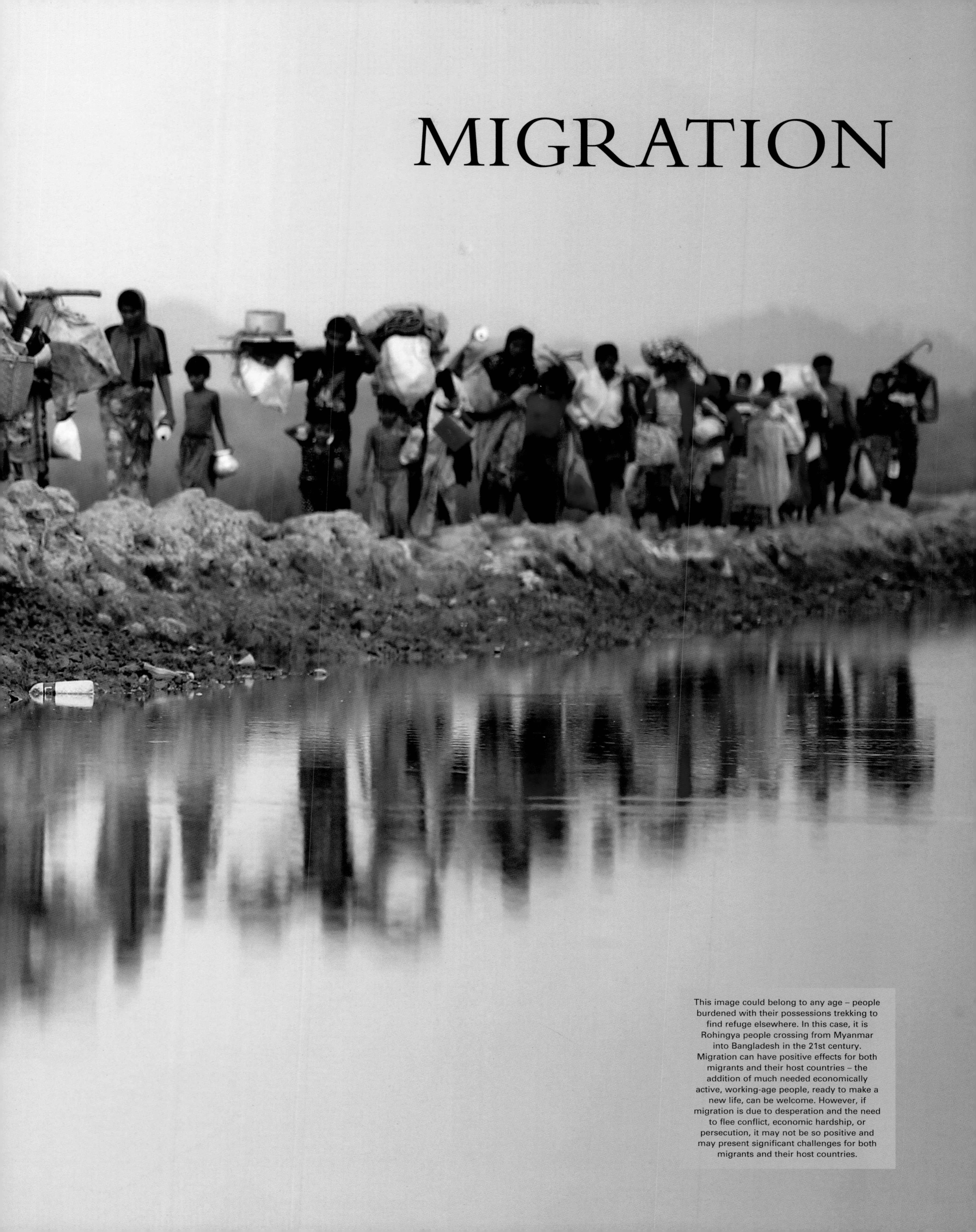

This image could belong to any age – people burdened with their possessions trekking to find refuge elsewhere. In this case, it is Rohingya people crossing from Myanmar into Bangladesh in the 21st century. Migration can have positive effects for both migrants and their host countries – the addition of much needed economically active, working-age people, ready to make a new life, can be welcome. However, if migration is due to desperation and the need to flee conflict, economic hardship, or persecution, it may not be so positive and may present significant challenges for both migrants and their host countries.

For more information:
90 Population
92 Cities
106 Levels of Income

Migration is the permanent or semi-permanent change in residence. It can be voluntary or forced, international or internal, long- or short-distance. Most voluntary migrants are moving for work, to retire, or for educational reasons. In contrast, forced migrations may be due to civil conflict, environmental damage, or persecution.

It is estimated that from 1500 to 1800 the world's population more than doubled. From then the growth rate increased dramatically and was unequally distributed. One consequence of this rise was an unprecedented intercontinental migration of people, fueled by both "push" and "pull" factors. The two maps below illustrate major global migrations since the Middle Ages.

Migration, both voluntary and involuntary continues. The broad geographical pattern remains fairly constant – movement is from low-income to higher-income countries, from the "Global South" to the north. The number of international migrants was estimated to be 272 million in 2019 – 3.5% of the world's population. With almost 75% of international migrants being of working age, the money they send home to families (remittances) is economically significant. On balance there are slightly more male than female migrants. India continues to be the largest source of international migrants, followed by Mexico and China. The top destination remains the USA – 51 million migrants in 2019 according to the UN.

▲ Ellis Island in New York was often the disembarkment point for immigrants to the USA. Over 12 million people passed through this immigration station in the 60 years it was open until its closure in 1954. This group was photographed in 1907. Like many who came before and after, they would be seeking a better life.

POPULATION MOVEMENTS 1500 – 1914

As the wider world became known to Europeans, many of them left their native countries in search of a better life for themselves and their families. Sometimes migrants left Europe in order to avoid persecution of various forms. The earliest of these European migrations was to the Americas. Later European settlers headed for South Africa and beyond, to Australia and New Zealand. Elsewhere in the world millions of Chinese and Japanese migrated in search of work, the majority to Southeast Asia but a sizable number to the west coast of North America.

The slave trade caused a massive involuntary migration of Africans to the Americas and Arabia.

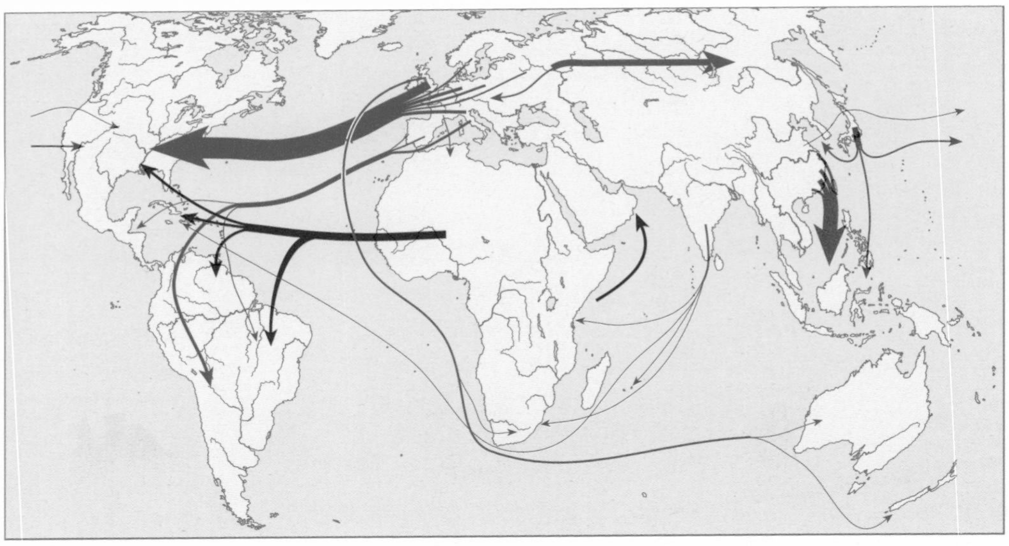

Migration originating from:

- Europe, Scandinavia, and western Russia
- Asia
- Africa

MAJOR WORLD MIGRATIONS

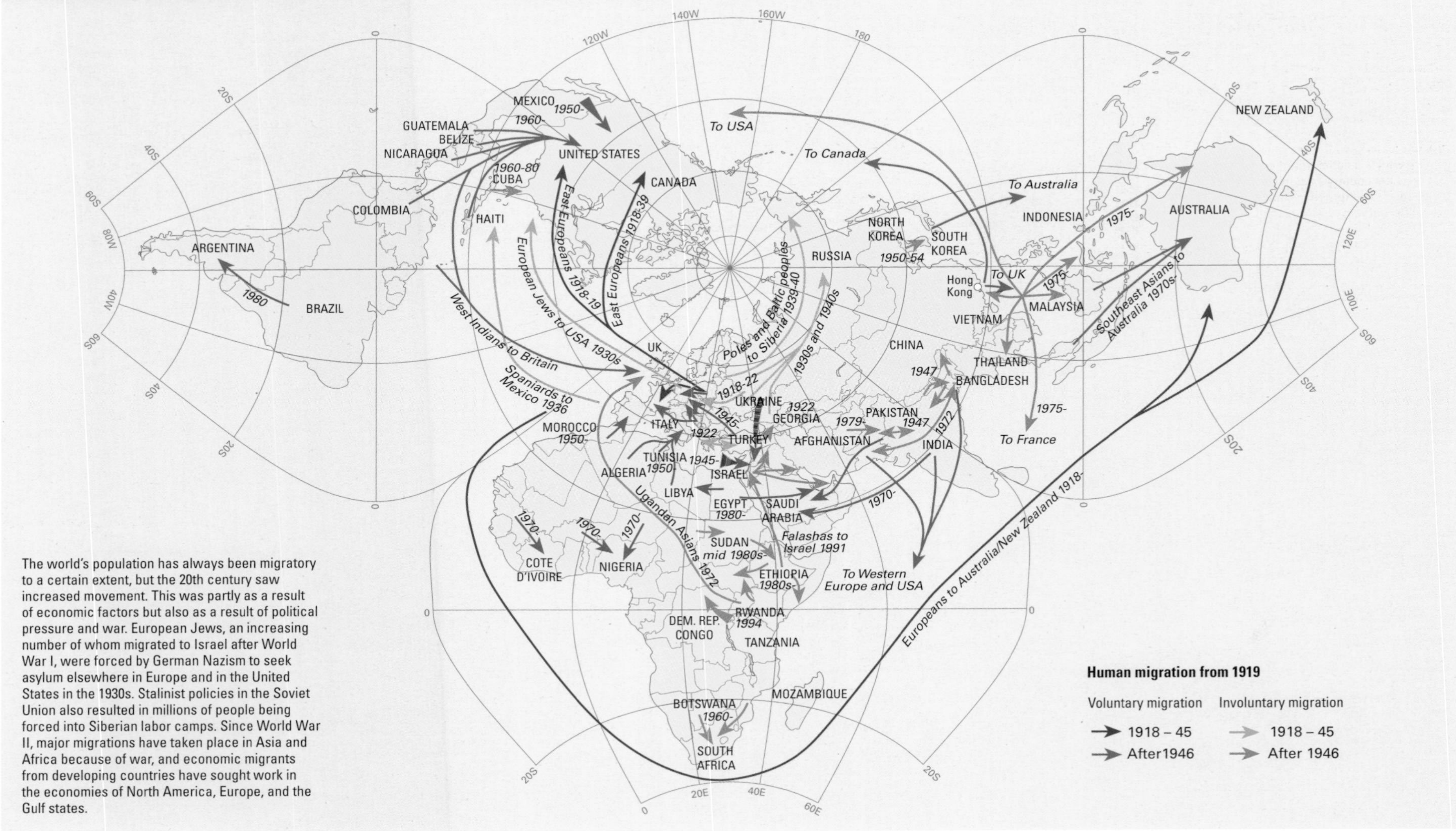

The world's population has always been migratory to a certain extent, but the 20th century saw increased movement. This was partly as a result of economic factors but also as a result of political pressure and war. European Jews, an increasing number of whom migrated to Israel after World War I, were forced by German Nazism to seek asylum elsewhere in Europe and in the United States in the 1930s. Stalinist policies in the Soviet Union also resulted in millions of people being forced into Siberian labor camps. Since World War II, major migrations have taken place in Asia and Africa because of war, and economic migrants from developing countries have sought work in the economies of North America, Europe, and the Gulf states.

NET MIGRATION

The net migration rate is the difference between the number of persons entering and leaving a country during a year per 1,000 persons (2021)

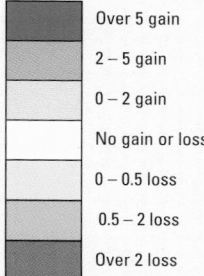

- Over 5 gain
- 2 – 5 gain
- 0 – 2 gain
- No gain or loss
- 0 – 0.5 loss
- 0.5 – 2 loss
- Over 2 loss
- No data available

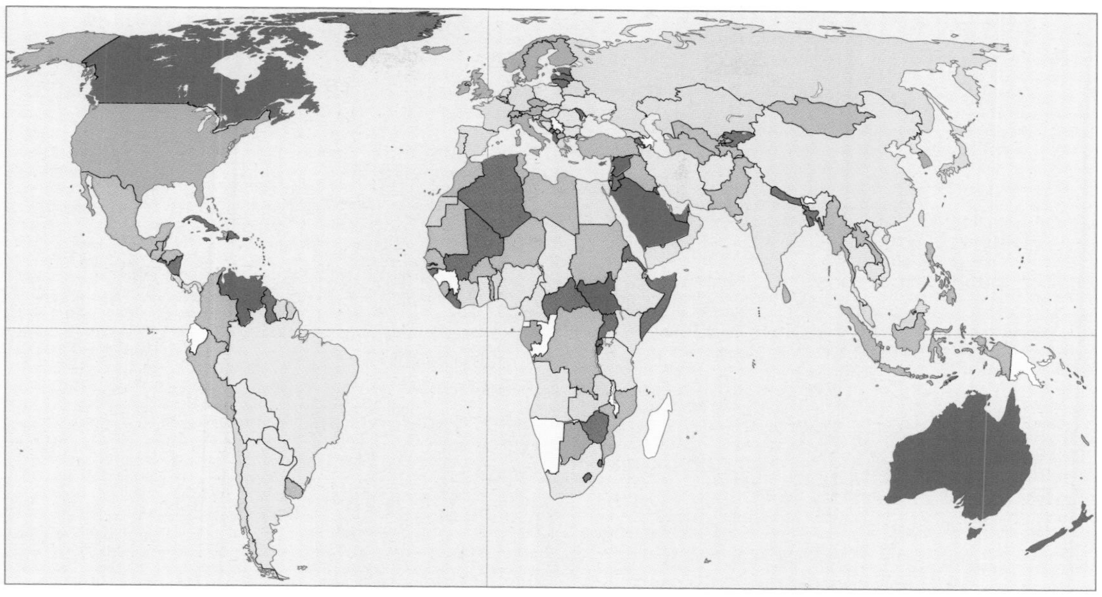

INTERNATIONAL MIGRANTS

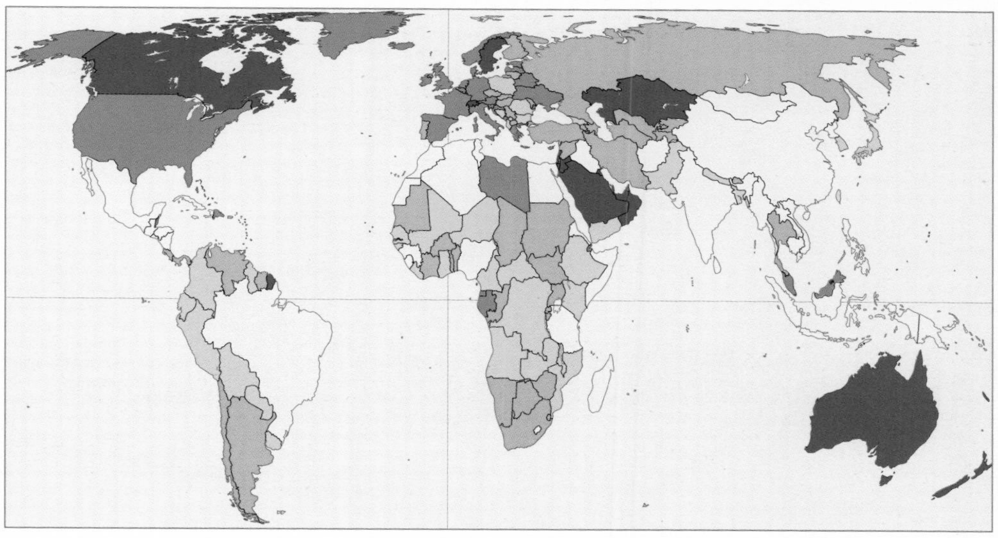

Migrant stock as percentage of total population (2019)

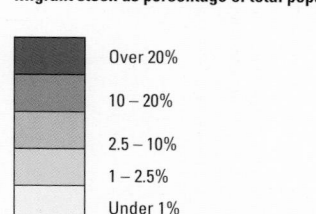

- Over 20%
- 10 – 20%
- 2.5 – 10%
- 1 – 2.5%
- Under 1%
- No data available

1. UAE 87.9%
2. Qatar 78.7%
3. Kuwait 72.1%
4. Monaco 68.0%
5. Liechtenstein 67.0%
6. Andorra 58.5%
7. Luxembourg 47.4%
8. Oman 46.0%
9. Bahrain 45.2%
10. Saudi Arabia 38.3%

POPULATION STRUCTURE

The population pyramids (right) show the relative mismatches between the population structures of the host countries and their migrant population. Mozambique, as an example of a low-income economy, has a relatively large population in its younger age group which is not mirrored by the migrants. As the host country's economy matures towards the pattern of Denmark, the differences are less marked.

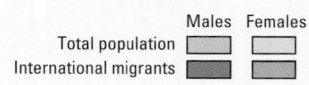

	Males	Females
Total population		
International migrants		

Source: UN DESA (2019a, 2019b)

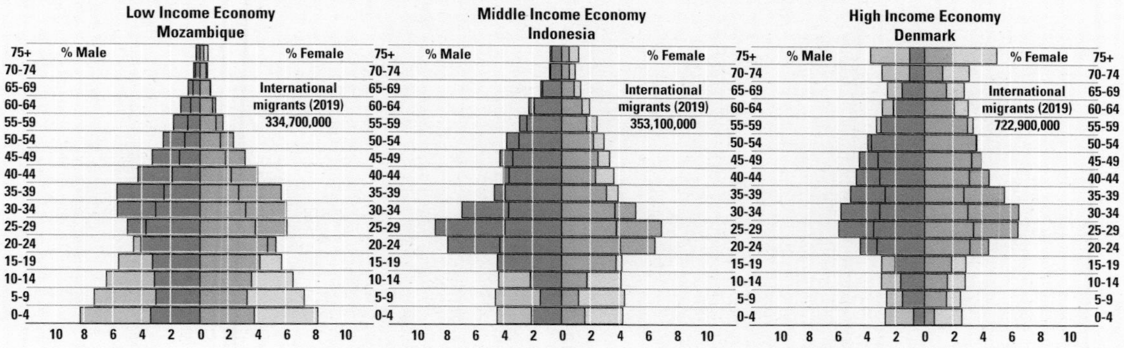

REMITTANCES

Money sent home by migrants as a percentage share of total GDP (2019)

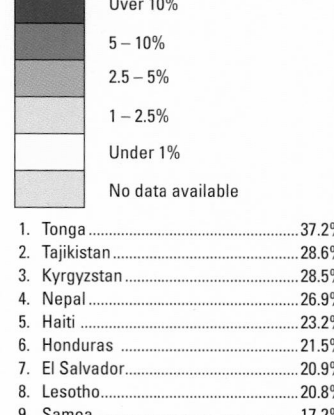

- Over 10%
- 5 – 10%
- 2.5 – 5%
- 1 – 2.5%
- Under 1%
- No data available

1. Tonga 37.2%
2. Tajikistan 28.6%
3. Kyrgyzstan 28.5%
4. Nepal 26.9%
5. Haiti 23.2%
6. Honduras 21.5%
7. El Salvador 20.9%
8. Lesotho 20.8%
9. Samoa 17.2%
10. Yemen 16.7%

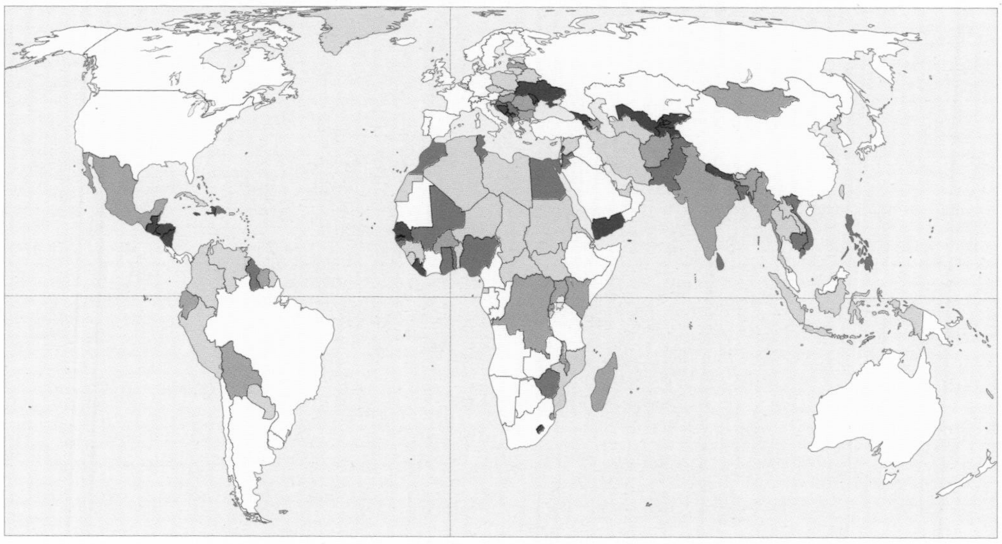

For more information:
94 Armed conflicts
Global Peace Index
95 International organizations
107 UN Sustainable Development Goals

Almost 80 million people are reported as being forcibly displaced by the United Nations Refugee Agency (UNHCR). Distressingly, 40% of this number are children below the age of 18. Within the world's forcibly displaced, 26 million are classified as refugees – a refugee is someone who has been forced to flee their own country, as to remain there would be unsafe. Some 68% of all refugees originate from just five countries – Syria, Venezuela, Afghanistan, South Sudan, and Myanmar. Most refugees stay in developing countries rather than richer countries. Developing countries host 85% of the world's refugees with the Least Developed Countries providing asylum to 27% of the total. Exceeding the refugee population, 46 million are classified as internally displaced people – those who remain within their own national borders but have had to leave their own homes due to conflict and violence. Although often referred to as refugees they do not conform to that legal definition. Exact numbers can be hard to establish, but it is estimated that between 70 and 80% of internally displaced people are women and children.

A number of themes related to refugees and forced displacement are explored here. In conclusion there is a summary of the situation regarding the return and resettlement of refugees.

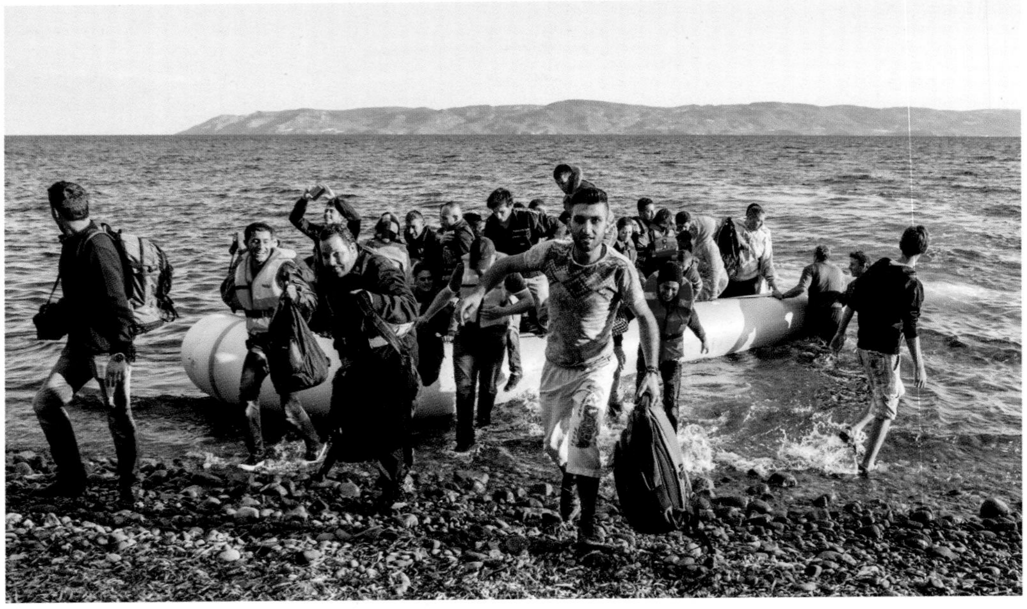

▲ Over-crowded and unsafe, small inflatable vessels such as this one have been a frequent sight in the Mediterranean in recent years bringing people from Asia to Europe. In this case it is refugees from Syria crossing from Turkey to the Greek island of Lesbos. Often, instead of finding freedom in Europe, such people are sent to detention camps to await processing of asylum claims. Economic migrants will also travel on the same routes, often exploited by those who arrange their passage.

REFUGEES

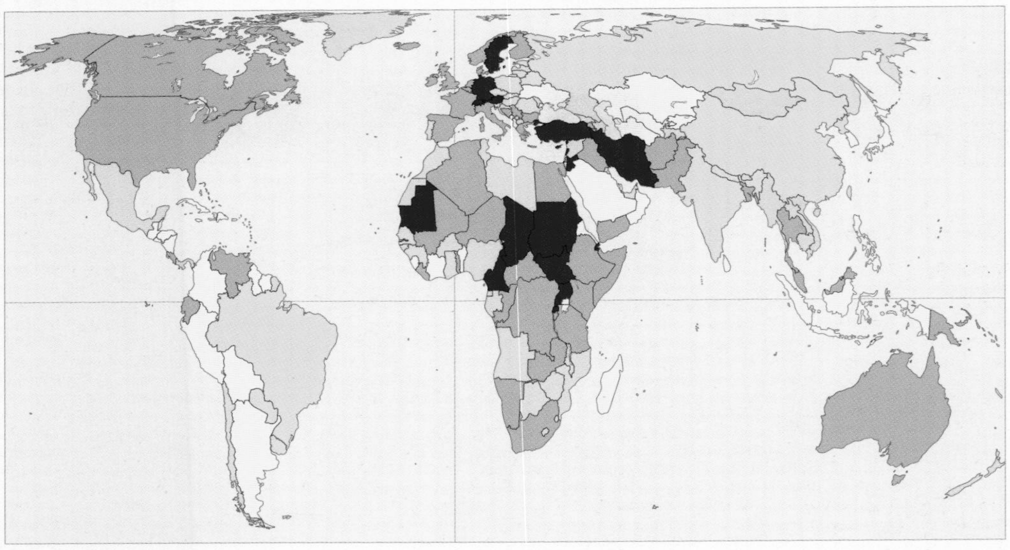

Total refugees* as a percentage of the population (2019)

- Over 1%
- 0.10 – 1%
- 0.01 – 0.10%
- Under 0.01%
- No data available

*includes people in a refugee-like situation

1. Lebanon 16.9%
2. Nauru 10.8%
3. Jordan 6.4%
4. Turkey 4.3%
5. Uganda 3.1%
6. South Sudan 2.8%
7. Chad 2.7%
8. Sweden 2.5%
9. Sudan 2.3%
10. Mauritania 2.2%

FORCED DISPLACEMENT

The number of people who have been forcibly displaced has risen in recent years to around one per cent of the world's total population. The chart here depicts this growth and the breakdown of the groups within those classified as "displaced" by the UN Refugee Agency (UNHCR). Some of the events which have led to this growth include the Syrian conflict, the arrival of refugees and migrants to Europe, war and security concerns (Afghanistan, Iraq, Libya, and Somalia), and recently the displacement of a large number of Venezuelans across Latin America and the Caribbean region.

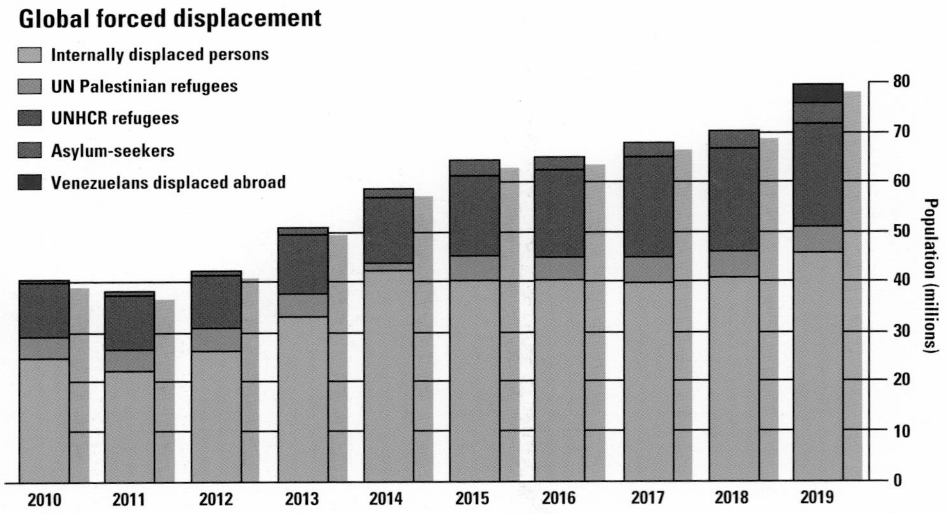

◄ Giving the appearance of a permanent settlement, this is the world's biggest refugee camp. Located near Cox's Bazar in Bangladesh, the Kutupalong camp houses more than 800,000 Rohingya people who were forced to flee their homes in Myanmar. Other large camps include Kakuma in Kenya, with 150,00 refugees mainly from South Sudan and Somalia; Dadaab (also in Kenya) with people mainly from Somalia; Za'atari in Jordan with refugees from Syria; and Um Rakuba in Sudan, looking after people fleeing violence in the Tigray region of Ethiopia.

ORIGIN AND DESTINATION OF REFUGEES

Syrians remain, by far, the largest nationality seeking asylum in another country. Asylum applications from Venezuelan refugees have grown rapidly in the past few years. The only European country to appear in the top ten of destination countries for refugees is Germany.

The map (right) shows the location of the countries that had the largest total numbers of refugees and those countries that were the origin of the largest volume of refugees in 2020. The figures are reflected in the bar charts below. The pie chart gives the breakdown of the refugee population by UN region.

Although accurate demographic data is difficult to gather, estimates are invaluable in assessing the effect, and needs, of refugee populations in the host countries. The UNHCR have used best estimates to produce the diagrams below right which show that the majority of displaced persons are of working age, and with the exception of Palestinian refugees, the balance is in favor of males over females.

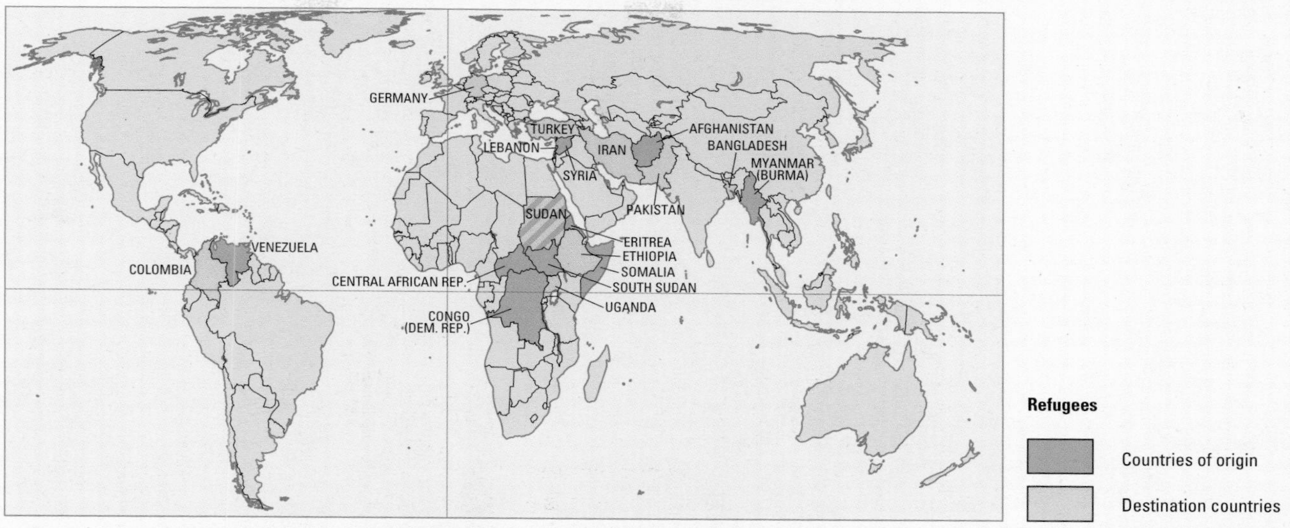

Refugee population by region (2020)

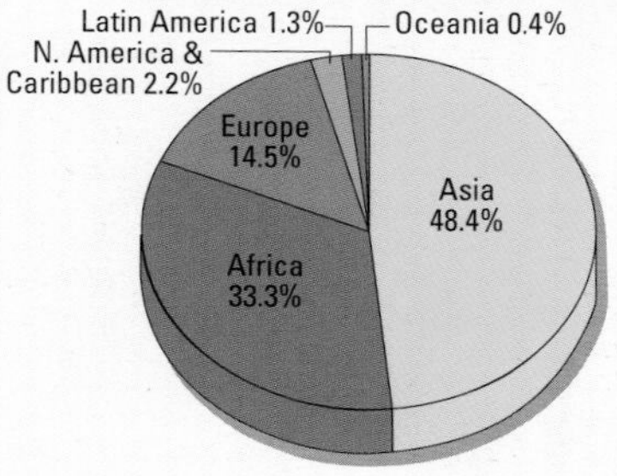

Sex and age structure of forcibly displaced populations

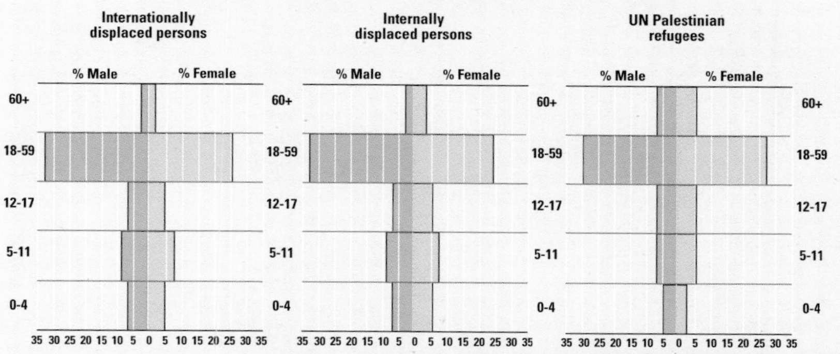

REFUGEES Total refugees and people in a refugee-like situation, in millions (2020)

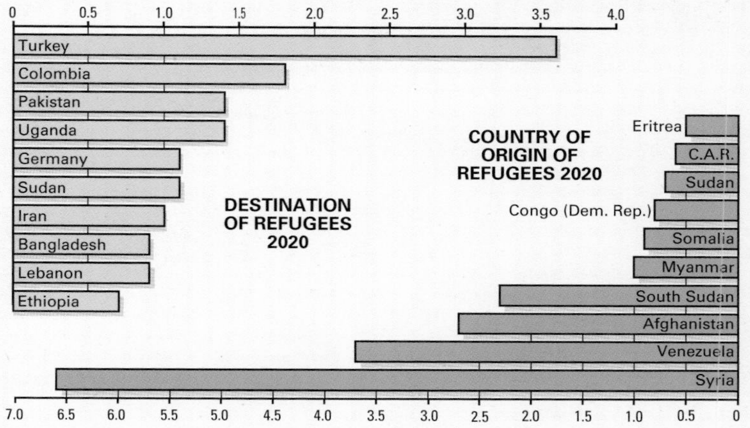

▼ Children walk to school wearing their blue backpacks with the UNICEF logo clearly visible. This is Kakuma refugee camp in Kenya, one of the world's largest. Over half a million refugees from more than 30 countries lived in Kenya in 2020. The camp at Kakuma was established in 1992 to host unaccompanied minors, mainly from Sudan. The perception amongst parts of the local community that camp residents have access to better facilities, thanks to aid agencies, has led to tensions.

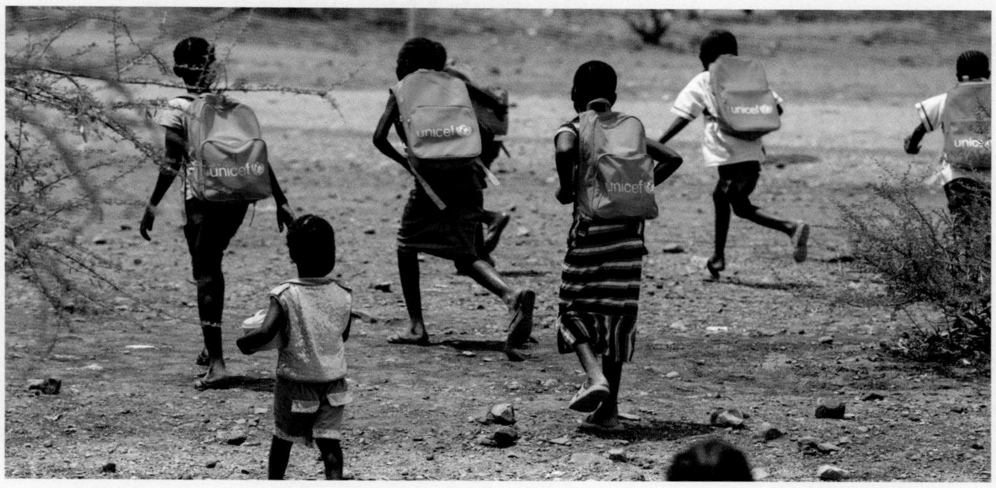

RETURN AND RESETTLEMENT

REFUGEE RETURNS (2010–2019)

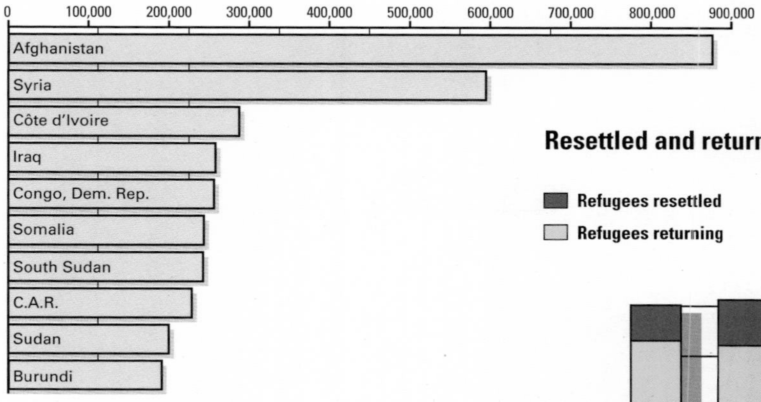

Resettled and returning refugees (2010 – 2019)

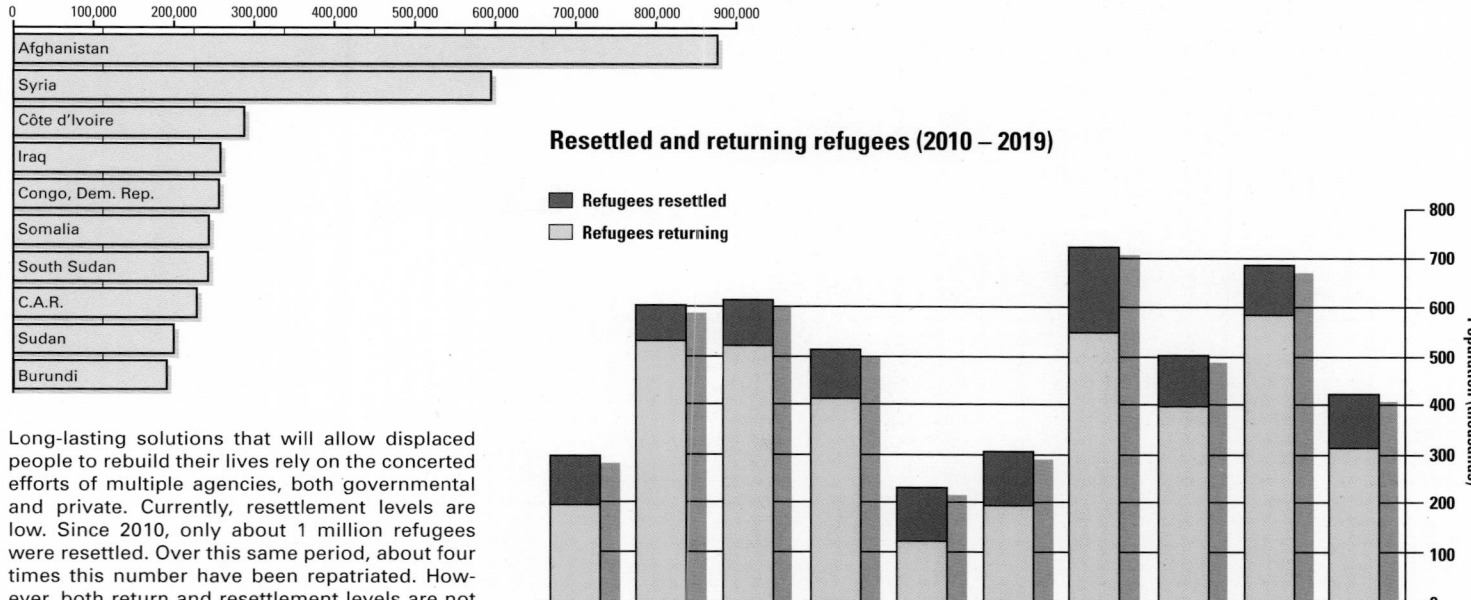

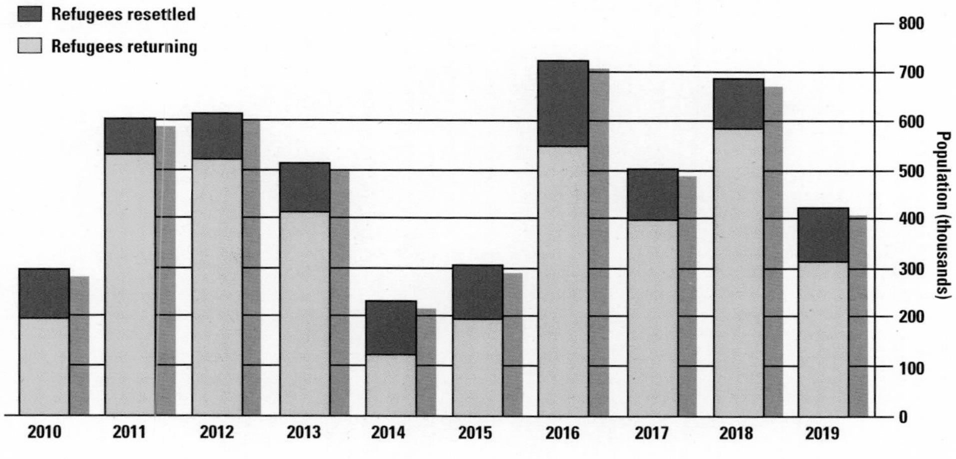

Long-lasting solutions that will allow displaced people to rebuild their lives rely on the concerted efforts of multiple agencies, both governmental and private. Currently, resettlement levels are low. Since 2010, only about 1 million refugees were resettled. Over this same period, about four times this number have been repatriated. However, both return and resettlement levels are not improving.

Nepal and Tibet are home to the spectacular Himalayan mountain range, the location of many of the world's highest mountains, including the highest of them all, Everest, which rises to 29,032 ft (8,849 m) above sea level. The Himalayas formed as a result of a collision between the Indian and Eurasian tectonic plates, which began 50 million years ago and continues to this day. The ongoing movement means that the Himalayas and the wider Tibetan Plateau continue to rise, although countered by weather and erosion. Glaciers snake around the high peaks and appear on this image as branching shapes that resemble plant roots. To find Everest, follow the line of the large glacier down from the top, just right of center, toward a dark triangle; Everest is at the bottom of the triangle. First climbed in 1953, Everest has since been conquered by thousands of climbers, despite the often deadly hazards of high winds, avalanches, and lack of oxygen.
[Map page 243] *CGG Satellite Mapping*

IMAGES OF EARTH

16 HELSINKI, FINLAND

Finland's capital and largest city, Helsinki lies on the northern shore of the Gulf of Finland. The coastline of this easternmost arm of the Baltic Sea is characterized by small bays and rocky islands, as can be seen in this image. Helsinki city center is in the lower middle of the photograph, just east of a bay crossed by several bridges. It is possible to make out a small white oval just above a lake in the city center. This is the Olympic Stadium. Built in functionalist style in the late 1930s, it was intended for the 1940 Olympic Games. Postponed because of World War II, the Games were finally held in Helsinki in 1952. Southwest of the stadium is the renowned Temppeliaukio church, which was excavated from solid rock, with only its copper-covered domed roof visible above ground. The 18th-century sea fortress Suomelinna lies on a cluster of islands southeast of the city. [Map page 121] *CGG Satellite Mapping*

The city of Brussels is visible as a roughly circular area in the middle of the image. It has an historic center, which radiates from the well-preserved Grand Place, and is home to many of the European Union's institutions. The large, forested region below center, right, is the Sonian Forest, known since the Middle Ages and prized for its beech and oak trees. The forest was the location of the Battle of Waterloo, in 1815. This battle marked the end of 23 years of intermittent warfare between France and the other powers of Europe, when the Duke of Wellington's troops, together with those of the Prussian army, defeated Napoleon Bonaparte. The actual battle site is now a little way outside the forest, toward the lower center of the image. The prominent white patch, bottom left, is a porphyry quarry. This hard, durable rock was traditionally used for making cobblestones.
[Map page 116] *CGG Satellite Mapping*

18 LISBON, PORTUGAL

Lisbon lies on the north bank of the Tagus estuary, where the river empties into the Atlantic Ocean after its c.600-mile (1,000-km) journey from the Sierra de Albarracín mountains in eastern Spain. The old city center, with its orange-roofed houses climbing up from the waterfront, lies between the two bridges that are just visible in the image. Behind Lisbon, to the north and west, are the Sintra mountains; the greenness of their vegetation can clearly be seen in contrast to the urban areas. On the far left of the image, the upper of the two promontories is the Cabo da Roca – the westernmost point in continental Europe. Lisbon's location made it a natural center for the European voyages of discovery in the 15th century. It was from here that the explorer and navigator Vasco da Gama set off in 1497 on his famous voyage around the Cape of Good Hope to India.

[Map page 195] *CGG Satellite Mapping*

The Dead Sea is a salt lake in the Jordan Rift Valley, fed from the north by the River Jordan, whose muddy waters can just be seen entering the lake near the top of this image. The Dead Sea's water level is the lowest point on the Earth's land surface. The lake is famous for its high salt content, which makes the water dense enough to support bathers. Photographs of tourists floating on the surface while reading newspapers are a familiar sight. Over the last 50 years or so, the water level has fallen dramatically as the amount of water entering from the River Jordan has decreased, mainly due to dams upstream. The lower water level has caused the Dead Sea to split in two. As can clearly be seen in the image, the shallower southern portion has been divided into evaporation pools for the extraction of salt.

[Map page 251] *CGG Satellite Mapping*

20 BAGHDAD, IRAQ

The Abbasid caliph al-Mansur founded Baghdad in 762. He built an imposing round city, which soon became a world-renowned center of Islamic civilization. Baghdad declined in importance from the 13th century, only regaining prominence in 1932 as capital of the newly independent Iraq. Baghdad is one of the most populous cities of the Middle East. It lies on both banks of the RiverTigris, with the older parts of the city on the west bank. The Tigris can clearly be seen flowing from the north and looping its way through the city until it is joined by the smaller Diyala River in the southeast. Just visible in this image is the Al-Shaheed Monument, which commemorates the soldiers who died in the Iran–Iraq War of the 1980s. Its giant bisected dome, covered in turquoise tiles, is the small bright circle on a patch of green – an artificial lake – in the east of the city.
[Map page 113] *CGG Satellite Mapping*

One of the world's most populous cities, Karachi is Pakistan's industrial and commercial center and its main seaport. It lies on the Arabian Sea, just west of the Indus River delta, on a large coastal plain. The mangrove forests of the delta region are visible lower right in the image, their green color contrasting with Karachi's main industrial region to its north, and the densely populated city above. Karachi was a small fishing village in the early 18th century, but it grew rapidly under British control in the 19th century thanks to its sheltered natural harbor, clearly visible lower left. The harbor is protected from monsoon winds by a sandspit that connects the mainland to Manora Point. Pakistan's largest airport – the Jinnah International Airport – can be seen below center right, and a short distance west from there is a small white oval, the National Stadium, site of many international cricket matches.

[Map page 123] *CGG Satellite Mapping*

22 GUANGZHOU, CHINA

Guangzhou, the capital of Guangdong province in southern China, is part of a vast urban area which more than fills this image. The rivers that are clearly visible flowing eastward through Guangzhou are heading toward the South China Sea, passing Hong Kong, which lies only about 80 miles (130 km) to the south. Guangzhou's location makes it easily accessible from the sea and inland, and it has long been a center for commerce, culture, and politics. It was the first Chinese city known to have been visited by European traders. Two branches of Zhu Jiang (or Pearl River) form a roughly oval shape just below the center of the image, and the city's central districts, and oldest areas, lie above the northern branch. Stretching away to the northeast are the forests and mountains of the Tianlu Forest Park, and, closest to the city's center, lies the Baiyun (White Cloud) Mountain. [Map page 121] *CGG Satellite Mapping*

Shanghai is the most populous city in China, and one of the most populous cities in the world. Already an important commercial center, it grew rapidly with the economic reforms of the 1990s to become an international hub for trade and finance, and one of the world's busiest container ports. It also has a rich cultural history, and its blend of old and new draws tourists from around the world. The Yangtse River flows across the top of the image, joining the Yellow Sea just to the east. The Huangpu winds through the city, dividing the historic center to the left from the ultra-modern Pudong Area on the right bank. Part of Changxing Island can be seen at the top of the image, a green contrast to the built-up city. Hongqiao – one of Shanghai's two international airports – is clearly visible at the bottom left.

[Map page 138] *CGG Satellite Mapping*

24 MOUNT FUJI, JAPAN

Mount Fuji is one of the world's most recognisable sights – a perfectly conical volcano, with a snow-capped peak, and verdant green slopes. It is Japan's highest mountain, reaching 12,388 ft (3,776 m) above sea level, and with a central crater that is about 1,600 ft (500 m) in diameter. Although it hasn't erupted since 1707, Mount Fuji is still considered to be an active volcano. Lava flows from early eruptions are responsible for the lakes that can be seen at intervals around the northern base of the mountain. The largest lake is Kawaguchiko, closest to the top of the image; to the lower right is Lake Ashinoko, which is part of the Fuji-Hakone-Izu National Park, famous for its hot springs. To Japanese people, Mount Fuji is considered sacred and to climb it is a religious experience, as witnessed by the many shrines and temples on its slopes.
[Map page 223] *CGG Satellite Mapping*

The striking feature in this image is the large natural harbor of Manila Bay, which lies on the southeast coast of Luzon, the largest island in the Philippines. Sheltering the harbor to the east is the rocky Bataan Peninsula with Mount Mariveles at its southern end. This large dormant volcano, visible lower left, marks the southern tip of the Zambales mountain range. The Bataan Peninsula and Corregidor Island, at the entrance to the bay, saw fierce battles between Japanese and US troops during World War II. A large urban area sprawls along the eastern coast of the bay. Manila, the capital of the Philippines, lies at the center of this conglomeration of cities, with the larger Quezon City to its north. The Pampanga River flows into Manila Bay from the northwest; its large swampy delta contrasts with the deeper blue waters of the bay.

[Map page 127] *CGG Satellite Mapping*

 TENERIFE, CANARY ISLANDS

The largest of Spain's Canary Islands, Tenerife lies in the Atlantic Ocean off northwest Africa. Its striking volcanic landscape together with its beaches and pleasant climate have made it a popular tourist destination, particularly for European visitors. The south central part of the island has been a National Park since 1954 and has the large Caldera de las Canadas crater at its heart. The summit of Mount Teide, Spain's highest peak, can be glimpsed in the image as a small white dot, its color coming from the dust deposited by sulfurous fumes. Tenerife's oldest city, San Cristobal de la Laguna, lies in the east of the island. It was founded in the late 15th century and contains many buildings of historical significance, reflecting its past as a center of cultural, artistic, and religious significance.
[Map page 153] *CGG Satellite Mapping*

Kampala lies on the northern shores of Lake Victoria, which occupies a shallow depression in a plateau that stretches between two branches of the Great Rift Valley. It is by the far the largest lake in Africa and is shared between Uganda, Tanzania, and Kenya. The lake's characteristically indented shoreline can be seen in this image, as can some of the rivers that wind sluggishly downhill toward the lake. Kampala is one of Africa's fastest growing cities, with a population that has more than doubled since the beginning of the century. It was originally built on seven hills but has since expanded over many more. It became the capital of Uganda in 1963 after the country gained independence from the United Kingdom. Kampala had long been an important settlement, however, serving as the center of power for the former kingdom of Buganda.
[Map page 268] *CGG Satellite Mapping*

28 PERTH, AUSTRALIA

Perth lies on the Indian Ocean in southwestern Australia. It is one of the world's most remote cities, with the ocean to the west and the deserts that make up the vast Australian outback to the east. It serves as the state capital of Western Australia. The two islands visible in this image are Rottnest Island and Garden Island. Rottnest, further offshore, is a nature reserve, popular for its sandy beaches, sheltered coves, salt lakes, and wildlife, including the quokka, a small marsupial famous for being appealingly photogenic. Perth was founded in 1829, on the estuary of the Swan River, when the British expanded their settlement in the region. After the discovery of gold, it grew rapidly – the population of Western Australia as a whole more than trebled between 1890 and 1900. These days, the Swan River is well known for its vineyards, which line the banks upstream from Perth.
[Map page 279] *CGG Satellite Mapping*

Toronto lies on the shores of Lake Ontario, one of the five Great Lakes of North America. It is Canada's most populous city, although not its capital, which is Ottawa, roughly 220 miles (350 km) to the northeast. Toronto's most famous landmark is the CN Tower, which lies slightly inland from the Harbour Front. It was built by the Canada National Railways and opened in 1976. With a height of 1,815 ft (553 m), it provides wonderful views over the surrounding area, sometimes as far as Niagara Falls. Toronto Island lies just offshore. It is actually a chain of 15 small interconnected islands, which, as can be seen in this image, shelter Toronto Harbour. Ferries travel to the islands and they are a popular spot for swimming and water sports. In the west of the image, below center, the five runways of Toronto's International Airport can just be made out.

[Map page 141] *CGG Satellite Mapping*

30 ORLANDO, USA

The city of Orlando in Florida is a popular tourist destination, best known for its many theme parks. Below center in the southwestern corner of the image is the most famous of them all, Disney World, which opened in 1971. Its success was a major contributing factor in Orlando's economic growth and increase in population over the following decades. Other theme parks soon followed, and Orlando is now one of the leading tourist centers in the world. Its large international airport can be seen on the right of the image, below center. The terrain of Orlando and the surrounding area is generally low and wet, and the city itself is dotted with numerous lakes and swamps, most of which are home to alligators. Top left is the southeastern corner of Orlando's largest lake, Apopka. Bottom right is the circular East Lake Tohopekaliga.
[Map page 133] *CGG Satellite Mapping*

The historic city of La Paz and its younger neighbor, El Alto, are in the center of this image. La Paz, Bolivia's seat of government and de facto capital, is right of center in a deep bowl-shaped canyon, with the snowcapped peaks of the Andes looming over it from the east. El Alto – and the airport that is visible in the image – lies immediately to the west of La Paz on the flatter land of the high Altiplano. This dry plateau region contrasts with the mountainous landscape seen to the north and east. The cities are home to one of the world's largest, urban cable-car networks. Opened in 2014, it is not only a practical form of public transport for La Paz's steep and overcrowded streets, it also connects the two city centers despite a difference in altitude of more than 1,300 ft (400 m). [Map page 330] *CGG Satellite Mapping*

GAZETTEER OF NATIONS

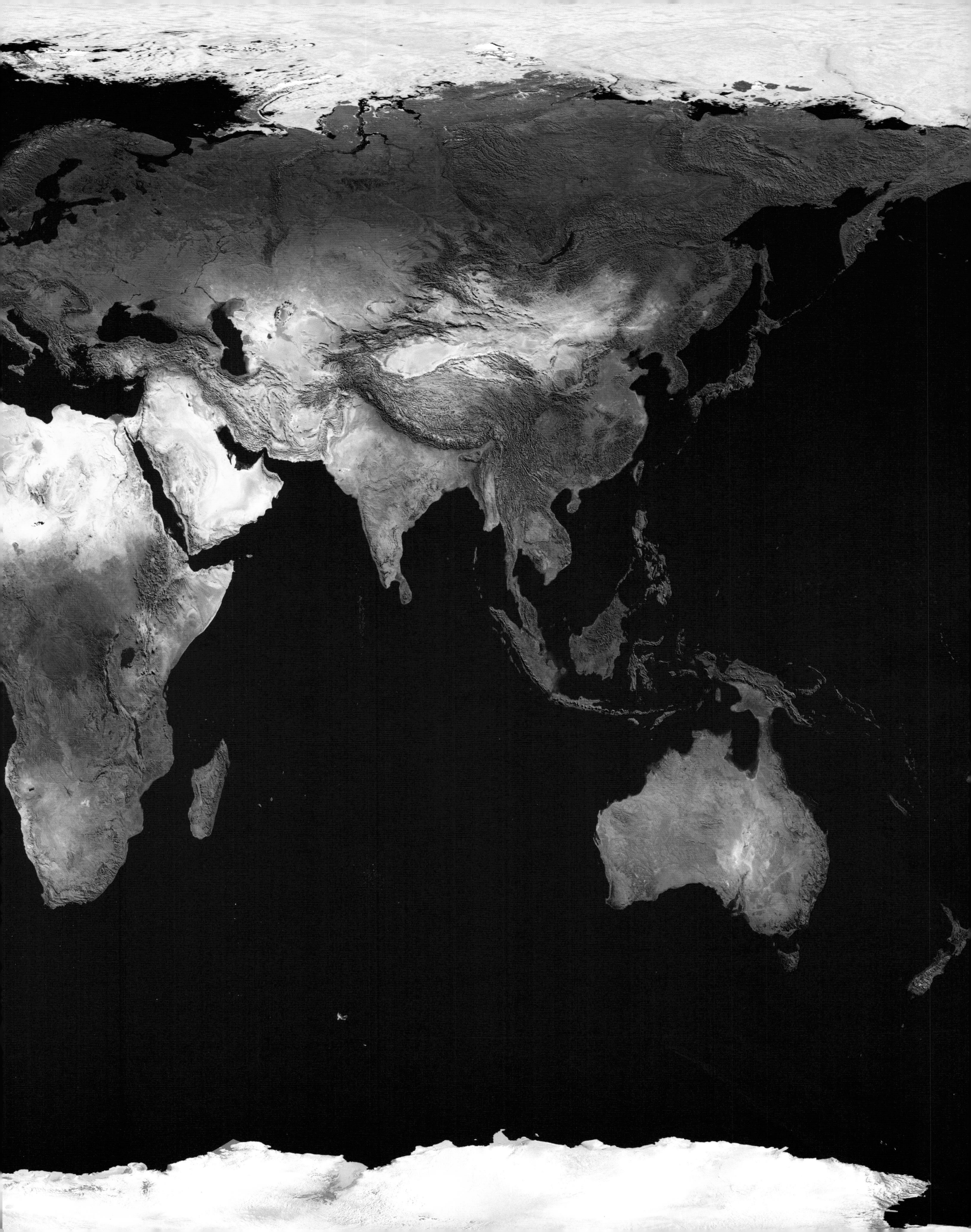

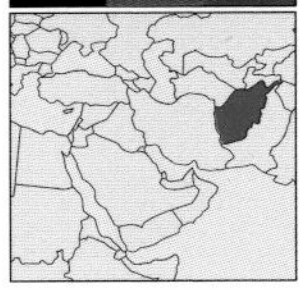

AFGHANISTAN

GEOGRAPHY The Republic of Afghanistan is a landlocked, mountainous country in southern Asia. The central highlands reach a height of more than 22,966 ft [7,000 m] in the east. The main range is the Hindu Kush. In winter, northerly winds bring cold, snowy weather to the mountains, but summers are hot and dry.

POLITICS & ECONOMY The modern history of Afghanistan began in 1747, with the unification of local tribes. In the 19th century, Russia and Britain struggled for control of the country. Following Britain's withdrawal in 1919, Afghanistan became fully independent. Soviet troops invaded in 1979 to support a socialist regime in Kabul, but they withdrew in 1989. By 2001, a group called the Taliban ("Islamic students") controlled 90% of the country. In 2001 an international force invaded Afghanistan, following the September 11 attacks on the US, and ousted the Taliban government. It regrouped as an insurgency force and became a deadly threat. In 2014 the NATO-led military force handed control to the Afghan security forces, although NATO troops remained. Presidential elections that year saw Ashraf Ghani elected, with his former rival Abdullah Abdullah as chief executive officer. The Taliban insurgency continued to grow, seizing control of more of the country, and the Islamic State emerged as a threat in the east. US and NATO troops are due to be withdrawn in 2021 after an agreement signed by the US and the Taliban in 2020.

Years of violent unrest and political instability, exacerbated by corruption associated with the illegal production of opium, have devastated the country's economy and infrastructure.

AREA 251,772 SQ MI [652,090 SQ KM] **POPULATION** 37,466,000
CAPITAL KABUL **GOVERNMENT** ISLAMIC REPUBLIC
ETHNIC GROUPS PASHTUN (PATHAN) 42%, TAJIK 27%, HAZARA 9%, UZBEK 9%, OTHERS 13%
LANGUAGES PASHTU, DARI/PERSIAN (BOTH OFFICIAL), UZBEK
RELIGIONS ISLAM (SUNNI MUSLIM 80%, SHI'ITE MUSLIM 19%), OTHERS 1%
CURRENCY AFGHANI = 100 PULS

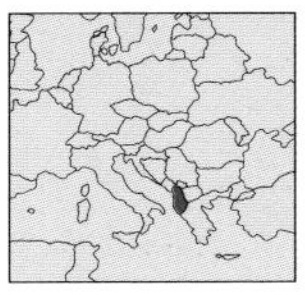

ALBANIA

GEOGRAPHY The Republic of Albania lies in the Balkan peninsula, facing the Adriatic Sea. About 70% of the land is mountainous, with most Albanians living on the western coastal lowlands. The coastal areas of Albania experience a typical Mediterranean climate, with fairly dry, sunny summers and cool, moist winters. The mountains have a severe climate, with heavy winter snowfalls.

POLITICS & ECONOMY Albania is one of Europe's poorest nations. A former Communist country, ruled for nearly 50 years by the Stalinist dictator Enver Hoxha, Albania adopted a multiparty system in the early 1990s. The transition to democracy has been hindered by poor infrastructure and widespread corruption. A center-right government was defeated in 2013 by a Socialist-led coalition, which has pledged to fight organised crime and crack down on the trafficking and production of illegal drugs.

Albania has been a member of NATO since 2009 and was granted EU candidate status in 2014. Agriculture employs more than 40% of the people. Albania has some oil, gas, and minerals; exports include footwear, chromite, copper, and nickel.

AREA 11,100 SQ MI [28,748 SQ KM] **POPULATION** 3,088,000
CAPITAL TIRANA **GOVERNMENT** MULTIPARTY REPUBLIC
ETHNIC GROUPS ALBANIAN 83%, GREEK 1%, MACEDONIAN, VLACH, ROMA
LANGUAGES ALBANIAN (OFFICIAL)
RELIGIONS ISLAM 57%, CHRISTIANITY 17% (ROMAN CATHOLIC 10%, ORTHODOX 7%)
CURRENCY LEK = 100 QINDARS

ALGERIA

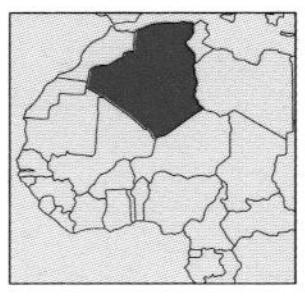

GEOGRAPHY The People's Democratic Republic of Algeria is Africa's largest country. Most Algerians live in the north, on the fertile coastal plains and hill country bordering the Mediterranean Sea. Four-fifths of Algeria is in the Sahara, the world's largest desert. The coast has a Mediterranean climate but the arid Sahara is hot by day and cold at night.

POLITICS & ECONOMY France ruled Algeria from 1830 until 1962, when the socialist FLN (National Liberation Front) formed a one-party government. Following the recognition of opposition parties in 1989, a Muslim group, the FIS (Islamic Salvation Front), won an election in 1991. The FLN canceled the elections and civil conflict broke out. About 100,000 people were killed in the 1990s. Abdelaziz Bouteflika served as president from 1999 to 2019, only standing down after widespread protests at his decision to run again. He was succeeded as president by his associate Abdelmadjid Tebboune.

Algeria's chief resources are oil and natural gas, which account for about 95% of export revenue. Its gas reserves are the largest in Africa. The challenge for the future is to diversify the economy. Cement, iron and steel, textiles, and vehicles are manufactured.

AREA 919,590 SQ MI [2,381,741 SQ KM] **POPULATION** 43,577,000
CAPITAL ALGIERS **GOVERNMENT** SOCIALIST REPUBLIC
ETHNIC GROUPS ARAB-BERBER 99%
LANGUAGES ARABIC AND BERBER (OFFICIAL), FRENCH **RELIGIONS** SUNNI MUSLIM 99% **CURRENCY** ALGERIAN DINAR = 100 SANTEEM

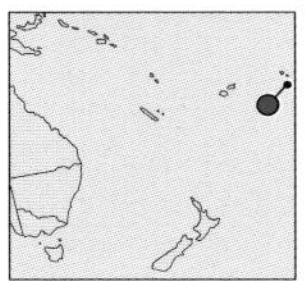

AMERICAN SAMOA

An "unincorporated territory" of the United States, American Samoa lies in the south-central Pacific Ocean.

AREA 77 SQ MI [199 SQ KM]
POPULATION 46,000 **CAPITAL** PAGO PAGO

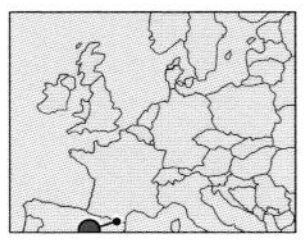

ANDORRA

In this prosperous mini-state, situated in the Pyrenees Mountains, tourism (especially winter sports) accounts for almost 80% of GDP. Most Andorrans live in the six valleys (the Valls) that drain into the River Valira.

AREA 181 SQ MI [468 SQ KM]
POPULATION 86,000 **CAPITAL** ANDORRA LA VELLA

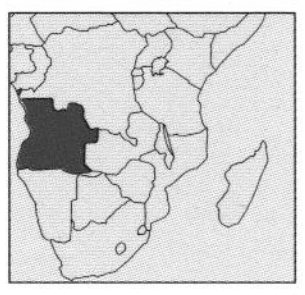

ANGOLA

GEOGRAPHY Situated in southwestern Africa, the Republic of Angola is the seventh largest country on the continent. Much of Angola lies on the South African plateau, with only a narrow coastal plain in the west.

Angola has a tropical climate, with temperatures of over 68°F [20°C] throughout the year, though the highest areas are cooler. The coast is dry, but the rainfall increases to the north and east.

POLITICS & ECONOMY Portugal controlled the coastal slave trade from the 17th century and extended its control inland in the 19th century. Independence, gained in 1975, was followed by 27 years of civil war which only finally ended when the rebel leader, Jonas Savimbi, was killed in 2002. Elections in 2008 began a transition toward a more democratic system. In 2017, after 38 years in power, Jose Eduardo dos Santos stood down as president and was replaced by former defence minister, Joao Lourenco. There is ongoing conflict with separatists in Cabinda.

Angola is a developing country, where 85% of the people are poor farmers. The main food crops are cassava and maize with coffee being exported. Angola's economy is heavily dependent on oil, with large reserves off the coast of Cabinda. Angola also mines diamonds and has reserves of copper and phosphates.

AREA 481,351 SQ MI [1,246,700 SQ KM] **POPULATION** 33,643,000
CAPITAL LUANDA **GOVERNMENT** MULTIPARTY REPUBLIC
ETHNIC GROUPS OVIMBUNDU 37%, KIMBUNDU 25%, BAKONGO 13%, OTHERS 25%
LANGUAGES PORTUGUESE (OFFICIAL), MANY OTHERS
RELIGIONS ROMAN CATHOLIC 41%, PROTESTANT 38%, OTHERS 9%, NONE 12%
CURRENCY KWANZA = 100 CÊNTIMOS

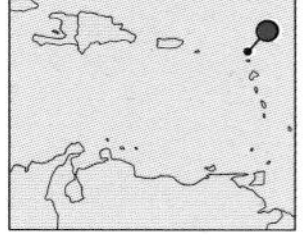

ANGUILLA

Formerly part of St Kitts and Nevis, Anguilla, the most northerly of the Leeward Islands, became a British dependency (now a British overseas territory) in 1980. The main sources of revenue are tourism and offshore banking, with lobster accounting for half of exports.

AREA 37 SQ MI [96 SQ KM]
POPULATION 18,000 **CAPITAL** THE VALLEY

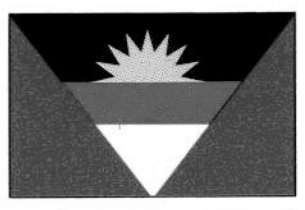
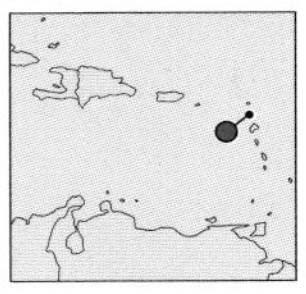

ANTIGUA & BARBUDA

This former British dependency became independent in 1981. Tourism and offshore banking are vital to its service-based economy. In 2017 Hurricane Irma devastated Barbuda.

AREA 171 SQ MI [442 SQ KM]
POPULATION 99,000 **CAPITAL** ST JOHN'S

ARGENTINA

GEOGRAPHY The Argentine Republic is South America's second largest and the world's eighth largest country. In the west, the high Andes range contains Mount Aconcagua, the highest peak in the Americas. In southern Argentina, the Andes Mountains overlook Patagonia, a plateau region. The fertile plain of the Pampas occupies the east-central area.

The climate varies from subtropical in the north to temperate in the south. Rainfall is abundant in the northeast but lower to the west and south. Patagonia is largely desert.

POLITICS & ECONOMY The earliest people were American Indians, but 86% of the people are now of European ancestry. After Spanish rule ended in 1816, Argentina experienced periods of regional instability and military rule. In 1982, Argentina's military regime invaded the Falkland (Malvinas) Islands, but Britain regained the islands later that year. In 1983 civilian rule was restored.

In 1991, Argentina was a founding member of the South American trade bloc Mercosur, but it has suffered from recurring economic crises. Government policies in response to an economic, social, and political crisis in 2001 barely allowed fitful recovery, and the country defaulted on repayment of its international debt in 2002 and 2014. Despite major market reforms following the election of Conservative Mauricio Macri in 2015, the World Bank downgraded Argentina's economy to "upper-middle-income" in 2019. In presidential elections that year, Macri was defeated by the center-left Peronist candidate Alberto Fernandez. Manufactures include food products, cars, and textiles. Oil is the main resource and the chief farm products are beef, soybeans, maize, and wheat. Exports include oil, meat, soybeans, wheat, and maize.

AREA 1,073,512 SQ MI [2,780,400 SQ KM] **POPULATION** 45,865,000
CAPITAL BUENOS AIRES **GOVERNMENT** FEDERAL REPUBLIC
ETHNIC GROUPS EUROPEAN 97%, MESTIZO, AMERINDIAN
LANGUAGES SPANISH (OFFICIAL)
RELIGIONS ROMAN CATHOLIC 92%, PROTESTANT 2%, JEWISH 2%, OTHERS
CURRENCY ARGENTINE PESO = 100 CENTAVOS

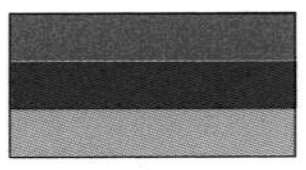
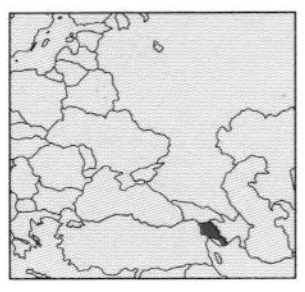

ARMENIA

GEOGRAPHY The Republic of Armenia is a landlocked country in southwestern Asia. Most of Armenia consists of a rugged plateau, crisscrossed by long faultlines which make the area prone to earthquakes. The highest point is Mount Aragats, at 13,419 ft [4,090 m] above sea level. The height of the land gives rise to severe winters and cool summers. The highest peaks are snow-capped, but the total yearly rainfall is generally low.

POLITICS & ECONOMY In 1920, Armenia became a Communist republic and, in 1922, it became, with Azerbaijan and Georgia, part of the Transcaucasian Republic within the Soviet Union. The three territories became separate Soviet Socialist Republics in 1936. After the breakup of the Soviet Union in 1991, Armenia became an independent republic. The ongoing dispute over Nagorno-Karabakh, an area enclosed by Azerbaijan where most people are Armenians, has caused conflict and instability which has hampered economic development. Protests in 2018 led to the appointment of Nikol Pashinyan of the My Step Alliance as prime minister. His rule was challenged in 2020 after he agreed to a ceasefire with Azerbaijan despite their gains in Nagorno-Karabakh.

Armenia's economy has suffered because of its former dependency on a centrally planned Soviet system. In 2015, the country joined the Russian-led Eurasian Customs Union, and in 2017 it signed a Comprehensive and Enhanced Partnership Agreement (CEPA) with the EU.

AREA 11,506 SQ MI [29,800 SQ KM] **POPULATION** 3,012,000
CAPITAL YEREVAN **GOVERNMENT** MULTIPARTY REPUBLIC
ETHNIC GROUPS ARMENIAN 98%, YEZIDI 1%
LANGUAGES ARMENIAN (OFFICIAL)
RELIGIONS ARMENIAN APOSTOLIC 95%
CURRENCY DRAM = 100 LUMA

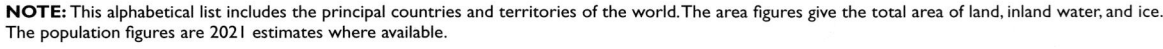

NOTE: This alphabetical list includes the principal countries and territories of the world. The area figures give the total area of land, inland water, and ice. The population figures are 2021 estimates where available.

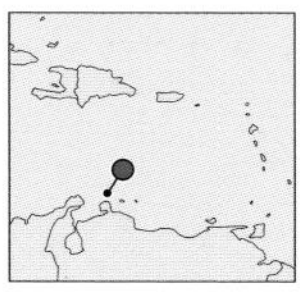

ARUBA

Formerly part of the Netherlands Antilles, Aruba (the most westerly of the Lesser Antilles) became a separate self-governing Dutch territory in 1986.

AREA 75 sq mi [193 sq km]
POPULATION 121,000 **CAPITAL** Oranjestad

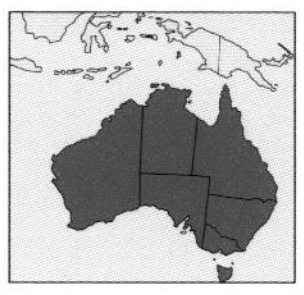

AUSTRALIA

GEOGRAPHY The Commonwealth of Australia, the world's sixth largest country, is also a continent. Australia is the flattest of the continents with its main highlands lying in the east. Here the Great Dividing Range separates the eastern coastal plains from the Central Plains. This range extends from Cape York Peninsula to Victoria in the far south. The longest rivers, the Murray and Darling, drain the southeastern part of the Central Plains. The Western Plateau makes up two-thirds of Australia. A few mountain ranges break the monotony of the generally flat landscape. Only 10% of Australia, notably the tropical north, the northeast coast and the southeast, has an average annual rainfall of more than 39 inches [1,000 mm]. Extreme weather events, including a prolonged drought in the Murray–Darling basin in the early 21st century and severe flooding in Queensland in 2010–12, cause periodic problems. Record-breaking temperatures in 2019 to 2020 led to devastating bush fires in southeast Australia.

POLITICS & ECONOMY The Aboriginal people of Australia entered the continent from Southeast Asia more than 50,000 years ago. The first European explorers were Dutch in the 17th century, but they did not settle. In 1770, the British Captain Cook explored the east coast and, in 1788, the first British settlement was established for convicts on the site of what is now Sydney. Whilst maintaining links with the British Isles, the last 50 years have seen people from other parts of Europe and, most recently, from Asia settling in the country. Ties with Britain were also weakened by Britain's membership of the European Union, and Australia has now forged stronger links with the nations of eastern Asia, especially China, Indonesia, and Japan. The issue of retaining the monarch of the UK as the head of state is a recurring theme but, in a referendum in 1999, the majority of Australians voted to remain a constitutional monarchy. The conservative Liberal–National coalition swept into power in 2013, ending six years of Labor Party rule.

Australia is a prosperous country. Crops can be grown on only 6% of the land, with dry pasture covering another 58%. Yet the country remains a major producer and exporter of farm products, particularly cattle, wheat, and wool. Grapes grown for wine-making are also important. The country is rich in a wide range of minerals, and Australia also produces oil and natural gas. Metals, minerals and farm products account for the bulk of exports. Australia's imports are mostly manufactured goods, though its own manufacturing industry is growing. The service sector contributes over 70% of total GDP.

AREA 2,988,885 sq mi [7,741,220 sq km] **POPULATION** 25,810,000
CAPITAL Canberra **GOVERNMENT** Federal constitutional monarchy
ETHNIC GROUPS Caucasian 92%, Asian 7%, Aboriginal 1%
LANGUAGES English (official) **RELIGIONS** Non-Christian 30%, Roman Catholic 23%, Protestant 23%, other Christian 6%
CURRENCY Australian dollar = 100 cents

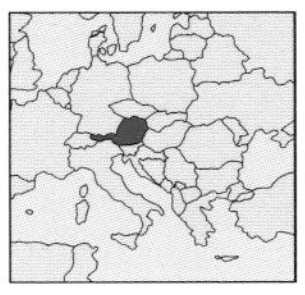

AUSTRIA

GEOGRAPHY Austria is a landlocked country at the heart of Europe. The River Danube flows across northern Austria on its way from Germany to the Black Sea. Southern Austria contains ranges of the Alps, reaching their highest point at Grossglockner, 12,457 ft [3,797 m] above sea level.

The climate is temperate in the west and more continental in the east. Winters are cold and snowy. Summers are warm and dry in the east.

POLITICS & ECONOMY Formerly part of the Austro-Hungarian Empire, Austria was annexed by Germany in 1938. In 1955, Austria became a neutral federal republic, later joining the European Union in 1995. In recent years, Austria has been governed by coalitions. In 2017 new chancellor Sebastian Kurz of the right-wing People's Party formed a coalition with the far-right Freedom Party. Following elections in 2019, he remained in power, now in coalition with the Green Party. Alexander Van der Bellen, allied with the Green Party, has been president since 2016.

Austria has a highly developed economy, with plenty of hydroelectric power and oil, gas, and coal reserves. Although manufacturing, metals, and metal products are important to the economy, banking, insurance services, and tourism predominate. Dairy and livestock farming are leading agricultural activities. Major crops include barley, potatoes, sugar beet, and wheat.

AREA 32,378 sq mi [83,859 sq km] **POPULATION** 8,885,000
CAPITAL Vienna **GOVERNMENT** Federal republic
ETHNIC GROUPS Austrian 81%, German, Bosnian, Turkish, others
LANGUAGES German (official) **RELIGIONS** Roman Catholic 57%, Eastern Orthodox 9%, Islam 8% **CURRENCY** Euro = 100 cents

AZERBAIJAN

GEOGRAPHY The Azerbaijani Republic is a country in the southwest of Asia, facing the Caspian Sea to the east. It includes the area of the Naxçivan Autonomous Republic, which is completely cut off from the rest of Azerbaijan by Armenian territory. The Caucasus Mountains border Russia in the north.

Azerbaijan has hot summers and cool winters. The plains are fairly dry, but the mountains are rainy.

POLITICS & ECONOMY For a short period after the Russian Revolution of 1917, Azerbaijanis set up an independent state before the area was occupied by Russian forces in 1920. In 1922, the Communists set up a Transcaucasian Republic consisting of Armenia, Azerbaijan, and Georgia under Russian control. In 1936, the three areas became separate Soviet Socialist Republics within the Soviet Union. In 1991, following the breakup of the Soviet Union, Azerbaijan became an independent nation again. Violent clashes with Armenia over the enclave of Nagorno-Karabakh escalated into war. A ceasefire in 1994 left Armenia in control of 20% of Azerbaijan's area, including Nagorno-Karabakh. A brief clash in 2020 resulted in Azerbaijan recapturing some territory.

Azerbaijan has huge oil reserves. Oil extraction and manufacturing, including refining, and the production of chemicals, are vital for the export earnings which are funding investment in the country's infrastructure. Problems remain with corruption, and the government, which has been led by members of the Aliyev family since 1993, has been accused of authoritarianism.

AREA 33,436 sq mi [86,600 sq km] **POPULATION** 10,282,000
CAPITAL Baku **GOVERNMENT** Federal multiparty republic
ETHNIC GROUPS Azeri 91%, Dagestani 2%, Russian 2%, Armenian, others **LANGUAGES** Azerbaijani (official), Lezgi, Russian, Armenian
RELIGIONS Islam 93%, Russian Orthodox 2%, Armenian Orthodox 2%
CURRENCY Azerbaijani manat = 100 qapik

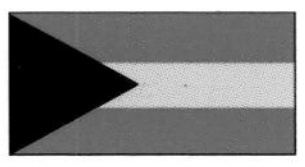
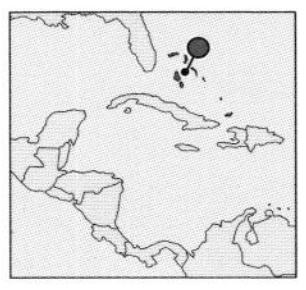

BAHAMAS, THE

A coral-limestone archipelago off the coast of Florida, The Bahamas became independent from Britain in 1973, and has since developed strong ties with the United States. Tourism and banking are major activities.

AREA 5,358 sq mi [13,878 sq km]
POPULATION 353,000 **CAPITAL** Nassau

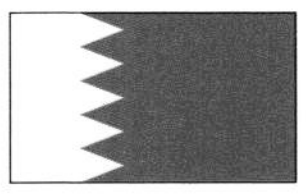
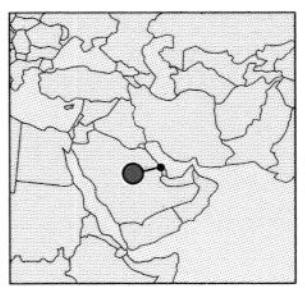

BAHRAIN

The Kingdom of Bahrain, an island nation in the Persian Gulf, became independent from the UK in 1971. An important financial services center, it is less dependent on oil than other Gulf states. Oil accounts for 60% of its exports. There have been protests by the Shia majority of the population claiming discrimination by the ruling Sunni minority.

AREA 268 sq mi [694 sq km]
POPULATION 1,527,000 **CAPITAL** Manama

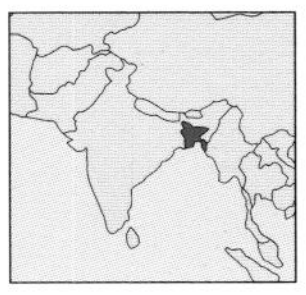

BANGLADESH

GEOGRAPHY The People's Republic of Bangladesh is one of the world's most densely populated countries. Apart from hilly regions in the far northeast and southeast, most of the land is flat and covered by fertile alluvium spread over the land by the Ganges, Brahmaputra, and Meghna rivers. These rivers overflow when they are swollen by the annual monsoon rains. Dry northerly winds blow in winter, but moist southerly winds bring heavy rain in summer. Bangladesh is likely to be badly affected by global rises in sea levels.

POLITICS & ECONOMY In 1947, British India was partitioned between the mainly Hindu India and the Muslim Pakistan. Pakistan consisted of two parts, West and East Pakistan, which were separated by about 1,000 mi [1,600 km] of Indian territory. Differences developed between West and East Pakistan and after a nine-month civil war, East Pakistan declared itself to be the new nation of Bangladesh in 1971. A famine in 1974 and military coup in 1975 were followed by political upheavals until a democratic parliamentary system of government was restored in 1991. The army briefly took control in 2007, but elections in 2008 returned Sheikh Hasina's Awami League to power. There has been a rise in Islamist extremism in recent years.

Bangladesh is one of the world's poorest countries. Its economy depends mainly on agriculture, and garment production.

AREA 55,598 sq mi [143,998 sq km] **POPULATION** 164,099,000
CAPITAL Dhaka **GOVERNMENT** Multiparty republic
ETHNIC GROUPS Bengali 98%, tribal groups
LANGUAGES Bengali (official), English **RELIGIONS** Islam 89%, Hinduism 10% **CURRENCY** Taka = 100 poishas

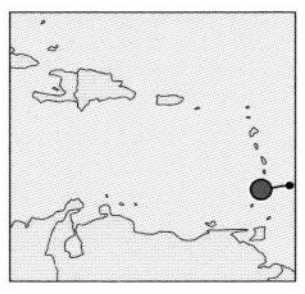

BARBADOS

The most easterly Caribbean country, Barbados became independent from the UK in 1966. A densely populated island, Barbados is prosperous by comparison with most Caribbean countries.

AREA 166 sq mi [430 sq km]
POPULATION 302,000 **CAPITAL** Bridgetown

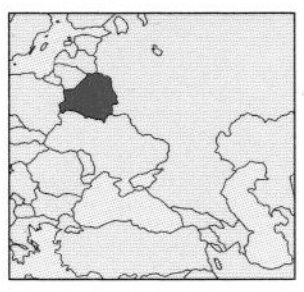

BELARUS

GEOGRAPHY The Republic of Belarus is a landlocked country in Eastern Europe. The land is low-lying and mostly flat. In the south, much of it is marshy and this area contains Europe's largest marsh and peat bog, the Pripet Marshes. The climate is affected by both the moderating influence of the Baltic Sea and continental conditions to the east. The winters are cold and the summers warm.

POLITICS & ECONOMY In 1918, Belarus (White Russia) became an independent republic, but Russia invaded the country and, in 1919, a Communist state was set up. In 1922, Belarus became a founder republic of the Soviet Union. In 1991, Belarus again became an independent republic, and though Belarus continued to support reunification with Russia, any surrender of sovereignty was not expected. Alexander Lukashenko, president since 1994, has been criticized for his autocratic rule, his poor record on human rights, and his disregard for freedom of speech. After his election to a sixth term in 2020, in elections widely believed to be rigged, thousands of protesters took to the streets.

Most economic activities in Belarus are under government control. From the 1990s, the economy stagnated, but 2017 onward saw signs of modest economic recovery. Mining and manufacturing are the most valuable activities.

AREA 80,154 sq mi [207,600 sq km] **POPULATION** 9,442,000
CAPITAL Minsk **GOVERNMENT** Multiparty republic
ETHNIC GROUPS Belarusian 84%, Russian 8%, Polish, Ukrainian, others
LANGUAGES Belarusian, Russian (both official)
RELIGIONS Eastern Orthodox 80%, others 20%
CURRENCY Belarusian ruble = 100 kapyeyka

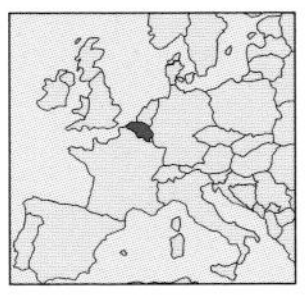

BELGIUM

GEOGRAPHY The Kingdom of Belgium is a densely populated country in Western Europe. Behind the coastline on the North Sea, which is 39 mi [63 km] long, lie its coastal plains. Central Belgium consists of low plateaux and the only highland region is the Ardennes in the southeast.

Belgium has a cool, temperate climate. Moist winds from the Atlantic Ocean bring fairly heavy rain, especially in the Ardennes.

POLITICS & ECONOMY In 1815, Belgium and the Netherlands united as the "low countries," but Belgium became independent in 1830. Belgium's economy was weakened by the two World Wars, but, from 1945, the country recovered quickly, first

through collaboration with the Netherlands and Luxembourg, which formed a customs union called Benelux, and later through its membership of the European Union.

Tension between the Dutch-speaking Flemings in the north and the French-speaking Walloons in the south is ongoing. In the 1970s, the government divided the country into three economic regions: Flanders, Wallonia, and bilingual Brussels. Belgium adopted a federal constitution in 1993, giving each region its own parliament. In 2020 Alexander De Croo became prime minister at the head of a seven-party coalition, ending a period of interim governments. Islamic State terrorists targeted Brussels in 2016, and there is concern over increasing Islamist extremism. King Philippe succeeded to the throne in 2013.

Belgium is a major trading nation. With few natural resources, it imports most materials used in manufacturing. Major products include chemicals, processed food, and steel. Flanders has a long history of textile production. Agriculture employs less than 2% of the people, but farmers produce most of the country's food. Barley and wheat are the major crops, followed by flax, hops, and potatoes. The most valuable agricultural activities are dairy farming and livestock rearing. Brussels is a major center for diplomacy.

AREA 11,787 sq mi [30,528 sq km] **POPULATION** 11,779,000
CAPITAL Brussels **GOVERNMENT** Federal constitutional monarchy
ETHNIC GROUPS Belgian 89% (Fleming 58%, Walloon 31%), others 11%
LANGUAGES Dutch, French, German (all official)
RELIGIONS Roman Catholic 75%, others 25%
CURRENCY Euro = 100 cents

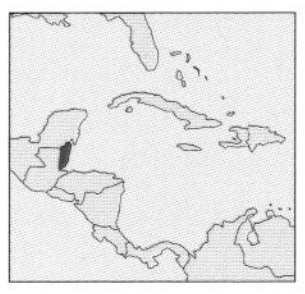

BELIZE

GEOGRAPHY Behind the southern coastal plain, the land rises to the Maya Mountains, which reach 3,674 ft [1,120 m] at Victoria Peak. The north is mostly low-lying and swampy. Temperatures are high all year round, while the average annual rainfall ranges from 51 inches [1,300 mm] in the north to over 150 inches [3,800 mm] in the south. Hurricanes caused much damage in the 1990s and 2000s, but tourist numbers have continued to increase.

POLITICS & ECONOMY From 1862, Belize (then called British Honduras) was a British colony. Full independence was achieved in 1981, but Guatemala, which had claimed the area since the early 19th century, opposed this. Relations improved in the 1990s, when Guatemala recognized Belize's independence although there are still tensions over a boundary dispute. In 2011, the United States added Belize and El Salvador to its list of illegal drug producers.

The World Bank classifies Belize as an "upper-middle-income" developing country. Its economy is based on agriculture, and sugarcane is the chief commercial crop. Other crops include bananas, citrus fruits, maize, and rice. Forestry, fishing, and tourism are other important economic activities, with the last being Belize's chief foreign earner.

AREA 8,867 sq mi [22,966 sq km] **POPULATION** 406,000
CAPITAL Belmopan **GOVERNMENT** Constitutional monarchy
ETHNIC GROUPS Mestizo 49%, Creole 25%, Mayan Indian 11%, Garifuna 6%, others 9%
LANGUAGES English (official), Spanish, Creole, Maya
RELIGIONS Roman Catholic 39%, Protestant 27%, others
CURRENCY Belizean dollar = 100 cents

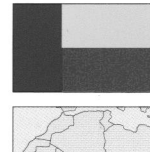

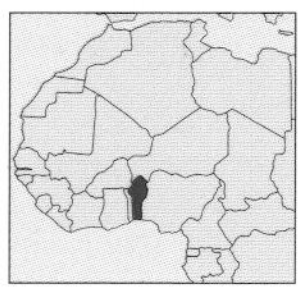

BENIN

GEOGRAPHY The Republic of Benin is one of Africa's smallest countries. It extends north–south for about 390 mi [620 km]. Lagoons line the short coastline, and the country has no natural harbors.

Benin has a hot, wet climate. The average annual temperature on the coast is about 77°F [25°C], and the average rainfall is around 52 inches [1,330 mm]. The inland plains are wetter than the coast.

POLITICS & ECONOMY After slavery was ended in the 19th century, the French gained influence in the area. Benin became self-governing in 1958 and fully independent as Dahomey in 1960. After much instability and many changes of government, a military group took over in 1972. The country, renamed Benin in 1975, became a one-party socialist state. Socialism was abandoned in 1989 and former coup leader Mathieu Kérékou served as president until 2006, when a former banker, Thomas Yayi Boni, was elected president. In 2016 elections, businessman Patrice Talon defeated the ruling party candidate.

Benin is classified by the World Bank as "lower-middle-income." Exports include cotton and palm products. Cocoa, nuts, and shea butter are also grown for export. The Port of Cotonou is vital to Benin's economy.

AREA 43,483 sq mi [112,622 sq km] **POPULATION** 13,302,000
CAPITAL Porto-Novo **GOVERNMENT** Multiparty republic
ETHNIC GROUPS Fon, Adja, Bariba, Yoruba, Fulani
LANGUAGES French (official), Fon, Adja, Yoruba
RELIGIONS Christianity 43%, traditional beliefs 30%, Islam 27%
CURRENCY CFA franc = 100 centimes

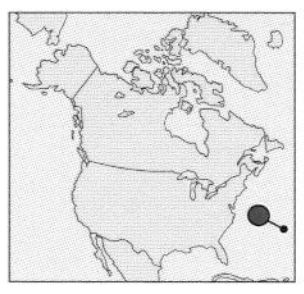

BERMUDA

A group of about 150 small islands situated 570 mi [920 km] east of the USA. Its main sources of revenue are tourism, international business, and offshore finance.

AREA 21 sq mi [53 sq km]
POPULATION 72,000 **CAPITAL** Hamilton

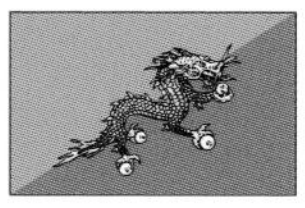
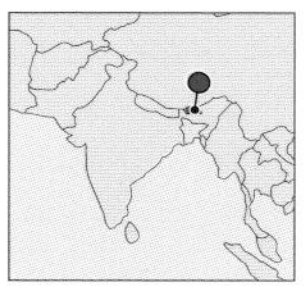

BHUTAN

GEOGRAPHY A mountainous, isolated Himalayan country located between India and Tibet. The climate is similar to that of Nepal, being dependent on altitude and affected by monsoonal winds.

POLITICS & ECONOMY The Wangchuk monarchy, in power since 1907, acted as both head of state and of government until 2008, when Bhutan held its first ever democratic elections and became a constitutional monarchy. This predominantly Buddhist country remains, even in the Asian context, both conservative and poor. Its economy is based on hydropower.

AREA 18,147 sq mi [47,000 sq km] **POPULATION** 857,000
CAPITAL Thimphu **GOVERNMENT** Constitutional monarchy
ETHNIC GROUPS Bhutanese 50%, Nepalese 35%
LANGUAGES Dzongkha (official) **RELIGIONS** Buddhism 75%, Hinduism 25% **CURRENCY** Ngultrum = 100 chhertum

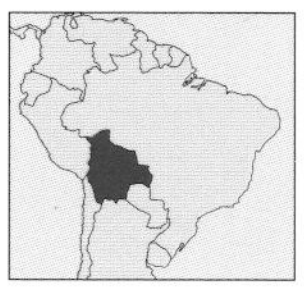

BOLIVIA

GEOGRAPHY The Plurinational State of Bolivia, as the country is officially called, is an isolated and landlocked South American country which straddles the Andes Mountains. The highest point is 21,391 ft [6,520 m] at Nevado Sajama in the west. About 40% of Bolivians live on the Altiplano, a high plateau in the Andes. The sparsely populated east consists of a vast lowland plain.

The Bolivian climate is greatly affected by altitude, with the Andean peaks permanently snow-covered and the eastern plains remaining hot and humid.

POLITICS & ECONOMY American Indians have lived in Bolivia for at least 10,000 years. The main groups today are the Aymara and Quechua people.

In the last 50 years, Bolivia has been ruled by a succession of civilian and military governments. Economic problems have led to a widening of the gap between rich and poor and, in 2005, Evo Morales, an Aymara farmer, was elected president. His policies of nationalization and redistributing wealth to peasants aroused opposition. Re-elected in 2009 and 2014, Morales advocated state control and nationalized energy production. In 2019, following a disputed election, Morales resigned. His former colleague Luis Arce won presidential elections in 2020.

Although one of South America's poorest countries, it has its second largest reserves of natural gas. Other resources include silver, tin, zinc, and lithium, but the main activity is agriculture. It is one of the world's largest cultivators of coca.

AREA 424,162 sq mi [1,098,581 sq km] **POPULATION** 11,759,000
CAPITAL La Paz (seat of government); Sucre (legal capital/seat of judiciary) **GOVERNMENT** Multiparty republic
ETHNIC GROUPS Mestizo 30%, Quechua 30%, Aymara 25%, White 15%
LANGUAGES Spanish, Aymara, Quechua (all official)
RELIGIONS Roman Catholic 95%
CURRENCY Boliviano = 100 centavos

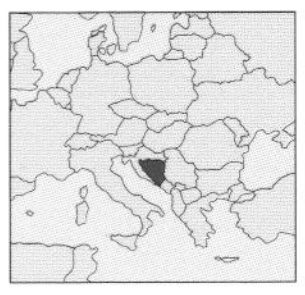

BOSNIA-HERZEGOVINA

GEOGRAPHY The Republic of Bosnia-Herzegovina is one of the seven republics to emerge from the former Federal People's Republic of Yugoslavia. Much of the country is mountainous or hilly, with an arid limestone plateau in the southwest. The River Sava, which forms most of the northern border with Croatia, is a tributary of the River Danube. Because of the country's odd shape, the coastline is limited to a short stretch of 13 mi [20 km] on the Adriatic coast. A Mediterranean climate, with dry, sunny summers and moist, mild winters, prevails only near the coast. Inland, the weather is more severe, with hot, dry summers and bitterly cold, snowy winters.

POLITICS & ECONOMY In 1918, Bosnia-Herzegovina became part of the Kingdom of the Serbs, Croats, and Slovenes, which was renamed Yugoslavia in 1929. Germany occupied the area during World War II (1939–45). From 1945, Communist governments ruled Yugoslavia as a federation containing six republics, one of which was Bosnia-Herzegovina. In the 1980s, the country faced problems as Communist policies proved unsuccessful.

In 1990, free elections were held in Bosnia-Herzegovina and the non-Communists won a majority. A Muslim, Alija Izetbegovic, was elected president. In 1991, Croatia and Slovenia, other parts of the former Yugoslavia, declared themselves independent. In 1992, Bosnia-Herzegovina held a vote on independence. Most Bosnian Serbs boycotted the vote, while the Muslims and Bosnian Croats voted in favor. Many Bosnian Serbs, opposed to independence, started a war against the non-Serbs. They soon occupied more than two-thirds of the land. The war spread when Croat forces seized other parts of the country.

In 1995, the country retained its external boundaries, but it was divided into two self-governing provinces – one Bosnian Serb and the other Muslim Croat. Stability was restored with the help of NATO, but the country remained divided. In December 2011, after 14 months of political crisis, Muslim Croat and Serb leaders agreed on the formation of a central government, with a federal presidency that rotates between a Serb, a Muslim, and a Croat. In 2016, the country formally requested membership of the European Union.

The infrastructure and economy were shattered by the war in the early 1990s, although some stability has been regained despite instances of corruption. The economy relies on exporting metals and receiving foreign aid. Farm products include fruits, maize, tobacco, vegetables, and wheat, but food has to be imported.

AREA 19,767 sq mi [51,197 sq km] **POPULATION** 3,825,000
CAPITAL Sarajevo **GOVERNMENT** Federal republic
ETHNIC GROUPS Bosnian 48%, Serb 37%, Croat 14%
LANGUAGES Bosnian, Serbian, Croatian
RELIGIONS Islam 40%, Serbian Orthodox 31%, Roman Catholic 15%, others 14% **CURRENCY** Convertible marka = 100 convertible pfenniga

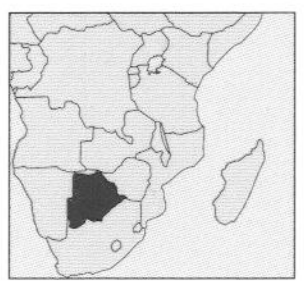

BOTSWANA

GEOGRAPHY The Republic of Botswana is a landlocked country in southern Africa. The Kalahari, a semidesert area covered mostly by grasses and thorn scrub, covers much of the country. Most of the south has no permanent streams but large depressions in the north form inland drainage basins. In one of them, the Okavango River, which rises in Angola, forms a large, swampy delta.

Temperatures are high in the summer months (October to April), but the winter months are much cooler. In winter, nighttime temperatures sometimes drop below freezing point. The average annual rainfall ranges from over 16 inches [400 mm] in the east to less than 8 inches [200 mm] in the southwest.

POLITICS & ECONOMY The earliest inhabitants of the region were the San, sometimes known as Bushmen. They had a nomadic way of life, hunting wild animals and collecting wild plant foods.

Britain ruled the area as the Bechuanaland Protectorate between 1885 and 1966. When the country became independent, it was renamed Botswana. Since then, the country has been a stable, multiparty democracy. In March 2018 Mokgweetsi Masisi was elected as the fifth president since independence. However, in a setback to development, the UN has said that around 22% of the adult population are infected with HIV/AIDS.

Since the 1960s Botswana's economy has grown quickly, and it is now classified by the World Bank as "upper-middle-income." It is the world's largest producer of diamonds. About 25% of the people depend on agriculture. Safari-based tourism is important.

AREA 224,606 sq mi [581,730 sq km] **POPULATION** 2,351,000
CAPITAL Gaborone **GOVERNMENT** Multiparty republic
ETHNIC GROUPS Tswana (or Setswana) 79%, Kalanga 11%, Basarwa 3%, others **LANGUAGES** English (official), Setswana
RELIGIONS Christianity 72%, Badimo 6%, others 2%
CURRENCY Pula = 100 thebe

BRAZIL

GEOGRAPHY The Federative Republic of Brazil is the world's fifth largest country. It contains three main regions. The Amazon basin in the north covers more than half of Brazil. The Amazon, the world's second longest river, has a far greater volume than any other river. The second region, the northeast, consists of a coastal plain and the sertão, which is the name for the inland plateaux and hill country. The main river in this region is the São Francisco.

The third region is made up of the plateaux in the southeast. This area, which covers about a quarter of the country, is the most developed and densely populated part of Brazil. Its main river is the Paraná, which flows south through Argentina.

Manaus, on the Amazon, has high temperatures all through the year. Rainfall is heavy, though the period from June to September is drier than the rest of the year. The capital, Brasília, and the city Rio de Janeiro in the south also have tropical climates, with much more marked dry seasons than Manaus. The far south has a temperate climate. The northeastern interior is the driest region, with an average annual rainfall of only 10 inches [250 mm] in places. Rainfall is also unreliable and severe droughts are common in this region.

POLITICS & ECONOMY The Portuguese explorer Pedro Alvarez Cabral claimed Brazil for Portugal in 1500. The Portuguese developed their colony by enslaving many local Amerindian people and introducing about 4 million African slaves. Brazil declared itself an independent empire in 1822 and a republic in 1889. From the 1930s, Brazil faced periods of military rule and widespread corruption. However, civilian rule was restored in 1985.

After two unpopular presidencies, financial stability was established under President Itamar Franco. One of the "BRICS" nations (Brazil, Russia, India, China, and South Africa), Brazil has a rapidly industrializing economy. But many people, including poor farmers and residents of the favelas (city slums), do not share in the country's economic boom. Poverty led to the election of President Luiz Inácio Lula da Silva (generally called "Lula") in 2002. In 2010, he was succeeded by Dilma Roussef. She was re-elected for a second term in 2014, but was impeached in 2016 over financial irregularities and convicted of fraud in early 2018. In October 2018 Jair Bolsonaro, a polarizing figure from the far-right of Brazilian politics, was elected president.

Brazil is Latin America's leading economy, with services and industry as the most important economic sectors. It is among the world's top producers of bauxite, chrome, gold, iron ore, manganese, and tin. It is also a major manufacturing country, and it is self-sufficient in oil.

Brazil is a major farming nation. Coffee is a leading export. Other products include bananas, citrus fruits, cocoa, maize, rice, soybeans, and sugarcane. Brazil is also South America's top producer of eggs, meat, and milk. The rate of deforestation remains a global concern, with the potential to accelerate global warming.

AREA 3,287,338 sq mi [8,514,215 sq km] **POPULATION** 213,445,000
CAPITAL Brasília **GOVERNMENT** Federal republic
ETHNIC GROUPS White 54%, Mixed 38%, Black 6%, others 2%
LANGUAGES Portuguese (official)
RELIGIONS Roman Catholic 80%
CURRENCY Real = 100 centavos

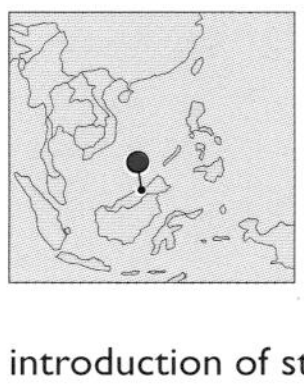

BRUNEI

The Islamic Sultanate of Brunei, a British protectorate until 1984, lies on the north coast of Borneo. The climate is tropical and rain forests cover large areas. Brunei is a prosperous country because of its oil and natural gas production, and the Sultan is said to be among the world's richest men. He has faced international criticism for his introduction of strict Islamic Sharia law in 2014.

AREA 2,226 sq mi [5,765 sq km]
POPULATION 471,000 **CAPITAL** Bandar Seri Begawan

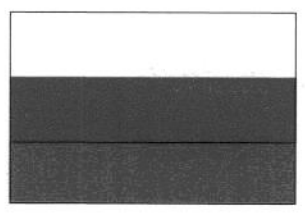

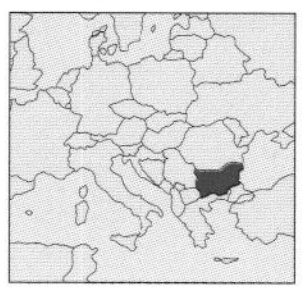

BULGARIA

GEOGRAPHY The Republic of Bulgaria is a country in the Balkan peninsula, facing the Black Sea in the east. The heart of Bulgaria is mountainous. The main ranges are the Balkan Mountains in the center and the Rhodope (or Rhodopi) Mountains in the south.

Summers are hot and winters are cold, though seldom severe. The rainfall is moderate.

POLITICS & ECONOMY Ottoman Turks ruled Bulgaria from 1396 and ethnic Turks still form a sizable minority in the country. In 1879, Bulgaria became a monarchy, and in 1908 it became fully independent. Bulgaria was an ally of Germany in World War I (1914–18) and again in World War II (1939–45). In 1944, Soviet troops invaded Bulgaria and, after the war, the monarchy was abolished and the country became a Communist ally of the Soviet Union. Reforms in the Soviet Union in the late 1980s led Bulgaria's government to introduce a multiparty system in 1990. A non-Communist government was elected in 1991, in the first free elections in 44 years. Throughout the 1990s, Bulgaria faced many problems and it sought to become aligned to the West. Bulgaria became a member of NATO in 2004 and a member of the European Union in 2007. Presidential elections in 2016 were won by Socialist-backed independent Ruman Radev, prompting early parliamentary elections and a coalition government.

Bulgaria's mineral deposits include brown coal, gold, and iron ore. Services and manufacturing are leading activities. Principal products include chemicals, processed foods, metal products, machinery, and textiles. Bulgaria has a growing economy, although it is hindered by corruption and the prevalence of organized crime.

AREA 42,823 sq mi [110,912 sq km] **POPULATION** 6,919,000
CAPITAL Sofia **GOVERNMENT** Multiparty republic
ETHNIC GROUPS Bulgarian 77%, Turkish 8%, Roma 4%, Macedonian, Armenian, others **LANGUAGES** Bulgarian (official), Turkish
RELIGIONS Eastern Orthodox 59%, Islam 8%, others
CURRENCY Lev = 100 stotinki

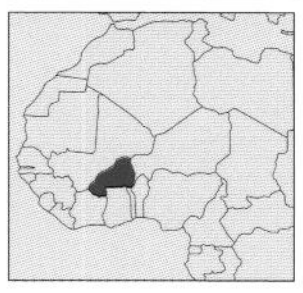

BURKINA FASO

GEOGRAPHY The Democratic People's Republic of Burkina Faso is a landlocked country, a little larger than the United Kingdom, in West Africa. However, Burkina Faso has only a quarter of the population of the UK. The country consists of a plateau, between about 650 ft and 2,300 ft [200 m to 700 m] above sea level. The plateau is cut by several, mainly seasonal, rivers.

The capital city, Ouagadougou, in central Burkina Faso, has high temperatures throughout the year. Most of the rain falls between May and September, but the rainfall is erratic and droughts are common.

POLITICS & ECONOMY The people of Burkina Faso are divided into two main groups: the Voltaic group which includes the Mossi, who form the largest single group, and the Bobo. The French conquered the Mossi capital of Ouagadougou in 1897 and made the area a protectorate. In 1919, it became a French colony called Upper Volta. After independence in 1960, Upper Volta became a, sometimes violent and unstable, one-party state. Following a coup in 1983, Thomas Sankara took power and, in 1984, renamed the country Burkina Faso. Long-term president Blaise Compaoré was ousted in 2014. Former PM Marc Kabore won the ensuing election. Terrorist attacks by Islamist groups are an increasing problem, leaving thousands of people internally displaced as a result.

Burkina Faso is one of the world's poorest countries and is very dependent on foreign aid. Most of the land is dry with thin soils. The country's main food crops are maize, millet, rice, and sorghum. Cotton, groundnuts (peanuts), and shea nuts, whose seeds produce a fat used to make cooking oil and soap, are grown for sale abroad.

The country has few resources and manufacturing is on a small scale. There are deposits of gold, manganese, and zinc, but lack of infrastructure hinders development. The country's key exports are cotton, gold, and livestock. Many young men seek jobs abroad in Ghana and Côte d'Ivoire and the money they send home to their families is important to the country's economy.

AREA 105,791 sq mi [274,000 sq km] **POPULATION** 21,383,000
CAPITAL Ouagadougou **GOVERNMENT** Multiparty republic
ETHNIC GROUPS Mossi 40%, Gurunsi, Senufo, Lobi, Bobo, Mande, Fulani
LANGUAGES French (official), Mossi, Fulani
RELIGIONS Islam 61%, Christianity 23%, traditional beliefs 16%
CURRENCY CFA franc = 100 centimes

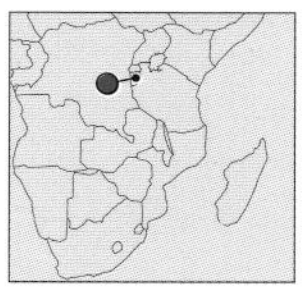

BURUNDI

GEOGRAPHY The Republic of Burundi is the fifth smallest country in mainland Africa. It is also the second most densely populated after its northern neighbor, Rwanda. Part of the Great African Rift Valley, which runs throughout eastern Africa into southwestern Asia, lies in western Burundi. It includes part of Lake Tanganyika. Bujumbura, the commercial capital, lies on the shore of Lake Tanganyika and has a warm climate. A dry season occurs from June to September, but the other months are fairly rainy. The mountains and plateaux to the east are cooler and wetter.

POLITICS & ECONOMY The Twa, a pygmy people, were the first known inhabitants of Burundi. About 1,000 years ago, the Hutu, a people who speak a Bantu language, gradually began to settle the area, pushing the Twa into remote areas.

From the 15th century, the Tutsi, a cattle-owning people from the northeast, gradually took over the country. The Hutu, though greatly outnumbering the Tutsi, were forced to serve the Tutsi overlords.

Germany conquered the area that is now Burundi and Rwanda in the late 1890s. This was followed by Belgian control during World War I (1914–18). Full independence was achieved in 1962. Since this time rivalry between the Hutu and Tutsi has led to periodic outbreaks of appalling violence, most notably in 1972 and 1993. Many thousands of civilians have been massacred. A ceasefire and power-sharing agreement was reached in 2001. Pierre Nkurunziza, a Hutu, led Burundi from 2005, although violent political unrest followed his election to a third term in 2015. Evariste Ndayishimiye, a fellow Hutu former rebel leader, succeeded him as president in 2020, although the election was widely believed to be flawed. In 2017 the International Criminal Court opened an investigation into human rights abuses in the country.

Burundi is one of the world's poorest countries. About 94% of the people live by farming, mostly at subsistence level. Livestock are raised and fishing is important. A lack of basic infrastructure and a poorly educated population are hindering development.

AREA 10,747 sq mi [27,834 sq km] **POPULATION** 12,241,000
CAPITAL Gitega (political); Bujumbura (commercial)
GOVERNMENT Republic **ETHNIC GROUPS** Hutu 85%, Tutsi 14%, Twa (Pygmy) 1% **LANGUAGES** French and Kirundi (both official)
RELIGIONS Roman Catholic 62%, traditional beliefs 23%, Islam 10%, Protestant 5% **CURRENCY** Burundi franc = 100 centimes

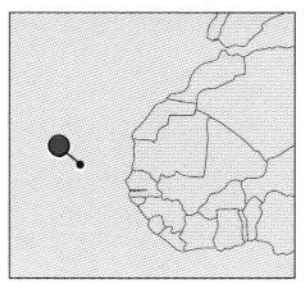

CABO VERDE

Cabo Verde consists of ten large and five small islands, and is situated 350 mi [560 km] west of Dakar in Senegal. The islands have a tropical climate, with high temperatures all year round. Cabo Verde became independent from Portugal in 1975 and is rated as a "lower-middle-income" country by the World Bank.

AREA 1,557 sq mi [4,033 sq km]
POPULATION 589,000 **CAPITAL** Praia

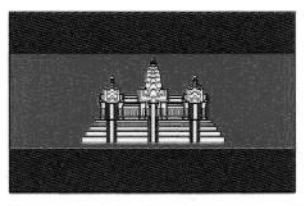

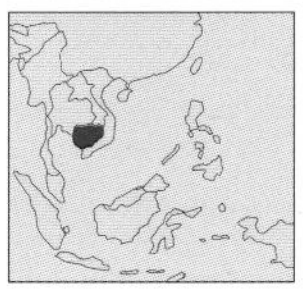

CAMBODIA

GEOGRAPHY The Kingdom of Cambodia is a country in Southeast Asia. Low mountains border the country except in the southeast. Most of Cambodia consists of plains drained by the River Mekong, which enters Cambodia from Laos in the north and exits through Vietnam in the southeast. The northwest contains Tonlé Sap (or Great Lake). In the dry season, this lake drains into the River Mekong. But in the wet season, the level of the Mekong rises and water flows in the opposite direction from the river into Tonlé Sap.

Cambodia has a tropical monsoon climate, with high temperatures throughout the year. The dry season, when winds blow from the north or northeast, runs from November to April. During the rainy season (May to October), moist winds blow from the south or southeast. The high humidity and heat often make conditions unpleasant. Rainfall is heaviest near the coast, and rather lower inland.

POLITICS & ECONOMY From 802 to 1432, the Khmer people ruled a great empire, which reached its peak in the 12th century. The Khmer capital was at Angkor. The Hindu stone temples built there and at nearby Angkor Wat form the world's largest group of religious buildings. France ruled the country between 1863 and 1954, when the country became an independent monarchy. The monarchy was abolished in 1970 and Cambodia became a republic.

In 1970, the Communists under Prime Minister Lon Nol staged a military coup and proclaimed the Khmer Republic, which plunged the country into a civil war. The Khmer Rouge under Pol Pot took control in 1975, renaming the country Kampuchea, and launched a reign of terror in which between 1 million and 2.5 million people were killed. In 1979, Vietnamese and Cambodian troops overthrew the Khmer Rouge government. Vietnam withdrew in 1989, and in 1991 Prince Sihanouk was recognized as head of state. In 1993 the monarchy was restored. In 2004, King Sihanouk abdicated and his son, Prince Norodom Sihamoni, became king. Hun Sen's Cambodian People's Party has been in power since 1998, and he has been prime minister since 1985. In 2017, the Supreme Court dissolved the only credible opposition party, leading to a predictable but controversial victory for Hun Sen's party in 2018 parliamentary elections.

Cambodia's economy, although devastated by war, has now had over 20 years of relative stability and growth, hindered by corruption. Garment manufacture, tourism, and construction are the main industries. Agriculture, mostly at subsistence levels, employs almost half the work force. In 2005 offshore oil reserves were discovered and there is potential to mine bauxite, iron, and gold.

AREA 69,898 sq mi [181,035 sq km] **POPULATION** 17,304,000
CAPITAL Phnom Penh **GOVERNMENT** Constitutional monarchy
ETHNIC GROUPS Khmer 90%, Vietnamese 5%, Chinese 1%, others
LANGUAGES Khmer (official), French, English
RELIGIONS Buddhism 96%, others 4% **CURRENCY** Riel = 10 kak

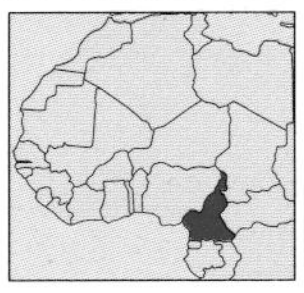

CAMEROON

GEOGRAPHY The Republic of Cameroon in West Africa derived its name from the Portuguese word camarões, or prawns. This name was used by Portuguese explorers who fished for prawns along the coast.

Behind the narrow coastal plains on the Gulf of Guinea, the land rises to a series of plateaux, with a mountainous region in the southwest where the volcano Mount Cameroun is situated.

The rainfall is heavy, especially in the highlands, but it becomes drier to the north. Temperatures are high on the coast, while the inland plateaux are cooler.

POLITICS & ECONOMY Germany lost Cameroon after World War I (1914–18). The country was then divided into two parts, one ruled by Britain and the other by France. In 1960, French Cameroon became the independent Cameroon Republic. In 1961, after a vote in British Cameroon, part of the territory joined the Cameroon Republic to become the Federal Republic of Cameroon – the other part joined Nigeria. It adopted the name Republic of Cameroon in 1984, but the country had two official languages. In 1995, partly to placate the English-speaking people, Cameroon became the 52nd member of the Commonwealth. A controversial amendment passed by parliament in 2008 has enabled President Paul Biya to run successfully for third and fourth terms in office in 2011 and 2018 respectively. The country has faced insurgency from Boko Haram since 2014, and increased unrest in the English-speaking provinces.

Cameroon's economy is based on agriculture, which employs 70% of the work force. The chief food crops include cassava, maize, millet, and plantains. Cocoa and coffee are exported, along with oil, timber, and bauxite. Cameroon has few manufacturing industries. In 2002, Cameroon's claim over the disputed oil-rich Bakassi peninsula was upheld and the handover by Nigeria completed in 2008. Despite a high literacy rate, economic development is marred by endemic corruption and years of authoritarian rule.

AREA 183,568 sq mi [475,442 sq km] **POPULATION** 28,524,000
CAPITAL Yaoundé **GOVERNMENT** Multiparty republic
ETHNIC GROUPS Cameroon Highlanders 31%, Bantu 27%, Kirdi 11%, Fulani 10%, others **LANGUAGES** French and English (both official)
RELIGIONS Christianity 40%, traditional beliefs 40%, Islam 20%
CURRENCY CFA franc = 100 centimes

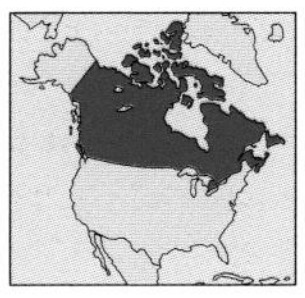

CANADA

GEOGRAPHY Canada is the world's second largest country after Russia but with only 15% of its population. Much of the land is too cold or too mountainous for human settlement. Around 90% of Canadians live within 124 mi [200 km] of the southern border.

Western Canada is rugged: it includes the Pacific ranges and the mighty Rocky Mountains. East of the Rockies are the interior plains. In the north lie the bleak Arctic islands, while to the south lie the densely populated lowlands around lakes Erie and Ontario and in the St Lawrence River valley. The melting of Arctic ice, attributed to global warming, has led to concern about international rights over the Arctic waters off northern Canada.

Canada has a cold climate. In winter, temperatures fall below freezing point throughout most of Canada. But the southwestern coast has a relatively mild climate. Along the Arctic Circle, mean temperatures are below freezing for seven months a year. The west and southeast have high rainfall, but the prairies are dry with 10 inches to 20 inches [250 mm to 500 mm] of rain every year.

POLITICS & ECONOMY Canada's first people, the ancestors of the Native Americans, or Indians, arrived in North America from Asia around 40,000 years ago. The Inuit (Eskimos) were later arrivals from Asia. Europeans first reached Canada in 1497 and soon Britain and France began to compete for control.

France gained an initial advantage, and the French founded Québec in 1608. The British later occupied eastern Canada and, in 1867, they passed the British North America Act, which set up the Dominion of Canada, which was made up of Québec, Ontario, Nova Scotia, and New Brunswick. Other areas were added, the last being Newfoundland in 1949. Canada is a constitutional monarchy, and the British monarch is Canada's head of state. The provinces have a high level of autonomy.

In 1995, the people of Québec voted narrowly against a move to make Québec a sovereign state. In 2006, the national parliament voted to recognize Québec as a nation within a united Canada – a symbolic act of reconciliation. Another major issue concerns the rights of Aboriginal minorities. In 1999, Canada created the territory of Nunavut for the Inuit population. Nunavut covers 64% of what was formerly the eastern part of the Northwest Territories. Nine years of Conservative party rule were ended in late 2015 with an emphatic election victory by the Liberal Party under Justin Trudeau.

Canada is a highly developed and prosperous country. Although farmland covers only 8% of the country, high levels of productivity mean that Canada is one of the world's leading producers of barley, wheat, meat, and milk. Forestry and fishing are also important. Canada is rich in natural resources, especially oil and natural gas, and is a major exporter of minerals. The country also produces copper, gold, iron ore, uranium, and zinc. Manufacturing is important in the urban areas, where over 80% of the people live. Manufactures include processed mineral and farm products, cars, chemicals, paper, and timber products. Although the USA is Canada's largest trading partner, increased levels of business involve Asian countries.

AREA 3,849,653 sq mi [9,970,610 sq km] **POPULATION** 37,943,000
CAPITAL Ottawa **GOVERNMENT** Federal multiparty constitutional monarchy **ETHNIC GROUPS** British origin 28%, French origin 23%, other European 15%, Amerindian/Inuit 2%, others
LANGUAGES English and French (both official)
RELIGIONS Roman Catholic 43%, Protestant 23%, Judaism, Islam, Hinduism **CURRENCY** Canadian dollar = 100 cents

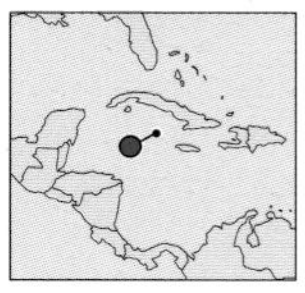

CAYMAN ISLANDS

The Cayman Islands are an overseas territory of the UK, consisting of three low-lying islands. Financial services are the main economic activity and the islands offer a secret tax haven to many companies and banks.

AREA 102 sq mi [264 sq km]
POPULATION 63,000 **CAPITAL** George Town

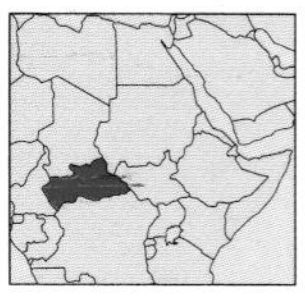

CENTRAL AFRICAN REPUBLIC

GEOGRAPHY The Central African Republic is a remote, landlocked country in the heart of Africa. It consists mostly of a plateau lying between 1,970 ft and 2,620 ft [600 m to 800 m] above sea level. The Oubangi drains the south, while the Chari (or Shari) River flows from the north to the Lake Chad basin. The climate is warm throughout the year, while the annual average rainfall in the capital Bangui totals 62 inches [1,600 mm]. The north is drier, with an average annual rainfall of about 31 inches [800 mm].

POLITICS & ECONOMY France set up an outpost at Bangui in 1889 and ruled the country as a colony from 1894. Known as Ubangi-Shari, the country was ruled by France as part of French Equatorial Africa until it gained independence in 1960.

Central African Republic became a one-party state in 1962, but army officers seized power in 1966. The head of the army, Jean-Bedel Bokassa, made himself emperor in 1976. The country was renamed the Central African Empire, but Bokassa was removed in 1979. The country again became a republic.

The election in 1993 ended 12 years of military rule. In 2003 General François Bozizé seized power; he was deposed in 2013 by rebel leader Michel Djotodia, who in turn resigned in 2014 following international pressure. The era was marked by frequent violent clashes between the government and rebel groups, and between Christian and Muslim fighters, which led to a breakdown in law and order and a refugee crisis. Faustin-Archange Touadera was elected president in 2016. Violent unrest continues, despite the government's efforts to make peace with the armed groups.

The World Bank classifies Central African Republic as a "low-income" developing country. Over 80% of the people are farmers. The main crops are bananas, maize, cassava, millet, and yams. Coffee, cotton, timber, and tobacco are produced for export. The country has significant natural resources including uranium and diamonds. Development has been impeded by the country's remote position, its poor transport system, and its untrained work force. The country depends heavily on aid.

AREA 240,534 sq mi [622,984 sq km] **POPULATION** 5,358,000
CAPITAL Bangui **GOVERNMENT** Multiparty republic
ETHNIC GROUPS Baya 33%, Banda 27%, Mandjia 13%, Sara 10%, Mboum 7%, Mbaka 4%, others **LANGUAGES** French (official), Sangho
RELIGIONS Traditional beliefs 35%, Protestant 25%, Roman Catholic 25%, Islam 15% **CURRENCY** CFA franc = 100 centimes

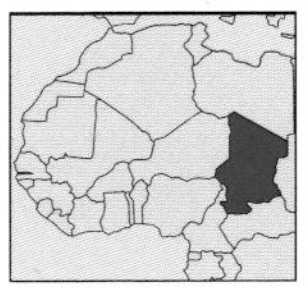

CHAD

GEOGRAPHY The Republic of Chad is a landlocked country in north-central Africa. It is Africa's fifth largest country and is over twice the size of France, the country which once ruled it as a colony.

Ndjamena in central Chad has a hot, tropical climate, with a marked dry season from November to April. The south of the country is wetter, with an average yearly rainfall of around 39 inches [1,000 mm]. The burning-hot desert in the north has an average yearly rainfall of less than 5 inches [130 mm].

POLITICS & ECONOMY Chad straddles two worlds. The north is populated by Muslim Arab and Berber peoples, while black Africans live in the south. Chad became independent from France in 1960, but the 1970s were marked by ethnic strife that led to conflict with Libya. Chad and Libya agreed a truce in 1987, and in 1994 the International Court of Justice ruled against Libya's claim to the Aozou Strip. From 2004 to 2010, Chadian forces clashed with pro-Sudanese militias as the conflict in Sudan's Darfur province spilled over the border. In 2016, Idriss Deby, in power since 1990, won a fifth term as president. He served until his death in 2021. The security situation is perilous, with the militant Islamist groups Boko Haram and Islamic State both active in the region, as well as inter-ethnic violence in the east.

One of the world's poorest countries, Chad has a large refugee population. Agriculture employs 80% of the work force. The main food crops are sorghum, millet, and yams. Chief exports include cotton, livestock, and oil, which it exports via a pipeline connecting its oilfields to the coast in Cameroon.

AREA 495,752 sq mi [1,284,000 sq km] **POPULATION** 17,414,000
CAPITAL Ndjamena **GOVERNMENT** Multiparty republic
ETHNIC GROUPS 200 distinct groups: mostly Muslim in the north and center; mostly Christian or animist in the south
LANGUAGES French and Arabic (both official), many others
RELIGIONS Islam 53%, Christianity 34%, animist 7%
CURRENCY CFA franc = 100 centimes

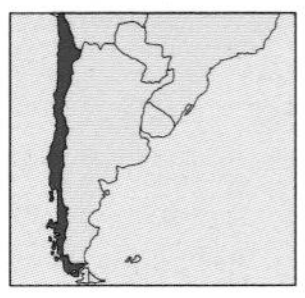

CHILE

GEOGRAPHY The Republic of Chile stretches about 2,650 mi [4,260 km] from north to south, although the maximum east–west distance is only about 267 mi [430 km]. The high Andes Mountains form Chile's eastern borders with Argentina and Bolivia. To the west are basins and valleys, with coastal uplands overlooking the shore. Most people live in the central valley, where the capital, Santiago, is situated. Earthquakes are common. In February 2010, an earthquake with a magnitude of 8.8 (the biggest in 50 years) struck central Chile, killing more than 400 people.

Santiago has a Mediterranean climate with hot, dry summers and mild, moist winters. The Atacama Desert in the north is extremely arid, while the south is cold and stormy.

POLITICS & ECONOMY Amerindian people reached the southern tip of South America 8,000 years ago. In 1520, Portuguese navigator Ferdinand Magellan was the first European to sight Chile and the country became a Spanish colony in the 1540s. Independent from 1818, Chile won mineral-rich areas from Peru and Bolivia during the War of the Pacific (1879–83).

In 1970, Salvador Allende became the first Communist leader to be elected democratically. He was overthrown in 1973 by army officers, who were supported by the CIA. General Augusto Pinochet then ruled as a dictator until 1989. Since then, government leaders have been democratically elected which has contributed to the country's prosperity and stability. Presidential elections in late 2017 saw a return to office for Sebastian Pinera.

According to the World Bank classifications, Chile has a "high-income" economy, one of the strongest in Latin America. Mining, especially copper, is important, with manufacturing and services the most valuable activities. Products include processed foods, iron and steel, transport equipment, and textiles. The chief crops are wheat, fruits, and maize; livestock products are also important. Chile's fishing industry is one of the world's largest. Its main exports are copper, fish, and fruit.

AREA 292,133 sq mi [756,626 sq km] **POPULATION** 18,308,000
CAPITAL Santiago **GOVERNMENT** Multiparty republic
ETHNIC GROUPS Mestizo 95%, Amerindian 4%
LANGUAGES Spanish (official), English, others **RELIGIONS** Roman Catholic 70%, Protestant 17% **CURRENCY** Chilean peso = 100 centavos

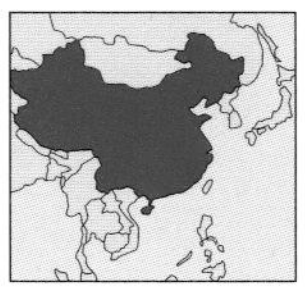

CHINA

GEOGRAPHY The People's Republic of China is the world's fourth largest country. Most people live in the east – on the coastal plains or in the fertile valleys of the Huang He (Hwang Ho or Yellow River), the Chang Jiang (Yangtse Kiang), which is Asia's longest river at 3,960 mi [6,380 km], and the Xi Jiang (Si Kiang). Western China is thinly populated. It includes the bleak Tibetan plateau, which is bounded by the Himalaya, the world's highest mountain range. Deserts include the Gobi along the Mongolian border and the Takla Makan in the far west. Earthquakes are common. Beijing has cold winters and warm summers with moderate rainfall. To the south, Shanghai has milder winters and more rain. The southeast has a wet, subtropical climate, but the west has a severe climate. Lhasa has very cold winters and a low rainfall.

POLITICS & ECONOMY China is one of the world's oldest civilizations, going back 3,500 years. Mongols conquered China in the 13th century, but Chinese rule was restored in 1368. The Manchu people of Mongolia ruled the country from 1644 to 1912, when the country became a republic.

War with Japan (1937–45) was followed by civil war between the nationalists and the Communists. The Communists triumphed in 1949, setting up the People's Republic of China. In the 1980s, following the death of the revolutionary leader Mao Zedong (Mao Tse-tung) in 1976, China encouraged formerly forbidden policies, namely private enterprise and foreign investment. But the Communist leaders have not permitted political freedom. Opponents are still harshly treated, with repressive measures in both Tibet and the Xinjiang Uighur Autonomous Region. Its record on human rights has been internationally criticized. Central control over Hong Kong has been increased, leading to widespread pro-democracy protests in 2019. Tensions remain between China and its neighbors over territorial disputes in the East and South China seas. In 2018 the Communist Party abolished the two-term presidential limit, opening the way for Xi Jinping, president since 2013, to remain in power indefinitely. In 2020 an outbreak of the Covid-19 virus, originating in China, caused a global health emergency.

China's economy expanded from the late 1970s when it moved from a centrally planned to a more market-oriented one, and many new industries were set up in the east. From 1989 until the global financial crisis in 2008, the economy grew by over 9% per year. It recovered quickly, and is now one of the world's largest economies. China has also made major investments overseas.

Agriculture employs around 30% of the work force. More than half the population lives in urban areas. Farm products include rice, sweet potatoes, tea, and wheat. Livestock farming is important, and China has the world's largest pig population. Resources include coal, iron ore, and other metals. Manufactures include cement, chemicals, fertilizers, machinery, cars, ships, and textiles. China is now a major producer of consumer goods, including computers, electrical machinery, and television sets. It is classified by the World Bank as an "upper-middle-income" economy but problems remain, such as pollution, inequality, and an inefficient state sector.

AREA 3,705,387 sq mi [9,596,961 sq km] **POPULATION** 1,397,898,000
CAPITAL Beijing **GOVERNMENT** Single-party Communist republic
ETHNIC GROUPS Han Chinese 92%, many others
LANGUAGES Mandarin Chinese (official) **RELIGIONS** Atheist (official)
CURRENCY Renminbi yuan = 10 jiao = 100 fen

COLOMBIA

GEOGRAPHY The Republic of Colombia, in northeastern South America, is the only country in the continent to have coastlines on both the Pacific Ocean and the Caribbean Sea. Colombia also contains the northernmost ranges of the Andes Mountains.

There is a tropical climate in the lowlands, but the altitude greatly affects the climate in the Andes. The capital, Bogotá, which stands on a plateau in the eastern Andes at about 9,200 ft [2,800 m] above sea level, has mild temperatures throughout the year. Rainfall is heavy, especially on the Pacific coast.

POLITICS & ECONOMY Amerindian people have lived in Colombia for thousands of years. But today, only a small proportion of the people are of unmixed Amerindian ancestry. Colombia emerged as a republic in 1886.

The 20th century was marred by civil war and violent conflict involving drug cartels and armed rebel groups. Andrés Pastrana, president in 1998–2002, tried to end the guerrilla war, but peace talks collapsed and conflict resumed. In 2016 the government and FARC (Revolutionary Armed Forces of Colombia) signed a peace agreement, with FARC formally dissolving itself as an armed group the following year. In 2018 Ivan Duque was elected president. The peace remains fragile.

Colombia is an oil producer, and its economy is vulnerable to fluctuations in oil prices and hindered by poor infrastructure. Agricultural products include sugarcane, bananas, and maize. It is one of the world's largest cultivators of coca. Petroleum, coffee, coal, gold, emeralds, and cut flowers are exported.

AREA 439,735 sq mi [1,138,914 sq km] **POPULATION** 50,356,000
CAPITAL Bogotá **GOVERNMENT** Multiparty republic
ETHNIC GROUPS Mestizo 58%, White 20%, Mixed 14%, Black 4%
LANGUAGES Spanish (official) **RELIGIONS** Roman Catholic 90%
CURRENCY Colombian peso = 100 centavos

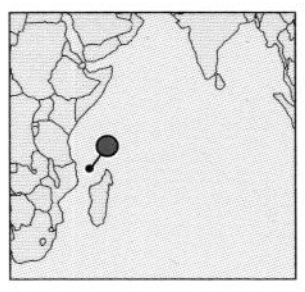

COMOROS

The Union of the Comoros consists of three large volcanic islands and some smaller ones lying at the north end of the Mozambique Channel in the Indian Ocean. France took over one of the islands, Mayotte, in 1843, and in 1886 the other islands came under French protection. They became independent in 1974, but Mayotte has remained French. Relations between the three remaining islands have been rocky. The constitution of 2001 granted greater autonomy to each island, with a rotating presidency. Changes to the constitution in 2018 undermined this system, and President Azali Assoumani, elected in 2016, was re-elected in 2019. Very dependent on foreign aid and remittances from abroad, Comoros is one of Africa's poorest nations. Exports include cloves, perfume oil, and vanilla.

AREA 863 sq mi [2,235 sq km]
POPULATION 864,000 **CAPITAL** Moroni

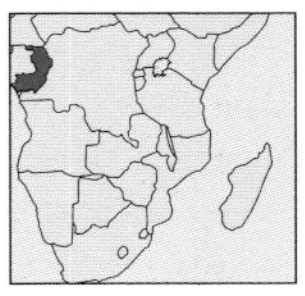

CONGO

GEOGRAPHY The Republic of the Congo is a country on the River Congo in west-central Africa. The equator runs through the center of the country. Congo has a narrow coastal plain on which its main port, Pointe Noire, stands. Behind the plain are uplands through which the River Kouilou-Niari has carved a fertile valley. Central Congo consists of high plains with the north comprising large swampy areas in the valleys of the tributaries of the River Congo.

Congo has a hot, wet equatorial climate. Brazzaville has a dry season between June and September. The coast is drier and cooler because of the cold offshore Benguela ocean current.

POLITICS & ECONOMY Part of the huge Kongo kingdom between the 15th and 18th centuries, the coast of the Congo later became a center of the European slave trade. The area came under French protection in 1880 and it was later governed as part of the larger region of French Equatorial Africa. The country remained under French control until 1960.

Congo became a one-party state in 1964 and a military group took over the government in 1968. In 1970, Congo declared itself a Communist country, though it continued to seek aid from Western countries. Multiparty elections were held in 1992, but the elected president, Pascal Lissouba, was overthrown in 1997 by former president Denis Sassou-Nguesso. Civil war broke out with a fragile peace being restored in 2002. Sassou-Nguesso, president for over 30 years, despite accusations of corruption and unfair elections, is one of Africa's longest serving leaders.

Despite being one of Africa's largest petroleum producers, poverty is widespread. Agriculture is an important activity, employing about 32% of the people, but many farmers produce little more than they need to feed their families. Major food crops include bananas, cassava, maize, and rice, while the leading cash crops are coffee and cocoa. Congo's main exports are oil (making up more than 90% of the total), timber, sugar, and diamonds. Manufacturing is still relatively unimportant, hampered by poor transport links, but it is gradually being developed.

AREA 132,046 sq mi [342,000 sq km] **POPULATION** 5,417,000
CAPITAL Brazzaville **GOVERNMENT** Republic
ETHNIC GROUPS Kongo 48%, Sangha 20%, Teke 17%, M'bochi 12%
LANGUAGES French (official), many others **RELIGIONS** Christianity 50%, animist 48%, Islam 2% **CURRENCY** CFA franc = 100 centimes

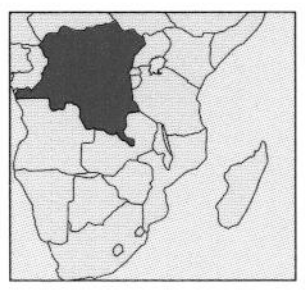

CONGO (DEMOCRATIC REPUBLIC OF THE)

GEOGRAPHY The Democratic Republic of the Congo, formerly known as Zaïre, is the world's 11th largest country. Much of the country lies within the drainage basin of the huge River Congo. The river reaches the sea at the country's short coastline, which is only 25 mi [40 km] long. Mountains rise in the east, where the country's borders run through lakes Tanganyika, Kivu, Edward, and Albert.

POLITICS & ECONOMY Portuguese navigators reached the coast in 1482, but the interior was not explored until the late 19th century. In 1885, the country, known as the Congo Free State, became the personal property of King Léopold II of Belgium and was then administered as a Belgian colony from 1908 until 1960.

The country, riven by ethnic rivalries, became a one-party state after a coup by President Mobutu in 1965. He renamed it Zaïre and held on to power for over 30 years. He was ousted in 1997 by Laurent Kabila, a rebel leader backed by Rwanda and Uganda, who gave the country its present name. Further rifts and violence continued until Kabila was assassinated in 2001. The presidency was taken over by his son Joseph, who negotiated the Pretoria Accord with Rwanda which called for an end to fighting and the establishment of a unity government. The country remains beset by violence. According to aid agencies more than 1.5 million people were internally displaced during 2017. Elections at the end of Kabila's term as president were twice delayed, but in 2019 opposition candidate Felix Tshisekedi became president.

The Democratic Republic of the Congo is one of the world's poorest countries. Decades of insurrection and instability have devastated what was once a relatively industrialized economy. It has a vast wealth of natural resources, much of it still to be exploited and, with foreign help, some reform is under way. The economy relies on mining: the country is the world's largest producer of cobalt and a major producer of copper and diamonds. However, the industry is plagued by financial irregularities. Agriculture, at subsistence level, employs 60% of the work force.

AREA 905,350 sq mi [2,344,858 sq km] **POPULATION** 105,045,000
CAPITAL Kinshasa **GOVERNMENT** Republic
ETHNIC GROUPS Over 200; the largest are Mongo, Luba, Kongo, Mangbetu-Azande **LANGUAGES** French (official), tribal languages
RELIGIONS Roman Catholic 50%, Protestant 20%, Islam 10%, others
CURRENCY Congolese franc = 100 centimes

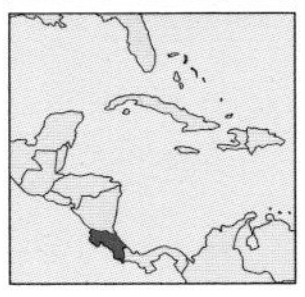

COSTA RICA

GEOGRAPHY The Republic of Costa Rica in Central America has coastlines on both the Pacific Ocean and the Caribbean Sea. Central Costa Rica consists of mountain ranges and plateaux with many volcanoes.

The coolest months of the year are December and January. The northeast trade winds bring heavy rain to the Caribbean coast,

while there are lower amounts of rainfall in the highlands and on the Pacific coastlands.

POLITICS & ECONOMY Christopher Columbus reached the Caribbean coast in 1502 and was followed by Spanish settlers. Spain ruled the country until 1821, when the Central American colonies broke away to join Mexico. In 1823, these states then split from Mexico and set up the Central American Federation. Later, this union broke up and Costa Rica became independent in 1838.

From the late 19th century onward, Costa Rica experienced a number of revolutions, with periods of dictatorship alternating with spells of democracy. In 1948, following a revolt, the armed forces were completely abolished and it remains without a standing army today. Since that year, Costa Rica has enjoyed a long period of consistent stable democracy. Center-left candidate and former Minister of Labor and Social Security, Carlos Alvarado, won the presidential elections of March 2018.

Costa Rica is one of the most prosperous countries in Central America. There are high educational standards, a high average life expectancy (about 77 years for men and 82 years for women), and the most developed welfare system in Central America. Agriculture employs 14% of the people. Costa Rica's natural resources include its forests and hydropower. Manufacturing is increasing, with the USA being Costa Rica's main trading partner. Ecotourism is a fast-growing industry. There are concerns, however, that the country is acting as a conduit for drugs and associated corruption.

AREA 19,730 SQ MI [51,100 SQ KM] **POPULATION** 5,151,000
CAPITAL SAN JOSÉ **GOVERNMENT** MULTIPARTY REPUBLIC
ETHNIC GROUPS WHITE (INCLUDING MESTIZO) 94%, BLACK 3%, AMERINDIAN 1%, CHINESE 1%, OTHERS **LANGUAGES** SPANISH (OFFICIAL), ENGLISH **RELIGIONS** ROMAN CATHOLIC 76%, EVANGELICAL PROTESTANT 14%
CURRENCY COSTA RICAN COLÓN = 100 CÉNTIMOS

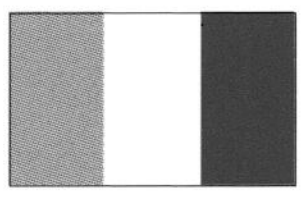

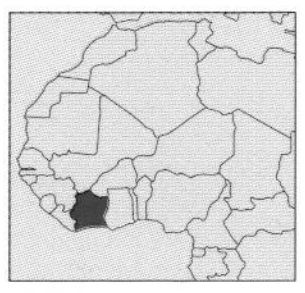

CÔTE D'IVOIRE (IVORY COAST)

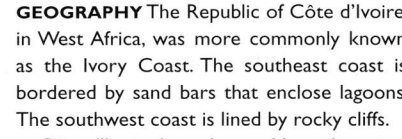

GEOGRAPHY The Republic of Côte d'Ivoire, in West Africa, was more commonly known as the Ivory Coast. The southeast coast is bordered by sand bars that enclose lagoons. The southwest coast is lined by rocky cliffs.

Côte d'Ivoire has a hot and humid tropical climate, with high temperatures all year. The south has two rainy seasons: between May and July, and from October to November. Inland, the rainfall decreases and the north has one dry and one rainy season.

POLITICS & ECONOMY From 1895, the Ivory Coast, as it was known, was governed as part of French West Africa.

Côte d'Ivoire became fully independent in 1960. Its first president, the pro-Western leader Félix Houphouët-Boigny, made Côte d'Ivoire a one-party state. Yamoussoukro, his birthplace, was named as the new capital in 1983. Houphouët-Boigny's uninterrupted period in office ended with his death in 1993. In 2000 Laurent Gbagbo was elected, restoring civilian rule after a military coup the previous year. An army rebellion in 2002 grew into civil war, resulting in the division of the country between the government-held south, and the north held by Muslim rebels. The country was reunited in 2007. Elections in 2010 were won by Alassane Outtara, but Gbagbo refused to stand down until 2011. Outtara won an overwhelming 84% of the vote in 2015's elections; his re-election in 2020 was controversial.

Agriculture employs 68% of the population and the country is the world's largest producer of cocoa beans. Coffee and palm oil are also important exports. Political instability and the lack of modern infrastructure are impeding economic growth.

AREA 124,503 SQ MI [322,463 SQ KM] **POPULATION** 28,088,000
CAPITAL YAMOUSSOUKRO **GOVERNMENT** MULTIPARTY REPUBLIC
ETHNIC GROUPS AKAN 42%, VOLTAIQUES 18%, NORTHERN MANDES 16%, KROUS 11%, SOUTHERN MANDES 10% **LANGUAGES** FRENCH (OFFICIAL), MANY NATIVE DIALECTS **RELIGIONS** ISLAM 39%, CHRISTIANITY 33%, TRADITIONAL BELIEFS 12% **CURRENCY** CFA FRANC = 100 CENTIMES

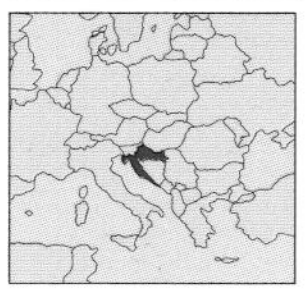

CROATIA

GEOGRAPHY The Republic of Croatia was one of the six republics that made up the former Communist country of Yugoslavia until it became independent in 1991. The region of Dalmatia borders the Adriatic Sea and here are found the coastal ranges of mountains, comprising large tracts of bare limestone. Most of the rest of the country consists of the fertile Pannonian plains.

The coastal area has a typical Mediterranean climate, with hot, dry summers and mild, moist winters. Inland, the climate becomes more continental. Winters are cold, while temperatures often soar to 100°F [38°C] in the summer months.

POLITICS & ECONOMY Once part of the Holy Roman empire, Croatia was an independent kingdom in the 10th and 11th centuries. In 1102, the crowns of Hungary and Croatia were joined, creating a union that lasted 800 years. In 1526, part of Croatia came under the Turkish Ottoman empire, while the rest fell under the control of the Austrian Habsburgs.

After Austria–Hungary was defeated in World War I (1914–18), Croatia became part of the new Kingdom of the Serbs, Croats, and Slovenes. This kingdom was renamed Yugoslavia in 1929. Germany occupied Yugoslavia during World War II (1939–45).

After the war, Communists took power with Josip Broz Tito as the country's leader. Despite ethnic differences between the people, Tito held Yugoslavia together until his death in 1980. In the 1980s, economic and ethnic problems, including a deterioration in relations with Serbia, threatened stability. In the 1990s, Yugoslavia split into five nations, one of which was Croatia, which declared itself independent in 1991.

After Serbia supplied arms to Serbs living in Croatia, war broke out between the two republics, causing great damage. Croatia lost more than 30% of its territory. In 1992, the United Nations sent a peacekeeping force to Croatia, which effectively ended the war with Serbia. In the same year, when war broke out in Bosnia-Herzegovina, Bosnian Croats occupied parts of the country. But in 1994, Croatia helped to end Croat–Muslim conflict in Bosnia-Herzegovina and, in 1995, after retaking some areas occupied by Serbs, it helped to draw up the Dayton Peace Accord, ending the civil war.

The conflict in the early 1990s badly disrupted the economy. Slow but steady economic growth in the early 2000s was thwarted by the recession of 2008, but picked up again from 2014 onward. Croatia acceded to membership of the EU in 2013. Problems remain with high unemployment and uneven regional development. Its intricate coastline and islands on the Adriatic Sea are a gift to the tourist industry. Croatia's main exports are manufactures, especially shipbuilding and machinery.

AREA 21,829 SQ MI [56,538 SQ KM] **POPULATION** 4,209,000
CAPITAL ZAGREB **GOVERNMENT** MULTIPARTY REPUBLIC
ETHNIC GROUPS CROAT 90%, SERB 5%, OTHERS
LANGUAGES CROATIAN 96% **RELIGIONS** ROMAN CATHOLIC 88%, ORTHODOX 4%, ISLAM 1%, OTHERS **CURRENCY** KUNA = 100 LIPAS

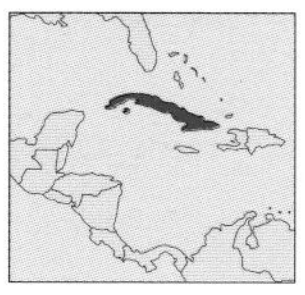

CUBA

GEOGRAPHY The Republic of Cuba is the largest island country in the Caribbean Sea. It consists of one large island, Cuba, the Isle of Youth (Isla de la Juventud), and about 1,600 small islets. Mountains and hills cover about a quarter of Cuba. The highest mountain range, the Sierra Maestra in the southeast, reaches 6,562 ft [2,000 m]. The rest of the land consists of gently rolling country or coastal plains, crossed by fertile valleys carved by the short, mostly shallow and narrow rivers.

POLITICS & ECONOMY Christopher Columbus discovered the island in 1492 and Spaniards began to settle there from 1511. Spanish rule ended in 1898, when the United States defeated Spain in the Spanish–American War. American influence in Cuba remained strong until 1959, when revolutionary forces under the leadership of Fidel Castro overthrew the dictatorship of Fulgencio Batista.

The United States opposed Castro's policies, when he turned to the Soviet Union for assistance. In 1962, a world crisis was averted when, under intense US pressure, the Soviet Union withdrew missile sites that could have been used to launch nuclear strikes against the United States. The breakup of the Soviet Union in 1991 damaged Cuba's economy and it worked to increase its trade with Latin America and China. Fidel Castro's brother, Raul, took over the leadership in 2008. He introduced reforms in 2009–12. In 2011, a new law allowed people to buy and sell private property. December 2014 saw the start of moves to normalize relations between Cuba and the US. During 2015, banking and diplomatic ties were re-established. The following year, some trade ties with the US were opened, as were diplomatic links with the EU. Fidel Castro died in April 2016. In 2017, the US government introduced new sanctions and travel restrictions. In April 2018 Raul Castro stood down and Miguel Díaz-Canel was named as president.

Sugarcane accounts for more than 60% of the country's exports. The other main crop is tobacco, and citrus fruits, rice, cattle, and milk production all make a contribution to the economy. Nickel oxide and pharmaceuticals are exported; tourism is also important.

AREA 42,803 SQ MI [110,861 SQ KM] **POPULATION** 11,032,000
CAPITAL HAVANA **GOVERNMENT** SOCIALIST REPUBLIC
ETHNIC GROUPS WHITE 65%, MESTIZO 25%, BLACK 10%
LANGUAGES SPANISH (OFFICIAL) **RELIGIONS** ROMAN CATHOLIC 27%, SANTERIA 13% **CURRENCY** CUBAN PESO = 100 CENTAVOS

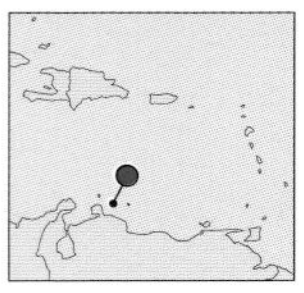

CURAÇAO

Part of the Netherlands Antilles until 2010, Curaçao is a self-governing territory within the Kingdom of the Netherlands. Oil refining, tourism, and trade are important.

AREA 171 SQ MI [444 SQ KM]
POPULATION 152,000 **CAPITAL** WILLEMSTAD

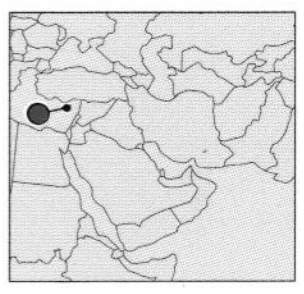

CYPRUS

GEOGRAPHY The Republic of Cyprus is an island nation in the northeastern Mediterranean Sea. Geographers regard it as part of Asia, but it resembles southern Europe in many ways. Its scenic mountain ranges include the southern Troodos Mountains, which reach 6,401 ft [1,951 m] at Mount Olympus, and the Kyrenia range in the north. Between them lies the Mesaoria plain. The climate is Mediterranean, with hot, dry summers and mild, moist winters.

POLITICS & ECONOMY Greeks settled on Cyprus around 3,200 years ago. From AD 330, the island was part of the Byzantine empire until, in the 1570s, Cyprus became part of the Turkish Ottoman empire. Turkish rule continued until 1878 when Cyprus was leased to Britain then went on to be proclaimed a colony in 1925. In the 1950s, Greek Cypriots, who made up four-fifths of the population, began a campaign for enosis (union) with Greece. Their leader was the Greek Orthodox Archbishop Makarios. A secret guerrilla force called EOKA attacked the British, who exiled Makarios in 1956; he returned to Cyprus in 1959.

Cyprus became an independent country in 1960, although Britain retained two military bases. Independent Cyprus had a constitution which provided for power-sharing between the Greek and Turkish Cypriots. But the constitution proved unworkable and fighting broke out between the two communities.

In 1974, Makarios was overthrown by Greek officers and Turkey invaded northern Cyprus. In 1979, the north was proclaimed the Turkish Republic of Northern Cyprus. The only country to recognize this state remains Turkey. In 2002, the European Union invited Cyprus to become a member in 2004. In 2004, the people voted on a UN plan to reunify Cyprus. The Turkish-Cypriots voted in favor, but the Greek-Cypriots voted against, unhappy at limits on their right to return to property located in the north. As a result, Cyprus was admitted to EU membership as a divided island. Talks on reunification continue, but progress is slow.

Cyprus got its name from the Greek word kypros, meaning copper. But little copper remains and the chief minerals today are asbestos and chromium. However, the most valuable activity in Cyprus is tourism. Manufactures include cement, clothes, and pharmaceuticals. Only around 4% of the population are involved in agriculture but 80% are employed in the service industry.

Problems due to the global financial crisis, and the south joining the euro in 2008, resulted in a contraction of the economy and a bailout from the EU at the beginning of 2013. Cypriot banks' substantial exposure to Greek debt is a cause for concern.

AREA 3,572 SQ MI [9,251 SQ KM] **POPULATION** 1,282,000
CAPITAL NICOSIA **GOVERNMENT** MULTIPARTY REPUBLIC
ETHNIC GROUPS GREEK CYPRIOT 77%, TURKISH CYPRIOT 18%, OTHERS
LANGUAGES GREEK AND TURKISH (BOTH OFFICIAL), ENGLISH
RELIGIONS GREEK ORTHODOX 78%, ISLAM 18%
CURRENCY EURO = 100 CENTS

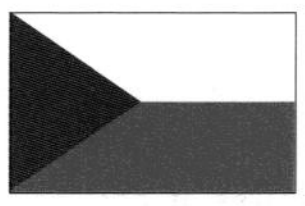

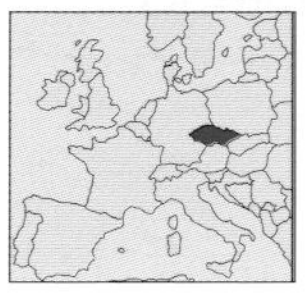

CZECHIA

GEOGRAPHY Until recently known as the Czech Republic, Czechia is the western three-fifths of the former country of Czechoslovakia. It contains two regions: Bohemia in the west and Moravia in the east. Mountains border much of the country in the west. The Bohemian basin in the north-center is a fertile lowland region, with Prague, the capital city, at its heart. Highlands cover much of the center of the country, with lowlands in the southeast.

The climate is influenced by the country's landlocked position in east-central Europe. Summers are warm and winters cold.

POLITICS & ECONOMY Czechoslovakia was born out of World War I (1914–18) and then occupied by Germany during World War II (1939–45). In 1948, Communist leaders took power and Czechoslovakia was allied to the Soviet Union. In the late 1980s, when democratic reforms were introduced in the Soviet Union, the Czechs also demanded change. Free elections were held in 1990, but differences between the Czechs and Slovaks led to the partitioning of the country (the "velvet divorce") on January 1, 1993. A former dissident, Vaclav Havel, became the first president. Czechia became a member of NATO in 1999 and a member of the European Union in 2004. In 2016, Parliament approved a new short form for the country's name, and the Czech Republic became Czechia. Milos Zeman won a second term as president in January 2018, campaigning on an anti-immigration stance.

Under Communist rule, Czechia became one of the most industrialized parts of Eastern Europe, and it remains a major producer of cars and machinery. It is classified by the World Bank as a "high-income" economy showing strong economic growth since the mid-2010s. The country has deposits of coal, uranium, and kaolin. Manufacturing employs about 38% of the work force.

AREA 30,450 SQ MI [78,866 SQ KM] **POPULATION** 10,703,000
CAPITAL PRAGUE **GOVERNMENT** MULTIPARTY REPUBLIC
ETHNIC GROUPS CZECH 64%, MORAVIAN 5%, SLOVAK 1%, POLISH, GERMAN, SILESIAN, GYPSY, HUNGARIAN, UKRAINIAN
LANGUAGES CZECH (OFFICIAL)
RELIGIONS ATHEIST 40%, ROMAN CATHOLIC 39%, PROTESTANT 4%, ORTHODOX 3%, OTHERS **CURRENCY** CZECH KORUNA = 100 HALER

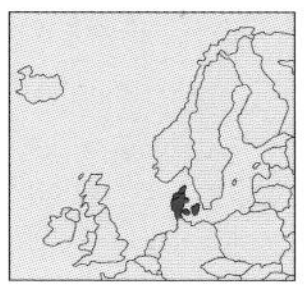

DENMARK

GEOGRAPHY The Kingdom of Denmark is the smallest country in Scandinavia. It consists of a peninsula, called Jutland (or Jylland), which is joined to Germany, and more than 400 islands, 89 of which are inhabited. The land is flat and mostly covered by rocks deposited by huge ice sheets during the last Ice Age. The highest point in Denmark is on Jutland. It is only 561 ft [171 m] above sea level. Denmark has a mild, moist climate, except during cold spells in winter when the Sound (Øresund) between Sjælland and Sweden may freeze over.

POLITICS & ECONOMY Once a Viking stronghold, Denmark formed a union with Norway and Sweden (which included Finland) in the 14th century. Sweden broke away in 1523, while Denmark lost Norway to Sweden in 1814. After 1945, Denmark joined NATO and became a member of the European Economic Community (now the European Union) in 1973. However, the country decided not to join the eurozone in a referendum in 2000. In 2009, Greenland joined the Færoe Islands in becoming a self-governing territory within the Danish realm.

Denmark is a prosperous country with a generous welfare system. Resources include oil and gas. Products include wind turbines, pharmaceuticals, machinery, processed food, and furniture. Meat and dairy farming, using intensively scientific methods, employs 3% of the people.

AREA 16,639 SQ MI [43,094 SQ KM] **POPULATION** 5,895,000
CAPITAL COPENHAGEN **GOVERNMENT** PARLIAMENTARY MONARCHY
ETHNIC GROUPS SCANDINAVIAN, INUIT, FÆROESE **LANGUAGES** DANISH (OFFICIAL), GREENLANDIC, ENGLISH, FÆROESE **RELIGIONS** EVANGELICAL LUTHERAN 75%, ISLAM 6% **CURRENCY** DANISH KRONE = 100 ØRE

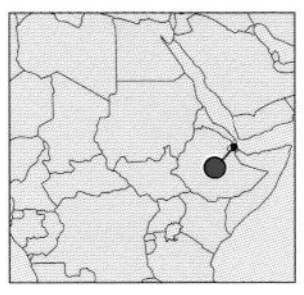

DJIBOUTI

GEOGRAPHY The Republic of Djibouti in eastern Africa occupies a strategic position where the Red Sea meets the Gulf of Aden. Djibouti has one of the world's hottest and driest climates.

POLITICS & ECONOMY Known as the French Territory of the Afars and Issas until 1977, Djibouti owes much of its importance to its rail link to Addis Ababa which allows it to function as a port for Ethiopia and other landlocked African states. It acts as a regional military base for the USA, France, China, Japan, and Italy, and is negotiating with Saudi Arabia and India. The current president, Ismail Omar Guelleh, has been in office since 1999. Djibouti is dominated by one political party, the People's Rally for Progress, with opposition parties having only limited freedom.

Djibouti is a poor country with few natural resources and the climate is unable to support much agriculture. Its economy is based largely on the revenue it gets from its port facilities and it relies heavily on foreign assistance. Unemployment is high at 40%.

AREA 8,958 SQ MI [23,200 SQ KM] **POPULATION** 938,000
CAPITAL DJIBOUTI **GOVERNMENT** MULTIPARTY REPUBLIC
ETHNIC GROUPS SOMALI 60%, AFAR 35% **LANGUAGES** ARABIC AND FRENCH (BOTH OFFICIAL) **RELIGIONS** ISLAM 94%, CHRISTIANITY 6%
CURRENCY DJIBOUTIAN FRANC

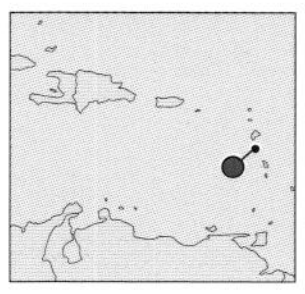

DOMINICA

The Commonwealth of Dominica, a former British colony, became independent in 1978. The island has a mountainous spine and, although less than 10% of the land is cultivated, agriculture employs 40% of the population. The economy has been over-reliant on growing bananas and Dominica is trying to develop its ecotourism business.

AREA 290 SQ MI [751 SQ KM] **POPULATION** 75,000 **CAPITAL** ROSEAU

DOMINICAN REPUBLIC

GEOGRAPHY Second largest of the Caribbean nations in both area and population, the Dominican Republic shares the island of Hispaniola with Haiti, with the Dominican Republic occupying the eastern two-thirds. The country is mountainous, and the hot and humid climate eases with altitude.

POLITICS & ECONOMY In 1492, Christopher Columbus landed on Hispaniola and Spaniards soon settled the island, followed by the French, who occupied the western third of the island (which is now Haiti). From 1930 to 1961, the country was ruled by the brutal dictator Rafael Trujillo. Political upheavals in the years that followed his assassination prompted the intervention of thousands of US troops. Faltering democracies and frequent natural disasters, primarily hurricanes, hampered the Dominican Republic's development in the late 20th century, but its economy has since grown rapidly. Tourism and the service industry are the mainstays of the economy. Sugarcane, coffee, rice, bananas, and cocoa are leading crops. Gold is mined.

AREA 18,730 SQ MI [48,511 SQ KM] **POPULATION** 10,597,000
CAPITAL SANTO DOMINGO **GOVERNMENT** MULTIPARTY REPUBLIC
ETHNIC GROUPS MULATTO 73%, WHITE 16%, BLACK 11%
LANGUAGES SPANISH (OFFICIAL) **RELIGIONS** ROMAN CATHOLIC 95%
CURRENCY DOMINICAN PESO = 100 CENTAVOS

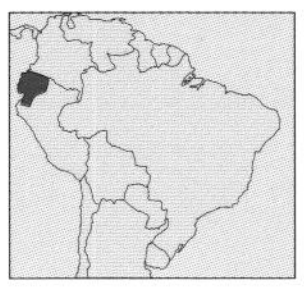

ECUADOR

GEOGRAPHY The Republic of Ecuador straddles the equator on the west coast of South America. Three ranges of the high Andes Mountains form the backbone of the country. Between the towering, snow-capped peaks of the mountains, some of which are volcanoes, lie a series of high plateaux, or basins. Nearly half of Ecuador's population live on these plateaux. The coast has a warm tropical climate, despite the cold offshore Peruvian Current. Inland, the altitude gives the plateaux spring-like weather throughout the year.

POLITICS & ECONOMY The Inca people of Peru conquered much of what is now Ecuador in the late 15th century and their language, Quechua, is still widely spoken. Spanish forces defeated the Incas in 1533 and took control of Ecuador until 1822.

In the 19th and 20th centuries, Ecuador suffered from political instability, while successive governments failed to tackle the country's social and economic problems. A war with Peru in 1941 led to a loss of territory. Economic crises in the early 21st century led to the adoption of the US dollar as the official currency. Rafael Correa, president since 2006, was succeeded by fellow left-winger Lenin Moreno in 2017. Attempts to stabilize the economy by introducing austerity measures, with support from the IMF, provoked large-scale protests in 2019, leading to the reining back of some subsidies.

The World Bank classifies Ecuador as an "upper-middle-income" developing country. Much dependent on its oil resources and the fluctuating world price of petrol, Ecuador has tried to diversify its economy. There is a wide disparity in the degree to which some stratas of society benefit from oil revenue: many live in poverty. Agriculture employs 28% of the people, and bananas, cocoa, and coffee are all important crops. Fishing, forestry, and manufacturing play a significant part in the economy.

AREA 109,483 SQ MI [283,561 SQ KM] **POPULATION** 17,093,000
CAPITAL QUITO **GOVERNMENT** MULTIPARTY REPUBLIC
ETHNIC GROUPS MESTIZO (MIXED WHITE/AMERINDIAN) 72%, MONTUBIO 7%, AFROECUADORIAN 7%, AMERINDIAN 7%, WHITE 6%
LANGUAGES SPANISH (OFFICIAL), QUECHUA, SHUAR
RELIGIONS ROMAN CATHOLIC 95% **CURRENCY** US DOLLAR = 100 CENTS

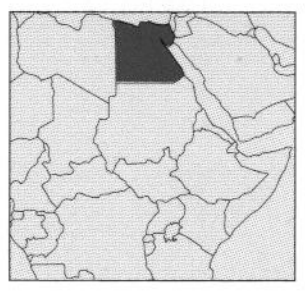

EGYPT

GEOGRAPHY The Arab Republic of Egypt is Africa's third largest country by population after Nigeria and Ethiopia, though it ranks 12th in area. Most of Egypt is desert. Almost all the people live either in the Nile Valley and its fertile delta or along the Suez Canal. This waterway, between the Mediterranean and Red seas, shortens the sea journey between the United Kingdom and India by 6,027 mi [9,700 km]. Recent attempts have been made to irrigate parts of the western desert.

Apart from the Nile Valley, Egypt can be divided into three other main regions. The Western and Eastern deserts are parts of the Sahara. The Sinai peninsula (Es Sina), to the east of the Suez Canal, is a mountainous desert region, falling geographically within Asia. It contains Egypt's highest peak, Gebel Katherîna (8,650 ft [2,637 m]); few people live in this area.

Egypt is a dry country. The low rainfall occurs, if at all, in winter and the country is one of the sunniest places on Earth.

POLITICS & ECONOMY Ancient Egypt, dating from around 5,000 years ago, was one of the great early civilizations. Throughout the country, pyramids, temples, and richly decorated tombs are memorials to its great achievements.

After Ancient Egypt declined, the country came under successive foreign rulers. The Arabs, who first occupied Egypt in the 7th century introducing their language and Islam, had a profound and lasting effect. Their influence was so great that most Egyptians now regard themselves as Arabs.

Egypt came under British rule in 1882, but it gained partial independence in 1922, becoming a monarchy. The monarchy was abolished in 1952, when Egypt became a republic, led by Gamal Abdel Nasser from 1954 to 1970. The creation of Israel in 1948 led Egypt into a series of wars. In 1979, it signed a peace treaty with Israel and regained the Sinai region, which it had lost in a war of 1967. Extremists opposed contacts with Israel and, in 1981, President Sadat, who had signed the treaty, was assassinated.

In February 2011, Hosni Mubarak, Egypt's president since 1981, was ousted following huge popular demonstrations. A Supreme Military Council took power and organized elections in 2011–12. President Muhammed Mursi from the formerly banned Muslim Brotherhood was elected in June 2012. Mursi was removed from power by the military in July 2013 and Abdel Fattah al-Sisi was elected in 2014. He was re-elected in March 2018, after credible opposing candidates withdrew or were arrested.

Egypt plays a major role in Arab affairs and is one of Africa's most industrialized countries, yet most of its people are poor. Oil and textiles are the country's main exports. Tourism is vitally important to the economy but is threatened by the rise in attacks by Islamist extremists. The country is struggling to support its rapidly growing population, and in an attempt to alleviate congestion in Cairo, a new Administrative Capital is being built to the east, although the project faces financial challenges.

AREA 386,659 SQ MI [1,001,449 SQ KM] **POPULATION** 106,437,000
CAPITAL CAIRO **GOVERNMENT** REPUBLIC
ETHNIC GROUPS EGYPTIANS/BEDOUINS/BERBERS 99%
LANGUAGES ARABIC (OFFICIAL), FRENCH, ENGLISH **RELIGIONS** ISLAM (MAINLY SUNNI MUSLIM) 90%, CHRISTIANITY (MAINLY COPTIC CHRISTIAN) AND OTHERS 10% **CURRENCY** EGYPTIAN POUND = 100 PIASTRES

EL SALVADOR

GEOGRAPHY The Republic of El Salvador is the only country in Central America not to have a coast on the Caribbean Sea. El Salvador has a narrow coastal plain along the Pacific Ocean. Behind the coastal plain, the coastal range is a zone of rugged mountains, including volcanoes, which overlooks a densely populated inland plateau. Beyond the plateau, the land rises to the sparsely populated interior highlands. The coast has a hot tropical climate, but inland this is moderated by the altitude. Rain is heavy between May and October.

POLITICS & ECONOMY Amerindians have lived in El Salvador for thousands of years. The ruins of Mayan pyramids, built between AD 100 and 1000, are still found in the western part of the country.

Spain first conquered the area in 1524, and ruled until 1821. In 1823, all the Central American countries, except for Panama, set up the Central American Federation, with El Salvador withdrawing in 1840 and declaring its independence in 1841. It suffered from instability throughout the 19th century. The 20th century saw more stable government, although from 1931 military dictatorships alternated with elected governments.

The country remained poor and in the 1970s protesters demanded that the government introduce reforms. Kidnappings and murders committed by left- and right-wing groups were common. A civil war broke out in 1979 between the US-backed government forces and left-wing guerrillas. A ceasefire was agreed in 1992. In 2011, the US added El Salvador and Belize to its list of countries considered to be major producers or transit routes of illegal drugs. Its murder rate is one of the world's highest.

The World Bank classifies El Salvador as a "lower-middle-income" economy. Often hit by natural disasters, the country relies heavily on remittances from abroad, especially the USA. About three-quarters of the country is farmed. Coffee, grown in the highlands, is the main export, followed by sugar and cotton, which grow on the coastal lowlands.

Area 8,124 sq mi [21,041 sq km] **Population** 6,528,000
Capital San Salvador **Government** Republic
Ethnic groups Mestizo (mixed White and Amerindian) 86%, White 13%, Amerindian 1% **Languages** Spanish (official) **Religions** Roman Catholic 57%, Protestant 21% **Currency** US dollar = 100 cents

EQUATORIAL GUINEA

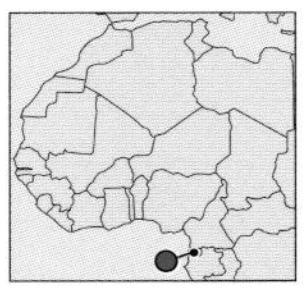

GEOGRAPHY The Republic of Equatorial Guinea is a small republic in west-central Africa. It consists of a mainland territory which makes up 90% of the land area, called Rio Muni, between Cameroon and Gabon, and five offshore islands in the Bight of Bonny, the largest of which is Bioko. The island of Annobon lies 350 mi [560 km] southwest of Rio Muni. Rio Muni consists mainly of hills and plateaux behind the coastal plains.

The climate is hot and humid. Bioko is mountainous, with the land rising to 9,869 ft [3,008 m], and hence it is particularly rainy. However, there is a marked dry season between the months of December and February. Mainland Rio Muni has a similar climate, though the rainfall diminishes inland.

POLITICS & ECONOMY Portuguese navigators reached the area in 1471. In 1778, Portugal granted Bioko, together with rights over Rio Muni, to Spain. In 1959, Spain made Bioko and Rio Muni provinces of overseas Spain and, in 1963, it gave them a degree of self-government. Equatorial Guinea became independent in 1968.

The first president of Equatorial Guinea, Francisco Macias Nguema, proved to be a tyrant. Overthrown in 1979, a Supreme Military Council then took control, led by Obiang Nguema. In 1991, a nominally democratic system was restored, with Obiang as president. He has been re-elected several times, most recently in 2016, in a series of flawed elections. Equatorial Guinea is widely recognized as one of Africa's worst abusers of human rights.

Substantial reserves of oil, discovered in 1996, fueled rapid economic growth and account for most of the country's export revenue. Despite being one of the largest oil producers in sub-Saharan Africa, poverty is widespread. Much of the population lives by subsistence farming. Crops include cassava, sweet potatoes, and bananas.

Area 10,830 sq mi [28,051 sq km] **Population** 857,000
Capital Malabo **Government** Republic
Ethnic groups Bubi (on Bioko), Fang (in Rio Muni)
Languages Spanish and French (both official)
Religions Christianity **Currency** CFA franc = 100 centimes

ERITREA

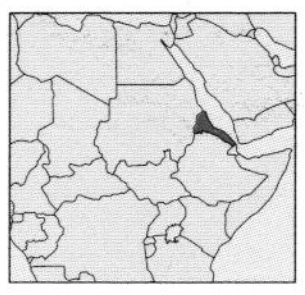

GEOGRAPHY The State of Eritrea consists of a hot, dry coastal plain facing the Red Sea, with a fairly mountainous area in the center. Most people live in the cooler highland area.

POLITICS & ECONOMY From the 1st century AD, Eritrea was part of the ancient Kingdom of Axum. The Ottoman Turks took over the area in the 16th century and it became an Italian colony in the 1880s. The Italians were driven out in 1941 and, in 1952, it became part of Ethiopia. A guerrilla struggle launched in 1961 ended in 1993, when Eritrea became independent. Economic recovery was hampered by conflict first with Yemen, over three islands in the Red Sea, and then with Ethiopia. A fragile peace has been negotiated and a treaty signed with Ethiopia in 2018. The country faces the huge task of reconstruction. Isaias Afwerki has been president since 1993. The UN has repeatedly accused the country's leaders of human rights violations and hundreds of thousands of people have fled.

Eritrea's main economic activities are farming and livestock rearing, both badly affected by chronic drought, with some manufacturing based around Asmara. Exploitation of the country's copper and gold resources may drive future economic growth.

Area 45,405 sq mi [117,600 sq km] **Population** 6,147,000
Capital Asmara **Government** Transitional government
Ethnic groups Tigrinya 55%, Tigre 30%, Saho 4%, Kunama 2%, others 9% **Languages** Tigrinya, Arabic, English (all official), others
Religions Islam, Coptic Christian, Roman Catholic
Currency Nakfa = 100 cents

ESTONIA

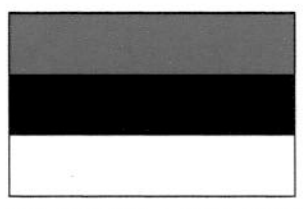

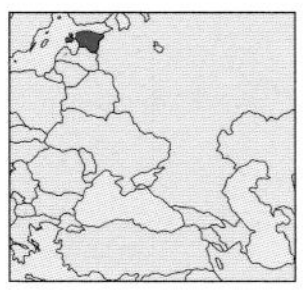

GEOGRAPHY The Republic of Estonia is the smallest of the three states on the Baltic Sea. Estonia consists of a generally flat plain which was covered by ice sheets during the Ice Age. The land is strewn with moraine (rocks deposited by the ice).

The country is dotted with more than 1,500 small lakes. The large Lake Peipus (Ozero Chudskoye) and the River Narva together make up much of Estonia's eastern border with Russia. The largest of the islands is Saaremaa (Ösel). The climate is fairly mild because of the moderating effects of the sea.

POLITICS & ECONOMY The ancestors of the Estonians, who are related to the Finns, settled in the area several thousand years ago. German crusaders, known as the Teutonic Knights, introduced Christianity in the early 13th century. By the 16th century, German noblemen owned much of the land in Estonia. In 1561, Sweden took the northern part of the country and Poland the south. From 1625, Sweden controlled the entire country until handing it over to Russia in 1721. Estonian nationalists campaigned for their independence from around the mid-19th century. Finally, Estonia was proclaimed independent in 1918.

In 1939, Germany and the Soviet Union agreed to take over parts of Eastern Europe. In 1940, Soviet forces occupied Estonia, but they were driven out by the Germans in 1941. Soviet troops returned in 1944 and Estonia became one of the 15 Soviet Socialist Republics of the Soviet Union. The Estonians strongly opposed Soviet rule and many of them were deported to Siberia.

Political changes in the Soviet Union in the late 1980s led to renewed demands for freedom. In 1990, the Estonian government declared the country independent and, finally, the Soviet Union recognized this act in September 1991.

Under Soviet rule, Estonia was the most prosperous of the three Baltic states. After independence, Estonia turned increasingly to the West, becoming a member of both the North Atlantic Treaty Organization and the European Union in 2004. In 2011, it joined the eurozone. From March 2017 NATO deployed armed forces to Estonia amid reports of a Russian troop build-up across the border. Estonia's resources include oil shale and its forests. Industries produce machinery, transport equipment, processed food, and petrochemical products. Major crops include wheat, barley, and rapeseed. Around a quarter of the population are of Russian origin and, due to official language requirements, they can be subject to discrimination.

Area 17,413 sq mi [45,100 sq km] **Population** 1,220,000
Capital Tallinn **Government** Multiparty republic
Ethnic groups Estonian 69%, Russian 26%, Ukrainian 2%, Belarusian 1%, Finnish 1% **Languages** Estonian (official), Russian
Religions Lutheran, Russian and Estonian Orthodox, Methodist, Baptist, Roman Catholic **Currency** Euro = 100 cents

ESWATINI

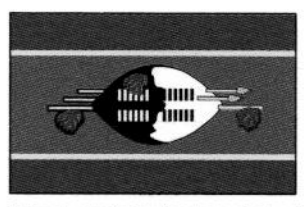

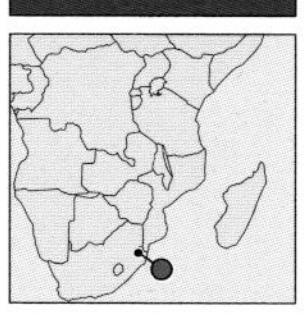

GEOGRAPHY Officially renamed in 2018 as the Kingdom of Eswatini, this is a small, land-locked country in southern Africa. The country has four regions which run north–south. In the west, the Highveld, with an average height of 3,950 ft [1,200 m], makes up 30% of Eswatini. The Middleveld, between 1,150 ft and 3,280 ft [350 m to 1,000 m], covers 28% of the country. The Lowveld, with an average height of 886 ft [270 m], covers another 33%. Finally, the Lebombo Mountains reach 2,600 ft [800 m] along the eastern border. The Lowveld is almost tropical, with average temperatures of 72°F [22°C] and low rainfall.

POLITICS & ECONOMY In 1894, Britain and the Boers of South Africa agreed to put Swaziland, as it was then known, under the control of the South African Republic (the Transvaal). But at the end of the Anglo–Boer War (1899–1902), Britain took control. In 1968, when it became fully independent as a constitutional monarchy, the head of state was King Sobhuza II. Sobhuza died in 1982 and was succeeded by his son, who, in 1986, became King Mswati III. Political parties are banned from participating in elections and Mswati rules by decree. In 2005, he signed a new constitution, but Eswatini remains an absolute monarchy. There have been pro-democracy protests in recent years.

This is a developing country. Farm products and processed food and drink, sugar, wood pulp, citrus fruits, and canned fruit are the leading exports. It is heavily dependent on South Africa and it shares two problems with its large neighbor – widespread poverty and the world's highest incidence of HIV/AIDS.

Area 6,704 sq mi [17,364 sq km] **Population** 1,113,000
Capital Mbabane (administrative); Lobamba (legislative)
Government Monarchy **Ethnic groups** African 97%, European 3%
Languages Siswati and English (both official)
Religions Zionist (a mix of Christianity and traditional beliefs) 40%, Roman Catholic 20%, Islam 10% **Currency** Lilangeni = 100 cents

ETHIOPIA

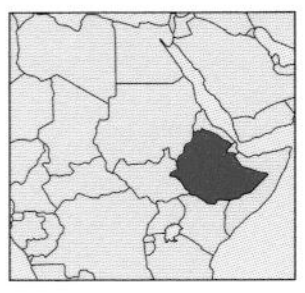

GEOGRAPHY Ethiopia is a landlocked country in northeastern Africa. The land is mainly mountainous, though there are extensive plains in the east, bordering southern Eritrea, and in the south, bordering Somalia. The highlands are divided into two blocks by an arm of the Great Rift Valley which runs throughout eastern Africa. North of the Rift Valley, the land is especially rugged, rising to 14,872 ft [4,533 m] at Ras Dashen. Southeast of Ras Dashen is Lake Tana, source of the River Abay (Blue Nile). The climate is affected by the altitude. The rainfall in the highlands is generally more than 39 inches [1,000 mm]. The lowlands are hot and arid.

POLITICS & ECONOMY Ethiopia was the home of an ancient monarchy, which became Christian in the 4th century. In the 7th century, Muslims gained control of the lowlands, but Christianity survived in the highlands. Ethiopia resisted attempts to colonize it, until Italy invaded in 1935. With help from the UK, the Italians were driven out in 1941 and Emperor Haile Selassie was put back on the throne. He reigned until deposed in a military coup in 1974.

In 1952, Eritrea was federated with Ethiopia. But in 1961, Eritrean nationalists demanded their freedom and began a long-lasting struggle for independence. The military pro-Soviet Derg regime (1974–91) presided over a period of violent conflict, drought, and famine. In 1995, Ethiopia was divided into nine provinces, reflecting its great ethnic diversity. Boundary disputes with Eritrea escalated into war in the late 1990s. A peace agreement was reached in 2001, but border incursions by both sides continued. In 2016, human rights protests broke out, leading to the resignation of PM Hailemariam Desalegn and his replacement by Abiy Ahmed in 2018. He signed a peace agreement with Eritrea the same year and reopened the border.

Ethiopia's agriculture-based economy is at the mercy of a fickle climate. Coffee and the drug "khat" are leading exports. Although still heavily dependent on foreign aid, Ethiopia has one of the fastest growing non-oil economies in Africa.

Area 426,370 sq mi [1,104,300 sq km] **Population** 110,871,000
Capital Addis Ababa **Government** Federation of nine provinces
Ethnic groups Oromo 34%, Amhara 27%, Somali 6%, Tigraway 6%, Sidama 4%
Languages Amharic (official), Oromo, many others
Religions Ethiopian Orthodox 43%, Islam 34%, Protestant 19%
Currency Birr = 100 santim

FALKLAND ISLANDS

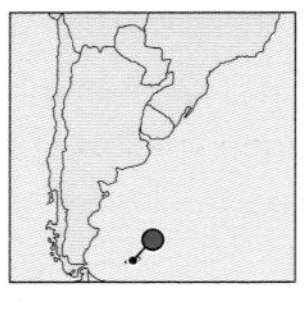

Comprising two main islands and over 200 small ones, the Falkland Islands lie 300 mi [480 km] from South America. Sheep farming and fishing are the main activities, though oil and diamonds are being sought. Argentina disputes Britain's sovereignty of the islands, but a referendum in 2013 resulted in an overwhelming vote to stay British.

Area 4,700 sq mi [12,173 sq km]
Population 3,000 **Capital** Stanley

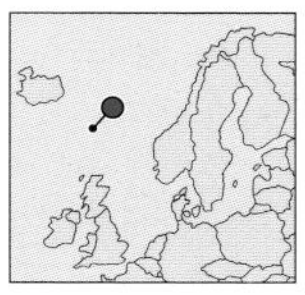

FÆROE ISLANDS

The Færoe Islands are a group of 18 volcanic islands and some reefs in the North Atlantic Ocean. The islands have been Danish since the 1380s, but they became largely self-governing in 1948. The islands are heavily reliant on fishing although the discovery of some oil may allow diversification in the future. Denmark still provides a subsidy.

AREA 540 sq mi [1,399 sq km]
POPULATION 52,000 **CAPITAL** Tórshavn

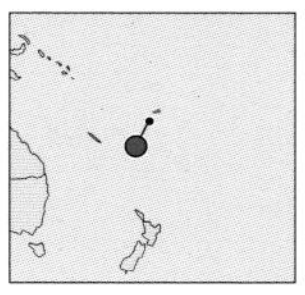

FIJI

The Republic of Fiji (the official name of Fiji since February 2011) consists of more than 800 Melanesian islands, the biggest being Viti Levu and Vanua Levu. The climate is tropical. A former British colony, Fiji became independent in 1970. Its recent history has been marred by tension between indigenous Fijians and the ethnic Indian community. Such political instability has harmed the economy, which relies on tourism and sugar.

AREA 7,056 sq mi [18,274 sq km] **POPULATION** 940,000 **CAPITAL** Suva

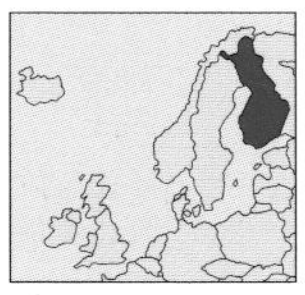

FINLAND

GEOGRAPHY The Republic of Finland is a beautiful country in northern Europe. In the south, behind the coastal lowlands where most Finns live, lies a region of sparkling lakes carved out by ice sheets in the Ice Age. The thinly populated northern uplands cover about two-fifths of the country.

Helsinki, the capital city, has warm summers, but the average temperatures between the months of December and March are below freezing. Snow covers the land in winter. The north has less precipitation than the south, but it is much colder.

POLITICS & ECONOMY Between 1150 and 1809, Finland was under Swedish rule and close links between the countries continue today. Swedish remains an official language in Finland and many towns have Swedish as well as Finnish names.

In 1809, Finland became a grand duchy of the Russian empire. It finally declared itself independent in 1917, following the Russian Revolution. But during World War II (1939–45), the Soviet Union declared war on Finland and took part of Finland's territory. Finland allied itself with Germany, but it lost more land to the Soviet Union at the end of the war.

After World War II, Finland became a neutral country and negotiated peace treaties with the Soviet Union. Finland also strengthened its relations with other northern European countries and became an associate member of the European Free Trade Association (EFTA) in 1961 and a full member in 1986. It then joined the European Union on January 1, 1995, adopting the euro as its currency in 2002.

Forests are the chief resource and wood, wood products, and paper once dominated the economy. They still make up about a quarter of exports, but, since World War II, Finland has set up many new industries, which employ around a quarter of the people. One of Finland's main advantages is a well-qualified work force who enjoy one of the highest rates of per capita income in Western Europe. Major exports include electrical equipment, machinery, and paper products. However, dealing with a growing aging population is a challenge to be met.

AREA 130,558 sq mi [338,145 sq km] **POPULATION** 5,587,000
CAPITAL Helsinki **GOVERNMENT** Multiparty republic
ETHNIC GROUPS Finnish 93%, Swedish 6%
LANGUAGES Finnish and Swedish (both official)
RELIGIONS Evangelical Lutheran 71% **CURRENCY** Euro = 100 cents

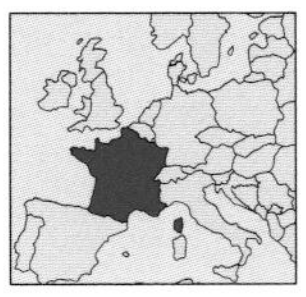

FRANCE

GEOGRAPHY The Republic of France is the largest country in Western Europe. The scenery is extremely varied. The Vosges Mountains overlook the Rhine valley in the northeast, the Jura Mountains and the Alps form the borders with Switzerland and Italy in the southeast, while the Pyrenees straddle France's border with Spain. The only large highland area entirely within France is the Massif Central between the Rhône–Saône valley and the basin of Aquitaine in southern France.

Brittany (Bretagne) and Normandy (Normande) form a scenic region. Fertile lowlands cover most of northern France, including the densely populated Paris basin. Another major lowland area, the Aquitanian basin, is in the southwest, while the Rhône–Saône valley and the Mediterranean lowlands are in the southeast.

The climate of France varies from west to east and from north to south. The west comes under the moderating influence of the Atlantic Ocean, giving generally mild weather. To the east, summers are warmer and winters colder. The climate also becomes warmer as one travels from north to south. The Mediterranean Sea coast has hot, dry summers and mild, moist winters. The Alps, Jura, and Pyrenees mountains have snowy winters. Winter sports centers are found in all three areas.

POLITICS & ECONOMY The Romans conquered France (then called Gaul) in the 50s BC. Roman rule began to decline in the 5th century AD and, in 486, the Frankish realm (as France was known) became independent under a Christian king, Clovis. In 800, Charlemagne, who had been king since 768, became emperor of the Romans. He extended France's boundaries, but in 843 his empire was divided into three parts and the area of France contracted. After the Norman invasion of England in 1066, large areas of France came under English rule, but this was all but ended in 1453.

France later became a powerful monarchy. But the French Revolution (1789–99) ended absolute rule by French kings. In 1799, Napoleon Bonaparte took power and fought a series of brilliant military campaigns before his final defeat in 1815. The monarchy was restored until 1848, when the Second Republic was founded. In 1852, Napoleon's nephew became Napoleon III, but the Third Republic was established in 1875. France was the scene of much fighting during World War I (1914–18) and World War II (1939–45), causing great loss of life and much damage to the economy.

In 1946, France adopted a new constitution, establishing the Fourth Republic. But political instability and costly colonial wars slowed France's post-war recovery. In 1958, Charles de Gaulle was elected president and he introduced a new constitution, giving the president extra powers and inaugurating the Fifth Republic.

Since the 1960s, France has made rapid economic progress, becoming one of the most prosperous nations in the European Union. But France's government faced a number of problems, including unemployment, pollution, and the growing number of elderly people. France is still facing economic challenges due to low growth and high public spending. A social issue concerns the large numbers of immigrants, including Muslims from North Africa, and in 2005, France was rocked by inter-ethnic violence. It has suffered several Islamist terrorist attacks since 2015.

In 2002, the euro replaced the franc as France's currency. In 2009, the right-wing president Nicolas Sarkozy announced that France would rejoin NATO. Presidential elections in 2017 were won by Emmanuel Macron. His proposed labor reforms sparked strikes in 2018, and price increases introduced to reduce the use of fossil fuels prompted violent street demonstrations by the "yellow shirts" from 2018 to 2019.

France is one of the world's most developed countries. Its principal natural resource is its fertile soil, and fast-flowing rivers offer the potential for much hydroelectric power. France is also one of the world's top manufacturing nations, and it has often innovated in bold and imaginative ways. The TGV and hypermarkets are typical examples. Paris is a world center of fashion industries. Manufactures include aircraft, cars, chemicals, electronic and metal products, machinery, processed food, steel, and textiles.

Agriculture employs about 3% of the people, but France is the largest producer of farm products in Western Europe, producing most of the food it needs. Wheat is the leading crop and livestock farming is of major importance. Fishing and forestry are leading industries, while tourism is a major activity.

AREA 212,934 sq mi [551,500 sq km] **POPULATION** 68,084,000
CAPITAL Paris **GOVERNMENT** Multiparty republic
ETHNIC GROUPS Celtic, Latin, Arab, Teutonic, Slavic
LANGUAGES French (official) **RELIGIONS** Roman Catholic 85%, Islam 8%, others **CURRENCY** Euro = 100 cents

FRENCH GUIANA

GEOGRAPHY French Guiana is the smallest country in mainland South America. The coastal plain is swampy in places, but some dry areas are cultivated. Inland lies a plateau, with the low Serra Tumucumaque in the south. Most of the rivers run north toward the Atlantic Ocean.

French Guiana has a hot, equatorial climate, with high temperatures throughout the year. The rainfall is heavy, especially between December and June, but the climate is dry between August and October. The northeast trade winds blow constantly across the country.

POLITICS & ECONOMY The first people to live in what is now French Guiana were Amerindians. Today, only a few of them survive in the interior. The first Europeans to explore the coast arrived in 1500, and they were followed by adventurers seeking El Dorado, the mythical city of gold. Cayenne was founded in 1637 by a group of French merchants and the area became a French colony in the late 17th century.

France used the colony as a penal settlement for political prisoners from the times of the French Revolution in the 1790s. From the 1850s to 1945, the country became notorious as a place where prisoners were harshly treated. Many of them died, unable to survive in the tropical conditions.

In 1946, French Guiana became an overseas department of France, and in 1974 it also became an administrative region. An independence movement developed in the 1980s, but most people want to retain their links with France. In 2010, the people voted in a referendum to reject plans for increased autonomy.

Although it has rich forest and mineral resources, such as bauxite (aluminum ore), French Guiana is a developing country. It depends greatly on France for money to run its services and the government is the country's biggest employer. Since 1968, Kourou, the European Space Agency's rocket-launching site, has earned money for France by sending communications satellites into space.

AREA 34,749 sq mi [90,000 sq km] **POPULATION** 250,000
CAPITAL Cayenne **GOVERNMENT** Overseas department of France
ETHNIC GROUPS Black or mixed 66%, East Indian/Chinese and Amerindian 12%, White 12%, others 10%
LANGUAGES French (official) **RELIGIONS** Roman Catholic
CURRENCY Euro = 100 cents

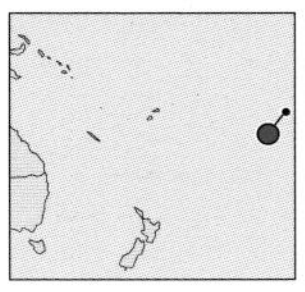

FRENCH POLYNESIA

French Polynesia consists of 130 islands, of which Tahiti is the most densely populated. It became a French protectorate in 1843 and has been an overseas "collectivity" since 2003. The links with France ensure a high standard of living. From the 1960s to the 1990s France tested nuclear weapons on the uninhabited atolls.

AREA 1,544 sq mi [4,000 sq km]
POPULATION 297,000 **CAPITAL** Papeete

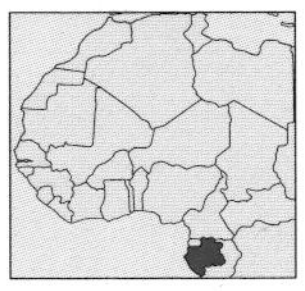

GABON

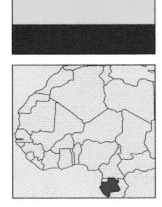

GEOGRAPHY The Gabonese Republic lies on the equator in west-central Africa. In area, it is a little larger than the United Kingdom, with a coastline 500 mi [800 km] long. Behind the narrow, partly lagoon-lined coastal plain, the land rises to hills, plateaux, and mountains divided by deep valleys carved by the River Ogooué and its tributaries.

Most of Gabon has an equatorial climate, with high temperatures and humidity throughout the year.

POLITICS & ECONOMY Gabon became a French colony in the 1880s, but it achieved full independence in 1960. In 1964, an attempted coup was put down when French troops intervened and crushed the revolt. In 1967, Bernard-Albert Bongo, who later renamed himself El Hadj Omar Bongo, became president and remained in power until his death in 2009, when he was succeeded by his son, Ali Ben Bongo Ondimba. In 2016 presidential elections, marred by violence and accusations of fraud, Ali Bongo won a second term.

Gabon's natural resources include its forests, oil and gas deposits, manganese, and uranium. Its economy is heavily dependent on oil, but falling oil revenue means that it has to diversify. Ecotourism is growing, but agriculture still employs about 60% of the work force. Many farmers produce little more than they need to support their families.

AREA 103,347 sq mi [267,668 sq km] **POPULATION** 2,285,000
CAPITAL Libreville **GOVERNMENT** Multiparty republic
ETHNIC GROUPS Four major Bantu tribes: Fang, Bapounou, Nzebi and Obamba **LANGUAGES** French (official), Fang, Myene, Nzebi, Bapounou/Eschira, Bandjabi
RELIGIONS Christianity 65%, animist, Islam
CURRENCY CFA franc = 100 centimes

GAMBIA, THE

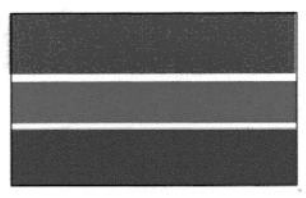

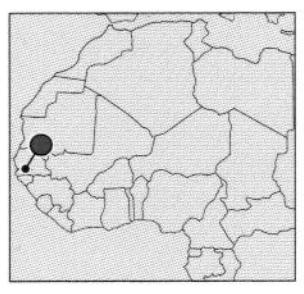

GEOGRAPHY The Republic of The Gambia is the smallest country in mainland Africa. It consists of a narrow strip of land bordering the River Gambia. The Gambia is almost entirely enclosed by Senegal, except along the short Atlantic coastline.

The Gambia has hot and humid summers, but winter temperatures (November to May) drop to around 61°F [16°C]. In the summer, moist southwesterlies bring rain, which is heaviest on the coast.

POLITICS & ECONOMY English traders established themselves on the River Gambia in the late 16th century and the country was a British colony from 1888 until independence in 1965.

In 1981, an attempted coup in The Gambia was put down with the help of Senegalese troops. Following this, in 1982, The Gambia and Senegal set up a defense alliance, called the Confederation of Senegambia, which was dissolved in 1989. In 1994, a military group led by Captain Yahya Jammeh overthrew the government of Sir Dawda Jawara. Jammeh remained in power until 2016, when he was defeated by Adama Barrow. Jammeh refused to accept the result and left only after neighboring countries undertook mediation and threatened armed intervention. Barrow's United Democratic Party won a landslide victory at parliamentary elections in 2017.

Agriculture is the chief activity, employing three-quarters of the population and accounting for around 20% of GDP. Food crops include cassava, millet, and sorghum, but groundnuts (peanuts) and groundnut products are the main exports. About one-third of the population live below the poverty line. Tourism is important to the economy, as are remittances sent back from overseas workers. Offshore oilfields were discovered in 2004 but this resource has yet to be developed.

AREA 4,361 sq mi [11,295 sq km] **POPULATION** 2,221,000
CAPITAL Banjul **GOVERNMENT** Republic
ETHNIC GROUPS Mandinka 42%, Fula 18%, Wolof 16%, Jola 10%, Serahuli 9%, others
LANGUAGES English (official), Mandinka, Wolof, Fula
RELIGIONS Islam 90%, Christianity 8%, traditional beliefs 2%
CURRENCY Dalasi = 100 bututs

GEORGIA

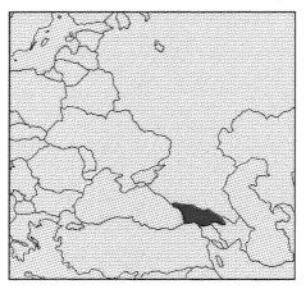

GEOGRAPHY Georgia is a country on the borders of Europe and Asia, facing the Black Sea. The land is rugged with the Caucasus Mountains forming its northern border.

The highest mountain in this range, Mount Elbrus (18,510 ft [5,642 m]), lies over the border in Russia. The Black Sea plains have hot summers and mild winters. The rainfall is heavy, though inland areas are drier.

POLITICS & ECONOMY The first Georgian state was set up nearly 2,500 years ago but has been overrun by a variety of conquering armies. From the 16th to the 18th centuries, Persia and the Turkish Ottoman empire struggled for control of the area, and in the late 18th century Georgia sought the protection of Russia. By the early 19th century, it was part of the Russian empire. After the Russian Revolution of 1917, Georgia declared its independence, but Russia invaded, making it part of the Soviet regime. Georgia declared itself independent in 1991 and it became a separate country when the Soviet Union was dissolved in 1991.

Georgia contains three regions populated by minority peoples: Abkhazia in the northwest, South Ossetia in north-central Georgia, and Ajaria in the southwest. Civil war broke out in South Ossetia in the early 1990s, while fierce fighting continued in Abkhazia until the late 1990s. In 2000, Georgia agreed to recognize Ajaria's autonomy in the country's constitution. In 2003, the pro-Western Mikhail Saakashvili was elected president following the "Rose Revolution." After Saakashvili's re-election in 2008, relations with Russia deteriorated. In August 2008, Georgia tried to retake South Ossetia by force. Russian troops counterattacked and drove Georgian troops out of South Ossetia and Abkhazia. Saakashvili resigned after parliamentary elections in 2012 were won by the opposition Georgian Dream coalition. They changed the presidency to a mainly ceremonial role and won a majority in 2016 elections. In 2019 Giorgi Gakharia became prime minister.

The World Bank classifies Georgia as an "upper-middle-income" economy. Agriculture is important, with products including barley, citrus fruits, grapes for wine-making, and tea. Livestock are reared. Manufactured products include vehicles and metals. Hydroelectricity provides most of Georgia's power needs but gas and oil have to be imported. Unemployment remains high.

AREA 26,911 sq mi [69,700 sq km] **POPULATION** 4,934,000
CAPITAL Tbilisi **GOVERNMENT** Multiparty republic
ETHNIC GROUPS Georgian 84%, Azeri 7%, Armenian 6%, Russian 1%, others 2%
LANGUAGES Georgian (official), Russian, Armenian, Azeri; Abkhaz (official in Abkhazia) **RELIGIONS** Georgian Orthodox 84%, Islam 10%, Armenian Gregorian 4% **CURRENCY** Lari = 100 tetri

GERMANY

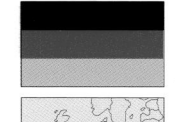

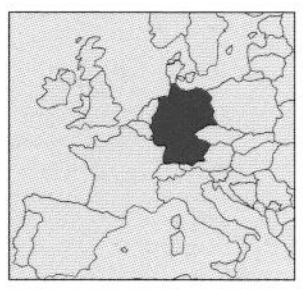

GEOGRAPHY The Federal Republic of Germany is the fourth largest country in Western Europe, after France, Spain, and Sweden. The North German Plain borders the North Sea in the northwest and the Baltic Sea in the northeast. Major rivers draining the plain include the Weser, Elbe, and Oder.

The central highlands include the Harz Mountains, the Thuringian Forest (Thüringer Wald), the Ore Mountains (Erzgebirge), and the Bohemian Forest (Böhmerwald) on the Czech border. The Bavarian Alps in the south contain Germany's highest peak, Zugspitze, at 9,718 ft [2,962 m] above sea level. The Black Forest (Schwarzwald) in the southwest overlooks the River Rhine. Northwestern Germany has a mild climate, but the Baltic coasts are cooler. To the south, the climate becomes more continental, especially in the highlands.

POLITICS & ECONOMY Germany and its allies were defeated in World War I (1914–18) and the country became a republic. Adolf Hitler came to power in 1933 and ruled as a dictator. His order to invade Poland led to the start of World War II (1939–45), which ended with Germany in ruins.

In 1945, Germany was divided into four military zones. In 1949, the American, British, and French zones were amalgamated to form the Federal Republic of Germany (West Germany), while the Soviet zone became the German Democratic Republic (East Germany), a Communist state. Berlin, which had also been partitioned, became a divided city. West Berlin was part of West Germany, while East Berlin became the capital of East Germany. Bonn was the capital of West Germany.

Tension between East and West mounted during the Cold War, but West Germany rebuilt its economy quickly. In East Germany, the recovery was less rapid. In the late 1980s, reforms in the Soviet Union led to unrest in East Germany. Free elections were held in East Germany in 1990 and, on October 3, 1990, Germany was reunited.

In the 1990s, the government faced many problems, especially those arising from reunification. In 1999, the parliament moved from Bonn to the reconstructed Reichstag building in Berlin. In 2005, Angela Merkel became Germany's first female Chancellor. Merkel's unpopular policy of welcoming asylum seekers adversely affected her party's showing in 2017 elections and boosted the vote of the far-right.

West Germany's "economic miracle" after World War II was greatly helped by foreign aid. Today, Germany is one of the world's major economic powers. It is a leading member of the European Union and the 19-member eurozone. Since 2011, it has helped to maintain the eurozone by supporting debt-ridden countries, such as Greece. The mainstay of its export-led economy is manufacturing. Exports include machinery, metals, chemicals, and vehicles. Germany has some coal, potash, and rock salt deposits, but it imports many industrial raw materials. Germany also imports food. Leading agricultural products include fruits, grapes for wine-making, potatoes, sugar beet, and vegetables. Livestock include beef cattle and pigs.

AREA 137,846 sq mi [357,022 sq km] **POPULATION** 79,903,000
CAPITAL Berlin **GOVERNMENT** Federal multiparty republic
ETHNIC GROUPS German 92%, Turkish 2%, Serbo-Croatian, Italian, Greek, Polish, Spanish **LANGUAGES** German (official)
RELIGIONS Protestant (mainly Lutheran) 34%, Roman Catholic 34%, Islam 4%, others **CURRENCY** Euro = 100 cents

GHANA

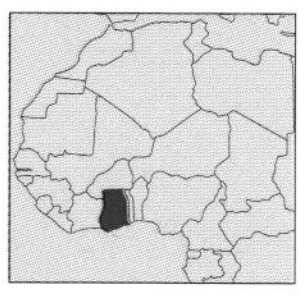

GEOGRAPHY The Republic of Ghana faces the Gulf of Guinea in West Africa, just north of the equator. In the southwest, behind the thickly populated southern coastal plains, which are lined with lagoons, lies a plateau region. Accra has a hot, tropical climate. Rain occurs all through the year, though Accra is drier than areas inland.

POLITICS & ECONOMY Portuguese explorers reached the area in 1471 and named it the Gold Coast. The area became a center of the slave trade in the 17th century until it was ended in the 1860s and, gradually, the British took control of the area. After independence in 1957 the country was renamed Ghana. Attempts were made to develop the economy by creating large state-owned manufacturing industries, but debt and corruption, together with falls in the price of cocoa, caused economic problems. Instability and frequent coups followed. In 1981, power was invested in a Provisional National Defense Council, led by Flight-Lieutenant Jerry Rawlings. The government steadied the economy and introduced reforms. Incumbent John Dramani Mahama lost to human rights lawyer Nana Akufo-Addo in the 2016 presidential elections.

The World Bank classifies Ghana as a "lower-middle-income" developing country, although the majority of the people are poor and farming employs 56% of the population. Ghana is benefiting from years of stable government and efficient administration and has one of Africa's fastest growing economies. It is exploiting recently discovered offshore oil reserves. Its other major exports are gold and cocoa.

AREA 92,098 sq mi [238,533 sq km] **POPULATION** 32,373,000
CAPITAL Accra **GOVERNMENT** Republic
ETHNIC GROUPS Akan 47%, Mole-Dagbon 17%, Ewe 14%, Ga-Dangme 7%, Gurma 6% **LANGUAGES** English (official), Asante, Ewe, Fante, Boron, Dagomba **RELIGIONS** Christianity 71%, Islam 18%, traditional beliefs 5% **CURRENCY** Cedi = 100 pesewas

GIBRALTAR

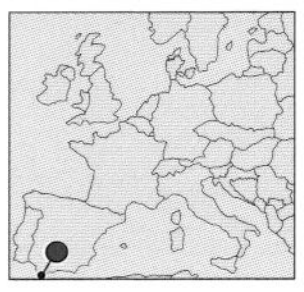

Gibraltar occupies a strategic position on the south coast of Spain where the Mediterranean meets the Atlantic. It was recognized as a British possession in 1713 and, despite Spanish claims, its population has consistently voted to retain its contacts with Britain.

AREA 2.3 sq mi [6 sq km]
POPULATION 30,000 **CAPITAL** Gibraltar Town

GREECE

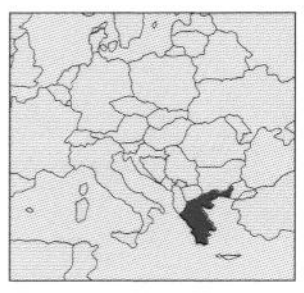

GEOGRAPHY The Hellenic Republic, as Greece is officially called, is a rugged country situated at the southern end of the Balkan peninsula. Olympus, at 9,570 ft [2,917 m], is the highest peak. Islands make up about a fifth of the land area. Low-lying areas in Greece have mild, moist winters and hot, dry summers. The east coast has more than 2,700 hours of sunshine a year and only about half of the rainfall of the west. The mountains have a much more severe climate, with snow on the higher slopes in winter.

POLITICS & ECONOMY Around 2,500 years ago, Greece became the birthplace of Western civilization, and Ancient Greek ruins and art still attract millions of tourists to the country. The first civilization, the Minoan, was centered on Crete. It flourished between about 3000 and 1400 BC. Following the end of the related Mycaenean period on the mainland (1580–1100 BC), a "dark age" lasted until about 800 BC. But from 750 BC, Greeks became rich traders and the city-state of Athens reached its peak in 461–431 BC. Greece became a Roman province in 146 BC and, in 365, it became part of the Byzantine empire.

The Byzantine empire fell to the Turks in 1453. But Greece became an independent monarchy in 1830. After World War II (1939–45), when Germany ruled Greece, a civil war broke out between Greek Communists and nationalists. It ended in 1949 and a military dictatorship seized power in 1967. The monarchy was abolished in 1973 and democracy was restored in 1974. Greece joined the European Community (now the European Union) in 1981 and, on January 1, 2002, the euro became the sole unit of currency. Greece suffered hugely following the international financial crisis of 2008, entering into three international bailout agreements. From 2018 there were signs of economic recovery.

Greece is one of the EU's less economically developed members. Manufactured products include processed food, cement, chemicals, metal products, textiles, and tobacco. Greece also mines lignite (brown coal), bauxite, and chromite. Crops include barley, grapes, dried fruits, olives, potatoes, sugar beet, and wheat. Livestock farming is important and tourism is a major industry.

AREA 50,949 sq mi [131,957 sq km] **POPULATION** 10,570,000
CAPITAL Athens **GOVERNMENT** Multiparty republic
ETHNIC GROUPS Greek 93% **LANGUAGES** Greek (official)
RELIGIONS Greek Orthodox 98%
CURRENCY Euro = 100 cents

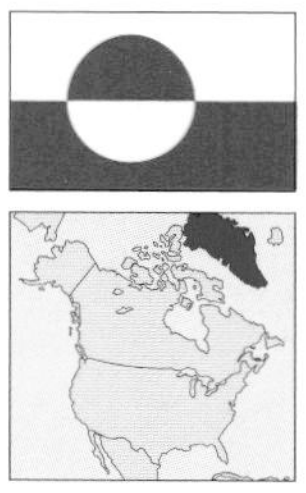

GREENLAND

Greenland is the world's largest island. With an ice sheet covering four-fifths of the land, settlements are confined to the coast. Greenland became a Danish possession in 1380. Full internal self-government was granted in 1981 and, in 2009, Greenland became a self-governing territory, though it remains dependent on Danish subsidies.

AREA 838,999 sq mi [2,175,600 sq km]
POPULATION 58,000 **CAPITAL** Nuuk

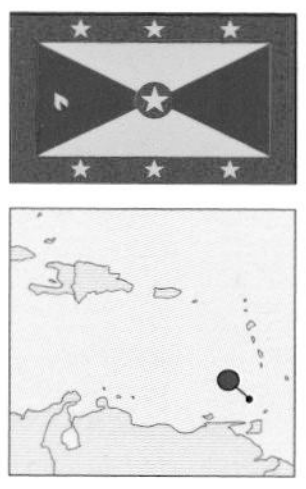

GRENADA

The most southerly of the Windward Islands in the Caribbean Sea, Grenada became independent from the UK in 1974. A military group seized power in 1983, when the prime minister was killed. US troops intervened and restored order and constitutional government.

AREA 133 sq mi [344 sq km]
POPULATION 114,000 **CAPITAL** St George's

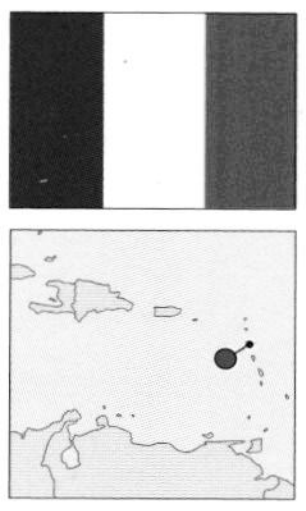

GUADELOUPE

Guadeloupe is a French overseas department which includes seven Caribbean islands, the largest of which is Basse-Terre. French aid has helped to maintain a reasonable standard of living for the people.

AREA 658 sq mi [1,705 sq km]
POPULATION 402,000 **CAPITAL** Basse-Terre

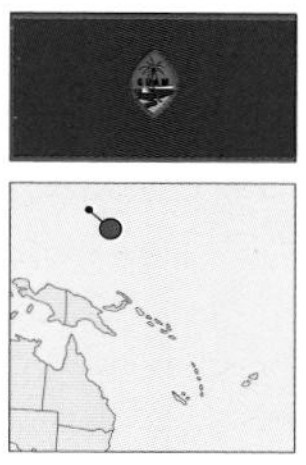

GUAM

Guam, a strategically important "unincorporated territory" of the USA, is the largest of the Mariana Islands in the Pacific Ocean. Its economy depends on US military spending.

AREA 212 sq mi [549 sq km]
POPULATION 169,000 **CAPITAL** Hagatna

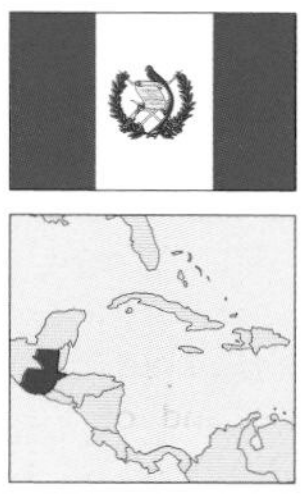

GUATEMALA

GEOGRAPHY The Republic of Guatemala in Central America contains a densely populated mountain region, with fertile soils. There are many volcanoes, some active. South of the mountains lie the thinly populated Pacific coastlands, while a large inland plain occupies the north. The lowlands of Guatemala are hot and rainy, but the central highlands are cooler and drier. Guatemala City has a pleasant, warm climate with a dry season between November and April.

POLITICS & ECONOMY Much of what is now Guatemala was part of the Maya empire which thrived between AD 300 and 900. Spain ruled the area from the 1520s until 1821, with Guatemala achieving full independence in 1839. Instability and periodic violence have marred its progress. Guatemala has a long-standing claim over Belize, but this was reduced in 1983 to the southern fifth of the country. Between 1960 and 1996, civil war occurred between left-wing groups, including many Amerindians, and government forces. Jimmy Morales served as president from 2015 till 2020, when conservative Alejandro Giammattei took office, amid voter discontent over corruption and unemployment.

Guatemala is an "upper-middle-income" economy with agriculture employing 31% of the population. Coffee, sugar, bananas, and beef are exported, and cardamom and cotton are also important. Maize is the main food crop. Poverty is endemic in the countryside, particularly among the indigenous population, with high rates of malnutrition, infant mortality, and illiteracy, as well as violence associated with drug trafficking.

AREA 42,042 sq mi [108,889 sq km] **POPULATION** 17,423,000
CAPITAL Guatemala City **GOVERNMENT** Republic
ETHNIC GROUPS Ladino (mixed Hispanic and Amerindian) 55%, Amerindian 43%, others 2%
LANGUAGES Spanish (official), Amerindian languages
RELIGIONS Roman Catholic, indigenous Mayan beliefs
CURRENCY Quetzal = 100 centavos

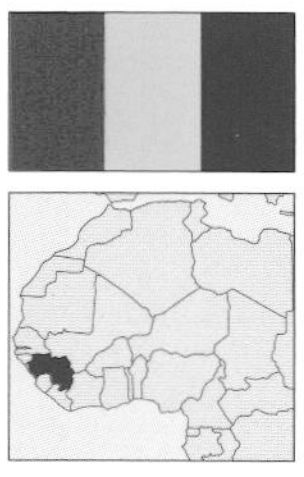

GUINEA

GEOGRAPHY The Republic of Guinea faces the Atlantic Ocean in West Africa. A flat, swampy plain borders the coast. Behind this plain, the land rises to a plateau region called Fouta Djallon. The Upper Niger Plains in the northeast are where the Niger, one of Africa's longest rivers, rises.

Guinea has a tropical climate and Conakry has its rainy period between May and November, the coolest season. In the dry season, hot harmattan winds blow from the Sahara.

POLITICS & ECONOMY Guinea came under the influence of several medieval African states, including Ancient Ghana and Ancient Mali. France began to control the area in the late 19th century with Guinea becoming independent in 1958. Its leaders pursued socialist policies but resorted to repressive measures to hold on to power. A military regime under Lansana Conté took over in 1984, but a multiparty system was restored in 1992. Following Conté's death in 2008, an army group led by Captain Mousa Dadis Camara seized power. But in 2010, Alpha Condé was elected president in Guinea's first democratic election since independence. He was re-elected in 2015.

Guinea is a "low-income" developing country. Its resources include bauxite (aluminum ore), diamonds, gold, iron ore, and uranium. Bauxite and alumina (processed bauxite) account for more than half of the country's exports. Agriculture employs more than 75% of the people, but most farmers are poor. Economic development is hampered by poor infrastructure.

AREA 94,925 sq mi [245,857 sq km] **POPULATION** 12,878,000
CAPITAL Conakry **GOVERNMENT** Multiparty republic
ETHNIC GROUPS Peuhl 40%, Malinke 30%, Soussou 20%, others 10%
LANGUAGES French (official)
RELIGIONS Islam 85%, Christianity 8%, traditional beliefs 7%
CURRENCY Guinean franc = 100 centimes

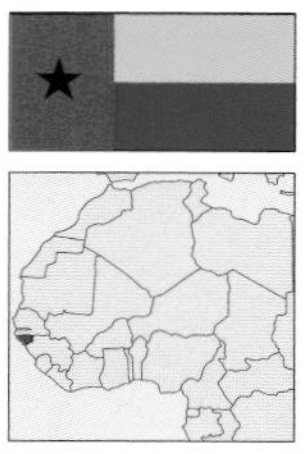

GUINEA-BISSAU

GEOGRAPHY The Republic of Guinea-Bissau, formerly known as Portuguese Guinea, is a small country in West Africa. The land is mostly low-lying, with a broad, swampy coastal plain and many flat offshore islands. The country has a tropical climate, with a dry season (December to May) and a wet season (June to November).

POLITICS & ECONOMY Portuguese explorers reached Guinea-Bissau in 1446 and the area became a center of the slave trade. From 1836, Portugal administered Guinea-Bissau with the Cape Verde Islands, but in 1879 the territories were separated.

In 1956, African nationalists in Portuguese Guinea (as Guinea-Bissau was then known) and Cape Verde founded the African Party for the Independence of Guinea and Cape Verde (PAIGC). The PAIGC began a guerrilla war in 1963 and, by 1968, it held two-thirds of the country. In 1972, a rebel National Assembly, elected by the people in the PAIGC-controlled area, voted to make the country independent as Guinea-Bissau.

The newly independent Guinea-Bissau faced many problems arising from its underdeveloped economy and its lack of trained people to work in the administration. One objective of the leaders of Guinea-Bissau was to unite their country with Cape Verde. But, in 1980, army leaders overthrew Guinea-Bissau's government. The Revolutionary Council, which took over, opposed unification with Cape Verde. Guinea-Bissau ceased to be a one-party state in 1991 and multiparty elections were held in 1994. Civil war and military coups followed until a civilian government was restored in 2004. Following another military coup in 2012, a government by Transitional National Council was established. Jose Mario Vaz was elected president in 2014, and his successor, Umaro Sissoco Embalo, in 2020, but political infighting and instability continues.

The economy is massively in debt and relies on foreign aid: Guinea-Bissau is one of the world's poorest countries. Agriculture employs 82% of the people. Crops include cashew nuts, coconuts, groundnuts (peanuts), maize, and rice. The country is a major hub for drug trafficking between Latin America and Europe.

AREA 13,948 sq mi [36,125 sq km] **POPULATION** 1,976,000
CAPITAL Bissau **GOVERNMENT** Republic
ETHNIC GROUPS Balanta 30%, Fula 20%, Manjaca 14%, Mandinga 13%, Papel 7% **LANGUAGES** Portuguese (official), Crioulo
RELIGIONS Islam 50%, traditional beliefs 40%, Christianity 10%
CURRENCY CFA franc = 100 centimes

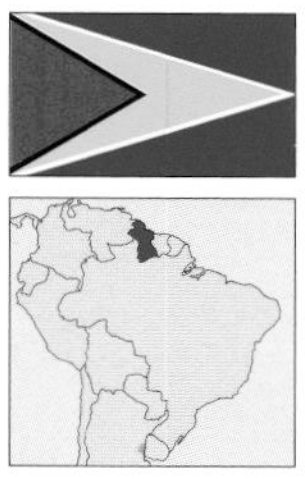

GUYANA

GEOGRAPHY The Cooperative Republic of Guyana faces the Atlantic Ocean in north-eastern South America. The coastal plain is flat and much of it is below sea level. The climate is hot and humid, though the interior highlands are cooler than the coast. Rainfall is heavy, occurring on more than 200 days a year.

POLITICS & ECONOMY Britain gained control of the area in 1814 and ruled British Guiana until its independence as Guyana in 1966. A black lawyer, Forbes Burnham, was the first prime minister. He served as president under a new constitution adopted in 1980, until his death in 1985. Ethnic tensions and political rivalries persisted between descendants of African slaves and those descended from Indians brought in by the British. In 2015 David Granger was elected president, ending 23 years of rule by the Indian-dominated People's Progressive Party. Granger initially declared victory in the 2020 election, but a recount established opposition candidate Irfaan Ali as the new president.

The discovery of substantial oil deposits has sparked interest from international oil companies. Oil revenue looks set to transform Guyana's economy. Other resources include gold, bauxite, forests, and fertile soils. Sugarcane and rice are leading crops.

AREA 83,000 sq mi [214,969 sq km] **POPULATION** 788,000
CAPITAL Georgetown **GOVERNMENT** Multiparty republic
ETHNIC GROUPS East Indian 43%, Black 30%, Amerindian 9%, others 18%
LANGUAGES English (official), Creole, Hindi, Urdu
RELIGIONS Christianity 57%, Hinduism 28%, Islam 7%, others 8%
CURRENCY Guyanese dollar = 100 cents

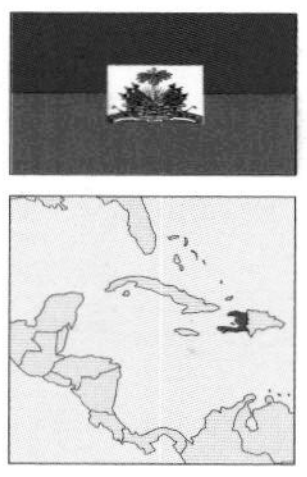

HAITI

GEOGRAPHY The Republic of Haiti occupies the western third of Hispaniola in the Caribbean. The land is mainly mountainous. The climate is hot and humid, though the northern highlands have more than twice as much rainfall as the southern coast.

POLITICS & ECONOMY Visited by Christopher Columbus in 1492, Haiti was later developed by the French. The country became independent in 1804, following a slave revolt led by Toussaint L'Ouverture. Haiti subsequently suffered from instability and violence, particularly under the dictatorial rule of "Papa Doc" and "Baby Doc" Duvalier from 1957 to 1986. Political instability continued in the following decades. Elections in 2016 were won by Jovenel Moise.

In January 2010, a massive earthquake killed up to 230,000 people and devastated the economy. Around 60% of the people live in poverty. The economy depends on agriculture and remittances from abroad.

AREA 10,714 sq mi [27,750 sq km] **POPULATION** 11,198,000
CAPITAL Port-au-Prince **GOVERNMENT** Multiparty republic
ETHNIC GROUPS Black 95%, Mixed/White 5%
LANGUAGES French and Creole (both official)
RELIGIONS Roman Catholic 80%, Protestant 16%, Voodoo
CURRENCY Gourde = 100 centimes

HONDURAS

GEOGRAPHY The Republic of Honduras is the second largest country in Central America. The northern coast, on the Caribbean Sea, extends for more than 373 mi [600 km], but the Pacific coast in the southeast is only about 50 mi [80 km] long. Honduras has a tropical climate, but the highlands are cooler. The rainiest months are between May and November. Hurricanes often hit the north coast. Hurricane Mitch in 1998 caused the worst destruction in modern times.

POLITICS & ECONOMY Once part of the Maya empire, the area was claimed for Spain by Christopher Columbus in 1502, and Spain ruled from 1625 until 1821. Honduras became part of the Central American Federation but withdrew in 1838.

In the 1890s, American companies developed plantations to grow bananas. Instability under successive military regimes slowed economic progress. From 1980, civilian governments friendly toward the United States ruled Honduras, but in 2008 it joined the "Bolivarian Alternative to the Americas," a left-wing alliance then headed by Venezuelan President Chavez. In 2014 Juan Orlando Hernández became president and was re-elected in a disputed election in 2017. He pledged to reduce the levels of drug-related gang violence.

Honduras is one of Central America's least industrialized countries with around 50% of its economy linked to the USA and very high levels of inequality. Its few resources include silver, lead, and zinc. Agriculture is the main activity. Bananas and coffee are exported and maize is the chief food crop. Products include processed food and textiles. Violent crime makes the country one of the least secure in Central America. It has one of the world's highest murder rates.

AREA 43,277 SQ MI [112,088 SQ KM] **POPULATION** 9,346,000
CAPITAL TEGUCIGALPA **GOVERNMENT** REPUBLIC
ETHNIC GROUPS MESTIZO 90%, AMERINDIAN 7%, BLACK (INCLUDING BLACK CARIB) 2%, WHITE 1%
LANGUAGES SPANISH (OFFICIAL), AMERINDIAN DIALECTS
RELIGIONS ROMAN CATHOLIC 97%
CURRENCY HONDURAN LEMPIRA = 100 CENTAVOS

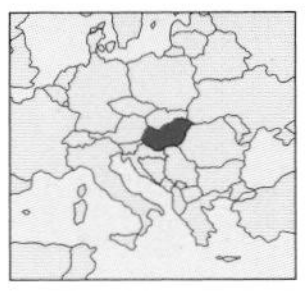

HUNGARY

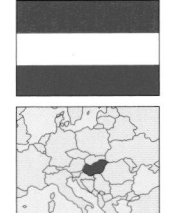

GEOGRAPHY Hungary is a landlocked country in central Europe. The land is mostly low-lying and drained by the Danube (Duna) and its tributary, the Tisza. Most of the land east of the Danube belongs to the region of the Great Plain (Nagy Alföld), which covers about half of Hungary.

Hungary lies far from the moderating influence of the sea, but it does contain Lake Balaton, the largest lake in central Europe. As a result of its position in the European landmass, summers are warmer and sunnier, and the winters colder than in Western Europe.

POLITICS & ECONOMY Following first an alliance, then occupation by Germany during World War II, Hungary was gradually taken over by a Communist government. From 1949, Hungary was an ally of the Soviet Union with Soviet troops crushing an anti-Communist revolt in 1956. But in the 1980s, reforms in the Soviet Union led to the growth of anti-Communist groups and, in 1989, Hungary adopted a new constitution making it a multiparty state and made moves toward a more free market economy. In 2004, Hungary became a member of both the North Atlantic Treaty Organization and the European Union. Right-wing prime minister Viktor Orban won a third term in power in April 2018 campaigning on an anti-immigrant, anti-Muslim ticket. Widespread protests followed.

Before World War II, Hungary's economy was based mainly on agriculture but the Communist era saw the introduction of many manufacturing industries. From the late 1980s, the increase in private ownership of businesses caused problems, including high rates of unemployment and inflation. High levels of government borrowing left the country vulnerable to the recession of 2008. Hungary's resources include bauxite, coal, and natural gas. Leading manufactures include vehicles, chemicals, and construction materials.

AREA 35,920 SQ MI [93,032 SQ KM] **POPULATION** 9,728,000
CAPITAL BUDAPEST **GOVERNMENT** MULTIPARTY REPUBLIC
ETHNIC GROUPS MAGYAR 92%, ROMA, GERMAN, SERB, ROMANIAN, SLOVAK
LANGUAGES HUNGARIAN (OFFICIAL)
RELIGIONS ROMAN CATHOLIC 52%, CALVINIST 16%, LUTHERAN 3%, OTHERS
CURRENCY FORINT = 100 FILLÉR

ICELAND

GEOGRAPHY The Republic of Iceland, in the North Atlantic Ocean, is closer to Greenland than Scotland. Iceland sits astride the Mid-Atlantic Ridge and it is slowly getting wider as the ocean is being stretched apart by continental drift.

Iceland has around 200 volcanoes, and eruptions are frequent. An eruption under the Vatnajökull ice cap in 1996 created a subglacial lake which subsequently burst, causing severe flooding. Geysers and hot springs are common, and in 2010 a volcanic eruption and its resulting ash cloud disrupted international air services. Ice caps and glaciers cover about an eighth of the land. The only habitable regions are the coastal lowlands. Despite its northerly position, Iceland's climate is moderated by the warm waters of the North Atlantic Drift. The port of Reykjavik is ice-free all year round.

POLITICS & ECONOMY Norwegian Vikings colonized Iceland in AD 874, and in 930 the settlers founded the world's oldest parliament, the Althing. Iceland joined forces with Norway in 1262. But when Norway united with Denmark in 1380, Iceland came under Danish rule. Iceland became a self-governing kingdom, still with links to Denmark, in 1918, and a fully independent republic in 1944. Elections in the fall of 2017, after the collapse of the previous government, led to Katrin Jakobsdottir of the Left-Green movement heading a broad coalition.

Iceland's fishing and fish processing industries dominate overseas trade. To protect this vital part of its economy, it has been involved in several fishing and whaling disputes. In 2013 it suspended its application to join the EU citing potential difficulties with fishing agreements. Barely 1% of the land is used to grow crops, but 23% of the country can be used for grazing sheep and cattle. Vegetables and fruit are grown in greenhouses, heated by water from the hot springs. Iceland's economy was particularly hard hit by the global financial crisis of 2008, but recovered steadily from the mid-2010s, helped by a growth in tourism. Other industries include aluminum smelting and geothermal power.

AREA 39,768 SQ MI [103,000 SQ KM] **POPULATION** 354,000
CAPITAL REYKJAVIK **GOVERNMENT** MULTIPARTY REPUBLIC
ETHNIC GROUPS ICELANDIC 97%, DANISH 1%
LANGUAGES ICELANDIC (OFFICIAL) **RELIGIONS** EVANGELICAL LUTHERAN 87%, OTHER PROTESTANT 4%, ROMAN CATHOLIC 2%, OTHERS
CURRENCY ICELANDIC KRÓNA

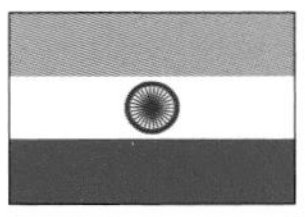
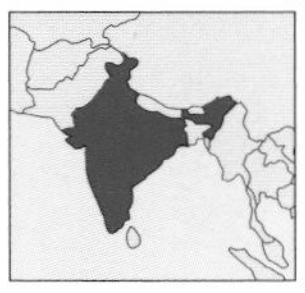

INDIA

GEOGRAPHY The Republic of India is the world's seventh largest country. In population, it ranks second only to China. The north is mountainous, with mountains and foothills of the Himalayan range. Rivers, such as the Brahmaputra and Ganges (Ganga), rise in the Himalaya and flow across the fertile northern plains. Southern India consists of the Deccan, an extensive plateau. The Deccan is bordered by two mountain ranges, the Western Ghats and the Eastern Ghats.

India has three main seasons. The cool season runs from October to February. The hot season runs from March to June. The rainy monsoon season starts in the middle of June and continues into September. Delhi has moderate rainfall, with about 25 inches [640 mm] a year. The southwestern coast and the north-east have far more rain. Darjeeling in the northeast has an average annual rainfall of 120 inches [3,040 mm]. But parts of the Thar Desert in the northwest have only 2 inches [50 mm] of rain.

POLITICS & ECONOMY In southern India, most of the people are descendants of the dark-skinned Dravidians, who were among India's earliest people. Most northerners are descendants of lighter-skinned Aryans who arrived around 3,500 years ago.

India was the birthplace of several major religions, including Hinduism, Buddhism, and Sikhism. Islam was introduced from about AD 1000. The Muslim Mughal empire was founded in 1526. From the 17th century, Britain began to gain influence and, from 1858 to 1947, India was ruled as part of the British empire. An independence movement began after the Sepoy Rebellion (1857–59), and in 1885 the Indian National Congress was formed. In 1920, Mohandas K. Gandhi became its leader. When independence was finally achieved in 1947, British India was divided into modern India and Muslim Pakistan. Partition was marred by mass slaughter as Hindus and Sikhs fled from Pakistan, and Indian Muslims poured into Pakistan. In the ensuing disputes, some 1 million people were killed.

India has 15 major languages and hundreds of minor ones, together with many religions. The country remains the world's largest democracy. It has faced many problems, especially with Pakistan, over the disputed territory of Jammu and Kashmir. Two wars in 1965 and 1972 failed to alter greatly the 1948 cease-fire lines. In the late 1980s, Kashmiri nationalists in the Indian-controlled area waged a campaign, demanding either integration into Pakistan or independence. India sent in troops and accused Pakistan of intervention. In the 1990s, Pakistani-backed guerrillas fought to break India's hold on the Srinagar valley, Kashmir's most populous region. Tension mounted following the testing of nuclear devices by both countries in 1998. Relations improved, but an attack on buildings in Mumbai in 2008, allegedly by Pakistanis, caused further tension. In 2009–11, the dispute with Maoists in central and eastern India flared up again. May 2014 parliamentary elections resulted in a landslide victory for the Hindu nationalist Bharatiya Janata Party, led by Narendra Modi, who promised to revitalize the economy.

Classified by the World Bank as "lower-middle-income," India's economy has fluctuated in the 21st century. It benefits from a young, educated population, many of whom speak English, but challenges include poor power generation, inadequate infrastructure, and discrimination against women.

Agriculture employs about 47% of the people, and services 31%. Crops include rice, wheat, millet, sorghum, peas, and beans. Cattle rearing is an important activity. Resources include coal, iron ore, and oil. Major products include iron and steel, machinery, refined petroleum, textiles, and information technology.

AREA 1,269,212 SQ MI [3,287,263 SQ KM] **POPULATION** 1,339,331,000
CAPITAL NEW DELHI **GOVERNMENT** MULTIPARTY FEDERAL REPUBLIC
ETHNIC GROUPS INDO-ARYAN (CAUCASOID) 72%, DRAVIDIAN 25%, OTHERS (MAINLY MONGOLOID) 3%
LANGUAGES HINDI, ENGLISH, TELUGU, BENGALI, MARATHI, TAMIL, URDU, GUJARATI, MALAYALAM, KANNADA, ORIYA, PUNJABI, ASSAMESE, KASHMIRI, SINDHI, AND SANSKRIT ARE ALL OFFICIAL LANGUAGES
RELIGIONS HINDUISM 80%, ISLAM 13%, CHRISTIANITY 2%, SIKHISM 2%, BUDDHISM, AND OTHERS **CURRENCY** INDIAN RUPEE = 100 PAISE

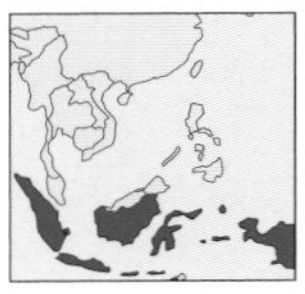

INDONESIA

GEOGRAPHY The Republic of Indonesia is an island nation in Southeast Asia. In all, Indonesia contains about 13,600 islands, fewer than 6,000 of which are inhabited. Three-quarters of the country is made up of five main areas: the islands of Sumatra, Java and Sulawesi (Celebes), together with Kalimantan (southern Borneo), and western New Guinea. The islands are generally mountainous and volcanic. The larger islands have extensive coastal lowlands. The climate is hot and humid, with a high rainfall. Only Java and the Sunda Islands have relatively dry seasons.

POLITICS & ECONOMY Indonesia is the world's most populous Muslim nation, though Islam was introduced as recently as the 15th century. It became a Dutch colony in 1799. After a long struggle, the Netherlands recognized Indonesia's independence in 1949. The economy has expanded, but ethnic and religious conflict has slowed down economic progress.

In the early 21st century, Indonesia was facing many problems, arising from widespread corruption in the government and the army. Separatists were operating in Aceh province in northern Sumatra and in West Papua, Christian–Muslim clashes led to loss of life in the Moluccas, and East (formerly Portuguese) Timor became an independent country. In December 2004, a tsunami killed more than 100,000 people. Aceh province was granted autonomy in 2006, but separatists in the Papua region continue to agitate for independence. Indonesia has suffered an increasing number of terrorist attacks from Islamist groups in recent years. In 2019 it was announced that Indonesia's capital would move to a yet-to-be-built city on Kalimantan. Its current capital, Jakarta, is one of the fastest sinking cities in the world and under threat from rising sea levels, as well as suffering from chronic traffic congestion.

Indonesia, a developing country, has a growing industrial sector hampered by inadequate infrastructure. It exports oil and natural gas, and mines tin and other minerals. Timber, textiles, rubber, coffee, and tea are also exported. Rice is the main food crop.

AREA 735,354 SQ MI [1,904,569 SQ KM] **POPULATION** 275,122,000
CAPITAL JAKARTA **GOVERNMENT** MULTIPARTY REPUBLIC
ETHNIC GROUPS JAVANESE 41%, SUNDANESE 15%, MADURESE 3%, MINANGKABAU 3%, BETAWI 2%, BUGIS 2%, BANTEN 2%, OTHERS 32%
LANGUAGES BAHASA INDONESIAN (OFFICIAL), MANY OTHERS
RELIGIONS ISLAM 86%, PROTESTANT 6%, ROMAN CATHOLIC 3%, HINDUISM 2%, BUDDHISM 1%
CURRENCY INDONESIAN RUPIAH

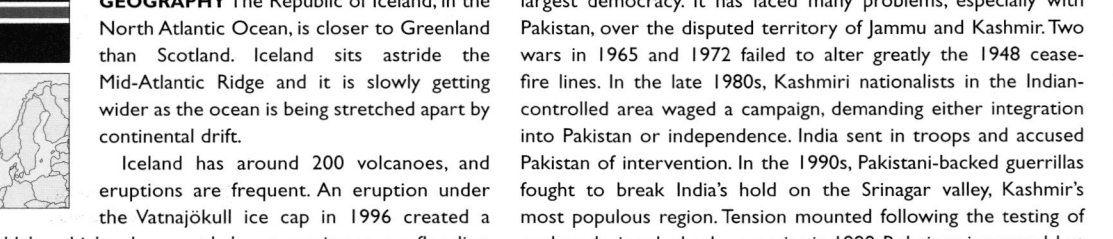

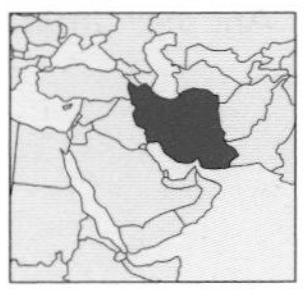

IRAN

GEOGRAPHY The Republic of Iran contains a barren central plateau which covers about half of the country. It includes the Dasht-e Kavir (Great Salt Desert) and the Dasht-e Lut (Great Sand Desert). The Elburz Mountains north of the plateau contain Iran's highest peak, Damavand, while narrow lowlands lie between the mountains and the Caspian Sea. West of the plateau are the Zagros Mountains, beyond which the land descends to the plains bordering the Persian Gulf.

Much of Iran has a severe, dry climate, with hot summers and cold winters. In Tehran, rain falls on only about 30 days in the year and the annual temperature range is more than 45°F [25°C]. The climate in the lowlands, however, is generally milder.

POLITICS & ECONOMY Iran was called Persia until 1935. The empire of Ancient Persia flourished between 550 and 350 BC. Islam was introduced in AD 641.

Britain and Russia competed for influence in the area in the 19th century, and in the early 20th century the British began to

develop the country's oil resources. In 1925, the Pahlavi family took power. Reza Khan became shah (king) and worked to modernize the country. The Pahlavi dynasty ended in 1979 when a religious leader, Ayatollah Ruhollah Khomeini, made Iran an Islamic republic. In 1980–88, Iran and Iraq fought a war over disputed borders. Khomeini died in 1989. In 2005, a hardliner, Mahmoud Ahmadinejad, was elected president. Iran's nuclear policies led to the application of international sanctions against it in 2009–12. The more moderate Hassan Rouhani was elected president in 2013 and re-elected in 2017. In 2015, after years of negotiations, a deal was agreed allowing for some economic sanctions to be lifted if Iran limited its nuclear activity. The following year UN inspectors reported satisfactory progress. In 2018, however, the US administration accused Iran of non-compliance and withdrew from the deal and renewed sanctions.

Iran's prosperity is based on its oil production and oil accounts for more than 80% of the country's exports. Agriculture is important and the main crops are wheat, barley, and fruit. Livestock farming and fishing are other important activities, although Iran has to import food.

AREA 636,368 SQ MI [1,648,195 SQ KM] **POPULATION** 85,889,000
CAPITAL TEHRAN **GOVERNMENT** ISLAMIC REPUBLIC
ETHNIC GROUPS PERSIAN 53%, AZERI 16%, KURD 10%, LUR 6%, ARAB 2%, BALOCH 2%, TURKMEN 2% **LANGUAGES** PERSIAN, TURKIC, KURDISH
RELIGIONS ISLAM 98% (SHI'ITE MUSLIM 89%)
CURRENCY IRANIAN RIAL = 100 DINARS

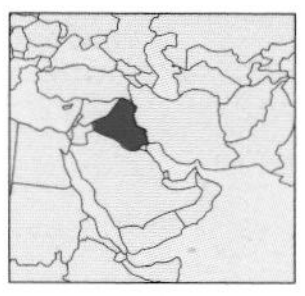

IRAQ

GEOGRAPHY The Republic of Iraq lies at the head of the Persian Gulf. Rolling deserts cover western and southwestern Iraq, with part of the Zagros Mountains in the northeast. The northern plains, across which flow the rivers Euphrates (Nahr al Furat) and Tigris (Nahr Dijlah), are dry. But the southern plains, including Mesopotamia and the delta of the Shatt al Arab, contain irrigated farmland, together with marshland.

The climate of Iraq ranges from temperate in the north to subtropical in the south. Baghdad, in central Iraq, has cool winters, with occasional frosts, and hot summers. The rainfall is generally low.

POLITICS & ECONOMY Mesopotamia was the home of several great civilizations, including Sumer, Babylon, and Assyria. It later became part of the Persian empire. Islam was introduced in AD 637 and Baghdad became the brilliant capital of the powerful Arab empire. But Mesopotamia declined after the Mongols invaded it in 1258. From 1534, Mesopotamia became part of the Turkish Ottoman empire. Britain invaded the area in 1916 and, in 1921, renamed the country Iraq and set up an Arab monarchy. Iraq finally became independent in 1932.

By the 1950s, oil dominated Iraq's economy. In 1952, Iraq agreed to take 50% of the profits of the foreign oil companies. This revenue enabled the government to pay for welfare services and development projects. Since 1958, when army officers killed the king and made Iraq a republic, Iraq has undergone turbulent times. In the 1960s, the Kurds, who live in northern Iraq and also in Iran, Turkey, Syria, and Armenia, pressed for self-rule. The government rejected their demands and war broke out. A peace treaty was signed in 1975, but conflict has continued.

In 1979, Saddam Hussein became Iraq's president. Under his leadership, Iraq invaded Iran in 1980, starting an eight-year war. Iraqi Kurds supported Iran and the Iraqi government attacked Kurdish villages with poison gas. In 1990, Iraqi troops occupied Kuwait, but an international force drove them out in 1991. From 1991, Iraqi troops attacked Shi'ite Marsh Arabs and Kurds. In 1998, Iraq's failure to permit UN inspectors, charged with disposing of Iraq's deadliest weapons, access to suspect sites led to the Western bombardment of Iraqi military sites. Another major offensive occurred in 2001. In March–April 2003, a coalition force headed by the United States invaded Iraq, overthrowing Saddam Hussein's regime. Despite ongoing sectarian violence, regular elections have been held since 2005. From 2013 Islamic State militants seized control of large parts of the country, with the loss of thousands of lives. By late 2017 they had largely been driven out by government troops with Kurdish and other allies. In 2019 large-scale protests over corruption and high unemployment led to the resignation of the prime minister and the appointment of Mustafa Al-Kadhimi in 2020.

Civil war, war damage, mismanagement, and UN sanctions have damaged the economy. Oil remains the main resource. Farmland covers about a fifth of the land. Products include barley, cotton, dates, fruit, livestock, wheat, and wool. But Iraq still has to import food. Manufactures include refined oil, petrochemicals, and consumer goods.

AREA 169,235 SQ MI [438,317 SQ KM] **POPULATION** 39,650,000
CAPITAL BAGHDAD **GOVERNMENT** PARLIAMENTARY DEMOCRACY
ETHNIC GROUPS ARAB 77%, KURDISH 19%, ASSYRIAN AND OTHERS
LANGUAGES ARABIC (OFFICIAL), KURDISH (OFFICIAL IN KURDISH AREAS), ASSYRIAN, ARMENIAN **RELIGIONS** ISLAM 97% (SHI'ITE MUSLIM 63%)
CURRENCY IRAQI DINAR = 1,000 FILS

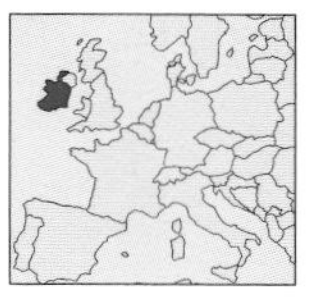

IRELAND

GEOGRAPHY Ireland occupies five-sixths of the island which is also called Ireland. The country consists of a large lowland region surrounded by a broken rim of low mountains. The uplands include the Mountains of Kerry where Carrauntoohill, Ireland's highest peak at 3,415 ft [1,041 m], is situated. The River Shannon is the longest in Ireland, flowing through three large lakes, loughs Allen, Ree, and Derg.

Ireland has a mild, rainy climate influenced by the warm North Atlantic Drift, whose effects are greatest in the west. However, Dublin in the east is cooler than places on the west coast.

POLITICS & ECONOMY In 1801, the Act of Union created the United Kingdom of Great Britain and Ireland. But Irish discontent intensified in the 1840s when a potato blight caused a famine in which a million people died and nearly a million emigrated. Britain was blamed for not having done enough to help. In 1916, an uprising in Dublin was crushed, but between 1919 and 1922 civil war broke out. In 1922, the Irish Free State was created as a Dominion in the British Commonwealth, but Northern Ireland remained part of the UK.

Ireland became a republic in 1949. In 1973, it became a member of the European Community (now the European Union) and, until the global financial crisis of 2008–9, it prospered. In 1998, Ireland took part in the negotiations to produce a constitutional settlement in Northern Ireland. Ireland agreed to give up its claim on Northern Ireland and, in 2007, a power-sharing government was set up in the north. From 2008–14 Irish politics was dominated by the fallout from the financial crisis. Questions now remain over the implications for Ireland, its economy, and its borders following the departure of the UK from the EU in 2020.

Major farm products include barley, cattle and dairy products, pigs, potatoes, poultry, sheep, mushrooms, and wheat. Fishing is important. Manufacturing and services are the main activities.

AREA 27,132 SQ MI [70,273 SQ KM] **POPULATION** 5,225,000
CAPITAL DUBLIN **GOVERNMENT** MULTIPARTY REPUBLIC
ETHNIC GROUPS IRISH 94% **LANGUAGES** IRISH (GAELIC) AND ENGLISH (BOTH OFFICIAL) **RELIGIONS** ROMAN CATHOLIC 92%, PROTESTANT 3%
CURRENCY EURO = 100 CENTS

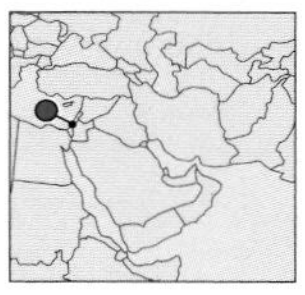

ISRAEL

GEOGRAPHY The State of Israel is a small country in the eastern Mediterranean. It includes a fertile coastal plain, where Israel's main industrial cities, Haifa (Hefa) and Tel Aviv-Jaffa, are situated. Inland lie the Judaeo-Galilean highlands, which run from northern Israel to the northern tip of the Negev Desert. To the east lies part of the Great Rift Valley, which contains the River Jordan, the Sea of Galilee, and the Dead Sea. Summers are hot and dry. Winters on the coast are mild and moist, but rainfall decreases from west to east and from north to south.

POLITICS & ECONOMY Israel is part of a region called Palestine. Some Jews have always lived in the area, though most modern Israelis are descendants of immigrants who began to settle there from the 1880s. Britain ruled Palestine from 1917. Large numbers of Jews escaping Nazi persecution arrived in the 1930s, provoking an Arab uprising against British rule. In 1947, the UN agreed to partition Palestine into an Arab and a Jewish state with the State of Israel coming into being in May 1948. Other Arab–Israeli wars in 1956, 1967, and 1973 led to land gains for Israel.

In 1978, Israel signed a treaty with Egypt which led to the return of the occupied Sinai peninsula to Egypt in 1979. Conflict continued between Israel and the PLO (Palestine Liberation Organization). In 1993, they agreed to establish Palestinian self-rule in two areas: the occupied Gaza Strip, and Jericho in the occupied West Bank. The agreement was extended in 1995 to include more than 30% of the West Bank. Israel's peace-making prime minister, Yitzhak Rabin, was assassinated the same year by a Jewish extremist. In 2005, Prime Minister Ariel Sharon handed over the Gaza Strip to the Palestinian Authority. Israeli forces clashed with Palestinians in Gaza and southern Lebanon in 2005–9. Talks in 2010 and 2013 between Israel and the Palestinian Authority collapsed. Increased violence along the Gaza border in 2018 led to attempts by the UN and Egypt to broker a long-term ceasefire. Disputes remain over the Golan Heights and Jewish settlements in the West Bank. A period of political stalemate ended in 2020 when Benjamin Netanyahu, prime minister since 2009, and Benny Gantz formed a national unity government.

Israel has developed a very diverse economy. Manufactures include chemicals, electronic equipment, plastics, processed food, scientific instruments, and textiles. Fruit and vegetables are major exports. Lacking natural resources, Israel has to import raw materials, crude oil, and grain. Offshore gas fields are being exploited.

AREA 7,954 SQ MI [20,600 SQ KM] **POPULATION** 8,787,000
CAPITAL JERUSALEM **GOVERNMENT** MULTIPARTY REPUBLIC
ETHNIC GROUPS JEWISH 76%, ARAB AND OTHERS 24%
LANGUAGES HEBREW AND ARABIC (BOTH OFFICIAL)
RELIGIONS JUDAISM 76%, ISLAM (MOSTLY SUNNI) 17%, CHRISTIANITY 2%, DRUZE AND OTHERS 5% **CURRENCY** NEW ISRAELI SHEKEL = 100 AGOROT

ITALY

GEOGRAPHY The Republic of Italy is famous for its history and traditions, its art and culture, and its beautiful scenery. Northern Italy is bordered in the north by the high Alps, with their many climbing and skiing resorts. The Alps overlook the northern plains – Italy's most fertile and densely populated region – drained by the River Po. The rugged Apennines form the backbone of southern Italy. Bordering the range are scenic hilly areas and coastal plains. Southern Italy contains a string of volcanoes, stretching from Vesuvius, through the Lipari Islands, to Etna on Sicily, the largest Mediterranean island. Northern Italy has cold, often snowy, winters, but the summer months are warm and sunny, with brief summer thunderstorms. Rainfall is abundant. The south has mild, moist winters and warm, dry summers.

POLITICS & ECONOMY Magnificent ruins throughout Italy testify to the glories of the ancient Roman empire, which was founded, according to legend, in 753 BC. Reaching its peak in the AD 100s, it finally collapsed in the 400s, although the Eastern Roman empire, also called the Byzantine empire, survived for another 1,000 years.

In the Middle Ages, Italy was split into many tiny states. These states made a great contribution to the Renaissance, the revival of art and learning, in the 14th to 16th centuries. Beautiful cities, such as Florence (Firenze) and Venice (Venézia), testify to the artistic achievements of this period.

Italy finally became a united kingdom in 1861, although the Papal Territories (a large area ruled by the Roman Catholic Church) were not added until 1870. The Pope and his successors disputed this takeover and it was not finally resolved until 1929, when the Vatican City was set up in Rome as a fully independent state.

Italy fought in World War I (1914–18) alongside the Allies – Britain, France, and Russia. In 1922, the dictator Benito Mussolini, leader of the Fascist Party, took power. Under Mussolini, Italy conquered Ethiopia. During World War II (1939–45), Italy at first fought on Germany's side against the Allies until late in 1943 it declared war on Germany. Italy became a republic in 1946. Playing an important part in European affairs, it was a founder member of the North Atlantic Treaty Organization (NATO) in 1949 and also, in 1958, of what has since become the European Union.

After the setting up of the European Union, Italy's economy developed quickly, despite problems such as greater prosperity in the north compared to the south. The greater economic development in the north forced many people to leave the poor south to find jobs in the north or abroad. Social problems, corruption at high levels of society, and a succession of weak coalition governments all contributed to instability. Between 1998 and 2011, power shifted between center-left and center-right coalitions. In 2016, constitutional changes aimed at creating more stable governments were rejected in a referendum, leading to prime minister Matteo Renzi's resignation. A populist coalition government took office in 2018.

Only 50 years ago, Italy was a mainly agricultural society, but it is now a leading industrial power. It lacks mineral resources, and imports most of the raw materials used in industry. Manufactures include textiles and clothing, processed food, machinery, cars, and chemicals. The chief industrial region is in the northwest.

Farmland covers around 47% of the land, of which 16% is pasture; forest and woodland cover another 31%. Major crops include citrus fruits, grapes which are used to make wine, olive oil, sugar beet, and vegetables. Livestock farming is important, though meat is imported.

AREA 116,339 sq mi [301,318 sq km] **POPULATION** 62,390,000
CAPITAL Rome **GOVERNMENT** Multiparty republic
ETHNIC GROUPS Italian 94%, German, French, Albanian, Slovene, Greek
LANGUAGES Italian (official), German, French, Slovene
RELIGIONS Predominantly Roman Catholic
CURRENCY Euro = 100 cents

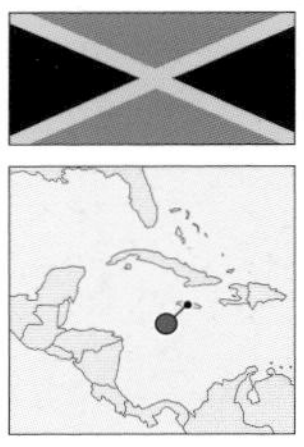

JAMAICA

GEOGRAPHY Jamaica is the third largest of the Caribbean islands. Half the country lies above 1,000 ft [300 m] and moist southeast trade winds bring rain to the central mountain range.

The "cockpit country" in the northwest of the island is an inaccessible limestone area of steep broken ridges and isolated basins.

POLITICS & ECONOMY Jamaica gained independence from Britain in 1962. Since then, power has alternated between the People's National Party and the Jamaica Labour Party and, despite some violence, there has been relative political stability. There is some support for becoming a republic. Problems arise from the drug trade, and the marked polarization of society between rich and poor. The murder rate is high. Tourism and sugarcane farming are important, with alumina and bauxite being exported.

AREA 4,244 sq mi [10,991 sq km] **POPULATION** 2,817,000
CAPITAL Kingston **GOVERNMENT** Constitutional monarchy
ETHNIC GROUPS Black 91%, Mixed 7%, East Indian 1%
LANGUAGES English (official), patois English
RELIGIONS Protestant 65%, Roman Catholic 3%
CURRENCY Jamaican dollar = 100 cents

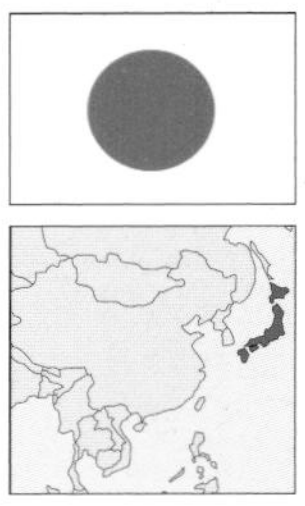

JAPAN

GEOGRAPHY Japan's four largest islands – Honshu, Hokkaido, Kyushu, and Shikoku – make up 98% of the country. But Japan contains thousands of small islands. The four largest islands are mainly mountainous, while many of the small islands are the tips of volcanoes. Japan has more than 150 volcanoes, about 60 of which are active. Volcanic eruptions, earthquakes and tsunamis (powerful sea waves) are common. In March 2011, a massive earthquake, the most powerful recorded in Japan (magnitude 9.0), struck Honshu in the northeast. The tremors and a tsunami caused great loss of life and severe damage to nuclear reactors at Fukushima, shutting down all nuclear power generation at that time.

The climate of Japan varies greatly from north to south. Hokkaido in the north has cold, snowy winters. At Sapporo, temperatures below 4°F [–20°C] have been recorded between December and March. But summers are warm, with temperatures sometimes exceeding 86°F [30°C]. Rain falls throughout the year, though Hokkaido is one of the driest parts of Japan. Tokyo has higher rainfall and temperatures, while the southern islands of Shikoku and Kyushu have warm temperate climates. Summers are long and hot; winters are cold.

POLITICS & ECONOMY In the late 19th century, Japan began a program of modernization. Under its new imperial leaders, it began to look for lands to conquer. In 1894–95, it fought a war with China and, in 1904–5, it defeated Russia. Soon its overseas empire included Korea and Taiwan. In 1930, Japan invaded Manchuria (northeast China), and in 1937 it began a war against China. In 1941, Japan launched an attack on the US base at Pearl Harbor in Hawai'i. This drew both Japan and the United States into World War II.

Japan surrendered in 1945 when the Americans dropped atomic bombs on two cities, Hiroshima and Nagasaki. The United States occupied Japan until 1952, during which time Japan adopted a democratic constitution. The emperor, who had previously been regarded as a god, became a constitutional monarch. In 2017, parliament passed a bill allowing the emperor to abdicate. Akihito stood down in favor of his son, Naruhito, in 2019.

From the 1960s, Japan rapidly built up new industries, but economic success brought problems, including housing shortages and pollution due to the rapid growth of cities. Other problems arise from an aging population.

The leading activities are manufacturing and services. Lacking natural resources, Japan imports most of the materials and fuels it needs, and its success has been based on its use of the latest technology, its skilled work force, its vigorous export policies, and the relatively low expenditure on defense. Exports include vehicles, machinery, electrical and electronic equipment, iron and steel, chemicals, textiles, and ships. Japan's economy suffered a stagnation in the 1990s. Signs of recovery from 2005 were shattered by the global financial crisis in 2008–9, and again by the 2011 earthquake and tsunami. The economy largely recovered with the economic reforms of Shinzo Abe (prime minister 2006–7 and 2012–20), becoming the world's third largest.

Japan is one of the world's top fishing nations and fish is an important source of protein for the Japanese. Because the land is so rugged, only 15% of the country can be farmed. Yet Japan produces about 70% of the food it needs. Rice is the chief crop, taking up about half of the total farmland.

AREA 145,880 sq mi [377,829 sq km] **POPULATION** 124,687,000
CAPITAL Tokyo **GOVERNMENT** Constitutional monarchy
ETHNIC GROUPS Japanese 99%, Chinese, Korean, Brazilian, and others
LANGUAGES Japanese (official)
RELIGIONS Shintoism and Buddhism 84% (most Japanese consider themselves to be both Shinto and Buddhist), others
CURRENCY Yen = 100 sen

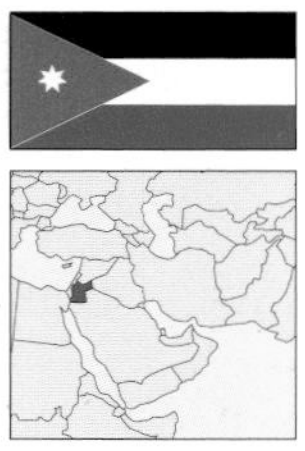

JORDAN

GEOGRAPHY The Hashemite Kingdom of Jordan is an Arab country in southwestern Asia. The Great Rift Valley in the west contains the River Jordan and the Dead Sea, which Jordan shares with Israel. East of the Rift Valley is the Transjordan plateau, where most Jordanians live. To the east and south lie vast areas of desert.

Amman has a much lower rainfall and longer dry season than the Mediterranean lands to the west. The Transjordan plateau, on which Amman stands, is a transition zone between the Mediterranean climate zone and the desert climate to the east.

POLITICS & ECONOMY In 1921, Britain created the territory of Transjordan east of the River Jordan. In 1923, Transjordan became self-governing, but Britain retained control of its defenses, finances, and foreign affairs. This territory became fully independent as Jordan in 1946. Jordan has suffered from instability arising from the Arab–Israeli conflict since the creation of the State of Israel in 1948. After the first Arab–Israeli War in 1948–49, Jordan acquired East Jerusalem and the fertile area of the West Bank. In 1967, Israel occupied this area. In Jordan, the presence of Palestinian refugees led to civil war in 1970–71.

In 1974, Arab leaders declared that the PLO (Palestine Liberation Organization) was the sole representative of the Palestinian people. In 1988, King Hussein of Jordan renounced Jordan's claims to the West Bank and passed responsibility for it to the PLO. Opposition parties were legalized in 1991 and elections were held in 1993. In October 1994, Jordan and Israel signed a peace treaty, ending a state of war that had lasted more than 40 years. Jordan's King Hussein commanded respect for his role in Middle Eastern affairs. He was succeeded by his eldest son, who became Abdullah II. The king has the power to dissolve parliament and appoint governments. He introduced modest political reforms in the wake of the pro-democracy protests that spread across the Middle East in 2011. More recently the government has been challenged by protests over economic reforms, particularly IMF-supported tax rises.

Jordan has an "upper-middle-income" economy. It lacks natural resources, apart from phosphates and potash, and depends on substantial aid. The country is facing economic challenges caused by the arrival of hundreds of thousands of refugees from civil war in Syria. Its tourism industry has been damaged by regional instability.

AREA 34,495 sq mi [89,342 sq km] **POPULATION** 10,910,000
CAPITAL Amman **GOVERNMENT** Constitutional monarchy
ETHNIC GROUPS Arab 98%, of which Palestinians make up roughly half
LANGUAGES Arabic (official)
RELIGIONS Islam (mostly Sunni) 92%, Christianity (mostly Greek Orthodox) 6%
CURRENCY Jordanian dinar = 100 Qirsh

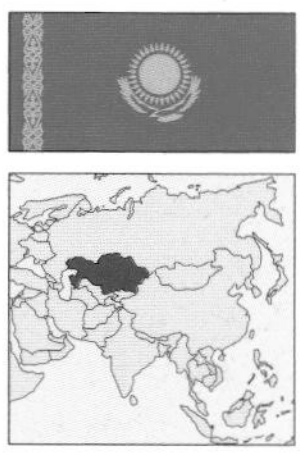

KAZAKHSTAN

GEOGRAPHY Kazakhstan is a large country in west-central Asia. In the west, the Caspian Sea lowlands include the Karagiye depression, which reaches 433 ft [132 m] below sea level. The lowlands extend eastward through the Aral Sea area. The north contains high plains, but the highest land is along the eastern and southern borders. These areas include parts of the Altai and Tian Shan mountain ranges. Eastern Kazakhstan contains several freshwater lakes, the largest of which is Lake Balkhash. The water in the rivers has been used for irrigation, causing ecological problems. For example, the Aral Sea, deprived of water, shrank from 25,830 sq mi [66,900 sq km] in 1960 to 6,630 sq mi [17,160 sq km] in 2004. Large areas are now barren desert, although a dam built in 2005 is reviving the north section.

Kazakhstan has an extreme climate. Winters are cold and snowy. The rainfall is generally low.

POLITICS & ECONOMY After the Russian Revolution of 1917, many Kazakhs wanted to make their country independent. But the Communists prevailed and in 1936 Kazakhstan became a republic of the Soviet Union, called the Kazakh Soviet Socialist Republic. During World War II and also after the war, the Soviet government moved many people from the west into Kazakhstan. From the 1950s, people were encouraged to work on a "Virgin Lands" project, which involved bringing large areas of grassland under cultivation.

Reforms in the Soviet Union in the 1980s led to its breakup in December 1991. Kazakhstan maintained contacts with Russia through the Commonwealth of Independent States (CIS). In 1997, the government moved its capital from Almaty to Aqmola (later renamed Astana), a town in the north. By the mid-2000s, the economy was in better shape than the other ex-Soviet republics in Central Asia, although President Nazarbayev, first elected in 1991, was criticized for his authoritarian rule. In 2007, constitutional changes enabled Nazarbayev to stand for the presidency as many times as he wished, and he was re-elected, virtually unopposed, in 2011 and 2015. After his unexpected resignation in 2019, the capital was renamed Nur-Sultan in his honor. Snap elections were won by his long-standing colleague Kassym-Jomart Tokayev.

The World Bank classifies Kazakhstan as an "upper-middle-income" developing country. Livestock farming, especially sheep and cattle, is an important activity, and major crops include barley, cotton, rice, and wheat. The country is rich in mineral resources, including coal and oil reserves, together with uranium, bauxite, copper, lead, tungsten, and zinc. Manufactures include chemicals, food products, machinery, and textiles. Oil is exported to Europe via a pipeline through Russia, and directly to China.

AREA 1,052,084 sq mi [2,724,900 sq km] **POPULATION** 19,246,000
CAPITAL Nur-Sultan **GOVERNMENT** Multiparty republic
ETHNIC GROUPS Kazakh 63%, Russian 24%, Uzbek 3%, Ukrainian 2%, others 8%
LANGUAGES Kazakh (official); Russian, the former official language, is widely spoken
RELIGIONS Islam 70%, Russian Orthodox 24%
CURRENCY Tenge = 100 tiyn

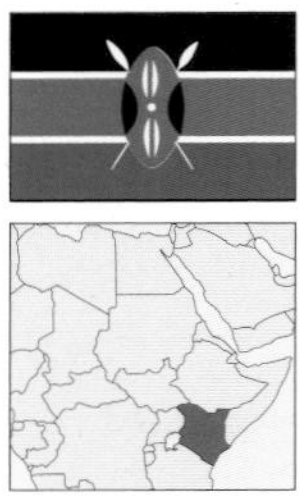

KENYA

GEOGRAPHY The Republic of Kenya is a country in East Africa which straddles the equator. Behind the narrow coastal plain on the Indian Ocean, the land rises to high plains and highlands, broken by volcanic mountains, including Mount Kenya, the country's highest peak at 17,057 ft [5,199 m]. Crossing the country is an arm of the Great Rift Valley, on the floor of which are several lakes, including Baringo, Magadi, Naivasha, Nakuru, and, on the northern frontier, Lake Turkana (formerly Lake Rudolf). Nairobi, in the southwestern highlands, has summer temperatures which are about 10°F [18°C] lower than humid Mombasa. Only about 15% of Kenya has a reliable annual rainfall of 31 inches [800 mm].

POLITICS & ECONOMY The Kenyan coast has been a trading center for more than 2,000 years. Britain took over the coast in 1895 and soon extended its influence inland. In the 1950s, a secret movement, called Mau Mau, launched an armed struggle against British rule. Although Mau Mau was eventually defeated, Kenya became independent in 1963.

Kenya was a one-party state for much of the time after 1963, with democracy restored in 1992. Elections in 2007 led to inter-ethnic violence when the opposition refused to accept the declared results. A deal was agreed by President Mwai Kibaki and Raila Odinga, who became prime minister. In 2011, Somali attacks and kidnappings in northern Kenya provoked Kenya to send forces into Somalia to try to combat the Islamist al-Shabab group, who nevertheless remain active in the country. Elections in August 2017 were declared void because of irregularities. The opposition boycotted the re-run and Uhuru Kenyatta was re-elected.

Many Kenyans are subsistence farmers. The chief food crop is maize. The main cash crops and the leading exports are tea and coffee. Manufactures include horticultural, food and petroleum products, and textiles. Oil was discovered in 2012. Tourism is important.

AREA 224,080 sq mi [580,367 sq km] **POPULATION** 54,685,000
CAPITAL Nairobi **GOVERNMENT** Multiparty republic
ETHNIC GROUPS Kikuyu 22%, Luhya 14%, Luo 13%, Kalenjin 12%, Kamba 11%, others
LANGUAGES Kiswahili and English (both official)
RELIGIONS Protestant 47%, Roman Catholic 23%, Islam 11%, others 19%
CURRENCY Kenyan shilling = 100 cents

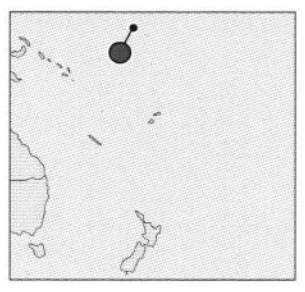

KIRIBATI

The Republic of Kiribati comprises three groups of coral atolls scattered over about 2 million sq mi [5 million sq km]. Kiribati straddles the equator and temperatures are high and the rainfall is abundant.

Formerly part of the British Gilbert and Ellice Islands, Kiribati became independent in 1979. The main export is copra and the country depends heavily on foreign aid. It is at risk from rising sea levels.

AREA 280 sq mi [726 sq km] **POPULATION** 113,000 **CAPITAL** Tarawa

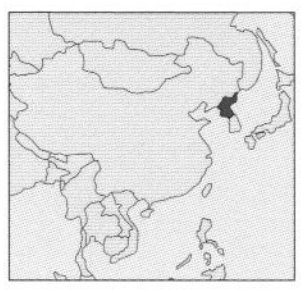

KOREA, NORTH

GEOGRAPHY The Democratic People's Republic of Korea occupies the northern part of the Korean peninsula. Mountains form the heart of the country, with the highest peak, Paektu-san, reaching 9,003 ft [2,744 m]. North Korea has a severe climate, with cold, snowy winters. In summer, winds from the oceans bring rain.

POLITICS & ECONOMY North Korea was created in 1945, when the peninsula, which had been a Japanese colony since 1910, was divided into two parts. Soviet forces occupied the north, with US forces in the south. Soviet occupation led to a Communist government being established in 1948 under the leadership of Kim Il Sung, who became a dictator, effectively founding the Kim dynasty.

The Korean War began in June 1950 when North Korean troops invaded the South. North Korea, aided by China and the Soviet Union, fought with South Korea, which was supported by troops from the United States and other UN members. The war ended in July 1953. An armistice was signed but no permanent peace treaty was agreed. The end of the Cold War in the late 1990s eased the situation. North and South Korea joined the United Nations in 1991, though North Korea remained isolated from most other countries. In 1993, North Korea withdrew from the Nuclear Non-Proliferation Treaty, arousing suspicions that it was developing nuclear weapons. Kim Il Sung died in 1994 and was succeeded by his son, Kim Jong Il. From 2003, the US accused North Korea of developing nuclear weapons, and it has since then carried out several tests, resulting in increased international isolation and tension. Kim Jong Il died in 2011, and his son, Kim Jong-Un, succeeded him. He expanded the nuclear program, but also appeared willing to negotiate with the US, although with no concrete results. In 2018 he became the first North Korean leader to enter South Korea.

North Korea's resources include coal, copper, iron ore, lead, and zinc. Manufactures include military products, chemicals, iron and steel, machinery, processed food, and textiles. Rice is the chief food crop, but food shortages have occurred in recent years.

AREA 46,540 sq mi [120,538 sq km] **POPULATION** 25,831,000
CAPITAL Pyŏngyang **GOVERNMENT** Single-party people's republic
ETHNIC GROUPS Korean 99% **LANGUAGES** Korean (official)
RELIGIONS Buddhism and Confucianism
CURRENCY North Korean won = 100 chon

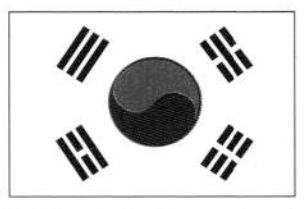
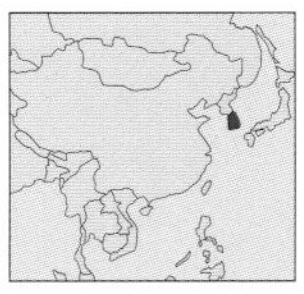

KOREA, SOUTH

GEOGRAPHY The Republic of Korea, as South Korea is officially known, occupies the southern part of the Korean peninsula. Mountains cover much of the country.

The southern and western coasts are major farming regions. Many islands are found along the west and south coasts. The largest of these is Jeju-do, which contains South Korea's highest peak, Hallasan, which rises to 6,398 ft [1,950 m].

Like North Korea, South Korea is chilled in winter by cold, dry winds from central Asia. Summers are hot and wet, especially in July and August.

POLITICS & ECONOMY After Japan's defeat in World War II (1939–45), North Korea was occupied by troops from the Soviet Union, while South Korea was occupied by United States forces. A National Assembly elected in 1948 in South Korea created the Republic of Korea, while North Korea became a Communist state. North Korea invaded the South in June 1950, sparking off the Korean War (1950–53). Despite the destruction caused by the war, South Korea under a series of rather authoritarian governments began to industrialize the economy between the 1960s and 1980s. In 1987, a new constitution permitted the election of presidents every five years. Tensions between South and North Korea continue, but at an historic meeting in 2018, South Korea's President Moon and North Korea's Kim Jon-Un agreed to work toward peace and reducing nuclear arms on the Korean peninsula.

Until the onset of the Asian financial crisis in 1997–98, South Korea had one of the world's fastest growing economies. Heavy industries produce chemicals, fertilizers, iron and steel, and ships, together with a wide range of consumer products, such as mobile phones, computers, cars, and television sets. The economy relies heavily on exports. Farming and fishing remain important. Rice is the chief crop, together with fruits, grains, and vegetables.

AREA 38,327 sq mi [99,268 sq km] **POPULATION** 51,715,000
CAPITAL Seoul **GOVERNMENT** Multiparty republic
ETHNIC GROUPS Korean 99% **LANGUAGES** Korean (official)
RELIGIONS No affiliation 43%, Christianity 32%, Buddhism 24%, others 1% **CURRENCY** South Korean won = 100 jeon

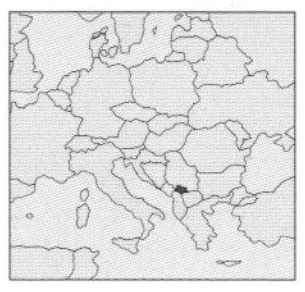

KOSOVO

GEOGRAPHY The Republic of Kosovo in the central Balkans, formerly part of Serbia, declared its independence in February 2008. Its independence was recognized by the United States and major EU countries, but Serbia, and its ally Russia, refused recognition. It is a landlocked country, consisting of a river basin bounded by uplands in the north and southwest. It has cold, snowy winters and hot, dry summers.

POLITICS & ECONOMY Most people are Albanian-speakers who are Muslims, but there is an important Christian Serb minority. In the early 13th century, Kosovo was part of the Serbian empire but, after 1389, it came under Muslim Turkish Ottoman rule.

Serbia regained control of Kosovo in 1912 and, in 1918, it became part of the Kingdom of Serbia. In 1946, it became part of the Socialist Federal Republic of Yugoslavia, becoming an autonomous province within the Republic of Serbia. In 1989, Serbia curtailed Kosovo's autonomy, while Albanian speakers declared their province independent. In 1995, the Albanian speakers set up the Kosovo Liberation Army, which launched an uprising against Serbia. In 1998, Serbia began repressive measures against Kosovo, resulting in massacres and ethnic cleansing of Albanian-speaking Kosovars. In 1999, NATO forces bombed Serbia and placed Kosovo under a temporary administration. Finally, the Kosovo Assembly declared its independence on February 17, 2008. Whilst Serbia still does not recognize Kosovo as an independent state, the two countries are engaged in diplomatic talks.

Kosovo is a poor country, with one of the lowest per capita incomes in Europe, although its economy is slowly improving. Many people are subsistence farmers and its industries suffer from lack of investment. The economy is highly dependent on international aid and remittances from Kosovans abroad.

AREA 4,203 sq mi [10,887 sq km] **POPULATION** 1,935,000
CAPITAL Pristina **GOVERNMENT** Republic **ETHNIC GROUPS** Albanian 92%, others 8% **LANGUAGES** Albanian and Serbian (both official), Turkish **RELIGIONS** Islam, Serbian Orthodox, Roman Catholic
CURRENCY Euro = 100 cents

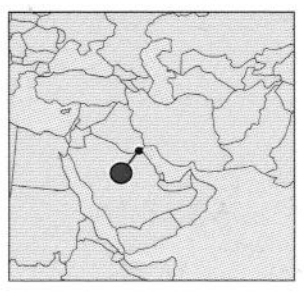

KUWAIT

GEOGRAPHY The State of Kuwait, at the northern end of the Persian Gulf, is an emirate. The land is low-lying and largely desert in nature. Summer temperatures are high but winters are cooler. Rainfall is low.

POLITICS & ECONOMY British influence began in 1775 and, in 1899, the local ruler concluded a treaty with Britain, agreeing to support British interests in return for protection. Kuwait became independent in 1961. Prosperity came from oil exports. Iraq invaded Kuwait in 1990, but it was liberated in 1991 by a coalition force. In 2004, the government announced legislation for women to vote and stand for parliament. In recent years there has been increasing unrest caused by militant Islamists, as well as tension between parliament and the ruling Al-Sabah family.

AREA 6,880 sq mi [17,818 sq km]
POPULATION 3,032,000 **CAPITAL** Kuwait City

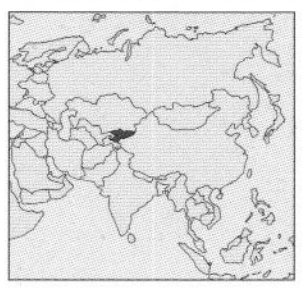

KYRGYZSTAN

GEOGRAPHY The Republic of Kyrgyzstan is a landlocked country between China, Tajikistan, Uzbekistan, and Kazakhstan. The country is mountainous, with spectacular scenery. The highest mountain, Pik Pobedy in the Tian Shan range, reaches 24,406 ft [7,439 m] in the east. The lowlands have warm summers and cold winters. But January temperatures in the mountains plummet to –18°F [–28°C]. Kyrgyzstan has a low annual rainfall.

POLITICS & ECONOMY In 1876, Kyrgyzstan became a province of Russia. In 1916, Russia crushed a rebellion among the Kyrgyz, and many subsequently fled to China. In 1922, the area became a self-governing region of the newly formed Soviet Union, but in 1936 it became one of the Soviet Socialist Republics. Under Communist rule, local customs and religious worship were suppressed, but education and health services were greatly improved.

In 1991, Kyrgyzstan became an independent country following the breakup of the Soviet Union. The Communist Party was dissolved, but the country maintained links with Russia. The first two elections as an independent state produced unpopular presidents who were swept from power and had to flee the country. In 2020, President Sooronbay Jeenbekov stepped down accused of rigging the presidential election. Sadyr Japarov was elected the following year.

As one of the poorest countries of the former Soviet Union, Kyrgyzstan sought to reform its Soviet-style economy in the 1990s. Classified as a "lower-middle-income" economy by the World Bank, agriculture and mining – mainly gold – are the principal activities. Major products include cotton, eggs, fruits, grain, tobacco, vegetables, and wool, but food is imported. Attracting foreign investment and legitimizing business practices will be vital to economic growth.

AREA 77,181 sq mi [199,900 sq km] **POPULATION** 6,019,000
CAPITAL Bishkek **GOVERNMENT** Multiparty republic
ETHNIC GROUPS Kyrgyz 65%, Uzbek 14%, Russian 13%
LANGUAGES Kyrgyz and Russian (both official) **RELIGIONS** Islam 75%, Russian Orthodox 20% **CURRENCY** Kyrgyzstani som = 100 tyiyn

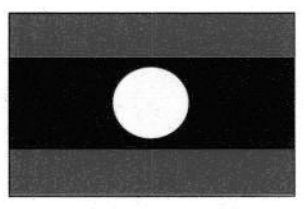
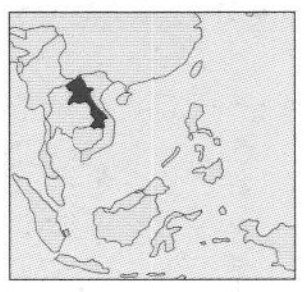

LAOS

GEOGRAPHY The Lao People's Democratic Republic is a landlocked country in Southeast Asia. Mountains and plateaux cover much of the country. Most people live on the plains bordering the River Mekong and its tributaries. This river, one of Asia's longest, forms much of the country's northwestern and southwestern borders.

Laos has a tropical monsoon climate. Winters are dry and sunny with winds blowing from the northeast. From April, the monsoon season starts with the arrival of moist southwesterly winds.

POLITICS & ECONOMY France made Laos a protectorate in the late 19th century and ruled it, with Cambodia and Vietnam, as part of French Indochina. Laos became an independent kingdom in 1954. After independence, a power struggle between royalist government forces and a pro-Communist group called Pathet Lao caused instability. A civil war broke out and continued into the 1970s. The Pathet Lao took control in 1975 and the king abdicated. In the 1990s, Laos started to open to the world and began tentative reforms. In 2011, a stock exchange was opened in Vientiane, as part of a gradual move toward capitalism.

Laos relies heavily on foreign aid. Agriculture employs nearly 73% of the population and accounts for about 20% of the gross domestic product. Rice is the main crop. Timber, coffee, copper, and gold are exported. The most valuable export is electricity, which is produced at hydroelectric power stations on the Mekong, although the environmental impact of the dams is a cause for concern.

AREA 91,428 sq mi [236,800 sq km] **POPULATION** 7,574,000
CAPITAL Vientiane **GOVERNMENT** Single-party republic
ETHNIC GROUPS Lao 55%, Khmou 11%, Hmong 8%, others 26%
LANGUAGES Lao (official), French, English **RELIGIONS** Buddhism 67%, traditional beliefs and others 33% **CURRENCY** Kip = 100 att

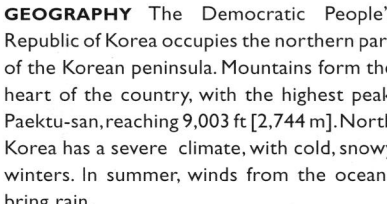

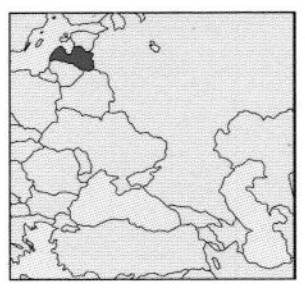

LATVIA

GEOGRAPHY The Republic of Latvia is one of three states on the southeastern corner of the Baltic Sea which were ruled as parts of the Soviet Union between 1940 and 1991. Latvia consists mainly of flat plains separated by low hills, composed of glacial moraine.

Riga has warm summers, but the winter months are sub-zero. The rainfall is moderate.

POLITICS & ECONOMY In 1800, Russia was in control of Latvia, but Latvians declared their independence after World War I. In 1940, under a German–Soviet pact, Soviet troops occupied Latvia, but they were driven out by the Germans in 1941. Soviet troops returned in 1944 and Latvia became part of the Soviet Union. Under Soviet rule, many Russian immigrants settled in Latvia and many Latvians feared that the Russians would become the dominant ethnic group.

In the late 1980s, when reforms were being introduced in the Soviet Union, Latvia's government ended absolute Communist rule and made Latvian the official language. In 1990, it declared the country to be independent, an act which was finally recognized by the Soviet Union in September 1991.

Latvia held the first free elections to its parliament (the Saeima) in 1993. Voting was limited only to citizens of Latvia on June 17, 1940, and their descendants. This meant that about 34% of Latvian residents were unable to vote. In 1994, Latvia restricted the naturalization of non-Latvians, including many Russian setlers, who were not allowed to vote or own land. However, in 1998, the government agreed that all children born since independence should have automatic citizenship. In 2004, Latvia became a member of the North Atlantic Treaty Organization and the European Union. Latvia was hit hard by the global financial crisis in 2009. It adopted the euro in January 2014.

The World Bank classifies Latvia as a "high-income" country. Manufactures include electronic goods, machinery, wood and wood products, processed food, and vehicles. About 30% of the land is used for agriculture, with crops including wheat, barley, potatoes, and rye.

AREA 24,942 sq mi [64,600 sq km] **POPULATION** 1,863,000
CAPITAL Riga **GOVERNMENT** Multiparty republic
ETHNIC GROUPS Latvian 59%, Russian 28%, Belarusian, Ukrainian, Polish, Lithuanian **LANGUAGES** Latvian (official), Russian, Lithuanian **RELIGIONS** Lutheran, Russian Orthodox, Roman Catholic
CURRENCY Euro = 100 cents

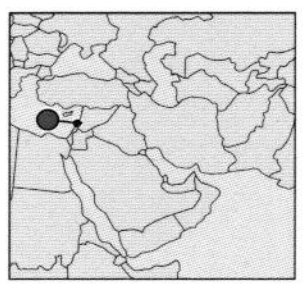

LEBANON

GEOGRAPHY The Republic of Lebanon is a country on the eastern shores of the Mediterranean Sea. Behind the coastal plain are the rugged Lebanon Mountains (Jabal Lubnan), which rise to 10,131 ft [3,088 m]. Another range, the Anti-Lebanon Mountains (Al Jabal Ash Sharqi), forms the eastern border with Syria. Between the two ranges is the Bekaa (Biqa) Valley, a fertile farming region. The coast has hot, dry summers and mild, wet winters. Heavy rain falls on the mountains, with snow at high altitudes.

POLITICS & ECONOMY Lebanon was ruled by Turkey from 1516 until World War I. France then took control from 1923 until independence in 1946. Muslims and Christians then agreed to share power, and Lebanon made rapid economic progress until the late 1950s, when development was slowed by periodic conflict between Sunni and Shia Muslims, Druze, and Christians. The situation was further complicated by the presence of Palestinian refugees, who used bases in Lebanon to attack Israel.

In 1975, civil war broke out as the many factions struggled for power. This led to intervention by Israel in the south and Syria in the north. UN peacekeeping forces arrived in 1978, but violence continued in the 1980s. Peace was restored in the 1990s, but, in 2005, the assassination of Rafik Hariri, former prime minister, was blamed on Syria. Under pressure, Syria withdrew its forces from Lebanon. In 2006, a 34-day conflict between Israeli troops and Hezbollah guerrillas caused devastation in southern Lebanon. The civil war in Syria had a destabilizing effect on Lebanon, with some violent clashes and increased social tensions. Refugees from Syria now make up one-third of the population.

Lebanon's civil war almost destroyed the valuable trade and financial services that had been Lebanon's chief source of income, together with tourism and manufacturing. The years 2011–17 were marked by slow economic growth. In 2018 Lebanon announced plans to explore potential offshore gas and oil reserves.

AREA 4,015 sq mi [10,400 sq km] **POPULATION** 5,261,000
CAPITAL Beirut **GOVERNMENT** Multiparty republic
ETHNIC GROUPS Arab 95%, Armenian 4%, others
LANGUAGES Arabic (official), French, English, Armenian
RELIGIONS Islam 60%, Christianity 39%
CURRENCY Lebanese pound = 100 piastres

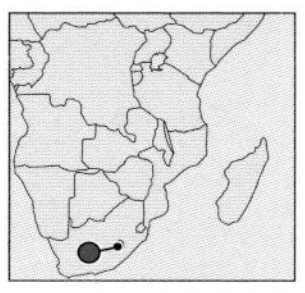

LESOTHO

GEOGRAPHY The Kingdom of Lesotho is a landlocked country, completely enclosed by South Africa. The land is mountainous, rising to 11,424 ft [3,482 m] on the northeastern border. The Drakensberg range covers most of the country.

The climate of Lesotho is greatly affected by the altitude, because most of the country lies above 4,920 ft [1,500 m]. Summers are warm but winters are cold. The rainfall averages about 28 inches [700 mm].

POLITICS & ECONOMY The political entity that eventually became Lesotho coalesced under King Moshoeshoe I in the 1820s who united various groups fleeing from tribal wars in southern Africa. Britain made the area a protectorate in 1868 and, in 1871, placed it under the British Cape Colony in South Africa. In 1884, Basutoland, as the area was called, was reconstituted as a British protectorate, where whites were not allowed to own land.

The country became independent in 1966 as the Kingdom of Lesotho, with Moshoeshoe II, great-grandson of Moshoeshoe I, as its king. Since independence, times have been turbulent with various factions, including the military, vying for power. There has been relative political stability since 1998, with prime ministerial power alternating between Pakalitha Mosisili (1998–2012, 2015–2017) and Thomas Thabane (2012–2015, 2017–20).

Lesotho faces many problems: agriculture is vulnerable to vagaries of the weather and the population has one of the highest rates of HIV/AIDS infection in the world. Poverty is widespread.

Lesotho lacks natural resources with agriculture employing 86% of the people, mostly at subsistence level. Remittances sent home by Basotho working abroad, mainly in South Africa, are important to the economy. Lesotho's main exports are textiles and diamonds, and it also exports water to South Africa.

AREA 11,720 sq mi [30,355 sq km] **POPULATION** 2,178,000
CAPITAL Maseru **GOVERNMENT** Constitutional monarchy
ETHNIC GROUPS Sotho 99% **LANGUAGES** Sesotho and English (both official) **RELIGIONS** Christianity 80%, traditional beliefs 20%
CURRENCY Loti = 100 lisente

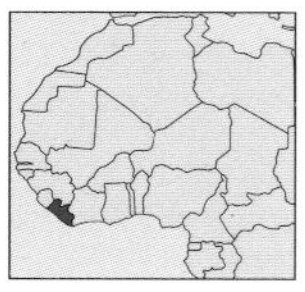

LIBERIA

GEOGRAPHY The Republic of Liberia is a country in West Africa. Behind the coastline, 311 mi [500 km] long, lies a narrow coastal plain. Beyond, the land rises to a plateau region, with the highest land along the border with Guinea. Liberia has a tropical climate with high temperatures and high humidity all through the year. Rainfall is abundant all year round, but there is a particularly wet period from June to November. Rainfall generally increases from east to west.

POLITICS & ECONOMY In the late 18th century, some white Americans in the United States wanted to help freed black slaves return to Africa. In 1816, they set up the American Colonization Society, which bought land in what is now Liberia.

In 1822, the Society landed former slaves at a settlement which they named Monrovia after US president Monroe. In 1847, Liberia became a fully independent republic with a constitution much like that of the United States. For many years, Americo-Liberians controlled the country's government with the American Firestone Company, which ran the rubber plantations, being especially influential. Other foreign companies readily exploited Liberia's mineral resources, including its huge iron-ore deposits.

In 1980, a military group composed of people from the local population killed the Americo-Liberian president, William R. Tolbert. An army sergeant, Samuel K. Doe, was made president. Elections held in 1985 resulted in victory for Doe. From 1989, the country was plunged into civil war between various ethnic groups. Doe was assassinated in 1990 and the struggle with rebel groups continued. West African peacekeeping forces arrived in Liberia and, in 1995, a ceasefire was agreed. A council of state was set up in 1997 and Charles Taylor became president. Taylor fled the country in 2003, and in 2006 he was extradited and faced war crimes charges, on several of which he was convicted in 2012. Following elections in 2005, Ellen Johnson-Sirleaf became Africa's first woman president. She was re-elected in 2011. Elections in 2017 were won by former soccer player George Weah.

Liberia's economy was devastated by the civil war and, more recently, by the regional outbreak of Ebola. Agriculture is important, but mostly at subsistence level. Food crops include cassava, rice, and sugarcane, while rubber, cocoa, and coffee are exported. The most valuable exports are rubber, iron ore, diamonds, and gold. Liberia also obtains revenue from its "flag of convenience" which is used by about 12% of the world's commercial shipping.

AREA 43,000 sq mi [111,369 sq km] **POPULATION** 5,214,000
CAPITAL Monrovia **GOVERNMENT** Multiparty republic
ETHNIC GROUPS Indigenous African tribes 95% (including Kpelle, Bassa, Grebo, Gio, Kru, Mano)
LANGUAGES English (official), ethnic languages
RELIGIONS Christianity 86%, Islam 12%, traditional beliefs and others 2% **CURRENCY** Liberian dollar = 100 cents

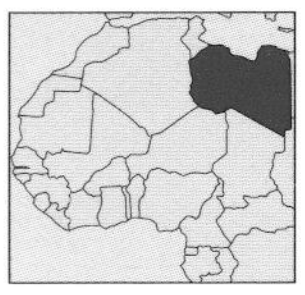

LIBYA

GEOGRAPHY Bordering the Mediterranean Sea, the State of Libya is the fourth largest country in Africa. Most people live on the coastal plains in the northeast and northwest. The Sahara, the world's largest desert, which occupies 95% of Libya, reaches the Mediterranean coast along the Gulf of Sidra (Khalij Surt).

The coastal plains in the northeast and northwest have Mediterranean climates, with hot, dry summers and mild, sometimes wet winters. Hot desert conditions prevail inland.

POLITICS & ECONOMY Italy took possession of Libya in 1911, but lost it during World War II. Britain and France jointly ruled Libya until 1951, when the country became independent.

In 1969, a military group headed by Colonel Muammar Gaddafi deposed the king and set up a military government. Under Gaddafi, the government took control of the economy and used money from oil exports to finance welfare services and development projects. Gaddafi was criticized for supporting terrorist groups around the world, and Libya became isolated from the mid-1980s.

From 2004, relations with the West improved and diplomatic links were restored with many nations, including the United States. However, in February 2011, the arrest of a human rights campaigner sparked off protests in Benghazi which rapidly spread. In October of that year, Gaddafi was killed and a National Transition Council was set up as the de facto government. Libya struggled to find peace and political stability, and by 2021 there were two main factions – the Government of National Accord based in Tripoli, and the "Libyan National Army" in the east. Islamic State also maintains a presence.

The discovery of oil and natural gas in 1959 led to a transformation of Libya's economy. This formerly poor country soon became Africa's richest in terms of its per capita income. But it remains a developing country, because oil accounts for nearly all of its export revenues. Agriculture is important, although Libya imports about 80% of its food. Crops include barley, citrus fruits, dates, olives, potatoes, and wheat, while cattle, sheep, and poultry are raised. Libya has oil refineries and petrochemical plants. Development and foreign investment await political stability.

AREA 679,358 sq mi [1,759,540 sq km] **POPULATION** 7,017,000
CAPITAL Tripoli **GOVERNMENT** Transitional
ETHNIC GROUPS Libyan Arab and Berber 97% **LANGUAGES** Arabic (official), Berber **RELIGIONS** Islam (Sunni Muslim) 97%
CURRENCY Libyan dinar = 1,000 dirhams

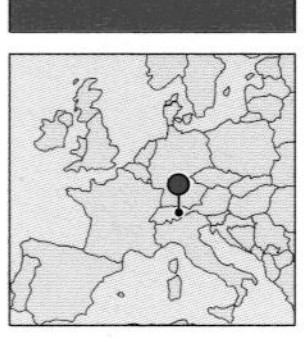

LIECHTENSTEIN

The tiny Principality of Liechtenstein is sandwiched between Switzerland and Austria. The River Rhine flows along its western border, while Alpine peaks rise in the east and south. The climate is relatively mild. Since 1924, Liechtenstein has been in a customs union with Switzerland. Taxation is low and the country is a haven for foreign companies. In 2004, the head of state Prince Hans-Adam II handed over the running of the country to his son, Prince Alois, though he remains titular head of state. In 2009, Liechtenstein agreed to share tax information with a number of countries in order to improve its reputation as a legitimate financial center.

AREA 62 sq mi [160 sq km] **POPULATION** 39,000 **CAPITAL** Vaduz

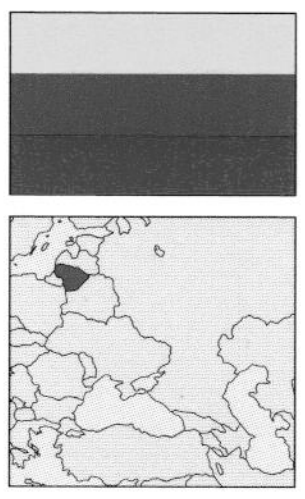

LITHUANIA

GEOGRAPHY The Republic of Lithuania is the southernmost of the three Baltic states which were ruled as part of the Soviet Union between 1940 and 1991. Much of the land is flat or gently rolling, with the highest land in the southeast.

Winters are cold and summers warm. The annual rainfall in the west is about 25 in [630 mm]. Eastern areas are drier.

POLITICS & ECONOMY The Lithuanian people were united into a single nation in the 12th century, and later joined a union with Poland. In 1795, Lithuania came under Russian rule. After World War I (1914–18), Lithuania declared itself independent, and in 1920 it signed a peace treaty with the Russians. In 1940, the Soviet Union occupied Lithuania, but was ousted by Germany a year later. After Soviet forces returned in 1944, Lithuania was integrated into the Soviet Union. However, Lithuanians resisted attempts to suppress their culture and steadfastly clung on to their language and staunch Catholic faith. In 1988, when the Soviet Union was introducing reforms, the Lithuanians demanded independence which was recognized by the Soviet Union in 1991.

Since 1991, Lithuania has sought to reform its economy and introduce a private enterprise system. Lithuania has also drawn closer to the West and, in 2004, it became a member of both the North Atlantic Treaty Organization and the European Union. Its first attempt to join the eurozone in 2007 was rejected due to high inflation but it adopted the euro in 2015.

The World Bank now classifies Lithuania as a "high-income" economy and it is growing faster than most other EU economies. Lithuania lacks natural resources. Manufacturing, based on imported materials, and services are the most valuable activities.

AREA 25,174 sq mi [65,200 sq km] **POPULATION** 2,712,000
CAPITAL Vilnius **GOVERNMENT** Multiparty republic
ETHNIC GROUPS Lithuanian 84%, Polish 6%, Russian 5%, Belarusian 1% **LANGUAGES** Lithuanian (official), Russian, Polish
RELIGIONS Mainly Roman Catholic **CURRENCY** Euro = 100 cents

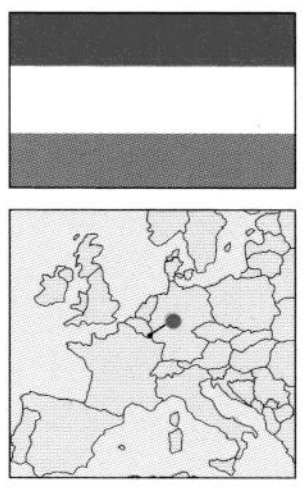

LUXEMBOURG

GEOGRAPHY The Grand Duchy of Luxembourg is one of the smallest and oldest countries in Europe. Luxembourg has a temperate climate. The south has warm summers and falls, when grapes ripen in sheltered southeastern valleys. Winters are sometimes severe, especially in upland areas.

POLITICS & ECONOMY Germany occupied Luxembourg in World Wars I and II. In 1944–45, northern Luxembourg was the scene of the Battle of the Bulge. In 1948, Luxembourg joined Belgium and the Netherlands in "Benelux," a customs union, and in the 1950s, it was one of the six founders of what is now the European Union. Its capital is a major financial center and contains several international agencies. In 2008, parliament restricted the monarch to a ceremonial role following the grand duke's refusal to sign a law allowing euthanasia.

Luxembourg has iron-ore reserves and has traditionally been a major steel producer. A decline in the industry prompted Luxembourg to diversify, particularly into financial services. Steel and other manufactures, including chemicals, rubber products, glass, and aluminum, continue to dominate the country's exports. The "LuxLeaks" scandal in 2009, which revealed advantageous tax arrangements for several multi-national companies, temporarily damaged Luxembourg's reputation.

AREA 998 sq mi [2,586 sq km] **POPULATION** 640,000
CAPITAL Luxembourg **GOVERNMENT** Constitutional monarchy (Grand Duchy) **ETHNIC GROUPS** Luxembourger 63%, Portuguese 13%, Italian, French, Belgian, Slavs **LANGUAGES** Luxembourgish (official), Portuguese, French, German **RELIGIONS** Roman Catholic 87%, others 13% **CURRENCY** Euro = 100 cents

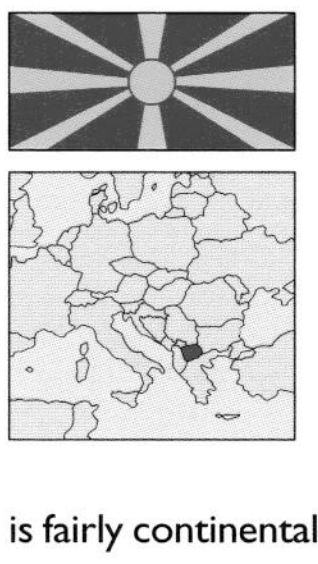

MACEDONIA, NORTH

GEOGRAPHY The Republic of North Macedonia is a country in southeastern Europe, which was once one of the six republics that made up the former Yugoslavia. This landlocked country is largely mountainous or hilly. North Macedonia has hot summers, though highland areas are cooler. Winters are cold and snowfalls are often heavy. The climate is fairly continental in character and rain occurs throughout the year.

POLITICS & ECONOMY Until the 20th century, North Macedonia's history was closely tied to the larger area of Macedonia, which included parts of northern Greece and southwestern Bulgaria. This region reached its peak in power at the time of Philip II (382–336 BC) and his son Alexander the Great (336–323 BC). After Alexander's death, his empire was split up and it gradually declined. The area became a Roman province in the 140s BC and part of the Byzantine empire from AD 395. In the 6th century, Slavs from eastern Europe settled in the area, followed by Bulgars from central Asia in the 9th century. The Byzantine empire regained control in 1018, but Serbia took Macedonia in the early 14th century. In 1371, the Ottoman Turks conquered the area and ruled it for more than 500 years.

In 1913, at the end of the Balkan Wars, the area was divided between Serbia, Bulgaria, and Greece. At the end of World War I, Serbian Macedonia became part of the Kingdom of the Serbs, Croats, and Slovenes, which was renamed Yugoslavia in 1929.

In the early 1990s, the country broke up into five separate republics with Macedonia declaring its independence in 1991. Greece objected to the use of the name Macedonia, which it considered to be a Greek name. It also objected to a symbol on Macedonia's flag and a reference in the constitution to the desire to reunite the three parts of the old Macedonia.

Macedonia adopted a new clause in its constitution rejecting any Macedonian claims on Greek territory and, in 1993, the United Nations accepted the new republic as a member under the name of the Former Yugoslav Republic of Macedonia (FYROM). By the end of 1993, all the countries of the EU, except Greece, were establishing diplomatic relations with the FYROM. In 1995, Greece lifted its trade ban when Macedonia agreed to redesign its flag. The issue over its name remained unresolved until 2018, when Macedonia and Greece agreed on the new name of the Republic of North Macedonia, paving the way for North Macedonia to apply for membership of the EU and NATO.

The World Bank describes North Macedonia as an "upper-middle-income" economy showing steady growth since independence due to conservative government financial policies working toward a more open economy. Manufactures dominate the country's exports. Coal is mined, but oil and natural gas are imported. The country is self-sufficient in its basic food needs and has a low rate of inflation, although it remains one of Europe's poorest economies and unemployment is high.

AREA 9,928 sq mi [25,713 sq km] **POPULATION** 2,128,000
CAPITAL Skopje **GOVERNMENT** Multiparty republic
ETHNIC GROUPS Macedonian 64%, Albanian 25%, Turkish 4%, Romanian 3%, Serb 2% **LANGUAGES** Macedonian and Albanian (official) **RELIGIONS** Macedonian Orthodox 65%, Islam 33%
CURRENCY Macedonian denar = 100 deni

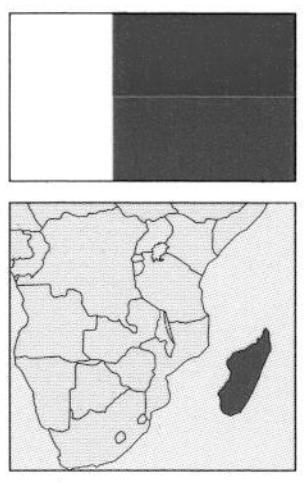

MADAGASCAR

GEOGRAPHY The Democratic Republic of Madagascar, in southeastern Africa, is an island nation, which has an area larger than France. Behind the narrow coastal plains in the east lies a highland zone, mostly between 2,000 ft and 4,000 ft [610 m to 1,220 m] above sea level. Broad plains border the Mozambique Channel in the west.

Temperatures in the highlands are moderated by the altitude. The winters (from April to September) are dry, but heavy rains occur in summer. The eastern coastlands are warm and humid. The west is drier, and the south and southwest are hot and dry. It has a unique fauna and flora.

POLITICS & ECONOMY People from Southeast Asia began to settle on Madagascar around 2,000 years ago. Subsequent influxes from Africa and Arabia added to the island's diverse heritage, culture, and language.

The island was a French colony from 1895 until it achieved independence as the Malagasy Republic in 1960. In 1972, army officers seized control and, in 1975, under the leadership of Lieutenant-Commander Didier Ratsiraka, the country was renamed Madagascar. In 2002, the country came close to civil war when Ratsiraka and his opponent, Marc Ravalomanana, both claimed victory in presidential elections. Ravalomanana became president, but he was deposed in 2009, in a move backed by the military and condemned internationally; Andry Rajoelina assumed power. Elections in 2013 were won by Hery Rajaonarimampiana, but Rajoelina returned to power after elections in 2018.

Madagascar is a poor country. Poverty and population growth impose pressure on the dwindling forests and the unique wildlife, as well as causing severe soil erosion. Farming, fishing, and forestry employ about 80% of the people. Food crops include bananas, cassava, rice, and sweet potatoes. Coffee and vanilla are exported.

AREA 226,657 sq mi [587,041 sq km] **POPULATION** 27,534,000
CAPITAL Antananarivo **GOVERNMENT** Republic
ETHNIC GROUPS Merina, Betsimisaraka, Betsileo, Tsimihety, Sakalava and others
LANGUAGES Malagasy and French (both official)
RELIGIONS Traditional beliefs 52%, Christianity 41%, Islam 7%
CURRENCY Malagasy ariary = 5 iraimbilanja

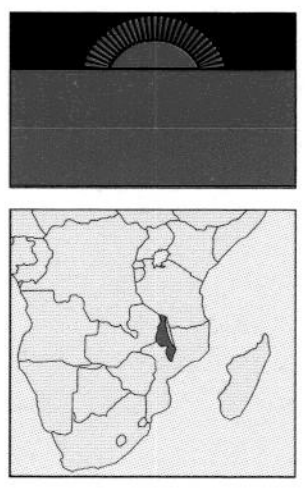

MALAWI

GEOGRAPHY The Republic of Malawi includes part of Lake Malawi, which is drained by the River Shire, a tributary of the River Zambezi. The land is mostly mountainous. The highest peak, Mulanje, reaches 9,849 ft [3,002 m] in the southeast.

While the low-lying areas of Malawi are hot and humid all year round, the uplands have more pleasant weather. Lilongwe has a warm and sunny climate. Frosts sometimes occur in July and August, in the middle of the long dry season.

POLITICS & ECONOMY Malawi, then called Nyasaland, became a British protectorate in 1891. In 1953, Britain established the Federation of Rhodesia and Nyasaland, which also included what are now Zambia and Zimbabwe. Black African opposition, led in Nyasaland by Dr Hastings Kamuzu Banda, led to the dissolution of the federation in 1963. In 1964, Nyasaland became independent as Malawi, with Banda as prime minister. Banda was an autocrat who maintained his control of the country by operating a one-party system and being made "president for life" in 1971 until he retired after elections in 1994. Bakili Muluzi became the first president after Banda and, despite Malawi aspiring toward more open government, subsequent administrations have been mired in accusations of corruption and treason.

Malawi is one of the world's poorest countries with more than half the population living below the poverty line. About 80% of the people are farmers, but many grow little more than they need to feed their families. Malawi is starting to exploit its uranium resources, but development is hampered by lack of infrastructure and the country's very high rates of HIV/AIDS infection.

AREA 45,747 sq mi [118,484 sq km] **POPULATION** 20,309,000
CAPITAL Lilongwe **GOVERNMENT** Multiparty republic
ETHNIC GROUPS Chewa, Lomwe, Yao, Ngoni, Tumbuka, Nyanja, Sena, Tonga, Ngonde and others
LANGUAGES Chichewa and English (both official)
RELIGIONS Christianity 68%, Islam 25%
CURRENCY Malawian kwacha = 100 tambala

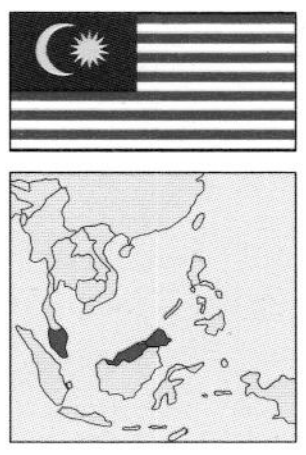

MALAYSIA

GEOGRAPHY The Federation of Malaysia consists of two main parts. Peninsular Malaysia, which is joined to mainland Asia, contains about 80% of the population. The other main regions, Sabah and Sarawak, are in northern Borneo, an island which Malaysia shares with Indonesia. Behind the coastal lowlands, the interior is mountainous.

Malaysia has a hot equatorial climate. The temperatures are high all through the year, though the mountains are much cooler than the lowland areas. Rainfall is heavy throughout the year.

POLITICS & ECONOMY Around 1,200 years ago, Indian traders introduced Hinduism and Buddhism into the Malay peninsula, while Arabs introduced Islam in the 15th century. Portuguese traders reached Melaka in 1509, but the Dutch took over in 1641. Britain became established in this region in 1786.

Japan occupied the area during World War II (1939–45), but it reverted to British rule in 1945. Malaya (Peninsular Malaysia) became independent in 1957. Malaysia was created in 1963, when Malaya, Singapore, Sabah, and Sarawak agreed to unite, but Singapore withdrew in 1965.

From 1981, Malaysia experienced rapid economic progress under the 22-year term of Prime Minister Mahathir bin Mohamad. Although not unaffected by global financial crises, the succeeding governments continued to develop a broad-based economy with an emphasis on manufacturing, tourism, and the service industry. From 2018 to 2020 Mahathir again served as prime minister.

The World Bank classifies Malaysia as an "upper-middle-income" developing country. Palm oil, rubber, and tin are major products. Manufactures include cars, chemicals, a wide range of electronic goods, plastics, textiles, rubber, and wood products.

AREA 127,320 sq mi [329,758 sq km] **POPULATION** 33,519,000
CAPITAL Kuala Lumpur; Putrajaya (administrative capital)
GOVERNMENT Federal constitutional monarchy
ETHNIC GROUPS Malay and other indigenous groups 61%, Chinese 24%, Indian 7%, others
LANGUAGES Malay (official), Chinese, English
RELIGIONS Islam, Buddhism, Daoism, Hinduism, Christianity, Sikhism
CURRENCY Ringgit = 100 sen

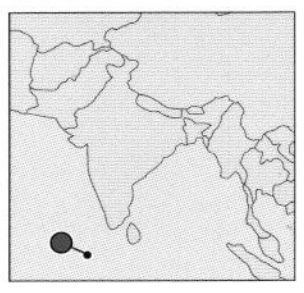

MALDIVES

The Republic of the Maldives consists of about 1,200 low-lying coral islands, south of India. The highest point is 79 ft [24 m], but most of the land is only 6 ft [1.8 m] above sea level, making it vulnerable to the effects of climate change. It became a British territory in 1887 and independent in 1965. It left the Commonwealth of Nations in 2016. Tourism and fishing are the main industries.

AREA 115 sq mi [298 sq km] **POPULATION** 391,000 **CAPITAL** Malé

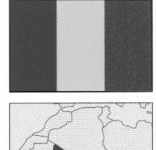

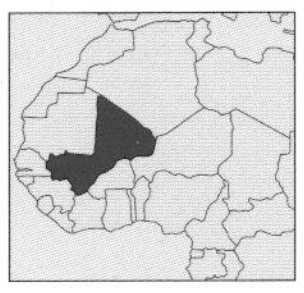

MALI

GEOGRAPHY The Republic of Mali is a landlocked country in northwestern Africa. The land is generally flat, with the highest land in the north. Northern Mali is hot and practically rainless. The south has enough rain for farming.

POLITICS & ECONOMY Between the 4th and 16th centuries, Mali was part of three African empires – Ancient Ghana, Ancient Mali and Songhay. However, after 1591, when Songhay was defeated by Morocco, the area was divided into small kingdoms. France ruled the area, then known as French Sudan, from 1893 until the country became independent as Mali in 1960.

The first socialist government was overthrown in 1968 by an army group led by Moussa Traoré, who was not ousted until 1991. Multiparty democracy was restored in 1992 with Alpha Oumar Konaré as president. He was succeeded by Ahmadou Touré in 2002. A Tuareg rebellion built in northern Mali, and the army overthrew Touré in 2012, accusing him of failing to deal with the situation. The ensuing chaos allowed Islamist terrorist groups to flourish in the north, and Mali called for French support as Islamist-held territory and attacks increased. Democracy returned with the election of Ibrahim Keita in 2013, but in 2020 he too was ousted by the military.

Mali is a very poor country and 70% of the land is desert or semidesert. Only about 2% of the land is used for growing crops, while 25% is used for grazing animals. Agriculture employs about 80% of the people, many of whom subsist by nomadic livestock rearing. Mali's chief exports are cotton and gold.

AREA 478,838 sq mi [1,240,192 sq km] **POPULATION** 20,138,000
CAPITAL Bamako **GOVERNMENT** Multiparty republic
ETHNIC GROUPS Mande 50% (Bambara, Malinke, Soninke), Peul 17%, Voltaic 12%, Songhai 6%, Tuareg and Moor 10%, others
LANGUAGES French (official), many African languages
RELIGIONS Islam 95%, traditional beliefs 3%, Christianity 2%
CURRENCY CFA franc = 100 centimes

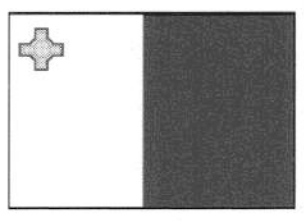
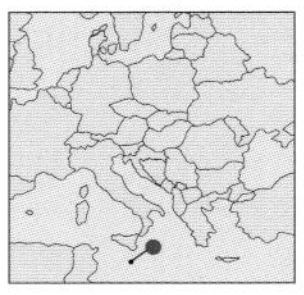

MALTA

GEOGRAPHY The Republic of Malta consists of two main islands, Malta and Gozo, with a third, much smaller island called Comino lying between the two large islands, and two islets. The climate is typically Mediterranean, with hot, dry summers and mild, moist winters.

POLITICS & ECONOMY Malta has fascinating Stone Age and Bronze Age remains. The islands later came under Phoenician, Greek, Carthaginian, Roman, and Arab rule. In about 1090, Malta fell under the Norman kings of Sicily and, from 1530, the Knights Hospitallers (also called the Knights of St John of Jerusalem). France took the islands in 1798, but the British drove them out in 1800. British rule was officially recognized in 1815.

During World War I (1914–18), Malta was an important naval base. In World War II (1939–45), Italian and German aircraft bombed the islands. In recognition of the islanders' bravery, the British King George VI awarded the George Cross to Malta in 1942: the emblem is incorporated into its flag. Malta became independent in 1964 and a republic in 1974. Since the 1980s Malta has pursued a policy of neutrality whilst maintaining links with Europe and the United States. It became a member of the European Union in May 2004, and adopted the euro as its official currency in 2008.

The World Bank classifies Malta as a "high-income" developing country. It lacks natural resources, and most people work in the former naval dockyards, which are now used for commercial shipbuilding and repair, in manufacturing industries, notably electronics, and in tourism and financial services.

Farming is difficult, because of the rocky soils. Crops include barley, fruits, potatoes, and wheat. Malta also has a small fishing industry. It is a major center for freight transshipment.

AREA 122 sq mi [316 sq km] **POPULATION** 461,000
CAPITAL Valletta **GOVERNMENT** Multiparty republic
ETHNIC GROUPS Maltese 96%, British 2%
LANGUAGES Maltese and English (both official)
RELIGIONS Roman Catholic 98%
CURRENCY Euro = 100 cents

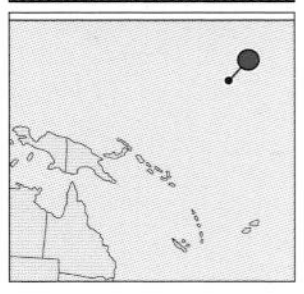

MARSHALL ISLANDS

The Republic of the Marshall Islands, a former US territory, became fully independent in 1991. This island nation, lying north of Kiribati in a region known as Micronesia, is heavily dependent on US aid. The main activities are agriculture and tourism.

AREA 70 sq mi [181 sq km]
POPULATION 79,000 **CAPITAL** Majuro

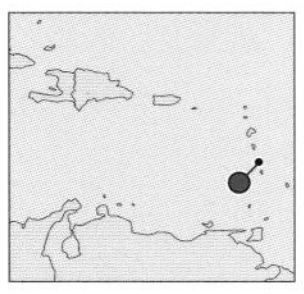

MARTINIQUE

Martinique, a volcanic island nation in the Caribbean, was colonized by France in 1635. It became a French overseas department in 1946. Tourism and agriculture are major activities. About 70% of Martinique's gross domestic product is provided by the French government, allowing for a good standard of living.

AREA 425 sq mi [1,102 sq km]
POPULATION 386,000 **CAPITAL** Fort-de-France

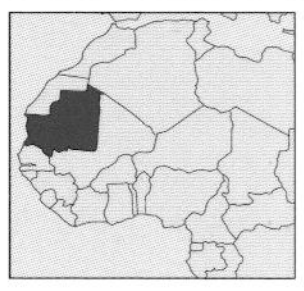

MAURITANIA

GEOGRAPHY The Islamic Republic of Mauritania in northwestern Africa is nearly twice the size of France. But France has almost 20 times as many people. Part of the world's largest desert, the Sahara, covers northern Mauritania and most Mauritanians live in the southwest. The amount of rainfall and the length of the rainy season increase from north to south. Much of the land is desert, but southwesterly winds bring summer rain to the south.

POLITICS & ECONOMY Originally part of the great African empires of Ghana and Mali, Mauritania became a French protectorate in 1903. In 1920, the country became a territory of French West Africa and a French colony. Mauritania finally became independent in 1960.

In 1976, Spain withdrew from Spanish (now Western) Sahara, a territory bordering Mauritania to the north. Morocco occupied the northern two-thirds of this territory, while Mauritania took the rest. Following this, Saharan guerrillas belonging to POLISARIO (the Popular Front for the Liberation of Saharan Territories) began an armed struggle for independence. In 1979, Mauritania withdrew from the southern part of Western Sahara, which was then occupied by Morocco. In 1984 Colonel Maaouya Ould Sid Ahmed Taya seized power in a coup and, despite allegations of fraudulent elections, remained president until he too was deposed in a coup in 2005. After a brief period of democracy, the military again seized control, in 2008, and its leader, Mohamed Ould Abdel Aziz, remained in power until 2019. The government has been largely successful in curbing Islamist terrorism in the country.

Mauritania is a "lower-middle-income" developing country. Nearly half of the population are engaged in agriculture and at the mercy of frequent droughts. The coastal waters provide good fishing grounds. In 2006, Mauritania became Africa's newest oil producer, when an offshore platform came online for the first time. Mauritania has extensive mineral deposits.

AREA 395,953 sq mi [1,025,520 sq km] **POPULATION** 4,079,000
CAPITAL Nouakchott **GOVERNMENT** Multiparty Islamic republic
ETHNIC GROUPS Mixed Moor/Black 40%, Moor 30%, Black 30%
LANGUAGES Arabic (official), Pulaar, Soninke, Wolof, French
RELIGIONS Islam **CURRENCY** Ouguiya = 5 khoums

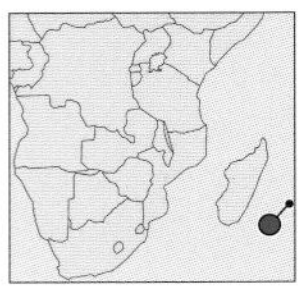

MAURITIUS

The Republic of Mauritius lies in the Indian Ocean east of Madagascar. It was previously ruled by France and Britain until it achieved independence in 1968. It became a republic in 1992. Sugar production is in decline with tourism and textiles vital to the economy. It has few natural resources.

AREA 788 sq mi [2,040 sq km]
POPULATION 1,386,000 **CAPITAL** Port Louis

MEXICO

GEOGRAPHY The United Mexican States, as Mexico is officially named, is the world's most populous Spanish-speaking country. Much of the land is mountainous, although most people live on the central plateau. Mexico contains two large peninsulas: Lower (or Baja) California in the northwest, and the flat Yucatán peninsula in the southeast.

The climate varies according to the altitude. The resort of Acapulco on the southwest coast has a dry and sunny climate. Mexico City, at about 7,546 ft [2,300 m] above sea level, is much cooler. Most rain occurs between June and September.

POLITICS & ECONOMY Once part of the Mayan and other indigenous empires, the region was colonized by Spain in the 16th century. In the mid-19th century, Mexico lost land to the United States, and between 1910 and 1921 violent revolutions created chaos. Reforms were introduced in the 1920s and, in 1929, the Institutional Revolutionary Party (PRI) was formed. The PRI ruled Mexico effectively as a one-party state until 2001. The new president, Vicente Fox, faced many problems. He was succeeded by Felipe Calderón in 2006, who prioritized a crackdown on the increasing gang violence related to drug trafficking. The left-winger Andres Manuel López Obrador was elected president in 2018.

The World Bank classifies Mexico as an "upper-middle-income" developing country. Agriculture is important. Food crops include beans, maize, rice, and wheat, while cash crops include coffee, cotton, fruits, and vegetables. Oil and oil products are major exports, while manufacturing is the most valuable activity. Mexico is the world's leading silver producer, and it also mines copper, gold, lead, zinc, and other minerals. Factories near the northern border assemble goods, such as car parts and electrical products, for US companies.

Hopes for the future lie in increasing cooperation with the US and Canada. In October 2018, a new trade deal – United States-Mexico-Canada Agreement (USMCA) – was negotiated. It was ratified in 2020.

AREA 756,061 sq mi [1,958,201 sq km] **POPULATION** 130,207,000
CAPITAL Mexico City **GOVERNMENT** Federal republic
ETHNIC GROUPS Mestizo 60%, Amerindian 30%, White 9%
LANGUAGES Spanish (official) **RELIGIONS** Roman Catholic 83%, Protestant 2%, others 15% **CURRENCY** Mexican peso = 100 centavos

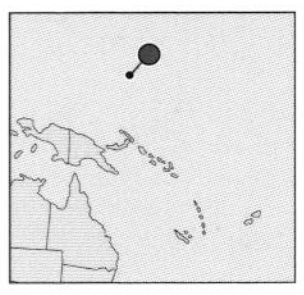

MICRONESIA

The Federated States of Micronesia, a former US territory in the western Pacific Ocean, became fully independent in 1991. The main exports are fish and agricultural products. Tourism is important.

AREA 271 sq mi [702 sq km]
POPULATION 102,000 **CAPITAL** Palikir

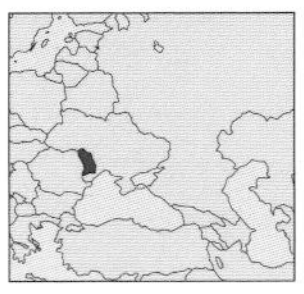

MOLDOVA

GEOGRAPHY The Republic of Moldova is a small country sandwiched between Ukraine and Romania. It was formerly one of the 15 republics that made up the Soviet Union.

Much of the land is hilly and the highest areas are located near the center of the country.

Moldova has a moderately continental climate, with warm summers and fairly cold winters when temperatures dip below freezing point. Most of the rain comes in the warmer months.

POLITICS & ECONOMY In the 14th century, the Moldavian people formed a state that comprised part of Romania and the historic region of Bessarabia. Following rule by the Ottoman Turks, Russia took control of Bessarabia in 1812. After World War I (1914–18), Bessarabia declared independence and voted to unite with Romania. This move was not recognized by Russia and in 1940 the area was annexed by the USSR. From 1944, the Moldovan Soviet Socialist Republic became part of the Soviet Union.

In 1989, the Moldovans asserted their independence and ethnicity by making Romanian the official language and, at the end of 1991, Moldova became an independent nation. But Trans-Dniester, an area east of the River Dniester inhabited by mainly Russian and Ukrainian speakers, has sought autonomy. In 2006, its people voted for independence and union with Russia, but this vote was not recognized internationally.

From 2001 to 2009 the Communist Party held power. Pro-Western coalitions ruled from 2010 to 2016, and Moldova signed its Association Agreement with the EU in 2014. Russia restricted some agricultural imports in response. A pro-Russian president, Igor Dodon, was elected in 2016, but defeated by the pro-European Maia Sandu in 2020.

In terms of its GNP per capita, Moldova is one of Europe's poorest countries. Agriculture is the leading activity and products include fruits, maize, tobacco, and wine. Moldova has few natural resources and it imports materials and fuels for its industries.

AREA 13,070 SQ MI [33,851 SQ KM] **POPULATION** 3,324,000
CAPITAL CHISINAU **GOVERNMENT** MULTIPARTY REPUBLIC
ETHNIC GROUPS MOLDOVAN/ROMANIAN 78%, UKRAINIAN 8%, RUSSIAN 6%, GAGAUZ 4%, OTHERS **LANGUAGES** MOLDOVAN/ROMANIAN (OFFICIAL), GAGAUZ, RUSSIAN **RELIGIONS** EASTERN ORTHODOX 98%
CURRENCY MOLDOVAN LEU = 100 BANI

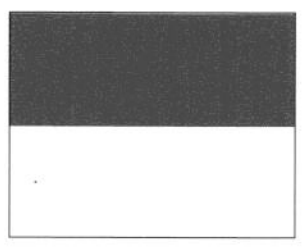

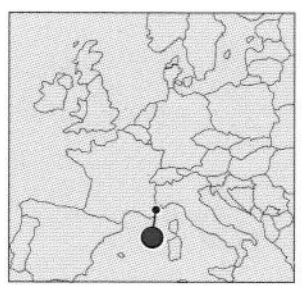

MONACO

The tiny Principality of Monaco consists of a narrow strip of coastline and a rocky peninsula on the French Riviera. Its considerable wealth is derived largely from banking, finance, gambling, recreation, and tourism. Monaco's citizens do not pay any income tax. The Grimaldi family have ruled the country for over 720 years with Prince Albert II as the current reigning monarch.

AREA 0.8 SQ MI [2 SQ KM] **POPULATION** 31,000 **CAPITAL** MONACO

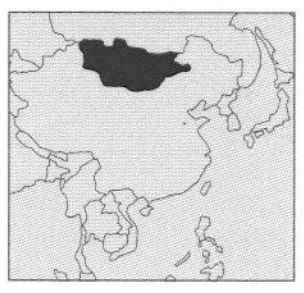

MONGOLIA

GEOGRAPHY The State of Mongolia is the world's largest landlocked country. It consists mainly of high plateaux, with a cold desert, the Gobi, in the southeast.

Ulan Bator lies on the northern edge of the desert plateau. It has bitterly cold winters. Summer temperatures are moderated by the altitude.

POLITICS & ECONOMY In the 13th century, Genghis Khan united the Mongolian peoples and built up a great empire. Under his grandson, Kublai Khan, the Mongol empire extended from Korea and China to eastern Europe and present-day Iraq.

The Mongol empire broke up in the late 14th century. In the early 17th century, Inner Mongolia came under Chinese control, and by the late 17th century Outer Mongolia had become a Chinese province. In 1911, the Mongolians drove the Chinese out of Outer Mongolia and made the area a Buddhist kingdom. But in 1924, under Russian influence, the Communist Mongolian People's Republic was set up. In 1990, the people demonstrated for more freedom, and free elections in June 1990 were won by the Communist Mongolian People's Revolutionary Party (MPRP). The Democratic Party coalition won in 1996, but the MPRP regained control in 2000. In 2009, the Democratic Party candidate, Tsakhiagiin Elbegdorj, was elected president. He was re-elected in 2013. In 2016 parliamentary elections, the Mongolian People's Party won a landslide. Presidential elections in 2017 were won by former martial arts star Khaltmaa Battulga of the Democratic Party.

The majority of the population were once nomads but, under Communist rule, most people were moved into permanent homes on government-owned farms. Livestock and animal products remain important, but minerals and fuels now account for more than three-fifths of Mongolia's exports. There is much mineral wealth yet to be exploited.

AREA 604,826 SQ MI [1,566,500 SQ KM] **POPULATION** 3,199,000
CAPITAL ULAN BATOR **GOVERNMENT** MULTIPARTY REPUBLIC
ETHNIC GROUPS KHALKHA MONGOL 95%, KAZAKH 5%
LANGUAGES KHALKHA MONGOLIAN (OFFICIAL), TURKIC, RUSSIAN
RELIGIONS TIBETAN BUDDHIST LAMAISM 53%
CURRENCY MONGOLIAN TÖGRÖG = 100 MÖNGÖS

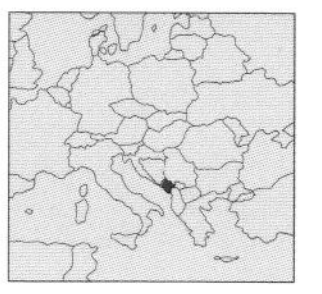

MONTENEGRO

The Republic of Montenegro, on the shores of the Adriatic Sea, became independent in 2006.

The coastal region has a Mediterranean climate. However, inland, the Dinaric Alps, which reach a height of 8,274 ft [2,522 m], have a more severe climate.

Serbia fell under Turkish rule in the 14th century, but Montenegro remained Christian. Montenegro was absorbed into Serbia in 1918 and it later became part of the Kingdom of the Serbs, Croats, and Slovenes, renamed as Yugoslavia in 1929. After World War II, Montenegro was recognized as one of the six republics of Yugoslavia. In the 1990s, as the other republics became independent, Montenegro remained with Serbia as the Federal Republic of Yugoslavia. It became independent in 2006.

In 2016, long-term prime minister Milo Djukanovich was replaced by Dusko Markovic. Two years later, Djukanovich, a pro-European, was elected president, a post he had also held from 1997–2002. Montenegro is a candidate for EU membership and joined NATO in 2017.

Manufacturing is the main activity, and steel and aluminum are major products. Farming and tourism are important. Montenegro became a member of the World Trade Organization in 2012.

AREA 5,415 SQ MI [14,026 SQ KM] **POPULATION** 607,000
CAPITAL PODGORICA **GOVERNMENT** REPUBLIC
ETHNIC GROUPS MONTENEGRIN 43%, SERB 32%, BOSNIAN 8%, ALBANIAN 5%, OTHERS **LANGUAGES** SERBIAN AND MONTENEGRIN (BOTH OFFICIAL), BOSNIAN, ALBANIAN **RELIGIONS** ORTHODOX, ISLAM, ROMAN CATHOLIC **CURRENCY** EURO = 100 CENTS

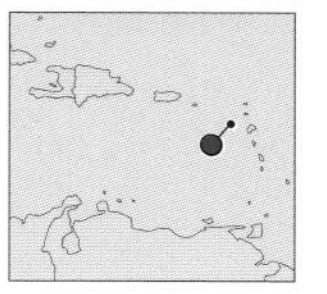

MONTSERRAT

Montserrat is a British overseas territory in the Caribbean Sea. The climate is tropical and hurricanes often cause much damage. Intermittent eruptions of the Soufrière Hills volcano between 1995 and 1998 led to the emigration of many people and the virtual destruction of Plymouth, the then capital. A new airport was opened in 2005. Volcanic activity continues.

AREA 39 SQ MI [102 SQ KM] **POPULATION** 5,000 **CAPITAL** BRADES

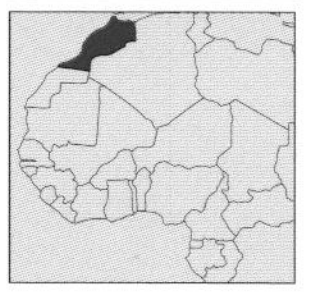

MOROCCO

GEOGRAPHY The Kingdom of Morocco lies in northwestern Africa. Behind the western coastal plain the land rises to a broad plateau and ranges of the Atlas Mountains. The High (Haut) Atlas contains the highest peak, Djebel Toubkal, at 13,665 ft [4,165 m]. East of the mountains, the land descends to the Sahara. The Canaries Current cools the Atlantic coast. Inland, summers are hot and dry. Winters are mild, with moderate rainfall. Snow often falls on the High Atlas Mountains.

POLITICS & ECONOMY The original people of Morocco were the Berbers, but, in the 680s, Arab invaders introduced Islam and the Arabic language. By the early 20th century, France and Spain controlled Morocco, which became an independent kingdom in 1956. Although Morocco is a constitutional monarchy, King Hassan II ruled the country in a generally authoritarian way, from his accession in 1961 to his death in 1999. His successor, Mohamed VI, faced several problems, including that of Western Sahara, which he claimed for Morocco (partly for its phosphate reserves), and the activities of Islamist extremists. After pro-democracy protests in 2011, a new constitution was introduced, granting the prime minister more power. A moderate Islamist party won a majority in parliamentary elections in 2011 and 2017.

Morocco is classified as a "lower-middle-income" developing country. It is one of the world's largest producers of phosphate rock, which is used to make fertilizer. Farming employs about 40% of Moroccans. Chief crops include barley, beans, citrus fruits, maize, olives, sugar beet, and wheat. Processed phosphates are exported, but most of Morocco's manufactures are for home consumption. Fishing and tourism are also important.

AREA 172,413 SQ MI [446,550 SQ KM] **POPULATION** 36,562,000
CAPITAL RABAT **GOVERNMENT** CONSTITUTIONAL MONARCHY
ETHNIC GROUPS ARAB-BERBER 99% **LANGUAGES** ARABIC (OFFICIAL), BERBER DIALECTS, FRENCH **RELIGIONS** ISLAM 99%
CURRENCY MOROCCAN DIRHAM = 100 SANTEEM

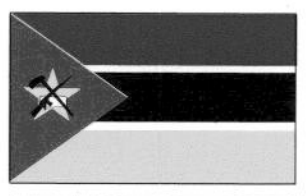

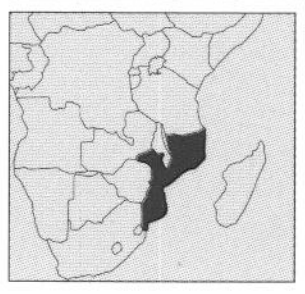

MOZAMBIQUE

GEOGRAPHY The Republic of Mozambique borders the Indian Ocean in southeastern Africa. The coastal plains are narrow in the north but broaden in the south. Inland lie plateaux and hills, which make up another two-fifths of the country. Mozambique has a mostly tropical climate. The capital, Maputo, which lies outside the tropics, has hot and humid summers, though the winters are mild and fairly dry.

POLITICS & ECONOMY In 1885, when the European powers divided Africa, Mozambique was recognized as a Portuguese colony. But black African opposition to European rule gradually increased. In 1961, the Front for the Liberation of Mozambique (FRELIMO) was founded to oppose Portuguese rule. In 1964, FRELIMO launched a guerrilla war, which continued for ten years, until Mozambique became independent in 1975.

After independence, Mozambique became a one-party state. Its government aided African nationalists in Rhodesia (now Zimbabwe) and South Africa. But the white governments of these countries helped an opposition group, the Mozambique National Resistance Movement (RENAMO), to lead an armed struggle against Mozambique's government. Civil war, combined with droughts, caused much suffering in the 1980s. In 1989, FRELIMO ended one-party rule and multiparty elections were held in 1994. In 1995 Mozambique became the 53rd member of the Commonwealth. In January 2015, Filipe Nyusi became the country's 4th president.

In the early 1990s, the UN rated Mozambique as one of the world's poorest countries, but from the second half of the 1990s there has been economic growth, although hampered by cycles of drought and flood. About 80% of the people are poor farmers. The development of Mozambique's large offshore natural gas reserves is threatened by Islamist terrorist activity in the north.

AREA 309,494 SQ MI [801,590 SQ KM] **POPULATION** 30,888,000
CAPITAL MAPUTO **GOVERNMENT** MULTIPARTY REPUBLIC
ETHNIC GROUPS INDIGENOUS TRIBAL GROUPS (SHANGAAN, CHOKWE, MANYIKA, SENA, MAKUA, OTHERS) 99% **LANGUAGES** PORTUGUESE (OFFICIAL), MANY OTHERS **RELIGIONS** ROMAN CATHOLIC 28%, PROTESTANT 28%, ISLAM 18% **CURRENCY** METICAL = 100 CENTAVOS

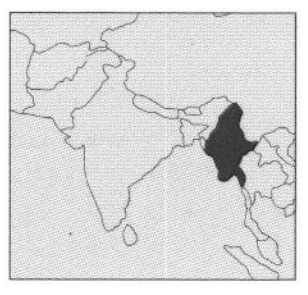

MYANMAR (BURMA)

GEOGRAPHY The Union of Burma has been officially known as the Union of Myanmar since 1989. Mountains border the country in the east and west, with the highest mountains in the north. Myanmar's highest mountain is Hkakabo Razi, which is 19,294 ft [5,881 m] high. Between these ranges are the fertile valleys of the Irrawaddy and Sittang rivers. The Irrawaddy delta is a leading rice-growing area.

Myanmar has a tropical monsoon climate with three seasons. The rainy season runs from late May to mid-October. A cool, dry season follows, between late October and the middle part of February. The hot season lasts from late February to mid-May. In May 2008, cyclone Nargis devastated the south, including the Irrawaddy delta, killing more than 80,000 people.

POLITICS & ECONOMY The ancestors of the country's main ethnic group today, the Burmese, arrived in the 9th century AD. They encroached on areas occupied since ancient times by a variety of indigenous tribes. Britain conquered Burma in the 19th century making it a province of British India until, in 1937, they granted Burma limited self-government. Japan then invaded and occupied Burma from 1942 until the end of World War II in 1945. Burma became a fully independent country in 1948. Revolts by Communists and various hill people led to instability in the 1950s. In 1962, Burma became a military dictatorship and, in 1974, a one-party state.

Elections in 1990 were won by the National League for Democracy (NLD), but the military ignored the results and placed the party's leader, Aung San Suu Kyi, under house arrest for much of the next 20 years. A military-backed civilian government took power in 2011, under President Thein Sein, marking the start of a gradual relaxation of the military's tight grip. NLD candidates, including Aung San Suu Kyi, won parliamentary seats the following year. The general elections in 2015 were a victory for the NLD, although

constitutional rules barred Aung San Suu Kyi from officially becoming president. In 2017 a violent military crackdown on minority ethnic groups, notably the Muslim Rohingya, led to the flight of up to a million Rohingya to Bangladesh. The UN termed the violence ethnic cleansing. In 2021 a military coup overthrew the civilian government. Pro-democracy protests immediately broke out, and the coup was condemned internationally.

Agriculture is the main activity, employing 70% of the people. The chief crop is rice with maize, pulses, oilseeds, and sugarcane also important. Myanmar's chief exports are natural gas, wood products, and rice. Myanmar has many mineral resources including oil and gas. The growth of tourism will depend on the stability of the country.

AREA 261,227 sq mi [676,578 sq km] **POPULATION** 57,069,000
CAPITAL Naypyidaw **GOVERNMENT** Multiparty republic
ETHNIC GROUPS Burman 68%, Shan 9%, Karen 7%, Rakhine 4%, Chinese, Indian, Mon
LANGUAGES Burmese (official); minority ethnic groups have their own languages **RELIGIONS** Buddhism 89%, Christianity, Islam
CURRENCY Kyat = 100 pyas

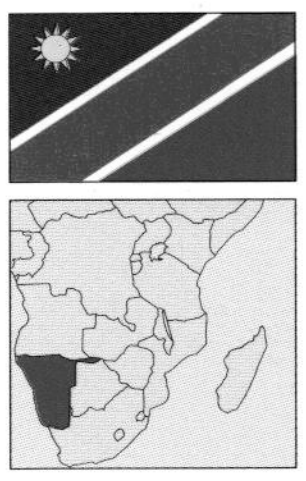

NAMIBIA

GEOGRAPHY When it was ruled by South Africa, the Republic of Namibia was known as South West Africa. The coastal region contains the arid Namib Desert, which is virtually uninhabited. Inland is a central plateau, bordered by a rugged spine of mountains stretching north–south. Eastern Namibia contains part of the Kalahari, a semidesert area extending into Botswana. Namibia has a warm and arid climate. Windhoek has an average annual rainfall of 15 inches [370 mm], which often occurs in thunderstorms during the hot summer.

POLITICS & ECONOMY During World War I, South African troops defeated the Germans who ruled what is now Namibia. After World War II, many people challenged South Africa's right to govern the territory, and a civil war began in the 1960s between African guerrillas and South African troops. A ceasefire was agreed in 1989 and Namibia became independent in 1990. In the 1990s, the government pursued a policy of "national reconciliation." An enclave on the coast, Walvis Bay (Walvisbaai), remained part of South Africa until 1994, when it was transferred to Namibia. In 2004, the nationalist leader, Sam Nujoma, president since 1990, retired. He was succeeded by Hifikepunye Pohamba, who in turn was followed by Hage Geingob after elections in 2014.

Namibia has reserves of diamonds, uranium, zinc, and copper. Agriculture employs around 30% of the people and much is at subsistence level. Fishing is important. Namibia has few industries and unemployment is high at around 34%. Potential offshore oil reserves are being explored. Tourism is expanding.

AREA 318,259 sq mi [824,292 sq km] **POPULATION** 2,678,000
CAPITAL Windhoek **GOVERNMENT** Multiparty republic
ETHNIC GROUPS Ovambo 50%, Kavango 9%, Herero 7%, Damara 7%, White 6%, Nama 5%
LANGUAGES English (official), Afrikaans, German, indigenous dialects
RELIGIONS Christianity 90% (Lutheran 51%)
CURRENCY Namibian dollar = 100 cents

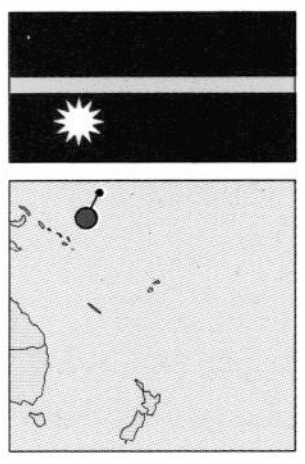

NAURU

Nauru is the world's smallest republic, located in the western Pacific Ocean. Independent since 1968, Nauru's prosperity is based on the mining of increasingly depleted reserves of phosphate. Since 2001, Australia has detained asylum-seekers on the island.

AREA 8 sq mi [21 sq km]
POPULATION 10,000 **CAPITAL** Yaren

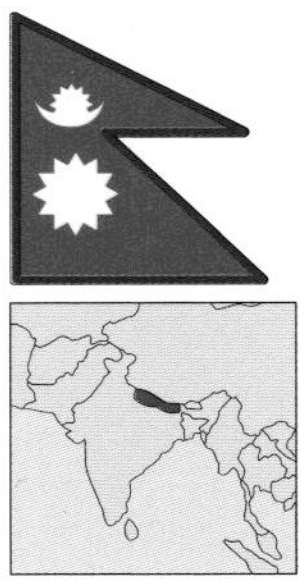

NEPAL

GEOGRAPHY Over three-quarters of Nepal lies in the Himalayan region, culminating in the world's highest peak (Mount Everest, or Sagarmatha in Nepali) at 29,032 ft [8,849 m]. As a result, climatic conditions vary widely according to the altitude.

POLITICS & ECONOMY Nepal was united in the late 18th century, although it remains a diverse patchwork of peoples. From the mid-19th century to 1951, power was held by the royal Rana family. The first democratic elections in 32 years were held in 1991, but, by the early 21st century, Nepal faced many problems, including an uprising of Maoist guerrillas. In 2005, King Gyanendra seized power but failed to stop the conflict. In 2006, the Maoists joined a provisional coalition government. In elections in April 2008, the Maoists became the largest single party. In May, Nepal became a republic after the abolition of the monarchy. A new constitution was adopted in 2015. Parliamentary elections in 2017 were won by a coalition of Communist and Maoist parties, and Khadga Prasad Sharma Oli became prime minister in 2018.

Agriculture is the main activity and poverty is rife in this overwhelmingly rural country. Nepal is heavily dependent on aid and remittances sent from abroad. Tourism is growing in importance. There are also ambitious plans to exploit the hydroelectric potential offered by the ferocious Himalayan rivers.

AREA 56,827 sq mi [147,181 sq km] **POPULATION** 30,425,000
CAPITAL Katmandu **GOVERNMENT** Multiparty republic
ETHNIC GROUPS Brahman, Chhetri, Newar, Gurung, Magar, Tamang, Sherpa, and others
LANGUAGES Nepali (official), local languages
RELIGIONS Hinduism 81%, Buddhism 11%, Islam 4%
CURRENCY Nepalese rupee = 100 paisa

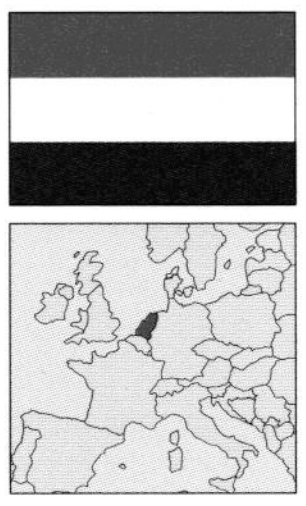

NETHERLANDS

GEOGRAPHY The Netherlands lies at the western end of the North European Plain, which extends to the Ural Mountains in Russia. Except for the far southeastern corner, the Netherlands is flat and about 40% lies below sea level at high tide. To prevent flooding, the Dutch have built dykes (sea walls) to hold back the waves. Large areas which were once under the sea, but which have been reclaimed, are known as polders. Because of its position on the North Sea, the Netherlands has a temperate climate, with mild, rainy winters.

POLITICS & ECONOMY Before the 16th century, the area that is now the Netherlands was under a succession of foreign rulers, including the Romans, the Germanic Franks, the French, and the Spanish. The Dutch declared their independence from Spain in 1581 and their status was finally recognized by Spain in 1648. In the 17th century, the Dutch built up a great overseas empire, especially in Southeast Asia. But in the early 18th century, the Dutch lost control of the seas to England.

France controlled the Netherlands from 1795 to 1813. In 1815, the Netherlands, then containing Belgium and Luxembourg, became an independent kingdom. Belgium broke away in 1830 and Luxembourg followed in 1890.

The Netherlands was neutral in World War I (1914–18), but was occupied by Germany in World War II (1939–45). After the war, the Netherlands Indies became independent as Indonesia. The Netherlands became active in West European affairs and, with Belgium and Luxembourg, it formed the customs union of Benelux in 1948. In 1949, it joined NATO (the North Atlantic Treaty Organization), and the European Coal and Steel Community (ECSC) in 1953. In 1957, it became a founder member of the European Economic Community (now the European Union), and, in 2002, it adopted the euro as its sole unit of currency. After a series of short-lived governments, Mark Rutte became prime minister in 2010 at the head of a coalition government. He retained his position following elections in 2012 and 2017, when the right-wing Freedom Party did not make the expected gains. His entire government resigned in 2021 over a childcare subsidies scandal. In 2013, after a 33-year reign, Queen Beatrix abdicated in favor of her son, Prince Willem Alexander.

2010 saw the dissolution of the Netherlands Antilles, an island territory in the Caribbean. Curaçao and St Maarten became nations in the Kingdom of the Netherlands. The small islands of Bonaire, St Eustatius, and Saba became special municipalities.

The Netherlands is a highly industrialized country and a major trading nation. Industry and commerce are the most valuable activities. Its resources include natural gas, some oil, and salt. Industrial products are wide-ranging, including machinery, chemicals, electronic equipment, and vehicles. Farming is scientific and yields are high; dairy farming is the leading activity. Major crops include barley, flowers and bulbs, potatoes, and sugar beet.

AREA 16,033 sq mi [41,526 sq km] **POPULATION** 17,337,000
CAPITAL Amsterdam; The Hague (seat of government)
GOVERNMENT Constitutional monarchy
ETHNIC GROUPS Dutch 81%, Indonesian, Turkish, Moroccan, and others **LANGUAGES** Dutch and Frisian (both official)
RELIGIONS Roman Catholic 30%, Protestant 20%, Islam 6%, others
CURRENCY Euro = 100 cents

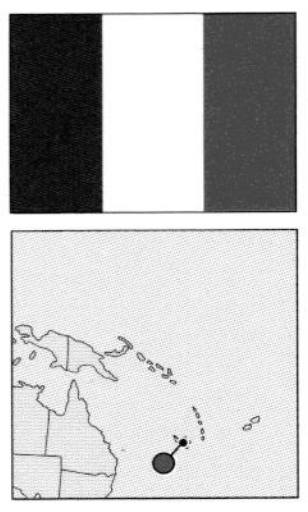

NEW CALEDONIA

New Caledonia is the most southerly of the Melanesian countries in the Pacific. It has been a French possession since 1853 and an Overseas Territory since 1958. In referendums in 2018 and 2020 the population voted against becoming independent. The country is rich in mineral resources, especially nickel.

AREA 7,172 sq mi [18,575 sq km] **POPULATION** 294,000 **CAPITAL** Nouméa

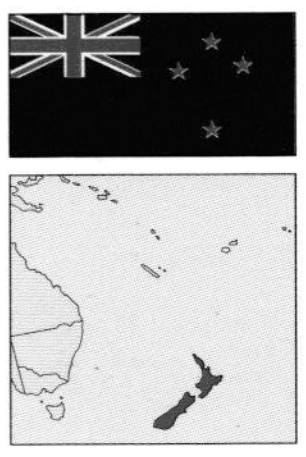

NEW ZEALAND

GEOGRAPHY New Zealand lies about 994 mi [1,600 km] southeast of Australia. It consists of two main islands and several other small ones. Much of North Island is volcanic. Active volcanoes include Ngauruhoe and Ruapehu. Hot springs and geysers are common, and steam from the ground is used to produce electricity. The Southern Alps, which contain the country's highest peak, Aoraki Mount Cook, at 12,217 ft [3,724 m], form the backbone of South Island. This island also has some large, fertile plains.

New Zealand lies on the geologically active "Pacific ring of fire." Most of the 14,000 earthquakes that occur every year have a magnitude of less than 5.0. But, in 2010 and 2011, two earthquakes, with magnitudes of 7.0 and 6.3 respectively, struck Christchurch on South Island, causing great damage. The 2011 earthquake resulted in a death toll of more than 180.

Auckland in the north has a warm, humid climate throughout the year. Wellington has cooler summers, while in Dunedin, in the southeast, temperatures sometimes dip below freezing in winter. The rainfall is heaviest on the western highlands.

POLITICS & ECONOMY Evidence suggests that early Maori settlers arrived in New Zealand more than 1,000 years ago. The Dutch navigator Abel Tasman reached New Zealand in 1642, but his discovery was not followed up. In 1769, the British Captain James Cook rediscovered the islands. During the early 19th century, British settlers arrived and, in 1840, under the Treaty of Waitangi, Britain took possession of the islands. From the 1870s, the Maoris were slowly integrated into colonial society.

In 1907, New Zealand became a self-governing dominion in the British Commonwealth. The country's economy developed quickly and the people became increasingly prosperous. However, after Britain joined the European Economic Community in 1973, New Zealand's exports to Britain shrank and the country had to reassess its economic and defense strategies and seek new markets. The world recession led the government to cut back on welfare spending in the 1990s. The preservation of Maori culture and rights are major issues as the Maoris, a Polynesian people, make up about 15% of the population. Other mainly Polynesian Pacific people make up another 7%. Ties with Britain have been reduced. In November 2008, the center-right National Party defeated the Labour Party in elections, and John Key served as prime minister 2008–16. Elections in 2017 resulted in a coalition between Jacinda Adern's Labour Party, the Greens and New Zealand First. She was emphatically re-elected in 2020. In 2019 the country was shocked by an anti-Islamic terrorist attack in Christchurch.

The economy once depended on agriculture, but manufacturing now employs more than twice as many people as farming. Tourism is important. Meat and dairy products are leading commodities. Sheep rearing has declined as the area under cattle, deer, and vines has expanded. New Zealand's economy is gradually recovering from a period of recession in 2008–9.

AREA 104,453 sq mi [270,534 sq km] **POPULATION** 4,991,000
CAPITAL Wellington **GOVERNMENT** Constitutional monarchy
ETHNIC GROUPS European 68%, Maori 15%, Asian 9%, Polynesian 7%
LANGUAGES English and Maori (both official)
RELIGIONS Anglican 24%, Presbyterian 18%, Roman Catholic 15%, others **CURRENCY** New Zealand dollar = 100 cents

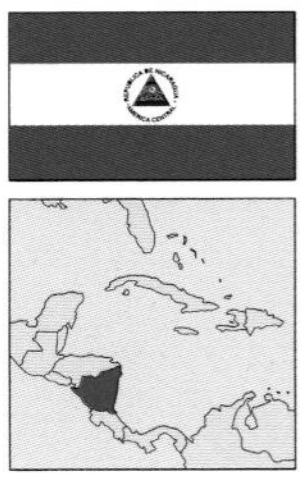

NICARAGUA

GEOGRAPHY The Republic of Nicaragua is a large country in Central America. In the east is a broad plain bordering the Caribbean Sea. The plain is drained by rivers that flow from the Central Highlands. The fertile western Pacific region contains about 40 volcanoes, many of which are active, and earthquakes are common.

Nicaragua has a tropical climate. Managua is hot throughout the year and there is a marked rainy season from May to October. In October 1998, Hurricane Mitch caused great devastation in Nicaragua. The Central Highlands and Caribbean region are cooler and wetter. The wettest region is the humid Caribbean plain.

POLITICS & ECONOMY In 1502, Christopher Columbus claimed the area for Spain, which ruled Nicaragua until 1821. By the early 20th century, the United States had considerable influence in the country and, in 1912, US forces entered Nicaragua. From 1927 to 1933, rebels under General Augusto César Sandino tried to drive US forces out of the country. In 1933, US marines set up a Nicaraguan army, the National Guard, to help to defeat the rebels. Its leader, Anastasio Somoza Garcia, had Sandino murdered in 1934, and from 1937 Somoza ruled as a dictator.

In the mid-1970s, many people began to protest against Somoza's rule and joined a guerrilla force, called the Sandinista National Liberation Front, named after General Sandino. The rebels defeated the Somoza regime in 1979. In the 1980s, US-supported forces, called the "Contras," launched a campaign against the Sandinista government. The US government opposed the Sandinista regime, under Daniel José Ortega Saavedra, claiming that it was a Communist dictatorship. A coalition, the National Opposition Union, defeated the Sandinistas in 1990. In 2001, the Sandinista candidate, Ortega, was defeated in presidential elections, but he was re-elected in 2006, 2011, and 2016. In 2018 he backed down from proposed reforms to the social security system after widespread and violent protests.

In the early 1990s, Nicaragua faced many problems in rebuilding its shattered economy. Agriculture employs about 28% of the people, producing coffee, beef, sugar, and bananas for export. Rice, sorghum, maize, and beans are the main food crops. Tourism has potential.

AREA 50,193 SQ MI [130,000 SQ KM] **POPULATION** 6,244,000
CAPITAL MANAGUA **GOVERNMENT** MULTIPARTY REPUBLIC
ETHNIC GROUPS MESTIZO 69%, WHITE 17%, BLACK 9%, AMERINDIAN 5%
LANGUAGES SPANISH (OFFICIAL)
RELIGIONS ROMAN CATHOLIC 59%, PROTESTANT 23%, OTHERS
CURRENCY NICARAGUAN CÓRDOBA = 100 CENTAVOS

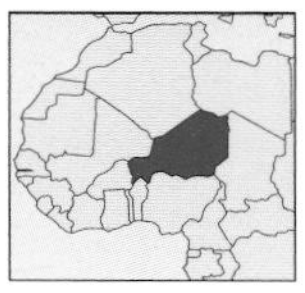

NIGER

GEOGRAPHY The Republic of Niger is a landlocked nation in north-central Africa. The northern plateaux lie in the desert area of the Sahara, while central Niger contains the rugged Aïr Mountains. The most fertile, densely populated region is the Niger valley.

Niger has a tropical climate and the south has a rainy season between June and September. The north is practically rainless.

POLITICS & ECONOMY Since independence in 1960, Niger, a French territory from 1900, has suffered severe droughts. Food shortages and the collapse of the traditional nomadic way of life of some of Niger's people have caused political instability. After a period of military rule, a multiparty constitution was adopted in 1992, but the military again seized power in 1996. The coup leader, Colonel Ibrahim Barre Mainassara, was elected president. He was assassinated in 1999, but parliamentary rule was restored. After a coup in 2010, Mahamadou Issoufou was elected president in 2011. After serving two terms, he stepped down in 2020 in Niger's first democratic transition of power. Islamist militants are an increasing problem.

Niger's chief resource is uranium and the country is one of the world's largest producers. The export of minerals accounts for 40% of total exports although there is much more to be exploited. Despite its considerable resources, Niger remains one of the world's poorest countries. Only 13% of the land can be used for crops but agriculture supports around 80% of the people.

AREA 489,189 SQ MI [1,267,000 SQ KM] **POPULATION** 23,606,000
CAPITAL NIAMEY **GOVERNMENT** MULTIPARTY REPUBLIC
ETHNIC GROUPS HAUSA 55%, DJERMA 21%, TUAREG 9%, FULA 8%, OTHERS **LANGUAGES** FRENCH (OFFICIAL), HAUSA, DJERMA
RELIGIONS ISLAM 80%, INDIGENOUS BELIEFS, CHRISTIANITY
CURRENCY CFA FRANC = 100 CENTIMES

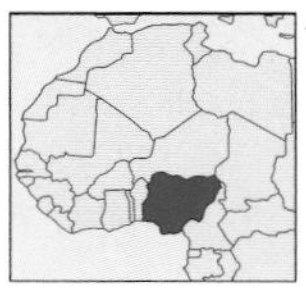

NIGERIA

GEOGRAPHY The Federal Republic of Nigeria is the most populous nation in Africa. The country's main rivers are the Niger and Benue, which meet in central Nigeria. North of the two river valleys are high plains and plateaux. The Lake Chad basin is in the north-east, with the Sokoto plains in the northwest. The south contains hilly uplands and plains, and has a hot, rainy climate. The north is drier and often hotter than the south.

POLITICS & ECONOMY Nigeria has a long artistic tradition. Major cultures include the Nok (500 BC to AD 200), the Ife, a major Yoruba culture which developed about 1,000 years ago, and the Benin (15th to 17th centuries). Britain gradually extended its influence over the area in the second half of the 19th century.

Nigeria became an independent nation in 1960 and a federal republic in 1963. A federal constitution dividing the country into regions was necessary because Nigeria contains more than 250 ethnic and linguistic groups, as well as several religious ones. Local rivalries have long been a threat to national unity, and six new states were created in 1996 in an attempt to overcome this. Civil war occurred between 1967 and 1970, when the people of the southeast attempted unsuccessfully to secede during the Biafran War. Between 1960 and 1998, Nigeria had only nine years of civilian government.

In 1998–99, civilian rule was restored but Nigeria faced many problems, including violence in the Niger delta region and religious conflict. From 2009 onward, northern Nigeria has been hit by violent attacks from the Islamist organization Boko Haram. 2015 saw Nigeria's first ever peaceful and democratic change of power from one party to another when Muhammadu Buhari was elected president. He was re-elected in 2019.

Nigeria is a developing country with great potential although most of the population currently live in poverty. Its chief natural resource is oil, which accounts for most of its exports. Agriculture employs 70% of the people and the country is a major producer of cocoa, palm oil and palm kernels, groundnuts (peanuts), and rubber. Industry is increasing and manufactures include cement, chemicals, fertilizers, textiles, and timber.

AREA 356,667 SQ MI [923,768 SQ KM] **POPULATION** 219,464,000
CAPITAL ABUJA **GOVERNMENT** FEDERAL MULTIPARTY REPUBLIC
ETHNIC GROUPS HAUSA AND FULANI 29%, YORUBA 21%, IBO (OR IGBO) 18%, IJAW 10%, KANURI 4%, MANY OTHERS
LANGUAGES ENGLISH (OFFICIAL), HAUSA, YORUBA, IBO
RELIGIONS ISLAM 50%, CHRISTIANITY 40%, TRADITIONAL BELIEFS 10%
CURRENCY NAIRA = 100 KOBO

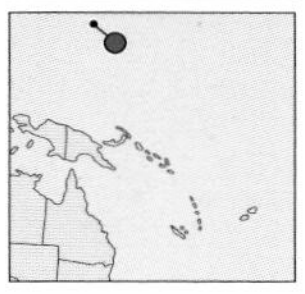

NORTHERN MARIANA ISLANDS

The Commonwealth of the Northern Mariana Islands contains 16 mountainous islands north of Guam in the western Pacific Ocean. In a 1975 plebiscite, the islanders voted for Commonwealth status in union with the United States, and in 1986 they were granted US citizenship.

AREA 179 SQ MI [464 SQ KM] **POPULATION** 52,000 **CAPITAL** SAIPAN

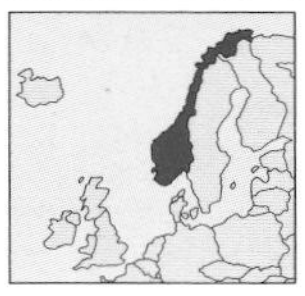

NORWAY

GEOGRAPHY The Kingdom of Norway forms the western part of the rugged Scandinavian peninsula. The deep inlets along the highly indented coastline were gouged out by glaciers during the Ice Age. The warm North Atlantic Drift off the coast of Norway moderates the climate, with mild winters and cool summers. Nearly all the ports are ice-free throughout the year. Inland, winters are colder and snow cover lasts for at least three months a year.

POLITICS & ECONOMY Norway was united with Denmark for over 400 years from the 14th century until 1814 when Denmark handed Norway over to Sweden. Denmark retained control of Norway's colonies – Greenland, Iceland and the Færoe Islands. The union with Sweden ended in 1903 and Norway became independent. Although Germany occupied Norway during World War II (1939–45), the country recovered quickly afterward and it now has one of the world's highest standards of living. In 1960, Norway and six other countries formed the European Free Trade Association (EFTA), but, in 1994, it voted against joining the European Union. Erna Solberg has been prime minister since 2013, heading a center-right coalition government. Harald V came to the throne in 1991.

Norway's chief resources and exports are offshore oil and natural gas, which are exploited via tightly regulated companies. To guard against the future decline of oil and gas production, a large sovereign wealth fund has been built up. Farmland covers only 3% of the land. Dairy farming, meat production, and fishing are important, but Norway has to import food. Norway has many industries powered by cheap hydroelectricity.

AREA 125,049 SQ MI [323,877 SQ KM] **POPULATION** 5,510,000
CAPITAL OSLO **GOVERNMENT** CONSTITUTIONAL MONARCHY
ETHNIC GROUPS NORWEGIAN 94% **LANGUAGES** NORWEGIAN (OFFICIAL)
RELIGIONS EVANGELICAL LUTHERAN 86%
CURRENCY NORWEGIAN KRONE = 100 ØRE

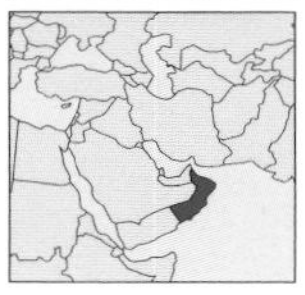

OMAN

GEOGRAPHY The Sultanate of Oman occupies the southeastern corner of the Arabian peninsula. It also includes the tip of the Musandam peninsula, overlooking the strategic Strait of Hormuz. Oman has a hot tropical climate. In Muscat, temperatures may reach 117°F [47°C] in the summer months.

POLITICS & ECONOMY Although strongly influenced by Britain since the end of the 18th century, Oman never became a colony. From 1970 when Qaboos ibn Said, the absolute ruler, overthrew his father in a bloodless coup, Oman followed a path of modernization. In 2000, Oman held elections to its consultative parliament and, in 2004, the Sultan appointed Oman's first woman minister. Anti-government demonstrations in 2011 led to the promise of more reforms. In 2020 Haitham bin Tariq Al Said succeeded to the throne on the death of Qaboos.

Oil and natural gas make up about 80% of Oman's exports; reserves are declining, and Oman is actively seeking to diversify its economy. Agriculture and fishing remain important. Crops include alfalfa, bananas, coconuts, dates, limes, tobacco, vegetables, and wheat, but Oman still has to import food. The tourist industry has grown rapidly in recent years.

AREA 119,498 SQ MI [309,500 SQ KM] **POPULATION** 3,695,000
CAPITAL MUSCAT **GOVERNMENT** MONARCHY WITH CONSULTATIVE COUNCIL
ETHNIC GROUPS ARAB, BALUCHI, INDIAN, PAKISTANI
LANGUAGES ARABIC (OFFICIAL), BALUCHI, ENGLISH **RELIGIONS** ISLAM (MAINLY IBADHI), CHRISTIAN 5%, HINDUISM 5% **CURRENCY** OMANI RIAL = 1,000 BAISA

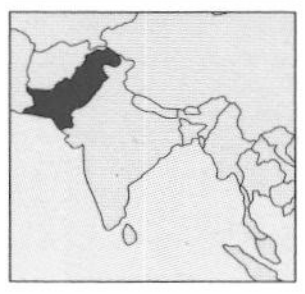

PAKISTAN

GEOGRAPHY The Islamic Republic of Pakistan contains high mountains, fertile plains, and rocky deserts. The Karakoram range, which contains K2, the world's second highest peak, lies in the northern part of Jammu and Kashmir, which is occupied by Pakistan but claimed by India. Other mountains rise in the west. Plains, drained by the River Indus and its tributaries, occupy much of eastern Pakistan. Arid areas include the Thar Desert and the Baluchistan plateau. Most of Pakistan has hot summers and mild winters, though the mountains are cold in winter. The rainfall is generally sparse.

POLITICS & ECONOMY Pakistan was the site of the Indus Valley civilization which developed about 4,500 years ago. However, Pakistan's modern history dates from 1947, when British India was divided into India and Pakistan. Muslim Pakistan was divided into two parts: East and West Pakistan, but East Pakistan broke away in 1971 to become Bangladesh. In 1948–49, 1965, and 1971, Pakistan and India clashed over Kashmir. In 1998, Pakistan responded in kind to India's nuclear weapons tests, but, in 2003–7, Pakistan and India launched a series of initiatives aimed at achieving peace.

Pakistan has been subject to alternating periods of military and civilian rule: the latter often characterized by inefficiency and corruption. The country's leaders have experienced turbulent times: Benazir Bhutto (daughter of the hanged prime minister, Zulfiqar Ali Bhutto) was twice dismissed as prime minister on charges of corruption in 1990 and 1996, and subsequently assassinated during an election campaign in 2007. Nawaz Sharif, prime minister from 2013 to 2017, resigned after corruption charges, and in 2018 former international cricketer Imran Khan became prime minister.

Both government and military struggle to control the Afghan border region where Taliban-linked extremists are active. Terrorist activity emanating from this region has hit targets elsewhere in the country. The Christian minority has also been targeted.

Lack of political stability has hindered economic development and discouraged foreign investment. The economy is agrarian, employing nearly half the population. Textiles are the main export and remittances from overseas workers are crucial.

AREA 307,372 SQ MI [796,095 SQ KM] **POPULATION** 238,181,000
CAPITAL ISLAMABAD **GOVERNMENT** FEDERAL REPUBLIC
ETHNIC GROUPS PUNJABI, SINDHI, PASHTUN (PATHAN), BALUCHI, MUHAJIR
LANGUAGES ENGLISH AND URDU (BOTH OFFICIAL), MANY OTHERS
RELIGIONS ISLAM 97%, CHRISTIANITY, HINDUISM
CURRENCY PAKISTANI RUPEE = 100 PAISA

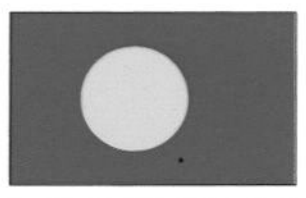

PALAU

The Republic of Palau became independent in 1994, after 47 years as a US-administered UN Trust Territory. The economy relies heavily on aid from the USA and Taiwan, tourism, fishing, and subsistence agriculture. The main crops include cassava, coconuts, and copra. Palau's low-lying islands are vulnerable to rising sea levels.

AREA 177 sq mi [459 sq km] **POPULATION** 22,000 **CAPITAL** Ngerulmud

PANAMA

GEOGRAPHY The Republic of Panama forms an isthmus linking Central America to South America. The Panama Canal, which is 50.7 mi [81.6 km] long, cuts across the isthmus. It has made the country a major transport hub.

Panama has a tropical climate. Temperatures are high, though the mountains are much cooler than the coastal plains. The main rainy season is between May and December.

POLITICS & ECONOMY Christopher Columbus landed in Panama in 1502 and Spain soon took the area. In 1821, Panama became independent from Spain and a province of Colombia.

In 1903, Colombia refused a request by the United States to build a canal. Panama revolted against Colombian rule, and became an independent state. The United States then began to build the canal, which was opened in 1914. The United States administered the Panama Canal Zone, a strip of land along the canal. But many Panamanians resented US influence and, in 1979, the Canal Zone was returned to Panama. Control of the canal itself was handed over by the USA to Panama on December 31, 1999.

Panama's government has changed many times since independence, and there have been periods of military dictatorships, including that of General Manuel Antonio Noriega in the 1980s. He was finally convicted of drug offences in the United States in 1992. In 2019 Laurentino Cortizo was elected president, promising to work to reduce corruption and inequality. The Panama Canal is an important source of revenue and, since 2016, new locks and channels have increased capacity and the size of ships that can be accommodated. The other main activity is agriculture, which employs 17% of the work force. The service industry accounts for nearly 80% of GDP. In 2011, the US Congress approved a long-stalled free-trade agreement with Panama.

AREA 29,157 sq mi [75,517 sq km] **POPULATION** 3,929,000
CAPITAL Panamá City **GOVERNMENT** Multiparty republic
ETHNIC GROUPS Mestizo 70%, Black and Mixed 14%, White 10%, Amerindian 6% **LANGUAGES** Spanish (official), English
RELIGIONS Roman Catholic 85%, Protestant 15%
CURRENCY US dollar; Balboa = 100 centésimos

PAPUA NEW GUINEA

GEOGRAPHY Papua New Guinea is an independent country in the Pacific Ocean, north of Australia. Papua New Guinea includes the eastern part of New Guinea, the Bismarck Archipelago, the northern Solomon Islands, the D'Entrecasteaux Islands, and the Louisiade Archipelago. The land is largely mountainous.

Papua New Guinea has a tropical climate, with high temperatures. Most of the rain occurs during the monsoon season (December–April). In the dry season, winds blow from the southeast.

POLITICS & ECONOMY The Dutch colonized western New Guinea (now part of Indonesia) in 1828, but it was not until 1884 that Germany appropriated northeastern New Guinea and Britain took the southeast. In 1906, Britain handed the southeast over to Australia when it became known as the Territory of Papua. When World War I broke out in 1914, Australia took German New Guinea, and in 1921 the League of Nations gave Australia a mandate to rule the area, which was named the Territory of New Guinea. In 1949, Papua and New Guinea were combined as one entity, becoming fully independent in 1975.

In the 1990s there was a secessionist revolt on the island of Bougainville, at the eastern end of the territory. A peace agreement in 2001 granted a degree of autonomy and in a non-binding referendum in 2019, the island voted in favor of independence.

There was political turmoil in 2011–12, when Prime Minister Michael Somare was replaced by Peter O'Neill, who was formally elected prime minister in August 2012. In 2019 O'Neill resigned amid accusations of corruption and was replaced by James Marape.

Agriculture employs 85% of the people, mostly at subsistence level. Mining is important with copper a major export. There are large reserves of natural gas and the development of production facilities to convert this to liquefied form for export could have a profound effect on the economy.

AREA 178,703 sq mi [462,840 sq km] **POPULATION** 7,400,000
CAPITAL Port Moresby **GOVERNMENT** Constitutional monarchy
ETHNIC GROUPS Papuan, Melanesian, Micronesian
LANGUAGES English, Tok Pisin, Hiri Motu (all official); more than 800 indigenous languages **RELIGIONS** Traditional beliefs 34%, Roman Catholic 22%, Lutheran 16% **CURRENCY** Kina = 100 toea

PARAGUAY

GEOGRAPHY The Republic of Paraguay is a landlocked country, and rivers, notably the Paraná, Pilcomayo (Brazo Sur), and Paraguay, form most of its borders. The flat region of the Gran Chaco lies in the northwest, while the southeast contains plains, hills, and plateaux. Northern Paraguay lies in the tropics, while the south is subtropical. Most of the country has a warm, humid climate.

POLITICS & ECONOMY Paraguayans achieved independence in 1811 after being part of a wider Spanish colonial possession since 1776. For many years, Paraguay was torn by internal strife and conflict with its neighbors. A war against Brazil, Argentina, and Uruguay (1865–70) led to the deaths of more than half of Paraguay's population, and a great loss of territory.

General Alfredo Stroessner took power in 1954 and ruled as a dictator until he was overthrown in 1989 (he died in exile in Brazil in 2006). The return of democracy in the years that followed often seemed precarious, because of rivalries between politicians and army leaders, together with economic problems arising partly from the financial crises experienced in neighboring Argentina and Brazil in 1999. In 2008, a former Roman Catholic bishop, Fernando Lugo, who was regarded as a champion of the poor, was elected president, ending more than six decades of rule by the Colorado Party. They returned to power, however, in the 2013 presidential election, which was won by Horacio Cartes, and in 2018, with the election of Mario Abdo Benítez.

Agriculture and forestry, employing about a fifth of the population, are important, and Paraguay is major exporter of soybeans. It produces hydroelectricity and exports power to its neighbors although it has few other natural resources. Paraguay remains a conduit for smuggling drugs.

AREA 157,047 sq mi [406,752 sq km] **POPULATION** 7,273,000
CAPITAL Asunción **GOVERNMENT** Multiparty republic
ETHNIC GROUPS Mestizo 95% **LANGUAGES** Spanish and Guaraní (both official) **RELIGIONS** Roman Catholic 90%, Protestant 6%
CURRENCY Guaraní = 100 céntimos

PERU

GEOGRAPHY The Republic of Peru lies in the tropics in western South America. A narrow coastal plain borders the Pacific Ocean in the west. Inland are ranges of the Andes Mountains, which rise to 22,205 ft [6,768 m] at Nevado Huascarán, an extinct volcano. East of the Andes lies the Amazon basin.

Lima, on the coastal plain, has an arid climate. The coastal region is chilled by the cold, offshore Humboldt Current. Rainfall increases inland and many mountains in the high Andes are snow-capped.

POLITICS & ECONOMY Spanish conquistadores conquered the Inca empire in Peru in the 1530s. In1820, an Argentinian, José de San Martín, led an army into Peru and declared it independent although Spain still held large areas. In 1823, the Venezuelan Simon Bolívar led another army into Peru which resulted in surrender by the Spanish in 1826. Peru suffered much instability throughout the 19th century.

Political turmoil continued in the 20th century, with several military coups. In 1980, when civilian rule was restored, a left-wing group called the Sendero Luminoso, or the "Shining Path," instigated guerrilla warfare against the government. From 1990 to 2000 Alberto Fujimori was president. He largely subdued the rebels, but his rule became increasingly authoritarian, and he was accused of human rights abuses. He fled the country in 2000 but was later extradited and found guilty of ordering killings and kidnappings. Allegations of corruption ended the terms of presidents Padro Pablo Kuczynski (2016–18) and his successor, Martin Vizcarra (2018–20).

Peru's economy benefits from a wide range of mineral resources, with copper, lead, and silver among the most valuable exports, but the environmental effect of mining is concerning. Fish products are exported. Although recent economic growth has been strong, lack of basic infrastructure prevents the spread of prosperity inland.

AREA 496,222 sq mi [1,285,216 sq km] **POPULATION** 32,201,000
CAPITAL Lima **GOVERNMENT** Constitutional republic
ETHNIC GROUPS Amerindian 45%, Mestizo 37%, White 15%
LANGUAGES Spanish and Quechua (both official), Aymara, other Amazonian languages **RELIGIONS** Roman Catholic 81%
CURRENCY Nuevo sol = 100 céntimos

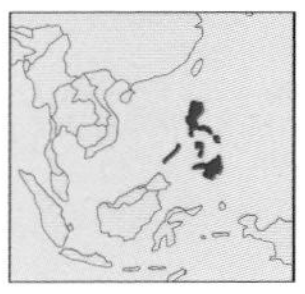

PHILIPPINES

GEOGRAPHY The Republic of the Philippines is an island nation in southeastern Asia. It includes about 7,100 islands, of which 2,770 are named and about 1,000 are inhabited. Luzon and Mindanao, the two largest islands, make up more than two-thirds of the country. The land is mainly mountainous.

The country has a hot tropical climate. The dry season runs from December to April. The rest of the year is wet. Much of the rainfall comes from the typhoons which periodically strike the east coast with devastating effect. In November 2013, Typhoon Haiyan, one of the strongest typhoons ever recorded, resulted in the deaths of over 6,000 people.

POLITICS & ECONOMY The first European to reach the Philippines was the Portuguese navigator Ferdinand Magellan in 1521. Spanish explorers claimed the region in 1565 when they established a settlement on Cebu. The Spaniards ruled the country until 1898, when the United States took over at the end of the Spanish–American War. Japan invaded the Philippines in 1941, but US forces returned in 1944. The country became fully independent as the Republic of the Philippines in 1946.

Since independence, the country's problems have included armed uprisings by left-wing guerrillas, Muslim separatist groups, crime, corruption, and unemployment. An outline peace plan was agreed in 2012 between the government and the Muslim rebel Moro Islamic Liberation Front, but other rebel groups persist, and Islamic State militants are an increasing problem in the south.

The dominant political figure in recent times was Ferdinand Marcos, who ruled in a dictatorial manner from 1965 to 1986. His most recent successor, elected in 2016, is the populist Rodrigo Duterte, whose harsh crackdown on drug dealers and users is popular domestically but has led to international claims of human rights abuses.

The Philippines is a developing country and is recovering steadily from the 2008 global financial crisis. Agriculture employs roughly 25% of the population. The main food crops are rice and maize, while bananas, cocoa, coffee, sugarcane, and tobacco are grown commercially. Shellfish and sea fishing are important, while manufacturing plays an increasingly significant part in the economy. Remittances from overseas workers make a large contribution and attempts are being made to encourage foreign investment.

AREA 115,830 sq mi [300,000 sq km] **POPULATION** 110,818,000
CAPITAL Manila **GOVERNMENT** Multiparty republic
ETHNIC GROUPS Tagalog 28%, Cebuano 13%, Ilocano 9%, Bisaya 8%, and others **LANGUAGES** Filipino (Tagalog) and English (both official), and eight major dialects
RELIGIONS Roman Catholic 83%, Protestant 9%, Islam 5%
CURRENCY Philippine peso = 100 centavos

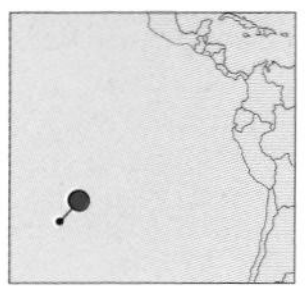

PITCAIRN

Pitcairn Island is a British overseas territory in the Pacific Ocean. Its inhabitants are descendants of the original settlers – nine mutineers from HMS Bounty and 18 Tahitians who arrived in 1790.

AREA 21 sq mi [55 sq km]
POPULATION 50 **CAPITAL** Adamstown

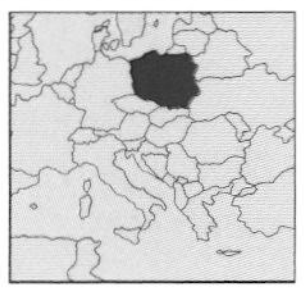

POLAND

GEOGRAPHY The Republic of Poland faces the Baltic Sea and behind its lagoon-fringed coast lies a broad plain. A plateau lies in the southeast, while the Sudeten Highlands straddle part of the border with Czechia. Part of the Carpathian Range (the Tatra) lies in the southeast.

Poland's climate is influenced by its position in Europe. Warm, moist air masses come from

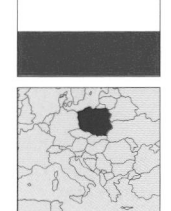

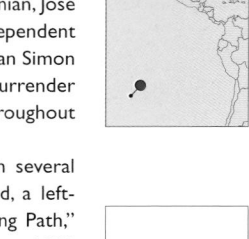

the west, while cold air masses come from the north and east. Summers are warm, but winters are cold and snowy.

POLITICS & ECONOMY Poland's boundaries have changed several times in the last 200 years, partly as a result of its geographical location between the powers of Germany and Russia. It disappeared from the map in the late 18th century, when the Polish state of the Grand Duchy of Warsaw was established. But in 1815, the country was partitioned between Austria, Prussia, and Russia. Poland became independent in 1918, but in 1939 it was divided between Germany and the Soviet Union. The country again became independent in 1945, when it lost land to Russia but gained some from Germany. Communists took power in 1948, but opposition mounted and eventually became focused through an organization called Solidarity.

A coalition government was formed between Solidarity and the Communists in 1989. In 1990, the Communist Party was dissolved and Lech Walesa, a trade unionist, became president. Facing many problems in developing a market economy, he was defeated in presidential elections in 1995. Poland joined NATO in 1999 and the European Union in 2004. In 2017 Mateusz Morawiecki of the conservative Law and Justice Party became prime minister. There were demonstrations by people fearing that new laws would curb democracy.

Poland's economy has grown strongly since the fall of Communism and especially since accession to the EU. It has large reserves of coal. Manufactures include chemicals, food, machinery, ships, steel, and textiles. Farming, although important, lacks investment and needs modernization.

AREA 124,807 sq mi [323,250 sq km] **POPULATION** 38,186,000
CAPITAL Warsaw **GOVERNMENT** Multiparty republic
ETHNIC GROUPS Polish 97%, German, Belarusian, Ukrainian
LANGUAGES Polish (official) **RELIGIONS** Roman Catholic 90%, Eastern Orthodox **CURRENCY** Zloty = 100 groszy

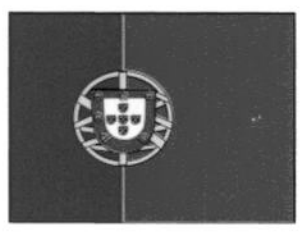

PORTUGAL

GEOGRAPHY The Republic of Portugal is the most westerly of Europe's mainland countries. The land rises from the coastal plains on the Atlantic Ocean to the western edge of the huge plateau, or Meseta, which occupies most of the Iberian peninsula. The climate is moderated by winds blowing from the Atlantic. Summers are cooler and winters are milder than in other Mediterranean lands. Portugal also contains two autonomous regions: the Azores and Madeira island groups.

POLITICS & ECONOMY Portugal became a separate country, independent of Spain, in 1143. In the 15th century, Portugal led the "Age of European Exploration" resulting in the growth of a large Portuguese empire. Portuguese power began to decline in the 16th century and, between 1580 and 1640, Portugal was ruled by Spain. In 1910 Portugal became a republic. Instability hampered progress and army officers seized power in 1926. In 1928, they chose Antonio de Salazar to be minister of finance.

Salazar became prime minister in 1932 and ruled as a dictator from 1933 until 1968. In 1974, army officers mounted a coup which led to free elections in 1978. Portugal joined the European Community (now the European Union) in 1986, and in 2002 joined the eurozone. In 2011–12, there was public unrest when the government introduced austerity measures in order to obtain an international financial bailout to help its weak economy. In 2014 Portugal was able to exit the international bailout, and from 2015 the center-left government has relaxed some of the measures.

Agriculture and fishing were the economic mainstays until the mid-20th century, when the economy started to diversify. Services and manufacturing are now the most valuable activities. Lagging behind the economies of other Western European countries, Portugal faces increasing competition from central Europe and Asia.

AREA 34,285 sq mi [88,797 sq km] **POPULATION** 10,264,000
CAPITAL Lisbon **GOVERNMENT** Multiparty republic
ETHNIC GROUPS Portuguese 99% **LANGUAGES** Portuguese (official)
RELIGIONS Roman Catholic 85%, Protestant
CURRENCY Euro = 100 cents

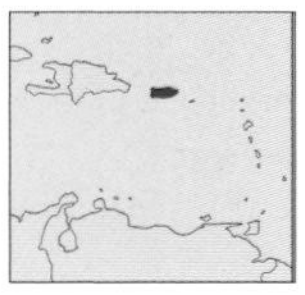

PUERTO RICO

The Commonwealth of Puerto Rico, a mainly mountainous island, is the easternmost of the Greater Antilles chain. The climate is hot and wet. Puerto Rico is a dependent territory of the United States and the people are US citizens. 2017's non-binding referendum resulted in a vote to become a US state, but the turnout was only 23%. Puerto Rico is the Caribbean's most industrialized country. The economy has been in recession since 2006, and many Puerto Ricans have emigrated to the US. Tourism is important, but manufacturing is the more valuable activity.

AREA 3,427 sq mi [8,875 sq km]
POPULATION 3,143,000 **CAPITAL** San Juan

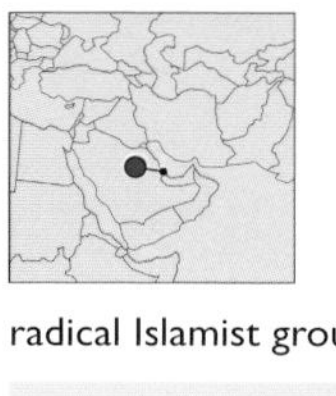

QATAR

The prosperous State of Qatar occupies a low, barren peninsula on the Persian Gulf. A British protectorate from 1916, Qatar became independent in 1971. Oil is the mainstay of the economy. In 2017 Saudi Arabia, the UAE, Egypt, and Bahrain implemented a blockade on Qatar over its alleged connections to radical Islamist groups. In 2019 Qatar withdrew from OPEC.

AREA 4,247 sq mi [11,000 sq km] **POPULATION** 2,480,000 **CAPITAL** Doha

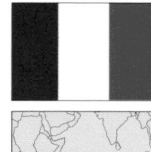

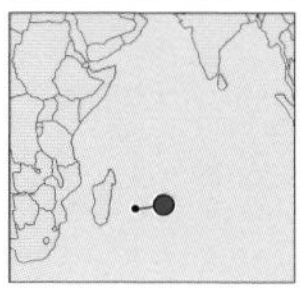

RÉUNION

Réunion is a French overseas department in the Indian Ocean. The land is mainly mountainous, though the lowlands are intensely cultivated. Sugar and sugar products are the main exports, but French aid, given to the island in return for its use as a military base, is important to the economy.

AREA 969 sq mi [2,510 sq km]
POPULATION 846,000 **CAPITAL** St-Denis

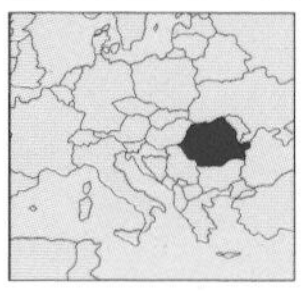

ROMANIA

GEOGRAPHY Romania is a country on the Black Sea in Eastern Europe. Eastern and southern Romania form part of the Danube river basin. The delta region, near the mouth of the Danube, where the river flows into the Black Sea, is one of Europe's finest wetlands. The southern part of the coast contains several resorts. At the heart of the country is the region of Transylvania, ringed in the east, south, and west by scenic mountains which are part of the Carpathian mountain system. Romania has hot summers and cold winters. Rainfall is heaviest in spring and early summer.

POLITICS & ECONOMY The entity that eventually coalesced into modern Romania was born out of the breakup of the Turkish empire in the late 18th century. In 1862 the regions of Wallachia and Moldavia were united under the new heading of Romania. After World War I (1914–18), Romania, which had fought on the side of the Allies, gained territory, including Transylvania, where most people were Romanians. This almost doubled the country's size and population. In 1939, Romania lost territory to Hungary, Bulgaria, and the Soviet Union. Occupied by Soviet troops in 1944, Romania regained northern Transylvania from Hungary in 1945. In 1947, Romania officially became a Communist country. It was ruled for decades by the dictator Ceausescu.

In 1990, Romania held its first free elections since the end of World War II. Initially the government was dominated by former Communists, led by Ion Iliescu, but there was a move toward the center-right at the elections in 1996. Iliescu again served as president from 2000 until 2004. Romania joined NATO in 2004 and the European Union in 2007. Klaus Iohannis of the center-right became president in December 2014.

The growth of Romania's post-communist economy was impeded by lack of reform, corruption, and then the international financial crisis of 2008, after which the government was forced to implement austerity measures which led to civil unrest. The economy recovered and is now classified by the World Bank as "high-income." Exports are increasing and include cars, industrial machinery, metals, textiles, and chemicals. Trade is mainly with other EU states especially Germany and Italy.

AREA 92,043 sq mi [238,391 sq km] **POPULATION** 21,230,000
CAPITAL Bucharest **GOVERNMENT** Multiparty republic
ETHNIC GROUPS Romanian 89%, Hungarian 7%, Roma 2%, Ukrainian **LANGUAGES** Romanian (official), Hungarian, Romany **RELIGIONS** Eastern Orthodox 87%, Protestant 7%, Roman Catholic 5% **CURRENCY** Leu = 100 bani

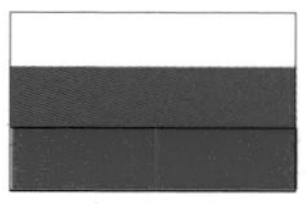
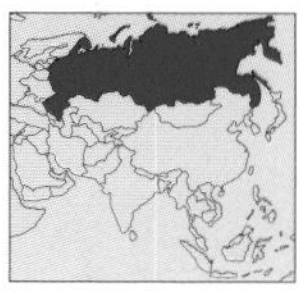

RUSSIA

GEOGRAPHY Russia is the world's largest country. About 25% lies west of the Ural Mountains in European Russia, where 80% of the population lives. It is mostly flat or undulating, but the land rises to the Caucasus Mountains in the south, where Russia's highest peak, Elbrus, at 18,510 ft [5,642 m], is found. Asian Russia, or Siberia, contains vast plains and plateaux, with mountains in the east and south. The Kamchatka peninsula in the far east has many active volcanoes. Russia contains several of the world's longest rivers. It also includes part of the world's largest inland body of water, the Caspian Sea, and Lake Baikal, the world's deepest lake.

Moscow has a continental climate, with cold, snowy winters and hot summers. Siberia has a harsher, drier climate.

POLITICS & ECONOMY In the 9th century AD, a state called Kievan Rus was founded by people known as the East Slavs. Kiev, now capital of Ukraine, became a major trading center, but, in 1237, Mongol armies conquered Russia and destroyed Kiev. Russia was part of the Mongol empire until the late 15th century with Moscow becoming the most important Russian city.

In the 16th century, Moscow's grand prince was retitled "tsar," and the first one, Ivan the Terrible, expanded the Russian territory. In 1613, Michael Romanov became tsar, founding a dynasty which ruled until 1917. In the 18th century, Tsar Peter the Great began to westernize Russia and, by 1812, when Napoleon failed to conquer the country, Russia was a major European power. However, in the 19th century demands for reform were growing.

In World War I (1914–18), the Russian people suffered great hardships and, in 1917, Tsar Nicholas II was forced to abdicate. In November 1917, the Bolsheviks seized power under Vladimir Lenin and set up the Union of Soviet Socialist Republics (also called the USSR or the Soviet Union).

From 1924, Joseph Stalin introduced a socialist economic program, suppressing all opposition. In 1939, the Soviet Union and Germany signed a non-aggression pact, but Germany invaded the Soviet Union in 1941. Soviet forces pushed the Germans back, occupying Eastern Europe. They reached Berlin in May 1945. From the late 1940s, tension between the Soviet Union and its allies and Western nations developed into a "Cold War." This continued until 1991, when the Soviet Union was dissolved.

The Soviet Union collapsed due to the failure of its economic policies. From 1991, Boris Yeltsin, president of the newly independent Russia, introduced democratic and economic reforms. He was succeeded by Vladimir Putin in 2000, who has held power ever since. Russia's size and diversity made national unity hard to achieve and secessionist movements instigated violent, sometimes fatal, incidents in Chechenia, Dagestan, Ingushetia, and Kabardino-Balkaria.

Relations with the West deteriorated from 2006, with Russia criticizing the expansion of NATO in Eastern Europe. In August 2008, Russia fought a short war against Georgia, which had attacked the secessionist region of South Ossetia. Political unrest in Ukraine allowed pro-Russian forces to seize Crimea in 2014. Further tensions with the West arose over Russia's support for the regime of Syria's President Assad. Putin's rule has become increasingly nationalistic and authoritarian, with tight control over political opposition and the media. He has been accused of poisoning his opponents with nerve agents. Thousands of protestors took to the streets in 2021 after opposition politician Alexei Navalny was arrested.

Russia's economy was thrown into disarray after the collapse of the Soviet Union, but is now classified as an "upper-middle-income" economy. It is underpinned by a wealth of natural resources: in particular, natural gas and coal. Gazprom, the state-run gas corporation, is a major supplier to Europe. Reliance on exporting such commodities makes the economy vulnerable to fluctuations in global prices. Future prosperity needs economic reform and investment in infrastructure.

Russia is a major producer of farm products. Crops include barley, flax, fruits, oats, rye, potatoes, sugar beet, sunflower seeds, vegetables, and wheat.

AREA 6,592,812 sq mi [17,075,400 sq km] **POPULATION** 142,321,000
CAPITAL Moscow **GOVERNMENT** Federal multiparty republic
ETHNIC GROUPS Russian 80%, Tatar 4%, Ukrainian 2%, Chuvash 1%, more than 100 others
LANGUAGES Russian (official), many others
RELIGIONS Mainly Russian Orthodox, Islam, Judaism
CURRENCY Russian ruble = 100 kopeks

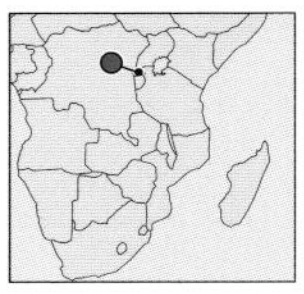

RWANDA

GEOGRAPHY The Republic of Rwanda is a small, landlocked country in east-central Africa. Lake Kivu and the River Ruzizi in the Great African Rift Valley form the country's western border.

Kigali stands on the central plateau of Rwanda. Here, temperatures are moderated by the altitude. Rainfall is abundant, but much heavier rain falls on the western uplands, while the Rift Valley floor is drier and warmer than the rest of Rwanda.

POLITICS & ECONOMY Germany conquered the area, called Ruanda-Urundi, in the 1890s. However, Belgium occupied the region during World War I (1914–18) and ruled it until 1961 when it became independent as a republic. This decision followed a rebellion by the majority Hutu people against the Tutsi monarchy which resulted in about 150,000 deaths. Many Tutsis fled to Uganda, where they formed a rebel army. Relations between Hutus and Tutsis deteriorated and, in 1994, between 500,000 and 800,000 people were massacred in Rwanda. After the Tutsis had restored order, Hutu rebels fled into the Democratic Republic of the Congo. In 2009, Rwanda became the 54th member of the Commonwealth. Paul Kagame has been president since 2000.

According to the World Bank, Rwanda is a "low-income" developing country with economic growth driven by exporting tea and coffee. Most people are poor farmers. Food crops include bananas, beans, cassava, and sorghum. Some cattle are raised.

AREA 10,169 sq mi [26,338 sq km] **POPULATION** 12,943,000
CAPITAL Kigali **GOVERNMENT** Republic
ETHNIC GROUPS Hutu 84%, Tutsi 15%, Twa 1%
LANGUAGES French, English and Kinyarwanda (all official)
RELIGIONS Roman Catholic 57%, Protestant 26%, Adventist 11%, Islam 5% **CURRENCY** Rwandan franc = 100 centimes

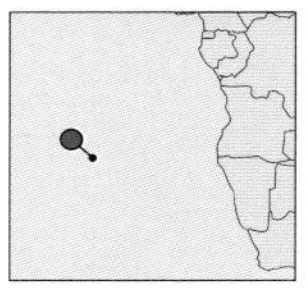

ST HELENA

St Helena, which became a British colony in 1834, is an isolated volcanic island in the South Atlantic Ocean. Now a British overseas territory, it is also the administrative center of Ascension and Tristan da Cunha.

AREA 47 sq mi [122 sq km]
POPULATION 8,000 **CAPITAL** Jamestown

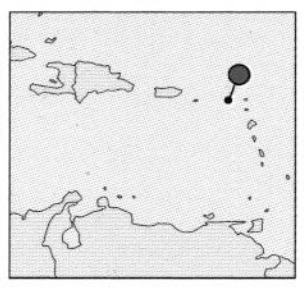

ST KITTS AND NEVIS

The Federation of St Kitts and Nevis comprises two well-watered volcanic islands, whose highest mountain rises to 3,793 ft [1,156 m]. The islands were the first in the Caribbean to be colonized by Britain (in 1623 and 1628), and they became an independent country in 1983. In 1998, a vote for the secession of Nevis fell short of the two-thirds majority required. Tourism, offshore finance, and service industries have replaced sugar as the principal earner.

AREA 101 sq mi [261 sq km]
POPULATION 54,000 **CAPITAL** Basseterre

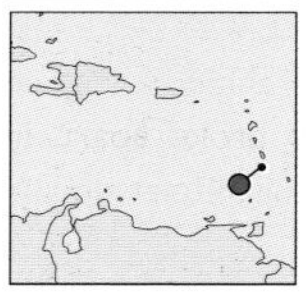

ST LUCIA

St Lucia, which became independent from Britain in 1979, is a mountainous, forested island of extinct volcanoes. It exports bananas and coconuts, and now attracts many tourists.

AREA 208 sq mi [539 sq km]
POPULATION 167,000 **CAPITAL** Castries

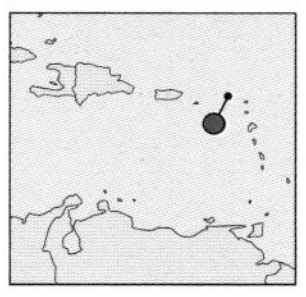

ST MAARTEN

Part of the Netherlands Antilles until 2010, the southern part of the island of St Maarten is a self-governing territory within the Kingdom of the Netherlands. In 2017, Hurricane Irma caused extensive damage.

AREA 13 sq mi [34 sq km]
POPULATION 33,000 **CAPITAL** Philipsburg

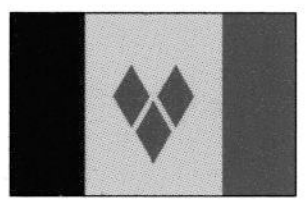

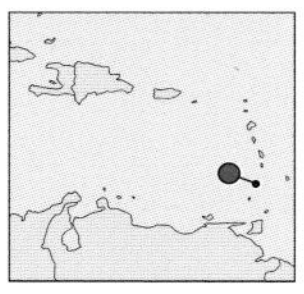

ST VINCENT AND THE GRENADINES

St Vincent and the Grenadines achieved its independence from Britain in 1979. Tourism is growing, but the territory is less prosperous than its neighbors. Its main export is bananas.

AREA 150 sq mi [388 sq km]
POPULATION 101,000 **CAPITAL** Kingstown

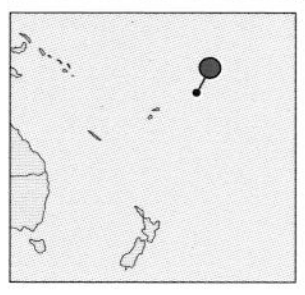

SAMOA

The Independent State of Samoa (formerly Western Samoa) comprises two main islands and several smaller ones in the south Pacific Ocean. Governed by New Zealand from 1920, it became independent in 1962. Exports include fish, coconut cream, and beer.

AREA 1,093 sq mi [2,831 sq km]
POPULATION 205,000 **CAPITAL** Apia

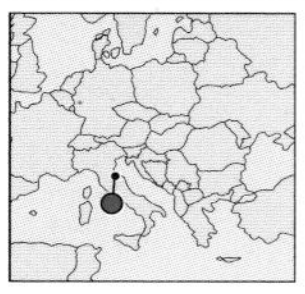

SAN MARINO

San Marino in northern Italy has been independent since 885 and a republic since the 14th century. It is the world's oldest republic. It has a friendship and cooperation treaty with Italy dating back to 1862. The state is governed by an elected council and has its own legal system. It has no armed forces and the police are "hired" from the Italian constabulary. The chief occupations are tourism, limestone quarrying, textiles, and wine-making.

AREA 24 sq mi [61 sq km] **POPULATION** 34,000 **CAPITAL** San Marino

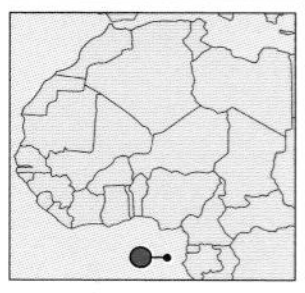

SÃO TOMÉ AND PRÍNCIPE

The Democratic Republic of São Tomé and Príncipe is a mountainous island territory west of Gabon. It became a colony of Portugal in 1522 and independent in 1975. The economy relies heavily on cocoa and foreign aid. Future growth depends on offshore oil.

AREA 372 sq mi [964 sq km] **POPULATION** 214,000 **CAPITAL** São Tomé

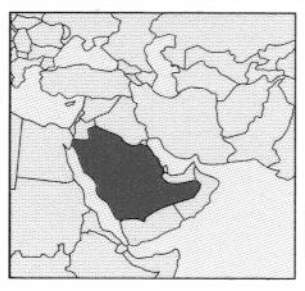

SAUDI ARABIA

GEOGRAPHY The Kingdom of Saudi Arabia occupies about three-quarters of the Arabian peninsula in southwest Asia. Deserts cover most of the land with mountains bordering the Red Sea plains in the west. In the north is the sandy Nafud Desert (An Nafud). In the south is the Rub' al Khali (the "Empty Quarter"), one of the world's bleakest deserts. Saudi Arabia has a hot dry climate. Summer temperatures in Riyadh often exceed 104°F [40°C].

POLITICS & ECONOMY Saudi Arabia contains the two holiest places in Islam – Mecca (or Makka), the birthplace of the Prophet Muhammad in AD 570, and Medina (Al Madinah), where he died in 632. These places are visited by huge numbers of pilgrims.

The monarch, King Salman, has supreme authority in this ultra-conservative country. In March 2015 Saudi Arabia began its controversial military involvement in Yemen, launching airstrikes against Houthi rebels. In 2017, Saudi Arabia, the UAE, Bahrain, and Egypt imposed a blockade on Qatar. The Crown Prince Muhammad bin Salman has introduced a few small reforms, including the re-opening of cinemas and overturning the ban on women driving.

Since 1933, oil has been the mainstay of the economy: the country has more than 18% of the world's known reserves. Oil products make up about 90% of exports. Irrigation and desalination projects have increased crop production. Problems have arisen from increasing unemployment, especially among the young, and moves are being made to diversify the economy.

AREA 829,995 sq mi [2,149,690 sq km] **POPULATION** 34,784,000
CAPITAL Riyadh **GOVERNMENT** Absolute monarchy with consultative assembly **ETHNIC GROUPS** Arab 90%, Afro-Asian 10%
LANGUAGES Arabic (official) **RELIGIONS** Islam 100%
CURRENCY Saudi riyal = 100 halalas

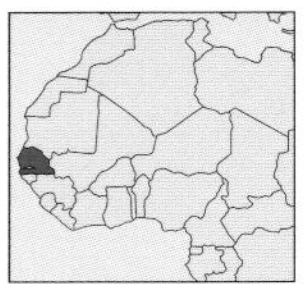

SENEGAL

GEOGRAPHY The Republic of Senegal is on the west coast of Africa. The volcanic Cape Verde (Cap Vert), on which Dakar stands, is the most westerly point in Africa. Plains cover most of Senegal, though the land rises gently in the southeast.

Dakar has a tropical climate, with a short rainy season between July and October.

POLITICS & ECONOMY In 1882, Senegal became a French colony, and from 1895 it was ruled as part of French West Africa, the capital of which, Dakar, developed as a major port and city.

In 1959, Senegal joined French Sudan (now Mali) to form the Federation of Mali. But Senegal withdrew in 1960 and became the separate Republic of Senegal. Its first president, Léopold Sédar Senghor, served until 1981, when he was succeeded by Abdou Diouf. However, in 2000, Diouf was defeated in elections by Abdoulaye Wade which peacefully ended the 40-year rule of the Socialist Party. Macky Sall was elected president in 2012. A ceasefire in 2014 ended a long-running separatist conflict in the southern province of Casamance.

Classified by the World Bank as a "lower-middle-income" country, Senegal is dependent on foreign aid and remittances from abroad. Agriculture employs 77% of the population, mainly at subsistence level. Food crops include groundnuts (peanuts), millet, and rice. Phosphates and fish are the chief resources, but there are plans to develop offshore oil reserves. Dakar is a busy port. Tourism is growing. Economic growth will depend on modernizing infrastructure and guaranteeing reliable power supplies.

AREA 75,954 sq mi [196,722 sq km] **POPULATION** 16,082,000
CAPITAL Dakar **GOVERNMENT** Multiparty republic
ETHNIC GROUPS Wolof 43%, Pular 24%, Serer 15%
LANGUAGES French (official), tribal languages
RELIGIONS Islam 94%, Christianity (mainly Roman Catholic) 5%, traditional beliefs 1%
CURRENCY CFA franc = 100 centimes

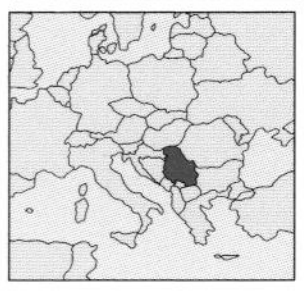

SERBIA

GEOGRAPHY The Republic of Serbia lies in the central Balkan peninsula. A landlocked country, it contains large, fertile lowlands drained by the River Danube and its tributaries, with uplands in the south. Most of Serbia has a continental climate, with cold, snowy winters and hot, dry summers. Heavy rains occur in the spring and the fall.

POLITICS & ECONOMY Around 1,500 years ago, South Slavs moved into the Balkan peninsula, and each group founded its own state. Serbia came under the Turkish Ottoman empire in the 15th century. In 1918, the South Slavs united as the Kingdom of the Serbs, Croats, and Slovenes, which was renamed Yugoslavia in 1929. Germany invaded in 1941, but Communist partisans, led by Josip Broz Tito, took power in 1945.

From 1945, the country became the Federal People's Republic of Yugoslavia. In 1991–92, the country split apart, with Bosnia-Herzegovina, Croatia, Macedonia and Slovenia proclaiming their independence. The remaining republics, Serbia and Montenegro, retained the name Yugoslavia. In 2003, these two republics agreed to form the loose Union of Serbia and Montenegro. In 2006, the Montenegrins voted for full independence, and Serbia and Montenegro became separate republics. In 2008, the province of Kosovo declared itself independent, an act which Serbia refused to recognize. In 2011, the European Commission recommended Serbia for European Union candidate status, but said talks could start only after it normalized ties with Kosovo. Accession talks started in January 2014 although Serbia still falls short of acknowledging Kosovo as fully independent.

Serbia's resources include coal, copper, gold, and other metals, together with oil and natural gas. The country relies on exports and manufacturing, with machinery, plastics, steel, textiles, and vehicles being important. Agriculture employs around one-fifth of the work force with crops including fruits, maize, potatoes, and wheat. There are serious challenges to development including unemployment and an aging population.

AREA 29,913 sq mi [77,474 sq km] **POPULATION** 6,974,000
CAPITAL Belgrade **GOVERNMENT** Republic
ETHNIC GROUPS Serb 83%, Hungarian 4%, others
LANGUAGES Serbian (official), Hungarian
RELIGIONS Serbian Orthodox, Roman Catholic, Islam, Protestant
CURRENCY New dinar = 100 paras

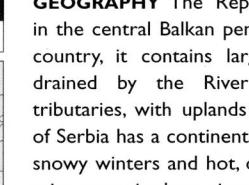

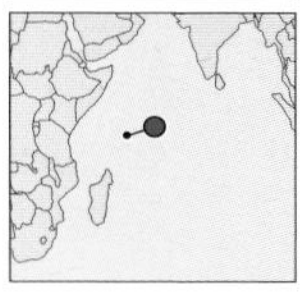

SEYCHELLES

The Republic of Seychelles in the western Indian Ocean achieved independence from Britain in 1976. Coconuts are the main cash crop, and fishing and tourism are important to the country's economy.

AREA 176 sq mi [455 sq km]
POPULATION 96,000 **CAPITAL** Victoria

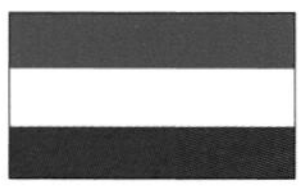
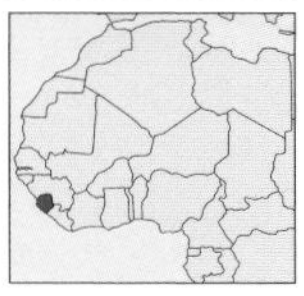

SIERRA LEONE

GEOGRAPHY The Republic of Sierra Leone in West Africa is about the same size as the country of Ireland. The coast contains several estuaries in the north, and extensive mangrove swamps. The most prominent feature is the mountainous Freetown (or Sierra Leone) peninsula.

Sierra Leone has a tropical climate, with heavy rainfall between April and November.

POLITICS & ECONOMY In the early 19th century, Freetown was established by British abolitionists as a destination for freed slaves. In 1961 it became independent from Britain, and a republic in 1971. The military seized power in 1992 and the following years of civil war resulted in tens of thousands of deaths and mutilations. The war ceased in 2002 with the intervention of the UK and a UN peacekeeping force. The last of the UN troops left the country in 2005, and elections were held in 2007. In 2010, the UN Security Council lifted the last remaining sanctions against Sierra Leone. In 2018 Julius Maada Bio of the People's Party was elected president.

Sierra Leone has a "low-income" economy, which, although showing signs of reasonable growth, has been hampered by the legacy of destruction left by the war, and by the outbreak of the Ebola virus in 2014–16. About 59% of the people live by subsistence farming. The leading exports are minerals, including iron ore and rutile (titanium ore), and diamonds. The trade in the latter as "blood diamonds" helped perpetuate the civil war and much diamond mining is still unlicensed.

AREA 27,699 sq mi [71,740 sq km] **POPULATION** 6,807,000
CAPITAL Freetown **GOVERNMENT** Multiparty republic **ETHNIC GROUPS** Native African tribes 90% **LANGUAGES** English (official), Mende, Temne, Limba **RELIGIONS** Islam 60%, traditional beliefs 30%, Christianity 10%
CURRENCY Leone = 100 cents

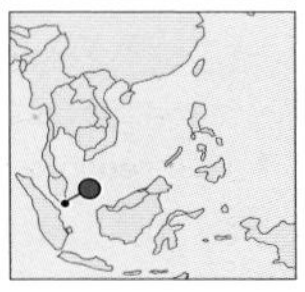

SINGAPORE

GEOGRAPHY The Republic of Singapore is an island country at the southern tip of the Malay peninsula. It consists of the large Singapore Island and 58 small islands, 20 of which are inhabited. The climate is hot and humid. Temperatures are high and rainfall is heavy throughout the year.

POLITICS & ECONOMY In 1819, Sir Thomas Stamford Raffles, agent of the British East India Company, made a treaty with the Sultan of Johor allowing the British to build a settlement on Singapore Island. Singapore soon became the leading British trading center in Southeast Asia and it later became a naval base. Japanese forces seized the island in 1942, but British rule was restored in 1945.

In 1963, Singapore became part of the Federation of Malaysia, which also included Malaya and the territories of Sabah and Sarawak on Borneo. In 1965, Singapore broke away and became independent.

The People's Action Party (PAP) has ruled Singapore since 1959. Its leader, Lee Kuan Yew, served as prime minister from 1959 until 1990, when he was succeeded by Goh Chok Tong. Lee Hsien Loong, son of Lee Kuan Yew, has been re-elected three times since becoming prime minister in 2004. The country is known for its conservative laws.

The World Bank classifies Singapore as a "high-income" economy, where a skilled work force has created a fast-growing economy. Trade and finance are major activities. Recovery was rapid after the global financial crisis in 2008–9. Manufactures include electronic products, machinery, scientific instruments, and ships. Petroleum products and manufactures are the main exports.

AREA 264 sq mi [683 sq km] **POPULATION** 5,866,000
CAPITAL Singapore City **GOVERNMENT** Multiparty republic
ETHNIC GROUPS Chinese 77%, Malay 14%, Indian 8%
LANGUAGES Chinese, Malay, Tamil and English (all official)
RELIGIONS Buddhism, Islam, Christianity, Hinduism
CURRENCY Singapore dollar = 100 cents

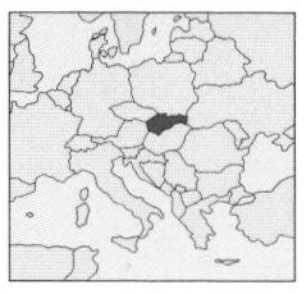

SLOVAKIA

GEOGRAPHY Slovakia is a predominantly mountainous country, consisting of part of the Carpathian range. The highest peak is Gerlachovsky in the Tatra Mountains, which reaches 8,711 ft [2,655 m]. The south is comprised of a fertile lowland. Slovakia has cold winters and warm summers. Kosice, in the east, has average temperatures ranging from 27°F [–3°C] in January to 68°F [20°C] in July. The highland areas are much colder. Snow or rain falls throughout the year. Kosice has an average annual rainfall of 24 inches [600 mm], the wettest months being July and August.

POLITICS & ECONOMY Slavic peoples settled here in the 5th century AD. They were subsequently conquered by Hungary, beginning a millennium of Hungarian rule and suppression of Slovak culture.

In 1867, Hungary and Austria united to form Austria–Hungary, of which the present-day Slovakia was a part. Austria–Hungary collapsed at the end of World War I (1914–18) and the Czech and Slovak people then united to form a new nation, Czechoslovakia. But Czech domination led to resentment by many Slovaks. In 1939, Slovakia declared itself independent, before Germany occupied the country. At the end of World War II, Slovakia again became part of Czechoslovakia.

The Communist Party took control in 1948 and although many people sought reform in the 1960s, they were crushed by the Russians. In the late 1980s, demands for democracy mounted and a non-Communist government took office in 1990. Elections in 1992 led to victory for the Movement for a Democratic Slovakia headed by a former Communist and nationalist, Vladimir Meciar, and Slovakia became independent in 1993.

Independence raised national aspirations among Slovakia's Magyar-speaking community which makes up about 10% of the population. Issues about the status of this minority group have soured relations with Hungary, and were not helped by the government making Slovak the only official language. Slovakia became a member of NATO and the European Union in 2004. On January 1, 2009, it became the 16th country to adopt the euro. In 2018, the murder of an investigative journalist who had reported on alleged fraud linked to the government shocked the nation, and led to victory for the anti-corruption OLaNO party in 2020 parliamentary elections.

Before 1948, Slovakia's economy was based on farming, but Communist governments developed manufacturing industries. From the late 1980s, many state-run businesses were privatized. Reforms following membership of the eurozone resulted in strong economic growth, driven by the export of cars, machinery, and electronic goods. About 40% of the land is cultivated and crops include sugar beet, wheat, and maize.

AREA 18,924 sq mi [49,012 sq km] **POPULATION** 5,436,000
CAPITAL Bratislava **GOVERNMENT** Multiparty republic
ETHNIC GROUPS Slovak 86%, Hungarian 10%
LANGUAGES Slovak (official), Hungarian
RELIGIONS Roman Catholic 69%, Protestant 11%, others
CURRENCY Euro = 100 cents

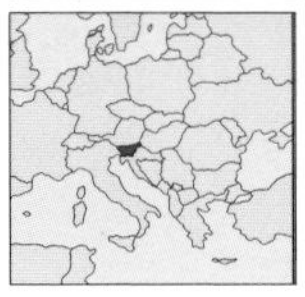

SLOVENIA

GEOGRAPHY The Republic of Slovenia was one of the six republics which made up the former Yugoslavia. Much of the land is mountainous, rising to 9,396 ft [2,864 m] at Mount Triglav in the Julian Alps (Julijske Alpe) in the northwest. Central Slovenia contains the limestone Karst region. The Postojna caves near Ljubljana are among the largest in Europe.

The coast has a mild Mediterranean climate, but inland the climate is more continental.

POLITICS & ECONOMY In the last 2,000 years, the Slovene people have been independent as a nation for less than 50 years. The Austrian Habsburgs ruled over the region from the 13th century until World War I when, in 1918, Slovenia became part of the Kingdom of the Serbs, Croats, and Slovenes (later called Yugoslavia). During World War II, Slovenia was invaded and partitioned between Italy, Germany, and Hungary, but, after the war, Slovenia again became part of Yugoslavia.

From the late 1960s, some Slovenes demanded independence, but the central government opposed the breakup of the country. In 1990, when Communist governments had collapsed throughout Eastern Europe, elections were held and a non-Communist coalition government was set up. Slovenia then declared itself independent. This led to fighting between Slovenes and the federal army, but Slovenia did not become a battlefield. Slovenia's independence was recognized in 1992 and a coalition led by the Liberal Democrats was elected. In 2004, Slovenia became a member of the North Atlantic Treaty Organization and the European Union. In 2013, the coalition government of Janez Jansa collapsed amidst criticisms of its austerity measures and allegations of corruption. In 2020, Jansa returned as prime minister, heading the anti-immigration SDS party and marking a shift to the right in Slovenian politics.

The reform of the formerly state-run economy caused problems for Slovenia. From 1993, the country made considerable economic progress although this stumbled in the European financial crisis of 2012 when tough austerity measures were unpopular. Recent economic growth has been strong.

Manufacturing and services are the strongest parts of the economy, and exports include chemicals, machinery and transport equipment, and textiles. Slovenia's natural resources include lead, lignite, and iron ore. Forests cover over 60% of the land. Maize, potatoes, and wheat are major crops; livestock are raised.

AREA 7,821 sq mi [20,256 sq km] **POPULATION** 2,102,000
CAPITAL Ljubljana **GOVERNMENT** Multiparty republic
ETHNIC GROUPS Slovene 83%, Croat 2%, Serb 2%, Hungarian, Bosnian **LANGUAGES** Slovenian (official), Serbo-Croatian
RELIGIONS Roman Catholic 58%
CURRENCY Euro = 100 cents

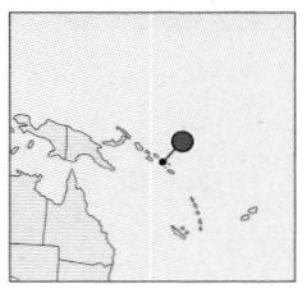

SOLOMON ISLANDS

The Solomon Islands, a chain of mainly volcanic islands in the Pacific Ocean extending for some 1,400 mi [2,250 km], were a British territory between 1893 and 1978. Most people are Melanesians, and the islands have a young population profile, with about 35% of the people aged under 15. The country is struggling to recover from five years of civil conflict and poverty is rife. Fish, coconuts, cocoa, and forestry products underpin the economy.

AREA 11,157 sq mi [28,896 sq km]
POPULATION 691,000 **CAPITAL** Honiara

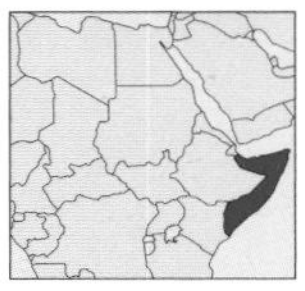

SOMALIA

GEOGRAPHY The Federal Republic of Somalia is in a region known as the "Horn of Africa." It is more than twice the size of Italy, the country which once ruled the southern part of Somalia. The most mountainous part of the country is in the north, behind the narrow coastal plains that border the Gulf of Aden. Rainfall is sparse, with the wettest regions in the south and northern mountains. Droughts are common and temperatures are generally high.

POLITICS & ECONOMY European powers became interested in the Horn of Africa in the 19th century. In 1884, Britain made the northern part of what is now Somalia a protectorate, while Italy took the south in 1905. The new boundaries divided the Somalis into five areas: the two Somalilands, Djibouti (which was taken by France in the 1880s), Ethiopia, and Kenya. Since then, many Somalis have wanted to create a Greater Somalia. Italy invaded British Somaliland in 1940, but was defeated in 1941. Britain ruled both Somalilands until 1950, when the UN asked Italy to take over the former Italian Somaliland for ten years. In 1960, the two Somalilands united to become Somalia.

Somalia has faced many problems. Economic difficulties led a military group to seize power in 1969. In the 1970s, Somalia supported an uprising of Somali-speaking people in the Ogaden region of Ethiopia. But, in 1988, Somalia and Ethiopia signed a peace treaty. In the 1990s, Somalia gradually broke apart. In 1991, the people in what was once British Somaliland set up the "Somaliland Republic," but it failed to get international recognition. The northeast, called Puntland, also seceded, while the south was riven by clan warfare. In 2004–5, a Somali parliament was set up in Kenya, moving to Baidoa, in Somalia, in 2006 (Mogadishu was regarded as unsafe). In 2006, Mogadishu was taken over by the Islamist Union of Islamic Courts, but government forces backed by Ethiopian troops defeated the Islamists. In 2012, the militant group al-Shabab was driven out of central Somalia, but continues to carry out attacks. President Mohamed Abdullahi Mohamed, elected in 2017, has indicated that he is willing to talk to the militants. Somali pirates are notorious for attacking international shipping in the area.

Somalia's economy has been shattered by war, droughts, and periodic floods. Many Somalis are nomads, who raise livestock.

Live animals, meat, and hides and skins are exported. Crops include bananas, citrus fruits, cotton, maize, and sugarcane.

AREA 246,199 sq mi [637,657 sq km] **POPULATION** 12,095,000
CAPITAL Mogadishu **GOVERNMENT** Single-party republic, military dominated **ETHNIC GROUPS** Somali 85%, Bantu, Arab
LANGUAGES Somali (official), Arabic **RELIGIONS** Islam (Sunni Muslim)
CURRENCY Somali shilling = 100 cents

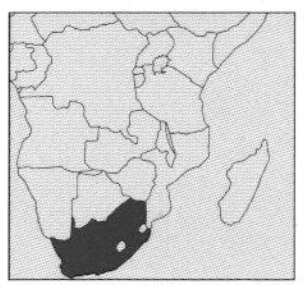

SOUTH AFRICA

GEOGRAPHY The Republic of South Africa comprises mainly of the southern part of the huge plateau which makes up most of southern Africa. The highest peaks are in the Drakensberg range. Part of the Namib Desert lies in the northwest. The area around Cape Town has a sunny climate with mild, rainy winters. Inland, large areas of the plateau are arid.

POLITICS & ECONOMY Early inhabitants in South Africa were the Khoisa, followed in the last 2,000 years by Bantu-speaking people. Their descendants include the Zulu, Xhosa, Sotho, and Tswana. The Dutch founded a settlement at the Cape in 1652, but Britain colonized the area in the early 19th century. The Dutch, called Boers or Afrikaners, resented British rule and moved inland. Rivalry between the groups led to Anglo–Boer Wars in 1880–81 and 1899–1902.

In 1910, the country was united as the Union of South Africa. In 1948, the National Party won power and introduced the policy of apartheid, under which non-whites could not vote and their human rights were strictly limited. Decades of protests followed, both in South Africa and abroad, as well as international sanctions. Multiracial elections were finally held in 1994 and Nelson Mandela, leader of the African National Congress (ANC), became president following 27 years in prison. The ANC has remained in power, under Thabo Mbeki, Jacob Zuma, who resigned in 2018 over allegations of corruption, and most recently Cyril Ramaphosa.

South Africa is Africa's most developed country and is one of the "BRICS" group of emerging global economic powers. However, most of the black people are poor, with farms still white-owned. Unemployment is high at 28% and it has nurtured an associated high crime rate. Natural resources include diamonds and gold; services, mining and manufacturing are valuable activities. Crops include maize, wheat, and sugarcane.

AREA 471,442 sq mi [1,221,037 sq km] **POPULATION** 56,979,000
CAPITAL Cape Town (legislative); Pretoria/Tshwane (administrative); Bloemfontein (judiciary) **GOVERNMENT** Multiparty republic
ETHNIC GROUPS Black 79%, White 10%, Colored 9%, Asian 2%
LANGUAGES Afrikaans, English, Ndebele, Pedi, Sotho, Swazi, Tsonga, Tswana, Venda, Xhosa and Zulu (all official)
RELIGIONS Christianity 68%, Islam 2%, Hinduism 1%
CURRENCY Rand = 100 cents

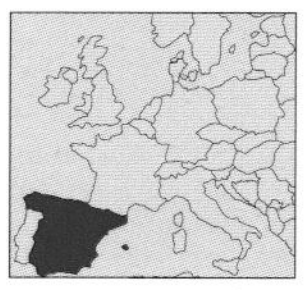

SPAIN

GEOGRAPHY The Kingdom of Spain is the second largest country in Western Europe after France. It shares the Iberian peninsula with the much smaller Portugal. The Meseta, an extensive plateau, covers most of Spain. It is mainly flat, but is crossed by the sierras, a series of mountain ranges.

The northern highlands include the Cantabrian Mountains (Cordillera Cantabrica) and the high Pyrenees, which form Spain's border with France. But Mulhacén, the highest peak on the Spanish mainland, is in the Sierra Nevada in the southeast. Spain also has fertile coastal plains. Other major lowlands include the Ebro river basin in the northeast and the Guadalquivir river basin in the southwest. Spain also encompasses the Balearic Islands in the Mediterranean Sea and the Canary Islands off the northwest coast of Africa.

The Meseta has a continental climate, with hot summers and cold winters, when temperatures often fall below freezing point. Snow frequently covers the mountain ranges on the Meseta. The Mediterranean coasts have hot, dry summers and mild winters.

POLITICS & ECONOMY In the early 16th century, Spain rose to be a world power. At its peak, it controlled much of Central and South America, parts of Africa, and the Philippines in Asia. Spain's influence began to decline in the late 16th century. Its sea power was destroyed by a British fleet in the Battle of Trafalgar (1805), and by the 20th century it was a poor country.

Spain became a republic in 1931, but the republicans were defeated in the Spanish Civil War (1936–39). General Francisco Franco became the country's dictator, though technically Spain remained a monarchy. On Franco's death in 1975, there was a peaceful transition to democracy, with Juan Carlos as king. In 2014 he abdicated in favor of his son Felipe.

Within Spain there are several groups, with their own languages and cultures, who have been vocal in their aim to run their own affairs. In the northern Basque region, the separatist group, ETA, waged a long-running terrorist campaign, finally announcing its complete disarmament in 2017.

Spain's regional makeup is complicated and the powers devolved to the regional parliaments since the 1970s are unevenly distributed. There are 17 regions, with Catalonia, the Basque Country, and Galicia having gained special status. A referendum in Catalonia in October 2017 led the regional government to declare independence. The central government swiftly cracked down and imposed direct rule.

Spain was badly affected by the global recession of 2008; sluggish economic growth and an unemployment rate of 26% in 2013 forced the country to undertake drastic austerity measures.

Agriculture employs only 4% of the population, as compared with 24% in industry and 72% in the service sector. Farmland occupies two-thirds of the land area. Manufactures include cars, chemicals, electronic goods, food, metal goods, and textiles. Spain lacks natural resources apart from some iron ore.

AREA 192,103 sq mi [497,548 sq km] **POPULATION** 47,261,000
CAPITAL Madrid **GOVERNMENT** Constitutional monarchy
ETHNIC GROUPS Composite of Mediterranean and Nordic types
LANGUAGES Castilian Spanish (official) 74%, Catalan 17%, Galician 7%, Basque 2% **RELIGIONS** Roman Catholic 94%, others 6% **CURRENCY** Euro = 100 cents

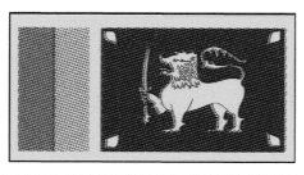

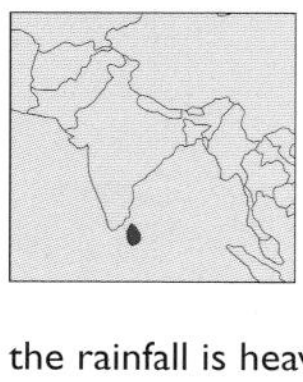

SRI LANKA

GEOGRAPHY The Democratic Socialist Republic of Sri Lanka is an island nation, separated from the southeast coast of India by the Palk Strait. The land is mostly low-lying, but a mountain region dominates the south-central part of the country.

The western part of Sri Lanka has a wet equatorial climate. Temperatures are high and the rainfall is heavy.

POLITICS & ECONOMY From the early 16th century, Ceylon (as Sri Lanka was then known) was ruled successively by the Portuguese, Dutch, and British. Independence was achieved in 1948 and the country was renamed Sri Lanka in 1972.

After independence, rivalries between the two main ethnic groups, the Buddhist Sinhalese and the minority Hindu Tamils, marred progress. In 1956 Solomon Bandaranaike was elected prime minister on a wave of Sinhalese nationalism, but he was assassinated in 1959 by an extremist Buddhist monk. He was succeeded by his wife, Sirimavo Bandaranaike, the world's first woman prime minister.

Conflict between Tamils and Sinhalese continued in the 1970s and 1980s. In 1987, India helped to engineer a ceasefire but withdrew its troops in 1990 after failing to subdue the main guerrilla group, the Tamil Tigers, who wanted to set up an independent Tamil homeland in the northeast. The Tamil Tigers were finally defeated in May 2009. In 2019, Islamist terrorists killed several hundred people in a series of suicide bombings.

In late 2004, a tsunami, caused by a sudden movement of the plates underlying the eastern Indian Ocean, struck parts of the coast of Sri Lanka, killing more than 30,000 people.

The end of the conflict with the Tamil Tigers was followed by strong economic growth. Agriculture employs about 30% of the people. Coconuts, rubber, spices, and tea are exported. Rice is the main food crop. Factories process farm products and manufacture textiles.

AREA 25,332 sq mi [65,610 sq km] **POPULATION** 23,044,000
CAPITAL Colombo (commercial); Sri Jayewardenepura Kotte (legislative)
GOVERNMENT Multiparty republic **ETHNIC GROUPS** Sinhalese 74%, Tamil 9%, Moor 7% **LANGUAGES** Sinhala and Tamil (both official)
RELIGIONS Buddhism 69%, Islam 8%, Hinduism 7%, Christianity 6%
CURRENCY Sri Lankan rupee = 100 cents

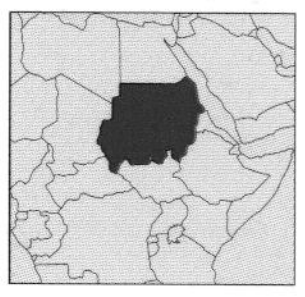

SUDAN

GEOGRAPHY The Republic of Sudan was Africa's largest country until 2011, when the people in the south voted to secede and form the new nation of South Sudan. Sudan is mainly arid, with part of the vast Sahara in the north. The main feature is the fertile River Nile valley, where most people live.

POLITICS & ECONOMY In the 19th century, Egypt gradually took control of Sudan. In 1881, a Muslim religious teacher, the Mahdi ("divinely appointed guide"), led a rebellion which was quashed, in 1898, by Britain and Egypt. In 1899, these two countries agreed to rule Sudan jointly as a condominium. After independence in 1952, the black Africans in the south feared domination by the Muslim north. They objected to Arabic becoming the sole official language and, in 1964, civil war broke out. The war ended in 1972, when the south was granted regional self-government.

In 1983, the announcement that Islamic law would apply throughout Sudan sparked off further resistance from the rebel Sudan People's Liberation Army (SPLA) in the south. In 1998, Sudan's government announced that it accepted the idea of a referendum. In 2005, a peace agreement was signed, and the referendum took place in 2011, when around 99% of the people in the south voted to set up their own country, South Sudan.

From 2003, conflict raged in the western province of Darfur, where government-backed militias battled with local rebel forces. A peace accord was agreed in 2010 but some conflict continues. In 2008, the International Criminal Court charged President al-Bashir with war crimes. In 2019 he was ousted and arrested by the military. A civilian-military transitional government was set up.

The majority of the population are poor and live by subsistence agriculture. Cotton, gum arabic, and sesame seeds are exported, but the most valuable exports are gold and oil products. More than 80% of the oil is produced in South Sudan, but Sudan has the infrastructure to exploit and export it.

AREA 728,222 sq mi [1,886,086 sq km] **POPULATION** 46,751,000
CAPITAL Khartoum **GOVERNMENT** Transitional
ETHNIC GROUPS Arab, Black, Beja, others **LANGUAGES** Arabic and English (both official), Nubian, Beja **RELIGIONS** Islam, traditional beliefs
CURRENCY Sudanese pound = 100 piastres

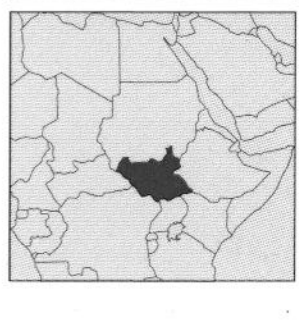

SUDAN, SOUTH

GEOGRAPHY The Republic of South Sudan is a landlocked country in east-central Africa. Much of the land is low-lying and drained by the White Nile and its tributaries. Mountains lie in the far south. The country has a wet tropical climate. Forests, swamps, and grasslands cover large areas.

POLITICS & ECONOMY South Sudan has about 200 ethnic groups. The South's deep cultural differences with the mainly Arab-Muslim north led to civil war (1964–1972 and 1983–2005). In January 2011, as part of the peace agreement, a referendum was held in which the vast majority of the people in the south voted for independence. Civil war broke out in 2013, displacing millions. Fighting was reduced after the president signed a power-sharing agreement in 2018. A transitional coalition government was formed in 2020, with Salva Kiir remaining as president and his former rival Riek Machar as vice president.

South Sudan has many mineral resources, including oil, but the country's infrastructure is undeveloped and poverty is widespread. Much of the population depends on subsistence agriculture.

AREA 239,285 sq mi [619,745 sq km] **POPULATION** 10,984,000
CAPITAL Juba **GOVERNMENT** Transitional Coalition
ETHNIC GROUPS Dinka, Kakwa, Bari, Azande, Shilluk, others
LANGUAGES English and Arabic (both official), local languages
RELIGIONS Traditional beliefs, Christianity
CURRENCY South Sudanese pound = 100 piastres

SURINAME

GEOGRAPHY The Republic of Suriname is sandwiched between French Guiana and Guyana in northeastern South America. The narrow coastal plain was once swampy, but it has been drained and now consists mainly of farmland. Inland lie hills and low mountains, which rise to 4,035 ft [1,230 m].

Suriname has a hot, wet and humid climate. Temperatures are high throughout the year.

POLITICS & ECONOMY In 1667, the British handed Suriname to the Dutch in return for New Amsterdam, an area that is now the state of New York. Slave revolts and Dutch neglect hampered development. In the early 19th century, Britain and the Netherlands disputed the ownership of the area with Britain relinquishing its claim in 1813. Slavery was abolished in 1863 and Indian and Indonesian laborers were introduced to work on the plantations.

Suriname became fully independent in 1975, but the economy was weakened when thousands of skilled people emigrated from

Suriname to the Netherlands. Following a coup in 1980, Suriname was ruled by a military dictator, Desiré ("Dési") Bouterse. Democracy was restored in 1988, but Bouterse returned to power from 2010 to 2020 at the head of the Mega Combination coalition. In 2019 he was convicted of the murders in 1982 of 15 of his political opponents.

Suriname's economy is based on gold mining and oil. It was badly affected by a decline in bauxite mining. Crops include rice and bananas, which are also exported. Fishing is important, and tourism has potential.

AREA 63,037 sq mi [163,265 sq km] **POPULATION** 615,000
CAPITAL Paramaribo **GOVERNMENT** Multiparty republic
ETHNIC GROUPS Hindustani/East Indian 37%, Creole (mixed White and Black) 31%, Javanese 15%, Black 10%, Amerindian 2%, Chinese 2%, others
LANGUAGES Dutch (official), Sranang Tongo
RELIGIONS Hinduism 27%, Protestant 25%, Roman Catholic 23%, Islam 20% **CURRENCY** Surinamese dollar= 100 cents

SWEDEN

GEOGRAPHY The Kingdom of Sweden is the largest of the countries of Scandinavia in both area and population. It shares the Scandinavian peninsula with Norway. The western part of the country, along the border with Norway, is mountainous. The highest point is Kebnekaise, which reaches 6,936 ft [2,114 m] in the northwest. The climate becomes increasingly severe from south to north.

POLITICS & ECONOMY Swedish Vikings plundered areas to the south and east between the 9th and 11th centuries. Sweden, Denmark, and Norway were united in 1397, but Sweden regained its independence in 1523. In 1809, Sweden lost Finland to Russia, but, in 1814, it gained Norway from Denmark. The union between Sweden and Norway was dissolved in 1905. Sweden remained neutral in World Wars I and II. Since 1945, Sweden has become a prosperous country and, in 1995, it joined the European Union. However, it did not adopt the euro, nor has it joined NATO.

Sweden has wide-ranging welfare provision but it comes at a high cost to the taxpayer. In 2006, a center-right alliance defeated the Social Democrats, who had governed for 65 of the previous 74 years. Stefan Löfven has been prime minister since 2014, heading a center-left minority government, and was re-elected in 2019 after losing a vote of no confidence the previous year.

Sweden is a highly developed industrial country: the economy is strong and unemployment low. Major products include steel and steel goods. Steel is used in the country's engineering industry to manufacture aircraft, cars, and machinery. Sweden has some of the world's richest iron ore deposits which are found near Kiruna in the far north. Most of this ore is exported, and Sweden has to import most of the materials needed by its own industries. Forestry is also important and hydroelectricity is a major source of energy.

AREA 173,731 sq mi [449,964 sq km] **POPULATION** 10,262,000
CAPITAL Stockholm **GOVERNMENT** Constitutional monarchy
ETHNIC GROUPS Swedish 91%, Finnish, Sami **LANGUAGES** Swedish (official), Finnish, Sami
RELIGIONS Lutheran 87%, Roman Catholic, Orthodox
CURRENCY Swedish krona = 100 öre

SWITZERLAND

GEOGRAPHY The Swiss Confederation is a landlocked country in Western Europe. Much of the land is mountainous. The Jura Mountains lie along Switzerland's western border with France, while the Swiss Alps make up about 60% of the country in the south and east. Four-fifths of the population live on the fertile Swiss plateau, which contains most of Switzerland's large cities.

The climate of Switzerland is generally temperate but varies greatly according to the altitude. The plateau has warm summers and cold, snowy winters. Rain occurs throughout the year.

POLITICS & ECONOMY In 1291, three small cantons (states) united to defend their freedom against the Habsburg rulers of the Holy Roman empire. They were Schwyz, Uri, and Unterwalden, and they called the confederation they formed "Switzerland." Switzerland expanded and, in the 14th century, defeated Austria in three wars of independence. After a defeat by the French in 1515, the Swiss adopted a policy of neutrality, which they still follow. In 1815, the Congress of Vienna expanded Switzerland to 22 cantons and guaranteed its neutrality. Switzerland's 23rd canton, Jura, was created in 1979 from part of Bern.

Since 1848, Switzerland has been governed by a Federal Council. Its seven members are elected to four-year terms and together form the country's head of state. Switzerland became a member of the United Nations in 2002, although it has remained outside the EU.

Switzerland's neutrality has helped it to become prosperous. Although lacking in natural resources, it is a wealthy, industrialized country. Products include chemicals, electrical equipment, machinery, precision instruments, processed food, watches, and textiles. Farmers produce about three-fifths of the country's food – the rest is imported. Crops include fruits, potatoes, and wheat. Tourism and banking are important. Swiss banks attract investors from all over the world.

AREA 15,940 sq mi [41,284 sq km] **POPULATION** 8,454,000
CAPITAL Bern **GOVERNMENT** Federal republic
ETHNIC GROUPS German 65%, French 18%, Italian 10%, Romansch 1%, others **LANGUAGES** German, French, Italian and Romansch (all official) **RELIGIONS** Roman Catholic 42%, Protestant 35% **CURRENCY** Swiss franc = 100 centimes

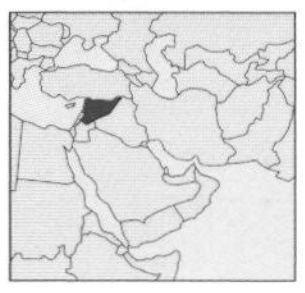

SYRIA

GEOGRAPHY The Syrian Arab Republic has a narrow coastal plain and is overlooked by a low mountain range which runs north–south. Another range, the Jabal ash Sharqi, runs along the border with Lebanon.

The coast has a Mediterranean climate, with dry, warm summers and wet, mild winters. The low mountains cut off Damascus from the sea. It has less rainfall than the coastal areas. To the east, the land becomes drier.

POLITICS & ECONOMY After the collapse of the Turkish Ottoman empire in World War I, Syria was governed by France until independence in 1946. In 1967 Syria lost the strategic Golan Heights to Israel. In 1970, Lieutenant-General Hafez al-Assad took power, establishing a stable but repressive regime. Hafez al-Assad died in 2000 and was succeeded by his son, Bashar al-Assad. From 2011, civil war, and the occupation of Syrian territory by jihadist militants, devastated the country with the number of deaths of civilians, rebels and government forces estimated at over half a million. By 2019, the government, with the help of Russian forces, had regained control of most of Syria's biggest cities, and the Islamic State had been reduced to a small enclave on the Iraqi border. The Kurds controlled territory in the northeast of the country, and Turkey in the north. The government has repeatedly been accused of using chemical warfare on its own citizens. Millions of people have been internally displaced or sought refuge elsewhere, and Syria remains in a state of crisis.

Syria's main resources are oil, hydroelectricity, and fertile land. However, the economy has been crippled by the civil war.

AREA 71,498 sq mi [185,180 sq km] **POPULATION** 20,384,000
CAPITAL Damascus **GOVERNMENT** Multiparty republic
ETHNIC GROUPS Arab 90%, Kurdish, Armenian, others
LANGUAGES Arabic (official), Kurdish, Armenian
RELIGIONS Sunni Muslim 74%, other Islam 16%
CURRENCY Syrian pound = 100 piastres

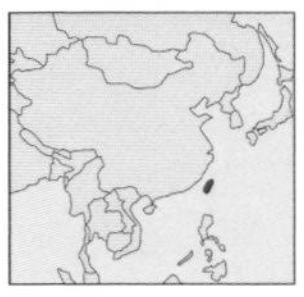

TAIWAN

GEOGRAPHY High mountain ranges run down the length of the island, with dense forest in many areas. The climate is warm, moist, and suitable for agriculture.

POLITICS & ECONOMY Chinese settlers occupied Taiwan from the 7th century. In 1895, Japan seized the territory from the Portuguese, who had named it Isla Formosa, or "beautiful island." China regained the island after World War II and, in 1949, it became the refuge of the Nationalists who had been driven out of China by the Communists. They set up the Republic of China, which, with US help, began to widen its economic base and develop manufacturing industries.

In the early 21st century, the Taiwanese declared full nationhood; however, China has never relinquished its claim of sovereignty over the island. Relations have improved since Taiwan and China signed a free-trade pact in 2010 although tensions still surface periodically. China is now Taiwan's main export market. Its major exports are electronic goods and petrochemicals.

AREA 13,900 sq mi [36,000 sq km] **POPULATION** 23,572,000
CAPITAL Taipei **GOVERNMENT** Unitary multiparty republic
ETHNIC GROUPS Taiwanese 84%, mainland Chinese 14%
LANGUAGES Mandarin Chinese (official), Min, Hakka
RELIGIONS Buddhism, Taoism, Christianity
CURRENCY New Taiwan dollar = 100 cents

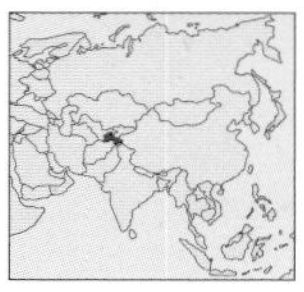

TAJIKISTAN

GEOGRAPHY The Republic of Tajikistan is one of the five central Asian republics that formed part of the former Soviet Union. Only 7% of the land is below 3,280 ft [1,000 m], while almost all of eastern Tajikistan is above 9,840 ft [3,000 m]. The highest point is Pik Imeni Ismail Samani (formerly known as Communism Peak or Pik Kommunizma), which reaches 24,590 ft [7,495 m]. The main ranges are the westward extension of the Tian Shan Range in the north and the snow-capped Pamirs in the southeast. Earthquakes are common throughout the country. The climate is continental, with hot, dry summers in the lower valleys and bitterly cold winters, especially in the mountains.

POLITICS & ECONOMY Russia conquered parts of Tajikistan in the late 19th century, and by 1920 Russia took complete control. In 1924, Tajikistan became part of the Uzbek Soviet Socialist Republic, but, in 1929, it was expanded, taking in some areas populated by Uzbeks, becoming the Tajik Soviet Socialist Republic.

While the Soviet Union began to introduce reforms during the 1980s, many Tajiks demanded freedom. In 1989, the Tajik government made Tajik the official language instead of Russian and, in 1990, it stated that its local laws overruled Soviet ones. Tajikistan became fully independent in 1991, following the breakup of the Soviet Union. In 1992, civil war broke out between the government, which was run by former Communists, and an alliance of democrats and Islamic forces. A ceasefire was agreed in 1996. In 2020, Emomali Rahmon, president since 1994, was re-elected for a fifth term. His rule has become increasingly autocratic and elections have been tainted by fraud, including his banning of the main opposition party in 2015.

Tajikistan is the poorest country in Central Asia and many people have left to work in Russia. Economic hardship has fueled rising interest in radical Islam. The country relies on Russia both economically and for security, but is fostering links with China. It struggles with its position on the drug transit route from neighboring Afghanistan. Cotton, grains, and fruits are the main crops. It produces aluminum, and has mineral resources and hydroelectric potential.

AREA 55,521 sq mi [143,100 sq km] **POPULATION** 8,991,000
CAPITAL Dushanbe **GOVERNMENT** Republic
ETHNIC GROUPS Tajik 80%, Uzbek 15%, Russian 1%, Kyrgyz 1%
LANGUAGES Tajik (official), Russian
RELIGIONS Islam (Sunni Muslim 95%, Shia Muslim 3%)
CURRENCY Somoni = 100 dirams

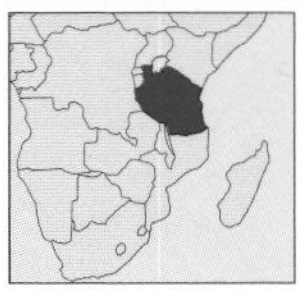

TANZANIA

GEOGRAPHY The United Republic of Tanzania consists of the former mainland country of Tanganyika and the island nation of Zanzibar, which also includes the island of Pemba. Behind a narrow coastal plain, most of Tanzania is a plateau, which is broken by arms of the Great African Rift Valley. In the west, this valley contains lakes Nyasa and Tanganyika. The highest peak is Kilimanjaro, Africa's highest mountain at 19,340 ft [5,895 m].

The coast has a hot and humid climate, with the greatest rainfall in April and May. The inland plateaux and mountains are cooler and less humid.

POLITICS & ECONOMY Mainland Tanganyika became a German territory in the 1880s, while Zanzibar and Pemba became a British protectorate in 1890. Following Germany's defeat in World War I, Britain took over Tanganyika, which remained a British territory until its independence in 1961. In 1964, Tanganyika and Zanzibar united to form the United Republic of Tanzania. The country's president from 1962 until 1985, Julius Nyerere, pursued socialist policies of self-help and egalitarianism. Many social reforms were successful, though the country failed to make economic progress. John Magufuli, president from 2015 until his death in 2021, attempted to improve the economy by developing the country's infrastructure.

Crops are grown on only 4% of the land, yet agriculture employs about 65% of the people and provides 65% of exports.

Food crops include bananas, cassava, and maize. Gold, coffee, tea, tobacco, and cashews are exported. Offshore gas fields have been discovered.

AREA 364,899 sq mi [945,090 sq km] **POPULATION** 62,093,000
CAPITAL Dodoma **GOVERNMENT** Multiparty republic
ETHNIC GROUPS Native African 99% (of which 95% are Bantu consisting of more than 130 tribes)
LANGUAGES Swahili (Kiswahili) and English (both official)
RELIGIONS Islam 35% (99% in Zanzibar), traditional beliefs 35%, Christianity 30%
CURRENCY Tanzanian shilling = 100 cents

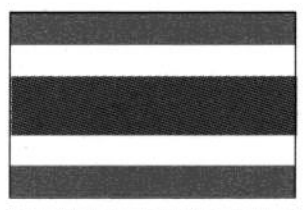
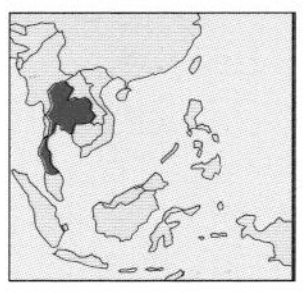

THAILAND

GEOGRAPHY The Kingdom of Thailand is one of the ten countries in Southeast Asia. The highest land is in the north, where Doi Inthanon, the highest peak, reaches 8,415 ft [2,565 m]. The Khorat plateau, in the north-east, makes up about 30% of the country and is the most heavily populated part of Thailand. In the south, Thailand shares the finger-like Malay peninsula with Burma and Malaysia.

Thailand has a tropical climate. Monsoon winds from the south-west bring heavy rains in May to October. Mountains shelter the central plains from the rain-bearing winds.

POLITICS & ECONOMY The first Thai state was set up in the 13th century and, by 1350, it included most of what is now Thailand. European contact began in the early 16th century, but their interference was unwelcome and, by the late 17th century, all Europeans were forced to leave. In 1782, a Thai General, Chao Phraya Chakkri, became king, founding a dynasty which continues today. The country became known as Siam. From the mid-19th century, contacts with the West were restored. In World War I, Siam supported the Allies against Germany and Austria–Hungary although in 1941 it was aligned with Japan against the UK and US.

After 1967, when Thailand became a member of ASEAN (Association of Southeast Asian Nations), its economy expanded rapidly. In 1997, with other eastern Asian economies, it suffered an economic recession. Thailand has also faced conflict in the south, where the government has clashed with minority Muslim groups. In 2001, Thaksin Shinawatra, a businessman, became prime minister. In 2006, his party won a majority, the result of a boycott by opposition parties. Following mass protests, a military junta took power until civilian rule was restored in 2007. In 2011, Thaksin's sister, Yingluck Shinawatra, was elected prime minister. Elections held in early 2014 were later declared invalid and the military took control, with General Prayuth Chan-ocha appointed prime minister. In disputed elections in 2019 his position was formally confirmed.

Classified as an "upper-middle-income country," Thailand has a well-developed infrastructure and an export-led economy. Agriculture employs 32% of the people and rice is the chief crop. Cassava, maize, rubber, sugarcane, and tobacco are also grown. Tin is mined, but the chief exports are manufactures and food products. Tourism plays a significant part in the economy.

AREA 198,114 sq mi [513,115 sq km] **POPULATION** 69,481,000
CAPITAL Bangkok **GOVERNMENT** Constitutional monarchy
ETHNIC GROUPS Thai 75%, Chinese 14%, others 11%
LANGUAGES Thai (official), English, ethnic and regional dialects
RELIGIONS Buddhism 95%, Islam, Christianity
CURRENCY Thai baht = 100 satang

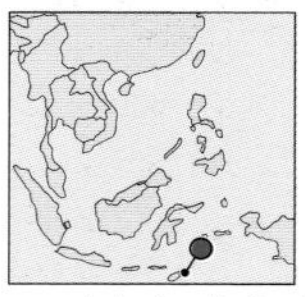

TIMOR-LESTE

The Republic of Timor-Leste (East Timor) is mainly rugged. Temperatures are generally high and the rainfall is moderate. Portugal, the ruling colonial power, withdrew in 1975 and Indonesia seized control. Brutal suppression by Indonesia led to a vote for independence in 1999, which came into force in 2002. Support from the UN and Australia was crucial in bringing stability and allowing reconstruction. In 2006, Timor-Leste and Australia signed a deal to share the revenue from oil and natural gas deposits under the Timor Sea. Its economy is now dominated by oil, and the challenge is to diversify. Agriculture employs 40% of the work force. Crops include rice, maize, cassava, and sweet potatoes.

AREA 5,743 sq mi [14,874 sq km] **POPULATION** 1,414,000 **CAPITAL** Dili

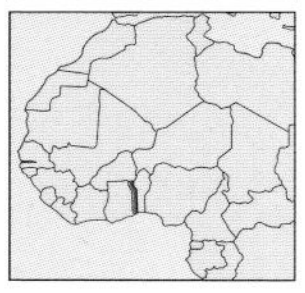

TOGO

GEOGRAPHY The Republic of Togo is a long, narrow country in West Africa. From north to south, it extends about 311 mi [500 km]. Its coastline on the Gulf of Guinea is only 40 mi [64 km] long and it is only 90 mi [145 km] at its widest point.

Togo's climate is generally tropical, and it has high temperatures all through the year. The main wet season is from March to July, with a minor wet season in October and November.

POLITICS & ECONOMY Togo became a German protectorate in 1884, but, in 1919, Britain took over the western third of the territory, while France took over the eastern two-thirds. In 1956, the people of British Togoland voted to join Ghana, while French Togoland became an independent republic in 1960.

A military regime took power in 1963. In 1967, General Gnassingbé Eyadéma became head of state, a position he maintained until his death in 2005. Elections held during this period were deemed unfair and were boycotted by opposition parties. His son, Faure Gnassingbé, took over as president, but international pressure forced him to step down. He was, however, elected later that year, and re-elected in 2010, 2015, and 2020. There are occasional protests against the family's rule.

Togo is a poor, developing country dependent on agriculture. Major food crops include cassava, maize, millet, and yams. Togo is one of the world's largest producers and exporters of phosphates. Economic growth will depend on reforms and foreign assistance.

AREA 21,925 sq mi [56,785 sq km] **POPULATION** 8,283,000
CAPITAL Lomé **GOVERNMENT** Multiparty republic
ETHNIC GROUPS Native African 99% (largest tribes are Ewe, Mina and Kabre) **LANGUAGES** French (official), African languages
RELIGIONS Traditional beliefs 51%, Christianity 29%, Islam 20%
CURRENCY CFA franc = 100 centimes

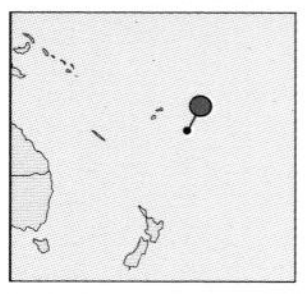

TONGA

The Kingdom of Tonga, a former British protectorate, became independent in 1970. Situated in the south Pacific Ocean, it contains more than 170 islands, 36 of which are inhabited. In 2010, Tonga held its first election for a popularly elected parliament. Agriculture is the main activity and unemployment is high.

AREA 251 sq mi [650 sq km] **POPULATION** 106,000 **CAPITAL** Nuku'alofa

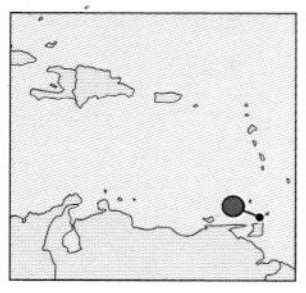

TRINIDAD AND TOBAGO

The Republic of Trinidad and Tobago became independent from Britain in 1962. These tropical islands, populated by people of African, Asian (mainly Indian) and European origin, are hilly and forested, though there are some fertile plains. Oil and natural gas production is the mainstay of the economy.

AREA 1,981 sq mi [5,130 sq km]
POPULATION 1,221,000 **CAPITAL** Port of Spain

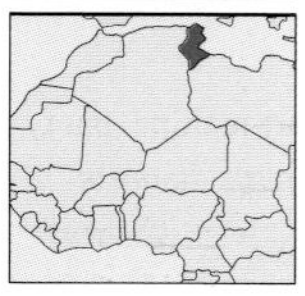

TUNISIA

GEOGRAPHY The Republic of Tunisia is the smallest country in North Africa. The mountains in the north are an eastward and comparatively low extension of the Atlas Mountains. To the north and east of the mountains lie fertile plains, especially between Sfax, Tunis, and Bizerte. In the south, low-lying regions contain the Chott Djerid, a vast salt pan, part of the Sahara.

Northern Tunisia has a Mediterranean climate, with dry, sunny summers, and mild winters with a moderate rainfall. The average yearly rainfall decreases toward the south.

POLITICS & ECONOMY Phoenicians first settled in what is now Tunisia in about 1100 BC. It later became of strategic importance to Romans, Arabs and Ottoman Turks, and was ruled by France from 1881 to 1956. The monarchy was abolished and Tunisia declared a republic in 1957, with the nationalist leader, Habib Bourguiba, as president. His government introduced reforms, including votes for women, but problems included unemployment among the middle class and fears that the ideas of Western visitors might undermine Muslim values. In 1987, the prime minister, Zine el Abidine Ben Ali, removed Bourguiba, and became president. He was re-elected five times until, in 2011, anti-government demonstrations forced him to flee the country. Kais Saied assumed the presidency in 2019.

The World Bank classifies Tunisia as a "lower-middle-income" developing country. The main resources and chief exports are phosphates and oil. Manufactured products include garments and processed foods. Fishing is important. The tourist industry has been hit hard by the fallout from Islamic State terrorist attacks in 2015.

AREA 63,170 sq mi [163,610 sq km] **POPULATION** 11,811,000
CAPITAL Tunis **GOVERNMENT** Multiparty republic
ETHNIC GROUPS Arab 98%, European 1% **LANGUAGES** Arabic (official), French **RELIGIONS** Islam 98%, Christianity 1%, others
CURRENCY Tunisian dinar = 1,000 millimes

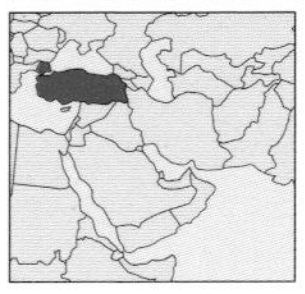

TURKEY

GEOGRAPHY The Republic of Turkey lies in two continents. European Turkey, also called Thrace, lies west of a waterway linking the Mediterranean and Black seas. Most of Asian Turkey consists of plateaux and mountains, which rise to 16,945 ft [5,165 m] at Mount Ararat, near the border with Armenia. Earthquakes are common. Central Turkey has a dry climate, with hot, sunny summers and cold winters. The west has a Mediterranean climate, but the Black Sea coast has cooler summers.

POLITICS & ECONOMY In AD 330, the Roman empire moved its capital to Byzantium, which it renamed Constantinople. Muslim Seljuk Turks from central Asia invaded Anatolia (Asian Turkey) in the 11th century. In the 14th century, another group of Turks, the Ottomans, conquered the area and, in 1453, they took Constantinople, renaming it Istanbul. The Ottomans built up a vast empire which collapsed during World War I (1914–18). Turkey became a republic in 1923 and Mustafa Kemal, or Atatürk ("father of the Turks"), began to modernize and secularize the country.

Turkey has enjoyed democracy since 1983 after a period of political instability and military coups. Elections in 1996 resulted in Turkey's first pro-Islamic government in more than 70 years. It was forced from power the following year, but after a period of secular government, pro-Islamic rule returned in 2002. Recep Tayyip Erdogan of the Islamic Justice and Development Party (AKP) served as prime minister from 2003 to 2014, and, despite some public concerns about his Islamist roots, president from 2014. A failed coup in 2016 was followed by a referendum on giving the president more powers. The result was a disputed narrow victory for Erdogan, who went on to win a further term as president in 2018.

Since the 1940s, Turkey has sought to strengthen its ties with Western powers. It joined NATO in 1951 and it applied to join the European Economic Community in 1987. Turkey's conflict with Greece, together with its invasion of northern Cyprus in 1974, has led many Europeans to treat its aspirations to full EU membership with caution. There is ongoing conflict with Kurdish nationalists in eastern Turkey. The war in Syria has increased tensions along the border, and Turkey has carried out several attacks on Kurdish areas of Syria and Iraq. There is concern about the country's record on human rights.

Turkey came close to economic collapse in 2002, but its recovery enabled it to withstand the global financial crisis in 2008, and bounce back by 2010–11. However, the economy is vulnerable to political instability in the region and investor confidence. Agriculture employs 20% of the people, with barley, cotton, fruits, nuts, maize, tobacco, and wheat being the major crops. Manufactures include petrochemicals, vehicles, and textiles.

AREA 299,156 sq mi [774,815 sq km] **POPULATION** 82,482,000
CAPITAL Ankara **GOVERNMENT** Multiparty republic
ETHNIC GROUPS Turkish 73%, Kurdish 18%
LANGUAGES Turkish (official), Kurdish, Arabic
RELIGIONS Islam (mainly Sunni Muslim) 99%
CURRENCY Turkish lira = 100 kurus

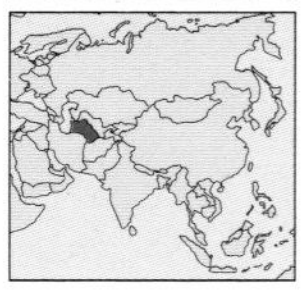

TURKMENISTAN

GEOGRAPHY The Republic of Turkmenistan is one of the five central Asian republics which once formed part of the former Soviet Union. Most of the land is low-lying, with mountains stretching along the southern and south-western borders. In the west lies the salty Caspian Sea. Most of Turkmenistan is arid and the Garagum (Kara Kum), Asia's largest sand

desert, covers about 80% of the country. Turkmenistan has a continental climate, with average annual rainfall varying from 3 inches [80 mm] in the desert to 12 inches [300 mm] in the mountains. Summer months are hot, but winter temperatures drop well below freezing point.

POLITICS & ECONOMY Just over 1,000 years ago, Turkic people settled in the lands east of the Caspian Sea and the name "Turkmen" dates from this time. Mongol armies conquered the area in the 13th century and Islam was introduced in the 14th century. Russia took over the area in the 1870s and 1880s. The area came under Communist rule in 1917 and, in 1924, it became the Turkmen Soviet Socialist Republic.

In the 1980s, when the Soviet Union began to introduce reforms, the Turkmen began to demand more freedom and, in 1991, asserted that their own laws held sway over those of Soviet Russia. In late 1991, Turkmenistan became fully independent although the country maintained ties with Russia through the Commonwealth of Independent States (CIS).

In 1992, Turkmenistan adopted a new constitution, allowing for the setting up of political parties, providing that they were not ethnic or religious in character. But, effectively, Turkmenistan remained a one-party state and, in 1992, Saparmurad Niyazov, the former Communist and at that time Democratic Party leader, was the only presidential candidate. In 1999, parliament declared Niyazov president for life. Niyazov died in 2006 and was succeeded by Gurbanguly Berdymukhamedov. He was returned to power in undemocratic elections in 2012 and 2017.

Faced with many economic problems, Turkmenistan began to look south rather than to the CIS for support. In 1992, it joined the Economic Cooperation Organization, which had been set up in 1985 by Iran, Pakistan, and Turkey. Oil and natural gas are the chief resources and most valuable exports. Gas pipelines to Iran opened in 1998 and 2010, but most is now exported to China via a pipeline opened in 2009. A pipeline to India, via Afghanistan and Pakistan, is under construction. Agriculture remains important, with cotton as the main commercial crop. Manufactures include cement, glass, petrochemicals, and textiles.

AREA 188,455 sq mi [488,100 sq km] **POPULATION** 5,580,000
CAPITAL Ashkhabad **GOVERNMENT** Single-party republic
ETHNIC GROUPS Turkmen 85%, Uzbek 5%, Russian 4%
LANGUAGES Turkmen (official), Russian, Uzbek
RELIGIONS Islam 89%, Eastern Orthodox 9%
CURRENCY Turkmen manat = 100 tenge

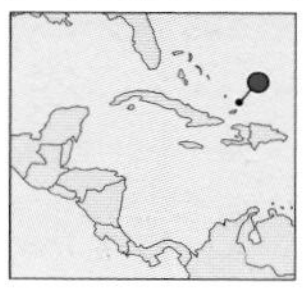

TURKS AND CAICOS ISLANDS

The Turks and Caicos Islands, a British territory since 1776, are a group of about 30 islands. Fishing, tourism, and offshore finance are the major economic activities.

AREA 166 sq mi [430 sq km]
POPULATION 57,000 **CAPITAL** Cockburn Town

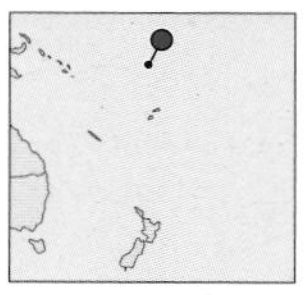

TUVALU

Tuvalu, formerly called the Ellice Islands, was a British territory from the 1890s until it became independent in 1978. It consists of nine low-lying coral atolls in the southern Pacific Ocean. Copra is the only significant export. It is vulnerable to rising sea levels.

AREA 10 sq mi [26 sq km]
POPULATION 11,000 **CAPITAL** Funafuti

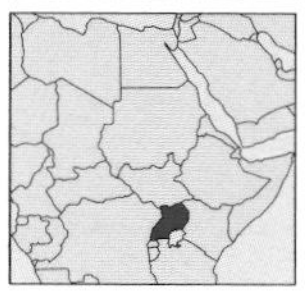

UGANDA

GEOGRAPHY The Republic of Uganda is a landlocked country on the East African plateau. It contains part of Lake Victoria, Africa's largest lake and a source of the River Nile, which occupies a shallow depression in the plateau. The equator runs through Uganda, and the country is warm throughout the year, though the high altitude moderates the temperature. The wettest regions are the lands to the north of Lake Victoria, where the capital, Kampala, is situated, and the western mountains, especially the high Ruwenzori range.

POLITICS & ECONOMY Little is known of the early history of Uganda. When Europeans first reached the area in the 19th century, many of the people were organized in kingdoms, the most powerful of which was Buganda, the home of the Baganda people. Britain took control of the country between 1894 and 1914, and administered it until independence in 1962.

In 1967, Uganda became a republic and Buganda's Kabaka (king), Sir Edward Mutesa II, was made president. But tensions between the Kabaka and the prime minister, Apollo Milton Obote, led to the dismissal of the Kabaka in 1966. Obote also abolished the traditional kingdoms, including Buganda. Obote was overthrown in 1971 by an army group led by General Idi Amin Dada. Amin ruled as a dictator: he forced most of the Asians who lived in Uganda to leave the country and had many of his opponents killed.

In 1978, a border dispute between Uganda and Tanzania led Tanzanian troops to enter Uganda. With help from Ugandan opponents of Amin, they overthrew Amin's government. In 1980, Obote led his party to victory in the elections, but following charges of fraud, Obote's opponents instigated a guerrilla war. A military group overthrew Obote in 1985, though strife continued until 1986, when Yoweri Museveni's National Resistance Movement seized power. In 1993, Museveni restored the traditional kingdoms. Elections were held in 1994, but political parties were forbidden. Museveni was re-elected five times between 1996 and 2016. From the late 1980s, Uganda faced the rebel Lord's Resistance Army in the north. Their brutal activities extended into the Central African Republic, the Democratic Republic of the Congo, and Sudan, but were substantially reduced by the mid-2010s. By 2017, more than a million South Sudanese fleeing civil war had sought refuge in Uganda.

Agriculture dominates the economy, employing over 70% of the work force. Chief exports are coffee and gold. Economic reforms and some investment in infrastructure have resulted in a strengthening of the economy. Challenges include corruption and rapid population growth. Newly discovered oil will be a valuable asset.

AREA 93,065 sq mi [241,038 sq km] **POPULATION** 44,712,000
CAPITAL Kampala **GOVERNMENT** Republic
ETHNIC GROUPS Baganda 17%, Ankole 8%, Basogo 8%, Iteso 8%, Bakiga 7%, Langi 6%, Rwanda 6%, Bagisu 5%, Acholi 4%, Lugbara 4%, and others
LANGUAGES English and Swahili (both official), Ganda
RELIGIONS Roman Catholic 42%, Protestant 42%, Islam 12%, traditional beliefs 4%
CURRENCY Ugandan shilling

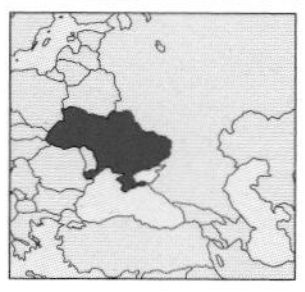

UKRAINE

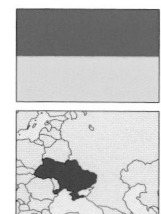

GEOGRAPHY Ukraine is the second largest country in Europe after Russia. It was formerly part of the Soviet Union, which split apart in 1991. This mostly flat country faces the Black Sea in the south. The Crimean peninsula includes a highland region overlooking Yalta. Ukraine has warm summers, but the winters are cold, becoming more severe from west to east. In the summer, the east is often warmer than the west. Most rain falls in the summer months.

POLITICS & ECONOMY Kiev was the original capital of the early Slavic civilization known as Kievan Rus. In the 17th and 18th centuries, parts of Ukraine came under Polish and Russian rule, but, by the late 18th century, Russia had gained most of Ukraine. In 1918, Ukraine gained independence, but only until 1922 when it became part of the Soviet Union.

In the 1980s, Ukrainian people demanded more say over their affairs and regained their independence in 1991. In the early 21st century, Ukraine has been pulled in two directions – either closer integration with Russia or with the EU. In 2005, the pro-Western leader Viktor Yushchenko was elected president. Economic problems, and political infighting, led to a Russian-leaning party, led by Viktor Yanukovych, winning most seats in parliament in 2006. An election in 2007 resulted in a pro-Western coalition government led by Yulia Tymoshenko. In 2010, the pro-Russian Viktor Yanukovych was declared winner of the presidential election, but in 2013–14 mass protests over his backtracking on a cooperation agreement with the EU forced him from power. Russia subsequently invaded, seized Crimea, and sent troops into other parts of eastern Ukraine, where unrest continues. The annexation of Crimea has not been recognized by Ukraine or the wider world. A pro-Western government has been in power since 2014. The actor Volodymyr Zelensky became president in 2019.

Manufacturing is the chief economic activity including iron and steel, machinery, and vehicles. Ukraine has large coalfields and its own hydroelectric and nuclear power plants, but the country imports oil and natural gas (much of it from Russia). Agriculture contributes 13% of GDP; export crops include maize, barley, wheat, and oil seeds.

AREA 233,089 sq mi [603,700 sq km] **POPULATION** 43,746,000
CAPITAL Kiev **GOVERNMENT** Multiparty republic
ETHNIC GROUPS Ukrainian 78%, Russian 17%, Belarusian, Moldovan, Bulgarian, Hungarian, Polish
LANGUAGES Ukrainian (official), Russian
RELIGIONS Mostly Ukrainian Orthodox
CURRENCY Hryvnia = 100 kopiykas

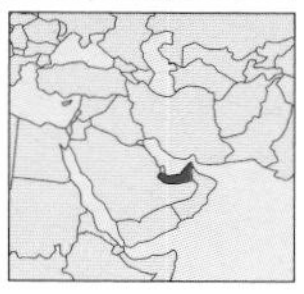

UNITED ARAB EMIRATES

The United Arab Emirates (UAE) were formed in 1971 when the seven Trucial States of the Persian Gulf (Abu Dhabi, Dubai, Sharjah, Ajman, Umm al Qawayn, Ra's al Khaymah, and Al Fujayrah) joined together. The economy of this hot and dry state depends on oil production, and the resulting revenues give the UAE one of the highest per capita GDPs in Asia. Tourism and finance are important sources of revenue.

AREA 32,278 sq mi [83,600 sq km]
POPULATION 9,875,000 **CAPITAL** Abu Dhabi

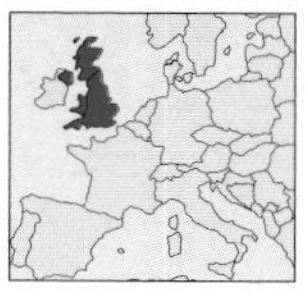

UNITED KINGDOM

GEOGRAPHY The United Kingdom (or UK) is a union of four countries. Three of them – England, Scotland, and Wales – make up Great Britain. The fourth country is Northern Ireland. The Isle of Man and the Channel Islands are not part of the UK. They are self-governing British dependencies.

The land is highly varied. Much of Scotland and Wales is mountainous, and the highest peak is Scotland's Ben Nevis at 4,411 ft [1,345 m]. England has some highland areas, including the Cumbrian Mountains (or Lake District) and the Pennine range in the north, but it also has extensive areas of fertile lowland. Northern Ireland is also a mixture of lowlands and uplands and it contains the UK's largest lake, Lough Neagh.

The UK has a mild climate, influenced by the warm North Atlantic Drift which is a continuation of the Gulf Stream originating from the Gulf of Mexico. Moist winds from the southwest bring rain, but the rainfall decreases from west to east. Winds from the east and north bring cold weather in winter.

POLITICS & ECONOMY In ancient times, Britain was invaded by many peoples, including Iberians, Celts, Romans, Angles, Saxons, Jutes, Norsemen, Danes, and the Normans, who arrived in 1066. King Edward I annexed Wales in 1282 and united it with England. Union with Scotland was achieved in 1707 and this created a country known as the United Kingdom of Great Britain.

Ireland came under Norman rule in the 11th century, and much of its later history was concerned with a struggle against English domination. In 1801, Ireland became part of the United Kingdom of Great Britain and Ireland. But in 1921, southern Ireland, where most of the people were Roman Catholics, broke away to become the Irish Free State. In Northern Ireland, where the majority of the people were Protestants, most people wanted to remain citizens of the United Kingdom. The country now became the United Kingdom of Great Britain and Northern Ireland.

The modern history of the UK began in the 18th century with the expansion of the British empire, despite the loss in 1783 of its 13 North American colonies. The other significant milestone occurred in the late 18th century, when the UK became the first country to industrialize its economy.

The 20th century was marked by the UK's involvement in both World War I (1914–18) and World War II (1939–45). The British empire then broke up, although the UK still administers many small, mainly island, territories around the world. The empire was transformed into the Commonwealth of Nations, a free association of independent countries which numbered 54 in 2020.

The UK was a founding member of NATO in 1949, and it has retained an important world role. In 2001, it played a prominent role in creating a broad alliance to counter international terrorism following attacks on the United States. It was also part of the coalition force which invaded Iraq in 2003. It became a member of the European Economic Community (now the European Union) in 1973. Whilst membership of the EU was important to the British economy, some feared a loss of British sovereignty and identity. A referendum in June 2016 on the UK's future in the EU resulted in a narrow vote to leave. Following long negotiations, the UK left at the end of January 2020.

Since the late 1990s some powers have been devolved to Scotland, Wales, and Northern Ireland. The Northern

Ireland Assembly has followed a fitful path since its establishment in 1998, and was suspended between 2017 and 2020. The National Assembly for Wales and the Scottish Parliament both opened in 1999. In a referendum on Scottish independence held in 2014, 55% of voters elected to stay within the UK.

The UK is a major industrial and trading nation. Natural resources include coal and iron ore, as well as dwindling reserves of oil and natural gas. It imports most of the materials for its industries. The UK also has to import food, because it produces only about two-thirds of the food it needs. In the first half of the 20th century, Britain was a major exporter of cars, ships, steel, and textiles. But many industries have suffered from competition from countries with lower labor costs. From 2008, Britain's economy was hit by a global financial crisis, which led the country into recession. Severe austerity measures were introduced. The country was particularly badly hit by the Covid-19 pandemic of 2020–21.

The UK is one of the world's most urbanized countries, and agriculture employs only 1% of the work force. Production is high because of the use of scientific methods and modern machinery. However, in the early 21st century, especially following the outbreak of foot-and-mouth disease in 2001, questions were raised about the future of rural industries. Major crops include barley, potatoes, sugar beet, and wheat. Sheep are the leading livestock, but beef and dairy cattle, pigs, and poultry are also important. Fishing is a major activity. It remains to be seen how the UK's economy will be affected by its departure from the EU.

Service industries play a major part in the UK's economy. Financial and insurance services bring in much-needed foreign exchange, while tourism has long been a major earner.

AREA 93,381 SQ MI [241,857 SQ KM] **POPULATION** 66,052,000
CAPITAL LONDON **GOVERNMENT** CONSTITUTIONAL MONARCHY
ETHNIC GROUPS ENGLISH 84%, SCOTTISH 9%, WELSH 5%, N. IRISH 3%, WEST INDIAN, INDIAN, PAKISTANI AND OTHERS
LANGUAGES ENGLISH (OFFICIAL), WELSH, GAELIC
RELIGIONS CHRISTIANITY (ANGLICAN, ROMAN CATHOLIC, PRESBYTERIAN, METHODIST), ISLAM, SIKHISM, HINDUISM, JUDAISM
CURRENCY POUND STERLING = 100 PENCE

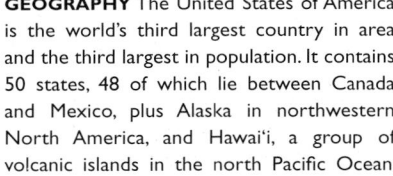

UNITED STATES OF AMERICA

GEOGRAPHY The United States of America is the world's third largest country in area and the third largest in population. It contains 50 states, 48 of which lie between Canada and Mexico, plus Alaska in northwestern North America, and Hawai'i, a group of volcanic islands in the north Pacific Ocean. Densely populated coastal plains lie to the east and south of the Appalachian Mountains. The central lowlands, drained by the Mississippi–Missouri rivers, stretch from the Appalachians to the Rocky Mountains in the west. The Pacific region contains fertile valleys, separated by mountain ranges.

The climate varies greatly, ranging from the Arctic cold of Alaska to the intense heat of Death Valley, a bleak desert in California. Of the 48 states between Canada and Mexico, winters are cold and snowy in the north, but mild in the south.

POLITICS & ECONOMY The first people in North America, the ancestors of the Native Americans (or American Indians), arrived perhaps 40,000 years ago from Asia. Although Vikings probably reached North America 1,000 years ago, European exploration proper did not begin until the late 15th century.

The first Europeans to settle in large numbers were the British, who founded settlements on the eastern coast in the early 17th century. British rule ended in the War of Independence (1775–83). The country expanded in 1803 when a vast territory in the south and west was acquired through the Louisiana Purchase, while the border with Mexico was fixed in the mid-19th century. The Civil War (1861–65) ended slavery and the serious threat that the nation might split into two parts. In the late 19th century, the West was opened up, while immigrants flooded in from Europe and elsewhere.

During the late 19th and early 20th centuries, industrialization led to the United States becoming the world's leading economic superpower and a pioneer in science and technology. It took on the mantle of the champion of Western democracy and, following the breakup of the Soviet Union, it became the world's only superpower. But the attacks on the country on September 11, 2001, revealed its vulnerability to terrorists and rogue states. The response was vigorous. In 2001, it attacked the Taliban government in Afghanistan, which was protecting al Qaeda terrorists. Then, in 2003, it led a coalition force to invade Iraq and overthrow Saddam Hussein.

In 2008, Democrat Barack Obama became the US's first black president. He prioritized the reform of health care. Bitterly fought elections in 2016 resulted in a win for Republican businessman Donald Trump. He served one term, during which he pursued an isolationist "America First" policy, imposing high import tariffs, cutting taxes, and discouraging immigration. Tension with the Middle East increased, notably with Iran, and he withdrew the US from the Paris Agreement aimed at tackling global warming. The Democrat Joe Biden achieved a narrow victory in the 2020 presidential election, promising to work toward uniting an increasingly divided nation and to re-engage with international diplomacy.

The US economy has long been one of the world's largest, but some authorities now see it being challenged by China. Recovery from the global financial crisis of 2008 has been slow. There is a wide disparity between rich and poor, and as many as 30 million Americans live below the poverty line. The US has been badly affected by the global outbreak of coronavirus in 2020, and the long-term effects on the economy are likely to be severe.

Natural resources include oil, natural gas, coal, metal ores, timber, and arable land. Manufacturing employs around 10% of the work force; major products include vehicles, food products, chemicals, machinery, printed goods, metal products, and scientific instruments. California, with its many high-tech electronics industries, is the top manufacturing state.

AREA 3,717,792 SQ MI [9,629,091 SQ KM] **POPULATION** 334,998,000
CAPITAL WASHINGTON, DC **GOVERNMENT** FEDERAL REPUBLIC
ETHNIC GROUPS WHITE 80%, AFRICAN AMERICAN 13%, ASIAN 4%, AMERINDIAN 1%, OTHERS
LANGUAGES ENGLISH, SPANISH, MORE THAN 30 OTHERS
RELIGIONS PROTESTANT 51%, ROMAN CATHOLIC 24%, JUDAISM 2%, MORMON 2%, ISLAM 1% **CURRENCY** US DOLLAR = 100 CENTS

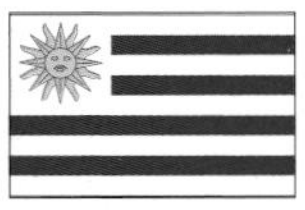

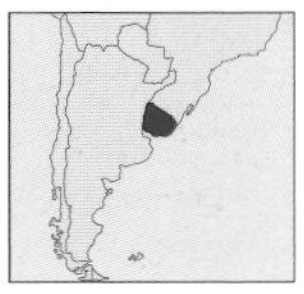

URUGUAY

GEOGRAPHY Uruguay is South America's second smallest independent country after Suriname. The land consists mainly of flat plains and hills. The River Uruguay, which forms the country's western border, flows into the Río de la Plata, a large estuary which leads into the South Atlantic Ocean.

Uruguay has a mild climate, with rain in every month, though droughts sometimes can occur. Summers are pleasantly warm and winters relatively mild.

POLITICS & ECONOMY In 1726, Spanish settlers founded Montevideo in order to halt the Portuguese gaining influence in the area. By the late 18th century, Spaniards had settled in most of the country and Uruguay became part of a colony called the Viceroyalty of La Plata, which also included Argentina, Paraguay, and parts of Bolivia, Brazil, and Chile. In 1820 Brazil annexed Uruguay, ending Spanish rule. In 1825, Uruguayans, supported by Argentina, began a struggle for independence.

Finally, in 1828, Brazil and Argentina recognized Uruguay as an independent republic. Social and economic developments were slow, but, from 1903, Uruguay became stable and democratic.

From the 1950s, economic problems incited unrest from terrorist groups, notably the Tupumaros, until the army took over the government in 1973. Military rule continued until elections were held in 1984. In the early 21st century, Uruguay faced economic problems, many of which were the result of the economic crisis in Argentina. Following the election of the country's first leftist president, Tabaré Vázquez, in 2005, Uruguay became increasingly liberal, with a generous welfare state and good levels of education. Vázquez served from 2005–10 and again from 2015–20.

The World Bank now classifies Uruguay as a "high-income" economy but, although it is one of the more prosperous countries in South America, there is still a minority underclass living in poverty. Agriculture employs 13% of the work force, and farm products, notably hides and leather goods, beef, and wool, are the main exports, while many manufacturing industries process farm products. Crops include maize, potatoes, wheat, and sugar beet. Uruguay depends largely on renewable power for energy, notably hydropower, wind and solar.

AREA 67,574 SQ MI [175,016 SQ KM] **POPULATION** 3,398,000
CAPITAL MONTEVIDEO **GOVERNMENT** MULTIPARTY REPUBLIC
ETHNIC GROUPS WHITE 88%, MESTIZO 8%, MULATTO OR BLACK 4%
LANGUAGES SPANISH (OFFICIAL)
RELIGIONS CHRISTIANITY 58% (ROMAN CATHOLIC 47%), OTHERS
CURRENCY URUGUAYAN PESO = 100 CENTÉSIMOS

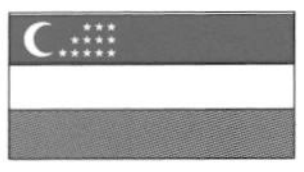

UZBEKISTAN

GEOGRAPHY The Republic of Uzbekistan is one of the five republics in Central Asia which were once part of the Soviet Union. Plains cover most of western Uzbekistan, with highlands in the east. The main rivers, the Amudarya and Syrdarya, drain into the Aral Sea. So much water has been taken from these rivers to irrigate the land to grow cotton that the Aral Sea has now shrunk to about a quarter of its size in 1960. The former lake area is now desert. Uzbekistan has cold winters and hot summers. The largely uninhabited Kyzyl Kum desert lies in central Uzbekistan.

POLITICS & ECONOMY Russia took the area in the 19th century. After the Russian Revolution of 1917, the Communists took over and, in 1924, they set up the Uzbek Soviet Socialist Republic. Under Communism, all aspects of Uzbek life were controlled and religious worship was discouraged, but education, health, housing, and transport were improved. In the late 1980s, the people demanded more autonomy, leading to independence in 1991 with the breakup of the Soviet Union.

Islam Karimov, leader of the People's Democratic Party (formerly the Communist Party), was first elected president in December 1991. Dissent was not tolerated and opposition leaders were arrested and accused of threatening national stability. Initially, Karimov's government allowed the US to use Uzbekistan as a base for its military campaign in Afghanistan, but relations cooled in 2005 and the US was asked to remove its troops. In an about-face in 2009, ties with Russia deteriorated and those with the US improved and they were again able to transport supplies through Uzbekistan to their troops. The United Nations has condemned the country's human rights record. Karimov remained in power until his death in 2016, when Prime Minister Shavjat Mirziyoyev was elected to replace him. Mirziyoyev has improved relations with neighboring countries and made moves to open up the economy.

The World Bank classifies Uzbekistan as a "lower-middle-income" developing country. Uzbekistan is one of the world's largest cotton exporters, although this has declined in recent years. The country produces coal, copper, gold, oil, and natural gas.

AREA 172,741 SQ MI [447,400 SQ KM] **POPULATION** 30,843,000
CAPITAL TASHKENT **GOVERNMENT** SOCIALIST REPUBLIC
ETHNIC GROUPS UZBEK 80%, RUSSIAN 5%, TAJIK 5%, KAZAKH 3%, TATAR 2%, KARA-KALPAK 2%
LANGUAGES UZBEK (OFFICIAL), RUSSIAN **RELIGIONS** ISLAM 88%, EASTERN ORTHODOX 9% **CURRENCY** UZBEKISTANI SUM = 100 TYIYN

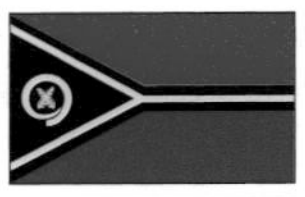

VANUATU

The Republic of Vanuatu, formerly the Anglo-French Condominium of the New Hebrides, became independent in 1980. It consists of a chain of 80 islands in the south Pacific Ocean. Its economy is based on agriculture, and it exports copra, beef and veal, timber, and cocoa.

AREA 4,706 SQ MI [12,189 SQ KM]
POPULATION 303,000 **CAPITAL** PORT-VILA

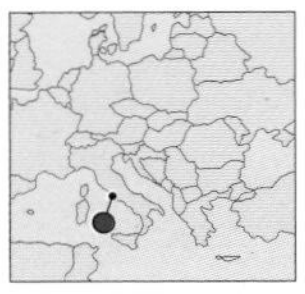

VATICAN CITY

Vatican City State, the world's smallest independent nation, is an enclave on the west bank of the River Tiber in Rome. It forms an independent base for the Holy See, the governing body of the Roman Catholic Church.

AREA 0.17 SQ MI [0.44 SQ KM]
POPULATION 1,000

VENEZUELA

GEOGRAPHY The Bolivarian Republic of Venezuela, in northern South America, contains the Maracaibo lowlands around the oil-rich Lake Maracaibo in the west. Andean ranges enclose the lowlands and extend across most of the northern part of the country. The Orinoco river basin, containing tropical grasslands called llanos, lies between the northern highlands and the Guiana Highlands in the southeast. The Orinoco is Venezuela's longest

river. Venezuela has a tropical climate. Rainfall is heaviest in the mountains, but much of the country has a dry season between December and April.

POLITICS & ECONOMY In the early 19th century, Venezuelans such as Simón Bolívar and Francisco de Miranda rebeled against Spanish colonial rule, leading to full independence in 1821.

The country has greatly benefited from its oil resources (first exploited in 1917) which are some of the world's largest. In 1960, Venezuela helped to form OPEC (the Organization of Petroleum Exporting Countries) and, in 1976, the government of Venezuela took control of the country's oil industry. In 1999, Hugo Chavez, who had staged an unsuccessful coup in 1992, was elected president, with social policies aimed at reducing poverty. He remained in office until his death in 2013 when he was succeeded by fellow socialist Nicolás Maduro. A severe economic downturn followed and Maduro's rule became increasingly autocratic. In 2018 he was re-elected, but the election was widely regarded as fraudulent. The result was declared invalid by the National Assembly, whose leader, Juan Guaidó, declared himself interim president in 2019. He is recognized as such by the EU, US and much of Latin America. Maduro, supported by the security forces, has refused to step down. The ongoing crisis has led to hyperinflation and shortages of food, medicines and electricity.

The political crisis, along with falling oil prices, devastated Venezuela's economy, which has long been dependent on petroleum refining and oil exports. But it is rich in natural resources, and other exports include iron ore, bauxite and aluminum. Beef cattle, dairy cattle, and poultry are raised. Crops include bananas, citrus fruits, coffee, and rice.

AREA 352,143 sq mi [912,050 sq km] **POPULATION** 29,069,000
CAPITAL Caracas **GOVERNMENT** Federal republic
ETHNIC GROUPS Spanish, Italian, Portuguese, Arab, German, African, indigenous people **LANGUAGES** Spanish (official), indigenous dialects **RELIGIONS** Roman Catholic 96%
CURRENCY Bolívar = 100 céntimos

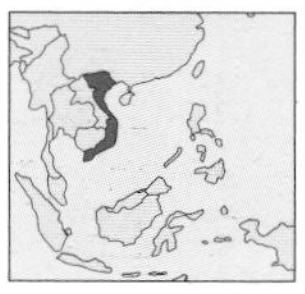

VIETNAM

GEOGRAPHY The Socialist Republic of Vietnam occupies an S-shaped strip of land facing the South China Sea in Southeast Asia. The coastal plains include two densely populated, fertile delta regions: the Red (Hong) delta facing the Gulf of Tonkin in the north, and the Mekong delta in the south.

Vietnam has a tropical climate, though the driest months of January to March are a little cooler than the wet, hot summer months, when monsoon winds blow from the southwest. Typhoons (cyclones or hurricanes) sometimes hit the coast, causing extensive flooding and much damage.

POLITICS & ECONOMY China dominated Vietnam for a thousand years before AD 939, when a Vietnamese state was founded. The French took over the area between the 1850s and 1880s, and they ruled Vietnam as part of French Indochina, which also included Cambodia and Laos.

Japan conquered Vietnam during World War II (1939–45). In 1946, war broke out between the Vietminh, a nationalist group, and the French colonial government. France withdrew in 1954 and Vietnam was divided into a Communist North Vietnam, led by the Vietminh leader, Ho Chi Minh, and a non-Communist South.

In 1957, a Communist insurgency, led by the Viet Cong, rebeled against South Vietnam's government, provoking a war that gradually escalated. The United States aided the South, but after it withdrew in 1975, South Vietnam surrendered. In 1976, the united Vietnam became a socialist republic. From the mid-1990s, diplomatic and trade relations were restored between the US and Vietnam, and the US is now its main trading partner. In 2007, Vietnam became a member of the World Trade Organization after 12 years of negotiations. The benefits of moves to modernize the economy have not been enjoyed by all groups in society: there is poverty in rural areas. Human rights issues remain a concern. Political power remains entirely in the hands of the ruling Communist Party.

Agriculture is the main activity although its share of economic output is diminishing. Rice and coffee are the main crops. Vietnam produces textiles, shoes, electronic goods, and phosphates.

AREA 128,065 sq mi [331,689 sq km] **POPULATION** 102,790,000
CAPITAL Hanoi **GOVERNMENT** Socialist republic
ETHNIC GROUPS Vietnamese 87%, Chinese, Hmong, Thai, Khmer, Cham, mountain groups
LANGUAGES Vietnamese (official), English, Chinese
RELIGIONS Buddhism, Christianity, indigenous beliefs
CURRENCY Dong = 10 hao = 100 xu

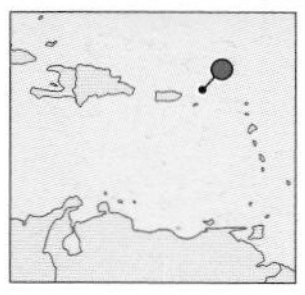

VIRGIN ISLANDS, BRITISH

The British Virgin Islands, the most northerly of the Lesser Antilles, are a British overseas territory, with a substantial measure of self-government.

AREA 58 sq mi [151 sq km]
POPULATION 38,000 **CAPITAL** Road Town

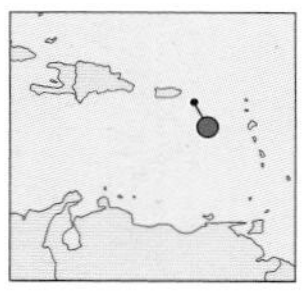

VIRGIN ISLANDS, US

The Virgin Islands of the United States, a group of three islands and 65 small islets, are a self-governing US territory, which was purchased from Denmark in 1917. Its residents are US citizens and they elect a non-voting delegate to the US House of Representatives.

AREA 134 sq mi [347 sq km]
POPULATION 106,000 **CAPITAL** Charlotte Amalie

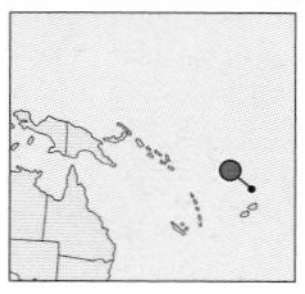

WALLIS AND FUTUNA

Wallis and Futuna, in the south Pacific Ocean, is the smallest and the poorest of France's overseas "collectivities." French aid is vital to an economy based on subsistence agriculture.

AREA 77 sq mi [200 sq km]
POPULATION 16,000 **CAPITAL** Mata-Utu

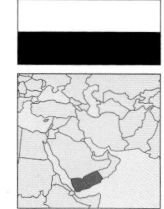

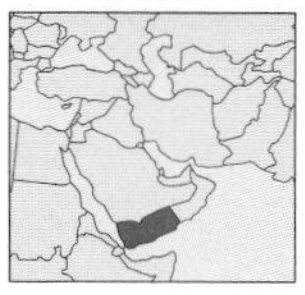

YEMEN

GEOGRAPHY The Republic of Yemen faces the Red Sea and the Gulf of Aden in the southwestern corner of the Arabian peninsula. Behind the narrow coastal plain along the Red Sea, the land rises to the mountains of the High Yemen. The climate ranges from hot and often humid conditions on the coast to the cooler highlands. Most of the country is arid. The south coasts are particularly hot and humid.

POLITICS & ECONOMY After World War I, northern Yemen, which had been ruled by Turkey, began to evolve into a separate state from the south, where Britain was in control. Britain withdrew in 1967 and a left-wing government took power in the south. In North Yemen, the monarchy was abolished in 1962 and the country became a republic.

Clashes occurred between the two factions but, in 1990, the two Yemens merged to form a single country. In the 2000s, the government faced conflict with Shi'ite northern rebels, called Houthis, al Qaeda supporters, and southern separatists. Protests in 2011 resulted in the resignation of President Ali Abdullah Saleh and a transfer of power to Abdrabbuh Mansour Hadi. The instability allowed the Houthi rebels to seize territory in the north. Civil war had taken hold by 2014. A Saudi-led coalition attacked the Houthi, while US drone strikes targeted Islamic State and al-Qaeda bases. However, the Houthi remain in control of much of the northwest of the country, including Sana'. The government is based in the city of Aden, where separatist unrest continues. The world's largest humanitarian crisis is unfolding, with a huge refugee crisis, thousands of civilian deaths, famine, and a major cholera outbreak.

Yemen is the poorest country in the Middle East, and its economy has been devastated by the civil war. Sheep are reared and crops such as barley, fruits, wheat, and vegetables are grown. Cash crops include khat, coffee, and cotton. Petroleum extraction is important to the economy, as are remittances from Yemenis abroad.

AREA 203,848 sq mi [527,968 sq km] **POPULATION** 30,399,000
CAPITAL Sana' **GOVERNMENT** Multiparty republic
ETHNIC GROUPS Predominantly Arab **LANGUAGES** Arabic (official)
RELIGIONS Islam **CURRENCY** Yemeni rial = 100 fils

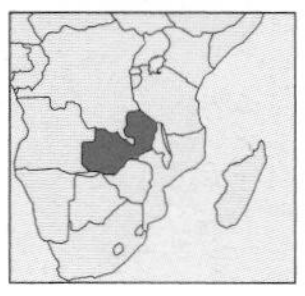

ZAMBIA

GEOGRAPHY The Republic of Zambia is a landlocked country in southern Africa. Zambia lies on the plateau that makes up most of the southern part of the continent. Much of the land is between 2,950 ft and 4,920 ft [900 m to 1,500 m] above sea level. The Muchinga Mountains in the northeast rise above this flat land. Lakes include Bangweulu, which is entirely within Zambia, together with parts of lakes Mweru and Tanganyika in the north. Zambia lies in the tropics, but temperatures are moderated by the altitude.

POLITICS & ECONOMY European contact with Zambia began in the 19th century, when the explorer David Livingstone crossed the River Zambezi. In the 1890s, the British South Africa Company, set up by Cecil Rhodes, the British financier and statesman, made treaties with local chiefs and gradually took over the area. In 1911, the Company named the area Northern Rhodesia and, in 1924, Britain took control of the country.

In 1953, Britain formed a federation of Northern Rhodesia, Southern Rhodesia (now Zimbabwe), and Nyasaland (now Malawi). Due to African opposition, the federation was dissolved in 1963 and Northern Rhodesia gained independence as Zambia in 1964. Kenneth Kaunda became president and remained in office for 27 years until Frederick Chiluba was elected in 1991. The current president, Edgar Lungu, took office in 2015.

Zambia's economy grew strongly in the early years of this century, until copper prices began to fall in 2015. Copper, however, remains the main resource, and the most valuable export. Zambia also produces cobalt, lead, zinc, and gemstones. China has invested heavily in Zambia's mining industry and infrastructure. Agriculture employs about 55% of the people. Food crops include cassava, fruits and vegetables, and maize. Cash crops include coffee, sugarcane, and tobacco.

AREA 290,586 sq mi [752,618 sq km] **POPULATION** 19,078,000
CAPITAL Lusaka **GOVERNMENT** Multiparty republic
ETHNIC GROUPS Native African (Bemba, Tonga, Maravi/Nyanja)
LANGUAGES English, Bemba, Kaonda, Nyanja and about 70 others
RELIGIONS Christianity 62%, Islam, Hinduism
CURRENCY Zambian kwacha = 100 ngwee

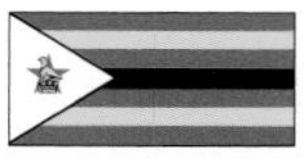
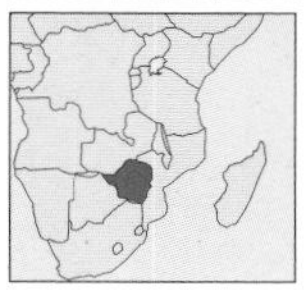

ZIMBABWE

GEOGRAPHY The Republic of Zimbabwe is a landlocked country in southern Africa. Most of the country lies on a high plateau between the Zambezi and Limpopo rivers, ranging from 2,950 ft to 4,920 ft [900 m to 1,500 m] above sea level. From October to March, the weather is hot and wet, but in the winter, daily temperatures can vary greatly.

POLITICS & ECONOMY The Shona people became dominant in the region about 1,000 years ago. The British South Africa Company, under the statesman Cecil Rhodes, occupied the area in the 1890s, after obtaining mineral rights from local chiefs. The area was named Rhodesia, and later Southern Rhodesia, becoming a self-governing British colony in 1923. Between 1953 and 1963, Southern and Northern Rhodesia (now Zambia) were united with Nyasaland (Malawi) in the Central African Federation.

In 1965, the European government of Southern Rhodesia (then called Rhodesia) declared their country independent, but Britain refused to accept this. After a civil war, the country became legally independent in 1980. Order was restored when the Shona prime minister, Robert Mugabe, brought his Ndebele rivals into his government. In 1987, Mugabe became the country's executive president.

From the late 1990s, Mugabe's government supported a violent campaign of land redistribution, seizing white-owned farms to be occupied by landless "war veterans." In elections in 2008, Mugabe lost to Morgan Tsvangirai, but intimidation of opposition supporters led Tsvangirai to withdraw from a run-off. In September 2008, a power-sharing government was set up, with Mugabe as president and Tsvangirai as prime minister. The election in 2013 saw Mugabe returned as president for the seventh time, and the post of prime minister was abolished. He was finally forced out by military intervention in late 2017 and replaced by his former vice-president Emmerson Mnangagwa, who went on to win a narrow victory in presidential elections in 2018.

In the 2000s, the economy collapsed and many people starved as a result of food shortages. The breakdown of public services led to a cholera epidemic. In 2009 the government allowed the use of foreign currencies in an effort to stem hyperinflation. Zimbabwe has valuable mineral reserves. Agriculture employs 66% of the work force. Maize is the main food crop. Cash crops include cotton, sugar, and tobacco. Cattle ranching is also important.

AREA 150,871 sq mi [390,757 sq km] **POPULATION** 14,830,000
CAPITAL Harare **GOVERNMENT** Multiparty republic
ETHNIC GROUPS Shona 82%, Ndebele 14%, other African groups 2%, mixed and Asian 1% **LANGUAGES** English, Shona, Ndebele
RELIGIONS Christianity, traditional beliefs
CURRENCY Multiple currencies

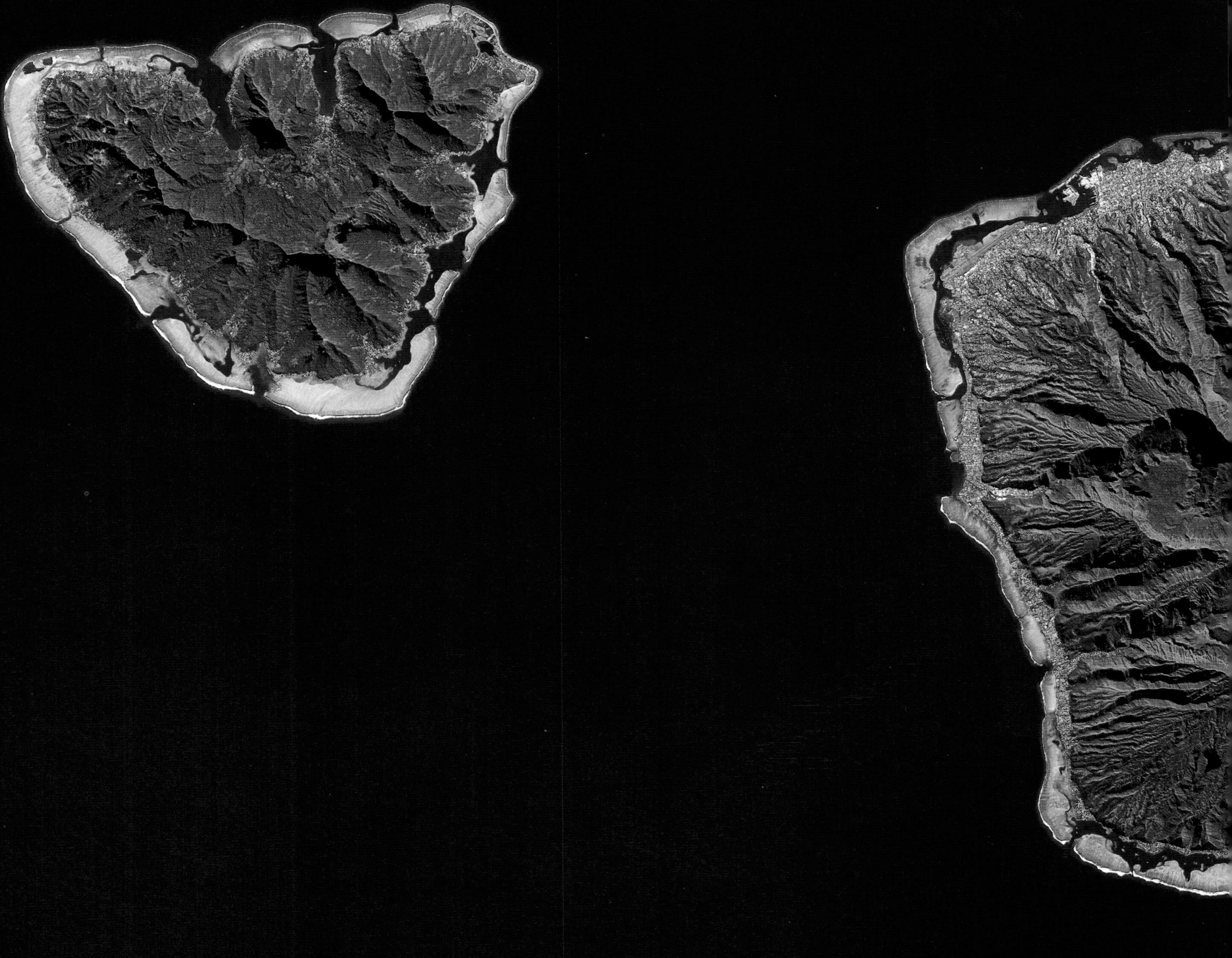

The islands of French Polynesia are dispersed over a wide area in the south Pacific Ocean. They were first settled in about 500 BC, at a time when seafarers from Southeast Asia were undertaking daring voyages as far afield as Hawaii, New Zealand, and the Easter Islands. Tahiti, the larger of the two islands in this striking image, and Moorea, to the northwest, are ancient eroded volcanic cones. In the case of Tahiti, two cones – the larger Tahiti Nui, and the smaller Tahiti Iti – are linked by a narrow isthmus. The verdant interiors of the islands are virtually uninhabited, with steep-sided valleys, jagged peaks, and fast-flowing streams. Coral reefs encircle the islands, protecting shallow lagoons of turquoise water, in which a huge variety of fish flourish. Visible on the northwestern shore of Tahiti is Papeete, the capital of French Polynesia and home to a large proportion of its population.
[Map page 289] *CGG Satellite Mapping*

WORLD GEOGRAPHY

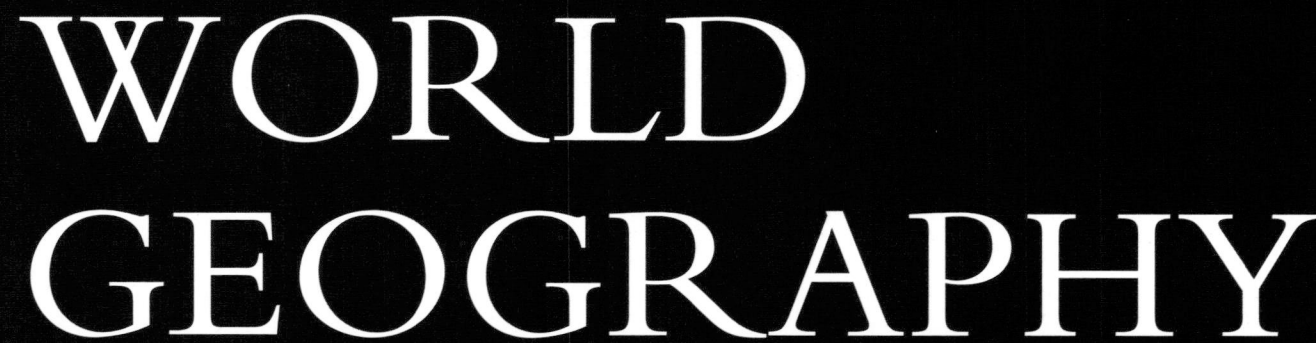

For more information:
70 Orbits of the planets
Planetary data

About 13.8 billion years ago, time and space began with the most colossal explosion in cosmic history: the so-called Big Bang that is believed to have initiated the Universe. According to current theory, in the first millionth of a second of its existence it expanded from a dimensionless point of infinite mass and density into a fireball about the size of our present Solar System – and it has been expanding ever since.

It took about 380,000 years for the primal fireball to cool enough for atoms to form. They were mostly hydrogen which is still the most abundant material in the Universe. The radiation from this era still pervades the Universe, though its subsequent expansion means that we see it at about 3° above absolute zero instead of its original 3,000°C. Observations of this faint background glow reveal slight fluctuations. It is these which appear to have become, over the next billion years or so, the large-scale structures in the present Universe. As well as the matter which we can see, there is evidence of a much greater quantity of dark matter whose nature remains unknown. Within knots of this dark matter, the first stars and galaxies formed, probably within the first billion years of the life of the Universe. Our own Galaxy was among them.

There were several generations of stars, each feeding on the wreckage of its extinct predecessors as well as the original galactic gas swirls. With each new generation, progressively larger atoms were forged in stellar furnaces, and the Galaxy's range of elements, once restricted to hydrogen and helium, grew larger. About 9 billion years after the Big Bang, a star formed on the outskirts of our Galaxy with enough matter left over to create a retinue of planets. Nearly 5 billion years after that, human beings evolved.

The Sun is one of more than 100 billion stars in the home galaxy alone. Our Galaxy, in turn, forms part of a local group consisting of approximately 80 similar structures, mostly small "dwarf" galaxies but a few large ones, and one – the Andromeda Galaxy – similar in size to our own. There are at least 100 billion galaxies in the Universe, many of which are members of huge galaxy clusters.

LIFE OF A STAR

For most of its existence, a star produces energy by the nuclear fusion of hydrogen into helium at its core. The duration of this hydrogen-burning period – known as the *main sequence* – depends on the star's mass; the greater the mass, the higher the core temperatures and the sooner the star's supply of hydrogen is exhausted. Dim, dwarf stars consume their hydrogen slowly, eking it out over billions of years. The Sun, like other stars of its mass, should spend about 10 billion years on the main sequence; since it was formed less than 5 billion years ago, it still has half its life left.

Once all of a star's core hydrogen has been fused into helium, nuclear activity moves outward into layers of unconsumed hydrogen. For a time, energy production sharply increases: the star grows hotter and expands enormously, turning into a so-called red giant. Its energy output will increase a thousandfold, and it will swell to a hundred times its former diameter.

After a few hundred million years, helium in the core will become sufficiently compressed to initiate a new cycle of nuclear fusion: from helium to carbon. The star will contract somewhat, before beginning its last expansion, in the Sun's case engulfing the Earth and perhaps Mars. In this bloated condition, the Sun's outer layers will break off into space, leaving a tiny inner core, mainly of carbon, that shrinks progressively under its own gravity. The white dwarf star thus formed can attain a density more than 10,000 times that of normal matter, with crushing surface gravity to match. Gradually, the nuclear fires will die down, and the Sun will reach its terminal stage: a black dwarf, emitting insignificant amounts of energy.

Black holes

However, stars more massive than the Sun may undergo a different transformation. The additional mass allows gravitational collapse to continue indefinitely: eventually, all the star's remaining matter shrinks to a point, and its density approaches infinity – a state that will not permit even subatomic structures to survive.

The star has become a *black hole*: an anomalous "singularity" in the fabric of space and time. Although vast coruscations of radiation will be emitted by any matter falling into its grasp, the singularity itself has an escape velocity that exceeds the speed of light, and nothing can ever be released from it. Within the boundaries of the black hole, the laws of physics are suspended.

GALACTIC STRUCTURES

▲ The galaxy cluster Abell 2744, nicknamed Pandora's Cluster for the wide range of galaxy phenomena within it. The brightest galaxies are ellipticals of various shapes, but spiral and barred spiral galaxies are also visible. The cross-shaped features on the star images are optical effects in the Hubble Space Telescope.

Many of the Universe's 100 billion galaxies show clear structural patterns, originally classified by the American astronomer Edwin Hubble in 1925. Spiral galaxies like our own have a central, almost spherical bulge and a surrounding disk composed of spiral arms. Barred spirals have a central bar of stars across the nucleus, with spiral arms trailing from the ends of the bar. Elliptical galaxies have a more uniform appearance, ranging from a flattened disk to a near sphere.

Most galaxies, however, have no obvious structure at all. Galaxies also vary enormously in size, from dwarf galaxies only 2,000 light years across to great assemblies of stars 80 or more times larger.

THE HOME GALAXY

The Sun and its planets are located in one of the spiral arms of the Galaxy, about 26,000 light years from the galactic center and orbiting around it in a period of about 220 million years. The center is invisible from the Earth, masked by vast, light-absorbing clouds of interstellar dust.

The Galaxy is probably around 12 billion years old and, like other spiral galaxies, has three distinct regions. The central bulge is about 30,000 light years in diameter. The disk in which the Sun is located is not much more than 1,000 light years thick, but approximately 130,000 light years from end to end. Around the Galaxy is the halo, a spherical zone 300,000 light years across, studded with globular star clusters and sprinkled with individual suns.

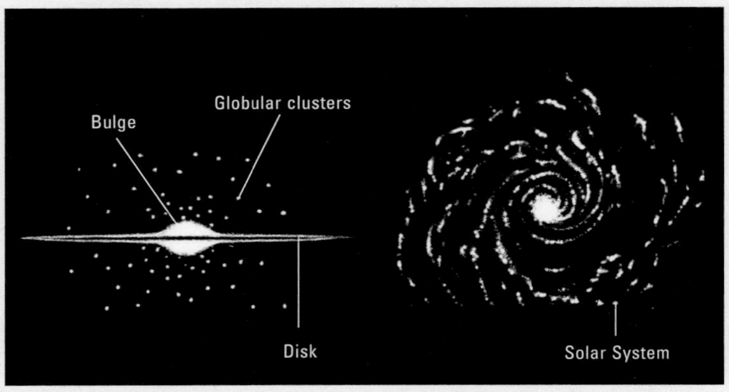

THE END OF THE UNIVERSE

The likely fate of the Universe is disputed. According to one theory (*top of diagram, below*), the expansion begun at the time of the Big Bang will continue "indefinitely," with aging galaxies moving farther and farther apart in an immense, dark graveyard.

Alternatively, gravity may overcome the expansion (*bottom of diagram*). Galaxies will fall back together until everything is again concentrated at a single point, followed by a new Big Bang and a new expansion, in an endlessly repeated cycle.

Observations of distant galaxies suggest that the expansion of the Universe is accelerating. This is attributed to a hypothetical dark energy filling the Universe, so continued expansion is considered likely.

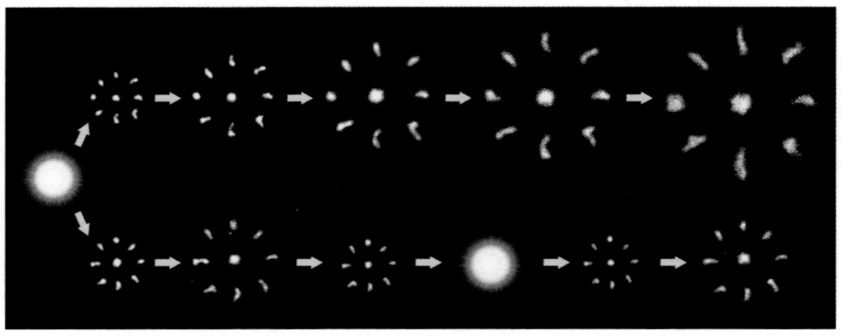

THE NEAREST STARS

The nearest stars, excluding the Sun, with their distance from Earth in light years*

Proxima Centauri	4.2	UV Ceti A & B	8.8	Procyon A & B	11.4
Alpha Centauri A & B	4.4	Ross 154	9.7	Struve 2398 A & B	11.5
Barnard's Star	6.0	Ross 248	10.3	Groombridge 34 A & B	11.6
Luhman 16 A & B	6.5	Epsilon Eridani	10.4	DX Cancri	11.7
WISE 0855-0714	7.3	HD 217987	10.7	Tau Ceti	11.8
Wolf 359	7.9	Ross 128	11.0	Epsilon Indi A & B	11.9
Lalande 21185	8.3	L789-6 A, B & C	11.1		
Sirius A & B	8.7	61 Cygni A & B	11.4		

* A light year is about 5,900 billion miles [9,500 billion km]

Many of the nearest stars, like Alpha Centauri A and B, are double stars, orbiting about their common center of gravity and to all intents and purposes equidistant from Earth. Many of them are dim objects including brown dwarfs: self-luminous objects which are intermediate in mass between planets and stars.

However, they include Sirius, the brightest star in the sky, and Procyon, the seventh brightest. Both are larger than the Sun; of the nearest stars, only Epsilon Eridani is similar in size and luminosity. Most of the other bright stars in the sky are within 500 light years of the Sun – a small fraction of the diameter of our Galaxy.

STAR CHARTS

NORTHERN HEMISPHERE SKY

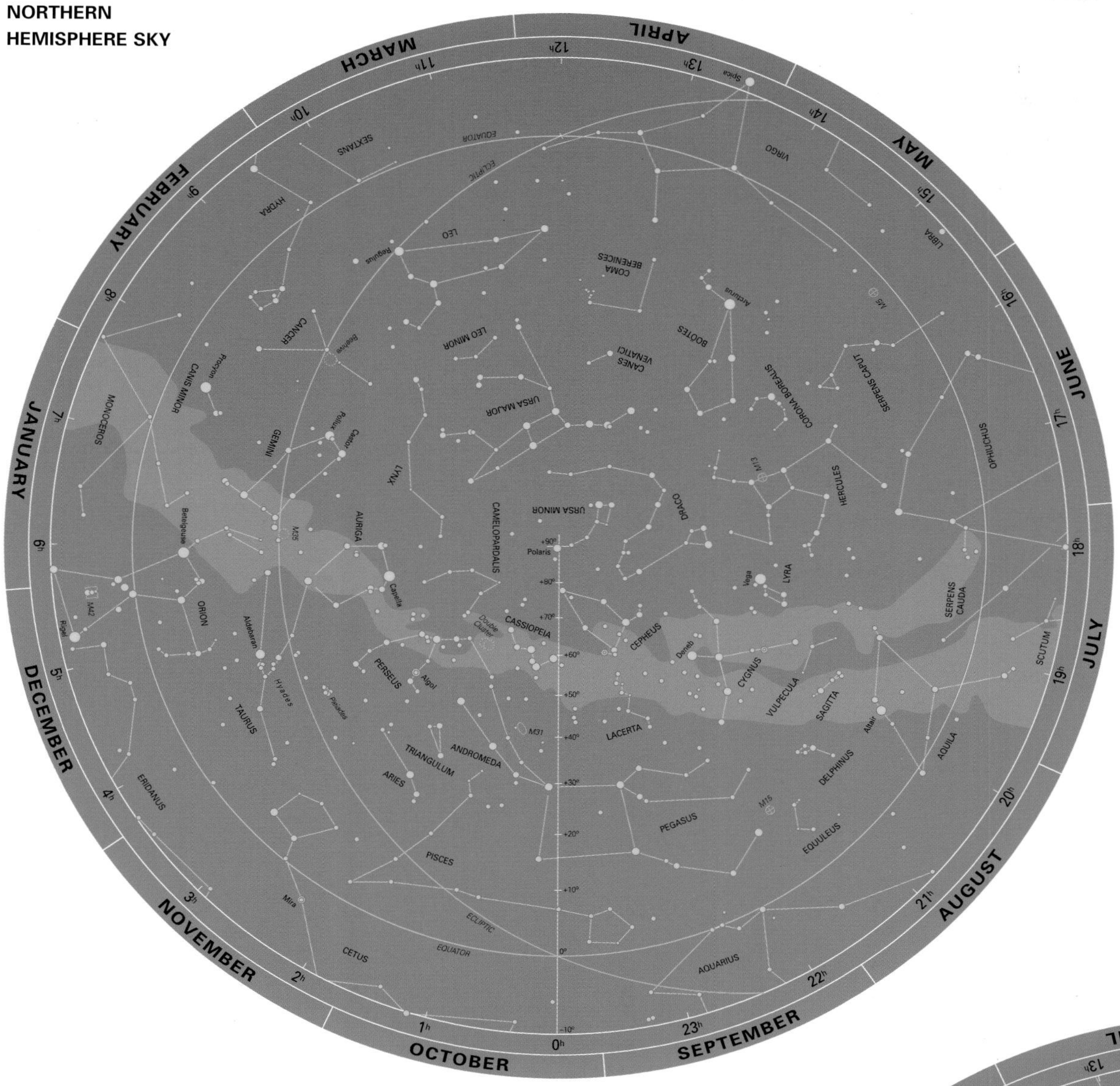

THE CONSTELLATIONS
The constellations and their English names

Andromeda	Andromeda	Lacerta	Lizard
Antlia	Air Pump	Leo	Lion
Apus	Bird of Paradise	Leo Minor	Little Lion
Aquarius	Water Carrier	Lepus	Hare
Aquila	Eagle	Libra	Scales
Ara	Altar	Lupus	Wolf
Aries	Ram	Lynx	Lynx
Auriga	Charioteer	Lyra	Lyre
Boötes	Herdsman	Mensa	Table Mountain
Caelum	Chisel	Microscopium	Microscope
Camelopardalis	Giraffe	Monoceros	Unicorn
Cancer	Crab	Musca	Fly
Canes Venatici	Hunting Dogs	Norma	Level
Canis Major	Great Dog	Octans	Octant
Canis Minor	Little Dog	Ophiuchus	Serpent Bearer
Capricornus	Sea Goat	Orion	Orion
Carina	Ship's Keel	Pavo	Peacock
Cassiopeia	Cassiopeia	Pegasus	Winged Horse
Centaurus	Centaur	Perseus	Perseus
Cepheus	Cepheus	Phoenix	Phoenix
Cetus	Whale	Pictor	Easel
Chamaeleon	Chameleon	Pisces	Fishes
Circinus	Compasses	Piscis Austrinus	Southern Fish
Columba	Dove	Puppis	Ship's Stern
Coma Berenices	Berenice's Hair	Pyxis	Mariner's Compass
Corona Australis	Southern Crown	Reticulum	Net
Corona Borealis	Northern Crown	Sagitta	Arrow
Corvus	Crow	Sagittarius	Archer
Crater	Cup	Scorpius	Scorpion
Crux	Southern Cross	Sculptor	Sculptor
Cygnus	Swan	Scutum	Shield
Delphinus	Dolphin	Serpens	Serpent
Dorado	Swordfish	Sextans	Sextant
Draco	Dragon	Taurus	Bull
Equuleus	Little Horse	Telescopium	Telescope
Eridanus	River Eridanus	Triangulum	Triangle
Fornax	Furnace	Triangulum Australe	Southern Triangle
Gemini	Twins	Tucana	Toucan
Grus	Crane	Ursa Major	Great Bear
Hercules	Hercules	Ursa Minor	Little Bear
Horologium	Clock	Vela	Ship's Sails
Hydra	Water Snake	Virgo	Virgin
Hydrus	Sea Serpent	Volans	Flying Fish
Indus	Indian	Vulpecula	Fox

SOUTHERN HEMISPHERE SKY

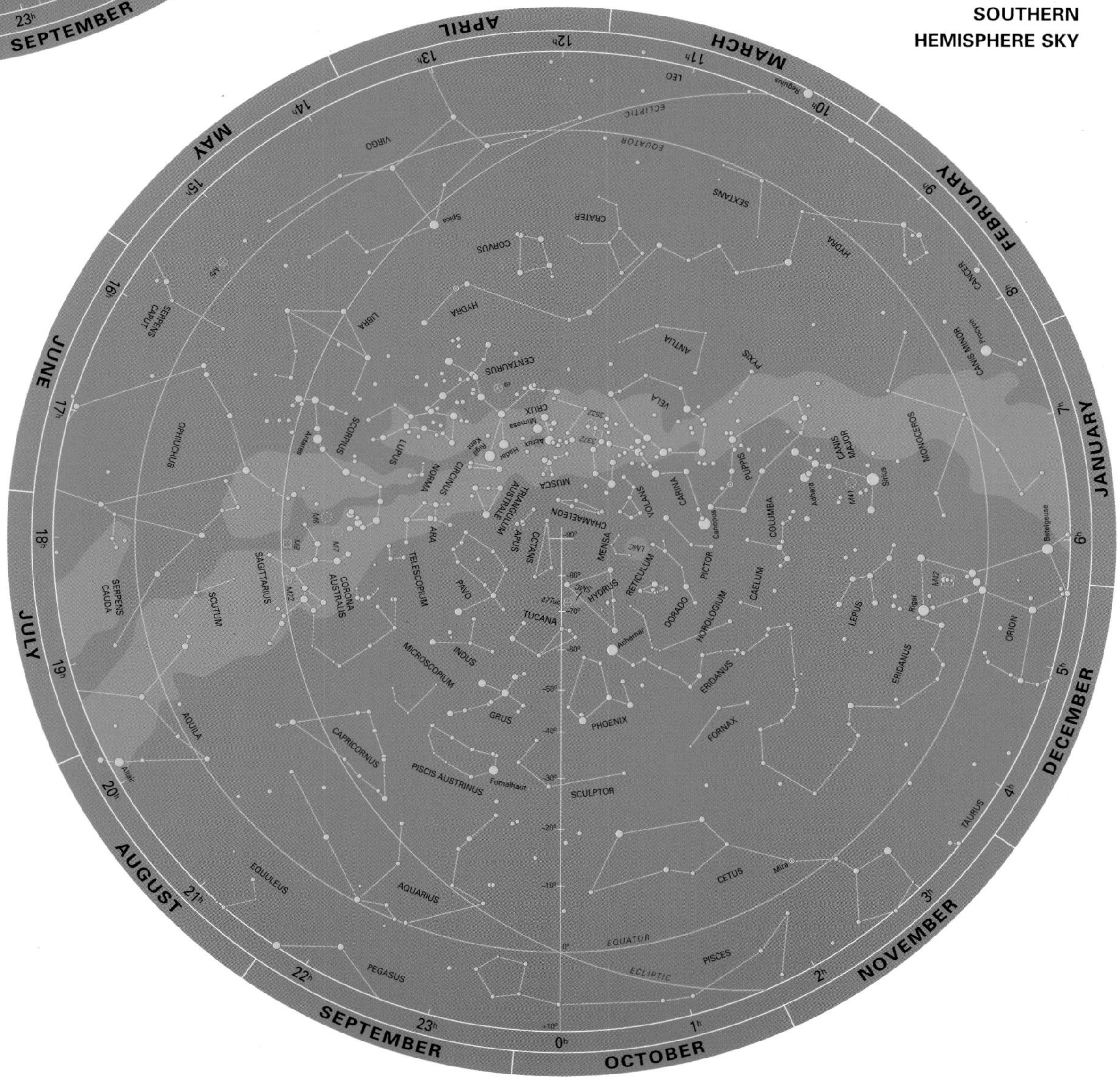

The charts on this page show the entire heavens divided into northern and southern hemispheres, with 10° of overlap between them around the perimeter of each one. However, the view from any particular location on Earth will be different, and will change both hourly as the Earth turns, and throughout the year as the Earth goes around the Sun.

The Sun's annual path through the heavens is known as the "ecliptic," and is shown here by an orange line. When the Sun is in the sky its light drowns out our view of the stars, so only that part of the heavens opposite the Sun is visible at a particular time. The sky's equivalent of longitude is known as "right ascension." As the stars appear to rotate around the Earth once every 24 hours, right ascension is measured eastward in hours and minutes, and is marked around the edge of the maps. The equivalent of latitude is "declination," measured in degrees north or south of the celestial equator, and shown by the vertical line on each chart.

Using the charts

At any place and time you can see half of the whole sky, assuming a flat horizon. If you were at one of the poles your view would be shown as a circle centered on the middle of the map for the appropriate hemisphere, with the horizon marked by the celestial equator. From all other locations the center of your view (your overhead point) will be at some other point on the map whose location changes with time. The closer you are to Earth's equator, the closer the center will be to the edge of the map and more stars in the opposite hemisphere will be visible.

So first choose the appropriate chart for your hemisphere and hold it with the month at the bottom. At 11 p.m., not allowing for Daylight Saving Time (Summer Time), your overhead point will be at the same declination as your geographical latitude and stars lower on the map will be due south (or north in the southern hemisphere). From latitude 50° in mid August, for example, your overhead point will be close to the star Deneb in the constellation of Cygnus. Stars on the opposite side of the map will be below your northern horizon, while stars below Deneb will be due south.

STAR MAGNITUDES
Apparent visual magnitudes

The magnitude scale of star brightnesses is developed from the system used by the Ancient Greeks in which the brightest stars were first magnitude and the faintest visible to the naked eye were sixth. Today the scale has a mathematical basis and extends, at the brightest end, through to negative magnitudes.

The Milky Way is shown in light blue on these charts.

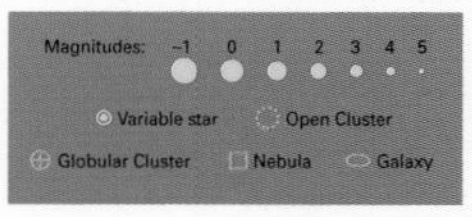

For more information:
68 The Home Galaxy
72 The seasons
Day and night
73 The Moon

Lying about halfway from the center of one of billions of galaxies that populate the observable Universe, our Solar System contains eight planets and their moons, at least five dwarf planets, innumerable asteroids, comets and other icy bodies, and a miscellany of dust and gas, all tethered by the immense gravitational field of the Sun, the star whose thermonuclear furnaces provide them all with heat and light.

The Solar System was formed about 5 billion years ago, when a spinning cloud of gas, mostly hydrogen but seeded with other heavier elements, condensed enough to ignite a nuclear reaction and create a star. The Sun still accounts for almost 99.9% of the system's total mass.

By composition as well as distance, the planetary array divides quite neatly in two: an inner system of four small, solid planets, including the Earth, and an outer system, from Jupiter to Neptune, of four much larger planets composed of lighter materials, such as gas, liquid, and ice. Lying mostly between the two groups is a scattering of rocky asteroids, numbering perhaps a million or more. They may be debris left over from the formation of the inner Solar System. In 2006, Pluto was demoted from its former status as a planet and is now regarded as a member of the Kuiper Belt of icy bodies at the fringes of the Solar System.

Much of the early history of science is the story of people trying to make sense of the wandering points of light that were all they knew of the planets. Now, men have stood on the Earth's Moon, space probes have landed on several bodies, and distant landscapes have been mapped with astonishing accuracy, transforming our knowledge of our celestial environment.

All the planets as far out as Saturn have now been studied by orbiting missions, while data on Uranus, Neptune, and dwarf planet Pluto have been obtained by flyby craft. Rovers have investigated parts of Mars and transmitted back detailed sample analyses. Several asteroids have been examined by flyby missions and landers, and samples of three asteroids have been returned to Earth for laboratory study.

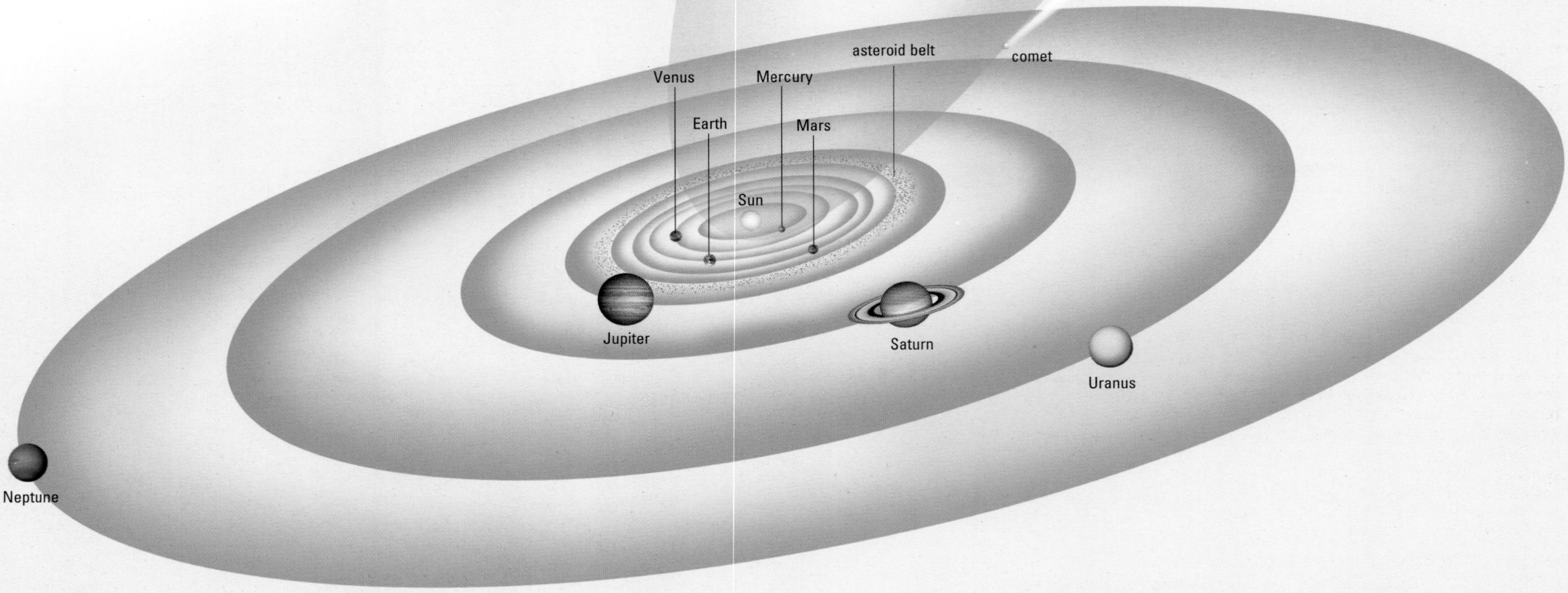

Diagram not drawn to scale

ORBITS OF THE PLANETS

The diagram above shows the Solar System as it might appear to an observer a few light-hours away in the direction of the constellation Hercules. Seen from such a position, above the plane of the ecliptic, all the planets revolve about the Sun in a counterclockwise direction. The perspective view exaggerates the elliptical form of all the planetary orbits: only Mercury follows a path that deviates noticeably from circularity.

The diagram also portrays the main asteroid belt between Mars and Jupiter, and the orbit of a comet. Comets reside in a vast spherical halo beyond the Solar System, and are occasionally diverted toward the Sun on highly elliptical orbits which may take many thousands of years to complete. Most, therefore, still await discovery, though there are a number of shorter-period comets which return regularly, such as Halley's Comet.

PLANETARY DATA

	Mean distance from Sun (million miles)	Mass (Earth = 1)	Period of orbit (Earth days/years)	Period of rotation (Earth days)	Equatorial diameter (miles)	Average density (water = 1)	Surface gravity (Earth = 1)	Number of known satellites*
Sun	*–*	*332,946*	*–*	*25.38*	*865,000*	*1.41*	*27.9*	*–*
Mercury	36.0	0.06	87.97d	58.65	3,032	5.43	0.38	0
Venus	67.2	0.82	224.7d	243.02	7,521	5.24	0.91	0
Earth	93.0	1.00	365.3d	1.00	7,926	5.51	1.00	1
Mars	141.6	0.11	687.0d	1.029	4,220	3.94	0.38	2
Jupiter	484.0	317.8	11.86y	0.411	88,848	1.33	2.36	79
Saturn	891.0	95.2	29.45y	0.428	74,900	0.69	0.91	82
Uranus	1,785.2	14.5	84.02y	0.720	31,764	1.27	0.89	27
Neptune	2,793.1	17.2	164.8y	0.673	30,776	1.64	1.13	14

Planetary days are given in sidereal days – that is, with respect to the stars rather than the Sun. The difference is caused by the movement of the planet in its orbit, so the interval between successive noons is slightly different from that between the rising of a particular star. The Earth's own sidereal day is 23h 56m in solar time. The equatorial diameters of most planets differ from their polar diameters as a consequence of their rotation, which is most marked in the case of Jupiter and Saturn, which are very noticeably flattened at the poles. Strictly speaking, the figures for surface gravity apply to the four inner planets only, as the outer planets have no solid surfaces. In their case, the figure is given for an arbitrary point in the atmosphere where the pressure is 1 bar.

** Number of known satellites at mid-2021*

THE PLANETS

Mercury is the closest planet to the Sun and hence the fastest-moving. It is very hot, with a cratered, wrinkled surface very similar to that of Earth's Moon. It is small and has low gravity, so there is no significant atmosphere.

Venus has much the same physical dimensions as Earth. Its dense atmosphere is composed of 97% carbon dioxide resulting in a runaway greenhouse effect that makes the surface, at 890°F, the hottest of all the planets in the Solar System. Radar mapping revealed a terrain consisting of highland regions and vast, rolling plains crossed by volcanic flows and dotted with craters. Discharges from volcanic regions could explain the sulfuric-acid rain detected by spacecraft. Soft-landers last less than an hour in Venus's fierce climate.

Earth seen from space is easily the most beautiful of the inner planets; it is also, and more objectively, the largest, as well as the only known home of life. Living things are the main reason why the Earth is able to retain a substantial proportion of reactive oxygen in its atmosphere; the oxygen in turn supports the life that constantly regenerates it. The Earth's natural satellite, the Moon, is believed to have been created when an asteroid struck our planet in its infancy.

Mars, smaller and cooler than the Earth, is nevertheless the most likely planet other than Earth where life may have formed. The planet was, at some stage in the distant past, a geologically active world with water on its surface: rivers, lakes, and even an ocean. Liquid water may well exist today, but trapped beneath its dusty, boulder-strewn surface. The Martian landscape features huge extinct volcanoes, a giant canyon system, craters, and sand dunes. Its thin atmosphere is mostly carbon dioxide, and its polar caps are of frozen carbon dioxide and water ice. It has two tiny moons, probably captured asteroids.

Jupiter has about three times the mass of all the other planets combined. The planet is mostly gas, under intense pressure in the lower atmosphere above a core of fiercely compressed hydrogen and helium. The upper layers form strikingly colored rotating belts, the outward sign of the intense storms created by Jupiter's rapid rotation. The Great Red Spot is a storm feature that has persisted for at least 130 years. Jupiter has at least 79 moons. Most are very small, but the four largest – Io, Europa, Ganymede, and Callisto – are fascinating worlds in their own right. Io is the most volcanically active world known, and Europa possesses an ocean deep below its icy surface. The planet also has a system of rings, though nowhere near as prominent as Saturn's.

Saturn is structurally similar to Jupiter, rotating fast enough to produce an obvious bulge at its equator. It is composed of 89% hydrogen and 11% helium, and has wind velocities in the outer atmosphere of 1,600 ft/sec. Ever since the invention of the telescope, Saturn's rings have been the feature that has most attracted observers. The rings consist of thousands of individual ringlets, composed of icy particles ranging in size from 30 feet down to microscopic. Titan, the largest of Saturn's 82 known moons, has a dense atmosphere.

Uranus was unknown to the ancients. Although it is faintly visible to the naked eye, it was not established as a planet until 1781. In its interior is probably a rocky core surrounded by frozen methane, water, and ammonia; the atmosphere is of hydrogen, helium, and some methane, which gives the planet its greenish-blue color. There is a system of thin, dark rings and a retinue of 27 moons, all but five of which are small.

Neptune is always more than 2.5 billion miles from Earth, and despite its diameter of over 31,000 miles, it can only be seen by telescope. Its discovery in 1846 was the result of mathematical predictions by astronomers seeking to explain irregularities in the orbit of Uranus. Like Uranus, it has a ring system; recent observations have revealed a total of 14 moons.

In 2006, following an increasing number of discoveries of objects orbiting the Sun of similar size to Pluto but at a greater distance, the International Astronomical Union issued for the first time a definition of a planet. A planet is defined as "a body orbiting the Sun, which is essentially round as a consequence of its gravity, and which does not share its orbital neighborhood with similar bodies." On this definition, Pluto is no longer classified as a planet, but is instead a member of a new category of "dwarf planet," which relaxes the last criterion but excludes bodies in orbit around another one.

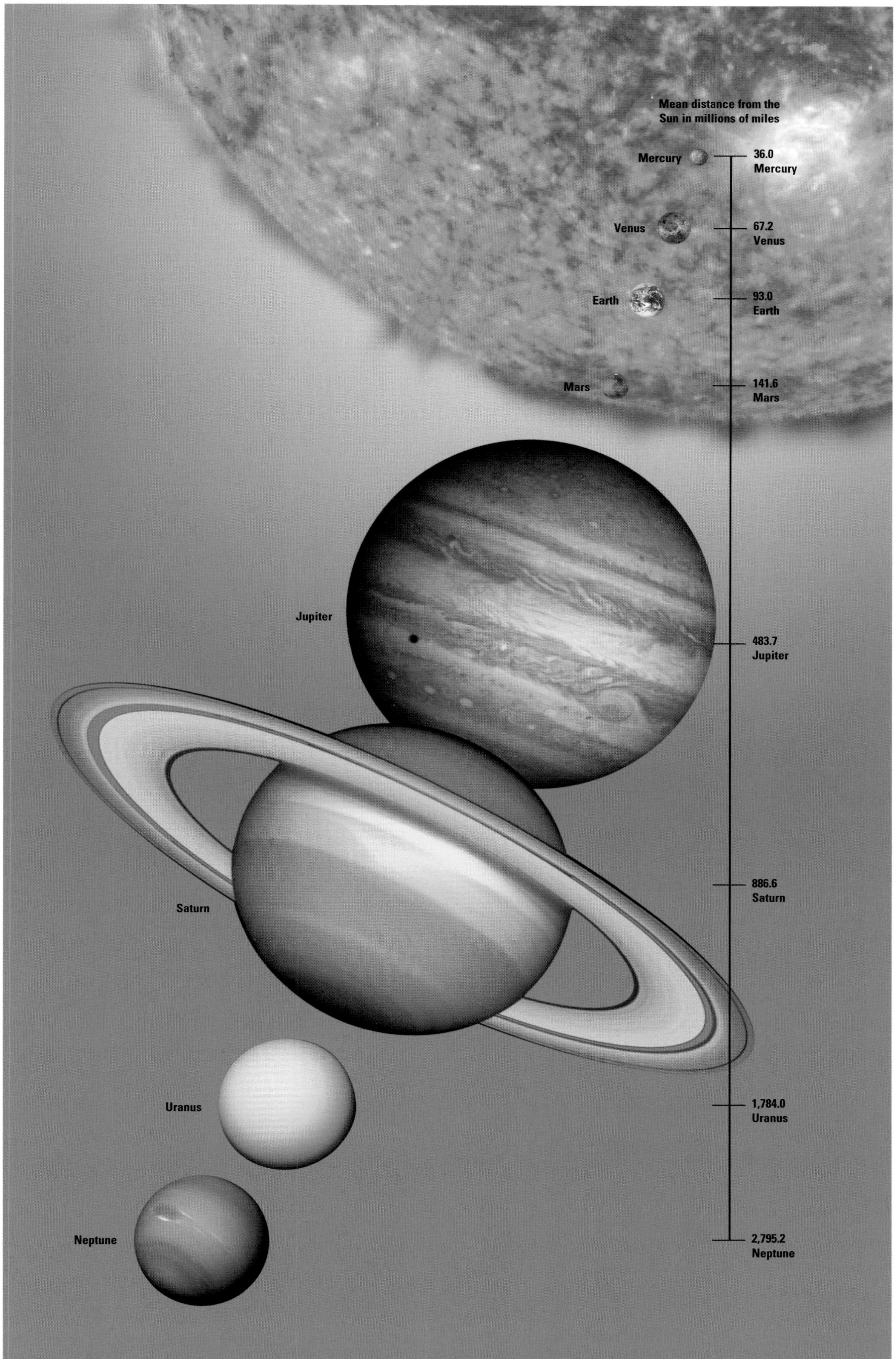

Diagrams not drawn to scale

For more information:
70 Orbits of the planets
76 Circulation of the air
78 Climate
84 Ocean currents

The basic units of time measurement are the day and the year. The day is one rotation of the Earth on its axis. Our present calendar is based on the solar year of 365.24 days, the time taken by the Earth to orbit the Sun. Calendars based on the movements of the Sun and Moon have been used since ancient times. The length of the year, reckoned by the Julian Calendar introduced by Julius Caesar, was about 11 minutes too long. The cumulative error was rectified in 1582 by the Gregorian Calendar, when Pope Gregory XIII decreed that the day following October 4 was October 15, and that century years did not count as leap years unless they were divisible by 400. England finally adopted the reformed calendar in 1752, when it was 11 days behind the European mainland.

The rotation of the Earth on its axis causes day and night. The Earth rotates through 360° every 24 hours, and the world is divided into 24 time zones centered on lines of longitude at 15° intervals.

The tilt of the Earth's axis, which is also called the "obliquity of the ecliptic," accounts for the seasons which are so familiar in the middle latitudes. However, geological evidence shows that, over long periods of time, climates change, and the advances and retreats of the ice during the Pleistocene Ice Age may have been caused by regular variations in the Earth's tilt, its orbit around the Sun, and changes in the season when it is closest to the Sun (perihelion).

THE SEASONS

Seasons occur because the Earth's axis is tilted at an angle of approximately 23½°. When the northern hemisphere is tilted to a maximum extent toward the Sun, on June 20 or 21, the Sun is overhead at the Tropic of Cancer (latitude 23½° North). This is midsummer, or the summer solstice, in the northern hemisphere.

On September 22 or 23, the Sun is overhead at the equator, and day and night are of equal length throughout the world. This is the autumnal equinox in the northern hemisphere.

On December 21 or 22, the Sun is overhead at the Tropic of Capricorn (23½° South), the winter solstice in the northern hemisphere. The overhead Sun then tracks north until, on March 20 or 21, it is overhead at the equator. This is the spring (vernal) equinox in the northern hemisphere.

In the southern hemisphere, the seasons are the reverse of those in the north.

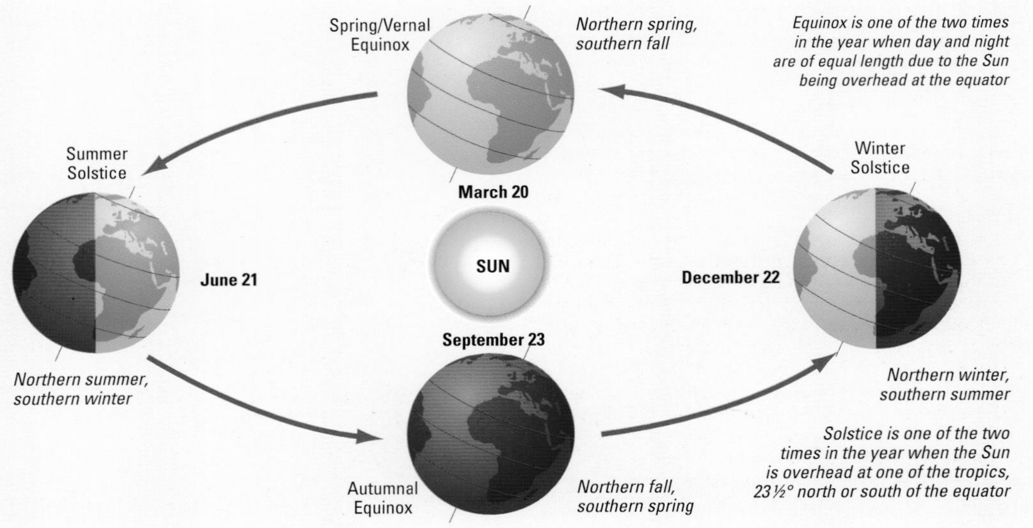

DAY AND NIGHT

The Sun appears to rise in the east, reach its highest point at noon, and then set in the west, to be followed by night. In reality, it is not the Sun that is moving but the Earth rotating from west to east. The moment when the Sun's upper limb first appears above the horizon is termed sunrise; the moment when the Sun's upper limb disappears below the horizon is sunset.

At the summer solstice in the northern hemisphere (June 21), the Arctic has total daylight and the Antarctic total darkness. The opposite occurs at the winter solstice (December 21 or 22). At the equator, the length of day and night are almost equal all year.

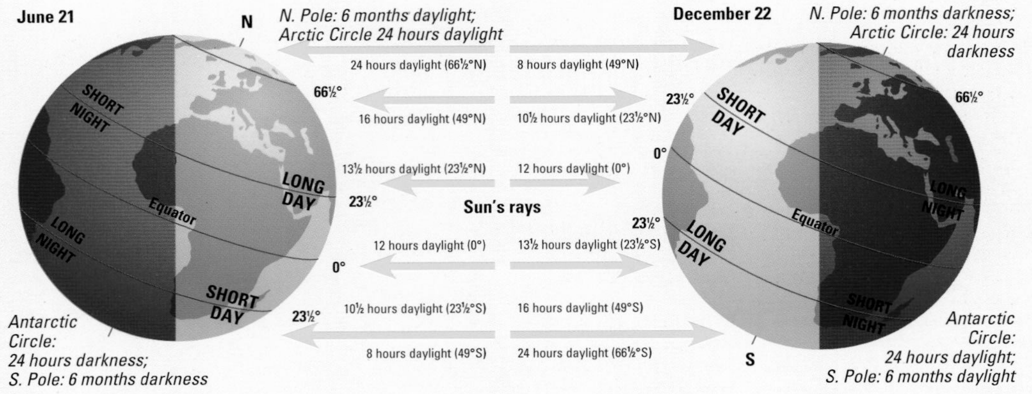

EARTH DATA

Aphelion (maximum distance from Sun):	94,500,000 miles
Perihelion (minimum distance from Sun):	91,400,000 miles
Angle of tilt (obliquity of the ecliptic):	23° 26′
Length of year – solar tropical (equinox to equinox):	365.24 days

Length of year:	365 days, 5 hours, 48 minutes, 45 seconds of mean solar time
Superficial area:	197,000,000 sq miles
Land surface:	57,500,000 sq miles (29.2%)
Water surface:	139,500,000 sq miles (70.8%)
Equatorial circumference:	24,901 miles

Polar circumference:	24,860 miles
Equatorial diameter:	7,926 miles
Polar diameter:	7,900 miles
Equatorial radius:	3,963 miles
Polar radius:	3,950 miles
Volume of the Earth:	$259{,}880 \times 10^6$ cu miles
Mass of the Earth:	5.97×10^{24} kg

SUNRISE AND SUNSET

The term "equinox" comes from the Latin for "equal night." At the spring and autumnal equinoxes, the Sun is vertically overhead at midday at the equator and all places on Earth have 12 hours of darkness and 12 hours of daylight. The graphs of sunrise and sunset show that these occasions occur on March 21 and on September 22 or 23. The graphs also show that, because the Sun remains high in the sky at the equator throughout the year, the length of day and night there remains roughly the same throughout the year, with sunrise around 6 a.m. and sunset around 6 p.m.

The further north or south one travels, the greater the difference between the number of hours of daylight and darkness. For example, the graph (*right*) shows that at latitude 60°N sunrise varies from just after 9 a.m. in midwinter (on December 22 or 23) to about 2.30 a.m. in midsummer (around the summer solstice on June 21). By contrast, the second graph (*far right*) shows that sunset at latitude 60°N occurs at about 2.45 p.m. in midwinter and 9.20 p.m. in midsummer.

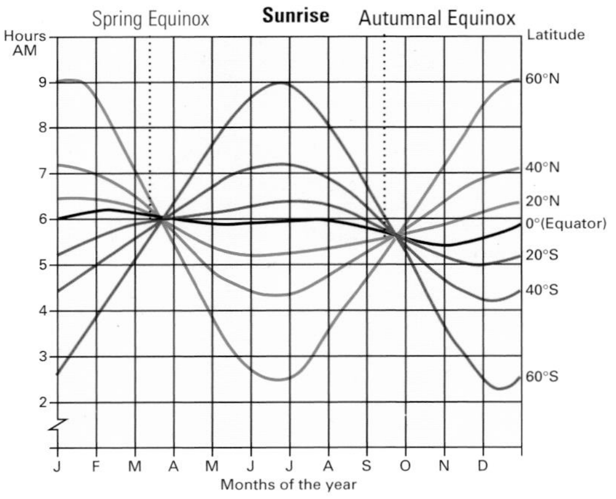

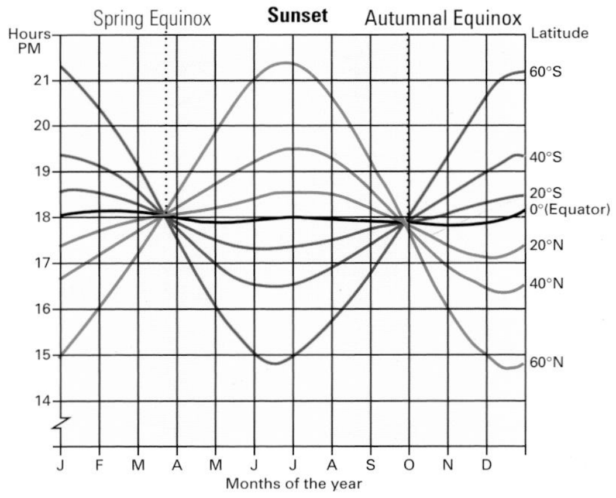

THE MOON

The Moon rotates more slowly than the Earth, taking just over 27 days to make one complete rotation on its axis. This corresponds to the Moon's orbital period around the Earth, and therefore the Moon always presents the same hemisphere toward us; some 41% of the Moon's far side is never visible from the Earth. The interval between one New Moon and the next is 29½ days – this is called a lunation, or lunar month. The Moon shines only by reflected sunlight, and emits no light of its own. During each lunation the Moon displays a complete cycle of phases, caused by the changing angle of illumination from the Sun.

PHASES OF THE MOON

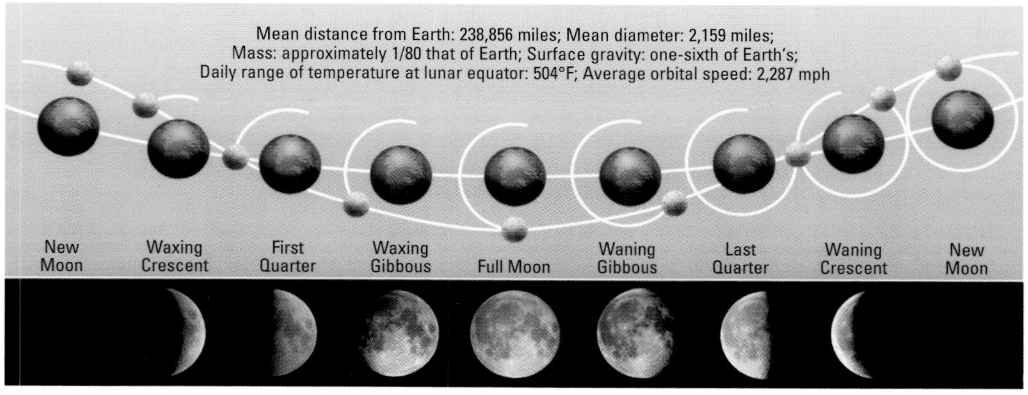

MOON DATA

Distance from Earth
The Moon orbits at a mean distance of 238,856 miles, at an average speed of 2,287 mph in relation to the Earth.

Size and mass
The average diameter of the Moon is 2,159 miles. It is 400 times smaller than the Sun but is about 400 times closer to the Earth, so we see them as the same size. The Moon has a mass of 7.35×10^{22} kg, with a density 3.344 times that of water.

Visibility
Only 59% of the Moon's surface is visible from the Earth over time. Sunlight reflected from the Moon takes 1.3 seconds to reach the Earth (the Sun itself is around 8½ light-minutes away).

Temperature
With the Sun overhead, the temperature on the lunar equator can reach 243°F [117°C]. At night it can sink to −261°F [−163°C].

ECLIPSES

When the Moon passes between the Sun and the Earth, the Sun becomes partially eclipsed (1). A partial eclipse becomes a total eclipse if the Moon proceeds to cover the Sun completely (2) and the dark central part of the lunar shadow touches the Earth. The broad geographical zone covered by the Moon's outer shadow (P) has only a very small central area (often less than 62 miles wide) that experiences totality. Totality can never last for more than 7½ minutes at maximum, but is usually much briefer than this. Lunar eclipses take place when the Moon moves through the shadow of the Earth, and can be partial or total. Any single location on Earth can experience a maximum of four solar and three lunar eclipses in any single year, while a total solar eclipse occurs an average of once every 360 years for any given location.

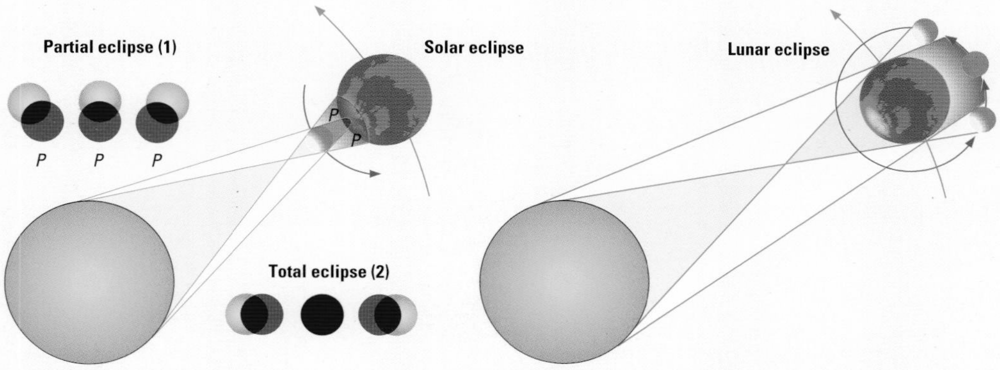

TIDES

The daily rise and fall of the ocean's tides are the result of the gravitational pull of the Moon and that of the Sun, though the effect of the latter is not as strong as that of the Moon. This effect is greatest on the hemisphere facing the Moon and causes a tidal "bulge." Spring tides occur when the Sun, Earth, and Moon are aligned; high tides are at their highest, and low tides fall to their lowest. When the Moon and Sun are farthest out of line (near the Moon's First and Last Quarters), neap tides occur, producing the smallest range between high and low tides.

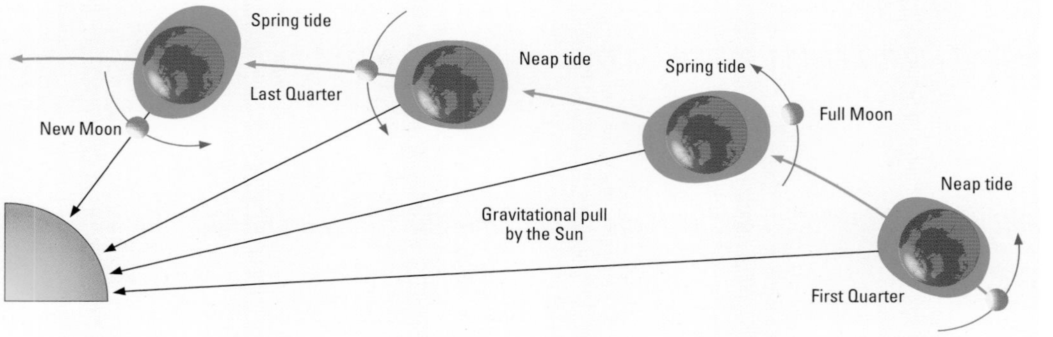

TIME ZONES

The Earth rotates through 360° in 24 hours, and so moves 15° every hour. The world is divided into 24 standard time zones, each centered on lines of longitude at 15° intervals. At the center of the first zone is the prime meridian, or Greenwich meridian. All places to the west of Greenwich are one hour behind for every 15° of longitude; places to the east are ahead by one hour for every 15°.

International Date Line
When it is 12 noon on the Greenwich meridian, 180° east it is midnight of the same day – while 180° west the day is just beginning. To overcome this, the International Date Line was established, approximately following the 180° meridian. Thus, if you were to travel eastward from Japan (140°E) to Hawai'i (160°W), you would pass from Sunday night into Sunday morning.

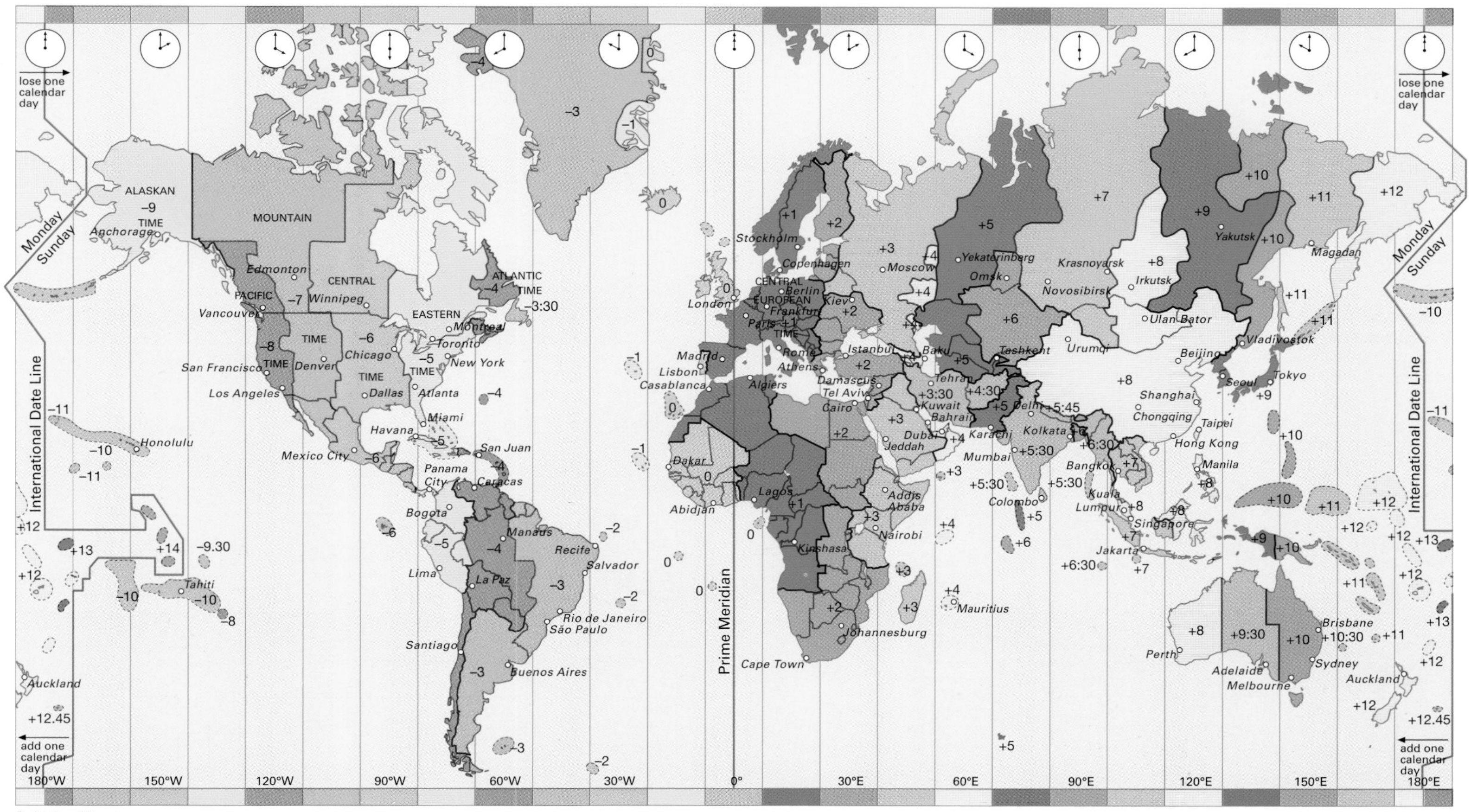

Projection: *Mercator*

10 Hours behind or ahead of UT or Coordinated Universal Time

Zones using UT (GMT)

Zones behind UT (GMT)

International boundaries

Zones ahead of UT (GMT)

Half-hour zones

Time-zone boundaries

International Date Line

Actual solar time when time at Greenwich is 12:00 (noon)

Note: Some of the above time zones are affected by the incidence of Daylight Saving Time in countries where it is adopted.

For more information:
98 Minerals

Every year, earthquakes and volcanic eruptions cause much destruction throughout the world. Such phenomena were once thought to be unconnected, but since the late 1960s, scientists have understood that these events are surface manifestations of the tremendous forces operating in the Earth's interior that are slowly but constantly changing the face of our planet.

The Earth is divided into three zones. The crust, a brittle, low-density zone, overlies the dense mantle. Separating the crust from the mantle is a distinct boundary called the Mohorovičić (or Moho) discontinuity. Enclosed by the mantle is the Earth's core, which consists mainly of iron and nickel.

Temperatures inside the Earth range from about 1,600°F in the upper mantle to perhaps 9,000°F in the core. Heat creates convection currents in a semimolten part of the mantle called the asthenosphere. Above the asthenosphere is the lithosphere, a solid layer about 40 miles thick, consisting of the crust and part of the mantle. The lithosphere is divided into rigid plates, moved around by the currents in the asthenosphere, a process named plate tectonics.

The Earth was formed around 4.6 billion years ago. Lighter elements floated toward the surface, where they formed crustal rocks. The oldest rocks so far discovered are about 4 billion years old, while the oldest fossils occur in rocks formed around 3.5 billion years ago. An explosion of life occurred at the start of the Cambrian period, 570 million years ago. The fossil record since the start of the Cambrian has enabled scientists to piece together the story of life on Earth.

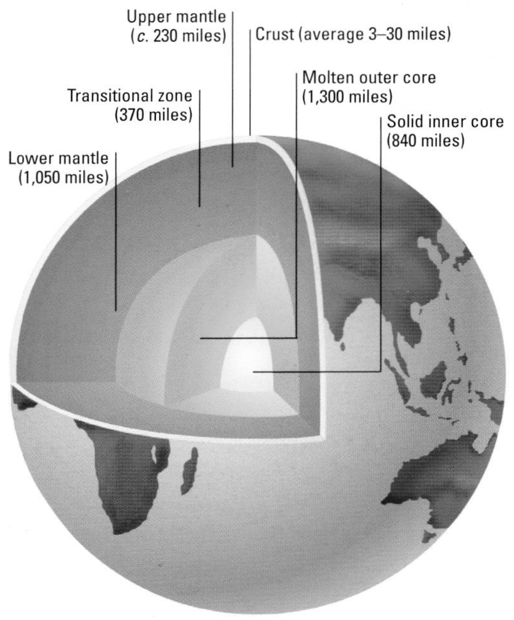

CONTINENTAL DRIFT

Trench
Rift
New ocean floor
Zones of slippage

In 1915, Alfred Wegener produced a series of world maps proposing that, around 200 million years ago, the continents had been joined together in a supercontinent that he called Pangaea. This land mass started to break up about 180 million years ago and the parts drifted to their present positions. In the 1950s and 1960s, evidence from studies of the ocean floor suggested that the low-density continents rest on huge slow-moving plates. The arrows on the present-day world map (*below*) show that the continents are still on the move.

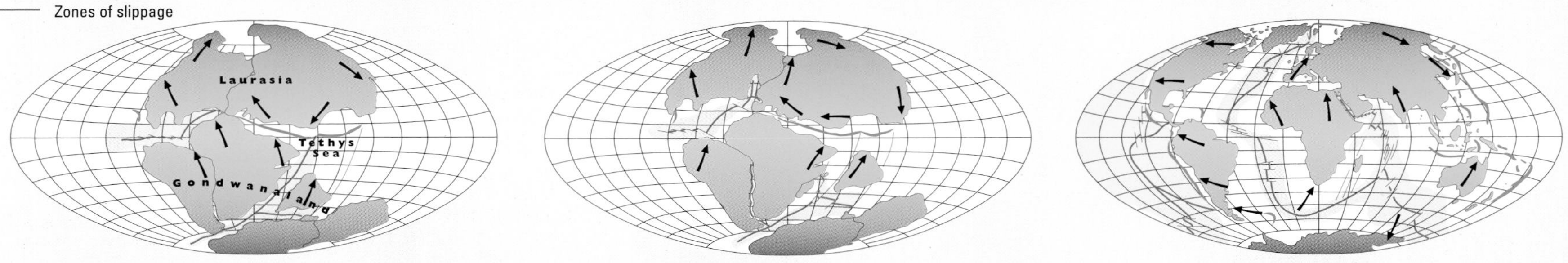

180 million years ago **135 million years ago** **Present day**

DISTRIBUTION OF VOLCANOES

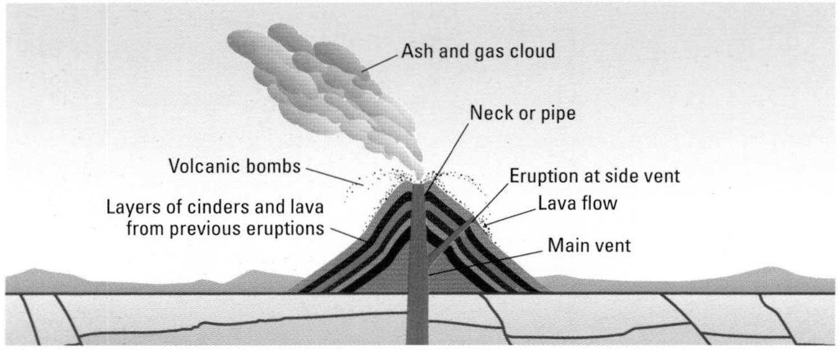

Volcanoes occur when hot liquefied rock beneath the Earth's crust is pushed up by pressure to the surface as molten lava. There are some 550 known active volcanoes, around 20 of which are erupting at any one time.

Submarine volcanoes
▲ Land volcanoes active since 1700
— Boundaries of tectonic plates

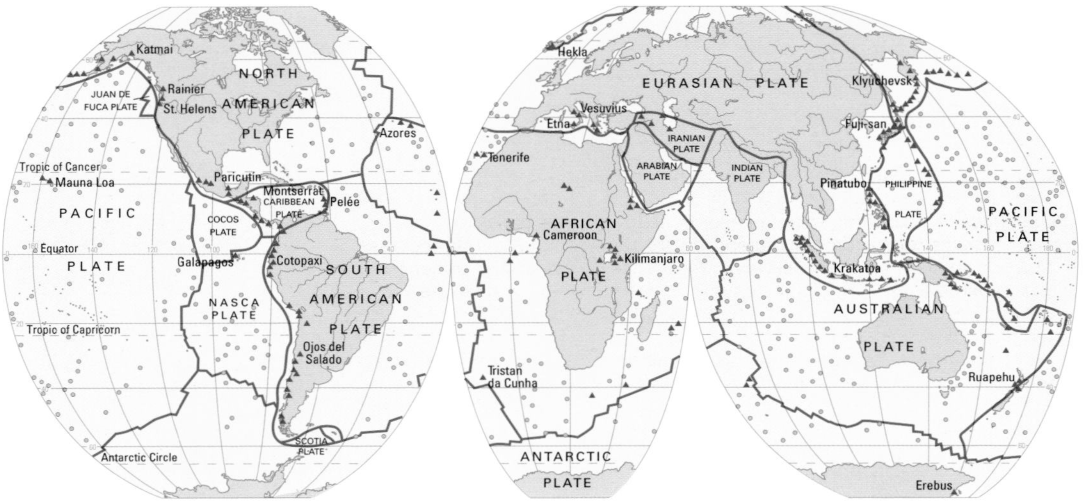

PLATE TECTONICS

The huge ridges that run through the oceans represent boundaries between plates. Here plates are diverging and molten magma from the mantle rises along a central rift valley to form new crustal rock. These ocean ridges, which are active zones where earthquakes and volcanic eruptions are common, are called constructive plate margins. Destructive plate margins, which occur when two contrasting plates converge, are marked by deep-ocean trenches as one plate is forced under the other. The descending plate is melted to produce the magma that fuels volcanoes alongside the trenches. Movements of descending plates are often sudden, triggering earthquakes in overlying continental areas.

Sea-floor spreading in the Atlantic Ocean and plate collision

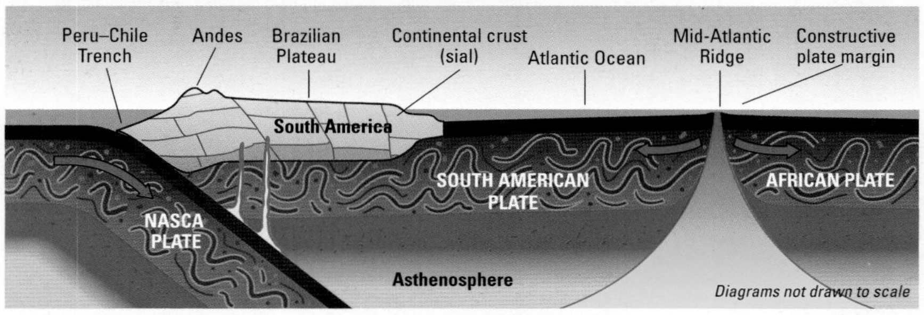

Sea-floor spreading in the Indian Ocean and continental plate collision

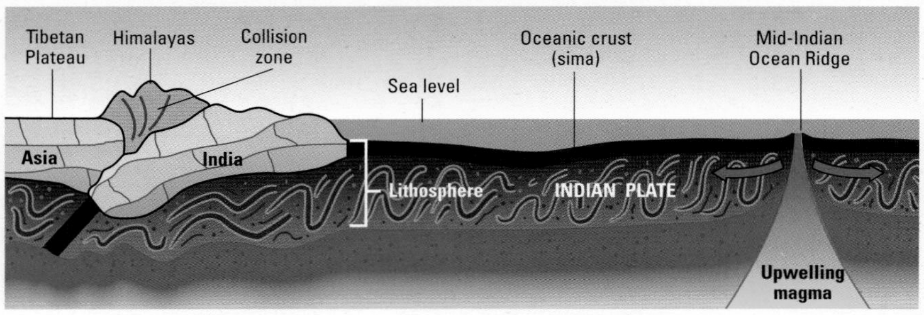

GEOLOGICAL TIME

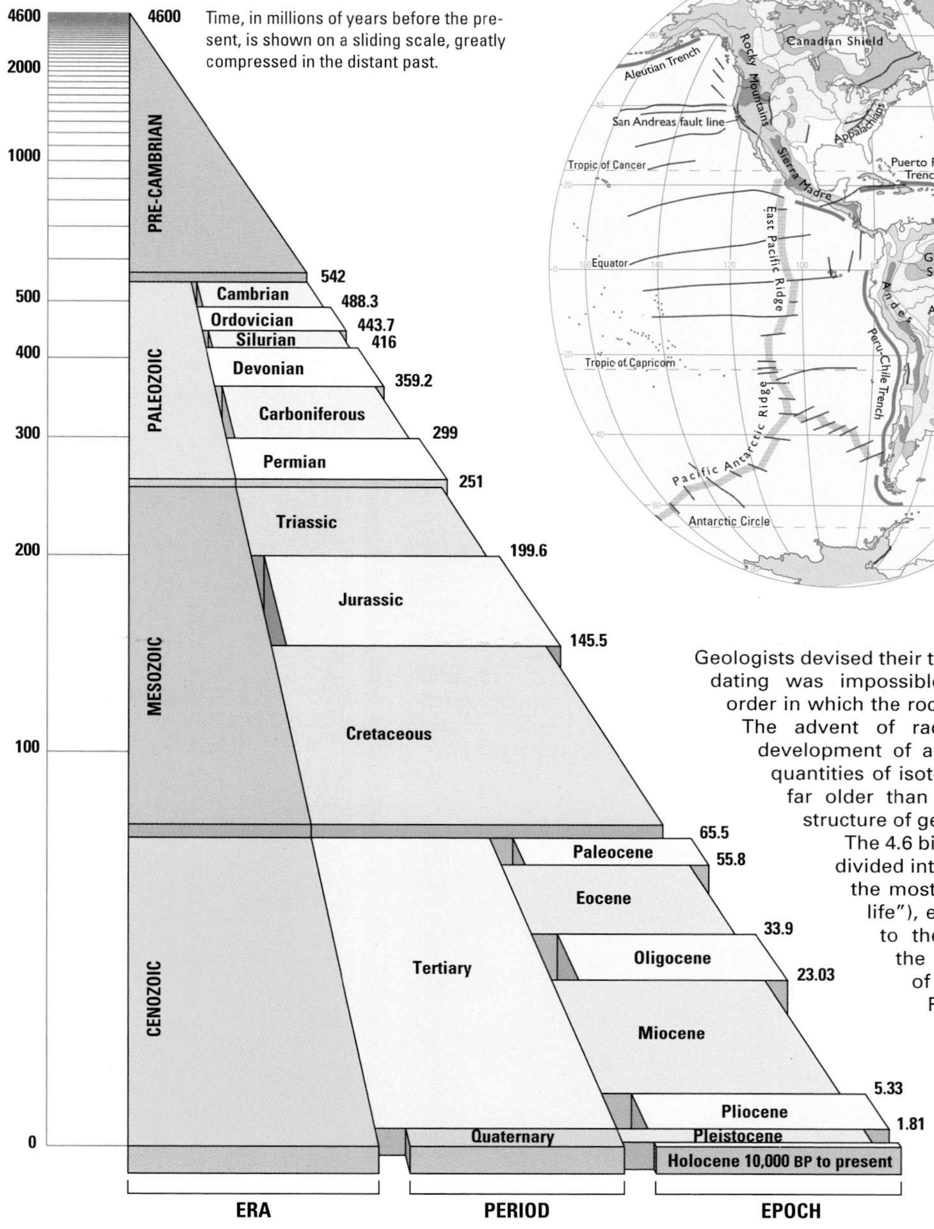

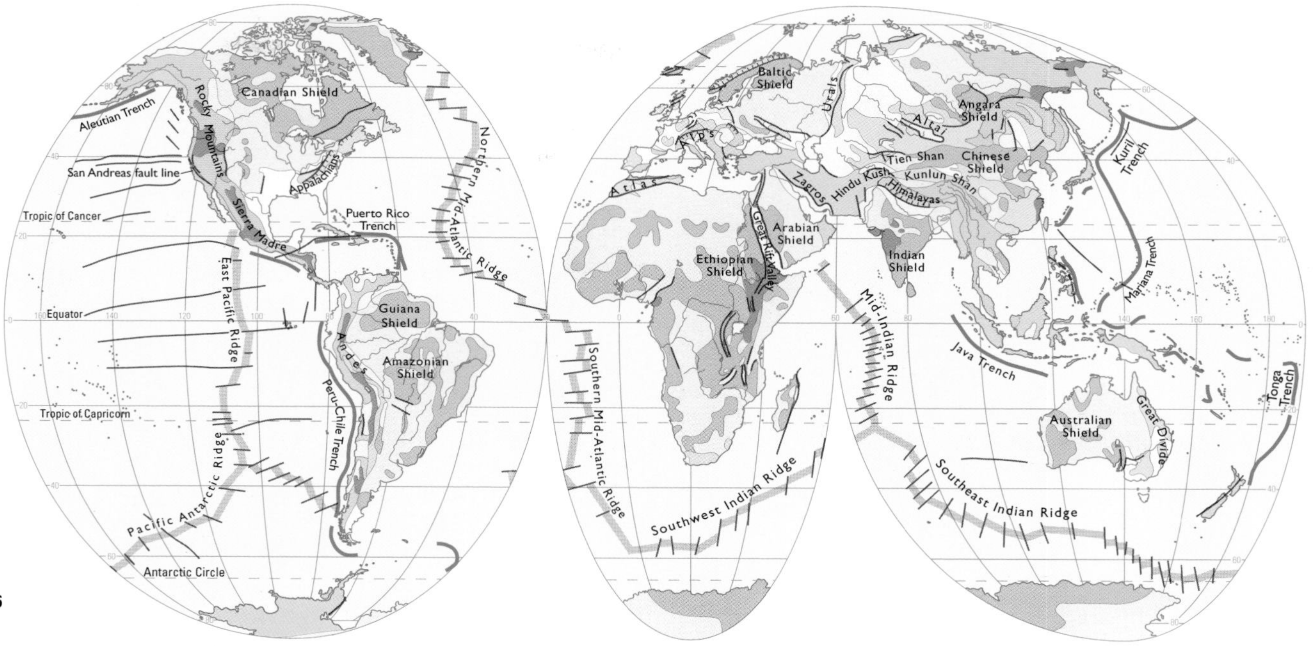

Geologists devised their timescale on the basis of relative, not calendar, ages. Accurate dating was impossible and estimates were often bitterly disputed, but the order in which the rocks were formed could be deduced from careful observation. The advent of radioactive dating – culminating in the 1950s with the development of a mass spectrometer capable of accurately measuring tiny quantities of isotopes – appears to have settled the arguments. The Earth is far older than geologists first imagined, but their painstakingly-created structure of geological time has withstood the advent of high technology.

The 4.6 billion (4,600 million) years since the formation of the Earth are divided into four great eras, further split into periods and, in the case of the most recent era, epochs. The present era is the Cenozoic ("new life"), extending backward through "middle life" and "ancient life" to the Pre-Cambrian, named after the Latin word for Wales, the location of some of the earliest known fossils. Most of the Earth's geological history is encompassed by the Pre-Cambrian: though traces of ancient life have since been found, it was largely the proliferation of fossils from the beginning of the Paleozoic era onward, some 570 million years ago, which first allowed precise subdivisions to be made.

Like the Cambrian, most are named after regions exemplifying a period's geology. Others – such as the Carboniferous ("coal-bearing") or the Cretaceous ("chalk-bearing") – are more directly descriptive.

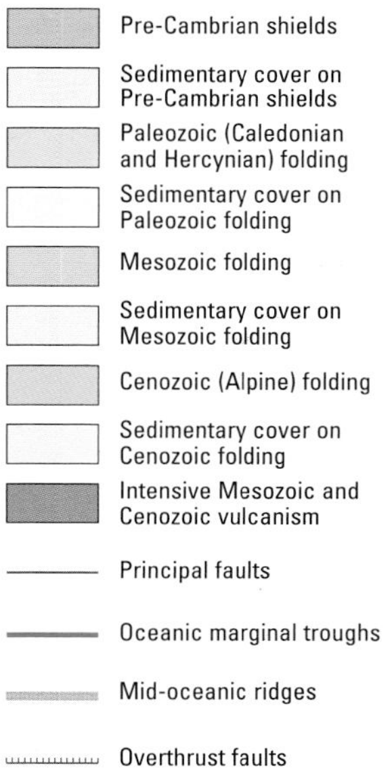

EARTHQUAKES

Earthquake magnitude is usually rated according to either the Richter scale or the Modified Mercalli scale, both devised by seismologists in the 1930s. The Richter scale measures absolute earthquake power with mathematical precision: each step upward represents a tenfold increase in the amplitude of the shockwave. Theoretically, there is no upper limit, but most of the largest earthquakes measured have been rated at between 8.8 and 8.9. The 12-point Mercalli scale, based on observed effects, is often more meaningful, ranging from I (earthquakes noticed only by seismographs) to XII (total destruction); intermediate points include V (people awakened at night; unstable objects overturned), VII (collapse of ordinary buildings; chimneys and monuments fall), and IX (conspicuous cracks in ground; serious damage to reservoirs).

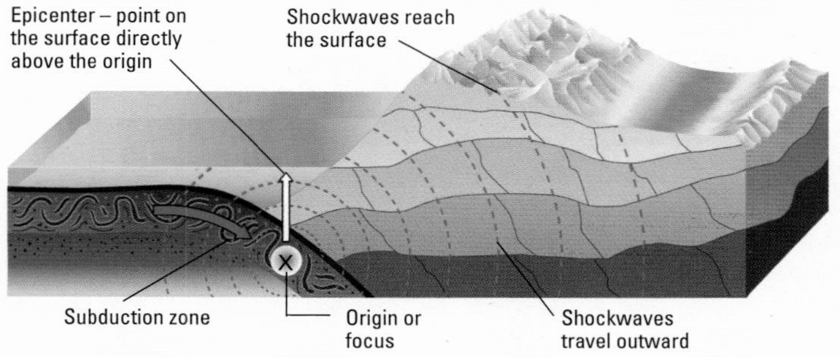

Notable Earthquakes Since 1900

Year	Location	Mag.	Deaths
1906	San Francisco, USA	8.3	3,000
1906	Valparaiso, Chile	8.6	22,000
1908	Messina, Italy	7.5	83,000
1915	Avezzano, Italy	7.5	30,000
1920	Gansu (Kansu), China	8.6	180,000
1923	Yokohama, Japan	8.3	143,000
1927	Nan Shan, China	8.3	200,000
1932	Gansu (Kansu), China	7.6	70,000
1934	Bihar, India/Nepal	8.4	10,700
1935	Quetta, India*	7.5	60,000
1939	Chillan, Chile	8.3	28,000
1939	Erzincan, Turkey	7.9	30,000
1960	S. W. Chile	9.5	2,200
1960	Agadir, Morocco	5.8	12,000
1962	Khorasan, Iran	7.1	12,230
1964	Anchorage, USA	9.2	125
1968	N. E. Iran	7.4	12,000
1970	N. Peru	7.8	70,000
1972	Managua, Nicaragua	6.2	5,000
1974	N. Pakistan	6.3	5,200
1976	Guatemala	7.5	22,500
1976	Tangshan, China	8.2	255,000
1978	Tabas, Iran	7.7	25,000
1980	El Asnam, Algeria	7.3	20,000
1985	Mexico City, Mexico	8.1	4,200
1988	N.W. Armenia	6.8	55,000
1990	N. Iran	7.7	36,000
1993	Maharashtra, India	6.4	30,000
1994	Los Angeles, USA	6.6	51
1995	Kobe, Japan	7.2	5,000
1995	Sakhalin, Russia	7.5	2,000
1998	Takhar, Afghanistan	6.1	4,200
1998	Rostaq, Afghanistan	7.0	5,000
1999	Izmit, Turkey	7.4	15,000
2001	Gujarat, India	7.7	14,000
2003	Bam, Iran	6.6	30,000
2004	Sumatra, Indonesia	9.0	250,000
2005	N. Pakistan	7.6	74,000
2006	Java, Indonesia	6.4	6,200
2007	S. Peru	8.0	600
2008	Sichuan, China	7.9	70,000
2010	Haiti	7.0	230,000
2011	Christchurch, NZ	6.3	182
2011	N. Japan	9.0	20,000
2015	Nepal	7.8	8,500
2016	Ecuador	7.8	668
2017	Chiapas, Mexico	8.2	98

* now Pakistan

Earthquakes are a series of rapid vibrations originating from the slipping or faulting of parts of the Earth's crust when stresses within build up to breaking point. They usually happen at depths varying from 5 to 20 miles. Severe earthquakes cause extensive damage when they take place in populated areas, destroying structures and severing communications. Most initial loss of life occurs due to secondary causes such as falling masonry, fires, and flooding.

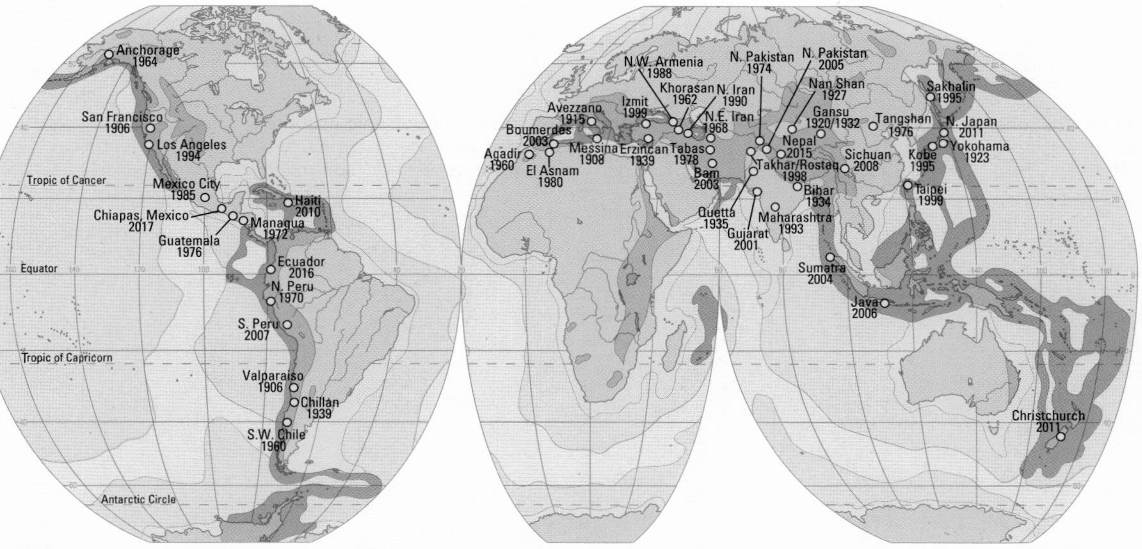

For more information:

79 Beaufort wind scale
Monsoon
80 Climate change
Global warming
84 Ocean currents

The atmosphere is a meteor shield, a radiation deflector, a thermal blanket, and a source of chemical energy for the Earth's diverse life forms. Five-sixths of its mass is in the lowest layer, the troposphere, which ranges in thickness from 11–6 miles between the equator and the poles. Powered by the Sun, the air is always on the move, flowing generally from high- to low-pressure areas. The troposphere is the layer where virtually all weather phenomena, including clouds, precipitation, and winds, occur. Above the troposphere is the stratosphere, which contains the important ozone layer and extends to about 30 miles above the Earth's surface. Beyond 60 miles, atmospheric density is lower than most laboratory vacuums.

STRUCTURE OF THE ATMOSPHERE

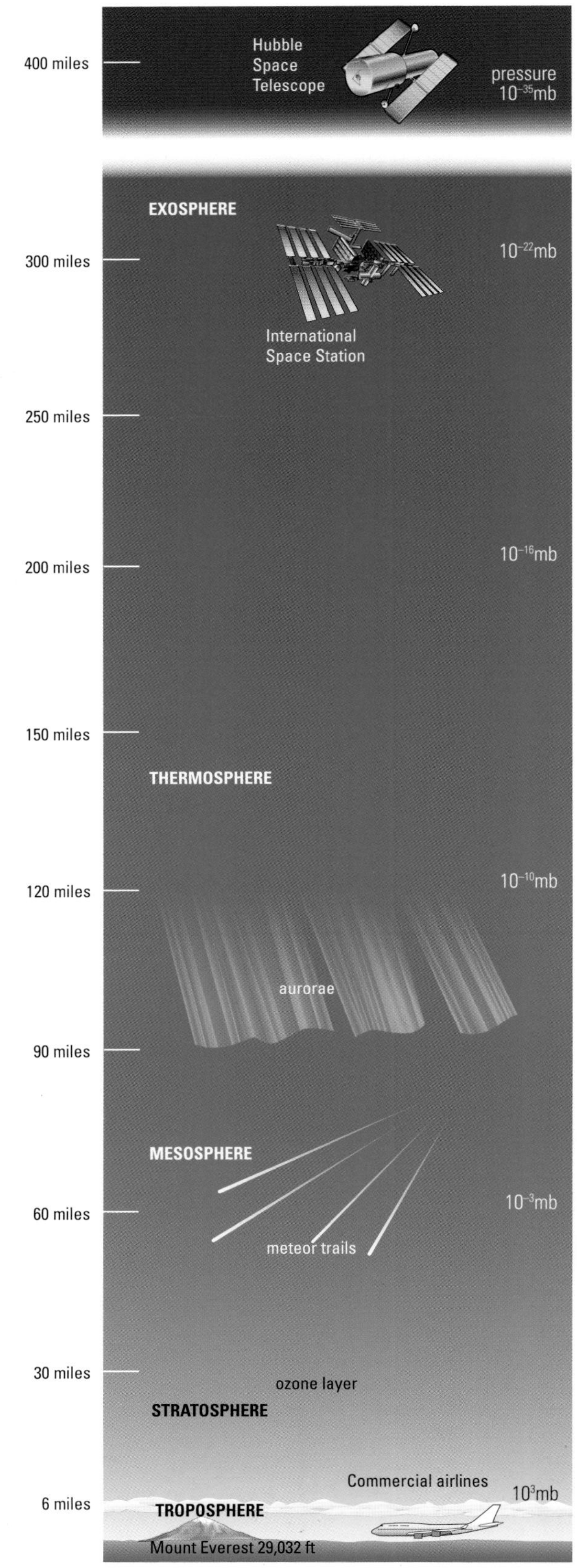

CIRCULATION OF THE AIR

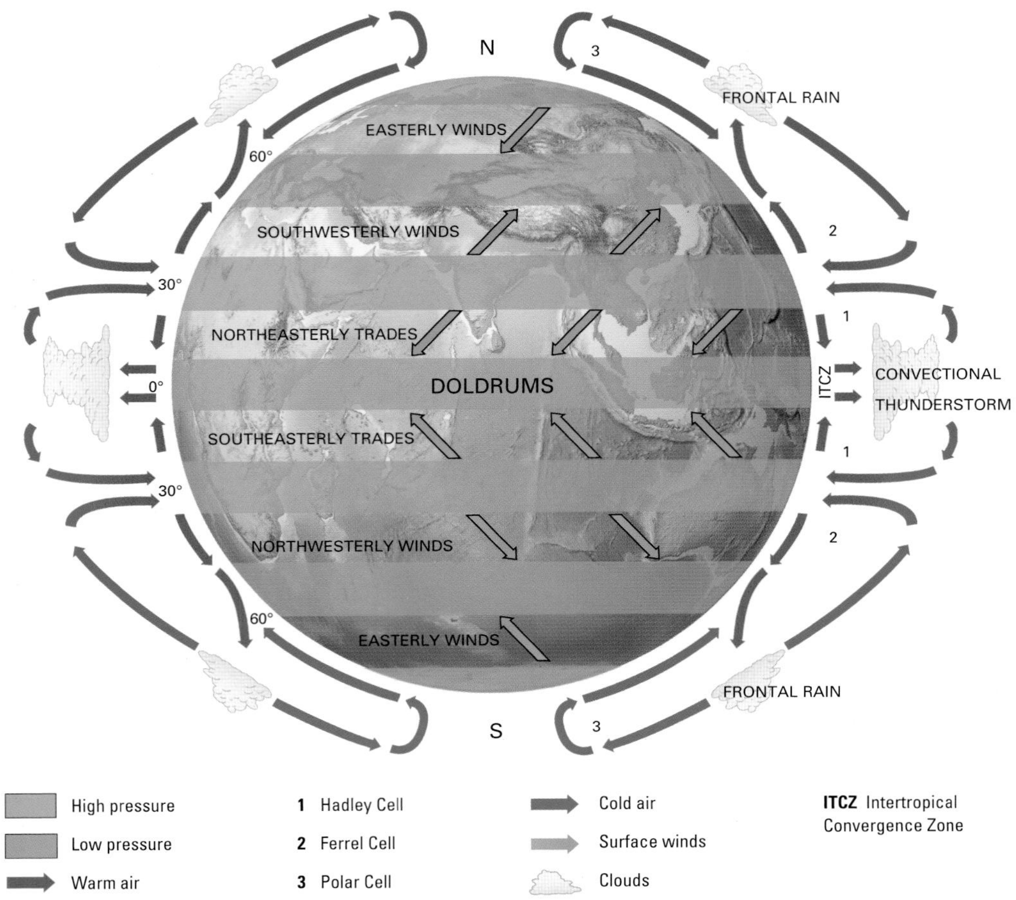

FRONTAL SYSTEMS

Depressions, also known as cyclones or lows, form on the polar front where relatively cold and dry polar air flows alongside warmer, moister subtropical air. They occur when the flow high above the polar front generates a surface inward-swirling circulation that moves along the polar front as a wave.

The warm front is the leading edge of the subtropical air that glides up and over the cooler air ahead of it. This gently ascending flow produces a characteristic sequence of clouds ahead of the warm front and a band of precipitation a few hundred miles wide immediately in advance of it. Conditions within the warm sector are often overcast with layer cloud and generally light rain or drizzle. The cloud sometimes breaks up downwind of hills.

Another band of precipitation often occurs just ahead of the cold front that is the leading edge of the cooler polar air. Cumulus clouds tend to occur in the air behind the cold front, producing scattered showers. The changes of temperature, wind direction, and cloud, etc, are illustrated by the diagram below.

CHEMICAL COMPOSITION

Gaseous composition of the principal atmospheric layers

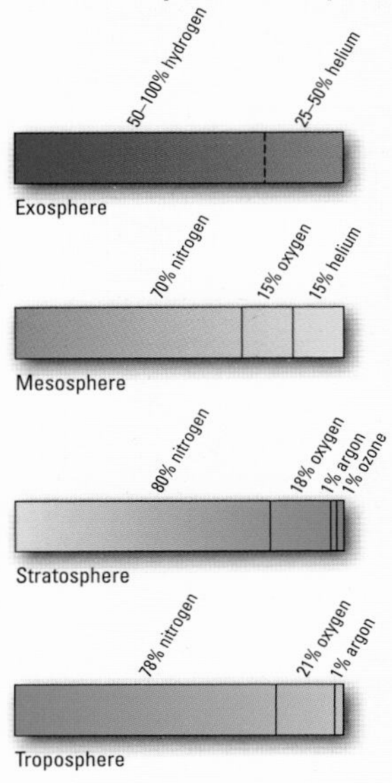

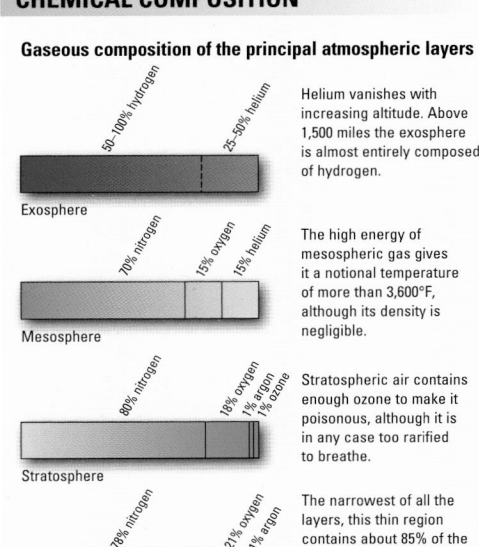

Helium vanishes with increasing altitude. Above 1,500 miles the exosphere is almost entirely composed of hydrogen.

The high energy of mesospheric gas gives it a notional temperature of more than 3,600°F, although its density is negligible.

Stratospheric air contains enough ozone to make it poisonous, although it is in any case too rarified to breathe.

The narrowest of all the layers, this thin region contains about 85% of the atmosphere's total mass and almost all of its water vapor. It is also the realm of the Earth's weather.

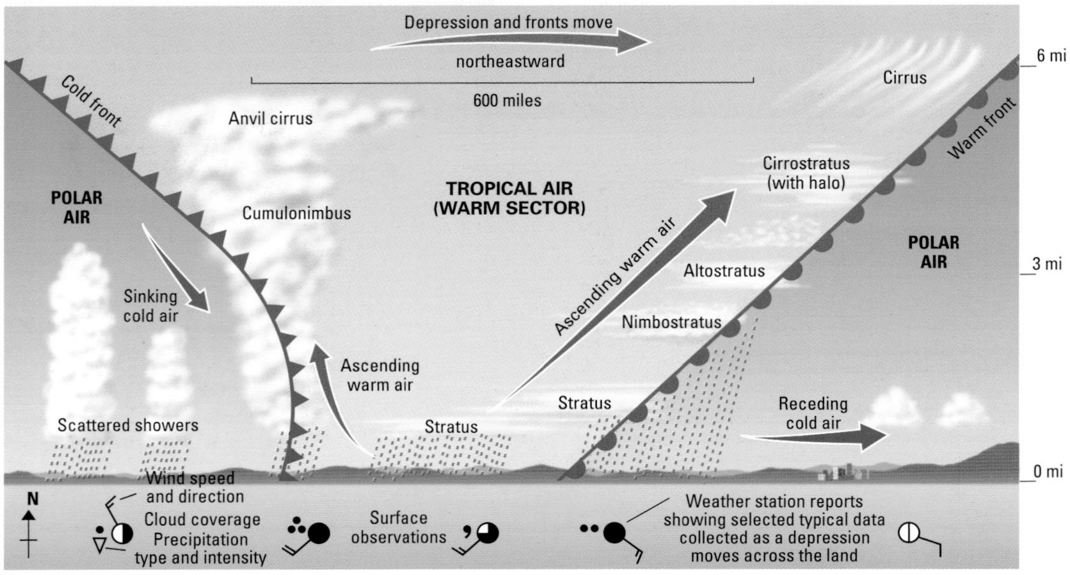

AIR MASSES

Air masses are large bodies of air where the variations of the main physical properties (that is, temperature and humidity) are relatively gentle. The term is generally applied only to the lower layers of the atmosphere, although air masses can cover areas of tens of thousands of square miles.

Air masses derive their temperature and humidity from the regions over which they lie. These regions are known as "source regions." The principal ones are:

- areas of relative calm, such as semipermanent high-pressure areas;
- areas where the surface is relatively uniform, including deserts, oceans, and ice-fields.

These are the "highs" marked on the map below.

As air masses move from their source regions, they may be changed due to the effects of the surface over which they move. These changes create "secondary air masses." For example, a warm air mass that travels over a cold surface is cooled and becomes more stable. Hence, it may form low cloud or fog, but is unlikely to produce much rain. By contrast, a cold air mass that passes over a warm surface is warmed and becomes less stable. The rising air is likely to produce more rain.

When two contrasting air masses meet, they form a "front." As warm air is lighter than cold, dense air, it begins to rise over it, condensing as it rises to form cloud and rain.

CLASSIFICATION OF CLOUDS

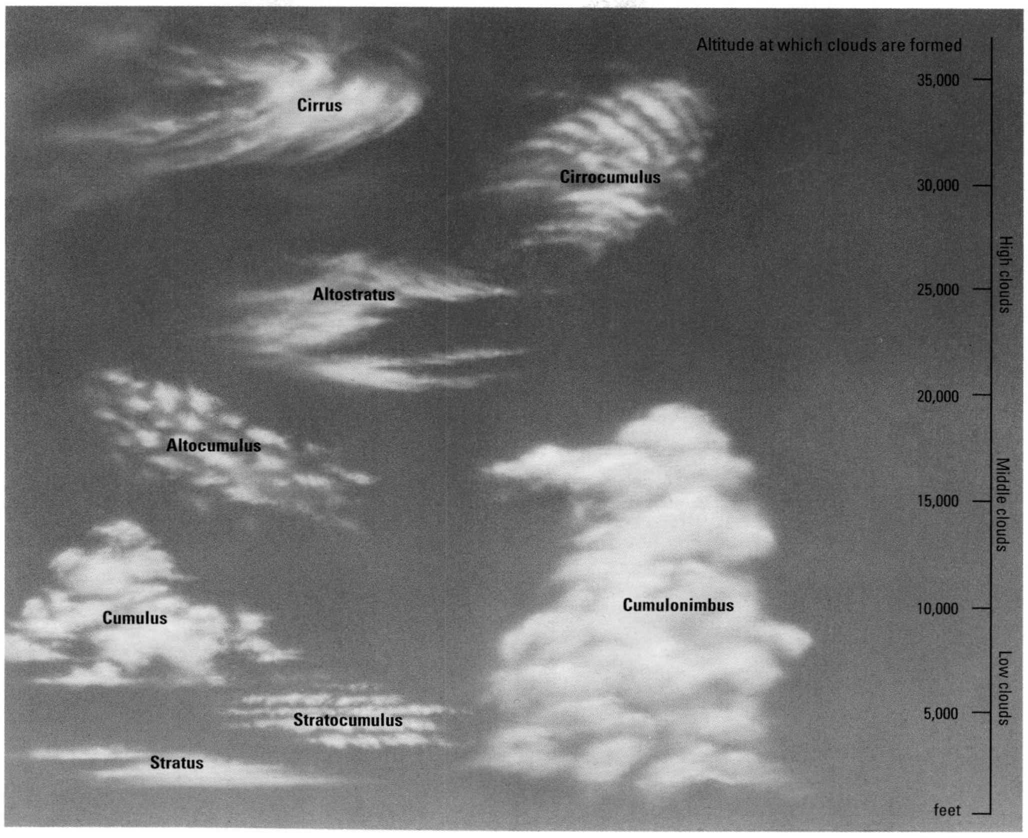

Clouds form when damp, usually rising, air is cooled. Thus they form when a wind rises to cross hills or mountains; when a mass of air rises over, or is pushed up by, another mass of denser air; or when local heating of the ground causes convection currents.

The first classification of clouds was developed by a London chemist, Luke Howard, in 1803, and it was later modified by the World Meteorological Organization. The types of clouds are classified according to altitude as high, middle, or low. The high ones, composed of ice crystals, are cirrus, cirrostratus, and cirrocumulus.

The middle clouds are altostratus – a gray or bluish striated, fibrous or uniform sheet producing light drizzle – and altocumulus, a thicker and fluffier version of cirrocumulus.

Low clouds include nimbostratus, a dark gray layer that brings rain or snow; cumulus, a detached heap, dark at the base; stratus, which forms dull, overcast skies at low levels; and stratocumulus, which consists of fluffy grayish-white layers.

Cumulonimbus, associated with storms and rains, heavy and dense with a flat base and a high, fluffy outline, can be tall enough to occupy middle as well as low altitudes.

PRESSURE AND SURFACE WINDS

JANUARY PRESSURE AND WINDS

Isobars are in millibars at sea level

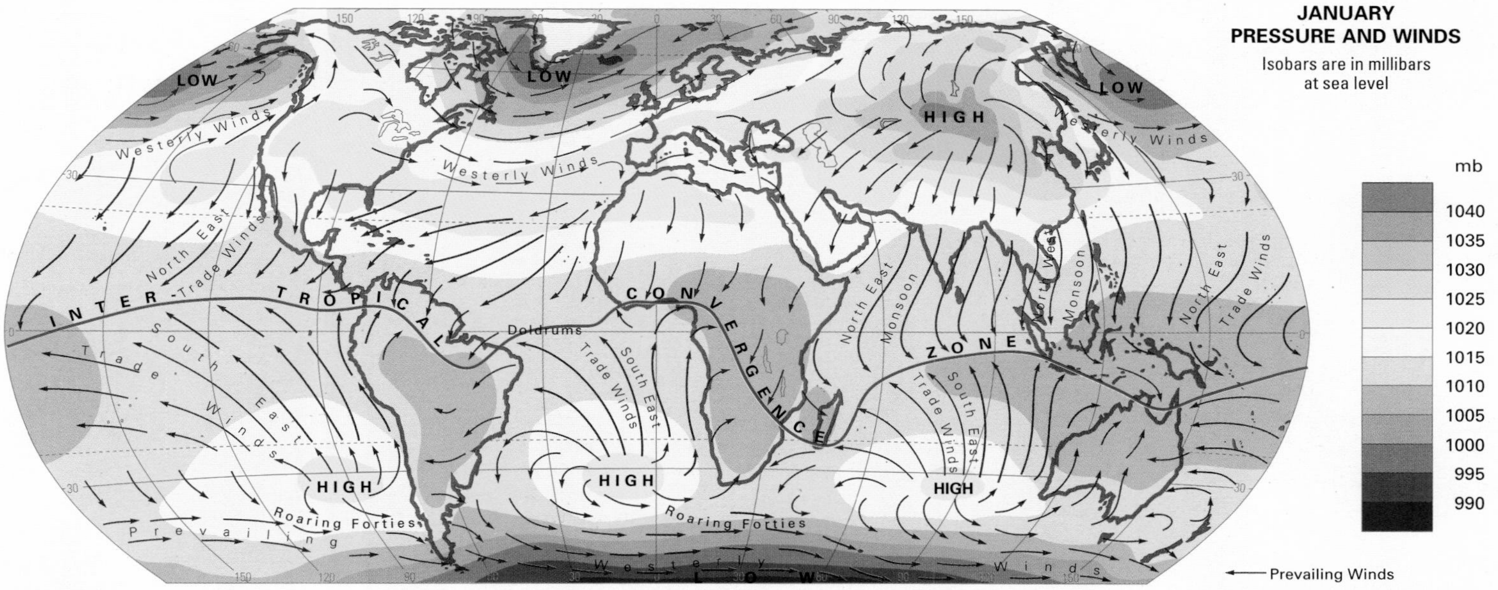

JULY PRESSURE AND WINDS

Isobars are in millibars at sea level

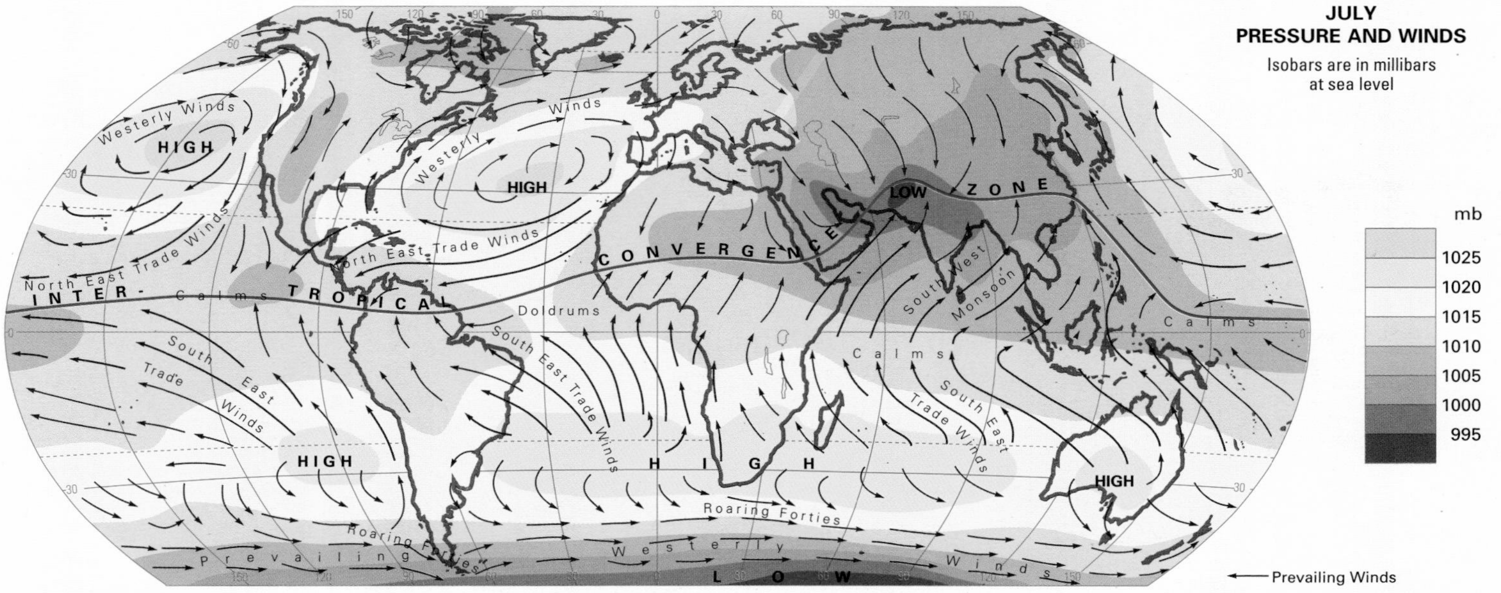

WEATHER RECORDS

Pressure and winds

Highest barometric pressure:
Agata, Siberia, 1,083.8 mb at altitude 862 ft [262 m], December 31, 1968.

Lowest barometric pressure:
Typhoon Tip, 300 mi [480 km] west of Guam, Pacific Ocean, 870 mb, October 12, 1979.

Highest recorded wind speed:
Bridge Creek, Oklahoma, USA, 318 mph [512 km/h], May 3, 1999. Measured by Doppler radar monitoring a tornado.

Windiest place:
Port Martin, Antarctica, where winds of more than 40 mph [64 km/h] occur for not less than 100 days a year.

Worst recorded storm:
Bangladesh (then East Pakistan) cyclone, November 13, 1970 – over 300,000 dead or missing. The 1991 cyclone, Bangladesh's and the world's second worst in terms of loss of life, killed an estimated 138,000 people.

Worst recorded tornado:
Tri-state tornado – Missouri/Illinois/Indiana, USA, March 18, 1925 – 695 deaths, lasted 3 hours with 219 mi [352 km] path length. A suspected tornado in Bangladesh on April 26, 1989, killed approximately 1,300 people.

For more information:

76 Circulation of the air
77 Classification of clouds
Pressure and winds
80 Climate change
Global warming
82 Hydrological cycle
83 Natural vegetation
84 Ocean currents

Weather is the day-to-day or hour-to-hour condition of the air, while climate is weather in the long term – the seasonal pattern of hot and cold, wet and dry, averaged over a long period.

Most classifications of climate are based on a system developed in the early 19th century by Vladimir Köppen, a Russian meteorologist. Using a code based on letters and a classification centered on two main features, temperature and precipitation, he identified five main climatic types: tropical (A), dry (B), warm temperate (C), cold temperate (D), and polar (E). A highland mountain climate (H) was added later to account for the variety of altitudinal climatic zones on high mountains. Each of these main regions was then further subdivided.

Latitude is a major factor in determining climate, but other factors add to the complexity. These include the differential heating of land and sea, the distance from the sea, the effect of mountains on winds, and the influence of ocean currents. For example, New York City, Naples, and the Gobi Desert share almost the same latitude, but their climates are very different.

During the last Ice Age, the Earth underwent alternating cold periods, called glacials, separated by warm interglacials. The Milankovich theory suggests such cycles may be caused by variations in the Earth's path around the Sun, changing from almost circular to elliptical every 95,000 years, and variations in the Earth's tilt from 21.5° to 24.5° every 42,000 years. Another factor is that the Earth is now closest to the Sun in the middle of winter in the northern hemisphere and furthest away in summer. But 12,000 years ago, at the height of the last glacial period, the northern winter fell with the Sun at its most distant.

Studies of these cycles suggest that we are now in an interglacial with a new glacial period on the way. However, scientists believe that global warming, largely a result of burning fossil fuels and deforestation, may be occurring much faster than the great, slow cycles of the Solar System.

Tropical rainy climates
All mean monthly temperatures above 64°F [18°C].

- **Af** Rain forest climate
- **Am** Monsoon climate
- **Aw** Savanna climate

Dry climates
Low rainfall combined with a wide range of temperatures.

- **BS** Steppe climate
- **BW** Desert climate

Warm temperate rainy climates
The mean temperature is below 64°F [18°C] but above 26°F [–3°C] and that of the warmest month is over 50°F [10°C].

- **Cw** Dry winter climate
- **Cs** Dry summer climate
- **Cf** Climate with no dry season

Cold temperate rainy climates
The mean temperature of the coldest month is below 26°F [–3°C] but that of the warmest month is still over 50°F [10°C].

- **Dw** Dry winter climate
- **Df** Climate with no dry season

Polar climates
The mean temperature of the warmest month is below 50°F [10°C], giving permanently frozen subsoil.

- **ET** Tundra climate

The mean temperature of the warmest month is below 32°F [0°C], giving permanent ice and snow.

- **EF** Polar climate

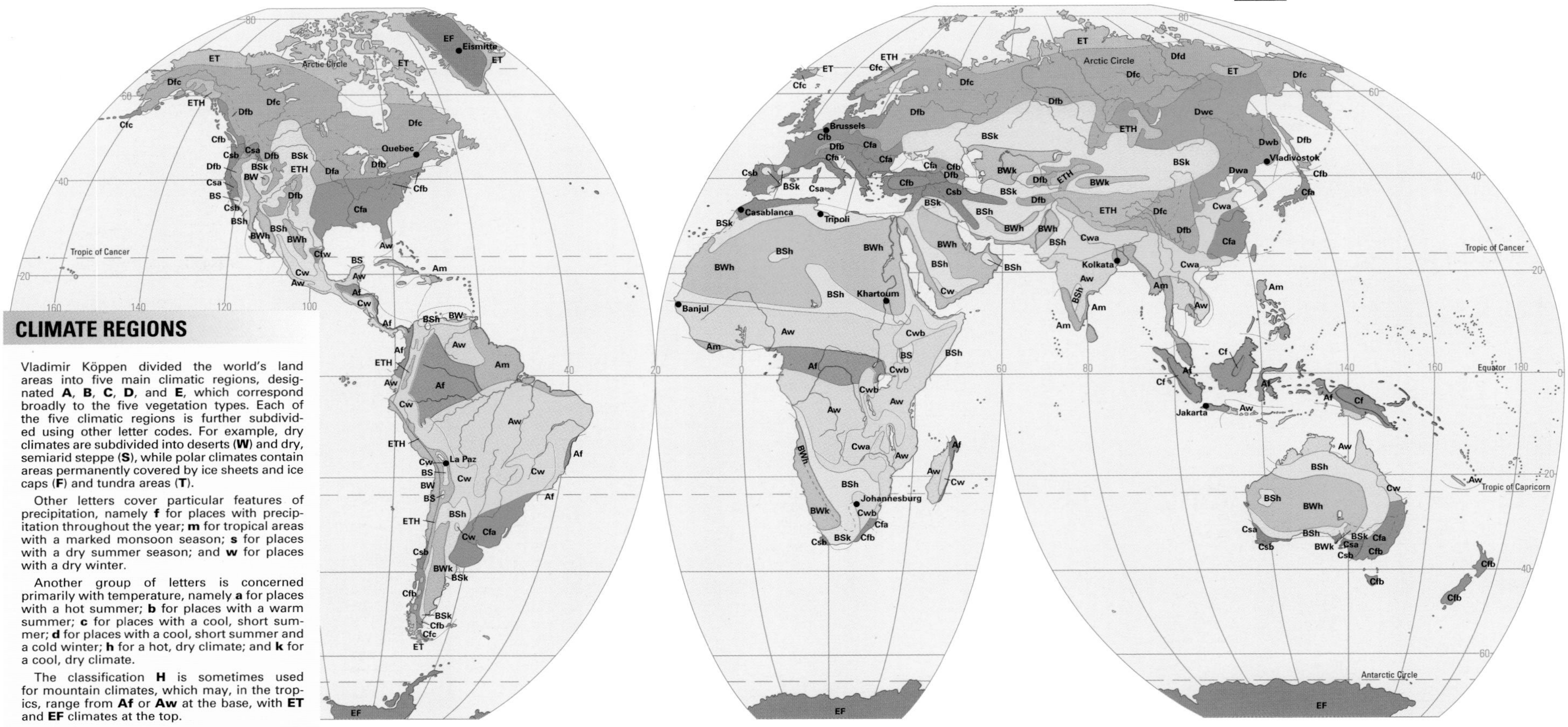

CLIMATE REGIONS

Vladimir Köppen divided the world's land areas into five main climatic regions, designated **A**, **B**, **C**, **D**, and **E**, which correspond broadly to the five vegetation types. Each of the five climatic regions is further subdivided using other letter codes. For example, dry climates are subdivided into deserts (**W**) and dry, semiarid steppe (**S**), while polar climates contain areas permanently covered by ice sheets and ice caps (**F**) and tundra areas (**T**).

Other letters cover particular features of precipitation, namely **f** for places with precipitation throughout the year; **m** for tropical areas with a marked monsoon season; **s** for places with a dry summer season; and **w** for places with a dry winter.

Another group of letters is concerned primarily with temperature, namely **a** for places with a hot summer; **b** for places with a warm summer; **c** for places with a cool, short summer; **d** for places with a cool, short summer and a cold winter; **h** for a hot, dry climate; and **k** for a cool, dry climate.

The classification **H** is sometimes used for mountain climates, which may, in the tropics, range from **Af** or **Aw** at the base, with **ET** and **EF** climates at the top.

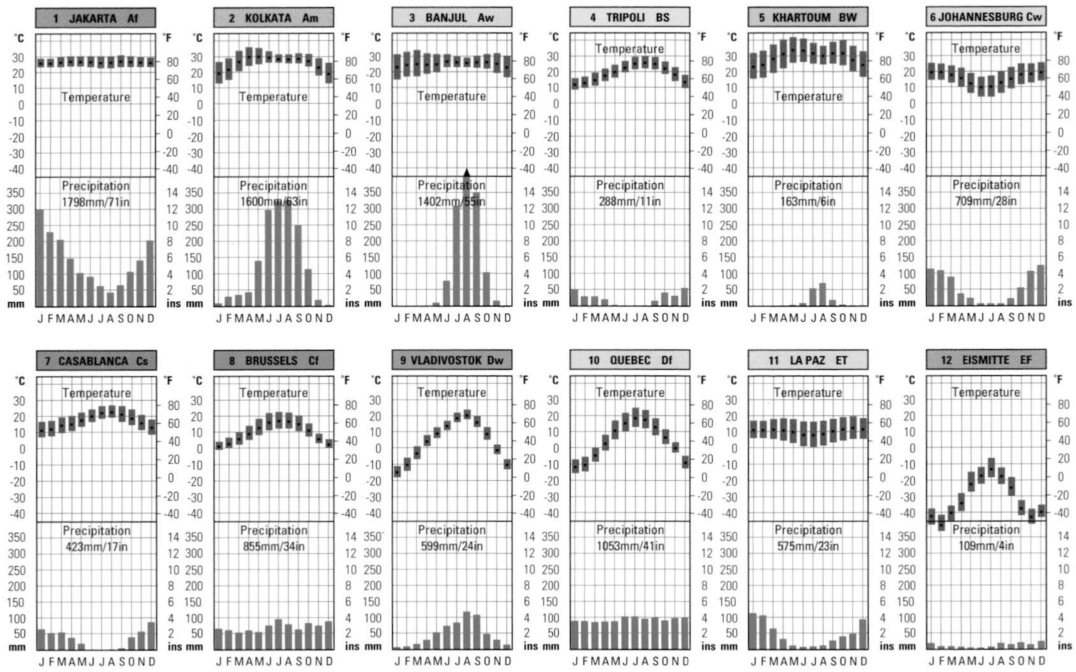

CLIMATE AND WEATHER TERMS

Anticyclone: area of high pressure with light winds and generally quiet weather.
Absolute humidity: mass of water vapor contained in a given volume of air.
Cloud cover: amount of cloud in the sky; measured in oktas (from 0–9), with 0 clear, and 9 "sky obscured."
Condensation: the conversion of water vapor into liquid.
Cyclone: violent storm resulting from counterclockwise rotation of winds in the northern hemisphere and clockwise in the southern: called hurricane in North America, typhoon in the Far East.
Depression: large area of low barometric pressure, a few thousand miles across.
Dew: deposition of small water droplets on the Earth's surface by direct condensation of water vapor.
Dew point: the temperature at which air becomes saturated by cooling at constant barometric pressure and absolute humidity.
Drizzle: precipitation drops between 0.01–0.02 inches [0.2 and 0.5 mm] in diameter.
Evaporation: conversion of water from liquid into vapor or moisture in the air.
Front: the dividing line between two air masses.
Frost: the surface deposition of water vapor as minute ice crystals, when temperature reaches the frost point.
Hail: variably-sized pieces of ice that fall in downdrafts from cumulonimbus clouds.
Humidity: amount of water vapor in the air.
Isobar: line joining places with the same barometric pressure.
Isotherm: line connecting places of equal temperature.
Lightning: massive electrical discharge released in thunderstorm from cloud to cloud or cloud to ground, the result of the top becoming positively charged and the bottom negatively charged.
Precipitation: measurable rain, snow, sleet, or hail.
Prevailing wind: most common direction of wind at a given location.
Rain: precipitation of liquid particles with diameter larger than 0.02 inches [0.5 mm].
Relative humidity: observed quantity of water vapor in a mass of air over the saturation value at a given temperature (as a percentage).
Snow: flake-like coagulations of ice crystals that fall from clouds in subzero temperatures.
Thunder: sound produced by the rapid expansion of air heated by lightning.
Tornado: rapidly-rotating funnel-shaped cloud or debris column that must reach the surface and be attached to a parent cumulonimbus cloud.

BEAUFORT WIND SCALE

Named after Admiral Sir Francis Beaufort, the 19th-century British naval officer who devised it, the Beaufort Scale assesses wind speed according to its effects. It was originally designed as an aid for sailors, but has since been adapted for use on the land. It is used internationally.

Scale	Wind speed mph	Wind speed km/h	Effect
0	0–1	0–1	**Calm** Smoke rises vertically
1	1–3	1–5	**Light air** Wind direction shown only by smoke drift
2	4–7	6–11	**Light breeze** Wind felt on face; leaves rustle; vanes moved by wind
3	8–12	12–19	**Gentle breeze** Leaves and small twigs in constant motion; wind extends small flag
4	13–18	20–28	**Moderate** Raises dust and loose paper; small branches move
5	19–24	29–38	**Fresh** Small trees in leaf sway; crested wavelets on inland waters
6	25–31	39–49	**Strong** Large branches move; difficult to use umbrellas; overhead wires whistle
7	32–38	50–61	**Near gale** Whole trees in motion; difficult to walk against wind
8	39–46	62–74	**Gale** Twigs break from trees; walking very difficult
9	47–54	75–88	**Strong gale** Slight structural damage
10	55–63	89–102	**Storm** Trees uprooted; serious structural damage
11	64–72	103–117	**Violent storm** Widespread damage
12	73+	118+	**Hurricane**

▲ In the Pacific Ocean, off Southeast Asia, Typhoon Haiyan developed into a Category 5 storm during November 2013. Moving westward, wind speeds of 170 mph (275 km/h) were recorded before it hit the Philippines. This makes it the strongest typhoon to make landfall, and over 6,000 people lost their lives.

THE MONSOON

Monsoon is the term given to the seasonal reversal of wind direction, most noticeably in Southeast Asia. It results from a combination of factors: the extreme heating and cooling of large land masses in relation to the less marked changes in temperature of the adjacent seas; the northward movement of the Intertropical Convergence Zone (ITCZ); and the effect of the Himalayas on the circulation of the air.

In March, winds blow outward from the mainland. But as the Sun and the ITCZ move northward, the land is intensely heated, and a low-pressure system develops. The southeast trade winds change direction and are sucked into the interior to become southwesterlies, bringing heavy rain. By November, the Sun and the ITCZ have again moved south and the wind directions are again reversed. Cool winds blow from the Asian interior to the sea, losing any moisture on the Himalayas before descending to the coast.

TEMPERATURE

Average temperature in January

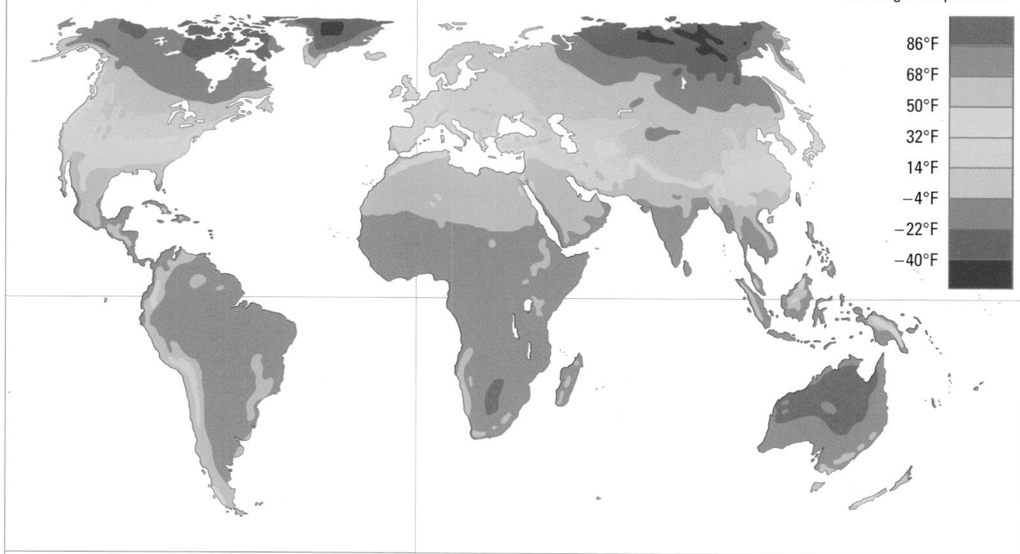

Average temperature in July

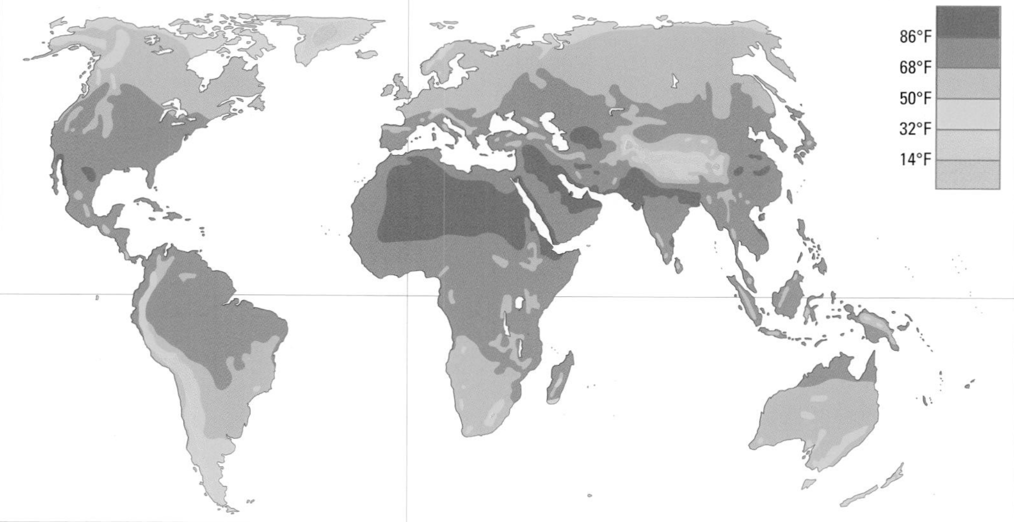

PRECIPITATION (RAINFALL AND SNOW)

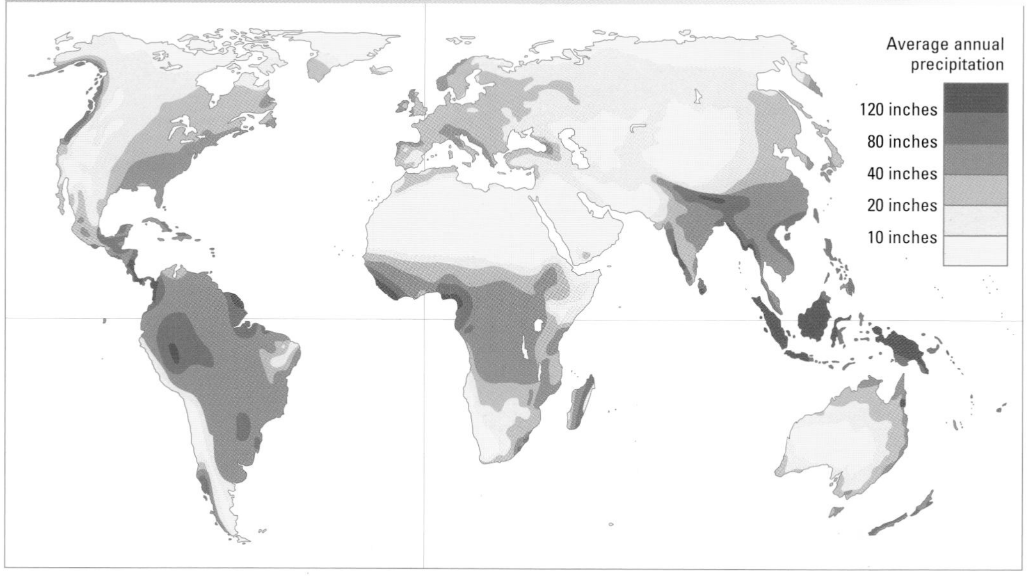

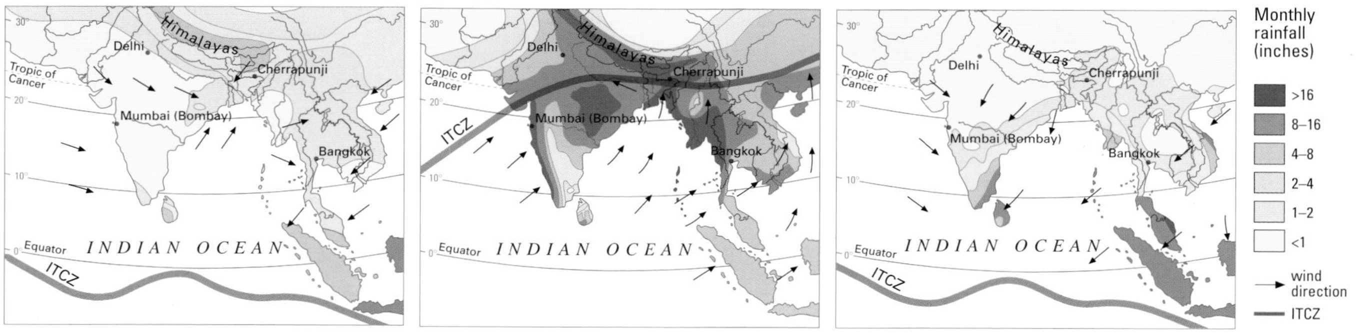

March – Start of the hot, dry season. The ITCZ is over the southern Indian Ocean.

July – The rainy season. The ITCZ has migrated northward; winds blow onshore.

November – The ITCZ has returned south. The offshore winds are cool and dry.

CLIMATE RECORDS

TEMPERATURE

Highest recorded temperature:
Death Valley, California, USA, 134°F [56.7°C], July 10, 1913.

Highest mean annual temperature:
Dallol, Ethiopia, 94°F [34.4°C], 1960–6.

Longest heatwave:
Marble Bar, W. Australia, 162 days over 100°F [38°C], October 23, 1923, to April 7, 1924.

Lowest recorded temperature (outside poles):
Verkhoyansk, Siberia, −93.6°F [−69.8°C], February 7, 1982. Verkhoyansk also registered the greatest annual range of temperature: −90°F to 98°F [−68°C to 37°C].

Lowest mean annual temperature:
Polus Nedostupnosti, Pole of Cold, Antarctica, −72°F [−57.8°C].

PRECIPITATION

Driest place:
Quillagua, N. Chile, mean annual rainfall 0.02 inches [0.5 mm], 1964–2001.

Wettest place (average):
Mt Wai'ale'ale, Hawai'i, USA, mean annual rainfall 459.8 inches [11,680 mm].

Wettest place (12 months):
Cherrapunji, Meghalaya, N.E. India, 1,042 inches [26,461 mm], August 1860 to August 1861. Cherrapunji also holds the record for rainfall in one month: 115 inches [2,930 mm], July 1861. (*See Monsoon maps below.*)

Wettest place (24 hours):
Fac Fac, Réunion, Indian Ocean, 71.9 inches [1,825 mm], March 15–16, 1952.

Heaviest hailstones:
Gopalganj, Bangladesh, up to 2.25 lb [1.02 kg], April 14, 1986 (killed 92 people).

Heaviest snowfall (continuous):
Bessans, Savoie, France, 68 inches [1,730 mm] in 19 hours, April 5–6. 1969.

Heaviest snowfall (season/year):
Mt Baker, Washington, USA, 1,140 inches [28,956 mm], June 1998 to June 1999.

For more information:
76 Atmosphere
78 Climate
84 Ocean currents

Ever since the Industrial Revolution began, the amount of carbon dioxide in the atmosphere has steadily increased. It is the result of burning fossil fuels, and the destruction of forests which absorb carbon dioxide. In the late 18th century, carbon dioxide made up about 280 parts per million by volume (ppmv). It has risen to over 416 ppmv in 2021.

Carbon dioxide is one of the "greenhouse gases" which also include CFCs (which also cause ozone depletion in the upper atmosphere), methane, and nitrous oxides. Another greenhouse gas is water vapor. The quantity of vapor in the atmosphere has increased during recent decades as an expression of increased evaporation. This enhances the greenhouse effect as a positive feedback.

Greenhouse gases are so-called because they absorb part of the Earth's radiation going out to space and re-radiate a proportion of it back down. This critically important natural process acts to insulate the Earth and is essential to life. Without it, our planet would be some 54°F [30°C] colder than it is. But the increase in the volume of carbon dioxide in particular has caused global temperatures to rise. These changes were detailed by the Intergovernmental Panel on Climate Change (IPCC) report in 2013. While computer projections are difficult to make, the IPCC report concluded that a rise in temperatures of between 2.7°F [1.5°C] (compared to the 1850–1900 global mean) and at least 3.6°F [2.0°C] is likely by 2100. Global warming will almost certainly alter weather patterns, causing food and water shortages in vulnerable parts of the world, massive floods, and a rise in sea levels of between 1.71 ft [0.52 m] and 3.22 ft [0.98 m].

While an international ban has been imposed on some greenhouse gases, their residence time in the atmosphere may have long-lasting consequences.

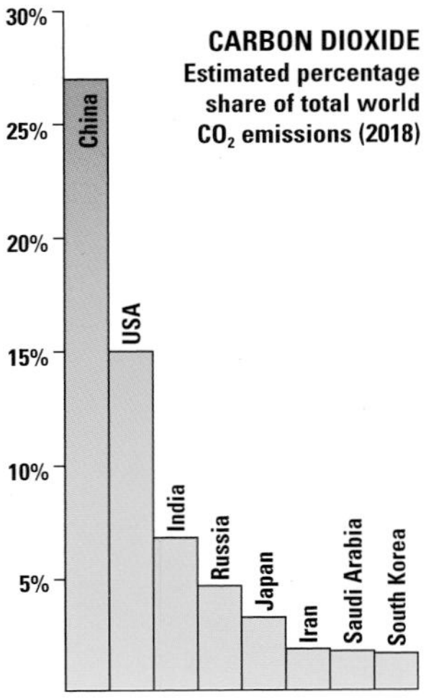

In 2018, the total world CO_2 emissions had reached over 37 billion tonnes. China remains the world's largest CO_2 emitter – accounting for more than one-quarter of all emissions.

GLOBAL WARMING

High atmospheric concentrations of heat-absorbing gases are a major cause in the rise of average surface temperatures worldwide – up by 1.78°F [0.99°C] between 1880 and 2016. Global warming is also likely to bring about a rise in sea levels that may flood some of the world's densely populated coastal areas (see panel at foot of page 81).

Evidence of global warming is attributed mainly to the "greenhouse effect," caused by the emission of certain gases, notably carbon dioxide, into the atmosphere. Despite international action to control emissions of some greenhouse gases, carbon dioxide levels are still rising.

Carbon dioxide emissions in tonnes per capita (2018)

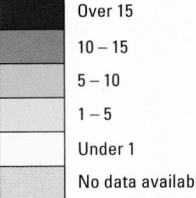

	Over 15
	10 – 15
	5 – 10
	1 – 5
	Under 1
	No data available

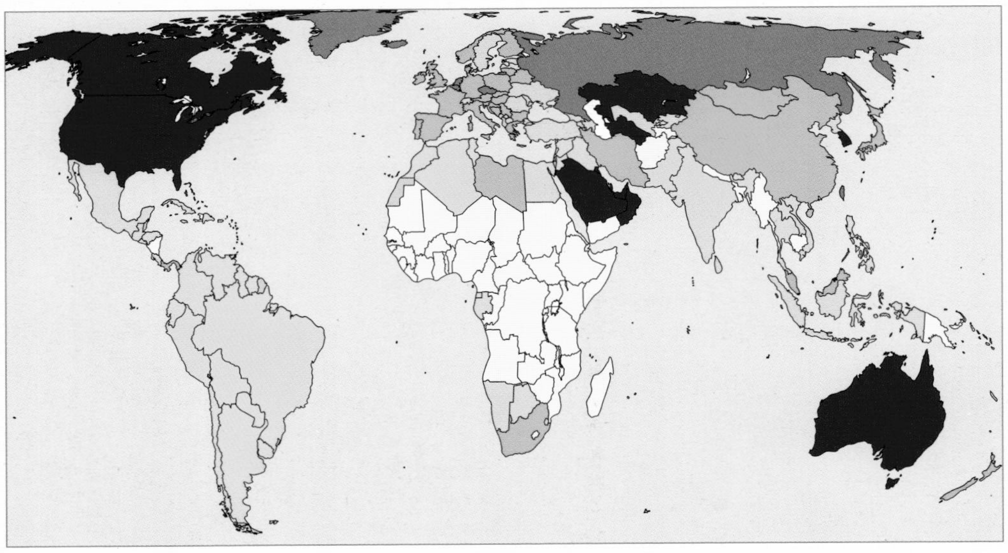

CLIMATE CHANGE

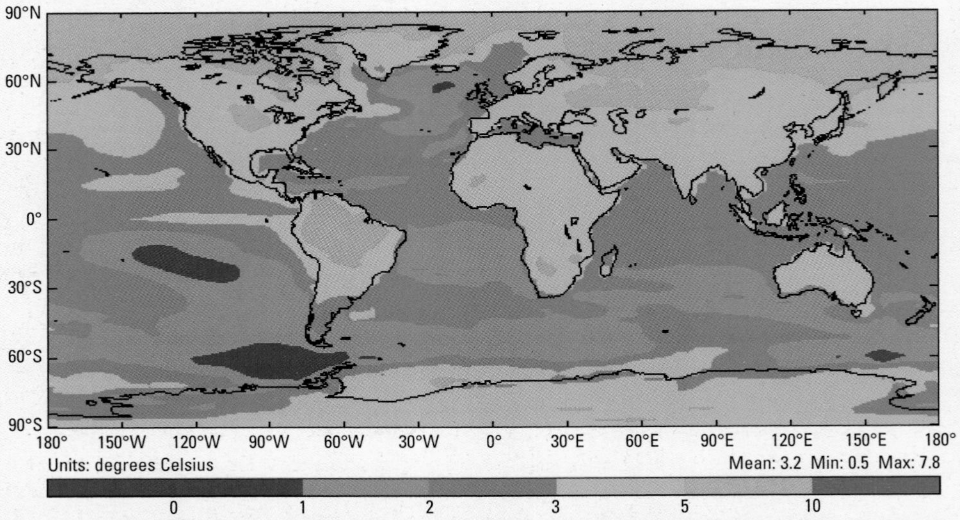

Annual average surface air temperature

The map summarizes the change in long-term mean values between the predicted average for the period from 2070 to 2100, and the observed average for 1960 to 1990. The predictions are from a long-term "run" of a "coupled" atmosphere-ocean computer model that represents the complex processes in the Earth's climate system. It assumes that the atmospheric concentration of carbon dioxide will increase more than twofold during the 21st century, assuming "medium growth" of the global economy, and that no measures to combat the emission of greenhouse gases are taken. Note that the predicted increase in average surface temperature suggests a warming across Britain and Ireland of between 3.6°F [2°C] in the north and west to possibly 7.2°F [4°C] in the southeast. Very broadly, the oceans and some adjacent continental areas are likely to see the smaller increases.

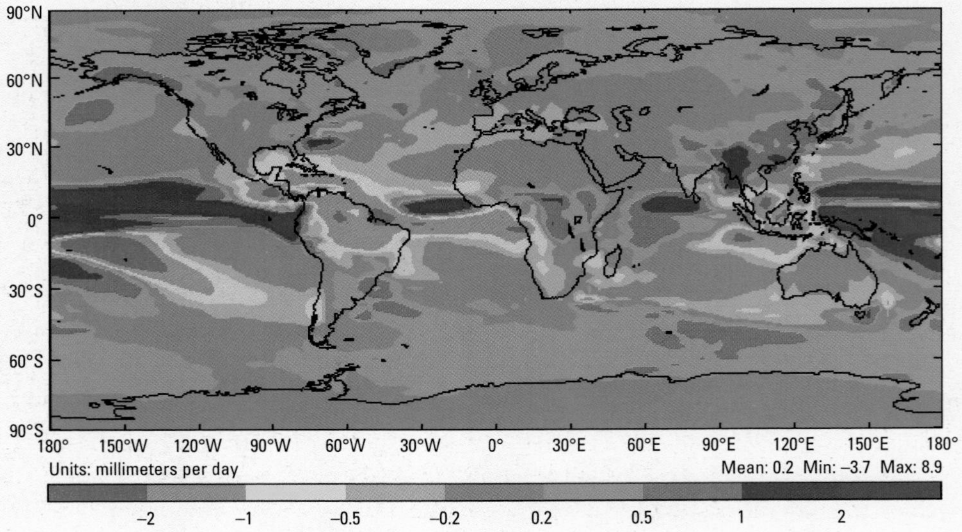

Annual average precipitation

Predictions from climate models always involve some degree of uncertainty. This is because our understanding of the climate system and its complex workings are imperfect, as are the model representations of the physical system. Additionally, we are unsure quite how the world will evolve economically and politically over the coming decades – although different scenarios are used in this regard. The map of predicted precipitation change indicates broadly, for example, an increase across Britain and Ireland. The largest increases of some 0.01–0.02 inches [0.2–0.5 mm] a day are anticipated to be over northern and western areas. This equates to some 3–7 inches [75–180 mm] a year.

It should be noted that both these maps mask quite significant seasonal detail, which is also predicted by the models.

ARCTIC SEA ICE

The fact that the Arctic sea ice is disappearing has been known for decades. The underlying cause is believed by all but a handful of climatologists to be global warming, brought about by greenhouse-gas emissions. At current rates of shrinkage, this looks likely to happen some time between 2020 and 2050.

The reason is that Arctic air is warming twice as fast as the atmosphere as a whole. While some of the causes of this are understood, others are not. The darkness of land and water compared to the reflectiveness of snow and ice means that when the snow and ice melt to reveal land or water, the area exposed absorbs more heat from the Sun and reflects less of it back into space. The result is a feedback loop that accelerates local warming.

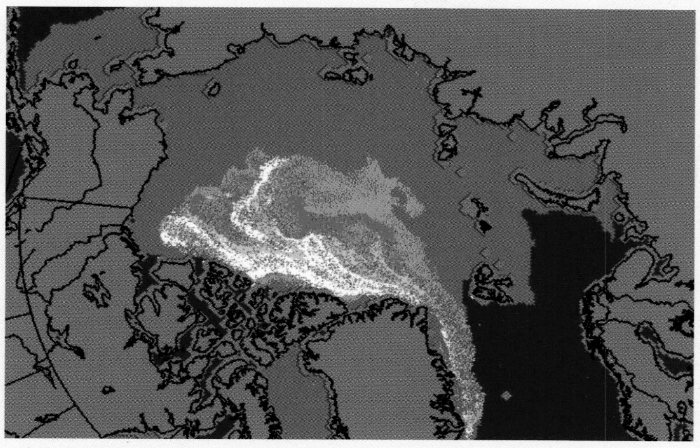

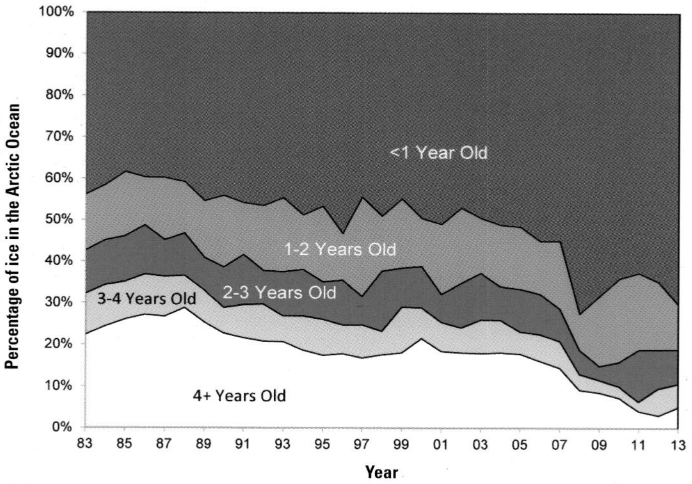

The diagram and map show that ice older than 1 year, which used to cover up to 60% of the Arctic Ocean, now covers only 30%. The oldest ice, over 4 years old, now comprises only 5% of the ice in the Arctic Ocean, whereas during the 1980s it covered roughly 25% of the region.

NSIDC courtesy J. Maslanik and M. Tschudi, University of Colorado

REGIONAL CLIMATE CHANGE

Climate modelers have produced simulations of global and continental surface temperature changes over the last century. This is done using only "natural forcing" by modeling the impact on atmospheric temperatures from known solar variability and volcanic eruptions. In addition, the same period of time is simulated by adding to natural forcing the impact of anthropogenic (human) influence due to measured changes in the concentration of greenhouse gases, particulate matter, etc.

The separate model "runs" are then compared with the observed temperature changes to illustrate which of the simulations matches the observations best.

This is a powerful means of verifying the relative roles of natural and human induced changes in atmospheric composition, and known solar output fluctuations on climate change.

► Climate model simulations for 1906 to 2009 using "natural forcings only" (blue bands) and "natural plus anthropogenic forcings" (pink bands). Regional decadal averages of observed temperature (black lines) are plotted as anomalies with respect to the 1880 to 1919 average. Blue and pink bands define the 5% to 95% range of possibilities for multiple runs for just natural forcings and natural plus anthropogenic forcings of the Coupled Model Intercomparison Project Phase 5.

Models using only natural forcings

Models using both natural and anthropogenic forcings

Observations
(dashed when spatial coverage is less than 50%)

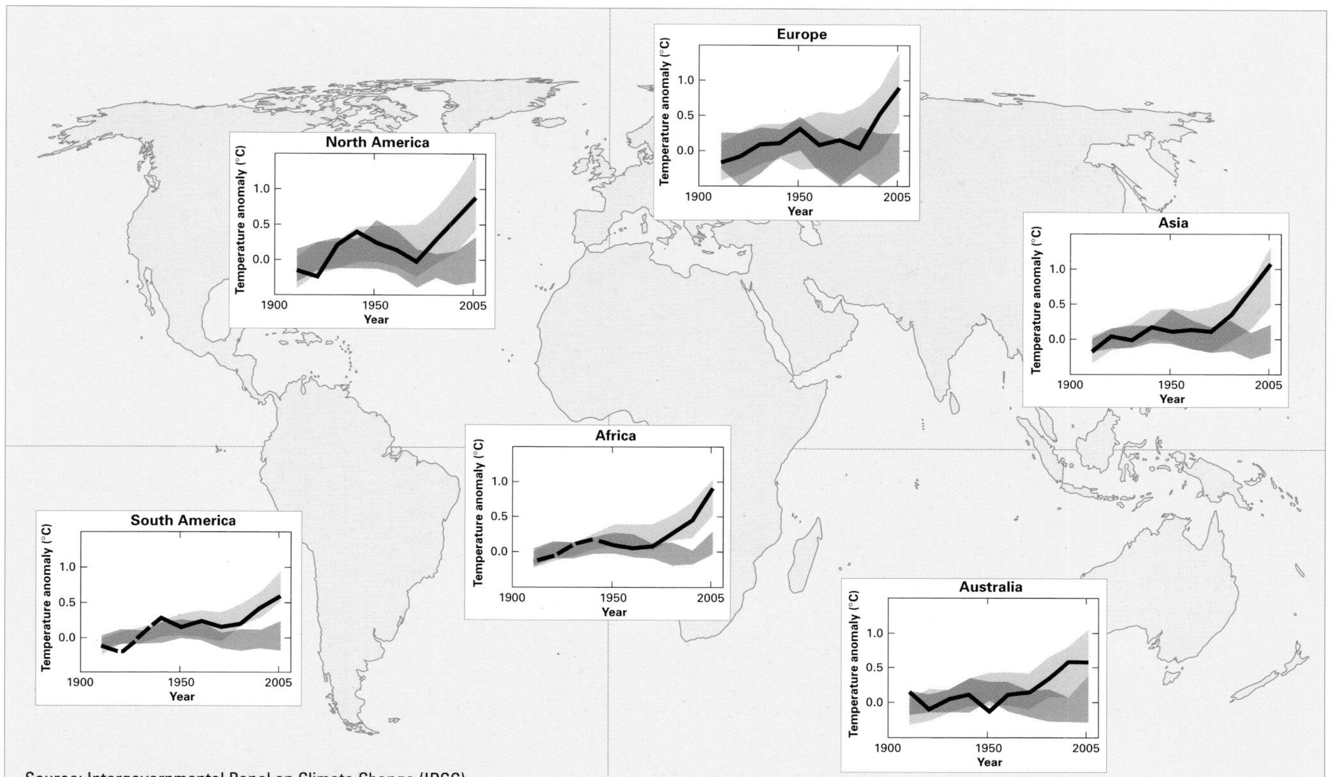

Source: Intergovernmental Panel on Climate Change (IPCC)

PROJECTED CHANGE IN GLOBAL WARMING

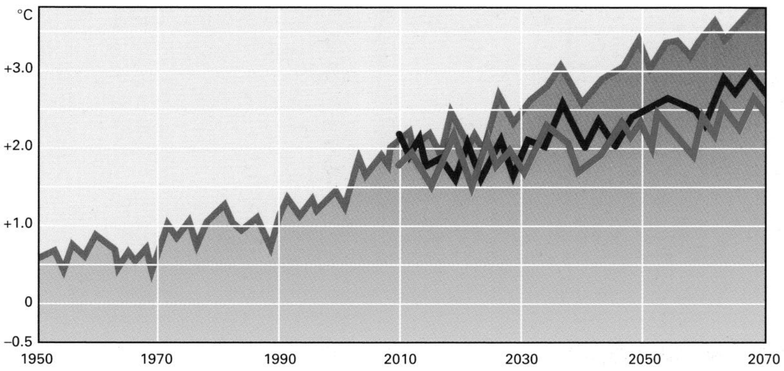

Rise in average temperatures assuming present trends in CO_2 emissions continue

Assuming some cuts are made in emissions

Assuming drastic cuts are made in emissions

Climate models are used to provide the best scientifically-based estimates of the future global climate. A typical method is to run the models for some decades ahead and then to compare the predicted average with a past 30-year period. A range of climate models are used, run with different scenarios that express the breadth of possibilities of, for example, industrial development and the degree of atmospheric pollution "clean-up" by industrial nations.

The diagram above shows global observed and predicted surface mean temperature change from 1950 to 2070 with three prediction scenarios. The first (red) assumes rapid economic growth and continued population increases. The second (blue) assumes some attempts are made to cut greenhouse gas emissions, while the green line involves the greater use of cleaner technologies, with global population peaking mid-century then declining.

RECENT AND FUTURE SEA LEVEL CHANGE

The rate at which global sea level has increased since about the middle of the 19th century exceeds the increase estimated over the last two thousand years. The recent change is one expression of the impact of global warming through a combination of glacier melt and thermal expansion of the ocean; it is estimated that these count for 75% of the total observed rise since the 1970s. A combination of tide-gauge records and, more recently, altimeter observations from satellites, indicate that the global average increase of sea level from 1901 to 2010 was 7.5 inches [190 mm] with an averaged global annual rise of 0.07 inches [1.7 mm] per year. This value has increased in recent periods from 0.08 inches [2.0 mm] per year (1971–2010) to 0.13 inches [3.2 mm] per year (1993–2010).

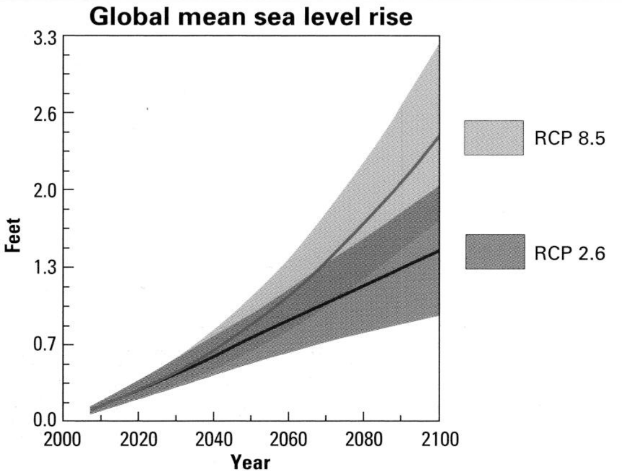

Source: Intergovernmental Panel on Climate Change (IPCC)

A combination of advanced global climate prediction models run through to 2100 produce an averaged forecast of the likely range of global mean sea level increase for two extreme CO_2, and other greenhouse gas, scenarios. The values on the graph are relative to the global mean conditions for the period 1986–2005. These "Representative Concentration Scenarios" (RCPs) vary from the lowest impact future (RCP 2.6) for which CO_2 concentration reaches 421 ppm by 2100, to the strongest impact (RCP 8.5) for which CO_2 increases to 936 ppm by 2100.

The upper and lower boundaries of the two bands of color on the graph show the predicted upper and lower possibilities of future sea level increase. The solid colored line is the median value that has 50% of estimates above it and 50% below. The low impact future indicates a median value of a 1.31 ft [0.4 m] increase by 2100 while the highest impact future is about double that at 2.46 ft [0.75 m].

For more information:
78 Climate regions
79 Precipitation
88 Biodiversity

Without the hydrological cycle, by which water is constantly recycled between the oceans, the atmosphere and the land, the continents would be barren. Precipitation enables plants to grow and soils to form, creating the world's natural vegetation regions and the ecosystems that support animal life.

Running water also plays a major role in shaping landforms. Yet in many parts of the world, people do not have safe water to drink and suffer from diseases caused by water-borne organisms and pollution. It is estimated that 770 million people lack access to safe water and more people have a mobile phone than a toilet.

Experts argue that world demand for water is increasing at about twice the rate of population growth. It is predicted that, by 2025, half the world's population will face water shortages. This could lead to conflict and even boundary wars – 300 major rivers cross national frontiers and access to their water is likely to be disputed.

THE HYDROLOGICAL CYCLE

The world's water balance is regulated by the constant recycling of water between the oceans, the atmosphere and the land. The movement of water between these three reservoirs is known as the "hydrological cycle." The oceans play a vital role in the hydrological cycle: 74% of the total precipitation falls over the oceans and 84% of the total evaporation comes from the oceans. Water vapor in the atmosphere circulates around the planet, transporting energy as well as the water itself. When the vapor cools, it falls as rain or snow. The whole cycle is driven by the Sun.

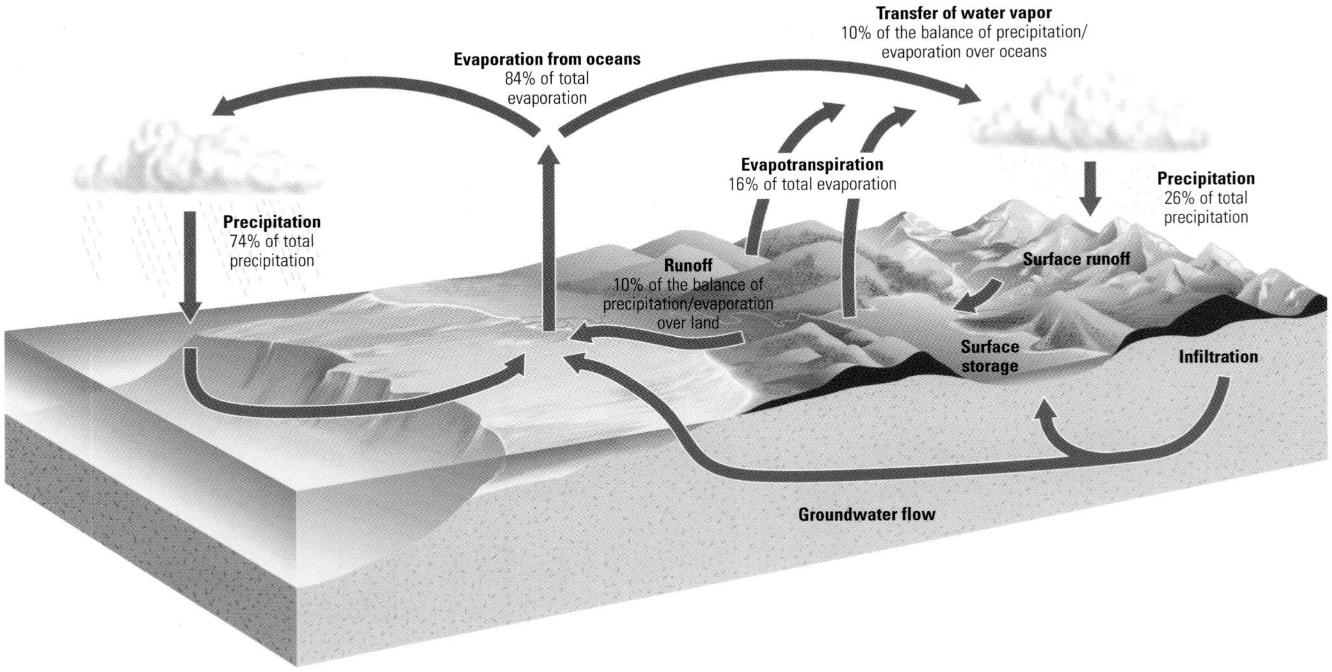

WATER DISTRIBUTION

The distribution of planetary water is shown by percentage. Oceans and ice caps together account for more than 99% of the total; the breakdown of the remainder is estimated.

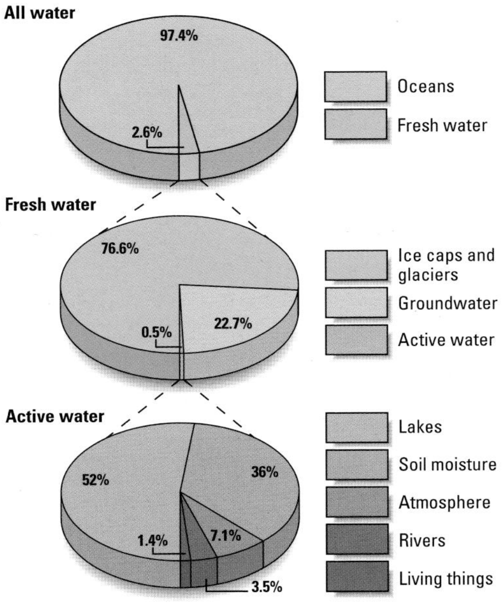

Almost all the world's water is 3,000 million years old, and all of it cycles endlessly through the hydrosphere, though at different rates. Water vapor circulates over days, even hours; deep-ocean water circulates over millennia; and ice-cap water remains solid for millions of years.

ANNUAL SEDIMENT YIELD

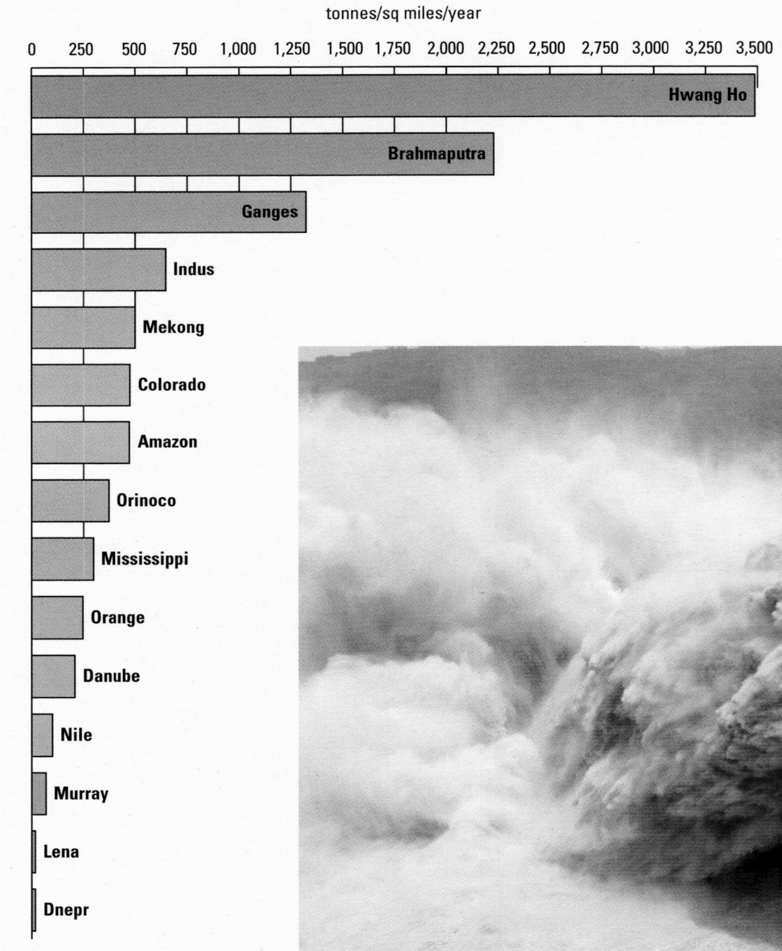

Around 20% of all land-derived sediment is carried by three Asian rivers: the Hwang Ho (Yellow River), the Brahmaputra, and the Ganges. Together, these three rivers carry around 3,000 million tonnes of sediment each year into the oceans. Sediment yield is affected by runoff and vegetation cover, and is steadily increasing due to large-scale deforestation, most notably in Southeast Asia and the Amazon basin. In these regions, deforesting the slopes allows the heavy tropical rains to wash away whatever thin and fragile soil there is, leading to severe erosion of the land.

▼ To prevent an excess of sediment building up and slowing the flow of the Hwang Ho (Yellow River), the river's mud, silt and sand is blasted downstream at an annual event at the Xiaolangdi Reservoir, near Jiyuan, in Henan province.

LONGEST RIVERS

		miles	km
Nile	Africa	4,160	6,695
Amazon	South America	4,010	6,450
Yangtse	Asia	3,960	6,380
Mississippi-Missouri	North America	3,710	5,971
Yenisey-Angara	Asia	3,445	5,550
Hwang Ho	Asia	3,395	5,464
Ob-Irtysh	Asia	3,360	5,410
Congo	Africa	2,900	4,670
Paraná-Plate	South America	2,796	4,500
Mekong	Asia	2,796	4,500
Amur	Asia	2,760	4,442
Lena	Asia	2,735	4,402
Irtysh	Asia	2,640	4,250
Mackenzie	North America	2,630	4,240
Niger	Africa	2,595	4,180
Yenisey	Asia	2,540	4,090
Missouri	North America	2,540	4,088
Mississippi	North America	2,350	3,782
Murray-Darling	Australia	2,330	3,750
Volga	Europe	2,300	3,700
Ob	Asia	2,285	3,680
Zambezi	Africa	2,200	3,540
Purus	South America	2,080	3,350
Madeira	South America	1,990	3,200
Yukon	North America	1,980	3,185
Indus	Asia	1,925	3,100
Darling	Australia	1,905	3,070
Rio Grande	North America	1,880	3,030
Brahmaputra	Asia	1,800	2,900
São Francisco	South America	1,800	2,900
Syrdarya	Asia	1,775	2,860
Danube	Europe	1,770	2,850
Salween	Asia	1,740	2,800
Paraná	South America	1,740	1,740
Tocantins	South America	1,710	2,750
Orinoco	South America	1,700	2,740
Euphrates	Asia	1,675	2,700
Murray	Australia	1,600	2,575
Paraguay	South America	1,580	2,550
Amudarya	Asia	1,575	2,540

WATER SCARCITY

Human populations require fresh water for many purposes – drinking, cooking, washing, farming, industry, recreation and energy production. Given population growth and rising standards of living in some areas, there will inevitably be increased pressure on this resource in certain places. Water scarcity can be physical and/or economic.

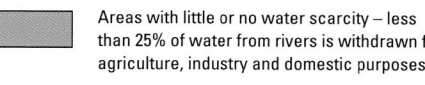

- Areas with little or no water scarcity – less than 25% of water from rivers is withdrawn for agriculture, industry and domestic purposes
- Areas with physical water scarcity – more than 75% of water from rivers is withdrawn for agriculture, industry and domestic purposes
- Areas approaching physical water scarcity – more than 60% of water from rivers is withdrawn and scarcity is expected in the near future
- Areas with economic water scarcity – less than 25% of water from rivers is withdrawn but human, institutional and financial problems limit access to water
- No data available

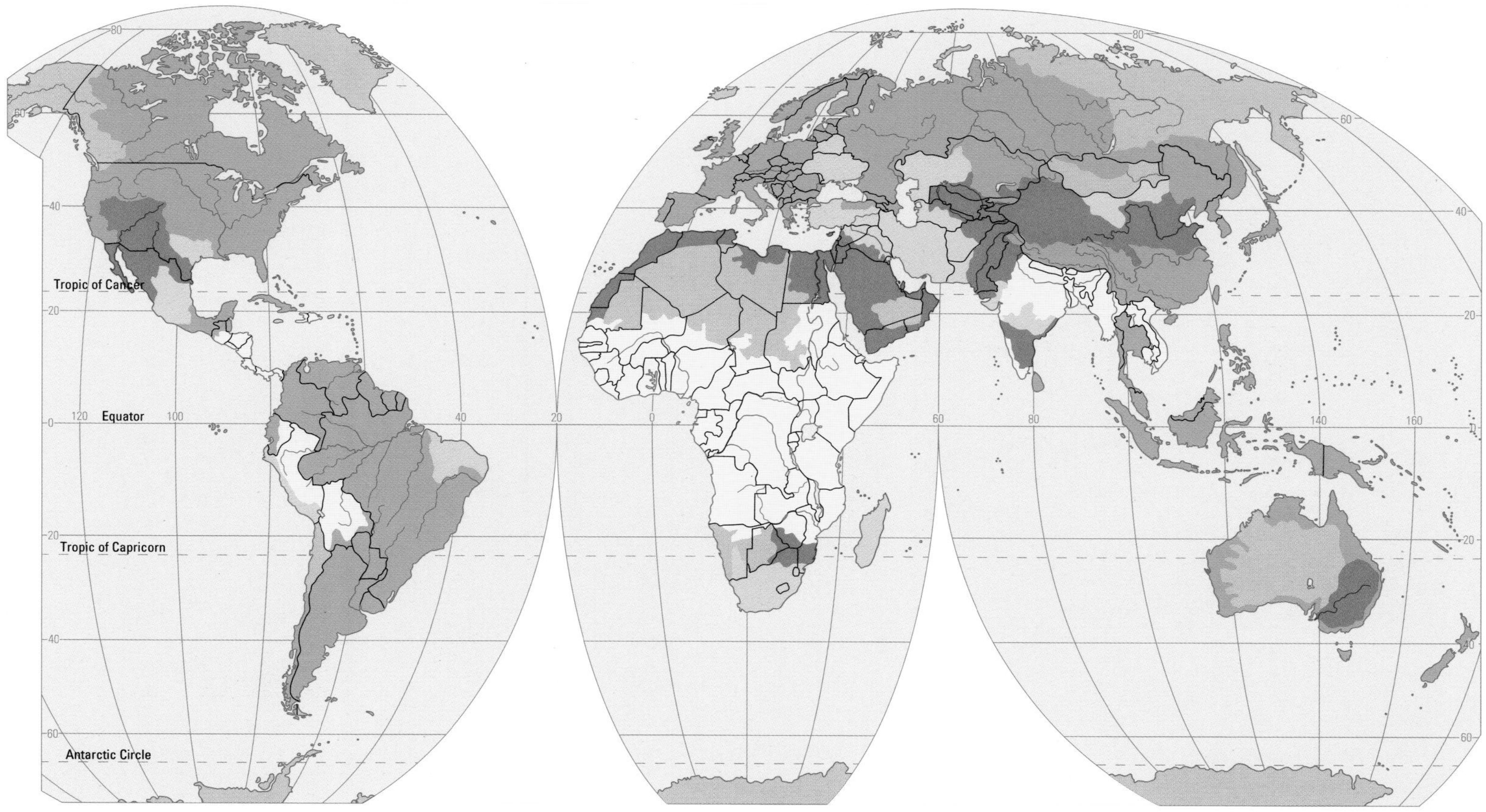

NATURAL VEGETATION

The map below illustrates the natural "climax vegetation" of a region, as dictated by its climate and topography. In most cases, human agricultural activity has drastically altered the pattern of the vegetation. The various vegetation regions support different kinds of animals and wildlife, and, in an undisturbed state, they are highly developed biological communities, or "biomes."

The blue line on the map represents the northern limit of tree growth, and the red lines indicate the northern and southern limits of palm growth. The majority of the numerous species are tropical or subtropical. Some, such as the coconut, date, sago, and oil palms, are important economically.

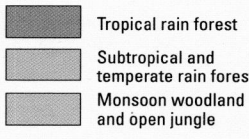

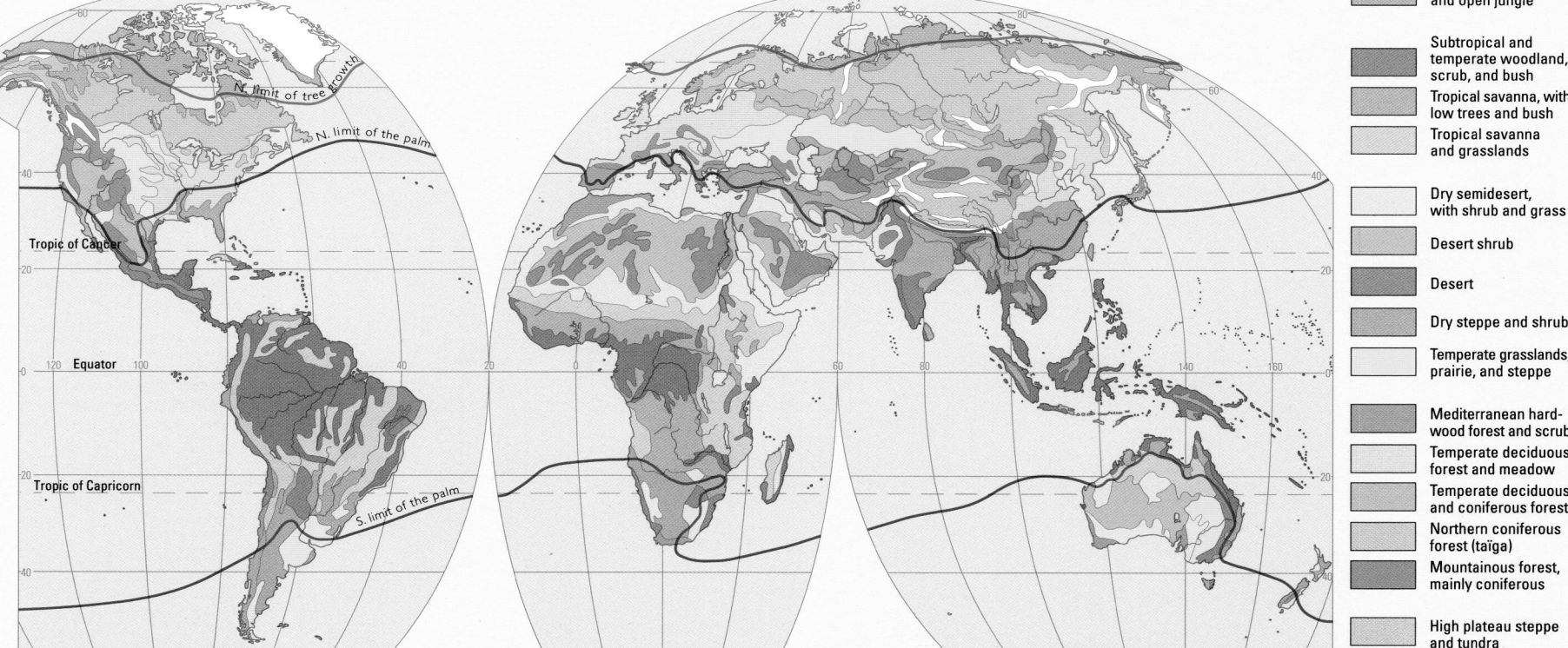

- Tropical rain forest
- Subtropical and temperate rain forest
- Monsoon woodland and open jungle
- Subtropical and temperate woodland, scrub, and bush
- Tropical savanna, with low trees and bush
- Tropical savanna and grasslands
- Dry semidesert, with shrub and grass
- Desert shrub
- Desert
- Dry steppe and shrub
- Temperate grasslands, prairie, and steppe
- Mediterranean hardwood forest and scrub
- Temperate deciduous forest and meadow
- Temperate deciduous and coniferous forest
- Northern coniferous forest (taïga)
- Mountainous forest, mainly coniferous
- High plateau steppe and tundra
- Arctic tundra
- Polar and mountainous ice desert

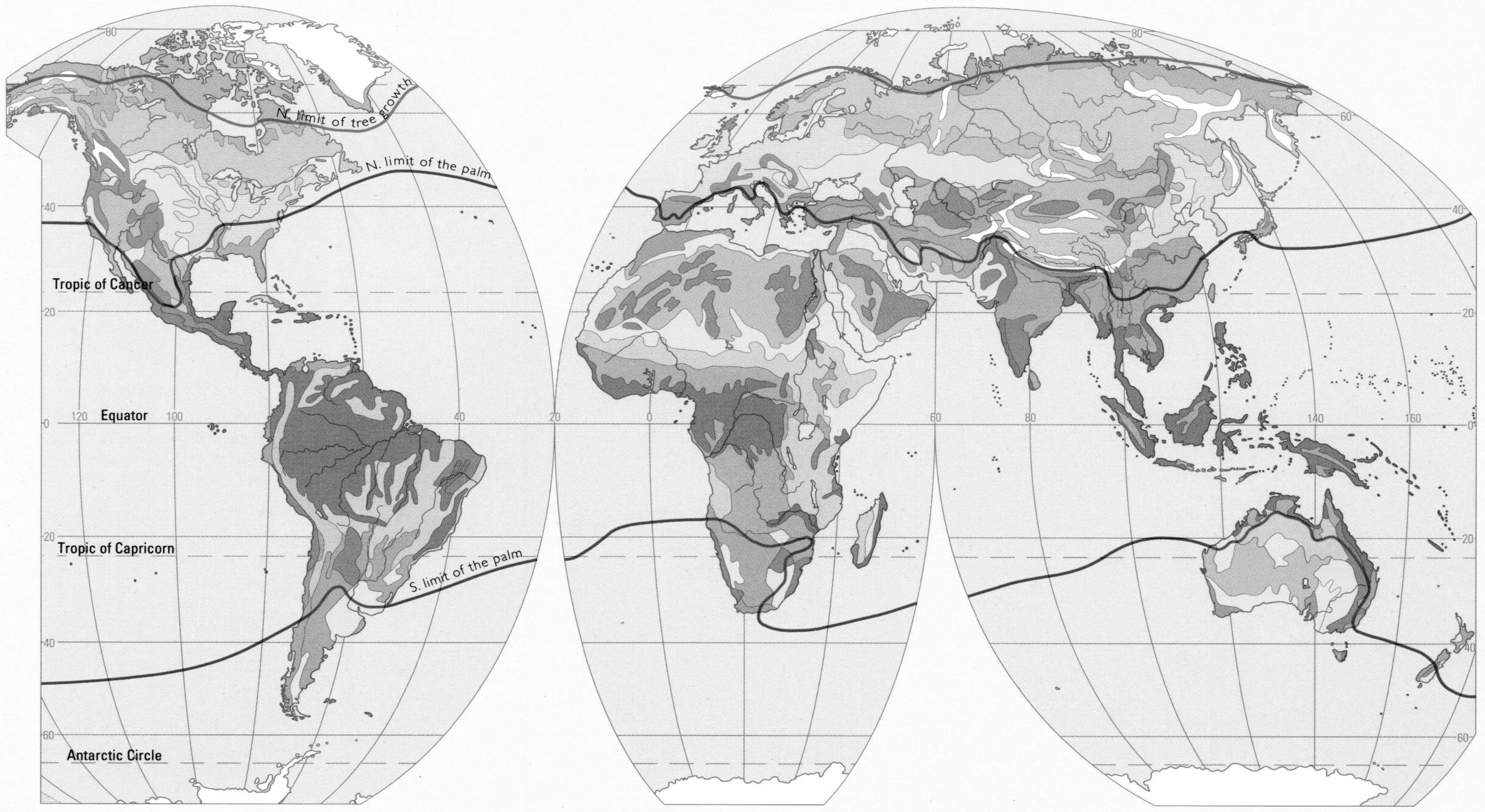

For more information:
79 Temperature and precipitation
80 Climate change and global warming
82 Water distribution

Oceans cover about 70% of the Earth's surface and are of great importance to humans in a number of ways. These include regulating global climates and providing a source of economic materials, such as food resources. In addition, oceans are important for leisure and recreation. They have also been described as the "highways in the globalized world." However, anthropogenic (man-made) stresses are changing the oceans faster than at almost any time in our planet's history.

Increasingly larger fishing fleets are now catching fewer large predatory fish but greater quantities of the smaller fish that are further down the food chain. The most prized food fish, such as cod and salmon, which tend to be top-level predators, are declining in numbers, leaving smaller, less desirable fish to be caught. Not only does this affect the type of fish available for human consumption, but it could also change marine ecosystems forever.

There are a number of possible strategies for the future, but there are clearly no simple solutions to the problems associated with such a politically, economically, and environmentally sensitive global industry. Fish resources could be conserved in a number of ways – for example, the protection of juveniles as well as policies to encourage breeding and discourage the marketing of illegal catches would help boost stocks. Catches could be restricted in order to match supply with demand and to protect sensitive species.

OCEANIC CONVEYOR BELTS

Oceanic convection occurs where cold, salty water from polar regions sinks into the depths and makes its way toward the Equator. The densest water is found in the Antarctic area. This cold, dense water sweeps round Antarctica at a depth of about 2.5 miles [4 km]. It then spreads into the deep basins of the Atlantic Ocean, the Pacific Ocean, and the Indian Ocean. Surface currents bring warm water to the North Atlantic from the Indian and Pacific Oceans. These waters give up their heat to cold winds, which blow from Canada across the North Atlantic. This water then sinks and starts the reverse convection of the deep ocean current. The amount of heat given up is about a third of the energy that is received from the Sun. Because the conveyor operates in this way, the North Atlantic is warmer than the North Pacific, so there is proportionally more evaporation there. The water left behind by evaporation contains more salt and it is therefore much denser, which causes it to sink. Eventually, this water is transported into the Pacific Ocean where it picks up more warm water, and thus its salinity and therefore its density is reduced.

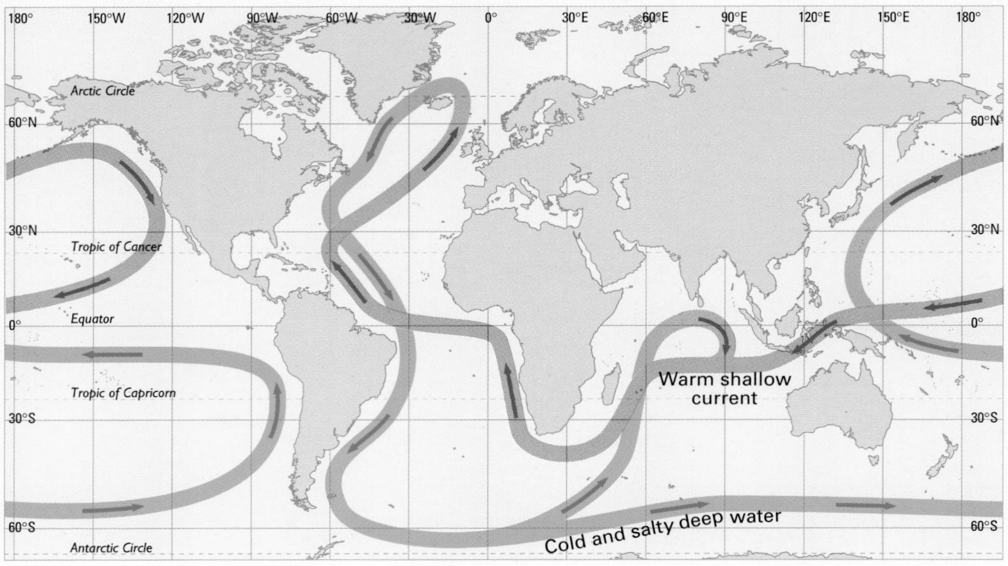

OCEAN CURRENTS

JANUARY CURRENTS
(Northern Hemisphere: winter)

Cold Warm Speed (knots)
Less than 0.5
0.5 – 1.0
Over 1.0

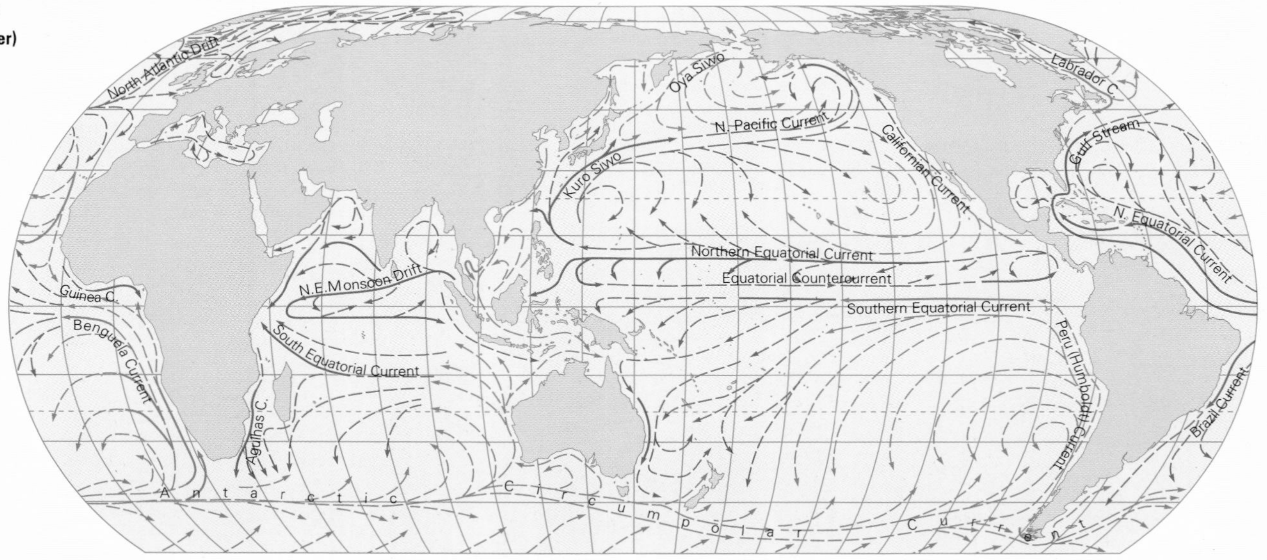

JULY CURRENTS
(Northern Hemisphere: summer)

Cold Warm Speed (knots)
Less than 0.5
0.5 – 1.0
Over 1.0

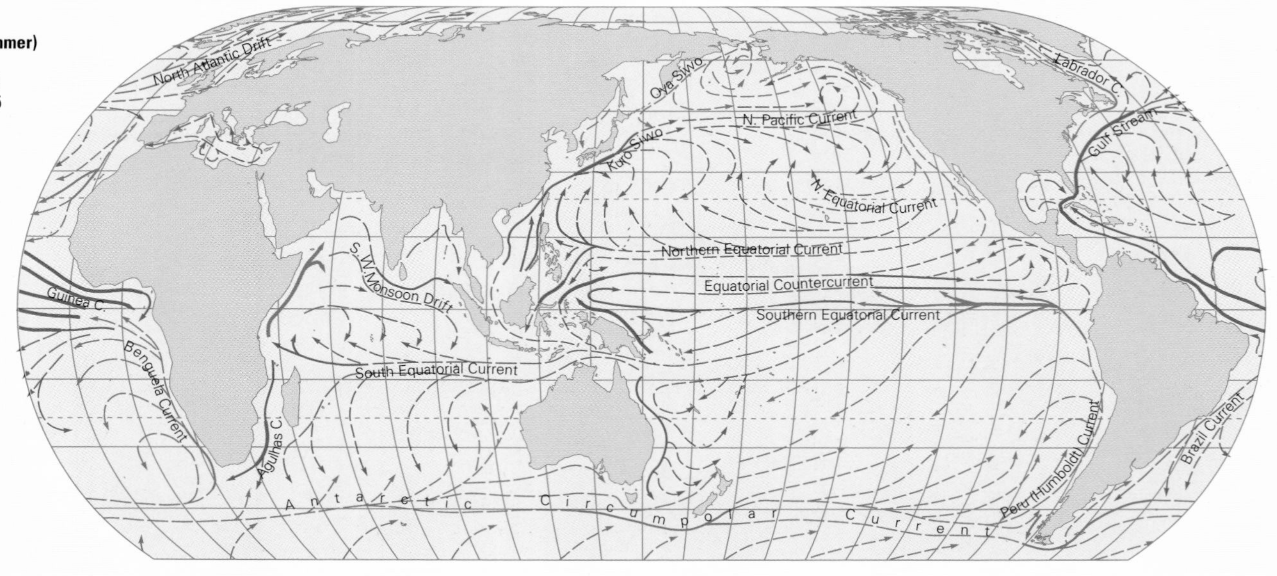

Moving immense quantities of energy as well as billions of tonnes of water every hour, the ocean currents are a vital part of the great heat engine that drives the Earth's climate. They themselves are produced by a twofold mechanism. At the surface, winds push huge masses of water before them; in the deep ocean below, an abrupt temperature gradient separates the churning surface waters from the still depths (*see the oceanic conveyor belt diagram above*).

Coriolis effect

The pattern of circulation of the great surface currents is determined by the displacement known as the "Coriolis effect." As the Earth turns, the vast mass of ocean water is deflected to one side. The deflection is most obvious near the Equator, where the Earth's surface is spinning eastward at 1,000 mph; currents moving poleward are curved clockwise in the northern hemisphere and counterclockwise in the southern hemisphere.

Ocean currents

The result is a system of spinning circles known as "gyres." Warm currents move constantly from the Equator toward the poles, while cold water moves in the reverse direction. In this way, ocean currents act like a thermostat, helping to regulate temperatures around the world.

Depending on the annual movements of the prevailing wind belts, some currents on or near the Equator may reverse their direction in the course of the year, a variation on which Asia's monsoon rains depend and whose occasional failure has brought disaster to millions of people.

FISHING

As stocks are overfished and dwindle, it is important to manage them carefully so that there are sufficient resources for future generations. The Marine Stewardship Council (MSC) is an international, non-profit organization set up to help make the seafood market sustainable. It oversees and manages the distinctive blue labeling system that tells consumers which species of fish they can buy without destroying stocks. This system is popular with large food retailers who wish to be seen supporting sustainable fish catches. It is estimated that over 30% of shoppers worldwide recognize the MSC ecolabel. However, only 8% of the world's fisheries are MSC certified.

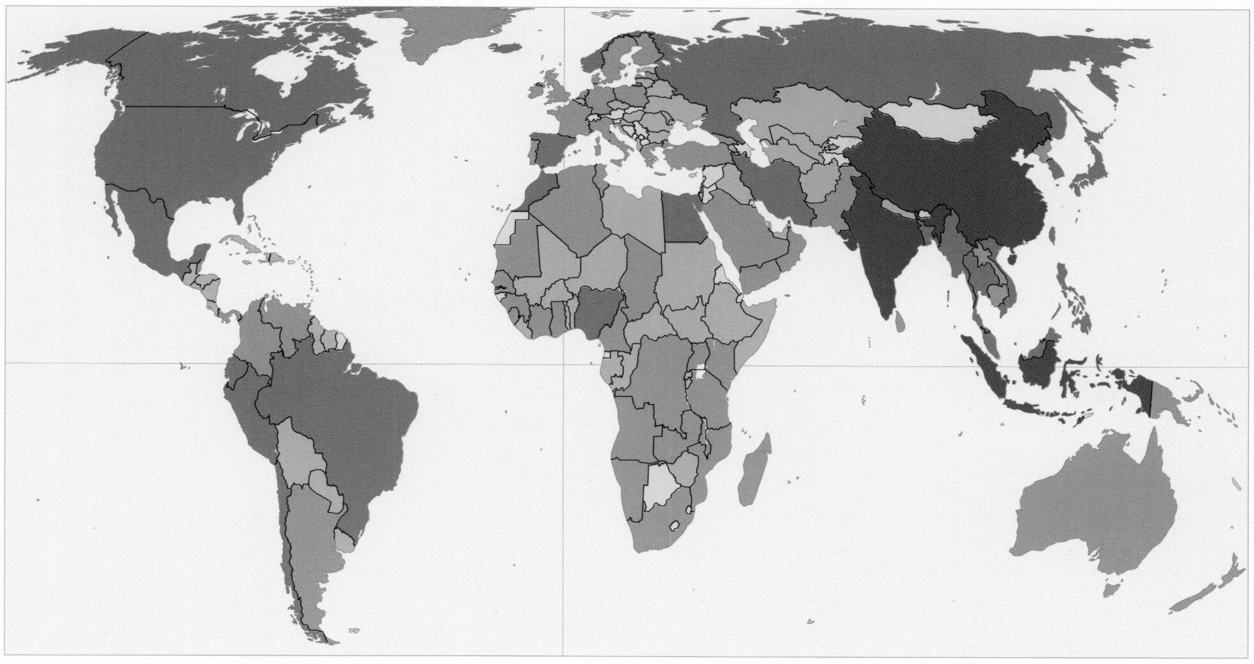

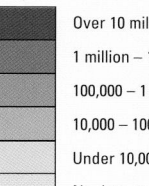

There has been a dramatic rise in world wild fish catches, from under 20 million tonnes in 1950 to an estimated 90.9 million tonnes in 2016, but this is now leveling off as the stocks become depleted and protection of fish stocks increases. Farmed fish totals rose from almost nothing in 1950 to 2019 where farmed fish overtook the wild catch. Currently, about 3 billion people get 20% of their animal protein from fishery products.

Total world fish catch in metric tonnes, inland and marine fishing (2018)

- Over 10 million
- 1 million – 10 million
- 100,000 – 1 million
- 10,000 – 100,000
- Under 10,000
- No data available

AQUACULTURE

▲ This aerial photo shows shrimp farms, near Mahajanga, in northwestern Madagascar. Shrimp farming is being used to stimulate the country's economy.

Aquaculture involves raising fish commercially, usually for food. In contrast, a fish hatchery releases juvenile fish into the wild for recreational fishing or to supplement a species' natural numbers. The most important fish species raised by fish farms are salmon, carp, tilapia, catfish, and cod. Salmon makes up 85% of the total sale of Norwegian fish farming. Farming was introduced when populations of wild Atlantic salmon in the North Atlantic and Baltic Sea crashed due to overfishing.

Technological costs are high, and include using drugs, such as antibiotics to keep fish healthy and steroids to improve growth. Breeding programs are also expensive. Outputs are high per hectare and per farmer, and efficiency is high also. However, environmental effects can be damaging. Salmon are carnivores and so need to be fed pellets made from other fish. It is possible that farmed salmon actually represent a net loss of protein in the global food supply, as it takes between 4–11 lbs [2–5 kg] of wild fish to grow 2 lbs [1 kg] of salmon. In contrast, most global aquaculture production (*c.* 85%) uses non-carnivorous fish species, such as tilapia and catfish, for domestic markets. Fish like herring, mackerel, sardine, and anchovy are used to produce the feed for farmed salmon, and so the production of salmon leads to the depletion of other fish species on a global scale.

Other environmental costs include the sea lice and disease that spread from farmed salmon into wild stocks, and pollution (created by uneaten food, faeces, and chemicals used to treat them) contaminating surrounding waters. Organic debris of this type, with steroids and other chemical waste, can contaminate coastal waters. In addition, the accidental escape of fish can affect local wild fish gene pools, when escaped fish interbreed with wild populations, reducing their genetic diversity, and potentially introducing non-natural genetic variation. In some parts of the world, escapees of farmed fish threaten native wild fish, as salmon is an alien species (for example, the salmon farming industry in British Columbia, Canada, has inadvertently introduced a non-native species – Atlantic salmon – into the Pacific Ocean).

However, the positive environmental benefits of not removing fish from wild stocks, but of growing them in farms, are great. Wild populations are allowed to breed and maintain stocks, whilst the farmed variety provides food.

▲ These floating aquaculture pens contain northern bluefin tuna in Baja California, Mexico. Small tuna are caught off-shore and moved to large enclosures.

PLASTIC

Yet more alarming for the health of the oceans and their wildlife is the plague of plastic. The UN Environment Programme estimated in 2006 that every square kilometer of sea held nearly 18,000 pieces of floating plastic. Much of it was, and is, in the central Pacific, where scientists believe as much as 100 million tonnes of plastic jetsam are suspended in two separate "gyres" of garbage over an area twice the size of the USA. This has been referred to as the Great Pacific Garbage Patch – about 90% of the plastic in the sea has been carried there by wind or water from land. It takes decades to sink or decompose.

▲ In the main, the plastic in the oceans comes from food and drink packaging. The larger pieces can be mistakenly eaten by animals such as seals and turtles and choke them. Smaller pieces are swallowed by fish which can then work their way up through the food chain to humans. Harm is also caused by the chemicals contained within plastics.

RESPONSES TO THE THREATS

In the case of the oceans, a conservative estimate of the cost of climate change is that by the year 2100 it will amount to nearly US $2 trillion annually, or about 0.4% of global GDP. Economists at the Stockholm Environment Institute arrived at the figure by looking at five measures: how much fisheries and tourism stood to lose, and what the economic impact would be of rising sea levels, more storms, and less carbon being absorbed by the oceans.

If the world continues to warm at its present rate and temperatures rise by 7.2°F [4°C] by 2100, the total will come to US $1.98 trillion. However, if drastic measures are taken to cut emissions and they rise by only 4°F [2.2°C], this figure will be US $612 billion. Governments worldwide were urged by the 1972 Stockholm Convention to control the dumping of waste in their oceans by implementing new laws. The United Nations met in London after this recommendation to begin the Convention on the Prevention of Marine Pollution by Dumping of Wastes and Other Matter, which was implemented in 1975. The International Maritime Organization was given responsibility for this convention and a Protocol was finally adopted in 1996, a major step in the regulation of ocean dumping.

The United Nations Convention on the Law of the Sea, signed in 1982 but only entering into force in 1994, established a framework of law for the oceans, including rules for deep-sea mining and economic exclusion zones extending 200 nautical miles around nation states.

For more information:
107 UN Sustainable Development Goals

Plastics have become an integral part of modern life. There is no denying their usefulness and living without them is hard to contemplate. Cheap to manufacture, they can be molded into myriad forms from simple plastic bags to aircraft parts. Most are produced from non-renewable resources – oil, natural gas, and coal. It has been estimated that 8.3 billion tonnes of plastic have been produced since the early 1950s. That in itself may not be a problem, providing any waste is carefully managed. However, it has become clear that waste in many cases is not managed adequately. Many plastic items lend themselves to being used once then thrown away. Again, if managed properly, and discarded items are collected and recycled, there may not be an issue. However, it is estimated that around 60% of plastics end up in either landfill or the environment. Carelessly thrown away on land and into water, plastics can be unsightly and cause great harm to wildlife.

According to the World Bank, the world generated 242 million tonnes of plastic waste in 2016. This equated to 12% of all solid waste produced and the majority originated in three regions: East Asia and the Pacific (57 million tonnes), Europe and Central Asia (45 million tonnes), and North America (35 million tonnes). It has been predicted that the amount of plastics produced will double in the next 20 years. The map below gives a picture of which countries generate the most plastic waste per head of population. But, as stated earlier, it is inadequately managed waste that is the root cause of problems of pollution. Unfortunately, it does appear that the majority of plastic waste is not currently managed in a responsible way. According to the Ellen MacArthur Foundation, up to 32% of all plastic packaging does not enter a collection system and is not recycled.

The effects of plastics in the oceans on wildlife are evident to see. Mammals and birds can become entangled in fishing nets and larger plastic items. Larger species such as marine turtles, seals, and whales are more prone to injury, or death, in this way. Birds in particular are susceptible to taking in small particles and it has been estimated that over 90% of all seabirds have ingested plastic. Broken down into microscopic particles, plastic is held in suspension in water and can be ingested by fish and ultimately humans.

Plastic waste is undeniably unsightly. Globally, three-quarters of beach litter is plastics, with drinks bottles being one of the largest components. Countries are beginning to control, collect, and recycle plastic waste, but much remains to be done.

▲ A now familiar sight – garbage left unsorted in a landfill dump. In this case, it is on the Greek island of Lesbos, but it is typical of many places where there is no, or inadequate, waste management or recycling. More developed, high-income countries have the resources, and an increasing public will, to invest in schemes to manage waste, and in particular plastic waste, more effectively. Good solutions require cooperation between commerce, government, and individuals.

PLASTIC WASTE

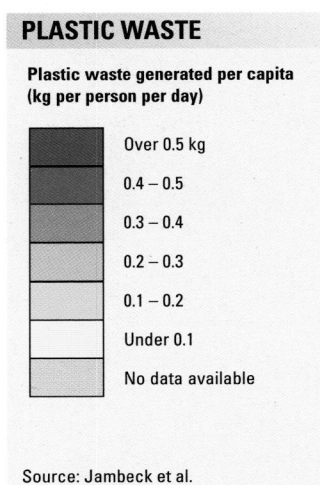

Plastic waste generated per capita (kg per person per day)

- Over 0.5 kg
- 0.4 – 0.5
- 0.3 – 0.4
- 0.2 – 0.3
- 0.1 – 0.2
- Under 0.1
- No data available

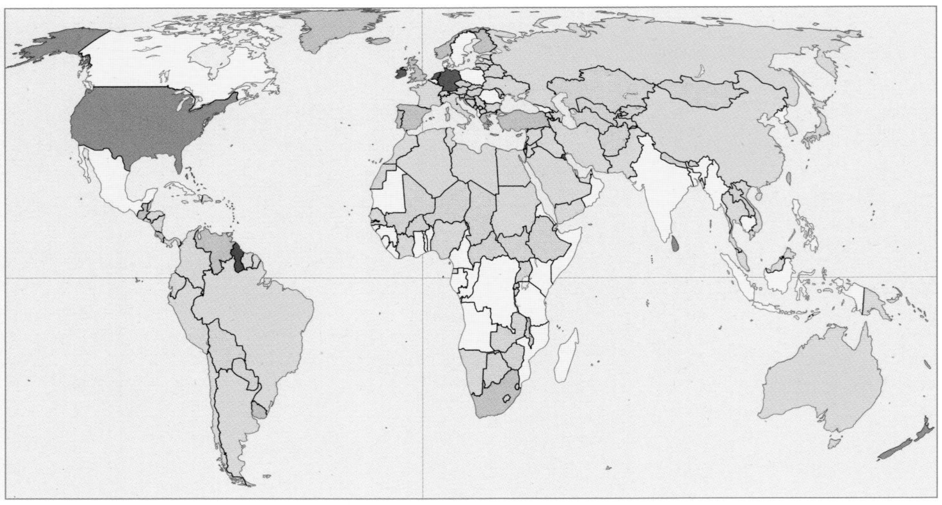

Source: Jambeck et al.

Highest plastic waste per capita (kg per day)	
Kuwait	0.69
Antigua & Barbuda	0.67
St Kitts & Nevis	0.65
Guyana	0.59
Barbados	0.57
St Lucia	0.52
Germany	0.49
Ireland	0.43

Lowest plastic waste per capita (kg per day)	
India	0.010
Mozambique	0.015
Madagascar	0.016
Tanzania	0.023
Brunei	0.026
Kenya	0.027
Guinea	0.030
Bangladesh	0.034

INADEQUATELY MANAGED PLASTIC WASTE

Share of a country's plastic waste inadequately managed

- 80 – 100%
- 60 – 80%
- 40 – 60%
- 20 – 40%
- 10 – 20%
- Under 10%
- No data available

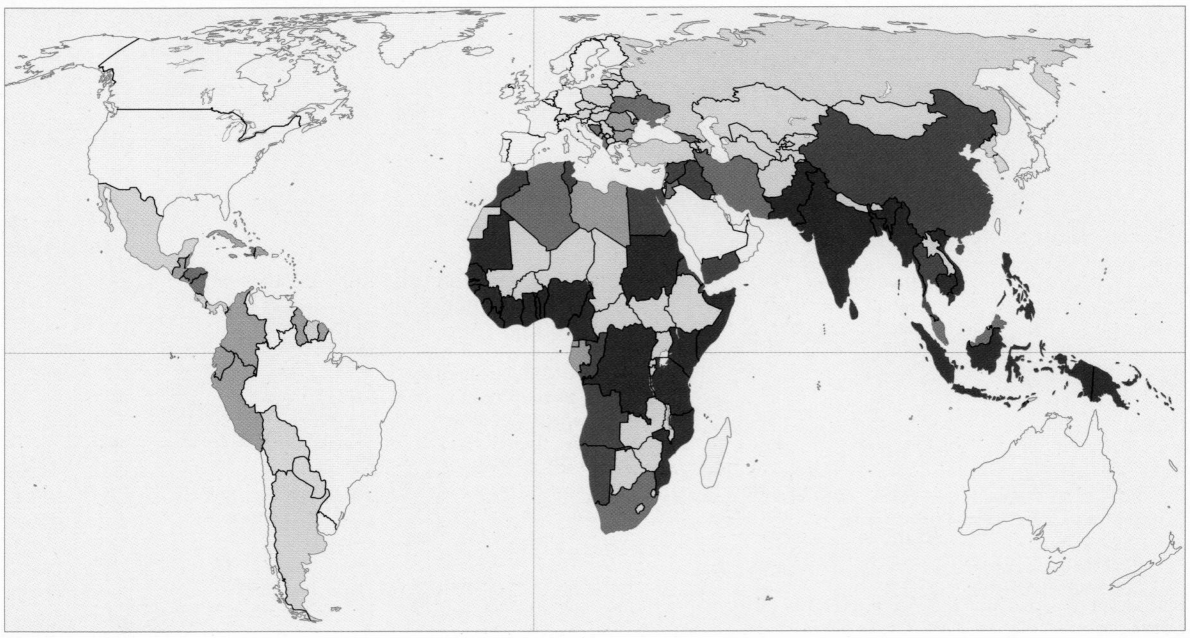

Source: Jambeck et al.

PLASTIC BOTTLES

Human behavior has to change to avoid scenes such as the one on the right. Plastic bottles make up a large part of discarded waste. The introduction of disposable plastic bottles, once seen as a great convenience, has turned into a major problem. Before their inception, drinks came in glass bottles and cans. It was the switch to using PET (polyethylene terephthalate) in the 1970s that provided lightweight plastic bottles that could be used successfully for carbonated drinks. Governments are now looking at ways to restrict the use of plastic bottles in the same way as they have tackled the issue of lightweight plastic bags. In some cities, facilities are being provided to allow people to refill reusable containers with safe drinking water. However, current global recycling rates remain low. Some manufacturers of drinks are now setting targets to ensure the materials they use are capable of being recycled and incorporating more recycled plastics into the manufacturing process. Efforts are being made to incorporate the cost of waste management strategies in the initial purchase price.

◀ This is not the type of image normally found in tourism brochures. Photographed in 2017, this is Kuta beach, Bali, Indonesia. The results of excessive numbers of visitors coupled with a lack of adequate waste management can be seen clearly.

MARINE SPECIES THREATENED BY PLASTIC POLLUTION

It is only in recent years that the threat to the marine environment, and its wildlife, has been fully realised. A report by the World Wide Fund for Nature (WWF) estimates that more than 1,400 marine species, including sea mammals and birds, are affected by plastic pollution. Danger not only comes from large items, such as bags and discarded fishing nets, but from microscopic particles that enter the food chain. The WWF also predicts that by 2050, 99% of all seabirds will have ingested plastic. Some of the most threatened species, and their associated threats, can be grouped under the headings shown here.

Fish, animals, and birds can confuse plastics with food. When they die, their stomachs have been found to be full of plastic. Sometimes the results are not readily visible, such as with baleen whales, which filter huge amounts of seawater with the result that microplastics, and chemicals, build up within their bodies. Humans are also threatened – microplastics work their way up the food chain. The geographical focus for this problem is again Southeast Asia with its fast-growing economies and pressures from burgeoning populations.

FISH

The smallest particles of plastic can enter the bodies of fish through their gills. Lodging in the body of fish, the particles will then be transferred to humans if the fish is eaten.

SEA TURTLES

Turtles can swallow plastic in mistake for food or can become entangled in netting. A study found that 50% of sea turtles had swallowed plastics that contributed to their deaths.

DOLPHINS/WHALES/SHARKS

Large sea mammals and sharks can accidently swallow large pieces of plastic in mistake for prey when hunting for food. Once the plastic is entangled in their guts, they can starve to death.

SEALS/SEALIONS

Curious seals can become dangerously entwined in discarded fishing lines and nets. If these get wrapped around their bodies, injuries and infections, or death, may follow.

SEA BIRDS

This penguin has become entrapped in plastic waste. Birds can swoop and take plastics from the ocean surface or dive deep into the water and mistake plastic for food.

THE FUTURE

The production of plastic has increased exponentially in the 70 years since the 1950s. To date, only a small part of this material has been recycled or incinerated. Can we collectively manage the 80% of material ever produced that is still in the environment? Given the global nature of pollution, international cooperation on an unprecedented scale is needed.

According to the WWF, effectively managing the situation requires a three-pronged attack: eliminate unnecessary plastics, vastly increase global plastic recovery, and move to sustainable plant-based sources for the remaining plastic.

Steps are now being taken in many places to reduce the use of single-use plastics – be it bottles or shopping bags. In some countries, fines are punitive with Kenya setting the highest, with the alternative of four years in jail for using, producing, or selling a plastic bag. Other countries are taking more measured steps, but the movement is spreading.

There is a growing intolerance from the public toward single-use plastics, often as the result of graphic publicity of the environmental consequences.

Plastic pollution is a complex problem that will require complex solutions. Its presence in the environment is rarely benign. The future will need commercial companies, governments, and individuals to cooperate. Improvements to waste management systems, government policies, and public engagement are the key to solutions.

◀ Single-use plastics, in particular bottles, are a major component of plastic pollution. In the US, 50 billion plastic bottles are produced per year – but only one quarter are recycled. Where facilities exist, bottles can be pressed, shredded, and recycled into new bottles.

For more information:
78 Climate
80 Climate change
Global warming
83 Natural vegetation

Biodiversity refers to the variety of living material. It includes the variety of species, the variety within the same species, and the variety of ecosystems within which species operate. Estimates of the number of species in the world vary from between 7 million and 80 million. The currently accepted total is about 14 million, yet only 2 million species have been formally identified.

Biodiversity is vital for human survival. It remains the basis for our food and most of our medicine. In less economically developed countries (LEDCs), over 20% of the food consumed is gathered from natural sources. At a global level, over 15% of animal protein consumed is from sea fish. More than 60% of the world's population rely on traditional medicines for their health care. In Mexico, the Popoluca Indians "farm" over 250 species of plant. Many medicines come from natural sources. Aspirin, for example, comes from an acid taken from the bark of willow trees. The anti-cancer drug "taxol" originates from the wild Pacific yew tree. It is estimated that the pharmaceuticals industry gains US $32 billion per year in profits from traditional remedies.

However, the loss of biodiversity is increasing at an accelerating rate. Up to 27,000 species a year may be lost, and the United Nations Environment Programme (UNEP) suggests that the current rate of extinction is 50–100 times greater than "normal," and believes that up to 25% of all the world's species may be lost by 2025. The main reasons for the decline are the introduction of alien species and habitat destruction. Human impact on biodiversity has brought about more extinctions than any other single factor since the extinction of the dinosaurs (65 million years ago).

Since 1600, 39% of animal extinctions have been due to the introduction of alien species, 36% from habitat destruction, and 23% from hunting or deliberate extermination. The introduction of rats, cats and other species has led to the extinction of many flightless birds in Polynesia. Plantation crops, such as rubber, often thrive best when taken away from their natural homes, since in the new lands there may not be the pests to control them. One noted example of extinction was caused by the introduction of the Nile perch into Lake Victoria, East Africa: introduced in the 1960s, it led to the extinction of some 50 species of cichlid fish within 20 years.

In 2021, over 16,306 species out of approximately 41,415 species on the IUCN (International Union for Conservation of Nature and Natural Resources) Red List of Threatened Species were in danger of extinction. This included one in four mammals, two in five amphibians, one in three coral and one in eight birds.

THREATENED SPECIES
Total number of threatened species for selected countries in each continent

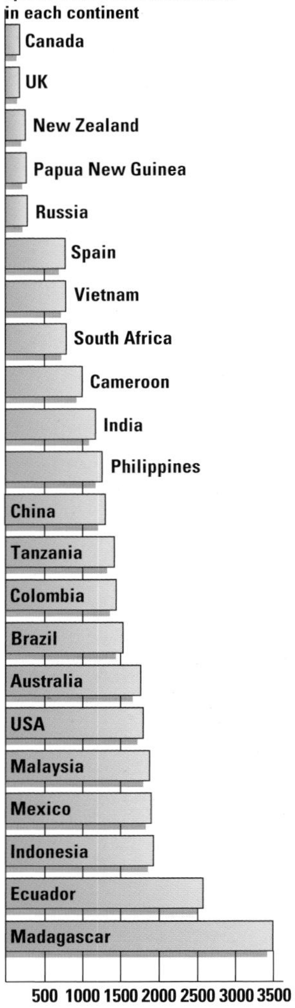

Source: IUCN Red List 2021

THREATENED MAMMAL SPECIES

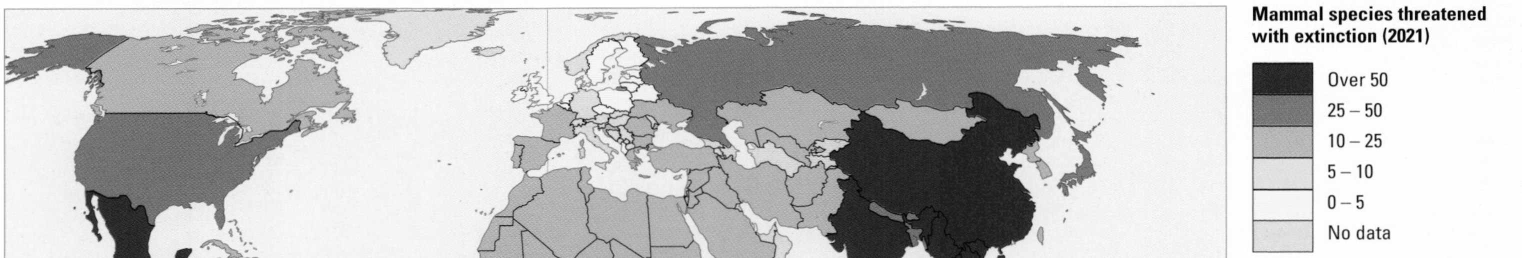

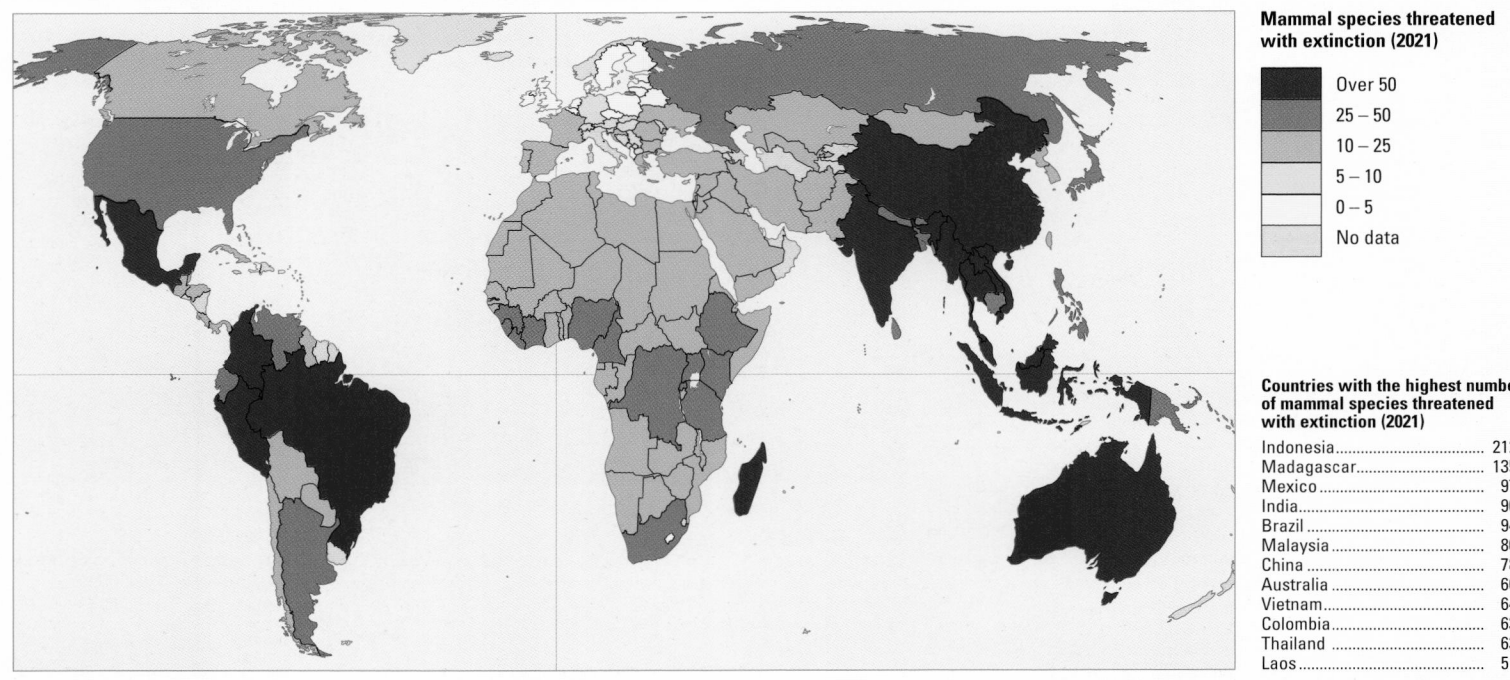

Countries with the highest number of mammal species threatened with extinction (2021)

Indonesia	212
Madagascar	135
Mexico	97
India	96
Brazil	94
Malaysia	80
China	78
Australia	66
Vietnam	64
Colombia	63
Thailand	63
Laos	51

BIODIVERSITY HOTSPOTS

Up to 75% of the world's most threatened mammals, birds and amphibians live in an area covering just 2.3% of the Earth's surface, and roughly half of all flowering plant species and 42% of land-based vertebrates exist in 36 biological hotspots.

Scientists argue that, with limited financial resources, governments and conservationists should prioritize by protecting the small total land areas that account for a very high percentage of global biodiversity. In 1999, scientists identified 25 such areas, mostly in the tropics, which were the center of global biodiversity.

The number of hotspots has risen to 36. These include the mountains of central Asia, the whole of Japan, the Horn of Africa including the Ethiopian highlands, and the Himalayas region. The hotspots once covered 15.7% of the Earth's surface, an area roughly the size of Russia and Australia combined – now they cover only 2.3% of the Earth's surface, an area slightly larger than India.

Over 70% of all mammals, 86% of all birds, and 92% of all amphibians are crammed into this small area of the world's total land mass. Madagascar and the Indian Ocean Islands hotspot was found to have very high concentrations of plant and vertebrate families that are found nowhere else on the globe.

Global warming could have a devastating effect on biodiversity hotspots such as the Amazonian and Indonesian rain forests. By 2100, between 12% and 39% of the land surface of the Earth will have a new climate. There are numerous species that will be unable to move in order to stay within their preferred climate range. These species will either have to evolve rapidly or die out.

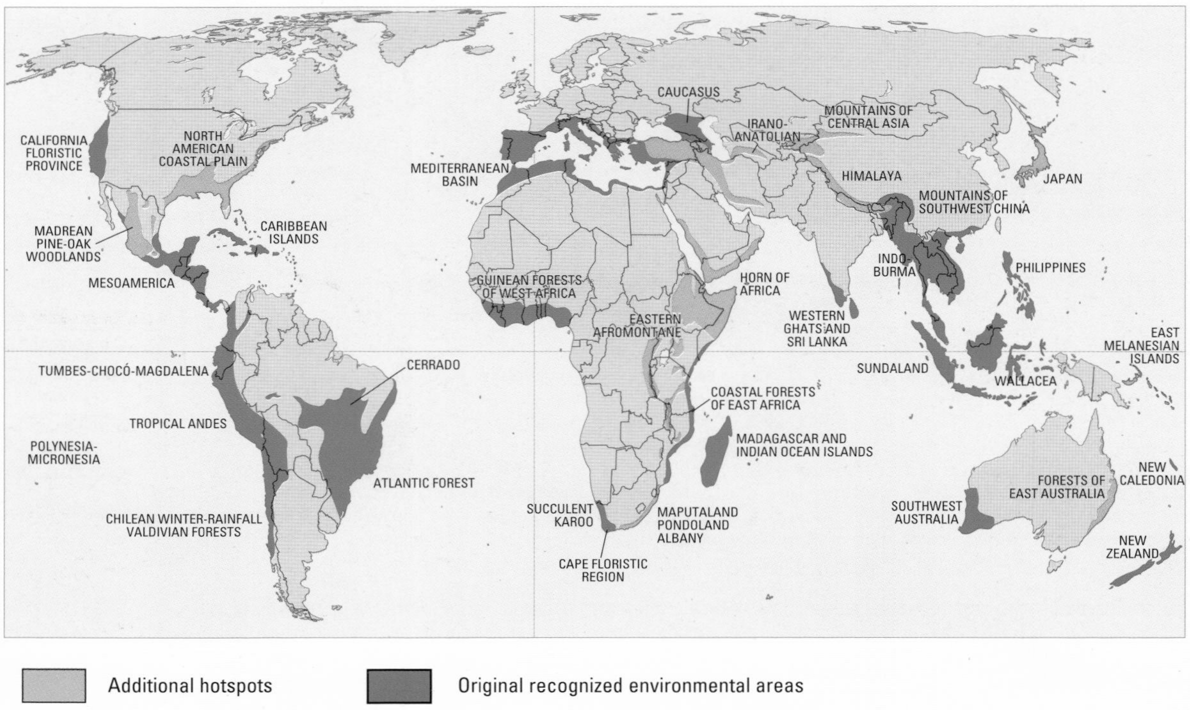

AUSTRALIA'S INTRODUCED SPECIES

Australia's native plants and animals adapted to life on an isolated continent over millions of years. Since European settlement in the 18th century they have had to compete with a range of species introduced by the settlers, which impact on the native species by predation, competition for food and shelter, destroying habitat, and by spreading diseases. Introduced species typically have few predators or fatal diseases, and some have very high reproductive rates.

Management and the prevention of the introduction of new invasive species are key environmental and agricultural policy issues for the Australian federal and state governments.

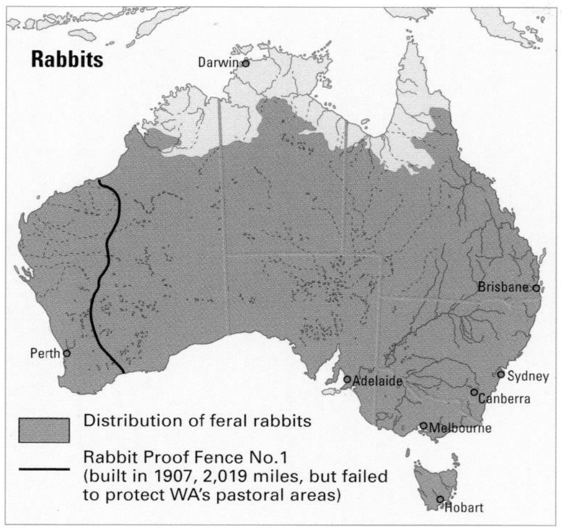

▲ Rabbits were introduced to Australia from England in 1859 for hunting, and quickly spread throughout the country. They are one of the most destructive introduced species in Australia, competing with native wildlife, damaging vegetation, and degrading the land.

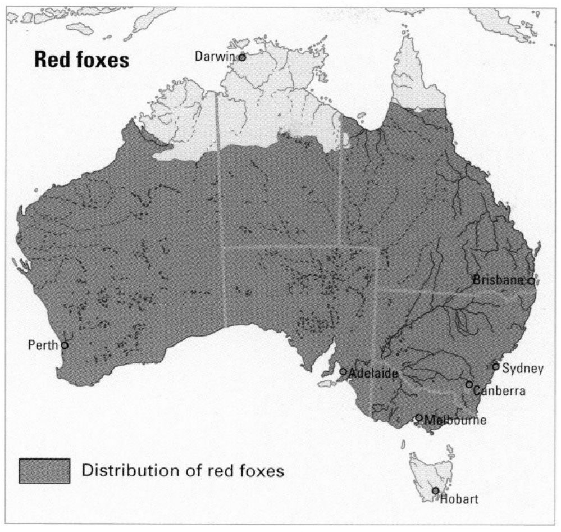

▲ The red fox was introduced from Europe for recreational hunting in 1855 and populations became established in the wild within 15 years. They prey on newborn lambs and have also been responsible for the decline of a number of native species.

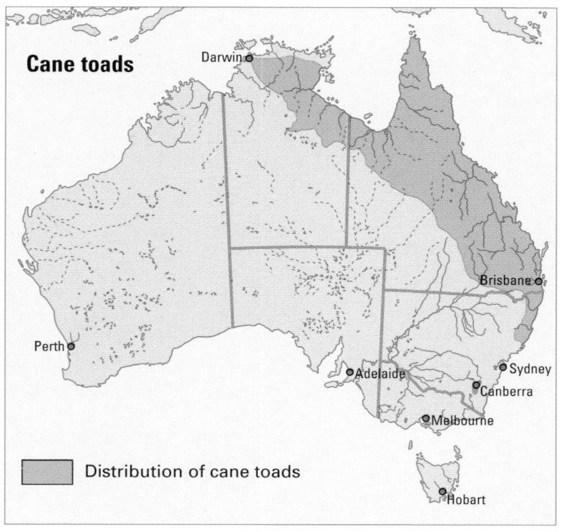

▲ Cane toads were introduced in 1935 to control beetles which were threatening the sugar-cane industry. However, this failed as both the toad and the beetle are still thriving. They adapted well to the Australian environment and with no natural predators they quickly spread. They eat small native wildlife and poison any predators.

THE VALUE OF NATURE

According to the National Ecosystem Assessment (NEA), lakes, forests, parks, and wildlife are a huge financial asset. Moreover, it is claimed that the natural world is vital for human existence, not only in providing food, water, and air, but also for the cultural and spiritual benefits that it provides.

Economic benefits include food production, which utilizes insects for pollination, earthworms for mixing the soil, and soil microbes for recycling nutrients. In the UK, for example, the value of pollinating insects has been calculated to be $727 million, and the value of wetlands, which help to provide clean water, at $2.5 billion. Globally, bees are believed to provide $368 billion worth of services, or about 9.5% of the total economic value of agriculture. One third of the food the world produces is dependent on bees for pollination.

Although the natural world provides many benefits including food supply, water supply, climate regulation, and breakdown of waste products, these are under-valued. Some of the benefits are non-quantifiable but include recreation and long-term health. Moreover, the way in which ecosystems have been used has changed over the last 60 years or so. Population increase and rising standards of living have contributed to a huge growth in agricultural production. It has also, however, contributed to the decline in ecosystem services, such as air, water, and soil quality.

Although some ecosystems are delivering services well, there are others which are showing long-term decline. Those that are in decline include marine fisheries, wild species diversity, and soil quality.

Ecosystems, and ecosystems services, constantly change as a result of demographic, economic, social, and cultural factors. For example, since the 1940s there has been intensification of agriculture at the expense of many habitats, including wetlands, forests, and grasslands.

Types of ecosystem service

Provisioning services

These are the services obtained from ecosystems such as food, fiber, fuel, and water from aquifers, rivers, and lakes. Goods can come from heavily managed ecosystems (intensive farms and fish farms) or from semi-natural ones (such as by hunting and fishing). Most of these food-producing ecosystems are land-based but some are water-based (aquaculture). Ecosystems also provide a variety of materials for construction and fuel including wood, charcoal, biofuels, and plant oils. They are also an important source of raw materials for the pharmaceuticals industry.

Supporting services

These are the essentials for life and include primary productivity, soil formation, and the cycling of nutrients. Ecosystems provide the conditions for growing food. Habitats provide all that an individual plant or animal needs to survive: food, water, nutrients, and shelter. Every habitat provides a variety of niches that can be essential for a species' lifecycle. For example, migratory birds depend on different habitats at different times of the year.

Ecosystems also help maintain genetic diversity (biodiversity) which is the variety of genetic materials between ecosystems, niches, and populations.

Regulating services

These are a diverse set of services and include pollination, regulation of pests and diseases, and production of goods. Other services include climate and climatic hazard regulation, and water quality regulation. For example, trees provide shade and influence water availability and, by removing air pollutants from the atmosphere, they improve air quality. Ecosystems influence global climate by storing and sequestering greenhouse gases such as carbon dioxide. As vegetation grows, it removes carbon dioxide and locks it in its tissue.

Ecosystems moderate extreme events: they act as buffers against natural disasters. Mangrove forests can help protect a shoreline against hurricane damage, and wetlands can absorb flood waters. Vegetation can help reduce soil erosion.

Insects and the wind help pollinate plants. Around 90 out of 115 leading food crops, such as cocoa and coffee, depend upon animal pollination.

Ecosystems are also important for the control of pests and vector-borne diseases. Birds, bats, wasps, frogs, and fungi are all examples of natural controls.

Cultural services

These occur when people interact with the environment and this provides cultural goods and benefits. Open spaces provide the opportunity for outdoor recreation, learning, and spiritual well-being. Recreation can lead to major improvements in physical and mental health. Also, tourism provides a major source of income to many countries.

▲ The wide variety of provisions on display in this Malaysian market are testament to the value of ecosystems for the supply of food.

▲ The destruction of large areas of vegetation can lessen the value of ecosystems. The deforested and drowned rain forest at Batang Ai, Sarawak, Malaysia, above, is the result of land being cleared for a hydroelectric power station.

The goods and services derived from mountains, moorlands, and heaths, and those from woodlands are shown in the table.

	Mountains, moorlands, and heaths	Woodlands
Provisioning	Food*	Timber*
	Fiber*	Species diversity*
	Fuel*	Fuelwood*
	Freshwater*	Fresh water*
Regulating	Climate regulation†	Climate regulation†
	Flood regulation†	Flood regulation†
	Wildfire regulation†	Erosion control†
	Water quality regulation†	Disease and pest control†
	Erosion control†	Wildfire regulation†
		Air and water quality regulation†
		Soil quality regulation†
		Noise regulation†
Cultural	Recreation and tourism*	Recreation and tourism*
	Aesthetic values*	Aesthetic values*
	Cultural heritage*	Cultural heritage*
	Spiritual values*	Employment*
	Education*	Education*
	Sense of place*	Sense of place*
	Health benefits*	Health benefits*

Key
Items marked * denote goods
Items marked † denote services

For more information:

92 Urbanization of the Earth
Urban population
93 Largest cities

In 8000 BC, following the development of agriculture, the world had an estimated population of 8 million and by AD 1000 it was about 300 million. The onset of the Industrial Revolution in the late 18th century led to a population explosion. The 1,000 million mark was passed by 1850, it doubled by the 1920s, and doubled again to 4,000 million by 1975.

In the 1990s, demographers estimated that the world's population, which passed the 7 billion mark in 2012, would reach 9.3 billion by 2050 and only level out in 2200, at a peak of around 11 billion. However, in the early 21st century, after the rate of population growth had shown signs of decline, the Institute for Applied Systems Analysis suggested that the world's population might peak at about 9 billion in 2070. Whatever the global projections, everyone agreed that the greatest population growth would be in the developing countries.

The developing world includes what the World Bank (2021) describes as low-income economies (per capita GNI of US $1,036 or less), lower-middle-income economies (per capita GNI of US $1,036 to US $4,045), and upper-middle-income economies (per capita GNI of US $4,045 to US $12,535). Most developing countries are in Africa, Asia, and Latin America. The developed world, made up of high-income, industrialized economies (per capita GNI of US $12,535 or more), contains Australasia, most of Europe and North America, and Japan.

In developing countries, a high proportion of the population is young and so these countries face high expenditure on health and education. In developed countries, the population pyramids are becoming top-heavy, with increasingly aging populations.

LARGEST NATIONS

The world's most populous nations, in millions (2021)

1.	China	1,398
2.	India	1,339
3.	USA	335
4.	Indonesia	275
5.	Pakistan	238
6.	Nigeria	220
7.	Brazil	213
8.	Bangladesh	164
9.	Russia	142
10.	Mexico	130
11.	Japan	125
12.	Philippines	111
13.	Ethiopia	111
14.	Egypt	106
15.	Congo (Dem. Rep.)	105
16.	Vietnam	103
17.	Iran	86
18.	Turkey	83
19.	Germany	80
20.	Thailand	70
21.	France	68
22.	UK	66
23.	Italy	62
24.	Tanzania	62
25.	Myanmar (Burma)	57

MOST CROWDED NATIONS

Population per square mile (2021)

1.	Monaco	40,030
2.	Singapore	22,562
3.	Bahrain	5,655
4.	Vatican City	5,000
5.	Malta	3,841
6.	Maldives	3,256
7.	Bangladesh	2,951
8.	Mauritius	1,755
9.	San Marino	1,712
10.	Barbados	1,704

LEAST CROWDED

Population per square mile (2021)

1.	Mongolia	5.3
2.	Namibia	8.4
3.	Australia	8.6
4.	Iceland	8.9
5.	Guyana	9.5
6.	Suriname	9.8
7.	Canada	9.9
8.	Mauritania	10.3
9.	Libya	10.3
10.	Botswana	10.4

POPULATION DENSITY

The places marked on the map reflect the size of the urban agglomerations and conurbations, rather than the actual city limits. San Francisco itself, for example, has an official population of less than a million people. All cities with more than 5 million inhabitants are named on the map.

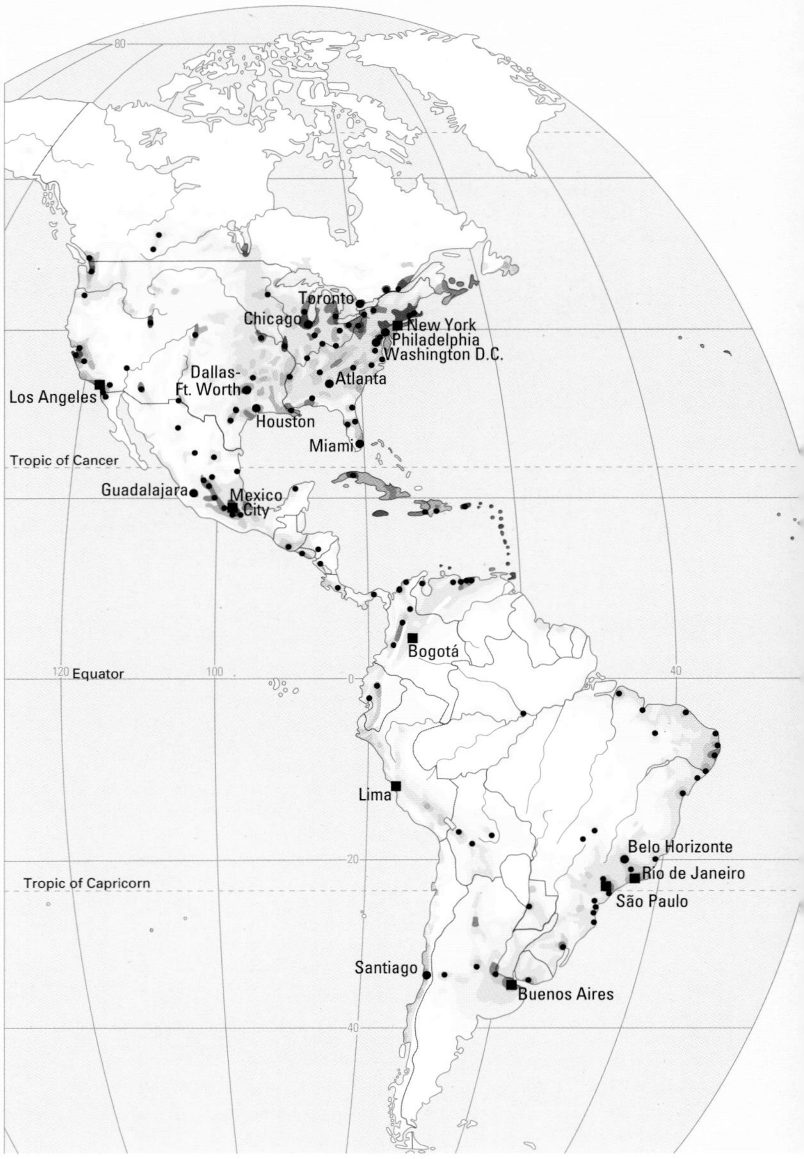

Inhabitants per square mile

- Over 500
- 250 – 500
- 125 – 250
- 65 – 125
- 15 – 65
- 8 – 15
- 3 – 8
- Under 3

Urban population

- ■ Over 10,000,000
- ● 5,000,000 – 10,000,000
- • 1,000,000 – 5,000,000

POPULATION CHANGE

The projected population change for the years 2004–2050

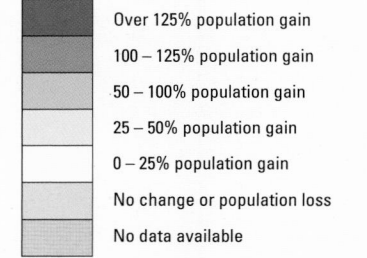

- Over 125% population gain
- 100 – 125% population gain
- 50 – 100% population gain
- 25 – 50% population gain
- 0 – 25% population gain
- No change or population loss
- No data available

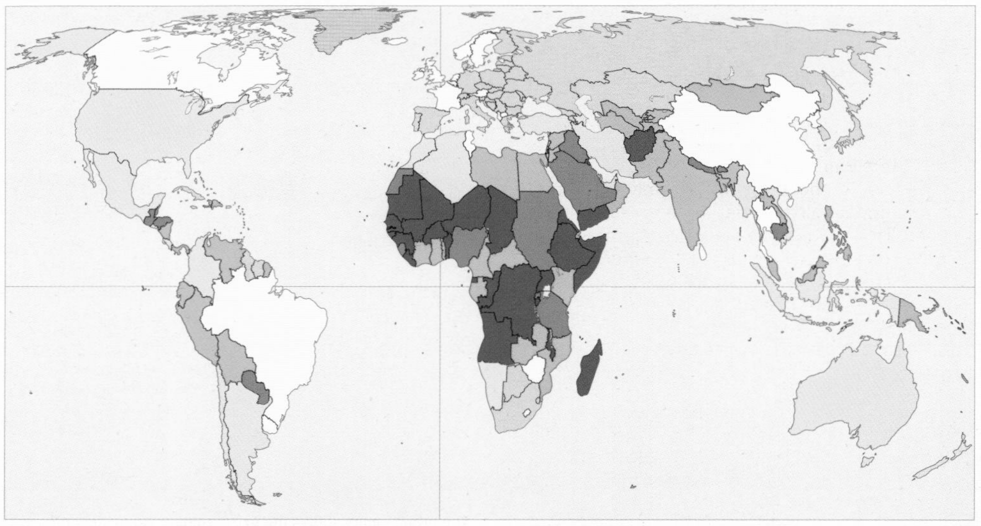

Based on estimates for the year 2050, below are listed the ten most populous nations in the world, in millions:

1.	India	1,628	6.	Pakistan	295
2.	China	1,437	7.	Bangladesh	280
3.	USA	420	8.	Brazil	221
4.	Indonesia	308	9.	Congo (Dem. Rep.)	181
5.	Nigeria	307	10.	Ethiopia	173

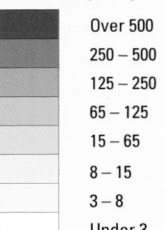

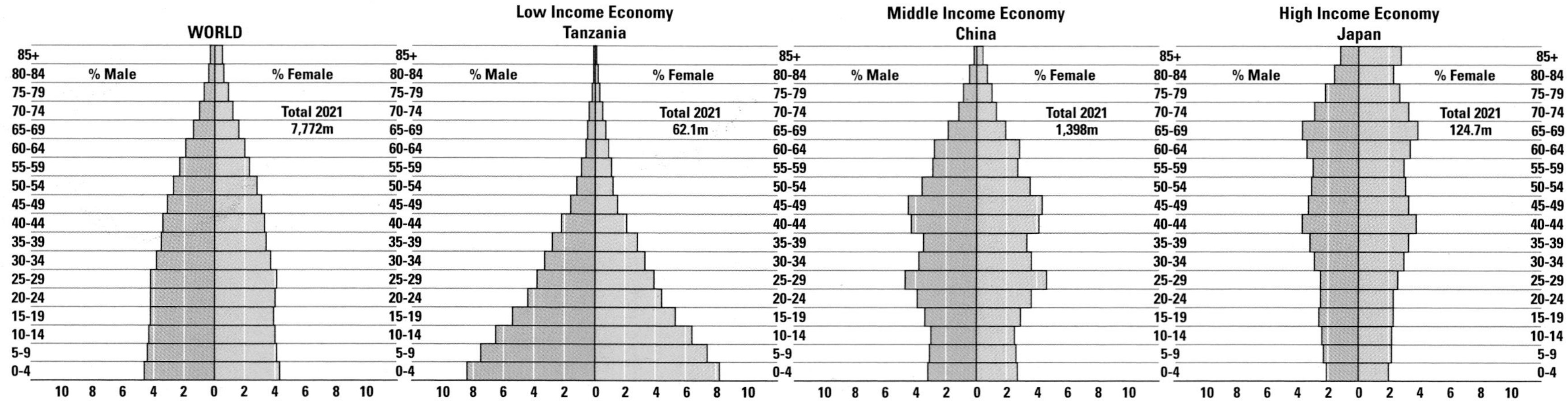

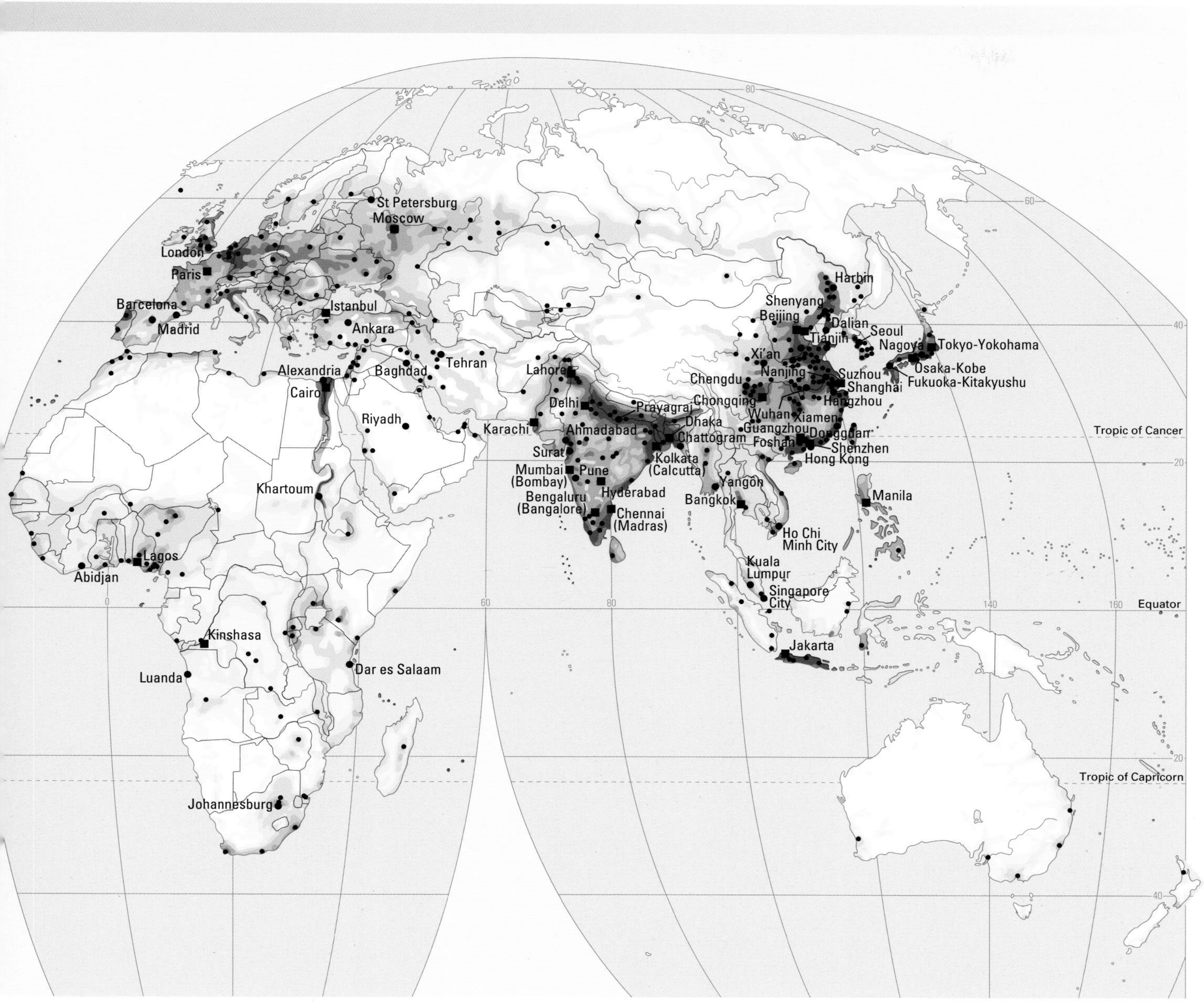

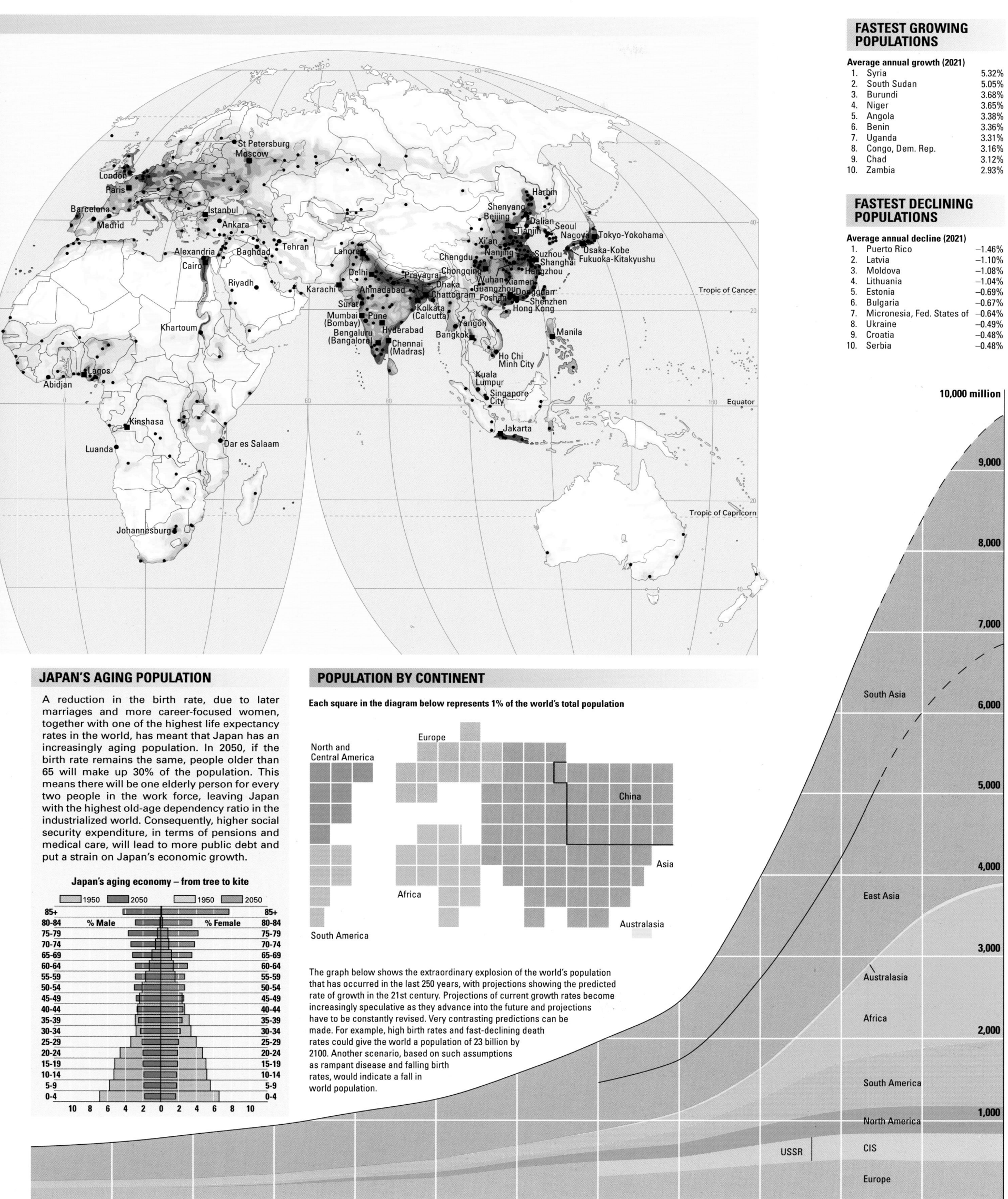

FASTEST GROWING POPULATIONS

Average annual growth (2021)

1.	Syria	5.32%
2.	South Sudan	5.05%
3.	Burundi	3.68%
4.	Niger	3.65%
5.	Angola	3.38%
6.	Benin	3.36%
7.	Uganda	3.31%
8.	Congo, Dem. Rep.	3.16%
9.	Chad	3.12%
10.	Zambia	2.93%

FASTEST DECLINING POPULATIONS

Average annual decline (2021)

1.	Puerto Rico	–1.46%
2.	Latvia	–1.10%
3.	Moldova	–1.08%
4.	Lithuania	–1.04%
5.	Estonia	–0.69%
6.	Bulgaria	–0.67%
7.	Micronesia, Fed. States of	–0.64%
8.	Ukraine	–0.49%
9.	Croatia	–0.48%
10.	Serbia	–0.48%

JAPAN'S AGING POPULATION

A reduction in the birth rate, due to later marriages and more career-focused women, together with one of the highest life expectancy rates in the world, has meant that Japan has an increasingly aging population. In 2050, if the birth rate remains the same, people older than 65 will make up 30% of the population. This means there will be one elderly person for every two people in the work force, leaving Japan with the highest old-age dependency ratio in the industrialized world. Consequently, higher social security expenditure, in terms of pensions and medical care, will lead to more public debt and put a strain on Japan's economic growth.

Japan's aging economy – from tree to kite

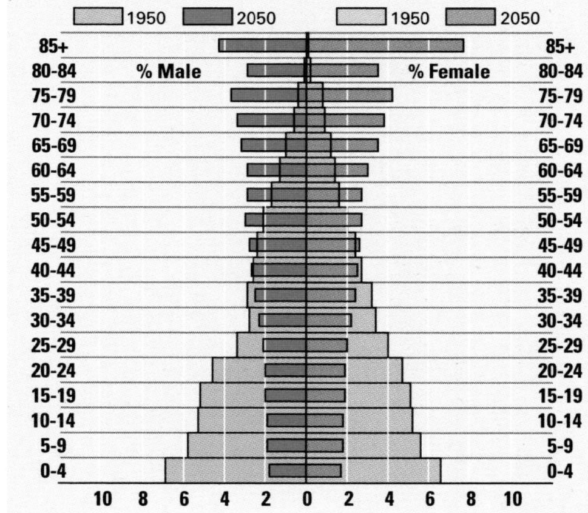

POPULATION BY CONTINENT

Each square in the diagram below represents 1% of the world's total population

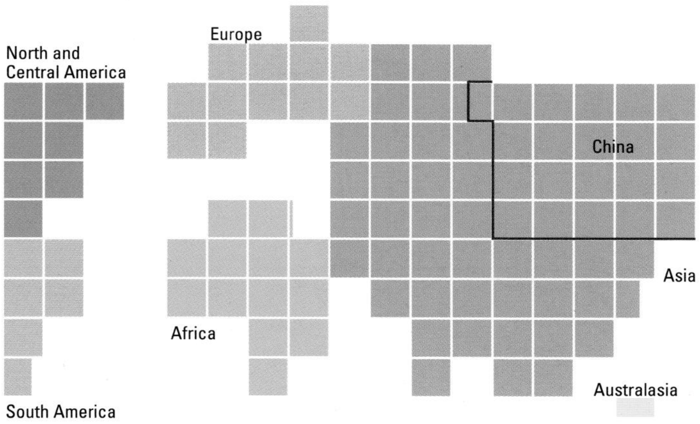

The graph below shows the extraordinary explosion of the world's population that has occurred in the last 250 years, with projections showing the predicted rate of growth in the 21st century. Projections of current growth rates become increasingly speculative as they advance into the future and projections have to be constantly revised. Very contrasting predictions can be made. For example, high birth rates and fast-declining death rates could give the world a population of 23 billion by 2100. Another scenario, based on such assumptions as rampant disease and falling birth rates, would indicate a fall in world population.

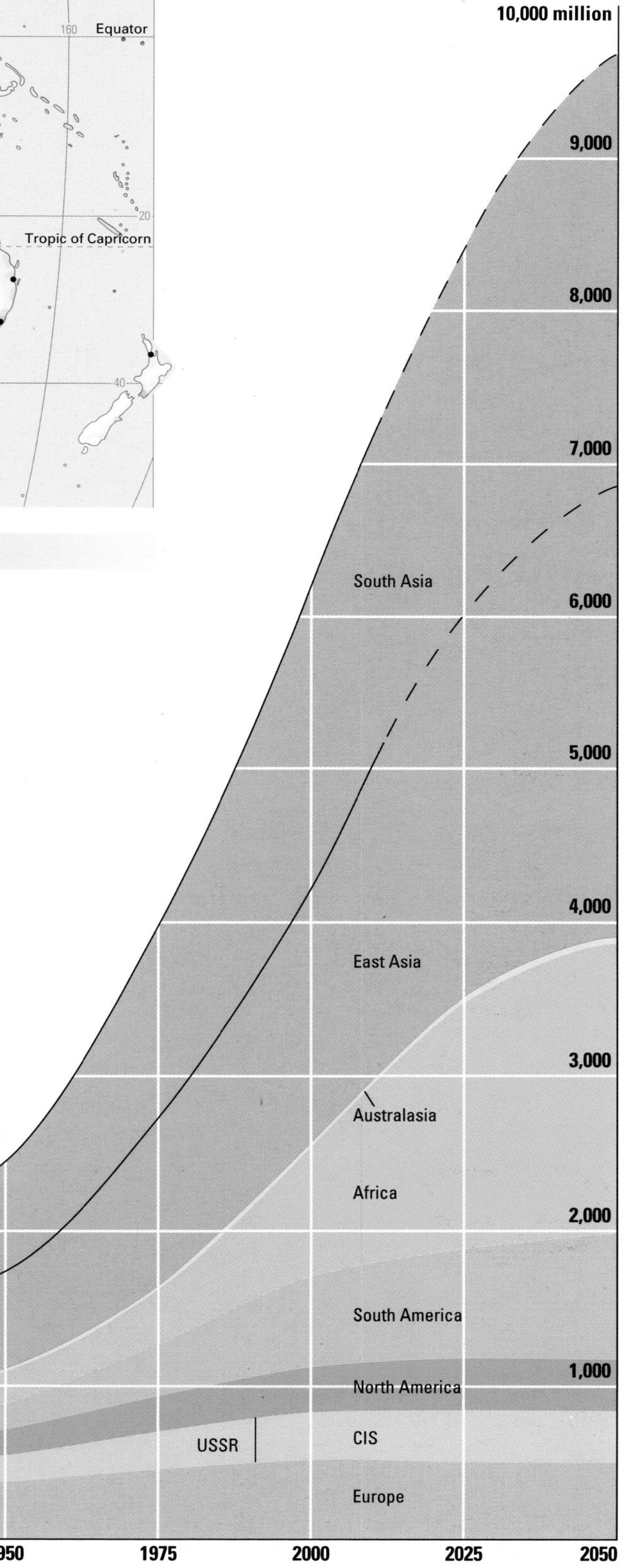

For more information:
80 Greenhouse gases
82 Water distribution
90 Population density
100 World trade

In 2008, for the first time in history, more than half of the world's population lived in urban areas. By 2050, it is thought that 5.3 billion people in the developing world will be living in an urban environment, with Asia having over 60% of the world's urban population and Africa almost 25%.

Urbanization is greatest in industrialized countries. For example, in 2010, 82% of the people in the USA lived in urban areas; but in low-income countries, which had nearly 40% of the world's population in the early 21st century, only 31% lived in urban areas.

A typical city in a developing country contains millions of people living, often illegally, in shanty towns (or "informal settlements"), while thousands live on the streets. Yet many of these shanty towns are healthier than the industrial cities of 19th-century Europe and North America. Indeed, surveys have shown that migrants to cities in developing countries are less likely to face poverty than they are in rural areas, while benefiting from greater access to healthcare services and education.

Modern cities face many problems today, including pollution, unemployment, and crime. Yet, with competent government, they are capable of generating the wealth they need to solve them, as well as making a major contribution to the nation's economy.

Megacities are cities with a population of over 10 million people. Megacities grow as a result of economic growth, rural to urban migration, and high rates of natural increase. As the cities grow, they swallow up rural areas and nearby towns. Some of these cities have populations that are bigger than those of entire countries – Mumbai, for example, has more people than Sweden and Norway combined.

Nevertheless, megacities contain between 4% and 7% of the world's total population, and grow at relatively slow rates, perhaps 1.5% per year. The first megacity was Tokyo, which now has a population of about 37 million (larger than Canada's population). By 2020, other megacities will include Mumbai, Delhi, Mexico City, São Paulo, New York, Dhaka, Karachi, and Lagos. Lagos has been growing at a very fast rate of 5% per annum and is expected to increase at this rate until after 2020. Usually, very large cities grow more slowly than medium-sized cities.

By 2020, all but four of the world's megacities will be in developing regions, 12 of them in Asia alone. The impact of megacities on their region is huge. For example, rapid economic growth and urbanization in China has had a negative impact on the urban environment. China contains 16 of the 20 most polluted cities in the world and is the largest producer of greenhouse gases.

Megacities are important for the generation of wealth – in more economically developed countries (MEDCs) urban areas generate over 80% of national economic output, while in less economically developed countries (LEDCs) it is over 40%. However, there are some aspects of megacities, such as crime and environmental issues, where they are less than attractive.

URBAN POPULATION

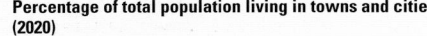

Percentage of total population living in towns and cities (2020)

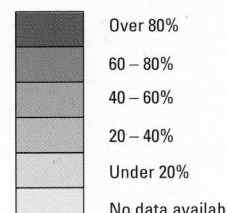

- Over 80%
- 60 – 80%
- 40 – 60%
- 20 – 40%
- Under 20%
- No data available

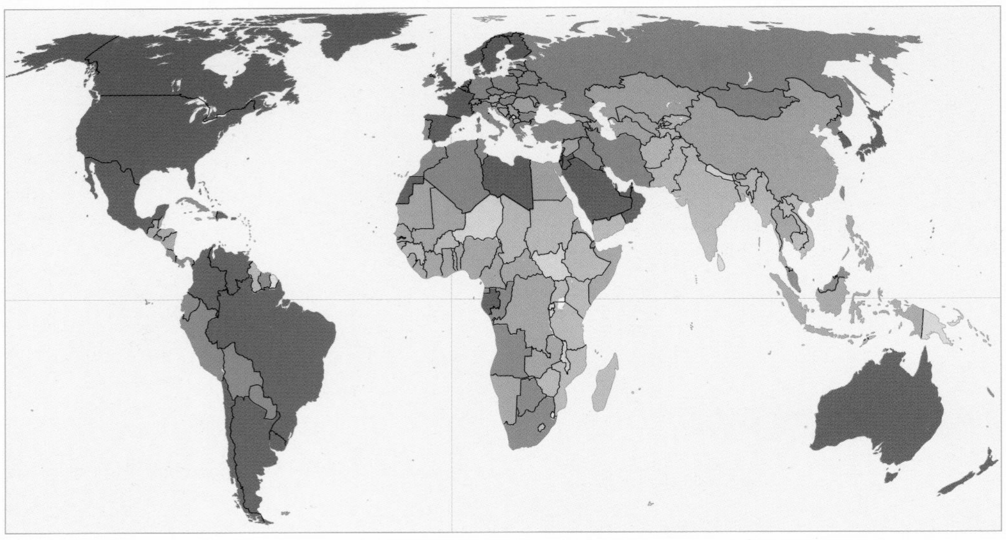

Most urbanized		Least urbanized	
Kuwait	100%	Papua New Guinea	13%
Monaco	100%	Burundi	14%
Singapore	100%	Liechtenstein	14%
Qatar	99%	Niger	17%
Belgium	98%	Malawi	17%

THE URBANIZATION OF THE EARTH

City-building, 1900–2005; each white spot represents a city of at least 1 million inhabitants

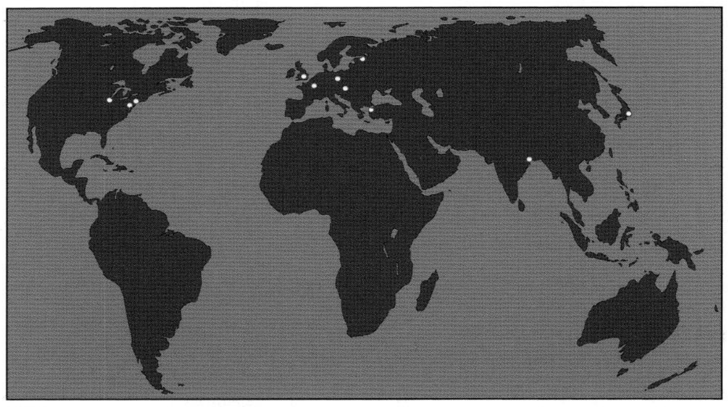

1900

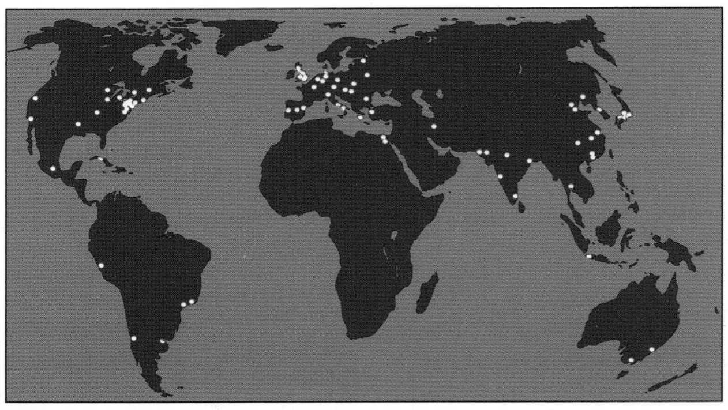

1950

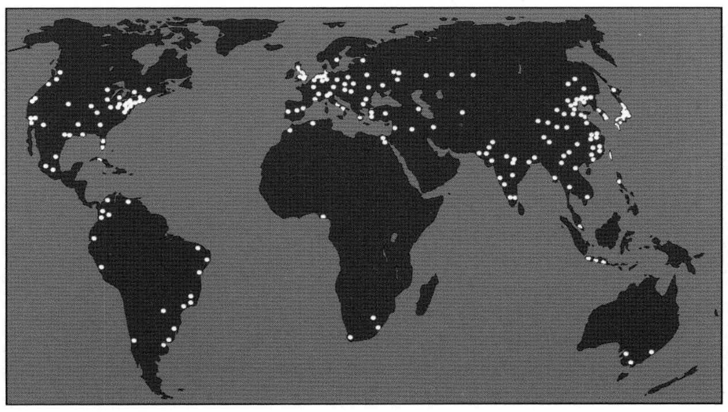

1975

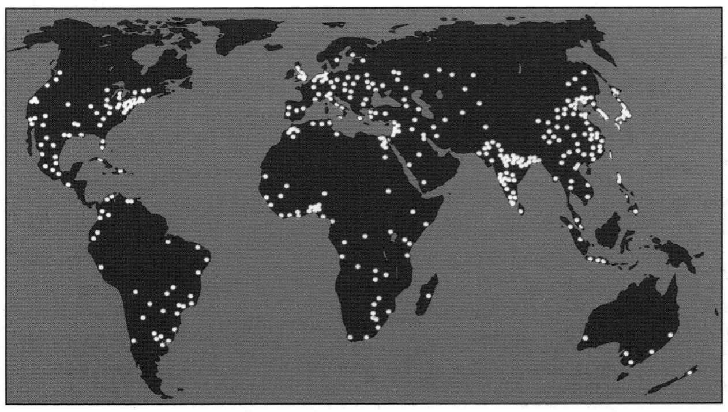

2005

URBANIZATION

The urban population of 3.7 billion people in 2012 was larger than the entire global population in 1947, 65 years earlier. Cities and urban areas are gaining an estimated 60 million people per year – over 1 million every week.

Urbanization rates vary across the world; the USA and UK have far lower rates of urbanization compared to less developed countries. This is because a high proportion of their populations already live in cities. The largest percentage increases in the urban population in the next decade will be in Africa and Asia. For example, Lagos in Nigeria increased from 675,000 inhabitants in 1960 to 14,368,000 in 2020.

Rapid urban growth reflects three factors:
1. Migration to cities from rural areas.
2. Natural population increases (births minus deaths).
3. Reclassification of previously rural areas as urban as they become built up and engulfed by urban sprawl.

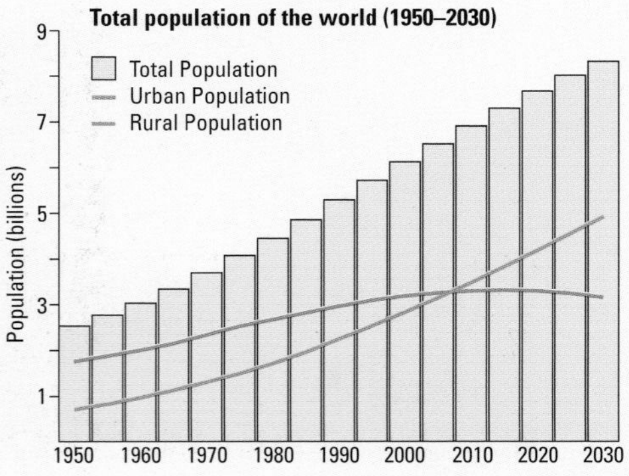

SLUM CITIES

The total number of slum dwellers in the world reached 1 billion in 2007, with one in every three city residents living in inadequate housing, with no or few basic services.

Urbanization in most developing countries has been proceeding so rapidly that local governments have been unable to provide the necessary services and housing to meet demand.

In some cities, many people make their homes in squatter settlements, or slums, which are frequently without basic services such as power, water, and sanitation. They are often on hazardous, dangerous or polluted land, and the building structures are inadequate and sometimes unsafe. Slum dwellers have limited access to credit and formal job markets due to stigmatization, discrimination, and geographical isolation.

Slums have a high concentration of poverty and social and economic deprivation, which may include broken families, unemployment, and economic, physical, and social exclusion. Yet these communities are often a dynamic part of the city's economy, keeping the wheels of the city turning in many different ways. Their inhabitants often take the initiative in setting up their own local government and self-help associations.

Some of the world's richest cities also have a homeless underclass, although calculating the numbers of people involved is problematic. Yet it is the case that homelessness and unemployment are currently affecting an increasing number of people in the developed world.

The locus of poverty is moving from the countryside to cities, in a process now recognized as the "urbanization of poverty."

Efforts to improve the living conditions of slum dwellers peaked during the 1980s. However, renewed concern about poverty has recently led governments to adopt specific targets on slums in the United Nations Millennium Declaration, which aims to improve the lives of at least 100 million slum dwellers by the year 2020.

SLUM FACTBOX

- A slum is defined by the UN as "a dilapidated area of a city characterized by substandard housing, squalor, and lacking in tenure security."
- 78% of the urban population in developing countries live in slums.
- More than 41% of Kolkata's slum households have lived there for more than 30 years.
- In most African cities between 40% and 70% of the city's population live in slums or squatter settlements.
- Slum populations in some parts of the world often include university lecturers, students, civil servants, and formal private-sector employees.
- The majority of slum households in Bangkok have a color television.
- Singapore is one of the few countries that successfully practises comprehensive public-sector housing development.
- Slums are the fastest growing human habitat in the world.

SUSTAINABLE CITIES

Large sprawling cities are often considered unsustainable because they consume huge amounts of resources and produce vast amounts of waste. The concept of "Sustainable Urban Development" is designed to meet the needs of the present generation without compromising the needs of future generations.

In the "compact" sustainable city, inputs are smaller and there is more recycling. Compact cities minimize the amount of distance traveled, use less space, require less infrastructure (pipes, cables, roads, etc), reduce urban sprawl, and the provision of public transport is easier. But if the compact city covers too large an area, it becomes congested, overcrowded, overpriced, and polluted. As a result, it then becomes unsustainable.

In order to achieve sustainability, a number of options are available:

- reducing the use of fossil fuels, e.g. by promoting public transport;
- keeping waste production to within levels that can be treated locally;
- providing sufficient green spaces;
- reusing and reclaiming land, e.g. brownfield sites;
- active involvement of the local community;
- conservation of non-renewable resources;
- using renewable resources.

CITY GROWTH

The growth of some of the world's largest cities in millions, 1950–2019

Comparisons of city populations over time are problematic due to changes in the definition of the city limits. These figures attempt to take such changes into consideration.

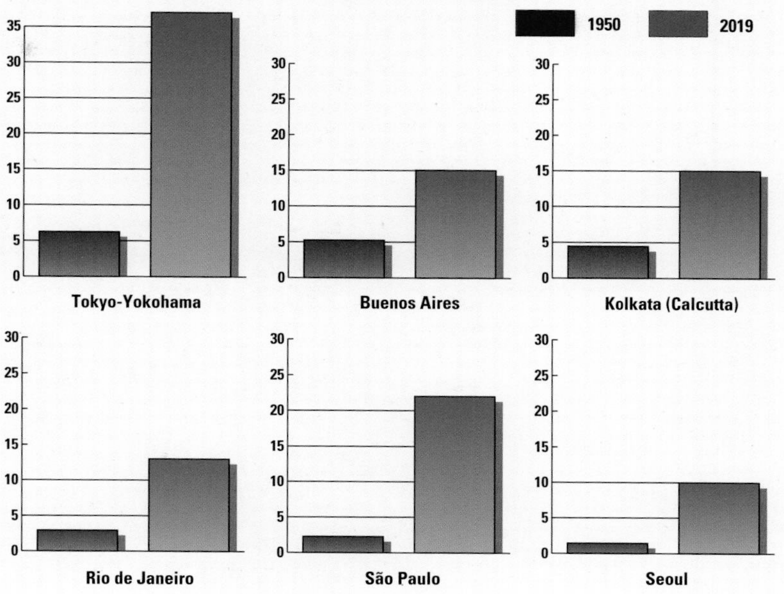

LARGEST CITIES

◄ Mt. Fuji stands sentinel over the futuristic skyline of the Shinjuku area of Tokyo, the world's most populous city. Originally a fishing village called Edo, the greater metropolitan area of Tokyo-Yokohama is now home to over 37 million people and is the capital of Japan.

In 2008, for the first time in history, the majority of the world's population lived in cities. Below is a list of the urban areas in the world with over 10 million inhabitants in 2020

1.	Tokyo–Yokohama	37.4
2.	Delhi	30.3
3.	Shanghai	27.1
4.	São Paulo	22.1
5.	Mexico City	21.8
6.	Dhaka	21.0
7.	Cairo	20.9
8.	Beijing	20.5
9.	Mumbai	20.4
10.	Osaka-Kobe	19.2
11.	New York	18.8
12.	Tianjin	18.6
13.	Karachi	16.1
14.	Chongqing	15.9
15.	Istanbul	15.2
16.	Buenos Aires	15.2
17.	Kolkata	14.9
18.	Lagos	14.4
19.	Kinshasa	14.3
20.	Manila	13.9
21.	Rio de Janeiro	13.5
22.	Guangzhou	13.3
23.	Lahore	12.6
24.	Moscow	12.5
25.	Los Angeles	12.4
26.	Shenzhen	12.4
27.	Bengaluru	12.3
28.	Paris	11.0
29.	Bogotá	11.0
30.	Chennai	11.0
31.	Jakarta	10.8
32.	Lima	10.7
33.	Bangkok	10.5
34.	Hyderabad	10.0

The population figures above are based on urban agglomerations rather than legal city limits. In some cases, where two adjacent cities have merged into one concentration, such as Tokyo–Yokohama, they have been regarded as a single unit.

URBAN ADVANTAGES

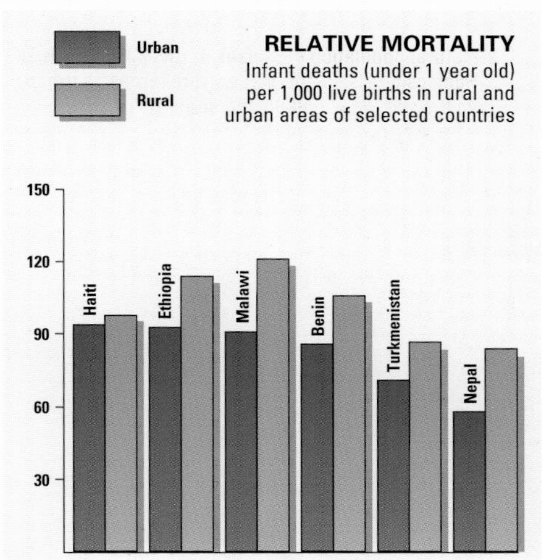

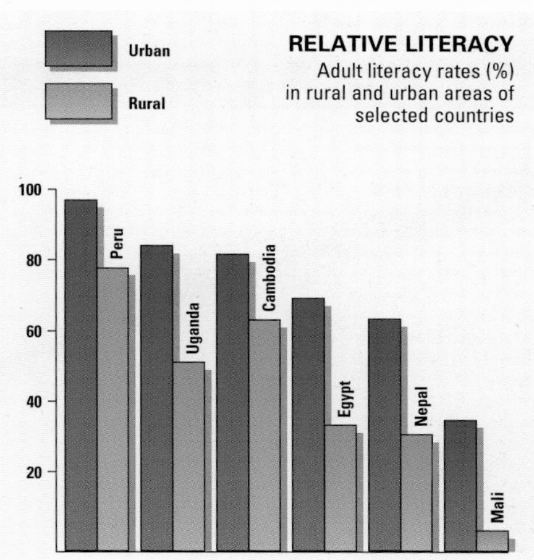

Despite overcrowding and poor housing, living standards in the developing world's cities are almost invariably better than in the surrounding countryside. Resources – financial, material, and administrative – are concentrated in the towns, which are usually also the centers of political activity and pressure. Governments – frequently unstable, and rarely established on a solid democratic base – are usually more responsive to urban discontent than to rural misery.

In many developing countries, especially in Africa, food prices are kept artificially low, thus appeasing the underemployed urban masses at the expense of agricultural development.

This imbalance encourages further cityward migration, helping to account for the astonishing rate of post-1950 urbanization and putting great strain on the ability of many nations to provide even modest improvements for their people.

For more information:
8 Migration

In the late 1980s, many people hoped that the end of the Cold War, following the collapse of Communist regimes in the former Soviet Union and Eastern Europe, would herald a new era of international stability. Instead, ethnic and religious antagonisms surfaced in many areas. Nationalist rivalries, suppressed under Communist rule, replaced ideological factors as the major cause of conflict. Since 2010, there has been accelerated political change, especially across North Africa and the Middle East.

Some countries are more likely to fail than others. Demographic stress is a major factor. Where there are large numbers of unemployed youths concentrated in large cities and a lack of growth, the chances of conflict escalate.

The causes of state failure and civil disintegration are multiple, but certain characteristics increase vulnerability. Extreme income and gender inequality increase the risk of discord. Corrupt governments that are widely regarded as illegitimate and ineffective are "at risk." Democracy, especially with a strong parliament, lowers the risk of state failure; autocracy increases it. Population pressure, exacerbated by internally displaced people, refugees, and food scarcity, contribute to state failure and civil unrest. Governments that fail to protect human rights are especially prone to fail.

The Arab Spring, a term given to the Arab Revolution, is a wave of demonstrations, protests, and wars that began in December 2010. A number of rulers have been forced from power in Tunisia, Egypt, Libya, and Yemen. In addition, there have been civil uprisings in Bahrain, Syria, and Ukraine. However, the major oil-rich nations (Saudi Arabia, UAE, Qatar, Kuwait, and Oman) have managed to keep their ruling families in power.

The protests have shared techniques of civil resistance in sustained campaigns involving strikes, demonstrations, marches, and rallies, but were also noticeable for their use of social media to organize and raise awareness of the situation.

Despite the words of John F. Kennedy, US President 1961–3, that "Mankind must put an end to war or war will put an end to mankind," in 2021 military conflicts are taking place around the world in countries such as Afghanistan, Somalia, Yemen, Pakistan, Mexico (the "drugs war"), South Sudan, Nigeria, Syria, Iraq, Libya, and Ukraine.

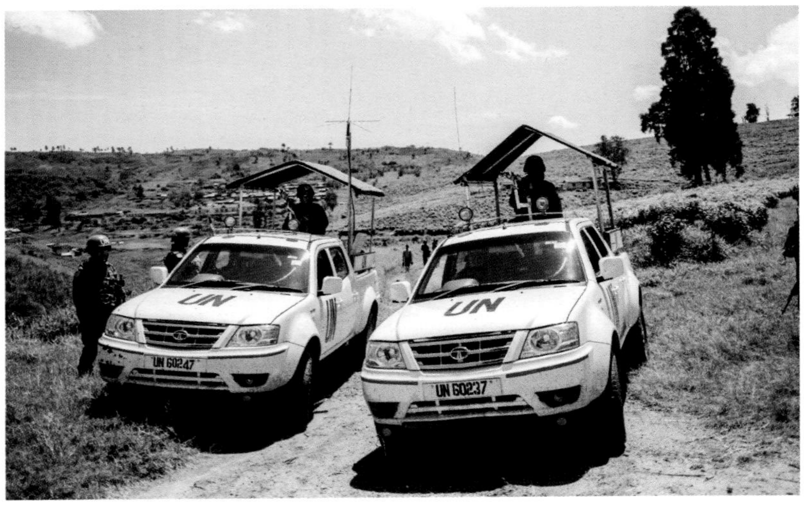

▲ UN peacekeepers in the Democratic Republic of the Congo. The UN is currently involved in 13 operations worldwide.

ARMED CONFLICTS

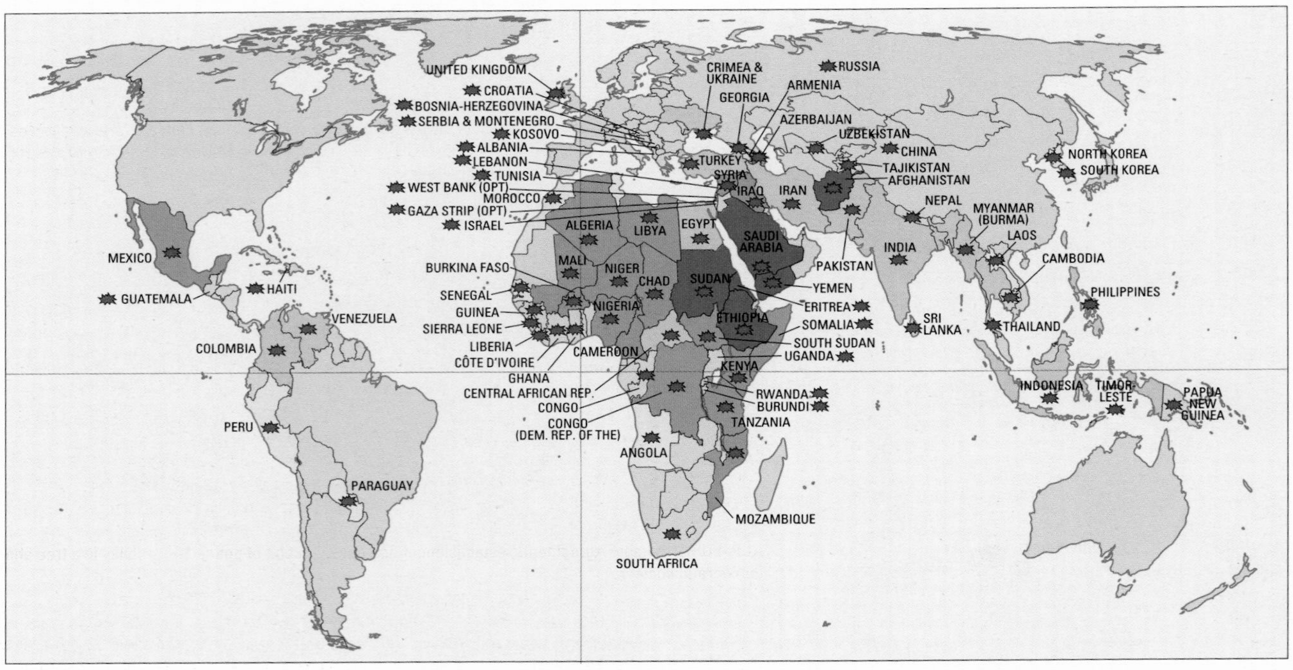

Current military and civilian deaths in countries with conflict, per year (2020)

- Over 10,000
- 1,000 – 10,000
- 100 – 1,000
- 0 – 100
- No conflict
- Countries with at least one armed conflict between 1994 and 2020

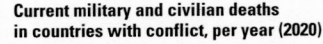

	Leading arms exporting countries (2020)	Leading recipients of arms deliveries (2020)
1	USA	India
2	Russia	Saudi Arabia
3	France	Australia
4	Germany	South Korea
5	Spain	Egypt
6	South Korea	China
7	Italy	Qatar
8	China	UK
9	Netherlands	Pakistan
10	UK	Japan

GLOBAL PEACE INDEX

The Global Peace Index (GPI) is an attempt to measure the relative position of nations' peacefulness. It quantifies: levels of security and safety; domestic and international conflict; and degree of militarization. Afghanistan is the least peaceful country with Libya and Ukraine showing the most deterioration.

Global Peace Index (2020)

- Under 1.500 (most peaceful)
- 1.501 – 2.000
- 2.001 – 2.500
- 2.501 – 3.000
- Over 3.001 (least peaceful)
- No data available

Five most peaceful countries		Five least peaceful countries	
Iceland	1.078	Afghanistan	3.644
New Zealand	1.198	Syria	3.539
Portugal	1.247	Iraq	3.487
Austria	1.275	South Sudan	3.447
Denmark	1.283	Yemen	3.411

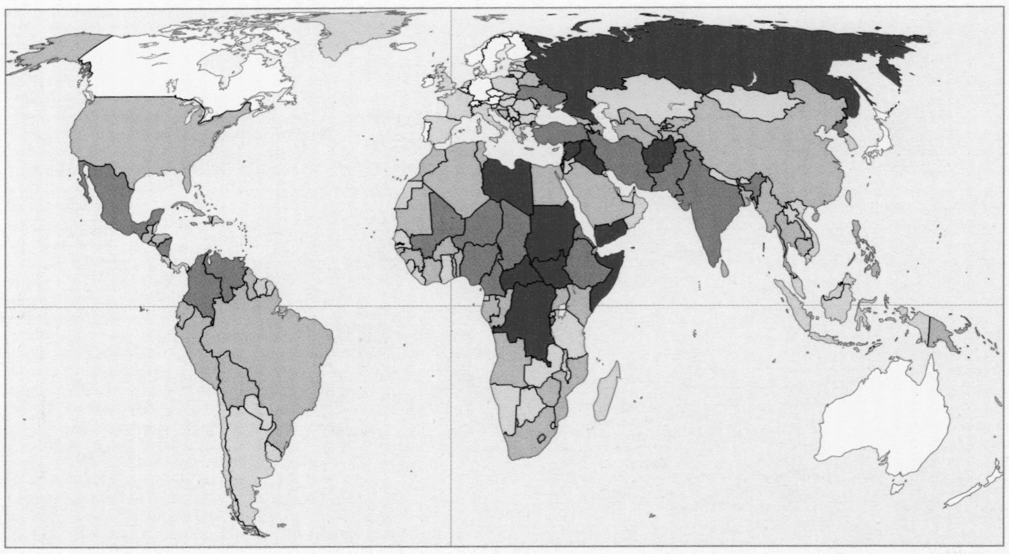

INTERNATIONAL ORGANIZATIONS

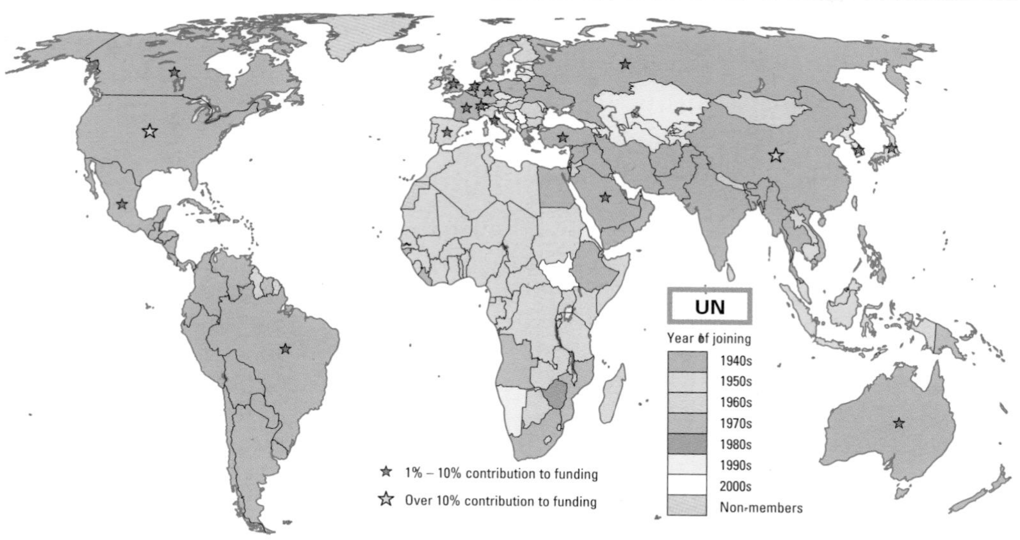

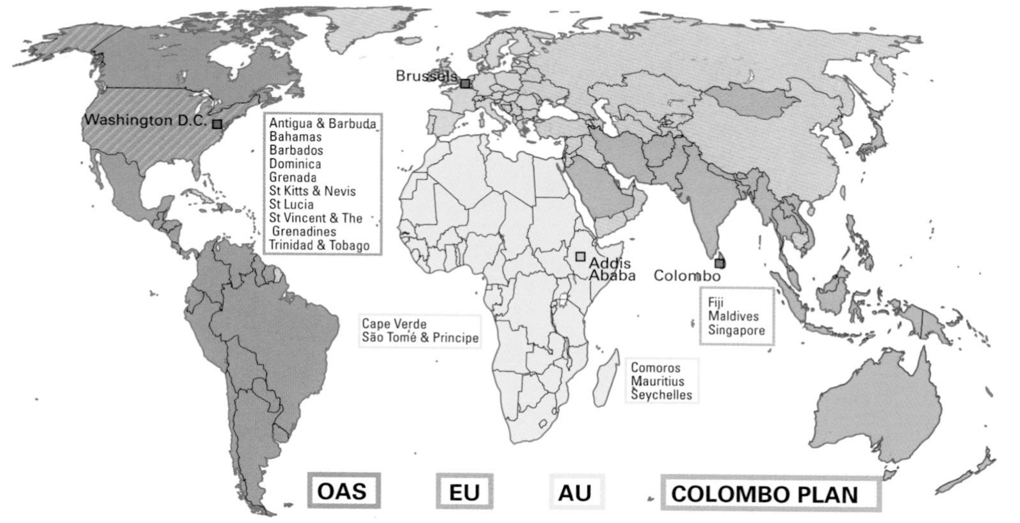

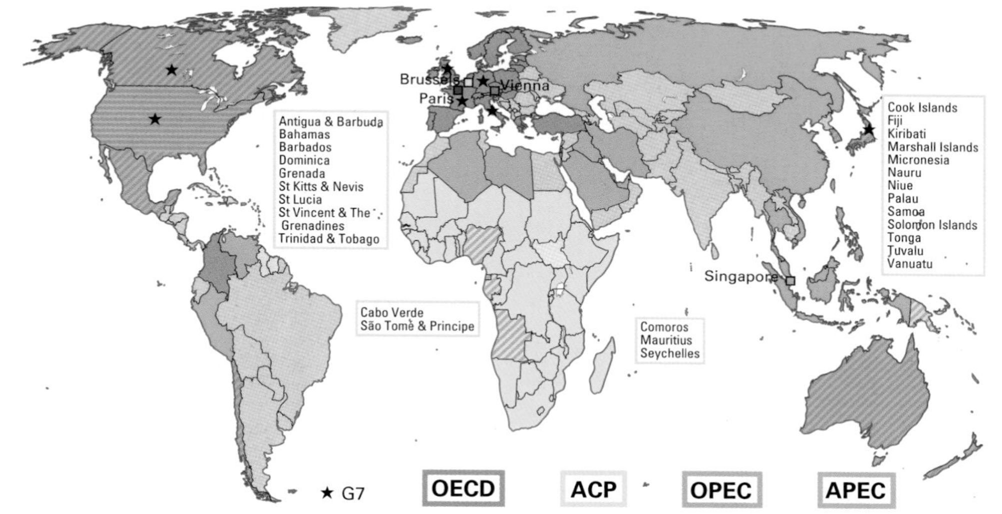

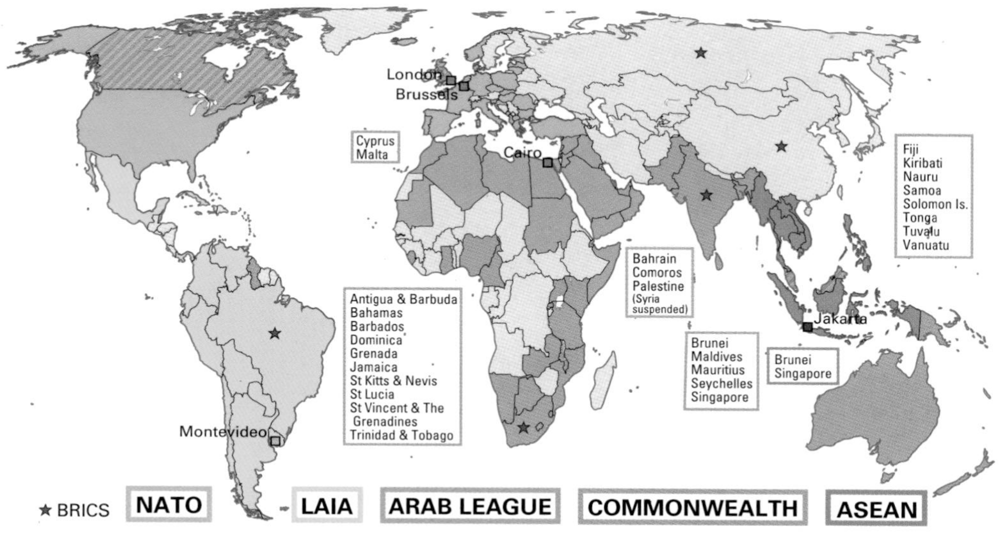

UNITED NATIONS

The creation of the United Nations in 1945 held out hope that the world's nations, tired of war, would have the means to control humanity's aggressive instincts. Although the UN lacks the power to halt conflicts, it has often helped to achieve negotiation. Economic pressures have led to another kind of cooperation, resulting in the creation of common markets and economic unions, such as ASEAN in Southeast Asia, the European Union, and NAFTA in North America.

The United Nations Organization was born as World War II drew to its conclusion. That body would replace the League of Nations, which, since its inception in 1920, had failed to curb the aggression of some of its member nations. At the United Nations Conference on International Organization held in San Francisco, the United Nations Charter was drawn up. Ratified by the Security Council and signed by the 51 original members, it came into effect on October 24, 1945.

The Charter set out the aims of the organization: to maintain peace and security, and to develop friendly relations between nations; to achieve international cooperation in solving economic, social, cultural, and humanitarian problems; to promote respect for human rights and fundamental freedoms; and to harmonize the activities of nations in order to achieve these common goals.

Membership From the original 51, membership of the UN has now grown to 193. There are only two independent states that are not members – Taiwan and the Vatican City. Official languages are Chinese, English, French, Russian, Spanish, and Arabic.

Funding The UN budget, now set yearly, for 2021 was US $3.2 billion. Contributions are assessed by the members' ability to pay, with the maximum 22% of the total (the USA's share), and the minimum 0.001%. The 27-member EU pays approximately 35% of the budget.

Peacekeeping The UN has been involved in 67 peacekeeping operations worldwide since 1948. They are involved in 13 operations in mid-2021.

OAS The **Organization of American States** was formed in 1948. It aims to promote social and economic cooperation between countries in the developed North America and developing Latin America.
EU The **European Union** evolved from the European Community in 1993. Cyprus, Czechia, Estonia, Hungary, Latvia, Lithuania, Malta, Poland, Slovakia, and Slovenia joined the EU in May 2004; Bulgaria and Romania joined in 2007; Croatia joined in 2013. The other 14 members of the EU are Austria, Belgium, Denmark, Finland, France, Germany, Greece, Ireland, Italy, Luxembourg, Netherlands, Portugal, Spain, and Sweden. The UK left the EU in 2020. Together, the 27 members aim to integrate economies, coordinate social developments, and bring about political union.
AU The **African Union** was set up in 2002, taking over from the Organization of African Unity (1963). It has 55 members. The main objectives of the OAU were, *inter alia*, to rid the continent of the remaining vestiges of colonization and apartheid; to promote unity and solidarity among African states; to coordinate and intensify cooperation for development; to safeguard the sovereignty and territorial integrity of member states; and to promote international cooperation within the framework of the United Nations.
COLOMBO PLAN Formed in 1951, its 27 members aim to promote economic and social development in Asia and the Pacific. Saudi Arabia joined in 2012.

G7 Group of seven leading industrialized nations, comprising Canada, France, Germany, Italy, Japan, the UK, and the USA. Periodic meetings are held to discuss major world issues, such as world recessions. The EU is also represented at meetings. Russian membership was suspended in 2014.
OECD The **Organization for Economic Co-operation and Development** (formed in 1961) comprises 37 major free-market economies. The "G7" is its "inner group" of leading industrial nations, comprising Canada, France, Germany, Italy, Japan, the UK, and the USA. The mission of the OECD is to promote policies that will improve the economic and social well-being of people around the world.
ACP The **African, Caribbean and Pacific Group of States** was formed in 1963. Members enjoy economic ties with the EU. The ACP Group's main objectives are sustainable development of its member states and their gradual integration into the global economy, which entails making poverty reduction a matter of priority; coordination of the activities of the ACP Group in the framework of the implementation of ACP–EU Partnership Agreements; establishment and consolidation of peace and stability in a free and democratic society.
OPEC The **Organization of Petroleum Exporting Countries** was formed in 1960. It controls about three-quarters of the world's oil supply. Its mission is to coordinate and unify the petroleum policies of its member countries, and to ensure the stabilization of oil markets in order to secure an efficient, economic, and regular supply of petroleum to consumers, a steady income to producers, and a fair return on capital for those investing in the petroleum industry. Qatar left in January 2019 and Ecuador left in 2020.
APEC Formed in 1989, the **Asia–Pacific Economic Cooperation** aims to enhance economic growth and prosperity for the region and to strengthen the Asia–Pacific community. APEC is the only intergovernmental grouping in the world operating on the basis of non-binding commitments, open dialog, and equal respect for the views of all participants. There are 21 member economies.

NATO The **North Atlantic Treaty Organization** (formed in 1949) continues despite the winding-up of the Warsaw Pact in 1991. Bulgaria, Estonia, Latvia, Lithuania, Romania, Slovakia, and Slovenia became members in 2004, and Albania and Croatia in 2009. Montenegro joined in 2017 and North Macedonia joined in 2020. Its main aim is to provide peace and security to its North Atlantic members through collective defense – an attack on one country is seen as an attack on all of NATO.
LAIA The **Latin American Integration Association** (formed in 1980) superceded the Latin American Free Trade Association formed in 1961. Its aim is to promote freer regional trade.
ARAB LEAGUE Formed in 1945, the Arab League aims to promote economic, social, political, and military cooperation. There are 22 member nations. Syria's membership was suspended in 2011.
COMMONWEALTH The **Commonwealth of Nations** evolved from the British Empire. Pakistan was suspended in 1999, but reinstated in 2004. Zimbabwe was suspended in 2002 and, in response to its continued suspension, Zimbabwe left the Commonwealth in 2003. Fiji was suspended in 2006 following a military coup. Rwanda joined the Commonwealth in 2009, as the 54th member state, becoming only the second country that was not formerly a British colony to be admitted to the group. The Gambia left between 2013 and 2018. Their objective is to build stronger democratic institutions and processes across the Commonwealth and to support economic growth in their member countries. There are currently 54 members.
ASEAN The **Association of Southeast Asian Nations** was formed in 1967. Cambodia joined in 1999. The aims of ASEAN include: to accelerate the economic growth, social progress, and cultural development in the region; to promote regional peace and stability; and to collaborate more effectively for the greater utilization of their agriculture and industries, the expansion of their trade, including the study of the problems of international commodity trade, the improvement of their transportation and communications facilities, and the raising of the living standards of their peoples.

For more information:
80 Global warming
Carbon dioxide
98 Minerals

Every year, the world's energy consumption is about the equivalent of what would come from burning 12,000 million tonnes of oil (12,000 MtOe) – a 20-fold increase since 1850. Two-fifths of this total actually comes from burning oil and most of the rest comes from coal and natural gas.

The oil crises in the 1970s precipitated concern over dependence on finite fossil fuels as the primary source of energy, and growing environmental awareness has added impetus to the search for alternative energy resources. Fossil fuel combustion damages the environment through the release of gases and particulate matter, but two other major sources of energy, hydroelectricity and nuclear power, are also controversial. Hydroelectricity production involves flooding large areas to create reservoirs, while nuclear power stations generate dangerous radioactive wastes and can cause major disasters. Nuclear power has been a growing source of energy, but the 2011 Japanese earthquake, with the consequent serious damage to the Fukushima nuclear power station, has caused many countries to rethink their energy strategies.

Alternative energy resources may soon provide a much larger proportion of the world's energy consumption. Solar and wind energy may become important in such countries as China and India, while tidal, wave, and geothermal energy all have potential in appropriate areas. Experts calculate that solar power could, in theory, supply between five and ten times the present electricity supply of developing countries.

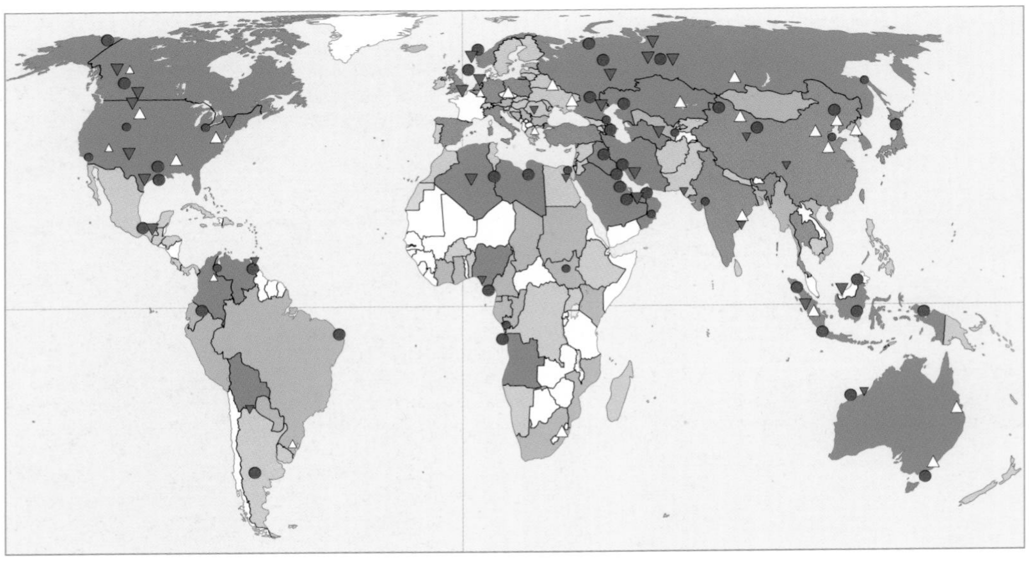

ENERGY BALANCE

Difference between energy production and consumption in millions of tonnes of oil equivalent (MtOe) (2019)

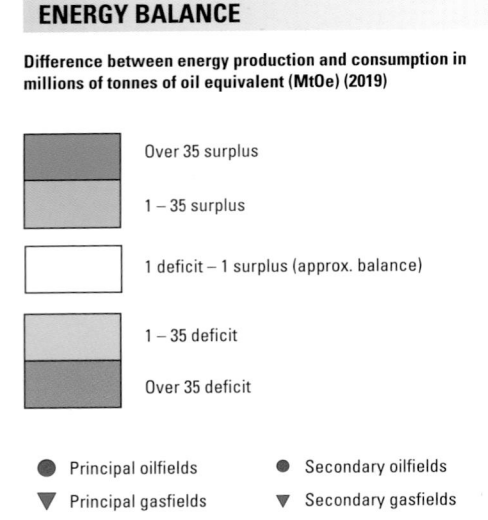

Over 35 surplus
1 – 35 surplus
1 deficit – 1 surplus (approx. balance)
1 – 35 deficit
Over 35 deficit

Principal oilfields
Principal gasfields
Principal coalfields
Secondary oilfields
Secondary gasfields
Secondary coalfields

ENERGY CONSUMPTION

Energy consumed by world regions, measured in million tonnes of oil equivalent in 2019. Total world consumption was 13,951 MtOe. Energy from commercially traded fuels, and modern renewables used to generate electricity, are included. Excluded are biomass fuels such as wood, peat and animal waste which, though important locally in some countries, are not always reliably documented statistically.

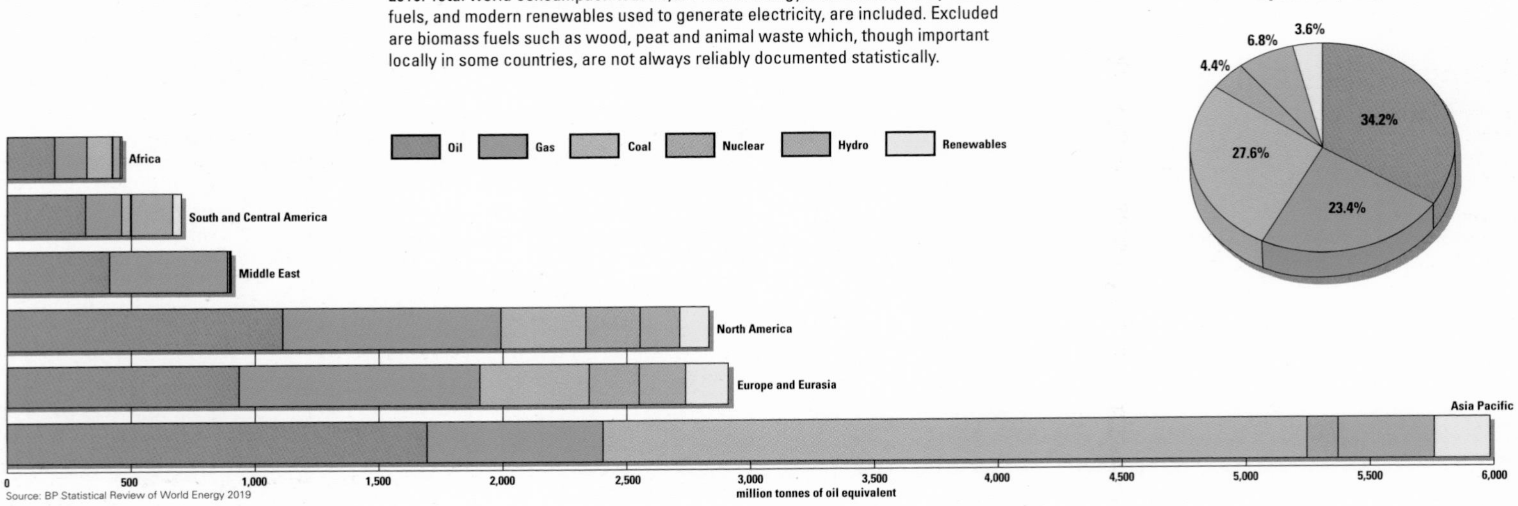

Source: BP Statistical Review of World Energy 2019

World energy consumption, by source (2019)

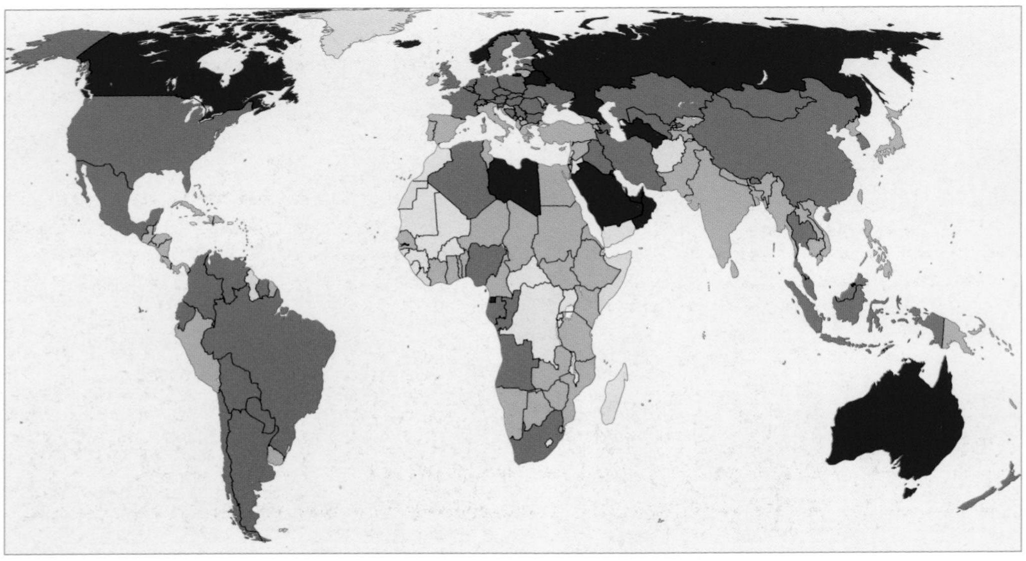

ENERGY PRODUCTION

Energy production in tonnes of oil equivalent per capita (2019)

Over 10
1 – 10
0.1 – 1
0 – 0.1
No data available

Highest energy producers, tonnes of oil equivalent per capita (2019)

Qatar	89.7
Kuwait	54.5
Norway	35.7
Brunei	34.9
Trinidad & Tobago	28.3

OIL MOVEMENTS

Major oil exporting regions

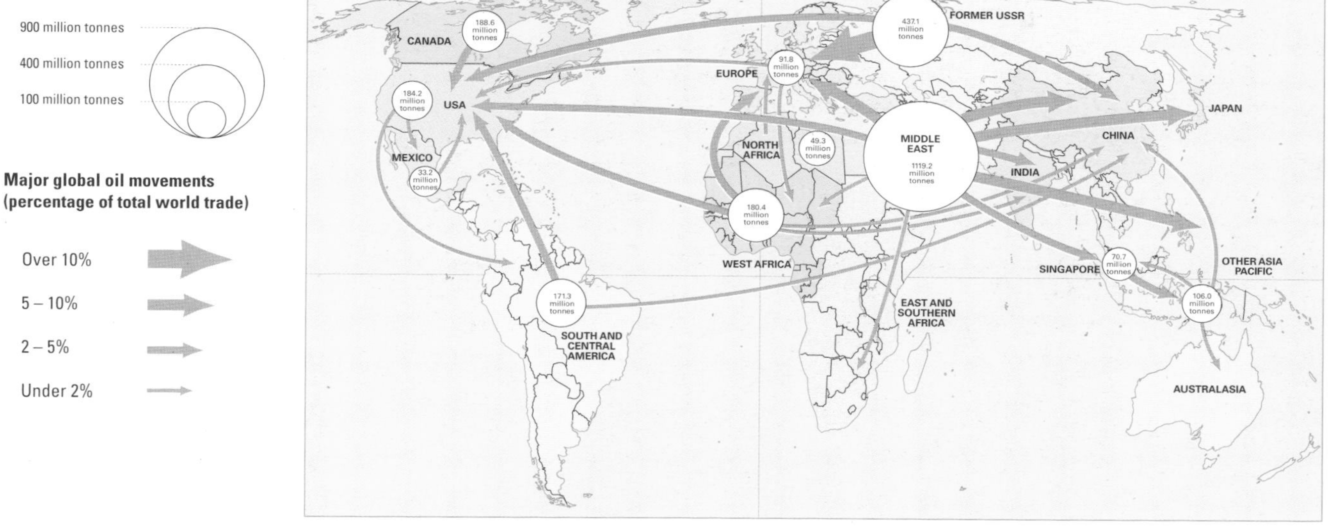

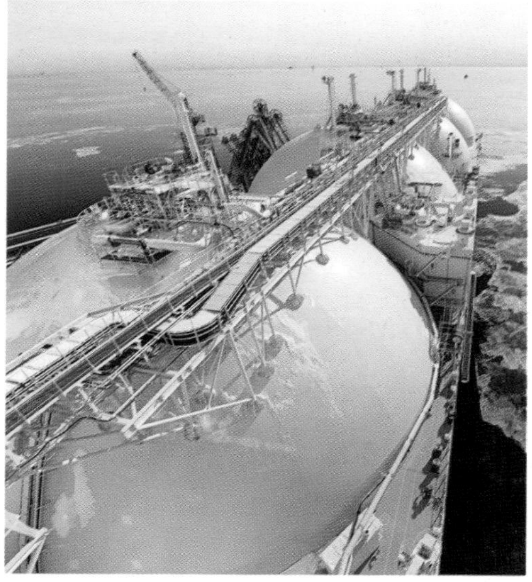

▲ A view over the tanks of the Liquefied Natural Gas (LNG) tanker Grand Aniva. LNG is natural gas that has been filtered and purified then cooled to -260°F (-162°C), which turns it into a liquid, 1/600th of its original volume, allowing it to be transported in special highly-insulated tanks on ships to markets around the world.

ENERGY RESERVES

WORLD OIL RESERVES

World oil reserves by region and country, billion tonnes (2019)

World total: 245 billion tonnes

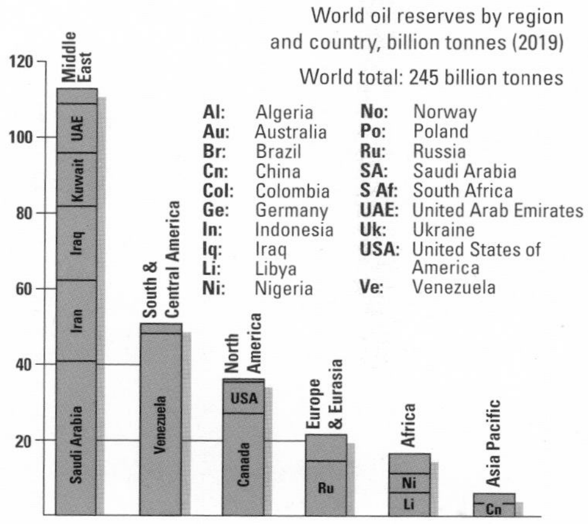

WORLD GAS RESERVES

World natural gas reserves by region and country, billion tonnes of oil equivalent (2019)

World total: 179 billion tonnes of oil equivalent

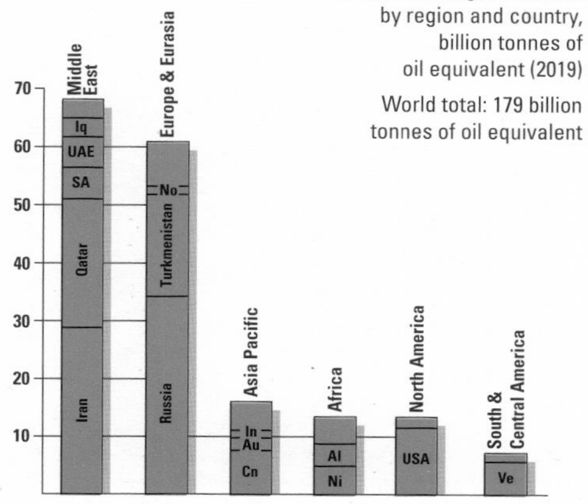

WORLD COAL RESERVES

World coal reserves (including lignite) by region and country, billion tonnes (2019)

World total: 1,071 billion tonnes

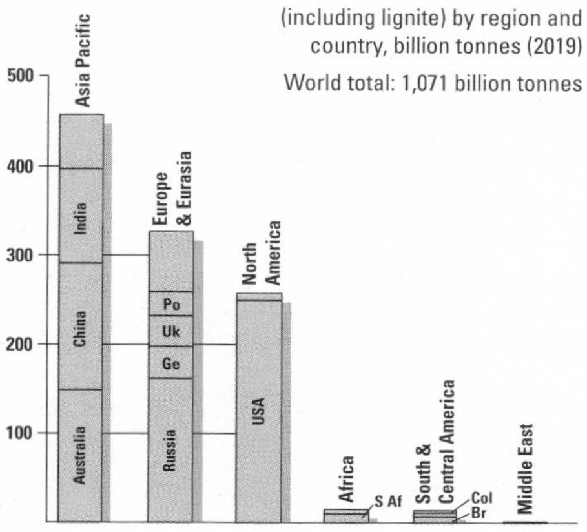

NUCLEAR POWER

Major producers by percentage of domestic electricity generation (2019)

Country	% of nuclear as proportion of domestic electricity	Country	% of nuclear as proportion of domestic electricity
1. France	71	11. Sweden	34
2. Slovakia	54	12. Armenia	28
3. Ukraine	54	13. South Korea	26
4. Hungary	49	14. Spain	21
5. Belgium	48	15. Russia	20
6. Switzerland	38	16. USA	20
7. Bulgaria	38	17. Romania	19
8. Slovenia	37	18. UK	16
9. Czechia	35	19. Canada	15
10. Finland	35	20. Taiwan	13

Although the 1980s were a bad time for the nuclear power industry, the industry picked up in the early 1990s. Despite this, growth has recently been curtailed whilst countries review their energy mix, in light of the March 2011 Japanese earthquake and tsunami that seriously damaged the Fukushima nuclear power station. Germany, for example, is phasing out its nuclear power production.

PEAK OIL

"Peak oil" refers to the peak of oil production. We depend on oil for many things: we use it for fuel, transport and heating, as a raw material in the plastics industry, and for fertilizer in food production. But as oil production decreases after peak oil, so will all of these, unless we can find new materials and alternatives.

Peak oil varies by country. The peak of oil discovery occurred in the 1960s, and by the 1980s the world was using more oil than was being discovered. Since then, the gap between use and discovery has been increasing, and many countries have now passed their peak oil production.

The International Energy Agency suggests that global peak oil will occur between 2013 and 2037. In contrast, the US Geological Survey suggests it will not occur until 2059. M. King Hubbert, who popularized the theory of peak oil, predicted that it would occur in 1995. It is claimed that in 1950 the world consumed 4 billion barrels of oil per annum, while the average discovery was 30 billion barrels per annum. Now, however, research suggests the figures are reversed: new discoveries are around 4 billion barrels per year, with an annual consumption of 30 billion barrels.

FRACKING

Hydraulic fracturing, commonly known as "fracking," releases natural gas or oil that is trapped in shale rock and is unobtainable by conventional techniques. This is accomplished by boring holes into the rock and injecting a liquid mix of chemicals under pressure, thus fracturing the rock and forcing the trapped oil or gas to the surface.

Just as nuclear scientists in the 1950s and 1960s believed that nuclear energy was going to be the answer to the world's energy needs, oil and gas producers believe that gas derived from shale could provide a plentiful supply of low-cost energy. As a result, shale gas could transform the pattern of energy trade in the world. Nevertheless, fracking has its critics and there may be problems related to the extraction of shale gas.

Shale is one of the most common forms of sedimentary rock on Earth. Significant reserves have been found in China, Argentina, the USA, and South Africa, and these are therefore having a new geopolitical influence. The world's gas trade has long been dominated by Russia, Qatar, and Algeria, but shale gas development has since taken off in the USA. In 2010, the USA replaced Russia as the world's largest gas producer and a new wave of gas producers may soon emerge.

However, as with the nuclear dawn, there are potential drawbacks with fracking. It may pollute soil and groundwater, release methane, produce toxic byproducts that have to be disposed of, and it may also trigger earthquakes.

HYDROELECTRICITY

Major producers by percentage of world total and by percentage of domestic electricity generation (2019)

Country	% of world total production	Country	% of hydroelectric as proportion of domestic electricity
1. China	27.2	1. Albania	100.0
2. Brazil	8.3	2. Paraguay	100.0
3. USA	7.9	3. Congo, Dem. Rep.	99.9
4. Canada	6.2	4. Nepal	99.8
5. Japan	3.8	5. Namibia	99.1
6. India	3.8	6. Zambia	97.2
7. Russia	3.8	7. Tajikistan	97.1
8. Norway	2.5	8. Norway	96.0
9. Turkey	2.2	9. Ethiopia	95.6
10. France	1.7	10. Kyrgyzstan	91.3

Countries heavily reliant on hydroelectricity are usually small and non-industrial: a high proportion of hydroelectric power more often reflects a modest energy budget than vast hydroelectric resources. The USA, for instance, produces only 6% of its domestic power requirements from hydroelectricity; yet that 6% amounts to almost half the hydropower generated by the whole of Africa.

ALTERNATIVE ENERGY RESOURCES

Solar: Each year the Sun bestows upon the Earth almost a million times as much energy as is locked up in all the planet's oil reserves, but only an insignificant fraction is trapped and used commercially. In a few installations around the world, mirrors focus the Sun's rays on to boilers, whose steam generates electricity by spinning turbines, and the use of photovoltaic panels in sunny climates has also started to become established.

Wind: Caused by uneven heating of the Earth, winds are themselves a form of solar energy. Windmills have been long used for wind power; recent models are often arranged in banks on wind-swept high ground or situated off coastlines. Wind-power figures are given in the table (*right*). Wind power contributes over 30% of all electricity generated in Denmark.

Tidal: The energy from tides is potentially enormous, although only a few installations have so far been built to exploit it. In theory, at least, waves and currents could also provide almost unimaginable power, and the thermal differences in the ocean depths are another huge well of potential energy. But work on extracting it is still at the experimental stage.

Geothermal: The Earth's temperature rises by 1°F for every 50 feet descent, with much steeper temperature gradients in geologically active areas. El Salvador, for example, produces 25% of its electricity from geothermal power stations, whilst the USA is the world's leading producer. Some of the oldest and most successful applications are in Iceland, where 87% of all households are heated by geothermal energy.

Biomass: The oldest of human fuels ranges from animal dung, still burned in cooking fires in much of North Africa and elsewhere, to sugarcane plantations feeding high-technology distilleries to produce ethanol for motor-vehicle engines. In Brazil and South Africa, plant ethanol provides up to 25% of motor fuel. Throughout the developing world, most biomass energy comes from firewood: although accurate figures are impossible to obtain, it may yield as much as 10% of the world's total energy consumption.

WIND POWER

World wind energy generating capacity, in megawatts

2000	17,800
2002	31,000
2003	39,300
2004	47,671
2005	58,982
2006	74,151
2007	93,927
2008	121,188
2009	157,899
2010	196,653
2011	238,035
2012	282,482
2013	318,105
2014	370,000
2015	434,856
2016	486,661
2017	540,000
2018	597,000
2019	650,785
2020	744,000

For more information:
74 Geology
101 Globalization

The use of metals played a vital part in the evolving technologies of early peoples. Copper first came into use around 10,000 years ago, bronze about 5,000 years ago, and iron 3,300 years ago. In the early stages of the Industrial Revolution, the location of coal, iron ore, and water power usually determined the location of new industries. But due to continuing improvements in transport, including oil pipelines, industries can now be located almost anywhere.

Minerals are distributed unevenly and some industrial countries, lacking their own mineral resources, import most of the raw materials they need. Some imports come from mineral-rich countries, such as Australia, but others come from developing countries, especially in Africa and South America. Most developing countries export unprocessed ores, losing out on the higher revenues gained from exporting metals.

Most minerals come from land deposits, because undersea deposits, with the exception of oil reserves under the continental shelves, have been inaccessible. But shortages of terrestrial minerals may one day encourage exploitation of the ocean floor.

► Bingham Canyon Mine in Utah, USA, is one of the largest open-pit mines in the world. It measures over 2.5 miles [4 km] wide and 3,900 ft [1,200 m] deep. Copper-containing rocks are excavated from the surface downward in terraces. These terraces are 50–80 ft [15–25 m] high and provide access for equipment to work the rock face whilst maintaining stability of the sloping pit walls.

Today's copper market is booming due to global demands from construction, telecommunications, and electronics companies. Over 17 million tonnes of copper have been mined from Bingham Canyon Mine to date, as well as gold, silver and other minerals.

URANIUM

Uranium was first discovered by the German chemist Martin Klaproth in 1789. In its pure state, uranium is an immensely heavy, white metal. Its main use is as a fuel in nuclear reactors and in nuclear weaponry, although depleted uranium is employed as a projectile in anti-missile cannons, where its mass ensures a lethal punch.

Uranium is very scarce: the main source is the rare ore pitchblende, which itself contains only 0.2% uranium oxide. This blackish, lustrous ore occurs in quartz veins. Only a minute fraction of that is the radioactive U^{235} isotope, though so-called breeder reactors can transmute the more common U^{238} into highly radioactive plutonium.

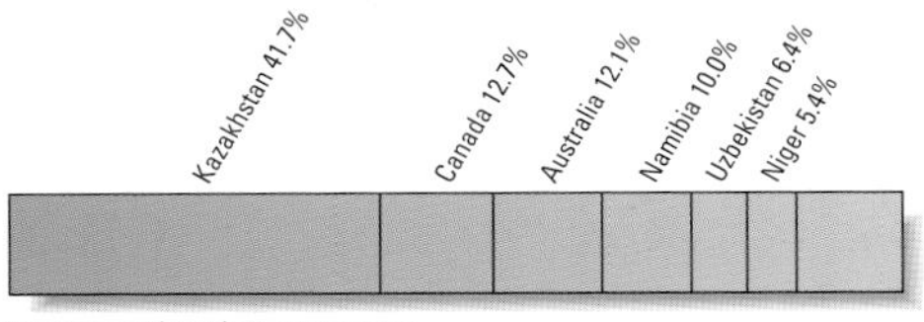

World total (2020): 54,752 tonnes

DIAMOND

Most of the world's diamond is found in kimberlite, or "blue ground," a basic igneous rock; erosion may wash the diamond from its kimberlite matrix and deposit it with sand or gravel on river beds. Only a small proportion of the world's diamond, the most flawless, is cut into gemstones – "diamonds"; most are used in industry, where the material's remarkable hardness and abrasion resistance find a use in cutting tools, drills, and dies. In 2020, the world's major producers were Russia (35.2%), Australia (22.2%), the Democratic Republic of the Congo (22.2%), Botswana (9.3%), South Africa (5.6%), and Zimbabwe (3.7%). Natural diamonds now account for about 3% of all industrial diamond output. Synthetic diamond production in centers such as China, Ireland, Japan, Russia, and the USA far exceeds it.

BLOOD DIAMONDS

Blood Diamonds, or "Conflict Diamonds," are stones that are produced in areas controlled by rebel forces that are opposed to internationally recognized governments. The rebels sell these diamonds, using the money to purchase arms or to fund their military actions. These diamonds are often the main source of funding for the rebels – however, arms merchants, smugglers, and dishonest diamond traders facilitate their actions.

The flow of Blood Diamonds originated mainly from Sierra Leone, Angola, Democratic Republic of Congo, Liberia, and Côte d'Ivoire. In 2003, the United Nations and other groups introduced a certification procedure known as the "Kimberley Process," to try to eradicate this practice. This procedure requires each nation to certify that all rough diamond exports are produced through legitimate mining and sales activity.

Over 80 countries participate in the agreement.

Aluminum: Produced mainly from its oxide, bauxite, which yields 25% of its weight in aluminum. The cost of refining and production is often too high for producer-countries to bear, so bauxite is largely exported. Lightweight and corrosion resistant, aluminum alloys are widely used in aircraft, vehicles, cans, and packaging.

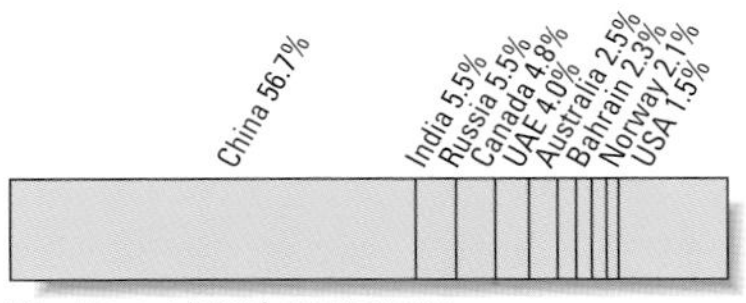

World total (2020): 65,200,000 tonnes

Copper: Derived from low-yielding sulfide ores, copper is an important export for several developing countries. An excellent conductor of heat and electricity, it forms part of most electrical items, and is used in the manufacture of brass and bronze. Major importers include Japan and Germany.

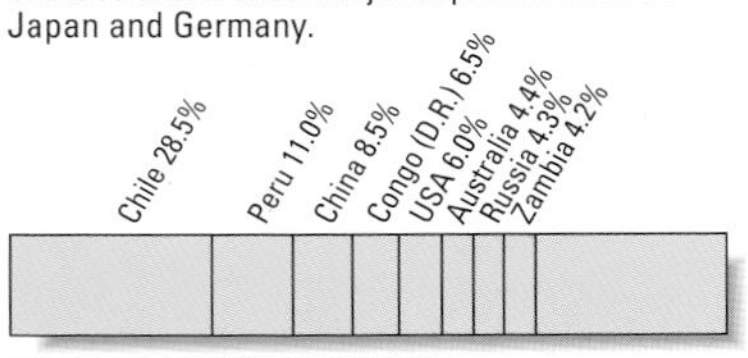

World total (2020): 20,000,000 tonnes

Lead: A soft metal, obtained mainly from galena (lead sulfide), which occurs in veins associated with iron, zinc, and silver sulfides. Its use in vehicle batteries accounts for the USA's prime consumer status; lead is also made into sheeting and piping. Its use as an additive to paints and petrol is decreasing.

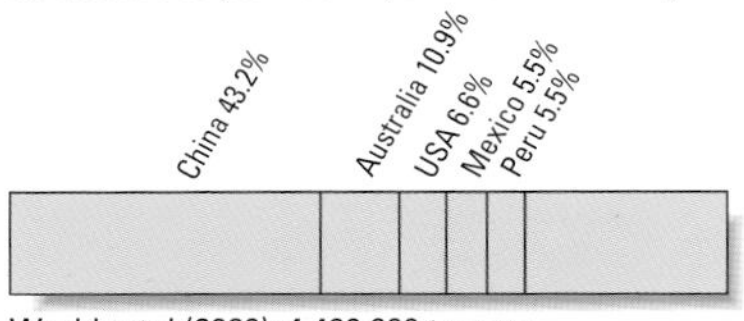

World total (2020): 4,400,000 tonnes

Mercury: The only metal that is liquid at normal temperatures, most is derived from its sulfide, cinnabar, found only in small quantities in volcanic areas. Apart from its value in thermometers and other instruments, most mercury production is used in anti-fungal and anti-fouling preparations, and to make detonators.

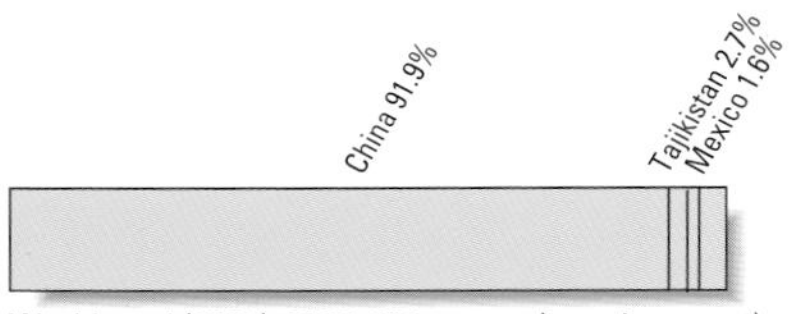

World total (2020): 3,700,000 tonnes (metal content)

Tin: Soft, pliable and non-toxic, used to coat "tin" (tin-plated steel) cans, in the manufacture of foils and in alloys. The principal tin-bearing mineral is cassiterite (SnO_2), found in ore formed from molten rock.

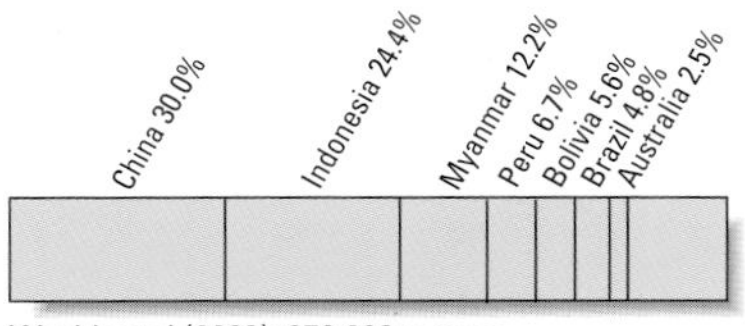

World total (2020): 270,000 tonnes

Zinc: Often found in association with lead ores, zinc is highly resistant to corrosion, and about 40% of the refined metal is used to plate sheet steel, particularly vehicle bodies – a process known as galvanizing. Zinc is also used in dry batteries, paints, and dyes.

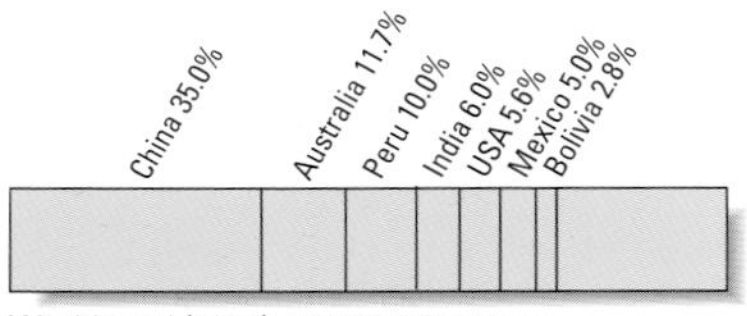

World total (2020): 12,000,000 tonnes

Gold: Regarded for centuries as the most valuable metal in the world and used to make coins, gold is still recognized as the monetary standard. A soft metal, it is alloyed to make jewelry; the electronics industry values its corrosion resistance and conductivity.

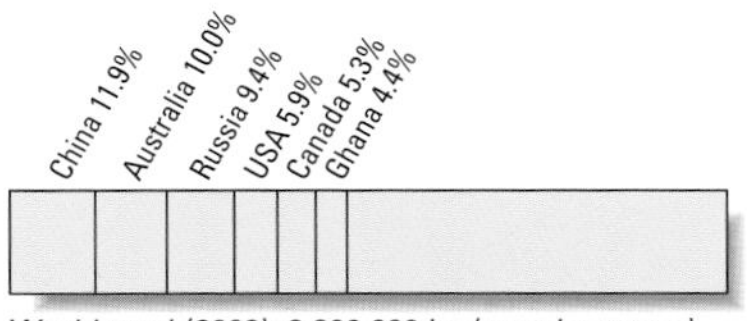

World total (2020): 3,200,000 kg (metal content)

Silver: Most silver comes from ores mined and processed for other metals (including lead and copper). Pure or alloyed with harder metals, it is used for jewelry and ornaments. Industrial use includes dentistry, electronics, photography, and as a chemical catalyst.

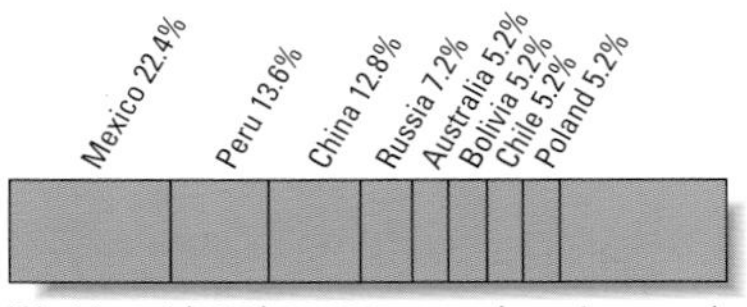

World total (2020): 25,000 tonnes (metal content)

DISTRIBUTION OF MINERALS

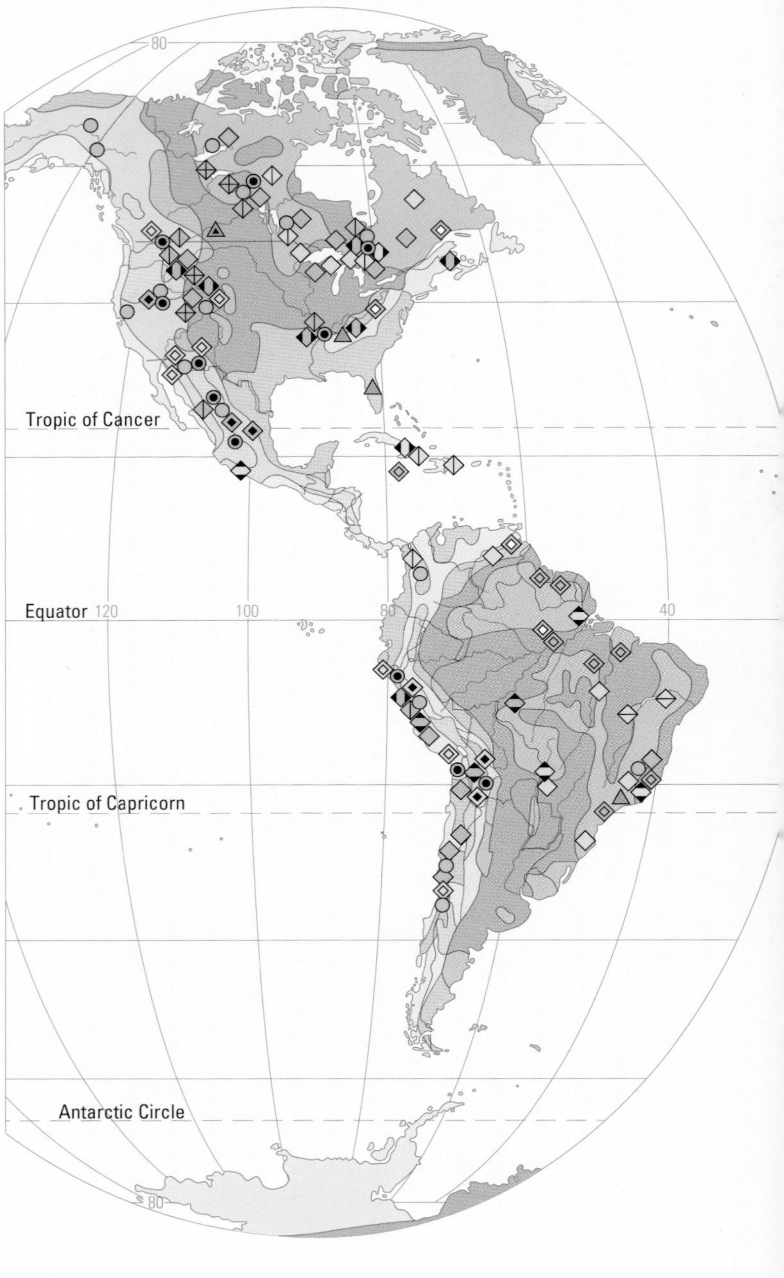

IRON ORE

Ever since the art of high-temperature smelting was discovered, some time in the second millennium BC, iron has been by far the most important metal known to man. The earliest iron plows transformed primitive agriculture and led to the first human population explosion, while iron weapons – or the lack of them – ensured the rise or fall of entire cultures.

Widely distributed around the world, iron ores usually contain 25–60% iron; blast furnaces process the raw product into pig-iron, which is then alloyed with carbon and other minerals to produce steels of various qualities. From the time of the Industrial Revolution, steel has been almost literally the backbone of modern civilization, the prime structural material on which all else is built.

Iron smelting usually developed close to the sources of ore and, later, to the coalfields that fueled the furnaces. Today, most ore comes from a few richly-endowed locations where large-scale mining is possible.

Iron and steel plants are generally built at coastal sites so that giant ore carriers, which account for a sizable proportion of the world's merchant fleet, can more easily discharge their cargoes.

World production of pig-iron (2020)

Total world production: 1,200 million tonnes

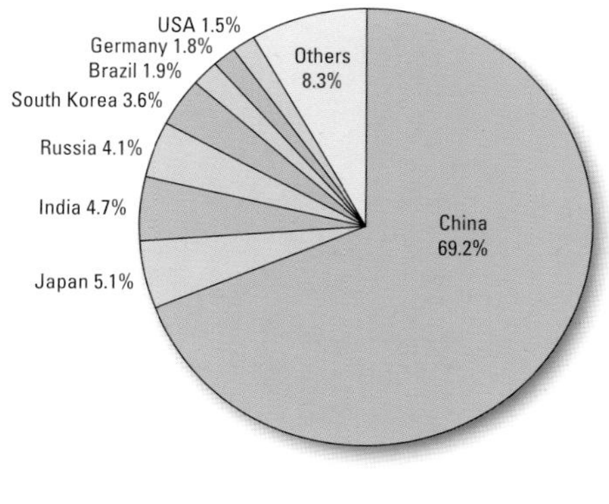

Iron ore

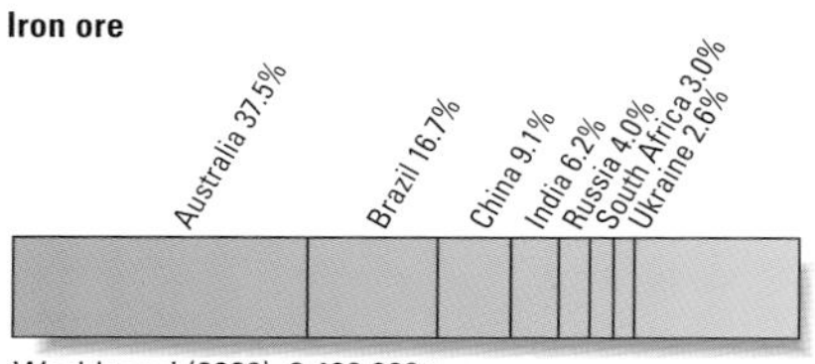

World total (2020): 2,400,000 tonnes

RARE EARTHS

Rare earth elements, or rare earth metals, are a set of 17 chemical elements, specifically the 15 lanthanides plus scandium and yttrium. Despite their name, rare earth elements are relatively plentiful, but are typically dispersed and not often found concentrated in economically exploitable ore deposits.

Until 1948, most of the world's rare earths were sourced from sand deposits in India and Brazil. Between the 1960s and the 1980s, the leading producer was California, USA. Today, China produces over 90% of the world's rare earth supply, although it only has less than 23% of proven reserves. The US Geological Survey is currently actively surveying southern Afghanistan for rare earth deposits under the protection of US military forces.

New demand has recently strained supply, and there is a growing concern that the world may soon face a shortage of the rare earths. In recent years, China has reduced its export quotas and halted production in some of its mines in order to conserve scarce resources and protect the environment.

A recently developed source of rare earths is electronic waste, and other wastes have rare earth components. Advances in recycling technology have made extraction of rare earths from these materials more feasible.

Rare earths are used as follows:

- **Neodymium** To make powerful magnets in loudspeakers and computer hard drives; also used in wind turbines and hybrid cars.
- **Lanthanum** In camera and telescope lenses.
- **Cerium** In catalytic converters in cars, and in the refining of oil.
- **Praseodymium** As an alloy, to create strong metals in aircraft engines.
- **Gadolinium** For X-ray machines, MRI scanning systems, and television screens.
- **Yttrium, terbium, europium** For television and computer screens, and for visual display units.

SCRAP METAL

Scrap metal has been an important source material for the manufacturing industry in domestic markets for decades, its value fluctuating according to the state of the local economy. Recently, however, with growing concern for the global environment and the rapid development of the economies in the Far East, the industry has become far more globalized. Container loads of processed-metal scrap from time-expired machinery in the Western world are now being exported to the Far East to be recycled. Processed-steel scrap accounts for almost half of the requirements for "furnace feed" for the world's steelmakers, and 40% of the world's copper requirements are derived from scrap.

Two major advantages of using scrap rather than refining mined ore are the energy and raw material savings that can be made. If 1 tonne of steel scrap is recycled, it saves 120 lb [54 kg] of limestone, 2,500 lb [1,130 kg] of iron ore and 1,400 lb [635 kg] of coal, with a consequent 86% reduction in air pollution, 40% saving in water use, and 76% reduction in water pollution. Huge energy savings, with consequent cuts in greenhouse-gas emissions, can also be made by using scrap.

As well as bulk minerals, such as those quoted above, alloys using nickel, chromium, tungsten, molybdenum, cobalt, and titanium, which are often only available in limited supplies and are expensive to produce, can also be recycled. The techniques involved to do this work are often very sophisticated, involving X-ray spectrometry and other computer-controlled methods, in order to recover high-value but low-volume metals from devices such as computers and televisions.

With companies having to take increased responsibility for their products, from manufacturing to sale and thence to their ultimate disposal at the end of their useful life, recycling scrap metals will become a much more important method of conserving the world's raw materials and preserving the environment in the future.

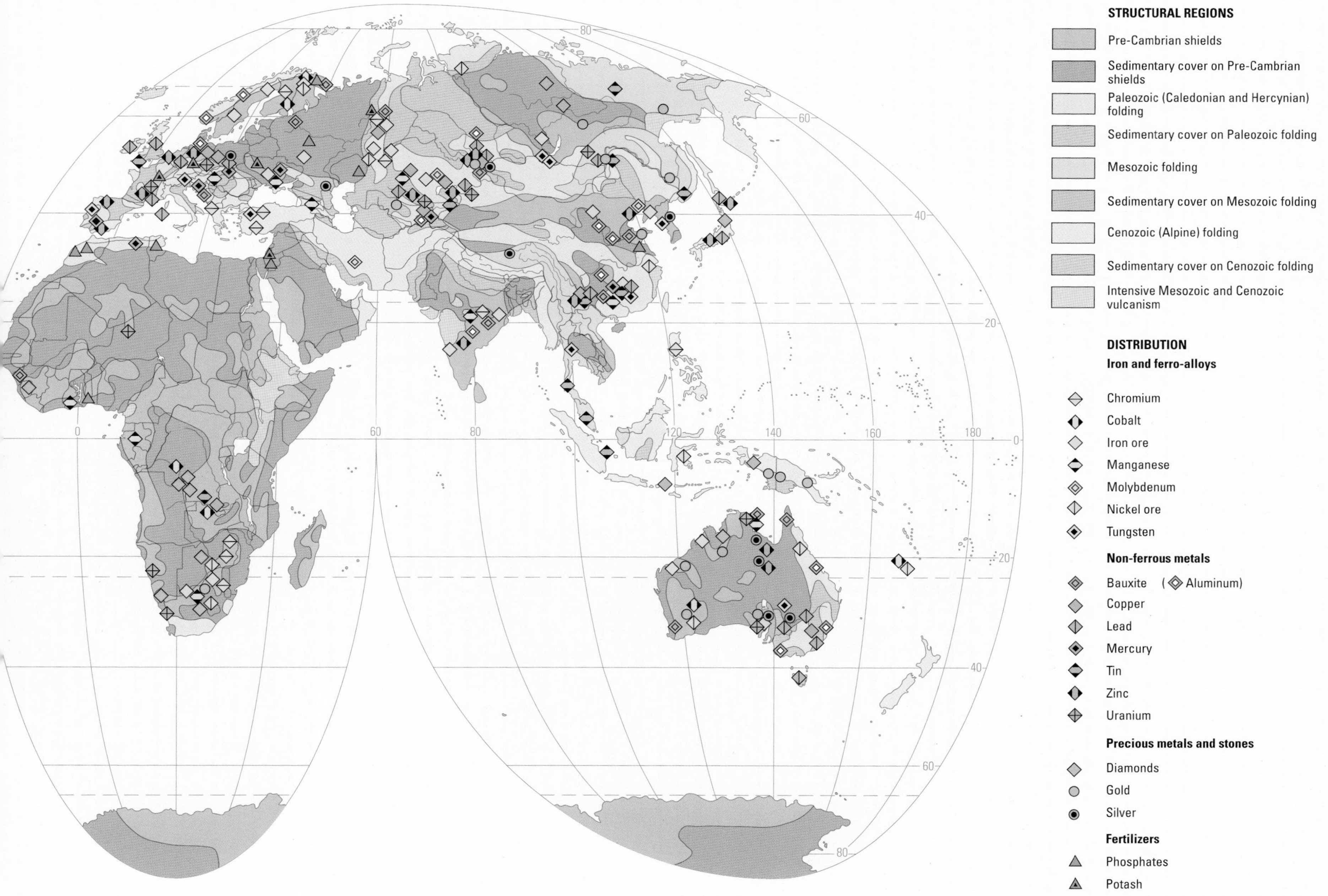

For more information:
97 Oil movements
98 Minerals
106 Levels of income

The Industrial Revolution, which began in Britain in the late 18th century, represented a major technological advance in the evolution of human society. It enabled a group of countries to become prosperous by replacing expensive human labor with increasingly sophisticated machinery. In economic terms, manufacturing is the transformation of raw materials, energy, labor, and machines into finished goods, which have a higher value than the various elements used in production.

The economies of countries can be compared by reference to their per capita Gross Domestic Products (GDPs), namely, the total value of goods and services produced within a country in a year, divided by the population. If this is calculated using Purchasing Power Parity (PPP) exchange rates, it better reflects the real state of the economy by taking into account differences in price levels in each country. The industrialized, or developed, countries accounted for 15% of the world's population in 2018 with an average per capita GDP of over US $45,000. On the other hand, low-income developing countries, with small industrial sectors, accounted for 77% of the world's population. Their per capita GDPs can be as low as $400.

Tanzania, with its low-income economy, had a per capita GDP in 2019 of US $2,660. Agriculture employs 80% of the people, while light industry together with services employ 20%. By contrast, Germany had a per capita GDP in 2019 of $54,000. Agriculture employs only 2% of the population, with 25% in industry and 74% in services. Germany's industrial sector differs greatly from Tanzania's, with its emphasis on vehicles, machinery, chemicals, and electronics.

Since the 1970s, some former developing countries in eastern Asia achieved rapid economic growth through industrialization. Despite setbacks in the late 1990s, they demonstrated that a developing industrial sector can transform an economy, which starts off with certain advantages, such as low labor costs. But economic success also depends on such factors as education to provide skills, and regulations that attract foreign investors. China, whose economy grew by more than 10% per year between 2002 and 2012, satisfies many of these criteria, though its record on human rights leaves much to be desired.

EMPLOYMENT

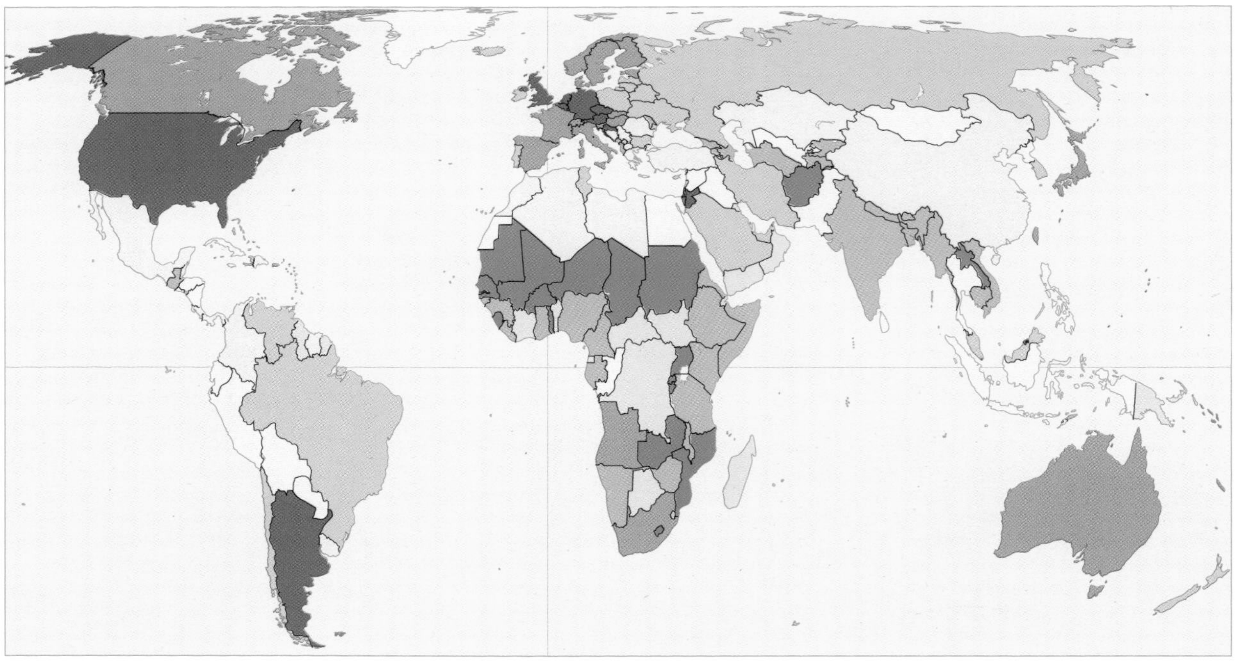

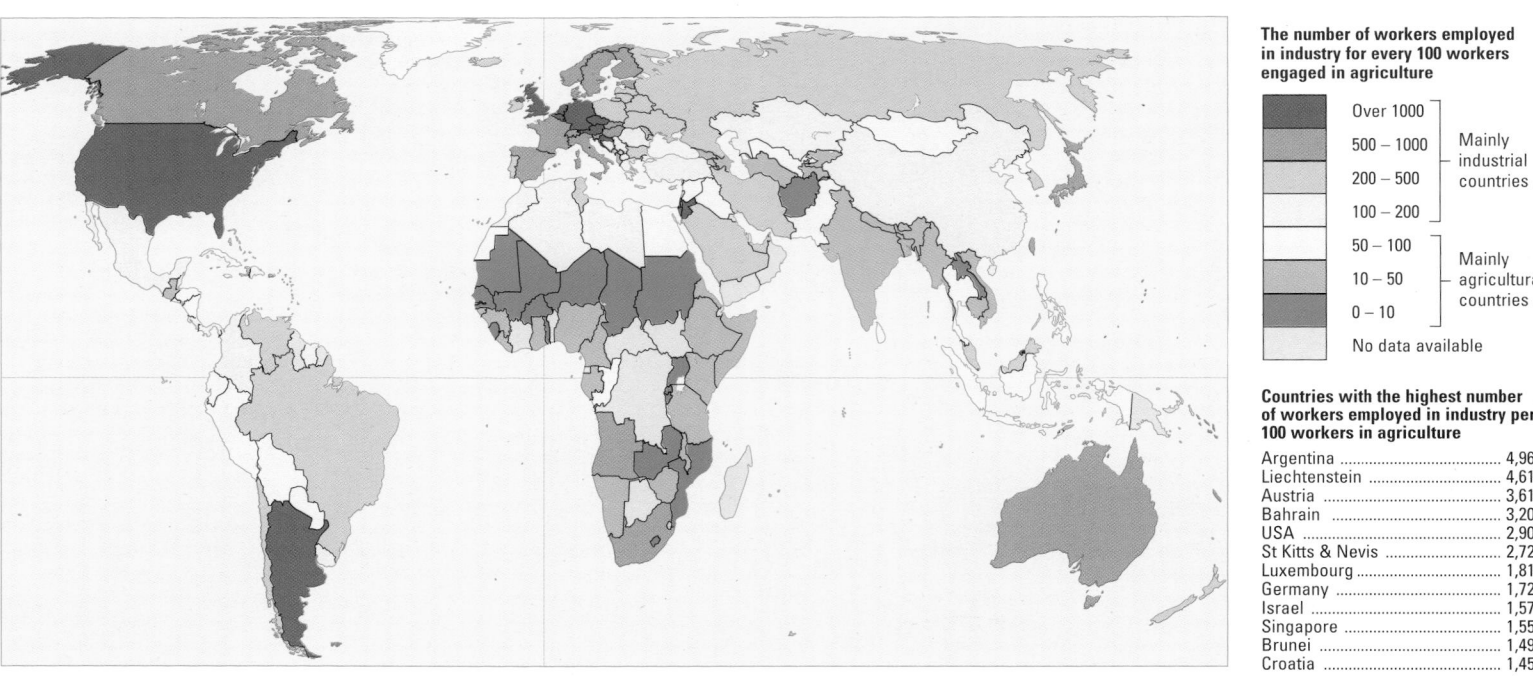

The number of workers employed in industry for every 100 workers engaged in agriculture

- Over 1000
- 500 – 1000
- 200 – 500
- 100 – 200

(Mainly industrial countries)

- 50 – 100
- 10 – 50
- 0 – 10

(Mainly agricultural countries)

- No data available

Countries with the highest number of workers employed in industry per 100 workers in agriculture

Argentina	4,960
Liechtenstein	4,613
Austria	3,614
Bahrain	3,200
USA	2,900
St Kitts & Nevis	2,727
Luxembourg	1,818
Germany	1,729
Israel	1,573
Singapore	1,550
Brunei	1,495
Croatia	1,453

DIVISION OF EMPLOYMENT

Distribution of workers between agriculture, industry and services, selected countries

The six countries selected illustrate the usual stages of economic development, from dependence on agriculture through industrial growth to the expansion of the service sector.

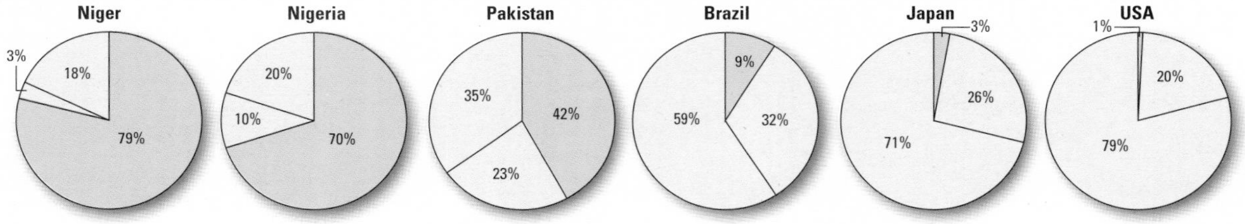

- Agriculture
- Industry
- Services

WORLD TRADE

Percentage share of total world exports by value (2019)

- Over 10% of world trade
- 1 – 10% of world trade
- 0.1 – 1.0% of world trade
- 0 – 0.1% of world trade
- No world trade
- No data available

International trade is dominated by a handful of powerful maritime nations: the members of "G7" (Canada, France, Germany, Italy, Japan, UK, and USA) and the "BRICS" nations (Brazil, Russia, India, China, and South Africa).

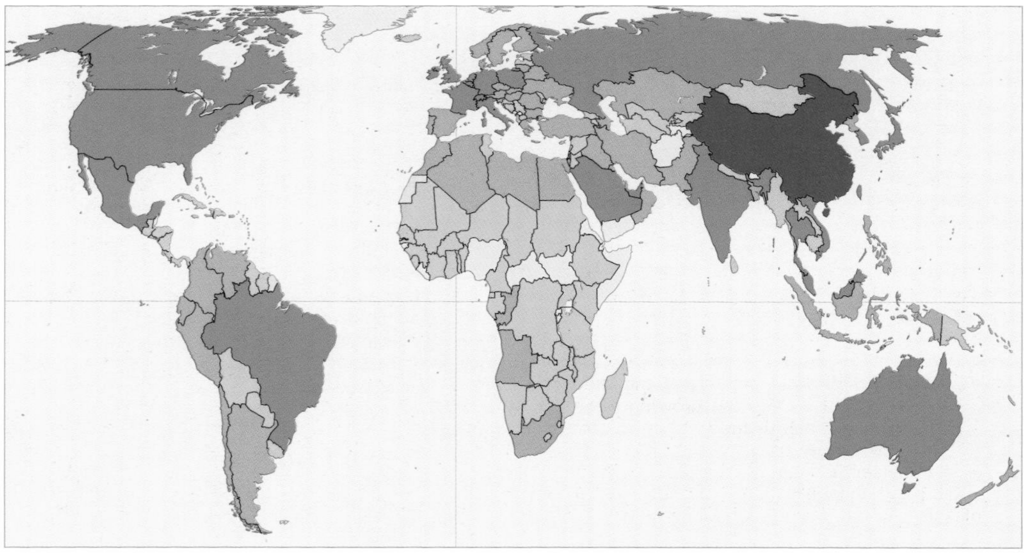

INDUSTRY AND TRADE

Manufactured goods (including machinery and transport) as a percentage of total exports (2019)

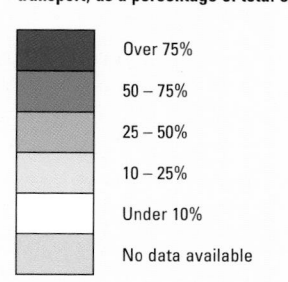

- Over 75%
- 50 – 75%
- 25 – 50%
- 10 – 25%
- Under 10%
- No data available

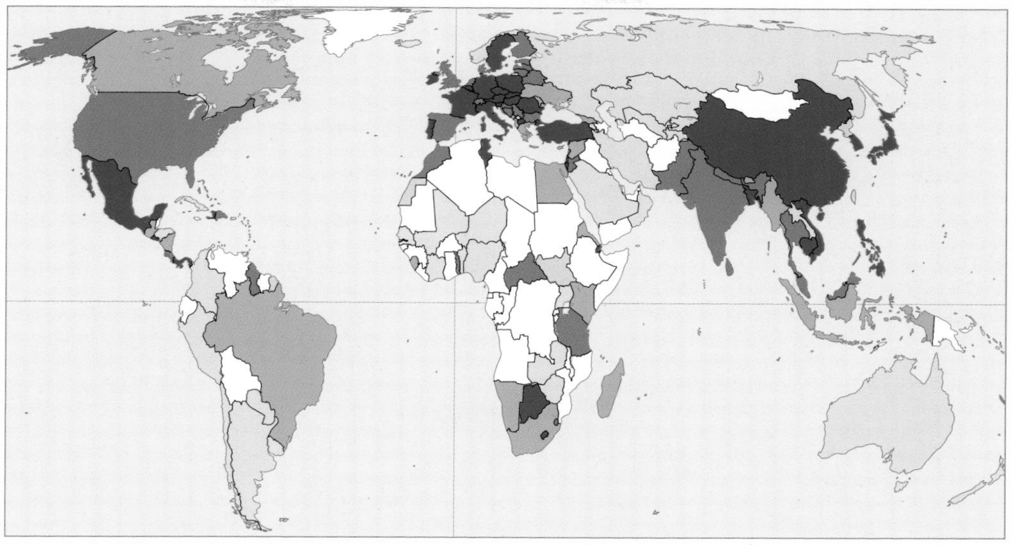

Countries most dependent on the export of manufactured goods (2019)

Bangladesh	96%
Botswana	96%
Panama	94%
China	93%
Israel	93%
Andorra	92%

UNEMPLOYMENT

Highest rates of unemployment, percentage of the labor force (2019)

1.	Burkina Faso	77%
2.	Syria	50%
3.	Senegal	48%
4.	Haiti	41%
5.	Kenya	40%
6.	Djibouti	40%
7.	Namibia	34%
8.	Venezuela	33%
9.	Kiribati	31%
10.	Libya	30%
11.	South Africa	29%
12.	Kosovo	29%
13.	Lesotho	28%
14.	Gabon	28%
15.	Eswatini	28%
16.	Yemen	27%
17.	Mozambique	25%
18.	Grenada	24%
19.	Afghanistan	24%
20.	Nauru	23%

IMPORTANCE OF SERVICE SECTOR

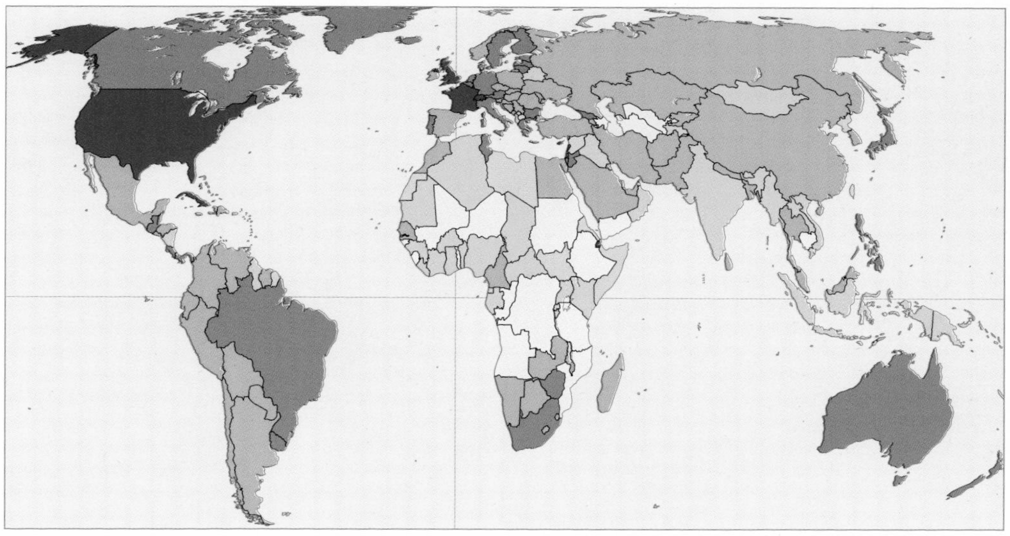

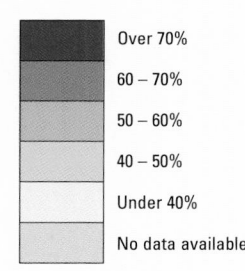

Percentage of total GDP from service sector (2019)

- Over 70%
- 60 – 70%
- 50 – 60%
- 40 – 50%
- Under 40%
- No data available

The service sector involves those parts of business such as accountancy, advertising, financial services, tourism, etc. No actual goods are produced, but high levels of income may be generated.

GLOBALIZATION

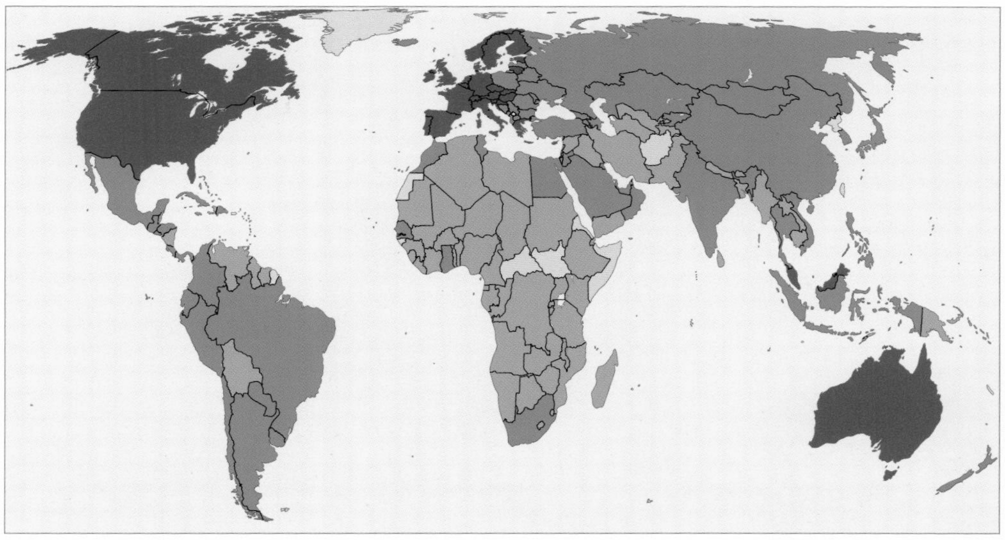

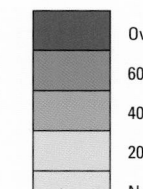

GLOBALIZATION INDEX
2020 KOF Globalization Index
(Rankings for 2018)

- Over 80
- 60 – 80
- 40 – 60
- 20 – 40
- No data available

The KOF index of globalization is named after the Swiss Federal Institute of Technology in Zürich, Switzerland, which devised it. Countries are scored on each of the three criteria below:

- **economic globalization**, characterized as long-distance flows of goods, capital and services, as well as information and perceptions that accompany market exchanges (this accounts for 38% of the globalization index);
- **political globalization**, characterized by a diffusion of government policies (this accounts for 23% of the globalization index);
- **social globalization**, expressed as the spread of ideas, information, images, and people (this accounts for the remaining 39% of the globalization index).

The higher values denote a greater level of globalization.

The concept of globalization developed in the 1960s after the Canadian academic Marshall McLuhan used the term "global village" to describe the breakdown of spatial barriers around the world. He argued that the similarities between places were greater than the differences between them, and that much of the world had been caught up in the same economic and social processes. He suggested that economic activities operated at a global scale and that other scales were becoming less important.

Today, globalization is defined by the International Monetary Fund (IMF) as "the growing interdependence of countries worldwide through the increasing volume and variety of cross-border transactions in goods and services and of international capital flows, and through the more rapid and widespread diffusion of technology." Essentially, it means that all countries, with the possible exception of North Korea, are increasingly bound in a global network of migration, trade, products and services, investment, and the diffusion of ideas and culture.

Globalization has occurred as a result of many factors, such as:

- improvements in transport and ICT, leading to a "shrinking" world;
- the desire to reach new markets;
- the attempt to tap cheap sources of labor;
- the expansion of economic activity to use resources from a wide range of locations;
- the rise of free-market economies and the spread of democratic governments;
- the role of trading blocs, free trade, and the impact of the World Trade Organization;
- the importance of multinational companies.

For more information:
73 Time zones
78 Climate

Tourism and travel is one of the world's largest economic sectors in terms of revenue generated. It has the potential to create prosperity in all parts of the world. Small economies in attractive areas are often completely dominated by tourism: in some Caribbean islands, for example, tourist spending provides over 90% of the total income and is the biggest foreign-exchange earner.

In 2019, the World Trade and Tourism Council reported that this sector, directly and indirectly, provided over 330 million jobs. This equates to 1 in 10 jobs around the world and this is predicted to grow in the coming years. In terms of the economic impact, the industry contributed 10.3% to global GDP in 2019 (US$8.9 trillion).

Increasingly, attention is being paid to the development potential of tourism in less developed countries. The United Nations General Assembly declared 2017 as the International Year of Sustainable Tourism for Development. This had the aim of raising awareness of the potential for economic growth, social inclusion and the preservation of culture and the environment. It is also seen as a contributing factor toward ensuring that tourism is fundamental to the implementation of the 17 UN Sustainable Development Goals (see page 107).

Even with new initiatives, challenges lie ahead. The Covid-19 pandemic of 2020/21 will have significant consequences.

AIR TRAVEL

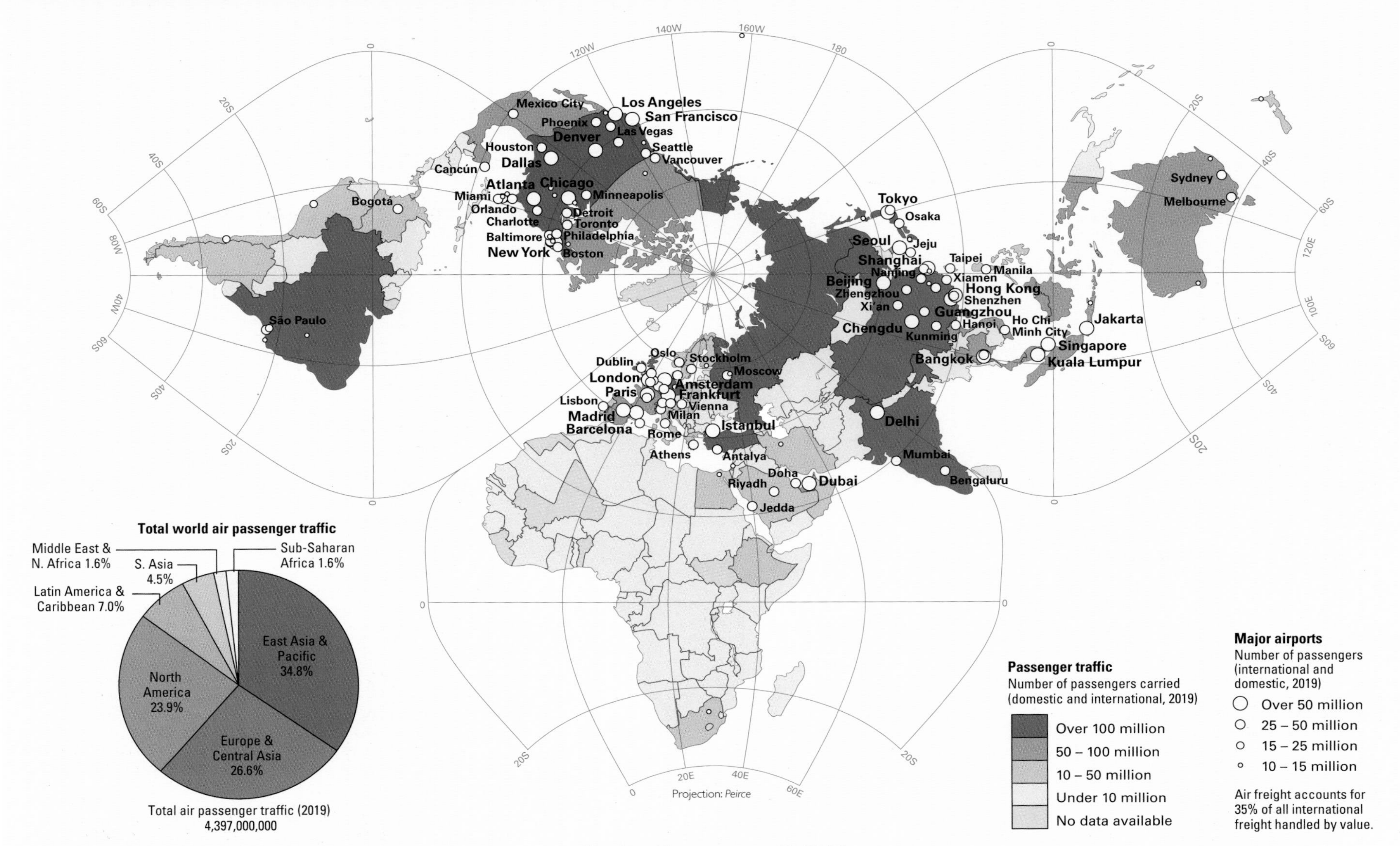

Total world passenger traffic (2019)

MAJOR AIRPORTS

WORLD'S BUSIEST AIRPORTS
Total passengers in millions (2019)

1.	Atlanta Hartsfield Intl. (ATL)	110.5
2.	Beijing Capital Intl. (PEK)	100.0
3.	Los Angeles Intl. (LAX)	88.1
4.	Tokyo Haneda (HND)	87.1
5.	Dubai Intl. (DXB)	86.4
6.	Chicago O'Hare Intl. (ORD)	84.4
7.	London Heathrow (LHR)	80.8
8.	Shanghai Pudong Intl. (PVG)	76.2
9.	Paris Charles de Gaulle (CDG)	76.2
10.	Dallas/Fort Worth (DFW)	75.1
11.	Guangzhou Baiyun (CAN)	73.4
12.	Amsterdam Schiphol (AMS)	71.7
13.	Hong Kong Intl. (HKG)	71.5
14.	Frankfurt (FRA)	70.6
15.	Denver (DEN)	69.9

Dubai International handles the most international passengers (88.9 million in 2018), followed by London's Heathrow (75.3 million).

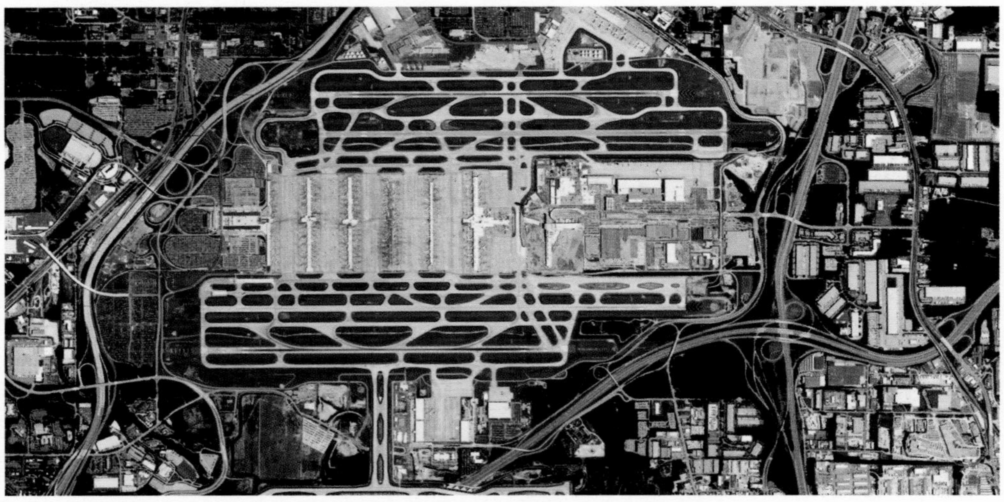

▲ Hartsfield-Jackson Atlanta International Airport, Georgia, USA, is the world's busiest airport.

IMPORTANCE OF TOURISM

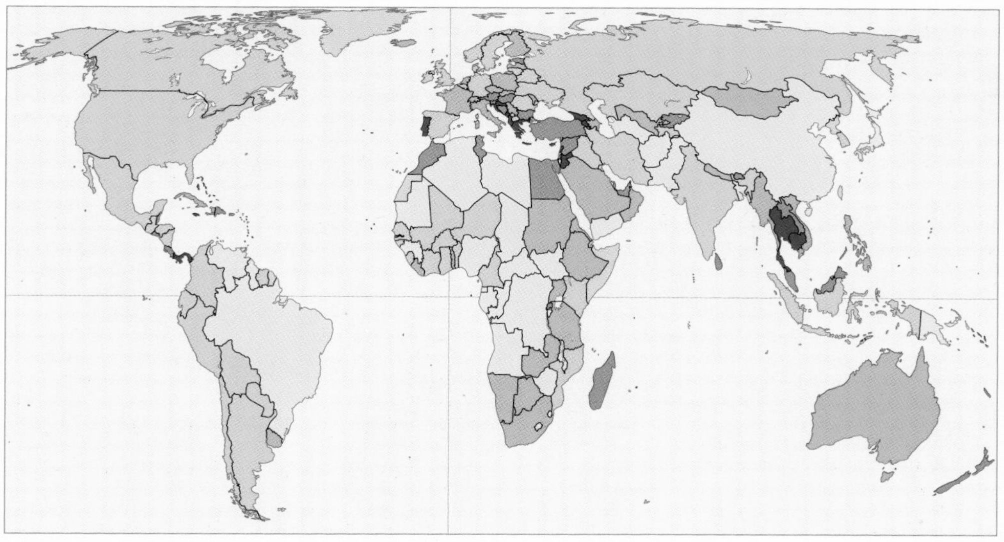

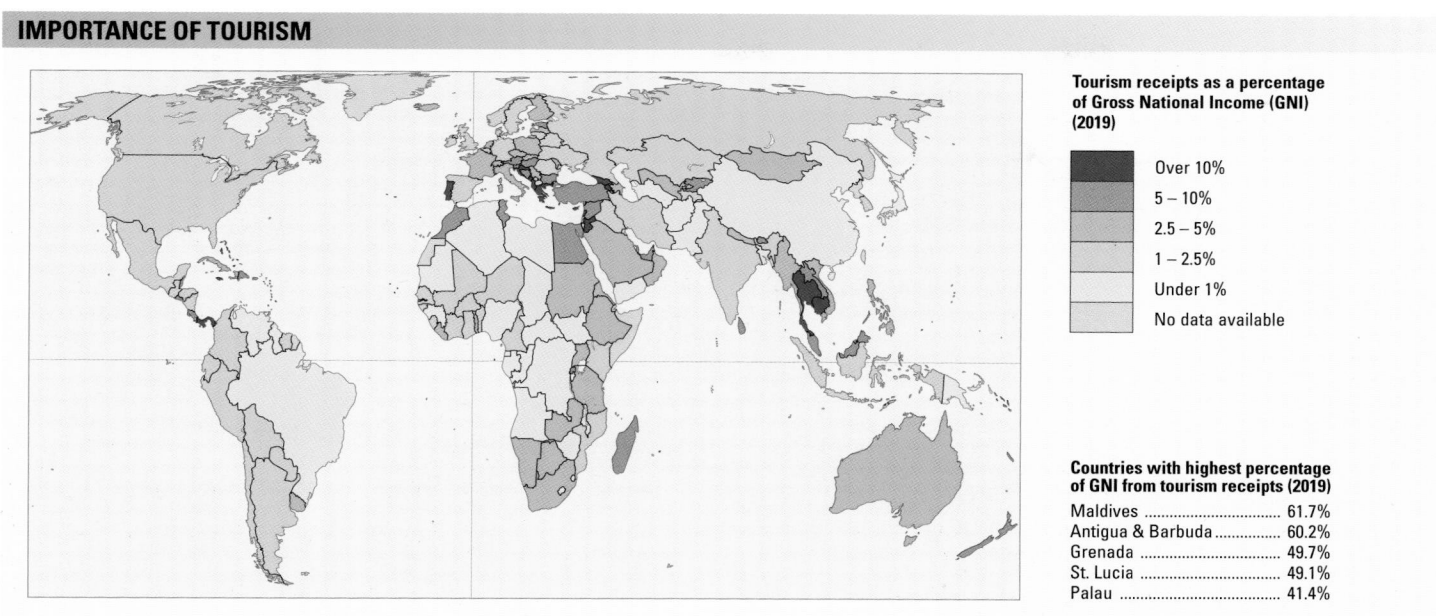

Tourism receipts as a percentage of Gross National Income (GNI) (2019)

- Over 10%
- 5 – 10%
- 2.5 – 5%
- 1 – 2.5%
- Under 1%
- No data available

Countries with highest percentage of GNI from tourism receipts (2019)

Maldives	61.7%
Antigua & Barbuda	60.2%
Grenada	49.7%
St. Lucia	49.1%
Palau	41.4%

TOURIST DESTINATIONS

UNESCO WORLD HERITAGE SITES 2019

Total sites = 1,121 (869 cultural, 213 natural and 39 mixed)

Region	Cultural sites	Natural sites	Mixed sites
Africa	53	38	5
Arab States	78	5	3
Asia & Pacific	189	67	12
Europe & North America	453	65	11
Latin America & Caribbean	96	38	8

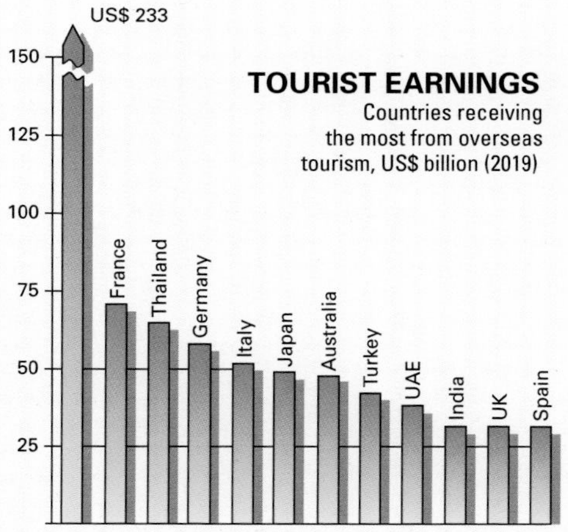

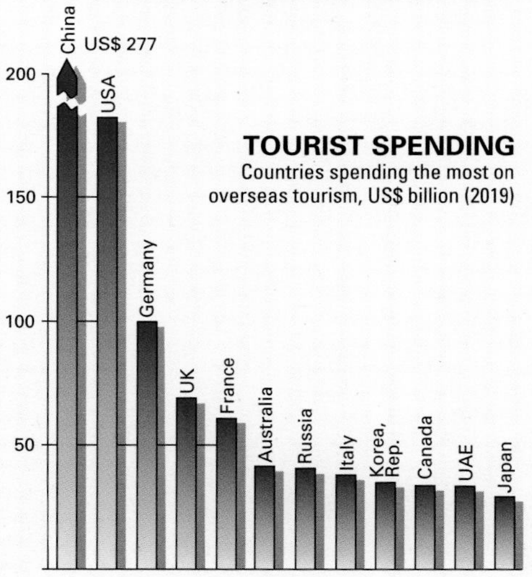

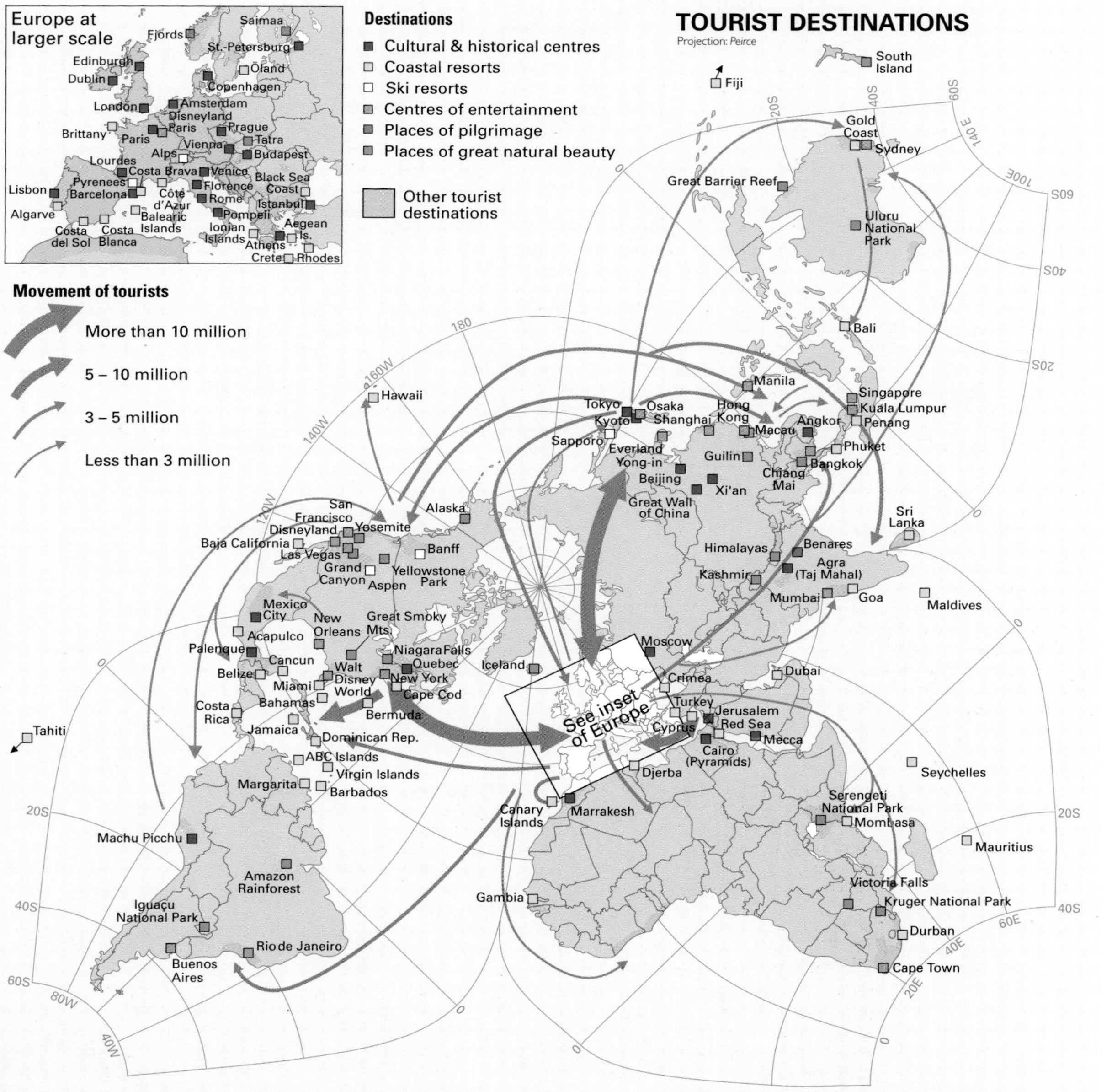

World's top tourism destinations

The UNWTO (United Nations World Tourism Organization) ranks countries by international tourism receipts (see top bar chart above) and international tourist arrivals (see table right). The USA continues to top the international tourism receipts ranking (233,400 million US$ in 2019) with France in second place. France has remained at the top of the list of main destinations for several years, with Spain rising to second place in 2017. In 2018, France recorded 89 million visitors and it is ranked third in terms of tourism earnings.

International tourist arrivals

		millions
1.	France	89.4
2.	Spain	82.8
3.	United States of America	79.6
4.	China	62.9
5.	Italy	62.1
6.	Turkey	45.8
7.	Mexico	41.4
8.	Germany	38.9
9.	Thailand	38.3
10.	United Kingdom	36.3

Visitors to the USA

		thousands
1.	Mexico	19,200
2.	Canada	12,300
3.	United Kingdom	4,900
4.	Japan	3,500
5.	China	3,000
6.	South Korea	2,200
8.	Brazil	2,200
7.	Germany	2,100
9.	France	1,800
10.	Australia	1,400

For more information:

82 Water distribution
93 Slum cities
Urban advantages
109 Distribution of spending

Until the late 1990s, when the full extent of the AIDS crisis emerged, average life expectancies at birth were rising almost everywhere. By 2011, they ranged from 81 years in high-income economies to 56 in sub-Saharan Africa. These figures represented an enormous advance on the situation in 1880, when citizens of Berlin had an estimated life expectancy of 30 years.

The ravages of AIDS have been greatest in southern Africa. One of the worst affected countries is Eswatini, where over 25% of the adult population were thought to be infected in 2009. Life expectancy fell from 61 years in 2000, to 32 years in 2009, but recovered to 59 years in 2021. In much of the world, average life expectancies are still increasing. The rises are attributed to improvements in agriculture and, hence, nutrition, as well as health education, improved sanitation and the quality of drinking water, together with advances in medicine.

Besides AIDS, the people of the developing world are subject to another affliction – malnutrition. The map below shows that in most of Africa, Asia, and Latin America, the average daily calorie supply per person is so low as to cause malnutrition. Malnutrition is a serious condition – among pregnant women it causes high rates of child mortality.

Deficiency diseases occur when people do not have a balanced diet. Protein deficiency causes stunting and kwashiorkor, which can be fatal, especially among young children, while vitamin deficiencies cause such illnesses as beri beri, pellagra, scurvy, and rickets. Iron deficiency causes anemia, while a lack of iodine causes mental retardation.

Infectious diseases, in association with deficient diets, continue to affect people in developing countries. Around the turn of the century, a WHO report stated that infectious diseases cause over 16 million deaths a year. Most of the victims are young and otherwise fit people in developing countries. The major killers are AIDS, cholera, dysentery, malaria, measles, pneumonia, respiratory infections, tuberculosis, and typhoid.

Infectious diseases are much less important as causes of death in developed countries, where cancer and circulatory diseases, such as atherosclerosis and hypertension, which cause strokes and heart attacks, are the most common causes of fatality. Because these diseases tend to kill older people, they are relatively less important in the developing countries where people have shorter lifespans.

Coronavirus disease 2019 (COVID-19) is a contagious disease which can lead to severe respiratory distress. First identified in China in 2019, it has spread worldwide. The maps on page 105 show a snapshot of the situation in early-2021.

▲ Almost 10% of the world's population does not have access to safe drinking water or adequate sanitation. This places a huge strain on the millions of mainly women and children who have to walk, collect, and carry drinkable water in order to survive. UNICEF is dedicated to help improve this situation and to react swiftly in the case of emergencies such as civil war, as with the case of this man in Liberia.

MALNUTRITION

Prevalence of undernourishment as a percentage of the population (2018)

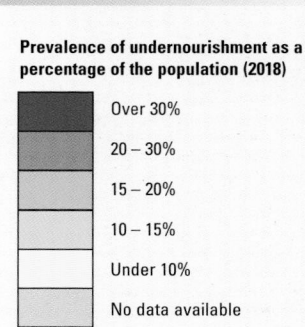

- Over 30%
- 20 – 30%
- 15 – 20%
- 10 – 15%
- Under 10%
- No data available

This map highlights the countries where, for a large part of the population, the food intake is insufficient to meet dietary energy requirements.

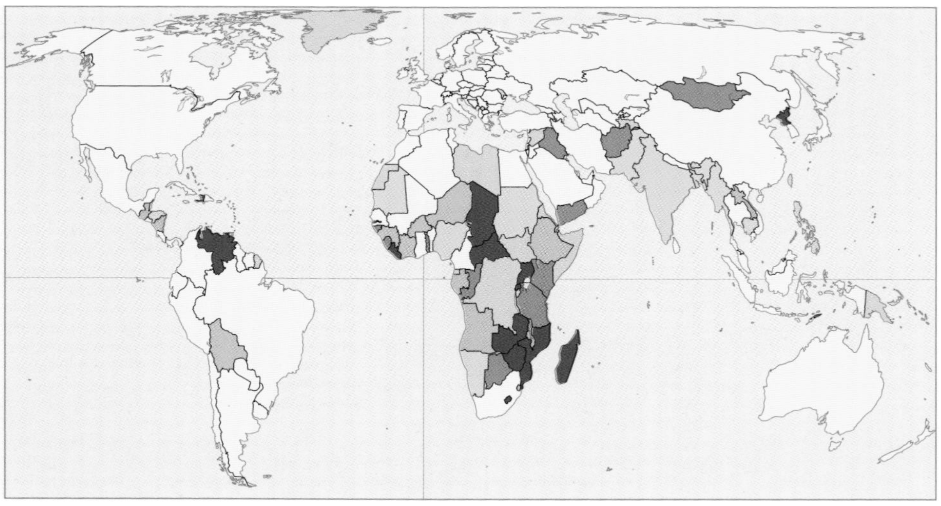

MATERNAL MORTALITY RATE

The number of mothers who died during pregnancy or childbirth per 100,000 live births

Countries with highest maternal mortality rate

South Sudan	1,150
Chad	1,140
Sierra Leone	1,120
Nigeria	917
Central African Republic	829
Somalia	829
Mauritania	766
Guinea-Bissau	667
Guyana	667
Liberia	661

The maternal mortality rate is the annual number of female deaths per 100,000 live births from any cause related to or aggravated by pregnancy or its management (excluding accidental or incidental causes).

INFANT MORTALITY

Number of babies who died under the age of one, per 1,000 live births (2021)

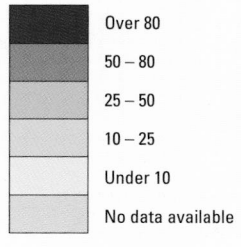

- Over 80
- 50 – 80
- 25 – 50
- 10 – 25
- Under 10
- No data available

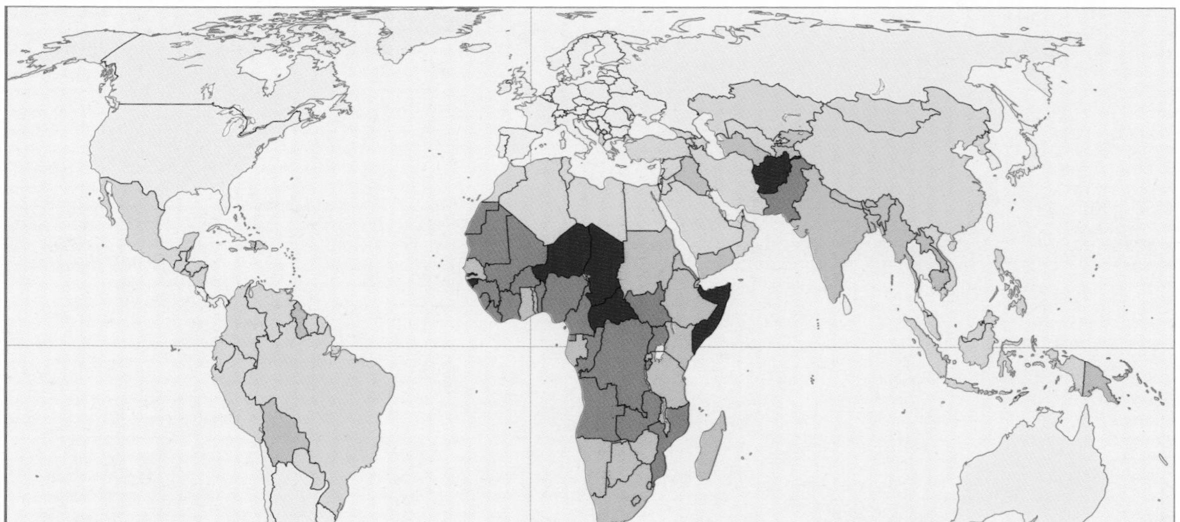

Highest infant mortality (deaths)

Afghanistan	110.6
Somalia	94.8
Central African Republic	86.3

Lowest infant mortality (deaths)

Monaco	1.8
Japan	2.0
Norway	2.1

EXPENDITURE ON HEALTH

Government health expenditure as a percentage of general government expenditure (2017)

- Over 20%
- 15 – 20%
- 10 – 15%
- 5 – 10%
- Under 5%
- No data available

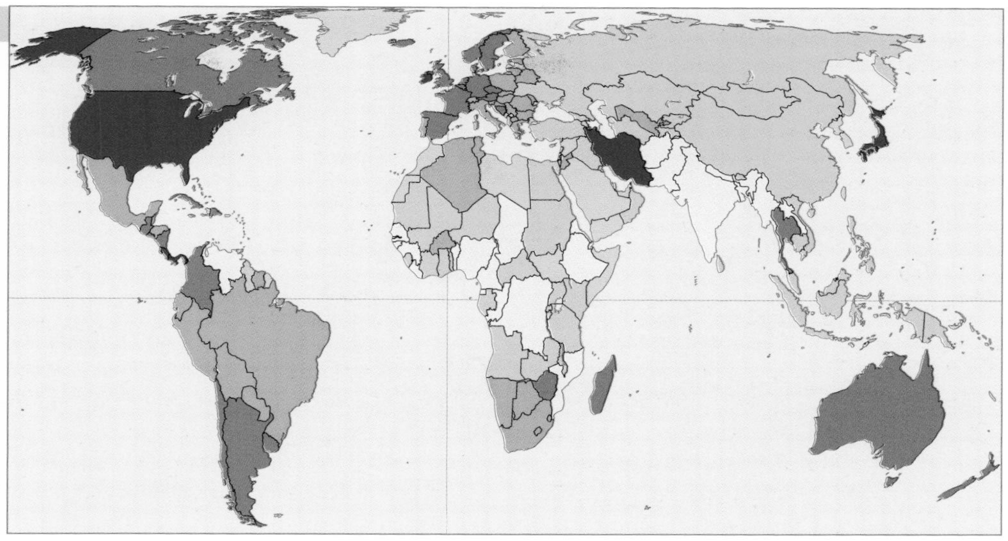

Countries with highest expenditure rate

Costa Rica	26.9%
Japan	23.6%
Iran	22.9%
USA	22.5%
Maldives	21.8%

CORONAVIRUS (COVID-19)

As of May 2021, the United Nations World Health Organization (WHO) estimated that there had been a cumulative total of over 154 million cases of Coronavirus (COVID-19) worldwide. This resulted in reports of over 3 million deaths. By this date it was estimated that more than 1,180 million doses of vaccine had been administered.

Confirmed cases by WHO region (May 2021)

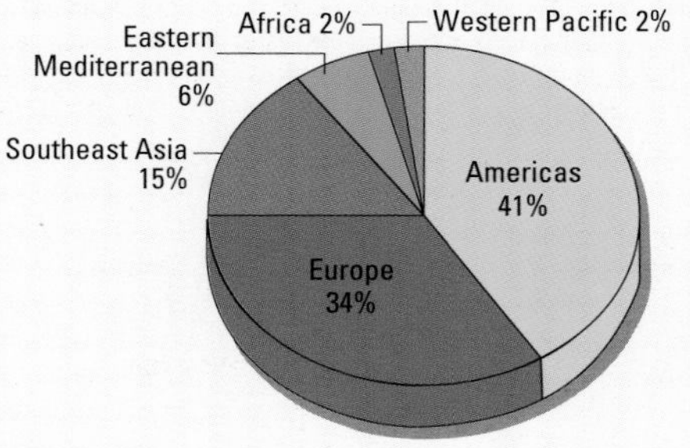

Confirmed deaths by WHO region (May 2021)

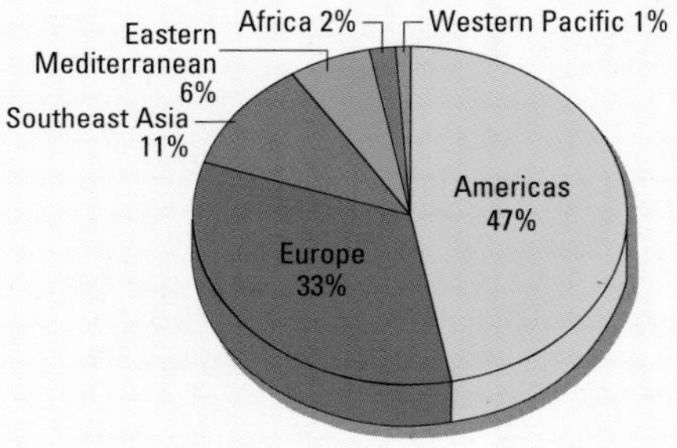

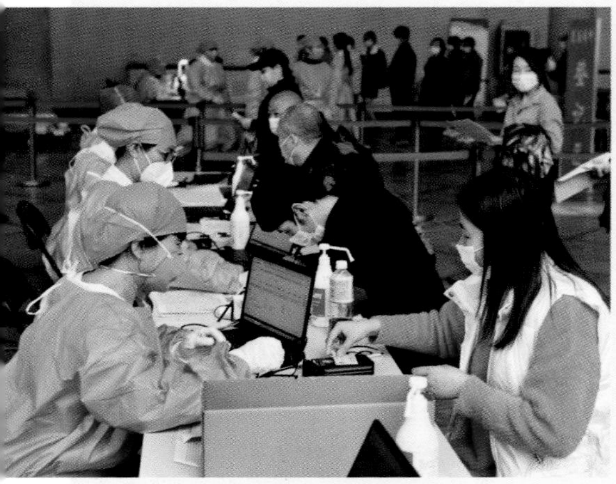

▲ An unprecedented vaccination programme is being implemented worldwide. Fair and equitable access to vaccines is critical to controlling the COVID-19 pandemic.

COVID-19 cases

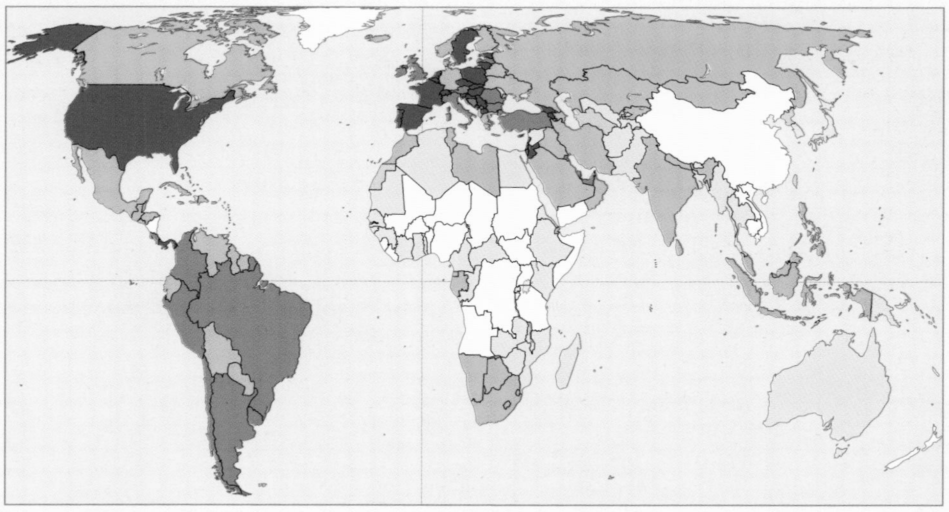

Cumulative total number of cases per 100,000 people (May 2021)

- Over 7,000
- 5,000 – 7,000
- 500 – 5,000
- 100 – 500
- Under 100
- No data available

Countries with highest number of cases per 100,000 people

Andorra	17,200
Montenegro	15,600
Czechia	15,300
Slovenia	11,600
Luxembourg	10,800

COVID-19 deaths

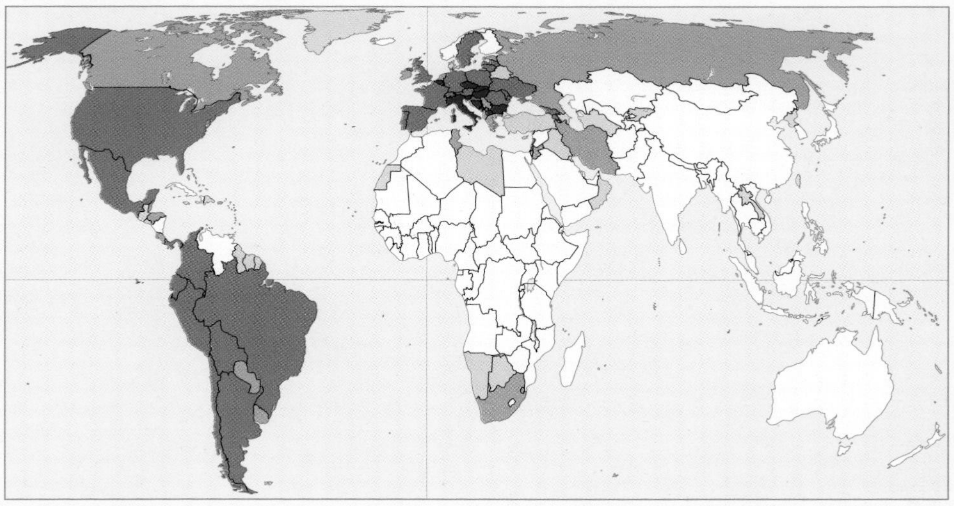

Cumulative total number of deaths per 100,000 people (May 2021)

- Over 200
- 100 – 200
- 50 – 100
- 25 – 50
- Under 25
- No data available

Countries with highest number of deaths per 100,000 people

Hungary	290
Czechia	280
Bosnia-Herzegovina	270
Montenegro	240
North Macedonia	240

COVID-19 vaccinations

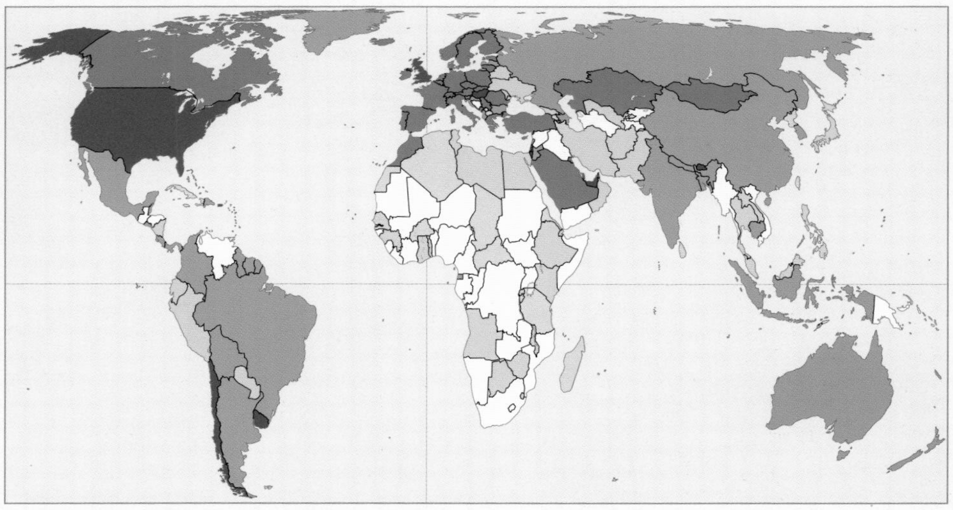

Cumulative total number of vaccinations per 100 people (May 2021)

- Over 50
- 25 – 50
- 5 – 25
- 1 – 5
- Under 1
- No data available

Countries with highest number of vaccinations per 100 people

Israel	99
Seychelles	99
United Arab Emirates	99
Chile	76
Maldives	76

Source: World Health Organization (www.covid19.who.int)

For more information:

101 Industrial output
100 World trade
109 Distribution of spending

Perhaps the most glaring differences in the world today are those between the rich and the poor. The World Bank divides countries into three main groups based on average economic production expressed in terms of per capita GNI (Gross National Income). They are the low-income economies (most African countries and much of Asia), the middle-income economies (most of Latin America and most of the former USSR), and the high-income economies of Canada, the United States, Western Europe, Japan, and Australia.

Per capita GNIs are a measure of the total goods and services produced by a country divided by the population, and then converted into US dollars at official exchange rates. They are useful indicators of a country's prosperity, though, like all statistics, they must be treated with care. For example, the prices for goods and services in China are far cheaper than they are in the United States. China's per capita GNI in 2019 was $10,390 (as compared with $65,850 in the USA), but the PPP (Purchasing Power Parity, which adjusts the figure for cost-of-living differences) estimate of China's per capita GNI was considerably higher at $16,760. Another problem with per capita GNIs is that they are averages, which often conceal wide internal variations.

The pattern of poverty varies from region to region. In Latin America, much progress has been made through industrialization, though startling inequalities still exist between rich and poor. China and other countries in eastern Asia, including South Korea and Taiwan, have followed Japan's example in pursuing export-led industrial policies. The success of China's Special Economic Zones, where foreign investment is encouraged, has led to a huge rise in China's per capita GNI.

In contrast to the dynamism of Asia, Africa lags behind as an impoverished continent. Corrupt governments, wasteful expenditures, civil wars, natural disasters, faulty national and international policy environments, high population growth, and the failure to break away from the neo-colonial trading patterns – all these contribute to keeping the majority of Africans impoverished. An initiative in some African countries has been to improve the infrastructure and develop tourism, creating employment and providing much-needed foreign currency. But the social and environmental cost of mass tourism needs to be taken seriously too.

The International Monetary Fund and the World Bank argue that real economic progress in Africa will be achieved only when African countries create market-friendly economies that encourage trade through export-led manufacturing, while at the same time strictly controlling public spending.

CONTINENTAL SHARES

Shares of population and of wealth (GNI) by continent

These generalized continental figures show the startling difference between rich and poor, but mask the successes or failures of individual countries. Japan, for example, with just over 3% of Asia's population, produces almost 19% of the continent's output. Within countries, the difference between rich and poor can also be startling. In Brazil, for example, the richest 20% of the population own 60% of the wealth.

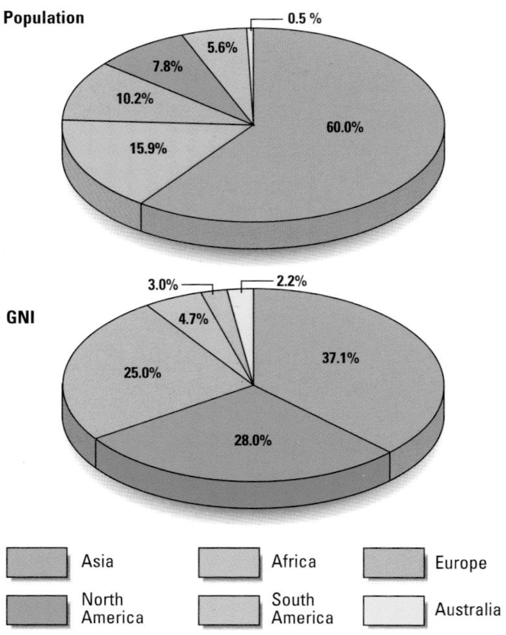

LEVELS OF INCOME

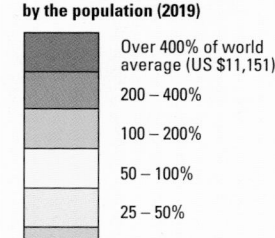

Gross National Income per capita: the value of total production divided by the population (2019)

Over 400% of world average (US $11,151)
200 – 400%
100 – 200%
50 – 100%
25 – 50%
10 – 25%
Under 10%
No data available

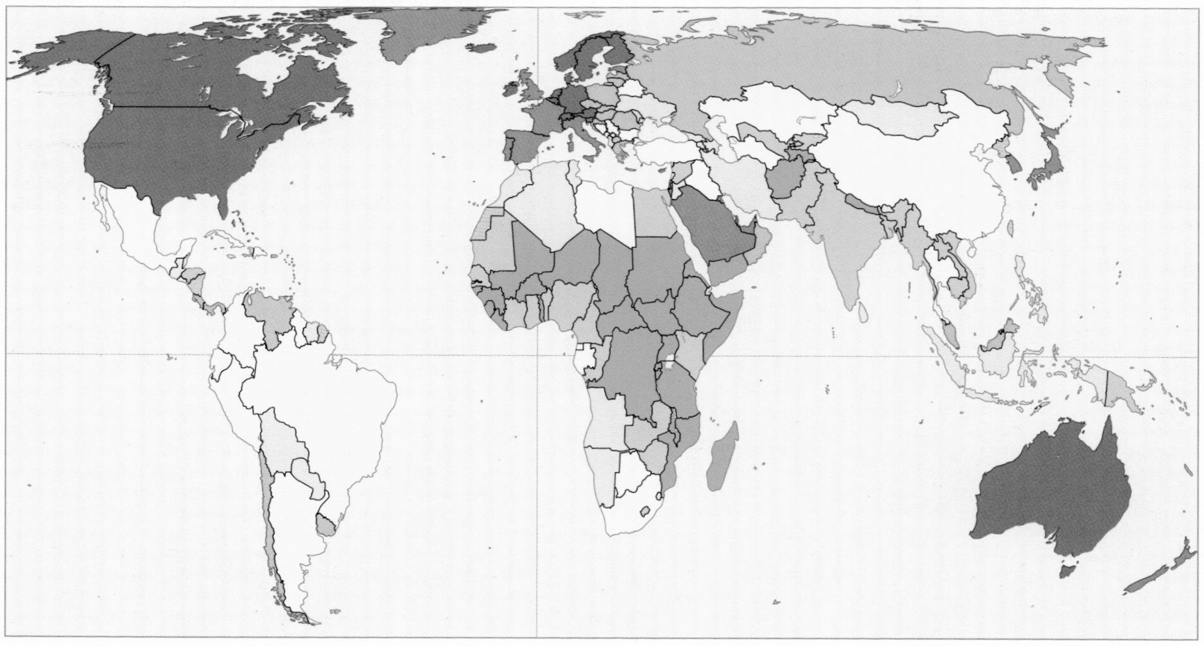

Richest countries (GNI per capita)

Switzerland	US $85,500
Norway	US $82,500
Luxembourg	US $73,910
Iceland	US $72,850
USA	US $65,850

Poorest countries (GNI per capita)

Somalia	US $130
Burundi	US $280
Malawi	US $380
Mozambique	US $490
Central African Rep.	US $520

INDICATORS

The gap between the world's rich and poor is now so great that it is difficult to illustrate on a single graph. Within each income group (as defined by the World Bank), however, comparisons have some meaning. The wealth gap in many developing countries, though, is wide, with a small, rich class and a large, impoverished majority, while many high-income countries contain an underclass of unemployed and homeless people.

HIGH INCOME

Number of motor vehicles, Internet users, and mobile phones for each 1,000 people, selected high-income countries

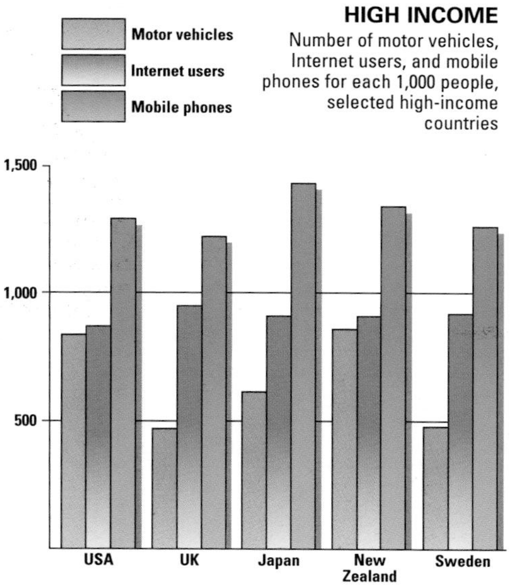

MIDDLE INCOME

Number of motor vehicles, Internet users, and mobile phones for each 1,000 people, selected middle-income countries

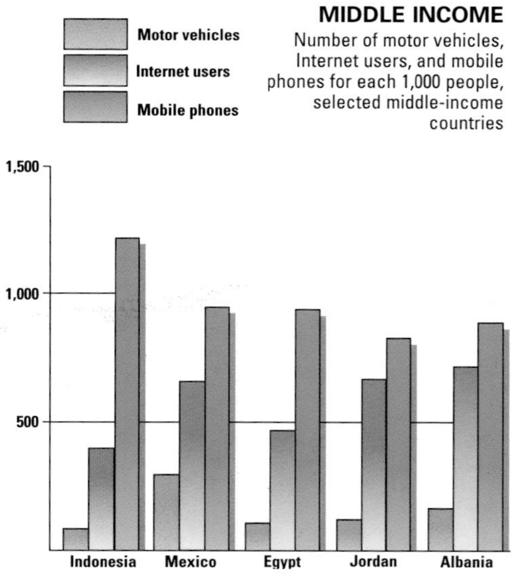

LOW INCOME

Number of motor vehicles, Internet users, and mobile phones for each 1,000 people, selected low-income countries

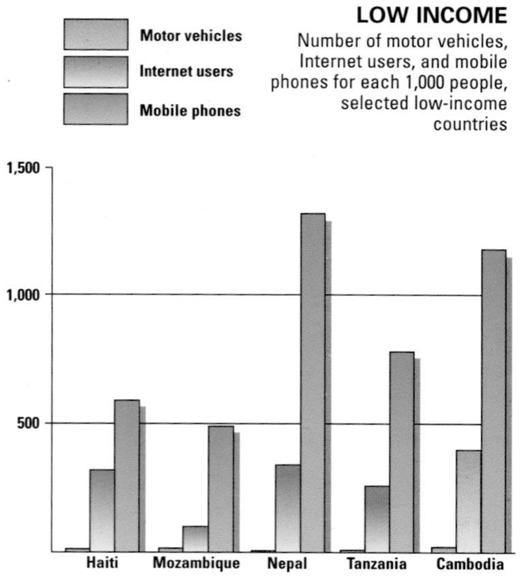

STATE FINANCE

Inflation rates (*shown on the map, right*) are an indication of a country's financial stability and, usually, of its prosperity. Annual inflation rates above 20% are usually marked by slow or even negative growth of the GNI. Above 50%, it becomes hyperinflation and an economy is left reeling.

In the late 1980s and early 1990s, many high-income countries had to contend with annual inflation rates of 10% or more, while Japan, the growth leader, had an average inflation rate of just 1.3% between 1985 and 1994.

Market-friendly policies, including low taxes and state spending, liberal trade policies, and a warm welcome for foreign investors, are major factors in countries that have enjoyed rapid economic growth in the decades since 1980. For example, the setting-up of Special Economic Zones in eastern China has led to a spectacular rise in that country's per capita GNI. However, an effective government remains a crucial factor in economic growth in most countries.

Other successful countries include South Korea and Singapore, although an Asian market crash in 1997 temporarily halted the dramatic economic expansion of these countries.

INFLATION

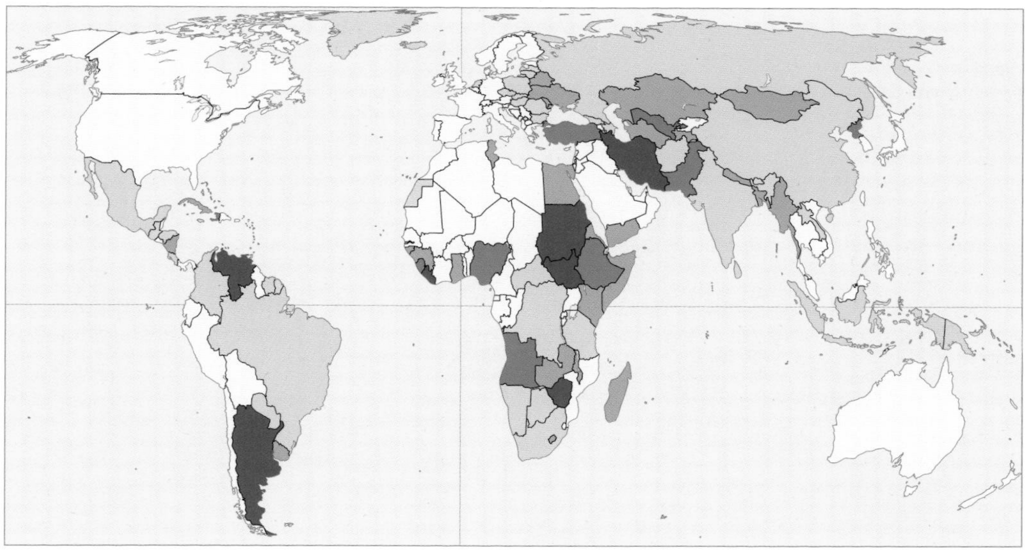

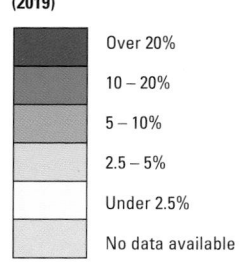

Average annual rate of inflation (2019)

- Over 20%
- 10 – 20%
- 5 – 10%
- 2.5 – 5%
- Under 2.5%
- No data available

Highest average inflation*

Zimbabwe	176%
South Sudan	56%
Argentina	54%

* Venezuela experienced hyperinflation in 2019

Lowest average inflation

Libya	-7.1%
Burundi	-4.0%
Burkina Faso	-3.9%

UNITED NATIONS SUSTAINABLE DEVELOPMENT GOALS

In 2000, the United Nations set out eight Millennium Development Goals (MDGs) that were to be achieved by 2015. The goals were:

1. To eradicate extreme poverty and hunger.
2. To achieve universal primary education.
3. To promote gender equality and empower women.
4. To reduce child mortality.
5. To improve maternal health.
6. To combat HIV/AIDS, malaria, and other diseases.
7. To ensure environmental sustainability.
8. To develop a global partnership for development.

Progress toward achieving these goals has been uneven: some countries achieved many of the goals, whereas others achieved few, if any. However, some targets have been met such as the MDG for poverty reduction. According to the 2015 MDG Report, the poverty rates and the number of people living in extreme poverty fell in every developing region – including sub-Saharan Africa, where rates were highest. In the developing regions, the proportion of people living on less than $1.25 a day fell from 47% in 1990 to 14% in 2015. In 2015, about 900 million fewer people than in 1990 lived in conditions of extreme poverty.

To follow on from the MDG, the Sustainable Development Goals (SDGs) were adopted by all the world's governments at the United Nations in September 2015. The aim is that they will guide global development for the 15 years until 2030. There are 17 goals – as illustrated by the official United Nations icons below. Although the SDGs are not legally binding, governments are expected to establish national frameworks in order to achieve them.

The ultimate aim is to go further than the MDGs and end all forms of poverty. It has been recognized that defeating poverty has to be coupled with strategies to encourage economic growth, and to address a range of social needs including education, health, social protection, and job opportunites, while tackling climate change and protecting the environment.

Progress will be monitored by using a set of global indicators, and annual reports will be published. There is, of course, a cost to achieving these goals. The more developed countries will have to provide development assistance to help the countries most in need.

It is acknowledged that climate change has affected public health, food and water security, migration, peace, and security. Collective action will have to be taken to mitigate the worst effects of climate change. Goal 13 (Climate Action) reflects the importance of this issue, and the hope is that it will be possible to limit the increases in global mean temperature to no more than 3.6°F [2.0°C] above pre-industrial levels.

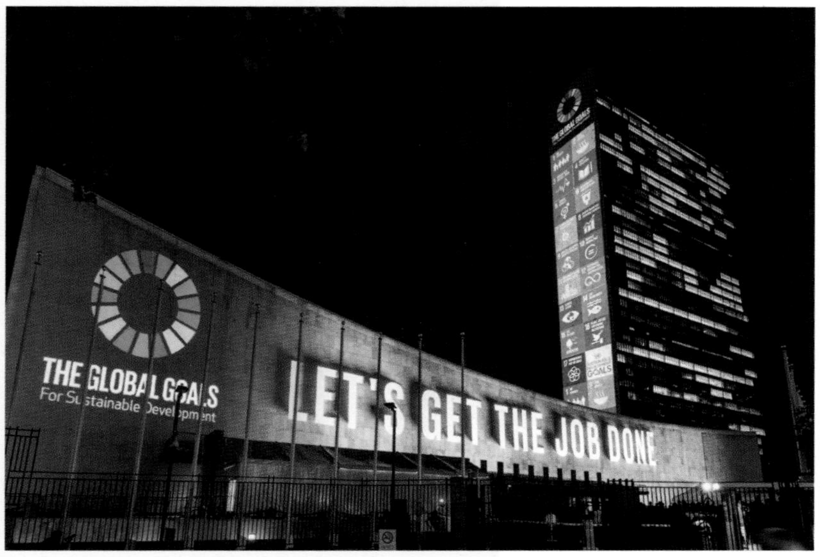

▲ To mark the 70th anniversary of the United Nations, and ahead of the United Nations Sustainable Development Summit in September 2015, massive projections of the icons for the 17 goals are seen on the façade of the General Assembly building in New York, United States. The aim was to raise awareness of the 2030 Agenda for Sustainable Development.

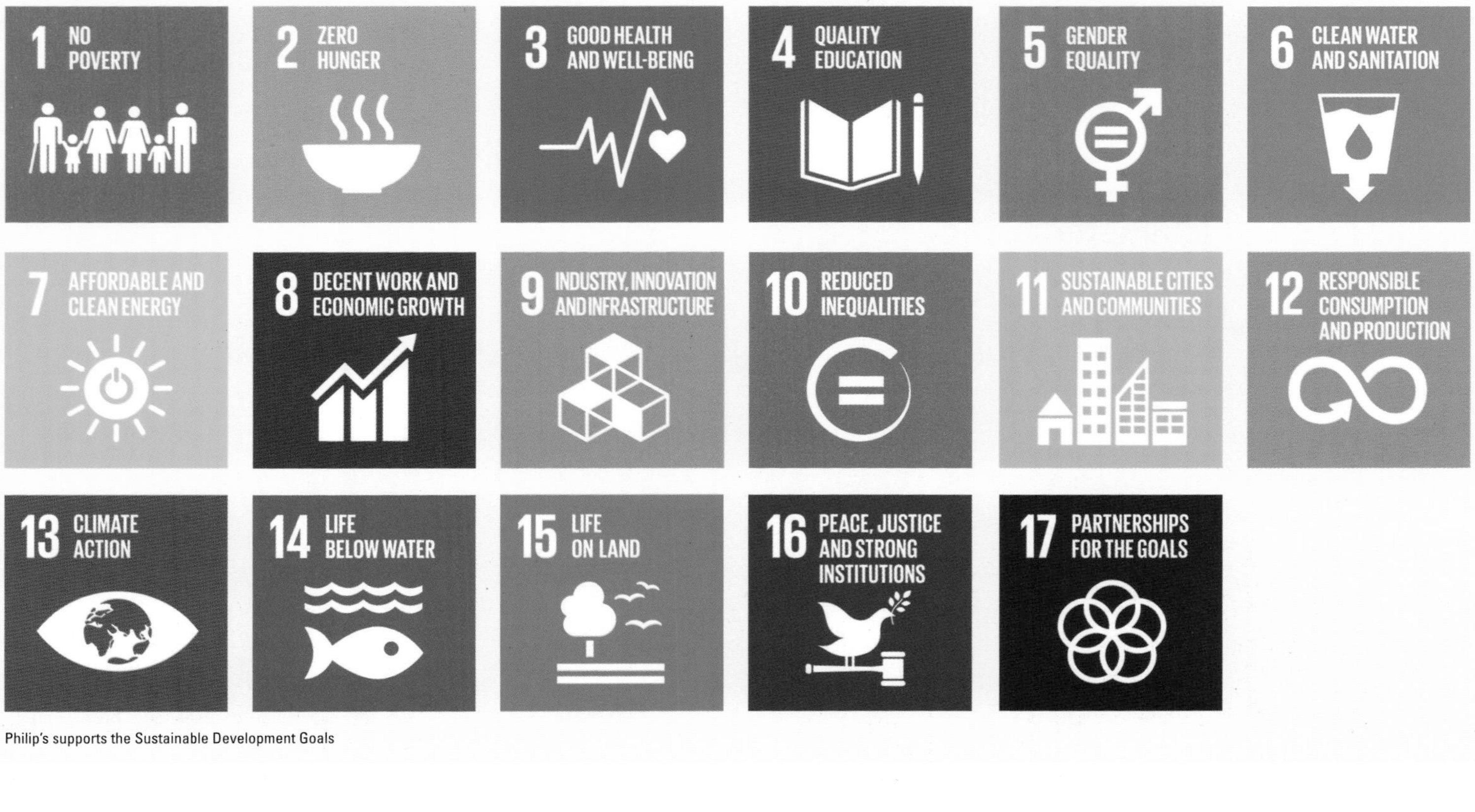

Philip's supports the Sustainable Development Goals

For more information:
82 Water supply
90 Population density
92 Urban population
93 Urban advantages
100 Employment
104 Infant mortality
106 Wealth

Wealth is a basic factor in determining standards of living. Everywhere, the rich have more of everything, including higher average life expectancies, while the poor have to spend most of their income on basic human needs, such as food and clothing. Yet poverty and wealth are relative terms: slum dwellers living on social security in an industrial society feel their poverty acutely, but have far more resources than an average African living in a rural area.

In 1990 the United Nations Development Programme published its first Human Development Index (HDI), an attempt to construct a comparative scale by which a simplified form of well-being might be measured. The HDI, expressed as a value between 0 and 0.999, combines figures for life expectancy and literacy with a wealth scale, based on Purchasing Power Parity.

The world's countries are divided into three groups: those with a high HDI (0.8 and above); those with a medium HDI (0.5 to 0.799); and those with a low HDI (below 0.5). In 2020, Norway and Switzerland were top in the world rankings and Niger was bottom. In fact, 34 of the 41 countries with a low HDI were from Africa. Besides having low per capita GNIs, the average life expectancy in these countries was 59 years, while the adult literacy rate was 36%. By comparison, the average life expectancy at birth in countries in the high HDI group was 79 years, while the literacy rate was 94%.

Comparisons between countries with similar per capita GNIs reveal the effects of government actions. For example, the World Bank classifies both India and China as low-income economies, but India's HDI at 0.647 is much lower than that of China, at 0.758. This reflects not only China's economic progress in the 1980s and 1990s, but also differences in average life expectancies (70 years in India and 76 years in China), and adult literacy rates (74% in India and 96% in China).

Disparities in standards of living exist not only between countries but also between individuals, groups, and regions within countries. For example, income distribution figures show that, in the United States, the poorest 10% of households receive less than 2% of the income.

Other contrasts exist in developing countries between rural communities, where incomes are low and basic services are often in short supply, and urban areas, where even those living in slums are generally better off than their rural neighbors. Other striking differences exist between men and women. For example, while adult literacy rates for men and women living in developed countries are more or less the same, large differences exist in many developing countries. In countries in the lowest HDI category, only 36% of women were literate, as compared with 58% of men.

Female education is a factor in population control, especially as women's fertility rates appear to fall in direct proportion to the amount of secondary education they receive. This point was acknowledged in 2004 by the UN Population Fund, which defined four main objectives relating to women and population control: the reduction of maternal, infant, and child mortality; better education, especially for girls; universal access to reproductive health services; and gender equality.

Statistical analysis presents many problems of interpretation, especially when trying to define such intangible factors as a sense of well-being. For example, education helps create wealth; but are rich countries wealthy because their people are well educated, or are they well educated because they are rich?

HUMAN DEVELOPMENT INDEX

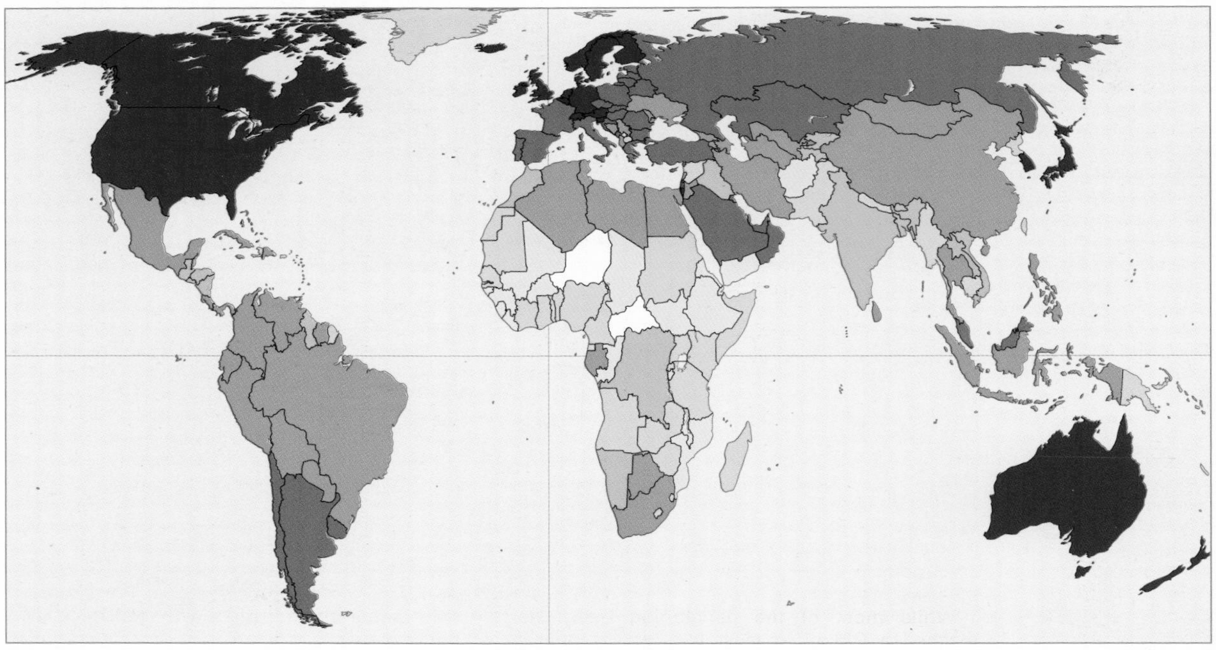

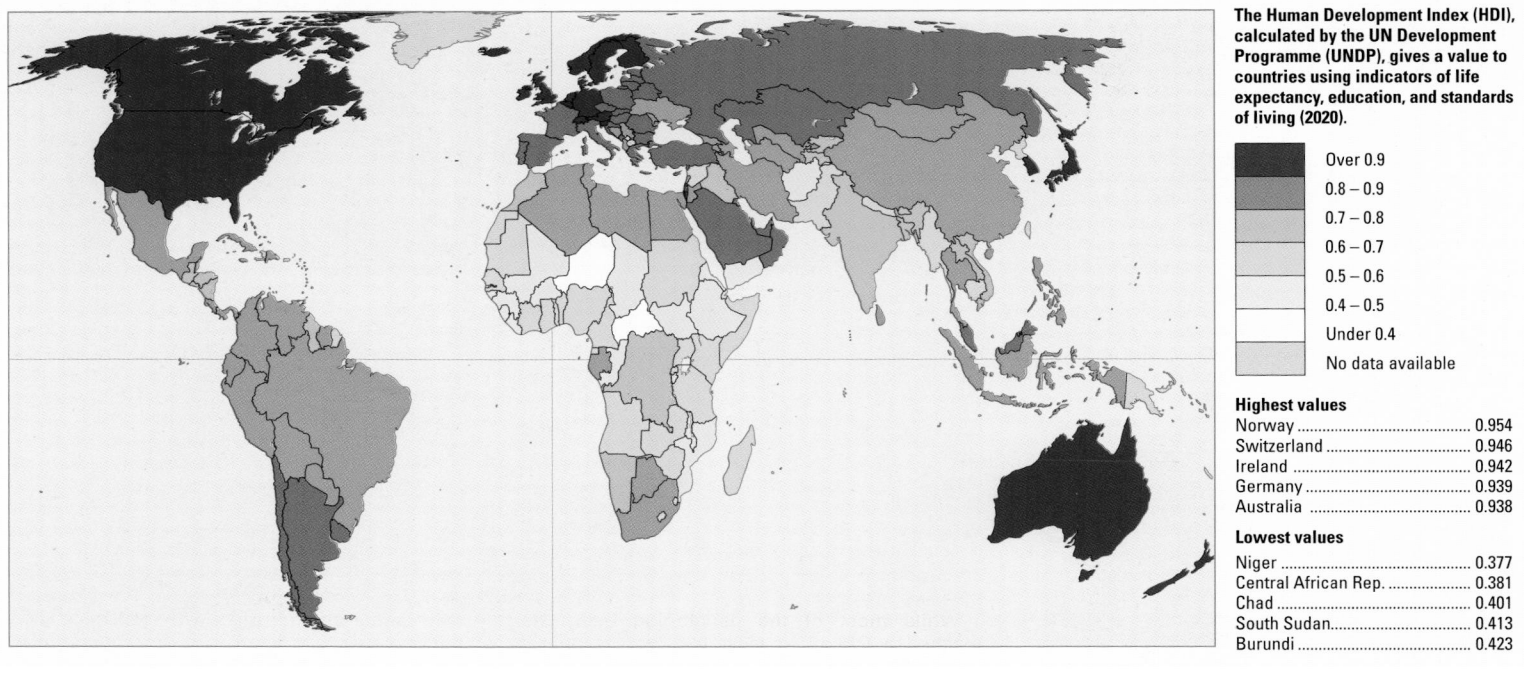

The Human Development Index (HDI), calculated by the UN Development Programme (UNDP), gives a value to countries using indicators of life expectancy, education, and standards of living (2020).

Highest values

Norway	0.954
Switzerland	0.946
Ireland	0.942
Germany	0.939
Australia	0.938

Lowest values

Niger	0.377
Central African Rep.	0.381
Chad	0.401
South Sudan	0.413
Burundi	0.423

EDUCATION

The developing countries made great efforts in the 1970s and 1980s to bring at least a basic education to their people. In all but the poorest nations, primary school enrolments rose above 60%. However, figures often include teenagers or young adults, and there are still 300 million children worldwide who receive no schooling at all. A lack of resources has restricted the development of secondary and higher education. Most primary school education is free in the poorer countries, but fees are often paid for secondary and higher education, thus heightening the differences between rich and poor.

PRIMARY
Percentage of age group in primary school, selected countries

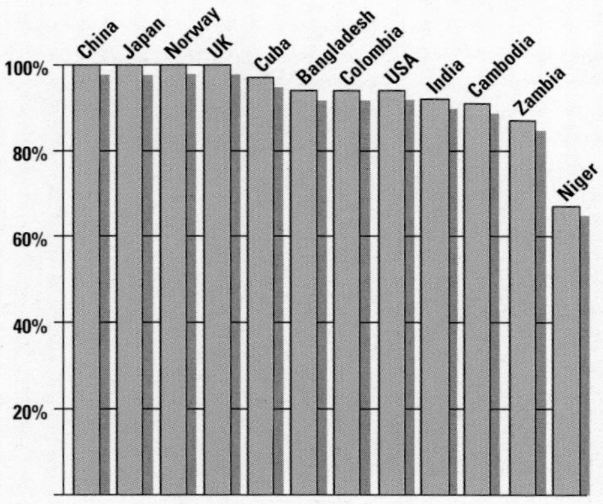

SECONDARY
Percentage of age group in secondary school, selected countries

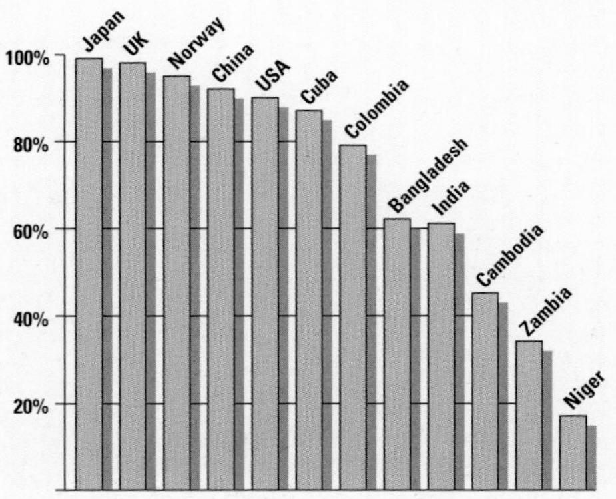

HIGHER
Percentage of age group in higher education, selected countries

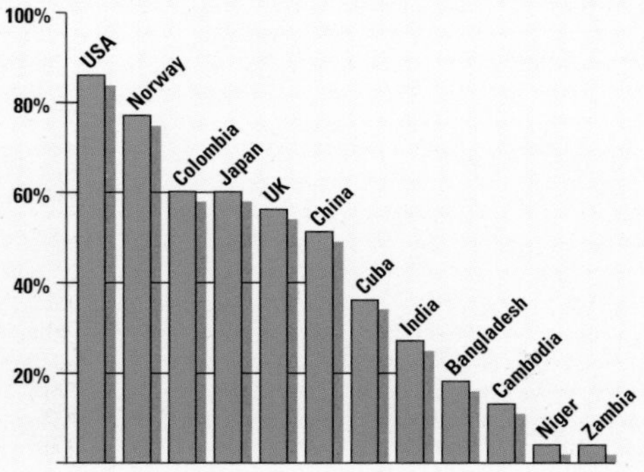

DISTRIBUTION OF SPENDING

Percentage share of household spending

A high proportion of the average income of households in developing nations is spent on basic needs such as food and clothing. In most Western countries food and clothing account for less than 25% of expenditure.

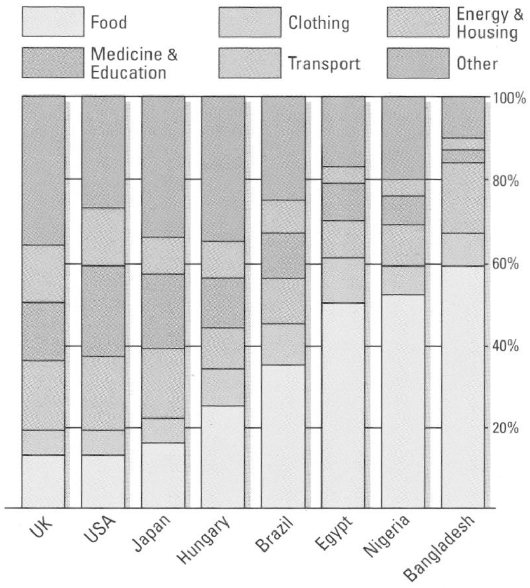

▲ These two images illustrate the reality of suburban life for people at either end of the economic scale. At the top is part of a huge area of "tract housing" in California, where large houses of a similar design are laid out by a developer, complete with gardens, drives, and swimming pools. Below, is a much more haphazard arrangement of home-built, rudimentary shelters, many without sanitation and most with no electricity, in Crossroads Township, outside Cape Town in South Africa.

FERTILITY AND EDUCATION

Fertility rates compared with female education, selected countries

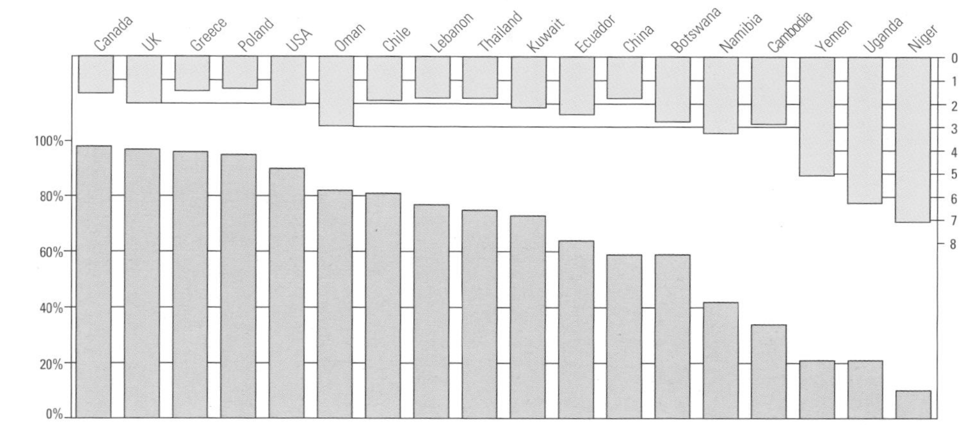

There seems to be a strong link between access to secondary education and the fertility rate. In developed countries, young girls have a high access to education and a low fertility rate. In contrast, in many developing countries women have a high fertility rate but lack access to education. This can be for a complex mix of social, economic, and cultural reasons. Despite a few high-profile examples of female politicians in different parts of the world, all evidence points to the continuing marginalization of women from the political and economic processes of decision-making. Female wages are, on average, only two-thirds of those of men.

GENDER INEQUALITY INDEX

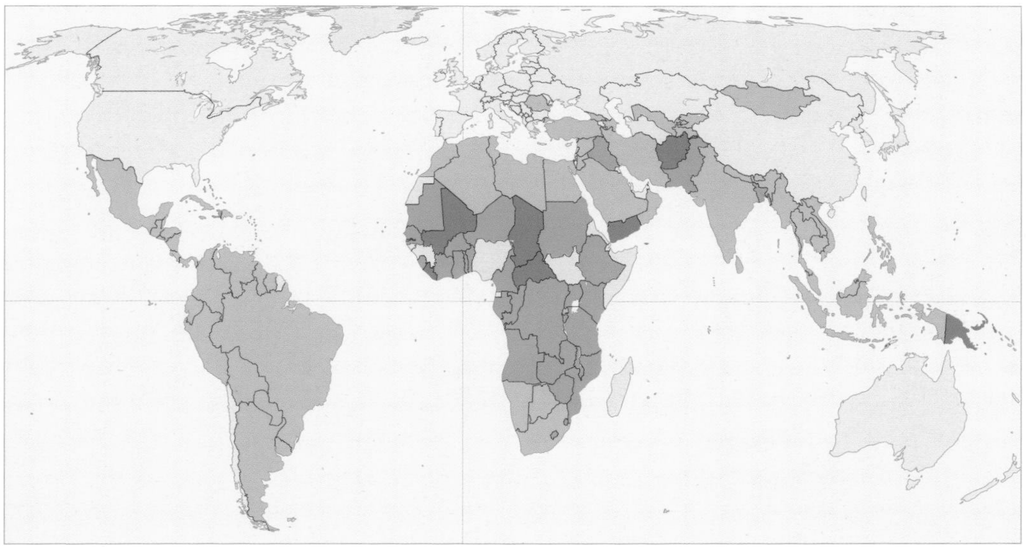

The Gender Inequality Index is a composite measure reflecting inequality in achievements between women and men in three categories: reproductive health, empowerment, and the labor market. It varies between 0, when women and men fare equally, and 1, when women or men fare poorly compared to the other in all categories (2019).

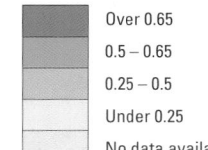

Most equal

Switzerland	0.025
Denmark	0.038
Sweden	0.039

Least equal

Yemen	0.795
Papua New Guinea	0.725
Chad	0.710

GENDER EQUALITY

The UN's Millennium Development Goal 3 was to "*Eliminate gender disparity in primary and secondary education*" in all levels of education no later than 2015. According to the 2015 Millennium Development Goal Report, achieving parity in education is an important step toward equal opportunity for men and women in the social, political, and economic domains. The Gender Parity Index (GPI) shows the ratio between the enrolment rate of girls and that of boys. The GPI grew from 91% in 1999 to 98% in 2015 for the developing regions as a whole – falling within the +/– 3-point margin of 100% that is the accepted measure for parity.

While most of the developing world had reached a GPI of at least 99% at the primary level by 2015, the Index was still lagging behind in Western Asia and sub-Saharan Africa. These two regions, however, have recorded the greatest progress. Between 1999 and 2015, girls' participation in primary education increased from 72% to 96% in sub-Saharan Africa, and from 87% to 97% in Western Asia.

Girls have shown the greatest progress at the secondary level of education. The GPI for secondary education in the developing world as a whole has risen from 78% in 1990 to 98% in 2015.

It is in tertiary education where the greatest disparities are to be found. Only one developing region, Western Asia, has achieved the target. The most extreme disparities at the expense of women are in sub-Saharan Africa and Southern Asia.

In general, countries with lower levels of national wealth tend to have more men enrolled in tertiary education than women, while the opposite occurs in countries with higher average incomes.

The GPI measures the rate of girls' school enrolment as a percentage of boys' enrolment in primary, secondary and tertiary education.

GENDER PARITY INDEX (GPI)

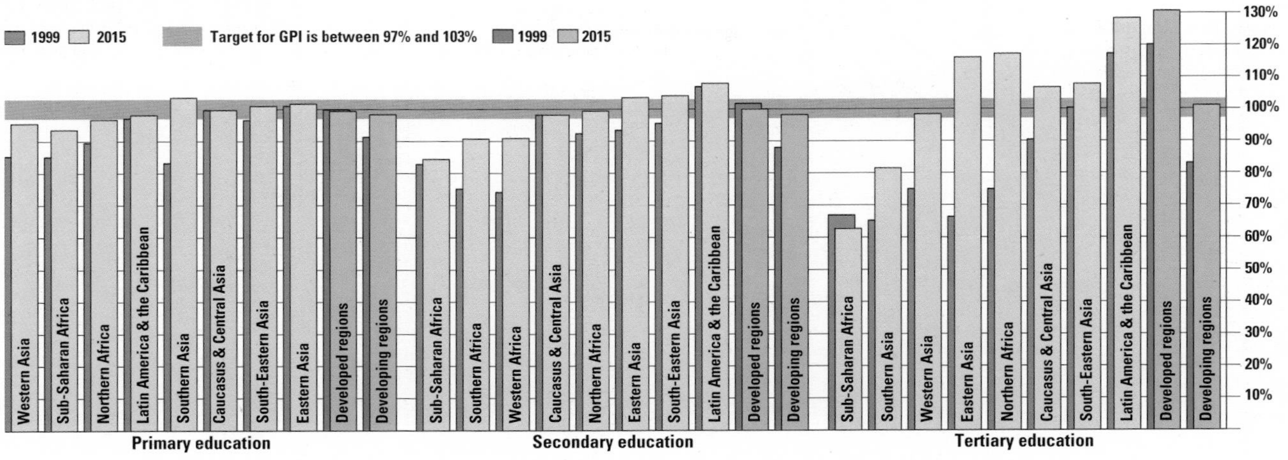

WORLD CITIES

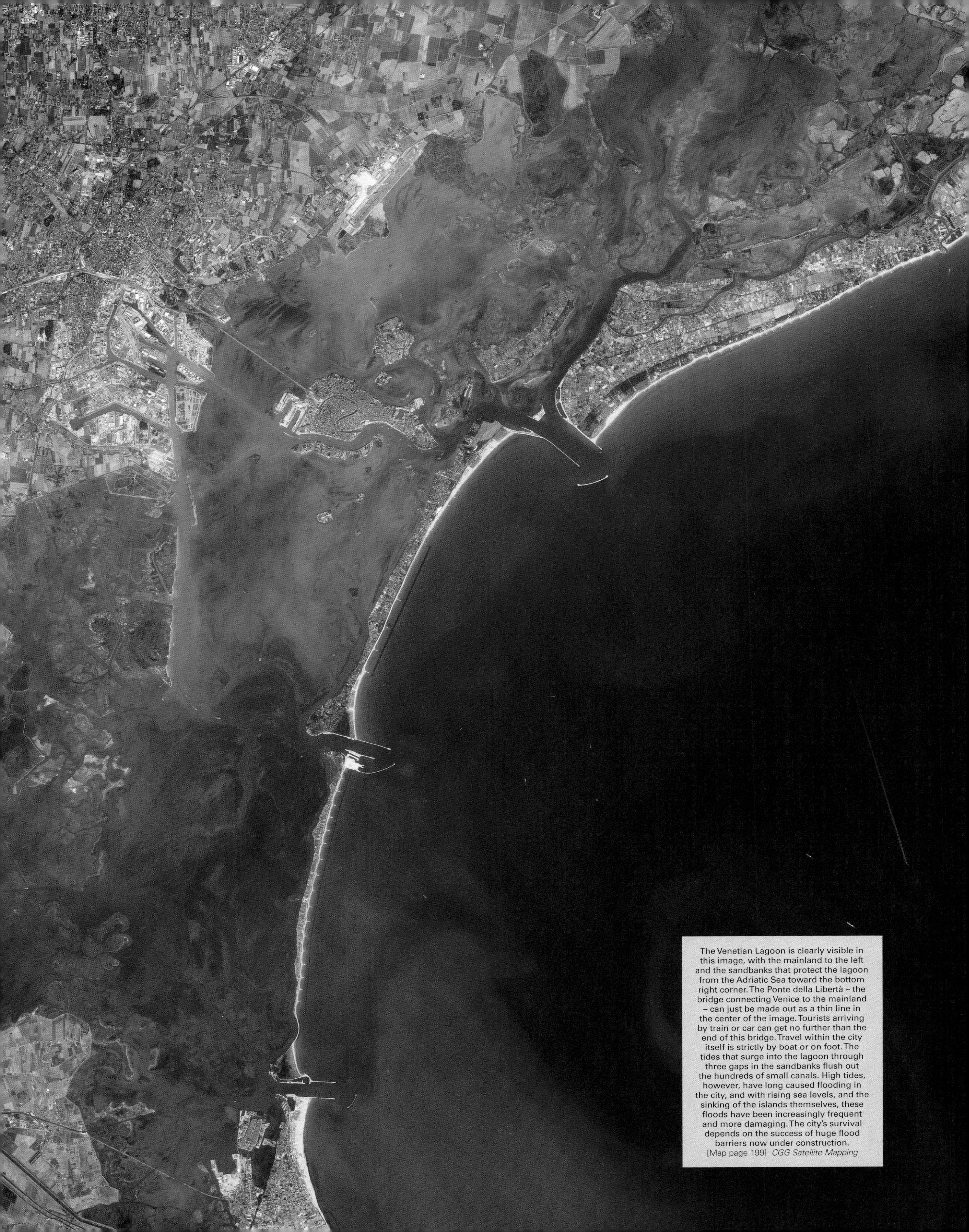

The Venetian Lagoon is clearly visible in this image, with the mainland to the left and the sandbanks that protect the lagoon from the Adriatic Sea toward the bottom right corner. The Ponte della Libertà – the bridge connecting Venice to the mainland – can just be made out as a thin line in the center of the image. Tourists arriving by train or car can get no further than the end of this bridge. Travel within the city itself is strictly by boat or on foot. The tides that surge into the lagoon through three gaps in the sandbanks flush out the hundreds of small canals. High tides, however, have long caused flooding in the city, and with rising sea levels, and the sinking of the islands themselves, these floods have been increasingly frequent and more damaging. The city's survival depends on the success of huge flood barriers now under construction.
[Map page 199] *CGG Satellite Mapping*

AMSTERDAM, NETHERLANDS

1 0 1 km 2 3 4 5
1 0 miles 1 2 3

CENTRAL AMSTERDAM

0 km 0.5
0 miles 0.25

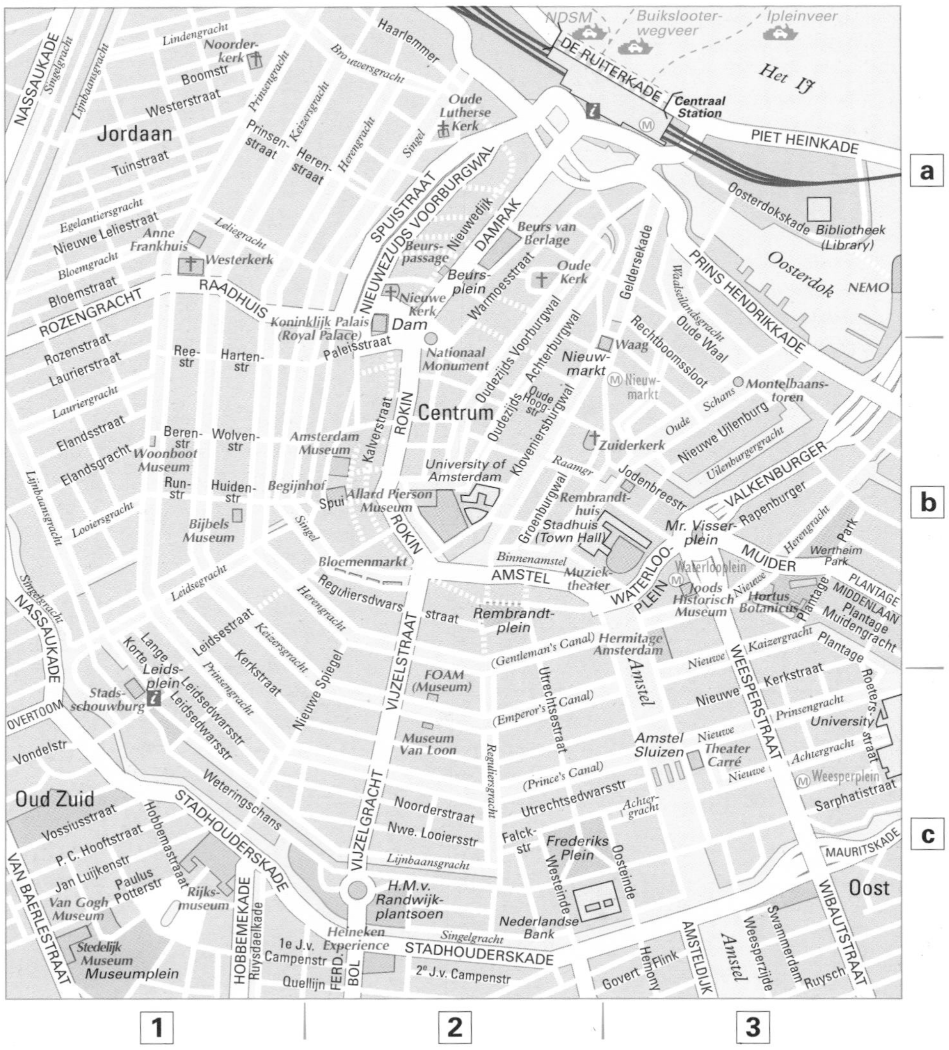

ATHENS, GREECE

1 0 1 km 2 3 4 5
1 0 miles 1 2 3

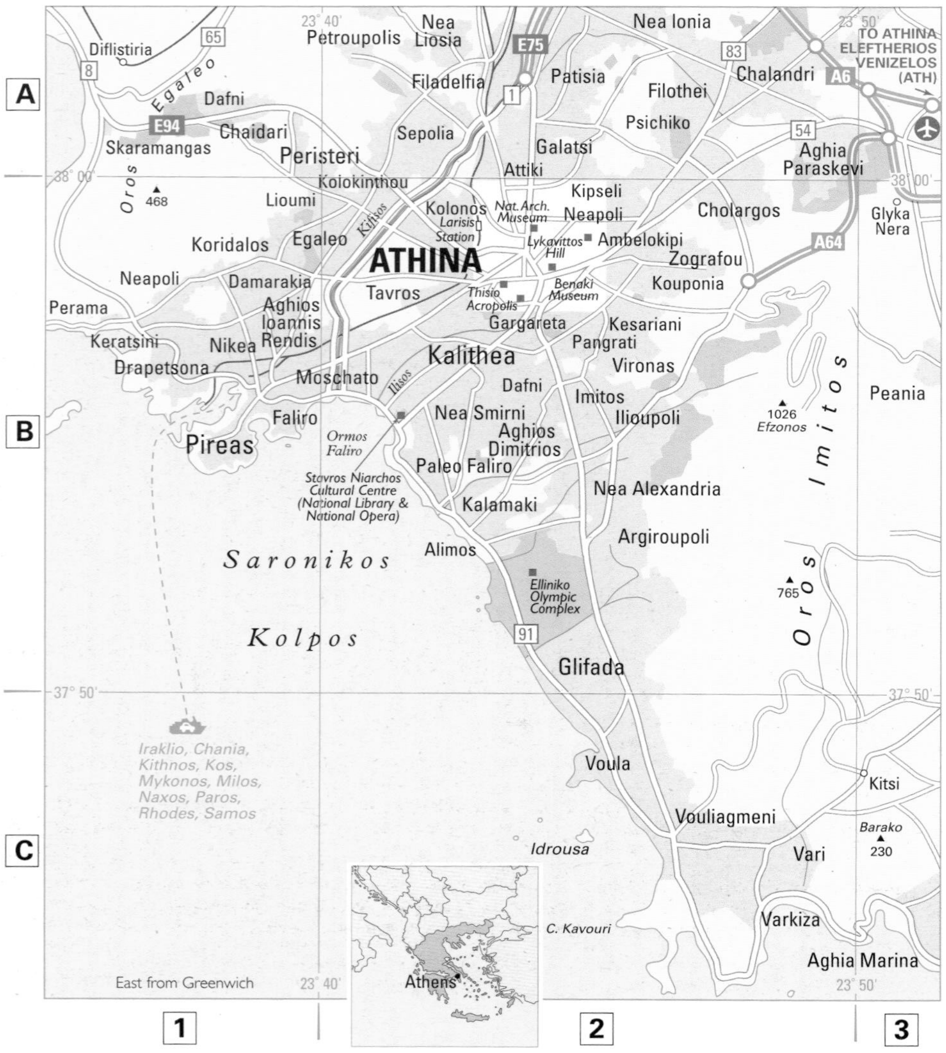

CENTRAL ATHENS

0 km 1
0 miles 0.5

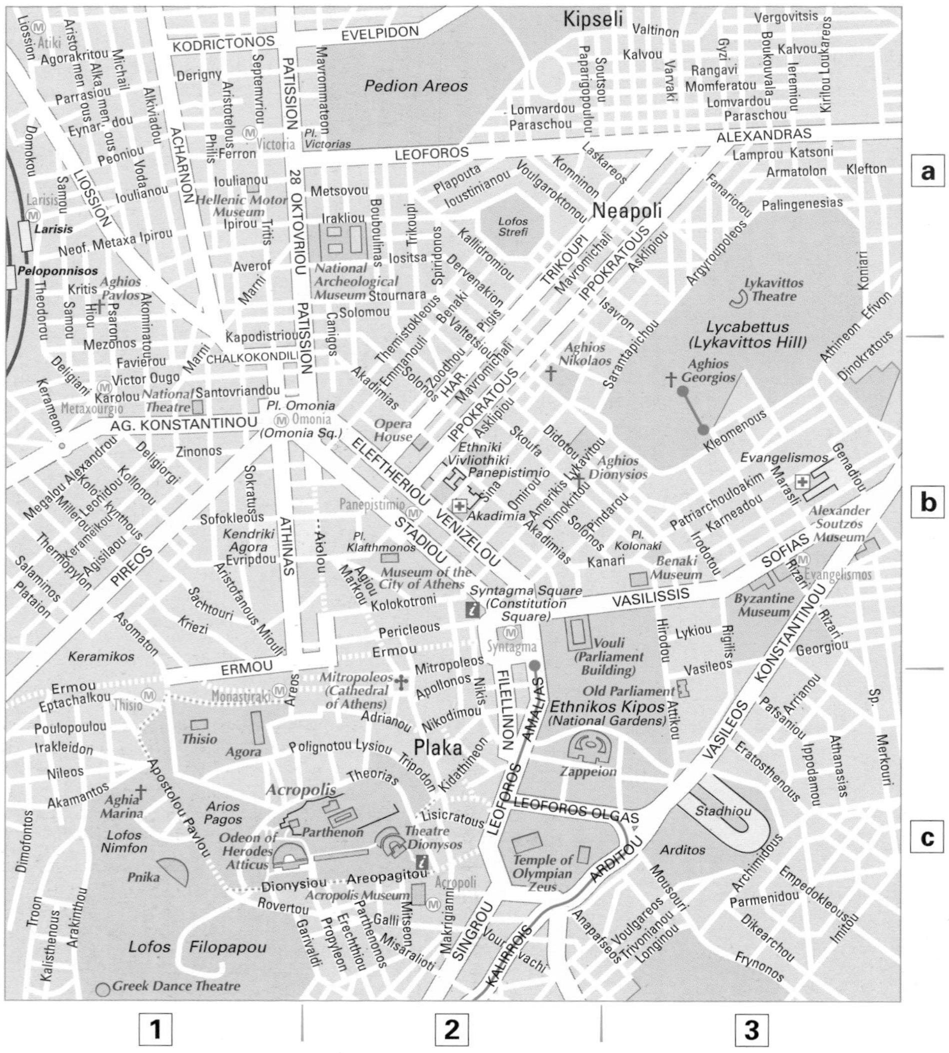

Tram Route

ATLANTA, GEORGIA

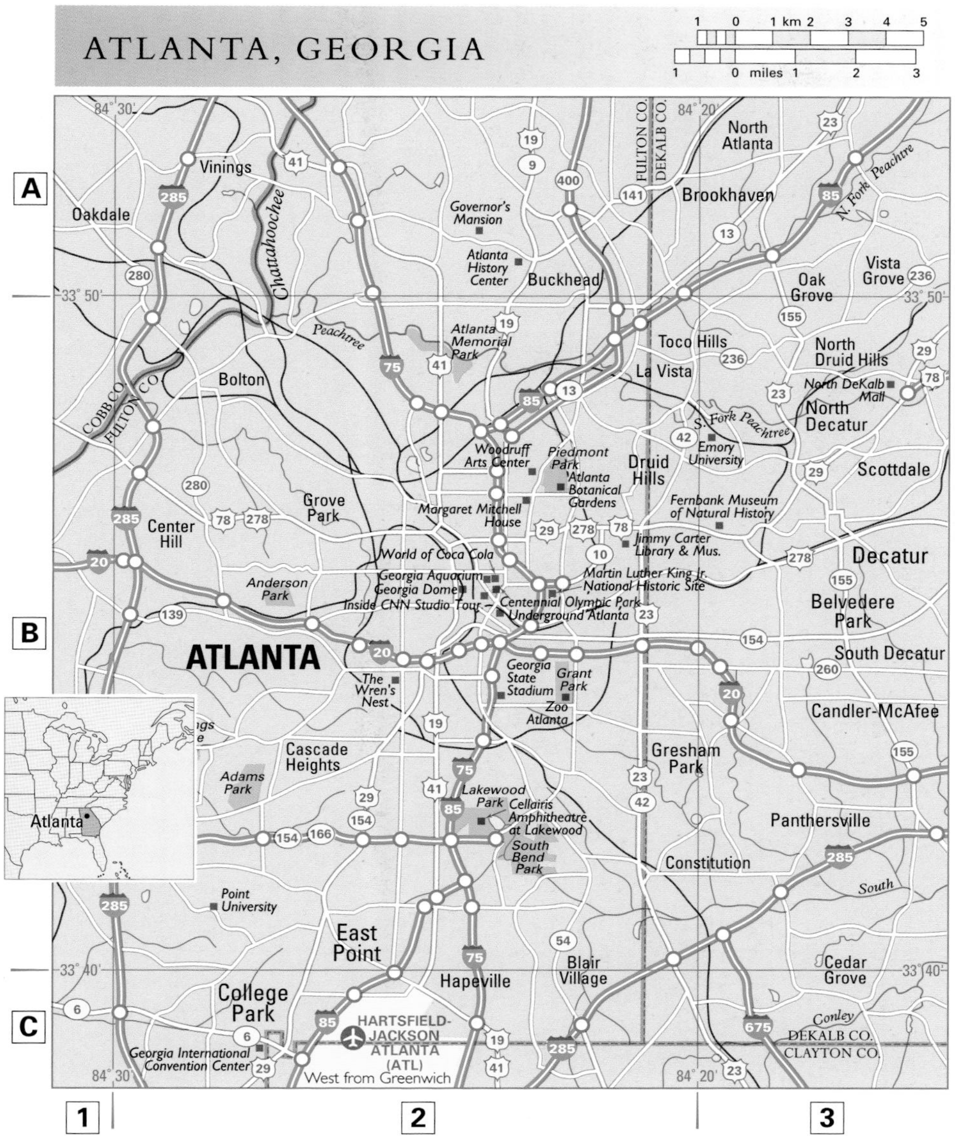

Interstate route numbers U.S. route numbers State route numbers

BAGHDAD, IRAQ

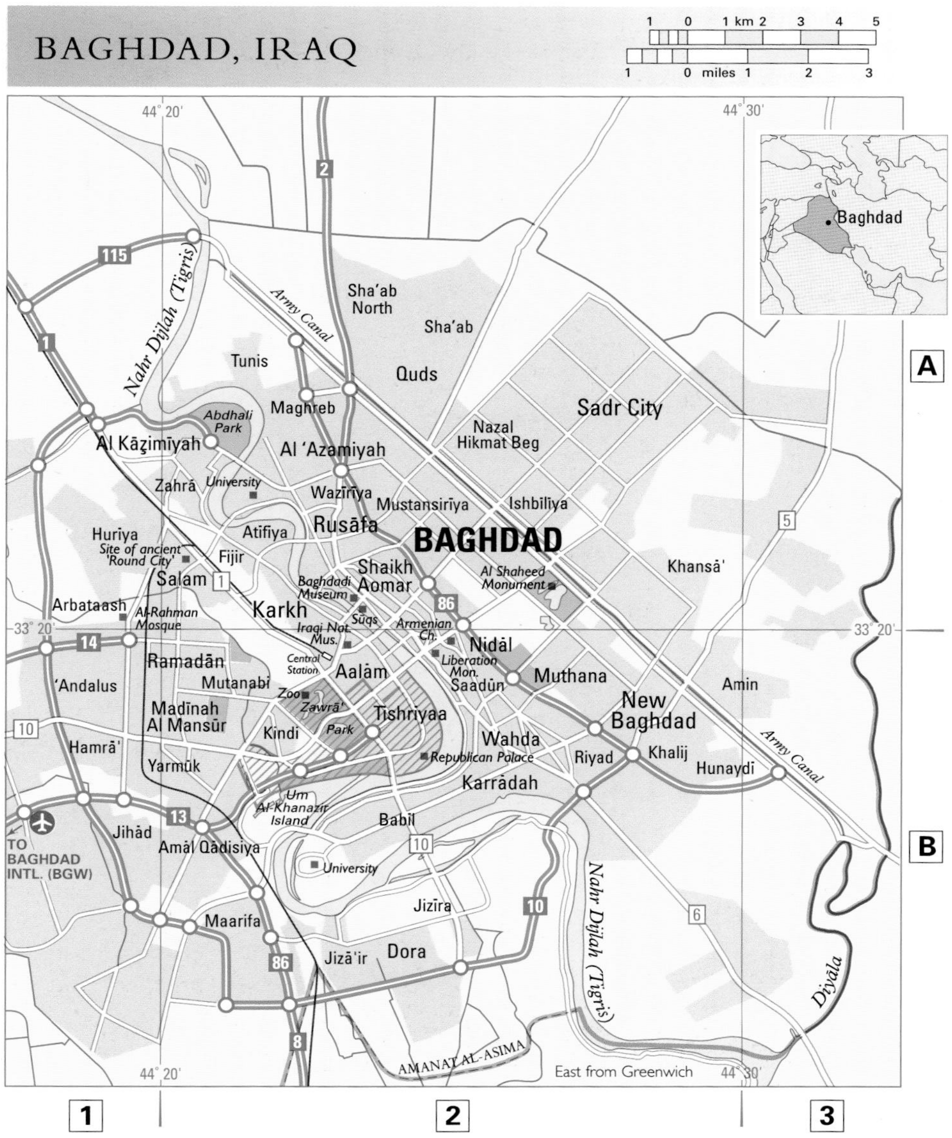

International Zone (Green Zone)

BANGKOK, THAILAND

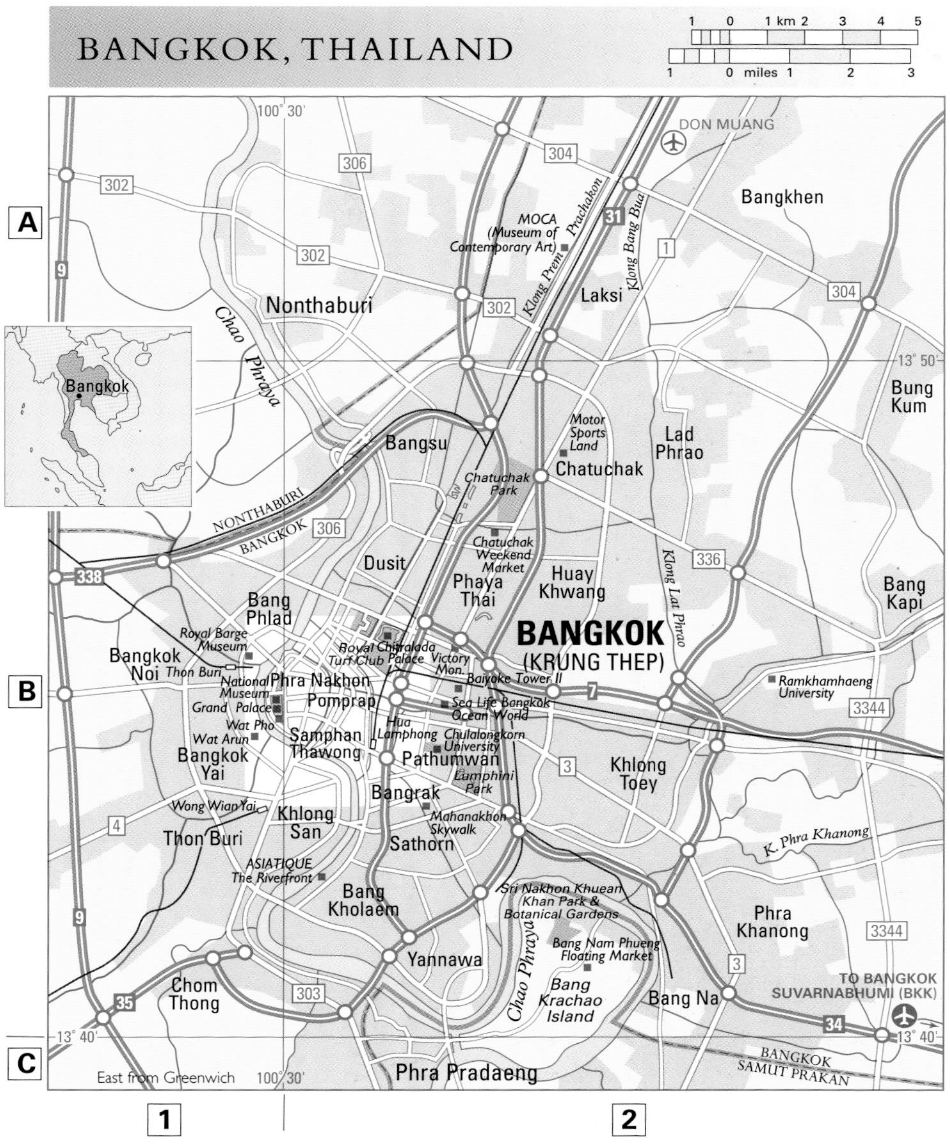

CENTRAL BANGKOK

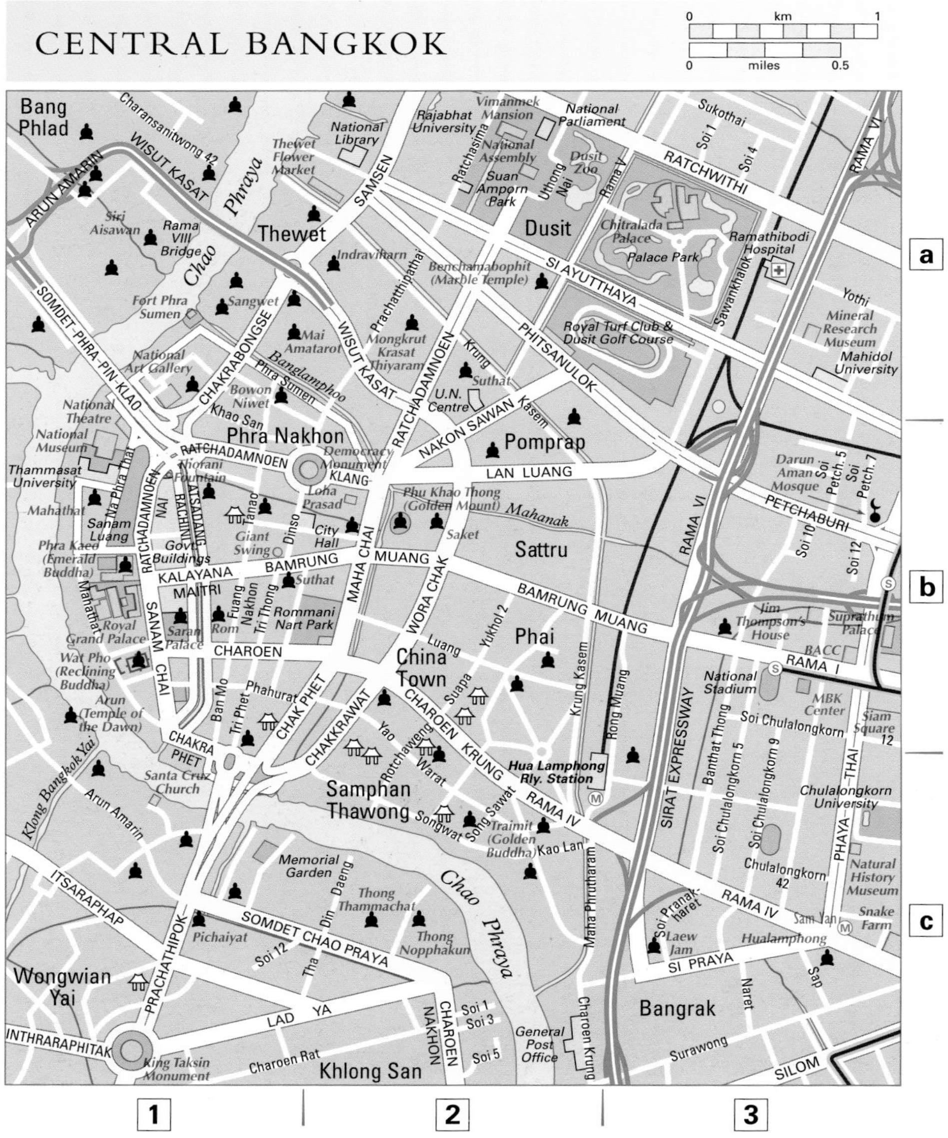

Skytrain Shrine Temple

BARCELONA, SPAIN

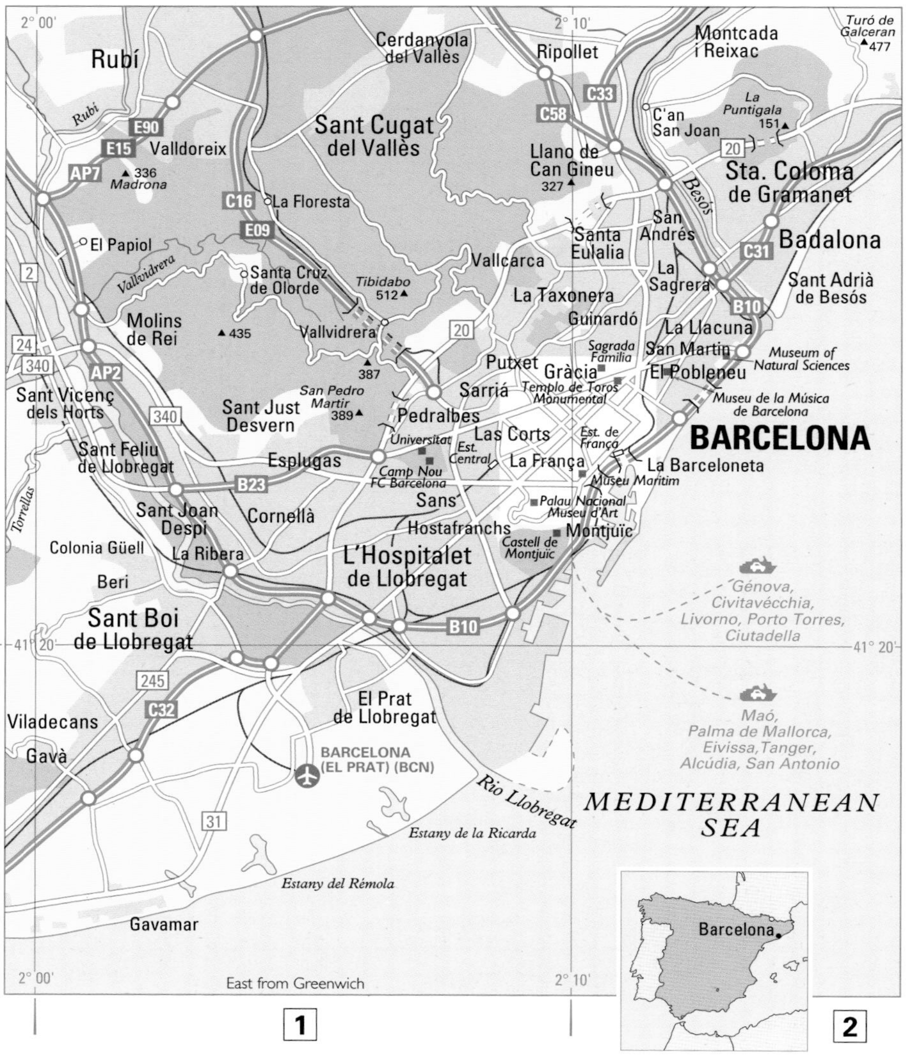

CENTRAL BARCELONA

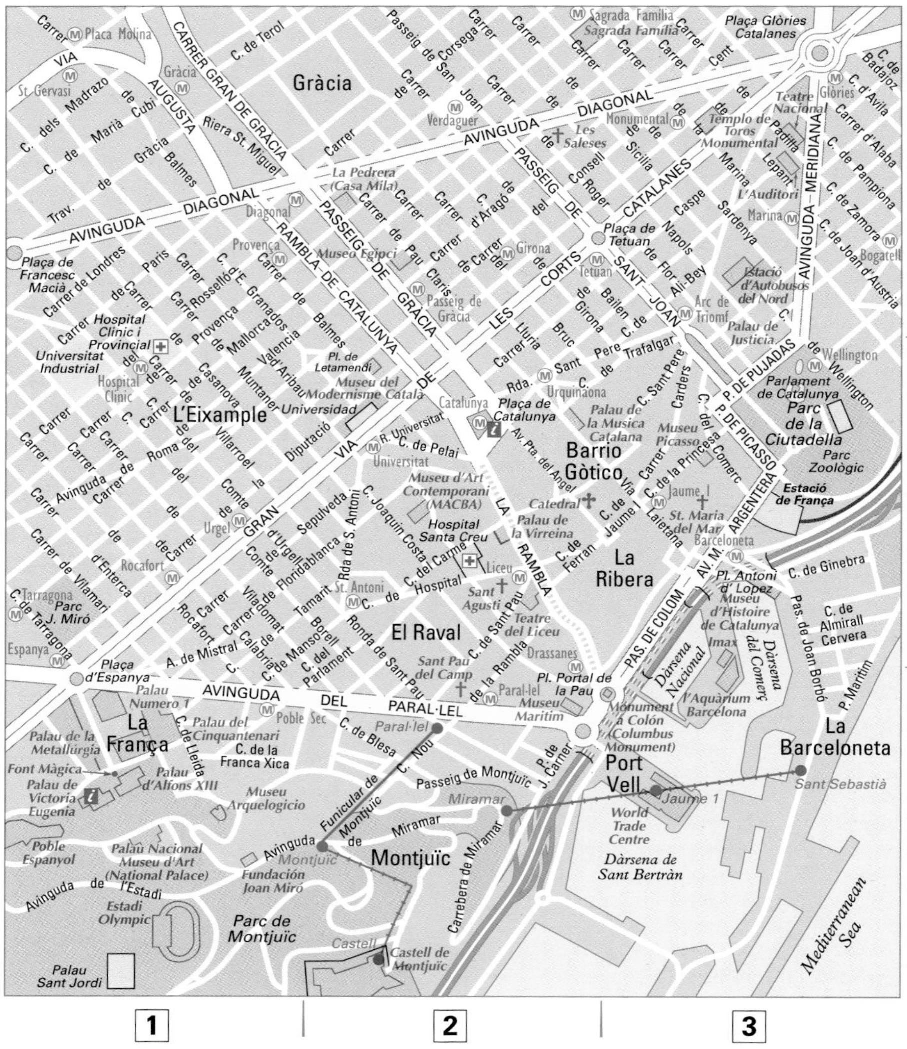

BEIJING, CHINA

CENTRAL BEIJING

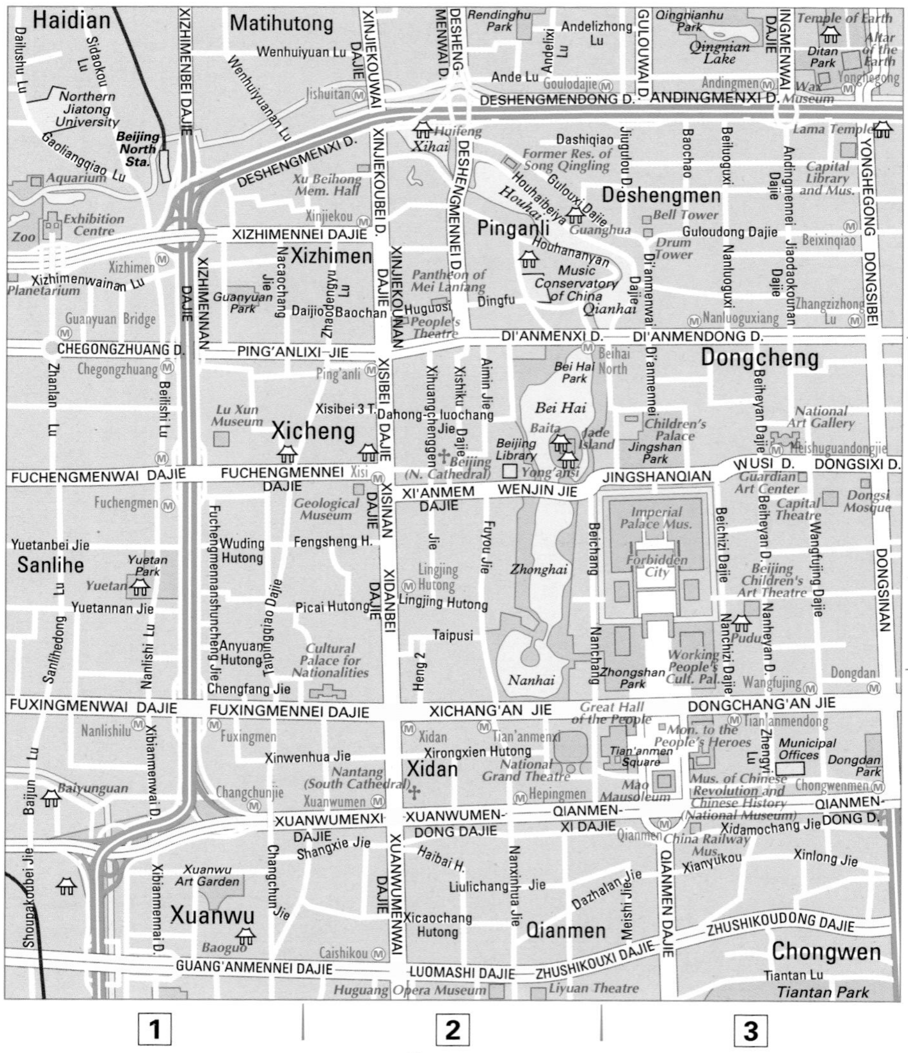

Temple

BERLIN, GERMANY

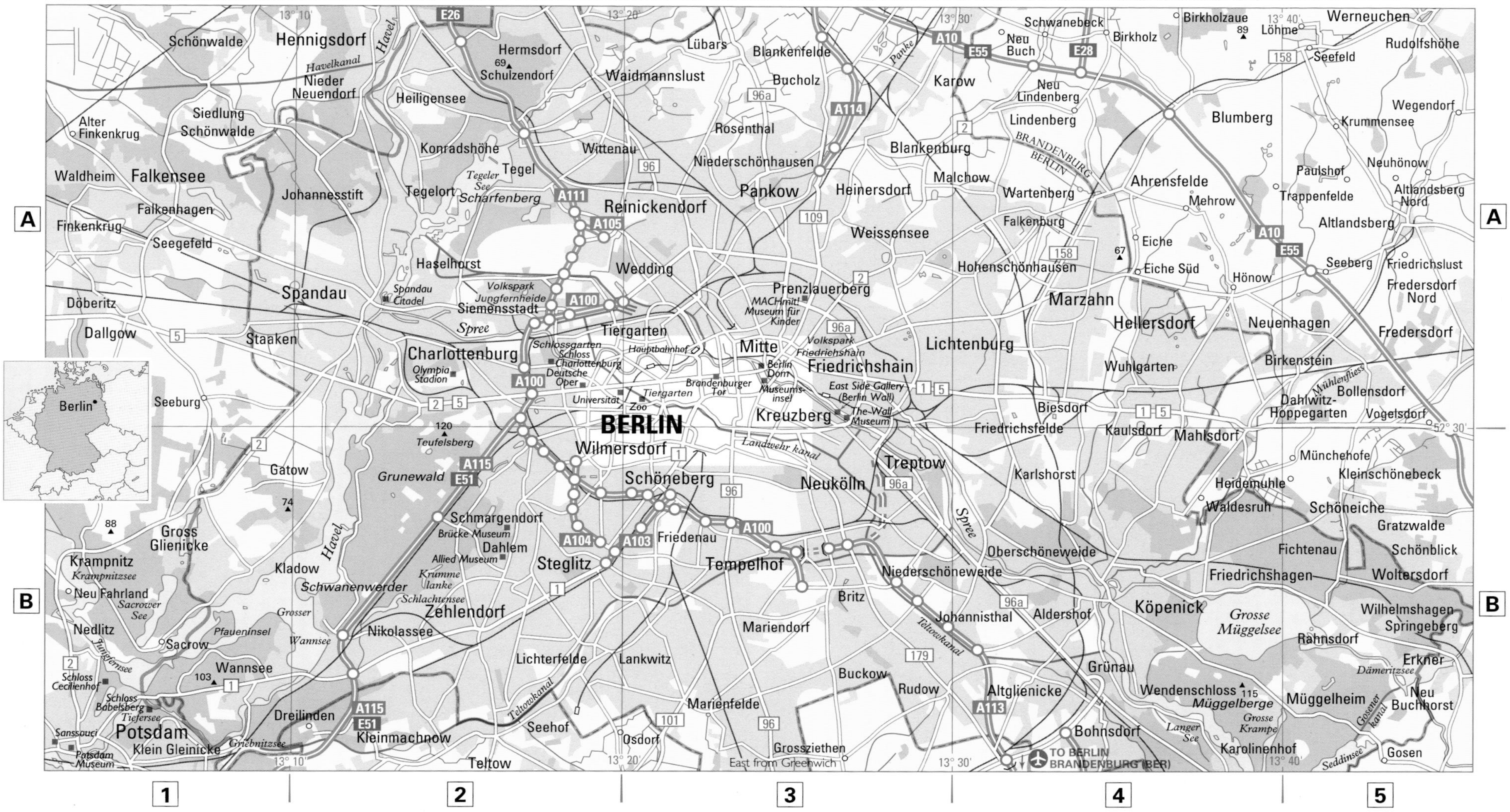

CENTRAL BERLIN

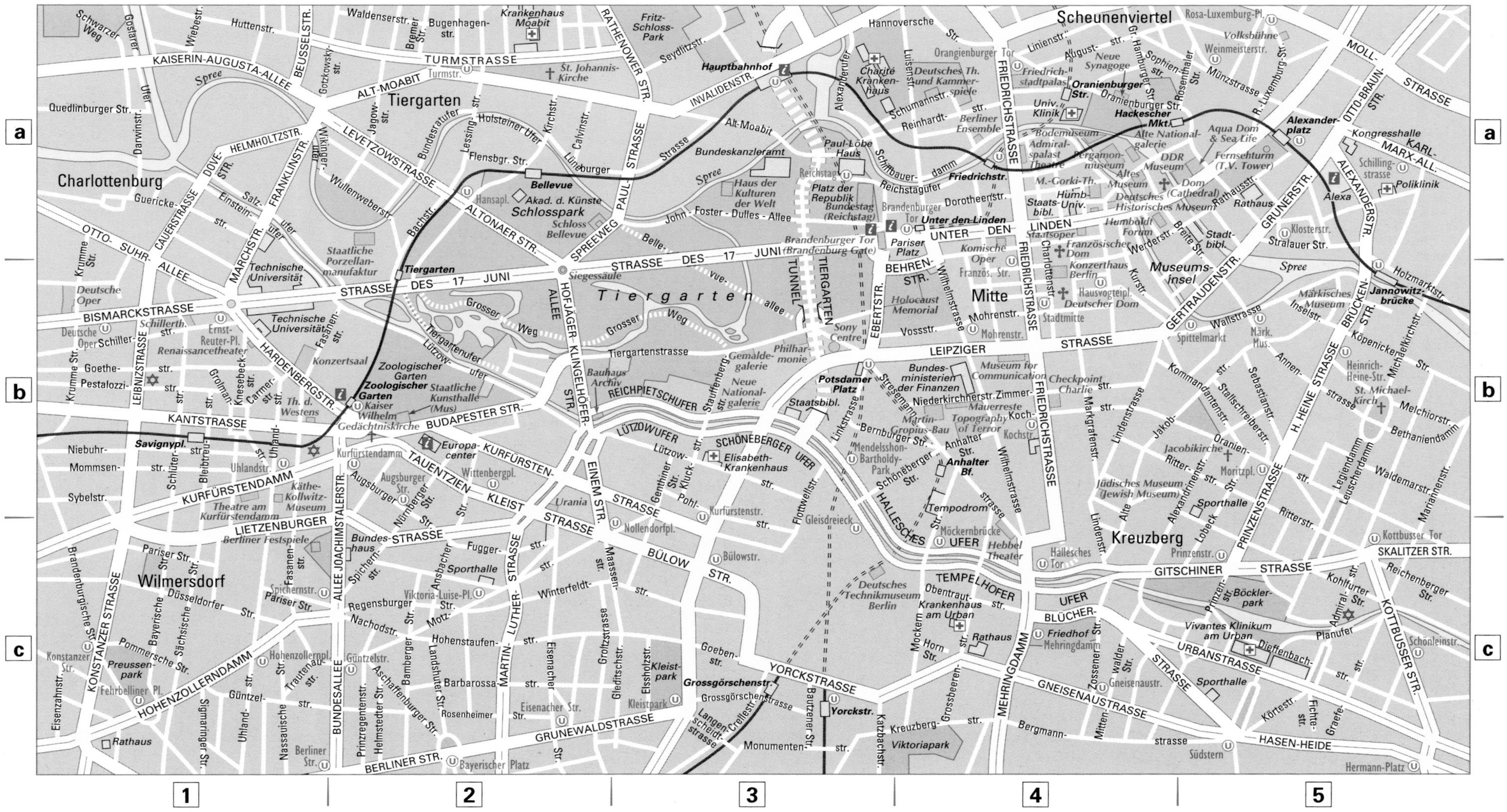

BOSTON, MASSACHUSETTS

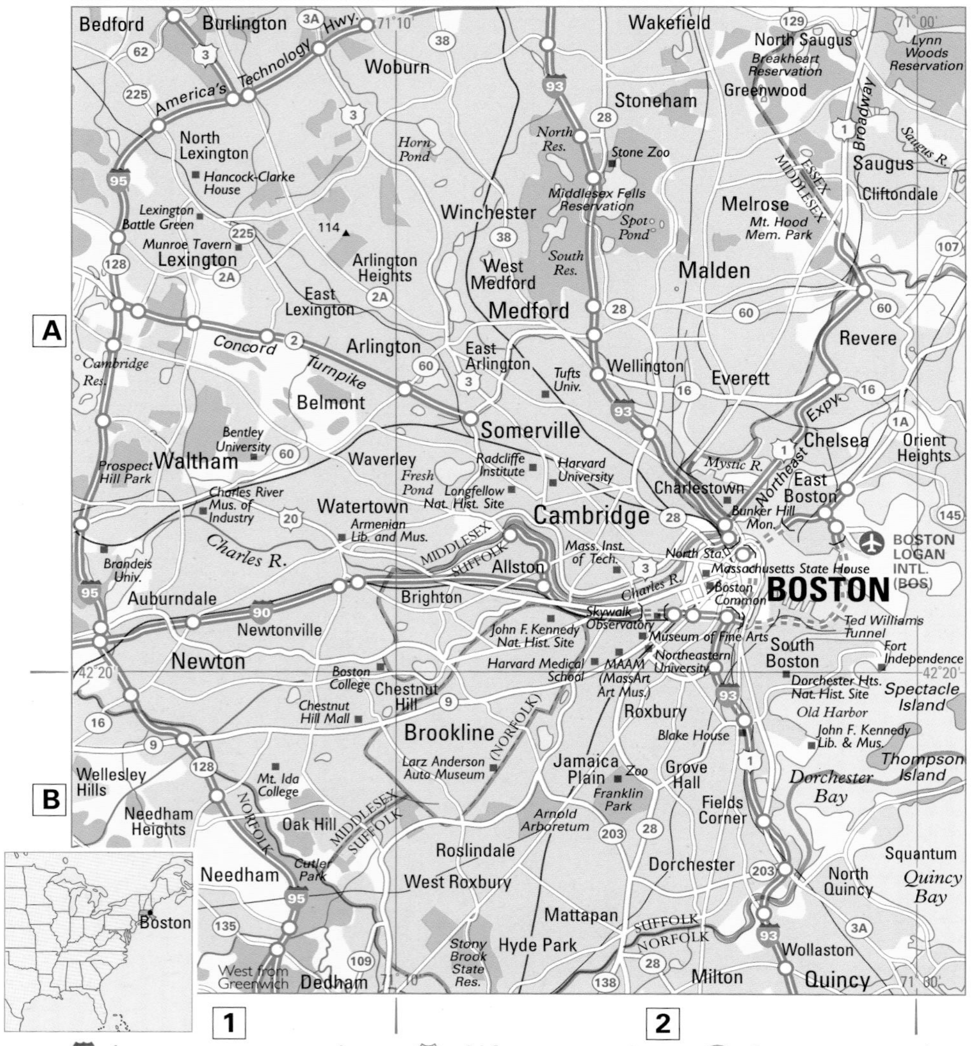

95 Interstate route numbers   20 U.S. route numbers   109 State route numbers

CENTRAL BOSTON

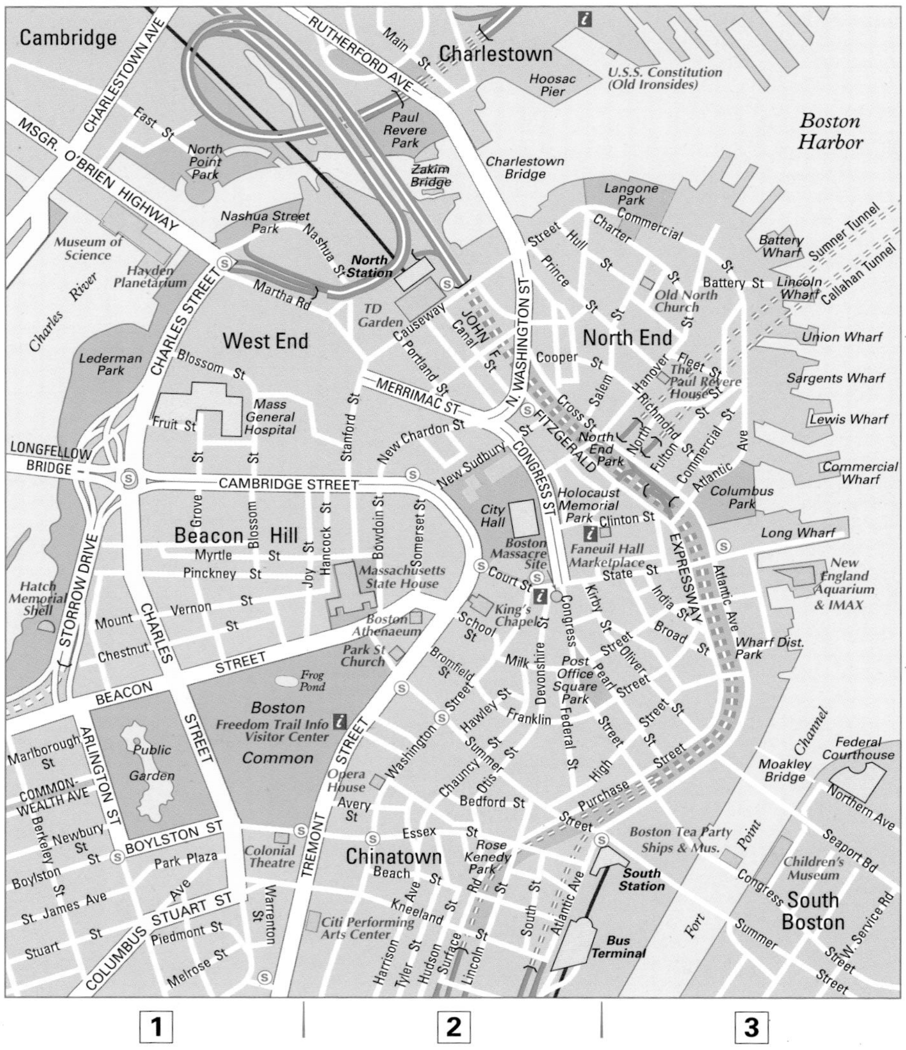

BRUSSELS, BELGIUM

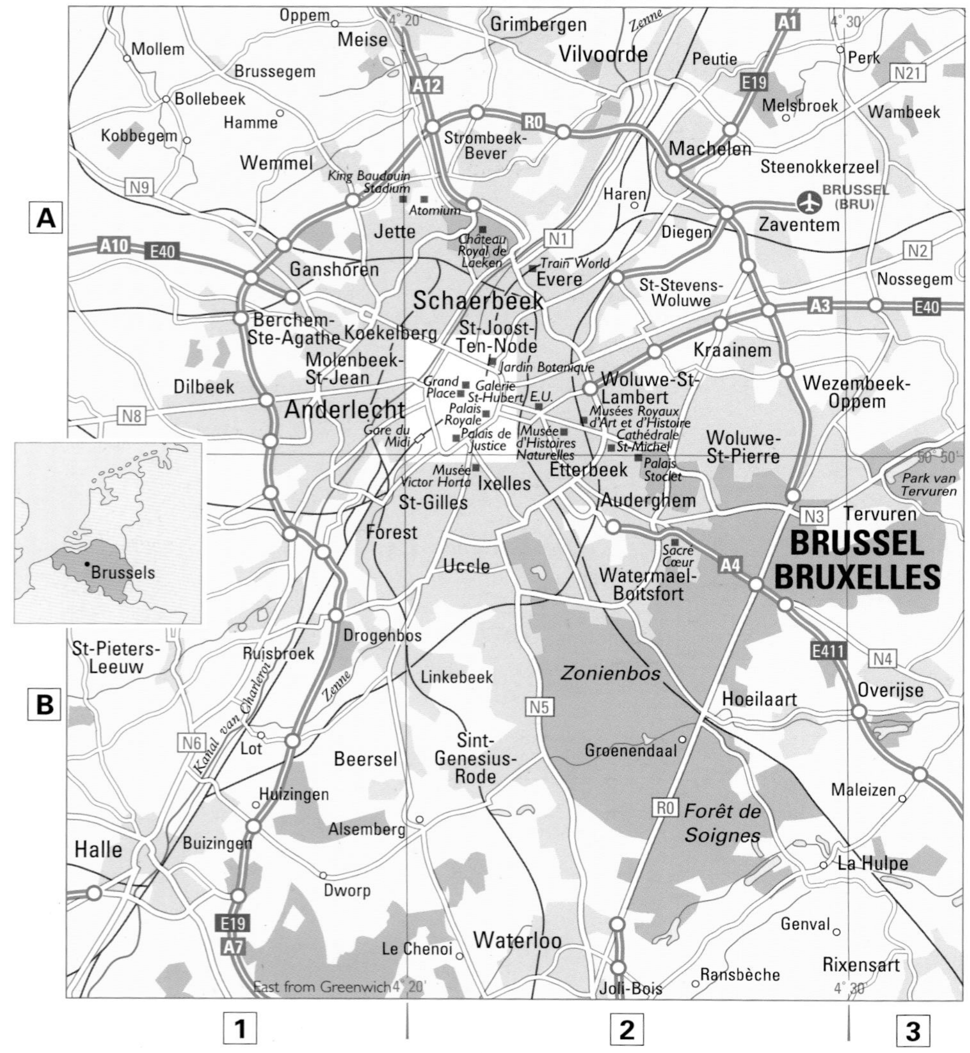

CENTRAL BRUSSELS

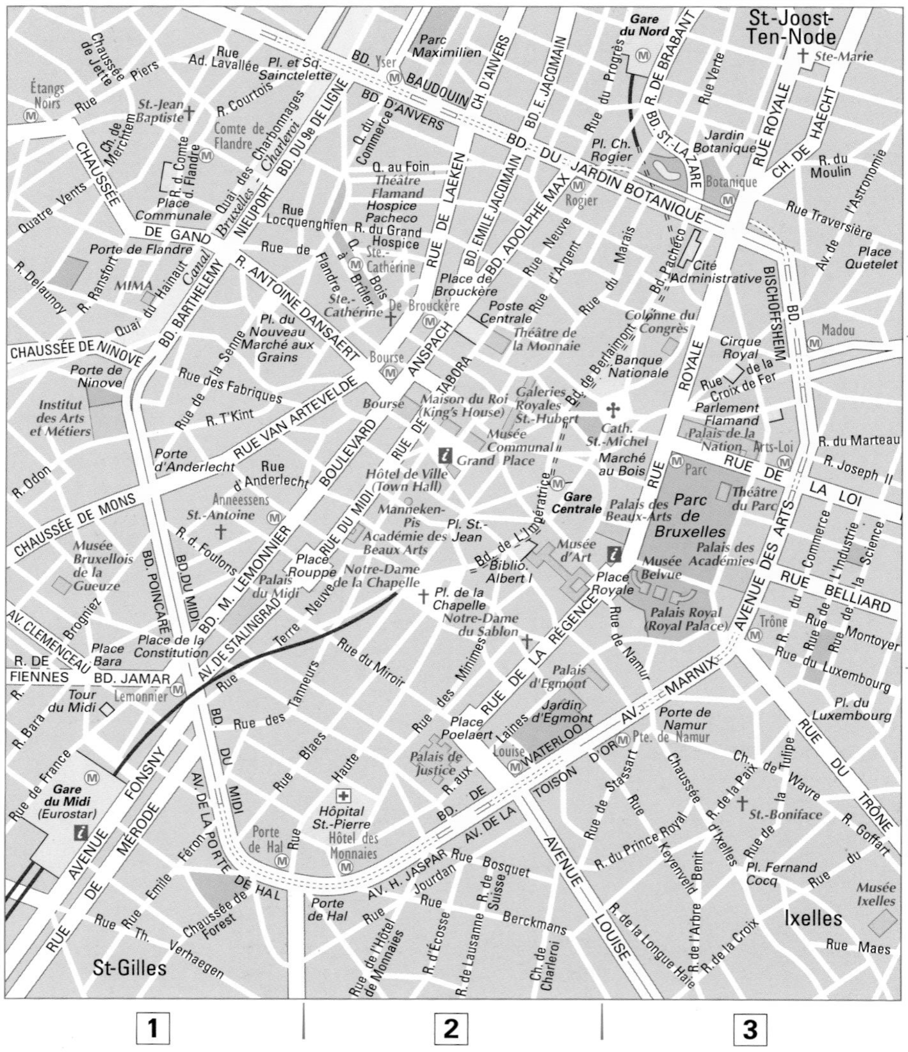

BUDAPEST, HUNGARY

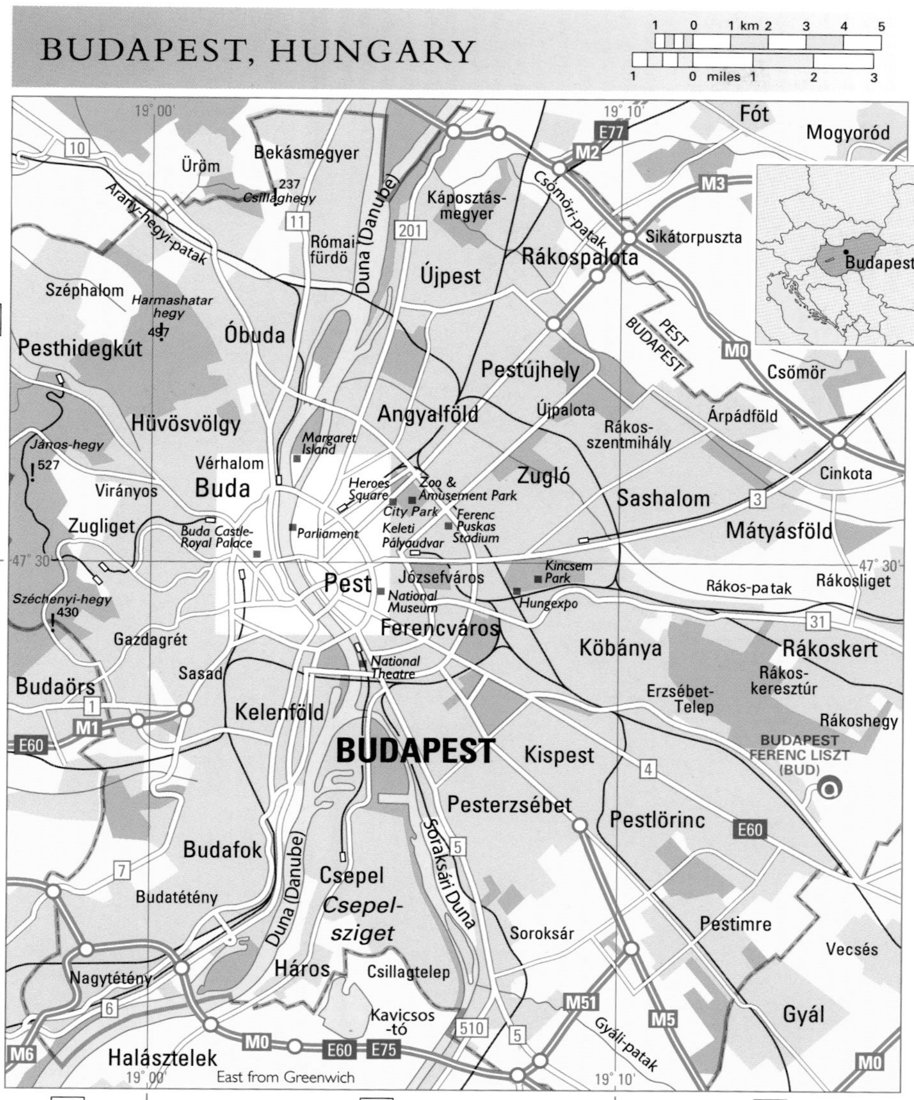

CENTRAL BUDAPEST

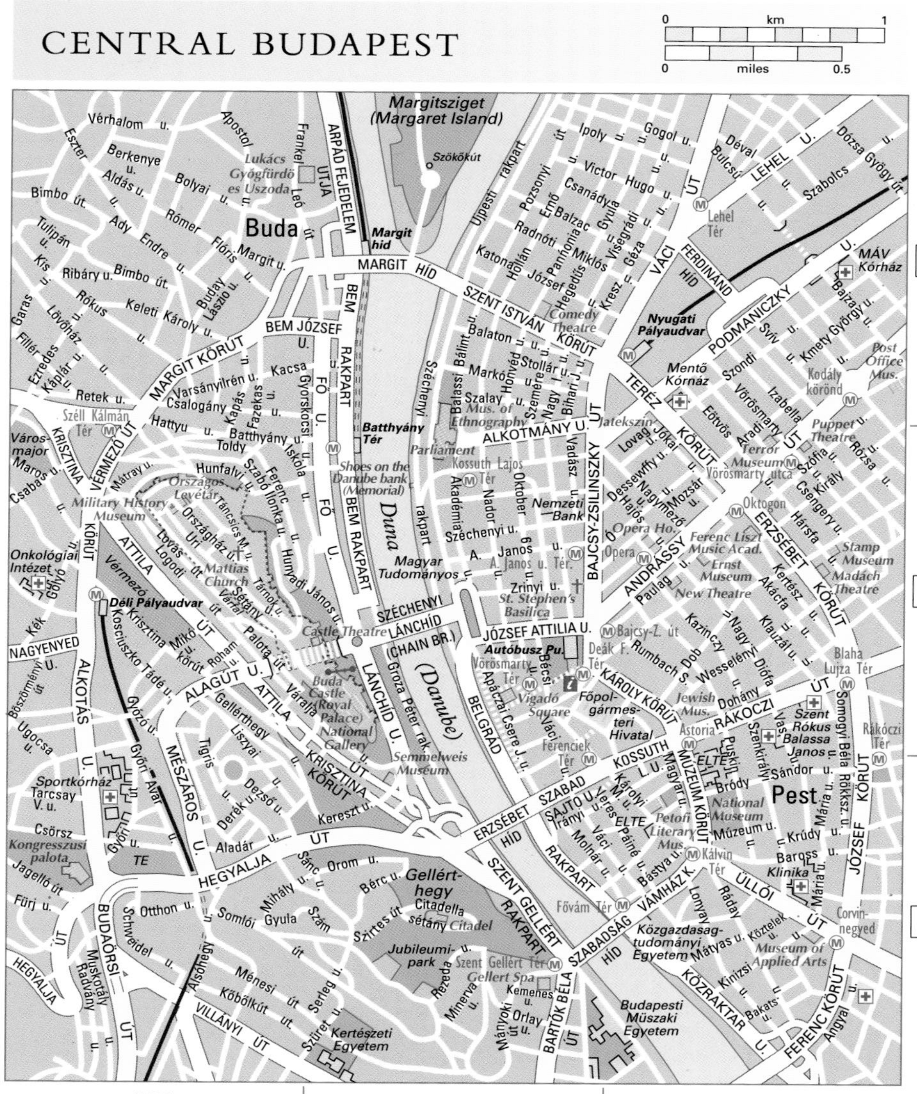

BUENOS AIRES, ARGENTINA

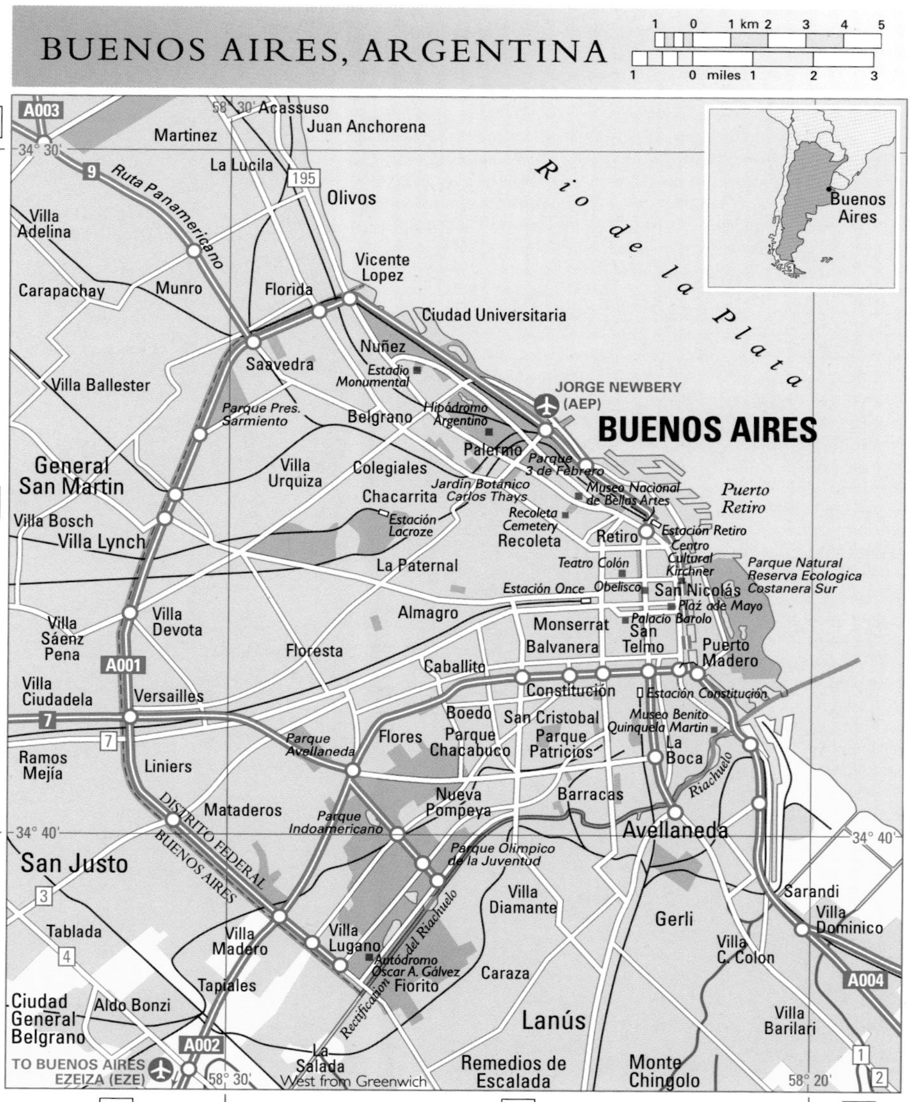

CAIRO, EGYPT

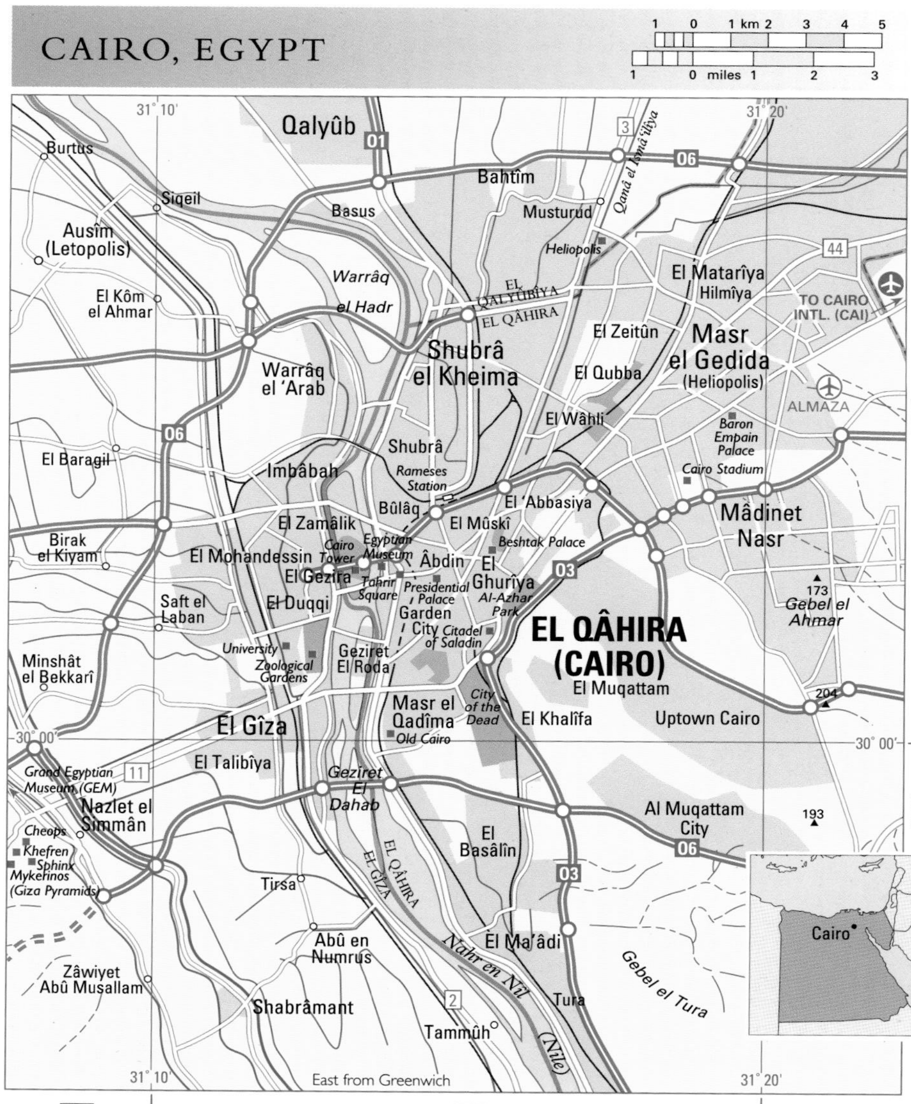

CAPE TOWN, SOUTH AFRICA

CENTRAL CAPE TOWN

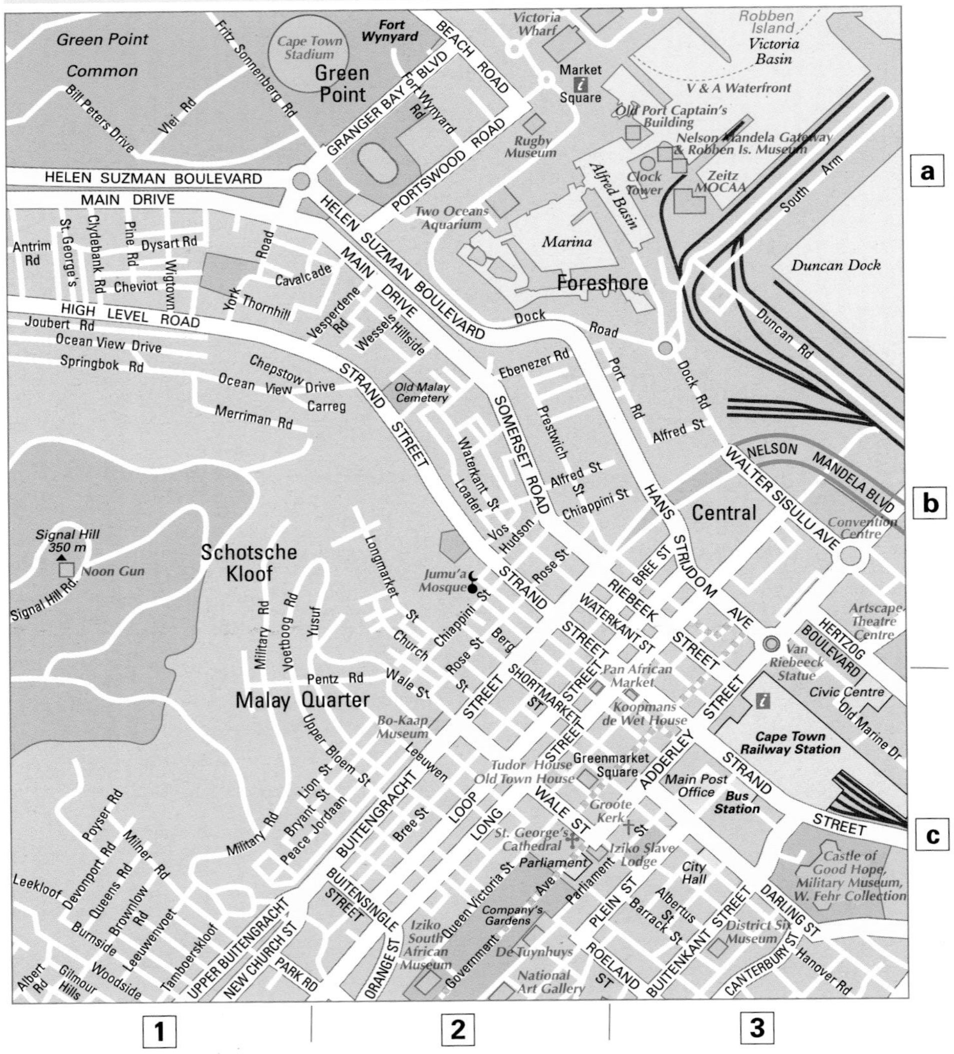

COPENHAGEN, DENMARK

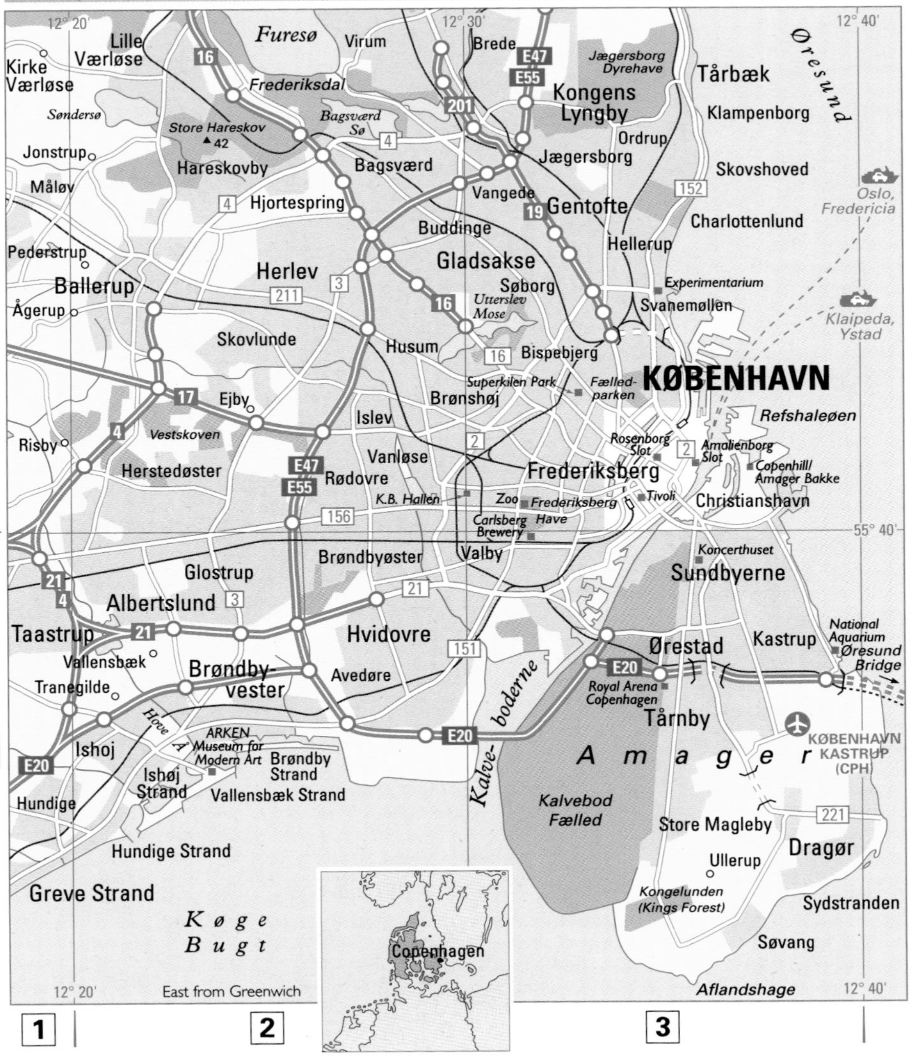

CENTRAL COPENHAGEN

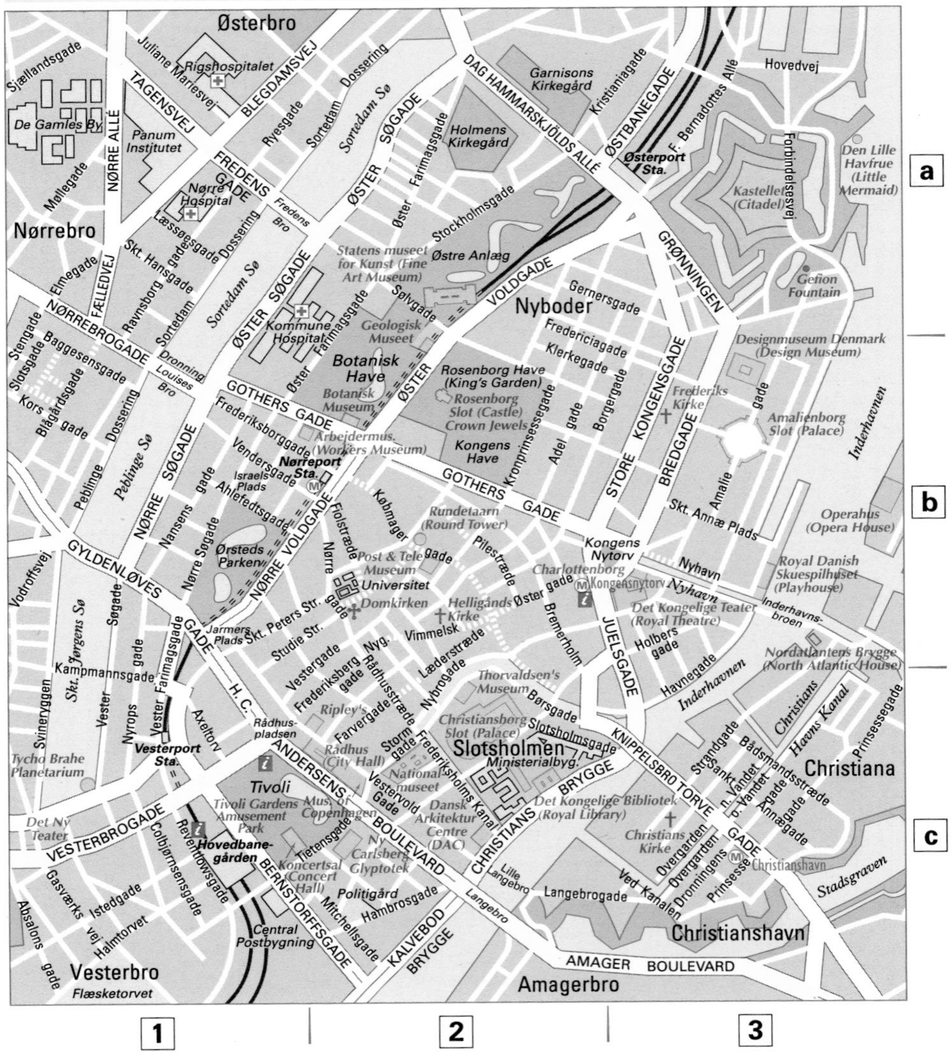

CENTRAL CHICAGO

0 km 0.5
0 miles 0.25

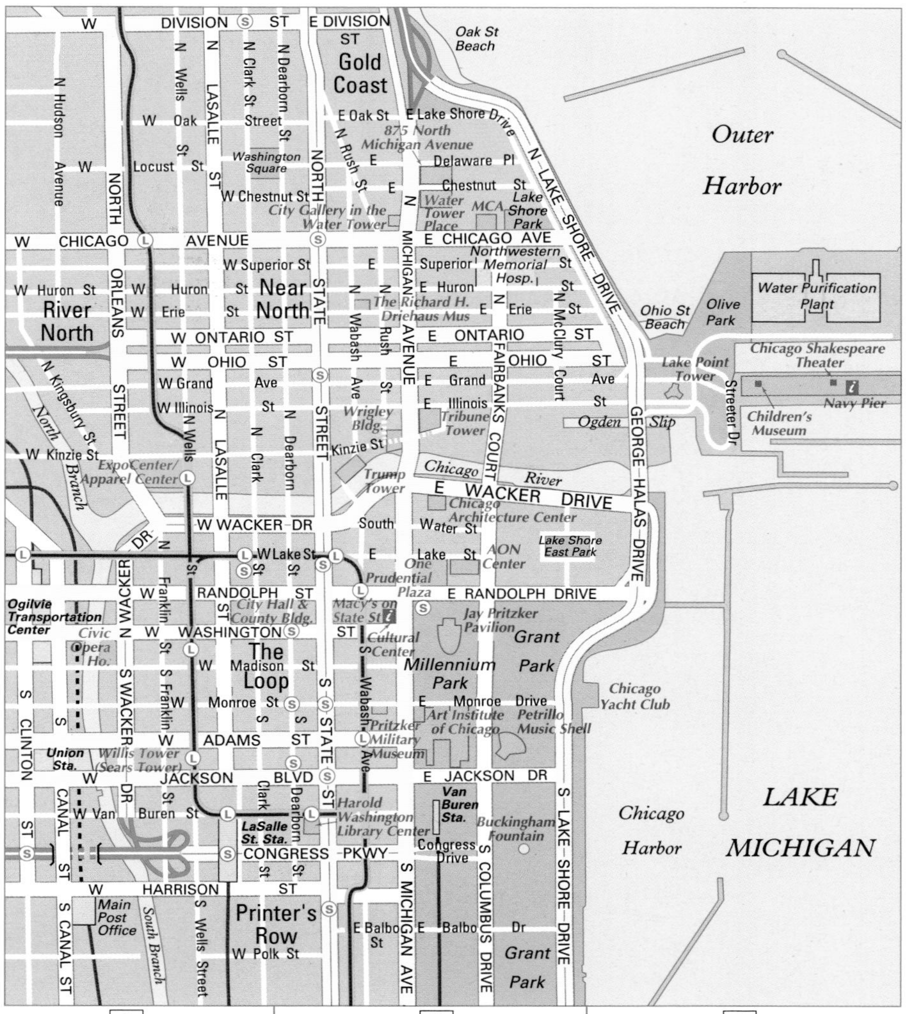

Elevated rail lines

DUBAI, U.A.E.

1 0 km 2 3 4 5
1 0 miles 1 2 3

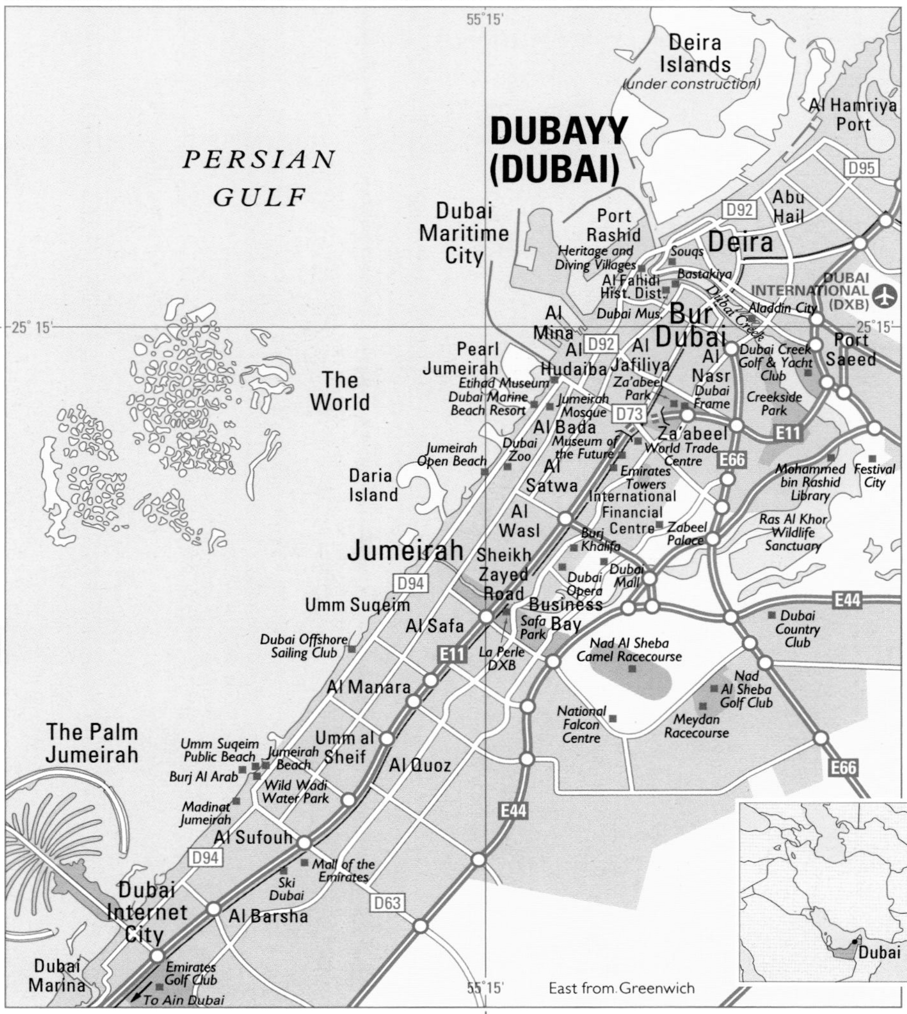

CHICAGO, ILLINOIS

1 0 1 km 2 3 4 5
1 0 miles 1 2 3

Interstate route numbers | U.S. route numbers | State route numbers

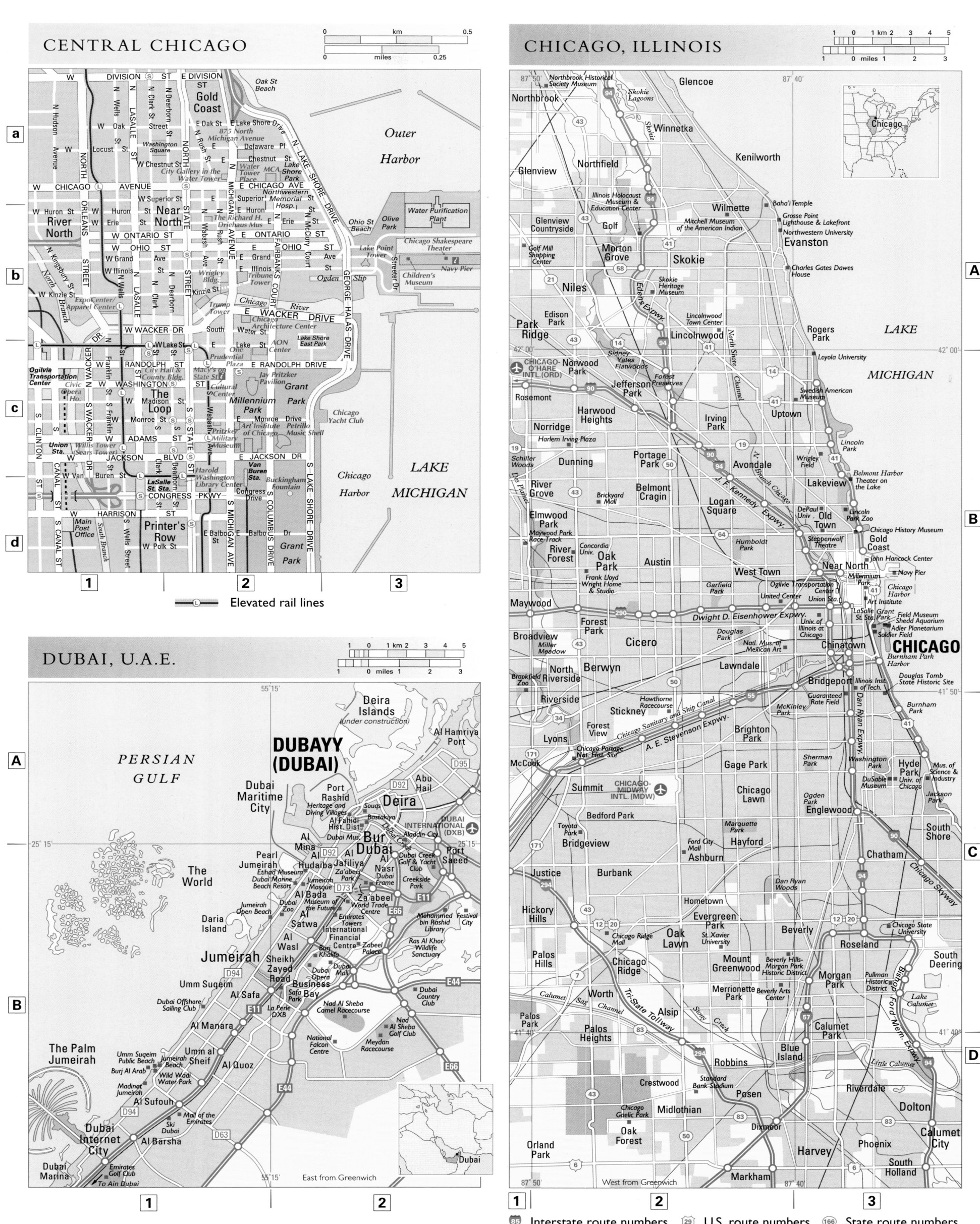

DALLAS–FORT WORTH, TEXAS

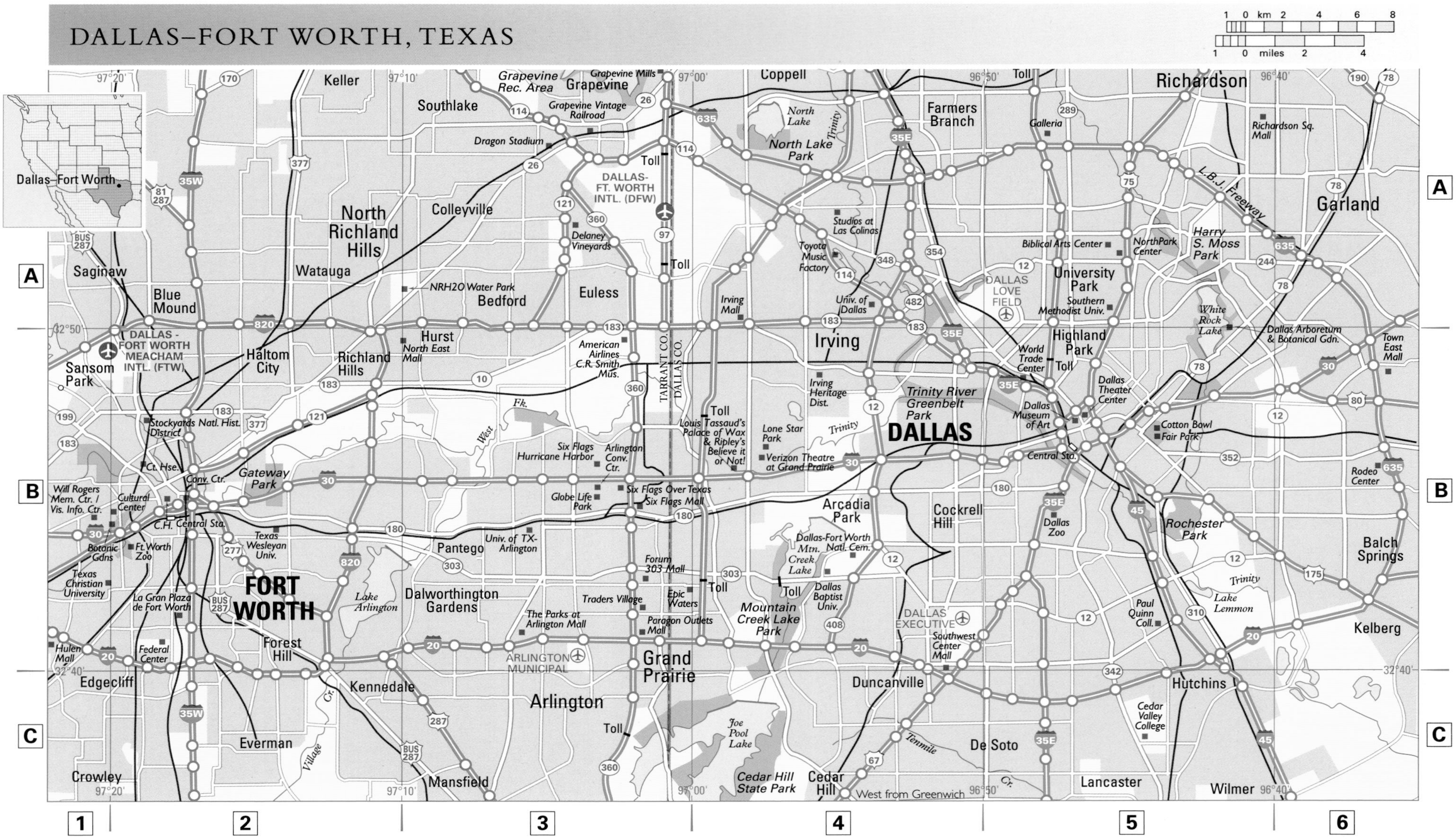

Interstate route numbers   U.S. route numbers   State route numbers

DELHI, INDIA

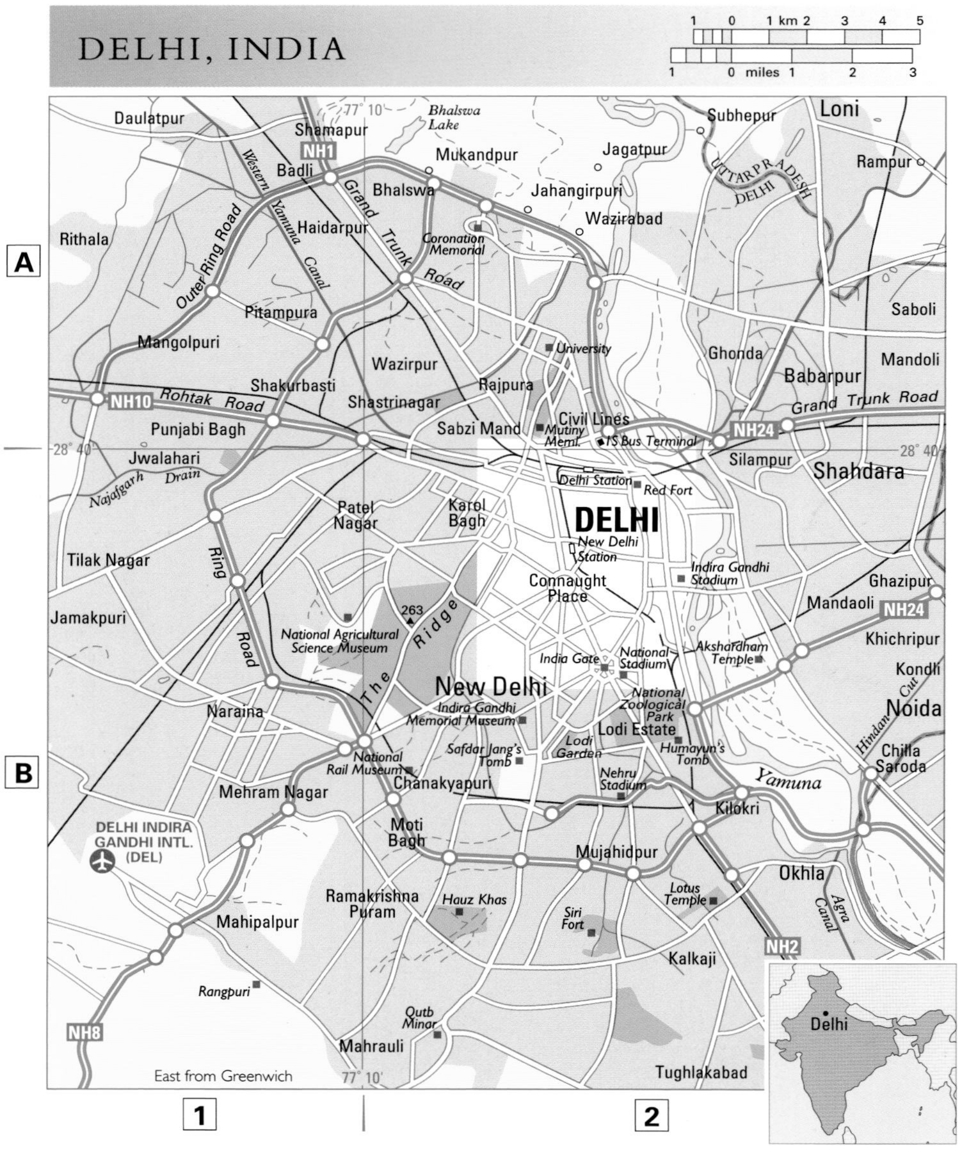

CENTRAL DELHI

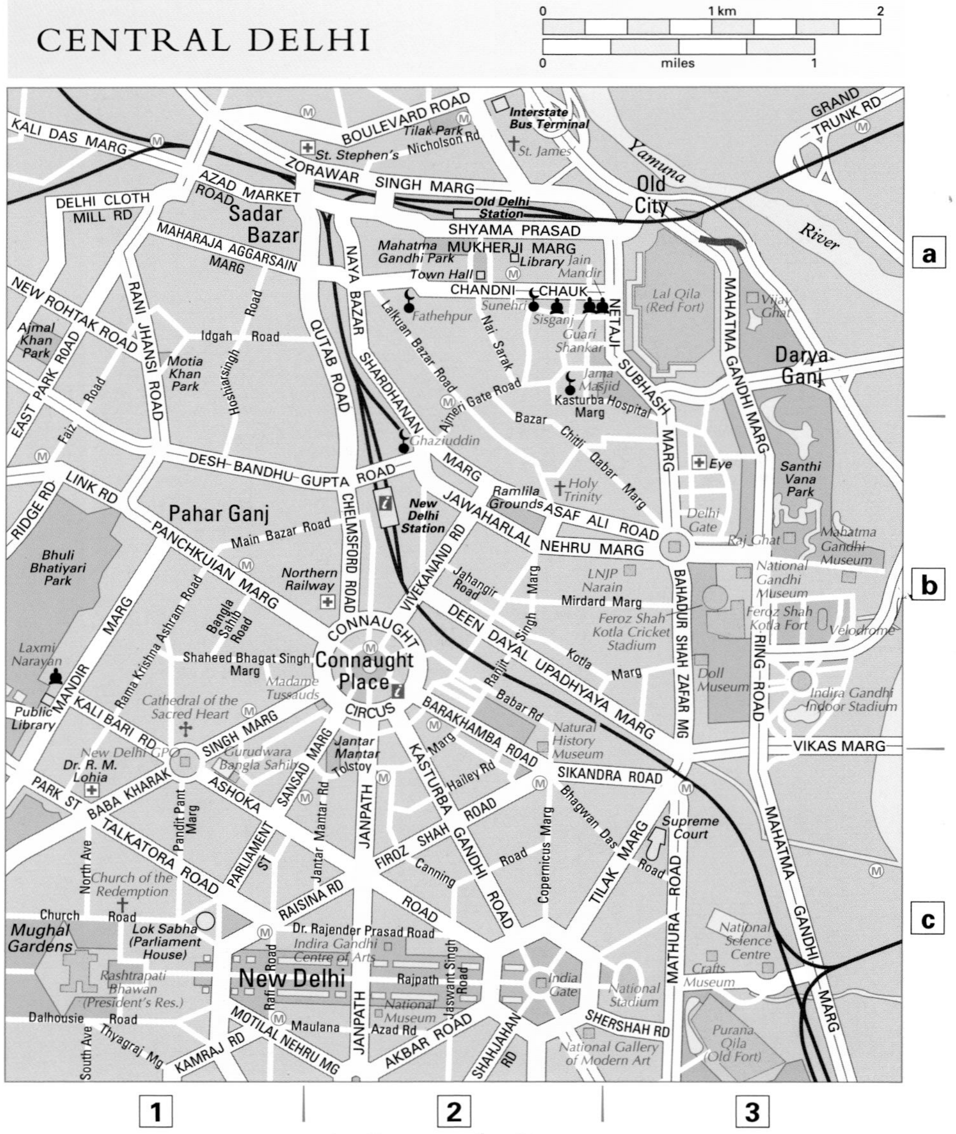

Shrine   Mosque

EDINBURGH, U.K.

CENTRAL EDINBURGH

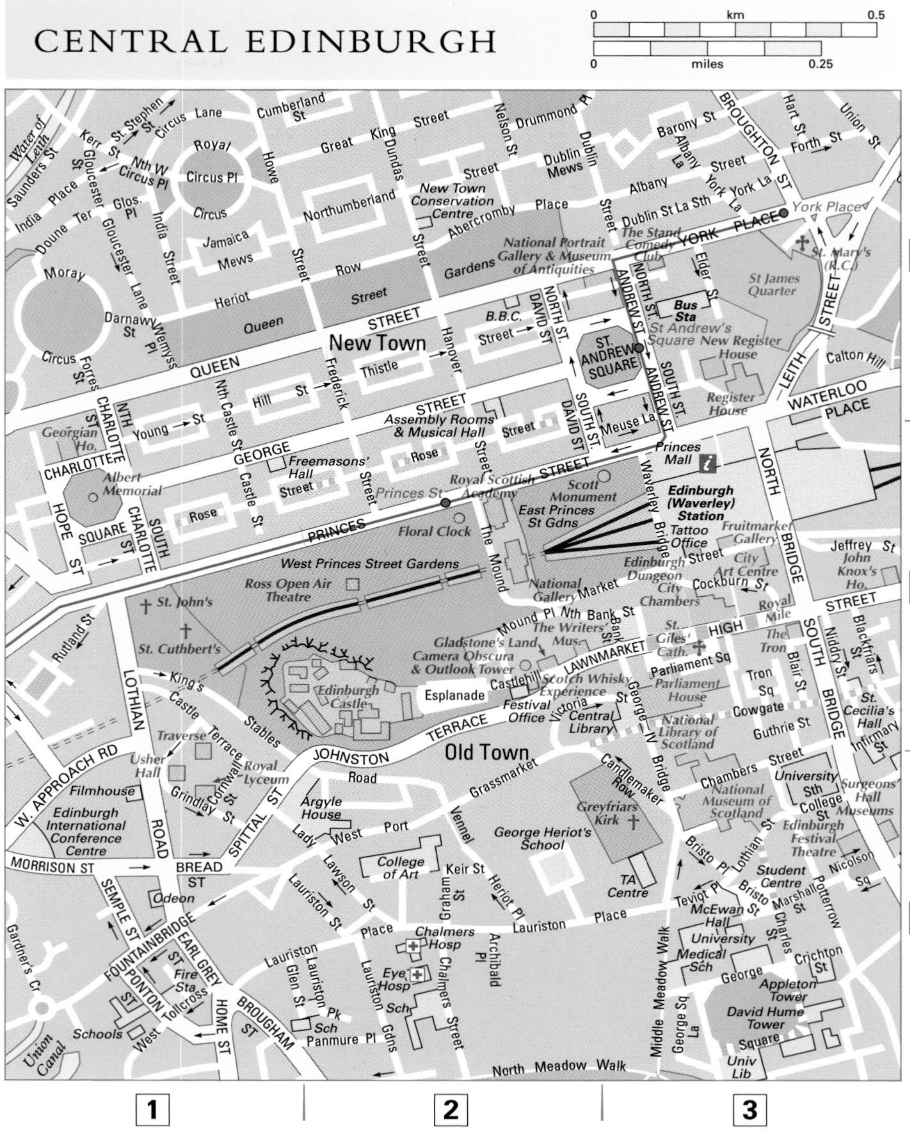

Tram Route

GUANGZHOU, CHINA

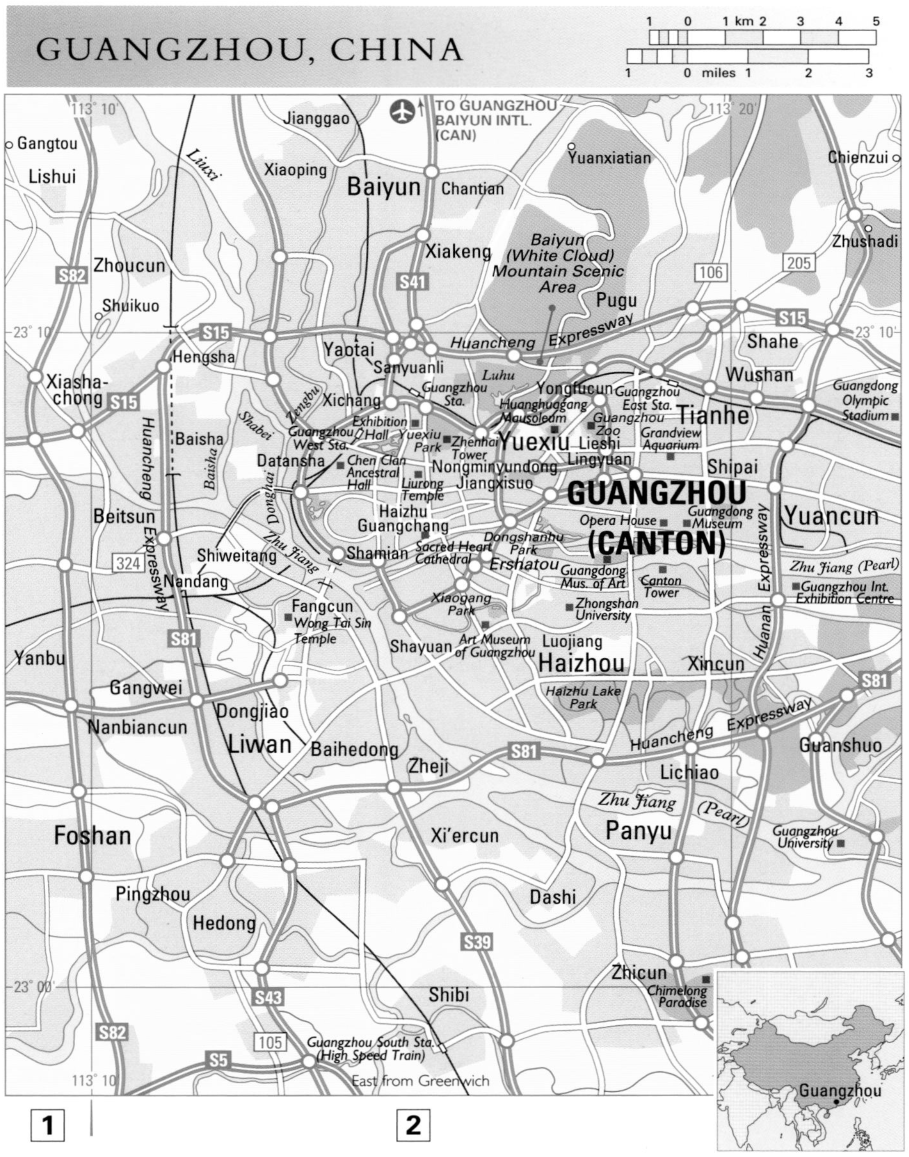

HELSINKI, FINLAND

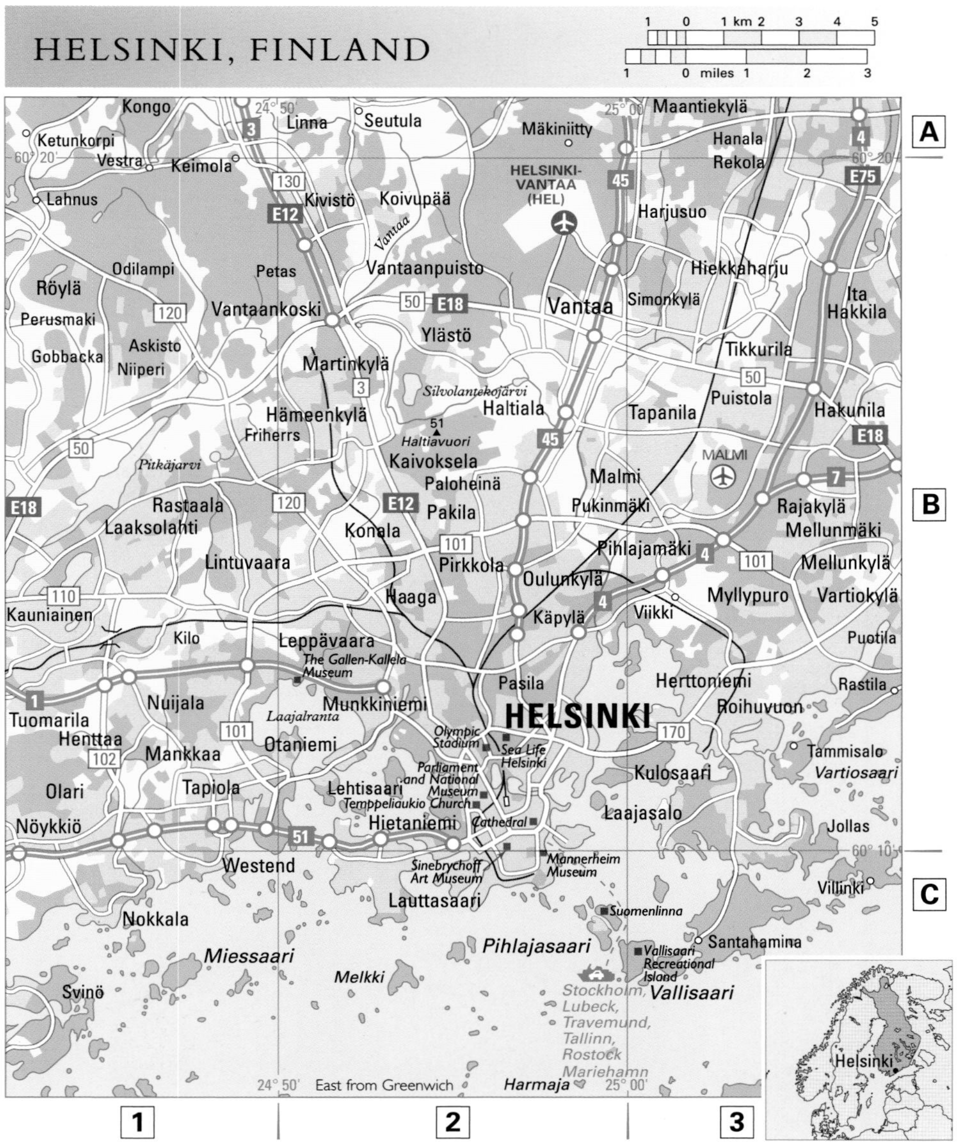

HONG KONG, CHINA

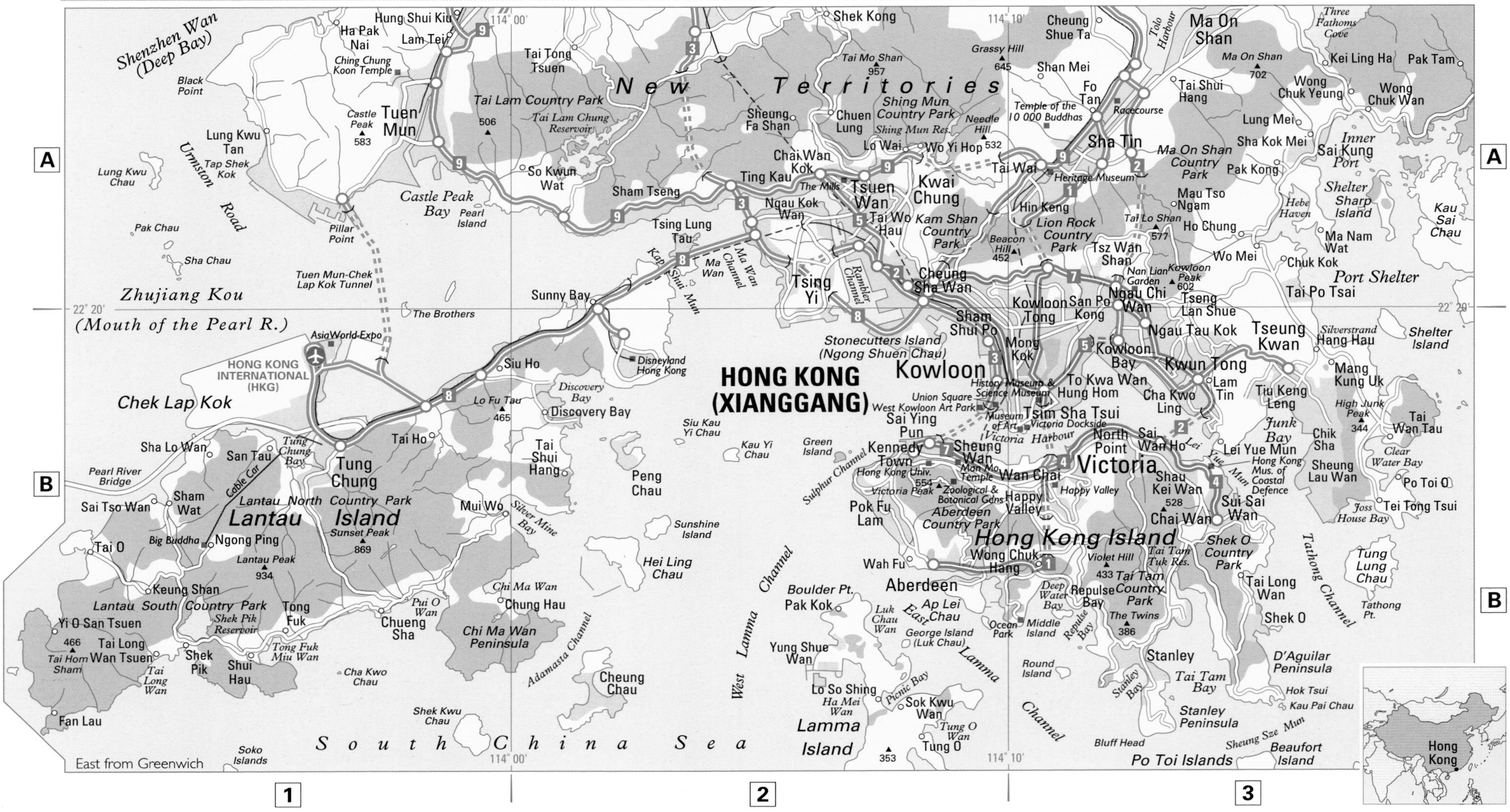

ISTANBUL, TURKEY

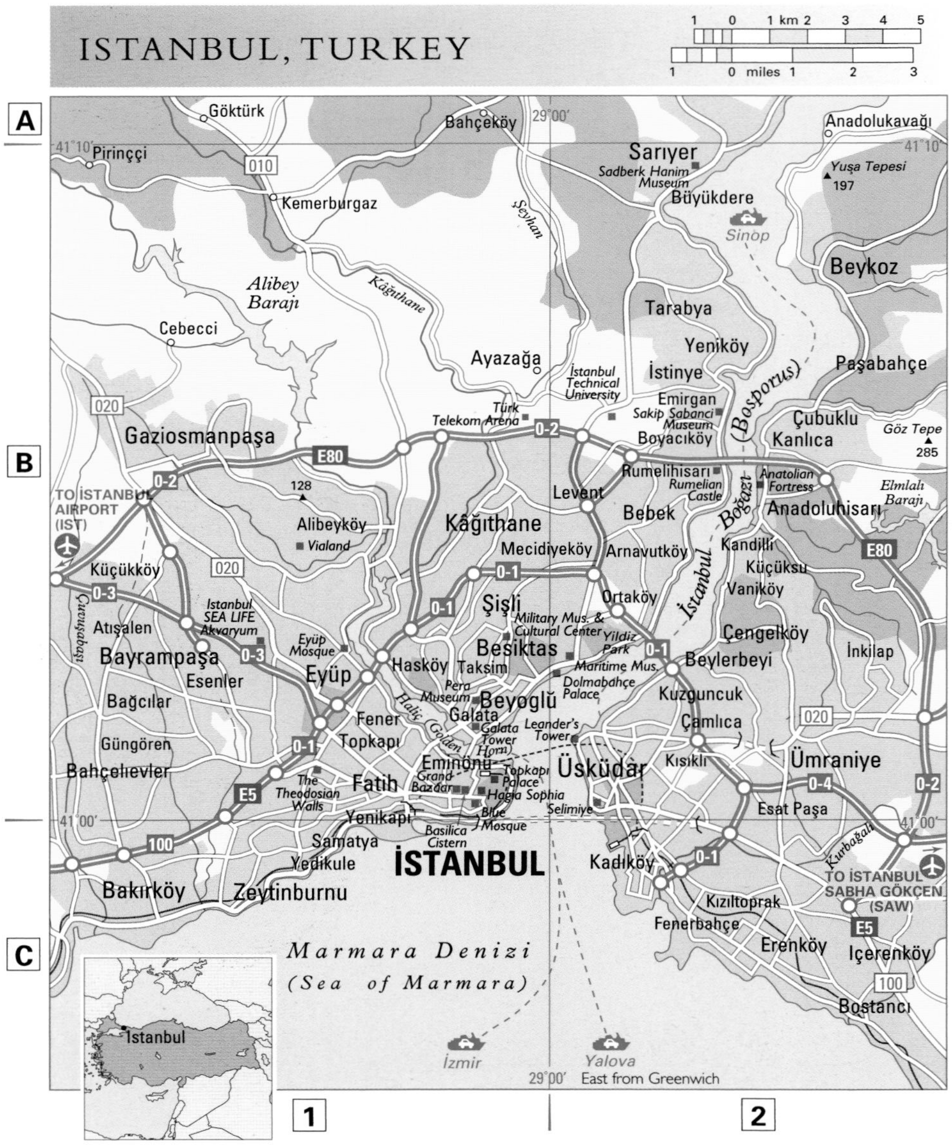

JAKARTA, INDONESIA

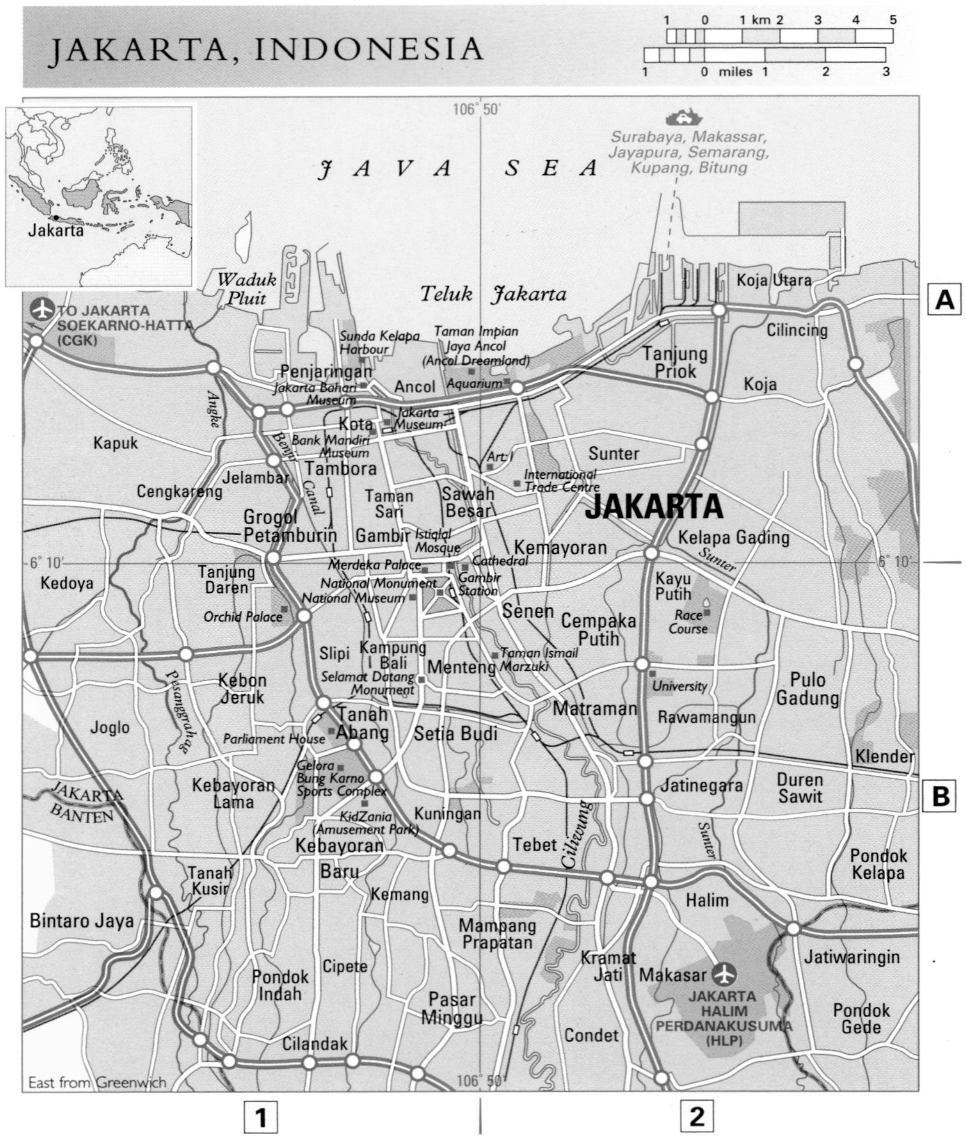

JERUSALEM, ISRAEL / W. BANK

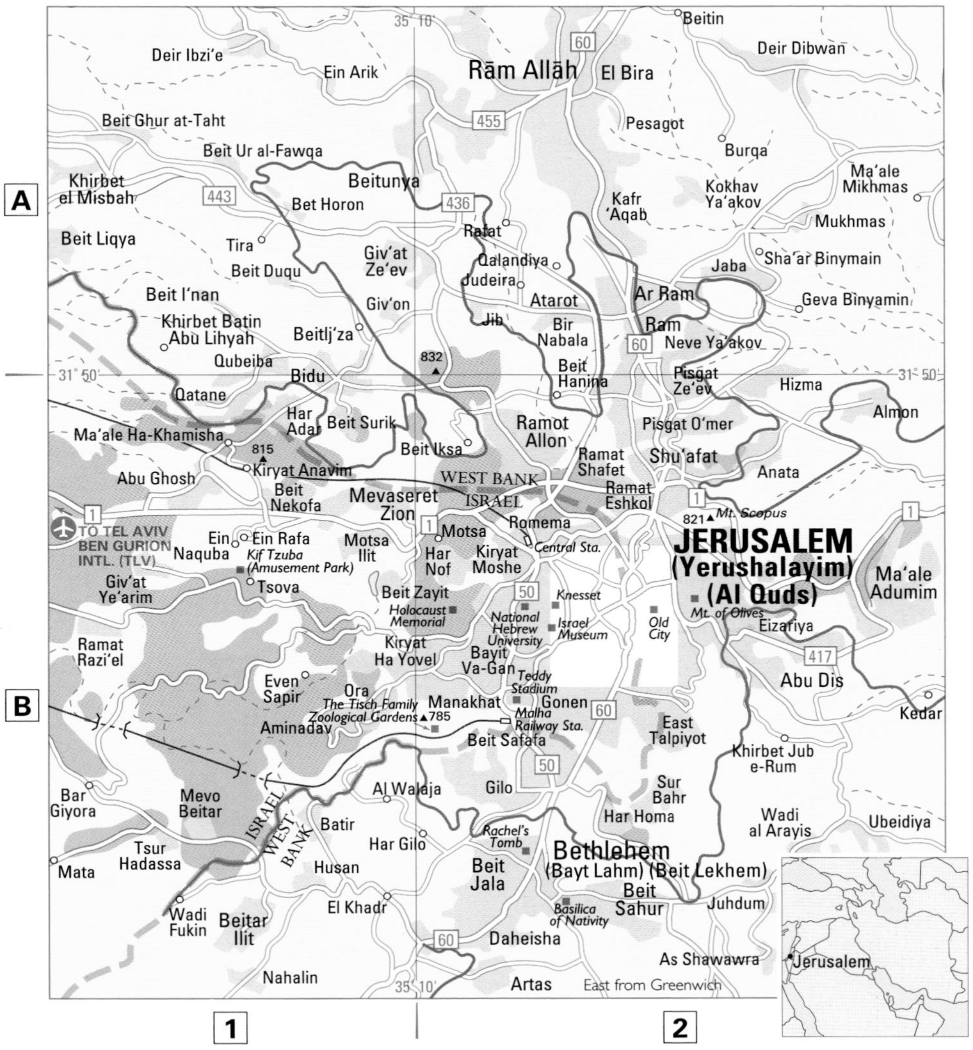

1949 Cease-fire line — Israeli security fence

CENTRAL JERUSALEM

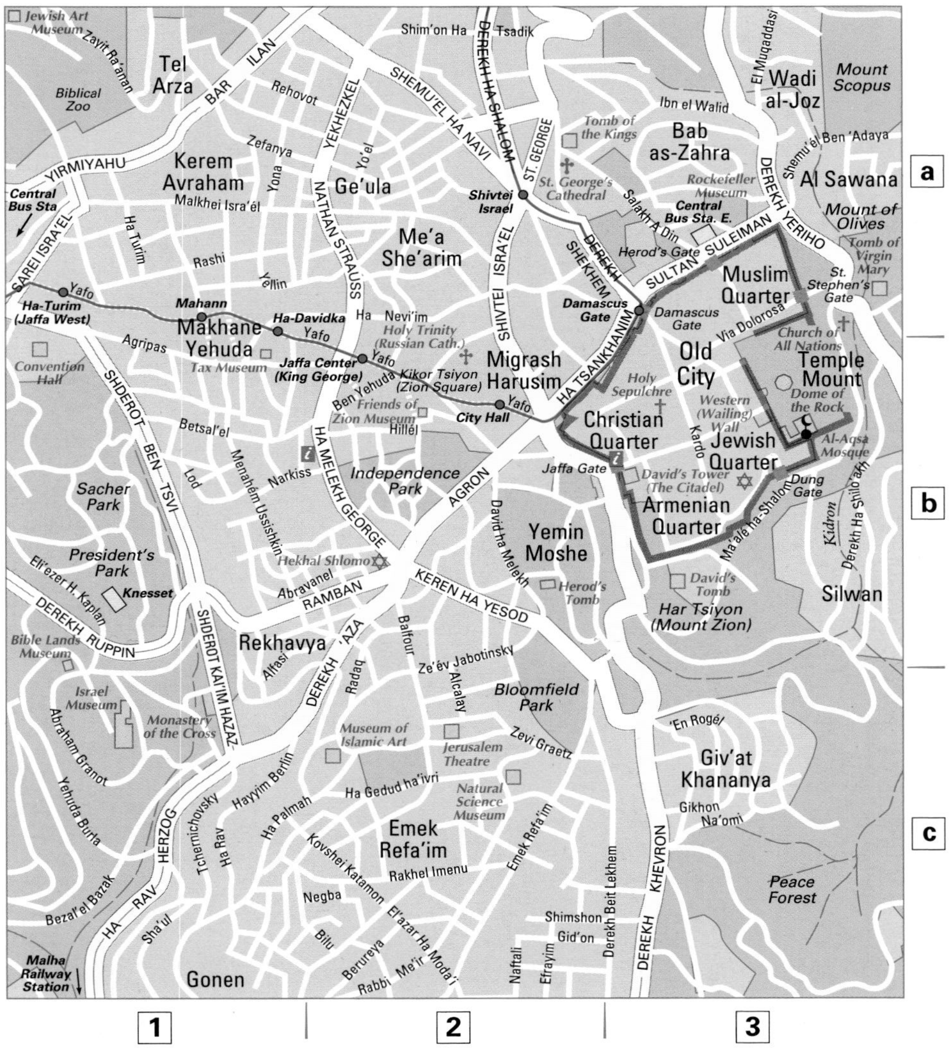

Light Railway

JOHANNESBURG, S. AFRICA

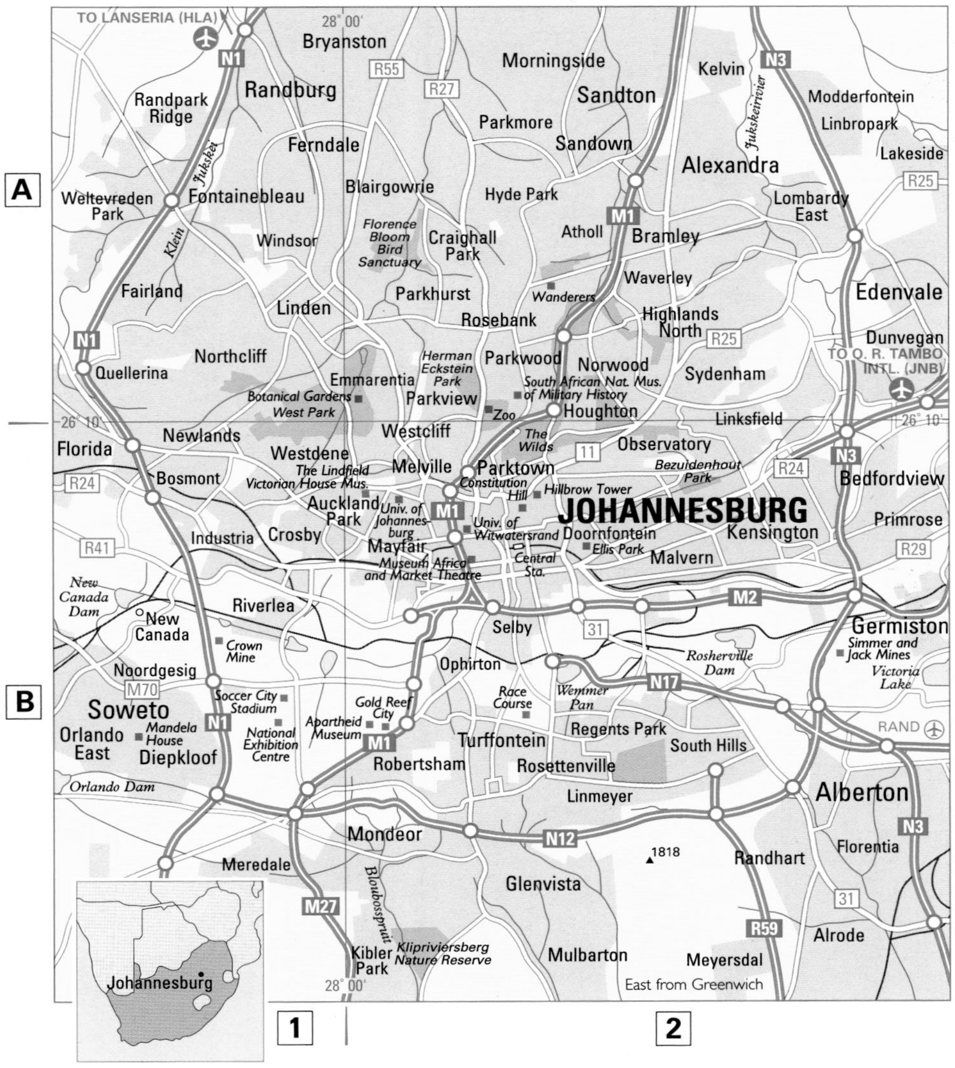

KARACHI, PAKISTAN

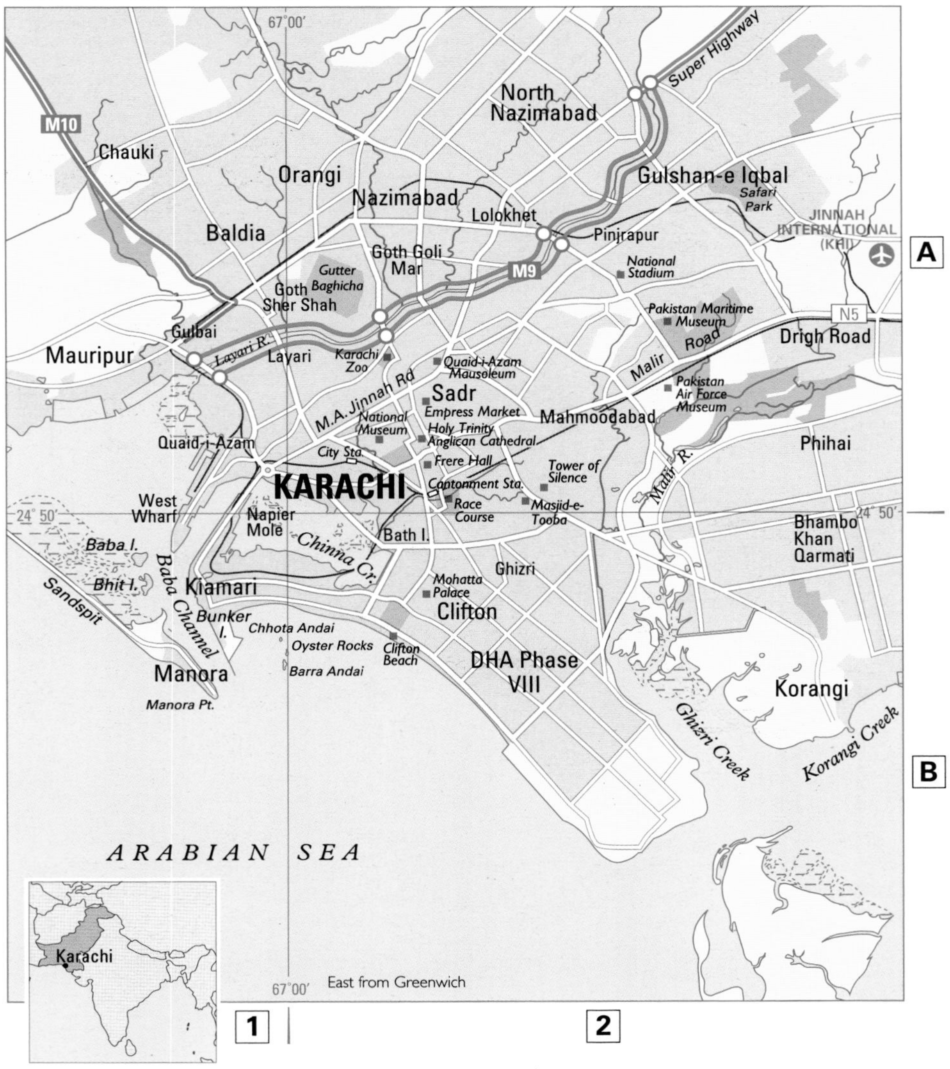

KOLKATA, INDIA

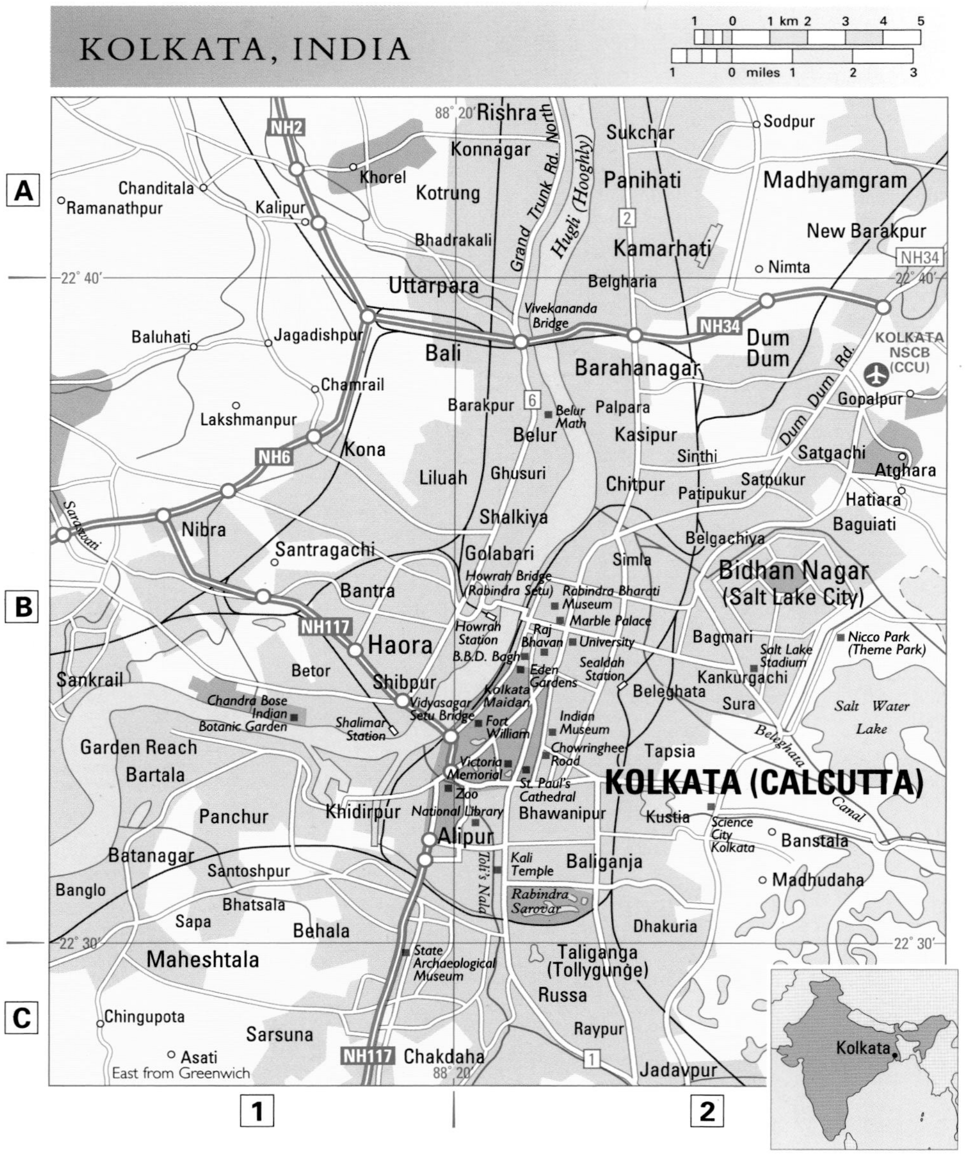

LAGOS, NIGERIA

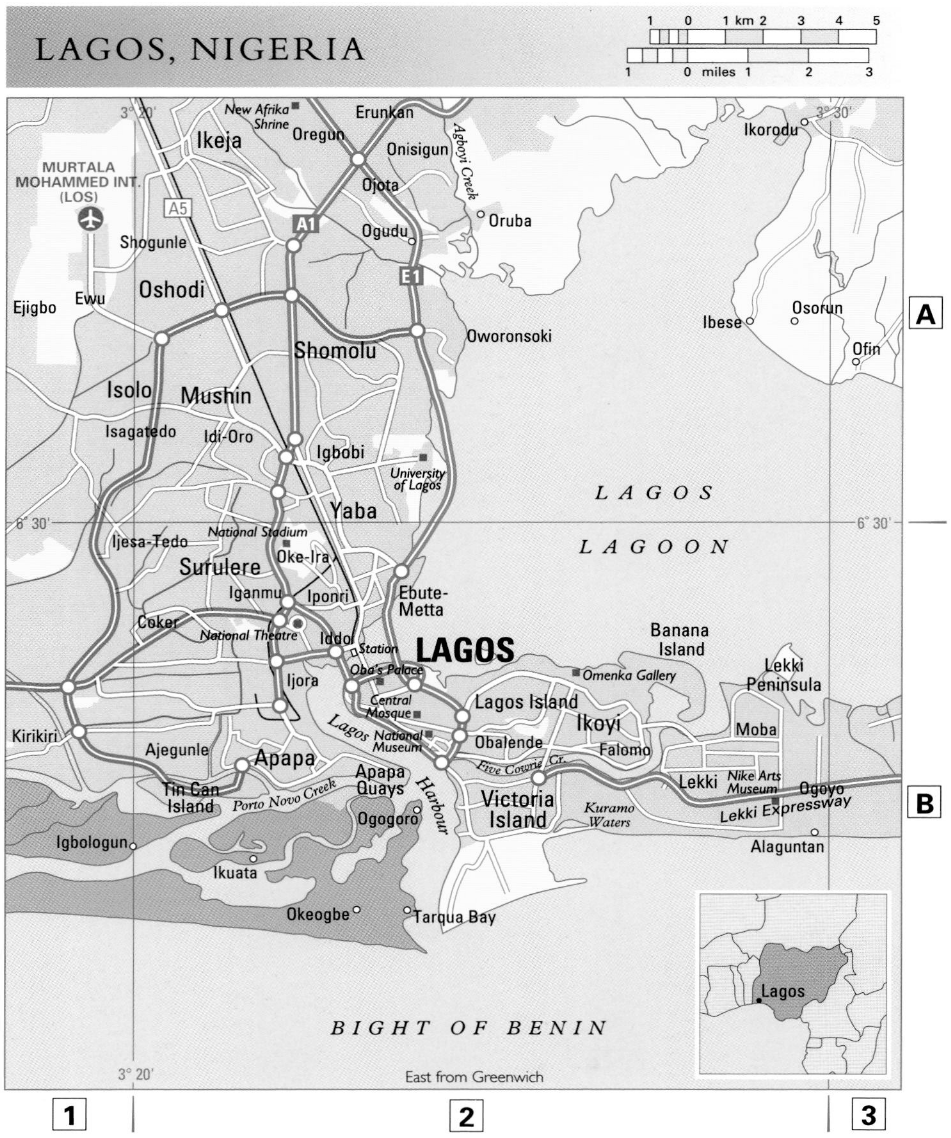

LAS VEGAS, NEVADA

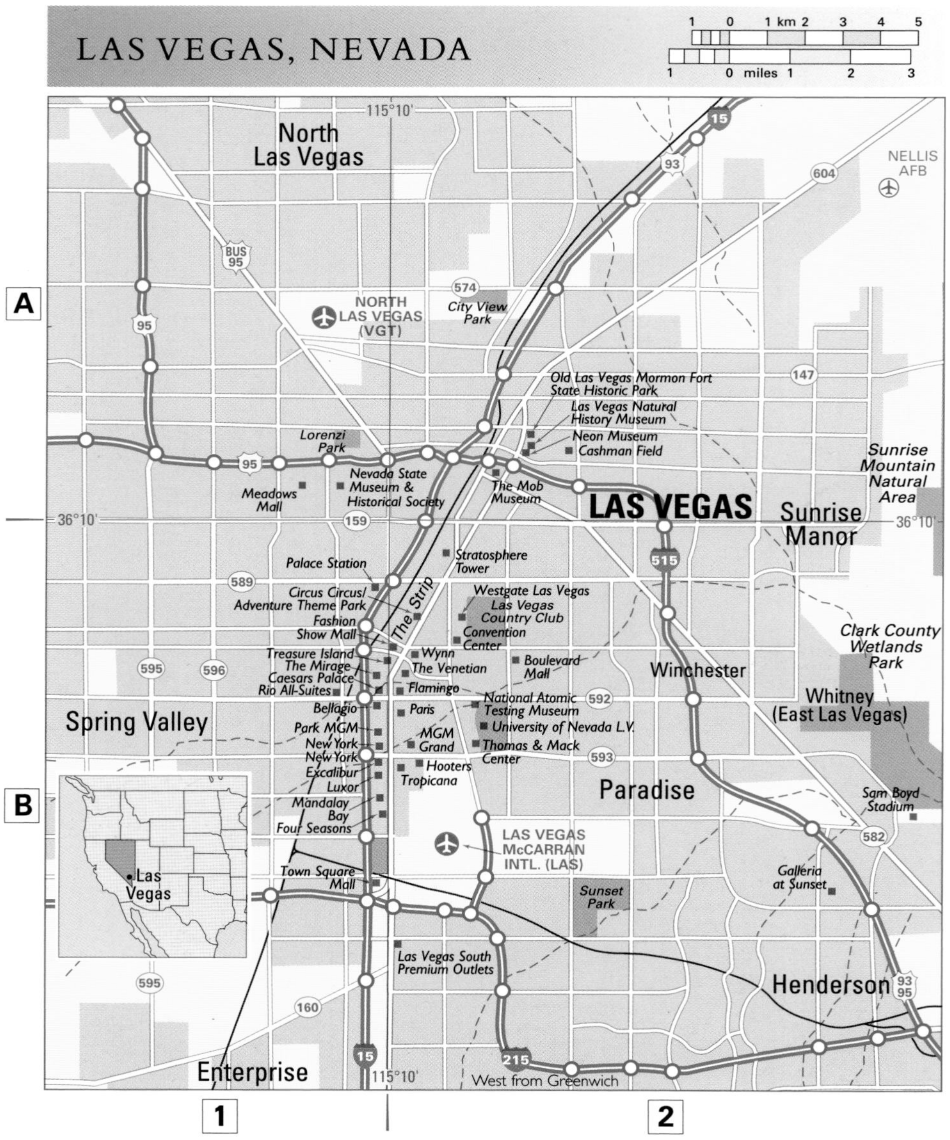

LIMA, PERU

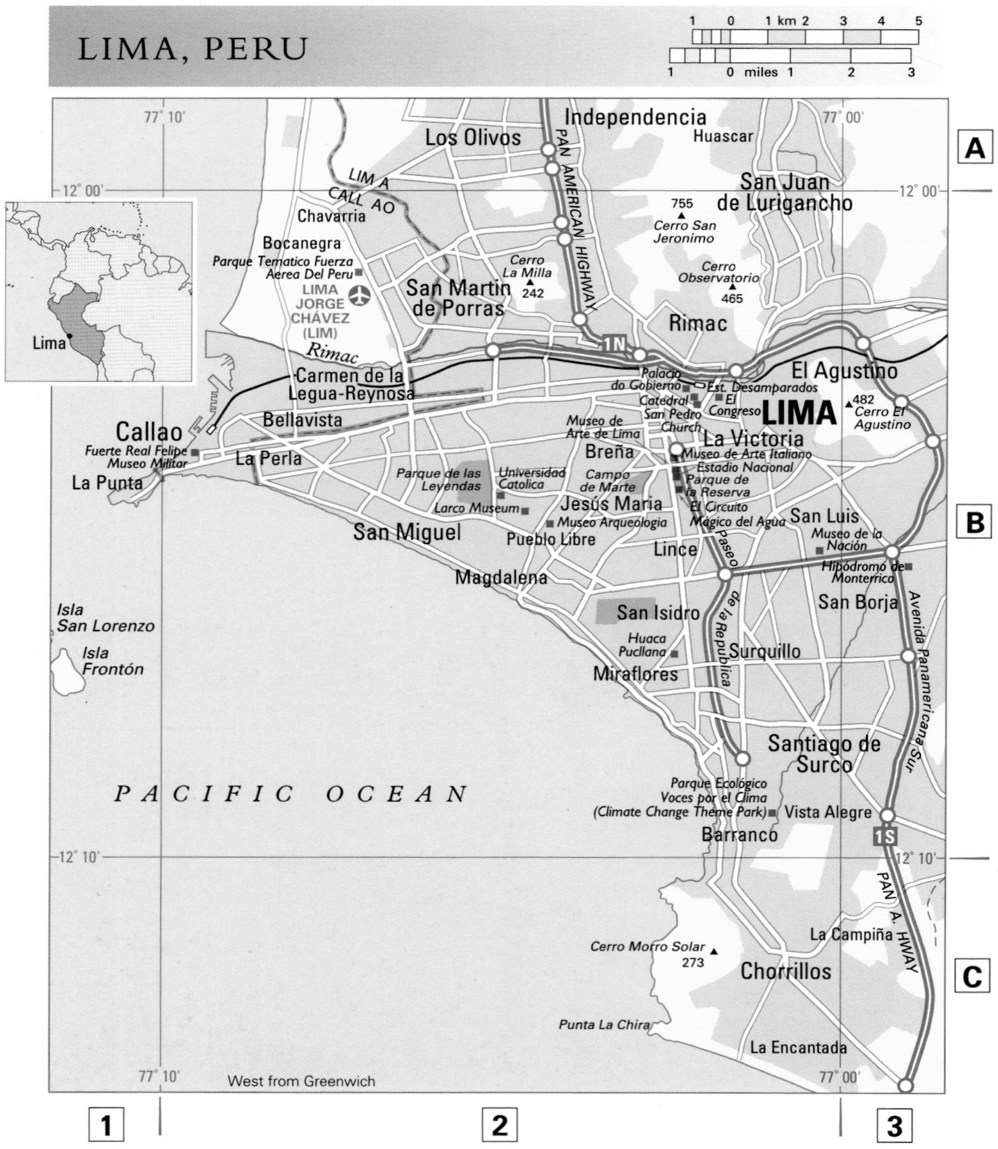

Interstate route numbers · U.S. route numbers · State route numbers

LONDON, U.K.

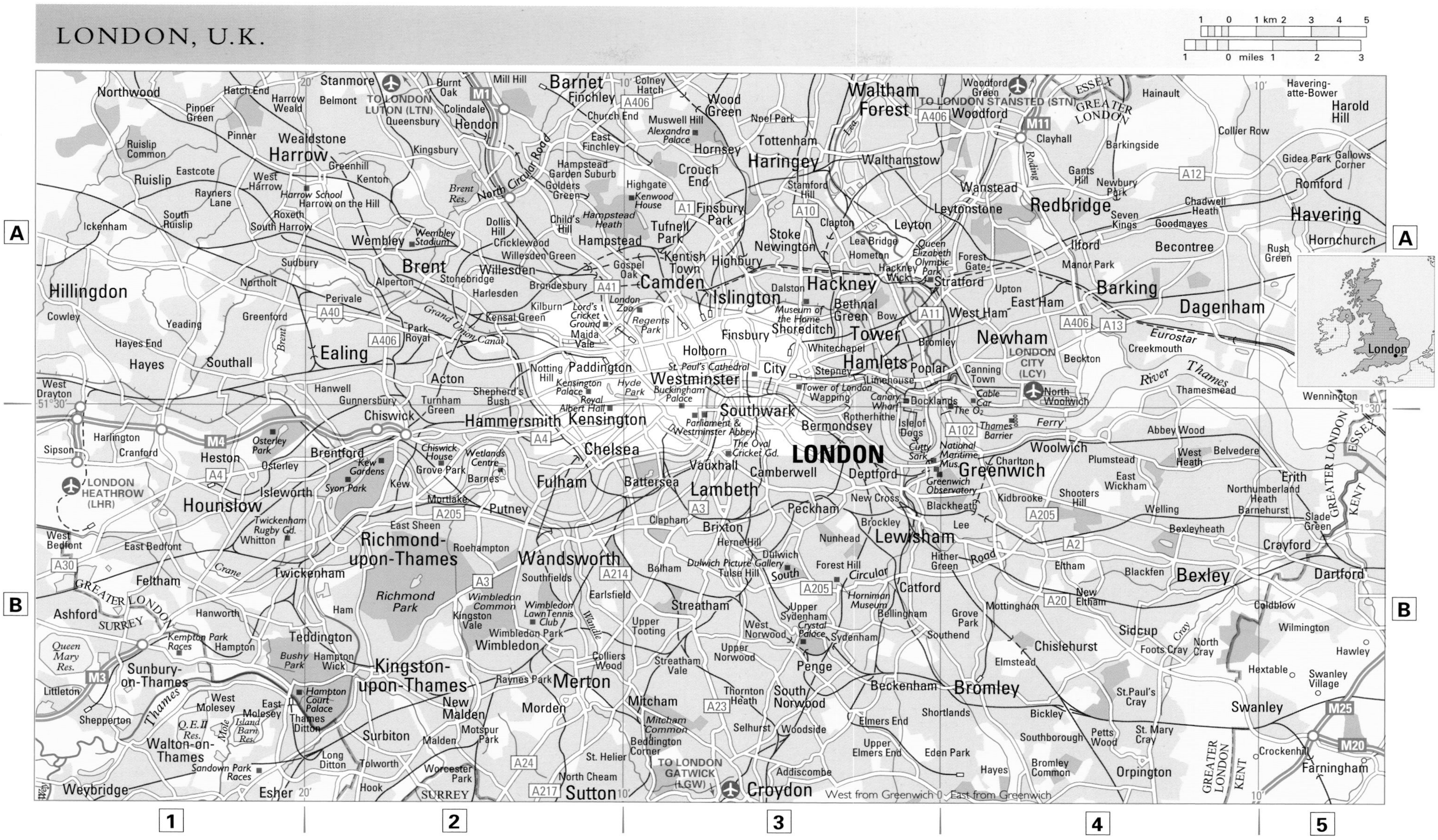

CENTRAL LONDON

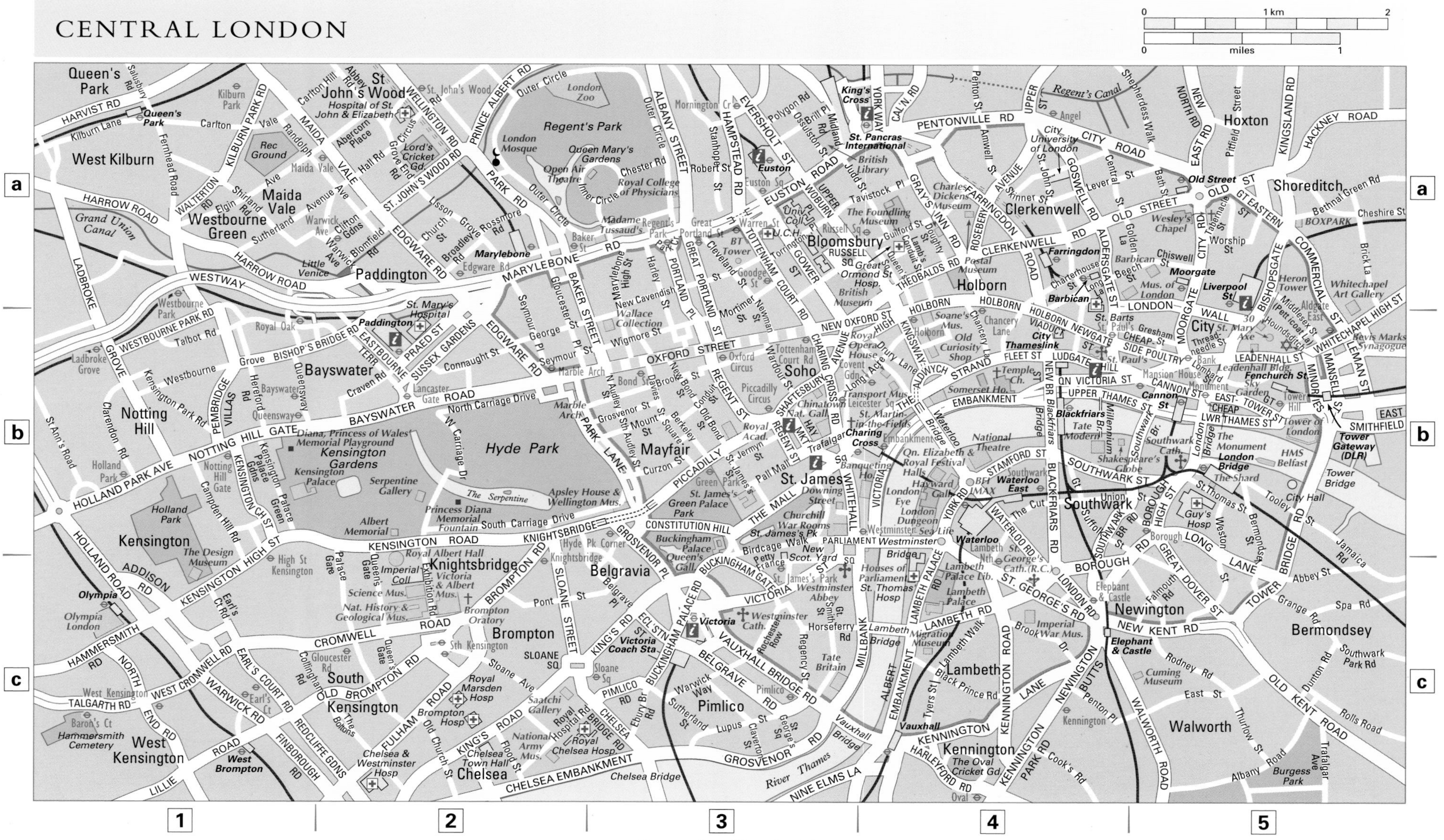

Congestion Charging Zone

LISBON, PORTUGAL

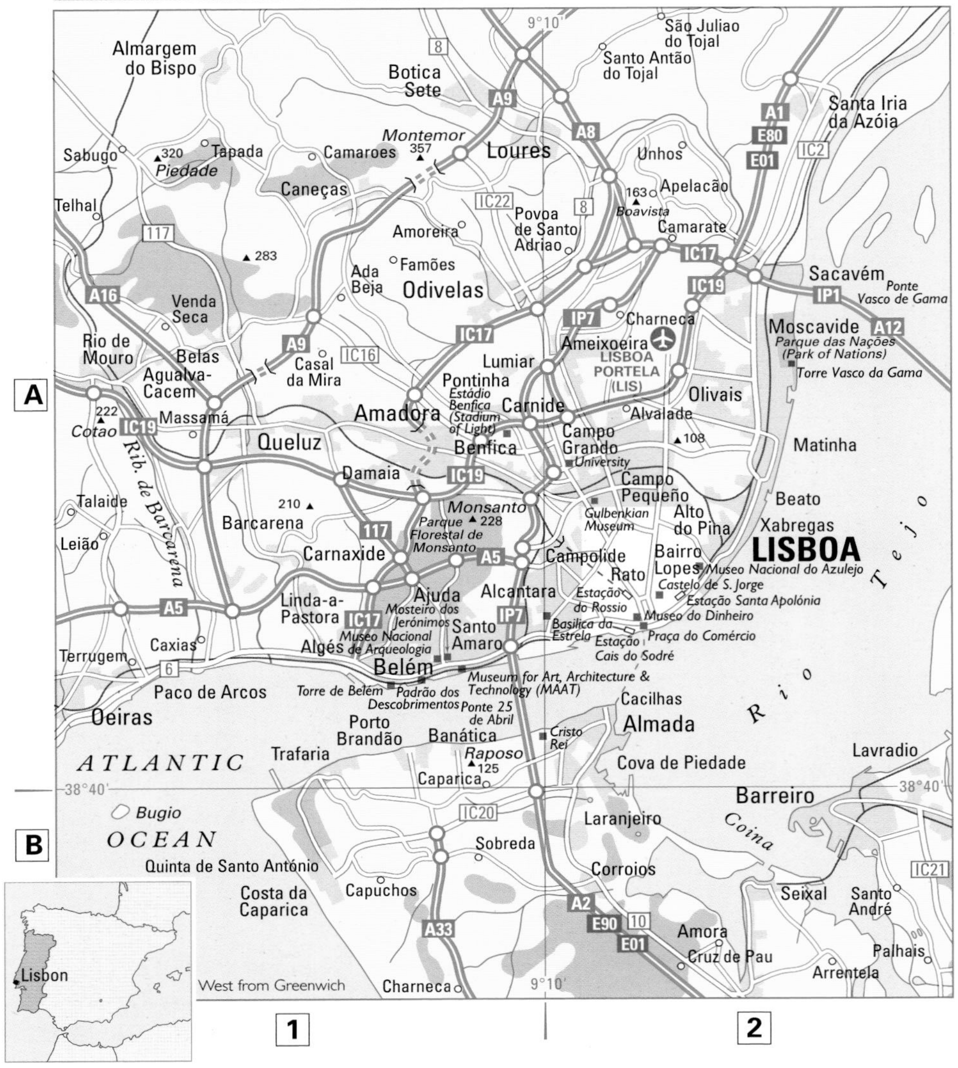

CENTRAL LISBON

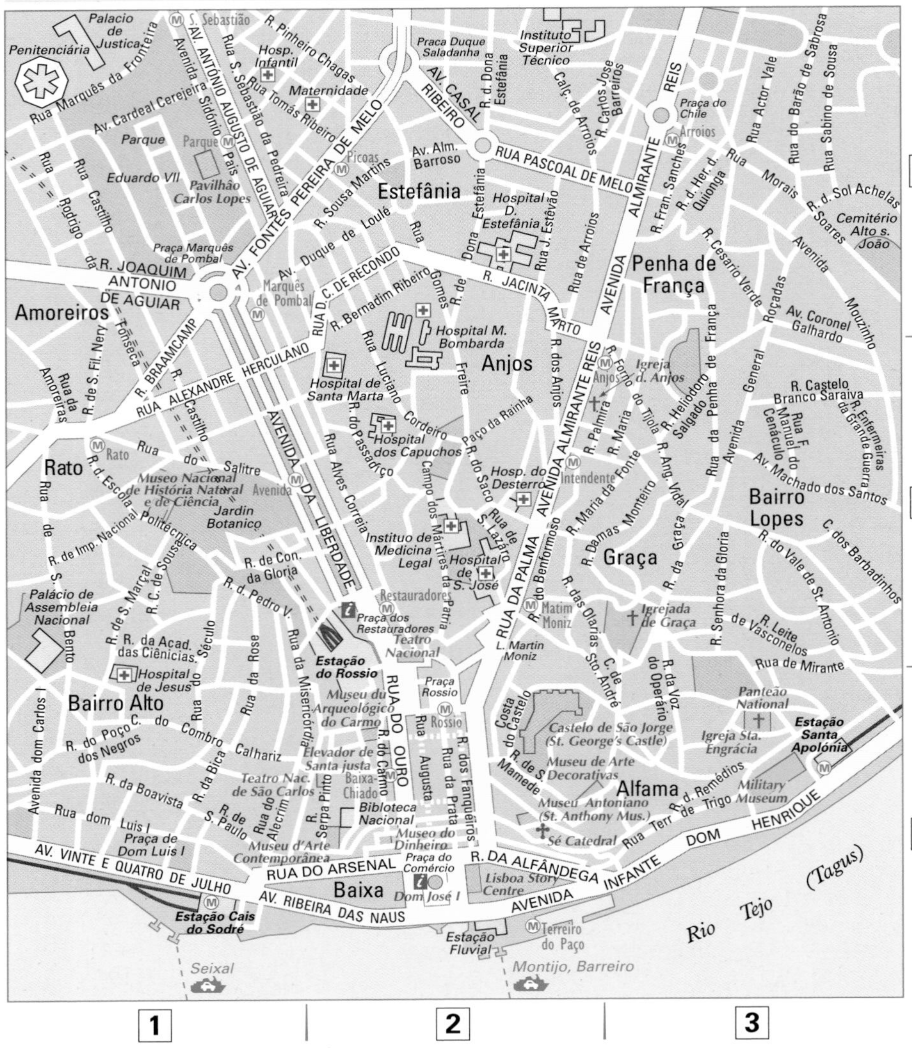

LOS ANGELES, CALIFORNIA

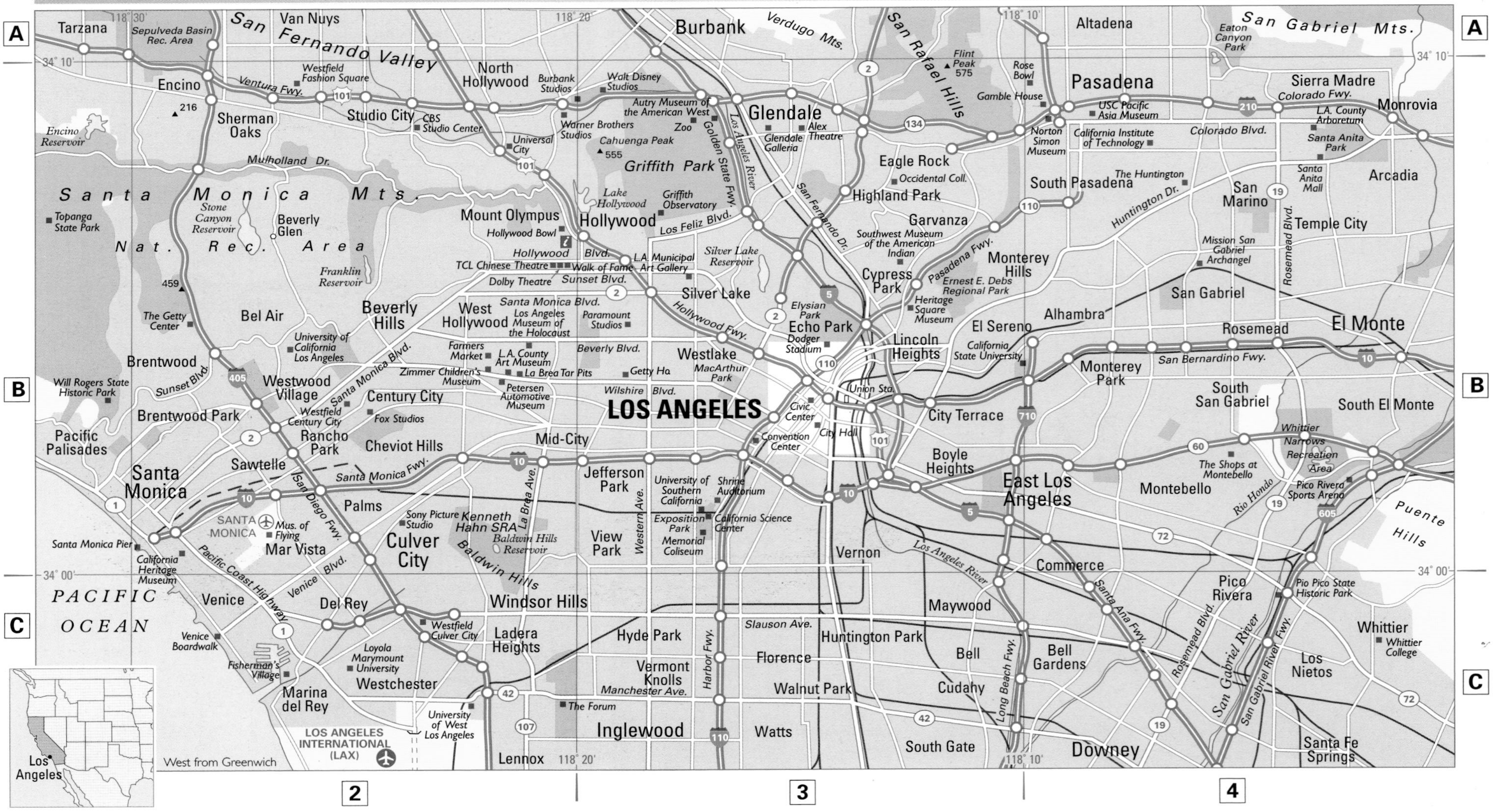

Interstate route numbers U.S. route numbers State route numbers

MADRID, SPAIN

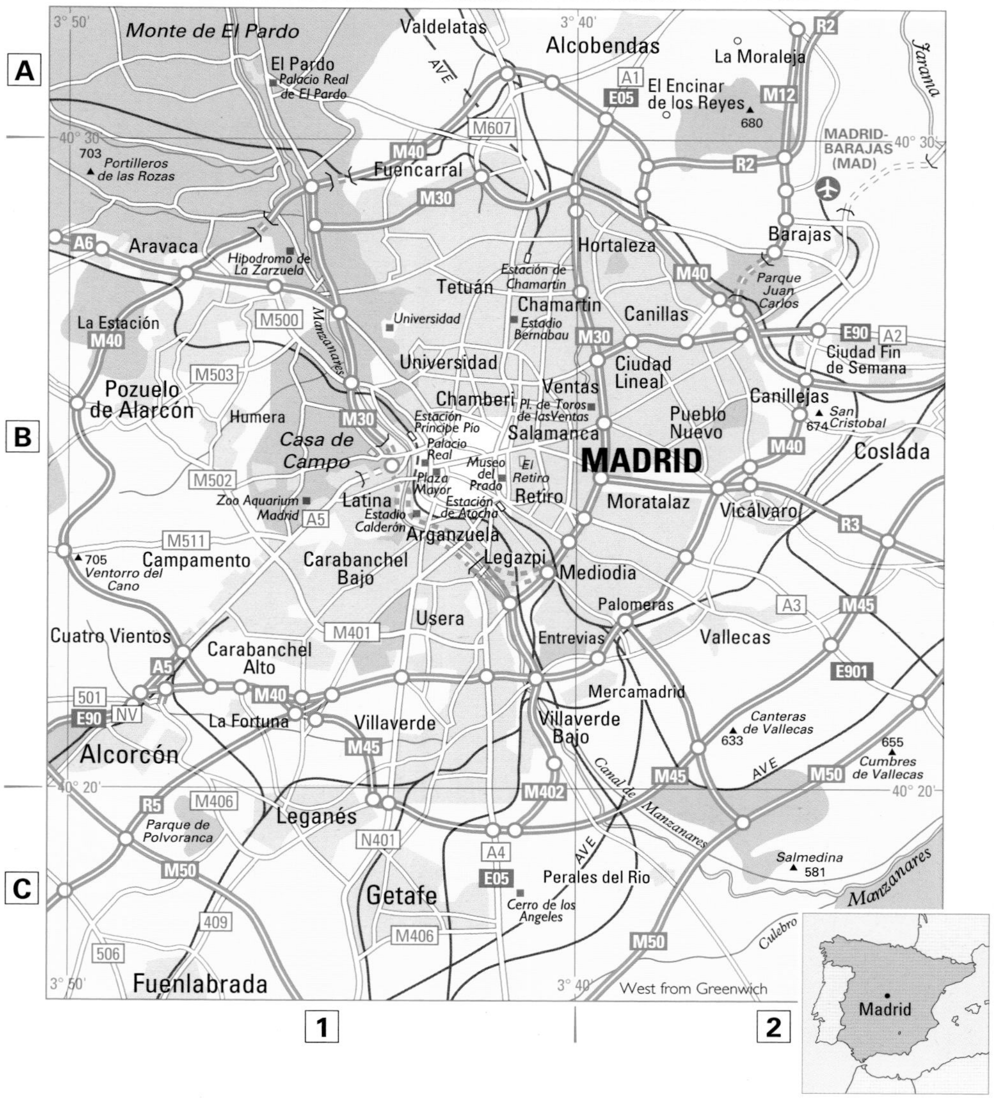

CENTRAL MADRID

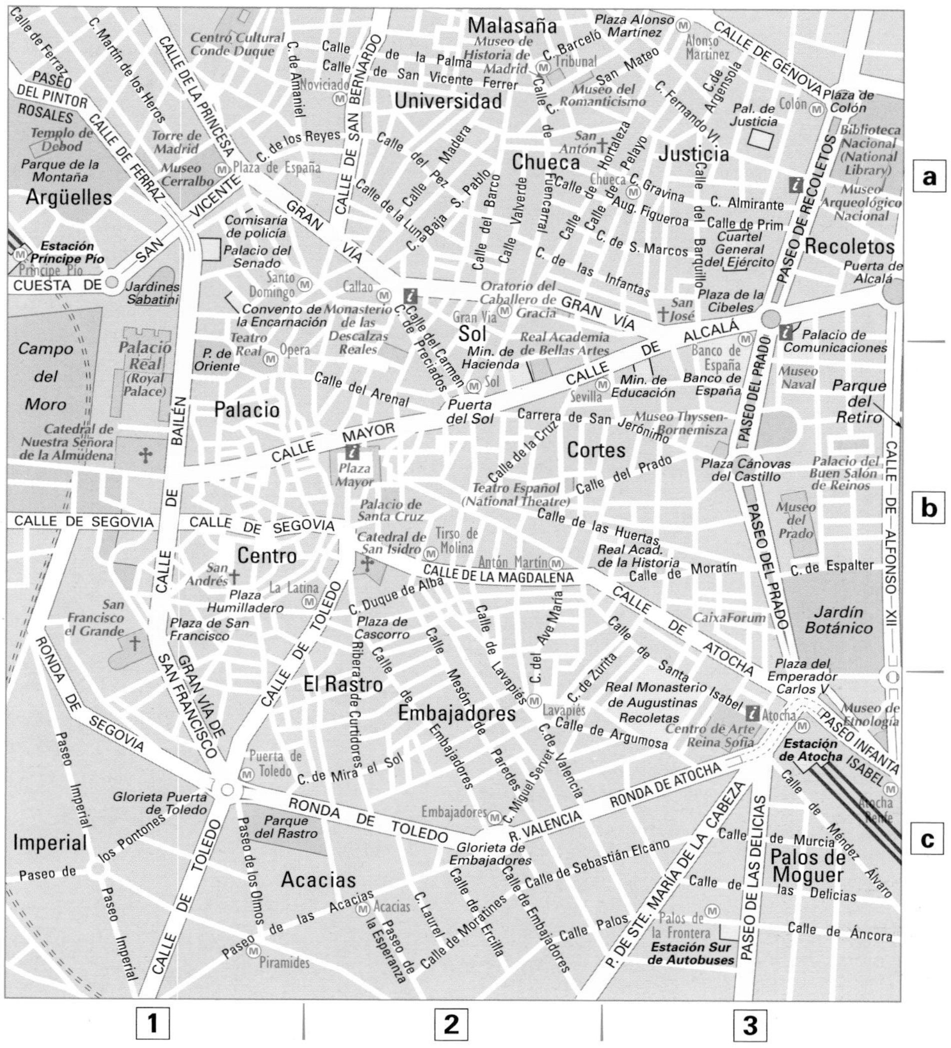

CENTRAL LOS ANGELES

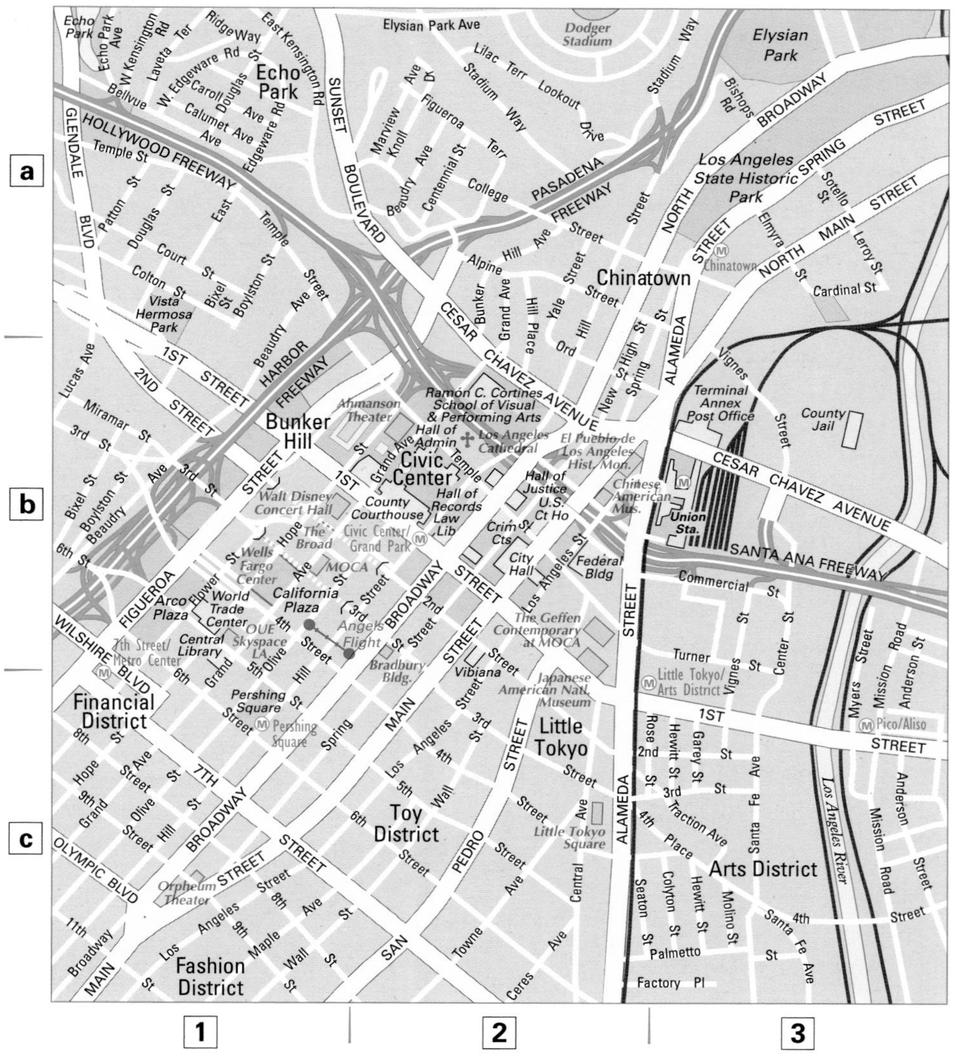

MANILA, PHILIPPINES

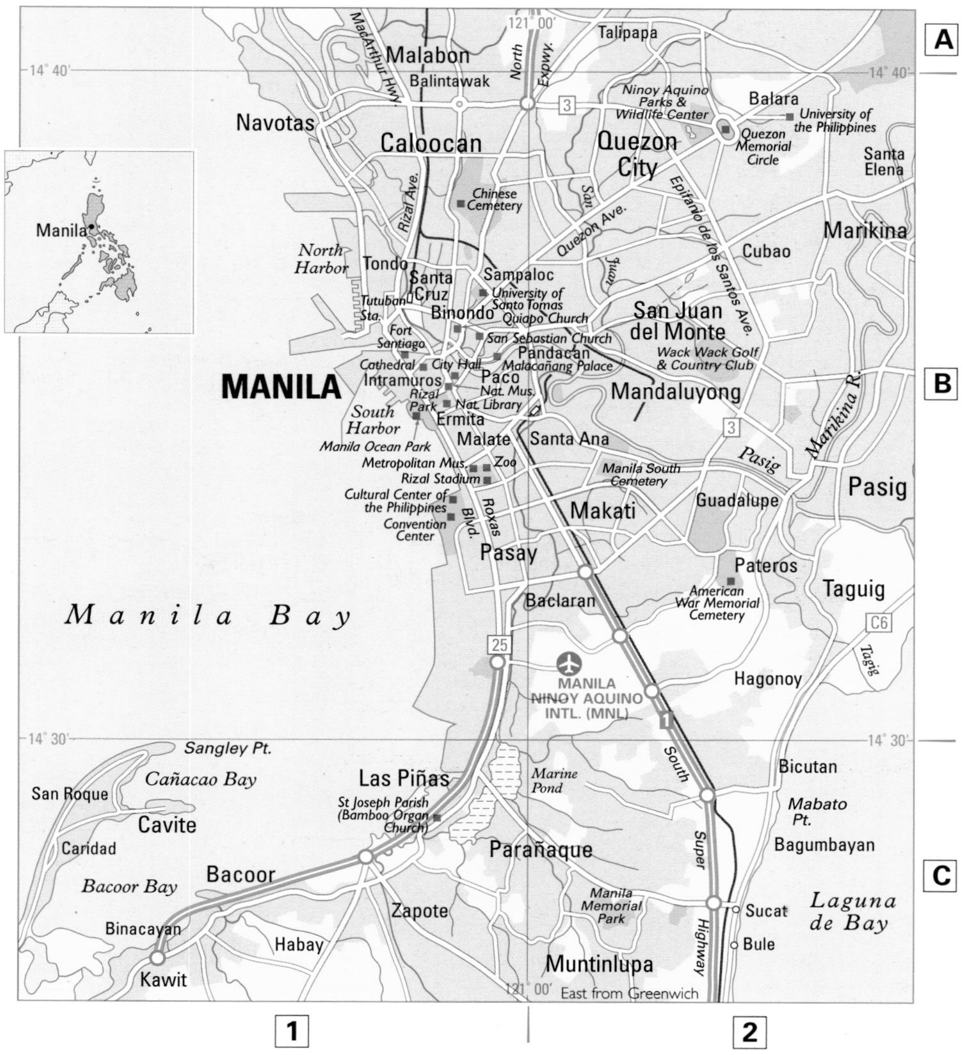

MEXICO CITY, MEXICO

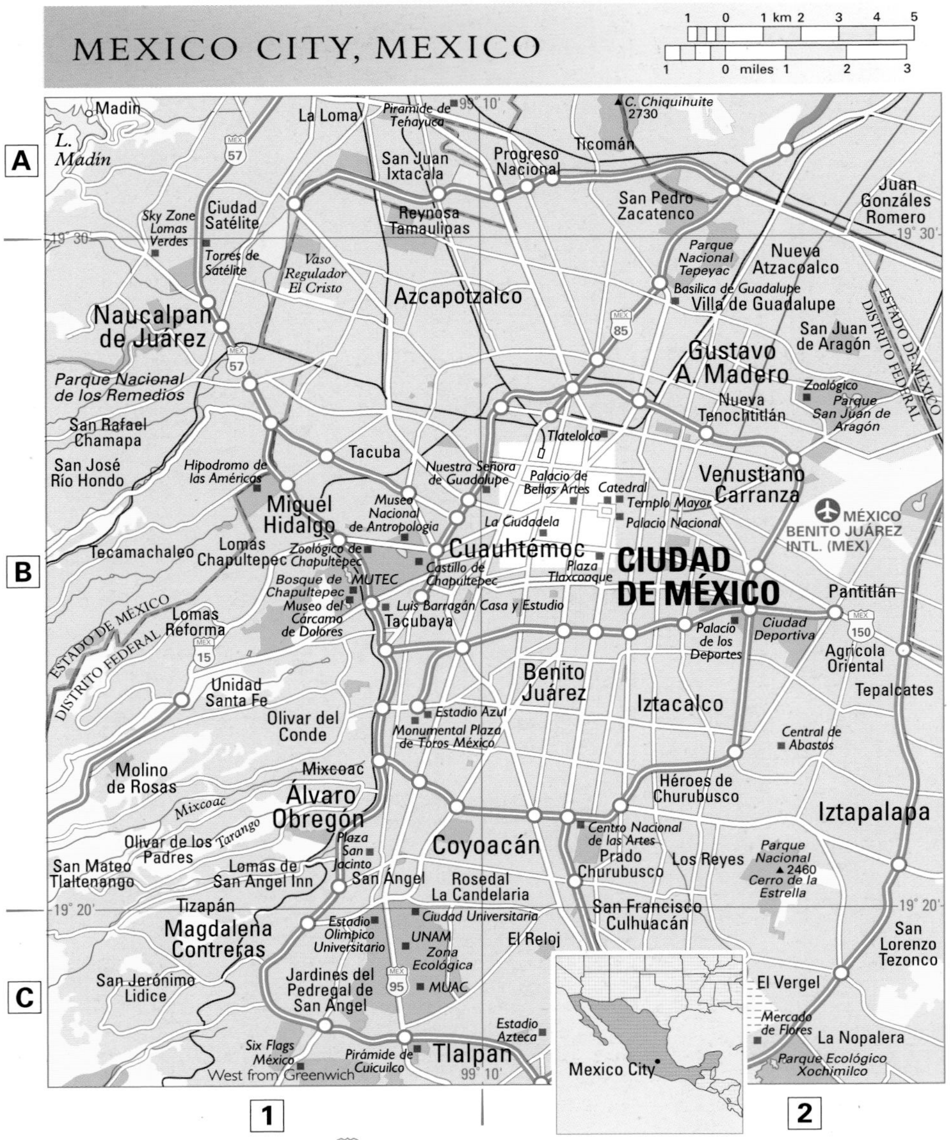

Federal route numbers

CENTRAL MEXICO CITY

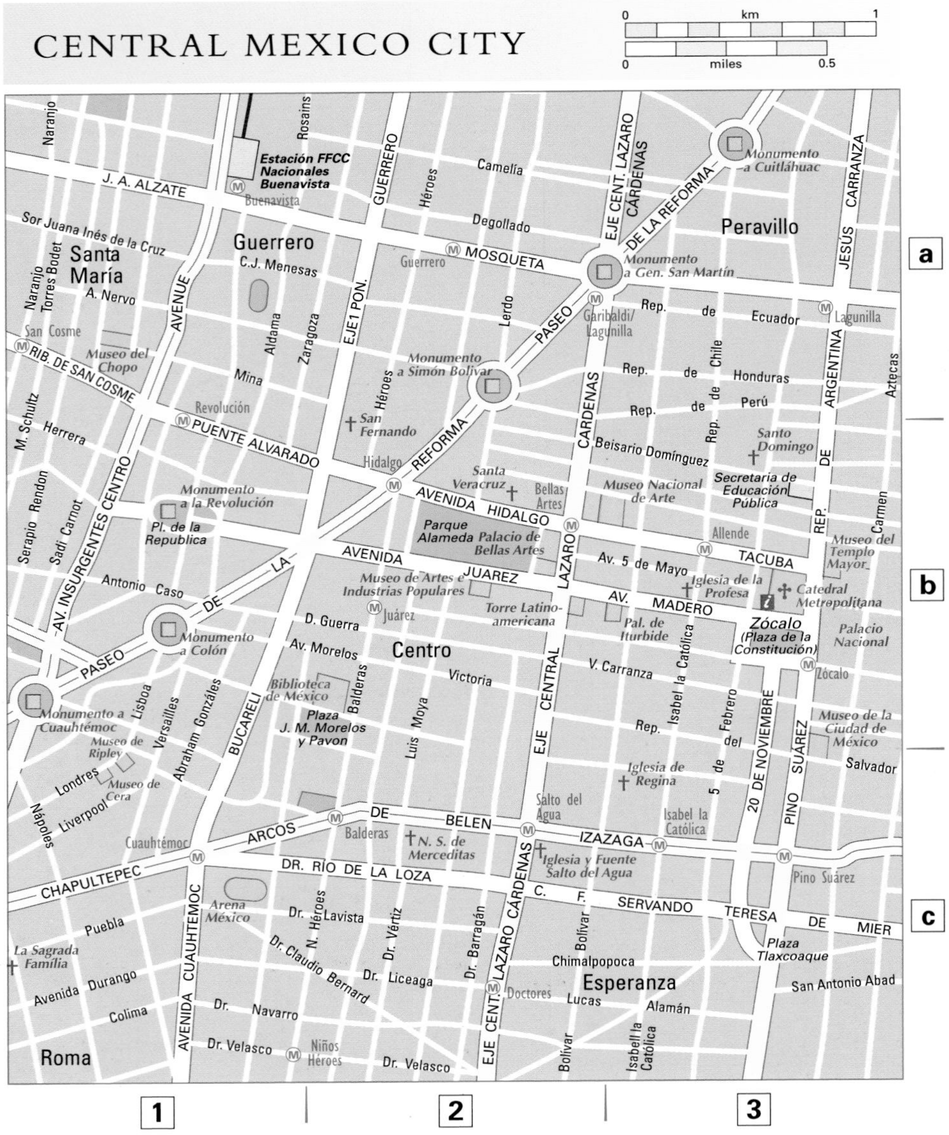

MELBOURNE, AUSTRALIA

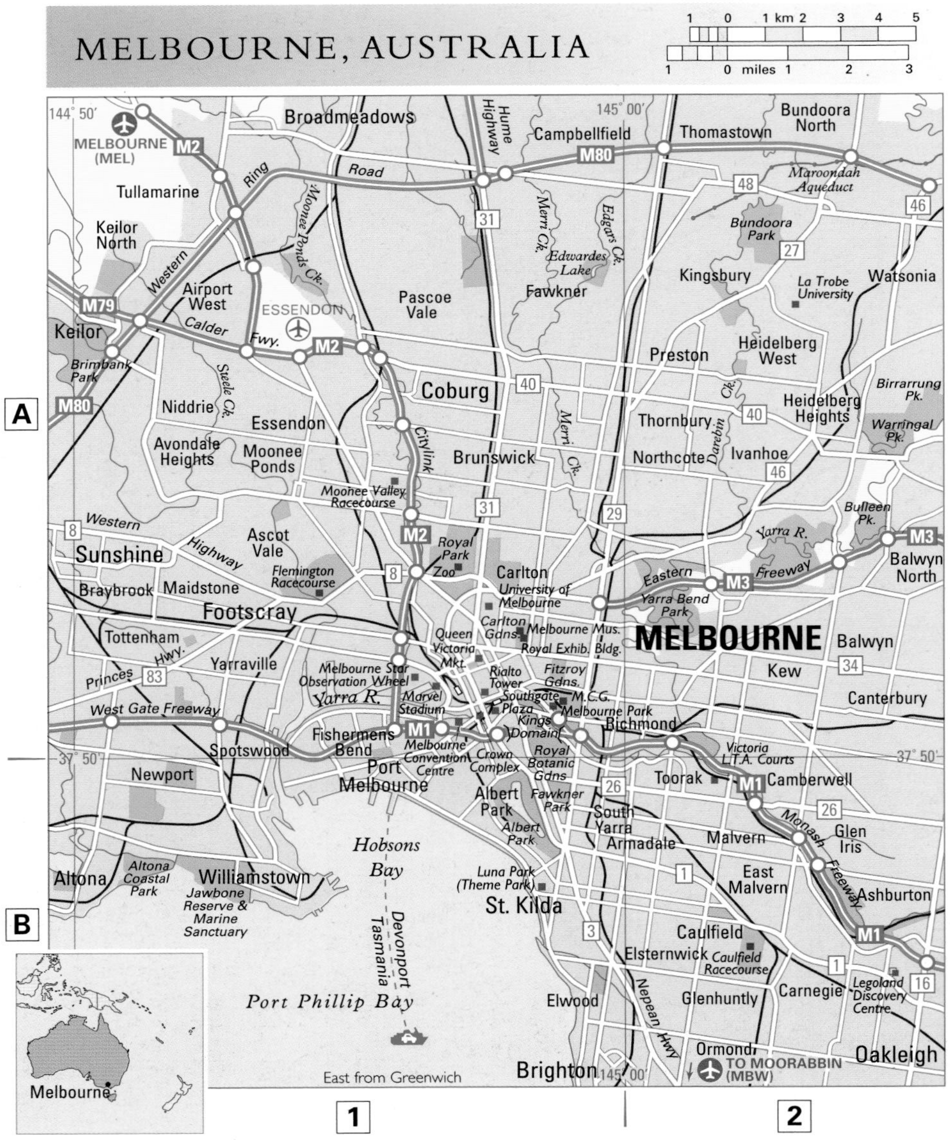

MILAN, ITALY

MIAMI, FLORIDA

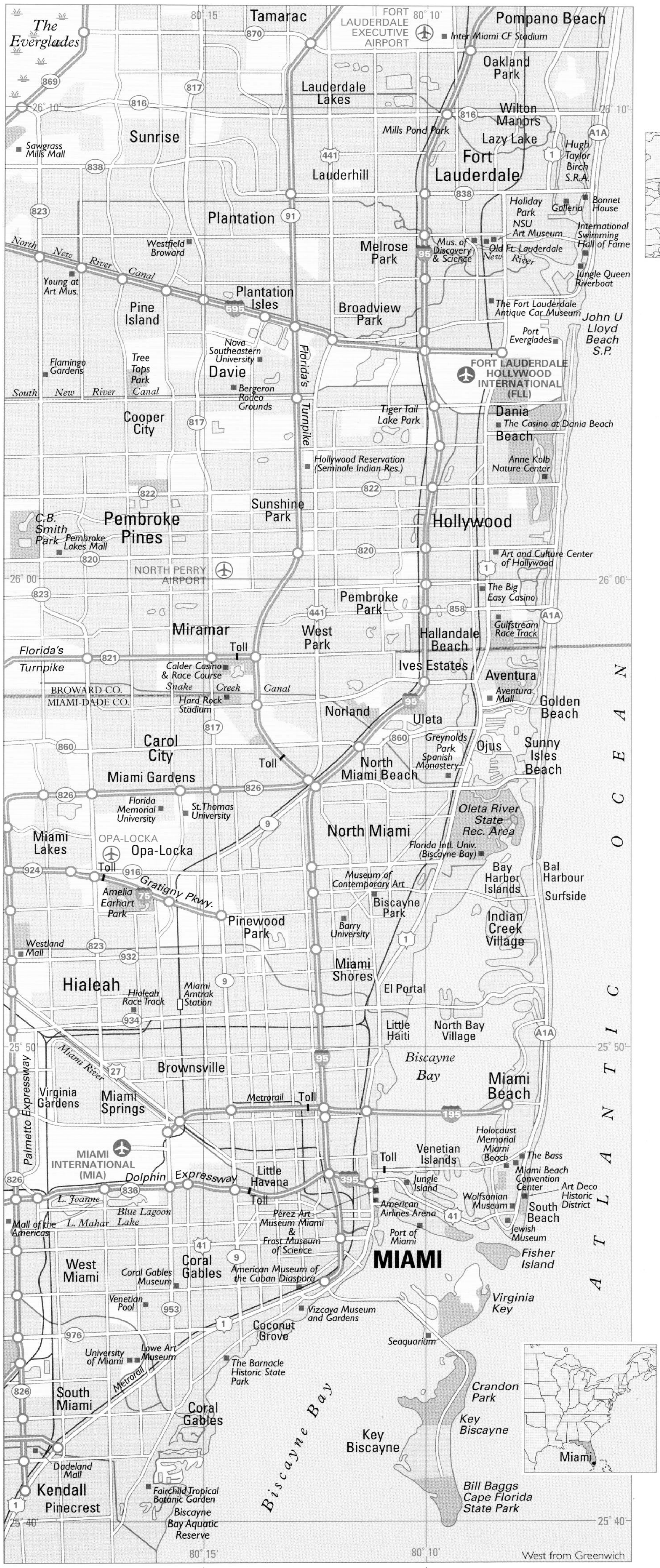

Interstate route numbers   U.S. route numbers   State route numbers

MOSCOW, RUSSIA

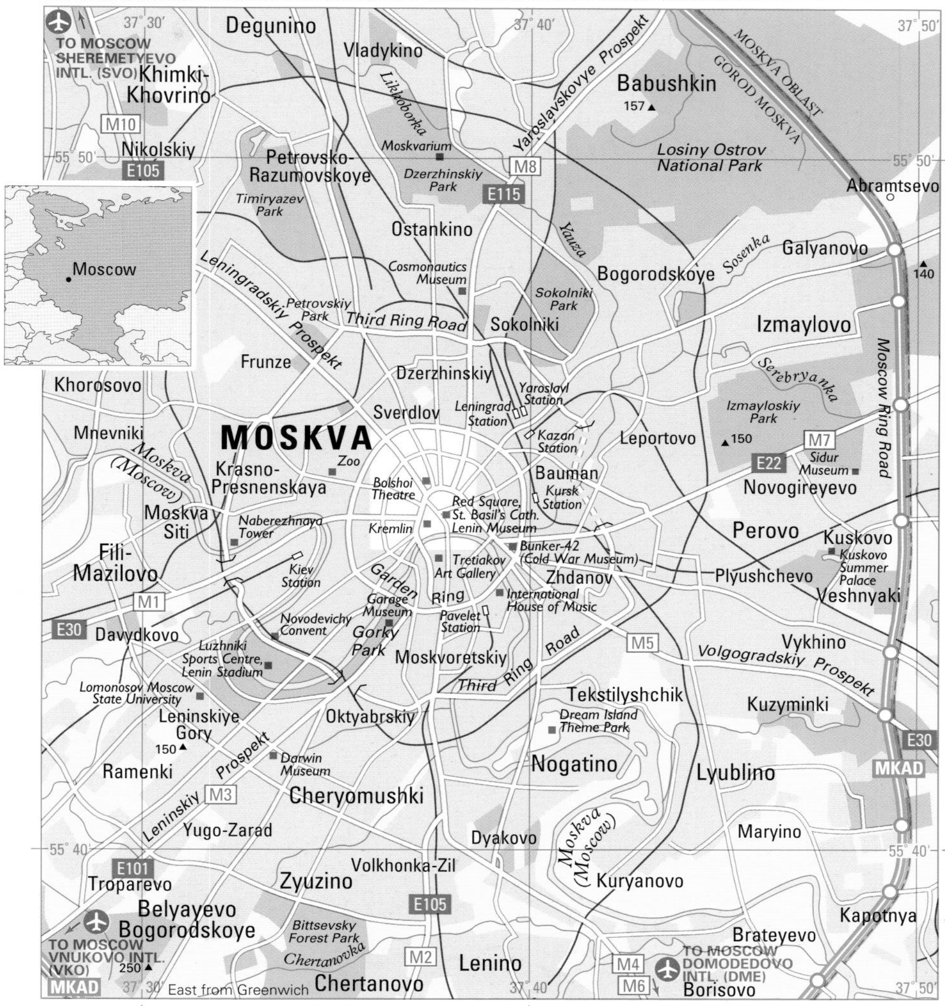

CENTRAL MOSCOW

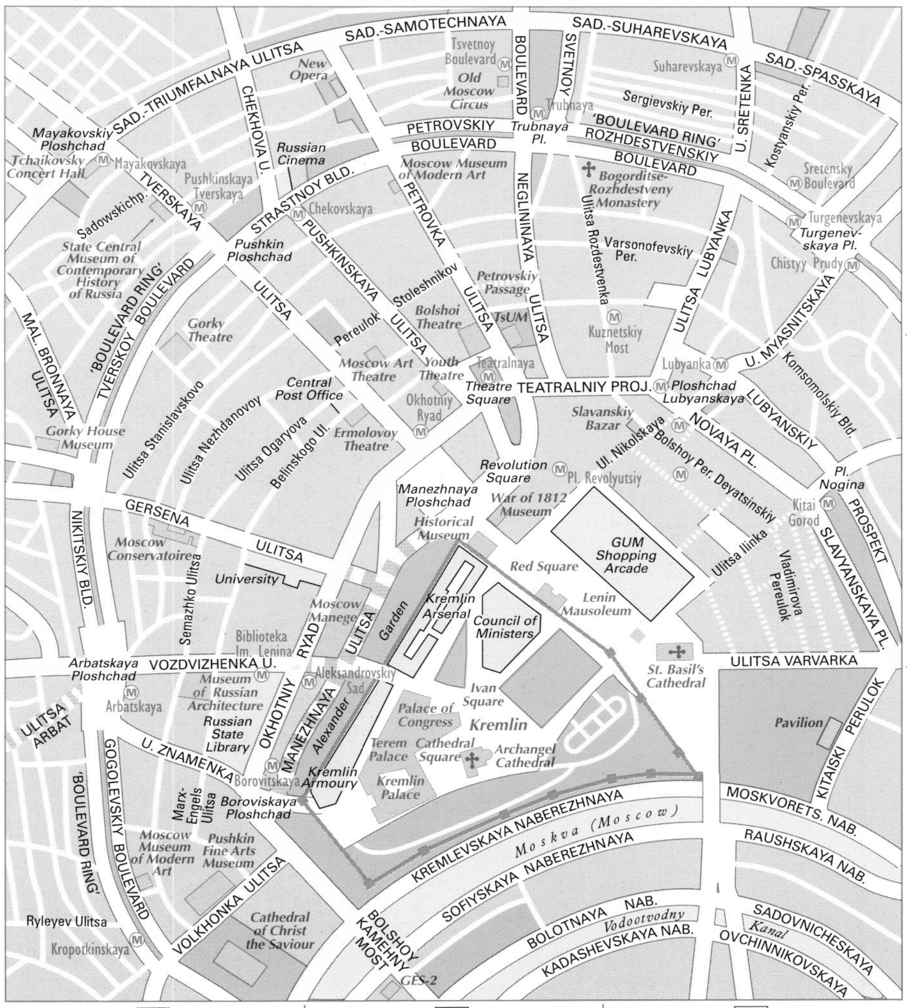

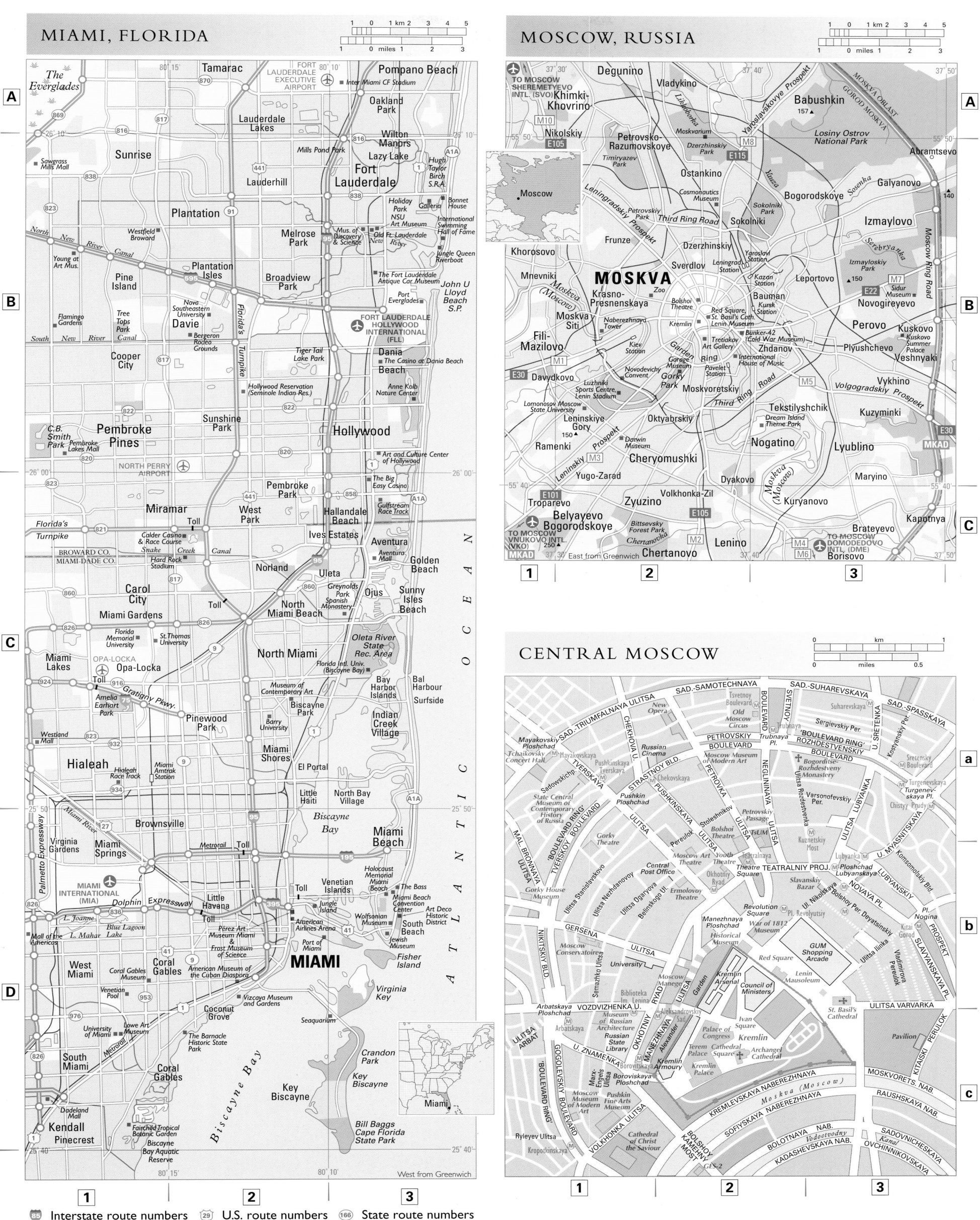

MONTRÉAL, CANADA

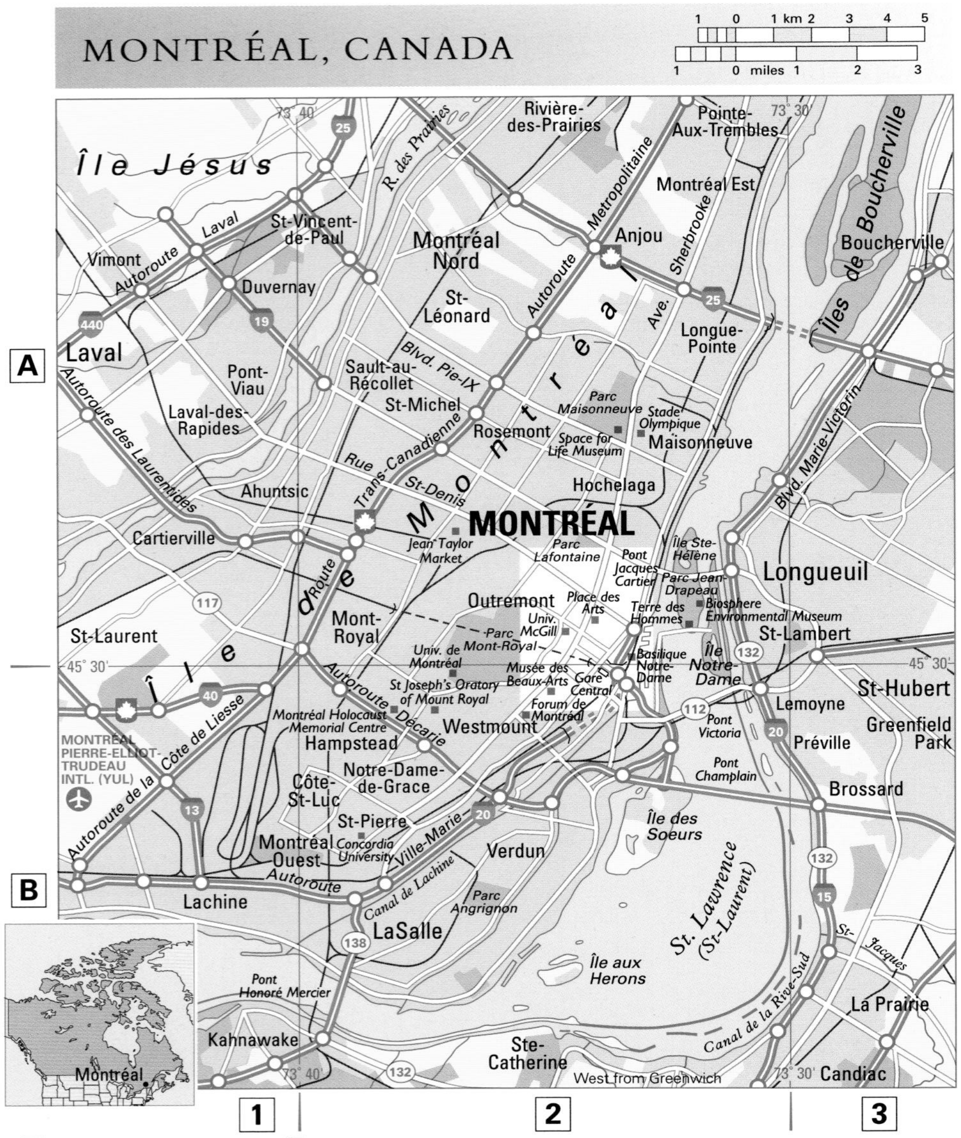

Trans-Canada route   13 Canadian autoroute numbers   166 Provincial route numbers

CENTRAL MONTRÉAL

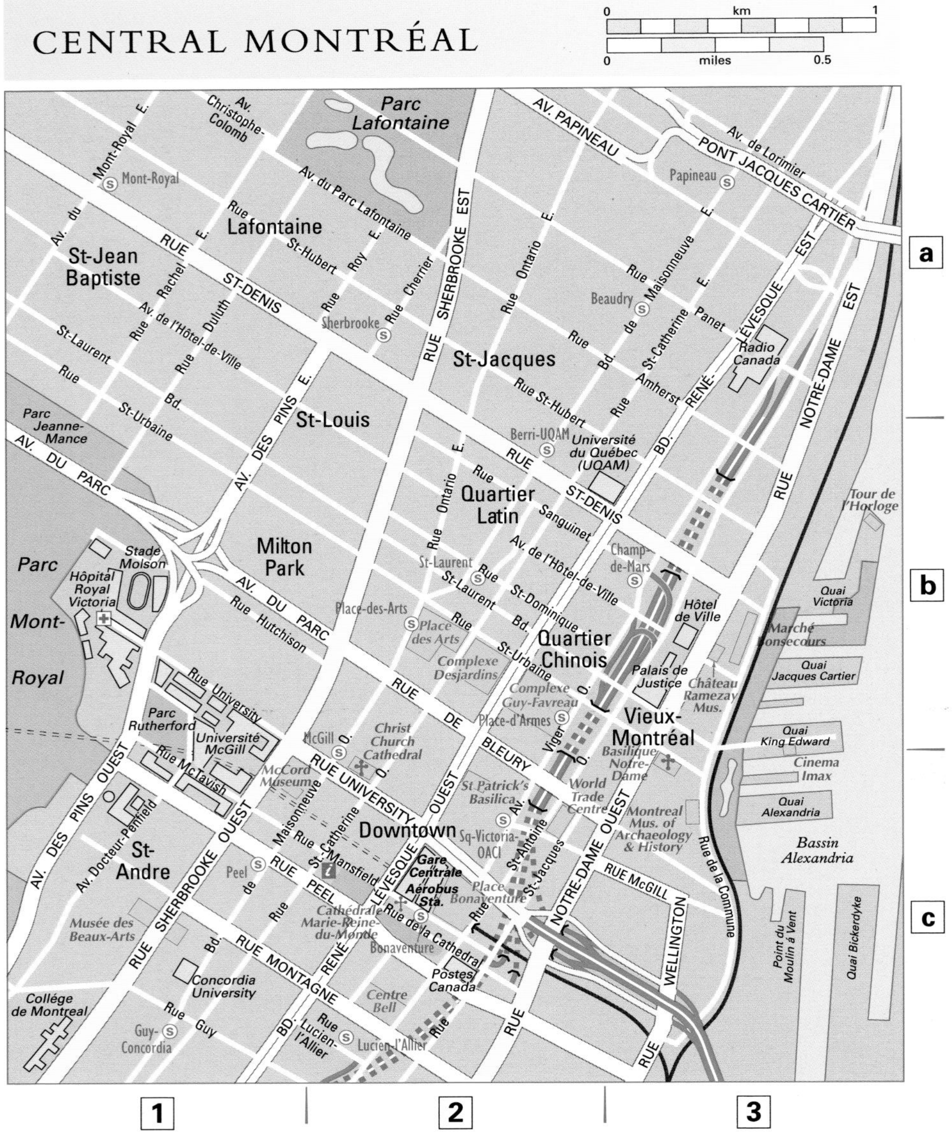

MUMBAI, INDIA

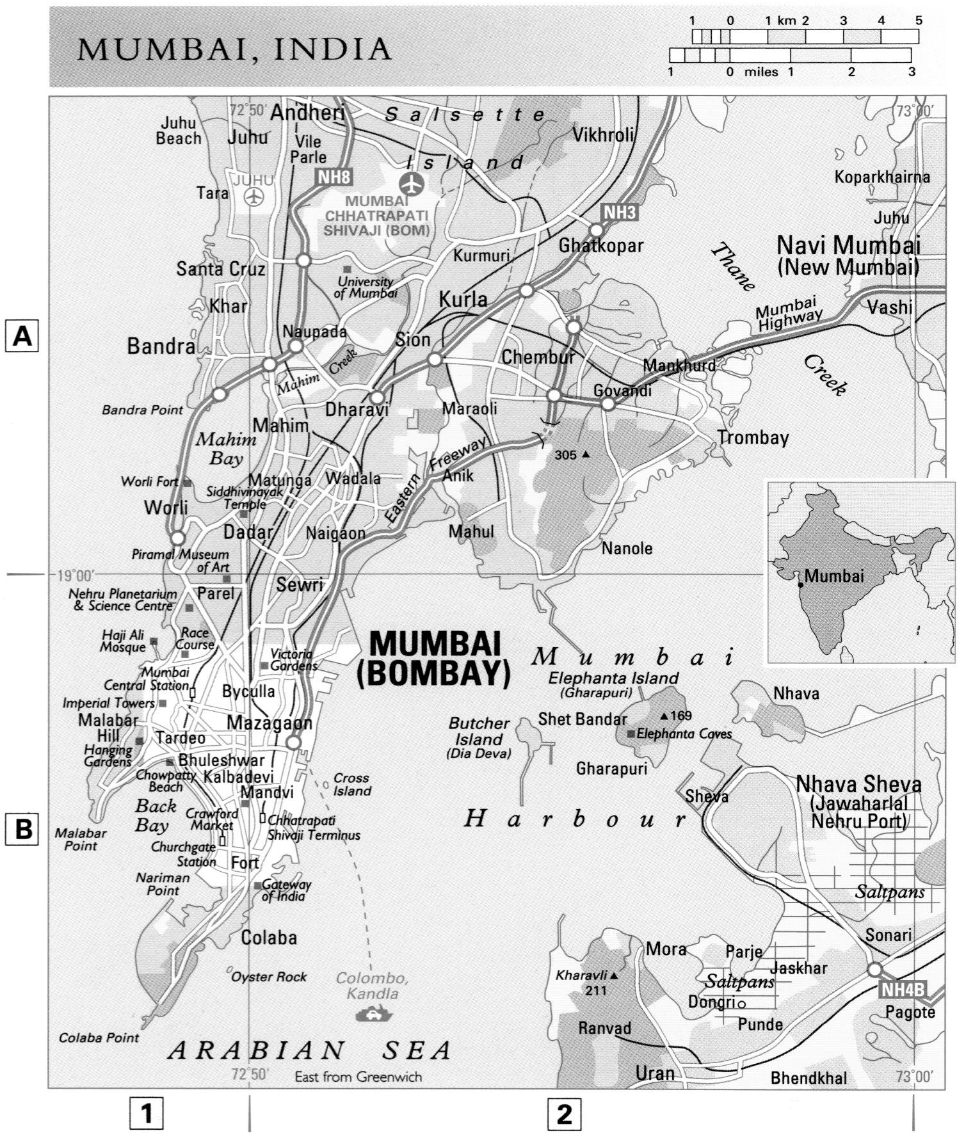

CENTRAL MUMBAI

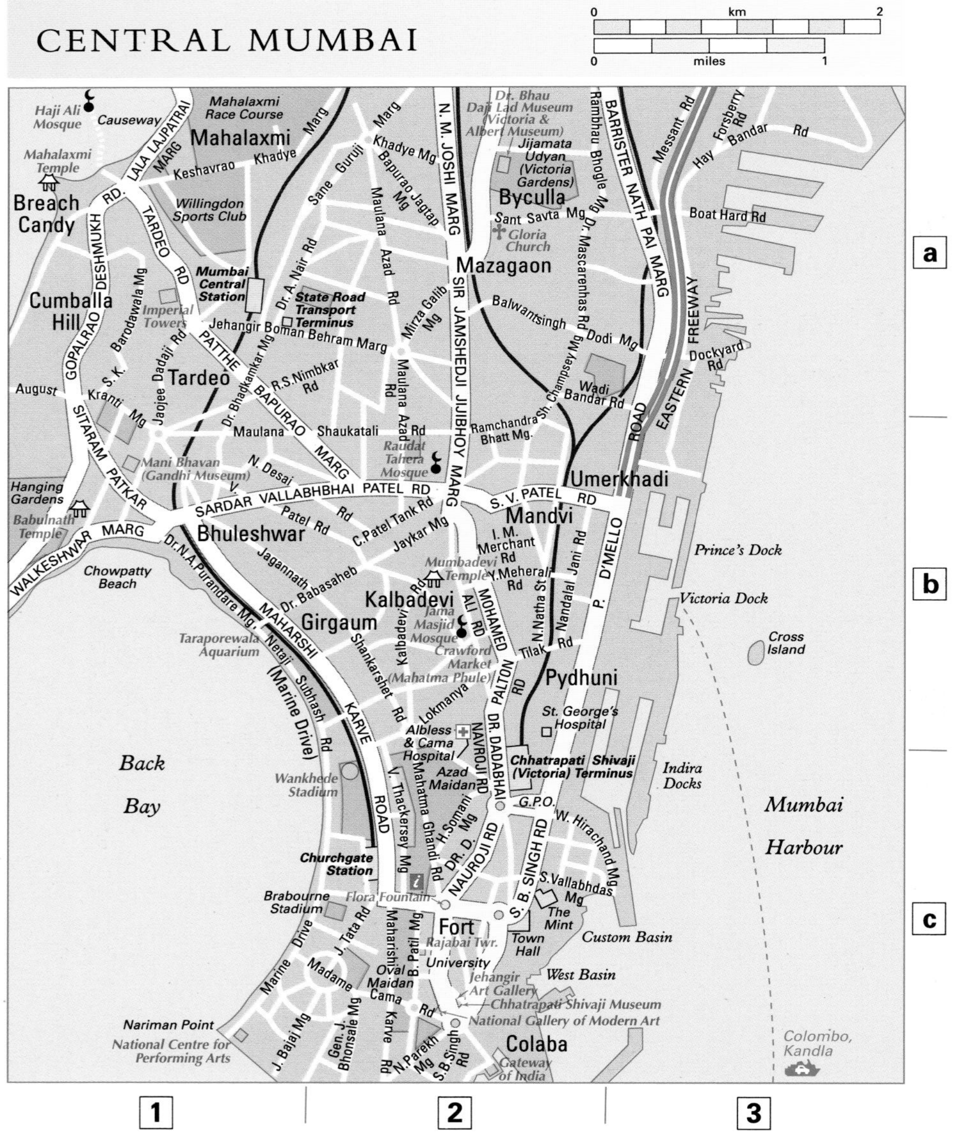

MUNICH, GERMANY

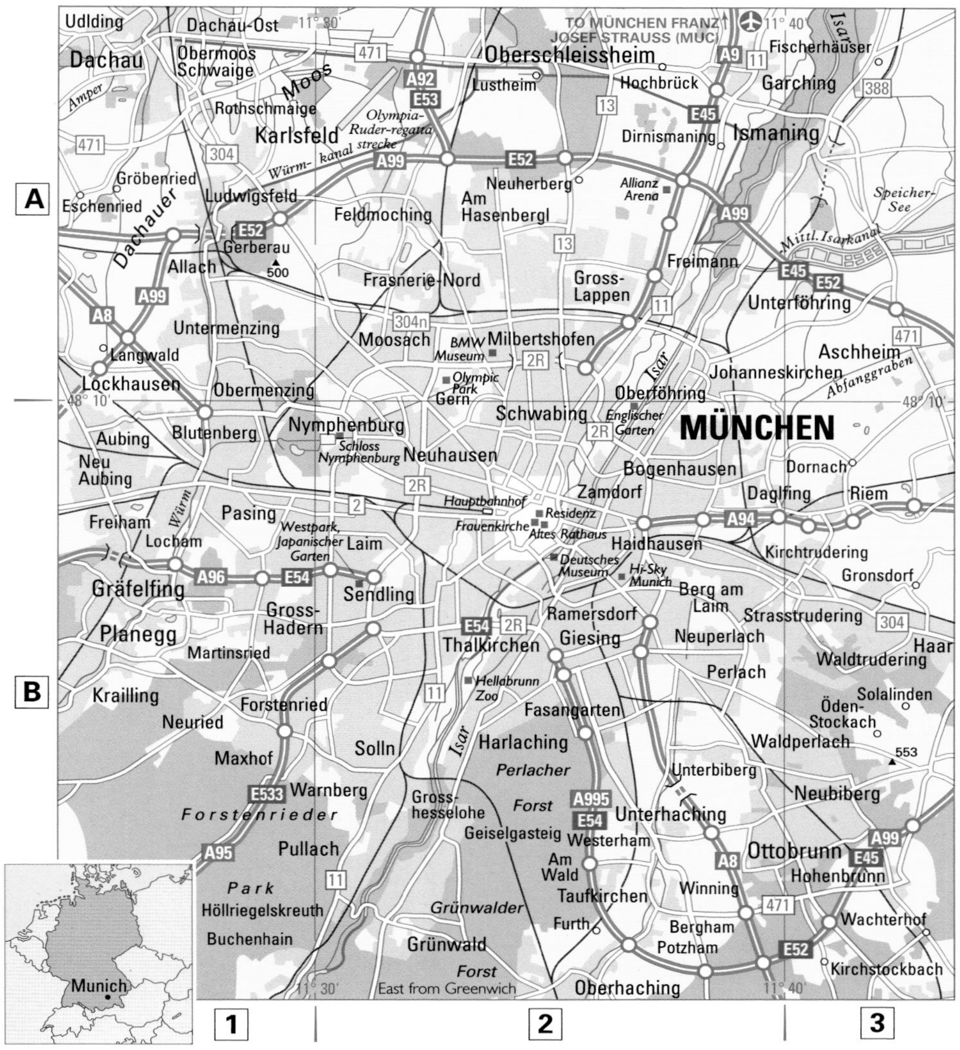

CENTRAL MUNICH

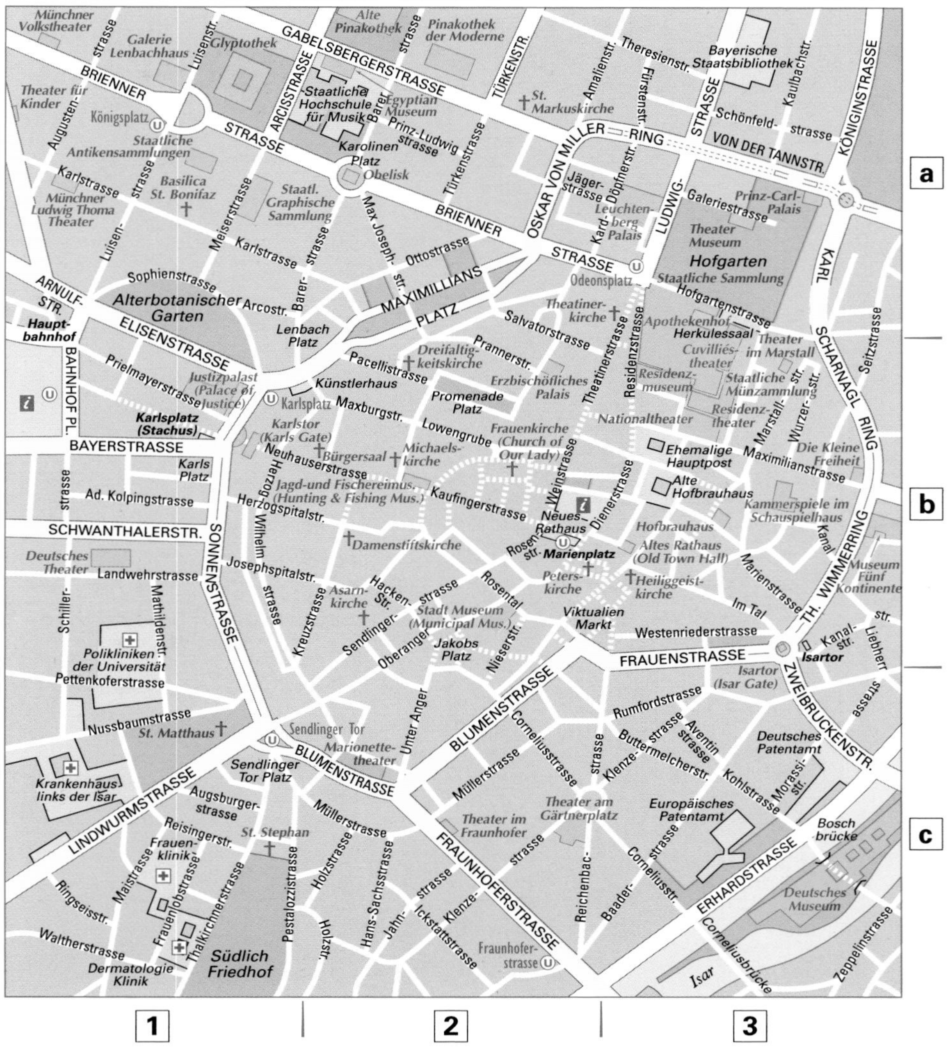

NEW ORLEANS, LOUISIANA

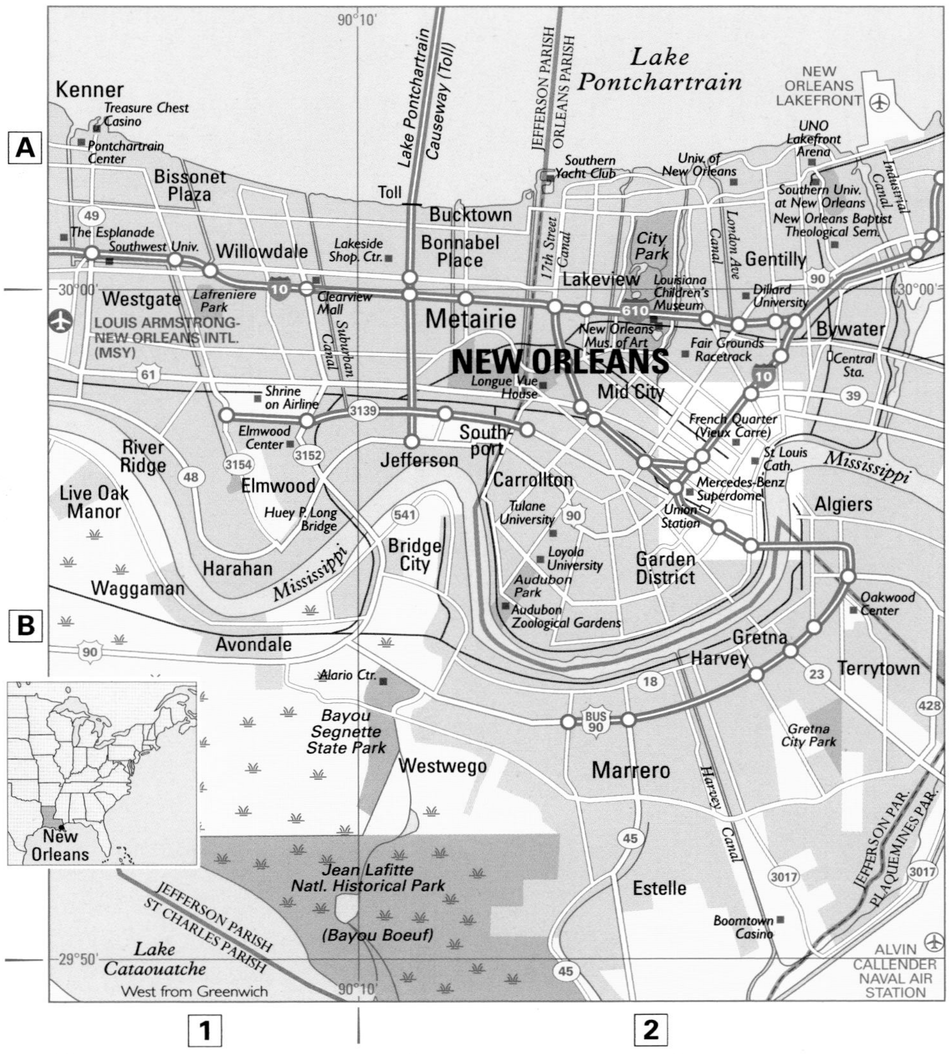

CENTRAL NEW ORLEANS

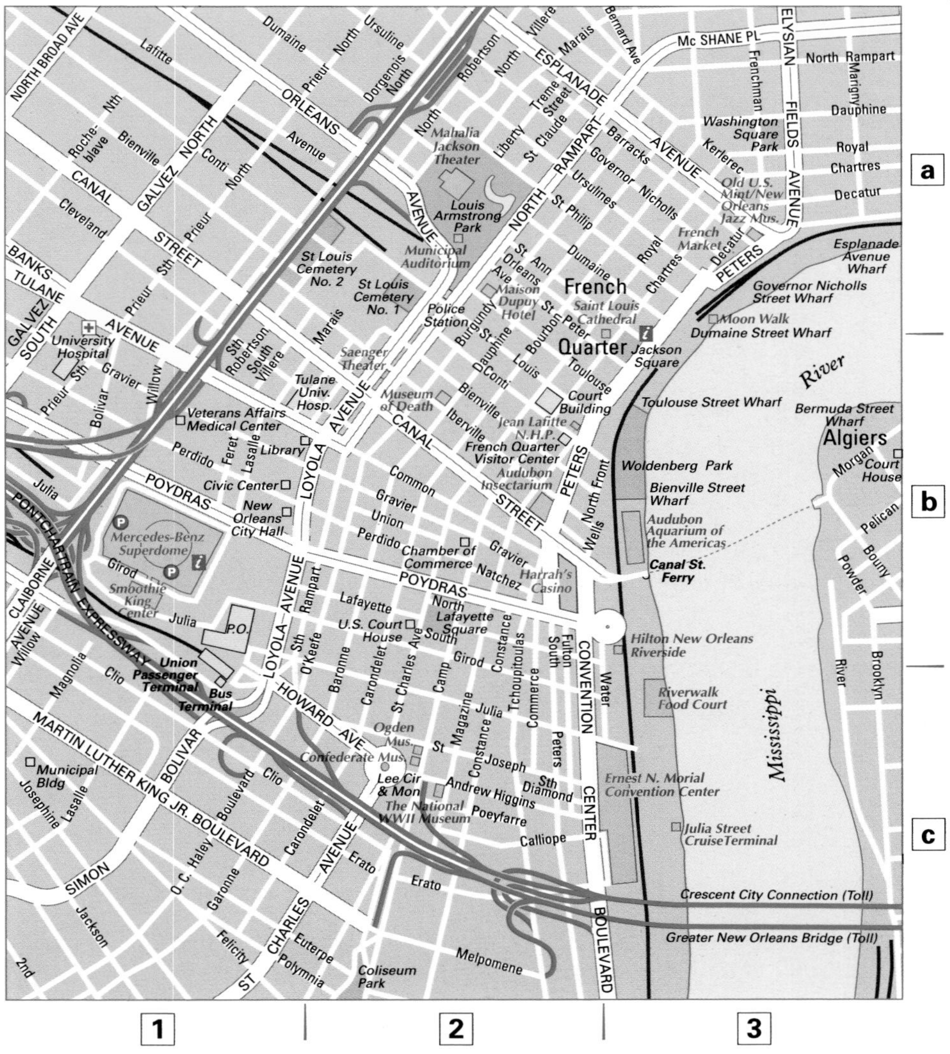

Interstate route numbers U.S. route numbers State route numbers

NEW YORK, NEW YORK

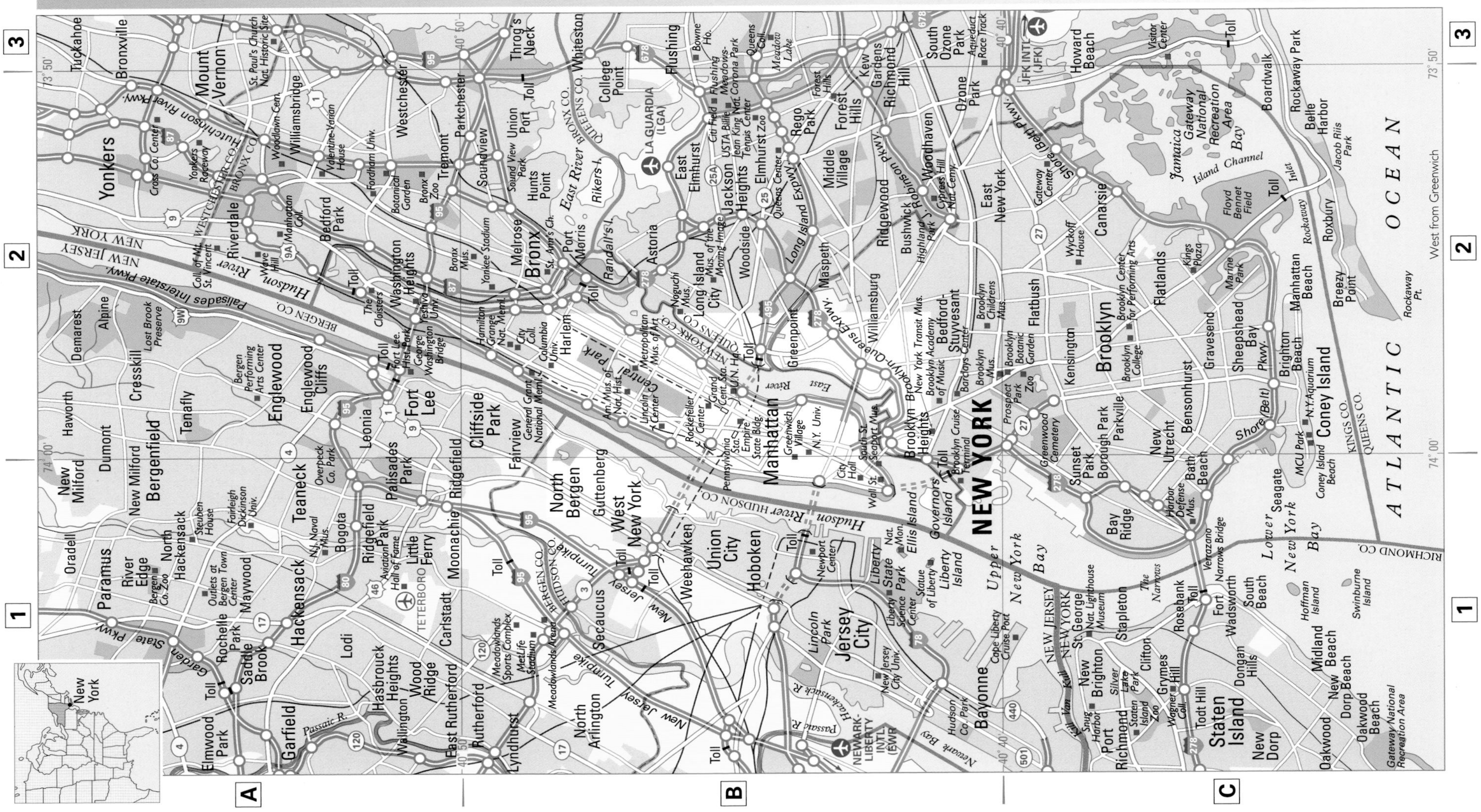

CENTRAL NEW YORK

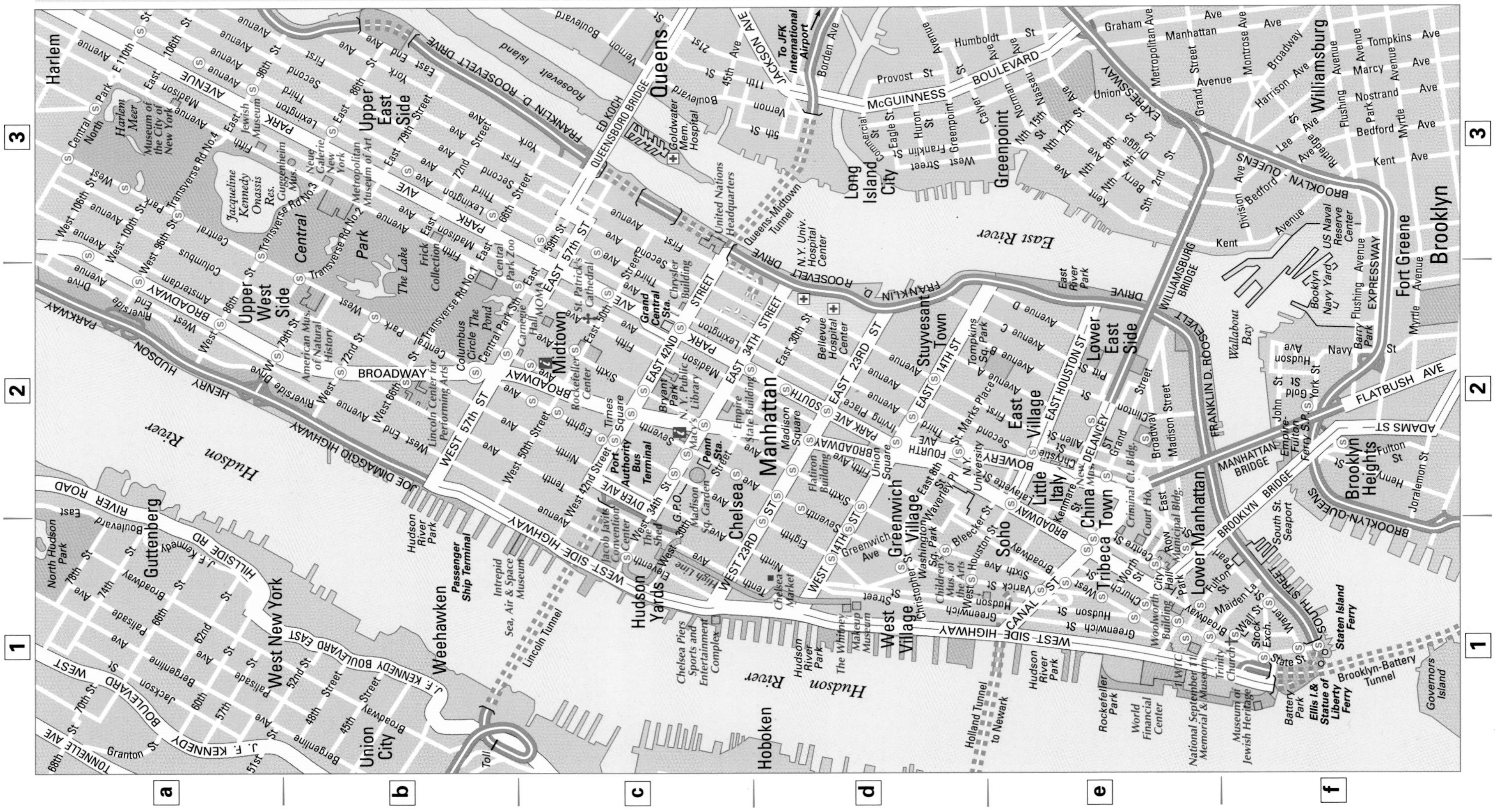

ORLANDO, FLORIDA

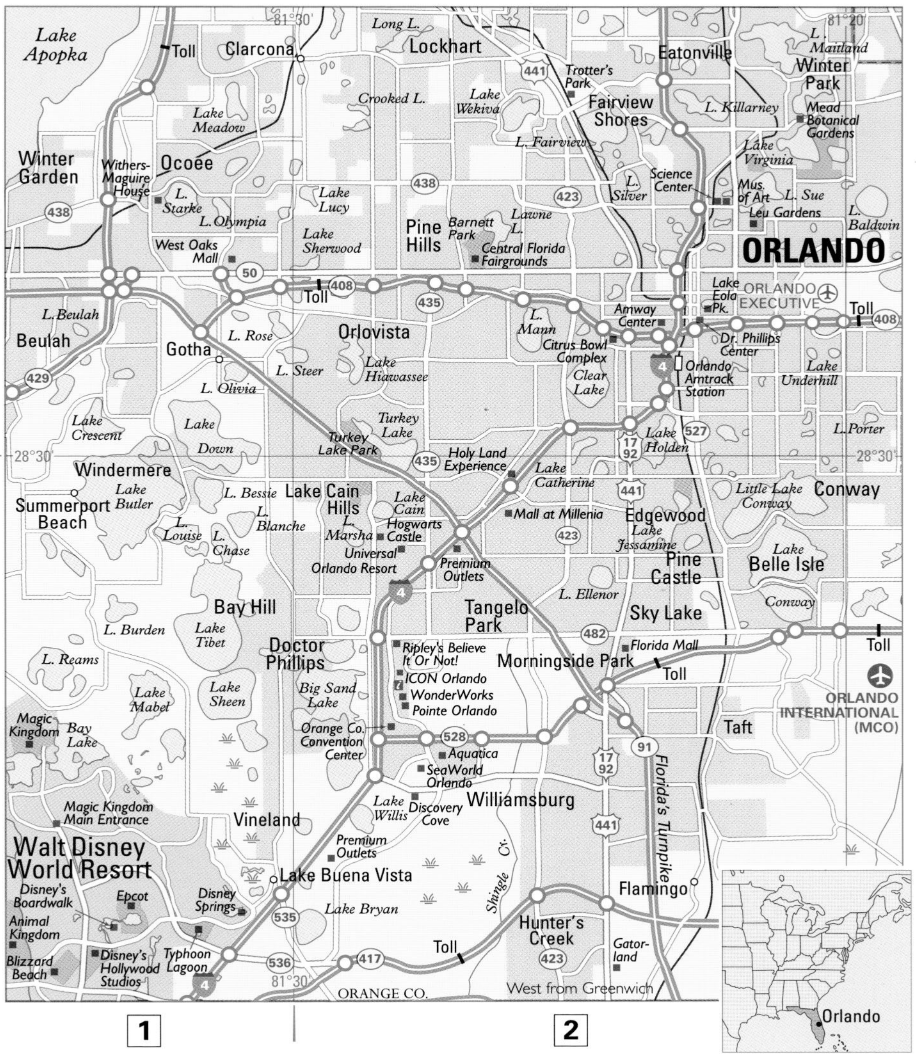

Interstate route numbers U.S. route numbers State route numbers

OSAKA, JAPAN

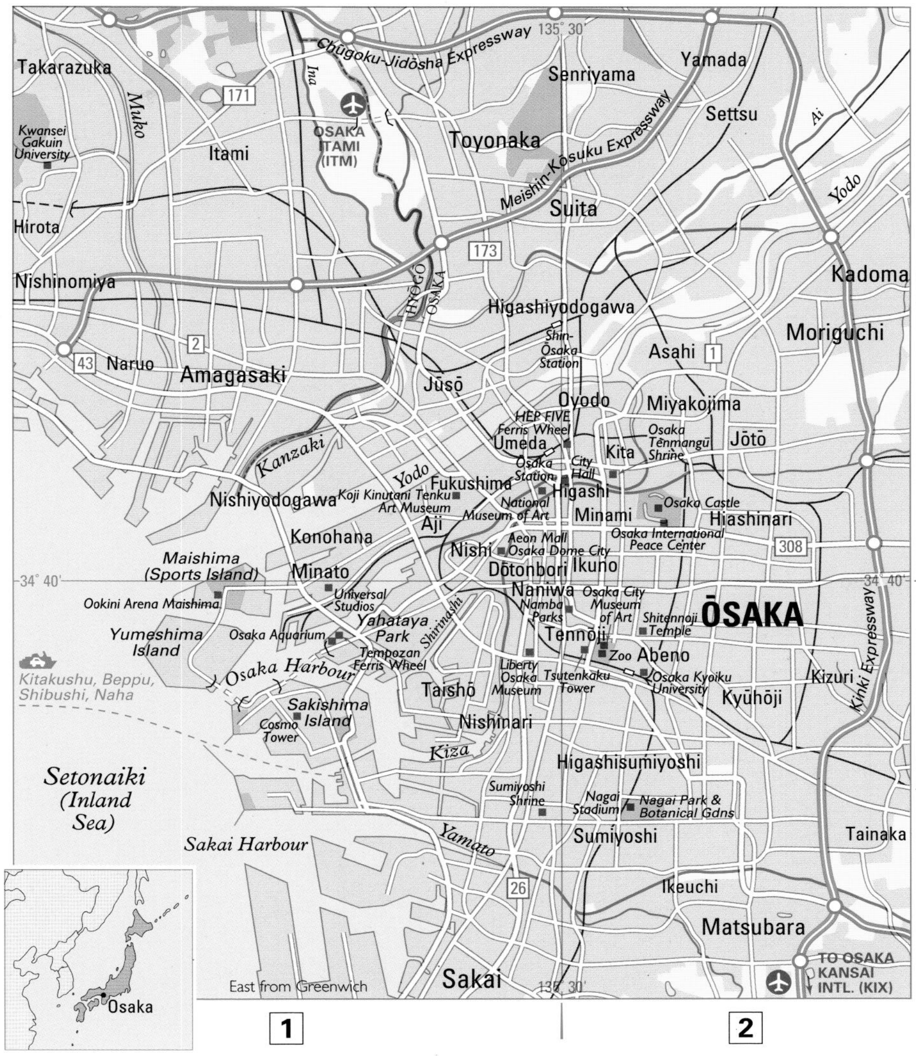

OSLO, NORWAY

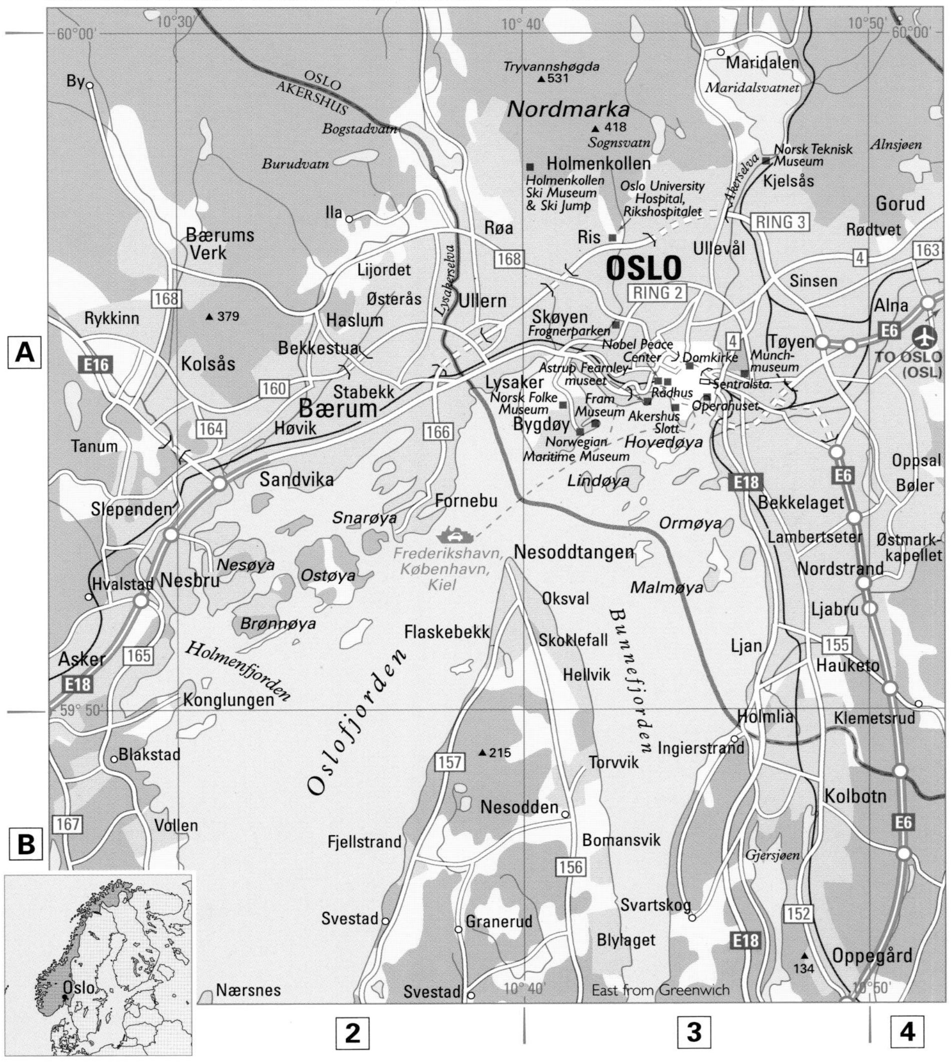

CENTRAL OSLO

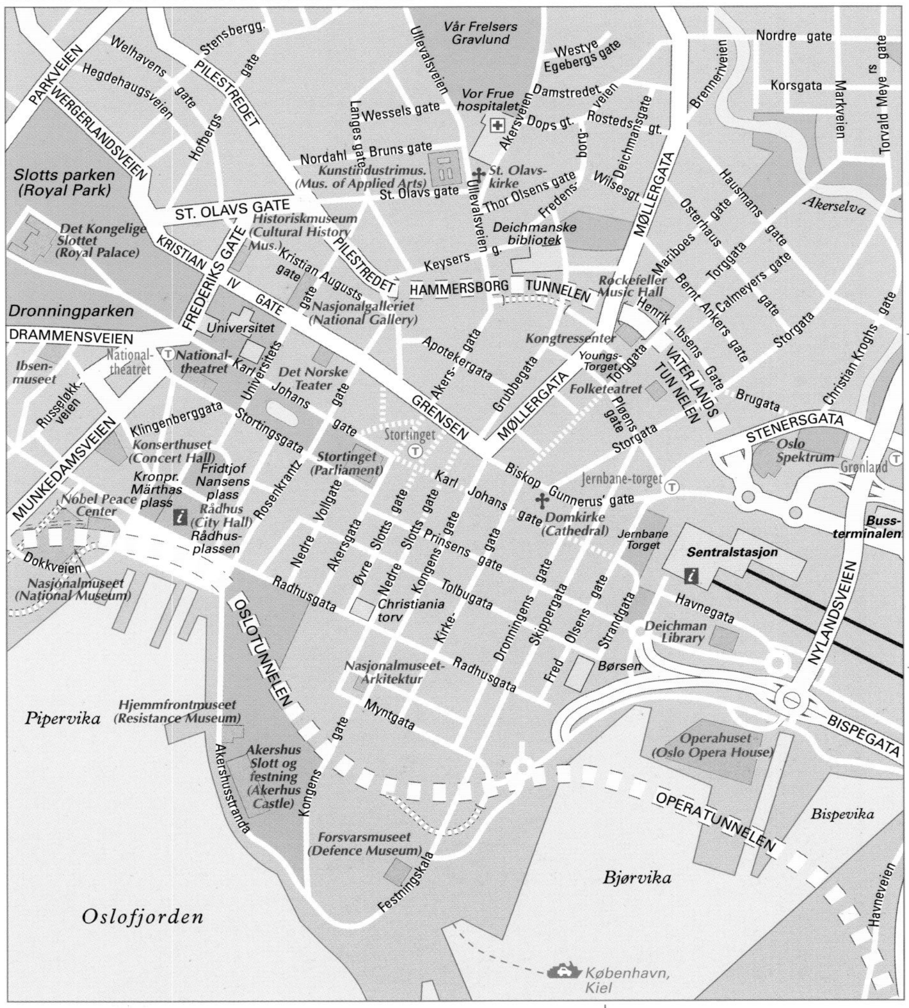

PARIS, FRANCE

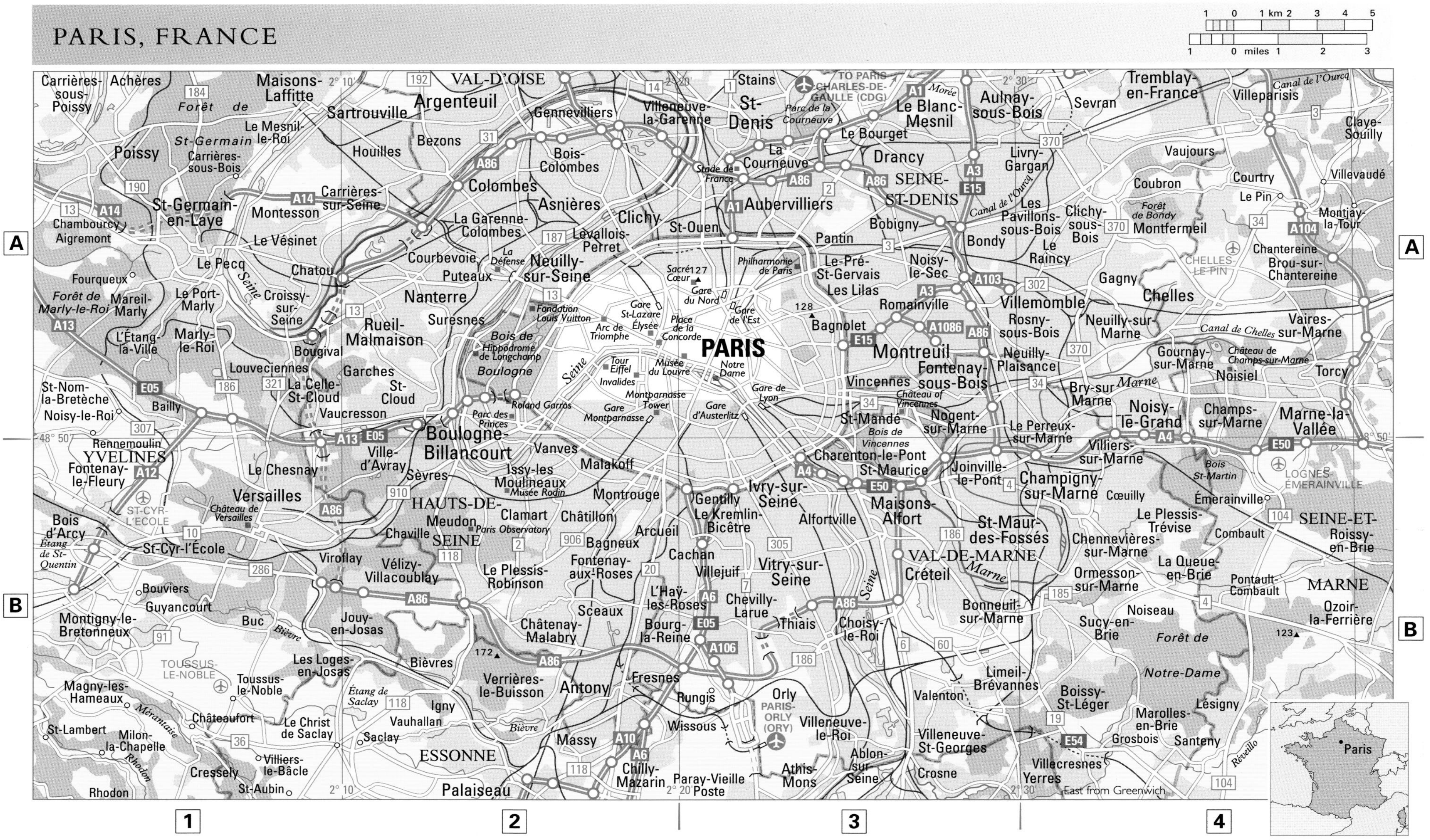

CENTRAL PARIS

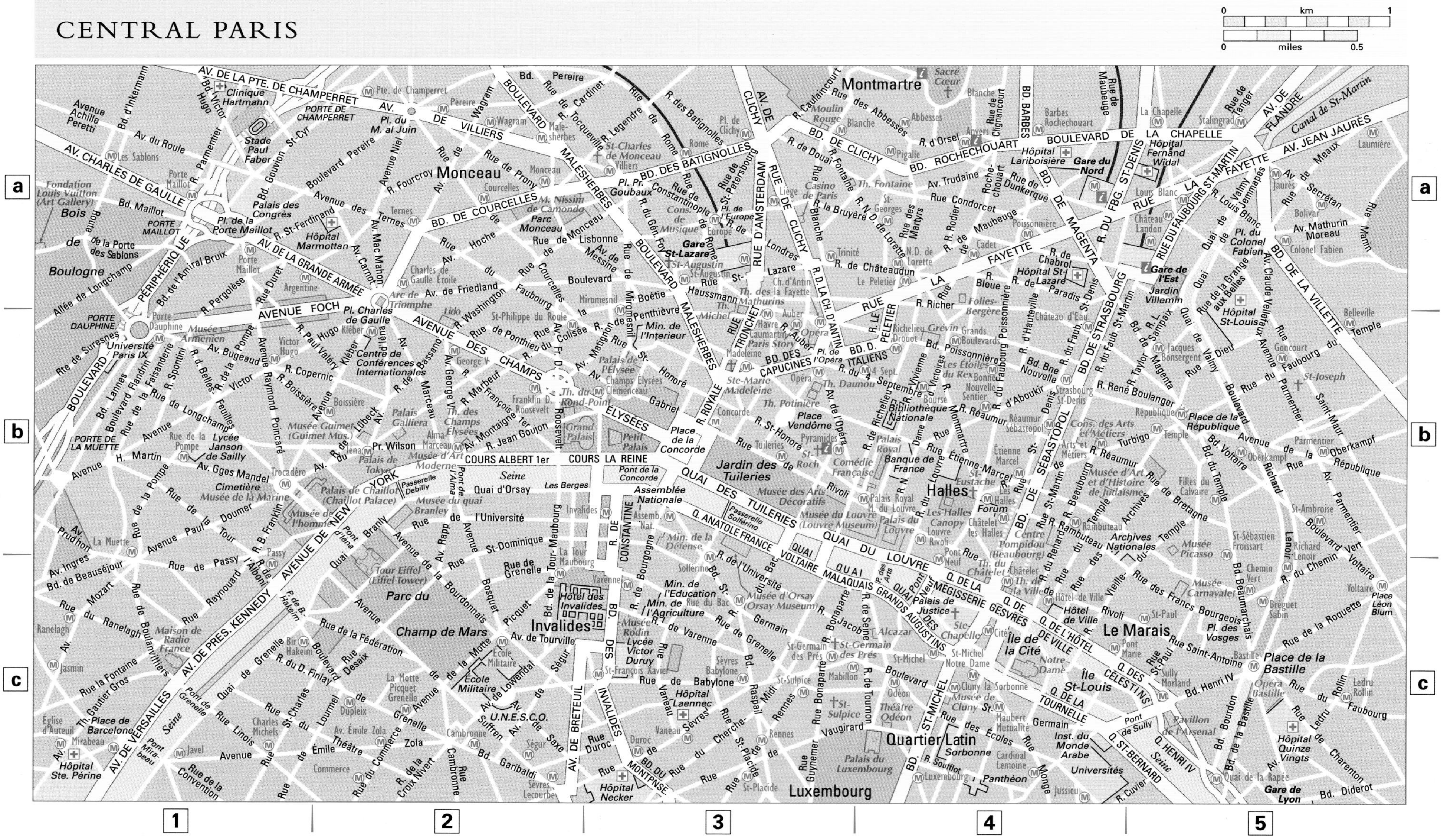

PRAGUE, CZECHIA

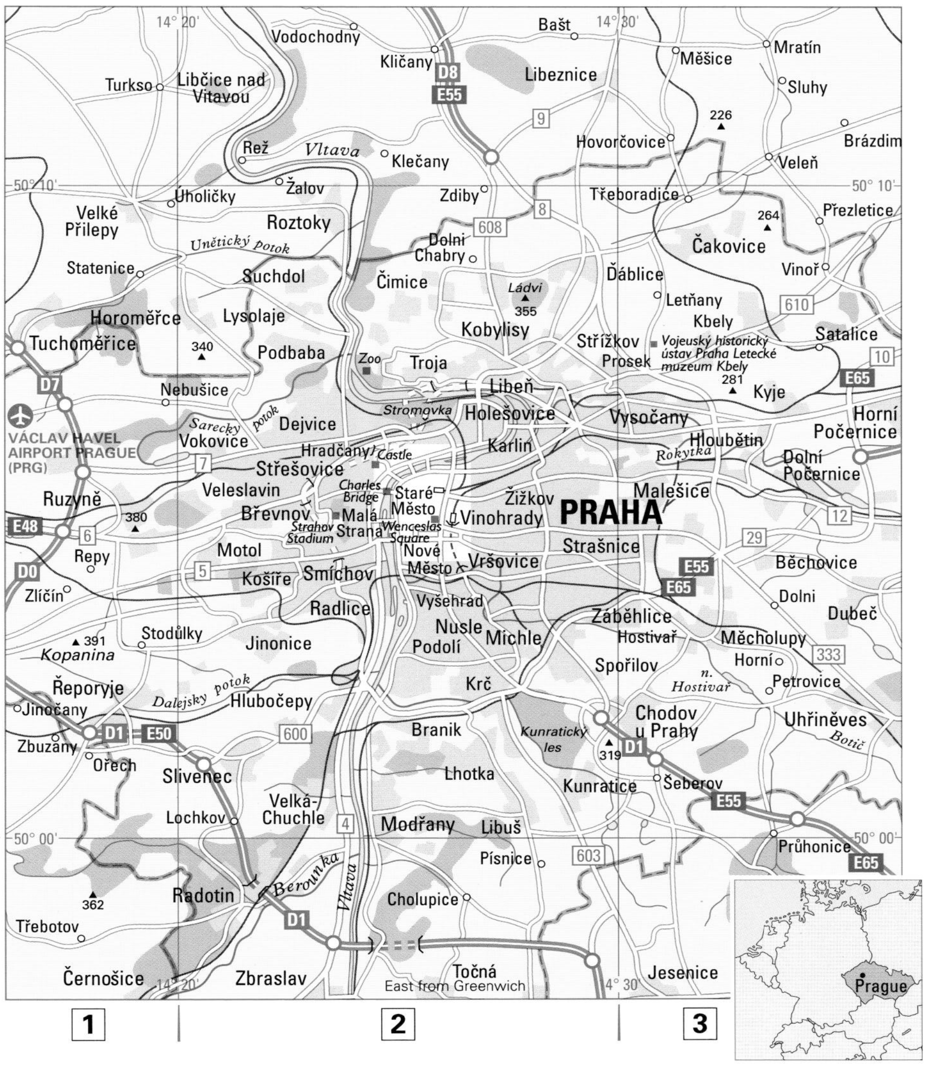

CENTRAL PRAGUE

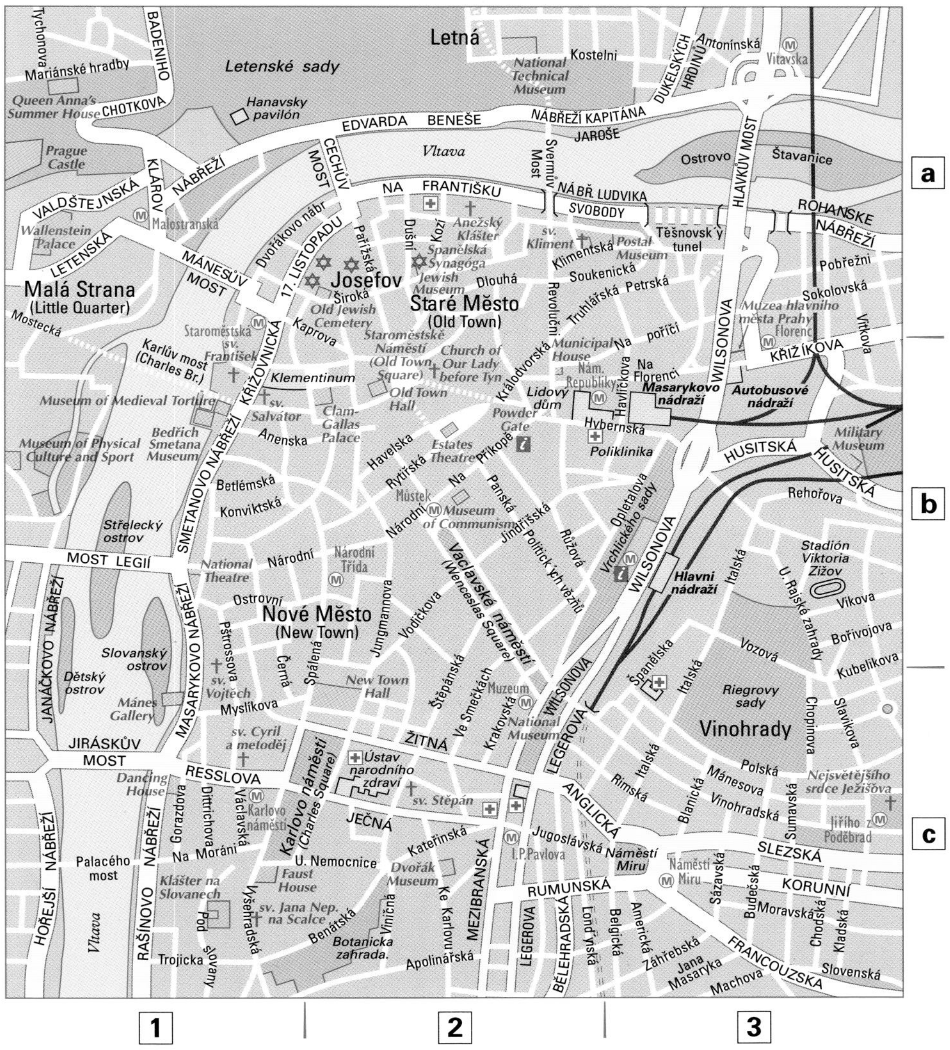

RIO DE JANEIRO, BRAZIL

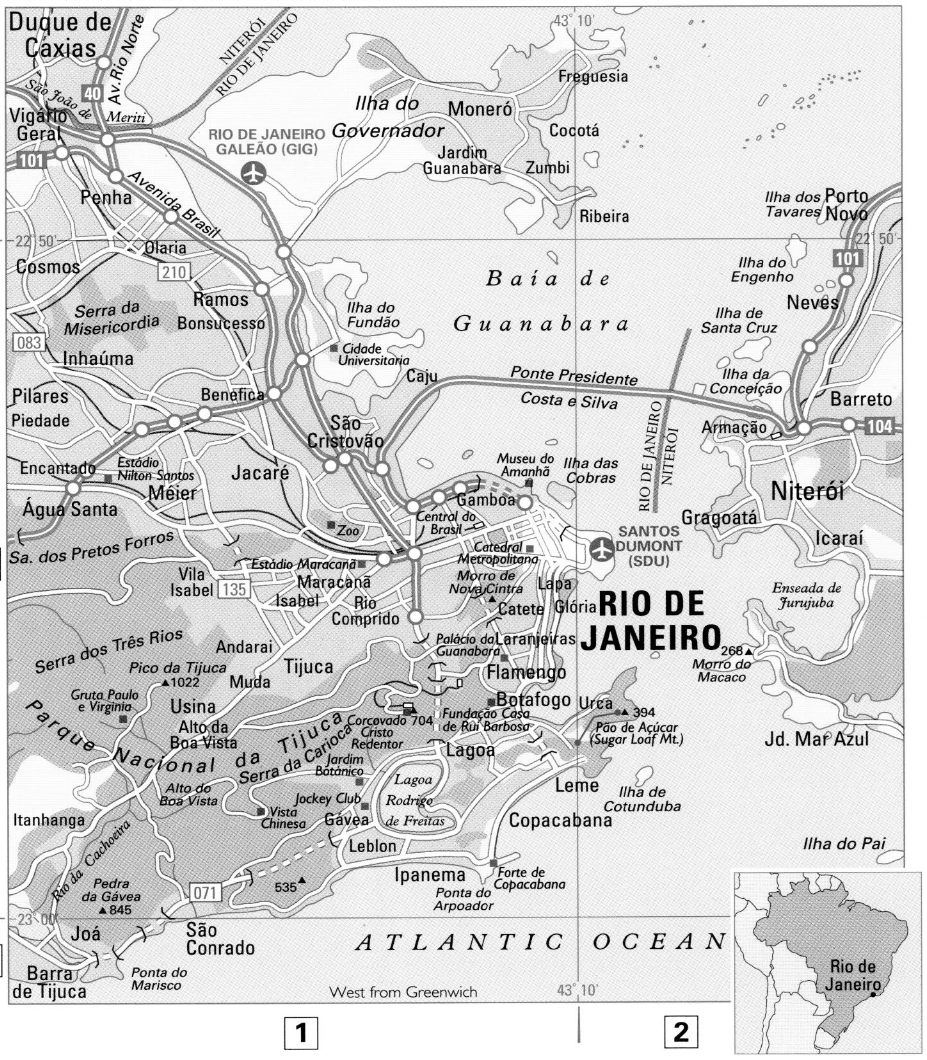

CENTRAL RIO DE JANEIRO

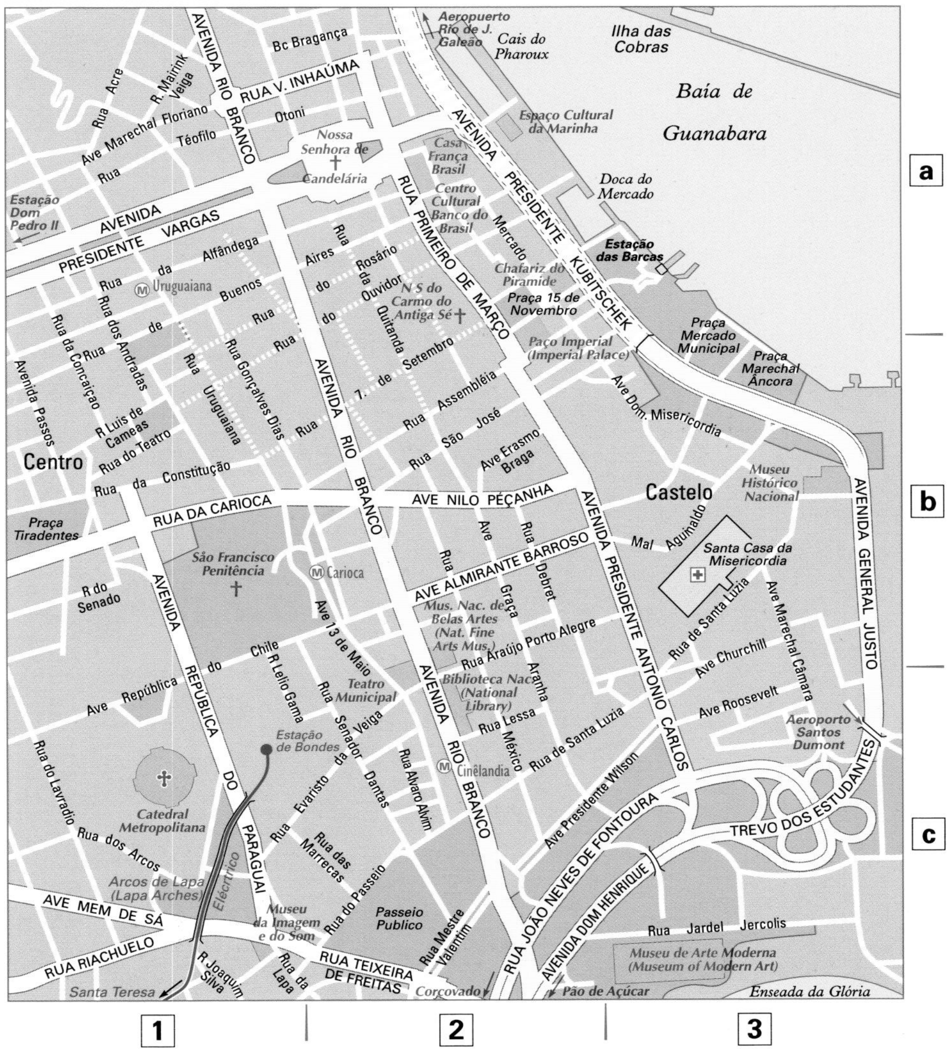

ROME, ITALY

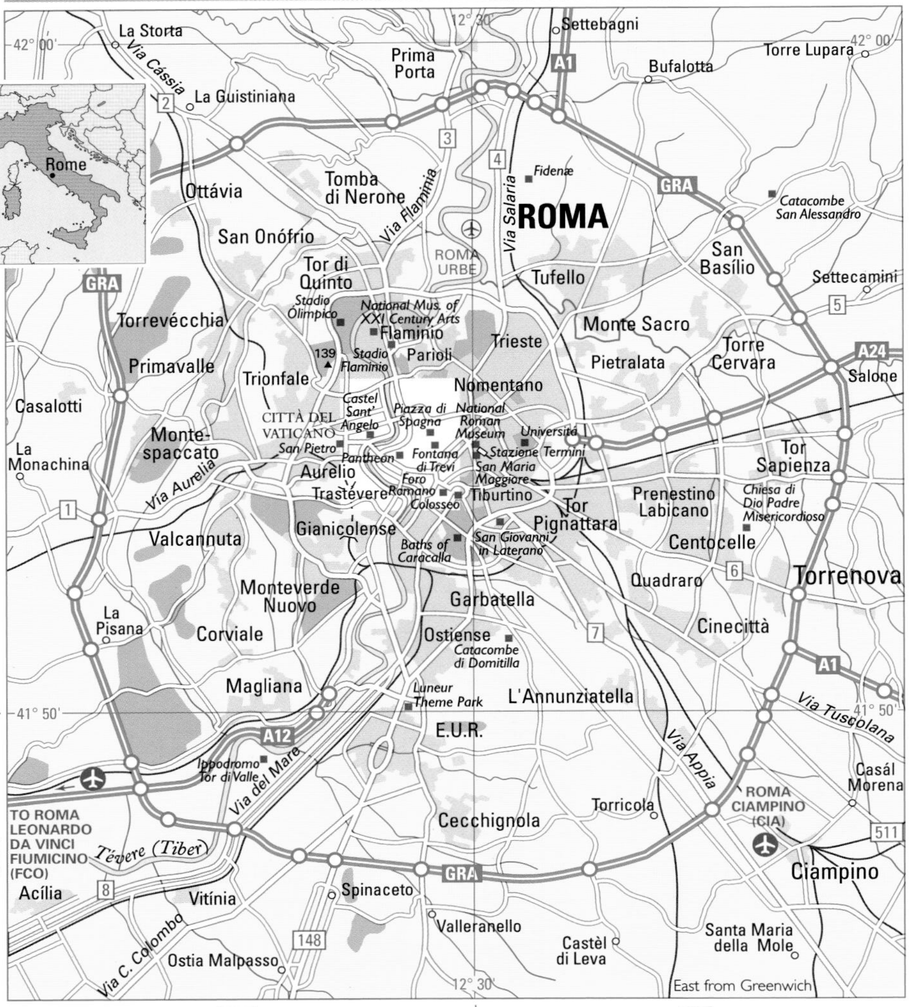

CENTRAL ROME

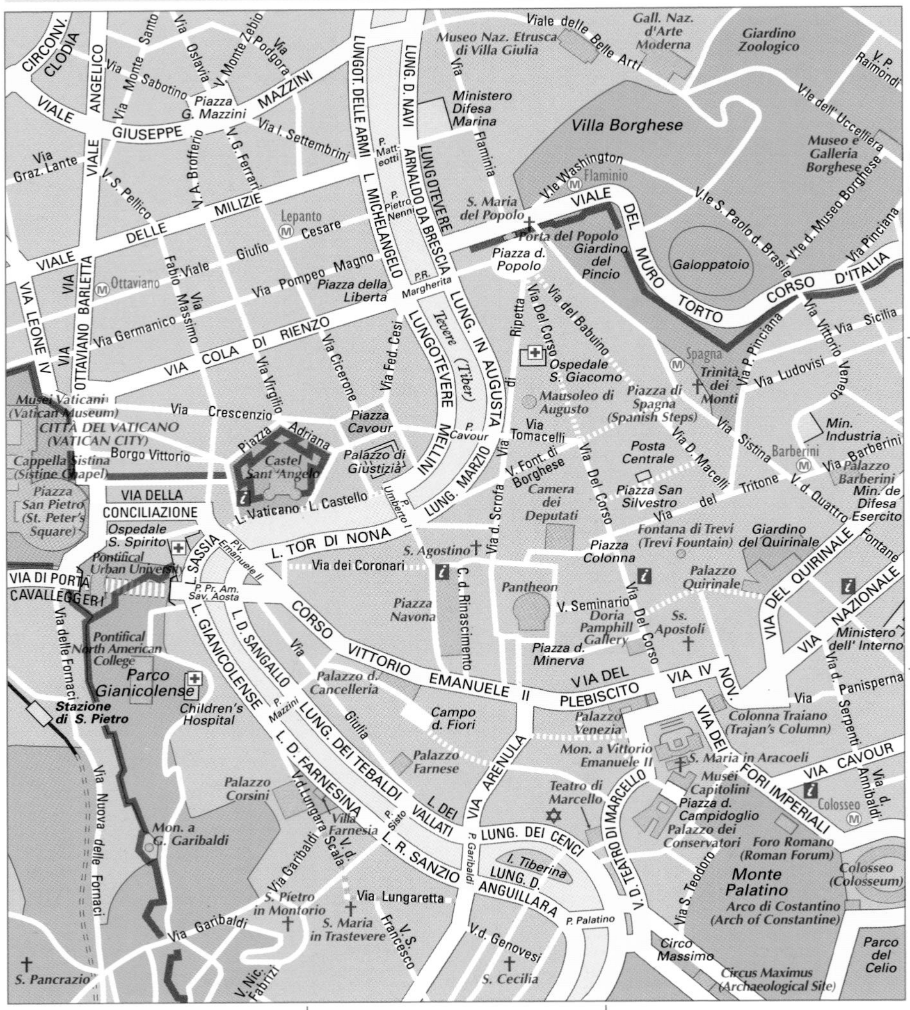

SAN FRANCISCO, CALIF.

CENTRAL SAN FRANCISCO

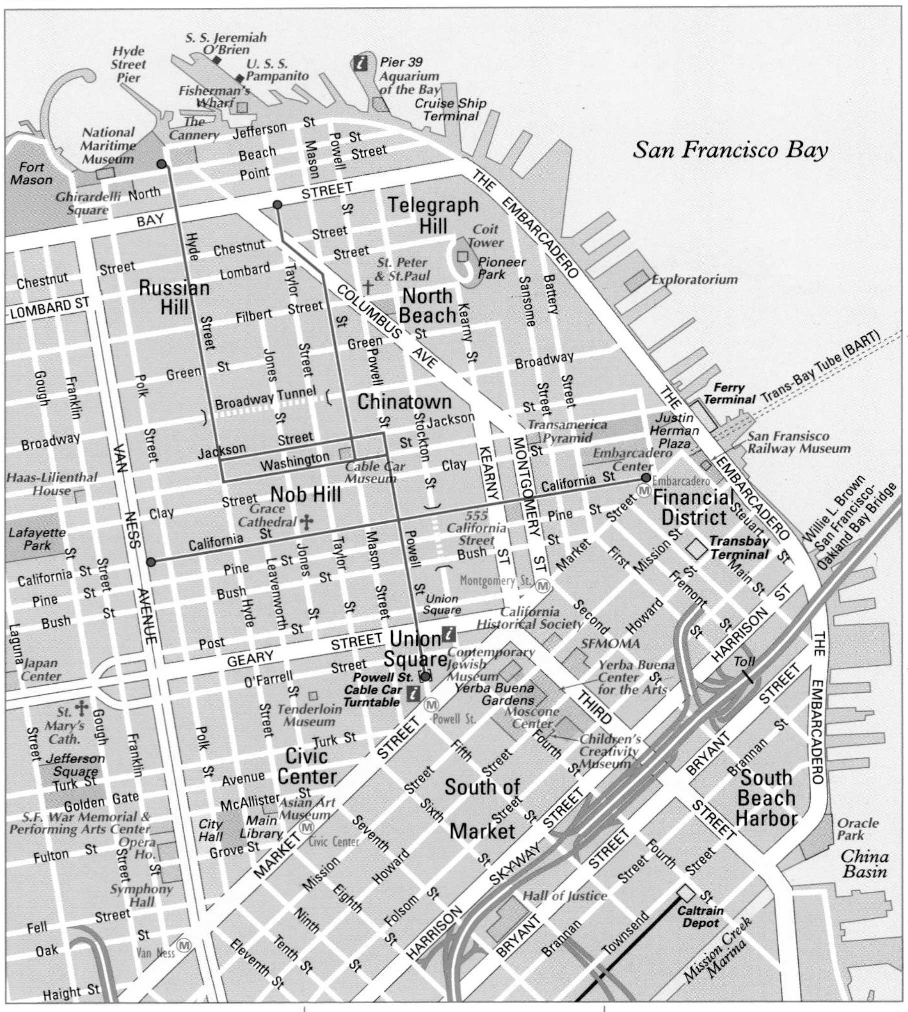

Interstate route numbers | U.S. route numbers | State route numbers

Cable Car route

ST PETERSBURG, RUSSIA

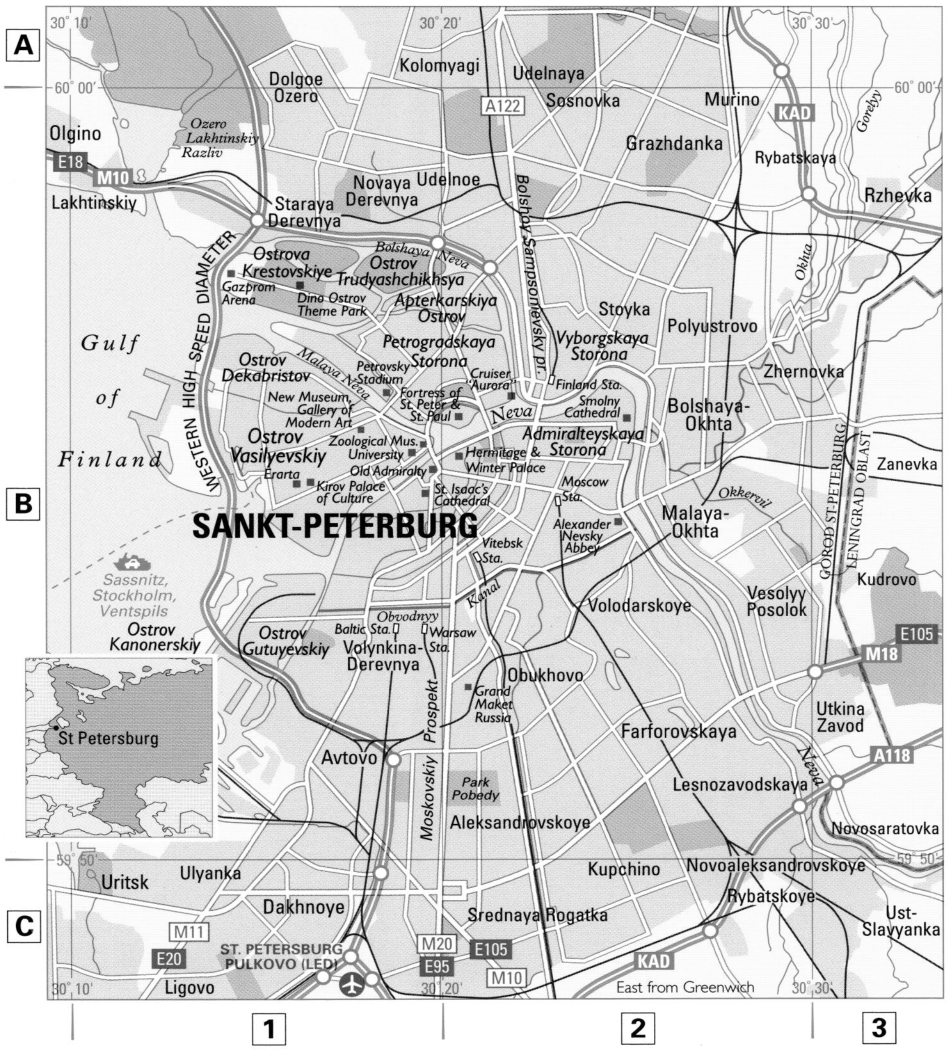

SANTIAGO, CHILE

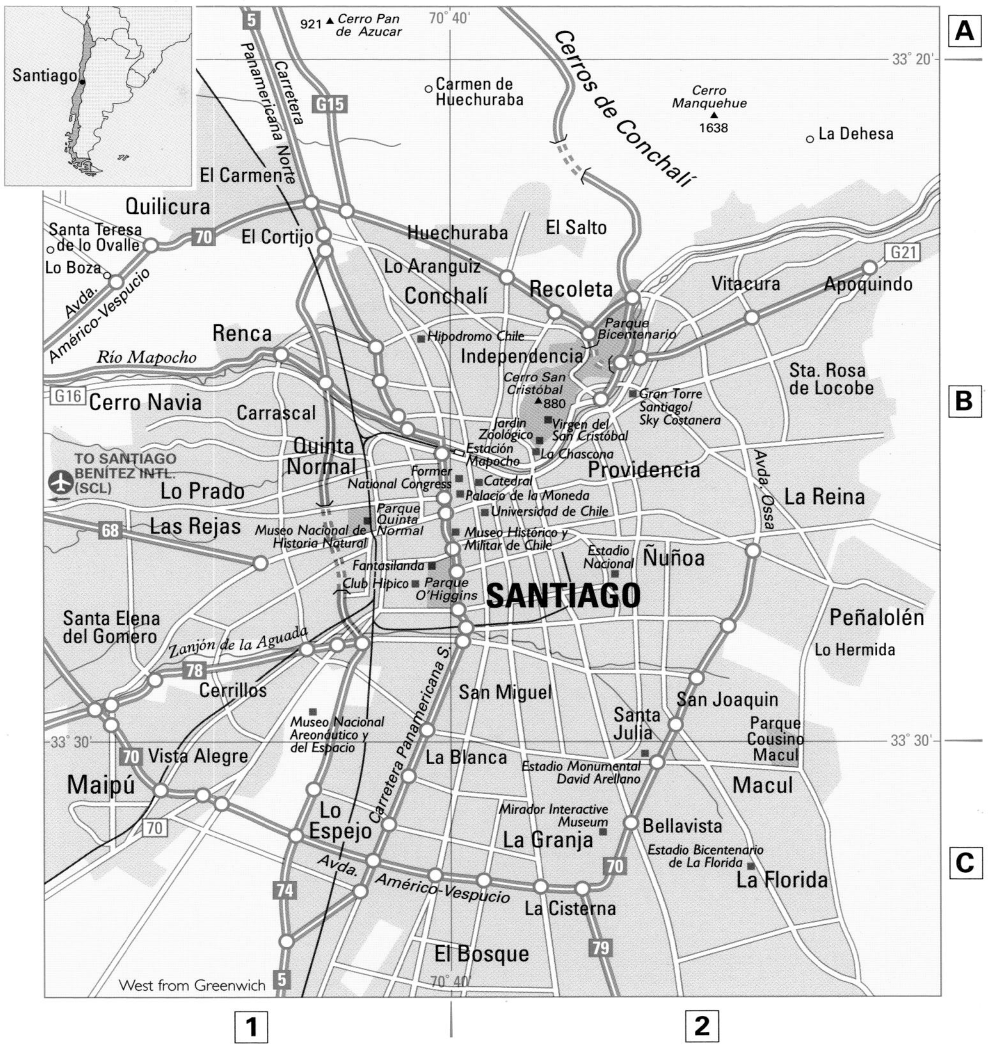

SÃO PAULO, BRAZIL

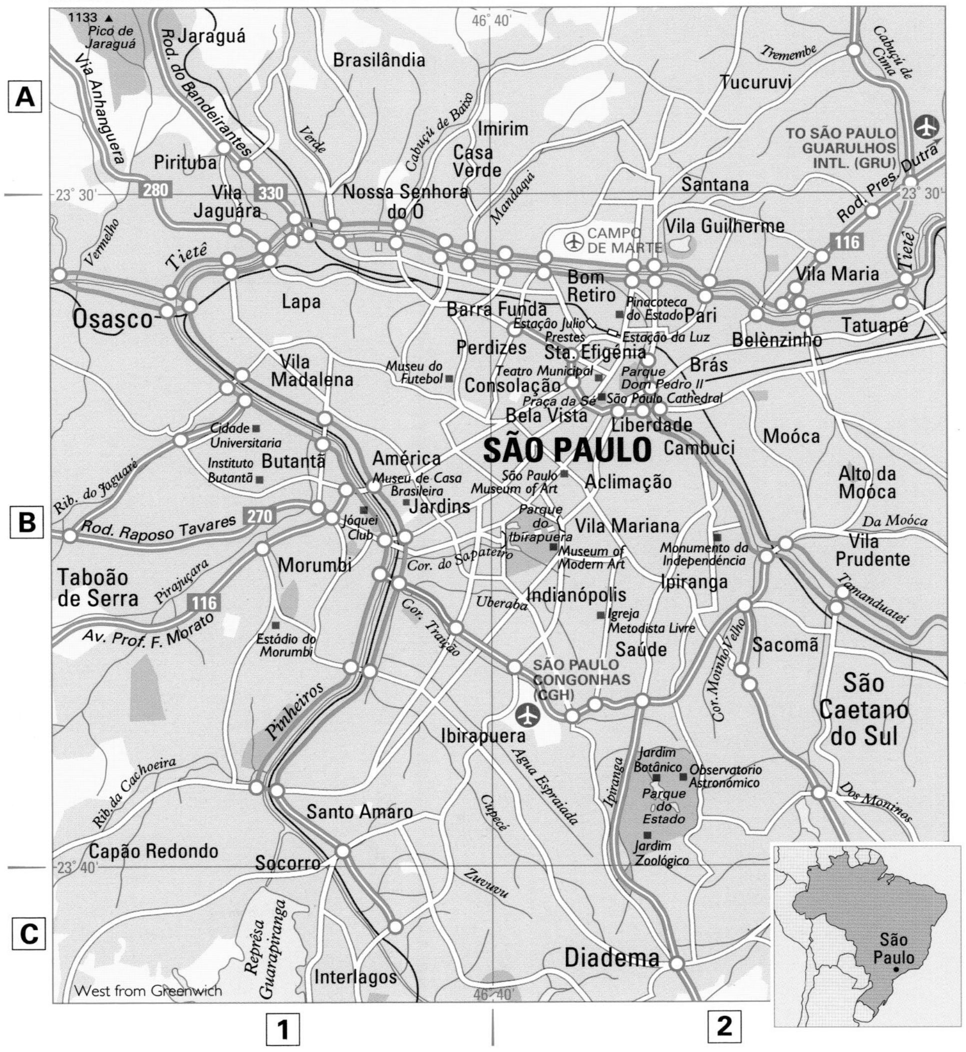

SEOUL, SOUTH KOREA

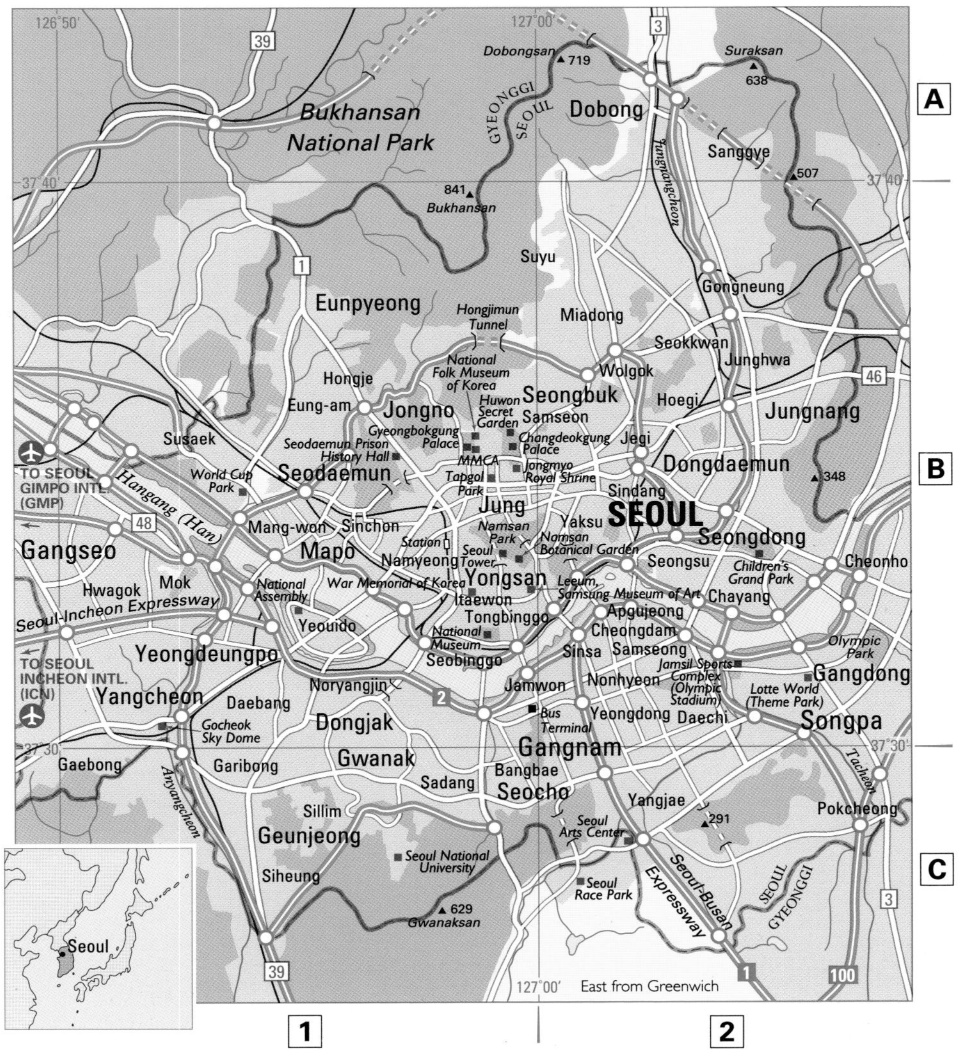

SHANGHAI, CHINA

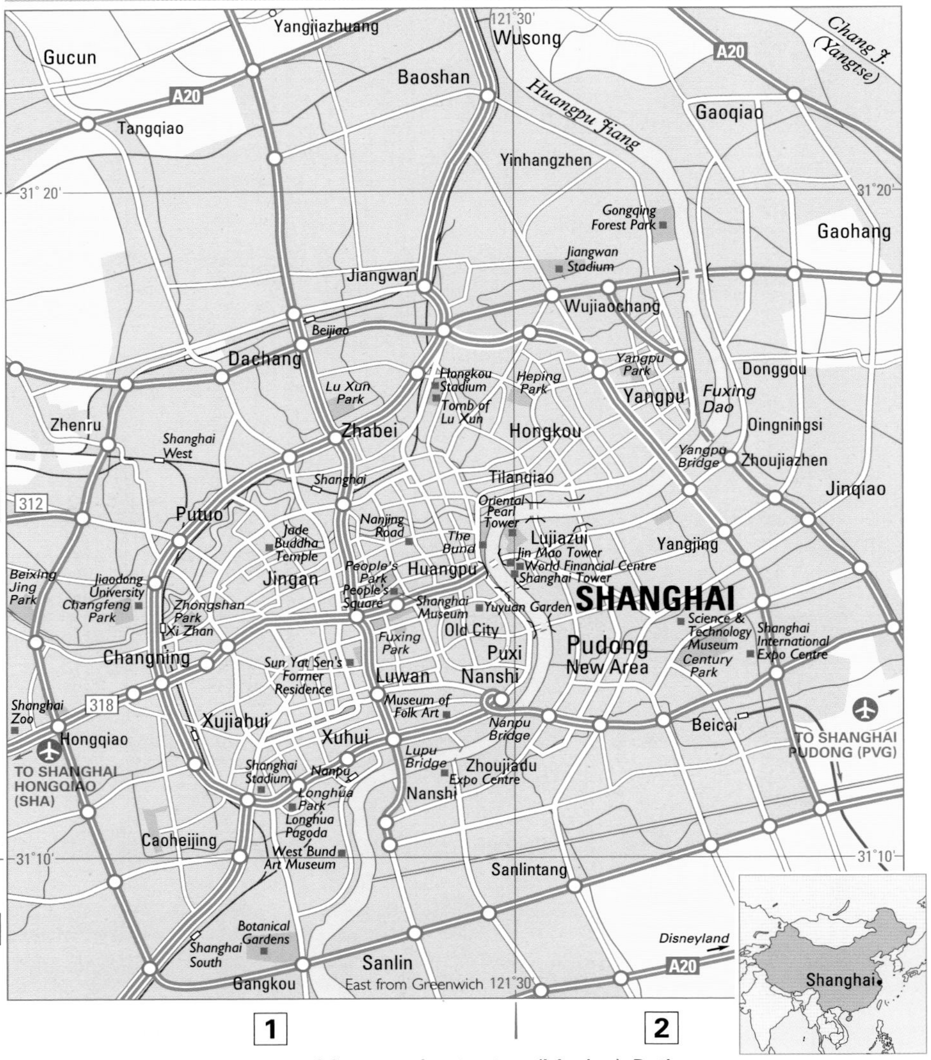

1 0 1 km 2 3 4 5
1 0 miles 1 2 3

—— Magnetic Levitation (Maglev) Railway

CENTRAL SINGAPORE

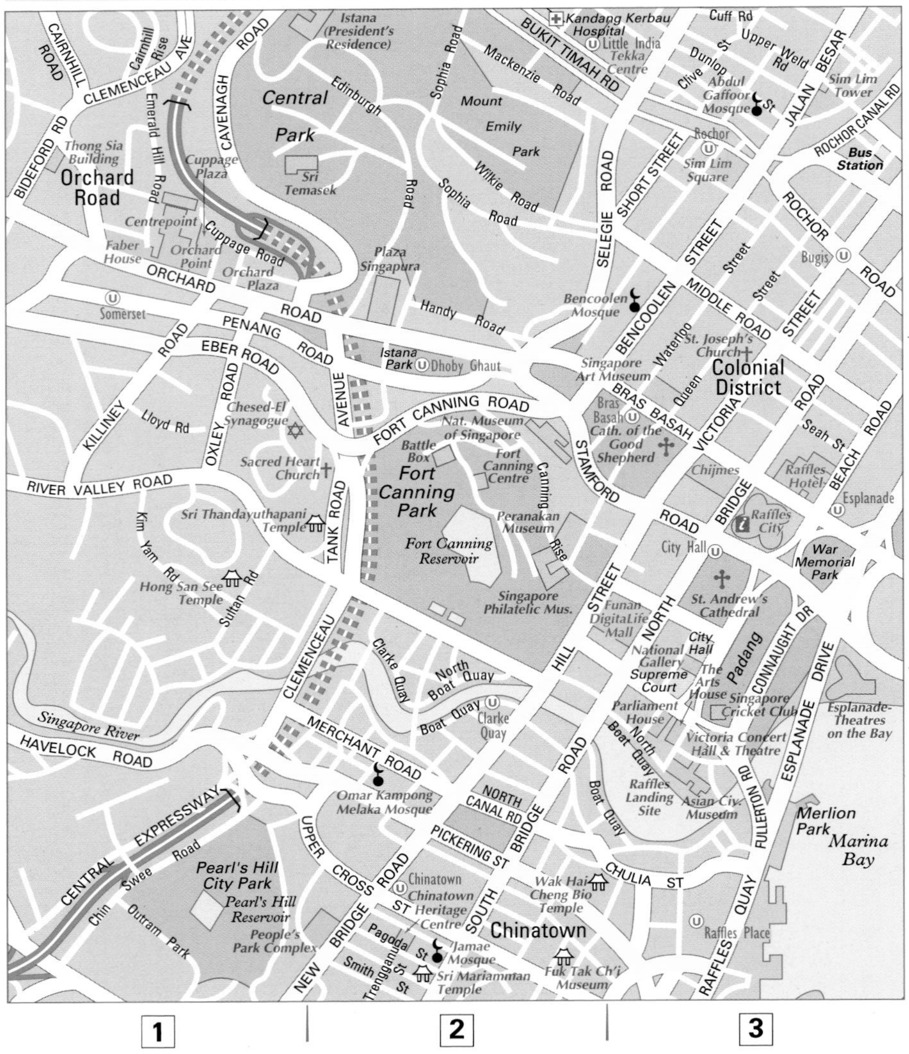

0 km 1
0 miles 0.5

SINGAPORE

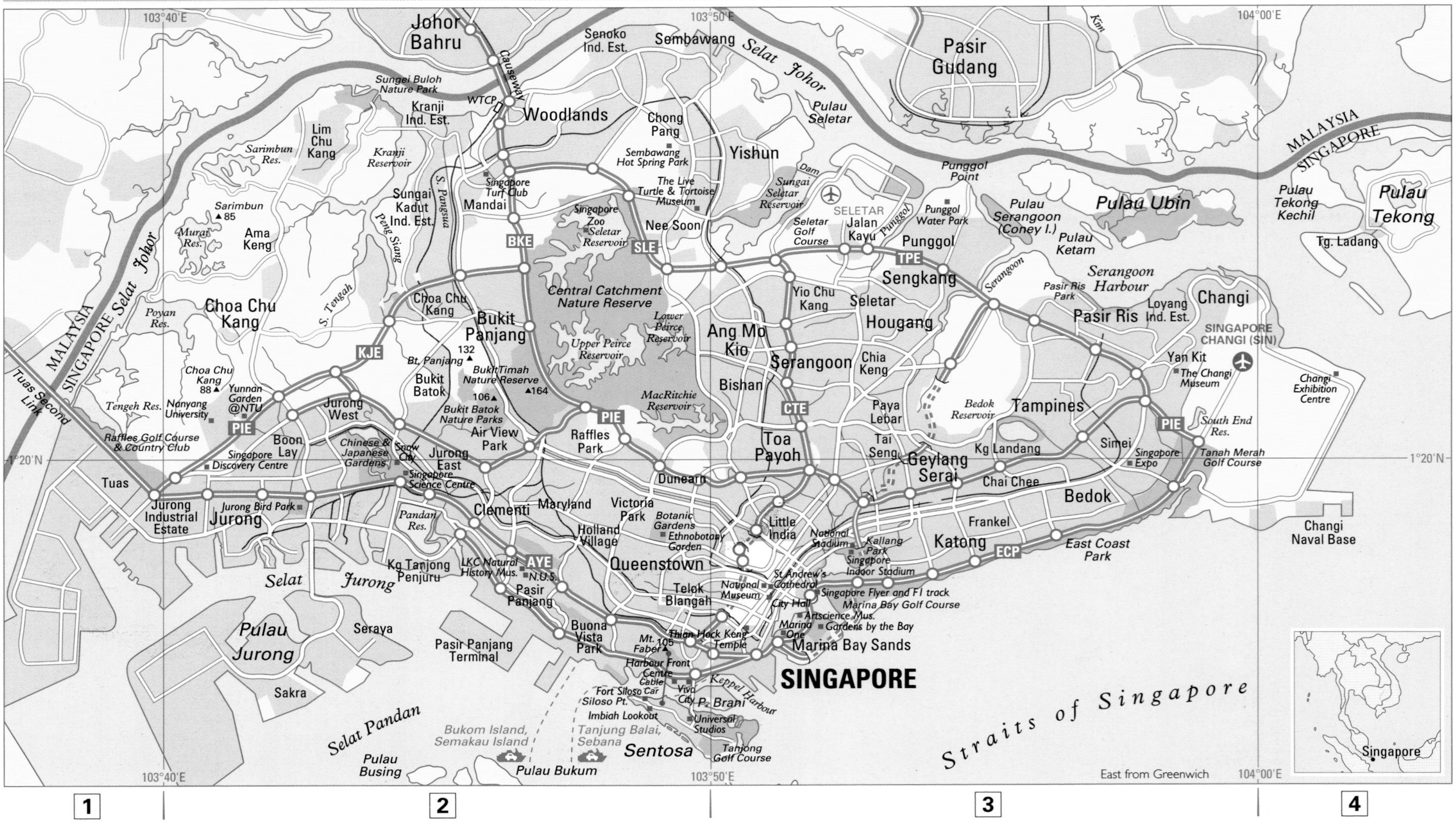

1 0 1 km 2 3 4 5
1 0 miles 1 2 3

STOCKHOLM, SWEDEN

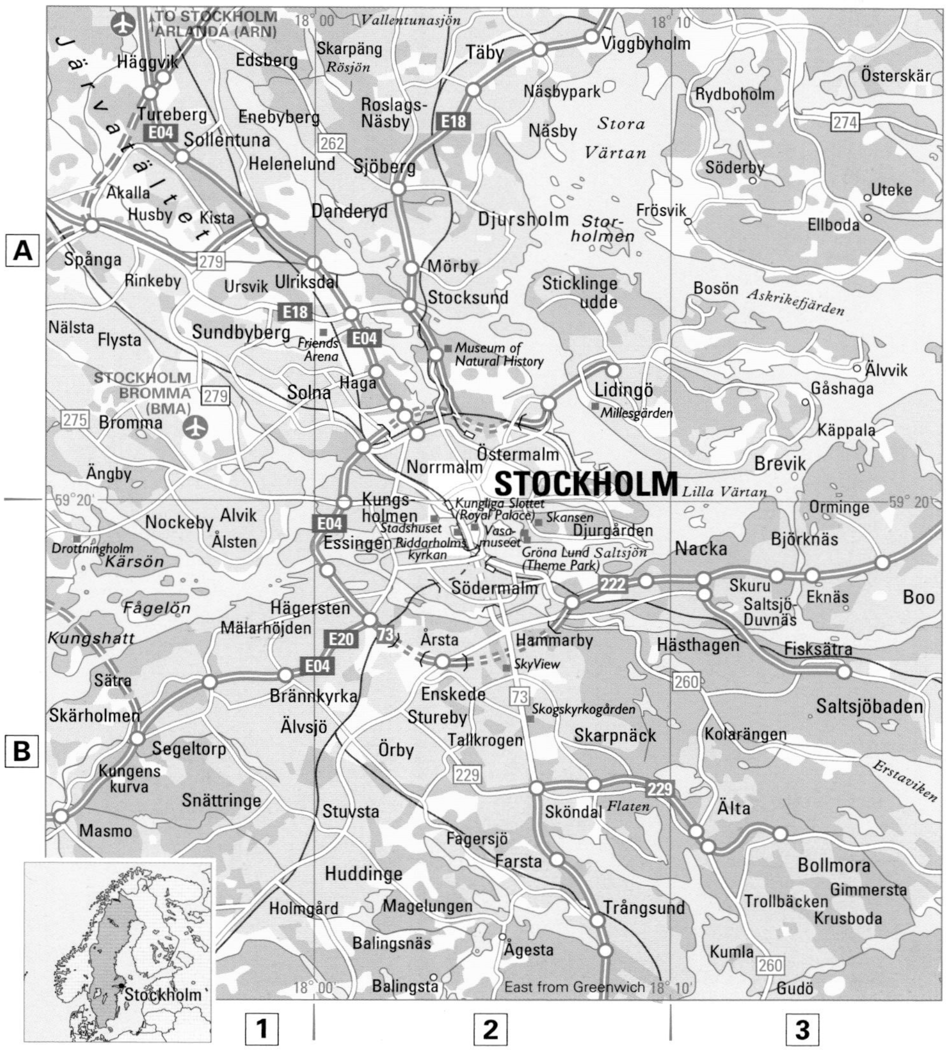

CENTRAL STOCKHOLM

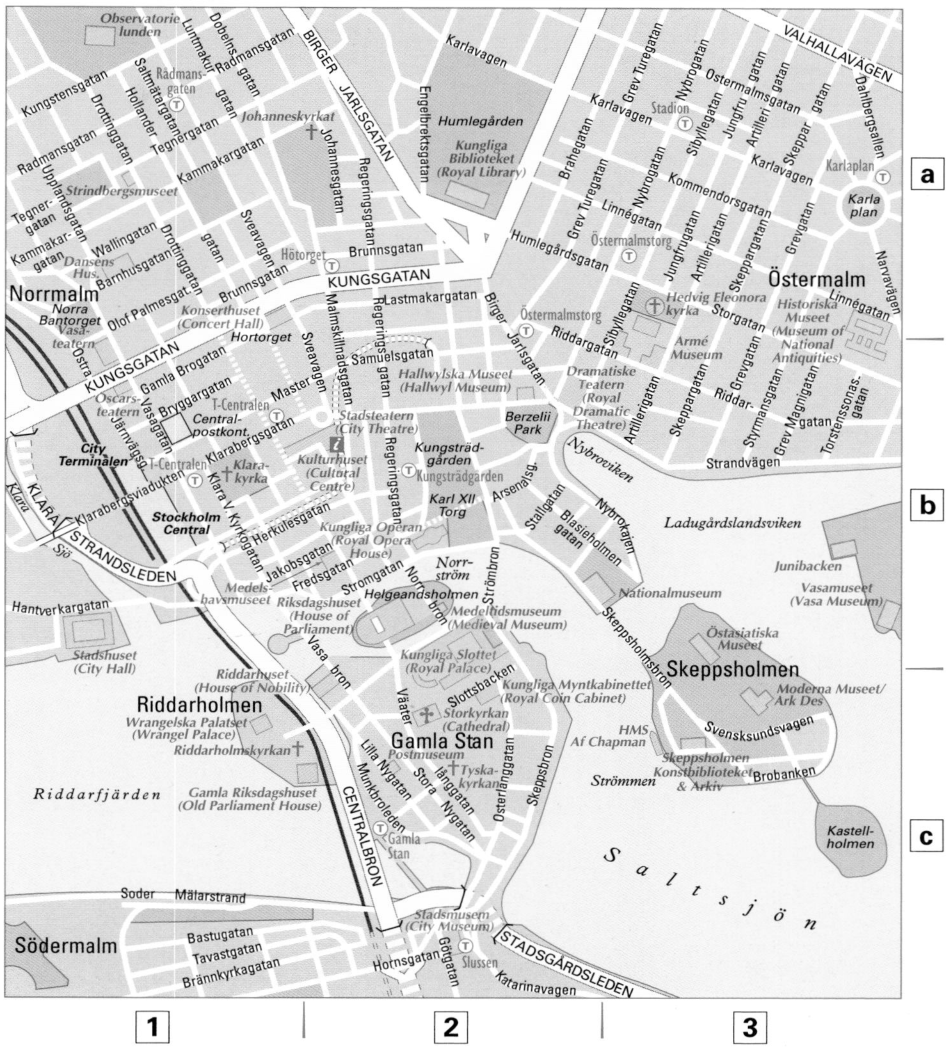

SYDNEY, AUSTRALIA

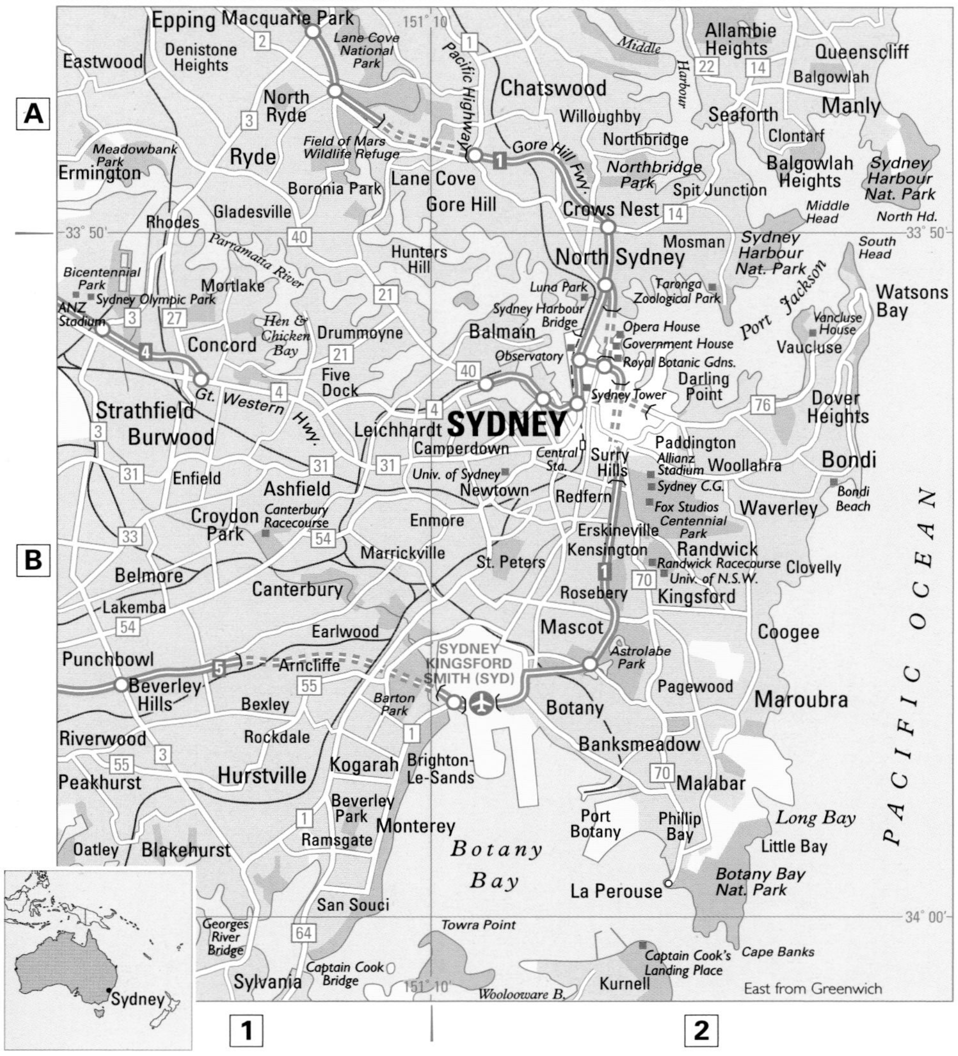

CENTRAL SYDNEY

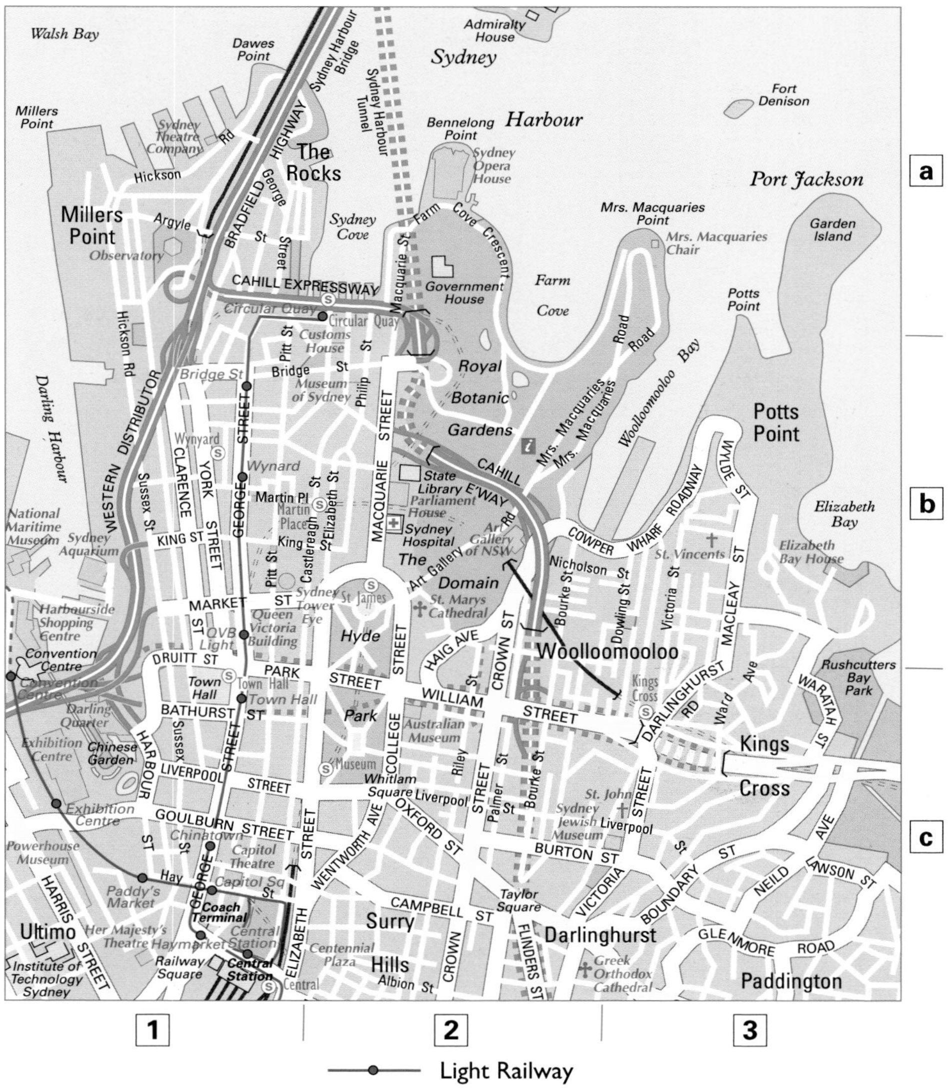

TOKYO, JAPAN

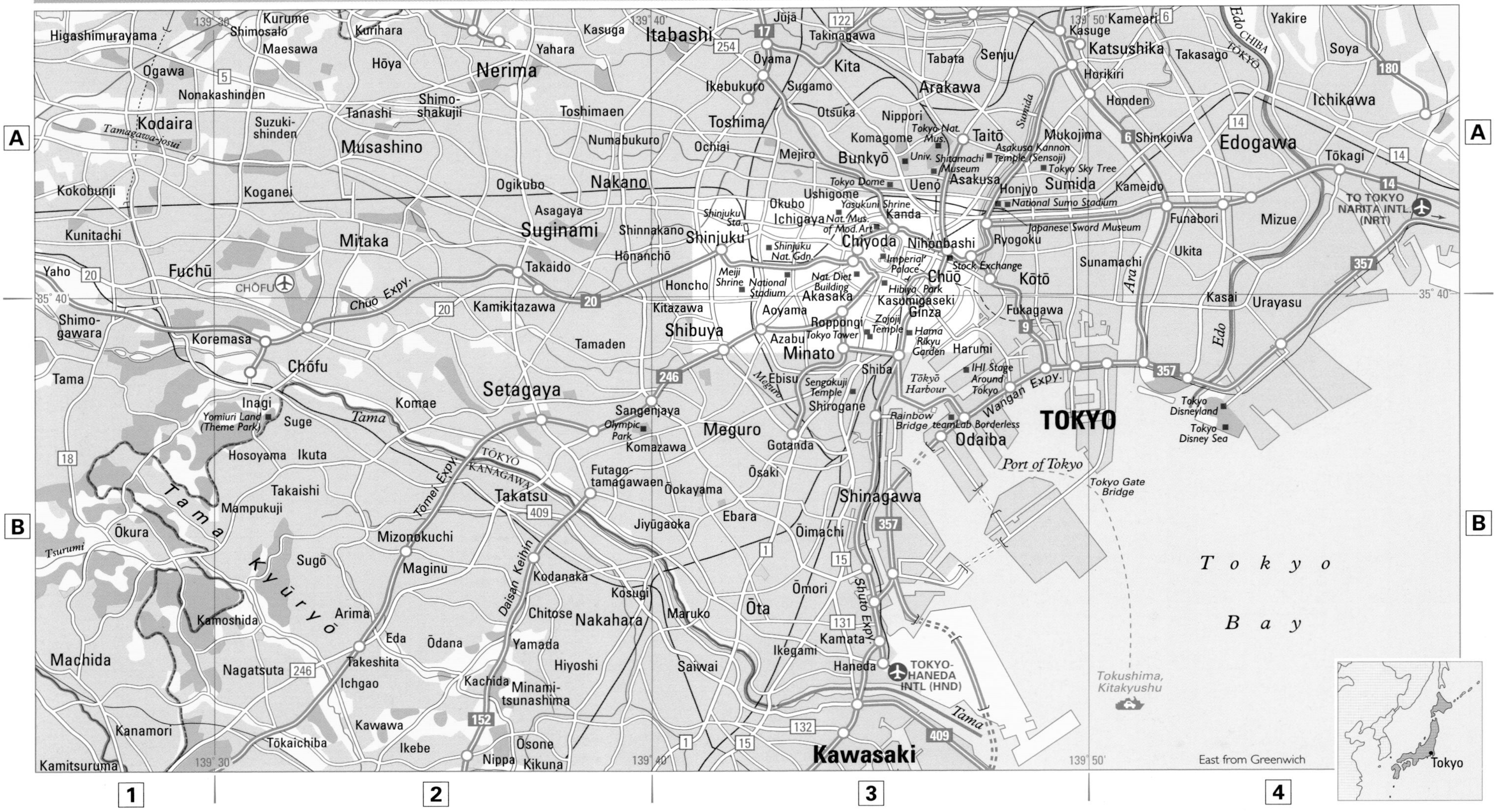
1 0 1 km 2 3 4 5
1 0 miles 1 2 3
Higashimurayama
Kurume
Shimosato
Kurihara
Maesawa
Hōya
Yahara
Kasuga
Itabashi
Jūjō
Takinagawa
Kameari
Kasuge
Yakire
Ogawa
Nonakashinden
Nerima
Ōyama
Kita
Tabata
Senju
Katsushika
Takasago
Soya
Kodaira
Suzuki-shinden
Tanashi
Shimo-shakujii
Toshimaen
Ikebukuro
Sugamo
Arakawa
Horikiri
Honden
Ichikawa
Musashino
Numabukuro
Toshima
Ōtsuka
Nippori
Taitō
Mukojima
Shinkoiwa
Edogawa
Ochiai
Mejiro
Bunkyō
Tokyo Nat. Mus.
Asakusa Kannon Temple (Sensoji)
Tokyo Sky Tree
Tōkagi
Kokobunji
Koganei
Ogikubo
Nakano
Ueno
Asakusa
Sumida
Kameido
Asagaya
Ushigome
Tokyo Dome
Honjyo
National Sumo Stadium
TO TOKYO NARITA INTL (NRT)
Kunitachi
Mitaka
Suginami
Shinnakano
Hōnanchō
Shinjuku
Ichigaya
Kanda
Japanese Sword Museum
Funabori
Mizue
Chiyoda
Nihonbashi
Ryogoku
Yaho
Fuchū
Takaido
Imperial Palace
Stock Exchange
Ukita
Chōfu
Chūō Expy.
Honcho
Meiji Shrine
National Stadium
Nat. Diet Building
Chūō
Kōtō
Sunamachi
Kamikitazawa
Akasaka
Kasumigaseki
Kasai
Urayasu
Shimo-gawara
Kitazawa
Aoyama
Hibiya Park
Ginza
Fukagawa
Koremasa
Tamaden
Shibuya
Roppongi
Tokyo Tower
Zojoji Temple
Hama Rikyu Garden
Harumi
Tama
Chōfu
Azabu
Minato
Setagaya
Ebisu
Shiba
IHI Stage Around Tokyo
Tokyo Disneyland
Tokyo Disney Sea
Inagi
Yomiuri Land (Theme Park)
Suge
Komae
Sangenjaya
Olympic Park
Sengakuji Temple
Shirogane
Tōkyō Harbour
Wangan Expy.
TOKYO
Hosoyama
Ikuta
Meguro
Gotanda
Rainbow Bridge
teamLab Borderless
Odaiba
Komazawa
Port of Tokyo
Takaishi
Futago-tamagawaen
Ōokayama
Ōsaki
Mampukuji
Takatsu
Tomei Expy.
TŌKYŌ KANAGAWA
Ebara
Shinagawa
Tokyo Gate Bridge
Ōkura
Tsurumi
Mizonokuchi
Jiyūgaoka
Ōimachi
Tokyo Bay
Sugō
Maginu
Kodanaka
Daisan Keihin
Kosugi
Ōmori
Kyūryō
Arima
Chitose
Nakahara
Maruko
Ōta
Kamoshida
Eda
Ōdana
Yamada
Shuto Expy.
Kamata
Machida
Takeshita
Hiyoshi
Saiwai
Ikegami
Haneda
TOKYO-HANEDA INTL (HND)
Tokushima, Kitakyushu
Nagatsuta
Ichgao
Kachida
Minami-tsunashima
Kanamori
Kawawa
Kawasaki
Tōkaichiba
Ikebe
Ōsone
Kamitsuruma
Nippa
Kikuna
East from Greenwich
Tokyo
139°30'
139°40'
139°50'
35°40'
A
B
1
2
3
4

CENTRAL TOKYO

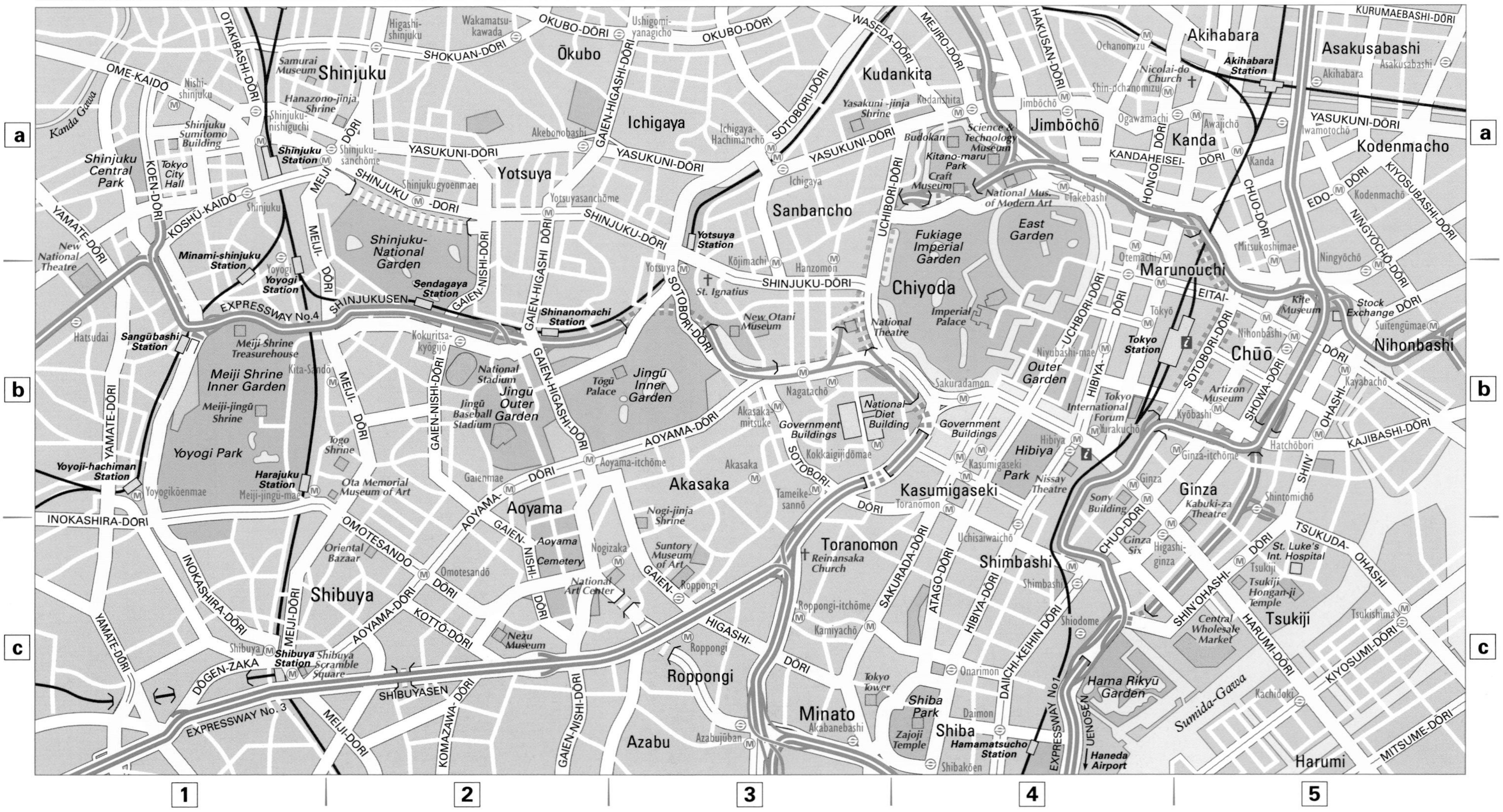
0 km 1
0 miles 0.5
Shinjuku
Ōkubo
Kudankita
Akihabara
Asakusabashi
Samurai Museum
Hanazono-jinja Shrine
Ichigaya
Yasukuni-jinja Shrine
Jimbōchō
Kanda
Kodenmacho
Shinjuku Central Park
Tokyo City Hall
Shinjuku Station
Yotsuya
Science & Technology Museum
Kitano-maru Park
Craft Museum
National Mus. of Modern Art
Sanbancho
Fukiage Imperial Garden
East Garden
Marunouchi
Shinjuku-National Garden
Sendagaya Station
Shinanomachi Station
Yotsuya Station
St. Ignatius
Chiyoda
Imperial Palace
Stock Exchange
Nihonbashi
Minami-shinjuku Station
Yoyogi Station
New Otani Museum
National Theatre
Chūō
Meiji Shrine Treasurehouse
Meiji Shrine Inner Garden
National Stadium
Jingū Outer Garden
Tōgū Palace
Jingū Inner Garden
Outer Garden
Tokyo Station
Tokyo International Forum
Meiji-jingū Shrine
Yoyogi Park
Jingū Baseball Stadium
Government Buildings
National Diet Building
Hibiya Park
Nissay Theatre
Ginza
Kabuki-za Theatre
Yoyogi-hachiman Station
Harajuku Station
Ota Memorial Museum of Art
Akasaka
Aoyama
Kasumigaseki
Sony Building
Ginza Six
Oriental Bazaar
Aoyama Cemetery
Nogi-jinja Shrine
Suntory Museum of Art
Toranomon
Reinansaka Church
Shimbashi
St. Luke's Int. Hospital
Tsukiji Hongan-ji Temple
Shibuya
National Art Center
Central Wholesale Market
Tsukiji
Nezu Museum
Shibuya Station
Shibuya Scramble Square
Roppongi
Tokyo Tower
Shiba Park
Hama Rikyū Garden
Minato
Zojoji Temple
Shiba
Hamamatsucho Station
Haneda Airport
Azabu
Harumi
Sumida-Gawa
EXPRESSWAY No.3
EXPRESSWAY No.4
EXPRESSWAY No.1
YASUKUNI-DŌRI
SHINJUKU-DŌRI
AOYAMA-DŌRI
MEIJI-DŌRI
INOKASHIRA-DŌRI
a
b
c
1
2
3
4
5

⊖ Toei Subway ⓜ Tokyo Metro

TEHRAN, IRAN

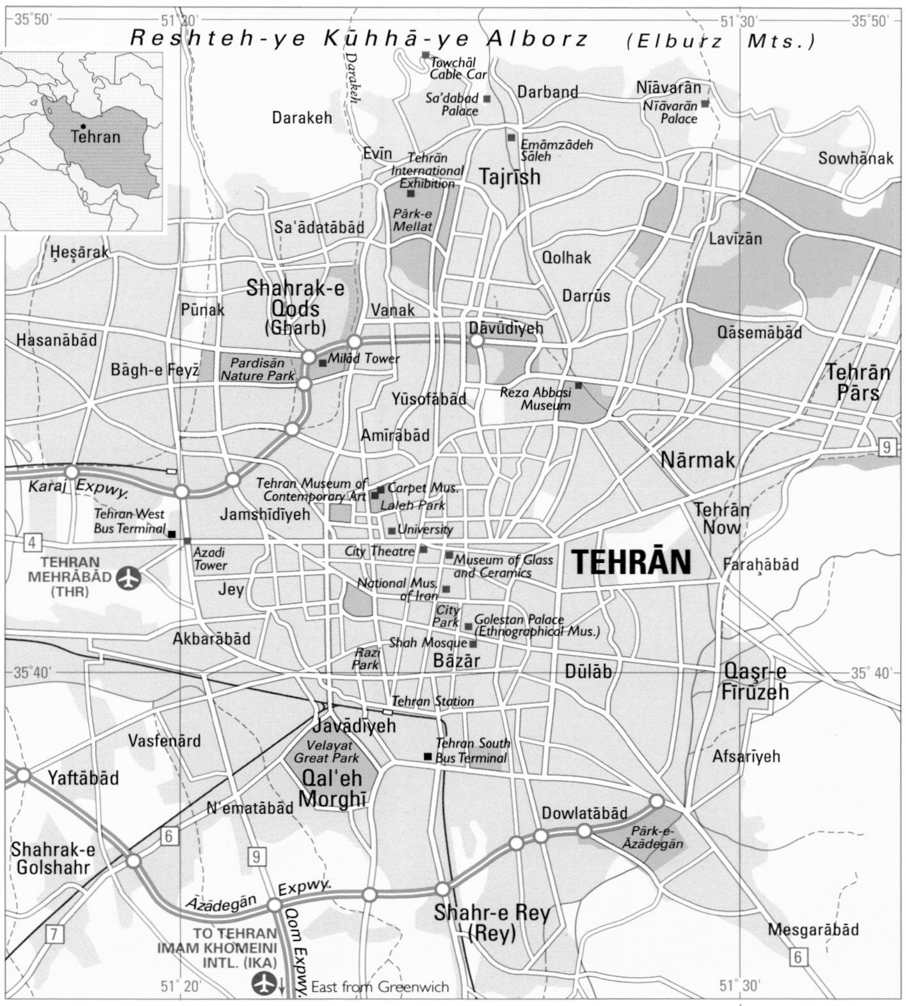

CENTRAL TORONTO

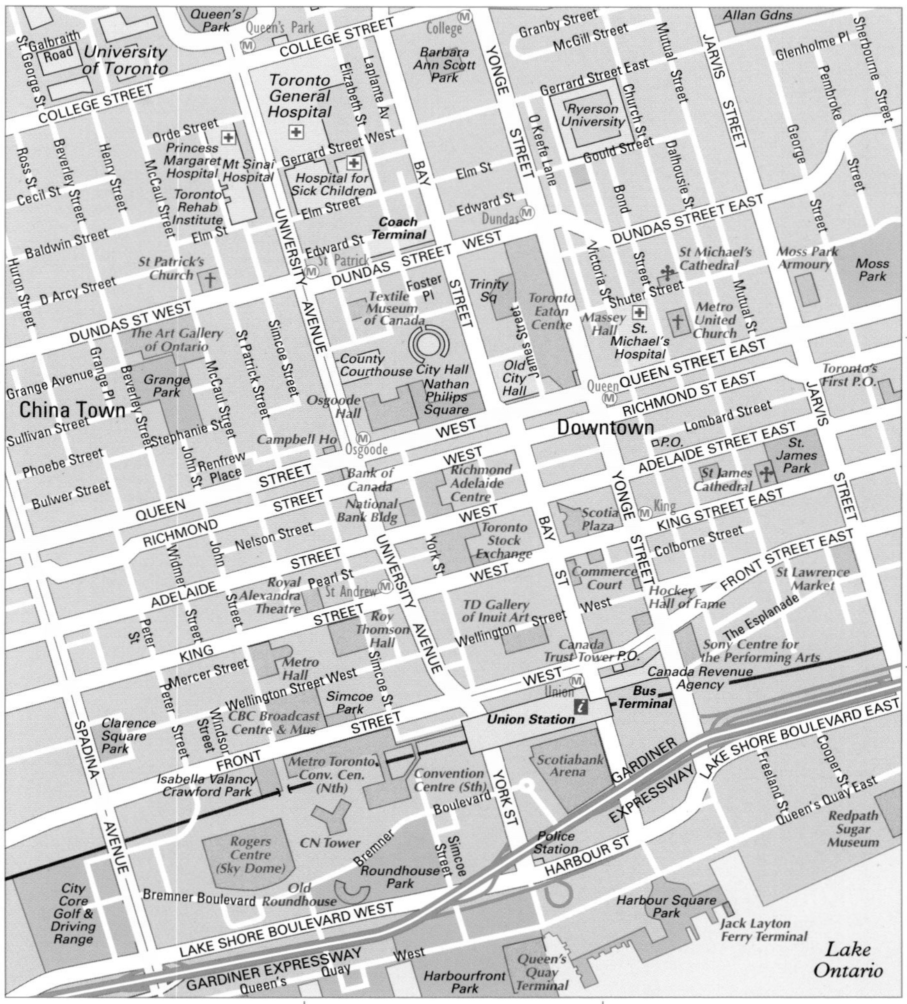

TORONTO, CANADA

(427) Provincial route numbers

CENTRAL VENICE

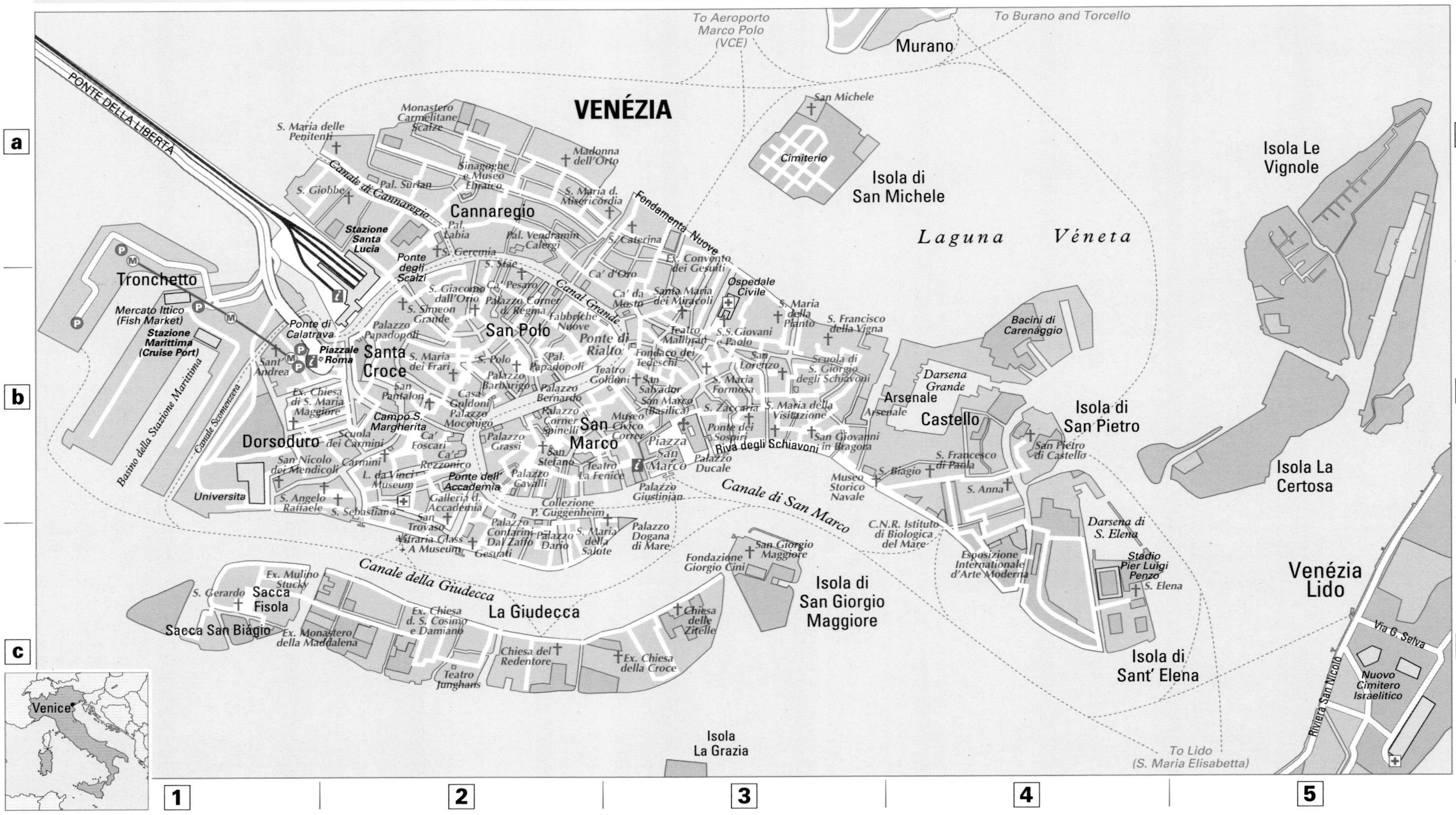

Car parks
Vaporetti (water buses)
Monorail (Venice People Mover)

VIENNA, AUSTRIA

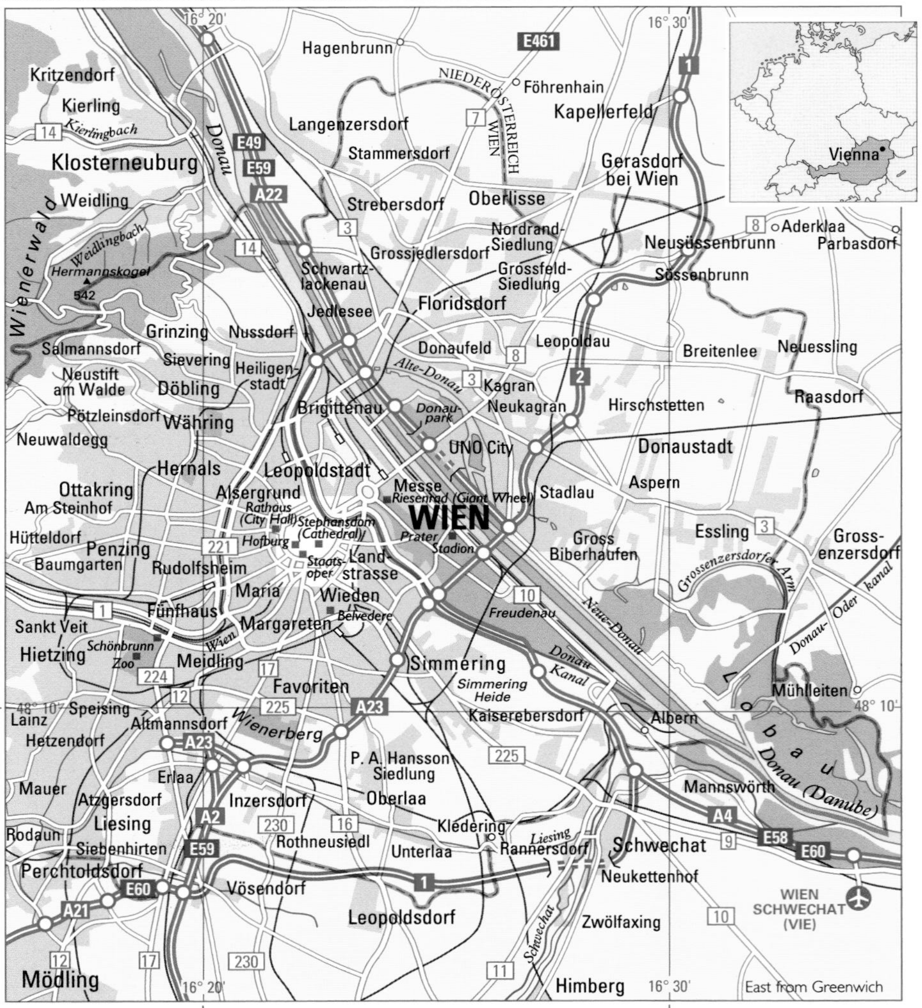

CENTRAL VIENNA

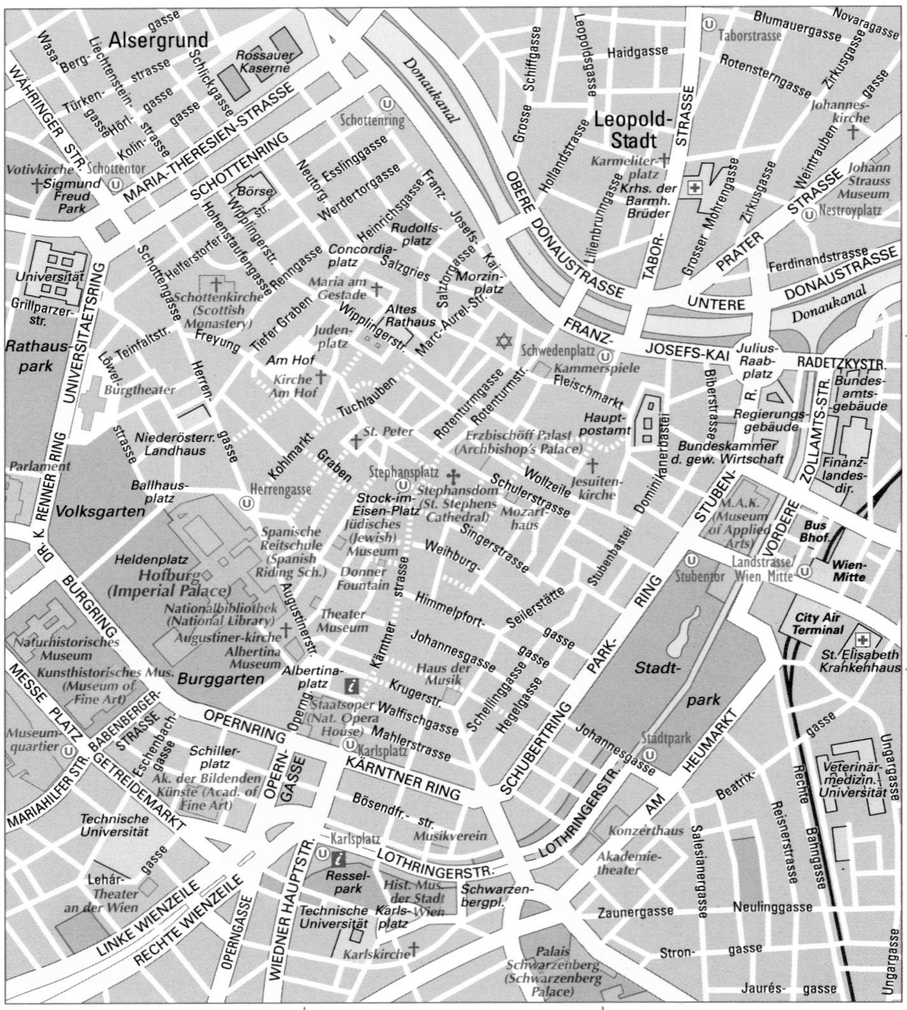

WARSAW, POLAND

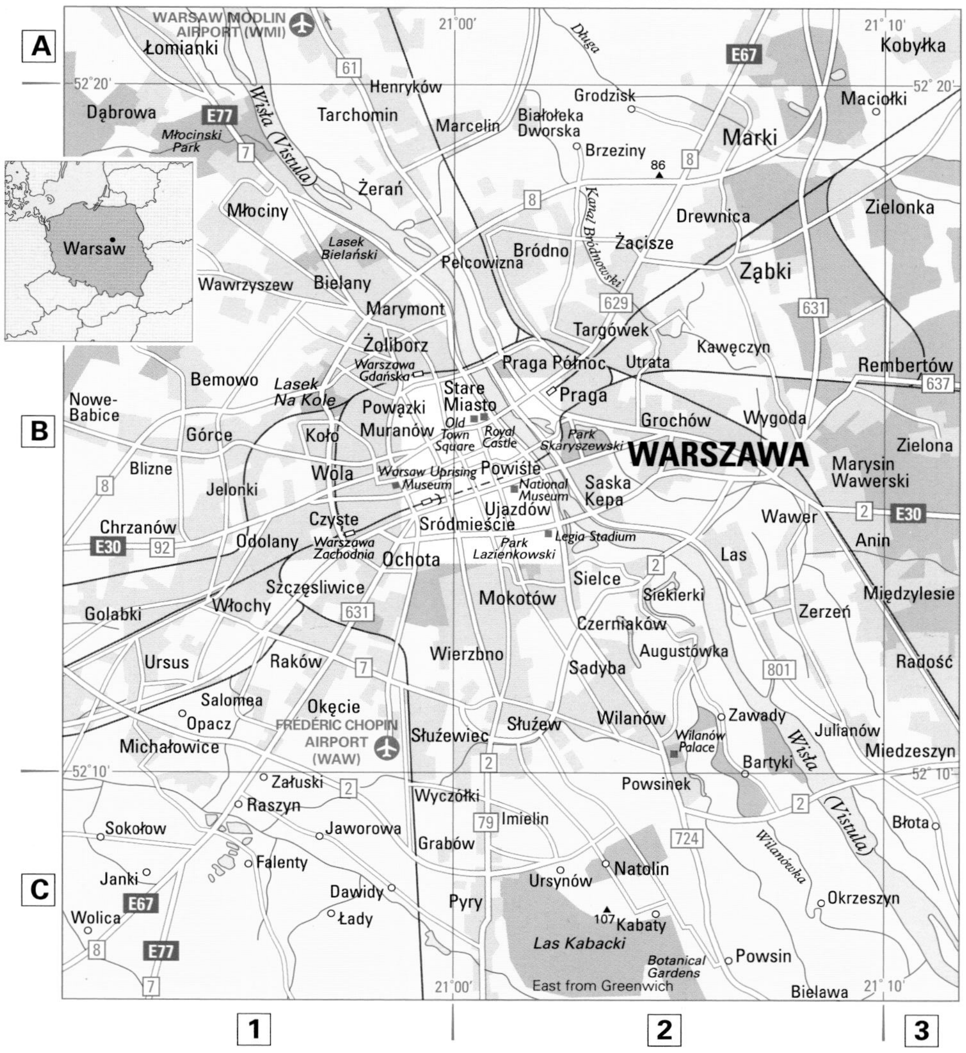

CENTRAL WARSAW

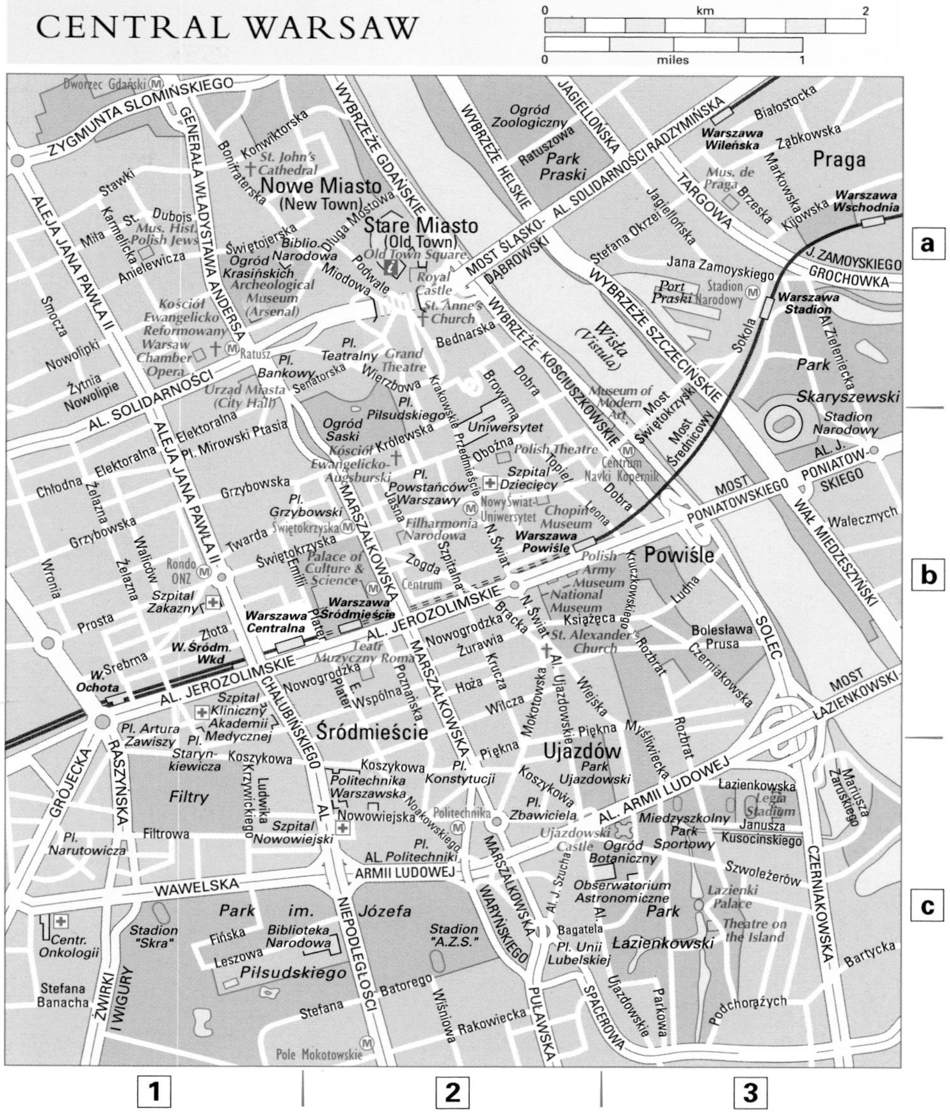

WASHINGTON D.C.

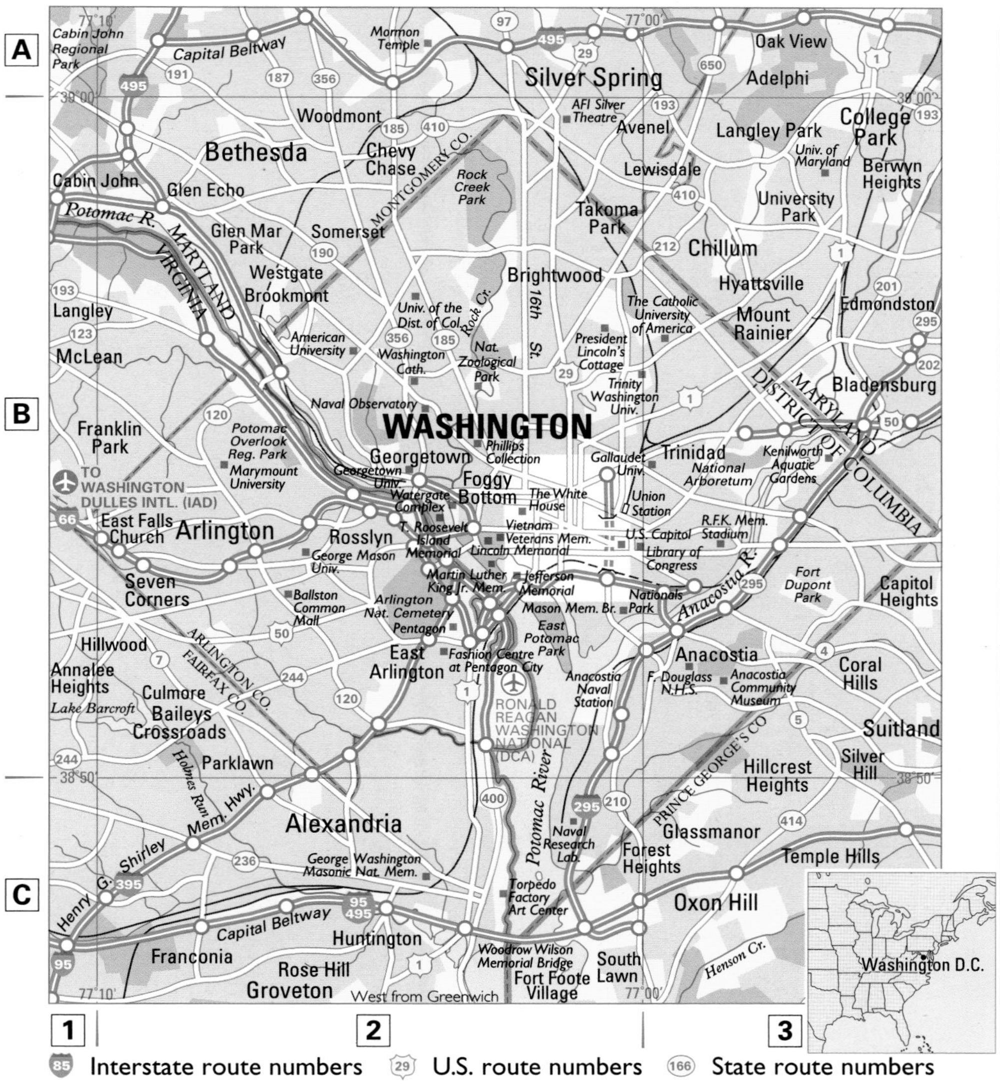

CENTRAL WASHINGTON

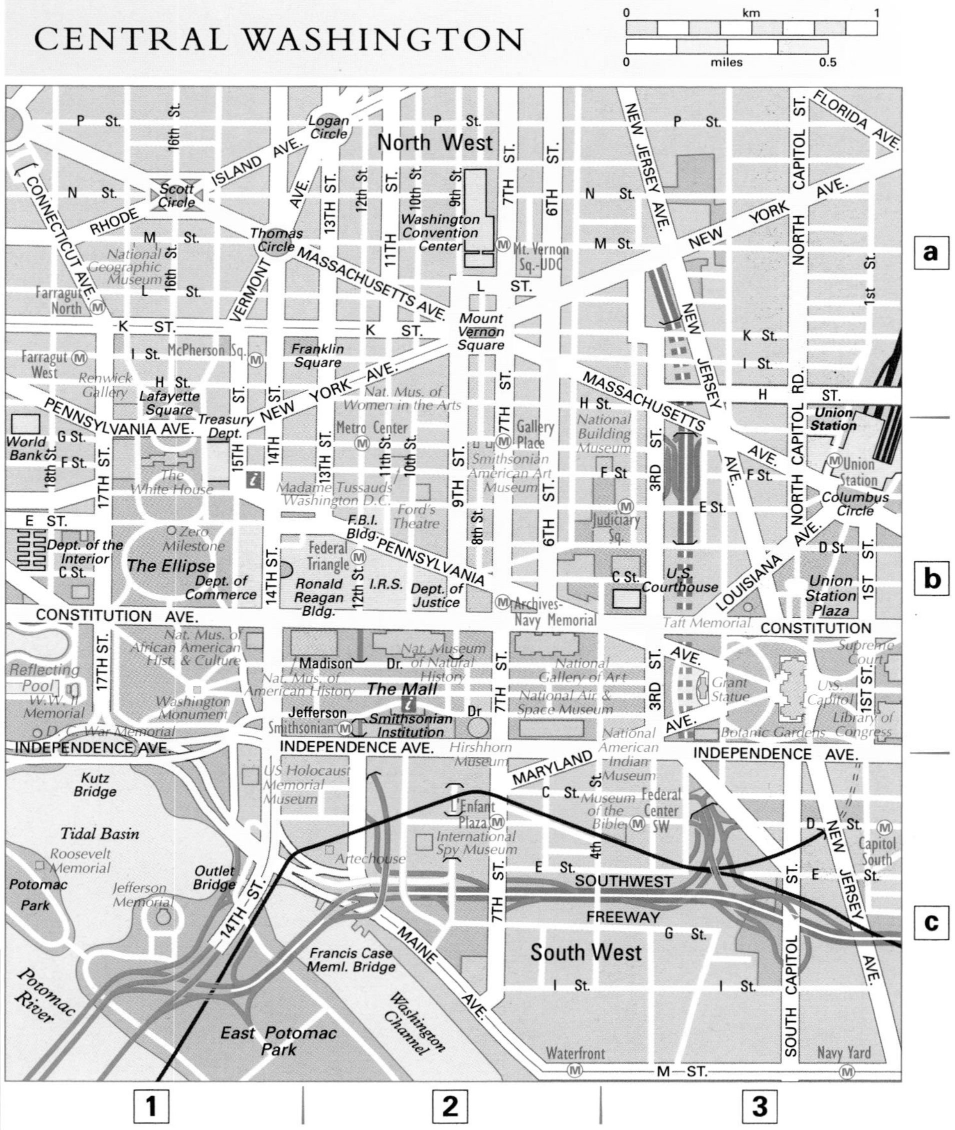

WORLD MAPS

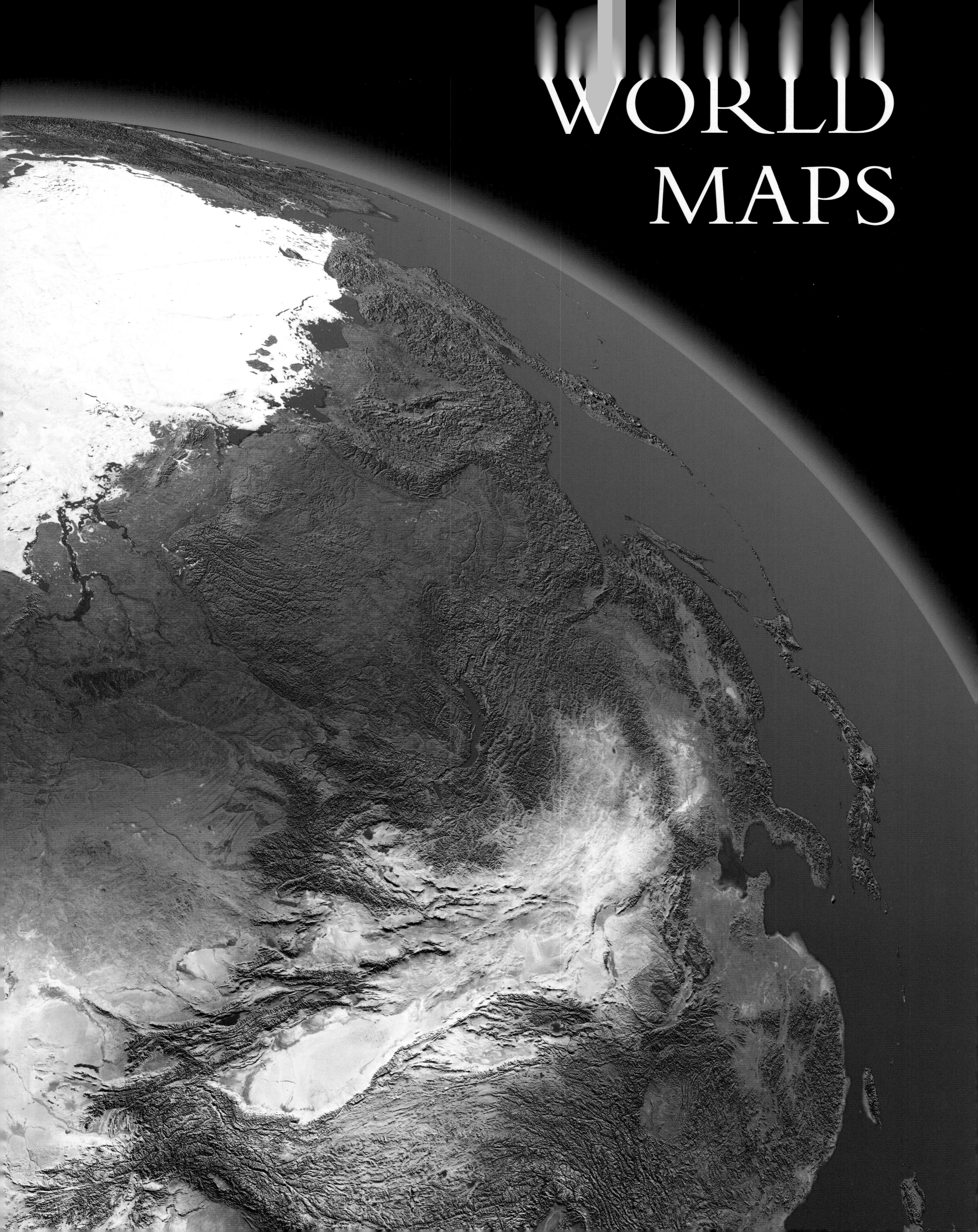

Equatorial Scale 1:76 000 000

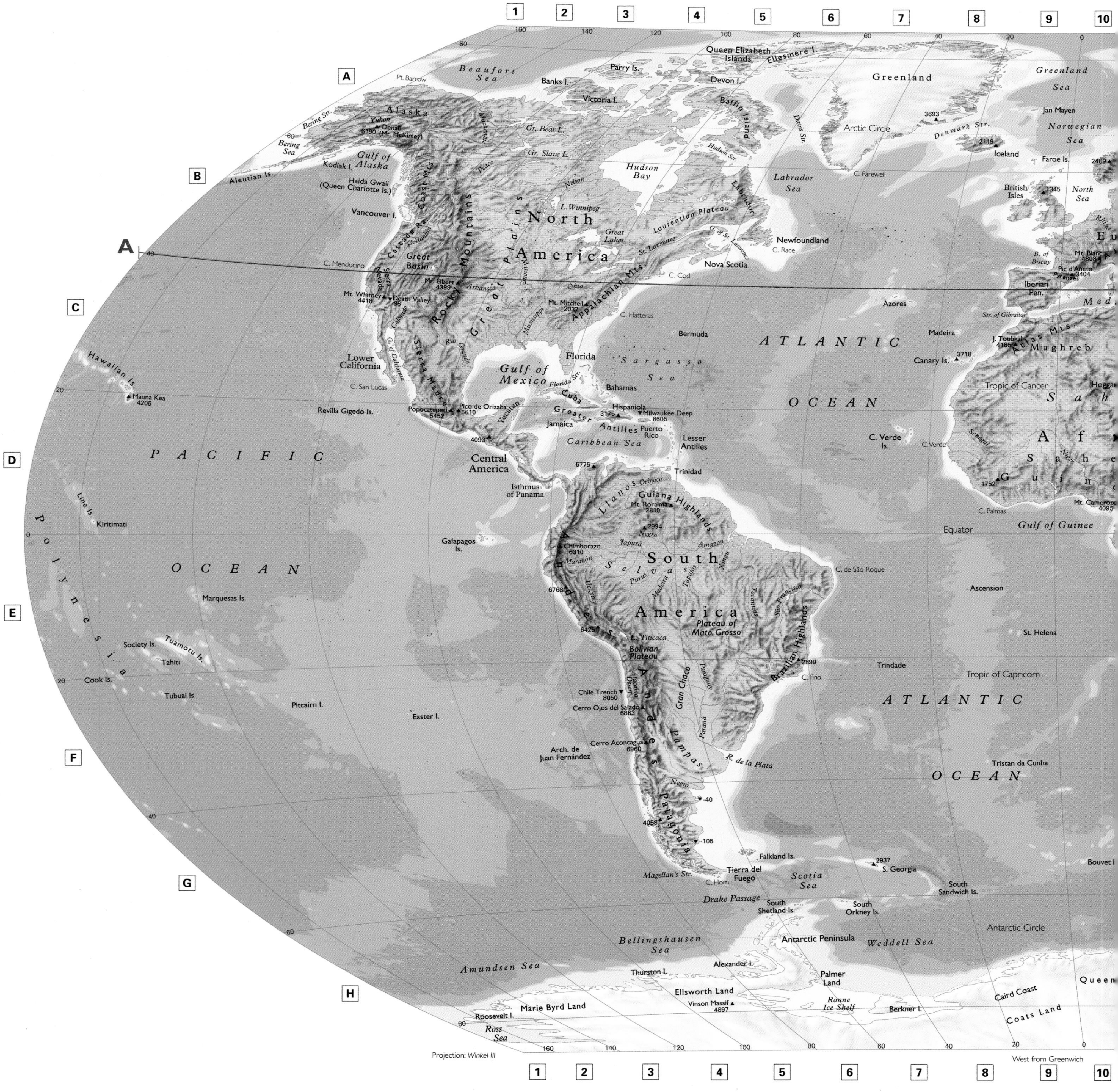

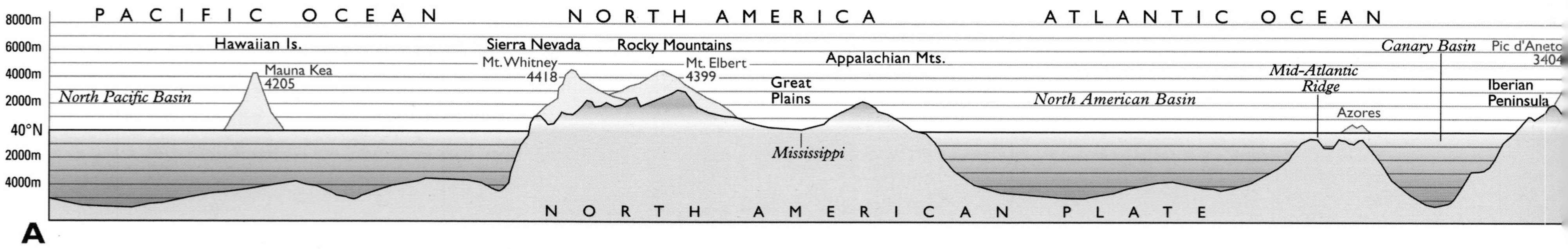

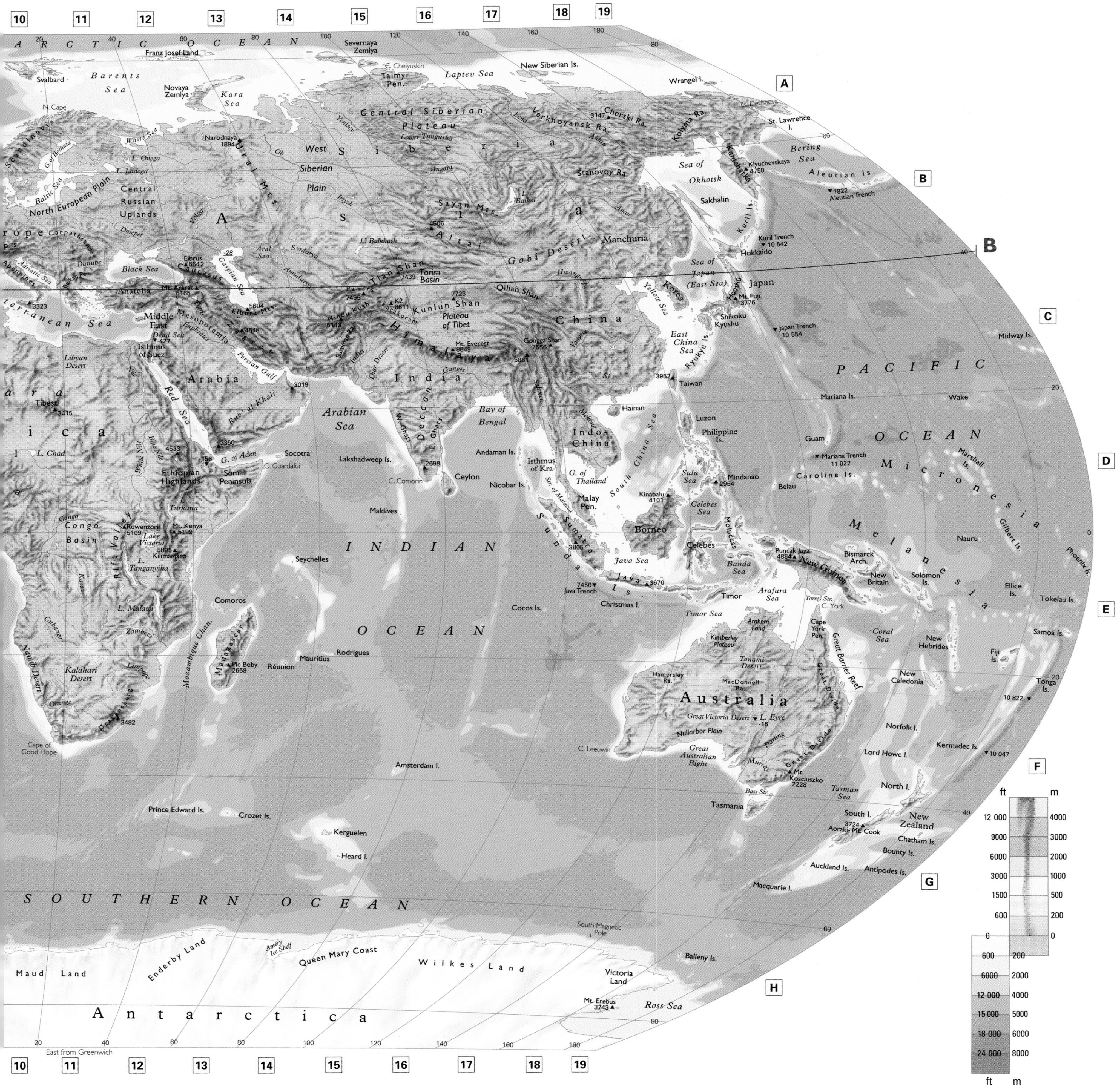
10
11
12
13
14
15
16
17
18
19
A R C T I C O C E A N
Franz Josef Land
Severnaya Zemlya
C. Chelyuskin
Taimyr Pen.
Laptev Sea
New Siberian Is.
Wrangel I.
Svalbard
Barents Sea
Novaya Zemlya
Kara Sea
N. Cape
Central Siberian Plateau
Lower Tunguska
Verkhoyansk Ra.
Cherski Ra.
3147
Kolyma Ra.
C. Dezhneva
St. Lawrence I.
Bering Sea
Aleutian Is.
7822
Aleutian Trench
Klyuchevskaya 4750
Kamchatka
Sea of Okhotsk
Sakhalin
Stanovoy Ra.
Scandinavia
G. of Bothnia
White Sea
L. Onega
L. Ladoga
Baltic Sea
North European Plain
Central Russian Uplands
Narodnaya 1894
Ural Mts.
West Siberian Plain
S i b e r i a
Ob
Yenisey
Lena
Aldan
Angara
Irtysh
Sayan Mts.
L. Baikal
Amur
A s i a
Europe
Carpathians
Dnieper
Volga
Danube
Adriatic Sea
Apennines
Balkan Pen.
Black Sea
Elbrus 5642
Caucasus
Caspian Sea
-28
Aral Sea
Syrdarya
Amudarya
L. Balkhash
4506
Altai
Gobi Desert
Manchuria
Kuril Is.
Kuril Trench 10 542
Hokkaido
Sea of Japan (East Sea)
Japan
Honshu
Mt. Fuji 3776
Shikoku
Kyushu
Korea
Yellow Sea
Hwang-He
Tian Shan
7439
Tarim Basin
Pamirs
7495
K2 8611
Karakoram
Hindu Kush
5143
Kunlun Shan
7723
Qilian Shan
Plateau of Tibet
Anatolia
Mt. Ararat 5165
5604
Elburz Mts.
Mesopotamia
Zagros Mts.
4548
Tigris
Euphrates
Mediterranean Sea
3323
Middle East
Dead Sea -427
Isthmus of Suez
Persian Gulf
Sulaiman Ra.
Indus
Thar Desert
Himalaya
Mt. Everest 8849
Gongga Shan 7556
5881
Ganges
Yangtze
C h i n a
East China Sea
Ryukyu Is.
3952
Taiwan
Japan Trench 10 554
Midway Is.
P A C I F I C
O C E A N
Libyan Desert
Nile
Sahara
Tibesti
3415
Arabia
Red Sea
Rub' al Khali
3019
Arabian Sea
I n d i a
Deccan
W. Ghats
E. Ghats
Bay of Bengal
Salween
Mekong
Hainan
Indo-China
Mariana Is.
Wake
Africa
L. Chad
Blue Nile
White Nile
4533
3350
-156
G. of Aden
Socotra
C. Guardafui
Ethiopian Highlands
Somali Peninsula
L. Turkana
Lakshadweep Is.
C. Comorin
2698
Ceylon
Andaman Is.
Nicobar Is.
Isthmus of Kra
G. of Thailand
South China Sea
Luzon
Philippine Is.
Guam
Mariana Trench 11 022
Marshall Is.
Micronesia
Sulu Sea
Mindanao
2954
Caroline Is.
Belau
Congo
Congo Basin
Ruwenzori 5109
Mt. Kenya 5199
Lake Victoria
5895 Kilimanjaro
Rift Valley
L. Tanganyika
Maldives
Str. of Malacca
Malay Pen.
Sumatra
Kinabalu 4101
Borneo
Celebes Sea
Celebes
Moluccas
Gilbert Is.
Nauru
Melanesia
Seychelles
I N D I A N
O C E A N
Sunda Is.
3805
Java Sea
Java
3670
7450
Java Trench
Banda Sea
Puncak Jaya 4884
New Guinea
Bismarck Arch.
New Britain
Solomon Is.
Phoenix Is.
Ellice Is.
Tokelau Is.
Kasai
L. Malawi
Comoros
Zambezi
Cubango
Namib Desert
Kalahari Desert
Limpopo
Orange
Drakensberg
3482
Cape of Good Hope
Mozambique Chan.
Madagascar
Pic Boby 2658
Réunion
Mauritius
Rodrigues
Cocos Is.
Christmas I.
Timor
Timor Sea
Arafura Sea
Torres Str.
C. York
Cape York Pen.
Arnhem Land
Kimberley Plateau
Tanami Desert
Hamersley Ra.
MacDonnell Ra.
Great Barrier Reef
Great Dividing Range
Coral Sea
New Hebrides
Fiji Is.
Samoa Is.
New Caledonia
Tonga Is.
10 822
A u s t r a l i a
Great Victoria Desert
L. Eyre -16
Nullarbor Plain
Great Australian Bight
C. Leeuwin
Darling
Murray
Mt. Kosciuszko 2228
Bass Str.
Tasmania
Norfolk I.
Lord Howe I.
Kermadec Is.
10 047
Tasman Sea
North I.
South I.
New Zealand
Aoraki Mt. Cook 3724
Chatham Is.
Bounty Is.
Antipodes Is.
Auckland Is.
Macquarie I.
Amsterdam I.
Prince Edward Is.
Crozet Is.
Kerguelen
Heard I.
S O U T H E R N O C E A N
South Magnetic Pole
Maud Land
Enderby Land
Amery Ice Shelf
Queen Mary Coast
Wilkes Land
Balleny Is.
Victoria Land
Mt. Erebus 3743
Ross Sea
A n t a r c t i c a
East from Greenwich
B
C
D
E
F
G
H
ft
m
12 000
9000
6000
3000
1500
600
0
4000
3000
2000
1000
500
200
0
600
6000
12 000
15 000
18 000
24 000
200
2000
4000
5000
6000
8000

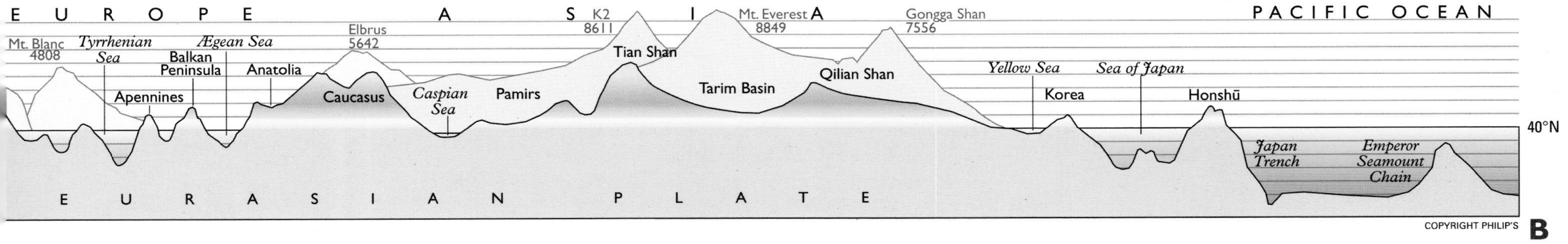
E U R O P E
A S I A
Mt. Blanc 4808
Tyrrhenian Sea
Balkan Peninsula
Ægean Sea
Apennines
Anatolia
Elbrus 5642
Caucasus
Caspian Sea
Pamirs
K2 8611
Tian Shan
Mt. Everest 8849
Tarim Basin
Gongga Shan 7556
Qilian Shan
Yellow Sea
Korea
Sea of Japan
Honshū
PACIFIC OCEAN
40°N
Japan Trench
Emperor Seamount Chain
E U R A S I A N P L A T E

B

 Equatorial Scale 1:76 000 000

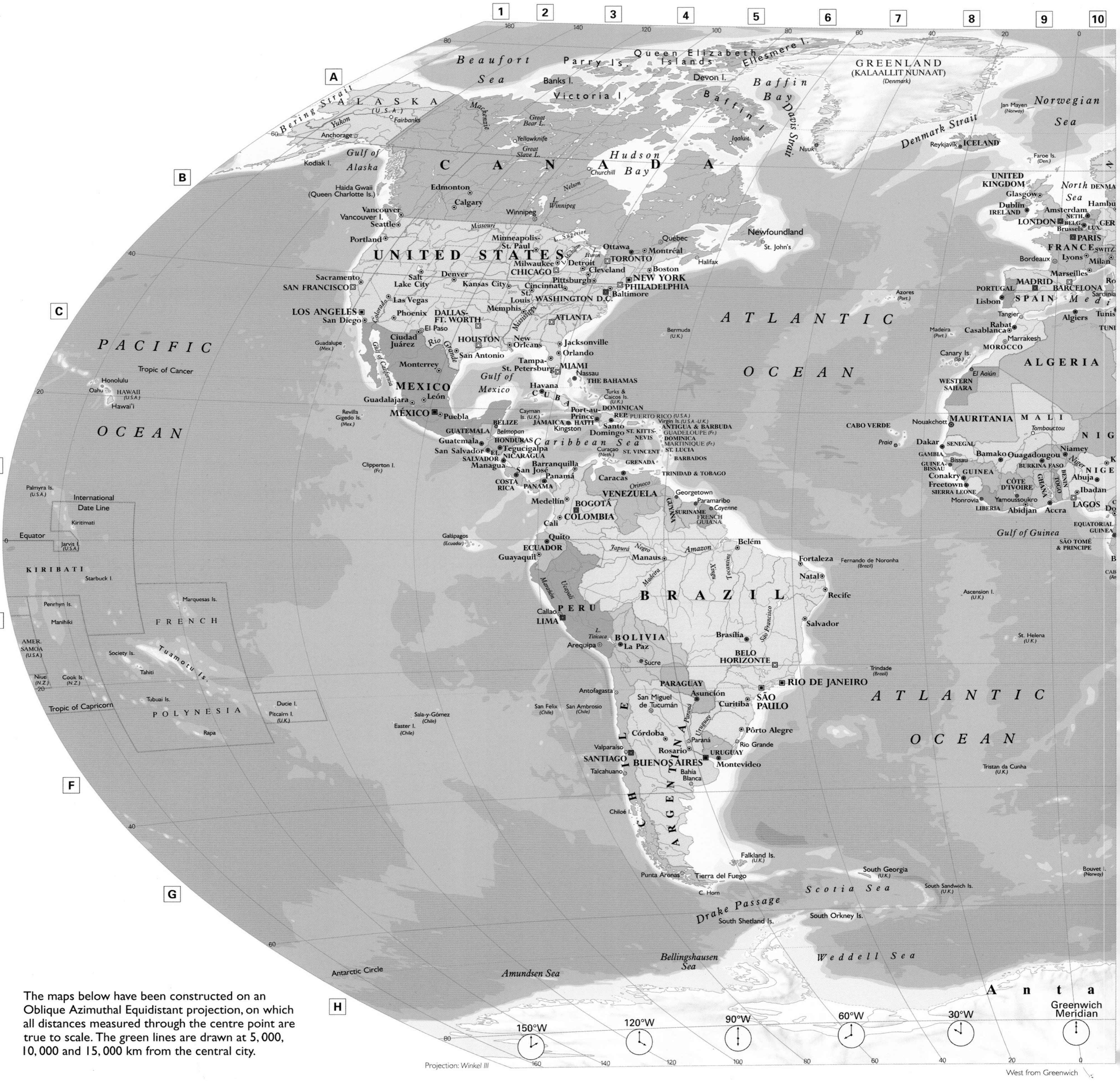

The maps below have been constructed on an Oblique Azimuthal Equidistant projection, on which all distances measured through the centre point are true to scale. The green lines are drawn at 5,000, 10,000 and 15,000 km from the central city.

MEXICO CITY
19° 26′N 99° 04′W

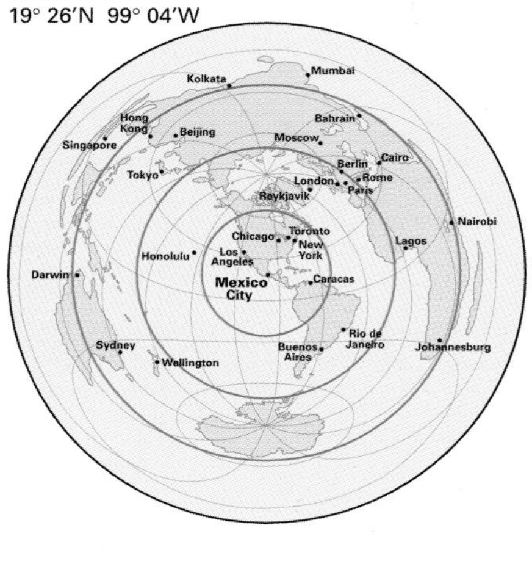

NEW YORK
40° 43′N 74° 00′W

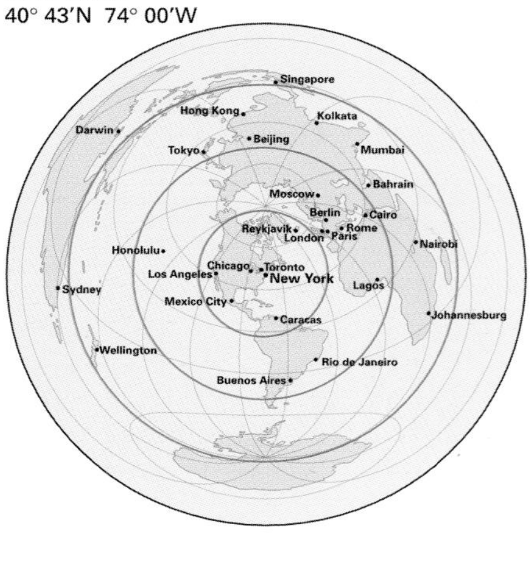

RIO DE JANEIRO
22° 50′S 43° 15′W

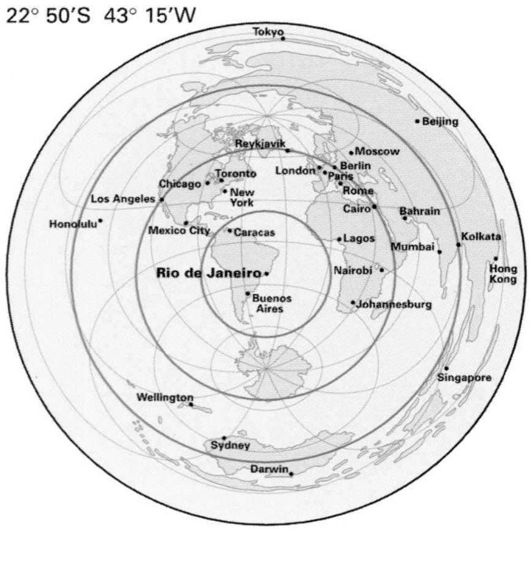

LONDON
51° 28′N 00° 27′W

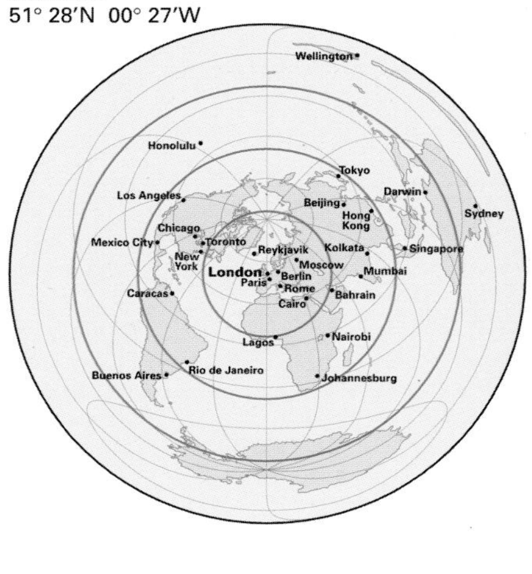

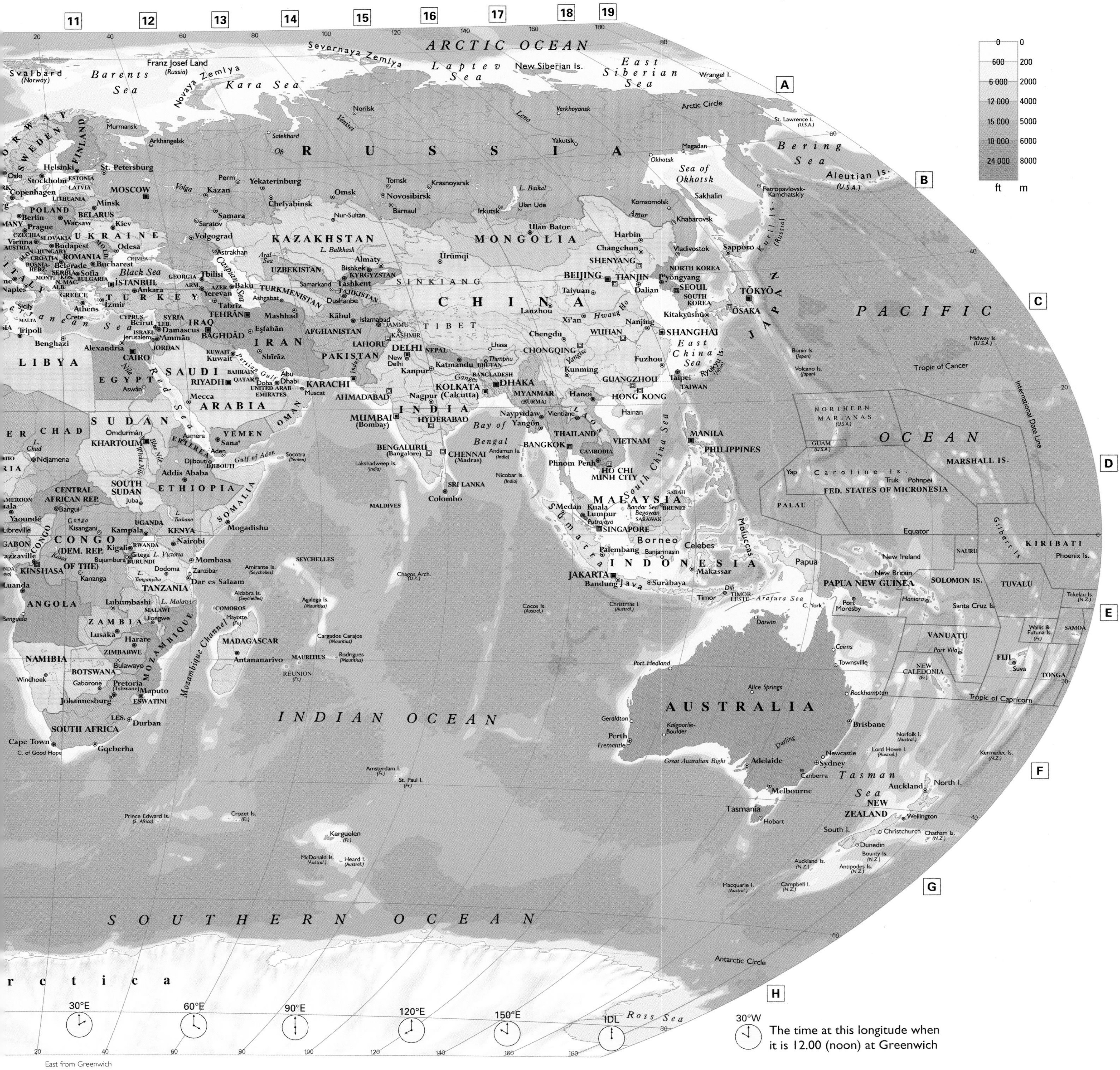

CAPE TOWN
33° 55′S 18° 35′E

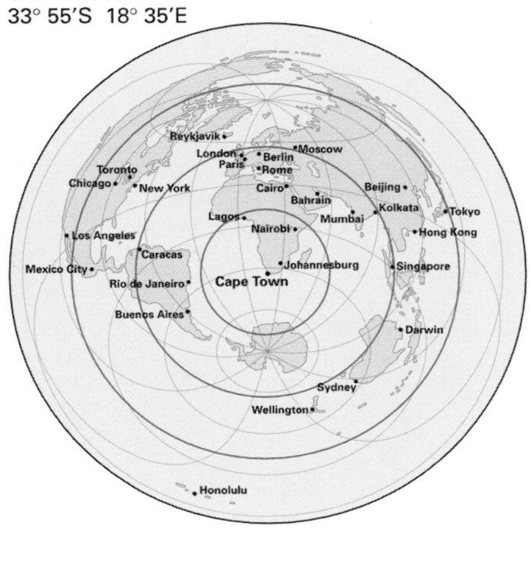

DELHI
28° 39′N 77° 13′E

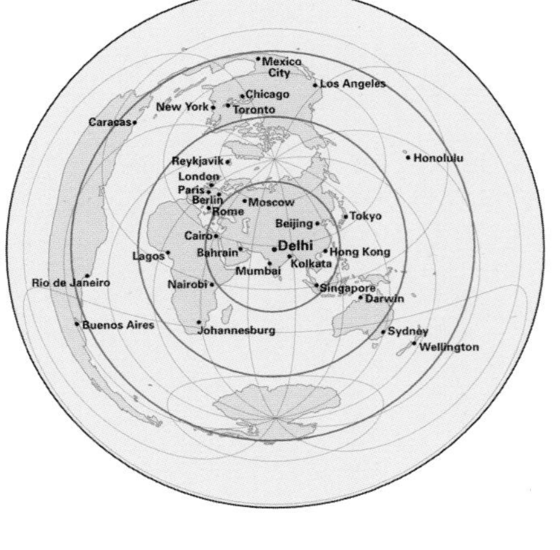

TOKYO
35° 33′N 139° 46′E

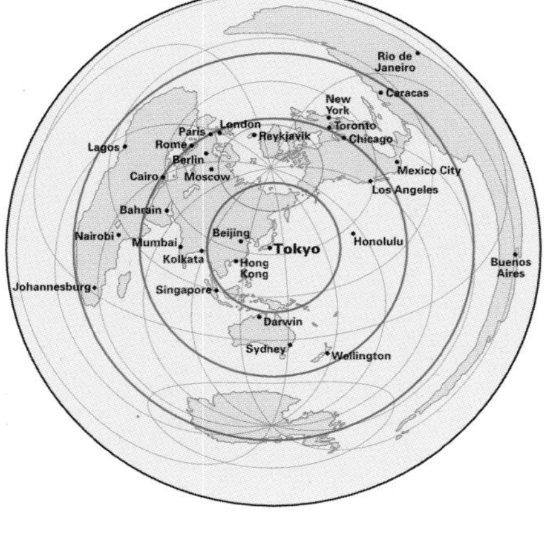

SYDNEY
33° 56′ S 151° 10′E

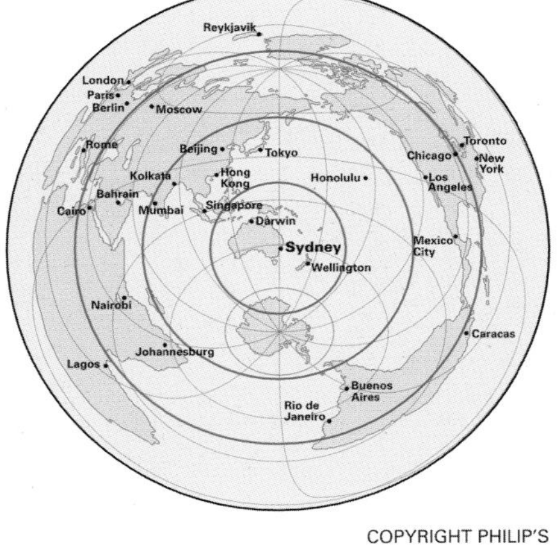

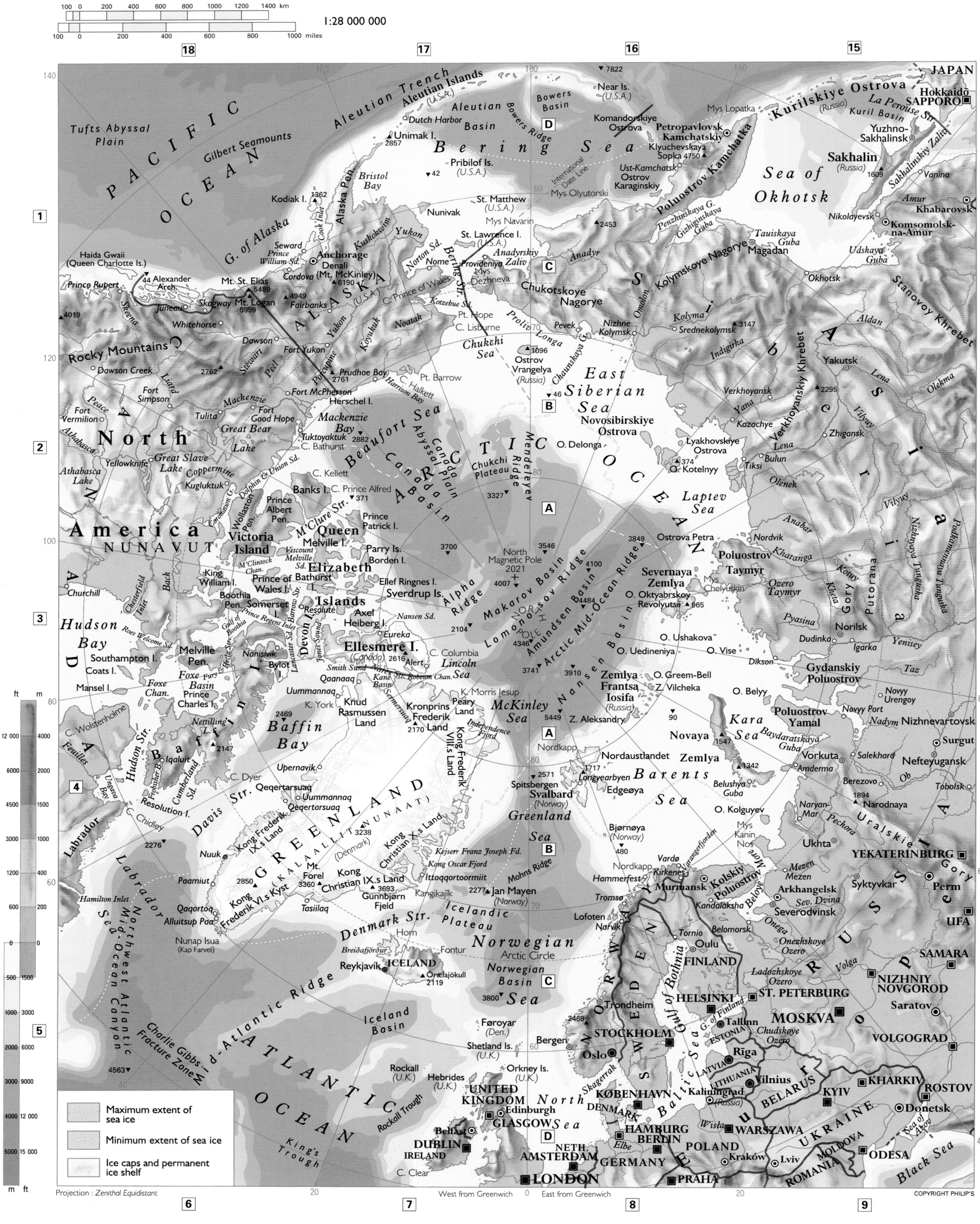
100 0 200 400 600 800 1000 1200 1400 km
100 0 200 400 600 800 1000 miles
1:28 000 000
18
17
16
15
1
2
3
4
5
14
13
12
11
10
6
7
8
9
PACIFIC OCEAN
Tufts Abyssal Plain
Gilbert Seamounts
Aleutian Trench
Aleutian Islands (U.S.A.)
Aleutian Basin
Bowers Basin
Bowers Ridge
Near Is. (U.S.A.)
Komandorskiye Ostrova
Bering Sea
Dutch Harbor
Unimak I.
Pribilof Is. (U.S.A.)
Bristol Bay
Kodiak I.
Alaska Pen.
Cook Inlet
Kuskokwim
Yukon
Nunivak
St. Matthew (U.S.A.)
St. Lawrence I. (U.S.A.)
Mys Navarin
International Date Line
Mys Olyutorski
Petropavlovsk Kamchatskiy
Klyuchevskaya Sopka 4750
Ust-Kamchatsk
Ostrov Karaginskiy
Poluostrov Kamchatka
Mys Lopatka
Kurilskiye Ostrova (Russia)
Kuril Basin
La Perouse Str.
JAPAN
Hokkaidō
SAPPORO
Yuzhno-Sakhalinsk
Sakhalin (Russia)
Sakhalinskiy Zaliv
Vanino
Sea of Okhotsk
Amur
Khabarovsk
Nikolayevsk
Komsomolsk-na-Amur
Penzhinskaya G.
Gizhiginskaya Guba
Tauiskaya Guba
Magadan
Udskaya Guba
Okhotsk
Stanovoy Khrebet
Aldan
Kolymskoye Nagorye
Omolon
Anadyr
Anadyrskiy Zaliv
Provideniya
Mys Dezhneva
Bering Str.
Chukotskoye Nagorye
G. of Alaska
Haida Gwaii (Queen Charlotte Is.)
Prince Rupert
Alexander Arch.
Seward
Prince William Sd.
Anchorage
Cordova
Denali (Mt. McKinley) 6190
Mt. St. Elias 5489
Mt. Logan 5959
Juneau
Skagway
Fairbanks
ALASKA (U.S.A.)
Norton Sd.
Nome
C. Prince of Wales
Kotzebue Sd.
Pt. Hope
C. Lisburne
Noatak
Koyukuk
Whitehorse
Skeena
Dawson
Fort Yukon
Porcupine
Rocky Mountains
Dawson Creek
Stewart
Pelt
Prudhoe Bay
Pt. Barrow
C. Halkett
Harrison Bay
Fort McPherson
Herschel I.
Fort Simpson
Liard
Mackenzie
Peace
Fort Vermilion
Tulita
Fort Good Hope
Great Bear Lake
Mackenzie Bay
Tuktoyaktuk
C. Bathurst
Beaufort Sea
Athabasca
Athabasca Lake
Yellowknife
Great Slave Lake
Coppermine
Kugluktuk
North America
NUNAVUT
CANADA
Dolphin & Union Sd.
Coronation G.
Wollaston Pen.
Prince Albert Pen.
C. Kellett
Banks I.
C. Prince Alfred
M'Clure Str.
Victoria Island
Queen Elizabeth Islands
Melville I.
Viscount Melville Sd.
Prince Patrick I.
Parry Is.
Borden I.
M'Clintock Chan.
King William I.
Chesterfield Inlet
Back
Churchill
Prince of Wales I.
Bathurst I.
Ellef Ringnes I.
Sverdrup Is.
Boothia Pen.
Somerset I.
Gulf of Boothia
Prince Regent Inlet
Barrow Str.
Resolute
Devon I.
Axel Heiberg I.
Nansen Sd.
Eureka
Hudson Bay
Roes Welcome Sd.
Melville Pen.
Southampton I.
Coats I.
Mansel I.
Foxe Basin
Foxe Chan.
Fury & Hecla Str.
Prince Charles I.
Nanisivik
Lancaster Sd.
Jones Sound
Bylot I.
Ellesmere I. (Canada)
Alert
C. Columbia
Lincoln Sea
Smith Sund
Qaanaaq
Kane Basin
Robeson Chan.
Uummannaq
K. York
Knud Rasmussen Land
Kronprins Frederik Land
Peary Land
K. Morris Jesup
Independence Fjord
Kong Frederik VIII.s Land
Baffin Bay
Baffin I.
Nettilling L.
C. Wolstenholme
Hudson Str.
Feuilles
Ungava Bay
Frobisher B.
Iqaluit
Cumberland Sd.
C. Dyer
Upernavik
Qeqertarsuaq
Resolution I.
C. Chidley
Labrador
Davis Str.
Kong Frederik IX.s Land
GREENLAND (KALAALLIT NUNAAT) (Denmark)
Kong Christian X.s Land
Kejser Franz Joseph Fd.
Kong Oscar Fjord
Ittoqqortoormiit
Mt. Forel 3360
Kong Christian IX.s Land
Kangikajik
Gunnbjørn Fjeld 3693
Tasiilaq
Nuuk
Paamiut
Kong Frederik VI.s Kyst
Qaqortoq
Alluitsup Paa
Nunap Isua (Kap Farvel)
Hamilton Inlet
Labrador Sea
Northwest Atlantic Mid-Ocean Canyon
Charlie Gibbs Fracture Zone
Mid-Atlantic Ridge
ATLANTIC OCEAN
Denmark Str.
Horn
Breiðafjörður
Fontur
Reykjavík
ICELAND
Öræfajökull 2119
Icelandic Plateau
Iceland Basin
Jan Mayen (Norway)
Mohns Ridge
Norwegian Sea
Norwegian Basin
Arctic Circle
Føroyar (Den.)
Shetland Is. (U.K.)
Orkney Is. (U.K.)
Rockall (U.K.)
Rockall Trough
Hebrides (U.K.)
King's Trough
UNITED KINGDOM
Edinburgh
GLASGOW
Belfast
DUBLIN
IRELAND
C. Clear
LONDON
North Sea
NETH.
AMSTERDAM
GERMANY
HAMBURG
BERLIN
Elbe
DENMARK
KØBENHAVN
Skagerrak
Bergen
Oslo
Trondheim
NORWAY
SWEDEN
STOCKHOLM
Gulf of Bothnia
Baltic Sea
G. of Finland
HELSINKI
FINLAND
Oulu
Tornio
Tallinn
ESTONIA
Rīga
LATVIA
LITHUANIA
Vilnius
Kaliningrad (Russia)
BELARUS
POLAND
Wisła
WARSZAWA
Kraków
PRAHA
Lviv
UKRAINE
KYIV
KHARKIV
ROSTOV
Donetsk
ODESA
MOLDOVA
ROMANIA
Sea of Azov
Black Sea
Chudskoye Ozero
ST. PETERBURG
MOSKVA
Ladozhskoye Ozero
Onezhskoye Ozero
Onega
NIZHNIY NOVGOROD
Volga
SAMARA
Saratov
VOLGOGRAD
UFA
Perm
YEKATERINBURG
Uralskie Gory
Syktyvkar
Arkhangelsk
Severodvinsk
Sev. Dvina
Mezen
Belomorsk
Kandalaksha
Beloye More
Murmansk
Kolskiy Poluostrov
Kirkenes
Vardø
Varangerfjorden
Hammerfest
Nordkapp
Tromsø
Narvik
Lofoten
Bjørnøya (Norway)
Greenland Sea
Spitsbergen
Svalbard (Norway)
Longyearbyen
Edgeøya
Nordaustlandet
Nordkapp
Barents Sea
Mys Kanin Nos
O. Kolguyev
Belushya Guba
Novaya Zemlya
Kara Sea
Baydaratskaya Guba
Vorkuta
Amderma
Salekhard
Naryan-Mar
Pechora
Ukhta
Narodnaya 1894
Ob
Berezovo
Tobolsk
Nefteyugansk
Surgut
Nizhnevartovsk
Nadym
Novyy Urengoy
Novyy Port
Poluostrov Yamal
Gydanskiy Poluostrov
Taz
Dikson
Dudinka
Igarka
Yenisey
Norilsk
Pyasina
Ozero Taymyr
Poluostrov Taymyr
Mys Chelyuskin
Khatanga
Nordvik
Anabar
Kotuy
Kheta
Gory Putorana
Nizhnyaya Tunguska
Podkamennaya Tunguska
Vilyuy
Olenek
Tiksi
Lena
Bulun
Zhigansk
Verkhoyanskiy Khrebet
Verkhoyansk
Yana
Kazachye
Yakutsk
Olekma
Lena
Indigirka
Srednekolymsk
Kolyma
Nizhne Kolymsk
Pevek
Chaunskaya G.
Proliv Longa
Chukchi Sea
Ostrov Vrangelya (Russia)
East Siberian Sea
Novosibirskiye Ostrova
O. Delonga
Lyakhovskiye Ostrova
Kotelnyy
Laptev Sea
Ostrova Petra
Severnaya Zemlya
O. Oktyabrskoy Revolyutsii
O. Ushakova
O. Uedineniya
O. Vise
O. Greem-Bell
Z. Vilcheka
Zemlya Frantsa Iosifa (Russia)
Z. Aleksandry
O. Belyy
SIBERIA
RUSSIA
EUROPE
ARCTIC OCEAN
Canada Basin
Canada Abyssal Plain
Chukchi Plateau
Mendeleyev Ridge
Alpha Ridge
Makarov Basin
Lomonosov Ridge
NORTH POLE
North Magnetic Pole 2021
Amundsen Basin
Arctic Mid-Ocean Ridge
Nansen Basin
McKinley Sea
Maximum extent of sea ice
Minimum extent of sea ice
Ice caps and permanent ice shelf
Projection : Zenithal Equidistant
West from Greenwich
East from Greenwich
COPYRIGHT PHILIP'S

1:28 000 000

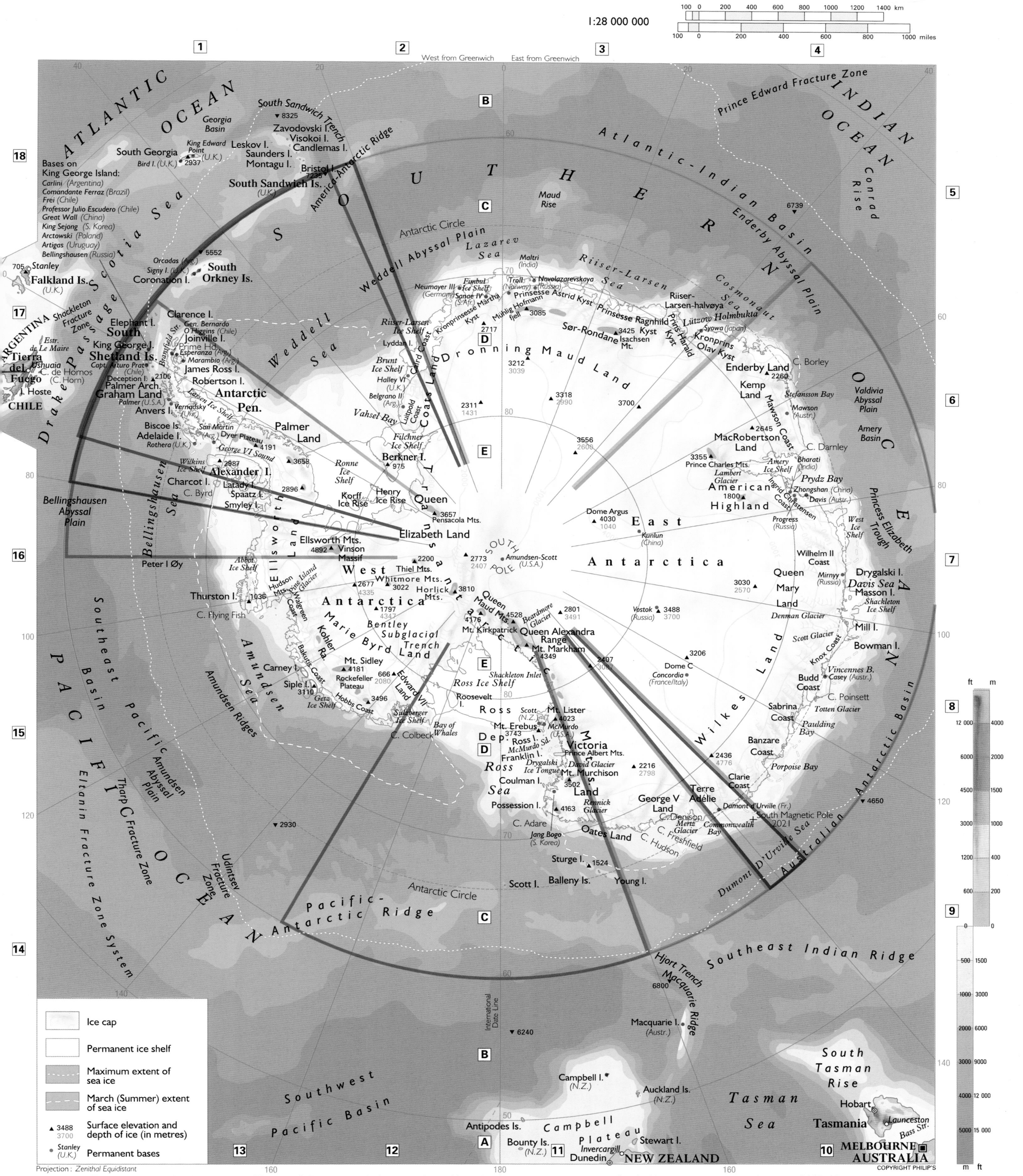

The Antarctic Treaty was signed in Washington in 1959 so that scientific and technical research could continue unhampered by international politics.

All territorial claims covering land areas south of latitude 60°S have been suspended. Those claims were:

Norwegian claim (Dronning Maud Land)
Australian claims
French claim (Terre Adélie)
New Zealand claim (Ross Dependency)
British claim
Argentine claim
Chilean claim

Equatorial Scale 1:41 000 000

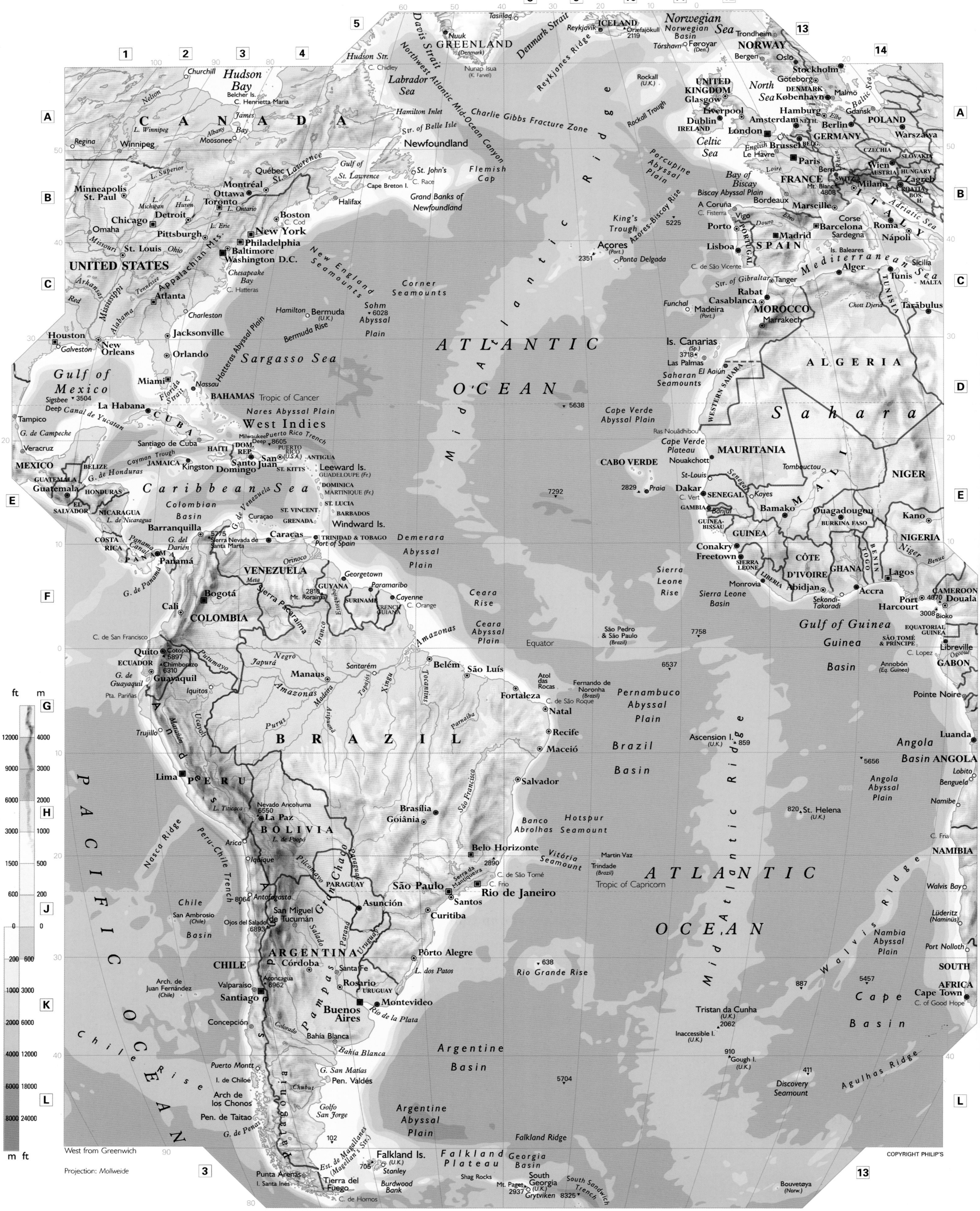

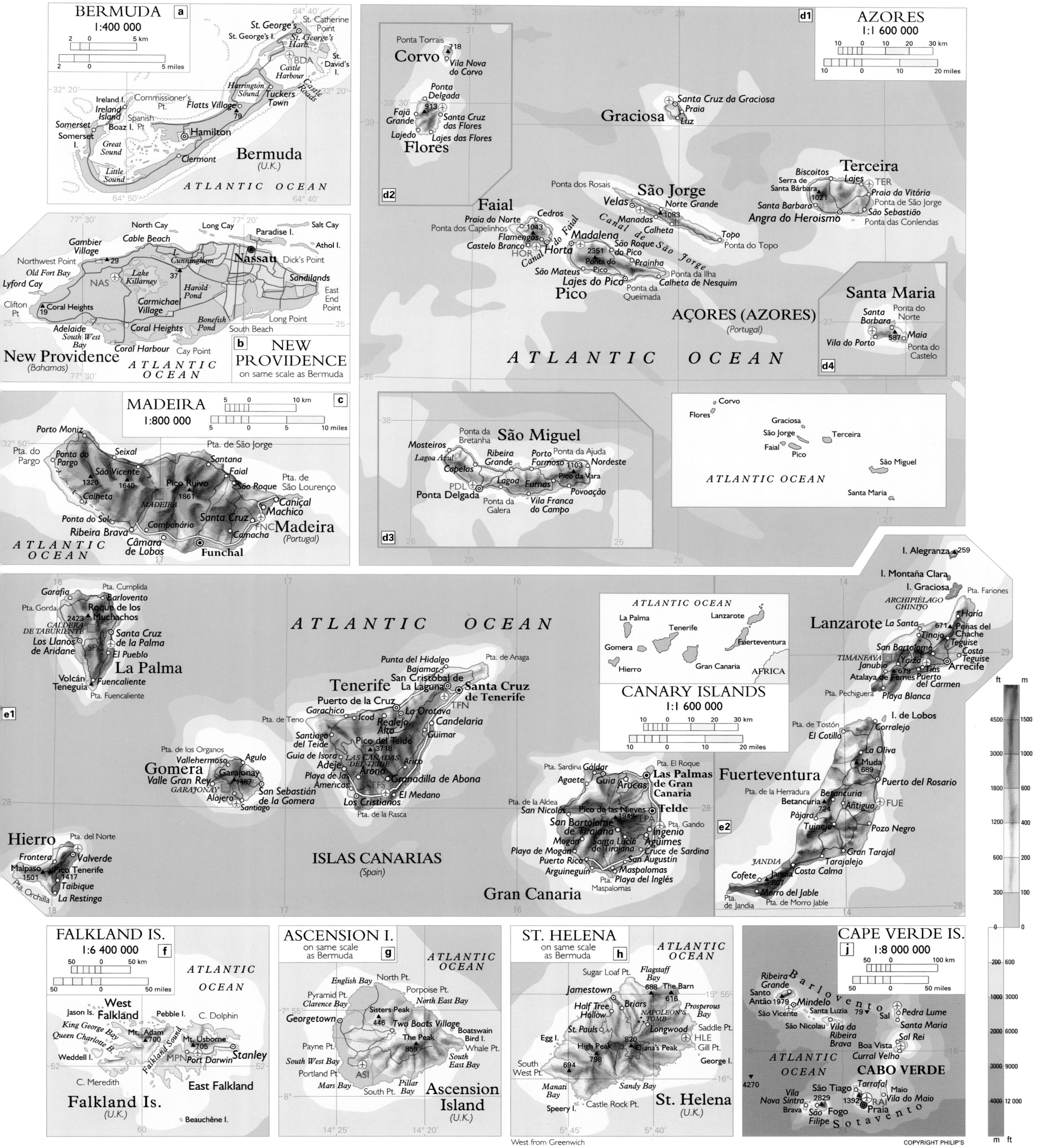
BERMUDA a
1:400 000
Bermuda
(U.K.)
St. George's
St. George's I.
St. Catherine Point
St. George's Harb.
St. David's I.
BDA
Castle Harbour
Castle Roads
Harrington Sound
Tuckers Town
Ireland I.
Commissioner's Pt.
Flatts Village
Ireland Island
Spanish Pt
Somerset
Boaz I.
Hamilton
Somerset I.
Great Sound
Clermont
Little Sound
ATLANTIC OCEAN
NEW PROVIDENCE b
on same scale as Bermuda
New Providence
(Bahamas)
North Cay
Long Cay
Salt Cay
Paradise I.
Athol I.
Cable Beach
Gambier Village
Northwest Point
Old Fort Bay
Lyford Cay
Nassau
Dick's Point
L. Cunningham
Lake Killarney
NAS
Harold Pond
Sandilands
East End Point
Clifton Pt
Coral Heights
Carmichael Village
Adelaide
South West Bay
Bonefish Pond
Long Point
South Beach
Coral Harbour
Cay Point
ATLANTIC OCEAN
MADEIRA c
1:800 000
Madeira
(Portugal)
Porto Moniz
Pta. do Pargo
Ponta do Pargo
Seixal
Pta. de São Jorge
Santana
São Vicente
Faial
Pico Ruivo
1861
São Roque
Pta. de São Lourenço
Calheta
Caniçal
Machico
Ponta do Sol
Santa Cruz
Ribeira Brava
Campanário
Camacha
FNC
Câmara de Lobos
Funchal
ATLANTIC OCEAN
AZORES d1
1:1 600 000
AÇORES (AZORES)
(Portugal)
Corvo
Ponta Torrais
Vila Nova do Corvo
Flores
Ponta Delgada
Fajã Grande
Santa Cruz das Flores
Lajedo
Lajes das Flores
Graciosa
Santa Cruz da Graciosa
Praia
Luz
Terceira
Biscoitos
Serra de Santa Bárbara
Lajes
TER
Praia da Vitória
Ponta de São Jorge
Santa Barbara
Angra do Heroismo
São Sebastião
Ponta das Conlendas
São Jorge
Ponta dos Rosais
Velas
Norte Grande
Manadas
Calheta
Topo
Ponta do Topo
Canal de São Jorge
Faial
Praia do Norte
Cedros
Ponta dos Capelinhos
Flamengos
Castelo Branco
HOR
Horta
Canal do Faial
Madalena
São Roque do Pico
Ponta do Pico
Prainha
São Mateus
Lajes do Pico
Ponta da Ilha
Calheta de Nesquim
Pico
Ponta da Queimada
Santa Maria
Santa Barbara
Ponta do Norte
Vila do Porto
Maia
Ponta do Castelo
São Miguel
Ponta da Bretanha
Mosteiros
Lagoa Azul
Ribeira Grande
Porto Formoso
Ponta da Ajuda
Nordeste
Capelas
Pico da Vara
Lagoa
Furnas
Povoação
PDL
Ponta Delgada
Ponta da Galera
Vila Franca do Campo
ATLANTIC OCEAN
CANARY ISLANDS
1:1 600 000
ISLAS CANARIAS
(Spain)
AFRICA
La Palma
Garafia
Pta. Cumplida
Barlovento
Pta. Gorda
Roque de los Muchachos
CALDERA DE TABURIENTE
Santa Cruz de la Palma
Los Llanos de Aridane
SPC
El Pueblo
Volcán Teneguía
Fuencaliente
Pta. Fuencaliente
Tenerife
Punta del Hidalgo
Bajamar
Pta. de Anaga
San Cristóbal de La Laguna
Santa Cruz de Tenerife
TFN
Puerto de la Cruz
Garachico
Pta. de Teno
Icod
La Orotava
Realejo Alto
Candelaria
Santiago del Teide
Pico del Teide
3718
Güimar
Guia de Isora
LAS CAÑADAS DEL TEIDE
Adeje
Arico
Playa de las Americas
Arona
Granadilla de Abona
TFS
El Medano
Los Cristianos
Pta. de la Rasca
Gomera
Pta. de los Organos
Vallehermoso
Agulo
Garajonay
Valle Gran Rey
GARAJONAY
San Sebastián de la Gomera
Alajero
Santiago
Hierro
Pta. del Norte
Frontera
Valverde
Malpaso
Pico Tenerife
Taibique
La Restinga
Pta. Orchilla
Gran Canaria
Pta. Sardina
Gáldar
Pta. El Roque
Agaete
Guia
Arucas
Las Palmas de Gran Canaria
Pta. de la Aldea
San Nicolás
Pico de las Nieves
LPA
Telde
San Bartolomé de Tirajana
Pta. Gando
Ingenio
Mogán
Santa Lucía de Tirajana
Agüimes
Playa de Mogán
Cruce de Sardina
Puerto Rico
San Augustin
Arguineguin
Maspalomas
Pta. Maspalomas
Playa del Inglés
Lanzarote
I. Alegranza
I. Montaña Clara
I. Graciosa
Pta. Fariones
ARCHIPIÉLAGO CHINIJO
Haría
La Santa
Peñas del Chache
Tinajo
Teguise
San Bartolomé
Costa Teguise
TIMANFAYA
Yaiza
Arrecife
Janubio
Tías
Atalaya de Femes
Puerto del Carmen
Pta. Pechiguera
Playa Blanca
Fuerteventura
I. de Lobos
Corralejo
Pta. de Tostón
El Cotillo
La Oliva
Muda
Pta. de la Herradura
Betancuria
Puerto del Rosario
FUE
Antigua
Pájara
Tuineje
Pozo Negro
JANDIA
Gran Tarajal
Tarajalejo
Costa Calma
Cofete
Jandia
Morro del Jable
Pta. de Jandia
Pta. de Morro Jable
ATLANTIC OCEAN
FALKLAND IS. f
1:6 400 000
Falkland Is.
(U.K.)
West Falkland
Jason Is.
Pebble I.
C. Dolphin
King George Bay
Queen Charlotte B.
Mt. Adam
Falkland Sound
Mt. Usborne
Weddell I.
MPN
Port Darwin
Stanley
C. Meredith
East Falkland
Beauchêne I.
ATLANTIC OCEAN
ASCENSION I. g
on same scale as Bermuda
Ascension Island
(U.K.)
English Bay
North Pt.
Porpoise Pt.
Pyramid Pt.
Clarence Bay
North East Bay
Sisters Peak
Georgetown
Two Boats Village
Boatswain Bird I.
The Peak
Whale Pt.
Payne Pt.
South West Bay
South East Bay
ASI
Portland Pt.
Mars Bay
South Pt.
Pillar Bay
ATLANTIC OCEAN
ST. HELENA h
on same scale as Bermuda
St. Helena
(U.K.)
Sugar Loaf Pt.
Flagstaff Bay
The Barn
Jamestown
Prosperous Bay
Half Tree Hollow
Briars
NAPOLEON'S TOMB
Longwood
St. Pauls
Saddle Pt.
HLE
Egg I.
High Peak
Diana's Peak
Gill Pt.
George I.
South West Pt.
Manati Bay
Sandy Bay
Speery I.
Castle Rock Pt.
ATLANTIC OCEAN
CAPE VERDE IS. j
1:8 000 000
CABO VERDE
Barlovento
Sotavento
Ribeira Grande
Santo Antão
Mindelo
São Vicente
Santa Luzia
Sal
Pedra Lume
Santa Maria
São Nicolau
Vila da Ribeira Brava
Sal Rei
Boa Vista
Curral Velho
Tarrafal
Maio
São Tiago
Vila do Maio
Vila Nova Sintra
Brava
São Filipe
Fogo
Praia
RAI
ATLANTIC OCEAN
West from Greenwich

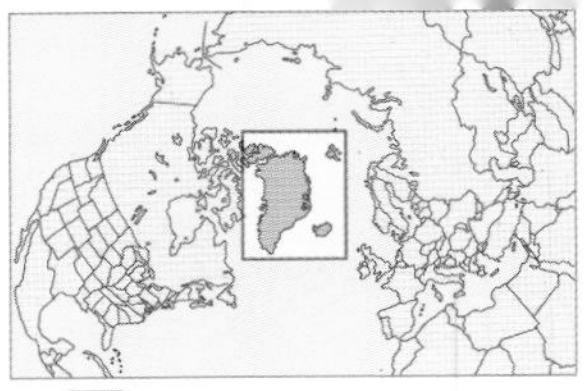

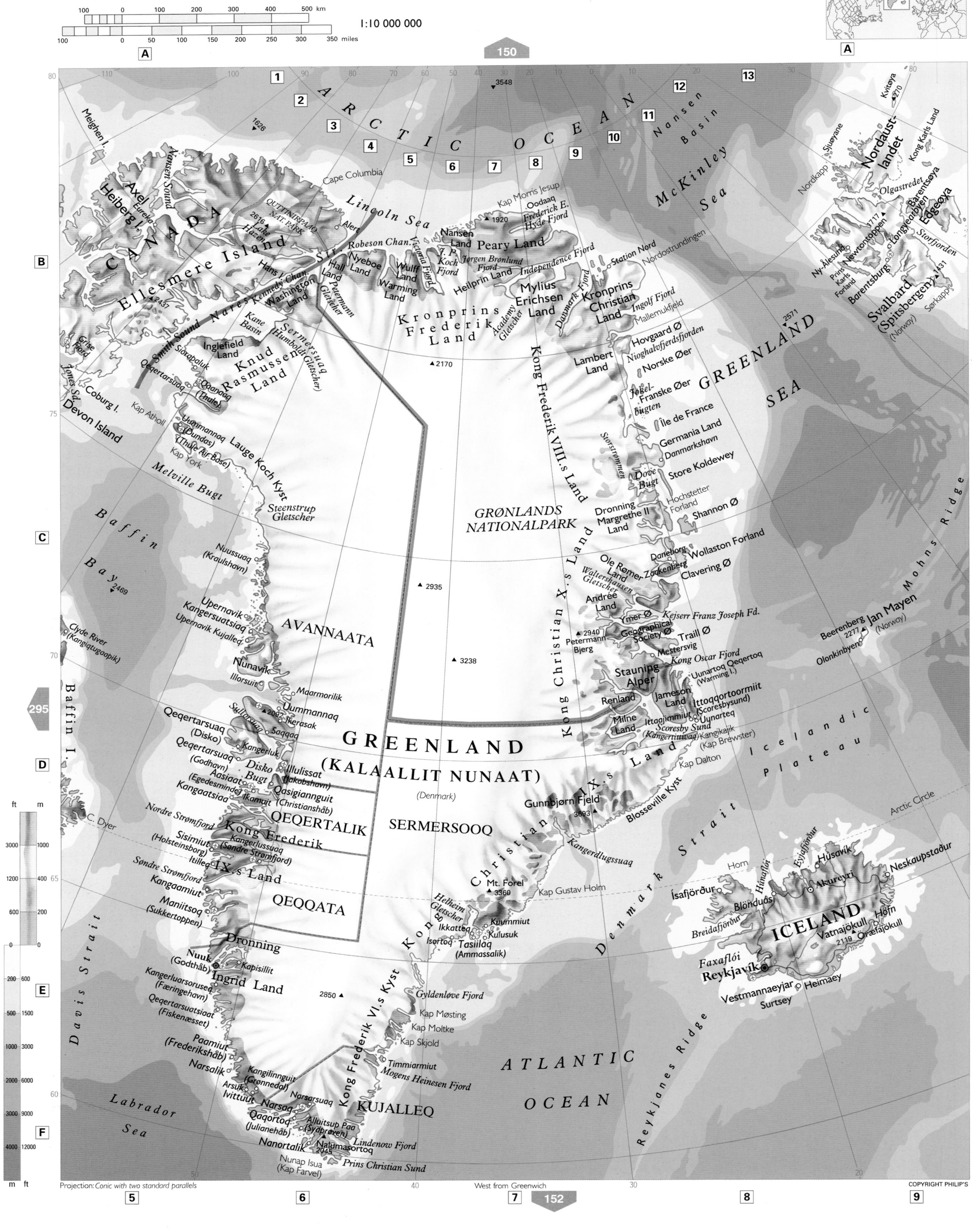

1:10 000 000
100 0 100 200 300 400 500 km
100 0 50 100 150 200 250 300 350 miles
ARCTIC OCEAN
Lincoln Sea
Cape Columbia
Kap Morris Jesup
Oodaaq
Frederick E. Hyde Fjord
Peary Land
Nansen Land
J. P. Koch Fjord
Jørgen Brønlund Fjord
Heilprin Land
Independence Fjord
Mylius Erichsen Land
Station Nord
Nordostrundingen
Kronprins Christian Land
Danmark Fjord
Ingolf Fjord
Mallemukfjeld
Academy Gletscher
Kronprins Frederik Land
Wulff Land
Warming Land
Nyeboe Land
Hall Land
Washington Land
Petermann Gletscher
Robeson Chan.
Victoria Fjord
Alert
QUTTINIRPAAQ NAT. PARK
Lake Hazen
Ellesmere Island
CANADA
Axel Heiberg I.
Eureka
Nansen Sound
Meighen I.
Hans I.
Kennedy Chan.
Nares Str.
Kane Basin
Smith Sound
Grise Fiord
Jones Sd.
Coburg I.
Devon Island
Inglefield Land
Siorapaluk
Qeqertarsuaq
Qaanaaq (Thule)
Knud Rasmussen Land
Sermersuaq Humboldt Gletscher
Kap Atholl
Uummannaq (Dundas) (Thule Air Base)
Kap York
Melville Bugt
Lauge Koch Kyst
Steenstrup Gletscher
Baffin Bay
Nuussuaq (Kraulshavn)
Upernavik
Kangersuatsiaq
Upernavik Kujalleq
Clyde River (Kangiqtugaapik)
AVANNAATA
Nunavik
Illorsuit
Maarmorilik
Uummannaq
Ikerasak
Saqqaq
Qeqertarsuaq (Disko)
Kangerluk
Disko Bugt
Qeqertarsuaq (Godhavn)
Ilulissat (Jakobshavn)
Qasigiannguit (Christianshåb)
Aasiaat (Egedesminde)
Ikamiut
Kangaatsiaq
QEQERTALIK
Nordre Strømfjord
Kong Frederik IX.s Land
Sisimiut (Holsteinsborg)
Kangerlussuaq (Søndre Strømfjord)
Itilleq
Søndre Strømfjord
Kangaamiut
Maniitsoq (Sukkertoppen)
QEQQATA
C. Dyer
Baffin I.
Davis Strait
Dronning Ingrid Land
Nuuk (Godthåb)
Kapisillit
Kangerluarsoruseq (Færingehavn)
Qeqertarsuatsiaat (Fiskenæsset)
Paamiut (Frederikshåb)
Narsalik
Kangilinnguit (Grønnedal)
Arsuk
Ivittuut
Narsarsuaq
Narsaq
Qaqortoq (Julianehåb)
Alluitsup Paa (Sydprøven)
Nanortalik
Nalumasortoq
Lindenow Fjord
Prins Christian Sund
Nunap Isua (Kap Farvel)
KUJALLEQ
Labrador Sea
Kong Frederik VI.s Kyst
Timmiarmiut
Mogens Heinesen Fjord
Kap Skjold
Kap Moltke
Kap Møsting
Gyldenløve Fjord
Kong Christian IX.s Land
Helheim Gletscher
Ikkatteq
Isortoq
Kuummiut
Kulusuk
Tasiilaq (Ammassalik)
Mt. Forel
Kap Gustav Holm
Kangerdlugssuaq
Gunnbjørn Fjeld
Blosseville Kyst
Kap Dalton
SERMERSOOQ
GREENLAND (KALAALLIT NUNAAT)
(Denmark)
GRØNLANDS NATIONALPARK
Kong Frederik VIII.s Land
Kong Christian X.s Land
Lambert Land
Hovgaard Ø
Nioghalvfjerdsfjorden
Norske Øer
Jøkelbugten
Franske Øer
Île de France
Germania Land
Danmarkshavn
Storstrømmen
Store Koldewey
Dove Bugt
Hochstetter Forland
Shannon Ø
Dronning Margrethe II Land
Daneborg
Zackenberg
Wollaston Forland
Clavering Ø
Ole Rømer Land
Waltershausen Gletscher
Andrée Land
Ymer Ø
Kejserr Franz Joseph Fd.
Geographical Society Ø
Traill Ø
Petermann Bjerg
Mestersvig
Kong Oscar Fjord
Stauning Alper
Uunartoq Qeqertoq (Warming I.)
Renland
Jameson Land
Milne Land
Ittoqqortoormiit (Scoresbysund)
Uunarteq
Ittajimmiut (Kangertittivaq)
Scoresby Sund
Kangikajik (Kap Brewster)
GREENLAND SEA
Icelandic Plateau
Denmark Strait
Arctic Circle
Mohns Ridge
Jan Mayen (Norway)
Beerenberg
Olonkinbyen
McKinley Sea
Nansen Basin
Svalbard (Spitsbergen) (Norway)
Nordaustlandet
Kvitøya
Kong Karls Land
Sjuøyane
Nordkapp
Olgastredet
Barentsøya
Edgeøya
Newtontoppen
Longyearbyen
Storfjorden
Ny-Ålesund
Prins Karls Forland
Barentsburg
Sørkapp
ICELAND
Ísafjörður
Horn
Húnaflói
Eyjafjörður
Húsavík
Akureyri
Neskaupstaður
Blönduós
Breiðafjörður
Vatnajökull
Höfn
Öræfajökull
Faxaflói
Reykjavík
Vestmannaeyjar
Heimaey
Surtsey
Reykjanes Ridge
ATLANTIC OCEAN
Projection: Conic with two standard parallels
West from Greenwich
COPYRIGHT PHILIP'S

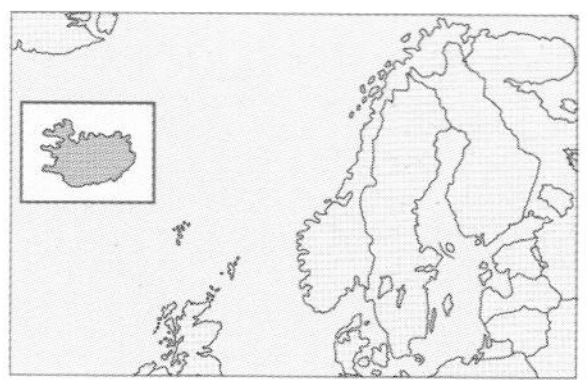

1:2 000 000

10 0 10 20 30 40 50 60 70 80 100 km

10 0 10 20 30 40 50 60 miles

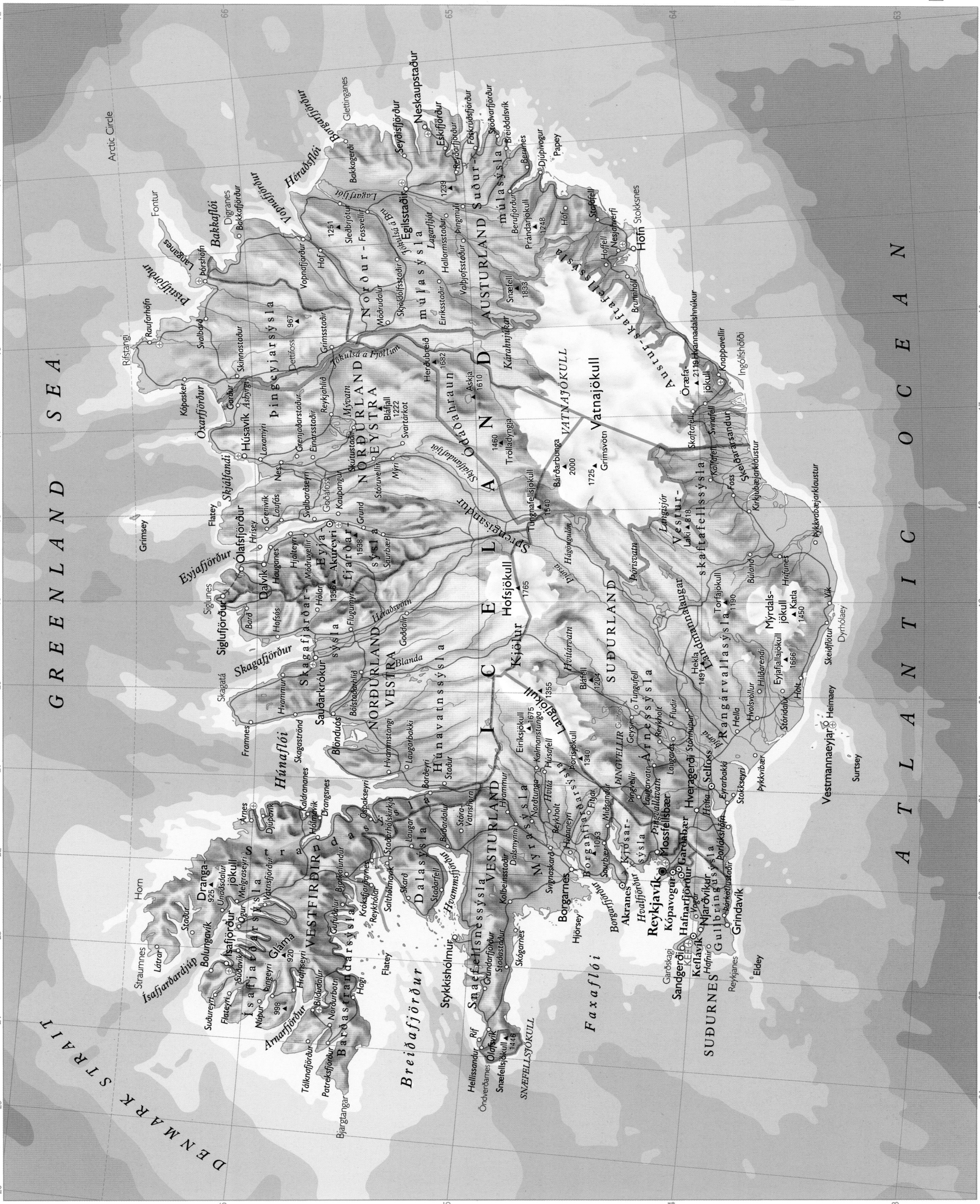

m ft
3000 1000
1200 400
600 200
300 100
0 0
50 150
100 300
200 600
500 1500
1000 3000

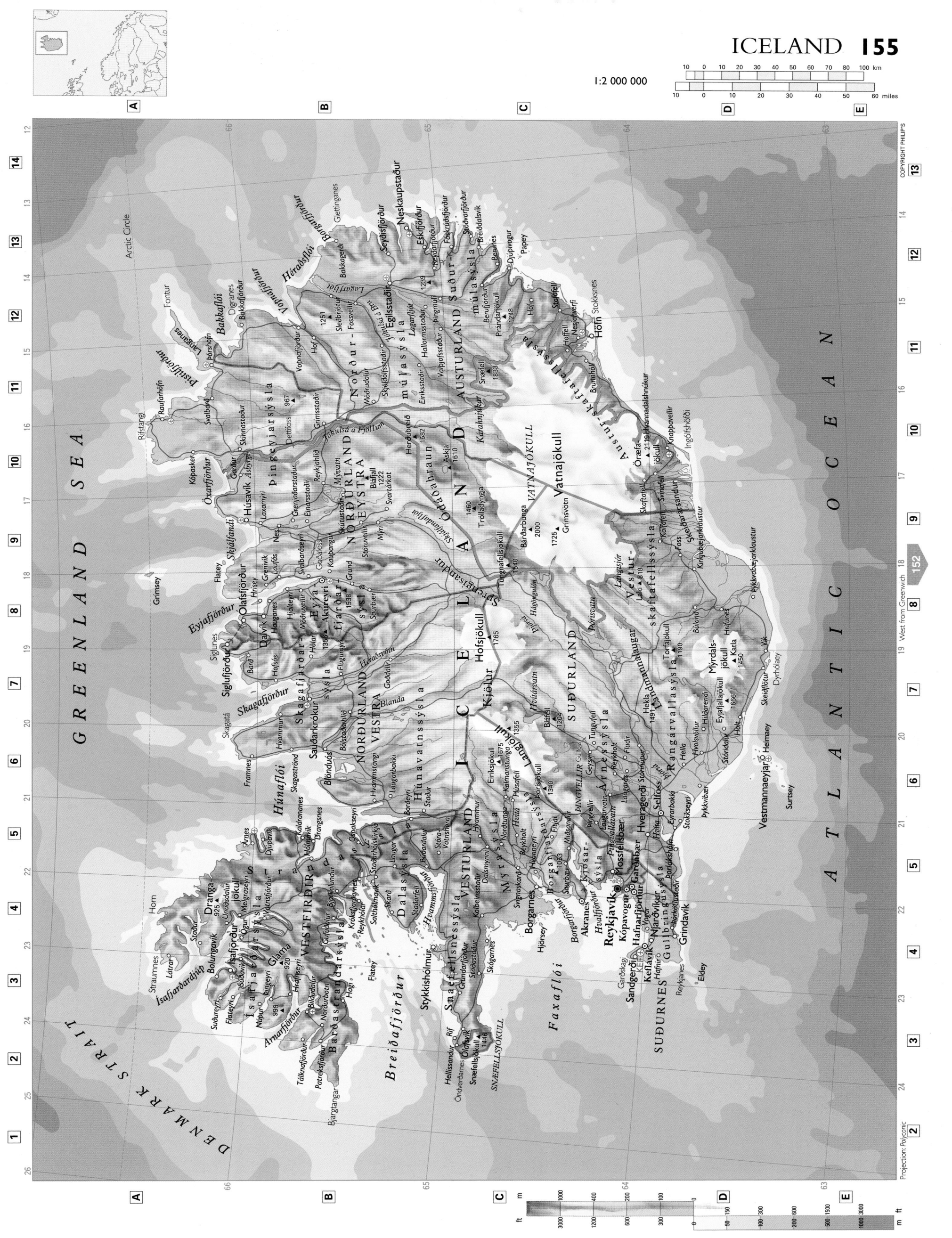

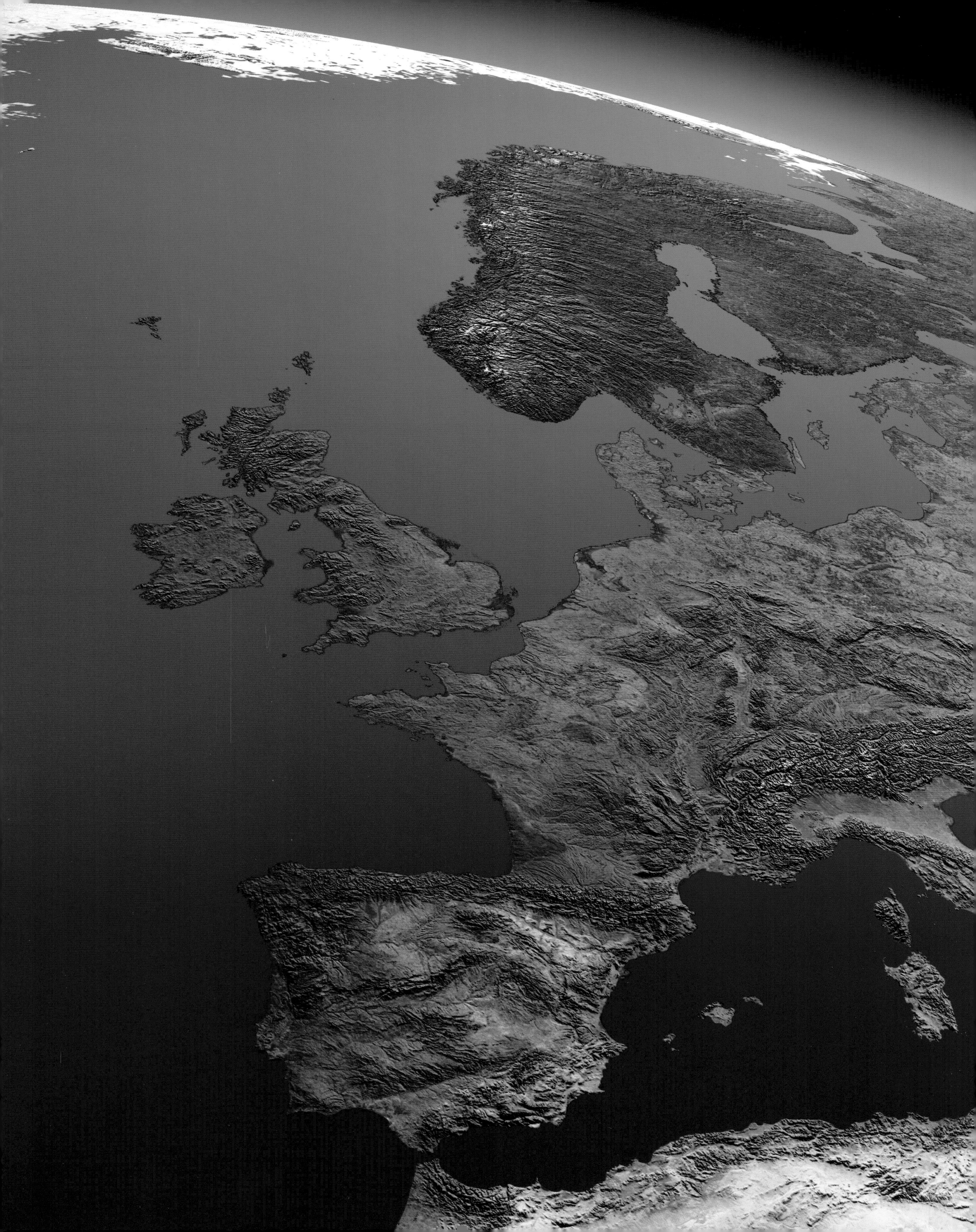

EUROPE

1:16 000 000

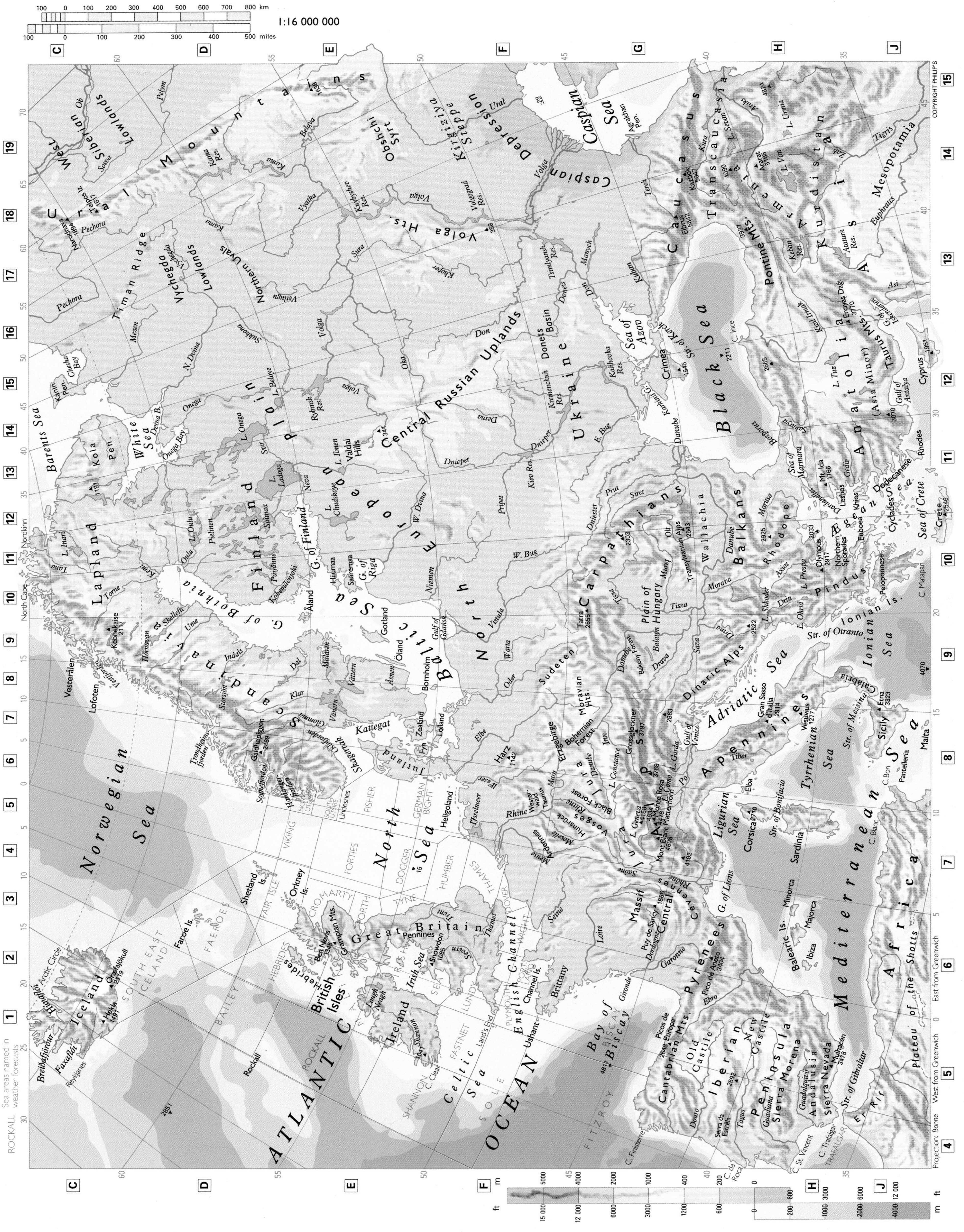
km
miles
Norwegian Sea
North Sea
Baltic Sea
Barents Sea
White Sea
ATLANTIC OCEAN
Bay of Biscay
Celtic Sea
English Channel
Irish Sea
Mediterranean Sea
Tyrrhenian Sea
Adriatic Sea
Ionian Sea
Aegean Sea
Sea of Crete
Black Sea
Sea of Azov
Caspian Sea
Caspian Depression
Ural Mountains
West Siberian Lowlands
Timan Ridge
Northern Uvals
Volga Hts.
Obshchi Syrt
Kirgiziya Steppe
Central Russian Uplands
North European Plain
Finland
Lapland
Scandinavia
Iceland
British Isles
Great Britain
Ireland
Iberian Peninsula
Pyrenees
Massif Central
Alps
Apennines
Carpathians
Transylvanian Alps
Plain of Hungary
Balkans
Rhodope
Pindus
Dinaric Alps
Caucasus
Transcaucasia
Armenia
Kurdistan
Anatolia (Asia Minor)
Taurus Mts.
Pontine Mts.
Mesopotamia
Crimea
Ukraine
Donets Basin
Wallachia
Africa
Plateau of the Shotts
Corsica
Sardinia
Sicily
Crete
Cyprus
Balearic Is.
G. of Bothnia
G. of Finland
Kattegat
Skagerrak
Jutland
Faroe Is.
Shetland Is.
Orkney Is.
Hebrides
Sea areas named in weather forecasts
Projection: Bonne
West from Greenwich
East from Greenwich
COPYRIGHT PHILIP'S
m
ft

1:16 000 000

100 0 100 200 300 400 500 600 700 800 km

100 0 100 200 300 400 500 miles

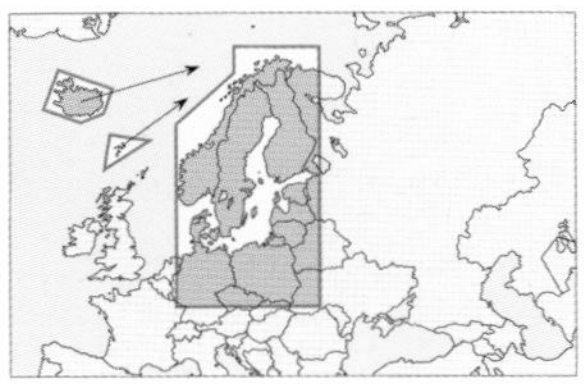

50 0 25 50 75 100 125 150 175 km

50 0 25 50 75 100 125 miles

1:4 800 000

BALTIC SEA
NORTH SEA
Skagerrak
Kattegat
Gulf of Finland
Gulf of Riga
Ålands hav
ESTONIA
LATVIA
LITHUANIA
BELARUS
POLAND
GERMANY
DENMARK
CZECHIA
UKRAINE
STOCKHOLM
OSLO
HELSINKI
TALLINN
Riga
Vilnius
MINSK
WARSZAWA (Warsaw)
BERLIN
PRAHA (Prague)
KØBENHAVN (Copenhagen)
HAMBURG
Gotland (Sweden)
Öland
Bornholm (Denmark)
Rügen
KALININGRAD (Russia)
Projection: Conical with two standard parallels
East from Greenwich
COPYRIGHT PHILIP'S

1:2 000 000

161
160
164

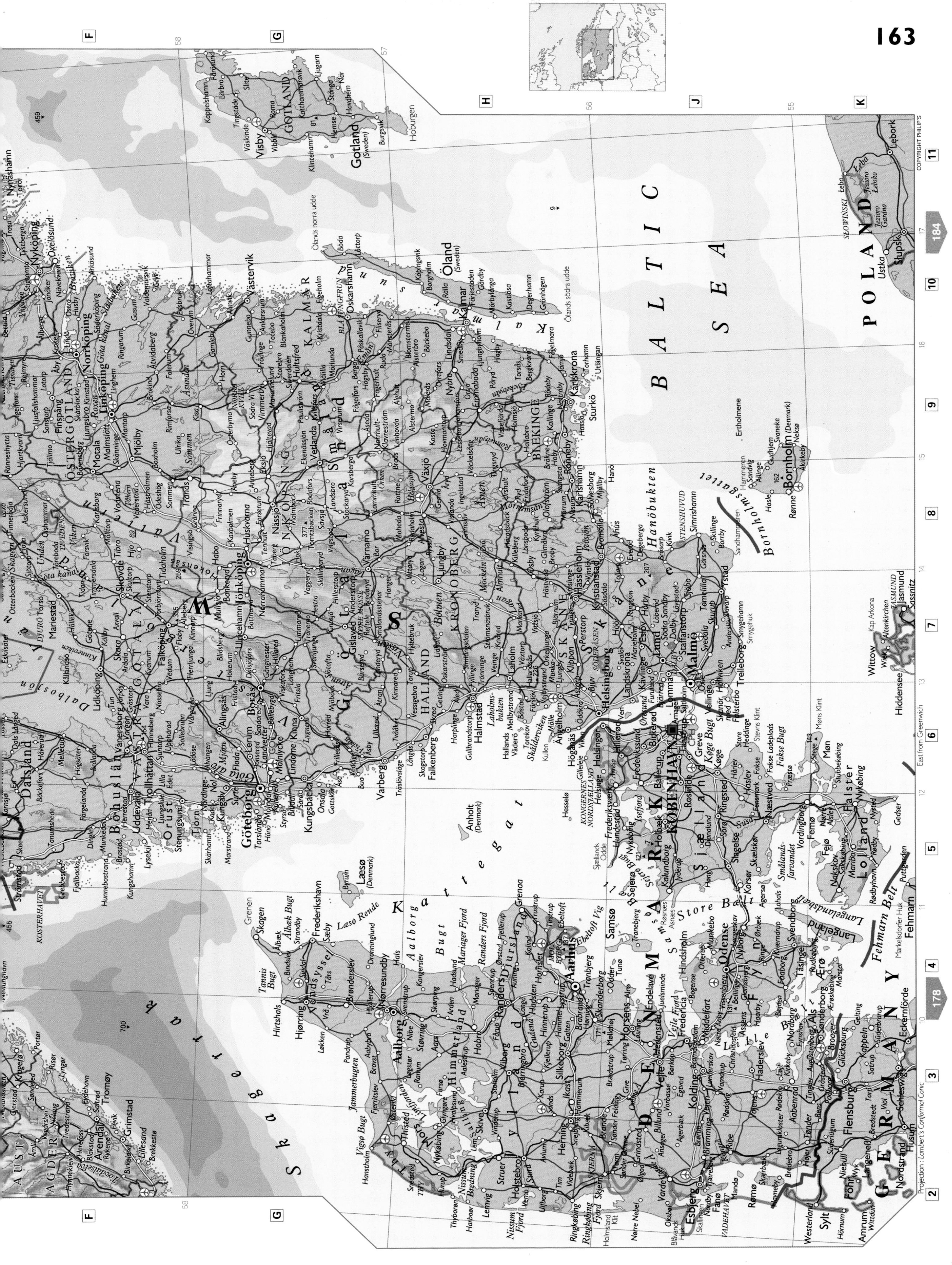

BALTIC SEA
POLAND
DENMARK
GERMANY
Skagerrak
Kattegat
KØBENHAVN
Göteborg
Malmö
Aarhus
Odense
Aalborg
Gotland (Sweden)
Öland (Sweden)
Bornholm (Denmark)
Anholt (Denmark)
Læsø (Denmark)
Sjælland
Lolland
Falster
Fyn
Jylland
Skåne
Småland
Halland
Blekinge
Kronoberg
Kalmar
Jönköping
Linköping
Norrköping
Helsingborg
Halmstad
Karlskrona
Kalmar
Växjö
Visby
Borås
Trollhättan
Uddevalla
Vänersborg
Esbjerg
Kolding
Vejle
Horsens
Randers
Herning
Flensburg
Kiel
Stralsund
Słupsk
Lębork
Ustka
Projection: Lambert's Conformal Conic
East from Greenwich
COPYRIGHT PHILIP'S
178
184

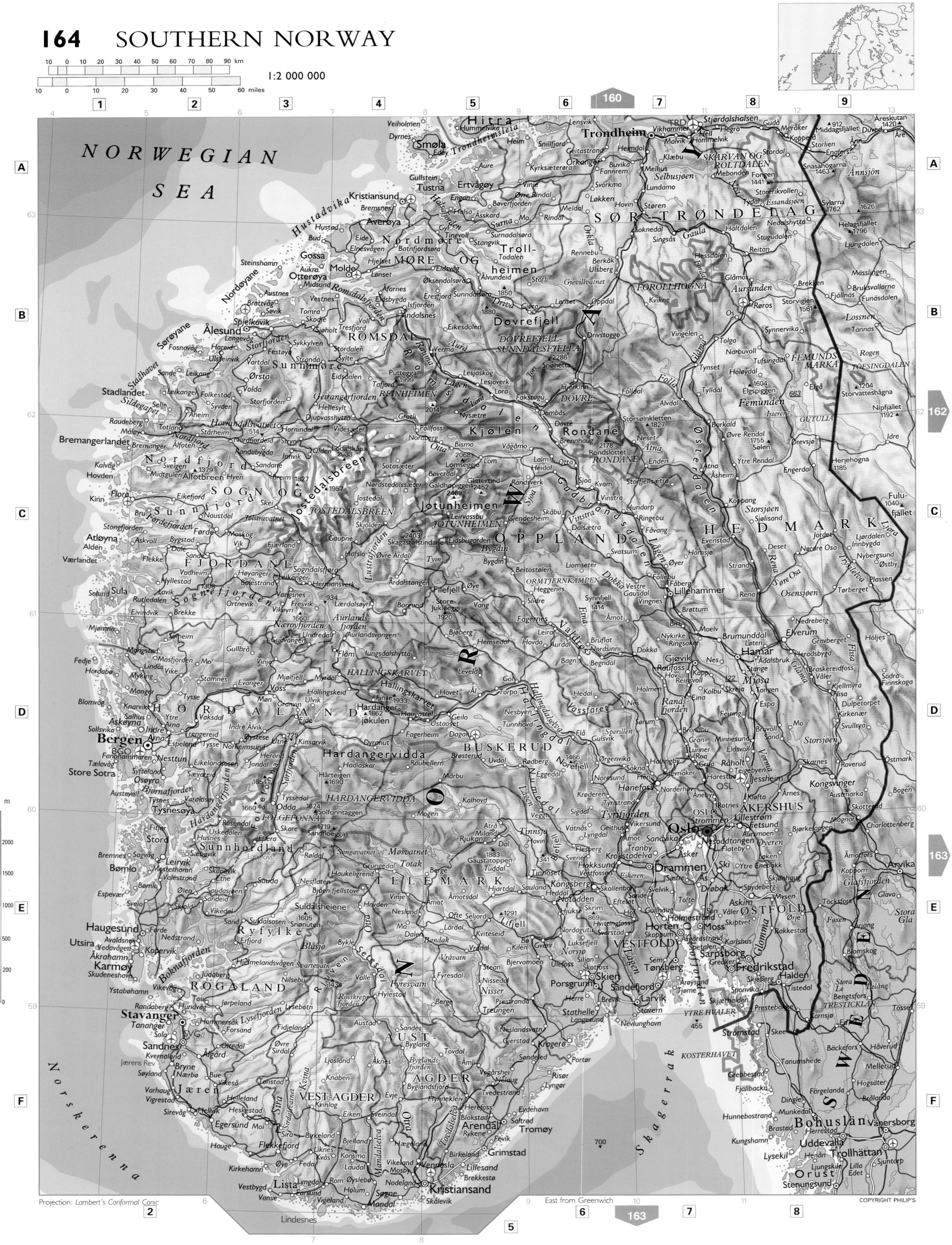
1:2 000 000
km
miles
NORWEGIAN SEA
Norskerenna
Skagerrak
SØR-TRØNDELAG
MØRE OG ROMSDAL
SOGN OG FJORDANE
HORDALAND
ROGALAND
VEST-AGDER
AUST-AGDER
TELEMARK
BUSKERUD
OPPLAND
HEDMARK
AKERSHUS
ØSTFOLD
VESTFOLD
NORWAY
SWEDEN
Trondheim
Kristiansund
Molde
Ålesund
Bergen
Haugesund
Stavanger
Sandnes
Kristiansand
Arendal
Skien
Drammen
Oslo
Lillehammer
Hamar
Fredrikstad
Halden
Jotunheimen
Hardangervidda
Jostedalsbreen
Dovrefjell
Rondane
Sognefjorden
Hardangerfjorden
Femunden
Mjøsa
Bohuslän
Projection: Lambert's Conformal Conic
East from Greenwich
COPYRIGHT PHILIP'S

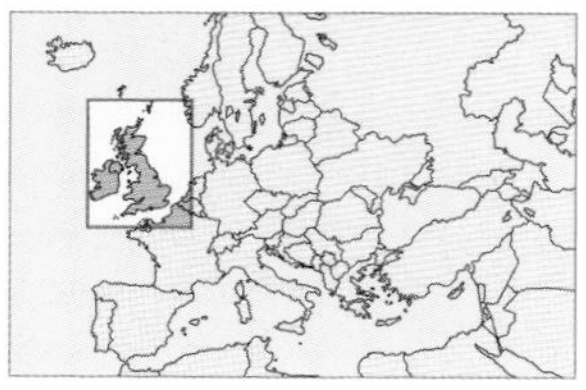

1:4 000 000
50 0 25 50 75 100 125 150 175 km
50 0 25 50 75 100 125 miles
ATLANTIC OCEAN
NORTH SEA
IRISH SEA
CELTIC SEA
English Channel
UNITED KINGDOM
IRELAND
SCOTLAND
ENGLAND
WALES
NORTHERN IRELAND
NORWAY
NETHERLANDS
BELGIUM
FRANCE
Shetland Is.
(U.K.)
Yell
Unst
Fetlar
Mainland
Lerwick
Foula
Fair Isle
Orkney Is.
Westray
Sanday
Stronsay
Kirkwall
Hoy
South Ronaldsay
Pentland Firth
North Rona
C. Wrath
Thurso
Wick
Helmsdale
Outer Hebrides
Flannan Is.
Stornoway
Lewis
Harris
St. Kilda
(U.K.)
North Uist
Benbecula
South Uist
Barra
North Minch
Inner Hebrides
Sea of the Hebrides
Skye
Portree
Rum
Eigg
Mallaig
Coll
Tiree
Iona
Mull
Tobermory
Colonsay
Jura
Islay
North West Highlands
Ullapool
Lairg
Golspie
Tain
Invergordon
Dingwall
Moray Firth
Inverness
Nairn
Elgin
Buckie
Banff
Fraserburgh
Peterhead
Huntly
Inverurie
Aberdeen
Stonehaven
CAIRNGORMS
Grampian Mts.
Glen Mor
L. Ness
Aviemore
Ben Nevis
Fort William
Ballater
Forfar
Montrose
Arbroath
Dundee
St. Andrews
Perth
Oban
L. Awe
L. Lomond
L. LOMOND & TROSSACHS
Stirling
Glenrothes
Kirkcaldy
Dunfermline
Dunbar
Dumbarton
Greenock
GLASGOW
Paisley
Cumbernauld
Edinburgh
East Kilbride
Hamilton
Irvine
Arran
Campbeltown
Kilmarnock
Ayr
Firth of Clyde
North Channel
Southern Uplands
Galashiels
Jedburgh
Hawick
Berwick-upon-Tweed
Cheviot Hills
Alnwick
NORTHUMBERLAND
Newcastle-upon-Tyne
South Shields
Sunderland
Gateshead
Durham
Hartlepool
Redcar
Middlesbrough
Stockton-on-Tees
N. YORK MOORS
Scarborough
Girvan
Dumfries
Annan
Hexham
Carlisle
Kirkcudbright
Stranraer
Mull of Galloway
Workington
Whitehaven
Cumbrian Mts.
LAKE DISTRICT
Barrow-in-Furness
Pennines
YORKSHIRE DALES
Darlington
Douglas
I. of Man
Lancaster
Harrogate
York
Leeds
Bradford
Bridlington
Beverley
Kingston upon Hull
Scunthorpe
Grimsby
Humber
Blackpool
Preston
Blackburn
Burnley
Keighley
Bolton
Halifax
Huddersfield
Barnsley
Doncaster
Rotherham
Sheffield
MANCHESTER
Oldham
Liverpool
Warrington
Stockport
Chesterfield
Lincoln
Louth
Skegness
Boston
The Wash
Cromer
THE BROADS
Great Yarmouth
Lowestoft
Norwich
King's Lynn
Anglesey
Holyhead
Bangor
Colwyn Bay
Chester
Crewe
Snowdon
Wrexham
Stoke-on-Trent
PEAK DISTRICT
Derby
Mansfield
Nottingham
Grantham
Pwllheli
SNOWDONIA
Stafford
Shrewsbury
Telford
Leicester
Nuneaton
Peterborough
Thetford
Cardigan Bay
Aberystwyth
Cambrian Mts.
Welshpool
Wolverhampton
BIRMINGHAM
Coventry
Corby
Ely
Bury St. Edmunds
Rugby
Northampton
Cambridge
Ipswich
Felixstowe
Redditch
Worcester
Royal Leamington Spa
Hereford
Bedford
Milton Keynes
Stevenage
Harwich
Colchester
Chelmsford
Fishguard
Carmarthen
BRECON BEACONS
Brecon
Cheltenham
Cotswold Hills
Gloucester
Oxford
Hemel Hempstead
Luton
Harlow
Haverfordwest
Milford Haven
Pembroke
PEMBROKESHIRE COAST
Llanelli
Swansea
Port Talbot
Neath
Merthyr Tydfil
Rhondda
Cwmbran
Newport
Cardiff
Barry
Bristol
Bath
High Wycombe
Watford
Slough
LONDON
Basildon
Southend-on-Sea
Thames
Bristol Channel
St. George's Channel
Swindon
Newbury
Reading
Basingstoke
Chatham
Margate
Canterbury
Maidstone
Dover
Ashford
Folkestone
Reigate
Guildford
Crawley
Weston-super-Mare
EXMOOR
Exmoor
Barnstaple
Taunton
Yeovil
Salisbury
Winchester
SOUTH DOWNS
Southampton
Fareham
Havant
Hastings
Eastbourne
Brighton
Worthing
Portsmouth
Isle of Wight
Newport
NEW FOREST
Bournemouth
Poole
Weymouth
Bude
Exeter
DARTMOOR
Dartmoor
Exmouth
Torbay
Plymouth
Newquay
Truro
St. Austell
Falmouth
Penzance
Land's End
Isles of Scilly
Str. of Dover
Tory I.
Malin Hd.
Buncrana
Arranmore
Letterkenny
GLENVEAGH
Lifford
Derry/Londonderry
Coleraine
Ballymena
Larne
Lough Neagh
Antrim
Bangor
Belfast
Lisburn
Craigavon
Omagh
Armagh
Newry
Donegal
Bundoran
Lower L. Erne
Enniskillen
Clones
Sligo
Ballina
Achill I.
Castlebar
L. Conn
Westport
Lough Mask
Connemara
Connaught
Roscommon
Leitrim
Cavan
Castleblaney
Dundalk
Drogheda
Boyne
Kells
Longford
Lough Ree
Mullingar
Athlone
Lough Corrib
Galway
Galway B.
Aran Is.
BURREN
Ballinasloe
Tullamore
Birr
Liffey
DUBLIN
Dun Laoghaire
Bray
Wicklow Mts.
Arklow
Leinster
Portlaoise
Athy
Carlow
Lough Derg
Ennis
Shannon
Limerick
Nenagh
Thurles
Kilkenny
Kilrush
Listowel
Tipperary
Munster
Clonmel
Carrick-on-Suir
Wexford
Rosslare
Tralee
Dingle
Killarney
Mallow
Waterford
Blackwater
Dungarvan
Carrauntoohill
Macgillycuddy's Reeks
Valencia I.
Cork
Cobh
Youghal
Bandon
Kinsale
Bantry
C. Clear
Alderney
C. de la Hague
Guernsey
St. Peter Port
Sark
Channel Is.
(U.K.)
Jersey
St. Helier
Cotentin
Pte. de Barfleur
Cherbourg-Octeville
Valognes
Bayeux
Caen
Trouville-sur-Mer
Lisieux
Le Havre
Bolbec
Fécamp
Dieppe
Pays de Caux
Rouen
Seine
Elbeuf
Le Tréport
Abbeville
Somme
Amiens
Picardie
St.-Quentin
Cambrai
Laon
Le Touquet-Paris-Plage
Boulogne-sur-Mer
C. Gris-Nez
Calais
Dunkerque
St.-Omer
Béthune
Bruay-la-Buissière
Lens
Valenciennes
LILLE
Tourcoing
Villeneuve d'Ascq
Tournai
Artois
Flandre
Oostende
Brugge
Gent
Zeebrugge
Antwerpen
Mechelen
BRUSSEL
(Bruxelles)
Vlissingen
Zeeland
Dordrecht
ROTTERDAM
Hoek van Holland
's-Gravenhage
(Den Haag)
Haarlem
Alkmaar
Den Helder
Texel
Askøyna
Bergen
Osøyro
Stord
Bømlo
Leirvik
Haugesund
Kopervik
Åkrahamn
Boknafjorden
Stavanger
Sandnes
Bryne
Nærbø
ft m
Projection: Conical with two standard parallels
West from Greenwich
East from Greenwich
COPYRIGHT PHILIP'S
161
171
176

1:1 600 000

Key to Northern Ireland districts on map

5. ANTRIM & NEWTOWNABBEY
6. ARMAGH, BANBRIDGE & CRAIGAVON
7. LISBURN & CASTLEREAGH
8. ARDS & NORTH DOWN

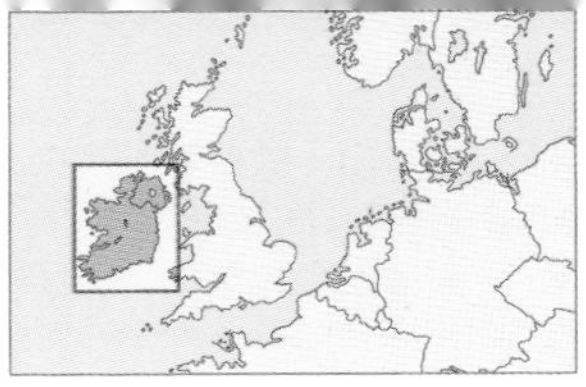

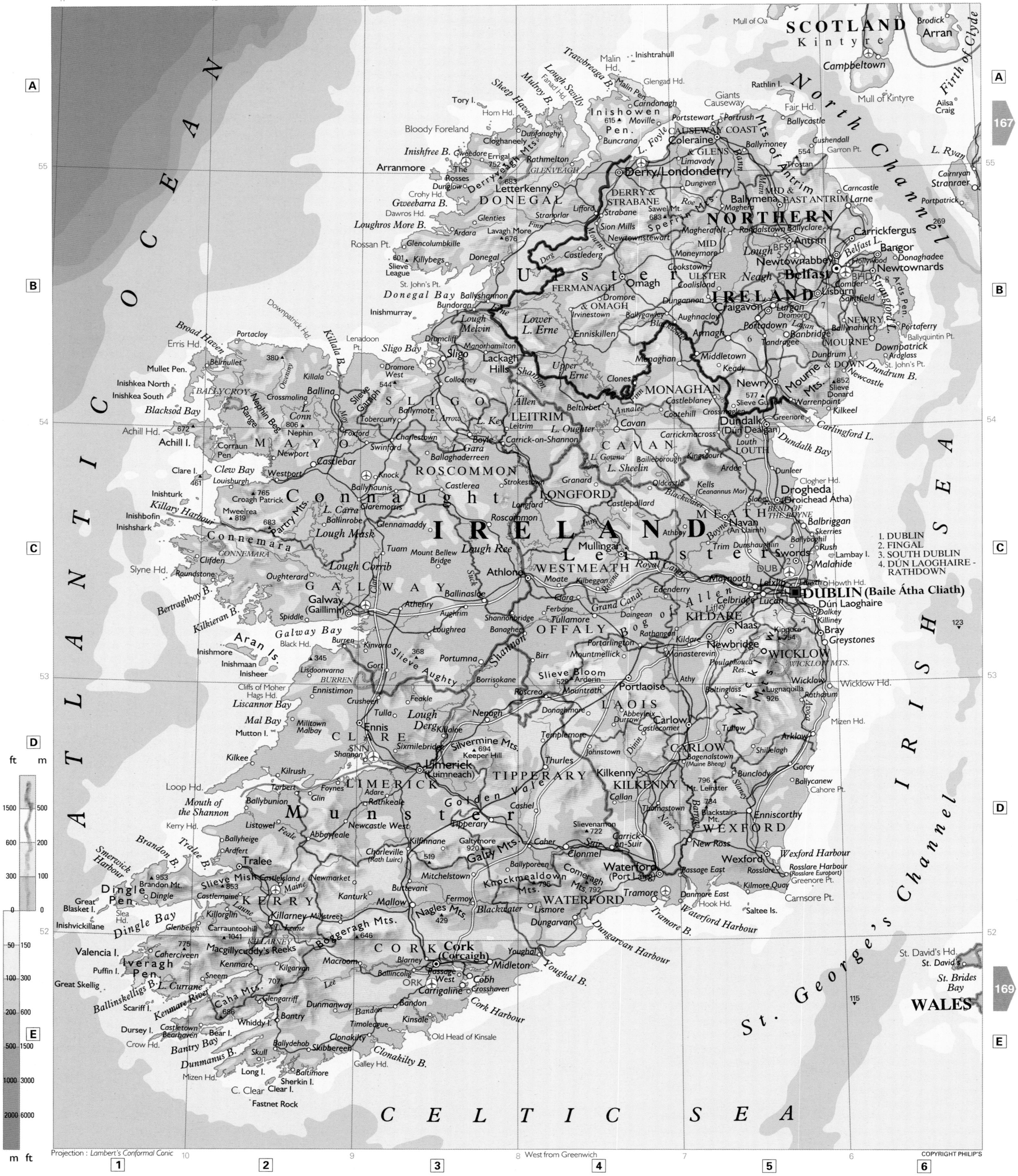

Projection : Lambert's Conformal Conic

West from Greenwich

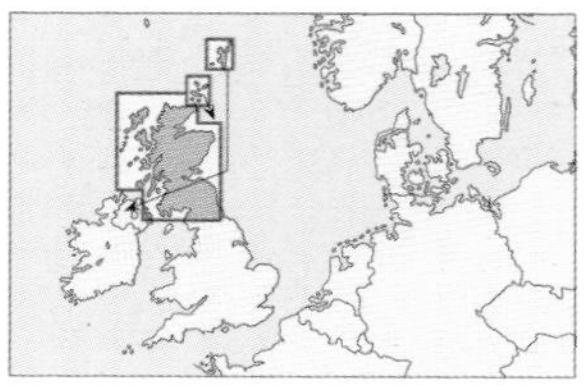

1:1 600 000

10 0 10 20 30 40 50 60 70 80 km

10 0 10 20 30 40 50 miles

10 0 10 20 30 40 50 60 70 80 km

1:1 600 000

10 0 10 20 30 40 50 miles

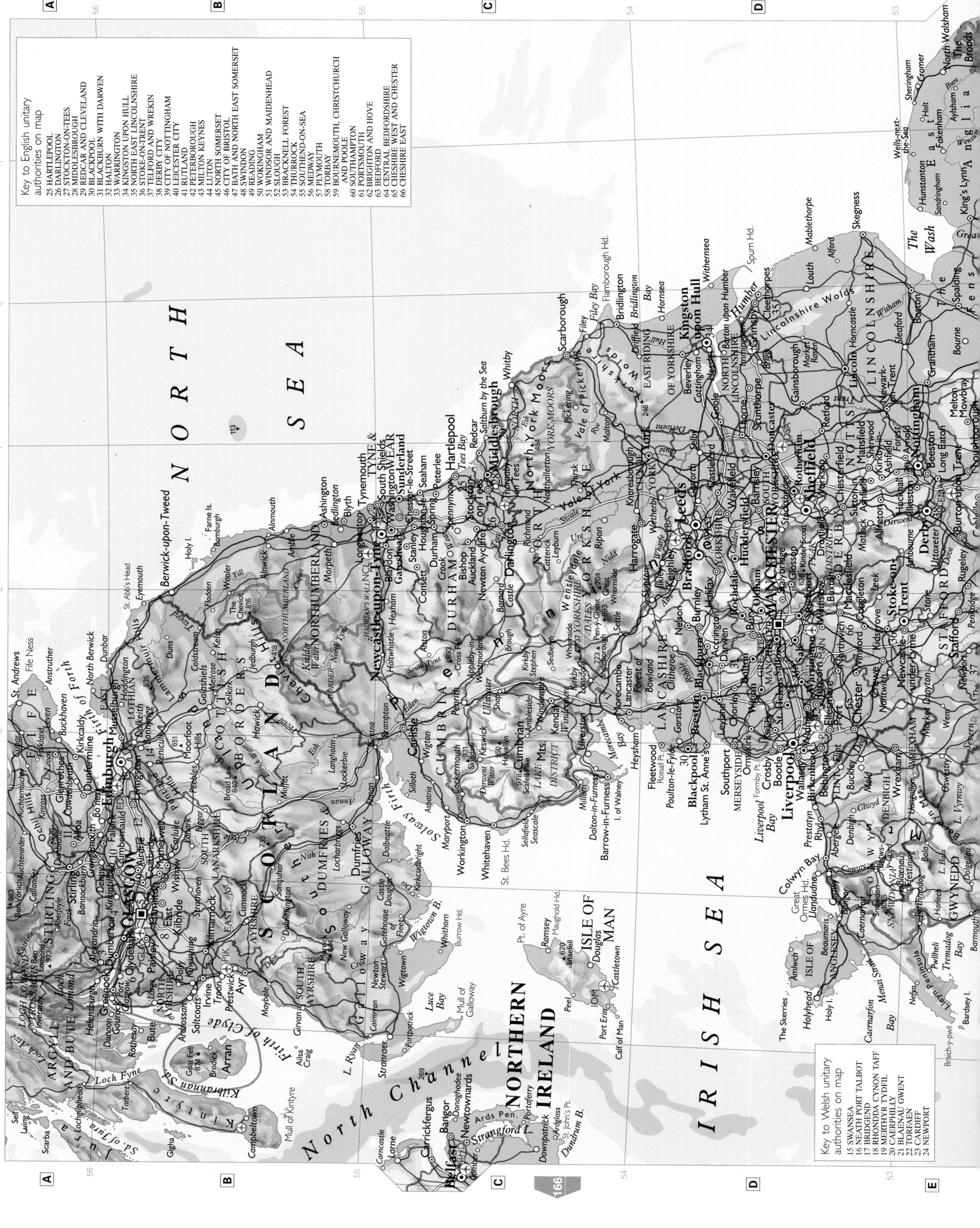

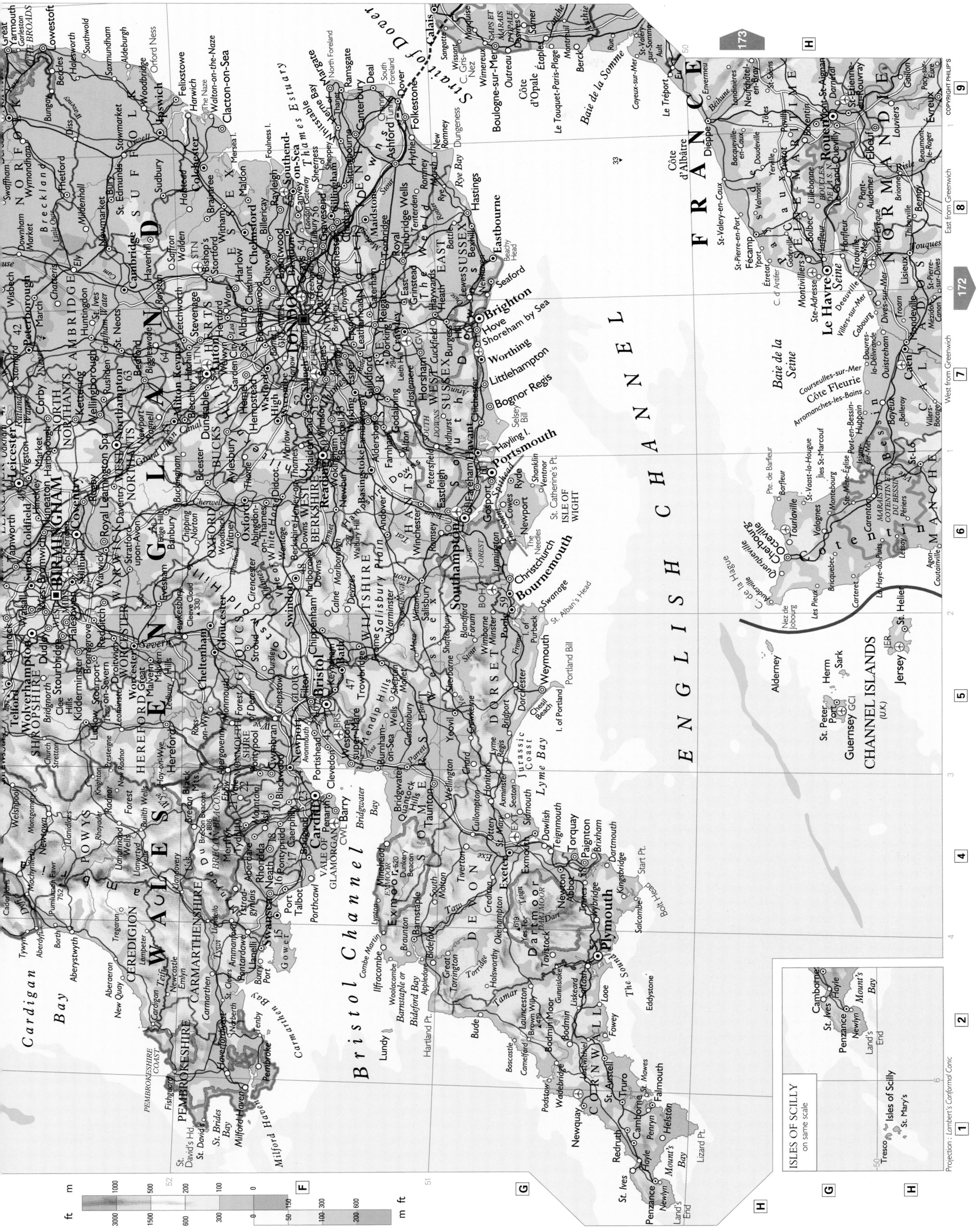

ENGLAND
WALES
FRANCE
ENGLISH CHANNEL
Bristol Channel
Cardigan Bay
Strait of Dover
Thames Estuary
Baie de la Seine
Baie de la Somme
Lyme Bay
CHANNEL ISLANDS (U.K.)
Jersey
Guernsey
Alderney
Sark
Herm
ISLE OF WIGHT
ISLES OF SCILLY on same scale
LONDON
BIRMINGHAM
Cardiff
Bristol
Southampton
Portsmouth
Brighton
Plymouth
Bournemouth
Le Havre
Rouen
Cherbourg-Octeville
Caen
Dieppe
Boulogne-sur-Mer
Calais
Dover
Exeter
Oxford
Cambridge
Gloucester
Swansea
Newport
Reading
Northampton
Leicester
Coventry
Wolverhampton
Ipswich
Norwich
Lowestoft
Great Yarmouth
Projection: Lambert's Conformal Conic
COPYRIGHT PHILIP'S
West from Greenwich
East from Greenwich
172
173
m
ft

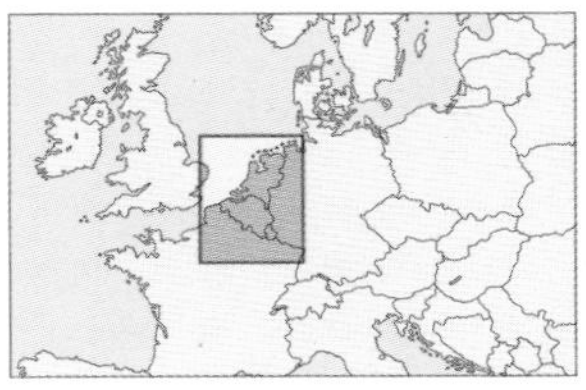

10 0 10 20 30 40 50 60 70 80 90 km

1:2 000 000

10 0 10 20 30 40 50 60 miles

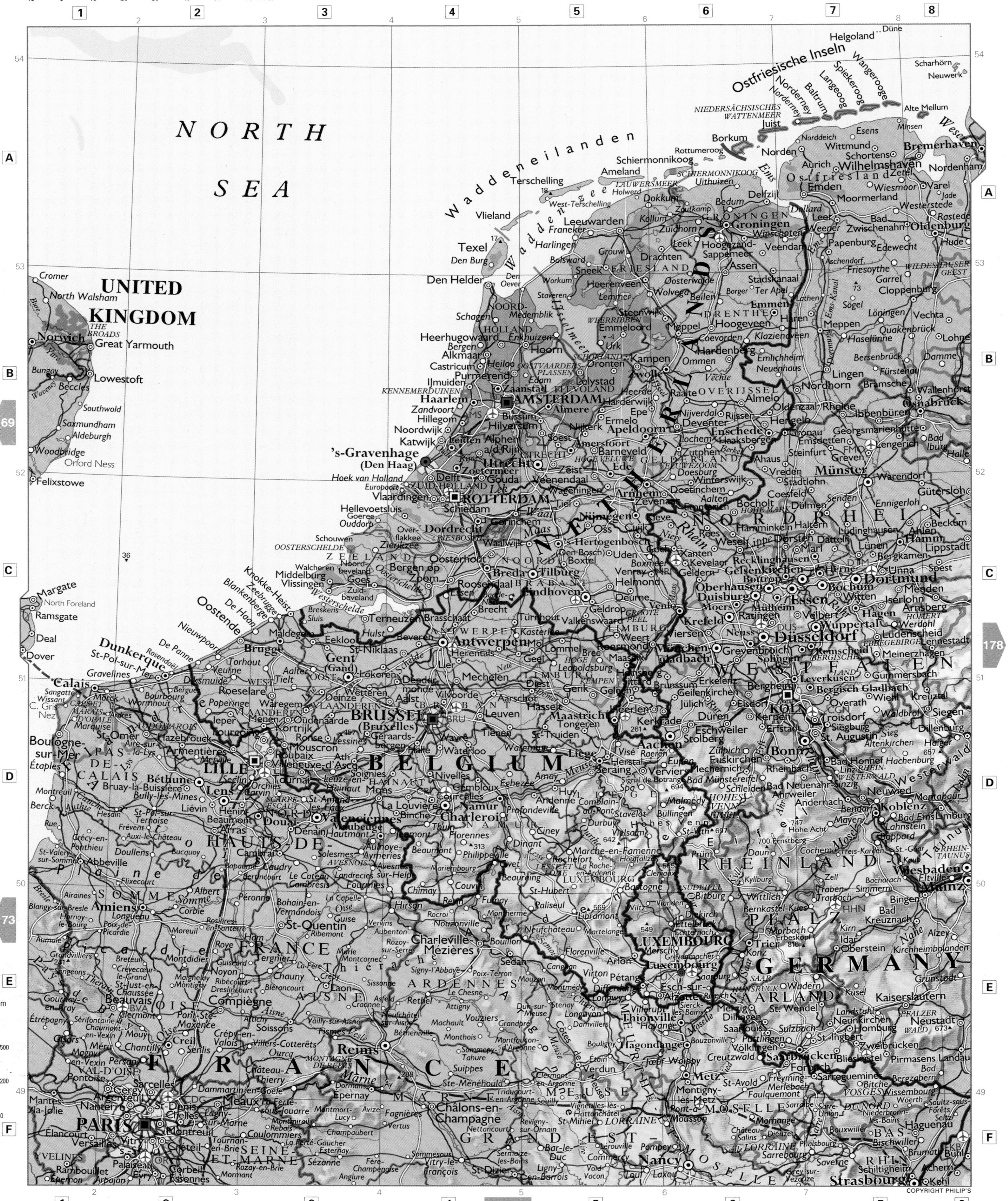

Underlined towns give their name to the administrative area in which they stand.

High-speed rail routes

173

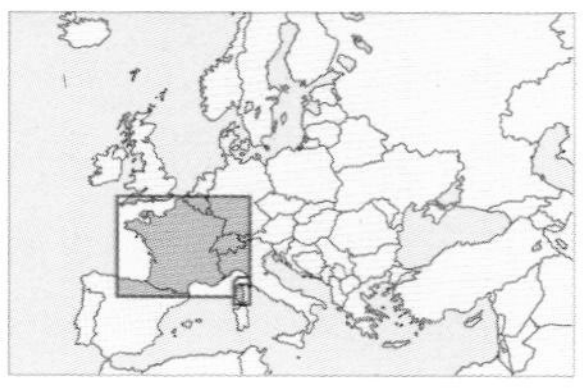

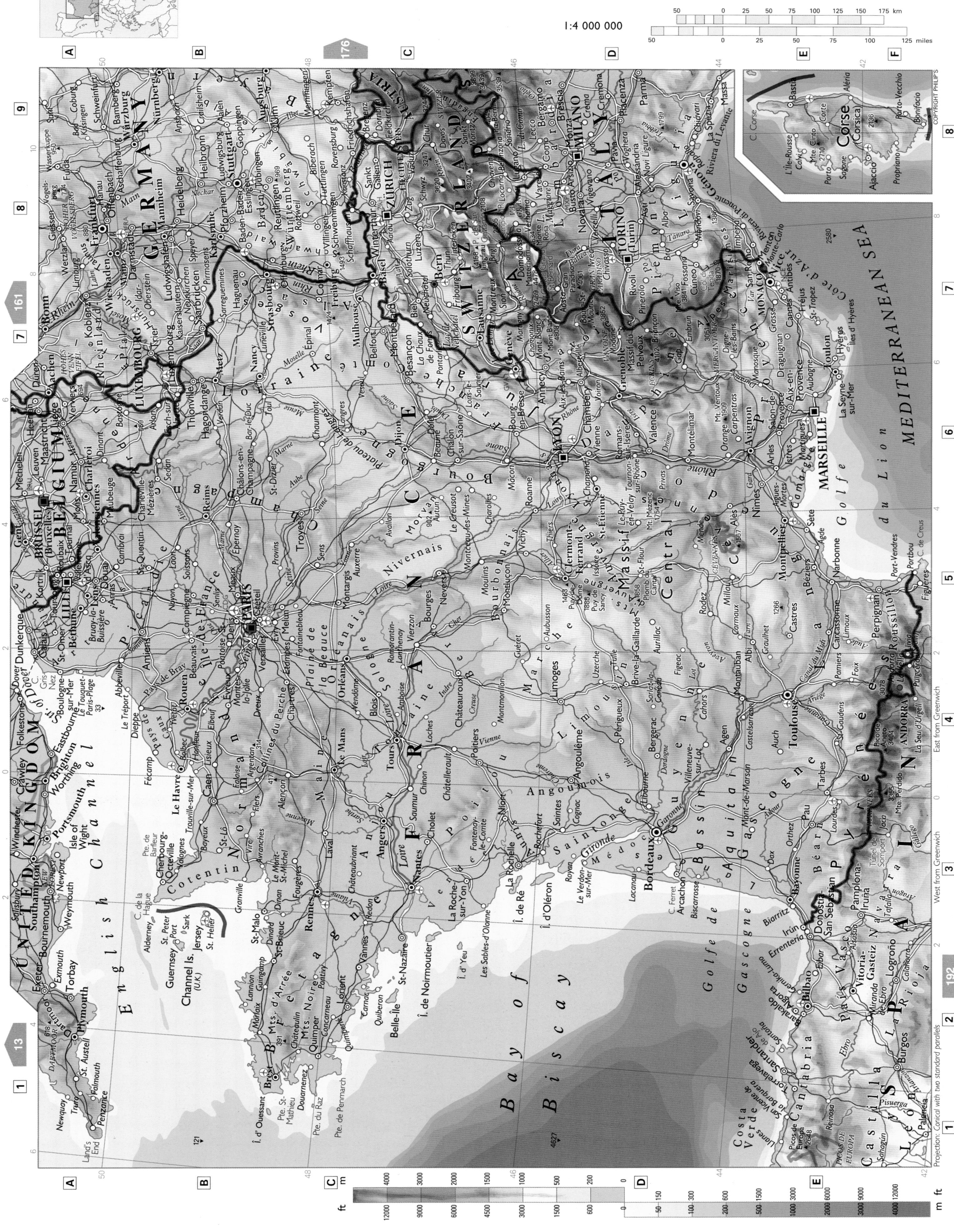
1:4 000 000
km
miles
FRANCE
UNITED KINGDOM
BELGIUM
LUXEMBOURG
GERMANY
SWITZERLAND
ITALY
SPAIN
ANDORRA
MONACO
AUSTRIA
PARIS
LYON
MARSEILLE
Bordeaux
Toulouse
Nantes
English Channel
Bay of Biscay
Golfe de Gascogne
MEDITERRANEAN SEA
Golfe du Lion
Massif Central
Corse (Corsica)
Projection: Conical with two standard parallels
East from Greenwich
West from Greenwich
COPYRIGHT PHILIPS
m
ft

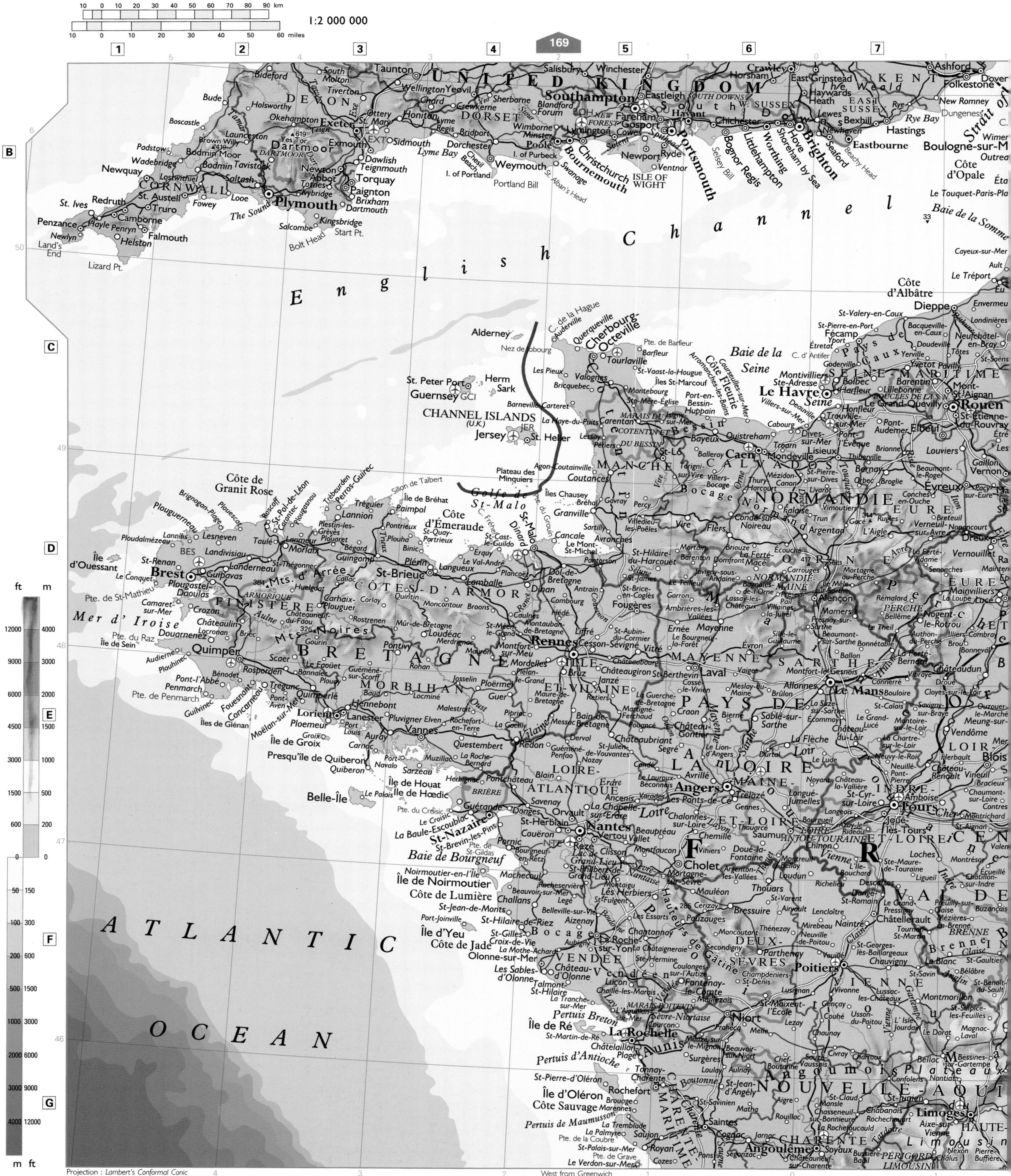

DÉPARTEMENTS IN THE PARIS AREA
1 Ville de Paris 2 Seine-St-Denis 3 Val-de-Marne 4 Hauts-de-Seine

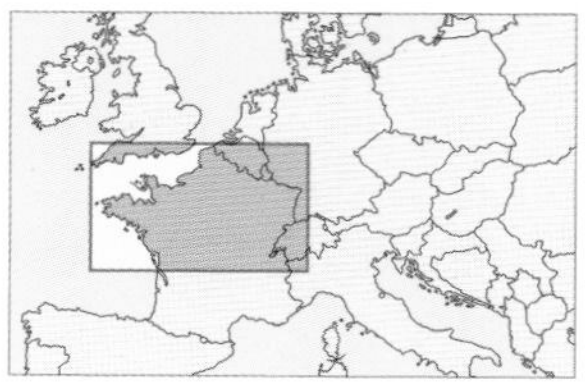

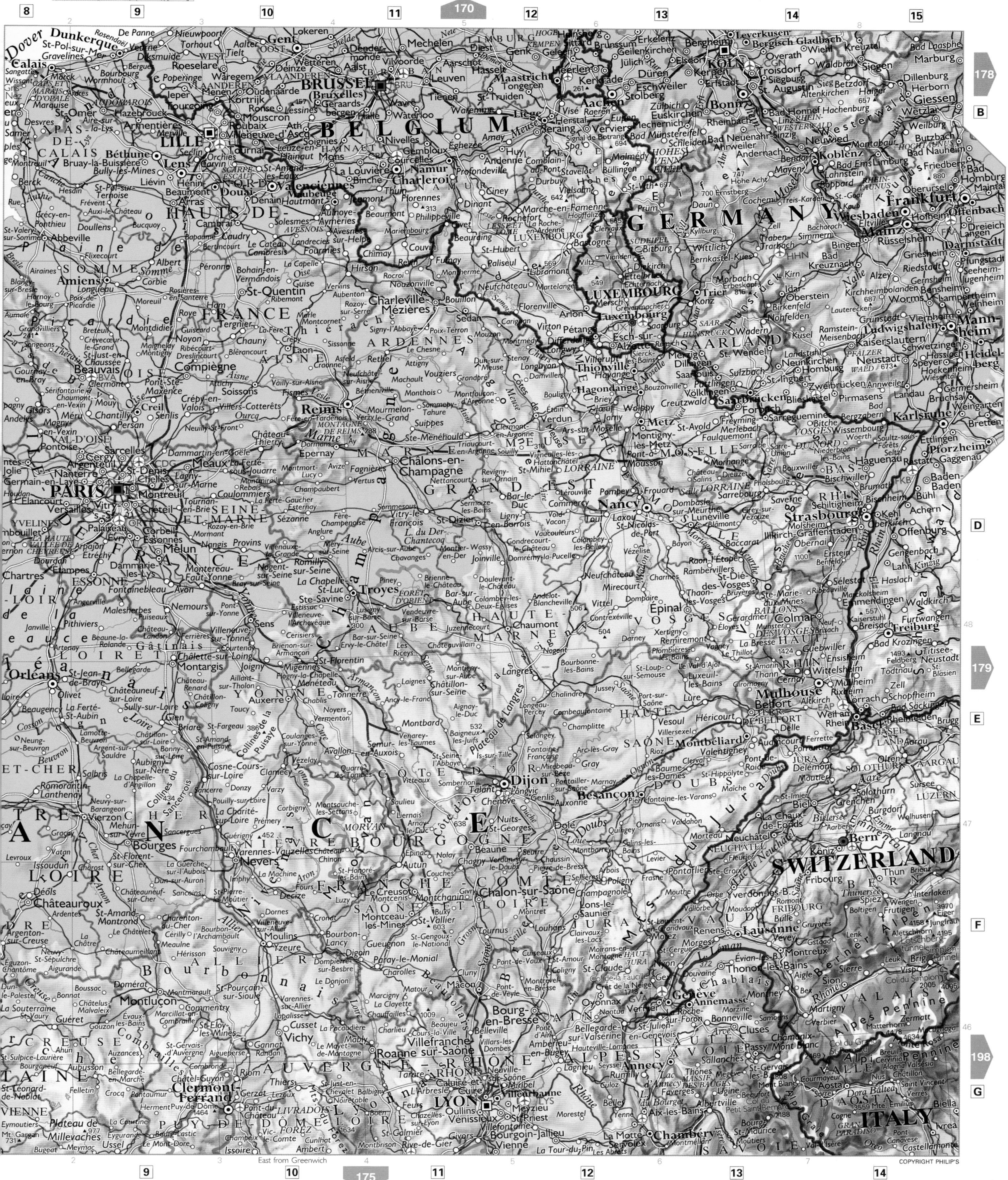

Underlined towns give their name to the administrative area in which they stand.

High-speed rail routes

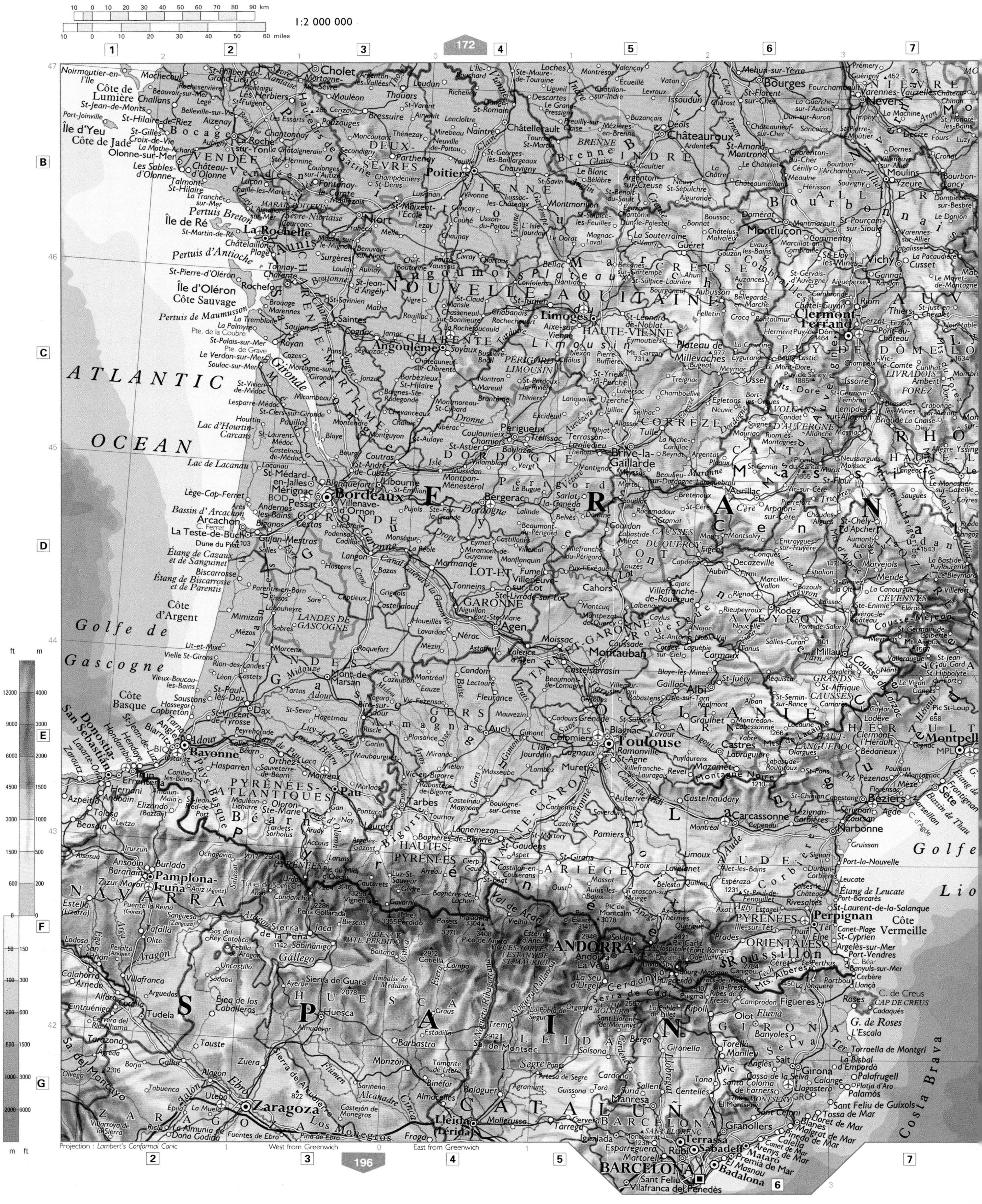
1:2 000 000
km
miles
172
196
ATLANTIC
OCEAN
Golfe de Gascogne
Golfe du Lion
NOUVELLE-AQUITAINE
OCCITANIE
AUVERGNE-RHÔNE-ALPES
ANDORRA
SPAIN
CATALUÑA
FRANCE
Bordeaux
Toulouse
Limoges
Clermont-Ferrand
Poitiers
La Rochelle
Bayonne
Pau
Perpignan
Zaragoza
Lleida (Lérida)
BARCELONA
Pamplona-Iruña
Donostia-San Sebastián
Huesca
Montpellier
Nantes
Bourges
Nevers
Angoulême
Périgueux
Agen
Montauban
Albi
Rodez
Carcassonne
Narbonne
Béziers
Projection : Lambert's Conformal Conic
West from Greenwich
East from Greenwich
ft
m

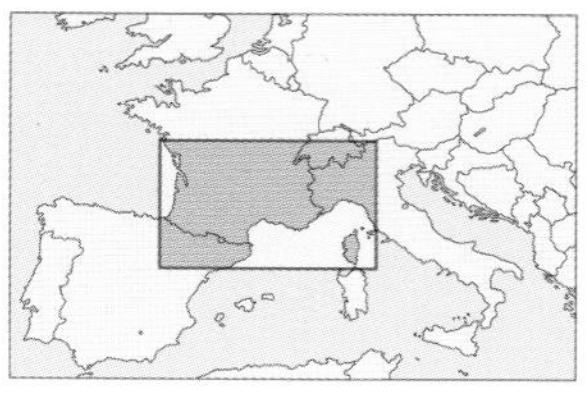

173

198

8
9
10
11
12
13
14
5
6
7
8
9
10
47
46
45
44
43
42
B
C
D
SWITZERLAND
FRANCE
ITALY
PIEMONTE
LOMBARDIA
VALAIS
GRAUBÜNDEN
TICINO
HAUTE-SAVOIE
SAVOIE
DRÔME
ARDÈCHE
VAUCLUSE
PROVENCE-ALPES-CÔTE D'AZUR
ALPES-DE-HAUTE-PROVENCE
ALPES-MARITIMES
BOUCHES-DU-RHÔNE
HAUTES-ALPES
VALLE D'AOSTA
LIGURIA
CORSE
HAUTE-CORSE
CORSE-DU-SUD
CÔTE D'AZUR
Côte d'Azur
Riviera di Ponente
Riviera di Levante
Golfo di Génova
LIGURIAN SEA
MEDITERRANEAN SEA
Alpes Pennines
Berner Alpen
Mts. du Jura
Dauphiné
Massif du Pelvoux
Alpi Marittime
Appennino Ligure
Arcipelago Toscano
Bern
Lausanne
Genève
Annecy
Chambéry
Grenoble
LYON
St-Étienne
Valence
Avignon
Nîmes
Arles
Aix-en-Provence
MARSEILLE
Toulon
Nice
MONACO
Cannes
Antibes
TORINO
MILANO
Genova
Savona
La Spezia
Livorno
Pisa
Parma
Piacenza
Novara
Alessandria
Cuneo
Bastia
Ajaccio
Elba
Gorgona
Capraia
Montecristo
Bonifacio
Porto-Vecchio
Bouches de Bonifacio
Maddalena
COPYRIGHT PHILIP'S
High-speed rail routes

161
165
171
192

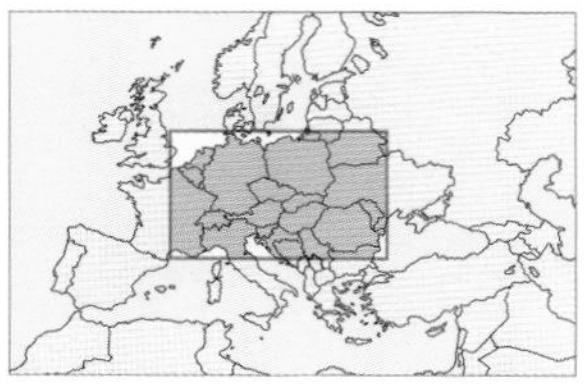

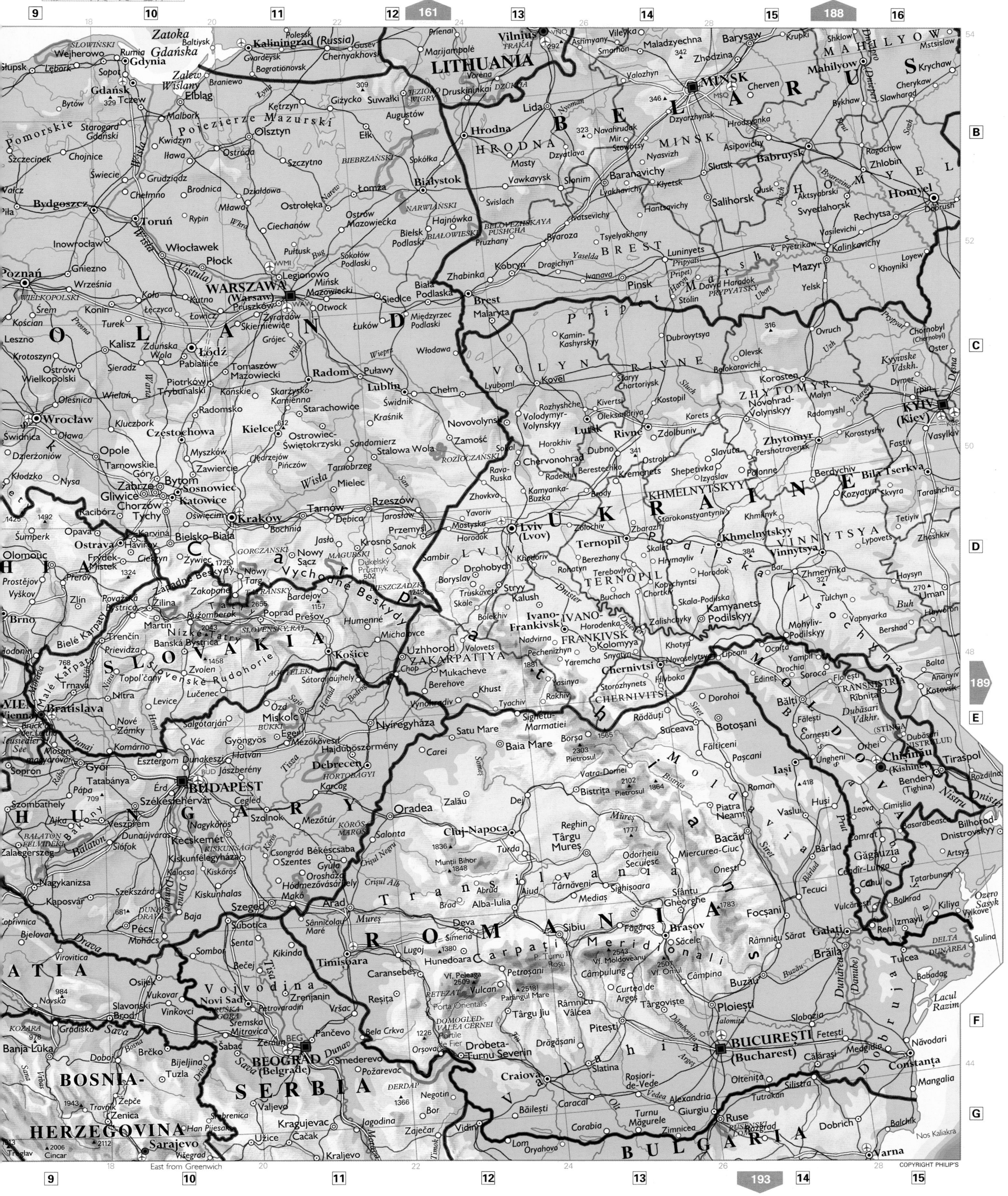
LITHUANIA
BELARUS
POLAND
UKRAINE
SLOVAKIA
HUNGARY
ROMANIA
MOLDOVA
SERBIA
BOSNIA-HERZEGOVINA
BULGARIA
CROATIA
Transilvania
Carpatii Meridionali
Podilska Vysochyna
Vojvodina
Moldavia
Walachia
Dobruja
Zatoka Gdańska
Pojezierze Mazurskie
Kaliningrad (Russia)
Vilnius
MINSK
Gdańsk
Gdynia
Elbląg
Olsztyn
Bydgoszcz
Toruń
Białystok
Hrodna
Brest
Pinsk
Babruysk
Homyel
Mahilyow
Baranavichy
Mazyr
Poznań
WARSZAWA (Warsaw)
Łódź
Radom
Lublin
Wrocław
Częstochowa
Kielce
Katowice
Kraków
Rzeszów
Opole
Ostrava
Lviv (Lvov)
Lutsk
Rivne
Ternopil
Khmelnytskyy
Vinnytsya
Zhytomyr
KYIV (Kiev)
Chernivtsi
Ivano-Frankivsk
Uzhhorod
Košice
Prešov
Žilina
Bratislava
BUDAPEST
Miskolc
Debrecen
Szeged
Pécs
Győr
Nyíregyháza
Oradea
Cluj-Napoca
Satu Mare
Baia Mare
Timişoara
Arad
Sibiu
Braşov
Iaşi
Bacău
Galaţi
Brăila
Ploieşti
BUCUREŞTI (Bucharest)
Craiova
Constanţa
CHIŞINĂU (Kishinev)
Tiraspol
BEOGRAD (Belgrade)
Novi Sad
Sarajevo
Varna
Ruse
Dunărea (Danube)
Wisła
Dnister
Prut
Buh
Siret
Mureş
Tisa
East from Greenwich
COPYRIGHT PHILIP'S

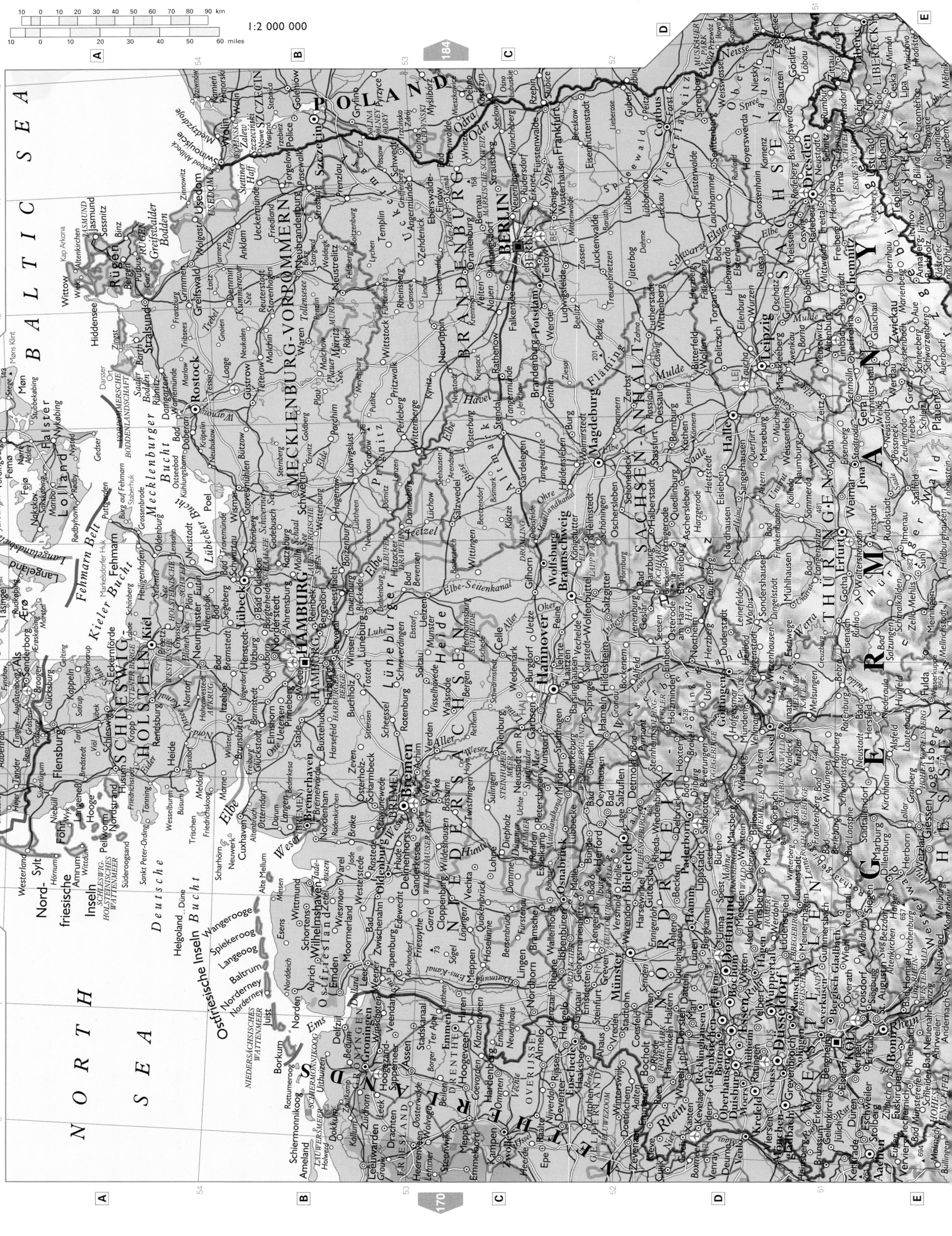

1:2 000 000
km
miles
184
163
170
NORTH SEA
BALTIC SEA
DENMARK
POLAND
GERMANY
NETHERLANDS
SCHLESWIG-HOLSTEIN
MECKLENBURG-VORPOMMERN
BRANDENBURG
NIEDERSACHSEN
SACHSEN-ANHALT
SACHSEN
THÜRINGEN
NORDRHEIN-WESTFALEN
HESSEN
BERLIN
HAMBURG
Bremen
Hannover
Kiel
Rostock
Schwerin
Magdeburg
Potsdam
Dresden
Leipzig
Erfurt
Düsseldorf
Köln
Bonn
Dortmund
Szczecin
Deutsche Bucht
Mecklenburger Bucht
Kieler Bucht
Fehmarn Belt
Lübecker Bucht
Ostfriesische Inseln
Nordfriesische Inseln
Lüneburger Heide

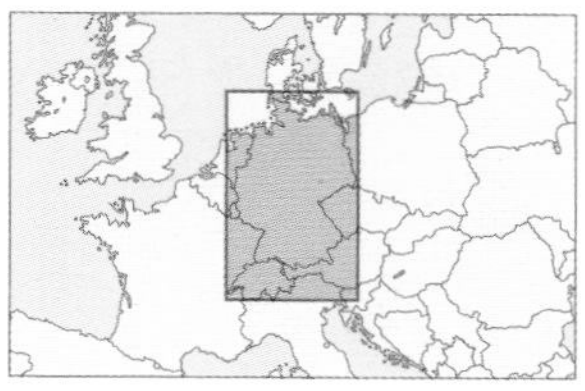

Underlined towns give their name to the administrative area in which they stand.
High-speed rail routes
Projection : Lambert's Conformal Conic
East from Greenwich
COPYRIGHT PHILIP'S
180
175
198
199
CZECHIA
SWITZERLAND
FRANCE
LUXEMBOURG
SLOVENIA
BAYERN
BADEN-WÜRTTEMBERG
SAARLAND
RHEINLAND-PFALZ
GRAND EST
PRAHA
MÜNCHEN
ZÜRICH
Bern
Stuttgart
Frankfurt

1:2 000 000
km
miles
Projection : Lambert's Conformal Conic
178
179
198
GERMANY
CZECHIA
AUSTRIA
SWITZERLAND
ITALY
SLOVENIA
THÜRINGEN
BAYERN
OBERFRANKEN
UNTERFRANKEN
MITTELFRANKEN
OBERPFALZ
NIEDERBAYERN
SCHWABEN
OBERBAYERN
KARLOVARSKÝ
PLZEŇSKÝ
STŘEDOČESKÝ
JIHOČESKÝ
LIBERECKÝ
ÚSTECKÝ
KRÁLOVÉHRADECKÝ
VYSOČINA
NIEDERÖSTERREICH
OBERÖSTERREICH
SALZBURG
STEIERMARK
KÄRNTEN
TIROL
VORARLBERG
TRENTINO-ALTO ADIGE
FRIULI-VENEZIA GIULIA
VÉNETO
LOMBARDIA
PRAHA
MÜNCHEN
ZAGREB
Dresden
Chemnitz
Erfurt
Nürnberg
Augsburg
Regensburg
Würzburg
Stuttgart
Salzburg
Linz
Innsbruck
Graz
Klagenfurt
Ljubljana
Trieste
Venézia
Bolzano
Trento
Vicenza
Brescia
Plzeň
České Budějovice
Liberec
Maribor
Golfo di Venézia
Bodensee
Donau
Inn
Vltava
Hohe Tauern
Niedere Tauern
Zillertaler Alpen
Karawanken
Karnische Alpen
Böhmerwald
Bayerischer Wald
Erzgebirge
Thüringer Wald
Šumava

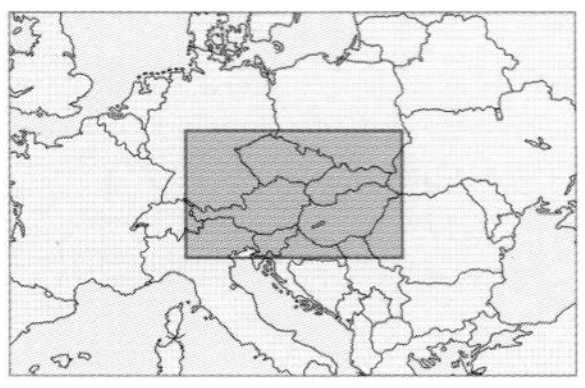

Underlined towns give their name to the administrative area in which they stand.

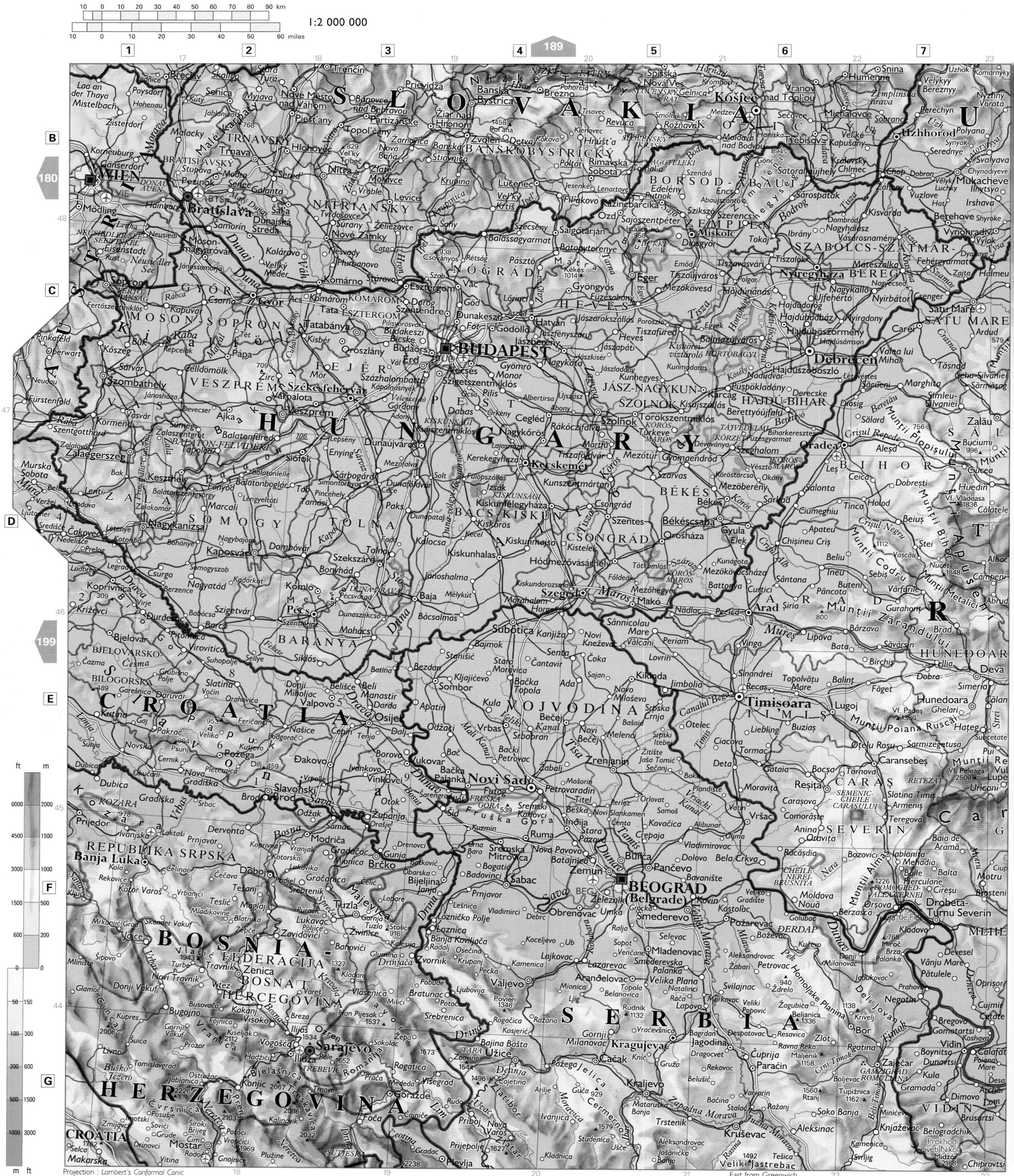

Projection : Lambert's Conformal Conic

East from Greenwich

Administrative divisions in Croatia:
1 Brodsko-Posavska
2 Koprivničko-Križevačka
4 Međimurska
5 Osječko-Baranjska
6 Požeško-Slavonska
8 Virovitičko-Podravska
9 Vukovarsko-Srijemska

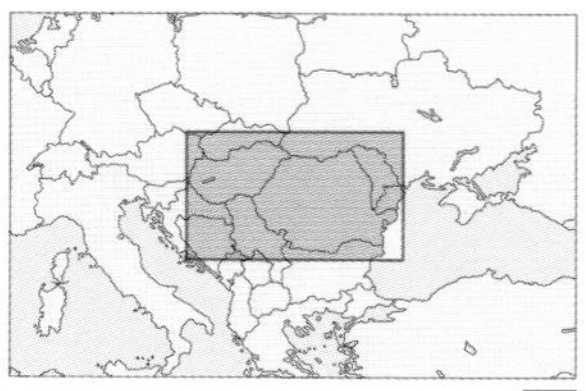

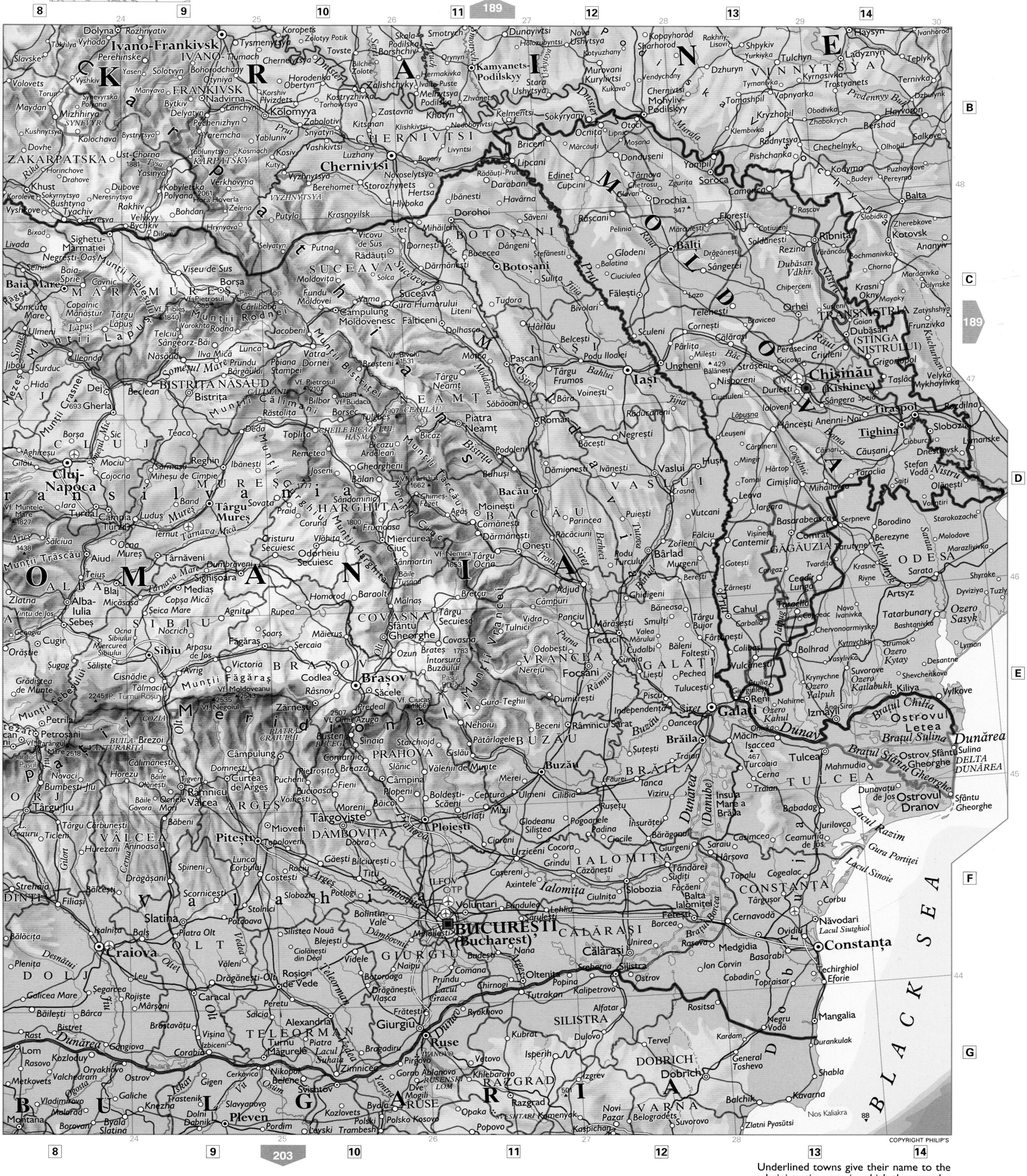

Underlined towns give their name to the administrative area in which they stand.

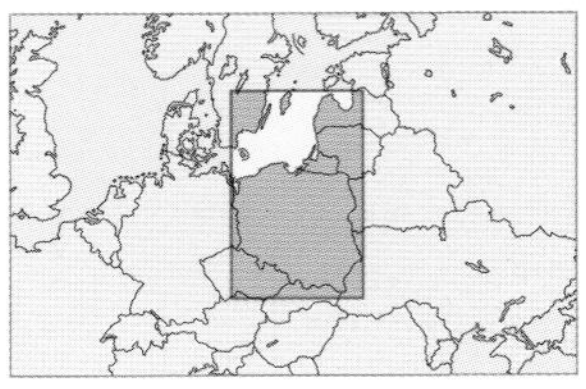

10 0 10 20 30 40 50 60 70 80 90 km

10 0 10 20 30 40 50 60 miles

1:2 000 000

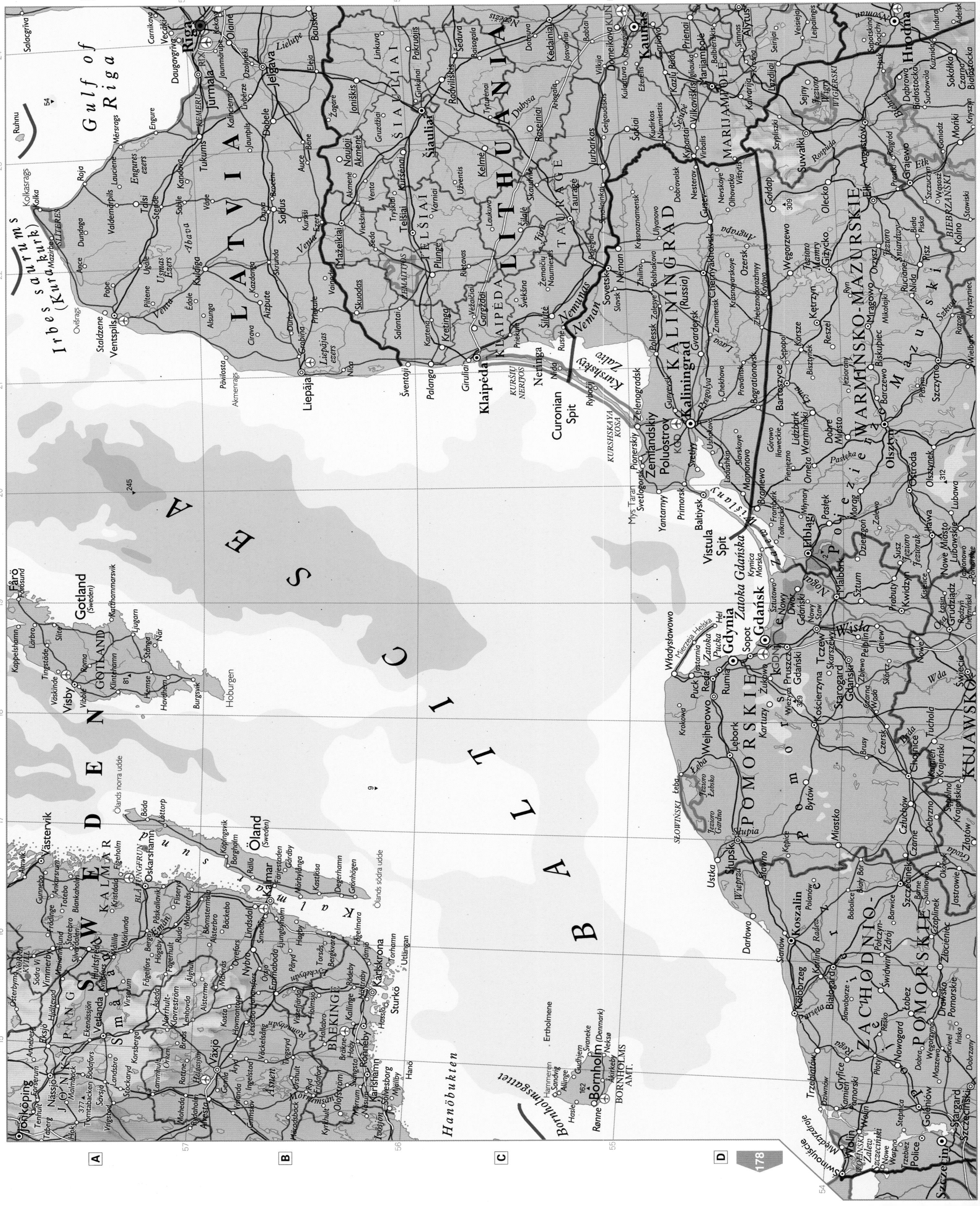

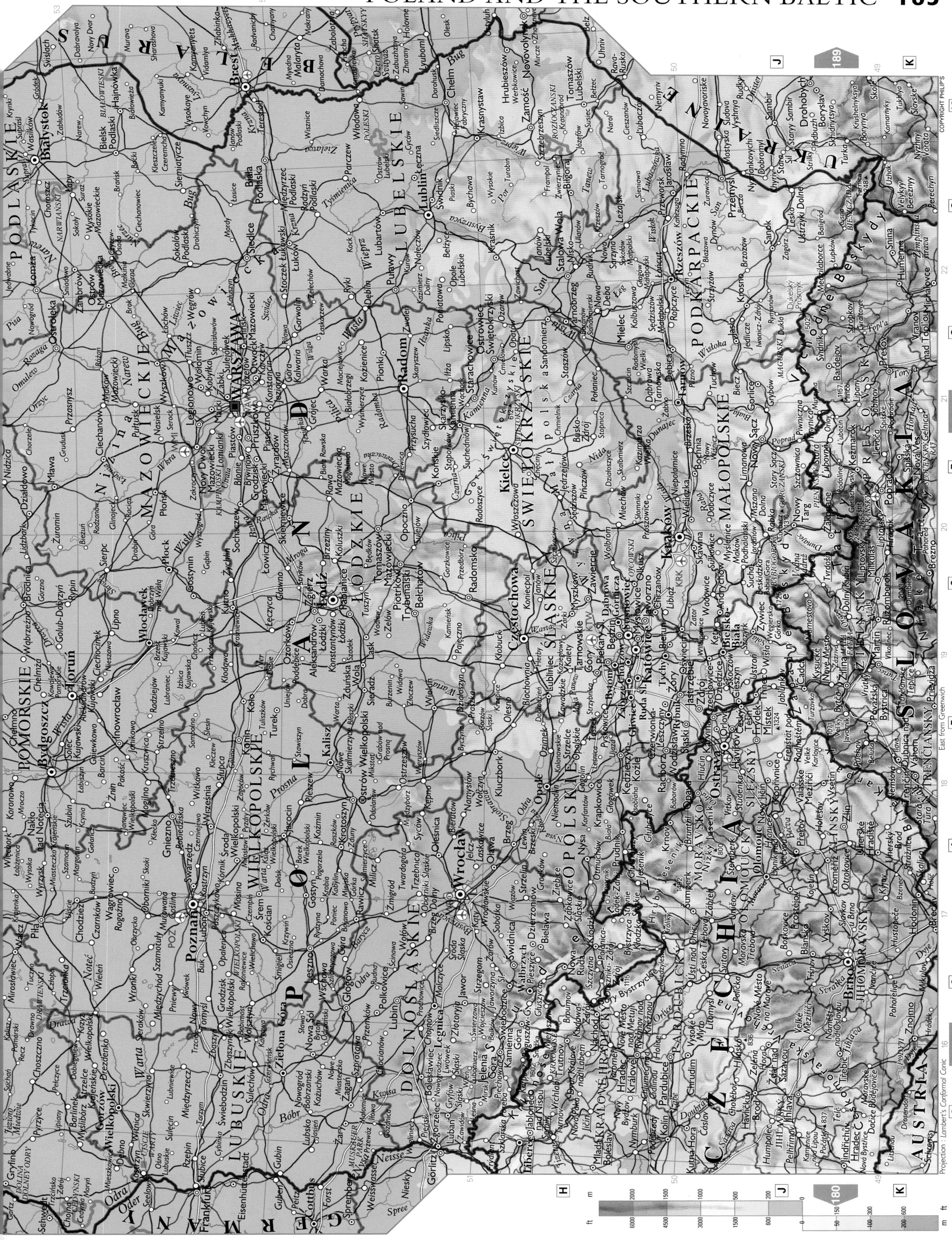

Underlined towns give their name to the administrative area in which they stand.

0 50 100 200 300 400 km
0 50 100 150 200 250 miles
1:8 000 000

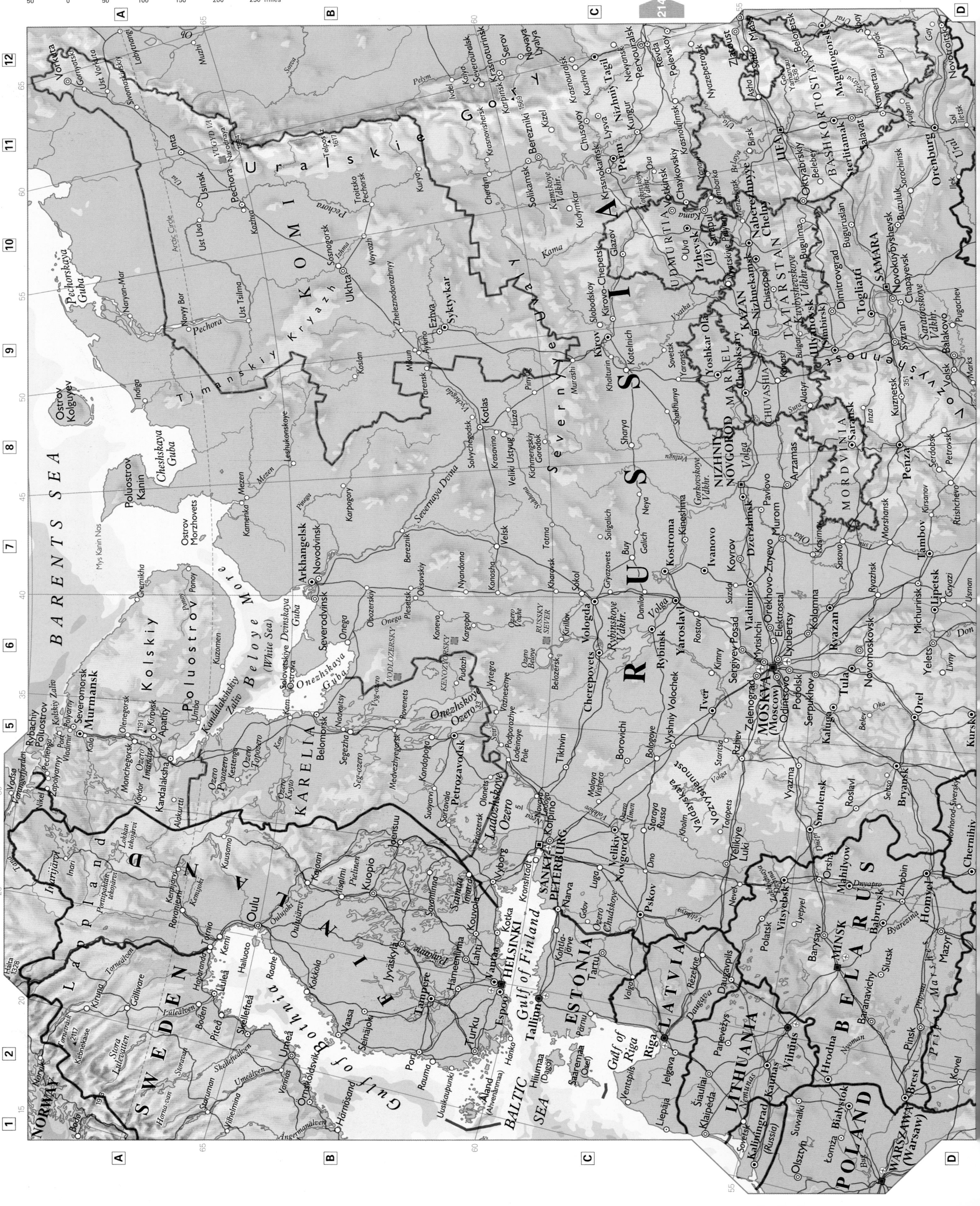

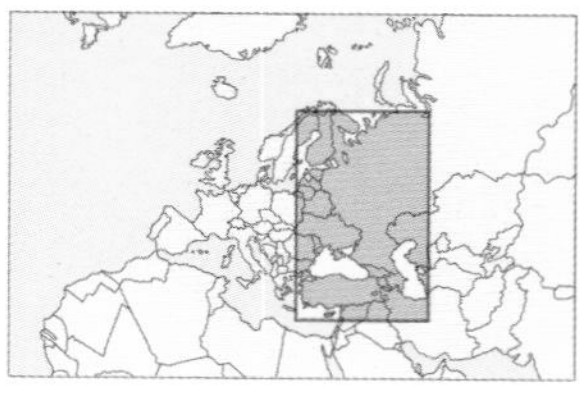

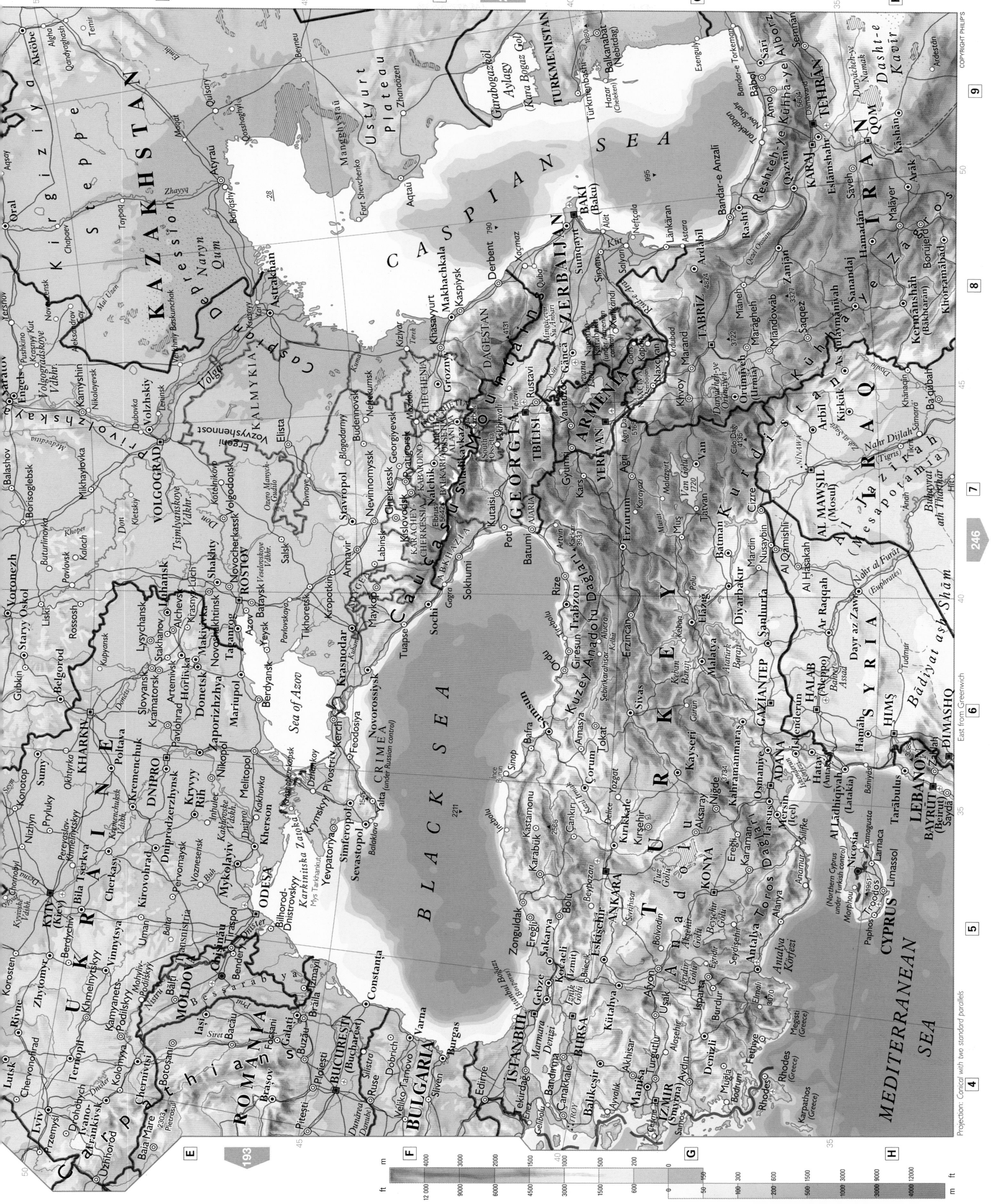
BLACK SEA
CASPIAN SEA
Sea of Azov
MEDITERRANEAN SEA
KAZAKHSTAN
UKRAINE
ROMANIA
MOLDOVA
BULGARIA
TURKEY
GEORGIA
ARMENIA
AZERBAIJAN
SYRIA
IRAQ
IRAN
LEBANON
CYPRUS
TURKMENISTAN
CRIMEA
KYIV (Kiev)
KHARKIV
DNIPRO
ODESA
CHIȘINĂU
BUCUREȘTI (Bucharest)
ISTANBUL
ANKARA
TBILISI
YEREVAN
BAKI (Baku)
TEHRĀN
VOLGOGRAD
ROSTOV
DIMASHQ
Caspian Depression
Ustyurt Plateau
Caucasus Mountains
Projection: Conical with two standard parallels
East from Greenwich
COPYRIGHT PHILIP'S
193
216
246

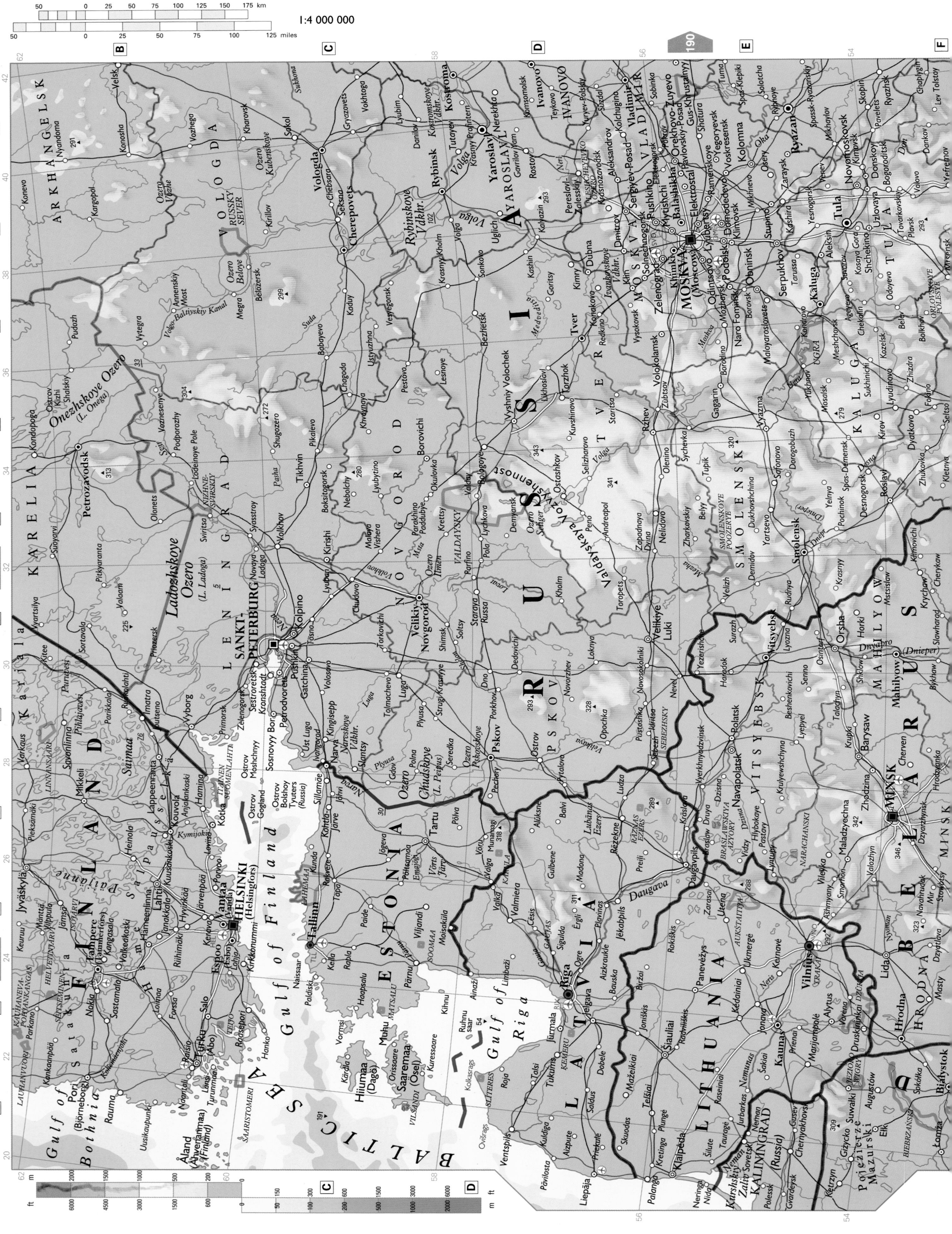
1:4 000 000
km
miles
BALTIC SEA
Gulf of Finland
Gulf of Riga
Gulf of Bothnia
FINLAND
ESTONIA
LATVIA
LITHUANIA
BELARUS
RUSSIA
KALININGRAD (Russia)
SANKT-PETERBURG
MOSKVA (Moscow)
HELSINKI (Helsingfors)
Tallinn
Riga
Vilnius
MINSK
Ladozhskoye Ozero (L. Ladoga)
Onezhskoye Ozero (L. Onega)
Ozero Chudskoye (L. Peipus)
Valdayskaya Vozvyshennost
186
190
160

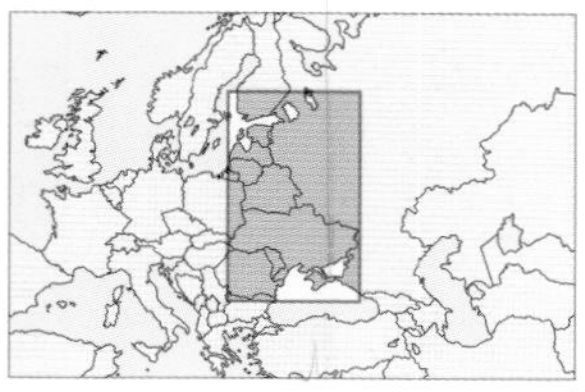

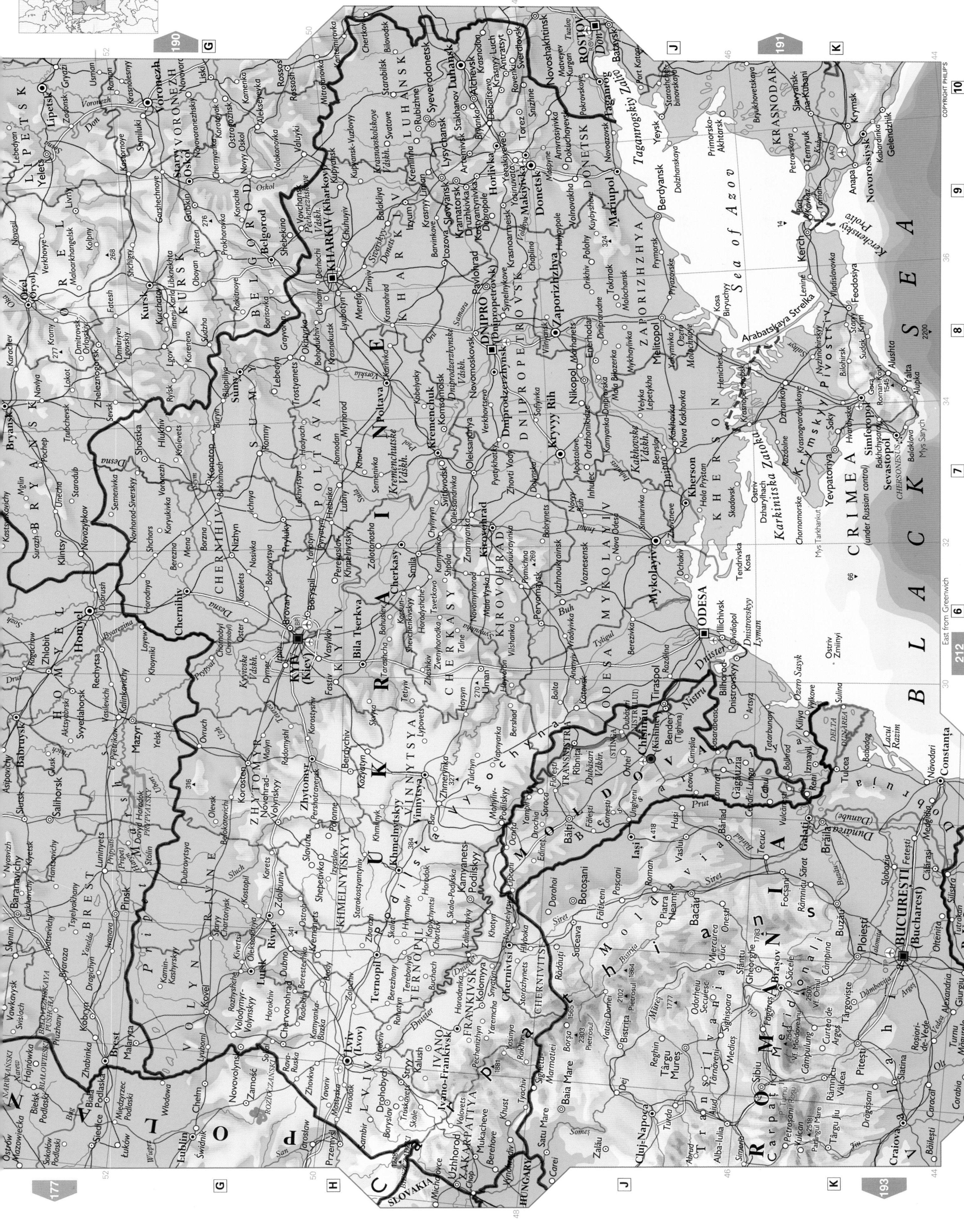
UKRAINE
MOLDOVA
ROMANIA
BULGARIA
CRIMEA
(under Russian control)
Sea of Azov
BLACK SEA
KYIV
(Kiev)
KHARKIV (Kharkov)
DNIPRO
(Dnipropetrovsk)
ODESA
CHIŞINĂU
BUCUREŞTI
(Bucharest)
ROSTOV
Donetsk
Luhansk
Zaporizhzhya
Mykolayiv
Kherson
Simferopol
Sevastopol
Lviv
(Lvov)
Chernihiv
Homyel
Voronezh
Kursk
Belgorod
Bryansk
Orel
(Oryol)
Lipetsk
Poltava
Vinnytsya
Zhytomyr
Rivne
Lutsk
Ternopil
Chernivtsi
Uzhhorod
Constanţa
Iaşi
Galaţi
Brăila
Ploieşti
Braşov
Craiova
Krasnodar
Novorossiysk
Mariupol
Kerch
Kryvyy Rih
Kremenchuk
Cherkasy
Sumy
Bila Tserkva
Khmelnytskyy
Ivano-Frankivsk
Brest
Pinsk
Mazyr
Tiraspol
East from Greenwich
Projection: Conical with two standard parallels
COPYRIGHT PHILIPS
190
191
193
177
212
G
H
J
K
6
7
8
9
10

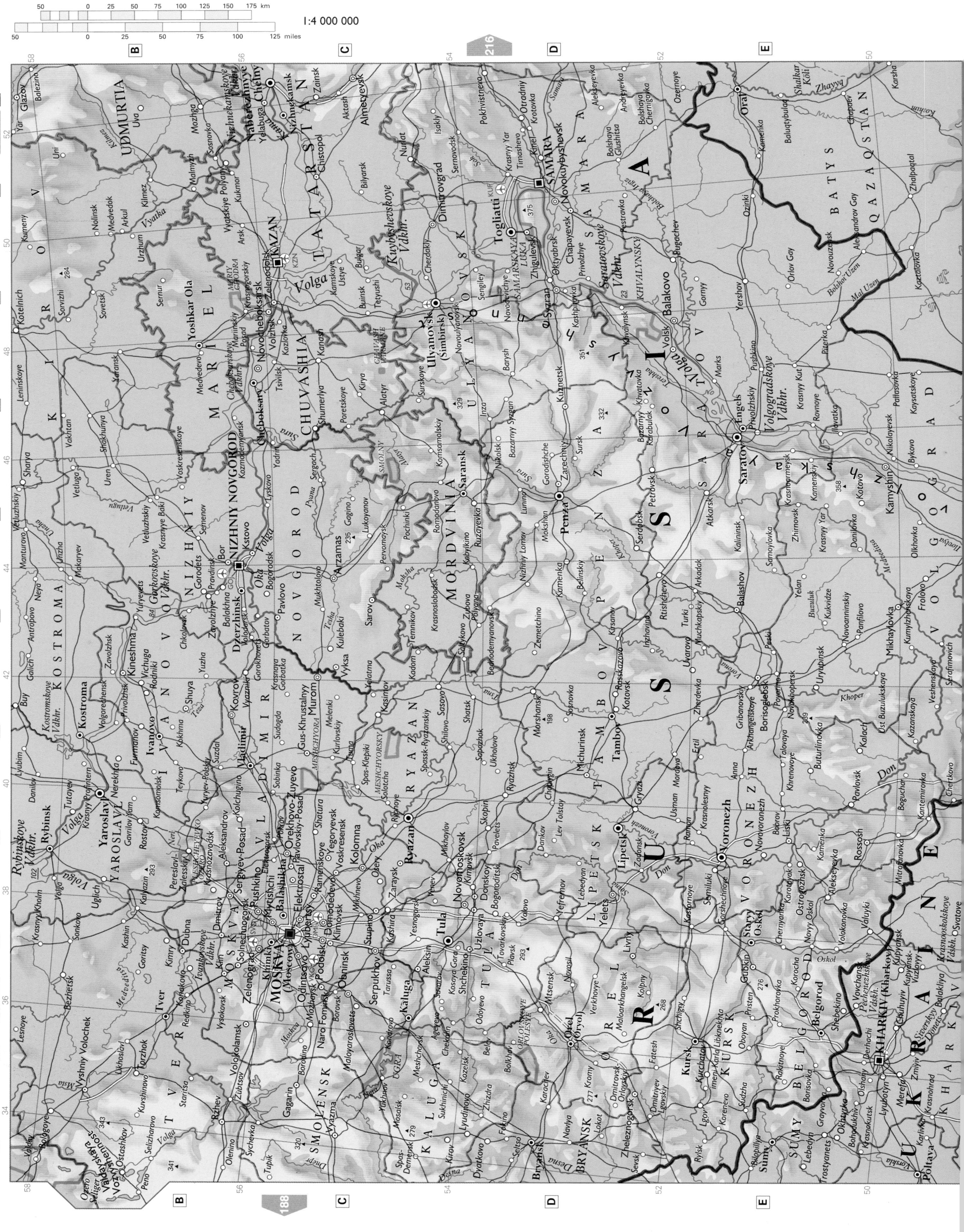

1:4 000 000
50 0 25 50 75 100 125 150 175 km
50 0 25 50 75 100 125 miles
216
214
188
MOSKVA (Moscow)
NIZHNIY NOVGOROD
KAZAN
SAMARA
Saratov
Voronezh
Ulyanovsk (Simbirsk)
Penza
Ryazan
Tula
Kaluga
Yaroslavl
Kostroma
Ivanovo
Vladimir
Tver
Oryol
Kursk
Belgorod
Lipetsk
Tambov
Bryansk
Kharkiv (Kharkov)
Togliatti
Saransk
Cheboksary
Yoshkar Ola
Naberezhnyye Chelny
TATARSTAN
CHUVASHIA
MORDVINIA
UDMURTIA
UKRAINE
QAZAQSTAN
RUSSIA
Volga
Oka
Don

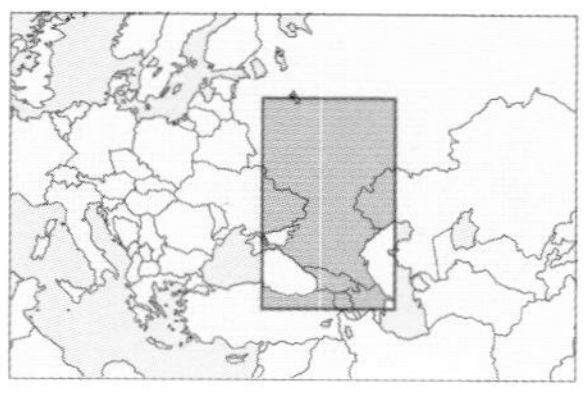

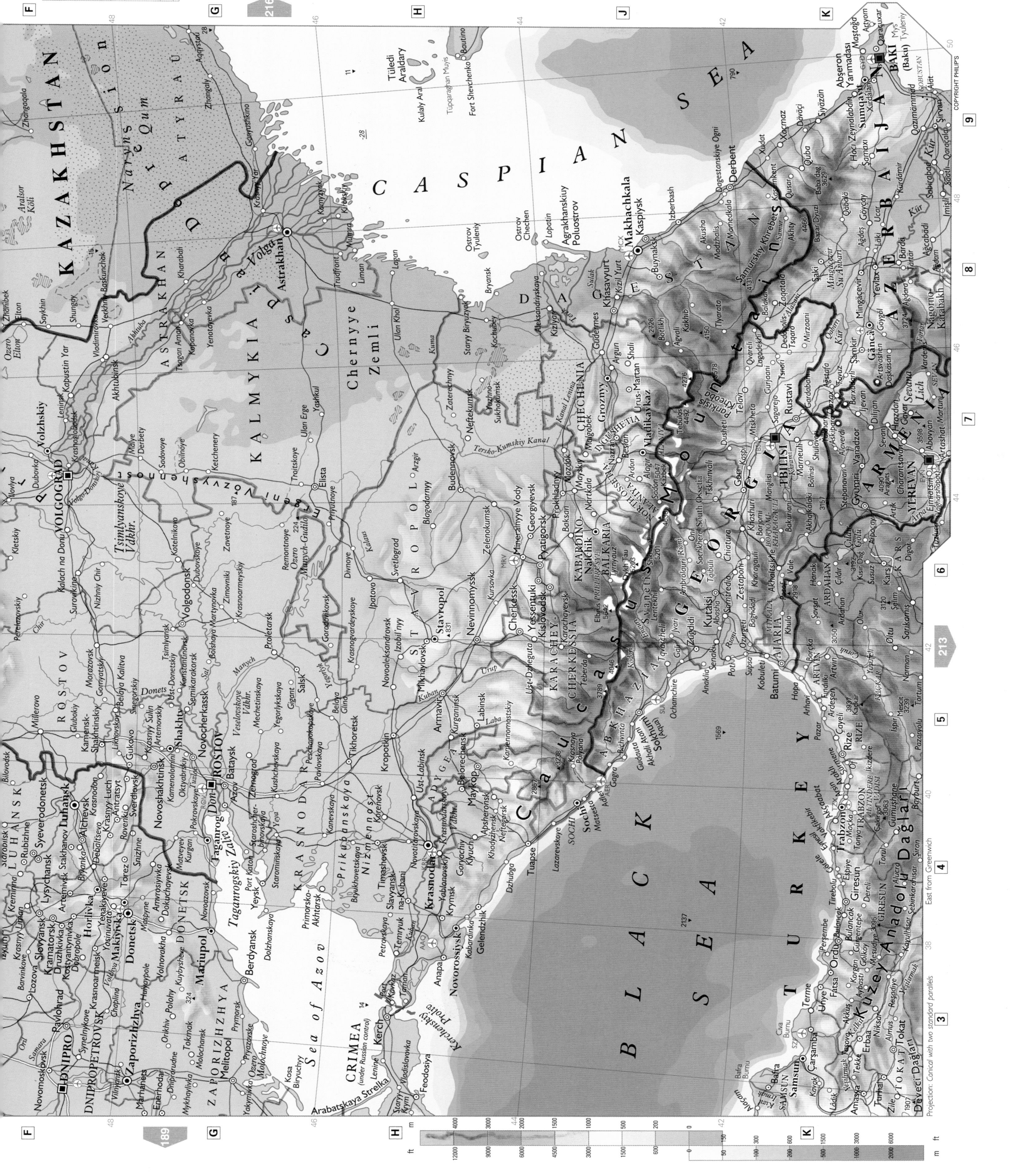
KAZAKHSTAN
CASPIAN SEA
BLACK SEA
Sea of Azov
CRIMEA
(under Russian control)
KALMYKIA
ASTRAKHAN
VOLGOGRAD
ROSTOV
KRASNODAR
STAVROPOL
DAGESTAN
CHECHENIA
GEORGIA
ARMENIA
AZERBAIJAN
TURKEY
Caucasus Mountains
Astrakhan
Volgograd
Rostov
Krasnodar
Stavropol
Makhachkala
Grozny
Sochi
Novorossiysk
Taganrog
Donetsk
Mariupol
Zaporizhzhya
Tbilisi
Yerevan
Baki (Baku)
Trabzon
Samsun
Volga
Kalmykia
Chernyye Zemli
216
213
189
Projection: Conical with two standard parallels
East from Greenwich
COPYRIGHT PHILIP'S

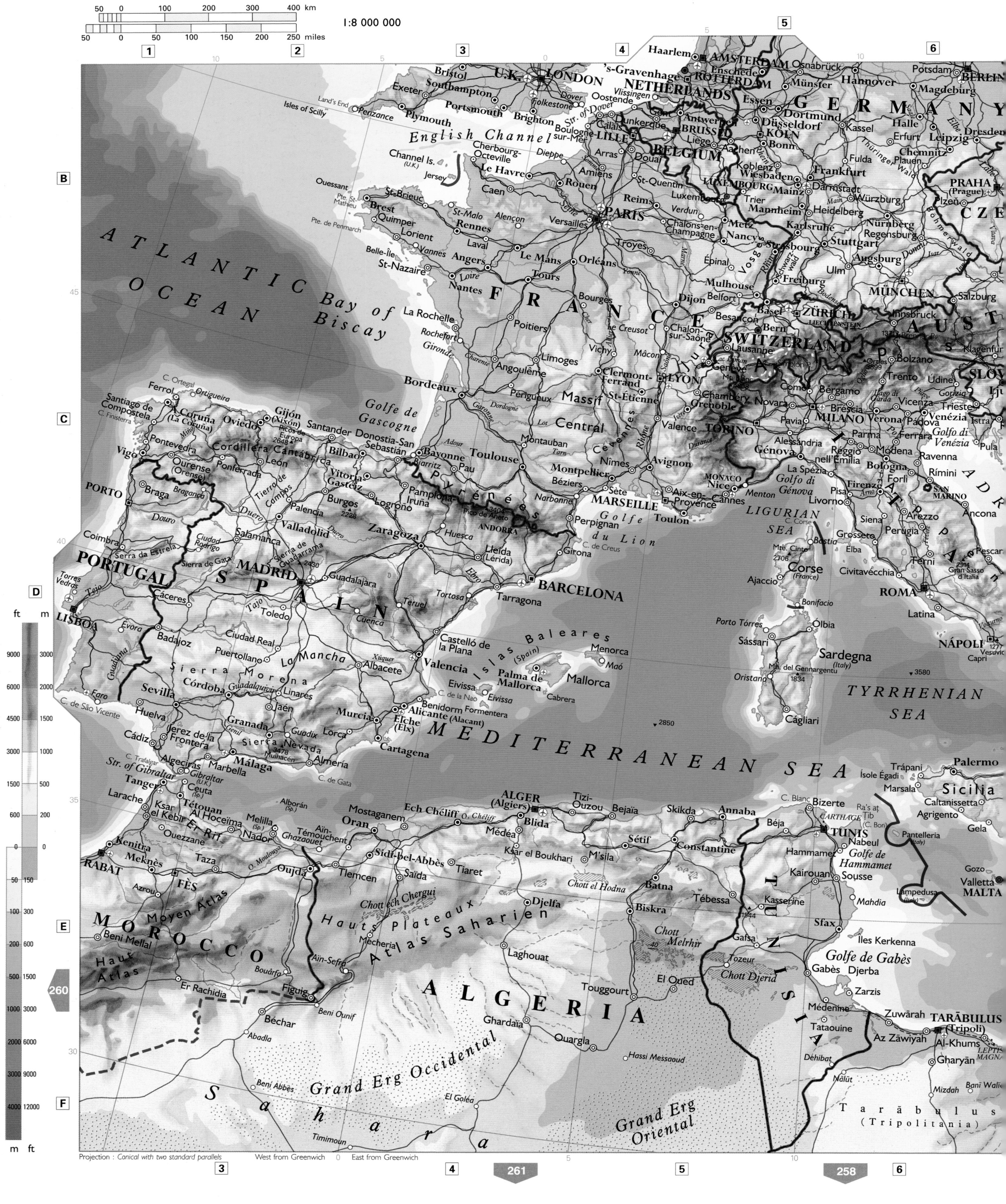
1:8 000 000
Projection : Conical with two standard parallels
West from Greenwich
East from Greenwich
ATLANTIC OCEAN
Bay of Biscay
Golfe de Gascogne
English Channel
MEDITERRANEAN SEA
TYRRHENIAN SEA
LIGURIAN SEA
Golfe du Lion
Islas Baleares (Spain)
Str. of Gibraltar
Str. of Dover
U.K.
LONDON
NETHERLANDS
AMSTERDAM
BELGIUM
BRUSSEL
LUXEMBOURG
GERMANY
BERLIN
FRANCE
PARIS
SWITZERLAND
Bern
ZÜRICH
LIECHTENSTEIN
AUSTRIA
ITALY
ROMA
MONACO
SAN MARINO
ANDORRA
SPAIN
MADRID
PORTUGAL
LISBOA
MOROCCO
RABAT
ALGERIA
ALGER (Algiers)
TUNISIA
TUNIS
MALTA
Valletta
TARĀBULUS (Tripoli)
Massif Central
Pyrénées
Alpes
Cordillera Cantábrica
Sierra Morena
Sierra Nevada
Moyen Atlas
Haut Atlas
Hauts Plateaux
Atlas Saharien
Grand Erg Occidental
Grand Erg Oriental
Sahara
Chott Melrhir
Chott Djerid
Corse (France)
Sardegna (Italy)
Sicilia
Mallorca
Menorca
Ibiza
Formentera
Golfe de Gabès
Golfe de Hammamet
Tarābulus (Tripolitania)
BARCELONA
MARSEILLE
LYON
TORINO
MILANO
NÁPOLI
Palermo
Cágliari
Valencia
Sevilla
Málaga
Granada
Bordeaux
Toulouse
Nantes
Oran
Constantine
Fès
Tanger

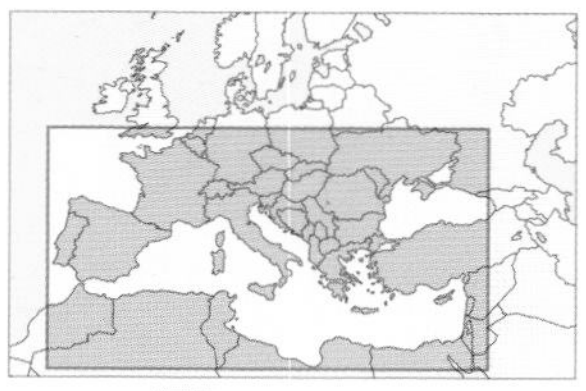

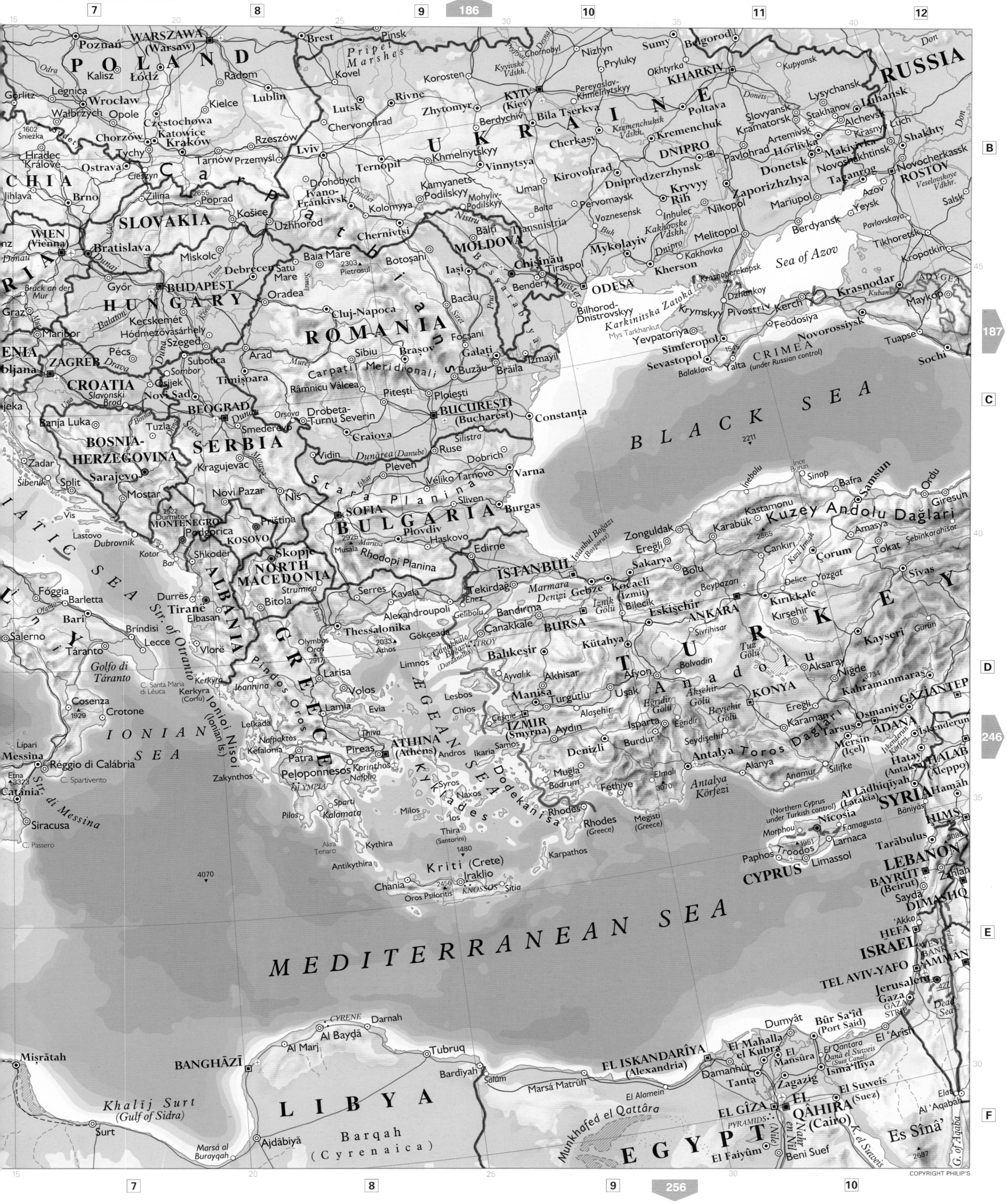

7
8
9
186
10
11
12
B
C
D
E
F
187
246
256
POLAND
WARSZAWA (Warsaw)
Poznań
Łódź
Kalisz
Radom
Lublin
Kielce
Wrocław
Legnica
Opole
Częstochowa
Katowice
Kraków
Rzeszów
Tarnów
Przemyśl
Chorzów
Tychy
Ostrava
Brno
Jihlava
Hradec Králové
SLOVAKIA
Bratislava
Žilina
Poprad
Košice
Uzhhorod
WIEN (Vienna)
HUNGARY
BUDAPEST
Győr
Miskolc
Debrecen
Kecskemét
Hódmezővásárhely
Szeged
Pécs
Maribor
ZAGREB
CROATIA
Osijek
Novi Sad
BEOGRAD
SERBIA
Smederevo
Kragujevac
Niš
Novi Pazar
BOSNIA-HERZEGOVINA
Banja Luka
Tuzla
Sarajevo
Mostar
Split
Zadar
Šibenik
MONTENEGRO
Podgorica
KOSOVO
Priština
Skopje
NORTH MACEDONIA
Bitola
ALBANIA
Tiranë
Durrës
Elbasan
Vlorë
Shkodër
ROMANIA
Cluj-Napoca
Oradea
Arad
Timișoara
Sibiu
Brașov
Iași
Bacău
Botoșani
Baia Mare
Satu Mare
Focșani
Galați
Brăila
Buzău
Ploiești
Pitești
Râmnicu Vâlcea
Craiova
Drobeta-Turnu Severin
BUCUREȘTI (Bucharest)
Constanța
Carpații Meridionali
MOLDOVA
Chișinău
Bălți
Tiraspol
Bender
UKRAINE
KYIV (Kiev)
Lviv
Lutsk
Rivne
Zhytomyr
Ternopil
Khmelnytskyy
Vinnytsya
Chernivtsi
Ivano-Frankivsk
Kolomyya
Kamyanets-Podilskyy
Bila Tserkva
Cherkasy
Uman
Kirovohrad
KHARKIV
Poltava
Kremenchuk
DNIPRO
Dniprodzerzhynsk
Kryvyy Rih
Zaporizhzhya
Nikopol
Donetsk
Mariupol
Luhansk
Horlivka
Mykolayiv
Kherson
ODESA
Melitopol
Berdyansk
Sumy
Nizhyn
Chornobyl
Korosten
Kovel
Brest
Pinsk
Pripet Marshes
CRIMEA (under Russian control)
Simferopol
Sevastopol
Yalta
Kerch
Feodosiya
Yevpatoriya
Sea of Azov
RUSSIA
ROSTOV
Novocherkassk
Taganrog
Shakhty
Krasnodar
Novorossiysk
Maykop
Tuapse
Sochi
BLACK SEA
BULGARIA
SOFIA
Plovdiv
Pleven
Ruse
Varna
Burgas
Stara Zagora
Haskovo
Veliko Tarnovo
Sliven
Dobrich
Vidin
Stara Planina
Rhodopi Planina
GREECE
ATHINA (Athens)
Thessaloniki
Larisa
Volos
Lamia
Patra
Pireas
Ioannina
Kalamata
Kerkyra (Corfu)
Peloponnesos
Kriti (Crete)
Iraklio
Chania
Rhodes (Greece)
AEGEAN SEA
Kyklades
Dodekanisa
TURKEY
İSTANBUL
ANKARA
İZMIR (Smyrna)
BURSA
KONYA
ADANA
GAZIANTEP
Kayseri
Samsun
Sivas
Eskişehir
Antalya
Mersin
Denizli
Kütahya
Zonguldak
Edirne
Tekirdağ
Çanakkale
Balıkesir
Manisa
Aydın
Isparta
Kahramanmaraş
Kuzey Andolu Dağlari
Toros Dağlari
Anadolu
Tuz Gölü
CYPRUS
Nicosia
Limassol
Larnaca
Paphos
SYRIA
HALAB (Aleppo)
LEBANON
BAYRŪT (Beirut)
DIMASHQ
ISRAEL
TEL AVIV-YAFO
Jerusalem
ʻAMMĀN
MEDITERRANEAN SEA
IONIAN SEA
ADRIATIC SEA
Bari
Brindisi
Lecce
Táranto
Salerno
Fóggia
Cosenza
Crotone
Messina
Réggio di Calábria
Catánia
Siracusa
LIBYA
BANGHĀZĪ
Mişrātah
Khalīj Surt (Gulf of Sidra)
Barqah (Cyrenaica)
Tubruq
Darnah
Al Bayḑā
Ajdābiyā
EGYPT
EL QÂHIRA (Cairo)
EL ISKANDARÎYA (Alexandria)
EL GÎZA
Bûr Saʻîd (Port Said)
El Suweis (Suez)
Marsá Matrûh
Munkhafed el Qattâra
COPYRIGHT PHILIP'S

1:2 000 000

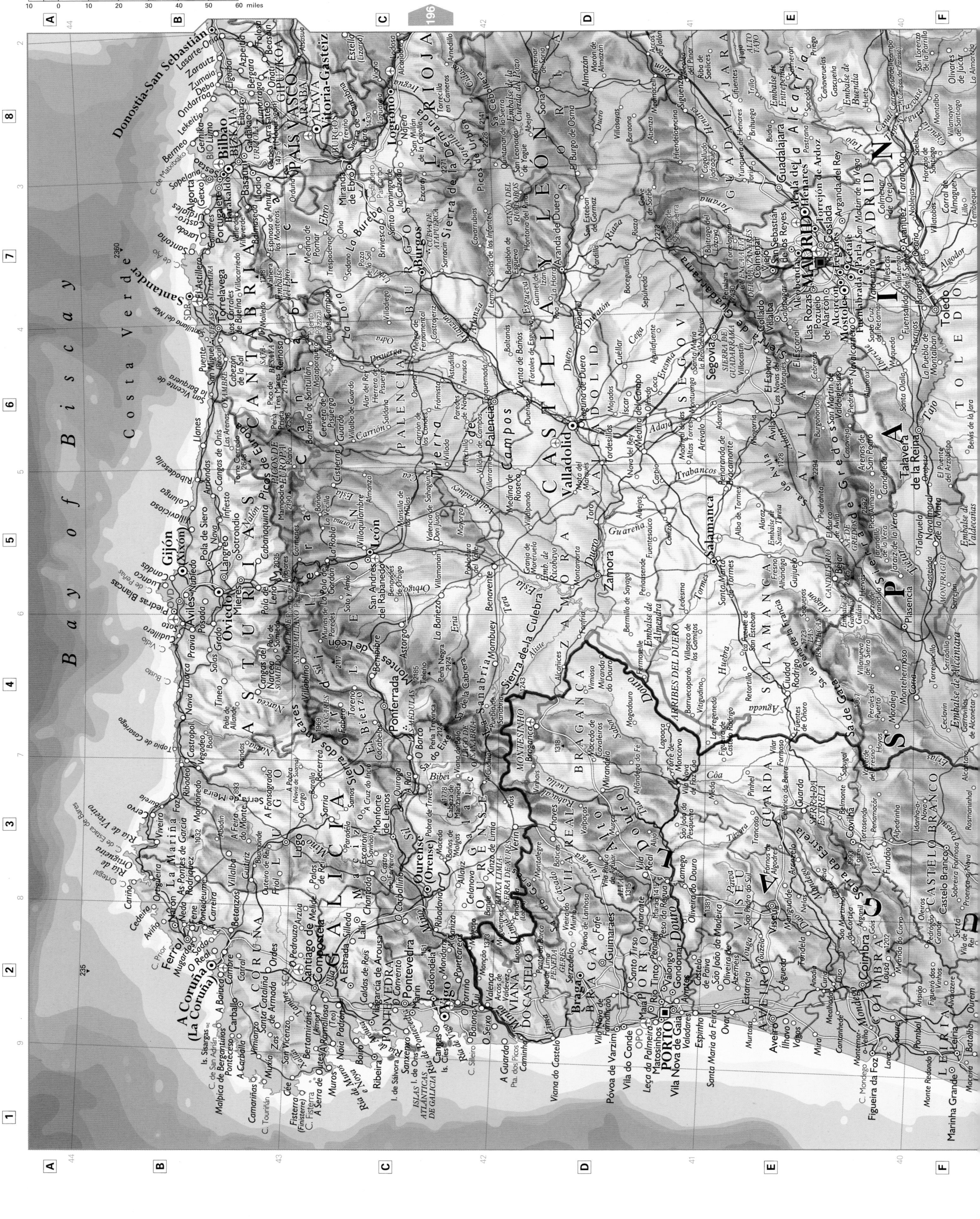

Bay of Biscay
Costa Verde
Donostia-San Sebastián
Bilbao
Vitoria-Gasteiz
PAÍS VASCO
Logroño
LA RIOJA
Santander
CANTABRIA
Gijón (Xixón)
Oviedo
ASTURIAS
León
Burgos
Palencia
Valladolid
CASTILLA Y LEÓN
Soria
Segovia
Ávila
Salamanca
Zamora
Guadalajara
MADRID
Toledo
Talavera de la Reina
Plasencia
Ponferrada
Lugo
Ourense (Orense)
GALICIA
A Coruña (La Coruña)
Ferrol
Santiago de Compostela
Pontevedra
Vigo
Braga
PORTO
Bragança
Guarda
Viseu
Aveiro
Coimbra

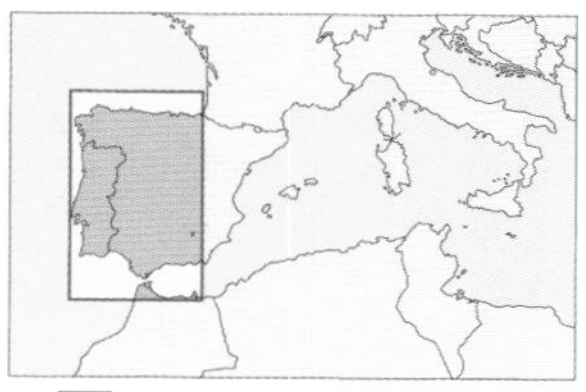

ATLANTIC OCEAN
MEDITERRANEAN SEA
Alboran Sea
Golfo de Cádiz
Costa de la Luz
Costa del Sol
EXTREMADURA
ANDALUCÍA
CASTILLA-LA MANCHA
PORTUGAL
MOROCCO
LISBOA
Sevilla
Córdoba
Granada
Málaga
Cádiz
Huelva
Badajoz
Cáceres
Jaén
Almería
Faro
Gibraltar (U.K.)
Strait of Gibraltar
Tanger (Tangier)
Ceuta (Sp.)
Melilla (Sp.)
High-speed rail routes
West from Greenwich
Projection : Lambert's Conformal Conic
COPYRIGHT PHILIP'S
197
260

10 0 10 20 30 40 50 60 70 80 90 km

10 0 10 20 30 40 50 60 miles

1:2 000 000

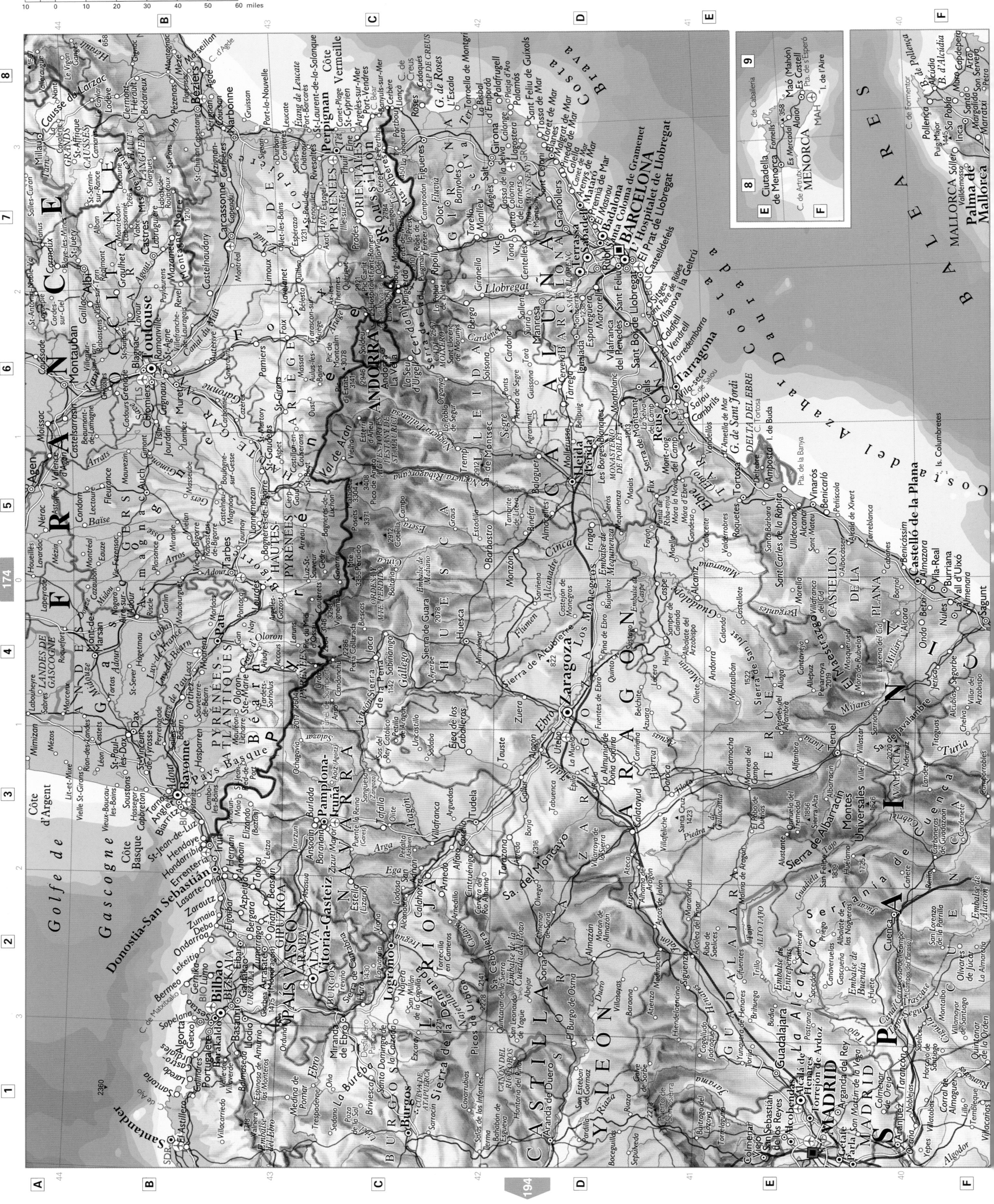

174

194

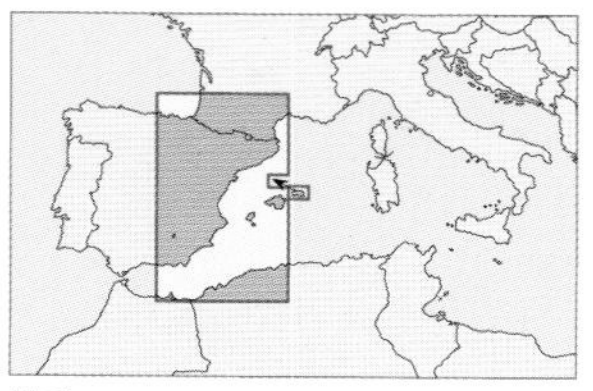

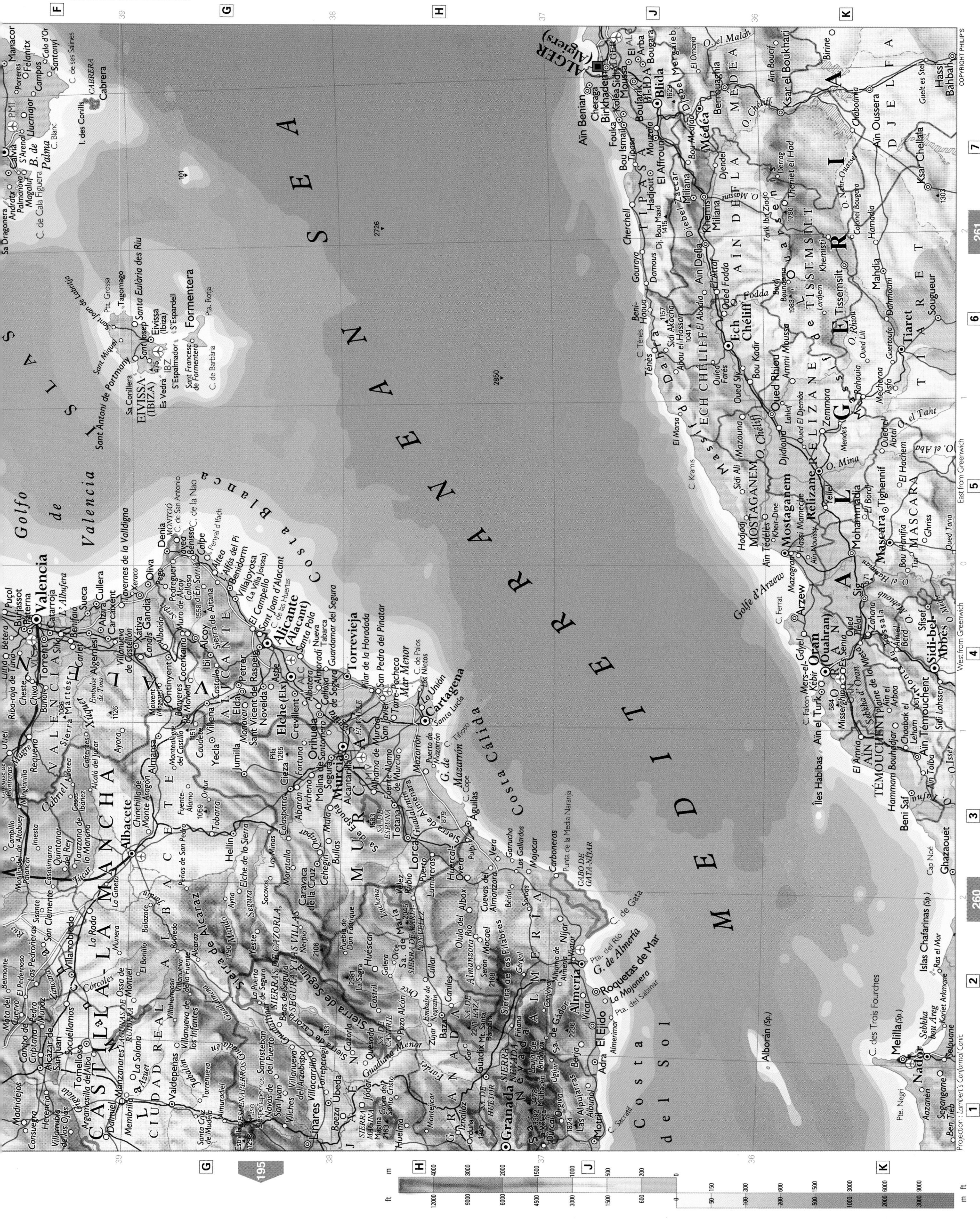
MEDITERRANEAN SEA
ISLAS
Golfo de Valencia
Costa Blanca
Costa Cálida
Costa del Sol
CASTILLA-LA MANCHA
MURCIA
ALMERÍA
GRANADA
ALBACETE
ALICANTE
VALENCIA
CIUDAD REAL
Valencia
Alicante (Alacant)
Murcia
Cartagena
Almería
Granada
Albacete
Eivissa (Ibiza)
Formentera
Cabrera
Palma
ALGER (Algiers)
Oran (Ouahran)
Mostaganem
Relizane
Ech Chélif
Blida
Médéa
Tiaret
Mascara
Sidi-bel-Abbès
Melilla (Sp.)
Nador
Alborán (Sp.)
High-speed rail routes
Projection : Lambert's Conformal Conic
COPYRIGHT PHILIP'S
195
260
261

10 0 10 20 30 40 50 60 70 80 90 km

10 0 10 20 30 40 50 60 miles

1:2 000 000

Projection : Lambert's Conformal Conic

East from Greenwich

m	4000	3000	2000	1500	1000	500	200	0
ft	12 000	9000	6000	4500	3000	1500	600	

ft	0	150	300	600	1500	3000	6000
m	0	50	100	200	500	1000	2000

Underlined towns give their name to the administrative area in which they stand.

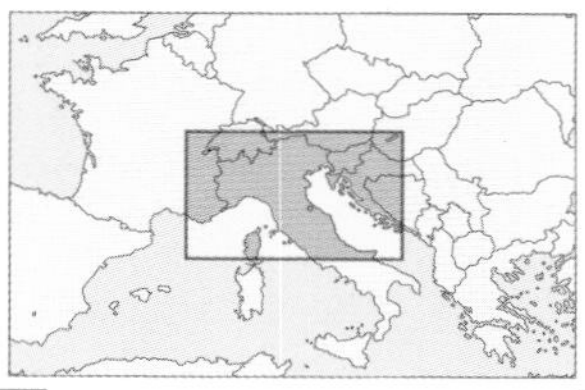

Administrative divisions in Croatia:

1 Brodsko-Posavska
2 Koprivničko-Križevačka
3 Krapinsko-Zagorska
4 Međimurska
6 Požeško-Slavonska
7 Varaždinska
8 Virovitičko-Podravska
10 Zagrebačka

High-speed rail routes

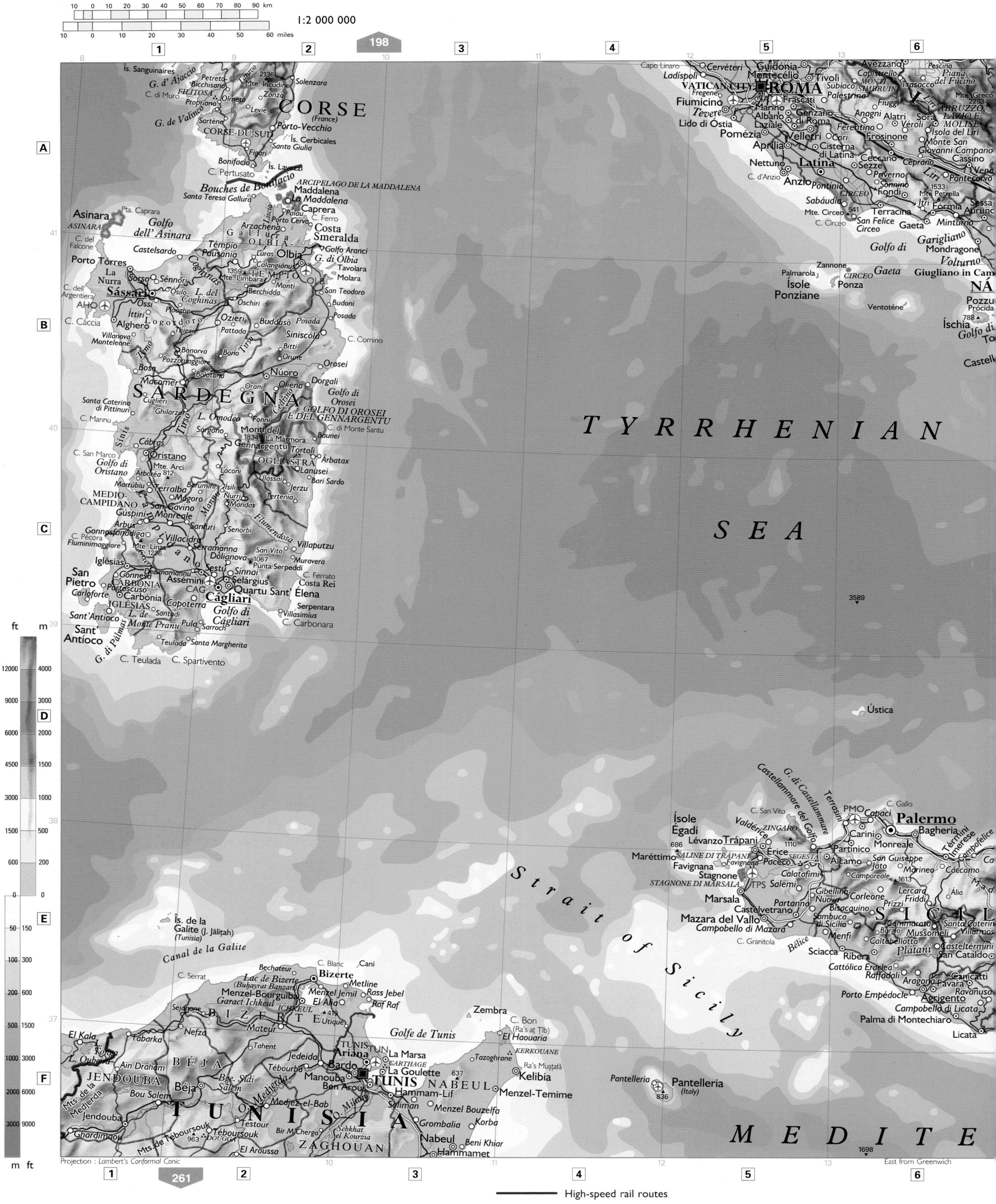

1:2 000 000
km
miles
198
261
CORSE
(France)
Solenzara
Porto-Vecchio
Bonifacio
Bouches de Bonifacio
ARCIPELAGO DE LA MADDALENA
Maddalena
La Maddalena
Caprera
Costa Smeralda
Asinara
Golfo dell' Asinara
Castelsardo
Porto Torres
Sássari
Alghero
Ólbia
G. di Ólbia
Tavolara
Siniscóla
Nùoro
Orosei
Golfo di Orosei
GOLFO DI OROSEI E DEL GENNARGENTU
Dorgali
SARDEGNA
Oristano
Golfo di Oristano
Monti del Gennargentu
Tortolì
Arbatax
OGLIASTRA
Lanusei
MEDIO-CAMPIDANO
Iglésias
CARBONIA IGLESIAS
Carbónia
San Pietro
Sant'Antíoco
Cágliari
Golfo di Cágliari
Quartu Sant' Élena
Villasimius
C. Carbonara
C. Teulada
C. Spartivento
Capo Linaro
Ladíspoli
Cerveteri
VATICAN CITY
ROMA
Fiumicino
Tívoli
Frascati
Lido di Óstia
Pomézia
Velletri
Aprília
Latina
Nettuno
Anzio
Frosinone
Cassino
Terracina
Fondi
Gaeta
Golfo di Gaeta
Formia
Mondragone
Giugliano in Campania
Ísole Ponziane
Ponza
Palmarola
Zannone
Ventotene
Íschia
Prócida
TYRRHENIAN SEA
3589
Ústica
G. di Castellammare
Castellammare del Golfo
Terrasini
Palermo
Bagheria
Carini
Monreale
Partinico
Ísole Égadi
Lévanzo
Trápani
Maréttimo
Favignana
Érice
Pàceco
Marsala
Salemi
Alcamo
Castelvetrano
Mazara del Vallo
Campobello di Mazara
Corleone
SICILIA
Sciacca
Agrigento
Porto Empédocle
Palma di Montechiaro
Licata
Strait of Sicily
Ís. de la Galite (Tunisia)
Canal de la Galite
C. Blanc
Bizerte
Lac de Bizerte
Menzel-Bourguiba
BIZERTE
Zembra
C. Bon
Golfe de Tunis
La Marsa
CARTHAGE
La Goulette
Ariana
Bardo
TUNIS
Ben Arous
Hammam-Lif
NABEUL
Kélibia
Menzel-Temime
Korba
Nabeul
Hammamet
Pantelleria (Italy)
836
Tabarka
Aïn Draham
BÉJA
Béja
JENDOUBA
Jendouba
Medjez-el-Bab
Téboursouk
ZAGHOUAN
TUNISIA
MEDITERRANEAN
1698
Projection : Lambert's Conformal Conic
East from Greenwich
High-speed rail routes

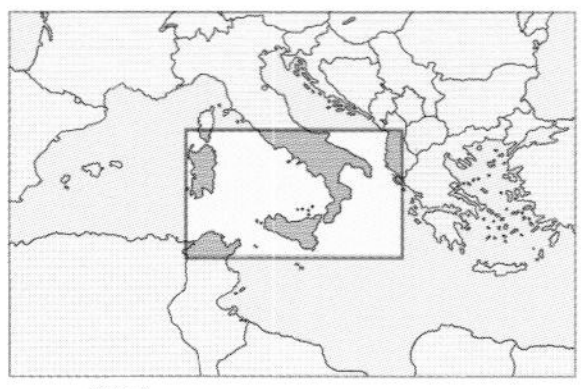

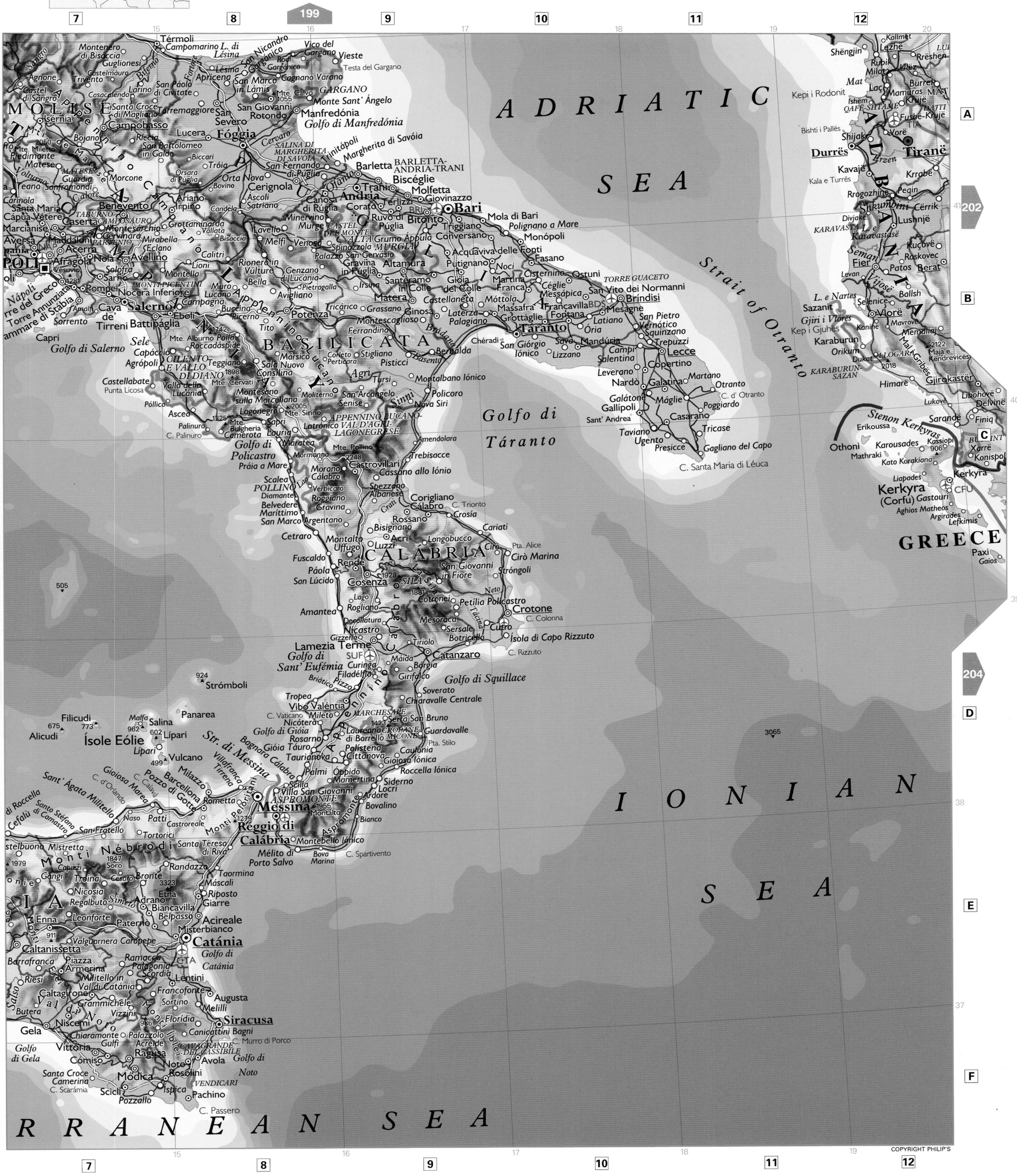

Underlined towns give their name to the administrative area in which they stand.

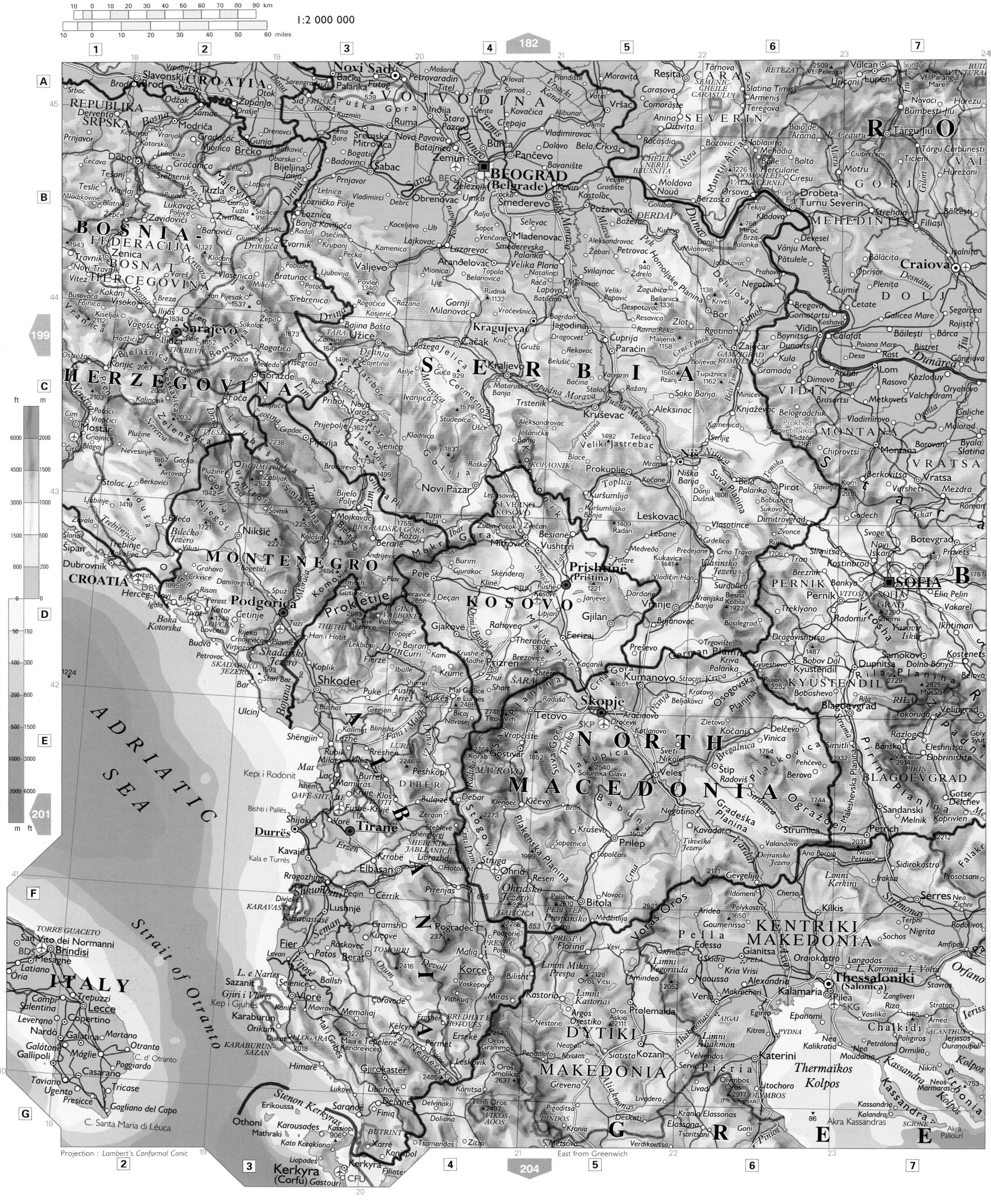
1:2 000 000
10 0 10 20 30 40 50 60 70 80 90 km
10 0 10 20 30 40 50 60 miles
182
199
201
204
SERBIA
KOSOVO
NORTH MACEDONIA
MONTENEGRO
ALBANIA
BOSNIA-HERZEGOVINA
FEDERACIJA BOSNA I HERCEGOVINA
REPUBLIKA SRPSKA
CROATIA
VOJVODINA
ITALY
ADRIATIC SEA
Strait of Otranto
KENTRIKI MAKEDONIA
DYTIKI MAKEDONIA
BEOGRAD (Belgrade)
Novi Sad
Sarajevo
Podgorica
Prishtinë (Priština)
Skopje
Tiranë
SOFIA
Thessaloniki (Salonica)
Craiova
Niš
Kragujevac
Durrës
Shkodër
Bitola
Brindisi
Lecce
Kerkyra (Corfu)
Thermaïkos Kolpos
Projection: Lambert's Conformal Conic
East from Greenwich

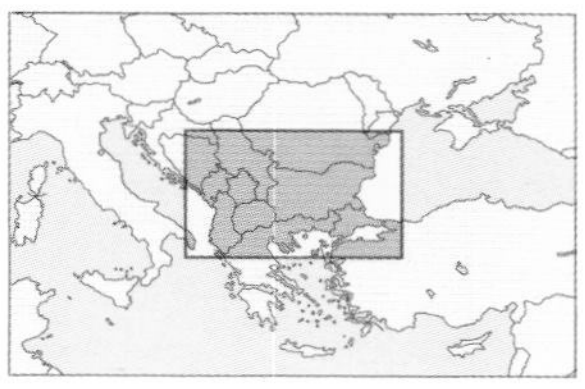

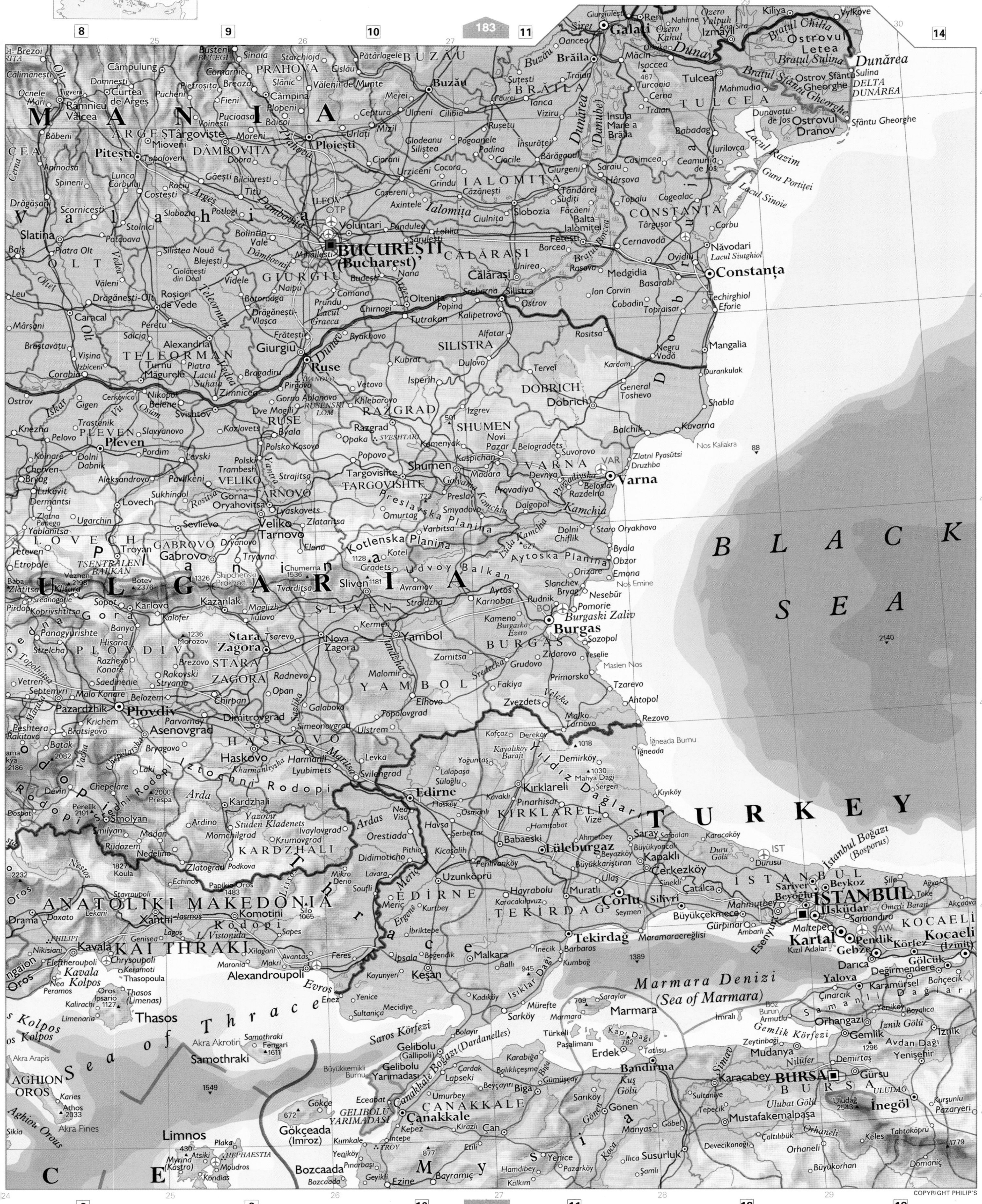
BLACK SEA
TURKEY
BULGARIA
ROMANIA
Walachia
Dobruja
Thrace
Sea of Thrace
Marmara Denizi
(Sea of Marmara)
BUCUREȘTI
(Bucharest)
ISTANBUL
Constanța
Varna
Burgas
Ruse
Pleven
Plovdiv
Stara Zagora
Veliko Tarnovo
Shumen
Dobrich
Sliven
Yambol
Haskovo
Kardzhali
Edirne
Kırklareli
Lüleburgaz
Tekirdağ
Çorlu
Çanakkale
Gelibolu
Bursa
Bandırma
Kocaeli
(İzmit)
Galați
Brăila
Tulcea
Buzău
Ploiești
Pitești
Giurgiu
Călărași
Silistra
Komotini
Xanthi
Alexandroupoli
Kavala
Thasos
Samothraki
Limnos
Gökçeada
(Imroz)
Bozcaada
İstanbul Boğazı
(Bosporus)
Çanakkale Boğazı (Dardanelles)
Dunărea
Dunav
DELTA DUNĂREA
Lacul Razim
Stara Planina
Rodopi
ANATOLIKI MAKEDONIA
KAI THRAKI
Nos Kaliakra
Nos Emine
Burgaski Zaliv
Saros Körfezi
Gemlik Körfezi
Uludağ
2543
COPYRIGHT PHILIP'S

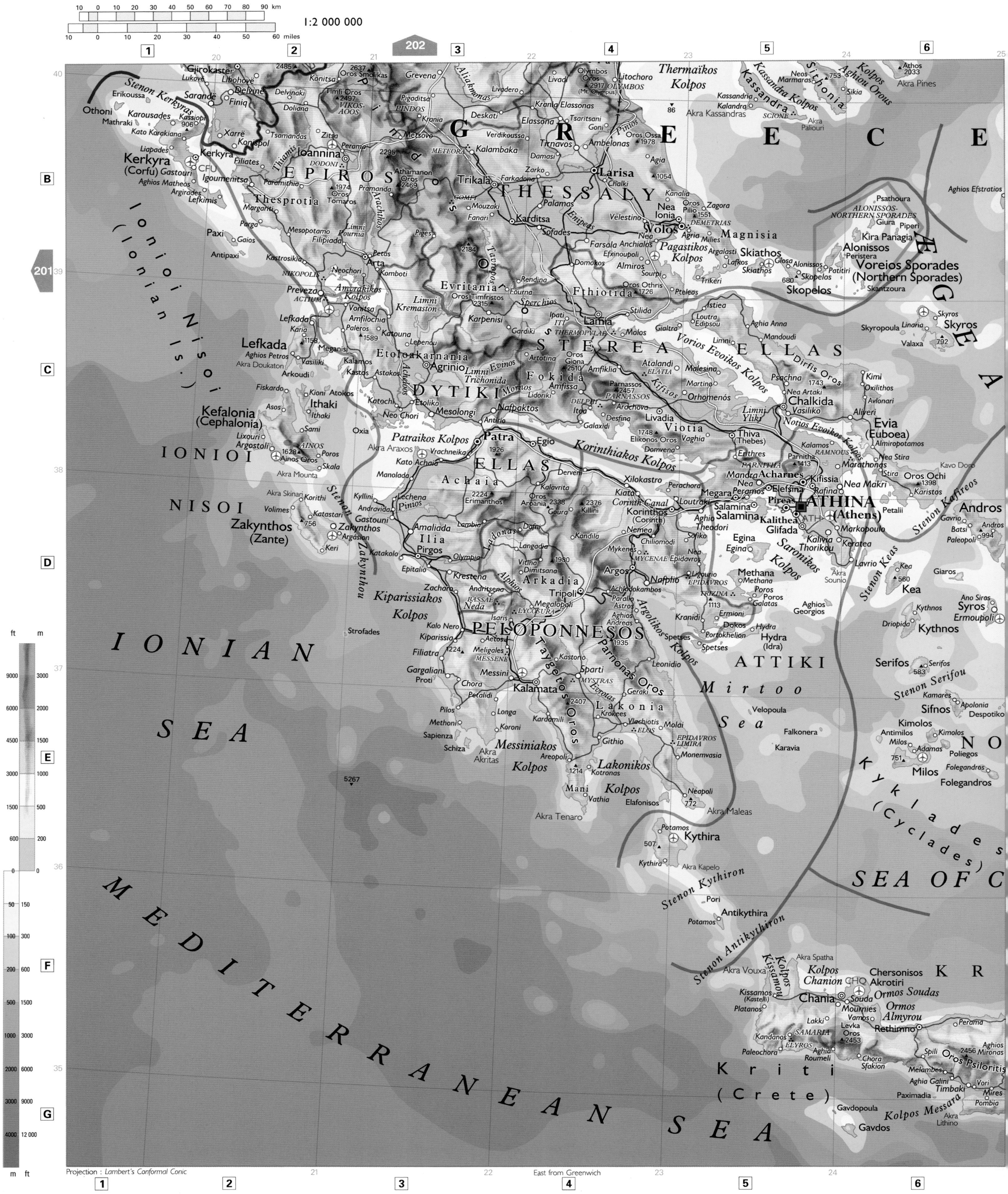
1:2 000 000
km
miles
202
201
1
2
3
4
5
6
B
C
D
E
F
G
Projection : Lambert's Conformal Conic
East from Greenwich
ft
m
G R E E C E
IONIAN SEA
MEDITERRANEAN SEA
SEA OF C
AEGEA
IONIOI NISOI
Ionioi Nisoi (Ionian Is.)
Stenon Kerkyras
Gjirokastër
Lukovë
Libohovë
Delvinë
Sarandë
Finiq
Xarrë
Konispol
Erikoussa
Othoni
Mathraki
Karousades
Kassiopi
Kato Korakiana
Liapades
Kerkyra (Corfu)
Gastouri
CFU
Kerkyra
Igoumenitsa
Filiates
Aghios Matheos
Argirades
Lefkimis
Paxi
Gaios
Antipaxi
Parga
Margariti
Thesprotia
Paramithia
Tsamandas
Zitsa
Ioannina
DODONI
Perama
Metsovo
EPIROS
Kastrosikia
NIKOPOLIS
Neochori
Arta
Petas
Komboti
Filipiada
Mesopotamo
Preveza
ACTIUM
Amvrakikos Kolpos
Vonitsa
Amfilochia
Paleros
Lefkada
Karia
Lefkada
Aghios Petros
Akra Doukaton
Vasiliki
Meganisi
Arkoudi
Fiskardo
Kioni
Atokos
Ithaki
Asos
Kefalonia (Cephalonia)
Sami
Lixouri
Argostoli
AINOS
Ainos Oros
Poros
Skala
Akra Mounta
Akra Skinari
Korithi
Volimes
Katastari
Zakynthos (Zante)
Zakynthos
Argasion
Keri
Stenon Zakynthou
Strofades
Kiparissiakos Kolpos
Oxia
Patraikos Kolpos
Patra
Akra Araxos
Vrachneika
Kato Achaia
Manolada
Kyllini
Lechena
Andravida
Gastouni
Pinios
Amaliada
Ilia
Pirgos
Katakolo
Olympia
Epitalio
Krestena
Zacharo
Andritsena
BASSAE
Neda
Kalo Nero
Kiparissia
Filiatra
Gargaliani
Proti
Chora
Petalidi
Pilos
Methoni
Sapienza
Schiza
Akra Akritas
Messiniakos Kolpos
Koroni
Longa
Kalamata
Messini
Meligales
MESSENE
Aetos
PELOPONNESOS
Megalopoli
LYCOSURA
Tripoli
Arkadia
Vitina
Dimitsana
Alfios
Langadia
Kalavrita
Achaia
Erimanthos
Ladonas
Aroania
Killini
Goura
Kandila
Nemea
Mykenes
MYCENAE
Argos
Nafplio
Ligourio
EPIDAVROS
Achladokambos
Astros
Paralio Astros
Aghios Andreas
Argolikos Kolpos
Leonidio
Parnonas Oros
Taygetos Oros
Kastoro
Sparti
MYSTRAS
Evrotas
Geraki
Lakonia
Krokees
Vlachiotis
Molai
ELOS
EPIDAVROS LIMIRA
Monemvasia
Githio
Kardamili
Areopoli
Mani
Vathia
Akra Tenaro
Lakonikos Kolpos
Elafonisos
Neapoli
Akra Maleas
Kythira
Potamos
Kythira
Akra Kapelo
Stenon Kythiron
Pori
Antikythira
Potamos
Stenon Antikythiron
Mirtoo Sea
ATTIKI
Velopoula
Falkonera
Karavia
Spetses
Kranidi
Ermioni
Dokos
Hydra
Hydra (Idra)
Portokhelion
Poros
Galatas
Methana
Troizina
TRIZINA
Aghios Georgios
Saronikos Kolpos
Aegina
Egina
Salamina
Salamis
Megara
Elefsina
Pireas
ATHINA (Athens)
Kalithea
Glifada
Thorikou
Kalivia
Keratea
Lavrio
Akra Sounio
Markopoulo
Rafina
Nea Makri
Marathonas
Kifissia
Acharnes
Parnitha
PARNITHA
Mandra
Perachora
Loutraki
Corinth Canal
Korinthos (Corinth)
Kiato
Xilokastro
Derveni
Egio
Korinthiakos Kolpos
Antirio
Nafpaktos
Mesolongi
Etoliko
Neo Chori
Katochi
Agrinio
Astakos
Kastos
Kalamos
Acheloos
Etoloakarnania
DYTIKI ELLAS
Limni Trichonida
Evinos
Mornos
Lidoriki
Fokida
Amfissa
Itea
Galaxidi
DELPHI
Desfina
Arachova
Parnassos
PARNASSOS
Distomo
Livadia
Viotia
Thiva (Thebes)
Erithres
Elikonos Oros
Vaghia
Domvena
Orhomenos
Martino
Kifisos
Atalandi
ELATIA
Malesino
Amfiklia
Giona
Artotina
STEREA ELLAS
Lamia
THERMOPYLAE
Ipati
Molos
Stilida
Karpenisi
Evritania
Timfristos
Sperchios
Gardiki
Limni Kremaston
Fourna
Rendina
Fthiotida
Othris
Pteleos
Domokos
Almiros
Sourpi
Farsala
Anchialos
Pagastikos Kolpos
Volos
Nea Ionia
Agria
Milies
Argalasti
Magnisia
Velestino
Pilio
DEMETRIAS
Zagora
Kanalia
Larisa
Chalki
Agia
Ambelonas
Tsaritsani
Elassona
Olympos
OLYMBOS
Litochoro
Pinios
Ossa
Deskati
Kalambaka
METEORA
Trikala
Farkadona
THESSALY
Palamas
Karditsa
Sofades
Mouzaki
Fanari
Pigés
Tavropos
Athamanon
Tomaros
Pramanda
Arachthos
Limni Pournia
Grevena
Pindos
Krania
Aliakmonas
Livadero
Konitsa
Smolikas
Timfi Oros
VIKOS-AOOS
Pigadtsa
Delvinaki
Doliana
Thermaikos Kolpos
Kassandra
Kassandria
Kalandra
SCIONE
Akra Kassandras
Akra Paliouri
Kassandras Kolpos
Sithonia
Neos Marmaras
Sikia
Aghiou Orous Kolpos
Athos
Akra Pines
Psathoura
ALONISSOS-NORTHERN SPORADES
Giura
Piperi
Kira Panagia
Alonissos
Peristera
Patitiri
Voreios Sporades (Northern Sporades)
Skopelos
Skantzoura
Skiathos
Trikeri
Lafkos
Glosa
Istiea
Loutra Edipsou
Aghia Anna
Mandoudi
Limni
Voreios Evoikos Kolpos
Psachna
Nea Artaki
Chalkida
Vasiliko
Dirfis Oros
Kimi
Oxilithos
Avlonari
Aliveri
Evia (Euboea)
Almiropotamos
Notios Evoikos Kolpos
Kalamos
RAMNOUS
Nea Stira
Stira
Kavo Doro
Oros Ochi
Karistos
Stenon Kafireos
Skyros
Skyropoula
Linaria
Valaxa
Aghios Efstratios
Andros
Gavrio
Batsi
Paleopoli
Petalii
Kea
Stenon Keas
Giaros
Syros
Ano Siros
Ermoupoli
Kythnos
Driopida
Serifos
Stenon Serifou
Sifnos
Kamares
Apolonia
Despotiko
Kimolos
Antimilos
Milos
Adamas
Poliegos
Folegandros
Kyklades (Cyclades)
Chersonisos Akrotiri
Kolpos Chanion
Akra Spatha
Kolpos Kissamou
Akra Vouxa
Kissamos (Kastelli)
Platanos
Chania
Souda
Ormos Soudas
Mournies
Vamos
Ormos Almyrou
Rethimno
Lakki
Levka Oros
SAMARIA
Kandanos
ELYROS
Aghia Roumeli
Paleochora
Chora Sfakion
Perama
Spili
Psiloritis
Melambes
Aghia Galini
Timbaki
Vori
Mires
Pombia
Paximadia
Kolpos Messara
Akra Lithino
Gavdopoula
Gavdos
Kriti (Crete)
K R
N O
5267

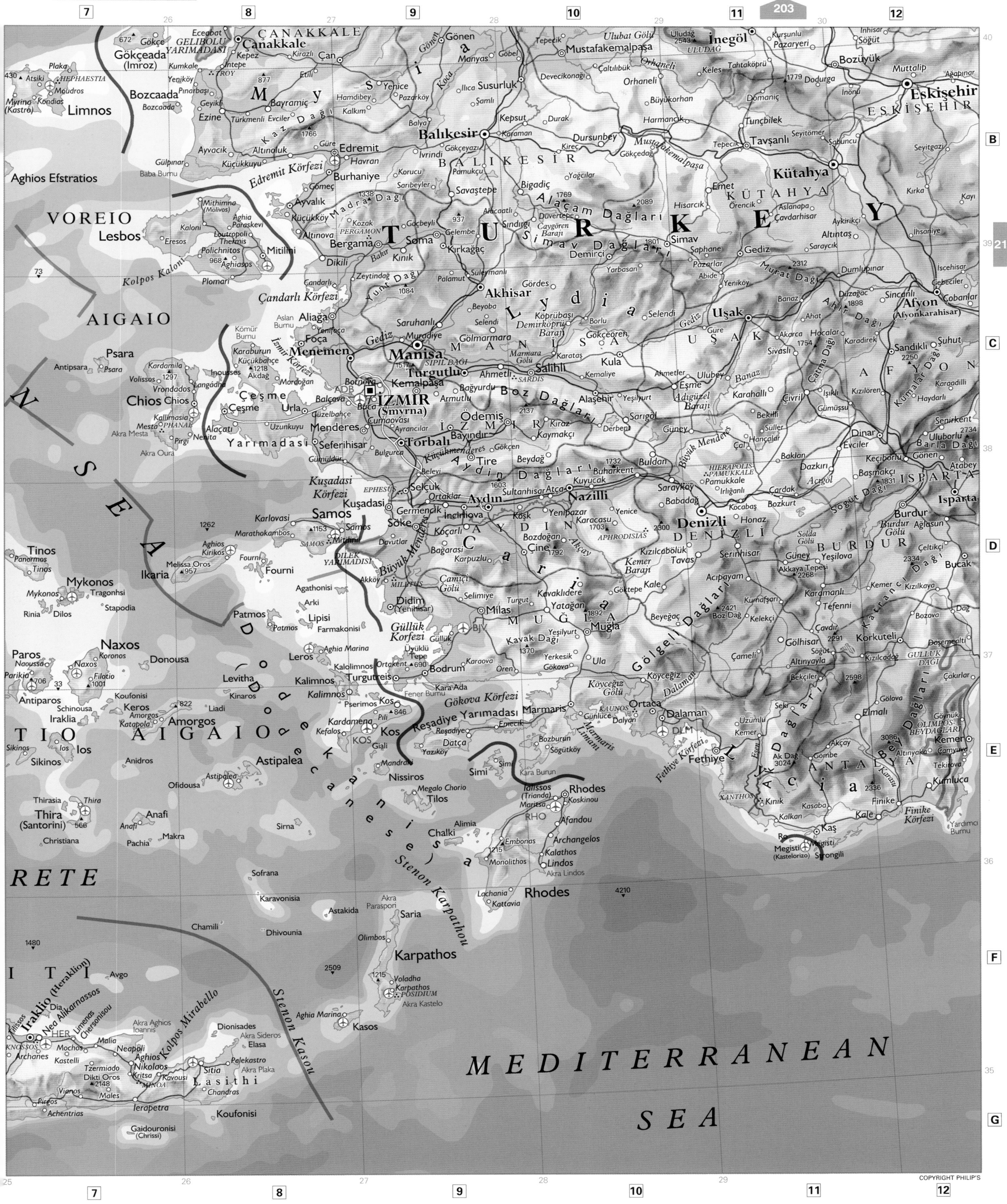
203
212
TURKEY
AIGAIO
AIGAIO NSEA
MEDITERRANEAN SEA
Lesbos
Limnos
Chios
Samos
Ikaria
Naxos
Paros
Mykonos
Tinos
Amorgos
Astipalea
Kos
Rhodes
Karpathos
Kasos
Thira (Santorini)
Dodecanese (Dodekanisa)
Stenon Karpathou
Stenon Kasou
İZMIR (Smyrna)
Manisa
Aydın
Denizli
Muğla
Bodrum
Marmaris
Fethiye
Kaş
Antalya
Isparta
Burdur
Afyon (Afyonkarahisar)
Uşak
Kütahya
Eskişehir
Balıkesir
Çanakkale
Bozcaada
Gökçeada (Imroz)
Edremit Körfezi
Çandarlı Körfezi
Kuşadasi Körfezi
Gökova Körfezi
Fethiye Körfezi
Iraklio (Heraklion)
Kolpos Mirabello
Lasithi
KRETE
VOREIO

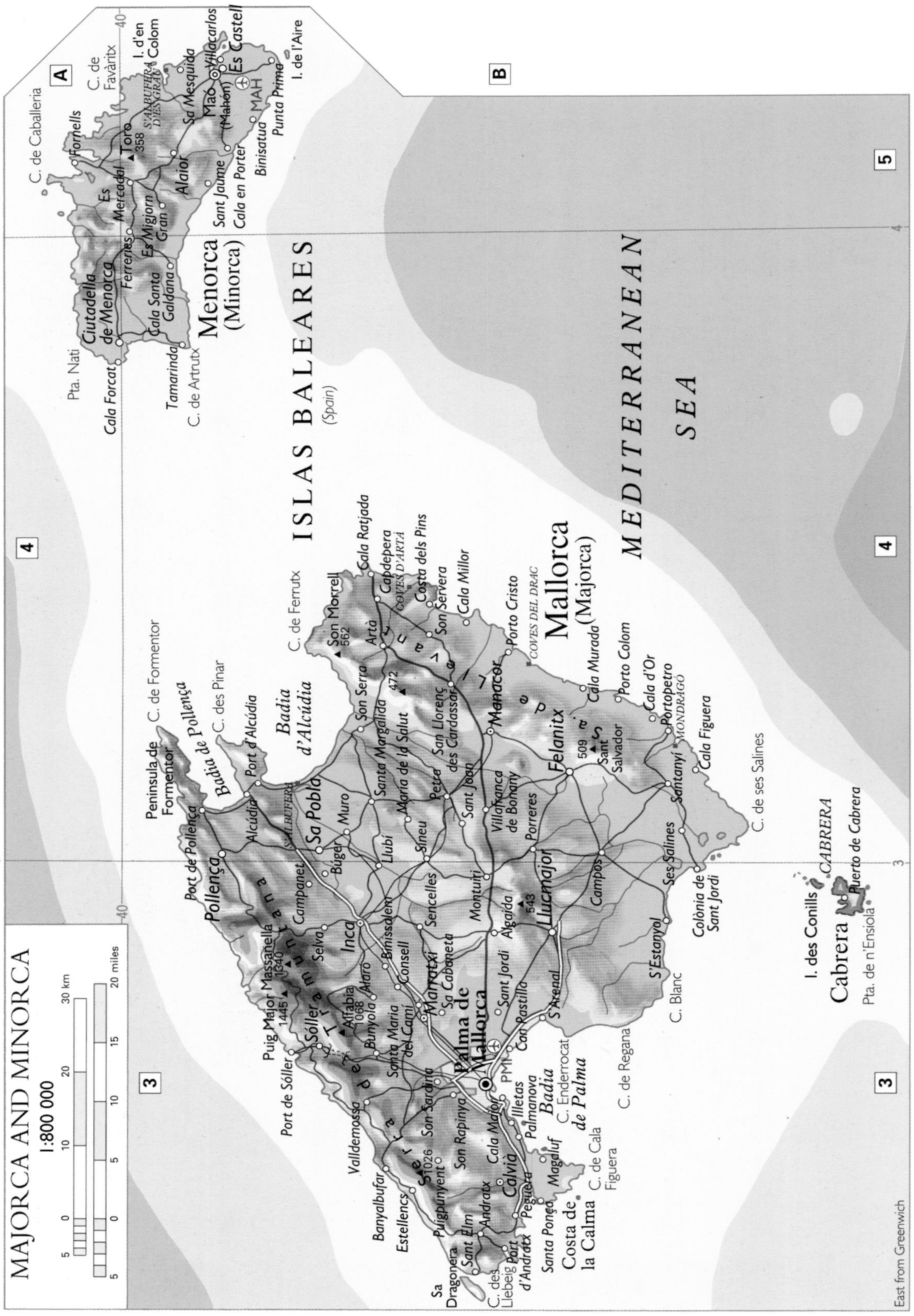
MAJORCA AND MINORCA
1:800 000
ISLAS BALEARES
(Spain)
MEDITERRANEAN SEA
Mallorca
(Majorca)
Menorca
(Minorca)
Palma de Mallorca
Cabrera
East from Greenwich

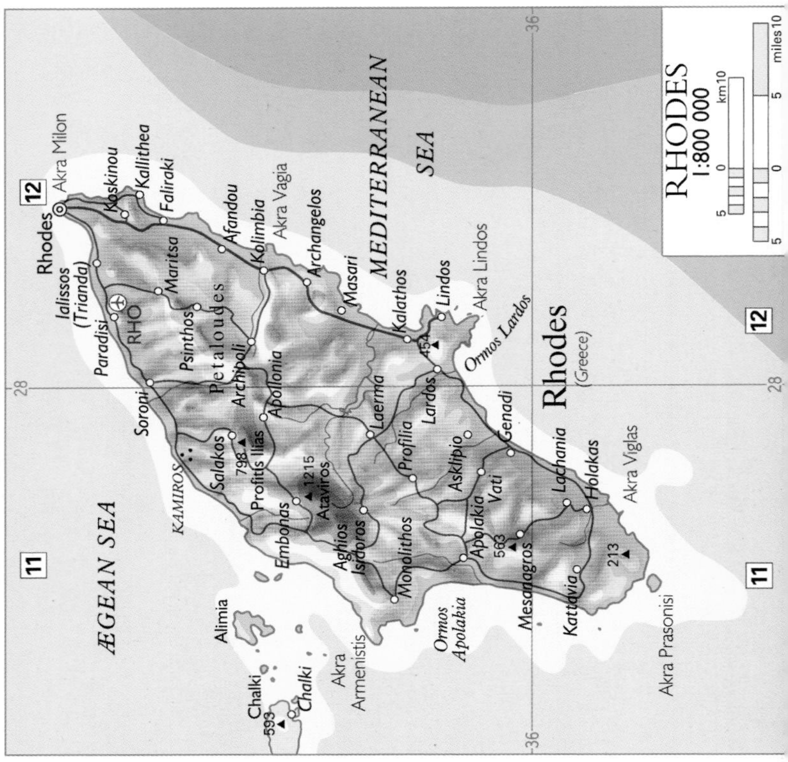
RHODES
1:800 000
Rhodes
(Greece)
ÆGEAN SEA
MEDITERRANEAN SEA

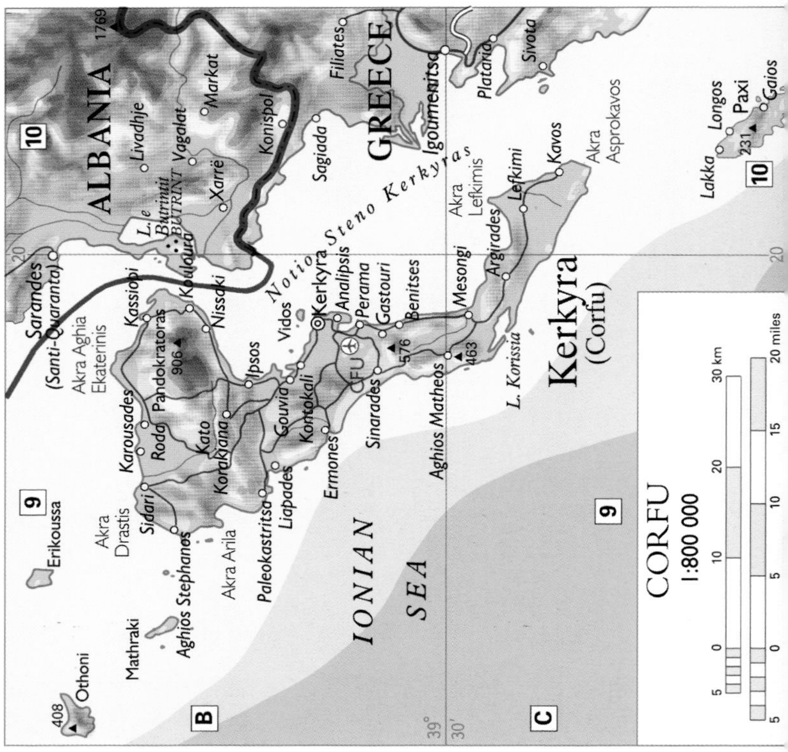
CORFU
1:800 000
Kerkyra
(Corfu)
ALBANIA
GREECE
IONIAN SEA

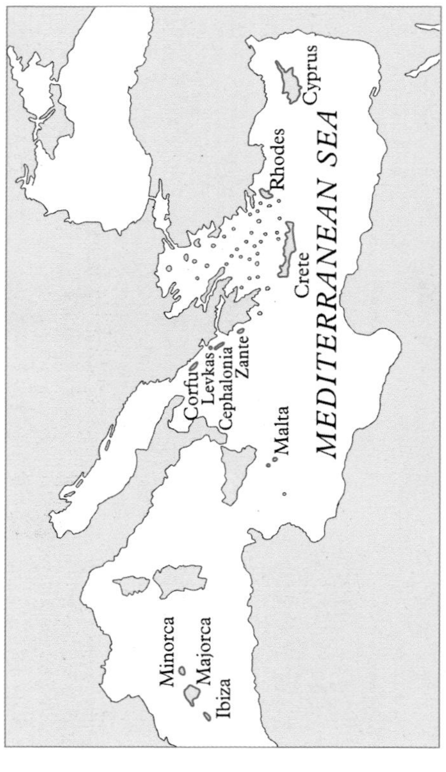
MEDITERRANEAN SEA
Minorca
Majorca
Ibiza
Malta
Corfu
Levkas
Cephalonia
Zante
Crete
Rhodes
Cyprus

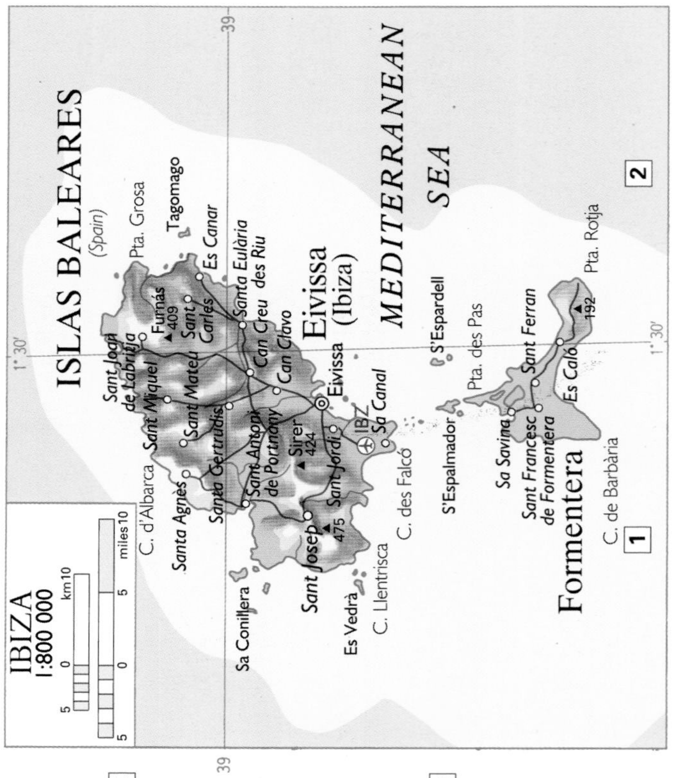
IBIZA
1:800 000
ISLAS BALEARES
(Spain)
MEDITERRANEAN SEA
Eivissa
(Ibiza)
Formentera

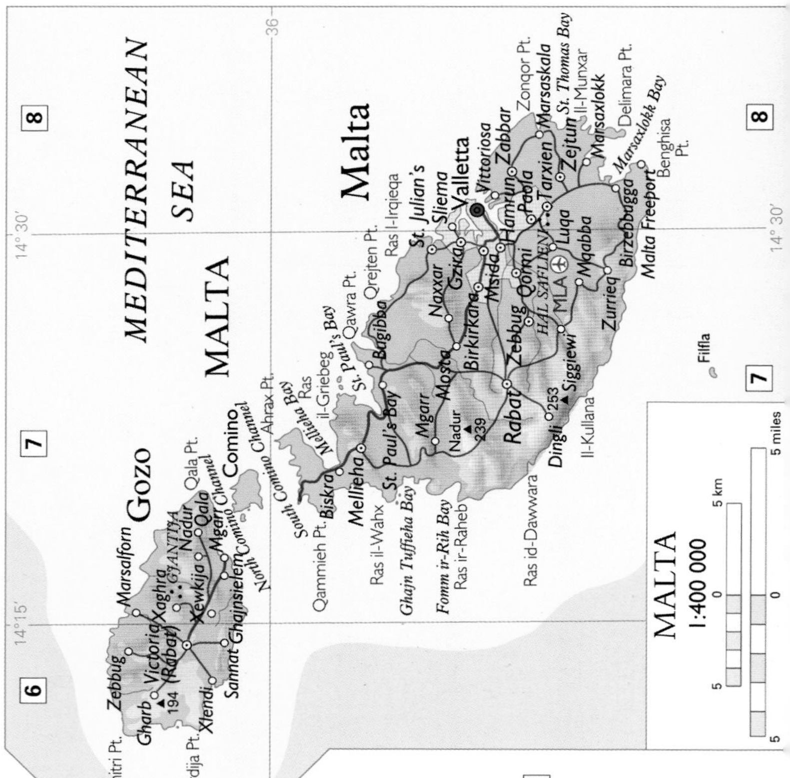
MALTA
1:400 000
MEDITERRANEAN SEA
MALTA
Malta
Gozo
Comino
Valletta

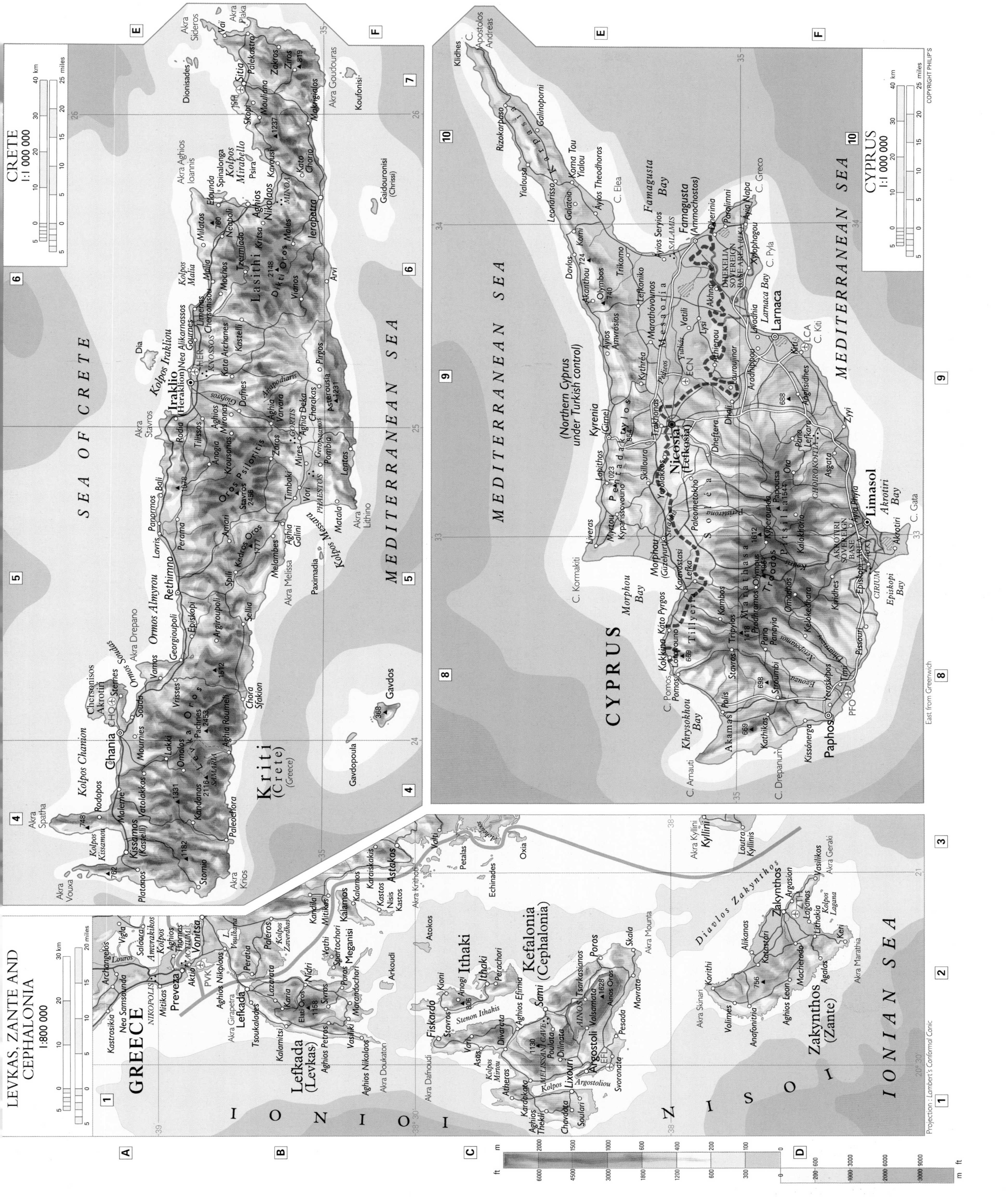
CRETE
1:1 000 000
CYPRUS
1:1 000 000
LEVKAS, ZANTE AND CEPHALONIA
1:800 000
SEA OF CRETE
MEDITERRANEAN SEA
IONIAN SEA
Kriti (Crete) (Greece)
CYPRUS
(Northern Cyprus under Turkish control)
GREECE
Lefkada (Levkas)
Kefalonia (Cephalonia)
Ithaki
Zakynthos (Zante)
Iraklio (Heraklion)
Chania
Rethimno
Nicosia (Lefkosia)
Limasol
Larnaca
Famagusta (Ammochostos)
Paphos
Projection : Lambert's Conformal Conic
East from Greenwich
COPYRIGHT PHILIP'S

ASIA

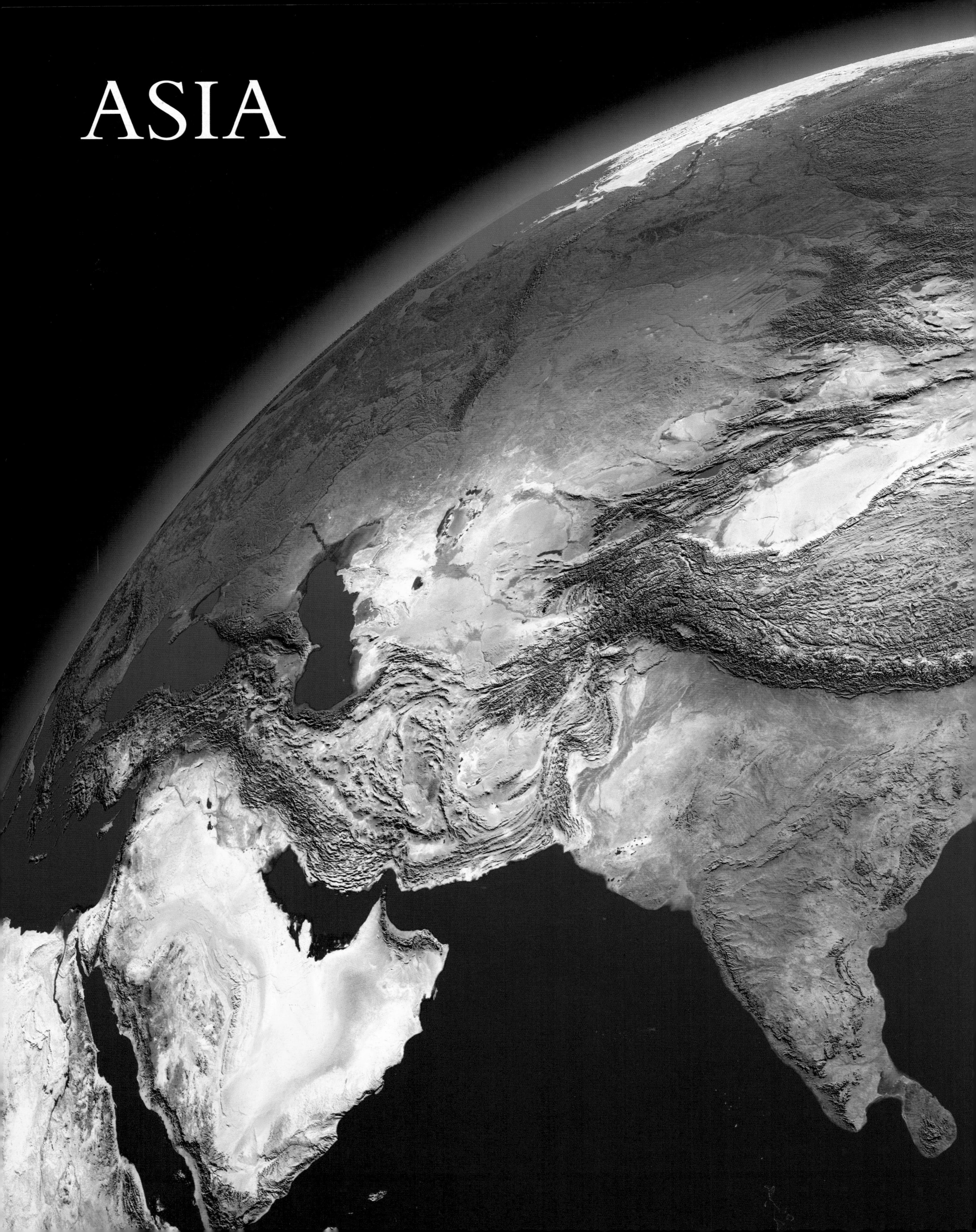

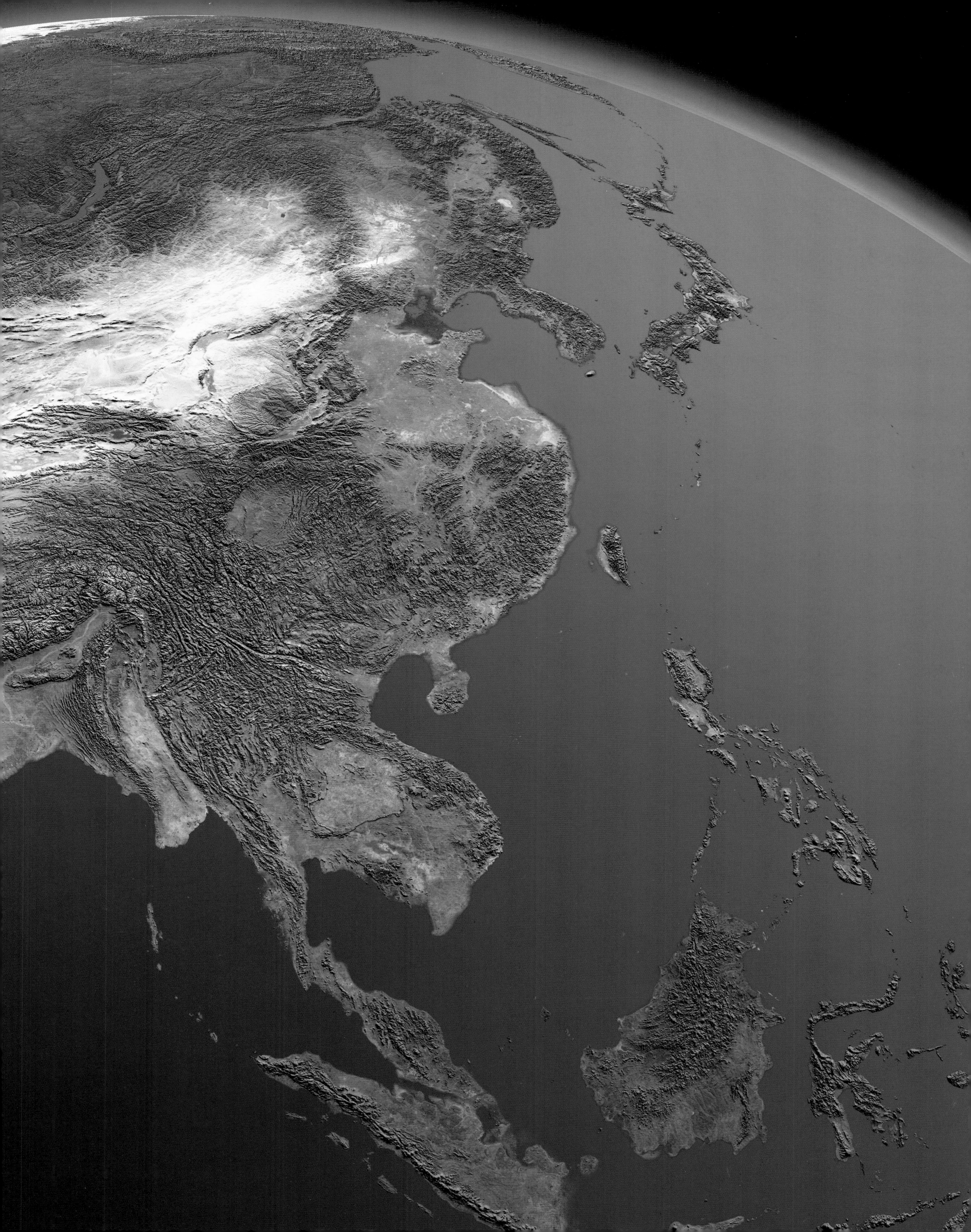

100 0 200 400 600 800 1000 1200 1400 km

100 0 200 400 600 800 1000 miles

1:40 000 000

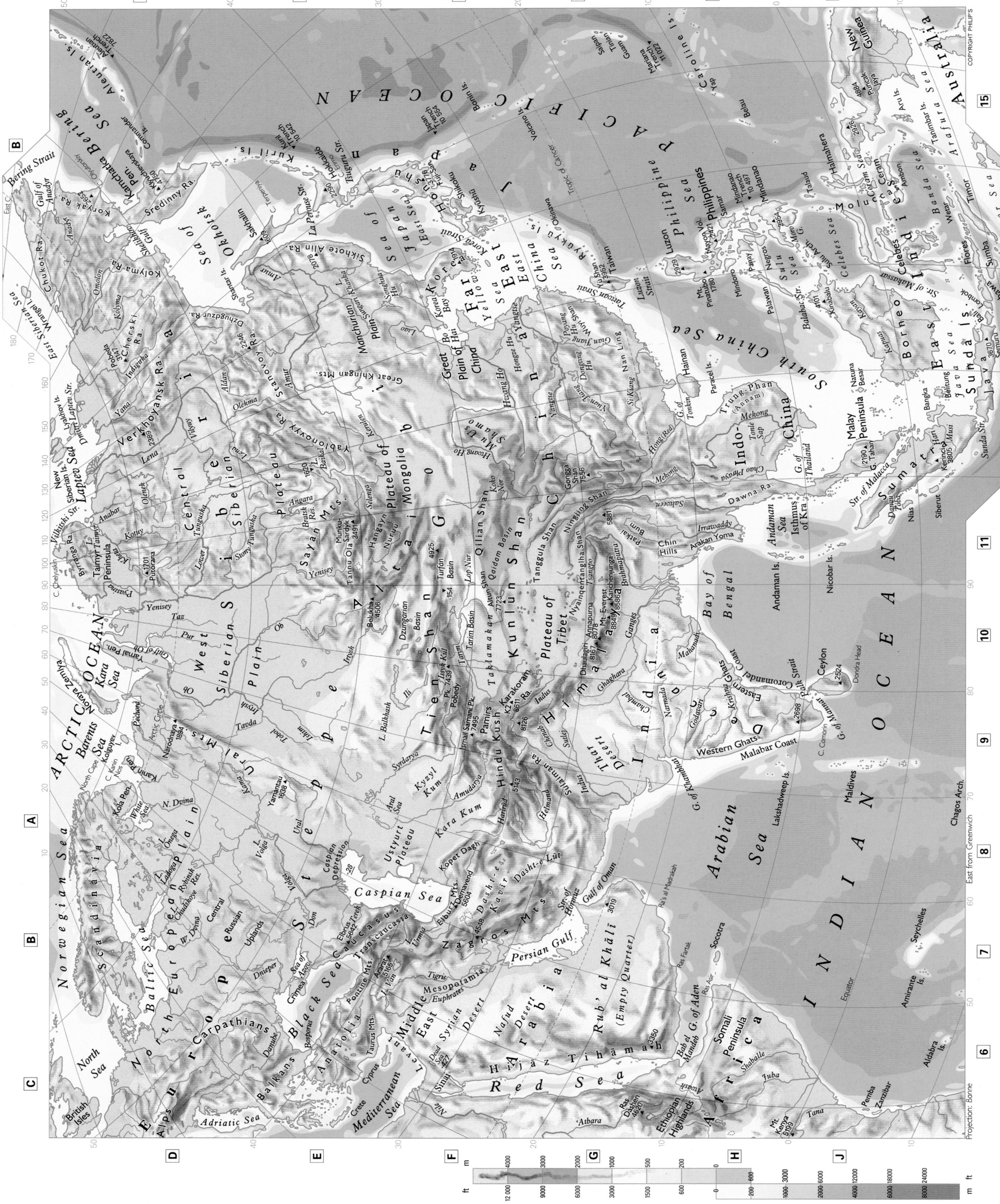

1:40 000 000

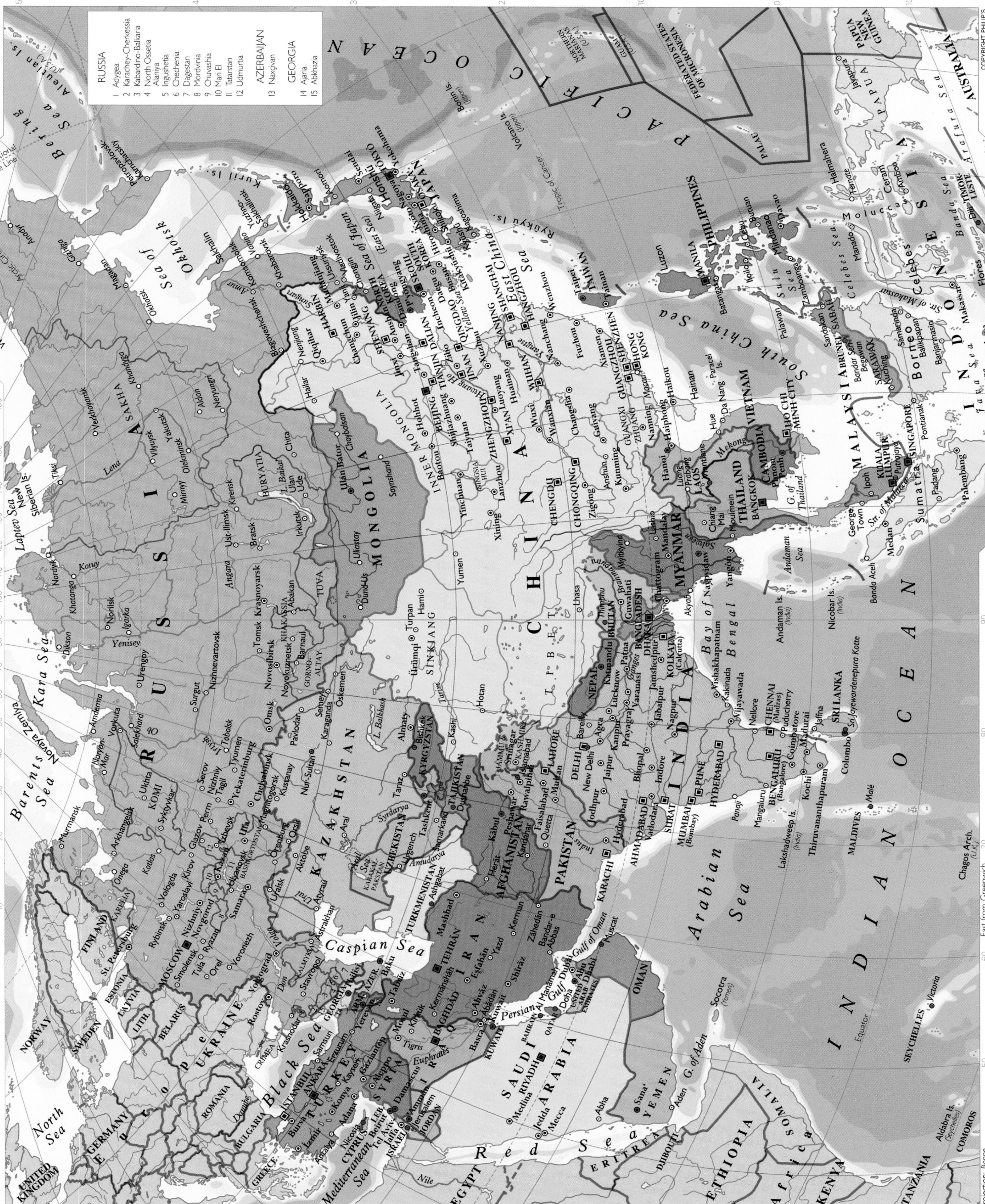
RUSSIA
1 Adygea
2 Karachey-Cherkessia
3 Kabardino-Balkaria
4 North Ossetia Alaniya
5 Ingushetia
6 Chechenia
7 Dagestan
8 Mordvinia
9 Chuvashia
10 Mari El
11 Tatarstan
12 Udmurtia
AZERBAIJAN
13 Naxçivan
GEORGIA
14 Ajaria
15 Abkhazia
RUSSIA
KAZAKHSTAN
MONGOLIA
CHINA
INDIA
PAKISTAN
AFGHANISTAN
IRAN
TURKEY
SAUDI ARABIA
YEMEN
OMAN
MYANMAR
THAILAND
CAMBODIA
VIETNAM
LAOS
PHILIPPINES
MALAYSIA
INDONESIA
JAPAN
NEPAL
BHUTAN
BANGLADESH
SRI LANKA
INDIAN OCEAN
PACIFIC OCEAN
Arabian Sea
Bay of Bengal
South China Sea
Caspian Sea
Black Sea
Red Sea
Capital Cities
Projection: Bonne
COPYRIGHT PHILIP'S

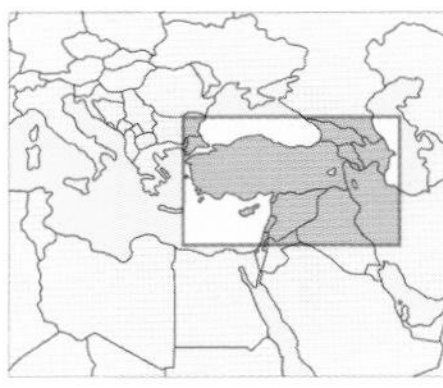

50 0 25 50 75 100 125 150 175 km

50 0 25 50 75 100 125 miles

1: 4 000 000

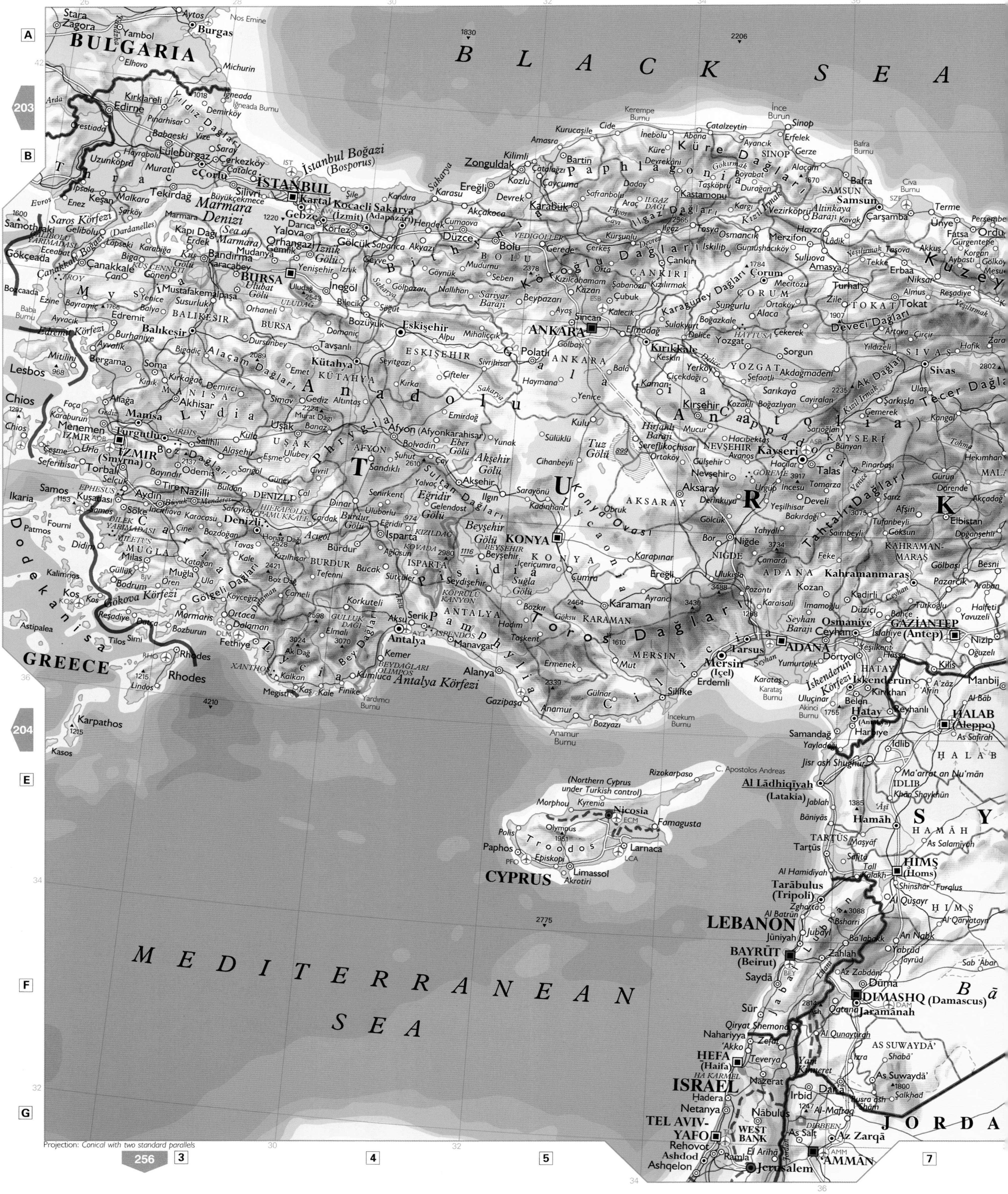

Projection: Conical with two standard parallels

189
203
204
256

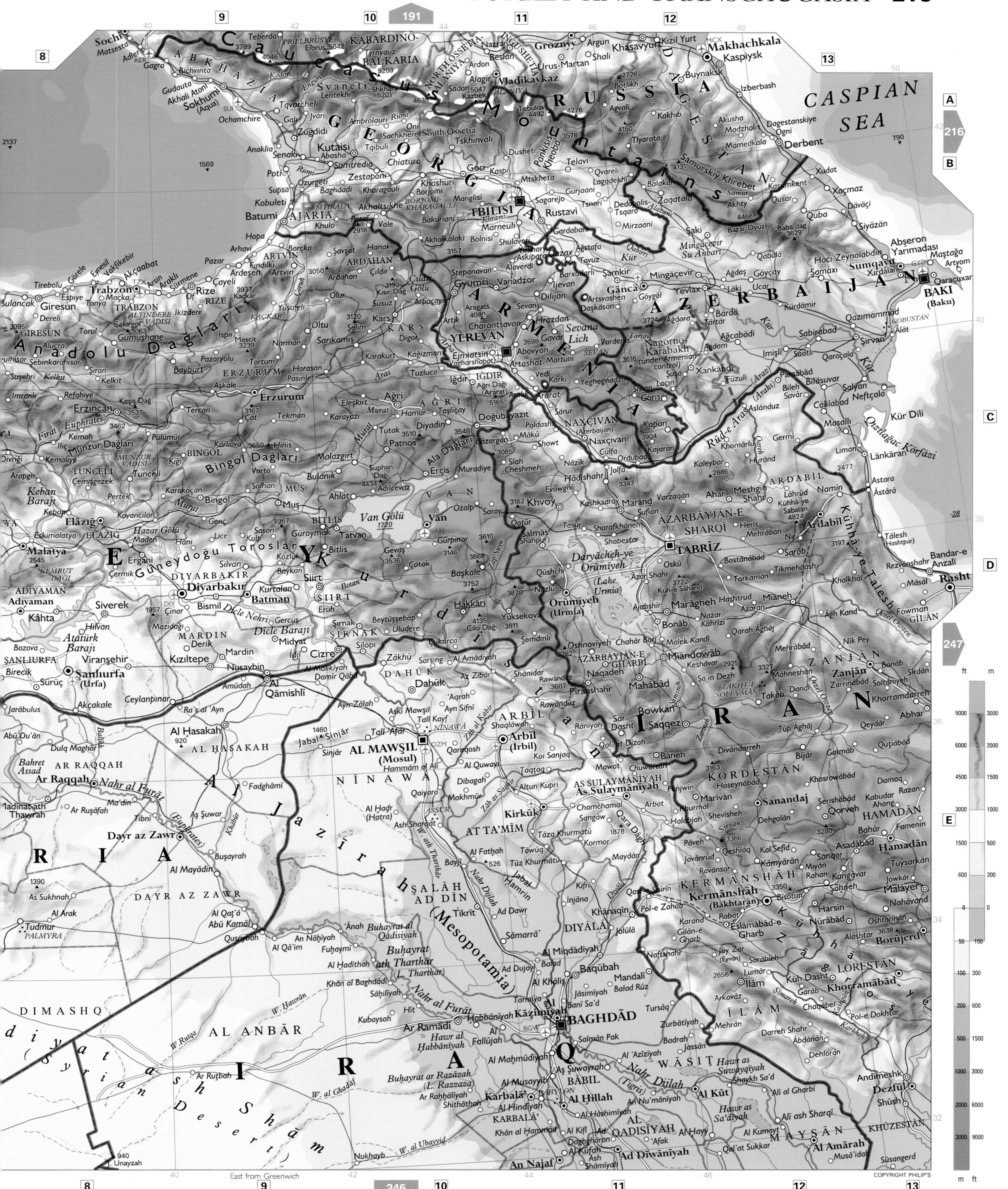

Underlined towns give their name to the administrative area in which they stand

100 0 100 200 300 400 500 600 700 800 km

1:16 000 000

100 0 100 200 300 400 500 miles

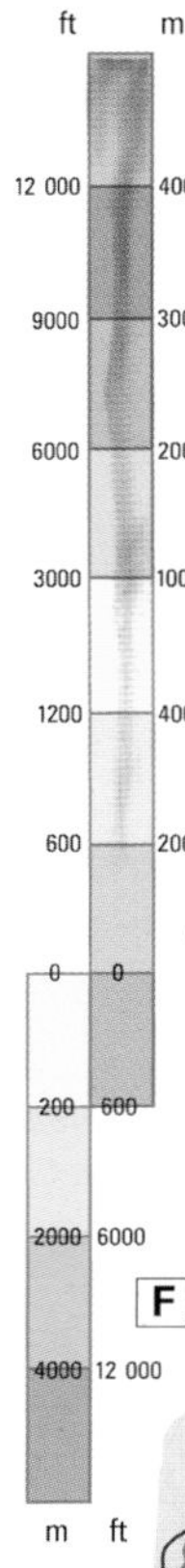

238 239

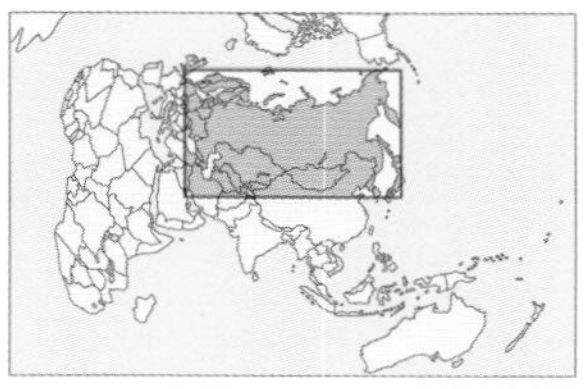

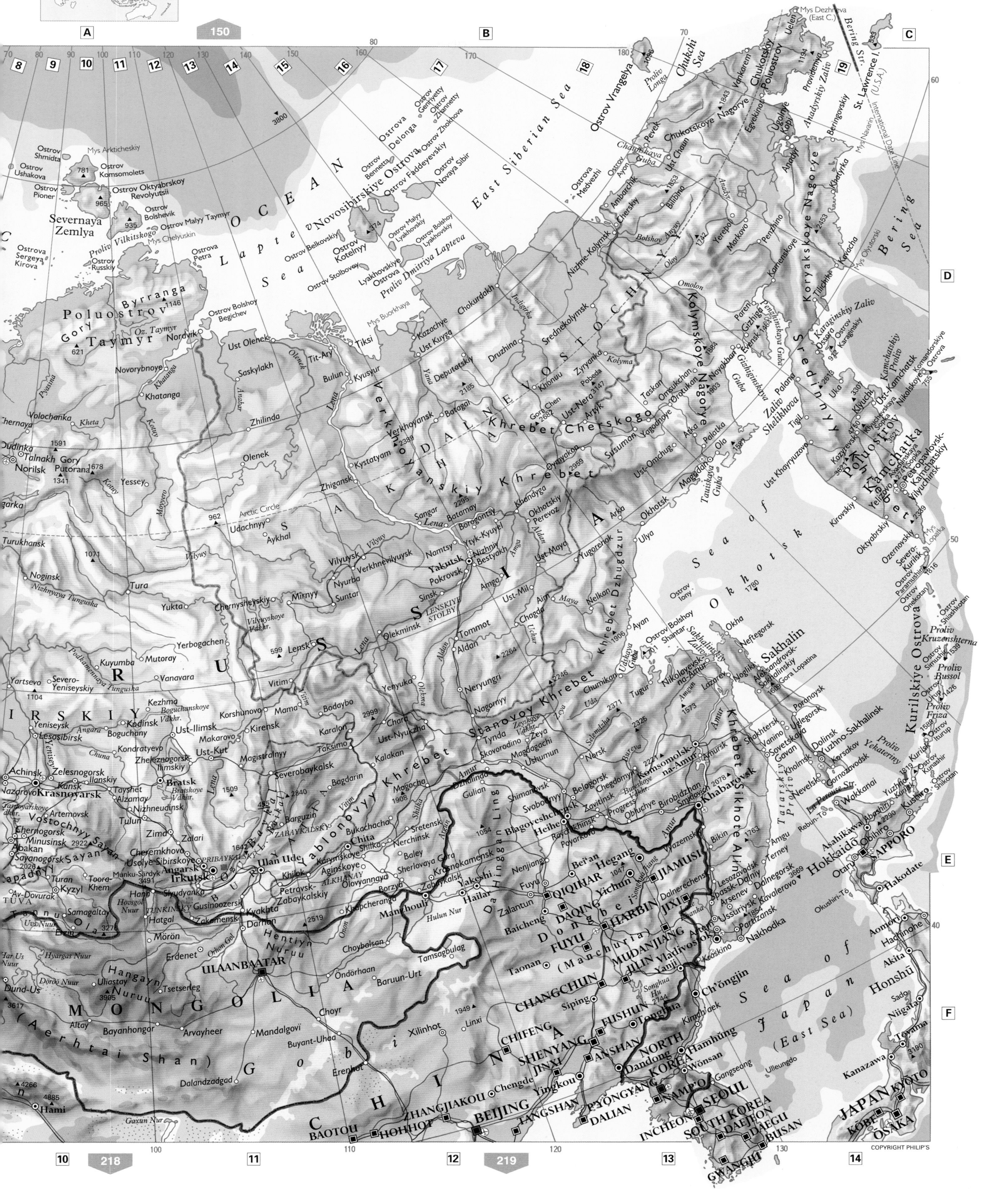
150
218
219
A
B
C
D
E
F
OCEAN
Laptev Sea
East Siberian Sea
Chukchi Sea
Bering Sea
Sea of Okhotsk
Sea of Japan (East Sea)
Severnaya Zemlya
Poluostrov Taymyr
Gory Byrranga
Novosibirskiye Ostrova
Ostrov Vrangelya
Chukotskoye Nagorye
Koryakskoye Nagorye
Kolymskoye Nagorye
Poluostrov Kamchatka
Sredinnyy Khrebet
Khrebet Cherskogo
Verkhoyanskiy Khrebet
DALNEVOSTOCHNY
Stanovoy Khrebet
Yablonovyy Khrebet
Sakhalin
Kurilskiye Ostrova
Hokkaido
Honshū
Arctic Circle
International Date Line
St. Lawrence I. (U.S.A.)
Bering Str.
RUSSIA
Yakutsk
Magadan
Petropavlovsk-Kamchatskiy
Norilsk
Krasnoyarsk
Irkutsk
Chita
Ulan Ude
Bratsk
Khabarovsk
Vladivostok
Komsomolsk-na-Amur
Blagoveshchensk
Yuzhno-Sakhalinsk
MONGOLIA
ULAANBAATAR
Gobi
Dongbei (Manchuria)
CHINA
HARBIN
QIQIHAR
CHANGCHUN
SHENYANG
BEIJING
NORTH KOREA
PYONGYANG
SOUTH KOREA
SEOUL
JAPAN
SAPPORO
KYOTO
OSAKA
Lena
Amur
Kolyma
Vilyuy
Aldan
Ozero Baykal
Da Hinggan Ling

1:8 000 000

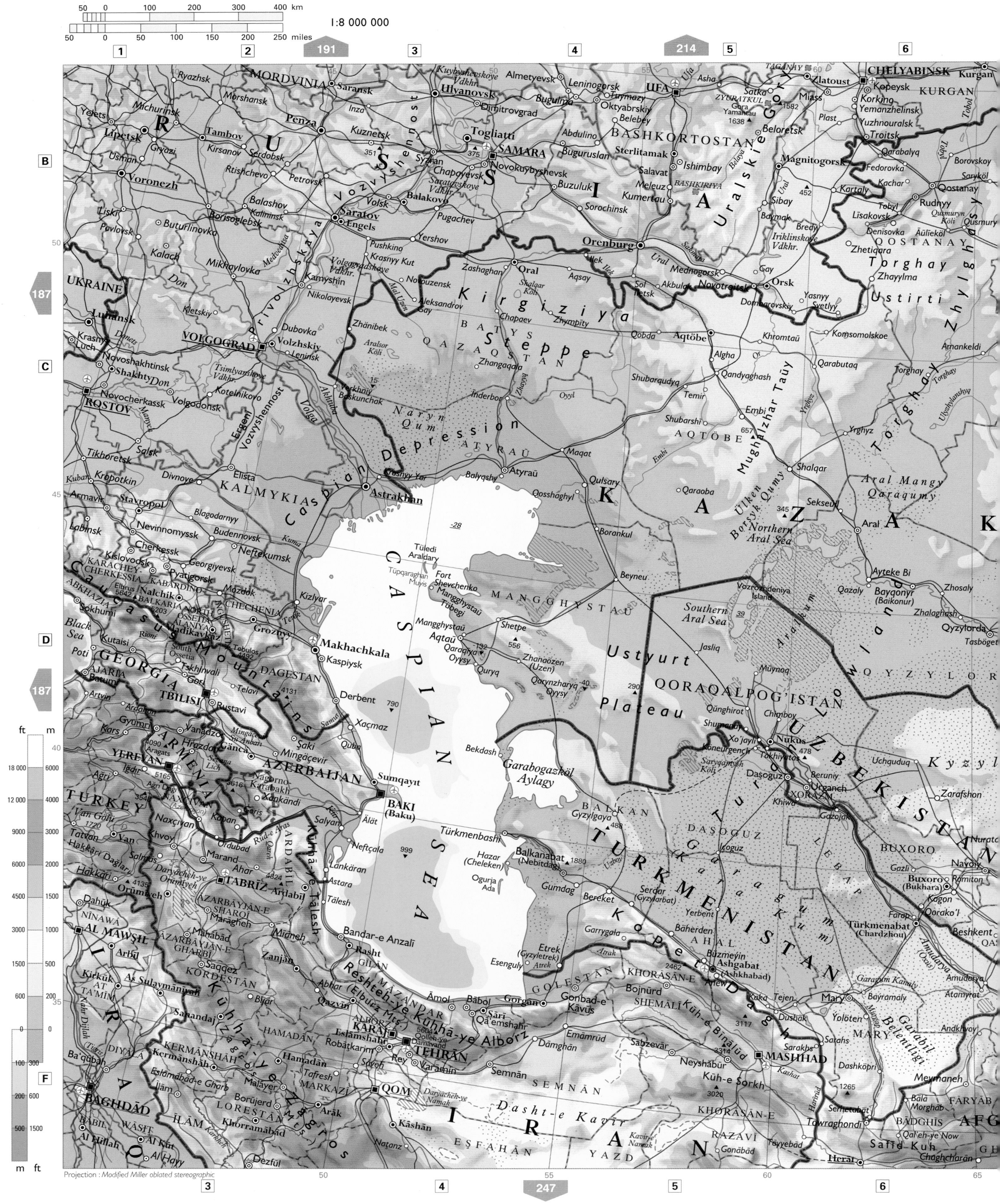

Projection : Modified Miller oblated stereographic

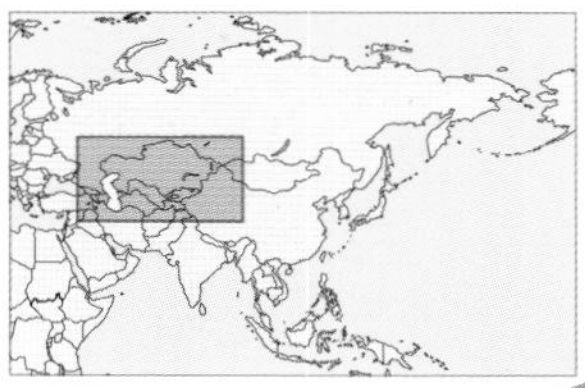

Underlined towns give their name to the administrative area in which they stand.

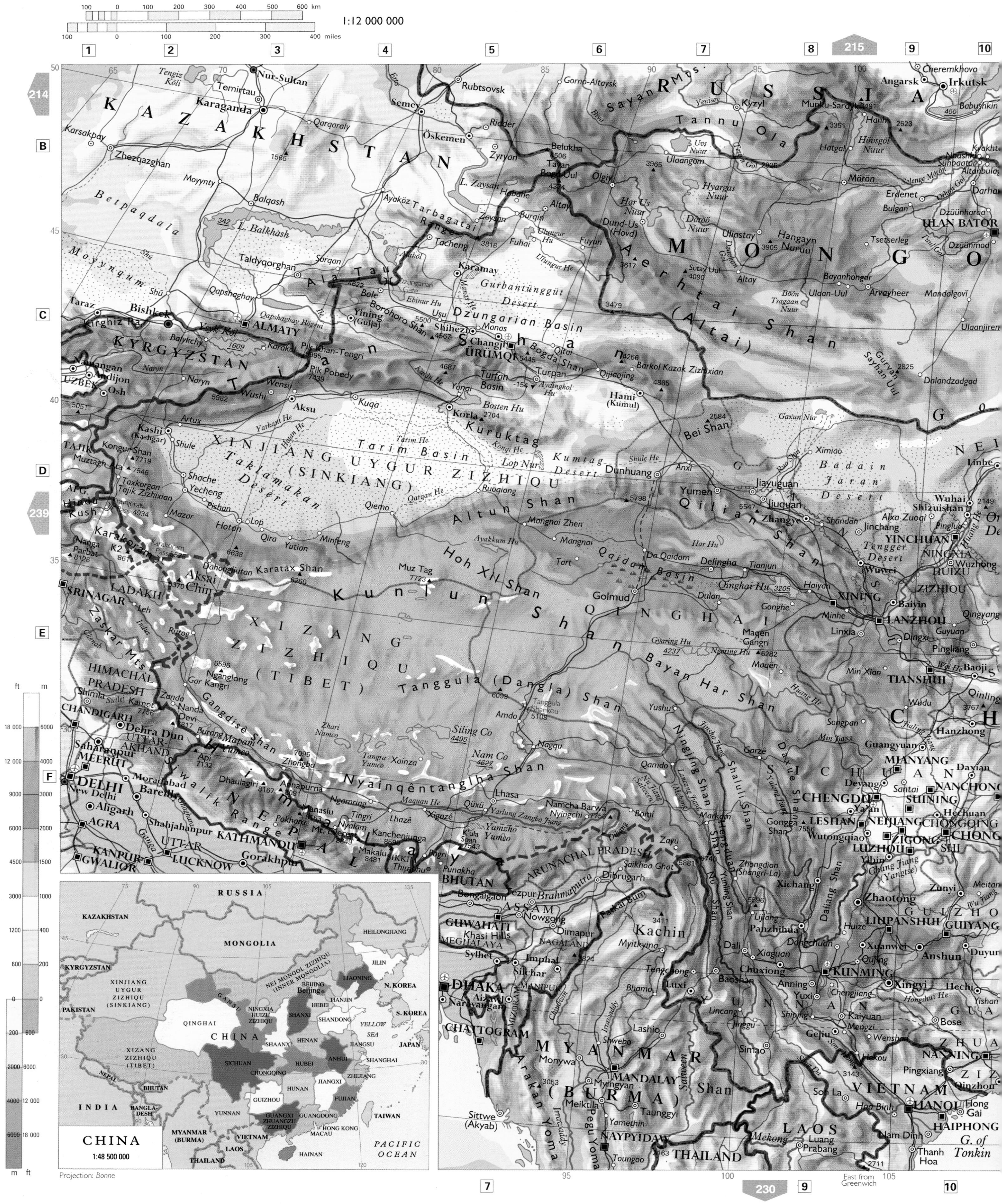
1:12 000 000
100 0 100 200 300 400 500 600 km
100 0 100 200 300 400 miles
215
214
239
230
ft m
18 000 6000
12 000 4000
9000 3000
6000 2000
4500 1500
3000 1000
1200 400
600 200
0 0
200 600
2000 6000
4000 12 000
6000 18 000
m ft
K A Z A K H S T A N
Nur-Sultan
Temirtau
Karaganda
Qarqaraly
Karsakpay
Zhezqazghan
Moyynty
Balqash
Betpaqdala
L. Balkhash
Moyynqum
Taldyqorghan
Sarqan
Qapshaghay
Taraz
Bishkek
ALMATY
Kirghiz Ra.
KYRGYZSTAN
Ysyk-Köl
Balykchy
Karakol
Naryn
Namangan
Andijon
Osh
UZBEK.
TAJIK.
Semey
Öskemen
Rubtsovsk
Ridder
Zyryan
L. Zaysan
Zaysan
Ayaköz
Tarbagatai Range
Tacheng
Ala Tau
Bole
Yining (Gulja)
Borohoro Shan
Karamay
Gurbantünggüt Desert
Dzungarian Basin
Shihezi
Changji
ÜRÜMQI
Manas
Bogda Shan
Turpan
Turfan Basin
Tian Shan
Pik Pobedy
Pik Khan-Tengri
Aksu
Wushi
Kuqa
Korla
Bosten Hu
Kuruktag
Kashi (Kashgar)
Artux
Shule
Kongur Shan
Muztagh Ata
Taxkorgan Tajik Zizhixian
Shache
Yecheng
Pishan
Hotan
Lop
Qira
Yutian
Minfeng
Qiemo
Ruoqiang
Tarim Basin
Taklamakan Desert
XINJIANG UYGUR ZIZHIQU (SINKIANG)
Lop Nur
Kumtag Desert
Dunhuang
Altun Shan
Mangnai Zhen
Mangnai
Qaidam Basin
Karakoram
K2
Nanga Parbat
Hindu Kush
AFG.
Aksai Chin
LADAKH
SRINAGAR
Leh
Rutog
Zaskar Mts.
HIMACHAL PRADESH
Shimla
CHANDIGARH
Dehra Dun
UTTARAKHAND
Saharanpur
MEERUT
DELHI
New Delhi
Aligarh
AGRA
KANPUR
GWALIOR
LUCKNOW
Bareilly
Moradabad
Shahjahanpur
UTTAR
Gorakhpur
KATHMANDU
NEPAL
Dhaulagiri
Annapurna
Manaslu
Mt. Everest
Makalu
Kanchenjunga
Himalaya
Siwalik Range
Kunlun Shan
Karatax Shan
Muz Tag
Hoh Xil Shan
XIZANG ZIZHIQU (TIBET)
Gangdise Shan
Nganglong Kangri
Gar Kangri
Zhongba
Siling Co
Nam Co
Tanggula (Dangla) Shan
Nyainqêntanglha Shan
Lhasa
Xigazê
Lhazê
Tingri
Qüxü
Yarlung Zangbo Jiang
Namcha Barwa
Nyingchi
Amdo
Nagqu
Qamdo
Bomi
Zayü
ARUNACHAL PRADESH
BHUTAN
Thimphu
Punakha
ASSAM
GUWAHATI
MEGHALAYA
Khasi Hills
Dimapur
NAGALAND
Imphal
MANIPUR
Silchar
Sylhet
Dibrugarh
DHAKA
Narayanganj
CHATTOGRAM
Aizawl
MIZORAM
Kachin
Myitkyina
MYANMAR (BURMA)
Bhamo
Lashio
Shwebo
Monywa
MANDALAY
Meiktila
Taunggyi
Yamethin
NAYPYIDAW
Toungoo
Sittwe (Akyab)
Arakan Yoma
Pegu Yoma
Shan
THAILAND
LAOS
Luang Prabang
VIETNAM
HANOI
Hai Phong
G. of Tonkin
Thanh Hoa
Nam Dinh
Son La
Hoa Binh
R U S S I A
Gorno-Altaysk
Sayan Mts.
Kyzyl
Tannu Ola
Belukha
Tavan Bogd Uul
Ölgiy
Ulaangom
Uvs Nuur
Hyargas Nuur
Har Us Nuur
Dund-Us (Hovd)
Dörgön Nuur
Uliastay
Hangayn Nuruu
Altay
Aerhtai Shan (Altai)
M O N G O L I A
Mörön
Hatgal
Hövsgöl Nuur
Erdenet
Bulgan
ULAN BATOR
Tsetserleg
Bayanhongor
Arvayheer
Mandalgovi
Ulaanjirem
Dalandzadgad
Gurvan Sayhan Uul
Irkutsk
Angarsk
Cheremkhovo
Babushkin
Gobi
Barkol Kazak Zizhixian
Hami (Kumul)
Bei Shan
Anxi
Yumen
Jiayuguan
Jiuquan
Zhangye
Qilian Shan
Badain Jaran Desert
Tengger Desert
Shandan
Jinchang
Wuwei
Alxa Zuoqi
YINCHUAN
NINGXIA HUIZU ZIZHIQU
Shizuishan
Wuhai
Delingha
Da Qaidam
Golmud
Qinghai Hu
Xining
LANZHOU
Baiyin
Linxia
Dingxi
Pingliang
Guyuan
Tianjun
Dulan
Gonghe
Minhe
QINGHAI
Maqên Gangri
Maqên
Gyaring Hu
Ngoring Hu
Bayan Har Shan
Yushu
Tianshui
Baoji
Qinling
Hanzhong
Wudu
Songpan
Min Jiang
Guangyuan
MIANYANG
Deyang
CHENGDU
Ya'an
Dadu He
Daxue Shan
SICHUAN
LESHAN
Gongga Shan
NEIJIANG
Santai
SUINING
NANCHONG
Dazhou
Hechuan
CHONGQING
ZIGONG
LUZHOU
Yibin
Chang Jiang (Yangtze)
Wutongqiao
Xichang
Daliang Shan
Zhaotong
LIUPANSHUI
GUIYANG
GUIZHOU
Zunyi
Anshun
Huize
Xuanwei
Qujing
KUNMING
Chuxiong
Dali
Xiaguan
Baoshan
Tengchong
Luxi
YUNNAN
Lincang
Simao
Jinggu
Anning
Yuxi
Kaiyuan
Mengzi
Gejiu
Wenshan
Hekou
Xingyi
Hechi
Bose
NANNING
Pingxiang
GUANGXI ZHUANGZU ZIZHIQU
Panzhihua
Lijiang
Zhongdian (Shangri-La)
Ningjing Shan
Shaluli Shan
Hengduan Shan
Nu Shan
Yunling Shan
Garzê
Markam
Salween
Mekong
Irrawaddy
Brahmaputra
Ganga
Indus
Sutlej
Projection: Bonne
East from Greenwich
RUSSIA
KAZAKHSTAN
MONGOLIA
KYRGYZSTAN
PAKISTAN
INDIA
NEPAL
BHUTAN
BANGLADESH
MYANMAR (BURMA)
THAILAND
LAOS
VIETNAM
N. KOREA
S. KOREA
JAPAN
TAIWAN
HEILONGJIANG
JILIN
LIAONING
NEI MONGOL ZIZHIQU (INNER MONGOLIA)
XINJIANG UYGUR ZIZHIQU (SINKIANG)
QINGHAI
GANSU
NINGXIA HUIZU ZIZHIQU
BEIJING
Beijing
TIANJIN
HEBEI
SHANXI
SHANDONG
HENAN
SHAANXI
JIANGSU
ANHUI
SHANGHAI
HUBEI
ZHEJIANG
SICHUAN
CHONGQING
XIZANG ZIZHIQU (TIBET)
HUNAN
JIANGXI
FUJIAN
GUIZHOU
YUNNAN
GUANGXI ZHUANGZU ZIZHIQU
GUANGDONG
HONG KONG
MACAU
HAINAN
CHINA
YELLOW SEA
PACIFIC OCEAN
CHINA 1:48 500 000

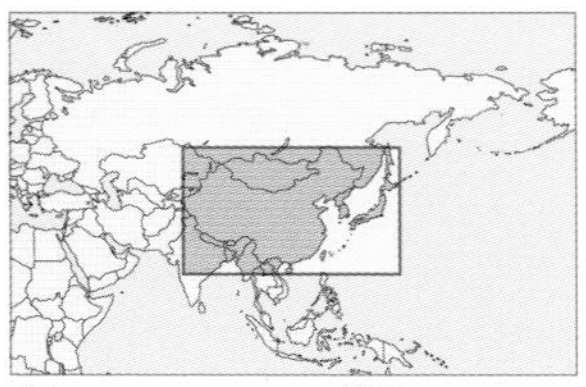

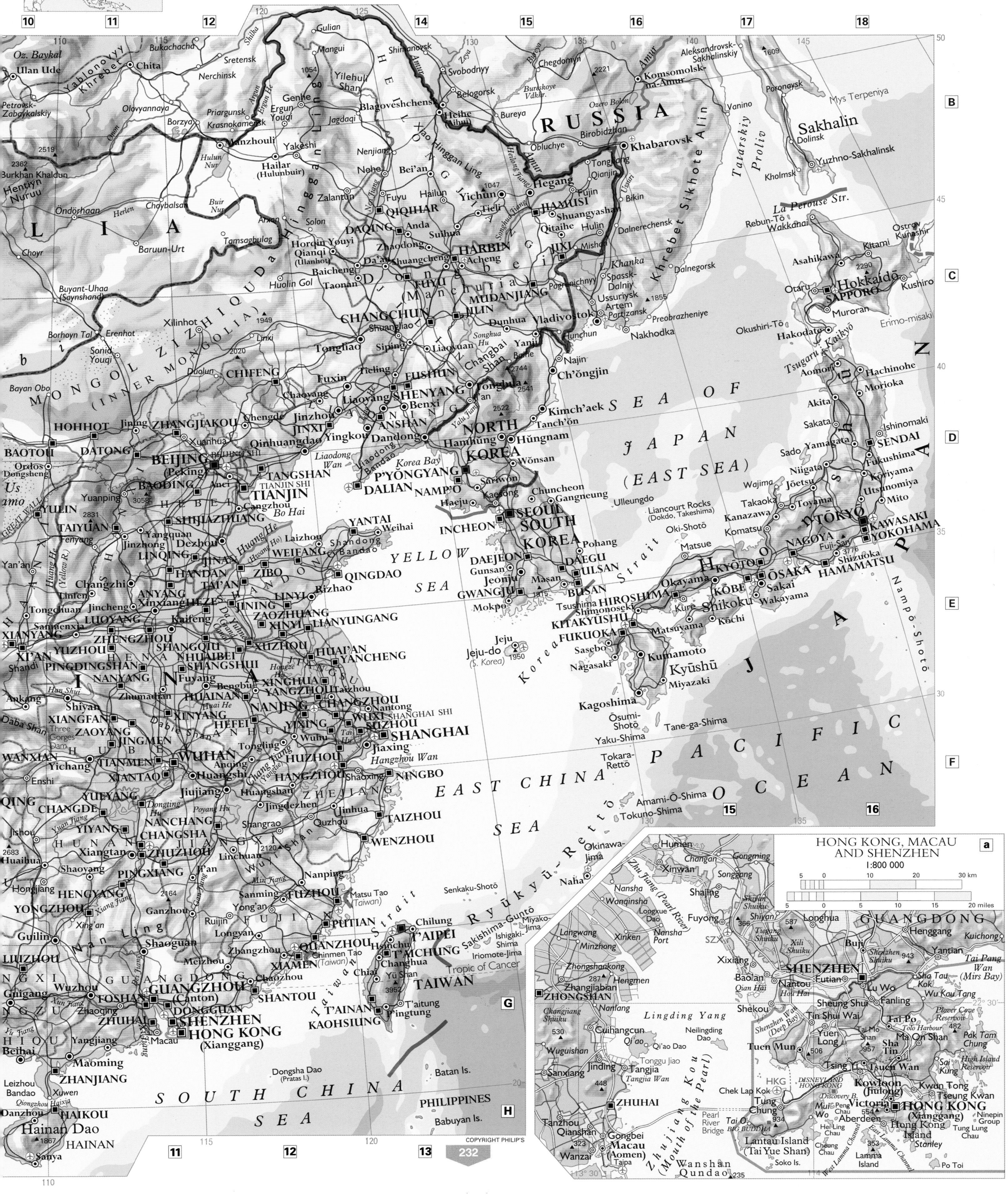

10
11
12
13
14
15
16
17
18
B
C
D
E
F
G
H
RUSSIA
MONGOLIA
CHINA
NORTH KOREA
SOUTH KOREA
JAPAN
TAIWAN
PHILIPPINES
SEA OF JAPAN (EAST SEA)
YELLOW SEA
EAST CHINA SEA
SOUTH CHINA SEA
PACIFIC OCEAN
Bo Hai
Korea Bay
Liaodong Wan
Hangzhou Wan
Korea Strait
Taiwan Strait
La Perouse Str.
Tatarskiy Proliv
Tsugaru-Kaikyō
Tropic of Cancer
HEILONGJIANG
JILIN
LIAONING
HEBEI
SHANDONG
HENAN
JIANGSU
ANHUI
HUBEI
HUNAN
JIANGXI
ZHEJIANG
FUJIAN
GUANGDONG
NEI MONGOL ZIZHIQU (INNER MONGOLIA)
Dongbei (Manchuria)
Oz. Baykal
Ulan Ude
Chita
Yablonovyy Khrebet
Bukachacha
Sretensk
Nerchinsk
Petrovsk-Zabaykalskiy
Olovyannaya
Borzya
Priargunsk
Krasnokamensk
Manzhouli
Hailar (Hulunbuir)
Yakeshi
Genhe
Ergun Youqi
Gulian
Mangui
Yilehuli Shan
Da Hinggan Ling
Xiao Hinggan Ling
Shimanovsk
Svobodnyy
Belogorsk
Blagoveshchensk
Heihe (Aihui)
Bureya
Chegdomyn
Komsomolsk-na-Amur
Aleksandrovsk-Sakhalinskiy
Poronaysk
Sakhalin
Mys Terpeniya
Dolinsk
Yuzhno-Sakhalinsk
Kholmsk
Vanino
Birobidzhan
Obluchye
Khabarovsk
Sikhote Alin
Hegang
Jiamusi
Shuangyashan
Qitaihe
Jixi
Mishan
Hulin
Dalnerechensk
Dalnegorsk
L. Khanka
Spassk-Dalniy
Ussuriysk
Artem
Partizansk
Vladivostok
Nakhodka
Preobrazheniye
Pogranichnyy
Nenjiang
Nehe
Bei'an
Hailun
Yichun
Tieli
Zalantun
Fuyu
Qiqihar
Anda
Suihua
Daqing
Zhaodong
Harbin
Acheng
Shuangcheng
Horqin Youyi Qianqi (Ulanhot)
Baicheng
Da'an
Taonan
Huolin Gol
Mudanjiang
Jilin
Changchun
Shuangliao
Siping
Liaoyuan
Tongliao
Dunhua
Yanji
Hunchun
Najin
Ch'ŏngjin
Kimch'aek
Tanch'ŏn
Hamhŭng
Hŭngnam
Wŏnsan
Changbai Shan
Tonghua
Fushun
Shenyang
Tieling
Fuxin
Liaoyang
Benxi
Anshan
Chaoyang
Jinzhou
Jinxi
Yingkou
Dandong
Liaodong Bandao
Dalian
P'yŏngyang
Namp'o
Sariwŏn
Haeju
Kaesŏng
Chuncheon
Gangneung
Ulleungdo
Liancourt Rocks (Dokdo, Takeshima)
Seoul
Incheon
Daejeon
Gunsan
Jeonju
Gwangju
Mokpo
Masan
Daegu
Ulsan
Pohang
Busan
Jeju
Jeju-do (S. Korea)
Tsushima
Chifeng
Xilinhot
Erenhot
Sonid Youqi
Baruun-Urt
Choybalsan
Öndörhaan
Herlen
Choyr
Buyant-Uhaa (Saynshand)
Borhoyn Tal
Bayan Obo
Hohhot
Baotou
Datong
Ordos (Dongsheng)
Zhangjiakou
Chengde
Beijing (Peking)
Qinhuangdao
Tangshan
Tianjin
Baoding
Cangzhou
Shijiazhuang
Taiyuan
Yulin
Yangquan
Jinzhong
Dezhou
Jinan
Weifang
Zibo
Qingdao
Yantai
Weihai
Shandong Bandao
Laizhou
Linqing
Handan
Tai'an
Linyi
Rizhao
Anyang
Xinxiang
Heze
Jining
Zaozhuang
Xinyi
Lianyungang
Changzhi
Linfen
Yan'an
Huang He (Yellow R.)
Luoyang
Zhengzhou
Kaifeng
Sanmenxia
Xianyang
Xi'an
Shangqiu
Huaibei
Xuzhou
Huai'an
Yancheng
Yuzhou
Pingdingshan
Nanyang
Fuyang
Bengbu
Huainan
Xinghua
Yangzhou
Taizhou
Nanjing
Changzhou
Nantong
Wuxi
Suzhou
Shanghai
Hefei
Xinyang
Zhumadian
Xiangfan
Shiyan
Ankang
Daba Shan
Three Gorges Dam
Zaoyang
Jingmen
Wanxian
Yichang
Tianmen
Wuhan
Xiantao
Huangshi
Anqing
Tongling
Wuhu
Yixing
Huzhou
Jiaxing
Hangzhou
Shaoxing
Ningbo
Chang Jiang (Yangtze)
Jiujiang
Huangshan
Jingdezhen
Jinhua
Quzhou
Taizhou
Wenzhou
Yueyang
Changde
Nanchang
Poyang Hu
Dongting Hu
Changsha
Yiyang
Xiangtan
Zhuzhou
Shangrao
Pingxiang
Ji'an
Hengyang
Yongzhou
Nanping
Fuzhou
Matsu Tao (Taiwan)
Sanming
Yong'an
Ganzhou
Putian
Quanzhou
Chinmen Tao (Taiwan)
Xiamen
Zhangzhou
Longyan
Meizhou
Chaozhou
Shantou
Guilin
Liuzhou
Wuzhou
Shaoguan
Guangzhou (Canton)
Foshan
Dongguan
Shenzhen
Hong Kong (Xianggang)
Zhuhai
Macau
Zhaoqing
Yangjiang
Maoming
Zhanjiang
Beihai
Leizhou Bandao
Haikou
Hainan Dao
Hainan
Sanya
Dongsha Dao (Pratas I.)
Batan Is.
Babuyan Is.
T'aipei
Chilung
Hsinchu
T'aichung
Changhua
Chiai
Yü Shan
T'ainan
Kaohsiung
P'ingtung
T'aitung
Senkaku-Shotō
Sakishima-Guntō
Ishigaki-Shima
Iriomote-Jima
Miyako-Jima
Ryūkyū-Rettō
Okinawa-Jima
Naha
Amami-Ō-Shima
Tokuno-Shima
Tokara-Rettō
Yaku-Shima
Tane-ga-Shima
Ōsumi-Shotō
Kagoshima
Kyūshū
Miyazaki
Kumamoto
Nagasaki
Sasebo
Fukuoka
Kitakyūshū
Shimonoseki
Hiroshima
Matsuyama
Kure
Okayama
Shikoku
Kōchi
Kōbe
Ōsaka
Kyōto
Sakai
Wakayama
Matsue
Oki-Shotō
Nagoya
Hamamatsu
Shizuoka
Fuji-San
Tōkyō
Kawasaki
Yokohama
Komatsu
Kanazawa
Takaoka
Toyama
Wajima
Jōetsu
Niigata
Sado
Yamagata
Utsunomiya
Mito
Kōriyama
Fukushima
Sendai
Ishinomaki
Sakata
Akita
Morioka
Aomori
Hachinohe
Hakodate
Okushiri-Tō
Muroran
Erimo-misaki
Sapporo
Otaru
Hokkaidō
Asahikawa
Kitami
Kushiro
Ostrov Kunashir
Rebun-Tō
Wakkanai
Nampō-Shotō
Honshū
HONG KONG, MACAU AND SHENZHEN
a
1:800 000
0
5
10
15
20
30 km
20 miles
Humen
Chang'an
Gongming
Xinwan
Songgang
Zhu Jiang (Pearl River)
Nansha
Shajing
Wanqingsha
Longxue Dao
Nansha Port
Fuyong
Shiyan
Shiyan Shuiku
Tiegang Shuiku
Xili Shuiku
Longhua
Guangdong
Henggang
Kuichong
Buji
Shenzhen Shuiku
Yantian
Tai Pang Wan (Mirs Bay)
Langwang
Minzhong
Xinken
Xixiang
Baolan
Qian Hai
Shenzhen
Futian
Nantou
Hou Hai
Sha Tau Kok
Lu Wo
Fanling
Wu Kau Tang
Plover Cove Reservoir
Tai Po
Tolo Harbour
Ma On Shan
Pak Tam Chung
High Island Reservoir
Sai Kung
Zhongshankong
Zhongshan
Hengmen
Zhangjiabian
Nanlang
Changjiang Shuiku
Lingding Yang
Neilingding Dao
Shekou
Shenzhen Wan (Deep Bay)
Sheung Shui
Tin Shui Wai
Yuen Long
Tai Mo Shan
Sha Tin
Tuen Mun
Tsing Yi
Tsuen Wan
Tseung Kwan
Kwun Tong
Cuihangcun
Qi'ao
Qi'ao Dao
Wuguishan
Sanxiang
Jinding
Tonggu Jiao
Tangjia
Tangjia Wan
Zhuhai
Zhujiang Kou (Mouth of the Pearl)
HKG
Disneyland Hong Kong
Chek Lap Kok
Tung Chung
Pearl River Bridge
Tai O
Big Buddha
Lantau Island (Tai Yue Shan)
Discovery B.
Mui Wo
Peng Chau
Hei Ling Chau
Kowloon (Jiulong)
Victoria
Hong Kong (Xianggang)
Aberdeen
Hong Kong Island
Stanley
Ninepin Group
Tung Lung Chau
Cheung Chau
Lamma Island
West Lamma Channel
East Lamma Channel
Po Toi
Soko Is.
Tanzhou
Qianshan
Gongbei
Macau (Aomen)
Taipa
Wanzai
Wanshan Qundao
22° 30'
113° 30'
COPYRIGHT PHILIP'S
232

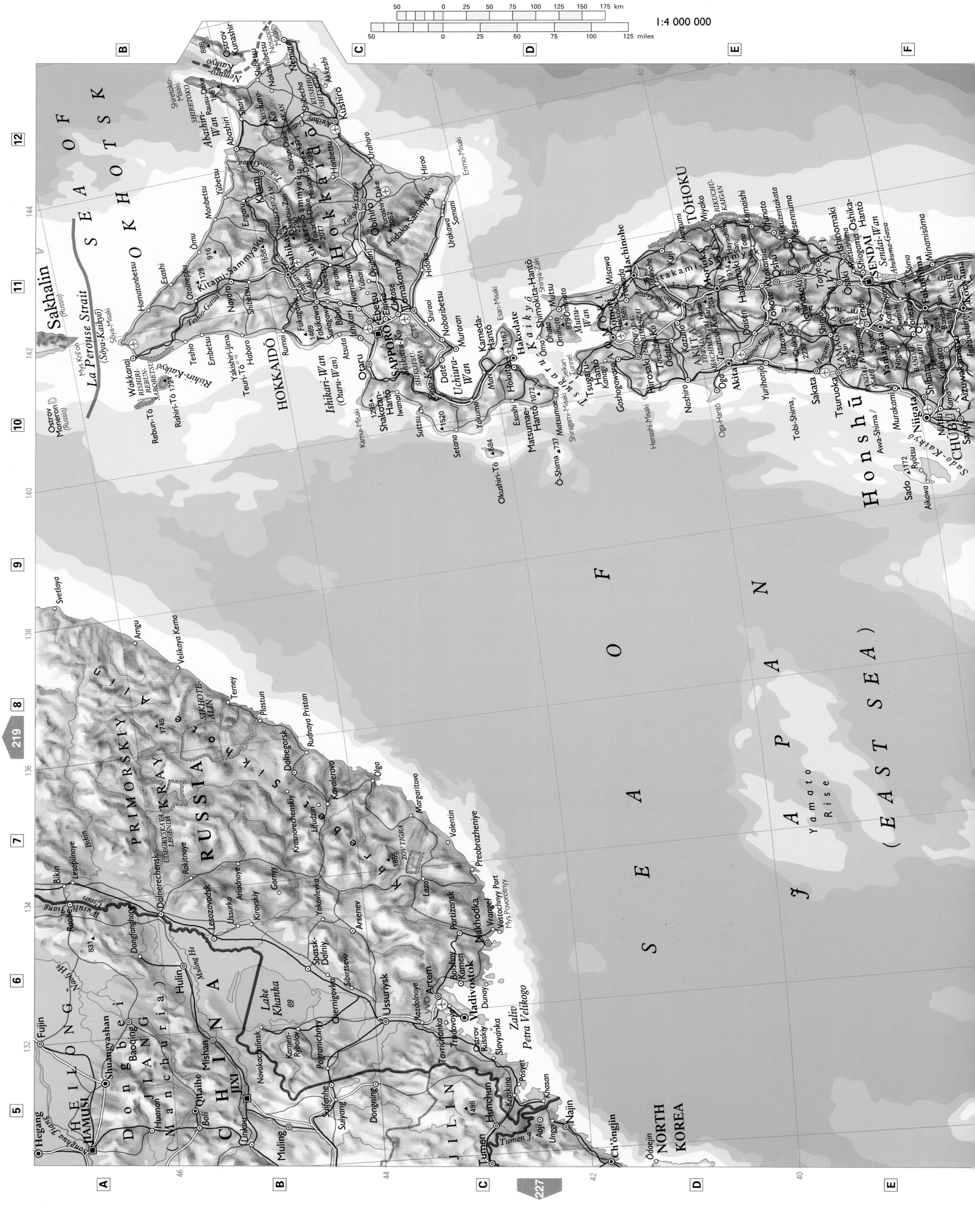
1:4 000 000
50 0 25 50 75 100 125 150 175 km
50 0 25 50 75 100 125 miles
SEA OF OKHOTSK
SEA OF JAPAN
(EAST SEA)
Sakhalin
(Russia)
La Perouse Strait
(Sōya-Kaikyō)
HOKKAIDŌ
Hokkaidō
SAPPORO
Hakodate
Kushiro
Asahikawa
Obihiro
Otaru
Muroran
Wakkanai
Abashiri
Kitami
Nemuro
Ishikari-Wan
Uchiura-Wan
Tsugaru-Kaikyō
Honshū
TŌHOKU
SENDAI
Sendai-Wan
Aomori
Morioka
Akita
Niigata
Yamagata
Fukushima
Sado
Yamato Rise
RUSSIA
PRIMORSKIY KRAY
Sikhote-Alin
Vladivostok
Ussuriysk
Nakhodka
Artem
Lake Khanka
Zaliv Petra Velikogo
CHINA
HEILONGJIANG
JILIN
JIXI
JIAMUSI
Manchuria
NORTH KOREA
Ch'ŏngjin
Tumen
Hunchun
Najin

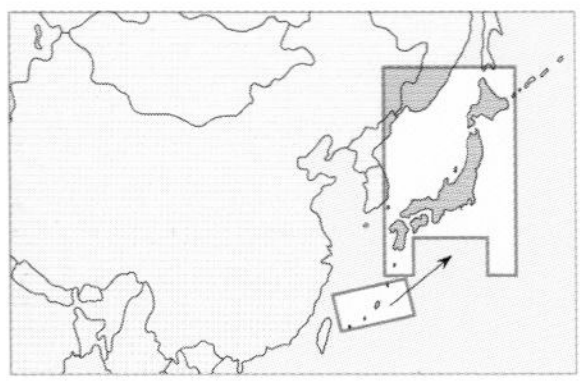

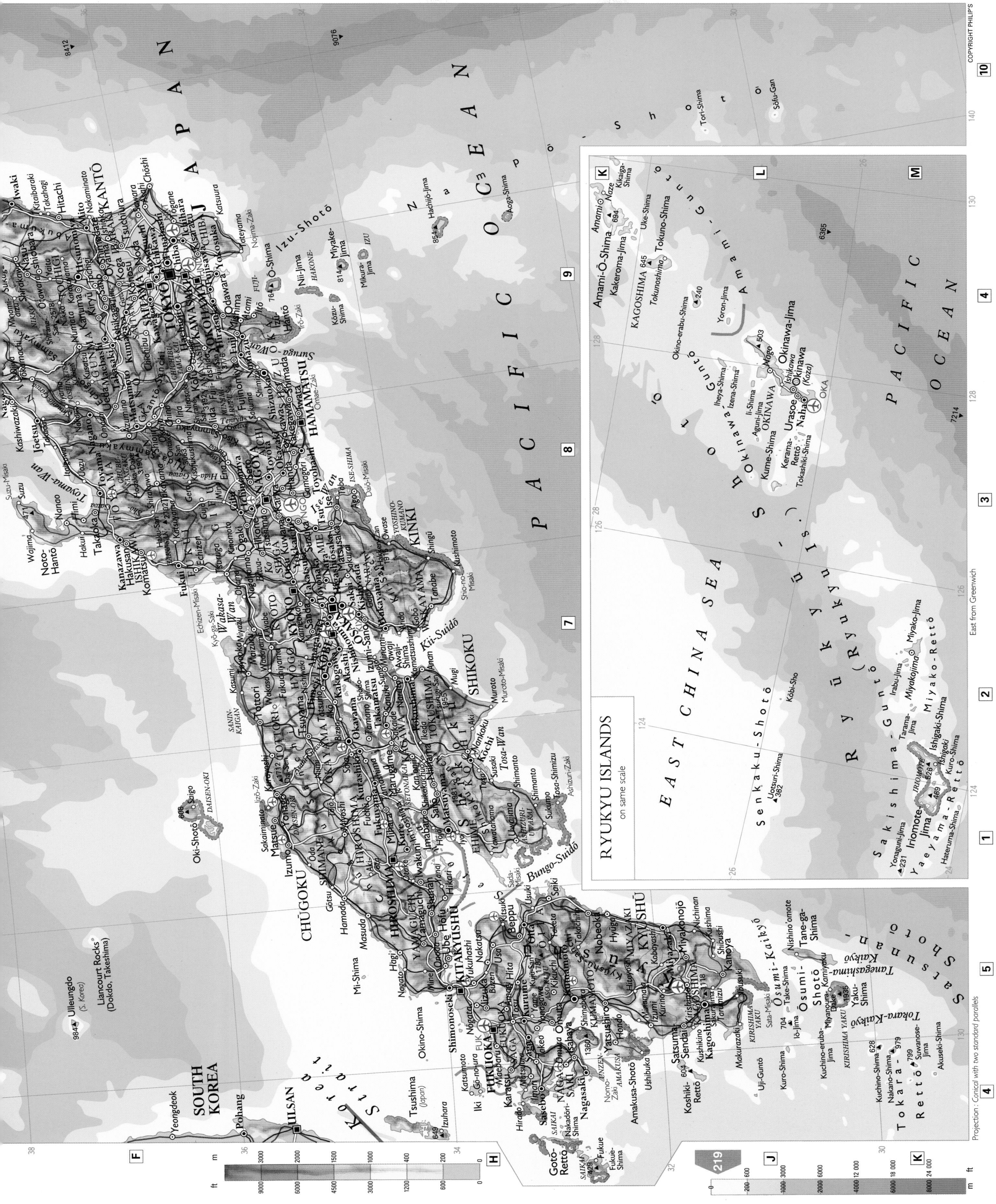
JAPAN
PACIFIC OCEAN
EAST CHINA SEA
RYUKYU ISLANDS
on same scale
Ryūkyū-Shotō (Ryukyu Is.)
SOUTH KOREA
Korea Strait
Izu-Shotō
Ogasawara-Shotō
Amami-Guntō
Okinawa-Shotō
Sakishima-Guntō
Senkaku-Shotō
Satsunan-Shotō
Tokara-Rettō
Tsushima
Oki-Shotō
Ulleungdo
Liancourt Rocks (Dokdo, Takeshima)
SHIKOKU
KYŪSHŪ
CHŪGOKU
KINKI
KANTŌ
TŌKYŌ
YOKOHAMA
KAWASAKI
NAGOYA
KYŌTO
ŌSAKA
KŌBE
HIROSHIMA
KITAKYŪSHŪ
FUKUOKA
NAGASAKI
KAGOSHIMA
HAMAMATSU
Okinawa
Naha
Bungo-Suidō
Kii-Suidō
Tosa-Wan
Suruga-Wan
Wakasa-Wan
Toyama-Wan
Ōsumi-Kaikyō
Tokara-Kaikyō
Tanegashima-Kaikyō
Projection: Conical with two standard parallels
East from Greenwich
COPYRIGHT PHILIP'S

1:2 000 000
km
miles
SEA OF JAPAN
(EAST SEA)
Oki-Shotō
Dōgo
Dōzen
Daimanji-San
Saigō
DAISEN-OKI
SOUTH KOREA
Yeongdeok
Heunghae
Pohang
224
Korea Strait
Honshu
CHŪGOKU-DISTRICT
Shimane-Hantō
Jizō-Zaki
Matsue
Sakaiminato
Yonago
Hirata
Taisha
Izumo
Yasugi
Daitō
Kisuki
Hi-no-Misaki
Dai-Sen
1729
TOTTORI
Tottori
Kurayoshi
Iwami
Kasumi
Toyooka
SANIN-KAIGAN
Hidaka
Suga-no-Sen
1510
Wadayama
Wakasa
Chizu
Ōda
Sanbe-San
1126
IWAMI GINZAN
Yunotsu
Gōtsu
Gō-Gawa
Hamada
SHIMANE
Dōgo-San
1269
Katsuyama
Tsuyama
Ochiai
Bingo-Ochiai
Niimi
Tōjō
OKAYAMA
Yamasaki
Nishiwaki
HYŌGO
Sayō
Yanahara
Kasai
Tatsuno
Himeji
Aioi
Takasago
Kakogawa
Akashi
Akō
Wake
Takahashi
Shōbara
Miyoshi
HIROSHIMA
Masuda
Akiōta
Yoshida
Fuchū
Ibara
Yakage
Sōja
Okayama
Kurashiki
Bizen
Saidaiji
Kannabe
Kōnkō
Fukuyama
Kasaoka
Onomichi
Mihara
Ieshima-Shotō
Harima-Nada
Shōdo-Shima
Tonoshō
Tamano
Mi-Shima
Ōmi-Shima
Hagi
Aono-Yama
908
Atō
Kanmuri-Yama
1339
Ōta-Gawa
Higashi-Hiroshima
HIROSHIMA
Hatsukaichi
Kaita
Kure
Takehara
In'noshima
Tsuno-Shima
Nagato
YAMAGUCHI
Yamaguchi
Hibiki-Nada
Toyoura
Mine
Ōgōri
San'yō
Hōfu
Tokuji
Shin-Nan'yō
Shūnan
Ōtake
Iwakuni
Hiroshima-Wan
Kudamatsu
Yanai
Hikari
Genkai-Nada
Shimonoseki
Onoda
Ube
KITAKYŪSHŪ
Suō-Nada
Naga-Shima
Iwai-Jima
Hime-Jima
Yashiro-Jima
Heigun-Tō
Kurahashi-Jima
Aki-Nada
Ōmi-Shima
Imabari
Hōjō
Tōyo
Saijō
Niihama
Hiuchi-Nada
Kan'onji
Onohara
Shikokuchūō
Marugame
Tadotsu
Zentsūji
Sakaide
Takamatsu
KAGAWA
Sanuki
Miki
Higashi-kagawa
Naruto
Naruto-Kaikyō
Awaji-Shima
Awaji
Sumoto
Minami-awaji
608
Kotohira
Sanyuki-Sammyaku
Itano
Tokushima
Ikeda
Mima
Yoshino-gawa
Komatsushima
TOKUSHIMA
Anan
Kii-Suidō
Iyo-Mishima
Matsuyama
Iyo
Ishizuchi-Yama
1981
Shikoku-Sanchi
Ōtoyo
Tsurugi-San
1955
1423
Gamoda-Saki
KŌCHI
Mugi
Iyo-Nada
Nagahama
Kuma
EHIME
Ozu
Uchiko
1562
Yawatahama
Uwa
Sada-Misaki-Hantō
Sada-Misaki
Sakawa
Ino
Nankoku
Kōchi
Kami
Noichi
Aki
Tōyō
Tosa
Susaki
Tosa-Wan
Muroto
Muroto-Misaki
Uwajima
Kihoku
Nishi-Tosa
Tsushima
Shimanto
Shikoku
SHIKOKU-DISTRICT
Saga
Mishō
Shimanto
Sukumo
865
Tosa-Shimizu
ASHIZURI-UWAKAI
Ashizuri-Zaki
Oki-no-Shima
Tsurumi-Saki
Bungo-Suidō
Hōgo-Kaikyō
Kara-Saki
Kamiagata
Kamitsushima
Tsushima
Mitsushima
Izuhara
649
Kō-Saki
Higashi-Suidō
Katsumoto
Iki
Gō-no-ura
Iki-Kaikyō
Ō-Shima
Munakata
Nakama
Fukuma
Koga
Nōgata
Miyata
Yukuhashi
FUKUOKA
Maebaru
Iizuka
Tagawa
Dazaifu
Kama
Buzen
Nakatsu
Futago-Yama
721
Kunisaki
Bungotakada
Usa
Kitsuki
Hiji
Kasuga
Chikushino
1200
Tsukushi-Sanchi
Sefuri-San
1055
Tosu
Amagi
Ōgōri
Kurume
Hita
Yufu-Dake
1584
Beppu
Beppu-Wan
Tsurusaki
Saganoseki
Ōita
ŌITA
Usuki
Kusu
Kurogi
ASO-KUJŪ
1787
Oguni
Kujū-San
Yobuko
Karatsu
Ikitsuki-Shima
Hirado
Matsuura
Imari
SAGA
Saga
Takeo
Taku
Ogi
Chikugo
Hirado-Shima
SAIKAI
Saza
Sasebo
Arita
Yame
Yanagawa
Kashima
Setaka
Ureshino
1076
Tara
Tara-Dake
Ariake-Kai
Ōmuta
Yamaga
Arao
Kikuchi
Aso
Kōshi
1592
Ichinomiya
Taketa
Tsukumi
Mie
Saiki
Kamae
Ōmura-Wan
Nishi-Sonogi-Hantō
NAGASAKI
Ōmura
Isahaya
Tamana
Kumamoto
Nagayo
Unzen-Dake
1360
Shimabara
Ozu
Aso-Zan
Sobo-Yama
1758
Nagasaki
Obama
UNZEN-AMAKUSA
KUMAMOTO
Uto
Matsubase
Takachiho
Nomo-Zaki
Tachibana-Wan
Kuchinotsu
Misumi
Kunimi-Dake
1739
Hinokage
Amakusa-Nada
Hondo
Matsushima
Kami-Jima
Yatsushiro
Nobeoka
Amakusa-Shotō
Shimo-Jima
UNZEN-AMAKUSA
Yatsushiro-Kai
Itsuki
Shiiba
Hyūga
Kyūshū-Sanchi
MIYAZAKI
Taragi
Hitoyoshi
Ushibuka
Minamata
Naga-Shima
Kyūshū
KYŪSHŪ-DISTRICT
Izumi
Akune
Ōkuchi
Ebino
Saito
Takanabe
Sadowara
Kami-Koshiki-Jima
Miyanojō
Yoshimatsu
Kobayashi
Kurino
Kirishima-Yama
1700
Miyazaki
KIRISHIMA-YAKU
Koshiki-Rettō
604
Satsuma-Sendai
Kushikino
Aira
Kirishima
Hayato
Miyakonojō
Shimo-Koshiki-Jima
Kagoshima
On-Take
Sakurajima
1118
Ijūin
Sōo
Nichinan
Aburatsu
Koshiki-Kaikyō
KAGOSHIMA
Fukiage
Noma-Saki
Kaseda
Satsuma-Hantō
Kagoshima-Wan
Tarumizu
Shibushi
Kanoya
Kushima
Kawanabe
Kiire
Ōsaki
Shibushi-Wan
Makurazaki
Bō-no-Misaki
Ibusuki
Kōyama
968
Kaimon-Dake
924
Yamagawa
Ōsumi-Hantō
KIRISHIMA YAKU
Sata-Misaki
Kyūshū Trench
5737
Projection: Lambert's Conformal Conic
Shinkansen lines

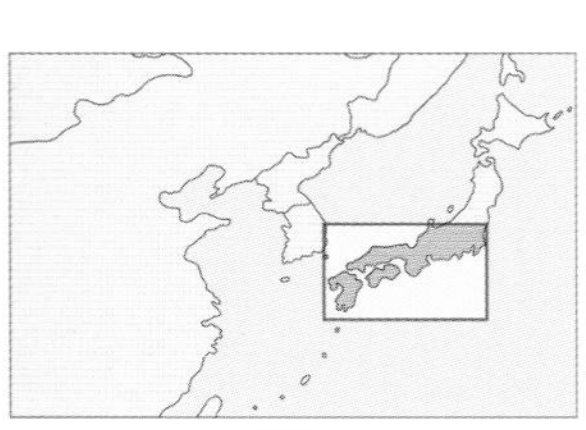

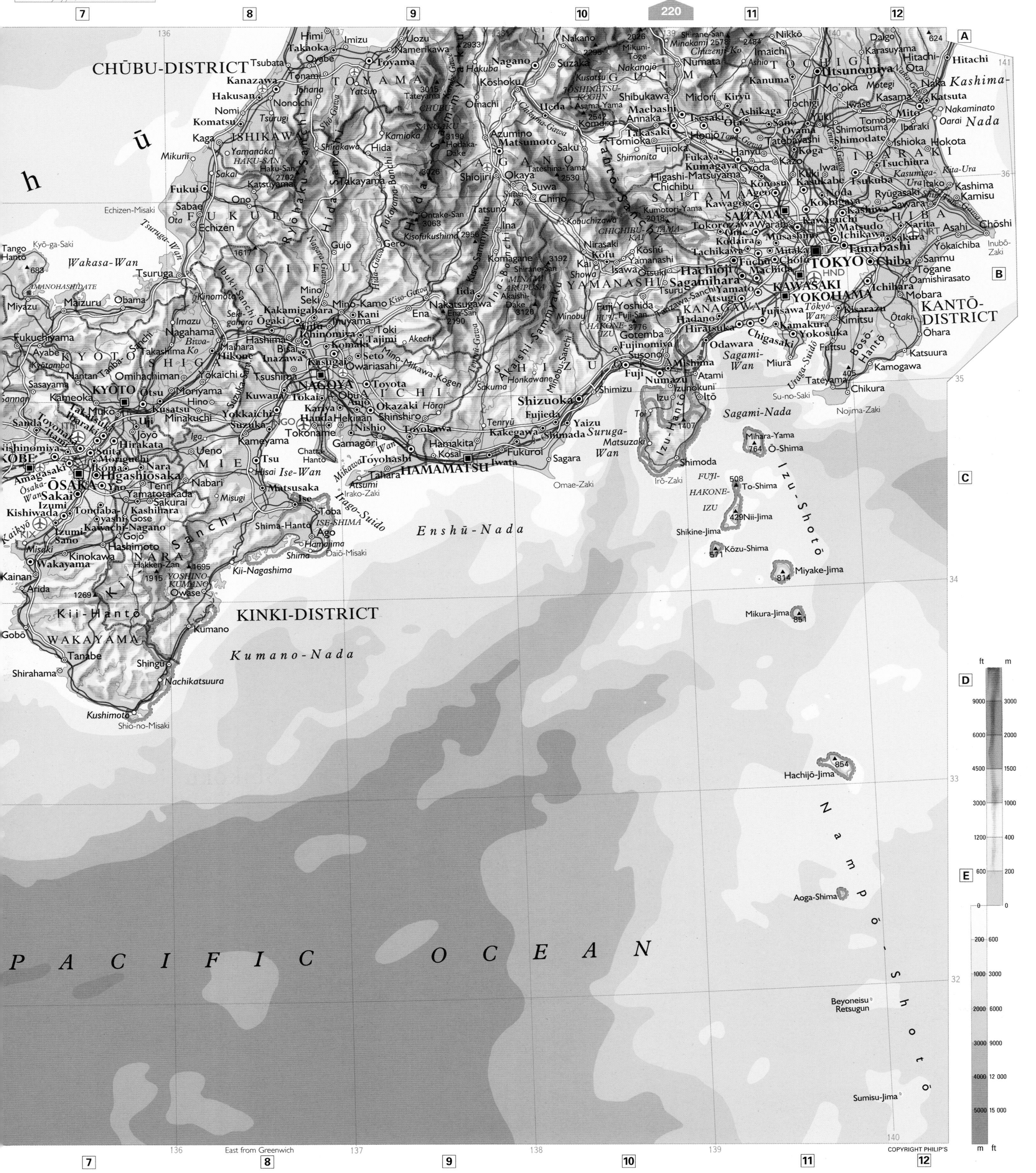
220
CHŪBU-DISTRICT
KINKI-DISTRICT
KANTŌ-DISTRICT
P A C I F I C O C E A N
Enshū-Nada
Kumano-Nada
Sagami-Nada
Wakasa-Wan
Ise-Wan
Suruga-Wan
Kii-Hantō
Izu-Hantō
Izu-Shotō
Nampō-shotō
TŌKYŌ
YOKOHAMA
KAWASAKI
NAGOYA
KYŌTO
ŌSAKA
KOBE
HAMAMATSU
Shizuoka
Chiba
Funabashi
SAITAMA
Utsunomiya
Maebashi
Nagano
Matsumoto
Kanazawa
Toyama
Fukui
Gifu
Tsu
Nara
Wakayama
Kōfu
Hachiōji
Sagamihara
Yokosuka
Numazu
Fuji
Odawara
Toyohashi
Okazaki
Toyota
Shimoda
Ō-Shima
Nii-Jima
Miyake-Jima
Mikura-Jima
Hachijō-Jima
Aoga-Shima
Beyoneisu Retsugun
Sumisu-Jima
East from Greenwich
COPYRIGHT PHILIP'S

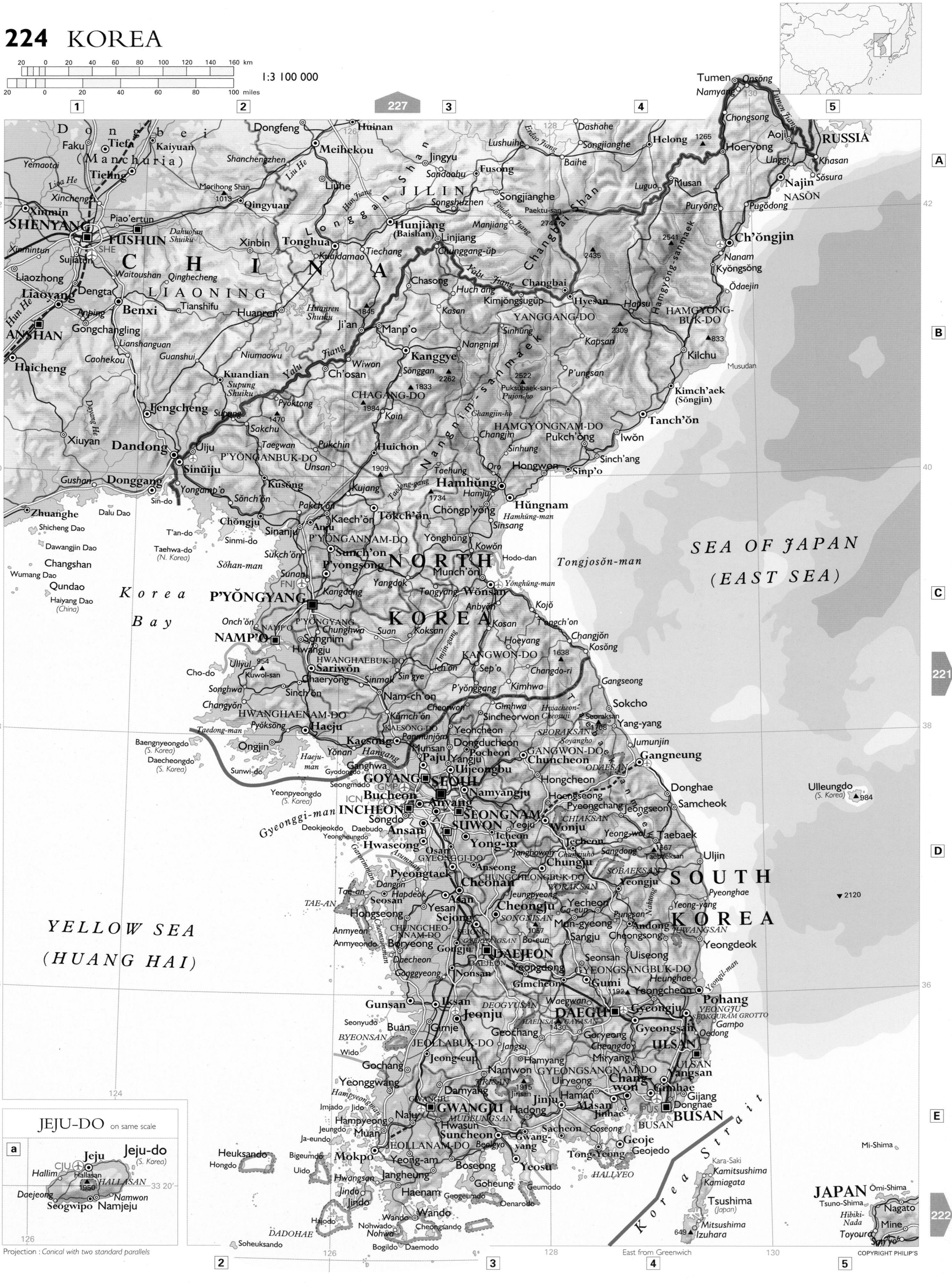

High-speed rail routes

1:1 400 000

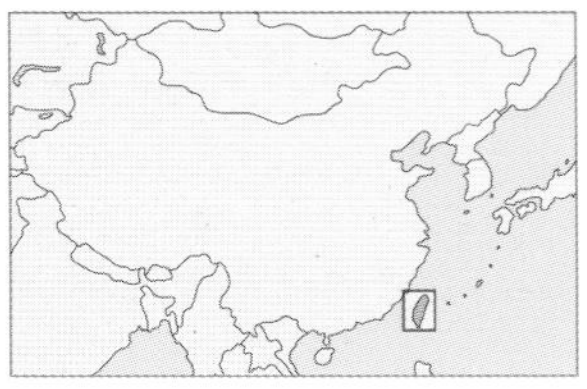

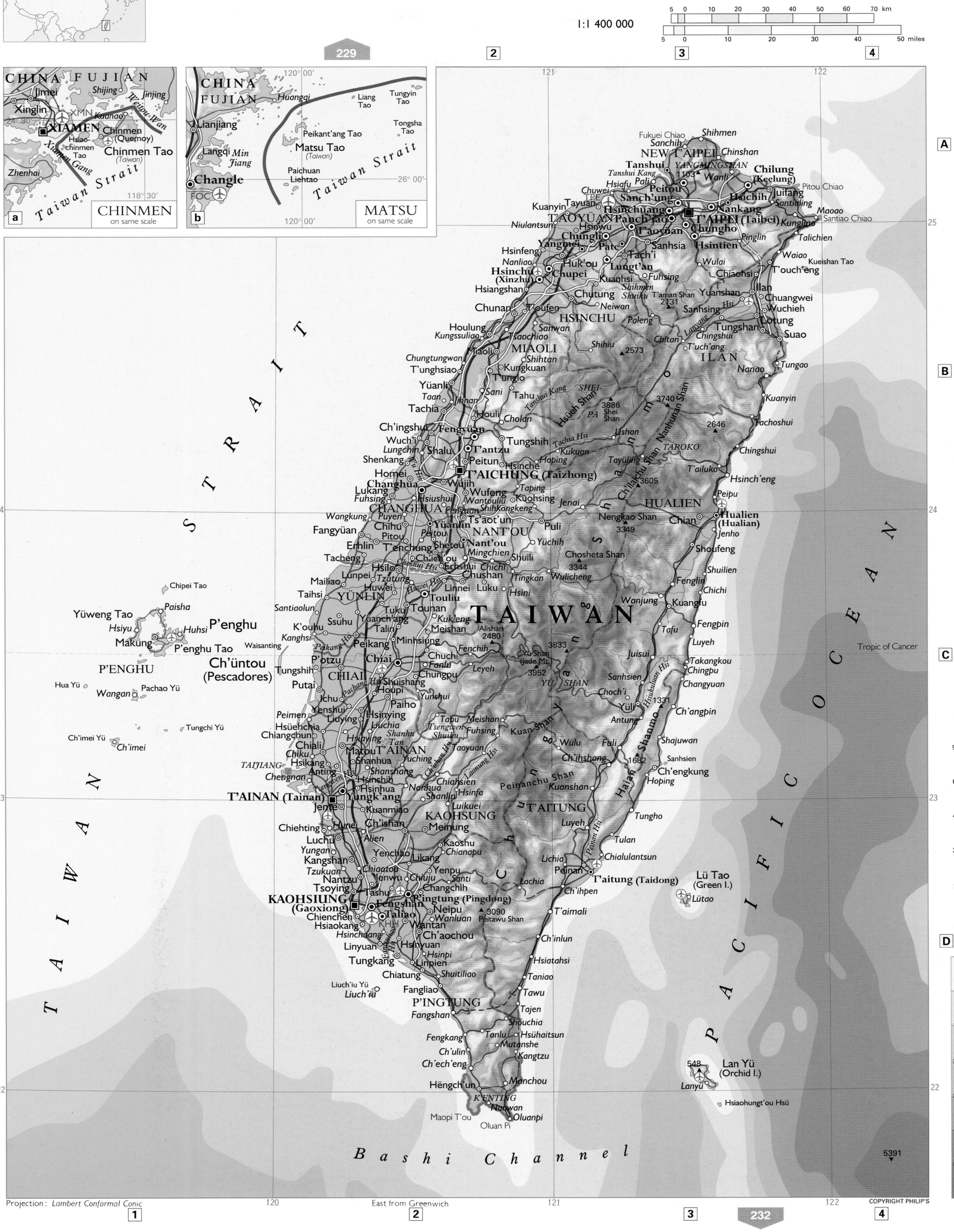

Projection: Lambert Conformal Conic

East from Greenwich

Taiwan High Speed Rail (THSR)

1:4 800 000

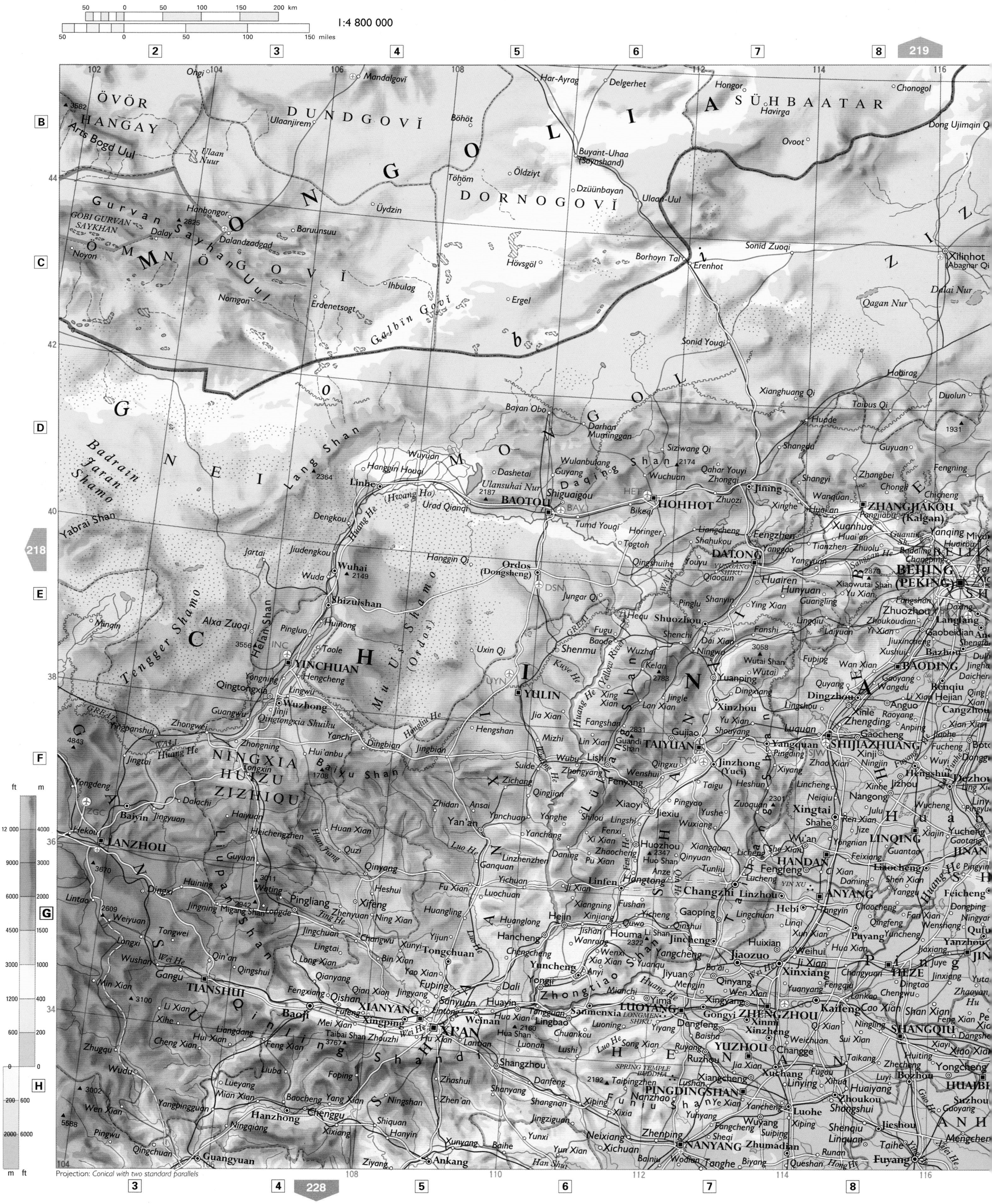

Projection: *Conical with two standard parallels*

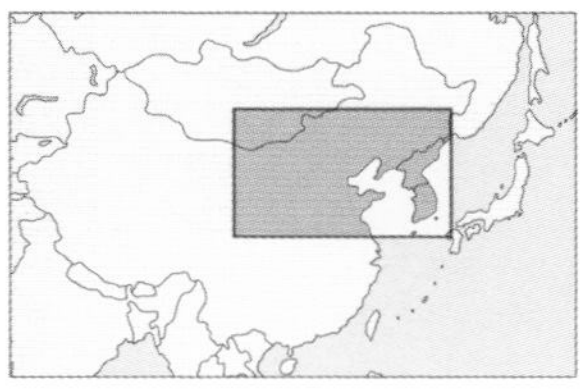

219
220
229
B
C
D
E
F
G
H
9
10
11
12
13
14
15
16
118
120
122
124
126
128
130
132
44
42
40
38
36
34
East from Greenwich
COPYRIGHT PHILIP'S
HARBIN
Bin Xian
Acheng
Horqin Youyi Qianqi
(Ulanhot)
Zhenlai
Baicheng
Da'an
Maoxing
Zhaoyuan
Shuangcheng
Taonan
Anguang
FUYU
Huolin Gol
Tuquan
Tongyu
Qian'an
Shenjingzi
Kaoshan
Nong'an
Dehui
Yushu
Wuchang
Shangzhi
Yimianpo
Linkou
Muling
JIXI
MUDANJIANG
Hailin
Ning'an
Suifenhe
Ussuriysk
Dongning
Vladivostok
Nakhodka
Artem
Zarubino
Posyet
Hunchun
Tumen
Yanji
Longjing
Helong
Antu
Dunhua
Jiaohe
JILIN
Yongji
Huadian
Panshi
Huinan
Jingyu
CHANGCHUN
Gongzhuling
Siping
Liaoyuan
Dongfeng
Meihekou
Tonghua
Hunjiang
Linjiang
Changbai
Hyesan
Jarud Qi
Xi Ujimqin Qi
Xebert
Tongliao
Bairin Zuoqi
Ar Horqin Qi
Kailu
Linxi
Bairin Youqi
Shuangliao
Jargalang
Changtu
Kangping
Ongniud Qi
Wutonghaolai
Hure Qi
Xiawa
Tiefa
Kaiyuan
Faku
Tieling
Qingyuan
CHIFENG
(Ulanhad)
Aohan Qi
Fuxin
Zhangwu
Xinmin
SHENYANG
FUSHUN
Benxi
Liaoyang
Anshan
Haicheng
Yingkou
Dashiqiao
Gaizhou
Dandong
Fengcheng
Xiuyan
Kuandian
Huanren
Beipiao
Chaoyang
Jianping
Lingyuan
Ningcheng
Jinzhou
Panjin
Huludao
Xingcheng
Suizhong
Liaodong Wan
Qinhuangdao
Qian'an
Zunhua
TANGSHAN
TIANJIN SHI
TIANJIN
Tanggu
Dagu
BO HAI
Bo Hai Haixia
Wafangdian
Pulandian
Jinzhou
Lüshun
DALIAN
(Lüda)
Zhuanghe
Changshan Qundao
(China)
Korea Bay
Miaodao Qundao
(China)
Penglai
Longkou
YANTAI
Weihai
Wendeng
Rongcheng
Laizhou Wan
Zhaoyuan
Laizhou
Shandong Bandao
Laiyang
Rushan
Haiyang
Laixi
Pingdu
WEIFANG
ZIBO
Jimo
QINGDAO
Jiaozhou
Zhucheng
Rizhao
Dongying
Binzhou
Huanghua
Huanghuagang
YELLOW SEA
(HUANG HAI)
Lianyungang
LIANYUNGANG
LINYI
ZAOZHUANG
XUZHOU
SUQIAN
Shuyang
HUAI'AN
YANCHENG
XINGHUA
Dongtai
Bengbu
Sheyang
NORTH KOREA
P'YŎNGYANG
NAMP'O
Sinŭiju
Kusŏng
Chŏngju
Anju
Sunch'ŏn
Kanggye
Manp'o
Hamhŭng
Hŭngnam
Sinp'o
Tanch'ŏn
Kimch'aek
(Sŏngjin)
Ch'ŏngjin
Kyŏngsŏng
Najin
Sŏsura
Unggi
Hoeryong
Musan
Paektu-san
2744
Wŏnsan
Tongjosŏn-man
Sariwŏn
Haeju
Kaesŏng
Ongjin
SEA OF JAPAN
(EAST SEA)
SOUTH KOREA
SEOUL
INCHEON
SUWON
SEONGNAM
GOYANG
Bucheon
Ansan
Anyang
Uijeongbu
Chuncheon
Hongcheon
Gangneung
Donghae
Samcheok
Wonju
Chungju
Cheongju
Cheonan
Gyeonggi-man
Seosan
DAEJEON
Gongju
Nonsan
Iksan
Gunsan
Jeonju
GWANGJU
Mokpo
Suncheon
Yeosu
Gwangyang
Jinju
Masan
Chang-won
BUSAN
Gimhae
ULSAN
Gyeongju
Pohang
DAEGU
Gumi
Andong
Yeongju
Uljin
Ulleungdo
(S. Korea)
Korea Strait
Tsushima
(Japan)
Izuhara
Jeju Haehyop
Jeju-do
(S. Korea)
Jeju
Hallasan
Seogwipo
Heuksando
(S. Korea)
Soheuksando
(S. Korea)
Baengnyeongdo
(S. Korea)
JAPAN
Karatsu
Sasebo
Nagasaki
Fukue-Shima
Nakadōri-Shima
Iki
RUSSIA
HEILONGJIANG
JILIN
LIAONING
SHANDONG
JIANGSU

1:4 800 000
50 0 50 100 150 200 km
50 0 50 100 150 miles
226
236
241
Projection: Conical with two standard parallels
GANSU
SHAANXI
SICHUAN
Sichuan Pendi
CHONGQING SHI
GUIZHOU
YUNNAN
GUANGXI
BURMA
KACHIN
MYANMAR
SHAN
LAOS
VIETNAM
THAILAND
Bac Phan
(Tonkin)
Gulf of Tonkin
CHENGDU
CHONGQING
KUNMING
GUIYANG
NANNING
HANOI
HAIPHONG
MIANYANG
NANCHONG
LESHAN
ZIGONG
LUZHOU
NEIJIANG
SUINING
WANXIAN
LIUPANSHUI
LIUZHOU
Panzhihua
Xichang
Lijiang
Dali
Baoshan
Qujing
Zunyi
Anshun
Kaili
Bose
Qinzhou
Beihai
Hanzhong
Guangyuan
Ya'an
Yibin
Ruili
Jinghong
Xishuangbanna
Ningjing Shan
Shaluli Shan
Daxue Shan
Qionglai Shan
Hengduan Shan
Yun Ling
Gaoligong Shan
Nu Shan
Daliang Shan
Wulian Feng
Wumeng Shan
Dalou Shan
Miao Ling
Ailao Shan
Wuliang Shan
Daba Shan
Jinsha Jiang (Yangtze)
Lancang Jiang (Mekong)
Nu Jiang (Salween)
Yalong Jiang
Min Jiang
Jialing Jiang
Chang Jiang (Yangtze)
Hong (Red)
Er Hai
Dian Chi
Fuxian Hu
Gongga Shan (Minya Konka) 7556
Sanxia Shuiku (Three Gorges Res.)
Longtan Shuiku
Jinping Bend Dams
GIANT PANDA NATIONAL PARK
HUANGLONG
JIUZHAIGOU
Leizhou Bandao
Weizhou Dao
Mekong
Salween

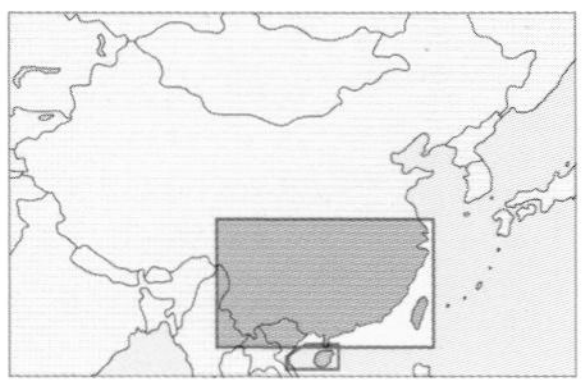

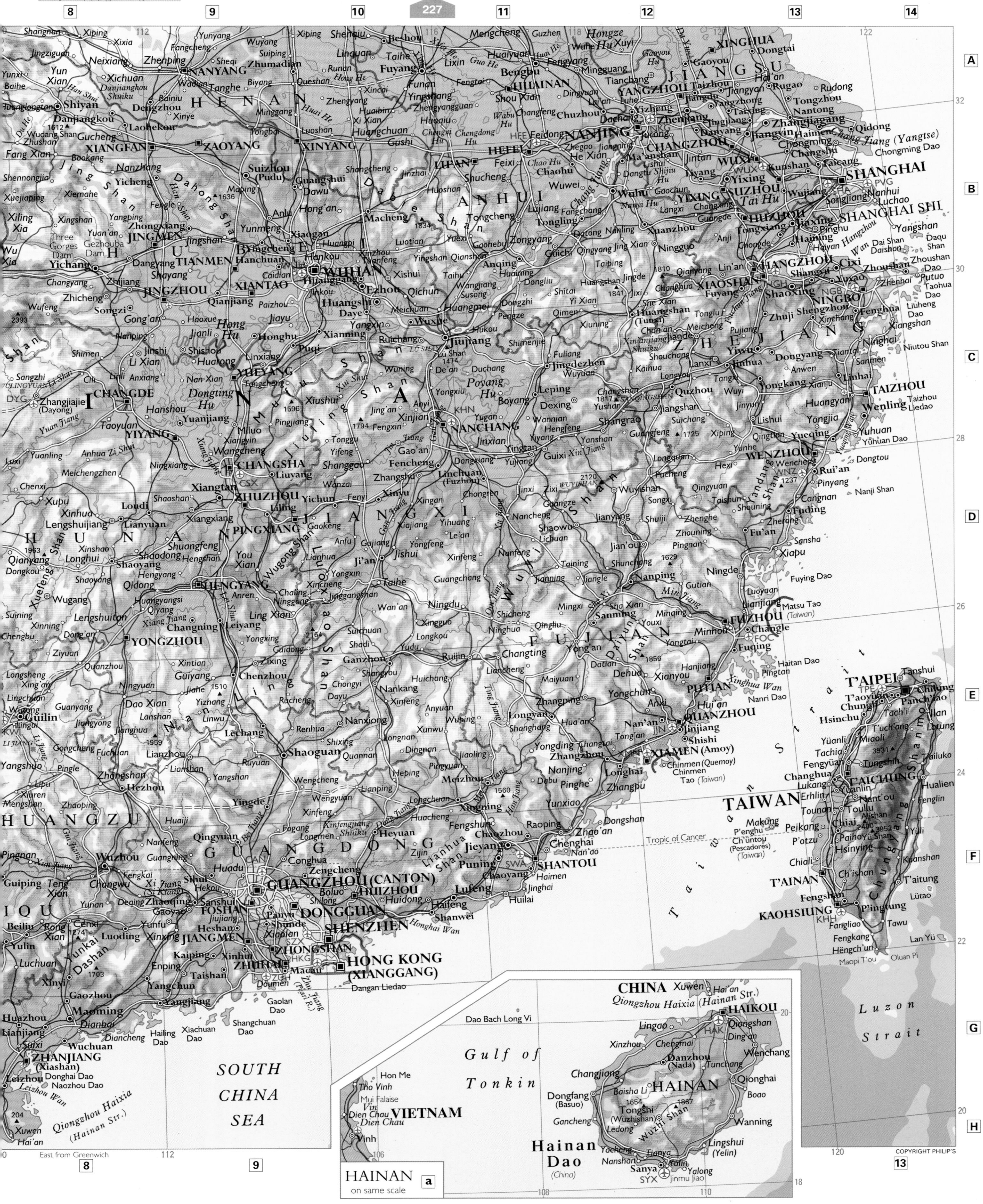
227
8
9
10
11
12
13
14
A
B
C
D
E
F
G
H
HENAN
ANHUI
JIANGSU
ZHEJIANG
JIANGXI
FUJIAN
HUNAN
GUANGDONG
TAIWAN
NANYANG
XIANGFAN
ZAOYANG
XINYANG
LU'AN
HEFEI
HUAINAN
NANJING
YANGZHOU
CHANGZHOU
WUXI
SHANGHAI
SHANGHAI SHI
HUZHOU
HANGZHOU
XIAOSHAN
NINGBO
JINGMEN
TIANMEN
XIANTAO
JINGZHOU
WUHAN
CHANGDE
YUEYANG
YIYANG
CHANGSHA
XHUZHOU
PINGXIANG
HENGYANG
YONGZHOU
NANCHANG
TAIZHOU
WENZHOU
FUZHOU
PUTIAN
QUANZHOU
XIAMEN (Amoy)
SHANTOU
GUANGZHOU (CANTON)
HUIZHOU
DONGGUAN
SHENZHEN
FOSHAN
JIANGMEN
ZHONGSHAN
ZHUHAI
HONG KONG (XIANGGANG)
Macau
ZHANJIANG (Xiashan)
T'AIPEI
T'AICHUNG
T'AINAN
KAOHSIUNG
Chang Jiang (Yangtze)
Dongting Hu
Poyang Hu
Tai Hu
Taiwan Strait
Tropic of Cancer
SOUTH CHINA SEA
Luzon Strait
Qiongzhou Haixia (Hainan Str.)
Zhu Jiang (Pearl R.)
East from Greenwich
COPYRIGHT PHILIP'S
CHINA
VIETNAM
Gulf of Tonkin
HAIKOU
HAINAN
Hainan Dao (China)
Sanya
HAINAN on same scale
a

1:10 000 000

MYANMAR
YANGON (Rangoon)
G. of Mottama
Mawlamyine
THAILAND
BANGKOK (Krung Thep)
SAMUT PRAKAN
Vientiane (Viangchan)
LAOS
VIETNAM
Da Nang
Hue
CAMBODIA
PHNOM PENH
Gulf of Thailand
THANH PHO HO CHI MINH (Saigon)
CAN THO
Paracel Islands
Macclesfield Bank
Scarborough Shoal
SOUTH CHINA SEA
Spratly Islands
ANDAMAN SEA
Malay Peninsula
MALAYSIA
PENINSULAR MALAYSIA
KUALA LUMPUR
SINGAPORE
BATAM
George Town
Ipoh
Straits of Malacca
Banda Aceh
MEDAN
Pekanbaru
Padang
Jambi
PALEMBANG
Bengkulu
Bandar Lampung
JAKARTA
BANDUNG
Semarang
SURABAYA
Denpasar
Kota Kinabalu
BRUNEI
Bandar Seri Begawan
SABAH
SARAWAK
Kuching
Pontianak
Banjarmasin
Samarinda
INDONESIA
Greater Sunda Islands
JAVA SEA
Jawa (Java)
INDIAN OCEAN
Java Trench
Kepulauan Mentawai
Nias
Siberut
Bangka
Belitung
Kepulauan Natuna
Kepulauan Anambas
Selat Karimata
Madura
Bali
Lombok
NUSA TENGGARA BARAT
Projection: Mercator
East from Greenwich

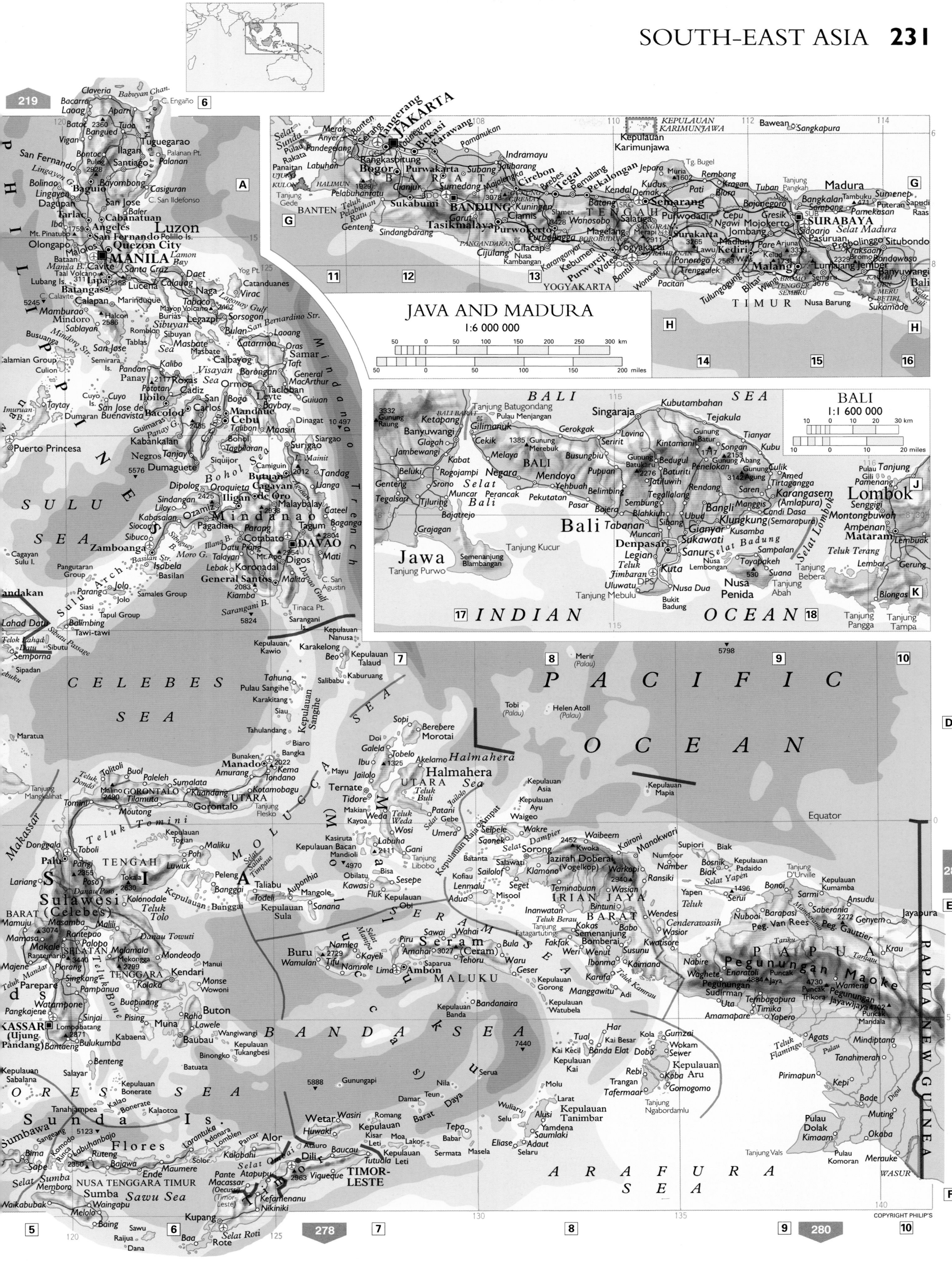

219 286 278 280

20 0 20 40 60 80 100 120 140 160 km

1:3 200 000

20 0 20 40 60 80 100 miles

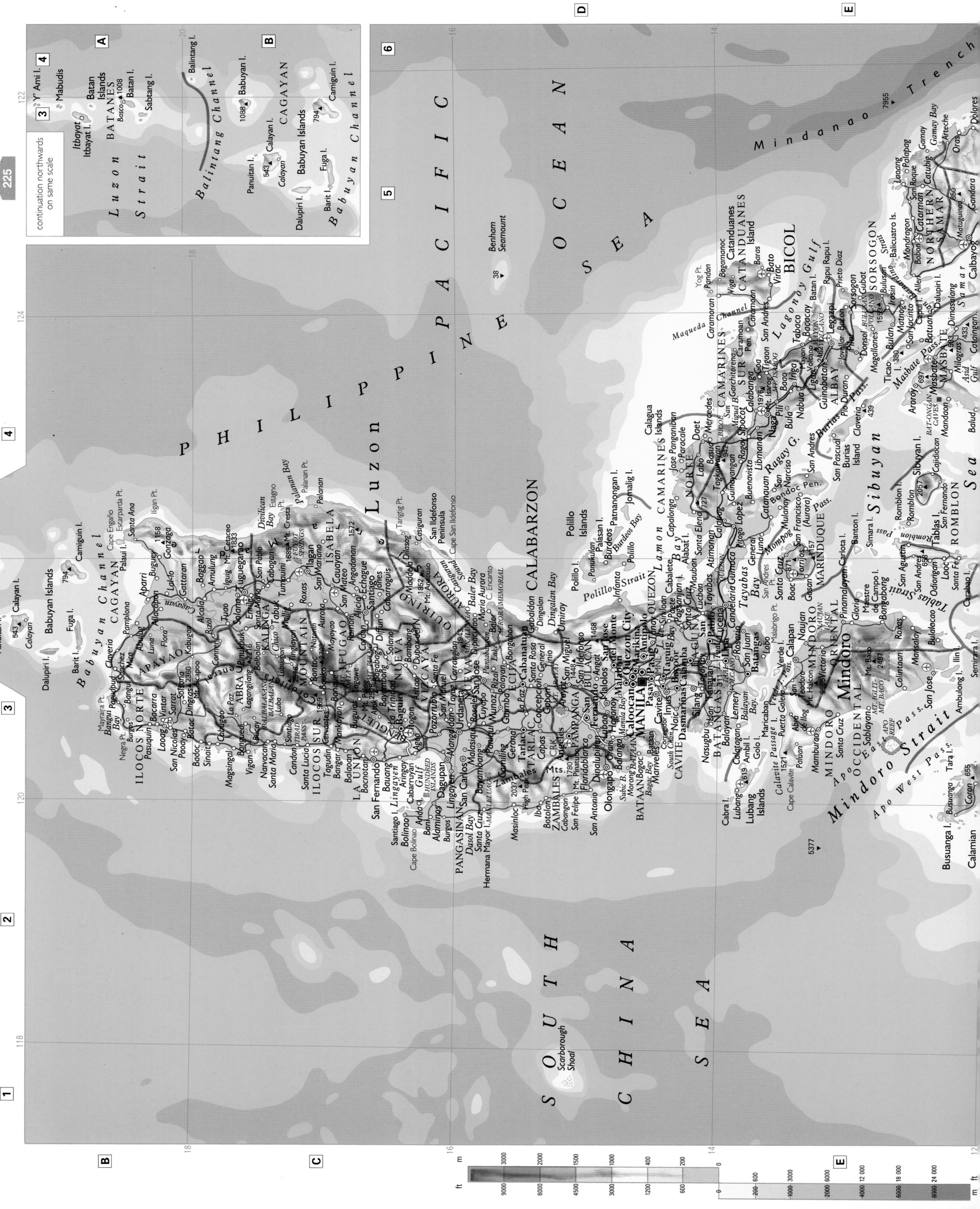

ft m
9000 3000
6000 2000
4500 1500
3000 1000
1200 400
600 200
0 0
200 600
1000 3000
2000 6000
4000 12 000
6000 18 000
8000 24 000
m ft

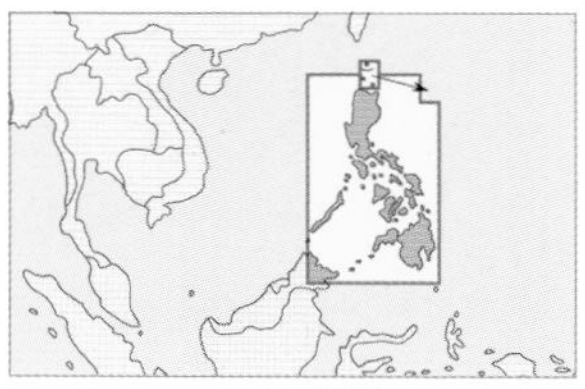

MIMAROPA
Palawan
Puerto Princesa
Cuyo Islands
Cuyo East Pass.
Cuyo West Pass.
Panay
Negros
VISAYAS
Cebu
Bohol
Leyte
SAMAR
EASTERN SAMAR
SOUTHERN LEYTE
DINAGAT ISLANDS
SURIGAO DEL NORTE
SURIGAO DEL SUR
CARAGA
AGUSAN DEL NORTE
AGUSAN DEL SUR
MISAMIS ORIENTAL
MISAMIS OCCIDENTAL
BUKIDNON
LANAO DEL NORTE
LANAO DEL SUR
DAVAO ORIENTAL
DAVAO DEL SUR
DAVAO OCCIDENTAL
Davao
Davao Gulf
NORTH COTABATO
SOUTH COTABATO
SULTAN KUDARAT
SARANGANI
SOCCSKSARGEN
MAGUINDANAO
BANGSAMORO
ZAMBOANGA DEL NORTE
ZAMBOANGA DEL SUR
ZAMBOANGA SIBUGAY
Zamboanga
Mindanao
Moro Gulf
Illana Bay
BASILAN
Basilan I.
SULU
Jolo
TAWI-TAWI
Sulu Archipelago
SULU SEA
CELEBES SEA
Bohol Sea
Visayan Sea
Camotes Sea
Leyte Gulf
Surigao Strait
Panay Gulf
Sibutu Passage
Balabac Str.
Palawan Passage
Tubbataha Reefs
Cagayan Sulu I.
Turtle Islands
MALAYSIA
SABAH
Borneo
Sandakan
Lahad Datu
Pulau Miangas (Indonesia)
Projection: Lambert Conformal Conic
East from Greenwich
COPYRIGHT PHILIP'S
231
235

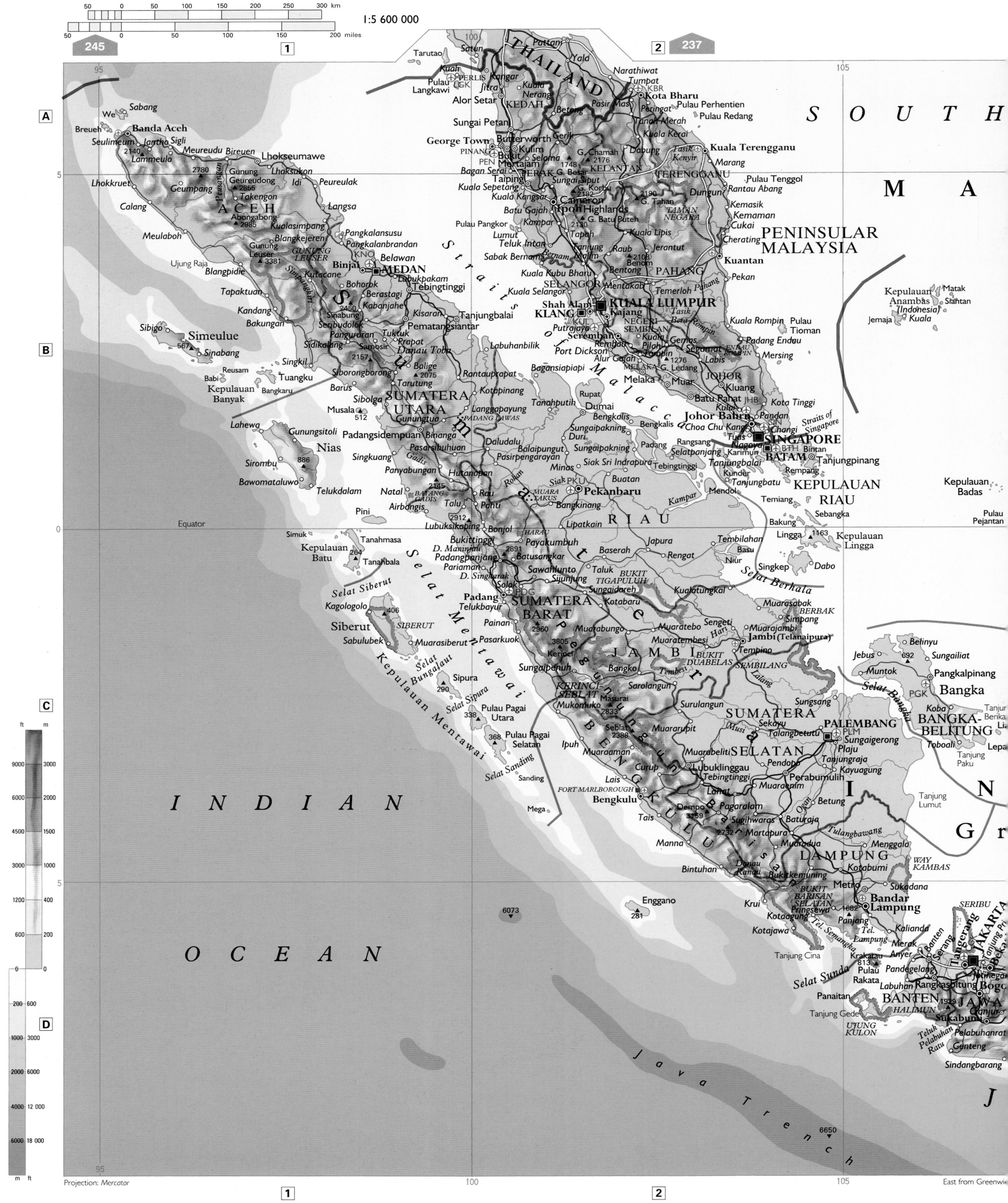
1:5 600 000
km
miles
245
237
Projection: Mercator
East from Greenwich
THAILAND
Pattani
Yala
Narathiwat
Tumpat
Kota Bharu
Satun
Tarutao
Kuah
Pulau Langkawi
PERLIS
Kangar
Jitra
Alor Setar
KEDAH
Sungai Petani
George Town
Butterworth
PINANG
Bukit Mertajam
Bagan Serai
Taiping
PERAK
Kuala Sepetang
Kuala Kangsar
Batu Gajah
Ipoh
Cameron Highlands
Kampar
Tapah
Lumut
Teluk Intan
Pulau Pangkor
Sabak Bernam
Kuala Kubu Bharu
SELANGOR
Kuala Selangor
Shah Alam
KLANG
KUALA LUMPUR
Kajang
Putrajaya
Seremban
NEGERI SEMBILAN
Port Dickson
Alur Gajah
MELAKA
Melaka
Muar
JOHOR
Kluang
Batu Pahat
Kota Tinggi
Johor Bahru
SINGAPORE
Straits of Singapore
BATAM
Bintan
Tanjungpinang
KELANTAN
TERENGGANU
Kuala Terengganu
Marang
Pulau Perhentian
Pulau Redang
Pulau Tenggol
Rantau Abang
Dungun
Kemasik
Kemaman
Cukai
Cherating
Kuantan
PAHANG
Pekan
Temerloh
Mentakab
Bentong
Raub
Jerantut
Kuala Lipis
TAMAN NEGARA
G. Tahan
2190
Kuala Rompin
Pulau Tioman
Mersing
Padang Endau
PENINSULAR MALAYSIA
SOUTH
M A
Kepulauan Anambas (Indonesia)
Matak
Siantan
Jemaja
Kuala
Kepulauan Badas
Pulau Pejantan
Straits of Malacca
Sabang
We
Banda Aceh
Breueh
Seulimeum
Jantho
Sigli
Meureudu
Bireuen
Lhokseumawe
Lhoksukon
Idi
Peureulak
Langsa
Lammeulo
Lhokkruet
Geumpang
Calang
ACEH
Takengon
Meulaboh
Gunung Leuser
3381
Kualasimpang
Blangkejeren
Ujung Raja
Blangpidie
Tapaktuan
Kandang
Bakungan
Simeulue
Sibigo
Sinabang
Singkil
Reusam
Babi
Tuangku
Kepulauan Banyak
Bangkaru
Binjai
MEDAN
Belawan
Pangkalansusu
Pangkalanbrandan
Lubukpakam
Tebingtinggi
Kutacane
Bohorok
Berastagi
Kabanjahe
Sinabung
Seribudolok
Kisaran
Tanjungbalai
Pematangsiantar
Pangururan
Tuktuk
Prapat
Danau Toba
Samosir
Sidikalang
Sibolga
Labuhanbilik
Balige
Tarutung
Barus
SUMATERA UTARA
Rantauprapat
Kotapinang
Musala
Lahewa
Gunungsitoli
Nias
Sirombu
Bawomataluwo
Telukdalam
Padangsidempuan
Gunungtua
Langgapayung
Sumatera
Sipirok
Panyabungan
Natal
Pini
Airbangis
Equator
Simuk
Tanahmasa
Kepulauan Batu
Tanahbala
Lubuksikaping
Bonjol
Bukittinggi
Payakumbuh
Padangpanjang
Batusangkar
Pariaman
Sawahlunto
Solok
Padang
Telukbayur
Painan
SUMATERA BARAT
Selat Siberut
Kagologolo
Siberut
Sabulubek
Muarasiberut
Selat Mentawai
Kepulauan Mentawai
Sipura
Selat Bungalaut
Selat Sipura
Pulau Pagai Utara
Pulau Pagai Selatan
Selat Sanding
Sanding
Mega
Dumai
Rupat
Bengkalis
Tanahputih
Bagansiapiapi
Duri
Sungaipakning
Balaipungut
Pasirpengarayan
Minas
Siak Sri Indrapura
Pekanbaru
Buatan
Bangkinang
Kampar
Lipatkain
RIAU
Japura
Rengat
Baserah
Taluk
Tembilahan
Kuala Enok
Selat Berhala
Singkep
Dabo
Lingga
Kepulauan Lingga
KEPULAUAN RIAU
Tanjungbalai
Kundur
Tanjungbatu
Sebangka
Kualatungkal
Muarasabak
Jambi (Telanaipura)
Muarabungo
Muaratebo
Muaratembesi
JAMBI
Bangko
Sarolangun
Sungaipenuh
Kerinci
3805
Mukomuko
Ipuh
Muaraaman
Lais
Bengkulu
FORT MARLBOROUGH
BENGKULU
Curup
Lubuklinggau
Tebingtinggi
Lahat
Pagaralam
Dempo
Tais
Manna
Bintuhan
Krui
Kotaagung
Kotajawa
Muararupit
Muarabeliti
SUMATERA SELATAN
Surulangun
Sekayu
Talangbetutu
PALEMBANG
Sungaigerong
Plaju
Tanjungraja
Kayuagung
Prabumulih
Muaraenim
Baturaja
Martapura
Muaradua
LAMPUNG
Kotabumi
Menggala
WAY KAMBAS
Metro
Sukadana
Bandar Lampung
Panjang
Kalianda
Tanjung Cina
Selat Sunda
Krakatau
Pulau Rakata
Panaitan
Tanjung Gede
UJUNG KULON
BANTEN
Serang
Banten
Tangerang
JAKARTA
Pandeglang
Labuhan
Rangkasbitung
Bogor
Sukabumi
Cianjur
Pelabuhanratu
Genteng
Sindangbarang
JAWA
Enggano
6073
Bangka
Pangkalpinang
Muntok
Belinyu
Sungailiat
Jebus
Selat Bangka
Koba
BANGKA-BELITUNG
Toboali
Tanjung Lumut
INDIAN OCEAN
Java Trench
6650

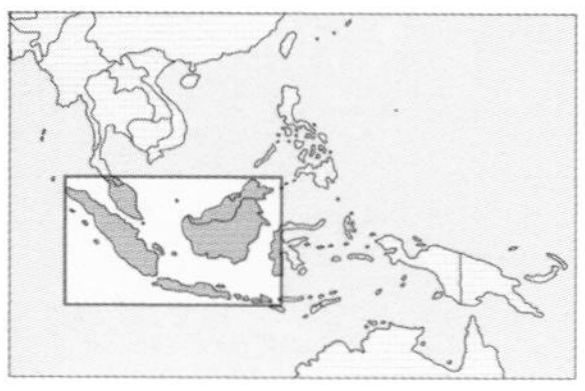

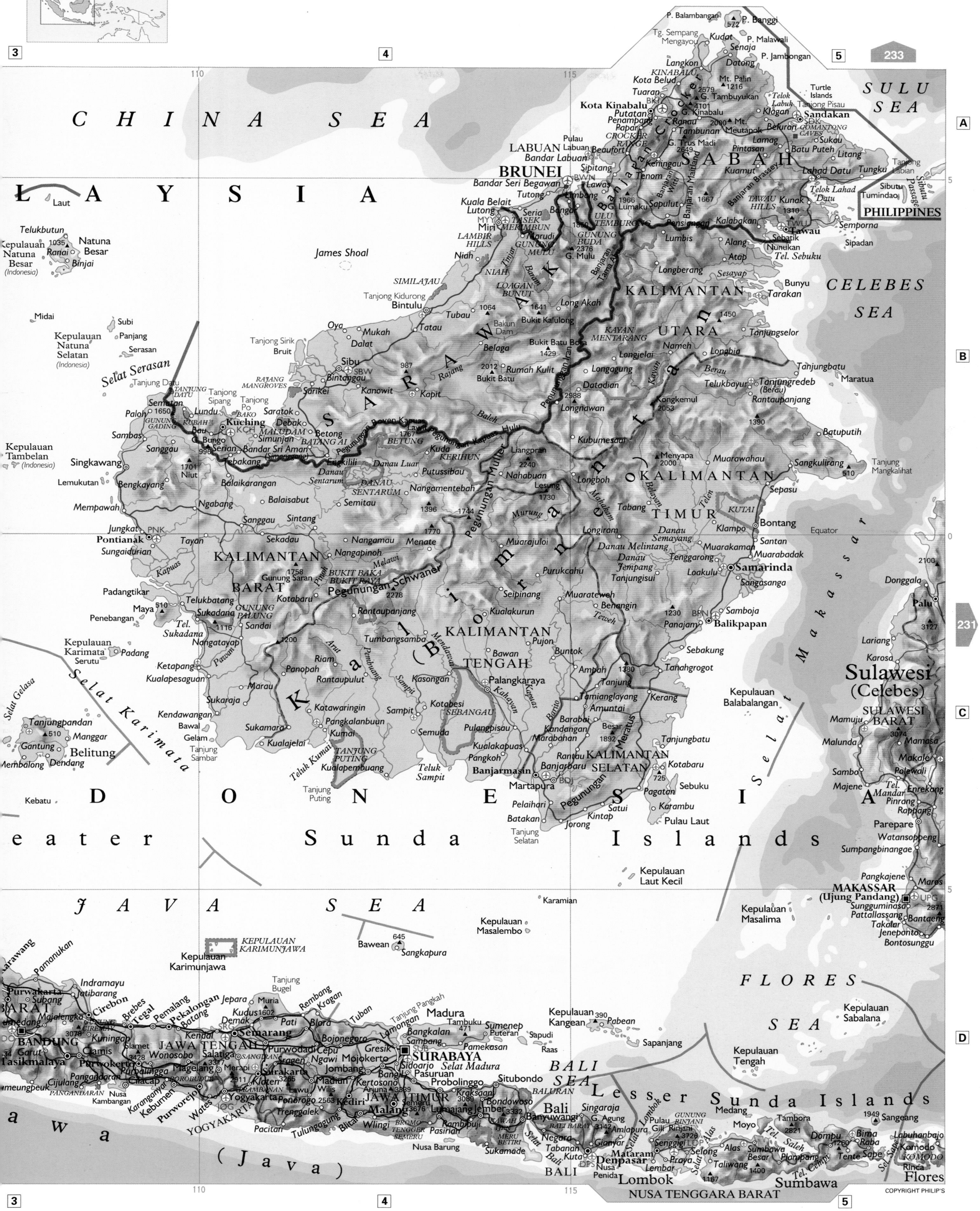
3
4
5
233
231
A
B
C
D
110
115
5
0
CHINA SEA
MALAYSIA
Laut
Telukbutun
Kepulauan Natuna Besar (Indonesia)
Natuna Besar
Ranai
Binjai
1035
James Shoal
Midai
Subi
Panjang
Serasan
Kepulauan Natuna Selatan (Indonesia)
Selat Serasan
Tanjung Datu
Kepulauan Tambelan (Indonesia)
Singkawang
Lemukutan
Bengkayang
Mempawah
Jungkat
Pontianak
Sungaidurian
Tayan
PNK
Paloh
Sambas
Sematan
Lundu
Kuching
KCH
Bau
Bungo
Serian
Simunjan
Bandar Sri Aman (Simanggang)
Sanggau
Tebakang
Niut
1701
1650
996
Balaikarangan
Balaisabut
Ngabang
Sanggau
Sekadau
Sintang
Tanjung Sipang
Tanjung Po
Saratok
Debak
Betong
Engkilili
Danau Sentarum
DANAU SENTARUM
Danau Luar
Putussibau
Nangamentebah
Semitau
SIMILAJAU
Tanjung Kidurong
Bintulu
Tanjung Sirik
Bruit
Oya
Mukah
Dalat
Sibu
SBW
Bintangau
Sarikei
Kanowit
Kapit
Tatau
Tubau
Belaga
Bakun Dam
Bukit Kalulong
Bukit Batu Bora
1429
1064
1641
987
2012
Rumah Kulit
Bukit Batu
Rajang
Baleh
SARAWAK
LAMBIR HILLS
Niah
NIAH
Miri
MYY
Marudi
LOAGAN BUNUT
Long Akah
G. Mulu
GUNUNG MULU
GUNUNG BUDA
2376
Lutong
Kuala Belait
Seria
TASEK MERIMBUN
Tutong
Bandar Seri Begawan
BRUNEI
BWN
LABUAN
Bandar Labuan
Pulau Labuan
Sipitang
Beaufort
Lawas
Limbang
Bangar
ULU TEMBURONG
1850
Tenom
Keningau
Sapulut
Lumaku
1966
Tinjar
Baram
Pegunungan Iran
Banjaran Tama Abu
Banjaran Crocker
Banjaran Witti
Banjaran Maitland
Banjaran Brassey
P. Balambangan
P. Banggi
572
Tg. Sempang Mengayau
Kudat
P. Malawali
Senaja
P. Jambongan
Langkon
KINABALU
Kota Belud
Tuaran
BKI
Kota Kinabalu
Putatan
Penampang
Papar
CROCKER RANGE
G. Kinabalu
4101
2579
G. Tambuyukan
Ranau
Tambunan
Mt. Palin
1216
Datong
Mt. Meutapok
2000
G. Trus Madi
2649
SABAH
Pintasan
Lamag
Beluran
Klagan
Telok Labuk
Tanjong Pisau
Turtle Islands
Sandakan
SDK
GOMANTONG CAVES
Sukau
Batu Puteh
Litang
Kuamut
Lahad Datu
Tungku
Tanjong Labian
Telok Lahad Datu
TAWAU HILLS
Kunak
1310
1667
Tawau
TWU
Semporna
Sibutu
Tumindao
Sibutu Passage
PHILIPPINES
SULU SEA
Sipadan
Sebatik
Nunukan
Tel. Sebuku
Kalabakan
Pensiangan
Lumbis
Alang
Atap
Sesayap
Longberang
KALIMANTAN UTARA
Tarakan
Bunyu
CELEBES SEA
1450
Tanjungselor
KAYAN MENTARANG
Nameh
Longjelai
Longbia
Longagung
Datodian
Kayan
Berau
Telukbayur
Tanjungredeb (Berau)
Rantaupanjang
Tanjungbatu
Maratua
Kongkemul
2053
2988
Longnawan
1390
Batuputih
Kubumesaai
Liangpran
Pegunungan Kapuas Hulu
Boven Kapuas
Lawit
1767
BETUNG KERIHUN
Kuda
2240
Nahabuan
Menyapa
2000
Muarawahau
Sangkulirang
510
Tanjung Mangkalihat
Lesung
1730
Longboh
Mahakam
Belayan
Telen
KALIMANTAN TIMUR
KUTAI
Sepasu
Tabang
Longiram
Bontang
Klampo
Equator
Santan
Muarabadak
Danau Semayang
Danau Melintang
Danau Jempang
Muarakaman
Tenggarong
Samarinda
Loakulu
Tanjungisui
Sangasanga
Pegunungan Muller
Murung
1744
1396
1770
Nangamau
Menate
Nangapinoh
Melawi
Muarajuloi
Purukcahu
Kalimantan (Borneo)
KALIMANTAN BARAT
Gunung Saran
1758
Pinoh
BUKIT BAKA BUKIT RAYA
Pegunungan Schwaner
2278
Kotabaru
Telukbatang
Padangtikar
Maya
510
Penebangan
Sukadana
Tel. Sukadana
GUNUNG PALUNG
1116
Sandai
Kapuas
Rantaupanjang
Seipinang
Kualakurun
Muaratewoh
Benangin
Teweh
1230
Panajam
BRN
Samboja
Balikpapan
Kepulauan Karimata
Serutu
Padang
Nangatayap
Pawan
1200
Tumbangsamba
Arut
Riam
Pembuang
Mendawai
KALIMANTAN TENGAH
Bawan
Pujon
Buntok
Ampah
1380
Sebakung
Tanahgrogot
Panopah
Rantaupulut
Kasongan
Palangkaraya
Kahayan
Kapuas
Barito
Tanjung
Tamianglayang
Amuntai
Kerang
Kepulauan Balabalangan
Selat Makasar
Ketapang
Kualapesaguan
Marau
Sukaraja
Kendawangan
Bawal
Gelam
Tanjung Sambar
Kotawaringin
Pangkalanbuun
Kumai
Sukamara
Kualajelai
Teluk Kumai
TANJUNG PUTING
Kualapembuang
Tanjung Puting
Sampit
Kotabesi
SEBANGAU
Semuda
Teluk Sampit
Pulangpisau
Kualakapuas
Pangkoh
Banjarmasin
Barabai
Kandangan
Marabahan
Besar
1892
Meratus
Rantau
Banjarbaru
BDJ
Martapura
KALIMANTAN SELATAN
Pegunungan Meratus
Tanjungbatu
Kotabaru
725
Pagatan
Sebuku
Karambu
Pulau Laut
Pelaihari
Batakan
Jorong
Kintap
Satui
Tanjung Selatan
Selat Gelasa
Selat Karimata
Tanjungpandan
Manggar
510
Gantung
Belitung
Membalong
Dendang
Kebatu
INDONESIA
Greater Sunda Islands
Kepulauan Laut Kecil
Karamian
Kepulauan Masalembo
JAVA SEA
KEPULAUAN KARIMUNJAWA
Kepulauan Karimunjawa
Bawean
645
Sangkapura
Kepulauan Masalima
Sulawesi (Celebes)
SULAWESI BARAT
2100
Donggala
Palu
3127
Lariang
Karosa
Mamuju
Malunda
3074
Mamasa
Makale
Polewali
Sambo
Majene
Tel. Mandar
Enrekang
Pinrang
Rappang
Parepare
Watansoppeng
Sumpangbinangae
Pangkajene
Maros
MAKASSAR (Ujung Pandang)
UPG
2871
Sungguminasa
Pattallassang
Bantaeng
Takalar
Jeneponto
Bontosunggu
FLORES SEA
Kepulauan Sabalana
Kepulauan Tengah
Karawang
Pamanukan
Subang
Purwakarta
Indramayu
Jatibarang
Cirebon
Majalengka
Brebes
Tegal
Pemalang
Pekalongan
Batang
BARAT
Sumedang
BANDUNG
Garut
Tasikmalaya
Kuningan
Slamet
3428
Ciamis
Purwokerto
Purbalingga
Wonosobo
JAWA TENGAH
Kendal
Semarang
Kudus
Jepara
Muria
1602
Tanjung Bugel
Demak
Pati
Rembang
Kragan
Blora
Tuban
Bojonegoro
Tanjung Pangkah
Madura
Tambuku
471
Sumenep
Puteran
Sapudi
Raas
Bangkalan
Sampang
Pamekasan
Kepulauan Kangean
390
Pabean
Sapanjang
Salatiga
Merapi
2911
Magelang
Purwodadi
Sragen
Surakarta
Klaten
Cepu
Ngawi
Mojokerto
Gresik
SURABAYA
SUB
Sidoarjo
Bangil
Pasuruan
Selat Madura
Probolinggo
Situbondo
Jombang
Madiun
Wilis
Kertosono
Arjuna
3339
Kediri
JAWA TIMUR
Semeru
3676
Malang
Lumajang
Jember
3332
Bondowoso
Banyuwangi
Ponorogo
Trenggalek
Tulungagung
Blitar
Wlingi
BROMO TENGGER SEMERU
Pasirian
Rambipuji
Nusa Barung
MERU BETIRI
Sukamade
BALURAN
Cilacap
Nusa Kambangan
PANGANDARAN
Cijulang
Pangandaran
Kebumen
Karanganyar
Purworejo
Wates
Yogyakarta
YOGYAKARTA
JOG
Lawu
3265
2563
Pacitan
Jawa (Java)
BALI SEA
Bali
Singaraja
G. Agung
3142
BALI BARAT
Negara
Tabanan
Kuta
Denpasar
DPS
Amlapura
Selat Bali
Selat Lombok
BALI
Nusa Penida
Lesser Sunda Islands
Pulau Gili
GUNUNG RINJANI
Rinjani
3726
Senggigi
Mataram
Praya
Selong
Lembar
Lombok
Selat Alas
Alas
1167
Sumbawa Besar
Taliwang
1400
Sumbawa
Medang
Moyo
Tel. Saleh
Tambora
2821
Dompu
Plampang
Tel. Cempi
Bima
Raba
1260
Tente
Sape
1949
Sangeang
Labuhanbajo
Komodo
KOMODO
Rinca
Flores
Selat Sape
NUSA TENGGARA BARAT

1:4 800 000
50 0 50 100 150 200 km
50 0 50 100 150 miles
Gulf of Tonkin
HAINAN
Hainan Dao
MYANMAR (BURMA)
THAILAND
CAMBODIA
LAOS
VIETNAM
YUNNAN
ANDAMAN SEA
BANGKOK
HANOI
VIENTIANE
NAY PYI TAW

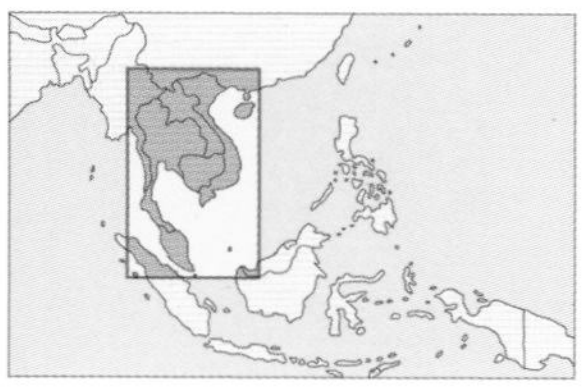

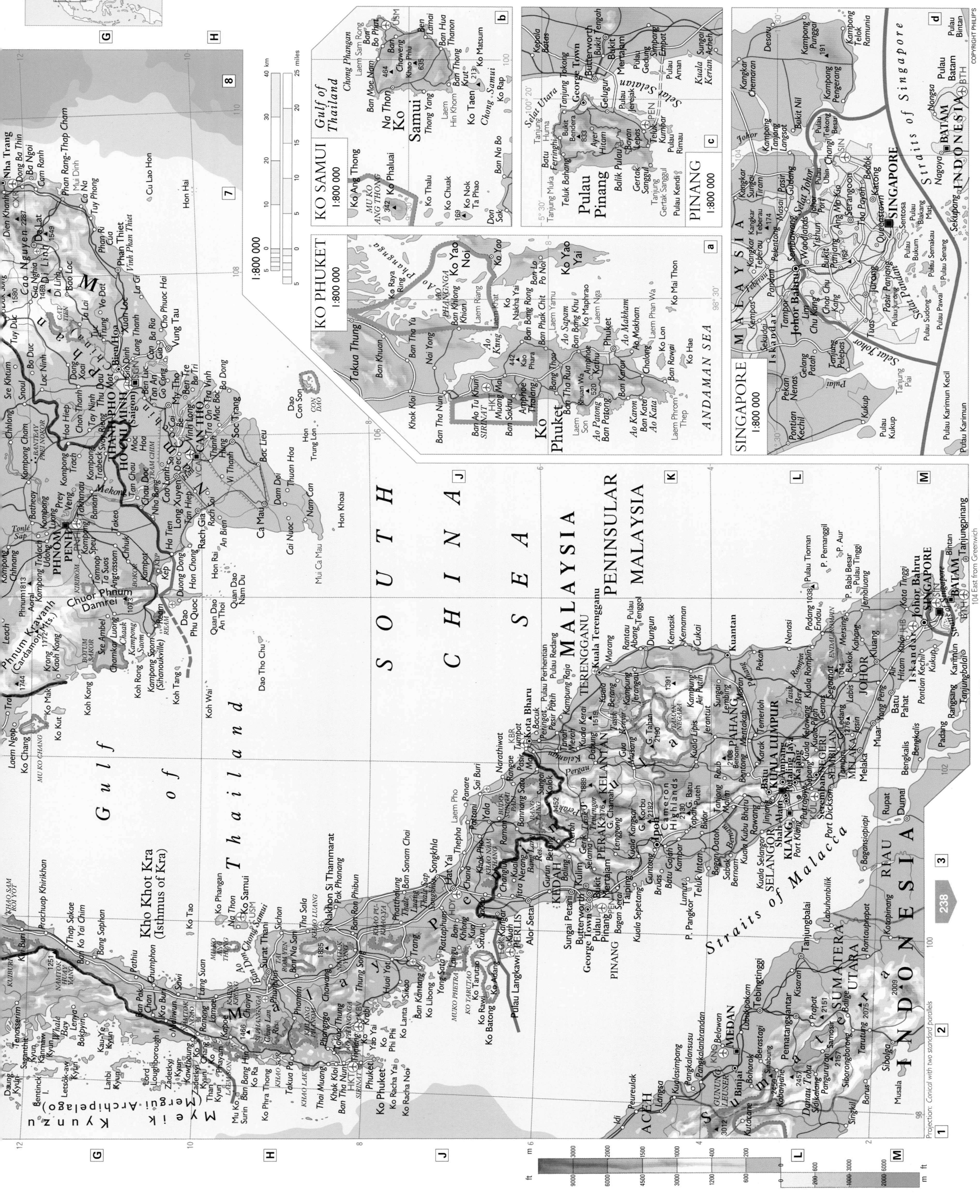
1:800 000
KO PHUKET
1:800 000
KO SAMUI
1:800 000
PINANG
1:800 000
SINGAPORE
1:800 000
Gulf of Thailand
ANDAMAN SEA
SOUTH CHINA SEA
Gulf of Thailand
Kho Khot Kra (Isthmus of Kra)
Straits of Malacca
MALAYSIA
PENINSULAR MALAYSIA
INDONESIA
SUMATERA UTARA
RIAU
ACEH
KELANTAN
TERENGGANU
PAHANG
PERAK
KEDAH
PERLIS
PINANG
SELANGOR
JOHOR
MELAKA
KUALA LUMPUR
SINGAPORE
PHNOM PENH
THANH PHO HO CHI MINH (Saigon)
CAN THO
MEDAN
Myeik Kyunzu (Mergui Archipelago)
Straits of Singapore
Projection: Conical with two standard parallels
104 East from Greenwich
238
COPYRIGHT PHILIP'S

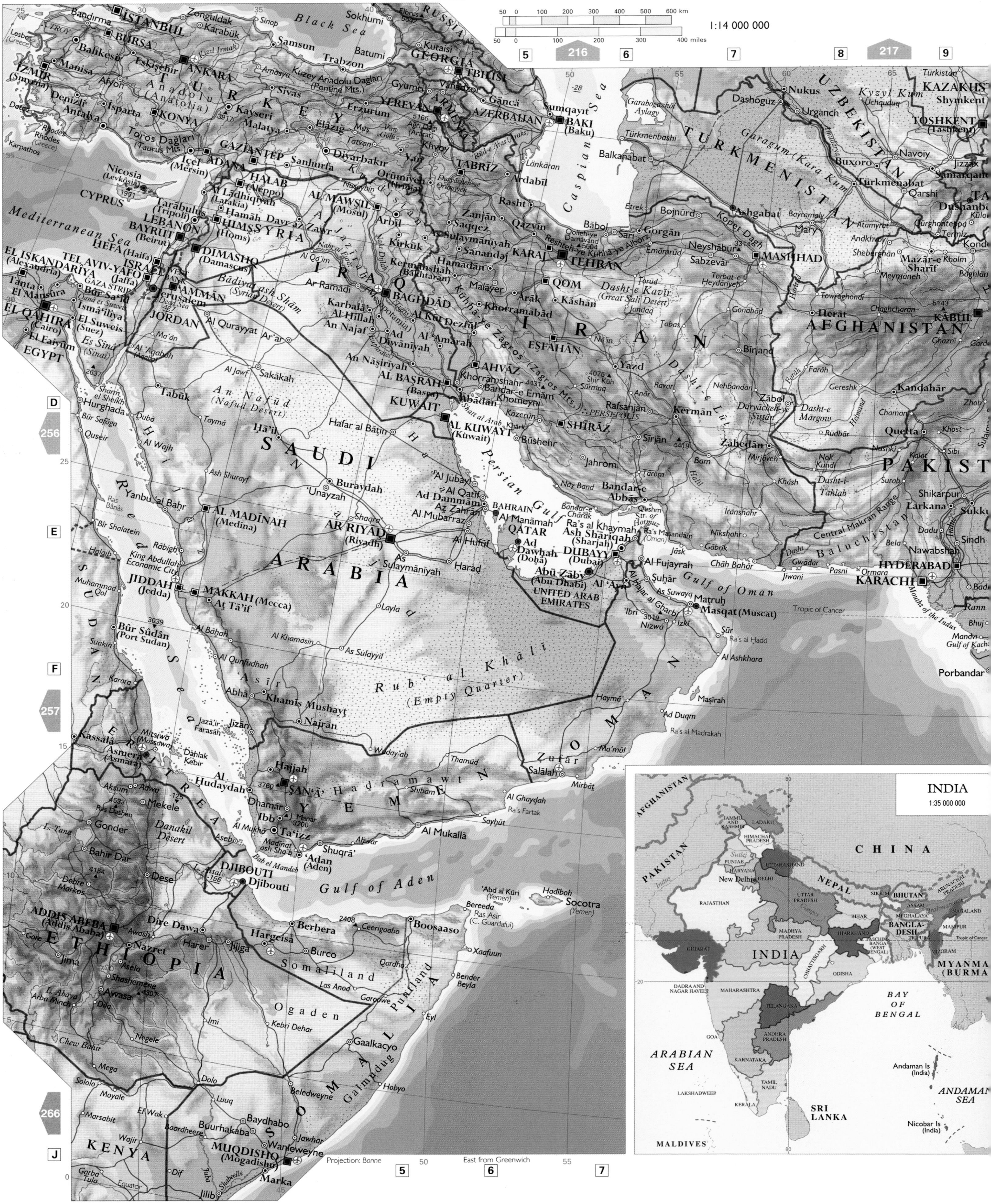
1:14 000 000
Black Sea
Caspian Sea
Mediterranean Sea
Persian Gulf
Gulf of Oman
Gulf of Aden
Tropic of Cancer
TURKEY
GEORGIA
ARMENIA
AZERBAIJAN
CYPRUS
LEBANON
SYRIA
ISRAEL
JORDAN
EGYPT
IRAQ
IRAN
KUWAIT
SAUDI ARABIA
BAHRAIN
QATAR
UNITED ARAB EMIRATES
OMAN
YEMEN
ERITREA
DJIBOUTI
ETHIOPIA
SOMALIA
KENYA
SUDAN
TURKMENISTAN
UZBEKISTAN
AFGHANISTAN
PAKISTAN
ISTANBUL
ANKARA
BAKI (Baku)
TEHRĀN
BAGHDĀD
DIMASHQ (Damascus)
BAYRŪT (Beirut)
'AMMĀN
EL QAHIRA (Cairo)
AR RIYĀD (Riyadh)
AL KUWAYT (Kuwait)
MAKKAH (Mecca)
JIDDAH (Jedda)
ŞAN'Ā'
Masqat (Muscat)
DUBAYY (Dubai)
Abū Zaby (Abu Dhabi)
ADDIS ABEBA (Addis Ababa)
MUQDISHO (Mogadishu)
KARACHI
Djibouti
Rub' al Khālī (Empty Quarter)
Socotra
Projection: Bonne
East from Greenwich
INDIA
1:35 000 000
CHINA
NEPAL
BHUTAN
BANGLADESH
SRI LANKA
MALDIVES
ARABIAN SEA
BAY OF BENGAL
ANDAMAN SEA
MYANMAR (BURMA)

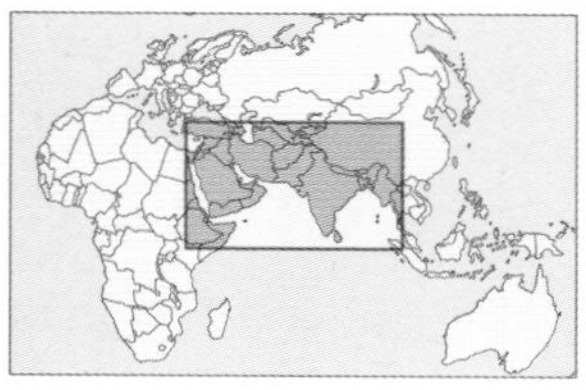

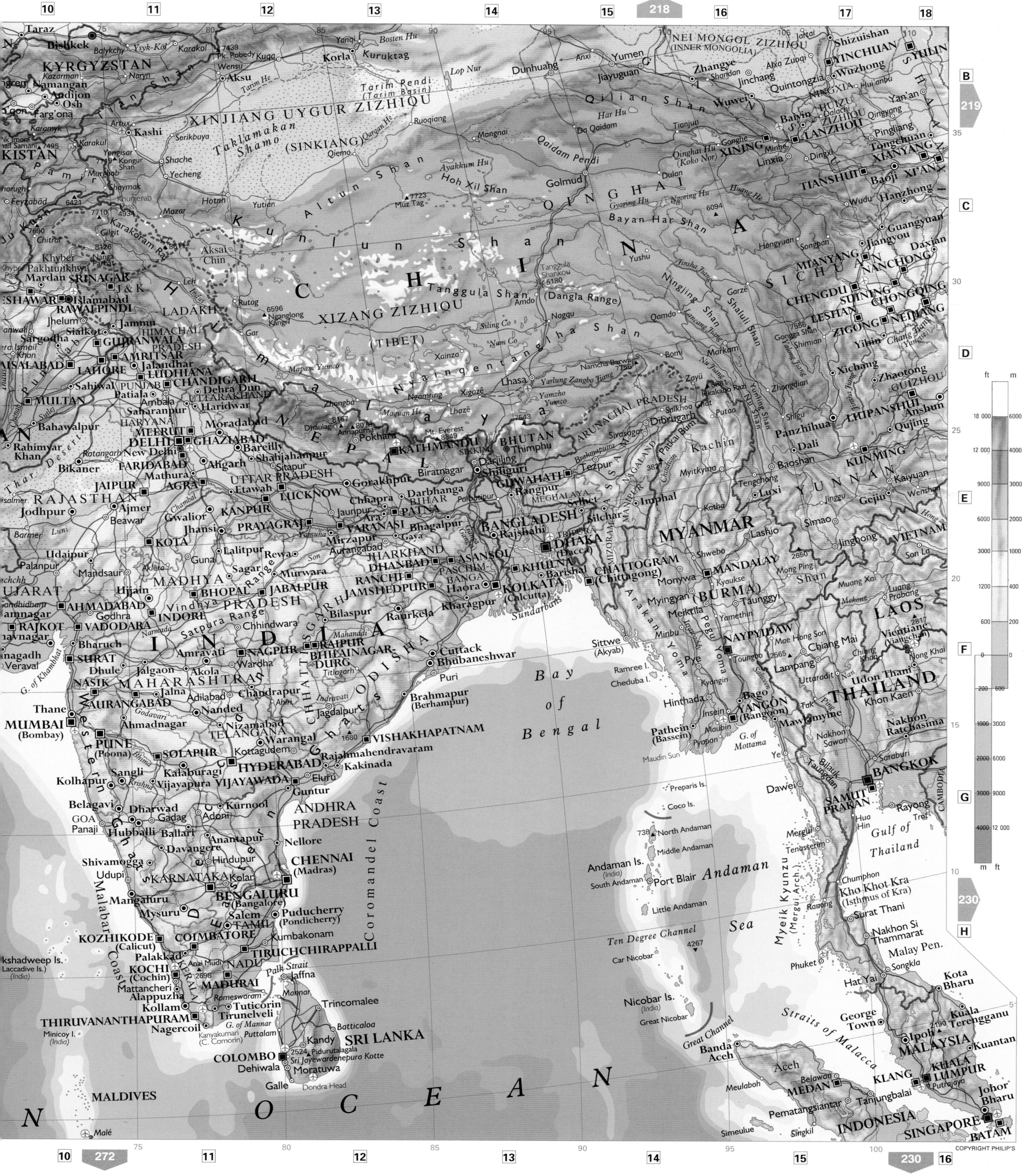
218
219
230
272
KYRGYZSTAN
Bishkek
XINJIANG UYGUR ZIZHIQU
(SINKIANG)
Tarim Pendi
(Tarim Basin)
Taklamakan Shamo
Kunlun Shan
Altun Shan
QINGHAI
Qaidam Pendi
Qilian Shan
NEI MONGOL ZIZHIQU
(INNER MONGOLIA)
CHINA
XIZANG ZIZHIQU
(TIBET)
Tanggula Shan
(Dangla Range)
Nyainqentanglha Shan
Himalaya
Karakoram Ra.
Kashi
Golmud
Lhasa
XINING
LANZHOU
XI'AN
CHENGDU
CHONGQING
KUNMING
SICHUAN
YUNNAN
GUIZHOU
ISLAMABAD
RAWALPINDI
LAHORE
SRINAGAR
KATHMANDU
NEPAL
Mt. Everest
8849
BHUTAN
Thimphu
DELHI
New Delhi
LUCKNOW
KANPUR
PRAYAGRAJ
VARANASI
PATNA
JAIPUR
RAJASTHAN
Thar Desert
AHMADABAD
INDORE
BHOPAL
MADHYA PRADESH
UTTAR PRADESH
BIHAR
JHARKHAND
KOLKATA
(Calcutta)
BANGLADESH
DHAKA
(Dacca)
CHATTOGRAM
(Chittagong)
INDIA
MAHARASHTRA
MUMBAI
(Bombay)
PUNE
(Poona)
NAGPUR
HYDERABAD
TELANGANA
ANDHRA PRADESH
ODISHA
VISHAKHAPATNAM
KARNATAKA
BENGALURU
(Bangalore)
CHENNAI
(Madras)
Coromandel Coast
Malabar Coast
Western Ghats
Eastern Ghats
Bay of Bengal
SRI LANKA
COLOMBO
Sri Jayewardenepura Kotte
MALDIVES
Malé
Lakshadweep Is.
(India)
MYANMAR
(BURMA)
MANDALAY
NAYPYIDAW
YANGON
(Rangoon)
Andaman Is.
(India)
Port Blair
Andaman Sea
Ten Degree Channel
Nicobar Is.
(India)
THAILAND
BANGKOK
Gulf of Thailand
LAOS
Vientiane
VIETNAM
MALAYSIA
KUALA LUMPUR
Straits of Malacca
SINGAPORE
INDONESIA
MEDAN
OCEAN
Kho Khot Kra
(Isthmus of Kra)
Malay Pen.

1:5 600 000

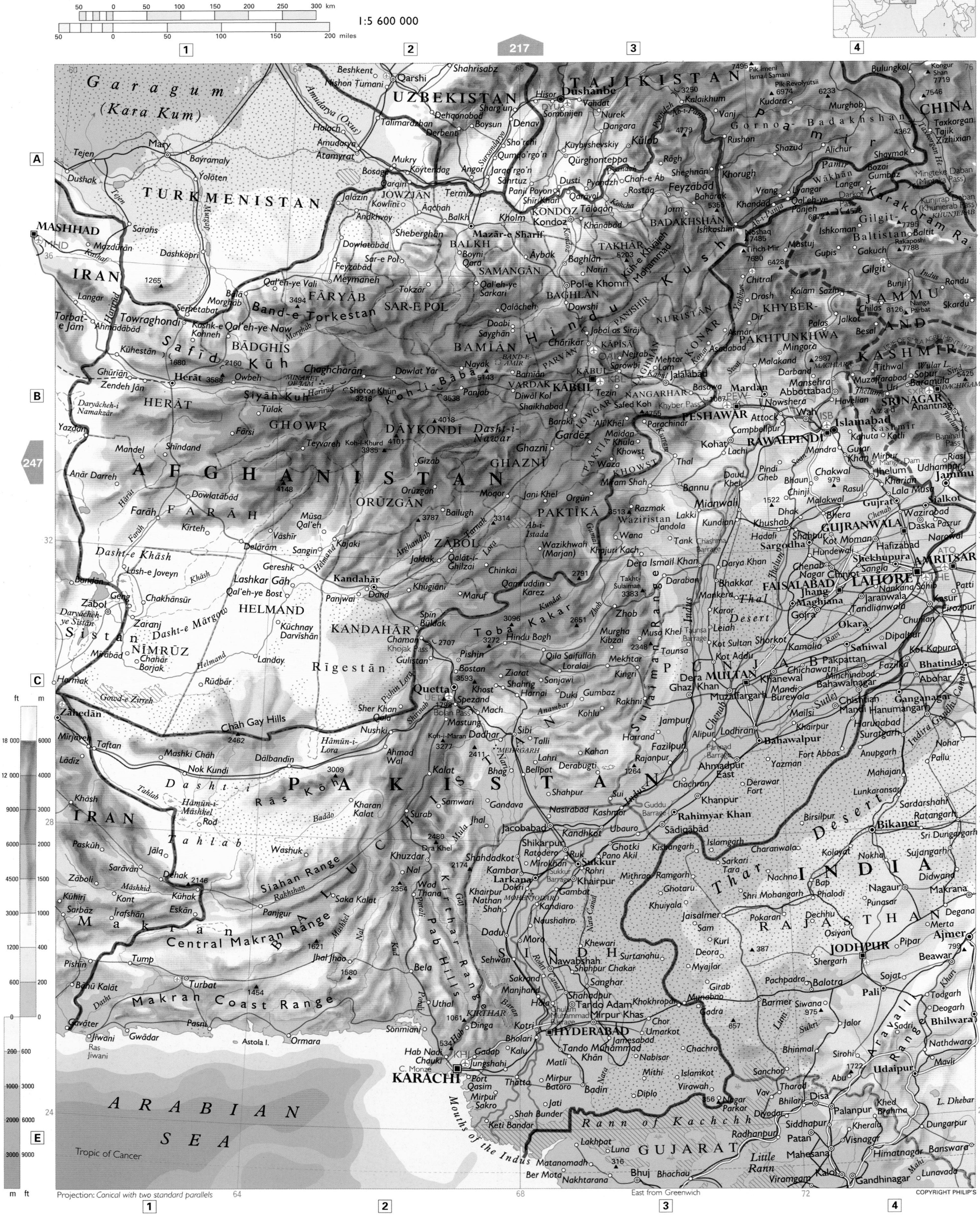

217
247
242
Garagum (Kara Kum)
UZBEKISTAN
TAJIKISTAN
TURKMENISTAN
CHINA
IRAN
AFGHANISTAN
PAKISTAN
INDIA
JAMMU AND KASHMIR
KHYBER-PAKHTUNKHWA
BALUCHISTAN
PUNJAB
SINDH
RAJASTHAN
GUJARAT
ARABIAN SEA
Tropic of Cancer
Hindu Kush
Safīd Kūh
Band-e Torkestan
Koh-i-Bābā
Siyāh Kūh
Pamir
Karakoram Ra.
Sulaiman Range
Toba Kakar
Kirthar Range
Pab Hills
Central Makran Range
Makran Coast Range
Siahan Range
Rās Koh
Dasht-i-Margow
Dasht-e Khāsh
Rīgestān
Thal Desert
Thar Desert
Rann of Kachchh
Mouths of the Indus
Dushanbe
Kābul
Islamabad
Rawalpindi
Peshawar
Lahore
Faisalabad
Multan
Quetta
Hyderabad
Karachi
Kandahār
Herāt
Mashhad
Mazār-e Sharif
Srinagar
Amritsar
Jodhpur
Bikaner
Ahmadabad
Zāhedān
Gwādar
Bahawalpur
Sukkur
Jammu
Mary
Qarshi
Projection: Conical with two standard parallels
East from Greenwich
COPYRIGHT PHILIP'S

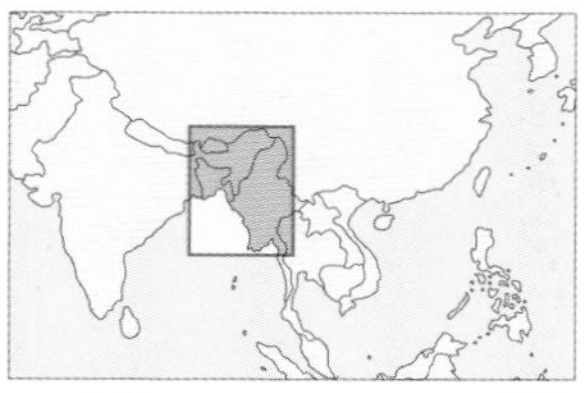

1:4 800 000

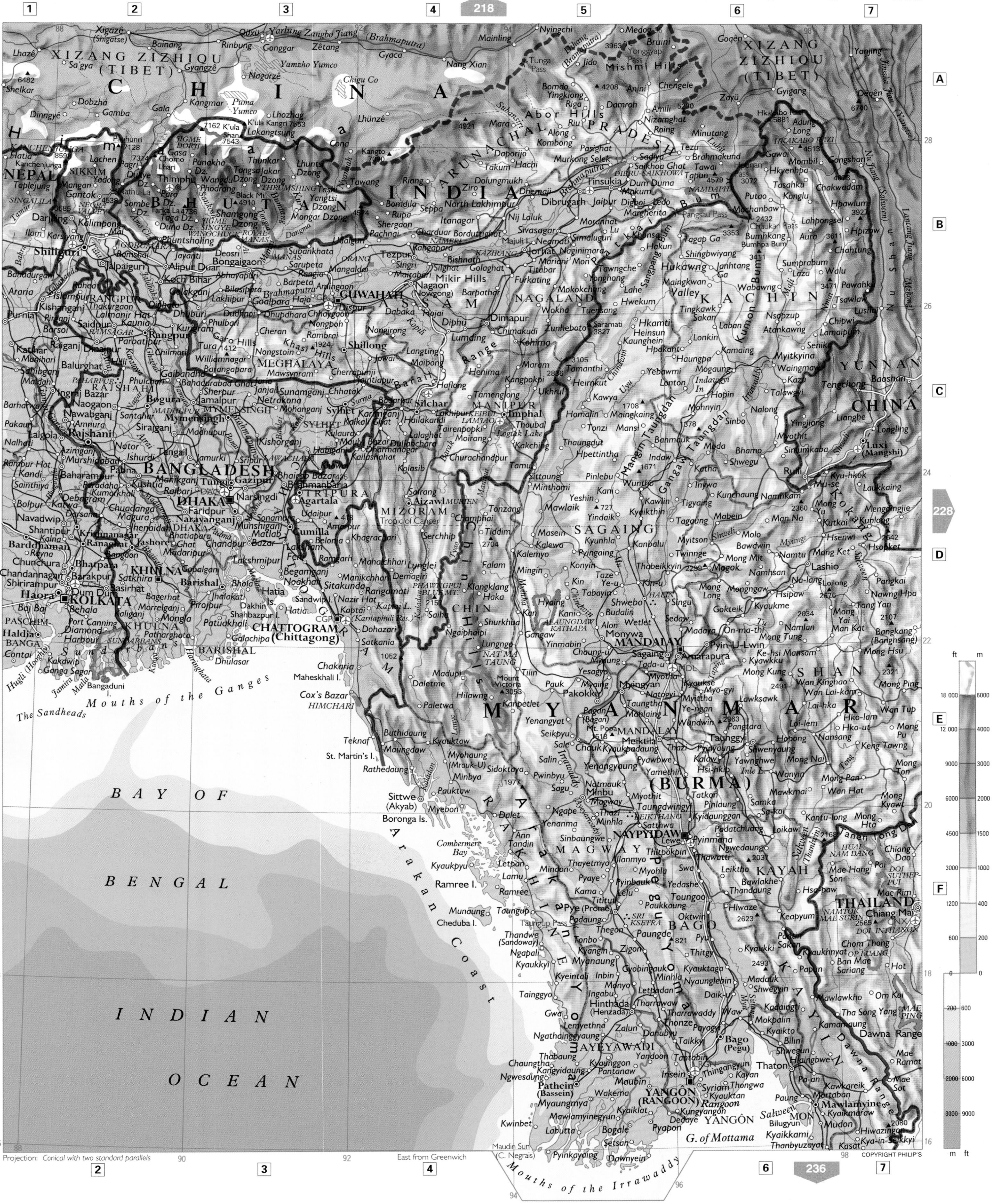
218
228
243
236
A
B
C
D
E
F
G
1
2
3
4
5
6
7
XIZANG ZIZHIQU (TIBET)
CHINA
NEPAL
SIKKIM
BHUTAN
INDIA
ARUNACHAL PRADESH
ASSAM
MEGHALAYA
NAGALAND
MANIPUR
MIZORAM
TRIPURA
BANGLADESH
DHAKA
RAJSHAHI
RANGPUR
MYMENSINGH
SYLHET
KHULNA
BARISHAL
CHATTOGRAM
Chattogram (Chittagong)
KOLKATA
Haora
Guwahati
Shillong
Imphal
Aizawl
Agartala
Thimphu
Gangtok
Darjiling
Shiliguri
Dibrugarh
Tropic of Cancer
MYANMAR (BURMA)
KACHIN
SAGAING
CHIN
MANDALAY
MAGWAY
RAKHINE
BAGO
AYEYAWADI
YANGÔN
SHAN
KAYAH
KAYIN
MON
NAYPYIDAW
Mandalay
Yangon (Rangoon)
Bago (Pegu)
Pathein (Bassein)
Mawlamyine
Sittwe (Akyab)
Lashio
Myitkyina
YUNNAN
THAILAND
Chiang Mai
Mouths of the Ganges
Mouths of the Irrawaddy
The Sandheads
BAY OF BENGAL
INDIAN OCEAN
Arakan Coast
G. of Mottama
Ramree I.
Cheduba I.
Arakan Yoma
Pegu Yoma
Mishmi Hills
Abor Hills
Mikir Hills
Khasi Hills
Garo Hills
Kumon Bum
Dawna Range
Projection: Conical with two standard parallels
East from Greenwich
COPYRIGHT PHILIP'S

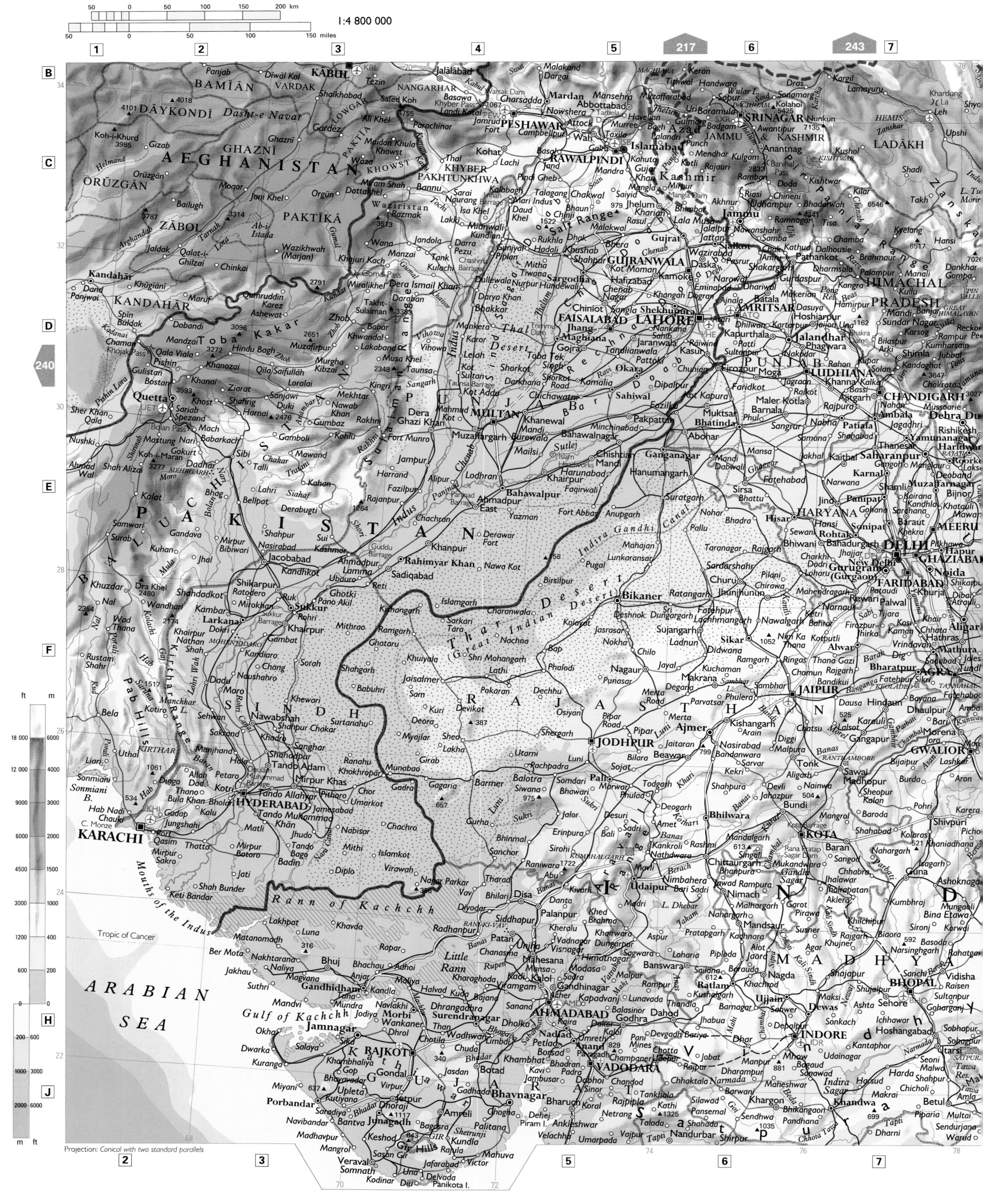

1:4 800 000
km
miles
AFGHANISTAN
PAKISTAN
ARABIAN SEA
BALUCHISTAN
PUNJAB
SINDH
RAJASTHAN
HARYANA
HIMACHAL PRADESH
KHYBER PAKHTUNKHWA
Azad Kashmir
JAMMU & KASHMIR
LADAKH
MADHYA PRADESH
Thar Desert
Great Indian Desert
Rann of Kachchh
Little Rann
Gulf of Kachchh
Mouths of the Indus
Tropic of Cancer
KABUL
ISLAMABAD
RAWALPINDI
PESHAWAR
LAHORE
FAISALABAD
GUJRANWALA
MULTAN
HYDERABAD
KARACHI
SRINAGAR
AMRITSAR
LUDHIANA
CHANDIGARH
DELHI
New Delhi
JAIPUR
JODHPUR
AHMADABAD
VADODARA
RAJKOT
INDORE
BHOPAL
KOTA
GWALIOR
Quetta
Kandahar
Sukkur
Bikaner
Ajmer
Udaipur
Projection: Conical with two standard parallels

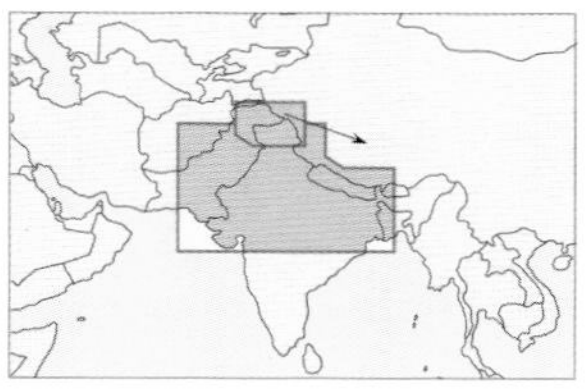

JAMMU AND KASHMIR
on same scale
East from Greenwich
CHINA
XIZANG ZIZHIQU (TIBET)
XINJIANG UYGUR ZIZHIQU (SINKIANG)
AFGHANISTAN
KHYBER PAKHTUNKHWA (N.W. FRONTIER)
Gilgit-Baltistan (Northern Areas)
PUNJAB
JAMMU & KASHMIR
LADĀKH
HIMACHAL PRADESH
UTTARAKHAND
NEPAL
UTTAR PRADESH
BIHAR
JHARKHAND
CHHATTISGARH
MADHYA PRADESH
PASCHIM BANGA
ODISHA
SIKKIM
BHUTAN
BANGLADESH
ASSAM
Aksai Chin
Karakoram Range
Ladakh Range
Zanskar Range
Kunlun Shan
Gangdisê Shan
Mahabharat Lekh
Kaimur Hills
Mouths of the Ganges
Mt. Everest (Chomolungma or Sagarmatha)
K2
Nanga Parbat
ISLAMABAD
RAWALPINDI
SRINAGAR
Jammu
LUCKNOW
KANPUR
PRAYAGRAJ (Allahabad)
VARANASI
PATNA
KATHMANDU
DHANBAD
ASANSOL
JAMSHEDPUR
RANCHI
KOLKATA
KHULNA
DHAKA
JABALPUR
THIMPHU
COPYRIGHT PHILIP'S

217
241
244

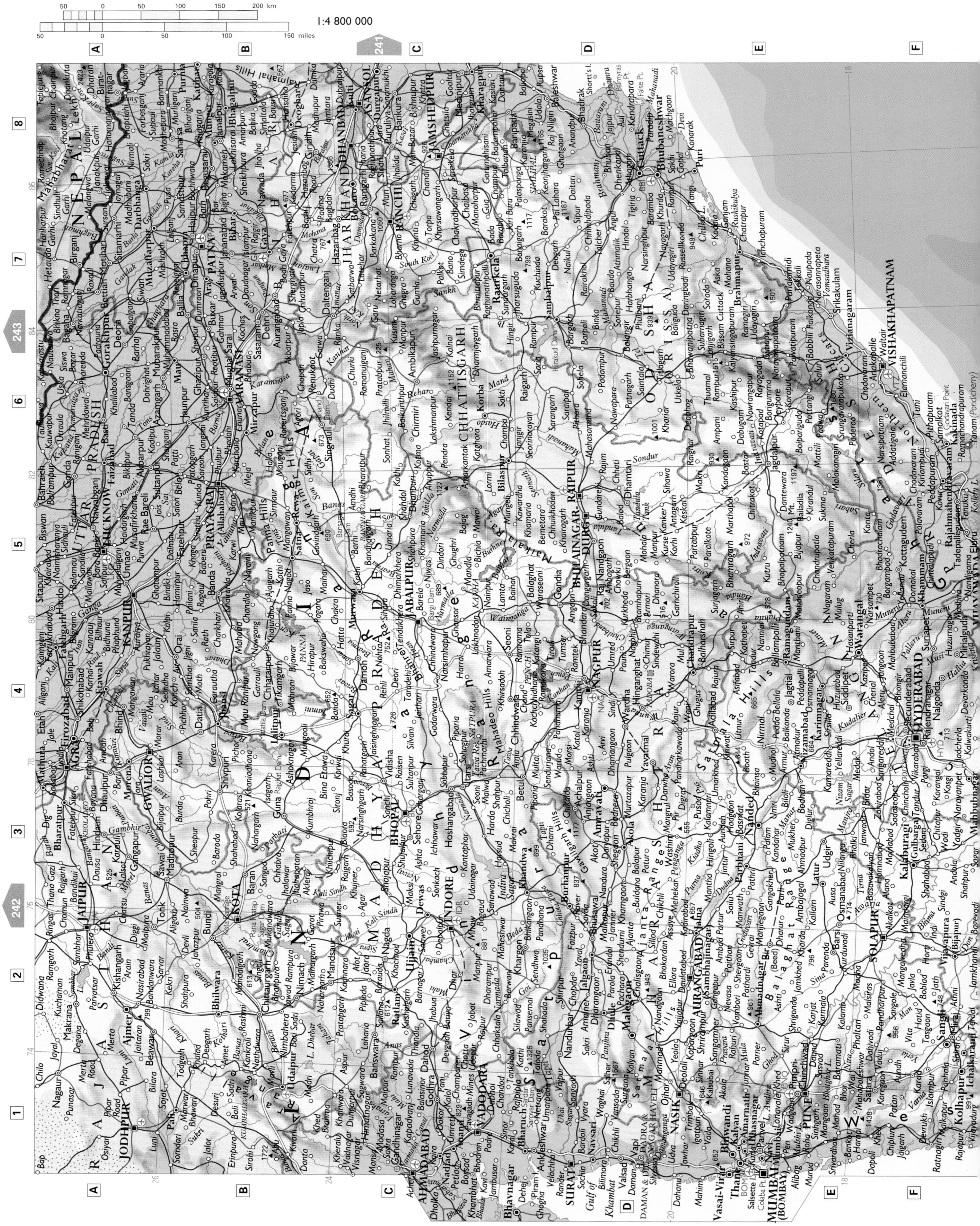
50 0 50 100 150 200 km
50 0 50 100 150 miles
1:4 800 000
241
242
243
A B C D E F
1 2 3 4 5 6 7 8
NEPAL
UTTAR PRADESH
BIHAR
JHARKHAND
CHHATTISGARH
ODISHA
MADHYA PRADESH
MAHARASHTRA
TELANGANA
RAJASTHAN
LUCKNOW
KANPUR
PRAYAGRAJ (Allahabad)
VARANASI
PATNA
GAYA
RANCHI
JAMSHEDPUR
ASANSOL
DHANBAD
CUTTACK
Bhubaneshwar
Puri
VISHAKHAPATNAM
Vizianagaram
Kakinada
Rajahmundry
RAIPUR
BHILAINAGAR-DURG
Bilaspur
Raurkela
Sambalpur
NAGPUR
JABALPUR
BHOPAL
INDORE
Ujjain
GWALIOR
AGRA
JAIPUR
KOTA
Ajmer
JODHPUR
Udaipur
AHMADABAD
VADODARA
SURAT
NASHIK
AURANGABAD
PUNE
MUMBAI (BOMBAY)
Thane
Kalyan
Bhiwandi
Kolhapur
Sangli
SOLAPUR
HYDERABAD
Secunderabad
Warangal
Nanded
Amravati
Akola
Chandrapur
Jalgaon
Dhule
Malegaon
Ahmadnagar
Kalaburagi (Gulbarga)
Bijapur (Vijayapura)
Bharuch
Bhavnagar
Dahod
Godhra
Ratlam
Mandsaur
Bhilwara
Sagar
Satna
Rewa
Mirzapur
Gorakhpur
Jhansi
Firozabad
Etawah
Bareilly
Darbhanga
Muzaffarpur
Bhagalpur
Deoghar
Hazaribag
Korba
Jagdalpur
Gulf of Khambat
Satpura Range
Vindhya Range
Maikala Range
Ajanta Range
Balaghat Range
Mahadeo Hills
Kaimur Hills
Satmala Hills
Eastern Ghats
Narmada
Godavari
Mahanadi
Chambal
Son
Betwa
Tapti
Wainganga
Penganga
Krishna
Bhima
Damodar
Subarnarekha
Brahmani
Indravati
Ganga
Ghaghara
Gomati

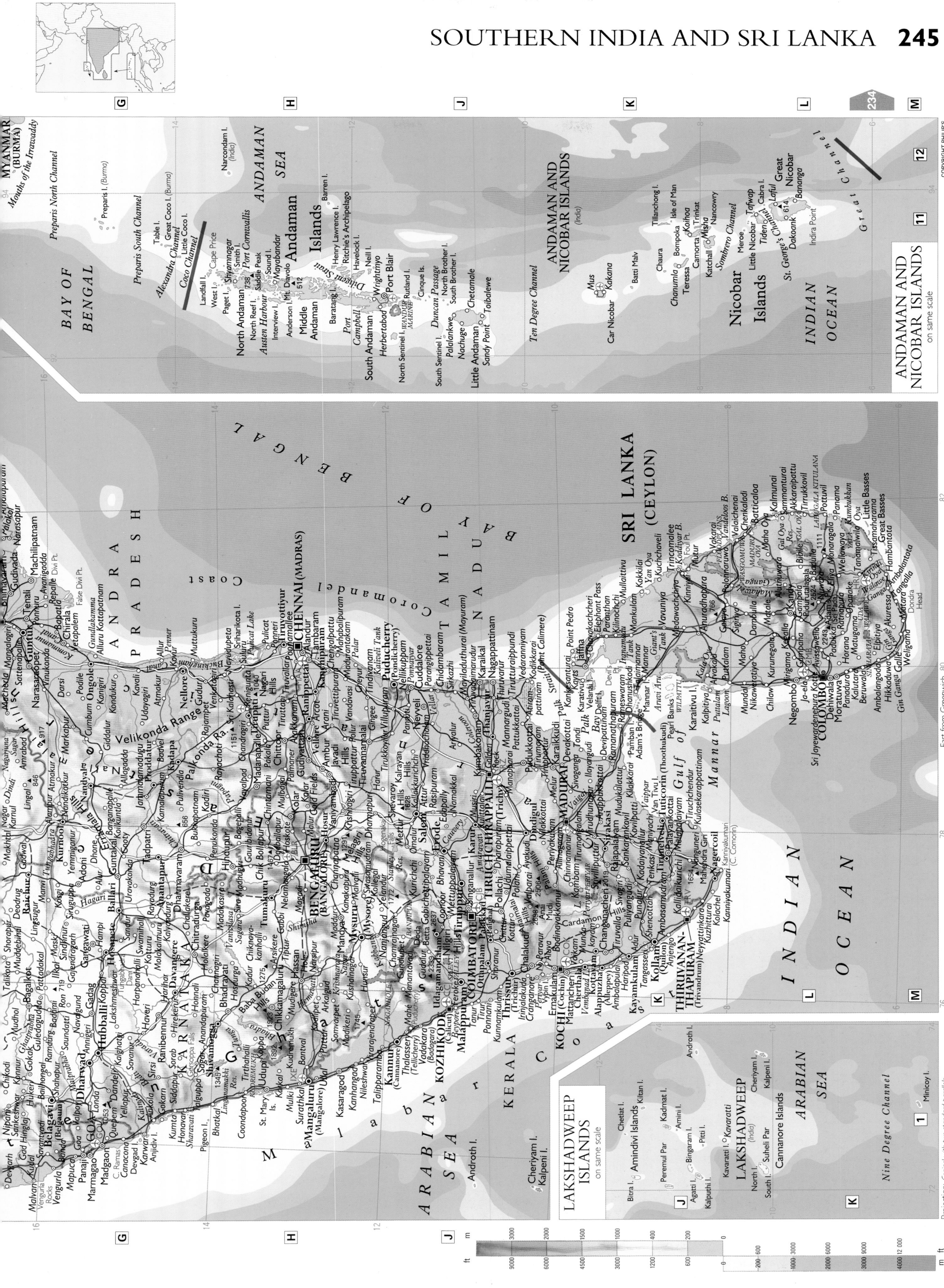
ANDHRA PRADESH
KARNATAKA
TAMIL NADU
KERALA
SRI LANKA (CEYLON)
BAY OF BENGAL
ARABIAN SEA
INDIAN OCEAN
Coromandel Coast
Gulf of Mannar
CHENNAI (MADRAS)
BENGALURU (BANGALORE)
COLOMBO
ANDAMAN AND NICOBAR ISLANDS on same scale
LAKSHADWEEP ISLANDS on same scale
ANDAMAN SEA
Andaman Islands
Nicobar Islands
Ten Degree Channel
Nine Degree Channel
East from Greenwich
Projection: Conical with two standard parallels
COPYRIGHT PHILIP'S

50 0 50 100 150 200 250 300 km

50 0 50 100 150 200 miles

1:5 600 000

213

212

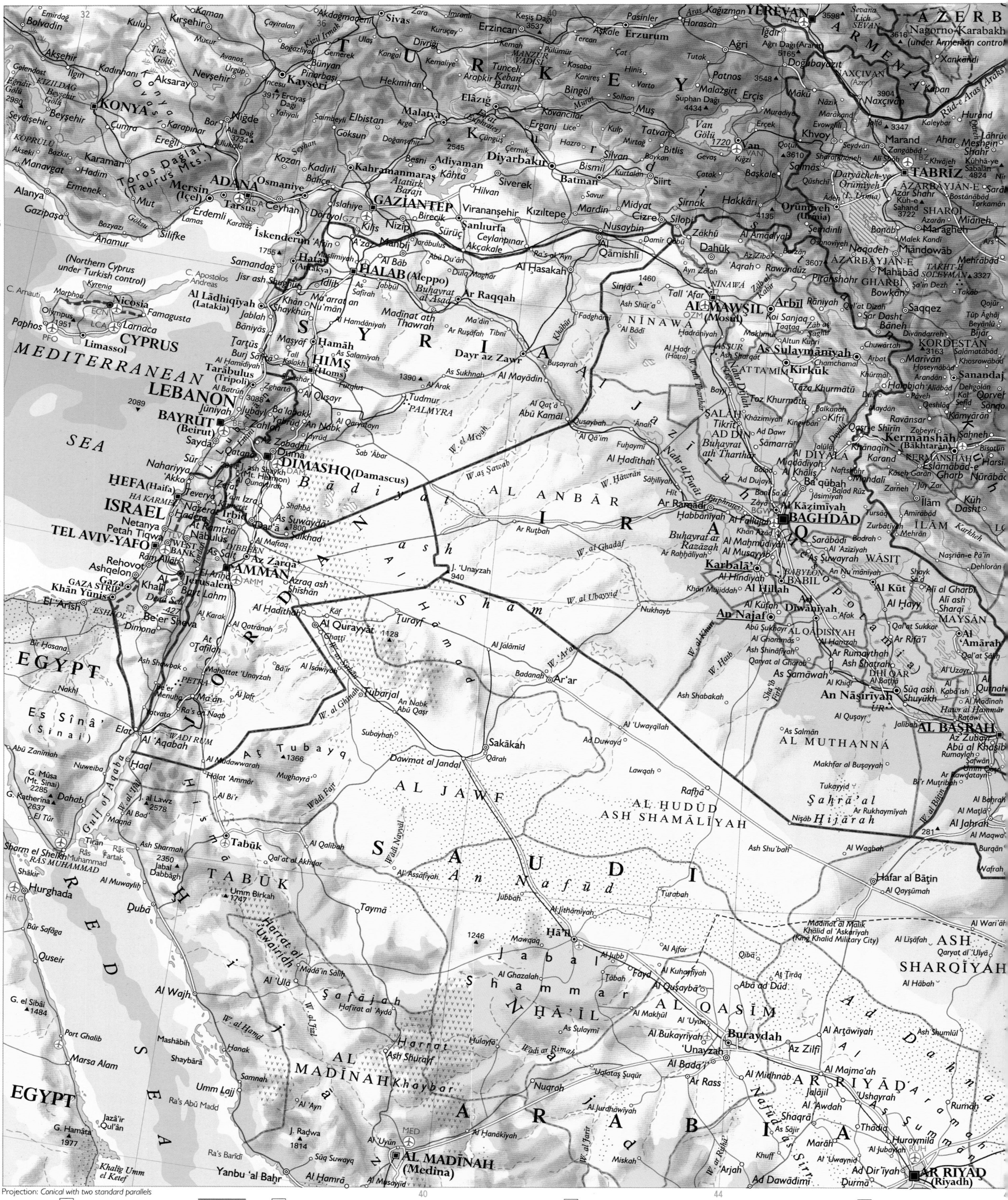

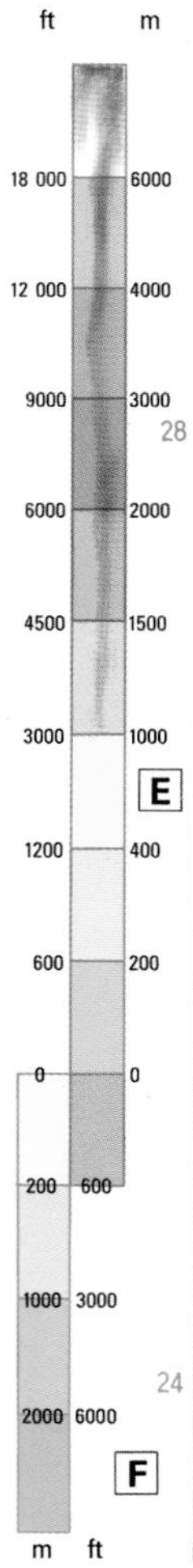

256

Projection: Conical with two standard parallels

248

Underlined towns in Iraq give their name to the administrative area in which they stand

Lava fields

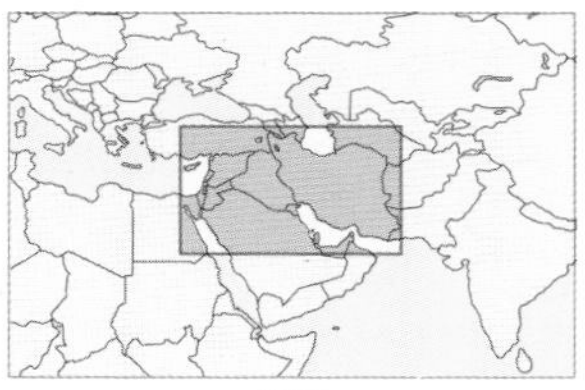

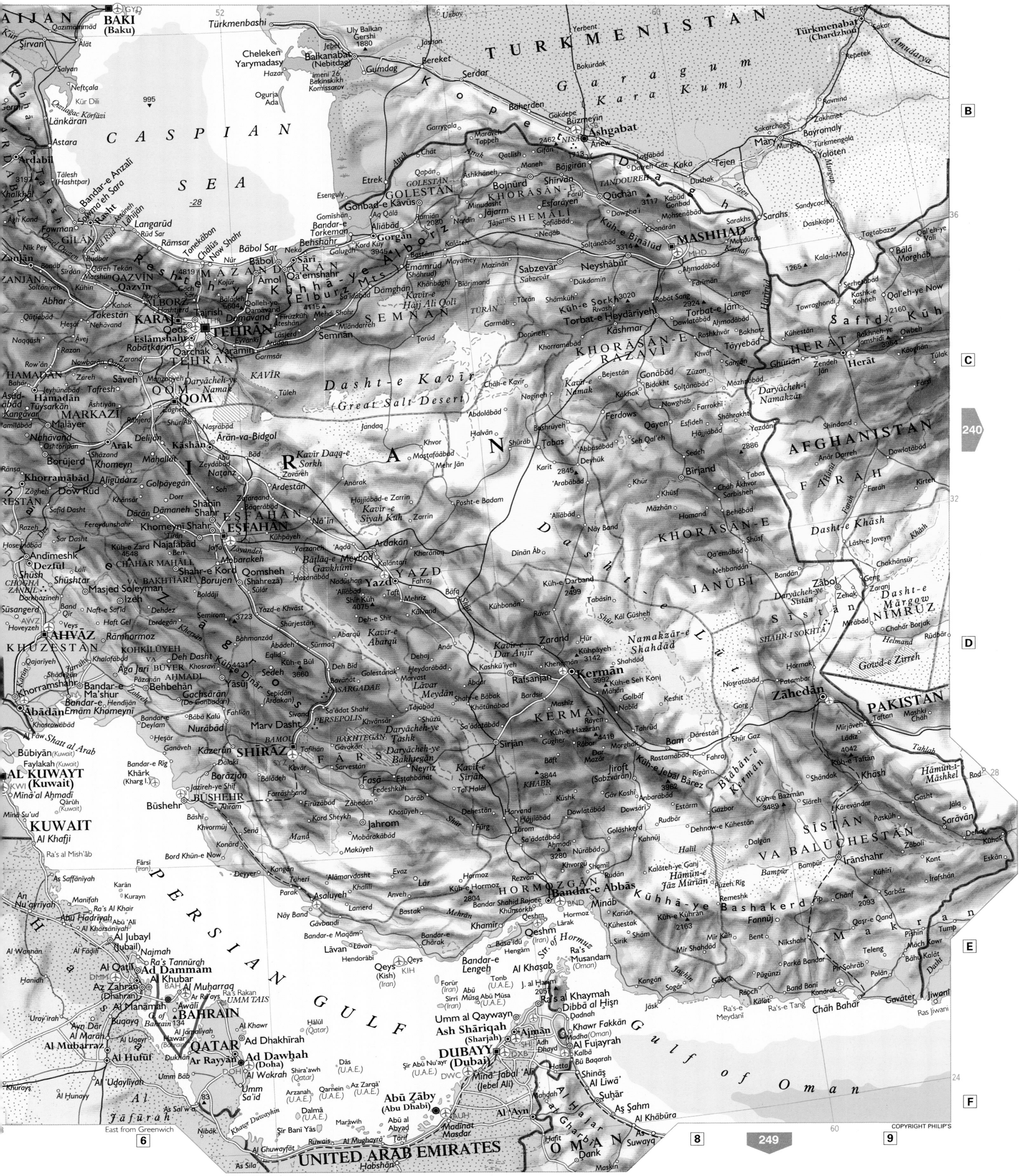
216
6
7
8
9
10
B
C
D
E
F
240
249
TURKMENISTAN
Garagum
(Kara Kum)
CASPIAN SEA
Kopet Dagh
BAKI (Baku)
Türkmenbashi
Balkanabat (Nebitdag)
Ashgabat
Türkmenabat (Chardzhou)
Mary
Bayramaly
Tejen
Serdar
GOLESTĀN
KHORĀSĀN-E SHEMĀLĪ
MASHHAD
Neyshābūr
Sabzevār
Gorgān
Sārī
Bābol
Qazvīn
Rasht
Ardabīl
Zanjān
Elburz Mts.
Reshteh-ye Kūhhā-ye Alborz
KARAJ
TEHRĀN
SEMNĀN
Semnān
Dasht-e Kavīr
(Great Salt Desert)
QOM
Qom
Hamadān
MARKAZĪ
Arāk
Kāshān
IRAN
ESFAHĀN
Eşfahān
YAZD
Yazd
Dasht-e Lūt
KHORĀSĀN-E RAZAVĪ
KHORĀSĀN-E JANŪBĪ
Bīrjand
Tabas
Kermān
KERMĀN
Sīrjān
Zāhedān
SĪSTĀN VA BALŪCHESTĀN
Zābol
AFGHANISTAN
HERĀT
Herāt
FARĀH
Farāh
NĪMRŪZ
PAKISTAN
AHVĀZ
KHUZESTĀN
Ābādān
Khorramshahr
Shīrāz
FĀRS
BŪSHEHR
Būshehr
HORMOZGĀN
Bandar-e Abbās
Zagros Mountains
PERSIAN GULF
Gulf of Oman
Str. of Hormuz
AL KUWAYT (Kuwait)
KUWAIT
BAHRAIN
Al Manāmah
QATAR
Ad Dawḩah (Doha)
Ad Dammām
Al Hufūf
DUBAYY (Dubai)
Abū Ẓaby (Abu Dhabi)
Ash Shāriqah (Sharjah)
Al Fujayrah
UNITED ARAB EMIRATES
OMAN
Al Ḩajar al Gharbī
Chāh Bahār
Makran
East from Greenwich
COPYRIGHT PHILIP'S

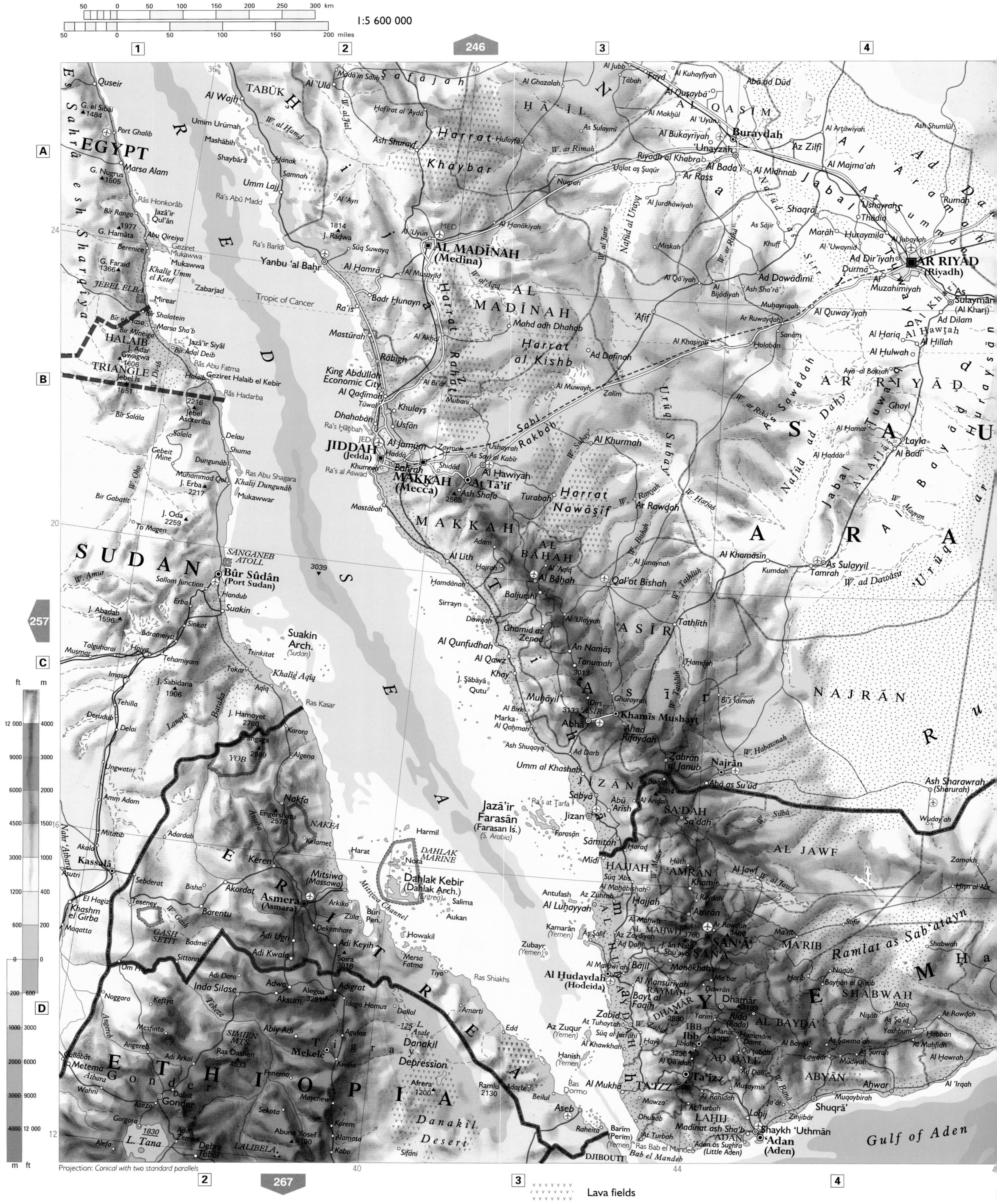

1:5 600 000
km
miles
246
267
257
1
2
3
4
A
B
C
D
ft
m
Projection: Conical with two standard parallels
Lava fields
Tropic of Cancer
RED SEA
EGYPT
SUDAN
ERITREA
ETHIOPIA
DJIBOUTI
YEMEN
SAUDI ARABIA
HALAIB TRIANGLE
Gulf of Aden
Bab el Mandeb
AL MADĪNAH (Medina)
AR RIYĀḌ (Riyadh)
JIDDAH (Jedda)
MAKKAH (Mecca)
At Ṭā'if
Buraydah
'Unayzah
Al Qunfudhah
Abhā
Khamīs Mushayt
Najrān
Jīzān
Ṣa'dah
Ṣan'ā'
Al Ḥudaydah (Hodeida)
Ta'izz
'Adan (Aden)
Mukalla
Būr Sûdân (Port Sudan)
Suakin
Kassalā
Asmera (Asmara)
Mitsiwa (Massawa)
Aksum
Mekele
Gonder
L. Tana
Danakil Depression
Danakil Desert
Jazā'ir Farasān (Farasan Is.)
Dahlak Kebir (Dahlak Arch.)
Suakin Arch.
Yanbu 'al Baḥr
King Abdullah Economic City
Ḥarrat Khaybar
Ḥarrat Rahaṭ
Ḥarrat al Kishb
Ḥarrat Nawāṣīf
NAJRĀN
AL JAWF
MA'RIB
SHABWAH
ABYĀN
Ramlat as Sab'atayn
Marsa Alam
Quseir
Al Wajh
Umm Lajj
Rābigh
Tabūk
Ḥā'il
Al Qaṣīm
'Asīr
Al Bāḥah
Qal'at Bishah
As Sulayyil
Ash Sharawrah
Dhamār
Ibb
Al Mukhā
Aseb

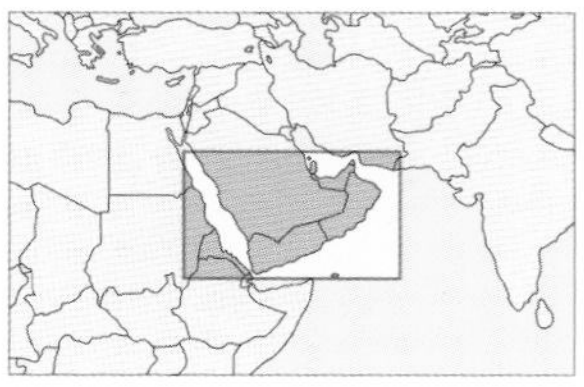

5 6 247 7 8

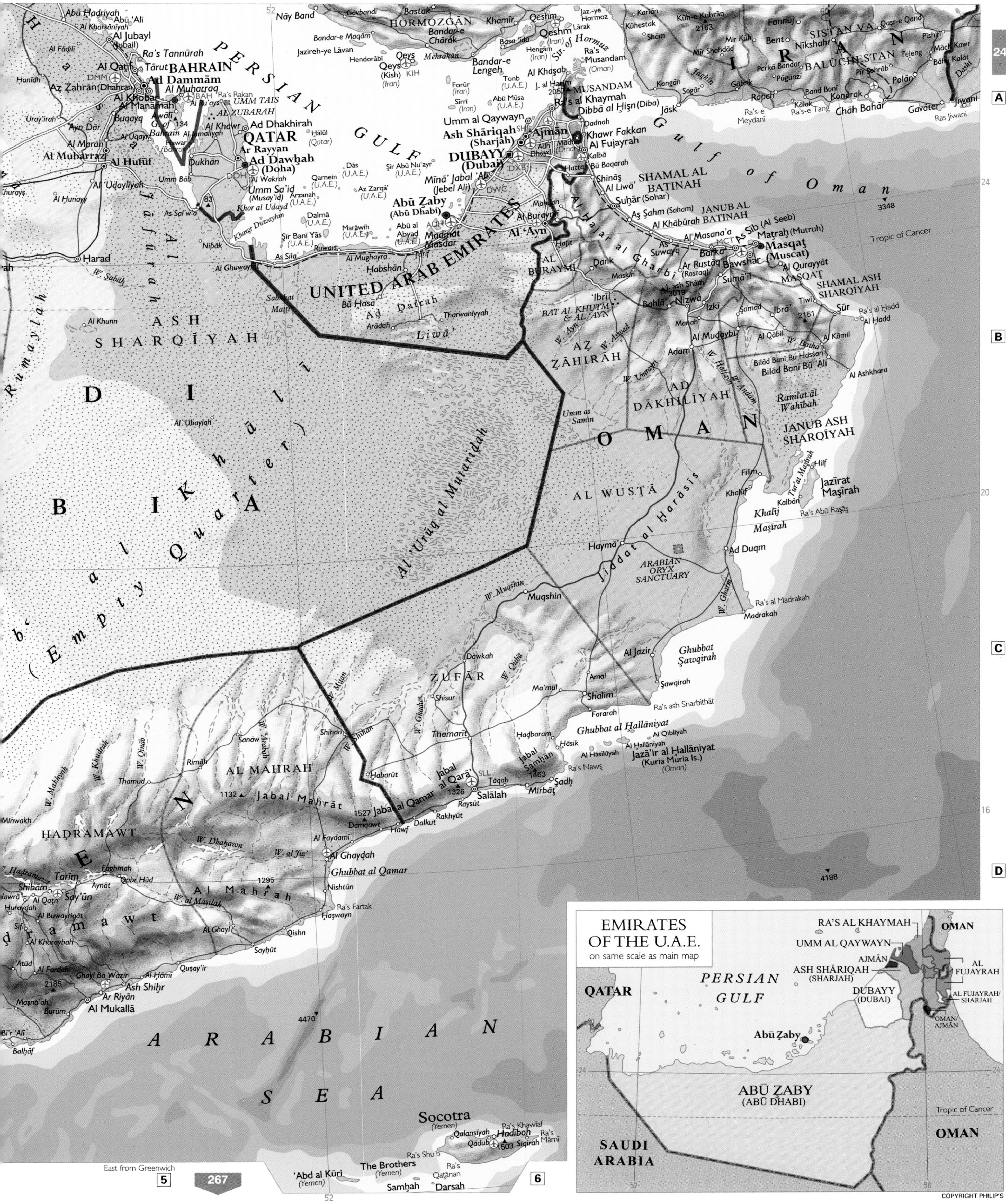
240
A
B
C
D
PERSIAN GULF
Gulf of Oman
ARABIAN SEA
IRAN
SISTAN VA BALUCHESTAN
HORMOZGAN
BAHRAIN
QATAR
UNITED ARAB EMIRATES
OMAN
YEMEN
Rub' al Khali (Empty Quarter)
ASH SHARQIYAH
AL BURAYMI
AZ ZAHIRAH
AD DAKHILIYAH
AL WUSTA
ZUFAR
AL MAHRAH
HADRAMAWT
MUSANDAM
SHAMAL AL BATINAH
JANUB AL BATINAH
MASQAT
SHAMAL ASH SHARQIYAH
JANUB ASH SHARQIYAH
Masqat (Muscat)
Abū Zaby (Abū Dhabi)
Ad Dawhah (Doha)
Al Manamah
Ad Dammām
Dubayy (Dubai)
Ash Shāriqah (Sharjah)
Ras al Khaymah
Al Fujayrah
Salālah
Al Mukallā
Tropic of Cancer
Liwā'
Jazīrat Maşīrah
Khalīj Maşīrah
Ad Duqm
ARABIAN ORYX SANCTUARY
Jiddat al Ḩarāsīs
Al 'Urūq al Mu'tariḑah
Jazā'ir al Ḩallānīyat (Kuria Muria Is.)
Ghubbat al Qamar
Socotra (Yemen)
The Brothers (Yemen)
'Abd al Kūrī (Yemen)
East from Greenwich
5
267
6
52
EMIRATES OF THE U.A.E.
on same scale as main map
RA'S AL KHAYMAH
UMM AL QAYWAYN
AJMĀN
ASH SHĀRIQAH (SHARJAH)
DUBAYY (DUBAI)
AL FUJAYRAH
AL FUJAYRAH/SHARJAH
OMAN/AJMĀN
OMAN
QATAR
PERSIAN GULF
Abū Ẓaby
ABŪ ẒABY (ABŪ DHABI)
Tropic of Cancer
SAUDI ARABIA
24
52
56

1:2 000 000

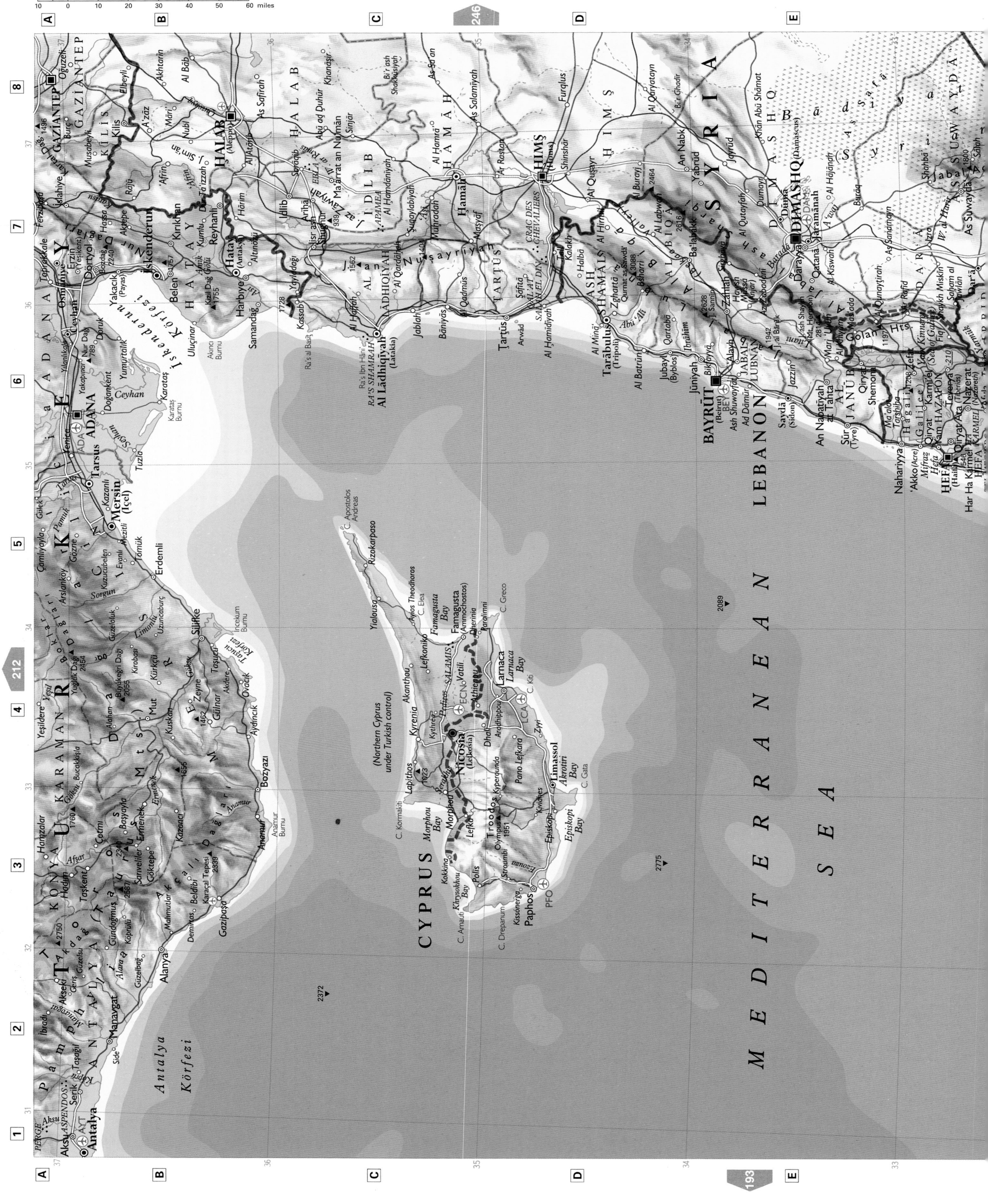

10 0 10 20 30 40 50 60 70 80 90 km
10 0 10 20 30 40 50 60 miles
MEDITERRANEAN SEA
CYPRUS
(Northern Cyprus under Turkish control)
Nicosia (Lefkosia)
Famagusta (Ammochostos)
Larnaca
Limassol
Paphos
Kyrenia
Morphou Bay
Famagusta Bay
Larnaca Bay
Akrotiri Bay
Episkopi Bay
Troodos
Olympus 1951
SYRIA
LEBANON
BAYRŪT (Beirut)
DIMASHQ (Damascus)
ḤIMṢ (Homs)
ḤALAB (Aleppo)
Ḥamāh
Al Lādhiqīyah (Latakia)
Ṭarābulus (Tripoli)
Ṭarṭūs
Ṣaydā (Sidon)
Ṣūr (Tyre)
Golan Hts
ADANA
GAZIANTEP
Mersin (İçel)
Tarsus
İskenderun
İskenderun Körfezi
Antalya
Antalya Körfezi
Alanya
Manavgat
Anamur
Silifke
HATAY
Hatay (Antakya)
Ceyhan
Karataş
Erdemli
Bozyazı
Gazipaşa
Jubayl (Byblos)

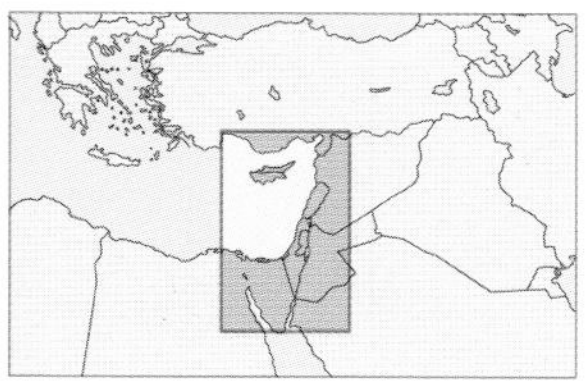

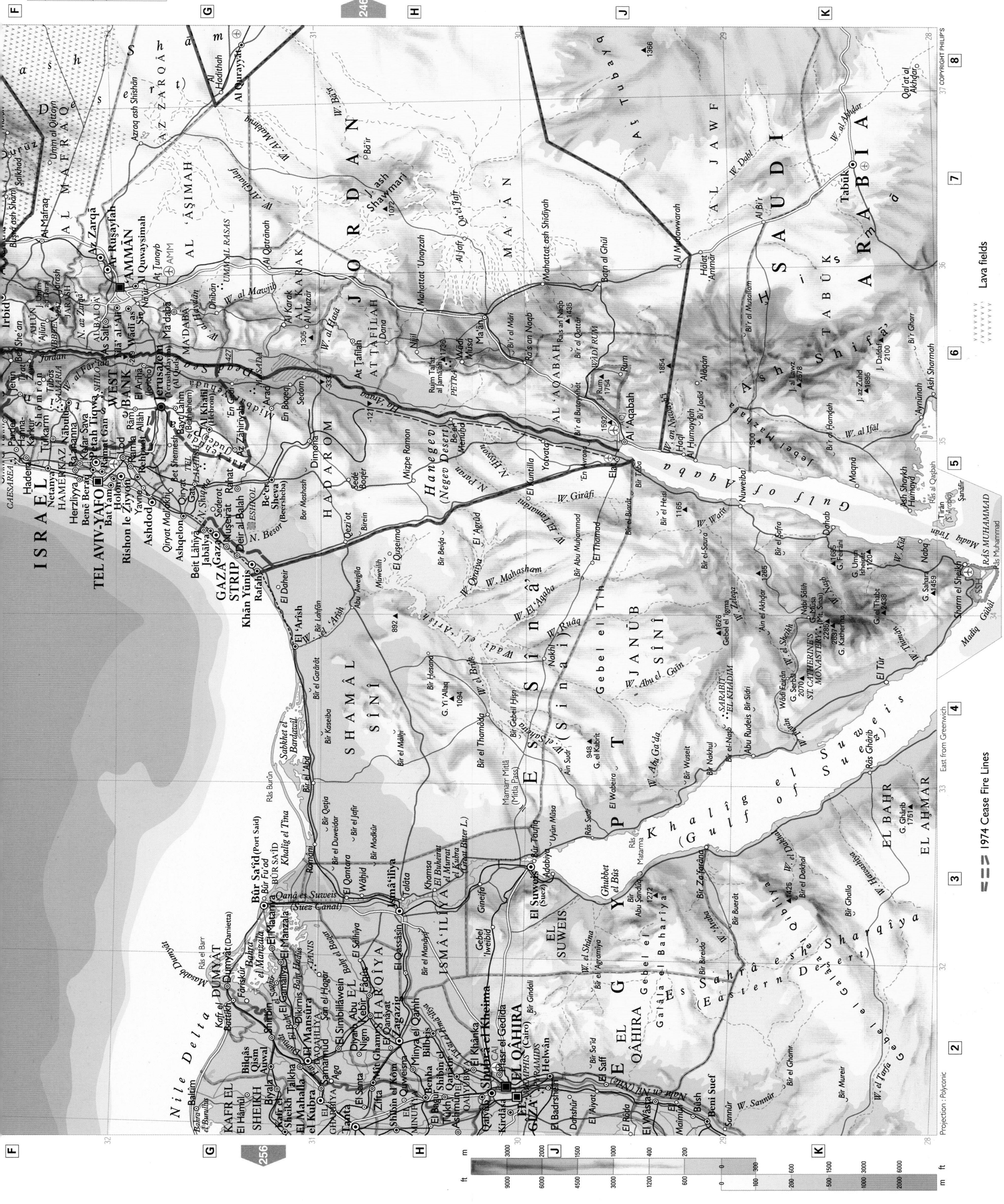

246
256
F
G
H
J
K
2
3
4
5
6
7
8
ISRAEL
JORDAN
SAUDI ARABIA
EGYPT
TEL AVIV-YAFO
Jerusalem
'AMMĀN
GAZA STRIP
WEST BANK
EL QÂHIRA (Cairo)
Bûr Sa'îd (Port Said)
Ismâ'ilîya
El Suweis (Suez)
Qanâ es Suweis (Suez Canal)
Al 'Aqabah
Elat
Tabūk
Haifa
Ashdod
Ashqelon
Be'er Sheva (Beersheba)
Khân Yûnis
Rafah
El 'Arîsh
Dimona
Ma'ān
Az Zarqā
Irbid
Dumyât (Damietta)
El Mansûra
Zagazig
Tanta
Helwân
GIZA
Beni Suef
Nile Delta
Gulf of Suez
Khalîg el Suweis
Gulf of Aqaba
Hanegev (Negev Desert)
Es Sînâ' (Sinai)
SHAMÂL SÎNÎ
JANÛB SÎNÎ
Gebel el Tîh
Es Sahrâ esh Sharqîya (Eastern Desert)
Ra's Muhammad
Sharm el Sheikh
St. Catherine's Monastery
Dead Sea
Jordan
Tîrân
Sanâfir
Projection : Polyconic
East from Greenwich
COPYRIGHT PHILIP'S
1974 Cease Fire Lines
Lava fields
m
ft
3000
2000
1500
1000
400
200
0
9000
6000
4500
3000
1200
600

AFRICA

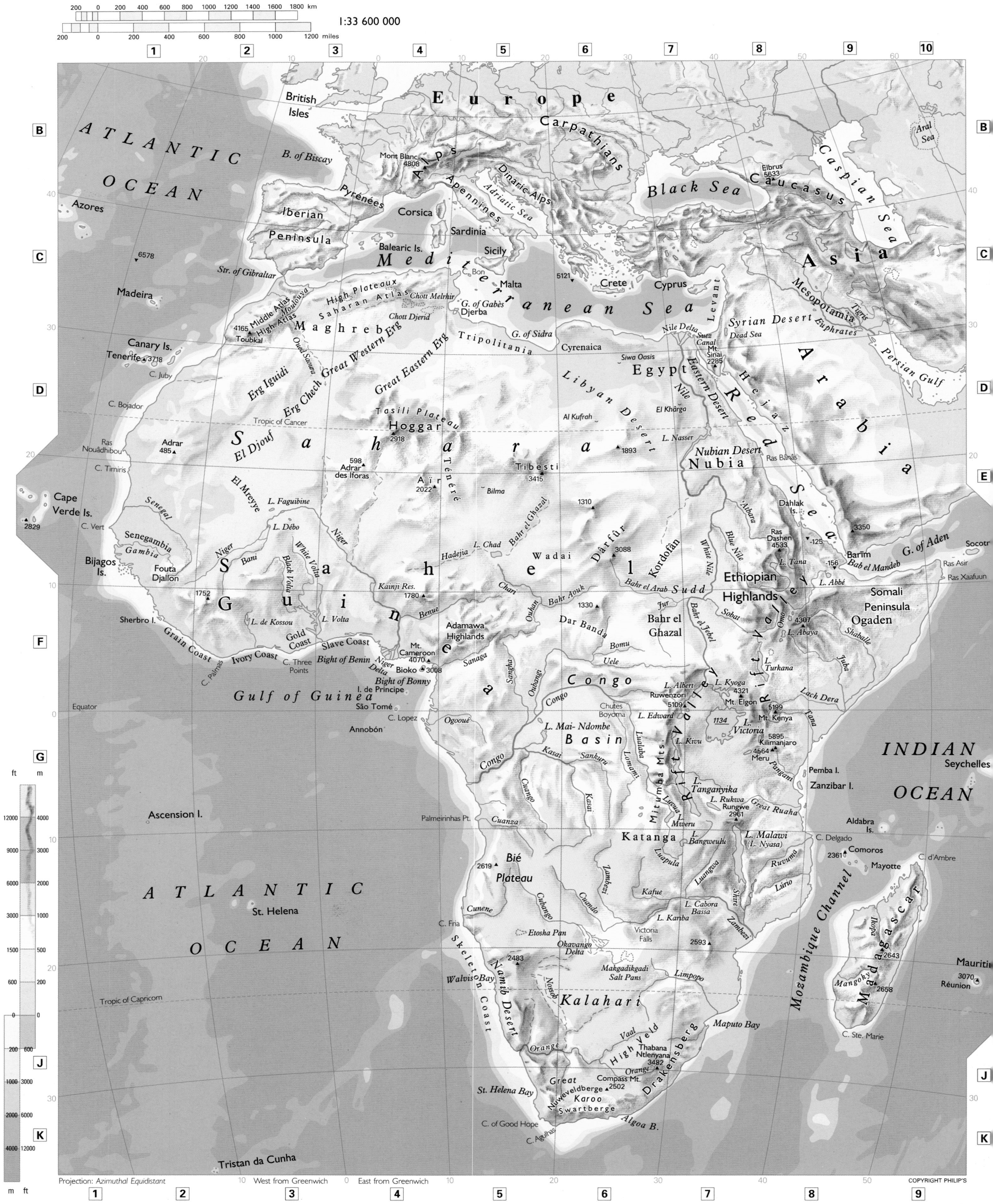

1:33 600 000
km
miles
Europe
British Isles
ATLANTIC OCEAN
Azores
B. of Biscay
Carpathians
Mont Blanc 4808
Alps
Pyrénées
Iberian Peninsula
Corsica
Sardinia
Apennines
Dinaric Alps
Adriatic Sea
Black Sea
Elbrus 5633
Caucasus
Caspian Sea
Aral Sea
Balearic Is.
Sicily
Malta
Crete
Cyprus
Mediterranean Sea
Str. of Gibraltar
6578
Madeira
C. Bon
5121
Asia
Mesopotamia
Tigris
Euphrates
Syrian Desert
Dead Sea
Levant
High Plateaux
Saharan Atlas
Chott Melrhir
Chott Djerid
G. of Gabès
Djerba
Middle Atlas
Moulouya
High Atlas
4165 Toubkal
Maghreb
Great Western Erg
Great Eastern Erg
Tripolitania
G. of Sidra
Cyrenaica
Nile Delta
Suez Canal
Mt. Sinai 2285
Persian Gulf
Arabia
Canary Is.
Tenerife 3718
C. Juby
Oued Saoura
Erg Iguidi
Erg Chech
Siwa Oasis
Egypt
Eastern Desert
Nile
Red Sea
Hejaz
Libyan Desert
C. Bojador
Tropic of Cancer
Tasili Plateau
Hoggar 2918
Al Kufrah
El Khârga
L. Nasser
Sahara
El Djouf
Adrar 485
Ras Nouâdhibou
1893
Nubian Desert
Nubia
Ras Banâs
C. Timiris
598 Adrar des Iforas
Aïr 2022
Ténéré
Tibesti 3415
Bilma
Cape Verde Is.
2829
C. Vert
El Mreyyé
L. Faguibine
1310
Atbara
Dahlak Is.
3350
Senegal
Senegambia
Gambia
L. Débo
Niger
White Volta
Black Volta
Bani
L. Chad
Bahr el Ghazal
Hadejia
Wadai
Dârfûr 3088
Kordofân
White Nile
Blue Nile
Ras Dashen 4533
-125
L. Tana
-156
Barīm
Bab el Mandeb
G. of Aden
Socotra
Ras Asir
Ras Xaafuun
Bijagos Is.
Fouta Djallon
Sahel
Kainji Res.
1780
Bahr el Arab
Sudd
Ethiopian Highlands
L. Abbé
Somali Peninsula
Ogaden
1752
Guinea
L. de Kossou
L. Volta
Benue
Chari
Bahr Aouk
Ouham
1330
Dar Banda
Jur
Bahr el Ghazal
Bahr el Jebel
Sobat
Omo
4307
L. Abaya
Shabeelle
Rift Valley
Sherbro I.
Grain Coast
Gold Coast
Slave Coast
Adamawa Highlands
Mt. Cameroon 4070
Ivory Coast
C. Palmas
C. Three Points
Bight of Benin
Niger Delta
Bioko 3008
Bight of Bonny
Sanaga
Sangha
Oubangi
Bomu
Uele
L. Turkana
Juba
I. de Principe
Gulf of Guinea
São Tomé
Equator
Congo
L. Albert
Ruwenzori 5109
L. Kyoga 4321
Mt. Elgon
Lach Dera
Chutes Boyoma
L. Edward
1134
5199 Mt. Kenya
Tana
C. Lopez
Annobón
Ogooué
L. Mai-Ndombe
Basin
Lualaba
L. Victoria
L. Kivu
5895 Kilimanjaro
4564 Meru
INDIAN OCEAN
Seychelles
Kasai
Sankuru
Lomami
Mitumba Mts.
Pangani
Pemba I.
Zanzibar I.
L. Tanganyika
L. Rukwa
Rungwe 2961
Great Ruaha
Cuango
Cuanza
Ascension I.
Palmeirinhas Pt.
Luvua
L. Mweru
Katanga
L. Bangweulu
L. Malawi (L. Nyasa)
Aldabra Is.
C. Delgado
2361 Comoros
Mayotte
C. d'Ambre
Bié Plateau
2619
Luapula
Lambezi
Ruvuma
Lúrio
ATLANTIC OCEAN
St. Helena
Cunene
Cubango
Cuando
Kafue
Luangwa
Shire
L. Cabora Bassa
L. Kariba
Zambezi
Mozambique Channel
Madagascar
Ihopo
2643
C. Fria
Skeleton Coast
Etosha Pan
Okavango Delta
Victoria Falls
2593
2483
Walvis Bay
Namib Desert
Nosob
Makgadikgadi Salt Pans
Limpopo
Mauritius
3070 Réunion
Mangoky
2658
Tropic of Capricorn
Kalahari
Vaal
High Veld
Thabana Ntlenyana 3482
Drakensberg
Maputo Bay
C. Ste. Marie
Orange
Great Compass Mt. 2502
Nuweveldberge
Karoo
Swartberge
St. Helena Bay
C. of Good Hope
C. Agulhas
Algoa B.
Tristan da Cunha
Projection: Azimuthal Equidistant
West from Greenwich
East from Greenwich
COPYRIGHT PHILIP'S
ft m
12000 4000
9000 3000
6000 2000
3000 1000
1500 500
600 200
0 0
200 600
1000 3000
2000 6000
4000 12000
m ft

1:33 600 000

200 0 200 400 600 800 1000 1200 1400 1600 1800 km

200 0 200 400 600 800 1000 1200 miles

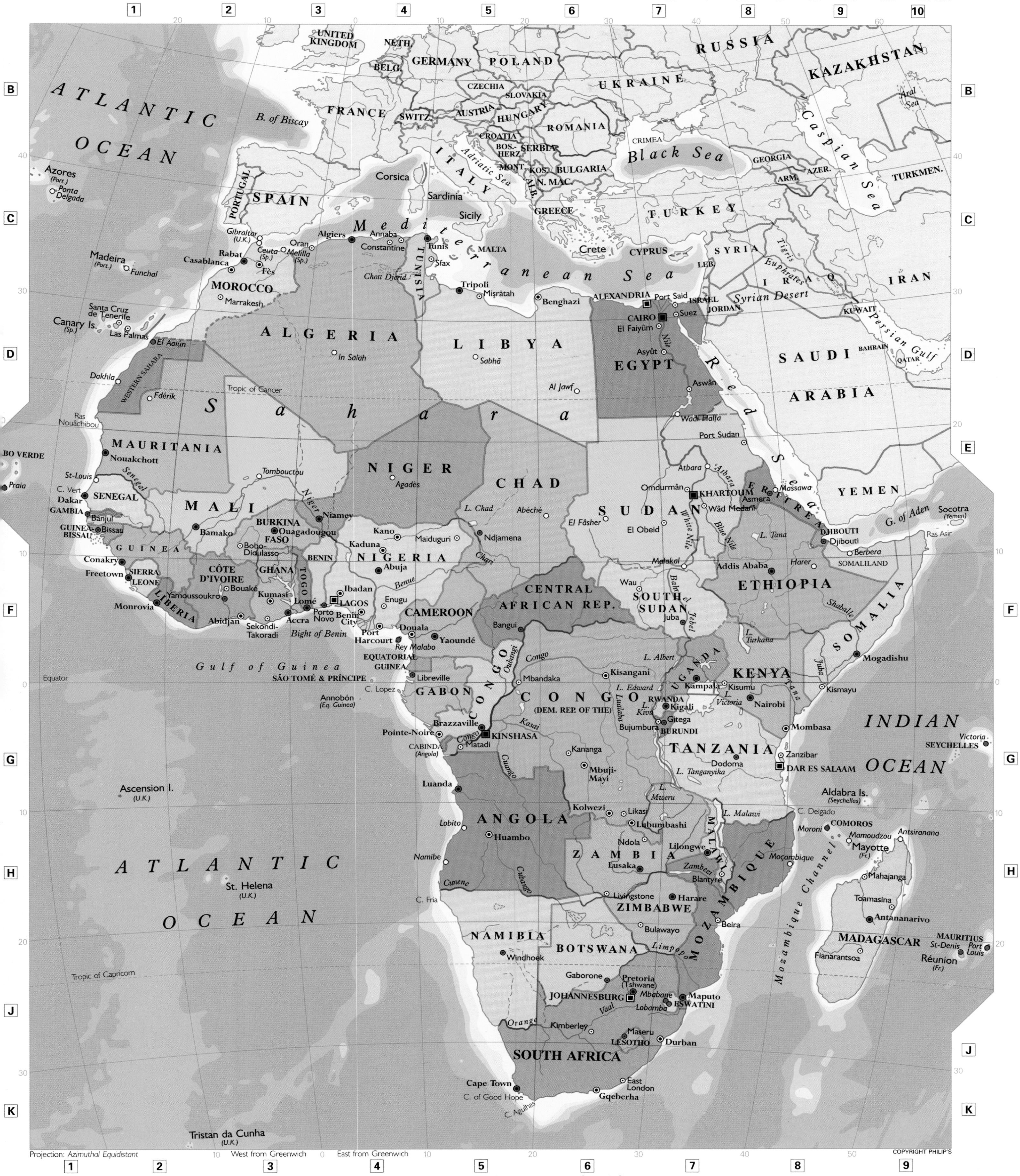

Dakar Capital Cities

1:6 400 000

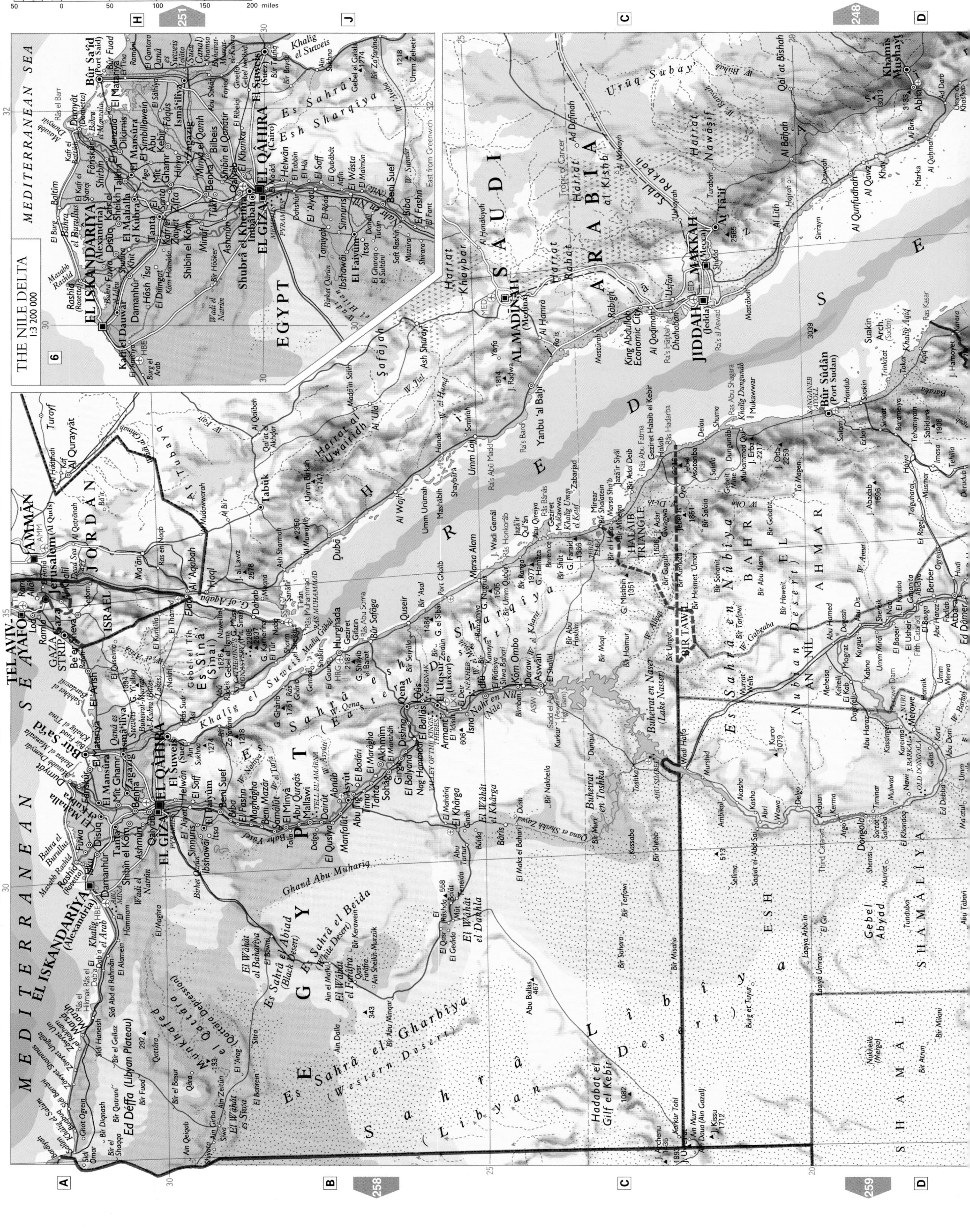
THE NILE DELTA
1:3 200 000
MEDITERRANEAN SEA
EL ISKANDARÎYA (Alexandria)
Bûr Sa'îd (Port Said)
EL QÂHIRA (Cairo)
EL GÎZA
EGYPT
SAUDI ARABIA
JORDAN
ISRAEL
AMMAN
Jerusalem
TEL AVIV-YAFO
GAZA STRIP
MAKKAH (Mecca)
JIDDAH (Jedda)
AL MADÎNAH (Medina)
RED SEA
Es Sahrâ el Gharbîya (Western Desert)
Es Sahrâ esh Sharqîya (Eastern Desert)
Sahrâ Lîbîya (Libyan Desert)
Aswân
Qena
El Uqsur (Luxor)
Asyût
Buheirat en Naser (Lake Nasser)
Wadi Halfa
Bûr Sûdân (Port Sudan)
HALAIB TRIANGLE
BIR TAWIL
Dongola
Berber
Atbara
Tabûk
Yanbu 'al Bahr
At Tâ'if
Abhâ
Khamîs Mushayt

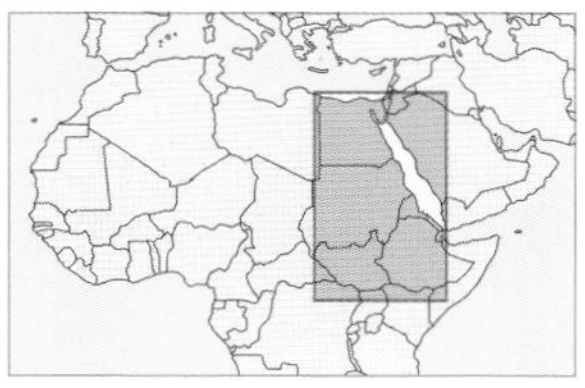

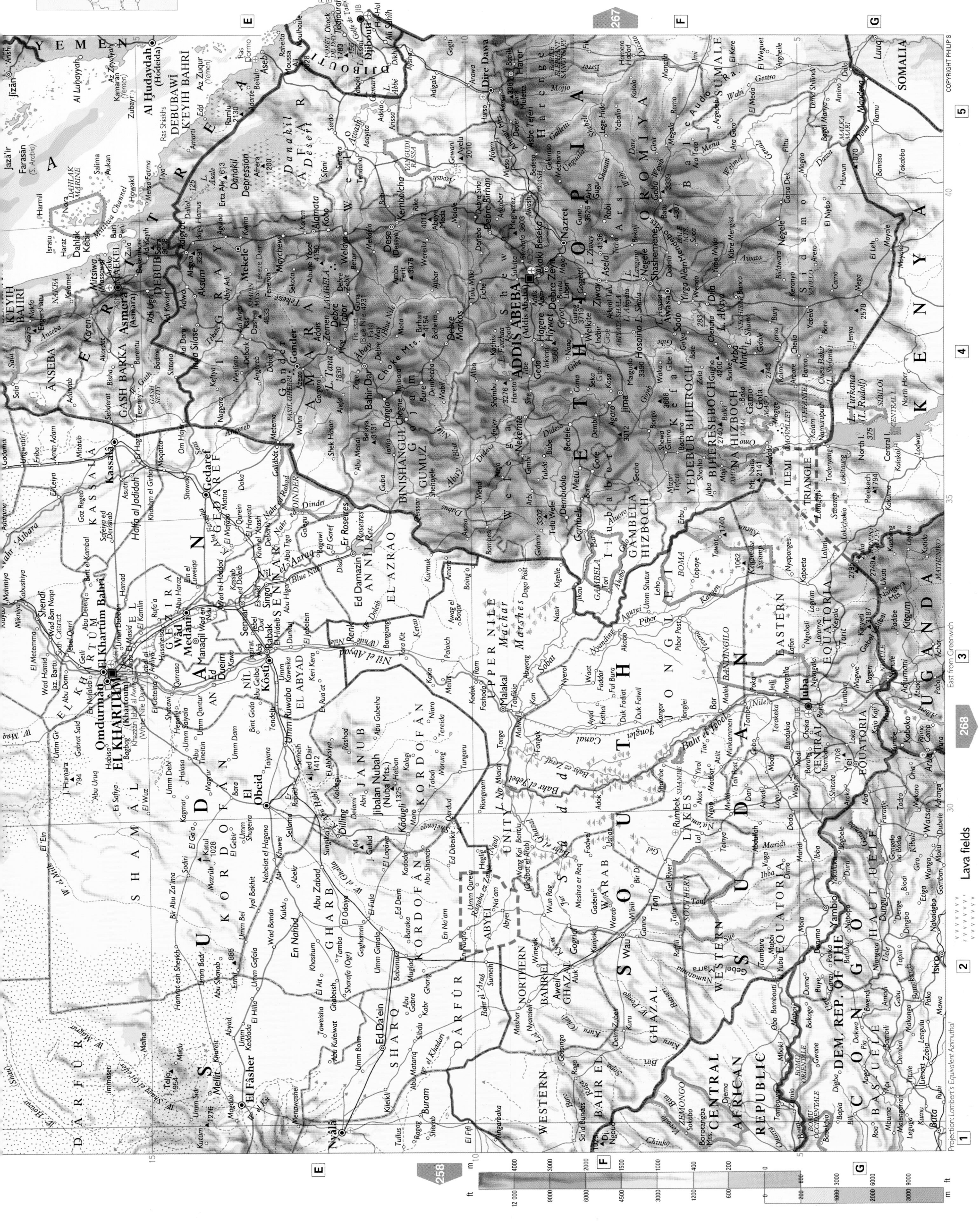
YEMEN
ERITREA
DJIBOUTI
ETHIOPIA
SOMALIA
KENYA
UGANDA
SOUTH SUDAN
SUDAN
CENTRAL AFRICAN REPUBLIC
DEM. REP. OF THE CONGO
ADDIS ABEBA
EL KHARTUM
Omdurman
Asmera
Juba
Lava fields
East from Greenwich
Projection: Lambert's Equivalent Azimuthal
COPYRIGHT PHILIP'S
267
268
258

50 0 50 100 150 200 250 300 km

1:6 400 000

50 0 50 100 150 200 miles

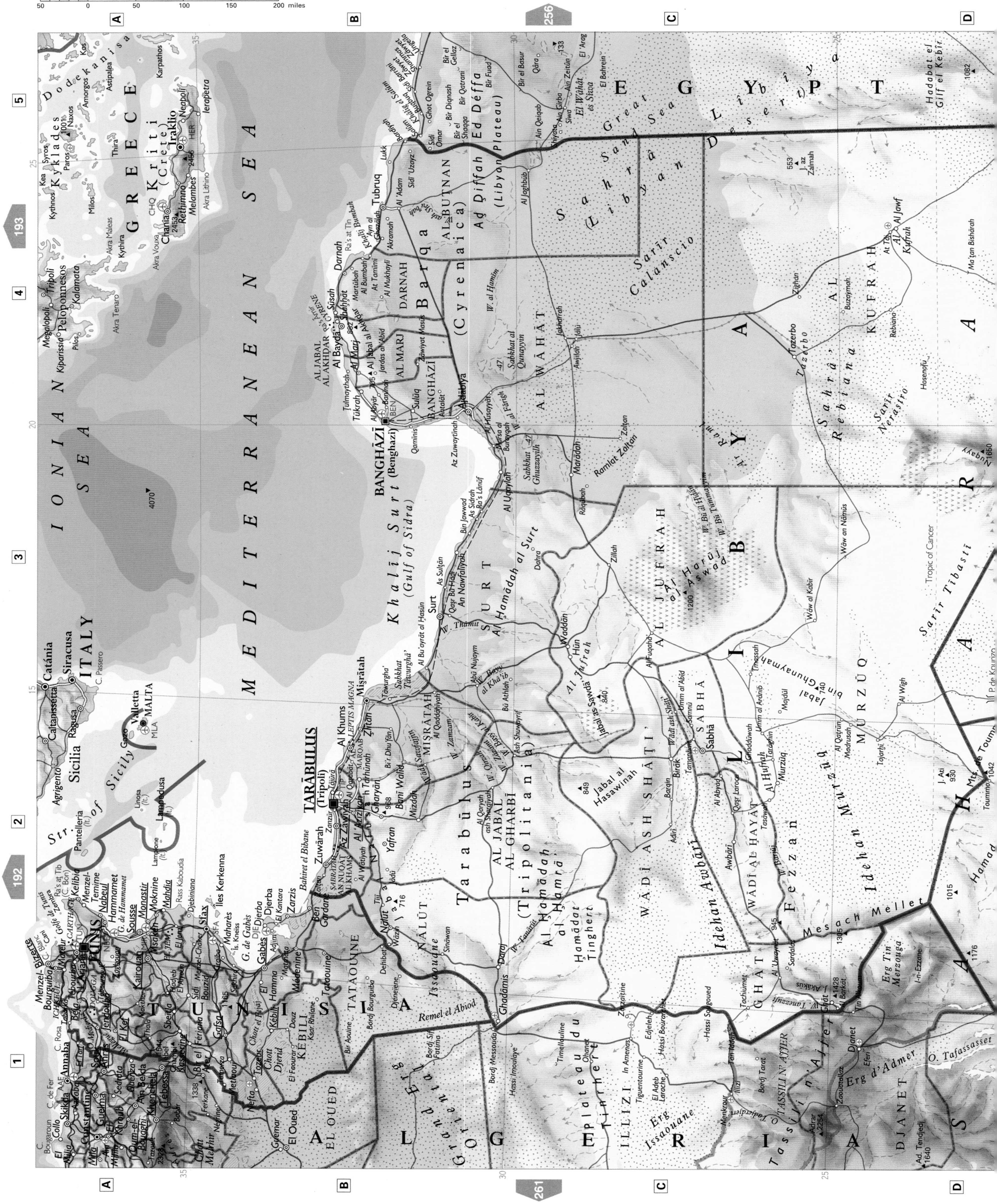

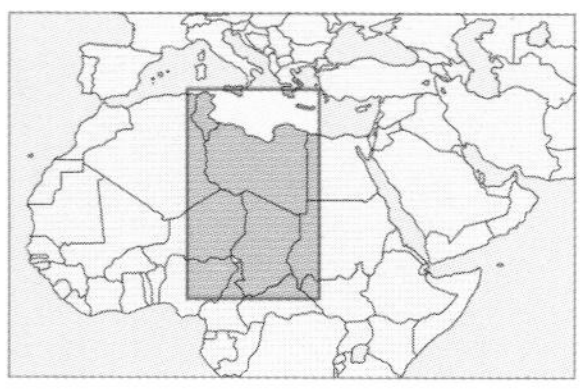

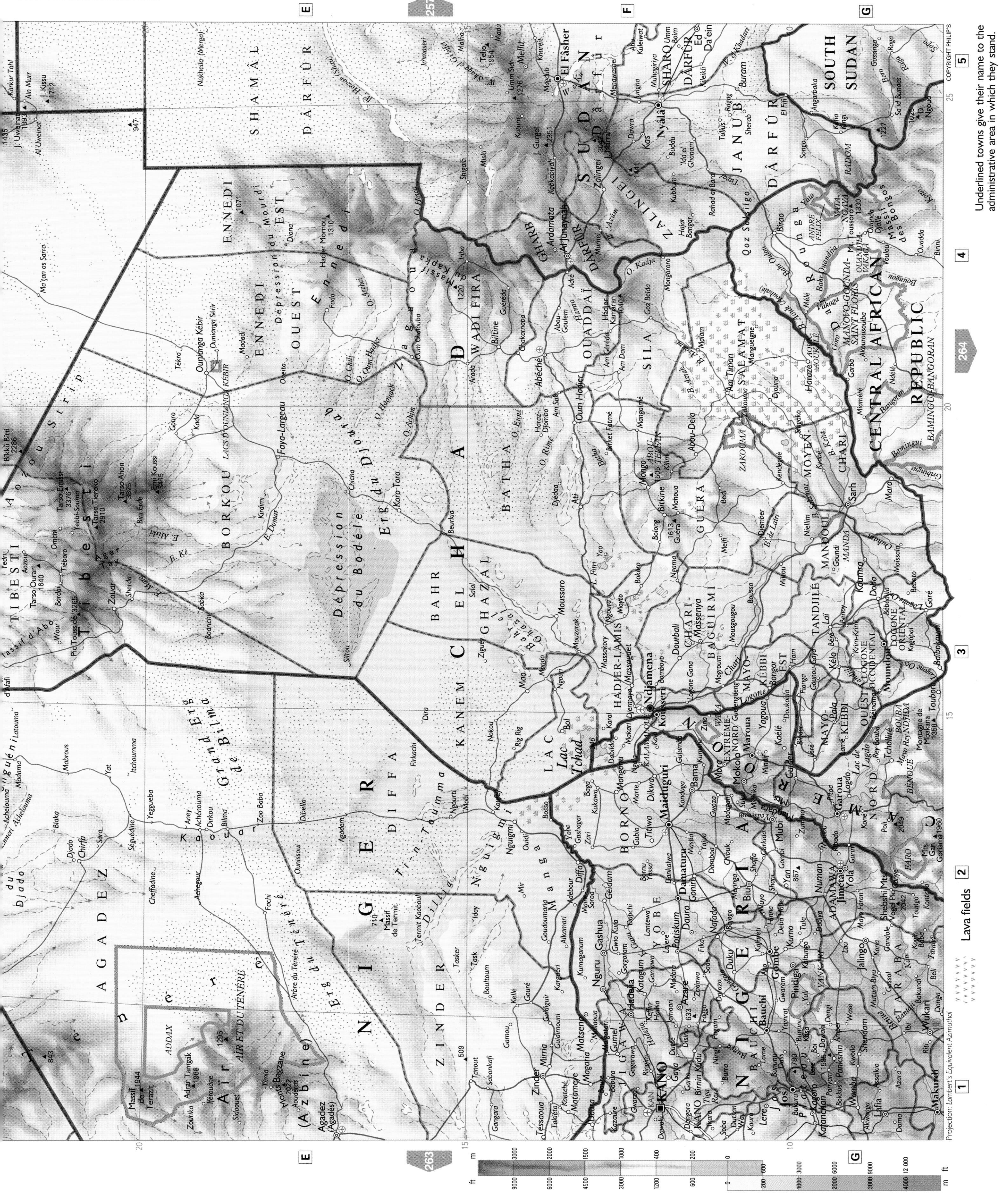

LIBYA
CHAD
NIGER
SUDAN
NIGERIA
CENTRAL AFRICAN REPUBLIC
SOUTH SUDAN
CAMEROON
TIBESTI
BORKOU
ENNEDI OUEST
ENNEDI EST
AGADEZ
DIFFA
ZINDER
KANEM
LAC
BATHA
OUADDAÏ
SILA
SALAMAT
GUÉRA
HADJER-LAMIS
CHARI-BAGUIRMI
MAYO-KEBBI EST
MAYO-KEBBI OUEST
TANDJILÉ
MANDOUL
MOYEN-CHARI
LOGONE ORIENTAL
LOGONE OCCIDENTAL
WADI FIRA
BAHR EL GHAZAL
SHAMAL DARFUR
GHARB DARFUR
JANUB DARFUR
SHARQ DARFUR
BORNO
YOBE
JIGAWA
KANO
BAUCHI
GOMBE
ADAMAWA
TARABA
PLATEAU
EXTRÊME-NORD
NORD
Lac Tchad
Ndjamena
Maiduguri
Kano
Zinder
Agadez
Faya-Largeau
Abéché
El Fasher
Nyala
Sarh
Moundou
Garoua
Maroua
Jos
Bauchi
Aïr
Ténéré
Grand Erg de Bilma
Erg du Djourab
Dépression du Bodélé
Emi Koussi 3415
Lava fields
Underlined towns give their name to the administrative area in which they stand.
Projection: Lambert's Equivalent Azimuthal
COPYRIGHT PHILIP'S
257
263
264
m
ft

50 0 50 100 150 200 250 300 km

1:6 400 000

50 0 50 100 150 200 miles

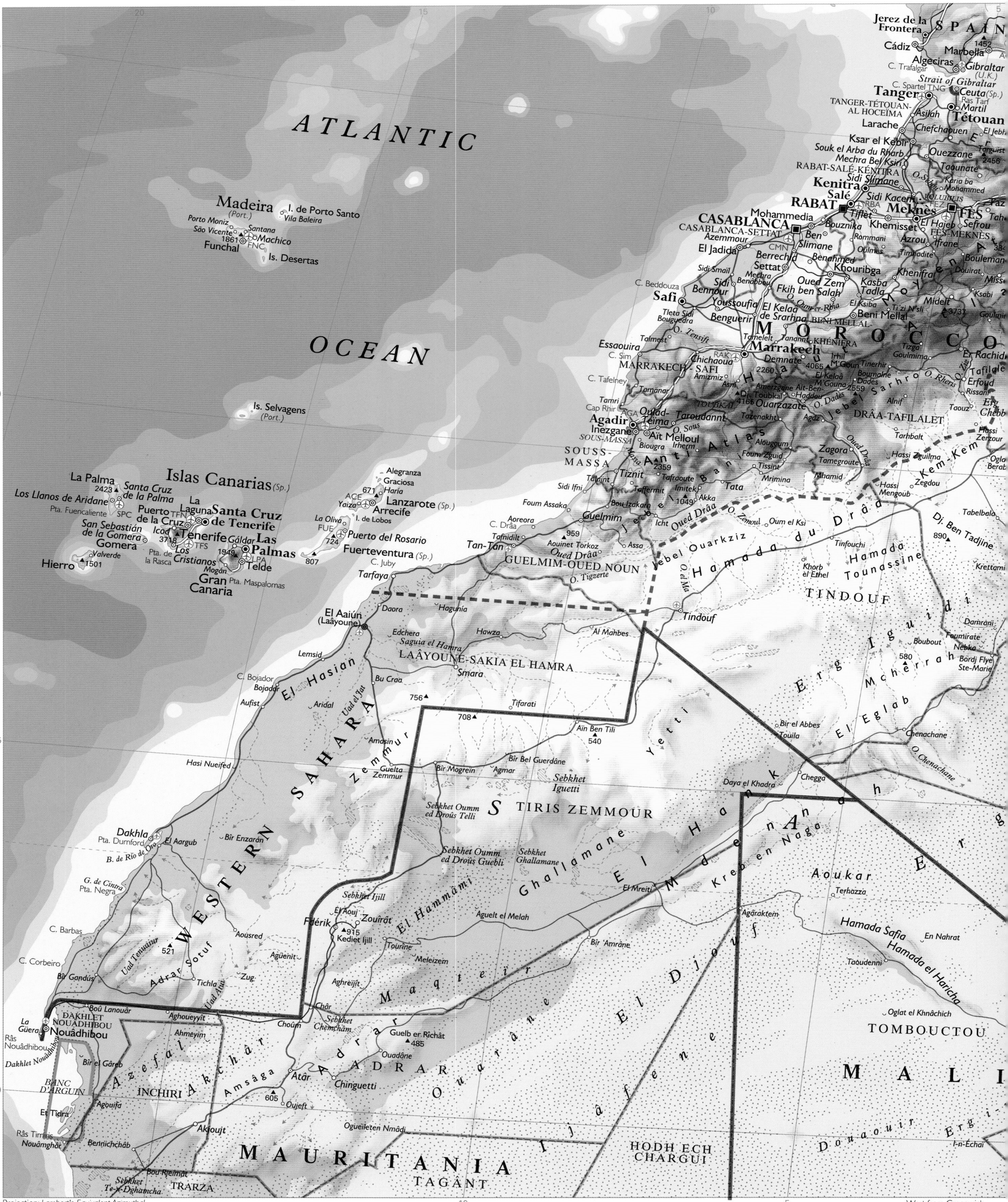

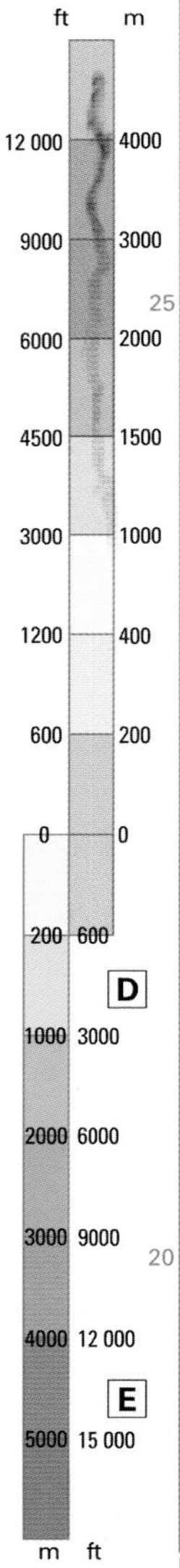

Projection: Lambert's Equivalent Azimuthal

West from Greenwich

Underlined towns give their name to the administrative area in which they stand

262

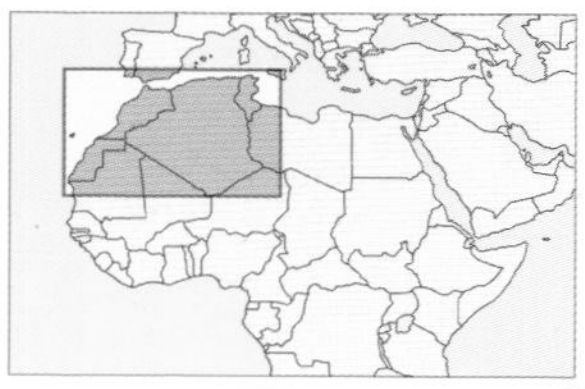

4 192 5 6 7 192

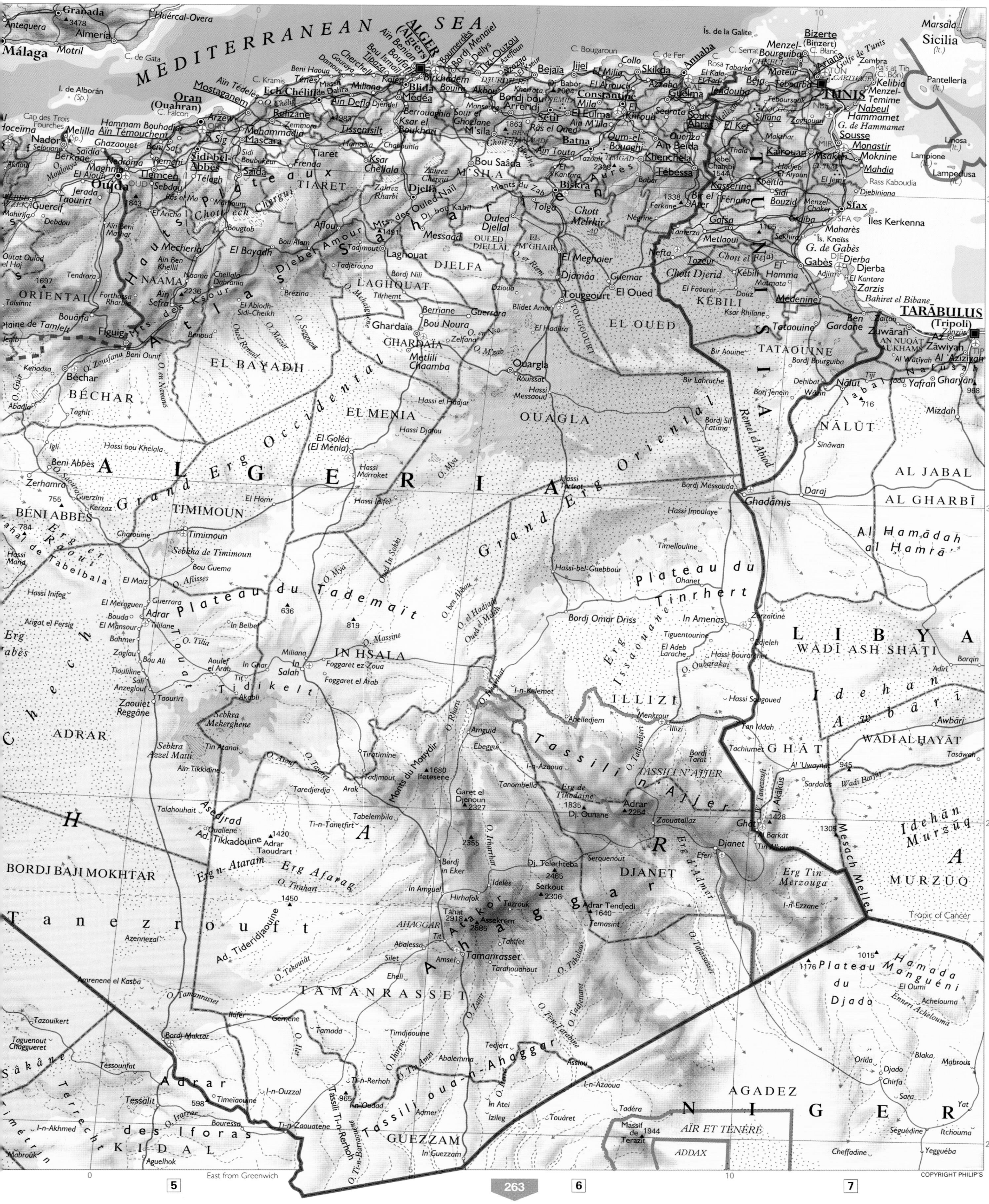

258
5 263 6 7

50 0 50 100 150 200 250 300 km

50 0 50 100 150 200 miles

1:6 400 000

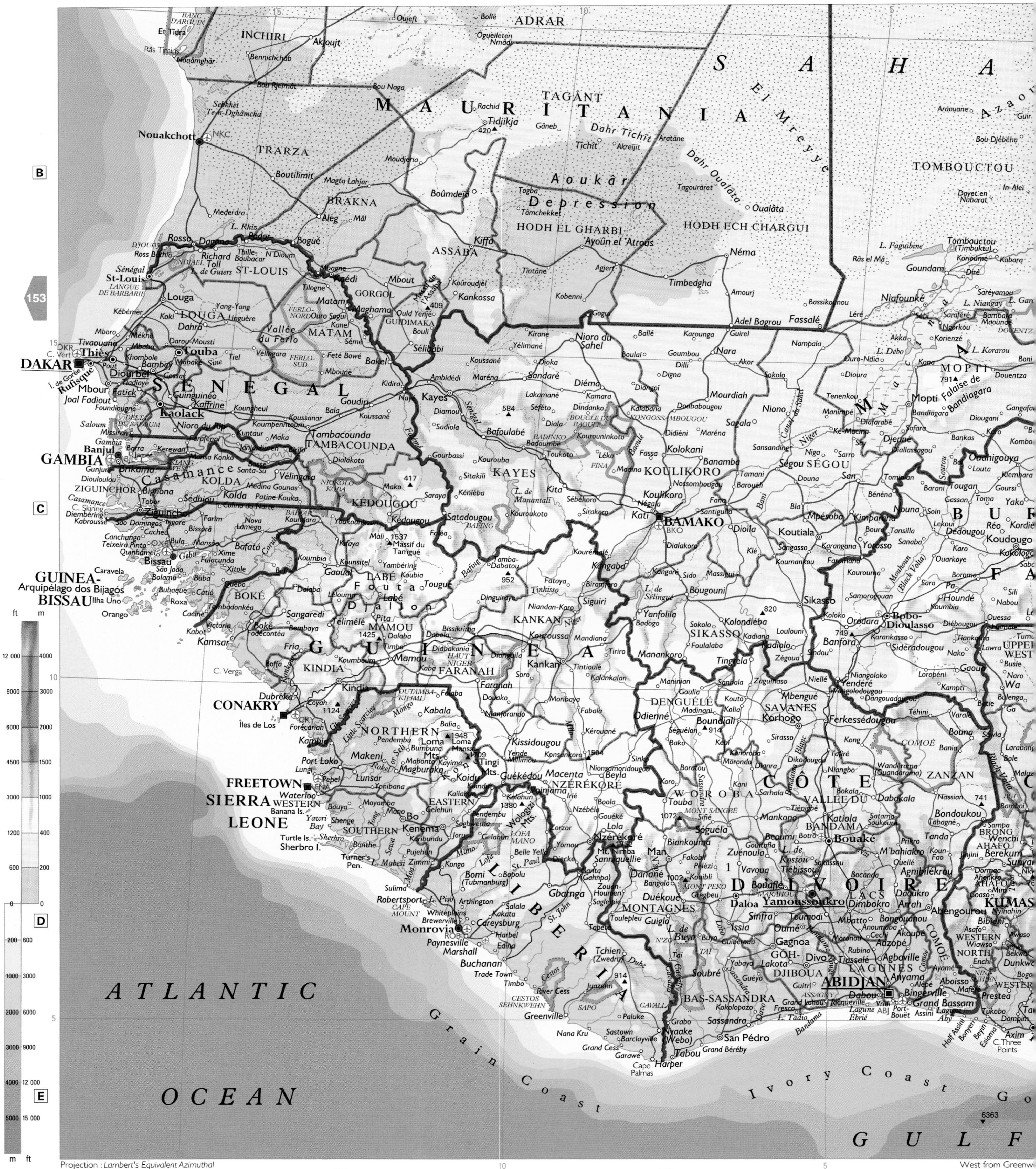

Underlined towns give their name to the administrative area in which they stand.

Administrative division in Côte d'Ivoire:
1 Sassandra-Marahoué

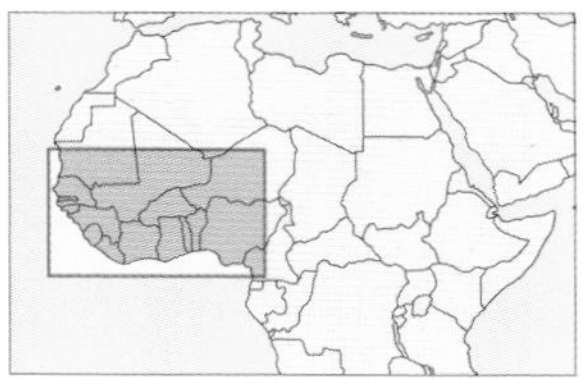

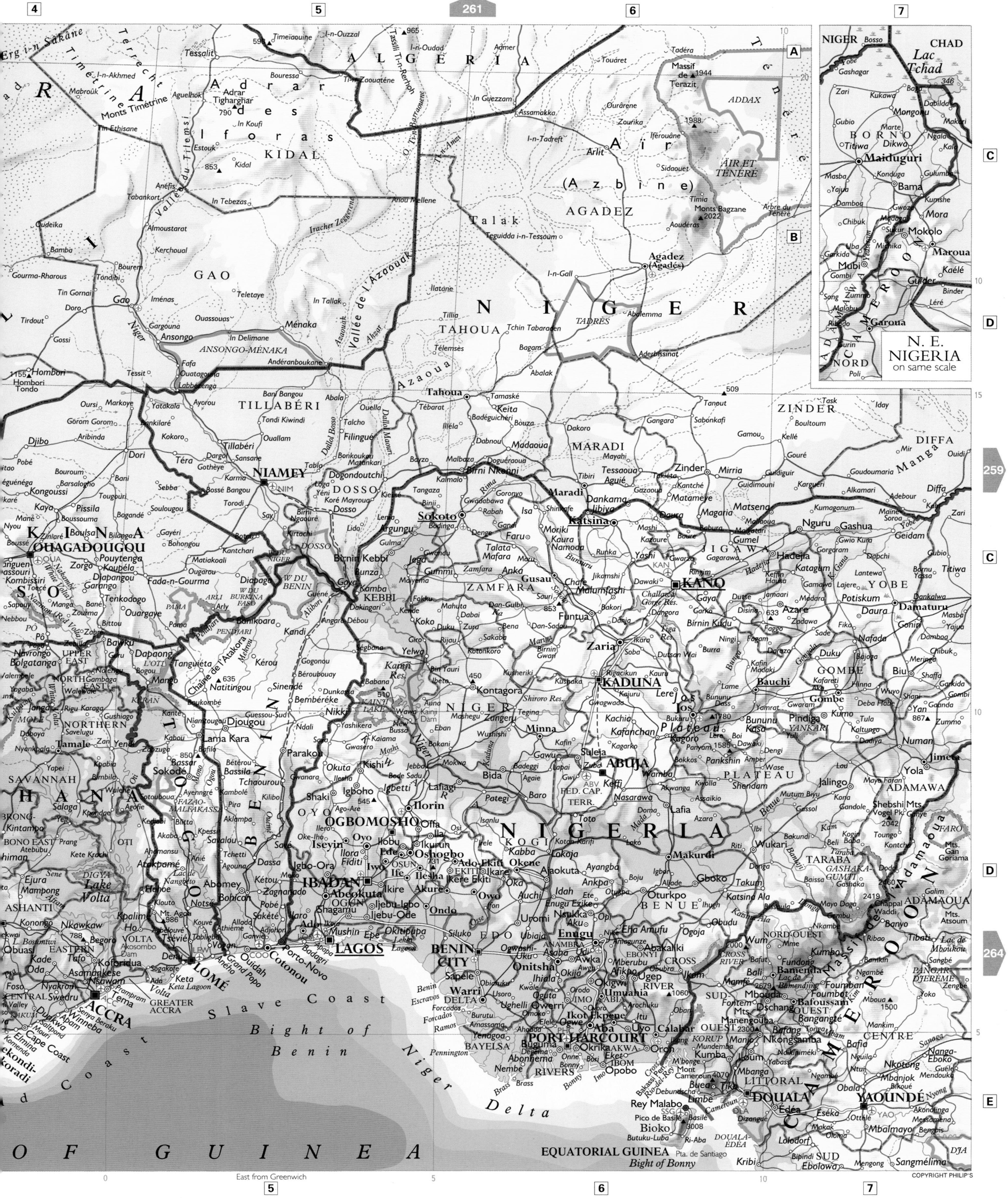
ALGERIA
NIGER
NIGERIA
BENIN
TOGO
GHANA
CAMEROON
CHAD
Lac Tchad
N. E. NIGERIA
on same scale
Adrar des Iforas
Aïr (Azbine)
AGADEZ
GAO
KIDAL
TAHOUA
TILLABÉRI
MARADI
ZINDER
DIFFA
DOSSO
NIAMEY
OUAGADOUGOU
ACCRA
LOMÉ
Cotonou
Porto-Novo
LAGOS
IBADAN
OGBOMOSHO
ABUJA
KADUNA
KANO
Zaria
Jos
Plateau
Sokoto
Katsina
Maiduguri
Enugu
BENIN CITY
PORT HARCOURT
DOUALA
YAOUNDÉ
Lake Volta
Slave Coast
Bight of Benin
Niger Delta
Bight of Bonny
OF GUINEA
EQUATORIAL GUINEA
East from Greenwich
COPYRIGHT PHILIP'S
261
259
264
4
5
6
7
A
B
C
D
E

50 0 50 100 150 200 250 300 km

50 0 50 100 150 200 miles

1:6 400 000

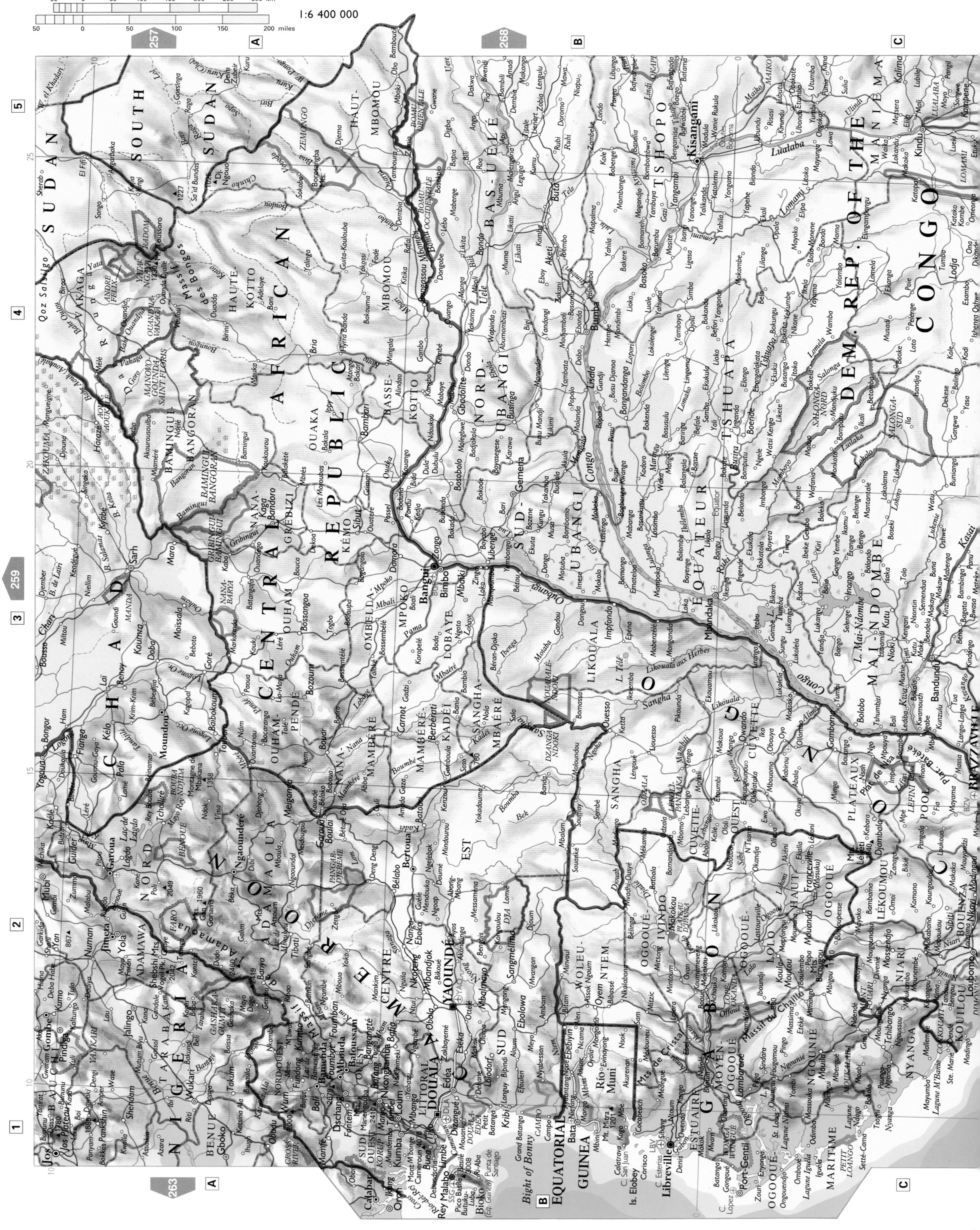

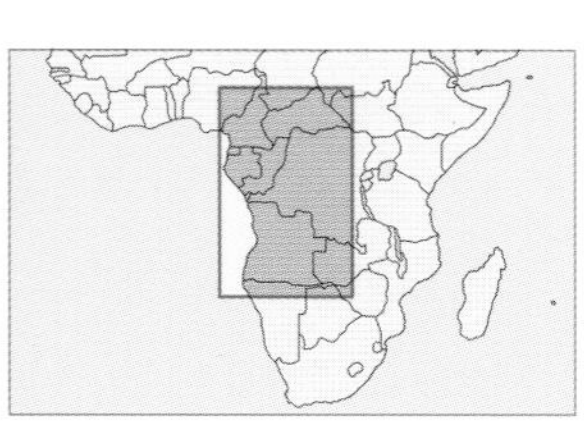

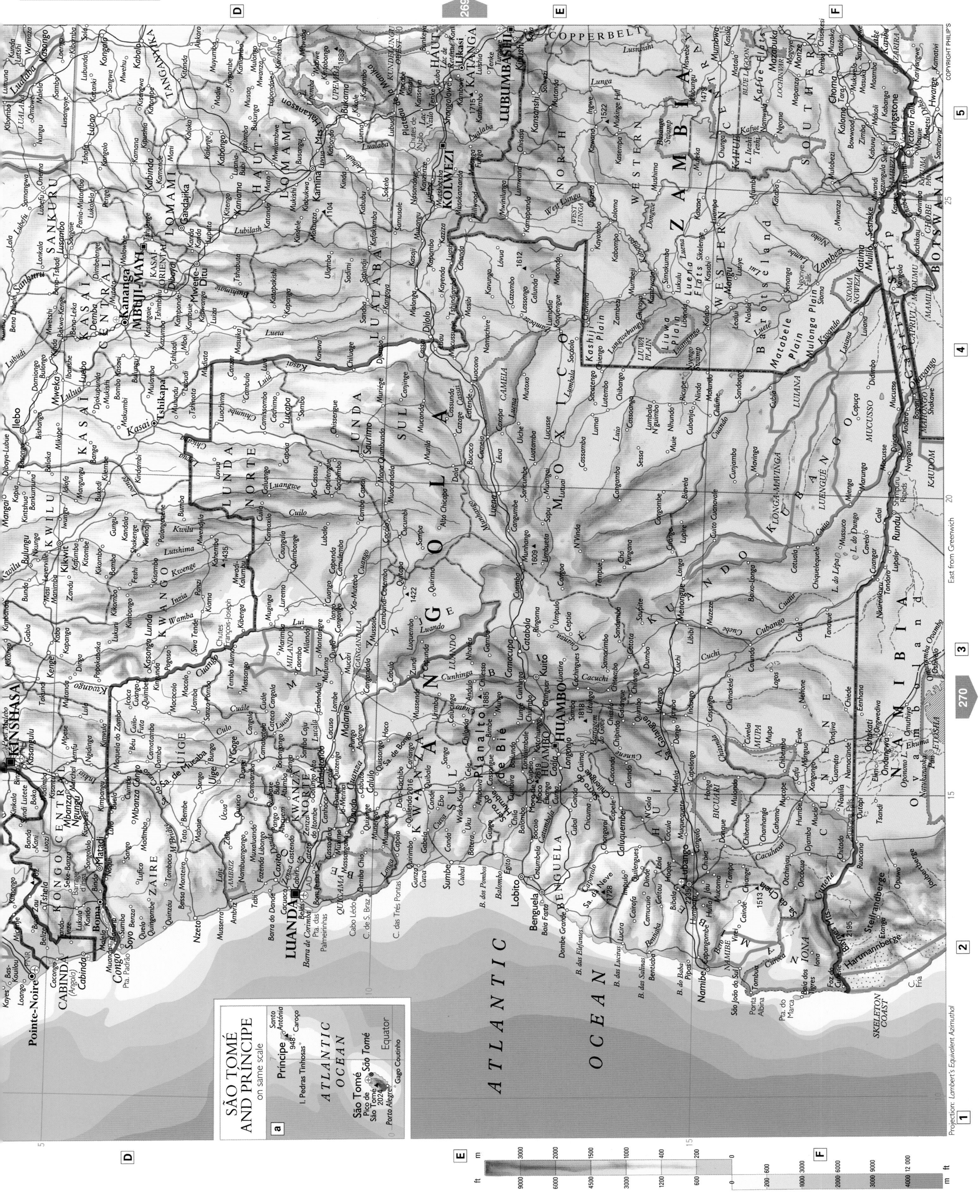
KINSHASA
LUANDA
HUAMBO
LUBUMBASHI
KOLWEZI
ATLANTIC
OCEAN
SÃO TOMÉ AND PRÍNCIPE
on same scale
Projection: Lambert's Equivalent Azimuthal
East from Greenwich
COPYRIGHT PHILIP'S
269
270

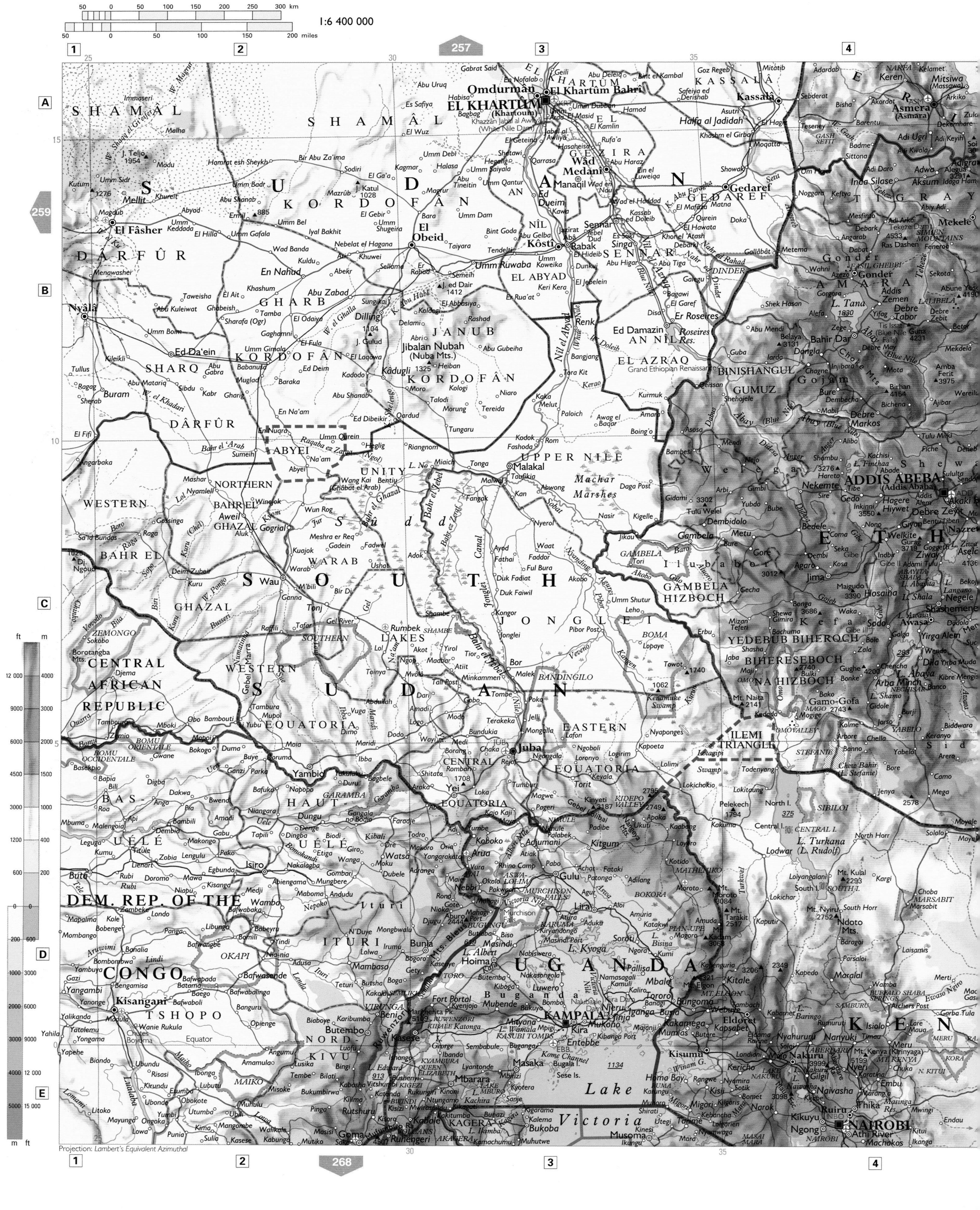
1:6 400 000
km
miles
257
259
268
SUDAN
SOUTH SUDAN
ETH
ERI
KEN
UGANDA
DEM. REP. OF THE CONGO
CENTRAL AFRICAN REPUBLIC
ABYEI
ILEMI TRIANGLE
EL KHARTUM
Omdurmân
El Khartûm Bahrî
Kassalâ
Asmera (Asmara)
Mitsiwa (Massawa)
Wad Medanî
Gedaref
El Obeid
Kôstî
El Fâsher
Nyâlâ
Ed Da'ein
Kâdugli
Malakal
Wau
Juba
ADDIS ABEBA
Gonder
Bahir Dar
Gambela
KAMPALA
NAIROBI
Kisangani
Gulu
Entebbe
Eldoret
Nakuru
Lake Victoria
L. Turkana (L. Rudolf)
L. Tana
L. Albert
L. Kyoga
Sudd
Machar Marshes
Equator
Projection: Lambert's Equivalent Azimuthal

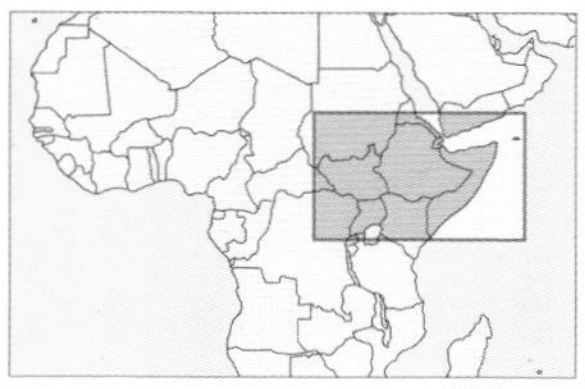

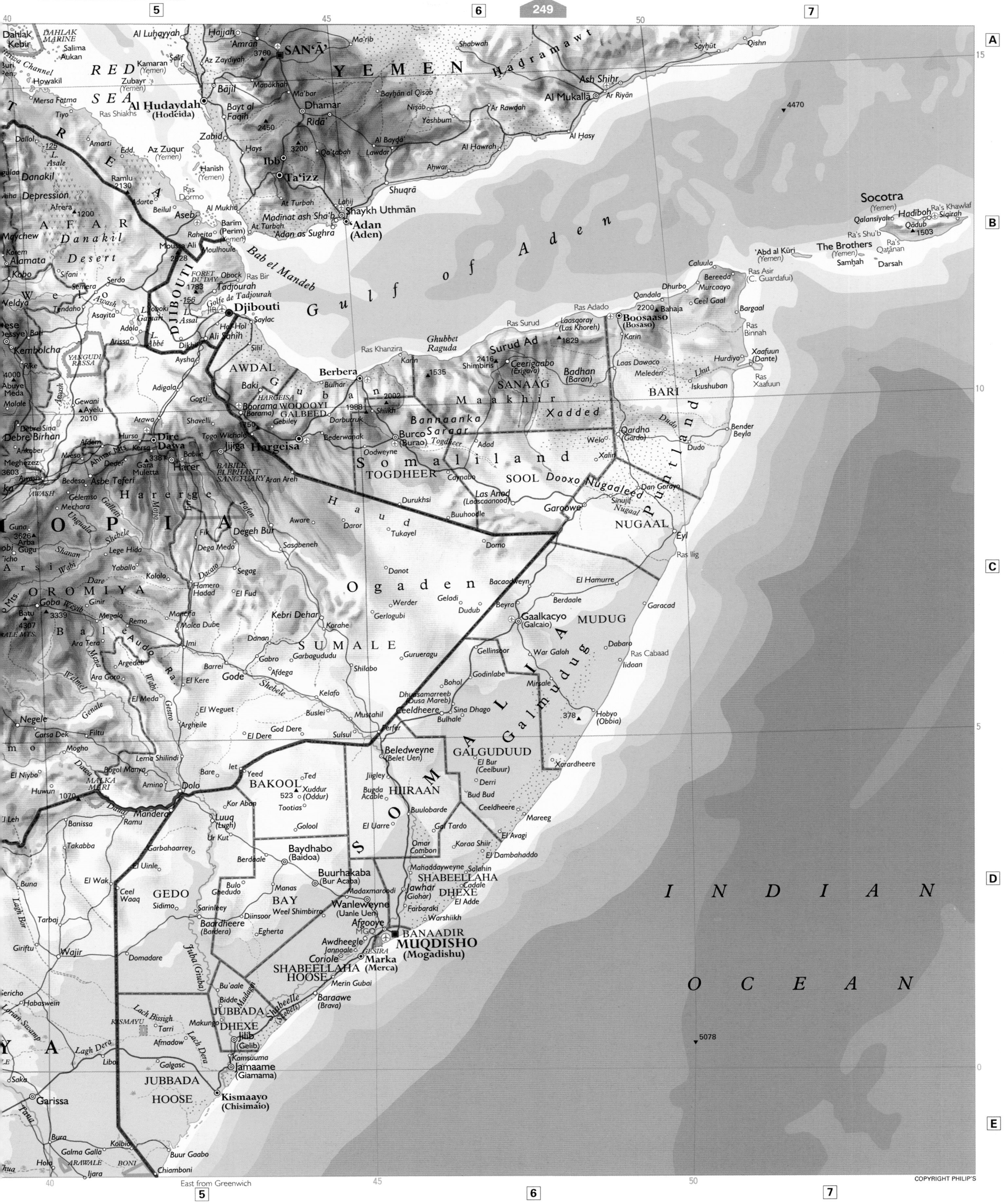
249
RED SEA
YEMEN
SAN'Ā'
Hadramawt
Al Hudaydah (Hodeida)
Dhamar
Ibb
Ta'izz
Adan (Aden)
Shaykh Uthmān
Al Mukallā
Ash Shihr
Sayhūt
Qishn
Shabwah
Ma'rib
Shuqrā
Zabid
Mocha
Bab el Mandeb
Gulf of Aden
Socotra (Yemen)
Hadiboh
Qalansiyah
The Brothers (Yemen)
'Abd al Kūri (Yemen)
Samhah
Darsah
Ras Asir (C. Guardafui)
DJIBOUTI
Djibouti
Tadjourah
Golfe de Tadjourah
Obock
L. Assal
Ali Sabih
Assab
Danakil Depression
Danakil Desert
AFAR
ERITREA
ETHIOPIA
Dire Dawa
Harer
Jijiga
Hargeisa
Berbera
Boorama (Borama)
Burco (Burao)
Ceerigaabo (Erigavo)
Laasqoray (Las Khoreh)
Boosaaso (Bosaso)
Qandala
Bargaal
Hurdiyo
Xaafuun (Dante)
Ras Xaafuun
Bender Beyla
Qardho (Gardo)
Garoowe
Eyl
Las Anod (Laascaanood)
Somaliland
Puntland
AWDAL
WOQOOYI GALBEED
TOGDHEER
SANAAG
BARI
SOOL
NUGAAL
MUDUG
GALGUDUUD
HIIRAAN
BAKOOL
BAY
GEDO
SHABEELLAHA DHEXE
SHABEELLAHA HOOSE
BANAADIR
JUBBADA DHEXE
JUBBADA HOOSE
Haud
Ogaden
SUMALE
OROMIYA
Harerge
Bale
Gaalkacyo (Galcaio)
Dhuusamarreeb (Dusa Mareb)
Hobyo (Obbia)
Beledweyne (Belet Uen)
Baydhabo (Baidoa)
Buurhakaba (Bur Acaba)
Afgooye
Wanlaweyne (Uanle Uen)
Jawhar (Giohar)
MUQDISHO (Mogadishu)
Marka (Merca)
Baraawe (Brava)
Jilib (Gelib)
Jamaame (Giamama)
Kismaayo (Chisimaio)
Luuq (Lugh)
Baardheere (Bardera)
Doolow
Mandera
Wajir
Garissa
Kebri Dehar
Gode
Degeh Bur
Negele
SOMALIA
INDIAN OCEAN
4470
5078
East from Greenwich
COPYRIGHT PHILIP'S

50 0 50 100 150 200 250 300 km

1:6 400 000

50 0 50 100 150 200 miles

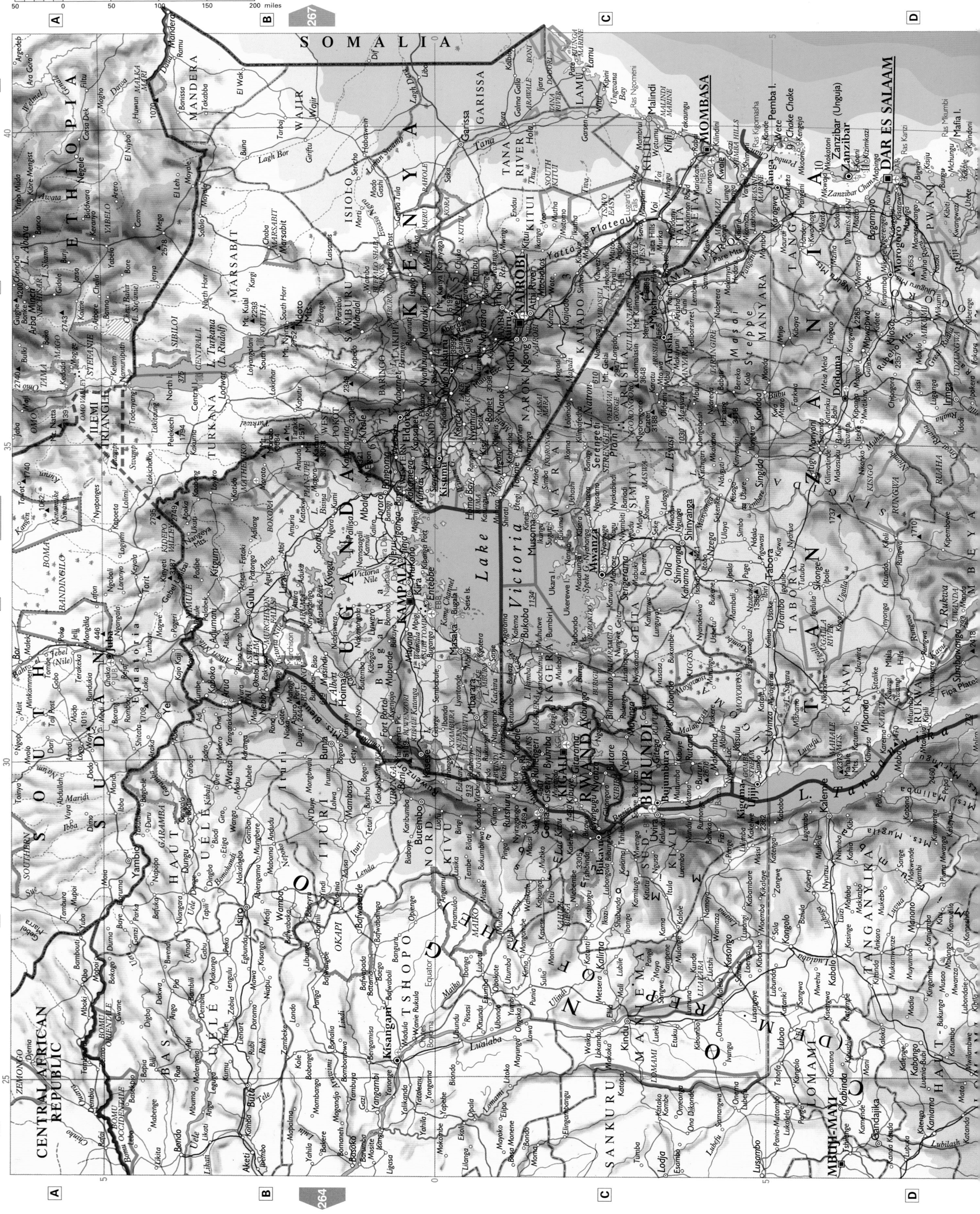

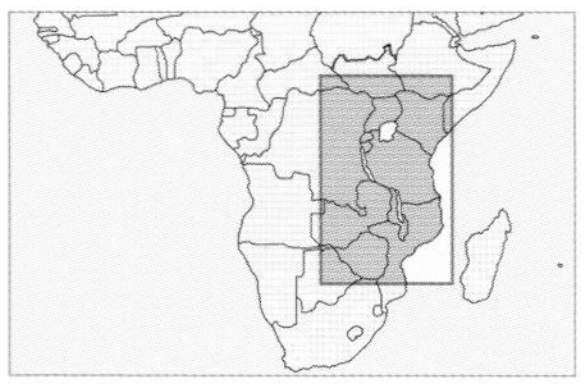

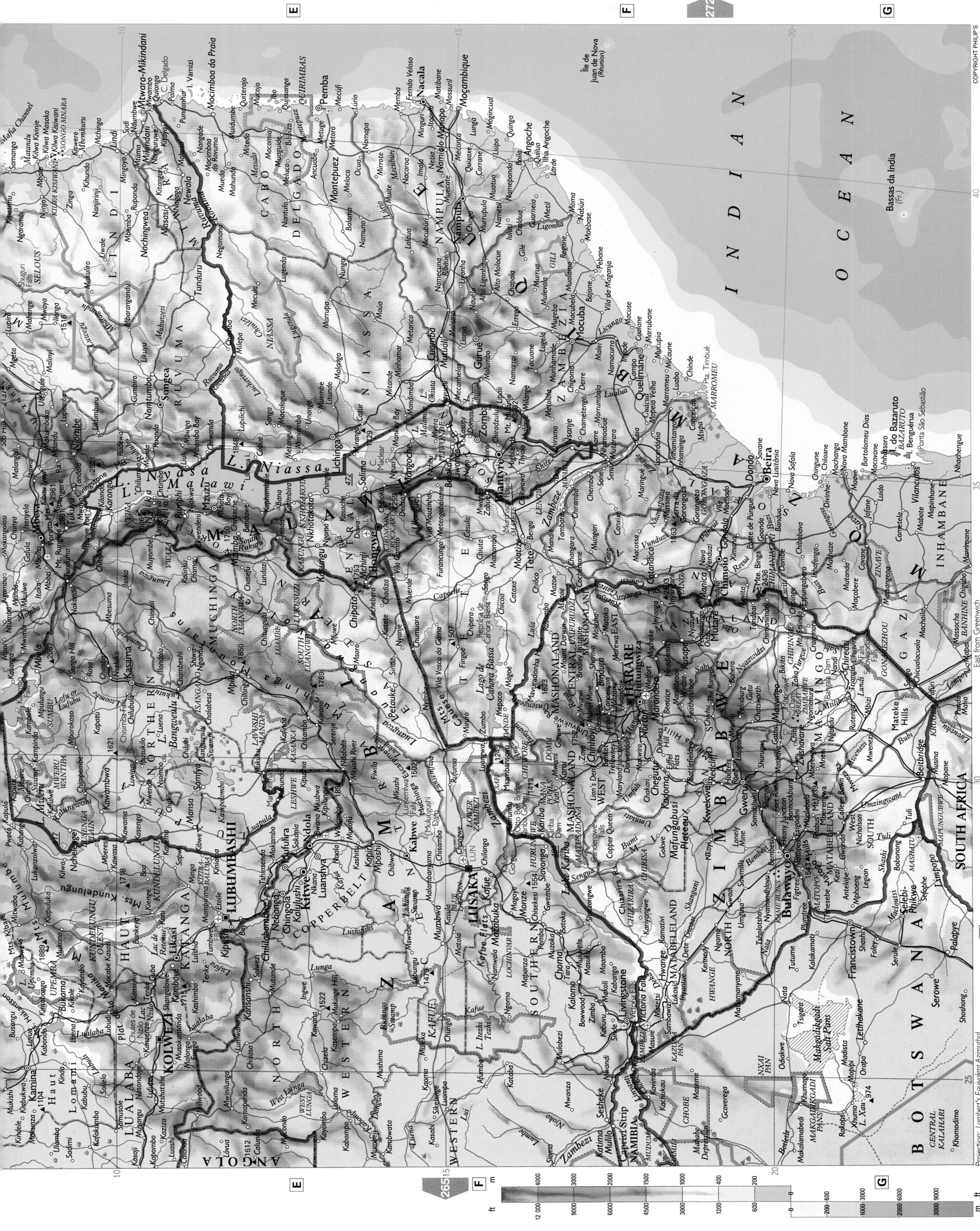
Administrative divisions in Kenya:
1 Elgeyo-Marakwet 3 Makueni 5 Tharaka Nithi 7 Uasin Gishu
2 Kirinyaga 4 Nyandarua 6 Trans-Nzoia
Administrative divisions in Tanzania:
8 North Pemba 10 North Zanzibar
9 South Pemba 11 South Zanzibar
Underlined towns give their name to the administrative area in which they stand.
Projection: Lambert's Equivalent Azimuthal
COPYRIGHT PHILIP'S
East from Greenwich
INDIAN OCEAN
ZAMBIA
ZIMBABWE
BOTSWANA
SOUTH AFRICA
MOÇAMBIQUE
NAMIBIA
ANGOLA
LUSAKA
HARARE
LUBUMBASHI

1:6 400 000

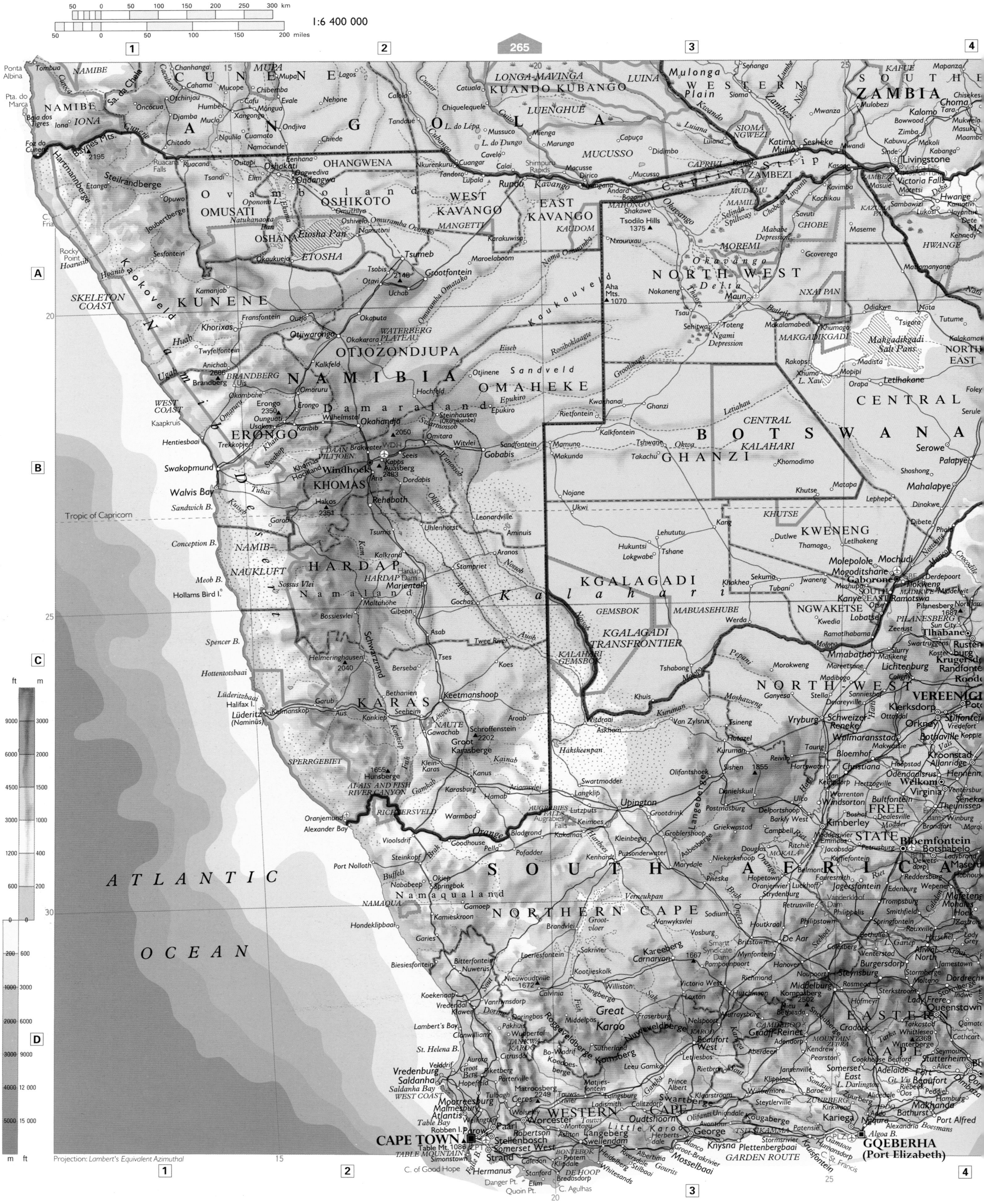

50 0 50 100 150 200 250 300 km
50 0 50 100 150 200 miles
265
ANGOLA
ZAMBIA
NAMIBIA
BOTSWANA
SOUTH AFRICA
ATLANTIC OCEAN
Tropic of Capricorn
NAMIBE
CUNENE
KUANDO KUBANGO
OHANGWENA
OSHIKOTO
OMUSATI
OSHANA
WEST KAVANGO
EAST KAVANGO
KUNENE
OTJOZONDJUPA
OMAHEKE
ERONGO
KHOMAS
HARDAP
KARAS
NORTH WEST
CENTRAL
GHANZI
KGALAGADI
KWENENG
NGWAKETSE
NORTHERN CAPE
WESTERN CAPE
EASTERN CAPE
FREE STATE
SKELETON COAST
Kaokoveld
Namib Desert
Damaraland
Namaland
Namaqualand
Kalahari
Great Karoo
Little Karoo
Okavango Delta
Makgadikgadi Salt Pans
Etosha Pan
Caprivi Strip
Windhoek
Walvis Bay
Swakopmund
Lüderitz
Keetmanshoop
Gaborone
Maun
Kimberley
Bloemfontein
CAPE TOWN
GQEBERHA (Port Elizabeth)
Livingstone
Victoria Falls
Orange
Okavango
Zambezi
C. of Good Hope
C. Agulhas
Projection: Lambert's Equivalent Azimuthal

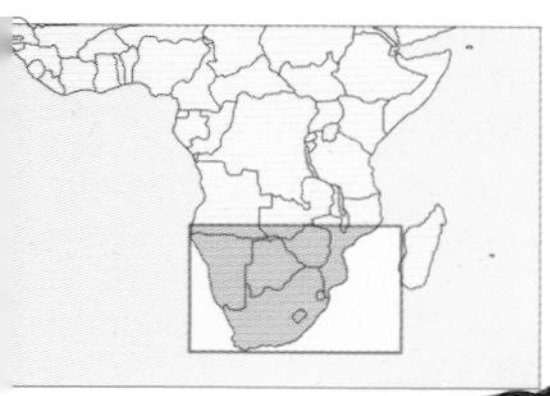

269
272
5
6
7
A
B
C
D
20
25
30
35
40
East from Greenwich
Tropic of Capricorn
MOZAMBIQUE CHANNEL
INDIAN OCEAN
ZIMBABWE
MOZAMBIQUE
MALAWI
ESWATINI
ZAMBEZIA
TETE
MASHONALAND CENTRAL
MASHONALAND EAST
MASHONALAND WEST
MANICA
SOFALA
INHAMBANE
GAZA
MASVINGO
MATABELELAND SOUTH
LIMPOPO
MPUMALANGA
KWAZULU NATAL
MAPUTO
HARARE
Chitungwiza
Bulawayo
Gweru
Kwekwe
Kadoma
Chinhoyi
Kariba
Marondera
Rusape
Mutare
Masvingo
Zvishavane
Beitbridge
Chimoio
Beira
Dondo
Quelimane
Mocuba
Angoche
I. Angoche
Tete
Chinde
Vilanculos
I. do Bazaruto
I. Benguérua
Inhambane
Maxixe
Xai-Xai
Chókwè
Chibuto
MAPUTO
Matola
Pen. Inhaca
Mbabane
Manzini
Polokwane
Phalaborwa
Mokopane
Thohoyandou
Louis Trichardt (Makhado)
Musina
PRETORIA (Tshwane)
JOHANNESBURG
Benoni
Springs
Nigel
Middelburg
Mbombela (Nelspruit)
Ermelo
Standerton
Newcastle
Vryheid
Ulundi
Ladysmith
Richards Bay
Empangeni
Pietermaritzburg
DURBAN
Umlazi
Umkomaas
Scottburgh
Port Shepstone
Margate
Kokstad
East London
Mthatha
LESOTHO
Île de Júan de Nova (Fr.)
Bassas da India (Fr.)
Île Europa (Fr.)
Lago de Cahora Bassa
Limpopo
Zambeze
L. St. Lucia
C. St. Lucia
L. Sibayi
B. de Maputo
C. das Correntes
Pta. da Barra Falsa
Pta. Timbué
Nova Sofala
I. Chiloane
Bartolomeu Dias
Save
Gorongosa
Sierra da Gorongoza
Inyangani
Drakensberg
Mt. aux Sources

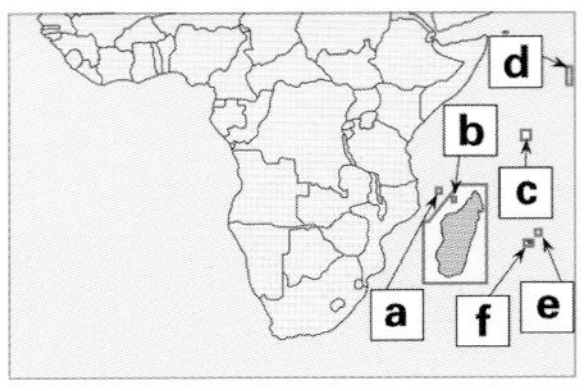

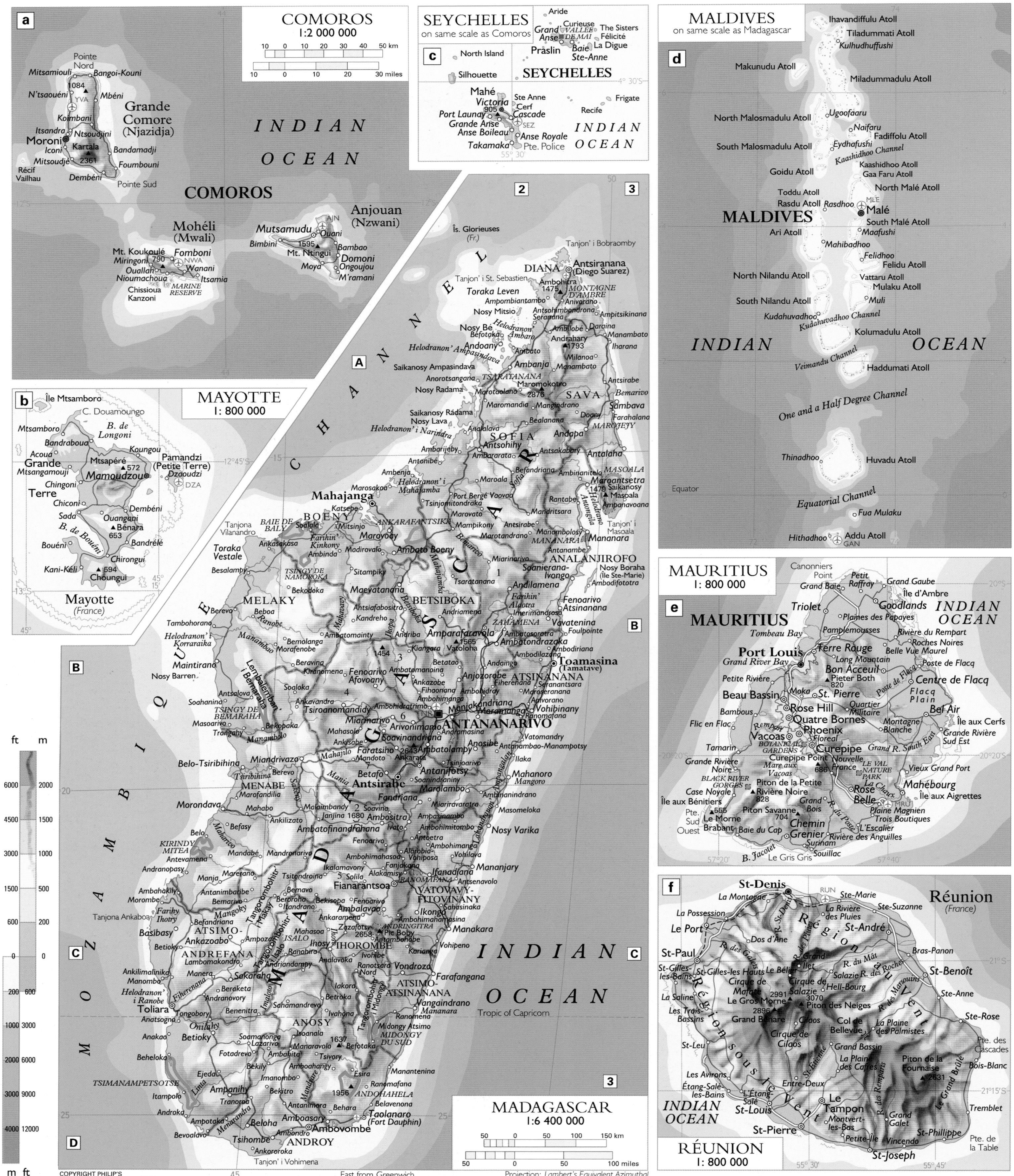

Administrative divisions in Madagascar:
1 Alaotra-Mangoro
2 Amoron'i Mania
3 Analamanga
4 Bongolava
5 Haute Matsiatra
6 Itasy
7 Vakinankaratra

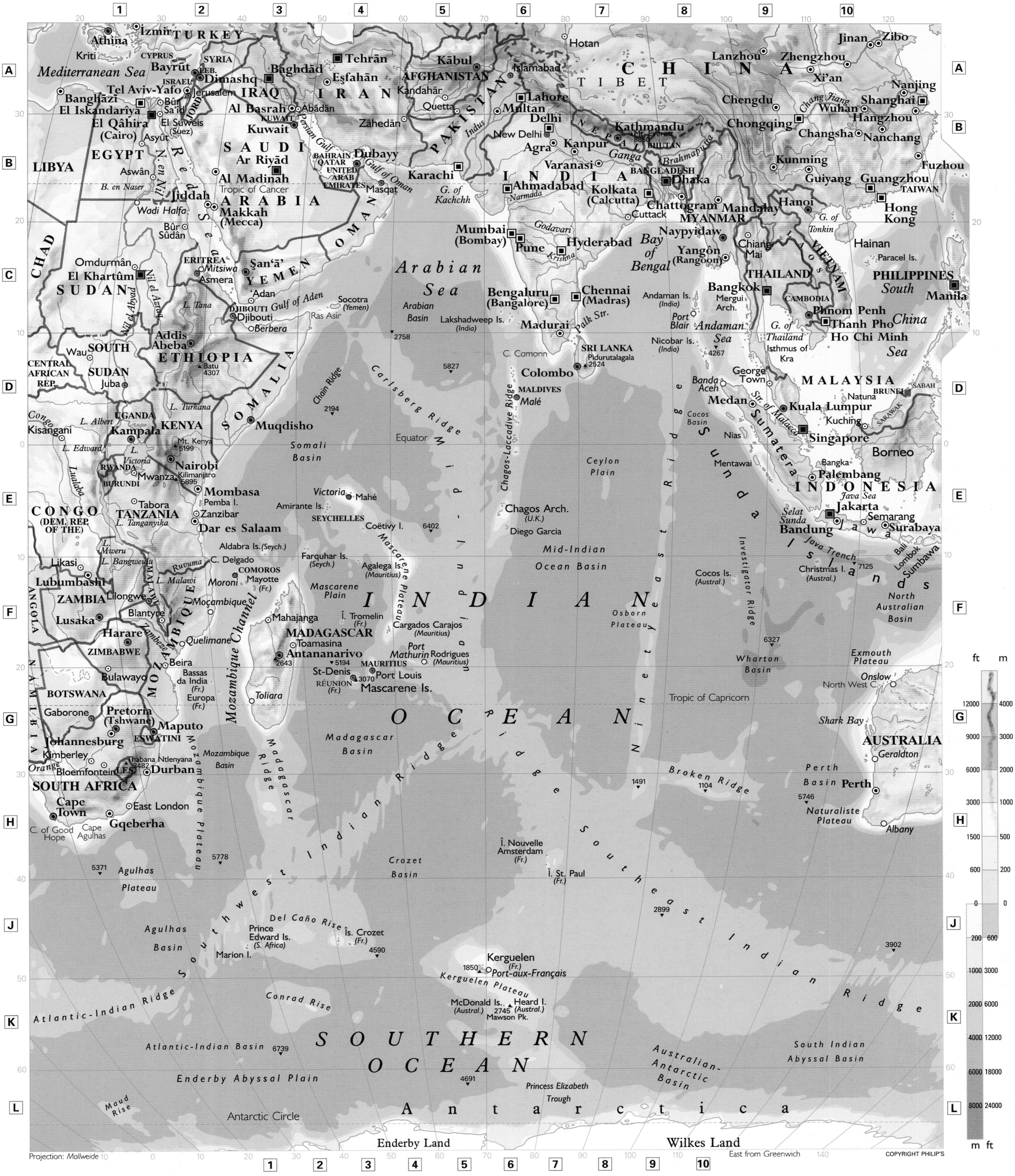

INDIAN OCEAN
Arabian Sea
Bay of Bengal
Andaman Sea
South China Sea
Mediterranean Sea
Red Sea
Persian Gulf
Gulf of Oman
Gulf of Aden
G. of Kachchh
G. of Tonkin
G. of Thailand
Java Sea
Mozambique Channel
Str. of Malacca
Palk Str.
SOUTHERN OCEAN
Antarctica
Enderby Land
Wilkes Land
Princess Elizabeth Trough
Antarctic Circle
Tropic of Cancer
Tropic of Capricorn
Equator
TURKEY
SYRIA
LEB.
ISRAEL
JORDAN
CYPRUS
IRAQ
IRAN
KUWAIT
BAHRAIN
QATAR
UNITED ARAB EMIRATES
SAUDI ARABIA
OMAN
YEMEN
ERITREA
DJIBOUTI
ETHIOPIA
SOMALIA
KENYA
UGANDA
RWANDA
BURUNDI
TANZANIA
SOUTH SUDAN
SUDAN
EGYPT
LIBYA
CHAD
CENTRAL AFRICAN REP.
CONGO (DEM. REP. OF THE)
ANGOLA
ZAMBIA
MALAWI
MOZAMBIQUE
ZIMBABWE
BOTSWANA
NAMIBIA
SOUTH AFRICA
LES.
ESWATINI
MADAGASCAR
COMOROS
SEYCHELLES
MAURITIUS
RÉUNION (Fr.)
AFGHANISTAN
PAKISTAN
INDIA
NEPAL
BHUTAN
BANGLADESH
SRI LANKA
MALDIVES
MYANMAR
THAILAND
LAOS
VIETNAM
CAMBODIA
MALAYSIA
BRUNEI
SABAH
SARAWAK
INDONESIA
PHILIPPINES
TAIWAN
CHINA
TIBET
AUSTRALIA
Athina
Izmir
Kriti
Bayrūt
Dimashq
Tel Aviv-Yafo
Jerusalem
Banghāzī
El Iskandarîya
El Qâhira (Cairo)
El Suweis (Suez)
Bûr Sa'îd
Asyût
Aswân
Wadi Halfa
Bûr Sûdân
Omdurmân
El Khartûm
Baghdād
Tehrān
Eşfahān
Al Basrah
Ābādān
Kuwait
Ar Riyād
Al Madinah
Jiddah
Makkah (Mecca)
Dubayy
Masqat
Zāhedān
Kābul
Kandahār
Quetta
Islamabad
Lahore
Multan
Karachi
Delhi
New Delhi
Agra
Kanpur
Varanasi
Kathmandu
Mt. Everest 8850
Dhaka
Ahmadabad
Kolkata (Calcutta)
Chattogram
Cuttack
Mumbai (Bombay)
Pune
Hyderabad
Bengaluru (Bangalore)
Chennai (Madras)
Madurai
C. Comorin
Colombo
Pidurutalagala 2524
Malé
Naypyidaw
Mandalay
Yangôn (Rangoon)
Chiang Mai
Bangkok
Phnom Penh
Thanh Pho Ho Chi Minh
Hanoi
Hotan
Lanzhou
Zhengzhou
Xi'an
Jinan
Zibo
Nanjing
Shanghai
Wuhan
Hangzhou
Chengdu
Chongqing
Changsha
Nanchang
Kunming
Guiyang
Guangzhou
Fuzhou
Hong Kong
Hainan
Manila
Paracel Is.
Kuala Lumpur
George Town
Banda Aceh
Medan
Singapore
Kuching
Natuna
Borneo
Palembang
Bangka
Jakarta
Bandung
Semarang
Surabaya
Selat Sunda
Jawa
Bali
Lombok
Sumbawa
Sumatera
Nias
Mentawai
Sunda Islands
Mergui Arch.
Isthmus of Kra
Andaman Is. (India)
Port Blair
Nicobar Is. (India)
Lakshadweep Is. (India)
Cocos Is. (Austral.)
Christmas I. (Austral.)
Onslow
North West C.
Exmouth Plateau
Shark Bay
Geraldton
Perth
Albany
Naturaliste Plateau
Perth Basin
North Australian Basin
Java Trench
Wau
Juba
Addis Abeba
Batu 4307
Djibouti
Berbera
Asmera
Mitsiwa
Şan'ā'
'Adan
Socotra (Yemen)
Ras Asir
Muqdisho
Kampala
Kisangani
Mt. Kenya 5199
Nairobi
Kilimanjaro 5895
Mwanza
Mombasa
Pemba I.
Zanzibar
Dar es Salaam
Tabora
L. Tanganyika
L. Victoria
L. Albert
L. Edward
L. Turkana
L. Tana
L. Mweru
L. Bangweulu
L. Malawi
Lualaba
Congo
Nil el Abyad
Nil el Azraq
Ruvuma
Zambeze
Orange
Likasi
Lubumbashi
Lilongwe
Blantyre
Lusaka
Harare
Bulawayo
Gaborone
Pretoria (Tshwane)
Johannesburg
Maputo
Kimberley
Bloemfontein
Thabana Ntlenyana 3482
Durban
East London
Cape Town
Gqeberha
C. of Good Hope
Cape Agulhas
Beira
Quelimane
Moçambique
C. Delgado
Moroni
Mayotte (Fr.)
Aldabra Is. (Seych.)
Farquhar Is. (Seych.)
Agalega Is. (Mauritius)
Coëtivy I.
Amirante Is.
Victoria
Mahé
Mahajanga
Toamasina
Antananarivo
Toliara
Bassas da India (Fr.)
Europa (Fr.)
Î. Tromelin (Fr.)
Cargados Carajos (Mauritius)
Port Mathurin
Rodrigues (Mauritius)
St-Denis
Port Louis
Mascarene Is.
Chagos Arch. (U.K.)
Diego Garcia
Î. Nouvelle Amsterdam (Fr.)
Î. St. Paul (Fr.)
Prince Edward Is. (S. Africa)
Marion I.
Îs. Crozet (Fr.)
Kerguelen (Fr.)
Port-aux-Français
McDonald Is. (Austral.)
Heard I. (Austral.)
Mawson Pk.
Arabian Basin
Somali Basin
Carlsberg Ridge
Chain Ridge
Mid-Indian Ridge
Chagos-Laccadive Ridge
Mascarene Plateau
Mascarene Plain
Mid-Indian Ocean Basin
Ceylon Plain
Cocos Basin
Ninetyeast Ridge
Investigator Ridge
Wharton Basin
Osborn Plateau
Broken Ridge
Madagascar Basin
Madagascar Ridge
Mozambique Basin
Mozambique Plateau
Southwest Indian Ridge
Southeast Indian Ridge
Crozet Basin
Del Caño Rise
Agulhas Plateau
Agulhas Basin
Conrad Rise
Kerguelen Plateau
Atlantic-Indian Ridge
Atlantic-Indian Basin
Enderby Abyssal Plain
Maud Rise
Australian-Antarctic Basin
South Indian Abyssal Basin
2758
5827
2194
6402
5194
3070
2643
4267
7125
6327
1491
1104
5746
5778
5371
2899
4590
1850
2745
6739
4691
3902
ft
m
12000
9000
6000
3000
1500
600
200
0
4000
3000
2000
1000
500
200
0
200
600
1000
3000
2000
6000
4000
12000
6000
18000
8000
24000
m ft
Projection: Mollweide
East from Greenwich
COPYRIGHT PHILIP'S

AUSTRALIA AND OCEANIA

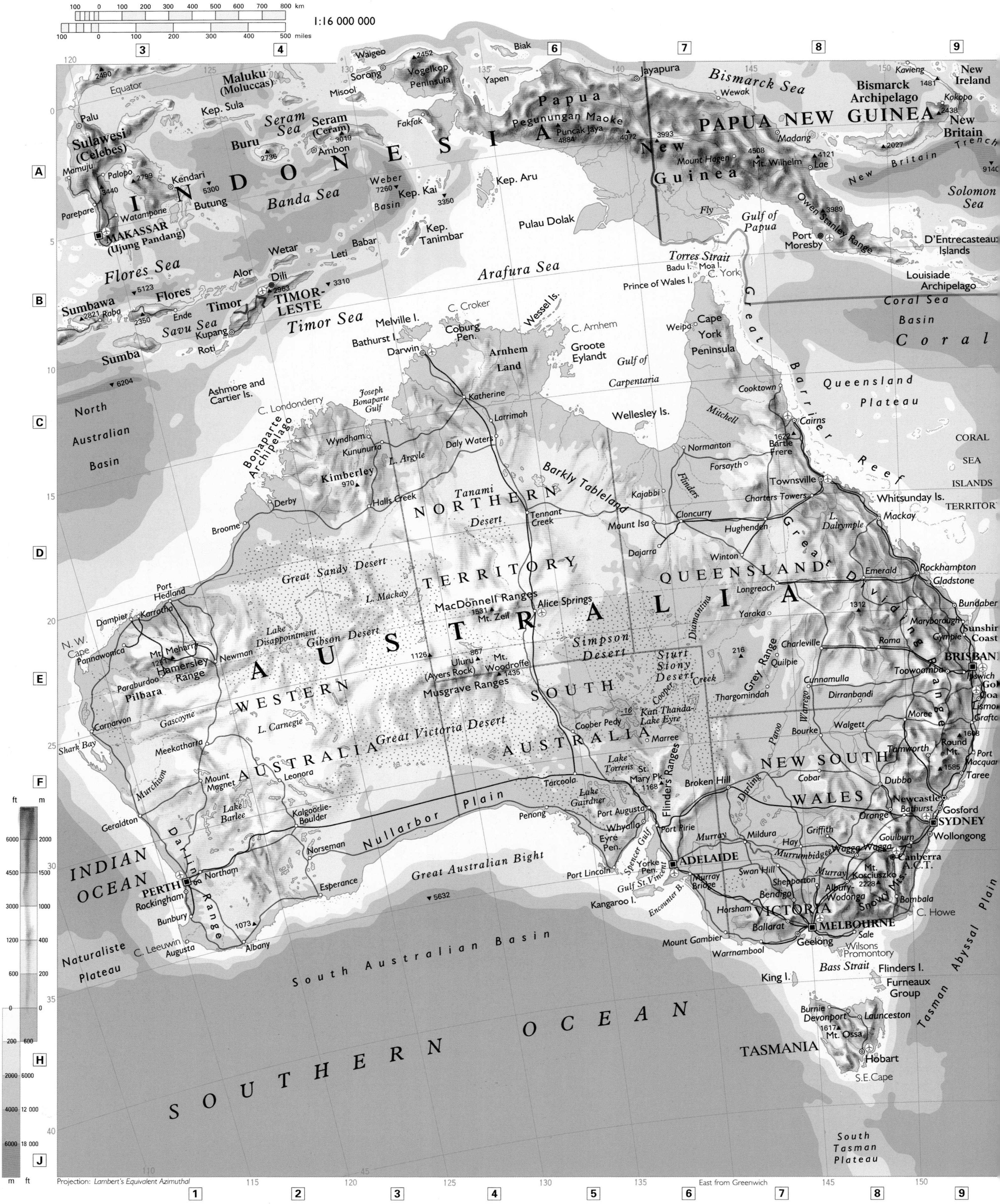
1:16 000 000
km
miles
INDONESIA
Maluku (Moluccas)
Sulawesi (Celebes)
Kep. Sula
Seram Sea
Seram (Ceram)
Buru
Ambon
Kendari
Butung
Banda Sea
Weber Basin
Kep. Kai
Kep. Aru
Kep. Tanimbar
MAKASSAR (Ujung Pandang)
Watampone
Parepare
Palopo
Mamuju
Palu
Equator
Waigeo
Sorong
Vogelkop Peninsula
Misool
Fakfak
Biak
Yapen
Jayapura
Papua
Pegunungan Maoke
Puncak Jaya
New Guinea
PAPUA NEW GUINEA
Bismarck Sea
Wewak
Madang
Mount Hagen
Mt. Wilhelm
Lae
Bismarck Archipelago
New Ireland
Kavieng
Kokopo
New Britain
New Britain Trench
Solomon Sea
Owen Stanley Range
Gulf of Papua
Port Moresby
Fly
D'Entrecasteaux Islands
Louisiade Archipelago
Pulau Dolak
Torres Strait
Badu I.
Moa I.
C. York
Prince of Wales I.
Arafura Sea
Flores Sea
Wetar
Babar
Leti
Alor
Dili
TIMOR-LESTE
Timor
Timor Sea
Flores
Ende
Sumbawa
Raba
Savu Sea
Kupang
Roti
Sumba
North Australian Basin
Ashmore and Cartier Is.
Coral Sea Basin
Coral
Queensland Plateau
CORAL SEA ISLANDS TERRITORY
Great Barrier Reef
Melville I.
Bathurst I.
Darwin
C. Croker
Coburg Pen.
Wessel Is.
C. Arnhem
Arnhem Land
Groote Eylandt
Gulf of Carpentaria
Cape York Peninsula
Weipa
Cooktown
Cairns
Bartle Frere
Mitchell
Wellesley Is.
Normanton
Forsayth
Flinders
Townsville
Charters Towers
Whitsunday Is.
Mackay
Joseph Bonaparte Gulf
C. Londonderry
Bonaparte Archipelago
Wyndham
Kununurra
L. Argyle
Kimberley
Halls Creek
Derby
Broome
Katherine
Larrimah
Daly Waters
Tanami Desert
NORTHERN TERRITORY
Barkly Tableland
Tennant Creek
Kajabbi
Cloncurry
Mount Isa
Dajarra
Hughenden
L. Dalrymple
Great Dividing Range
Winton
QUEENSLAND
Longreach
Emerald
Rockhampton
Gladstone
Bundaberg
Maryborough
Sunshine Coast
Gympie
Roma
Yaraka
Charleville
Quilpie
Grey Range
Toowoomba
BRISBANE
Ipswich
Cunnamulla
Dirranbandi
Thargomindah
Sturt Stony Desert
Cooper Creek
Diamantina
Warrego
Paroo
Great Sandy Desert
L. Mackay
MacDonnell Ranges
Mt. Zeil
Alice Springs
Lake Disappointment
Gibson Desert
Simpson Desert
AUSTRALIA
Uluru (Ayers Rock)
Mt. Woodroffe
Musgrave Ranges
SOUTH AUSTRALIA
Kati Thanda-Lake Eyre
Coober Pedy
Marree
Great Victoria Desert
L. Carnegie
WESTERN AUSTRALIA
Port Hedland
Dampier
Karratha
N. W. Cape
Pannawonica
Mt. Meharry
Hamersley Range
Newman
Paraburdoo
Pilbara
Carnarvon
Gascoyne
Shark Bay
Meekatharra
Murchison
Mount Magnet
Leonora
Lake Barlee
Kalgoorlie-Boulder
Geraldton
Darling Range
Northam
PERTH
Rockingham
Bunbury
Norseman
Esperance
Albany
Augusta
C. Leeuwin
Naturaliste Plateau
INDIAN OCEAN
Nullarbor Plain
Great Australian Bight
Tarcoola
Lake Gairdner
Lake Torrens
St. Mary Pk.
Flinders Ranges
Penong
Port Augusta
Whyalla
Eyre Pen.
Port Lincoln
Spencer Gulf
Yorke Pen.
Gulf St. Vincent
Kangaroo I.
Port Pirie
ADELAIDE
Encounter B.
Murray Bridge
Broken Hill
Bourke
Walgett
Moree
Cobar
Darling
NEW SOUTH WALES
Tamworth
Round Mt.
Port Macquarie
Taree
Dubbo
Newcastle
Bathurst
Orange
Gosford
SYDNEY
Wollongong
Murray
Mildura
Hay
Griffith
Murrumbidgee
Wagga Wagga
Goulburn
Canberra
A.C.T.
Mt. Kosciuszko
Snowy Mts.
Swan Hill
Shepparton
Bendigo
Albury-Wodonga
Bombala
C. Howe
Horsham
VICTORIA
Ballarat
MELBOURNE
Geelong
Sale
Mount Gambier
Warrnambool
Wilsons Promontory
Bass Strait
King I.
Flinders I.
Furneaux Group
Burnie
Devonport
Launceston
Mt. Ossa
TASMANIA
Hobart
S.E.Cape
Tasman Abyssal Plain
South Tasman Plateau
South Australian Basin
SOUTHERN OCEAN
Projection: Lambert's Equivalent Azimuthal
East from Greenwich
ft
m

Ontong Java Plateau
Solomon Rise
Melanesia
Bougainville
Mt. Balbi
2743
Shortland Is.
Choiseul
1067
Vella Lavella
New Georgia Is.
SOLOMON ISLANDS
Santa Isabel
1219
Vangunu
Russell Is.
Florida Is.
Malaita
1432
Honiara
2439
Guadalcanal
Makira (San Cristóbal)
1250
Pocklington Reef
Bellona
Rennell
South Solomon Trench
7223
Reef Is.
Duff Is.
Nendo
Santa Cruz Is.
Vanikoro
9165
Fataka
Tikopia
Vitiaz Trench
Sea
Is. Torres
Vanua Lava
Is. Banks
Gaua
Espíritu Santo
1879
VANUATU (New Hebrides)
Malakula
863
Epi
Shepherd Is.
Port Vila
Efate
Erromango
1084
Tanna
7569
Aneityum
West Fiji Basin
Îles D'Entrecasteaux
Îles Chesterfield
Îles Bélep
New Caledonia (Fr.)
1628
Î. Lifou
Î. Maré
La Foa
Nouméa
Yaté
Î. des Pins
Îles Loyauté
South New Hebrides Trench
Î. Matthew
Ceve-i-Ra
Lord Howe Seamount Chain
New Caledonia Basin
Norfolk Ridge
PACIFIC OCEAN
5303
South Fiji Basin
Norfolk I. (Austral.)
Norfolk Basin
Lord Howe I. (Austral.)
734
Lord Howe Rise
Trough
Tasman Sea
5267
Challenger Plateau
North C.
Kaitaia
Whangarei
AUCKLAND
North Island
Hamilton
Bay of Plenty
Tauranga
Rotorua
Gisborne
New Plymouth
Ruapehu
2797
Napier
NEW ZEALAND
Wanganui
Palmerston North
Masterton
Nelson
Cook Strait
Blenheim
Wellington
Greymouth
South Island
Aoraki Mt. Cook
3724
Southern Alps
Christchurch
Chatham Rise
Timaru
Queenstown
Dunedin
Invercargill
Stewart I.
Chatham I.
Chatham Is. (N.Z.)
Pitt I.
Tabiteuea
Beru
Nikunau
Onotoa
Tamana
Gilbert Is.
Arorae
KIRIBATI
Baker I. (U.S.A.)
Equator
International Date Line
Winslow Reef
6195
McKean
Abariringa
Enderbury
Birnie
Phoenix Is.
Nikumaroro
Rawaki
Orona
Manra
Carondelet Reef
Namumea
Nanumanga
Niutao
Nui
Vaitupu
TUVALU (Ellice Is.)
Funafuti
Fongafale
Nukulaelae
Niulakita
Atafu
Tokelau Is. (N.Z.)
Nukunonu
Fakaofo
Rotuma
Mata-Utu
Uvea
Wallis & Futuna (Fr.)
Horn
Alofi
SAMOA
Savai'i
1858
Apia
'Upolu
Pago Pago
American Samoa (U.S.A.)
Tutuila
Niuafo'ou
Niua Group
Niuatoputapu
Vanua Levu
1031
Taveuni
Viti Levu
1323
Suva
FIJI
Kadavu
Lau Group
Lau Ridge
Vava'u Group
Late
Lau Basin
Ha'apai Group
TONGA
Alofi
Niue (N.Z.)
Nuku'alofa
Tongatapu Group
Eua
Ata
10 882
Tonga Trench
Tropic of Capricorn
Raoul I.
Kermadec Is. (N.Z.)
Macauley I.
Curtis I.
10 047
Kermadec Trench
Colville Ridge
Southwest Pacific Basin
International Date Line
West from Greenwich
COPYRIGHT PHILIP'S

50 0 50 100 150 200 250 300 km

1:6 400 000

50 0 50 100 150 200 miles

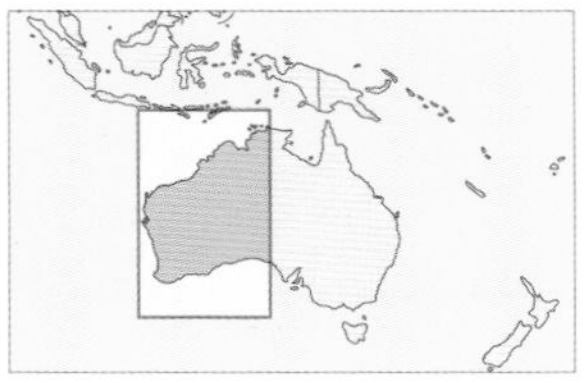

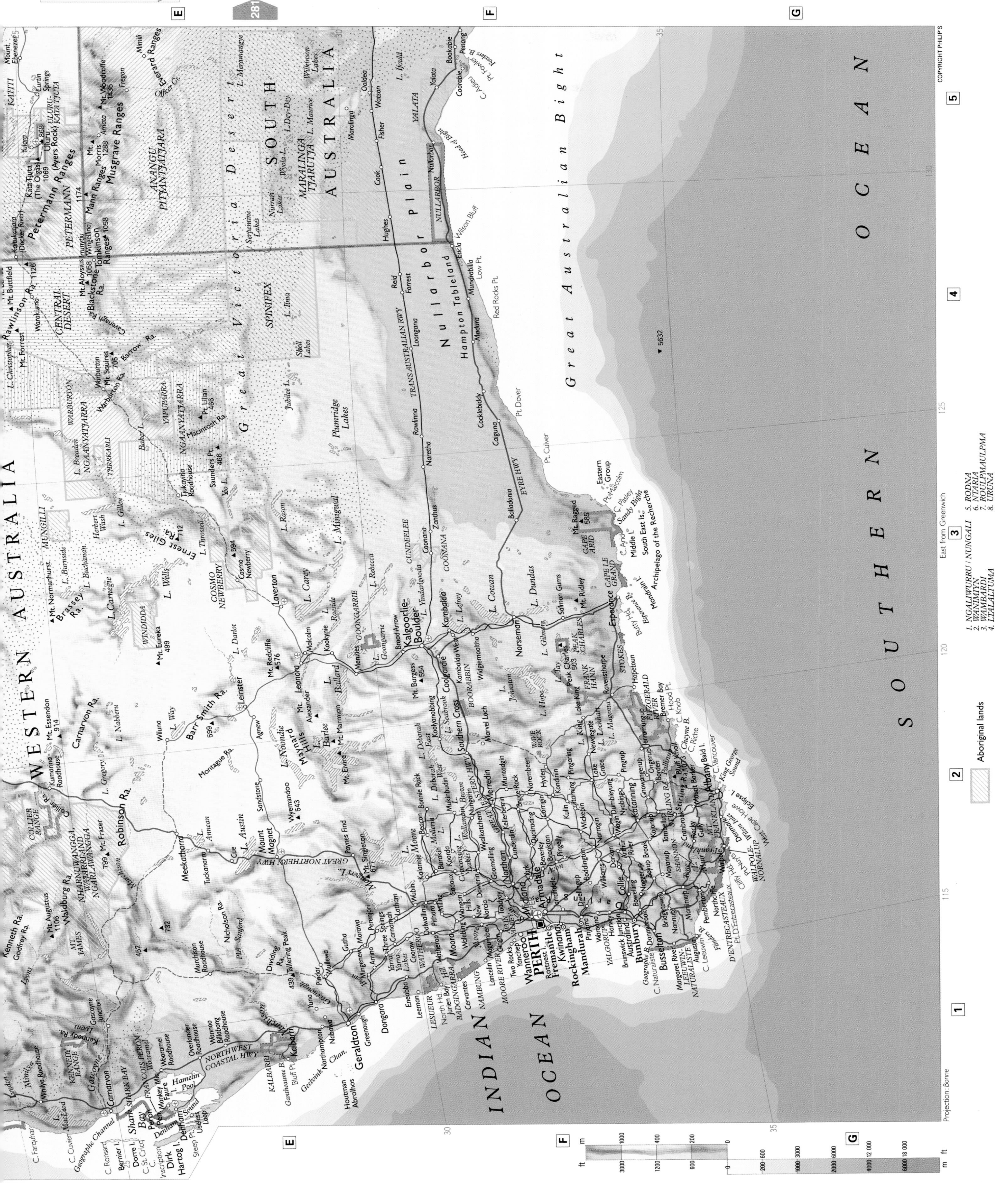
WESTERN AUSTRALIA
SOUTH AUSTRALIA
Great Victoria Desert
Nullarbor Plain
Great Australian Bight
SOUTHERN OCEAN
INDIAN OCEAN
PERTH
Fremantle
Rockingham
Mandurah
Bunbury
Busselton
Albany
Esperance
Geraldton
Kalgoorlie-Boulder
Coolgardie
Kambalda
Norseman
Leonora
Laverton
Meekatharra
Mount Magnet
Carnarvon
Denham
Kalbarri
Northam
Merredin
Southern Cross
Eucla
Madura
Cocklebiddy
Balladonia
Hampton Tableland
TRANS AUSTRALIAN RWY
EYRE HWY
GREAT NORTHERN HWY
NORTHWEST COASTAL HWY
Aboriginal lands
East from Greenwich
Projection: Bonne
COPYRIGHT PHILIP'S
1. NGALIWURRU / NUNGALI
2. WANIMIYN
3. WAMBARDI
4. LTALALTUMA
5. RODNA
6. NTARIA
7. ROULPMAULPMA
8. URUNA

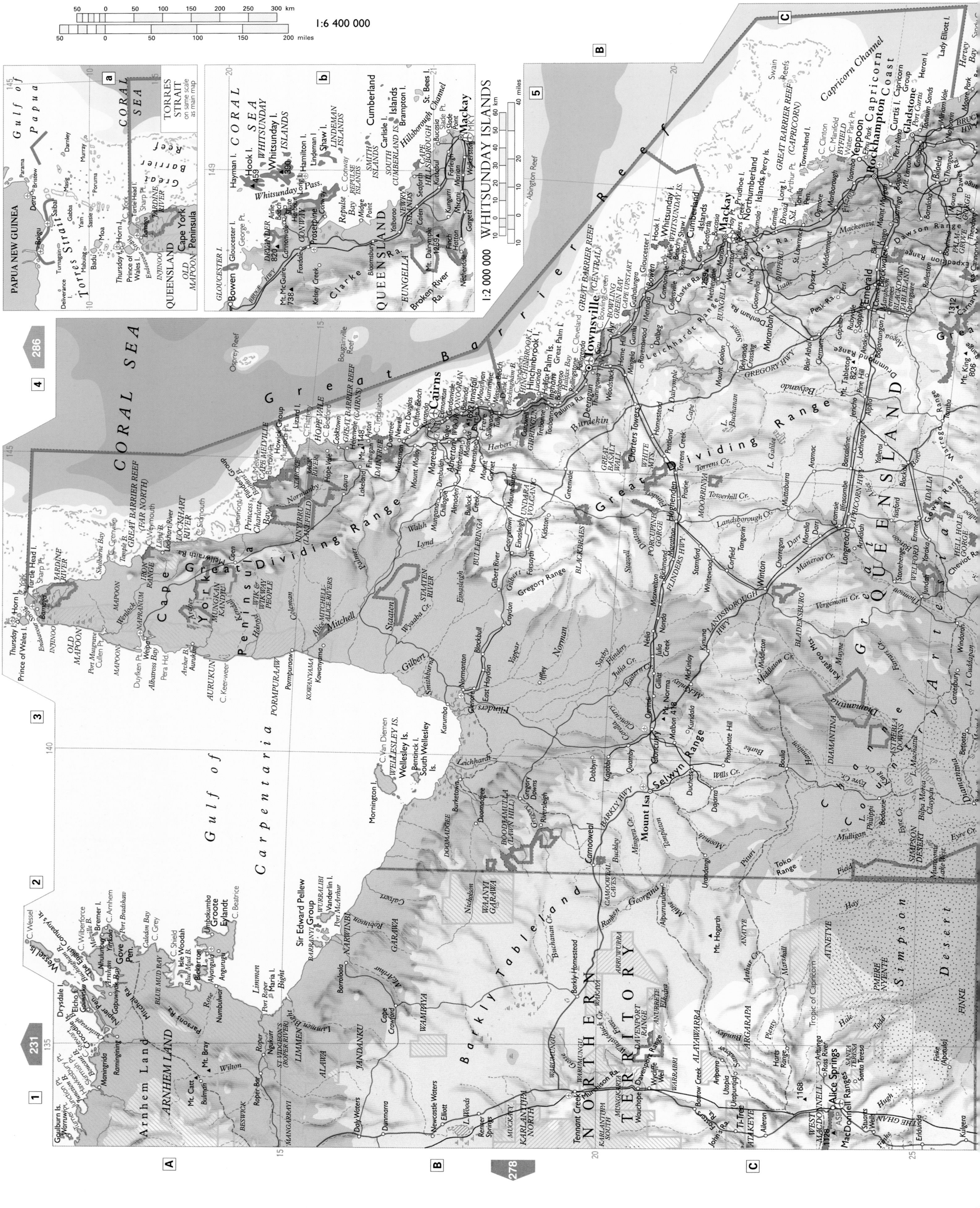
1:6 400 000
1:2 000 000
WHITSUNDAY ISLANDS
TORRES STRAIT on same scale as main map
CORAL SEA
Gulf of Carpentaria
Gulf of Papua
PAPUA NEW GUINEA
Torres Strait
Cape York Peninsula
Great Dividing Range
Great Barrier Reef
QUEENSLAND
NORTHERN TERRITORY
Barkly Tableland
Simpson Desert
Great Artesian Basin
Arnhem Land
Cairns
Townsville
Mackay
Rockhampton
Gladstone
Mount Isa
Alice Springs
Tennant Creek
Longreach
Charters Towers
Emerald
Cloncurry
Hughenden
Winton
Normanton
Tropic of Capricorn
Capricorn Channel
Whitsunday I.
Groote Eylandt
Sir Edward Pellew Group
Wellesley Is.
Mornington I.
Selwyn Range
Gregory Range
Leichhardt Range
Clarke Ra.
Dawson Range
Mitchell
Burdekin
Flinders
Gilbert
Diamantina
Georgina
MacDonnell Ranges

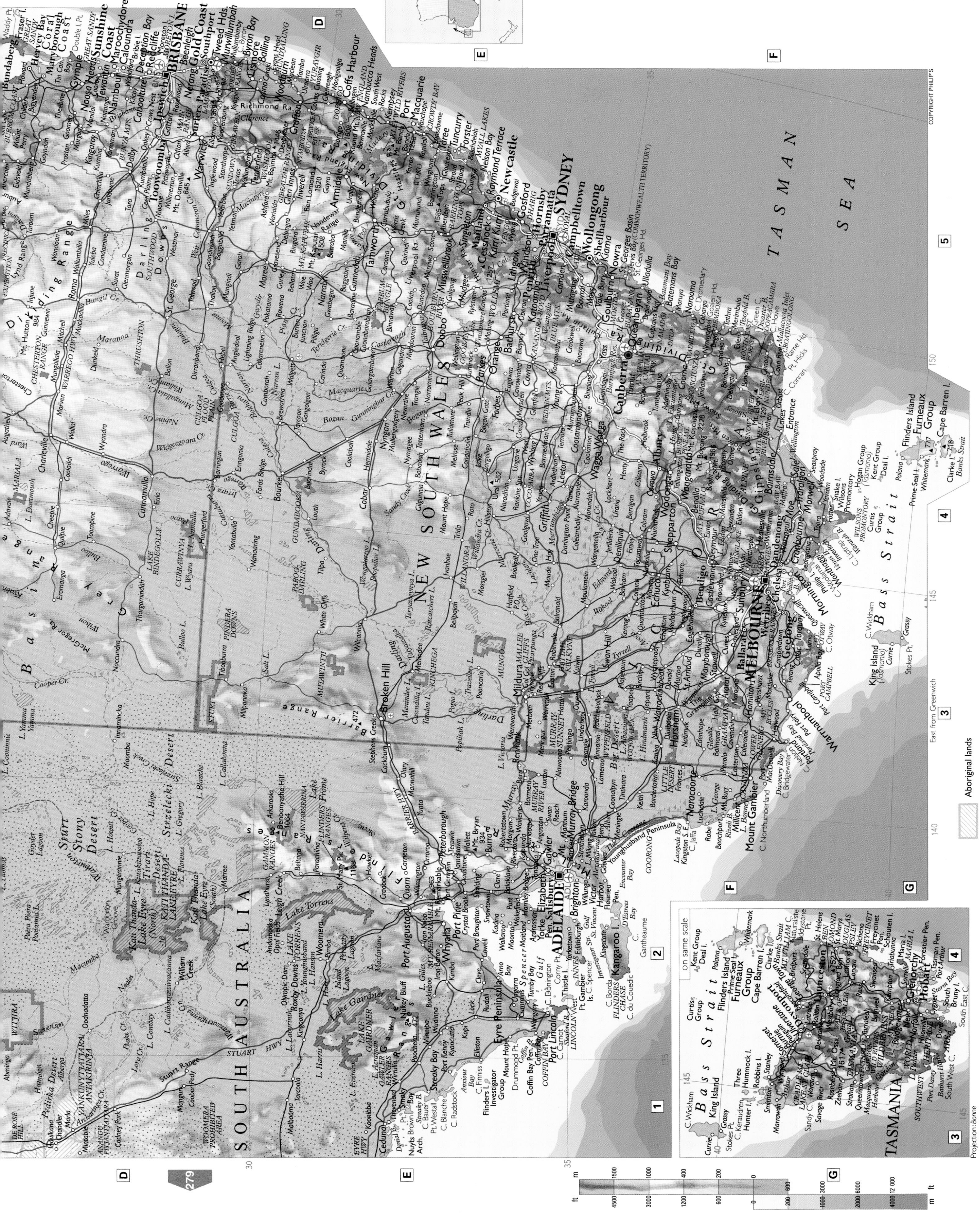
NEW SOUTH WALES
SOUTH AUSTRALIA
TASMAN SEA
Bass Strait
TASMANIA
SYDNEY
BRISBANE
MELBOURNE
ADELAIDE
Canberra
Hobart
Newcastle
Wollongong
Gold Coast
Sunshine Coast
Broken Hill
Kangaroo I.
King Island
Flinders Island
Lake Eyre
Lake Torrens
Lake Gairdner
Great Dividing Range
Grey Range
Strzelecki Desert
Sturt Stony Desert
Eyre Peninsula
Aboriginal lands
Projection: Bonne
East from Greenwich
on same scale
COPYRIGHT PHILIP'S
279

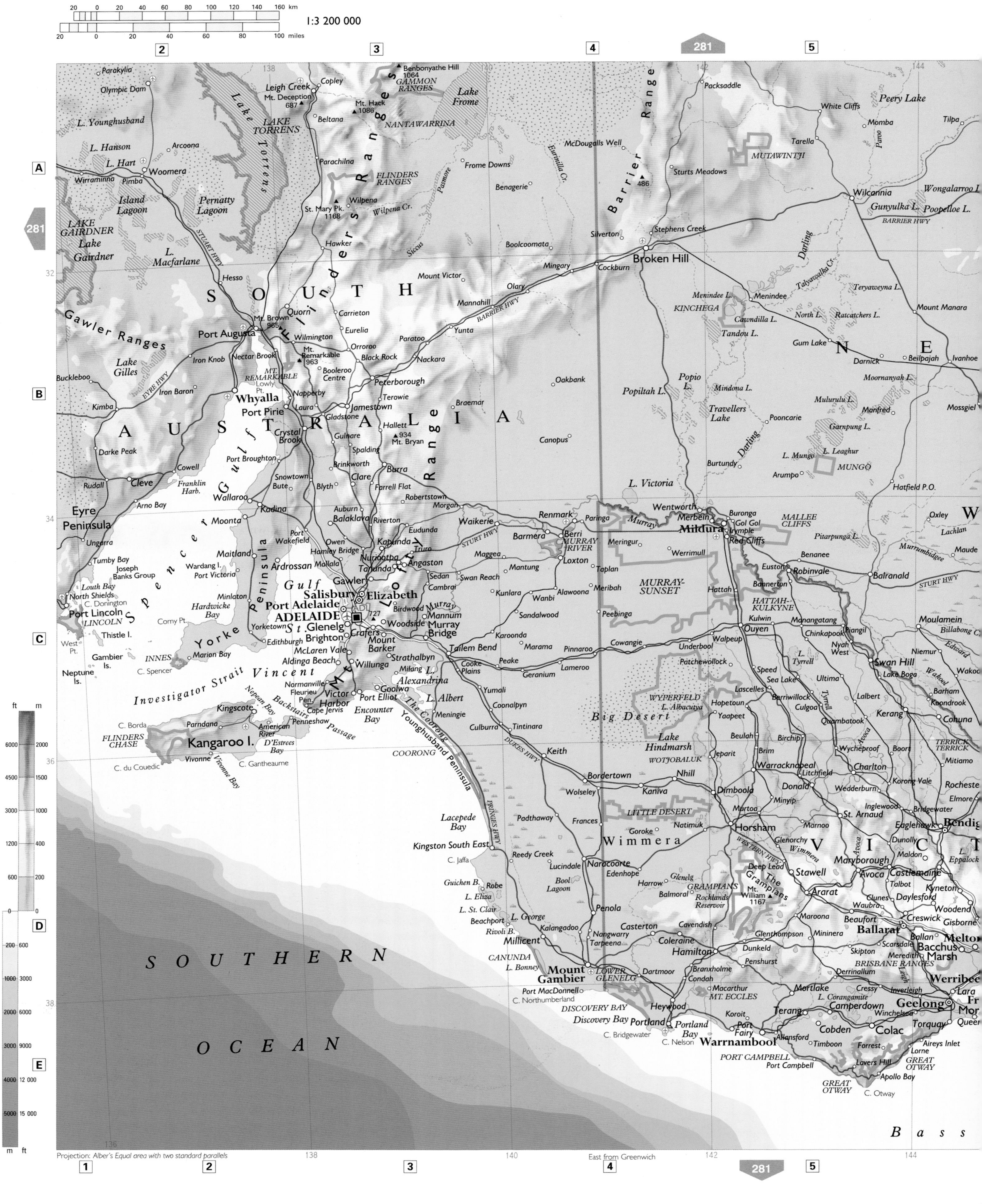
1:3 200 000
km
miles
281
SOUTH AUSTRALIA
NEW
VIC
Lake Torrens
LAKE TORRENS
Lake Frome
Lake Gairdner
LAKE GAIRDNER
L. Younghusband
L. Hanson
L. Hart
Island Lagoon
Pernatty Lagoon
L. Macfarlane
Flinders Ranges
FLINDERS RANGES
GAMMON RANGES
NANTAWARRINA
Barrier Range
Gawler Ranges
Lake Gilles
MT. REMARKABLE
Mt. Lofty Ranges
Spencer Gulf
Gulf St Vincent
Eyre Peninsula
Yorke Peninsula
Investigator Strait
Backstairs Passage
Nepean Bay
Encounter Bay
Kangaroo I.
FLINDERS CHASE
D'Estrees Bay
Vivonne Bay
C. du Couedic
C. Borda
C. Gantheaume
Lake Alexandrina
L. Albert
The Coorong
COORONG
Younghusband Peninsula
Lacepede Bay
Big Desert
LITTLE DESERT
WYPERFELD
MURRAY-SUNSET
HATTAH-KULKYNE
MUTAWINTJI
KINCHEGA
MUNGO
MALLEE CLIFFS
MURRAY RIVER
GRAMPIANS
The Grampians
Wimmera
Lake Hindmarsh
WOTJOBALUK
LOWER GLENELG
MT. ECCLES
CANUNDA
PORT CAMPBELL
GREAT OTWAY
DISCOVERY BAY
Discovery Bay
Portland Bay
SOUTHERN OCEAN
Bass
Darling
Murray
Murrumbidgee
Lachlan
Peery Lake
L. Victoria
Popiltah L.
Popio L.
Menindee L.
Travellers Lake
Leigh Creek
Copley
Beltana
Parachilna
Wilpena
Hawker
Quorn
Port Augusta
Whyalla
Port Pirie
Port Lincoln
Woomera
Kimba
Cleve
Cowell
Wallaroo
Kadina
Moonta
Clare
Burra
Peterborough
Jamestown
Gawler
Salisbury
Elizabeth
Port Adelaide
ADELAIDE
Glenelg
Brighton
Murray Bridge
Victor Harbor
Goolwa
Kingscote
Renmark
Berri
Loxton
Waikerie
Morgan
Broken Hill
Silverton
Wilcannia
Menindee
Wentworth
Mildura
Red Cliffs
Ouyen
Robinvale
Balranald
Swan Hill
Kerang
Cohuna
Keith
Bordertown
Naracoorte
Penola
Millicent
Mount Gambier
Kingston South East
Robe
Horsham
Nhill
Kaniva
Dimboola
Stawell
Ararat
Hamilton
Portland
Heywood
Warrnambool
Port Fairy
Terang
Camperdown
Colac
Cobden
Ballarat
Castlemaine
Maryborough
Daylesford
Bacchus Marsh
Melton
Geelong
Werribee
Torquay
Lorne
Apollo Bay
C. Otway
C. Nelson
C. Bridgewater
Stuart Hwy
Eyre Hwy
Barrier Hwy
Sturt Hwy
Dukes Hwy
Princes Hwy
Western Hwy
Projection: Alber's Equal area with two standard parallels
East from Greenwich

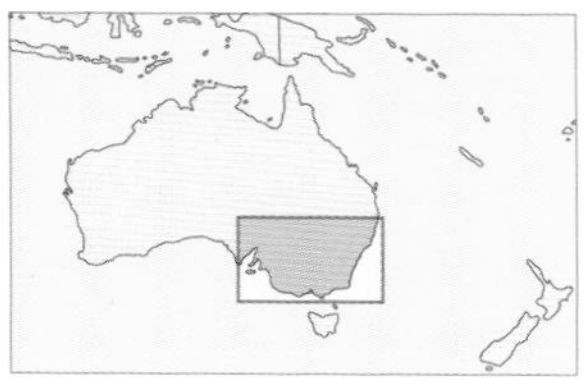

6
7
8
9
281
10
A
B
C
D
E
146
148
150
152
32
34
36
38
East from Greenwich
W O S O U T H
A L E S
V I C T O R I A
TASMAN SEA
Strait
Great Dividing Range
Liverpool Plains
Liverpool Range
Hunter Range
Hastings Range
Blue Mts.
Cullarin Range
Gourock Ra.
Snowy Mts.
Bowen Mts.
Gippsland
SYDNEY
Canberra
MELBOURNE
AUSTRALIAN CAPITAL TERRITORY
NSW JERVIS BAY (Commonwealth Territory)
Newcastle
Wollongong
Port Kembla
Shellharbour
Kiama
Nowra
Goulburn
Bathurst
Orange
Dubbo
Tamworth
Armidale
Coffs Harbour
Port Macquarie
Taree
Forster
Maitland
Cessnock
Gosford
Hornsby
Manly
Parramatta
Fairfield
Liverpool
Penrith
Katoomba
Lithgow
Campbelltown
Sutherland
Queanbeyan
Batemans Bay
Moruya
Narooma
Bega
Merimbula
Eden
Albury
Wodonga
Wagga Wagga
Griffith
Leeton
Narrandera
Cootamundra
Young
Cowra
Parkes
Forbes
Condobolin
Cobar
Nyngan
Bourke
Coonamble
Gunnedah
Mudgee
Wellington
Deniliquin
Echuca
Shepparton
Wangaratta
Benalla
Bairnsdale
Lakes Entrance
Sale
Traralgon
Morwell
Moe
Warragul
Dandenong
Pakenham
Wonthaggi
Wilsons Promontory
Lake Cargelligo
Lake Burrendong
L. Hume
L. Eucumbene
L. Eildon
L. Wellington
Mt. Kosciuszko 2228
Mt. Bogong 1986
Mt. Buller 1804
Mt. Jagungal 2060
Bimberi Pk. 1913
Mt. Ellery 1297
Barrington Tops 1585
Round Mt. 1608
Mt. Banda Banda 1263
KOSCIUSZKO
WOLLEMI
YENGO
NATTAI
DHARAWAL
ROYAL
MORTON
BUDAWANG
DEUA
WADBILLIGA
ALPINE
CROAJINGOLONG
WILSONS PROMONTORY
BARRINGTON TOPS
OXLEY WILD RIVERS
NEW ENGLAND
WARRUMBUNGLE
GOULBURN RIVER
BLUE MTS.
KANANGRA-BOYD
C. Howe
Green C.
C. Conran
Pt. Hicks
Rame Hd.
Hogan Group
South East Pt.
Aboriginal lands
COPYRIGHT PHILIP'S

1:2 800 000

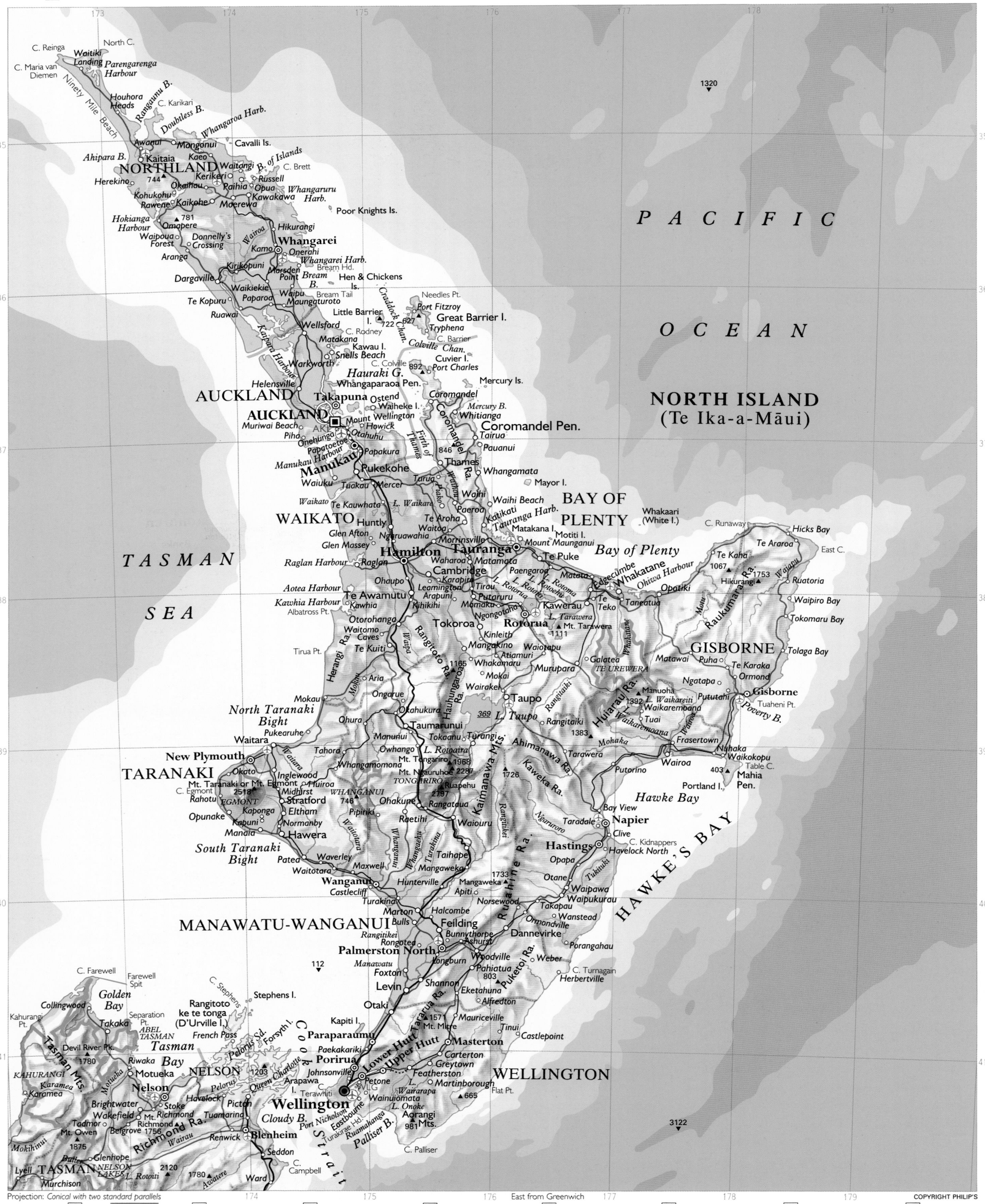

Projection: Conical with two standard parallels

East from Greenwich

285

1:2 800 000

10 0 20 40 60 80 100 120 140 km

10 0 20 40 60 80 100 miles

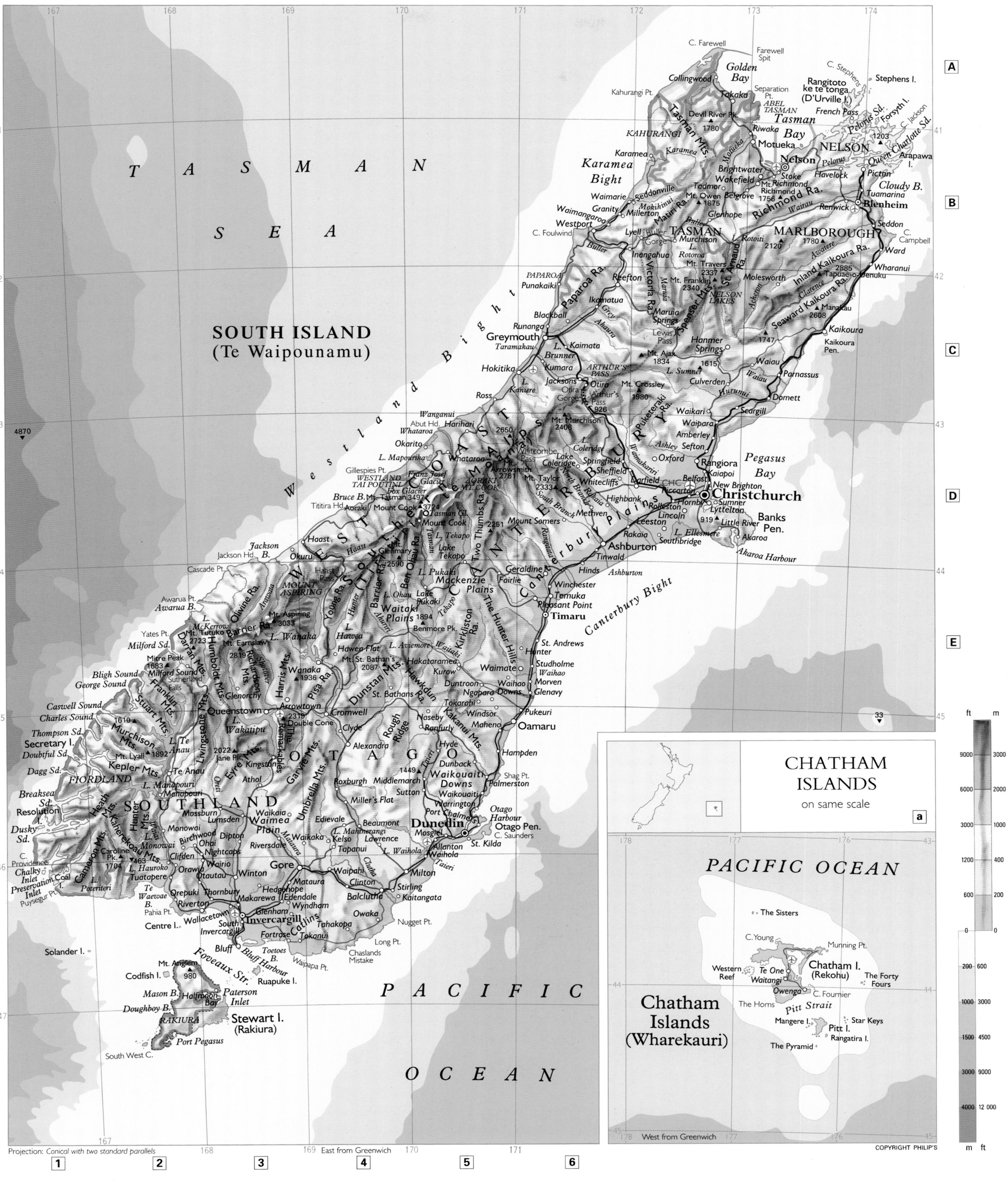

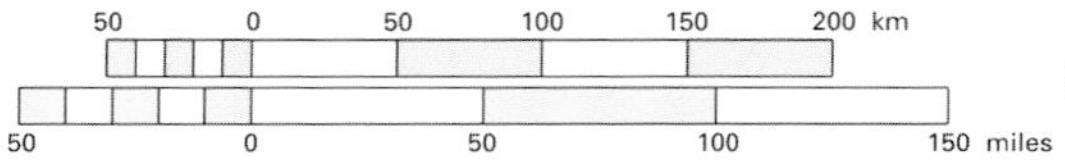

1:5 200 000

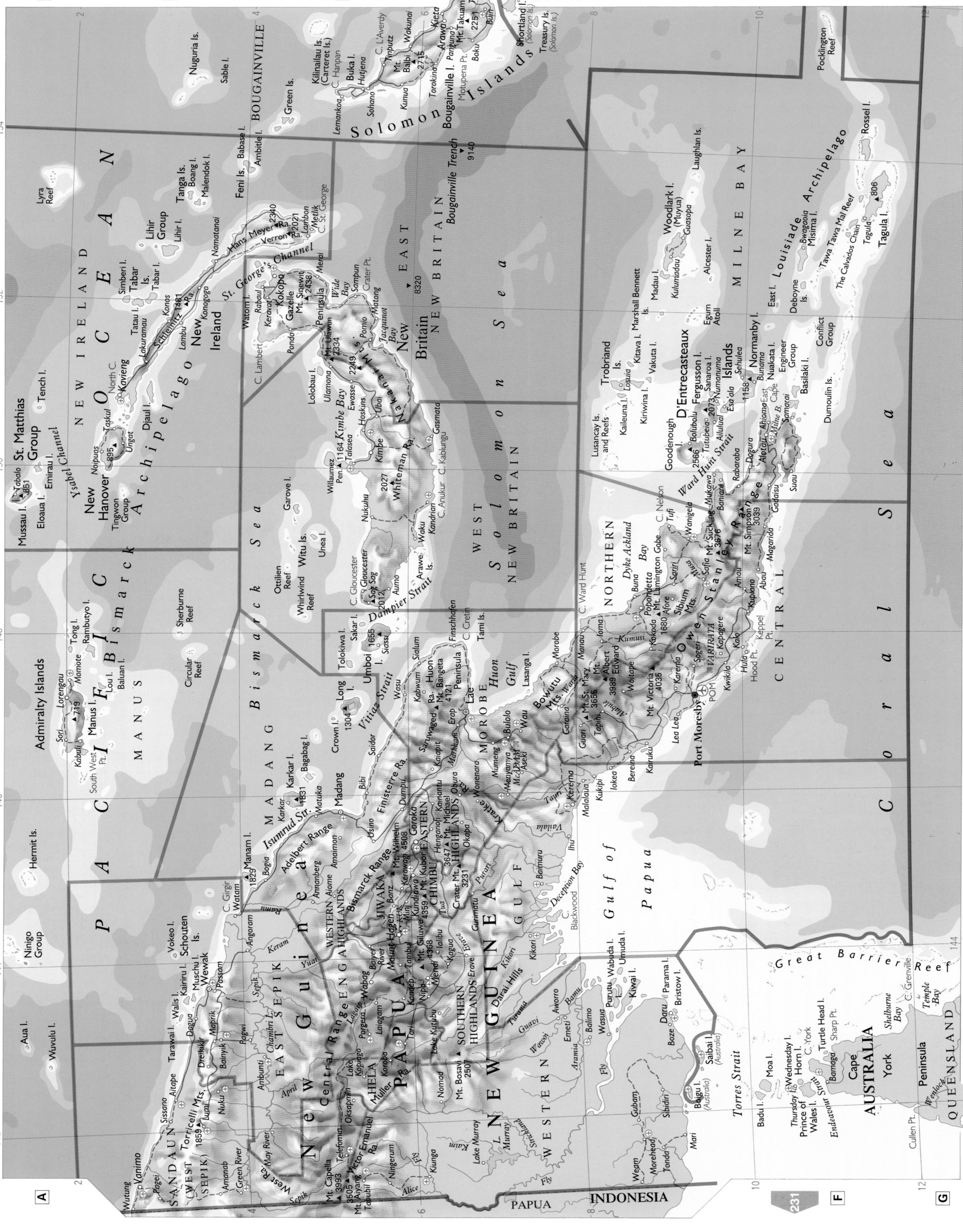
PACIFIC OCEAN
Bismarck Sea
Bismarck Archipelago
Solomon Sea
Coral Sea
Gulf of Papua
Huon Gulf
Admiralty Islands
Manus I.
New Hanover
New Ireland
New Britain
Bougainville I.
Buka I.
Solomon Islands
Trobriand Is.
Woodlark I. (Muyua)
D'Entrecasteaux Islands
Louisiade Archipelago
Rossel I.
Port Moresby
Lae
Madang
Wewak
Rabaul
Kokopo
Kavieng
Goroka
Mount Hagen
Mt. Wilhelm 4508
Owen Stanley Range
Central Range
Bismarck Range
New Guinea
PAPUA
INDONESIA
AUSTRALIA
Torres Strait
Great Barrier Reef
Cape York Peninsula
QUEENSLAND
SANDAUN (WEST SEPIK)
EAST SEPIK
MADANG
MOROBE
CENTRAL
NORTHERN
MILNE BAY
WESTERN
GULF
SOUTHERN HIGHLANDS
WESTERN HIGHLANDS
EASTERN HIGHLANDS
CHIMBU
ENGA
HELA
JIWAKA
MANUS
NEW IRELAND
EAST NEW BRITAIN
WEST NEW BRITAIN
BOUGAINVILLE
Fly
Sepik
Bougainville Trench 9140
New Britain Trench 8320
Projection: Lambert Conformal Conic
East from Greenwich
COPYRIGHT PHILIP'S
Tracks

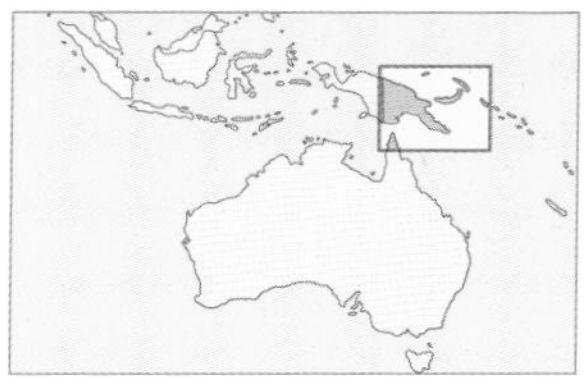

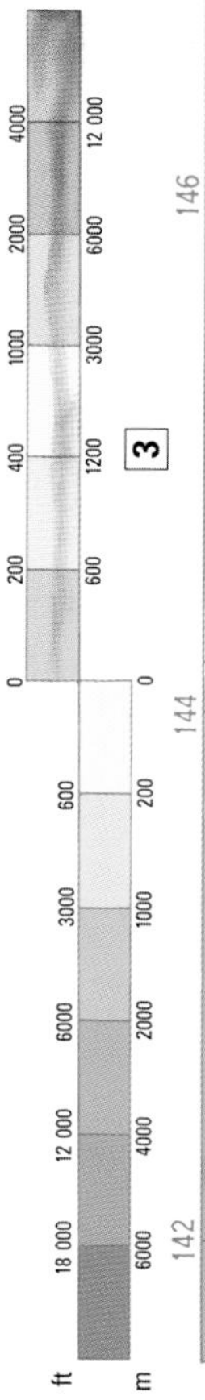

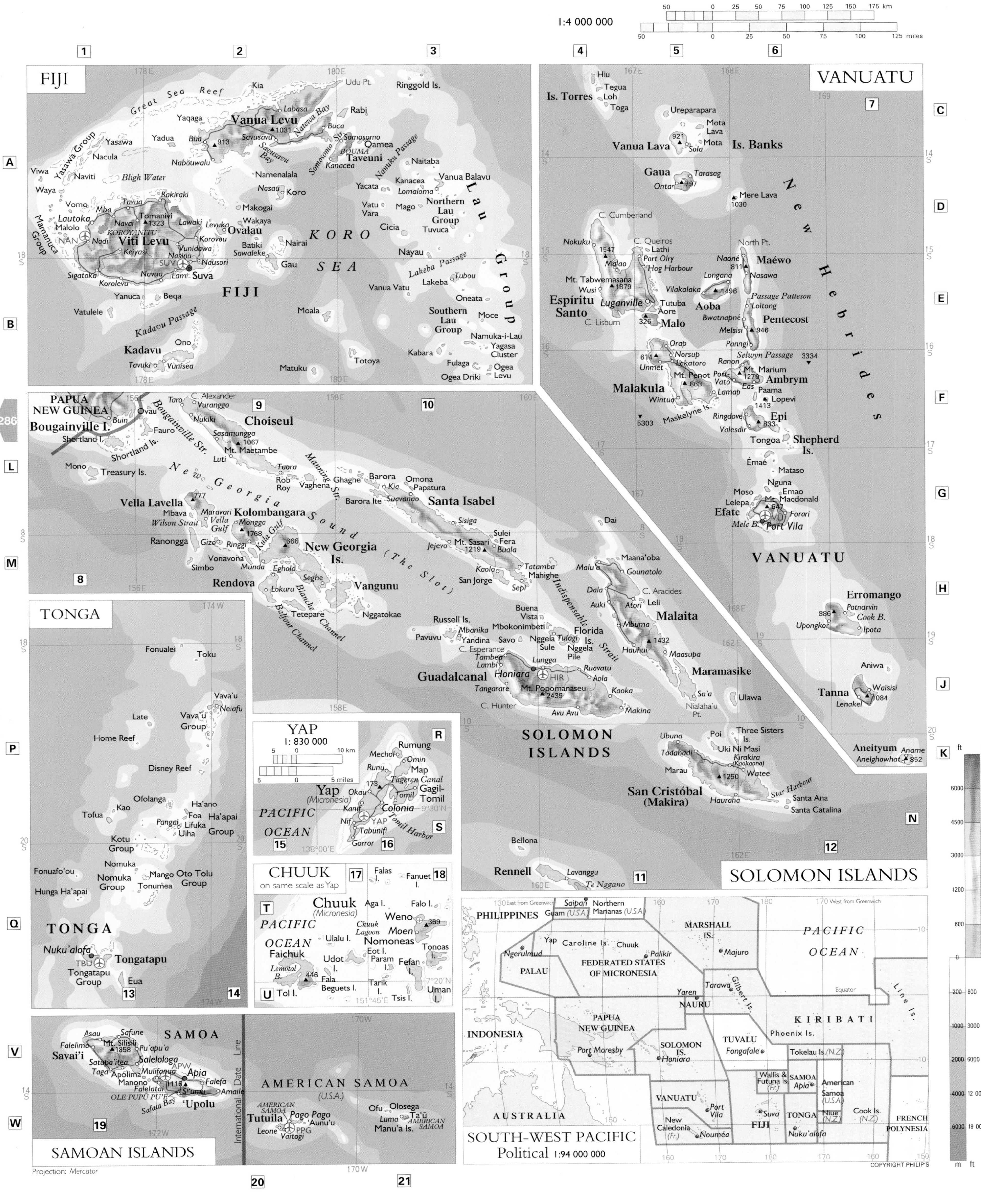
1:4 000 000
km
miles
FIJI
Great Sea Reef
Kia
Udu Pt.
Ringgold Is.
Labasa
Vanua Levu
Natewa Bay
Rabi
Yaqaga
Yasawa Group
Yasawa
Yadua
Bua
Savusavu
Savusavu Bay
Buca
Somosomo
Somosomo Str.
Qamea
BOUMA
Taveuni
Kanacea
Nacula
Nabouwalu
Naitaba
Nanuku Passage
Viwa
Naviti
Bligh Water
Namenalala
Vanua Balavu
Waya
Nasau
Koro
Yacata
Kanacea
Lomaloma
Vomo
Rakiraki
Makogai
Vatu Vara
Mago
Northern Lau Group
Tavua
Mba
Tomanivi
Lautoka
Malolo
Navai
KOROYANITU
Lawaki
Levuka
Wakaya
Ovalau
Cicia
Tuvuca
Mamanuca Group
NAN
Nadi
Viti Levu
Korovou
Batiki
Nairai
KORO SEA
Keiyasi
Vunidawa
Sawaleke
Nayau
Lau Group
Nasinu
SUV
Nausori
Gau
Lakeba Passage
Sigatoka
Navua
Lami
Suva
Tubou
Korolevu
Lakeba
Vanua Vatu
Yanuca
Beqa
FIJI
Oneata
Vatulele
Moala
Southern Lau Group
Moce
Kadavu Passage
Namuka-i-Lau
Ono
Yagasa Cluster
Kadavu
Totoya
Kabara
Tavuki
Vunisea
Matuku
Fulaga
Ogea Levu
Ogea Driki
178E
180E
18 S
VANUATU
Hiu
Tegua
Is. Torres
Loh
Toga
Ureparapara
Mota Lava
Vanua Lava
Sola
Mota
Is. Banks
Gaua
Tarasag
Ontar
Mere Lava
New Hebrides
C. Cumberland
Nokuku
C. Queiros
Lathi
Port Olry
Hog Harbour
North Pt.
Naone
Maéwo
Nasawa
Mt. Tabwemasana
Wusi
Longana
Vilakalaka
Aoba
Passage Patteson
Loltong
Espíritu Santo
Luganville
Tutuba
Aore
Malo
C. Lisburn
Bwatnapné
Pentecost
Melsisi
Panngi
Orap
Norsup
Lakatoro
Selwyn Passage
Unmet
Ranon
Mt. Marium
Malakula
Mt. Penot
Port Vato
Ambrym
Wintua
Eas
Paama
Lamap
Lopevi
Maskelyne Is.
Ringdove
Epi
Valesdir
Tongoa
Shepherd Is.
Émae
Mataso
Nguna
Moso
Emao
Lelepa
Mt. Macdonald
Efate
VLI
Forari
Mele B.
Port Vila
VANUATU
Erromango
Potnarvin
Cook B.
Upongkor
Ipota
Aniwa
Waisisi
Tanna
Lenakel
Aneityum
Aname
Anelghowhat
PAPUA NEW GUINEA
Bougainville I.
Buin
Ovau
Taro
C. Alexander
Vuranggo
Choiseul
Shortland I.
Fauro
Bougainville Str.
Nukiki
Sasamungga
Mt. Maetambe
Shortland Is.
Luti
Mono
Treasury Is.
New Georgia Sound (The Slot)
Taora
Manning Str.
Rob Roy
Ghaghe
Vaghena
Barora
Omona
Kia
Papatura
Barora Ite
Suavanao
Santa Isabel
Vella Lavella
Mbava
Maravari
Vella Gulf
Kolombangara
Wilson Strait
Mongga
Sisiga
Kula Gulf
Ranongga
Gizo
Ringgi
Sulei
Fera
Buala
Jejevo
Mt. Sasari
New Georgia Is.
Vonavona
Simbo
Munda
Egholo
Kaolo
Tatamba
Mahighe
Malu'u
Maana'oba
Gounatolo
Rendova
Seghe
San Jorge
Sepi
Indispensable Strait
Vangunu
Lokuru
Blanche Channel
C. Aracides
Dala
Leli
Dai
Auki
Atori
Malaita
Tetepare
Ngatokae
Russell Is.
Buena Vista
Mbanika
Mbokonimbeti
Mbuma
Balfour Channel
Pavuvu
Yandina
Savo
Ngela Tulagi
Florida Is.
Hauhui
C. Esperance
Sule
Ngela Pile
Maasupa
Tambea
Lambi
Lungga
Ruavatu
Maramasike
Guadalcanal
Honiara
HIR
Aola
Tangarare
Mt. Popomanaseu
Kaoka
Sa'a
Ulawa
C. Hunter
Avu Avu
Makina
Nialaha'u Pt.
SOLOMON ISLANDS
Ubuna
Poi
Three Sisters Is.
Todahadi
Uki Ni Masi
Kirakira (Kaokaona)
Marau
Wanoni
San Cristóbal (Makira)
Hauraha
Star Harbour
Santa Ana
Santa Catalina
Bellona
Rennell
Lavanggu
Te Nggano
SOLOMON ISLANDS
156E
158E
160E
162E
8 S
10 S
TONGA
Fonualei
Toku
Vava'u
Neiafu
Late
Vava'u Group
Home Reef
Disney Reef
Ofolanga
Ha'ano
Kao
Foa
Ha'apai
Tofua
Pangai
Lifuka
Uiha
Ha'apai Group
Kotu Group
Nomuka
Fonuafo'ou
Nomuka Group
Mango
Oto Tolu Group
Hunga Ha'apai
Tonumea
TONGA
Nuku'alofa
TBU
Tongatapu
Tongatapu Group
Eua
174W
YAP
1: 830 000
km
miles
Rumung
Mechol
Omin
Runu
Map
Fageren Canal
Gagil-Tomil
Yap (Micronesia)
Okau
Tomil
Kanif
Colonia
PACIFIC OCEAN
YAP
Nif
Tabunifi
Gorror
Tomil Harbor
138°00'E
9°30'N
CHUUK
on same scale as Yap
Falas I.
Fanuet I.
Chuuk (Micronesia)
Aga I.
Falo I.
Chuuk Lagoon
Weno
Moen
PACIFIC OCEAN
Ulalu I.
Nomoneas
Tonoas I.
Faichuk
Eot I.
Udot I.
Param I.
Fefen I.
Lemotol B.
Fala Beguets I.
Tarik I.
Tol I.
Tsis I.
Uman I.
151°45'E
7°20'N
SAMOA
Asau
Safune
Falelima
Mt. Silisili
Pu'apu'a
Savai'i
Satupa'itea
Salelologa
APW
Apia
Taga
Apolima
Mulifanua
Manono
Falelatai
Falefa
Si'umu
Amaile
OLE PUPŪ PU'E
Safata Bay
'Upolu
International Date Line
AMERICAN SAMOA (U.S.A.)
AMERICAN SAMOA
Tutuila
Pago Pago
'Aunu'u
Leone
PPG
Vaitogi
Ofu
Olosega
Luma
Ta'ū
Manu'a Is.
SAMOAN ISLANDS
170W
172W
14 S
SOUTH-WEST PACIFIC
Political 1:94 000 000
East from Greenwich
West from Greenwich
PHILIPPINES
Saipan
Guam (U.S.A.)
Northern Marianas (U.S.A.)
MARSHALL IS.
PACIFIC OCEAN
Yap
Caroline Is.
Chuuk
Palikir
Ngerulmud
Majuro
PALAU
FEDERATED STATES OF MICRONESIA
Tarawa
Gilbert Is.
Yaren
NAURU
Equator
Line Is.
INDONESIA
PAPUA NEW GUINEA
KIRIBATI
Phoenix Is.
SOLOMON IS.
Honiara
TUVALU
Fongafale
Port Moresby
Tokelau Is. (N.Z.)
Wallis & Futuna Is. (Fr.)
SAMOA
Apia
American Samoa (U.S.A.)
VANUATU
Port Vila
Suva
FIJI
TONGA
Niue (N.Z.)
Cook Is. (N.Z.)
AUSTRALIA
New Caledonia (Fr.)
Nouméa
Nuku'alofa
FRENCH POLYNESIA
ft
m
Projection: Mercator
COPYRIGHT PHILIP'S

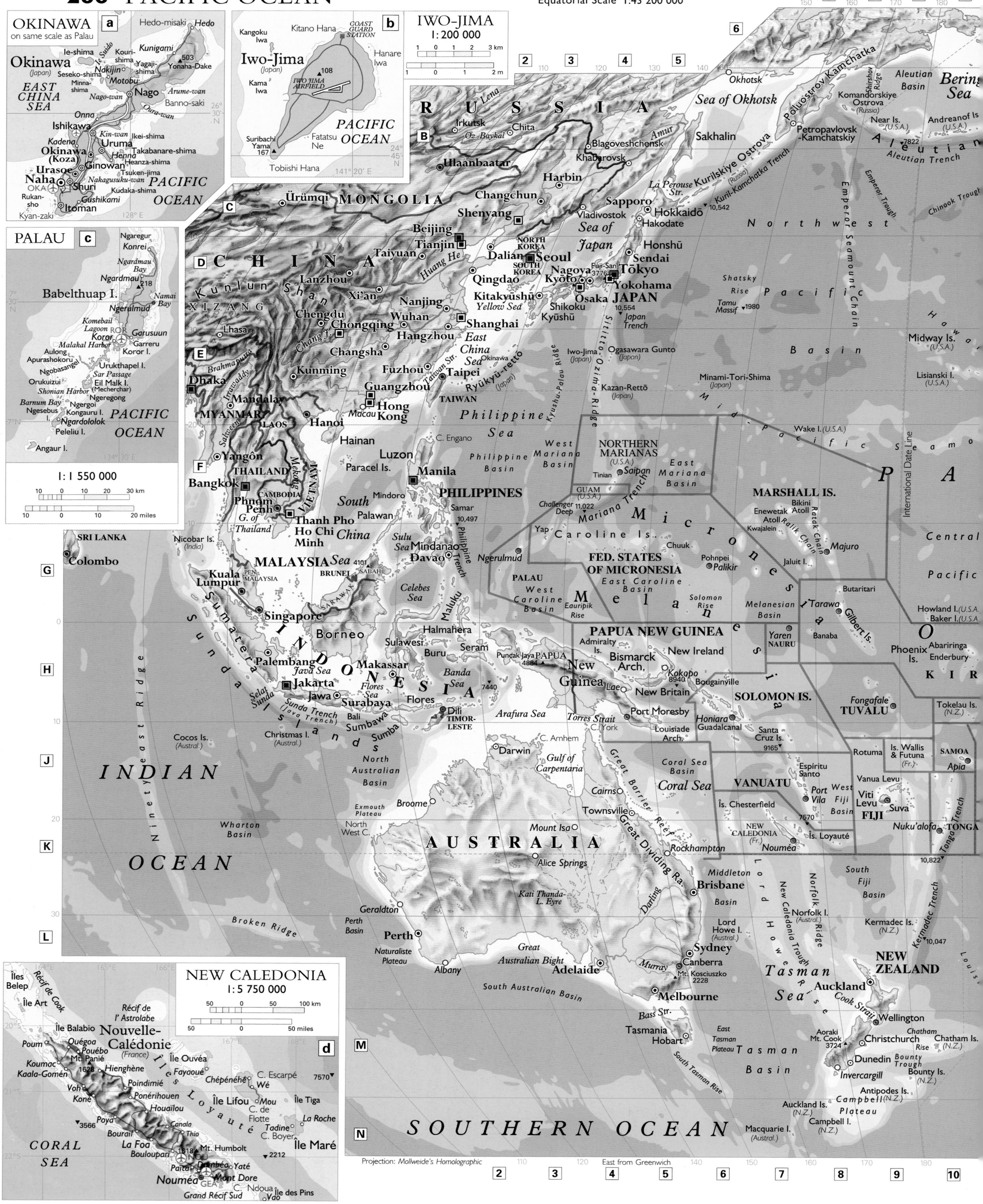
Equatorial Scale 1:43 200 000
OKINAWA a
on same scale as Palau
Okinawa (Japan)
EAST CHINA SEA
Hedo-misaki
Hedo
Kunigami
Yonaha-Dake
Motobu
Nago
Banno-saki
Ishikawa
Kadena
Okinawa (Koza)
Uruma
Ginowan
Urasoe
Naha
Shuri
Itoman
Kyan-zaki
PACIFIC OCEAN
IWO-JIMA
1:200 000
Iwo-Jima (Japan)
Kitano Hana
Kangoku Iwa
Hanare Iwa
Kama Iwa
Suribachi Yama 167
Fatatsu Ne
Tobiishi Hana
PACIFIC OCEAN
PALAU c
Babelthuap I.
Ngaregur
Konrei
Ngardmau Bay
Ngerulmud
Namai Bay
Komebail Lagoon
Koror
Garusuun
Koror I.
Urukthapel I.
Eil Malk I.
Ngeregong
Peleliu I.
Angaur I.
PACIFIC OCEAN
1:1 550 000
RUSSIA
Lena
Irkutsk
Oz. Baykal
Chita
Amur
Blagoveshchensk
Khabarovsk
Ulaanbaatar
Harbin
Sea of Okhotsk
Okhotsk
Sakhalin
Poluostrov Kamchatka
Petropavlovsk-Kamchatskiy
Bering Sea
Aleutian Basin
Komandorskiye Ostrova (Russia)
Near Is. (U.S.A.)
Andreanof Is (U.S.A.)
Aleutian Trench
Kurilskiye Ostrova (Russia)
Kuril-Kamchatka Trench
La Perouse Str.
Ürümqi
MONGOLIA
Changchun
Shenyang
Vladivostok
Sapporo
Hokkaido
Hakodate
Sea of Japan
Beijing
Tianjin
Taiyuan
Huang He
NORTH KOREA
Dalian
Seoul
SOUTH KOREA
Honshū
Sendai
Tōkyo
Yokohama
Nagoya
Kyōto
Ōsaka
JAPAN
Kitakyūshū
Shikoku
Kyūshū
CHINA
Kunlun Shan
XIZANG
Lanzhou
Xi'an
Qingdao
Yellow Sea
Nanjing
Chengdu
Chongqing
Wuhan
Shanghai
Hangzhou
Chang Jiang
Lhasa
Changsha
East China Sea
Kunming
Fuzhou
Taipei
TAIWAN
Ryūkyū-rettō (Japan)
Brahmaputra
Dhaka
Irrawaddy
Mandalay
MYANMAR
LAOS
Hanoi
Guangzhou
Hong Kong
Macau
Hainan
Yangôn
THAILAND
Bangkok
CAMBODIA
Phnom Penh
VIETNAM
Mekong
Thanh Pho Ho Chi Minh
G. of Thailand
South China Sea
Paracel Is.
Luzon
Manila
PHILIPPINES
Mindoro
Palawan
Samar
Mindanao
Davao
Philippine Trench
Philippine Sea
Philippine Basin
Kyushu-Palau Ridge
Shichito-Iozima Ridge
Iwo-Jima (Japan)
Ogasawara Gunto (Japan)
Kazan-Rettō (Japan)
Japan Trench
Shatsky Rise
Tamu Massif
Northwest Pacific Basin
Emperor Seamount Chain
Emperor Trough
Chinook Trough
Midway Is. (U.S.A.)
Minami-Tori-Shima (Japan)
Lisianski I. (U.S.A.)
Mid-Pacific Seamounts
Wake I. (U.S.A.)
NORTHERN MARIANAS (U.S.A.)
Saipan
Tinian
GUAM (U.S.A.)
West Mariana Basin
East Mariana Basin
Mariana Trench
Challenger Deep 11,022
MARSHALL IS.
Bikini Atoll
Enewetak Atoll
Kwajalein
Ratak Chain
Ralik Chain
Majuro
Jaluit I.
International Date Line
Micronesia
Caroline Is.
Yap
Chuuk
Pohnpei
Palikir
FED. STATES OF MICRONESIA
East Caroline Basin
Ngerulmud
PALAU
West Caroline Basin
Eauripik Rise
Melanesia
Solomon Rise
Melanesian Basin
Tarawa
Gilbert Is.
Butaritari
Banaba
Howland I. (U.S.A.)
Baker I. (U.S.A.)
Central Pacific
Phoenix Is.
Abariringa
Enderbury
KIR
SRI LANKA
Colombo
Nicobar Is. (India)
MALAYSIA
Kuala Lumpur
PEN. MALAYSIA
BRUNEI
SABAH
SARAWAK
Sulu Sea
Celebes Sea
Singapore
Sumatera
Borneo
INDONESIA
Palembang
Java Sea
Jakarta
Jawa
Surabaya
Bali
Makassar
Sulawesi
Halmahera
Maluku
Buru
Seram
Banda Sea
Flores Sea
Flores
Sumbawa
Sumba
Dili
TIMOR-LESTE
Selat Sunda
Sunda Trench (Java Trench)
Sunda Islands
Arafura Sea
Puncak Jaya 4884
PAPUA
New Guinea
Lae
PAPUA NEW GUINEA
Admiralty Is.
Bismarck Arch.
New Ireland
Kokopo
New Britain
Bougainville
SOLOMON IS.
Port Moresby
Honiara
Guadalcanal
Torres Strait
C. York
Louisiade Arch.
Santa Cruz Is.
Yaren
NAURU
TUVALU
Fongafale
Tokelau Is. (N.Z.)
Rotuma
Is. Wallis & Futuna (Fr.)
SAMOA
Apia
Vanua Levu
Viti Levu
Suva
FIJI
West Fiji Basin
VANUATU
Espíritu Santo
Port Vila
Coral Sea Basin
Coral Sea
Îs. Chesterfield
NEW CALEDONIA (Fr.)
Nouméa
Îs. Loyauté
Nuku'alofa
TONGA
Tonga Trench
Christmas I. (Austral.)
Cocos Is. (Austral.)
INDIAN OCEAN
Ninetyeast Ridge
North Australian Basin
Wharton Basin
Exmouth Plateau
North West C.
Broome
Darwin
C. Arnhem
Gulf of Carpentaria
Great Barrier Reef
Cairns
Townsville
Mount Isa
AUSTRALIA
Alice Springs
Great Dividing Ra.
Rockhampton
Kati Thanda-L. Eyre
Darling
Brisbane
Middleton Basin
Geraldton
Perth Basin
Perth
Broken Ridge
Naturaliste Plateau
Albany
Great Australian Bight
Adelaide
Murray
Sydney
Canberra
Mt. Kosciuszko 2228
Melbourne
South Australian Basin
Bass Str.
Tasmania
Hobart
East Tasman Plateau
South Tasman Rise
Lord Howe I. (Austral.)
Lord Howe Rise
New Caledonia Trough
Norfolk Ridge
Norfolk I. (Austral.)
Tasman Sea
Tasman Basin
South Fiji Basin
Kermadec Is. (N.Z.)
Kermadec Trench
NEW ZEALAND
Auckland
Cook Strait
Wellington
Aoraki Mt. Cook 3724
Christchurch
Chatham Rise
Chatham Is. (N.Z.)
Dunedin
Bounty Trough
Invercargill
Bounty Is. (N.Z.)
Antipodes Is. (N.Z.)
Campbell Plateau
Auckland Is. (N.Z.)
Campbell I. (N.Z.)
Macquarie I. (Austral.)
SOUTHERN OCEAN
Projection: Mollweide's Homolographic
East from Greenwich
NEW CALEDONIA
1:5 750 000
Îles Belep
Récif de Cook
Île Art
Récif de l'Astrolabe
Île Balabio
Nouvelle-Calédonie (France)
Poum
Ouégoa
Pouébo
Mt. Panié
Koumac
Kaala-Gomén
Hienghène
Île Ouvéa
Fayaoué
Chépénéhé
C. Escarpé
Wé
Voh
Poindimié
Koné
Ponérihouen
Houailou
Île Lifou
C. de Flotte
Île Tiga
Poya
Canala
Thio
Tadine
C. Boyer
La Roche
Île Maré
Bourail
La Foa
Boulouparis
Mt. Humbolt
Païta
Dumbéa
Yaté
Mont Dore
Nouméa
C. Ndoua
Île des Pins
Vao
Grand Récif Sud
CORAL SEA

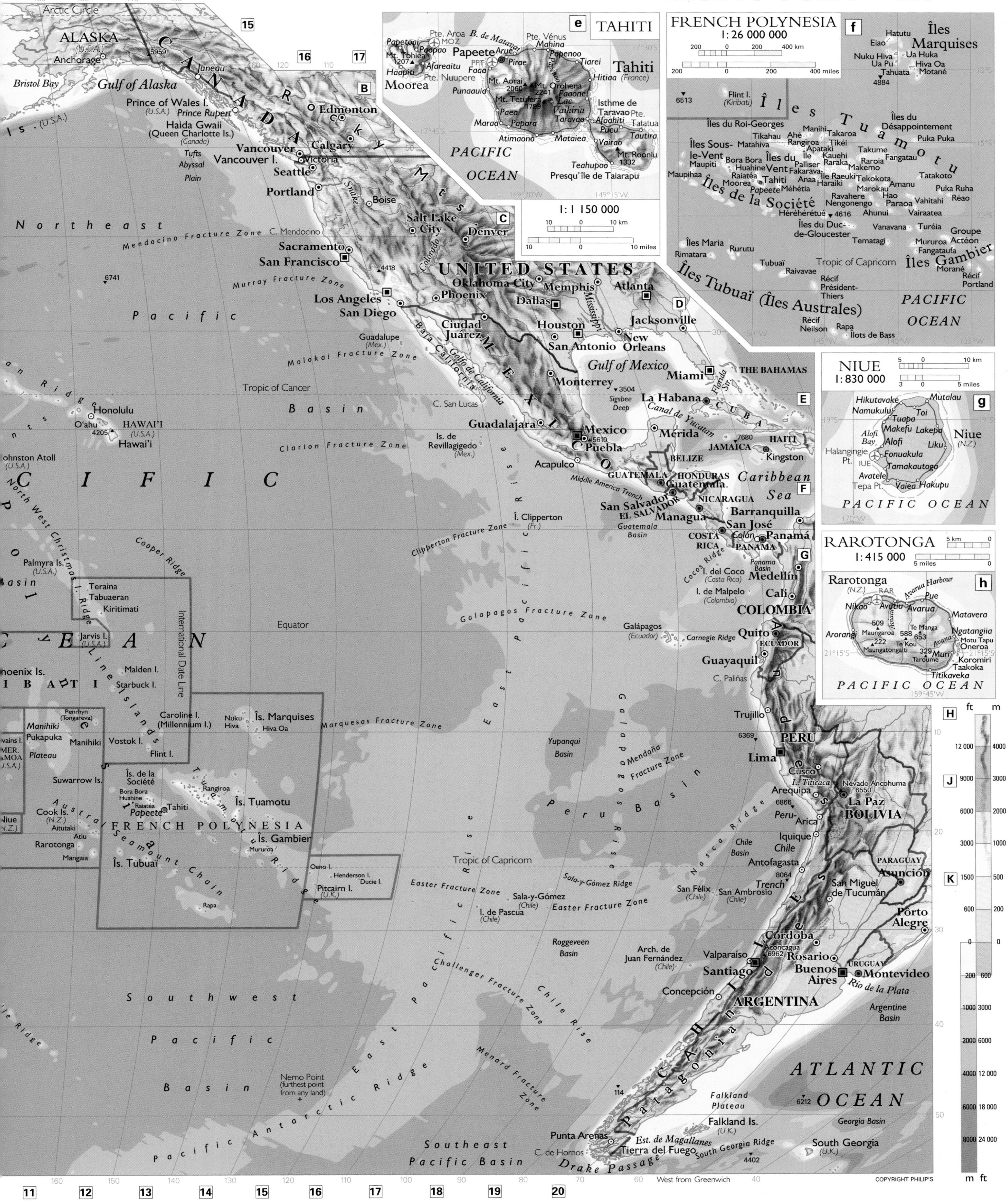
Arctic Circle
ALASKA
(U.S.A.)
Anchorage
Bristol Bay
Gulf of Alaska
Juneau
CANADA
ROCKY MTS.
Prince of Wales I.
(U.S.A.)
Prince Rupert
Haida Gwaii
(Queen Charlotte Is.)
(Canada)
Tufts Abyssal Plain
Edmonton
Calgary
Vancouver
Vancouver I.
Victoria
Seattle
Portland
Snake
Boise
Salt Lake City
Denver
Colorado
Northeast
Mendocino Fracture Zone
C. Mendocino
Sacramento
San Francisco
4418
6741
Murray Fracture Zone
UNITED STATES
Oklahoma City
Memphis
Atlanta
Mississippi
Dallas
Los Angeles
Phoenix
San Diego
Pacific
Jacksonville
Ciudad Juárez
Houston
New Orleans
San Antonio
Guadalupe
(Mex.)
Molokai Fracture Zone
Baja California
Golfo de California
MEXICO
Gulf of Mexico
Miami
THE BAHAMAS
Florida Str.
Monterrey
3504
Sigsbee Deep
Tropic of Cancer
Honolulu
O'ahu
HAWAI'I
(U.S.A.)
4205
Hawai'i
Basin
C. San Lucas
La Habana
Canal de Yucatán
CUBA
Guadalajara
Mexico
5610
Puebla
Mérida
7680
HAITI
JAMAICA
Kingston
BELIZE
Is. de Revillagigedo
(Mex.)
Clarion Fracture Zone
Johnston Atoll
(U.S.A.)
PACIFIC
North West Christmas I. Ridge
Acapulco
GUATEMALA
Guatemala
HONDURAS
Caribbean Sea
Middle America Trench
San Salvador
EL SALVADOR
NICARAGUA
Managua
Barranquilla
Guatemala Basin
San José
COSTA RICA
Colón
Panamá
PANAMA
Î. Clipperton
(Fr.)
Clipperton Fracture Zone
Cooper Ridge
Palmyra Is.
(U.S.A.)
Teraina
Tabuaeran
Kiritimati
International Date Line
Cocos Ridge
I. del Coco
(Costa Rica)
Panama Basin
Medellín
I. de Malpelo
(Colombia)
Cali
COLOMBIA
Galapagos Fracture Zone
Equator
Jarvis I.
(U.S.A.)
OCEAN
Line Islands
Galápagos
(Ecuador)
Carnegie Ridge
Quito
ECUADOR
Guayaquil
C. Paliñas
Malden I.
Starbuck I.
Phoenix Is.
KIRIBATI
Penrhyn
(Tongareva)
Manihiki
Pukapuka
Manihiki Plateau
Caroline I.
(Millennium I.)
Nuku Hiva
Îs. Marquises
Hiva Oa
Marquesas Fracture Zone
Vostok I.
Flint I.
Trujillo
East Pacific Rise
Galapagos Rise
Yupanqui Basin
6369
PERU
Lima
Mendaña Fracture Zone
Peru Basin
Cusco
L. Titicaca
Nevado Ancohuma
6550
Arequipa
6866
La Paz
BOLIVIA
Peru-Chile Trench
Arica
Iquique
Chile Basin
Antofagasta
Suwarrow Is.
Îs. de la Société
Bora Bora
Huahine
Raiatea
Papeete
Tahiti
Rangiroa
Îs. Tuamotu
Cook Is.
(N.Z.)
Aitutaki
Atiu
Rarotonga
Mangaia
FRENCH POLYNESIA
Austral Seamount Chain
Îs. Gambier
Mururoa
Tuamotu Ridge
Îs. Tubuaï
Rapa
Oeno I.
Henderson I.
Ducie I.
Pitcairn I.
(U.K.)
Tropic of Capricorn
Easter Fracture Zone
Sala-y-Gómez Ridge
Sala-y-Gómez
(Chile)
I. de Pascua
(Chile)
Nasca Ridge
8064
Trench
San Félix
(Chile)
San Ambrosio
(Chile)
San Miguel de Tucumán
PARAGUAY
Asunción
Porto Alegre
Roggeveen Basin
Arch. de Juan Fernández
(Chile)
Córdoba
Aconcagua
6962
Valparaíso
Rosario
Santiago
Buenos Aires
URUGUAY
Montevideo
Río de la Plata
Concepción
ARGENTINA
Argentine Basin
Challenger Fracture Zone
Chile Rise
Southwest Pacific Basin
Pacific Antarctic Ridge
Menard Fracture Zone
Nemo Point
(furthest point from any land)
ANDES
Patagonia
114
ATLANTIC OCEAN
Falkland Plateau
6212
Falkland Is.
(U.K.)
Georgia Basin
Punta Arenas
Est. de Magallanes
Tierra del Fuego
South Georgia Ridge
South Georgia
(U.K.)
4402
C. de Hornos
Drake Passage
Southeast Pacific Basin
West from Greenwich
TAHITI
e
Pte. Aroa
MOZ
B. de Matavai
Pte. Vénus
Mahina
Papetoai
Paopao
Mt. Tohiea
1207
Afareaitu
Haapiti
Pte. Nuupere
Moorea
Papeete
Arue
PPT
Faaa
Pirae
Papenoo
Tiarei
Tahiti
(France)
Hitiaa
Punaauia
Mt. Aorai
2066
Mt. Orohena
2241
Faaone
Mt. Tetufera
1799
Vaihiria
Lac
Paea
Papara
Taravao
Isthme de Taravao
Pte. Tatatua
Maraa
Afaahiti
Pueu
Tautira
Atimaono
Mataiea
Vairao
Mt. Rooniu
1332
PACIFIC OCEAN
Teahupoo
Presqu'île de Taiarapu
1: 1 150 000
FRENCH POLYNESIA
1: 26 000 000
f
Hatutu
Eiao
Îles Marquises
Nuku Hiva
Ua Pu
Ua Huka
Hiva Oa
Tahuata
Motane
4884
6513
Flint I.
(Kiribati)
Îles Tuamotu
Îles du Roi-Georges
Îles du Désappointement
Tikahau
Ahé
Manihi
Takaroa
Mataiva
Rangiroa
Tikéi
Puka Puka
Îles Sous-le-Vent
Apataki
Takume
Maupiti
Bora Bora
Îles du Vent
Kauehi
Raroia
Fangatau
Huahine
Palliser
Raraka
Makemo
Maupihaa
Raiatea
Tahiti
Fakarava
Anaa
Île Raeuki
Tekokota
Tatakoto
Moorea
Haraiki
Amanu
Papeete
Méhétia
Marokau
Puka Ruha
Îles de la Société
Ravahere
Hao
Réao
Nengonengo
Paraoa
Vahitahi
Hérèhérétué
4616
Ahunui
Vairaatea
Îles du Duc-de-Gloucester
Vanavana
Turéia
Groupe Actéon
Tematagi
Mururoa
Îles Maria
Fangataufa
Rimatara
Rurutu
Tubuaï
Tropic of Capricorn
Îles Gambier
Morané
Raivavae
Récif Président-Thiers
Récif Portland
Îles Tubuaï (Îles Australes)
PACIFIC OCEAN
Récif Neilson
Rapa
Îlots de Bass
NIUE
1: 830 000
g
Hikutavake
Mutalau
Namukulu
Toi
Tuapa
Makefu
Lakepa
Alofi Bay
Alofi
Liku
Niue
(N.Z.)
Halangingie Pt.
IUE
Fonuakula
Tamakautoga
Avatele
Tepa Pt.
Vaiea
Hakupu
PACIFIC OCEAN
RAROTONGA
1: 415 000
h
Rarotonga
(N.Z.)
RAR
Avarua Harbour
Pue
Nikao
Avatiu
Avarua
Matavera
509
Te Manga
Ngatangiia
Arorangi
Maungaroa
588
653
Motu Tapu
222
Te Kou
Oneroa
Maungatongaiti
329
Muri
Koromiri
Taroume
Taakoka
Titikaveka
PACIFIC OCEAN
COPYRIGHT PHILIP'S

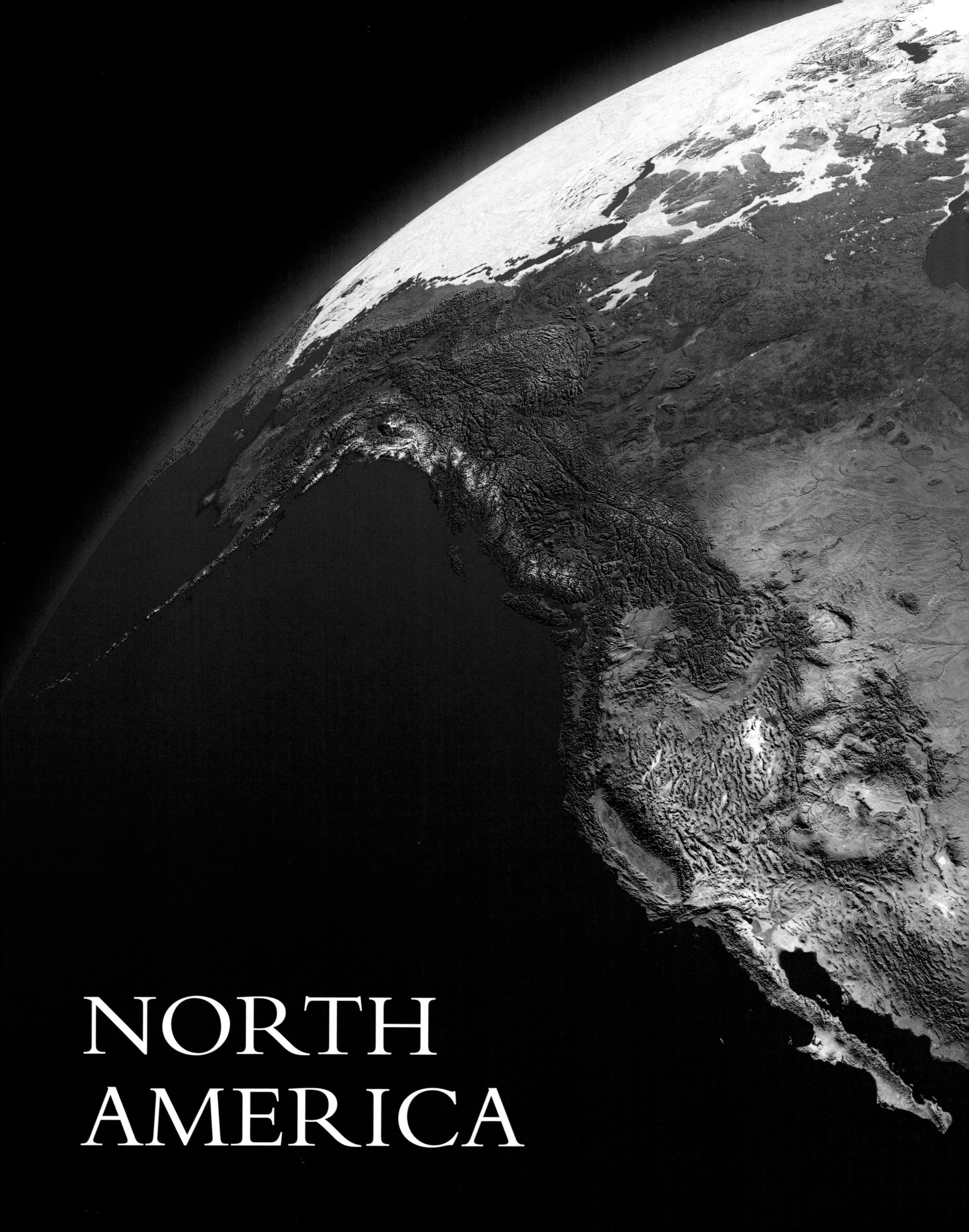

NORTH AMERICA

100 0 200 400 600 800 1000 1200 1400 km

1:28 000 000

100 0 200 400 600 800 1000 miles

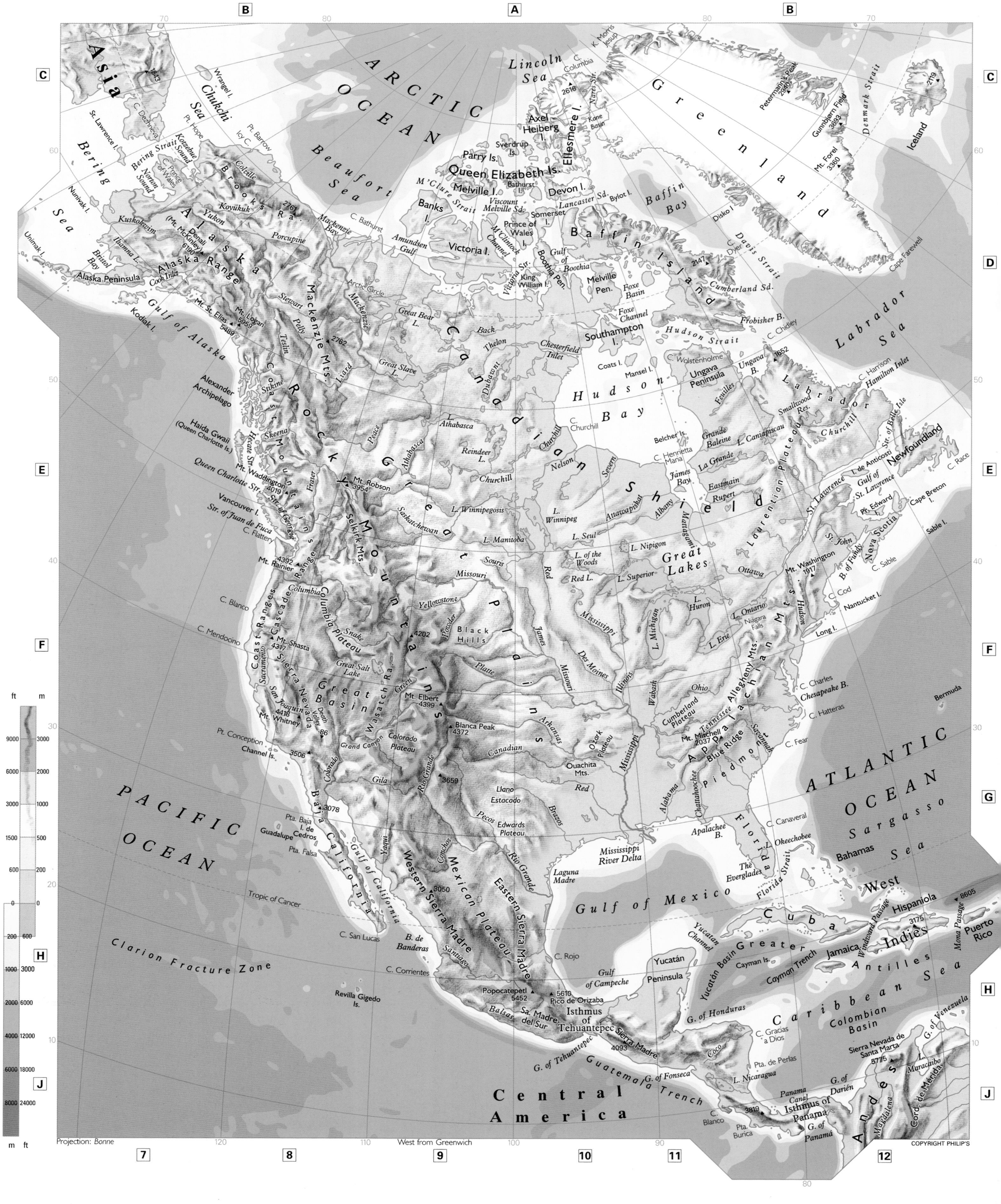

1:28 000 000

100 0 200 400 600 800 1000 1200 1400 km

100 0 200 400 600 800 1000 miles

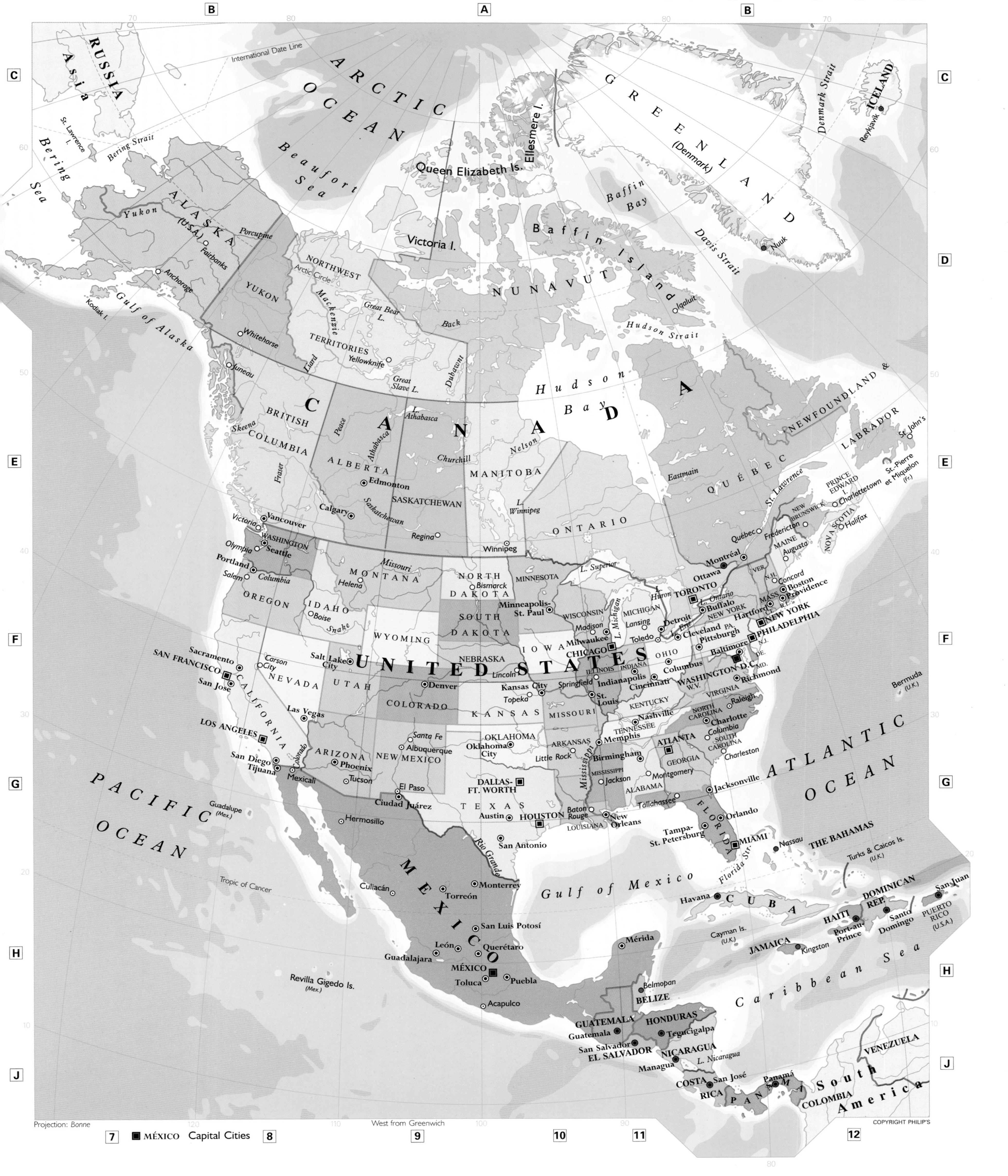

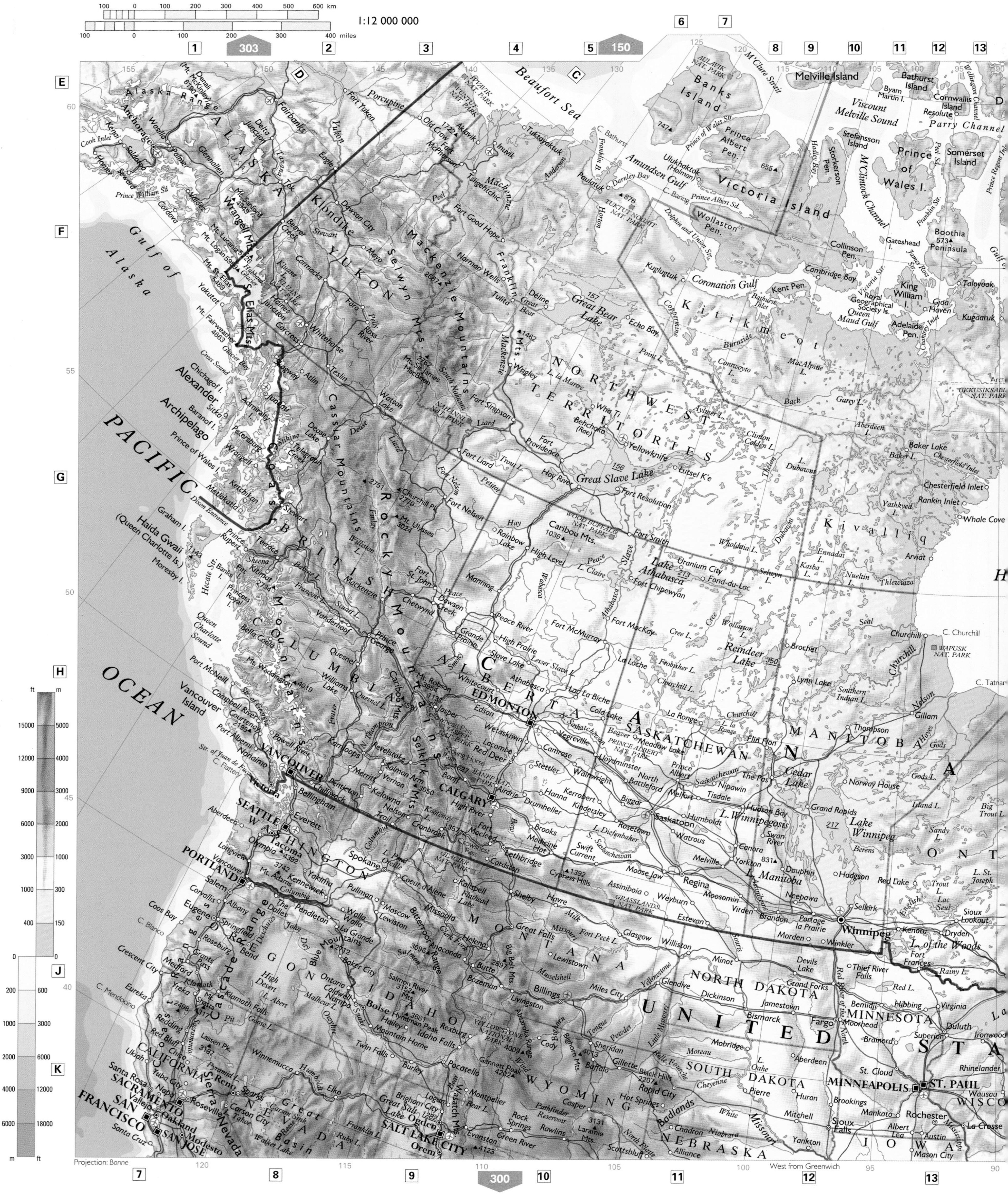
1:12 000 000
km
miles
Projection: Bonne
West from Greenwich
PACIFIC
OCEAN
Beaufort Sea
Gulf of Alaska
ALASKA
YUKON
NORTHWEST TERRITORIES
BRITISH COLUMBIA
ALBERTA
SASKATCHEWAN
MANITOBA
Kitikmeot
Kivalliq
UNITED STATES
WASHINGTON
OREGON
IDAHO
MONTANA
WYOMING
NORTH DAKOTA
SOUTH DAKOTA
NEBRASKA
MINNESOTA
IOWA
NEVADA
CALIFORNIA
Rocky Mountains
Mackenzie Mountains
Selwyn Mts.
Cassiar Mountains
Coast Mountains
Columbia Mountains
Alaska Range
Banks Island
Victoria Island
Melville Island
Prince of Wales I.
Somerset Island
Boothia Peninsula
King William I.
Amundsen Gulf
Coronation Gulf
Great Bear Lake
Great Slave Lake
Lake Athabasca
Reindeer Lake
Lake Winnipeg
Cedar Lake
L. Winnipegosis
L. Manitoba
Lake of the Woods
Vancouver Island
Haida Gwaii (Queen Charlotte Is.)
Alexander Archipelago
Anchorage
Fairbanks
Whitehorse
Dawson City
Inuvik
Yellowknife
Fort McMurray
EDMONTON
CALGARY
VANCOUVER
Victoria
Prince George
Prince Rupert
Saskatoon
Regina
Winnipeg
Churchill
SEATTLE
PORTLAND
Spokane
Boise
SALT LAKE CITY
MINNEAPOLIS
ST. PAUL
SACRAMENTO
SAN FRANCISCO
SAN JOSE
Reno
Billings
Bismarck
Fargo

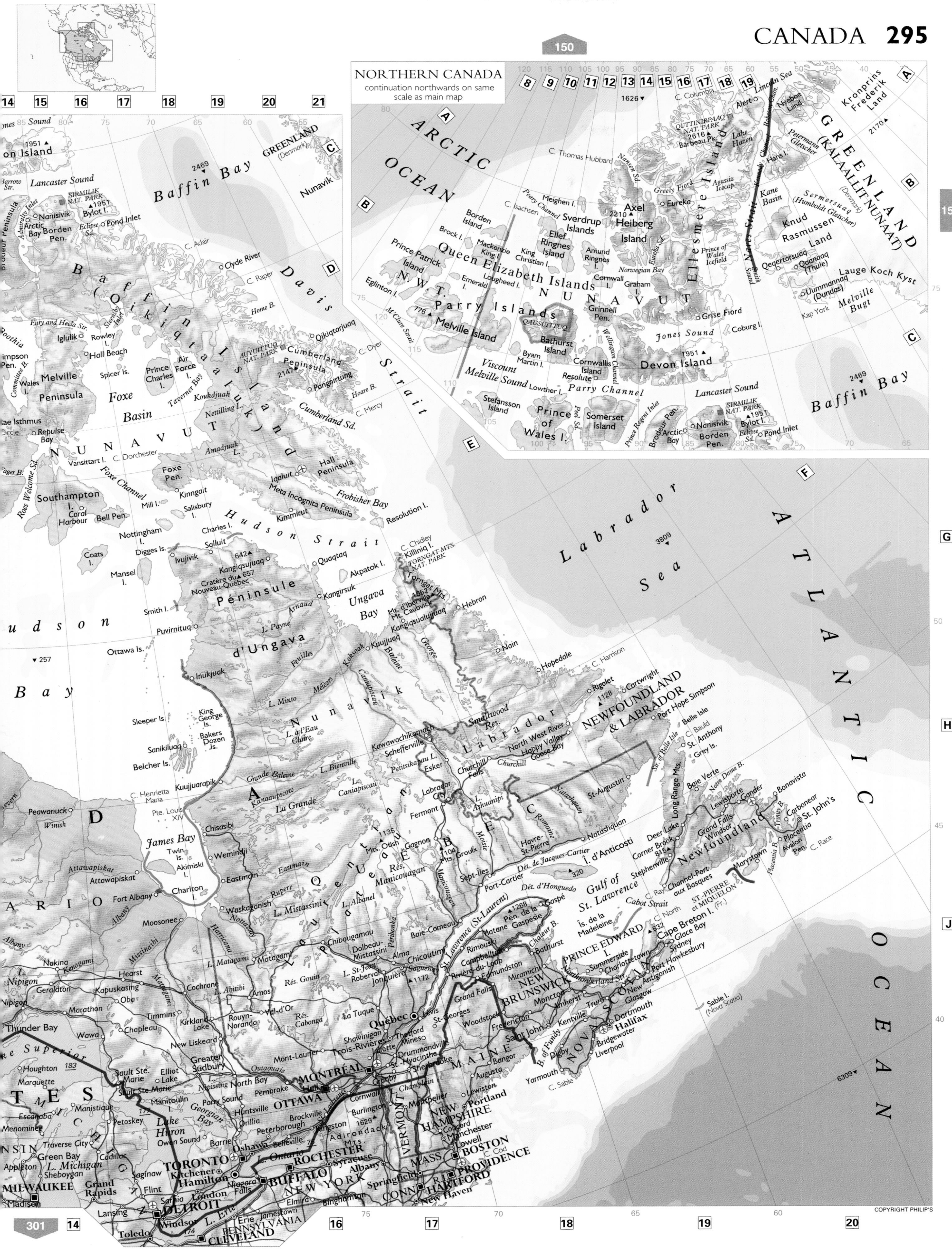
NORTHERN CANADA
continuation northwards on same scale as main map
ARCTIC OCEAN
Queen Elizabeth Islands
Parry Islands
Melville Island
Prince Patrick Island
Eglinton I.
Emerald I.
Mackenzie King I.
Borden Island
Brock I.
King Christian I.
Lougheed I.
Ellef Ringnes Island
Amund Ringnes I.
Meighen I.
Sverdrup Islands
Axel Heiberg Island
Ellesmere Island
Eureka
Grise Fiord
Alert
Lincoln Sea
C. Columbia
QUTTINIRPAAQ NAT. PARK
Barbeau Pk.
Lake Hazen
Greely Fiord
Agassiz Icecap
C. Thomas Hubbard
Nansen Sd.
C. Isachsen
Peary Channel
Cornwall I.
Graham I.
Norwegian Bay
Grinnell Pen.
Jones Sound
Coburg I.
Devon Island
Bathurst Island
QAUSUITTUQ
Byam Martin I.
Cornwallis Island
Resolute
Wellington Channel
Viscount Melville Sound
Lowther I.
Parry Channel
Stefansson Island
Prince of Wales I.
Peel Sd.
Somerset Island
Prince Regent Inlet
Lancaster Sound
Brodeur Pen.
Arctic Bay
Nanisivik
Borden Pen.
SIRMILIK NAT. PARK
Bylot I.
Eclipse Sd.
Pond Inlet
Baffin Bay
Kane Basin
Nares Strait
Smith Sound
Kennedy Channel
Robeson Chan.
Hans I.
Petermann Gletscher
Nyeboe Land
Kronprins Frederik Land
GREENLAND (KALAALLIT NUNAAT) (Denmark)
Sermersuaq (Humboldt Gletscher)
Knud Rasmussen Land
Qeqertarsuaq
Qaanaaq (Thule)
Uummannaq (Dundas)
Kap York
Melville Bugt
Laube Koch Kyst
N.W.T.
NUNAVUT
M'Clure Strait
Baffin Island (Qikiqtaaluk)
Davis Strait
Clyde River
C. Adair
C. Raper
Home B.
Qikiqtarjuaq
C. Dyer
Cumberland Peninsula
AUYUITTUQ NAT. PARK
Pangnirtung
Cumberland Sd.
Hoare B.
C. Mercy
Fury and Hecla Str.
Steensby Inlet
Igluik
Rowley I.
Hall Beach
Spicer Is.
Prince Charles I.
Air Force I.
Foxe Basin
Melville Peninsula
Koukdjuak
Nettilling L.
Amadjuak L.
Taverner Bay
Repulse Bay
Vansittart I.
C. Dorchester
Foxe Pen.
Foxe Channel
Southampton I.
Coral Harbour
Bell Pen.
Roes Welcome Sd.
Mill I.
Kinngait
Salisbury I.
Iqaluit
Hall Peninsula
Meta Incognita Peninsula
Frobisher Bay
Kimmirut
Resolution I.
Hudson Strait
Nottingham I.
Charles I.
Digges Is.
Salluit
Ivujivik
Coats I.
Mansel I.
Kangiqsujuaq
Cratère du Nouveau-Québec
Quaqtaq
Akpatok I.
C. Chidley
Killinig I.
TORNGAT MTS. NAT. PARK
Torngat Mts.
Péninsule d'Ungava
Kangirsuk
Ungava Bay
Mt. d'Iberville
Mt. Caubvick
Kangiqsualujjuaq
Hebron
Smith I.
Puvirnituq
Arnaud
L. Payne
Kuujjuaq
Nain
Ottawa Is.
Hudson Bay
Inukjuak
Feuilles
Koksoak
Baleine
George
Hopedale
C. Harrison
Labrador Sea
ATLANTIC OCEAN
L. Minto
Mélèzes
Caniapiscau
Nunavik
Rigolet
Cartwright
NEWFOUNDLAND & LABRADOR
Port Hope Simpson
Sleeper Is.
King George Is.
Bakers Dozen Is.
L. à l'Eau Claire
Smallwood Res.
Labrador
North West River
Happy Valley-Goose Bay
Belle Isle
C. Bauld
St. Anthony
Str. of Belle Isle
Grey Is.
Sanikiluaq
Belcher Is.
Kawawachikamach
Schefferville
Pettsikapau L.
Esker
Churchill Falls
Churchill
Grande Baleine
L. Bienville
Kuujjuarapik
C. Henrietta Maria
Pte. Louis XIV
Kanaaupscow
La Grande
L. Caniapiscau
Labrador City
Fermont
L. Ashuanipi
Natashquan
St-Augustin
Long Range Mts.
Baie Verte
Notre Dame B.
Lewisporte
Gander
Bonavista
Trinity B.
Carbonear
St. John's
Grand Falls-Windsor
Newfoundland
Deer Lake
Corner Brook
Stephenville
Placentia
Placentia B.
Avalon Pen.
C. Race
Marystown
Peawanuck
Winisk
James Bay
Chisasibi
Twin Is.
Akimiski I.
Wemindji
Eastmain
Charlton I.
Mts. Otish
Mts. Groulx
Rés. Manicouagan
Gagnon
Moisie
Romaine
Havre-St-Pierre
Natashquan
Î. d'Anticosti
Dét. de Jacques-Cartier
Dét. d'Honguedo
Sept-Îles
Port-Cartier
Gulf of St. Lawrence
Cabot Strait
Channel-Port aux Basques
C. Ray
ST-PIERRE et MIQUELON (Fr.)
Attawapiskat
Fort Albany
Albany
Moosonee
Waskaganish
Rupert
L. Mistassini
L. Albanel
Nottaway
Harricana
Chibougamau
Dolbeau-Mistassini
Peribonka
Baie-Comeau
Manicouagan
St. Lawrence (St-Laurent)
Pén. de la Gaspésie
Gaspé
Matane
Rimouski
Îs. de la Madeleine
C. North
Cape Breton I.
Glace Bay
Sydney
Port Hawkesbury
PRINCE EDWARD I.
Summerside
Charlottetown
Northumberland Str.
New Glasgow
Antigonish
Chaleur B.
Bathurst
Campbellton
Rivière-du-Loup
Edmundston
Miramichi
NEW BRUNSWICK
Moncton
Amherst
Truro
Grand Falls
Fredericton
Saint John
Woodstock
B. of Fundy
Kentville
Dartmouth
Halifax
Bridgewater
Liverpool
NOVA SCOTIA
Digby
Yarmouth
C. Sable
Sable I. (Nova Scotia)
Alma
Chicoutimi
Saguenay
Jonquière
Roberval
L. St-Jean
Rés. Gouin
L. Matagami
Matagami
Laurentides
QUEBEC
Nakina
Kenogami
Nipigon
L. Nipigon
Geraldton
Hearst
Kapuskasing
Cochrane
L. Abitibi
Amos
Val-d'Or
Rouyn-Noranda
Kirkland Lake
Rés. Cabonga
La Tuque
Québec
Lévis
St-Georges
Thetford Mines
Shawinigan
Trois-Rivières
Drummondville
Joliette
St-Hyacinthe
Sherbrooke
Granby
Marathon
Thunder Bay
Wawa
Timmins
Chapleau
Mattagami
Missinaibi
New Liskeard
Mont-Laurier
Greater Sudbury
L. Superior
Houghton
Marquette
Sault Ste. Marie
Elliot Lake
L. Nipissing
North Bay
Outaouais
MONTRÉAL
Pembroke
OTTAWA
Cornwall
Burlington
Montpelier
Champlain
MAINE
Augusta
Bangor
Lewiston
Portland
NEW HAMPSHIRE
Concord
Manchester
Lowell
BOSTON
C. Cod
VERMONT
MASS.
PROVIDENCE
R.I.
HARTFORD
CONN.
New Haven
Springfield
Albany
Syracuse
Adirondack Mts.
Kingston
Brockville
Belleville
Peterborough
Oshawa
Barrie
Orillia
Huntsville
Parry Sound
Georgian Bay
Manitoulin I.
Owen Sound
Lake Huron
L. Ontario
TORONTO
Kitchener
Hamilton
Niagara Falls
ROCHESTER
BUFFALO
NEW YORK
Elmira
Binghamton
Jamestown
Erie
L. Erie
PENNSYLVANIA
CLEVELAND
Toledo
Windsor
DETROIT
London
Sarnia
Flint
Saginaw
Lansing
Grand Rapids
MICHIGAN
L. Michigan
Traverse City
Cadillac
Petoskey
Manistique
Escanaba
Menominee
Green Bay
Sheboygan
Appleton
WISCONSIN
MILWAUKEE
Madison
UNITED STATES
ONTARIO
CANADA
NUNAVUT
Greenland (Denmark)
Nunavik
Sirmilik Nat. Park
COPYRIGHT PHILIP'S

1:5 600 000

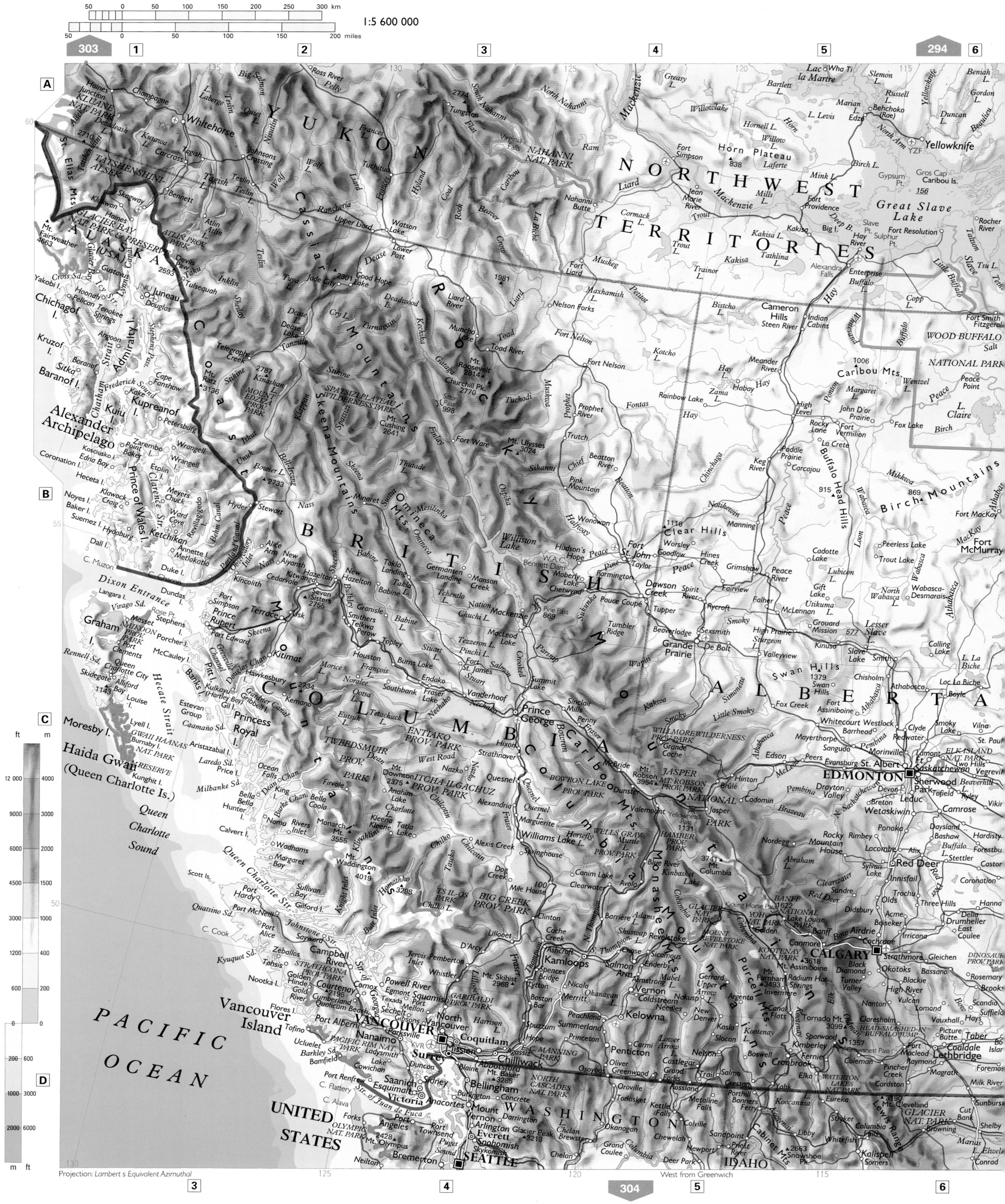

50 0 50 100 150 200 250 300 km
50 0 50 100 150 200 miles
303
294
304
YUKON
NORTHWEST TERRITORIES
BRITISH COLUMBIA
ALBERTA
ALASKA
WASHINGTON
IDAHO
UNITED STATES
PACIFIC OCEAN
Cassiar Mountains
Coast Mountains
Rocky Mountains
Skeena Mountains
Omineca Mts.
Cariboo Mts.
Columbia Mts.
Monashee Mts.
Purcell Mts.
Birch Mountains
Caribou Mts.
Clear Hills
Swan Hills
Horn Plateau
Great Slave Lake
Alexander Archipelago
Haida Gwaii (Queen Charlotte Is.)
Queen Charlotte Sound
Hecate Strait
Dixon Entrance
Vancouver Island
Graham I.
Moresby I.
Prince of Wales I.
Baranof I.
Chichagof I.
Admiralty I.
Whitehorse
Yellowknife
Juneau
Ketchikan
Prince Rupert
Prince George
Kamloops
Kelowna
Vancouver
Victoria
Nanaimo
Surrey
Coquitlam
Seattle
Bellingham
EDMONTON
CALGARY
Red Deer
Lethbridge
Grande Prairie
Fort Nelson
Fort St. John
Dawson Creek
Fort McMurray
Hay River
Fort Simpson
Fort Smith
Peace
Liard
Mackenzie
Fraser
Stikine
Skeena
Athabasca
Projection: Lambert's Equivalent Azimuthal
West from Greenwich
ft m
12 000 4000
9000 3000
6000 2000
4500 1500
3000 1000
1200 400
600 200
0 0
200 600
1000 3000
2000 6000
m ft

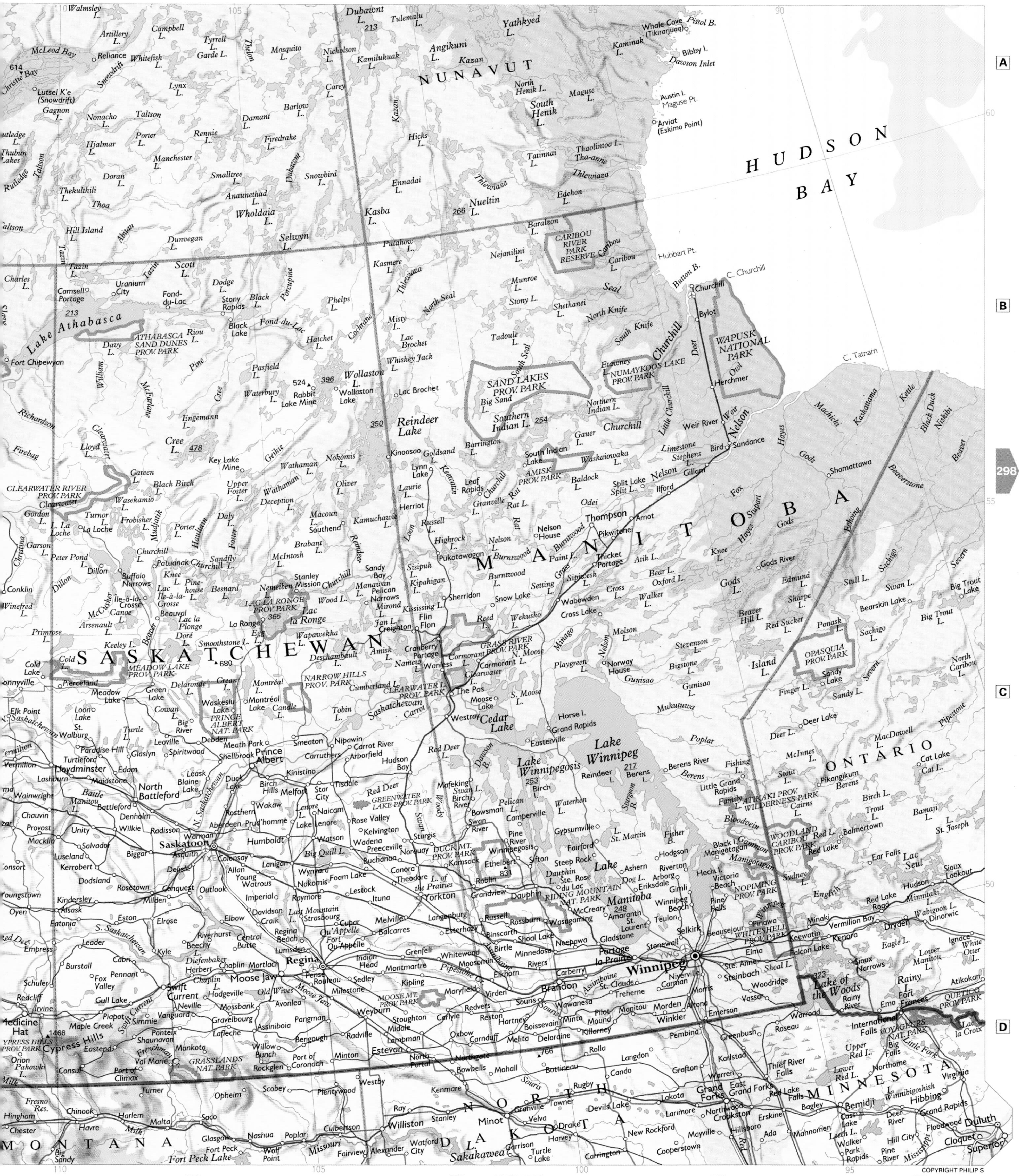
7
8
9
10
11
A
B
C
D
298
308
NUNAVUT
HUDSON BAY
MANITOBA
SASKATCHEWAN
ONTARIO
MINNESOTA
NORTH DAKOTA
MONTANA
Lake Athabasca
Reindeer Lake
Wollaston L.
Southern Indian L.
Lake Winnipeg
Lake Winnipegosis
Lake Manitoba
Cedar Lake
Lake of the Woods
Lac la Ronge
Cree L.
Yathkyed L.
Nueltin L.
Kasba L.
Dubawnt L.
WAPUSK NATIONAL PARK
SAND LAKES PROV. PARK
CARIBOU RIVER PARK RESERVE
ATHABASCA SAND DUNES PROV. PARK
PRINCE ALBERT NAT. PARK
RIDING MOUNTAIN NAT. PARK
GRASSLANDS NAT. PARK
VOYAGEURS NAT. PARK
QUETICO PROV. PARK
OPASQUIA PROV. PARK
WOODLAND CARIBOU PROV. PARK
Churchill
C. Churchill
C. Tatnam
Hubbart Pt.
Whale Cove (Tikirarjuaq)
Arviat (Eskimo Point)
Fort Chipewyan
Uranium City
Thompson
Flin Flon
The Pas
Gillam
Prince Albert
North Battleford
Lloydminster
Saskatoon
Regina
Moose Jaw
Swift Current
Yorkton
Brandon
Winnipeg
Portage la Prairie
Dauphin
Estevan
Weyburn
Kenora
Dryden
Fort Frances
International Falls
Grand Forks
Minot
Williston
Bemidji
Duluth
Superior
Medicine Hat
Cypress Hills
COPYRIGHT PHILIP S

50 0 50 100 150 200 250 300 km

1:5 600 000

50 0 50 100 150 200 miles

1 2 3 4 5

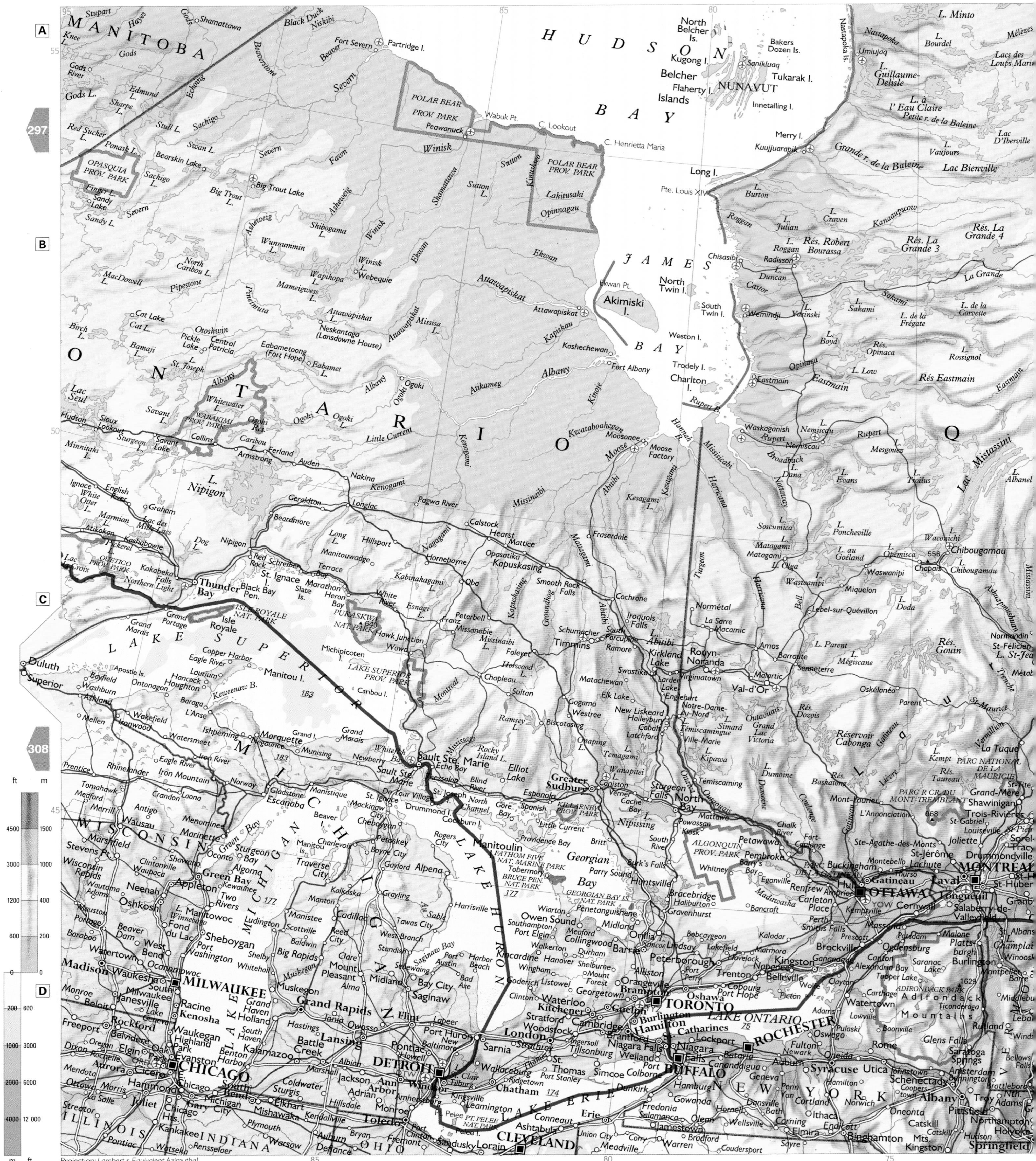

297
308
309

6 295 7 8 9

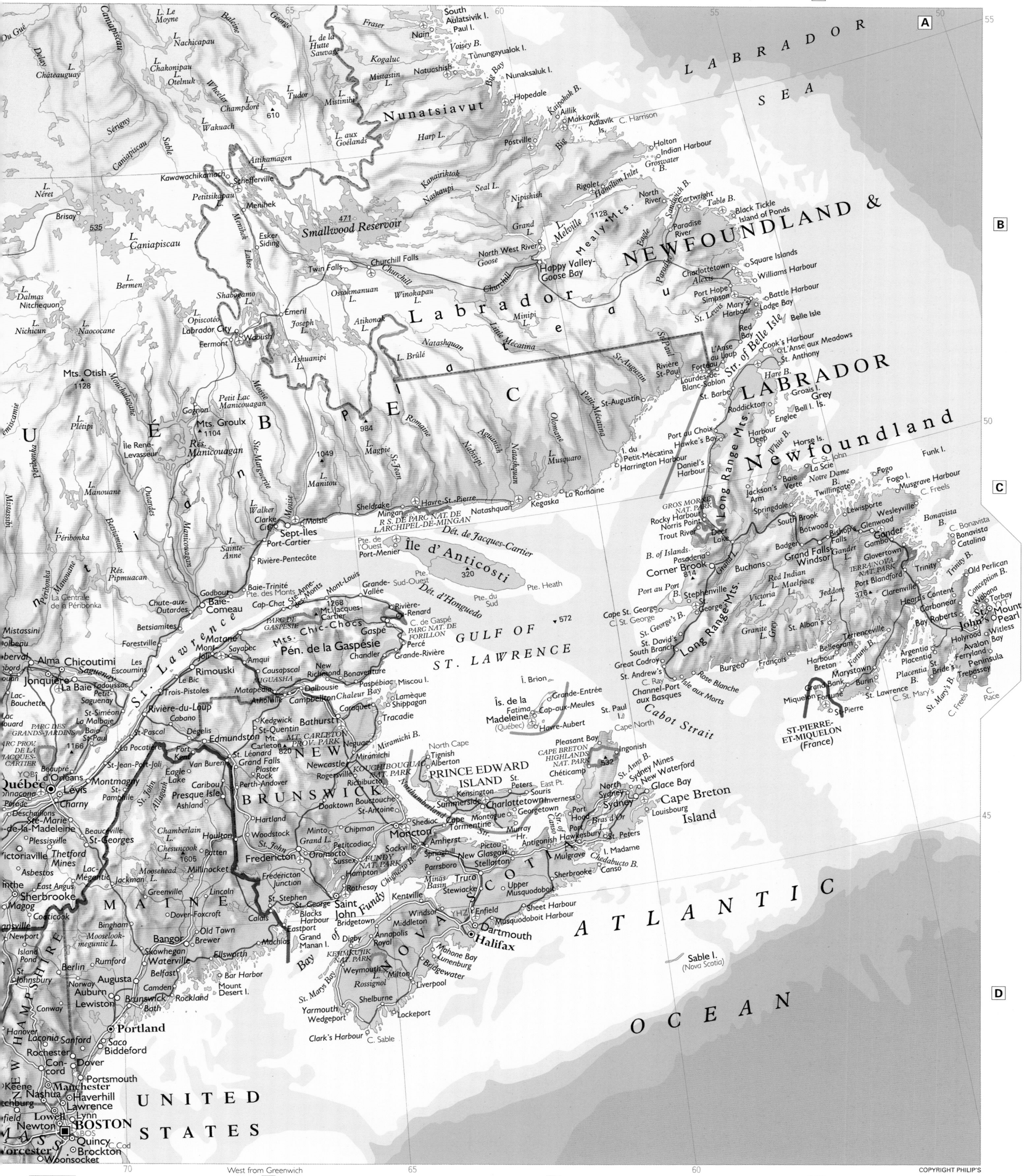
A
B
C
D
LABRADOR SEA
NEWFOUNDLAND & LABRADOR
Labrador
Newfoundland
Q U É B E C
Nunatsiavut
Smallwood Reservoir
Churchill Falls
Happy Valley-Goose Bay
Mealy Mts.
Labrador City
Wabush
Fermont
Schefferville
Mts. Otish
Rés. Manicouagan
Mts. Groulx
Sept-Îles
Port-Cartier
Baie-Comeau
Havre-St-Pierre
Île d'Anticosti
Dét. de Jacques-Cartier
Dét. d'Honguedo
Str. of Belle Isle
Long Range Mts.
Corner Brook
Gander
Grand Falls-Windsor
Stephenville
St. John's
Avalon Peninsula
Cabot Strait
ST-PIERRE-ET-MIQUELON (France)
GULF OF ST. LAWRENCE
Îs. de la Madeleine
Mts. Chic-Chocs
Pén. de la Gaspésie
Gaspé
Rimouski
Chicoutimi
Jonquière
Saguenay
St. Lawrence
Québec
Lévis
Edmundston
NEW BRUNSWICK
Fredericton
Moncton
Saint John
Bathurst
PRINCE EDWARD ISLAND
Charlottetown
Summerside
NOVA SCOTIA
Halifax
Dartmouth
Truro
Sydney
Cape Breton Island
Bay of Fundy
Sable I. (Nova Scotia)
MAINE
Bangor
Augusta
Portland
Lewiston
Sherbrooke
NEW HAMPSHIRE
Manchester
BOSTON
UNITED STATES
ATLANTIC OCEAN
C. Sable
C. Race
C. Cod
West from Greenwich
70
65
60
55
50
45

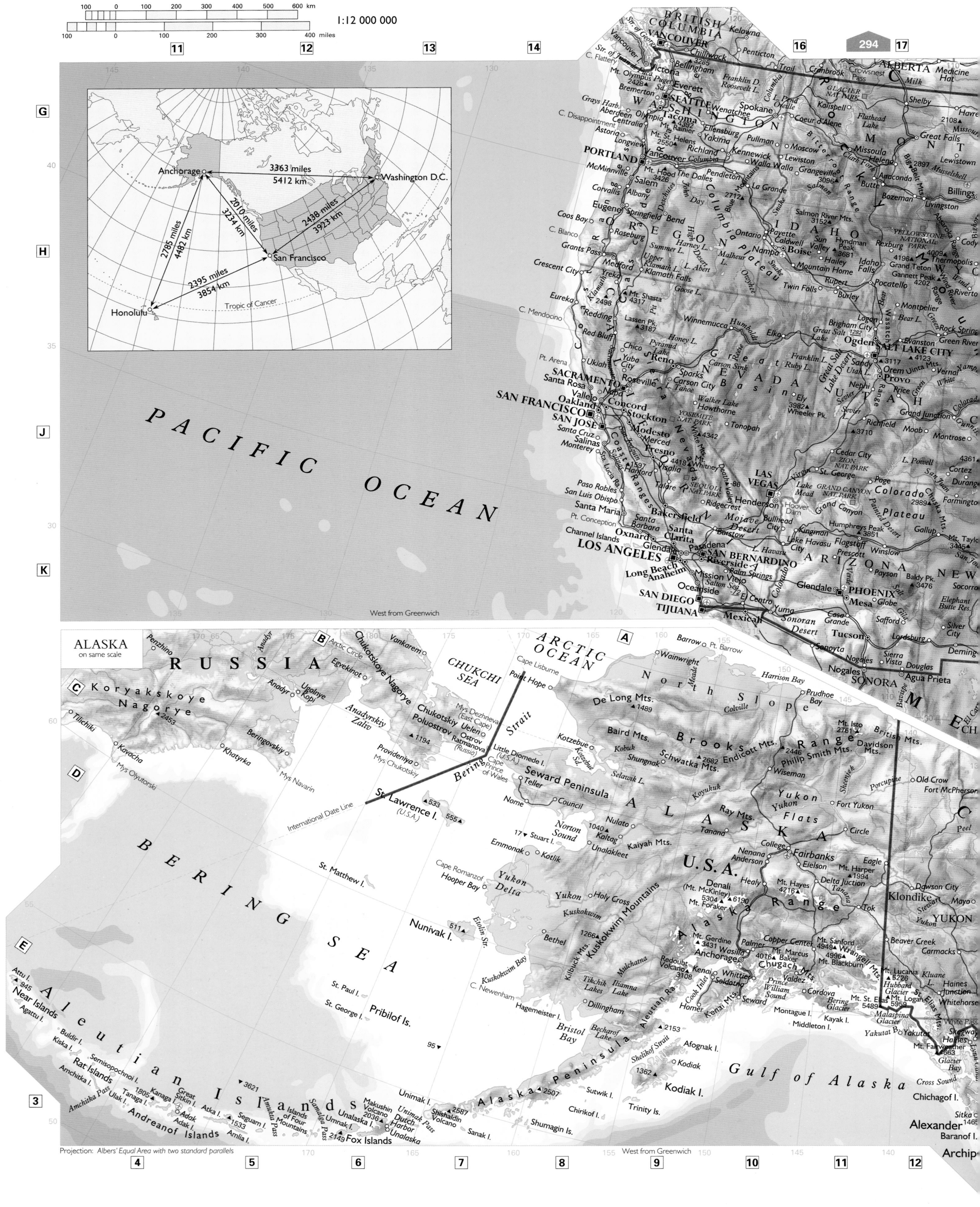

Projection: Albers' Equal Area with two standard parallels

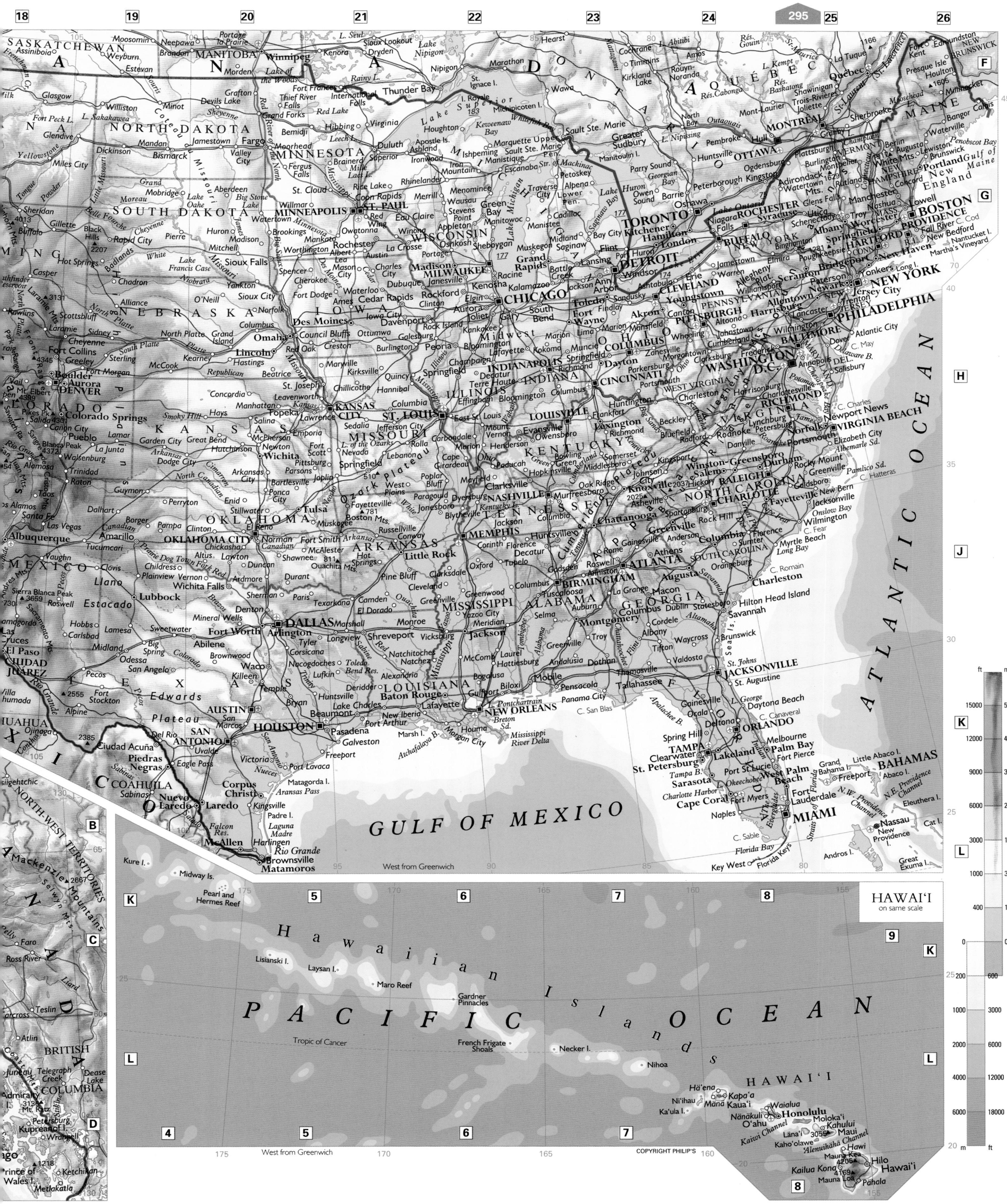
295
SASKATCHEWAN
MANITOBA
ONTARIO
QUÉBEC
NEW BRUNSWICK
NORTH DAKOTA
SOUTH DAKOTA
NEBRASKA
KANSAS
OKLAHOMA
TEXAS
MINNESOTA
IOWA
MISSOURI
ARKANSAS
LOUISIANA
WISCONSIN
MICHIGAN
ILLINOIS
INDIANA
OHIO
KENTUCKY
TENNESSEE
MISSISSIPPI
ALABAMA
GEORGIA
FLORIDA
SOUTH CAROLINA
NORTH CAROLINA
VIRGINIA
WEST VIRGINIA
PENNSYLVANIA
NEW YORK
MAINE
VERMONT
NEW HAMPSHIRE
MASS.
CONN.
NEW JERSEY
MARYLAND
DEL.
WASHINGTON D.C.
BAHAMAS
BRITISH COLUMBIA
COAHUILA
CIUDAD JUÁREZ
Winnipeg
Thunder Bay
MINNEAPOLIS
ST. PAUL
MILWAUKEE
CHICAGO
DETROIT
TORONTO
MONTRÉAL
OTTAWA
Québec
BOSTON
PROVIDENCE
HARTFORD
NEW YORK
PHILADELPHIA
BALTIMORE
PITTSBURGH
CLEVELAND
BUFFALO
ROCHESTER
COLUMBUS
CINCINNATI
INDIANAPOLIS
LOUISVILLE
ST. LOUIS
KANSAS CITY
Des Moines
Omaha
Lincoln
Denver
Colorado Springs
Albuquerque
OKLAHOMA CITY
Tulsa
Wichita
DALLAS
Fort Worth
AUSTIN
SAN ANTONIO
HOUSTON
NEW ORLEANS
MEMPHIS
NASHVILLE
ATLANTA
BIRMINGHAM
CHARLOTTE
RALEIGH
RICHMOND
VIRGINIA BEACH
JACKSONVILLE
ORLANDO
TAMPA
MIAMI
Nassau
GULF OF MEXICO
ATLANTIC OCEAN
PACIFIC OCEAN
Hawaiian Islands
HAWAI‘I
Honolulu
Hilo
Kaua‘i
O‘ahu
Maui
Hawai‘i
Midway Is.
Kure I.
Pearl and Hermes Reef
Lisianski I.
Laysan I.
Maro Reef
Gardner Pinnacles
French Frigate Shoals
Necker I.
Nihoa
Tropic of Cancer
West from Greenwich
HAWAI‘I on same scale
COPYRIGHT PHILIP'S
ft
m
15000
12000
9000
6000
3000
1000
400
0
200
2000
4000
5000
4000
3000
2000
1000
300
150
600
6000
12000
18000

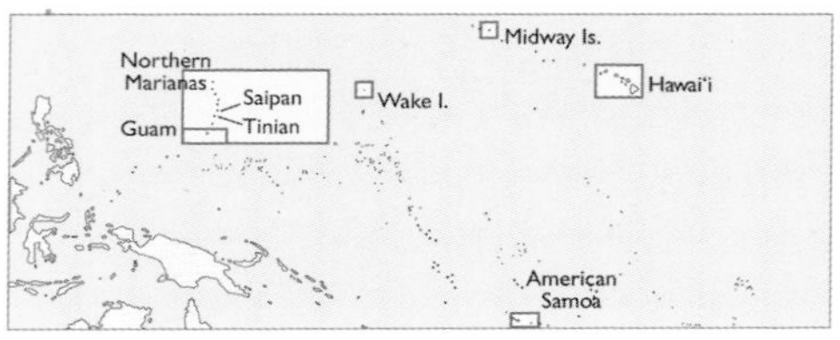
Midway Is.
Northern Marianas
Saipan
Tinian
Guam
Wake I.
Hawaiʻi
American Samoa

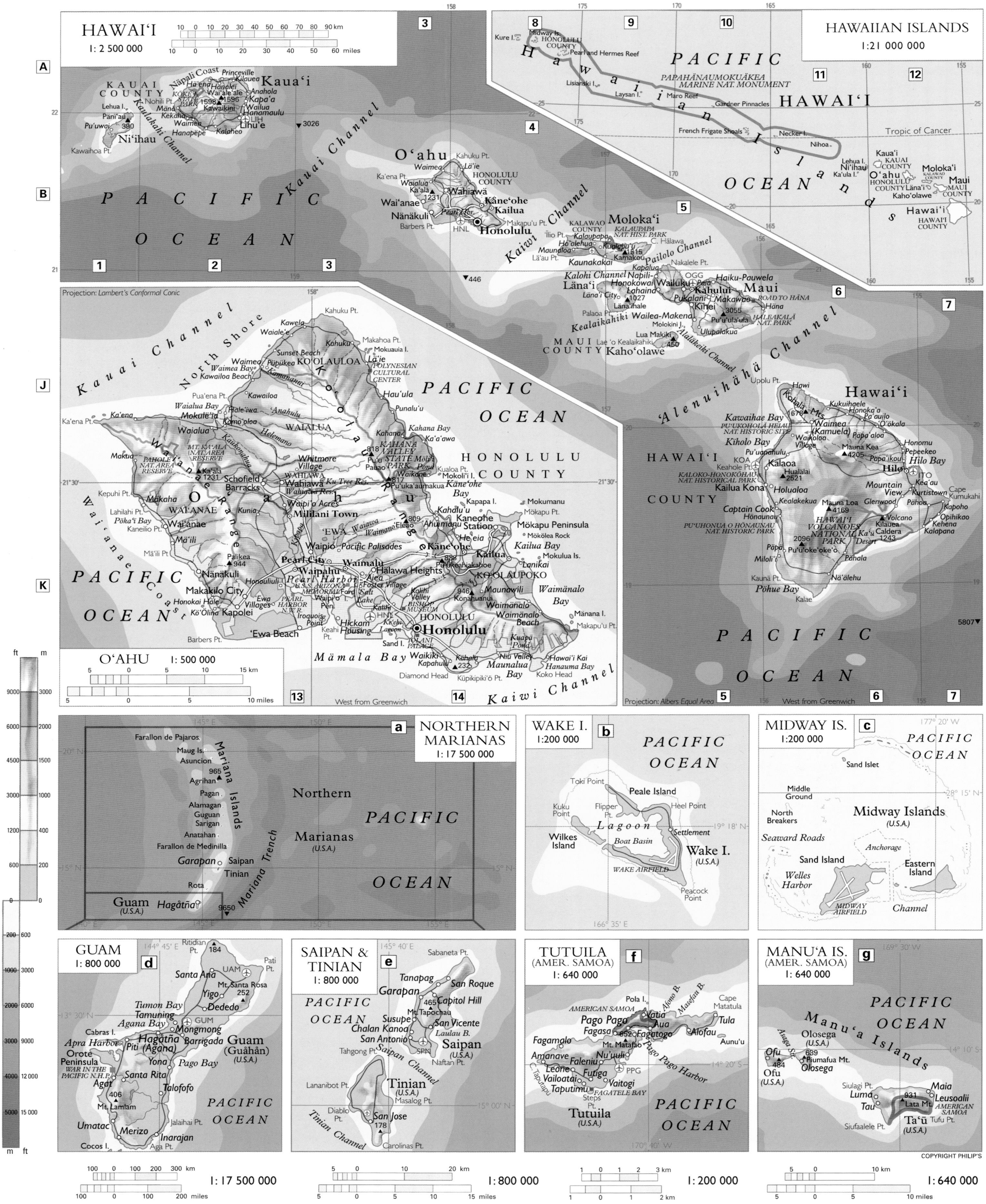
HAWAIʻI
1: 2 500 000
HAWAIIAN ISLANDS
1:21 000 000
PACIFIC OCEAN
PAPAHĀNAUMOKUĀKEA MARINE NAT. MONUMENT
Hawaiian Islands
Kure I.
Midway Is.
HONOLULU COUNTY
Pearl and Hermes Reef
Lisianski I.
Laysan I.
Maro Reef
Gardner Pinnacles
French Frigate Shoals
Necker I.
Nihoa
Tropic of Cancer
KAUAI COUNTY
Kauaʻi
Niʻihau
Lehua I.
Kaʻula I.
Oʻahu
Molokaʻi
KALAWAO COUNTY
Lānaʻi
MAUI COUNTY
Maui
Kahoʻolawe
Hawaiʻi
HAWAIʻI COUNTY
Nāpali Coast
Princeville
Kilauea
Haʻena
Hanalei
Anahola
Kapaʻa
Wailua
Hanamaulu
Līhuʻe
Kalaheo
Hanapēpē
Waimea
Kekaha
Mānā
Kawaikini
Waiʻaleʻale
Pāniʻau
Puʻuwai
Kawaihoa Pt.
Kaulakahi Channel
Kauai Channel
Kaiwi Channel
Kahuku Pt.
Lāʻie
Waimea
Waialua
Kaʻala
Kaʻena Pt.
Wahiawā
Waiʻanae
Nānākuli
Barbers Pt.
Pearl Hbr.
HNL
Honolulu
Kāneʻohe
Kailua
Makapuʻu Pt.
KALAUPAPA NAT. HIST. PARK
ʻIlio Pt.
Hoʻolehua
Kualapuʻu
Maunaloa
Lāʻau Pt.
Kaunakakai
Kamakou
C. Hālawa
Pailolo Channel
Nakalele Pt.
Kalohi Channel
Kapalua
Napili-Honokowai
Lāhainā
Lānaʻi City
Lānaʻihale
Palaoa Pt.
OGG
Haiku-Pauwela
Paia
Wailuku
Kahului
Pukalani
Makawao
Kīhei
ROAD TO HĀNA
Hāna
Puʻuʻulaʻula
HALEAKALĀ NAT. PARK
Ulupalakua
Wailea-Makena
Molokini I.
Kealaikahiki Channel
Lae ʻo Kealaikahiki
Lua Makika
ʻAlalākeiki Channel
ʻAlenuihāhā Channel
Upolu Pt.
Hawi
Kohala Mts.
Kukuihaele
Honokaʻa
Paʻauilo
ʻŌʻōkala
Kawaihae Bay
PUʻUKOHOLĀ HEIAU NAT. HISTORIC SITE
Waimea (Kamuela)
Waikoloa Village
Pāpaʻaloa
Kīholo Bay
Puʻuanahulu
Mauna Kea
Honomu
Pepeekeo
Pāpaʻikou
Hilo
Hilo Bay
Keahole Pt.
KOA
Kalaoa
KALOKO-HONOKŌHAU NAT. HISTORICAL PARK
Hualālai
Kailua Kona
Holualoa
ITO
Keaʻau
Mountain View
Kurtistown
Cape Kumukahi
Kealakekua
Captain Cook
Hōnaunau
Mauna Loa
Glenwood
Pāhoa
Kapoho
PUʻUHONUA O HŌNAUNAU NAT. HISTORIC PARK
HAWAIʻI VOLCANOES NATIONAL PARK
Volcano
Kilauea Caldera
Opihikao
Kehena
Kalapana
Kaʻū Desert
Puʻuokeʻokeʻo
Pāpā
Miloliʻi
Pahala
Nāʻālehu
Kaunā Pt.
Pōhue Bay
Kalae
Projection: Lambert's Conformal Conic
Projection: Albers Equal Area
West from Greenwich
OʻAHU
1: 500 000
Kauai Channel
North Shore
Kawela
Waialeʻe
Kahuku
Sunset Beach
Pūpūkea
KOʻOLAULOA
Makahoa Pt.
Mokuauia I.
POLYNESIAN CULTURAL CENTER
Waimea Bay
Kawailoa Beach
Kamananui
Hauʻula
Punaluʻu
Puaʻena Pt.
Kawailoa
Waialua Bay
Mokulēʻia
Haleʻiwa
Kamoʻoloa
ʻAnahulu
WAIALUA
Helemano
Kahana Bay
Kaʻaʻawa
Kahanaʻiki
KAHANA VALLEY STATE PARK
Makua
MT. KAʻALA NAT. AREA RESERVE
PAHOLE NAT. AREA RESERVE
Waiʻanae Range
Koʻolau Range
Whitmore Village
Puʻu Pauao
Mōliʻi Pond
Kualoa Pt.
Mokoliʻi I.
Waikāne
Puʻukaʻaumakua
Schofield Barracks
Wahiawā Res.
Ku Tree Res.
Kepuhi Pt.
Mākaha
Waipiʻo Acres
Mililani Town
Kapapa I.
Mokumanu
Mōkapu Pt.
Kahaluʻu
Lahilahi Pt.
Pōkaʻī Bay
Kaneilio Pt.
Māʻili
Māʻili Pt.
Kunia
ʻEWA
Waiawa
Waimano
ʻEleao
ʻAhuimanu
Kaneohe Station
Mōkapu Peninsula
Mōkōlea Rock
Heʻeia
Kailua Bay
Mokulua Is.
Lanikai
Palikea
Waipio
Pacific Palisades
Pearl City
Waimalu
Waipahu
Pearl Harbor
U.S.S. ARIZONA MEMORIAL
Hālawa Heights
ʻAiea
Foster Village
Puʻukonahakoe
KOʻOLAUPOKO
Maunawili
Konahuanui
Waimānalo Bay
Mānana I.
Waimānalo Beach
Makapuʻu Pt.
Waiʻanae Coast
Makakilo City
Honolulu
Honokai Hale
Kō ʻOlina
Kapolei
Ewa Villages
PEARL HARBOR N.W.R.
Iroquois Point
Waipiʻo Pen.
Ford Island
Salt Lake
Kalihi Valley
BISHOP MUSEUM
Kalihi
Hickam Housing
Keʻehi Lagoon
Keahi Pt.
Sand I.
ʻIOLANI PALACE
Kuapā Pond
Niu Valley
Hawaiʻi Kai
Hanauma Bay
Koko Head
Maunalua Bay
Kūpikipikiʻō Pt.
Diamond Head
Waikīkī
Kapahulu
Kāhala
Māmala Bay
ʻEwa Beach
Barbers Pt.
Hōnouliuli
NORTHERN MARIANAS
1: 17 500 000
Farallon de Pajaros
Maug Is.
Asuncion
Agrihan
Pagan
Alamagan
Guguan
Sarigan
Anatahan
Farallon de Medinilla
Mariana Islands
Garapan
Saipan
Tinian
Rota
Mariana Trench
Guam (U.S.A.)
Hagåtña
Northern Marianas (U.S.A.)
WAKE I.
1:200 000
Toki Point
Peale Island
Heel Point
Kuku Point
Flipper Pt.
Lagoon
Settlement
Wilkes Island
Boat Basin
Wake I. (U.S.A.)
WAKE AIRFIELD
Peacock Point
MIDWAY IS.
1:200 000
Sand Islet
Middle Ground
North Breakers
Midway Islands (U.S.A.)
Seaward Roads
Anchorage
Sand Island
Welles Harbor
Eastern Island
MIDWAY AIRFIELD
Channel
GUAM
1: 800 000
Ritidian Pt.
Pati Pt.
UAM
Santa Ana
Mt. Santa Rosa
Yigo
Dededo
Tumon Bay
Tamuning
GUM
Agana Bay
Mongmong
Cabras I.
Apra Harbor
Hagåtña (Agana)
Piti
Barrigada
Guam (Guåhån) (U.S.A.)
Orote Peninsula
WAR IN THE PACIFIC N.H.P.
Yona
Pago Bay
Agat
Santa Rita
Talofofo
Mt. Lamlam
Umatac
Merizo
Jalaihai Pt.
Inarajan
Cocos I.
Aga Pt.
SAIPAN & TINIAN
1: 800 000
Sabaneta Pt.
Tanapag
San Roque
Garapan
Capitol Hill
Mt. Tapochau
Susupe
San Vicente
Chalan Kanoa
Laulau B.
San Antonio
Saipan (U.S.A.)
SPN
Tahgong Pt.
Naftan Pt.
Saipan Channel
Lananibot Pt.
Tinian (U.S.A.)
Masalog Pt.
Diablo Pt.
San Jose
Tinian Channel
Carolinas Pt.
TUTUILA (AMER. SAMOA)
1: 640 000
Pola I.
Afono B.
Masefau B.
Cape Matatula
AMERICAN SAMOA
Pago Pago
Vatia
Aua
Tula
Fagasa
Fagatogo
Alofau
Mt. Matafao
Aunuʻu
Fagamalo
Pago Pago Harbor
Amanave
Nuʻuuli
Faleniu
PPG
Leone
Futiga
Vailoatai
Vaitogi
Taputimu
C. Taputapu
Steps Pt.
FAGATELE BAY
Tutuila (U.S.A.)
MANUʻA IS. (AMER. SAMOA)
1: 640 000
Manuʻa Islands
Asaga Str.
Ofu
Olosega (U.S.A.)
Piumafua Mt.
Ofu (U.S.A.)
Siulagi Pt.
Maia
Luma
Tau
Lata Mt.
Leusoalii
AMERICAN SAMOA
Taʻū (U.S.A.)
Tufu Pt.
Siufaalele Pt.
COPYRIGHT PHILIP'S
1: 17 500 000
1: 800 000
1: 200 000
1: 640 000

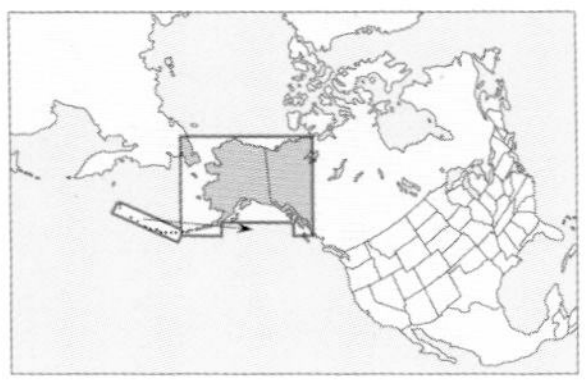

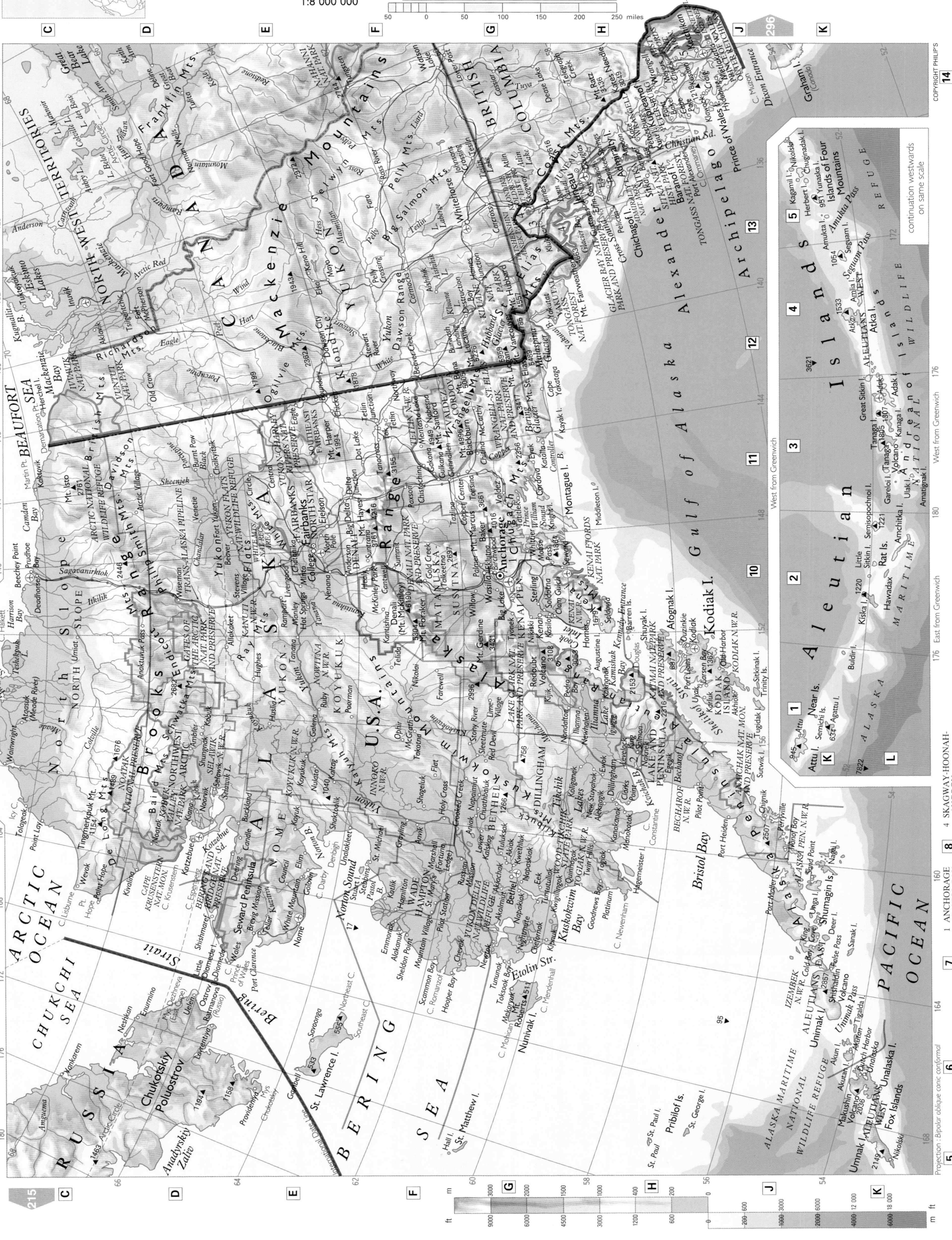
1:8 000 000
km
miles
ARCTIC OCEAN
CHUKCHI SEA
BEAUFORT SEA
BERING SEA
PACIFIC OCEAN
Gulf of Alaska
Bristol Bay
Norton Sound
Bering Strait
RUSSIA
CANADA
U.S.A.
ALASKA
YUKON
NORTH WEST TERRITORIES
BRITISH COLUMBIA
Brooks Range
Alaska Range
Mackenzie Mountains
Alexander Archipelago
Aleutian Islands
Kodiak I.
Anchorage
Fairbanks
Juneau
Nome
Barrow
Denali (Mt. McKinley)
Chukotskiy Poluostrov
St. Lawrence I.
Nunivak I.
Pribilof Is.
continuation westwards on same scale
County boundaries
1 ANCHORAGE
2 BRISTOL BAY
3 HAINES
4 SKAGWAY-HOONAH-ANGOON
5 KETCHIKAN GATEWAY
Projection: Bipolar oblique conic conformal
COPYRIGHT PHILIP'S
West from Greenwich
East from Greenwich
294
296
215

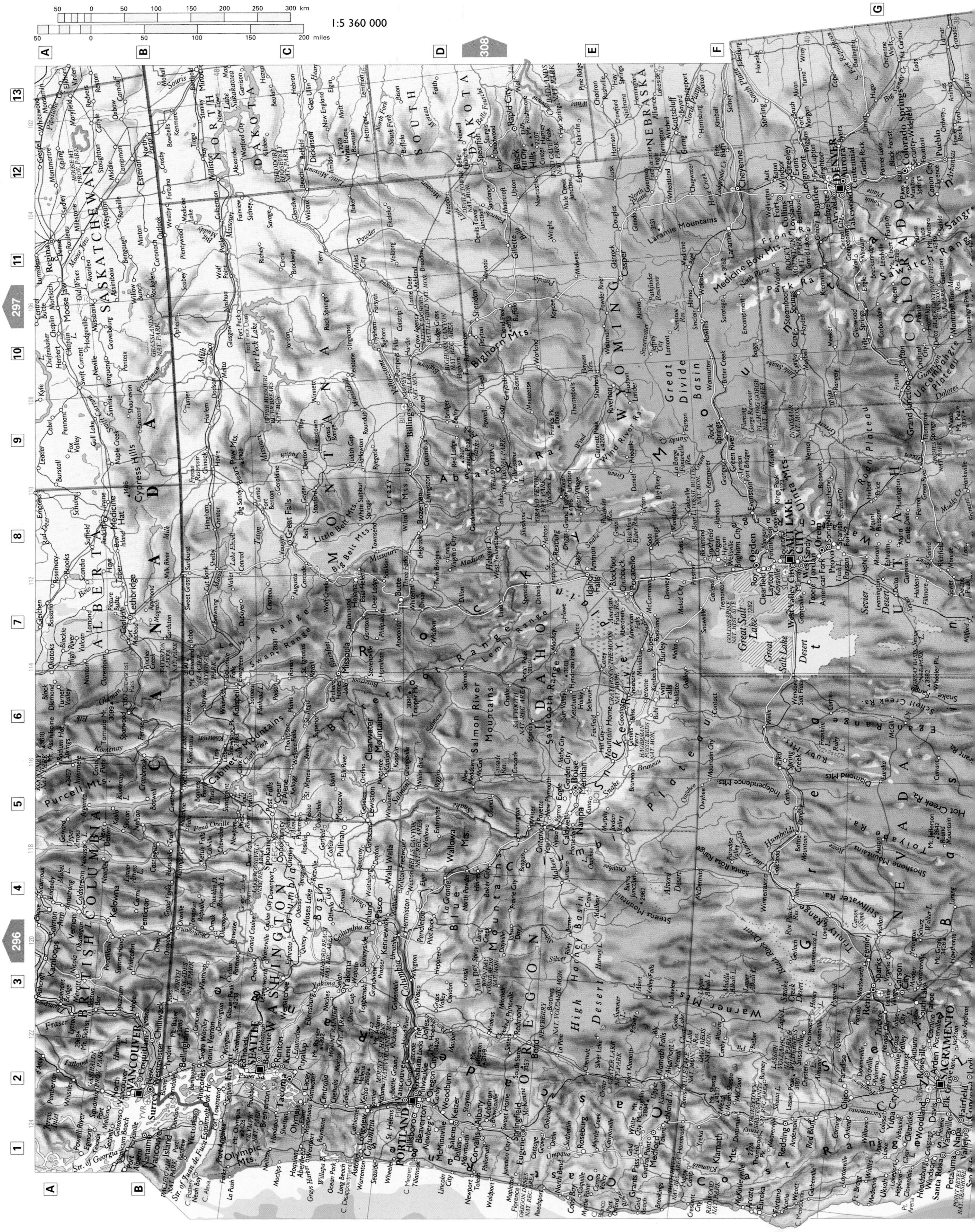
50 0 50 100 150 200 250 300 km
1:5 360 000
50 0 50 100 150 200 miles
308
297
296
ALBERTA
SASKATCHEWAN
BRITISH COLUMBIA
MONTANA
NORTH DAKOTA
SOUTH DAKOTA
WYOMING
NEBRASKA
COLORADO
IDAHO
UTAH
NEVADA
WASHINGTON
OREGON
CANADA
DENVER
SALT LAKE CITY
SEATTLE
PORTLAND
VANCOUVER
SACRAMENTO
Great Salt Lake
Great Salt Lake Desert
Great Divide Basin
Bighorn Mts.
Laramie Mountains
Medicine Bow Mts.
Snake River Plain
Blue Mountains
Salmon River Mountains
Sawtooth Range
Bitterroot Range
Uinta Mts.
Wind River Ra.
High Desert
Columbia Basin
Cypress Hills
Purcell Mts.
Olympic Mts.

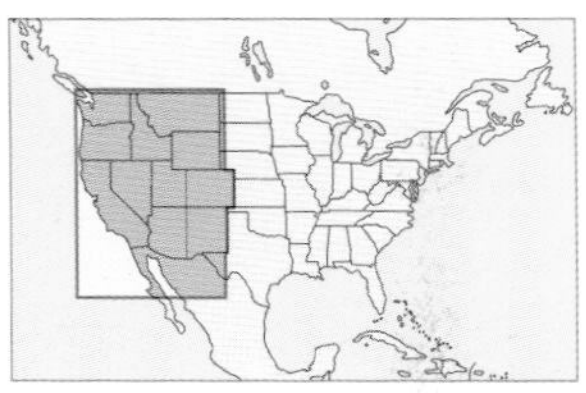

PACIFIC OCEAN
Golfo de California
ARIZONA
NEW MEXICO
TEXAS
CHIHUAHUA
SONORA
BAJA CALIFORNIA
BAJA CALIFORNIA SUR
MEXICO
Colorado Plateau
Sierra Nevada
Mojave Desert
Sonoran Desert
LOS ANGELES
SAN DIEGO
TIJUANA
PHOENIX
Tucson
Albuquerque
LAS VEGAS
CIUDAD JUÁREZ
El Paso
Chihuahua
Hermosillo
Ciudad Obregón
SAN FRANCISCO
SAN JOSE
Isla Guadalupe (Mexico)
Cedros Trench
Lava fields
West from Greenwich
COPYRIGHT PHILIP'S
Projection: Albers' Equal Area with two standard parallels
m 3000 2000 1500 1000 400 200 0 200 1000 2000 4000
ft 9000 6000 4500 3000 1200 600 0 600 3000 6000 12 000
314
318

1:2 000 000
10 0 10 20 30 40 50 60 70 80 90 km
10 0 10 20 30 40 50 60 miles
WESTERN WASHINGTON REGION
on same scale
PACIFIC OCEAN
BRITISH COLUMBIA
CANADA
Vancouver Island
Strait of Georgia
Strait of Juan de Fuca
VANCOUVER
Victoria
Bellingham
Everett
SEATTLE
Tacoma
Olympia
Olympic Mountains
OLYMPIC NATIONAL PARK
WASHINGTON
Mt. Rainier 4392
MT. RAINIER NAT. PARK
Mt. St. Helens 2550
Mt. Adams 3742
Aberdeen
Longview
Vancouver
PORTLAND
OREGON
Astoria
Reno
Carson City
Lake Tahoe
Sierra Nevada
YOSEMITE NATIONAL PARK
KINGS CANYON NATIONAL PARK
SEQUOIA NATIONAL PARK
White Mts.
Inyo Mts.
Mono Lake
SACRAMENTO
Sacramento Valley
San Joaquin Valley
Stockton
Modesto
Merced
Fresno
Visalia
Tulare
Hanford
Madera
SAN FRANCISCO
Oakland
SAN JOSE
Santa Cruz
Monterey
Salinas
Salinas Valley
Santa Clara Valley
Santa Lucia Range
Diablo Range
Coast Ranges
Santa Rosa
Napa
Vallejo
Paso Robles
Morro Bay
Pahute Mesa

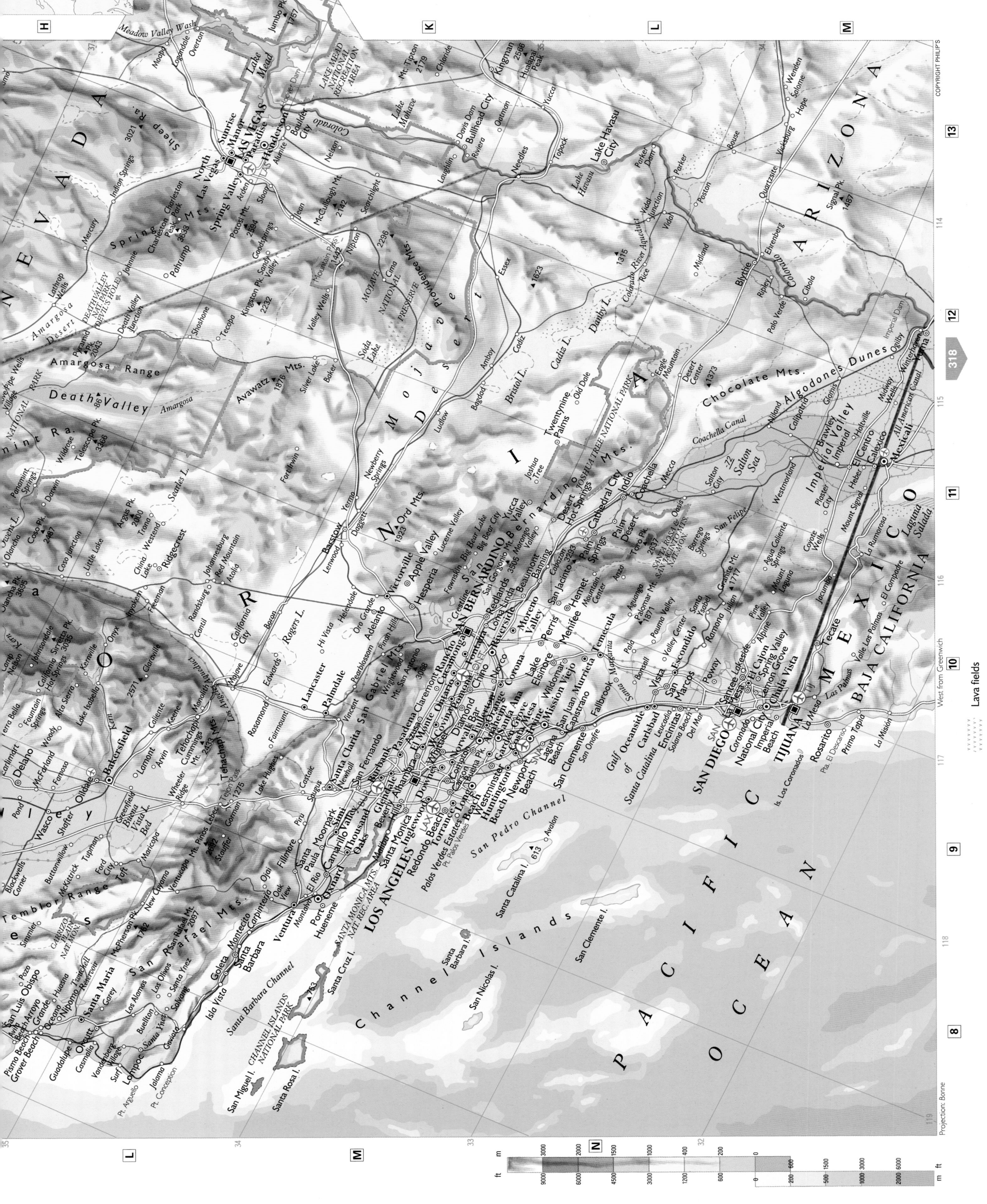
NEVADA
ARIZONA
CALIFORNIA
MEXICO
BAJA CALIFORNIA
PACIFIC OCEAN
Mojave Desert
Death Valley
Amargosa Range
Channel Islands
San Pedro Channel
Santa Barbara Channel
Gulf of Santa Catalina
Salton Sea
Chocolate Mts.
Algodones Dunes
LAS VEGAS
Henderson
Lake Mead
Kingman
Needles
Lake Havasu City
Blythe
Yuma
Barstow
Victorville
Hesperia
SAN BERNARDINO
Riverside
Palm Springs
Indio
El Centro
Calexico
Mexicali
Bakersfield
Lancaster
Palmdale
LOS ANGELES
Santa Monica
Long Beach
Anaheim
Santa Ana
Oxnard
Ventura
Santa Barbara
Santa Maria
Lompoc
San Luis Obispo
Oceanside
Escondido
SAN DIEGO
Chula Vista
TIJUANA
Tecate
Rosarito
Santa Catalina I.
San Clemente I.
San Nicolas I.
Santa Cruz I.
Santa Rosa I.
San Miguel I.
Lava fields
West from Greenwich
Projection: Bonne
COPYRIGHT PHILIP'S
318

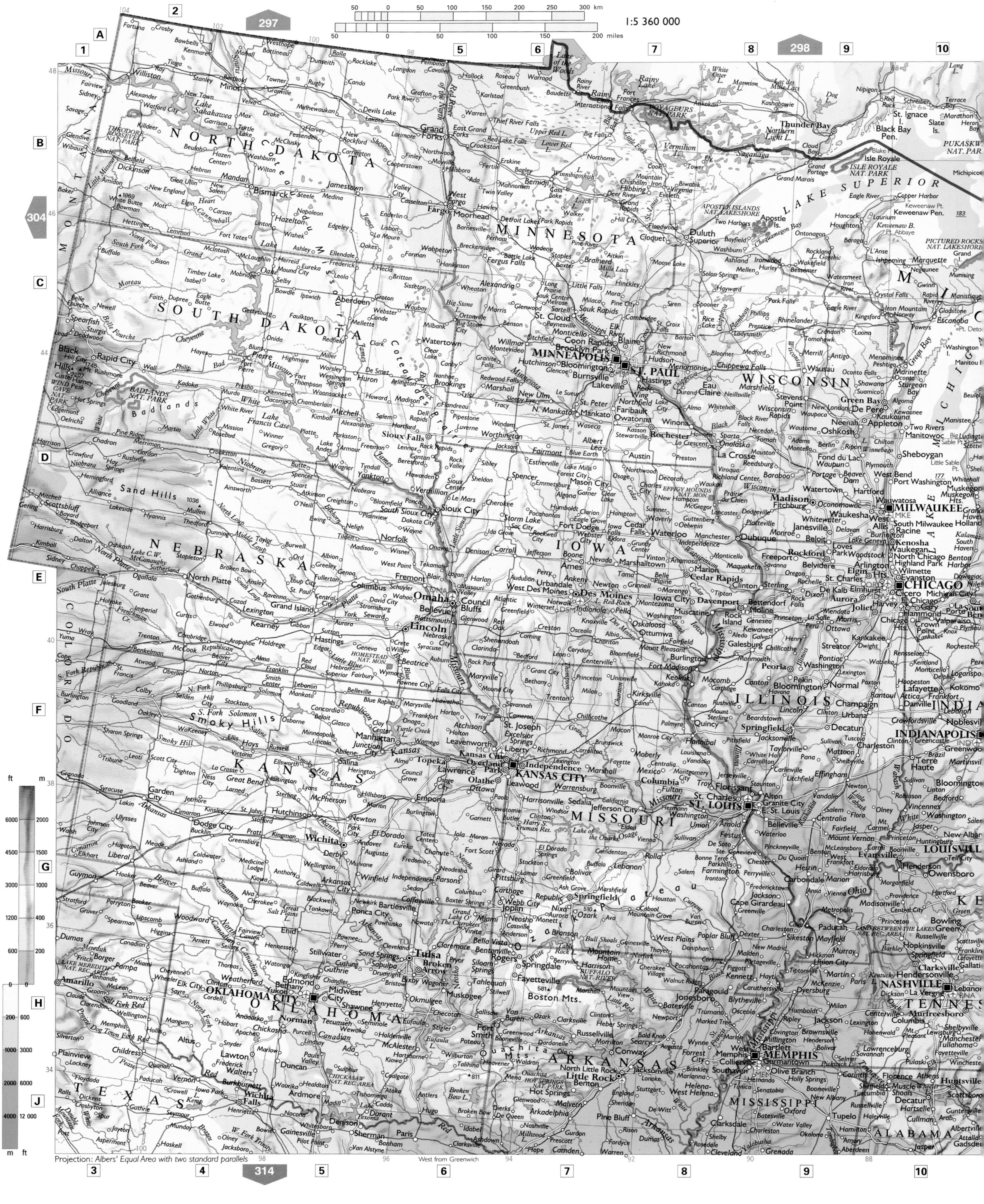

Projection: Albers' Equal Area with two standard parallels

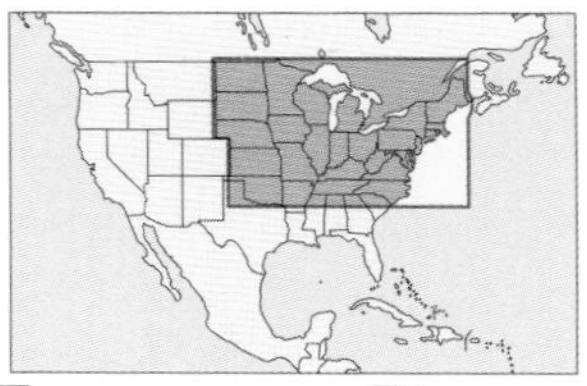

298
299
315
ONTARIO
QUÉBEC
CANADA
LAKE HURON
LAKE ERIE
LAKE ONTARIO
Georgian Bay
MICHIGAN
OHIO
PENNSYLVANIA
NEW YORK
WEST VIRGINIA
VIRGINIA
NORTH CAROLINA
SOUTH CAROLINA
GEORGIA
KENTUCKY
TENNESSEE
MARYLAND
DELAWARE
NEW JERSEY
VERMONT
NEW HAMPSHIRE
MAINE
MA.
CT.
R.I.
NEW BRUNS.
Gulf of Maine
ATLANTIC OCEAN
Allegheny Plateau
Cumberland Plateau
APPALACHIAN MTS.
Blue Ridge
TORONTO
MONTREAL
OTTAWA
Québec
DETROIT
CLEVELAND
PITTSBURGH
BUFFALO
ROCHESTER
COLUMBUS
CINCINNATI
PHILADELPHIA
NEW YORK
BOSTON
HARTFORD
PROVIDENCE
BALTIMORE
WASHINGTON D.C.
RICHMOND
VIRGINIA BEACH
RALEIGH
CHARLOTTE
ATLANTA
Portland
COPYRIGHT PHILIP'S

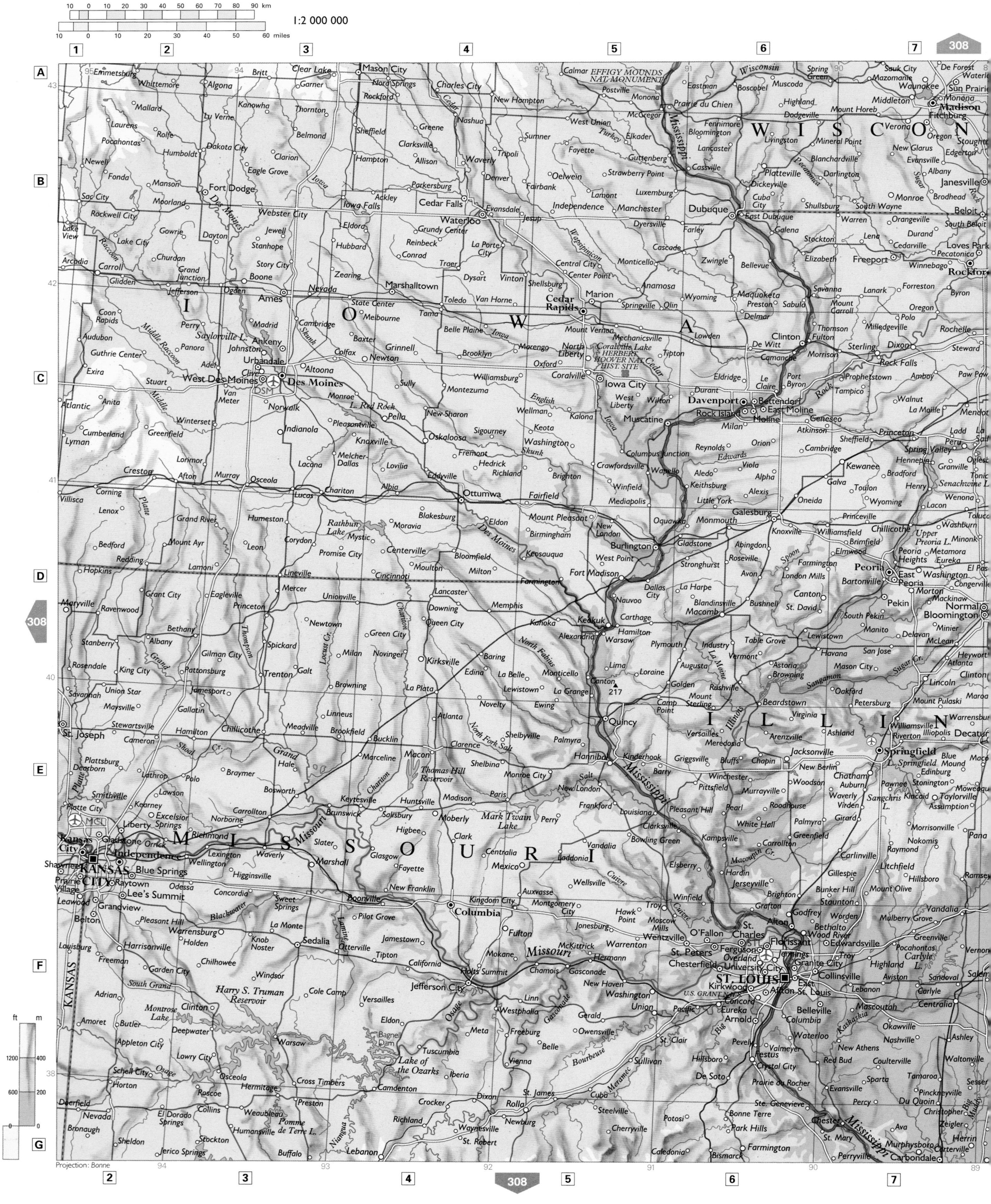
1:2 000 000
km
miles
308
IOWA
WISCONSIN
ILLINOIS
MISSOURI
KANSAS
Emmetsburg
Whittemore
Algona
Britt
Clear Lake
Mason City
Nora Springs
Charles City
Calmar
EFFIGY MOUNDS NAT. MONUMENT
Postville
Eastman
Prairie du Chien
Boscobel
Spring Green
Muscoda
Sauk City
Mazomanie
De Forest
Waunakee
Sun Prairie
Monona
Madison
Fitchburg
Middleton
Highland
Dodgeville
Mount Horeb
Verona
Oregon
Stoughton
New Glarus
Evansville
Edgerton
Janesville
Beloit
South Beloit
Rockford
Garner
Rockford
Kanowha
Thornton
Mallard
Lu Verne
Laurens
Rolfe
Pocahontas
Humboldt
Dakota City
Clarion
Belmond
Sheffield
Greene
Nashua
New Hampton
Monona
McGregor
West Union
Elkader
Fennimore
Bloomington
Lancaster
Livingston
Mineral Point
Blanchardville
Platteville
Darlington
Dickeyville
Cuba City
Shullsburg
South Wayne
Monroe
Brodhead
Albany
Newell
Fonda
Eagle Grove
Clarksville
Allison
Hampton
Waverly
Tripoli
Sumner
Fayette
Guttenberg
Strawberry Point
Oelwein
Cassville
Parkersburg
Denver
Fairbank
Lamont
Luxemburg
Manson
Fort Dodge
Moorland
Sac City
Rockwell City
Webster City
Iowa Falls
Ackley
Cedar Falls
Waterloo
Evansdale
Jesup
Independence
Manchester
Dubuque
East Dubuque
Galena
Warren
Orangeville
Lake View
Gowrie
Dayton
Jewell
Eldora
Grundy Center
Reinbeck
Dyersville
Farley
Stockton
Lena
Durand
Cedarville
Loves Park
Lake City
Stanhope
Hubbard
Conrad
La Porte City
Cascade
Elizabeth
Freeport
Winnebago
Pecatonica
Arcadia
Carroll
Churdan
Grand Junction
Story City
Zearing
Traer
Dysart
Vinton
Central City
Center Point
Monticello
Zwingle
Bellevue
Glidden
Jefferson
Boone
Ogden
Ames
Nevada
Marshalltown
Shellsburg
Marion
Cedar Rapids
Anamosa
Wyoming
Maquoketa
Savanna
Lanark
Forreston
Byron
State Center
Toledo
Van Horne
Springville
Olin
Preston
Sabula
Mount Carroll
Oregon
Coon Rapids
Perry
Madrid
Cambridge
Melbourne
Tama
Belle Plaine
Mount Vernon
Mechanicsville
Lowden
Delmar
Clinton
Thomson
Fulton
Milledgeville
Polo
Rochelle
Audubon
Panora
Saylorville L.
Ankeny
Baxter
Grinnell
Marengo
North Liberty
Coralville Lake
HERBERT HOOVER NAT. HIST. SITE
Tipton
De Witt
Camanche
Morrison
Sterling
Dixon
Steward
Guthrie Center
Johnston
Urbandale
Colfax
Newton
Brooklyn
Oxford
Rock Falls
Exira
Stuart
Adel
Clive
West Des Moines
Des Moines
Altoona
Williamsburg
Coralville
Iowa City
Eldridge
Le Claire
Port Byron
Prophetstown
Amboy
Paw Paw
Van Meter
Monroe
Sully
Montezuma
Durant
Davenport
Bettendorf
Tampico
Anita
Atlantic
Winterset
Norwalk
L. Red Rock
Pella
New Sharon
English
Wellman
Kalona
West Liberty
Wilton
Rock Island
Moline
East Moline
Walnut
La Moille
Mendota
Cumberland
Lyman
Greenfield
Indianola
Pleasantville
Oskaloosa
Sigourney
Keota
Washington
Muscatine
Milan
Geneseo
Atkinson
Princeton
Ladd
Peru
Knoxville
Melcher-Dallas
Fremont
Hedrick
Richland
Columbus Junction
Reynolds
Orion
Cambridge
Sheffield
Spring Valley
Lorimor
Lacona
Lovilia
Crawfordsville
Aledo
Viola
Kewanee
Hennepin
Granville
Creston
Afton
Murray
Osceola
Eddyville
Brighton
Wapello
Winfield
Keithsburg
Alpha
Bradford
Galva
Toulon
Henry
Villisca
Corning
Lucas
Chariton
Albia
Ottumwa
Fairfield
Mediapolis
Little York
Alexis
Oneida
Wyoming
Wenona
Lenox
Grand River
Humeston
Rathbun Lake
Moravia
Blakesburg
Eldon
Mount Pleasant
New London
Galesburg
Oquawka
Monmouth
Knoxville
Princeville
Williamsfield
Chillicothe
Lacon
Washburn
Upper Peoria L.
Minonk
Bedford
Mount Ayr
Leon
Corydon
Mystic
Promise City
Centerville
Birmingham
Burlington
Gladstone
Abingdon
Brimfield
Elmwood
Peoria
Metamora
Peoria Heights
Eureka
Redding
Lamoni
Moulton
Bloomfield
Milton
Keosauqua
West Point
Stronghurst
Roseville
Farmington
Hopkins
Lineville
Cincinnati
Farmington
Fort Madison
Dallas City
La Harpe
Avon
London Mills
Bartonville
East Peoria
Washington
Congerville
Maryville
Grant City
Eagleville
Mercer
Princeton
Unionville
Lancaster
Downing
Memphis
Nauvoo
Blandinsville
Macomb
Bushnell
Canton
St. David
Pekin
Morton
Mackinaw
Normal
Bloomington
Ravenwood
Bethany
Newtown
Green City
Queen City
Kahoka
Keokuk
Carthage
Hamilton
Warsaw
Alexandria
South Pekin
Manito
Minier
Stanberry
Albany
Gilman City
Spickard
Milan
Novinger
Kirksville
Baring
Plymouth
Industry
Table Grove
Lewistown
Delavan
McLean
Heyworth
Atlanta
Rosendale
King City
Pattonsburg
Trenton
Galt
Edina
La Belle
Monticello
Lima
Loraine
Vermont
Astoria
Havana
San Jose
Mason City
Clinton
Browning
La Plata
Lewistown
La Grange
Canton
Augusta
Golden
Rushville
Oakford
Lincoln
Savannah
Union Star
Jamesport
Novelty
Ewing
Camp Point
Mount Sterling
Beardstown
Petersburg
Mount Pulaski
Maysville
Gallatin
Linneus
Atlanta
Quincy
Virginia
Williamsville
Riverton
Illiopolis
Decatur
St. Joseph
Stewartsville
Hamilton
Chillicothe
Meadville
Brookfield
Bucklin
Shelbyville
Palmyra
Versailles
Meredosia
Arenzville
Ashland
Springfield
Cameron
Clarence
Macon
Hannibal
Kinderhook
Griggsville
Bluffs
Chapin
Jacksonville
Plattsburg
Dearborn
Hale
Marceline
Shelbina
Thomas Hill Reservoir
Monroe City
Barry
New Berlin
Chatham
Auburn
Blue Mound
Lathrop
Polo
Braymer
Bosworth
Paris
Salt
New London
Winchester
Pittsfield
Murrayville
Woodson
Pawnee
Stonington
Edinburg
Moweaqua
Smithville
Lawson
Keytesville
Huntsville
Madison
Waverly
Kincaid
Taylorville
Assumption
Sangchris L.
Platte City
Kearney
Excelsior Springs
Carrollton
Norborne
Brunswick
Salisbury
Moberly
Mark Twain Lake
Perry
Frankford
Louisiana
Pleasant Hill
Pearl
Roodhouse
Virden
Girard
MCI
Liberty
Gladstone
Richmond
Higbee
Clark
Clarksville
White Hall
Palmyra
Kansas City
Independence
Orrick
Slater
Centralia
Vandalia
Bowling Green
Kampsville
Greenfield
Morrisonville
Nokomis
Shawnee
Lexington
Waverly
Marshall
Glasgow
Mexico
Laddonia
Carrollton
Carlinville
Raymond
Prairie Village
Blue Springs
Wellington
Fayette
Elsberry
Hardin
Litchfield
Hillsboro
Raytown
Odessa
Higginsville
Jerseyville
Gillespie
Leawood
Lee's Summit
Concordia
Sweet Springs
Boonville
New Franklin
Auxvasse
Kingdom City
Montgomery City
Winfield
Brighton
Bunker Hill
Mount Olive
Belton
Grandview
Pleasant Hill
Pilot Grove
Columbia
Hawk Point
Troy
Moscow Mills
Grafton
Godfrey
Staunton
Worden
Vandalia
Warrensburg
La Monte
Knob Noster
Sedalia
Jamestown
Fulton
Jonesburg
Wentzville
O'Fallon
St. Charles
Alton
Bethalto
Wood River
Mulberry Grove
Louisburg
Harrisonville
Holden
Otterville
Tipton
Mokane
McKittrick
Warrenton
St. Peters
Ferguson
Florissant
Edwardsville
Greenville
Pocahontas
Carlyle L.
Freeman
Chilhowee
California
Holts Summit
Missouri
Hermann
Chesterfield
Overland
University City
Jennings
Granite City
Troy
Highland
Garden City
Windsor
Jefferson City
Chamois
Gasconade
New Haven
Kirkwood
ST. LOUIS
East St. Louis
Collinsville
Aviston
Sandoval
South Grand
Harry S. Truman Reservoir
Cole Camp
Versailles
Linn
Washington
U.S. GRANT N.H.S.
Affton
Lebanon
Carlyle
Adrian
Montrose Lake
Clinton
Westphalia
Union
Pacific
Eureka
Concord
Belleville
Mascoutah
Centralia
Amoret
Butler
Eldon
Gerald
Arnold
Columbia
Okawville
Deepwater
Meta
Freeburg
Owensville
Waterloo
Nashville
Ashley
Appleton City
Warsaw
Bagnell Dam
Tuscumbia
Belle
St. Clair
Pevely
Valmeyer
New Athens
Lowry City
Lake of the Ozarks
Vienna
Bourbeuse
Sullivan
Hillsboro
Festus
Crystal City
Red Bud
Coulterville
Waltonville
Schell City
Horton
Osceola
Iberia
De Soto
Prairie du Rocher
Sparta
Tamaroa
Cross Timbers
Hermitage
Camdenton
Evansville
Pinckneyville
Deerfield
Roscoe
Preston
Crocker
Dixon
St. James
Cuba
Ste. Genevieve
Percy
Du Quoin
Nevada
El Dorado Springs
Collins
Weaubleau
Pomme de Terre L.
Richland
Rolla
Steelville
Potosi
Bonne Terre
Chester
Christopher
Zeigler
Bronaugh
Humansville
Waynesville
Newburg
Cherryville
Park Hills
Ava
Herrin
Sheldon
Stockton
St. Robert
Farmington
St. Mary
Murphysboro
Carterville
Jerico Springs
Buffalo
Lebanon
Caledonia
Bismarck
Perryville
Carbondale
Mississippi
Missouri
Des Moines
Iowa
Cedar
Skunk
Rock
Illinois
Sangamon
Osage
Gasconade
Meramec
Kaskaskia
Big Muddy
Grand
Chariton
Platte
Thompson
Salt
North Fabius
La Moine
Spoon
Macoupin Cr.
Cuivre
Blackwater
Niangua
Middle Raccoon
Raccoon
Wapsipinicon
Turkey
Pecatonica
Sugar
Edwards
Locust Cr.
North Fork Salt
Shoal Cr.
Big
217
ft
m
1200
600
400
200
0
Projection: Bonne
95
94
93
92
91
90
89
43
42
41
40
38
1
2
3
4
5
6
7
A
B
C
D
E
F
G

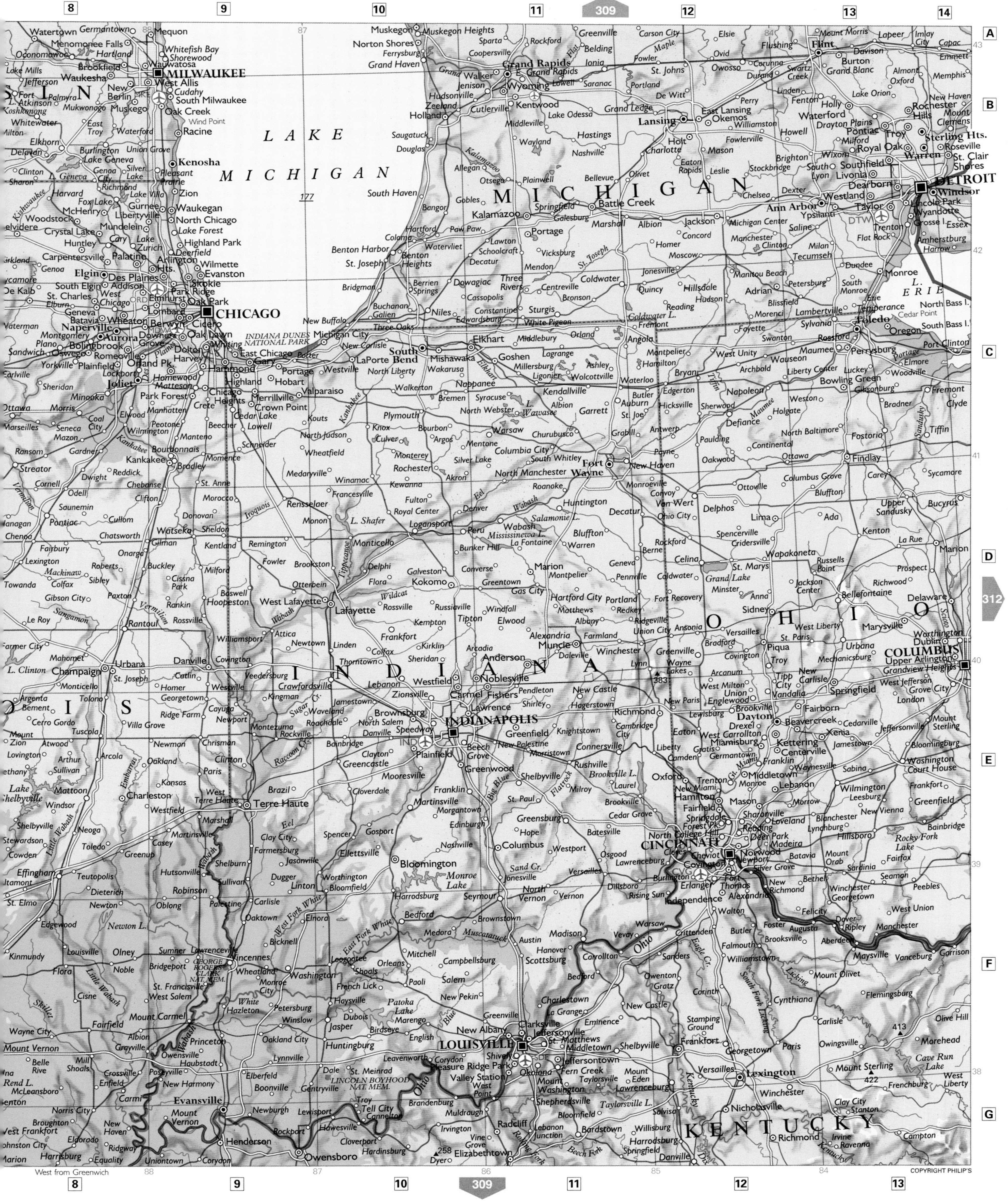
8
9
10
11
309
12
13
14
A
B
C
D
E
F
G
312
LAKE MICHIGAN
177
MICHIGAN
INDIANA
OHIO
KENTUCKY
L. ERIE
MILWAUKEE
CHICAGO
DETROIT
Windsor
INDIANAPOLIS
COLUMBUS
CINCINNATI
LOUISVILLE
Grand Rapids
Lansing
Flint
Ann Arbor
Kalamazoo
Battle Creek
Jackson
Toledo
South Bend
Fort Wayne
Elkhart
Gary
Hammond
Joliet
Aurora
Naperville
Elgin
Waukegan
Kenosha
Racine
Champaign
Urbana
Kokomo
Lafayette
West Lafayette
Muncie
Anderson
Terre Haute
Bloomington
Evansville
Owensboro
Henderson
Lexington
Frankfort
Dayton
Springfield
Hamilton
Lima
Findlay
Fostoria
Marion
Richmond
Columbus
Madison
Vincennes
Danville
Kankakee
Monroe
INDIANA DUNES NATIONAL PARK
GEORGE ROGERS CLARK NAT. MEM.
LINCOLN BOYHOOD NAT. MEM.
Wind Point
Cedar Point
Ohio
Wabash
Kankakee
Kalamazoo
St. Joseph
Maumee
White
East Fork White
Monroe Lake
Taylorsville L.
Coldwater L.
Grand Lake
Newton L.
Lake Shelbyville
383
258
413
422
43
42
41
40
39
38
87
86
85
84
88
West from Greenwich
COPYRIGHT PHILIP'S

1:2 000 000

10 0 10 20 30 40 50 60 70 80 90 km

10 0 10 20 30 40 50 60 miles

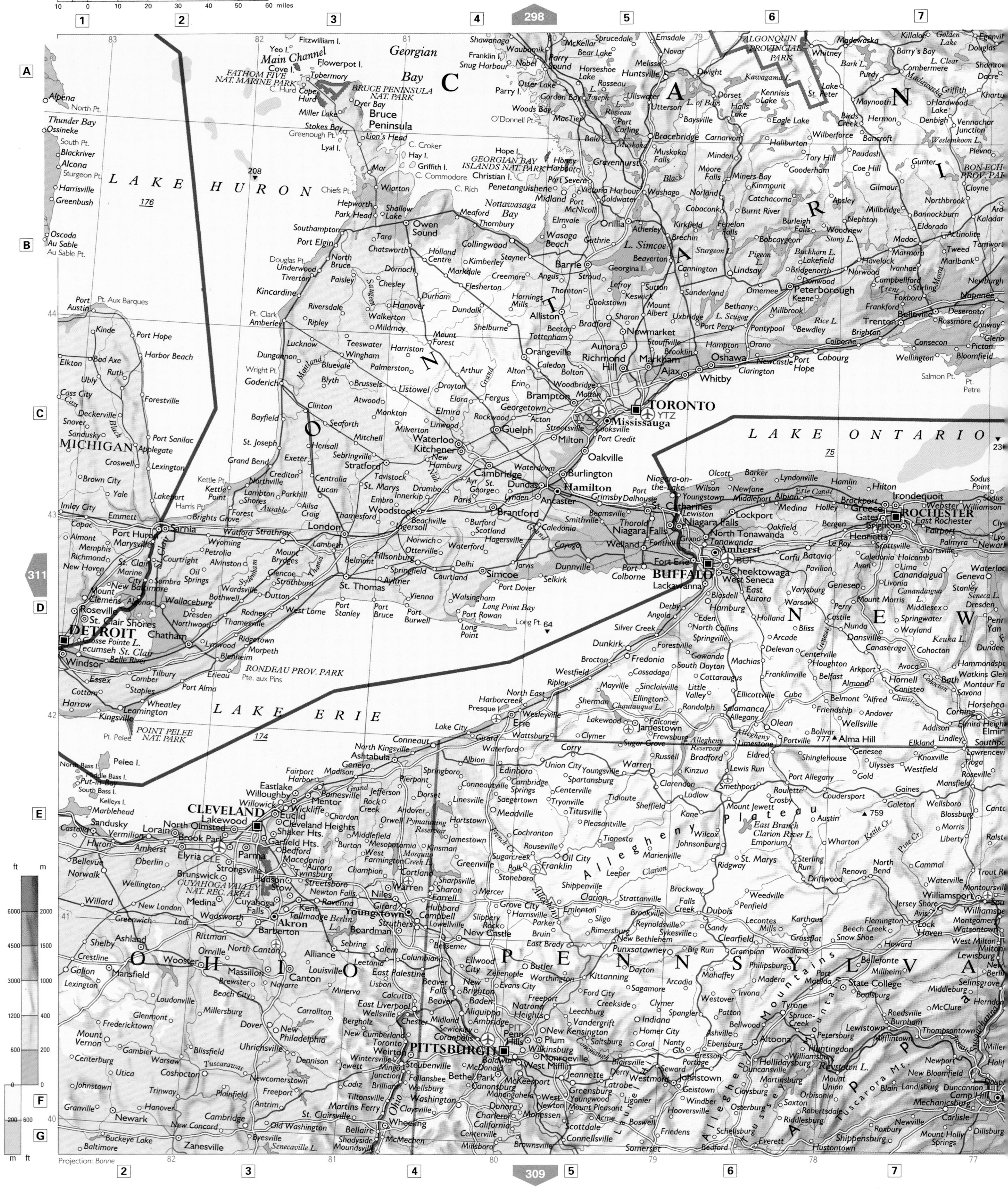

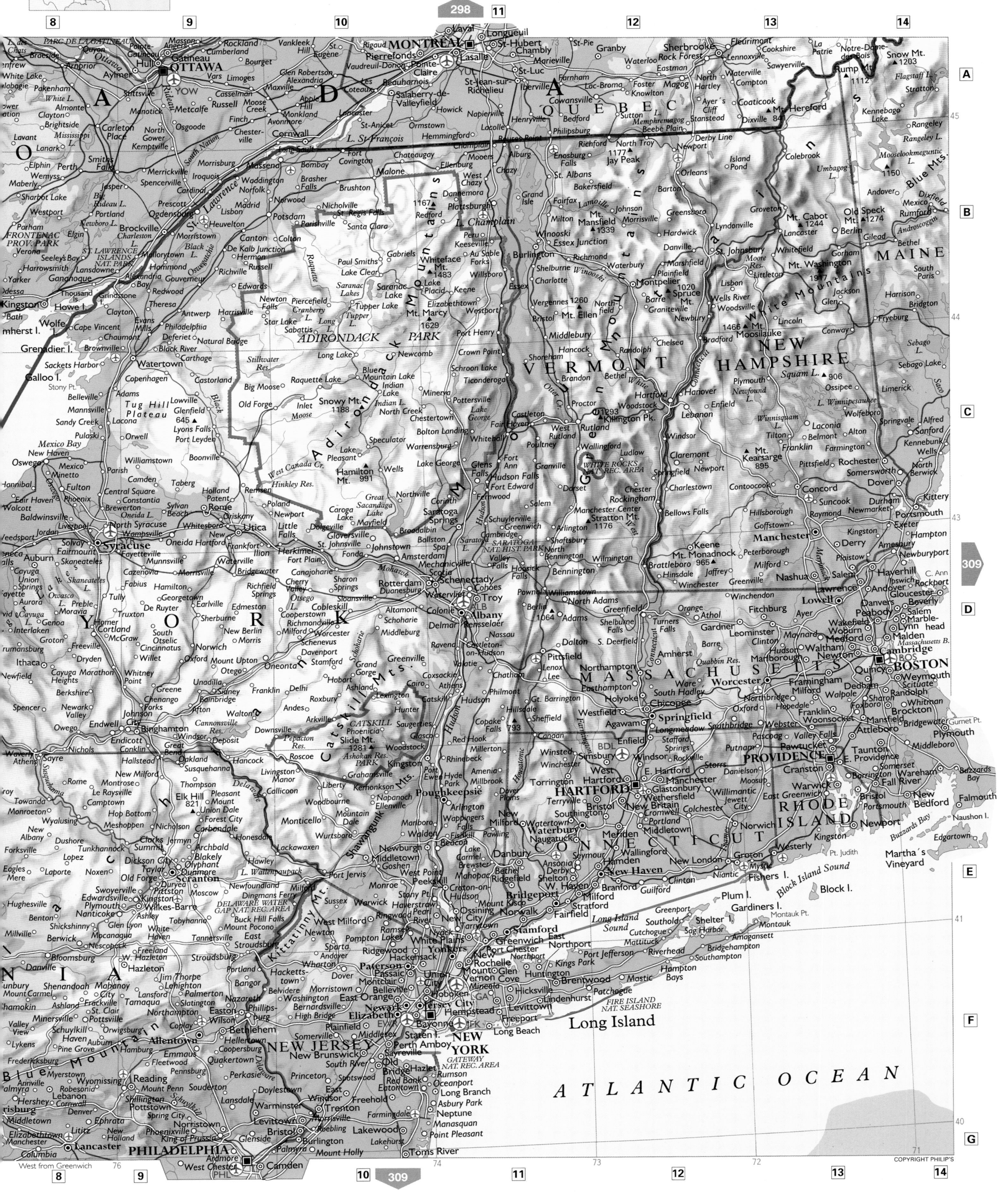
298
309
QUEBEC
MONTREAL
OTTAWA
MAINE
NEW HAMPSHIRE
VERMONT
MASSACHUSETTS
CONNECTICUT
RHODE ISLAND
NEW JERSEY
NEW YORK
ADIRONDACK PARK
Adirondack Mountains
Green Mountains
White Mountains
Catskill Mts.
Long Island
ATLANTIC OCEAN
Boston
Albany
Hartford
Providence
Philadelphia
Syracuse
Springfield
Worcester
Manchester
Burlington
Montpelier
Concord
Cape Cod
Martha's Vineyard
Block Island Sound
Long Island Sound
L. Champlain
West from Greenwich
COPYRIGHT PHILIP'S

1:5 360 000

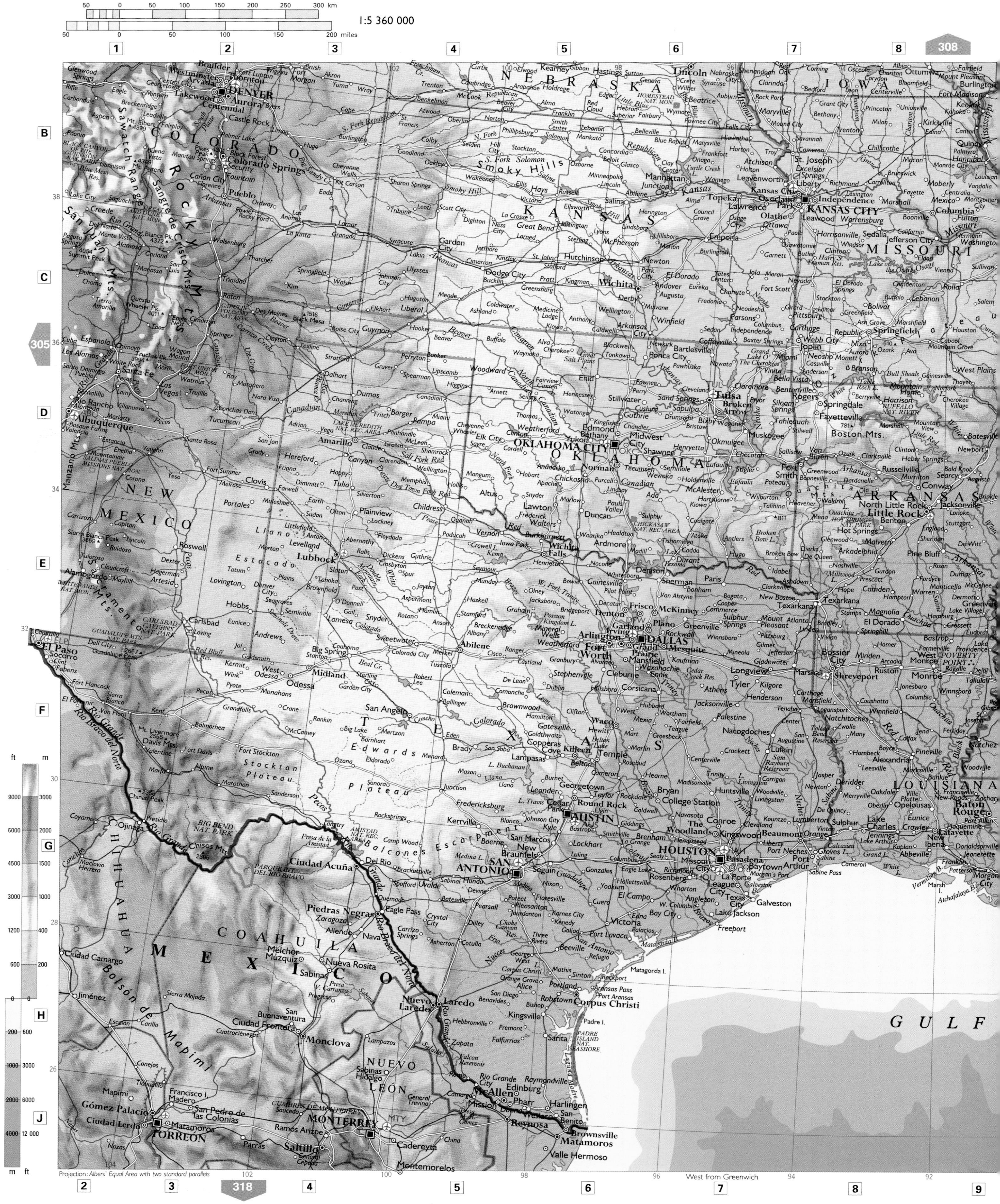

50 0 50 100 150 200 250 300 km
50 0 50 100 150 200 miles
308
305
318
NEBRASKA
IOWA
KANSAS
MISSOURI
COLORADO
Rocky Mts
Sangre de Cristo Mts.
Sawatch Range
San Juan Mts.
OKLAHOMA
ARKANSAS
NEW MEXICO
TEXAS
LOUISIANA
MEXICO
COAHUILA
CHIHUAHUA
NUEVO LEÓN
GULF
Llano Estacado
Edwards Plateau
Stockton Plateau
Balcones Escarpment
Ozark Plateau
Ouachita Mts.
Boston Mts.
Smoky Hills
Bolsón de Mapimí
Sacramento Mts.
Rio Grande
Rio Bravo del Norte
Red
Arkansas
Canadian
Pecos
Brazos
Colorado
DENVER
Colorado Springs
Pueblo
Albuquerque
Santa Fe
El Paso
Lubbock
Amarillo
Midland
Odessa
Abilene
San Angelo
Wichita
Wichita Falls
Topeka
KANSAS CITY
Lincoln
Tulsa
OKLAHOMA CITY
DALLAS
Fort Worth
Arlington
AUSTIN
SAN ANTONIO
HOUSTON
Galveston
Corpus Christi
Laredo
Nuevo Laredo
Brownsville
Matamoros
McAllen
Reynosa
MONTERREY
Saltillo
Monclova
Piedras Negras
Ciudad Acuña
TORREON
Gómez Palacio
Ciudad Lerdo
Shreveport
Little Rock
Fort Smith
Springfield
Baton Rouge
Lake Charles
Beaumont
Texarkana
Waco
Tyler
Projection: Albers' Equal Area with two standard parallels
West from Greenwich
ft m
9000 3000
6000 2000
4500 1500
3000 1000
1200 400
600 200
0 0
200 600
1000 3000
2000 6000
4000 12 000
m ft

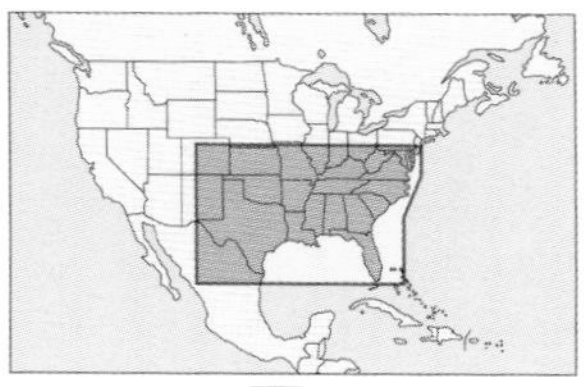

309
320
ILLINOIS
INDIANA
OHIO
PENNSYLVANIA
MARYLAND
DELAWARE
WEST VIRGINIA
VIRGINIA
KENTUCKY
TENNESSEE
NORTH CAROLINA
SOUTH CAROLINA
GEORGIA
ALABAMA
MISSISSIPPI
FLORIDA
THE BAHAMAS
ATLANTIC OCEAN
GULF OF MEXICO
PITTSBURGH
PHILADELPHIA
COLUMBUS
INDIANAPOLIS
CINCINNATI
BALTIMORE
WASHINGTON D.C.
ST. LOUIS
LOUISVILLE
RICHMOND
VIRGINIA BEACH
NASHVILLE
MEMPHIS
RALEIGH
CHARLOTTE
ATLANTA
BIRMINGHAM
NEW ORLEANS
JACKSONVILLE
ORLANDO
TAMPA
MIAMI
Appalachian Mountains
Cumberland Plateau
Blue Ridge
Mississippi River Delta
Florida Keys
Str. of Florida
Florida Bay
DRY TORTUGAS NAT. PARK
EVERGLADES NAT. PARK
BISCAYNE NAT. PARK
Northwest Providence Channel
Northeast Providence Channel
COPYRIGHT PHILIP'S

1:2 000 000

ATLANTIC
OCEAN
SOUTH CAROLINA
GEORGIA
ALABAMA
Sea Islands
ATLANTA
Columbia
Charleston
Savannah
Augusta
Macon
Columbus
Montgomery
Tallahassee
JACKSONVILLE
Okefenokee Swamp
315

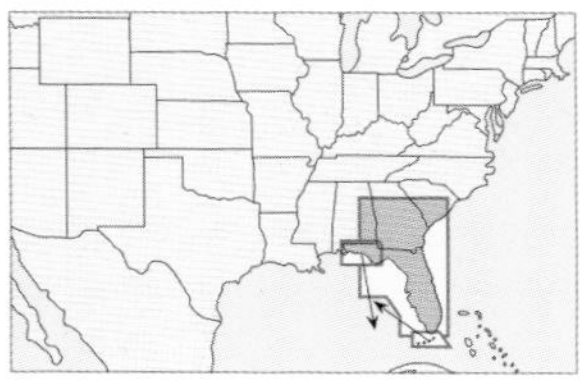

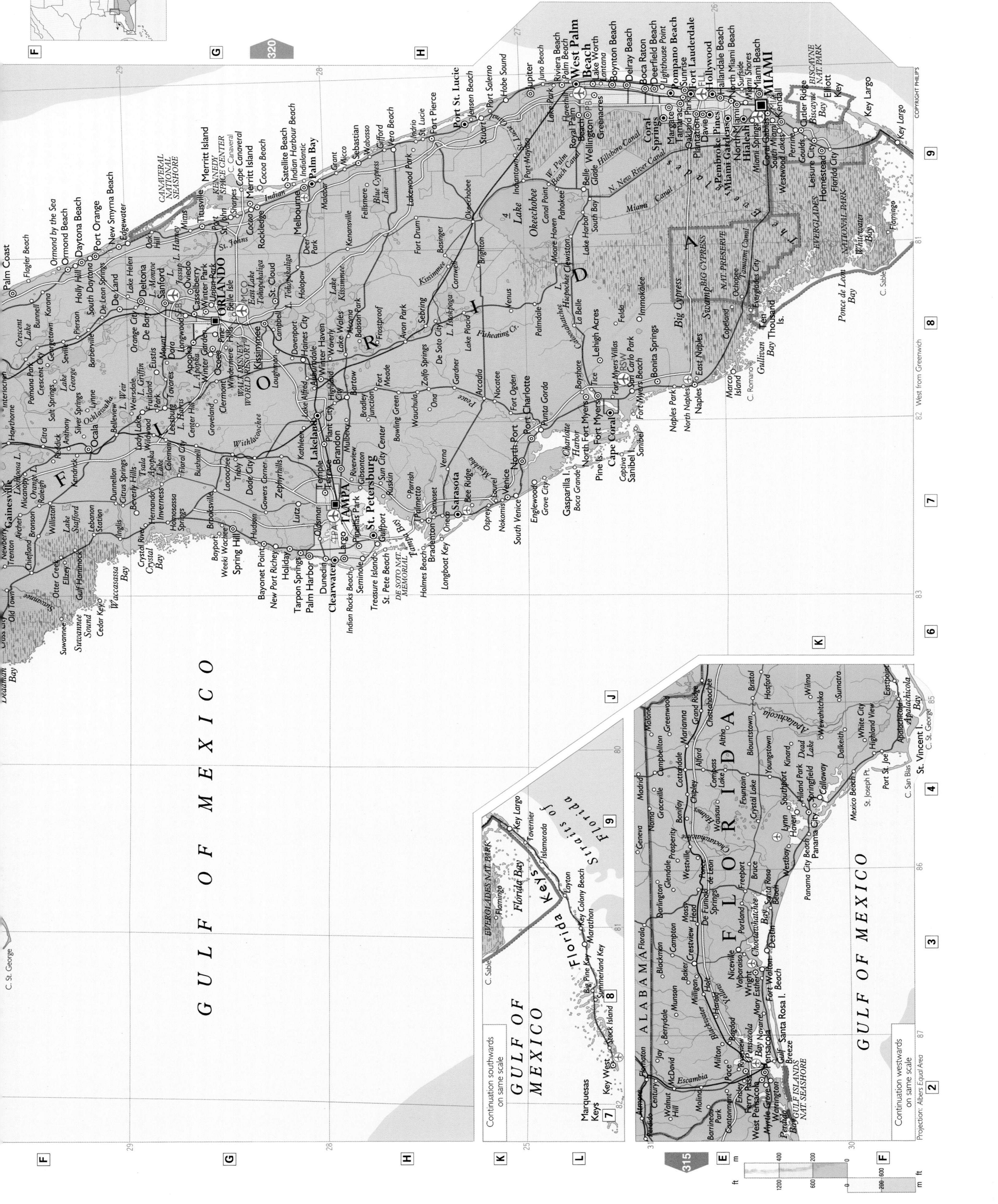
GULF OF MEXICO
FLORIDA
ALABAMA
MIAMI
ORLANDO
TAMPA
St. Petersburg
Clearwater
Lakeland
Gainesville
Ocala
Daytona Beach
West Palm Beach
Fort Lauderdale
Hollywood
Fort Myers
Cape Coral
Naples
Sarasota
Bradenton
Melbourne
Palm Bay
Port St. Lucie
Fort Pierce
Kissimmee
Lake Okeechobee
Big Cypress Swamp
EVERGLADES NATIONAL PARK
Florida Bay
Florida Keys
Straits of Florida
Key West
Key Largo
Pensacola
Panama City
Apalachicola Bay
Continuation southwards on same scale
Continuation westwards on same scale
Projection: Albers Equal Area
COPYRIGHT PHILIPS
West from Greenwich
320
315

50 0 50 100 150 200 250 300 km

50 0 50 100 150 200 miles

1:6 400 000

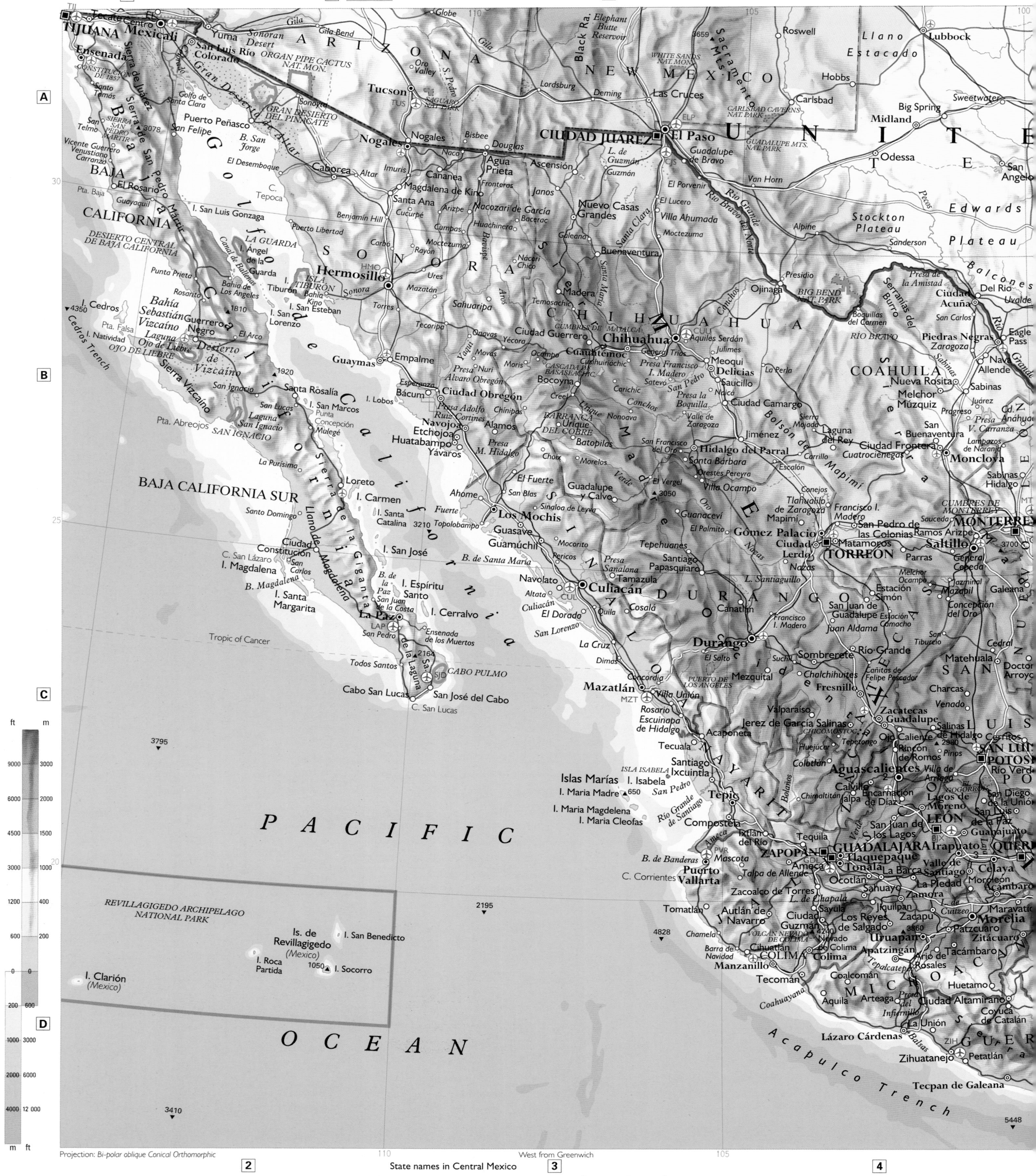

Projection: *Bi-polar oblique Conical Orthomorphic*

West from Greenwich

State names in Central Mexico

1 DISTRITO FEDERAL 2 AGUASCALIENTES 3 GUANAJUATO 4 HIDALGO 5 MÉXICO 6 MORELOS 7 QUERÉTARO 8 TLAXCALA

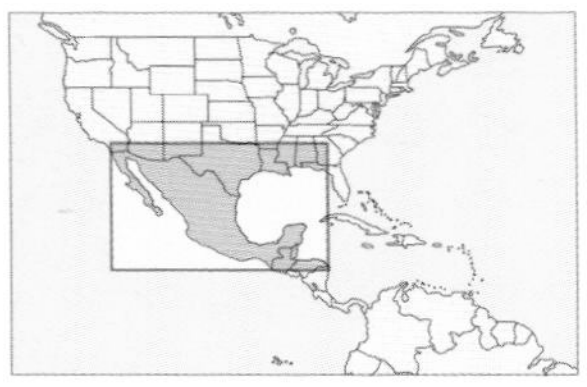

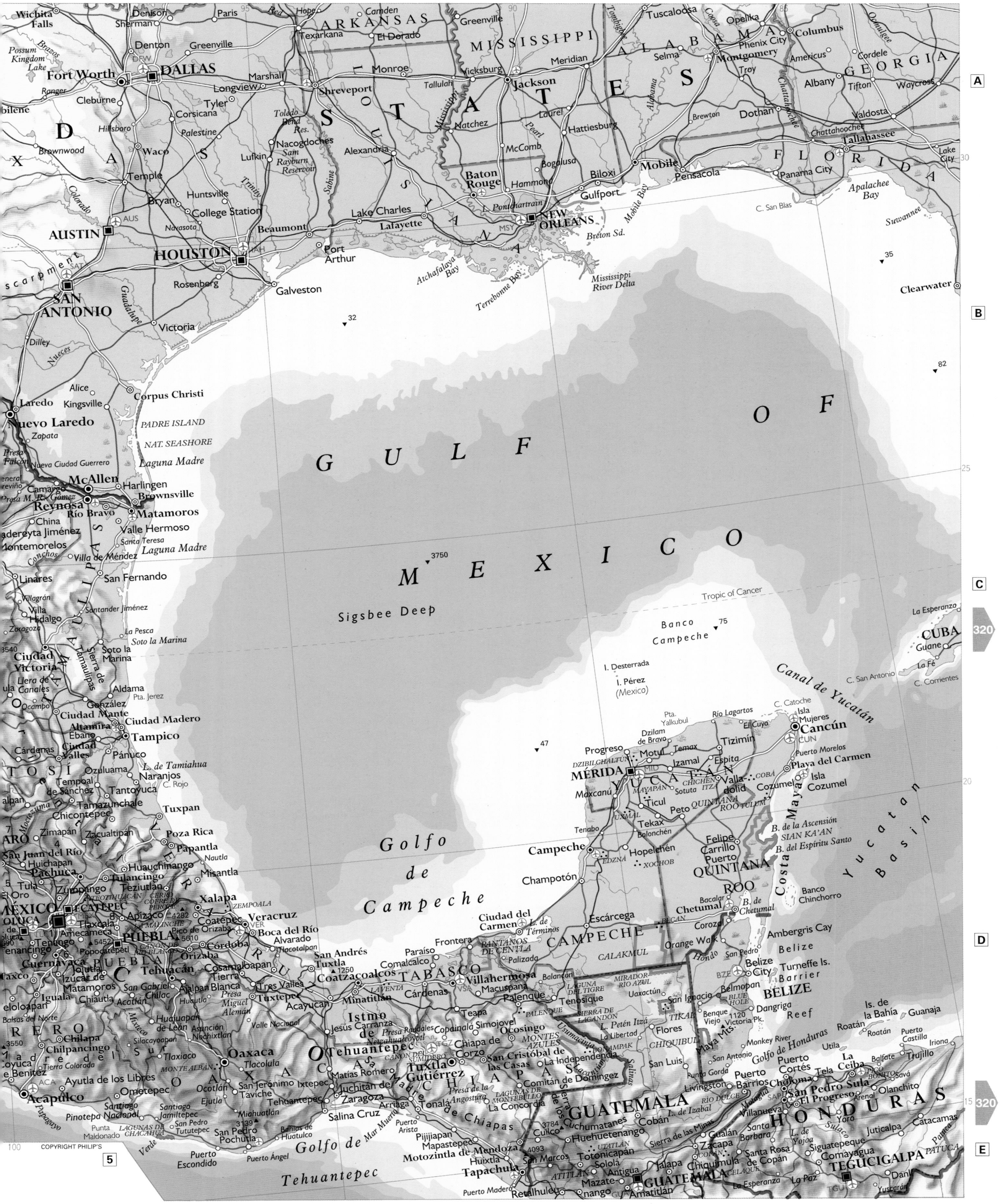
5
6
7
8
315
A
B
C
D
E
320
GULF OF MEXICO
Sigsbee Deep
Golfo de Campeche
Banco Campeche
Tropic of Cancer
Canal de Yucatán
Yucatan Basin
Costa Maya
ARKANSAS
MISSISSIPPI
ALABAMA
GEORGIA
FLORIDA
LOUISIANA
UNITED STATES
TEXAS
TAMAULIPAS
VERACRUZ
PUEBLA
OAXACA
CHIAPAS
TABASCO
CAMPECHE
YUCATÁN
QUINTANA ROO
GUATEMALA
BELIZE
HONDURAS
CUBA
DALLAS
Fort Worth
Wichita Falls
Sherman
Denison
Denton
Paris
Texarkana
Camden
El Dorado
Greenville
Tuscaloosa
Opelika
Columbus
Phenix City
Montgomery
Selma
Meridian
Jackson
Vicksburg
Monroe
Shreveport
Tallulah
Marshall
Longview
Tyler
Corsicana
Waco
Temple
Cleburne
Hillsboro
Brownwood
Palestine
Nacogdoches
Lufkin
Alexandria
Natchez
McComb
Laurel
Hattiesburg
Bogalusa
Hammond
Baton Rouge
Biloxi
Gulfport
Mobile
Pensacola
Panama City
Tallahassee
Dothan
Albany
Tifton
Valdosta
Waycross
Americus
Cordele
Troy
Brewton
Lake City
Apalachee Bay
C. San Blas
Suwannee
Clearwater
NEW ORLEANS
L. Pontchartrain
Lake Charles
Lafayette
Beaumont
Port Arthur
Galveston
HOUSTON
AUSTIN
SAN ANTONIO
Huntsville
College Station
Bryan
Navasota
Rosenberg
Victoria
Breton Sd.
Mississippi River Delta
Atchafalaya Bay
Terrebonne Bay
Corpus Christi
Alice
Kingsville
Laredo
Nuevo Laredo
Zapata
PADRE ISLAND NAT. SEASHORE
Laguna Madre
McAllen
Harlingen
Brownsville
Reynosa
Río Bravo
Matamoros
Valle Hermoso
Linares
San Fernando
Soto la Marina
Ciudad Victoria
Aldama
González
Ciudad Mante
Altamira
Ciudad Madero
Tampico
Pánuco
Naranjos
Tuxpan
Poza Rica
Papantla
Misantla
Xalapa
Veracruz
Boca del Río
Alvarado
Córdoba
Orizaba
Tehuacán
PUEBLA
Tlaxcala
MÉXICO
Pachuca
Cuernavaca
Iguala
Chilpancingo
Acapulco
Oaxaca
Tuxtepec
Cosamaloapan
San Andrés Tuxtla
Coatzacoalcos
Minatitlán
Acayucan
Istmo de Tehuantepec
Juchitán de Zaragoza
Salina Cruz
Tehuantepec
Golfo de Tehuantepec
Puerto Escondido
Pochutla
Tuxtla Gutiérrez
San Cristóbal de las Casas
Comitán de Domínguez
Tonalá
Tapachula
Villahermosa
Cárdenas
Paraíso
Frontera
Ciudad del Carmen
L. de Términos
Champotón
Campeche
Escárcega
Calakmul
Chetumal
Bacalar
Felipe Carrillo Puerto
Mérida
Progreso
Motul
Izamal
Tizimín
Valladolid
Ticul
Peto
Maxcanú
Hopelchén
Cancún
Isla Mujeres
Playa del Carmen
Cozumel
Isla Cozumel
C. Catoche
Río Lagartos
I. Desterrada
I. Pérez (Mexico)
Banco Chinchorro
Ambergris Cay
Belize City
Belmopan
Dangriga
Orange Walk
Corozal
San Ignacio
Flores
Tikal
Sayaxché
Puerto Barrios
Livingston
L. de Izabal
Cobán
Huehuetenango
Quetzaltenango
GUATEMALA
Antigua
Puerto Cortés
San Pedro Sula
Tela
La Ceiba
Trujillo
Roatán
Is. de la Bahía
Guanaja
Comayagua
TEGUCIGALPA
Juticalpa
Catacamas
Olanchito
Golfo de Honduras
La Esperanza
Guane
C. San Antonio
C. Corrientes
3750
4282
5452
5610
4093
3784
COPYRIGHT PHILIP'S
100

316
JAMAICA
a
JAMAICA
1:1 600 000
CARIBBEAN SEA
Montego Bay
Falmouth
Runaway Bay
St. Ann's Bay
Ocho Rios
Oracabessa
Port Maria
Lucea
Negril
Savanna-la-Mar
Black River
Santa Cruz
Mandeville
May Pen
Spanish Town
Portmore
Kingston
Port Antonio
Morant Bay
Yallahs
CORNWALL
MIDDLESEX
SURREY
Christiana
Linstead
Bog Walk
Old Harbour
Hayes
Porus
Highgate
Annotto Bay
BLUE MOUNTAINS
West from Greenwich
A
FLORIDA
U. S. A.
West Palm Beach
Fort Myers
Boca Raton
Fort Lauderdale
Cape Coral
Naples
C. Romano
Hialeah
MIAMI
EVERGLADES NAT. PARK
C. Sable
Florida Bay
Dry Tortugas (U.S.A.)
Key West
Florida Keys
Straits of Florida
Santaren Channel
Great Bahama Bank
Grand Bahama
Freeport
West End
Little Abaco
Hope Town
Marsh Harbour
Abaco
Northwest Providence Channel
Northeast Providence Channel
Bimini
Berry Is.
Nicolls Town
Andros Town
Andros
Nassau
New Providence
Eleuthera
Governor's Harbour
Exuma Sound
Great Exuma
Great Guana Cay
Cay Sal Bank
4
B
Gulf of Mexico
LA HABANA (Havana)
Matanzas
Santa Cruz del Norte
Canal Nicholás
Arch. de Sabana
Cárdenas
Sagua la Grande
Pinar del Río
Bahía Honda
Guanajay
San Antonio de los Baños
Batabanó
Güines
Cienfuegos
Santa Clara
Caibarién
Trinidad
Sancti Spíritus
Ciego de Ávila
Morón
Nuevitas
Camagüey
Florida
Las Tunas
Holguín
Bayamo
Manzanillo
Sierra Maestra
Pico Turquino
Santiago de Cuba
Golfo de Guacanayabo
Arch. de Jardines de la Reina
Golfo de Batabanó
Nueva Gerona
I. de la Juventud
Arch. de los Canarreos
C. Corrientes
C. San Antonio
Canal de Yucatán
Yucatan Basin
Cayman Islands (U.K.)
George Town
Grand Cayman
Cayman Brac
Little Cayman
Cayman Trench
Misteriosa Bank
Is. Santanilla (Swan Islands) (Honduras)
Pedro Bank
Pedro Cays (Jamaica)
Rosalind Bank
Serranilla Bank
Banco Gorda
Bajo Nuevo (Colombia)
C A R I B
C
Greater Antilles
MÉRIDA
Progreso
Dzilam de Bravo
Motul
Izamal
Tizimín
Río Lagartos
C. Catoche
Isla Mujeres
Cancún
Puerto Morelos
Playa del Carmen
Cozumel
Isla Cozumel
Valladolid
Maxcanú
Ticul
Tekax
Peto
YUCATÁN
Campeche
Champotón
Ciudad del Carmen
Escárcega
Felipe Carrillo Puerto
QUINTANA ROO
B. de la Ascensión
SIAN KA'AN
B. del Espíritu Santo
Costa Maya
Bacalar
Chetumal
Corozal
Orange Walk
Banco Chinchorro
Ambergris Cay
San Pedro
Belize City
Turneffe Is.
Belmopan
BELIZE
Dangriga
Barrier Reef
Maya Mts.
Victoria Peak
MEXICO
CAMPECHE
CALAKMUL
L. de Términos
Palizada
Balancán
Tenosique
PALENQUE
Ocosingo
Comitán de Domínguez
L. Petén Itzá
Flores
TIKAL
San Luis
Sebol
Punta Gorda
Livingston
Puerto Barrios
Puerto Cortés
Golfo de Honduras
Is. de la Bahía
Roatán
Guanaja
Utila
Tela
La Ceiba
Trujillo
Iriona
C. Camarón
GUATEMALA
Huehuetenango
Cobán
Totonicapán
Quetzaltenango
Sololá
Antigua
GUATEMALA
Escuintla
Chiquimula
Zacapa
L. de Izabal
San Pedro Sula
Choloma
El Progreso
HONDURAS
Santa Rosa de Copán
Juticalpa
Catacamas
Comayagua
TEGUCIGALPA
Danlí
Yuscarán
Choluteca
Santa Ana
Sonsonate
Ahuachapán
SAN SALVADOR
EL SALVADOR
Usulután
San Miguel
La Unión
Acajutla
Nueva San Salvador
Cojutepeque
Zacatecoluca
Laguna de Caratasca
Puerto Lempira
C. Gracias a Dios
Puerto Cabo Gracias á Dios
Mosquitia
Coco (Segovia)
Cayos Miskitos (Nicaragua)
Puerto Cabezas
Pta. Gorda
Bonanza
Siuna
Prinzapolca
La Barra
I. de Providencia (Colombia)
Cayos Roncador (Colombia)
San Andrés
I. de San Andrés (Colombia)
Cayos de Albuquerque (Colombia)
Is. del Maíz (Nicaragua)
Costa de Mosquitos
NICARAGUA
Estelí
Ocotal
Somoto
Jinotega
Matagalpa
Chinandega
Corinto
León
L. de Managua
MANAGUA
Masaya
Granada
Tipitapa
Boaco
Juigalpa
Santo Domingo
Rama
El Bluff
Bluefields
Cord. de Yolaina
Jinotepe
Rivas
Lago de Nicaragua
I. de Ometepe
San Juan del Sur
San Carlos
San Juan del Norte
B. de San Juan del Norte
Pta. Mono
G. de Fonseca
G. de Papagayo
Guanacaste
Liberia
Santa Cruz
Nicoya
Pen. de Nicoya
G. de Nicoya
Puntarenas
Alajuela
SAN JOSÉ
Cartago
Limón
COSTA RICA
Volcán Irazú
Puerto Quepos
B. de Coronado
Ciudad Cortés
Golfito
San Vito
Pen. de Osa
G. Dulce
Pta. Burica
Chiriquí Grande
Bocas del Toro
L. de Chiriquí
David
Puerto Armuelles
G. de Chiriquí
I. de Coiba
I. de Cébaco
I. Jicarón
Santiago
Penonomé
Chitré
Pen. de Azuero
Las Tablas
Pedasí
Colón
Portobelo
Nombre de Dios
Archipiélago de San Blas
Golfo del Darién
PANAMÁ
La Chorrera
Golfo de Panamá
Arch. de las Perlas
San Miguel
La Palma
Yaviza
El Real de Sta María
DARIÉN
Jaqué
Isthmus of Panama
Serranía de Tabasará
Serranía del Darién
CARTAGENA
I. de San Bernardo
PACIFIC OCEAN
Guatemala Trench
E
319
D
1
2
3
4
328
CARIBBEAN SEA
Colón
Cativá
Cristobal
Chagres
Gatún
Gatún Locks
Gatún Dam
PANAMA
El Limón
L. Alajuela
Lago Gatún
Escobal
Gamboa
Chilibre
Gaillard Cut
Pedro Miguel Locks
Miraflores Locks
L. Miraflores
Paraíso
Arraiján
San Miguelito
Balboa
PANAMA
La Chorrera
PACIFIC OCEAN
PANAMA CANAL
1:800 000
c
■ Place of interest
Projection: Conical with two standard parallels
1:6 400 000
km
miles

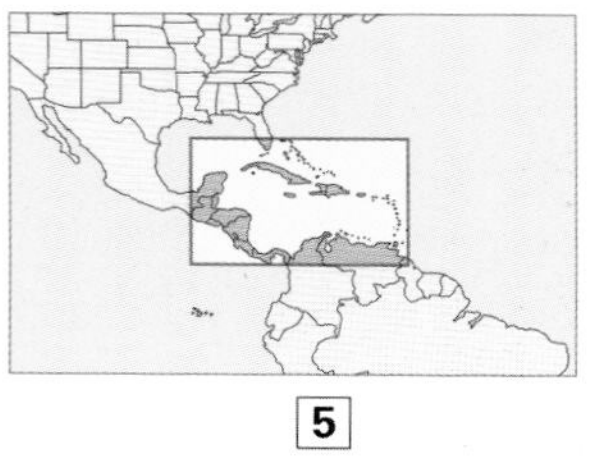
5

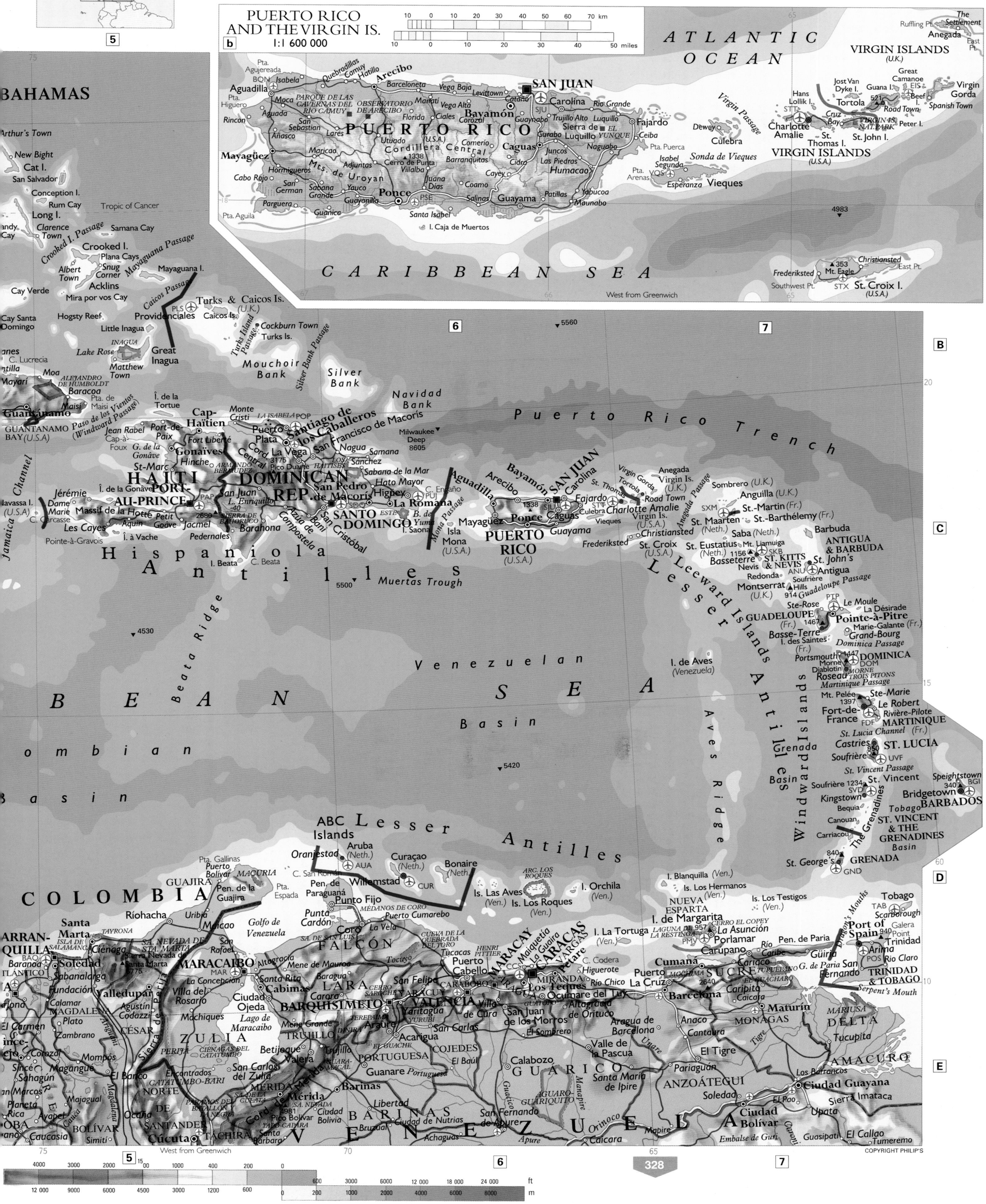
PUERTO RICO
AND THE VIRGIN IS.
b 1:1 600 000
km
miles
ATLANTIC OCEAN
VIRGIN ISLANDS (U.K.)
VIRGIN ISLANDS (U.S.A.)
SAN JUAN
PUERTO RICO (U.S.A.)
Cordillera Central
Arecibo
Aguadilla
Mayagüez
Ponce
Bayamón
Carolina
Caguas
Guayama
Humacao
Fajardo
Culebra
Vieques
Virgin Passage
Sonda de Vieques
Charlotte Amalie
Tortola
Road Town
Virgin Gorda
Anegada
St. Croix I. (U.S.A.)
Christiansted
Frederiksted
I. Caja de Muertos
CARIBBEAN SEA
West from Greenwich
BAHAMAS
Tropic of Cancer
Turks & Caicos Is. (U.K.)
Cockburn Town
Great Inagua
Mouchoir Bank
Silver Bank
Navidad Bank
Puerto Rico Trench
Milwaukee Deep 8605
HAITI
PORT-AU-PRINCE
Cap-Haïtien
Gonaïves
DOMINICAN REP.
SANTO DOMINGO
Santiago de los Caballeros
San Francisco de Macorís
La Romana
Hispaniola
Mona Passage
Windward Passage
Jamaica Channel
Antilles
Muertas Trough
Beata Ridge
Venezuelan Basin
SEA
Colombian Basin
Leeward Islands
Lesser Antilles
Aves Ridge
Windward Islands
Grenada Basin
Anguilla (U.K.)
St.-Martin (Fr.)
St. Maarten (Neth.)
St.-Barthélemy (Fr.)
Saba (Neth.)
St. Eustatius (Neth.)
ST. KITTS & NEVIS
Basseterre
ANTIGUA & BARBUDA
St. John's
Montserrat (U.K.)
GUADELOUPE (Fr.)
Pointe-à-Pitre
Basse-Terre
Marie-Galante (Fr.)
DOMINICA
Roseau
MARTINIQUE
Fort-de-France
ST. LUCIA
Castries
ST. VINCENT & THE GRENADINES
Kingstown
BARBADOS
Bridgetown
GRENADA
St. George's
I. de Aves (Venezuela)
ABC Islands
Aruba (Neth.)
Oranjestad
Curaçao (Neth.)
Willemstad
Bonaire (Neth.)
Lesser Antilles
COLOMBIA
Barranquilla
Santa Marta
Riohacha
Cúcuta
Golfo de Venezuela
MARACAIBO
Lago de Maracaibo
CARACAS
Valencia
Barquisimeto
Maracay
Cumaná
Barcelona
Maturín
Ciudad Bolívar
Ciudad Guayana
I. de Margarita
Port of Spain
TRINIDAD & TOBAGO
Tobago
Serpent's Mouth
Dragon's Mouths
Orinoco
VENEZUELA
COPYRIGHT PHILIP'S
328
ft
m

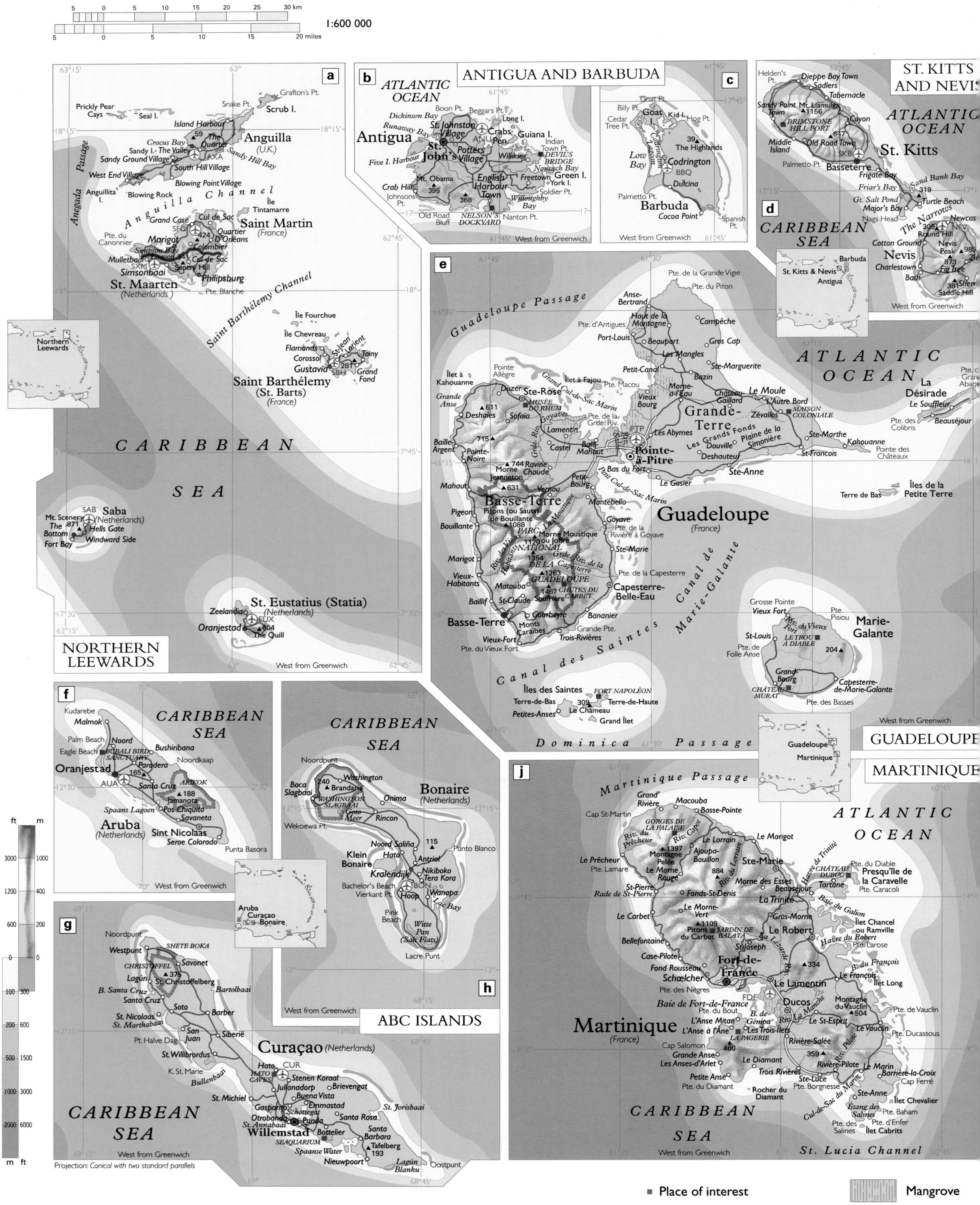
5 0 5 10 15 20 25 30 km
5 0 5 10 15 20 miles
1:600 000
NORTHERN LEEWARDS
a
Grafton's Pt.
Scrub I.
Prickly Pear Cays
Snake Pt.
Seal I.
Island Harbour
Anguilla
(U.K.)
Crocus Bay
The Quarter
Sandy I.
The Valley
Sandy Ground Village
AXA
Sandy Hill Bay
South Hill Village
West End Village
Anegada Passage
Blowing Point Village
Anguillita I.
Blowing Rock
Anguilla Channel
Île Tintamarre
Cul de Sac
Grand Case
Saint Martin
(France)
SFG
Pte. du Canonnier
Marigot
Quartier d'Orléans
Colombier
Simpson Bay
SXM
Mulletbaai
Cul de Sac
Simsonbaai
Sentry Hill
Philipsburg
St. Maarten
(Netherlands)
Pte. Blanche
Saint Barthélemy Channel
Île Fourchue
Île Chevreau
Flamands
St-Jean
Lorient
Corossol
Toiny
Gustavia
SBH
Grand Fond
Saint Barthélemy
(St. Barts)
(France)
Northern Leewards
CARIBBEAN SEA
SAB
Saba
(Netherlands)
Mt. Scenery
The Bottom
Hells Gate
Windward Side
Fort Bay
St. Eustatius (Statia)
(Netherlands)
Zeelandia
EUX
Oranjestad
The Quill
West from Greenwich
b
ANTIGUA AND BARBUDA
ATLANTIC OCEAN
Boon Pt.
Beggars Pt.
Dickinson Bay
Long I.
Runaway Bay
St. Johnston Village
Crabs Pen
Guiana I.
Antigua
ANU
St. John's
Potters Village
Indian Town Pt.
Five I. Harbour
Willikies
DEVIL'S BRIDGE
Nonsuch Bay
Crab Hill
Mt. Obama
English Harbour Town
Freetown
Green I.
York I.
Johnsons Pt.
Soldier Pt.
Willoughby Bay
Old Road Bluff
NELSON'S DOCKYARD
Nanton Pt.
West from Greenwich
c
Goat Pt.
Billy Pt.
Goat I.
Kid I.
Hog Pt.
Cedar Tree Pt.
Codrington Lagoon
The Highlands
Low Bay
Codrington
BBQ
Dulcina
Palmetto Pt.
Barbuda
Cocoa Point
Spanish Pt.
West from Greenwich
d
ST. KITTS AND NEVIS
Helden's Pt.
Dieppe Bay Town
Sadlers
Tabernacle
Sandy Point Town
Mt. Liamuiga
ATLANTIC OCEAN
BRIMSTONE HILL FORT
Cayon
Middle Island
Old Road Town
St. Kitts
SKB
Palmetto Pt.
Basseterre
Frigate Bay
Sand Bank Bay
Friar's Bay
Gt. Salt Pond
Turtle Beach
Major's Bay
The Narrows
Nags Head
CARIBBEAN SEA
Newcastle
Round Hill
Cotton Ground
Nevis Peak
Nevis
Charlestown
Fig Tree
Bath
Saddle Hill
St. Kitts & Nevis
Barbuda
Antigua
West from Greenwich
e
Pte. de la Grande Vigie
Pte. du Piton
Anse-Bertrand
Guadeloupe Passage
Haut de la Montagne
Campêche
Pte. d'Antigues
Port-Louis
Beauport
Gros Cap
Les Mangles
Petit-Canal
Ste-Marguerite
ATLANTIC OCEAN
Îlet à Kahouanne
Pointe Allègre
Îlet à Fajou
Pte. Macou
Bazin
Morne-à-l'Eau
Grand Cul-de-Sac Marin
Dozer
Ste-Rose
MUSÉE DU RHUM
Vieux Bourg
Château Gaillard
Le Moule
La Désirade
Grande Anse
Deshaies
Sofaïa
L'Autre Bord
MAISON COLONIALE
Le Souffleur
Pte. de la Grde. Riv.
Grande-Terre
Zévallos
Pte. des Colibris
Beauséjour
Lamentin
PTP
Les Abymes
Les Grands Fonds
Plaine de la Simonière
Ste-Marthe
Baille-Argent
Pointe-Noire
Castel
Baie Mahault
Pointe-à-Pitre
Douville
Deshauteur
Kahouanne
St-François
Pointe des Châteaux
Ravine Chaude
Morne Jeanneton
Bas du Fort
Ste-Anne
Mahaut
Vernou
Petit-Bourg
Petit Cul-de-Sac Marin
Le Gosier
Terre de Bas
Îles de la Petite Terre
Basse-Terre
Montebello
Guadeloupe
(France)
Pigeon
Pitons (ou Sauts) de Bouillante
Goyave
Bouillante
Pte. de la Rivière à Goyave
PARC NATIONAL DE LA GUADELOUPE
Morne Moustique ou Joffre
Ste-Marie
Marigot
Grde. Riv. de la Capesterre
Vieux-Habitants
Pte. de la Capesterre
Capesterre-Belle-Eau
Matouba
CHUTES DU CARBET
Baillif
St-Claude
Soufrière
Canal de Marie-Galante
Basse-Terre
Gourbeyre
Bananier
Grosse Pointe
Pte. Pisiou
Vieux Fort
Marie-Galante
Monts Caraïbes
Grande Pte.
Riv. du Vieux Fort
Vieux-Fort
Trois-Rivières
St-Louis
LE TROU À DIABLE
Pte. du Vieux Fort
Canal des Saintes
Pte. de Folle Anse
Grand Bourg
Îles des Saintes
FORT NAPOLÉON
Capesterre-de-Marie-Galante
Terre-de-Bas
Terre-de-Haute
CHÂTEAU MURAT
Le Chameau
Pte. des Basses
Petites-Anses
Grand Îlet
Dominica Passage
West from Greenwich
Guadeloupe
Martinique
GUADELOUPE
MARTINIQUE
f
Kudarebe
CARIBBEAN SEA
Malmok
Palm Beach
Noord
Bushiribana
Eagle Beach
BUBALI BIRD SANCTUARY
Noordkaap
Paradera
Oranjestad
AUA
Santa Cruz
ARIKOK
Spaans Lagoen
Pos Chiquito
Savaneta
Aruba
(Netherlands)
Sint Nicolaas
Seroe Colorado
Punta Basora
West from Greenwich
h
CARIBBEAN SEA
Noordpunt
Boca Slagbaai
Washington
Brandaris
WASHINGTON SLAGBAAI
Onima
Bonaire
(Netherlands)
Gotomeer
Rincon
Wekoewa Pt.
Noord Saliña
Punto Blanco
Hato
Klein Bonaire
Antriol
Kralendijk
Nikiboko
Tera Kora
Bachelor's Beach
BON
Vierkant Pt.
Hoop
Wanapa
Lac Bay
Pink Beach
Witte Pan
(Salt Flats)
Lacre Punt
Aruba
Curaçao
Bonaire
West from Greenwich
ABC ISLANDS
g
Noordpunt
Westpunt
SHETE BOKA
CHRISTOFFEL
Savonet
Lagún
St. Christoffelberg
B. Santa Cruz
Bartolbaai
Santa Cruz
Soto
St. Nicolaas
St. Marthabaai
Barber
San Juan
Siberië
Pt. Halve Dag
St. Willibrordus
Curaçao (Netherlands)
Hato
CUR
HATO CAVES
K. St. Marie
Stenen Koraal
Bullenbaai
Julianadorp
Brievengat
Buena Vista
St. Michiel
Emmastad
St. Jorisbaai
Gasparito
Schottegat
Santa Rosa
Otrobanda
Punda
St. Annabaai
Santa Barbara
Willemstad
Bottelier
SEAQUARIUM
Tafelberg
CARIBBEAN SEA
Spaanse Water
Nieuwpoort
Lagún Blanku
Oostpunt
West from Greenwich
j
Martinique Passage
Grand' Rivière
Macouba
Basse-Pointe
Cap St-Martin
GORGES DE LA FALAISE
ATLANTIC OCEAN
Riv. du Prêcheur
Riv. Capot
Le Lorrain
Le Marigot
Montagne Pelée
Ajoupa-Bouillon
Le Prêcheur
Pte. Lamare
Le Morne Rouge
Ste-Marie
Havre de Trinité
Pte. du Diable
CHÂTEAU DUBUC
Presqu'île de la Caravelle
St-Pierre
Morne des Esses
Rade de St-Pierre
Fonds-St-Denis
Beauséjour
Tartane
Pte. Caracoli
La Trinité
Le Morne-Vert
Baie du Galion
Le Carbet
Gros-Morne
Îlet Chancel ou Ramville
Pitons du Carbet
JARDIN DE BALATA
Le Robert
Havre du Robert
Bellefontaine
St-Joseph
Pte. Larose
Case-Pilote
Fort-de-France
B. du François
Fond Rousseau
Le François
Schœlcher
Le Lamentin
Îlet Long
Pte. des Nègres
FDF
Baie de Fort-de-France
Ducos
Montagne du Vauclin
Pte. du Bout
Pte. de Vauclin
Martinique
(France)
B. de Génipa
L'Anse Mitan
L'Anse à l'Âne
Les Trois-Îlets
Le St-Esprit
Le Vauclin
LA PAGERIE
Rivière-Salée
Pte. Ducassous
Cap Salomon
Grande Anse
Les Anses-d'Arlet
Le Diamant
Rivière-Pilote
Le Marin
Barrière-la-Croix
Petite Anse
Trois Rivières
Ste-Luce
Cap Ferré
Pte. du Diamant
Rocher du Diamant
Pte. Borgnesse
Ste-Anne
CARIBBEAN SEA
Cul-de-Sac du Marin
Îlet Chevalier
Étang des Salines
Pte. Baham
Pte. d'Enfer
Pte. des Salines
Îlet Cabrits
St. Lucia Channel
West from Greenwich
ft m
Projection: Conical with two standard parallels
Place of interest
Mangrove

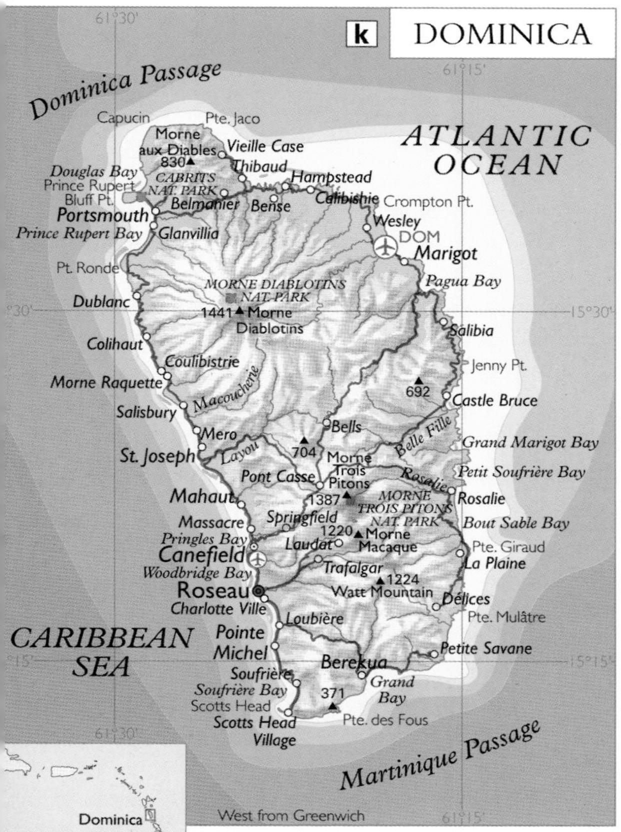
k
DOMINICA
Dominica Passage
ATLANTIC OCEAN
CARIBBEAN SEA
Martinique Passage
Capucin
Pte. Jaco
Morne aux Diables 830
Vieille Case
Thibaud
CABRITS NAT. PARK
Douglas Bay
Prince Rupert Bluff Pt.
Portsmouth
Prince Rupert Bay
Belmanier
Bense
Hampstead
Calibishie
Crompton Pt.
Wesley
DOM
Marigot
Pagua Bay
Glanvillia
Pt. Ronde
Dublanc
MORNE DIABLOTINS NAT. PARK
1441 Morne Diablotins
Salibia
Colihaut
Coulibistrie
Jenny Pt.
Morne Raquette
692
Castle Bruce
Salisbury
Mero
Bells
Grand Marigot Bay
St. Joseph
704
Morne Trois Pitons
Petit Soufrière Bay
Pont Casse
Rosalie
Mahaut
1387
MORNE TROIS PITONS NAT. PARK
Massacre
Springfield
Bout Sable Bay
Pringles Bay
1220
Laudat
Morne Macaque
Pte. Giraud
Canefield
La Plaine
Woodbridge Bay
Trafalgar
1224
Roseau
Watt Mountain
Délices
Charlotte Ville
Loubière
Pte. Mulâtre
Pointe Michel
Petite Savane
Berekua
Soufrière
Soufrière Bay
371
Grand Bay
Scotts Head
Scotts Head Village
Pte. des Fous
West from Greenwich
Dominica
St. Lucia

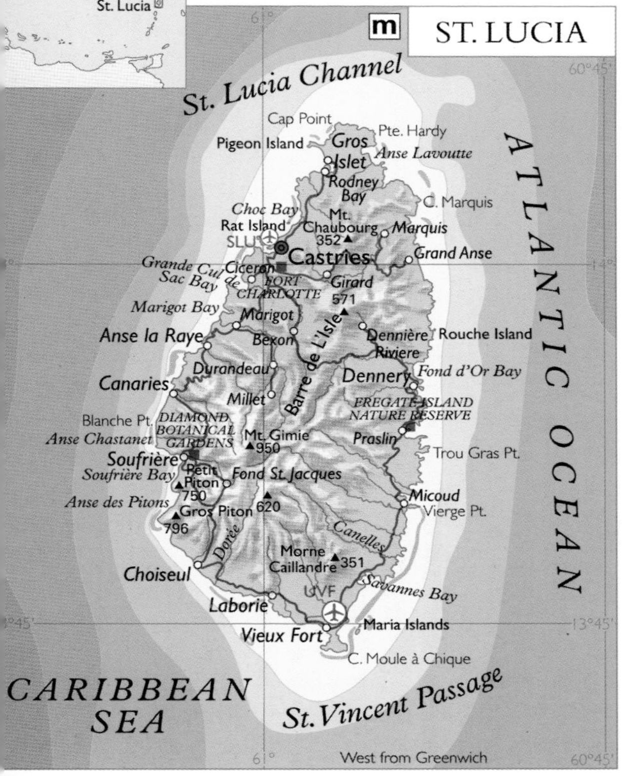
m
ST. LUCIA
St. Lucia Channel
ATLANTIC OCEAN
CARIBBEAN SEA
St. Vincent Passage
Cap Point
Pte. Hardy
Pigeon Island
Gros Islet
Anse Lavoutte
Rodney Bay
C. Marquis
Choc Bay
Rat Island
Mt. Chaubourg
Marquis
SLU
352
Castries
Grand Anse
Grande Cul de Sac Bay
Cicéron
FORT CHARLOTTE
571
Girard
Marigot Bay
Marigot
Anse la Raye
Bexon
Dennière Rivière
Rouche Island
Durandeau
Dennery
Fond d'Or Bay
Canaries
Millet
Barre de l'Isle
FREGATE ISLAND NATURE RESERVE
Blanche Pt.
DIAMOND BOTANICAL GARDENS
Mt. Gimie
950
Praslin
Anse Chastanet
Soufrière
Trou Gras Pt.
Soufrière Bay
Petit Piton 750
Fond St. Jacques
Anse des Pitons
Gros Piton
620
Micoud
Vierge Pt.
796
Morne Caillandre
351
Choiseul
Laborie
Savannes Bay
UVF
Vieux Fort
Maria Islands
C. Moule à Chique
West from Greenwich

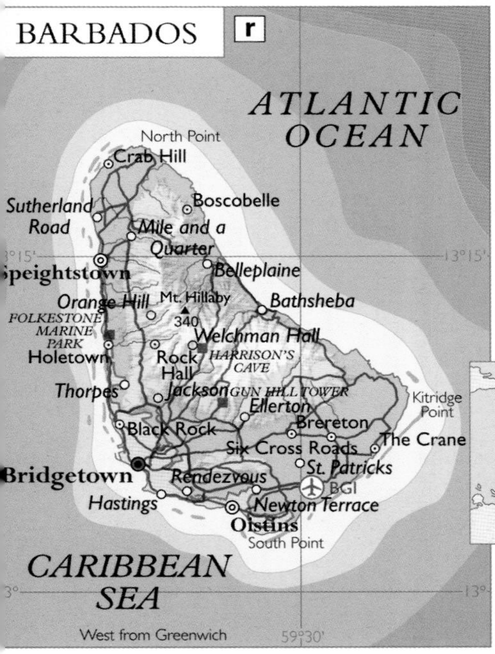
BARBADOS
r
ATLANTIC OCEAN
CARIBBEAN SEA
North Point
Crab Hill
Boscobelle
Sutherland Road
Mile and a Quarter
Speightstown
Belleplaine
Orange Hill
Mt. Hillaby
340
Bathsheba
FOLKESTONE MARINE PARK
Holetown
Welchman Hall
Rock Hall
HARRISON'S CAVE
Thorpes
Jackson
GUN HILL TOWER
Ellerton
Kitridge Point
Black Rock
Brereton
The Crane
Six Cross Roads
St. Patricks
Bridgetown
Rendezvous
Hastings
Newton Terrace
BGI
Oistins
South Point
West from Greenwich

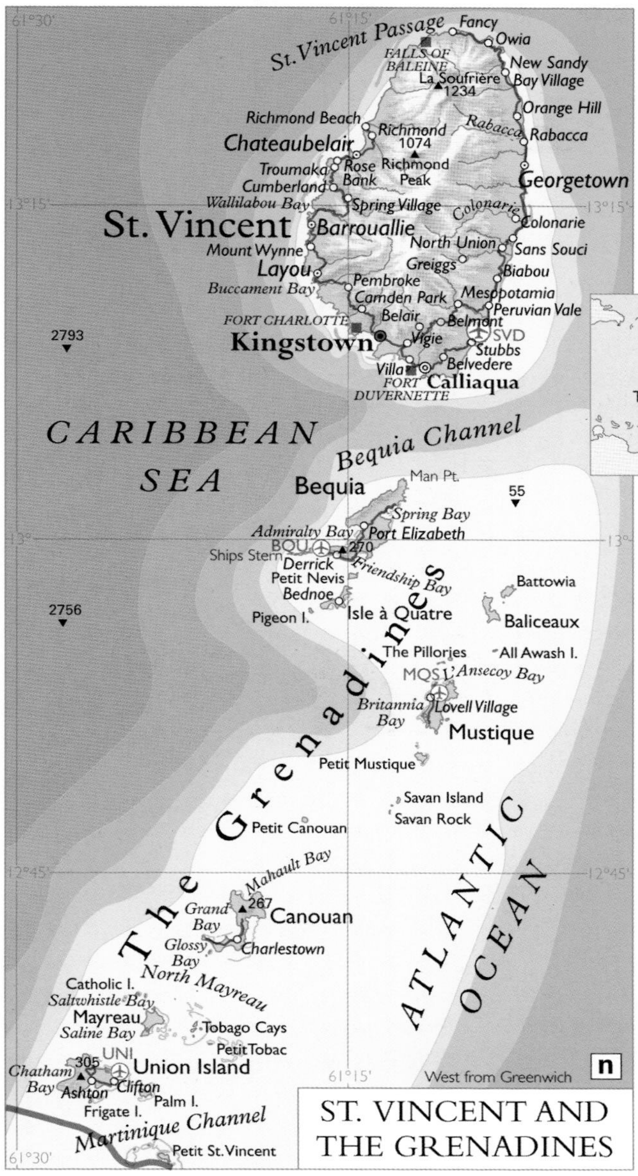
St. Vincent Passage
Fancy
Owia
FALLS OF BALEINE
New Sandy Bay Village
La Soufrière 1234
Orange Hill
Richmond Beach
Rabacca
Chateaubelair
Richmond 1074
Troumaka
Rose Bank
Richmond Peak
Georgetown
Cumberland
Wallilabou Bay
Spring Village
Colonarie
St. Vincent
Barrouallie
North Union
Sans Souci
Mount Wynne
Layou
Greiggs
Biabou
Buccament Bay
Pembroke
Camden Park
Mesopotamia
Peruvian Vale
FORT CHARLOTTE
Belair
Belmont
SVD
Kingstown
Vigie
Stubbs
Villa
Belvedere
FORT DUVERNETTE
Calliaqua
2793
CARIBBEAN SEA
Bequia Channel
Bequia
Man Pt.
55
Spring Bay
Admiralty Bay
BQU
Port Elizabeth
Ships Stern
270
Derrick
Petit Nevis
Friendship Bay
Bednoe
Battowia
Pigeon I.
Isle à Quatre
Baliceaux
2756
The Pillories
All Awash I.
MQS
L'Ansecoy Bay
Britannia Bay
Lovell Village
Mustique
Petit Mustique
Savan Island
Savan Rock
The Grenadines
Petit Canouan
ATLANTIC OCEAN
Mahault Bay
Grand Bay
267
Canouan
Glossy Bay
Charlestown
North Mayreau
Catholic I.
Saltwhistle Bay
Mayreau
Saline Bay
Tobago Cays
Petit Tobac
Chatham Bay
305
UNI
Union Island
Ashton
Clifton
Palm I.
Frigate I.
Martinique Channel
Petit St. Vincent
West from Greenwich
n
ST. VINCENT AND THE GRENADINES
Montserrat
St. Vincent & The Grenadines
Grenada

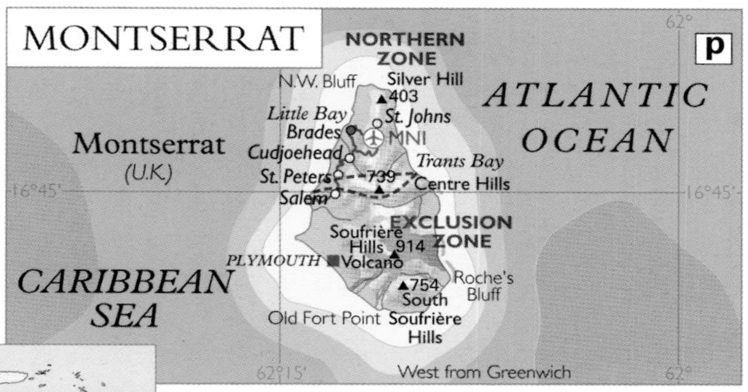
MONTSERRAT
NORTHERN ZONE
p
Montserrat (U.K.)
N.W. Bluff
Silver Hill
403
ATLANTIC OCEAN
Little Bay
St. Johns
Brades
MNI
Cudjoehead
Trants Bay
St. Peters
739
Centre Hills
Salem
EXCLUSION ZONE
Soufrière Hills 914
PLYMOUTH
Volcano
CARIBBEAN SEA
754
Roche's Bluff
South Soufrière Hills
Old Fort Point
West from Greenwich

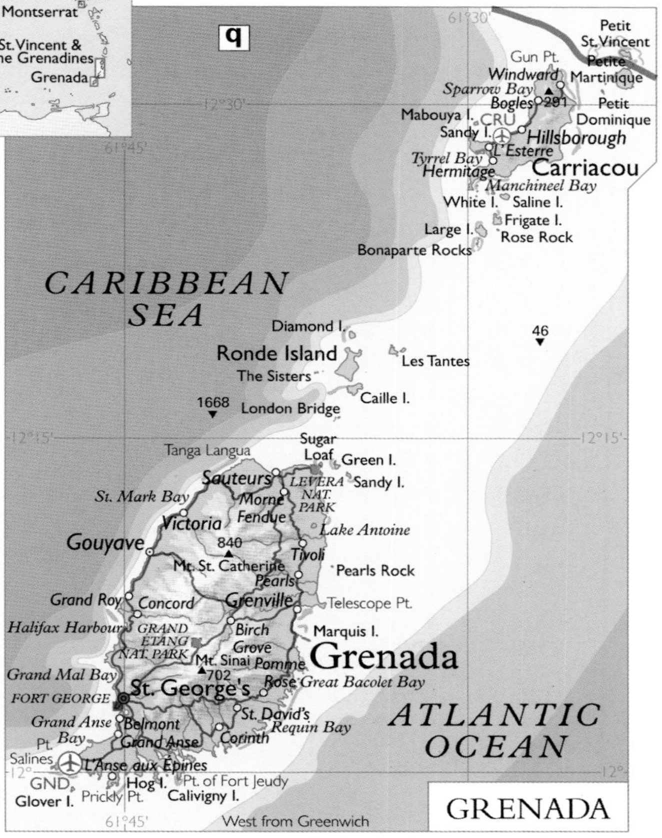
q
Petit St. Vincent
Gun Pt.
Windward
Petite Martinique
Sparrow Bay
Bogles
291
Petit Dominique
Mabouya I.
Sandy I.
CRU
Hillsborough
Tyrrel Bay
Hermitage
L'Esterre
Carriacou
Manchineel Bay
White I.
Saline I.
Large I.
Frigate I.
Rose Rock
Bonaparte Rocks
CARIBBEAN SEA
Diamond I.
46
Ronde Island
Les Tantes
The Sisters
Caille I.
1668
London Bridge
Tanga Langua
Sugar Loaf
Green I.
Sauteurs
LEVERA NAT. PARK
Sandy I.
St. Mark Bay
Morne Fendue
Victoria
Lake Antoine
Gouyave
840
Tivoli
Mt. St. Catherine
Pearls Rock
Pearls
Grand Roy
Concord
Grenville
Telescope Pt.
Halifax Harbour
GRAND ETANG NAT. PARK
Birch Grove
Marquis I.
Mt. Sinai
Pomme Rose
Grenada
702
Grand Mal Bay
FORT GEORGE
St. George's
Great Bacolet Bay
Grand Anse Bay
Belmont
St. David's
Requin Bay
Grand Anse
Corinth
ATLANTIC OCEAN
Saline Pt.
L'Anse aux Epines
GND
Hog I.
Pt. of Fort Jeudy
Glover I.
Prickly Pt.
Calivigny I.
West from Greenwich
GRENADA

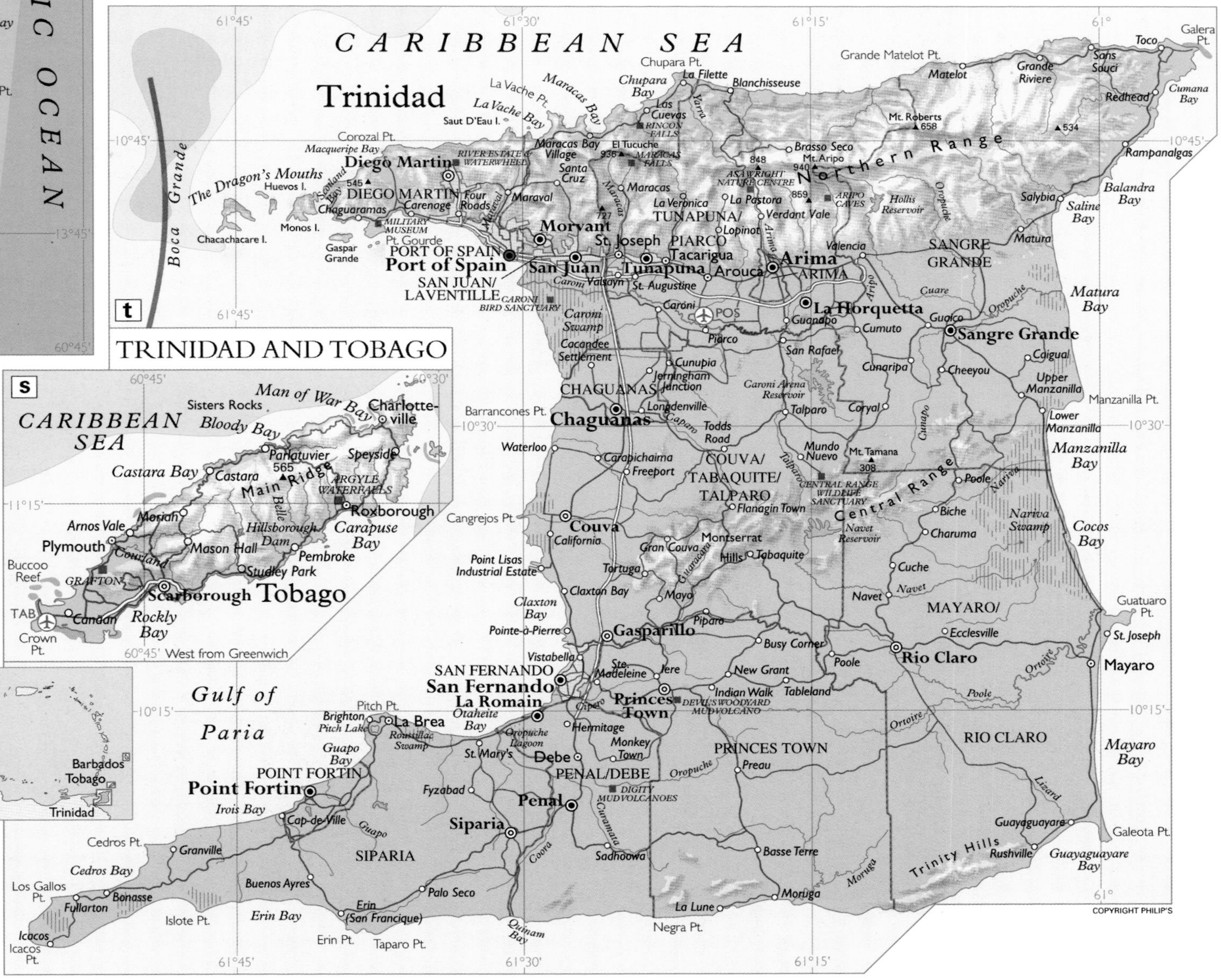
CARIBBEAN SEA
Trinidad
Chupara Pt.
La Filette
Blanchisseuse
Grande Matelot Pt.
Galera Pt.
Toco
Matelot
Grande Riviere
Sans Souci
Redhead
Cumana Bay
Chupara Bay
Maracas Bay
La Vache Pt.
La Vache Bay
Saut D'Eau I.
Las Cuevas
RINCON FALLS
Mt. Roberts 658
534
Corozal Pt.
Maracas Bay Village
El Tucuche 936
MARACAS FALLS
Brasso Seco
Mt. Aripo
940
Northern Range
Rampanalgas
Macqueripe Bay
Diego Martin
RIVER ESTATE WATERWHEEL
848
ASA WRIGHT NATURE CENTRE
Balandra Bay
The Dragon's Mouths
Huevos I.
Santa Cruz
Maracas
La Pastora
859
ARIPO CAVES
Hollis Reservoir
Salybia
Boca Grande
545
DIEGO MARTIN
Four Roads
La Veronica
Verdant Vale
Saline Bay
Chaguaramas
Carenage
Maraval
TUNAPUNA/PIARCO
Monos I.
MILITARY MUSEUM
Morvant
Lopinot
Matura
Chacachacare I.
Gaspar Grande
Pt. Gourde
PORT OF SPAIN
St. Joseph
Tacarigua
Valencia
SANGRE GRANDE
Port of Spain
San Juan
Tunapuna
Arouca
Arima
ARIMA
SAN JUAN/LAVENTILLE
Valsayn
St. Augustine
CARONI BIRD SANCTUARY
Caroni
POS
La Horquetta
Matura Bay
Caroni Swamp
Piarco
Guanapo
Cumuto
Guaico
Sangre Grande
Cacandee Settlement
San Rafael
Coigual
Cunupia
Cunaripo
Cheeyou
Jerningham Junction
Upper Manzanilla
CHAGUANAS
Caroni Arena Reservoir
Manzanilla Pt.
Barrancones Pt.
Chaguanas
Talparo
Coryal
Lower Manzanilla
Todds Road
Waterloo
Mundo Nuevo
Mt. Tamana 308
Manzanilla Bay
Carapichaima
Freeport
COUVA/TABAQUITE/TALPARO
CENTRAL RANGE WILDLIFE SANCTUARY
Central Range
Poole
Flanagin Town
Nariva Swamp
Cangrejos Pt.
Couva
Biche
California
Navet Reservoir
Charuma
Cocos Bay
Montserrat Hills
Point Lisas Industrial Estate
Gran Couva
Tabaquite
Tortuga
Cuche
Claxton Bay
Navet
Guatuaro Pt.
MAYARO/RIO CLARO
Mayo
Pipiaro
Gasparillo
Pointe-a-Pierre
Busy Corner
Ecclesville
Vistabella
Rio Claro
St. Joseph
SAN FERNANDO
Ste. Madeleine
Poole
Mayaro
San Fernando
New Grant
La Romain
Princes Town
Indian Walk
Tableland
Gulf of Paria
DEVIL'S WOODYARD MUD VOLCANO
Pitch Pt.
Brighton
La Brea
Oropuche Lagoon
Rousillac Swamp
Hermitage
Monkey Town
RIO CLARO
Mayaro Bay
Guapo Bay
St. Mary's
Debe
PRINCES TOWN
POINT FORTIN
PENAL/DEBE
Preau
Point Fortin
Irois Bay
Fyzabad
DIGITY MUD VOLCANOES
Penal
Siparia
Cap-de-Ville
Guayaguayare
Cedros Pt.
Granville
SIPARIA
Basse Terre
Galeota Pt.
Trinity Hills
Rushville
Cedros Bay
Sadhoowa
Guayaguayare Bay
Buenos Ayres
Los Gallos Pt.
Bonasse
Palo Seco
Moriga
Fullarton
Erin (San Francique)
La Lune
Icacos
Islote Pt.
Erin Bay
Quinam Bay
Negra Pt.
Icacos Pt.
Erin Pt.
Taparo Pt.
COPYRIGHT PHILIP'S
t
TRINIDAD AND TOBAGO
s
Man of War Bay
Charlotteville
CARIBBEAN SEA
Sisters Rocks
Bloody Bay
Parlatuvier
Speyside
565
Castara Bay
Castara
Main Ridge
ARGYLE WATERFALLS
Moriah
Roxborough
Arnos Vale
Hillsborough Dam
Carapuse Bay
Plymouth
Mason Hall
Pembroke
Buccoo Reef
Studley Park
GRAFTON
Scarborough
Tobago
TAB
Canaan
Rockly Bay
Crown Pt.
West from Greenwich
Barbados
Tobago
Trinidad

Coral reef

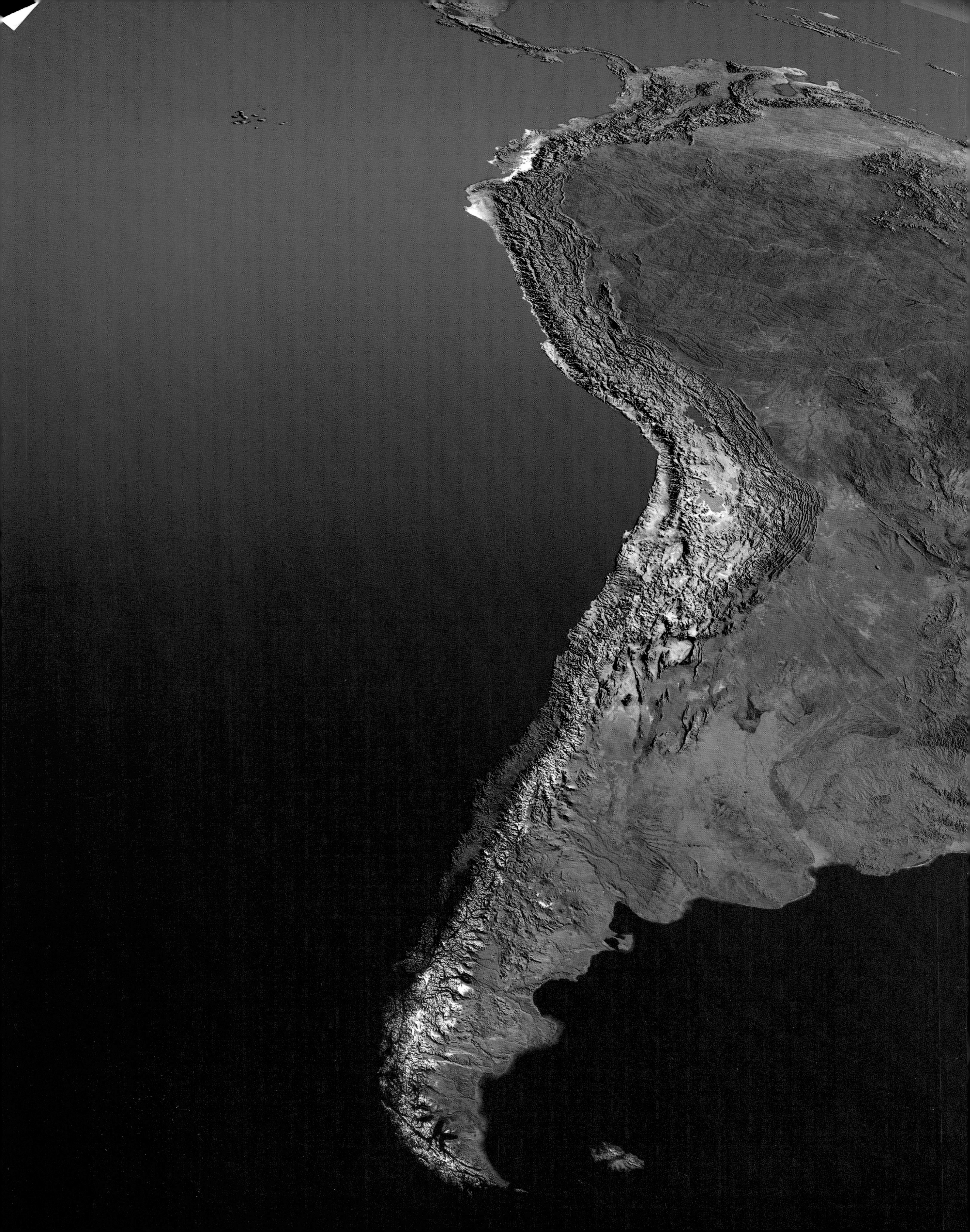

SOUTH AMERICA

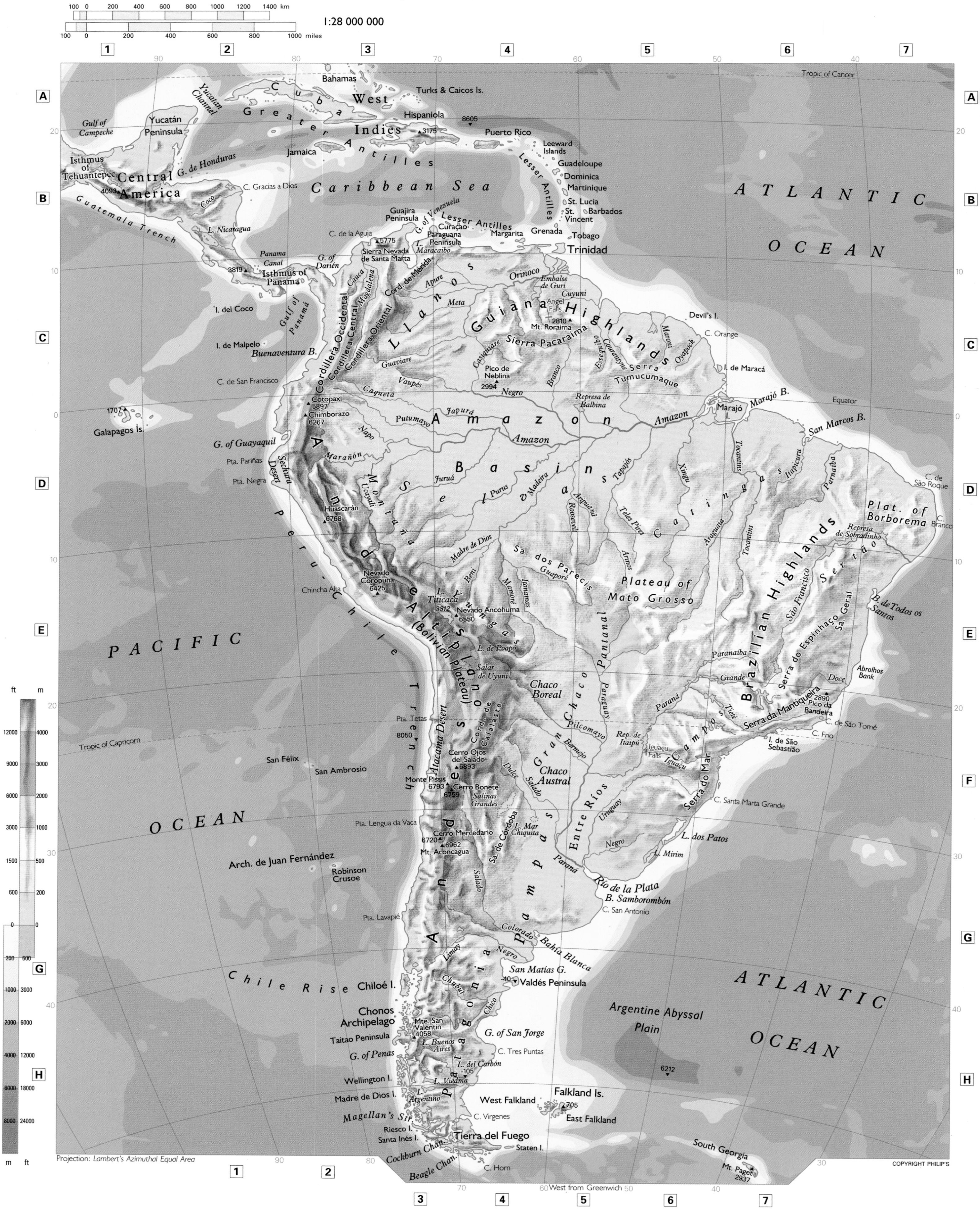
1:28 000 000
km
miles
Tropic of Cancer
Bahamas
Turks & Caicos Is.
Cuba
West
Greater
Indies
Antilles
Hispaniola
8605
3175
Puerto Rico
Yucatan Channel
Gulf of Campeche
Yucatán Peninsula
Isthmus of Tehuantepec
Central America
G. de Honduras
4093
Jamaica
Leeward Islands
Lesser Antilles
Guadeloupe
Dominica
Martinique
St. Lucia
St. Vincent
Barbados
Grenada
Tobago
Trinidad
C. Gracias a Dios
Caribbean Sea
ATLANTIC OCEAN
Guatemala Trench
Coco
L. Nicaragua
Guajira Peninsula
G. of Venezuela
Lesser Antilles
Curaçao
Paraguana Peninsula
Margarita
L. Maracaibo
C. de la Aguja
5775
Sierra Nevada de Santa Marta
Panama Canal
3819
Isthmus of Panama
G. of Darién
Cauca
Magdalena
Cord. de Mérida
Apure
Orinoco
Embalse de Guri
Cuyuni
Angel Falls
Llanos
Meta
Guiana Highlands
2810
Mt. Roraima
Sierra Pacaraima
Devil's I.
C. Orange
Maroni
Oyapock
Essequibo
Courantyne
Serra Tumucumaque
I. de Maracá
I. del Coco
Gulf of Panamá
I. de Malpelo
Buenaventura B.
Cordillera Occidental
Cordillera Central
Cordillera Oriental
Guaviare
Casiquiare
Pico de Neblina
2994
Vaupés
Branco
Negro
Caquetá
Represa de Balbina
C. de San Francisco
Cotopaxi
5897
Chimborazo
6267
1707
Galapagos Is.
Japurá
Putumayo
Amazon
Marajó I.
Marajó B.
Equator
San Marcos B.
Napo
G. of Guayaquil
Marañón
Sechura Desert
Pta. Pariñas
Pta. Negra
Juruá
Basin
Purus
Madeira
Tapajós
Xingu
Tocantins
Itapicuru
Parnaíba
C. de São Roque
Plat. of Borborema
C. Branco
Montaña
Selvas
Ucayali
Huascarán
6768
Aripuanã
Roosevelt
Teles Pires
Caatinga
Araguaia
Tocantins
Represa de Sobradinho
Peru-Chile Trench
Andes
Madre de Dios
Sa. dos Parecis
Guaporé
Arinos
Brazilian Highlands
Sertão
Beni
Mamoré
Itonamas
Plateau of Mato Grosso
São Francisco
Nevado Coropuna
6425
Chincha Alta
L. Titicaca
3812
Nevado Ancohuma
6550
Yungas
B. de Todos os Santos
Altiplano (Bolivian Plateau)
L. de Poopó
Pantanal
Serra do Espinhaço
Sa. Geral
PACIFIC
Salar de Uyuni
Chaco Boreal
Paranaíba
Grande
Doce
Abrolhos Bank
Paraguay
Paraná
Tietê
2890
Pico da Bandeira
Serra da Mantiqueira
C. de São Tomé
C. Frio
Pta. Tetas
8050
Atacama Desert
Cord. de Calalaste
Gran Chaco
Pilcomayo
Bermejo
Rep. de Itaipú
Iguaçu Falls
Iguaçu
Campos
I. de São Sebastião
Tropic of Capricorn
San Félix
San Ambrosio
Cerro Ojos del Salado
6893
Monte Pissis
6793
Cerro Bonete
6759
Salinas Grandes
Dulce
Salado
Chaco Austral
Entre Ríos
Uruguay
Serra do Mar
C. Santa Marta Grande
OCEAN
Pta. Lengua da Vaca
Cerro Mercedario
6720
6962
Mt. Aconcagua
L. Mar Chiquita
Sa. de Córdoba
Negro
L. dos Patos
L. Mirim
Arch. de Juan Fernández
Robinson Crusoe
Salado
Pampas
Paraná
Río de la Plata
B. Samborombón
C. San Antonio
Pta. Lavapié
Colorado
Bahía Blanca
Limay
Negro
Patagonia
Chile Rise
Chiloé I.
San Matías G.
40
Valdés Peninsula
ATLANTIC OCEAN
Chubut
Chico
Argentine Abyssal Plain
Chonos Archipelago
Mte. San Valentín
4058
Taitao Peninsula
G. of San Jorge
L. Buenos Aires
C. Tres Puntas
G. of Penas
L. del Carbón
-105
6212
Wellington I.
L. Viedma
Madre de Dios I.
L. Argentino
West Falkland
Falkland Is.
705
East Falkland
Magellan's Str.
C. Virgenes
Riesco I.
Santa Inés I.
Tierra del Fuego
Staten I.
Cockburn Chan.
Beagle Chan.
C. Horn
South Georgia
Mt. Paget
2937
Projection: Lambert's Azimuthal Equal Area
West from Greenwich
COPYRIGHT PHILIP'S
ft
m
12000
9000
6000
3000
1500
600
0
200
1000
2000
4000
6000
8000
4000
3000
2000
1000
500
200
600
3000
12000
18000
24000

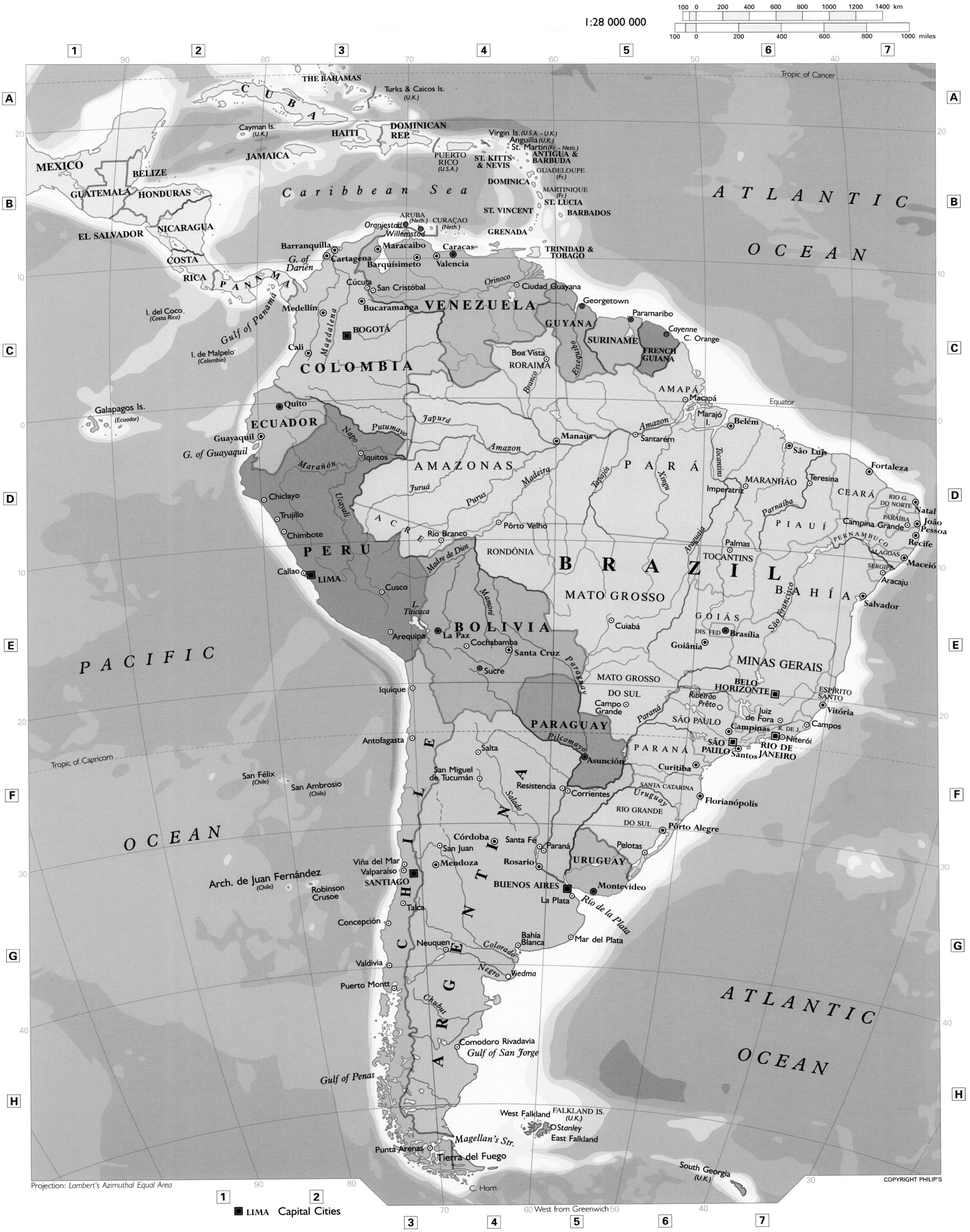
1:28 000 000
THE BAHAMAS
Turks & Caicos Is. (U.K.)
CUBA
Cayman Is. (U.K.)
HAITI
DOMINICAN REP.
JAMAICA
MEXICO
BELIZE
GUATEMALA
HONDURAS
EL SALVADOR
NICARAGUA
COSTA RICA
PANAMA
Caribbean Sea
PUERTO RICO (U.S.A.)
Virgin Is. (U.S.A. - U.K.)
Anguilla (U.K.)
St. Martin (Fr. - Neth.)
ST. KITTS & NEVIS
ANTIGUA & BARBUDA
GUADELOUPE (Fr.)
DOMINICA
MARTINIQUE (Fr.)
ST. LUCIA
ST. VINCENT
BARBADOS
GRENADA
TRINIDAD & TOBAGO
ARUBA (Neth.)
CURAÇAO (Neth.)
Oranjestad
Willemstad
ATLANTIC OCEAN
Barranquilla
Cartagena
G. of Darién
Maracaibo
Barquísimeto
Caracas
Valencia
Cúcuta
San Cristóbal
Orinoco
Ciudad Guayana
Medellín
Bucaramanga
VENEZUELA
Georgetown
GUYANA
Paramaribo
SURINAME
Cayenne
C. Orange
FRENCH GUIANA
I. del Coco (Costa Rica)
Gulf of Panamá
I. de Malpelo (Colombia)
BOGOTÁ
Cali
Magdalena
COLOMBIA
Boa Vista
RORAIMA
Branco
Essequibo
AMAPÁ
Macapá
Equator
Galapagos Is. (Ecuador)
Quito
ECUADOR
Guayaquil
G. of Guayaquil
Napo
Putumayo
Japurá
Amazon
Marajó I.
Belém
Manaus
Santarém
São Luís
Iquitos
Marañón
AMAZONAS
PARÁ
Tapajós
Xingu
Tocantins
Fortaleza
MARANHÃO
Teresina
CEARÁ
Imperatriz
RIO G. DO NORTE
Natal
Chiclayo
Ucayali
Juruá
Purus
Madeira
ACRE
Pôrto Velho
Rio Branco
Parnaíba
PIAUÍ
PARAÍBA
João Pessoa
Campina Grande
Recife
PERNAMBUCO
Trujillo
Chimbote
PERU
Madre de Dios
RONDÔNIA
Palmas
TOCANTINS
Araguaia
ALAGOAS
Maceió
SERGIPE
Aracaju
Callao
LIMA
Cusco
BRAZIL
MATO GROSSO
BAHÍA
Salvador
São Francisco
Mamoré
L. Titicaca
Arequipa
La Paz
BOLIVIA
Cochabamba
Santa Cruz
Cuiabá
GOIÁS
DIS. FED.
Brasília
Goiânia
MINAS GERAIS
PACIFIC OCEAN
Sucre
Paraguay
MATO GROSSO DO SUL
BELO HORIZONTE
ESPÍRITO SANTO
Vitória
Iquique
Campo Grande
Ribeirão Prêto
Juiz de Fora
Paraná
SÃO PAULO
Campinas
R. DE J.
Niterói
Campos
PARAGUAY
Antofagasta
Salta
Pilcomayo
SÃO PAULO
Santos
RIO DE JANEIRO
Tropic of Capricorn
Asunción
PARANÁ
Curitiba
San Félix (Chile)
San Ambrosio (Chile)
San Miguel de Tucumán
Resistencia
Corrientes
SANTA CATARINA
Florianópolis
Salado
Uruguay
RIO GRANDE DO SUL
Pôrto Alegre
Córdoba
Santa Fé
Paraná
San Juan
Pelotas
URUGUAY
Viña del Mar
Valparaíso
SANTIAGO
Mendoza
Rosario
Arch. de Juan Fernández (Chile)
Robinson Crusoe
BUENOS AIRES
Montevideo
La Plata
Rio de la Plata
Talca
Concepción
Bahía Blanca
Mar del Plata
Neuquen
Colorado
Valdivia
Negro
Viedma
Puerto Montt
CHILE
ARGENTINA
Chubut
Comodoro Rivadavia
Gulf of San Jorge
Gulf of Penas
West Falkland
FALKLAND IS. (U.K.)
Stanley
East Falkland
Magellan's Str.
Punta Arenas
Tierra del Fuego
C. Horn
South Georgia (U.K.)
Projection: Lambert's Azimuthal Equal Area
West from Greenwich
LIMA Capital Cities
COPYRIGHT PHILIP'S

50 0 50 100 150 200 250 300 km

1:6 400 000

50 0 50 100 150 200 miles

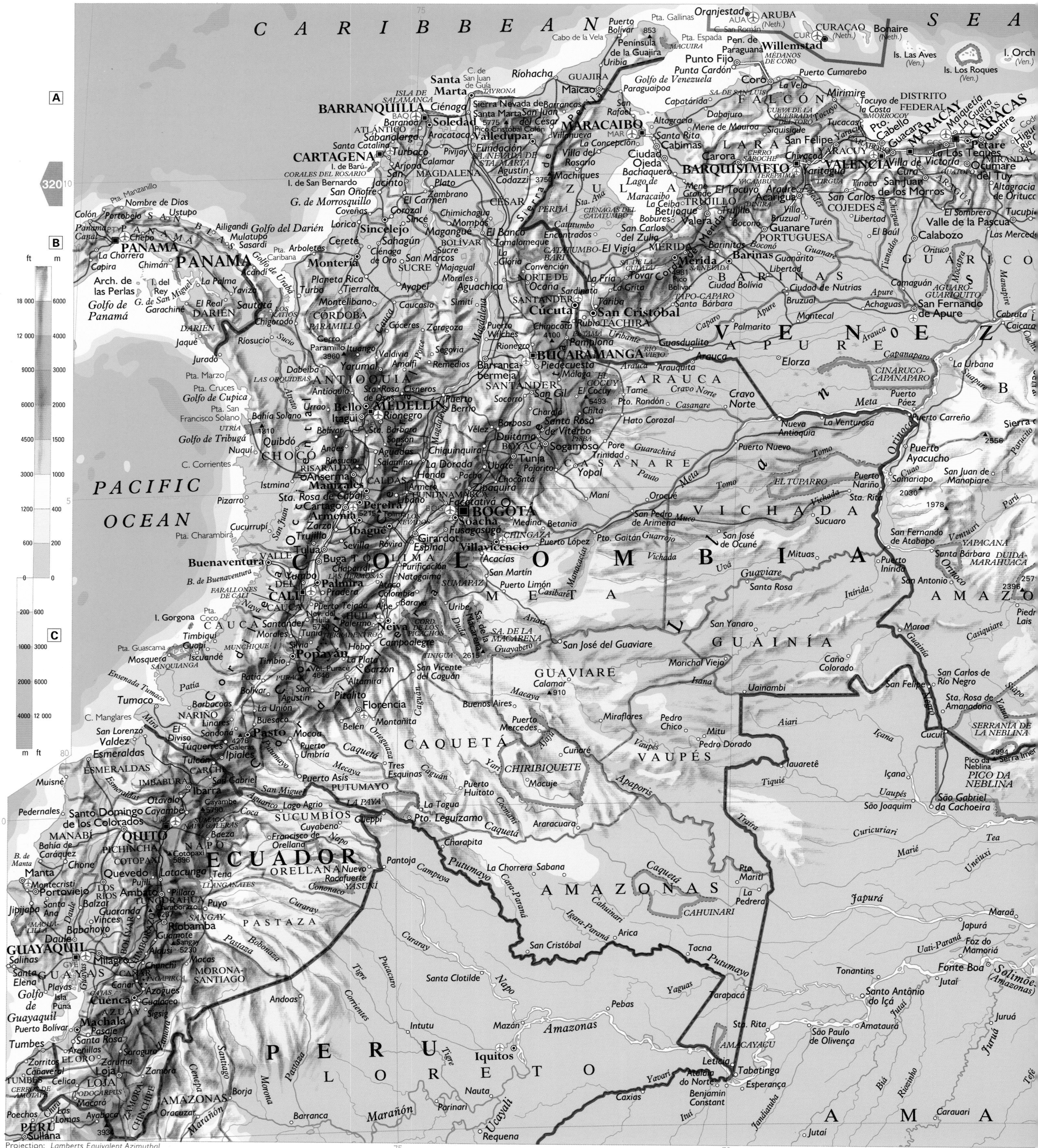

Projection: *Lamberts Equivalent Azimuthal*

1
2
330
3
4

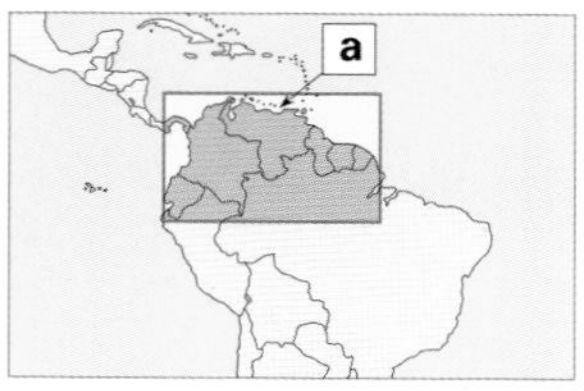

Administrative divisions in Guyana

1 POMEROON-SUPENAAM
2 ESSEQUIBO ISLANDS - WEST DEMERARA
3 DEMERARA-MAHAICA
4 MAHAICA-BERBICE
5 EAST BERBICE - CORENTYNE

332

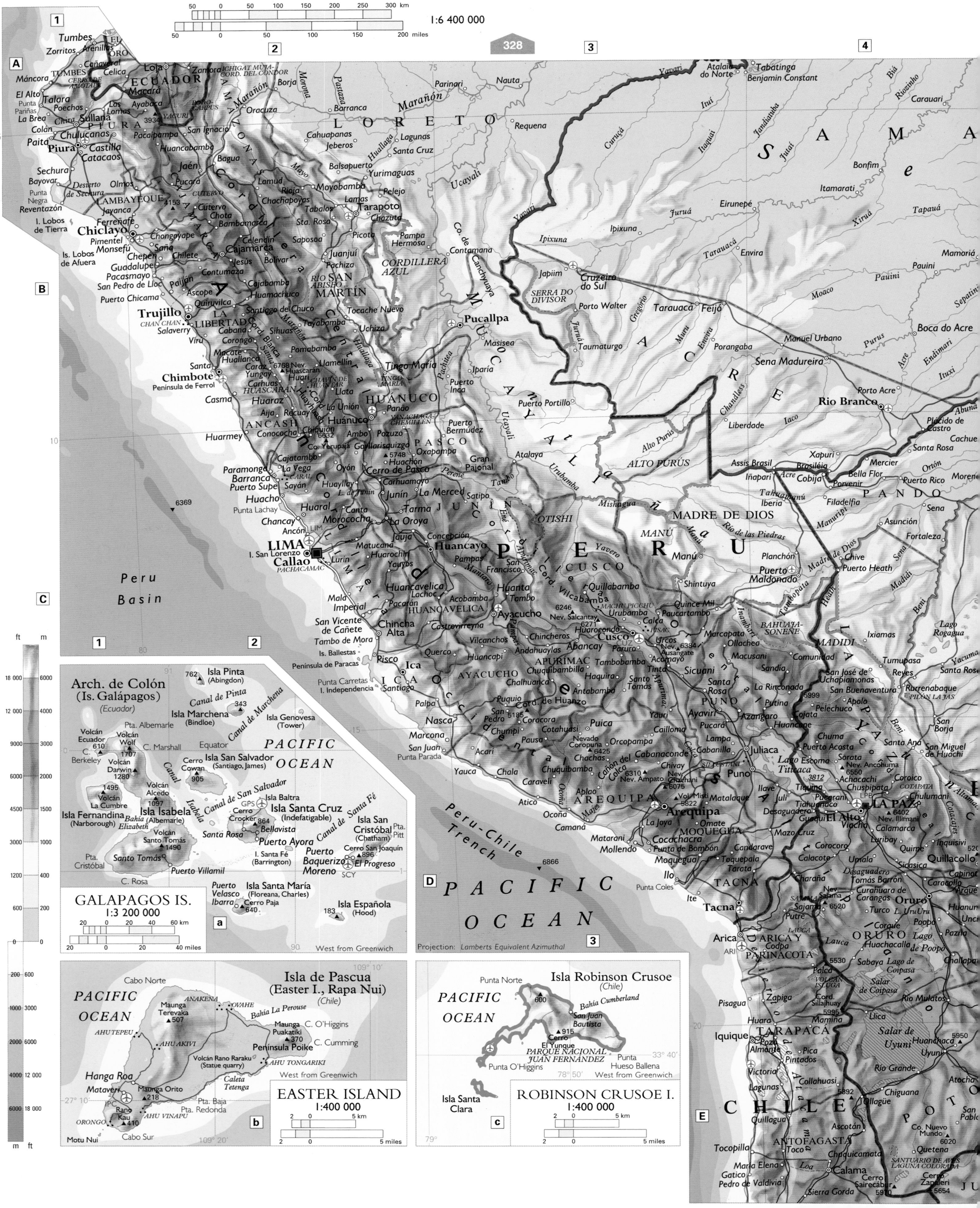
1:6 400 000
km
miles
328
ECUADOR
PERU
LORETO
AMAZONAS
SAN MARTÍN
LA LIBERTAD
ANCASH
HUÁNUCO
PASCO
JUNÍN
LIMA
HUANCAVELICA
AYACUCHO
APURÍMAC
CUSCO
MADRE DE DIOS
PUNO
AREQUIPA
MOQUEGUA
TACNA
ICA
UCAYALI
PIURA
LAMBAYEQUE
CAJAMARCA
TUMBES
ACRE
PANDO
LA PAZ
ORURO
ARICA Y PARINACOTA
TARAPACA
ANTOFAGASTA
CHILE
Lima
Callao
Trujillo
Chiclayo
Piura
Chimbote
Huancayo
Ayacucho
Cusco
Arequipa
Tacna
Arica
Iquique
Puno
Juliaca
Pucallpa
Rio Branco
La Paz
Oruro
Calama
Tocopilla
Peru Basin
Peru-Chile Trench
PACIFIC OCEAN
Lago Titicaca
Salar de Uyuni
Projection: Lamberts Equivalent Azimuthal
Arch. de Colón (Is. Galápagos) (Ecuador)
PACIFIC OCEAN
Isla Isabela (Albemarle)
Isla Santa Cruz (Indefatigable)
Isla San Cristóbal (Chatham)
Isla Fernandina (Narborough)
Isla San Salvador (Santiago, James)
Isla Santa María (Floreana, Charles)
Isla Española (Hood)
Isla Pinta (Abingdon)
Isla Marchena (Bindloe)
Isla Genovesa (Tower)
Puerto Ayora
Puerto Baquerizo Moreno
GALAPAGOS IS.
1:3 200 000
West from Greenwich
a
Isla de Pascua (Easter I., Rapa Nui) (Chile)
PACIFIC OCEAN
Hanga Roa
Cabo Norte
Cabo Sur
EASTER ISLAND
1:400 000
b
Isla Robinson Crusoe (Chile)
PACIFIC OCEAN
Punta Norte
Bahía Cumberland
San Juan Bautista
El Yunque
PARQUE NACIONAL JUAN FERNÁNDEZ
Punta O'Higgins
Punta Hueso Ballena
Isla Santa Clara
ROBINSON CRUSOE I.
1:400 000
c

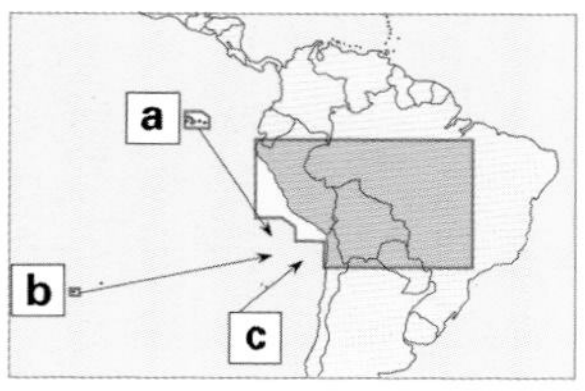

329

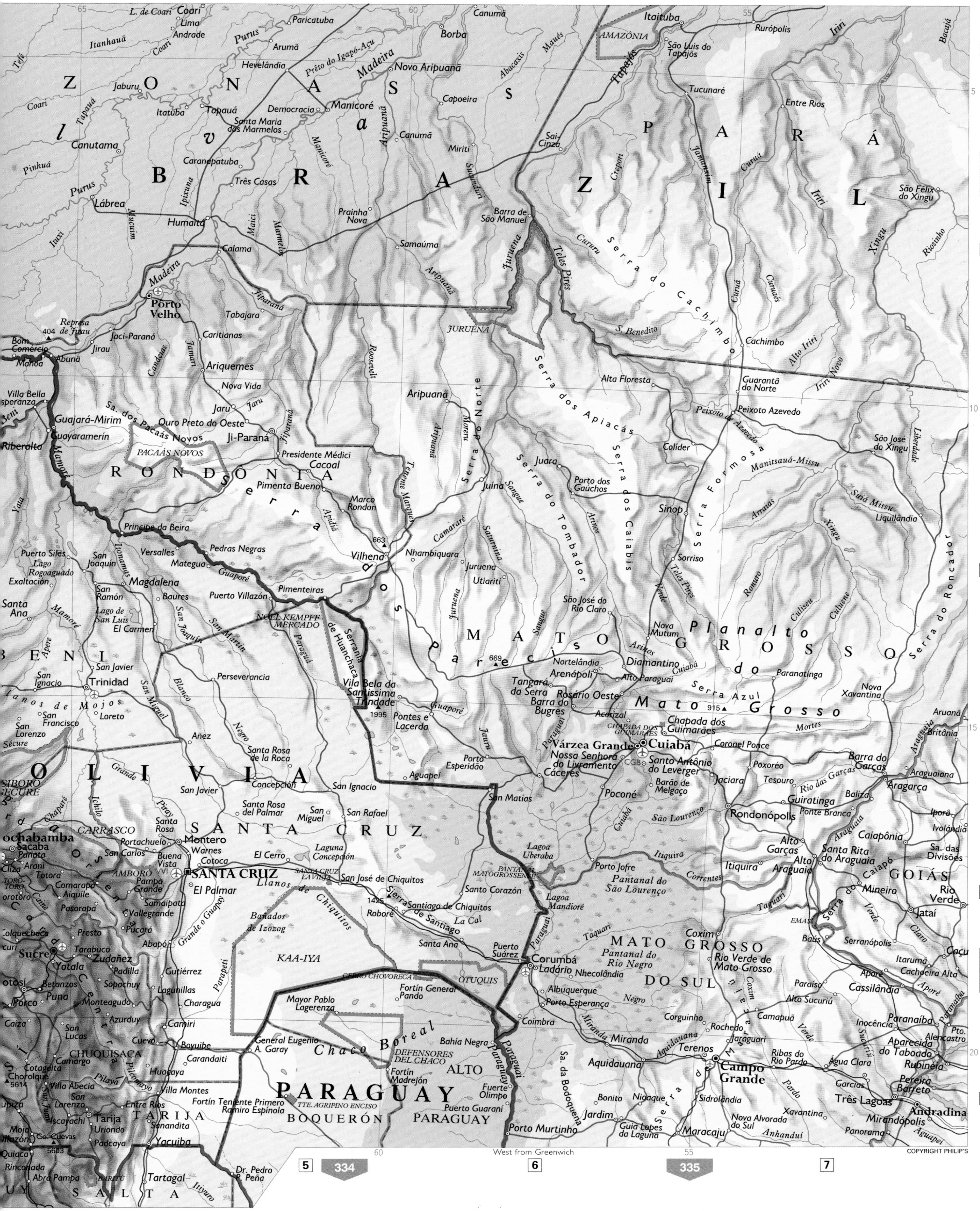

332
333
334
335

50 0 50 100 150 200 250 300 km
1:6 400 000
50 0 50 100 150 200 miles

328
331

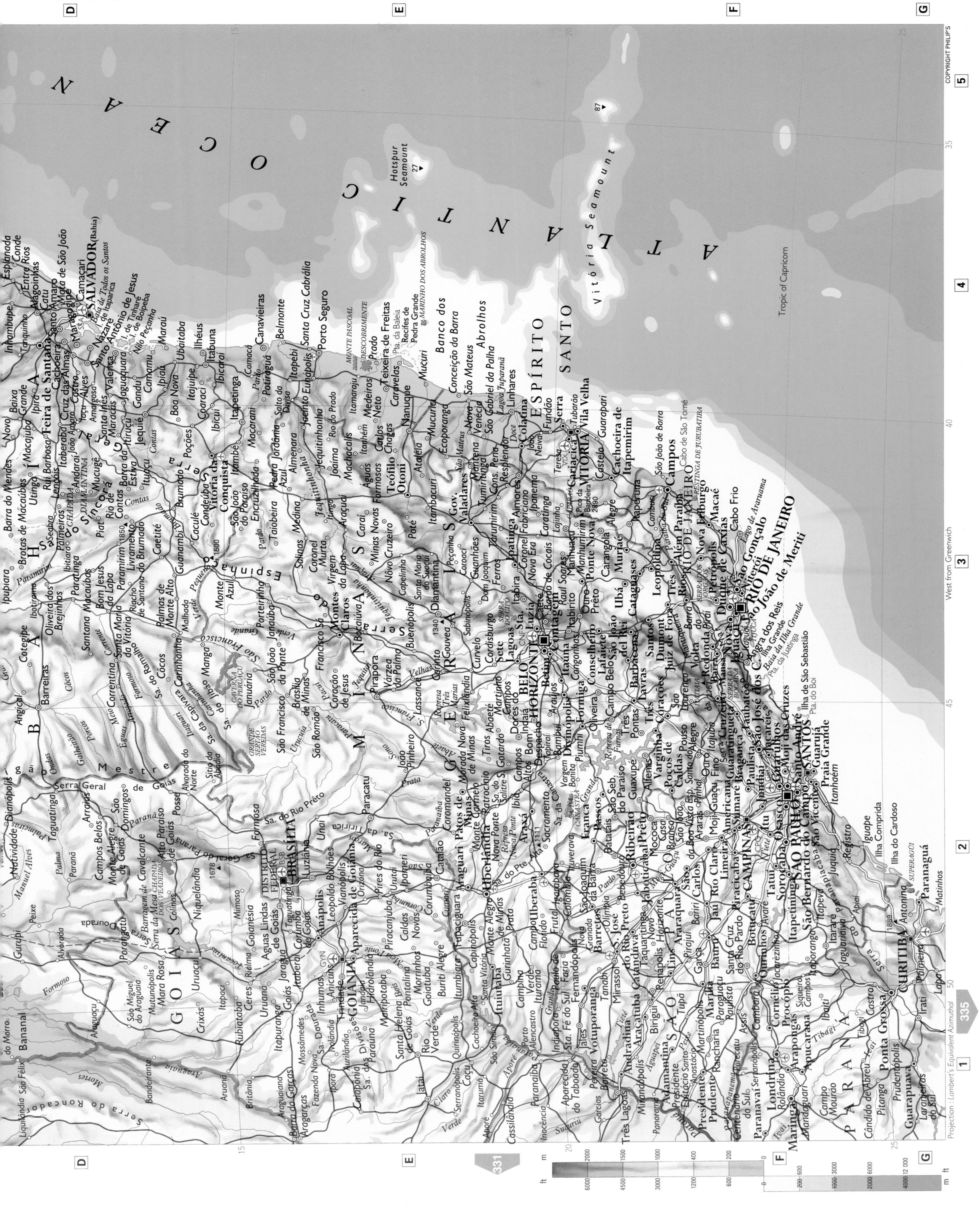
A T L A N T I C O C E A N
Hotspur Seamount
Vitória Seamount
Tropic of Capricorn
West from Greenwich
Projection : Lambert's Equivalent Azimuthal
COPYRIGHT PHILIP'S
SALVADOR (Bahia)
BRASÍLIA
GOIÂNIA
BELO HORIZONTE
VITÓRIA
RIO DE JANEIRO
SÃO PAULO
CURITIBA
CAMPINAS
SANTOS
DISTRITO FEDERAL
GOIÁS
BAHIA
MINAS GERAIS
ESPÍRITO SANTO
SÃO PAULO
PARANÁ
Banco dos Abrolhos
Serra do Espinhaço
Serra Geral de Goiás
Cabo Frio
331
335

50 0 50 100 150 200 250 300 km

1:6 400 000

50 0 50 100 150 200 miles

330

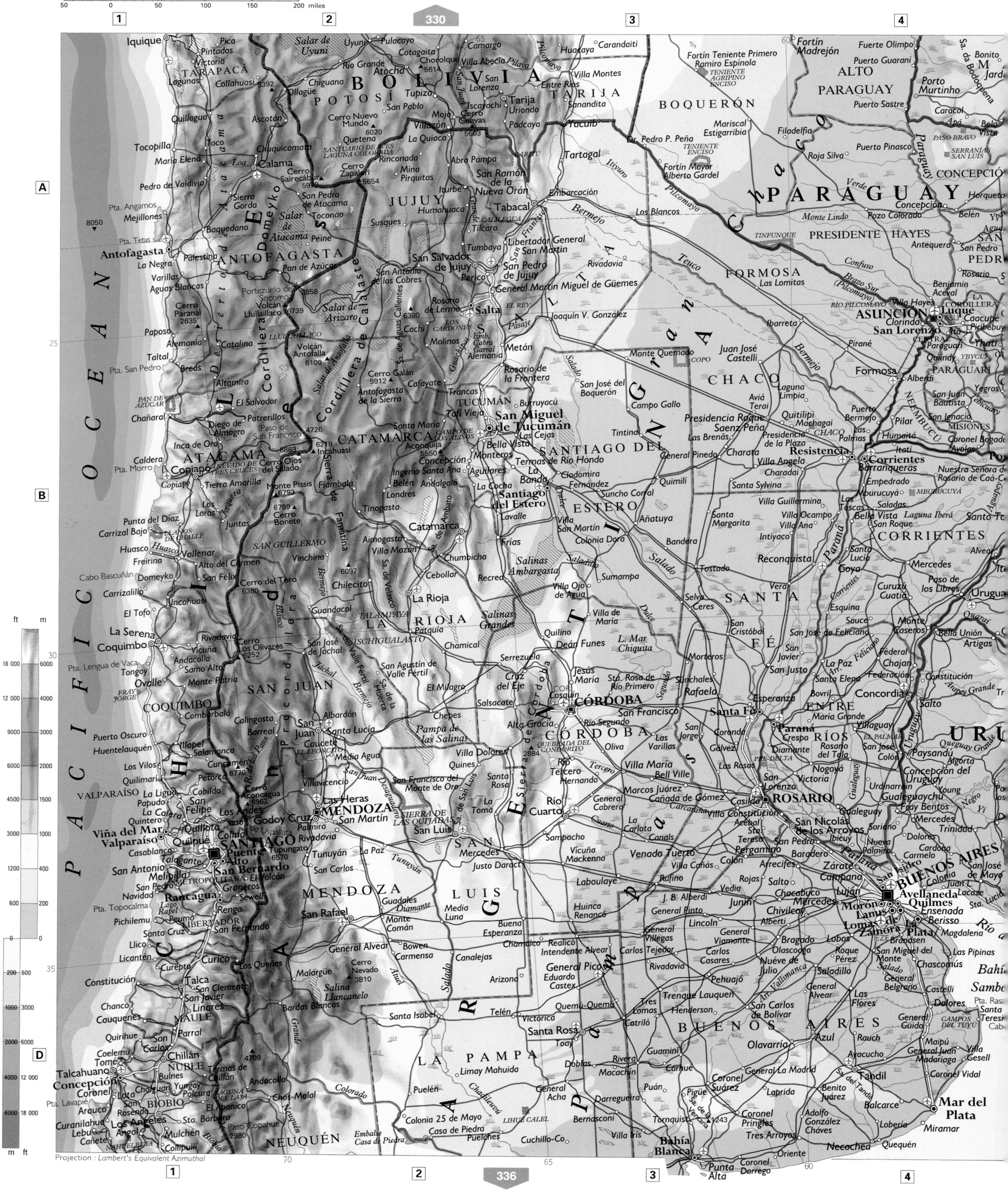

336

BELO HORIZONTE
Betim
Contagem
333
VITÓRIA
Vila Velha
RIO DE JANEIRO
Niterói
São Gonçalo
Duque de Caxias
Nova Iguaçu
Petrópolis
Nova Friburgo
Macaé
Cabo Frio
Campos
Cachoeiro de Itapemirim
Juiz de Fora
Volta Redonda
Barra Mansa
Taubaté
São José dos C.
SÃO PAULO
GUARULHOS
Santo André
São Bernardo do Campo
SANTOS
Guarujá
Praia Grande
São Vicente
Osasco
Sorocaba
Jundiaí
CAMPINAS
Piracicaba
Limeira
Americana
Rio Claro
Ribeirão Prêto
São Carlos
Araraquara
Bauru
Marília
Presidente Prudente
Londrina
Maringá
Apucarana
Ponta Grossa
CURITIBA
Paranaguá
JOINVILLE
Blumenau
Itajaí
São José
FLORIANÓPOLIS
Ilha de Santa Catarina
Criciúma
Tubarão
Laguna
Cabo Santa Marta Grande
Lages
Caxias do Sul
Novo Hamburgo
São Leopoldo
Canoas
PORTO ALEGRE
Viamão
Lagoa dos Patos
Pelotas
Rio Grande
Bagé
Santa Maria
Cascavel
Foz do Iguaçu
Ciudad del Este
Encarnación
MONTEVIDEO
Maldonado
Pta. del Este
Chuy
Lagoa Mirim
Lagoa Mangueira
Tropic of Capricorn
B R A Z I L
P A R A N Á
SANTA CATARINA
R I O G R A N D E D O S U L
S Ã O P A U L O
A T L A N T I C
O C E A N
5304
25
30
35
55
50
45
40
West from Greenwich
5
6
7
A
B
C
D
COPYRIGHT PHILIP'S

1:6 400 000

334
335
LA PAMPA
BUENOS AIRES
NEUQUÉN
RÍO NEGRO
CHUBUT
SANTA CRUZ
TIERRA DEL FUEGO
LA ARAUCANIA
LOS RÍOS
LOS LAGOS
MAGALLANES Y ANTÁRTICA CHILENA
ARGENTINA
CHILE
Andes
Temuco
Valdivia
Osorno
Puerto Montt
San Carlos de Bariloche
Neuquén
Bahía Blanca
Viedma
Golfo San Matías
Península Valdés
Puerto Madryn
Trelew
Rawson
Esquel
Comodoro Rivadavia
Golfo San Jorge
Puerto Deseado
Puerto San Julián
Puerto Santa Cruz
Bahía Grande
Río Gallegos
Puerto Natales
Punta Arenas
Isla Grande de Tierra del Fuego
Ushuaia
Río Grande
Cabo de Hornos (Cape Horn)
Isla de Chiloé
Archipiélago de los Chonos
Golfo de Penas
Estrecho de Magallanes (Magellan's Strait)
I. de los Estados (Staten I.)
FALKLAND ISLANDS (U.K.) (ISLAS MALVINAS)
West Falkland
East Falkland
Stanley
Burdwood Bank
ATLANTIC OCEAN
PACIFIC OCEAN
Projection : Lambert s Equivalent Azimuthal
West from Greenwich

GEOGRAPHICAL GLOSSARY

This is a list of the geographical terms from various foreign languages that are found in the place names on the maps and in the index. Each is followed by the language and its English meaning.

Afr. Afrikaans
Alb. Albanian
Amh. Amharic
Ar. Arabic
Belo. Belorussian
Berb. Berber
Bulg. Bulgarian
Burm. Burmese
Cam. Cambodian
Cat. Catalan
Chin. Chinese
Czec. Czech
Dan. Danish
Dut. Dutch
Est. Estonian
Fin. Finnish
Fr. French
Gae. Gaelic
Ger. German
Gr. Greek
Heb. Hebrew
Hin. Hindi
Hung. Hungarian
I.-C. Indo-Chinese
Ice. Icelandic
It. Italian
Indo. Indonesian
Jap. Japanese
Kaz. Kazakh
Kor. Korean
Kyrg. Kyrgyz
Lapp. Lapp (Sami)
Lat. Latvian
Lith. Lithuanian
Malag. Malagasy
Mong. Mongolian
Nor. Norway
Pash. Pashto
Per. Persian
Pol. Polish
Port. Portuguese
Rom. Romanian
Russ. Russian
Sin. Sinhalese
Ser.-Cr. Serbo-Croat
Slov. Slovene
Som. Somali
Span. Spanish
Swe. Swedish
Tib. Tibetan
Turk. Turkish
Ukr. Ukrainian
Viet. Vietnamese

-á *Ice.* river
-å *Dan., Nor., Swe.* stream
-abad *Farsi, Russ.* town
Abyad *Ar.* white mountain
Ada, Adasi *Turk.* island
Addis *Amh.* new
Adrar *Ar., Berb.* mountains
Aiguille *Fr.* peak
Aïn, Aîn (A.) *Ar.* spring
Åkra *Gr.* cape, point
Akrotiri *Gr.* cape, point
Alb *Ger.* mountains
Albufera *Span.* lagoon
-ålen *Nor.* islands
Alpen *Ger.* mountain ranges
Alpes *Fr.* mountains
Alpi *It.* mountains
Alt *Ger.* old
Alta, Alto *Port.* high, upper
Altos *Span.* mountains
-älv, -älven *Swe.* stream, river
Amtskommune (Amt.) *Dan.* first-order administrative division
-ån *Swe.* river
Anse *Fr.* bay
Ao *Thai* bay
Appennino *It.* mountain range
Archipel *Fr.* archipelago
Archipiélago (Arch.) *Span.* archipelago
Arcipèlago *It.* archipelago
Arquipélago (Arq.) *Port.* archipelago
Arrecife *Span.* reef
Arroyo (Arr.) *Span.* stream
-ås, -åsen *Nor., Swe.* hill
Ayios *Gr.* island
Ayn *Ar.* well, waterhole

Baai, -baai *Afr., Dut.* bay
Bāb *Ar.* gate, strait
Bäck, -bäcken *Swe.* stream
Back, -backen, *Swe.* hill
Bad, -baden *Ger.* spa
Badia *Cat.* bay
Bādiyah, Bādiyat *Ar.* desert
Bæk *Dan.* stream
Bælt *Dan.* strait
Baharu *Malay* new
Bahía (B.) *Span.* bay
Bahiret *Ar.* lagoon
Bahr *Ar.* sea, lake, river
Bahra Bahrat *Ar.* lake
Baía (B.) *Port.* bay
Baie (B.) *Fr.* bay
Baixa, Baixo *Port.* lower
Baja, Bajo *Span.* lower
Bakke *Nor.* hill
Bala *Farsi* upper
Ballon *Fr.* dome
Baltă *Rom.* marsh, lake
Ban *Lao, Thai* village
-Bana *Jap.* cape
Banc *Fr.* bank
Banco *Span.* bank
Bandao *Chin.* peninsula
Bandar *Ar., Malay* port, harbour
Bandar *Farsi* bay
Banja *Ser.-Cr.* spa, resort
Banjaran *Malay* mountain range
Baraji *Turk.* dam
Barat *Indo., Malay* western
Barrage (Barr.) *Fr.* dam
Barragem (Barr.) *Port.* dam, reservoir
Bas, basse *Fr.* lower
Bassin *Fr.* basin
-batang *Indo.* river
Baṭlaq *Farsi* marsh
Batu *Malay* mountain
Bayt *Heb.* house, village
Bazar *Hin.* market, bazaar
-beek *Afr., Dut.* river
Be'er *Heb.* well
Bei *Chin.* north, northern
Beinn, Ben *Gae.* mountain
Beit *Heb.* village
Belaya, Belo, Beloye, Belyy *Russ.* white
Belogorye *Russ.* hills, mountain range
Bender *Som.* harbour
Berg(e), -berg(e) *Afr., Ger.* mountain(s)
-berg, -en, -et *Nor., Swe.* hill, mountain, rock
Besar *Indo., Malay* big
Bet *Heb.* house, village
Bir, Bîr, Bi'r *Ar.* well
Birkat, Birket *Ar.* lake, marsh, well
Bishti *Alb.* cape
-bjerg *Dan.* hill, point
Blaenau *Welsh* upland
-bo *Chin.* lake
Boca *Port., Span.* river mouth, inlet
Bodden *Ger.* bay, inlet
Bogaz, Boğazı *Turk.* channel, strait
Bogd *Mong.* mountain range
Bois *Fr.* woods
Boka *Ser.-Cr.* gulf, inlet
Bolshoi, Bolshaya, Bolshoye (Bol.) *Russ.* great, large
Bordj (Bj.) *Ar.* fort
-borg *Dan., Nor., Swe.* castle, fort
Bory *Pol.* woods
Bosque *Span.* woods
-botn *Nor.* valley floor
Bouche(s) *Fr.* mouth(s)
Braţul *Rom.* distributary stream, branch
-bre, -breen *Nor.* glacier
Bredning *Dan.* bay
Brücke *Ger.* bridge
-brug *Dut.* bridge
-brunn *Swe.* well, spring
Bucht *Ger.* bay
Bugt *Dan.* bay
-bugten *Dan.* bay
Buheirat *Ar.* lake, reservoir
Bukit *Malay* hill
-bukt, -a *Nor.* bay
-bukten *Swe.* bay
-bulag *Mong.* spring
Bulag *Chin.* lake
Bulu *Malay* mountain
Bum *Burm.* mountain
Bûr *Ar.* port
Burg. *Ar.* fort
Burg, -burg *Ger.* castle
Burnu, Burun *Turk.* cape
Butt *Gae.* promontory
Büyük *Turk.* big
-by *Dan., Nor., Swe.* town
-byen *Nor., Swe.* town

Cabeza *Span.* peak, hill
Cabo (C.) *Port., Span.* headland, cape
Cachoeira *Port.* waterfall
Cala Cat. *It.* bay
Camp Port. *Span.* land, field
Câmpia *Rom.* plain
Campo *It., Port., Span.* plain
Campos *Span.* upland
Canal (Can.) *Fr., Port., Span.* canal, channel
Canale (Can.) *It.* channel
Canalul (Can.) *Ser.-Cr.* canal
Cao Nguyen *Thai* plateau, tableland
Cap (C.) *Cat., Fr.* cape
Capo (C) *It.* cape
Carn *Gae.* hill
Carse *Gae.* valley
Catarata *Port., Span.* cataract
Cauce *Span.* intermittent stream
Causse *Fr.* limestone plateau
Cay, Cayi, -cay, -cayi *Turk.* river
Cayo(s) *Span.* rock(s), islet(s)
Cefn *Welsh* hill
Cerro *Span.* hill, peak
Česká, Český, České *Czec.* Czech
Chaco *Span.* jungle
Chaîne(s) *Fr.* mountain range(s)
Chang *Chin.* mountain
Chapa *Span.* hills, upland
Chapada *Port.* hills, upland
Chaung *Burm.* stream, river
Chi *Chin.* small lake
-ch'ŏn *Kor.* river
-chŏsuji *Kor.* reservoir
Chott *Ar.* salt lake, depression
Chu *Tib.* river
Chute *Fr.* waterfall
Città *It.* city
Ciudad *Span.* city
Co *Tib.* lake
Cochilla (Coch.) *Port.* hills
Col *Fr., It.* pass
Colina(s) *Span.* hill(s)
Colle *It.* pass
Colline(s) *Fr.* hill(s)
Conca *It.* plain, basin
Cordillera (Cord.) *Span.* mountain range
Costa *It., Port., Span.* coast
Côte *Fr.* coast, slope, hill
Coteaux *Fr.* hills
Cuchilla *Span.* hills
Cuenca *Span.* river basin
Cu-Lao *Viet.* island

Da *Chin.* big
Da *Viet.* river
Daban *Mong.* pass
Dağ(ı) *Turk.* mountain(s)
Dāgh *Farsi* mountain
Dağları *Turk.* mountain range
-dai, -daichi *Jap.* plateau
-Dake *Jap.* mountain
-dal, -e *Dan., Swe.* valley
-dal, -en *Swe., Nor.* valley, stream
Dalay Mong. large lake
-dalur, -dalur *Ice.* valley
-damm, -en *Swe.* lake
Danau *Malay* lake
Dao *Chin., Viet.* island
Dar *Ar.* region
Darya *Russ.* river
Daryācheh *Farsi* marshy lake, lake
Dasht *Farsi* desert, steppe
Daung *Burm.* mountain, hill
Dayr *Ar.* monastery
Debre *Amh.* hill
Deli *Ser.-Cr.* mountain
Deniz, -i *Turk.* sea
Département (Dépt.) *Fr.* first-order administrative division
Dere *Turk.* stream
Desierto (Des.) *Span.* desert
Détroit *Fr.* strait
Dhar *Ar.* region, mountain range
Diep *Dut.* channel
Dijk *Dut.* dyke
Ding *Chin.* mountain
Dingzi *Chin.* hill, mountain
Djebel (Dj.) *Ar.* mountain
-djúp *Ice.* fjord
-djupet *Swe.* channel, sound
-Do *Jap., Kor.* island
Dolina *Russ.* valley
Dolna, Dolni *Bulg.* lower
Dolna, Dolne, Dolny *Russ.* lower
Dolní *Czec.* lower
Dolok (D.) *Malay* mountain
-dong *Kor.* village, town
Dong *Chin.* east, eastern
Donja, Donji *Ser.-Cr.* lower
-dorf *Ger.* village
-dorp *Afr.* village
-drif *Afr.* ford
-dybet *Dan.* marine channel
Dzong *Tib.* town, settlement
Dzüün *Mong.* east, eastern

-egga *Nor.* peak
-eiland, -en (eil.) *Afr., Dut.* island(s)
Eilean *Gae.* island
-elv, -a *Nor.* river
Embalse *Span.* reservoir
'Emeq *Heb.* plain, valley
Ensenada *Span.* bay
Erg *Ar.* sand desert
Estero *Span.* estuary
Estrada *Span.* bay
Estrecho *Span.* strait
Estuaire *Fr.* estuary
Estuario *Span.* estuary
Étang *Fr.* lagoon, lake
-ey, -jar *Ice.* island(s)
-ežeras *Lith.* lake
-ezers *Lat.* lake

Falaise *Fr.* cliff
-fallet *Swe.* waterfall
Farihy *Malag.* lake
Faro *Span.* lighthouse
-feld *Ger.* field
-fell *Ice.* mountain, hill
Feng *Chin.* mountain range
Fiume (F.) *It.* river
-fjäll, -en, -et *Swe.* hill(s), mountain(s), ridge
-fjärden *Swe.* fjord
Fjeld *Dan.* mountain
-fjell, -et *Nor.* mountain range
-fjord, -en *Dan., Nor., Swe.* fjord
-fjörður *Ice.* fjord, bay, inlet
Fleuve (Fl.) *Fr.* river
-flói *Ice.* bay, marshy country
Fluss (F.) *Ger.* river
Foce, Foci *It.* mouth(s)
Folyó (F.) *Hung.* river
-fonn *Nor.* glacier
-fontein *Afr.* fountain, spring
Forêt *Fr.* forest
-fors, -en *Swe.* waterfall, rapids
-foss, -en *Ice., Nor.* waterfall
Forst *Ger.* forest
Foum *Ar.* pass
Fuente *Span.* source
-furt *Ger.* ford
Fylke *Nor.* first-order administrative division

-gang *Chin.* bay, harbour
-gang *Kor.* river
Ganga *Hin., Sin.* river
Gangri *Tib.* mountain
Gaoyuan *Chin.* plateau
-gat *Dan.* sound
-Gata *Jap.* lake
-gau *Ger.* district
-Gawa *Jap.* river
Gebel (G.) *Ar.* mountain
Gebirge (Geb.) *Ger.* hills, mountains
Gezirat, Geziret *Ar.* island
Ghat *Hin.* range of hills
Ghiol *Rom.* lake
Ghubbat *Ar.* bay, inlet
Gjiri *Alb.* bay
Gjol *Alb.* lagoon, lake
Glava (Gl.) *Ser.-Cr.* mountain, peak
Glen *Gae.* valley
Gletscher (Gl.) *Ger.* glacier
Gobi *Mong.* desert
Gol *Mong.* river
Göl *Azeri, Turk.* lake
Golfe (G.) *Fr.* gulf
Golfo (G.) *It., Span.* gulf
Gölü *Turk.* lake
Gomba *Tib.* settlement
Gora, Góra *Bulg., Russ., Ser.-Cr., Pol.* mountain
Gorje *Ser.-Cr.* hills, mountains
Gorno *Russ.* mountainous
-gorod *Russ.* small town
Gory, Góry *Pol., Russ.* mountain
-grad *Bulg. Russ., Ser.-Cr.* town, city
-grada *Russ.* ridge
Gran *It., Span.* big, great
Grand, -e *Fr.* big, great
Groot (Gt.) *Afr., Dut.* big, great
Gross, -e, -en, -er *Ger.* big, great(er)
Grupo *Span.* group
Gruppo *It.* group
Guan *Chin.* pass
Guba (G.) *Russ.* bay
-Guntō *Jap.* island group
Gunong, Gunung (G.) *Indo., Malay* mountain
Gură *Rom.* passage

Hadabat *Ar.* plateau
Hadjer *Ar.* mountain
-hafen *Ger.* harbour, port
Haff *Ger.* bay, lagoon
Hai *Chin.* lake, sea
Haixia *Chin.* channel, strait
Halbinsel *Ger.* peninsula
Halvø *Dan.* peninsula
Halvøya *Nor.* peninsula
Hāmad, Hamada, Hammādah, Hammādat *Ar.* stony desert, plateau
-hamn *Swe., Nor.* harbour, anchorage
Hāmūn *Farsi* marsh, lake
-Hantō *Jap.* peninsula
Har(e) *Heb.* hill(s), mountain(s)
Hassi (Hi.) *Ar.* well
-haug *Nor.* hill
Hav, Havet *Nor., Swe.* sea
-havn *Dan., Nor.* bay, harbour
Havre *Fr.* harbour
Hawd *Ar.* oasis
Hawr *Ar.* lake, marsh
He *Chin.* river
-hegység *Hung.* hills, forest
Heide *Ger.* heath, moor
Helodranon' *Malag.* bay
Higashi *Jap.* east, eastern
-ho *Kor.* lake
-hø *Nor.* peak
Hoch *Ger.* high
Hochland *Afr.* highland
Hoek, -hoek *Afr., Dut.* cape, point
-höfn *Ice.* harbour, port
-hög, -en, -högar, -högarna *Swe.* hill(s), peak, mountain
Höhe *Ger.* height
Hohen *Ger.* high, upper
-hoi *Chin.* bay
-høj, -e *Dan.* hills
-holm, -holme, -holmen *Dan., Nor., Swe.* island
Hon *Viet.* island
Hoog *Dut.* high
Hora *Czec., Ukr.* mountain
-horn *Ger.* peak
Hory *Czec.* mountains, hills
-hot *Mong.* town
-hoved *Dan.* point, headland, peninsula
-hrad *Czec.* town
Hráun *Ice.* lava
-hsi *Chin.* river
-hsia *Chin.* gorge, strait
-hsien *Chin.* district
Hu *Chin.* lake, reservoir
Huk *Dan., Ger.* cape
-huk *Swe.* cape
Huken *Nor.* cape

Idd *Ar.* well
Idehan *Ar., Berb.* sandy plain, dunes
-ike *Jap.* lake
Île(s) (I(s).) *Fr.* island(s)
Ilha(s) (I(s).) *Port.* island(s)
imeni *Russ.* 'in the name of'
Inish *Gae.* island
Insel(n) (I.) *Ger.* island(s)
Irmak *Turk.* river
'Irq *Ar.* dunes
Isla(s) (I(s).) *Span.* island(s)
Iso *Fin.* big, great
Isol, -a, -e (I.) *It.* island(s)
Isthme *Fr.* isthmus
Istmo *Span.* isthmus
-iwa *Jap.* island

Jabal *Ar.* mountain range
Järv *Est.* lake
järvi *Fin.* lake, bay, pond
-jaur, -javre *Lapp.* lake
Jazā'ir *Ar.* islands
Jazīra, jazīrat *Ar.* island
Jazireh *Farsi* island
Jebel *Ar.* mountain
Jezero *Ser.-Cr.* lake
Jezioro *Pol.* lake
Jiang *Chin.* river
Jiao *Chin.* cape
-Jima *Jap.* island
Jøkulen *Nor.* glacier, ice cap
-joki *Fin.* river
-jökull *Ice.* glacier, ice cap
Jūras Līcis *Lat.* bay, gulf

Kaap (K.) *Afr.* cape
-kai *Jap.* bay, channel, sea
-kaikyō *Jap.* strait
-kaise *Lapp.* mountain
kalnas *Lith.* hill
Kamennyy *Russ.* stony
Kampong *Cam.* village
Kampung *Malay* village
-kanaal *Dut.* canal
Kanal *Dan.* channel, gulf
Kanal *Ger., Swe.* canal
-kanal *Ser.-Cr.* channel, canal
Kanava *Fin.* canal
Kang *Kor.* river, bay
Kap (K.) *Dan., Ger.* cape, point
-kapp *Nor.* cape, point
-kaupstaður *Ice.* market town
-kaupunki *Fin.* town
Kavīr *Farsi* salt desert
Kébir *Ar.* great
Kecil *Malay* lesser, little
Kefar *Heb.* village, hamlet
-Ken *Jap.* first-order administrative division
Kep, -i (K.) *Alb.* cape
Kepulauan (Kep.) *Indo., Malay* archipelago
Keski- *Fin.* middle, central
Khalīg, Khalīj *Ar.* gulf
-khamba *Tib.* source, spring
Khawr *Ar.* bay, channel, wadi
Khlong *Thai* river
Kho Khot *Thai* isthmus
Khōr *Farsi* bay, estuary
Khrebet *Russ.* mountain range
Kita- *Jap.* north
Klein,-e, -er *Ger.* small
-klint *Dan.* cliff
Klintar *Swe.* hills
-kloof *Afr.* gorge, pass
Knude *Dan.* point
-Ko *Jap.* lake
Ko *Thai* island
-kōchi *Jap.* mountainous region
-kōgen *Jap.* plateau
Kohi *Pash.* mountains
Kol *Kaz., Kyrg.* lake
Kólpos *Gr., Turk.* gulf, bay
Kolymskoye *Russ.* mountain range
Kompong *Malay* landing place
-kop *Afr.* hill
-kopf *Ger.* hill
-köping *Swe.* market town
Körfäzi *Azeri* gulf
Körfezi *Turk.* gulf
Kosa *Russ., Ukr.* spit
-koski *Fin.* rapids
-kraal *Afr.* native village
-kraj *Czec., Pol., Ser.-Cr.* region
Krasnyy *Russ.* red
Kryazh *Russ.* ridge, hills
Kuala *Malay* bay
-kuan *Chin.* pass
Kūh(ha) *Farsi* mountain(s)
Kul *Russ.* lake
-kulle *Swe.* hill
Kum *Russ.* sandy desert
Kumpu *Fin.* hill
Kwe *Burm.* bay, gulf
-kylä *Fin.* village
Kyst, -en *Dan., Nor.* coast
Kyun(zu) *Burm.* island(s)

La *Tib.* pass
-laagte *Afr.* watercourse

Lääni *Fin.* first-order administrative division
Lac (L.) *Fr.* lake
Lacul (L.) *Rom.* lake, lagoon
Lago (L.) *It., Port., Span.* lake, lagoon
Lagoa (L.) *Port.* lagoon
Lagos *Port., Span.* lakes
Laguna (L.) *It., Span.* lagoon, lake
Lagune (L.) *Fr.* lake
-laht *Est.* bay
Lahti *Fin.* bay, gulf, cove
Lakhti *Russ.* bay, gulf
Lam *Thai* river
Lampi *Fin.* lake
Län *Swe.* first-order administrative division
Land *Ger.* first-order administrative division
-land *Dan.* region
-land *Afr., Nor.* land, province
Lande *Fr.* heath
Laut *Indo.* sea
Law *Gae.* hill, mountain
Līcis *Lat.* gulf
Lido *It.* beach, shore
Liedao *Chin.* islands
Lilla *Swe.* small
Lille *Dan., Nor.* small
Liman *Russ.* bay, gulf
Límni (L.) *Gr.* lake
Ling *Chin.* mountain range
-linna *Fin.* fort
Llano *Span.* prairie, plain
Llyn *Welsh* lake
Loch (L.) *Gae.* lake, inlet
Lough (L.) *Gae.* lake, inlet
Lum *Alb.* river
Lund *Dan.* forest
-lund, -en *Swe.* wood(s)
-luoto *Fin.* island

-maa *Est.* island
Madīnat *Ar.* town, city
Madiq *Ar.* strait
Maja *Alb.* mountains
-mäki *Fin.* hill, hillside
Mal *Alb.* mountain
Maloye, Malyy, Malyya *Russ.* little, small
Mala, Mali, Malo *Ser.-Cr.* little, small
Malaya *Belo.* small
Malé *Czec., Slovak* small
Mali *Alb.* mountain
-man *Kor.* bay
Mar *Span.* lagoon, sea
Marais *Fr.* marsh
Mare *It.* sea
Mare *Rom.* great
Marisma *Span.* marsh
-mark *Dan., Nor.* land
Marsâ *Ar.* anchorage, bay, inlet
Masabb *Ar.* river mouth, estuary
Massif *Fr.* upland, mountains
Mato *Port.* forest
Mazar *Farsi* shrine, tomb
Meer, -meer *Afr., Dut., Ger.* lake, sea
-men *Chin.* bay, gorge, channel
Mesto *Ser.-Cr., Czec.* town
Mezzo *It.* middle
Midbar *Heb.* wilderness
Mierzeja *Pol.* spit
Mifraz *Heb.* bay
Mina *Ar.* port
Minami *Jap.* south, southern
-misaki *Jap.* cape, point
Mittel *Ger.* central, middle
-mo *Nor., Swe.* heath, island
-mon *Swe.* heath
Mong *Burm.* town
Mont(s) (Mt(s).) *Fr.* hill(s), mountain(s)
Montagna (Mt.) *It.* mountain
Montagne(s) (Mt(s).) *Fr.* hill(s), mountain(s)
Montaña(s) (Mt(s).) *Span.* mountain(s)
Montanyes *Cat.* mountains
Monte(s) (Mte(s).) *It., Port., Span.* mountain(s)
Monti (Mti.) *It.* mountains
More *Russ.* sea
Mörön *Mong.* river
Moyen *Fr.* central, middle
Muang *Malay* town
Mui *Viet.* cape
Mull *Gae.* promontory
Mund, -mund *Afr.* mouth
Munkhafed *Ar.* depression
Munte (Mte.) *Rom.* mount
Munți(i) (Mti.) *Rom.* mountain(s)
Muong *Malay* village
Myit *Burm.* river
Myitwanya *Burm.* mouths of river
Mynydd *Welsh* mountain
-myr *Nor., Swe.* swamp
-mýri *Ice.* swamp
Mys (M.) *Russ.* cape

-Nada *Jap.* bay, gulf
-næs *Dan.* point, cape
Nafūd *Ar.* sandy desert
Nagorye *Russ.* hills, mountains
Nagy *Hung.* big
Nahal (N.) *Heb.* river
Nahr (N.) *Ar.* river, stream
Najd *Ar.* plateau, pass
Nakhon *Thai* town
Nam *Kor., Viet.* river
-nam *Kor.* south
Namakzār *Per.* salt flat
Nan *Chin.* south, southern
-nao *Chin.* lake
-näs *Swe.* cape
Neder *Dut.* lower
Nedre *Nor.* lower
Nei *Chin.* inner
Nek *Afr.* pass
-nes *Ice., Nor.* cape
Ness, -ness *Gae.* promontory, cape
Nevada, Nevado *Span.* snow-capped mountain
Nez *Fr.* cape
Nieder *Ger.* lower
-niemi *Fin.* cape, point, peninsula, island
Nieuw, -e *Dut.* new
Nishi *Jap.* west, western
Nisos, Nisoi *Gr.* island(s)
Nizhneye, Nizhniy *Russ.* lower
Nizina *Belo., Pol.* lowland
Nizmennost *Russ.* plain, lowland
Nízní *Czec.* lower
Noord *Dut.* north, northern
Nord *Fr.* north, northern
Norra *Swe.* north, northern
Nørre *Dan.* north, northern
Norte *Port., Span.* north, northern
Nos *Bulg., Russ.* cape, point
Nosy *Malag.* island
Nouveau, Nouvelle *Fr.* new
Nova, Novi *Bulg., Port., Serb.-Cr.* new
Novaya, Novo, Novoye, Novyy *Russ.* new
Nové, Novy *Czec., Slovak* new
Novo *Port.* new
Nowa, Nowe, Nowy *Pol.* new
Nudo *Span.* mountain
Nueva, Nuevo *Span.* new
Nur *Chin.* lake
Nur *Tib.* peak
Nuruu *Mong.* mountain range
Nusa *Indo.* island
Nuur *Mong.* lake
Ny *Dan., Nor., Swe.* new

-ø *Dan., Nor.* island
-ö *Swe.* island,
-öar, -na *Swe.* islands
Ober *Ger., Ukr.* upper
Oblast *Russ.* administrative division
Öbör *Mong.* inner
Occidental *Fr., Span.* western
-odde *Dan., Nor.* point, peninsula, cape
Oeste *Span.* west, western
Oglat *Ar.* well
Oji *Alb.* bay
Ojo *Span.* spring
-Oki *Jap.* bay
-ön *Swe.* island
Ondör *Mong.* upper
Oost(er) *Dut.* east(ern)
Orașu *Rom.* city
Ord *Gae.* point
Óri *Gr.* mountains
Oriental, -e *Fr., Span.* east, eastern
Órmos *Gr.* bay
Óros *Gr.* mountain(s)
Ort *Ger.* point, cape
Ost *Ger.* east
Øst(er) *Den., Nor.* east(ern)
Öst(ra) *Swe.* east(ern)
Ostriv *Ukr.* island
Ostrov(a) *Russ.* island(s)
Otok(i) *Ser.-Cr.* island(s)
Ouabi, Ouadi (O.) *Ar.* dry watercourse, wadi
Oud, -e *Dut.* old
Oued, -i (O.) *Ar.* watercourse
Ouest *Fr.* west, western
Ouzan *Farsi* river
Ova, -si *Turk.* plains, lowlands
Over- *Dan., Dut.* upper
Över-, Övre *Nor., Swe.* upper
-øy, -a *Nor.* island(s)
Oya *Hin.* point
Oya *Sin.* river
Ozero, Ozera (Oz.) *Russ., Ukr.* lake(s)

-pää *Fin.* hill(s), mountain
Pahta *Lapp.* hill
Pampa(s) *Span.* plain(s)
Pantanal *Port.* marsh
Pantano *Span.* reservoir
Pantao *Chin.* peninsula
Parbat *Urdu* mountain
Pas *Fr.* strait
Paso (P.) *Span.* pass
Passage *Fr.* channel
Passe *Fr.* channel
Passo (P.) *It.* pass
Pasul (P.) *Rom.* pass
Patam *Hin.* small village
Patna, -patnam *Hin.* small village
Pegunungan *Indo., Malay* mountain range
Pei, -pei *Chin.* north
Pélagos *Gr.* sea
Pen *Welsh* hill
Peña *Span.* rock, peak
Pendi *Chin.* basin, depression
Péninsule *Fr.* peninsula
Penisola (Pen.) *It.* peninsula
Pereval (Per.) *Russ.* pass
Pervo-, Pervyy- *Russ.* first
Pertuis *Fr.* channel, strait
Peski *Russ.* sand desert
Petit, -e *Fr.* small
Phanom *Thai* mountain
Phnum *Cam.* mountain
Phou *Lao.* mountain
Phu *Thai, Viet.* mountain
Piano *It.* plain
Pic *Cat., Fr.* peak
Pico(s) *Span.* peak(s)
-piggen *Dan.* peak
Pik *Russ.* peak
Pingyuan *Chin.* plain
Pique *Fr.* peak
Piton *Fr.* peak
Pivostriv *Ukr.* peninsula
Piz, Pizzo *It.* peak
Plage *Fr.* beach
Plaine *Fr.* plain
Planalto *Port.* plateau
Planina (Pl.) *Bulg., Ser.-Cr.* mountain range
Plato *Russ., Bulg.* plateau
Playa *Span.* beach
-po *Chin.* lake, wetland
Pointe (Pte.) *Fr.* point, cape
Pojezierze *Pol.* lakes
Polder *Dut.* reclaimed farmland
-pólis *Gr.* city, town
Poluostrov (Pov.) *Russ.* peninsula
Połwysep *Pol.* peninsula
Pont *Fr.* bridge
Ponta (Pta.) *Port.* point, cape
Ponte *Port.* bridge
Poort *Afr.* passage, gate
-poort *Dut.* port
Porta *Port.* pass
Porțile *Rom.* gate
Portillo *Span.* pass
Porto *It., Port., Span.* port
Potámi, Potamós *Gr.* river
Pradesh *Hin.* state
Praia *Port.* beach, shore
Presa *Span.* reservoir
Presqu'île *Fr.* peninsula
Prokhod *Bulg.* pass
Proliv *Russ.* strait
Promontorio *Span.* promontory
Průsmyk (Pr.) *Czec.* pass
Pueblo *Span.* village
Puerto (Pto.) *Span.* port
Puig *Cat.* peak
Pulau (P.) *Indo., Malay* island
Puna *Span.* desert plateau
Puncak *Indo.* peak
Punta (Pta.) *It., Span.* point, peak
Puy *Fr.* peak

Qal'at *Ar.* fort
Qanat *Ar.* canal
Qasr *Ar.* fort
Qiryat *Heb.* town
Qiuling *Chin.* plateau
Qolleh *Farsi* mountain
-qundao *Chin.* islands

Rach *Viet.* river
Rags *Lat.* cape
Rambla *Cat.* river
Ramlat *Ar.* sandy desert
Rão (R.) *Port.* river
Rann *Hin.* swampy region
Rao *I.-C.* river
Ras *Amh., Ar., Farsi* cape, point
Récif(s) *Fr.* reef(s)
Recife(s) *Port.* reef(s)
Reka *Bulg.* river
Repede *Rom.* rapids
Reprêsa *Port.* reservoir
Reshteh *Farsi* mountain range
-rettō *Jap.* group of islands, chain
Ria *Port., Span.* estuary, bay
Ribeirão (R.) *Port.* river
Ribera (R.) *Span.* river bank
Rijeka *Ser.-Cr.* river
Rio (R.) *Port., Span.* river
Rivier (R.) *Afr., Dut.* river
Riviera *It.* coastal plain, coast
Rivière (R.) *Fr.* river
Roca *Span.* rock
Rocca *It.* rock, peak
Roche *Fr.* rock
Rt *Ser.-Cr.* cape, point
Rubh', Rubha *Gae.* cape, point
-rück *Ger.* ridge
Rūd *Farsi* stream, river
Rudohorie *Slovak* mountains
Rzeka (R.) *Pol.* river

-saar *Est.* island
-saari *Fin.* island
Sabkhat, Sabkhet *Ar.* salt flats
Sadd *Ar.* dam
Sagar,-a *Hin., Urdu* lake
Sahrâ *Ar.* desert
-Saki *Jap.* cape, point
Salar *Span.* salt flat
Salina(s) *Span.* salt marsh(es)
-salmi *Fin.* strait, sound, lake, channel
Saltsjöbad *Swe.* resort
-Sammyaku *Jap.* mountain range
Samut *Thai* gulf
San (S.) *It., Port., Span.* saint
-San *Jap., Kor.* hill, mountain
-Sanchi *Jap.* mountain range
Sankt (St.) *Ger., Russ.* saint
-sanmaek *Kor.* mountain range
-sanmyaku *Jap.* mountain range
Santa (Sta.) *It., Port., Span.* saint
Santo (Sto.) *It. Port., Span.* saint
São (S.) *Port.* saint
Sarīr *Ar.* desert
Sasso *It.* mountain
Satu *Rom.* village
Saurums *Lat.* strait
Sebkha, Sebkhet *Ar.* salt flat
See, -see *Ger.* lake
-şehir *Turk.* town
Selat *Indo., Malay* strait
Selatan *Indo.* southern
-selkä *Fin.* bay, lake, ridge, hills
Selo *Ser.-Cr., Russ.* village
Selva *Port., Span.* forest, wood
Seno *Span.* bay, sound
Serir *Ar.* stony desert
Serra (Sa.) *Cat., Port.* range of hills
Serranía *Span.* mountain ridge
Severo, Severnaya, Severnoye, Severnyy (Sev.) *Russ.* north, northern
Sfântu *Rom.* saint
Shahr, -shahr *Farsi* city, town
Shamo *Chin.* desert
Shan *Chin.* hills, mountains
Shankou *Chin.* pass
Shanmo *Chin.* mountain range
Sharm *Ar.* bay
Shatt *Ar.* river mouth, estuary
-Shima *Jap.* island
Shimāli *Ar.* northern
-Shotō *Jap.* group of islands
-shui *Chin.* river
-shuiku *Chin.* reservoir
Sierra (Sa.) *Span.* mountain range
-sjö, -sjön, -sjø *Swe., Nor.* lake
-sjøen *Dan.* sea
-sjór *Ice.* lake
-sker *Ice.* island
-skär *Swe.* island, rock, cape
-skog, -skogen *Nor., Swe.* wood(s)
-skov *Dan.* forest
Slieve *Gae.* hill, mountain
Sø *Dan., Nor.* lake
Söder, Södra *Swe.* south, southern
Sør *Nor.* south, southern
Solonchak *Russ.* salt lake, marsh
Sønder, Søndra *Dan.* south, southern
Song *Viet.* river
Souk *Ar.* market
-spitze *Ger.* peak, mountain
-spruit *Afr.* stream
Sredna, Sredno *Bulg.* middle, central
Sredne, Sredneye *Russ.* middle, central
Srednja *Ser.-Cr.* middle, central
-stad *Afr., Nor., Swe.* town
-stadt *Ger.* town
-staður *Ice.* town
Stara, Stari *Ser.-Cr.* old
Stará, Staré, Stary *Czec.* old
Staraya, Staroye, Staryy *Russ.* old
Stare, Staro, Stary *Ukr.* old
Stausee *Ger.* reservoir
Stenón *Gr.* strait, pass
Step *Russ.* steppe
Stor, -a *Swe.* big
Store *Dan.* big
-strand *Dan., Ger., Nor., Swe.* beach
-strede *Nor.* straits
Strelka *Russ.* spit
-strete *Nor.* straits
Stretto (Str.) *It.* strait
Strædet (Str.) *Dan.* strait
-ström, -strömmen *Swe.* stream(s)
-stroom *Afr.* large river
Sud *Fr.* south, southern
Süd, -er *Ger.* south, southern
Suid *Afr.* south, southern
-Suidō *Jap.* strait, channel
Sul *Port.* south, southern
Sûn *Burm.* cape
-sund, -et *Dan., Swe., Nor.* sound, estuary, inlet
Sungai *Indo., Malay* river
Sur *Span.* south, southern
Sveti *Bulg.* saint
Syd *Dan., Swe.* south, southern
Sýsla *Ice.* first-order administrative division

-tag *Uighur* mountain
Tai -tai *Chin.* tower
-Take *Jap.* mountain
Tal *Mong.* plain, steppe
-tal *Ger.* valley
Tall *Ar.* hills
Tanjona *Malag.* cape, point
Tanjung, Tanjong (Tg.) *Indo., Malay.* cape, point
Tao *Chin.* island
Tasik *Malay* lake
Tassili *Ar.* rocky plateau
Tau *Russ.* mountain range
Taung *Burm.* mountain
Taungdan. *Burm.* mountain range
Taunggya *Burm.* pass
-tekojärvi *Fin.* reservoir
Teluk *Indo., Malay* bay, gulf
Ténéré *Berb.* desert
Tengah *Indo.* middle, central
-thal *Ger.* valley
Thok *Tib.* town
Tien *Chin.* lake, marsh
Tierra *Span.* land, country
Timur *Indo.* eastern
-tind *Nor.* peak
-ting *Chin.* mountain
Tjärn, -en, -et *Swe.* lake
-Tō *Jap.* island
Tong *Kor.* village, town
Tong *Burm., Thai, Kor.* mountain range
Tonlé *Cam.* lake
Top *Dut.* peak
-topp, -en *Nor.* peak
-träsk *Swe.* lake, swamp
Tsangpo *Tib.* large river
Tso *Tib.* lake
Tsu *Jap.* entrance, bay
Tsui *Chin.* cape, point
Tulur *Ar.* hill
-tunturi *Fin.* hill(s), mountain(s), ridge

Uad *Ar.* dry watercourse, wadi
Über *Ger.* upper
-udde, -udden *Swe.* point, cape
Uebi *Som.* river
Ujung *Indo., Malay* cape
Unter- *Ger.* lower
Us *Mong.* water
Ust, Ustye *Russ.* river mouth
Utara *Indo.* north, northern
Uttar *Hin.* north, northern
Uul *Mong., Russ.* mountain range

-vaara *Fin.* hill, mountain ridge, peak
Vaart *Dut.* canal
-våg *Nor.* bay
Val *Fr., Port., Span.* valley
Valea *Rom.* valley
-vall, -en *Swe.* mountain
Valle *It., Span.* valley
Vallée *Fr.* valley
Valli *It.* lake, lagoon
-város *Hung.* town
-varre *Nor.* mountain
Väst, Västra *Swe.* west, western
-vatn *Ice., Nor.* lake
-vatnet *Nor.* lake
-vatten, vattnet *Swe.* lake
-vecchio *It.* old
Vechi *Rom.* old
-ved, -veden *Swe.* hills
Veld, -veld *Afr.* field
Velha, Velho *Port.* old
Velika, Velike, Veliki, Veliko *Ser.-Cr., Slov.* big, large
Velikaya, Velikiy *Russ.* big, large
Velká, Velké, Velký *Czec.* big, large
Verkhne, Verkhniy *Russ.* upper
-vesi *Fin.* water, lake, bay, sound, strait
Vest, Vester, Vestre *Dan., Nor.* west, western
-vidda *Nor.* plateau
Vieille, Vieux *Fr.* old
Vieja, Vejo *Span.* old
Vig *Dan.* bay, inlet, cove, lagoon, lake
-vík *Ice.* bay
-vik, -a, -en *Nor., Swe.* bay, gulf, inlet, lake
Vila *Port.* small town
Villa *Span.* town
Ville *Fr.* town
Vinh *Viet.* bay
Vîrful (Vf.) *Rom.* peak, mountain
-viz *Hung.* river
-víztároló *Hung.* reservoir
-vlei *Afr.* lake, salt pan
-vliet *Dut.* canal
-vloer *Afr.* salt pan
Vodokhranilishche (Vdkhr.) *Russ.* reservoir
Vodoskovyshche (Vdskh.) *Ukr.* reservoir
Volcán (Vol.) *Span.* volcano, mountain
Vorota *Russ.* pass, channel, strait
Vostochno, Vostochnyy *Russ.* east, eastern
-vötn *Ice.* lakes
Vozvyshennost *Russ.* heights, uplands
Vozyera *Belo.* lake
Vrata *Bulg.* gate, pass
Vrchovina *Czec.* mountainous country
Vrch(y) *Czec.* mountain (range)
Vung *Viet.* bay, gulf
-vuori *Fin.* mountain, hill
Vychodné *Slovak* east, eastern
Vysochyna *Ukr.* upland

-waard *Dut.* polder
Wadi (W.) *Ar.* dry watercourse
Wâhât *Ar.* oasis
Wald *Ger.* forest, mountains
-Wan *Chin., Jap.* bay, harbour
Wāw *Ar.* well
Webi *Amh.* river
Wes *Afr.* west, western
Wielka, Wielki, Wielko *Pol.* big, large
Woestyn *Afr.* desert
Wysoka, Wysoki *Pol.* upper
Wyżyna *Pol.* plateau

Xi *Chin.* river
Xia *Chin.* gorge, strait
Xiao *Chin.* small

Yam *Heb.* sea
-Yama *Jap.* mountain
-yan *Chin.* gorge, island
Yang *Chin.* bay, sea, sound
Yangi *Russ.* new
Yazovir *Bulg.* reservoir
Yeni *Turk.* new
Yli *Fin.* upper
Ynys *Welsh* island
Yoma *Burm.* mountain range
Ytre-, Ytter- *Nor., Swe.* outer
-yuan *Chin.* stream
Yugo- *Ser.-Cr.* south, southern
Yunhe *Chin.* canal
Yuzhni, Yuzhno *Russ.* south, southern

-Zaki *Jap.* point
Zalew *Pol.* lagoon, swamp
Zaliv *Russ.* bay, gulf
-Zan *Jap.* mountain
Zangbo *Tib.* stream, river
Zapadnaya, Zapadno, Zapadnyi (Zap.) *Russ.* west, western
Zatoka *Pol., Ukr.* bay, gulf
-zee *Dut.* lake, sea
Zemlya *Russ.* land, island(s)
Zhang *Chin.* mountain
-zhou *Chin.* island
Zhong *Chin.* middle, central
Zhou *Chin.* island
Zizhiqu *Chin.* autonomous region
Zuid, Zuider *Dut.* south, southern

INDEX TO WORLD MAPS

HOW TO USE THE INDEX

The index contains the names of all the principal places and features shown on the World and City Maps. Each name is followed by an additional entry in italics giving the country or region within which it is located. The alphabetical order of names composed of two or more words is governed primarily by the first word, then by the second, and then by the country or region name that follows. This is an example of the rule:

Mir *Niger*	14°5N 11°59E	**259** F2
Mīr Kūh *Iran*	26°22N 58°55E	**247** E8
Mīr Shahdād *Iran*	26°15N 58°29E	**247** E8
Mira *Italy*	45°26N 12°8E	**199** C9

Physical features composed of a proper name (Erie) and a description (Lake) are positioned alphabetically by the proper name. The description is positioned after the proper name and is usually abbreviated:

Erie, L. *N. Amer.* 42°15N 81°0W **312** D4

Where a description forms part of a settlement or administrative name, however, it is always written in full and put in its true alphabetical position:

Mount Olive *U.S.A.* 39°4N 89°44W **310** E7

Names beginning with M' and Mc are indexed as if they were spelled Mac. Names beginning St. are alphabetized under Saint, but Sankt, Sint, Sant', Santa and San are all spelt in full and are alphabetized accordingly. If the same place name occurs two or more times in the index and all are in the same country, each is followed by the name of the administrative subdivision in which it is located.

The geographical co-ordinates which follow each name in the index give the latitude and longitude of each place. The first co-ordinate indicates latitude – the distance north or south of the Equator. The second co-ordinate indicates longitude – the distance east or west of the Greenwich Meridian. Both latitude and longitude are measured in degrees and minutes (there are 60 minutes in a degree). Latitude and longitude references are not used on the Central Area City Maps.

The latitude is followed by N(orth) or S(outh) and the longitude by E(ast) or W(est).

The number in bold type which follows the geographical co-ordinates refers to the number of the map page where that feature or place will be found. This is usually the largest scale at which the place or feature appears.

The letter and figure that are immediately after the page number give the grid square on the map page, within which the feature is situated. The letter represents the latitude and the figure the longitude. A lower-case letter immediately after the page number refers to an inset map on that page.

In some cases the feature itself may fall within the specified square, while the name is outside. This is usually the case only with features that are larger than a grid square.

Rivers are indexed to their mouths or confluences, and carry the symbol → after their names. The following symbols are also used in the index: ■ country, ☒ overseas territory or dependency, □ first-order administrative area, ☆ U.S. county, △ national park, ⌂ other park (provincial park, nature reserve or game reserve), ⚙ Australian aboriginal land, ▲ U.S. Indian reservation, ✈ (LHR) principal airport (and location identifier).

HOW TO PRONOUNCE PLACE NAMES

English-speaking people usually have no difficulty in reading and pronouncing correctly English place names. However, foreign place name pronunciations may present many problems. Such problems can be minimized by following some simple rules. However, these rules cannot be applied to all situations, and there will be many exceptions.

1. In general, stress each syllable equally, unless your experience suggests otherwise.
2. Pronounce the letter 'a' as a broad 'a' as in 'arm'.
3. Pronounce the letter 'e' as a short 'e' as in 'elm'.
4. Pronounce the letter 'i' as a cross between a short 'i' and long 'e', as the two 'i's in 'California'.
5. Pronounce the letter 'o' as an intermediate 'o' as in 'soft'.
6. Pronounce the letter 'u' as an intermediate 'u' as in 'sure'.
7. Pronounce consonants hard, except in the Romance-language areas where 'g's are likely to be pronounced softly like 'j' in 'jam'; 'j' itself may be pronounced as 'y'; and 'x's may be pronounced as 'h'.
8. For names in mainland China, pronounce 'q' like the 'ch' in 'chin', 'x' like the 'sh' in 'she', 'zh' like the 'j' in 'jam', and 'z' as if it were spelled 'dz'. In general, pronounce 'a' as in 'father', 'e' as in 'but', 'i' as in 'keep', 'o' as in 'or', and 'u' as in 'rule'.

Moreover, English has no diacritical marks (accent and pronunciation signs), although some languages do. The following is a brief and general guide to the pronunciation of those most frequently used in the principal Western European languages.

		Pronunciation as in
French	é	day and shows that the 'e' is to be pronounced; e.g. Orléans.
	è	mare
	î	used over any vowel and does not affect pronunciation; shows contraction of the name, usually omission of 's' following a vowel.
	ç	's' before 'a', 'o' and 'u'.
	ë, ï, ü	over 'e', 'i' and 'u' when they are used with another vowel and shows that each is to be pronounced.
German	ä	fate
	ö	fur
	ü	no English equivalent; like French 'tu'.
Italian	à, é	over vowels and indicates stress.
Portuguese	ã, õ	vowels pronounced nasally.
	ç	boss
	á	shows stress.
	ô	shows that a vowel has an 'i' or 'u' sound combined with it.
Spanish	ñ	canyon
	ü	pronounced as 'w' and separately from adjoining vowels.
	á	usually indicates that this is a stressed vowel.

ABBREVIATIONS

A.C.T. – Australian Capital Territory
A.R. – Autonomous Region
Afghan. – Afghanistan
Afr. – Africa
Ala. – Alabama
Alta. – Alberta
Amer. – America(n)
Ant. – Antilles
Arch. – Archipelago
Ariz. – Arizona
Ark. – Arkansas
Atl. Oc. – Atlantic Ocean
B. – Baie, Bahía, Bay, Bucht, Bugt
B.C. – British Columbia
Bangla. – Bangladesh
Barr. – Barrage
Bos.-H. – Bosnia-Herzegovina
C. – Cabo, Cap, Cape, Coast
C.A.R. – Central African Republic
C. Prov. – Cape Province
Calif. – California
Cat. – Catarata
Cent. – Central
Chan. – Channel
Colo. – Colorado
Conn. – Connecticut
Cord. – Cordillera
Cr. – Creek
D.C. – District of Columbia
Del. – Delaware
Dem. – Democratic
Dep. – Dependency
Des. – Desert
Dét. – Détroit
Dist. – District
Dj. – Djebel
Dom. Rep. – Dominican Republic
E. – East
El Salv. – El Salvador
Eq. Guin. – Equatorial Guinea
Est. – Estrecho
Falk. Is. – Falkland Is.
Fd. – Fjord
Fla. – Florida
Fr. – French
G. – Golfe, Golfo, Gulf, Guba, Gebel
Ga. – Georgia
Gt. – Great, Greater
Guinea-Biss. – Guinea-Bissau
H.K. – Hong Kong
H.P. – Himachal Pradesh
Hants. – Hampshire
Harb. – Harbor, Harbour
Hd. – Head
Hts. – Heights
I.(s). – Île, Ilha, Insel, Isla, Island, Isle
Ill. – Illinois
Ind. – Indiana
Ind. Oc. – Indian Ocean
J. – Jabal, Jebel
Jaz. – Jazīrah
Junc. – Junction
K. – Kap, Kapp
Kans. – Kansas
Kep. – Kepulauan
Ky. – Kentucky
L. – Lac, Lacul, Lago, Lagoa, Lake, Limni, Loch, Lough
La. – Louisiana
Ld. – Land
Liech. – Liechtenstein
Lux. – Luxembourg
Mad. P. – Madhya Pradesh
Madag. – Madagascar
Man. – Manitoba
Mass. – Massachusetts
Md. – Maryland
Me. – Maine
Medit. S. – Mediterranean Sea
Mich. – Michigan
Minn. – Minnesota
Miss. – Mississippi
Mo. – Missouri
Mont. – Montana
Mozam. – Mozambique
Mt.(s) – Mont, Montaña, Mountain
Mte. – Monte
Mti. – Monti
N. – Nord, Norte, North, Northern, Nouveau, Nahal, Nahr
N.B. – New Brunswick
N.C. – North Carolina
N. Cal. – New Caledonia
N. Dak. – North Dakota
N.H. – New Hampshire
N.I. – North Island
N.J. – New Jersey
N. Mex. – New Mexico
N.S. – Nova Scotia
N.S.W. – New South Wales
N.W.T. – North West Territory
N.Y. – New York
N.Z. – New Zealand
Nac. – Nacional
Nat. – National
Nebr. – Nebraska
Neths. – Netherlands
Nev. – Nevada
Nfld. & L. – Newfoundland and Labrador
Nic. – Nicaragua
O. – Oued, Ouadi
Occ. – Occidentale
Okla. – Oklahoma
Ont. – Ontario
Or. – Orientale
Oreg. – Oregon
Os. – Ostrov
Oz. – Ozero
P. – Pass, Passo, Pasul, Pulau
P.E.I. – Prince Edward Island
Pa. – Pennsylvania
Pac. Oc. – Pacific Ocean
Papua N.G. – Papua New Guinea
Pass. – Passage
Peg. – Pegunungan
Pen. – Peninsula, Péninsule
Phil. – Philippines
Pk. – Peak
Plat. – Plateau
Prov. – Province, Provincial
Pt. – Point
Pta. – Ponta, Punta
Pte. – Pointe
Qué. – Québec
Queens. – Queensland
R. – Rio, River
R.I. – Rhode Island
Ra. – Range
Raj. – Rajasthan
Recr. – Recreational, Récréatif
Reg. – Region
Rep. – Republic
Res. – Reserve, Reservoir
Rhld-Pfz. – Rheinland-Pfalz
S. – South, Southern, Sur
Si. Arabia – Saudi Arabia
S.C. – South Carolina
S. Dak. – South Dakota
S.I. – South Island
S. Leone – Sierra Leone
Sa. – Serra, Sierra
Sask. – Saskatchewan
Scot. – Scotland
Sd. – Sound
Sev. – Severnaya
Sib. – Siberia
Sprs. – Springs
St. – Saint
Sta. – Santa
Ste. – Sainte
Sto. – Santo
Str. – Strait, Stretto
Switz. – Switzerland
Tas. – Tasmania
Tenn. – Tennessee
Terr. – Territory, Territoire
Tex. – Texas
Tg. – Tanjung
Trin. & Tob. – Trinidad & Tobago
U.A.E. – United Arab Emirates
U.K. – United Kingdom
U.S.A. – United States of America
Univ. – University, Université, Universidad
Ut. P. – Uttar Pradesh
Va. – Virginia
Vdkhr. – Vodokhranilishche
Vdskh. – Vodoskhovyshche
Vf. – Vírful
Vic. – Victoria
Vol. – Volcano
Vt. – Vermont
W. – Wadi, West
W. Va. – West Virginia
Wall. & F. Is. – Wallis and Futuna Is.
Wash. – Washington
Wis. – Wisconsin
Wlkp. – Wielkopolski
Wyo. – Wyoming
Yorks. – Yorkshire

A

A 'Âli an Nîl = Upper Nile □ South Sudan 9°30N 33°0E 257 F3
A Baiuca Spain 43°19N 8°29W 194 B2
A Baña = San Vicenzo Spain 42°58N 8°46W 194 C2
A Cañiza Spain 42°13N 8°16W 194 C2
A Carballa Spain 43°13N 8°54W 194 B2
A Carreira Spain 43°21N 8°12W 194 B2
A Coruña Spain 43°20N 8°25W 194 B2
A Coruña □ Spain 43°10N 8°30W 194 B2
A Cruz do Incio Spain 42°39N 7°21W 194 C3
A Estrada Spain 42°43N 8°27W 194 C2
A Feira do Monte Spain 43°12N 7°34W 194 B3
A Fonsagrada Spain 43°8N 7°4W 194 B3
A Guarda Spain 41°56N 8°52W 194 D2
A Gudiña Spain 42°4N 7°8W 194 C3
A Pobre Spain 42°58N 7°3W 194 C3
A Ramallosa Spain 42°45N 8°30W 194 C2
A Rúa Spain 42°24N 7°6W 194 C3
A Serra de Outes Spain 42°52N 8°55W 194 C2
A Shau Vietnam 16°6N 107°22E 236 D6
A.N.R. Robinson Int. ✈ (TAB) Trin. & Tob. 11°9N 60°50W 323 s
A.N.Z. Stadium Sydney, Australia 33°51S 151°5E 139 B1
A.R.M.M. = Bangsamoro □ Phil. 8°0N 123°0E 233 H3
Aabenraa Denmark 55°3N 9°25E 163 J3
Aabybro Denmark 57°10N 9°44E 163 G3
Aachen Germany 50°45N 6°6E 178 E2
Aalām Iraq 33°19N 44°23E 113 B2
Aalborg Denmark 57°2N 9°54E 163 G3
Aalborg Bugt Denmark 56°50N 10°35E 163 H4
Aalen Germany 48°51N 10°6E 179 G6
Aalestrup Denmark 56°42N 9°29E 163 H3
Aalsmeer Neths. 52°16N 4°46E 112 B1
Aalst Belgium 50°56N 4°2E 170 D4
Aalten Neths. 51°56N 6°35E 170 C6
Aalter Belgium 51°5N 3°28E 170 C3
Äänekoski Finland 62°36N 25°44E 160 E21
Aarau Switz. 47°23N 8°4E 179 H4
Aarberg Switz. 47°2N 7°16E 179 H3
Aare → Switz. 47°33N 8°14E 179 H4
Aargau □ Switz. 47°26N 8°10E 179 H4
Aarhus Denmark 56°8N 10°11E 163 H4
Aarlen = Arlon Belgium 49°42N 5°49E 170 E5
Aars Denmark 56°48N 9°30E 163 H3
Aarschot Belgium 50°59N 4°49E 170 D4
Aasiaat Greenland 68°43N 52°56W 154 D5
Ab-i-Istada Afghan. 32°29N 67°55E 240 B3
Ab-i-Panja = Pyandzh → Asia 37°6N 68°20E 240 A2
Aba Sichuan, China 32°59N 101°42E 228 A3
Aba Dem. Rep. of the Congo 3°58N 30°17E 268 B3
Aba Nigeria 5°10N 7°19E 263 D6
Âbâ, Jazîrat Sudan 13°30N 32°31E 257 E3
Abacaxis → Brazil 3°54S 58°47W 329 D6
Abaco The Bahamas 26°25N 77°10W 320 A4
Abadab, J. Sudan 18°54N 35°56E 256 D4
Ābādān Iran 30°22N 48°20E 247 D6
Abade Ethiopia 9°22N 38°3E 257 F4
Ābādeh Iran 31°8N 52°40E 247 D7
Abadín Spain 43°21N 7°29W 194 B3
Abadla Algeria 31°2N 2°45W 261 B4
Abaeté Brazil 19°9S 45°27W 333 E2
Abaeté → Brazil 18°2S 45°12W 333 E2
Abaetetuba Brazil 1°40S 48°50W 332 B2
Abagnar Qi = Xilinhot China 43°52N 116°2E 226 C9
Abah, Tanjung Indonesia 8°46S 115°38E 231 K18
Abai Paraguay 25°58S 55°54W 335 B4
Abakaliki Nigeria 6°22N 8°2E 263 D6
Abakan Russia 53°40N 91°10E 217 B12
Abala Congo 1°17S 15°35E 264 C3
Abala Niger 14°56N 3°22E 263 C5
Abalak Niger 15°22N 6°21E 263 B6
Abalemma Algeria 20°51N 5°59E 261 D6
Abalemma Niger 16°12N 7°50E 263 B6
Abalessa Algeria 22°58N 4°47E 261 D5
Abana Turkey 41°59N 34°1E 212 B6
Abancay Peru 13°35S 72°55W 330 C3
Abang, Gunung Indonesia 8°16S 115°25E 231 J18
Abanga → Gabon 0°20S 10°30E 264 C2
Abano Terme Italy 45°22N 11°46E 199 C8
Abapó Bolivia 18°48S 63°25W 331 D5
Abarán Spain 38°12N 1°23W 197 G3
Abariringa Kiribati 2°50S 171°40W 277 A16
Abarqū Iran 31°10N 53°20E 247 D7
Abasha Georgia 42°11N 42°13E 191 J6
Abashiri Japan 44°0N 144°15E 220 B12
Abashiri-Wan Japan 44°0N 144°30E 220 C12
Abau Papua N. G. 10°11S 148°46E 286 F5
Abaújszántó Hungary 48°16N 21°12E 182 B6
Abava → Latvia 57°6N 21°54E 184 A8
Ābay = Nîl el Azraq → Sudan 15°38N 32°31E 257 D3
Abay Kazakhstan 49°38N 72°53E 217 C8
Abaya, L. Ethiopia 6°30N 37°50E 257 F4
Abaza Russia 52°39N 90°6E 217 B12
Abba C.A.R. 5°20N 15°11E 264 A3
Abbadia di Fiastra ⌓ Italy 43°12N 13°24E 199 E10
Abbadia San Salvatore Italy 42°53N 11°41E 199 F8
'Abbāsābād Iran 33°34N 58°23E 247 C8
Abbay = Nîl el Azraq → Sudan 15°38N 32°31E 257 D3
Abbaye, Pt. U.S.A. 46°58N 88°8W 308 B9
Abbazia = Opatija Croatia 45°21N 14°17E 199 C11
Abbé, L. Ethiopia 11°8N 41°47E 257 E5
Abbeville Somme, France 50°6N 1°49E 173 B8
Abbeville Ala., U.S.A. 31°34N 85°15W 316 D4
Abbeville Ga., U.S.A. 31°59N 83°18W 316 D6
Abbeville La., U.S.A. 29°58N 92°8W 314 G8
Abbeville S.C., U.S.A. 34°11N 82°23W 316 A7
Abbey Wood U.K. 51°29N 0°7E 125 B4
Abbeyfeale Ireland 52°23N 9°18W 166 D2
Abbeyleix Ireland 52°54N 7°22W 166 D4
Abbiategrasso Italy 45°24N 8°54E 198 C5
Abbot Ice Shelf Antarctica 73°0S 92°0W 151 D16
Abbotsford Canada 49°5N 122°20W 296 D4
Abbottabad Pakistan 34°10N 73°15E 242 B5
Abbou, O. ben → Algeria 28°32N 5°14E 261 C6
ABC Islands W. Indies 12°15N 69°0W 322 g
Abcoude Neths. 52°17N 4°59E 112 B2
Abd al Kūrī Yemen 12°5N 52°20E 249 D6
Ābdānān Iran 32°56N 47°28E 213 F12
Ābdar Iran 30°16N 55°19E 247 D7
Âbdîn Egypt 30°2N 31°14E 117 A2
'Abdolābād Iran 34°12N 56°30E 247 C8
Abdulino Russia 53°42N 53°40E 216 B4
Abdullah South Sudan 5°30N 29°55E 257 F3
Abdulpur Bangla. 24°15N 88°59E 243 G13
Abéché Chad 13°50N 20°35E 259 F4
Abejar Spain 41°48N 2°47W 196 D2
Abekr Sudan 12°45N 28°50E 257 E2
Abel Tasman △ N.Z. 40°59S 173°3E 285 A8
Abengourou Côte d'Ivoire 6°42N 3°27W 262 D4
Abeno Japan 34°38N 135°31E 133 B2
Abenójar Spain 38°53N 4°21W 195 G6
Åbenrå = Aabenraa Denmark 55°3N 9°25E 163 J3
Abensberg Germany 48°48N 11°51E 179 G7
Abeokuta Nigeria 7°3N 3°19E 263 D5
Aberaeron U.K. 52°15N 4°15W 169 E3
Aberayron = Aberaeron U.K. 52°15N 4°15W 169 E3
Aberchirder U.K. 57°34N 2°37W 167 D6
Abercorn = Mbala Zambia 8°46S 31°24E 269 D3
Abercorn Australia 25°12S 151°5E 281 D5
Abercrombie River △ Australia 34°5S 149°40E 283 C8
Aberdare U.K. 51°43N 3°27W 169 F4
Aberdare △ Kenya 0°22S 36°44E 268 C4
Aberdare Ra. Kenya 0°15S 36°50E 268 C4
Aberdaugleddau = Milford Haven U.K. 51°42N 5°7W 169 F2
Aberdeen N.S.W., Australia 32°9S 150°56E 283 B9
Aberdeen Sask., Canada 52°20N 106°8W 297 C7
Aberdeen Hong Kong, China 22°14N 114°8E 122 B2
Aberdeen Eastern Cape, S. Africa 32°28S 24°2E 270 D3
Aberdeen Aberd. City, U.K. 57°9N 2°5W 167 D6
Aberdeen Idaho, U.S.A. 42°57N 112°50W 304 E7
Aberdeen Md., U.S.A. 39°31N 76°10W 309 F15
Aberdeen Miss., U.S.A. 33°49N 88°33W 315 E10
Aberdeen Ohio, U.S.A. 38°39N 83°46W 311 F13
Aberdeen S. Dak., U.S.A. 45°28N 98°29W 308 C4
Aberdeen Wash., U.S.A. 46°59N 123°50W 306 D3
Aberdeen City □ U.K. 57°10N 2°10W 167 D6
Aberdeen Country Park ⌓ Hong Kong, China 22°16N 114°9E 122 B2
Aberdeen L. Canada 64°30N 99°0W 294 E12
Aberdeenshire □ U.K. 57°17N 2°36W 167 D6
Aberdour U.K. 56°3N 3°18W 121 A2
Aberdour Castle U.K. 56°3N 3°18W 121 A2
Aberdovey = Aberdyfi U.K. 52°33N 4°3W 169 E3
Aberdyfi U.K. 52°33N 4°3W 169 E3
Aberfeldy U.K. 56°37N 3°51W 167 E5
Aberfoyle U.K. 56°11N 4°23W 167 E4
Abergavenny U.K. 51°49N 3°1W 169 F4
Abergele U.K. 53°17N 3°35W 168 D4
Abergwaun = Fishguard U.K. 52°0N 4°58W 169 E3
Aberhonddu = Brecon U.K. 51°57N 3°23W 169 F4
Abermaw = Barmouth U.K. 52°44N 4°4W 168 E3
Abernathy U.S.A. 33°50N 101°51W 314 E4
Aberpennar = Mountain Ash U.K. 51°40N 3°23W 169 F4
Abert, L. U.S.A. 42°38N 120°14W 304 E3
Abertawe = Swansea U.K. 51°37N 3°57W 169 F4
Aberteifi = Cardigan U.K. 52°5N 4°40W 169 E3
Aberystwyth U.K. 52°25N 4°5W 169 E3
Abfanggraben → Germany 48°10N 11°41E 131 A3
Abhā Si. Arabia 18°0N 42°34E 248 C3
Abhar Iran 36°9N 49°13E 213 D13
Abhayapuri India 26°24N 90°38E 241 B3
Abia □ Nigeria 5°30N 7°35E 263 D6
Abiad, Es Sahrâ el Egypt 28°0N 28°0E 256 B2
Abide Turkey 38°55N 29°20E 205 C11
Abidiya Sudan 18°18N 34°3E 256 D3
Abidjan Côte d'Ivoire 5°26N 3°58W 262 D4
Abidjan □ Côte d'Ivoire 5°20N 4°0W 262 D4
Abilene Kans., U.S.A. 38°55N 97°13W 308 F5
Abilene Tex., U.S.A. 32°28N 99°43W 314 E5
Abingdon Ill., U.S.A. 40°48N 90°24W 310 D6
Abingdon Va., U.S.A. 36°43N 81°59W 309 G13
Abingdon, I. = Pinta, I. Ecuador 0°35N 90°44W 330 a
Abingdon-on-Thames U.K. 51°40N 1°17W 169 F6
Abington Reef Australia 18°0S 149°35E 280 B4
Abiod, Remel el Tunisia 31°45N 9°35E 261 B6
Abisko △ Sweden 68°18N 18°44E 160 B18
Abitau → Canada 59°53N 109°3W 297 B7
Abitibi → Canada 51°3N 80°55W 298 B3
Abitibi, L. Canada 48°40N 79°40W 298 C4
Abiy Adi Ethiopia 13°39N 39°3E 257 E4
Abiyata, L. Ethiopia 7°37N 38°36E 266 C4
Abiyata-Shala △ Ethiopia 7°40N 38°37E 257 F4
Abkhaz Republic = Abkhazia □ Georgia 43°12N 41°5E 191 J5
Abkhazia □ Georgia 43°12N 41°5E 191 J5
Ablon-sur-Seine France 48°43N 2°25E 134 B3
Abminga Australia 26°8S 134°51E 281 D1
Abnûb Egypt 27°18N 31°4E 256 B3
Åbo = Turku Finland 60°30N 22°19E 188 B2
Abo, Massif d' Chad 21°41N 16°8E 259 D3
Abohar India 30°10N 74°10E 242 D6
Aboisso Côte d'Ivoire 5°30N 3°5W 262 D4
Abolo Congo 0°8N 14°16E 264 B2
Abomey Benin 7°10N 2°5E 263 D5
Abong-Mbang Cameroon 4°0N 13°8E 264 B2
Abongabong Indonesia 4°15N 96°48E 234 B1
Abonnema Nigeria 4°41N 6°49E 263 E6
Abony Hungary 47°12N 20°3E 182 C5
Abor Hills India 28°25N 94°46E 241 A5
Aborlan Phil. 9°26N 118°33E 233 G2
Aboso Ghana 5°23N 1°57W 262 D4
Abou-Deïa Chad 11°20N 19°20E 259 F3
Abou-Goulem Chad 13°37N 21°38E 259 F4
Abou-Telfan ⌓ Chad 12°2N 18°58E 259 F3
Abovyan Armenia 40°16N 44°37E 191 K7
Aboyne U.K. 57°4N 2°47W 167 D6
Abra □ Phil. 17°35N 120°45E 232 C3
Abra de Ilog Phil. 13°27N 120°44E 232 E3
Abra Pampa Argentina 22°43S 65°42W 334 A2
Abraham L. Canada 52°15N 116°35W 296 C5
Abramtsevo Russia 55°49N 37°49E 129 B3
Abrantes Portugal 39°24N 8°7W 195 F2
Abreojos, Pta. Mexico 26°50N 113°40W 318 B2
Abri Esh Shamâliya, Sudan 20°50N 30°27E 256 C3
Abri Janub Kordofân, Sudan 11°40N 30°21E 257 E3
Abrolhos, Banco dos Brazil 18°0S 38°0W 333 E4
Abrud Romania 46°19N 23°5E 182 D8
Abruzzo □ Italy 42°15N 14°0E 199 F10
Absaroka Range U.S.A. 44°45N 109°50W 304 D9
Abşeron Yarımadası Azerbaijan 40°28N 49°57E 191 K9
Abtenau Austria 47°33N 13°21E 180 D6
Abu India 24°41N 72°50E 242 G5
Abū aḑ Ḑuhūr Syria 35°44N 37°2E 250 C8
Abū al Abyad U.A.E. 24°11N 53°50E 247 E7
Abū al Khaşīb Iraq 30°25N 48°0E 246 D5
Abū 'Alī Si. Arabia 27°20N 49°27E 247 E6
Abū 'Alī → Lebanon 34°25N 35°50E 250 D6
Abū 'Arīsh Si. Arabia 16°53N 42°48E 248 C3
Abu 'Aweigîla Egypt 30°50N 34°7E 251 H5
Abu Ballas Egypt 24°26N 27°36E 256 C2
Abu Deleiq Sudan 15°57N 33°48E 257 D3
Abu Dhabi = Abū Z̧āby U.A.E. 24°28N 54°22E 247 E7
Abu Dis Sudan 19°12N 33°38E 256 D3
Abu Dis West Bank 31°46N 35°16E 123 B2
Abu Dom Sudan 16°18N 32°25E 257 D3
Abū Du'ān Syria 36°25N 38°15E 213 D8
Abu el Gaīn, W. → Egypt 29°35N 33°30E 251 J4
Abû en Numrus Egypt 29°57N 31°12E 117 B2
Abu Fatma, Ras Sudan 22°25N 36°25E 256 C4
Abu Gabra Sudan 11°2N 26°50E 257 E2
Abu Ga'da, W. → Egypt 29°15N 32°53E 251 J3
Abu Gelba Sudan 13°11N 31°52E 257 E3
Abu Ghosh Israel 31°48N 35°6E 123 B1
Abu Gubeiha Sudan 11°30N 31°15E 257 E3
Abu Habl, Khawr → Sudan 12°37N 31°0E 257 E3
Abū Ḩadrīyah Si. Arabia 27°20N 48°58E 247 E6
Abu Hail U.A.E. 25°17N 55°20E 119 A2
Abu Hamed Sudan 19°32N 33°13E 256 D3
Abu Haraz An Nîl el Azraq, Sudan 18°1N 33°58E 256 D3
Abu Haraz El Gezira, Sudan 14°35N 33°30E 257 E3
Abu Haraz Esh Shamâliya, Sudan 19°8N 32°18E 256 D3
Abu Higar Sudan 12°50N 33°59E 257 E3
Abū Kamāl Syria 34°30N 41°0E 213 E9
Abu Kebîr Egypt 30°43N 31°40E 251 H2
Abu Kuleiwat Sudan 12°20N 26°0E 257 E2
Abū Madd, Ra's Si. Arabia 24°50N 37°7E 246 E3
Abu Matariq Sudan 10°59N 26°9E 257 E2
Abu Mena = Abu Mina Egypt 30°51N 29°40E 256 H6
Abu Mendi Ethiopia 11°48N 35°42E 257 E4
Abu Mina Egypt 30°51N 29°40E 256 H6
Abū Mūsā U.A.E. 25°52N 55°3E 247 E7
Abū Nujaym Libya 30°35N 15°24E 258 B3
Abū Qaşr Si. Arabia 30°21N 38°34E 246 D3
Abu Qireiya Egypt 24°5N 35°28E 256 C4
Abu Qurqâs Egypt 28°1N 30°44E 256 B3
Abū Raşāş, Ra's Oman 20°10N 58°38E 249 B7
Abu Rudeis Egypt 28°54N 33°11E 251 K4
Abu Shagara, Ras Sudan 21°4N 37°19E 256 C4
Abu Shanab Janub Kordofân, Sudan 10°47N 29°32E 266 B2
Abu Shanab Shamâl Kordofân, Sudan 13°58N 27°49E 257 E2
Abu Simbel Egypt 22°18N 31°40E 256 C3
Abu Soma, Râs Egypt 26°51N 33°58E 256 B3
Abū Şukhayr Iraq 31°54N 44°30E 213 G11
Abu Sultân Egypt 30°24N 32°21E 256 H8
Abu Tabari Sudan 17°32N 28°32E 256 D2
Abu Tig Egypt 27°4N 31°15E 256 B3
Abu Tiga Sudan 12°47N 34°12E 257 E3
Abu Tineitin Sudan 14°24N 31°1E 257 E3
Abu Uruq Sudan 15°52N 30°25E 257 D3
Abu Zabad Sudan 12°25N 29°10E 257 E2
Abū Z̧āby U.A.E. 24°28N 54°22E 247 E7
Abū Zeydābād Iran 33°54N 51°45E 247 C6
Abufari Brazil 5°25S 62°59W 331 B5
Abuja Nigeria 9°5N 7°32E 263 D6
Abukuma-Gawa → Japan 38°6N 140°52E 220 E10
Abukuma-Sammyaku Japan 37°30N 140°45E 220 F10
Abulug Phil. 18°27N 121°27E 232 B3
Abumombazi Dem. Rep. of the Congo 3°42N 22°10E 264 B4
Abunã Brazil 9°40S 65°20W 331 B4
Abunã → Brazil 9°41S 65°20W 331 B4
Abune Yosef Ethiopia 12°5N 39°12E 257 E4
Aburatsu Japan 31°34N 131°24E 222 F3
Aburo Dem. Rep. of the Congo 2°4N 30°53E 268 B3
Abut Hd. N.Z. 43°7S 170°15E 285 D5
Abuye Meda Ethiopia 10°30N 39°49E 257 E4
Abuyog Phil. 10°45N 125°0E 233 F5
Abwong South Sudan 9°2N 32°14E 257 F3
Åby Sweden 58°40N 16°10E 163 F10
Aby, Lagune Côte d'Ivoire 5°15N 3°14W 262 D4
Abyad Sudan 13°47N 26°24E 257 E2
Abyān □ Yemen 13°50N 46°0E 248 D4
Abyei Sudan 9°36N 28°26E 257 F2
Abyei ⊠ Sudan 9°30N 28°30E 257 F2
Ābyek Iran 36°4N 50°33E 247 B6
Acacías Colombia 3°59N 73°46W 328 C3
Acacias Madrid, Spain 127 c2
Academy Gletscher Greenland 82°2N 34°0W 154 A7
Acadia △ U.S.A. 44°20N 68°13W 309 C19
Açailândia Brazil 4°57S 47°30W 332 B2
Acajutla El Salv. 13°36N 89°50W 320 D2
Acámbaro Mexico 20°2N 100°44W 318 D4
Acandí Colombia 8°32N 77°14W 328 B2
Acanthus Greece 40°27N 23°47E 202 F7
Acaponeta Mexico 22°30N 105°22W 318 C3
Acapulco Mexico 16°51N 99°55W 319 D5
Acapulco Trench Pac. Oc. 12°0N 88°0W 318 D4
Acará Brazil 1°57S 48°11W 332 B2
Acaraí, Serra Brazil 1°50N 57°50W 329 C6
Acarai Mts. = Acaraí, Serra Brazil 1°50N 57°50W 329 C6
Acaraú Brazil 2°53S 40°7W 332 B3
Acari Brazil 6°31S 36°38W 332 C4
Acarí Peru 15°25S 74°36W 330 D3
Acarigua Venezuela 9°33N 69°12W 328 B4
Acassuso Argentina 34°29S 58°30W 117 A2
Acatlán Mexico 18°12N 98°3W 319 D5
Acayucán Mexico 17°57N 94°55W 319 D6
Accademia, Galleria dell' Venice, Italy 142 b2
Accademia, Ponte dell' Venice, Italy 142 b2
Accéglio Italy 44°28N 7°0E 198 D4
Accomac U.S.A. 37°43N 75°40W 309 G16
Accous France 43°0N 0°36W 174 E3
Accra Ghana 5°35N 0°6W 263 D4
Accrington U.K. 53°45N 2°22W 168 D5
Acebal Argentina 33°20S 60°50W 334 C3
Aceh □ Indonesia 4°15N 97°30E 234 B1
Acerra Italy 40°57N 14°22E 201 B7
Aceuchal Spain 38°39N 6°30W 195 G4
Achacachi Bolivia 16°3S 68°43W 330 D4
Achaguas Venezuela 7°46N 68°14W 328 B4
Achaia Greece 38°5N 21°45E 204 C3
Achalpur India 21°22N 77°32E 244 D3
Achao Chile 42°28S 73°30W 336 B2
Acharnes Greece 38°5N 23°44E 204 C5
Achegour Niger 19°10N 11°54E 259 E2
Acheloos → Greece 38°19N 21°7E 204 C3
Achelouma Niger 22°12N 12°50E 259 D2
Achelouma, Enneri → Niger 21°55N 13°35E 259 D2
Acheng China 45°30N 126°58E 227 B14
Achenkirch Austria 47°32N 11°45E 180 D4
Achénouma Niger 19°7N 12°55E 259 E2
Achensee Austria 47°26N 11°45E 180 D4
Achentrias Greece 34°59N 25°13E 205 G7
Acher India 23°10N 72°32E 242 H5
Achères France 48°57N 2°3E 134 A1
Achern Germany 48°37N 8°4E 179 G4
Acheron → N.Z. 42°16S 173°4E 285 C8
Achill Hd. Ireland 53°58N 10°15W 166 C1
Achill I. Ireland 53°58N 10°1W 166 C1
Achim Germany 53°1N 9°3E 178 B5
Achinsk Russia 56°20N 90°20E 215 D10
Achladokambos Greece 37°31N 22°35E 204 D4
Achouka Gabon 0°52S 9°45E 264 C2
Acıgöl Turkey 37°50N 29°50E 205 D11
Acília Italy 41°47N 12°21E 136 C1
Acıpayam Turkey 37°26N 29°22E 205 D11
Acireale Italy 37°37N 15°10E 201 E8
Ackerman U.S.A. 33°19N 89°11W 315 E10
Ackley U.S.A. 42°33N 93°3W 310 B3
Acklins The Bahamas 22°30N 74°0W 321 B5
Aclimação Brazil 23°34S 46°37W 137 B2
Acme Alta., Canada 51°33N 113°30W 296 C6
Acme Pa., U.S.A. 40°8N 79°26W 312 F5
Acobamba Peru 12°52S 74°35W 330 C3
Acomayo Peru 13°55S 71°38W 330 C3
Aconcagua, Cerro Argentina 32°39S 70°0W 334 C2
Aconquija, Mt. Argentina 27°0S 66°0W 334 B2
Acopiara Brazil 6°6S 39°27W 332 C4
Açores, Is. dos Atl. Oc. 38°0N 27°0W 153 d1
Acorizal Brazil 15°12S 56°22W 331 D6
Acornhoek S. Africa 24°37S 31°2E 271 B5
Acoua Mayotte 12°43S 45°4E 272 b
Acquapendente Italy 42°44N 11°52E 199 F8
Acquasanta Terme Italy 42°46N 13°24E 199 F10
Acquasparta Italy 42°41N 12°33E 199 F9
Acquaviva delle Fonti Italy 40°54N 16°50E 201 B9
Ácqui Terme Italy 44°41N 8°28E 198 D5
Acraman, L. Australia 32°2S 135°23E 281 E2
Acre = 'Akko Israel 32°55N 35°4E 250 F6
Acre □ Brazil 9°1S 71°0W 330 B3
Acre → Brazil 8°45S 67°22W 330 B4
Acri Italy 39°29N 16°23E 201 C9
Acropolis Athens, Greece 112 c2
Acs Hungary 47°42N 18°2E 182 C3
Actæon Mt. = Diana's Peak St. Helena 15°58S 5°42W 153 h
Actéon, Groupe French Polynesia 21°20S 136°30W 289 f
Actinolite Canada 44°32N 77°19W 312 B7
Actium Greece 38°57N 20°45E 207 B2
Acton Ont., Canada 43°38N 80°3W 312 C4
Acton London, U.K. 51°30N 0°16W 125 A2
Açu Brazil 5°34S 36°54W 332 C4
Açúcar, Pão de Brazil 22°56S 43°9W 135 B2
Acul = Vidin Bulgaria 43°59N 22°50E 202 C6
Acworth U.S.A. 34°4N 84°41W 316 A5
Ad Dafinah Si. Arabia 23°18N 41°58E 248 B3
Aḑ Ḑafrah U.A.E. 23°30N 54°30E 249 B6
Ad Daghghāran Iraq 32°8N 44°55E 213 G11
Aḑ Ḑaḩī Yemen 15°13N 43°4E 248 D3
Ad Dahnā Si. Arabia 24°30N 48°10E 249 A5
Ad Dākhilīyah □ Oman 22°30N 57°30E 249 B7
Aḑ Ḑālī' Yemen 13°42N 44°44E 248 D4
Aḑ Ḑālī' □ Yemen 13°42N 44°44E 248 D4
Ad Dammām Si. Arabia 26°20N 50°5E 247 E6
Ad Dāmūr Lebanon 33°43N 35°27E 250 E6
Ad Darb Si. Arabia 18°2N 43°7E 248 C3
Ad Dawādimī Si. Arabia 24°35N 44°15E 246 E5
Ad Dawḩah Qatar 25°15N 51°35E 247 E6
Ad Dawr Iraq 34°27N 43°47E 213 E10
Ad Dhakhīrah Qatar 25°44N 51°33E 247 E6
Aḑ Ḑiffah Libya 30°30N 24°30E 258 B4
Ad Dilam Si. Arabia 23°55N 47°10E 248 B4
Ad Dir'īyah Si. Arabia 24°44N 46°35E 246 E5
Ad Dīwānīyah Iraq 32°0N 45°0E 213 F11
Ad Dujayl Iraq 33°51N 44°14E 213 F11
Ad Duqm Oman 19°39N 57°42E 249 C7
Ad Duwayd Si. Arabia 30°15N 42°17E 246 D4
Ada Ghana 5°44N 0°40E 263 D5
Ada Serbia 45°49N 20°9E 182 E5
Ada Minn., U.S.A. 47°18N 96°31W 308 B5
Ada Ohio, U.S.A. 40°46N 83°49W 311 D13
Ada Okla., U.S.A. 34°46N 96°41W 314 D6
Ada Beja Portugal 38°47N 9°13W 126 A1
Adad Somalia 9°27N 46°49E 267 C6
Adado, Ras Somalia 11°19N 48°39E 267 B6
Adair, C. Canada 71°30N 71°34W 295 C17
Adaja → Spain 41°32N 4°52W 194 D6
Adak U.S.A. 51°45N 176°45W 303 L3
Adak I. U.S.A. 51°45N 176°45W 303 L3
Ådalsbruk Norway 60°43N 11°19E 164 D8
Adam Oman 22°15N 57°28E 249 B7
Adam, Mt. Falk. Is. 51°34S 60°4W 153 f
Adama = Nazret Ethiopia 8°32N 39°22E 257 F4
Adamantina Brazil 21°42S 51°4W 333 F1
Adamaoua □ Cameroon 6°30N 13°30E 263 D7
Adamaoua, Massif de l' Cameroon 7°20N 12°20E 263 D7
Adamasta Channel Hong Kong, China 22°14N 114°1E 122 B2
Adamawa □ Nigeria 9°20N 12°30E 263 D7
Adamawa Highlands = Adamaoua, Massif de l' Cameroon 7°20N 12°20E 263 D7
Adamello, Mte. Italy 46°9N 10°30E 198 B7
Adamello ⌓ Italy 46°4N 10°28E 198 B7
Adami Tulu Ethiopia 7°53N 38°41E 257 F4
Adaminaby Australia 36°0S 148°45E 283 D8
Adams Mass., U.S.A. 42°38N 73°7W 313 D11
Adams N.Y., U.S.A. 43°49N 76°1W 313 C8
Adams Wis., U.S.A. 43°57N 89°49W 308 D9
Adams, Mt. U.S.A. 46°12N 121°30W 306 D5
Adam's Bridge Sri Lanka 9°15N 79°40E 245 K4
Adams L. Canada 51°10N 119°40W 296 C5
Adams Park U.S.A. 33°43N 84°27W 113 B2
Adam's Peak Sri Lanka 6°48N 80°30E 245 L5
Adamuz Spain 38°2N 4°32W 195 G6
'Adan Yemen 12°45N 45°0E 248 D4
Adana Turkey 37°0N 35°16E 250 B6
Adana □ Turkey 37°0N 35°30E 250 B6
Adanero Spain 40°56N 4°36W 194 E6
Adang, Ko Thailand 6°33N 99°18E 237 J2
Adapazarı = Sakarya Turkey 40°48N 30°25E 212 B4
Adar Gwagwa, J. Sudan 22°15N 35°20E 256 C4
Adarama Sudan 17°10N 34°52E 257 D3
Adare Ireland 52°34N 8°47W 166 D3
Adare, C. Antarctica 71°0S 171°0E 151 D11
Adarte Eritrea 13°18N 42°8E 257 E5
Adaut Indonesia 8°8S 131°7E 231 F8
Adavale Australia 25°52S 144°32E 281 D3
Adda → Italy 45°8N 9°53E 198 C6
Addatigala India 17°31N 82°3E 244 F6
Addax ⌓ Niger 19°17N 9°22E 259 E1
Addis Ababa = Addis Abeba Ethiopia 9°2N 38°42E 257 F4
Addis Abeba Ethiopia 9°2N 38°42E 257 F4
Addis Alem Ethiopia 9°0N 38°17E 257 F4
Addis Zemen Ethiopia 12°7N 37°47E 257 E4
Addiscombe U.K. 51°22N 0°4W 125 B3
Addison Ill., U.S.A. 41°55N 88°0W 311 C8
Addison N.Y., U.S.A. 42°1N 77°14W 312 D7
Addo S. Africa 33°32S 25°45E 270 D4
Addo △ S. Africa 33°30S 25°50E 270 D4
Addu Atoll Maldives 0°38S 73°10E 272 d
Adebour Niger 13°17N 11°50E 259 F2
Ādeh Iran 37°42N 45°11E 246 B5
Adeje Canary Is. 28°7N 16°43W 153 e1
Adel Ga., U.S.A. 31°8N 83°25W 316 D6
Adel Iowa, U.S.A. 41°37N 94°1W 310 C2
Adel Bagrou Mauritania 15°29N 6°57W 262 B3
Adelaide S. Austral., Australia 34°52S 138°30E 282 C3
Adelaide Eastern Cape, S. Africa 32°42S 26°20E 270 D4
Adelaide I. Antarctica 67°15S 68°30W 151 C17
Adelaide Pen. Canada 68°15N 97°30W 294 D12
Adelaide River Australia 13°15S 131°7E 278 B5
Adelaide Village The Bahamas 25°0N 77°31W 153 b
Adelanto U.S.A. 34°35N 117°22W 307 L9
Adelaye C.A.R. 7°7N 22°49E 264 A4
Adele I. Australia 15°32S 123°9E 278 C3
Adélie, Terre Antarctica 68°0S 140°0E 151 C10
Adelie Land = Adélie, Terre Antarctica 68°0S 140°0E 151 C10
Adelong Australia 35°16S 148°4E 283 C8
Adelphi U.S.A. 39°0N 76°58W 143 A3
Adelsk Belarus 53°24N 23°47E 184 E10
Adelunga Toghi Uzbekistan 42°7N 70°58E 217 D8
Ademuz Spain 40°5N 1°13W 196 E3
Aden = 'Adan Yemen 12°45N 45°0E 248 D4
Aden, G. of Ind. Oc. 12°30N 47°30E 267 B6
Adendorp S. Africa 32°15S 24°30E 270 D3
Aderbissinat Niger 15°34N 7°54E 263 B6
Aderklaa Austria 48°17N 16°32E 142 A3
Adh Dhayd U.A.E. 25°17N 55°53E 247 E7
Adhoi India 23°26N 70°32E 242 H4
Adi Indonesia 4°15S 133°30E 231 E8
Adi Arkai Ethiopia 13°35N 37°57E 257 E4
Adi Daro Ethiopia 14°20N 38°14E 257 E4
Adi Keyih Eritrea 14°51N 39°22E 257 E4
Adi Kwala Eritrea 14°38N 38°48E 257 E4
Adi Ugri Eritrea 14°58N 38°48E 257 E4
Adieu, C. Australia 32°0S 132°10E 279 F5
Adieu Pt. Australia 15°14S 124°35E 278 C3
Adigala Ethiopia 10°24N 42°15E 257 E5
Adige → Italy 45°9N 12°20E 199 C9
Adigrat Ethiopia 14°20N 39°26E 257 E4
Adıgüzel Barajı Turkey 38°13N 29°14E 205 C11
Adilabad India 19°33N 78°20E 244 E4
Adilcevaz Turkey 38°47N 42°43E 213 C10
Adīrī Libya 27°32N 13°2E 258 C2
Adirondack ⌓ U.S.A. 44°0N 74°20W 313 C10
Adirondack Mts. U.S.A. 44°0N 74°0W 313 C10
Adis Abeba = Addis Abeba Ethiopia 9°2N 38°42E 257 F4
Adıyaman Turkey 37°45N 38°16E 213 D8
Adıyaman □ Turkey 37°30N 38°10E 213 D8
Adjim Tunisia 33°47N 10°50E 258 B2
Adjohon Benin 6°41N 2°32E 263 D5
Adjud Romania 46°7N 27°10E 183 D12
Adjumani Uganda 3°20N 31°50E 268 B3
Adjuntas Puerto Rico 18°10N 66°43W 321 b
Adlavik Is. Canada 55°0N 58°40W 299 B8
Adler Russia 43°28N 39°52E 191 J4
Adler Planetarium Chicago, U.S.A. 41°51N 87°36W 119 B3
Admer Algeria 20°21N 5°27E 261 D6
Admer, Erg d' Algeria 24°0N 9°5E 261 D6
Admiralteyskaya Storona Russia 59°56N 30°20E 137 B2
Admiralty G. Australia 14°20S 125°55E 278 B4
Admiralty Gulf ☼ Australia 14°16S 125°52E 278 B4
Admiralty I. U.S.A. 57°30N 134°30W 296 B2
Admiralty Inlet Canada 72°30N 86°0W 295 C14
Admiralty Is. Papua N. G. 2°0S 147°0E 286 B4
Admiralty Island ⌓ U.S.A. 57°40N 134°10W 303 H14
Adnan Menderes, İzmir ✈ (ADB) Turkey 38°23N 27°6E 205 C9
Ado Nigeria 6°36N 2°56E 263 D5
Ado-Ekiti Nigeria 7°38N 5°12E 263 D6
Adok South Sudan 8°10N 30°20E 257 F3
Adola Ethiopia 11°14N 41°44E 257 E5
Adolfo González Chaves Argentina 38°2S 60°5W 334 D3
Adolfo Ruiz Cortines, Presa Mexico 27°15N 109°6W 318 B3
Adonara Indonesia 8°15S 123°5E 231 F6
Adoni India 15°33N 77°18E 245 G3
Adony Hungary 47°6N 18°52E 182 C3
Adour → France 43°32N 1°32W 174 E2
Adra India 23°30N 86°42E 243 H12
Adra Spain 36°43N 3°3W 195 J7
Adrano Italy 37°40N 14°50E 201 E7
Adrar Algeria 27°51N 0°19W 261 C4
Adrar □ Algeria 27°0N 1°0W 261 C5
Adrar □ Mauritania 20°10N 10°0W 260 D3
Adrar des Iforas Africa 19°40N 1°40E 261 D5
Adré Chad 13°40N 22°20E 259 F4
Ádria Italy 45°3N 12°3E 199 C9
Adrian Ga., U.S.A. 32°33N 82°35W 316 C7
Adrian Mich., U.S.A. 41°54N 84°2W 311 C12
Adrian Mo., U.S.A. 38°24N 94°21W 310 F2
Adrian Tex., U.S.A. 35°16N 102°40W 314 D3
Adrianople = Edirne Turkey 41°40N 26°34E 203 E10
Adriatic Sea Medit. S. 43°0N 16°0E 193 C7
Adua Indonesia 1°45S 129°50E 231 E7
Adung Long Myanmar 28°7N 97°42E 241 A6
Adur India 9°8N 76°40E 245 K3
Adwa Ethiopia 14°15N 38°52E 257 E4
Adygea □ Russia 45°0N 40°0E 191 H5
Adzhar Republic = Ajaria □ Georgia 41°30N 42°0E 191 K6
Adzhibakul = Qazımämmäd Azerbaijan 40°3N 49°0E 191 K9
Adzopé Côte d'Ivoire 6°7N 3°49W 262 D4
Aegae = Aigai Greece 40°28N 22°19E 202 F6
Ægean Sea Medit. S. 38°30N 25°0E 205 C7
Aerhtai Shan Mongolia 46°40N 92°45E 217 C12
Ærø Denmark 54°52N 10°25E 163 K4
Ærøskøbing Denmark 54°53N 10°24E 163 K4
Aetdia-Akarnania = Etoloakarnania Greece 38°45N 21°18E 204 C3
Aetos Greece 37°15N 21°50E 204 D3
Afaahiti Tahiti 17°45S 149°17W 289 e
Afafi, Massif d' Niger 22°11N 15°10E 259 D3
'Afak Iraq 32°4N 45°15E 213 F11
Afandou Greece 36°18N 28°12E 206 E12
Afar □ Ethiopia 12°0N 41°0E 257 E5
Afarag, Erg Algeria 23°50N 2°47E 261 D5
Afareaitu Moorea 17°33S 149°47W 289 e
Åfarnes Norway 62°40N 7°32E 164 B4
Afdega Ethiopia 6°4N 43°30E 267 C5
Afdem Ethiopia 9°28N 41°0E 267 C5
Áffori Italy 45°31N 9°10E 128 A2
Affton U.S.A. 38°33N 90°20W 310 F6
Afghanistan ■ Asia 33°0N 65°0E 240 B2
Afgooye Somalia 2°7N 44°59E 267 D5
'Afīf Si. Arabia 23°53N 42°56E 248 B3
Afikpo Nigeria 5°53N 7°54E 263 D6
Aflandshage Denmark 55°33N 12°35E 118 B3
Aflisses, O. → Algeria 28°40N 0°50E 261 C5
Aflou Algeria 34°7N 2°3E 261 B5
Afmadow Somalia 0°31N 42°4E 267 D5
Afogados da Ingàzeira Brazil 7°45S 37°39W 332 C4
Afognak I. U.S.A. 58°15N 152°30W 303 G9
Afono B. Amer. Samoa 14°15S 170°38W 302 f
Afore Papua N. G. 9°9S 148°23E 286 E5
Afragóla Italy 40°55N 14°18E 201 B7
Afram → Ghana 7°0N 0°52W 263 D4
Afrera Ethiopia 13°16N 41°5E 257 E5
Africa 10°0N 20°0E 254 E6
'Afrīn Syria 36°32N 36°50E 250 B7
'Afrīn → Syria 36°20N 36°35E 250 B7
Afşar → Turkey 37°2N 32°35E 250 A3
Afsarīyeh Iran 35°39N 51°30E 141 B2
Afşin Turkey 38°14N 36°55E 212 C7
Afton Iowa, U.S.A. 41°2N 94°12W 310 C2
Afton N.Y., U.S.A. 42°14N 75°32W 313 D9
Afton Wyo., U.S.A. 42°44N 110°56W 304 E8
Afuá Brazil 0°15S 50°20W 329 D7
'Afula Israel 32°37N 35°17E 250 F6
Afumba Zambia 15°38S 24°56E 265 F4
Afyon Turkey 38°45N 30°33E 205 C12
Afyon □ Turkey 38°25N 30°30E 205 C12
Afyonkarahisar = Afyon Turkey 38°45N 30°33E 205 C12
Aga Egypt 30°55N 31°10E 256 H7
Aga I. Micronesia 7°29N 151°43E 287 T18
Āgā Jarī Iran 30°42N 49°50E 247 D6
Agadem Niger 16°50N 13°11E 259 E2
Agadés = Agadez Niger 16°58N 7°59E 259 E1
Agadez Niger 16°58N 7°59E 259 E1
Agadir Morocco 30°28N 9°55W 260 B3
Agaete Canary Is. 28°6N 15°43W 153 e1
Agaie Nigeria 9°1N 6°18E 263 D6
Agalas Greece 37°43N 20°47E 207 D2
Agalega Is. Mauritius 11°0S 57°0E 273 F4
Agana = Hagåtña Guam 13°28N 144°45E 302 d
Agana B. Guam 13°29N 144°45E 302 d
Ağapınar Turkey 39°48N 30°47E 205 B12
Agar India 23°40N 76°2E 242 H7
Agar → India 21°0N 82°57E 244 D6
Agâraktem Mali 23°8N 6°22W 260 D3
Agaro Ethiopia 7°50N 36°38E 257 F4
Agartala India 23°50N 91°23E 241 D3
Agăş Romania 46°28N 26°15E 183 D11
Agassiz Canada 49°14N 121°46W 296 D4
Agassiz Icecap Canada 80°15N 76°0W 295 A16
Agat Guam 13°25N 144°40E 302 d
Agats Indonesia 5°33S 138°0E 231 F9
Agatti I. India 10°50N 72°12E 245 J1
Agattu I. U.S.A. 52°25N 173°35E 303 K1
Agawam U.S.A. 42°5N 72°37W 313 D12
Agbélouvé Togo 6°35N 1°14E 263 D5
Agboville Côte d'Ivoire 5°55N 4°15W 262 D4
Agboyi Cr. → Nigeria 6°33N 3°24E 124 A2
Ağcabädi Azerbaijan 40°5N 47°27E 191 K8
Ağdam Azerbaijan 40°0N 46°58E 191 K8
Ağdara Azerbaijan 40°13N 46°49E 191 K8
Ağdaş Azerbaijan 40°44N 47°22E 191 K8
Agde France 43°19N 3°28E 174 E7
Agde, C. d' France 43°16N 3°28E 174 E7
Agdz Morocco 30°47N 6°30W 260 B3
Agdzhabedi = Ağcabädi Azerbaijan 40°5N 47°27E 191 K8
Agen France 44°12N 0°38E 174 D4
Ageo Japan 35°58N 139°36E 223 B11
Ager Tay Chad 20°0N 17°41E 259 E3
Agerbæk Denmark 55°36N 8°48E 163 J2
Agersø Denmark 55°13N 11°12E 163 J5
Ågerup Denmark 55°43N 12°19E 118 A1
Ågesta Sweden 59°12N 18°6E 139 B2
Ageyevo Russia 54°10N 36°27E 188 E9
Aggteleki △ Hungary 48°27N 20°36E 182 B5
Āgh Kand Iran 37°15N 48°4E 213 D13
Aghathonisi Greece 37°28N 27°0E 205 D8
Aghia Anna Greece 38°52N 23°24E 204 C5
Aghia Deka Greece 35°3N 24°58E 207 E5
Aghia Ekaterinis, Akra Greece 39°50N 19°50E 206 B9
Aghia Galini Greece 35°6N 24°41E 207 E5
Aghia Marina Athina, Greece 37°48N 23°51E 112 C3
Aghia Marina Kasos, Greece 35°27N 26°53E 205 F8
Aghia Marina Leros, Greece 37°11N 26°48E 205 D8
Aghia Paraskevi Athina, Greece 38°1N 23°49E 112 A2
Aghia Paraskevi Voreio Aigaio, Greece 39°14N 26°21E 205 B8
Aghia Roumeli Greece 35°14N 23°58E 207 E4
Aghia Varvara Greece 35°8N 25°1E 207 E6
Aghiasos Greece 39°5N 26°23E 205 B8
Aghio Theodori Greece 37°55N 23°9E 204 D5
Aghion Oros = Athos Greece 40°9N 24°22E 203 F8
Aghion Oros □ Greece 40°25N 24°6E 203 F8
Aghios Andreas Greece 37°21N 22°45E 204 D4
Aghios Dimitrios Greece 37°53N 23°44E 112 B2
Aghios Efimia Greece 38°18N 20°36E 207 C2
Aghios Efstratios Greece 39°34N 24°58E 204 B6
Aghios Georgios Greece 37°28N 23°57E 204 D5
Aghios Ioannis, Akra Greece 35°20N 25°40E 207 E6
Aghios Ioannis Rendis Greece 37°57N 23°39E 112 B1
Aghios Isidoros Greece 36°9N 27°51E 206 E11
Aghios Kirikos Greece 37°34N 26°17E 205 D8
Aghios Leon Greece 37°47N 20°43E 207 D2
Aghios Matheos Greece 39°30N 19°47E 206 C9
Aghios Mironas Greece 35°15N 25°1E 207 E6
Aghios Nikolaos Etoloakarnania, Greece 38°52N 20°48E 207 B2
Aghios Nikolaos Kriti, Greece 35°11N 25°41E 207 E6
Aghios Nikolaos Lefkada, Greece 38°36N 20°34E 207 B2
Aghios Petros Greece 38°40N 20°36E 207 B2
Aghios Stephanos Greece 39°46N 19°39E 206 B9
Aghios Thekli Greece 38°15N 20°23E 207 C1
Aghios Thomas Greece 38°58N 20°47E 207 B2
Aghiou Orous, Kolpos Greece 40°6N 24°0E 202 F7
Aghireşu Romania 46°53N 23°15E 183 D8
Aghoueyyît Mauritania 21°10N 15°6W 260 D1
Aghreïjît Mauritania 21°58N 12°11W 260 D2
Agia Greece 39°43N 22°45E 204 B4
Agincourt Canada 43°47N 79°16W 141 A3
Aginskoye Russia 51°6N 114°32E 215 D12
Agjert Mauritania 16°23N 9°17W 262 B3
Ağlasun Turkey 37°39N 30°31E 205 D12
Agly → France 42°46N 3°3E 174 F7
Agmar Mauritania 25°18N 10°50W 260 C2
Agnew Australia 28°1S 120°31E 279 E3
Agnibilékrou Côte d'Ivoire 7°10N 3°11W 262 D4
Agnita Romania 45°59N 24°40E 183 E9
Agnone Italy 41°48N 14°22E 199 G11
Ago Japan 34°20N 136°51E 223 C8
Ago-Are Nigeria 8°30N 3°25E 263 D5
Agofie Ghana 8°27N 0°15E 263 D5
Agogna → Italy 45°4N 8°54E 198 C5
Agoitz = Aoiz Spain 42°46N 1°22W 196 C3
Agön Sweden 61°34N 17°23E 162 C11
Agon-Coutainville France 49°2N 1°34W 172 C5
Agoo Phil. 16°20N 120°22E 232 C3
Agora Athens, Greece 112 c1
Ágordo Italy 46°18N 12°2E 199 B9
Agori India 24°33N 82°57E 243 G10
Agouifa Mauritania 19°57N 16°10W 260 E1
Agouna Benin 7°39N 1°47E 263 D5
Agout → France 43°47N 1°41E 174 E5
Agra India 27°17N 77°58E 242 F7
Agra Canal India 28°33N 77°17E 120 B2
Agrakhanskiuy Poluostrov Russia 43°42N 47°36E 191 J8
Agram = Zagreb Croatia 45°50N 15°58E 199 C12
Agramunt Spain 41°48N 1°6E 196 D6
Ágreda Spain 41°51N 1°55W 196 D3
Ağri Turkey 39°44N 43°3E 213 C10
Ağri □ Turkey 39°45N 43°5E 213 C10
Agri → Italy 40°13N 16°44E 201 B9
Ağrı Dağı Turkey 39°50N 44°15E 213 C11
Ağri Karakose = Ağri Turkey 39°44N 43°3E 213 C10
Agria Greece 39°20N 23°1E 204 B5
Agricola Oriental Mexico 19°23N 99°4W 128 B2
Agrigento Italy 37°19N 13°34E 200 E6
Agrihan N. Marianas 18°46N 145°40E 302 a
Agrinio Greece 38°37N 21°27E 204 C3
Agrópoli Italy 40°21N 14°59E 201 B7
Ağstafa Azerbaijan 41°7N 45°27E 191 K7
Água Branca Brazil 5°50S 42°40W 332 C3
Agua Caliente Mexico 32°29N 116°59W 307 N10
Agua Caliente Springs U.S.A. 32°56N 116°19W 307 N10
Água Clara Brazil 20°25S 52°45W 331 E7
Água Espraiada → Brazil 23°36S 46°41W 137 B2
Agua Fria ⌓ U.S.A. 34°14N 112°0W 305 J8
Agua Hechicera Mexico 32°28N 116°15W 307 N10
Água Preta → Brazil 1°41S 63°48W 329 D5
Agua Prieta Mexico 31°18N 109°34W 318 A3
Aguachica Colombia 8°19N 73°38W 328 B3
Aguada Puerto Rico 18°23N 67°11W 321 b
Aguada Cecilio Argentina 40°51S 65°51W 336 B3
Aguadas Colombia 5°40N 75°38W 328 B2
Aguadilla Puerto Rico 18°26N 67°10W 321 C6
Aguadulce Panama 8°15N 80°32W 320 E3
Agualva-Cacem Portugal 38°46N 9°15W 126 A1
Aguanga U.S.A. 33°27N 116°51W 307 M10
Aguanish Canada 50°14N 62°2W 299 B7
Aguanish → Canada 50°13N 62°5W 299 B7
Aguapeí Brazil 16°12S 59°43W 331 D6
Aguapeí → Brazil 21°0S 51°0W 333 F1

Aguapey → Argentina 29°7S 56°36W 334 B4
Aguaray Guazú →
Paraguay 24°47S 57°19W 334 A4
Aguarico → Ecuador 0°59S 75°11W 328 D2
Aguaro-Guariquito △
Venezuela 8°20N 66°35W 328 B4
Aguas → Spain 41°20N 0°30W 196 D4
Aguas Blancas Chile 24°15S 69°55W 334 A2
Aguas Calientes, Sierra de
Argentina 25°26S 66°40W 334 B2
Águas Formosas Brazil 17°5S 40°57W 333 E3
Águas Lindas de Goiás
Brazil 15°46S 48°15W 333 E2
Aguascalientes Mexico 21°53N 102°18W 318 C4
Aguascalientes □ Mexico 22°0N 102°20W 318 C4
Aguateca Guatemala 16°25N 90°11W 320 C1
Agudo Spain 38°59N 4°52W 195 G6
Águeda Portugal 40°34N 8°27W 194 E2
Agueda → Spain 41°2N 6°56W 194 D4
Aguelhok Mali 19°29N 0°52E 261 E5
Aguelt el Melah
Mauritania 23°3N 10°40W 260 D2
Agüenit W. Sahara 22°11N 13°8W 260 D2
Aguié Niger 13°31N 7°46E 263 C6
Aguila, Punta Puerto Rico 17°57N 67°13W 321 b
Aguilafuente Spain 41°13N 4°7W 194 D6
Aguilar de Campóo Spain 42°47N 4°15W 194 C6
Aguilar de la Frontera
Spain 37°31N 4°40W 195 H6
Aguilares Argentina 27°26S 65°35W 334 B2
Águilas Spain 37°23N 1°35W 197 H3
Agüimes Canary Is. 27°58N 15°27W 153 e1
Aguja, C. de la Colombia 11°18N 74°12W 328 A3
Agujereada, Pta.
Puerto Rico 18°30N 67°8W 321 b
Agulaa Ethiopia 13°40N 39°40E 257 E4
Agulhas, C. S. Africa 34°52S 20°0E 270 D3
Agulhas Ridge Atl. Oc. 42°0S 15°0E 152 L13
Agulo Canary Is. 28°11N 17°12W 153 e1
Agung, Gunung
Indonesia 8°20S 115°28E 231 J18
Aguni-Jima Japan 26°30N 127°10E 221 L3
Agur Uganda 2°28N 32°55E 268 B3
Agurei → South Sudan 7°45N 33°0E 257 F3
Agusan → Phil. 9°0N 125°30E 233 G5
Agusan del Norte □ Phil. 9°20N 125°10E 233 G5
Agusan del Sur □ Phil. 8°30N 125°30E 233 G5
Agustin Codazzi Colombia 10°2N 73°14W 328 A3
Agutaya I. Phil. 11°9N 120°58E 233 F3
Ağva Turkey 41°8N 29°51E 203 E13
Agvali Russia 42°36N 46°8E 191 J8
Aha Mts. Botswana 19°45S 21°0E 270 A3
Ahad Rifaydah Si. Arabia 17°50N 42°50E 248 C3
Ahafo □ Ghana 7°0N 2°20W 262 D4
Ahaggar Algeria 23°0N 6°30E 261 D6
Ahaggar △ Algeria 23°0N 4°50E 261 D5
Ahai Dam China 27°21N 100°30E 228 D3
Ahal □ Turkmenistan 37°0N 57°0E 216 E5
Ahamansu Ghana 7°38N 0°35E 263 D5
Ahar Iran 38°35N 47°0E 213 C12
Ahat Turkey 38°39N 29°47E 205 C11
Ahaura → N.Z. 42°21S 171°34E 285 C6
Ahaus Germany 52°4N 7°0E 178 C2
Ahé French Polynesia 14°30S 146°18W 289 f
Åheim Norway 62°2N 5°13E 164 B2
Ahelledjem Algeria 26°37N 6°58E 261 C6
Ahimanawa Ra. N.Z. 39°3S 176°30E 284 F5
Ahioma Papua N. G. 10°20S 150°33E 286 F6
Ahipara B. N.Z. 35°5S 173°5E 284 B2
Ahir Dağı Turkey 38°45N 30°10E 205 C12
Ahiri India 19°30N 80°0E 244 E5
Ahlat Turkey 38°45N 42°29E 213 C10
Ahlen Germany 51°45N 7°53E 178 D3
Ahmad Wal Pakistan 29°18N 65°58E 242 E1
Ahmadabad India 23°0N 72°40E 242 H5
Aḥmadābād Khorāsān, Iran 35°3N 60°50E 247 C9
Aḥmadābād Khorāsān,
Iran 35°49N 59°42E 247 C8
Aḥmadī Iran 27°56N 56°42E 247 E8
Ahmadnagar India 19°7N 74°46E 244 E2
Ahmadpur India 18°40N 76°57E 244 E3
Ahmadpur East Pakistan 29°12N 71°10E 242 E4
Ahmadpur Lamma
Pakistan 28°19N 70°3E 242 E4
Ahmanson Theater Los Angeles, U.S.A. 127 b2
Ahmar, Mts. Ethiopia 9°20N 41°15E 257 F5
Ahmedabad = Ahmadabad
India 23°0N 72°40E 242 H5
Ahmednagar = Ahmadnagar
India 19°7N 74°46E 244 E2
Ahmetbey Turkey 41°26N 27°34E 203 E11
Ahmetler Turkey 38°28N 29°5E 205 C11
Ahmetli Turkey 38°32N 27°57E 205 C9
Ahmeyim Mauritania 20°51N 14°25W 260 D2
Ahoada Nigeria 5°8N 6°36E 263 D6
Ahome Mexico 25°55N 109°11W 318 B3
Ahon, Tarso Chad 20°23N 18°18E 259 D3
Ahoskie U.S.A. 36°17N 76°59W 315 C16
Ahr → Germany 50°32N 7°16E 178 E3
Ahram Iran 28°52N 51°16E 247 D6
Ahrax Pt. Malta 36°0N 14°22E 206 F7
Ahrensbök Germany 54°2N 10°35E 178 A6
Ahrensburg Germany 53°40N 10°13E 178 B6
Ahrensfelde Germany 52°34N 13°34E 115 A4
Ahtopol Bulgaria 42°6N 27°56E 203 D11
Ahu Akivi Chile 27°7S 109°24W 330 b
Ahu Tepeu Chile 27°6S 109°25W 330 b
Ahu Tongariki Chile 27°8S 109°17W 330 b
Ahu Vinapu Chile 27°10S 109°25W 330 b
Ahuachapán El Salv. 13°54N 89°52W 320 D2
'Āhuimanu U.S.A. 21°26N 157°50W 302 K14
Ahun France 46°4N 2°5E 173 F9
Ahuntsic Canada 45°32N 73°41W 130 A1
Ahunui French Polynesia 19°39S 140°25W 289 f
Ahuriri → N.Z. 44°31S 170°12E 285 E5
Åhus Sweden 55°56N 14°18E 163 J8
Ahvāz Iran 31°20N 48°40E 247 D6
Ahvenanmaa = Åland
Finland 60°15N 20°0E 161 F19
Aḥwar Yemen 13°30N 46°40E 248 D4
Ahzar → Mali 15°30N 3°20E 263 B5
Ai → India 26°26N 90°44E 241 B3
Ai → Ōsaka, Japan 34°46N 135°35E 133 A2
Ai-Ais Namibia 27°54S 17°59E 270 C2
Ai-Ais and Fish River Canyon △
Namibia 24°45S 17°15E 270 B2
Aiari → Brazil 1°22N 68°36W 328 C4
Aichach Germany 48°27N 11°8E 179 G7
Aichi □ Japan 35°0N 137°15E 223 C9
'Aiea U.S.A. 21°23N 157°56W 302 K14
Aigai Greece 40°28N 22°19E 202 F6
Aigle Switz. 46°18N 6°58E 179 J2
Aignay-le-Duc France 47°40N 4°43E 173 E11
Aigoual, Mt. France 44°8N 3°35E 174 D7
Aigre France 45°54N 0°1E 174 C4
Aigremont France 48°54N 2°1E 134 A1
Aigrettes, Île aux Mauritius 20°25S 57°43E 272 e
Aiguá Uruguay 34°13S 54°46W 335 C5
Aigueperse France 46°3N 3°13E 173 F10
Aigues → France 44°7N 4°43E 175 D8
Aigues-Mortes France 43°35N 4°12E 175 E8
Aigues-Mortes, G. d' France 43°31N 4°3E 175 E8
Aigües-Tortes i Estany de St.
Maurici △ Spain 42°38N 0°31E 196 C4
Aiguilles France 44°47N 6°51E 175 D10
Aiguillon France 44°18N 0°21E 174 D4
Aigurande France 46°27N 1°49E 173 F8
Aihui = Heihe China 50°10N 127°30E 219 A14
Aija Peru 9°50S 77°45W 330 B2
Aikawa Japan 38°2N 138°15E 220 E9
Aiken U.S.A. 33°34N 81°43W 316 B8
Ailao Shan China 24°0N 101°20E 228 F3
Aileron Australia 22°39S 133°20E 280 C1
Ailey U.S.A. 32°11N 82°34W 316 C7
Ailigandi Panama 9°14N 78°1W 328 B2
Aillant-sur-Tholon France 47°52N 3°20E 173 E10
Aillik Canada 55°11N 59°18W 299 A8
Ailsa Craig Ont., Canada 43°8N 81°33W 312 C3
Ailsa Craig S. Ayrs., U.K. 55°15N 5°6W 167 F3
Ailuluai Papua N. G. 9°38S 150°35E 286 E6
Aim Russia 59°0N 133°55E 215 D14
Aimogasta Argentina 28°33S 66°50W 334 B2
Aimorés Brazil 19°30S 41°4W 333 E3
Ain □ France 46°5N 5°20E 173 F12
Ain → France 45°45N 5°11E 175 C9
Aïn Beïda Algeria 35°50N 7°29E 261 A6
Aïn Ben Khellil Algeria 33°15N 0°49W 261 B4
Aïn Ben Tili Mauritania 25°59N 9°27W 260 C3
Aïn Beni Mathar Morocco 34°1N 2°0W 261 B4
Aïn Benian Algeria 36°48N 2°55E 261 A5
Ain Dalla Egypt 27°20N 27°23E 256 B2
Aïn Defla Algeria 36°16N 1°58E 261 A5
Aïn Defla □ Algeria 36°10N 2°10E 261 A5
Ain el Akhḍar Egypt 28°50N 33°55E 251 K4
Ain el Mafki Egypt 27°30N 28°15E 256 B2
Ain Girba Egypt 29°20N 25°14E 256 B2
Aïn M'lila Algeria 36°2N 6°35E 261 A6
Ain Murr Sudan 21°50N 25°9E 256 C2
Ain Qeiqab Egypt 29°42N 24°55E 256 B1
Aïn Salah = In Salah
Algeria 27°10N 2°32E 261 C5
Aïn Sefra Algeria 32°47N 0°37W 261 B4
Ain Sheikh Murzûk
Egypt 26°47N 27°45E 256 B2
Ain Sudr Egypt 29°50N 33°6E 251 J4
Ain Sukhna Egypt 29°32N 32°20E 256 J8
Aïn Tédelès Algeria 36°0N 0°21E 261 A5
Aïn Témouchent Algeria 35°16N 1°8W 261 A4
Aïn Témouchent □ Algeria 35°20N 1°5W 261 A4
Aïn Tikkidine Algeria 25°33N 1°24E 261 C5
Aïn Touta Algeria 35°26N 5°54E 261 A6
Ain Zeitûn Egypt 29°10N 25°48E 256 B2
Aïn Zorah Morocco 34°37N 3°32W 261 B4
Ainaži Latvia 57°50N 24°24E 188 D3
Ainos Oros Greece 38°9N 20°40E 207 C2
Ainsworth U.S.A. 42°33N 99°52W 308 D4
Aintab = Gaziantep Turkey 37°6N 37°23E 250 A8
Aioi Japan 34°48N 134°28E 222 C6
Aiome Papua N. G. 5°8S 144°44E 286 C3
Aipe Colombia 3°13N 75°15W 328 C2
Aiquile Bolivia 18°10S 65°10W 331 D4
Aïr Niger 18°30N 8°0E 259 E1
Air Canada Centre Toronto, Canada 141 c2
Aïr et Ténéré △ Niger 18°12N 9°56E 263 B6
Air Force I. Canada 67°58N 74°5W 295 D17
Air Hitam Malaysia 1°55N 103°11E 237 M4
Air View Park Singapore 1°20N 103°46E 138 A2
Aira Japan 31°43N 130°43E 222 F2
Airaines France 49°58N 1°55E 173 C8
Airão Brazil 1°56S 61°22W 329 D5
Airbangis Indonesia 0°12N 99°22E 234 B1
Airdrie Alta., Canada 51°18N 114°2W 296 C6
Airdrie N. Lanarks., U.K. 55°52N 3°57W 167 F5
Aire → Meuse, France 49°18N 4°54E 173 C11
Aire → N. Yorks., U.K. 53°43N 0°55W 168 D7
Aire, I. de l' Spain 39°48N 4°16E 206 B5
Aire-sur-la-Lys France 50°37N 2°22E 173 B9
Aire-sur-l'Adour France 43°42N 0°15W 174 E3
Aireys Inlet Australia 38°29S 144°5E 282 E6
Airlie Beach Australia 20°16S 148°43E 280 b
Airport West Australia 37°42S 144°52E 128 A1
Airvault France 46°50N 0°8W 172 F6
Aisch → Germany 49°49N 10°58E 179 F6
Aisne □ France 49°42N 3°40E 173 C10
Aisne → France 49°26N 2°50E 173 C9
Ait India 25°54N 79°14E 243 G8
Aït Ben Haddou Morocco 31°3N 7°7W 260 B3
Aït Melloul Morocco 30°20N 9°30W 260 B3
Aitana, Sierra de Spain 38°35N 0°24W 197 G4
Aitape Papua N. G. 3°11S 142°22E 286 B2
Aitkin U.S.A. 46°32N 93°42W 308 B7
Aitutaki Cook Is. 18°52S 159°45W 289 J12
Aiuaba Brazil 6°38S 40°7W 332 C3
Aiud Romania 46°19N 23°44E 183 D8
Aix-en-Provence France 43°32N 5°27E 175 E9
Aix-la-Chapelle = Aachen
Germany 50°45N 6°6E 178 E2
Aix-les-Bains France 45°41N 5°53E 175 C9
Aixe-sur-Vienne France 45°47N 1°9E 174 C5
Aiyang, Mt. Papua N. G. 5°10S 141°20E 286 C1
Aíyina = Egina Greece 37°45N 23°26E 204 D5
Aizawl India 23°40N 92°44E 241 D4
Aizenay France 46°44N 1°38W 172 F5
Aizkraukle Latvia 56°36N 25°11E 188 D3
Aizpute Latvia 56°43N 21°40E 184 B8
Aizuwakamatsu Japan 37°30N 139°56E 220 F9
Ajabshīr Iran 37°28N 45°54E 213 D11
Ajaccio France 41°55N 8°40E 175 G12
Ajaccio, G. d' France 41°52N 8°40E 175 G12
Ajai △ Uganda 2°52N 31°16E 268 B3
Ajaigarh India 24°52N 80°16E 243 G9
Ajajú → Colombia 0°59N 72°20W 328 C3
Ajalpan Mexico 18°22N 97°15W 319 D5
Ajanta India 20°30N 75°48E 244 D2
Ajanta Ra. India 20°28N 75°50E 244 D2
Ajaokuta Nigeria 7°28N 6°42E 263 D6
Ajari Rep. = Ajaria □
Georgia 41°30N 42°0E 191 K6
Ajaria □ Georgia 41°30N 42°0E 191 K6
Ajasse Nigeria 8°4N 4°52E 263 D5
Ajax Canada 43°50N 79°1W 312 C5
Ajax, Mt. N.Z. 42°35S 172°5E 285 C7
Ajdābiyā Libya 30°54N 20°4E 258 B4
Ajdovščina Slovenia 45°54N 13°54E 199 C10
Ajegunle Nigeria 6°26N 3°20E 124 B2
Aji Japan 34°40N 135°27E 133 A1
Ajibar Ethiopia 10°35N 38°36E 257 E4
Ajitgarh India 30°47N 76°41E 242 D7
Ajka Hungary 47°4N 17°31E 182 C2
'Ajlūn Jordan 32°18N 35°47E 251 F6
'Ajmān U.A.E. 25°25N 55°30E 247 E7
Ajmer India 26°28N 74°37E 242 F6
Ajnala India 31°50N 74°48E 242 D6
Ajo U.S.A. 32°22N 112°52W 305 K7
Ajo, C. de Spain 43°31N 3°35W 194 B7
Ajoupa-Bouillon Martinique 14°49N 61°7W 322 j
Ajuda Brazil 38°42N 9°12W 126 A1
Ajuda, Pta. da Azores 37°52N 25°19W 153 d3
Ajuy Phil. 11°10N 123°1E 233 F4
Ak Dağ Turkey 36°30N 29°32E 205 E11
Ak Dağlar Turkey 39°32N 36°12E 212 C7
Ak Dağları Turkey 36°30N 29°30E 205 E11
Ak-Dovurak Russia 51°11N 90°36E 217 B11
Ak-Mechet = Qyzylorda
Kazakhstan 44°48N 65°28E 216 D7
Ak-Mednet = Chornomorske
Ukraine 45°30N 32°40E 189 K7
Ak-Sheikh = Razdolnoye
Ukraine 45°46N 33°29E 189 K7
Akaba Togo 8°10N 1°2E 263 D5
Akabira Japan 43°33N 142°5E 220 C11
Akabli Algeria 26°49N 1°31E 261 C5
Akademika Obrucheva, Khrebet
Russia 51°50N 96°0E 217 B13
Akagera △ Rwanda 1°31S 30°33E 268 C3
Akaishi-Dake Japan 35°27N 138°9E 223 B10
Akaishi-Sammyaku
Japan 35°25N 138°10E 223 B10
Akaki Beseka Ethiopia 8°55N 38°45E 257 F4
Akākūs, J. Libya 25°20N 10°30E 258 C2
Akalkot India 17°32N 76°13E 244 F3
Akalla Sweden 59°24N 17°55E 139 A1
Akamas Cyprus 35°3N 32°18E 207 E8
Akan △ Japan 43°20N 144°20E 220 C12
Akanthou Cyprus 35°22N 33°45E 207 E9
Akarca Turkey 38°35N 29°35E 205 C11
Akaroa N.Z. 43°49S 172°59E 285 D7
Akaroa Harbour N.Z. 43°50S 172°55E 285 D7
Akasaka Tokyo, Japan 140 b3
Akasha Sudan 21°10N 30°32E 256 C3
Akashi Japan 34°45N 134°58E 222 C6
Akbarābād Iran 35°40N 51°20E 141 A2
Akbarpur Bihar, India 24°39N 83°58E 243 G10
Akbarpur Ut. P., India 26°25N 82°32E 243 F10
Akbou Algeria 36°31N 4°31E 261 A5
Akbulak Russia 51°1N 55°37E 216 B5
Akçaabat Turkey 41°1N 39°34E 213 B8
Akçadağ Turkey 38°27N 37°43E 212 C7
Akçakale Turkey 36°41N 38°56E 213 D8
Akçakoca Turkey 41°5N 31°8E 212 B4
Akçalı Dağları Turkey 36°18N 33°21E 250 B4
Akçaova Turkey 41°3N 29°57E 203 E13
Akçay Turkey 36°36N 29°45E 205 E11
Akçay → Turkey 37°50N 28°15E 205 D10
Akchâr Mauritania 20°20N 14°28W 260 D2
Akchi-Karasu = Toktogul
Kyrgyzstan 41°50N 72°50E 217 D8
Akdağ Antalya, Turkey 37°0N 32°0E 250 B3
Akdağ İzmir, Turkey 38°33N 26°30E 205 C8
Akdağmadeni Turkey 39°39N 35°53E 212 C6
Akdere Turkey 36°14N 33°46E 250 B4
Akdoğan = Lysi Cyprus 35°6N 33°41E 207 E9
Akechi Japan 35°18N 137°23E 223 B9
Akelamo Indonesia 1°35N 129°40E 231 D7
Åkernes = Åknes Norway 58°45N 7°30E 164 F4
Åkers styckebruk Sweden 59°15N 17°5E 162 E11
Åkersberga Sweden 59°29N 18°18E 162 E12
Akershus □ Norway 60°0N 11°10E 164 D8
Akershus Slott Oslo, Norway 133 c1
Akeru → India 17°25N 80°5E 244 F5
Aketi Dem. Rep. of the Congo 2°38N 23°47E 264 B4
Akhali Atoni Georgia 43°7N 40°50E 191 J5
Akhalkalaki Georgia 41°27N 43°25E 191 K6
Akhaltsikhe Georgia 41°40N 43°0E 191 K6
Akhḍar, W. al →
Si. Arabia 28°36N 36°28E 251 K7
Akhiok U.S.A. 56°57N 154°10W 303 H9
Akhisar Turkey 38°56N 27°48E 205 C9
Akhmîm Egypt 26°31N 31°47E 256 B3
Akhna Cyprus 35°3N 33°47E 207 E9
Akhnur India 32°52N 74°45E 243 C6
Akhtarīn Syria 36°31N 37°20E 250 B8
Akhtopol = Ahtopol
Bulgaria 42°6N 27°56E 203 D11
Akhtuba → Russia 47°41N 46°55E 191 G8
Akhtubinsk Russia 48°13N 46°7E 191 F8
Akhty Russia 41°30N 47°45E 191 K8
Akhtyrka = Okhtyrka
Ukraine 50°25N 35°0E 189 G8
Aki Japan 33°30N 133°54E 222 D5
Aki-Nada Japan 34°5N 132°40E 222 C4
Akiachak U.S.A. 60°55N 161°26W 303 F7
Akiak U.S.A. 60°55N 161°13W 303 F7
Akiéni Gabon 1°11S 13°53E 264 C2
Akihabara Tokyo, Japan 140 a5
Akimiski I. Canada 52°50N 81°30W 298 B3
Akıncı Burnu Turkey 36°19N 35°46E 250 B6
Akıncılar = Louroujina
Cyprus 35°0N 33°28E 207 F9
Akiōta Japan 34°36N 132°19E 222 C4
Åkirkeby Denmark 55°4N 14°55E 163 J8
Akita Japan 39°45N 140°7E 220 E10
Akita □ Japan 39°40N 140°30E 220 E10
Akjoujt Mauritania 19°45N 14°15W 262 B2
Akka Mali 15°24N 4°11W 262 B4
Akka Morocco 29°22N 8°9W 260 C3
Akkaraipattu Sri Lanka 7°13N 81°51E 245 L5
Akkaya Tepesi Turkey 37°25N 29°18E 205 D11
Akkerman = Bilhorod-
Dnistrovskyy Ukraine 46°11N 30°23E 189 J6
Akkeshi Japan 43°2N 144°51E 220 C12
'Akko Israel 32°55N 35°4E 250 F6
Akköy Turkey 37°29N 27°15E 205 D9
Akkuş Turkey 40°47N 37°0E 212 B7
Aklampa Benin 8°15N 2°10E 263 D5
Aklan □ Phil. 11°50N 122°30E 233 F4
Aklavik Canada 68°12N 135°0W 294 D4
Aklera India 24°26N 76°32E 242 G7
Akmenė Lithuania 56°15N 22°45E 184 B9
Akmenrags Latvia 56°50N 21°4E 184 B8
Akmolinsk = Nur-Sultan
Kazakhstan 51°10N 71°30E 217 B8
Akmonte = Almonte
Spain 37°13N 6°38W 195 H4
Åknes Norway 58°45N 7°30E 164 F4
Aknoul Morocco 34°40N 3°55W 261 B4
Akō Japan 34°45N 134°24E 222 C6
Ako Nigeria 10°19N 10°48E 263 C7
Akobo South Sudan 7°47N 33°1E 257 F3
Akobo → Ethiopia 7°48N 33°3E 257 F3
Akola Maharashtra, India 20°42N 77°2E 244 D3
Akola Maharashtra, India 19°32N 74°3E 244 E2
Akolmiut U.S.A. 60°55N 162°20W 303 F7
Akonolinga Cameroon 3°50N 12°18E 263 E7
Akor Mali 14°59N 6°58W 262 C3
Akordat Eritrea 15°30N 37°40E 257 D4
Akosombo Dam Ghana 6°20N 0°5E 263 D5
Akot India 21°10N 77°10E 244 D3
Akot South Sudan 6°31N 30°9E 257 F3
Akoupé Côte d'Ivoire 6°23N 3°54W 262 D4
Akourousoulba C.A.R. 8°58N 20°46E 264 A4
Akpatok I. Canada 60°25N 68°8W 295 E18
Åkrahamn Norway 59°15N 5°10E 164 E2
'Akramah Libya 32°2N 23°41E 258 B4
Akranes Iceland 64°19N 22°5W 155 C4
Akreïjit Mauritania 18°19N 9°11W 262 B3
Akritas, Akra Greece 36°43N 21°54E 204 E3
Akron Colo., U.S.A. 40°10N 103°13W 304 F12
Akron Ind., U.S.A. 41°2N 86°1W 311 C10
Akron Ohio, U.S.A. 41°5N 81°31W 312 E3
Akrotiri Cyprus 34°36N 32°57E 207 F8
Akrotiri, Akra Greece 40°26N 25°27E 203 F9
Akrotiri Bay Cyprus 34°35N 33°10E 207 F9
Aksai Chin China 35°15N 79°55E 243 B8
Aksaray Turkey 38°25N 34°2E 212 C6
Aksaray □ Turkey 38°20N 33°45E 212 C5
Aksay = Aqsay Kazakhstan 51°11N 53°0E 187 D9
Akşehir Turkey 38°18N 31°30E 212 C4
Akşehir Gölü Turkey 38°30N 31°25E 212 C4
Akseki Turkey 37°2N 31°47E 250 A2
Akstafa = Ağstafa
Azerbaijan 41°7N 45°27E 191 K7
Aksu Xinjiang Uygur, China 41°5N 80°10E 217 D10
Aksu Turkey 36°57N 30°50E 250 B1
Aksu → Turkey 36°52N 30°57E 250 B1
Aksu He → China 40°26N 80°59E 217 D10
Aksum Ethiopia 14°5N 38°40E 257 E4
Aktash Russia 55°2N 52°3E 190 C11
Aktepe Turkey 36°42N 36°27E 250 B7
Aktio Greece 38°57N 20°46E 207 B2
Akto China 39°5N 75°59E 217 E9
Aktsyabrski Belarus 52°38N 28°53E 177 B15
Aktyubinsk = Aqtöbe
Kazakhstan 50°17N 57°10E 187 D10
Aku Nigeria 6°40N 7°18E 263 D6
Akula Dem. Rep. of the Congo 2°22N 20°12E 264 B4
Akun I. U.S.A. 54°11N 165°32W 303 J6
Akune Japan 32°1N 130°12E 222 E2
Akure Nigeria 7°15N 5°5E 263 D6
Akurenan Eq. Guin. 1°2N 10°40E 264 B2
Akuressa Sri Lanka 6°5N 80°29E 245 L5
Akureyri Iceland 65°40N 18°6W 155 B8
Akuseki-Shima Japan 29°27N 129°37E 221 K4
Akusha Russia 42°18N 47°30E 191 J8
Akutan U.S.A. 54°8N 165°46W 303 J6
Akutan I. U.S.A. 54°7N 165°55W 303 J6
Akwa-Ibom □ Nigeria 4°30N 7°30E 263 E6
Akwanga Nigeria 8°55N 8°23E 263 D6
Akyab = Sittwe Myanmar 20°18N 92°45E 241 E4
Akyazı Turkey 40°40N 30°38E 212 B4
Ål Norway 60°38N 8°33E 164 D5
Al Abyaḍ Libya 26°49N 14°1E 258 C2
Al Abyār Libya 32°9N 20°29E 258 B4
Al 'Adam Libya 31°51N 23°55E 258 B4
Al 'Adan = 'Adan Yemen 12°45N 45°0E 248 D4
Al Aḥsā = Hasa Si. Arabia 25°50N 49°0E 247 E6
Al Ajfar Si. Arabia 27°26N 43°0E 246 E4
Al Akhḍar, al Jabal Libya 32°30N 21°30E 258 B4
Al Amādīyah Iraq 37°5N 43°30E 213 D10
Al 'Amārah Iraq 31°55N 47°15E 213 G12
Al Anbār □ Iraq 33°25N 42°0E 246 C4
Al 'Aqabah Jordan 29°31N 35°0E 251 J6
Al 'Aqabah □ Jordan 29°30N 35°0E 251 J6
Al 'Aqīq Si. Arabia 20°39N 41°25E 248 B3
Al Arak Syria 34°38N 38°35E 213 E8
Al 'Aramah Si. Arabia 25°30N 46°0E 246 E5
Al 'Ariḍah Si. Arabia 17°3N 43°5E 248 C3
Al 'Arṭāwīyah Si. Arabia 26°31N 45°20E 246 E5
Al Ashkhara Oman 21°50N 59°30E 249 B7
Al 'Āṣimah □ Jordan 31°40N 36°30E 251 G7
Al 'Assāfīyah Si. Arabia 28°17N 38°59E 246 D3
Al Atārib Syria 36°9N 36°49E 250 B7
Al 'Awdah Si. Arabia 25°32N 45°41E 246 E5
Al 'Ayn Si. Arabia 25°4N 38°6E 246 E3
Al 'Ayn U.A.E. 24°15N 55°45E 247 E7
Al 'Aẓamīyah Iraq 33°22N 44°22E 113 A2
Al 'Azīzīyah Iraq 32°54N 45°4E 213 F11
Al 'Azīzīyah Libya 32°30N 13°1E 258 B2
Al Bāb Syria 36°23N 37°29E 250 B8
Al Bad' Si. Arabia 28°28N 35°1E 246 D2
Al Bada U.A.E. 25°13N 55°16E 119 B2
Al Bada'i' Si. Arabia 26°2N 43°33E 246 E4
Al Bādī Iraq 35°56N 41°32E 246 C4
Al Badī' Si. Arabia 22°0N 46°35E 248 B4
Al Bāḥah Si. Arabia 20°1N 41°28E 256 C5
Al Bāḥah □ Si. Arabia 20°30N 41°30E 248 B3
Al Baḥrah Kuwait 29°40N 47°52E 246 D5
Al Baḥral Mayyit = Dead Sea
Asia 31°30N 35°30E 251 G6
Al Balqā' □ Jordan 32°5N 35°45E 251 F6
Al Barkāt Libya 24°56N 10°14E 258 D2
Al Barsha U.A.E. 25°6N 55°11E 119 B1
Al Bārūk, J. Lebanon 33°39N 35°40E 250 E6
Al Baṣrah Iraq 30°30N 47°50E 246 D5
Al Baṭḥā Iraq 31°6N 45°53E 246 D5
Al Batrūn Lebanon 34°15N 35°40E 250 D6
Al Bayāḍ Si. Arabia 22°0N 47°0E 248 B4
Al Bayḍā Libya 32°50N 21°44E 258 B4
Al Bayḍā' Yemen 14°5N 45°42E 248 D4
Al Bayḍā' □ Yemen 14°5N 45°42E 248 D4
Al Bi'ār Si. Arabia 22°39N 39°40E 248 B2
Al Biqā Lebanon 34°10N 36°10E 250 D7
Al Biqā □ Lebanon 34°0N 36°5E 250 E7
Al Bi'r Si. Arabia 28°51N 36°16E 251 K7
Al Birk Si. Arabia 18°13N 41°33E 248 C3
Al Bu'ayrāt al Ḥasūn
Libya 31°24N 15°44E 258 B3
Al Bukayrīyah Si. Arabia 26°9N 43°40E 246 E4
Al Bumbah Libya 32°24N 23°8E 258 B4
Al Burayj Syria 34°15N 36°46E 250 D7
Al Buraymī □ Oman 23°50N 55°50E 249 B6
Al Buṭnān □ Libya 31°40N 24°30E 258 B4
Al Buwayiqāt Yemen 15°22N 48°30E 249 D5
Al Faḍilī Si. Arabia 26°58N 49°10E 247 E6
Al Fallūjah Iraq 33°20N 43°55E 213 F10
Al Fatḥah Iraq 35°3N 43°33E 213 E10
Al Fāw Iraq 30°0N 48°30E 247 D6
Al Faydamī Yemen 16°25N 52°26E 249 C6
Al Fujayrah U.A.E. 25°7N 56°18E 247 E8
Al Ghadaf, W. → Jordan 31°26N 36°43E 251 G7
Al Ghammās Iraq 31°45N 44°37E 246 D5
Al Gharīb Libya 32°35N 21°11E 258 B4
Al Ghayḍah Yemen 16°13N 52°11E 249 C6
Al Ghayl Yemen 15°30N 50°54E 249 D5
Al Ghazālah Si. Arabia 26°48N 41°19E 246 E4
Al Ghuwayfāt U.A.E. 24°10N 51°38E 247 E6
Al Ḥadd Oman 22°32N 59°48E 249 B7
Al Ḥaddār Si. Arabia 21°58N 45°57E 248 B4
Al Ḥadīthah Iraq 34°0N 41°13E 213 E10
Al Ḥadīthah Si. Arabia 31°28N 37°8E 246 D3
Al Ḥaḍr Iraq 35°35N 42°44E 213 E10
Al Ḥaffah Syria 35°36N 36°1E 250 C7
Al Ḥājānah Syria 33°20N 36°33E 250 E7
Al Ḥajar al Gharbī Oman 24°10N 56°15E 247 E8
Al Ḥallānīyah Oman 17°30N 56°1E 249 C7
Al Ḥāmad Si. Arabia 31°30N 39°30E 246 D3
Al Ḥamar Si. Arabia 22°26N 46°12E 248 B4
Al Ḥamdānīyah Syria 35°25N 36°50E 250 C7
Al Ḥāmī Yemen 14°48N 49°49E 249 D5
Al Ḥamīdīyah Syria 34°42N 35°57E 250 D6
Al Ḥammār Iraq 30°57N 46°51E 246 D5
Al Ḥamrā' Si. Arabia 24°2N 38°55E 246 E3
Al Ḥamrā' Syria 35°19N 37°5E 250 C8
Al Ḥamrā', al Ḥamādah
Libya 29°30N 12°0E 258 C2
Al Hamriya Port U.A.E. 25°18N 55°20E 119 A2
Al Ḥamzah Iraq 31°43N 44°58E 246 D5
Al Ḥanākīyah Si. Arabia 24°51N 40°31E 246 E4
Al Ḥarīq Si. Arabia 23°29N 46°27E 248 B4
Al Harūj al Aswad Libya 27°0N 17°10E 258 C3
Al Ḥasakah Syria 36°35N 40°45E 213 D9
Al Ḥasakah □ Syria 36°40N 40°50E 213 D9
Al Hāshimīyah Iraq 32°22N 44°39E 213 G11
Al Hāsikīyah Oman 17°28N 55°36E 249 C6
Al Hawīyah Ash Sharqīyah,
Si. Arabia 24°45N 49°6E 249 A5
Al Ḥawīyah Makkah,
Si. Arabia 21°26N 40°30E 248 B3
Al Ḥawrah Yemen 13°50N 47°35E 248 D4
Al Ḥawṭah = Laḥij Yemen 13°4N 44°53E 248 D4
Al Ḥawṭah Si. Arabia 23°30N 47°0E 248 B4
Al Ḥayy Iraq 32°5N 46°5E 213 F12
Al Ḥazm = Al Jawf Yemen 16°10N 44°37E 248 C4
Al Ḥillah Iraq 32°30N 44°25E 213 F11
Al Ḥillah Si. Arabia 23°35N 46°50E 248 B4
Al Hindīyah Iraq 32°30N 44°10E 213 F11
Al Hirmil Lebanon 34°26N 36°24E 250 D7
Al Hoceïma Morocco 35°8N 3°58W 261 A4
Al Hudaiba U.A.E. 25°14N 55°16E 119 B2
Al Ḥudaydah Yemen 14°50N 43°0E 248 D3
Al Ḥudaydah □ Yemen 14°50N 43°0E 248 D3
Al Ḥudūd ash Shamālīyah □
Si. Arabia 29°10N 42°30E 246 D4
Al Ḥufrah Libya 25°32N 14°1E 258 C2
Al Hufūf Si. Arabia 25°25N 49°45E 247 E6
Al Ḥulwah Si. Arabia 23°24N 46°48E 248 B4
Al Ḥumayḍah Si. Arabia 29°14N 34°56E 251 J5
Al Ḥunayy Si. Arabia 25°58N 48°45E 247 E6
Al Ḥurayḍah Yemen 15°36N 48°11E 249 D5
Al Husayyāt Libya 30°24N 20°37E 258 B4
Al 'Irqah Yemen 13°39N 47°22E 248 D4
Al Īsāwīyah Si. Arabia 30°43N 37°59E 246 D3
Al Ittihad = Madīnat ash Sha'b
Yemen 12°50N 45°0E 248 D4
Al Jabal al Akhḍar □
Libya 32°30N 21°41E 258 B4
Al Jabal al Gharbī □ Libya 31°26N 12°59E 258 B2
Al Jafiliya U.A.E. 25°14N 55°17E 119 B2
Al Jafr Jordan 30°18N 36°14E 251 H7
Al Jāfūrah Si. Arabia 25°0N 50°15E 247 E7
Al Jaghbūb Libya 29°42N 24°38E 258 C4
Al Jahrah Kuwait 29°25N 47°40E 246 D5
Al Jalāmīd Si. Arabia 31°20N 40°6E 246 D3
Al Jamalīyah Qatar 25°37N 51°5E 247 E6
Al Janūb □ Lebanon 33°20N 35°20E 250 E6
Al Jawf Libya 24°10N 23°24E 258 D4
Al Jawf Yemen 16°10N 44°37E 248 C4
Al Jawf □ Si. Arabia 29°30N 39°30E 246 D3
Al Jawf □ Yemen 16°15N 45°0E 248 C4
Al Jazair = Algeria ■ Africa 28°30N 2°0E 261 C5
Al Jazirah Iraq 33°30N 44°0E 213 E10
Al Jithāmīyah Si. Arabia 27°41N 41°43E 246 E4
Al Jubayl Si. Arabia 27°0N 49°50E 247 E6
Al Jubaylah Si. Arabia 24°55N 46°25E 246 E5
Al Jubb Si. Arabia 27°11N 42°17E 246 E4
Al Jufrah Libya 29°10N 16°0E 258 C3
Al Jufrah □ Libya 27°30N 17°30E 258 C3
Al Jumūm Si. Arabia 21°37N 39°42E 248 B2
Al Junaynah Sudan 13°27N 22°45E 259 F4
Al Kabā'ish Iraq 30°58N 47°0E 246 D5
Al Kāmil Oman 22°13N 59°12E 249 B7
Al Karak Jordan 31°11N 35°42E 251 G6
Al Karak □ Jordan 31°0N 36°0E 251 H7
Al Kāẓimīyah Iraq 33°22N 44°18E 213 F11
Al Khābūrah Oman 23°57N 57°5E 247 F8
Al Khafji Si. Arabia 28°24N 48°29E 247 E6
Al Khalīl West Bank 31°32N 35°6E 251 G6
Al Khāliṣ Iraq 33°49N 44°32E 213 F11
Al Khamāsīn Si. Arabia 20°29N 44°46E 248 B4
Al Kharj Si. Arabia 24°0N 47°0E 248 B4
Al Kharsānīyah Si. Arabia 27°13N 49°18E 247 E6
Al Khaṣab Oman 26°14N 56°15E 247 E8
Al Khāṣirah Si. Arabia 23°30N 43°47E 248 B3
Al Khawr Qatar 25°41N 51°30E 247 E6
Al Khiḍr Iraq 31°12N 45°33E 246 D5
Al Khiyām Lebanon 33°20N 35°36E 250 E6
Al Khubar Si. Arabia 26°17N 50°12E 247 E6
Al Khums Libya 32°40N 14°17E 258 B2
Al Khurmah Si. Arabia 21°54N 42°3E 248 B3
Al Kifl Iraq 32°13N 44°22E 213 G11
Al Kiswah Syria 33°23N 36°14E 250 E7
Al Kūfah Iraq 32°2N 44°24E 213 F11
Al Kufrah Libya 24°17N 23°15E 258 D4
Al Kuhayfīyah Si. Arabia 27°12N 43°3E 246 E4
Al Kumayt Iraq 32°2N 46°52E 213 G12
Al Kūt Iraq 32°30N 46°0E 213 F11
Al Kuwayt Kuwait 29°30N 48°0E 246 D5
Al Labwah Lebanon 34°11N 36°20E 250 D7
Al Lādhiqīyah Syria 35°30N 35°45E 250 C6
Al Lādhiqīyah □ Syria 35°45N 36°0E 250 C7
Al Līth Si. Arabia 20°9N 40°15E 248 B3
Al Liwā' Oman 24°31N 56°36E 247 E8
Al Luḥayyah Yemen 15°45N 42°40E 248 D3
Al Madīnah Iraq 30°57N 47°16E 246 D5
Al Madīnah Si. Arabia 24°35N 39°52E 246 E3
Al Madīnah □ Si. Arabia 23°50N 40°30E 248 B3
Al Mafraq Jordan 32°17N 36°14E 251 F7
Al Mafraq □ Jordan 32°17N 36°15E 251 F7
Al Maghreb = Morocco ■
N. Afr. 32°0N 5°50W 260 B3
Al Maḥābishah Yemen 15°55N 43°24E 248 D3
Al Mahbes W. Sahara 27°10N 9°50W 260 C3
Al Maḥfidh Yemen 14°5N 46°55E 248 D4
Al Maḥmūdīyah Iraq 33°3N 44°21E 213 F11
Al Mahrah Yemen 16°0N 51°20E 249 D5
Al Mahrah □ Yemen 17°0N 52°0E 249 C6
Al Maḥwīt Yemen 15°29N 43°33E 248 D3
Al Majma'ah Si. Arabia 25°57N 45°22E 246 E5
Al Makhruq, W. → Jordan 31°28N 37°0E 251 G8
Al Makḥūl Si. Arabia 26°37N 42°39E 246 E4
Al Mālikīyah Syria 37°10N 42°8E 213 D10
Al Manāmah Bahrain 26°10N 50°30E 247 E6
Al Manara U.A.E. 25°9N 55°14E 119 B1
Al Maqwa' Kuwait 29°10N 47°59E 246 D5
Al Marāḥ Si. Arabia 25°35N 49°35E 247 E6
Al Marāwi'ah Yemen 14°50N 43°9E 248 D3
Al Marj Libya 32°25N 20°30E 258 B4
Al Marj □ Libya 32°0N 21°0E 258 B4
Al Marqab □ Libya 32°32N 14°35E 258 B2
Al Masana'a Oman 23°46N 57°39E 249 B7
Al Maṭlā Kuwait 29°24N 47°40E 246 D5
Al Mawṣil Iraq 36°15N 43°5E 213 D10
Al Mayādin Syria 35°1N 40°27E 213 E9
Al Mazār Jordan 31°4N 35°41E 251 G6
Al Midhnab Si. Arabia 25°50N 44°18E 246 E5
Al Minā' Lebanon 34°24N 35°49E 250 D6
Al Mina U.A.E. 25°15N 55°16E 119 B2
Al Miqdādīyah Iraq 34°0N 45°0E 213 E11
Al Mubarraz Si. Arabia 25°30N 49°40E 247 E6
Al Mudawwarah Jordan 29°19N 36°0E 251 J7
Al Muḍaybī Oman 22°34N 58°7E 249 B7
Al Mughayrā' U.A.E. 24°5N 53°32E 247 E7
Al Muḥarraq Bahrain 26°15N 50°40E 247 E6
Al Mukallā Yemen 14°33N 49°2E 249 D5
Al Mukhā Yemen 13°18N 43°15E 248 D3
Al Mukhaylī Libya 32°10N 22°17E 258 B4
Al Musayjīd Si. Arabia 24°5N 39°5E 246 E3
Al Musayyib Iraq 32°49N 44°20E 213 F11
Al Muthanná □ Iraq 30°30N 45°15E 246 D5
Al Muwayh Si. Arabia 22°41N 41°37E 256 C5
Al Muwayliḥ Si. Arabia 27°40N 35°30E 246 E2
Al Muzāḥimīyah
Si. Arabia 24°29N 46°18E 248 A4
Al Nasr U.A.E. 25°15N 55°19E 119 B2
Al Owuho = Otukpa Nigeria 7°9N 7°41E 263 D6
Al Qābil Oman 22°34N 58°42E 249 B7
Al Qaddāḥīyah Libya 31°15N 15°9E 258 B3
Al Qaḍīmah Si. Arabia 22°20N 39°13E 248 B2
Al Qādisīyah □ Iraq 32°0N 45°0E 246 D5
Al Qadmūs Syria 35°5N 36°10E 250 C7
Al Qaḥmah Si. Arabia 18°0N 41°41E 248 C3
Al Qā'idah Yemen 13°45N 44°10E 248 D4
Al Qā'im Iraq 34°21N 41°7E 213 E9
Al Qā'iyah Si. Arabia 24°33N 43°15E 248 A3
Al Qalībah Si. Arabia 28°24N 37°42E 246 D3
Al Qāmishlī Syria 37°2N 41°14E 213 D9
Al Qardāḥah Syria 35°27N 36°3E 250 C7
Al Qaryah ash Sharqīyah
Libya 30°28N 13°40E 258 B2
Al Qaryatayn Syria 34°12N 37°13E 250 D8
Al Qaṣabāt Libya 32°39N 14°1E 258 B2
Al Qaṣīm □ Si. Arabia 26°0N 43°0E 246 E4
Al Qaṭ'ā Syria 34°40N 40°48E 213 E9
Al Qaṭīf Si. Arabia 26°35N 50°0E 247 E6
Al Qaṭn Yemen 15°51N 48°26E 249 D5
Al Qatrānah Jordan 31°12N 36°6E 251 G7
Al Qaṭrūn Libya 24°56N 15°3E 258 D3
Al Qawz Si. Arabia 18°58N 41°26E 248 C3
Al Qayṣūmah Si. Arabia 28°20N 46°7E 246 D5
Al Qiblīyah Oman 17°30N 56°20E 249 C7
Al Quds = Jerusalem
Israel/West Bank 31°47N 35°10E 123 B2
Al Qunayṭirah Syria 33°5N 35°45E 250 F6
Al Qunfudhah Si. Arabia 19°3N 41°4E 248 C3
Al Quoz U.A.E. 25°8N 55°14E 119 B1
Al Qurayyāt Oman 23°17N 58°53E 249 B7
Al Qurayyāt Si. Arabia 31°20N 37°20E 251 G8
Al Qurḥ Yemen 16°44N 51°29E 249 C5
Al Qurnah Iraq 31°1N 47°25E 246 D5
Al Quṣayr Iraq 30°39N 45°50E 246 D5
Al Quṣayr Syria 34°31N 36°34E 250 D7
Al Qutayfah Syria 33°44N 36°36E 250 E7
Al Quway'īyah Si. Arabia 24°3N 45°15E 248 A4
Al Quwayr Iraq 36°2N 43°29E 213 D10
Al Quwaysimah Jordan 31°55N 35°57E 251 G6
Al Safa U.A.E. 25°10N 55°14E 119 B1
Al Satwa U.A.E. 25°13N 55°16E 119 B2
Al Seeb = As Sīb Oman 23°41N 58°11E 249 B7
Al Sufouh U.A.E. 25°7N 55°12E 119 B1
Al 'Ubaylah Si. Arabia 21°59N 50°57E 249 B5
Al 'Uḍaylīyah Si. Arabia 25°8N 49°18E 247 E6
Al 'Ulā Si. Arabia 26°35N 38°0E 246 E3
Al 'Ulayyah Si. Arabia 19°39N 41°54E 248 C3
Al Uqaylah ash Sharqīgah
Libya 30°12N 19°10E 258 B3
Al 'Uqayr Si. Arabia 25°40N 50°15E 247 E6
Al 'Urūq al Mutariḍah
Si. Arabia 21°0N 53°30E 249 B6
Al 'Uwaynāt Libya 25°47N 10°33E 261 C7
Al 'Uwaynid Si. Arabia 24°50N 46°0E 246 E5
Al 'Uwayqīlah Si. Arabia 30°30N 42°10E 246 D4
Al Uweinat Libya 21°34N 24°50E 259 D4
Al 'Uyūn Ḥijāz, Si. Arabia 24°33N 39°35E 246 E3
Al 'Uyūn Najd, Si. Arabia 26°30N 43°50E 246 E4
Al 'Uzayr Iraq 31°19N 47°25E 246 D5
Al Wāḥāt □ Libya 29°0N 22°0E 258 C4
Al Wajh Si. Arabia 26°10N 36°30E 246 E3
Al Wakrah Qatar 25°10N 51°40E 247 E6
Al Walaja West Bank 31°44N 35°9E 123 B1
Al Waqbah Si. Arabia 28°48N 45°33E 246 D5
Al Wari'āh Si. Arabia 27°51N 47°25E 246 E5
Al Wasl U.A.E. 25°12N 55°16E 119 B2
Al Wāṭīyah Libya 32°28N 11°57E 258 B2
Al Wīgh Libya 24°16N 15°30E 258 D3
Al Wusṭā □ Oman 20°0N 57°0E 249 C7
Al Yaman = Yemen ■ Asia 15°0N 44°0E 248 D4
Ala Italy 45°45N 11°0E 198 C8
Ala Archa △ Kyrgyzstan 42°32N 74°28E 217 D8
Ala Dağ Turkey 37°44N 35°9E 246 B2
Ala Dağları Turkey 39°15N 43°33E 213 C10
Ala Tau Asia 45°30N 80°40E 217 C10
Ala Tau Shankou = Dzungarian
Gate Asia 45°10N 82°0E 217 C10
Alabama □ U.S.A. 33°0N 87°0W 315 E11
Alabama → U.S.A. 31°8N 87°57W 315 F11
Alabaster U.S.A. 33°15N 86°49W 315 E11
Alabat I. Phil. 14°7N 122°3E 232 D4
Alabel Phil. 6°4N 125°16E 233 H5
Alabule → Papua N. G. 8°31S 146°56E 286 E4
Alaca Turkey 40°10N 34°51E 212 B6
Alacaatlı Turkey 39°15N 28°3E 205 B10
Alaçam Turkey 41°36N 35°36E 212 B6
Alaçam Dağları Turkey 39°18N 28°49E 205 B10
Alacant = Alicante Spain 38°23N 0°30W 197 G4
Alaçatı Turkey 38°15N 26°22E 205 C8
Alachua U.S.A. 29°47N 82°30W 316 F7
Alaejos Spain 41°18N 5°13W 194 D5
Alaer China 40°30N 81°16E 217 D10
Alagir Russia 43°3N 44°14E 191 J7
Alagna Valsésia Italy 45°51N 7°56E 198 C4
Alagoa de Baixo = Sertânia
Brazil 8°5S 37°20W 332 C4
Alagoa Grande Brazil 7°3S 35°35W 332 C4
Alagoas = Marechal Deodoro
Brazil 9°43S 35°54W 332 C4
Alagoas □ Brazil 9°0S 36°0W 332 C4
Alagoinhas Brazil 12°7S 38°20W 333 D4
Alagón Spain 41°46N 1°12W 196 D3
Alagón → Spain 39°44N 6°53W 194 F4
Alaguntan Nigeria 6°25N 3°29E 124 B2
Alagyoz = Aragats
Armenia 40°30N 44°15E 191 K7
Alahan Turkey 36°46N 33°19E 250 B4
Alaheaieatnu = Altaelva →
Norway 69°54N 23°17E 160 B20
Alai Range Asia 39°45N 72°0E 217 E8
Alaior Spain 39°57N 4°8E 206 B5
Alajero Canary Is. 28°3N 17°13W 153 e1
Alajuela Costa Rica 10°2N 84°8W 320 D3
Alajuela, L. Panama 9°14N 79°34W 320 c
Alakamisy Madag. 21°19S 47°14E 272 C2
Alakanuk U.S.A. 62°41N 164°37W 303 E6
Alaknanda → India 30°8N 78°36E 243 D8
Alaköl Kazakhstan 46°0N 81°5E 217 C10
Alakurtti Russia 66°58N 30°25E 160 C24
'Alaläkeiki Channel
U.S.A. 20°30N 156°30W 302 C5
Alalapura Suriname 2°20N 56°25W 329 C6
Alalaú → Brazil 0°30S 61°9W 329 D5
Alamagan N. Marianas 17°36N 145°50E 302 a
Alamarvdasht Iran 27°37N 52°59E 247 E7
Alamata Ethiopia 12°25N 39°33E 257 E4
Alameda Calif., U.S.A. 37°46N 122°15W 136 B3
Alameda N. Mex.,
U.S.A. 35°11N 106°37W 305 J10
Alameda, Parque Mexico City, Mexico 128 b2
Alameda Memorial State Beach
Park U.S.A. 37°45N 122°16W 136 B3
Alaminos Phil. 16°10N 119°59E 232 C2
Alamo Ga., U.S.A. 32°9N 82°47W 316 C7
Alamo Nev., U.S.A. 37°22N 115°10W 307 H11
Alamogordo U.S.A. 32°54N 105°57W 305 K11
Alamos Mexico 27°1N 108°56W 318 B3
Alamosa U.S.A. 37°28N 105°52W 305 H11
Alampur India 15°55N 78°6E 245 G4
Åland Finland 60°15N 20°0E 161 F19
Aland India 17°36N 76°35E 244 F3
Alandroal Portugal 38°41N 7°24W 195 G3
Ålands hav Europe 60°0N 19°30E 161 G18
Älandsbro Sweden 62°40N 17°51E 162 B11
Alandur India 13°0N 80°15E 245 H5
Alang Indonesia 4°7N 117°0E 235 B5
Alange, Embalse d' Spain 38°45N 6°18W 195 G4
Alanís Spain 38°3N 5°43W 195 G5
Alaniya = North Ossetia-Alaniya □
Russia 43°30N 44°30E 191 J7
Alaniya △ Russia 42°55N 44°30E 191 J7
Alanya Turkey 36°38N 32°0E 250 B3
Alaotra, Farihin' Madag. 17°30S 48°30E 272 B2
Alaotra-Mangoro □
Madag. 17°50S 48°25E 272 B2
Alapaha U.S.A. 31°23N 83°13W 316 D6
Alapayevsk Russia 57°52N 61°42E 214 D7
Alappuzha India 9°30N 76°28E 245 K3
'Alāqán Si. Arabia 29°10N 35°21E 251 J6
Alar del Rey Spain 42°38N 4°20W 194 C6
Alara → Turkey 36°38N 31°39E 250 B2
Alaraz Spain 40°45N 5°17W 194 E5
Alarcón, Embalse de Spain 39°36N 2°10W 196 F2
Alaró Spain 39°42N 2°47E 206 B3
Alarobia-Vohiposa Madag. 20°59S 47°9E 272 C2
Alas Indonesia 8°29S 117°0E 235 D5
Alas, Selat Indonesia 8°40S 116°40E 235 D5
Alaşehir Turkey 38°23N 28°30E 205 C10
Alashtar Iran 33°51N 48°15E 213 F13
Alaska □ U.S.A. 64°0N 154°0W 303 D9
Alaska, G. of Pac. Oc. 58°0N 145°0W 303 G11
Alaska Maritime Nat. Wildlife
Refuge ⌓ U.S.A. 52°0N 174°0W 303 L4
Alaska Peninsula U.S.A. 56°0N 159°0W 303 H8
Alaska Peninsula Nat. Wildlife
Refuge ⌓ U.S.A. 56°0N 159°0W 303 J8
Alaska Range U.S.A. 62°50N 151°0W 303 E10
Alássio Italy 44°0N 8°10E 198 E5
Älät Azerbaijan 39°58N 49°25E 191 L9
Alatau Shan = Ala Tau
Asia 45°30N 80°40E 217 C10
Alatri Italy 41°43N 13°21E 199 G10
Alatyr Russia 54°55N 46°35E 190 C8
Alatyr → Russia 54°52N 46°36E 190 C8
Alaungdaw Kathapa △
Myanmar 22°30N 94°30E 241 D5
Alausi Ecuador 2°0S 78°50W 328 D2
Álava = Araba/Álava □
Spain 42°48N 2°28W 196 C2

Alava, C. U.S.A. 48°10N 124°44W 306 B2
Alaverdi Armenia 41°15N 44°37E 191 K7
Alavo = Alavus Finland 62°35N 23°36E 160 E20
Alavus Finland 62°35N 23°36E 160 E20
Alawa ◎ Australia 15°42S 134°39E 280 B1
Alawoona Australia 34°45S 140°30E 282 C4
Alayawarra ◎ Australia 22°0S 134°30E 280 C1
'Alayh Lebanon 33°46N 35°33E 250 E6
Alayköy = Yerolakkos Cyprus 35°11N 33°15E 207 E9
Alazani ➔ Azerbaijan 41°5N 46°40E 191 K8
Alba Italy 44°42N 8°2E 198 D5
Alba □ Romania 46°10N 23°30E 183 D8
Alba Adriatica Italy 42°50N 13°56E 199 F10
Alba de Tormes Spain 40°50N 5°30W 194 E5
Alba-Iulia Romania 46°8N 23°39E 183 D8
Albac Romania 46°28N 22°58E 182 D7
Albacete Spain 39°0N 1°50W 197 F3
Albacete □ Spain 38°50N 2°0W 197 G3
Albacutya, L. Australia 35°45S 141°58E 282 C4
Ålbæk Denmark 57°36N 10°25E 163 G4
Ålbæk Bugt Denmark 57°35N 10°40E 163 G4
Albaida Spain 38°51N 0°31W 197 G4
Albalate de las Nogueras Spain 40°22N 2°18W 196 E2
Albalate del Arzobispo Spain 41°6N 0°31W 196 D4
Alban France 43°53N 2°28E 174 E6
Albanel, L. Canada 50°55N 73°12W 298 B5
Albania ■ Europe 41°0N 20°0E 202 E4
Albano Laziale Italy 41°44N 12°39E 199 G9
Albany W. Austral., Australia 35°1S 117°58E 279 G2
Albany Ga., U.S.A. 31°35N 84°10W 316 D5
Albany Ind., U.S.A. 40°18N 85°14W 311 D11
Albany Mo., U.S.A. 40°15N 94°20W 310 D2
Albany N.Y., U.S.A. 42°39N 73°45W 313 D11
Albany Oreg., U.S.A. 44°38N 123°6W 304 D2
Albany Tex., U.S.A. 32°44N 99°18W 314 E5
Albany Wis., U.S.A. 42°42N 89°26W 310 B7
Albany ➔ Canada 52°17N 81°31W 298 B3
Albarca, C. d' Spain 39°4N 1°22E 206 C1
Albardón Argentina 31°20S 68°30W 334 C2
Albarracín Spain 40°25N 1°26W 196 E3
Albarracín, Sierra de Spain 40°30N 1°30W 196 E3
Albatera Spain 38°11N 0°52W 197 G4
Albâtre, Côte d' France 49°55N 0°50E 172 C7
Albatross B. Australia 12°45S 141°30E 280 A3
Albatross Pt. N.Z. 38°7S 174°44E 284 E3
Albay □ Phil. 13°13N 123°33E 232 E4
Albegna ➔ Italy 42°30N 11°11E 199 F8
Albemarle U.S.A. 35°21N 80°12W 315 D14
Albemarle, I. = Isabela, I. Ecuador 0°30S 91°4W 330 a
Albemarle, Pta. Ecuador 0°11N 91°21W 330 a
Albemarle Sd. U.S.A. 36°5N 76°0W 315 C16
Albenga Italy 44°3N 8°13E 198 D5
Alberche ➔ Spain 39°58N 4°46W 194 F6
Alberdi Paraguay 26°14S 58°20W 334 B4
Albères, Mts. France 42°28N 2°56E 174 F6
Ålberga Sweden 58°44N 16°35E 163 F10
Alberga ➔ Australia 27°6S 135°33E 281 D2
Albern Austria 48°9N 16°29E 142 B2
Albersdorf Germany 54°8N 9°17E 178 A5
Albert France 50°0N 2°38E 173 C9
Albert, L. Africa 1°30N 31°0E 268 B3
Albert, L. S. Austral., Australia 35°30S 139°10E 282 C3
Albert Edward, Mt. Papua N. G. 8°20S 147°24E 286 E4
Albert Edward Ra. Australia 18°17S 127°57E 278 C4
Albert Lea U.S.A. 43°39N 93°22W 308 D7
Albert Nat. Park = Virunga △ Dem. Rep. of the Congo 0°5N 29°38E 268 B2
Albert Nile ➔ Uganda 3°36N 32°2E 268 B3
Albert Park Australia 37°51S 144°58E 128 B1
Albert Town Jamaica 18°17N 77°33W 320 a
Albert Town The Bahamas 22°37N 74°33W 321 B5
Alberta □ Canada 54°40N 115°0W 296 C6
Alberti Argentina 35°1S 60°16W 334 D3
Albertinia S. Africa 34°11S 21°34E 270 D3
Albertirsa Hungary 47°14N 19°37E 182 C4
Alberto de Agostini △ Chile 54°38S 71°37W 336 D2
Alberton P.E.I., Canada 46°50N 64°0W 299 C7
Alberton Gauteng, S. Africa 26°15S 28°7E 123 B2
Albertslund Denmark 55°39N 12°21E 118 B2
Albertville = Kalemie Dem. Rep. of the Congo 5°55S 29°9E 268 D2
Albertville Savoie, France 45°40N 6°22E 175 C10
Albertville Ala., U.S.A. 34°16N 86°13W 315 D11
Albi France 43°56N 2°9E 174 E6
Albia U.S.A. 41°2N 92°48W 310 C4
Albina Suriname 5°37N 54°15W 329 B7
Albina, Ponta Angola 15°52S 11°44E 265 F2
Albino Italy 45°46N 9°47E 198 C6
Albion Ill., U.S.A. 38°23N 88°4W 311 F8
Albion Ind., U.S.A. 41°24N 85°25W 311 C11
Albion Mich., U.S.A. 42°15N 84°45W 311 B12
Albion Nebr., U.S.A. 41°42N 98°0W 308 E4
Albion Pa., U.S.A. 41°53N 80°22W 312 E4
Albocácer Spain 40°21N 0°1E 196 E5
Albolote Spain 37°14N 3°39W 195 H7
Alborán Medit. S. 35°57N 3°0W 195 K7
Alboran Sea Medit. S. 36°0N 3°30W 195 K7
Alborea Spain 39°17N 1°24W 197 F3
Ålborg = Aalborg Denmark 57°2N 9°54E 163 G3
Ålborg Bugt = Aalborg Bugt Denmark 56°50N 10°35E 163 H4
Alborz □ Iran 36°0N 50°50E 247 B6
Alborz, Reshteh-ye Kūhhā-ye Iran 36°0N 52°0E 247 C7
Albox Spain 37°23N 2°8W 197 H2
Albstadt Germany 48°13N 9°1E 179 G5
Albuera Phil. 10°55N 124°42E 233 F5
Albufeira Portugal 37°5N 8°15W 195 H2
Albula ➔ Switz. 46°38N 9°28E 179 J5
Albuñol Spain 36°48N 3°11W 195 J7
Albuquerque Brazil 19°23S 57°26W 331 D6
Albuquerque N. Mex., U.S.A. 35°5N 106°39W 305 J10
Albuquerque, Cayos de Caribbean 12°10N 81°50W 320 D3
Alburg U.S.A. 44°59N 73°18W 313 B11
Alburno, Mte. Italy 40°33N 15°17E 201 B8
Alburquerque Spain 39°15N 6°59W 195 F4
Albury Australia 36°3S 146°56E 283 D7
Alby Sweden 62°30N 15°28E 162 B9
Alcácer do Sal Portugal 38°22N 8°33W 195 G2
Alcáçovas Portugal 38°23N 8°9W 195 G2
Alcala Phil. 17°54N 121°39E 232 C3
Alcalá de Guadaira Spain 37°20N 5°50W 195 H5
Alcalá de Henares Spain 40°28N 3°22W 194 E7
Alcalá de los Gazules Spain 36°29N 5°43W 195 J5
Alcalá de Xivert Spain 40°19N 0°13E 196 E5
Alcalá del Júcar Spain 39°12N 1°26W 197 F3
Alcalá del Río Spain 37°31N 5°59W 195 H5
Alcalá del Valle Spain 36°54N 5°10W 195 J5
Alcalá la Real Spain 37°27N 3°57W 195 H7
Álcamo Italy 37°59N 12°55E 200 E5
Alcanadre Spain 42°24N 2°7W 196 C2
Alcanadre ➔ Spain 41°43N 0°12W 196 D4
Alcanar Spain 40°33N 0°28E 196 E5
Alcanede Portugal 39°25N 8°49W 195 F2
Alcanena Portugal 39°27N 8°40W 195 F2
Alcañices Spain 41°41N 6°21W 194 D4
Alcañiz Spain 41°2N 0°8W 196 D4
Alcântara Brazil 2°20S 44°30W 332 B3
Alcantara Lisboa, Portugal 38°43N 9°10W 126 A1
Alcántara Spain 39°41N 6°57W 194 F4
Alcántara, Embalse de Spain 39°44N 6°50W 194 F4
Alcantarilla Spain 37°59N 1°12W 197 H3
Alcaracejos Spain 38°24N 4°58W 195 G6
Alcaraz Spain 38°40N 2°29W 197 G2
Alcaraz, Sierra de Spain 38°40N 2°20W 197 G2
Alcatraz I. U.S.A. 37°49N 122°25W 136 B2
Alcaudete Spain 37°35N 4°5W 195 H6
Alcázar de San Juan Spain 39°24N 3°12W 195 F7
Alcazarquivir = Ksar el Kebir Morocco 35°0N 6°0W 260 B3
Alcedo, Volcán Ecuador 0°24S 91°6W 330 a
Alchevsk Ukraine 48°30N 38°45E 189 H10
Alcira = Alzira Spain 39°9N 0°30W 197 F4
Alcobaça = Tucuruí Brazil 3°42S 49°44W 332 B2
Alcobaça Portugal 39°32N 8°58W 195 F2
Alcobendas Spain 40°32N 3°38W 127 A2
Alcolea del Pinar Spain 41°2N 2°28W 196 D2
Alcoma U.S.A. 27°54N 81°29W 317 H8
Alcorcón Spain 40°20N 3°48W 127 B1
Alcoutim Portugal 37°25N 7°28W 195 H3
Alcova U.S.A. 42°34N 106°43W 304 E10
Alcoy Spain 38°43N 0°30W 197 G4
Alcubierre, Sierra de Spain 41°45N 0°22W 196 D4
Alcublas Spain 39°48N 0°43W 196 F4
Alcúdia Spain 39°51N 3°7E 206 B4
Alcúdia, B. d' Spain 39°47N 3°15E 206 B4
Alcúdia, Serra de la Spain 38°34N 4°30W 195 G6
Aldabra Is. Seychelles 9°22S 46°28E 255 G8
Aldama Mexico 22°55N 98°4W 319 C5
Aldan Russia 58°40N 125°30E 215 D13
Aldan ➔ Russia 63°28N 129°35E 215 C13
Aldea, Pta. de la Canary Is. 28°0N 15°50W 153 e1
Aldeburgh U.K. 52°10N 1°37E 169 E9
Alden Norway 61°19N 4°45E 164 C1
Alder Pk. U.S.A. 35°53N 121°22W 306 K5
Alderney U.K. 49°42N 2°11W 169 H5
Aldershof Germany 52°26N 13°32E 115 B4
Aldershot U.K. 51°15N 0°44W 169 F7
Alderwood Canada 43°36N 79°32W 141 B1
Aldinga Beach Australia 35°17S 138°27E 282 C3
Aldo Bonzi Argentina 34°42S 58°31W 117 C1
Åled Sweden 56°44N 12°57E 163 H6
Aledo U.S.A. 41°12N 90°45W 310 C6
Alefa Ethiopia 11°55N 36°55E 257 E4
Aleg Mauritania 17°3N 13°55W 262 B2
Alegranza Canary Is. 29°23N 13°32W 260 C2
Alegranza, I. Canary Is. 29°23N 13°32W 153 e2
Alegre Brazil 20°50S 41°30W 333 F3
Alegrete Brazil 29°40S 56°0W 335 B4
Aleknagik U.S.A. 59°17N 158°36W 303 G8
Aleksandriya = Oleksandriya Kirovohrad, Ukraine 48°42N 33°3E 189 H7
Aleksandriya = Oleksandriya Rivne, Ukraine 50°37N 26°19E 177 C14
Aleksandriyskaya Russia 43°58N 47°14E 191 J8
Aleksandropol = Gyumri Armenia 40°47N 43°50E 191 K6
Aleksandrov Russia 56°23N 38°44E 188 D10
Aleksandrov Gay Russia 50°9N 48°34E 190 E9
Aleksandrovac Serbia 43°28N 21°3E 202 C5
Aleksandrovac Serbia 44°28N 21°13E 202 B5
Aleksandrovka = Oleksandrivka Ukraine 48°55N 32°20E 189 H7
Aleksandrovka = Ordzhonikidze Ukraine 47°39N 34°3E 189 J8
Aleksandrovo Bulgaria 43°14N 24°51E 203 C8
Aleksandrovsk = Belogorsk Russia 51°0N 128°20E 215 D13
Aleksandrovsk = Polyarny Russia 69°8N 33°20E 160 B25
Aleksandrovsk = Zaporizhzhya Ukraine 47°50N 35°10E 189 J8
Aleksandrovsk-Grushevsky = Shakhty Russia 47°40N 40°16E 191 G5
Aleksandrovsk-Sakhalinskiy Russia 50°50N 142°20E 219 A17
Aleksandrovskoye Russia 59°51N 30°20E 137 B2
Aleksandrów Kujawski Poland 52°53N 18°43E 185 F5
Aleksandrów Łódzki Poland 51°49N 19°17E 185 G6
Aleksandry, Zemlya Russia 80°25N 48°0E 214 A5
Alekseyevka Samara, Russia 52°35N 51°17E 190 D10
Alekseyevka Voronezh, Russia 50°43N 38°40E 189 G10
Alekseyevsk = Svobodnyy Russia 51°20N 128°0E 215 D13
Alekseyevskoye = Qazyghurt Kazakhstan 41°45N 69°23E 217 D7
Aleksin Russia 54°31N 37°9E 188 E9
Aleksinac Serbia 43°31N 21°42E 202 C5
Além Paraíba Brazil 21°52S 42°41W 333 F3
Alemania Argentina 25°40S 65°30W 334 B2
Alemania Chile 25°10S 69°55W 334 B2
Alen Eq. Guin. 1°58N 11°19E 264 B2
Alençon France 48°27N 0°4E 172 D7
'Alenuihāhā Channel U.S.A. 20°30N 156°0W 302 C5
Alépé Côte d'Ivoire 5°29N 3°40W 262 D4
Aleppo = Ḩalab Syria 36°10N 37°15E 250 B8
Alerce Andino △ Chile 41°33S 72°29W 336 B2
Alerce Costero △ Chile 40°10S 73°30W 336 B2
Aléria France 42°5N 9°26E 175 F13
Alert Canada 83°2N 60°0W 295 A20
Aleru India 17°39N 79°3E 244 F4
Alès France 44°9N 4°5E 175 D8
Aleşd Romania 47°3N 22°22E 182 C7
Alessándria Italy 44°54N 8°37E 198 D5
Ålesund Norway 62°28N 6°12E 164 B3
Alet-les-Bains France 42°59N 2°14E 174 F6
Aletschhorn Switz. 46°28N 8°0E 179 J4
Aleutian Basin Pac. Oc. 57°0N 177°0E 288 B9
Aleutian Is. Pac. Oc. 52°0N 175°0W 303 K3
Aleutian Range U.S.A. 60°0N 154°0W 303 G9
Aleutian Trench Pac. Oc. 48°0N 180°0E 150 D17
Alexander Ga., U.S.A. 33°1N 81°53W 316 B8
Alexander N. Dak., U.S.A. 47°51N 103°39W 308 B2
Alexander, C. Solomon Is. 6°34S 156°32E 287 L9
Alexander, Mt. Australia 28°58S 120°16E 279 E3
Alexander Arch. U.S.A. 56°0N 136°0W 303 J14
Alexander Bay S. Africa 28°40S 16°30E 270 C2
Alexander City U.S.A. 32°56N 85°58W 316 C4
Alexander I. Antarctica 69°0S 70°0W 151 C17
Alexander Nevsky Abbey Russia 59°54N 30°23E 137 B2
Alexander Soutzos Museum Athens, Greece 112 b3
Alexandra Vic., Australia 37°8S 145°40E 283 D6
Alexandra N.Z. 45°14S 169°25E 285 F4
Alexandra Singapore, Singapore 1°17N 103°49E 138 B2
Alexandra Gauteng, S. Africa 26°6S 28°5E 123 A2
Alexandra Channel Myanmar 14°7N 93°13E 245 G11
Alexandra Falls Canada 60°29N 116°18W 296 A5
Alexandretta = İskenderun Turkey 36°32N 36°10E 250 B7
Alexandria = El Iskandarîya Egypt 31°13N 29°58E 256 H6
Alexandria B.C., Canada 52°35N 122°27W 296 C4
Alexandria Ont., Canada 45°19N 74°38W 313 A10
Alexandria Romania 43°57N 25°24E 183 G10
Alexandria Eastern Cape, S. Africa 33°38S 26°28E 270 D4
Alexandria W. Dunb., U.K. 55°59N 4°35W 167 F4
Alexandria Ind., U.S.A. 40°16N 85°41W 311 D11
Alexandria Ky., U.S.A. 38°58N 84°23W 311 F12
Alexandria La., U.S.A. 31°18N 92°27W 314 F8
Alexandria Minn., U.S.A. 45°53N 95°22W 308 C6
Alexandria Mo., U.S.A. 40°27N 91°28W 310 D5
Alexandria S. Dak., U.S.A. 43°39N 97°47W 308 D5
Alexandria Va., U.S.A. 38°49N 77°5W 143 C2
Alexandria Bay U.S.A. 44°20N 75°55W 313 B9
Alexandrina, L. Australia 35°25S 139°10E 282 C3
Alexandroupoli Greece 40°50N 25°54E 203 F9
Alexis U.S.A. 41°4N 90°33W 310 C6
Alexis ➔ Canada 52°33N 56°8W 299 B8
Alexis Creek Canada 52°10N 123°20W 296 C4
Aley ➔ Russia 52°51N 83°36E 217 B10
Aleysk Russia 52°40N 83°0E 217 B10
Alfabia Spain 39°44N 2°44E 206 B3
Alfama Lisbon, Portugal 126 c3
Alfambra Spain 40°33N 1°5W 196 E3
Alfândega da Fé Portugal 41°20N 6°59W 194 D4
Alfaro Spain 42°10N 1°50W 196 C3
Alfatar Bulgaria 43°59N 27°13E 203 C11
Alfeld Germany 51°59N 9°50E 178 D5
Alfenas Brazil 21°20S 46°10W 335 A6
Alföld Hungary 46°30N 20°0E 182 D5
Alfonsine Italy 44°30N 12°3E 199 D9
Alford Aberds., U.K. 57°14N 2°41W 167 D6
Alford Lincs., U.K. 53°15N 0°10E 168 D8
Alford Fla., U.S.A. 30°42N 85°24W 316 E4
Alfortville France 48°48N 2°24E 134 B3
Alfred Maine, U.S.A. 43°29N 70°43W 313 C14
Alfred N.Y., U.S.A. 42°16N 77°48W 312 D7
Alfredton N.Z. 40°41S 175°54E 284 G4
Alfreton U.K. 53°6N 1°24W 168 D6
Alfta Sweden 61°21N 16°4E 162 C10
Algaida Spain 39°33N 2°53E 206 B3
Algar Spain 36°40N 5°39W 195 J5
Ålgård Norway 58°46N 5°53E 164 F2
Algarinejo Spain 37°19N 4°9W 195 H6
Algarve Portugal 36°58N 8°20W 195 J2
Algeciras Spain 36°9N 5°28W 195 J5
Algemesí Spain 39°11N 0°27W 197 F4
Alger Algeria 36°42N 3°8E 261 A5
Alger ✕ (ALG) Algeria 36°45N 3°10E 197 J8
Alger ✕ (ALG) Algeria 36°39N 3°13E 197 J8
Algeria ■ Africa 28°30N 2°0E 261 C5
Algés Portugal 38°42N 9°13W 126 A1
Algha Kazakhstan 49°53N 57°20E 187 E10
Alghero Italy 40°33N 8°19E 200 B1
Älghult Sweden 57°0N 15°35E 163 G9
Algiers = Alger Algeria 36°42N 3°8E 261 A5
Algiers U.S.A. 29°56N 90°2W 131 B2
Algoa B. S. Africa 33°50S 25°45E 270 D4
Algodonales Spain 36°54N 5°24W 195 J5
Algodones Dunes U.S.A. 32°50N 115°5W 307 N11
Algodor ➔ Spain 39°55N 3°53W 194 F7
Algoma U.S.A. 44°36N 87°26W 308 C10
Algona U.S.A. 43°4N 94°14W 310 A2
Algonac U.S.A. 42°37N 82°32W 312 D2
Algonquin △ Canada 45°50N 78°30W 298 C4
Algorta Spain 43°21N 2°59W 196 B2
Algorta Uruguay 32°25S 57°23W 334 C4
Alhama de Almería Spain 36°57N 2°34W 195 J8
Alhama de Aragón Spain 41°18N 1°54W 196 D3
Alhama de Granada Spain 37°0N 3°59W 195 H7
Alhama de Murcia Spain 37°51N 1°25W 197 H3
Alhambra U.S.A. 34°5N 118°7W 126 B4
Alhaurín el Grande Spain 36°39N 4°41W 195 J6
Alhucemas = Al Hoceïma Morocco 35°8N 3°58W 261 A4
'Alī al Gharbī Iraq 32°30N 46°45E 213 F12
'Alī ash Sharqī Iraq 32°7N 46°44E 213 F12
Äli Bayramlı = Şirvan Azerbaijan 39°59N 48°52E 191 L9
'Alī Khēl Afghan. 33°57N 69°43E 242 C3
Ali Sahîh Djibouti 11°10N 42°44E 257 E5
Alī Shāh Iran 38°9N 45°50E 246 B5
Ália Italy 37°47N 13°43E 200 E6
'Alīābād Golestān, Iran 36°40N 54°33E 247 B7
'Alīābād Khorāsān, Iran 32°30N 57°30E 247 C8
'Alīābād Kordestān, Iran 35°4N 46°58E 246 C5
'Alīābād Yazd, Iran 31°41N 53°49E 247 D7
Aliade Nigeria 7°18N 8°29E 263 D6
Aliaga Spain 40°40N 0°42W 196 E4
Aliağa Turkey 38°47N 26°59E 205 C8
Aliakmonas ➔ Greece 40°30N 22°36E 202 F6
Alibag India 18°38N 72°56E 244 E1
Alibey Turkey 41°3N 28°56E 122 B1
Alibey Barajı Turkey 41°8N 28°53E 122 B1
Alibeyköy Turkey 41°4N 28°56E 122 B1
Alibo Ethiopia 9°52N 37°5E 257 F4
Alibori ➔ Benin 11°56N 3°17E 263 C5
Alibunar Serbia 45°5N 20°57E 182 E5
Alicante Spain 38°23N 0°30W 197 G4
Alicante □ Spain 38°30N 0°37W 197 G4
Alicante ✕ (ALC) Spain 38°14N 0°36W 197 G4
Alice Eastern Cape, S. Africa 32°48S 26°55E 270 D4
Alice Tex., U.S.A. 27°45N 98°5W 314 H5
Alice ➔ Queens., Australia 24°2S 144°50E 280 C3
Alice ➔ Queens., Australia 15°35S 142°20E 280 B3
Alice ➔ Papua N. G. 6°10S 141°8E 286 D1
Alice, Punta Italy 39°24N 17°9E 201 C10
Alice Arm Canada 55°29N 129°31W 296 B3
Alice Springs Australia 23°40S 133°50E 280 C1
Alicedale S. Africa 33°15S 26°4E 270 D4
Aliceville U.S.A. 33°8N 88°9W 315 E10
Alicia Bohol, Phil. 9°54N 124°26E 233 G5
Alicia Isabela, Phil. 16°46N 121°42E 232 C3
Alicudi Italy 38°33N 14°20E 201 D7
Alien Taiwan 22°52N 120°19E 225 D2
Aliganj India 27°30N 79°10E 243 F8
Aligarh Raj., India 25°55N 76°15E 242 G7
Aligarh Ut. P., India 27°55N 78°10E 242 F8
Alīgūdarz Iran 33°25N 49°45E 247 C6
Alijó Portugal 41°16N 7°27W 194 D3
Alikanas Greece 37°51N 20°47E 207 D2
Alima ➔ Congo 1°36S 16°36E 264 C3
Alimia Greece 36°16N 27°43E 206 E11
Alimodian Phil. 10°49N 122°26E 233 F4
Alimos Greece 37°52N 23°43E 112 B2
Alindao C.A.R. 5°2N 21°13E 264 A4
Alingsås Sweden 57°56N 12°31E 163 G6
Alipur Paschimbanga, India 22°43N 88°12E 124 B1
Alipur Pakistan 29°25N 70°55E 242 E4
Alipur Duar India 26°30N 89°35E 241 D2
Aliquippa U.S.A. 40°37N 80°15W 312 F4
Alishan Taiwan 23°31N 120°48E 225 D2
Aliste ➔ Spain 41°34N 5°58W 194 D5
Alitus = Alytus Lithuania 54°24N 24°3E 188 E3
Aliveri Greece 38°24N 24°2E 204 C6
Aliwal North S. Africa 30°45S 26°45E 270 D4
Alix Canada 52°24N 113°11W 296 C6
Aljezur Portugal 37°18N 8°49W 195 H2
Aljustrel Portugal 37°55N 8°10W 195 H2
Alkamari Niger 13°27N 11°10E 259 F2
Alkhanay △ Russia 51°0N 113°30E 215 D12
Alkmaar Neths. 52°37N 4°45E 170 B4
All American Canal U.S.A. 32°45N 115°15W 307 N11
Allacapan Phil. 18°15N 121°35E 232 B3
Allach Germany 48°11N 11°27E 131 A1
Allada Benin 6°41N 2°9E 263 D5
Allagadda India 15°8N 78°30E 245 G4
Allagash ➔ U.S.A. 47°5N 69°3W 309 B19
Allah Dad Pakistan 25°38N 67°34E 242 G2
Allahabad = Prayagraj India 25°25N 81°58E 243 G9
Allakaket U.S.A. 66°34N 152°39W 303 C9
Allambie Heights Australia 33°46S 151°15E 139 A2
Allan Canada 51°53N 106°4W 297 C7
Allanche France 45°14N 2°57E 174 C6
Allanmyo Myanmar 19°30N 95°17E 241 F5
Allanridge S. Africa 27°45S 26°40E 270 C4
Allansford Australia 38°26S 142°39E 282 E5
Allanton N.Z. 45°55S 170°15E 285 F5
Allaqi, Wadi ➔ Egypt 23°7N 32°47E 256 C3
Allariz Spain 42°11N 7°50W 194 C3
Allassac France 45°15N 1°29E 174 C5
Allatoona L. U.S.A. 34°10N 84°44W 316 A5
Ålleberg Sweden 58°8N 13°36E 163 F7
Allegan U.S.A. 42°32N 85°51W 311 B11
Allegany U.S.A. 42°6N 78°30W 312 D6
Allegheny ➔ U.S.A. 40°27N 80°1W 312 F5
Allegheny Mts. U.S.A. 38°15N 80°10W 309 F13
Allegheny Plateau U.S.A. 41°30N 78°30W 309 E14
Allegheny Res. U.S.A. 41°50N 79°0W 312 E6
Allègre France 45°12N 3°41E 174 C7
Allègre, Pte. Guadeloupe 16°22N 61°46W 322 e
Allen Argentina 38°58S 67°50W 336 A3
Allen Phil. 12°30N 124°17E 232 E5
Allen, Bog of Ireland 53°15N 7°0W 166 C5
Allen, L. Ireland 54°8N 8°4W 166 B3
Allendale U.S.A. 33°1N 81°18W 316 B8
Allende Mexico 28°20N 100°51W 318 B4
Allenstein = Olsztyn Poland 53°48N 20°29E 184 E7
Allentown U.S.A. 40°37N 75°29W 313 F9
Allentsteig Austria 48°41N 15°20E 180 C8
Alleppey = Alappuzha India 9°30N 76°28E 245 K3
Allepuz Spain 40°29N 0°44W 196 E4
Aller ➔ Germany 52°56N 9°12E 178 C5
Allermuir Hill U.K. 55°53N 3°14W 121 B2
Alley, The Jamaica 17°48N 77°17W 320 a
Alliance Suriname 5°50N 54°50W 329 B7
Alliance Nebr., U.S.A. 42°6N 102°52W 308 D2
Alliance Ohio, U.S.A. 40°55N 81°6W 312 F3
Allianz Arena Munich, Germany 48°13N 11°37E 131 A2
Allier □ France 46°25N 2°40E 173 F9
Allier ➔ France 46°57N 3°4E 173 F10
Alliford Bay Canada 53°12N 131°58W 296 C2
Alligator Pond Jamaica 17°52N 77°34W 320 a
Allinagaram India 10°2N 77°30E 245 J3
Allinge Denmark 55°17N 14°50E 163 J8
Allison U.S.A. 42°45N 92°48W 310 B4
Alliston Canada 44°9N 79°52W 312 B5
Alloa U.K. 56°7N 3°47W 167 E5
Allones France 48°20N 1°40E 172 D8
Allora Australia 28°2S 152°0E 281 D5
Allos France 44°15N 6°38E 175 D10
Allston U.S.A. 42°21N 71°7W 116 A2
Alluitsup Paa Greenland 60°30N 45°35W 154 E6
Allur India 14°40N 80°4E 245 G5
Alluru Kottapatnam India 15°24N 80°7E 245 G5
Alma Qué., Canada 48°35N 71°40W 299 C5
Alma Ga., U.S.A. 31°33N 82°28W 316 D7
Alma Kans., U.S.A. 39°1N 96°17W 308 F5
Alma Mich., U.S.A. 43°23N 84°39W 309 D11
Alma Nebr., U.S.A. 40°6N 99°22W 308 E4
Alma Wis., U.S.A. 44°20N 91°55W 308 C8
Alma Ata = Almaty Kazakhstan 43°15N 76°57E 217 D9
Alma Hill U.S.A. 42°2N 78°0W 312 D7
Almacelles Spain 41°43N 0°27E 196 D5
Almada Portugal 38°41N 9°8W 126 A2
Almaden Queens., Australia 17°22S 144°40E 280 B3
Almadén Spain 38°49N 4°52W 195 G6
Almagro Argentina 34°38S 58°24W 117 B2
Almagro I. Phil. 11°55N 124°18E 233 F5
Almalyk = Olmaliq Uzbekistan 40°50N 69°35E 217 D7
Almanor, L. U.S.A. 40°14N 121°9W 304 F3
Almansa Spain 38°51N 1°5W 197 G3
Almanza Spain 42°39N 5°3W 194 C5
Almanzor, Pico Spain 40°15N 5°18W 194 E5
Almanzora ➔ Spain 37°14N 1°46W 197 H3
Almargem do Bispo Portugal 38°49N 9°17W 126 A1
Almas Brazil 11°33S 47°9W 333 D2
Almaş, Munţii Romania 44°49N 22°12E 182 F7
Almaty Kazakhstan 43°15N 76°57E 217 D9
Almaty □ Kazakhstan 44°30N 78°0E 217 D9
Almazán Spain 41°30N 2°30W 196 D2
Almazora Spain 39°57N 0°3W 196 F4
Almeirim Brazil 1°30S 52°34W 329 D7
Almeirim Portugal 39°12N 8°37W 195 F2
Almelo Neths. 52°22N 6°42E 170 B6
Almenar de Soria Spain 41°43N 2°12W 196 D2
Almenara Brazil 16°11S 40°42W 333 E3
Almenara Spain 39°46N 0°14W 196 F4
Almenara, Sierra de Spain 37°34N 1°32W 197 H3
Almendra, Embalse de Spain 41°10N 6°5W 194 D4
Almendralejo Spain 38°41N 6°26W 195 G4
Almere Neths. 52°20N 5°15E 170 B5
Almería Spain 36°52N 2°27W 195 J8
Almería □ Spain 37°20N 2°20W 197 H2
Almería, G. de Spain 36°41N 2°28W 197 J2
Almetyevsk Russia 54°53N 52°20E 190 C11
Älmhult Sweden 56°33N 14°8E 163 H8
Almirante Panama 9°10N 82°30W 320 E3
Almirante G. Brown, Parque Argentina 34°40S 58°28W 117 C2
Almirante Montt, G. Chile 51°52S 72°50W 336 D2
Almiropotamos Greece 38°16N 24°11E 204 C6
Almiros Greece 39°11N 22°45E 204 B4
Almodôvar Portugal 37°31N 8°2W 195 H2
Almodóvar del Campo Spain 38°43N 4°10W 195 G6
Almodóvar del Río Spain 37°48N 5°1W 195 H5
Almon West Bank 31°49N 35°17E 123 B2
Almond U.S.A. 42°19N 77°44W 312 D7
Almond ➔ U.K. 55°58N 3°18W 121 B2
Almont U.S.A. 42°55N 83°3W 312 D1
Almonte Ont., Canada 45°14N 76°12W 313 A8
Almonte Spain 37°13N 6°38W 195 H4
Almora India 29°38N 79°40E 243 E8
Almoradí Spain 38°7N 0°46W 197 G4
Almorox Spain 40°14N 4°24W 194 E6
Almoustarat Mali 17°35N 0°8E 263 B5
Älmsta Sweden 59°58N 18°50E 162 E12
Almudévar Spain 42°3N 0°35W 196 C4
Almuñécar Spain 36°43N 3°41W 195 J7
Almunge Sweden 59°53N 18°3E 162 E12
Almuradiel Spain 38°32N 3°28W 195 G7
Almus Turkey 40°22N 36°54E 212 B7
Almvik Sweden 57°49N 16°30E 163 G10
Almyrou, Ormos Greece 35°23N 24°20E 207 E5
Alna Norway 59°55N 10°50E 133 A4
Alness U.K. 57°41N 4°16W 167 D4
Alnif Morocco 31°10N 5°8W 260 B3
Alnmouth U.K. 55°24N 1°37W 168 B6
Alnsjøen Norway 59°57N 10°51E 133 A4
Alnwick U.K. 55°24N 1°42W 168 B6
Alofau Amer. Samoa 14°16S 170°36W 302 f
Alofi Niue 19°1S 169°55W 289 g
Alofi, I. Wall. & F. Is. 14°27S 178°5W 277 C15
Alofi B. Niue 19°1S 169°56W 289 g
Aloi Uganda 2°16N 33°10E 268 B3
Alon Myanmar 22°12N 95°5E 241 D5
Along India 28°10N 94°46E 241 A5
Alonissos Greece 39°8N 23°50E 204 B5
Alonissos-Northern Sporades △ Greece 39°15N 24°5E 204 B6
Alor Indonesia 8°15S 124°30E 231 F6
Alor Setar Malaysia 6°7N 100°22E 237 J3
Álora Spain 36°49N 4°46W 195 J6
Alosno Spain 37°33N 7°7W 195 H3
Alost = Aalst Belgium 50°56N 4°2E 170 D4
Alot India 23°56N 75°40E 242 H6
Alotau Papua N. G. 10°16S 150°30E 286 F6
Alougoum Morocco 30°17N 6°56W 260 B3
Aloum Cameroon 2°16N 10°34E 264 B2
Aloysius, Mt. Australia 26°0S 128°38E 279 E4
Alpaugh U.S.A. 35°53N 119°29W 306 K7
Alpe Apuane ⌂ Italy 44°4N 10°15E 198 D7
Alpedrinha Portugal 40°6N 7°27W 194 E3
Alpena U.S.A. 45°4N 83°27W 312 A1
Alpercatas ➔ Brazil 6°2S 44°19W 332 C3
Alperton U.K. 51°32N 0°17W 125 A2
Alpes-de-Haute-Provence □ France 44°8N 6°10E 175 D10
Alpes-Maritimes □ France 43°55N 7°10E 175 E11
Alpha Queens., Australia 23°39S 146°37E 280 C4
Alpha Ill., U.S.A. 41°12N 90°23W 310 C6
Alpha Ridge Arctic 84°0N 118°0W 150 A2
Alpharetta U.S.A. 34°5N 84°18W 316 A5
Alphen aan den Rijn Neths. 52°7N 4°40E 170 B4
Alphios ➔ Greece 37°40N 21°33E 204 D3
Alpiarça Portugal 39°15N 8°35W 195 F2
Alpine Ariz., U.S.A. 33°51N 109°9W 305 K9
Alpine Calif., U.S.A. 32°50N 116°46W 307 N10
Alpine N.J., U.S.A. 40°57N 73°57W 132 A2
Alpine Tex., U.S.A. 30°22N 103°40W 314 F3
Alpine △ Australia 36°56S 148°10E 283 D7
Alps Europe 46°30N 9°30E 176 E5
Alpu Turkey 39°46N 30°58E 212 C4
Alpurrurulam Australia 20°59S 137°50E 280 C2
Alqueta, Barragem do Portugal 38°20N 7°25W 195 G3
Alrø Denmark 55°52N 10°5E 163 J4
Alrode S. Africa 26°17S 28°7E 123 B2
Als Denmark 54°59N 9°55E 163 K3
Alsace France 48°15N 7°25E 171 B7
Alsask Canada 51°21N 109°59W 297 C7
Alsasua Spain 42°54N 2°10W 196 C2
Alsek ➔ U.S.A. 59°10N 138°12W 296 B1
Alsemberg Belgium 50°44N 4°20E 116 B2
Alsergrund Austria 48°13N 16°21E 142 A2
Alsfeld Germany 50°44N 9°16E 178 E5
Alsip U.S.A. 41°40N 87°44W 119 C2
Alsta Norway 65°58N 12°40E 160 D15
Ålsten Sweden 59°19N 17°57E 139 B1
Alsterbro Sweden 56°57N 15°55E 163 H9
Alstermo Sweden 56°58N 15°38E 163 H9
Alston U.K. 54°49N 2°25W 168 C5
Alta Finnmark, Norway 69°57N 23°10E 160 B20
Älta Sweden 59°15N 18°11E 139 B3
Alta, Sierra Spain 40°31N 1°30W 196 E3
Alta Floresta Brazil 9°57S 55°58W 331 B6
Alta Gracia Argentina 31°40S 64°30W 334 C3
Alta Murgia △ Italy 40°55N 16°30E 201 B9
Alta Sierra U.S.A. 35°42N 118°33W 307 K8
Altadena U.S.A. 34°11N 118°8W 126 A4
Altaelva ➔ Norway 69°54N 23°17E 160 B20
Altafjorden Norway 70°5N 23°5E 160 A20
Altagracia Nueva Esparta, Venezuela 11°6N 63°57W 329 a
Altagracia Zulia, Venezuela 10°45N 71°30W 328 A3
Altagracia de Orituco Venezuela 9°52N 66°23W 328 B4
Altai = Aerhtai Shan Mongolia 46°40N 92°45E 217 C12
Altai = Gorno-Altay □ Russia 51°0N 86°0E 217 B11
Altai △ Russia 50°30N 85°30E 217 B11
Altamachi ➔ Bolivia 16°8S 66°50W 330 D4
Altamaha ➔ U.S.A. 31°20N 81°20W 316 D8
Altamira Brazil 3°12S 52°10W 329 D7
Altamira Chile 25°47S 69°51W 334 B2
Altamira Colombia 2°3N 75°47W 328 C2
Altamira Tamaulipas, Mexico 22°24N 97°55W 319 C5
Altamira, Cuevas de Spain 43°20N 4°5W 194 B6
Altamont Ill., U.S.A. 39°4N 88°45W 311 E9
Altamont N.Y., U.S.A. 42°42N 74°2W 313 D10
Altamura Italy 40°49N 16°33E 201 B9
Altanbulag Mongolia 50°16N 106°30E 218 A10
Altar Mexico 30°43N 111°44W 318 A2
Altar, Gran Desierto de Mexico 31°50N 114°10W 318 B2
Altata Mexico 24°40N 107°55W 318 C3
Altavas Phil. 11°32N 122°29E 233 F4
Altavista U.S.A. 37°6N 79°17W 309 G14
Altay Xinjiang Uygur, China 47°48N 88°10E 217 C11
Altay Mongolia 46°22N 96°15E 218 B8
Altdorf Switz. 46°52N 8°36E 179 J4
Alte-Donau ➔ Austria 48°14N 16°25E 142 A2
Alte Mellum Germany 53°43N 8°10E 178 B4
Altea Spain 38°38N 0°2W 197 G4
Altenberg Germany 50°45N 13°45E 178 E9
Altenbruch Germany 53°49N 8°46E 178 B4
Altenburg Germany 50°59N 12°25E 178 E8
Altenkirchen Mecklenburg-Vorpommern, Germany 54°38N 13°22E 178 A9
Altenkirchen Rhld-Pfz., Germany 50°41N 7°39E 178 E3
Altenmarkt Austria 47°43N 14°39E 180 D7
Alter do Chão Brazil 2°31S 54°57W 329 D6
Alter do Chão Portugal 39°12N 7°40W 195 F3
Alter Finkenkrug Germany 52°35N 13°3E 115 A1
Altes Rathaus Munich, Germany 131 b3
Altglienicke Germany 52°25N 13°32E 115 B4
Altha U.S.A. 30°34N 85°8W 316 E4
Altınkaya Barajı Turkey 41°18N 35°30E 212 B6
Altınoluk Turkey 39°34N 26°45E 205 B8
Altınova Turkey 39°12N 26°47E 205 B8
Altınözü Turkey 36°7N 36°14E 250 B7
Altıntaş Turkey 39°4N 30°7E 205 B12
Altınyaka Turkey 36°33N 30°20E 205 E12
Altınyayla Turkey 37°0N 29°33E 205 D11
Altiplano Bolivia 17°0S 68°0W 330 D4
Altkirch France 47°37N 7°15E 173 E14
Altlandsberg Germany 52°33N 13°43E 115 A5
Altlandsberg Nord Germany 52°34N 13°43E 115 A5
Altmannsdorf Austria 48°9N 16°18E 142 B2
Altmark Germany 52°45N 11°30E 178 C7
Altmühl ➔ Germany 48°54N 11°52E 179 G7
Altmühltal △ Germany 48°55N 11°15E 179 G7
Altmunster Austria 47°54N 13°45E 180 D6
Alto Adige = Trentino-Alto Adige □ Italy 46°30N 11°20E 199 B8
Alto Alegre Brazil 2°50N 61°20W 329 C5
Alto Araguaia Brazil 17°15S 53°20W 333 E1
Alto Chicapa Angola 10°52S 19°17E 265 E3
Alto Cuchumatanes = Cuchumatanes, Sierra de los Guatemala 15°35N 91°25W 320 C1
Alto Cuito = Tempué Angola 13°27S 18°49E 265 E3
Alto da Boa Vista Brazil 22°57S 43°16W 135 B1
Alto da Moóca Brazil 23°34S 46°33W 137 B2
Alto del Carmen Chile 28°46S 70°30W 334 B1
Alto do Pina Portugal 38°44N 9°7W 126 A2
Alto Douro Portugal 41°6N 7°47W 194 D3
Alto Garças Brazil 16°56S 53°32W 331 D7
Alto Garda Bresciano ⌂ Italy 45°42N 10°38E 198 C7
Alto Iriri ➔ Brazil 8°50S 53°25W 331 B7
Alto Ligonha Mozam. 15°30S 38°11E 269 F4
Alto Molocue Mozam. 15°50S 37°35E 269 F4
Alto Paraguai Brazil 14°30S 56°31W 331 C6
Alto Paraguay □ Paraguay 21°0S 58°30W 334 A4
Alto Paraíso de Goiás Brazil 14°7S 47°31W 333 D2
Alto Paraná □ Paraguay 25°30S 54°50W 335 B5
Alto Parnaíba Brazil 9°6S 45°57W 332 C2
Alto Purús ➔ Peru 9°12S 70°28W 330 B3
Alto Río Senguerr Argentina 45°2S 70°50W 336 C2
Alto Santo Brazil 5°31S 38°15W 332 C4
Alto Sucuriú Brazil 19°19S 52°47W 331 D7
Alto Tajo ⌂ Spain 40°44N 2°30W 196 E2
Alton Ont., Canada 43°54N 80°5W 312 C4
Alton Hants., U.K. 51°9N 0°59W 169 F7
Alton Ill., U.S.A. 38°53N 90°11W 310 F6
Alton N.H., U.S.A. 43°27N 71°13W 313 C13
Altona Vic., Australia 37°51S 144°49E 128 B1
Altona Man., Canada 49°6N 97°33W 297 D9
Altoona Ala., U.S.A. 34°2N 86°20W 316 A3
Altoona Iowa, U.S.A. 41°39N 93°28W 310 C3
Altoona Pa., U.S.A. 40°31N 78°24W 312 F6
Altos Brazil 5°3S 42°28W 332 C3
Altötting Germany 48°12N 12°39E 179 G8
Altsasu = Alsasua Spain 42°54N 2°10W 196 C2
Altstätten Switz. 47°22N 9°33E 179 H5
Altun Kupri Iraq 35°45N 44°9E 213 E11
Altun Shan China 38°30N 88°0E 217 E11
Alturas U.S.A. 41°29N 120°32W 304 F3
Altus U.S.A. 34°38N 99°20W 314 D5
Altyn-Emel △ Kazakhstan 44°40N 78°26E 217 D9
Alubijid Phil. 8°35N 124°29E 233 G5
Alucra Turkey 40°22N 38°47E 213 B8
Aluk South Sudan 8°25N 27°30E 257 F2
Alūksne Latvia 57°24N 27°3E 188 D4
Alunda Sweden 60°4N 18°5E 162 D12
Alunite U.S.A. 35°59N 114°55W 307 K12
Aluoro ➔ Ethiopia 8°26N 33°24E 257 F3
Alupka Ukraine 44°23N 34°2E 189 K8
Alur India 15°24N 77°15E 245 E3
Alur Gajah Malaysia 2°23N 102°13E 234 B2
Alushta Ukraine 44°40N 34°25E 189 K8
Alusi Indonesia 7°35S 131°40E 231 F8
Alustante Spain 40°36N 1°40W 196 E3
Alutgama Sri Lanka 6°26N 79°59E 245 L4
Alutnuwara Sri Lanka 7°19N 80°59E 245 L5
Aluva India 10°8N 76°24E 245 J3
Alva U.S.A. 36°48N 98°40W 314 C5
Alvaiázere Portugal 39°49N 8°23W 194 F2
Alvalade Portugal 38°45N 9°8W 126 A2
Älvängen Sweden 57°58N 12°8E 163 G6
Alvão △ Portugal 41°22N 7°48W 194 D3
Alvarado Veracruz, Mexico 18°46N 95°46W 319 D5
Alvarado Tex., U.S.A. 32°24N 97°13W 314 E6
Alvarães Brazil 3°12S 64°50W 329 D5
Alvaro Obregón, Presa Mexico 27°52N 109°52W 318 B3
Alvdal Norway 62°6N 10°37E 164 B7
Älvdalen Sweden 61°13N 14°4E 162 C8
Alvear Argentina 29°5S 56°30W 334 B4
Alverca Portugal 38°56N 9°1W 195 G1
Alvesta Sweden 56°54N 14°35E 163 H8
Alvik Sweden 59°19N 17°58E 139 B1
Alvin Callendar Naval Air Station U.S.A. 29°50N 90°1W 131 B2
Alvinston Canada 42°49N 81°52W 312 D3
Alvito Portugal 38°15N 7°58W 195 G3
Älvkarleby Sweden 60°34N 17°26E 162 D11
Alvorado Brazil 12°28S 49°6W 333 D2
Alvord Desert U.S.A. 42°30N 118°25W 304 E4
Älvros Sweden 62°3N 14°38E 162 B8
Älvsbyn Sweden 65°40N 21°0E 160 D19
Älvsjö Sweden 59°16N 18°0E 139 B2
Ålvundeid Norway 62°45N 8°33E 164 B5
Älvvik Sweden 59°21N 18°15E 139 A3
Alwar India 27°38N 76°34E 242 F7
Alwaye = Aluva India 10°8N 76°24E 245 J3
Alxa Zuoqi China 38°50N 105°40E 226 E3
Alyangula Australia 13°55S 136°30E 280 A2
Alyata = Älät Azerbaijan 39°58N 49°25E 191 L9
Alyth U.K. 56°38N 3°13W 167 E5
Alytus Lithuania 54°24N 24°3E 188 E3
Alzada U.S.A. 45°2N 104°25W 304 D11
Alzamay Russia 55°33N 98°39E 215 D10
Alzey Germany 49°45N 8°7E 179 F4
Alzira Spain 39°9N 0°30W 197 F4
Am Dam Chad 12°40N 20°35E 259 F4
Am Géréda Chad 12°53N 21°14E 259 F4
Am Hasenbergl Germany 48°12N 11°33E 131 A2
Am Sak Chad 13°39N 20°8E 259 F4
Am Steinhof Austria 48°12N 16°17E 142 A1
Am Timan Chad 11°0N 20°10E 259 F4
Am Wald Germany 48°3N 11°36E 131 B2
Ama Keng Singapore 1°23N 103°41E 138 A2
Amacayacu △ Colombia 3°21S 70°8W 328 D3
Amada Gaza C.A.R. 4°46N 15°9E 264 B3
Amådalen Sweden 61°20N 14°44E 162 C8
Amadeus, L. Australia 24°54S 131°0E 279 D5
Amadi Dem. Rep. of the Congo 3°40N 26°40E 268 B2
Amadi South Sudan 5°29N 30°25E 257 F3
Amadjuak L. Canada 65°0N 71°8W 295 E17
Amadora Portugal 38°45N 9°13W 126 A1
Amagansett U.S.A. 40°59N 72°9W 313 F12
Amagasaki Japan 34°42N 135°23E 133 A1
Amager Denmark 55°36N 12°35E 118 B3
Amagi Japan 33°25N 130°39E 222 D2
Amagunze Nigeria 6°20N 7°40E 263 D6
Amahai Indonesia 3°20S 128°55E 231 E7
Amaile Samoa 13°59S 171°22W 287 V20
Amaimon Papua N. G. 5°12S 145°30E 286 C3
Amaiun-Maia Spain 43°12N 1°29W 196 B3
Amakusa = Hondo Japan 32°27N 130°12E 222 E2
Amakusa-Nada Japan 32°35N 130°5E 222 E2
Amakusa-Shotō Japan 32°15N 130°10E 222 E2
Amal Oman 18°21N 55°39E 249 C6
Åmål Sweden 59°3N 12°42E 162 E6
Amâl Qādisiya Iraq 33°16N 44°20E 113 B2
Amalapuram India 16°35N 81°55E 245 F5
Amalfi Colombia 6°55N 75°4W 328 B2
Amalfi Italy 40°38N 14°36E 201 B7
Amaliada Greece 37°47N 21°22E 204 D3
Amalienborg Slot Copenhagen, Denmark 118 b3
Amalner India 21°5N 75°5E 244 D2
Amamapare Indonesia 4°53S 136°38E 231 E9
Amambaí Brazil 23°5S 55°13W 335 A4
Amambaí ➔ Brazil 23°22S 53°56W 335 A5
Amambay □ Paraguay 23°0S 56°0W 334 A4
Amambay, Cordillera de S. Amer. 23°0S 55°45W 335 A4
Amami Japan 28°22N 129°27E 221 K4
Amami-Guntō Japan 27°16N 129°21E 221 L4
Amami-Ō-Shima Japan 28°16N 129°21E 221 K4
Aman, Pulau Malaysia 5°16N 100°24E 237 c
Amana ➔ Venezuela 9°45N 62°39W 329 B5
Amaná, L. Brazil 2°35S 64°40W 329 D5
Amanab Papua N. G. 3°40S 141°14E 286 B1
Amanat ➔ India 24°7N 84°4E 243 G11
Amanave Amer. Samoa 14°20S 170°50W 302 f
Amanda Park U.S.A. 47°28N 123°55W 306 C3
Amankeldi Kazakhstan 50°10N 65°10E 216 B7
Amanohashidate Japan 35°40N 135°15E 223 B7

Amantea *Italy* 39°8N 16°4E **201** C9
Amanu *French Polynesia* 17°48S 140°46W **289** f
Amapá *Brazil* 2°5N 50°50W **329** C7
Amapá □ *Brazil* 1°40N 52°0W **329** C7
Amapari = Ferreira Gomes *Brazil* 0°48N 51°8W **329** C7
Amara *Sudan* 10°25N 34°10E **257** E3
Amara □ *Ethiopia* 12°30N 37°30E **257** E4
Amaração = Luis Correia *Brazil* 3°0S 41°35W **332** B3
Amarante *Brazil* 6°14S 42°50W **332** C3
Amarante *Portugal* 41°16N 8°5W **194** D2
Amarante do Maranhão *Brazil* 5°36S 46°45W **332** C2
Amaranth *Canada* 50°36N 98°43W **297** C9
Amarapura *Myanmar* 21°54N 96°3E **241** E6
Amaravati ➔ *India* 11°0N 78°15E **245** J4
Amareleja *Portugal* 38°12N 7°13W **195** G3
Amargosa *Brazil* 13°2S 39°36W **333** D4
Amargosa ➔ *U.S.A.* 36°14N 116°51W **307** J10
Amargosa Desert *U.S.A.* 36°40N 116°30W **307** J10
Amargosa Range *U.S.A.* 36°20N 116°45W **307** J10
Amari *Greece* 35°13N 24°40E **207** E5
Amarillo *U.S.A.* 35°13N 101°50W **314** D4
Amarkantak *India* 22°40N 81°45E **243** H9
'Amârna, Tell el *Egypt* 27°38N 30°52E **256** B3
Amarnath *India* 19°12N 73°22E **244** E1
Amaro, Mte. *Italy* 42°5N 14°5E **199** F11
Amarpur *Bihar, India* 25°5N 87°0E **243** G12
Amarpur *Tripura, India* 23°31N 91°39E **241** D3
Amarti *Eritrea* 14°17N 41°6E **257** E5
Amarwara *India* 22°18N 79°10E **243** H8
Amasin *W. Sahara* 25°45N 13°20W **260** C2
Amasra *Turkey* 41°45N 32°23E **212** B5
Amassama *Nigeria* 5°1N 6°2E **263** D6
Amasya *Turkey* 40°40N 35°50E **212** B6
Amasya □ *Turkey* 40°40N 35°50E **212** B6
Amata *S. Austral., Australia* 26°9S 131°9E **279** E5
Amata *Piemonte, Italy* 45°34N 9°8E **128** A1
Amataurá *Brazil* 3°29S 68°6W **328** D4
Amatignak I. *U.S.A.* 51°16N 179°6W **303** L3
Amatikulu *S. Africa* 29°3S 31°33E **271** C5
Amatitlán *Guatemala* 14°29N 90°38W **320** D1
Amatrice *Italy* 42°38N 13°17E **199** F10
Amau *Papua N. G.* 10°2S 148°34E **286** F5
Amay *Belgium* 50°33N 5°19E **170** D5
Amazon = Amazonas ➔ *S. Amer.* 0°5S 50°0W **329** D8
Amazonas □ *Brazil* 5°0S 65°0W **331** B5
Amazonas □ *Peru* 5°0S 78°0W **330** B2
Amazonas □ *Venezuela* 3°30N 66°0W **328** C4
Amazonas ➔ *S. Amer.* 0°5S 50°0W **329** D8
Amba Ferit *Ethiopia* 10°55N 38°50E **257** E4
Ambad *India* 19°38N 75°50E **244** E2
Ambae = Aoba *Vanuatu* 15°25S 167°50E **287** E5
Ambagarh Chowki *India* 20°47N 80°43E **244** D5
Ambah *India* 26°43N 78°13E **242** F8
Ambahakily *Madag.* 21°36S 43°41E **272** C1
Ambahita *Madag.* 24°1S 45°16E **272** C2
Ambajogal *India* 18°44N 76°23E **244** E3
Ambala *India* 30°23N 76°56E **242** D7
Ambalangoda *Sri Lanka* 6°15N 80°5E **245** L5
Ambalantota *Sri Lanka* 6°7N 81°1E **245** L5
Ambalapulai *India* 9°25N 76°25E **245** K3
Ambalavao *Madag.* 21°50S 46°56E **272** C2
Ambam *Cameroon* 2°20N 11°15E **264** B2
Ambanja *Madag.* 13°40S 48°27E **272** A2
Ambararata *Madag.* 15°3S 48°33E **272** B2
Ambarchik *Russia* 69°40N 162°20E **215** C17
Ambarijeby *Madag.* 14°56S 47°41E **272** A2
Ambarlı *Turkey* 40°58N 28°40E **203** E12
Ambaro, Helodranon' *Madag.* 13°23S 48°38E **272** A2
Ambasamudram *India* 8°43N 77°25E **245** K3
Ambato *Ecuador* 1°5S 78°42W **328** D2
Ambato *Madag.* 13°24S 48°29E **272** A2
Ambato, Sierra de *Argentina* 28°25S 66°10W **334** B2
Ambato Boeny *Madag.* 16°28S 46°43E **272** B2
Ambatofinandrahana *Madag.* 20°33S 46°48E **272** C2
Ambatolampy *Madag.* 19°20S 47°35E **272** B2
Ambatomainty *Madag.* 17°41S 45°40E **272** B2
Ambatomanoina *Madag.* 18°18S 47°37E **272** B2
Ambatondrazaka *Madag.* 17°55S 48°28E **272** B2
Ambatosoratra *Madag.* 17°37S 48°31E **272** B2
Ambelokipi *Greece* 37°58N 23°47E **112** B2
Ambelonas *Greece* 39°45N 22°22E **204** B4
Ambenja *Madag.* 15°17S 46°58E **272** B2
Amberg *Germany* 49°26N 11°52E **179** F7
Ambergris Cay *Belize* 18°0N 87°55W **320** C2
Ambérieu-en-Bugey *France* 45°57N 5°20E **175** C9
Amberley *Ont., Canada* 44°2N 81°42W **312** B3
Amberley *N.Z.* 43°9S 172°44E **285** D7
Ambert *France* 45°33N 3°44E **174** C7
Ambidédi *Mali* 14°35N 11°47W **262** C2
Ambikapur *India* 23°15N 83°15E **243** H10
Ambikol *Sudan* 21°20N 30°50E **256** C3
Ambil I. *Phil.* 13°48N 120°18E **232** E3
Ambilobé *Madag.* 13°10S 49°3E **272** A2
Ambinanindrano *Madag.* 20°5S 48°23E **272** C2
Ambinanitelo *Madag.* 15°21S 49°35E **272** B2
Ambinda *Madag.* 16°25S 45°52E **272** B2
Ambitle I. *Papua N. G.* 4°5S 153°37E **286** C7
Amble *U.K.* 55°20N 1°36W **168** B6
Ambler *U.S.A.* 67°5N 157°52W **303** C8
Ambleside *U.K.* 54°26N 2°58W **168** C5
Ambo *Peru* 10°5S 76°10W **330** C2
Amboahangy *Madag.* 24°15S 46°22E **272** C2
Amboasary *Madag.* 25°1S 46°5E **272** D2
Ambodifototra *Madag.* 16°59S 49°52E **272** B2
Ambodilazana *Madag.* 18°6S 49°10E **272** B2
Ambodiriana *Madag.* 17°55S 49°18E **272** B2
Ambohidratrimo *Madag.* 18°50S 47°26E **272** B2
Ambohidray *Madag.* 18°36S 48°18E **272** B2
Ambohimahamasina *Madag.* 21°56S 47°11E **272** C2
Ambohimahasoa *Madag.* 21°7S 47°13E **272** C2
Ambohimanga *Analamanga, Madag.* 18°45S 47°33E **272** B2
Ambohimanga *Vatovavy-Fitovinany, Madag.* 20°52S 47°36E **272** C2
Ambohimitombo *Madag.* 20°43S 47°26E **272** C2
Ambohitra *Madag.* 12°30S 49°10E **272** A2
Amboise *France* 47°24N 1°2E **172** E8
Amboiva *Angola* 11°33S 14°43E **265** E2
Ambon *Indonesia* 3°43S 128°12E **231** E7
Ambondro *Madag.* 25°13S 45°44E **272** D2
Amboró ⌓ *Bolivia* 17°39S 64°3W **331** D5
Amboseli, L. *Kenya* 2°40S 37°10E **268** C4
Amboseli ⌓ *Kenya* 2°37S 37°13E **268** C4
Ambositra *Madag.* 20°31S 47°25E **272** C2
Ambovombe *Madag.* 25°11S 46°5E **272** D2
Amboy *Calif., U.S.A.* 34°33N 115°45W **307** L11
Amboy *Ill., U.S.A.* 41°44N 89°20W **310** C7
Amboyna Cay *S. China Sea* 7°50N 112°50E **230** C4
Ambre, Île d' *Mauritius* 20°2S 57°41E **277** e
Ambridge *U.S.A.* 40°36N 80°14W **312** F4
Ambriz *Angola* 7°48S 13°8E **265** D2
Ambriz ⌓ *Angola* 7°56S 10°27E **265** D2
Ambrolauri *Georgia* 42°31N 43°9E **213** A10
Ambrym *Vanuatu* 16°15S 168°10E **287** F6
Ambulong I. *Phil.* 12°13N 121°1E **232** E3
Ambunti *Papua N. G.* 4°13S 142°52E **286** C2
Ambur *India* 12°48N 78°43E **245** H4
Amchitka I. *U.S.A.* 51°32N 179°0E **303** L2
Amderma *Russia* 69°45N 61°30E **214** C7
Amdhi *India* 23°51N 81°27E **243** H9
Amdo *China* 32°20N 91°40E **218** E7
Ameca *Mexico* 20°33N 104°2W **318** C4
Ameca ➔ *Mexico* 20°41N 105°18W **318** C3
Amecameca de Juárez *Mexico* 19°8N 98°46W **319** D5
Amed *Indonesia* 8°19S 115°39E **231** J18
Ameixoeira *Portugal* 38°46N 9°8W **126** A2
Ameland *Neths.* 53°27N 5°45E **170** A5
Amélia *Italy* 42°33N 12°25E **199** F9
Amelia City *U.S.A.* 30°35N 81°28W **316** E8
Amelia Earhart Park *U.S.A.* 25°53N 80°16W **129** C1
Amelia I. *U.S.A.* 30°40N 81°25W **316** E8
Amendolara *Italy* 39°57N 16°35E **201** C9
Amenia *U.S.A.* 41°51N 73°33W **313** E11
América *Brazil* 23°35S 46°41W **137** B1
America-Antarctica Ridge *S. Ocean* 59°0S 16°0W **151** B2
American Falls *U.S.A.* 42°47N 112°51W **304** E7
American Falls Res. *U.S.A.* 42°47N 112°52W **304** E7
American Fork *U.S.A.* 40°23N 111°48W **304** F8
American Highland *Antarctica* 73°0S 75°0E **151** D6
American Indian Museum *Washington, D.C., U.S.A.* **143** b3
American Museum of Natural History *New York, U.S.A.* **132** b2
American River *Australia* 35°47S 137°46E **282** C2
American Samoa ☑ *Pac. Oc.* 14°20S 170°0W **302** f
American Samoa ⌓ *Amer. Samoa* 14°15S 170°28W **302** g
American Univ. *U.S.A.* 38°56N 77°5W **143** B2
Americana *Brazil* 22°45S 47°20W **335** A6
Americus *U.S.A.* 32°4N 84°14W **316** C5
Amerigo Vespucci, Firenze ✕ (FLR) *Italy* 43°49N 11°13E **199** E8
Amerika = Nakhodka *Russia* 42°53N 132°54E **220** C6
Amersfoort *Neths.* 52°9N 5°23E **170** B5
Amersfoort *Mpumalanga, S. Africa* 26°59S 29°53E **271** C4
Amery Basin *S. Ocean* 68°15S 74°30E **151** C6
Amery Ice Shelf *Antarctica* 69°30S 72°0E **151** C6
Amerzgane *Morocco* 31°4N 7°14W **260** B3
Ames = Bertamirans *Spain* 42°54N 8°38W **194** C2
Ames *U.S.A.* 42°2N 93°37W **310** C3
Amesbury *U.S.A.* 42°51N 70°56W **313** D14
Amet *India* 25°18N 73°56E **242** G5
Amfiklia *Greece* 38°38N 22°35E **204** C4
Amfilochia *Greece* 38°52N 21°9E **204** C3
Amfipoli *Greece* 40°48N 23°52E **202** F7
Amfissa *Greece* 38°32N 22°22E **204** C4
Amga *Russia* 60°50N 132°0E **215** C14
Amga ➔ *Russia* 62°38N 134°32E **215** C14
Amgaon *India* 21°22N 80°22E **244** D5
Amgu *Russia* 45°45N 137°15E **220** B8
Amguid *Algeria* 26°26N 5°22E **261** C6
Amgun ➔ *Russia* 52°56N 139°38E **215** D14
Amherst = Kyaikkami *Myanmar* 16°4N 97°34E **241** G6
Amherst *N.S., Canada* 45°48N 64°8W **299** C7
Amherst *Mass., U.S.A.* 42°23N 72°31W **313** D12
Amherst *N.Y., U.S.A.* 42°59N 78°48W **312** D6
Amherst *Ohio, U.S.A.* 41°24N 82°14W **312** E2
Amherst I. *Canada* 44°8N 76°43W **313** B8
Amherstburg *Canada* 42°6N 83°6W **311** B13
Amiata, Mte. *Italy* 42°53N 11°37E **199** F8
Amidon *U.S.A.* 46°29N 103°19W **308** B2
Amiens *France* 49°54N 2°16E **173** C9
Amik Gölü *Turkey* 36°22N 36°17E **250** B7
Amili *India* 28°25N 95°52E **241** A5
Amin *Iraq* 33°19N 44°29E **113** B2
Aminadav *Israel* 31°45N 35°8E **123** B1
Amindeo *Greece* 40°42N 21°42E **202** F5
Amindivi Is. *India* 11°23N 72°23E **245** J1
Amingaon *India* 26°11N 91°40E **241** B3
Amini I. *India* 11°6N 72°45E **245** J1
Amino *Ethiopia* 4°25N 41°52E **257** G5
Aminuis *Namibia* 23°43S 19°21E **270** B2
Āmir, Ra's *Libya* 32°57N 21°43E **258** B4
Amīrābād *Īlām, Iran* 33°20N 46°16E **246** C5
Amīrābād *Tehrān, Iran* 35°43N 51°24E **141** A2
Amirante Is. *Seychelles* 6°0S 53°0E **210** J7
Amisk ⌓ *Canada* 56°43N 98°0W **297** B9
Amisk L. *Canada* 54°35N 102°15W **297** C8
Amistad, Presa de la *Mexico* 29°26N 101°3W **318** B4
Amistad ⌓ *U.S.A.* 29°32N 101°12W **314** G4
Amite *U.S.A.* 30°44N 90°30W **315** F9
Amizmiz *Morocco* 31°12N 8°15W **260** B3
Amla *India* 21°56N 78°7E **242** J8
Amlapura *Indonesia* 8°27S 115°37E **231** J18
Åmli *Norway* 58°45N 8°32E **164** F5
Amlia I. *U.S.A.* 52°4N 173°30W **303** K4
Amlwch *U.K.* 53°24N 4°20W **168** D3
Amm Adam *Sudan* 16°20N 36°1E **257** D4
'Ammān *Jordan* 31°57N 35°52E **251** G6
Ammanford *U.K.* 51°48N 3°59W **169** F4
Ammassalik = Tasiilaq *Greenland* 65°40N 37°20W **154** D7
Ammerån ➔ *Sweden* 63°9N 16°13E **162** A10
Ammersee *Germany* 48°0N 11°7E **179** G7
Ammochostos = Famagusta *Cyprus* 35°8N 33°55E **207** E9
Ammon *U.S.A.* 43°28N 111°58W **304** E8
Amnat Charoen *Thailand* 15°51N 104°38E **236** E5
Amnura *Bangla.* 24°37N 88°25E **243** G13
Amo Jiang ➔ *China* 23°0N 101°50E **228** F3
Āmol *Iran* 36°23N 52°20E **247** B7
Amora *Portugal* 38°37N 9°6W **126** B2
Amoreira *Portugal* 38°48N 9°11W **126** A1
Amoret *U.S.A.* 38°15N 94°35W **310** F2
Amorgos *Greece* 36°50N 25°57E **205** E7
Amoron'i Mania □ *Madag.* 20°0S 46°0E **272** C2
Amory *U.S.A.* 33°59N 88°29W **315** E10
Amos *Canada* 48°35N 78°5W **298** C4
Åmot *Buskerud, Norway* 59°57N 9°54E **164** E6
Åmot *Oppland, Norway* 61°0N 10°2E **164** D7
Åmot *Telemark, Norway* 59°34N 8°0E **164** E5
Åmot *Sweden* 60°58N 16°27E **162** D10
Åmotfors *Sweden* 59°47N 12°22E **162** E6
Åmotsdal *Norway* 59°37N 8°26E **164** E5
Amour, Djebel *Algeria* 33°42N 1°37E **261** B5
Amoy = Xiamen *China* 24°25N 118°4E **229** E12
Ampah *Indonesia* 1°46S 115°7E **235** C5
Ampanavoana *Madag.* 15°41S 50°22E **272** B3
Ampang *Malaysia* 3°8N 101°45E **237** L3
Ampangalana, Lakandranon' *Madag.* 22°48S 47°50E **272** C2
Ampani *India* 19°35N 82°38E **244** E6
Ampanihy *Madag.* 24°40S 44°45E **272** C1
Amparafaravola *Madag.* 17°35S 48°13E **272** B2
Ampasinambo *Madag.* 20°31S 48°0E **272** C2
Ampasindava, Helodranon' *Madag.* 13°40S 48°15E **272** A2
Ampasindava, Saikanosy *Madag.* 13°42S 47°55E **272** A2
Ampato, Nevado *Peru* 15°40S 71°56W **330** D3
Ampenan *Indonesia* 8°34S 116°4E **231** K18
Amper *Nigeria* 9°25N 9°40E **263** D6
Amper ➔ *Bayern, Germany* 48°29N 11°55E **179** G7
Amper ➔ *Oberbayern, Germany* 48°14N 11°25E **131** A1
Ampezzo *Italy* 46°25N 12°48E **199** B9
Amphitrite Group *S. China Sea* 16°50N 112°20E **230** A4
Amphoe Kathu *Thailand* 7°55N 98°21E **237** a
Amphoe Thalang *Thailand* 8°1N 98°20E **237** a
Ampitsikinana *Madag.* 12°57S 49°49E **272** A2
Ampombiantambo *Madag.* 12°42S 48°57E **272** A2
Amposta *Spain* 40°43N 0°34E **196** E5
Ampotaka *Madag.* 25°3S 44°41E **272** D1
Ampoza *Madag.* 22°20S 44°44E **272** C1
Amqui *Canada* 48°28N 67°27W **299** C6
Amrabad *India* 16°23N 78°50E **245** F4
'Amrān *Yemen* 15°41N 43°55E **248** D3
'Amrān □ *Yemen* 15°41N 43°55E **248** D3
Amraoti = Amravati *India* 20°55N 77°45E **244** D3
Amravati *India* 20°55N 77°45E **244** D3
Amreli *India* 21°35N 71°17E **242** J4
Amrenene el Kasba *Algeria* 22°10N 0°30E **261** D5
Amritsar *India* 31°35N 74°57E **242** D6
Amroha *India* 28°53N 78°30E **243** E8
Amrum *Germany* 54°38N 8°21E **178** A4
Amsāga *Mauritania* 20°7N 14°10W **260** D2
Amsel *Algeria* 22°47N 5°29E **261** D6
Amstel *Amsterdam, Neths.* **112** b2
Amstel ➔ *Amsterdam, Neths.* **112** b3
Amstel-Drecht-Kanaal *Neths.* 52°18N 4°54E **112** B2
Amstelveen *Neths.* 52°18N 4°51E **112** B2
Amsterdam *Neths.* 52°23N 4°54E **112** A2
Amsterdam *N.Y., U.S.A.* 42°56N 74°11W **313** D10
Amsterdam ✕ (AMS) *Neths.* 52°18N 4°45E **112** B1
Amsterdam Arena *Neths.* 52°19N 4°56E **112** B2
Amsterdam I. = Nouvelle Amsterdam, Î. *Ind. Oc.* 38°30S 77°30E **273** H6
Amsterdam-Rijnkanaal *Neths.* 52°17N 5°1E **112** B3
Amsterdam Zuidoost *Neths.* 52°18N 4°58E **112** B2
Amsterdamse Bos *Neths.* 52°19N 4°50E **112** B1
Amstetten *Austria* 48°7N 14°51E **180** C7
'Amūdah *Syria* 37°6N 40°55E **213** D9
Amudarya *Turkmenistan* 37°53N 65°15E **216** E7
Amudarya ➔ *Uzbekistan* 43°58N 59°34E **216** D5
Amukta I. *U.S.A.* 52°30N 171°16W **303** K5
Amukta Pass *U.S.A.* 52°0N 171°0W **303** K5
Amulung *Phil.* 17°50N 121°43E **232** C3
Amund Ringnes I. *Canada* 78°20N 96°25W **295** B12
Amundsen Abyssal Plain *S. Ocean* 65°0S 125°0W **151** C14
Amundsen Basin *Arctic* 87°30N 80°0E **150** A
Amundsen Gulf *Canada* 71°0N 124°0W **294** C7
Amundsen Ridges *S. Ocean* 69°15S 123°0W **151** C14
Amundsen-Scott *Antarctica* 90°0S 166°0E **151** E
Amundsen Sea *Antarctica* 72°0S 115°0W **151** D15
Amungen *Sweden* 61°10N 15°40E **162** C9
Amuntai *Indonesia* 2°28S 115°25E **235** C5
Amur ➔ *Russia* 52°56N 141°10E **215** D15
Amur, W. ➔ *Sudan* 18°56N 33°34E **256** D3
Amurang *Indonesia* 1°5N 124°40E **231** D6
Amurrio *Spain* 43°3N 3°0W **196** B1
Amursk *Russia* 50°14N 136°54E **215** D14
Amusco *Spain* 42°10N 4°28W **194** C6
Amvrakikos Kolpos *Greece* 39°0N 20°55E **204** C2
Amvrosiyivka *Ukraine* 47°43N 38°30E **189** J10
Amyderya = Amudarya ➔ *Uzbekistan* 43°58N 59°34E **216** D5
An Bang, Dao = Amboyna Cay *S. China Sea* 7°50N 112°50E **230** C4
An Bien *Vietnam* 9°45N 105°0E **237** H5
An Hoa *Vietnam* 15°40N 108°5E **236** E7
An Khe *Vietnam* 13°57N 108°51E **236** F7
An Nabatīyah at Tahta *Lebanon* 33°23N 35°27E **250** E6
An Nabk *Syria* 34°2N 36°44E **250** D7
An Nafūd *Si. Arabia* 28°15N 41°0E **246** D4
An Nāḩīyah *Iraq* 34°26N 41°33E **213** E9
An Najaf *Iraq* 32°3N 44°15E **213** G11
An Namāş *Si. Arabia* 19°7N 42°8E **248** C3
An Nāşirīyah *Iraq* 31°0N 46°15E **246** D5
An Nawfaliyah *Libya* 30°54N 17°58E **258** B3
An Nhon = Binh Dinh *Vietnam* 13°55N 109°7E **236** F7
An Nîl □ *Sudan* 19°30N 33°0E **256** D3
An Nîl el Abyad □ *Sudan* 14°0N 32°15E **257** E3
An Nîl el Azraq □ *Sudan* 11°30N 34°30E **257** E3
An Nu'ayrīyah *Si. Arabia* 27°30N 48°30E **247** E6
An Nu'mānīyah *Iraq* 32°32N 45°25E **213** F11
An Nuqat al Khams □ *Libya* 32°42N 11°57E **258** B2
An Ros = Rush *Ireland* 53°31N 6°6W **166** C5
An Thoi, Quan Dao *Vietnam* 9°58N 104°0E **237** H5
Åna-Sira *Norway* 58°17N 6°25E **164** F3
Anaa *French Polynesia* 17°25S 145°30W **289** f
Anabar ➔ *Russia* 73°8N 113°36E **215** B12
Anaco *Venezuela* 9°27N 64°28W **329** B5
Anaconda *U.S.A.* 46°8N 112°57W **304** C7
Anacortes *U.S.A.* 48°30N 122°37W **306** B4
Anacostia *U.S.A.* 38°51N 76°59W **143** B3
Anacostia ➔ *U.S.A.* 38°52N 77°1W **143** B3
Anacuao, Mt. *Phil.* 16°16N 121°53E **232** C3
Anadarko *U.S.A.* 35°4N 98°15W **314** D5
Anadia *Brazil* 9°42S 36°18W **332** C4
Anadia *Portugal* 40°26N 8°27W **194** E2
Anadolu *Turkey* 39°0N 30°0E **212** C5
Anadoluhisarı *Turkey* 41°4N 29°3E **122** B2
Anadolukavağı *Turkey* 41°10N 29°7E **122** A2
Anadyr *Russia* 64°35N 177°20E **215** C18
Anadyr ➔ *Russia* 64°55N 176°5E **215** C18
Anadyrskiy Zaliv *Russia* 64°0N 180°0E **215** C19
Anafi *Greece* 36°22N 25°48E **205** E7
Anafonitria *Greece* 37°51N 20°39E **207** D2
Anaga, Pta. de *Canary Is.* 28°34N 16°9W **153** e1
Anagni *Italy* 41°44N 13°9E **199** G10
'Ānah *Iraq* 34°25N 42°0E **213** E10
Anaheim *U.S.A.* 33°50N 117°55W **307** M9
Anahim Lake *Canada* 52°28N 125°18W **296** C3
Anahola *U.S.A.* 22°9N 159°19W **302** A2
'Anahulu ➔ *U.S.A.* 21°37N 158°6W **302** J13
Anai Mudi *India* 10°12N 77°4E **245** J3
Anaichak ⌓ *U.S.A.* 56°50N 158°15W **303** H8
Anaimalai Hills *India* 10°20N 76°40E **245** J3
Anajás *Brazil* 0°59S 49°57W **332** B2
Anajatuba *Brazil* 3°16S 44°37W **332** B3
Anakao *Madag.* 23°40S 43°39E **272** C1
Anakapalle *India* 17°42N 83°6E **244** F6
Anakena *Chile* 27°5S 109°20W **330** b
Anakie *Australia* 23°32S 147°45E **280** C4
Anaklia *Georgia* 42°22N 41°35E **191** J5
Anaktuvuk Pass *U.S.A.* 68°8N 151°45W **303** B10
Analalava *Madag.* 14°35S 48°0E **272** A2
Analamanga □ *Madag.* 18°0S 47°30E **272** B2
Analanjirofo □ *Madag.* 16°35S 49°25E **272** B2
Analavoka *Madag.* 22°23S 46°30E **272** C2
Analipsis *Greece* 39°36N 19°55E **206** B9
Anamã *Brazil* 3°35S 61°22W **329** D5
Anambar ➔ *Pakistan* 30°15N 68°50E **242** D3
Anambas, Kepulauan *Indonesia* 3°20N 106°30E **234** B3
Anambas Is. = Anambas, Kepulauan *Indonesia* 3°20N 106°30E **234** B3
Anambra □ *Nigeria* 6°20N 7°0E **263** D6
Anamé *Vanuatu* 20°8S 169°47E **287** K7
Anamosa *U.S.A.* 42°7N 91°17W **310** B5
Anamur *Turkey* 36°8N 32°58E **250** B3
Anamur ➔ *Turkey* 36°5N 32°53E **250** B3
Anamur Burnu *Turkey* 36°2N 32°47E **250** B3
Anan *Japan* 33°54N 134°40E **222** D6
Anand *India* 22°32N 72°59E **242** H5
Anandapuram *India* 14°5N 75°12E **245** G2
Anandpur *India* 21°16N 86°13E **244** D8
Ananes *Greece* 36°33N 24°9E **204** E6
Anangu Pitjantjatjara ◎ *Australia* 27°0S 132°0E **279** E5
Ananindeua *Brazil* 1°22S 48°22W **332** B2
Anantapur *India* 14°39N 77°42E **245** G3
Anantnag *India* 33°45N 75°10E **243** C6
Ananyiv *Ukraine* 47°44N 29°58E **183** C14
Anapa *Russia* 44°55N 37°25E **189** K9
Anapodiaris ➔ *Greece* 34°59N 25°20E **207** F6
Anápolis = Simão Dias *Brazil* 10°44S 37°49W **332** D4
Anápolis *Brazil* 16°15S 48°50W **333** E2
Anapu ➔ *Brazil* 1°53S 50°53W **329** D7
Anār *Iran* 30°55N 55°13E **247** D7
Anār Darreh *Afghan.* 32°46N 61°39E **240** B1
Anārak *Iran* 33°25N 53°40E **247** C7
Anarisfjällen *Sweden* 63°6N 13°10E **162** A7
Anas ➔ *India* 23°26N 74°0E **242** H6
Añasco *Puerto Rico* 18°17N 67°8W **321** b
Anata *West Bank* 31°49N 35°16E **123** B2
Anatahan *N. Marianas* 16°21N 145°40E **302** a
Anatolia = Anadolu *Turkey* 39°0N 30°0E **212** C5
Anatoliki Makedonia kai Thraki □ *Greece* 41°10N 24°30E **203** E8
Anatsogno *Madag.* 23°33S 43°46E **272** C1
Añatuya *Argentina* 28°20S 62°50W **334** B3
Anatye ◎ *Australia* 22°29S 137°3E **280** C2
Anauá ➔ *Brazil* 0°58N 61°21W **329** C5
Anaunethad L. *Canada* 60°55N 104°25W **297** A8
Anavilhanas, Arquipélago das *Brazil* 2°42S 60°45W **329** D5
Anbyŏn *N. Korea* 39°1N 127°35E **224** C3
Ancares, Sierra dos *Spain* 42°51N 6°52W **194** C4
Ancares ⌓ *Spain* 42°50N 6°40W **194** C4
Ancash □ *Peru* 9°30S 77°45W **330** B2
Ancaster *Canada* 43°13N 79°59W **312** C5
Ancenis *France* 47°21N 1°10W **172** E5
Anchieta = Piatã *Brazil* 13°9S 41°48W **333** D3
Anch'ing = Anqing *China* 30°30N 117°3E **229** B11
Ancho, Canal *Chile* 50°0S 74°20W **336** D2
Anchor Bay *U.S.A.* 38°48N 123°34W **306** G3
Anchorage *U.S.A.* 61°13N 149°54W **303** F10
Anchorage ✕ (ANC) *U.S.A.* 61°10N 150°0W **303** F10
Anchuras *Spain* 39°29N 4°50W **195** F6
Anchuthengu *India* 8°40N 76°46E **245** K3
Anci *China* 39°20N 116°40E **226** E9
Ancohuma, Nevado *Bolivia* 16°0S 68°50W **330** D4
Ancol *Indonesia* 6°7S 106°49E **122** A1
Ancón *Peru* 11°50S 77°10W **330** C2
Ancona *Italy* 43°38N 13°30E **199** E10
Ancud *Chile* 42°0S 73°50W **336** B2
Ancud, G. de *Chile* 42°0S 73°0W **336** B2
Ancy-le-Franc *France* 47°46N 4°10E **173** E11
Anda *Heilongjiang, China* 46°24N 125°19E **219** B14
Anda *Phil.* 16°17N 119°57E **232** C2
Andacollo *Argentina* 37°10S 70°42W **334** D1
Andacollo *Chile* 30°14S 71°6W **334** C1
Andahuaylas *Peru* 13°40S 73°25W **330** C3
Andaingo *Madag.* 18°12S 48°17E **272** B2
Andalgalá *Argentina* 27°40S 66°30W **334** B2
Åndalsnes *Norway* 62°35N 7°43E **164** B4
Andalucía □ *Spain* 37°35N 5°0W **195** H6
'Andalus *Iraq* 33°19N 44°18E **113** B1
Andalusia = Andalucía □ *Spain* 37°35N 5°0W **195** H6
Andalusia *U.S.A.* 31°18N 86°29W **315** F11
Andaman & Nicobar Is. □ *India* 10°0N 93°0E **245** K11
Andaman Is. *Ind. Oc.* 12°30N 92°45E **245** H11
Andaman Sea *Ind. Oc.* 13°0N 96°0E **230** B1
Andamooka *Australia* 30°27S 137°9E **281** E2
Andapa *Madag.* 14°39S 49°39E **272** A2
Andara *Namibia* 18°2S 21°9E **270** A3
Andaraí *Bahia, Brazil* 12°48S 41°20W **333** D3
Andaraí *Rio de J., Brazil* 22°56S 43°14W **135** B1
Andelot-Blancheville *France* 48°15N 5°18E **173** D12
Andenes *Norway* 69°19N 16°18E **160** B17
Andenne *Belgium* 50°28N 5°5E **170** D5
Andéranboukane *Mali* 15°26N 3°2E **263** B5
Anderlecht *Belgium* 50°50N 4°19E **116** A1
Andermatt *Switz.* 46°38N 8°35E **179** J4
Andernach *Germany* 50°26N 7°24E **178** E3
Andernos-les-Bains *France* 44°44N 1°6W **174** D2
Andersen Air Force Base ✕ (UAM) *Guam* 13°35N 144°55E **302** d
Anderslöv *Sweden* 55°26N 13°19E **163** J7
Anderson *Vic., Australia* 38°31S 145°26E **283** E6
Anderson *Alaska, U.S.A.* 64°25N 149°15W **303** D10
Anderson *Calif., U.S.A.* 40°27N 122°18W **304** F2
Anderson *Ind., U.S.A.* 40°10N 85°41W **311** D11
Anderson *Mo., U.S.A.* 36°39N 94°27W **308** G6
Anderson *S.C., U.S.A.* 34°31N 82°39W **315** D13
Anderson ➔ *Canada* 69°42N 129°0W **294** D6
Anderson I. *India* 12°46N 92°43E **245** H11
Anderson Park *U.S.A.* 33°45N 84°27W **113** B2
Andersonville *U.S.A.* 32°12N 84°9W **316** C5
Andersonville ⌓ *U.S.A.* 32°12N 84°1W **316** C5
Anderstorp *Sweden* 57°19N 13°39E **163** G7
Andes *Colombia* 5°39N 75°54W **328** B2
Andes *N.Y., U.S.A.* 42°12N 74°47W **313** D10
Andes, Cord. de los *S. Amer.* 20°0S 68°0W **330** E4
Andfjorden *Norway* 69°10N 16°20E **160** B17
Andhra, L. *India* 18°54N 73°32E **244** E1
Andhra Pradesh □ *India* 18°0N 79°0E **244** F4
Andijon *Uzbekistan* 41°10N 72°15E **217** B8
Andijon □ *Uzbekistan* 40°45N 72°20E **217** B8
Andikithira = Antikythira *Greece* 35°52N 23°15E **204** F5
Andilamena *Madag.* 17°1S 48°35E **272** B2
Andīmeshk *Iran* 32°27N 48°21E **213** F13
Andimilos = Antimilos *Greece* 36°47N 24°12E **204** E6
Anding = Anting *Taiwan* 23°7N 120°14E **225** C2
Andingmen *China* 39°55N 116°23E **114** B2
Andiparos = Antiparos *Greece* 37°0N 25°3E **205** D7
Andipaxoi = Antipaxi *Greece* 39°9N 20°13E **204** B2
Andipsara = Antipsara *Greece* 38°30N 25°29E **205** C7
Andizhan = Andijon *Uzbekistan* 41°10N 72°15E **217** B8
Andkhvoy *Afghan.* 36°52N 65°8E **240** A2
Andoain *Spain* 43°13N 2°1W **196** B2
Andoany *Madag.* 13°25S 48°16E **272** A2
Andoas *Peru* 2°55S 76°25W **328** D2
Andohahela ⌓ *Madag.* 24°4S 46°44E **272** C2
Andol *India* 17°51N 78°4E **244** F4
Andola *India* 16°57N 76°50E **244** F3
Andong *S. Korea* 36°40N 128°43E **224** D4
Andorra *Spain* 40°59N 0°28W **196** E4
Andorra ■ *Europe* 42°30N 1°30E **174** F5
Andorra La Vella *Andorra* 42°31N 1°32E **174** F5
Andover *Hants., U.K.* 51°12N 1°29W **169** F6
Andover *Kans., U.S.A.* 37°43N 97°7W **308** G5
Andover *Maine, U.S.A.* 44°38N 70°45W **313** B14
Andover *Mass., U.S.A.* 42°40N 71°8W **313** D13
Andover *N.J., U.S.A.* 40°59N 74°45W **313** F10
Andover *N.Y., U.S.A.* 42°10N 77°48W **312** D7
Andover *Ohio, U.S.A.* 41°36N 80°34W **312** E4
Andøya *Norway* 69°10N 15°50E **160** B16
Andrade *Brazil* 4°40S 63°45W **329** D5
Andradina *Brazil* 20°54S 51°23W **333** F1
Andrahary *Madag.* 13°37S 49°17E **272** A2
Andramasina *Madag.* 19°11S 47°35E **272** B2
Andranopasy *Madag.* 21°17S 43°44E **272** C1
Andranovory *Madag.* 23°8S 44°10E **272** C1
Andratx *Spain* 39°39N 2°25E **206** B3
Andravida *Greece* 37°54N 21°16E **204** D3
André Félix ⌓ *C.A.R.* 9°29N 23°18E **264** A4
Andreanof Is. *U.S.A.* 51°30N 176°0W **303** L4
Andreapol *Russia* 56°40N 32°17E **188** D7
Andrée Land *Greenland* 73°40N 26°0W **154** C8
Andrews *S.C., U.S.A.* 33°27N 79°34W **315** E15
Andrews *Tex., U.S.A.* 32°19N 102°33W **314** E3
Andreyev = Jędrzejów *Poland* 50°35N 20°15E **185** H7
Andreyevka *Russia* 52°19N 51°55E **190** D10
Ándria *Italy* 41°13N 16°17E **201** A9
Andriamena *Madag.* 17°26S 47°30E **272** B2
Andriandampy *Madag.* 22°45S 45°41E **272** C2
Andriba *Madag.* 17°30S 46°58E **272** B2
Andrijevica *Montenegro* 42°45N 19°48E **202** D3
Andringitra ⌓ *Madag.* 22°13S 46°55E **272** C2
Andritsena *Greece* 37°29N 21°52E **204** D3
Androka *Madag.* 24°58S 44°2E **272** C1
Andropov = Rybinsk *Russia* 58°5N 38°50E **188** C10
Andros *Greece* 37°50N 24°57E **204** D6
Andros *The Bahamas* 24°30N 78°0W **320** B4
Andros Town *The Bahamas* 24°43N 77°47W **320** B4
Androth I. *India* 10°50N 73°41E **245** J1
Androy □ *Madag.* 25°10S 46°10E **272** D3
Andrychów *Poland* 49°51N 19°18E **185** J6
Andselv *Norway* 69°4N 18°34E **160** B18
Andújar *Spain* 38°3N 4°5W **195** G6
Andulo *Angola* 11°25S 16°45E **265** E3
Åneby *Akershus, Norway* 60°5N 10°51E **164** D7
Aneby *Sweden* 57°48N 14°49E **163** G8
Anéfis *Mali* 18°2N 0°36E **263** B5
Anegada *Br. Virgin Is.* 18°45N 64°20W **321** C7
Anegada, B. *Argentina* 40°20S 62°20W **336** B4
Anegada Passage *W. Indies* 18°15N 63°45W **321** C7
Anéno *Togo* 6°12N 1°34E **263** D5
Aneityum *Vanuatu* 20°12S 169°45E **287** K7
Anelghowhat *Vanuatu* 20°19S 169°43E **287** K7
Añelo *Argentina* 38°20S 68°45W **336** A3
Anenni-Noi *Moldova* 46°53N 29°15E **183** D14
Aneto, Pico de *Spain* 42°37N 0°40E **196** C5
Änew *Turkmenistan* 37°52N 58°31E **216** E5
Aney *Niger* 19°15N 12°50E **259** E2
Añez *Bolivia* 15°40S 63°10W **331** D5
Anfu *China* 27°21N 114°40E **229** D10
Ang Mo Kio *Singapore* 1°23N 103°50E **138** A3
Ang Thong *Thailand* 14°35N 100°31E **236** E3
Ang Thong, Ko *Thailand* 9°37N 99°41E **237** b
Ang Thong, Mu Ko ⌓ *Thailand* 9°40N 99°43E **237** b
Angadanan *Phil.* 16°45N 121°45E **232** C3
Angamos, Punta *Chile* 23°1S 70°32W **334** A1
Angara ➔ *Russia* 58°5N 94°20E **215** D10
Angara-Débou *Benin* 11°19N 3°3E **263** C5
Angarbaka *South Sudan* 9°44N 24°44E **257** F1
Angarsk *Russia* 52°30N 104°0E **218** A9
Angas Hills *Australia* 23°0S 127°50E **278** D4
Angaston *Australia* 34°30S 139°8E **282** C3
Angat *Phil.* 14°56N 121°2E **232** D3
Angaur I. *Palau* 6°54N 134°9E **288** c
Ängby *Sweden* 59°20N 17°53E **139** A1
Ånge *Sweden* 62°31N 15°35E **162** B9
Ángel, Salto = Angel Falls *Venezuela* 5°57N 62°30W **329** B5
Ángel de la Guarda, I. *Mexico* 29°20N 113°25W **318** B2
Angel Falls *Venezuela* 5°57N 62°30W **329** B5
Angel I. *U.S.A.* 37°52N 122°25W **136** A2
Angel Island State Park ⌓ *U.S.A.* 37°52N 122°25W **136** A2
Angeles *Phil.* 15°9N 120°33E **232** D3
Ängelholm *Sweden* 56°15N 12°50E **163** H6
Angels Camp *U.S.A.* 38°4N 120°32W **306** G6
Ängelsberg *Sweden* 59°58N 16°0E **162** E10
Anger ➔ *Ethiopia* 9°37N 36°6E **257** F4
Angerburg = Węgorzewo *Poland* 54°13N 21°43E **184** D8
Angereb *Ethiopia* 13°11N 37°7E **257** E4
Angereb ➔ *Ethiopia* 13°45N 36°40E **257** E4
Ångermanälven ➔ *Sweden* 63°0N 17°20E **162** A11
Ångermanland *Sweden* 63°36N 17°45E **160** E17
Angermünde *Germany* 53°0N 14°0E **178** B9
Angers *Qué., Canada* 45°31N 75°29W **313** A9
Angers *Maine-et-Loire, France* 47°30N 0°35W **172** E6
Angerville *France* 48°19N 2°0E **173** D9
Ängesån ➔ *Sweden* 66°16N 22°47E **160** C20
Angical *Brazil* 12°0S 44°42W **333** D3
Angikuni L. *Canada* 62°12N 99°59W **297** A9
Angke, Kali ➔ *Indonesia* 6°6S 106°46E **122** A1
Angkor *Cambodia* 13°22N 103°50E **236** F4
Angledool *Australia* 29°5S 147°55E **281** D4
Anglem, Mt. *N.Z.* 46°45S 167°53E **285** G2
Anglès *Spain* 41°57N 2°38E **196** D7
Anglesey *U.K.* 53°17N 4°20W **168** D3
Anglesey, Isle of □ *U.K.* 53°16N 4°18W **168** D3
Anglet *France* 43°29N 1°31W **174** E2
Angleton *U.S.A.* 29°10N 95°26W **314** G7
Anglin ➔ *France* 46°42N 0°52E **174** B4
Anglisidhes *Cyprus* 34°51N 33°27E **207** F9
Anglure *France* 48°35N 3°50E **173** D10
Angmagssalik = Tasiilaq *Greenland* 65°40N 37°20W **154** D7
Ango *Dem. Rep. of the Congo* 4°10N 26°5E **268** B2
Angoche *Mozam.* 16°8S 39°55E **269** F4
Angoche, I. *Mozam.* 16°20S 39°50E **269** F4
Angol *Chile* 37°56S 72°45W **334** D1
Angola *Ind., U.S.A.* 41°38N 85°0W **311** C12
Angola *N.Y., U.S.A.* 42°38N 79°2W **312** D5
Angola ■ *Africa* 12°0S 18°0E **265** E3
Angola Abyssal Plain *Atl. Oc.* 15°0S 2°0E **152** H12
Angola Basin *Atl. Oc.* 15°0S 3°0E **152** H12
Angoon *U.S.A.* 57°30N 134°35W **303** H14
Angora = Ankara *Turkey* 39°57N 32°54E **212** C5
Angoram *Papua N. G.* 4°4S 144°4E **286** C3
Angoulême *France* 45°39N 0°10E **174** C4
Angoumois *France* 45°50N 0°25E **174** C4
Angra do Heroísmo *Azores* 38°39N 27°13W **153** d1
Angra dos Reis *Brazil* 23°0S 44°10W **335** A7
Angrapa ➔ *Russia* 54°37N 21°54E **184** D8
Angren *Uzbekistan* 41°1N 70°12E **217** B8
Angtassom *Cambodia* 11°1N 104°41E **237** G5
Angu *Dem. Rep. of the Congo* 3°23N 24°30E **264** B4
Anguang *China* 45°15N 123°45E **227** B12
Anguilla ☑ *W. Indies* 18°14N 63°5W **322** a
Anguilla I. *Anguilla* 18°9N 63°11W **322** a
Angul *India* 20°51N 85°6E **244** D7
Anguo *China* 38°28N 115°15E **226** E8
Angurugu *Australia* 14°0S 136°25E **280** A2
Angus *Canada* 44°19N 79°53W **312** B5
Angus □ *U.K.* 56°46N 2°56W **167** E6
Angwa ➔ *Zimbabwe* 16°0S 30°23E **271** A5
Angyalföld *Hungary* 47°32N 19°5E **117** A2
Anhanduí ➔ *Brazil* 21°46S 52°9W **335** A5
Anholt *Denmark* 56°42N 11°33E **163** H5
Anhua *China* 28°23N 111°12E **229** C8
Anhui □ *China* 32°0N 117°0E **229** B11
Anhwei = Anhui □ *China* 32°0N 117°0E **229** B11
Aniak *U.S.A.* 61°35N 159°32W **303** F8
Anichab *Namibia* 21°0S 14°46E **270** B1
Anicuns *Brazil* 16°28S 49°58W **333** E2
Anidros *Greece* 36°38N 25°43E **205** E7
Anié *Togo* 7°42N 1°8E **263** D5
Anik *India* 19°1N 72°53E **130** A2
Anil *Brazil* 2°32S 44°14W **332** B3
Animas ➔ *U.S.A.* 36°43N 108°13W **305** H9
Anin *Myanmar* 15°36N 97°50E **236** E1
Anin *Warszawa, Poland* 52°13N 21°9E **123** B2
Anina *Romania* 45°6N 21°51E **182** E6
Anini *India* 28°47N 95°53E **241** A5
Anini-y *Phil.* 10°25N 121°55E **233** F3
Aninoasa *Romania* 44°47N 24°10E **183** F9
Añisoc *Eq. Guin.* 1°51N 10°46E **264** B2
Anita *U.S.A.* 41°27N 94°46W **310** C2
Anivorano *Atsinanana, Madag.* 18°44S 48°58E **272** B2
Anivorano *Diana, Madag.* 12°44S 49°14E **272** A2
Aniwa *Vanuatu* 19°17S 169°35E **287** J7
Anjalankoski *Finland* 60°45N 26°51E **188** B4
Anjangaon *India* 21°10N 77°20E **244** D3
Anjar = Hawsh Mūssá *Lebanon* 33°45N 35°55E **250** E6
Anjar *India* 23°6N 70°10E **242** H4
Anjengo = Anchuthengu *India* 8°40N 76°46E **245** K3
Anji *China* 30°46N 119°40E **229** B12
Anjidiv I. *India* 14°40N 74°10E **245** G2
Anjō *Japan* 34°57N 137°5E **223** C9
Anjou *Qué., Canada* 45°36N 73°33W **130** A2
Anjou *Maine-et-Loire, France* 47°20N 0°15W **172** E6
Anjouan *Comoros Is.* 12°15S 44°20E **272** a
Anjouan ✕ (AJN) *Comoros Is.* 12°9S 44°26E **272** a
Anjozorobe *Madag.* 18°22S 47°52E **272** B2
Anju *N. Korea* 39°36N 125°40E **224** C2
Anka *Nigeria* 12°13N 5°58E **263** C6
Ankaboa, Tanjona *Madag.* 21°58S 43°20E **272** C1
Ankang *China* 32°40N 109°1E **226** H5
Ankara *Turkey* 39°57N 32°54E **212** C5
Ankara □ *Turkey* 39°55N 32°50E **212** C5
Ankarafantsika ⌓ *Madag.* 16°8S 47°5E **272** B2
Ankaramena *Madag.* 21°57S 46°39E **272** C2
Ankarata *Madag.* 19°20S 47°30E **272** B2
Ankarsrum *Sweden* 57°41N 16°20E **163** G10
Ankasakasa *Madag.* 16°21S 44°52E **272** B1
Ankavandra *Madag.* 18°46S 45°18E **272** B2
Ankazoabo *Madag.* 22°18S 44°31E **272** C1
Ankazobe *Madag.* 18°20S 47°10E **272** B2
Ankeny *U.S.A.* 41°44N 93°36W **310** C3
Ankhialo = Pomorie *Bulgaria* 42°32N 27°41E **203** D11
Ankilimalinika *Madag.* 22°58S 43°45E **272** C1
Ankilizato *Madag.* 20°25S 45°1E **272** C2
Anking = Anqing *China* 30°30N 117°3E **229** B11
Ankisabe *Madag.* 19°17S 46°29E **272** B2
Anklam *Germany* 53°51N 13°41E **178** B9
Ankleshwar *India* 21°38N 73°3E **244** D1
Ankober *Ethiopia* 9°35N 39°40E **257** F4
Ankola *India* 14°40N 74°18E **245** G2
Ankoro *Dem. Rep. of the Congo* 6°45S 26°55E **268** D2
Ankororoka *Madag.* 25°30S 45°11E **272** D2
Ankpa *Nigeria* 7°22N 7°38E **263** D6
Anlong *China* 25°2N 105°27E **228** E5
Anlong Veng *Cambodia* 14°14N 104°5E **236** E5
Anlu *China* 31°15N 113°45E **229** B9
Anmyeondo *S. Korea* 36°25N 126°25E **224** D3
Ann *Myanmar* 19°48N 94°0E **241** F5
Ånn *Sweden* 63°19N 12°33E **162** A6
Ann, C. *U.S.A.* 42°38N 70°35W **313** D14
Ann Arbor *U.S.A.* 42°17N 83°45W **311** B13
Anna *Russia* 51°28N 40°23E **190** E5
Anna *Ill., U.S.A.* 37°28N 89°15W **308** G9
Anna *Ohio, U.S.A.* 40°24N 84°11W **311** D12
Anna Regina *Guyana* 7°10N 58°30W **329** B6
Annaba *Algeria* 36°50N 7°46E **261** A6
Annaba □ *Algeria* 36°12N 7°45E **261** A6
Annaberg-Buchholz *Germany* 50°34N 13°0E **178** E9
Annai *Guyana* 3°57N 59°8W **329** C6
Annaka *Japan* 36°19N 138°54E **223** A10
Annalee ➔ *Ireland* 54°2N 7°24W **166** B4
Annalee Heights *U.S.A.* 38°51N 77°10W **143** B1
Annam = Trung Phan *Vietnam* 17°0N 109°0E **236** D6
Annamitique, Chaîne *Asia* 17°0N 106°0E **236** D6
Annan *U.K.* 54°59N 3°16W **167** G5
Annan ➔ *U.K.* 54°58N 3°16W **167** G5
Annanberg *Papua N. G.* 4°52S 144°42E **286** C3
Annapolis *U.S.A.* 38°59N 76°30W **309** F15
Annapolis Royal *Canada* 44°44N 65°32W **299** D6
Annapurna *Nepal* 28°34N 83°50E **243** E10
Anne Frankhuis *Amsterdam, Neths.* **112** a1
Annean, L. *Australia* 26°54S 118°14E **279** E2
Anneberg *Sweden* 57°44N 14°49E **163** G8
Annecy *France* 45°55N 6°8E **175** C10
Annecy, Lac d' *France* 45°52N 6°10E **175** C10
Annemasse *France* 46°12N 6°16E **173** F13
Annenfeld = Şämkir *Azerbaijan* 40°50N 46°0E **191** K8
Annenskiy Most *Russia* 60°45N 37°10E **188** B9
Annette I. *U.S.A.* 55°9N 131°28W **296** B2
Annette Island ▲ *U.S.A.* 55°9N 131°28W **303** J15
Annigeri *India* 15°26N 75°26E **245** G2
Anning *China* 24°55N 102°26E **228** E4
Anniston *U.S.A.* 33°39N 85°50W **316** B4
Annobón *Atl. Oc.* 1°25S 5°36E **255** G4
Annonay *France* 45°15N 4°40E **175** C8
Annot *France* 43°58N 6°38E **175** E10
Annotto B. *Jamaica* 18°17N 76°45W **320** a
Annotto Bay *Jamaica* 18°16N 76°47W **320** a
Ånnsjön *Sweden* 63°19N 12°33E **162** A6
Annville *U.S.A.* 40°20N 76°31W **313** F8
Annweiler *Germany* 49°12N 7°57E **179** F3
Ano Poroia *Greece* 41°17N 23°2E **202** E7
Ano Siros *Greece* 37°29N 24°56E **204** D6
Anogi *Greece* 38°25N 20°40E **207** C2
Anogia *Greece* 35°16N 24°52E **207** E5
Anorotsangana *Madag.* 13°56S 47°55E **272** A2
Anosibe *Madag.* 19°26S 48°13E **272** B2
Anosy □ *Madag.* 24°10S 46°10E **272** C2
Anou Mellene *Mali* 17°29N 0°33E **263** B5
Anoumaba *Côte d'Ivoire* 6°23N 4°38W **262** D4
Anping *Hebei, China* 38°15N 115°30E **226** E8
Anping *Liaoning, China* 41°5N 123°30E **224** B1
Anpu Gang *China* 21°25N 109°50E **228** G7
Anqing *China* 30°30N 117°3E **229** B11
Anqiu *China* 36°25N 119°10E **227** F10
Anren *China* 26°43N 113°18E **229** D9
Ansager *Denmark* 55°43N 8°45E **163** J2
Ansai *China* 36°50N 109°20E **226** F5
Ansan *S. Korea* 37°21N 126°52E **224** D3
Ansbach *Germany* 49°28N 10°34E **179** F6
Anse-Bertrand *Guadeloupe* 16°28N 61°32W **322** e
Anse Boileau *Seychelles* 4°43S 55°29E **272** c
Anse la Raye *St. Lucia* 13°55N 61°3W **323** m
Anse Royale *Seychelles* 4°44S 55°31E **272** c
Ānseba □ *Eritrea* 16°30N 37°0E **257** D4
Anseba ➔ *Eritrea* 16°0N 38°30E **257** D4

Anseong S. Korea 37°0N 127°16E 224 D3
Anserma Colombia 5°13N 75°48W 328 B2
Ansfelden Austria 48°12N 14°17E 180 C7
Anshan China 41°5N 122°58E 224 B1
Anshun China 26°18N 105°57E 228 D5
Ansião Portugal 39°56N 8°27W 194 F2
Ansley U.S.A. 41°18N 99°23W 308 E4
Ansó Spain 42°51N 0°48W 196 C4
Ansoáin Spain 42°50N 1°38W 196 C3
Anson U.S.A. 32°45N 99°54W 314 E5
Anson B. Australia 13°20S 130°6E 278 B5
Ansongo Mali 15°25N 0°35E 263 B5
Ansongo-Ménaka △ Mali 15°3N 1°37E 263 B5
Ansonia Conn., U.S.A. 41°21N 73°5W 313 E11
Ansonia Ohio, U.S.A. 40°13N 84°38W 311 D12
Anstruther U.K. 56°14N 2°41W 167 E6
Ansudu Indonesia 2°11S 139°22E 231 E9
Antabamba Peru 14°40S 73°0W 330 C3
Antagarh India 20°6N 81°9E 244 D5
Antakya = Hatay Turkey 36°14N 36°10E 250 B7
Antalaha Madag. 14°57S 50°20E 272 A3
Antalāt Libya 31°8N 20°42E 258 B4
Antalya Turkey 36°52N 30°45E 250 B1
Antalya □ Turkey 36°50N 30°45E 250 B1
Antalya ✈ (AYT) Turkey 36°54N 30°47E 212 D4
Antalya Körfezi Turkey 36°15N 31°30E 250 B2
Antambohobe Madag. 22°20S 46°47E 272 C2
Antanambao-Manampotsy Madag. 19°29S 48°34E 272 B2
Antanambe Madag. 16°26S 49°52E 272 B2
Antananarivo Madag. 18°55S 47°31E 272 B2
Antananarivo □ Madag. 19°0S 47°0E 272 B2
Antanifotsy Madag. 19°39S 47°19E 272 B2
Antanimbaribe Madag. 21°30S 44°48E 272 C1
Antanimora Madag. 24°49S 45°40E 272 C2
Antarctic Pen. Antarctica 67°0S 60°0W 151 C18
Antarctica 90°0S 0°0 151 E3
Antécume Pata Fr. Guiana 3°17N 54°4W 329 C7
Antelope Zimbabwe 21°2S 28°31E 269 G2
Antep = Gaziantep Turkey 37°6N 37°23E 250 A8
Antequera Paraguay 24°8S 57°7W 334 A4
Antequera Spain 37°5N 4°33W 196 H6
Antero, Mt. U.S.A. 38°41N 106°15W 304 G10
Antevamena Madag. 21°2S 44°8E 272 C1
Anthony Fla., U.S.A. 29°18N 82°7W 317 F7
Anthony Kans., U.S.A. 37°9N 98°2W 308 G4
Anthony N. Mex., U.S.A. 32°0N 106°36W 305 K10
Anti Atlas Morocco 30°0N 8°30W 260 C3
Anti-Lebanon = Sharqi, Al Jabal ash Lebanon 33°40N 36°10E 250 E7
Antibes France 43°34N 7°6E 175 E11
Antibes, C. d' France 43°31N 7°7E 175 E11
Anticosti, Î. d' Canada 49°30N 63°0W 299 C7
Antifer, C. d' France 49°41N 0°10E 172 C7
Antigo U.S.A. 45°9N 89°9W 308 C9
Antigonish Canada 45°38N 61°58W 299 C7
Antigua Canary Is. 28°24N 14°1W 153 e2
Antigua Guatemala 14°34N 90°41W 320 D1
Antigua W. Indies 17°0N 61°50W 322 b
Antigua & Barbuda ■ W. Indies 17°20N 61°48W 322 b
Antigua Intl. ✈ (ANU) Antigua & B. 17°8N 61°47W 322 b
Antigues, Pte. d' Guadeloupe 16°26N 61°32W 322 e
Antikythira Greece 35°52N 23°15E 204 F5
Antilla Cuba 20°40N 75°50W 320 B4
Antilles = West Indies Cent. Amer. 15°0N 65°0W 321 D7
Antimilos Greece 36°47N 24°12E 204 E6
Anting Taiwan 23°7N 120°14E 225 C2
Antioch = Hatay Turkey 36°14N 36°10E 250 B7
Antioch U.S.A. 38°1N 121°48W 306 G5
Antioche, Pertuis d' France 46°6N 1°20W 174 B2
Antioquia Colombia 6°40N 75°55W 328 B2
Antioquia □ Colombia 7°0N 75°30W 328 B2
Antiparos Greece 37°0N 25°3E 205 D7
Antipaxi Greece 39°9N 20°13E 204 B2
Antipodes Is. Pac. Oc. 49°45S 178°40E 288 M9
Antipolo Phil. 14°35N 121°10E 232 D3
Antipsara Greece 38°30N 25°29E 205 C7
Antique □ Phil. 11°10N 122°5E 233 F4
Antirio Greece 38°20N 21°46E 204 C3
Antlers U.S.A. 34°14N 95°37W 314 D7
Antoetra Madag. 20°46S 47°20E 272 C2
Antofagasta Chile 23°50S 70°30W 334 A1
Antofagasta □ Chile 24°0S 69°0W 334 A2
Antofagasta de la Sierra Argentina 26°5S 67°20W 334 B2
Antofalla Argentina 25°30S 68°5W 334 B2
Antofalla, Salar de Argentina 25°40S 67°45W 334 B2
Antoine, L. Grenada 12°11N 61°36W 323 q
Anton U.S.A. 33°49N 102°10W 314 E3
Antongila, Helodrano Madag. 15°30S 49°50E 272 B2
Antonibé Madag. 15°7S 47°24E 272 B2
Antonina Brazil 25°26S 48°42W 335 B6
Antonio B. Won Pat Int. ✈ (GUM) Guam 13°29N 144°48E 302 d
Antonio Carlos Jobim Int. ✈ (GIG) Brazil 22°49S 43°15W 135 A1
António Enes = Angoche Mozam. 16°8S 39°55E 269 F4
Antony France 48°44N 2°17E 134 B2
Antrain France 48°28N 1°30W 172 D5
Antratsyt Ukraine 48°7N 39°5E 189 H10
Antrim Antrim, U.K. 54°43N 6°14W 166 B5
Antrim Ohio, U.S.A. 40°7N 81°21W 312 F3
Antrim, Mts. of U.K. 55°3N 6°14W 166 A5
Antrim & Newtownabbey □ U.K. 54°40N 6°11W 166 B5
Antrim Plateau Australia 18°8S 128°20E 278 C4
Antriol Bonaire 12°12N 68°16W 322 h
Antrodoco Italy 42°25N 13°5E 199 F10
Antropovo Russia 58°24N 43°6E 190 A6
Antsakabary Madag. 15°3S 48°56E 272 B2
Antsalova Madag. 18°40S 44°37E 272 B1
Antsenavolo Madag. 21°24S 48°3E 272 C2
Antsiafabositra Madag. 17°18S 46°57E 272 B2
Antsirabe Sofia, Madag. 15°57S 48°58E 272 B2
Antsirabe Vakinankaratra, Madag. 19°55S 47°2E 272 B2
Antsiranana Madag. 12°25S 49°20E 272 A2
Antsohihy Madag. 14°50S 47°59E 272 A2
Antsohimbondrona Seranana Madag. 13°7S 48°48E 272 A2
Antu China 42°30N 128°20E 227 C15
Antufash Yemen 15°42N 42°25E 248 D3
Antung Taiwan 23°18N 121°20E 225 C3
Antwerp = Antwerpen Belgium 51°13N 4°25E 170 C4
Antwerp N.Y., U.S.A. 44°12N 75°37W 313 B9
Antwerp Ohio, U.S.A. 41°11N 84°45W 311 C12
Antwerpen Belgium 51°13N 4°25E 170 C4
Antwerpen □ Belgium 51°15N 4°40E 170 C4
Anukur, C. Papua N. G. 6°18S 149°37E 286 D5
Anupgarh India 29°10N 73°10E 242 E5
Anuppur India 23°6N 81°41E 243 H9
Anuradhapura Sri Lanka 8°22N 80°28E 245 K5
Anurrete ○ Australia 20°50S 135°38E 280 C2
Anveh Iran 27°23N 54°11E 247 E7
Anvers = Antwerpen Belgium 51°13N 4°25E 170 C4
Anvers I. Antarctica 64°30S 63°40W 151 C17
Anvik U.S.A. 62°39N 160°13W 302 C6
Anwen China 29°4N 120°26E 229 C13
Anxi Fujian, China 25°2N 118°12E 229 E12
Anxi Gansu, China 40°30N 95°43E 218 C8
Anxian China 31°40N 104°25E 228 B5
Anxiang China 29°27N 112°11E 229 C9
Anxious B. Australia 33°24S 134°45E 281 E1
Anyama Côte d'Ivoire 5°30N 4°3W 262 D4
Anyang Henan, China 36°5N 114°21E 226 F8
Anyang S. Korea 37°23N 126°55E 224 C2
Anyer Indonesia 6°4S 105°53E 234 D3
Anyi Jiangxi, China 28°49N 115°25E 229 C10
Anyi Shanxi, China 35°2N 111°2E 226 G6
Anyuan China 25°9N 115°21E 229 E10
Anyue China 30°9N 105°50E 228 B5
Anza U.S.A. 33°35N 116°39W 307 M10
Anze China 36°10N 112°12E 226 F7
Anzegloud Algeria 26°50N 0°1E 261 C5
Anzhero-Sudzhensk Russia 56°10N 86°0E 214 D9
Ánzio Italy 41°27N 12°37E 200 A5
Anzoátegui □ Venezuela 9°0N 64°30W 329 B5
Ao Makham Thailand 7°50N 98°24E 237 a
Ao Phangnga △ Thailand 8°10N 98°32E 237 a
Aoba Vanuatu 15°25S 167°50E 287 E5
Aoga-Shima Japan 32°28N 139°46E 223 E11
Aohan Qi China 43°18N 119°43E 227 C10
Aoiz Spain 42°46N 1°22W 196 C3
Aoji N. Korea 42°31N 130°23E 224 A5
Aola Solomon Is. 9°30S 160°30E 287 M11
Aomen = Macau China 22°12N 113°33E 229 F9
Aomori Japan 40°45N 140°45E 220 D10
Aomori □ Japan 40°45N 140°40E 220 D10
AON Center Chicago, U.S.A. 119 b2
tAonach, An = Nenagh Ireland 52°52N 8°11W 166 D3
Aonla India 28°16N 79°11E 243 E8
Aono-Yama Japan 34°28N 131°48E 222 C3
Aorai, Mt. Tahiti 17°34S 149°30W 289 e
Aoraki Mount Cook N.Z. 43°36S 170°9E 285 D5
Aoral, Phnum Cambodia 12°0N 104°15E 237 G5
Aorangi Ra. N.Z. 41°28S 175°22E 284 H4
Aore Vanuatu 15°35S 167°10E 287 E5
Aoreora Morocco 28°51N 10°53W 260 C2
Aosta Italy 45°45N 7°20E 198 C4
Aotea Harbour N.Z. 38°0S 174°50E 284 E3
Aotearoa = New Zealand ■ Oceania 40°0S 176°0E 284 G5
Aoudéras Niger 17°45N 8°20E 259 E1
Aouinet Torkoz Morocco 28°31N 9°46W 260 C3
Aouk, Bahr → Africa 8°51N 18°53E 259 G3
Aouk-Aoukalé △ C.A.R. 9°52N 21°25E 264 A4
Aoukar Mali 23°50N 2°45W 260 D4
Aoukâr Mauritania 17°40N 10°0W 262 B3
Aoulef el Arab Algeria 26°55N 1°2E 261 C5
Aousred W. Sahara 22°32N 14°17W 260 D2
Aoyama Tokyo, Japan 140 b2
Aozou Chad 21°45N 17°28E 259 D3
Aozou, Couloir d' Chad 22°0N 19°0E 259 D3
Ap Lei Chau Hong Kong, China 22°14N 114°9E 122 B2
Apá → S. Amer. 22°6S 58°2W 334 A4
Apache U.S.A. 34°54N 98°22W 314 D5
Apache Junction U.S.A. 33°25N 111°33W 305 K8
Apalachee B. U.S.A. 30°0N 84°0W 316 E5
Apalachicola U.S.A. 29°43N 84°59W 316 F5
Apalachicola → U.S.A. 29°43N 84°58W 316 F5
Apalachicola B. U.S.A. 29°40N 85°0W 316 F3
Apam Ghana 5°19N 0°42W 263 D4
Apamea Syria 35°31N 36°28E 250 C7
Apapa Nigeria 6°26N 3°21E 124 B2
Apapa Quays Nigeria 6°26N 3°23E 124 B2
Apaporis → Colombia 1°23S 69°25W 328 D4
Aparados da Serra △ Brazil 29°10S 50°8W 335 B5
Aparecida = Bertolínia Brazil 7°38S 43°57W 332 C3
Aparecida de Goiânia Brazil 16°45S 49°16W 333 E2
Aparecida do Taboado Brazil 20°5S 51°5W 333 F1
Aparri Phil. 18°22N 121°38E 232 B3
Aparurén Venezuela 5°6N 62°8W 329 B5
Apataki French Polynesia 15°26S 146°20W 289 f
Apateu Romania 46°36N 21°47E 182 D6
Apatin Serbia 45°40N 19°0E 182 E4
Apatity Russia 67°34N 33°22E 160 C25
Apatou Fr. Guiana 5°9N 54°20W 329 B7
Apatula = Finke Australia 25°34S 134°35E 280 D1
Apatzingán Mexico 19°5N 102°21W 318 D4
Apayao □ Phil. 18°10N 121°10E 232 B3
Apelacão Portugal 38°48N 9°7W 126 A2
Apeldoorn Neths. 52°13N 5°57E 170 B5
Apen Germany 53°13N 7°48E 178 B3
Apennines = Appennini Italy 44°30N 10°0E 198 D7
Apenrade = Aabenraa Denmark 55°3N 9°25E 163 J3
Apere → Bolivia 13°44S 65°18W 331 C4
Apgujeong S. Korea 37°32N 127°2E 137 B2
Aphrodisias Turkey 37°42N 28°46E 205 D10
Api Nepal 30°0N 80°57E 218 F5
Apia Samoa 13°50S 171°50W 287 V20
Apiacás, Serra dos Brazil 9°50S 57°0W 331 B6
Apiaí Brazil 24°31S 48°50W 333 F2
Apiaú → Brazil 2°39N 61°12W 329 C5
Apiaú, Serra do Brazil 2°30N 62°0W 329 C5
Apidiá → Brazil 11°39S 61°11W 331 C5
Apies → S. Africa 25°15S 28°8E 271 C4
Apinajé Brazil 11°31S 48°18W 333 D2
Apiti N.Z. 39°58S 175°54E 284 F4
Apizaco Mexico 19°25N 98°8W 319 D5
Aplao Peru 16°0S 72°40W 330 D3
Apo, Mt. Phil. 6°53N 125°14E 233 H5
Apo East Pass. Phil. 12°40N 120°40E 232 E3
Apo Reef △ Phil. 12°50N 120°50E 232 E3
Apo West Pass. Phil. 12°31N 120°22E 232 E3
Apodi Brazil 5°39S 37°48W 332 C4
Apoera Suriname 5°12N 57°10W 329 B6
Apolakia Greece 36°5N 27°48E 206 E11
Apolakia, Ormos Greece 36°5N 27°45E 206 E11
Apolda Germany 51°2N 11°32E 178 D7
Apolima Samoa 13°49S 172°9W 287 V19
Apollo Bay Australia 38°45S 143°40E 282 E5
Apollonia = Sūsah Libya 32°52N 21°59E 258 B4
Apollonia Greece 36°15N 27°58E 206 E11
Apolo Bolivia 14°30S 68°30W 330 C4
Apolonia Greece 36°58N 24°43E 204 E6
Apónguao → Venezuela 4°48N 61°36W 329 C5
Apopa El Salv. 13°48N 89°10W 320 D2
Apopka U.S.A. 28°40N 81°31W 317 G8
Apopka, L. U.S.A. 28°37N 81°37W 133 A1
Apoquindo Chile 33°24S 70°32W 137 B2
Aporé Brazil 18°58S 52°1W 331 D7
Aporé → Brazil 19°27S 50°57W 333 E1
Aporema Brazil 1°14N 50°49W 332 A1
Apostle Is. U.S.A. 47°0N 90°40W 308 B8
Apostle Islands △ U.S.A. 46°55N 91°0W 308 B8
Apóstoles Argentina 28°0S 56°0W 335 B4
Apostolos Andreas, C. Cyprus 35°42N 34°35E 207 E10
Apostolovo Ukraine 47°39N 33°39E 189 J7
Apoteri Guyana 4°2N 58°32W 329 C6
Appalachian Mts. U.S.A. 38°0N 80°0W 309 G14
Åppelbo Sweden 60°29N 14°1E 162 D8
Appenino Lucano-Val d'Agri-Lagonegrese △ Italy 40°5N 16°10E 201 B9
Appennino Tosco-Emiliano △ Italy 44°10N 10°25E 198 D7
Appennini Italy 44°30N 10°0E 198 D7
Appennino Ligure Italy 44°30N 9°0E 198 D6
Appenzell-Ausser Rhoden □ Switz. 47°23N 9°23E 179 H5
Appenzell-Inner Rhoden □ Switz. 47°20N 9°25E 179 H5
Appiano Italy 46°28N 11°15E 199 B8
Apple Hill Canada 45°13N 74°46W 313 A10
Apple Valley U.S.A. 34°32N 117°14W 307 L9
Appleby-in-Westmorland U.K. 54°35N 2°29W 168 C5
Appledore U.K. 51°3N 4°13W 169 F3
Appleton U.S.A. 44°16N 88°25W 308 C9
Appleton City U.S.A. 38°11N 94°2W 310 F2
Appleton Rum Distillery Jamaica 18°10N 77°44W 320 a
Appling U.S.A. 33°33N 82°19W 316 B7
Apra Harbor Guam 13°26N 144°40E 302 d
Apricena Italy 41°47N 15°27E 199 G12
April → Papua N. G. 4°18S 142°26E 286 C2
Aprilia Italy 41°36N 12°39E 200 A5
Apsheronsk Russia 44°28N 39°42E 191 H4
Apsley Canada 44°45N 78°6W 312 B6
Apt France 43°53N 5°24E 175 E9
Apterkarskiy Ostrov Russia 59°57N 30°20E 137 B2
Apuane, Alpi Italy 44°7N 10°14E 198 D7
Apuaú Brazil 2°25S 60°53W 329 D5
Apucarana Brazil 23°55S 51°33W 335 A5
Apulia = Púglia □ Italy 41°15N 16°15E 201 A9
Apurashokoru Palau 7°16N 134°17E 288 c
Apurauan Phil. 9°35N 118°20E 233 G2
Apure □ Venezuela 7°10N 68°50W 328 B4
Apure → Venezuela 7°37N 66°25W 328 B4
Apurímac □ Peru 14°0S 73°0W 330 C3
Apurímac → Peru 12°17S 73°56W 330 C3
Apuseni, Munţii Romania 46°30N 22°45E 182 D7
Āq Qālā Iran 37°10N 54°30E 247 B7
Aqaba = Al 'Aqabah Jordan 29°31N 35°0E 251 F4
Aqaba, G. of Red Sea 29°0N 34°40E 251 K5
'Aqabah, Khalīj al = Aqaba, G. of Red Sea 29°0N 34°40E 251 K5
Aqadyr Kazakhstan 48°17N 74°50E 217 C8
Āqchah Afghan. 36°56N 66°11E 240 A2
'Aqdā Iran 32°26N 53°37E 247 C7
Aqiq Sudan 18°14N 38°12E 256 D4
Aqīq, Khalīg Sudan 18°20N 38°10E 256 D4
'Aqīq, W. al → Si. Arabia 20°16N 41°40E 248 B3
Aqköl Kazakhstan 51°59N 70°56E 217 B8
Aqmola = Nur-Sultan Kazakhstan 51°10N 71°30E 217 B8
Aqmola □ Kazakhstan 51°30N 70°0E 217 B8
'Aqrah Iraq 36°46N 43°45E 213 D10
Aqsay Kazakhstan 51°11N 53°0E 187 D9
Aqshataū Kazakhstan 47°59N 74°3E 217 C8
Aqsū Ongtüstik Qazaqstan, Kazakhstan 42°25N 69°50E 217 D7
Aqsū Pavlodar, Kazakhstan 52°2N 76°55E 217 B9
Aqsūgek Kazakhstan 44°37N 74°30E 217 D8
Aqtaū Mangghystaū, Kazakhstan 43°39N 51°12E 187 F9
Aqtaū Qaraghandy, Kazakhstan 50°14N 73°3E 217 B8
Aqtöbe Kazakhstan 50°17N 57°10E 187 D10
Aqtoghay Kazakhstan 46°57N 79°40E 217 C9
Aqua = Sokhumi Georgia 43°0N 41°0E 191 J5
Aquarium of the Americas New Orleans, U.S.A. 131 b3
Aquidauana Brazil 20°30S 55°50W 331 E6
Aquidauana → Brazil 19°44S 56°50W 331 D6
Aquila Mexico 18°36N 103°30W 318 D4
Aquileia Italy 45°46N 13°22E 199 C10
Aquiles Serdán Mexico 28°36N 105°53W 318 B3
Aquin Haiti 18°16N 73°24W 321 C5
Aquitain, Bassin France 44°0N 0°30W 171 D3
Ar Horqin Qi China 43°45N 120°0E 227 C11
Ar Kazimiyah Iraq 33°22N 44°20E 113 B1
Ar Rafid Syria 32°57N 35°52E 250 F6
Ar Raḩḩālīyah Iraq 32°44N 43°23E 213 F10
Ar Rāhidah Yemen 13°23N 44°19E 248 D4
Ar Ram West Bank 31°51N 35°15E 123 A2
Ar Ramādī Iraq 33°25N 43°20E 213 F10
Ar Raml Libya 26°45N 19°40E 258 C3
Ar Ramthā Jordan 32°34N 36°0E 251 F7
Ar Raqqah Syria 35°59N 39°8E 213 E8
Ar Raqqah □ Syria 36°20N 39°10E 213 D8
Ar Rashidiya = Er Rachidia Morocco 31°58N 4°20W 260 B4
Ar Rass Si. Arabia 25°50N 43°40E 246 E4
Ar Rastan Syria 34°55N 36°43E 250 D7
Ar Rawḑah Si. Arabia 21°16N 42°50E 248 B3
Ar Rawḑah Şan'ā', Yemen 15°26N 44°13E 248 D4
Ar Rawḑah Shabwah, Yemen 14°28N 47°17E 248 D4
Ar Rayyan Qatar 25°17N 51°25E 247 E6
Ar Rifā'ī Iraq 31°50N 46°10E 246 D5
Ar Riyāḑ Si. Arabia 24°41N 46°42E 246 E5
Ar Riyāḑ □ Si. Arabia 23°0N 45°50E 248 B4
Ar Riyān Yemen 14°39N 49°19E 249 D5
Ar Rmäs, W. → Syria 35°47N 36°50E 250 C7
Ar Ru'ays Qatar 26°8N 51°12E 247 E6
Ar Rukhaymīyah Iraq 29°22N 45°38E 246 D5
Ar Rumaythah Iraq 31°31N 45°12E 246 D5
Ar Ruşāfah Syria 35°45N 38°49E 213 E8
Ar Ruşayfah Jordan 32°1N 36°1E 251 F7
Ar Rustāq Oman 23°23N 57°26E 249 B7
Ar Ruṭbah Iraq 33°0N 40°15E 213 F9
Ar Ruwaydah Si. Arabia 23°40N 44°40E 248 B4
Ara India 25°35N 84°32E 243 G11
Ara Japan 35°41N 139°50E 140 A4
Ara → Spain 42°26N 0°9E 196 C5
Ara Goro Ethiopia 5°48N 41°18E 257 F5
Ara Tera Ethiopia 6°38N 40°57E 257 F5
Arab U.S.A. 34°19N 86°30W 315 D11
'Arab, Bahr el → South Sudan 9°0N 29°30E 257 F2
Arab, Khalîg el Egypt 30°55N 29°0E 256 A2
Arab, Shatt al → Asia 29°57N 48°34E 247 D6
'Araba, W. → Egypt 28°19N 33°31E 256 J8
'Arabābād Iran 33°2N 57°41E 247 C8
'Arabah, W. → Yemen 18°5N 51°26E 249 C5
Araban Turkey 37°28N 37°44E 212 D7
Arabatskaya Strelka Ukraine 45°40N 35°0E 189 K8
Araba/Álava □ Spain 42°48N 2°28W 196 C2
Arabba Italy 46°30N 11°52E 199 B8
Arabelo Venezuela 4°55N 64°13W 329 C5
Arabi U.S.A. 31°50N 83°44W 316 D6
Arabia Asia 25°0N 45°0E 210 F6
Arabian Basin Ind. Oc. 11°30N 65°0E 273 C5
Arabian Desert = Sharqîya, Es Sahrâ esh Egypt 27°30N 32°30E 256 B3
Arabian Gulf = Persian Gulf Asia 27°0N 50°0E 247 E6
Arabian Sea Ind. Oc. 16°0N 65°0E 238 F9
Arabistan = Khūzestān □ Iran 31°0N 49°0E 247 D6
Araç Turkey 41°15N 33°21E 212 B5
Aracaju Brazil 10°55S 37°4W 332 D4
Aracataca Colombia 10°38N 74°9W 328 A3
Aracati Brazil 4°30S 37°44W 332 B4
Araçatuba Brazil 21°10S 50°30W 335 A5
Araceli Phil. 10°33N 119°59E 233 F2
Aracena Spain 37°53N 6°38W 195 H4
Aracena, Sierra de Spain 37°50N 6°50W 195 H4
Arachova Greece 38°28N 22°35E 204 C4
Arachthos → Greece 39°20N 21°4E 204 B3
Aracides, C. Solomon Is. 8°21S 161°0E 287 M11
Aračinovo N. Macedonia 42°1N 21°34E 202 D5
Araçuaí Brazil 16°52S 42°4W 333 E3
Araçuaí → Brazil 16°46S 42°2W 333 E3
'Arad Israel 31°15N 35°12E 251 G6
Arad Romania 46°10N 21°20E 182 D6
Arad □ Romania 46°20N 22°0E 182 D6
Arada Chad 15°0N 20°20E 259 F4
Arādān Iran 35°21N 52°30E 247 C7
Aradhippou Cyprus 34°57N 33°36E 207 F9
Arafura Sea E. Indies 9°0S 135°0E 288 H5
Aragarças Brazil 15°55S 52°15W 331 D7
Aragats Armenia 40°30N 44°15E 191 K7
Aragon U.S.A. 34°2N 85°3W 316 A4
Aragón □ Spain 41°25N 0°40W 196 D4
Aragón → Spain 42°13N 1°44W 196 C3
Aragona Italy 37°24N 13°37E 200 E6
Aragua □ Venezuela 10°0N 67°10W 328 B4
Aragua de Barcelona Venezuela 9°28N 64°49W 329 B5
Araguacema Brazil 8°50S 49°20W 332 C2
Araguaçu = Paraguaçu Paulista Brazil 22°22S 50°35W 335 A5
Araguaçu Brazil 12°49S 49°51W 333 D2
Araguaia → Brazil 5°21S 48°41W 332 C2
Araguaia △ Brazil 10°30S 50°0W 332 D2
Araguaiana Brazil 15°43S 51°51W 331 D7
Araguaína Brazil 7°12S 48°12W 332 C2
Araguari Brazil 18°38S 48°11W 333 E2
Araguari → Brazil 1°15N 49°55W 329 C8
Araguatins Brazil 5°38S 48°7W 332 C2
Arahal Spain 37°15N 5°33W 195 H5
Arain India 26°27N 75°2E 242 F6
Araioses Brazil 2°53S 41°55W 332 B3
Arak Algeria 25°20N 3°45E 261 C5
Arāk Iran 34°0N 49°40E 247 C6
Araka South Sudan 4°20N 30°23E 257 G3
Arakan = Rakhine □ Myanmar 19°0N 94°15E 241 F5
Arakan Coast Myanmar 19°0N 94°0E 241 F4
Arakan Yoma Myanmar 20°0N 94°40E 241 F5
Arakawa Japan 35°44N 139°48E 140 A3
Arakkonam India 13°7N 79°43E 245 H4
Araklı Turkey 41°6N 40°2E 213 B9
Araks = Aras, Rūd-e → Asia 40°5N 48°29E 213 B13
Araks → Iran 39°10N 47°10E 216 E3
Aral Kazakhstan 46°41N 61°45E 216 C6
Aral Mangy Qaraqumy Kazakhstan 46°50N 63°10E 216 C6
Aral Sea Asia 45°0N 58°20E 216 C5
Aral Tengizi = Aral Sea Asia 45°0N 58°20E 216 C5
Aralık Turkey 39°52N 44°31E 213 C11
Aralkum Asia 44°30N 60°35E 216 D6
Aralsk = Aral Kazakhstan 46°41N 61°45E 216 C6
Aralskoye More = Aral Sea Asia 45°0N 58°20E 216 C5
Aralsor, Ozero = Aralsor Köli Kazakhstan 49°5N 48°12E 191 F9
Aralsor Köli Kazakhstan 49°5N 48°12E 191 F9
Aramac Australia 22°58S 145°14E 280 C4
Aramia → Papua N. G. 7°55S 143°22E 286 D2
Aran → India 19°55N 78°12E 244 E4
Aran, Val de Spain 42°50N 0°55E 196 C5
Aran Areh Ethiopia 9°2N 43°54E 267 C5
Aran I. = Arranmore Ireland 55°0N 8°30W 166 A3
Aran Is. Ireland 53°6N 9°38W 166 C2
Aranda de Duero Spain 41°39N 3°42W 194 D7
Arandān Iran 35°23N 46°55E 246 C5
Aranđelovac Serbia 44°18N 20°34E 202 B4
Aranga N.Z. 35°44S 173°40E 284 B2
Arani Bolivia 17°34S 65°46W 331 D4
Arani India 12°43N 79°19E 245 H4
Aranjuez Spain 40°1N 3°40W 194 E7
Aranos Namibia 24°9S 19°7E 270 B2
Aransas Pass U.S.A. 27°55N 97°9W 314 H6
Arany-hegyi-patak → Hungary 47°34N 19°4E 117 A2
Aranyaprathet Thailand 13°41N 102°30E 236 F4
Arao Japan 32°59N 130°25E 222 E2
Araouane Mali 18°55N 3°30W 262 B4
Arapahoe U.S.A. 40°18N 99°54W 308 E4
Arapari Brazil 5°34S 49°15W 332 C2
Arapawa I. N.Z. 41°11S 174°17E 285 B9
Arapey Grande → Uruguay 30°55S 57°49W 334 C4
Arapgir Turkey 39°5N 38°30E 213 C8
Arapiraca Brazil 9°45S 36°39W 332 C4
Arapis, Akra Greece 40°27N 24°0E 203 F8
Arapongas Brazil 23°29S 51°28W 335 A5
Arapuni N.Z. 38°4S 175°39E 284 E4
Ar'ar Si. Arabia 30°59N 41°2E 246 D4
Araracuara Colombia 0°24S 72°17W 328 D3
Araranguá Brazil 29°0S 49°30W 335 B6
Araraquara Brazil 21°50S 48°0W 333 F2
Araras Brazil 22°22S 47°23W 333 F2
Ararás, Serra das Brazil 25°0S 53°10W 335 B5
Ararat Armenia 39°48N 44°50E 213 C11
Ararat Vic., Australia 37°16S 142°58E 282 D5
Ararat, Mt. = Ağrı Dağı Turkey 39°50N 44°15E 213 C11
Arari Brazil 3°28S 44°47W 332 B3
Araria India 26°9N 87°33E 243 F12
Araripe, Chapada do Brazil 7°20S 40°0W 332 C4
Araripina Brazil 7°33S 40°34W 332 C3
Araruama, L. de Brazil 22°53S 42°12W 333 F3
Araruna Brazil 6°52S 35°44W 332 C4
Aras, Rūd-e → Asia 40°5N 48°29E 213 B13
Aratāne Mauritania 18°24N 8°32W 262 B3
Araticu = Oeiras do Pará Brazil 1°58S 49°51W 329 D8
Arauca Colombia 7°0N 70°40W 328 B3
Arauca □ Colombia 6°40N 71°0W 328 B3
Arauca → Venezuela 7°24N 66°35W 328 B4
Arauco Chile 37°16S 73°25W 334 D1
Araújos Brazil 19°56S 45°14W 333 E2
Arauquita Colombia 7°2N 71°25W 328 B3
Araure Venezuela 9°34N 69°13W 328 B4
Aravaca Spain 40°27N 3°47W 127 B1
Aravalli Range India 25°0N 73°30E 242 G5
Arawa Ethiopia 9°57N 41°58E 257 F5
Arawale △ Kenya 1°24S 40°9E 268 C5
Arawe Is. Papua N. G. 6°6S 149°6E 286 D5
Arawhata → N.Z. 44°0S 168°40E 285 E3
Araxá Brazil 19°35S 46°55W 333 E2
Araxos, Akra Greece 38°13N 21°20E 204 C3
Araya, Pen. de Venezuela 10°40N 64°0W 329 A5
Arayat Phil. 15°10N 120°46E 232 D3
Arba Gugu Ethiopia 8°40N 40°15E 257 F5
Arba Minch Ethiopia 6°0N 37°30E 257 F4
Arbat Iraq 35°25N 45°35E 213 E11
Arbataash Iraq 33°20N 44°19E 113 A1
Árbatax Italy 39°56N 9°42E 200 C2
Arbi Ethiopia 9°4N 35°7E 257 F4
Arbīl Iraq 36°15N 44°5E 213 D11
Arbīl □ Iraq 36°20N 44°20E 213 D11
Arboga Sweden 59°24N 15°52E 162 E9
Arbois France 46°55N 5°46E 173 F12
Arboletes Colombia 8°51N 76°26W 328 B2
Arbore Ethiopia 5°3N 36°50E 257 F4
Arboréa Italy 39°46N 8°35E 200 C1
Arborfield Canada 53°6N 103°39W 297 C8
Arborg Canada 50°54N 97°13W 297 C9
Arbre du Ténéré Niger 17°50N 10°4E 259 E2
Arbroath U.K. 56°34N 2°35W 167 E6
Arbuckle U.S.A. 39°1N 122°3W 306 F4
Arbus Italy 39°30N 8°33E 200 C1
Arc → France 45°34N 6°12E 175 C10
Arc de Triomphe Paris, France 134 a2
Arc-lès-Gray France 47°28N 5°34E 173 E12
Arcachon France 44°40N 1°10W 174 D2
Arcachon, Bassin d' France 44°42N 1°10W 174 D2
Arcade U.S.A. 42°32N 78°25W 312 D6
Arcadia = Arkadia Greece 37°30N 22°20E 204 D4
Arcadia Calif., U.S.A. 34°7N 118°1W 126 B4
Arcadia Fla., U.S.A. 27°13N 81°52W 317 H8
Arcadia Ind., U.S.A. 40°11N 86°1W 311 D10
Arcadia Iowa, U.S.A. 42°5N 95°3W 310 B1
Arcadia La., U.S.A. 32°33N 92°55W 314 E8
Arcadia Pa., U.S.A. 40°47N 78°51W 312 F6
Arcadia Park U.S.A. 32°44N 96°56W 120 B4
Arcanum U.S.A. 39°59N 84°33W 311 E12
Arcata U.S.A. 40°52N 124°5W 304 F1
Arcévia Italy 43°30N 12°56E 199 E9
Archanes Greece 35°16N 25°11E 205 F7
Archangel = Arkhangelsk Russia 64°38N 40°36E 186 B7
Archangelos Preveza, Greece 39°6N 20°42E 207 A2
Archangelos Rhodes, Greece 36°13N 28°7E 206 E12
Archar Bulgaria 43°50N 22°54E 202 C6
Archbald U.S.A. 41°30N 75°32W 313 E9
Archbold U.S.A. 41°31N 84°18W 311 C12
Archena Spain 38°9N 1°16W 197 G3
Archenu, J. Libya 22°15N 24°45E 259 D4
Archer U.S.A. 29°32N 82°32W 317 F7
Archer → Australia 13°28S 141°41E 280 A3
Archer B. Australia 13°20S 141°30E 280 A3
Archer Bend = Mungkan Kandju △ Australia 13°35S 142°52E 280 A3
Archers Post Kenya 0°35N 37°35E 268 B4
Arches △ U.S.A. 38°45N 109°25W 304 G9
Archidona Spain 37°6N 4°22W 196 H6
Archipel-de-Mingan △ Canada 50°13N 63°10W 299 B7
Archipiélago Chinijo △ Canary Is. 29°20N 13°30W 153 e2
Archipiélago Los Roques △ Venezuela 11°50N 66°44W 321 D6
Archives Navy Memorial Washington, D.C., U.S.A. 143 b2
Arci, Mte. Italy 39°47N 8°45E 200 C1
Arcidosso Italy 42°52N 11°33E 199 F8
Arcila = Asilah Morocco 35°29N 6°0W 260 A3
Arcipelago de la Maddalena △ Italy 41°14N 9°24E 200 A2
Arcipelago Toscano △ Italy 42°45N 10°15E 198 F7
Arcis-sur-Aube France 48°32N 4°10E 173 D11
Arckaringa Cr. → Australia 28°10S 135°22E 281 D2
Arco Italy 45°55N 10°53E 198 C7
Arco Idaho, U.S.A. 43°38N 113°18W 304 E7
Arco Plaza Los Angeles, U.S.A. 127 b1
Arcola U.S.A. 39°41N 88°19W 311 E8
Arcoona Australia 31°2S 137°1E 282 A2
Arcos de Jalón Spain 41°12N 2°16W 196 D2
Arcos de la Frontera Spain 36°45N 5°49W 195 J5
Arcos de Valdevez Portugal 41°55N 8°22W 194 D2
Arcot India 12°53N 79°20E 245 H4
Arcoverde Brazil 8°25S 37°4W 332 C4
Arcozelo Portugal 40°32N 7°47W 194 E3
Arctic Bay Canada 73°1N 85°7W 295 C14
Arctic Mid-Ocean Ridge Arctic 87°0N 90°0E 150 A
Arctic Ocean Arctic 78°0N 160°0W 150 B18
Arctic Red River = Tsiigehtchic Canada 67°15N 134°0W 294 D5
Arctic Village U.S.A. 68°8N 145°32W 303 B11
Arctowski Antarctica 62°30S 58°0W 151 C18
Arcueil France 48°48N 2°19E 134 B2
Arda → Bulgaria 41°40N 26°30E 203 E10
Arda → Italy 45°2N 10°2E 198 C7
Ardabīl Iran 38°15N 48°18E 213 C13
Ardabīl □ Iran 38°15N 48°20E 247 B6
Ardahan Turkey 41°7N 42°41E 213 B10
Ardahan □ Turkey 41°10N 42°50E 213 B10
Ardakān = Sepīdān Iran 30°20N 52°5E 247 D7
Ardakān Iran 32°19N 53°59E 247 C7
Ardala Sweden 58°22N 13°19E 163 F7
Ardales Spain 36°53N 4°51W 195 J6
Ardalstangen Norway 61°14N 7°43E 164 C4
Ardamata Sudan 13°29N 22°28E 259 F4
Ardara Ireland 54°46N 8°25W 166 B3
Ardas → Greece 41°40N 26°30E 203 E10
Ardèche □ France 44°42N 4°16E 175 D8
Ardèche → France 44°16N 4°39E 175 D8
Ardee Ireland 53°52N 6°33W 166 C5
Arden Ont., Canada 44°43N 76°56W 312 B8
Arden Denmark 56°46N 9°52E 163 H3
Arden Calif., U.S.A. 38°36N 121°33W 306 G5
Arden Nev., U.S.A. 36°1N 115°14W 307 J11
Ardenne Belgium 49°50N 5°5E 170 E5
Ardennes = Ardenne Belgium 49°50N 5°5E 170 E5
Ardennes □ France 49°35N 4°40E 173 C11
Ardentes France 46°45N 1°50E 173 F8
Arderin Ireland 53°2N 7°39W 166 C4
Ardeşen Turkey 41°12N 41°2E 213 B9
Ardestān Iran 33°20N 52°25E 247 C7
Ardfert Ireland 52°20N 9°47W 166 D2
Ardglass U.K. 54°16N 5°36W 166 B6
Ardhéa = Aridea Greece 40°58N 22°3E 202 F6
Ardila → Portugal 38°12N 7°28W 195 G3
Ardino Bulgaria 41°34N 25°9E 203 E9
Ardivachar Pt. U.K. 57°23N 7°26W 167 D1
Ardlethan Australia 34°22S 146°53E 283 C7
Ardmore Okla., U.S.A. 34°10N 97°8W 314 D6
Ardmore Pa., U.S.A. 40°2N 75°17W 313 F9
Ardnamurchan, Pt. of U.K. 56°43N 6°14W 167 E2
Ardnave Pt. U.K. 55°53N 6°20W 167 F2
Ardon Russia 43°10N 44°18E 191 J7
Ardore Italy 38°11N 16°10E 201 D9
Ardres France 50°50N 1°59E 173 B8
Ardrossan S. Austral., Australia 34°26S 137°53E 282 C2
Ardrossan N. Ayrs., U.K. 55°39N 4°49W 167 F4
Ards & North Down □ U.K. 54°32N 5°39W 166 B6
Ards Pen. U.K. 54°33N 5°34W 166 B6
Ardud Sudan 19°54N 30°20E 256 D3
Ardud Romania 47°37N 22°52E 182 C7
Åre Sweden 63°22N 13°15E 162 A7
Arecibo Puerto Rico 18°29N 66°43W 321 C6
Areia Branca Brazil 5°0S 37°0W 332 B4
Arena, Pt. U.S.A. 38°57N 123°44W 306 G3
Arena I. Phil. 9°14N 120°45E 233 G3
Arenal Honduras 15°21N 86°50W 320 C2
Arenales, Cerro Chile 47°5S 73°40W 336 C2
Arenápolis Brazil 14°26S 56°49W 331 C6
Arenas = Las Arenas Spain 43°17N 4°50W 194 B6
Arenas, Pta. Venezuela 10°58N 64°24W 329 a
Arenas de San Pedro Spain 40°12N 5°5W 194 E5
Arendal Norway 58°28N 8°46E 164 F5
Arendsee Germany 52°52N 11°27E 178 C7
Arenillas Ecuador 3°33S 80°10W 328 D1
Arensburg = Kuressaare Estonia 58°15N 22°30E 188 C2
Arenys de Mar Spain 41°35N 2°33E 196 D7
Arenzano Italy 44°24N 8°41E 198 D5
Arenzville U.S.A. 39°53N 90°22W 310 E6
Areopoli Greece 36°40N 22°22E 204 E4
Arequipa Peru 16°20S 71°30W 330 D3
Arequipa □ Peru 16°0S 72°50W 330 D3
Arere Brazil 0°16S 53°52W 329 D7
Arero Ethiopia 4°41N 38°50E 257 G4
Arès France 44°47N 1°8W 174 D2
Arese Italy 45°33N 9°4E 128 A1
Arévalo Spain 41°3N 4°43W 194 D6
Arezzo Italy 43°25N 11°53E 199 E8
Arga Turkey 38°21N 37°59E 246 B3
Arga → Spain 42°18N 1°47W 196 C3
Argalasti Greece 39°13N 23°13E 204 B5
Argamasilla de Alba Spain 39°8N 3°5W 195 F7
Argamasilla de Calatrava Spain 38°44N 4°4W 195 G6
Arganda del Rey Spain 40°19N 3°26W 194 E7
Arganil Portugal 40°13N 8°3W 194 E2
Arganzuela Spain 40°23N 3°42W 127 B1
Argao Phil. 9°52N 123°36E 233 G4
Argarapa ○ Australia 22°20S 134°58E 280 C1
Argasi Greece 37°45N 20°56E 207 D2
Argedeb Ethiopia 6°11N 41°13E 257 F5
Argelès-Gazost France 43°0N 0°6W 174 E3
Argelès-sur-Mer France 42°34N 3°1E 174 F7
Argens → France 43°24N 6°44E 175 E10
Argent, Côte d' France 44°15N 1°30W 174 D2
Argent-sur-Sauldre France 47°33N 2°25E 173 E9
Argenta = North Little Rock U.S.A. 34°45N 92°16W 314 D8
Argenta B.C., Canada 50°11N 116°56W 296 C5
Argenta Italy 44°37N 11°50E 199 D8
Argenta Ill., U.S.A. 39°59N 88°49W 311 E8
Argentan France 48°45N 0°1W 172 D6
Argentário, Mte. Italy 42°24N 11°9E 199 F8
Argentat France 45°6N 1°56E 174 C5
Argentera Italy 44°12N 7°5E 198 D4
Argenteuil France 48°56N 2°15E 134 A2
Argentia Canada 47°18N 53°58W 299 C9
Argentiera, C. dell' Italy 40°44N 8°8E 200 B1
Argentina ■ S. Amer. 35°0S 66°0W 327 G4
Argentine Abyssal Plain Atl. Oc. 46°0S 52°0W 152 L6
Argentine Basin Atl. Oc. 45°0S 45°0W 152 L7
Argentino, L. Argentina 50°10S 73°0W 336 D2
Argenton-les-Vallées France 46°59N 0°27W 172 F6
Argenton-sur-Creuse France 46°36N 1°30E 173 F8
Argeş □ Romania 45°0N 24°45E 183 F9
Argeş → Romania 44°5N 26°38E 183 F11
Arghandab → Afghan. 31°30N 64°15E 242 D1
Argheile Ethiopia 5°19N 42°4E 257 F5
Argirades Greece 39°27N 19°58E 206 C9
Argiroupoli Athina, Greece 37°52N 23°44E 112 B2
Argiroupoli Kriti, Greece 35°17N 24°20E 207 E5
Argo Sudan 19°28N 30°30E 256 D3
Argolikos Kolpos Greece 37°20N 22°52E 204 D4
Argonne France 49°10N 5°0E 173 C12
Argos Greece 37°40N 22°43E 204 D4
Argos Ind., U.S.A. 41°14N 86°15W 311 C10
Argos Orestiko Greece 40°27N 21°18E 202 F5
Argostoli Greece 38°11N 20°29E 207 C2
Argostoliou, Kolpos Greece 38°10N 20°27E 207 C1
Arguedas Spain 42°11N 1°36W 196 C3
Argüelles Madrid, Spain 127 a1
Arguello, Pt. U.S.A. 34°35N 120°39W 307 L6
Arguineguín Canary Is. 27°46N 15°41W 153 e1
Argun Russia 43°18N 45°52E 191 J7
Argun → Russia 53°20N 121°28E 219 A13
Argungu Nigeria 12°40N 4°31E 263 C5
Argus Pk. U.S.A. 35°52N 117°26W 307 K9
Argyle ✈ (SVD) St. Vincent 13°9N 61°9W 323 n
Argyle, L. Australia 16°20S 128°40E 278 C4
Argyle Waterfalls Trin. & Tob. 11°15N 60°35W 323 s
Argyll & Bute □ U.K. 56°13N 5°28W 167 E3
Arhavi Turkey 41°21N 41°18E 213 B9
Århus = Aarhus Denmark 56°8N 10°11E 163 H4
Ari Atoll Maldives 3°53N 72°50E 272 d
Aria N.Z. 38°33S 175°0E 284 E4
Ariadnoye Russia 45°8N 134°25E 220 B7
Ariamsvlei Namibia 28°9S 19°51E 270 C2
Ariana, L' Tunisia 36°52N 10°12E 258 A2
Ariana, L' □ Tunisia 36°50N 10°5E 261 A6
Ariano Irpino Italy 41°9N 15°5E 201 A8
Ariari → Colombia 2°35N 72°47W 328 C3
Aribinda Burkina Faso 14°17N 0°52W 263 C4
Arica Chile 18°32S 70°20W 330 D3
Arica Colombia 2°0S 71°50W 328 D3
Arica y Parinacota □ Chile 17°40S 69°50W 330 D4
Arico Canary Is. 28°9N 16°29W 153 e1
Arid, C. Australia 34°1S 123°10E 279 F3
Arida Japan 34°5N 135°8E 223 C7
Aridal W. Sahara 25°59N 13°54W 260 C2
Aride Seychelles 4°13S 55°40E 272 c
Aridea Greece 40°58N 22°3E 202 F6
Ariège □ France 42°56N 1°30E 174 F5
Ariège → France 43°30N 1°25E 174 E5
Aries → Romania 46°24N 23°20E 183 D8
Arigat el Fersig Algeria 27°35N 2°7W 261 C4
Arihā Israel 31°51N 35°27E 256 A4
Arīḩā Syria 35°49N 36°35E 250 C7
Arikok △ Aruba 12°31N 69°56W 322 f
Arila, Akra Greece 39°43N 19°39E 206 B9
Arilje Serbia 43°44N 20°7E 202 C4
Arima Kanagawa, Japan 35°33N 139°33E 140 B2
Arima Trin. & Tob. 10°38N 61°17W 323 t
Arima → Trin. & Tob. 10°35N 61°16W 323 t
Aringay Phil. 16°26N 120°21E 232 C3
Arinos → Brazil 10°25S 58°20W 331 C6
Ario de Rosales Mexico 19°12N 101°43W 318 D4
Ariogala Lithuania 55°16N 23°28E 184 C10
Arios Pagos Athens, Greece 112 c1
Aripo → Trin. & Tob. 10°35N 61°14W 323 t
Aripo, Mt. Trin. & Tob. 10°45N 61°15W 323 t
Aripo Caves Trin. & Tob. 10°43N 61°14W 323 t
Aripuanã Brazil 9°25S 60°30W 331 B5
Aripuanã → Brazil 5°7S 60°25W 331 B5
Ariquemes Brazil 9°55S 63°6W 331 B5
Arisaig U.K. 56°55N 5°51W 167 E3
Arish, W. el → Egypt 31°9N 33°49E 256 A3
Arissa Ethiopia 11°10N 41°35E 257 E5
Aristazabal I. Canada 52°40N 129°10W 296 C3
Arita Japan 33°11N 129°54E 222 D1
Aritao Phil. 16°18N 121°2E 232 C3
Ariton U.S.A. 31°36N 85°43W 316 D4
Arivonimamo Madag. 19°1S 47°11E 272 B2
Ariyalur India 11°8N 79°8E 245 J4
Ariza Spain 41°19N 2°3W 196 D2
Arizaro, Salar de Argentina 24°40S 67°50W 334 A2
Arizona Argentina 35°45S 65°25W 334 D2
Arizona □ U.S.A. 34°0N 112°0W 305 J8
Arizpe Mexico 30°20N 110°10W 318 A2
'Arjah Si. Arabia 24°43N 44°17E 246 E5
Årjäng Sweden 59°24N 12°8E 162 E6
Arjeplog Sweden 66°3N 17°54E 160 C17
Arjeplouvve = Arjeplog Sweden 66°3N 17°54E 160 C17
Arjona Colombia 10°14N 75°22W 328 A2
Arjona Spain 37°56N 4°4W 195 H6
Arjuna Indonesia 7°49S 112°34E 235 G15
Arka Russia 60°15N 142°0E 215 C15
Arkadak Russia 51°58N 43°30E 190 E6
Arkadelphia U.S.A. 34°7N 93°4W 314 D8
Arkadia Greece 37°30N 22°20E 204 D4
Arkaig, L. U.K. 56°59N 5°10W 167 E3
Arkalgud India 12°46N 76°3E 245 H3
Arkalyk = Arqalyk Kazakhstan 50°13N 66°50E 217 B7
Arkansas □ U.S.A. 35°0N 92°30W 314 D8
Arkansas → U.S.A. 33°47N 91°4W 314 E9
Arkansas City U.S.A. 37°4N 97°2W 308 G5
Arkaroola Australia 30°20S 139°22E 281 E2
Arkavāz Iran 33°22N 46°35E 213 F12

Arken Denmark 55°36N 12°23E 118 B2
Arkhangelsk Russia 64°38N 40°36E 186 B7
Arkhangelskoye Russia 51°32N 40°58E 190 E5
Arki Greece 37°24N 26°44E 205 D8
Arki India 31°9N 76°58E 242 D7
Arkiko Eritrea 15°33N 39°30E 257 D4
Arklow Ireland 52°48N 6°10W 166 D5
Arkona, Kap Germany 54°42N 13°26E 178 A9
Arkösund Sweden 58°29N 16°56E 163 F10
Arkoudi Greece 38°33N 20°43E 207 B2
Arkport U.S.A. 42°24N 77°42W 312 D7
Arktitcheskiy, Mys Russia 81°10N 95°0E 215 A10
Arkul Russia 57°17N 50°3E 190 B10
Arkville U.S.A. 42°9N 74°37W 313 D10
Årla Sweden 59°17N 16°40E 162 E10
Arlanda, Stockholm ✕ (ARN) Sweden 59°41N 17°56E 139 A1
Arlanza → Spain 42°6N 4°9W 194 C6
Arlanzón → Spain 42°3N 4°17W 194 C6
Arlbergpass Austria 47°9N 10°12E 180 D3
Arlbergtunnel Austria 47°9N 10°12E 180 D3
Arles France 43°41N 4°40E 175 E8
Arli Burkina Faso 11°35N 1°28E 263 C5
Arli △ Burkina Faso 11°35N 1°28E 263 C5
Arlington Free State, S. Africa 28°1S 27°53E 271 C4
Arlington Ga., U.S.A. 31°26N 84°44W 316 D5
Arlington Mass., U.S.A. 42°24N 71°10W 116 A1
Arlington N.Y., U.S.A. 41°42N 73°54W 313 E11
Arlington Oreg., U.S.A. 45°43N 120°12W 304 D3
Arlington S. Dak., U.S.A. 44°22N 97°8W 308 C5
Arlington Tex., U.S.A. 32°44N 97°6W 120 C3
Arlington Va., U.S.A. 38°53N 77°7W 143 B2
Arlington Vt., U.S.A. 43°5N 73°9W 313 C11
Arlington Wash., U.S.A. 48°12N 122°8W 306 B4
Arlington, L. U.S.A. 32°43N 97°11W 120 B2
Arlington Heights Ill., U.S.A. 42°5N 87°59W 311 B9
Arlington Heights Mass., U.S.A. 42°25N 71°10W 116 A1
Arlington Municipal ✕ (JLH) U.S.A. 32°39N 97°5W 120 B3
Arlington Nat. Cemetery U.S.A. 38°52N 77°4W 143 B2
Arlon Belgium 49°42N 5°49E 170 E5
Arlparra Australia 22°11S 134°30E 280 C1
Arltunga Australia 23°26S 134°41E 280 C1
Armação Brazil 22°52S 43°6W 135 B2
Armação de Pêra Portugal 37°6N 8°22W 195 H2
Armadale Vic., Australia 37°51S 145°0E 128 B2
Armadale W. Austral., Australia 32°9S 116°0E 279 F2
Armagh U.K. 54°21N 6°39W 166 B5
Armagh, Bansbridge & Craigavon □ U.K. 54°20N 6°28W 166 B5
Armagnac France 43°50N 0°10E 174 E4
Armançon → France 47°59N 3°30E 173 E10
Armando Bermudez △ Dom. Rep. 19°3N 71°0W 321 C5
Armant Egypt 25°37N 32°32E 256 B3
Armatree Australia 31°26S 148°28E 283 A8
Armavir Russia 45°2N 41°7E 191 H5
Armenia Colombia 4°35N 75°45W 328 C2
Armenia ■ Asia 40°20N 45°0E 191 K7
Armenian Quarter Jerusalem 123 b3
Armeniş Romania 45°13N 22°17E 182 E7
Armenistis, Akra Greece 36°8N 27°42E 206 E11
Armentières France 50°40N 2°50E 173 B9
Armero Colombia 4°58N 74°54W 328 C3
Armidale Australia 30°30S 151°40E 283 A9
Armilla Spain 37°9N 3°37W 195 H7
Armori India 20°28N 79°59E 244 D4
Armorique ⌂ France 48°22N 3°50W 172 D3
Armour U.S.A. 43°19N 98°21W 308 D4
Armour Heights Canada 43°45N 79°25W 141 A2
Armstrong B.C., Canada 50°25N 119°10W 296 C5
Armstrong Ont., Canada 50°18N 89°4W 298 B2
Armur India 18°48N 78°16E 244 E4
Armutlu Bursa, Turkey 40°31N 28°50E 203 F12
Armutlu İzmir, Turkey 38°24N 27°34E 205 C9
Arnarfjörður Iceland 65°48N 23°40W 155 B3
Arnaud → Canada 59°59N 69°46W 295 F18
Arnauti, C. Cyprus 35°6N 32°17E 207 E8
Arnay-le-Duc France 47°10N 4°27E 173 E11
Arncliffe Australia 33°56S 151°8E 139 B1
Arnea Greece 40°30N 23°38E 202 F7
Arnedillo Spain 42°13N 2°14W 196 C2
Arnedo Spain 42°12N 2°5W 196 C2
Årnes Iceland 66°1N 21°31W 155 A5
Årnes Akershus, Norway 60°7N 11°28E 164 D8
Árnessýsla Iceland 64°15N 20°30W 155 C6
Arnett U.S.A. 36°8N 99°46W 314 C5
Arnhem Neths. 51°58N 5°55E 170 C5
Arnhem, C. Australia 12°20S 137°30E 280 A2
Arnhem B. Australia 12°20S 136°10E 280 A2
Arnhem Land Australia 13°10S 134°30E 280 A1
Arnhem Land ◎ Australia 12°50S 134°50E 280 A1
Arnissa Greece 40°47N 21°49E 202 F5
Arno → Italy 43°41N 10°17E 198 E7
Arno Bay Australia 33°54S 136°34E 282 B2
Arnold Notts., U.K. 53°1N 1°7W 168 D6
Arnold Calif., U.S.A. 38°15N 120°21W 306 G6
Arnold Mo., U.S.A. 38°26N 90°23W 310 F6
Arnold Arboretum U.S.A. 42°18N 71°8W 116 B2
Arnoldstein Austria 46°33N 13°43E 180 E6
Arnon → France 47°13N 2°1E 173 E9
Arnos Vale Trin. & Tob. 11°13N 60°45W 323 s
Arnot Canada 55°56N 96°41W 297 B9
Arnøya Norway 70°9N 20°40E 160 A19
Arnprior Canada 45°26N 76°21W 313 A8
Arnsberg Germany 51°24N 8°5E 178 D4
Arnsberger Wald ⌂ Germany 51°25N 8°20E 178 D4
Arnstadt Germany 50°50N 10°56E 178 E6
Arnswalde = Choszczno Poland 53°7N 15°25E 185 E2
Aro → Venezuela 8°1N 64°11W 329 B5
Aroa, Pte. Moorea 17°28S 149°46W 289 e
Aroab Namibia 26°41S 19°39E 270 C2
Aroania Oros Greece 37°56N 22°12E 204 D4
Aroche Spain 37°56N 6°57W 195 H4
Arochuku Nigeria 5°21N 7°54E 263 D6
Aroeiras Brazil 7°31S 35°41W 332 C4
Arolsen Germany 51°23N 9°2E 178 D5
Aron India 25°57N 77°56E 242 G6
Aron → France 46°50N 3°28E 173 F10
Arona Canary Is. 28°6N 16°40W 153 e1
Arona Italy 45°46N 8°34E 198 C5
Arorae Kiribati 2°38S 176°49E 277 A14
Arorangi Cook Is. 21°13S 159°49W 289 h
Aroroy Phil. 12°31N 123°24E 232 E4
Aros → Mexico 29°9N 107°57W 318 B3
Arouca Trin. & Tob. 10°38N 61°20W 323 t
Arousa, Ría de → Spain 42°28N 8°57W 194 C2
Årøysund Norway 59°10N 10°27E 164 E7
Arpa → Asia 39°28N 44°56E 213 C11
Arpaçay Turkey 40°50N 43°19E 213 B10
Árpádföld Hungary 47°32N 19°8E 117 A3
Arpajon France 48°36N 2°15E 173 D9
Arpajon-sur-Cère France 44°53N 2°28E 174 D6
Arpaşu de Jos Romania 45°47N 24°37E 183 E9
Arqalyk Kazakhstan 50°13N 66°50E 217 B7
Arque Bolivia 17°48S 66°23W 330 D4
Arrah = Ara India 25°35N 84°32E 243 G11
Arrah Côte d'Ivoire 6°40N 3°58W 262 D4
Arraias Brazil 12°56S 46°57W 333 D2
Arraias → Mato Grosso, Brazil 11°10S 53°35W 331 C7
Arraias → Pará, Brazil 7°30S 49°20W 332 C2
Arraijan Panama 8°56N 79°36W 320 c
Arraiolos Portugal 38°44N 7°59W 195 G3
Arran U.K. 55°34N 5°12W 167 F3
Arranmore Ireland 55°0N 8°30W 166 A3
Arras France 50°17N 2°46E 173 B9
Arrasate Spain 43°4N 2°30W 196 B2
Arrats → France 44°6N 0°52E 174 E4
Arreau France 42°54N 0°22E 174 F4
Arrecife Canary Is. 28°57N 13°37W 153 e2
Arrecifes Argentina 34°6S 60°9W 334 C3
Arrée, Mts. d' France 48°26N 3°55W 172 D3
Arrentela Portugal 38°37N 9°6W 126 B2
Arresø Denmark 55°58N 12°6E 163 J6
Arriaga Mexico 16°14N 93°54W 319 D6
Arribes del Duero ⌂ Spain 41°11N 6°39W 194 D4
Arrilalah Australia 23°43S 143°54E 280 C3
Arrino Australia 29°30S 115°40E 279 E2
Arriondas Spain 43°23N 5°11W 194 B5
Arrojado → Brazil 13°24S 44°20W 333 D3
Arromanches-les-Bains France 49°20N 0°38W 172 C6
Arronches Portugal 39°8N 7°16W 195 F3
Arros → France 43°40N 0°2W 174 E3
Arrow, L. Ireland 54°3N 8°19W 166 B3
Arrowsmith, Mt. N.Z. 43°20S 170°55E 285 D5
Arrowtown N.Z. 44°57S 168°50E 285 E3
Arroyo de la Luz Spain 39°30N 6°38W 195 F4
Arroyo del Puerco = Arroyo de la Luz Spain 39°30N 6°38W 195 F4
Arroyo Grande U.S.A. 35°7N 120°35W 307 K6
Arroyo Seco Park U.S.A. 34°6N 118°11W 126 B3
Ars Iran 37°9N 47°46E 246 B5
Ars-sur-Moselle France 49°5N 6°4E 173 C13
Arsenale Venice, Italy 142 b4
Arsenault L. Canada 55°6N 108°32W 297 B7
Arsenev Russia 44°10N 133°15E 220 B6
Arsi Ethiopia 7°45N 39°0E 257 F4
Arsiero Italy 45°48N 11°21E 199 C8
Arsikere India 13°15N 76°15E 245 H3
Arsin Turkey 41°8N 39°55E 213 B8
Arsk Russia 56°10N 49°50E 190 B9
Arslanköy Turkey 37°0N 34°17E 250 B5
Årsta Sweden 59°17N 18°3E 139 B2
Arsunda Sweden 60°31N 16°45E 162 D10
Art, Î. N. Cal. 19°43S 163°38E 288 d
Arta Greece 39°8N 21°2E 204 B3
Artà Spain 39°41N 3°21E 206 B4
Artà, Coves d' Spain 39°40N 3°24E 206 B4
Artas West Bank 31°41N 35°11E 123 B2
Artashat Armenia 40°0N 44°35E 213 B11
Arteaga Mexico 18°28N 102°25W 318 D4
Arteche Phil. 12°17N 125°22E 232 E5
Arteixo = A Baiuca Spain 43°19N 8°29W 194 B2
Artem = Artyom Azerbaijan 40°28N 50°20E 191 K10
Artem Russia 43°22N 132°13E 220 C6
Artemivsk = Bakhmut Ukraine 48°35N 38°0E 189 H9
Artemovsk Russia 54°45N 93°35E 215 D10
Artemovskiy Russia 57°45N 40°16E 191 G5
Artenay France 48°5N 1°50E 173 D8
Artern Germany 51°22N 11°18E 178 D7
Artesa de Segre Spain 41°54N 1°3E 196 D6
Artesia = Mosomane Botswana 24°2S 26°19E 270 B4
Artesia U.S.A. 32°51N 104°24W 305 K11
Arthington Liberia 6°35N 10°45W 262 D2
Arthur Ont., Canada 43°50N 80°32W 312 C4
Arthur Ill., U.S.A. 39°43N 88°28W 311 E8
Arthur → Australia 41°2S 144°40E 281 G3
Arthur Cr. → Australia 22°30S 136°25E 280 C2
Arthur Pt. Australia 22°7S 150°3E 280 C5
Arthur River Australia 33°20S 117°2E 279 F2
Arthur's Pass N.Z. 42°54S 171°35E 285 C6
Arthur's Pass △ N.Z. 42°53S 171°42E 285 C6
Arthur's Seat U.K. 55°56N 3°9W 121 B3
Arthur's Town The Bahamas 24°38N 75°42W 321 B4
Artigas = Rio Branco Uruguay 32°40S 53°40W 335 C5
Artigas Antarctica 62°30S 58°0W 151 C18
Artigas Uruguay 30°20S 56°30W 334 C4
Artik Armenia 40°38N 43°58E 191 K6
Artillery L. Canada 63°9N 107°52W 297 A7
Artois France 50°20N 2°30E 173 B9
Artotina Greece 38°42N 22°2E 204 C4
Artova Turkey 40°5N 36°28E 212 B7
Artrutx, C. de Spain 39°55N 3°49E 206 B4
Arts, Place des Montréal, Canada 130 b2
Arts Bogd Uul Mongolia 44°40N 102°20E 226 B2
Artsvashen Armenia 40°38N 45°30E 213 B11
Artsyz Ukraine 46°4N 29°26E 183 D14
Artux China 39°40N 76°10E 217 E9
Artvin Turkey 41°14N 41°44E 213 B9
Artvin □ Turkey 41°10N 41°50E 213 B9
Aru, Kepulauan Indonesia 6°0S 134°30E 231 F8
Aru Is. = Aru, Kepulauan Indonesia 6°0S 134°30E 231 F8
Arua Uganda 3°1N 30°58E 268 B3
Aruanã Brazil 14°54S 51°10W 333 D1
Aruba ☑ W. Indies 12°30N 70°0W 322 f
Arudy France 43°7N 0°28W 174 E3
Arué Tahiti 17°31S 149°30W 289 e
Arumã Brazil 4°44S 62°8W 329 D5
Arume-wan Japan 26°35N 128°8E 288 a
Arumpo Australia 33°48S 142°55E 282 B5
Arun Bangkok, Thailand 113 b1
Arun → Nepal 26°55N 87°10E 243 F12
Arun → W. Susx., U.K. 50°49N 0°33W 169 G7
Arunachal Pradesh □ India 28°0N 95°0E 241 B5
Aruppukkottai India 9°31N 78°8E 245 K4
Arusha Tanzania 3°20S 36°40E 268 C4
Arusha □ Tanzania 3°20S 36°30E 268 C4
Arusha △ Tanzania 3°16S 36°47E 268 C4
Arusha Chini Tanzania 3°32S 37°20E 268 C4
Arut → Indonesia 2°42S 111°34E 235 C4
Aruvi → Sri Lanka 8°48N 79°53E 245 K4
Aruwimi → Dem. Rep. of the Congo 1°13N 23°36E 264 B4
Arvada Colo., U.S.A. 39°48N 105°5W 304 G11
Arvada Wyo., U.S.A. 44°39N 106°8W 304 D10
Arvakalu Sri Lanka 8°20N 79°58E 245 K4
Arvayheer Mongolia 46°15N 102°48E 218 B9
Arve → France 46°11N 6°8E 173 F13
Arvi Kriti, Greece 34°59N 25°28E 207 F6
Arvi India 20°59N 78°16E 244 D4
Arviat Canada 61°6N 93°59W 297 A10
Arvidsjaur Sweden 65°35N 19°10E 160 D18
Arvika Sweden 59°40N 12°36E 162 E6
Arvin U.S.A. 35°12N 118°50W 307 K8
Arwad Syria 34°51N 35°51E 250 D6
Arwal India 25°15N 84°41E 243 G11
Arxan China 47°11N 119°57E 219 B12
Åryd Sweden 56°49N 14°59E 163 H8
Arys Kazakhstan 42°26N 68°48E 217 D7
Arzachena Italy 41°5N 9°23E 200 A2
Arzamas Russia 55°27N 43°55E 190 C6
Arzanah U.A.E. 24°47N 52°34E 247 E7
Arzew Algeria 35°50N 0°23W 261 A4
Arzgir Russia 45°18N 44°23E 191 H7
Arzignano Italy 45°31N 11°20E 199 C8
Arzúa Spain 42°56N 8°9W 194 C2
Aš Czechia 50°13N 12°12E 180 A5
Ås Akershus, Norway 59°40N 10°48E 164 E7
Ås Sweden 63°15N 14°34E 162 A8
As Pontes de García Rodríguez Spain 43°27N 7°50W 194 B3
As Sa'an Syria 35°16N 37°22E 250 C8
As Safā Syria 33°10N 37°0E 250 E8
As Saffānīyah Si. Arabia 27°55N 48°50E 247 E6
As Safirah Syria 36°5N 37°21E 250 B8
Aş Şahm Oman 24°10N 56°53E 247 E8
Aş Şa'īd Yemen 14°15N 46°50E 248 D4
As Sājir Si. Arabia 25°11N 44°36E 246 E5
As Salamīyah Syria 35°1N 37°2E 250 C8
Aş Şalīf Yemen 15°18N 42°41E 248 D3
As Salmān Iraq 30°30N 44°32E 246 D5
As Salṭ Jordan 32°2N 35°43E 251 F6
As Salwa'a Qatar 24°23N 50°50E 247 E6
As Samāwah Iraq 31°15N 45°15E 246 D5
As Sanamayn Syria 33°3N 36°10E 250 E7
As Sawādah Si. Arabia 22°24N 44°28E 248 B4
Aş Şawma'ah Yemen 14°5N 45°48E 248 D4
As Sayl al Kabīr Si. Arabia 21°38N 40°25E 248 B3
As Shawawra West Bank 31°41N 35°15E 123 B2
As Sīb Oman 23°41N 58°11E 249 B7
As Sila' U.A.E. 24°4N 51°45E 247 E6
As Sukhnah Syria 34°52N 38°52E 213 E8
As Sulaymānīyah Iraq 35°35N 45°29E 213 E11
As Sulaymānīyah Si. Arabia 24°9N 47°18E 248 A4
As Sulaymānīyah □ Iraq 35°50N 45°30E 213 E11
As Sulaymī Si. Arabia 26°17N 41°21E 246 E4
As Sulayyil Si. Arabia 20°27N 45°34E 248 B4
As Sulṭān Libya 31°4N 17°8E 258 B3
As Summān Si. Arabia 25°0N 47°0E 246 E5
Aş Şurrah Yemen 13°57N 46°14E 248 D4
Aş Şuwar Syria 35°30N 40°38E 213 E9
As Suwaydā' Syria 32°40N 36°30E 250 F7
As Suwaydā' □ Syria 32°45N 36°45E 250 F7
As Suwayq Oman 23°51N 57°26E 247 F8
Aş Şuwayrah Iraq 32°55N 45°0E 213 F11
Åsa Sweden 57°21N 12°8E 163 G6
Asa Wright Nature Centre Trin. & Tob. 10°43N 61°17W 323 t
Asab Namibia 25°30S 18°0E 270 C2
Asaba Nigeria 6°12N 6°38E 263 D6
Asad, Buḩayrat al Syria 36°0N 38°15E 213 D8
Asadābād Iran 34°47N 48°7E 213 E13
Asafo Ghana 6°20N 2°40W 262 D4
Asaga Str. Amer. Samoa 14°10S 169°37W 302 g
Asagaya Japan 35°41N 139°38E 140 A2
Asahi Chiba, Japan 35°43N 140°39E 223 B12
Asahi Ōsaka, Japan 34°43N 135°31E 133 A2
Asahi-Gawa → Japan 34°36N 133°58E 222 C5
Asahigawa = Asahikawa Japan 43°46N 142°22E 220 C11
Asahikawa Japan 43°46N 142°22E 220 C11
Asakusa Japan 35°42N 139°47E 140 A3
Asakusabashi Tokyo, Japan 140 a5
Asale, L. Ethiopia 14°0N 40°20E 257 E5
Asaluyeh Iran 27°29N 52°37E 247 E7
Asama-Yama Japan 36°24N 138°31E 223 A10
Asamankese Ghana 5°50N 0°40W 263 D4
Asan S. Korea 36°48N 127°1E 224 D3
Asan → India 26°37N 78°24E 243 F8
Asansol India 23°40N 87°1E 243 H12
Åsarna Sweden 62°39N 14°22E 162 B8
Asati India 22°28N 88°15E 124 C1
Asau Samoa 13°27S 172°33W 287 V19
Asayita Ethiopia 11°35N 41°23E 257 E5
Asba Littoria = Asbe Teferi Ethiopia 9°4N 40°49E 257 F5
Asbe Teferi Ethiopia 9°4N 40°49E 257 F5
Asbesberge S. Africa 29°0S 23°0E 270 C3
Asbestos Canada 45°47N 71°58W 299 C5
Asbury Park U.S.A. 40°13N 74°1W 313 F10
Åsby Sweden 57°14N 12°18E 163 G6
Ásbyrgi Iceland 66°0N 16°30W 155 A10
Ascea Italy 40°8N 15°11E 201 B8
Ascensión Mexico 31°6N 107°59W 318 A3
Ascensión, B. de la Mexico 19°40N 87°30W 319 D7
Ascension I. Atl. Oc. 7°57S 14°23W 153 g
Ascension I. ✕ (ASI) Ascension I. 7°58S 14°23W 153 g
Aschach an der Donau Austria 48°22N 14°2E 180 C7
Aschaffenburg Germany 49°58N 9°6E 179 F5
Aschendorf Germany 53°3N 7°19E 178 B3
Aschersleben Germany 51°45N 11°29E 178 D7
Aschheim Germany 48°10N 11°42E 131 A3
Asciano Italy 43°14N 11°33E 199 E8
Áscoli Piceno Italy 42°51N 13°34E 199 F10
Áscoli Satriano Italy 41°11N 15°32E 201 A8
Ascope Peru 7°46S 79°8W 330 B2
Ascot Vale Australia 37°46S 144°53E 128 A1
Ascotán Chile 21°45S 68°17W 334 A2
Ascuncion Phil. 7°35N 125°45E 233 H5
Aseb Eritrea 13°0N 42°40E 257 E5
Åseda Sweden 57°10N 15°20E 163 G9
Asedjrad Algeria 24°51N 1°29E 261 D5
Aseki Papua N. G. 7°21S 146°12E 286 D4
Asela Ethiopia 8°0N 39°0E 257 F4
Åsen Sweden 61°17N 13°50E 162 C7
Asenovgrad Bulgaria 42°1N 24°51E 203 D8
Asfeld France 49°27N 4°5E 173 C11
Asfûn el Matâ'na Egypt 25°26N 32°30E 256 B3
Aşgabat = Ashgabat Turkmenistan 37°58N 58°24E 247 B8
Åsgårdstrand Norway 59°22N 10°27E 164 E7
Asgata Cyprus 34°46N 33°15E 207 F9
Ash Fork U.S.A. 35°13N 112°29W 305 J7
Ash Grove U.S.A. 37°19N 93°35W 308 G7
Ash Shabakah Iraq 30°49N 43°39E 246 D4
Ash Shafa Si. Arabia 21°27N 39°49E 248 B2
Ash Shamāl □ Lebanon 34°25N 36°0E 250 D7
Ash Shāmīyah Iraq 31°55N 44°35E 213 G11
Ash Sha'rā' Si. Arabia 24°16N 44°11E 248 A4
Ash Shāriqah U.A.E. 25°23N 55°26E 247 E7
Ash Sharmah Si. Arabia 28°1N 35°16E 251 K6
Ash Sharqāt Iraq 35°27N 43°16E 213 E10
Ash Sharqīyah □ Si. Arabia 23°0N 50°0E 249 B6
Ash Shaṭrah Iraq 31°30N 46°10E 246 D5
Ash Shawbak Jordan 30°32N 35°34E 246 D2
Ash Shaykh Ḩumayd Si. Arabia 28°6N 34°33E 251 K5
Ash Shifā' Si. Arabia 28°30N 35°30E 251 K6
Ash Shiḩr Yemen 14°45N 49°36E 249 D5
Ash Shināfīyah Iraq 31°35N 44°39E 246 D5
Ash Shu'bah Si. Arabia 28°54N 44°44E 246 D5
Ash Shumlūl Si. Arabia 26°31N 47°20E 246 E5
Ash Shuqayq Si. Arabia 17°44N 42°1E 248 C3
Ash Shūr'a Iraq 35°58N 43°13E 246 C4
Ash Shurayf Si. Arabia 25°43N 39°14E 246 E3
Ash Shuwayfāt Lebanon 33°45N 35°30E 250 E6
Ash Shuwayrif Libya 29°59N 14°16E 258 C2
Asha Russia 55°0N 57°16E 186 D10
Ashanti □ Ghana 7°30N 1°30W 263 D4
Ashbourne U.K. 53°2N 1°43W 168 D6
Ashbridge's Bay Park Canada 43°40N 79°18W 141 B3
Ashburn Ga., U.S.A. 31°43N 83°39W 316 D6
Ashburn Ill., U.S.A. 41°45N 87°43W 119 C2
Ashburton N.Z. 43°53S 171°48E 285 D6
Ashburton Vic., Australia 37°51S 145°4E 128 B2
Ashburton → Australia 21°40S 114°56E 278 D1
Ashburton, North Branch → N.Z. 43°54S 171°44E 285 D6
Ashburton, South Branch → N.Z. 43°54S 171°44E 285 D6
Ashcroft Canada 50°40N 121°20W 296 C4
Ashdod Israel 31°49N 34°35E 251 G5
Ashdown U.S.A. 33°40N 94°8W 314 E7
Asheboro U.S.A. 35°43N 79°49W 315 D15
Åsheim Norway 61°42N 11°11E 164 C8
Ashern Canada 51°11N 98°21W 297 C9
Asherton U.S.A. 28°27N 99°46W 314 G5
Asheville U.S.A. 35°36N 82°33W 315 D13
Ashewat Pakistan 31°22N 68°32E 242 D3
Asheweig → Canada 54°17N 87°12W 298 B2
Ashfield Australia 33°53S 151°7E 139 B1
Ashford N.S.W., Australia 29°15S 151°3E 281 D5
Ashford Kent, U.K. 51°8N 0°53E 169 F8
Ashford Surrey, U.K. 51°25N 0°26W 125 B1
Ashford Ala., U.S.A. 31°11N 85°14W 316 D4
Ashgabat Turkmenistan 37°58N 58°24E 247 B8
Ashhurst N.Z. 40°16S 175°45E 284 G4
Ashibetsu Japan 43°31N 142°11E 220 C11
Ashikaga Japan 36°28N 139°29E 223 A11
Ashington U.K. 55°11N 1°33W 168 B6
Ashio Japan 36°38N 139°27E 223 A11
Ashizuri-Uwakai △ Japan 32°56N 132°32E 222 E4
Ashizuri-Zaki Japan 32°44N 133°0E 222 E5
Ashkarkot Afghan. 33°3N 67°58E 242 C2
Ashkhabad = Ashgabat Turkmenistan 37°58N 58°24E 247 B8
Āshkhāneh Iran 37°26N 56°55E 247 B8
Ashland Ala., U.S.A. 33°16N 85°50W 316 B4
Ashland Ill., U.S.A. 39°53N 90°1W 310 E7
Ashland Kans., U.S.A. 37°11N 99°46W 308 G4
Ashland Ky., U.S.A. 38°28N 82°38W 309 F12
Ashland Maine, U.S.A. 46°38N 68°24W 309 B19
Ashland Mont., U.S.A. 45°36N 106°16W 304 D10
Ashland Ohio, U.S.A. 40°52N 82°19W 312 F2
Ashland Oreg., U.S.A. 42°12N 122°43W 304 E2
Ashland Pa., U.S.A. 40°45N 76°22W 313 F8
Ashland Va., U.S.A. 37°46N 77°29W 309 G15
Ashland Wis., U.S.A. 46°35N 90°53W 308 B8
Ashley Ill., U.S.A. 38°20N 89°11W 310 F7
Ashley Ind., U.S.A. 41°32N 85°4W 311 C11
Ashley N. Dak., U.S.A. 46°2N 99°22W 308 B4
Ashley Pa., U.S.A. 41°12N 75°55W 313 E9
Ashley → N.Z. 43°17S 172°44E 285 D7
Ashmore and Cartier Is. Ind. Oc. 12°15S 123°0E 278 B3
Ashmore Reef Australia 12°14S 123°5E 278 B3
Ashmûn Egypt 30°18N 30°58E 255 H1
Ashmyany Belarus 54°26N 25°52E 177 A13
Ashokan Res. U.S.A. 41°56N 74°13W 313 E10
Ashoknagar India 24°34N 77°43E 244 B3
Ashqelon Israel 31°42N 34°35E 251 G5
Ashraf = Behshahr Iran 36°45N 53°35E 247 B7
Ashta India 23°1N 76°43E 242 H7
Ashtabula U.S.A. 41°52N 80°47W 312 E4
Ashti Maharashtra, India 21°12N 78°11E 244 D4
Ashti Maharashtra, India 18°50N 75°15E 244 E2
Āshtiyān Iran 34°31N 50°0E 247 C6
Ashton Western Cape, S. Africa 33°50S 20°5E 270 D3
Ashton Idaho, U.S.A. 44°4N 111°27W 304 D8
Ashuanipi, L. Canada 52°45N 66°15W 299 B6
Ashuapmushuan → Canada 48°37N 72°20W 299 C5
Ashur = Assur Iraq 35°27N 43°15E 213 E10
Ashville Ala., U.S.A. 33°50N 86°15W 316 B3
Ashville Fla., U.S.A. 30°37N 83°39W 316 E6
Ashville Pa., U.S.A. 40°34N 78°33W 312 F6
'Āṣī → Asia 36°1N 35°59E 250 B6
Asia 45°0N 75°0E 210 E9
Asia, Kepulauan Indonesia 1°0N 131°13E 231 D8
Asiago Italy 45°52N 11°30E 199 C8
AsiaWorld-Expo Hong Kong, China 22°19N 113°57E 122 B1
Asid G. Phil. 12°10N 123°29E 232 E4
Asidonhoppo Suriname 3°50N 55°30W 329 C6
Asifabad India 19°20N 79°24E 244 E4
Asilah Morocco 35°29N 6°0W 260 A3
Asinara Italy 41°4N 8°16E 200 A1
Asinara, G. dell' Italy 41°0N 8°30E 200 A1
Asino Russia 57°0N 86°0E 214 D9
Asipovichy Belarus 53°19N 28°33E 177 B15
'Asīr Si. Arabia 18°40N 42°30E 248 C3
Asir, Ras Somalia 11°55N 51°10E 267 B7
Aska India 19°2N 84°42E 244 E7
Aşkale Turkey 39°55N 40°41E 213 C9
Asker Norway 59°50N 10°29E 164 E7
Askersund Sweden 58°53N 14°55E 163 F8
Askham S. Africa 26°59S 20°47E 270 C3
Askī Mawşil Iraq 36°30N 42°45E 213 D10
Askim Norway 59°35N 11°10E 164 E8
Askio, Oros Greece 40°25N 21°35E 202 F5
Askisto Finland 60°16N 24°47E 121 B1
Askja Iceland 65°3N 16°48W 155 B10
Asklipio Greece 36°4N 27°56E 206 E11
Askøyna Norway 60°29N 5°10E 164 D2
Askrikefjärden Sweden 59°22N 18°13E 139 A3
Askvoll Norway 61°21N 5°4E 164 C2
Asl Egypt 29°33N 32°44E 256 B3
Aslan Burnu Turkey 38°44N 26°45E 205 C8
Aslanapa Turkey 39°13N 29°52E 205 B11
Asländuz Iran 39°26N 47°24E 213 C12
Asmār Afghan. 35°10N 71°27E 242 B4
Asmara = Asmera Eritrea 15°19N 38°55E 257 D4
Asmera Eritrea 15°19N 38°55E 257 D4
Asnæs Denmark 55°40N 11°0E 163 J4
Åsnen Sweden 56°37N 14°45E 163 H8
Asni Morocco 31°17N 7°58W 260 B3
Asnières France 48°54N 2°16E 134 A2
Aso Japan 32°55N 131°5E 222 E3
Aso Kujū △ Japan 32°53N 131°6E 222 E3
Aso-Zan Japan 32°53N 131°6E 222 E3
Asola Italy 45°13N 10°24E 198 C7
Asos Greece 38°22N 20°33E 207 C2
Asosa Ethiopia 10°3N 34°32E 257 E3
Asoteriba, Jebel Sudan 21°51N 36°30E 256 C4
Asouf, O. → Algeria 25°40N 2°8E 261 C5
Aspatria U.K. 54°47N 3°19W 168 C4
Aspe Spain 38°20N 0°40W 197 G4
Aspen U.S.A. 39°11N 106°49W 304 G10
Aspendos Turkey 36°54N 31°7E 250 B2
Aspermont U.S.A. 33°8N 100°14W 314 E4
Aspet France 43°1N 0°48E 174 E4
Aspiring, Mt. N.Z. 44°23S 168°46E 285 E3
Aspres-sur-Buëch France 44°32N 5°44E 175 D9
Asprokavos, Akra Greece 39°21N 20°6E 206 C10
Aspromonte △ Italy 38°9N 15°58E 201 D8
Aspur India 23°58N 74°7E 242 H6
Asquith Canada 52°8N 107°13W 297 C7
Assa Morocco 28°35N 9°6W 260 C3
Assab = Aseb Eritrea 13°0N 42°40E 257 E5
Assâba □ Mauritania 16°40N 11°40W 262 B2
Assâba, Massif de l' Mauritania 16°10N 11°45W 262 B2
Assagny △ Côte d'Ivoire 5°10N 4°48W 262 D4
Assago Italy 45°24N 9°7E 128 B1
Assaikio Nigeria 8°34N 8°55E 263 D6
Assal, L. Djibouti 11°40N 42°26E 257 E5
Assam □ India 26°0N 93°0E 241 C4
Assamakka Niger 19°21N 5°38E 263 B6
Assateague Island ⌂ U.S.A. 38°15N 75°10W 309 F16
Assaye India 20°15N 75°53E 244 D2
Asse Belgium 50°24N 4°10E 170 D4
Assekrem Algeria 23°16N 5°49E 261 D6
Asséminі Italy 39°17N 9°0E 200 C1
Assen Neths. 53°0N 6°35E 170 A6
Assendelft Neths. 52°28N 4°45E 112 A1
Assens Denmark 55°16N 9°55E 163 J3
Assiano Italy 45°27N 9°3E 128 B1
Assini Côte d'Ivoire 5°9N 3°17W 262 D4
Assiniboia Canada 49°40N 105°59W 297 D7
Assiniboine → Canada 49°53N 97°8W 297 D9
Assiniboine, Mt. Canada 50°52N 115°39W 296 C5
Assiou Algeria 21°7N 7°36E 261 D6
Assis Brazil 22°40S 50°20W 335 A5
Assis Brasil Brazil 10°55S 69°32W 330 C4
Assisi Italy 43°4N 12°37E 199 E9
Åsskard Norway 63°1N 8°30E 164 A5
Assok Ngoum Gabon 1°45N 11°39E 264 B2
Assumption U.S.A. 39°31N 89°3W 310 E7
Assur Iraq 35°27N 43°15E 213 E10
Assynt, L. U.K. 58°10N 5°3W 167 C3
Astaffort France 44°4N 0°40E 174 D4
Astakida Greece 35°53N 26°50E 205 F8
Astakos Greece 38°32N 21°5E 207 B3
Astana = Nur-Sultan Kazakhstan 51°10N 71°30E 217 B8
Āstāneh Iran 37°17N 49°59E 247 B6
Astapovo = Lev Tolstoy Russia 53°13N 39°29E 188 F10
Astara Azerbaijan 38°30N 48°50E 213 C13
Āstārā Iran 38°20N 48°52E 213 C13
Astarabad = Gorgān Iran 36°55N 54°30E 247 B7
Asterousia Greece 34°59N 25°3E 207 F6
Asti Italy 44°54N 8°12E 198 D5
Astipalea Greece 36°32N 26°22E 205 E8
Astola I. Pakistan 25°7N 63°51E 240 D1
Astorga Davao del S., Phil. 6°54N 125°27E 233 H5
Astorga Spain 42°29N 6°8W 194 C4
Astoria Ill., U.S.A. 40°14N 90°21W 310 D6
Astoria N.Y., U.S.A. 40°46N 73°55W 132 B2
Astoria Oreg., U.S.A. 46°11N 123°50W 306 D3
Åstorp Sweden 56°6N 12°55E 163 H6
Astrakhan Russia 46°25N 48°5E 191 G9
Astrakhan □ Russia 47°45N 46°20E 191 G8
Astrebla Downs Australia 24°12S 140°34E 280 C3
Astrolabe, Récifs de l' N. Cal. 19°48S 165°37E 288 d
Astrolabe Park Australia 33°57S 151°12E 139 B2
Astudillo Spain 42°12N 4°22W 194 C6
Asturias □ Spain 43°15N 6°0W 194 B5
Asturias ✕ (OVD) Spain 43°33N 6°3W 194 B4
Asumman S. Korea 37°4N 126°40E 224 D3
Asunción Bolivia 11°46S 67°50W 330 C4
Asunción N. Marianas 19°40N 145°24E 302 a
Asunción Paraguay 25°10S 57°30W 334 B4
Asunción Nochixtlán Mexico 17°28N 97°14W 319 D5
Åsunden Sweden 58°0N 15°51E 163 F9
Asutri Sudan 15°25N 35°45E 257 D4
Aswa → Uganda 3°43N 31°55E 268 B3
Aswa-Lolim ⌂ Uganda 2°43N 31°35E 268 B3
Aswad, Ra's al Si. Arabia 21°20N 39°0E 248 B2
Aswân Egypt 24°4N 32°57E 256 C3
Aswan High Dam = Sadd el Aali Egypt 23°54N 32°54E 256 C3
Asyût Egypt 27°11N 31°4E 256 B3
Asyûti, Wadi → Egypt 27°11N 31°16E 256 B3
Aszód Hungary 47°39N 19°28E 182 C4
At-Bashy Kyrgyzstan 41°10N 75°48E 217 D9
At Ṭafīlah Jordan 30°45N 35°30E 251 H6
At Ṭafīlah □ Jordan 30°45N 35°30E 251 H6
Aṭ Ṭā'if Si. Arabia 21°5N 40°27E 248 B3
At Tāj Libya 24°13N 23°18E 258 D4
At Ta'mīm □ Iraq 35°30N 44°20E 246 C5
At Tamīmī Libya 32°20N 23°4E 258 B4
Aṭ Ṭirāq Si. Arabia 27°19N 44°33E 246 E5
Aṭ Ṭubayq Si. Arabia 29°30N 37°0E 251 J8
At Tuhaytah Yemen 14°18N 43°15E 248 D3
Aṭ Ṭunayb Jordan 31°48N 35°57E 251 G6
At Turbah Lahij, Yemen 12°40N 43°30E 248 D3
At Turbah Ta'izz, Yemen 13°13N 44°7E 248 D4
Atabey Turkey 37°57N 30°39E 205 D12
Atacama □ Chile 27°30S 70°0W 334 B2
Atacama, Desierto de Chile 24°0S 69°20W 334 A2
Atacama, Salar de Chile 23°30S 68°20W 334 A2
Ataco Colombia 3°35N 75°23W 328 C2
Atafu Pac. Oc. 8°32S 172°31W 277 B16
Atakeye ⊙ Australia 22°30S 133°45E 278 D5
Atakor Algeria 23°27N 5°31E 261 D6
Atakpamé Togo 7°31N 1°13E 263 D5
Atalaia do Norte Brazil 4°20S 70°12W 328 D3
Atalandi Greece 38°39N 22°58E 204 C4
Atalaya Peru 10°45S 73°50W 330 C3
Atalaya de Femes Canary Is. 28°56N 13°47W 153 e2
Ataléia Brazil 18°3S 41°6W 333 E3
Atami Japan 35°5N 139°4E 223 B11
Atamyrat Turkmenistan 37°50N 65°12E 217 E7
Atankawng Myanmar 25°50N 97°47E 241 C6
Atap Indonesia 3°51N 117°1E 235 B5
Atapupu, Cueva de Spain 42°22N 3°32W 194 C7
Atapupu Indonesia 9°0S 124°51E 231 F6
'Ataq Yemen 14°33N 46°47E 248 D4
Atâr Mauritania 20°30N 13°5W 260 D2
Atarum, Erg n- Algeria 23°57N 2°0E 261 D5
Atarfe Spain 37°13N 3°40W 195 H7
Atari Pakistan 30°56N 74°2E 242 D6
Atarot West Bank 31°52N 35°13E 123 A2
Atarot ✕ (JRS) West Bank 31°52N 35°14E 123 A2
Atascadero U.S.A. 35°29N 120°40W 306 K6
Atasū Kazakhstan 48°30N 71°0E 217 C8
Atatürk, İstanbul ✕ (IST) Turkey 40°59N 28°49E 203 F12
Atatürk Barajı Turkey 37°28N 38°30E 213 D8
Atauro Timor-Leste 8°10S 125°30E 231 F7
Ataviros Greece 36°12N 27°50E 206 E11
Atbara Sudan 17°42N 33°59E 256 D3
'Atbara, Nahr → Sudan 17°40N 33°56E 256 D3
Atbasar Kazakhstan 51°48N 68°20E 217 B7
Atbashi = At-Bashy Kyrgyzstan 41°10N 75°48E 217 D9
Atça Turkey 37°53N 28°13E 205 D10
Atchafalaya B. U.S.A. 29°25N 91°25W 314 G9
Atchison U.S.A. 39°34N 95°7W 308 F6
Atebubu Ghana 7°47N 1°0W 263 D4
Ateca Spain 41°20N 1°49W 196 D3
Aterno → Italy 42°11N 13°51E 199 F10
Āteshān Iran 35°35N 52°37E 247 C7
Atesine, Alpi Italy 46°55N 11°30E 199 B8
Atessa Italy 42°4N 14°27E 199 F11
Atfîh Egypt 29°25N 31°15E 256 J7
Atghara India 22°37N 88°26E 124 B2
Ath Belgium 50°38N 3°47E 170 D3
Athabasca Canada 54°45N 113°20W 296 C6
Athabasca → Canada 58°40N 110°50W 297 B6
Athabasca, L. Canada 59°15N 109°15W 297 B7
Athabasca Sand Dunes ⌂ Canada 59°4N 108°43W 297 B7
Athagarh India 20°32N 85°37E 244 D7
Athamanon Oros Greece 39°30N 21°26E 204 B3
Athboy Ireland 53°36N 6°56W 166 C5
Athena U.S.A. 29°59N 83°30W 316 F6
Athenry Ireland 53°18N 8°44W 166 C3
Athens = Athina Greece 37°58N 23°43E 112 B2
Athens Ala., U.S.A. 34°48N 86°58W 315 D11
Athens Ga., U.S.A. 33°57N 83°23W 316 B6
Athens N.Y., U.S.A. 42°16N 73°49W 313 D11
Athens Ohio, U.S.A. 39°20N 82°6W 309 F12
Athens Pa., U.S.A. 41°57N 76°31W 313 E8
Athens Tenn., U.S.A. 35°27N 84°36W 315 D12
Athens Tex., U.S.A. 32°12N 95°51W 314 E7
Atheras Greece 38°19N 20°25E 207 C1
Atherley Canada 44°37N 79°20W 312 B5
Atherton Australia 17°17S 145°30E 280 B4
Athi River Kenya 1°28S 36°58E 268 C4
Athiéme Benin 6°37N 1°40E 263 D5
Athienou Cyprus 35°3N 33°32E 207 D12
Athina Greece 37°58N 23°43E 112 B2
Athina ✕ (ATH) Greece 37°56N 23°56E 112 A3
Athínai = Athina Greece 37°58N 23°43E 112 B2
Athis-Mons France 48°42N 2°23E 134 B3
Athlone Westmeath, Ireland 53°25N 7°56W 166 C4
Athlone Western Cape, S. Africa 33°57S 18°30E 118 A2
Athmalik India 20°43N 84°32E 244 D7
Athni India 16°44N 75°6E 244 F2
Athol N.Z. 45°30S 168°35E 285 F3
Athol Mass., U.S.A. 42°36N 72°14W 313 D12
Athol I. The Bahamas 25°5N 77°16W 153 b
Atholl S. Africa 26°7S 28°3E 123 A2
Atholl, Forest of U.K. 56°51N 3°50W 167 E5
Atholl, Kap Greenland 76°25N 69°30W 154 B4
Atholville Canada 47°59N 66°43W 299 C6
Athos Greece 40°9N 24°22E 203 F8
Athy Ireland 53°0N 7°0W 166 C5
Ati Chad 13°13N 18°20E 259 F3
Ati Sudan 13°5N 29°2E 257 E2
Ati, J. Libya 23°24N 14°21E 258 D2
Atiak Uganda 3°12N 32°2E 268 B3
Atiamuri N.Z. 38°24S 176°5E 284 E5
Atico Peru 16°14S 73°40W 330 D3
Atienza Spain 41°12N 2°52W 196 D2
Atiffiya Iraq 33°21N 44°21E 113 A2
Atiit South Sudan 6°10N 30°35E 257 F3
Atik L. Canada 55°15N 96°0W 297 B9
Atikaki ⌂ Canada 51°30N 95°31W 297 C9
Atikameg → Canada 52°30N 82°46W 298 B3
Atikokan Canada 48°45N 91°37W 298 C1
Atikonak L. Canada 52°40N 64°32W 299 B7
Atimaono Tahiti 17°46S 149°28W 289 e
Atimonan Phil. 14°0N 121°55E 232 D3
'Ātinah, W. → Oman 18°23N 53°28E 249 C6
Atirampattinam India 10°28N 79°20E 245 J4
Atişalen Turkey 41°3N 28°52E 122 B1
Atitlán △ Guatemala 14°38N 91°10W 320 D1
Atiu Cook Is. 20°0S 158°10W 289 J12
Atka Russia 60°50N 151°48E 215 C16
Atka Alaska, U.S.A. 52°12N 174°12W 303 K4
Atka I. U.S.A. 52°7N 174°30W 303 K4
Atkarsk Russia 51°55N 45°2E 190 E7
Atkinson Ga., U.S.A. 31°13N 81°47W 316 D8
Atkinson Ill., U.S.A. 41°25N 90°1W 310 C6
Atkinson Nebr., U.S.A. 42°32N 98°59W 308 D4
Atlanta Ga., U.S.A. 33°45N 84°23W 113 B2
Atlanta Ill., U.S.A. 40°16N 89°14W 310 D7
Atlanta Mo., U.S.A. 39°54N 92°29W 310 E4
Atlanta Tex., U.S.A. 33°7N 94°10W 314 E7
Atlanta Hartsfield-Jackson Int. ✕ (ATL) U.S.A. 33°38N 84°26W 113 C2
Atlanta History Center U.S.A. 33°45N 84°22W 113 B2
Atlanta Zoo U.S.A. 33°44N 84°22W 113 B2
Atlantic U.S.A. 41°24N 95°1W 310 C2
Atlantic Beach U.S.A. 30°20N 81°24W 316 E8
Atlantic City U.S.A. 39°21N 74°27W 309 F16
Atlantic-Indian Basin Antarctica 60°0S 30°0E 151 B4
Atlantic Ocean 0°0 20°0W 152 F8
Atlántico □ Colombia 10°45N 75°0W 328 A3
Atlantis S. Africa 33°34S 18°29E 270 D2
Atlas Mts. = Haut Atlas Morocco 32°30N 5°0W 260 B4
Atlin Canada 59°31N 133°41W 296 B2
Atlin, L. Canada 59°26N 133°45W 296 B2
Atlin ⌂ Canada 59°10N 134°30W 296 B2
Atløyna Norway 61°21N 4°58E 164 C1
Atmakur Andhra Pradesh, India 14°37N 79°40E 245 G4
Atmakur Andhra Pradesh, India 15°53N 78°35E 245 G4
Atmakur Telangana, India 18°45N 78°39E 244 E4
Atmore U.S.A. 31°2N 87°29W 317 D2
Atna Norway 61°44N 10°49E 164 C7
Atna → Norway 61°44N 10°49E 164 C7
Atō Japan 34°25N 131°40E 222 C3
Atocha Bolivia 20°56S 66°14W 330 E4
Atok Phil. 16°35N 120°41E 232 C3
Atoka U.S.A. 34°23N 96°8W 314 D6
Atokos Greece 38°28N 20°49E 207 C2
Atolia U.S.A. 35°19N 117°37W 307 K9
Atomium Belgium 50°54N 4°20E 116 A2
Atongo-Bakari C.A.R. 5°49N 21°35E 264 A4
Atori Solomon Is. 8°42S 160°59E 287 M11
Atqasuk U.S.A. 70°28N 157°24W 303 A8
Atqasuk → U.S.A. 70°52N 155°55W 303 A9
Atrå Norway 59°59N 8°45E 164 E5
Atrai → Bangla. 24°7N 89°22E 241 C2
Atrak = Atrek → Turkmenistan 37°35N 53°58E 247 B8
Åtran Sweden 57°7N 12°57E 163 G6
Åtran → Sweden 56°53N 12°30E 163 H6
Atrato → Colombia 8°17N 76°58W 328 B2
Atrauli India 28°2N 78°20E 242 E8
Atrek → Turkmenistan 37°35N 53°58E 247 B8
Atri Italy 42°35N 13°58E 199 F10
Atsiki Greece 39°56N 25°13E 205 B7
Atsimo-Andrefana □ Madag. 23°25S 43°50E 272 C1
Atsimo-Atsinanana □ Madag. 22°50S 47°50E 272 C2
Atsinanana □ Madag. 18°40S 49°0E 272 B2
Atsoum, Mts. Cameroon 6°41N 12°57E 263 D7
Atsugi Japan 35°25N 139°21E 223 B11
Atsumi Japan 34°35N 137°4E 223 C9
Atsuta Japan 43°24N 141°26E 220 C10
Attalla U.S.A. 34°1N 86°6W 316 A3
Attapeu Laos 14°48N 106°50E 236 E6
Attapulgus U.S.A. 30°45N 84°29W 316 E5
Attawapiskat Canada 52°56N 82°24W 298 B3
Attawapiskat → Canada 52°57N 82°18W 298 B3
Attawapiskat L. Canada 52°18N 87°54W 298 B2
Attersee Austria 47°55N 13°32E 180 D6
Attica = Attiki □ Greece 37°10N 23°40E 204 D5
Attica Ind., U.S.A. 40°18N 87°15W 311 D9
Attica Ohio, U.S.A. 41°4N 82°53W 312 E2
Attichy France 49°25N 3°3E 173 C10
Attigny France 49°28N 4°35E 173 C11
Attikamagen L. Canada 55°0N 66°30W 299 B6
Attiki Greece 38°0N 23°43E 112 A2
Attiki □ Greece 37°10N 23°40E 204 D5
Attleboro U.S.A. 41°57N 71°17W 313 E13
Attock Pakistan 33°52N 72°20E 242 C5
Attopu = Attapeu Laos 14°48N 106°50E 236 E6
Attu U.S.A. 52°56N 173°15E 303 K1
Attu I. U.S.A. 52°55N 172°55E 303 K1
Attunga Australia 30°55S 150°50E 283 A9
Attur India 11°35N 78°30E 245 J4
'Atūd Yemen 13°54N 46°2E 248 D4
Atuel → Argentina 36°17S 66°50W 334 D2
Atura Uganda 2°7N 32°20E 268 B3
Åtvidaberg Sweden 58°12N 16°0E 163 F10
Atwater U.S.A. 37°21N 120°37W 306 H6
Atwood Ont., Canada 43°40N 81°1W 312 C3
Atwood Ill., U.S.A. 39°48N 88°28W 311 E8
Atwood Kans., U.S.A. 39°48N 101°3W 308 F3
Atyraū Kazakhstan 47°5N 52°0E 187 E9
Atzgersdorf Austria 48°8N 16°18E 142 B1
Au Sable U.S.A. 44°25N 83°20W 312 B1
Au Sable → U.S.A. 44°25N 83°20W 309 C12
Au Sable Forks U.S.A. 44°27N 73°41W 313 B11
Au Sable Pt. U.S.A. 44°20N 83°20W 312 B1
Au Vent, Région Réunion 21°0S 55°35E 272 f
Aua Amer. Samoa 14°17S 170°40W 302 f
Auas Honduras 15°29N 84°20W 320 C3
Auasberg Namibia 22°37S 17°13E 270 B2
Aubagne France 43°17N 5°37E 175 E9
Aube □ France 48°15N 4°10E 173 D11

Aube → France 48°34N 3°43E 173 D10
Aubenas France 44°37N 4°24E 175 D8
Aubenton France 49°50N 4°12E 173 C11
Auberry U.S.A. 37°7N 119°29W 306 H7
Aubervilliers France 48°54N 2°22E 134 A3
Aubigny-sur-Nère France 47°30N 2°24E 173 E9
Aubin France 44°33N 2°15E 174 D6
Aubing Germany 48°9N 11°25E 131 B1
Aubrac, Mts. d' France 44°40N 3°2E 174 D7
Auburn S. Austral., Australia 34°1S 138°42E 282 C3
Auburn Ala., U.S.A. 32°36N 85°29W 316 C4
Auburn Calif., U.S.A. 38°54N 121°4W 306 G5
Auburn Ill., U.S.A. 39°36N 89°45W 310 E7
Auburn Ind., U.S.A. 41°22N 85°4W 311 C11
Auburn Maine, U.S.A. 44°6N 70°14W 309 C18
Auburn N.Y., U.S.A. 42°56N 76°34W 313 D8
Auburn Nebr., U.S.A. 40°23N 95°51W 308 E6
Auburn Pa., U.S.A. 40°36N 76°6W 313 F8
Auburn Wash., U.S.A. 47°18N 122°14W 306 C4
Auburn Ra. Australia 25°15S 150°30E 281 D5
Auburndale Fla., U.S.A. 28°4N 81°48W 317 G8
Auburndale Mass., U.S.A. 42°20N 71°14W 116 A1
Aubusson France 45°57N 2°11E 174 C6
Auce Latvia 56°28N 22°53E 184 B9
Auch France 43°39N 0°36E 174 E4
Auchendinny U.K. 55°51N 3°11W 121 B2
Auchi Nigeria 7°6N 6°13E 263 D6
Auchterarder U.K. 56°18N 3°41W 167 E5
Auchtermuchty U.K. 56°18N 3°13W 167 E5
Auckland N.Z. 36°52S 174°46E 284 C3
Auckland □ N.Z. 36°50S 175°0E 284 C3
Auckland Int. ✕ (AKL) N.Z. 37°0S 174°50E 284 C3
Auckland Is. Pac. Oc. 50°40S 166°5E 288 N8
Auckland Park S. Africa 26°11S 28°0E 123 B2
Aude □ France 43°8N 2°28E 174 E6
Aude → France 43°13N 3°14E 174 E7
Auden Canada 50°14N 87°53W 298 B2
Auderghem Belgium 50°49N 4°26E 116 B2
Auderville France 49°43N 1°57W 172 C5
Audierne France 48°1N 4°34W 172 D2
Audincourt France 47°30N 6°50E 173 E13
Audo Ra. Ethiopia 6°20N 41°50E 257 F5
Audomarois ⌓ France 50°50N 2°30E 173 B9
Audubon U.S.A. 41°43N 94°56W 310 C2
Audubon Park U.S.A. 29°55N 90°8W 131 B2
Aue Germany 50°35N 12°41E 178 E8
Auerbach Germany 50°30N 12°24E 178 E8
Aufist W. Sahara 25°44N 14°39W 260 C2
Augathella Australia 25°48S 146°35E 281 D4
Aughnacloy U.K. 54°25N 6°59W 166 B5
Aughrim Ireland 53°18N 8°19W 166 C3
Augrabies Falls S. Africa 28°35S 20°20E 270 C3
Augrabies Falls △ S. Africa 28°40S 20°22E 270 C3
Augsburg Germany 48°25N 10°52E 179 G6
Augsburg-Westliche Wälder ⌓ Germany 48°22N 10°40E 179 G6
August Town Jamaica 17°59N 76°44W 320 a
Augusta W. Austral., Australia 34°19S 115°9E 279 F2
Augusta Italy 37°13N 15°13E 201 E8
Augusta Ark., U.S.A. 35°17N 91°22W 314 D9
Augusta Ga., U.S.A. 33°28N 81°58W 316 B8
Augusta Ill., U.S.A. 40°14N 90°57W 310 D6
Augusta Kans., U.S.A. 37°41N 96°59W 308 G5
Augusta Ky., U.S.A. 38°47N 84°0W 311 F12
Augusta Maine, U.S.A. 44°19N 69°47W 309 C19
Augusta Mont., U.S.A. 47°30N 112°24W 304 C7
Augusta, Mausoleo di Rome, Italy 136 b2
Augustenborg Denmark 54°57N 9°53E 163 K3
Augustine I. U.S.A. 59°22N 153°26W 303 G9
Augusto Cardosa = Metangula Mozam. 12°40S 34°50E 269 E3
Augustów Poland 53°51N 23°0E 184 E9
Augustówka Poland 52°11N 21°5E 143 B2
Augustus, Mt. Australia 24°20S 116°50E 279 D2
Augustus I. Australia 15°20S 124°30E 278 C3
Aujuittuq = Grise Fiord Canada 76°25N 82°57W 295 B15
Aukan Eritrea 15°29N 40°50E 257 D5
Auki Solomon Is. 8°45S 160°42E 287 M11
Aukra Norway 62°47N 6°55E 164 B3
Aukrug ⌓ Germany 54°5N 9°45E 178 A5
Aukštaitija △ Lithuania 55°15N 26°0E 161 J22
Aukum U.S.A. 38°34N 120°43W 306 G6
Aul India 20°41N 86°39E 244 D8
Aulavik △ Canada 73°42N 119°55W 294 C8
Auld, L. Australia 22°25S 123°50E 278 D3
Äūlīeköl Kazakhstan 52°32N 62°45E 216 B6
Aulifeltet Norway 60°30N 11°21E 162 D5
Auliye-Ata = Taraz Kazakhstan 42°54N 71°22E 217 D8
Aulla Italy 44°12N 9°58E 198 D6
Aulnay France 46°2N 0°22W 174 B3
Aulnay-sous-Bois France 48°56N 2°29E 134 A3
Aulne → France 48°17N 4°16W 172 D2
Aulnoye-Aymeries France 50°12N 3°50E 173 B10
Aulong Palau 7°16N 134°17E 288 c
Ault Somme, France 50°8N 1°26E 172 B8
Ault Colo., U.S.A. 40°35N 104°44W 304 F11
Aulus-les-Bains France 42°49N 1°19E 174 F5
Aumale = Sour el Ghozlane Algeria 36°10N 3°45E 261 A5
Aumale France 49°46N 1°46E 173 C8
Aumo Papua N. G. 5°44S 148°30E 286 C5
Aumont-Aubrac France 44°43N 3°17E 174 D7
Auna Nigeria 10°9N 4°42E 263 C5
Aundah India 19°32N 77°3E 244 E3
Aundh India 17°33N 74°23E 244 F2
Auning Denmark 56°26N 10°22E 163 H4
Aunis France 46°5N 0°50W 174 B3
Aunu'u Amer. Samoa 14°20S 170°31W 302 f
Auponhia Indonesia 1°58S 125°27E 231 E7
Aups France 43°37N 6°15E 175 E10
Aur, Pulau Malaysia 2°35N 104°10E 237 L5
Aura Myanmar 26°59N 97°57E 241 B6
Auraiya India 26°28N 79°33E 243 F8
Aurangabad Bihar, India 24°45N 84°18E 243 G11
Aurangabad Maharashtra, India 19°50N 75°23E 244 E2
Auray France 47°40N 2°59W 172 E4
Aurdal Norway 60°55N 9°26E 164 D6
Aure Norway 63°16N 8°33E 164 A5
Aurelio Italy 41°54N 12°26E 136 B1
Aurès Algeria 35°8N 6°30E 261 A6
Aurich Germany 53°28N 7°28E 178 B3
Aurilândia Brazil 16°44S 50°28W 333 E1
Aurillac France 44°55N 2°26E 174 D6
Aurlandsfjorden Norway 61°3N 7°1E 164 C4
Aurlandsvangen Norway 60°55N 7°12E 164 D4
Auronzo di Cadore Italy 46°33N 12°26E 199 B9
Aurora = Maéwo Vanuatu 15°10S 168°10E 287 E6
Aurora = San Francisco Phil. 13°21N 122°31E 232 E4
Aurora Ont., Canada 44°0N 79°28W 312 C5
Aurora Isabela, Phil. 16°59N 121°38E 232 C3
Aurora Zamboanga del S., Phil. 7°57N 123°36E 233 H4
Aurora Western Cape, S. Africa 32°40S 18°29E 270 D2
Aurora Colo., U.S.A. 39°43N 104°49W 304 G11
Aurora Ill., U.S.A. 41°45N 88°19W 311 C8
Aurora Mo., U.S.A. 36°58N 93°43W 308 G7
Aurora N.Y., U.S.A. 42°45N 76°42W 313 D8
Aurora Nebr., U.S.A. 40°52N 98°0W 308 E5
Aurora Ohio, U.S.A. 41°21N 81°20W 312 E3
Aurora □ Phil. 15°30N 121°30E 232 D3
Aurora Memorial △ Phil. 15°40N 121°20E 232 D3
Aursmoen Norway 59°55N 11°26E 164 E8
Aursunden Norway 62°40N 11°40E 164 B8
Aurukun Australia 13°20S 141°45E 280 A3
Aurukun ◎ Australia 13°36S 141°48E 280 A3
Aus Namibia 26°35S 16°12E 270 C2
Ausa India 18°15N 76°30E 244 E3
Ausable → Canada 43°19N 81°46W 312 C3
Auschwitz = Oświęcim Poland 50°2N 19°11E 185 H6
Ausîm Egypt 30°7N 31°8E 117 A1
Auski Roadhouse Australia 22°22S 118°41E 278 D2
Auspitz = Hustopeče Czechia 48°57N 16°43E 181 C9
Aussig = Ústí nad Labem Czechia 50°41N 14°3E 180 A7
Aust-Agder □ Norway 58°45N 8°0E 164 F4
Austad Norway 58°58N 7°37E 164 F4
Austen Harbour India 12°55N 92°45E 245 H11
Austerlitz = Slavkov u Brna Czechia 49°10N 16°52E 181 B9
Austerlitz, Gare d' Paris, France 48°50N 2°22E 134 A3
Austevoll Norway 60°5N 5°13E 164 D2
Austin Ill., U.S.A. 41°53N 87°45W 119 B2
Austin Ind., U.S.A. 38°45N 85°49W 311 F11
Austin Minn., U.S.A. 43°40N 92°58W 308 D7
Austin Nev., U.S.A. 39°30N 117°4W 304 G5
Austin Pa., U.S.A. 41°38N 78°6W 312 E6
Austin Tex., U.S.A. 30°17N 97°45W 314 F6
Austin, L. Australia 27°40S 118°0E 279 E2
Austin I. Canada 61°10N 94°0W 297 A10
Austmarka Norway 60°6N 12°21E 164 D9
Austnes Norway 62°38N 6°16E 164 B3
Austra Norway 65°8N 11°55E 160 D14
Austral Is. = Tubuaï, Îs. French Polynesia 25°0S 150°0W 289 f
Austral Seamount Chain Pac. Oc. 24°0S 150°0W 289 K13
Australia ■ Oceania 23°0S 135°0E 276 E3
Australian-Antarctic Basin S. Ocean 60°0S 120°0E 151 C9
Australian Capital Territory □ Australia 35°30S 149°0E 283 C8
Australind Australia 33°17S 115°42E 279 F2
Austria ■ Europe 47°0N 14°0E 180 E7
Austur-skaftafellssýsla Iceland 64°15N 16°0W 155 C10
Austurland □ Iceland 64°55N 15°30W 155 C11
Austvågøya Norway 68°20N 14°40E 160 B16
Autazes Brazil 3°35S 59°8W 329 D6
Auterive France 43°21N 1°29E 174 E5
Authie → France 50°22N 1°38E 173 B8
Authon-du-Perche France 48°12N 0°54E 172 D7
Autlán de Navarro Mexico 19°46N 104°22W 318 D4
Autry Museum of the American West U.S.A. 34°9N 118°17W 126 B3
Autun France 46°58N 4°17E 173 F11
Auvergne France 45°20N 3°15E 171 D5
Auvergne, Mts. d' France 45°20N 2°55E 174 C6
Auvergne -Rhône-Alpes □ France 45°30N 5°0E 175 C8
Auvézère → France 45°12N 0°50E 174 C4
Auxerre France 47°48N 3°32E 173 E10
Auxi-le-Château France 50°15N 2°8E 173 B9
Auxonne France 47°10N 5°20E 173 E12
Auxvasse U.S.A. 39°1N 91°54W 310 E5
Auyuittuq △ Canada 67°30N 66°0W 295 D18
Auzances France 46°2N 2°30E 173 F9
Auzangate, Nevado Peru 13°47S 71°13W 330 C3
Av-Dovurak Russia 51°17N 91°35E 215 D10
Ava Ill., U.S.A. 37°53N 89°30W 310 G7
Ava Mo., U.S.A. 36°57N 92°40W 308 G7
Avachinskaya Sopka Russia 53°15N 158°50E 215 D16
Avaldsnes Norway 59°21N 5°20E 164 E2
Avallon France 47°30N 3°53E 173 E10
Avalon U.S.A. 33°21N 118°20W 307 M8
Avalon Pen. Canada 47°30N 53°20W 299 C9
Avana → Cook Is. 21°14S 159°43W 289 h
Avanavero Suriname 4°51N 57°22W 329 C6
Avanigadda India 16°0N 80°56E 245 G5
Avannaata □ Greenland 74°0N 50°0W 154 C5
Avanos Turkey 38°43N 34°51E 212 C6
Avantas Greece 40°57N 25°56E 203 F9
Avaré Brazil 23°4S 48°58W 335 A6
Avarua Cook Is. 21°12S 159°46W 289 h
Avarua Harb. Cook Is. 21°12S 159°46W 289 h
Avatele Cook Is. 19°6S 169°55W 289 g
Avatiu Cook Is. 21°12S 159°47W 289 h
Avawatz Mts. U.S.A. 35°40N 116°30W 307 K10
Avdan Dağı Turkey 40°23N 29°46E 203 F13
Avedøre Denmark 55°37N 12°27E 118 B2
Aveiro Brazil 3°10S 55°5W 329 D6
Aveiro Portugal 40°37N 8°38W 194 E2
Aveiro □ Portugal 40°40N 8°35W 194 E2
Āvej Iran 35°40N 49°15E 247 C6
Avellaneda Argentina 34°40S 58°22W 117 C2
Avellino Italy 40°54N 14°47E 201 B7
Avenal U.S.A. 36°0N 120°8W 306 K6
Avenel U.S.A. 38°59N 76°59W 143 B3
Aventura U.S.A. 25°57N 80°8W 129 C3
Averøya Norway 63°0N 7°35E 164 A4
Aversa Italy 40°58N 14°12E 201 B7
Avery U.S.A. 47°15N 115°49W 304 C6
Aves, I. de W. Indies 15°45N 63°55W 321 C7
Aves, Is. las Venezuela 12°0N 67°30W 321 D6
Aves Laguna Colorada, Santuario de ⌓ Bolivia 22°30S 67°30W 330 E4
Aves Ridge W. Indies 14°0N 63°30W 321 D7
Avesnes-sur-Helpe France 50°8N 3°55E 173 B10
Avesnois ⌓ France 50°10N 3°45E 173 B10
Avesta Sweden 60°9N 16°10E 162 D10
Aveyron □ France 44°22N 2°45E 174 D6
Aveyron → France 44°5N 1°16E 174 D5
Avezzano Italy 42°2N 13°25E 199 F10
Avgo Greece 35°33N 25°37E 205 F7
Aviá Terai Argentina 26°45S 60°50W 334 B3
Aviano Italy 46°4N 12°36E 199 B9
Aviatu → Cook Is. 21°12S 159°49W 289 h
Aviemore U.K. 57°12N 3°50W 167 D5
Aviemore, L. N.Z. 44°37S 170°18E 285 E5
Avigliana Italy 45°5N 7°23E 198 C4
Avigliano Italy 40°44N 15°43E 201 B8
Avignon France 43°57N 4°50E 175 E8
Ávila Spain 40°39N 4°43W 194 E6
Ávila □ Spain 40°30N 5°0W 194 E6
Ávila, Sierra de Spain 40°40N 5°15W 194 E5
Avila Beach U.S.A. 35°11N 120°44W 307 K6
Avilés Spain 43°35N 5°57W 194 B5
Aviño Spain 43°36N 8°8W 194 B2
Avintes Portugal 41°7N 8°33W 194 D2
Avis Portugal 39°4N 7°53W 195 F3
Avis Pa., U.S.A. 41°11N 77°19W 312 E7
Avísio → Italy 46°7N 11°5E 198 B8
Avissawella Sri Lanka 6°56N 80°11E 245 L5
Aviston U.S.A. 38°36N 89°36W 310 F7
Aviz = Avis Portugal 39°4N 7°53W 195 F3
Avize France 48°59N 4°1E 173 D11
Avlona = Vlorë Albania 40°32N 19°28E 202 F3
Avlonari Greece 38°31N 24°8E 204 C6
Avlum Denmark 56°16N 8°47E 163 H2
Avoca Vic., Australia 37°5S 143°26E 282 D5
Avoca N.Y., U.S.A. 42°25N 77°25W 312 D7
Avoca → Vic., Australia 35°40S 143°43E 282 C5
Avoca → Wicklow, Ireland 52°48N 6°10W 166 D5
Avola B.C., Canada 51°45N 119°19W 296 C5
Avola Italy 36°56N 15°7E 201 F8
Avon Ill., U.S.A. 40°40N 90°26W 310 D6
Avon N.Y., U.S.A. 42°55N 77°45W 312 D7
Avon → W. Austral., Australia 31°40S 116°7E 279 F2
Avon → Bristol, U.K. 51°29N 2°41W 169 F5
Avon → Dorset, U.K. 50°44N 1°46W 169 G6
Avon → Warks., U.K. 52°0N 2°8W 169 E5
Avon Park U.S.A. 27°36N 81°31W 317 H8
Avondale Ill., U.S.A. 41°56N 87°41W 119 B2
Avondale La., U.S.A. 29°54N 90°12W 131 B1
Avondale Zimbabwe 17°43S 30°58E 269 F3
Avondale Heights Australia 37°45S 144°52E 128 A1
Avonlea Canada 50°0N 105°0W 297 D8
Avonmore Canada 45°10N 74°58W 313 A10
Avonmouth U.K. 51°30N 2°42W 169 F5
Avramov Bulgaria 42°45N 26°38E 203 D10
Avranches France 48°40N 1°20W 172 D5
Avre → France 48°47N 1°22E 172 D8
Avrig Romania 45°43N 24°21E 183 E9
Avrillé France 47°30N 0°35W 172 E6
Avtovac Bos.-H. 43°9N 18°35E 202 C2
Avtovo Russia 59°51N 30°16E 137 B1
Avu Avu Solomon Is. 9°50S 160°22E 287 M11
Awa-Shima Japan 38°27N 139°14E 220 E9
Awag el Baqar South Sudan 10°10N 33°10E 257 E3
A'waj → Syria 33°23N 36°20E 250 E7
Awaji Japan 34°28N 134°56E 222 C6
Awaji-Shima Japan 34°30N 134°50E 222 C6
'Awālī Bahrain 26°0N 50°30E 247 E6
Awantipur India 33°55N 75°3E 243 C6
Awanui N.Z. 35°4S 173°17E 284 B2
Aware Ethiopia 8°16N 44°9E 267 C5
Awarja → India 17°5N 76°15E 244 F3
Awarua B. N.Z. 44°28S 168°4E 285 E3
Awarua Pt. N.Z. 44°15S 168°5E 285 E3
Awasa Ethiopia 7°2N 38°28E 257 F4
Awasa, L. Ethiopia 7°0N 38°30E 257 F4
Awash Ethiopia 9°1N 40°10E 257 F5
Awash → Ethiopia 11°45N 41°5E 257 E5
Awash △ Ethiopia 9°8N 40°0E 257 F5
Awaso Ghana 6°15N 2°22W 262 D4
Awat China 40°35N 80°24E 217 D10
Awatere → N.Z. 41°37S 174°10E 285 B9
Awbārī Libya 26°46N 12°57E 258 C2
Awbārī, Idehan Libya 27°10N 11°30E 258 C2
Awdal □ Somalia 10°30N 43°30E 267 B5
Awdheegle Somalia 1°59N 44°50E 267 D5
Awe, L. U.K. 56°17N 5°16W 167 E3
Aweil South Sudan 8°42N 27°20E 257 F2
Awgu Nigeria 6°4N 7°24E 263 D6
Awjilah Libya 29°8N 21°7E 258 C4
Awka Nigeria 6°12N 7°5E 263 D6
Aworro Papua N. G. 7°43S 143°11E 286 D2
Awsard Mauritania 22°37N 14°22W 260 D2
Ax-les-Thermes France 42°44N 1°50E 174 F5
Axat France 42°48N 2°13E 174 F6
Axe → U.K. 50°42N 3°4W 169 F5
Axel Heiberg I. Canada 80°0N 90°0W 295 B14
Axim Ghana 4°51N 2°15W 262 E4
Axinim Brazil 4°2S 59°22W 329 D6
Axintele Romania 44°37N 26°47E 183 F11
Axioma Brazil 6°45S 64°31W 331 B5
Axios → Greece 40°57N 22°35E 202 F6
Axminster U.K. 50°46N 3°0W 169 G4
Axson U.S.A. 31°17N 82°44W 316 D7
Axvall Sweden 58°23N 13°34E 163 F7
Ay France 49°3N 4°1E 173 C11
Ayaantang Eq. Guin. 1°58N 10°24E 264 B2
Ayabaca Peru 4°40S 79°53W 330 A2
Ayabe Japan 35°20N 135°20E 223 B7
Ayacucho Argentina 37°5S 58°20W 334 D4
Ayacucho Peru 13°0S 74°0W 330 C3
Ayacucho □ Peru 14°0S 74°0W 330 C3
Ayaguz = Ayaköz Kazakhstan 48°10N 80°10E 217 C10
Ayakkum Hu China 37°30N 89°20E 217 E11
Ayaköz Kazakhstan 48°10N 80°10E 217 C10
Ayaköz → Kazakhstan 46°40N 79°14E 217 C9
Ayakudi India 10°28N 77°56E 245 J3
Ayala Phil. 6°57N 121°57E 233 H3
Ayamé Côte d'Ivoire 5°35N 3°9W 262 D4
Ayamonte Spain 37°12N 7°24W 195 H3
Ayan Russia 56°30N 138°16E 215 D14
Ayancık Turkey 41°57N 34°35E 212 B6
Ayangba Nigeria 7°31N 7°8E 263 D6
Ayapel Colombia 8°19N 75°9W 328 B2
Ayas Turkey 40°2N 32°21E 212 B5
Ayaviri Peru 14°50S 70°35W 330 C3
Ayazağa Turkey 41°6N 28°59E 122 B1
Āybak Afghan. 36°15N 68°5E 240 A3
Aybastı Turkey 40°41N 37°23E 212 B7
Aydarko'l Ko'li Uzbekistan 40°50N 67°10E 217 D7
Aydın Turkey 37°51N 27°51E 212 D2
Aydin □ Turkey 37°50N 28°0E 205 D9
Aydin Dağları Turkey 38°0N 28°0E 205 D10
Aydıncık Turkey 36°9N 33°21E 250 B4
Aydingkol Hu China 42°40N 89°15E 217 D11
Ayelu Ethiopia 10°5N 40°42E 257 E5
Ayenngré Togo 8°40N 1°1E 263 D5
Ayer U.S.A. 42°34N 71°35W 313 D13
Ayer Chawan, Pulau Singapore 1°16N 103°41E 138 B2
Ayer Hitam Malaysia 5°24N 100°16E 237 c
Ayer Merbau, Pulau Singapore 1°16N 103°42E 138 B2
Ayerbe Spain 42°17N 0°41W 196 C4
Ayer's Cliff Canada 45°10N 72°3W 313 A12
Ayers Rock = Uluru Australia 25°23S 131°5E 279 E5
Ayeyarwady = Ayeyawadi → Myanmar 15°50N 95°6E 241 G5
Ayeyawadi → Myanmar 15°50N 95°6E 241 G5
Áyia Napa Cyprus 34°59N 34°0E 207 F10
Áyia Phyla Cyprus 34°43N 33°1E 207 F9
Áyios Amvrósios Cyprus 35°20N 33°35E 207 E9
Áyios Seryios Cyprus 35°12N 33°53E 207 E9
Áyios Theodhoros Cyprus 35°22N 34°1E 207 E10
Áyios Yeóryios = Aghios Georgios Greece 37°28N 23°57E 204 D5
Aykhal Russia 66°0N 111°30E 215 C12
Aykino Russia 62°15N 49°56E 186 B8
Aykirikçi Turkey 39°8N 30°9E 205 B12
Aylesbury U.K. 51°49N 0°49W 169 F7
Aylmer Canada 42°46N 80°59W 312 D4
Aylmer, L. Canada 64°5N 108°30W 294 E10
'Ayn al Ghazālah Libya 32°10N 23°20E 258 B4
Ayn Dār Si. Arabia 25°55N 49°10E 247 E7
Ayn Sifnī Iraq 36°41N 43°20E 213 D10
Ayn Zālah Iraq 36°45N 42°35E 213 D10
Ayna Spain 38°34N 2°3W 197 G2
Aynāt Yemen 16°4N 49°9E 249 C5
'Aynūnah Si. Arabia 28°5N 35°8E 251 K6
Ayod South Sudan 8°7N 31°26E 257 F3
Ayolas Paraguay 27°10S 56°59W 334 B4
Ayon, Ostrov Russia 69°50N 169°0E 215 C17
Ayora Spain 39°3N 1°3W 197 F3
Ayorou Niger 14°53N 1°0E 263 C5
Ayos Cameroon 3°53N 12°31E 264 B2
'Ayoûn el 'Atroûs Mauritania 16°38N 9°37W 262 B3
Ayr Queens., Australia 19°35S 147°25E 280 B4
Ayr Ont., Canada 43°17N 80°27W 312 C4
Ayr S. Ayrs., U.K. 55°28N 4°38W 167 F4
Ayr → U.K. 55°28N 4°38W 167 F4
Ayrancı Turkey 37°21N 33°41E 212 D5
Ayrancılar Turkey 38°15N 27°18E 205 C9
Ayre, Pt. of I. of Man 54°25N 4°21W 168 C3
Ayribaba Turkmenistan 37°50N 66°34E 217 E7
Aysén □ Chile 46°30S 73°0W 336 C2
Aysha Ethiopia 10°50N 42°23E 257 E5
Ayteke Bi Kazakhstan 45°48N 62°6E 216 C6
Ayton Australia 15°56S 145°22E 280 B4
Aytos Bulgaria 42°42N 27°16E 203 D11
Aytoska Planina Bulgaria 42°45N 27°30E 203 D11
Ayu, Kepulauan Indonesia 0°35N 131°5E 231 D8
Ayutla Guatemala 14°40N 92°10W 320 D1
Ayutla de los Libres Mexico 16°54N 99°13W 319 D5
Ayutthaya = Phra Nakhon Si Ayutthaya Thailand 14°25N 100°30E 236 E3
Ayvacık Turkey 39°36N 26°24E 212 C2
Ayvalık Turkey 39°20N 26°46E 205 B8
Az Zabadānī Syria 33°43N 36°5E 250 E7
Aẓ Ẓāhirāh □ Oman 22°40N 56°0E 249 B7
Aẓ Ẓāhirīyah West Bank 31°25N 34°58E 251 G5
Aẓ Ẓahrān Si. Arabia 26°10N 50°7E 247 E6
Az Zarqā Jordan 32°5N 36°4E 251 F7
Az Zarqā' U.A.E. 24°53N 53°4E 247 E7
Az Zāwiyah Libya 32°52N 12°56E 258 B2
Az Zāwiyah □ Libya 32°44N 12°43E 261 B7
Az Zaydīyah Yemen 15°20N 43°1E 248 D3
Az Zībār Iraq 36°52N 44°4E 213 D11
Az Zilfī Si. Arabia 26°12N 44°52E 246 E5
Az Zubayr Iraq 30°26N 47°40E 246 D5
Az Zuhrah Yemen 15°44N 43°0E 248 D3
Az Zuqur Yemen 14°0N 42°45E 248 D3
Az Zuwaytīnah Libya 30°58N 20°7E 258 B4
Azabu Tokyo, Japan 140 c3
Azad Kashmir □ Pakistan 33°50N 73°50E 243 C5
Azahar, Costa del Spain 40°0N 0°5E 196 F5
Azambuja Portugal 39°4N 8°51W 195 F2
Azamgarh India 26°5N 83°13E 243 F10
Azangaro Peru 14°55S 70°13W 330 C3
Azaoua Niger 15°50N 4°0E 263 B5
Azaouad Mali 19°0N 3°0W 262 B4
Azaouak → Mali 15°30N 3°18E 263 B5
Azaouak, Vallée de l' Mali 15°50N 3°20E 263 B5
Āzār Shahr Iran 37°45N 45°59E 213 D11
Azara Nigeria 8°22N 9°12E 263 D6
Azarān Iran 37°25N 47°16E 213 D12
Azärbayjan = Azerbaijan ■ Asia 40°20N 48°0E 191 K9
Āzarbāyjān-e Gharbī □ Iran 37°0N 44°30E 246 B5
Āzarbāyjān-e Sharqī □ Iran 37°20N 47°0E 246 B5
Azare Nigeria 11°55N 10°10E 263 C7
Azay-le-Rideau France 47°16N 0°30E 172 E7
A'zāz Syria 36°36N 37°4E 250 B8
Azazga Algeria 36°48N 4°22E 261 A5
Azbine = Aïr Niger 18°30N 8°0E 259 E1
Azcapotzalco Mexico 19°28N 99°10W 128 B1
Azefal Mauritania 21°0N 14°45W 260 D2
Azeffoun Algeria 36°51N 4°26E 261 A5
Azemmour Morocco 33°20N 9°20W 260 B3
Azennezal Algeria 22°58N 0°43E 261 D5
Azerbaijan ■ Asia 40°20N 48°0E 191 K9
Azezo Ethiopia 12°28N 37°15E 257 E4
Azkoien = Peralta Spain 42°20N 1°48W 196 C3
Aznalcóllar Spain 37°32N 6°17W 195 H4
Azogues Ecuador 2°35S 78°0W 328 D2
Azores = Açores, Is. dos Atl. Oc. 38°0N 27°0W 153 d1
Azores-Biscay Rise Atl. Oc. 42°0N 20°0W 152 B9
Azoum, B. → Chad 10°53N 20°15E 259 F4
Azov Russia 47°3N 39°25E 191 G4
Azov, Sea of Europe 46°0N 36°30E 189 J9
Azovskoye More = Azov, Sea of Europe 46°0N 36°30E 189 J9
Azpeitia Spain 43°12N 2°19W 196 B2
Azrak, B. → Chad 10°52N 20°35E 259 F4
Azraq ash Shīshān Jordan 31°50N 36°49E 251 G7
Azrou Morocco 33°28N 5°19W 260 B3
Aztec U.S.A. 36°49N 107°59W 305 H10
Azteca, Estadia Mexico 19°19N 99°9W 128 C2
Azua de Compostela Dom. Rep. 18°25N 70°44W 321 C5
Azuaga Spain 38°16N 5°39W 195 G5
Azuara Spain 41°15N 0°53W 196 D4
Azuay □ Ecuador 2°55S 79°0W 328 D2
Azucar, Cerro Pan de Chile 33°19S 70°41W 137 A1
Azuer → Spain 39°8N 3°36W 195 F7
Azuero, Pen. de Panama 7°30N 80°30W 320 E3
Azuga Romania 45°27N 25°33E 183 E10
Azul Argentina 36°42S 59°43W 334 D4
Azul, Lagoa Azores 37°52N 25°47W 153 d3
Azul, Serra Brazil 14°50S 54°50W 331 C7
Azumino Japan 36°20N 137°50E 223 A9
Azur, Côte d' France 43°25N 7°10E 175 E11
Azurduy Bolivia 19°59S 64°29W 331 D5
Azusa U.S.A. 34°8N 117°52W 307 L9
Azzaba Algeria 36°48N 7°6E 261 A6
Azzano Décimo Italy 45°52N 12°56E 199 C9
Azzel Matti, Sebkra Algeria 26°10N 0°43E 261 C5

B

Ba Be △ Vietnam 22°25N 105°37E 236 A5
Ba Don Vietnam 17°45N 106°26E 236 D6
Ba Dong Vietnam 9°40N 106°33E 237 H6
Ba Ngoi Vietnam 11°54N 109°10E 237 G7
Ba Ria Vietnam 10°30N 107°10E 237 G6
Ba Tri Vietnam 10°2N 106°36E 237 G6
Ba Vi △ Vietnam 21°1N 105°22E 236 B5
Ba Xian = Bazhou China 39°8N 116°22E 226 E9
Baa Indonesia 10°50S 123°0E 278 B3
Baalbek = Ba'labakk Lebanon 34°0N 36°10E 250 E7
Baambrugge Neths. 52°15N 4°59E 112 B2
Baamonde Spain 43°7N 7°44W 194 B3
Baao Phil. 13°27N 123°22E 232 E4
Baardheere Somalia 2°20N 42°27E 267 D5
Baarle-Nassau Belgium 51°27N 4°56E 170 C4
Bab el Mandeb Red Sea 12°35N 43°25E 248 D3
Baba Bulgaria 42°44N 23°59E 202 D7
Baba, B. do Angola 14°50S 12°14E 265 E2
Bābā, Koh-i- Afghan. 34°30N 67°0E 240 B2
Baba Budan Hills India 13°30N 75°44E 245 H2
Baba Burnu Turkey 39°29N 26°2E 205 B8
Baba Channel Pakistan 24°48N 66°58E 123 B1
Baba dag Azerbaijan 41°0N 48°19E 191 K9
Baba I. Pakistan 24°49N 66°57E 123 B1
Bābā Kalū Iran 30°7N 50°49E 247 D6
Babaçulândia Brazil 7°13S 47°46W 332 C2
Babadag Romania 44°53N 28°44E 183 F13
Babadağ Turkey 37°49N 28°52E 205 D10
Babaeski Turkey 41°26N 27°6E 203 E11
Babahoyo Ecuador 1°40S 79°30W 328 D2
Babai = Sarju → India 27°21N 81°23E 243 F9
Babai → Nepal 28°10N 82°21E 243 E10
Babak Phil. 7°8N 125°41E 233 H5
Babana Nigeria 10°31N 3°46E 263 C5
Babanusa Sudan 11°20N 27°48E 257 E2
Babar Algeria 35°10N 7°6E 261 A6
Babar Indonesia 8°0S 129°30E 231 F7
Babar Pakistan 31°7N 69°32E 242 D3
Babarkach Pakistan 29°45N 68°0E 242 E3
Babarpur India 28°41N 77°16E 120 A2
Babase I. Papua N. G. 4°0S 153°42E 286 B7
Babayevo Russia 59°24N 35°55E 188 C8
Babb U.S.A. 48°51N 113°27W 304 B7
Babelthuap Palau 7°30N 134°30E 288 c
Babenhausen Germany 49°57N 8°57E 179 F4
Băbeni Romania 44°59N 24°11E 183 F9
Baberu India 25°33N 80°43E 243 G9
Babi Indonesia 2°5N 96°39E 234 B1
Babi Besar, Pulau Malaysia 2°25N 103°59E 237 L4
Babia Gora Europe 49°38N 19°38E 185 J6
Babian Jiang → China 22°55N 101°47E 228 F3
Bābil □ Iraq 32°30N 44°30E 246 C5
Babile Ethiopia 9°16N 42°11E 257 F5
Babile ⌓ Ethiopia 8°45N 42°20E 267 C5
Babimost Poland 52°10N 15°49E 185 F2
Babinda Australia 17°20S 145°56E 280 B4
Babine Canada 55°22N 126°37W 296 B3
Babine → Canada 55°45N 127°44W 296 B3
Babine L. Canada 54°48N 126°0W 296 C3
Babiogórski △ Poland 49°38N 19°39E 185 J6
Babo Indonesia 2°30S 133°30E 231 E8
Babócsa Hungary 46°2N 17°21E 182 D2
Bābol Iran 36°40N 52°50E 247 B7
Bābol Sar Iran 36°45N 52°45E 247 B7
Babor, Dj. Algeria 36°31N 5°25E 261 A6
Baborów Poland 50°7N 18°1E 185 H5
Baboua C.A.R. 5°49N 14°58E 264 A2
Babruysk Belarus 53°10N 29°15E 177 B15
Babson Park U.S.A. 27°49N 81°32W 317 H8
Babuhri India 26°49N 69°43E 242 F3
Babuna N. Macedonia 41°30N 21°40E 202 E5
Babura Nigeria 12°51N 8°59E 263 C6
Babusar Pass Pakistan 35°12N 73°59E 243 B5
Babushkin Russia 55°51N 37°42E 129 A3
Babušnica Serbia 43°7N 22°27E 202 C6
Babuyan Phil. 10°0N 118°54E 233 F2
Babuyan Chan. Phil. 18°40N 121°30E 232 B3
Babuyan I. Phil. 19°32N 121°57E 232 B3
Babuyan Is. Phil. 19°10N 121°40E 232 B3
Babylon Iraq 32°34N 44°22E 213 F11
Bač Serbia 45°29N 19°17E 182 E4
Bâc → Moldova 46°55N 29°26E 183 D14
Bac Can Vietnam 22°8N 105°49E 228 F5
Bac Giang Vietnam 21°16N 106°11E 228 G6
Bac Lieu Vietnam 9°17N 105°43E 237 H5
Bac Ninh Vietnam 21°13N 106°4E 228 G6
Bac Phan Vietnam 22°0N 105°0E 228 G5
Bacaadweyn Somalia 7°15N 47°40E 267 C6
Bacabal Brazil 4°15S 44°45W 332 B3
Bacacay Phil. 13°18N 123°47E 232 E4
Bacajá → Brazil 3°25S 51°50W 329 D7
Bacalar Mexico 18°43N 88°27W 319 D7
Bacan, Kepulauan Indonesia 0°35S 127°30E 231 E7
Bacarra Phil. 18°15N 120°37E 232 B3
Bacău Romania 46°35N 26°55E 183 D11
Bacău □ Romania 46°30N 26°45E 183 D11
Baccarat France 48°28N 6°42E 173 D13
Bacchus Marsh Australia 37°43S 144°27E 282 D6
Bacerac Mexico 30°18N 108°50W 318 A3
Băceşti Romania 46°50N 27°11E 183 D12
Bach Long Vi, Dao Vietnam 20°10N 107°40E 236 B6
Bach Ma △ Vietnam 16°11N 107°49E 236 D6
Bachaquero Venezuela 9°56N 71°8W 328 B3
Bacharach Germany 50°3N 7°44E 179 E3
Bachelor's Beach Bonaire 12°11N 68°18W 322 h
Bachhwara India 25°35N 85°54E 243 G11
Bachu China 39°46N 78°34E 217 E9
Bachuma Ethiopia 6°48N 35°53E 257 F4
Bačina Serbia 43°42N 21°23E 202 C5
Back → Canada 65°10N 104°0W 294 D11
Back B. India 18°56N 72°48E 130 B1
Bačka Palanka Serbia 45°17N 19°27E 182 E4
Bačka Topola Serbia 45°49N 19°39E 182 E4
Bäckebo Sweden 56°53N 16°4E 163 H10
Bäckefors Sweden 58°48N 12°9E 163 F6
Bäckhammar Sweden 59°10N 14°11E 162 E8
Bački Petrovac Serbia 45°29N 19°32E 182 E4
Backnang Germany 48°56N 9°26E 179 G5
Backstairs Passage Australia 35°40S 138°5E 282 C3
Baclaran Phil. 14°31N 121°0E 127 B2
Bacnotan Phil. 16°43N 120°21E 232 C3
Baco, Mt. Phil. 12°49N 121°10E 232 E3
Bacolod Phil. 10°40N 122°57E 233 F4
Bacon Phil. 13°3N 124°3E 232 E5
Baconton U.S.A. 31°23N 84°10W 316 D5
Bacoor Phil. 14°27N 120°56E 127 C1
Bacoor B. Phil. 14°27N 120°54E 127 C1
Bacqueville-en-Caux France 49°47N 1°0E 172 C8
Bács-Kiskun □ Hungary 46°43N 19°30E 182 D4
Bácsalmás Hungary 46°8N 19°17E 182 D4
Bacuag = Placer Phil. 9°36N 125°38E 233 G5
Bacuit = El Nido Phil. 11°10N 119°25E 233 F2
Bacuk Malaysia 6°4N 102°25E 237 J4
Bácum Mexico 27°33N 110°5W 318 B2
Bād Iran 33°41N 52°1E 247 C7
Bad → U.S.A. 44°21N 100°22W 308 C3
Bad Aussee Austria 47°43N 13°45E 180 D6
Bad Axe U.S.A. 43°48N 83°0W 312 C2
Bad Bergzabern Germany 49°6N 7°59E 179 F3
Bad Berleburg Germany 51°2N 8°26E 178 D4
Bad Bevensen Germany 53°5N 10°35E 178 B6
Bad Bramstedt Germany 53°55N 9°53E 178 B5
Bad Brückenau Germany 50°18N 9°47E 179 E5
Bad Doberan Germany 54°6N 11°53E 178 A7
Bad Driburg Germany 51°43N 9°1E 178 D5
Bad Ems Germany 50°20N 7°43E 179 E3
Bad Frankenhausen Germany 51°21N 11°5E 178 D7
Bad Freienwalde Germany 52°46N 14°1E 178 C10
Bad Goisern Austria 47°38N 13°38E 180 D6
Bad Harzburg Germany 51°52N 10°34E 178 D6
Bad Hersfeld Germany 50°52N 9°42E 178 E5
Bad Hofgastein Austria 47°17N 13°6E 180 D6
Bad Homburg Germany 50°13N 8°38E 179 E4
Bad Honnef Germany 50°38N 7°13E 178 E3
Bad Iburg Germany 52°10N 8°3E 178 C4
Bad Ischl Austria 47°44N 13°38E 180 D6
Bad Kissingen Germany 50°11N 10°4E 179 E6
Bad Königshofen Germany 50°17N 10°28E 179 E6
Bad Kreuznach Germany 49°50N 7°51E 179 F3
Bad Krozingen Germany 47°54N 7°42E 179 H3
Bad Kudowa = Kudowa-Zdrój Poland 50°27N 16°15E 185 H3
Bad Laasphe Germany 50°56N 8°25E 178 E4
Bad Landeck = Lądek-Zdrój Poland 50°21N 16°53E 185 H3
Bad Langensalza Germany 51°5N 10°38E 178 D6
Bad Lauterberg Germany 51°38N 10°28E 178 D6
Bad Leonfelden Austria 48°31N 14°18E 180 C7
Bad Liebenwerda Germany 51°31N 13°24E 178 D9
Bad Mergentheim Germany 49°28N 9°42E 179 F5
Bad Münstereifel Germany 50°33N 6°46E 178 E2
Bad Nauheim Germany 50°21N 8°43E 179 E4
Bad Neuenahr-Ahrweiler Germany 50°32N 7°5E 178 E3
Bad Neustadt Germany 50°18N 10°13E 179 E6
Bad Oeynhausen Germany 52°12N 8°46E 178 C4
Bad Oldesloe Germany 53°48N 10°22E 178 B6
Bad Orb Germany 50°12N 9°22E 179 E5
Bad Polzin = Polanica-Zdrój Poland 50°24N 16°32E 185 H3
Bad Pyrmont Germany 51°59N 9°16E 178 D5
Bad Reichenhall Germany 47°43N 12°54E 179 H8
Bad Reinerz = Duszniki-Zdrój Poland 50°24N 16°24E 185 H3
Bad Säckingen Germany 47°33N 7°56E 179 H3
Bad Salzuflen Germany 52°5N 8°45E 178 C4
Bad Salzungen Germany 50°48N 10°14E 178 E6
Bad Sankt Leonhard Austria 46°58N 14°47E 180 E7
Bad Schönfliess = Trzcińsko Zdrój Poland 52°58N 14°35E 185 F1
Bad Schwartau Germany 53°55N 10°41E 178 B6
Bad Segeberg Germany 53°56N 10°17E 178 B6
Bad Tölz Germany 47°45N 11°34E 179 H7
Bad Urach Germany 48°29N 9°23E 179 G5
Bad Vöslau Austria 47°58N 16°12E 181 D9
Bad Waldsee Germany 47°55N 9°45E 179 H5
Bad Wildungen Germany 51°6N 9°7E 178 D5
Bad Wimpfen Germany 49°13N 9°11E 179 F5
Bad Windsheim Germany 49°36N 10°25E 179 F6
Bad Zwischenahn Germany 53°12N 8°1E 178 B4
Bada Barabil India 22°7N 85°24E 243 H11
Badagara = Vadakara India 11°35N 75°40E 245 J2
Badagri Nigeria 6°25N 2°55E 263 D5
Badain Jaran Shamo China 40°23N 102°0E 218 C9
Badajós, L. Brazil 3°15S 62°50W 329 D5
Badajoz Spain 38°50N 6°59W 195 G4
Badajoz □ Spain 38°40N 6°30W 195 G4
Badakhshān □ Afghan. 36°30N 71°0E 240 A3
Badaling China 40°20N 116°0E 226 D9
Badalona Spain 41°26N 2°15E 114 A2
Badalzai Afghan. 29°50N 65°35E 242 E1
Badami India 15°55N 75°41E 245 G2
Badampahar India 22°10N 86°10E 244 C8
Badanah Si. Arabia 30°58N 41°30E 246 D4
Badarinath India 30°45N 79°30E 243 D8
Badarpur India 24°54N 92°36E 241 C4
Badas, Kepulauan Indonesia 0°45N 107°5E 234 B3
Baddo → Pakistan 28°0N 64°20E 240 D2
Bade = Pate Taiwan 24°56N 121°17E 225 B3
Bade Indonesia 7°10S 139°35E 231 F9
Badeggi Nigeria 9°1N 6°8E 263 D6
Badéguichéri Niger 14°30N 5°22E 263 C6
Baden Austria 48°1N 16°13E 181 C9
Baden Switz. 47°28N 8°18E 179 H4
Baden Pa., U.S.A. 40°38N 80°14W 312 F4
Baden-Baden Germany 48°44N 8°13E 179 G4
Baden-Württemberg □ Germany 48°20N 8°40E 179 G4
Badgam India 34°1N 74°45E 243 B6
Badgastein Austria 47°7N 13°9E 180 D6
Badger Nfld. & L., Canada 49°0N 56°4W 299 C8
Badger Calif., U.S.A. 36°38N 119°1W 306 J7
Bādghīs □ Afghan. 35°0N 63°0E 240 B1
Badgingarra △ Australia 30°23S 115°22E 279 F2
Badhan = Buraan Somalia 10°14N 48°44E 267 B6
Badhoevedorp Neths. 52°20N 4°47E 112 A1
Badia Polésine Italy 45°5N 11°29E 199 C8
Badian Phil. 9°55N 123°24E 233 G4
Badiar △ Guinea 13°37N 13°11W 262 C2
Badin Pakistan 24°38N 68°54E 242 G3
Badinka ⌓ Mali 13°31N 9°28W 262 C3
Badjokola Dem. Rep. of the Congo 3°54N 20°17E 264 B4
Badlands U.S.A. 43°55N 102°30W 308 D2
Badlands △ U.S.A. 43°38N 102°56W 308 D2
Badli India 28°44N 77°8E 120 A1
Badme Africa 14°43N 37°48E 248 D2
Badnera India 20°48N 77°44E 244 D3
Badoc Phil. 17°56N 120°28E 232 C3
Badogo Mali 11°2N 8°13W 262 C3
Badoumbé Mali 13°42N 10°15W 262 C2
Badr Ḥunayn Si. Arabia 23°44N 38°46E 248 B2
Badrah Iraq 33°6N 45°58E 213 F11
Badrain Jaran Shamo China 40°40N 103°20E 226 D2
Badrinath India 30°44N 79°29E 243 D8
Badu Australia 10°7S 142°11E 280 a
Badulla Sri Lanka 7°1N 81°7E 245 L5
Badung, Bukit Indonesia 8°49S 115°10E 231 K18
Badung, Selat Indonesia 8°40S 115°22E 231 K18
Badvel India 14°45N 79°3E 245 G4
Baena Spain 37°37N 4°20W 195 H6
Baengnyeongdo S. Korea 37°57N 124°40E 224 D2
Baerami Australia 32°27S 150°27E 283 B9
Bærum Norway 59°54N 10°36E 133 A2
Baetov Kyrgyzstan 41°13N 74°54E 217 D8
Baeza Ecuador 0°25S 77°53W 328 D2
Baeza Spain 37°57N 3°25W 195 H7
Bafang Cameroon 5°9N 10°11E 263 D7
Bafatá Guinea-Biss. 12°8N 14°40W 262 C2
Baffin B. N. Amer. 72°0N 64°0W 292 B13
Baffin I. Canada 68°0N 75°0W 295 D17
Bafia Cameroon 4°40N 11°10E 263 E7
Bafilo Togo 9°22N 1°22E 263 D5
Bafing → Mali 13°49N 10°50W 262 C2
Bafing △ Mali 12°38N 10°28W 262 C2
Bafliyūn Syria 36°37N 36°59E 246 B3
Bafoulabé Mali 13°50N 10°55W 262 C2
Bafoussam Cameroon 5°28N 10°25E 263 D7
Bāfq Iran 31°40N 55°25E 247 D7
Bafra Turkey 41°34N 35°54E 212 B6
Bafra Burnu Turkey 41°45N 36°2E 212 B7
Bāft Iran 29°15N 56°38E 247 D8
Bafut Cameroon 6°6N 10°2E 263 D7
Bafwasende Dem. Rep. of the Congo 1°3N 27°5E 268 B2
Bagabag Phil. 16°30N 121°15E 232 C3
Bagabag I. Papua N. G. 4°48S 146°14E 286 C4
Bagac Phil. 14°36N 120°23E 232 D3
Bagac B. Phil. 14°36N 120°20E 232 D3
Bagaha India 27°6N 84°5E 244 A7
Bagalkot India 16°10N 75°40E 245 F2
Bagam Niger 15°43N 6°35E 263 B6
Bagamanoc Phil. 13°57N 124°17E 232 E5
Bagamoyo Tanzania 6°28S 38°55E 268 D4
Bagan = Pagan Myanmar 21°10N 94°52E 241 E5
Bagan Datoh Malaysia 3°59N 100°47E 237 L3
Bagan Serai Malaysia 5°1N 100°32E 237 K3
Baganga Phil. 7°34N 126°33E 233 H6
Bagani Namibia 18°7S 21°41E 270 A3
Bagansiapiapi Indonesia 2°12N 100°50E 234 B2
Bagasra India 21°30N 71°0E 242 J4
Bagata Dem. Rep. of the Congo 3°44S 17°57E 264 C3
Bagaud India 22°19N 75°53E 242 H6
Bagawi Sudan 12°20N 34°18E 257 E3
Bagbag Sudan 15°23N 31°30E 257 D3
Bağcılar Turkey 41°2N 28°49E 122 B1
Bagdad Calif., U.S.A. 34°35N 115°53W 307 L11
Bagdad Fla., U.S.A. 30°36N 87°2W 317 E2
Bagdarin Russia 54°26N 113°36E 215 D12
Bagé Brazil 31°20S 54°15W 335 C5
Bagenalstown Ireland 52°42N 6°58W 166 D5
Bagepalli India 13°47N 77°47E 245 H3
Bagerhat Bangla. 22°40N 89°47E 241 D2
Bageshwar India 29°51N 79°46E 243 E8
Bagevadi India 16°35N 75°58E 244 F2
Baggao Phil. 17°56N 121°46E 232 C3
Bággio Italy 45°27N 9°6E 128 B1
Baggs U.S.A. 41°2N 107°39W 304 F10
Bagh Pakistan 33°59N 73°45E 243 C5
Bāgh-e-Feyz Iran 35°44N 51°19E 141 A1
Baghain → India 25°32N 81°1E 243 G9
Baghdād Iraq 33°20N 44°23E 113 A2
Baghdad Int. ✕ (BGW) Iraq 33°15N 44°14E 113 B1
Baghdadi Georgia 42°5N 42°49E 213 A10
Bagheria Italy 38°5N 13°30E 200 D6
Baghlān Afghan. 32°12N 68°46E 240 A3
Baghlān □ Afghan. 36°0N 68°30E 240 B3

Bagley U.S.A. 47°32N 95°24W 308 B6
Baglung Nepal 28°16N 83°36E 243 E10
Bagmari India 22°34N 88°23E 124 B2
Bagn Norway 60°49N 9°34E 164 D6
Bagnara Cálabra Italy 38°17N 15°48E 201 D8
Bagnasco Italy 44°18N 8°2E 198 D5
Bagnell Dam U.S.A. 38°14N 92°36W 310 F4
Bagnères-de-Bigorre France 43°5N 0°9E 174 E4
Bagnères-de-Luchon France 42°47N 0°38E 174 F4
Bagneux France 48°47N 2°18E 134 B2
Bagni di Lucca Italy 44°1N 10°35E 198 D7
Bagno di Romagna Italy 43°50N 11°57E 199 E8
Bagnoles-de-l'Orne France 48°32N 0°25W 172 D6
Bagnolet France 48°52N 2°25E 134 A3
Bagnols-sur-Cèze France 44°10N 4°36E 175 D8
Bagnorea = Bagnorégio Italy 42°37N 12°5E 199 F9
Bagnorégio Italy 42°37N 12°5E 199 F9
Bago Myanmar 17°20N 96°29E 241 G6
Bago Phil. 10°32N 122°50E 233 F4
Bago □ Myanmar 17°30N 96°30E 241 G6
Bagodar India 24°5N 85°52E 243 G11
Bagram ✈ (OAI) Afghan. 34°57N 69°14E 240 B3
Bagrationovsk Russia 54°23N 20°39E 184 D7
Bagrdan Serbia 44°5N 21°11E 202 B5
Bagsværd Denmark 55°45N 12°27E 118 A2
Bagsværd Sø Denmark 55°46N 12°28E 118 A2
Bagua Peru 5°35S 78°22W 330 B2
Baguiati India 22°36N 88°25E 124 B2
Baguio Phil. 16°26N 120°34E 232 C3
Bagumbayan Phil. 14°28N 121°3E 127 C2
Bağyurdu Turkey 38°25N 27°41E 205 C9
Bagzane, Monts Niger 17°43N 8°45E 259 E1
Bahabón de Esgueva Spain 41°52N 3°43W 194 D7
Bahadurabad Ghat Bangla. 25°11N 89°44E 241 C2
Bahadurganj India 26°16N 87°49E 243 F12
Bahadurgarh India 28°40N 76°57E 242 E7
Baha'i Temple U.S.A. 42°4N 87°41W 119 A2
Bahaja Somalia 11°16N 49°50E 267 B6
Baham, Pte. Martinique 14°24N 60°50W 322 j
Bahama, Canal Viejo de W. Indies 22°10N 77°30W 320 B4
Bahamas, The ■ N. Amer. 24°0N 75°0W 321 B5
Bahār Iran 34°54N 48°26E 213 E13
Bahārak Afghan. 37°0N 70°53E 240 A3
Baharampur India 24°2N 88°27E 243 G13
Bahariya, El Wâhât al Egypt 28°0N 28°50E 256 B2
Baharu Pandan = Pandan Malaysia 1°32N 103°46E 237 d
Bahawalnagar Pakistan 30°0N 73°15E 242 E5
Bahawalpur Pakistan 29°24N 71°40E 242 E4
Bahçe Turkey 37°13N 36°34E 212 D7
Bahçecik Turkey 40°41N 29°44E 203 F13
Bahçeköy Turkey 41°10N 28°59E 122 A1
Bahçelievler Turkey 41°0N 28°50E 122 B1
Baheli Phil. 10°0N 118°47E 233 F2
Bäherden Turkmenistan 38°25N 57°26E 247 B8
Baheri India 28°45N 79°34E 243 E8
Bahgul → India 27°45N 79°36E 243 F8
Bahi Tanzania 5°58S 35°21E 268 D4
Bahi Swamp Tanzania 6°10S 35°0E 268 D4
Bahia = Salvador Brazil 13°0S 38°30W 333 D4
Bahia □ Brazil 12°0S 42°0W 333 D3
Bahía, Is. de la Honduras 16°45N 86°15W 320 C2
Bahía Blanca Argentina 38°35S 62°13W 334 D3
Bahía de Caráquez Ecuador 0°40S 80°27W 328 D1
Bahía de Los Angeles Mexico 28°56N 113°34W 318 B2
Bahía Honda Cuba 22°54N 83°10W 320 B3
Bahía Kino Mexico 28°47N 111°58W 318 B2
Bahía Laura Argentina 48°10S 66°30W 336 C3
Bahía Mansa Chile 40°33S 73°46W 336 B2
Bahía Negra Paraguay 20°5S 58°5W 331 E6
Bahía Solano Colombia 6°14N 77°25W 328 B2
Bahir Dar Ethiopia 11°37N 37°10E 257 E4
Bahlā' Oman 22°58N 57°18E 249 B7
Bahmanzād Iran 31°15N 51°47E 247 D6
Bahmer Algeria 27°32N 0°10W 261 C4
Bahr el Ahmar □ Sudan 20°0N 35°0E 256 D4
Bahr el Ghazal = Kanem □ Chad 15°0N 15°0E 259 F3
Bahr el Jebel = Central Equatoria □ South Sudan 4°0N 31°0E 257 G3
Bahraich India 27°38N 81°37E 243 F9
Bahrain ■ Asia 26°0N 50°35E 247 E6
Bahror India 27°51N 76°20E 242 F7
Bahtīm Egypt 30°8N 31°16E 117 A2
Bāhū Kalāt Iran 25°43N 61°25E 247 E9
Bai Mali 13°35N 3°28W 262 C4
Bai Bung, Mui = Ca Mau, Mui Vietnam 8°38N 104°44E 237 H5
Bai Thuong Vietnam 19°54N 105°23E 236 C5
Baia de Aramă Romania 45°0N 22°50E 182 E7
Baía dos Tigres Angola 16°40S 11°47E 265 F2
Baía Farta Angola 12°40S 13°11E 265 E2
Baia Mare Romania 47°40N 23°35E 183 C8
Baia-Sprie Romania 47°41N 23°43E 183 C8
Baião Brazil 2°40S 49°40W 332 B2
Baïbokoum Chad 7°46N 15°43E 259 G3
Baicheng Jilin, China 45°38N 122°42E 227 B12
Baicheng Xinjiang Uygur, China 41°46N 81°52E 217 D10
Băicoi Romania 45°3N 25°52E 183 E10
Baidoa = Baydhabo Somalia 3°8N 43°30E 267 D5
Baie-Comeau Canada 49°12N 68°10W 299 C6
Baie de Baly △ Madag. 16°2S 45°15E 272 B2
Baie du Cap Mauritius 20°29S 57°22E 272 e
Baie-Mahault Guadeloupe 16°16N 61°35W 322 e
Baie-St-Paul Canada 47°28N 70°32W 299 C5
Baie Ste-Anne Seychelles 4°18S 55°45E 272 c
Baie-Trinité Canada 49°25N 67°20W 299 C6
Baie Verte Canada 49°55N 56°12W 299 C8
Baignes-Ste-Radegonde France 45°23N 0°25W 174 C3
Baigneux-les-Juifs France 47°31N 4°39E 173 E11
Baihar India 22°6N 80°33E 243 H9
Baihe = Paiho Taiwan 23°21N 120°25E 225 C2
Baihe Hubei, China 32°50N 110°5E 229 A8
Baihe Jilin, China 42°27N 128°9E 227 C15
Baihedong China 23°4N 113°14E 121 B2
Baihetan Dam China 27°11N 102°54E 228 D4
Ba'ījī Iraq 35°0N 43°30E 213 E10
Baijnath India 29°55N 79°37E 243 E8
Baikal, L. = Baykal, Oz. Russia 53°0N 108°0E 215 D11
Baikonur = Bayqonyr Kazakhstan 45°40N 63°20E 216 C6
Baikunthpur India 23°15N 82°33E 243 H10
Bailadila, Mt. India 18°43N 81°15E 244 E5
Baile Átha Cliath = Dublin Ireland 53°21N 6°15W 166 C5
Baile Átha Fhirdhia = Ardee Ireland 53°52N 6°33W 166 C5
Baile Átha Í = Athy Ireland 53°0N 7°0W 166 C5
Baile Átha Luain = Athlone Ireland 53°25N 7°56W 166 C4
Baile Átha Troim = Trim Ireland 53°33N 6°48W 166 C5
Baile Brigín = Balbriggan Ireland 53°37N 6°11W 166 C5
Băile Govora Romania 45°5N 24°11E 183 E9
Băile Herculane Romania 44°53N 22°26E 182 F7
Băile Olăneşti Romania 45°12N 24°14E 183 E9
Baile Sear = Baleshare U.K. 57°31N 7°22W 167 D1
Băile Tuşnad Romania 46°9N 25°51E 183 D10
Bailén Spain 38°8N 3°48W 195 G7
Băileşti Romania 44°1N 23°20E 183 F8
Baileys Crossroads U.S.A. 38°50N 77°6W 143 B2
Bailhongal India 15°55N 74°53E 245 G2
Bailieborough Ireland 53°56N 6°59W 166 C5
Bailique, Ilha Brazil 1°2N 49°58W 332 A2
Baille-Argent Guadeloupe 16°15N 61°48W 322 e
Baillif Guadeloupe 16°1N 61°44W 322 e
Bailly France 48°50N 2°4E 134 A1
Bailugh Afghan. 32°40N 66°47E 240 B2
Bailundo = Luau Angola 10°40S 22°10E 265 E4
Bailundo Angola 12°10S 15°50E 265 E3
Baima China 33°0N 100°26E 228 A3
Baimuru Papua N. G. 7°35S 144°51E 286 D3
Bain-de-Bretagne France 47°50N 1°40W 172 E5
Bainbridge Ga., U.S.A. 30°55N 84°35W 316 E5
Bainbridge Ind., U.S.A. 39°46N 86°49W 311 E10
Bainbridge N.Y., U.S.A. 42°18N 75°29W 313 D9
Bainbridge Ohio, U.S.A. 39°14N 83°16W 311 E13
Bainbridge Island U.S.A. 47°38N 122°32W 306 C4
Baine China 42°0N 128°0E 219 C14
Baing Indonesia 10°14S 120°34E 231 F6
Bainiu China 32°50N 112°15E 229 A9
Bainyik Papua N. G. 3°40S 143°4E 286 B2
Baiona Spain 42°6N 8°52W 194 C2
Bā'ir Jordan 30°45N 36°55E 251 H7
Bā'ir, W. → Jordan 30°59N 37°24E 251 H8
Baird Mts. U.S.A. 67°0N 160°0W 303 C7
Bairiki = Tarawa Kiribati 1°30N 173°0E 288 G9
Bairin Youqi China 43°30N 118°35E 227 C10
Bairin Zuoqi China 43°58N 119°15E 227 C10
Bairnsdale Australia 37°48S 147°36E 283 D7
Bairro Alto Lisbon, Portugal 126 c1
Bairro Lopes Lisbon, Portugal 126 b3
Bais Phil. 9°35N 123°7E 233 G4
Baisha Guangdong, China 23°8N 113°11E 121 B2
Baisha Henan, China 34°20N 112°32E 226 G7
Baisha Li China 19°12N 109°20E 229 a
Baishan = Hunjiang China 41°54N 126°26E 224 B3
Baishan China 42°43N 127°14E 227 C14
Baissa Nigeria 7°14N 10°38E 263 D7
Baitadi Nepal 29°35N 80°25E 243 E9
Baitarani → India 20°45N 86°48E 244 D8
Baixa Lisbon, Portugal 126 c2
Baixa Grande Brazil 11°57S 40°11W 333 D3
Baixa Limia-Sierra do Xurés ⌂ Spain 41°59N 8°2W 194 D2
Baixo-Longa Angola 15°41S 18°45E 265 F3
Baiyer River Papua N. G. 5°32S 144°9E 286 C3
Baiyin China 36°45N 104°14E 226 F3
Baiyü China 31°16N 98°50E 228 B2
Baiyu Shan China 37°15N 107°30E 226 F4
Baiyuda Sudan 17°35N 32°7E 256 D3
Baiyun China 23°11N 113°16E 121 A2
Baiyun Mountain Scenic Area ⌂ China 23°11N 113°17E 121 A2
Baj Baj India 22°30N 88°5E 243 H13
Baja Hungary 46°12N 18°59E 182 D3
Baja, Pta. Easter I., Chile 27°10S 109°22W 330 b
Baja, Pta. Baja Calif., Mexico 29°58N 115°49W 318 B1
Baja California Mexico 31°10N 115°12W 318 A1
Baja California □ Mexico 30°0N 115°0W 318 B2
Baja California Sur □ Mexico 25°50N 111°50W 318 B2
Bajag India 22°40N 81°21E 243 H9
Bajamar Canary Is. 28°33N 16°20W 153 e1
Bajana India 23°7N 71°49E 242 H4
Bajatrejo Indonesia 8°29S 114°19E 231 J17
Bajawa Indonesia 8°47S 120°59E 231 F6
Bajera Indonesia 8°31S 115°2E 231 J18
Bajgīrān Iran 37°36N 58°24E 247 B8
Bājil Yemen 15°4N 43°17E 248 D3
Bajimba, Mt. Australia 29°17S 152°6E 281 D5
Bajina Bašta Serbia 43°58N 19°35E 202 C3
Bajmok Serbia 45°57N 19°24E 182 E4
Bajo Boquete Panama 8°46N 82°27W 320 E3
Bajo Caracoles Argentina 47°27S 70°56W 336 C2
Bajo Nuevo Caribbean 15°40N 78°50W 320 C4
Bajoga Nigeria 10°57N 11°20E 263 C7
Bajool Australia 23°40S 150°35E 280 C5
Bak Hungary 46°43N 16°51E 182 D1
Bakala C.A.R. 6°15N 20°20E 264 A4
Bakar Croatia 45°18N 14°32E 199 C11
Bakassi Pen. Cameroon 4°42N 8°20E 263 E6
Bakel Senegal 14°56N 12°20W 262 C2
Baker Calif., U.S.A. 35°16N 116°4W 307 K10
Baker Fla., U.S.A. 30°48N 86°41W 317 E3
Baker Mont., U.S.A. 46°22N 104°17W 304 C11
Baker, Canal Chile 47°45S 74°45W 336 C2
Baker, L. Canada 64°0N 96°0W 294 E12
Baker, Mt. U.S.A. 48°50N 121°49W 304 B3
Baker City U.S.A. 44°47N 117°50W 304 D5
Baker I. Pac. Oc. 0°10N 176°35W 277 A15
Baker I. Alaska, U.S.A. 55°20N 133°40W 296 B2
Baker L. Australia 26°54S 126°5E 279 E4
Baker Lake Canada 64°20N 96°3W 294 E12
Bakere Dem. Rep. of the Congo 1°36N 23°50E 264 B4
Bakerhill U.S.A. 31°47N 85°18W 316 D4
Bakers Creek Australia 21°13S 149°7E 280 C4
Bakers Dozen Is. Canada 56°45N 78°45W 298 A4
Bakersfield Calif., U.S.A. 35°23N 119°1W 307 K8
Bakersfield Vt., U.S.A. 44°45N 72°48W 313 B12
Bakharden = Bäherden Turkmenistan 38°25N 57°26E 247 B8
Bakhchysaray Ukraine 44°40N 33°45E 189 K7
Bakhmach Ukraine 51°10N 32°45E 189 G7
Bakhmut Ukraine 48°35N 38°0E 189 H9
Bākhtarān = Kermānshāh Iran 34°23N 47°0E 213 E12
Bākhtarān = Kermānshāh □ Iran 34°0N 46°30E 246 C5
Bakhtegān, Daryācheh-ye Iran 29°40N 53°50E 247 D7
Bakhtegān △ Iran 29°51N 53°40E 247 D7
Baki = Krasnyye Baki Russia 57°8N 45°10E 190 B7
Bakı Azerbaijan 40°29N 49°56E 191 K9
Baki Somalia 10°30N 43°8E 267 B5
Bakır → Turkey 38°55N 27°0E 205 C9
Bakırdağı Turkey 38°13N 35°46E 212 C6
Bakırköy Turkey 40°58N 28°52E 122 C1
Bakkafjörður Iceland 66°2N 14°48W 155 A12
Bakkaflói Iceland 66°10N 14°45W 155 A12
Bakkagerði Iceland 65°31N 13°49W 155 B13
Baklan Turkey 38°0N 29°36E 205 C11
Bako Côte d'Ivoire 9°8N 7°40W 262 D3
Bako Ethiopia 5°51N 36°33E 257 F4
Bako △ Malaysia 1°43N 110°28E 235 B4
Bakony Hungary 47°10N 17°30E 182 C2
Bakony Forest = Bakony Hungary 47°10N 17°30E 182 C2
Bakool □ Somalia 4°0N 44°0E 267 D5
Bakori Nigeria 11°34N 7°25E 263 C6
Bakouma C.A.R. 5°40N 22°56E 264 A4
Baksan Russia 43°42N 43°32E 191 J6
Bakswaho India 24°15N 79°18E 243 G8
Baku = Bakı Azerbaijan 40°29N 49°56E 191 K9
Bakun Dam Malaysia 2°50N 113°50E 235 B4
Bakundi Nigeria 8°2N 10°45E 263 D7
Bakung Indonesia 0°5N 104°26E 234 B2
Bakungan Indonesia 2°55N 97°28E 234 B1
Bakuriani Georgia 41°44N 43°31E 213 B10
Bakutis Coast Antarctica 74°0S 120°0W 151 D15
Bakwa-Kenge Dem. Rep. of the Congo 4°51S 22°4E 265 C4
Bakwanga = Mbuji-Mayi Dem. Rep. of the Congo 6°9S 23°40E 265 D4
Baky = Bakı Azerbaijan 40°29N 49°56E 191 K9
Bal Harbor U.S.A. 25°53N 80°7W 129 C3
Bala Ont., Canada 45°1N 79°37W 312 A5
Bala Senegal 14°1N 13°8W 262 C2
Balâ Turkey 39°32N 33°6E 212 C5
Bala Gwynedd, U.K. 52°54N 3°36W 168 E4
Bala, L. U.K. 52°53N 3°37W 168 E4
Bālā Morghāb Afghan. 35°35N 63°20E 240 B1
Balabac Phil. 7°59N 117°4E 233 H1
Balabac I. Phil. 8°0N 117°0E 233 H1
Balabac Str. E. Indies 7°53N 117°5E 230 C5
Balabagh Afghan. 34°25N 70°12E 242 B4
Ba'labakk Lebanon 34°0N 36°10E 250 E7
Balabalangan, Kepulauan Indonesia 2°20S 117°30E 235 C5
Balabio, Î. N. Cal. 20°7S 164°11E 288 d
Bălăciţa Romania 44°23N 23°8E 183 F8
Balad Iraq 34°0N 44°9E 213 F11
Balad Rūz Iraq 33°42N 45°5E 213 F11
Bālādeh Fārs, Iran 29°17N 51°56E 247 D6
Bālādeh Māzandaran, Iran 36°12N 51°48E 247 B6
Balaghat India 21°49N 80°12E 244 D5
Balaghat Ra. India 18°50N 76°30E 244 E3
Balaguer Spain 41°50N 0°50E 196 D5
Balaikarangan Indonesia 0°49N 110°25E 235 B4
Balaipungut Indonesia 1°3N 101°17E 234 B2
Balaisabut Indonesia 0°28N 110°49E 235 B4
Balaka Dem. Rep. of the Congo 4°52S 19°57E 265 C3
Balakän Azerbaijan 41°43N 46°24E 191 K8
Balakété C.A.R. 6°56N 19°56E 264 A3
Balakhna Russia 56°25N 43°32E 190 B6
Balaklava S. Austral., Australia 34°7S 138°22E 282 C3
Balaklava Ukraine 44°30N 33°30E 189 K7
Balakliya Ukraine 49°28N 36°55E 189 H9
Balakovo Russia 52°4N 47°55E 190 D8
Balamau India 27°10N 80°21E 243 F9
Balamban Phil. 10°30N 123°43E 233 F4
Balambangan, Pulau Malaysia 7°17N 116°55E 235 A5
Bălan Romania 46°39N 25°49E 183 D10
Balancán Mexico 17°48N 91°32W 319 D6
Balanda = Kalininsk Russia 51°30N 44°40E 190 E7
Balandra B. Trin. & Tob. 10°42N 61°0W 323 t
Balanga Phil. 14°41N 120°32E 232 D3
Balangala Dem. Rep. of the Congo 0°30N 19°56E 264 B3
Balangiga Phil. 11°7N 125°23E 233 F5
Balangir India 20°43N 83°35E 244 D6
Balaoan Phil. 16°49N 120°24E 232 C3
Balapur India 20°40N 76°45E 244 D3
Balara Phil. 14°39N 121°3E 127 B2
Balashikha Russia 55°48N 37°58E 188 E9
Balashov Russia 51°30N 43°10E 190 E6
Balasinor India 22°57N 73°23E 242 H5
Balasore = Baleshwar India 21°35N 87°3E 244 D8
Balassagyarmat Hungary 48°4N 19°15E 182 B4
Balât Egypt 25°36N 29°19E 256 B2
Balaton Hungary 46°50N 17°40E 182 D2
Balaton-Felvidéki △ Hungary 46°52N 17°30E 182 D2
Balatonboglár Hungary 46°46N 17°40E 182 D2
Balatonfüred Hungary 46°58N 17°54E 182 D2
Balatonszentgyörgy Hungary 46°41N 17°19E 182 D2
Balayan Phil. 13°57N 120°44E 232 E3
Balayan B. Phil. 13°51N 120°48E 232 E3
Balazote Spain 38°54N 2°9W 197 G2
Balbalan Phil. 17°27N 121°12E 232 C3
Balbalasang-Balbalan △ Phil. 17°23N 121°1E 232 C3
Balbi, Mt. Papua N. G. 5°55S 154°58E 286 C8
Balbieriškis Lithuania 54°32N 23°53E 184 D10
Balbigny France 45°49N 4°11E 175 C8
Balbina Brazil 1°58S 59°29W 329 D6
Balbina, Represa de Brazil 2°0S 59°30W 329 D6
Balboa Panama 8°57N 79°34W 320 c
Balbriggan Ireland 53°37N 6°11W 166 C5
Balcarce Argentina 38°0S 58°10W 334 D4
Balcarres Canada 50°50N 103°35W 297 C8
Bălceşti Romania 44°37N 23°57E 183 F8
Balch Springs U.S.A. 32°43N 96°37W 120 B6
Balchik Bulgaria 43°28N 28°11E 203 C12
Balclutha N.Z. 46°15S 169°45E 285 G4
Balcones Escarpment U.S.A. 29°30N 99°15W 314 G5
Balçova Turkey 38°22N 27°4E 205 C9
Bald I. Australia 34°57S 118°27E 279 F2
Bald Knob U.S.A. 35°19N 91°34W 314 D9
Baldenburg = Biały Bór Poland 53°53N 16°51E 184 E3
Baldia Pakistan 24°54N 66°58E 123 A1
Baldock L. Canada 56°33N 97°57W 297 B9
Baldwin Fla., U.S.A. 30°18N 81°59W 316 E8
Baldwin Mich., U.S.A. 43°54N 85°51W 309 D11
Baldwin Pa., U.S.A. 40°21N 79°58W 312 F5
Baldwin, L. U.S.A. 28°34N 81°19W 133 A3
Baldwin Hills U.S.A. 34°0N 118°21W 126 B2
Baldwin Hills Res. U.S.A. 34°0N 118°21W 126 B2
Baldwinsville U.S.A. 43°10N 76°20W 313 C8
Baldy Peak U.S.A. 33°54N 109°34W 305 K9
Bale Croatia 45°4N 13°46E 199 C10
Bale Oromīya, Ethiopia 6°57N 40°8E 257 F5
Bale Oromīya, Ethiopia 6°20N 41°30E 257 F5
Bale Mts. △ Ethiopia 6°59N 39°52E 257 F4
Baleares, Is. Spain 39°30N 3°0E 206 B4
Balearic Is. = Baleares, Is. Spain 39°30N 3°0E 206 B4
Baleh → Malaysia 2°1N 113°1E 235 B4
Baleia, Pta. da Brazil 17°40S 39°7W 333 E4
Baleine → Canada 58°15N 67°40W 299 A6
Baleine, Petite R. de la → Canada 56°0N 76°45W 298 A4
Băleni Romania 45°48N 27°51E 183 E12
Baler Phil. 15°46N 121°34E 232 D3
Baler B. Phil. 15°50N 121°35E 232 D3
Baleshare U.K. 57°31N 7°22W 167 D1
Baleshwar India 21°35N 87°3E 244 D8
Balestrand Norway 61°11N 6°31E 164 C3
Baley Russia 51°36N 116°37E 215 D12
Balezino Russia 58°2N 53°6E 190 B11
Balfate Honduras 15°48N 86°25W 320 C2
Balfour Channel Solomon Is. 8°43S 157°27E 287 M9
Balgo Australia 20°9S 127°58E 278 D4
Balgowlah Australia 33°47S 151°16E 139 A3
Balgowlah Heights Australia 33°48S 151°16E 139 A2
Balham U.K. 51°26N 0°8W 125 B3
Balharshah India 19°50N 79°23E 244 E4
Bali Cameroon 5°54N 10°0E 263 D7
Bali Dem. Rep. of the Congo 2°50S 16°12E 264 C3
Bali Kriti, Greece 35°25N 24°47E 207 E5
Bali Paschimbanga, India 22°38N 88°20E 124 B1
Bali Raj., India 25°11N 73°17E 242 G5
Bali Indonesia 8°20S 115°0E 231 J18
Bali □ Indonesia 8°20S 115°0E 231 J17
Bali, Selat Indonesia 8°18S 114°25E 231 J17
Bali Barat △ Indonesia 8°12S 114°35E 231 J17
Bali Sea Indonesia 8°0S 115°0E 231 J18
Balia S. Leone 9°22N 11°1W 262 D2
Baliapal India 21°40N 87°17E 244 D8
Baliceaux St. Vincent 12°57N 61°8W 323 n
Balicuatro Is. Phil. 12°39N 124°24E 232 E5
Baliganja India 22°31N 88°22E 124 B2
Balige Indonesia 2°14N 99°7E 234 B1
Baligród Poland 49°20N 22°17E 185 J9
Baliguda India 20°12N 83°55E 244 D6
Balik Pulau Malaysia 5°21N 100°14E 237 c
Balıkesir Turkey 39°39N 27°53E 205 B9
Balıkesir □ Turkey 39°45N 28°0E 205 B9
Balīkh → Syria 35°52N 39°12E 213 E8
Balıklıçeşme Turkey 40°18N 27°5E 203 F11
Balikpapan Indonesia 1°10S 116°55E 235 C5
Balimbing Phil. 5°5N 119°58E 233 J2
Balimo Papua N. G. 8°6S 142°57E 286 E2
Baling Malaysia 5°41N 100°55E 237 K3
Balingasag Phil. 8°45N 124°47E 233 G5
Balinge Sweden 59°57N 17°33E 162 E11
Balingen Germany 48°16N 8°51E 179 G4
Balingsnäs Sweden 59°13N 18°0E 139 B2
Balingsta Sweden 59°12N 18°3E 139 B2
Balinsasayao Twin Lakes △ Phil. 9°21N 123°9E 233 G4
Balinţ Romania 45°48N 21°54E 182 E6
Balintang Channel Phil. 19°49N 121°40E 232 B3
Balintang I. Phil. 19°58N 122°9E 232 B4
Balintawak Phil. 14°39N 120°59E 127 B1
Baliza Brazil 16°0S 52°20W 331 D7
Baljurashī Si. Arabia 19°51N 41°33E 248 C3
Balkan □ Turkmenistan 40°0N 54°30E 216 D5
Balkan Mts. = Stara Planina Bulgaria 43°15N 23°0E 202 C7
Balkanabat Turkmenistan 39°30N 54°22E 247 B7
Balkh Afghan. 36°44N 66°47E 217 E7
Balkh □ Afghan. 36°50N 67°0E 240 A2
Balkhash = Balqash Kazakhstan 46°50N 74°50E 214 E8
Balkhash, Ozero = Balqash Köli Kazakhstan 46°0N 74°50E 217 C8
Balkonda India 18°52N 78°21E 244 E4
Ballachulish U.K. 56°41N 5°8W 167 E3
Balladonia Australia 32°27S 123°51E 279 F3
Ballaghaderreen Ireland 53°55N 8°34W 166 C3
Ballan Australia 37°35S 144°13E 282 D6
Ballarat Australia 37°33S 143°50E 282 D5
Ballard, L. Australia 29°20S 120°40E 279 E3
Ballari India 15°10N 76°56E 245 G3
Ballater U.K. 57°3N 3°3W 167 D5
Ballé Mali 15°18N 8°33W 262 B3
Ballena, Pta. Venezuela 11°11N 63°47W 329 a
Ballenas, Canal de Mexico 29°10N 113°29W 318 B2
Balleny Is. Antarctica 66°30S 163°0E 151 C11
Balleroy France 49°11N 0°50W 172 C6
Ballerup Denmark 55°43N 12°21E 118 A2
Ballestas, Is. Peru 13°44S 76°25W 330 C2
Ballı Turkey 40°50N 27°3E 203 F11
Ballia India 25°46N 84°12E 243 G11
Ballina N.S.W., Australia 28°50S 153°31E 281 D5
Ballina Mayo, Ireland 54°7N 9°9W 166 B2
Ballinasloe Ireland 53°20N 8°13W 166 C3
Ballincollig Ireland 51°53N 8°33W 166 E3
Ballinger U.S.A. 31°45N 99°57W 314 F5
Ballinrobe Ireland 53°38N 9°13W 166 C2
Ballinskelligs B. Ireland 51°48N 10°13W 166 E1
Ballon France 48°10N 0°14E 172 D7
Ballons des Vosges ⌂ France 48°0N 7°0E 173 E14
Ballsh Albania 40°36N 19°44E 202 F3
Ballston Spa U.S.A. 43°0N 73°51W 313 D11
Ballyboghil Ireland 53°32N 6°16W 166 C5
Ballybunion Ireland 52°31N 9°40W 166 D2
Ballycanew Ireland 52°37N 6°19W 166 D5
Ballycastle U.K. 55°12N 6°15W 166 A5
Ballyclare U.K. 54°46N 6°0W 166 B5
Ballycroy △ Ireland 54°5N 9°50W 166 B2
Ballydehob Ireland 51°34N 9°28W 166 E2
Ballygawley U.K. 54°27N 7°2W 166 B4
Ballyhaunis Ireland 53°46N 8°46W 166 C3
Ballyheigue Ireland 52°23N 9°49W 166 D2
Ballymena U.K. 54°52N 6°17W 166 B5
Ballymoney U.K. 55°5N 6°31W 166 A5
Ballymote Ireland 54°5N 8°31W 166 B3
Ballynahinch U.K. 54°24N 5°54W 166 B6
Ballyporeen Ireland 52°16N 8°6W 166 D3
Ballyquintin Pt. U.K. 54°20N 5°30W 166 B6
Ballyshannon Ireland 54°30N 8°11W 166 B3
Balmaceda Chile 46°0S 71°50W 336 C2
Balmain Australia 33°51S 151°11E 139 B2
Balmaseda Spain 43°11N 3°12W 196 B1
Balmazújváros Hungary 47°37N 21°21E 182 C6
Balmertown Canada 51°4N 93°41W 297 C10
Balmoral Australia 37°15S 141°48E 282 D4
Balmorhea U.S.A. 30°59N 103°45W 314 F3
Balneário Camboriú Brazil 26°59S 48°38W 335 B6
Balochistan = Baluchistan □ Pakistan 27°30N 65°0E 240 D2
Balod India 20°44N 81°13E 244 D5
Balombo Angola 12°21S 14°46E 265 E2
Balombo → Angola 11°57S 13°46E 265 E2
Balonne → Australia 28°47S 147°56E 281 D4
Balotra India 25°50N 72°14E 242 G5
Balpyq Bī Kazakhstan 44°52N 78°12E 217 D9
Balqash Kazakhstan 46°50N 74°50E 214 E8
Balqash Köli Kazakhstan 46°0N 74°50E 217 C8
Balrampur India 27°30N 82°20E 243 F10
Balranald Australia 34°38S 143°33E 282 C5
Balş Romania 44°22N 24°5E 183 F9
Balsapuerto Peru 5°48S 76°33W 330 B2
Balsas Maranhão, Brazil 7°15S 44°35W 332 C3
Balsas → Tocantins, Brazil 9°58S 47°52W 332 C2
Balsas → Michoacan, Mexico 17°55N 102°10W 318 D4
Balsas del Norte Mexico 18°0N 99°46W 319 D5
Bålsta Sweden 59°35N 17°30E 162 E11
Balta Romania 44°54N 22°38E 182 F7
Balta Ukraine 47°56N 29°45E 183 C14
Balta Ialomiţei Romania 44°20N 27°55E 183 F12
Baltakōl Kazakhstan 43°7N 67°46E 217 D7
Baltanás Spain 41°56N 4°15W 194 D6
Bălţi Moldova 47°48N 27°58E 183 C12
Baltic Sea Europe 57°0N 19°0E 161 H18
Baltīm Egypt 31°35N 31°10E 256 H7
Baltimore Cork, Ireland 51°29N 9°22W 166 E2
Baltimore Md., U.S.A. 39°17N 76°36W 309 F15
Baltimore Ohio, U.S.A. 39°51N 82°36W 312 G2
Baltimore-Washington Int. ✈ (BWI) U.S.A. 39°10N 76°40W 309 F15
Baltinglass Ireland 52°56N 6°43W 166 D5
Baltit Pakistan 36°15N 74°40E 243 A6
Baltiysk Russia 54°41N 19°58E 184 D6
Baltiyskiy = Paldiski Estonia 59°23N 24°9E 188 C3
Baltra, I. Ecuador 0°26S 90°16W 330 a
Baltrum Germany 53°43N 7°24E 178 B3
Baluan I. Papua N. G. 2°33S 147°17E 286 B4
Baluchistan □ Pakistan 27°30N 65°0E 240 D2
Balud Phil. 12°2N 123°12E 232 E4
Baluhati India 22°39N 88°15E 124 B1
Baluqtybulaq Kazakhstan 50°51N 51°8E 190 E10
Baluran △ Indonesia 7°50S 114°23E 235 D4
Balurghat India 25°15N 88°44E 241 C2
Balut I. Phil. 5°24N 125°23E 233 J5
Balvanera Argentina 34°37S 58°23W 117 B2
Balvi Latvia 57°8N 27°15E 188 D4
Balwyn Australia 37°48S 145°4E 128 A2
Balwyn North Australia 37°47S 145°4E 128 A2
Balya Turkey 39°44N 27°35E 205 B9
Balykchy Kyrgyzstan 42°26N 76°12E 217 D9
Balyqshy Kazakhstan 47°4N 51°52E 187 E9
Balzar Ecuador 2°2S 79°54W 328 D2
Bam Iran 29°7N 58°14E 247 D8
Bama Guangxi Zhuangzu, China 24°8N 107°12E 228 E6
Bama Nigeria 11°33N 13°41E 263 C7
Bamaga Australia 10°50S 142°25E 280 A3
Bamaji L. Canada 51°9N 91°25W 298 B1
Bamako Mali 12°34N 7°55W 262 C3
Bamba Dem. Rep. of the Congo 5°45S 18°23E 265 D3
Bamba Mali 17°5N 1°24W 263 B4
Bambama Congo 2°32S 13°32E 264 C2
Bambamarca Peru 6°36S 78°32W 330 B2
Bambang Phil. 16°23N 121°6E 232 C3
Bambannan I. Phil. 5°37N 120°17E 233 J3
Bambao Comoros Is. 12°11S 44°31E 272 a
Bambara Maoundé Mali 13°26N 4°3W 262 B4
Bambari C.A.R. 5°40N 20°35E 264 A4
Bambaroo Australia 18°50S 146°10E 280 B4
Bambaya Guinea 10°55N 13°38W 262 D2
Bamberg Bayern, Germany 49°54N 10°54E 179 F6
Bamberg S.C., U.S.A. 33°18N 81°2W 316 B8
Bambesi Ethiopia 9°45N 34°40E 257 F3
Bambey Senegal 14°42N 16°28W 262 C1
Bambili Dem. Rep. of the Congo 3°40N 26°0E 268 B2
Bambinga Dem. Rep. of the Congo 3°43S 18°53E 264 C3
Bambio C.A.R. 3°55N 16°57E 264 B3
Bamboi Ghana 8°13N 2°1W 262 D4
Bamboo Avenue Jamaica 18°6N 77°47W 320 a
Bambous Mauritius 20°15S 57°24E 272 e
Bambouti C.A.R. 5°24N 27°12E 264 A5
Bambuí Brazil 20°1S 45°58W 333 F2
Bamburgh U.K. 55°37N 1°43W 168 B6
Bamenda Cameroon 5°57N 10°11E 263 D7
Bamendjing, L. de Cameroon 5°50N 10°30E 263 D7
Bamfield Canada 48°45N 125°10W 296 D3
Bāmīān Afghan. 34°49N 67°49E 240 B2
Bāmīān □ Afghan. 35°0N 67°0E 240 B2
Bamiancheng China 43°15N 124°2E 227 C13
Bamingui C.A.R. 7°34N 20°11E 264 A3
Bamingui → C.A.R. 8°33N 19°5E 264 A3
Bamingui-Bangoran □ C.A.R. 8°30N 20°0E 264 A4
Bamingui-Bangoran △ C.A.R. 8°30N 19°46E 264 A3
Bamkin Cameroon 6°3N 11°27E 263 D7
Bamou △ Iran 29°45N 52°35E 247 D7
Bampūr Iran 27°15N 60°21E 247 E9
Bampūr → Iran 27°24N 59°0E 247 E8
Bamu → Papua N. G. 8°1S 143°33E 286 E2
Ban Burkina Faso 14°5N 2°27W 262 C4
Ban Ao Tu Khun Thailand 8°9N 98°20E 237 a
Ban Ban Laos 19°31N 103°30E 236 C4
Ban Bang Hin Thailand 9°32N 98°35E 237 H2
Ban Bang Khu Thailand 7°57N 98°23E 237 a
Ban Bang Rong Thailand 8°3N 98°25E 237 a
Ban Bo Phut Thailand 9°33N 100°2E 237 b
Ban Chaweng Thailand 9°32N 100°3E 237 b
Ban Chiang Thailand 17°32N 103°21E 236 D4
Ban Chiang Thailand 17°30N 103°10E 236 D4
Ban Chiang Klang Thailand 19°25N 100°55E 236 C3
Ban Choho Thailand 15°2N 102°9E 236 E4
Ban Dan Lan Hoi Thailand 17°0N 99°35E 236 D2
Ban Don = Surat Thani Thailand 9°6N 99°20E 237 H2
Ban Don Vietnam 12°53N 107°48E 236 F6
Ban Don, Ao → Thailand 9°20N 99°25E 237 H2
Ban Dong Thailand 19°30N 100°59E 236 C3
Ban Hong Thailand 18°18N 98°50E 236 C2
Ban Hua Thanon Thailand 9°26N 100°1E 237 b
Ban Kantang Thailand 7°25N 99°31E 237 J2
Ban Karon Thailand 7°51N 98°18E 237 a
Ban Kata Thailand 7°50N 98°18E 237 a
Ban Keun Laos 18°22N 102°35E 236 C4
Ban Khai Thailand 12°46N 101°18E 236 F3
Ban Kheun Laos 20°13N 101°7E 236 B3
Ban Khlong Khian Thailand 8°10N 98°26E 237 a
Ban Khlong Kua Thailand 6°57N 100°8E 237 J3
Ban Khuan Thailand 8°20N 98°25E 237 a
Ban Ko Yai Chim Thailand 11°17N 99°26E 237 G2
Ban Laem Thailand 13°13N 99°59E 236 F2
Ban Lamai Thailand 9°28N 100°3E 237 b
Ban Lao Ngam Laos 15°28N 106°10E 236 E6
Ban Le Kathe Thailand 15°49N 98°53E 236 E2
Ban Lo Po Noi Thailand 8°1N 98°34E 237 a
Ban Mae Chedi Thailand 19°11N 99°31E 236 C2
Ban Mae Nam Thailand 9°34N 100°0E 237 b
Ban Mae Sariang Thailand 18°10N 97°56E 236 C1
Ban Mê Thuôt = Buon Ma Thuot Vietnam 12°40N 108°3E 236 F7
Ban Mi Thailand 15°3N 100°32E 236 E3
Ban Muang Mo Laos 19°4N 103°58E 236 C4
Ban Na Bo Thailand 9°19N 99°41E 237 b
Ban Na San Thailand 8°53N 99°52E 237 H2
Ban Na Tong Laos 20°56N 101°47E 236 B3
Ban Nam Bac Laos 20°38N 102°20E 236 B4
Ban Nammi Laos 17°7N 105°40E 236 D5
Ban Nong Bok Laos 17°5N 104°48E 236 D5
Ban Nong Pling Thailand 15°40N 100°10E 236 E3
Ban Pak Chan Thailand 10°32N 98°51E 237 G2
Ban Patong Thailand 7°54N 98°18E 237 a
Ban Phai Thailand 16°4N 102°44E 236 D4
Ban Phak Chit Thailand 8°0N 98°24E 237 a
Ban Pong Thailand 13°50N 99°55E 236 F2
Ban Rawai Thailand 7°47N 98°20E 237 a
Ban Ron Phibun Thailand 8°9N 99°51E 237 H2
Ban Sakhu Thailand 8°4N 98°18E 237 a
Ban Sanam Chai Thailand 7°33N 100°25E 237 J3
Ban Tak Thailand 17°2N 99°4E 236 D2
Ban Tako Thailand 14°5N 102°40E 236 E4
Ban Tha Dua Thailand 17°59N 98°39E 236 D2
Ban Tha Nun Thailand 8°12N 98°18E 237 a
Ban Tha Rua Thailand 7°59N 98°22E 237 a
Ban Tha Yu Thailand 8°17N 98°22E 237 a
Ban Thong Krut Thailand 9°25N 99°57E 237 b
Ban Xien Kok Laos 20°54N 100°39E 236 B3
Ban Yen Nhan Vietnam 20°57N 106°2E 236 B6
Banā, W. → Yemen 13°3N 45°24E 248 D4
Banaadir □ Somalia 2°7N 45°24E 267 D6
Banaba Kiribati 0°45S 169°50E 288 H8
Banagher Ireland 53°11N 7°59W 166 C3
Banalia Dem. Rep. of the Congo 1°32N 25°5E 268 B2
Banam Cambodia 11°20N 105°17E 237 G5
Banamba Mali 13°29N 7°22W 262 C3
Banana Dem. Rep. of the Congo 6°1S 12°25E 265 D2
Banana Is. S. Leone 8°7N 13°15W 262 D2
Banana Island Nigeria 6°28N 3°27E 124 B2
Bananal, I. do Brazil 11°30S 50°30W 333 D1
Bananga India 6°57N 93°54E 245 L11
Bananier Guadeloupe 16°0N 61°36W 322 e
Banaras = Varanasi India 25°22N 83°0E 243 G10
Banas → Gujarat, India 23°45N 71°25E 242 H4
Banas → Mad. P., India 24°15N 81°30E 243 G9
Bânâs, Ras Egypt 23°57N 35°59E 256 C4
Banática Portugal 38°40N 9°11W 126 A1
Banaue Phil. 16°55N 121°4E 232 C3
Banaz Turkey 38°46N 29°46E 205 C11
Banaz → Turkey 38°12N 29°14E 205 C11
Banbridge U.K. 54°22N 6°16W 166 B5
Banbury U.K. 52°4N 1°20W 169 E6
Banc d'Arguin △ Mauritania 20°10N 16°20W 260 D1
Banchory U.K. 57°3N 2°29W 167 D6
Banco Ethiopia 6°12N 38°13E 257 F4
Banco do Brasil, Centro Cultural Rio de J., Brazil 135 a2
Bancoran Phil. 7°45N 118°30E 233 H2
Bancroft = Chililabombwe Zambia 12°18S 27°43E 269 E2
Bancroft Canada 45°3N 77°51W 312 A7
Band Romania 46°30N 24°25E 183 D9
Band Bonī Iran 25°30N 59°33E 247 E8
Band-e Amīr Afghan. 34°50N 67°10E 240 B2
Band-e Torkestan Afghan. 35°30N 64°0E 240 B2
Band Qīr Iran 31°39N 48°53E 247 D6
Banda Cameroon 3°58N 14°32E 264 B2
Banda Mad. P., India 24°3N 78°57E 243 G8
Banda Maharashtra, India 15°49N 73°52E 245 G1
Banda Ut. P., India 25°30N 80°26E 243 G9
Banda, Kepulauan Indonesia 4°37S 129°50E 231 E7
Banda Aceh Indonesia 5°35N 95°20E 234 A1
Banda Banda, Mt. Australia 31°10S 152°28E 283 A10
Banda Elat Indonesia 5°40S 133°5E 231 F8
Banda Is. = Banda, Kepulauan Indonesia 4°37S 129°50E 231 E7
Banda Kani Dem. Rep. of the Congo 4°48S 13°52E 265 C2
Banda Sea Indonesia 6°0S 130°0E 231 F8
Bandai-Asahi △ Japan 37°38N 140°5E 220 F10
Bandai-San Japan 37°36N 140°4E 220 F10
Bandak Norway 59°23N 8°29E 164 E5
Bandama → Côte d'Ivoire 6°32N 4°30W 262 D3
Bandama Blanc → Côte d'Ivoire 6°55N 5°30W 262 D4
Bandama Rouge → Côte d'Ivoire 6°55N 5°30W 262 D4
Bandamadji Comoros Is. 11°47S 43°26E 272 a
Bandān Iran 31°23N 60°44E 247 D9
Bandanaira Indonesia 4°32S 129°54E 231 E7
Bandanwara India 26°9N 74°38E 242 F6
Bandar = Machilipatnam India 16°12N 81°8E 245 F5
Bandar-e Abbās Iran 27°15N 56°15E 247 E8
Bandar-e Anzalī Iran 37°30N 49°30E 213 D13
Bandar-e Bushehr = Būshehr Iran 28°55N 50°55E 247 D6
Bandar-e Chārak Iran 26°45N 54°20E 247 E7
Bandar-e Deylam Iran 30°5N 50°10E 247 D6
Bandar-e Emām Khomeynī Iran 30°30N 49°5E 247 D6
Bandar-e Lengeh Iran 26°35N 54°58E 247 E7
Bandar-e Maqām Iran 26°56N 53°29E 247 E7
Bandar-e Ma'shur Iran 30°35N 49°10E 247 D6
Bandar-e Rīg Iran 29°29N 50°38E 247 D6
Bandar-e Torkeman Iran 37°0N 54°10E 247 B7
Bandar Labuan Malaysia 5°20N 115°14E 235 A5
Bandar Lampung Indonesia 5°20S 105°10E 234 D3
Bandar Maharani = Muar Malaysia 2°3N 102°34E 237 L4
Bandar Penggaram = Batu Pahat Malaysia 1°50N 102°56E 237 M4
Bandar Seri Begawan Brunei 4°52N 115°0E 235 B4
Bandar Shahid Rajaee Iran 27°7N 56°4E 247 E8
Bandar Sri Aman Malaysia 1°15N 111°32E 235 B4
Bandawe Malawi 11°58S 34°5E 269 E3
Bande Spain 42°3N 7°58W 194 C3
Bandeira, Pico da Brazil 20°26S 41°47W 333 F3
Bandeirante Brazil 13°41S 50°48W 333 D1
Bandera Argentina 28°55S 62°20W 334 B3
Banderas, B. de Mexico 20°40N 105°25W 318 C3
Bandhavgarh India 23°40N 81°2E 243 H9
Bandhavgarh △ India 23°45N 81°10E 244 C5
Bandi → India 26°12N 75°47E 242 F6
Bandi → India 19°2N 80°28E 244 E5
Bandiagara Mali 14°12N 3°29W 262 C4
Bandiagara, Falaise de Mali 14°14N 3°29W 262 D4
Bandikui India 27°3N 76°34E 242 F7
Bandingilo △ South Sudan 5°26N 32°17E 257 F3
Bandipur △ India 11°45N 76°30E 245 J3
Bandırma Turkey 40°20N 28°0E 203 F11
Bandjarmasin = Banjarmasin Indonesia 3°20S 114°35E 235 C4
Bandol France 43°8N 5°46E 175 E9
Bandon Ireland 51°44N 8°44W 166 E3
Bandon → Ireland 51°43N 8°37W 166 E3
Bandra India 19°3N 72°49E 130 A1
Bandra Pt. India 19°2N 72°49E 130 A1
Bandraboua Mayotte 12°42S 45°8E 272 b
Bandrélé Mayotte 12°54S 45°11E 272 b
Bandula Mozam. 19°0S 33°7E 269 F3
Bandundu Dem. Rep. of the Congo 3°15S 17°22E 264 C3
Bandung Indonesia 6°54S 107°36E 235 D3
Bané Burkina Faso 11°42N 0°15W 263 C4
Băneasa Romania 45°56N 27°55E 183 E12
Bāneh Iran 35°59N 45°53E 213 E11
Banes Cuba 21°0N 75°42W 320 B4
Banff Alta., Canada 51°10N 115°34W 296 C5
Banff Aberds., U.K. 57°40N 2°33W 167 D6
Banff △ Canada 51°30N 116°15W 296 C5
Banfora Burkina Faso 10°40N 4°40W 262 C4
Bang Fai → Laos 16°57N 104°45E 236 D5
Bang Hieng → Laos 16°10N 105°10E 236 D5
Bang Kapi Thailand 13°45N 100°38E 113 B2
Bang Krathum Thailand 16°34N 100°18E 236 D3
Bang Lang △ Thailand 5°58N 101°19E 237 K3
Bang Lang Res. Thailand 6°6N 101°17E 237 J3
Bang Mun Nak Thailand 16°2N 100°23E 236 D3
Bang Na Thailand 13°40N 100°36E 113 B2
Bang Pa In Thailand 14°14N 100°35E 236 E3
Bang Phlad Bangkok, Thailand 113 a1
Bang Rakam Thailand 16°45N 100°7E 236 D3
Bang Saphan Thailand 11°14N 99°28E 237 G2
Bang Thao Thailand 7°59N 98°18E 237 a
Banga Angola 8°43S 15°13E 265 D3
Banga Dem. Rep. of the Congo 5°25S 20°28E 265 D4
Banga Aklan, Phil. 11°38N 122°20E 233 F4
Banga S. Cotabato, Phil. 6°21N 124°47E 233 H5
Bangaduni I. India 21°34N 88°52E 241 E2
Bangala Dam Zimbabwe 21°7S 31°25E 269 G3
Bangalore = Bengaluru India 12°59N 77°40E 245 H3
Banganapalle India 15°19N 78°14E 245 G4
Banganga → India 27°6N 77°25E 242 F6
Bangangté Cameroon 5°8N 10°32E 263 D7
Bangaon India 23°0N 88°47E 243 H13
Bangar Brunei 4°43N 115°4E 235 B4
Bangar La Union, Phil. 16°54N 120°25E 232 C3
Bangassou C.A.R. 4°55N 23°7E 264 B4
Bangbae S. Korea 37°29N 126°59E 137 C1
Bangeta, Mt. Papua N. G. 6°21S 147°3E 286 D4
Banggai Indonesia 1°34S 123°30E 231 E6
Banggai, Kepulauan Indonesia 1°40S 123°30E 231 E6
Banggai Arch. = Banggai, Kepulauan Indonesia 1°40S 123°30E 231 E6
Banggi, Pulau Malaysia 7°17N 117°12E 235 A5
Banghāzī Libya 32°11N 20°3E 258 B4
Banghāzī □ Libya 32°7N 20°4E 258 B4
Bangil Indonesia 7°36S 112°50E 235 D4
Bangjang South Sudan 11°23N 32°41E 257 E3
Bangka Sulawesi, Indonesia 1°50N 125°5E 231 D7
Bangka Sumatera, Indonesia 2°0S 105°50E 234 C3
Bangka, Selat Indonesia 2°30S 105°30E 234 C3
Bangka-Belitung □ Indonesia 2°30S 107°0E 234 C3
Bangkalan Indonesia 7°2S 112°46E 235 D4
Bangkang Myanmar 22°4N 99°1E 228 F2
Bangkaru Indonesia 2°4N 97°7E 234 B1

Bangkhen Thailand 13°52N 100°36E 113 A2
Bangkinang Indonesia 0°18N 101°5E 234 B2
Bangko Indonesia 2°5S 102°9E 234 C2
Bangkok Thailand 13°45N 100°35E 113 B2
Bangkok, Bight of Thailand 12°55N 100°30E 236 F3
Bangkok Don Muang Int. ✈ (BKK) Thailand 13°53N 100°36E 113 A2
Bangkok Noi Thailand 13°45N 100°29E 113 B1
Bangkok Yai Thailand 13°43N 100°29E 113 B1
Bangla = Paschimbanga □ India 23°0N 88°0E 243 H13
Bangladesh ■ Asia 24°0N 90°0E 241 D3
Bangli Indonesia 8°27S 115°21E 231 J18
Banglo India 22°31N 88°14E 124 B1
Bangoi-Kouni Comoros Is. 11°22S 43°21E 272 a
Bangolo Côte d'Ivoire 7°1N 7°29W 262 D3
Bangong Co China 33°45N 78°43E 243 C8
Bangor Gwynedd, U.K. 53°14N 4°8W 168 D3
Bangor Newry M. & D., U.K. 54°40N 5°40W 166 B6
Bangor Maine, U.S.A. 44°48N 68°46W 309 C19
Bangor Mich., U.S.A. 42°18N 86°7W 311 B10
Bangor Pa., U.S.A. 40°52N 75°13W 313 F9
Bangoran ➜ C.A.R. 8°42N 19°6E 264 A3
Bangrak Thailand 13°43N 100°31E 113 B2
Bangsamoro □ Phil. 8°0N 123°0E 233 H3
Bangsu Thailand 13°49N 100°31E 113 B2
Bangu Dem. Rep. of the Congo 0°3S 19°12E 264 C3
Bangued Phil. 17°40N 120°37E 232 C3
Bangui C.A.R. 4°23N 18°35E 264 B3
Bangui Phil. 18°32N 120°46E 232 B3
Bangui B. Phil. 18°33N 120°43E 232 B3
Banguru Dem. Rep. of the Congo 0°30N 27°10E 268 B2
Bangweulu, L. Zambia 11°0S 30°0E 269 E3
Bangweulu Swamp Zambia 11°20S 30°15E 269 E3
Banhine △ Mozam. 22°49S 32°55E 271 B5
Bani Burkina Faso 13°43N 0°10W 263 C4
Bani C.A.R. 7°6N 22°50E 264 A4
Baní Dom. Rep. 18°16N 70°22W 321 C5
Bani Phil. 16°11N 119°52E 232 C2
Bani ➜ Mali 14°30N 4°12W 262 C4
Bani, Jebel Morocco 29°16N 8°0W 260 C3
Bani Bangou Niger 15°3N 2°42E 263 B5
Banī Sa'd Iraq 33°34N 44°32E 213 F11
Banī Walīd Libya 31°36N 13°53E 258 B2
Bania C.A.R. 4°1N 16°7E 264 B3
Bania Côte d'Ivoire 9°4N 3°6W 262 D4
Baniara Papua N. G. 9°44S 149°54E 286 E5
Banihal Pass India 33°30N 75°12E 243 C6
Banikoara Benin 11°18N 2°26E 263 C5
Banīnah Libya 32°0N 20°12E 258 B4
Banissa Kenya 3°55N 40°19E 266 B5
Bāniyās Syria 35°10N 36°0E 250 C7
Banja Luka Bos.-H. 44°49N 17°11E 182 F2
Banjar India 31°38N 77°21E 242 D7
Banjar ➜ India 22°36N 80°22E 243 H9
Banjarbaru Indonesia 3°25S 114°49E 235 C4
Banjarmasin Indonesia 3°20S 114°35E 235 C4
Banjul Gambia 13°28N 16°40W 262 C1
Bank London, U.K. 125 b5
Banka India 24°53N 86°55E 243 G12
Bankas Mali 14°4N 3°31W 262 C4
Bankeryd Sweden 57°53N 14°6E 163 G8
Banket Zimbabwe 17°27S 30°19E 269 F3
Bankilaré Niger 14°35N 0°44E 263 C5
Bankot India 17°58N 73°2E 244 F1
Banks U.S.A. 31°49N 85°51W 316 D4
Banks, C. Australia 34°0S 151°16E 139 C2
Banks I. = Moa Australia 10°11S 142°16E 280 a
Banks I. B.C., Canada 53°20N 130°0W 296 C3
Banks I. N.W.T., Canada 73°15N 121°30W 294 C7
Banks Is. Vanuatu 13°50S 167°30E 287 C5
Banks L. U.S.A. 31°2N 83°6W 316 D6
Banks Pen. N.Z. 43°45S 173°15E 285 D8
Banks Str. Australia 40°40S 148°10E 281 G4
Banksmeadow Australia 33°57S 151°12E 139 B2
Bankumuna Dem. Rep. of the Congo 4°28S 19°57E 265 C3
Bankura India 23°11N 87°18E 243 H12
Bankya Bulgaria 42°43N 23°8E 202 D7
Banmankhi India 25°53N 87°11E 243 G12
Banmauk Myanmar 24°24N 95°51E 241 C5
Bann ➜ Armagh B. & C., U.K. 54°30N 6°31W 166 B5
Bann ➜ Caus. C. & Glens, U.K. 55°8N 6°41W 166 A5
Bannaanka Saraar Somalia 9°25N 46°17E 267 C6
Bannalec France 47°57N 3°42W 172 E3
Bannang Sata Thailand 6°16N 101°16E 237 J3
Bannerton Australia 34°42S 142°47E 282 C5
Banning U.S.A. 33°56N 116°53W 307 M10
Banningville = Bandundu Dem. Rep. of the Congo 3°15S 17°22E 264 C3
Banno Ethiopia 4°51N 37°24E 257 G4
Banno-saki Japan 26°33N 128°8E 288 a
Bannockburn Ont., Canada 44°39N 77°33W 312 B7
Bannockburn Stirling, U.K. 56°5N 3°55W 167 E5
Bannockburn Zimbabwe 20°17S 29°48E 269 G2
Bannu Pakistan 33°0N 70°18E 240 B3
Bano India 22°40N 84°55E 243 H11
Bañolas = Banyoles Spain 42°16N 2°44E 196 C7
Banon France 44°2N 5°38E 175 D9
Baños de la Encina Spain 38°10N 3°46W 195 G7
Baños de Molgas Spain 42°15N 7°40W 194 C3
Bánovce nad Bebravou Slovakia 48°44N 18°16E 181 C11
Banovići Bos.-H. 44°25N 18°32E 182 F3
Banqiao = Panch'iao Taiwan 25°1N 121°27E 225 A3
Bansagar Dam India 24°11N 81°17E 244 B5
Bansalan Phil. 6°55N 125°13E 233 H5
Bansgaon India 26°33N 83°21E 243 F10
Banská Bystrica Slovakia 48°46N 19°14E 181 C12
Banská Štiavnica Slovakia 48°25N 18°55E 181 C11
Bansko Bulgaria 41°52N 23°28E 202 E7
Banskobystrický □ Slovakia 48°20N 19°0E 181 C12
Banstala India 22°31N 88°24E 124 B2
Banswara India 23°32N 74°24E 242 H6
Bantaeng Indonesia 5°32S 119°56E 235 D5
Bantaji ➜ Nigeria 8°6N 10°5E 263 D7
Bantayan Phil. 11°10N 123°43E 233 F4
Bantayan I. Phil. 11°13N 123°44E 233 F4
Banteay Prei Nokor Cambodia 11°56N 105°40E 237 G5
Banten Indonesia 6°5S 106°8E 234 D3
Banten □ Indonesia 6°30S 106°0E 234 D3
Banton I. Phil. 12°56N 122°4E 232 E4
Bantra India 22°35N 88°18E 124 B1
Bantry Ireland 51°41N 9°27W 166 E2
Bantry B. Ireland 51°37N 9°44W 166 E2
Bantva India 21°29N 70°12E 242 J4
Bantval India 12°55N 75°0E 245 H2
Banya Bulgaria 42°33N 24°50E 203 D8
Banya, Pta. de la Spain 40°33N 0°36E 196 E5
Banyak, Kepulauan Indonesia 2°10N 97°10E 234 B1
Banyalbufar Spain 39°42N 2°31E 206 B3
Banyeres de Mariola Spain 38°43N 0°38W 197 G4
Banyo Cameroon 6°52N 11°45E 263 D7
Banyoles Spain 42°16N 2°44E 196 C7
Banyuls-sur-Mer France 42°28N 3°8E 174 F7
Banyuwangi Indonesia 8°13S 114°21E 231 J17
Banz Papua N. G. 5°47S 144°37E 286 C3
Banza Dem. Rep. of the Congo 0°28N 20°10E 264 B4
Banzare Coast Antarctica 68°0S 125°0E 151 C9
Banzyville = Mobayi Dem. Rep. of the Congo 4°15N 21°8E 264 B4
Bao Ha Vietnam 22°11N 104°21E 228 F5
Bao Lac Vietnam 22°57N 105°40E 236 A5
Bao Loc Vietnam 11°32N 107°48E 237 G6
Bao'an China 22°34N 113°52E 219 a
Baocheng China 33°12N 106°56E 228 A6
Baode China 39°1N 111°5E 226 E6
Baodi China 39°38N 117°20E 227 E9
Baoding China 38°50N 115°28E 226 E8
Baoji China 34°20N 107°5E 226 G4
Baojing China 28°45N 109°41E 228 C7
Baokang China 31°54N 111°12E 229 B8
Baoro C.A.R. 5°40N 15°58E 264 A3
Baoshan Shanghai, China 31°24N 121°28E 138 A1
Baoshan Yunnan, China 25°10N 99°5E 228 E2
Baotou China 40°32N 110°2E 226 D6
Baotow = Baotou China 40°32N 110°2E 226 D6
Baoulé ➜ Mali 12°36N 9°45W 262 C3
Baoxing China 30°24N 102°50E 228 B4
Baoying China 33°17N 119°20E 227 H10
Baoyou = Ledong China 18°41N 109°5E 229 a
Bap India 27°23N 72°18E 242 F5
Bapatla India 15°55N 80°30E 245 G5
Bapaume France 50°7N 2°50E 173 B9
Baqar, Bahr el ➜ Egypt 31°7N 32°6E 251 G3
Bāqerābād Iran 33°2N 51°58E 247 C6
Ba'qūbah Iraq 33°45N 44°50E 213 F11
Baquedano Chile 23°20S 69°52W 334 A2
Bar Montenegro 42°8N 19°6E 202 D3
Bar Ukraine 49°4N 27°40E 177 D14
Bar Bigha India 25°21N 85°47E 243 G11
Bar Giyora Israel 31°45N 35°5E 123 B1
Bar Harbor U.S.A. 44°23N 68°13W 309 C19
Bar-le-Duc France 48°47N 5°10E 173 D12
Bar-sur-Aube France 48°14N 4°40E 173 D11
Bar-sur-Seine France 48°7N 4°20E 173 D11
Bara India 25°16N 81°43E 243 G9
Bâra Romania 47°2N 27°3E 183 C12
Bara Sudan 13°42N 30°22E 266 B3
Bara Banki India 26°55N 81°12E 243 F9
Baraawe Somalia 1°20N 44°8E 267 D5
Barabai Indonesia 2°32S 115°34E 235 C5
Baraboo U.S.A. 43°28N 89°45W 308 D9
Baracoa Cuba 20°20N 74°30W 321 B5
Baradā ➜ Syria 33°33N 36°34E 250 E7
Baradero Argentina 33°52S 59°29W 334 C4
Baradine Australia 30°56S 149°4E 283 A8
Baraga U.S.A. 46°47N 88°30W 308 B9
Bărăganul Romania 44°49N 27°31E 183 F12
Baragoi Kenya 1°47N 36°47E 268 B4
Barah ➜ India 27°42N 77°5E 242 F6
Barahanagar India 22°39N 88°22E 124 B2
Barahona Dom. Rep. 18°13N 71°7W 321 C5
Barail Range India 25°15N 93°20E 241 C4
Barajas Spain 40°28N 3°34W 127 B2
Barajas, Madrid ✈ (MAD) Spain 40°26N 3°34W 127 B2
Barak ➜ India 24°52N 92°34E 241 C4
Baraka Sudan 10°59N 27°59E 257 E2
Baraka ➜ Sudan 18°13N 37°35E 256 D4
Barakaldo Spain 43°18N 2°59W 196 B2
Barakar ➜ India 24°7N 86°14E 243 G12
Barakee △ Australia 31°37S 151°53E 283 A9
Barakī Afghan. 33°56N 68°55E 240 B3
Barakot India 21°33N 84°59E 243 J11
Barakpur India 22°47N 88°21E 124 A2
Baralaba Australia 24°13S 149°50E 280 C4
Baralla Spain 42°53N 7°15W 194 C3
Baralzon L. Canada 60°0N 98°3W 297 B9
Baram ➜ Malaysia 4°35N 113°58E 235 B4
Baramati India 18°11N 74°33E 244 E2
Baramba India 20°25N 85°23E 244 D7
Barameiya Sudan 18°32N 36°38E 256 D4
Baramula India 34°15N 74°20E 243 B6
Baran India 25°9N 76°40E 242 G7
Baran ➜ Pakistan 25°13N 68°17E 242 G3
Barañain Spain 42°48N 1°40W 196 C3
Baranavichy Belarus 53°10N 26°0E 177 B14
Barani Burkina Faso 13°9N 3°51W 262 C4
Baranoa Colombia 10°48N 74°55W 328 A3
Baranof U.S.A. 57°5N 134°50W 296 B2
Baranof I. U.S.A. 57°0N 135°0W 303 H14
Baranów Sandomierski Poland 50°29N 21°30E 185 H8
Baranowicze = Baranavichy Belarus 53°10N 26°0E 177 B14
Baranya □ Hungary 46°0N 18°15E 182 E3
Barão de Cocais Brazil 19°56S 43°28W 333 E3
Barão de Grajaú Brazil 6°45S 43°1W 332 C3
Barão de Melgaço Mato Grosso, Brazil 16°14S 55°52W 331 D6
Barão de Melgaço Rondônia, Brazil 11°50S 60°45W 331 C5
Baraolt Romania 46°5N 25°34E 183 D10
Baraona Spain 41°17N 2°39W 196 D2
Barapasi Indonesia 2°15S 137°5E 231 E9
Barapina = Panguna Papua N. G. 6°21S 155°25E 286 D8
Baras Phil. 13°40N 124°22E 232 E5
Barasat India 22°46N 88°31E 243 H13
Barat Daya, Kepulauan Indonesia 7°30S 128°0E 231 F7
Barataria B. U.S.A. 29°20N 89°55W 315 G10
Barauda India 23°33N 75°15E 242 H6
Baraut India 29°13N 77°7E 242 E7
Baraya Colombia 3°10N 75°4W 328 C2
Barbacan = Roxas Phil. 10°20N 119°21E 233 F2
Barbacena Brazil 21°15S 43°56W 333 F3
Barbacoas Colombia 1°45N 78°0W 328 C2
Barbados ■ W. Indies 13°10N 59°30W 323 r
Barbalha Brazil 7°19S 39°17W 332 C4
Barban Croatia 45°5N 14°2E 199 C11
Barbària, C. de Spain 38°39N 1°24E 206 D1
Barbarigo, Palazzo Venice, Italy 142 b2
Barbaros Turkey 40°54N 27°27E 203 F11
Barbas, C. W. Sahara 22°20N 16°42W 260 D1
Barbastro Spain 42°2N 0°5E 196 C5
Barbate Spain 36°13N 5°56W 195 J5
Barbaza Phil. 11°12N 122°2E 233 F4
Barbeau Pk. Canada 81°54N 75°1W 295 A16
Barber Curaçao 12°17N 69°4W 322 g
Barberini, Palazzo Rome, Italy 136 b3
Barberino di Mugello Italy 44°0N 11°15E 199 E8
Barbers Pt. U.S.A. 21°18N 158°7W 302 K13
Barberton Mpumalanga, S. Africa 25°42S 31°2E 271 C5
Barberton Ohio, U.S.A. 41°1N 81°39W 312 E3
Barberville U.S.A. 29°11N 81°26W 317 F8
Barbezieux-St-Hilaire France 45°28N 0°9W 174 C3
Barbican London, U.K. 125 a4
Barbosa Colombia 5°57N 73°37W 328 B3
Barbourville U.S.A. 36°52N 83°53W 309 G12
Barbuda W. Indies 17°30N 61°40W 322 c
Bârca Romania 43°59N 23°36E 183 G8
Barcaldine Australia 23°43S 145°6E 280 C4
Barcarena Brazil 1°30S 48°40W 332 B2
Barcarena Lisboa, Portugal 38°43N 9°16W 126 A1
Barcarena, Rib. de ➜ Portugal 38°41N 9°16W 126 A1
Barcarrota Spain 38°31N 6°51W 195 G4
Barce = Al Marj Libya 32°25N 20°30E 258 B4
Barcellona Pozzo di Gotto Italy 38°9N 15°13E 201 D8
Barcelona Spain 41°22N 2°10E 114 A2
Barcelona Venezuela 10°10N 64°40W 329 A5
Barcelona □ Spain 41°30N 2°0E 196 D7
Barcelona, El Prat ✈ (BCN) Spain 41°18N 2°5E 114 B1
Barceloneta Puerto Rico 18°27N 66°32W 321 b
Barcelonette France 44°23N 6°40E 175 D10
Barcelos Brazil 1°0S 63°0W 329 D5
Barcin Poland 52°52N 17°55E 185 F4
Barclayville Liberia 4°48N 8°10W 262 E3
Barcoo ➜ Australia 25°30S 142°50E 280 D3
Barcroft, L. U.S.A. 38°52N 77°9W 143 B2
Barcs Hungary 45°58N 17°28E 182 E2
Barczewo Poland 53°50N 20°42E 184 E7
Bärdä Azerbaijan 40°25N 47°10E 191 K8
Barda del Medio Argentina 38°45S 68°11W 336 A3
Bardaï Chad 21°25N 17°0E 259 D3
Bardas Blancas Argentina 35°49S 69°45W 334 D2
Bardawīl, Sabkhet el Egypt 31°10N 33°15E 251 G4
Barddhaman India 23°14N 87°39E 243 H12
Bardejov Slovakia 49°18N 21°15E 181 B14
Bardera = Baardheere Somalia 2°20N 42°27E 267 D5
Barðo Iceland 66°3N 19°8W 155 A7
Bárðarbunga Iceland 64°38N 17°32W 155 C9
Barðastrandarsýsla Iceland 65°40N 23°0W 155 B3
Bardi Italy 44°38N 9°44E 198 D6
Bardīyah Libya 31°45N 25°5E 258 B5
Bardoli India 21°12N 73°5E 244 D1
Bardolino Italy 45°33N 10°43E 198 C7
Bardonécchia Italy 45°5N 6°42E 198 C3
Bardsey I. U.K. 52°45N 4°47W 168 E3
Bardstown U.S.A. 37°49N 85°28W 311 G11
Bare Ethiopia 4°37N 42°43E 267 D5
Bareilly India 28°22N 79°27E 243 E8
Barela India 23°6N 80°3E 243 H9
Barellan Australia 34°16S 146°24E 283 C7
Barentin France 49°33N 0°58E 172 C7
Barenton France 48°38N 0°50W 172 D6
Barents Sea Arctic 73°0N 39°0E 150 B9
Barentsøya Svalbard 78°25N 21°20E 154 B13
Barentu Eritrea 15°2N 37°35E 257 D4
Barfleur France 49°40N 1°17W 172 C5
Barfleur, Pte. de France 49°42N 1°16W 172 C5
Barfurush = Bābol Iran 36°40N 52°50E 247 B7
Barga Italy 44°4N 10°29E 198 D7
Bargaal Somalia 11°25N 51°0E 267 B7
Bargara Australia 24°50S 152°25E 280 C5
Bargarh India 21°20N 83°37E 244 D6
Bargas Spain 39°56N 4°3W 194 F6
Barge Italy 44°43N 7°20E 198 D4
Bargi Dam India 22°59N 80°0E 244 C5
Bargo Australia 34°18S 150°35E 283 C9
Bargteheide Germany 53°44N 10°14E 178 B6
Barguzin Russia 53°37N 109°37E 215 D11
Barh India 25°29N 85°46E 243 G11
Barhaj India 26°18N 83°44E 243 F10
Barham Australia 35°36S 144°8E 282 C6
Barharwa India 24°52N 87°47E 243 G12
Barhi India 24°15N 85°25E 243 G11
Bari Dem. Rep. of the Congo 3°20N 19°25E 264 B3
Bari India 26°39N 77°39E 242 F7
Bari Italy 41°8N 16°51E 201 A9
Bari □ Somalia 10°0N 50°0E 267 B6
Bari Doab Pakistan 30°20N 73°0E 242 D5
Bari Sadri India 24°28N 74°30E 242 G6
Bari Sardo Italy 39°50N 9°38E 200 C2
Bariadi Tanzania 2°48S 34°0E 268 C3
Barīdī, Ra's Si. Arabia 24°17N 37°31E 246 E3
Barīm Yemen 12°39N 43°25E 248 D3
Barima ➜ Guyana 8°33N 60°25W 329 B5
Barima-Waini □ Guyana 7°34N 59°40W 329 B6
Barinas Venezuela 8°36N 70°15W 328 B3
Barinas □ Venezuela 8°10N 69°50W 328 B4
Baring U.S.A. 40°15N 92°12W 310 D4
Baring, C. Canada 70°0N 117°30W 294 D8
Baringa Dem. Rep. of the Congo 0°45N 20°52E 264 B4
Baringo Kenya 0°38N 36°16E 266 D4
Baringo □ Kenya 0°40N 36°0E 268 B4
Baringo, L. Kenya 0°47N 36°16E 268 B4
Barinitas Venezuela 8°45N 70°25W 328 B3
Baripada India 21°57N 86°45E 244 D8
Bariri Brazil 22°4S 48°44W 333 F2
Bârîs Egypt 24°42N 30°31E 256 C3
Barisal = Barishal Bangla. 22°45N 90°20E 241 D3
Barisan, Pegunungan Indonesia 3°30S 102°15E 234 C2
Barishal Bangla. 22°45N 90°20E 241 D3
Barishal □ Bangla. 22°45N 90°20E 241 D3
Barit I. Phil. 18°51N 121°15E 232 B3
Barito ➜ Indonesia 4°0S 114°50E 235 C4
Baritú △ Argentina 23°43S 64°40W 334 A3
Barjac France 44°20N 4°22E 175 D8
Barjols France 43°34N 6°2E 175 E10
Barjūj, Wadi ➜ Libya 25°26N 12°12E 258 C2
Bark L. Canada 45°27N 77°51W 312 A7
Barka = Baraka ➜ Sudan 18°13N 37°35E 256 D4
Barkā' Oman 23°40N 58°0E 249 B7
Barkakana India 23°37N 85°29E 243 H11
Barkal, J. Sudan 18°32N 31°50E 256 D3
Barkald Norway 61°59N 10°53E 164 C7
Barkam China 31°51N 102°28E 228 B4
Barker U.S.A. 43°20N 78°33W 312 C6
Barking U.K. 51°32N 0°5E 125 A4
Barkingside U.K. 51°35N 0°4E 125 A4
Barkley, L. U.S.A. 37°1N 88°14W 315 C10
Barkley Sound Canada 48°50N 125°10W 296 D3
Barkly East S. Africa 30°58S 27°33E 270 D4
Barkly Homestead Australia 19°52S 135°50E 280 B2
Barkly Tableland Australia 17°50S 136°40E 280 B2
Barkly West S. Africa 28°5S 24°31E 270 C3
Barkol Kazak Zizhixian China 43°37N 93°2E 218 C7
Barla Dağı Turkey 38°5N 30°40E 205 C12
Bârlad Romania 46°15N 27°38E 183 D12
Bârlad ➜ Romania 45°38N 27°32E 183 E12
Barlee, L. Australia 29°15S 119°30E 279 E2
Barlee, Mt. Australia 24°38S 128°13E 279 D4
Barletta Italy 41°19N 16°17E 201 A9
Barlinek Poland 53°0N 15°15E 185 F2
Barlovento Cabo Verde 17°0N 25°0W 153 j
Barlovento Canary Is. 28°48N 17°48W 153 e1
Barlow L. Canada 62°0N 103°0W 297 A8
Barmedman Australia 34°9S 147°21E 283 C7
Barmer India 25°45N 71°20E 242 G4
Barmera Australia 34°15S 140°28E 282 C4
Barmouth U.K. 52°44N 4°4W 168 E3
Barmstedt Germany 53°47N 9°46E 178 B5
Barn, The St. Helena 15°55S 5°40W 153 h
Barna ➜ India 25°21N 83°3E 243 G10
Barnagar India 23°7N 75°19E 242 H6
Barnala India 30°23N 75°33E 242 D6
Barnard ➜ Australia 31°34S 151°25E 283 A9
Barnard Castle U.K. 54°33N 1°55W 168 C6
Barnato Australia 31°38S 145°0E 283 A6
Barnaul Russia 53°20N 83°40E 217 B10
Barnes N.S.W., Australia 36°2S 144°49E 282 D6
Barnes London, U.K. 51°28N 0°14W 125 B2
Barnesville Ga., U.S.A. 33°3N 84°9W 316 B5
Barnesville Minn., U.S.A. 46°43N 96°28W 308 B5
Barnet U.K. 51°39N 0°11W 125 A2
Barnet □ U.K. 51°38N 0°9W 169 F7
Barneveld Neths. 52°7N 5°36E 170 B5
Barneville-Cartevert France 49°23N 1°46W 172 C5
Barnhart U.S.A. 31°8N 101°10W 314 F4
Barnsley U.K. 53°34N 1°27W 168 D6
Barnstable U.S.A. 41°42N 70°18W 309 E18
Barnstaple U.K. 51°5N 4°4W 169 F3
Barnstaple Bay = Bideford Bay U.K. 51°5N 4°20W 169 F3
Barnum B. Palau 7°6N 134°15E 288 c
Barnwell U.S.A. 33°15N 81°23W 316 B8
Baro Nigeria 8°35N 6°18E 263 D6
Baro ➜ Ethiopia 8°26N 33°13E 257 F3
Barobo Phil. 8°33N 126°7E 233 G6
Baroda = Vadodara India 22°20N 73°10E 242 H5
Baroda India 25°29N 76°35E 242 G7
Baroe S. Africa 33°13S 24°33E 270 D3
Baron Empain Palace Egypt 30°5N 31°20E 117 A2
Baron Ra. Australia 23°30S 127°45E 278 D4
Barong China 31°3N 99°20E 228 B2
Barora Solomon Is. 7°30S 158°20E 287 L10
Barora Ite Solomon Is. 7°36S 158°24E 287 L10
Barotse = Western □ Zambia 15°0S 24°4E 265 F4
Barotseland Zambia 15°0S 24°0E 265 F4
Barouéli Mali 13°4N 6°50W 262 C3
Barpali India 21°11N 83°35E 244 D6
Barpathar India 26°17N 93°53E 241 B4
Barpeta India 26°20N 91°10E 241 B3
Barqa Libya 27°0N 23°0E 258 B4
Barqin Libya 27°33N 13°34E 258 C2
Barques, Pt. Aux U.S.A. 44°4N 82°58W 312 B2
Barquisimeto Venezuela 10°4N 69°19W 328 A4
Barr, Ras el Egypt 31°32N 31°50E 256 H7
Barr Smith Range Australia 27°4S 120°20E 279 E3
Barra Brazil 11°5S 43°10W 332 D3
Barra Gambia 13°28N 16°32W 262 C1
Barra W. Isles, U.K. 57°0N 7°29W 167 E1
Barra, Pta. Mozam. 23°48S 35°32E 271 B6
Barra, Sd. of U.K. 57°4N 7°25W 167 D1
Barra Andai Pakistan 24°47N 66°59E 123 B2
Barra Bonita = Ibaiti Brazil 23°50S 50°10W 333 F1
Barra da Estiva Brazil 13°38S 41°19W 333 D3
Barra de Navidad Mexico 19°12N 104°41W 318 D4
Barra de São Manuel Brazil 7°19S 58°5W 331 B6
Barra do Bugres Brazil 15°0S 57°11W 331 D6
Barra do Corda Brazil 5°30S 45°10W 332 C2
Barra do Dande Angola 8°28S 13°22E 265 D2
Barra do Garças Brazil 15°54S 52°16W 331 D7
Barra do Mendes Brazil 11°43S 42°4W 333 D3
Barra do Piraí Brazil 22°30S 43°50W 333 F3
Barra Falsa, Pta. da Mozam. 22°58S 35°37E 271 B6
Barra Funda Brazil 23°31S 46°39W 137 B2
Barra Hd. U.K. 56°47N 7°40W 167 E1
Barra Mansa Brazil 22°35S 44°12W 333 F3
Barraba Australia 30°21S 150°35E 283 A9
Barracão do Barreto Brazil 8°48S 58°24W 331 B6
Barracas Argentina 34°39S 58°24W 117 B2
Barracas al Sur = Avellaneda Argentina 34°40S 58°22W 117 C2
Barrackpur = Barakpur India 22°47N 88°21E 124 A2
Barrafranca Italy 37°22N 14°12E 201 E7
Barrage de Petit-Saut Fr. Guiana 5°3N 53°3W 329 B7
Barrāmīya Egypt 25°4N 33°47E 256 B3
Barranca Lima, Peru 10°45S 77°50W 330 C2
Barranca Loreto, Peru 4°50S 76°50W 328 D2
Barranca del Cobre △ Mexico 27°18N 107°40W 318 B3
Barrancabermeja Colombia 7°0N 73°50W 328 B3
Barrancas Colombia 10°57N 72°50W 328 A3
Barrancas Venezuela 8°55N 62°5W 329 B5
Barranco Peru 12°9S 77°2W 124 B2
Barrancos Pt. Trin. & Tob. 10°31N 61°28W 323 t
Barrancos Portugal 38°10N 6°58W 195 G4
Barranqueras Argentina 27°30S 59°0W 334 B4
Barranquilla Colombia 11°0N 74°50W 328 A3
Barranquitas Puerto Rico 18°11N 66°19W 321 b
Barras Brazil 4°15S 42°18W 332 B3
Barras Colombia 1°45S 73°13W 328 D3
Barraute Canada 48°26N 77°38W 298 C4
Barre Mass., U.S.A. 42°25N 72°6W 313 D12
Barre Vt., U.S.A. 44°12N 72°30W 313 B12
Barre de L'Isle Ridge St. Lucia 13°55N 60°58W 323 m
Barreal Argentina 31°33S 69°28W 334 C2
Barrei Ethiopia 6°10N 42°49E 267 C5
Barreiras Brazil 12°8S 45°0W 333 D3
Barreirinha Brazil 2°47S 57°3W 329 D6
Barreirinhas Brazil 2°30S 42°50W 332 B3
Barreiro Portugal 38°39N 9°5W 126 B2
Barreiros Brazil 8°49S 35°12W 332 C4
Barrême France 43°57N 6°23E 175 E10
Barren, Nosy Madag. 18°25S 43°40E 272 B1
Barren I. India 12°16N 93°51E 245 H11
Barren Is. U.S.A. 58°55N 152°15W 303 G9
Barreto Brazil 22°50S 43°15W 132 B2
Barretos Brazil 20°30S 48°35W 333 F2
Barrhead Canada 54°10N 114°24W 296 C6
Barrie Canada 44°24N 79°40W 312 B5
Barrier, C. N.Z. 36°25S 175°32E 284 C4
Barrier Ra. N.S.W., Australia 31°0S 141°30E 282 A4
Barrier Ra. Otago, N.Z. 44°15S 169°32E 285 E4
Barrier Ra. W. Coast, N.Z. 44°30S 168°30E 285 E3
Barrière Canada 51°12N 120°7W 296 C4
Barrière-la-Croix Martinique 14°27N 60°51W 322 j
Barrigada Guam 13°28N 144°48E 302 d
Barrineau Park U.S.A. 30°42N 87°26W 317 E2
Barrington U.S.A. 41°44N 71°18W 313 E13
Barrington, I. = Santa Fé, I. Ecuador 0°49S 90°5W 330 a
Barrington L. Canada 56°55N 100°15W 297 B8
Barrington Tops Australia 32°6S 151°28E 283 B9
Barrington Tops △ Australia 32°4S 151°25E 283 B9
Barringun Australia 29°1S 145°41E 281 D4
Barrit-Luluno = Luba Phil. 17°19N 120°42E 232 C3
Barron U.S.A. 45°24N 91°51W 308 C8
Barrouallie St. Vincent 13°14N 61°17W 323 n
Barroui = Salisbury Dominica 15°26N 61°27W 323 k
Barrow U.S.A. 71°18N 156°47W 303 A8
Barrow ➜ Ireland 52°25N 6°58W 166 D5
Barrow, Pt. U.S.A. 71°23N 156°29W 303 A8
Barrow Creek Australia 21°30S 133°55E 280 C1
Barrow I. Australia 20°45S 115°20E 278 D2
Barrow-in-Furness U.K. 54°7N 3°14W 168 C4
Barrow Pt. Australia 14°20S 144°40E 280 A3
Barrow Ra. Australia 26°0S 127°40E 279 E4
Barrow Str. Canada 74°20N 95°0W 295 C13
Barruecopardo Spain 41°4N 6°40W 194 D4
Barruelo de Santullán Spain 42°54N 4°17W 194 C6
Barry V. of Glam., U.K. 51°24N 3°16W 169 F4
Barry Ill., U.S.A. 39°42N 91°2W 310 E5
Barry's Bay Canada 45°29N 77°41W 312 A7
Barsalogho Burkina Faso 13°25N 1°3W 263 C4
Barsat Pakistan 36°10N 72°45E 243 A5
Barsham Syria 35°21N 40°33E 213 E9
Barshatas Kazakhstan 48°10N 78°39E 217 C9
Barsi India 18°10N 75°50E 244 E2
Barsinghausen Germany 52°18N 9°28E 178 C5
Barsoi India 25°48N 87°57E 241 C1
Barstow U.S.A. 34°54N 117°1W 307 L9
Bartala India 22°32N 88°15E 124 B1
Bartenstein = Bartoszyce Poland 54°15N 20°55E 184 D7
Bartfeld = Bardejov Slovakia 49°18N 21°15E 181 B14
Barth Germany 54°22N 12°42E 178 A8
Bartica Guyana 6°25N 58°40W 329 B6
Bartın Turkey 41°38N 32°21E 212 B5
Bartle Frere Australia 17°27S 145°50E 280 B4
Bartlesville U.S.A. 36°45N 95°59W 314 C7
Bartlett Calif., U.S.A. 36°29N 118°2W 306 J8
Bartlett Tenn., U.S.A. 35°12N 89°52W 315 D10
Bartlett, L. Canada 63°5N 118°20W 296 A5
Bartolbaai Curaçao 12°20N 69°2W 322 g
Bartolo = Betanzos Bolivia 19°34S 65°27W 331 D4
Bartolomeu Dias Mozam. 21°10S 35°8E 269 G4
Barton Phil. 10°24N 119°8E 233 F2
Barton Vt., U.S.A. 44°45N 72°11W 313 B12
Barton Park Australia 33°56S 151°9E 139 B1
Barton-upon-Humber U.K. 53°41N 0°25W 168 D7
Bartonville U.S.A. 40°39N 89°39W 310 D7
Bartoszyce Poland 54°15N 20°55E 184 D7
Bartow Fla., U.S.A. 27°54N 81°50W 317 H8
Bartow Ga., U.S.A. 32°53N 82°29W 316 C7
Bartycki Poland 52°10N 21°6E 143 C2
Barú, I. de Colombia 10°15N 75°35W 328 A2
Barú, Volcan Panama 8°55N 82°35W 320 E3
Barumba Dem. Rep. of the Congo 1°3N 23°37E 268 B1
Barumbu Dem. Rep. of the Congo 1°14N 23°31E 264 B4
Barúmini Italy 39°42N 8°59E 200 C1
Barung, Nusa Indonesia 8°30S 113°30E 235 D4
Barus Indonesia 2°0N 98°24E 234 B1
Baruth Germany 52°3N 13°30E 178 C9
Baruun Urt Mongolia 46°46N 113°15E 219 B11
Baruunsuu Mongolia 43°43N 105°35E 226 C3
Barvinkove Ukraine 48°57N 37°0E 189 H9
Bärwalde = Barwice Poland 53°44N 16°21E 184 E3
Barwani India 22°2N 74°57E 242 H6
Barwice Poland 53°44N 16°21E 184 E3
Barwick U.S.A. 30°54N 83°44W 316 E6
Barxudarlı Azerbaijan 41°0N 45°14E 213 B11
Barycz ➜ Poland 51°42N 16°15E 185 G3
Barysaw Belarus 54°17N 28°28E 177 A15
Barysh Russia 53°39N 47°8E 190 D8
Barzān Iraq 36°55N 44°3E 246 B5
Bârzava Romania 46°7N 21°59E 182 D6
Bas du Fort Guadeloupe 16°13N 61°30W 322 e
Bas-Kouilou Congo 4°28S 11°42E 265 C2
Bas-Rhin □ France 48°40N 7°30E 173 D14
Bas-Sassandra □ Côte d'Ivoire 5°30N 7°0W 262 D3
Bas-Uélé □ Dem. Rep. of the Congo 3°30N 25°0E 264 B4
Bašaid Serbia 45°38N 20°25E 182 E5
Bāsa'īdū Iran 26°35N 55°20E 247 E7
Basal Pakistan 33°33N 72°13E 242 C5
Basankusu Dem. Rep. of the Congo 1°5N 19°50E 264 B3
Basarabeasca Moldova 46°21N 28°58E 183 D13
Basarabi Romania 44°10N 28°26E 183 F13
Basarabia = Bessarabiya Moldova 47°0N 28°10E 177 E15
Basauri Spain 43°13N 2°53W 196 B2
Basavakalyan India 17°52N 76°57E 244 F3
Basawa Afghan. 34°15N 70°50E 242 B4
Basco Phil. 20°27N 121°58E 232 A3
Bascuñán, C. Chile 28°52S 71°35W 334 B1
Basekpio Dem. Rep. of the Congo 4°43N 24°36E 264 B4
Basel Switz. 47°35N 7°35E 179 H3
Basel-Landschaft □ Switz. 47°26N 7°45E 179 H3
Basento ➜ Italy 40°20N 16°49E 201 B9
Baserah Indonesia 0°25S 101°43E 234 C2
Basey Phil. 11°17N 125°4E 233 F5
Bashākerd, Kūhhā-ye Iran 26°42N 58°35E 247 E8
Bashanta = Gorodovikovsk Russia 46°8N 41°58E 191 G5
Bashaw Canada 52°35N 112°58W 296 C6
Bāshī Iran 28°41N 51°4E 247 D6
Bashi Channel Asia 21°25N 121°30E 225 E2
Bashkand = Artsvashen Armenia 40°38N 45°30E 213 B11
Bashkir Republic = Bashkortostan □ Russia 54°0N 57°0E 186 D10
Bashkiriya △ Russia 52°58N 56°30E 216 B5
Bashkortostan □ Russia 54°0N 57°0E 186 D10
Bashtanivka Ukraine 45°46N 29°29E 183 E14
Basibasy Madag. 22°10S 43°40E 272 C1
Basilaki I. Papua N. G. 10°35S 151°0E 286 F6
Basilan □ Phil. 6°33N 122°4E 233 H3
Basilan I. Phil. 6°35N 122°0E 233 H4
Basilan Str. Phil. 6°50N 122°0E 233 H4
Basildon U.K. 51°34N 0°28E 169 F8
Basilé Eq. Guin. 3°42N 8°48E 263 E6
Basilé, Pico de Eq. Guin. 3°36N 8°49E 263 E6
Basilicata □ Italy 40°30N 16°30E 201 B9
Basim = Washim India 20°3N 77°0E 244 D3
Basin U.S.A. 44°23N 108°2W 304 D9
Basinger U.S.A. 27°23N 81°2W 317 H8
Basingstoke U.K. 51°15N 1°5W 169 F6
Basirhat Bangla. 22°40N 88°54E 241 D2
Basīt, Ra's al Syria 35°51N 35°48E 250 C6
Baška Croatia 44°58N 14°45E 199 D11
Başkale Turkey 38°2N 43°59E 213 C10
Baskatong, Rés. Canada 46°46N 75°50W 298 C4
Basle = Basel Switz. 47°35N 7°35E 179 H3
Basle Euroairport ✈ (BSL) France 47°36N 7°33E 173 E14
Başmakçı Turkey 37°54N 30°1E 205 D12
Basmat India 19°15N 77°12E 244 E3
Basoda India 23°52N 77°54E 242 H7
Basoko Dem. Rep. of the Congo 1°16N 23°40E 264 B4
Basongo Dem. Rep. of the Congo 4°15S 20°20E 265 C4
Basora, Pta. Aruba 12°25N 69°51W 322 f
Basque, Côte France 43°50N 2°0W 174 E2
Basque, Pays France 43°15N 1°20W 174 E2
Basque Provinces = País Vasco □ Spain 42°50N 2°45W 196 C2
Basra = Al Başrah Iraq 30°30N 47°50E 246 D5
Bass, Îs. de French Polynesia 27°55S 143°26W 289 f
Bass Str. Australia 39°15S 146°30E 281 F4
Bassae Greece 37°26N 21°53E 204 D3
Bassano Canada 50°48N 112°20W 296 C6
Bassano del Grappa Italy 45°46N 11°44E 199 C8
Bassar Togo 9°19N 0°57E 263 D5
Bassas da India Ind. Oc. 22°0S 39°0E 269 G4
Basse-Kotto □ C.A.R. 5°0N 21°30E 264 A4
Basse-Pointe Martinique 14°52N 61°8W 322 j
Basse Santa-Su Gambia 13°13N 14°15W 262 C2
Basse-Terre Guadeloupe 16°0N 61°44W 322 e
Basse Terre Trin. & Tob. 10°7N 61°19W 323 t
Bassein = Pathein Myanmar 16°45N 94°30E 241 G5
Basses, Pte. des Guadeloupe 15°52N 61°17W 322 e
Basses-Alpes = Alpes-de-Haute-Provence □ France 44°8N 6°10E 175 D10
Basses-Pyrénées = Pyrénées-Atlantiques □ France 43°10N 0°50W 174 E3
Basseterre St. Kitts & Nevis 17°17N 62°43W 322 d
Bassett U.S.A. 42°35N 99°32W 308 D4
Bassi India 30°44N 76°21E 242 D7
Bassigny France 48°0N 5°30E 173 E12
Bassikounou Mauritania 15°55N 6°1W 262 B3
Bassila Benin 9°1N 1°46E 263 D5
Bassum Germany 52°50N 8°42E 178 C4
Båstad Sweden 56°25N 12°51E 163 H6
Bastak Iran 27°15N 54°25E 247 E7
Baştām Iran 36°29N 55°4E 247 B7
Bastar India 19°15N 81°40E 244 E5
Bastelica France 42°1N 9°3E 175 F13
Basti India 26°52N 82°55E 243 F10
Bastia France 42°40N 9°30E 175 F13
Bastille, Place de la Paris, France 134 c5
Bastogne Belgium 50°1N 5°43E 170 D5
Bastrop La., U.S.A. 32°47N 91°55W 314 E9
Bastrop Tex., U.S.A. 30°7N 97°19W 314 F6
Basu Indonesia 0°18S 103°52E 234 C2
Basud Phil. 14°4N 122°58E 232 D4
Basuo = Dongfang China 18°50N 108°33E 229 a
Basus Egypt 30°7N 31°12E 117 A2
Basutoland = Lesotho ■ Africa 29°40S 28°0E 271 C4
Başyayla Turkey 36°45N 32°40E 250 B3
Bat al Khutm & Al 'Ayn Oman 23°16N 56°44E 249 B7
Bat-ongan Caves Phil. 12°20N 123°15E 232 E4
Bat Yam Israel 32°2N 34°44E 251 F5
Bata Eq. Guin. 1°57N 9°50E 264 B1
Bata Romania 46°1N 22°4E 182 D7
Bataan □ Phil. 14°40N 120°25E 232 D3
Bataan △ Phil. 14°45N 120°27E 232 D3
Batabanó Cuba 22°41N 82°18W 320 B3
Batabanó, G. de Cuba 22°30N 82°30W 320 B3
Batac Phil. 18°3N 120°34E 232 B3
Batagai Russia 67°38N 134°38E 215 C14
Batajnica Serbia 44°54N 20°17E 202 B4
Batak Bulgaria 41°57N 24°12E 203 E8
Batakan Indonesia 4°5S 114°38E 235 C4
Batala India 31°48N 75°12E 242 D6
Batalha Portugal 39°40N 8°50W 194 F2
Batalpashinsk = Cherkessk Russia 44°15N 42°5E 191 H6
Batam Indonesia 1°10N 104°2E 237 d
Batama Dem. Rep. of the Congo 0°58N 26°33E 268 B2
Batamay Russia 63°30N 129°15E 215 C13
Batan I. Albay, Phil. 13°15N 124°0E 232 E4
Batan I. Batanes, Phil. 20°26N 121°58E 232 A3
Batan Is. Phil. 20°30N 122°0E 232 A3
Batanagar India 22°31N 88°15E 124 B1
Batanes □ Phil. 20°40N 121°55E 232 A3
Batang Sichuan, China 30°1N 99°0E 228 B2
Batang Indonesia 6°55S 109°45E 235 D3
Batang Ai △ Malaysia 1°32N 112°2E 235 B4
Batang Gadis △ Indonesia 0°28N 99°12E 234 B1
Batanga Gabon 0°21S 9°18E 264 C1
Batangafo C.A.R. 7°25N 18°20E 264 A3
Batangas Phil. 13°35N 121°10E 232 E3
Batangas □ Phil. 13°40N 121°5E 232 E3
Batanta Indonesia 0°55S 130°40E 231 E8
Batarasa Phil. 8°40N 117°37E 233 G1
Batas I. Phil. 11°10N 119°36E 233 F2
Batatais Brazil 20°54S 47°37W 335 A6
Batavia = Jakarta Indonesia 6°9S 106°52E 122 A2
Batavia Ill., U.S.A. 41°51N 88°19W 311 C8
Batavia N.Y., U.S.A. 43°0N 78°11W 312 D6
Batavia Ohio, U.S.A. 39°5N 84°11W 311 E12
Bataysk Russia 47°3N 39°45E 189 J10
Batbakara = Amankeldi Kazakhstan 50°10N 65°10E 216 B7
Batchelor Australia 13°4S 131°1E 278 B5
Batdambang Cambodia 13°7N 103°12E 236 F4
Batéké, Plateau Congo 3°30S 15°45E 264 C3
Batemans B. Australia 35°40S 150°12E 283 C9
Batemans Bay Australia 35°44S 150°11E 283 C9
Batesburg-Leesville U.S.A. 33°54N 81°33W 316 B8
Batesville Ark., U.S.A. 35°46N 91°39W 314 D9
Batesville Ind., U.S.A. 39°18N 85°13W 311 E11
Batesville Miss., U.S.A. 34°19N 89°57W 315 D10
Batesville Tex., U.S.A. 28°58N 99°37W 314 G5
Bath Ont., Canada 44°11N 76°47W 313 B8
Bath St. Kitts & Nevis 17°8N 62°37W 322 d
Bath Bath & N.E. Somerset, U.K. 51°23N 2°22W 169 F5
Bath Maine, U.S.A. 43°55N 69°49W 309 D19
Bath N.Y., U.S.A. 42°20N 77°19W 312 D5
Bath & North East Somerset □ U.K. 51°21N 2°27W 169 F5
Bath Beach U.S.A. 40°36N 74°0W 132 C1
Bath I. Pakistan 24°49N 67°1E 123 B2
Batha □ Chad 14°0N 19°30E 259 F3
Batha ➜ Chad 12°47N 17°34E 259 F3
Batheay Cambodia 11°59N 104°57E 237 G5
Bathsheba Barbados 13°13N 59°32W 323 r
Bathurst = Banjul Gambia 13°28N 16°40W 262 C1
Bathurst N.S.W., Australia 33°25S 149°31E 283 B8
Bathurst N.B., Canada 47°37N 65°43W 299 C6
Bathurst Eastern Cape, S. Africa 33°30S 26°50E 270 D4
Bathurst, C. Canada 70°34N 128°0W 294 C6
Bathurst B. Australia 14°16S 144°25E 280 A3
Bathurst Harb. Australia 43°15S 146°10E 281 G4
Bathurst I. N. Terr., Australia 11°30S 130°10E 278 B5
Bathurst I. Nunavut, Canada 76°0N 100°30W 295 B11
Bathurst Inlet Canada 66°50N 108°1W 294 D10
Bati Ethiopia 11°10N 40°0E 257 E5
Batie Burkina Faso 9°53N 2°53W 262 D4
Batiki Fiji 17°48S 179°10E 287 A2
Batir West Bank 31°43N 35°8E 123 B1
Batken Kyrgyzstan 40°3N 70°50E 217 D8
Batken □ Kyrgyzstan 39°50N 71°0E 217 E8
Batlow Australia 35°31S 148°9E 283 C8
Batman Turkey 37°55N 41°5E 213 D9
Batn al Ghūl Jordan 29°36N 35°56E 251 J6
Batna Algeria 35°34N 6°15E 261 A6
Batna □ Algeria 35°30N 5°55E 261 A6
Batnfjordsøra Norway 62°53N 7°42E 164 B4
Bato Catanduanes, Phil. 13°36N 124°18E 232 E5
Bato Leyte, Phil. 10°13N 124°48E 233 F5
Bato Bato Phil. 5°6N 119°49E 233 J2
Batoala Gabon 0°48N 13°27E 264 B2
Batobato = San Isidro Phil. 6°50N 126°5E 233 H6
Batočina Serbia 44°7N 21°5E 202 B5
Batoka Zambia 16°45S 27°15E 269 F2
Baton Rouge U.S.A. 30°27N 91°11W 314 F9
Batong, Ko Thailand 6°32N 99°12E 237 J2
Bátonyterenye Hungary 47°59N 19°50E 182 C4
Batopilas Mexico 27°1N 107°44W 318 B3
Batouri Cameroon 4°30N 14°25E 264 B2
Batovany = Partizánske Slovakia 48°38N 18°23E 181 C11
Båtsfjord Norway 70°38N 29°39E 160 A23
Batsi Greece 37°52N 24°47E 204 D6
Battambang = Batdambang Cambodia 13°7N 103°12E 236 F4
Battersea U.K. 51°28N 0°9W 125 B3
Battery Park New York, U.S.A. 132 f1
Batti Malv India 8°50N 92°51E 245 K11
Batticaloa Sri Lanka 7°43N 81°45E 245 L5
Battipáglia Italy 40°37N 14°58E 201 B7
Battle U.K. 50°55N 0°30E 169 G8
Battle ➜ Canada 52°43N 108°15W 297 C7
Battle Creek U.S.A. 42°19N 85°11W 311 B11
Battle Ground U.S.A. 45°47N 122°32W 306 E4
Battle Harbour Canada 52°16N 55°35W 299 B8

Battle Lake U.S.A. 46°17N 95°43W 308 B6
Battle Mountain U.S.A. 40°38N 116°56W 304 F5
Battlefields Zimbabwe 18°37S 29°47E 269 F2
Battleford Canada 52°45N 108°15W 297 C7
Battonya Hungary 46°16N 21°3E 182 D6
Batu Ethiopia 6°55N 39°45E 257 F4
Batu Malaysia 3°15N 101°40E 237 L3
Batu, Bukit Malaysia 2°16N 113°43E 235 B4
Batu, Kepulauan Indonesia 0°30S 98°25E 234 C1
Batu Bora, Bukit Malaysia 2°43N 114°43E 235 B4
Batu Ferringhi Malaysia 5°28N 100°15E 237 c
Batu Gajah Malaysia 4°28N 101°3E 237 K3
Batu Is. = Batu, Kepulauan Indonesia 0°30S 98°25E 234 C1
Batu Pahat Malaysia 1°50N 102°56E 237 M4
Batu Puteh Malaysia 5°25N 117°55E 235 A5
Batu Puteh, Gunung Malaysia 4°15N 101°31E 237 K3
Batuan Phil. 12°25N 123°46E 232 E4
Batuata Indonesia 6°12S 122°42E 231 F6
Batugondang, Tanjung Indonesia 8°6S 114°29E 231 J17
Batukaru, Gunung Indonesia 8°20S 115°5E 231 J18
Batulaki Phil. 5°34N 125°19E 233 J5
Batuli = San Isidro Phil. 6°50N 126°5E 233 H6
Batumi Georgia 41°39N 41°44E 191 K5
Batuputih Indonesia 1°24N 118°28E 235 B5
Batur, Gunung Indonesia 8°14S 115°23E 231 J18
Batura Sar Pakistan 36°30N 74°31E 243 A6
Baturaja Indonesia 4°11S 104°15E 234 C2
Baturité Brazil 4°28S 38°45W 332 B4
Baturiti Indonesia 8°19S 115°11E 231 J18
Batusangkar Indonesia 0°27S 100°35E 234 C2
Batys Qazaqstan □ Kazakhstan 50°0N 50°0E 216 C3
Bau Malaysia 1°25N 110°9E 235 B4
Bauang Phil. 16°31N 120°20E 232 C3
Baubau Indonesia 5°25S 122°38E 231 F6
Baucau Timor-Leste 8°27S 126°27E 231 F7
Bauchi Nigeria 10°22N 9°48E 263 C6
Bauchi □ Nigeria 10°30N 10°0E 263 C7
Baud France 47°52N 3°1W 172 E3
Bauda India 20°50N 84°25E 244 D7
Baudette U.S.A. 48°43N 94°36W 308 A6
Bauer, C. Australia 32°44S 134°4E 281 E1
Bauerwitz = Baborów Poland 50°7N 18°1E 185 H5
Bauguen = Salcedo Phil. 11°9N 125°40E 233 F5
Bauhinia Australia 24°35S 149°18E 280 C4
Baukau = Baucau Timor-Leste 8°27S 126°27E 231 F7
Bauko Phil. 17°0N 120°52E 232 C3
Baulai → Bangla. 24°22N 91°1E 241 C3
Bauld, C. Canada 51°38N 55°26W 295 G20
Bauman Russia 55°45N 37°40E 129 B3
Baume-les-Dames France 47°22N 6°22E 173 E13
Baumgarten Austria 48°12N 16°17E 142 A1
Baunatal Germany 51°14N 9°24E 178 D5
Baunei Italy 40°2N 9°40E 200 B2
Baure Nigeria 12°52N 8°50E 263 C6
Baures Bolivia 13°35S 63°35W 331 C5
Bauru Brazil 22°10S 49°0W 335 A6
Baús Brazil 18°22S 52°47W 331 D7
Bausi India 24°48N 87°1E 243 G12
Bauska Latvia 56°24N 24°15E 184 B11
Bautino Kazakhstan 44°35N 50°14E 191 H10
Bautzen Germany 51°10N 14°26E 178 D10
Bauya S. Leone 8°12N 12°38W 262 D2
Bavānāt Iran 30°28N 53°27E 247 D7
Bavanište Serbia 44°49N 20°55E 182 F5
Bavaria = Bayern □ Germany 48°50N 12°0E 179 G7
Båven Sweden 59°0N 16°56E 162 E10
Bavispe → Mexico 29°15N 109°11W 318 B3
Baw Baw △ Australia 37°50S 146°17E 283 D7
Bawal Indonesia 7°52S 111°13E 235 D4
Bawan Indonesia 1°42S 113°55E 235 C4
Bawdwin Myanmar 23°5N 97°20E 241 D6
Bawean Indonesia 5°46S 112°35E 235 D4
Bawku Ghana 11°3N 0°19W 263 C4
Bawlakhe Myanmar 19°11N 97°21E 241 F6
Bawolung China 28°50N 101°16E 228 C3
Bawomataluwo Indonesia 0°38N 97°44E 234 B1
Baxley U.S.A. 31°47N 82°21W 316 D7
Baxter Iowa, U.S.A. 41°49N 93°9W 310 C3
Baxter Minn., U.S.A. 46°21N 94°17W 308 B6
Baxter Springs U.S.A. 37°2N 94°44W 308 G6
Baxter State ⌂ U.S.A. 46°5N 68°57W 309 B19
Bay □ Somalia 3°0N 43°30E 267 D5
Bay, L. U.S.A. 28°25N 81°34W 133 A2
Bay, Laguna de Phil. 14°20N 121°11E 232 D3
Bay City Mich., U.S.A. 43°36N 83°54W 309 D12
Bay City Tex., U.S.A. 28°59N 95°58W 314 G7
Bay Harbor Islands U.S.A. 25°53N 80°7W 129 C3
Bay Hill U.S.A. 28°28N 81°30W 133 B1
Bay Is. = Bahía, Is. de la Honduras 16°45N 86°15W 320 C2
Bay Minette U.S.A. 30°53N 87°46W 315 F11
Bay of Plenty □ N.Z. 38°0S 177°0E 284 D5
Bay Ridge U.S.A. 40°37N 74°1W 132 C1
Bay Roberts Canada 47°36N 53°16W 299 C9
Bay St. Louis U.S.A. 30°19N 89°20W 315 F10
Bay Springs U.S.A. 31°59N 89°17W 315 F10
Bay View N.Z. 39°25S 176°50E 284 F5
Baya Dem. Rep. of the Congo 11°53S 27°25E 269 E2
Bayambang Phil. 15°49N 120°27E 232 D3
Bayamo Cuba 20°20N 76°40W 320 B4
Bayamón Puerto Rico 18°24N 66°9W 321 C6
Bayan Har Shan China 34°0N 98°0E 218 E8
Bayan Hot = Alxa Zuoqi China 38°50N 105°40E 226 E3
Bayan Lepas Malaysia 5°17N 100°16E 237 c
Bayan Obo China 41°52N 109°59E 226 D5
Bayan-Ovoo = Erdenetsogt Mongolia 42°55N 106°5E 226 C4
Bayan-Tumen = Choybalsan Mongolia 48°4N 114°30E 219 B11
Bayana India 26°55N 77°18E 242 F7
Bayanaūyl Kazakhstan 50°45N 75°45E 217 B9
Bayanbulak ⌂ China 42°20N 84°0E 217 D10
Bayanhongor Mongolia 46°8N 102°43E 218 B9
Bayard N. Mex., U.S.A. 32°46N 108°8W 305 K9
Bayard Nebr., U.S.A. 41°45N 103°20W 308 E2
Bayawan Phil. 9°46N 122°45E 233 G4
Baybay Phil. 10°40N 124°55E 233 F5
Bayburt Turkey 40°15N 40°20E 213 B9
Bayburt □ Turkey 40°35N 39°25E 213 B8
Baydaratskaya Guba Russia 69°0N 67°30E 214 C7
Baydhabo Somalia 3°8N 43°30E 267 D5
Bayelsa □ Nigeria 4°30N 6°0E 263 E6
Bayerische Alpen Germany 47°35N 11°30E 179 H7
Bayerische Rhön ⌂ Germany 50°15N 10°5E 179 E6
Bayerischer Spessart ⌂ Germany 49°58N 10°15E 179 F6
Bayerischer Wald Germany 48°56N 12°50E 179 G8
Bayern □ Germany 48°50N 12°0E 179 G7
Bayeux France 49°17N 0°42W 172 C6
Bayfield Ont., Canada 43°34N 81°42W 312 C3
Bayfield Wis., U.S.A. 46°49N 90°49W 308 B8
Bayḩān al Qişāb Yemen 15°48N 45°44E 248 D4
Bayındır Turkey 38°13N 27°39E 205 C9
Bayit Va-Gan Israel 31°46N 35°11E 123 B2
Baykal, Oz. Russia 53°0N 108°0E 215 D11
Baykan Turkey 38°7N 41°44E 213 C9
Baymak Russia 52°36N 58°19E 186 D10
Baynes Mts. Namibia 17°15S 13°0E 270 A1
Bayombong Phil. 16°30N 121°10E 232 C3
Bayon France 48°30N 6°20E 173 D13
Bayona = Baiona Spain 42°6N 8°52W 194 C2
Bayonet Point U.S.A. 28°20N 82°41W 317 G7
Bayonne Pyrénées-Atlantiques, France 43°30N 1°28W 174 E2
Bayonne N.J., U.S.A. 40°40N 74°6W 132 B1
Bayou Boeuf U.S.A. 29°50N 90°10W 131 B1
Bayou Segnette State Park ⌂ U.S.A. 29°53N 90°10W 131 B2
Bayovar Peru 5°50S 81°0W 330 B1
Bayport U.S.A. 28°32N 82°39W 317 G7
Bayqonyr Kazakhstan 45°40N 63°20E 216 C6
Bayram-Ali = Baýramaly Turkmenistan 37°37N 62°10E 247 B9
Baýramaly Turkmenistan 37°37N 62°10E 247 B9
Bayramiç Turkey 39°48N 26°36E 205 B8
Bayrampaşa Turkey 41°1N 28°56E 122 B1
Bayreuth Germany 49°56N 11°35E 179 F7
Bayrischzell Germany 47°41N 12°0E 179 H8
Bayrūt Lebanon 33°53N 35°31E 250 E6
Bays, L. of Canada 45°15N 79°4W 312 A5
Bayshore Calif., U.S.A. 37°42N 122°24W 136 B2
Bayshore Fla., U.S.A. 26°43N 81°50W 317 J8
Baysville Canada 45°9N 79°7W 312 A5
Bayswater London, U.K. 125 b2
Bayt al Faqīh Yemen 14°31N 43°19E 248 D3
Bayt Lahm West Bank 31°43N 35°12E 123 B2
Baytik Shan China 45°15N 90°50E 217 C12
Baytown U.S.A. 29°43N 94°59W 314 G7
Bayugan Phil. 8°43N 125°42E 233 G5
Bayuquan China 40°16N 122°8E 227 D12
Bayview U.S.A. 37°44N 122°23W 136 B2
Bayville = Kirkwood S. Africa 33°22S 25°15E 270 D4
Bayy al Kabir, W. Libya 31°10N 15°53E 258 B3
Bayy al Khā'ib, Wādī → Libya 30°55N 15°29E 258 B3
Bayzo Niger 13°52N 4°35E 263 C5
Baza Spain 37°30N 2°47W 195 H8
Bāzār Iran 35°40N 51°25E 141 A2
Bazar Dyuzi Russia 41°12N 47°50E 191 K8
Bazardüzü = Bazar Dyuzi Russia 41°12N 47°50E 191 K8
Bāzargān Iran 39°22N 44°26E 213 C11
Bazargic = Dobrich Bulgaria 43°37N 27°49E 203 C11
Bazarny Karabulak Russia 52°20N 46°29E 190 D8
Bazarnyy Syzgan Russia 53°45N 46°40E 190 D8
Bazaruto, I. do Mozam. 21°40S 35°28E 271 B6
Bazaruto △ Mozam. 21°42S 35°26E 271 B6
Bazas France 44°27N 0°13W 174 D3
Bazhong China 31°52N 106°46E 228 B6
Bazhou China 39°8N 116°22E 226 E9
Bazin Guadeloupe 16°22N 61°26W 322 e
Bazmān, Kūh-e Iran 28°4N 60°1E 247 D9
Baztan = Elizondo Spain 43°12N 1°30W 196 B3
Bé, Nosy Madag. 13°25S 48°15E 272 A2
Beach U.S.A. 46°58N 104°0W 308 B2
Beach City U.S.A. 40°39N 81°35W 312 F3
Beachport Australia 37°29S 140°0E 282 D4
Beachville Canada 43°5N 80°49W 312 C4
Beachy Hd. U.K. 50°44N 0°15E 169 G8
Beacon W. Austral., Australia 30°26S 117°52E 279 F2
Beacon N.Y., U.S.A. 41°30N 73°58W 313 E11
Beacon Hill Hong Kong, China 22°21N 114°10E 122 A3
Beacon Hill Boston, U.S.A. 116 b1
Beaconsfield Australia 41°11S 146°48E 281 G4
Beagle, Canal S. Amer. 55°0S 68°30W 336 E3
Beagle Bay Australia 16°58S 122°40E 278 C3
Beagle Bay ✪ Australia 16°53S 122°40E 278 C3
Beagle G. Australia 12°15S 130°25E 278 B5
Béal an Átha = Ballina Ireland 54°7N 9°9W 166 B2
Béal Átha na Sluaighe = Ballinasloe Ireland 53°20N 8°13W 166 C3
Bealanana Madag. 14°33S 48°44E 272 A2
Beals Cr. → U.S.A. 32°10N 100°51W 314 E4
Beamsville Canada 43°12N 79°28W 312 C5
Bear → Calif., U.S.A. 38°56N 121°36W 306 G5
Bear → Utah, U.S.A. 41°30N 112°8W 300 G17
Béar, C. France 42°31N 3°8E 174 F7
Bear I. = Bjørnøya Arctic 74°30N 19°0E 150 B8
Bear I. Ireland 51°38N 9°50W 166 E2
Bear L. Man., Canada 55°8N 96°0W 297 B9
Bear L. Utah, U.S.A. 41°59N 111°21W 304 F8
Bear Lake Canada 45°27N 79°35W 312 A5
Beardmore Canada 49°36N 87°57W 298 C2
Beardmore Glacier Antarctica 84°30S 170°0E 151 E11
Beardstown U.S.A. 40°1N 90°26W 310 E6
Bearma → India 24°20N 79°51E 243 G8
Béarn France 43°20N 0°30W 174 E3
Bearpaw Mts. U.S.A. 48°12N 109°30W 304 B9
Bearskin Lake Canada 53°58N 91°2W 298 B1
Beas → India 31°10N 74°59E 242 D6
Beas de Segura Spain 38°15N 2°53W 195 G8
Beasain Spain 43°3N 2°11W 196 B2
Beata, C. Dom. Rep. 17°40N 71°30W 321 C5
Beata, I. Dom. Rep. 17°34N 71°31W 321 C5
Beata Ridge W. Indies 16°0N 72°30W 321 C5
Beato Portugal 38°44N 9°5W 126 A2
Beatrice Nebr., U.S.A. 40°16N 96°45W 308 E5
Beatrice Zimbabwe 18°15S 30°55E 269 F3
Beatrice, C. Australia 14°20S 136°55E 280 A2
Beatton → Canada 56°15N 120°45W 296 B4
Beatton River Canada 57°26N 121°20W 296 B4
Beatty U.S.A. 36°54N 116°46W 306 J10
Beau Bassin Mauritius 20°13S 57°27E 272 e
Beauaraba = Pittsworth Australia 27°41S 151°37E 281 D5
Beaucaire France 43°48N 4°39E 175 E8
Beauce, Plaine de la France 48°10N 1°45E 173 D8
Beauceville Canada 46°13N 70°46W 299 C5
Beauchêne, I. Falk. Is. 52°55S 59°15W 153 f
Beaudesert Australia 27°59S 153°0E 281 D5
Beaufort Vic., Australia 37°25S 143°25E 282 D5
Beaufort Savoie, France 45°44N 6°34E 175 C10
Beaufort Malaysia 5°30N 115°40E 235 A5
Beaufort N.C., U.S.A. 34°43N 76°40W 315 D16
Beaufort S.C., U.S.A. 32°26N 80°40W 316 C9
Beaufort Sea Arctic 72°0N 140°0W 292 B5
Beaufort West S. Africa 32°18S 22°36E 270 D3
Beaugency France 47°47N 1°38E 173 E8
Beauharnois Canada 45°20N 73°52W 313 A11
Beaujeu France 46°10N 4°35E 173 F11
Beaujolais France 46°0N 4°22E 173 F11
Beaulieu → Canada 62°3N 113°11W 296 A6
Beaulieu-sur-Dordogne France 44°58N 1°50E 174 D5
Beaulieu-sur-Mer France 43°42N 7°20E 175 E11
Beauly U.K. 57°30N 4°28W 167 D4
Beauly → U.K. 57°29N 4°27W 167 D4
Beaumaris U.K. 53°16N 4°6W 168 D3
Beaumont Belgium 50°15N 4°14E 170 D4
Beaumont N.Z. 45°50S 169°33E 285 F4
Beaumont Calif., U.S.A. 33°57N 116°59W 307 M9
Beaumont Tex., U.S.A. 30°5N 94°6W 314 F7
Beaumont-de-Lomagne France 43°53N 1°0E 174 E5
Beaumont-du-Périgord France 44°45N 0°46E 174 D4
Beaumont-le-Roger France 49°4N 0°47E 172 C7
Beaumont-sur-Sarthe France 48°13N 0°8E 172 D7
Beaumonte Heights Canada 43°45N 79°34W 141 A1
Beaune France 47°2N 4°50E 173 E11
Beaune-la-Rolande France 48°4N 2°25E 173 D9
Beauport Guadeloupe 16°25N 61°30W 322 e
Beaupré Canada 47°3N 70°54W 299 C5
Beaupréau France 47°12N 1°0W 172 E6
Beauraing Belgium 50°7N 4°57E 170 D4
Beaurepaire France 45°22N 5°1E 175 C9
Beausejour Man., Canada 50°5N 96°35W 297 C9
Beauséjour Guadeloupe 16°18N 61°4W 322 e
Beauséjour Martinique 14°44N 60°57W 322 j
Beauvais France 49°25N 2°8E 173 C9
Beauval Canada 55°9N 107°37W 297 B7
Beauvoir-sur-Mer France 46°55N 2°2W 172 F4
Beauvoir-sur-Niort France 46°12N 0°30W 174 B3
Beaver Alaska, U.S.A. 66°22N 147°24W 303 C11
Beaver Okla., U.S.A. 36°49N 100°31W 314 C4
Beaver Pa., U.S.A. 40°42N 80°19W 312 F4
Beaver Utah, U.S.A. 38°17N 112°38W 304 G7
Beaver → B.C., Canada 59°52N 124°20W 296 B4
Beaver → Ont., Canada 55°55N 87°48W 298 A2
Beaver → Sask., Canada 55°26N 107°45W 297 B7
Beaver → Okla., U.S.A. 36°35N 99°30W 314 C5
Beaver City U.S.A. 40°8N 99°50W 308 E4
Beaver Creek Canada 63°0N 141°0W 294 E3
Beaver Dam U.S.A. 43°28N 88°50W 308 D9
Beaver Falls U.S.A. 40°46N 80°20W 312 F4
Beaver Hill L. Canada 54°5N 94°50W 297 C10
Beaver I. U.S.A. 45°40N 85°33W 309 C11
Beavercreek U.S.A. 39°43N 84°11W 311 E12
Beaverhill L. Canada 53°27N 112°32W 296 C6
Beaverlodge Canada 55°11N 119°29W 296 B5
Beaverstone → Canada 54°59N 89°25W 298 B2
Beaverton Ont., Canada 44°26N 79°9W 312 B5
Beaverton Oreg., U.S.A. 45°29N 122°48W 306 E4
Beawar India 26°3N 74°18E 242 F6
Bebedouro Brazil 21°0S 48°25W 335 A6
Bebek Turkey 41°4N 29°2E 122 B2
Bebera, Tanjung Indonesia 8°44S 115°51E 231 K18
Bebington U.K. 53°22N 3°0W 168 D4
Beboa Madag. 17°22S 44°33E 272 B1
Beboto Chad 8°16N 16°56E 259 G3
Bebra Germany 50°58N 9°48E 178 E5
Becán Mexico 18°34N 89°31W 319 D7
Bécancour Canada 46°20N 72°26W 309 B17
Beccles U.K. 52°27N 1°35E 169 E9
Bečej Serbia 45°36N 20°3E 182 E5
Beceni Romania 45°23N 26°48E 183 E11
Becerreá Spain 42°51N 7°10W 194 C3
Béchar Algeria 31°38N 2°18W 261 B4
Béchar □ Algeria 31°30N 2°20W 261 B4
Becharof L. U.S.A. 57°56N 156°23W 303 H8
Becharof Nat. Wildlife Refuge ⌂ U.S.A. 58°0N 156°15W 303 H8
Becharre = Bsharri Lebanon 34°15N 36°0E 250 D7
Běchovice Czechia 50°4N 14°36E 135 B3
Bechuanaland = Botswana ■ Africa 22°0S 24°0E 270 B3
Bechyně Czechia 49°17N 14°29E 180 B7
Beckenham U.K. 51°24N 0°1W 125 B3
Bečkerek = Zrenjanin Serbia 45°22N 20°23E 182 E5
Beckley U.S.A. 37°47N 81°11W 309 G13
Beckton U.K. 51°30N 0°4E 125 A4
Beckum Germany 51°45N 8°3E 178 D4
Beclean Romania 47°11N 24°11E 183 C9
Becontree U.K. 51°33N 0°7E 125 A4
Bečov nad Teplou Czechia 50°5N 12°49E 180 A5
Bečva → Czechia 49°31N 17°20E 181 B10
Bédar Spain 37°11N 1°59W 197 H3
Bédarieux France 43°37N 3°10E 174 E7
Beddington Corner U.K. 51°23N 0°9W 125 B3
Beddouza, C. Morocco 32°33N 9°9W 260 B3
Bedeau = Râs el Ma Algeria 34°26N 0°50W 261 B4
Bedele Ethiopia 8°31N 36°23E 257 F4
Bederkesa Germany 53°37N 8°50E 178 B4
Bederwanak Somalia 9°34N 44°23E 267 C5
Bedeso Ethiopia 9°58N 40°52E 257 F5
Bedford Qué., Canada 45°7N 72°59W 313 A12
Bedford Eastern Cape, S. Africa 32°40S 26°10E 270 D4
Bedford Beds., U.K. 52°8N 0°28W 169 E7
Bedford Ind., U.S.A. 38°52N 86°29W 311 F10
Bedford Iowa, U.S.A. 40°40N 94°44W 310 D2
Bedford Ky., U.S.A. 38°36N 85°19W 311 F11
Bedford Mass., U.S.A. 42°27N 71°15W 116 A1
Bedford Ohio, U.S.A. 41°23N 81°32W 312 E3
Bedford Pa., U.S.A. 40°1N 78°30W 312 F6
Bedford Tex., U.S.A. 32°50N 97°8W 120 A3
Bedford Va., U.S.A. 37°20N 79°31W 309 G14
Bedford □ U.K. 52°4N 0°28W 169 E7
Bedford, C. Australia 15°14S 145°21E 280 B4
Bedford Park Ill., U.S.A. 41°46N 87°46W 119 C2
Bedford Park N.Y., U.S.A. 40°52N 73°52W 132 A2
Bedford Stuyvesant U.S.A. 40°41N 73°56W 132 B2
Bedford View S. Africa 26°10S 28°7E 123 B2
Bedi Chad 11°6N 18°33E 259 F3
Będków Poland 51°36N 19°44E 185 G6
Bednja → Croatia 46°20N 16°52E 199 B13
Bednodemyanovsk Russia 53°55N 43°15E 190 D6
Bedok Singapore 1°19N 103°56E 138 B3
Bedok, Res. Singapore 1°20N 103°56E 138 A3
Bedónia Italy 44°30N 9°38E 198 D6
Bedourie Australia 24°30S 139°30E 280 C2
Bedti → India 14°50N 74°44E 245 G2
Bedugul Indonesia 8°17S 115°10E 231 J18
Bedum Neths. 53°18N 6°36E 170 A6
Będzin Poland 50°19N 19°7E 185 H6
Bee Ridge U.S.A. 27°17N 82°29W 317 H7
Beebe Plain Canada 45°1N 72°9W 313 A12
Beech Creek U.S.A. 41°5N 77°36W 312 E7
Beech Fork → U.S.A. 37°46N 85°41W 311 G11
Beech Grove U.S.A. 39°43N 86°5W 311 E10
Beecher U.S.A. 41°21N 87°38W 311 C9
Beechey Point U.S.A. 70°29N 149°9W 303 A10
Beechworth Australia 36°22S 146°43E 283 D7
Beechy Canada 50°53N 107°24W 297 C7
Beed = Bir India 19°4N 75°46E 244 E2
Beef I. Br. Virgin Is. 18°26N 64°30W 321 b
Beelitz Germany 52°14N 12°58E 178 C8
Beenleigh Australia 27°43S 153°10E 281 D5
Be'er Menuha Israel 30°19N 35°8E 251 H6
Be'er Sheva Israel 31°15N 34°48E 251 G5
Beerenberg Norway 71°0N 8°20W 154 C10
Beersel Belgium 50°46N 4°18E 116 B1
Beersheba = Be'er Sheva Israel 31°15N 34°48E 251 G5
Beeskow Germany 52°10N 14°15E 178 C10
Beestekraal S. Africa 25°23S 27°38E 271 C4
Beeston U.K. 52°56N 1°14W 168 E6
Beeton Canada 44°5N 79°47W 312 B5
Beetzendorf Germany 52°42N 11°6E 178 C7
Beeville U.S.A. 28°24N 97°45W 314 G6
Befale Dem. Rep. of the Congo 0°25N 20°45E 264 B4
Befandriana Atsimo-Andrefana, Madag. 21°55S 44°0E 272 C1
Befandriana Sofia, Madag. 15°16S 48°32E 272 B2
Befasy Madag. 20°33S 44°23E 272 C1
Befori Dem. Rep. of the Congo 0°8N 22°22E 264 B4
Befotaka Atsimo-Atsinanana, Madag. 23°49S 47°0E 272 C2
Befotaka Diana, Madag. 13°15S 48°16E 272 A2
Bega Australia 36°41S 149°51E 283 D8
Bega, Canalul Romania 45°37N 20°46E 182 E5
Begamganj Bangla. 22°56N 91°6E 241 D3
Bégard France 48°38N 3°18W 172 D3
Beğendik Turkey 40°55N 26°34E 203 F10
Beggars Pt. Antigua & B. 17°10N 61°48W 322 b
Begndal Norway 60°49N 9°46E 164 D6
Begoro Ghana 6°23N 0°23W 263 D4
Begusarai India 25°24N 86°9E 243 G12
Behābād Iran 32°24N 59°47E 247 C8
Behala India 22°30N 88°18E 124 B1
Behara Madag. 24°55S 46°20E 272 C2
Behbehān Iran 30°30N 50°15E 247 D6
Behchoko Canada 62°50N 116°3W 296 A5
Beheloka Madag. 23°54S 43°40E 272 C1
Behm Canal U.S.A. 55°10N 131°0W 296 B2
Behshahr Iran 36°45N 53°35E 247 B7
Bei Hai Beijing, China 114 b2
Bei Hai Park Beijing, China 114 b2
Bei Jiang → China 23°2N 112°58E 229 F9
Bei Shan China 41°30N 96°0E 218 C8
Bei'an China 48°10N 126°20E 219 B14
Beibei China 29°47N 106°22E 228 C6
Beicai China 31°11N 121°32E 138 B2
Beichuan China 31°55N 104°39E 228 B5
Beida, Es Sahrâ al Egypt 27°50N 28°45E 256 B2
Beigang = Peikang Taiwan 23°34N 120°18E 225 C2
Beihai China 21°28N 109°6E 228 G7
Beijing China 39°53N 116°21E 114 B1
Beijing Capital Int. ✕ (PEK) China 40°5N 116°35E 226 D9
Beijing Shi □ China 39°55N 116°20E 226 E9
Beijing Zoo Beijing, China 114 a1
Beikthano Myanmar 20°0N 95°23E 241 F5
Beilau = Pilawa Poland 51°57N 21°32E 185 G8
Beilen Neths. 52°52N 6°27E 170 B6
Beiliu China 22°41N 110°21E 229 F8
Beilngries Germany 49°2N 11°28E 179 F7
Beilpajah Australia 32°54S 143°52E 282 B5
Beilul Eritrea 13°2N 42°20E 257 E5
Béinamar Chad 8°40N 15°23E 259 G3
Beinan = Peinan Taiwan 22°47N 121°7E 225 D3
Beinn na Faoghla = Benbecula U.K. 57°26N 7°21W 167 D1
Beipan Jiang → China 24°55N 106°5E 228 E6
Beipiao China 41°52N 120°32E 227 D11
Beira Mozam. 19°50S 34°52E 269 F3
Beirut = Bayrūt Lebanon 33°53N 35°31E 250 E6
Beiseker Canada 51°23N 113°32W 296 C6
Beit Duqu West Bank 31°51N 35°6E 123 A1
Beit Ghur at-Taht West Bank 31°54N 35°5E 123 A1
Beit Ghur el-Fawqa West Bank 31°53N 35°5E 123 A1
Beit Hanina West Bank 31°50N 35°12E 123 B2
Beit Ij'za West Bank 31°51N 35°9E 123 A1
Beit Iksa West Bank 31°49N 35°11E 123 B2
Beit I'nan West Bank 31°51N 35°7E 123 A1
Beit Jala West Bank 31°43N 35°11E 123 B2
Beit Lāhīyā Gaza Strip 31°33N 34°30E 251 G5
Beit Lahm = Bayt Lahm West Bank 31°43N 35°12E 123 B2
Beit Liqya West Bank 31°52N 35°4E 123 A1
Beit Nekofa Israel 31°49N 35°7E 123 B1
Beit Sahur West Bank 31°42N 35°13E 123 B2
Beit Sofafa West Bank 31°45N 35°12E 123 B2
Beit Surik West Bank 31°50N 35°9E 123 B1
Beit Ur al-Fawqa West Bank 31°53N 35°7E 123 A1
Beit Zayit Israel 31°47N 35°9E 123 B1
Beitaipingzhuan China 39°57N 116°20E 114 B1
Beitaolaizhao China 44°58N 125°58E 227 B13
Beitar Ilit West Bank 31°42N 35°7E 123 B1
Beitbridge Zimbabwe 22°12S 30°0E 269 G3
Beitin West Bank 31°56N 35°14E 123 A2
Beitou = Peitou Taiwan 25°11N 121°27E 225 A3
Beitsun China 23°7N 113°10E 121 B2
Beitun China 47°22N 87°4E 217 D11
Beitunya West Bank 31°53N 35°10E 123 A2
Beiuş Romania 46°40N 22°21E 182 D7
Beixing Jing Park China 31°14N 121°21E 138 B1
Beizhen = Binzhou China 37°20N 118°2E 227 F10
Beizhen China 41°38N 121°54E 227 D11
Beizhengzhen China 44°31N 123°30E 227 B12
Beja Portugal 38°2N 7°53W 195 G3
Béja Tunisia 36°43N 9°12E 258 A1
Beja □ Portugal 37°55N 7°55W 195 H3
Béja □ Tunisia 36°40N 9°29E 261 A6
Bejaïa Algeria 36°42N 5°2E 261 A6
Bejaïa □ Algeria 36°40N 4°55E 261 A5
Béjar Spain 40°23N 5°46W 194 E5
Bejestān Iran 34°30N 58°5E 247 C8
Bek-Budi = Qarshi Uzbekistan 38°53N 65°48E 217 E7
Bekaa Valley = Al Biqā Lebanon 34°10N 36°10E 250 D7
Bekasi Indonesia 6°14S 106°59E 234 D3
Békásmegyer Hungary 47°35N 19°3E 117 A2
Bekçiler Turkey 36°56N 29°44E 205 E11
Bekdash Turkmenistan 41°34N 52°32E 216 D4
Békés Hungary 46°47N 21°9E 182 D6
Békés □ Hungary 46°45N 21°0E 182 D6
Békéscsaba Hungary 46°40N 21°5E 182 D6
Bekilli Turkey 38°17N 29°27E 205 C11
Bekily Madag. 24°13S 45°19E 272 C2
Bekisopa Madag. 21°40S 45°54E 272 C2
Bekitro Madag. 24°33S 45°18E 272 C2
Bekkelaget Norway 59°53N 10°47E 133 A3
Bekkestua Norway 59°55N 10°35E 133 A2
Bekodoka Madag. 16°58S 45°7E 272 B2
Bekoji Ethiopia 7°40N 39°17E 257 F4
Bekok Malaysia 2°20N 103°7E 237 L4
Bekopaka Madag. 19°9S 44°48E 272 B1
Bekwai Ghana 6°30N 1°34W 263 D4
Bel Air Mauritius 20°15S 57°44E 272 e
Bel Air Calif., U.S.A. 34°4N 118°27W 126 B2
Bela India 25°50N 82°0E 243 G10
Bela Pakistan 26°12N 66°20E 242 F2
Bela Aliança = Rio do Sul Brazil 27°13S 49°37W 335 B6
Bela Bela S. Africa 24°51S 28°19E 271 B4
Bela Crkva Serbia 44°55N 21°27E 182 F6
Bela Palanka Serbia 43°13N 22°17E 202 C6
Bela Vista Mato Grosso do Sul, Brazil 22°12S 56°20W 334 A4
Bela Vista São Paulo, Brazil 23°33S 46°38W 137 B2
Bela Vista Mozam. 26°10S 32°44E 271 C5
Bélabo Cameroon 4°56N 13°18E 264 B2
Bélâbre France 46°34N 1°8E 174 B5
Belaga Malaysia 2°42N 113°47E 235 B4
Belagavi India 15°55N 74°35E 245 G2
Belalcázar Spain 38°35N 5°10W 195 G5
Belan → India 24°2N 81°45E 243 G9
Bélanger Canada 45°35N 73°42W 130 A1
Belanovica Serbia 44°15N 20°23E 202 B4
Belarus ■ Europe 53°30N 27°0E 177 B14
Belas Angola 8°55S 13°9E 265 D2
Belas Lisboa, Portugal 38°46N 9°17W 126 A1
Belau = Palau ■ Palau 7°30N 134°30E 288 c
Belavenona Madag. 24°50S 47°4E 272 C2
Belawan Indonesia 3°33N 98°32E 234 B1
Belaya Ethiopia 11°25N 36°8E 257 E4
Belaya → Russia 54°40N 56°0E 186 C9
Belaya Glina Russia 46°5N 40°48E 191 G5
Belaya Kalitva Russia 48°13N 40°50E 191 F5
Belaya Tserkov = Bila Tserkva Ukraine 49°45N 30°10E 177 D16
Belaya Zemlya, Ostrova Russia 81°36N 62°18E 214 A7
Belayan → Indonesia 0°14S 116°36E 235 C5
Belceşti Romania 47°19N 27°7E 183 C12
Bełchatów Poland 51°21N 19°22E 185 G6
Belcher Is. Canada 56°15N 78°45W 298 A3
Belchite Spain 41°18N 0°43W 196 D4
Belden U.S.A. 40°2N 121°17W 306 E5
Beldibi Turkey 36°25N 32°26E 250 B3
Belding U.S.A. 43°6N 85°14W 311 A11
Belebey Russia 54°7N 54°7E 186 D9
Beledweyne Somalia 4°30N 45°5E 267 D6
Beleghata India 22°33N 88°22E 124 B2
Belém = Palmeirais Brazil 6°0S 43°0W 332 C3
Belém Brazil 1°20S 48°30W 332 B2
Belém Lisboa, Portugal 38°41N 9°12W 126 A1
Belém, Torre de Portugal 38°41N 9°12W 126 A1
Belém de São Francisco Brazil 8°46S 38°58W 332 C4
Belén Argentina 27°40S 67°5W 334 B2
Belén Colombia 1°26N 75°56W 328 C2
Belén Paraguay 23°30S 57°6W 334 A4
Belen Turkey 36°31N 36°10E 250 B7
Belen N. Mex., U.S.A. 34°40N 106°46W 305 J10
Belene Bulgaria 43°39N 25°10E 203 C9
Belènzinho Brazil 23°32S 46°34W 137 B2
Belep, Îs. N. Cal. 19°45S 163°40E 288 d
Bélesta France 42°55N 1°56E 174 F5
Belet Uen = Beledweyne Somalia 4°30N 45°5E 267 D6
Belev Russia 53°50N 36°5E 188 F9
Belevi Turkey 38°0N 27°28E 205 C9
Belfair U.S.A. 47°27N 122°50W 306 C4
Belfast = eMakhazeni S. Africa 25°42S 30°2E 271 C5
Belfast N.Z. 43°27S 172°39E 285 D7
Belfast Antrim, U.K. 54°37N 5°56W 166 B6
Belfast Maine, U.S.A. 44°26N 69°1W 309 C19
Belfast N.Y., U.S.A. 42°21N 78°7W 312 D6
Belfast L. U.K. 54°40N 5°50W 166 B6
Belfield U.S.A. 46°53N 103°12W 308 B2
Belfort France 47°38N 6°50E 173 E13
Belfort, Territoire de □ France 47°40N 6°55E 173 E13
Belfry U.S.A. 45°9N 109°1W 304 D9
Belgachiya India 22°36N 88°23E 124 B2
Belgard = Białogard Poland 54°2N 15°58E 184 D2
Belgaum = Belagavi India 15°55N 74°35E 245 G2
Belgharia India 22°39N 88°22E 124 B2
Belgian Congo = Congo, Dem. Rep. of the ■ Africa 3°0S 23°0E 265 C4
Belgioioso Italy 45°10N 9°19E 198 C6
Belgium ■ Europe 50°30N 5°0E 170 D4
Belgodère France 42°35N 9°1E 175 F13
Belgorod Russia 50°35N 36°35E 189 G9
Belgorod □ Russia 50°45N 36°45E 189 G9
Belgorod-Dnestrovskiy = Bilhorod-Dnistrovskyy Ukraine 46°11N 30°23E 189 J6
Belgrade = Beograd Serbia 44°50N 20°37E 202 B4
Belgrade U.S.A. 45°47N 111°11W 304 D8
Belgrano Argentina 34°33S 58°27W 117 B2
Belgrano II Antarctica 77°52S 34°37W 151 D1
Belgravia London, U.K. 125 c3
Belgrove N.Z. 41°27S 172°59E 285 B7
Belhaven U.S.A. 35°33N 76°37W 315 D16
Béli Guinea-Biss. 11°51N 13°56W 262 C2
Beli Nigeria 7°52N 10°55E 263 D7
Beli Drim → Europe 42°6N 20°25E 202 D4
Beli Manastir Croatia 45°45N 18°36E 182 E3
Beli Timok → Serbia 43°53N 22°14E 202 C6
Bélice → Italy 37°35N 12°55E 200 E5
Belimbing Indonesia 8°24S 115°2E 231 J18
Bélinga Gabon 1°10N 13°2E 264 B2
Belinskiy Russia 53°0N 43°25E 190 D6
Belinyu Indonesia 1°35S 105°50E 234 C3
Beliton Is. = Belitung Indonesia 3°10S 107°50E 235 C3
Belitung Indonesia 3°10S 107°50E 235 C3
Beliu Romania 46°30N 22°0E 182 D6
Belize Angola 4°39S 12°46E 265 C2
Belize ■ Cent. Amer. 17°0N 88°30W 320 C2
Belize Barrier Reef Belize 17°9N 88°3W 319 D7
Belize City Belize 17°25N 88°10W 320 C2
Beljakovci N. Macedonia 42°6N 21°59E 202 D5
Beljanica Serbia 44°8N 21°43E 202 B5
Belkovskiy, Ostrov Russia 75°32N 135°44E 215 B14
Bell Calif., U.S.A. 33°58N 118°11W 126 C3
Bell Fla., U.S.A. 29°45N 82°52W 316 F7
Bell → Canada 49°48N 77°38W 298 C4
Bell Gardens U.S.A. 33°58N 118°9W 126 C4
Bell I. Canada 50°46N 55°35W 299 B8
Bell-Irving → Canada 56°12N 129°5W 296 B3
Bell Peninsula Canada 63°50N 82°0W 295 E15
Bell Tower Beijing, China 114 a3
Bell Ville Argentina 32°40S 62°40W 334 C3
Bella Italy 40°45N 15°32E 201 B8
Bella Bella Canada 52°10N 128°10W 296 C3
Bella Coola Canada 52°25N 126°40W 296 C3
Bella Flor Bolivia 11°9S 67°49W 330 C4
Bella Unión Uruguay 30°15S 57°40W 334 C4
Bella Vista Corrientes, Argentina 28°33S 59°0W 334 B4
Bella Vista Tucuman, Argentina 27°10S 65°25W 334 B2
Bella Vista Ark., U.S.A. 36°28N 94°16W 308 G6
Bellac France 46°7N 1°3E 174 B5
Bellágio Italy 45°59N 9°15E 198 C6
Bellaire U.S.A. 40°1N 80°45W 312 F4
Bellária Italy 44°9N 12°28E 199 D9
Bellata Australia 29°53S 149°46E 281 D4
Bellavista Santiago, Chile 33°31S 70°35W 137 C2
Bellavista Galápagos Is., Ecuador 0°41S 90°18W 330 a
Bellavista Lima, Peru 12°4S 77°8W 124 B2
Belle U.S.A. 38°17N 91°43W 310 F5
Belle → Trin. & Tob. 11°14N 60°37W 323 s
Belle Fille → Dominica 15°25N 61°16W 323 k
Belle Fourche U.S.A. 44°40N 103°51W 308 C2
Belle Fourche → U.S.A. 44°26N 102°18W 308 C2
Belle Glade U.S.A. 26°41N 80°40W 317 J9
Belle Harbor U.S.A. 40°34N 73°51W 132 C2
Belle-Île France 47°20N 3°10W 172 E3
Belle Isle Nfld. & L., Canada 51°57N 55°25W 299 B8
Belle Isle Fla., U.S.A. 28°27N 81°12W 317 G8
Belle Isle, Str. of Canada 51°30N 56°30W 299 B8
Belle Plaine U.S.A. 41°54N 92°17W 310 C4
Belle Rive U.S.A. 38°14N 88°45W 311 F8
Belle River Canada 42°18N 82°43W 312 D2
Belle Vue Maurel Mauritius 20°7S 57°39E 272 e
Belle Yella Liberia 7°24N 10°0W 262 D3
Belledonne France 45°20N 6°10E 175 C10
Bellefontaine Martinique 14°39N 61°10W 322 j
Bellefontaine Ohio, U.S.A. 40°22N 83°46W 311 D13
Bellefonte U.S.A. 40°55N 77°47W 312 F7
Bellegarde France 47°59N 2°26E 173 E9
Bellegarde-en-Marche France 45°59N 2°18E 174 C6
Bellegarde-sur-Valserine France 46°4N 5°50E 173 F12
Bellême France 48°22N 0°34E 172 D7
Belleoram Canada 47°31N 55°25W 299 C8
Belleplaine Barbados 13°15N 59°34W 323 r
Belleview U.S.A. 29°4N 82°3W 317 F7
Belleville Ont., Canada 44°10N 77°23W 312 B7
Belleville Rhône, France 46°7N 4°45E 173 F11
Belleville Ill., U.S.A. 38°31N 89°59W 310 F7
Belleville Kans., U.S.A. 39°50N 97°38W 308 F5
Belleville N.J., U.S.A. 40°47N 74°9W 313 F10
Belleville N.Y., U.S.A. 43°46N 76°10W 313 C8
Belleville-sur-Vie France 46°46N 1°25W 172 F5
Bellevue Idaho, U.S.A. 43°28N 114°16W 304 E6
Bellevue Iowa, U.S.A. 42°16N 90°26W 310 B6
Bellevue Mich., U.S.A. 42°27N 85°1W 311 B11
Bellevue Nebr., U.S.A. 41°9N 95°54W 308 E6
Bellevue Ohio, U.S.A. 41°17N 82°51W 312 E2
Bellevue Wash., U.S.A. 47°37N 122°12W 306 C4
Bellevue, Col de Réunion 21°9S 55°36E 272 f
Bellevue, Schloss Berlin, Germany 115 a2
Belley France 45°46N 5°41E 175 C9
Bellin = Kangirsuk Canada 60°0N 70°0W 295 F18
Bellinge Denmark 55°20N 10°20E 163 J4
Bellingen Australia 30°25S 152°50E 283 A10
Bellingham London, U.K. 51°25N 0°1W 125 B3
Bellingham Wash., U.S.A. 48°46N 122°29W 306 B4
Bellingshausen Abyssal Plain S. Ocean 64°0S 90°0W 151 C16
Bellingshausen Sea Antarctica 66°0S 80°0W 151 C17
Bellinzona Switz. 46°11N 9°1E 179 J5
Bello Colombia 6°20N 75°33W 328 B2
Bellona Solomon Is. 11°17S 159°47E 287 N10
Bellows Falls U.S.A. 43°8N 72°27W 313 C12
Bellpat Pakistan 29°0N 68°5E 242 E3
Bellpuig Spain 41°37N 1°1E 196 D6
Bells Dominica 15°25N 61°21W 323 k
Belluno Italy 46°9N 12°13E 199 B9
Bellville U.S.A. 32°9N 81°59W 316 C8
Bellwood U.S.A. 40°36N 78°20W 312 F6
Belmanier Dominica 15°35N 61°24W 323 k
Bélmez Spain 38°17N 5°17W 195 G5
Belmond U.S.A. 42°51N 93°37W 310 B3
Belmont N.S.W., Australia 33°4S 151°42E 283 B9
Belmont Ont., Canada 42°53N 81°5W 312 D3
Belmont Grenada 12°2N 61°45W 323 q
Belmont Northern Cape, S. Africa 29°28S 24°22E 270 C3
Belmont London, U.K. 51°36N 0°18W 125 A2
Belmont Mass., U.S.A. 42°23N 71°10W 116 A1
Belmont N.Y., U.S.A. 42°14N 78°2W 312 D6
Belmont Cragin U.S.A. 41°55N 87°45W 119 B2
Belmont Harbor U.S.A. 41°56N 87°38W 119 B3
Belmonte Brazil 16°0S 39°0W 333 E4
Belmonte Portugal 40°21N 7°20W 194 E3
Belmonte Spain 39°34N 2°43W 197 F2
Belmopan Belize 17°18N 88°30W 320 C2
Belmore Australia 33°55S 151°5E 139 B1
Belmullet Ireland 54°14N 9°58W 166 B2
Belo Dem. Rep. of the Congo 0°32S 23°13E 264 C4
Belo Madag. 20°44S 44°0E 272 C1
Belo Horizonte Brazil 19°55S 43°56W 333 E3
Belo Jardim Brazil 8°20S 36°26W 332 C4
Belo Monte Brazil 3°5S 51°46W 329 D7
Belo-Tsiribihina Madag. 19°40S 44°30E 272 B1
Belogorsk = Bilohirsk Ukraine 45°3N 34°35E 189 K8
Belogorsk Russia 51°0N 128°20E 215 D13
Belogradchik Bulgaria 43°53N 22°42E 202 C6
Belogradets Bulgaria 43°22N 27°18E 203 C11
Beloha Madag. 25°10S 45°3E 272 D2
Beloit Kans., U.S.A. 39°28N 98°6W 308 F4
Beloit Wis., U.S.A. 42°31N 89°2W 310 B7
Belokalitvenskaya = Belaya Kalitva Russia 48°13N 40°50E 191 F5
Belokorovichi Ukraine 51°7N 28°2E 177 C15
Belomorsk Russia 64°35N 34°54E 186 B5
Belondo Dem. Rep. of the Congo 0°19S 19°31E 264 C3
Belonge Dem. Rep. of the Congo 2°7S 19°33E 264 C3
Belonia India 23°15N 91°30E 241 D3
Belopolye = Bilopillya Ukraine 51°14N 34°20E 189 G8
Belorechensk Russia 44°46N 39°52E 191 H4
Beloretsk Russia 53°58N 58°24E 186 D10
Belorussia = Belarus ■ Europe 53°30N 27°0E 177 B14
Beloshchelye = Naryan-Mar Russia 67°42N 53°12E 186 A9
Beloslav Bulgaria 43°11N 27°42E 203 C11
Belotsarsk = Kyzyl Russia 51°50N 94°30E 217 B12
Beloūsovka Kazakhstan 50°8N 82°31E 217 B10
Belovezhskaya Pushcha = Białowieski △ Poland 52°43N 23°50E 185 F10
Belovo Bulgaria 42°13N 24°1E 203 D8
Belovo Russia 54°30N 86°0E 217 B11
Beloyarskiy Russia 63°42N 66°40E 214 C7
Beloye, Ozero Russia 60°10N 37°35E 188 B9
Beloye More Russia 66°30N 38°0E 186 A6
Belozem Bulgaria 42°12N 25°2E 203 D9
Belozersk Russia 60°1N 37°45E 188 B9
Belpasso Italy 37°35N 14°58E 201 E7
Belpre U.S.A. 39°17N 81°34W 309 F13
Belrain India 28°23N 80°55E 243 E9
Belt U.S.A. 47°23N 110°55W 304 C8
Beltana Australia 30°48S 138°25E 282 A3
Belterra Brazil 2°45S 55°0W 329 D7
Beltinci Slovenia 46°37N 16°20E 199 B13
Belton Mo., U.S.A. 38°49N 94°32W 310 F2
Belton Tex., U.S.A. 31°3N 97°28W 314 F6
Belton L. U.S.A. 31°6N 97°28W 314 F6
Beltsy = Bălţi Moldova 47°48N 27°58E 183 C12
Belturbet Ireland 54°6N 7°26W 166 B4
Belukha Russia 49°50N 86°50E 217 C11
Belur India 22°37N 88°21E 124 B2
Beluran Malaysia 5°48N 117°35E 235 A5
Beluša Slovakia 49°5N 18°17E 181 B11
Belushya Guba Russia 71°32N 52°19E 214 B6
Belušić Serbia 43°50N 21°10E 202 C5
Belvedere St. Vincent 13°8N 61°11W 323 n
Belvedere London, U.K. 51°29N 0°9E 125 B4
Belvedere Calif., U.S.A. 37°52N 122°27W 136 A2
Belvedere Maríttimo Italy 39°37N 15°52E 201 C8
Belvedere Park U.S.A. 33°45N 84°16W 113 B3
Belvès France 44°46N 1°0E 174 D5
Belvidere Ill., U.S.A. 42°15N 88°50W 311 B8
Belvidere N.J., U.S.A. 40°50N 75°5W 313 F9
Belvís de la Jara Spain 39°45N 4°57W 194 F6
Bely Bychek = Chagoda Russia 59°10N 35°15E 188 C8
Belyando → Australia 21°38S 146°50E 280 C4
Belyando Crossing Australia 21°32S 146°51E 280 C4
Belyayevo Bogorodskoye Russia 55°39N 37°31E 129 C2
Belyuen Australia 12°34S 130°42E 278 B5
Belyy Russia 55°49N 33°3E 188 E7
Belyy, Ostrov Russia 73°30N 71°0E 214 B8
Belyy Yar Russia 58°26N 84°39E 214 D9
Belyye Vody = Aqsū Kazakhstan 42°25N 69°50E 217 D7
Belz Ukraine 50°23N 24°1E 185 H11
Bełżec Poland 50°23N 23°26E 185 H10
Belzig Germany 52°8N 12°35E 178 C8
Belzoni U.S.A. 33°11N 90°29W 315 E9
Bełżyce Poland 51°11N 22°17E 185 G9
Bemaraha, Lembalemban' i Madag. 18°40S 44°45E 272 B1
Bemarivo Madag. 21°45S 44°45E 272 C1
Bemarivo → Sava, Madag. 14°9S 50°9E 272 A3
Bemarivo → Sofia, Madag. 15°27S 47°40E 272 B2
Bemavo Madag. 21°33S 45°25E 272 C2
Bembe Angola 7°3S 14°25E 265 D2
Bembéréke Benin 10°11N 2°43E 263 C5
Bembesi Zimbabwe 20°0S 28°58E 269 G2
Bembesi → Zimbabwe 18°57S 27°47E 269 F2
Bembézar → Spain 37°45N 5°13W 195 H5
Bembibre Spain 42°37N 6°25W 194 C4
Bemboka △ Australia 36°35S 149°41E 283 D8

Bement U.S.A. 39°55N 88°34W 311 E8
Bemetara India 21°42N 81°32E 243 J9
Bemidji U.S.A. 47°28N 94°53W 308 B6
Bemolanga Madag. 17°44S 45°6E 272 B2
Bemowo Poland 52°15N 20°53E 143 B1
Ben Iran 32°32N 50°45E 247 C6
Ben Boyd △ Australia 37°0S 149°55E 283 D8
Ben Cruachan U.K. 56°26N 5°8W 167 E3
Ben Dearg U.K. 57°47N 4°56W 167 D4
Ben En △ Vietnam 19°37N 105°30E 236 C5
Ben Gardane Tunisia 33°11N 11°11E 258 B2
Ben Halls Gap △ Australia 31°37S 151°1E 283 A9
Ben Hope U.K. 58°25N 4°36W 167 C4
Ben Lawers U.K. 56°32N 4°14W 167 E4
Ben Lomond N.S.W., Australia 30°1S 151°43E 281 E5
Ben Lomond Tas., Australia 41°38S 147°42E 281 G4
Ben Lomond Stirling, U.K. 56°11N 4°38W 167 E4
Ben Lomond △ Australia 41°33S 147°39E 281 G4
Ben Luc Vietnam 10°39N 106°29E 237 G6
Ben Macdhui U.K. 57°4N 3°40W 167 D5
Ben Mhor U.K. 57°15N 7°18W 167 D1
Ben More Argyll & Bute, U.K. 56°26N 6°1W 167 E2
Ben More Stirling, U.K. 56°23N 4°32W 167 E4
Ben More Assynt U.K. 58°8N 4°52W 167 C4
Ben Nevis U.K. 56°48N 5°1W 167 E3
Ben Ohau Ra. N.Z. 44°1S 170°4E 285 E5
Ben Quang Vietnam 17°3N 106°55E 236 D6
Ben Slimane Morocco 33°38N 7°7W 260 B3
Ben Tadjine, Djebel Algeria 29°0N 3°30W 260 C4
Ben Tre Vietnam 10°14N 106°23E 237 G6
Ben Vorlich U.K. 56°21N 4°14W 167 E4
Ben Wyvis U.K. 57°40N 4°35W 167 D4
Bena Nigeria 11°20N 5°50E 263 C6
Bena-Dibele Dem. Rep. of the Congo 4°4S 22°50E 265 C4
Bena-Leka Dem. Rep. of the Congo 5°8S 22°10E 265 D4
Bena-Tshadi Dem. Rep. of the Congo 4°40S 22°49E 265 C4
Benaco, L. di = Garda, L. di Italy 45°40N 10°41E 198 C7
Benagerie Australia 31°25S 140°22E 282 A4
Benahmed Morocco 33°4N 7°9W 260 B3
Benaki Museum Athens, Greece 112 b3
Benalla Australia 36°30S 146°0E 283 D7
Benalmádena Spain 36°36N 4°34W 195 J6
Benambra, Mt. Australia 36°31S 147°34E 283 D7
Benanee Australia 34°31S 142°52E 282 C5
Benangin Indonesia 0°58S 115°19E 235 C5
Benara Mayotte 12°53S 45°9E 272 b
Benares = Varanasi India 25°22N 83°0E 243 G10
Bénat, C. France 43°5N 6°22E 175 E10
Benavente Portugal 38°59N 8°49W 195 G2
Benavente Spain 42°2N 5°43W 194 C5
Benavides U.S.A. 27°36N 98°25W 314 H5
Benavides de Órbigo Spain 42°30N 5°54W 194 C5
Benbecula U.K. 57°26N 7°21W 167 D1
Benbonyathe Hill Australia 30°25S 139°11E 282 A3
Bend U.S.A. 44°4N 121°19W 304 D3
Bendale Canada 43°45N 79°13W 141 A3
Bendela Dem. Rep. of the Congo 3°18S 17°36E 264 C3
Bendemeer Australia 30°53S 151°8E 283 A9
Bender Beyla Somalia 9°30N 50°48E 267 C7
Bendery Moldova 46°50N 29°30E 183 D14
Bendigo Australia 36°40S 144°15E 282 D6
Bendin = Będzin Poland 50°19N 19°7E 185 H6
Bendorf Germany 50°25N 7°35E 178 E3
Bendsburg = Będzin Poland 50°19N 19°7E 185 H6
Benē Beraq Israel 32°6N 34°51E 251 F5
Beneditinos Brazil 5°27S 42°22W 332 C3
Benedito Leite Brazil 7°13S 44°34W 332 C3
Benefica Brazil 22°52S 43°14W 135 B1
Bénéna Mali 13°9N 4°17W 262 C4
Benenitra Madag. 23°27S 45°5E 272 C2
Benešov Czechia 49°46N 14°41E 180 B7
Benevento Italy 41°8N 14°45E 201 A7
Benfeld France 48°22N 7°34E 173 D14
Benfica Portugal 38°45N 9°11W 126 A1
Beng Mealea Cambodia 13°28N 104°14E 236 F5
Benga Mozam. 16°11S 33°40E 269 F3
Bengal = Pashchimbanga □ India 23°0N 88°0E 243 H13
Bengal, Bay of Ind. Oc. 15°0N 90°0E 239 F14
Bengaluru India 12°59N 77°40E 245 H3
Bengbis Cameroon 3°27N 12°36E 263 E7
Bengbu China 32°58N 117°20E 229 A11
Benghazi = Banghāzī Libya 32°11N 20°3E 258 B4
Benghisa Point Malta 35°49N 14°33E 206 F8
Bengkalis Indonesia 1°30N 102°10E 237 M4
Bengkayang Indonesia 0°49N 109°28E 235 B3
Bengkulu Indonesia 3°50S 102°12E 234 C2
Bengkulu □ Indonesia 3°48S 102°16E 234 C2
Bengo Dem. Rep. of the Congo 2°11S 19°56E 264 C3
Bengo □ Angola 9°0S 13°10E 265 D2
Bengough Canada 49°25N 105°10W 297 D7
Bengtsfors Sweden 59°2N 12°14E 162 E6
Benguela Angola 12°37S 13°25E 265 E2
Benguela □ Angola 13°0S 13°30E 265 E2
Benguerir Morocco 32°16N 7°56W 260 B3
Benguérua, I. Mozam. 21°58S 35°28E 271 B6
Benguet □ Phil. 16°30N 120°40E 232 C3
Benha Egypt 30°26N 31°8E 256 H7
Benham Seamount Pac. Oc. 15°40N 124°30E 232 D5
Beni Dem. Rep. of the Congo 0°30N 29°27E 268 B2
Beni □ Bolivia 14°0S 65°0W 331 C5
Beni → Bolivia 10°23S 65°24W 331 C4
Béni Abbès Algeria 30°5N 2°5W 261 B4
Béni Abbès □ Algeria 29°0N 3°0W 261 C4
Beni Hammad Algeria 35°49N 4°47E 261 A5
Beni Haoua Algeria 36°30N 1°30E 261 A5
Beni Mazâr Egypt 28°32N 30°44E 256 B3
Beni Mellal Morocco 32°21N 6°21W 260 B3
Beni Mellal-Khenifra □ Morocco 32°20N 6°29W 260 B3
Beni Ounif Algeria 32°0N 1°10W 261 B4
Beni Saf Algeria 35°17N 1°15W 261 A4
Beni Suef Egypt 29°5N 31°6E 256 J7
Beniah L. Canada 63°23N 112°17W 296 A6
Benicarló Spain 40°23N 0°23E 196 E5
Benicássim Spain 40°3N 0°4E 196 E5
Benidorm Spain 38°33N 0°9W 197 G4
Benin ■ Africa 10°0N 2°0E 263 D5
Benin → Nigeria 5°45N 5°4E 263 D6
Benin, Bight of W. Afr. 5°0N 3°0E 263 E5
Benin City Nigeria 6°20N 5°31E 263 D6
Benissa Spain 38°43N 0°3E 197 G5
Benítez Int. ✈ (SCL) Santiago, Chile 33°33S 70°42W 137 B1
Bénitiers, Île aux Mauritius 20°24S 57°20E 272 e
Benito Juárez Argentina 37°40S 59°43W 334 D4
Benito Juárez Int. ✈ (MEX) Mexico 19°25N 99°5W 128 B2
Benitses Greece 39°32N 19°55E 206 B9
Benjamin Aceval Paraguay 24°58S 57°34W 334 A4
Benjamin Constant Brazil 4°40S 70°15W 328 D3
Benjamin Hill Mexico 30°9N 111°7W 318 A2
Benkelman U.S.A. 40°3N 101°32W 308 E3
Benkovac Croatia 44°2N 15°37E 199 D12
Benmore Pk. N.Z. 44°25S 170°8E 285 E5
Bennett Canada 59°51N 135°0W 296 B2
Bennett, L. Australia 22°50S 131°2E 278 D5
Bennetta, Ostrov Russia 76°21N 148°56E 215 B15
Bennettsville U.S.A. 34°37N 79°41W 315 D15
Bennichchâb Mauritania 19°32N 15°12W 262 B1
Bennington N.H., U.S.A. 43°0N 71°55W 313 D11
Bennington Vt., U.S.A. 42°53N 73°12W 313 D11
Beno Dem. Rep. of the Congo 3°41S 17°49E 264 C3
Bénodet France 47°53N 4°7W 172 E2
Benom Malaysia 3°50N 102°6E 237 L4
Benoni S. Africa 26°11S 28°18E 271 C4
Benoud Algeria 32°20N 0°16E 261 B5
Bénoué △ Cameroon 8°30N 13°55E 264 A2
Benoy Chad 8°59N 16°19E 259 G3
Benque Viejo del Carmen Belize 17°5N 89°8W 320 C2
Bense Dominica 15°35N 61°22W 323 k
Bensheim Germany 49°40N 8°38E 179 F4
Benson Ariz., U.S.A. 31°58N 110°18W 305 L8
Benson Minn., U.S.A. 45°19N 95°36W 308 C6
Bensonhurst U.S.A. 40°35N 73°59W 132 C2
Bent Iran 26°20N 59°31E 247 E8
Benteng Indonesia 6°10S 120°30E 231 F6
Bentiaba Angola 14°15S 12°21E 265 E2
Bentinck I. Queens., Australia 17°3S 139°35E 280 B2
Bentinck I. Myanmar 11°45N 98°3E 237 G2
Bentiu South Sudan 9°10N 29°55E 257 F2
Bentley Subglacial Trench Antarctica 80°0S 115°0W 151 E15
Bento Gonçalves Brazil 29°10S 51°31W 335 B5
Benton Ark., U.S.A. 34°34N 92°35W 314 D8
Benton Calif., U.S.A. 37°48N 118°32W 306 H8
Benton Ill., U.S.A. 38°0N 88°55W 310 G8
Benton Pa., U.S.A. 41°12N 76°23W 313 E8
Benton Harbor U.S.A. 42°6N 86°27W 311 B10
Benton Heights U.S.A. 42°7N 86°24W 311 B10
Bentong Malaysia 3°31N 101°55E 237 L3
Bentonville U.S.A. 36°22N 94°13W 314 C7
Bentu Liben Ethiopia 8°32N 38°21E 257 F4
Benue □ Nigeria 7°20N 8°45E 263 D6
Benue → Nigeria 7°48N 6°46E 263 D6
Benxi China 41°20N 123°48E 224 B1
Benza Dem. Rep. of the Congo 4°49S 13°17E 265 D2
Benzdorp Suriname 3°44N 54°5W 329 C7
Beo Indonesia 4°25N 126°50E 231 D7
Beograd Serbia 44°50N 20°37E 202 B4
Beograd ✈ (BEG) Serbia 43°49N 20°17E 202 C4
Beolgyo S. Korea 34°51N 127°21E 224 E3
Beoumi Côte d'Ivoire 7°45N 5°23W 262 D3
Beppu Japan 33°15N 131°30E 222 D3
Beppu-Wan Japan 33°18N 131°34E 222 D3
Beqa Fiji 18°23S 178°8E 287 B2
Beqaa Valley = Al Biqā Lebanon 34°10N 36°10E 250 D7
Bequia St. Vincent 13°0N 61°15W 323 n
Ber Mota India 23°27N 68°34E 242 H3
Bera, Tasik Malaysia 3°5N 102°38E 237 L4
Berach → India 25°15N 75°2E 242 G6
Beraketa Madag. 23°7S 44°25E 272 C1
Béran-Djoko Congo 3°15N 17°0E 264 B3
Berane Montenegro 42°51N 19°52E 202 D3
Berastagi Indonesia 3°11N 98°31E 237 L2
Berat Albania 40°43N 19°59E 202 F3
Berau = Tanjungredeb Indonesia 2°9N 117°29E 235 B5
Berau → Indonesia 2°10N 117°42E 235 B5
Berau, Teluk Indonesia 2°30S 132°30E 231 E8
Beravina Madag. 18°10S 45°14E 272 B2
Berbak △ Indonesia 1°27S 104°19E 234 C2
Berber Sudan 18°0N 34°0E 256 D3
Berbera Somalia 10°30N 45°2E 267 B6
Berbérati C.A.R. 4°15N 15°40E 264 B3
Berbice → Guyana 6°20N 57°32W 329 B6
Berceto Italy 44°31N 9°51E 198 D6
Berchem-Ste-Agathe Belgium 50°52N 4°17E 116 A1
Berchidda Italy 40°47N 9°10E 200 B2
Berchtesgaden Germany 47°38N 13°0E 179 H8
Berchtesgaden △ Germany 47°34N 12°55E 179 H8
Berck France 50°25N 1°36E 173 B8
Berdaale Bay, Somalia 7°4N 47°51E 267 C6
Berdaale Mudug, Somalia 3°14N 43°11E 267 D5
Berdichev = Berdychiv Ukraine 49°57N 28°30E 177 D15
Berdsk Russia 54°47N 83°2E 217 B10
Berdyansk Ukraine 46°45N 36°50E 189 J9
Berdychiv Ukraine 49°57N 28°30E 177 D15
Béré Chad 9°20N 16°9E 259 G3
Berea U.S.A. 37°34N 84°17W 309 G11
Berebere Indonesia 2°25N 128°45E 231 D7
Bereeda Somalia 11°45N 51°0E 267 B7
Berehomet Ukraine 48°10N 25°19E 183 B10
Berehove Ukraine 48°15N 22°35E 182 B7
Bereina Papua N. G. 8°39S 146°30E 286 E4
Bereket Turkmenistan 39°16N 55°32E 247 B7
Berekua Dominica 15°14N 61°19W 323 k
Berekum Ghana 7°29N 2°34W 262 D4
Berenice Egypt 24°2N 35°25E 256 C4
Berens → Canada 52°25N 97°2W 297 C9
Berens I. Canada 52°18N 97°18W 297 C9
Berens River Canada 52°25N 97°0W 297 C9
Beresfield Australia 32°50S 151°40E 283 B9
Beresford U.S.A. 43°5N 96°47W 308 D5
Berestechko Ukraine 50°22N 25°5E 177 C13
Berești Romania 46°6N 27°50E 183 D12
Beretău → Romania 47°10N 21°50E 182 C6
Berettyó → Hungary 46°59N 21°7E 182 D6
Berettyóújfalu Hungary 47°13N 21°33E 182 C6
Berevo Melaky, Madag. 17°14S 44°17E 272 B1
Berevo Menabe, Madag. 19°44S 44°58E 272 B1
Bereza = Byaroza Belarus 52°31N 24°51E 177 B13
Berezhany Ukraine 49°26N 24°58E 177 D13
Berezina = Byarezina → Belarus 52°33N 30°14E 177 B16
Berezivka Ukraine 47°14N 30°55E 189 J6
Berezna Ukraine 51°35N 31°46E 189 G6
Bereznik Russia 62°51N 42°40E 186 B7
Berezniki Russia 59°24N 56°46E 186 C10
Berezovo Russia 64°0N 65°0E 214 C7
Berezyne Ukraine 46°14N 29°12E 183 D14
Berg am Laim Germany 48°7N 11°38E 131 B2
Berga Spain 42°6N 1°48E 196 C6
Berga Kalmar, Sweden 57°14N 16°3E 163 G10
Bergama Turkey 39°8N 27°11E 205 B9
Bérgamo Italy 45°41N 9°43E 198 C6
Bergaon India 20°41N 80°27E 244 D5
Bergara Spain 43°9N 2°28W 196 B2
Bergby Sweden 60°57N 17°2E 162 D11
Berge Norway 59°34N 8°10E 162 E2
Bergedorf Germany 53°28N 10°6E 178 B6
Bergeforsen Sweden 62°32N 17°23E 162 B11
Bergen Mecklenburg-Vorpommern, Germany 54°25N 13°25E 178 A9
Bergen Niedersachsen, Germany 52°49N 9°57E 178 C5
Bergen Neths. 52°40N 4°43E 170 B4
Bergen Hordaland, Norway 60°20N 5°20E 164 D2
Bergen N.Y., U.S.A. 43°5N 77°57W 312 C7
Bergen ✈ (BGO) Norway 60°17N 5°19E 164 D2
Bergen op Zoom Neths. 51°28N 4°18E 170 C4
Bergenfield U.S.A. 40°55N 73°59W 132 A2
Bergerac France 44°51N 0°30E 174 D4
Bergham Germany 48°2N 11°37E 131 B2
Bergheim Germany 50°57N 6°38E 178 E2
Bergholz U.S.A. 40°31N 80°53W 312 F4
Bergisch Gladbach Germany 50°59N 7°8E 178 E3
Bergisches Land ⌓ Germany 51°0N 7°30E 178 E3
Bergkamen Germany 51°37N 7°38E 178 D3
Bergkvara Sweden 56°23N 16°5E 163 H10
Berghamra Sweden 59°38N 18°37E 162 E12
Bergsjö Sweden 61°59N 17°3E 162 C11
Bergstadt = Leśnica Poland 50°26N 18°11E 185 H5
Bergstrasse-Odenwald ⌓ Germany 49°45N 5°55E 179 F1
Bergues France 50°58N 2°24E 173 B9
Bergviken Sweden 61°15N 16°40E 162 C10
Bergville S. Africa 28°52S 29°18E 271 C4
Bergvliet S. Africa 34°2S 18°25E 118 B1
Berhala, Selat Indonesia 1°0S 104°15E 234 C2
Berhampore = Baharampur India 24°2N 88°27E 243 G13
Berhampur = Brahmapur India 19°15N 84°54E 244 E7
Berheci → Romania 45°58N 27°28E 183 E12
Beri Spain 41°20N 2°1E 114 A1
Berikat, Tanjung Indonesia 2°34S 106°52E 234 C3
Bering Glacier U.S.A. 60°20N 143°30W 303 F12
Bering Land Bridge ⌓ U.S.A. 66°20N 165°0W 303 C6
Bering Sea Pac. Oc. 58°0N 171°0W 292 D2
Bering Strait Pac. Oc. 65°30N 169°0W 303 D5
Beringovskiy Russia 63°3N 179°19E 215 C18
Berisso Argentina 34°56S 57°50W 334 C4
Berja Spain 36°50N 2°56W 195 J8
Berkåk Norway 62°50N 10°0E 164 B6
Berkane Morocco 34°52N 2°20W 261 B4
Berkeley U.S.A. 37°51N 122°16W 136 A3
Berkeley, C. Ecuador 0°1N 91°35W 330 a
Berkner I. Antarctica 79°30S 50°0W 151 D18
Berkovitsa Bulgaria 43°16N 23°8E 202 C7
Berkshire U.S.A. 42°19N 76°11W 313 D8
Berkshire Downs U.K. 51°33N 1°29W 169 F6
Berlanga Spain 38°17N 5°50W 195 G5
Berlenga, I. Portugal 39°25N 9°30W 195 F1
Berlengas = Valença do Piauí Brazil 6°20S 41°45W 332 C3
Berlin = Kitchener Canada 43°27N 80°29W 312 C4
Berlin Germany 52°31N 13°23E 115 A3
Berlin Ga., U.S.A. 31°4N 83°37W 316 D6
Berlin Md., U.S.A. 38°20N 75°13W 309 F16
Berlin N.H., U.S.A. 44°28N 71°11W 313 B13
Berlin N.Y., U.S.A. 42°42N 73°23W 313 D11
Berlin Wis., U.S.A. 43°58N 88°57W 308 D9
Berlin □ Germany 52°30N 13°20E 178 C9
Berlin Brandenburg ✈ (BER) Germany 52°22N 13°30E 115 B4
Berlin Dom Germany 52°31N 13°24E 115 A3
Berlin L. U.S.A. 41°3N 81°0W 312 E4
Berlinchen = Barlinek Poland 53°0N 15°15E 185 F2
Bermagui Australia 36°25S 150°4E 283 D9
Bermeja, Sierra Spain 36°30N 5°11W 195 J5
Bermejo → Formosa, Argentina 26°51S 58°23W 334 B4
Bermejo → San Juan, Argentina 32°30S 67°30W 334 C2
Bermejo, Paso = Uspallata, P. de Argentina 32°37S 69°22W 334 C2
Bermen, L. Canada 53°35N 68°55W 299 B6
Bermeo Spain 43°25N 2°47W 196 B2
Bermillo de Sayago Spain 41°22N 6°8W 194 D4
Bermondsey U.K. 51°29N 0°3W 125 B3
Bermuda ⧄ Atl. Oc. 32°18N 64°45W 153 a
Bermuda Rise Atl. Oc. 32°30N 65°0W 152 C5
Bern Switz. 46°57N 7°28E 179 J3
Bern □ Switz. 46°45N 7°40E 179 J3
Bernabeu, Estadio Spain 40°27N 3°41W 127 B1
Bernal Heights U.S.A. 37°44N 122°24W 136 B2
Bernalda Italy 40°24N 16°41E 201 B9
Bernalillo U.S.A. 35°18N 106°33W 305 J10
Bernam → Malaysia 3°45N 101°5E 234 B2
Bernardo, Palazzo Venice, Italy 142 b2
Bernardo de Irigoyen Argentina 26°15S 53°40W 335 B5
Bernardo O'Higgins ⌓ Chile 48°50S 75°36W 336 C1
Bernardsville U.S.A. 40°43N 74°34W 313 F10
Bernasconi Argentina 37°55S 63°44W 334 D3
Bernau Bayern, Germany 47°47N 12°22E 179 H8
Bernau Brandenburg, Germany 52°40N 13°35E 178 C9
Bernay France 49°5N 0°35E 172 C7
Bernburg Germany 51°47N 11°44E 178 D7
Berndorf Austria 47°59N 16°1E 180 D9
Berne = Bern Switz. 46°57N 7°28E 179 J3
Berne = Bern □ Switz. 46°45N 7°40E 179 J3
Berne U.S.A. 40°39N 84°57W 311 D12
Berner Alpen Switz. 46°27N 7°35E 179 J3
Berneray U.K. 57°43N 7°11W 167 D1
Bernier I. Australia 24°50S 113°12E 279 D1
Bernina, Piz Switz. 46°20N 9°54E 179 J5
Bernkastel-Kues Germany 49°55N 7°3E 179 F3
Bernstadt = Bierutów Poland 51°7N 17°32E 185 G4
Bernstein = Pełczyce Poland 53°3N 15°16E 185 E2
Bero → Angola 15°10S 12°9E 265 F2
Beroroha Madag. 21°40S 45°10E 272 C2
Béroubouay Benin 10°34N 2°46E 263 C5
Beroun Czechia 49°57N 14°5E 180 B7
Berounka → Czechia 50°0N 14°22E 180 B7
Berovo N. Macedonia 41°38N 22°51E 202 E6
Berre, Étang de France 43°27N 5°5E 175 E9
Berre-l'Étang France 43°27N 5°10E 175 E9
Berrechid Morocco 33°18N 7°36W 260 B3
Berri Australia 34°14S 140°35E 282 C4
Berriane Algeria 32°50N 3°46E 261 B5
Berridale Australia 36°22S 148°48E 283 D8
Berrien Springs U.S.A. 41°57N 86°20W 311 C10
Berrigan Australia 35°38S 145°49E 283 C6
Berriwillock Australia 35°36S 142°59E 282 C5
Berrouaghia Algeria 36°10N 2°53E 261 A5
Berry N.S.W., Australia 34°46S 150°43E 283 C9
Berry France 46°50N 2°0E 173 F8
Berry Is. The Bahamas 25°40N 77°50W 320 A4
Berrydale U.S.A. 30°53N 87°3W 317 E2
Berryessa, L. U.S.A. 38°31N 122°6W 306 G4
Berryville U.S.A. 36°22N 93°34W 314 C8
Berseba Namibia 26°0S 17°46E 270 C2
Bersenbrück Germany 52°34N 7°56E 178 C3
Bershad Ukraine 48°22N 29°31E 183 B14
Bertamirans Spain 42°54N 8°38W 194 C2
Berthold U.S.A. 48°19N 101°44W 308 A3
Berthoud U.S.A. 40°19N 105°5W 304 F11
Bertincourt France 50°5N 2°58E 173 B9
Bertolinia Brazil 7°38S 43°57W 332 C3
Bertoua Cameroon 4°30N 13°45E 264 B2
Bertraghboy B. Ireland 53°22N 9°54W 166 C2
Bertys = Balqash Kazakhstan 46°50N 74°50E 214 E8
Beru Kiribati 1°20S 176°0E 277 A14
Berufjörður Iceland 64°48N 14°29W 155 C12
Beruniy Uzbekistan 41°41N 60°45E 216 D6
Beruri Brazil 3°54S 61°22W 329 D5
Beruwala Sri Lanka 6°30N 80°0E 245 L4
Berwick U.S.A. 41°3N 76°14W 313 E8
Berwick-upon-Tweed U.K. 55°46N 2°0W 168 B6
Berwyn U.S.A. 41°50N 87°47W 119 B2
Berwyn Heights U.S.A. 38°59N 76°55W 143 B3
Berwyn Mts. U.K. 52°54N 3°26W 168 E4
Beryslav Ukraine 46°50N 33°30E 189 J7
Berzasca Romania 44°39N 21°58E 182 F6
Berzence Hungary 46°12N 17°11E 182 D2
Besal Pakistan 35°4N 73°56E 243 B5
Besalampy Madag. 16°43S 44°29E 272 B1
Besançon France 47°15N 6°2E 173 E13
Besar Indonesia 2°40S 116°0E 235 C5
Besar, Gunung Malaysia 5°10N 101°18E 234 A2
Beshenkovichi Belarus 55°2N 29°29E 188 E5
Besianë Kosovo 42°54N 21°10E 202 D5
Beşiktaş Turkey 41°2N 29°0E 122 B2
Beška Serbia 45°8N 20°6E 182 E5
Beslan Russia 43°15N 44°28E 191 J7
Besna Kobila Serbia 42°31N 22°10E 202 D6
Besnard L. Canada 55°25N 106°0W 297 B7
Besni Turkey 37°41N 37°52E 212 D7
Besor, N. → Egypt 31°28N 34°22E 251 G5
Besós → Spain 41°24N 2°13E 114 A2
Bessa Monteiro Angola 7°7S 13°44E 265 D2
Bessarabiya Moldova 47°0N 28°10E 177 E15
Bessarabka = Basarabeasca Moldova 46°21N 28°58E 183 D13
Bessèges France 44°18N 4°8E 175 D8
Bessemer Ala., U.S.A. 33°24N 86°58W 315 E11
Bessemer Mich., U.S.A. 46°29N 90°3W 308 B8
Bessemer Pa., U.S.A. 40°59N 80°30W 312 F4
Bessie, L. U.S.A. 28°29N 81°31W 133 B1
Bessin France 49°18N 1°0W 172 C6
Bessines-sur-Gartempe France 46°6N 1°22E 174 B5
Beswick Australia 14°34S 132°53E 278 B5
Beswick ✪ Australia 14°31S 132°51E 278 B5
Bet Horon West Bank 31°52N 35°7E 123 A1
Bet She'an Israel 32°30N 35°30E 251 F6
Bet Shemesh Israel 31°44N 35°0E 251 G6
Betafo Madag. 19°50S 46°51E 272 B2
Betamba Dem. Rep. of the Congo 2°17S 21°24E 264 C4
Betancuria Canary Is. 28°25N 14°3W 153 e2
Betancuria, Mt. Canary Is. 28°25N 14°6W 153 e2
Betania Colombia 4°22N 72°54W 328 C3
Betanzos Bolivia 19°34S 65°27W 331 D4
Betanzos Spain 43°15N 8°12W 194 B2
Bétaré Oya Cameroon 5°40N 14°5E 264 A2
Betatao Madag. 18°11S 47°52E 272 B2
Bétera Spain 39°35N 0°28W 197 F4
Bétérou Benin 9°12N 2°16E 263 D5
Bethal S. Africa 26°27S 29°28E 271 C4
Bethalto U.S.A. 38°55N 90°2W 310 F6
Bethanien Namibia 26°31S 17°8E 270 C2
Bethany Ont., Canada 44°11N 78°34W 312 B6
Bethany Ill., U.S.A. 39°39N 88°45W 311 E8
Bethany Mo., U.S.A. 40°16N 94°2W 310 D2
Bethany Okla., U.S.A. 35°31N 97°38W 314 D6
Bethel Alaska, U.S.A. 60°48N 161°45W 303 F7
Bethel Conn., U.S.A. 41°22N 73°25W 313 E11
Bethel Maine, U.S.A. 44°25N 70°47W 313 B14
Bethel Ohio, U.S.A. 38°58N 84°5W 311 F12
Bethel Vt., U.S.A. 43°50N 72°38W 313 C12
Bethel Park U.S.A. 40°19N 80°2W 312 F4
Béthenville France 49°18N 4°23E 173 C11
Bethesda U.S.A. 38°59N 77°6W 143 B2
Bethlehem = Bayt Lahm West Bank 31°43N 35°12E 123 B2
Bethlehem Free State, S. Africa 28°14S 28°18E 271 C4
Bethlehem Pa., U.S.A. 40°37N 75°23W 313 F9
Bethnal Green U.K. 51°31N 0°2W 125 A3
Bethulie S. Africa 30°30S 25°59E 270 D4
Béthune France 50°30N 2°38E 173 B9
Béthune → France 49°53N 1°4E 172 C8
Bethungra Australia 34°45S 147°51E 283 C7
Betijoque Venezuela 9°23N 70°44W 328 B3
Betim Brazil 19°58S 44°13W 333 E3
Betioky Atsimo-Andrefana, Madag. 23°48S 44°20E 272 C1
Betioky Atsimo-Andrefana, Madag. 22°27S 43°43E 272 C1
Betong Malaysia 1°24N 111°31E 235 B4
Betong Thailand 5°45N 101°5E 237 K3
Betoota Australia 25°45S 140°42E 280 D3
Betor Ethiopia 11°37N 39°2E 257 E4
Betor Paschimbanga, India 22°34N 88°17E 124 B1
Bétou Congo 3°2N 18°32E 264 B3
Betpaqdala Kazakhstan 45°45N 70°30E 217 C8
Betroka Madag. 23°16S 46°0E 272 C2
Betsiamites Canada 48°56N 68°40W 299 C6
Betsiamites → Canada 48°56N 68°38W 299 C6
Betsiboka □ Madag. 17°0S 46°50E 272 B2
Betsiboka → Madag. 16°3S 46°36E 272 B2
Bettendorf U.S.A. 41°32N 90°30W 310 C6
Bettiah India 26°48N 84°33E 243 F11
Bettna Sweden 58°55N 16°38E 163 F10
Béttola Italy 44°47N 9°36E 198 D6
Betul India 21°58N 77°59E 244 D3
Betung Indonesia 3°58S 104°34E 234 C2
Betung Kerihun ⌓ Indonesia 1°11N 113°38E 235 B4
Betws-y-Coed U.K. 53°5N 3°48W 168 D4
Betxi Spain 39°56N 0°12W 196 F4
Betzdorf Germany 50°46N 7°52E 178 E3
Béu Angola 6°15S 15°32E 265 D3
Beuil France 44°6N 6°59E 175 D10
Beulah Vic., Australia 35°58S 142°29E 282 C5
Beulah Fla., U.S.A. 28°32N 81°34W 133 A1
Beulah Mich., U.S.A. 44°38N 86°6W 308 C10
Beulah N. Dak., U.S.A. 47°16N 101°47W 308 B3
Beulah, L. U.S.A. 28°32N 81°33W 133 A1
Beurkia Chad 15°20N 17°56E 259 E3
Beurs van Berlage Amsterdam, Neths. 112 a2
Beuthen = Bytom Poland 50°25N 18°54E 185 H5
Beuthen an der Oder = Bytom Odrzański Poland 51°44N 15°48E 185 G2
Beuvron → France 47°29N 1°15E 172 E8
Beveren Belgium 51°12N 4°16E 170 C4
Beverley W. Austral., Australia 32°9S 116°56E 279 F2
Beverley E. Riding, U.K. 53°51N 0°26W 168 D7
Beverley Hills Australia 33°56S 151°5E 139 B1
Beverley Park Australia 33°58S 151°8E 139 B1
Beverly Ill., U.S.A. 41°42N 87°39W 119 C3
Beverly Mass., U.S.A. 42°33N 70°53W 313 D14
Beverly Arts Center U.S.A. 41°41N 87°40W 119 C2
Beverly Glen U.S.A. 34°6N 118°26W 126 B2
Beverly Hills Calif., U.S.A. 34°5N 118°24W 126 B2
Beverly Hills Fla., U.S.A. 28°55N 82°28W 317 G7
Beverly Hills-Morgan Park Historic District U.S.A. 41°41N 87°40W 119 C2
Beverungen Germany 51°39N 9°22E 178 D5
Bevoalavo Madag. 25°13S 44°26E 272 D2
Bewas → India 23°59N 79°21E 243 H8
Bewdley Canada 44°5N 78°19W 312 B6
Bex Switz. 46°15N 7°1E 179 J3
Bexhill U.K. 50°51N 0°29E 169 G8
Bexley Australia 33°56S 151°7E 139 B1
Bexley □ U.K. 51°27N 0°9E 125 B4
Bexleyheath U.K. 51°27N 0°8E 125 B4
Bexon St. Lucia 13°57N 60°59W 323 m
Bey Dağları Turkey 36°38N 30°29E 205 E12
Beyānlū Iran 36°0N 47°51E 246 C5
Beyazköy Turkey 41°21N 27°42E 203 E11
Beyçayırı Turkey 40°15N 26°55E 203 F10
Beydağ Turkey 38°5N 28°13E 205 C10
Beyeğaç Turkey 37°14N 28°53E 205 D10
Beyin Ghana 5°1N 2°41W 262 D4
Beykoz Turkey 41°7N 29°7E 122 B2
Beyla Guinea 8°30N 8°38W 262 D3
Beylerbeyi Turkey 41°2N 29°2E 122 B2
Beynat France 45°8N 1°44E 174 C5
Beyneu Kazakhstan 45°18N 55°9E 187 E10
Beyoba Turkey 38°48N 27°47E 205 C9
Beyoğlu Turkey 41°1N 28°58E 122 B1
Beyoneisu Retsugan Japan 31°55N 139°55E 223 F11
Beypazarı Turkey 40°10N 31°56E 212 B4
Beypore → India 11°10N 75°47E 245 J2
Beyra Somalia 6°57N 47°19E 267 C6
Beyşehir Turkey 37°41N 31°45E 212 D4
Beyşehir Gölü Turkey 37°41N 31°33E 212 D4
Beytüşşebap Turkey 37°35N 43°10E 213 D10
Bezdan Serbia 45°50N 18°57E 182 E3
Bezhetsk Russia 57°47N 36°39E 188 D9
Béziers France 43°20N 3°12E 174 E7
Bezons France 48°56N 2°13E 134 A2
Bezuidenhout Park S. Africa 26°10S 28°5E 123 B2
Bezwada = Vijayawada India 16°31N 80°39E 244 F5
Bhabua India 25°3N 83°37E 243 G10
Bhachau India 23°20N 70°16E 242 H4
Bhadar → Gujarat, India 22°17N 72°20E 242 H5
Bhadar → Gujarat, India 21°27N 69°47E 242 J3
Bhadarwah India 32°58N 75°46E 243 C6
Bhadgaon = Bhaktapur Nepal 27°38N 85°24E 243 F11
Bhadohi India 25°25N 82°34E 243 G10
Bhadra India 29°8N 75°14E 242 E6
Bhadra → India 14°0N 75°20E 245 H2
Bhadrachalam India 17°40N 80°53E 244 F5
Bhadrak India 21°10N 86°30E 244 D8
Bhadrakali India 22°40N 88°20E 124 A2
Bhadran India 22°19N 72°6E 242 H5
Bhadravati India 13°49N 75°40E 245 H2
Bhag Pakistan 29°2N 67°49E 242 E2
Bhagalpur India 25°10N 87°0E 243 G12
Bhagirathi → Paschimbanga, India 23°25N 88°23E 243 H13
Bhagirathi → Uttarakhand, India 30°8N 78°35E 243 D8
Bhainsa India 19°10N 77°58E 244 E3
Bhairab → Bangla. 22°51N 89°34E 243 H13
Bhairab Bazar Bangla. 24°4N 90°58E 241 C3
Bhakkar Pakistan 31°40N 71°5E 242 D4
Bhakra Dam India 31°30N 76°45E 242 D7
Bhaktapur Nepal 27°38N 85°24E 243 F11
Bhalki India 18°2N 77°13E 244 E3
Bhalswa India 28°44N 77°10E 120 A2
Bhambo Khan Qarmati Pakistan 24°49N 67°7E 123 B2
Bhamo Myanmar 24°15N 97°15E 241 C6
Bhamragarh India 19°30N 80°40E 244 E5
Bhandara India 21°5N 79°42E 244 D4
Bhanpura India 24°31N 75°44E 242 G6
Bhanrer Ra. India 23°40N 79°45E 243 H8
Bhaptiahi India 26°19N 86°44E 243 F12
Bharat = India ■ Asia 20°0N 78°0E 239 F11
Bharati Antarctica 69°24S 76°11E 151 C6
Bharatpur Chhattisgarh, India 23°44N 81°46E 243 H9
Bharatpur Raj., India 27°15N 77°30E 242 F7
Bharatpur Nepal 27°34N 84°10E 243 F11
Bharno India 23°14N 84°53E 243 H11
Bharraig = Barra U.K. 57°0N 7°29W 167 E1
Bharraig, Caolas = Barra, Sd. of U.K. 57°4N 7°25W 167 D1
Bharuch India 21°47N 73°0E 244 D1
Bhatarsaigh = Vatersay U.K. 56°55N 7°32W 167 E1
Bhatghar L. India 18°10N 73°48E 244 E1
Bhatiapara Ghat Bangla. 23°13N 89°42E 241 D2
Bhatinda India 30°15N 74°57E 242 D6
Bhatkal India 13°58N 74°35E 245 H2
Bhatpara India 22°50N 88°25E 243 H13
Bhatsala India 22°52N 88°16E 124 B1
Bhattu India 29°36N 75°19E 242 E6
Bhaun Pakistan 32°55N 72°40E 242 C5
Bhaunagar = Bhavnagar India 21°45N 72°10E 244 D1
Bhavani India 11°27N 77°43E 245 J3
Bhavnagar India 21°45N 72°10E 244 D1
Bhawanipatna India 19°55N 83°10E 244 E6
Bhawanipur India 22°32N 88°21E 124 B2
Bhawari India 25°42N 73°4E 242 G5
Bhayavadar India 21°51N 70°15E 242 J4
Bhearnaraigh = Berneray U.K. 57°43N 7°11W 167 D1
Bhendkhal India 18°52N 72°59E 130 B2
Bhera Pakistan 32°29N 72°57E 242 C5
Bheri → Nepal 28°47N 81°18E 243 E9
Bhikangaon India 21°52N 75°57E 242 J6
Bhilai = Bhilainagar-Durg India 21°13N 81°26E 244 D5
Bhilainagar-Durg India 21°13N 81°26E 244 D5
Bhilsa = Vidisha India 23°28N 77°53E 242 H7
Bhilwara India 25°25N 74°38E 242 G6
Bhima → India 16°25N 77°17E 244 F3
Bhimavaram India 16°30N 81°30E 245 F5
Bhimbar Pakistan 32°59N 74°3E 243 C6
Bhind India 26°30N 78°46E 243 F8
Bhinga India 27°43N 81°56E 243 F9
Bhinmal India 25°0N 72°15E 242 G5
Bhisho S. Africa 32°50S 27°23E 270 D4
Bhit I. Pakistan 24°49N 67°0E 123 B1
Bhiwandi India 19°20N 73°0E 244 E1
Bhiwani India 28°50N 76°9E 242 E7
Bhogava → India 22°26N 72°20E 242 H5
Bhojpur Nepal 27°10N 87°3E 243 F12
Bhokardan India 20°16N 75°46E 244 D2
Bhola Bangla. 22°45N 90°35E 241 D3
Bholari Pakistan 25°19N 68°13E 242 G3
Bhongir India 17°30N 78°56E 244 F4
Bhopal India 23°20N 77°30E 242 H7
Bhopalpatnam India 18°52N 80°23E 244 E5
Bhor India 18°12N 73°53E 244 E1
Bhuban India 20°53N 85°50E 244 D7
Bhubaneshwar India 20°15N 85°50E 244 D7
Bhuj India 23°15N 69°49E 242 H3
Bhuleshwar Mumbai, India 130 b2
Bhumiphol Res. Thailand 17°20N 98°40E 236 D2
Bhusawal India 21°3N 75°46E 244 D2
Bhutan ■ Asia 27°25N 90°30E 241 B3
Biá → Brazil 3°28S 67°23W 328 D4
Biafra, B. of = Bonny, Bight of Africa 3°30N 9°20E 263 E6
Biak Indonesia 1°10S 136°6E 231 E9
Biała Poland 50°24N 17°40E 185 H4
Biała → Poland 50°3N 20°55E 185 H7
Biała Piska Poland 53°37N 22°5E 184 E9
Biała Podlaska Poland 52°4N 23°6E 185 F10
Biała Rawska Poland 51°48N 20°29E 185 G7
Białobrzegi Poland 51°39N 20°58E 185 G7
Białogard Poland 54°2N 15°58E 184 D2
Białołeka Dworska Poland 52°19N 21°1E 143 B2
Białowieski △ Poland 52°43N 23°50E 185 F10
Białowieża Poland 52°41N 23°49E 185 F10
Biały Bór Poland 53°53N 16°51E 184 E3
Białystok Poland 53°10N 23°10E 185 E10
Biancavilla Italy 37°38N 14°52E 201 E7
Bianco Italy 38°5N 16°9E 201 D9
Biankouma Côte d'Ivoire 7°50N 7°40W 262 D3
Biaora India 23°56N 76°56E 242 H7
Bīārjmand Iran 36°6N 55°53E 247 B7
Biaro Indonesia 2°5N 125°26E 231 D7
Biarritz France 43°29N 1°33W 174 E2
Biasca Switz. 46°22N 8°58E 179 J4
Biavela Angola 14°43S 19°47E 265 E3
Biba Egypt 28°55N 31°0E 256 J7
Bibai Japan 43°19N 141°52E 220 C10
Bibala Angola 14°44S 13°24E 265 E2
Bibane, Bahiret el Tunisia 33°16N 11°13E 258 B2
Bibassé Gabon 1°27N 11°37E 264 B2
Bibbiena Italy 43°42N 11°49E 199 E8
Bibby I. Canada 61°55N 93°0W 297 A10
Bibei → Spain 42°24N 7°13W 194 C3
Biberach Germany 48°5N 9°47E 179 G5
Bibi Papua N. G. 5°30S 146°2E 286 C4
Bibiani Ghana 6°30N 2°8W 262 D4
Bibile Sri Lanka 7°10N 81°25E 245 L5
Bibungwa Dem. Rep. of the Congo 2°40S 28°15E 268 C2
Bicaj Albania 41°58N 20°25E 202 E4
Bicaz Romania 46°53N 26°5E 183 D11
Bicazu Ardelean Romania 46°51N 25°56E 183 D10
Biccari Italy 41°23N 15°12E 201 A8
Bicentennial Park N.S.W., Australia 33°51S 151°5E 139 B1
Bicentennial Park Calif., U.S.A. 34°1N 118°17W 126 B4
Bicester U.K. 51°54N 1°9W 169 F6
Biche Trin. & Tob. 10°26N 61°8W 323 t
Bichena Ethiopia 10°28N 38°10E 257 E4
Bicheno Australia 41°52S 148°18E 281 G4
Bichia India 22°27N 80°42E 243 H9
Bichvinta Georgia 43°9N 40°21E 191 J5
Bickerton I. Australia 13°45S 136°10E 280 A2
Bickley U.K. 51°23N 0°3E 125 B4
Bicknell U.S.A. 38°47N 87°19W 311 F9
Bicol □ Phil. 13°30N 124°0E 232 E5
Bicol △ Phil. 13°55N 122°58E 232 E4
Bicske Hungary 47°29N 18°38E 182 C3
Bicuari △ Angola 15°14S 14°45E 265 F2
Bicutan Phil. 14°30N 121°3E 127 C2
Bid = Bir India 19°4N 75°46E 244 E2
Bida Dem. Rep. of the Congo 4°55N 19°56E 264 B3
Bida Nigeria 9°3N 5°58E 263 D6
Bidar India 17°55N 77°35E 244 F3
Bidde Somalia 0°58N 42°37E 267 D5
Biddeford U.S.A. 43°30N 70°28W 309 D18
Biddwara Ethiopia 5°11N 38°34E 257 F4
Bideford U.K. 51°1N 4°13W 169 F3
Bideford Bay U.K. 51°5N 4°20W 169 F3
Bidhan Nagar India 22°35N 88°25E 124 B2
Bidhuna India 26°49N 79°31E 243 F8
Bīdokht Iran 34°20N 58°46E 247 C8
Bidor Malaysia 4°6N 101°15E 237 K3
Bidu West Bank 31°50N 35°9E 123 B1
Bidyadanga Australia 18°45S 121°43E 278 C3
Bidzar Cameroon 9°54N 14°7E 264 A2
Bie Sweden 59°5N 16°12E 162 E10
Bié □ Angola 12°30S 17°0E 265 E3
Bié, Planalto de Angola 12°0S 16°0E 265 E3
Bieber U.S.A. 41°7N 121°8W 304 F3
Biebrza → Poland 53°13N 22°25E 185 E9
Biebrzański △ Poland 53°36N 22°45E 184 E9
Biecz Poland 49°44N 21°15E 185 J8
Biel Switz. 47°8N 7°14E 179 H3
Bielany Poland 52°17N 20°57E 143 B1
Bielawa Dolnośląskie, Poland 50°43N 16°37E 185 H3
Bielawa Warszawa, Poland 52°8N 21°9E 143 C2
Bielefeld Germany 52°1N 8°33E 178 C4
Bielersee Switz. 47°6N 7°5E 179 H3
Bielitz = Bielsko-Biała Poland 49°50N 19°2E 185 J6
Biella Italy 45°34N 8°3E 198 C5
Bielsk Podlaski Poland 52°47N 23°12E 185 F10
Bielsko-Biała Poland 49°50N 19°2E 185 J6
Bien Hoa Vietnam 10°57N 106°49E 237 G6
Bienne = Biel Switz. 47°8N 7°14E 179 H3
Bienvenida Spain 38°18N 6°12W 195 G4
Bienvenue Fr. Guiana 3°0N 52°30W 329 C7
Bienville, L. Canada 55°5N 72°40W 298 A5
Bierné France 47°48N 0°33W 172 E6
Bierun Poland 50°6N 19°6E 185 H6
Bierutów Poland 51°7N 17°32E 185 G4
Biesbosch △ Neths. 51°45N 4°48E 170 C4
Biescas Spain 42°37N 0°20W 196 C4
Biesdorf Germany 52°30N 13°33E 115 A4
Biese → Germany 52°53N 11°46E 178 C7
Biesiesfontein S. Africa 30°57S 17°58E 270 D2
Bieszczadzki △ Poland 49°5N 22°43E 185 J9
Bietigheim-Bissingen Germany 48°58N 9°8E 179 G5
Bièvre → France 48°44N 2°9E 134 B1
Bièvres France 48°45N 2°13E 134 B2
Bieżuń Poland 52°58N 19°55E 185 F6
Biferno → Italy 41°59N 15°2E 199 G12
Bifoum Gabon 0°20S 10°23E 264 C2
Big → Nfld. & L., Canada 54°50N 58°55W 299 B8
Big → Mo., U.S.A. 38°28N 90°37W 310 F6
Big B. = Awarua B. N.Z. 44°28S 168°4E 285 E3
Big B. Canada 55°43N 60°35W 299 A7
Big Bear City U.S.A. 34°16N 116°51W 307 L10
Big Bear Lake U.S.A. 34°15N 116°56W 307 L10
Big Belt Mts. U.S.A. 46°30N 111°25W 304 C8
Big Bend Eswatini 26°50S 31°58E 271 C5
Big Bend △ U.S.A. 29°20N 103°5W 314 G3
Big Black → U.S.A. 32°3N 91°4W 315 E9
Big Blue → Ind., U.S.A. 39°12N 85°56W 311 E11
Big Blue → Kans., U.S.A. 39°35N 96°34W 308 F5
Big Buddha Hong Kong, China 22°15N 113°54E 122 B1
Big Buddha Hong Kong, China 22°15N 113°54E 219 a
Big Creek U.S.A. 37°11N 119°14W 306 H7
Big Creek ⌓ Canada 51°18N 123°10W 296 C4
Big Cypress ⌓ U.S.A. 26°0N 81°10W 317 J8
Big Cypress Swamp U.S.A. 26°15N 81°30W 317 J8
Big Delta U.S.A. 64°10N 145°51W 303 D11
Big Desert Australia 35°45S 141°10E 281 F3
Big Falls U.S.A. 48°12N 93°48W 308 A7
Big Fork → U.S.A. 48°31N 93°43W 308 A7
Big Horn Mts. = Bighorn Mts. U.S.A. 44°25N 107°0W 304 D10
Big I. Canada 61°7N 116°45W 296 A5
Big Lake Alaska, U.S.A. 61°20N 150°20W 303 F10
Big Lake Tex., U.S.A. 31°12N 101°28W 314 F4
Big Moose U.S.A. 43°49N 74°58W 313 C10
Big Muddy → U.S.A. 37°33N 89°32W 310 G8
Big Muddy Cr. → U.S.A. 48°8N 104°36W 304 B11
Big Pine U.S.A. 37°10N 118°17W 306 H8
Big Pine Key U.S.A. 24°40N 81°21W 317 L8
Big Piney U.S.A. 42°32N 110°7W 304 E8
Big Quill L. Canada 51°55N 104°30W 297 C8
Big Rapids U.S.A. 43°42N 85°29W 309 D11
Big Rideau L. Canada 44°40N 76°15W 313 B8
Big River Canada 53°50N 107°0W 297 C7
Big Run U.S.A. 40°57N 78°55W 312 F6
Big Sable Pt. U.S.A. 44°3N 86°1W 308 C10
Big Salmon → Canada 61°52N 134°55W 296 A2
Big Sand L. Man., Canada 57°45N 99°45W 297 B9
Big Sand L. Fla., U.S.A. 28°25N 81°29W 133 B2
Big Sandy U.S.A. 48°11N 110°7W 304 B8
Big Sandy → U.S.A. 38°25N 82°36W 309 F12
Big Sandy Cr. = Sandy Cr. → U.S.A. 41°51N 109°47W 304 F9
Big Sandy Cr. → U.S.A. 38°7N 102°29W 304 G12
Big Satilla Cr. → U.S.A. 31°27N 82°3W 316 D7
Big Sioux → U.S.A. 42°29N 96°27W 308 D5
Big South Fork ⌓ U.S.A. 36°27N 84°47W 315 C12
Big Spring U.S.A. 32°15N 101°28W 314 E4
Big Stone City U.S.A. 45°18N 96°28W 308 C5
Big Stone Gap U.S.A. 36°52N 82°47W 309 G12
Big Stone L. U.S.A. 45°18N 96°27W 308 C5
Big Sur U.S.A. 36°15N 121°48W 306 J5
Big Timber U.S.A. 45°50N 109°57W 304 D9
Big Trout L. Canada 53°40N 90°0W 298 B2
Big Trout Lake Canada 53°45N 90°0W 298 B2
Biğa Turkey 40°13N 27°14E 203 F11
Biga → Turkey 40°20N 27°14E 203 F11
Bigadiç Turkey 39°22N 28°7E 205 B10
Biganos France 44°39N 0°59W 174 D3
Bigeumdo S. Korea 34°45N 126°56E 224 E3

Biggar *Sask., Canada* 52°4N 108°0W **297** C7
Biggar *S. Lanarks., U.K.* 55°38N 3°32W **167** F5
Bigge I. *Australia* 14°35S 125°10E **278** B4
Biggenden *Australia* 25°31S 152°4E **281** D5
Biggleswade *U.K.* 52°5N 0°14W **169** E7
Biggs *U.S.A.* 39°25N 121°43W **306** F5
Bighorn *U.S.A.* 46°10N 107°27W **304** C10
Bighorn ➜ *U.S.A.* 46°10N 107°28W **304** C10
Bighorn Canyon ⌓ *U.S.A.* 45°10N 108°0W **304** D10
Bighorn L. *U.S.A.* 44°55N 108°15W **304** D9
Bighorn Mts. *U.S.A.* 44°25N 107°0W **304** D10
Bigi *Dem. Rep. of the Congo* 3°2N 22°25E **264** B4
Bignona *Senegal* 12°52N 16°14W **262** C1
Bigorre *France* 43°10N 0°5E **174** E4
Bigstone L. *Canada* 53°42N 95°44W **297** D9
Biguglia, Étang de *France* 42°36N 9°29E **175** F13
Bigwa *Tanzania* 7°10S 39°10E **268** D4
Bihać *Bos.-H.* 44°49N 15°57E **199** D12
Bihar *India* 25°5N 85°40E **243** G11
Bihar □ *India* 25°0N 86°0E **243** G12
Biharamulo *Tanzania* 2°25S 31°25E **268** C3
Biharamulo ⌓ *Tanzania* 2°24S 31°26E **268** C3
Bihariganj *India* 25°44N 86°59E **243** G12
Biharkeresztes *Hungary* 47°8N 21°44E **182** C6
Bihor □ *Romania* 47°0N 22°10E **182** D7
Bihor, Munţii *Romania* 46°29N 22°47E **182** D7
Bijagós, Arquipélago dos *Guinea-Biss.* 11°15N 16°10W **262** C1
Bijaipur *India* 26°2N 77°20E **242** F7
Bijapur = Vijayapura *India* 16°50N 75°55E **244** F2
Bijapur *India* 18°50N 80°50E **244** E5
Bījār *Iran* 35°52N 47°35E **213** E12
Bijauri *Nepal* 28°6N 82°20E **243** E10
Bijawar *India* 24°38N 79°30E **243** G8
Bijbels Museum *Amsterdam, Neths.* **112** b1
Bijela *Montenegro* 42°28N 18°39E **202** D2
Bijeljina *Bos.-H.* 44°46N 19°14E **182** F4
Bijelo Polje *Montenegro* 43°1N 19°45E **202** C3
Bijie *China* 27°20N 105°16E **228** D5
Bijlmermeer *Neths.* 52°19N 4°59E **112** B2
Bijnor *India* 29°27N 78°11E **242** E8
Bikaner *India* 28°2N 73°18E **242** E5
Bikapur *India* 26°30N 82°7E **243** F10
Bikeqi *China* 40°43N 111°20E **226** D6
Bikfayyā *Lebanon* 33°55N 35°41E **250** E6
Bikié *Congo* 3°7S 13°52E **264** C2
Bikin *Russia* 46°50N 134°20E **220** A7
Bikin ➜ *Russia* 46°51N 134°2E **220** A7
Bikini Atoll *Marshall Is.* 12°0N 167°30E **288** F8
Bikita *Zimbabwe* 20°6S 31°41E **271** B5
Bīkkū Bīttī *Libya* 22°0N 19°12E **259** D3
Bikoro *Dem. Rep. of the Congo* 0°48S 18°15E **264** C3
Bikoué *Cameroon* 3°55N 11°50E **263** E7
Bila Tserkva *Ukraine* 49°45N 30°10E **177** D16
Bilād Banī Bū 'Alī *Oman* 22°1N 59°19E **249** B7
Bilād Banī Bu Hassan *Oman* 22°5N 59°17E **249** B7
Bilanga *Burkina Faso* 12°40N 0°1W **263** C4
Bilara *India* 26°14N 73°53E **242** F5
Bilasipara *India* 26°13N 90°14E **241** B3
Bilaspur *Chhattisgarh, India* 22°2N 82°15E **243** H10
Bilaspur *Punjab, India* 31°19N 76°50E **242** D7
Biläsuvar *Azerbaijan* 39°27N 48°32E **213** C13
Bilauk Taungdan *Thailand* 13°0N 99°0E **236** F2
Bilauri *Nepal* 28°41N 80°21E **243** E9
Bilbao *Spain* 43°16N 2°56W **196** B2
Bilbao ✈ (BIO) *Spain* 43°18N 2°57W **196** B2
Bilbeis *Egypt* 30°25N 31°34E **256** H7
Bilbo = Bilbao *Spain* 43°16N 2°56W **196** B2
Bilbor *Romania* 47°6N 25°30E **183** C10
Bilche-Zolote *Ukraine* 48°47N 25°53E **183** B10
Bilciureşti *Romania* 44°44N 25°48E **183** F10
Bildudalur *Iceland* 65°41N 23°36W **155** B3
Bilé Karpaty *Europe* 49°5N 18°0E **181** B11
Bileća *Bos.-H.* 42°53N 18°27E **202** D2
Bilecik *Turkey* 40°5N 30°5E **212** B4
Bilecik □ *Turkey* 40°0N 30°0E **212** B3
Bilećko Jezero *Bos.-H.* 42°48N 18°28E **202** D2
Bileh Savār *Iran* 39°21N 48°21E **213** C13
Bilgoraj *Poland* 50°33N 22°42E **185** H9
Bilgram *India* 27°11N 80°2E **243** F9
Bilhaur *India* 26°51N 80°5E **243** F9
Bilhorod-Dnistrovskyy *Ukraine* 46°11N 30°23E **189** J6
Bili ➜ *Dem. Rep. of the Congo* 4°9N 22°29E **264** B4
Bilibino *Russia* 68°3N 166°20E **215** C17
Bilibiza *Mozam.* 12°30S 40°20E **269** E5
Bilimora *India* 20°45N 72°57E **244** D1
Bilin *Myanmar* 17°14N 97°15E **241** G6
Biliran *Phil.* 11°28N 124°28E **233** F5
Biliran □ *Phil.* 11°35N 124°28E **233** F5
Bilisht *Albania* 40°37N 21°2E **202** F5
Bill Baggs Cape Florida State Recr. Area ⌓ *U.S.A.* 25°40N 80°9W **129** D3
Billabong Cr. ➜ *Australia* 35°5S 144°2E **282** C6
Billdal *Sweden* 57°35N 11°57E **163** G5
Billiluna *Australia* 19°37S 127°41E **278** C4
Billings *U.S.A.* 45°47N 108°30W **304** D9
Billiton Is. = Belitung *Indonesia* 3°10S 107°50E **235** C3
Billsta *Sweden* 63°20N 18°28E **162** A12
Billund *Denmark* 55°44N 9°6E **163** J3
Billy Pt. *Antigua & B.* 17°44N 61°52W **322** c
Bilma *Niger* 18°50N 13°30E **259** E2
Bilma, Grand Erg de *Niger* 18°30N 14°0E **259** E2
Bilo Gora *Croatia* 45°53N 17°15E **182** E2
Biloela *Australia* 24°24S 150°31E **280** C5
Bilohirsk *Ukraine* 45°3N 34°35E **189** K8
Biloku *Guyana* 1°50N 58°25W **329** C6
Biloli *India* 18°46N 77°44E **244** E3
Bilopillya *Ukraine* 51°14N 34°20E **189** G8
Bilovodsk *Ukraine* 49°13N 39°36E **189** H10
Biloxi *U.S.A.* 30°24N 88°53W **315** F10
Bilpa Morea Claypan *Australia* 25°0S 140°0E **280** D3
Bilqās Qism Auwal *Egypt* 31°12N 31°21E **251** G2
Bilston *U.K.* 55°52N 3°10W **121** B2
Biltine *Chad* 14°40N 20°50E **259** F4
Bilugyun *Myanmar* 16°24N 97°32E **241** G6
Bilyarsk *Russia* 54°58N 50°22E **190** C10
Bim Son *Vietnam* 20°4N 105°51E **236** B5
Bima *Indonesia* 8°22S 118°49E **235** D5
Bimban *Egypt* 24°24N 32°54E **256** C3
Bimbe *Angola* 11°50S 15°50E **265** E3
Bimberi Pk. *Australia* 35°44S 148°51E **283** C8
Bimbila *Ghana* 8°54N 0°5E **263** D5
Bimbini *Comoros Is.* 12°11S 44°14E **272** a
Bimbo *C.A.R.* 4°15N 18°33E **264** B3
Bimini *The Bahamas* 25°42N 79°25W **320** A4
Bin Ghunaymah, Jabal *Libya* 25°0N 15°30E **258** D3
Bin Jawwād *Libya* 30°47N 18°4E **258** B3
Bin Xian *Heilongjiang, China* 45°42N 127°32E **227** B14
Bin Xian *Shaanxi, China* 35°2N 108°4E **226** G5
Bin Yauri *Nigeria* 10°46N 4°45E **263** C5
Bina-Etawah *India* 24°13N 78°14E **242** G8
Binalbagan *Phil.* 10°12N 122°50E **233** F4
Binacayan *Phil.* 14°27N 120°55E **127** C1
Binalong *Australia* 34°40S 148°39E **283** C8
Bīnālūd, Kūh-e *Iran* 36°30N 58°30E **247** B8
Binanga *Indonesia* 1°24N 99°46E **234** B1
Binangonan de Lampon = Infanta *Phil.* 14°45N 121°39E **232** D3
Binatang = Bintangau *Malaysia* 2°10N 111°40E **235** B4
Binche *Belgium* 50°26N 4°10E **170** D4
Binchuan *China* 25°42N 100°38E **228** E3
Binda *Dem. Rep. of the Congo* 5°52S 13°14E **265** D2
Binder *Chad* 9°56N 14°27E **259** G2
Bindki *India* 26°2N 80°36E **243** F9
Bindloe, I. = Marchena, I. *Ecuador* 0°19N 90°29W **330** a
Bindoy *Phil.* 9°48N 123°5E **233** G4
Bindslev *Denmark* 57°33N 10°11E **163** G4
Bindura *Zimbabwe* 17°18S 31°18E **269** F3
Binéfar *Spain* 41°51N 0°18E **196** D5
Bingara *Australia* 29°52S 150°36E **281** D5
Bingaram I. *India* 10°56N 72°17E **245** J1
Bingen *Germany* 49°57N 7°55E **179** F3
Bingerau = Węgrów *Poland* 52°24N 22°0E **185** F9
Bingerville *Côte d'Ivoire* 5°18N 3°49W **262** D4
Bingham *U.S.A.* 45°3N 69°53W **309** C19
Binghamton *U.S.A.* 42°6N 75°55W **313** D9
Bingo-Ochiai *Japan* 34°59N 133°8E **222** C4
Bingöl *Turkey* 38°53N 40°29E **213** C9
Bingöl □ *Turkey* 38°55N 40°30E **213** C9
Bingöl Dağları *Turkey* 39°16N 41°9E **213** C9
Bingsjö *Sweden* 61°1N 15°39E **162** C9
Binh Dinh *Vietnam* 13°55N 109°7E **236** F7
Binh Son *Vietnam* 15°20N 108°40E **236** E7
Binhai *China* 34°2N 119°49E **227** G10
Bini Erde *Chad* 20°6N 18°1E **259** D3
Binic *France* 48°46N 2°50W **172** D4
Binisatua *Spain* 39°50N 4°11E **206** B5
Binishangul Gumuz □ *Ethiopia* 11°0N 35°30E **257** E4
Binissalem *Spain* 39°41N 2°50E **206** B3
Binjai *Kepulauan Riau, Indonesia* 3°48N 108°13E **235** B3
Binjai *Sumatera Utara, Indonesia* 3°20N 98°30E **234** B1
Binji *Nigeria* 13°10N 4°55E **263** C5
Binka *India* 21°2N 83°48E **244** D6
Binnah, Ras *Somalia* 11°9N 51°10E **267** B7
Binnaway *Australia* 31°28S 149°24E **283** A8
Binondo *Phil.* 14°36N 120°58E **127** B1
Binongko *Indonesia* 5°57S 124°2E **231** F6
Binscarth *Canada* 50°37N 101°17W **297** C8
Bint Goda *Sudan* 13°17N 31°33E **257** E3
Bintan *Indonesia* 1°0N 104°0E **234** B2
Bintangau *Malaysia* 2°10N 111°40E **235** B4
Bintaro Jaya *Indonesia* 6°16S 106°44E **122** B1
Bintuhan *Indonesia* 4°48S 103°22E **234** C2
Bintulu *Malaysia* 3°10N 113°0E **235** B4
Bintuni *Indonesia* 2°7S 133°32E **231** E8
Binyang *China* 23°12N 108°47E **228** F7
Binz *Germany* 54°24N 13°35E **178** A9
Binza *Dem. Rep. of the Congo* 4°21S 15°14E **265** C3
Binzert = Bizerte *Tunisia* 37°15N 9°50E **258** A1
Binzhou *China* 37°20N 118°2E **227** F10
Biobío □ *Chile* 37°30S 72°20W **334** D1
Biobío ➜ *Chile* 36°49S 73°10W **334** D1
Biograd na Moru *Croatia* 43°56N 15°29E **199** E12
Biogradska Gora △ *Montenegro* 42°55N 19°40E **202** D3
Bioko *Eq. Guin.* 3°30N 8°40E **263** E6
Biokovo *Croatia* 43°23N 17°0E **199** E14
Biougra *Morocco* 30°15N 9°14W **260** B3
Bipindi *Cameroon* 3°6N 10°30E **263** E7
Bir *India* 19°4N 75°46E **244** E2
Bîr, Ras *Djibouti* 12°0N 43°20E **257** E5
Bîr Abu Hashim *Egypt* 23°42N 34°6E **256** C3
Bîr Abu Minqar *Egypt* 26°33N 27°33E **256** B2
Bi'r Abū Muḩammad *Egypt* 29°44N 34°14E **251** J5
Bîr Abu Sandûq *Egypt* 29°24N 32°30E **251** J3
Bîr Adal Deib *Sudan* 22°35N 36°10E **256** C4
Bi'r al Butayyihāt *Jordan* 29°47N 35°20E **251** J6
Bi'r al Ḩamdah *Si. Arabia* 28°30N 34°55E **251** K5
Bi'r al Mārī *Jordan* 30°4N 35°33E **251** H6
Bi'r al Musallam *Si. Arabia* 28°56N 35°38E **251** K6
Bi'r al Qattār *Jordan* 29°47N 35°32E **251** J6
Bîr 'Ali *Yemen* 14°1N 48°20E **249** D5
Bîr 'Amrâne *Mauritania* 22°45N 8°39W **260** D3
Bîr Aouine *Tunisia* 32°25N 9°18E **258** B1
Bîr 'Asal *Egypt* 25°55N 34°20E **256** B3
Bi'r ash Shakkūsīyah *Syria* 35°23N 37°26E **250** C8
Bîr Atrun *Sudan* 18°15N 26°40E **256** D2
Bîr Beiḍa *Egypt* 30°25N 34°29E **251** H5
Bîr Bel Guerdâne *Mauritania* 25°24N 10°31W **260** C2
Bîr Bireida *Egypt* 29°8N 32°7E **251** J3
Bîr Buerât *Egypt* 28°59N 32°11E **251** K3
Bi'r Dhu'fān *Libya* 31°59N 14°32E **258** B2
Bîr Di South *Sudan* 7°34N 28°49E **257** F2
Bîr Diqnash *Egypt* 31°3N 25°23E **256** A2
Bîr el Abbes *Algeria* 26°7N 6°9W **260** C3
Bîr el 'Abd *Egypt* 31°2N 33°0E **251** G4
Bîr el 'Agramîya *Egypt* 29°38N 31°50E **251** J2
Bîr el Ater *Algeria* 34°46N 8°3E **261** B6
Bîr el Basur *Egypt* 29°51N 25°49E **256** B2
Bîr el Biarât *Egypt* 29°30N 34°43E **251** J5
Bîr el Dakhal *Egypt* 28°39N 32°23E **251** K3
Bîr el Duweidar *Egypt* 30°56N 32°32E **251** H3
Bîr el Garârât *Egypt* 31°3N 33°34E **251** G4
Bîr el Gâreb *Mauritania* 20°33N 16°12W **260** D1
Bîr el Gellaz *Egypt* 30°50N 26°40E **256** A2
Bîr el Gharr *Egypt* 28°43N 31°20E **251** K2
Bîr el Heisi *Egypt* 29°22N 34°36E **251** J5
Bîr el Jafir *Egypt* 30°50N 32°41E **251** H3
Bîr el Mâlḩi *Egypt* 30°38N 33°19E **251** H4
Bîr el Manâyif *Egypt* 30°31N 32°12E **251** H3
Bîr el-Naṣb *Egypt* 29°3N 33°22E **251** J4
Bîr el Ṣafra *Egypt* 28°45N 34°21E **251** K5
Bîr el-Saura *Egypt* 29°9N 34°30E **251** J5
Bîr el Shaqqa *Egypt* 30°54N 25°1E **256** A2
Bîr el Thamâda *Egypt* 30°12N 33°27E **251** H4
Bîr Enzarân *W. Sahara* 23°53N 14°32W **260** D2
Bîr Fuad *Egypt* 30°35N 26°28E **256** A2
Bîr Gandús *W. Sahara* 21°36N 16°30W **260** D1
Bîr Gebeil Ḩiṣn *Egypt* 30°2N 33°18E **251** H4
Bi'r Ghadīr *Syria* 34°6N 37°3E **250** D8
Bîr Ghalla *Egypt* 28°23N 32°19E **251** K3
Bi'r Gharr *Si. Arabia* 28°7N 35°32E **251** K6
Bîr Gindali *Egypt* 29°55N 31°40E **251** J2
Bîr Haimur *Egypt* 22°45N 33°40E **256** C3
Bîr Ḩasana *Egypt* 30°29N 33°46E **251** H4
Bîr Hôôker *Egypt* 30°22N 30°21E **256** H7
Bi'r Īdimah *Si. Arabia* 18°31N 44°12E **248** C4
Bi'r Jadīd *Si. Arabia* 29°10N 35°6E **251** J6
Bîr Kanayis *Egypt* 24°59N 33°15E **256** C3
Bîr Kaseiba *Egypt* 31°0N 33°17E **251** H4
Bîr Kerawein *Egypt* 27°10N 28°25E **256** B2
Bîr Lahfân *Egypt* 31°0N 33°51E **251** H4
Bîr Lahrache *Algeria* 32°1N 8°12E **261** B6
Bîr Madkûr *Egypt* 30°44N 32°33E **251** H3
Bîr Maql *Egypt* 23°7N 33°40E **256** C3
Bîr Mineiga *Sudan* 22°47N 35°12E **256** C4
Bîr Misaha *Egypt* 22°13N 27°59E **256** C2
Bîr Mogreïn *Mauritania* 25°10N 11°25W **260** C2
Bîr Mureir *Egypt* 28°25N 33°16E **251** K4
Bîr Murr *Egypt* 23°28N 30°10E **256** C3
Bi'r Muṭribah *Kuwait* 29°54N 47°17E **246** D5
Bîr Nabala *West Bank* 31°51N 35°12E **252** B4
Bîr Nakheila *Egypt* 24°1N 30°50E **256** C3
Bîr Nakhul *Egypt* 29°5N 33°16E **251** J4
Bîr Qaṭia *Egypt* 30°58N 32°45E **251** H3
Bîr Qatrani *Egypt* 30°55N 26°10E **256** A2
Bîr Ranga *Egypt* 24°25N 35°15E **256** C4
Bîr Sahara *Egypt* 22°54N 28°40E **256** C2
Bîr Sa'îd *Egypt* 29°38N 31°24E **251** J2
Bîr Seiyâla *Egypt* 26°10N 33°50E **256** B3
Bîr Shalatein *Egypt* 23°5N 35°25E **256** C4
Bîr Shebb *Egypt* 22°25N 29°40E **256** C2
Bîr Shût *Egypt* 23°50N 35°15E **256** C4
Bîr Sidri *Egypt* 28°53N 33°28E **251** K4
Bîr Tâba *Egypt* 29°29N 34°53E **251** J5
Bîr Terfawi *Egypt* 22°57N 28°55E **256** C2
Bir Umm Qubûr *Egypt* 24°35N 34°2E **256** C3
Bîr Ungât *Egypt* 22°8N 33°48E **256** C3
Bi'r Wuseit *Egypt* 29°14N 33°1E **251** J4
Bîr Za'farâna *Egypt* 29°10N 32°40E **256** J8
Bîr Zeidûn *Egypt* 25°45N 33°40E **256** B3
Birāk *Libya* 27°31N 14°20E **258** C2
Birak el Kiyam *Egypt* 30°2N 31°9E **117** A1
Biramféro *Guinea* 11°40N 9°10W **262** C3
Birao *C.A.R.* 10°20N 22°47E **264** A4
Biratnagar *Nepal* 26°27N 87°17E **243** F12
Birawa *Dem. Rep. of the Congo* 2°20S 28°48E **268** C2
Birch ➜ *Canada* 58°28N 112°17W **296** B6
Birch Cliff *Canada* 43°41N 79°16W **141** A3
Birch Grove *Grenada* 12°6N 61°40W **323** q
Birch Hills *Canada* 52°59N 105°25W **297** C7
Birch I. *Canada* 52°26N 99°54W **297** C9
Birch L. *N.W.T., Canada* 62°4N 116°33W **296** A5
Birch L. *Ont., Canada* 51°23N 92°18W **298** B1
Birch Mts. *Canada* 57°30N 113°10W **296** B6
Birch River *Canada* 52°24N 101°6W **297** C8
Birchip *Australia* 35°56S 142°55E **282** C5
Birchiş *Romania* 45°58N 22°9E **182** E7
Birchwood *N.Z.* 45°55S 167°53E **285** F2
Birchwood *Alaska, U.S.A.* 61°24N 149°28W **303** F10
Bird *Canada* 56°30N 94°13W **297** B10
Bird I. = Aves, I. de *W. Indies* 15°45N 63°55W **321** C7
Bird I. *S. Georgia* 54°0S 38°3W **151** B1
Birds Creek *Canada* 45°6N 77°52W **312** A7
Birdseye *U.S.A.* 38°19N 86°42W **311** F10
Birdsville *Australia* 25°51S 139°20E **280** D2
Birdum Cr. ➜ *Australia* 15°14S 133°0E **278** C5
Birdwood *Australia* 34°51S 138°58E **282** C3
Birecik *Turkey* 37°2N 38°0E **213** D8
Birein *Israel* 30°50N 34°28E **251** H5
Bireuen *Indonesia* 5°14N 96°39E **234** A1
Birganj *Nepal* 27°1N 84°52E **243** F11
Birgu = Vittoriosa *Malta* 35°54N 14°31E **206** F8
Birhan *Ethiopia* 10°45N 38°4E **266** B4
Biri *Norway* 60°58N 10°35E **164** D7
Biri ➜ *South Sudan* 7°56N 26°33E **257** F2
Birifo *Gambia* 13°30N 14°0W **262** C2
Birigüi *Brazil* 21°18S 50°16W **335** A5
Birini *C.A.R.* 7°51N 22°24E **264** A4
Bīrjand *Iran* 32°53N 59°13E **247** C8
Birka *Sweden* 59°20N 17°32E **162** E11
Birkeland *Norway* 58°24N 7°12E **164** F4
Birkenfeld *Germany* 49°38N 7°9E **179** F3
Birkenhead *U.K.* 53°23N 3°2W **168** D4
Birkenstein *Germany* 52°31N 13°40E **115** A5
Birkerød *Denmark* 55°50N 12°25E **163** J6
Birket Fatmé *Chad* 12°55N 19°7E **259** F3
Birket Qârûn *Egypt* 29°30N 30°40E **256** J7
Birkfeld *Austria* 47°21N 15°45E **180** D8
Birkhadem *Algeria* 36°43N 3°3E **261** A5
Birkholz *Germany* 52°37N 13°34E **115** A4
Birkholzaue *Germany* 52°38N 13°36E **115** A4
Birkirkara *Malta* 35°54N 14°28E **206** F7
Bîrlad = Bârlad *Romania* 46°15N 27°38E **183** D12
Birmingham *W. Mids., U.K.* 52°29N 1°52W **169** E6
Birmingham *Ala., U.S.A.* 33°31N 86°48W **315** E11
Birmingham *Iowa, U.S.A.* 40°53N 91°57W **310** D5
Birmingham Int. ✈ (BHX) *U.K.* 52°26N 1°45W **169** E6
Birmitrapur *India* 22°24N 84°46E **244** C7
Birni Ngaouré *Niger* 13°5N 2°51E **263** C5
Birni Nkonni *Niger* 13°55N 5°15E **263** C6
Birnie *Kiribati* 3°35S 171°31W **277** A16
Birnin Gwari *Nigeria* 11°0N 6°45E **263** C6
Birnin Kebbi *Nigeria* 12°32N 4°12E **263** C5
Birnin Kudu *Nigeria* 11°30N 9°29E **263** C6
Birobidzhan *Russia* 48°50N 132°50E **219** B15
Birougou, Mts. *Gabon* 1°51S 12°20E **264** C2
Birr *Ireland* 53°6N 7°54W **166** C4
Birrarrung Park *Australia* 37°45S 145°4E **128** A2
Birrie ➜ *Australia* 29°43S 146°37E **281** D4
Birsilpur *India* 28°11N 72°15E **242** E5
Birsk *Russia* 55°25N 55°30E **186** C10
Birstall *U.K.* 52°41N 1°7W **169** E6
Birtle *Canada* 50°30N 101°5W **297** C8
Biruychiy *Ukraine* 46°10N 35°0E **189** J8
Biržai *Lithuania* 56°11N 24°45E **188** D3
Birzebbugga *Malta* 35°50N 14°32E **206** F8
Birzhi = Madona *Latvia* 56°53N 26°5E **188** D4
Birzula = Kotovsk *Ukraine* 47°45N 29°35E **177** E15
Bisa *Indonesia* 1°15S 127°28E **231** E7
Bisáccia *Italy* 41°1N 15°22E **201** A8
Bisacquino *Italy* 37°42N 13°15E **200** E6
Bisai *Japan* 35°16N 136°44E **223** B8
Bisalpur *India* 28°14N 79°48E **243** E8
Bisbee *U.S.A.* 31°27N 109°55W **305** L9
Biscarrosse *France* 44°22N 1°20W **174** D2
Biscarrosse et de Parentis, Étang de *France* 44°21N 1°10W **174** D2
Biscay, B. of *Atl. Oc.* 45°0N 2°0W **171** D1
Biscay Abyssal Plain *Atl. Oc.* 45°0N 8°0W **152** B11
Biscayne ⌓ *U.S.A.* 25°25N 80°12W **317** K9
Biscayne B. *U.S.A.* 25°40N 80°12W **317** K9
Biscayne Bay Aquatic Reserve *U.S.A.* 25°40N 80°16W **129** E2
Biscayne Park *U.S.A.* 25°52N 80°10W **129** C2
Bisceglie *Italy* 41°14N 16°30E **201** A9
Bischheim *France* 48°37N 7°46E **173** D14
Bischoflack = Škofja Loka *Slovenia* 46°9N 14°19E **199** B11
Bischofsburg = Biskupiec *Poland* 53°53N 20°58E **184** E7
Bischofshofen *Austria* 47°26N 13°14E **180** D6
Bischofswerder = Ujazd *Poland* 50°23N 18°21E **185** H5
Bischofstein = Bisztynek *Poland* 54°8N 20°53E **184** D7
Bischofswerda *Germany* 51°7N 14°10E **178** D10
Bischwiller *France* 48°46N 7°50E **173** D14
Biscoe Is. *Antarctica* 66°0S 67°0W **151** C17
Biscoitos *Azores* 38°47N 27°15W **153** d1
Biscotasing *Canada* 47°18N 82°9W **298** C3
Biševo *Croatia* 42°57N 16°3E **199** F13
Bisha *Eritrea* 15°30N 37°31E **257** D4
Bishah, W. ➜ *Si. Arabia* 21°24N 43°26E **248** B3
Bishan *China* 29°33N 106°12E **228** C6
Bishanga *Dem. Rep. of the Congo* 4°31S 21°25E **265** C4
Bishkek *Kyrgyzstan* 42°54N 74°46E **217** D8
Bishnath *India* 26°40N 93°10E **241** B4
Bishnupur *India* 23°8N 87°20E **243** H12
Bisho = Bhisho *S. Africa* 32°50S 27°23E **270** D4
Bishoftu = Debre Zeyit *Ethiopia* 8°50N 39°0E **257** F4
Bishop *Calif., U.S.A.* 37°22N 118°24W **306** H8
Bishop *Ga., U.S.A.* 33°49N 83°26W **316** B6
Bishop *Tex., U.S.A.* 27°35N 97°48W **314** H6
Bishop Auckland *U.K.* 54°39N 1°40W **168** C6
Bishop Lavis *S. Africa* 33°56S 18°35E **118** A2
Bishop Museum *U.S.A.* 21°20N 157°52W **302** K14
Bishop's Falls *Canada* 49°2N 55°30W **299** C8
Bishop's Stortford *U.K.* 51°52N 0°10E **169** F8
Bishopscourt *S. Africa* 33°59S 18°27E **118** A1
Bisignano *Italy* 39°31N 16°17E **201** C9
Bisina, L. *Uganda* 1°38N 33°56E **268** B3
Biskra *Algeria* 34°50N 5°44E **261** B6
Biskra *Malta* 35°58N 14°21E **206** F7
Biskra □ *Algeria* 34°40N 5°25E **261** B6
Biskupiec *Poland* 53°53N 20°58E **184** E7
Bislig *Phil.* 8°12N 126°18E **233** G6
Bismarck *Mo., U.S.A.* 37°46N 90°38W **310** G6
Bismarck *N. Dak., U.S.A.* 46°48N 100°47W **308** B3
Bismarck Arch. *Papua N. G.* 2°30S 150°0E **286** B6
Bismarck Ra. *Papua N. G.* 5°35S 145°0E **286** C3
Bismarck Sea *Papua N. G.* 4°10S 146°50E **286** C4
Bismarckburg = Kasanga *Tanzania* 8°30S 31°10E **269** D3
Bismark *Germany* 52°40N 11°33E **178** C7
Bismil *Turkey* 37°51N 40°40E **213** D9
Bismo *Norway* 61°54N 8°15E **164** C5
Biso *Uganda* 1°44N 31°26E **268** B3
Bison *U.S.A.* 45°31N 102°28W **308** C2
Bīsotūn *Iran* 34°23N 47°26E **213** E12
Bispebjerg *Denmark* 55°42N 12°31E **118** A3
Bispgården *Sweden* 63°2N 16°40E **162** A10
Bissagos = Bijagós, Arquipélago dos *Guinea-Biss.* 11°15N 16°10W **262** C1
Bissam Cuttack *India* 19°31N 83°31E **244** E6
Bissau *Guinea-Biss.* 11°45N 15°45W **262** C1
Bissaula *Nigeria* 7°0N 10°27E **263** D7
Bissigh, Lach ➜ *Somalia* 0°45N 41°33E **267** D5
Bissikrima *Guinea* 10°50N 10°58W **262** C2
Bissonet Plaza *U.S.A.* 30°1N 90°13W **131** A1
Bissorã *Guinea-Biss.* 12°16N 15°35W **262** C1
Bistcho L. *Canada* 59°45N 118°50W **296** B5
Bistreţ *Romania* 43°54N 23°23E **183** G8
Bistrica = Ilirska-Bistrica *Slovenia* 45°34N 14°14E **199** C11
Bistriţa *Romania* 47°9N 24°35E **183** C9
Bistriţa ➜ *Romania* 46°30N 26°57E **183** D11
Bistriţa Năsăud □ *Romania* 47°15N 24°30E **183** C9
Bistriţei, Munţii *Romania* 47°15N 25°40E **183** C10
Biswan *India* 27°29N 81°2E **243** F9
Bisztynek *Poland* 54°8N 20°53E **184** D7
Bita ➜ *C.A.R.* 6°26N 24°43E **264** A4
Bitam *Gabon* 2°5N 11°25E **264** B2
Bitburg *Germany* 49°58N 6°31E **179** F2
Bitche *France* 49°2N 7°25E **173** C14
Bithynia *Turkey* 40°40N 31°0E **212** B4
Bitkine *Chad* 11°59N 18°13E **259** F3
Bitlis *Turkey* 38°20N 42°3E **213** C10
Bitlis □ *Turkey* 38°20N 42°5E **213** C10
Bitola *N. Macedonia* 41°1N 21°20E **202** E5
Bitolj = Bitola *N. Macedonia* 41°1N 21°20E **202** E5
Bitonto *Italy* 41°6N 16°41E **201** A9
Bitra I. *India* 11°33N 72°9E **245** J1
Bitter Creek *U.S.A.* 41°33N 108°33W **304** F9
Bitter L. = Buheirat-Murrat-el-Kubra *Egypt* 30°18N 32°26E **256** H8
Bitterfeld-Wolfen *Germany* 51°37N 12°20E **178** D8
Bitterfontein *S. Africa* 31°1S 18°32E **270** D2
Bitterroot ➜ *U.S.A.* 46°52N 114°7W **304** C6
Bitterroot Range *U.S.A.* 46°0N 114°20W **304** C6
Bitterwater *U.S.A.* 36°23N 121°0W **306** J6
Bitti *Italy* 40°29N 9°23E **200** B2
Bittou *Burkina Faso* 11°17N 0°18W **263** C4
Bitsevsky Forest Park *Russia* 55°38N 37°35E **129** C2
Biu *Nigeria* 10°40N 12°3E **263** C7
Bivolari *Romania* 47°31N 27°27E **183** C12
Bivolu, Vf. *Romania* 47°16N 25°58E **183** C10
Biwa-Ko *Japan* 35°15N 136°10E **223** B8
Biwabik *U.S.A.* 47°32N 92°21W **308** B7
Bixad *Romania* 47°56N 23°28E **183** C8
Bixby *U.S.A.* 35°57N 95°53W **314** D7
Biya ➜ *Russia* 52°25N 85°0E **217** B11
Biyala *Egypt* 31°10N 31°13E **251** G2
Biyang *China* 32°38N 113°21E **229** A9
Biysk *Russia* 52°40N 85°0E **217** B11
Bizana *S. Africa* 30°50S 29°52E **271** D4
Bizen *Japan* 34°43N 134°8E **222** C6
Bizerte *Tunisia* 37°15N 9°50E **258** A1
Bizerte □ *Tunisia* 37°5N 9°35E **261** A6
Bizkaia □ *Spain* 43°15N 2°45W **196** B2
Bjåen fjellstove *Norway* 59°37N 7°26E **164** E4
Bjargtangar *Iceland* 65°30N 24°30W **155** B2
Bjarkalundur *Iceland* 65°33N 22°9W **155** B4
Bjärnum *Sweden* 56°17N 13°43E **163** H7
Bjästa *Sweden* 63°12N 18°29E **162** A12
Bjelasica *Montenegro* 42°50N 19°40E **202** D3
Bjelašnica *Bos.-H.* 43°43N 18°9E **182** G3
Bjelland *Norway* 58°23N 7°32E **164** F4
Bjelovar *Croatia* 45°56N 16°49E **199** C13
Bjerringbro *Denmark* 56°23N 9°39E **163** H3
Bjervamoen *Norway* 59°17N 9°5E **164** E6
Bjøberg *Norway* 60°56N 8°13E **164** D5
Björbo *Sweden* 60°27N 14°44E **162** D8
Bjørkelangen *Norway* 59°53N 11°34E **164** E8
Björkhage *Sweden* 60°2N 17°33E **162** D11
Björknäs *Sweden* 59°19N 18°12E **139** B3
Björkö *Sweden* 59°45N 19°2E **162** E13
Bjørnafjorden *Norway* 60°7N 5°28E **164** D2
Björneborg = Pori *Finland* 61°29N 21°48E **188** B1
Björneborg *Sweden* 59°14N 14°16E **162** E8
Bjørnevatn *Norway* 69°40N 30°0E **160** B24
Bjørnøya *Arctic* 74°30N 19°0E **150** B8
Bjursås *Sweden* 60°44N 15°25E **162** D9
Bjuv *Sweden* 56°5N 12°55E **163** H6
Bla *Mali* 12°56N 5°47W **262** C3
Blå Jungfrun △ *Sweden* 57°16N 16°47E **163** G10
Blace *Serbia* 43°18N 21°17E **202** C5
Blachownia *Poland* 50°49N 18°56E **185** H5
Black = Da ➜ *Vietnam* 21°15N 105°20E **228** G5
Black ➜ *Ont., Canada* 44°42N 79°19W **312** B5
Black ➜ *Alaska, U.S.A.* 66°42N 144°42W **303** C11
Black ➜ *Ariz., U.S.A.* 33°44N 110°13W **305** K8
Black ➜ *Ark., U.S.A.* 35°38N 91°20W **314** D9
Black ➜ *La., U.S.A.* 31°16N 91°50W **314** F9
Black ➜ *Mich., U.S.A.* 42°59N 82°27W **312** D2
Black ➜ *N.Y., U.S.A.* 43°59N 76°4W **313** C8
Black ➜ *Wis., U.S.A.* 43°57N 91°22W **308** D8
Black Bay Pen. *Canada* 48°38N 88°21W **298** C2
Black Birch L. *Canada* 56°53N 107°45W **297** B7
Black Canyon of the Gunnison ⌓ *U.S.A.* 38°40N 107°35W **304** G10
Black Cr. ➜ *Canada* 43°40N 79°30W **141** A2
Black Creek Pioneer Village *Canada* 43°46N 79°30W **141** A1
Black Desert = Abiad, Es Sahrâ el *Egypt* 28°0N 28°0E **256** B2
Black Diamond = Pittsburg *U.S.A.* 38°2N 121°53W **306** G5
Black Diamond *Canada* 50°45N 114°14W **296** C6
Black Duck ➜ *Canada* 56°51N 89°2W **298** A2
Black Forest = Schwarzwald *Germany* 48°30N 8°20E **179** G4
Black Forest *U.S.A.* 39°0N 104°43W **304** G11
Black Hd. *Ireland* 53°9N 9°16W **166** C2
Black Hills *U.S.A.* 44°0N 103°45W **308** D2
Black I. *Canada* 51°12N 96°30W **297** C9
Black L. *Sask., Canada* 59°12N 105°15W **297** B7
Black L. *Mich., U.S.A.* 45°28N 84°16W **309** C11
Black L. *N.Y., U.S.A.* 44°31N 75°36W **313** B9
Black Lake *Canada* 59°11N 105°20W **297** B7
Black Mesa *U.S.A.* 36°58N 102°58W **314** C3
Black Mountain *Australia* 30°18S 151°39E **283** A9
Black Mt. = Mynydd Du *U.K.* 51°52N 3°50W **169** F4
Black Mt. *Bhutan* 27°20N 90°25E **241** B3
Black Mts. *U.K.* 51°55N 3°7W **169** F4
Black Range *U.S.A.* 33°15N 107°50W **305** K10
Black River *Jamaica* 18°0N 77°50W **320** a
Black River *N.Y., U.S.A.* 44°0N 75°47W **313** C9
Black River B. *Jamaica* 18°0N 77°51W **320** a
Black River Falls *U.S.A.* 44°18N 90°51W **308** C8
Black River Gorges *Mauritius* 20°24S 57°25E **272** e
Black Rock *S. Australi., Australia* 32°50S 138°44E **282** B3
Black Rock *Barbados* 13°7N 59°37W **323** r
Black Rock Desert *U.S.A.* 41°10N 118°50W **304** F4
Black Sea *Eurasia* 43°30N 35°0E **187** F6
Black Tickle *Canada* 53°28N 55°45W **299** B8
Black Volta ➜ *Africa* 8°41N 1°33W **262** D4
Black Warrior ➜ *U.S.A.* 32°32N 87°51W **315** E11
Blackall *Australia* 24°25S 145°45E **280** C4
Blackball *N.Z.* 42°22S 171°26E **285** C6
Blackbraes △ *Australia* 19°10S 144°10E **280** B3
Blackbull *Australia* 17°55S 141°45E **280** B3
Blackburn *U.K.* 53°45N 2°29W **168** D5
Blackburn, Mt. *U.S.A.* 61°44N 143°26W **303** F12
Blackburn with Darwen □ *U.K.* 53°45N 2°29W **168** D5
Blackdown Tableland △ *Australia* 23°52S 149°8E **280** C4
Blackfen *U.K.* 51°26N 0°6E **125** B4
Blackfoot *U.S.A.* 43°11N 112°21W **304** E7
Blackfoot ➜ *U.S.A.* 46°52N 113°53W **304** C7
Blackfoot Res. *U.S.A.* 42°55N 111°39W **304** E8
Blackheath *U.K.* 51°28N 0°0 **125** B4
Blackman *U.S.A.* 30°56N 86°38W **317** E3
Blackpool *U.K.* 53°49N 3°3W **168** D4
Blackpool □ *U.K.* 53°49N 3°3W **168** D4
Blackriver *U.S.A.* 44°46N 83°17W **312** B1
Blacks Harbour *Canada* 45°3N 66°49W **299** C6
Blacksburg *U.S.A.* 37°14N 80°25W **309** G13
Blackshear *U.S.A.* 31°18N 82°14W **316** D7
Blackshear, L. *U.S.A.* 31°51N 83°56W **316** D6
Blacksod B. *Ireland* 54°6N 10°0W **166** B1
Blackstairs Mt. *Ireland* 52°33N 6°48W **166** D5
Blackstone *U.S.A.* 37°5N 78°0W **309** G14
Blackstone Ra. *Australia* 26°0S 128°30E **279** E4
Blackville *U.S.A.* 33°22N 81°16W **316** B8
Blackwater = West Road ➜ *Canada* 53°18N 122°53W **296** C4
Blackwater *Australia* 23°35S 148°53E **280** C4
Blackwater ➜ *Meath, Ireland* 53°39N 6°41W **166** C4
Blackwater ➜ *Waterford, Ireland* 52°4N 7°52W **166** D4
Blackwater ➜ *Armagh B. & C., U.K.* 54°31N 6°35W **166** B5
Blackwater ➜ *Fla., U.S.A.* 30°36N 87°2W **317** E2
Blackwater ➜ *Mo., U.S.A.* 38°56N 92°57W **310** F4
Blackwell *U.S.A.* 36°48N 97°17W **314** C6
Blackwells Corner *U.S.A.* 35°37N 119°47W **307** K7
Blackwood *U.K.* 51°39N 3°12W **169** F4
Blackwood, C. *Papua N. G.* 7°49S 144°31E **286** D3
Bladensburg *U.S.A.* 38°55N 76°55W **143** B3
Bladensburg △ *Australia* 22°30S 142°59E **280** C3
Blaenau Ffestiniog *U.K.* 53°0N 3°56W **168** E4
Blaenau Gwent □ *U.K.* 51°48N 3°12W **169** F4
Bláfell *Iceland* 64°30N 19°51W **155** C7
Bláfjall *Iceland* 65°26N 16°50W **155** B10
Blåfjella-Skjækerfjella △ *Norway* 64°15N 13°8E **160** D15
Blagaj *Bos.-H.* 43°16N 17°55E **202** C1
Blagnac *France* 43°37N 1°23E **174** E5
Blagnac, Toulouse ✈ (TLS) *France* 43°37N 1°22E **174** E5
Blagodarnyy *Russia* 45°7N 43°37E **191** H6
Blagoevgrad *Bulgaria* 42°2N 23°5E **202** D7
Blagoevgrad □ *Bulgaria* 42°2N 23°5E **202** D7
Blagoveshchensk *Russia* 50°20N 127°30E **219** A14
Blahkiuh *Indonesia* 8°31S 115°12E **231** J18
Blain *Loire-Atlantique, France* 47°29N 1°45W **172** E5
Blain *Pa., U.S.A.* 40°20N 77°31W **312** F7
Blaine *Minn., U.S.A.* 45°10N 93°13W **308** C7
Blaine *Wash., U.S.A.* 48°59N 122°45W **306** B4
Blaine Lake *Canada* 52°51N 106°52W **297** C7
Blair *U.S.A.* 41°33N 96°8W **308** E5
Blair Athol *Australia* 22°42S 147°31E **280** C4
Blair Atholl *U.K.* 56°46N 3°50W **167** E5
Blair Village *U.S.A.* 33°46N 84°23W **113** C2
Blairgowrie *Gauteng, S. Africa* 26°6S 28°0E **123** A2
Blairgowrie *Perth & Kinr., U.K.* 56°35N 3°21W **167** E5
Blairsden *U.S.A.* 39°47N 120°37W **306** F6
Blairsville *U.S.A.* 40°26N 79°16W **312** F5
Blaj *Romania* 46°10N 23°57E **183** D8
Blaka *Niger* 21°21N 12°47E **259** D2
Blakang Mati, Pulau *Singapore* 1°15N 103°50E **237** d
Blake House *U.S.A.* 42°19N 71°3W **116** B2
Blake Pt. *U.S.A.* 48°11N 88°25W **308** A9
Blakehurst *Australia* 33°59S 151°6E **139** B1
Blakely *Ga., U.S.A.* 31°23N 84°56W **316** D5
Blakely *Pa., U.S.A.* 41°28N 75°37W **313** E9
Blakesburg *U.S.A.* 40°58N 92°38W **310** D4
Blakstad *Akershus, Norway* 59°49N 10°28E **133** B1
Blakstad *Aust-Agder, Norway* 58°30N 8°39E **164** F5
Blambangan, Semenanjung *Indonesia* 8°42S 114°29E **231** K17
Blâmont *France* 48°35N 6°50E **173** D13
Blanc, C. *Spain* 39°21N 2°51E **206** B3
Blanc, C. *Tunisia* 37°15N 9°56E **258** A1
Blanc, Mont *Europe* 45°48N 6°50E **175** C10
Blanca, B. *Argentina* 39°10S 61°30W **336** A4
Blanca, Costa *Spain* 38°25N 0°10W **197** G4
Blanca Peak *U.S.A.* 37°35N 105°29W **305** H11
Blanchardville *U.S.A.* 42°49N 89°52W **310** B7
Blanche, C. *Australia* 33°1S 134°9E **281** E1
Blanche, L. *S. Austral., Australia* 29°15S 139°40E **281** D2
Blanche, L. *W. Austral., Australia* 22°25S 123°17E **278** D3
Blanche, L. *Fla., U.S.A.* 28°28N 81°30W **133** B1
Blanche, Pte. *St. Lucia* 13°53N 61°5W **323** m
Blanche, Pte. *St.-Maarten* 18°0N 63°2W **322** a
Blanche Channel *Solomon Is.* 8°30S 157°30E **287** M9
Blanchester *U.S.A.* 39°17N 83°59W **311** E13
Blanchisseuse *Trin. & Tob.* 10°48N 61°18W **323** t
Blanco *Western Cape, S. Africa* 33°55S 22°23E **270** D3
Blanco *Tex., U.S.A.* 30°6N 98°25W **314** F5
Blanco ➜ *Argentina* 30°20S 68°42W **334** C2
Blanco ➜ *Bolivia* 12°30S 64°18W **331** C5
Blanco, C. *Costa Rica* 9°34N 85°8W **320** E2
Blanco, C. *Oreg., U.S.A.* 42°51N 124°34W **304** E1
Blanco, Pta. *Bonaire* 12°13N 68°14W **322** h
Blanda ➜ *Iceland* 65°37N 20°9W **155** B6
Blandford Forum *U.K.* 50°51N 2°9W **169** G5
Blanding *U.S.A.* 37°37N 109°29W **305** H9
Blandinsville *U.S.A.* 40°33N 90°52W **310** D6
Blanes *Spain* 41°40N 2°48E **196** D7
Blangkejeren *Indonesia* 3°59N 97°20E **234** B1
Blangpidie *Indonesia* 3°44N 96°49E **234** B1
Blangy-sur-Bresle *France* 49°55N 1°37E **173** C8
Blanice ➜ *Czechia* 49°10N 14°5E **180** B7
Blankaholm *Sweden* 57°36N 16°31E **163** G10
Blankenberge *Belgium* 51°20N 3°9E **170** C3
Blankenburg *Berlin, Germany* 52°35N 13°27E **115** A3
Blankenburg *Sachsen-Anhalt, Germany* 51°47N 10°57E **178** D6
Blankenfelde *Germany* 52°37N 13°23E **115** A3
Blanku, L. *Curaçao* 12°2N 68°47W **322** g
Blanquefort *France* 44°55N 0°38W **174** D3
Blanquilla, I. *Venezuela* 11°51N 64°37W **321** D7
Blanquillo *Uruguay* 32°53S 55°37W **335** C4
Blansko *Czechia* 49°22N 16°40E **181** B9
Blantyre *Malawi* 15°45S 35°0E **269** F4
Blarney *Ireland* 51°56N 8°33W **166** E3
Blasdell *U.S.A.* 42°48N 78°50W **312** D6
Blåsjø *Norway* 59°20N 6°50E **164** E3
Błaszki *Poland* 51°38N 18°30E **185** G5
Blatná *Czechia* 49°25N 13°52E **180** B6
Blåvands Huk *Denmark* 55°33N 8°4E **163** J2
Blaydon *U.K.* 54°58N 1°42W **168** C6
Blaye *France* 45°8N 0°40W **174** C3
Blaye-les-Mines *France* 44°1N 2°8E **174** D6
Blayney *Australia* 33°32S 149°14E **283** B8
Blaze, Pt. *Australia* 12°56S 130°11E **278** B5
Błażowa *Poland* 49°53N 22°7E **185** J9
Blechhammer = Blachownia *Poland* 50°49N 18°56E **185** H5
Bleckede *Germany* 53°17N 10°43E **178** B6
Bled *Slovenia* 46°27N 14°7E **199** B11
Blefjell *Norway* 59°48N 9°10E **164** E6
Bleiburg *Austria* 46°35N 14°49E **180** E7
Blejeşti *Romania* 44°19N 25°27E **183** F10
Blekinge *Sweden* 56°25N 15°20E **161** H16
Blekinge □ *Sweden* 56°20N 15°20E **163** H9
Blenheim *Ont., Canada* 42°20N 82°0W **312** D3
Blenheim *N.Z.* 41°38S 173°57E **285** B8
Bléone ➜ *France* 44°5N 6°0E **175** D10
Blérancourt *France* 49°31N 3°9E **173** C10
Bletchley *U.K.* 51°59N 0°44W **169** F7
Bleus, Monts *Dem. Rep. of the Congo* 1°30N 30°30E **268** B3
Blida *Algeria* 36°30N 2°49E **261** A5
Blida □ *Algeria* 36°35N 3°0E **261** A5
Blidet Amor *Algeria* 32°59N 5°58E **261** B6
Blidö *Sweden* 59°37N 18°53E **162** E12
Blidsberg *Sweden* 57°56N 13°30E **163** G7
Blieskastel *Germany* 49°14N 7°12E **179** F3
Bligh Sound *N.Z.* 44°47S 167°32E **285** E2
Bligh Water *Fiji* 17°0S 178°0E **287** A2
Blind River *Canada* 46°10N 82°58W **298** C3
Blinisht *Albania* 41°52N 19°59E **202** E3
Bliss *Idaho, U.S.A.* 42°56N 114°57W **304** E6
Bliss *N.Y., U.S.A.* 42°34N 78°15W **312** D6
Blissfield *Mich., U.S.A.* 41°50N 83°52W **311** C13
Blissfield *Ohio, U.S.A.* 40°24N 81°58W **312** F3
Blitar *Indonesia* 8°5S 112°11E **235** D4
Blitchton *U.S.A.* 32°12N 81°26W **316** C8
Blitta *Togo* 8°23N 1°6E **263** D5
Blizne *Poland* 52°14N 20°52E **143** B1
Block I. *U.S.A.* 41°11N 71°35W **313** E13
Block Island Sd. *U.S.A.* 41°15N 71°40W **313** E13
Bloemenmarkt *Amsterdam, Neths.* **112** b2
Bloemfontein *S. Africa* 29°6S 26°7E **270** C4
Bloemhof *S. Africa* 27°38S 25°32E **270** C4
Blois *France* 47°35N 1°20E **172** E8
Blomskog *Sweden* 59°16N 12°2E **162** E6
Blomstermåla *Sweden* 56°59N 16°21E **163** H10
Blönduós *Iceland* 65°40N 20°12W **155** B6
Blongas *Indonesia* 8°53S 116°2E **231** K19
Blonie *Poland* 52°12N 20°37E **185** F7
Bloodvein ➜ *Canada* 51°47N 96°43W **297** C9
Bloody B. *Trin. & Tob.* 11°18N 60°38W **323** s
Bloody Foreland *Ireland* 55°10N 8°17W **166** A3
Bloom = Chicago Heights *U.S.A.* 41°30N 87°38W **311** C9
Bloomer *U.S.A.* 45°6N 91°29W **308** C8
Bloomfield *Ont., Canada* 43°59N 77°14W **312** C7
Bloomfield *Ind., U.S.A.* 39°1N 86°57W **311** E10
Bloomfield *Iowa, U.S.A.* 40°45N 92°25W **310** D4
Bloomfield *Ky., U.S.A.* 37°55N 85°19W **311** G11
Bloomfield *N. Mex., U.S.A.* 36°43N 107°59W **305** H10
Bloomfield *Nebr., U.S.A.* 42°36N 97°39W **308** D5
Bloomingburg *U.S.A.* 39°36N 83°24W **311** E13
Bloomington *Ill., U.S.A.* 40°28N 89°0W **310** D8
Bloomington *Ind., U.S.A.* 39°10N 86°32W **311** E10
Bloomington *Minn., U.S.A.* 44°50N 93°17W **308** C7
Bloomington *Wis., U.S.A.* 42°53N 90°55W **310** B6
Bloomsburg *U.S.A.* 41°0N 76°27W **313** F8
Bloomsbury *Australia* 20°48S 148°38E **280** b
Bloomsbury *London, U.K.* **125** a3
Blora *Indonesia* 6°57S 111°25E **235** D4
Blossburg *U.S.A.* 41°41N 77°4W **312** E7
Blosseville Kyst *Greenland* 68°50N 26°30W **154** D8
Blota *Poland* 52°9N 21°11E **143** C3
Blouberg *S. Africa* 23°8S 28°59E **271** B4
Blountstown *U.S.A.* 30°27N 85°3W **316** E4
Blowing Point Village *Anguilla* 18°11N 63°6W **322** a
Blowing Rock *Anguilla* 18°9N 63°10W **322** a
Bludenz *Austria* 47°10N 9°50E **180** D2
Blue ➜ *U.S.A.* 38°11N 86°19W **311** F10
Blue Cypress L. *U.S.A.* 27°44N 80°45W **317** H9
Blue Earth *U.S.A.* 43°38N 94°6W **308** D6
Blue Hole *Jamaica* 18°10N 76°24W **320** a
Blue Hole △ *Belize* 17°9N 88°40W **320** C2
Blue Island *U.S.A.* 41°40N 87°40W **119** D2
Blue Lagoon △ *Zambia* 15°28S 27°26E **269** F2
Blue Lagoon L. *U.S.A.* 25°46N 80°17W **129** D1
Blue Mesa Res. *U.S.A.* 38°28N 107°20W **304** G10
Blue Mosque = Sultanahme Camil *Turkey* 41°0N 28°58E **122** B1
Blue Mound *Ill., U.S.A.* 39°42N 89°7W **310** E7
Blue Mound *Tex., U.S.A.* 32°51N 97°20W **120** A2
Blue Mountain Lake *U.S.A.* 43°51N 74°27W **313** C10
Blue Mountain Pk. *Jamaica* 18°3N 76°36W **320** a
Blue Mountains and John Crow Mountains △ *Jamaica* 18°5N 76°34W **320** a
Blue Mt. *U.S.A.* 40°30N 76°30W **313** F8
Blue Mts. *N.S.W., Australia* 33°40S 150°15E **283** B9
Blue Mts. *Jamaica* 18°3N 76°36W **320** a
Blue Mts. *Maine, U.S.A.* 44°50N 70°35W **313** B14
Blue Mts. *Oreg., U.S.A.* 45°0N 118°20W **304** D4
Blue Mts. △ *Australia* 34°2S 150°15E **283** C9
Blue Mud B. *Australia* 13°30S 136°0E **280** A2
Blue Mud Bay ⚬ *Australia* 13°25S 136°2E **280** A2
Blue Nile = Nîl el Azraq ➜ *Sudan* 15°38N 32°31E **257** D3
Blue Nile Falls = Tis Issat *Ethiopia* 11°25N 37°45E **257** E4
Blue Rapids *U.S.A.* 39°41N 96°39W **308** F5
Blue Ridge *U.S.A.* 36°40N 80°50W **309** G13
Blue River *Canada* 52°6N 119°18W **296** C5
Blue Springs *U.S.A.* 39°1N 94°17W **310** E2
Bluefield *U.S.A.* 37°15N 81°17W **309** G13
Bluefields *Nic.* 12°20N 83°50W **320** D3
Bluevale *Canada* 43°51N 81°15W **312** C3
Bluff *Queens., Australia* 23°35S 149°4E **280** C4
Bluff *N.Z.* 46°37S 168°20E **285** G3
Bluff *Utah, U.S.A.* 37°17N 109°33W **305** H9
Bluff Harbour *N.Z.* 46°36S 168°21E **285** G3
Bluff Hd. *Hong Kong, China* 22°11N 114°12E **122** B3
Bluff Knoll *Australia* 34°24S 118°15E **279** F2
Bluff Pt. *Australia* 27°50S 114°5E **279** E1
Bluffers Park *Canada* 43°43N 79°14W **141** A3
Bluffs *U.S.A.* 39°45N 90°32W **310** E6
Bluffton *Ga., U.S.A.* 31°31N 84°52W **316** D5
Bluffton *Ind., U.S.A.* 40°44N 85°11W **311** D11
Bluffton *Ohio, U.S.A.* 40°54N 83°54W **311** D13
Bluffton *S.C., U.S.A.* 32°14N 80°52W **316** C9

Blumberg Germany 52°36N 13°39E 115 A4
Blumenau = Stettler Canada 52°19N 112°40W 296 C6
Blumenau Brazil 27°0S 49°0W 335 B6
Blunt U.S.A. 44°31N 99°59W 308 C4
Blunt Pt. U.S.A. 37°51N 122°25W 136 A2
Blutenberg Germany 48°9N 11°27E 131 B1
Bly U.S.A. 42°24N 121°3W 304 E3
Blyde River Canyon ⌓ S. Africa 24°37S 31°2E 271 B5
Blylaget Norway 59°46N 10°41E 133 B3
Blyth S. Austral., Australia 33°49S 138°28E 282 B3
Blyth Ont., Canada 43°44N 81°26W 312 C3
Blyth Northumberland, U.K. 55°8N 1°31W 168 B6
Blythe Calif., U.S.A. 33°37N 114°36W 307 M12
Blythe Ga., U.S.A. 33°17N 82°12W 316 B7
Blytheville U.S.A. 35°56N 89°55W 315 D10
Bø Telemark, Norway 59°25N 9°3E 164 E6
Bo S. Leone 7°55N 11°50W 262 D2
Bo Duc Vietnam 11°58N 106°50E 237 G6
Bo-eun S. Korea 36°29N 127°43E 224 D3
Bo Hai China 39°0N 119°0E 227 E10
Bo Hai Haixia Asia 38°25N 121°10E 227 E11
Bo-Kaap Museum Cape Town, S. Africa 118 c2
Bō-no-Misaki Japan 31°15N 130°13E 222 F2
Bo Xian = Bozhou China 33°55N 115°41E 226 H8
Boa Esperança Brazil 3°21N 61°23W 329 C5
Boa Esperança, Represa Brazil 6°50S 43°50W 332 C3
Boa Nova Brazil 14°22S 40°10W 333 D3
Boa Viagem Brazil 5°7S 39°44W 332 C4
Boa Vista = Tocantinópolis Brazil 6°20S 47°25W 332 C2
Boa Vista Brazil 2°48N 60°30W 329 C5
Boa Vista Cabo Verde 16°0N 22°49W 153 j
Boa Vista, Alto do Brazil 22°58S 43°16W 135 B1
Boa Vista do Erechim = Erechim Brazil 27°35S 52°15W 335 B5
Boac Phil. 13°27N 121°50E 232 E3
Boaco Nic. 12°29N 85°35W 320 D2
Bo'ai China 35°10N 113°3E 226 G7
Boal Spain 43°25N 6°49W 194 B4
Boali C.A.R. 4°48N 18°7E 264 B3
Boalsburg U.S.A. 40°47N 77°49W 312 F7
Boane Mozam. 26°6S 32°19E 271 C5
Boang I. Papua N. G. 3°23S 153°18E 286 B7
Boao China 19°8N 110°34E 229 a
Boardman U.S.A. 41°2N 80°40W 312 E4
Boardwalk U.S.A. 40°34N 73°49W 132 C3
Boath India 19°20N 78°20E 244 E4
Boatswain Bird I. Ascension I. 7°56S 14°18W 153 g
Boavista Portugal 38°48N 9°8W 126 A2
Boayan I. Phil. 10°34N 119°9E 233 F2
Boaz I. Bermuda 32°18N 64°51W 153 a
Bob Marley Mausoleum Jamaica 18°18N 77°18W 320 a
Bobadah Australia 32°19S 146°41E 283 B7
Bobai China 22°17N 109°59E 228 F7
Bobbili India 18°35N 83°30E 244 E6
Bóbbio Italy 44°46N 9°23E 198 D6
Bobcaygeon Canada 44°33N 78°33W 312 B6
Bobigny France 48°54N 2°26E 134 A3
Boblad India 17°13N 75°26E 244 F2
Böblingen Germany 48°40N 9°1E 179 G5
Bobo-Dioulasso Burkina Faso 11°8N 4°13W 262 C4
Bobolice Poland 53°58N 16°37E 184 E3
Bobon Phil. 12°32N 124°34E 232 E5
Bobonaza → Ecuador 2°36S 76°38W 328 D2
Bobonong Botswana 21°58S 28°20E 271 B4
Boboshevo Bulgaria 42°9N 23°0E 202 D7
Bobov Dol Bulgaria 42°20N 23°0E 202 D6
Bóbr → Poland 52°4N 15°4E 185 F2
Bobraomby, Tanjon' i Madag. 12°40S 49°10E 272 A2
Bobrov Russia 51°5N 40°2E 190 E5
Bobrovytsya Ukraine 50°45N 31°23E 189 G6
Bobruysk = Babruysk Belarus 53°10N 29°15E 177 B15
Bobrynets Ukraine 48°4N 32°5E 189 H7
Bobures Venezuela 9°15N 71°11W 328 B3
Boby, Pic Madag. 22°12S 46°55E 272 C2
Boca de Pozo Venezuela 11°0N 64°23W 329 a
Boca del Río Veracruz, Mexico 19°5N 96°4W 319 D5
Boca del Río Venezuela 10°58N 64°11W 329 a
Boca do Acre Brazil 8°50S 67°27W 330 B4
Boca do Jari Brazil 1°7S 51°58W 329 D7
Boca Grande Fla., U.S.A. 26°45N 82°16W 317 J7
Boca Grande Venezuela 8°40N 60°40W 329 B5
Boca Raton U.S.A. 26°21N 80°5W 317 J9
Boca Slagbaai Bonaire 12°16N 68°24W 322 h
Bocaiúva Brazil 17°7S 43°49W 333 E3
Bocanda Côte d'Ivoire 7°5N 4°31W 262 D4
Bocanegra Peru 12°1S 77°7W 124 B2
Bocaranga C.A.R. 7°0N 15°35E 264 A3
Bocas del Dragón = Dragon's Mouths Trin. & Tob. 11°0N 61°50W 323 t
Bocas del Toro Panama 9°15N 82°20W 320 E3
Boceguillas Spain 41°20N 3°39W 194 D7
Bochkarevo = Belogorsk Russia 51°0N 128°20E 215 D13
Bochmanivka Ukraine 47°40N 29°34E 183 C14
Bochnia Poland 49°58N 20°27E 185 J7
Bocholt Germany 51°50N 6°36E 178 D2
Bochum = Senwabarana S. Africa 23°17S 29°7E 271 B4
Bochum Germany 51°28N 7°13E 178 D3
Bockenem Germany 52°1N 10°8E 178 C6
Boćki Poland 52°39N 23°3E 185 F10
Bocognano France 42°5N 9°4E 175 F13
Bocoio Angola 12°28S 14°10E 265 E2
Boconó Venezuela 9°15N 70°16W 328 B3
Boconó → Venezuela 8°43N 69°34W 328 B4
Bocoyna Mexico 27°52N 107°35W 318 B3
Bocşa Romania 45°21N 21°47E 182 E6
Boda C.A.R. 4°19N 17°26E 264 B3
Boda Dalarna, Sweden 61°1N 15°13E 162 C9
Böda Kalmar, Sweden 57°15N 17°3E 163 G11
Boda Västernorrland, Sweden 62°52N 16°39E 162 B10
Bodafors Sweden 57°48N 14°23E 163 G8
Bodaybo Russia 57°50N 114°0E 215 D12
Boddam U.K. 59°56N 1°17W 167 B7
Boddington Australia 32°50S 116°30E 279 F2
Bode Sadu Nigeria 9°0N 4°47E 263 D5
Bodega Bay U.S.A. 38°20N 123°3W 306 G3
Boden Sweden 65°50N 21°42E 160 D19
Bodensee Europe 47°35N 9°25E 179 H5
Bodenteich Germany 52°50N 10°42E 178 C6
Bodh Gaya India 24°41N 84°59E 243 G11
Bodhan India 18°40N 77°44E 244 E3
Bodinayakkanur India 10°2N 77°10E 245 J3
Bodinga Nigeria 12°58N 5°10E 263 C6
Bodmin U.K. 50°28N 4°43W 169 G3
Bodmin Moor U.K. 50°33N 4°36W 169 G3
Bodø Norway 67°17N 14°24E 160 C16
Bodoquena, Serra da Brazil 21°0S 56°50W 331 E6
Bodoupa C.A.R. 5°43N 17°36E 264 A3
Bodrichi Chad 19°11N 15°54E 259 E3
Bodrog → Hungary 48°11N 21°22E 182 B6
Bodrum Turkey 37°3N 27°30E 205 D9
Boduna Dem. Rep. of the Congo 5°5N 19°44E 264 A3
Bódva → Hungary 48°19N 20°45E 182 B5
Boedo Argentina 34°38S 58°26W 117 B2
Boembé Congo 2°54S 15°39E 264 C3
Boën France 45°44N 4°1E 175 C8
Boende Dem. Rep. of the Congo 0°24S 21°12E 264 C4
Boeny □ Madag. 15°45S 46°20E 272 B2
Boeotia = Viotia Greece 38°20N 23°0E 204 C5
Boerne U.S.A. 29°47N 98°44W 314 G5
Boesmans → S. Africa 33°42S 26°39E 270 D4
Boffa Guinea 10°16N 14°3W 262 C2
Bog Walk Jamaica 18°6N 77°1W 320 a
Bogal, Lagh → Kenya 0°41N 40°57E 267 D5
Bogale Myanmar 16°17N 95°24E 241 G5
Bogalusa U.S.A. 30°47N 89°52W 315 F10
Bogan → Australia 30°20S 146°55E 283 A7
Bogan Gate Australia 33°7S 147°49E 283 B7
Bogandé Burkina Faso 13°2N 0°8W 263 C4
Bogangolo C.A.R. 5°34N 18°15E 264 A3
Bogantungan Australia 23°41S 147°17E 280 C4
Bogata U.S.A. 33°28N 95°13W 314 E7
Bogatić Serbia 44°51N 19°30E 202 B3
Boğazkale Turkey 40°2N 34°37E 212 B6
Boğazlıyan Turkey 39°11N 35°14E 212 C6
Bogbonga Dem. Rep. of the Congo 1°36N 19°24E 264 B3
Bogda Shan China 43°35N 89°40E 217 D11
Bogen Sweden 60°4N 12°33E 162 D6
Bogenhausen Germany 48°8N 11°36E 131 B2
Bogense Denmark 55°34N 10°5E 163 J4
Bogetići Montenegro 42°41N 18°58E 202 D2
Boggabilla Australia 28°36S 150°24E 281 D5
Boggabri Australia 30°45S 150°5E 283 A9
Boggeragh Mts. Ireland 52°2N 8°55W 166 D3
Boghari = Ksar el Boukhari Algeria 35°51N 2°52E 261 A5
Bogia Papua N. G. 4°9S 145°0E 286 C3
Bogildo S. Korea 34°9N 126°32E 224 E3
Boglan = Solhan Turkey 38°57N 41°3E 213 C9
Bogles Grenada 12°30N 61°26W 323 q
Bognes Norway 68°13N 16°5E 160 B17
Bognor Regis U.K. 50°47N 0°40W 169 G7
Bogo Phil. 11°3N 124°0E 233 F4
Bogodukhov = Bohodukhiv Ukraine 50°9N 35°33E 189 G8
Bogol Manya Ethiopia 4°34N 41°29E 257 G5
Bogong, Mt. Australia 36°47S 147°17E 283 D7
Bogor Indonesia 6°36S 106°48E 234 D3
Bogoroditsk Russia 53°47N 38°8E 188 F10
Bogorodsk Russia 56°4N 43°30E 190 B6
Bogorodskoye = Kamskoye Ustye Russia 55°10N 49°20E 190 C9
Bogorodskoye = Leninskoye Russia 58°23N 47°3E 190 A8
Bogorodskoye Russia 55°48N 37°42E 129 B3
Bogoslovsky = Karpinsk Russia 59°45N 60°1E 186 C11
Bogoso Ghana 5°38N 2°3W 262 D4
Bogotá Colombia 4°34N 74°0W 328 C3
Bogota N.J., U.S.A. 40°52N 74°2W 132 A1
Bogotol Russia 56°15N 89°50E 214 D9
Bogou Togo 10°40N 0°12E 263 C5
Bogra = Bogura Bangla. 24°51N 89°22E 241 C2
Bogstadvatnet Norway 59°58N 10°37E 133 A2
Boguchanskoye Vdkhr. Russia 58°42N 99°9E 215 D10
Boguchany Russia 58°40N 97°30E 215 D10
Boguchar Russia 49°55N 40°32E 190 F5
Bogué Mauritania 16°45N 14°10W 262 B2
Bogura Bangla. 24°51N 89°22E 241 C2
Boguszów-Gorce Poland 50°45N 16°12E 185 H3
Bohain-en-Vermandois France 49°59N 3°28E 173 C10
Bohdan Ukraine 48°2N 24°22E 183 B9
Bohemian Forest = Böhmerwald Germany 49°8N 13°14E 179 F9
Bohena Cr. → Australia 30°17S 149°42E 283 A8
Bohinjska Bistrica Slovenia 46°17N 14°1E 199 B11
Böhmerwald Germany 49°8N 13°14E 179 F9
Böhmisch-Brod = Český Brod Czechia 50°4N 14°52E 180 A7
Böhmisch-Leipa = Česká Lípa Czechia 50°45N 14°30E 180 A7
Böhmisch-Trübau = Česká Třebová Czechia 49°54N 16°27E 181 B9
Bohmte Germany 52°22N 8°19E 178 C4
Bohnsdorf Germany 52°23N 13°34E 115 B4
Bohodukhiv Ukraine 50°9N 35°33E 189 G8
Bohol Somalia 5°45N 46°9E 267 C6
Bohol □ Phil. 9°50N 124°10E 233 G5
Bohol Sea Phil. 9°0N 124°0E 233 G5
Bohol Str. Phil. 9°45N 123°40E 233 G4
Bohongou Burkina Faso 12°30N 0°40E 263 C5
Böhönye Hungary 46°25N 17°28E 182 D2
Bohorodchany Ukraine 48°48N 24°32E 183 B9
Bohorok Indonesia 3°30N 98°12E 237 L2
Böhöt Mongolia 45°13N 108°16E 226 B5
Bohu China 41°58N 86°37E 217 D11
Bohuslän Sweden 58°25N 12°0E 163 F5
Bohuslev Ukraine 49°33N 30°56E 189 H6
Boi Nigeria 9°35N 9°27E 263 D6
Boi, Pta. do Brazil 23°55S 45°15W 335 A6
Boiaçu Brazil 0°27S 61°46W 329 D5
Boigu Australia 9°16S 142°13E 280 a
Boigu I. Australia 9°15S 142°14E 286 E2
Boileau, C. Australia 17°40S 122°7E 278 C3
Boim Brazil 2°49S 55°10W 329 D6
Boing'o South Sudan 9°58N 33°44E 257 F3
Boipariguda India 18°46N 82°26E 244 E6
Boipeba, I. de Brazil 13°39S 38°55W 333 D4
Boiro Spain 42°39N 8°54W 194 C2
Bois → Brazil 18°35S 50°2W 333 E1
Bois-Blanc Réunion 21°11S 55°49E 272 f
Bois-Colombes France 48°55N 2°16E 134 A2
Bois-d'Arcy France 48°48N 2°1E 134 B1
Boise U.S.A. 43°37N 116°13W 304 E5
Boise City U.S.A. 36°44N 102°31W 314 C3
Boissevain Canada 49°15N 100°5W 297 D8
Boissy-St-Léger France 48°44N 2°31E 134 B4
Bóite → Italy 46°5N 12°5E 199 B9
Boitzenburg Germany 53°16N 13°35E 178 B9
Boizenburg Germany 53°23N 10°43E 178 B6
Bojador W. Sahara 23°56N 15°49W 260 D1
Bojador, C. W. Sahara 26°0N 14°30W 260 C2
Bojana → Albania 41°52N 19°22E 202 E3
Bojano Italy 41°29N 14°29E 201 A7
Bojanowo Poland 51°43N 16°42E 185 G3
Bøjden Denmark 55°6N 10°7E 163 J4
Bojnūrd Iran 37°30N 57°20E 247 B8
Bojonegoro Indonesia 7°11S 111°54E 235 D4
Boju Nigeria 7°22N 7°55E 263 D6
Boka Serbia 45°22N 20°52E 182 E5
Boka Kotorska Montenegro 42°23N 18°32E 202 D2
Bokada Dem. Rep. of the Congo 4°8N 19°23E 264 B3
Bokala Côte d'Ivoire 8°31N 4°33W 262 D4
Bokala Dem. Rep. of the Congo 3°8S 17°4E 264 C3
Bokani Nigeria 9°28N 5°10E 263 D6
Bokaro India 23°46N 85°55E 243 H11
Bokatola Dem. Rep. of the Congo 0°38S 18°46E 264 C3
Boké Guinea 10°56N 14°17W 262 C2
Bokela Dem. Rep. of the Congo 1°10S 21°59E 264 C4
Bokenda Dem. Rep. of the Congo 1°16N 21°22E 264 B4
Bokhara → Australia 29°55S 146°42E 281 D4
Bokkos Nigeria 9°17N 9°1E 263 D6
Boklar Dağları Turkey 37°5N 33°55E 250 A4
Boknafjorden Norway 59°14N 5°40E 164 E2
Boko Congo 4°46S 14°36E 265 C2
Bokode Dem. Rep. of the Congo 3°55N 19°30E 264 B3
Bokolo Gabon 2°40S 10°10E 264 C2
Bokondo Dem. Rep. of the Congo 0°15N 22°32E 264 B4
Bokor △ Cambodia 10°50N 104°1E 237 G5
Bokora ⌓ Uganda 2°12N 31°32E 268 B3
Bokoro Chad 12°25N 17°14E 259 F3
Bokota Dem. Rep. of the Congo 0°56S 22°24E 264 C4
Bokote Dem. Rep. of the Congo 0°12S 21°8E 264 C4
Bokpyin Myanmar 11°18N 98°42E 237 G2
Boksitogorsk Russia 59°22N 33°50E 188 C7
Boku Papua N. G. 6°34S 155°21E 286 D8
Bokungu Dem. Rep. of the Congo 0°35S 22°50E 264 C4
Bol Chad 13°30N 14°40E 259 F2
Bol Croatia 43°18N 16°38E 199 E13
Bolama Guinea-Biss. 11°30N 15°30W 262 C1
Bolan → Pakistan 28°38N 67°42E 242 E2
Bolan Pass Pakistan 29°50N 67°20E 240 C2
Bolaños → Mexico 21°12N 104°5W 318 C4
Bolaños de Calatrava Spain 38°54N 3°40W 195 G7
Bolayır Turkey 40°31N 26°45E 203 F10
Bolbec France 49°30N 0°30E 172 C7
Boldājī Iran 31°56N 51°3E 247 D6
Boldeşti-Scăeni Romania 45°3N 26°2E 183 E11
Boldinasco Italy 45°29N 9°8E 128 B1
Bole Xinjiang Uygur, China 44°55N 81°37E 217 C10
Bole Ethiopia 6°36N 37°20E 257 F4
Bole Ghana 9°3N 2°23W 262 D4
Bolekhiv Ukraine 49°0N 23°57E 177 D12
Boleko Dem. Rep. of the Congo 1°35S 19°50E 264 C3
Bøler Norway 59°53N 10°50E 133 A4
Bolesławiec Poland 51°17N 15°37E 185 G2
Bolgatanga Ghana 10°44N 0°53W 263 C4
Bolgrad = Bolhrad Ukraine 45°40N 28°32E 183 E13
Bolhrad Ukraine 45°40N 28°32E 183 E13
Bolia Dem. Rep. of the Congo 1°36S 18°22E 264 C3
Bolinao Phil. 16°23N 119°54E 232 C2
Bolinao, C. Phil. 16°23N 119°55E 232 C2
Bolingbroke U.S.A. 32°57N 83°48W 316 C6
Bolingbrook U.S.A. 41°42N 88°4W 311 C8
Bolingo Dem. Rep. of the Congo 3°31S 21°43E 264 C4
Bolintin-Vale Romania 44°27N 25°46E 183 F10
Bolívar Antioquía, Colombia 5°50N 76°1W 328 B2
Bolívar Cauca, Colombia 2°0N 77°0W 328 C2
Bolívar Peru 7°18S 77°48W 330 B2
Bolivar Mo., U.S.A. 37°37N 93°25W 308 G7
Bolivar N.Y., U.S.A. 42°4N 78°10W 312 D6
Bolivar Tenn., U.S.A. 35°12N 89°0W 315 D10
Bolívar □ Colombia 9°0N 74°40W 328 B3
Bolívar □ Ecuador 1°15S 79°5W 328 D2
Bolívar □ Venezuela 6°20N 63°30W 329 B5
Bolivia ■ S. Amer. 17°6S 64°0W 331 D5
Bolivian Plateau = Altiplano Bolivia 17°0S 68°0W 330 D4
Boljevac Serbia 43°51N 21°58E 202 C5
Bolkhov Russia 53°25N 36°0E 188 F9
Bolków Poland 50°55N 16°6E 185 H3
Bollate Italy 45°32N 9°7E 128 A1
Bollebeek Belgium 50°55N 4°14E 116 A1
Bollebygd Sweden 57°40N 12°35E 163 G6
Bollène France 44°18N 4°45E 175 D8
Bollensdorf Germany 52°30N 13°42E 115 A5
Bollmora Sweden 59°14N 18°14E 139 B3
Bollnäs Sweden 61°21N 16°24E 162 C10
Bollon Australia 28°2S 147°29E 281 D4
Bollstabruk Sweden 62°59N 17°40E 162 B11
Bolmen Sweden 56°55N 13°40E 163 H7
Bolnisi Georgia 41°26N 44°32E 191 K7
Bolobo Dem. Rep. of the Congo 2°6S 16°20E 264 C3
Bologna Italy 44°29N 11°20E 199 D8
Bologna ✕ (BLQ) Italy 44°34N 11°16E 199 D8
Bologoye Russia 57°55N 34°5E 188 D8
Bolomba Dem. Rep. of the Congo 0°35N 19°0E 264 B3
Bolombo → Dem. Rep. of the Congo 1°32N 21°14E 264 B4
Bolonchén Mexico 20°1N 89°45W 319 D7
Bolondo Dem. Rep. of the Congo 2°12S 18°42E 264 C3
Bolong Chad 12°3N 17°45E 259 F3
Bolong Phil. 7°6N 122°14E 233 H4
Bolongongo Angola 8°28S 15°16E 265 D3
Bolótana Italy 40°20N 8°52E 200 B1
Boloven, Cao Nguyen Laos 15°10N 106°30E 236 E6
Bolpur India 23°40N 87°45E 243 H12
Bolsena Italy 42°39N 11°59E 199 F8
Bolsena, L. di Italy 42°36N 11°56E 199 F8
Bolshakovo Russia 54°53N 21°40E 184 D8
Bolshaya Chernigovka Russia 52°6N 50°52E 190 D10
Bolshaya Garmanda = Evensk Russia 62°12N 159°30E 215 C16
Bolshaya Glushitsa Russia 52°28N 50°30E 190 D10
Bolshaya Martynovka Russia 47°19N 41°37E 191 G5
Bolshaya Okhta Russia 59°56N 30°26E 137 B2
Bolshaya Tsaryovshchina = Volzhskiy Russia 48°56N 44°46E 191 F7
Bolshaya Vradiyevka Ukraine 47°50N 30°40E 189 J6
Bolshevik, Ostrov Russia 78°30N 102°0E 215 B11
Bolshoi Theatre Russia 129 b2
Bolshoy Anyuy → Russia 68°30N 160°49E 215 C17
Bolshoy Begichev, Ostrov Russia 74°20N 112°30E 215 B12
Bolshoy Kamen Russia 43°7N 132°19E 220 C6
Bolshoy Kavkas = Caucasus Mountains Eurasia 42°50N 44°0E 191 J7
Bolshoy Lyakhovskiy, Ostrov Russia 73°35N 142°0E 215 B15
Bolshoy Tokmak = Tokmak Kyrgyzstan 42°49N 75°15E 217 D9
Bolshoy Tyuters, Ostrov Russia 59°51N 27°13E 188 C4
Bólstaðarhlíð Iceland 65°31N 19°49W 155 B7
Bolsward Neths. 53°3N 5°32E 170 A5
Bolt Head U.K. 50°12N 3°48W 169 G4
Boltaña Spain 42°28N 0°4E 196 C5
Boltigen Switz. 46°38N 7°24E 179 J3
Bolton Ont., Canada 43°54N 79°45W 312 C5
Bolton Gt. Man., U.K. 53°35N 2°26W 168 D5
Bolton Georgia, U.S.A. 33°48N 84°28W 113 B2
Bolton Landing U.S.A. 43°32N 73°35W 313 C11
Bolu Turkey 40°45N 31°35E 212 B4
Bolu □ Turkey 40°40N 31°30E 212 B4
Bolubolu Papua N. G. 9°21S 150°20E 286 E6
Bolungavík Iceland 66°9N 23°15W 155 A3
Boluo China 23°3N 114°21E 229 F10
Bolvadin Turkey 38°45N 31°4E 212 C4
Bolzano Italy 46°31N 11°22E 199 B8
Bom Comércio Brazil 9°45S 65°54W 331 B4
Bom Conselho Brazil 9°10S 36°41W 332 C4
Bom Despacho Brazil 19°43S 45°15W 333 E2
Bom Jesus Angola 9°11S 13°34E 265 D2
Bom Jesus Brazil 9°4S 44°22W 332 C3
Bom Jesus da Gurguéia, Serra Brazil 9°0S 43°0W 332 C3
Bom Jesus da Lapa Brazil 13°15S 43°25W 333 D3
Bom Retiro Brazil 23°31S 46°38W 137 B2
Boma Dem. Rep. of the Congo 5°50S 13°4E 265 D2
Boma △ South Sudan 7°0N 34°0E 257 F3
Bomaderry Australia 34°52S 150°37E 283 C9
Bomandjokou Congo 0°34N 14°23E 264 B2
Bomaneh Dem. Rep. of the Congo 1°18N 23°47E 264 B4
Bomassa Congo 2°12N 16°12E 264 B3
Bomate Dem. Rep. of the Congo 2°14N 25°15E 264 C3
Bombala Australia 36°56S 149°15E 283 D8
Bombarral Portugal 39°15N 9°9W 195 F1
Bombay = Mumbai India 18°56N 72°50E 130 B2
Bombay U.S.A. 44°56N 74°34W 313 B10
Bombedor, Pta. Venezuela 9°53N 61°37W 329 G9
Bomberai, Semenanjung Indonesia 3°0S 133°0E 231 E8
Bombo Kasani Dem. Rep. of the Congo 5°51S 21°54E 265 D4
Bomboma Dem. Rep. of the Congo 2°25N 18°55E 264 B3
Bombombwa Dem. Rep. of the Congo 1°40N 25°40E 268 B2
Bomboyo Chad 12°1N 15°28E 259 F3
Bomdila India 27°18N 92°22E 241 B4
Bomdo India 28°44N 94°54E 241 A5
Bomet Kenya 0°47S 35°21E 266 E4
Bomi China 29°50N 95°45E 218 F8
Bomi Liberia 7°1N 10°38W 262 D2
Bomili Dem. Rep. of the Congo 1°45N 27°5E 268 B2
Bømlo Norway 59°37N 5°13E 164 E2
Bomokandi → Dem. Rep. of the Congo 3°39N 26°8E 268 B2
Bomongo Dem. Rep. of the Congo 1°27N 18°21E 264 B3
Bompoka India 8°15N 93°13E 245 K11
Bomputu Dem. Rep. of the Congo 0°23S 20°6E 264 C4
Bomst = Babimost Poland 52°10N 15°49E 185 F2
Bomu → C.A.R. 4°40N 22°30E 264 B4
Bomu Occidentale ⌓ Dem. Rep. of the Congo 4°48N 24°17E 264 B4
Bomu Orientale ⌓ Dem. Rep. of the Congo 5°0N 25°50E 264 B2
Bon, C. = Ra's aṭ Tib Tunisia 37°1N 11°2E 258 A2
Bon Acceuil Mauritius 20°10S 57°39E 272 e
Bon Echo ⌓ Canada 44°55N 77°16W 312 B7
Bon Sar Pa Vietnam 12°24N 107°35E 236 F6
Bona, Mt. U.S.A. 61°23N 141°45W 303 F12
Bonāb Āzarbājān-e Sharqī, Iran 37°20N 46°4E 213 D12
Bonāb Zanjān, Iran 36°35N 48°41E 213 D13
Bonaigarh India 21°50N 84°57E 243 J11
Bonaire Ga., U.S.A. 32°33N 83°36W 316 C6
Bonaire W. Indies 12°10N 68°15W 322 h
Bonampak Mexico 16°44N 91°5W 319 D6
Bonang Australia 37°11S 148°41E 283 D8
Bonanza Nic. 13°54N 84°35W 320 D3
Bonaparte Arch. Australia 14°0S 124°30E 278 B3
Bonaparte Rocks Grenada 12°24N 61°30W 323 q
Boñar Spain 42°52N 5°19W 194 C5
Bonar Bridge U.K. 57°54N 4°20W 167 D4
Bonasse Trin. & Tob. 10°5N 61°54W 323 t
Bonaventure Canada 48°5N 65°32W 299 C6
Bonaventure, Place Montréal, Canada 130 c2
Bonavista Canada 48°40N 53°5W 299 C9
Bonavista, C. Canada 48°42N 53°5W 299 C9
Bonavista B. Canada 48°45N 53°25W 299 C9
Bondeno Italy 44°53N 11°25E 199 D8
Bondi Australia 33°53S 151°16E 139 B2
Bondo Équateur, Dem. Rep. of the Congo 1°22S 23°54E 264 C4
Bondo Orientale, Dem. Rep. of the Congo 3°55N 23°53E 264 B4
Bondoc Pen. Phil. 13°26N 122°33E 232 E4
Bondokodi Indonesia 9°33S 119°0E 278 A2
Bondoukou Côte d'Ivoire 8°2N 2°47W 262 D4
Bondowoso Indonesia 7°55S 113°49E 235 D4
Bondy France 48°54N 2°28E 134 A3
Bondy, Forêt de France 48°54N 2°33E 134 A4
Bône = Annaba Algeria 36°50N 7°46E 261 A6
Bone, Teluk Indonesia 4°10S 120°50E 231 E6
Bonefish Pond The Bahamas 24°59N 77°23W 153 b
Bonerate Indonesia 7°25S 121°5E 231 F6
Bonerate, Kepulauan Indonesia 6°30S 121°10E 231 F6
Bo'ness U.K. 56°1N 3°37W 167 E5
Bonete, Cerro Argentina 27°55S 68°40W 334 B2
Bonfim = Senhor-do-Bonfim Brazil 10°30S 40°10W 332 D3
Bonfim Brazil 3°33N 59°25W 329 C6
Bong Son = Hoai Nhon Vietnam 14°28N 109°1E 236 E7
Bonga Ethiopia 7°15N 36°14E 257 F4
Bongabon Phil. 15°38N 121°8E 232 D3
Bongabong Phil. 12°45N 121°29E 232 E3
Bongaigaon India 26°28N 90°34E 241 B3
Bongandanga Dem. Rep. of the Congo 1°24N 21°3E 264 B4
Bongao Phil. 5°2N 119°46E 233 J2
Bongo Dem. Rep. of the Congo 1°47S 17°41E 264 C3
Bongo, Sa. de Angola 10°3S 15°15E 265 E3
Bongo I. Phil. 7°20N 124°3E 233 H5
Bongolava □ Madag. 18°45S 46°0E 272 B2
Bongor Chad 10°35N 15°20E 259 F3
Bongos, Massif des C.A.R. 8°40N 22°25E 264 A4
Bongouanou Côte d'Ivoire 6°42N 4°15W 262 D4
Bonham U.S.A. 33°35N 96°11W 314 E6
Boni Mali 15°3N 2°10W 262 B4
Boni ⌓ Kenya 1°35S 41°18E 268 C5
Bonifacio France 41°24N 9°10E 175 G13
Bonifacio, Bouches de Medit. S. 41°12N 9°15E 200 A2
Bonifacio Monument Phil. 14°38N 120°58E 127 B1
Bonifay U.S.A. 30°47N 85°41W 316 E4
Bonin Is. = Ogasawara Gunto Pac. Oc. 27°0N 142°0E 288 E6
Bonita Springs U.S.A. 26°21N 81°47W 317 J8
Bonito Brazil 21°8S 56°28W 331 E6
Bonjol Indonesia 0°1S 100°13E 234 C2
Bonke Ethiopia 6°5N 37°16E 257 F4
Bonkoukou Niger 14°0N 3°15E 263 C5
Bonn Germany 50°46N 7°6E 178 E3
Bonnabel Place U.S.A. 30°0N 90°8W 131 A2
Bonnat France 46°20N 1°54E 173 F8
Bonne Terre U.S.A. 37°55N 90°33W 310 G6
Bonneau U.S.A. 33°16N 79°58W 316 B10
Bonners Ferry U.S.A. 48°42N 116°19W 304 B5
Bonnétable France 48°11N 0°25E 172 D7
Bonneuil-sur-Marne France 48°46N 2°30E 134 B4
Bonneval France 45°22N 7°3E 175 C11
Bonneval-sur-Arc France 48°11N 1°24E 172 D8
Bonneville France 46°4N 6°24E 173 F13
Bonney, L. Australia 37°50S 140°20E 282 D4
Bonnie Doon Australia 37°2S 145°53E 283 D6
Bonnie Rock Australia 30°29S 118°22E 279 F2
Bonnington U.K. 55°54N 3°25W 121 B1
Bonny Nigeria 4°25N 7°13E 263 E6
Bonny → Nigeria 4°20N 7°10E 263 E6
Bonny, Bight of Africa 3°30N 9°20E 263 E6
Bonny Hills Australia 31°36S 152°51E 283 A10
Bonny-sur-Loire France 47°33N 2°50E 173 E9
Bonnyrigg U.K. 55°53N 3°6W 167 F5
Bonnyrigg and Lasswade U.K. 55°52N 3°6W 121 B3
Bonnyville Canada 54°20N 110°45W 297 C6
Bono Italy 40°25N 9°2E 200 B2
Bono East □ Ghana 7°50N 1°0W 263 D4
Bonoi Indonesia 1°45S 137°41E 231 E9
Bonorva Italy 40°25N 8°46E 200 B1
Bonsall U.S.A. 33°16N 117°14W 307 M9
Bonsucesso Brazil 22°51S 43°15W 135 B1
Bontang Indonesia 0°10N 117°30E 235 B5
Bontebok △ S. Africa 34°5S 20°28E 270 D3
Bonteheuwel S. Africa 33°57S 18°33E 118 A2
Bonthe S. Leone 7°30N 12°33W 262 D2
Bontoc Phil. 17°7N 120°58E 232 C3
Bontosunggu Indonesia 5°41S 119°42E 235 D5
Bonyeri Ghana 5°1N 2°46W 262 D4
Bonyhád Hungary 46°18N 18°32E 182 D3
Bonython Ra. Australia 23°40S 128°45E 278 D4
Boo Sweden 59°20N 18°16E 139 A3
Booderee △ Australia 35°12S 150°42E 283 C9
Boodjamulla △ Australia 18°15S 138°6E 280 B2
Bookabie Australia 31°50S 132°41E 279 F5
Booke Dem. Rep. of the Congo 2°34S 22°3E 264 C4
Booker U.S.A. 36°27N 100°32W 314 C4
Bool Lagoon Australia 37°7S 140°40E 282 D4
Boola Guinea 8°22N 8°41W 262 D3
Boolcoomata Australia 31°57S 140°33E 282 A4
Booleroo Centre Australia 32°53S 138°21E 282 B3
Booligal Australia 33°58S 144°53E 283 B6
Boon Pt. Antigua & B. 17°10N 61°50W 322 b
Böön Tsagaan Nuur Mongolia 45°35N 99°9E 218 B8
Boonah Australia 27°58S 152°41E 281 D5
Boone Iowa, U.S.A. 42°4N 93°53W 310 B3
Boone N.C., U.S.A. 36°13N 81°41W 315 C14
Booneville Ark., U.S.A. 35°8N 93°55W 314 D8
Booneville Miss., U.S.A. 34°39N 88°34W 315 D10
Boonville Calif., U.S.A. 39°1N 123°22W 306 F3
Boonville Ind., U.S.A. 38°3N 87°16W 311 F9
Boonville Mo., U.S.A. 38°58N 92°44W 310 F4
Boonville N.Y., U.S.A. 43°29N 75°20W 313 C9
Boorabbin △ Australia 31°30S 120°10E 279 F3
Boorama Somalia 9°55N 43°7E 267 C5
Boorindal Australia 30°22S 146°11E 281 E4
Boorowa Australia 34°28S 148°44E 283 C8
Boort Australia 36°7S 143°46E 282 D5
Boosaaso Somalia 11°12N 49°18E 267 B6
Boothia, Gulf of Canada 71°0N 90°0W 294 C14
Boothia Pen. Canada 71°0N 94°0W 294 C13
Bootle U.K. 53°28N 3°1W 168 D4
Booué Gabon 0°5S 11°55E 264 C2
Bopako Dem. Rep. of the Congo 1°53N 21°13E 264 B4
Bopolu Liberia 7°4N 10°29W 262 D2
Boppard Germany 50°13N 7°35E 179 E3
Boquerón □ Paraguay 23°0S 60°0W 331 E6
Boquilla, Presa de la Mexico 27°31N 105°30W 318 B3
Boquillas del Carmen Mexico 29°11N 102°58W 318 B4
Bor Czechia 49°41N 12°45E 180 B5
Bor Russia 56°28N 43°59E 190 B7
Bor Serbia 44°5N 22°7E 202 B6
Bor South Sudan 6°10N 31°40E 257 F3
Bor Sweden 57°9N 14°10E 163 G8
Bor Turkey 37°54N 34°32E 212 D6
Bor, Lagh → Kenya 1°18N 40°40E 267 D5
Bor Mashash Israel 31°7N 34°50E 251 G5
Bor u Ceske Lipy = Nový Bor Czechia 50°46N 14°35E 180 A7
Bora Bora French Polynesia 16°30S 151°45W 289 f
Borah Peak U.S.A. 44°8N 113°47W 304 D7
Boraha, Nosy Madag. 16°50S 49°55E 272 B2
Borang South Sudan 4°50N 30°59E 257 G3
Borangapara India 25°14N 90°14E 241 C3
Borankul Kazakhstan 46°11N 54°25E 216 C4
Borås Sweden 57°43N 12°56E 163 G6
Borāzjān Iran 29°22N 51°10E 247 D6
Borba Brazil 4°12S 59°34W 329 D6
Borba Portugal 38°50N 7°26W 195 G3
Borbon Phil. 10°50N 124°2E 233 F5
Borborema, Planalto da Brazil 7°0S 37°0W 332 C4
Borča Serbia 44°52N 20°28E 202 B4
Borcea Romania 44°20N 27°45E 183 F12
Borchalo = Marneuli Georgia 41°30N 44°48E 191 K7
Borçka Turkey 41°25N 41°41E 213 B9
Bord Khūn-e Now Iran 28°3N 51°28E 247 D6
Borda, C. Australia 35°45S 136°34E 282 C2
Bordeaux France 44°50N 0°36W 174 D3
Bordeaux ✕ (BOD) France 44°50N 0°35W 174 D3
Borden Australia 34°3S 118°12E 279 F2
Borden-Carleton Canada 46°18N 63°47W 299 C7
Borden I. Canada 78°30N 111°30W 295 B9
Borden Pen. Canada 73°0N 83°0W 295 C15
Borden Springs U.S.A. 33°56N 85°28W 316 B4
Border Ranges △ Australia 28°24S 152°56E 281 D5
Borders = Scottish Borders □ U.K. 55°35N 2°50W 167 F6
Bordertown Australia 36°19S 140°45E 282 D4
Borðeyri Iceland 65°12N 21°6W 155 B5
Bordighera Italy 43°46N 7°39E 198 E4
Bordj Badji Mokhtar □ Algeria 24°0N 1°0W 261 D4
Bordj bou Arreridj Algeria 36°4N 4°45E 261 A5
Bordj Bourguiba Tunisia 32°12N 10°2E 258 B2
Bordj Flye Ste-Marie Algeria 27°19N 2°32W 260 C4
Bordj in Eker Algeria 24°9N 5°3E 261 D6
Bordj Menaïel Algeria 36°46N 3°43E 261 A5
Bordj Messouda Algeria 30°12N 9°25E 261 B6
Bordj Mokhtar Algeria 21°20N 0°56E 261 D5
Bordj Nili Algeria 33°28N 3°2E 261 B5
Bordj Omar Driss Algeria 28°10N 6°40E 261 C6
Bordj Sif Fatima Algeria 31°6N 8°41E 261 B6
Bordj Tarat Algeria 25°55N 9°3E 261 C6
Borduttighat India 26°57N 93°58E 241 B4
Bore Ethiopia 4°39N 37°39E 257 G4
Borehamwood U.K. 51°40N 0°15W 169 F7
Borek Wielkopolski Poland 51°54N 17°11E 185 G4
Borensberg Sweden 58°34N 15°17E 163 F9
Borgå = Porvoo Finland 60°24N 25°40E 188 B3
Borgampad India 17°39N 80°52E 244 F5
Borgarfjarðarsýsla Iceland 64°30N 21°30W 155 C5
Borgarfjörður Austurland Iceland 65°33N 13°47W 155 B13
Borgarfjörður Vesturland Iceland 64°30N 22°0W 155 C4
Borgarnes Iceland 64°32N 21°55W 155 C5
Børgefjellet Norway 65°20N 13°45E 160 D15
Borger Neths. 52°54N 6°44E 170 B6
Borger Tex., U.S.A. 35°39N 101°24W 314 D4
Borgholm Sweden 56°52N 16°39E 163 H10
Bórgia Italy 38°49N 16°30E 201 D9
Borgnesse, Pte. Martinique 14°26N 60°54W 322 j
Borgo San Dalmazzo Italy 44°20N 7°30E 198 D4
Borgo San Donnino = Fidenza Italy 44°52N 10°3E 198 D7
Borgo San Lorenzo Italy 43°57N 11°23E 199 E8
Borgo Val di Taro Italy 44°29N 9°46E 198 D6
Borgo Valsugana Italy 46°3N 11°27E 199 B8
Borgomanero Italy 45°42N 8°28E 198 C5
Borgorose Italy 42°11N 13°13E 199 F10
Borgosésia Italy 45°43N 8°16E 198 C5
Borgotaro = Borgo Val di Taro Italy 44°29N 9°46E 198 D6
Borgund Norway 61°3N 7°48E 164 C4
Borhoyn Tal Mongolia 43°50N 111°58E 226 C6
Bori Nigeria 4°42N 7°21E 263 E6
Borigumma India 19°3N 82°33E 244 E6
Borikhane Laos 18°33N 103°43E 236 C4
Borisoglebsk Russia 51°27N 42°5E 190 E6
Borisov = Barysaw Belarus 54°17N 28°28E 177 A15
Borisovgrad = Parvomay Bulgaria 42°8N 25°17E 203 D9
Borisovka Russia 50°36N 36°1E 189 G9
Borisovo Russia 55°38N 37°44E 129 C3
Borj Jeneïn Tunisia 31°45N 10°9E 258 B2
Borja Peru 4°20S 77°40W 328 D2
Borja Spain 41°48N 1°34W 196 D3
Borjas Blancas = Les Borges Blanques Spain 41°31N 0°52E 196 D5
Borjomi Georgia 41°48N 43°28E 191 K6
Børkop Denmark 55°39N 9°39E 163 J3
Borkou Chad 18°15N 18°50E 259 E3
Borkou □ Chad 18°0N 18°0E 259 E3
Borkum Germany 53°34N 6°40E 178 B2
Borlänge Sweden 60°29N 15°26E 162 D9
Borle India 19°2N 72°54E 130 A2
Borley, C. Antarctica 66°15S 52°30E 151 C5
Borlu Turkey 38°44N 28°27E 205 C10
Bormida → Italy 44°23N 8°13E 198 D5
Bórmio Italy 46°28N 10°22E 198 B7
Borna Germany 51°7N 12°29E 178 D8
Borne Sulinowo Poland 53°32N 16°36E 184 E3
Borneo E. Indies 1°0N 115°0E 235 B4
Bornholm Denmark 55°10N 15°0E 163 J8
Bornholmsgattet Europe 55°15N 14°20E 163 J8
Borno □ Nigeria 11°30N 13°0E 263 C7
Bornos Spain 36°48N 5°42W 195 J5
Bornova Turkey 38°27N 27°14E 205 C9
Bornu Yassa Nigeria 12°14N 12°25E 263 C7
Boro → South Sudan 8°52N 26°11E 257 F2
Borobudur △ Indonesia 7°36S 110°12E 231 G14
Borobudur Indonesia 7°40S 110°11E 235 D4
Borocay I. Phil. 11°58N 121°55E 233 F3
Borodino Russia 55°31N 35°40E 188 E8
Borodino Ukraine 46°18N 29°15E 183 D14
Borogontsy Russia 62°42N 131°8E 215 C14
Borohoro Shan China 44°6N 83°10E 217 D10
Boromo Burkina Faso 11°45N 2°58W 262 C4
Boron U.S.A. 35°0N 117°39W 307 L9
Boronga Is. Myanmar 19°58N 93°6E 241 F4
Borongan Phil. 11°37N 125°26E 233 F5
Boronia Park Australia 33°49S 151°8E 139 A1
Borotangba Mts. C.A.R. 6°30N 25°0E 257 F2
Borotou Côte d'Ivoire 8°46N 7°30W 262 D3
Borovan Bulgaria 43°27N 23°45E 202 C7
Borovichi Russia 58°25N 33°55E 188 C7
Borovsk Russia 55°12N 36°24E 188 E9
Borovskoy Kazakhstan 53°48N 64°9E 216 B6
Borrby Sweden 55°27N 14°10E 163 J8
Borrego Springs U.S.A. 33°15N 116°23W 307 M10
Borriol Spain 40°4N 0°4W 196 E4
Borrisokane Ireland 53°0N 8°7W 166 D3
Borroloola Australia 16°4S 136°17E 280 B2
Borşa Cluj, Romania 46°56N 23°40E 183 D8
Borşa Maramureş, Romania 47°41N 24°50E 183 C9
Borsad India 22°25N 72°54E 242 H5
Borsec Romania 46°57N 25°34E 183 D10
Borshchiv Ukraine 48°48N 26°3E 183 B11
Borsod-Abaúj-Zemplén □ Hungary 48°20N 21°0E 182 B6
Bort-les-Orgues France 45°24N 2°29E 174 C6
Bortala = Bole China 44°55N 81°37E 217 C10
Borth U.K. 52°29N 4°2W 169 E3
Börtnan Sweden 62°45N 13°50E 162 B7
Borūjerd Iran 33°55N 48°50E 213 F13
Boryeong S. Korea 36°21N 126°36E 224 D3
Borynya Ukraine 49°4N 23°0E 185 J10
Boryslav Ukraine 49°18N 23°28E 185 J10
Boryspil Ukraine 50°21N 30°59E 189 G6
Borzhomi = Borjomi Georgia 41°48N 43°28E 191 K6
Borzna Ukraine 51°18N 32°26E 189 G7
Borzya Russia 50°24N 116°31E 219 A12
Bosa Italy 40°18N 8°30E 200 B1
Bosa Monene Dem. Rep. of the Congo 1°16S 23°40E 264 C4
Bosaga Turkmenistan 37°33N 65°41E 240 A2
Bosambi Dem. Rep. of the Congo 2°24N 22°39E 264 B4
Bosanska Dubica = Dubica Bos.-H. 45°10N 16°50E 199 C13
Bosanska Gradiška = Gradiška Bos.-H. 45°10N 17°15E 182 E2
Bosanska Kostajnica = Kostajnica Bos.-H. 45°11N 16°33E 199 C13
Bosanska Krupa Bos.-H. 44°53N 16°10E 199 D13
Bosanski Brod = Brod Bos.-H. 45°10N 18°0E 182 E2
Bosanski Novi = Novi Grad Bos.-H. 45°2N 16°22E 199 C13
Bosanski Petrovac Bos.-H. 44°35N 16°21E 199 D13
Bosanski Šamac = Šamac Bos.-H. 45°3N 18°29E 182 E3
Bosansko Grahovo Bos.-H. 44°12N 16°26E 199 D13
Bosavi, Mt. Papua N. G. 6°30S 142°49E 286 D2
Boscastle U.K. 50°41N 4°42W 169 G3
Boscobel U.S.A. 43°8N 90°42W 310 A6
Boscobelle Barbados 13°17N 59°35W 323 r
Bose China 23°53N 106°35E 228 F6
Boseki Dem. Rep. of the Congo 2°34S 19°38E 264 C3
Boseong S. Korea 34°46N 127°5E 224 E3
Boshan China 36°28N 117°49E 227 F9
Boshof S. Africa 28°31S 25°13E 270 C4
Boshrūyeh Iran 33°50N 57°30E 247 C8
Bosilegrad Serbia 42°30N 22°27E 202 D6
Boskovice Czechia 49°29N 16°40E 181 B9
Bosmont S. Africa 26°10S 27°57E 123 B1
Bosna → Bos.-H. 45°4N 18°29E 182 E3
Bosna i Hercegovina = Bosnia-Herzegovina ■ Europe 44°0N 18°0E 182 G2
Bosnia-Herzegovina ■ Europe 44°0N 18°0E 182 G2
Bosnik Indonesia 1°5S 136°10E 231 E9
Bōsō-Hantō Japan 35°20N 140°20E 223 B12
Bosobolo Dem. Rep. of the Congo 4°15N 19°50E 264 B3
Bosön Sweden 59°22N 18°11E 139 A3
Bosporus = İstanbul Boğazı Turkey 41°5N 29°3E 122 B2
Bosque Farms U.S.A. 35°51N 106°42W 305 J10
Bosra = Buşra ash Shām Syria 32°30N 36°25E 251 F7
Bossangoa C.A.R. 6°35N 17°30E 264 A3
Bossé Bangou Niger 13°20N 1°18E 263 C5
Bossembélé C.A.R. 5°25N 17°40E 264 A3
Bossemtélé C.A.R. 5°41N 16°38E 264 A3
Bossier City U.S.A. 32°31N 93°44W 314 E8
Bossiesvlei Namibia 25°1S 16°44E 270 C2
Bosso Niger 13°43N 13°19E 259 F2
Bosso, Dallol → Niger 12°25N 2°50E 263 C5
Bostan Pakistan 30°26N 67°2E 242 D2
Bostānābād Iran 37°50N 46°50E 213 D12
Bostancı Turkey 40°57N 29°5E 122 C2
Bosten Hu China 41°55N 87°40E 217 D11
Boston Phil. 7°52N 126°22E 233 H6
Boston Lincs., U.K. 52°59N 0°2W 168 E7
Boston Ga., U.S.A. 30°47N 83°47W 316 E6
Boston Mass., U.S.A. 42°22N 71°3W 116 A2
Boston Bar Canada 49°52N 121°30W 296 D4
Boston Bay Jamaica 18°9N 76°22W 320 a
Boston Common Boston, U.S.A. 116 c1
Boston Logan Int. ✕ (BOS) U.S.A. 42°22N 71°1W 116 A2
Boston Mts. U.S.A. 35°42N 93°15W 314 D8
Boston Tea Party Ship & Museum Boston, U.S.A. 116 c3

Bostwick U.S.A. 29°46N 81°38W 316 F8
Bosumtwi, L. Ghana 6°30N 1°25W 263 D4
Bosusulu Dem. Rep. of the Congo 0°50N 20°45E 264 B4
Bosut → Croatia 45°20N 18°45E 182 E3
Boswell B.C., Canada 49°28N 116°45W 296 D5
Boswell Ind., U.S.A. 40°31N 87°23W 311 D9
Boswell Pa., U.S.A. 40°10N 79°2W 312 F5
Bosworth U.S.A. 39°28N 93°20W 310 E3
Botad India 22°15N 71°40E 242 H4
Botafogo Brazil 22°56S 43°10W 135 B1
Botan → Turkey 37°57N 42°2E 213 D10
Botanic Gardens Washington, D.C., U.S.A. 143 b3
Botanisk Have Copenhagen, Denmark 118 b2
Botany Australia 33°56S 151°12E 139 B2
Botany B. Australia 33°58S 151°11E 139 B2
Botany Bay △ Australia 34°0S 151°14E 139 B2
Botene Laos 17°35N 101°12E 236 D3
Botera Angola 11°37S 14°16E 265 E2
Botev Bulgaria 42°44N 24°52E 203 D8
Botevgrad Bulgaria 42°55N 23°47E 202 D7
Bothaville S. Africa 27°23S 26°34E 270 C4
Bothnia, G. of Europe 62°0N 20°0E 160 F19
Bothwell Tas., Australia 42°20S 147°1E 281 G4
Bothwell Ont., Canada 42°38N 81°52W 312 D3
Botič → Czechia 50°4N 14°26E 135 B3
Botica Sete Portugal 38°49N 9°10W 126 A1
Boticas Portugal 41°41N 7°40W 194 D3
Botletle → Botswana 20°10S 23°15E 270 B3
Botlikh Russia 42°39N 46°11E 191 J8
Botna → Moldova 46°45N 29°34E 183 D14
Botola Dem. Rep. of the Congo 1°17S 18°13E 264 C3
Botolan Phil. 15°17N 120°1E 232 D3
Botoroaga Romania 44°8N 25°32E 183 F10
Botoşani Romania 47°42N 26°41E 183 C11
Botoşani □ Romania 47°50N 26°50E 183 C11
Botou Burkina Faso 12°42N 1°59E 263 C5
Botou China 38°4N 116°34E 226 E9
Botricello Italy 38°56N 16°51E 201 D9
Botro Côte d'Ivoire 7°51N 5°19W 262 D3
Botshabelo S. Africa 29°14S 26°44E 270 C4
Botswana ■ Africa 22°0S 24°0E 270 B3
Bottelier Curaçao 12°6N 68°54W 322 g
Bottineau U.S.A. 48°50N 100°27W 308 A3
Bottnaryd Sweden 57°47N 13°50E 163 G7
Bottom, The Saba 17°38N 63°15W 322 a
Bottopassi Suriname 4°14N 55°27W 329 C6
Bottrop Germany 51°31N 6°58E 178 D2
Botucatu Brazil 22°55S 48°30W 335 A6
Botum Sakor △ Cambodia 11°5N 103°15E 237 G4
Botwood Canada 49°6N 55°23W 299 C8
Bou Alam Algeria 33°50N 1°26E 261 B5
Bou Ali Algeria 27°11N 0°4W 261 C4
Bou Djébéha Mali 18°25N 2°45W 262 B4
Bou Guema Algeria 28°49N 0°19E 261 C5
Bou Ismaïl Algeria 36°38N 2°42E 261 A5
Bou Izakarn Morocco 29°12N 9°46W 260 C3
Boû Lanouâr Mauritania 21°12N 16°34W 260 D1
Boû Naga Mauritania 18°49N 13°20W 262 B2
Bou Noura Algeria 32°29N 3°43E 261 B5
Boû Rjeïmât Mauritania 19°4N 15°3W 262 B1
Bou Saâda Algeria 35°11N 4°9E 261 A5
Bou Salem Tunisia 36°45N 9°2E 258 A1
Bouaflé Côte d'Ivoire 7°1N 5°47W 262 D3
Bouaké Côte d'Ivoire 7°40N 5°2W 262 D3
Bouanga Congo 2°7S 16°8E 264 C3
Bouar C.A.R. 6°0N 15°40E 264 A3
Bouârfa Morocco 32°32N 1°58W 261 B4
Bouba Ndjida △ Cameroon 8°50N 14°45E 264 A2
Boubout Algeria 27°26N 4°30W 260 C4
Bouca C.A.R. 6°45N 18°25E 264 A3
Boucaut B. Australia 12°0S 134°25E 280 A1
Boucherville Canada 45°36N 73°28W 130 A3
Boucherville, Îs. de Canada 45°36N 73°28W 130 A3
Bouches-du-Rhône □ France 43°37N 5°2E 175 E9
Boucle de Baoulé △ Mali 13°53N 9°0W 262 C3
Boucles de la Seine Normande ⌂ France 49°32N 0°35E 172 C7
Bouctouche Canada 46°30N 64°45W 299 C7
Bouda Algeria 27°50N 0°27W 261 C4
Boudenib Morocco 31°59N 3°31W 260 B4
Bouéni Mayotte 12°54S 45°4E 272 b
Bouéni, B. de Mayotte 12°55S 45°7E 272 b
Bouenza □ Congo 4°30S 13°0E 264 C2
Boufarik Algeria 36°34N 2°58E 261 A5
Bougainville □ Papua N. G. 4°0S 155°0E 286 B8
Bougainville, C. Australia 13°57S 126°4E 278 B4
Bougainville I. Papua N. G. 6°0S 155°0E 277 B10
Bougainville Reef Australia 15°30S 147°5E 280 B4
Bougainville Str. Solomon Is. 6°40S 156°10E 287 L9
Bougaroun, C. Algeria 37°6N 6°30E 261 A6
Bougie = Bejaïa Algeria 36°42N 5°2E 261 A6
Bougival France 48°51N 2°8E 134 A1
Bougouni Mali 11°30N 7°20W 262 C3
Bougtob Algeria 34°2N 0°5E 261 B5
Bouillante Guadeloupe 16°8N 61°46W 322 e
Bouillante, Pitons de Guadeloupe 16°8N 61°43W 322 e
Bouillon Belgium 49°44N 5°3E 170 E5
Bouïra Algeria 36°20N 3°59E 261 A5
Bouïra □ Algeria 36°15N 3°55E 261 A5
Boukombé Benin 10°13N 1°9E 263 C5
Boulal Mali 15°8N 8°21W 262 B3
Boulazac France 45°10N 0°47E 174 C4
Boulder Colo., U.S.A. 40°1N 105°17W 304 F11
Boulder Mont., U.S.A. 46°14N 112°7W 304 C7
Boulder City U.S.A. 35°58N 114°49W 307 K12
Boulder Creek U.S.A. 37°7N 122°7W 306 H4
Boulder Dam = Hoover Dam U.S.A. 36°1N 114°44W 307 K12
Boulder Pt. Hong Kong, China 22°14N 114°6E 122 B2
Boulembo Gabon 1°26S 12°0E 264 C2
Bouli Mauritania 15°17N 12°18W 262 B2
Boulia Australia 22°52S 139°51E 280 C2
Bouligny France 49°17N 5°45E 173 C12
Boulogne → France 47°12N 1°47W 172 E5
Boulogne, Bois de France 48°51N 2°14E 134 A2
Boulogne-Billancourt France 48°50N 2°14E 134 A2
Boulogne-sur-Gesse France 43°18N 0°38E 174 E4
Boulogne-sur-Mer France 50°42N 1°36E 173 B8
Bouloire France 47°59N 0°45E 172 E7
Boulou → C.A.R. 6°45N 24°16E 264 A4
Boulouli Mali 15°30N 9°25W 262 B3
Bouloupari N. Cal. 21°52S 166°4E 288 d
Boulouposse Congo 1°58S 12°40E 264 C2
Boulsa Burkina Faso 12°39N 0°34W 263 C4
Boultoum Niger 14°45N 10°25E 259 F2
Bouma △ Fiji 16°50S 179°52W 287 A2
Boumalne Dadès Morocco 31°25N 6°0W 260 B3
Boumba → Cameroon 2°2N 15°12E 264 B3
Boumbé → C.A.R. 4°4N 15°23E 264 B3
Boûmdeïd Mauritania 17°25N 11°50W 262 B2
Boumerdès Algeria 36°46N 3°28E 261 A5
Boumerdès □ Algeria 36°45N 3°40E 261 A5
Boun Neua Laos 21°38N 101°54E 236 B3
Boun Tai Laos 21°23N 101°58E 236 B3
Bouna Côte d'Ivoire 9°10N 3°0W 262 D4
Boundary U.S.A. 64°5N 141°1W 303 D12
Boundary Peak U.S.A. 37°51N 118°21W 306 H8
Boundiali Côte d'Ivoire 9°30N 6°20W 262 D3
Boungou → C.A.R. 8°21N 23°48E 264 A4
Bountiful U.S.A. 40°53N 111°52W 304 F8
Bounty Is. Pac. Oc. 48°0S 178°30E 288 M9
Bounty Trough Pac. Oc. 46°0S 178°0E 288 M9
Boura Mali 12°25N 4°33W 262 C4
Bourail N. Cal. 21°34S 165°30E 288 d
Bourbeuse → U.S.A. 38°24N 90°53W 310 F6
Bourbon U.S.A. 41°18N 86°7W 311 C10
Bourbon-Lancy France 46°37N 3°45E 173 F10
Bourbon-l'Archambault France 46°36N 3°4E 173 F10
Bourbon Street New Orleans, U.S.A. 131 b2
Bourbonnais Allier, France 46°28N 3°0E 173 F10
Bourbonnais Ill., U.S.A. 41°9N 87°52W 311 C9
Bourbonne-les-Bains France 47°54N 5°45E 173 E12
Bourbourg France 50°56N 2°12E 173 B9
Bourdel L. Canada 56°43N 74°10W 298 A5
Bourem Mali 17°0N 0°24W 263 B4
Bouressa Mali 20°0N 2°15E 261 E5
Bourg France 45°3N 0°34W 174 C3
Bourg-Argental France 45°18N 4°32E 175 C8
Bourg-de-Péage France 45°2N 5°3E 175 C9
Bourg-en-Bresse France 46°13N 5°12E 173 F12
Bourg-la-Reine France 48°46N 2°19E 134 B2
Bourg-Lastic France 45°39N 2°35E 174 C6
Bourg-Madame France 42°26N 1°55E 174 F5
Bourg-St-Andéol France 44°23N 4°39E 175 D8
Bourg-St-Maurice France 45°35N 6°46E 175 C10
Bourganeuf France 45°57N 1°45E 174 C5
Bourgas = Burgas Bulgaria 42°33N 27°29E 203 D11
Bourges France 47°9N 2°25E 173 E9
Bourget Canada 45°26N 75°9W 313 A9
Bourget, Lac du France 45°44N 5°52E 175 C9
Bourgneuf, B. de France 47°3N 2°10W 172 E4
Bourgneuf-en-Retz France 47°2N 1°58W 172 E5
Bourgogne France 47°0N 4°50E 171 C6
Bourgogne -Franche-Comté □ France 47°0N 5°0E 173 E11
Bourgoin-Jallieu France 45°36N 5°17E 175 C9
Bourgueil France 47°17N 0°10E 172 E7
Bourke Australia 30°8S 145°55E 281 E4
Bourne U.K. 52°47N 0°22W 168 E7
Bournemouth U.K. 50°43N 1°52W 169 G6
Bournemouth, Christchurch & Poole □ U.K. 50°43N 1°52W 169 G6
Bouroum Burkina Faso 13°37N 0°39W 263 C4
Bouse U.S.A. 33°56N 114°0W 307 M13
Boussac France 46°22N 2°13E 173 F9
Boussé Burkina Faso 12°39N 1°53W 263 C4
Bousso Chad 10°34N 16°52E 259 F3
Boussouma Burkina Faso 12°52N 1°13W 263 C4
Bout, Pte. du Martinique 14°33N 61°3W 322 j
Bout Stable Bay Dominica 15°21N 61°15W 323 k
Boutilimit Mauritania 17°45N 14°40W 262 B2
Boutonne → France 45°54N 0°50W 174 C3
Bouvet I. = Bouvetøya Antarctica 54°26S 3°24E 152 M12
Bouvetøya Antarctica 54°26S 3°24E 152 M12
Bouviers France 48°46N 2°4E 134 B1
Bouxwiller France 48°49N 7°27E 173 D14
Bouza Niger 14°29N 6°2E 263 C6
Bouznika Morocco 33°46N 7°6W 260 B3
Bouzonville France 49°17N 6°32E 173 C13
Bova Marina Italy 37°56N 15°55E 201 E8
Bovalino Italy 38°10N 16°10E 201 D9
Bovanenkovo Russia 70°22N 68°40E 214 B7
Bovec Slovenia 46°20N 13°33E 199 B10
Boven Kapuas, Pegunungan Malaysia 1°25N 113°15E 235 B4
Bovenkerk Neths. 52°18N 4°51E 112 B2
Bovenkerker Polder Neths. 52°16N 4°52E 112 B2
Boverdal Norway 61°44N 8°20E 164 C5
Bøverfjorden Norway 63°1N 8°32E 164 A5
Bovill U.S.A. 46°51N 116°24W 304 C5
Bovino Italy 41°15N 15°20E 201 A8
Bovisa Italy 45°30N 9°10E 128 A2
Bovril Argentina 31°21S 59°26W 334 C4
Bow U.K. 51°31N 0°1W 125 A3
Bow → Canada 49°57N 111°41W 296 C6
Bow Island Canada 49°50N 111°23W 304 B8
Bowbells U.S.A. 48°48N 102°15W 308 A2
Bowdle U.S.A. 45°27N 99°39W 308 C4
Bowdon U.S.A. 33°32N 85°15W 316 B4
Bowdon Junction U.S.A. 33°40N 85°9W 316 B4
Bowelling Australia 33°25S 116°30E 279 F2
Bowen Argentina 35°0S 67°31W 334 D2
Bowen Queens., Australia 20°0S 148°16E 280 J6
Bowen Mts. Australia 37°0S 147°50E 283 D7
Bowers Basin Pac. Oc. 53°45N 176°0E 150 D16
Bowers Ridge Pac. Oc. 54°0N 180°0E 150 D17
Bowery New York, U.S.A. 132 e2
Bowie Ariz., U.S.A. 32°19N 109°29W 305 K9
Bowie Tex., U.S.A. 33°34N 97°51W 314 E6
Bowkān Iran 36°31N 46°12E 213 D12
Bowland, Forest of U.K. 54°0N 2°30W 168 D5
Bowling Green Fla., U.S.A. 27°38N 81°50W 317 H8
Bowling Green Ky., U.S.A. 36°59N 86°27W 308 G10
Bowling Green Mo., U.S.A. 39°21N 91°12W 310 E5
Bowling Green Ohio, U.S.A. 41°23N 83°39W 311 C13
Bowling Green, C. Australia 19°19S 147°25E 280 B4
Bowling Green Bay △ Australia 19°26S 146°57E 280 B4
Bowman N. Dak., U.S.A. 46°11N 103°24W 308 B2
Bowman S.C., U.S.A. 33°21N 80°41W 316 B9
Bowman I. Antarctica 65°0S 104°0E 151 C8
Bowmanville = Clarington Canada 43°55N 78°41W 312 C6
Bowmore U.K. 55°45N 6°17W 167 F2
Bowral Australia 34°26S 150°27E 283 C9
Bowraville Australia 30°37S 152°52E 281 E5
Bowron → Canada 54°3N 121°50W 296 C4
Bowron Lake ⌂ Canada 53°10N 121°5W 296 C4
Bowser L. Canada 56°30N 129°30W 296 B3
Bowsman Canada 52°14N 101°12W 297 C8
Bowutu Mts. Papua N. G. 7°45S 147°10E 286 D4
Bowwood Zambia 17°5S 26°20E 269 F2
Box Cr. → Australia 34°10S 143°50E 281 E3
Boxholm Sweden 58°12N 15°3E 163 F9
Boxmeer Neths. 51°38N 5°56E 170 C5
Boxtel Neths. 51°36N 5°20E 170 C5
Boyabat Turkey 41°28N 34°47E 212 B6
Boyabo Dem. Rep. of the Congo 3°43N 18°46E 264 B3
Boyacá □ Colombia 5°30N 72°30W 328 B3
Boyacıköy Turkey 41°5N 29°2E 122 B2
Boyalıca Turkey 40°29N 29°33E 203 F13
Boyang China 29°0N 116°38E 229 C11
Boyany Ukraine 48°17N 26°8E 183 B11
Boyasegese Dem. Rep. of the Congo 3°29N 20°33E 264 B4
Boyce U.S.A. 31°23N 92°40W 314 F8
Boyd U.S.A. 30°11N 83°37W 316 E6
Boyd Conservation Area Canada 43°49N 79°35W 141 A1
Boyd L. Canada 52°46N 76°42W 298 B4
Boyenge Dem. Rep. of the Congo 0°14N 18°55E 264 B3
Boyer, C. N. Cal. 21°37S 168°6E 288 d
Boyera Dem. Rep. of the Congo 0°40S 19°23E 264 C3
Boyle Alta., Canada 54°35N 112°49W 296 C6
Boyle Roscommon, Ireland 53°59N 8°18W 166 C3
Boyle Heights U.S.A. 34°1N 118°12W 126 B3
Boyne → Ireland 53°43N 6°15W 166 C5
Boyne, Bend of the Ireland 53°41N 6°27W 166 C5
Boyne City U.S.A. 45°13N 85°1W 309 C11
Boyni Qara Afghan. 36°20N 67°0E 240 A2
Boynitsa Bulgaria 43°58N 22°32E 202 C6
Boynton Beach U.S.A. 26°32N 80°4W 317 J9
Boyoma, Chutes Dem. Rep. of the Congo 0°35N 25°23E 264 B5
Boysen Res. U.S.A. 43°25N 108°11W 304 E9
Boysun Uzbekistan 38°12N 67°12E 240 A2
Boyup Brook Australia 33°50S 116°23E 279 F2
Boz Burun Turkey 40°32N 28°46E 203 F12
Boz Dağ Turkey 37°18N 29°11E 205 D11
Boz Dağları Turkey 38°20N 28°0E 205 C10
Bozai Gumbaz Afghan. 37°8N 74°0E 240 A4
Bozburun Turkey 36°43N 28°4E 205 E10
Bozcaada Turkey 39°49N 26°3E 212 C2
Bozdağ Turkey 36°50N 36°22E 250 B7
Bozdoğan Turkey 37°40N 28°17E 205 D10
Boze Papua N. G. 9°3S 143°3E 286 E2
Bozeman U.S.A. 45°41N 111°2W 304 D8
Bozen = Bolzano Italy 46°31N 11°22E 199 B8
Bozene Dem. Rep. of the Congo 2°56N 19°12E 264 B3
Boževac Serbia 44°32N 21°24E 202 B5
Bozhou China 33°55N 115°41E 226 H8
Bozkır Turkey 37°11N 32°14E 212 D5
Bozkurt Turkey 37°50N 29°37E 205 D11
Bozouls France 44°28N 2°43E 174 D6
Bozoum C.A.R. 6°25N 16°35E 264 A3
Bozova Antalya, Turkey 37°13N 30°18E 205 D12
Bozova Sanliurfa, Turkey 37°21N 38°32E 213 D8
Bozovici Romania 44°56N 22°0E 182 F7
Bozüyük Turkey 39°54N 30°3E 205 B12
Bozyazı Turkey 36°6N 33°0E 250 B4
Bra Italy 44°42N 7°51E 198 D4
Braås Sweden 57°4N 15°3E 163 G9
Brabant □ Belgium 50°46N 4°30E 170 D4
Brabant L. Canada 55°58N 103°43W 297 B8
Brabrand Denmark 56°9N 10°7E 163 H4
Brač Croatia 43°20N 16°40E 199 E13
Bracadale, L. U.K. 57°20N 6°30W 167 D2
Bracciano Italy 42°6N 12°10E 199 F9
Bracciano, L. di Italy 42°7N 12°14E 199 F9
Bracebridge Canada 45°2N 79°19W 312 A5
Bracieux France 47°30N 1°30E 172 E8
Bräcke Sweden 62°45N 15°26E 162 B9
Brackettville U.S.A. 29°19N 100°25W 314 G4
Bracki Kanal Croatia 43°24N 16°40E 199 E13
Bracknell U.K. 51°25N 0°43W 169 F7
Bracknell Forest □ U.K. 51°25N 0°44W 169 F7
Brad Romania 46°10N 22°50E 182 D7
Brádano → Italy 40°23N 16°51E 201 B9
Bradbury Building Los Angeles, U.S.A. 127 b2
Bradenton U.S.A. 27°30N 82°34W 317 H7
Brades Montserrat 16°47N 62°13W 323 p
Bradford Ont., Canada 44°7N 79°34W 312 B5
Bradford W. Yorks., U.K. 53°47N 1°45W 168 D6
Bradford Ill., U.S.A. 41°11N 89°39W 310 C7
Bradford Ohio, U.S.A. 40°8N 84°27W 311 D12
Bradford Pa., U.S.A. 41°58N 78°38W 312 E6
Bradford Vt., U.S.A. 43°59N 72°9W 313 C12
Bradley Ark., U.S.A. 33°6N 93°39W 314 E8
Bradley Calif., U.S.A. 35°52N 120°48W 306 K6
Bradley Ill., U.S.A. 41°9N 87°52W 311 C9
Bradley Institute Zimbabwe 17°7S 31°25E 269 F3
Bradley Junction U.S.A. 27°48N 81°59W 317 H8
Bradner U.S.A. 41°20N 83°26W 311 C13
Brady U.S.A. 31°9N 99°20W 314 F5
Brædstrup Denmark 55°58N 9°37E 163 J3
Braemar Australia 33°12S 139°35E 282 B3
Braepark U.K. 55°58N 3°18W 121 B2
Braeside Canada 45°28N 76°24W 313 A8
Braeton Jamaica 17°57N 76°53W 320 a
Braga Portugal 41°35N 8°25W 194 D2
Braga □ Portugal 41°30N 8°30W 194 D2
Bragadiru Romania 43°46N 25°31E 183 G10
Bragado Argentina 35°2S 60°27W 334 D3
Bragança Brazil 1°0S 47°2W 332 B2
Bragança Portugal 41°48N 6°50W 194 D4
Bragança □ Portugal 41°30N 6°45W 194 D4
Bragança Paulista Brazil 22°55S 46°32W 335 A6
Bragg's Spur = West Memphis U.S.A. 35°8N 90°10W 315 D9
Brahestad = Raahe Finland 64°40N 24°28E 160 D21
Brahmakund India 27°52N 96°22E 241 B6
Brahmanbaria Bangla. 23°58N 91°15E 241 D3
Brahmani → India 20°39N 86°46E 244 D8
Brahmapur India 19°15N 84°54E 244 E7
Brahmaputra → Asia 23°40N 90°35E 241 D3
Braich-y-pwll U.K. 52°47N 4°46W 168 E3
Braid U.K. 55°55N 3°11W 121 B2
Braidwood Australia 35°27S 149°49E 283 C8
Brăila Romania 45°19N 27°59E 183 E12
Brăila □ Romania 45°5N 27°30E 183 E12
Brainerd U.S.A. 46°22N 94°12W 308 B6
Braintree Essex, U.K. 51°53N 0°34E 169 F8
Braintree Mass., U.S.A. 42°13N 71°0W 313 D14
Brak → S. Africa 29°35S 22°55E 270 C3
Brake Germany 53°20N 8°28E 178 B4
Brakel Germany 51°42N 9°11E 178 D5
Brakna □ Mauritania 17°0N 13°20W 262 B2
Bräkne-Hoby Sweden 56°14N 15°6E 163 H9
Brakwater Namibia 22°28S 17°3E 270 B2
Brålanda Sweden 58°34N 12°21E 163 F6
Bramberg Germany 50°6N 10°40E 179 E6
Bramdrupdam Denmark 55°31N 9°28E 163 J3
Bramhapuri India 20°36N 79°52E 244 D4
Bramley S. Africa 26°7S 28°4E 123 A2
Bramming Denmark 55°28N 8°42E 163 J2
Brämön Sweden 62°14N 17°40E 162 B11
Brampton Ont., Canada 43°45N 79°45W 312 C5
Brampton Cumb., U.K. 54°57N 2°44W 168 C5
Brampton I. Australia 20°49S 149°16E 280 b
Bramsche Germany 52°24N 7°59E 178 C3
Branchville U.S.A. 33°15N 80°49W 316 B9
Branco → Brazil 1°20S 61°50W 329 D5
Branco, C. Brazil 7°9S 34°47W 332 C5
Brandaris Bonaire 12°16N 68°23W 322 h
Brandberg Namibia 21°10S 14°33E 270 B1
Brandberg △ Namibia 21°10S 14°30E 270 B1
Brandbu Norway 60°26N 10°28E 164 D7
Brande Denmark 55°57N 9°8E 163 J3
Brandeis Univ. U.S.A. 42°21N 71°17W 116 A1
Brandenburg = Neubrandenburg Germany 53°33N 13°15E 178 B9
Brandenburg Brandenburg, Germany 52°25N 12°33E 178 C8
Brandenburg Ky., U.S.A. 38°0N 86°10W 311 G10
Brandenburg □ Germany 52°50N 13°0E 178 C9
Brandenburger Tor Germany 52°30N 13°21E 115 A3
Brandfort S. Africa 28°40S 26°30E 270 C4
Brando France 42°47N 9°27E 175 F13
Brandon Man., Canada 49°50N 99°57W 297 D9
Brandon Fla., U.S.A. 27°56N 82°17W 317 H7
Brandon Vt., U.S.A. 43°48N 73°6W 313 C11
Brandon B. Ireland 52°17N 10°8W 166 D1
Brandon Mt. Ireland 52°15N 10°15W 166 D1
Brandsen Argentina 35°10S 58°15W 334 D4
Brandvlei S. Africa 30°25S 20°30E 270 D3
Brandýs nad Labem Czechia 50°10N 14°40E 180 A7
Branford Conn., U.S.A. 41°17N 72°49W 313 E12
Branford Fla., U.S.A. 29°58N 82°56W 316 F7
Brani, Pulau Singapore 1°15N 103°50E 138 B3
Braniewo Poland 54°25N 19°50E 184 D6
Branik Czechia 50°1N 14°25E 135 B2
Brännkyrka Sweden 59°17N 18°0E 139 B2
Bransfield Str. Antarctica 63°0S 59°0W 151 C18
Brańsk Poland 52°45N 22°50E 185 F9
Branson U.S.A. 36°39N 93°13W 308 G7
Brantford Canada 43°10N 80°15W 312 C4
Brantley U.S.A. 31°35N 86°16W 316 D3
Brantôme France 45°22N 0°39E 174 C4
Branxholme Australia 37°52S 141°49E 282 D4
Branxton Australia 32°38S 151°21E 283 B9
Branzi Italy 46°1N 9°46E 198 B6
Brás Amazonas, Brazil 2°5S 58°10W 329 D6
Brás São Paulo, Brazil 23°32S 46°36W 137 B2
Bras d'Or L. Canada 45°50N 60°50W 299 C7
Bras-Panon Réunion 20°59S 55°41E 272 f
Brasher Falls U.S.A. 44°49N 74°47W 313 B10
Brasil = Brazil ■ S. Amer. 12°0S 50°0W 327 E6
Brasil, Planalto Brazil 18°0S 46°30W 326 E6
Brasil Novo Brazil 3°19S 52°38W 329 D7
Brasilândia Brazil 23°28S 46°42W 137 A1
Brasiléia Brazil 11°0S 68°45W 330 C4
Brasilia Distrito Federal, Brazil 15°47S 47°55W 333 E2
Brasilia Minas Gerais, Brazil 16°12S 44°26W 333 E3
Brasilia △ Brazil 15°41S 48°8W 333 E2
Brasilia Int. ✈ (BSB) Brazil 15°52S 47°55W 333 E2
Brasilia Legal Brazil 3°49S 55°36W 329 D6
Braskereidfoss Norway 60°44N 11°46E 164 D8
Braslaw Belarus 55°38N 27°0E 188 E4
Braslawskiya Azyory △ Belarus 55°36N 27°3E 188 E4
Braslovče Slovenia 46°21N 15°3E 199 B12
Braşov Romania 45°38N 25°35E 183 E10
Braşov □ Romania 45°45N 25°15E 183 E10
Brass Nigeria 4°35N 6°14E 263 E6
Brass → Nigeria 4°15N 6°13E 263 E6
Brassac-les-Mines France 45°24N 3°20E 174 C7
Brasschaat Belgium 51°19N 4°27E 170 C4
Brassey, Banjaran Malaysia 5°0N 117°15E 235 B5
Brassey Ra. Australia 25°8S 122°15E 279 E3
Brasso Seco Trin. & Tob. 10°45N 61°16W 323 t
Brasstown Bald U.S.A. 34°53N 83°49W 315 D13
Brastad Sweden 58°23N 11°30E 163 F5
Brastavățu Romania 43°55N 24°24E 183 G9
Bratan = Morozov Bulgaria 42°30N 25°10E 203 D9
Brateş Romania 45°50N 26°4E 183 E11
Brateyevo Russia 55°39N 37°45E 129 C3
Bratislava Slovakia 48°10N 17°7E 181 C10
Bratislava M.R. Štefánik ✈ (BTS) Slovakia 48°11N 17°12E 181 C10
Bratislavský □ Slovakia 48°15N 17°20E 181 C10
Bratsberg = Telemark □ Norway 59°25N 8°30E 164 E5
Bratsigovo Bulgaria 42°1N 24°22E 203 D8
Bratsk Russia 56°10N 101°30E 215 D11
Bratskoye Vdkhr. Russia 56°0N 101°40E 215 D11
Brattleboro U.S.A. 42°51N 72°34W 313 D12
Brattvåg Norway 62°37N 6°25E 164 B3
Bratunac Bos.-H. 44°13N 19°21E 182 F4
Braunau am Inn Austria 48°15N 13°3E 180 C6
Braunsberg = Braniewo Poland 54°25N 19°50E 184 D6
Braunschweig Germany 52°15N 10°31E 178 C6
Braunton U.K. 51°7N 4°10W 169 F3
Brava = Baraawe Somalia 1°20N 44°8E 267 D5
Brava Cabo Verde 15°0N 24°40W 153 j
Brava, Costa Spain 41°30N 3°0E 196 D8
Bravicea Moldova 47°22N 28°27E 183 C13
Bråviken Sweden 58°38N 16°32E 163 F10
Bravo del Norte, Rio = Grande, Rio → N. Amer. 25°58N 97°9W 314 J6
Brawley U.S.A. 32°59N 115°31W 307 N11
Bray Ireland 53°13N 6°7W 166 C5
Bray, Mt. Australia 14°0S 134°30E 280 A1
Bray, Pays de France 49°46N 1°26E 173 C8
Bray-sur-Seine France 48°25N 3°14E 173 D10
Braybrook Australia 37°46S 144°51E 128 A1
Braymer U.S.A. 39°35N 93°48W 310 E3
Brázdim Czechia 50°10N 14°35E 135 A3
Brazeau → Canada 52°55N 115°14W 296 C5
Brazil Ind., U.S.A. 39°32N 87°8W 311 E9
Brazil ■ S. Amer. 12°0S 50°0W 327 E6
Brazil Basin Atl. Oc. 15°0S 25°0W 152 H9
Brazilian Highlands = Brasil, Planalto Brazil 18°0S 46°30W 326 E6
Brazo Sur → S. Amer. 25°21S 57°42W 334 B4
Brazos → U.S.A. 28°53N 95°23W 314 G7
Brazzaville Congo 4°9S 15°12E 265 C3
Brčko Bos.-H. 44°54N 18°46E 182 F3
Brda → Poland 53°8N 18°8E 185 E5
Brdy Czechia 49°43N 13°55E 180 B6
Bré = Bray Ireland 53°13N 6°7W 166 C5
Breach Candy Mumbai, India 130 a1
Breaden, L. Australia 25°51S 125°28E 279 E4
Breakheart Reservation U.S.A. 42°28N 71°1W 116 A2
Breaksea Sd. N.Z. 45°35S 166°35E 285 F1
Bream B. N.Z. 35°56S 174°28E 284 B3
Bream Hd. N.Z. 35°51S 174°36E 284 B3
Bream Tail N.Z. 36°3S 174°36E 284 C3
Breas Chile 25°29S 70°24W 334 B1
Breaza Romania 45°11N 25°40E 183 E10
Brebes Indonesia 6°52S 109°3E 235 D3
Brechin Ont., Canada 44°32N 79°10W 312 B5
Brechin Angus, U.K. 56°44N 2°39W 167 E6
Brecht Belgium 51°21N 4°38E 170 C4
Breckenridge Colo., U.S.A. 39°29N 106°3W 304 G10
Breckenridge Minn., U.S.A. 46°16N 96°35W 308 B5
Breckenridge Tex., U.S.A. 32°45N 98°54W 314 E5
Breckland U.K. 52°30N 0°40E 169 E8
Brecknock, Pen. Chile 54°35S 71°30W 336 D2
Břeclav Czechia 48°46N 16°53E 181 C9
Brecon U.K. 51°57N 3°23W 169 F4
Brecon Beacons U.K. 51°53N 3°26W 169 F4
Brecon Beacons ⌂ U.K. 51°50N 3°30W 169 F4
Breda Neths. 51°35N 4°45E 170 C4
Bredaryd Sweden 57°10N 13°45E 163 G7
Bredasdorp S. Africa 34°33S 20°2E 270 D3
Bredbo Australia 35°58S 149°10E 283 C8
Brede Denmark 55°47N 12°30E 118 A3
Bredebro Denmark 55°4N 8°50E 163 J2
Bredhat e Hotovës △ Albania 40°18N 20°25E 202 F4
Bredstedt Germany 54°37N 8°55E 178 A4
Bredy Russia 52°26N 60°21E 216 B6
Bree Belgium 51°8N 5°35E 170 C5
Breezy Point U.S.A. 40°33N 73°56W 132 D2
Brega = Marsa al Burayqah Libya 30°24N 19°37E 258 B3
Bregalnica → N. Macedonia 41°43N 22°9E 202 E6
Bregenz Austria 47°30N 9°45E 180 D2
Bregovo Bulgaria 44°9N 22°39E 202 B6
Bréhal France 48°53N 1°30W 172 D5
Bréhat, Î. de France 48°51N 3°0W 172 D4
Breiðafjörður Iceland 65°15N 23°15W 160 D2
Breiðdalsvík Iceland 64°44N 14°0W 155 C13
Breil-sur-Roya France 43°56N 7°31E 175 E11
Breim Norway 61°44N 6°25E 164 C3
Breisach Germany 48°1N 7°36E 179 G3
Breitenlee Austria 48°15N 16°30E 142 A3
Brejinho de Nazaré Brazil 11°1S 48°34W 333 D2
Brejo Brazil 3°41S 42°47W 332 B3
Brekke Norway 61°1N 5°26E 164 C2
Brekken Norway 62°40N 11°51E 164 B8
Brekkestø Norway 58°11N 8°22E 164 F5
Bremanger Norway 61°51N 4°58E 164 C1
Bremangerlandet Norway 61°51N 5°0E 164 C1
Bremen Bremen, Germany 53°4N 8°47E 178 B4
Bremen Ga., U.S.A. 33°43N 85°9W 316 B4
Bremen Ind., U.S.A. 41°27N 86°9W 311 C10
Bremen □ Germany 53°4N 8°50E 178 B4
Bremer Bay Australia 34°21S 119°20E 279 F2
Bremer I. Australia 12°5S 136°45E 280 A2
Bremerhaven Germany 53°33N 8°36E 178 B4
Bremersdorp = Manzini Eswatini 26°30S 31°25E 271 C5
Bremerton U.S.A. 47°34N 122°37W 306 C4
Bremervörde Germany 53°29N 9°8E 178 B5
Bremnes Norway 59°47N 5°8E 164 E2
Bremsnes Norway 63°6N 7°40E 164 A4
Breña Peru 12°3S 77°3W 124 B2
Brenes Spain 37°32N 5°54W 195 H5
Brenham U.S.A. 30°10N 96°24W 314 F6
Brenne France 46°44N 1°14E 174 B5
Brenne ⌂ France 46°40N 1°15E 174 B5
Brennerpass Austria 47°2N 11°30E 180 D4
Brennhaug Norway 61°54N 9°21E 164 C6
Breno Italy 45°57N 10°18E 198 C7
Brent U.S.A. 32°56N 87°10W 315 E11
Brent □ U.K. 51°33N 0°16W 125 A2
Brent Res. U.K. 51°34N 0°14W 125 A2
Brenta → Italy 45°11N 12°18E 199 C9
Brentford U.K. 51°28N 0°18W 125 B2
Brentwood Essex, U.K. 51°37N 0°19E 169 F8
Brentwood Calif., U.S.A. 34°3N 118°28W 126 B2
Brentwood Calif., U.S.A. 37°56N 121°42W 306 H5
Brentwood N.Y., U.S.A. 40°47N 73°15W 313 F11
Brentwood Park U.S.A. 34°3N 118°29W 126 B2
Brera Italy 45°28N 9°11E 128 B2
Brereton Barbados 13°7N 59°30W 323 r
Bréscia Italy 45°33N 10°15E 198 C7
Breskens Neths. 51°23N 3°33E 170 C3
Breslau = Wrocław Poland 51°5N 17°5E 185 G4
Bresle → France 50°4N 1°22E 172 B8
Bressanone Italy 46°43N 11°39E 199 B8
Bressay U.K. 60°9N 1°6W 167 A7
Bresse France 46°50N 5°10E 173 F12
Bresso Italy 45°32N 9°11E 128 A2
Bressuire France 46°51N 0°30W 172 F6
Brest Belarus 52°10N 23°40E 177 B12
Brest Finistère, France 48°24N 4°31W 172 D2
Brest □ Belarus 52°30N 26°10E 177 B13
Brest-Litovsk = Brest Belarus 52°10N 23°40E 177 B12
Bretagne □ France 48°10N 3°0W 172 D3
Bretanha, Pta. da Azores 37°54N 25°47W 153 d3
Bretçu Romania 46°7N 26°18E 183 D11
Bretenoux France 44°54N 1°51E 174 D5
Breteuil Eure, France 48°50N 0°57E 172 D7
Breteuil Oise, France 49°38N 2°18E 173 C9
Breton Canada 53°7N 114°28W 296 C6
Breton, Pertuis France 46°17N 1°25W 174 B2
Breton Sd. U.S.A. 29°35N 89°15W 315 G10
Brett, C. N.Z. 35°10S 174°20E 284 B3
Bretten Germany 49°2N 8°42E 179 F4
Breueh Indonesia 5°44N 95°3E 234 A1
Breuil-Cervinia Italy 45°56N 7°38E 198 C4
Brevard U.S.A. 35°14N 82°44W 315 D13
Breves Brazil 1°40S 50°29W 332 B1
Brevig Mission U.S.A. 65°20N 166°29W 303 D6
Brevik Telemark, Norway 59°4N 9°42E 164 E6
Brevik Stockholm, Sweden 59°20N 18°12E 139 A3
Břevnov Czechia 50°4N 14°22E 135 B2
Brewarrina Australia 30°0S 146°51E 281 E4
Brewer U.S.A. 44°48N 68°46W 309 C19
Brewer, Mt. U.S.A. 36°44N 118°28W 306 J8
Brewerville Liberia 6°26N 10°47W 262 D2
Brewster N.Y., U.S.A. 41°24N 73°36W 313 E11
Brewster Ohio, U.S.A. 40°43N 81°36W 312 F3
Brewster Wash., U.S.A. 48°6N 119°47W 304 B4
Brewster, Kap = Kangikajik Greenland 70°7N 22°0W 154 C8
Brewton U.S.A. 31°7N 87°4W 315 F11
Breyten S. Africa 26°16S 30°0E 271 C5
Breza Bos.-H. 44°2N 18°16E 182 F3
Brežice Slovenia 45°54N 15°35E 199 C12
Brézina Algeria 33°4N 1°14E 261 B5
Březnice Czechia 49°32N 13°57E 180 B6
Breznik Bulgaria 42°44N 22°55E 202 D6
Brezno Slovakia 48°50N 19°40E 181 C12
Brezoi Romania 45°21N 24°15E 183 E9
Brezovicë Kosovo 42°15N 21°3E 202 D5
Brezovo Bulgaria 42°21N 25°5E 203 D9
Bria C.A.R. 6°30N 21°58E 264 A4
Briançon France 44°54N 6°39E 175 D10
Briare France 47°38N 2°45E 173 E9
Briars Pt. St. Helena 15°56S 5°43W 153 h
Briático Italy 38°43N 16°2E 201 D9
Bribie I. Australia 27°0S 153°10E 281 D5
Bribri Costa Rica 9°38N 82°50W 320 E3
Briceni Moldova 48°22N 27°6E 183 B12
Brickyard, The U.S.A. 41°55N 87°47W 119 B2
Bricquebec France 49°28N 1°38W 172 C5
Bridge City U.S.A. 29°55N 90°9W 131 B2
Bridge of Sighs = Sospiri, Ponte dei Venice, Italy 142 b3
Bridgehampton U.S.A. 40°56N 72°19W 313 F12
Bridgend U.K. 51°30N 3°34W 169 F4
Bridgend □ U.K. 51°36N 3°36W 169 F4
Bridgenorth Canada 44°23N 78°23W 312 B6
Bridgeport Calif., U.S.A. 38°15N 119°14W 306 G7
Bridgeport Conn., U.S.A. 41°11N 73°12W 313 E11
Bridgeport Ill., U.S.A. 41°50N 87°38W 119 B3
Bridgeport Ill., U.S.A. 38°43N 87°46W 311 F9
Bridgeport N.Y., U.S.A. 43°9N 75°58W 313 C9
Bridgeport Nebr., U.S.A. 41°40N 103°6W 308 E2
Bridgeport Tex., U.S.A. 33°13N 97°45W 314 E6
Bridger U.S.A. 45°18N 108°55W 304 D9
Bridgeton U.S.A. 39°26N 75°14W 309 F16
Bridgetown W. Austral., Australia 33°58S 116°7E 279 F2
Bridgetown Barbados 13°6N 59°37W 323 r
Bridgetown N.S., Canada 44°55N 65°18W 299 D6
Bridgetown Western Cape, S. Africa 33°58S 18°33E 118 A2
Bridgeview U.S.A. 41°45N 87°48W 119 C2
Bridgewater Tas., Australia 42°44S 147°14E 281 G4
Bridgewater Vic., Australia 36°36S 143°59E 282 D5
Bridgewater N.S., Canada 44°25N 64°31W 299 D7
Bridgewater Mass., U.S.A. 41°59N 70°58W 313 E14
Bridgewater N.Y., U.S.A. 42°53N 75°15W 313 D9
Bridgewater, C. Australia 38°23S 141°23E 282 E4
Bridgman U.S.A. 41°57N 86°33W 311 C10
Bridgnorth U.K. 52°32N 2°25W 169 E5
Bridgton U.S.A. 44°3N 70°42W 313 B14
Bridgwater U.K. 51°8N 2°59W 169 F5
Bridgwater B. U.K. 51°15N 3°15W 169 F4
Bridlington U.K. 54°5N 0°12W 168 C7
Bridlington B. U.K. 54°4N 0°10W 168 C7
Bridport Tas., Australia 40°59S 147°23E 281 G4
Bridport Dorset, U.K. 50°44N 2°45W 169 G5
Briec France 48°6N 4°0W 172 D2
Brieg = Brzeg Poland 50°52N 17°30E 185 H4
Brienne-le-Château France 48°24N 4°30E 173 D11
Brienon-sur-Armançon France 47°59N 3°38E 173 E10
Brienz Switz. 46°46N 8°2E 179 J4
Brienzersee Switz. 46°44N 7°53E 179 J3
Brier Cr. → U.S.A. 32°44N 81°26W 316 C8
Brière ⌂ France 47°22N 2°13W 172 E4
Brievengat Curaçao 12°9N 68°54W 322 g
Brig Switz. 46°18N 7°59E 179 J3
Brigg U.K. 53°34N 0°28W 168 D7
Brigham City U.S.A. 41°31N 112°1W 304 F7
Bright Australia 36°42S 146°56E 283 D7
Brighton S. Austral., Australia 35°5S 138°30E 282 C3
Brighton Vic., Australia 37°55S 144°59E 128 B1
Brighton Ont., Canada 44°2N 77°44W 312 B7
Brighton Trin. & Tob. 10°15N 61°39W 323 t
Brighton Brighton & Hove, U.K. 50°49N 0°7W 169 G7
Brighton Fla., U.S.A. 27°14N 81°6W 317 H8
Brighton Ill., U.S.A. 39°2N 90°8W 310 E6
Brighton Iowa, U.S.A. 41°10N 91°49W 310 C5
Brighton Mass., U.S.A. 42°21N 71°9W 116 A2
Brighton Mich., U.S.A. 42°32N 83°47W 311 B13
Brighton N.Y., U.S.A. 43°8N 77°34W 312 C7
Brighton Beach U.S.A. 40°34N 73°57W 132 C2
Brighton-Le-Sands Australia 33°57S 151°9E 139 B1
Brighton Park U.S.A. 41°48N 87°41W 119 C2
Brightside Canada 45°7N 76°29W 313 A8
Brightwater N.Z. 41°22S 173°9E 285 B8
Brightwood U.S.A. 38°57N 77°1W 143 B2
Brigittenau Austria 48°14N 16°22E 142 A2
Brignogan-Plage France 48°40N 4°20W 172 D2
Brignoles France 43°25N 6°5E 175 E10
Brihuega Spain 40°45N 2°52W 196 E2
Brikama Gambia 13°15N 16°45W 262 C1
Brilliant U.S.A. 40°15N 80°39W 312 F4
Brilon Germany 51°23N 8°35E 178 D4
Brim Australia 36°3S 142°27E 282 D5
Brimbank Park Australia 37°43S 144°50E 128 A1
Brimfield U.S.A. 40°50N 89°53W 310 D7
Brimstone Hill Fort St. Kitts & Nevis 17°20N 62°50W 322 d
Brindabella △ Australia 35°14S 148°5E 283 C8
Bríndisi Italy 40°39N 17°55E 201 B10
Brinje Croatia 44°59N 15°9E 199 D12
Brinkley U.S.A. 34°53N 91°12W 314 D9
Brinkworth Australia 33°42S 138°26E 282 B3
Brinnon U.S.A. 47°41N 122°54W 306 C4
Brinson U.S.A. 30°59N 84°44W 316 E5
Brion, Î. Canada 47°46N 61°26W 299 C7
Brionne France 49°11N 0°43E 172 C7
Brionski Croatia 44°55N 13°45E 199 D10
Brioude France 45°18N 3°24E 174 C7
Briouze France 48°42N 0°23W 172 D6
Brisay Canada 54°26N 70°31W 299 B5
Brisbane Queens., Australia 27°25S 153°2E 281 D5
Brisbane Calif., U.S.A. 37°40N 122°23W 136 B2
Brisbane → Australia 27°24S 153°9E 281 D5
Brisbane ✈ (BNE) Australia 27°35S 153°7E 281 D5
Brisbane Ranges △ Australia 37°47S 144°16E 282 D6
Brisbane Water △ Australia 33°26S 151°13E 283 B9
Brisighella Italy 44°13N 11°46E 199 D8
Bristol Bristol, U.K. 51°26N 2°35W 169 F5
Bristol Conn., U.S.A. 41°40N 72°57W 313 E12
Bristol Fla., U.S.A. 30°26N 84°59W 316 E5
Bristol Pa., U.S.A. 40°6N 74°51W 313 F10
Bristol R.I., U.S.A. 41°40N 71°16W 313 E13
Bristol Tenn., U.S.A. 36°36N 82°11W 315 C13
Bristol Vt., U.S.A. 44°8N 73°4W 313 B11
Bristol, City of □ U.K. 51°27N 2°36W 169 F5
Bristol B. U.S.A. 58°0N 160°0W 303 H8
Bristol Channel U.K. 51°18N 4°30W 169 F3
Bristol I. Antarctica 58°45S 28°0W 151 B1
Bristol L. U.S.A. 34°28N 115°41W 307 L11
Bristow U.S.A. 35°50N 96°23W 314 D6
Bristow I. Papua N. G. 9°8S 143°14E 286 E2
Britain = Great Britain Europe 54°0N 2°15W 158 E5
Britânia Brazil 15°14S 51°9W 331 D7
British Central Africa = Malawi ■ Africa 11°55S 34°0E 269 E3
British Columbia □ Canada 55°0N 125°15W 296 C3
British East Africa = Kenya ■ Africa 1°0N 38°0E 268 B4
British Guiana = Guyana ■ S. Amer. 5°0N 59°0W 329 C6
British Honduras = Belize ■ Cent. Amer. 17°0N 88°30W 320 C2
British Indian Ocean Terr. = Chagos Arch. ☑ Ind. Oc. 6°0S 72°0E 273 E6
British Isles Europe 54°0N 4°0W 165 D5
British Mts. N. Amer. 68°50N 140°0W 300 B12
British Museum London, U.K. 125 a3
British Virgin Is. ☑ W. Indies 18°30N 64°30W 321 C7
Brits S. Africa 25°37S 27°48E 271 C4
Britstown S. Africa 30°37S 23°30E 270 D3
Britt Ont., Canada 45°46N 80°34W 298 C3
Britt Iowa, U.S.A. 43°6N 93°48W 310 A3
Brittany = Bretagne □ France 48°10N 3°0W 172 D3
Britton U.S.A. 45°48N 97°45W 308 C5
Britz Germany 52°26N 13°27E 115 B3
Brive-la-Gaillarde France 45°10N 1°32E 174 C5
Briviesca Spain 42°32N 3°19W 194 C7
Brixen = Bressanone Italy 46°43N 11°39E 199 B8
Brixham U.K. 50°23N 3°31W 169 G4
Brixton U.K. 51°27N 0°8W 125 B3
Brnaze Croatia 43°41N 16°40E 199 E13
Brnenský = Jihomoravský □ Czechia 49°5N 16°30E 181 B9
Brno Czechia 49°10N 16°35E 181 B9
Broach = Bharuch India 21°47N 73°0E 244 D1
Broad → Ga., U.S.A. 33°59N 82°39W 316 B7
Broad → S.C., U.S.A. 34°1N 81°4W 315 D14
Broad Arrow Australia 30°23S 121°15E 279 F3
Broad B. U.K. 58°14N 6°18W 167 C2
Broad Haven Ireland 54°20N 9°55W 166 B2
Broad Law U.K. 55°30N 3°21W 167 F5
Broad Pk. = Faichan Kangri India 35°48N 76°34E 243 B7
Broad Sd. Australia 22°0S 149°45E 280 C4
Broadalbin U.S.A. 43°4N 74°12W 313 C10
Broadback → Canada 51°21N 78°52W 298 B4
Broadford Australia 37°14S 145°4E 283 D6
Broadhurst Ra. Australia 22°30S 122°30E 278 D3
Broadmeadows Australia 37°40S 144°55E 128 A1
Broadmoor U.S.A. 37°41N 122°29W 136 B2
Broads, The U.K. 52°45N 1°30E 168 E9
Broadus U.S.A. 45°27N 105°25W 304 D11
Broadview U.S.A. 41°51N 87°52W 119 B1
Broadview Park U.S.A. 26°5N 80°12W 129 B2
Broadway New York, U.S.A. 132 d2
Broager Denmark 54°53N 9°40E 163 K3
Broby Sweden 56°15N 14°4E 163 H8
Brocēni Latvia 56°42N 22°32E 184 B9
Brochet Canada 57°53N 101°40W 297 B8
Brochet, L. Canada 58°36N 101°35W 297 B8
Brock I. Canada 77°52N 114°19W 295 B9
Brocken Germany 51°47N 10°37E 178 D6
Brocklehurst Australia 32°9S 148°38E 283 B8
Brocklesby Australia 35°49S 146°40E 283 C7
Brockley U.K. 51°27N 0°2W 125 B3
Brockport U.S.A. 43°13N 77°56W 312 C7
Brockton U.S.A. 42°5N 71°1W 313 D13
Brockville Canada 44°35N 75°41W 313 B9
Brockway Mont., U.S.A. 47°18N 105°45W 304 C11
Brockway Pa., U.S.A. 41°15N 78°47W 312 E6
Brocton U.S.A. 42°23N 79°26W 312 D5
Brod Bos.-H. 45°10N 18°0E 182 E2
Brod N. Macedonia 41°32N 21°17E 202 E5
Brodarevo Serbia 43°14N 19°44E 202 C3
Brodeur Pen. Canada 72°30N 88°10W 295 C14
Brodhead U.S.A. 42°37N 89°22W 310 B7
Brodick U.K. 55°35N 5°9W 167 F3

Brodnica Poland 53°15N 19°25E 185 E6
Bródno Poland 52°17N 21°1E 143 B2
Bródnowski, Kanal Poland 52°17N 21°3E 143 B2
Brody Ukraine 50°5N 25°10E 177 C13
Broek Neths. 52°26N 5°0E 112 A2
Brogan U.S.A. 44°15N 117°31W 304 D5
Broglie France 49°2N 0°30E 172 C7
Brok Poland 52°43N 21°52E 185 F8
Broken Arrow U.S.A. 36°3N 95°48W 314 C7
Broken Bow Nebr., U.S.A. 41°24N 99°38W 308 E4
Broken Bow Okla., U.S.A. 34°2N 94°44W 314 D7
Broken Bow Lake U.S.A. 34°9N 94°40W 314 D7
Broken Hill = Kabwe Zambia 14°30S 28°29E 269 E2
Broken Hill Australia 31°58S 141°29E 282 A4
Broken River Ra. Australia 21°0S 148°22E 280 b
Brokind Sweden 58°13N 15°42E 163 F9
Brokopondo Suriname 5°3N 54°59W 329 B7
Bromberg = Bydgoszcz Poland 53°10N 18°0E 185 E5
Bromley ☐ U.K. 51°24N 0°2E 125 B4
Bromley Common U.K. 51°22N 0°2E 125 B4
Bromma Sweden 59°21N 17°55E 139 A1
Bromma ✈ (BMA) Sweden 59°21N 17°56E 139 A1
Bromo, Gunung Indonesia 7°56N 112°57E 231 H15
Bromo Tengger Semeru △ Indonesia 7°56S 112°57E 235 D4
Bromölla Sweden 56°5N 14°28E 163 H8
Brompton London, U.K. 125 c2
Bromsgrove U.K. 52°21N 2°2W 169 E5
Bronaugh U.S.A. 37°41N 94°28W 310 G2
Brøndby Strand Denmark 55°36N 12°25E 118 B2
Brøndbyøster Denmark 55°39N 12°26E 118 B2
Brøndbyvester Denmark 55°37N 12°23E 118 B2
Brønderslev Denmark 57°16N 9°57E 163 G3
Brondesbury U.K. 51°32N 0°12W 125 A2
Brong-Ahafo ☐ Ghana 7°50N 2°0W 262 D4
Broni Italy 45°4N 9°16E 198 C6
Bronkhorstspruit S. Africa 25°46S 28°45E 271 C4
Brønnøya Norway 59°51N 10°32E 133 A2
Brønnøysund Norway 65°28N 12°14E 160 D15
Brønshøj Denmark 55°41N 12°29E 118 A2
Bronson Fla., U.S.A. 29°27N 82°39W 317 F7
Bronson Mich., U.S.A. 41°52N 85°12W 311 C11
Bronte Italy 37°47N 14°50E 201 E7
Bronwood U.S.A. 31°50N 84°22W 316 D5
Bronxville U.S.A. 40°56N 73°49W 132 A3
Brook Park U.S.A. 41°23N 81°48W 312 E4
Brooke's Point Phil. 8°47N 117°50E 233 G1
Brookfield Mo., U.S.A. 39°47N 93°4W 310 E3
Brookfield Wis., U.S.A. 43°4N 88°9W 311 A8
Brookfield Zoo U.S.A. 41°50N 87°50W 119 B1
Brookhaven Georgia, U.S.A. 33°52N 84°19W 113 A2
Brookhaven Miss., U.S.A. 31°35N 90°26W 315 F9
Brookings Oreg., U.S.A. 42°3N 124°17W 304 E1
Brookings S. Dak., U.S.A. 44°19N 96°48W 308 C5
Brookland = West Columbia U.S.A. 33°59N 81°4W 316 B8
Brooklet U.S.A. 32°23N 81°40W 316 C8
Brooklin Canada 43°55N 78°55W 312 C6
Brookline U.S.A. 42°19N 71°8W 116 B2
Brooklyn Western Cape, S. Africa 33°54S 18°29E 118 A1
Brooklyn Iowa, U.S.A. 41°44N 92°27W 310 C4
Brooklyn N.Y., U.S.A. 40°37N 73°57W 132 C2
Brooklyn-Battery Tunnel New York, U.S.A. 132 f1
Brooklyn Bridge New York, U.S.A. 132 f2
Brooklyn Heights New York, U.S.A. 132 f2
Brooklyn Park U.S.A. 45°6N 93°23W 308 C7
Brookmont U.S.A. 38°57N 77°7W 143 B2
Brooks Canada 50°35N 111°55W 296 C6
Brooks Range U.S.A. 68°0N 152°0W 303 C9
Brookston U.S.A. 40°36N 86°52W 311 D10
Brooksville Fla., U.S.A. 28°33N 82°23W 317 G7
Brooksville Ky., U.S.A. 38°41N 84°4W 311 F12
Brookton Australia 32°22S 117°0E 279 F2
Brookville Ind., U.S.A. 39°25N 85°1W 311 E12
Brookville Ohio, U.S.A. 39°50N 84°24W 311 E12
Brookville Pa., U.S.A. 41°10N 79°5W 312 E5
Brookville L. U.S.A. 39°28N 85°0W 311 E11
Broom, L. U.K. 57°55N 5°15W 167 D3
Broome Australia 18°0S 122°15E 278 C3
Broons France 48°20N 2°16W 172 D4
Brora U.K. 58°0N 3°52W 167 C5
Brora → U.K. 58°0N 3°51W 167 C5
Brørup Denmark 55°29N 9°1E 163 J2
Brösarp Sweden 55°43N 14°6E 163 J8
Brosna → Ireland 53°14N 7°58W 166 C4
Brossard Canada 45°27N 73°28W 130 B3
Broşteni Mehedinţi, Romania 44°45N 22°59E 182 F7
Broşteni Suceava, Romania 47°14N 25°43E 183 C10
Brøsterud Norway 60°28N 8°34E 164 D5
Brotas de Macaúbas Brazil 12°0S 42°38W 333 D3
Brothers U.S.A. 43°49N 120°36W 304 E3
Brothers, The Hong Kong, China 22°20N 113°58E 122 A1
Brothers, The Yemen 12°8N 53°10E 249 D6
Brøttum Norway 61°2N 10°34E 164 C7
Brou France 48°13N 1°11E 172 D8
Brou-sur-Chantereine France 48°53N 2°37E 134 A4
Brouage France 45°52N 1°4W 174 C2
Brough U.K. 54°32N 2°18W 168 C5
Brough Hd. U.K. 59°8N 3°20W 167 B5
Broughton U.S.A. 37°56N 88°27W 311 G8
Broughton Island = Qikiqtarjuaq Canada 67°33N 63°0W 295 D19
Broumov Czechia 50°35N 16°20E 181 A9
Brovary Ukraine 50°34N 30°48E 189 G6
Brovst Denmark 57°6N 9°31E 163 G3
Brown Canada 43°48N 79°14W 141 A3
Brown, L. Australia 31°5S 118°15E 279 F2
Brown, Mt. Australia 32°30S 138°0E 282 B3
Brown, Pt. Australia 32°32S 133°50E 281 E1
Brown City U.S.A. 43°13N 82°59W 312 C2
Brown Willy U.K. 50°35N 4°37W 169 G3
Brownfield U.S.A. 33°11N 102°17W 314 E3
Browning Ill., U.S.A. 40°8N 90°22W 310 D6
Browning Mo., U.S.A. 40°3N 93°12W 310 D3
Browning Mont., U.S.A. 48°34N 113°1W 304 B7
Brown's Town Jamaica 18°24N 77°22W 320 a
Brownsburg U.S.A. 39°51N 86°24W 311 E10
Brownstown U.S.A. 38°53N 86°3W 311 F10
Brownsville Fla., U.S.A. 25°49N 80°15W 129 D1
Brownsville Oreg., U.S.A. 44°24N 122°59W 304 D2
Brownsville Pa., U.S.A. 40°1N 79°53W 312 F5
Brownsville Tenn., U.S.A. 35°36N 89°16W 315 D10
Brownsville Tex., U.S.A. 25°54N 97°30W 314 J6
Brownsweg Suriname 5°5N 55°15W 329 B6
Brownville U.S.A. 44°0N 75°59W 313 C9
Brownwood U.S.A. 31°43N 98°59W 314 F5
Browse I. Australia 14°7S 123°33E 278 B3
Broxton U.S.A. 31°38N 82°53W 316 D7
Bru Norway 61°32N 5°11E 164 C2
Bruas Malaysia 4°30N 100°47E 237 K3
Bruay-la-Buissière France 50°29N 2°33E 173 B9
Bruce U.S.A. 30°28N 85°58W 316 E4
Bruce, Mt. Australia 22°37S 118°8E 278 D2
Bruce B. N.Z. 43°35S 169°42E 285 D4
Bruce Pen. Canada 45°0N 81°30W 312 B3
Bruce Peninsula △ Canada 45°14N 81°36W 312 A3
Bruce Rock Australia 31°52S 118°8E 279 F2
Bruche → France 48°34N 7°43E 173 D14
Bruchsal Germany 49°7N 8°35E 179 F4
Bruck an der Leitha Austria 48°1N 16°47E 181 C9
Bruck an der Mur Austria 47°24N 15°16E 180 D8
Brue → U.K. 51°13N 2°59W 169 F5
Bruflat Norway 60°53N 9°37E 164 D6
Bruges = Brugge Belgium 51°13N 3°13E 170 C3
Brugg Switz. 47°29N 8°11E 179 H4
Brugge Belgium 51°13N 3°13E 170 C3
Brughério Italy 45°33N 9°17E 128 A2
Bruin U.S.A. 41°3N 79°43W 312 E5
Bruini India 29°10N 96°11E 241 A6
Bruit, Pulau Malaysia 2°35N 111°20E 235 B4
Brûk, W. el → Egypt 30°15N 33°50E 251 H4
Bruksvallarna Sweden 62°38N 12°27E 162 B6
Brûlé Canada 53°15N 117°58W 296 C5
Brûlé, L. Canada 53°35N 64°4W 299 B7
Brûlon France 47°58N 0°15W 172 E6
Brumado Brazil 14°14S 41°40W 333 D3
Brumado → Brazil 14°13S 41°40W 333 D3
Brumath France 48°43N 7°40E 173 D14
Brumunddal Norway 60°53N 10°56E 164 D7
Brundidge U.S.A. 31°43N 85°49W 316 D4
Bruneau U.S.A. 42°53N 115°48W 304 E6
Bruneau → U.S.A. 42°56N 115°57W 304 E6
Bruneck = Brunico Italy 46°48N 11°56E 199 B8
Brunei = Bandar Seri Begawan Brunei 4°52N 115°0E 235 B4
Brunei ■ Asia 4°50N 115°0E 235 B4
Brunflo Sweden 63°5N 14°50E 162 A8
Brunico Italy 46°48N 11°56E 199 B8
Brünn = Brno Czechia 49°10N 16°35E 181 B9
Brunnen Switz. 46°59N 8°37E 179 J4
Brunner, L. N.Z. 42°37S 171°27E 285 C6
Brunnhóll Iceland 64°17N 15°26W 155 C11
Brunnsberg Sweden 61°17N 13°56E 162 C8
Brunsbüttel Germany 53°53N 9°6E 178 B5
Brunssum Neths. 50°57N 5°59E 170 D5
Brunswick = Braunschweig Germany 52°15N 10°31E 178 C6
Brunswick Vic., Australia 37°45S 144°57E 128 A1
Brunswick Ga., U.S.A. 31°10N 81°30W 316 D8
Brunswick Maine, U.S.A. 43°55N 69°58W 309 D19
Brunswick Md., U.S.A. 39°19N 77°38W 309 F15
Brunswick Mo., U.S.A. 39°26N 93°8W 310 E3
Brunswick Ohio, U.S.A. 41°14N 81°51W 312 E3
Brunswick, Pen. de Chile 53°30S 71°30W 336 D2
Brunswick B. Australia 15°15S 124°50E 278 C3
Brunswick Junction Australia 33°15S 115°50E 279 F2
Brunt Ice Shelf Antarctica 75°30S 25°0W 151 D2
Bruntál Czechia 49°59N 17°27E 181 B10
Brus Laguna Honduras 15°47N 84°35W 320 C3
Brusa = Bursa Turkey 40°15N 29°5E 203 F13
Brusartsi Bulgaria 43°40N 23°5E 202 C7
Brush U.S.A. 40°15N 103°37W 304 F12
Brushton U.S.A. 44°50N 74°31W 313 B10
Brusio Switz. 46°14N 10°8E 179 J6
Brusque Brazil 27°5S 49°0W 335 B6
Brussegem Belgium 50°56N 4°16E 116 A1
Brussel Belgium 50°51N 4°21E 116 A2
Brussel ✈ (BRU) Belgium 50°54N 4°29E 116 A2
Brussels = Brussel Belgium 50°51N 4°21E 116 A2
Brussels Canada 43°44N 81°15W 312 C3
Brusy Poland 53°53N 17°43E 184 E4
Bruthen Australia 37°42S 147°50E 283 D7
Bruvoll Norway 60°27N 11°29E 164 D8
Bruxelles = Brussel Belgium 50°51N 4°21E 116 A2
Bruyères France 48°10N 6°40E 173 D13
Bruz France 48°1N 1°46W 172 D5
Bruzzano Italy 45°31N 9°10E 128 A2
Brwinów Poland 52°9N 20°40E 185 F7
Bry-sur-Marne France 48°50N 2°32E 134 A4
Bryagovo Bulgaria 41°58N 25°8E 203 E9
Bryan Ohio, U.S.A. 41°28N 84°33W 311 C12
Bryan Tex., U.S.A. 30°40N 96°22W 314 F6
Bryan, L. U.S.A. 28°22N 81°29W 133 B2
Bryan, Mt. Australia 33°30S 139°5E 282 B3
Bryanka Ukraine 48°32N 38°45E 189 H10
Bryansk Bryansk, Russia 53°13N 34°25E 189 F8
Bryansk Dagestan, Russia 44°20N 47°10E 191 H8
Bryansk ☐ Russia 53°10N 33°10E 189 F7
Bryanston S. Africa 26°4S 28°0E 123 A1
Bryant Park New York, U.S.A. 132 c2
Bryce Canyon ⌂ U.S.A. 37°30N 112°10W 305 H7
Bryne Norway 58°44N 5°38E 164 F2
Bryson City U.S.A. 35°26N 83°27W 315 D13
Bryukhovetskaya Russia 45°48N 39°0E 189 K10
Brza Palanka Serbia 44°28N 22°27E 202 B6
Brzeg Poland 50°52N 17°30E 185 H4
Brzeg Dolny Poland 51°16N 16°41E 185 G3
Brześć Kujawski Poland 52°36N 18°55E 185 F5
Brzešć nad Bugiem = Brest Belarus 52°10N 23°40E 177 B12
Brzesko Poland 49°59N 20°34E 185 J7
Brzeziny Łódzkie, Poland 51°49N 19°42E 185 G6
Brzeziny Warszawa, Poland 52°19N 21°1E 143 B2
Brzozów Poland 49°41N 22°3E 185 J9
Bsharri Lebanon 34°15N 36°0E 250 A5
Bū al Ḩīdān, W. → Libya 27°25N 19°22E 258 C3
Bū Athlah Libya 30°9N 15°39E 258 B2
Bū Baqarah U.A.E. 25°35N 56°25E 247 E8
Bū Craa W. Sahara 26°45N 12°50W 260 C2
Bū Ḩasā U.A.E. 23°30N 53°20E 247 F7
Bū Tummayyim, W. → Libya 26°56N 19°13E 258 C3
Bua Fiji 16°48S 178°37E 287 A2
Bua Sweden 57°14N 12°7E 163 G6
Bua → Malawi 12°45S 34°16E 269 E3
Bua Yai Thailand 15°33N 102°26E 236 E4
Bu'aale Somalia 1°5N 42°35E 267 D5
Buad I. Phil. 11°40N 124°51E 233 F5
Buala Solomon Is. 8°10S 159°35E 287 M10
Buan S. Korea 35°44N 126°44E 224 E3
Buapinang Indonesia 4°40S 121°30E 231 E6
Buatan Indonesia 0°44N 101°49E 234 B2
Buayan = General Santos Phil. 6°5N 125°14E 233 H5
Buba Guinea-Biss. 11°40N 14°59W 262 C2
Bubali Bird Sanctuary Aruba 12°33N 70°2W 322 f
Bubanda Dem. Rep. of the Congo 4°14N 19°38E 264 B3
Bubanza Burundi 3°6S 29°23E 268 C2
Bubaque Guinea-Biss. 11°16N 15°51W 262 C1
Bube Ethiopia 8°46N 35°48E 257 F4
Bubeneč Czechia 50°6N 14°24E 135 B2
Bubi → Zimbabwe 22°20S 31°7E 271 B5
Būbiyān Kuwait 29°45N 48°15E 247 D6
Buc France 48°46N 2°7E 134 B1
Buca Fiji 16°38S 179°52E 287 A2
Buca Turkey 38°22N 27°11E 205 C9
Bucaco Angola 11°26S 20°10E 266 D3
Bucak Turkey 37°28N 30°36E 205 D12
Bucakkışla Turkey 36°57N 33°1E 250 B4
Bucaramanga Colombia 7°0N 73°0W 328 B3
Bucas Grande I. Phil. 9°40N 125°57E 233 G6
Bucasia Australia 21°2S 149°10E 280 b
Bucay Phil. 17°32N 120°43E 232 C3
Buccaneer Arch. Australia 16°7S 123°20E 278 C3
Buccino Italy 40°38N 15°22E 201 B8
Buccoo Reef Trin. & Tob. 11°10N 60°51W 323 s
Bucecea Romania 47°47N 26°28E 183 C11
Bucegi ⌂ Romania 45°25N 25°25E 183 E10
Buchach Ukraine 49°5N 25°25E 177 D13
Buchan Vic., Australia 37°30S 148°12E 283 D8
Buchan Aberds., U.K. 57°32N 2°21W 167 D6
Buchan Ness U.K. 57°29N 1°46W 167 D7
Buchanan Sask., Canada 51°40N 102°45W 297 C8
Buchanan Liberia 5°57N 10°2W 262 D2
Buchanan Ga., U.S.A. 33°48N 85°11W 316 B4
Buchanan Mich., U.S.A. 41°50N 86°22W 311 C10
Buchanan, L. Queens., Australia 21°35S 145°52E 280 C4
Buchanan, L. W. Austral., Australia 25°33S 123°2E 279 E3
Buchanan, L. Tex., U.S.A. 30°45N 98°25W 314 F5
Buchanan Cr. → Australia 19°13S 136°33E 280 B2
Buchans Canada 48°50N 56°52W 299 C8
Bucharest = Bucureşti Romania 44°27N 26°10E 183 F11
Buchen Germany 49°32N 9°20E 179 F5
Buchenhain Germany 48°1N 11°29E 131 B1
Bucheon S. Korea 37°28N 126°45E 224 D3
Buchholz Berlin, Germany 52°36N 13°25E 115 A3
Buchholz Niedersachsen, Germany 53°19N 9°52E 178 B5
Buchloe Germany 48°1N 10°44E 179 G6
Buchon, Pt. U.S.A. 35°15N 120°54W 306 K6
Buciumi Romania 47°3N 23°1E 182 C8
Buck Hill Falls U.S.A. 41°11N 75°16W 313 E9
Bückeburg Germany 52°16N 9°7E 178 C5
Buckeye Lake U.S.A. 39°55N 82°29W 312 G2
Buckhannon U.S.A. 39°0N 80°8W 309 F13
Buckhaven U.K. 56°11N 3°3W 167 E5
Buckhead U.S.A. 33°51N 84°24W 113 A2
Buckhorn L. Canada 44°29N 78°23W 312 B6
Buckie U.K. 57°41N 2°58W 167 D6
Buckingham Qué., Canada 45°37N 75°24W 298 C4
Buckingham Bucks., U.K. 51°59N 0°57W 169 F7
Buckingham B. Australia 12°10S 135°40E 280 A2
Buckingham Canal India 14°0N 80°5E 245 H5
Buckingham Fountain Chicago, U.S.A. 119 d2
Buckingham Palace London, U.K. 125 b3
Buckinghamshire ☐ U.K. 51°53N 0°55W 169 F7
Buckland U.S.A. 65°59N 161°8W 303 D7
Buckland Hd. Australia 14°26S 127°52E 278 B4
Buckleboo Australia 32°54S 136°12E 282 B2
Buckley Flints., U.K. 53°10N 3°5W 168 D4
Buckley Ill., U.S.A. 40°36N 88°2W 311 D8
Buckley → Australia 20°10S 138°49E 280 C2
Bucklin Kans., U.S.A. 37°33N 99°38W 308 G4
Bucklin Mo., U.S.A. 39°47N 92°53W 310 E4
Buckow Germany 52°25N 13°26E 115 B3
Bucks L. U.S.A. 39°54N 121°12W 306 F5
Bucktown U.S.A. 30°1N 90°8W 131 A2
Buco Zau Angola 4°46S 12°33E 265 C2
Bucquoy France 50°9N 2°43E 173 B9
Bucureşti Romania 44°27N 26°10E 183 F11
Bucureşti Otopeni ✈ (OTP) Romania 44°30N 26°11E 183 F11
Bucyrus U.S.A. 40°48N 82°59W 311 D14
Bud Norway 62°55N 6°55E 164 B3
Bud Bud Somalia 4°11N 46°28E 267 D6
Buda Hungary 47°30N 19°2E 117 A2
Buda Castle = Budavárpalota Budapest, Hungary 117 b2
Budacu, Vf. Romania 47°7N 25°41E 183 C10
Budafok Hungary 47°25N 19°2E 117 B2
Budai = Putai Taiwan 23°23N 120°9E 225 C2
Budalin Myanmar 22°20N 95°10E 241 D5
Budaörs Hungary 47°27N 18°57E 117 B1
Budapest Hungary 47°29N 19°3E 117 B2
Budapest ☐ Hungary 47°29N 19°5E 182 C4
Budapest Ferenc Liszt ✈ (BUD) Hungary 47°26N 19°14E 117 B3
Budatétény Hungary 47°25N 19°1E 117 B2
Budaun India 28°5N 79°10E 243 E8
Budavárpalota Budapest, Hungary 117 b2
Budawang △ Australia 35°10S 150°12E 283 C9
Budd Coast Antarctica 68°0S 112°0E 151 C8
Buddenbrock = Brodnica Poland 53°15N 19°25E 185 E6
Budderoo △ Australia 35°40S 150°41E 283 C9
Buddinge Denmark 55°44N 12°30E 118 A3
Buddusò Italy 40°35N 9°15E 200 B2
Bude U.K. 50°49N 4°34W 169 G3
Budennovsk Russia 44°50N 44°10E 191 H7
Budeşti Romania 44°13N 26°30E 183 F11
Budeyi Ukraine 48°3N 29°16E 183 B14
Budge Budge = Baj Baj India 22°30N 88°5E 243 H13
Budgewoi Australia 33°13S 151°34E 283 B9
Búðardalur Iceland 65°7N 21°46W 155 B5
Budia Spain 40°38N 2°46W 196 E2
Büdingen Germany 50°16N 9°7E 179 E5
Budjala Dem. Rep. of the Congo 2°50N 19°40E 264 B3
Budo-Sungai Padi △ Thailand 6°19N 101°42E 237 J3
Budokan Tokyo, Japan 140 a4
Budoni Italy 40°40N 9°45E 200 B2
Búdrio Italy 44°32N 11°32E 199 D8
Budszentmihály = Tiszavasvári Hungary 47°58N 21°18E 182 C6
Budva Montenegro 42°17N 18°50E 202 D2
Budweis = České Budějovice Czechia 48°55N 14°25E 180 C7
Budyonnovka = Novoazovsk Ukraine 47°15N 38°4E 189 J10
Budzyń Poland 52°54N 16°59E 185 F3
Bue Norway 58°40N 5°58E 164 F2
Buea Cameroon 4°10N 9°9E 263 E6
Buela Angola 5°54S 14°40E 265 D2
Buellton U.S.A. 34°37N 120°12W 307 L6
Buena Esperanza Argentina 34°45S 65°15W 334 C2
Buena Park U.S.A. 33°52N 117°59W 307 M9
Buena Vista Bolivia 17°27S 63°40W 331 D5
Buena Vista Curaçao 12°8N 68°57W 322 g
Buena Vista Solomon Is. 8°52S 160°3E 287 M11
Buena Vista Colo., U.S.A. 38°51N 106°8W 304 G10
Buena Vista Ga., U.S.A. 32°19N 84°31W 316 C5
Buena Vista Va., U.S.A. 37°44N 79°21W 309 G14
Buena Vista Lake Bed U.S.A. 35°12N 119°18W 307 K7
Buenaventura Colombia 3°53N 77°4W 328 C2
Buenaventura Chihuahua, Mexico 29°51N 107°29W 318 B3
Buenaventura, B. de Colombia 3°48N 77°17W 328 C2
Buenavista Agusan del N., Phil. 8°59N 125°24E 233 G5
Buenavista Quezon, Phil. 13°35N 122°34E 232 E4
Buendia, Embalse de Spain 40°25N 2°43W 196 E2
Buenópolis Brazil 17°54S 44°11W 333 E3
Buenos Aires Argentina 34°36S 58°22W 117 B2
Buenos Aires Colombia 1°36N 73°18W 328 C3
Buenos Aires Costa Rica 9°10N 83°20W 320 E3
Buenos Aires ☐ Argentina 36°30S 60°0W 334 D4
Buenos Aires, L. = General Carrera, L. S. Amer. 46°35S 72°0W 336 C2
Buenos Aires Ezeiza ✈ (EZE) Argentina 34°49S 58°32W 117 C1
Buenos Ayres Trin. & Tob. 10°6N 61°41W 323 t
Buesaco Colombia 1°23N 77°9W 328 C2
Bufalotta Italy 41°59N 12°33E 136 B2
Buff Bay Jamaica 18°14N 76°40W 320 a
Buffalo Mo., U.S.A. 37°39N 93°6W 310 G3
Buffalo N.Y., U.S.A. 42°53N 78°53W 312 D6
Buffalo Okla., U.S.A. 36°50N 99°38W 314 C5
Buffalo S. Dak., U.S.A. 45°35N 103°33W 308 C2
Buffalo Wyo., U.S.A. 44°21N 106°42W 304 D10
Buffalo → Alta., Canada 60°5N 115°5W 296 A5
Buffalo → S. Africa 28°43S 30°37E 271 C5
Buffalo ⌂ U.S.A. 36°14N 92°36W 314 C8
Buffalo Head Hills Canada 57°25N 115°55W 296 B5
Buffalo L. Alta., Canada 52°27N 112°54W 296 C6
Buffalo L. N.W.T., Canada 60°12N 115°25W 296 A5
Buffalo Narrows Canada 55°51N 108°29W 297 B7
Buffalo Springs ⌂ Kenya 0°32N 37°35E 268 B4
Buffels → S. Africa 29°36S 17°3E 270 C2
Buford U.S.A. 34°7N 83°59W 316 A6
Bug = Buh → Ukraine 46°59N 31°58E 189 J6
Bug → Poland 52°31N 21°5E 185 F8
Buga Colombia 4°0N 76°15W 328 C2
Bugala I. Uganda 0°40S 32°20E 268 C3
Buganda Uganda 0°0 31°30E 268 C3
Buganga Uganda 0°3S 32°0E 268 C3
Bugasong Phil. 11°3N 122°4E 233 F4
Bugda Acable Somalia 4°4N 45°15E 267 D6
Bugeat France 45°36N 1°55E 174 C5
Bugel, Tanjung Indonesia 6°26S 111°3E 235 D4
Búger Spain 39°45N 2°59E 206 B3
Bugibba Malta 35°57N 14°25E 206 F7
Bugio Portugal 38°39N 9°18W 126 B1
Bugojno Bos.-H. 44°2N 17°25E 182 F2
Bugsuk I. Phil. 8°12N 117°18E 233 G1
Buguey Phil. 18°17N 121°50E 232 B3
Buguias Phil. 16°43N 120°50E 232 C3
Bugulma Russia 54°33N 52°48E 186 D9
Buguma Nigeria 4°42N 6°55E 263 E6
Bugungu ⌂ Uganda 2°17N 31°50E 268 B3
Buguruslan Russia 53°39N 52°26E 186 D9
Buh → Ukraine 46°59N 31°58E 189 J6
Buharkent Turkey 37°58N 28°44E 205 D10
Buheirat-Murrat-el-Kubra Egypt 30°18N 32°26E 256 H8
Buhera Zimbabwe 19°18S 31°29E 271 A5
Bühl Baden-W., Germany 48°40N 8°8E 179 G4
Buhl Idaho, U.S.A. 42°36N 114°46W 304 E6
Buhuşi Romania 46°41N 26°45E 183 D11
Bui △ Ghana 8°21N 2°21W 262 D4
Buiksloot Neths. 52°24N 4°55E 112 A2
Buila-Vanturariţa △ Romania 45°15N 24°0E 183 E8
Builth Wells U.K. 52°9N 3°25W 169 E4
Buin Papua N. G. 6°48S 155°42E 286 D8
Buinsk Russia 55°0N 48°18E 190 C9
Buíque Brazil 8°37S 37°9W 332 C4
Buir Nur Mongolia 47°50N 117°42E 219 B12
Buis-les-Baronnies France 44°17N 5°16E 175 D9
Buitenveldert Neths. 52°20N 4°53E 112 B2
Buitenzorg = Bogor Indonesia 6°36S 106°48E 234 D3
Buitrago del Lozoya Spain 40°58N 3°38W 194 E7
Buizingen Belgium 50°44N 4°15E 116 B1
Bujalance Spain 37°54N 4°23W 195 H6
Bujanovac Serbia 42°28N 21°44E 202 D5
Bujaraloz Spain 41°29N 0°10W 196 D4
Buje Croatia 45°24N 13°39E 199 C10
Buji China 22°37N 114°5E 219 a
Bujumbura Burundi 3°16S 29°18E 268 C2
Bük Hungary 47°22N 16°45E 182 C1
Buk Poland 52°21N 16°30E 185 F3
Buka I. Papua N. G. 5°10S 154°35E 286 C8
Bukachacha Russia 52°55N 116°50E 215 D12
Bukama Dem. Rep. of the Congo 9°10S 25°50E 269 D2
Bukavu Dem. Rep. of the Congo 2°20S 28°52E 268 C2
Bukene Tanzania 4°15S 32°48E 268 C3
Bukhansan S. Korea 37°38N 126°58E 137 B1
Bukhara = Buxoro Uzbekistan 39°48N 64°25E 216 E6
Bukhoro = Buxoro Uzbekistan 39°48N 64°25E 216 E6
Bukhtarma Res. = Zaysan Köli Kazakhstan 48°0N 83°0E 217 C10
Bukidnon ☐ Phil. 8°0N 125°0E 233 G5
Bukima Tanzania 1°50S 33°25E 268 C3
Bukit Baka Bukit Raya △ Indonesia 0°43S 112°40E 235 C4
Bukit Barisan Selatan △ Indonesia 5°8S 104°4E 234 D2
Bukit Batok Singapore 1°22N 103°45E 138 A2
Bukit Bendera Malaysia 5°25N 100°15E 237 c
Bukit Duabelas △ Indonesia 2°3S 102°48E 234 C2
Bukit Mertajam Malaysia 5°22N 100°28E 237 c
Bukit Nil Malaysia 1°22N 104°12E 237 d
Bukit Panjang Singapore 1°23N 103°46E 138 A2
Bukit Panjang Nature Reserve ⌂ Singapore 1°22N 103°45E 138 A2
Bukit Tengah Malaysia 5°22N 100°25E 237 c
Bukit Tigapuluh △ Indonesia 1°15S 102°25E 234 C2
Bukit Timah Nature Reserve ⌂ Singapore 1°20N 103°47E 138 A2
Bukitkemuning Indonesia 4°51S 104°33E 234 C2
Bukittinggi Indonesia 0°20S 100°20E 234 C2
Bükk Hungary 48°0N 20°30E 182 B5
Bukkapatnam India 14°14N 77°46E 245 G3
Bükki △ Hungary 48°3N 20°30E 182 B5
Bukoba Tanzania 1°20S 31°49E 268 C3
Bukum, Pulau Singapore 1°14N 103°46E 138 B2
Bukuru Nigeria 9°42N 8°48E 263 D6
Bukuya Uganda 0°40N 31°52E 268 B3
Būl, Kuh-e Iran 30°48N 52°45E 247 D7
Bula Guinea-Biss. 12°7N 15°43W 262 C1
Bula Indonesia 3°6S 130°30E 231 E8
Bula Camarines S., Phil. 13°28N 123°16E 232 E4
Bula-Atumba Angola 8°41S 14°52E 265 D2
Bulabog-Putian △ Phil. 11°2N 122°4E 233 F4
Bulacan ☐ Phil. 15°0N 121°5E 232 D3
Bülach Switz. 47°31N 8°32E 179 H4
Bŭlaevo Kazakhstan 54°54N 70°26E 217 B8
Bulahdelah Australia 32°23S 152°13E 283 B10
Bulalacao Phil. 12°31N 121°26E 232 E3
Bulan Phil. 12°40N 123°52E 232 E4
Bulancak Turkey 40°56N 38°14E 213 B8
Búland Iceland 63°46N 18°30W 155 D8
Bulanık Turkey 39°4N 42°14E 213 C10
Bûlâq El Khârga, Egypt 25°10N 30°38E 256 B3
Bûlâq El Qâhira, Egypt 30°3N 31°14E 117 A2
Bulawayo Zimbabwe 20°7S 28°32E 269 G2
Buldan Turkey 38°2N 28°50E 205 C10
Buldana India 20°30N 76°18E 244 D3
Buldir I. U.S.A. 52°21N 175°56E 303 K1
Buldon Phil. 7°33N 124°25E 233 H5
Bule Phil. 14°26N 121°2E 127 C2
Bulenga Ghana 9°56N 2°12W 262 D4
Bulgan Mongolia 48°45N 103°34E 218 B9
Bulgar Russia 54°57N 49°4E 190 C9
Bulgaria ■ Europe 42°35N 25°30E 203 D9
Bulgheria, Monte Italy 40°4N 15°26E 201 B8
Bulgurca Turkey 38°9N 27°9E 205 C9
Bulhale Somalia 5°20N 46°29E 267 D6
Bulhar Somalia 10°25N 44°30E 267 B5
Buli, Teluk Indonesia 0°48N 128°25E 231 D7
Buliluyan, C. Phil. 8°20N 117°15E 233 G1
Bulki Ethiopia 6°11N 36°31E 257 F4
Bulkley → Canada 55°15N 127°40W 296 B3
Bull Head Jamaica 18°10N 77°16W 320 a
Bull Savanna Jamaica 17°53N 77°35W 320 a
Bull Shoals L. U.S.A. 36°22N 92°35W 314 C8
Bullaque → Spain 38°59N 4°17W 195 G6
Bullard U.S.A. 32°38N 83°30W 316 C6
Bullas Spain 38°2N 1°40W 197 G3
Bulle Switz. 46°37N 7°3E 179 J3
Bullen Park Australia 37°46S 145°4E 128 A2
Bullenbaai Curaçao 12°11N 69°2W 322 g
Buller → N.Z. 41°44S 171°36E 285 B6
Buller, Mt. Australia 37°10S 146°28E 283 D7
Buller Gorge N.Z. 41°40S 172°10E 285 B7
Bullering △ Australia 17°39S 143°56E 280 B3
Bullhead City U.S.A. 35°8N 114°32W 307 K12
Bulli Australia 34°15S 150°57E 283 C9
Büllingen Belgium 50°25N 6°16E 170 D6
Bullock Creek Australia 17°43S 144°31E 280 B3
Bulloo → Australia 28°43S 142°30E 281 D3
Bulloo L. Australia 28°43S 142°25E 281 D3
Bulls N.Z. 40°10S 175°24E 284 G4
Bully-les-Mines France 50°27N 2°44E 173 B9
Bulman Australia 13°39S 134°20E 280 A1
Bulnes Chile 36°42S 72°19W 334 D1
Bulo Ghedudo Somalia 2°52N 43°1E 267 D5
Bulolo Papua N. G. 7°10S 146°40E 286 D4
Bulongo Dem. Rep. of the Congo 4°45S 21°30E 265 C4
Bulqizë Albania 41°30N 20°21E 202 E4
Bulsar = Valsad India 20°40N 72°58E 244 D1
Bultfontein S. Africa 28°18S 26°10E 270 C4
Buluan Phil. 6°44N 124°47E 233 H5
Buluan, L. Phil. 6°40N 124°49E 233 H5
Bulukumba Indonesia 5°33S 120°11E 231 F6
Bulun Russia 70°37N 127°30E 215 B13
Bulungkol China 38°36N 74°58E 227 E8
Bulungu Bandundu, Dem. Rep. of the Congo 4°33S 18°36E 265 C3
Bulungu Kasai-Occ., Dem. Rep. of the Congo 6°4S 21°54E 265 D4
Bulusan Phil. 12°45N 124°8E 232 E5
Bulusan Vol. Phil. 12°46N 124°3E 232 E5
Bumba Bandundu, Dem. Rep. of the Congo 6°58S 19°19E 265 D3
Bumba Équateur, Dem. Rep. of the Congo 2°13N 22°30E 264 B4
Bumbah, Khalīj Libya 32°20N 23°15E 258 B4
Bumbeşti-Jiu Romania 45°10N 23°24E 183 E8
Bumbiri I. Tanzania 1°40S 31°55E 268 C3
Bumbuna S. Leone 9°2N 11°49W 262 D2
Bumhkang Myanmar 26°51N 97°40E 241 B6
Bumhpa Bum Myanmar 26°51N 97°14E 241 B6
Bumi → Zimbabwe 17°0S 28°20E 269 F2
Bumthang = Jakar Dzong Bhutan 27°33N 90°43E 241 B3
Bumtang → Bhutan 26°56N 90°53E 241 B3
Buna Dem. Rep. of the Congo 3°14S 18°59E 264 C3
Buna North Eastern, Kenya 2°58N 39°30E 268 B4
Buna Papua N. G. 8°42S 148°27E 286 E5
Bunaken Indonesia 1°37N 124°46E 231 D6
Bunama Papua N. G. 10°9S 151°9E 286 F7
Bunawan Phil. 8°12N 125°57E 233 G5
Bunazi Tanzania 1°3S 31°23E 268 C3
Bunbury Australia 33°20S 115°35E 279 F2
Bunclody Ireland 52°39N 6°40W 166 D5
Buncrana Ireland 55°8N 7°27W 166 A4
Bund, The China 31°14N 121°30E 138 B1
Bunda Dem. Rep. of the Congo 4°58S 14°29E 265 C3
Bundaberg Australia 24°54S 152°22E 281 C5
Bundanoon Australia 34°40S 150°16E 283 C9
Bünde Germany 52°11N 8°35E 178 C4
Bundestag = Reichstag Berlin, Germany 115 a3
Bundey → Australia 21°46S 135°37E 280 C2
Bundi India 25°30N 75°35E 242 G6
Bundjalung △ Australia 29°16S 153°21E 281 D5
Bundoora North Australia 37°41S 145°2E 128 A2
Bundoora Park Australia 37°42S 145°2E 128 A2
Bundoran Ireland 54°28N 8°18W 166 B3
Bundukia South Sudan 5°14N 30°55E 257 F3
Bundure Australia 35°10S 146°1E 283 C7
Bung Kan Thailand 18°23N 103°37E 236 C4
Bunga → Nigeria 11°23N 9°56E 263 C6
Bungalaut, Selat Indonesia 2°0S 99°25E 234 C1
Bungay U.K. 52°27N 1°28E 169 E9
Bungendore Australia 35°14S 149°30E 283 C8
Bungil Cr. → Australia 27°5S 149°5E 281 D4
Bungle Bungle = Purnululu △ Australia 17°20S 128°20E 278 C4
Bungo Angola 7°26S 15°33E 265 D3
Bungo, Gunung Malaysia 1°16N 110°9E 235 B4
Bungo-Suidō Japan 33°0N 132°15E 222 E4
Bungoma Kenya 0°34N 34°34E 268 B3
Bungotakada Japan 33°35N 131°25E 222 D3
Bungu Tanzania 7°35S 39°0E 268 D4
Bunia Dem. Rep. of the Congo 1°35N 30°20E 268 B3
Bunianga Dem. Rep. of the Congo 3°28S 20°11E 264 C4
Bunji Pakistan 35°45N 74°40E 243 B6
Bunker Hill Ill., U.S.A. 39°3N 89°57W 310 E7
Bunker Hill Ind., U.S.A. 40°40N 86°6W 311 D10
Bunker Hill Memorial U.S.A. 42°22N 71°4W 116 A2
Bunker I. Pakistan 24°48N 66°57E 123 B1
Bunkie U.S.A. 30°57N 92°11W 314 F8
Bunkyō Japan 35°42N 139°45E 140 A3
Bunnefjorden Norway 59°50N 10°44E 133 A3
Bunnell U.S.A. 29°28N 81°16W 317 F8
Bunnythorpe N.Z. 40°16S 175°39E 284 G4
Buñol Spain 39°25N 0°47W 197 F4
Bunsuru → Nigeria 13°21N 6°23E 263 C5
Buntok Indonesia 1°40S 114°58E 235 C4
Bunumu Dass Nigeria 10°5N 9°31E 263 C6
Bunumu Kasa Nigeria 9°51N 9°32E 263 D6
Bunya Mts. △ Australia 26°51S 151°34E 281 D5
Bünyan Turkey 38°51N 35°51E 212 C6
Bunyola Spain 39°41N 2°42E 206 B3
Bunyu Indonesia 3°35N 117°50E 235 B5
Bunza Nigeria 12°8N 4°0E 263 C5
Bunzlau = Bolesławiec Poland 51°17N 15°37E 185 G2
Buol Indonesia 1°15N 121°32E 231 D6
Buon Brieng Vietnam 13°9N 108°12E 236 F7
Buon Ho Vietnam 12°57N 108°18E 236 F7
Buon Ma Thuot Vietnam 12°40N 108°3E 236 F7
Buona Vista Park Singapore 1°16N 103°47E 138 B2
Buong Long Cambodia 13°44N 106°59E 236 F6
Buorkhaya, Mys Russia 71°50N 132°40E 215 B14
Buqayq Si. Arabia 26°0N 49°45E 247 E6
Buqbuq Egypt 31°29N 25°29E 256 A2
Bur Acaba = Buurhakaba Somalia 3°12N 44°20E 267 D5
Bur Dubai U.A.E. 25°15N 55°17E 119 A2
Bûr Fuad Egypt 31°15N 32°20E 256 H8
Bûr Safâga Egypt 26°43N 33°57E 246 E2
Bûr Sa'îd Egypt 31°16N 32°18E 256 H8
Bûr Sûdân Sudan 19°32N 37°9E 256 D4
Bûr Taufiq Egypt 29°54N 32°32E 256 J8
Bura Kenya 1°4S 39°58E 268 C4
Buraan Somalia 10°14N 48°44E 267 B6
Burakin Australia 30°31S 117°10E 279 F2
Buram Sudan 10°51N 25°9E 257 E2
Burang China 30°15N 81°10E 218 E5
Burao = Burco Somalia 9°32N 45°32E 267 C6
Burāq Syria 33°11N 36°29E 250 E7
Burathum Nepal 28°4N 84°50E 243 E11
Burauen Phil. 10°58N 124°53E 233 F5
Buraydah Si. Arabia 26°20N 43°59E 246 E4
Burbank Calif., U.S.A. 34°12N 118°18W 126 A3
Burbank Ill., U.S.A. 41°44N 87°46W 119 C2
Burç Turkey 36°59N 37°8E 250 B8
Burcher Australia 33°30S 147°16E 283 B7
Burco Somalia 9°32N 45°32E 267 C6
Burda India 25°50N 77°35E 242 G7
Burdekin → Australia 19°38S 147°25E 280 B4
Burden, L. U.S.A. 28°27N 81°33W 133 B1
Burdeos Phil. 14°50N 121°58E 232 D3
Burdeos B. Phil. 14°44N 122°6E 232 D4
Burdur Turkey 37°45N 30°17E 205 D12
Burdur ☐ Turkey 37°45N 30°0E 205 D12
Burdur Gölü Turkey 37°44N 30°10E 205 D12
Burdwan = Barddhaman India 23°14N 87°39E 243 H12
Burdwood Bank Atl. Oc. 54°0S 59°0W 336 D5
Bure Gojam, Ethiopia 10°40N 37°4E 257 E4
Bure Ilubabor, Ethiopia 8°19N 35°8E 257 F4
Bure → U.K. 52°38N 1°43E 168 E9
Burela Spain 43°39N 7°24W 194 B3
Büren Germany 51°33N 8°35E 178 D4
Bureskoye Vdkhr. Russia 50°16N 130°20E 215 D14
Bureya → Russia 49°27N 129°30E 215 E13
Burford Canada 43°7N 80°27W 312 C4
Burg Germany 52°16N 11°51E 178 C7
Burg auf Fehmarn Germany 54°28N 11°9E 178 A7
Burg el Arab Egypt 30°54N 29°32E 256 H6
Burg et Tuyur Sudan 20°55N 27°56E 256 C2
Burg Stargard Germany 53°29N 13°18E 178 B9
Burgas Bulgaria 42°33N 27°29E 203 D11
Burgas ☐ Bulgaria 42°30N 27°20E 203 D11
Burgaski Zaliv Bulgaria 42°30N 27°39E 203 D11
Burgdorf Niedersachsen, Germany 52°27N 10°1E 178 C6
Burgdorf Switz. 47°3N 7°37E 179 H3
Burgenland ☐ Austria 47°20N 16°20E 181 D9
Burgeo Canada 47°37N 57°38W 299 C8
Burgersdorp S. Africa 31°0S 26°20E 270 D4
Burgess, Mt. Australia 30°50S 121°5E 279 F3
Burghausen Germany 48°9N 12°49E 179 G8
Burghead U.K. 57°43N 3°30W 167 D5
Búrgio Italy 37°36N 13°17E 200 E6
Burglengenfeld Germany 49°12N 12°2E 179 F8
Burgohondo Spain 40°26N 4°47W 194 E6
Burgos Ilocos N., Phil. 18°31N 120°39E 232 B3
Burgos Pangasinan, Phil. 16°4N 119°52E 232 C2
Burgos Spain 42°21N 3°41W 194 C7
Burgos ☐ Spain 42°21N 3°42W 194 C7
Burgstädt Germany 50°54N 12°49E 178 E8
Burgsvik Sweden 57°3N 18°19E 163 G12
Burguillos del Cerro Spain 38°23N 6°35W 195 G4
Burgundy = Bourgogne France 47°0N 4°50E 171 C6
Burhaniye Turkey 39°30N 26°58E 205 B8
Burhanpur India 21°18N 76°14E 244 D3
Burhi Gandak → India 25°20N 86°37E 243 G12
Burhner → India 22°43N 80°31E 243 H9
Buri Pen. Eritrea 15°25N 39°55E 257 D4
Burias I. Phil. 12°55N 123°5E 232 E4
Burias Pass. Phil. 13°0N 123°15E 232 E4
Buriás, Pta. Costa Rica 8°3N 82°51W 320 E3
Burien U.S.A. 47°28N 122°20W 306 C4
Burigi, L. Tanzania 2°2S 31°22E 268 C3
Burigi ⌂ Tanzania 2°20S 31°6E 268 C3
Burim Kosovo 42°45N 20°24E 202 D4
Burin Canada 47°1N 55°14W 299 C8
Buriram Thailand 15°0N 103°0E 236 E4
Buriti Alegre Brazil 18°9S 49°3W 333 E2
Buriti Bravo Brazil 5°50S 43°50W 332 C3
Buriti dos Lopes Brazil 3°10S 41°52W 332 B3
Burj Al Arab U.A.E. 25°8N 55°11E 119 B1
Burj Khalifa Dubai, U.A.E. 25°12N 55°16E 119 B2
Burji Ethiopia 5°29N 37°51E 257 F4
Burkburnett U.S.A. 34°6N 98°34W 314 D5
Burke → Australia 23°12S 139°33E 280 C2
Burke Chan. Canada 52°10N 127°30W 296 C3
Burketown Australia 17°45S 139°33E 280 B2
Burkhan Khaldun Mongolia 48°45N 108°40E 219 B10
Burkina Faso ■ Africa 12°0N 1°0W 262 C4
Burk's Falls Canada 45°37N 79°24W 298 C4
Burlada Spain 42°49N 1°36W 196 C3
Burleigh Falls Canada 44°33N 78°12W 312 B6
Burley U.S.A. 42°32N 113°48W 304 E7
Burlingame U.S.A. 37°35N 122°21W 306 H4
Burlington Ont., Canada 43°18N 79°45W 312 C5
Burlington Colo., U.S.A. 39°18N 102°16W 304 G12
Burlington Iowa, U.S.A. 40°49N 91°14W 310 D5
Burlington Kans., U.S.A. 38°12N 95°45W 308 F6
Burlington Ky., U.S.A. 39°2N 84°43W 311 E12
Burlington Mass., U.S.A. 42°30N 71°13W 116 A1
Burlington N.C., U.S.A. 36°6N 79°26W 315 C15
Burlington N.J., U.S.A. 40°4N 74°51W 313 F10
Burlington Vt., U.S.A. 44°29N 73°12W 313 B11
Burlington Wash., U.S.A. 48°28N 122°20W 306 B4
Burlington Wis., U.S.A. 42°41N 88°17W 311 B8
Burma = Myanmar ■ Asia 21°0N 96°30E 241 E6
Burnaby I. Canada 52°25N 131°19W 296 C2
Burnet U.S.A. 30°45N 98°14W 314 F5
Burney U.S.A. 40°53N 121°40W 304 F3
Burnham U.S.A. 40°38N 77°34W 312 F7
Burnham-on-Sea U.K. 51°14N 3°0W 169 F5
Burnham Park U.S.A. 41°49N 87°35W 119 C3
Burnham Park Harbor U.S.A. 41°51N 87°36W 119 B3
Burnhamthorpe Canada 43°37N 79°35W 141 B1
Burnie Australia 41°4S 145°56E 281 G4
Burnley U.K. 53°47N 2°14W 168 D5
Burns U.S.A. 43°35N 119°3W 304 E4
Burns Junction U.S.A. 42°47N 117°51W 304 E5
Burns Lake Canada 54°14N 125°45W 296 C3
Burnside → Canada 66°51N 108°4W 294 D10
Burnside, L. Australia 25°22S 123°0E 279 E3
Burnsville U.S.A. 44°47N 93°17W 308 C7
Burnt Oak U.K. 51°36N 0°15W 125 A2
Burnt Paw U.S.A. 66°54N 143°44W 303 C12
Burnt River Canada 44°41N 78°42W 312 B6
Burntisland U.K. 56°4N 3°13W 121 A2
Burntwood → Canada 56°8N 96°34W 297 B9
Burntwood L. Canada 55°22N 100°26W 297 B8
Burnwynd U.K. 55°54N 3°23W 121 B1
Buronga Australia 34°18S 142°20E 282 C5
Burqa West Bank 31°54N 35°15E 123 A2
Burqān Kuwait 29°0N 47°57E 246 D5
Burqin China 47°43N 87°0E 217 C11
Burra S. Austral., Australia 33°40S 138°55E 282 B3
Burra Nigeria 11°0N 8°56E 263 C6
Burragorang, L. Australia 33°52S 150°37E 283 B9
Burray U.K. 58°51N 2°54W 167 C6
Burrel Albania 41°36N 20°1E 202 E4
Burren △ Ireland 53°9N 9°5W 166 C2
Burren Junction Australia 30°7S 148°58E 281 E4
Burrendong, L. Australia 32°45S 149°10E 283 B8
Burriana Spain 39°50N 0°4W 196 F5
Burrinjuck, L. Australia 35°0S 148°36E 283 C8
Burro, Serranías del Mexico 28°56N 102°5W 318 B4
Burrow Hd. U.K. 54°41N 4°24W 167 G4
Burrowa-Pine Mountain △ Australia 36°6S 147°45E 283 D7
Burrum Coast △ Australia 25°13S 152°36E 281 D5
Burruyacú Argentina 26°30S 64°40W 334 B3
Burry Port U.K. 51°41N 4°15W 169 F3
Bursa Turkey 40°15N 29°5E 203 F13
Bursa ☐ Turkey 40°10N 29°5E 212 B3
Burseryd Sweden 57°12N 13°17E 163 G7
Burstall Canada 50°39N 109°54W 297 C7
Burton Mich., U.S.A. 43°0N 83°40W 311 B13
Burton Ohio, U.S.A. 41°28N 81°8W 312 E3
Burton S.C., U.S.A. 32°26N 80°43W 316 C9
Burton, L. Canada 54°45N 78°20W 298 B4
Burton upon Trent U.K. 52°48N 1°38W 168 E6
Burtundy Australia 33°45S 142°15E 282 B5
Burtus Egypt 30°8N 31°8E 117 A1
Buru Indonesia 3°30S 126°30E 231 E7
Buruanga Phil. 11°51N 121°53E 233 F3
Burudvatn Norway 59°58N 10°35E 133 A2
Burullus, Bahra el Egypt 31°25N 31°0E 256 H7
Burūm Yemen 14°22N 48°59E 249 D5
Burûn, Râs Egypt 31°14N 33°7E 251 G4
Burundi ■ Africa 3°15S 30°0E 268 C3
Burunny = Tsagan Aman Russia 47°34N 46°43E 191 G8
Bururi Burundi 3°57S 29°37E 268 C2

Burutu Nigeria 5°20N 5°29E 263 D6
Burwell U.S.A. 41°47N 99°8W 308 E4
Burwick U.K. 58°45N 2°58W 167 C5
Burwood Australia 33°52S 151°5E 139 B1
Bury U.K. 53°35N 2°17W 168 D5
Bury St. Edmunds U.K. 52°15N 0°43E 169 E8
Buryatia □ Russia 53°0N 110°0E 215 D12
Būrylbaytal Kazakhstan 44°56N 74°0E 217 D8
Buryn Ukraine 51°13N 33°50E 189 G7
Burzenin Poland 51°28N 18°47E 185 G5
Busa, Mt. Phil. 6°8N 124°39E 233 H5
Busalla Italy 44°34N 8°57E 198 D5
Busan S. Korea 35°5N 129°0E 224 E4
Busanga Dem. Rep. of the Congo 0°53S 22°7E 264 C4
Busango Swamp Zambia 14°15S 25°45E 269 E2
Busaso = Boosaaso Somalia 11°12N 49°18E 267 B6
Buşayrah Syria 35°9N 40°26E 213 E9
Busca Italy 44°31N 7°29E 198 D4
Bûsh Egypt 29°9N 31°8E 251 J2
Bushat Albania 41°58N 19°34E 202 E3
Būshehr Iran 28°55N 50°55E 247 D6
Būshehr □ Iran 28°20N 51°45E 247 D6
Bushenyi Uganda 0°35S 30°10E 268 C3
Bushimaie → Dem. Rep. of the Congo 6°2S 23°45E 265 D4
Bushire = Būshehr Iran 28°55N 50°55E 247 D6
Bushiribana Aruba 12°33N 69°58W 322 f
Bushnell Fla., U.S.A. 28°40N 82°7W 317 G7
Bushnell Ill., U.S.A. 40°33N 90°31W 310 D6
Bushtyna Ukraine 48°3N 23°28E 183 B8
Bushwick U.S.A. 40°41N 73°54W 132 B2
Bushy Park U.K. 51°24N 0°20W 125 B1
Busie Ghana 10°29N 2°22W 262 C4
Business Bay U.A.E. 25°11N 55°16E 119 B2
Businga Dem. Rep. of the Congo 3°16N 20°59E 264 B4
Büsingen Germany 47°42N 8°41E 179 H4
Busira = Tshuapa → Dem. Rep. of the Congo 0°14S 20°42E 264 C4
Buskerud □ Norway 60°20N 9°0E 164 D5
Busko-Zdrój Poland 50°28N 20°42E 185 H7
Buslei Ethiopia 5°28N 44°25E 267 C5
Busovača Bos.-H. 44°6N 17°53E 182 F2
Buşra ash Shām Syria 32°30N 36°25E 251 F7
Busselton Australia 33°42S 115°15E 279 F2
Busseri → South Sudan 7°41N 28°3E 257 F2
Busseto Italy 44°59N 10°2E 198 D7
Bussière-Badil France 45°39N 0°36E 174 C4
Bussol, Proliv Russia 46°30N 151°0E 215 E16
Bussolengo Italy 45°28N 10°51E 198 C7
Bussum Neths. 52°16N 5°10E 170 B5
Bustamante, B. Argentina 45°5S 66°18W 336 C3
Buşteni Romania 45°24N 25°32E 183 E10
Busto, C. Spain 43°34N 6°28W 194 B4
Busto Arsízio Italy 45°37N 8°51E 198 C5
Busu Djanoa Dem. Rep. of the Congo 1°43N 21°23E 264 B4
Busu Kwanga Dem. Rep. of the Congo 1°48N 20°21E 264 B4
Busu Mandji Dem. Rep. of the Congo 2°52N 21°14E 264 B4
Busuanga Phil. 12°14N 119°52E 232 E2
Busuanga I. Phil. 12°10N 120°0E 232 E2
Büsum Germany 54°7N 8°51E 178 A4
Busungbiu Indonesia 8°16S 114°58E 231 J17
Busy Corner Trin. & Tob. 10°18N 61°17W 323 t
Buta Dem. Rep. of the Congo 2°50N 24°53E 264 B4
Butantã Brazil 23°34S 46°42W 137 B1
Butare Rwanda 2°31S 29°52E 268 C2
Butaritari Kiribati 3°30N 174°0E 288 G9
Butcher I. India 18°57N 72°53E 130 B2
Bute S. Austral., Australia 33°51S 138°0E 282 B3
Bute Scotland, U.K. 55°48N 5°2W 167 F3
Bute Inlet Canada 50°40N 124°53W 296 C4
Butemba Uganda 1°9N 31°37E 268 B3
Butembo Dem. Rep. of the Congo 0°9N 29°18E 268 B2
Buteni Romania 46°19N 22°7E 182 D7
Butera Italy 37°11N 14°11E 201 E7
Butere Kenya 0°13N 34°30E 268 B3
Butha-Buthe Lesotho 28°47S 28°14E 271 C4
Buthidaung Myanmar 20°52N 92°32E 241 E4
Butiaba Uganda 1°50N 31°20E 268 B3
Butler Ga., U.S.A. 32°33N 84°14W 316 C5
Butler Ind., U.S.A. 41°26N 84°52W 311 C12
Butler Ky., U.S.A. 38°47N 84°22W 311 F12
Butler Mo., U.S.A. 38°16N 94°20W 310 F2
Butler Pa., U.S.A. 40°52N 79°54W 312 F5
Butler, L. U.S.A. 28°29N 81°33W 133 B1
Buton Indonesia 5°0S 122°45E 231 E6
Bütow = Bytów Poland 54°10N 17°30E 184 D4
Butrint Albania 39°45N 20°1E 206 B10
Butrint △ Albania 39°45N 20°1E 202 G4
Butrintit, L. e Albania 39°43N 20°5E 206 B10
Butte Mont., U.S.A. 46°0N 112°32W 304 C7
Butte Nebr., U.S.A. 42°58N 98°51W 308 D4
Butte Creek → U.S.A. 39°12N 121°56W 306 F5
Butterworth = Gcuwa S. Africa 32°20S 28°11E 271 D4
Butterworth Malaysia 5°24N 100°23E 237 c
Buttevant Ireland 52°14N 8°40W 166 D3
Buttfield, Mt. Australia 24°45S 128°9E 279 D4
Button B. Canada 58°45N 94°23W 297 B10
Buttonwillow U.S.A. 35°24N 119°28W 307 K7
Butty Hd. Australia 33°54S 121°39E 279 F3
Butuan Phil. 8°57N 125°33E 233 G5
Butuan B. Phil. 9°4N 125°21E 233 G5
Butuku-Luba Eq. Guin. 3°29N 8°33E 263 E6
Butung = Buton Indonesia 5°0S 122°45E 231 E6
Buturlinovka Russia 50°50N 40°35E 190 E5
Butwal Nepal 27°33N 83°31E 243 F10
Butzbach Germany 50°25N 8°40E 179 E4
Bützow Germany 53°50N 11°58E 178 B7
Buuhoodle Somalia 8°20N 46°25E 267 C6
Buulobarde Somalia 3°50N 45°33E 267 D6
Buur Gaabo Somalia 1°13S 41°51E 267 E5
Buurhakaba Somalia 3°12N 44°20E 267 D5
Buvika Norway 63°18N 10°11E 164 A7
Buxa Duar India 27°45N 89°35E 243 F13
Buxar India 25°34N 83°58E 243 G10
Buxoro Uzbekistan 39°48N 64°25E 216 E6
Buxtehude Germany 53°28N 9°39E 178 B5
Buxton U.K. 53°16N 1°54W 168 D6
Buxy France 46°44N 4°40E 173 F11
Buy Russia 58°28N 41°28E 190 A5
Buyant-Uhaa Mongolia 44°55N 110°11E 226 B6
Buynaksk Russia 42°48N 47°7E 191 J8
Buyo Côte d'Ivoire 6°21N 7°5W 262 D3
Buyo, L. de Côte d'Ivoire 6°16N 7°10W 262 D3
Büyük Menderes → Turkey 37°28N 27°11E 205 D9
Büyükçekmece Turkey 41°2N 28°35E 203 E12
Büyükdere Turkey 41°9N 29°2E 122 B2
Büyükeğri Dağı Turkey 36°45N 33°33E 250 B4
Büyükkariştiran Turkey 41°18N 27°33E 203 E11
Büyükkemikli Burnu Turkey 40°18N 26°14E 203 F10
Büyükkonuk = Komi Cyprus 35°24N 34°0E 207 E9
Büyükorhan Turkey 39°46N 28°56E 205 B10
Büyükyoncalı Turkey 41°20N 27°55E 203 E11
Buyun Shan China 40°4N 122°43E 227 D12
Buzançais France 46°54N 1°25E 172 F8
Buzău Romania 45°10N 26°50E 183 E11
Buzău □ Romania 45°20N 26°30E 183 E11
Buzău → Romania 45°26N 27°44E 183 E12
Buzău, Pasul Romania 45°35N 26°12E 183 E11
Buzaymah Libya 24°55N 22°2E 258 D4
Buzen Japan 33°35N 131°5E 222 D3
Buzet Croatia 45°24N 13°58E 199 C10
Buzi → Mozam. 19°50S 34°43E 269 F3
Buziaş Romania 45°38N 21°36E 182 E6
Büzmeýin Turkmenistan 38°3N 58°12E 247 B8
Buzuluk Russia 52°48N 52°12E 186 D9
Buzuluk → Russia 50°15N 42°7E 190 E6
Buzzards Bay U.S.A. 41°45N 70°37W 313 E14
Bwagaoia Papua N. G. 10°40S 152°52E 286 F7
Bwana Mkubwa Zambia 13°8S 28°38E 269 E2
Bwasa Dem. Rep. of the Congo 3°55S 18°24E 264 C3
Bwatnapné Vanuatu 15°41S 168°9E 287 E6
Bwindi △ Uganda 1°2S 29°42E 268 C2
Byakar Dzong = Jakar Dzong Bhutan 27°33N 90°43E 241 B3
Byala Ruse, Bulgaria 43°28N 25°44E 203 C9
Byala Varna, Bulgaria 42°53N 27°55E 203 D11
Byala Slatina Bulgaria 43°26N 23°58E 202 C7
Byam Martin I. Canada 75°15N 104°15W 295 B11
Byarezina → Belarus 52°33N 30°14E 177 B16
Byaroza Belarus 52°31N 24°51E 177 B13
Byblos = Jubayl Lebanon 34°5N 35°39E 250 D6
Bychawa Poland 51°1N 22°36E 185 G9
Byculla India 18°58N 72°50E 130 B2
Byczyna Poland 51°7N 18°12E 185 G5
Bydgoszcz Poland 53°10N 18°0E 185 E5
Byelorussia = Belarus ■ Europe 53°30N 27°0E 177 B14
Byeonsan △ S. Korea 35°40N 126°30E 224 E3
Byers U.S.A. 39°43N 104°14W 304 G11
Byesville U.S.A. 39°58N 81°32W 312 G3
Byfield △ Australia 22°52S 150°45E 280 C5
Bygdin Norway 61°21N 8°32E 164 C5
Bygdøy Norway 59°54N 10°40E 133 A3
Bygland Norway 58°50N 7°48E 164 F4
Byglandsfjorden Norway 58°44N 7°50E 164 F4
Bygstad Norway 61°23N 5°40E 164 C2
Bykhaw Belarus 53°31N 30°14E 177 B16
Bykhov = Bykhaw Belarus 53°31N 30°14E 177 B16
Bykle Norway 59°20N 7°22E 164 E4
Bykovo Russia 49°50N 45°25E 190 F7
Bylas U.S.A. 33°8N 110°7W 305 K8
Bylot Canada 58°25N 94°8W 297 B10
Bylot I. Canada 73°13N 78°34W 295 C16
Byram U.S.A. 32°11N 90°15W 315 E9
Byrd, C. Antarctica 69°38S 76°7W 151 C17
Byrock Australia 30°40S 146°27E 283 A7
Byron Ga., U.S.A. 32°39N 83°46W 316 C6
Byron Ill., U.S.A. 42°8N 89°15W 310 B7
Byron, C. Australia 28°43S 153°38E 281 D5
Byron Bay Australia 28°43S 153°37E 281 D5
Byrranga, Gory Russia 75°0N 100°0E 215 B11
Byrranga Mts. = Byrranga, Gory Russia 75°0N 100°0E 215 B11
Byrum Denmark 57°16N 11°0E 163 G5
Byske Sweden 64°57N 21°11E 160 D19
Byskeälven → Sweden 64°57N 21°13E 160 D19
Bystrytsya Ukraine 48°27N 24°14E 183 B9
Bystrzyca → Dolnośląskie, Poland 51°12N 16°55E 185 G3
Bystrzyca → Lubelskie, Poland 51°21N 22°46E 185 G9
Bystrzyca Kłodzka Poland 50°19N 16°39E 185 H3
Bytča Slovakia 49°13N 18°34E 181 B11
Bytkiv Ukraine 48°38N 24°28E 183 B9
Bytom Poland 50°25N 18°54E 185 H5
Bytom Odrzański Poland 51°44N 15°48E 185 G2
Bytów Poland 54°10N 17°30E 184 D4
Byumba Rwanda 1°35S 30°4E 268 C3
Bywater U.S.A. 29°58N 90°2W 131 B2
Byzantine Museum = Vizandino, Moussio Athens, Greece 112 b3
Bzenec Czechia 48°58N 17°18E 181 C10
Bzura → Poland 52°25N 20°15E 185 F7

C

C.B.S. Fox Studios U.S.A. 34°9N 118°24W 126 B2
C.N. Tower Toronto, Canada 141 c1
C.W. McConaughy, L. U.S.A. 41°14N 101°40W 308 E3
Ca → Vietnam 18°45N 105°45E 236 C5
Ca' da Mosto Venice, Italy 142 b3
Ca' d'Oro Venice, Italy 142 b2
Ca' Foscari Venice, Italy 142 b2
Ca Mau Vietnam 9°7N 105°8E 237 H5
Ca Mau, Mui Vietnam 8°38N 104°44E 237 H5
Ca Na Vietnam 11°20N 108°54E 237 G7
Ca' Pesaro Venice, Italy 142 b2
Ca' Rezzonico Venice, Italy 142 b2
Caacupé Paraguay 25°23S 57°5W 334 B4
Caaguazú △ Paraguay 26°5S 55°31W 335 B4
Caála Angola 12°46S 15°30E 265 E3
Caamaño Sd. Canada 52°55N 129°25W 296 C3
Caapiranga Brazil 3°18S 61°13W 329 D5
Caazapá Paraguay 26°8S 56°19W 334 B4
Caazapá □ Paraguay 26°10S 56°0W 335 B4
Cabaad, Ras Somalia 6°18N 49°4E 267 C6
Cabadbaran Phil. 9°10N 125°38E 233 G5
Cabagan Phil. 17°26N 121°46E 232 C3
Cabalete I. Phil. 14°16N 121°49E 232 D3
Cabalian = San Juan Phil. 10°16N 125°10E 233 F5
Caballito Argentina 34°37S 58°25W 117 B2
Cabana Peru 8°25S 78°5W 330 B2
Cabana de Bergantiños = A Carballa Spain 43°13N 8°54W 194 B2
Cabanaconde Peru 15°38S 71°58W 330 D3
Cabañaquinta Spain 43°10N 5°38W 194 B5
Cabanatuan Phil. 15°30N 120°58E 232 D3
Cabañeros ⌓ Spain 39°18N 4°35W 195 F6
Cabanes Spain 40°9N 0°2E 196 E5
Cabangon Phil. 15°10N 120°3E 232 D3
Cabanilla Peru 15°36S 70°28W 330 D3
Cabano Canada 47°40N 68°56W 299 C6
Čabar Croatia 45°36N 14°39E 199 C11
Cabarroguis Phil. 16°50N 121°30E 232 C3
Cabarruyan I. Phil. 16°18N 119°59E 232 C2
Cabazon U.S.A. 33°55N 116°47W 307 M10
Cabedelo Brazil 7°0S 34°50W 332 C5
Cabeza del Buey Spain 38°44N 5°13W 195 G5
Cabezón de la Sal Spain 43°18N 4°14W 194 B6
Cabhán, An = Cavan Ireland 54°0N 7°22W 166 B4
Cabildo Chile 32°30S 71°5W 334 C1
Cabimas Venezuela 10°23N 71°25W 328 A3
Cabin John U.S.A. 38°58N 77°10W 143 B1
Cabin John Regional Park ⌓ U.S.A. 39°0N 77°10W 143 A1
Cabinda Angola 5°33S 12°11E 265 D2
Cabinda □ Angola 5°0S 12°30E 265 D2
Cabinet Mts. U.S.A. 48°10N 115°50W 304 B6
Cabiri Angola 8°52S 13°39E 265 D2
Cable Beach The Bahamas 25°4N 77°24W 153 b
Cabo Blanco Argentina 47°15S 65°47W 336 C3
Cabo de Gata-Níjar ⌓ Spain 36°51N 2°6W 197 J2
Cabo de Hornos △ Chile 55°42S 67°20W 336 E3
Cabo de Santo Agostinho Brazil 8°20S 34°55W 332 C5
Cabo Frio Brazil 22°51S 42°3W 333 F3
Cabo Pantoja Peru 1°0S 75°10W 328 D2
Cabo Pulmo △ Mexico 23°20N 109°28W 318 C3
Cabo Raso Argentina 44°20S 65°15W 336 B3
Cabo Rojo Puerto Rico 18°5N 67°9W 321 b
Cabo San Lucas Mexico 22°53N 109°54W 318 C3
Cabo Verde ■ Atl. Oc. 16°0N 24°0W 153 j
Cabo Yubi = Tarfaya Morocco 27°55N 12°55W 260 C2
Cabonga, Réservoir Canada 47°20N 76°40W 298 C4
Cabool U.S.A. 37°7N 92°6W 308 G7
Caboolture Australia 27°5S 152°58E 281 D5
Cabora Bassa Dam = Cahora Bassa, Lago de Mozam. 15°20S 32°50E 269 F3
Caborca Mexico 30°37N 112°6W 318 A2
Cabot, Mt. U.S.A. 44°30N 71°25W 313 B13
Cabot Hd. Canada 45°14N 81°17W 312 A3
Cabot Str. Canada 47°15N 59°40W 299 C8
Cabourg France 49°17N 0°7W 172 C6
Cabra Spain 37°30N 4°28W 195 H6
Cabra del Santo Cristo Spain 37°42N 3°16W 195 H7
Cabra I. India 7°18N 93°50E 245 L11
Cabra I. Phil. 13°53N 120°2E 232 E3
Cábras Italy 39°56N 8°32E 200 C1
Cabras I. Guam 13°27N 144°44E 302 d
Cabrera Spain 39°8N 2°57E 206 B3
Cabrera, Sierra de la Spain 42°12N 6°40W 194 C4
Cabrera △ Spain 39°13N 2°53E 197 F7
Cabri Canada 50°35N 108°25W 297 C7
Cabriel → Spain 39°14N 1°3W 197 F3
Cabrits, Î. Martinique 14°23N 60°52W 322 j
Cabrits △ Dominica 15°35N 61°26W 323 k
Cabruta Venezuela 7°50N 66°10W 328 B4
Cabuçú de Baixo → Brazil 23°30S 46°40W 137 A1
Cabuçú de Cima → Brazil 23°30S 46°33W 137 A2
Cabugao Phil. 17°48N 120°27E 232 C3
Cabulauan Is. Phil. 11°25N 120°8E 233 F3
Cabulo Angola 10°18S 16°22E 265 E3
Caburan = Jose Abad Santos Phil. 5°55N 125°39E 233 J5
Cabuta Angola 9°48S 14°58E 265 D2
Cabuyaro Colombia 4°18N 72°49W 328 C3
Cacabelos Spain 42°36N 6°44W 194 C4
Caçador Brazil 26°47S 51°0W 335 B5
Čačak Serbia 43°54N 20°20E 202 C4
Cacandee Settlement Trin. & Tob. 10°33N 61°26W 323 t
Cacao Fr. Guiana 4°33N 52°26W 329 C7
Caçapava do Sul Brazil 30°30S 53°30W 335 C5
Cáccamo Italy 37°56N 13°40E 200 E6
Cacém Portugal 38°46N 9°18W 195 G1
Cáceres Brazil 16°5S 57°40W 331 D6
Cáceres Colombia 7°35N 75°20W 328 B2
Cáceres Spain 39°26N 6°23W 195 F4
Cáceres □ Spain 39°45N 6°0W 194 F5
Cachan France 48°47N 2°19E 134 B2
Cache Bay Canada 46°22N 80°0W 298 C4
Cache Cr. → U.S.A. 38°42N 121°42W 306 G5
Cache Creek Canada 50°48N 121°19W 296 C4
Cacheu Guinea-Biss. 12°14N 16°8W 262 C1
Cachi Argentina 25°5S 66°10W 334 B2
Cachimbo Brazil 8°57S 54°54W 331 B7
Cachimbo, Serra do Brazil 9°30S 55°30W 331 B6
Cachimo Angola 8°21S 21°24E 265 D4
Cachinal de la Sierra Chile 24°58S 69°32W 334 A2
Cachingues Angola 13°5S 16°43E 265 E3
Cachoeira = Solonópole Brazil 5°44S 39°1W 332 C4
Cachoeira Brazil 12°30S 39°0W 333 D4
Cachoeira, Rib. da → Brazil 23°38S 46°43W 137 B1
Cachoeira Alta Brazil 18°48S 50°58W 333 E1
Cachoeira do Sul Brazil 30°3S 52°53W 335 C5
Cachoeiro de Itapemirim Brazil 20°51S 41°7W 333 F3
Cachoeiro do Arari Brazil 1°1S 48°58W 332 B2
Cachopo Portugal 37°20N 7°49W 195 H3
Cachuela Esperanza Bolivia 10°32S 65°38W 331 C4
Cacilhas Portugal 38°41N 9°8W 126 A2
Cacine Guinea-Biss. 11°8N 14°57W 262 C1
Cacoal Brazil 11°32S 61°18W 331 C5
Cacólo Angola 10°9S 19°21E 265 E3
Caconda Angola 13°48S 15°8E 265 E3
Cacongo Angola 5°11S 12°5E 265 D2
Caçu Brazil 18°37S 51°4W 333 E1
Cacuaco Angola 8°47S 13°21E 265 D2
Cacuchi → Angola 14°26S 16°46E 265 E3
Cacula Angola 14°29S 14°10E 265 E2
Caculé Brazil 14°30S 42°13W 333 D3
Caculuvar → Angola 16°47S 14°56E 265 F2
Cacuso Angola 9°25S 15°45E 265 D3
Cadale Somalia 2°45N 46°19E 267 D6
Cadaqués Spain 42°17N 3°17E 196 C8
Čadca Slovakia 49°26N 18°45E 181 B11
Caddo U.S.A. 34°7N 96°16W 314 D6
Cader Idris U.K. 52°42N 3°53W 169 E4
Cadereyta de Jiménez Mexico 25°36N 100°0W 318 B5
Cades U.S.A. 33°47N 79°47W 316 B10
Cadí, Serra del Spain 42°17N 1°42E 196 C6
Cadí-Moixeró ⌓ Spain 42°17N 1°44W 196 C3
Cadibarrawirracanna, L. Australia 28°52S 135°27E 281 D2
Cadillac Gironde, France 44°38N 0°20W 174 D3
Cadillac Mich., U.S.A. 44°15N 85°24W 309 C11
Cadiz Phil. 10°57N 123°15E 233 F4
Cádiz Spain 36°30N 6°20W 195 J4
Cadiz Calif., U.S.A. 34°30N 115°28W 307 L11
Cadiz Ohio, U.S.A. 40°22N 81°0W 312 F4
Cádiz □ Spain 36°36N 5°45W 195 J5
Cádiz, G. de Spain 36°40N 7°0W 195 J3
Cadiz L. U.S.A. 34°18N 115°24W 307 L11
Cadley U.S.A. 33°32N 82°40W 316 B7
Cadney Park Australia 27°55S 134°3E 281 D1
Cadomin Canada 53°2N 117°20W 296 C5
Cadotte Lake Canada 56°26N 116°23W 296 B5
Cadours France 43°44N 1°2E 174 E5
Cadoux Australia 30°46S 117°7E 279 F2
Cadwell U.S.A. 32°20N 83°3W 316 C6
Caen France 49°10N 0°22W 172 C6
Caerdydd = Cardiff U.K. 51°29N 3°10W 169 F4
Caerfyrddin = Carmarthen U.K. 51°52N 4°19W 169 F3
Caergybi = Holyhead U.K. 53°18N 4°38W 168 D3
Caernarfon U.K. 53°8N 4°16W 168 D3
Caernarfon B. U.K. 53°4N 4°40W 168 D3
Caernarvon = Caernarfon U.K. 53°8N 4°16W 168 D3
Caerphilly U.K. 51°35N 3°13W 169 F4
Caerphilly □ U.K. 51°37N 3°12W 169 F4
Caesarea Israel 32°30N 34°53E 251 F5
Caeté Brazil 19°55S 43°40W 333 E3
Caetité Brazil 13°50S 42°32W 333 D3
Cafayate Argentina 26°2S 66°0W 334 B2
Cafu Angola 16°30S 15°8E 265 F3
Cagayan □ Phil. 18°0N 121°50E 232 C3
Cagayan → Phil. 18°25N 121°42E 232 B3
Cagayan de Oro Phil. 8°30N 124°40E 233 G5
Cagayan Is. Phil. 9°40N 121°16E 233 G3
Cagayan Sulu I. Phil. 7°1N 118°30E 233 H2
Cagli Italy 43°33N 12°39E 199 E9
Cágliari Italy 39°13N 9°7E 200 C2
Cágliari, G. di Italy 39°8N 9°11E 200 C2
Cagnano Varano Italy 41°49N 15°47E 199 G12
Cagnes-sur-Mer France 43°40N 7°9E 175 E11
Caguán → Colombia 0°8S 74°18W 328 D3
Caguas Puerto Rico 18°14N 66°2W 321 C6
Caha Mts. Ireland 51°45N 9°40W 166 E2
Cahama Angola 16°17S 14°19E 265 F2
Caherciveen Ireland 51°56N 10°14W 166 E1
Cahir Ireland 52°22N 7°56W 166 D4
Cahora Bassa, Lago de Mozam. 15°20S 32°50E 269 F3
Cahore Pt. Ireland 52°33N 6°12W 166 D5
Cahors France 44°27N 1°27E 174 D5
Cahuapanas Peru 5°15S 77°0W 330 B2
Cahuenga Pk. U.S.A. 34°8N 118°19W 126 B3
Cahuinari → Colombia 1°21S 70°44W 328 D3
Cahuinari △ Colombia 1°20S 71°10W 328 D3
Cahul Moldova 45°50N 28°15E 183 E13
Cai Bau, Dao Vietnam 21°10N 107°27E 228 G6
Cai Be Vietnam 10°20N 106°2E 237 G6
Cai Nuoc Vietnam 8°56N 105°1E 237 H5
Caia Mozam. 17°51S 35°24E 269 F4
Caiabis, Serra dos Brazil 11°30S 56°30W 331 C6
Caianda Angola 11°2S 23°31E 265 E4
Caiapó, Serra do Brazil 17°0S 52°0W 331 D7
Caiapônia Brazil 16°57S 51°49W 331 D7
Caibarién Cuba 22°30N 79°30W 320 B4
Caibiran Phil. 11°34N 124°35E 233 F5
Caiçara = Alvarães Brazil 3°12S 64°50W 329 D5
Caicara Bolívar, Venezuela 7°38N 66°10W 328 B4
Caicara Monagas, Venezuela 9°52N 63°38W 329 B5
Caicó Brazil 6°20S 37°0W 332 C4
Caicos Is. Turks & Caicos 21°40N 71°40W 321 B5
Caicos Passage W. Indies 22°45N 72°45W 321 B5
Caidian China 30°35N 114°2E 229 B10
Caiguna Australia 32°16S 125°29E 279 F4
Caillandre, Morne St. Lucia 13°46N 60°57W 323 m
Caille I. Grenada 12°16N 61°34W 323 q
Cailloma Peru 15°9S 71°45W 330 D3
Cain, L. U.S.A. 28°28N 81°28W 133 B2
Căinari Moldova 46°41N 29°3E 183 D14
Cainde Angola 15°29S 13°24E 265 F2
Caine → Bolivia 18°23S 65°21W 331 D4
Caird Coast Antarctica 75°0S 25°0W 151 D1
Cairn Gorm U.K. 57°7N 3°39W 167 D5
Cairngorm Mts. U.K. 57°6N 3°42W 167 D5
Cairngorms △ U.K. 57°10N 3°50W 167 D5
Cairnryan U.K. 54°59N 5°1W 167 G3
Cairns Australia 16°57S 145°45E 280 B4
Cairns L. Canada 51°42N 94°30W 297 C10
Cairo = El Qâhira Egypt 30°2N 31°13E 117 A2
Cairo Ga., U.S.A. 30°52N 84°13W 316 E5
Cairo Ill., U.S.A. 37°0N 89°11W 308 G9
Cairo N.Y., U.S.A. 42°18N 74°0W 313 D10
Cairo Int. ✕ (CAI) Egypt 30°7N 31°24E 117 A3
Cairo Montenotte Italy 44°23N 8°16E 198 D5
Cairofa Angola 14°3S 12°54E 265 E2
Caiseal = Cashel Ireland 52°30N 7°53W 166 D4
Caisleán an Bharraigh = Castlebar Ireland 53°52N 9°18W 166 C2
Caithness U.K. 58°25N 3°35W 167 C5
Caithness, Ord of U.K. 58°8N 3°36W 167 C5
Caitou Angola 14°28S 13°7E 265 E2
Caiuás = Rio Brilhante Brazil 21°48S 54°33W 335 A5
Caiundo Angola 15°50S 17°28E 265 F3
Caiza Bolivia 20°2S 65°40W 331 E4
Caja de Muertos, I. Puerto Rico 17°54N 66°32W 321 b
Cajabamba Peru 7°38S 78°4W 330 B2
Cajamarca Peru 7°5S 78°28W 330 B2
Cajamarca □ Peru 6°15S 78°50W 330 B2
Cajamarquilla = Bolívar Peru 7°18S 77°48W 330 B2
Cajapió Brazil 2°58S 44°48W 332 B3
Cajarc France 44°29N 1°50E 174 D5
Cajas △ Ecuador 2°48S 79°15W 328 D2
Cajatambo Peru 10°30S 77°2W 330 C2
Cajazeiras Brazil 6°52S 38°30W 332 C4
Čajetina Serbia 43°47N 19°42E 202 C3
Cajidiocan Phil. 12°22N 122°41E 232 E4
Caju Brazil 22°52S 43°12W 135 B1
Çakirgol Turkey 40°33N 39°40E 213 B8
Çakırlar Turkey 36°52N 30°33E 205 E12
Čakovec Croatia 46°23N 16°26E 199 B13
Čakovice Czechia 50°9N 14°31E 135 B3
Çal Turkey 38°4N 29°23E 205 C11
Cala Spain 37°59N 6°21W 195 H4
Cala → Spain 37°38N 6°5W 195 H4
Cala Cadolar, Punta de = Rotja, Pta. Spain 38°38N 1°35E 206 D2
Cala d'Or Spain 39°23N 3°14E 206 B4
Cala en Porter Spain 39°52N 4°8E 206 B5
Cala Figuera Spain 39°20N 3°10E 206 B4
Cala Figuera, C. de Spain 39°27N 2°31E 206 B3
Cala Forcat Spain 40°0N 3°47E 206 B4
Cala Major Spain 39°33N 2°37E 206 B3
Cala Mezquida = Sa Mesquida Spain 39°55N 4°16E 206 B5
Cala Millor Spain 39°35N 3°22E 206 B4
Cala Murada Spain 39°27N 3°17E 206 B4
Cala Ratjada Spain 39°43N 3°27E 206 B4
Cala Santa Galdana Spain 39°56N 3°58E 206 B4
Calabanga Phil. 13°42N 123°17E 232 E4
Calabar Nigeria 4°57N 8°20E 263 E6
Calabarzon □ Phil. 15°30N 121°0E 232 D3
Calabogie Canada 45°18N 76°43W 313 A8
Calabozo Venezuela 9°0N 67°28W 328 B4
Calábria □ Italy 39°0N 16°30E 201 C9
Calábria △ Italy 39°6N 16°35E 201 C9
Calaburras, Pta. de Spain 36°30N 4°38W 195 J6
Calaceite Spain 41°1N 0°11E 196 D5
Calacoto Bolivia 17°16S 68°38W 330 D4
Calacuccia France 42°21N 9°1E 175 F13
Calafat Romania 43°58N 22°59E 182 G7
Calafell Spain 41°11N 1°34E 196 D6
Calagnaan I. Phil. 11°29N 123°12E 233 F4
Calagua Is. Phil. 14°30N 122°55E 232 D4
Calahorra Spain 42°18N 1°59W 196 C3
Calai Angola 17°47S 19°41E 265 F3
Calais Pas-de-Calais, France 50°57N 1°56E 173 B8
Calais Maine, U.S.A. 45°11N 67°17W 309 C20
Calakmul ⌓ Mexico 18°14N 89°48W 319 D7
Calalaste, Cord. de Argentina 25°0S 67°0W 334 B2
Calama Brazil 8°0S 62°50W 331 B5
Calama Chile 22°30S 68°55W 334 A2
Calamar Bolívar, Colombia 10°15N 74°55W 328 A3
Calamar Vaupés, Colombia 1°58N 72°32W 328 C3
Calamarca Bolivia 16°55S 68°9W 330 D4
Calamba Cavite, Phil. 14°13N 121°10E 232 D3
Calamba Mis. Occ., Phil. 8°35N 123°39E 233 G4
Calamian Group Phil. 11°50N 119°55E 233 F2
Calamocha Spain 40°50N 1°17W 196 E3
Calamonte Spain 38°53N 6°23W 195 G4
Călan Romania 45°44N 22°59E 182 E7
Calañas Spain 37°40N 6°53W 195 H4
Calanda Spain 40°56N 0°15W 196 E4
Calandagan I. Phil. 10°39N 120°15E 233 F3
Calandula Angola 9°6S 15°57E 265 D3
Calang Indonesia 4°37N 95°37E 234 B1
Calangiánus Italy 40°56N 9°11E 200 B2
Calanques △ France 43°14N 5°30E 175 E9
Calanscio, Sarīr Libya 27°30N 22°30E 258 C4
Calapan Phil. 13°25N 121°7E 232 E3
Călăraşi Moldova 47°16N 28°19E 183 C13
Călăraşi Romania 44°12N 27°20E 183 F12
Călăraşi □ Romania 44°10N 27°0E 183 F12
Calasparra Spain 38°14N 1°41W 197 G3
Calatafimi Italy 37°55N 12°52E 200 E5
Calatagan Phil. 13°50N 120°38E 232 E3
Calatayud Spain 41°20N 1°40W 196 D3
Călăţele Romania 46°46N 23°1E 182 D8
Calato = Kalathos Greece 36°9N 28°8E 206 E12
Calatrava Eq. Guin. 1°6N 9°25E 264 B1
Calatrava Phil. 10°35N 123°28E 233 F4
Calatrava, Ponte di Venice, Italy 142 b1
Calauag Phil. 13°55N 122°15E 232 E4
Calavà, C. Italy 38°11N 14°55E 201 D7
Calavite, C. Phil. 13°26N 120°20E 232 E3
Calavite Pass. Phil. 13°36N 120°25E 232 E3
Calayan Phil. 19°16N 121°28E 232 B3
Calayan I. Phil. 19°20N 121°27E 232 B3
Calbayog Phil. 12°4N 124°38E 232 E5
Calbiga Phil. 11°38N 125°0E 233 F5
Calca Peru 13°22S 72°0W 330 C3
Calcasieu L. U.S.A. 29°55N 93°18W 314 G8
Calcium U.S.A. 44°1N 75°50W 313 B9
Calcutta = Kolkata India 22°34N 88°21E 124 B2
Calcutta U.S.A. 40°40N 80°34W 312 F4
Caldaro Italy 46°25N 11°14E 199 B8
Caldas □ Colombia 5°15N 75°30W 328 B2
Caldas da Rainha Portugal 39°24N 9°8W 195 F1
Caldas de Reis Spain 42°36N 8°39W 194 C2
Caldas Novas Brazil 17°45S 48°38W 333 E2
Calder → U.K. 53°44N 1°22W 168 D6
Caldera Chile 27°5S 70°55W 334 B1
Caldera de Taburiente △ Canary Is. 28°43N 17°52W 153 e1
Caldwell Idaho, U.S.A. 43°40N 116°41W 304 E5
Caldwell Kans., U.S.A. 37°2N 97°37W 308 G5
Caldwell Tex., U.S.A. 30°32N 96°42W 314 F6
Caledon Ont., Canada 43°51N 79°51W 312 C5
Caledon Western Cape, S. Africa 34°14S 19°26E 270 D2
Caledon → S. Africa 30°31S 26°5E 270 D4
Caledon B. Australia 12°45S 137°0E 280 A2
Caledonia Ont., Canada 43°7N 79°58W 312 C5
Caledonia Mo., U.S.A. 37°45N 90°46W 310 G6
Caledonia N.Y., U.S.A. 42°58N 77°51W 312 D7
Calella Spain 41°37N 2°40E 196 D7
Calemba Angola 16°0S 15°44E 270 A2
Calen Australia 20°56S 148°48E 280 b
Calenzana France 42°31N 8°51E 175 F12
Caleta Olivia Argentina 46°25S 67°25W 336 C3
Caletones Chile 34°6S 70°27W 334 C1
Calexico U.S.A. 32°40N 115°30W 307 N11
Calf of Man I. of Man 54°3N 4°48W 168 C3
Calgary Canada 51°0N 114°10W 296 C6
Calheta Azores 38°36N 28°1W 153 d1
Calheta Madeira 32°44N 17°11W 153 c
Calheta de Nesquim Azores 38°24N 28°5W 153 d1
Calhoun U.S.A. 34°30N 84°57W 315 D12
Calhoun Falls U.S.A. 34°6N 82°36W 316 A7
Cali Colombia 3°25N 76°35W 328 C2
Calibishie Dominica 15°35N 61°21W 323 k
Calicoan I. Phil. 10°59N 125°48E 233 F5
Calicut = Kozhikode India 11°15N 75°43E 245 J2
Cálida, Costa Spain 37°30N 1°30W 197 H3
Caliente U.S.A. 37°37N 114°31W 305 H6
California Trin. & Tob. 10°24N 61°28W 323 t
California Mo., U.S.A. 38°38N 92°34W 310 F4
California Pa., U.S.A. 40°4N 79°54W 312 F5
California □ U.S.A. 37°30N 119°30W 306 H7
California, Baja, T.N. = Baja California □ Mexico 30°0N 115°0W 318 B2
California, Baja, T.S. = Baja California Sur □ Mexico 25°50N 111°50W 318 B2
California, G. de Mexico 27°0N 111°0W 318 B2
California City U.S.A. 35°10N 117°55W 307 K9
California Hot Springs U.S.A. 35°51N 118°41W 307 K8
California Institute of Technology Los Angeles, U.S.A. 34°8N 118°8W 126 B4
California Los Angeles, Univ. of U.S.A. 34°4N 118°27W 126 B2
California Plaza Los Angeles, U.S.A. 127 b1
California State Univ. U.S.A. 34°4N 118°10W 126 B3
Călilabad Azerbaijan 39°12N 48°29E 213 C13
Calilegua △ Argentina 25°36S 64°50W 334 B3
Călimăneşti Romania 45°14N 24°20E 183 E9
Călimani, Munţii Romania 47°12N 25°0E 183 C10
Călimani △ Romania 47°7N 25°10E 183 C10
Calingasta Argentina 31°15S 69°30W 334 C2
Calinog Phil. 11°7N 122°32E 233 F4
Calintaan Phil. 12°35N 120°57E 232 E3
Calipatria U.S.A. 33°8N 115°31W 307 M11
Calistoga U.S.A. 38°35N 122°35W 306 G4
Calitri Italy 40°54N 15°26E 201 B8
Calitzdorp S. Africa 33°33S 21°42E 270 D3
Calivigny I. Grenada 12°0N 61°43W 323 q
Callabonna, L. Australia 29°40S 140°5E 281 D3
Callac France 48°25N 3°27W 172 D3
Callahan U.S.A. 30°34N 81°50W 316 E8
Callahan Tunnel Boston, U.S.A. 116 a3
Callan Ireland 52°32N 7°24W 166 D4
Callander U.K. 56°15N 4°13W 167 E4
Callang = San Manuel Phil. 16°4N 120°40E 232 C3
Callao Peru 12°3S 77°8W 124 B2
Callaway U.S.A. 30°8N 85°36W 316 E4
Calliaqua St. Vincent 13°8N 61°12W 323 n
Callicoon U.S.A. 41°46N 75°3W 313 E9
Calling Lake Canada 55°15N 113°12W 296 B6
Calliope Australia 24°0S 151°16E 280 C5
Callosa de Segura Spain 38°7N 0°53W 197 G4
Callosa d'En Sarrià Spain 38°40N 0°8W 197 G4
Calma, Costa de la Spain 39°28N 2°26E 206 B3
Calmar U.S.A. 43°11N 91°52W 310 A5
Calne U.K. 51°26N 2°0W 169 F6
Calola Angola 16°25S 17°48E 265 F3
Calolbon = San Andres Phil. 13°36N 124°6E 232 E5
Calonge Spain 41°52N 3°5E 196 D8
Caloocan Phil. 14°39N 120°58E 127 B1
Caloosahatchee → U.S.A. 26°31N 82°1W 317 J7
Calore → Italy 41°11N 14°28E 201 A7
Caloundra Australia 26°45S 153°10E 281 D5
Calpe Spain 38°39N 0°3E 197 G5
Calpella U.S.A. 39°14N 123°12W 306 F3
Calpine U.S.A. 39°40N 120°27W 306 F6
Calstock Canada 49°47N 84°9W 298 C3
Caltabellotta Italy 37°34N 13°13E 200 E6
Caltagirone Italy 37°14N 14°31E 201 E7
Caltanissetta Italy 37°29N 14°4E 201 E7
Çaltılıbük Turkey 39°57N 28°36E 203 G12
Caluango Angola 8°20S 19°39E 265 D3
Calubian Phil. 11°27N 124°26E 233 F5
Calucinga Angola 11°18S 16°12E 265 E3
Caluire-et-Cuire France 45°48N 4°52E 173 G11
Calulo Angola 10°1S 14°56E 265 E2
Calumet, L. U.S.A. 41°41N 87°35W 119 C3
Calumet City U.S.A. 41°37N 87°32W 119 D3
Calumet Park U.S.A. 41°40N 87°39W 119 C3
Calumet Sag Channel → U.S.A. 41°40N 87°47W 119 C2
Calunda Angola 12°7S 23°36E 265 E4
Caluquembe Angola 13°47S 14°44E 265 E2
Caluso Italy 45°18N 7°53E 198 C4
Caluula Somalia 11°50N 50°45E 267 B7
Caluya I. Phil. 11°55N 121°34E 233 F3
Calvados □ France 49°5N 0°15W 172 C6
Calvados Chain, The Papua N. G. 11°10S 152°45E 286 F7
Calvairate Italy 45°27N 9°13E 128 B2
Calvert → Australia 16°17S 137°44E 280 B2
Calvert I. Canada 51°30N 128°0W 296 C3
Calvert Ra. Australia 24°0S 122°30E 278 D3
Calvi France 42°34N 8°45E 175 F12
Calvià Spain 39°34N 2°31E 206 B3
Calvillo Mexico 21°51N 102°43W 318 C4
Calvinia S. Africa 31°28S 19°45E 270 D2
Calvo, Mte. Italy 41°44N 15°46E 199 G12
Calwa U.S.A. 36°42N 119°46W 306 J7
Calzada Almuradiel = Almuradiel Spain 38°32N 3°28W 195 G7
Calzada de Calatrava Spain 38°42N 3°46W 195 G7
Cam → U.K. 52°21N 0°16E 169 E8
Cam Lam = Ba Ngoi Vietnam 11°54N 109°10E 237 G7
Cam Pha Vietnam 21°7N 107°18E 228 G6
Cam Ranh Vietnam 11°54N 109°12E 237 G7
Cam Xuyen Vietnam 18°15N 106°0E 236 C6
Camabatela Angola 8°20S 15°26E 265 D3
Camacã Brazil 15°24S 39°30W 333 E4
Camaçari Brazil 12°41S 38°18W 333 D4
Camacha Madeira 32°41N 16°49W 153 c
Camacupa Angola 11°58S 17°22E 265 E3
Camaguán Venezuela 8°6N 67°36W 328 B4
Camagüey Cuba 21°20N 77°55W 320 B4
Camagüey, Arch. de Cuba 22°18N 78°0W 320 B4
Camaiore Italy 43°56N 10°18E 198 E7
Camamu Brazil 13°57S 39°7W 333 D4
Camaná Peru 16°30S 72°50W 330 D3
Camanche U.S.A. 41°47N 90°15W 310 C6
Camanche Res. U.S.A. 38°14N 121°1W 306 G6
Camapuã Brazil 19°30S 54°5W 331 D7
Camaquã Brazil 30°51S 51°49W 335 C5
Camaquã → Brazil 31°17S 51°47W 335 C5
Câmara de Lobos Madeira 32°39N 16°59W 153 c
Camararé → Brazil 12°15S 58°55W 331 C6
Camarat, C. France 43°12N 6°41E 175 E10
Camarate Portugal 38°48N 9°7W 126 A2
Çamardı Turkey 37°49N 34°58E 212 D6
Camarès France 43°49N 2°53E 174 E6
Camaret-sur-Mer France 48°16N 4°37W 172 D2
Camargo Bolivia 20°38S 65°15W 331 E4
Camargo Tamaulipas, Mexico 26°19N 98°50W 319 B5
Camargue France 43°34N 4°34E 175 E8
Camargue ⌓ France 43°30N 4°40E 175 E8
Camarillo U.S.A. 34°13N 119°2W 307 L7
Camariñas Spain 43°8N 9°12W 194 B1
Camarines Norte □ Phil. 14°10N 122°45E 232 D4
Camarines Sur □ Phil. 13°40N 123°20E 232 E4
Camaroes Portugal 38°49N 9°14W 126 A1
Camarón, C. Honduras 16°0N 85°5W 320 C2
Camarones Argentina 44°50S 65°40W 336 B3
Camarones, B. Argentina 44°45S 65°35W 336 B3
Camas Spain 37°24N 6°2W 195 H4
Camas Wash., U.S.A. 45°35N 122°24W 306 E4
Camas Valley U.S.A. 43°2N 123°40W 304 E2
Camatambo Angola 6°31S 15°21E 265 D3
Camataquí = Villa Abecia Bolivia 21°0S 68°18W 334 A2
Camaxilo Angola 8°21S 18°56E 265 D3
Camba Cassai Angola 9°47S 19°9E 265 D3
Camballin Australia 17°59S 124°12E 278 C3
Cambamba Angola 8°53S 14°44E 265 D2
Cambará Brazil 23°2S 50°5W 335 A5
Cambay = Khambhat India 22°23N 72°33E 242 H5
Cambay, G. of = Khambhat, G. of India 20°45N 72°30E 239 E10
Camberwell Vic., Australia 37°50S 145°5E 128 B2
Camberwell London, U.K. 51°28N 0°5W 125 B3
Cambil Spain 37°40N 3°33W 195 H7
Cambo Angola 10°55S 20°6E 265 D3
Cambo-les-Bains France 43°22N 1°23W 174 E2
Cambodia ■ Asia 12°15N 105°0E 236 F5
Camborne U.K. 50°12N 5°19W 169 G2
Cambrai S. Austral., Australia 34°40S 139°16E 282 C3
Cambrai Nord, France 50°11N 3°14E 173 B10
Cambre Spain 43°17N 8°20W 194 B2
Cambria U.S.A. 35°34N 121°5W 306 K5
Cambrian Mts. U.K. 52°3N 3°57W 169 E4
Cambridge Ont., Canada 43°23N 80°15W 312 C4
Cambridge Jamaica 18°18N 77°54W 320 a
Cambridge N.Z. 37°54S 175°29E 284 D4
Cambridge Cambs., U.K. 52°12N 0°8E 169 E8
Cambridge Ill., U.S.A. 41°18N 90°12W 310 C6
Cambridge Iowa, U.S.A. 41°54N 93°32W 310 C3
Cambridge Mass., U.S.A. 42°23N 71°7W 116 A2
Cambridge Minn., U.S.A. 45°34N 93°13W 308 C7
Cambridge N.Y., U.S.A. 43°2N 73°22W 313 C11
Cambridge Nebr., U.S.A. 40°17N 100°10W 308 E3
Cambridge Ohio, U.S.A. 40°2N 81°35W 312 F3
Cambridge Bay Canada 69°10N 105°0W 294 D11
Cambridge City U.S.A. 39°49N 85°10W 311 E11
Cambridge G. Australia 14°55S 128°15E 278 B4
Cambridge Springs U.S.A. 41°48N 80°4W 312 E4
Cambridgeshire □ U.K. 52°25N 0°7W 169 E7
Cambrils Spain 41°8N 1°3E 196 D6
Cambuci Rio de J., Brazil 21°35S 41°55W 333 F3
Cambuci São Paulo, Brazil 23°33S 46°47W 137 B2
Cambulo Angola 7°49S 21°15E 265 D4
Cambundi-Catembo Angola 10°10S 17°35E 265 E3
Camdeboo △ S. Africa 32°28S 24°25E 270 D3
Camden N.S.W., Australia 34°1S 150°43E 283 C9
Camden Ala., U.S.A. 31°59N 87°17W 315 F11
Camden Ark., U.S.A. 33°35N 92°50W 314 E8
Camden Maine, U.S.A. 44°13N 69°4W 309 C19
Camden N.J., U.S.A. 39°55N 75°7W 313 G9
Camden N.Y., U.S.A. 43°20N 75°45W 313 C9
Camden Ohio, U.S.A. 39°38N 84°39W 311 E12
Camden S.C., U.S.A. 34°16N 80°36W 315 D14
Camden □ U.K. 51°32N 0°8W 125 A3
Camden Bay U.S.A. 70°10N 145°15W 303 A11
Camden Sd. Australia 15°27S 124°25E 278 C3
Camdenton U.S.A. 38°1N 92°45W 310 F4
Cameia △ Angola 12°5S 21°40E 265 E4
Camelford U.K. 50°37N 4°42W 169 G3
Çameli Turkey 37°5N 29°24E 205 D11
Camenca Moldova 48°3N 28°42E 183 B13
Camerino Italy 43°8N 13°4E 199 E10
Camerón Chile 53°38S 69°39W 336 D3
Cameron Ariz., U.S.A. 35°53N 111°25W 305 J8
Cameron La., U.S.A. 29°48N 93°20W 314 G8
Cameron Mo., U.S.A. 39°44N 94°14W 310 E2
Cameron S.C., U.S.A. 33°34N 80°43W 316 B9
Cameron Tex., U.S.A. 30°51N 96°59W 314 F6
Cameron Highlands Malaysia 4°27N 101°22E 237 K3
Cameron Hills Canada 59°48N 118°0W 296 B5
Cameron Mts. N.Z. 46°1S 167°0E 285 G2
Cameroon ■ Africa 6°0N 12°30E 264 A2
Camerota Italy 40°2N 15°22E 201 B8
Cameroun → Cameroon 4°0N 9°35E 263 E6
Cameroun, Mt. Cameroon 4°13N 9°10E 263 E6
Cametá Brazil 2°12S 49°30W 332 B2
Çamiçi Gölü Turkey 37°29N 27°28E 205 D9
Camiguin □ Phil. 9°11N 124°42E 233 G5
Camiguin I. Phil. 18°56N 121°55E 232 B3
Camiling Phil. 15°42N 120°24E 232 D3
Camilla U.S.A. 31°14N 84°12W 316 D5
Caminha Portugal 41°50N 8°50W 194 D2
Camino U.S.A. 38°44N 120°41W 306 G6
Camiranga Brazil 1°48S 46°17W 332 B2
Camiri Bolivia 20°3S 63°31W 331 E5
Camissombo Angola 8°7S 20°38E 265 D4
Camlıbel = Myrtou Cyprus 35°18N 33°4E 207 E9
Çamlıca Turkey 41°1N 29°3E 122 B2
Çamlıyayla Turkey 37°10N 34°36E 250 A5
Cammal U.S.A. 41°24N 77°28W 312 E7
Cammarata Italy 37°38N 13°38E 200 E6
Cammin = Kamień Pomorski Poland 53°57N 14°43E 184 E1
Camo Ethiopia 4°29N 38°24E 266 D4
Camocim Brazil 2°55S 40°50W 332 B3
Camonica, Val Italy 46°0N 10°20E 198 B7
Camooweal Australia 19°56S 138°7E 280 B2
Camooweal Caves △ Australia 20°1S 138°11E 280 C2

Camopi Fr. Guiana 3°12N 52°17W 329 C7
Camopi → Fr. Guiana 3°10N 52°20W 329 C7
Camorta India 8°8N 93°30E 245 K11
Camotes Is. Phil. 10°40N 124°24E 233 F5
Camotes Sea Phil. 10°30N 124°15E 233 F5
Camp Coulter = Powell U.S.A. 44°45N 108°46W 304 D9
Camp Hill Ala., U.S.A. 32°48N 85°39W 316 C4
Camp Hill Pa., U.S.A. 40°14N 76°55W 312 F8
Camp Nelson U.S.A. 36°8N 118°39W 307 J8
Camp Nou F.C. Barcelona Spain 41°22N 2°7E 114 A1
Camp Pendleton U.S.A. 33°13N 117°24W 307 M9
Camp Point U.S.A. 40°3N 91°4W 310 D5
Camp Springs U.S.A. 38°48N 76°55W 143 C3
Camp Verde U.S.A. 34°34N 111°51W 305 J8
Camp Wood U.S.A. 29°40N 100°1W 314 G4
Campagna Italy 40°40N 15°6E 201 B8
Campamento Spain 40°23N 3°46W 127 B1
Campana Argentina 34°10S 58°55W 334 C4
Campana, I. Chile 48°20S 75°20W 336 C1
Campanário Madeira 32°39N 17°2W 153 c
Campanario Spain 38°52N 5°36W 195 G5
Campanet Spain 39°46N 2°58E 206 B3
Campánia □ Italy 41°0N 14°30E 201 B7
Campas del Tuyú △ Argentina 36°17S 56°50W 334 D4
Campbell Northern Cape, S. Africa 28°48S 23°44E 270 C3
Campbell Calif., U.S.A. 37°17N 121°57W 306 H5
Campbell Fla., U.S.A. 28°16N 81°27W 317 G8
Campbell Ohio, U.S.A. 41°5N 80°37W 312 E4
Campbell, C. N.Z. 41°47S 174°18E 285 B9
Campbell I. Pac. Oc. 52°30S 169°0E 288 N8
Campbell L. Canada 63°14N 106°55W 297 E7
Campbell Plateau S. Ocean 50°0S 170°0E 151 A11
Campbell River Canada 50°5N 125°20W 296 C3
Campbellfield Australia 37°41S 144°57E 128 A1
Campbellford Canada 44°18N 77°48W 312 B7
Campbellpur Pakistan 33°46N 72°26E 242 C5
Campbellsburg U.S.A. 38°39N 86°16W 311 F10
Campbellsville U.S.A. 37°21N 85°20W 309 G11
Campbellton N.B., Canada 47°57N 66°43W 299 C6
Campbellton Fla., U.S.A. 30°57N 85°24W 316 E4
Campbelltown = Bluff N.Z. 46°37S 168°20E 285 G3
Campbelltown Australia 34°4S 150°49E 283 C9
Campbeltown U.K. 55°26N 5°36W 167 F3
Campêche Guadeloupe 16°26N 61°26W 322 e
Campeche Campeche, Mexico 19°51N 90°32W 319 D6
Campeche □ Mexico 19°0N 90°30W 319 D6
Campeche, Banco Mexico 22°30N 88°0W 319 C7
Campeche, Golfo de Mexico 19°30N 93°0W 319 D6
Câmpeni Romania 46°22N 23°3E 182 D8
Camperdown N.S.W., Australia 33°53S 151°11E 139 B2
Camperdown Vic., Australia 38°14S 143°9E 282 E5
Camperville Canada 51°59N 100°9W 297 C8
Campi Salentina Italy 40°24N 18°1E 201 B11
Câmpia Turzii Romania 46°34N 23°53E 183 D8
Campidano Italy 39°30N 8°47E 200 C1
Campidoglio, Piazza de Rome, Italy 136 c3
Campiglia Maríttima Italy 43°4N 10°37E 198 E7
Campillo de Altobuey Spain 39°36N 1°49W 197 F3
Campillos Spain 37°4N 4°51W 195 H6
Câmpina Romania 45°10N 25°45E 183 E10
Campina Grande Brazil 7°20S 35°47W 332 C4
Campina Verde Brazil 19°31S 49°28W 333 E2
Campinas Brazil 22°50S 47°0W 335 A6
Campione Italy 45°58N 8°58E 175 C12
Campli Italy 42°43N 13°41E 199 F10
Campo = Ntem → Cameroon 2°21N 9°49E 264 B2
Campo Cameroon 2°22N 9°50E 264 B1
Campo Spain 42°25N 0°24E 196 C5
Campo, Casa de Spain 40°25N 3°45W 127 B1
Campo △ Cameroon 2°23N 10°5E 264 B2
Campo Belo Brazil 20°52S 45°16W 333 F2
Campo de Criptana Spain 39°24N 3°7W 195 F7
Campo de Diauarum Brazil 11°12S 53°14W 331 C7
Campo de Gibraltar Spain 36°15N 5°25W 195 J5
Campo de los Alisos △ Argentina 27°15S 66°0W 334 B2
Campo Florido Brazil 19°47S 48°35W 333 E2
Campo Formoso = Campo Florido Brazil 19°47S 48°35W 333 E2
Campo Formoso Brazil 10°30S 40°20W 332 D3
Campo Grande Brazil 20°25S 54°40W 331 E7
Campo Grando Portugal 38°45N 9°9W 126 A2
Campo Maior Brazil 4°50S 42°12W 332 B3
Campo Maior Portugal 39°2N 7°7W 195 F3
Campo Mourão Brazil 24°3S 52°22W 335 A5
Campo Pequeño Portugal 38°44N 9°8W 126 A2
Campo Santa Margherita Venice, Italy 142 b2
Campo Túres Italy 46°53N 11°55E 199 B8
Campoalegre Colombia 2°41N 75°20W 328 C2
Campobasso Italy 41°34N 14°39E 201 A7
Campobello di Licata Italy 37°15N 13°55E 200 E6
Campobello di Mazara Italy 37°38N 12°45E 200 E5
Campofelice di Roccella Italy 37°59N 13°53E 200 E6
Campolide Portugal 38°43N 9°9W 126 A2
Campomarino Italy 41°57N 15°2E 199 G12
Camporeale Italy 37°54N 13°6E 200 E6
Camporrobles Spain 39°39N 1°24W 196 F3
Campos Brazil 21°50S 41°20W 333 F3
Campos Spain 39°26N 3°1E 206 B4
Campos Altos Brazil 19°47S 46°10W 333 E2
Campos Belos Brazil 13°10S 47°3W 333 D2
Campos del Paraíso = Carrascosa del Campo Spain 40°2N 2°45W 196 E2
Campos Novos Brazil 27°21S 51°50W 335 B5
Campos Sales Brazil 7°4S 40°23W 332 C3
Camprodon Spain 42°19N 2°23E 196 C7
Camps Bay S. Africa 33°57S 18°23E 118 A1
Campton Fla., U.S.A. 30°53N 86°31W 317 E3
Campton Ga., U.S.A. 33°52N 83°43W 316 B6
Campton Ky., U.S.A. 37°44N 83°33W 311 G13
Camptonville U.S.A. 39°27N 121°3W 306 F5
Camptown U.S.A. 41°44N 76°14W 313 E8
Câmpulung Romania 45°17N 25°3E 183 E10
Câmpulung Moldovenesc Romania 47°32N 25°30E 183 C10
Câmpuri Romania 46°0N 26°50E 183 D11
Campuya → Peru 1°40S 73°30W 328 D3
Campville U.S.A. 29°40N 82°7W 316 F7
Camrose Canada 53°0N 112°50W 296 C6
Camsell Portage Canada 59°37N 109°15W 297 B7
Camucuio Angola 14°7S 13°15E 265 E2
Camuy Puerto Rico 18°29N 66°51W 321 b
Çamyuva Turkey 36°30N 30°30E 205 E12
Çan Turkey 40°2N 27°3E 203 F11
Can Clavo Spain 38°57N 1°27E 206 D1
Can Creu Spain 38°58N 1°28E 206 D1
Can Gio Vietnam 10°25N 106°58E 237 G6
Can Pastilla Spain 39°32N 2°42E 206 B3
C'an San Joan Spain 41°28N 2°11E 114 A2
Can Tho Vietnam 10°2N 105°46E 237 G5
Canaan Trin. & Tob. 11°9N 60°49W 323 s
Canaan Conn., U.S.A. 42°2N 73°20W 313 D11
Canaan Hill Jamaica 18°23N 77°14W 320 a
Cañacao B. Phil. 14°29N 120°54E 127 C1
Canacona India 15°1N 74°4E 245 G2
Canada ■ N. Amer. 60°0N 100°0W 294 G11
Canada Abyssal Plain Arctic 80°0N 140°0W 150 B18
Canada Basin Arctic 75°0N 145°0W 150 B18
Cañada de Gómez Argentina 32°40S 61°30W 334 C3
Canadian U.S.A. 35°55N 100°23W 314 D4
Canadian → U.S.A. 35°28N 95°3W 314 D7
Canadian Shield Canada 53°0N 75°0W 292 D12
Canadys U.S.A. 33°3N 80°37W 316 B9
Canajoharie U.S.A. 42°54N 74°35W 313 D10
Çanakkale Turkey 40°8N 26°24E 203 F10
Çanakkale □ Turkey 40°10N 26°25E 203 F10
Çanakkale Boğazı Turkey 40°17N 26°32E 203 F10
Canal Flats Canada 50°10N 115°48W 296 C5
Canal Grande Venice, Italy 142 b2
Canal Point U.S.A. 26°52N 80°38W 317 J9
Canal Street New Orleans, U.S.A. 131 b2
Canala N. Cal. 21°32S 165°57E 288 d
Canalejas Argentina 35°15S 66°34W 334 D2
Canals Argentina 33°35S 62°53W 334 C3
Canals Spain 38°58N 0°35W 197 G4
Canandaigua U.S.A. 42°54N 77°17W 312 D7
Canandaigua L. U.S.A. 42°47N 77°19W 312 D7
Cananea Mexico 31°0N 110°18W 318 A2
Cañar Ecuador 2°33S 78°56W 328 D2
Cañar □ Ecuador 2°30S 79°0W 328 D2
Canarias, Is. Atl. Oc. 28°30N 16°0W 153 e1
Canaries St. Lucia 13°55N 61°4W 323 m
Canarreos, Arch. de los Cuba 21°35N 81°40W 320 B3
Canarsie U.S.A. 40°38N 73°53W 132 C2
Canary Is. = Canarias, Is. Atl. Oc. 28°30N 16°0W 153 e1
Canary Wharf U.K. 51°30N 0°1W 125 A3
Canaseraga U.S.A. 42°27N 77°45W 312 D7
Canastra, Serra da Brazil 20°0S 46°20W 333 F2
Canatlán Mexico 24°31N 104°47W 318 C4
Cañaveral Peru 3°56S 80°39W 328 D1
Canaveral, C. U.S.A. 28°27N 80°32W 317 G9
Canaveral △ U.S.A. 28°28N 80°34W 317 G9
Cañaveruelas Spain 40°24N 2°38W 196 E2
Canavieiras Brazil 15°39S 39°0W 333 E4
Canbelego Australia 31°32S 146°18E 283 A7
Canberra Australia 35°15S 149°8E 283 D8
Canby Calif., U.S.A. 41°27N 120°52W 304 F3
Canby Minn., U.S.A. 44°43N 96°16W 308 C5
Canby Oreg., U.S.A. 45°16N 122°42W 306 E4
Cancale France 48°40N 1°50W 172 D5
Cancelleria, Palazzo dei Rome, Italy 136 c2
Canche → France 50°31N 1°39E 173 B8
Canchungo = Teixeira Pinto Guinea-Biss. 12°3N 16°0W 262 C1
Canchungo Guinea-Biss. 12°26N 16°5W 262 C1
Canchyuaya, Cordillera de Peru 7°30S 74°0W 330 B3
Cancún Mexico 21°8N 86°44W 319 C7
Candanchú Spain 42°47N 0°32W 196 C4
Candarave Peru 17°15S 70°13W 330 D3
Çandarlı Turkey 38°56N 26°56E 205 C8
Çandarlı Körfezi Turkey 38°52N 26°55E 205 C8
Candás Spain 43°35N 5°45W 194 B5
Candé France 47°34N 1°2W 172 E5
Candeias → Brazil 8°39S 63°31W 331 B5
Candela Italy 41°8N 15°31E 201 A8
Candelaria Argentina 27°29S 55°44W 335 B4
Candelaria Canary Is. 28°22N 16°22W 153 e1
Candelaria Phil. 13°56N 121°25E 232 E3
Candelario △ Spain 40°20N 5°46W 194 E5
Candeleda Spain 40°10N 5°14W 194 E5
Candelo Australia 36°47S 149°43E 283 D8
Candi Dasa Indonesia 8°30S 115°34E 231 J18
Candia = Iraklio Greece 35°20N 25°12E 207 E6
Candia, Sea of = Crete, Sea of Greece 36°0N 25°0E 205 E7
Candiac Canada 45°23N 73°29W 130 B3
Cândido de Abreu Brazil 24°35S 51°20W 333 F1
Cândido Mendes Brazil 1°27S 45°43W 332 B2
Candle U.S.A. 65°55N 161°56W 303 D7
Candle L. Canada 53°50N 105°18W 297 C7
Candlemas I. Antarctica 57°3S 26°40W 151 B1
Candler-McAfee U.S.A. 33°44N 84°16W 113 B3
Cando U.S.A. 48°32N 99°12W 308 A4
Candon Phil. 17°12N 120°27E 232 C3
Canea = Chania Greece 35°30N 24°4E 207 E5
Caneças Portugal 38°48N 9°13W 126 A1
Canefield Dominica 15°20N 61°24W 323 k
Canela Brazil 10°15S 48°25W 332 D2
Canelles → St. Lucia 13°47N 60°55W 323 m
Canelli Italy 44°43N 8°17E 198 D5
Canelones Uruguay 34°32S 56°17W 335 C4
Canet de Mar Spain 41°35N 2°35E 196 D7
Canet-Plage France 42°41N 3°2E 174 F7
Cañete Chile 37°50S 73°30W 334 D1
Cañete Spain 40°3N 1°54W 196 E3
Cañete de las Torres Spain 37°53N 4°19W 195 H6
Cangamba Angola 13°40S 19°54E 265 E3
Cangandala Angola 9°45S 16°33E 265 D3
Cangandala △ Angola 9°53S 16°42E 265 D3
Cangas Spain 42°16N 8°47W 194 C2
Cangas de Onís Spain 43°21N 5°8W 194 B5
Cangas de Tineo = Cangas del Narcea Spain 43°10N 6°32W 194 B4
Cangas del Narcea Spain 43°10N 6°32W 194 B4
Cangnan China 27°30N 120°23E 229 D13
Cangoa Angola 13°8S 18°30E 265 E3
Cangola Angola 7°58S 15°53E 265 D3
Cangolo Angola 15°0S 13°52E 265 E2
Cangombe Angola 14°24S 19°59E 265 E3
Cangongo Angola 9°24S 17°30E 265 D3
Cangshan China 34°50N 118°2E 227 G10
Canguaretama Brazil 6°20S 35°5W 332 C4
Canguçu Brazil 31°22S 52°43W 335 C5
Canguçu, Serra do Brazil 31°20S 52°40W 335 C5
Cangumbe Angola 11°58S 19°12E 265 E3
Cangxi China 31°47N 105°59E 228 B5
Cangyuan China 23°12N 99°14E 228 F2
Cangzhou China 38°19N 116°52E 226 E9
Canhoca Angola 9°15S 14°41E 265 D2
Cani, I. Tunisia 36°21N 10°5E 258 A2
Caniapiscau → Canada 56°40N 69°30W 299 A6
Caniapiscau, L. Canada 54°10N 69°55W 299 B6
Caniçal Madeira 32°44N 16°43W 153 c
Canicattì Italy 37°21N 13°51E 200 E6
Canicattini Bagni Italy 37°2N 15°4E 201 E8
Canigao Channel Phil. 10°15N 124°42E 233 F5
Canigou France 42°31N 2°27E 174 F6
Caniles Spain 37°26N 2°43W 195 H8
Canillas Spain 40°27N 3°38W 127 B2
Canillejas Spain 40°26N 3°36W 127 B2
Canim Lake Canada 51°47N 120°54W 296 C4
Canindé Brazil 4°22S 39°19W 332 B4
Canindé → Brazil 6°15S 42°52W 332 C3
Canindeyu □ Paraguay 24°10S 55°0W 335 A5
Canino Italy 42°28N 11°45E 199 F8
Canisteo U.S.A. 42°16N 77°36W 312 D7
Canisteo → U.S.A. 42°7N 77°8W 312 D7
Cañitas de Felipe Pescador Mexico 23°36N 102°43W 318 C4
Cañizal Spain 41°12N 5°22W 194 D5
Canjáyar Spain 37°1N 2°44W 195 H8
Canjinge Angola 10°12S 21°17E 265 E4
Çankırı Turkey 40°40N 33°37E 212 B5
Çankırı □ Turkey 40°40N 33°30E 212 B5
Cankuzo Burundi 3°10S 30°31E 268 C3
Canlaon Phil. 10°22N 123°12E 233 F4
Canlaon Volcano Phil. 10°25N 123°8E 233 F4
Canmore Canada 51°7N 115°18W 296 C5
Cann River Australia 37°35S 149°7E 283 D8
Canna U.K. 57°3N 6°33W 167 D2
Cannanore = Kannur India 11°53N 75°27E 245 J2
Cannanore Is. India 10°30N 72°30E 245 J1
Cannaregio Venice, Italy 142 a2
Cannaregio, Canale di Venice, Italy 142 a2
Cannelton U.S.A. 37°55N 86°45W 311 G10
Cannery, The San Francisco, U.S.A. 136 a1
Cannes France 43°32N 7°1E 175 E11
Canning Town = Port Canning India 22°23N 88°40E 243 H13
Canning Town U.K. 51°30N 0°1E 125 A4
Cannington Canada 44°20N 79°2W 312 B5
Cannóbio Italy 46°4N 8°42E 198 B5
Cannock U.K. 52°41N 2°1W 169 E5
Cannonball → U.S.A. 46°26N 100°35W 308 B3
Cannondale Mt. Australia 25°13S 148°57E 280 D4
Cannonsville Res. U.S.A. 42°4N 75°22W 313 D9
Cannonvale Australia 20°17S 148°43E 280 b
Caño Colorado Colombia 2°18N 68°22W 328 C4
Canoas Brazil 29°56S 51°11W 335 B5
Canoe L. Canada 55°10N 108°15W 297 B7
Cañon City U.S.A. 38°27N 105°14W 304 G11
Cañón de Río Blanco △ Mexico 18°43N 97°15W 319 D5
Cañón del Río Lobos △ Spain 41°46N 3°28W 194 D7
Canonnier, Pte. du St.-Martin 18°4N 63°7W 322 a
Canonniers Pt. Mauritius 20°2S 57°32E 272 e
Canoochee → U.S.A. 31°59N 81°19W 316 D8
Canopus Australia 33°29S 140°42E 282 B4
Canora Canada 51°40N 102°30W 297 C8
Canosa di Púglia Italy 41°13N 16°4E 201 A9
Canouan St. Vincent 12°43N 61°20W 323 p
Canowindra Australia 33°35S 148°38E 283 B8
Canso Canada 45°20N 61°0W 299 C7
Canso, Str. of Canada 45°37N 61°22W 299 C7
Canta Peru 11°29S 76°37W 330 C2
Cantabria □ Spain 43°10N 4°0W 194 B7
Cantabria, Sierra de Spain 42°40N 2°30W 196 C2
Cantabrian Mts. = Cantábrica, Cordillera Spain 43°0N 5°10W 194 C5
Cantábrica, Cordillera Spain 43°0N 5°10W 194 C5
Cantal □ France 45°5N 2°45E 174 C6
Cantal, Plomb du France 45°3N 2°45E 174 C6
Cantanhede Portugal 40°20N 8°36W 194 E2
Cantaura Venezuela 9°19N 64°21W 329 B5
Cantavieja Spain 40°31N 0°25W 196 E4
Čantavir Serbia 45°55N 19°46E 182 E4
Cantemir Moldova 46°17N 28°14E 183 D13
Canteras de Vallecas Spain 40°20N 3°37W 127 B2
Canterbury = Invermere Canada 50°30N 116°2W 296 C5
Canterbury N.S.W., Australia 33°55S 151°7E 139 B1
Canterbury Queens., Australia 25°23S 141°53E 280 D3
Canterbury Vic., Australia 37°49S 145°4E 128 A2
Canterbury Kent, U.K. 51°16N 1°6E 169 F9
Canterbury □ N.Z. 43°45S 171°19E 285 D6
Canterbury Bight N.Z. 44°16S 171°55E 285 E6
Canterbury Plains N.Z. 43°55S 171°22E 285 D6
Cantil U.S.A. 35°18N 117°58W 307 K9
Cantilan Phil. 9°20N 125°58E 233 G5
Cantillana Spain 37°36N 5°50W 195 H5
Canto do Buriti Brazil 8°7S 42°58W 332 C3
Canton = Guangzhou China 23°6N 113°13E 121 B2
Canton Ga., U.S.A. 34°14N 84°29W 315 D12
Canton Ill., U.S.A. 40°33N 90°2W 310 D6
Canton Miss., U.S.A. 32°37N 90°2W 315 E9
Canton Mo., U.S.A. 40°8N 91°32W 310 D5
Canton N.Y., U.S.A. 44°36N 75°10W 313 B9
Canton Ohio, U.S.A. 40°48N 81°23W 312 F3
Canton Pa., U.S.A. 41°39N 76°51W 312 E8
Canton S. Dak., U.S.A. 43°18N 96°35W 308 D5
Canton L. U.S.A. 36°6N 98°35W 314 C5
Canton Tower China 23°6N 113°19E 121 B2
Cantonment U.S.A. 30°37N 87°20W 317 E2
Cantù Italy 45°44N 9°8E 198 C6
Cantwell U.S.A. 63°24N 148°57W 303 E10
Canudos Brazil 7°13S 58°5W 331 B6
Canumã Amazonas, Brazil 4°2S 59°4W 329 D6
Canumã Amazonas, Brazil 6°8S 60°10W 331 B5
Canumã → Brazil 3°55S 59°10W 331 A6
Canunda △ Australia 37°42S 140°16E 282 D4
Canutama Brazil 6°30S 64°20W 331 B5
Canutillo U.S.A. 31°55N 106°36W 314 F1
Canvey Island U.K. 51°31N 0°37E 169 F8
Canyon U.S.A. 34°59N 101°55W 314 D4
Canyon De Chelly △ U.S.A. 36°10N 109°20W 305 H9
Canyonlands △ U.S.A. 38°15N 110°0W 305 G9
Canyons of the Ancients △ U.S.A. 37°30N 108°55W 305 H9
Canyonville U.S.A. 42°56N 123°17W 304 E2
Canzar Angola 7°35S 21°34E 265 D4
Cao Bang Vietnam 22°40N 106°15E 228 F6
Cao He → China 40°10N 124°32E 227 D13
Cao Lanh Vietnam 10°27N 105°38E 237 G5
Cao Xian China 34°50N 115°35E 226 G8
Caofeidian China 38°56N 118°32E 227 E10
Caoheijing China 31°10N 121°25E 138 B1
Caombo Angola 8°42S 16°33E 265 D3
Cáorle Italy 45°36N 12°53E 199 C9
Cap-aux-Meules Canada 47°23N 61°52W 299 C7
Cap-Chat Canada 49°6N 66°40W 299 C6
Cap-de-la-Madeleine Canada 46°22N 72°31W 298 C5
Cap-de-Ville Trin. & Tob. 10°9N 61°42W 323 t
Cap-Haïtien Haiti 19°40N 72°20W 321 C5
Cap I. Phil. 5°57N 120°6E 233 J3
Cap Pt. St. Lucia 14°7N 60°57W 323 m
Capac U.S.A. 43°1N 82°56W 312 C2
Capáccio Italy 40°25N 15°5E 201 B8
Capaci Italy 38°10N 13°14E 200 D6
Capaia Angola 8°27S 20°13E 265 D4
Capalonga Phil. 14°20N 122°30E 232 D4
Capanaparo → Venezuela 7°1N 67°7W 328 B4
Capanema Brazil 1°12S 47°11W 332 B2
Capangombe Angola 15°6S 13°8E 265 F2
Capánnori Italy 43°50N 10°34E 198 E7
Capão Redondo Brazil 23°39S 46°45W 137 B1
Caparaó △ Brazil 20°25S 41°46W 333 F3
Caparica Portugal 38°40N 9°9W 126 A2
Caparica, Costa da Portugal 38°38N 9°15W 126 B1
Caparo → Trin. & Tob. 10°31N 61°28W 323 t
Capas Phil. 15°38N 120°28E 232 D3
Capatárida Venezuela 11°11N 70°37W 328 A3
Capayas Phil. 10°28N 119°39E 233 F2
Capbreton France 43°39N 1°26W 174 E2
Capdenac France 44°34N 2°5E 174 D6
Capdepera Spain 39°42N 3°26E 206 B4
Cape → Australia 20°59S 146°51E 280 C4
Cape Arid △ Australia 33°58S 123°13E 279 F3
Cape Barren I. Australia 40°25S 148°15E 281 G4
Cape Basin Atl. Oc. 38°0S 7°0W 152 K12
Cape Breton Highlands △ Canada 46°50N 60°40W 299 C7
Cape Breton I. Canada 46°0N 60°30W 299 C7
Cape Canaveral U.S.A. 28°24N 80°36W 317 G9
Cape Charles U.S.A. 37°16N 76°1W 309 G15
Cape Coast Ghana 5°5N 1°15W 263 D4
Cape Cod △ U.S.A. 41°56N 70°6W 309 E18
Cape Coral U.S.A. 26°33N 81°57W 317 J8
Cape Crawford Australia 16°41S 135°43E 280 B2
Cape Dorset = Kinngait Canada 64°14N 76°32W 295 E16
Cape Fear → U.S.A. 33°53N 78°1W 315 E15
Cape Flats S. Africa 34°3S 18°33E 118 B2
Cape Girardeau U.S.A. 37°19N 89°32W 308 G9
Cape Hatteras △ U.S.A. 35°30N 75°28W 315 D17
Cape Hillsborough △ Australia 20°54S 149°2E 280 b
Cape Jervis Australia 35°40S 138°5E 282 C3
Cape Krusenstern △ U.S.A. 67°30N 163°30W 303 C7
Cape Lambert Australia 20°36S 117°11E 278 D2
Cape Le Grand △ Australia 33°54S 122°26E 279 F3
Cape Lisburne = Wevok U.S.A. 68°53N 166°13W 303 B6
Cape Lookout △ U.S.A. 35°45N 76°25W 315 D16
Cape May U.S.A. 38°56N 74°56W 309 F16
Cape May Point U.S.A. 38°56N 74°58W 309 F16
Cape Melville △ Australia 14°26S 144°28E 280 A3
Cape Mount △ Liberia 6°44N 11°24W 262 D2
Cape Pole U.S.A. 55°58N 133°48W 303 J14
Cape Range △ Australia 22°3S 114°0E 278 D1
Cape St. George Canada 48°28N 59°14W 299 C8
Cape Tormentine Canada 46°8N 63°47W 299 C7
Cape Town S. Africa 33°55S 18°22E 118 A1
Cape Town Int. ✈ (CPT) S. Africa 33°58S 18°35E 118 A2
Cape Upstart △ Australia 19°45S 147°48E 280 B4
Cape Verde Abyssal Plain Atl. Oc. 23°0N 26°0W 152 D9
Cape Verde Is. = Cabo Verde ■ Atl. Oc. 16°0N 24°0W 153 j
Cape Verde Is. Atl. Oc. 16°0N 24°0W 153 j
Cape Verde Plateau Atl. Oc. 18°0N 20°0W 152 E10
Cape Vincent U.S.A. 44°8N 76°20W 313 B8
Cape Yakataga U.S.A. 60°4N 142°26W 303 F12
Cape York Peninsula Australia 12°0S 142°30E 286 F2
Capela Brazil 10°30S 37°0W 332 D4
Capelas Azores 37°50N 25°41W 153 d3
Capele Angola 13°39S 14°53E 265 E2
Capelengue Angola 8°53S 19°42E 265 D3
Capelinha Brazil 17°42S 42°31W 333 E3
Capelinhos, Pta. dos Azores 38°36N 28°50W 153 d1
Capella Australia 23°2S 148°1E 280 C4
Capella, Mt. Papua N. G. 5°4S 141°8E 286 C1
Capelongo Angola 14°54S 15°8E 265 E3
Capenda Camulemba Angola 9°24S 18°27E 265 D3
Capendu France 43°11N 2°31E 174 E6
Capertree Australia 33°6S 149°58E 283 B8
Capestang France 43°20N 3°2E 174 E7
Capesterre, Grande Rivière de la → Guadeloupe 16°3N 61°33W 322 e
Capesterre, Pte. de la Guadeloupe 16°3N 61°33W 322 e
Capesterre-Belle-Eau Guadeloupe 16°4N 61°36W 322 e
Capesterre-de-Marie-Galante Guadeloupe 15°53N 61°14W 322 e
Capim → Brazil 1°40S 47°47W 332 B2
Capinópolis Brazil 18°41S 49°35W 333 E2
Capinota Bolivia 17°43S 66°14W 330 D4
Capira Panama 8°45N 79°53W 328 B2
Capistrello Italy 41°57N 13°23E 199 G10
Capitan U.S.A. 33°35N 105°35W 305 K11
Capitán Aracena, I. Chile 54°10S 71°20W 336 D2
Capitán Arturo Prat Antarctica 63°0S 61°0W 151 C17
Capitán Pastene Chile 38°13S 73°1W 336 A2
Capitão de Campos Brazil 4°40S 41°55W 332 B3
Capitol Heights U.S.A. 38°52N 76°55W 143 B3
Capitol Hill N. Marianas 15°13N 145°45E 302 e
Capitol Reef △ U.S.A. 38°15N 111°10W 305 G8
Capitola U.S.A. 36°59N 121°57W 306 J5
Capitolini, Musei Rome, Italy 136 c3
Capivara, Serra da Brazil 14°35S 45°0W 333 D3
Capiz □ Phil. 11°35N 122°30E 233 F4
Capizzi Italy 37°51N 14°29E 201 E7
Capoche → Mozam. 15°35S 33°0E 269 F3
Capodichino, Nápoli ✈ (NAP) Italy 40°53N 14°16E 201 B7
Capodistria = Koper Slovenia 45°31N 13°44E 199 C10
Capoeira Brazil 5°37S 59°33W 331 B6
Capolo Angola 10°22S 14°7E 265 E2
Caporetto = Kobarid Slovenia 46°15N 13°30E 199 B10
Caporolo → Angola 12°56S 12°58E 265 E2
Capot → Martinique 14°50N 61°5W 322 j
Capoterra Italy 39°11N 8°58E 200 C1
Cappadocia Turkey 39°0N 35°0E 212 C6
Capps U.S.A. 30°24N 83°54W 316 E6
Capraia Italy 43°2N 9°50E 198 E6
Caprara, Pta. Italy 41°7N 8°19E 200 A1
Caprarola Italy 42°19N 12°14E 199 F9
Caprera Italy 41°12N 9°28E 200 A2
Capri Italy 40°33N 14°14E 201 B7
Capricorn Coast Australia 23°16S 150°49E 280 C5
Capricorn Group Australia 23°30S 151°55E 280 C5
Capricorn Ra. Australia 23°20S 116°50E 278 D2
Caprino Veronese Italy 45°36N 10°47E 198 C7
Caprivi △ Namibia 17°55S 22°37E 270 A3
Caprivi Strip Namibia 18°0S 23°0E 270 A3
Caps et Marais d'Opale △ France 50°40N 2°0E 173 B9
Captain Cook U.S.A. 19°30N 155°55W 302 D6
Captain Cook Bridge Australia 34°0S 151°7E 139 C1
Captain Cook Landing Place Park Australia 34°1S 151°14E 139 C2
Captains Flat Australia 35°35S 149°27E 283 C8
Captieux France 44°18N 0°16W 174 D3
Captiva U.S.A. 26°31N 82°11W 317 J7
Capuça Angola 17°22S 21°18E 265 F4
Capuchos Portugal 38°38N 9°16W 126 B1
Capucin Dominica 15°38N 61°28W 323 k
Capul I. Phil. 12°26N 124°10E 232 E5
Capulin Volcano △ U.S.A. 36°47N 103°58W 314 C3
Capunda Angola 10°41S 17°23E 265 E3
Caquetá □ Colombia 1°0N 74°0W 328 C3
Caquetá → Colombia 1°15S 69°15W 328 D4
Car Nicobar India 9°10N 92°47E 245 K11
Cara-Paraná → Colombia 1°45S 73°13W 328 D3
Carabanchel Alto Spain 40°22N 3°44W 127 B1
Carabanchel Bajo Spain 40°23N 3°44W 127 B1
Carabao I. Phil. 12°4N 121°56E 232 E3
Carabobo □ Venezuela 10°10N 68°5W 328 A4
Caracal Romania 44°8N 24°22E 183 F9
Caracarai Brazil 1°50N 61°8W 329 C5
Caracas Venezuela 10°30N 66°55W 328 A4
Caracol Belize 16°45N 89°6W 320 C2
Caracol Mato Grosso do Sul, Brazil 22°18S 57°1W 334 A4
Caracol Piauí, Brazil 9°15S 43°22W 332 C3
Caracoli, Pte. Martinique 14°45N 60°52W 322 j
Caracollo Bolivia 17°39S 67°10W 330 D4
Caraga Phil. 7°20N 126°34E 233 H6
Caraga □ Phil. 9°40N 125°30E 233 G6
Caragabal Australia 33°49S 147°45E 283 B7
Caráglio Italy 44°25N 7°26E 198 D4
Carahue Chile 38°43S 73°12W 336 A2
Caraí Brazil 17°12S 41°42W 333 E3
Caraïbes, Mts. Guadeloupe 15°58N 61°41W 322 e
Carajás Brazil 2°57S 51°22W 332 C1
Carajás, Serra dos Brazil 6°0S 51°30W 332 C1
Caral Peru 10°53S 77°31W 330 C2
Caramoan Phil. 13°46N 123°52E 232 E4
Caramoan Pen. Phil. 13°47N 123°44E 232 E4
Caramoran Phil. 14°0N 124°8E 232 D5
Caranapatuba Brazil 6°38S 62°34W 331 B5
Carandaiti Bolivia 20°45S 63°4W 331 E5
Carangola Brazil 20°44S 42°5W 333 F3
Caransebeş Romania 45°28N 22°18E 182 E7
Carantec France 48°40N 3°55W 172 D3
Carapachay Argentina 34°31S 58°32W 137 B1
Carapichaima Trin. & Tob. 10°28N 61°27W 323 t
Carapo → Barinas, Venezuela 7°46N 70°23W 328 B3
Carapo → Bolívar, Venezuela 7°30N 64°0W 329 B5
Carapuse B. Trin. & Tob. 11°14N 60°35W 323 s
Caraquet Canada 47°48N 64°57W 299 C6
Caraş Severin □ Romania 45°10N 22°10E 182 E7
Caraşova Romania 45°11N 21°51E 182 E6
Caratasca, L. de Honduras 15°20N 83°40W 320 C3
Caratinga Brazil 19°50S 42°10W 333 E3
Carauari Brazil 4°52S 66°54W 328 D4
Caraúbas Brazil 5°43S 37°33W 332 C4
Caravaca de la Cruz Spain 38°8N 1°52W 197 G3
Caravággio Italy 45°30N 9°38E 198 C6
Caravela Guinea-Biss. 11°30N 16°30W 262 C1
Caravelas Brazil 17°45S 39°15W 333 E4
Caraveli Peru 15°45S 73°25W 330 D3
Caravelle, Presqu'île de la Martinique 14°46N 60°48W 322 j
Caraz Peru 9°3S 77°47W 330 B2
Caraza Argentina 34°41S 58°25W 117 C2
Carazinho Brazil 28°16S 52°46W 335 B5
Carbalia Moldova 45°52N 28°27E 183 E13
Carballino = O Carballiño Spain 42°26N 8°5W 194 C2
Carballo Spain 43°13N 8°41W 194 B2
Carberry Canada 49°50N 99°25W 297 D9
Carbet, Chutes du Guadeloupe 16°2N 61°38W 322 e
Carbet, Pitons du Martinique 14°40N 61°7W 322 j
Carbó Mexico 29°42N 110°58W 318 B2
Carbón, L. del Argentina 49°35S 68°21W 336 C3
Carbonara, C. Italy 39°6N 9°31E 200 C2
Carbondale Colo., U.S.A. 39°24N 107°13W 304 G10
Carbondale Ill., U.S.A. 37°44N 89°13W 310 G7
Carbondale Pa., U.S.A. 41°35N 75°30W 313 E9
Carbonear Canada 47°42N 53°13W 299 C9
Carboneras Spain 36°59N 1°53W 197 J3
Carboneras de Guadazaón Spain 39°54N 1°50W 196 F3
Carbónia Italy 39°10N 8°30E 200 C1
Carbonne France 43°18N 1°11E 174 E5
Carcabuey Spain 37°27N 4°17W 195 H6
Carcagente = Carcaixent Spain 39°8N 0°28W 197 F4
Carcaixent Spain 39°8N 0°28W 197 F4
Carcajou Canada 57°47N 117°6W 296 B5
Carcar Phil. 10°6N 123°38E 233 F4
Carcarana → Argentina 32°27S 60°48W 334 C3
Carcasse, C. Haiti 18°30N 74°28W 321 C5
Carcassonne France 43°13N 2°20E 174 E6
Carchi □ Ecuador 0°45N 78°0W 328 C2
Carcoar Australia 33°36S 149°8E 283 B8
Carcross Canada 60°13N 134°45W 296 A2
Çardak Çanakkale, Turkey 40°22N 26°43E 203 F10
Çardak Denizli, Turkey 37°49N 29°39E 205 D11
Cardamon Hills India 9°30N 77°15E 245 K3
Cardamon Mts. = Kravanh, Chuor Phnum Cambodia 12°0N 103°32E 237 G4
Cardeña Spain 38°16N 4°20W 195 G6
Cárdenas Cuba 23°0N 81°30W 320 B3
Cárdenas San Luis Potosí, Mexico 22°0N 99°38W 319 C5
Cárdenas Tabasco, Mexico 17°59N 93°22W 319 D6
Cardener → Spain 41°41N 1°51E 196 D6
Cardenete Spain 39°46N 1°41W 196 F3
Cardiel, L. Argentina 48°55S 71°10W 336 C2
Cardiff U.K. 51°29N 3°10W 169 F4
Cardiff □ U.K. 51°31N 3°12W 169 F4
Cardiff-by-the-Sea U.S.A. 33°1N 117°17W 307 M9
Cardigan U.K. 52°5N 4°40W 169 E3
Cardigan B. U.K. 52°30N 4°30W 169 E3
Cardinal Canada 44°47N 75°23W 313 B9
Cardón, Punta Venezuela 11°37N 70°14W 328 A3
Cardona Spain 41°56N 1°40E 196 D6
Cardona Uruguay 33°53S 57°18W 334 C4
Cardoso, Ilha do Brazil 25°8S 47°58W 335 B5
Cardston Canada 49°15N 113°20W 296 D6
Cardwell Australia 18°14S 146°2E 280 B4
Careen L. Canada 57°0N 108°11W 297 B7
Carei Romania 47°40N 22°29E 182 C7
Careiro Brazil 3°12S 59°45W 329 D6
Careme = Ciremai Indonesia 6°55S 108°27E 231 G13
Carenage Trin. & Tob. 10°41N 61°36W 323 t
Carentan France 49°19N 1°15W 172 C5
Carey Idaho, U.S.A. 43°19N 113°57W 304 E7
Carey Ohio, U.S.A. 40°57N 83°23W 311 D13
Carey, L. Australia 29°0S 122°15E 279 E3
Carey L. Canada 62°12N 102°55W 297 A8
Careysburg Liberia 6°34N 10°30W 262 D2
Cargados Carajos Ind. Oc. 17°0S 59°0E 273 F4
Cargèse France 42°7N 8°35E 175 F12
Carhaix-Plouguer France 48°18N 3°36W 172 D3
Carhuamayo Peru 10°51S 76°4W 330 C2
Carhuas Peru 9°15S 77°39W 330 B2
Carhué Argentina 37°10S 62°50W 334 D3
Caria Turkey 37°20N 28°10E 205 D10
Cariacica Brazil 20°16S 40°25W 333 F3
Cariaco Venezuela 10°29N 63°33W 329 A5
Cariango Angola 10°37S 15°20E 265 E3
Cariati Italy 39°30N 16°57E 201 C9
Caribbean Sea W. Indies 15°0N 75°0W 320 C4
Cariboo Mts. Canada 53°0N 121°0W 296 C4
Caribou U.S.A. 46°52N 68°1W 309 B19
Caribou → Man., Canada 59°20N 94°44W 297 B10
Caribou → N.W.T., Canada 61°27N 125°45W 296 A3
Caribou I. Canada 47°22N 85°49W 298 C2
Caribou Is. Canada 61°55N 113°15W 296 A6
Caribou L. Man., Canada 59°21N 96°10W 297 B9
Caribou L. Ont., Canada 50°25N 89°5W 298 B2
Caribou Mts. Canada 59°12N 115°40W 296 B5
Caribou River △ Canada 59°35N 96°35W 297 B9
Caribrod = Dimitrovgrad Serbia 43°2N 22°48E 202 C6
Carichic Mexico 27°56N 107°3W 318 B3
Caridad Phil. 14°28N 120°53E 127 C1
Carigara Phil. 11°18N 124°41E 233 F5
Carigara B. Phil. 11°22N 124°37E 233 F5
Carignan France 49°38N 5°10E 173 C12
Carignano Italy 44°55N 7°40E 198 D4
Carinda Australia 30°28S 147°41E 283 A7
Cariñena Spain 41°20N 1°13W 196 D3
Carinhanha Brazil 14°15S 44°46W 333 D3
Carinhanha → Brazil 14°20S 43°47W 333 D3
Carini Italy 38°8N 13°11E 200 D6
Cariño Spain 43°45N 7°52W 194 B3
Carinola Italy 41°11N 13°58E 200 A6
Carinthia = Kärnten □ Austria 46°52N 13°30E 180 E6
Carioca, Sa. da Brazil 22°57S 43°13W 135 B1
Caripito Venezuela 10°8N 63°6W 329 A5
Cariré Brazil 3°57S 40°27W 332 B3
Caritianas Brazil 9°20S 63°6W 331 B5
Carles Phil. 11°34N 123°8E 233 F4
Carlet Spain 39°14N 0°31W 197 F4
Carleton, Mt. Canada 47°23N 66°53W 299 C6
Carleton Place Canada 45°8N 76°9W 313 A8
Carletonville S. Africa 26°23S 27°22E 270 C4
Cârlibaba Romania 47°35N 25°8E 183 C10
Carlin U.S.A. 40°43N 116°7W 304 F5
Carlingford L. U.K. 54°3N 6°9W 166 B5
Carlini Base Antarctica 62°30S 58°0W 151 C18
Carlinville U.S.A. 39°17N 89°53W 310 E7
Carlisle Cumb., U.K. 54°54N 2°56W 168 C5
Carlisle Ind., U.S.A. 38°58N 87°24W 311 F9
Carlisle Ky., U.S.A. 38°19N 84°1W 311 F12
Carlisle Pa., U.S.A. 40°12N 77°12W 312 F7
Carlisle I. Australia 20°49S 149°18E 280 b
Carlit, Pic France 42°35N 1°55E 174 F5
Carloforte Italy 39°8N 8°18E 200 C1
Carlos Casares Argentina 35°32S 61°20W 334 D3
Carlos Chagas Brazil 17°43S 40°45W 333 E3
Carlos Tejedor Argentina 35°25S 62°25W 334 D3
Carlota I. Phil. 13°1N 121°53E 232 E3
Carlow Ireland 52°50N 6°56W 166 D5
Carlow □ Ireland 52°43N 6°50W 166 D5
Carlsbad = Karlovy Vary Czechia 50°13N 12°51E 180 A5
Carlsbad Calif., U.S.A. 33°10N 117°21W 307 M9
Carlsbad N. Mex., U.S.A. 32°25N 104°14W 305 K11
Carlsbad Caverns △ U.S.A. 32°10N 104°35W 305 K11
Carlsberg Ridge Ind. Oc. 1°0N 66°0E 273 D5
Carlstadt U.S.A. 40°50N 74°6W 132 A1
Carlton Australia 37°47S 144°57E 128 A1
Carlton Gardens Australia 37°48S 144°58E 128 A1
Carluke U.K. 55°45N 3°50W 167 F5
Carlyle Sask., Canada 49°40N 102°20W 297 D8
Carlyle Ill., U.S.A. 38°37N 89°22W 310 F7
Carlyle L. U.S.A. 38°37N 89°21W 310 F7
Carmacks Canada 62°5N 136°16W 294 E4
Carmagnola Italy 44°51N 7°43E 198 D4
Carman Canada 49°30N 98°0W 297 D9
Carmarthen U.K. 51°52N 4°19W 169 F3
Carmarthen B. U.K. 51°40N 4°30W 169 F3
Carmarthenshire □ U.K. 51°55N 4°13W 169 F3
Carmaux France 44°3N 2°10E 174 D6
Carmel Ind., U.S.A. 39°58N 86°7W 311 E10
Carmel N.Y., U.S.A. 41°26N 73°41W 313 E11
Carmel, Mt. = Ha Karmel, Har Israel 32°44N 35°3E 250 F5
Carmel-by-the-Sea U.S.A. 36°33N 121°55W 306 J5
Carmel Valley U.S.A. 36°29N 121°43W 306 J5
Carmelitane Scalze, Monastero Venice, Italy 142 a2
Carmelo Uruguay 34°0S 58°20W 334 C4
Carmen Bolivia 11°40S 67°51W 330 C4
Carmen Paraguay 27°13S 56°12W 335 B4
Carmen Bohol, Phil. 9°50N 124°12E 233 G5
Carmen Cebu, Phil. 10°35N 124°1E 233 F5
Carmen N. Cotabato, Phil. 7°13N 124°45E 233 H5
Carmen Venezuela 1°16N 66°52W 328 C4
Carmen, I. Mexico 25°57N 111°12W 318 B2
Carmen de Huechuraba Chile 33°20S 70°40W 137 B1
Carmen de la Legua -Reynosa Peru 12°3S 77°7W 124 B2
Carmen de Patagones Argentina 40°50S 63°0W 336 B4
Cármenes Spain 42°58N 5°34W 194 C5
Carmensa Argentina 35°15S 67°40W 334 D2
Carmi B.C., Canada 49°36N 119°8W 296 D5
Carmi Ill., U.S.A. 38°5N 88°10W 311 F8
Carmichael Village The Bahamas 25°0N 77°26W 153 b
Carmila Australia 21°55S 149°24E 280 C4
Carmini, Scuola dei Venice, Italy 142 b2
Carmona Costa Rica 10°0N 85°15W 320 E2
Carmona Spain 37°28N 5°42W 195 H5
Carn Ban U.K. 57°7N 4°15W 167 D4
Carn Eige U.K. 57°17N 5°8W 167 D3
Carnac France 47°35N 3°6W 172 E3
Carnamah Australia 29°41S 115°53E 279 E2
Carnarvon W. Austral., Australia 24°51S 113°42E 279 D1
Carnarvon Ont., Canada 45°3N 78°41W 312 A6
Carnarvon Northern Cape, S. Africa 30°56S 22°8E 270 D3
Carnarvon △ Australia 24°54S 148°2E 280 C4
Carnarvon Ra. Queens., Australia 25°15S 148°30E 280 D4
Carnarvon Ra. W. Austral., Australia 25°20S 120°45E 279 E3
Carnatic India 9°40N 77°50E 245 K3
Carnation U.S.A. 47°39N 121°55W 306 C5
Carnaxide Portugal 38°43N 9°14W 126 A1
Carncastle U.K. 54°54N 5°53W 166 B6
Carndonagh Ireland 55°16N 7°15W 166 A4
Carnduff Canada 49°10N 101°50W 297 D8
Carnegie Vic., Australia 37°53S 145°3E 128 B2
Carnegie U.S.A. 40°24N 80°5W 312 F4
Carnegie, L. Australia 26°5S 122°30E 279 E3
Carnegie Hall New York, U.S.A. 132 c2
Carnegie Ridge Pac. Oc. 1°0S 87°0W 289 H19
Carney I. Antarctica 74°0S 121°0W 151 D14
Carnic Alps = Karnische Alpen Europe 46°36N 13°0E 180 E6
Carniche Alpi = Karnische Alpen Europe 46°36N 13°0E 180 E6
Carnide Portugal 38°45N 9°10W 126 A1
Carnot C.A.R. 4°59N 15°56E 264 B3
Carnot, C. Australia 34°57S 135°38E 281 E2
Carnot B. Australia 17°20S 122°15E 278 C3
Carnoustie U.K. 56°30N 2°42W 167 E6
Carnsore Pt. Ireland 52°10N 6°22W 166 D5
Caro U.S.A. 43°29N 83°24W 309 D12
Caroço São Tomé & Príncipe 1°32N 7°27E 265 a
Caroga Lake U.S.A. 43°8N 74°28W 313 C10
Carol City U.S.A. 25°56N 80°14W 129 C1
Carolina Brazil 7°10S 47°30W 332 C2
Carolina Puerto Rico 18°23N 65°58W 321 C6
Carolina Mpumalanga, S. Africa 26°5S 30°6E 271 C5
Carolinas Pt. N. Marianas 14°55N 145°38E 302 e
Caroline I. Kiribati 9°58S 150°13W 289 H12
Caroline Is. Micronesia 8°0N 150°0E 288 G6
Caroline Pk. N.Z. 45°57S 167°15E 285 F2
Carollton U.S.A. 29°57N 90°8W 131 B2
Carondelet Reef Kiribati 5°33S 173°50E 277 B16
Caroni Trin. & Tob. 10°34N 61°23W 323 t
Caroni → Trin. & Tob. 10°37N 61°30W 323 t
Caroní → Venezuela 8°21N 62°43W 329 B5
Caroni Arena Res. Trin. & Tob. 10°33N 61°15W 323 t
Caroni Bird Sanctuary Trin. & Tob. 10°36N 61°28W 323 t
Caroni Swamp Trin. & Tob. 10°36N 61°27W 323 t
Caronie = Nébrodi, Monti Italy 37°54N 14°35E 201 E7
Caroona Australia 31°24S 150°26E 283 A9
Carora Venezuela 10°19N 70°5W 328 A3
Carpathians Europe 49°30N 21°0E 177 D11
Carpaţii Meridionali Romania 45°30N 25°0E 183 E9
Carpentaria, G. of Australia 14°0S 139°0E 280 A2
Carpentersville U.S.A. 42°6N 88°17W 311 B8
Carpentras France 44°3N 5°2E 175 D9
Carpi Italy 44°47N 10°53E 198 D7
Carpina Brazil 7°51S 35°15W 332 C4
Cărpineni Moldova 46°46N 28°22E 183 D13
Carpinteria U.S.A. 34°24N 119°31W 307 L7
Carpio Spain 41°13N 5°7W 194 D5
Carr Boyd Ra. Australia 16°15S 128°35E 278 C4
Carra, L. Ireland 53°41N 9°14W 166 C2
Carrabelle U.S.A. 29°51N 84°40W 316 F5

Carraig Mhachaire Rois = Carrickmacross Ireland 53°59N 6°43W 166 C5
Carraig na Siúire = Carrick-on-Suir Ireland 52°21N 7°24W 166 D4
Carral Spain 43°14N 8°21W 194 B2
Carranglan Phil. 15°58N 121°4E 232 D3
Carranya ◇ Australia 19°13S 127°46E 278 C4
Carrara Italy 44°5N 10°6E 198 D7
Carrascal Santiago, Chile 33°25S 70°42W 137 B1
Carrascal Phil. 9°22N 125°56E 233 G5
Carrasco △ Bolivia 17°23S 64°59W 331 D5
Carrascosa del Campo Spain 40°2N 2°45W 196 E2
Carrauntoohill Ireland 52°0N 9°45W 166 D2
Carretas, Punta Peru 14°12S 76°17W 330 C2
Carriacou Grenada 12°29N 61°26W 323 q
Carrick-on-Shannon Ireland 53°57N 8°7W 166 C3
Carrick-on-Suir Ireland 52°21N 7°24W 166 D4
Carrickfergus U.K. 54°43N 5°49W 166 B6
Carrickmacross Ireland 53°59N 6°43W 166 C5
Carrières-sous-Bois France 48°56N 2°6E 134 A1
Carrières-sous-Poissy France 48°56N 2°2E 134 A1
Carrières-sur-Seine France 48°55N 2°11E 134 A2
Carrieton Australia 32°25S 138°31E 282 B3
Carrigaline Ireland 51°48N 8°23W 166 E3
Carrillo Mexico 26°54N 103°55W 318 B4
Carrington U.S.A. 47°27N 99°8W 308 B4
Carrión → Spain 41°53N 4°32W 194 D6
Carrión de los Condes Spain 42°20N 4°37W 194 C6
Carrizal Bajo Chile 28°5S 71°20W 334 B1
Carrizalillo Chile 29°5S 71°30W 334 B1
Carrizo Cr. → U.S.A. 36°55N 103°55W 305 H12
Carrizo Plain ⌓ U.S.A. 35°11N 119°47W 306 K7
Carrizo Springs U.S.A. 28°31N 99°52W 314 G5
Carrizozo U.S.A. 33°38N 105°53W 305 K11
Carroll U.S.A. 42°4N 94°52W 310 B2
Carrollton Ga., U.S.A. 33°35N 85°5W 316 B4
Carrollton Ill., U.S.A. 39°18N 90°24W 310 E6
Carrollton Ky., U.S.A. 38°41N 85°11W 311 F11
Carrollton Mo., U.S.A. 39°22N 93°30W 310 E3
Carrollton Ohio, U.S.A. 40°34N 81°5W 312 F3
Carron → U.K. 57°53N 4°22W 167 D4
Carron, L. U.K. 57°22N 5°35W 167 D3
Carrot → Canada 53°50N 101°17W 297 C8
Carrot River Canada 53°17N 103°35W 297 C8
Carrouges France 48°34N 0°10W 172 D6
Carrù Italy 44°29N 7°52E 198 D4
Carruthers Canada 52°52N 109°16W 297 C7
Carsa Dek Ethiopia 5°13N 39°50E 257 F4
Çarşamba Turkey 41°11N 36°44E 212 B7
Carsòli Italy 42°6N 13°5E 199 F10
Carson Calif., U.S.A. 33°49N 118°16W 307 M8
Carson N. Dak., U.S.A. 46°25N 101°34W 308 B3
Carson → U.S.A. 39°45N 118°40W 306 F8
Carson City Mich., U.S.A. 43°11N 84°51W 311 A12
Carson City Nev., U.S.A. 39°10N 119°46W 306 F7
Carson Sink U.S.A. 39°50N 118°25W 304 G4
Carstensz Pyramid = Jaya, Puncak Indonesia 3°57S 137°17E 231 E9
Cartagena Colombia 10°25N 75°33W 328 A2
Cartagena Spain 37°38N 0°59W 197 H4
Cartago Colombia 4°45N 75°55W 328 C2
Cartago Costa Rica 9°50N 83°55W 320 E3
Cártama Spain 36°43N 4°39W 195 J6
Cartaxo Portugal 39°10N 8°47W 195 F2
Cartaya Spain 37°16N 7°9W 195 H3
Carter Bar U.K. 55°21N 2°29W 167 F6
Carteret Is. = Kilinailau Is. Papua N. G. 4°45S 155°20E 286 C8
Cartersville U.S.A. 34°10N 84°48W 316 A5
Carterton N.Z. 41°2S 175°31E 284 H4
Carterville U.S.A. 37°46N 89°5W 310 G7
Carthage Tunisia 36°52N 10°20E 200 F3
Carthage Ill., U.S.A. 40°25N 91°8W 310 D5
Carthage Mo., U.S.A. 37°11N 94°19W 308 G6
Carthage N.Y., U.S.A. 43°59N 75°37W 313 C9
Carthage Tex., U.S.A. 32°9N 94°20W 314 E7
Cartier I. Australia 12°31S 123°29E 278 B3
Cartierville Canada 45°31N 73°42W 130 A1
Cartwright Canada 53°41N 56°58W 299 B8
Caruachi, Represa de Venezuela 8°9N 62°50W 329 B5
Caruaru Brazil 8°15S 35°55W 332 C4
Carúpano Venezuela 10°39N 63°15W 329 A5
Caruray Phil. 10°20N 119°0E 233 F2
Carutapera Brazil 1°13S 46°1W 332 B2
Caruthersville U.S.A. 36°11N 89°39W 308 G9
Carvalho Brazil 2°16S 51°29W 329 D7
Carvin France 50°30N 2°57E 173 B9
Carvoeiro Brazil 1°30S 61°59W 329 D5
Carvoeiro, C. Portugal 39°21N 9°24W 195 F1
Cary Ill., U.S.A. 42°13N 88°14W 311 B8
Cary N.C., U.S.A. 35°47N 78°46W 315 D15
Cas-gwent = Chepstow U.K. 51°38N 2°41W 169 F5
Casa, Pas de la = Envalira, Port d' Europe 42°33N 1°43E 196 C6
Casa Branca Brazil 21°46S 47°4W 333 F2
Casa Branca Portugal 38°29N 8°12W 195 G2
Casa de Piedra Argentina 38°5S 67°28W 334 D2
Casa de Piedra, Embalse Argentina 38°5S 67°32W 334 D2
Casa Grande U.S.A. 32°53N 111°45W 305 K8
Casa Loma Canada 43°41N 79°24W 141 A2
Casa Nova Brazil 9°25S 41°5W 332 C3
Casa Verde Brazil 23°29S 46°40W 137 A1
Casablanca Chile 33°20S 71°25W 334 C1
Casablanca Morocco 33°36N 7°36W 260 B3
Casablanca-Settat □ Morocco 33°0N 8°0W 260 B3
Casacalenda Italy 41°44N 14°51E 199 G11
Casal da Mira Portugal 38°47N 9°14W 126 A1
Casal Morena Italy 41°49N 12°37E 136 C2
Casalbordino Italy 42°9N 14°35E 199 F11
Casale Monferrato Italy 45°8N 8°27E 198 C5
Casalmaggiore Italy 44°59N 10°26E 198 D7
Casalotti Italy 41°54N 12°22E 136 B1
Casalpusterlengo Italy 45°11N 9°39E 198 C6
Casamance Senegal 13°0N 15°30W 262 C1
Casamance → Senegal 12°33N 16°46W 262 C1
Casanare □ Colombia 5°30N 72°0W 328 B3
Casanare → Colombia 6°2N 69°51W 328 B4
Casarano Italy 40°0N 18°10E 201 B11
Casares Spain 36°27N 5°16W 195 J5
Casas Ibáñez Spain 39°17N 1°30W 197 F3
Casasimarro Spain 39°22N 2°3W 197 F2
Casatejada Spain 39°54N 5°40W 194 F5
Casavieja Spain 40°17N 4°46W 194 E6
Cascada de Basaseachic △ Mexico 28°9N 108°15W 318 B3
Cascade Seychelles 4°39S 55°29E 272 c
Cascade Idaho, U.S.A. 44°31N 116°2W 304 D5
Cascade Iowa, U.S.A. 42°18N 91°0W 310 B6
Cascade Mont., U.S.A. 47°16N 111°42W 304 C8
Cascade Heights U.S.A. 33°43N 84°26W 113 B2
Cascade Locks U.S.A. 45°40N 121°54W 306 E5
Cascade Pt. N.Z. 44°1S 168°20E 285 E3
Cascade Ra. U.S.A. 47°0N 121°30W 306 D5
Cascade Res. U.S.A. 44°32N 116°3W 304 D5
Cascades, Pte. des Réunion 21°9S 55°51E 272 f
Cascais Portugal 38°41N 9°25W 195 G1
Cascavel Ceará, Brazil 4°7S 38°14W 332 B4
Cascavel Paraná, Brazil 24°57S 53°28W 335 A5
Cáscina Italy 43°41N 10°33E 198 E7
Casco B. U.S.A. 43°45N 70°0W 309 D19
Case Noyale Mauritius 20°23S 57°22E 272 e
Case-Pilote Martinique 14°38N 61°9W 322 j
Caselle Torinese Italy 45°10N 7°39E 198 C4
Caserta Italy 41°4N 14°20E 201 A7
Casey Antarctica 66°0S 76°0E 151 C8
Casey Ill., U.S.A. 39°18N 87°59W 311 E9
Caseyr, Raas = Asir, Ras Somalia 11°55N 51°10E 267 B7
Cashel Ireland 52°30N 7°53W 166 D4
Casibare → Colombia 3°48N 72°18W 328 C3
Casiguran Phil. 16°22N 122°7E 232 C4
Casiguran Sound Phil. 16°6N 121°58E 232 C3
Casilda Argentina 33°10S 61°10W 334 C3
Casim = General Toshevo Bulgaria 43°42N 28°6E 203 C12
Casimcea Romania 44°45N 28°23E 183 F13
Casino Australia 28°52S 153°3E 281 D5
Casiquiare → Venezuela 2°1N 67°7W 328 C4
Casitas Peru 3°54S 80°39W 330 A1
Čáslav Czechia 49°54N 15°22E 180 B8
Casma Peru 9°30S 78°20W 330 B2
Casmalia U.S.A. 34°50N 120°32W 307 L6
Casnewydd = Newport U.K. 51°35N 3°0W 169 F5
Cásola Valsénio Italy 44°12N 11°40E 199 D8
Cásoli Italy 42°7N 14°18E 199 F11
Caspe Spain 41°14N 0°1W 196 D4
Casper U.S.A. 42°51N 106°19W 304 E10
Caspian Depression Eurasia 47°0N 48°0E 191 G9
Caspian Sea Eurasia 43°0N 50°0E 187 F9
Cass City U.S.A. 43°36N 83°10W 312 C1
Cass Lake U.S.A. 47°23N 94°37W 308 B6
Cassà de la Selva Spain 41°53N 2°52E 196 D7
Cassadaga U.S.A. 42°20N 79°19W 312 D5
Cassai Angola 10°33S 21°59E 265 E4
Cassai → Angola 3°2S 16°57E 265 E4
Cassamba Angola 13°6S 20°18E 265 E4
Cassano allo Iónio Italy 39°47N 16°20E 201 C9
Casselberry U.S.A. 28°41N 81°20W 317 G8
Casselman Canada 45°19N 75°5W 313 A9
Casselton U.S.A. 46°54N 97°13W 308 B5
Cassiar Mts. Canada 59°30N 130°30W 296 B2
Cassilândia Brazil 19°9S 51°45W 331 D7
Cassilis Australia 32°3S 149°58E 283 B8
Cassinga Angola 15°5S 16°4E 265 F3
Cassino Italy 41°30N 13°49E 200 A6
Cassis France 43°14N 5°32E 175 E9
Cassoalala Angola 9°30S 14°22E 265 D2
Cassoango Angola 13°42S 20°56E 265 E3
Cassongue Angola 11°53S 15°2E 265 E3
Cassopolis U.S.A. 41°55N 86°1W 311 C10
Cassunda Angola 10°57S 21°3E 265 E4
Cassville Mo., U.S.A. 36°41N 93°52W 308 G7
Cassville Wis., U.S.A. 42°43N 90°59W 310 B6
Castagneto Carducci Italy 43°9N 10°36E 198 E7
Castaic U.S.A. 34°30N 118°38W 307 L8
Castalia U.S.A. 41°24N 82°49W 312 E2
Castanhal Brazil 1°18S 47°55W 332 B2
Castara Trin. & Tob. 11°17N 60°42W 323 s
Castara B. Trin. & Tob. 11°17N 60°42W 323 s
Casteddu = Cágliari Italy 39°13N 9°7E 200 C2
Castéggio Italy 45°0N 9°7E 198 C6
Castejón de Monegros Spain 41°37N 0°15W 196 D4
Castel Guadeloupe 16°15N 61°35W 322 e
Castèl del Monte Italy 41°5N 16°16E 201 A9
Castèl di Lèva Italy 41°46N 12°33E 136 C2
Castèl di Sangro Italy 41°47N 14°6E 199 G11
Castèl San Giovanni Italy 45°4N 9°26E 198 C6
Castèl San Pietro Terme Italy 44°24N 11°35E 199 D8
Castèl Sant' Angelo Rome, Italy 136 b1
Castelbuono Italy 37°56N 14°5E 201 E7
Castelfidardo Italy 43°28N 13°33E 199 E10
Castelfiorentino Italy 43°36N 10°58E 198 E7
Castelfranco Véneto Italy 45°40N 11°55E 199 C8
Casteljaloux France 44°19N 0°6E 174 D4
Castell-Nedd = Neath U.K. 51°39N 3°48W 169 F4
Castellabate Italy 40°17N 14°57E 201 B7
Castellammare, G. di Italy 38°8N 12°54E 200 D5
Castellammare del Golfo Italy 38°1N 12°53E 200 D5
Castellammare di Stábia Italy 40°42N 14°29E 201 B7
Castellamonte Italy 45°23N 7°42E 198 C4
Castellane France 43°50N 6°31E 175 E10
Castellaneta Italy 40°38N 16°56E 201 B9
Castelli Argentina 36°7S 57°47W 334 D4
Castello Venice, Italy 142 b4
Castelló de la Plana Spain 39°58N 0°3W 196 F4
Castellón de la Plana □ Spain 40°15N 0°5W 196 E4
Castellote Spain 40°48N 0°15W 196 E4
Castelmáuro Italy 41°50N 14°43E 199 G11
Castelnau-de-Médoc France 45°2N 0°48W 174 C3
Castelnau-Magnoac France 43°17N 0°31E 174 E4
Castelnaudary France 43°20N 1°58E 174 E5
Castelnovo ne' Monti Italy 44°26N 10°24E 198 D7
Castelnuovo di Val di Cécina Italy 43°12N 10°59E 198 E7
Castelo = Manuel Urbano Brazil 8°53S 69°18W 330 B4
Castelo Brazil 20°33S 41°14W 333 F3
Castelo, Pta. do Azores 36°56N 25°1W 153 d4
Castelo Branco Azores 38°31N 28°44W 153 d1
Castelo Branco Portugal 39°50N 7°31W 194 F3
Castelo Branco □ Portugal 39°52N 7°45W 194 F3
Castelo de Paiva Portugal 41°2N 8°16W 194 D2
Castelo de Vide Portugal 39°25N 7°27W 195 F3
Castelo do Piauí Brazil 5°20S 41°33W 332 C3
Castelrosso = Megisti Greece 36°8N 29°34E 205 E11
Castelsardo Italy 40°55N 8°43E 200 B1
Castelsarrasin France 44°2N 1°7E 174 D5
Casteltérmini Italy 37°32N 13°39E 200 E6
Castelvetrano Italy 37°41N 12°47E 200 E5
Castendo Angola 8°39S 14°10E 265 D2
Casterton Australia 37°30S 141°30E 282 D4
Castets France 43°52N 1°6W 174 E2
Castiglion Fiorentino Italy 43°20N 11°55E 199 E8
Castiglione = Bou Ismaïl Algeria 36°38N 2°42E 261 A5
Castiglione del Lago Italy 43°7N 12°3E 199 E9
Castiglione della Pescáia Italy 42°46N 10°53E 198 F7
Castiglione delle Stiviere Italy 45°23N 10°29E 198 C7
Castilblanco Spain 39°17N 5°5W 195 F5
Castile U.S.A. 42°38N 78°3W 312 D6
Castilla Peru 5°12S 80°38W 330 B1
Castilla, Playa de Spain 37°0N 6°33W 195 J4
Castilla-La Mancha □ Spain 39°30N 3°30W 195 F7
Castilla y Leon □ Spain 42°0N 5°0W 194 D6
Castillo de Locubín Spain 37°32N 3°56W 195 H7
Castillo de San Marcos ⌓ U.S.A. 29°54N 81°19W 316 F8
Castillon-en-Couserans France 42°56N 1°1E 174 F5
Castillonès France 44°39N 0°37E 174 D4
Castillos Uruguay 34°12S 53°52W 335 C5
Castle Bruce Dominica 15°26N 61°16W 323 k
Castle Dale U.S.A. 39°13N 111°1W 304 G8
Castle Douglas U.K. 54°56N 3°56W 167 G5
Castle Harbour Bermuda 32°21N 64°40W 153 a
Castle Mt. Jamaica 18°8N 76°22W 320 a
Castle of Good Hope Cape Town, S. Africa 118 c3
Castle Peak B. Hong Kong, China 22°23N 113°58E 122 A1
Castle Pk. Hong Kong, China 22°23N 113°57E 122 A1
Castle Roads Bermuda 32°20N 64°40W 153 a
Castle Rock Colo., U.S.A. 39°22N 104°51W 304 G11
Castle Rock Wash., U.S.A. 46°17N 122°54W 306 D4
Castle Rock Pt. St. Helena 16°1S 5°45W 153 h
Castlebar Ireland 53°52N 9°18W 166 C2
Castlebay U.K. 56°57N 7°31W 167 E1
Castleblayney Ireland 54°7N 6°44W 166 B5
Castlecliff N.Z. 39°57S 175°5E 284 F4
Castlecomer Ireland 52°48N 7°14W 166 D4
Castlederg U.K. 54°42N 7°36W 166 B4
Castleford U.K. 53°43N 1°21W 168 D6
Castlegar Canada 49°20N 117°40W 296 D5
Castleisland Ireland 52°14N 9°28W 166 D2
Castlemaine Vic., Australia 37°2S 144°12E 282 D6
Castlemaine Kerry, Ireland 52°10N 9°42W 166 D2
Castlepoint N.Z. 40°54S 176°15E 284 G5
Castlepollard Ireland 53°41N 7°19W 166 C4
Castlerea Ireland 53°46N 8°29W 166 C3
Castlereagh → Australia 30°12S 147°32E 283 A7
Castlereagh B. Australia 12°10S 135°10E 280 A2
Castleton U.S.A. 43°37N 73°11W 313 C11
Castleton Corners U.S.A. 40°36N 74°8W 132 C1
Castleton-on-Hudson U.S.A. 42°31N 73°45W 313 D11
Castletown I. of Man 54°5N 4°38W 168 C3
Castletown Bearhaven Ireland 51°39N 9°55W 166 E2
Castor Canada 52°15N 111°50W 296 C6
Castor → Canada 53°24N 78°58W 298 B4
Castorland U.S.A. 43°53N 75°31W 313 C9
Castres France 43°37N 2°13E 174 E6
Castricum Neths. 52°33N 4°40E 170 B4
Castries St. Lucia 14°2N 60°58W 323 m
Castril Spain 37°48N 2°46W 195 H8
Castro Brazil 24°45S 50°0W 335 A6
Castro Chile 42°30S 73°50W 336 B2
Castro Alves Brazil 12°46S 39°33W 333 D4
Castro del Río Spain 37°41N 4°29W 195 H6
Castro-Urdiales Spain 43°23N 3°11W 194 B7
Castro Valley U.S.A. 37°41N 122°5W 306 H4
Castro Verde Portugal 37°41N 8°4W 195 H2
Castrogiovanni = Enna Italy 37°34N 14°16E 201 E7
Castrojeriz Spain 42°17N 4°9W 194 C6
Castropol Spain 43°32N 7°0W 194 B4
Castroreale Italy 38°6N 15°12E 201 D8
Castrovillari Italy 39°49N 16°12E 201 C9
Castroville U.S.A. 36°46N 121°45W 306 J5
Castrovirreyna Peru 13°20S 75°18W 330 C2
Castuera Spain 38°43N 5°37W 195 G5
Caswell Sound N.Z. 44°59S 167°8E 285 E2
Çat Turkey 39°40N 41°3E 213 C9
Cat Ba, Dao Vietnam 20°50N 107°0E 236 B6
Cat Ba △ Vietnam 20°47N 107°3E 236 B6
Cat I. The Bahamas 24°30N 75°30W 321 B4
Cat L. Canada 51°40N 91°50W 298 B1
Cat Lake Canada 51°40N 91°50W 298 B1
Cat Tien △ Vietnam 11°25N 107°17E 237 G6
Čata Slovakia 47°58N 18°38E 181 D11
Catabola Angola 12°9S 17°16E 265 E3
Catacamas Honduras 14°54N 85°56W 320 D2
Catacaos Peru 5°20S 80°45W 330 B1
Cataguases Brazil 21°23S 42°39W 333 F3
Catagupan Phil. 8°1N 116°58E 233 G1
Cataingan Phil. 12°0N 124°0E 232 E4
Çatak Turkey 38°1N 43°8E 213 C10
Çatalağzı Turkey 41°30N 31°59E 212 B4
Catalão Brazil 18°10S 47°57W 333 E2
Çatalca Turkey 41°8N 28°27E 203 E12
Catalina Nfld. & L., Canada 48°31N 53°4W 299 C9
Catalina Chile 25°13S 69°43W 334 B2
Catalina Ariz., U.S.A. 32°30N 110°50W 305 K8
Catalonia = Cataluña □ Spain 41°40N 1°15E 196 D6
Cataluña □ Spain 41°40N 1°15E 196 D6
Çatalzeytin Turkey 41°57N 34°12E 212 B6
Catamarca Argentina 28°30S 65°50W 334 B2
Catamarca □ Argentina 27°0S 65°50W 334 B2
Catanauan Phil. 13°36N 122°19E 232 E4
Catanduanes □ Phil. 13°50N 124°20E 232 E5
Catanduva Brazil 21°5S 48°58W 335 A6
Catánia Italy 37°30N 15°6E 201 E8
Catánia, G. di Italy 37°24N 15°8E 201 E8
Cataño Puerto Rico 18°27N 66°7W 321 b
Catanzaro Italy 38°54N 16°35E 201 D9
Cataouatche, L. U.S.A. 29°50N 90°14W 131 B1
Catarman Camiguin, Phil. 9°8N 124°40E 233 G5
Catarman N. Samar, Phil. 12°28N 124°35E 232 E5
Catatumbo → Venezuela 9°21N 71°45W 328 B3
Cataula U.S.A. 32°39N 84°52W 316 C5
Catbalogan Phil. 11°46N 124°53E 233 F5
Catchacoma Canada 44°44N 78°19W 312 B6
Cateco Cangola Angola 8°28S 15°51E 265 D3
Cateel Phil. 7°47N 126°24E 233 H6
Cateel B. Phil. 7°54N 126°25E 233 H6
Catembe Mozam. 26°0S 32°33E 271 C5
Catende Angola 11°14S 21°30E 265 E4
Catende Brazil 8°40S 35°43W 332 C4
Caterham U.K. 51°15N 0°4W 169 F7
Catete Angola 9°6S 13°43E 265 D2
Catete Rio de J., Brazil 22°54S 43°10W 135 B1
Catford U.K. 51°26N 0°1W 125 B3
Cathair na Mart = Westport Ireland 53°48N 9°31W 166 C2
Cathcart N.S.W., Australia 36°52S 149°24E 283 D8
Cathcart Eastern Cape, S. Africa 32°18S 27°10E 270 D4
Cathedral City U.S.A. 33°47N 116°28W 307 M10
Cathedral Rock △ Australia 30°24S 152°15E 283 A10
Catherine, L. U.S.A. 28°30N 81°24W 133 B2
Cathlamet U.S.A. 46°12N 123°23W 306 D3
Catió Guinea-Biss. 11°17N 15°15W 262 C1
Catismiña Venezuela 4°5N 63°40W 329 C5
Catita Brazil 9°31S 43°1W 332 C3
Cativa Panama 9°21N 79°49W 320 c
Catlettsburg U.S.A. 38°25N 82°36W 309 F12
Catlin U.S.A. 40°4N 87°42W 311 D9
Catlins N.Z. 46°22S 169°17E 285 G4
Çatma Dağı Turkey 38°25N 29°50E 205 C11
Catmon Phil. 10°43N 124°1E 233 F5
Catoche, C. Mexico 21°35N 87°5W 319 C7
Catolé do Rocha Brazil 6°21S 37°45W 332 C4
Catota Angola 13°57S 17°30E 265 E3
Cátria, Mte. Italy 43°28N 12°42E 199 E9
Catriló Argentina 36°26S 63°24W 334 D3
Catrimani Brazil 0°27N 61°41W 329 C5
Catrimani → Brazil 0°28N 61°44W 329 C5
Catskill U.S.A. 42°14N 73°52W 313 D11
Catskill △ U.S.A. 42°8N 74°39W 313 D10
Catskill Mts. U.S.A. 42°10N 74°25W 313 D10
Catt, Mt. Australia 13°49S 134°23E 280 A1
Cattaraugus U.S.A. 42°20N 78°52W 312 D6
Cattaro = Kotor Montenegro 42°25N 18°47E 202 D2
Catterick U.K. 54°23N 1°37W 168 C6
Cattólica Italy 43°58N 12°44E 199 E9
Cattólica Eraclea Italy 37°26N 13°24E 200 E6
Catu Brazil 12°21S 38°23W 333 D4
Catuala Angola 16°25S 19°2E 265 F3
Catuane Mozam. 26°48S 32°18E 271 C5
Catubig Phil. 12°24N 125°3E 232 E5
Catumbela Angola 12°25S 13°34E 265 E2
Catumbela → Angola 12°29S 13°28E 265 E2
Catur Mozam. 13°45S 35°30E 269 E4
Catwick Is. = Hon Hai Vietnam 10°0N 109°0E 237 H7
Cauayan Isabela, Phil. 16°56N 121°46E 232 C3
Cauayan Neg. Occ., Phil. 9°58N 122°37E 233 G4
Caubvick, Mt. = Iberville, Mt. d' Canada 58°50N 63°50W 295 F19
Cauca □ Colombia 2°30N 76°50W 328 C2
Cauca → Colombia 8°54N 74°28W 328 B3
Caucaia Brazil 3°40S 38°35W 332 B4
Caucasia Colombia 8°0N 75°12W 328 B2
Caucasus Mountains Eurasia 42°50N 44°0E 191 J7
Caucete Argentina 31°38S 68°20W 334 C2
Caudete Spain 38°42N 1°2W 197 G3
Caudry France 50°7N 3°22E 173 B10
Cauese Mts. Mozam. 15°14S 30°33E 269 F3
Caulfield Australia 37°52S 145°1E 128 B2
Caulnes France 48°18N 2°10W 172 D4
Caulónia Italy 38°23N 16°24E 201 D9
Caungula Angola 8°26S 18°38E 265 D3
Cauquenes Chile 36°0S 72°22W 334 D1
Caura → Venezuela 7°38N 64°53W 329 B5
Caurés → Brazil 1°21S 62°20W 329 D5
Cauresi → Mozam. 17°8S 33°0E 269 F3
Căușani Moldova 46°38N 29°25E 183 D14
Causapscal Canada 48°19N 67°12W 299 C6
Causeway Coast & Glens □ U.K. 55°5N 6°33W 166 A5
Caussade France 44°10N 1°33E 174 D5
Causse-Méjean France 44°18N 3°42E 174 D7
Causses du Quercy ⌓ France 44°35N 1°35E 174 D5
Cauterets France 42°52N 0°8W 174 F3
Cauvery → India 11°9N 78°52E 245 J4
Caux, Pays de France 49°38N 0°35E 172 C7
Cava de' Tirreni Italy 40°42N 14°42E 201 B7
Cávado → Portugal 41°32N 8°48W 194 D2
Cavagrande del Cassibile ⌓ Italy 36°58N 15°6E 201 F8
Cavaillon France 43°50N 5°2E 175 E9
Cavalaire-sur-Mer France 43°10N 6°33E 175 E10
Cavalcante Brazil 13°48S 47°30W 333 D2
Cavalese Italy 46°17N 11°27E 199 B8
Cavalier U.S.A. 48°48N 97°37W 308 A5
Cavalla = Cavally → Africa 4°22N 7°32W 262 E3
Cavalla △ Liberia 5°8N 7°20W 262 D3
Cavalli, Palazzo Venice, Italy 142 b2
Cavalli Is. N.Z. 35°0S 173°58E 284 B2
Cavally → Africa 4°22N 7°32W 262 E3
Cavan Ireland 54°0N 7°22W 166 B4
Cavan □ Ireland 54°1N 7°16W 166 C4
Cavárzere Italy 45°8N 12°5E 199 C9
Cavazzuccherina = Jésolo Italy 45°32N 12°38E 199 C9
Çavdarhisar Turkey 39°12N 29°37E 205 B11
Çavdır Turkey 37°10N 29°42E 205 D11
Cave Creek U.S.A. 33°50N 111°57W 305 K8
Cave Run L. U.S.A. 38°5N 83°25W 311 F13
Cave Spring U.S.A. 34°6N 85°20W 316 A4
Cavalleria, C. de Spain 40°5N 4°5E 206 A6
Cavenagh Ra. Australia 26°12S 127°55E 279 E4
Cavendish Australia 37°31S 142°2E 282 D5
Caverna do Peruaçu △ Brazil 15°0S 44°35W 333 E3
Caviana, I. Brazil 0°10N 50°10W 329 C7
Cavili I. Phil. 9°16N 120°49E 233 G3
Cavite Phil. 14°29N 120°54E 127 C1
Cavite □ Phil. 14°15N 120°50E 232 D3
Caviúna = Rolândia Brazil 23°18S 51°23W 335 A5
Cavnic Romania 47°40N 23°52E 183 C8
Cavour Italy 44°47N 7°22E 198 D4
Cavtat Croatia 42°35N 18°13E 202 D2
Cawayan Phil. 11°56N 123°46E 233 F4
Cawayanon = Vintar Phil. 18°14N 120°39E 232 B3
Cawndilla L. Australia 32°30S 142°15E 282 B5
Cawnpore = Kanpur India 26°28N 80°20E 243 F9
Caxias Brazil 4°55S 43°20W 332 B3
Caxias Lisboa, Portugal 38°42N 9°16W 126 A1
Caxias do Sul Brazil 29°10S 51°10W 335 B5
Caxito Angola 8°30S 13°30E 265 D2
Caxopa Angola 11°52S 20°52E 265 E4
Çay Turkey 38°35N 31°1E 212 C4
Cay Pt. The Bahamas 24°59N 77°25W 153 b
Cay Sal Bank The Bahamas 23°45N 80°0W 320 B4
Cayambe Napo, Ecuador 0°2N 77°59W 328 C2
Cayambe Quito, Ecuador 0°3N 78°8W 328 C2
Cayce U.S.A. 33°58N 81°4W 316 B8
Çaycuma Turkey 41°25N 32°4E 212 B5
Çayeli Turkey 41°5N 40°45E 213 B9
Cayenne Fr. Guiana 5°5N 52°18W 329 B7
Cayenne □ Fr. Guiana 5°2N 52°37W 329 C7
Cayey Puerto Rico 18°7N 66°10W 321 b
Caygören Barajı Turkey 39°15N 28°12E 205 B10
Cayiralan Turkey 39°17N 35°38E 212 C6
Çayırova = Áyios Theodhoros Cyprus 35°22N 34°1E 207 E10
Caylus France 44°15N 1°47E 174 D5
Cayman Brac Cayman Is. 19°43N 79°49W 320 C4
Cayman Is. ☒ W. Indies 19°40N 80°30W 320 C3
Cayman Trench Caribbean 17°0N 83°0W 320 C3
Caynabo Somalia 9°0N 46°25E 267 C6
Cayon St. Kitts & Nevis 17°21N 62°52W 322 d
Cayres France 44°55N 3°48E 174 D7
Cayuga Ont., Canada 42°59N 79°50W 312 D5
Cayuga Ind., U.S.A. 39°57N 87°28W 311 E9
Cayuga N.Y., U.S.A. 42°54N 76°44W 313 D8
Cayuga Heights U.S.A. 42°27N 76°29W 313 D8
Cayuga L. U.S.A. 42°41N 76°41W 313 D8
Cazage Angola 11°2S 20°45E 265 E4
Cazalla de la Sierra Spain 37°56N 5°45W 195 H5
Căzănești Romania 44°36N 27°3E 183 F12
Cazaubon France 43°56N 0°3W 174 E3
Cazaux et de Sanguinet, Étang de France 44°29N 1°10W 174 D2
Cazenovia U.S.A. 42°56N 75°51W 313 D9
Cazères France 43°13N 1°5E 174 E5
Cazin Bos.-H. 44°57N 15°57E 199 D12
Čazma Croatia 45°45N 16°39E 199 C13
Cazombo Angola 11°54S 22°56E 265 E4
Cazorla Spain 37°55N 3°2W 195 H7
Cazorla, Sierra de Spain 38°5N 2°55W 195 G8
Cea → Spain 42°0N 5°36W 194 C5
Ceadîr-Lunga Moldova 46°3N 28°51E 183 D13
Ceahlău △ Romania 46°58N 25°55E 183 D10
Ceamurlia de Jos Romania 44°43N 28°47E 183 F13
Ceanannus Mor = Kells Ireland 53°44N 6°53W 166 C5
Ceará = Fortaleza Brazil 3°45S 38°35W 332 B4
Ceará □ Brazil 5°0S 40°0W 332 C4
Ceara Abyssal Plain Atl. Oc. 0°0 36°30W 332 B4
Ceará-Mirim Brazil 5°38S 35°25W 332 C4
Ceara Rise Atl. Oc. 4°30N 43°30W 152 F7
Ceatharlach = Carlow Ireland 52°50N 6°56W 166 D5
Ceauru, L. Romania 44°58N 23°11E 183 F8
Cébaco, I. de Panama 7°33N 81°9W 320 E3
Cebeci Turkey 41°7N 28°52E 122 B1
Cebollar Argentina 29°10S 66°35W 334 B2
Cebollera, Sierra Spain 42°0N 2°30W 196 D2
Cebreros Spain 40°27N 4°28W 194 E6
Cebu Phil. 10°18N 123°54E 233 F4
Cebu □ Phil. 10°20N 123°40E 233 F4
Čečava Bos.-H. 44°42N 17°44E 182 F2
Ceccano Italy 41°34N 13°20E 200 A6
Cecchignola Italy 41°48N 12°29E 136 C2
Cece Hungary 46°46N 18°39E 182 D3
Cechi Côte d'Ivoire 6°15N 4°25W 262 D4
Cecil Plains Australia 27°30S 151°11E 281 D5
Cecilienhof, Schloss Germany 52°35N 13°5E 115 B1
Cécina Italy 43°19N 10°31E 198 E7
Cécina → Italy 43°18N 10°29E 198 E7
Ceclavín Spain 39°50N 6°45W 194 F4
Cedar → U.S.A. 41°17N 91°21W 310 C5
Cedar City U.S.A. 37°41N 113°4W 305 H7
Cedar Creek Res. U.S.A. 32°11N 96°4W 314 E6
Cedar Falls Iowa, U.S.A. 42°32N 92°27W 310 B4
Cedar Falls Wash., U.S.A. 47°25N 121°45W 306 C5
Cedar Grove Georgia, U.S.A. 33°40N 84°16W 113 C3
Cedar Grove Ind., U.S.A. 39°22N 84°56W 311 E12
Cedar Hill U.S.A. 32°35N 96°57W 120 C4
Cedar Hill State Park ⌓ U.S.A. 32°36N 96°59W 120 C4
Cedar Key U.S.A. 29°8N 83°2W 317 F6
Cedar L. Canada 53°10N 100°0W 297 C9
Cedar Lake U.S.A. 41°22N 87°26W 311 C9
Cedar Park U.S.A. 30°30N 97°49W 314 F6
Cedar Point U.S.A. 41°44N 83°21W 311 C13
Cedar Rapids U.S.A. 41°59N 91°40W 310 C5
Cedar Tree Pt. Antigua & B. 17°42N 61°53W 322 c
Cedartown U.S.A. 34°1N 85°15W 316 A4
Cedarvale Canada 55°1N 128°22W 296 B3
Cedarvale Park Canada 43°42N 79°36W 141 A2
Cedarville KwaZulu Natal, S. Africa 30°23S 29°3E 271 D4
Cedarville Ill., U.S.A. 42°23N 89°38W 310 B7
Cedarville Ohio, U.S.A. 39°44N 83°49W 311 E13
Cedeira Spain 43°39N 8°2W 194 B2
Cedral Mexico 23°50N 100°45W 318 C4
Cedrino → Italy 40°11N 9°24E 200 B2
Cedro Brazil 6°34S 39°3W 332 C4
Cedros Azores 38°38N 28°42W 153 d1
Cedros, I. Mexico 28°12N 115°15W 318 B1
Cedros B. Trin. & Tob. 10°16N 61°54W 323 t
Cedros Pt. Trin. & Tob. 10°7N 61°49W 323 t
Ceduna Australia 32°7S 133°46E 281 E1
Cedynia Poland 52°53N 14°12E 185 F1
Cée Spain 42°57N 9°10W 194 C1
Ceel Gaal Somalia 10°58N 50°20E 267 B7
Ceel Waaq Kenya 2°49N 40°56E 267 D5
Ceelbuur = El Bur Somalia 4°40N 46°37E 267 D6
Ceeldheere Galguduud, Somalia 5°30N 47°8E 267 D6
Ceeldheere Galguduud, Somalia 5°22N 46°11E 267 C6
Ceerigaabo Somalia 10°35N 47°20E 267 B6
Cefalù Italy 38°2N 14°1E 201 D7
Cega → Spain 41°33N 4°46W 194 D6
Cegléd Hungary 47°11N 19°47E 182 C4
Céglie Messápica Italy 40°39N 17°31E 201 B10
Cehegín Spain 38°6N 1°48W 197 G3
Ceheng China 24°58N 105°48E 228 E5
Cehu-Silvaniei Romania 47°24N 23°9E 183 C8
Ceiba Puerto Rico 18°16N 65°39W 321 b
Ceica Romania 46°53N 22°10E 182 D7
Ceira → Portugal 40°13N 8°16W 194 E2
Çekerek Turkey 40°4N 35°29E 212 B6
Cekik Indonesia 8°12S 114°27E 231 J17
Cela Angola 11°25S 15°7E 265 E3
Čelákovice Czechia 50°10N 14°46E 180 A7
Celano Italy 42°5N 13°33E 199 F10
Celanova Spain 42°9N 7°58W 194 C3
Celaque △ Honduras 14°30N 88°43W 320 D2
Celaya Mexico 20°31N 100°37W 318 C4
Celbridge Ireland 53°20N 6°32W 166 C5
Celebes = Sulawesi Indonesia 2°0S 120°0E 235 C5
Celebes Sea Indonesia 3°0N 123°0E 231 D6
Celendín Peru 6°52S 78°10W 330 B2
Celestial Mts. = Tian Shan Asia 40°30N 76°0E 217 D9
Čelić Bos.-H. 44°43N 18°49E 182 F3
Celica Ecuador 4°7S 79°59W 328 D2
Celina U.S.A. 40°33N 84°35W 311 D12
Celinac Bos.-H. 44°44N 17°22E 182 F2
Celje Slovenia 46°16N 15°18E 199 B12
Celldömölk Hungary 47°16N 17°10E 182 C2
Celle Germany 52°37N 10°4E 178 C6
Celorico da Beira Portugal 40°38N 7°24W 194 E3
Celtic Sea Atl. Oc. 50°9N 9°34W 165 F2
Çeltikçi Turkey 37°32N 30°29E 205 D12
Çemişgezek Turkey 39°3N 38°56E 213 C8
Cempaka Putih Indonesia 6°10S 106°51E 122 B2
Cempi, Teluk Indonesia 8°44S 118°22E 235 D5
Cenderawasih, Teluk Indonesia 3°0S 135°20E 231 E9
Cenepa → Peru 4°40S 78°10W 328 D2
Çengelköy Turkey 41°2N 29°3E 122 B2
Cengkareng Indonesia 6°9S 106°45E 122 A1
Cengong China 27°13N 108°44E 228 D7
Ceno → Italy 44°43N 10°5E 198 D7
Centallo Italy 44°30N 7°35E 198 D4
Centelles Spain 41°50N 2°14E 196 D7
Centenário do Sul Brazil 22°48S 51°36W 333 F1
Centennial U.S.A. 39°34N 104°52W 304 G11
Centennial Olympic Park Atlanta, U.S.A. 33°46N 84°23W 113 B2
Centennial Park Sydney, Australia 33°53S 151°14E 139 B2
Center N. Dak., U.S.A. 47°7N 101°18W 308 B3
Center Tex., U.S.A. 31°48N 94°11W 314 F7
Center Hill Fla., U.S.A. 28°38N 82°3W 317 G7
Center Hill Georgia, U.S.A. 33°46N 84°29W 113 B2
Center Point U.S.A. 42°12N 91°47W 310 B5
Centerburg U.S.A. 40°18N 82°42W 312 F2
Centerville Calif., U.S.A. 36°44N 119°30W 306 J7
Centerville Iowa, U.S.A. 40°44N 92°52W 310 D4
Centerville Ohio, U.S.A. 39°38N 84°8W 311 E12
Centerville Pa., U.S.A. 40°3N 79°59W 312 F5
Centerville Tenn., U.S.A. 35°47N 87°28W 315 D11
Centerville Tex., U.S.A. 31°16N 95°59W 314 F7
Cento Italy 44°43N 11°17E 199 D8
Centocelle Italy 41°52N 12°34E 136 B2
Centraal Station Amsterdam, Neths. 112 a3
Central = Tsentralnyy □ Russia 52°0N 40°0E 214 D4
Central Brazil 11°8S 42°8W 332 D3
Central Alaska, U.S.A. 65°35N 144°48W 303 D11
Central □ Botswana 22°0S 26°30E 270 B4
Central □ Ghana 5°30N 1°0W 263 D4
Central □ Malawi 13°30S 33°30E 269 E3
Central □ Papua N. G. 10°0S 148°0E 286 F5
Central □ Zambia 14°25S 28°50E 269 E2
Central, Cordillera Bolivia 18°30S 64°55W 331 D5
Central, Cordillera Colombia 5°0N 75°0W 328 C3
Central, Cordillera Costa Rica 10°10N 84°5W 320 D3
Central, Cordillera Dom. Rep. 19°15N 71°0W 321 C5
Central, Cordillera Peru 7°0S 77°30W 330 B2
Central, Cordillera Phil. 17°20N 120°57E 232 C3
Central, Cordillera Puerto Rico 18°8N 66°35W 321 b
Central, Gare Montréal, Canada 130 c2
Central African Empire = Central African Rep. ■ Africa 7°0N 20°0E 264 A4
Central African Rep. ■ Africa 7°0N 20°0E 264 A4
Central America America 12°0N 85°0W 292 H11
Central Australia ◇ Australia 22°30S 128°30E 278 D4
Central Bedfordshire □ U.K. 52°5N 0°20W 169 E7
Central Butte Canada 50°48N 106°31W 297 C7
Central City Colo., U.S.A. 39°48N 105°31W 304 G11
Central City Iowa, U.S.A. 42°12N 91°32W 310 B5
Central City Ky., U.S.A. 37°18N 87°7W 308 G10
Central City Nebr., U.S.A. 41°7N 98°0W 308 E4
Central Desert ◇ Australia 19°56S 130°46E 278 C5
Central Equatoria □ South Sudan 4°0N 31°0E 257 G3
Central I. Kenya 3°30N 36°0E 268 B4
Central Island △ Kenya 2°33N 36°1E 268 B4
Central Japan Int. ✈ (NGO) Japan 34°53N 136°45E 223 C8
Central Kalahari ⌓ Botswana 22°36S 23°58E 270 B3
Central Makran Range Pakistan 26°30N 64°15E 240 D2
Central Pacific Basin Pac. Oc. 8°0N 175°0W 288 G10
Central Park New York, U.S.A. 132 a3
Central Park Zoo New York, U.S.A. 132 b2
Central Patricia Canada 51°30N 90°9W 298 B1
Central Point U.S.A. 42°23N 122°55W 304 E2
Central Provinces = Madhya Pradesh □ India 22°50N 78°0E 242 J8
Central Ra. Papua N. G. 5°0S 143°0E 286 C2
Central Ra. Trin. & Tob. 10°25N 61°15W 323 t
Central Range Wildlife Sanctuary ⌓ Trin. & Tob. 10°27N 61°14W 323 t
Central Russian Uplands Europe 54°0N 36°0E 158 E13
Central Siberian Plateau Russia 65°0N 105°0E 210 B12
Central Square U.S.A. 43°17N 76°9W 313 C8
Central Village Jamaica 17°59N 76°55W 320 a
Centralia Ont., Canada 43°17N 81°28W 312 C3
Centralia Ill., U.S.A. 38°32N 89°8W 310 F7
Centralia Mo., U.S.A. 39°13N 92°8W 310 E4
Centralia Wash., U.S.A. 46°43N 122°58W 306 D4
Centre U.S.A. 34°9N 85°41W 316 A4
Centre □ Cameroon 4°45N 12°0E 263 E7
Centre de Flacq Mauritius 20°12S 57°43E 272 e
Centre -Val de Loire □ France 47°30N 1°30E 172 E8
Centreville Mich., U.S.A. 41°55N 85°32W 311 C11
Centreville N.Y., U.S.A. 42°28N 78°14W 312 D6
Centreville Pa., U.S.A. 41°44N 79°45W 312 E5
Century U.S.A. 30°58N 87°16W 317 E2
Century City U.S.A. 34°3N 118°25W 126 B2
Cenxi China 22°57N 110°57E 229 F8
Čeotina → Bos.-H. 43°36N 18°50E 202 C2
Cephalonia = Kefalonia Greece 38°15N 20°30E 207 C2
Čepin Croatia 45°32N 18°34E 182 E3
Ceprano Italy 41°33N 13°31E 200 A6
Ceptia Angola 12°56S 17°35E 265 E3
Ceptura Romania 45°1N 26°21E 183 E11
Cepu Indonesia 7°9S 111°35E 235 D4
Ceram = Seram Indonesia 3°10S 129°0E 231 E7
Ceram Sea = Seram Sea Indonesia 2°30S 128°30E 231 E7
Cerbère France 42°26N 3°10E 174 F7
Cerbicales, Îs. France 41°33N 9°22E 175 G13
Cercal Portugal 37°48N 8°40W 195 H2
Cerdanya Spain 42°22N 1°35E 196 C6
Cerdanyola del Vallès Spain 41°27N 2°8W 114 A1
Cère → France 44°55N 1°49E 174 D5
Cerea Italy 45°12N 11°13E 199 C8
Ceredigion □ U.K. 52°16N 4°15W 169 E3
Ceres Argentina 29°55S 61°55W 334 B3
Ceres Brazil 15°17S 49°35W 333 E2
Ceres Western Cape, S. Africa 33°21S 19°18E 270 D2
Ceres Calif., U.S.A. 37°35N 120°57W 306 H6
Cerésio, L. di = Lugano, L. di Switz. 46°0N 9°0E 198 C6
Céret France 42°30N 2°42E 174 F6
Cereté Colombia 8°53N 75°48W 328 B2
Cerf Seychelles 4°38S 55°40E 272 c
Cerfs, Îs. aux Mauritius 20°16S 57°47E 272 e
Cergy France 49°2N 2°4E 173 C9
Cerignola Italy 41°17N 15°53E 201 A8
Cerigo = Kythira Greece 36°8N 23°0E 204 E5
Cerillos Chile 33°29S 70°42W 137 B1
Cérilly France 46°37N 2°50E 173 F9
Cerisiers France 48°8N 3°30E 173 D10
Cerizay France 46°50N 0°40W 172 F6
Çerkeş Turkey 40°49N 32°52E 212 B5
Çerkezköy Turkey 41°17N 28°0E 203 E12
Cerknica Slovenia 45°48N 14°21E 199 C11
Cerkovica Bulgaria 43°41N 24°50E 203 C8
Cermerno Serbia 43°35N 20°25E 202 C4
Çermik Turkey 38°8N 39°26E 213 C8
Cerna Romania 45°4N 28°17E 183 E13
Cerna → Romania 44°38N 23°58E 183 F8
Cernauti = Chernivtsi Ukraine 48°15N 25°52E 183 B10
Cernavodă Romania 44°22N 28°3E 183 F13
Cernay France 47°44N 7°10E 173 E14
Černík Croatia 45°17N 17°22E 182 E2
Cerralvo, I. Mexico 24°15N 109°55W 318 C3
Cërrik Albania 41°2N 19°58E 202 E3
Cerritos Mexico 22°25N 100°16W 318 C4
Cerro Chato Uruguay 33°6S 55°8W 335 C4
Cerro Chovoreca △ Paraguay 19°19S 59°7W 331 D6
Cerro Cofre de Perote △ Mexico 19°29N 97°8W 319 D5
Cerro Corá △ Paraguay 22°35S 56°2W 335 A4
Cerro de la Estrella △ Mexico 19°23N 99°5W 128 B2
Cerro de los Angeles Spain 40°18N 3°41W 127 C1
Cerro de Pasco Peru 10°45S 76°10W 330 C2
Cerro El Copey △ Venezuela 11°1N 63°54W 329 a
Cerro Gordo U.S.A. 39°53N 88°44W 311 E8
Cerro Hoya △ Panama 7°17N 80°45W 320 E3
Cerro Navia Chile 33°25S 70°42W 137 B1
Cerro Saroche △ Venezuela 10°8N 69°38W 328 A4
Cerro Sombrero Chile 52°45S 69°15W 336 D3
Cerros Colorados, Embalse Argentina 38°30S 68°50W 336 A3
Certaldo Italy 43°33N 11°2E 198 E8
Cervantes Phil. 17°0N 120°44E 232 C3
Cervaro → Italy 41°30N 15°52E 201 A8
Cervati, Monte Italy 40°17N 15°29E 201 B8
Cerventes Australia 30°31S 115°3E 279 F2
Cervera Spain 41°40N 1°16E 196 D6
Cervera de Pisuerga Spain 42°51N 4°30W 194 C6
Cervera del Río Alhama Spain 42°2N 1°58W 196 C3
Cervéteri Italy 42°0N 12°6E 199 F9
Cérvia Italy 44°15N 12°22E 199 D9
Cervignano del Friuli Italy 45°49N 13°20E 199 C10
Cervinara Italy 41°1N 14°37E 201 A7
Cervione France 42°20N 9°29E 175 F13
Cervo Spain 43°40N 7°24W 194 B3
Cesano Boscone Italy 45°26N 9°5E 128 B1
César □ Colombia 9°0N 73°30W 328 B3
Cesarò Italy 37°50N 14°38E 201 E7
Cesate Italy 45°35N 9°4E 128 A1
Cesena Italy 44°8N 12°15E 199 D9
Cesenático Italy 44°12N 12°24E 199 D9
Cēsis Latvia 57°18N 25°15E 188 D3
Česká Lípa Czechia 50°45N 14°30E 180 A7
Česká Rep. = Czechia ■ Europe 50°0N 15°0E 180 B8

Česká Třebová Czechia 49°54N 16°27E 181 B9
České Budějovice Czechia 48°55N 14°25E 180 C7
České Švýcarsko △ Czechia 50°50N 14°15E 180 A7
České Velenice Czechia 48°45N 14°57E 180 C7
Českobudějovický = Jihočeský □ Czechia 49°8N 14°35E 180 B7
Českomoravská Vrchovina Czechia 49°30N 15°40E 180 B8
Český Brod Czechia 50°4N 14°52E 180 A7
Český Krumlov Czechia 48°43N 14°21E 180 C7
Český Těšín Czechia 49°45N 18°39E 181 B11
Česma → Croatia 45°35N 16°29E 199 C13
Çeşme Turkey 38°20N 26°23E 205 C8
Çeşme Yarımadası Turkey 38°20N 26°30E 205 C8
Cessnock Australia 32°50S 151°21E 283 B9
Cesson-Sévigné France 48°7N 1°36W 172 D5
Cestas France 44°44N 0°41W 174 D3
Cestos → Liberia 5°40N 9°10W 262 D3
Cestos Sehnkwehn △ Liberia 5°40N 9°10W 262 D3
Cetaceo, Mt. Phil. 17°42N 122°3E 232 C4
Cetate Romania 44°7N 23°2E 182 F8
Cetatea-Albă = Bilhorod-Dnistrovskyy Ukraine 46°11N 30°23E 189 J6
Cetin Grad Croatia 45°9N 15°45E 199 C12
Cetina → Croatia 43°26N 16°42E 199 E13
Cetinje Montenegro 42°23N 18°59E 202 D2
Çetmı Turkey 36°52N 32°38E 250 B3
Cetraro Italy 39°31N 15°55E 201 C8
Ceuta N. Afr. 35°52N 5°18W 260 A3
Ceva Italy 44°23N 8°2E 198 D5
Ceve-i-Ra Fiji 21°46S 174°31E 277 E13
Cévennes France 44°10N 3°50E 174 D7
Cévennes △ France 44°15N 3°45E 174 D7
Ceyhan Turkey 37°4N 35°47E 250 A6
Ceyhan → Turkey 36°38N 35°40E 250 B6
Ceylanpınar Turkey 36°50N 40°2E 213 D9
Ceylon = Sri Lanka ■ Asia 7°30N 80°50E 245 L5
Ceylon Plain Ind. Oc. 4°0S 82°0E 273 E7
Cèze → France 44°6N 4°43E 175 D8
Cha-am Thailand 12°48N 99°58E 236 F2
Cha Kwo Ling Hong Kong, China 22°18N 114°13E 122 B3
Chá Pungana Angola 13°44S 18°39E 265 E3
Chabanais France 45°52N 0°48E 174 C4
Chabeuil France 44°54N 5°3E 175 D9
Chablais France 46°20N 6°36E 173 F13
Chablis France 47°47N 3°48E 173 E10
Chabounia Algeria 35°30N 2°38E 261 A5
Chacabuco Argentina 34°40S 60°27W 334 C3
Chacachacare Venezuela 10°58N 64°9W 329 a
Chacachacare I. Trin. & Tob. 10°41N 61°45W 323 t
Chacao, Canal Chile 41°47S 73°42W 336 B2
Chacarrita Argentina 34°35S 58°27W 117 B2
Chachani, Nevado Peru 16°11S 71°31W 330 D3
Chachapoyas Peru 6°15S 77°50W 330 B2
Chachasp Peru 15°30S 72°15W 330 D3
Chachoengsao Thailand 13°42N 101°5E 236 F3
Chachran Pakistan 28°55N 70°30E 242 E4
Chachro Pakistan 25°5N 70°15E 242 G4
Chaco □ Argentina 26°30S 61°0W 334 B3
Chaco □ Paraguay 26°0S 60°0W 334 B4
Chaco → U.S.A. 36°46N 108°39W 305 H9
Chaco △ Argentina 27°0S 59°30W 334 B4
Chaco Culture ⌓ U.S.A. 36°3N 107°58W 305 H10
Chacon, C. U.S.A. 54°42N 132°0W 296 C2
Chad ■ Africa 15°0N 17°15E 259 F3
Chad, L. = Tchad, L. Chad 13°30N 14°30E 259 F2
Chadileuvú → Argentina 37°46S 66°0W 334 D2
Chadiza Zambia 14°45S 32°27E 269 E3
Chadron U.S.A. 42°50N 103°0W 308 D2
Chadwell Heath U.K. 51°34N 0°8E 125 A4
Chadyr-Lunga = Ceadîr-Lunga Moldova 46°3N 28°51E 183 D13
Chae Hom Thailand 18°43N 99°35E 236 C2
Chae Son △ Thailand 18°42N 99°20E 236 C2
Chaem → Thailand 18°11N 98°38E 236 C2
Chaeryŏng N. Korea 38°24N 125°36E 224 C2
Chafe Nigeria 11°59N 6°50E 263 C6
Chagai Hills = Chāh Gay Hills Afghan. 29°30N 64°0E 240 C2
Chagang-do □ N. Korea 40°50N 126°30E 224 B3
Chagda Russia 58°45N 130°38E 215 D14
Chagdo Kangri China 34°15N 84°10E 217 F10
Chaghcharān Afghan. 34°31N 65°15E 240 B2
Chagne Ethiopia 10°57N 36°30E 266 B4
Chagny France 46°57N 4°45E 173 F11
Chagoda Russia 59°10N 35°15E 188 C8
Chagos Arch. ☒ Ind. Oc. 6°0S 72°0E 273 E6
Chagos-Laccadive Ridge Ind. Oc. 3°0N 73°0E 273 D6
Chagres → Panama 9°10N 79°40W 320 c
Chagres △ Panama 9°33N 79°37W 320 c
Chaguanas Trin. & Tob. 10°30N 61°26W 323 t
Chaguaramas Trin. & Tob. 10°41N 61°38W 323 t
Chāh Ākhvor Iran 32°41N 59°40E 247 C8
Chāh Bahar Iran 25°20N 60°40E 247 E9
Chāh-e Āb Afghan. 37°23N 69°48E 240 A3
Chāh-e Kavīr Iran 34°29N 56°52E 247 C8
Chāh Gay Hills Afghan. 29°30N 64°0E 240 C2
Chahār Borj Iran 37°6N 45°59E 213 D11
Chahār Borjak Afghan. 30°17N 62°3E 240 C1
Chahār Mahāll va Bakhtīarī □ Iran 32°0N 49°0E 247 C6
Chahtung Myanmar 26°41N 98°10E 241 B7
Chai Badan Thailand 15°12N 101°8E 236 E3
Chai Chee Singapore 1°19N 103°46E 138 B3
Chai Wan Hong Kong, China 22°16N 114°14E 122 B3
Chai Wan Kok Hong Kong, China 22°22N 114°6E 122 A2
Chaibasa India 22°42N 85°49E 243 H11
Chaidari Greece 38°2N 23°38E 112 A1
Chaillé-les-Marais France 46°25N 1°2W 174 B2
Chaillot, Palais de Paris, France 134 b2
Chaillu, Massif du Gabon 2°32S 11°10E 264 C2
Chain Ridge Ind. Oc. 6°0N 54°0E 273 D4
Chainat Thailand 15°11N 100°8E 236 E3
Chainpur Nepal 27°17N 87°19E 243 F12
Chaires U.S.A. 30°26N 84°7W 316 E5
Chaitén Chile 42°55S 72°43W 336 B2
Chaiya Thailand 9°23N 99°14E 237 H2
Chaiyaphum Thailand 15°48N 102°2E 236 E4
Chaj Doab Pakistan 32°15N 73°0E 242 C5
Chajari Argentina 30°42S 58°0W 334 C4
Chak Amru Pakistan 32°22N 75°11E 242 C6
Chaka South Sudan 4°49N 31°14E 257 G3
Chakar → Pakistan 29°29N 68°2E 242 E3
Chakari Zimbabwe 18°5S 29°51E 271 A4
Chakaria Bangla. 21°45N 92°5E 241 E4
Chakarnaba Chad 14°13N 20°51E 259 F4
Chakdaha India 22°28N 88°19E 124 C1
Chake Chake Tanzania 5°15S 39°45E 268 D4
Chakhānsūr Afghan. 31°10N 62°0E 240 C1
Chakonipau, L. Canada 56°18N 68°30W 299 A6
Chakradharpur India 22°45N 85°40E 243 H11
Chakrata India 30°42N 77°51E 242 D7
Chakwadam Myanmar 27°29N 98°31E 241 B7
Chakwal Pakistan 32°56N 72°53E 242 C5
Chala Peru 15°48S 74°20W 330 D3
Chalais France 45°16N 0°3E 174 C4
Chalakudi India 10°18N 76°20E 245 J3
Chalan Kanoa N. Marianas 15°9N 145°42E 302 e
Chalandri Greece 38°3N 23°48E 112 A2
Chalchihuites Mexico 23°29N 103°53W 318 C4
Chalcis = Chalkida Greece 38°27N 23°42E 204 C5
Châlette-sur-Loing France 48°1N 2°44E 173 D9
Chaleur B. Canada 47°55N 65°30W 299 C6
Chalfant U.S.A. 37°32N 118°21W 306 H8
Chalhuanca Peru 14°15S 73°15W 330 C3
Chalindrey France 47°43N 5°26E 173 E12
Chaling China 26°58N 113°30E 229 D9
Chalisgaon India 20°30N 75°10E 244 D2
Chalk River Canada 46°1N 77°27W 298 C4
Chalkar, Ozero = Shalkar Köli Kazakhstan 50°35N 51°47E 190 E10
Chalki Dodekanisa, Greece 36°17N 27°35E 205 E9
Chalki Thessaly, Greece 39°36N 22°30E 204 B4
Chalkida Greece 38°27N 23°42E 204 C5
Chalkidiki Greece 40°25N 23°20E 202 F7
Chalky Inlet N.Z. 46°3S 166°31E 285 G1
Chalkyitsik U.S.A. 66°39N 143°43W 303 C12
Challakere India 14°19N 76°39E 245 G3
Challans France 46°50N 1°52W 172 F5
Challapata Bolivia 18°53S 66°50W 330 D4
Challawa Gorge Res. Nigeria 11°54N 8°25E 263 C6
Challenger Deep Pac. Oc. 11°30N 142°0E 288 F6
Challenger Fracture Zone Pac. Oc. 35°0S 105°0W 289 L17
Challis U.S.A. 44°30N 114°14W 304 D6
Chalmette U.S.A. 29°56N 89°57W 315 G10
Chaloem Rattanakosin △ Thailand 14°40N 99°17E 236 E2
Chalon-sur-Saône France 46°48N 4°50E 173 F11
Chalong Thailand 7°50N 98°22E 237 a
Chalonnes-sur-Loire France 47°20N 0°45W 172 E6
Châlons-en-Champagne France 48°58N 4°20E 173 D11
Chálten, Cerro = Fitz Roy, Cerro Argentina 49°17S 73°5W 336 C2
Châlus Haute-Vienne, France 45°39N 0°58E 174 C4
Chālūs Iran 36°38N 51°26E 247 B6
Cham Germany 49°13N 12°39E 179 F8
Cham, Cu Lao Vietnam 15°57N 108°30E 236 E7
Chama U.S.A. 36°54N 106°35W 305 H10
Chamah, Gunung Malaysia 5°13N 101°35E 234 A2
Chamaicó Argentina 35°3S 64°58W 334 D3
Chaman Pakistan 30°58N 66°25E 240 C2
Chamartin Spain 40°27N 3°40W 127 B1
Chamba India 32°35N 76°10E 242 C7
Chamba Tanzania 11°37S 37°0E 269 E4
Chambal → India 26°29N 79°15E 243 F8
Chamberi Spain 40°26N 3°42W 127 B1
Chamberlain U.S.A. 43°49N 99°20W 308 D4
Chamberlain → Australia 15°30S 127°54E 278 C4
Chamberlain L. U.S.A. 46°14N 69°19W 309 B19
Chambers U.S.A. 35°11N 109°26W 305 J9
Chambersburg U.S.A. 39°56N 77°40W 309 F15
Chambéry France 45°34N 5°55E 175 C9
Chambi, Jebel Tunisia 35°11N 8°39E 261 A6
Chamblee U.S.A. 33°53N 84°18W 316 B5
Chambly Canada 45°27N 73°17W 313 A11
Chambord Canada 48°25N 72°6W 299 C5
Chamboulive France 45°26N 1°42E 174 C5
Chambourcy France 48°54N 2°2E 134 A1
Chambri L. Papua N. G. 4°15S 143°10E 286 C2
Chamchamal Iraq 35°32N 44°50E 213 E11
Chamela Mexico 19°32N 105°5W 318 D3
Chamical Argentina 30°22S 66°27W 334 C2
Chamili Greece 35°50N 26°15E 205 F8
Chamkar Luong Cambodia 11°0N 103°45E 237 G4
Chamois U.S.A. 38°41N 91°46W 310 F5
Chamoli India 30°24N 79°21E 243 D8
Chamonix-Mont Blanc France 45°55N 6°51E 175 C10
Chamouchuane = Ashuapmushuan → Canada 48°37N 72°20W 298 C5
Champ de Mars, Parc du Paris, France 134 c2
Champa India 22°2N 82°43E 243 H10
Champagne Canada 60°49N 136°30W 296 A1
Champagne France 48°40N 4°20E 173 D11
Champagnole France 46°45N 5°55E 173 F12
Champaign U.S.A. 40°7N 88°15W 311 D8
Champaner India 22°29N 73°32E 242 H5
Champassak Laos 14°53N 105°52E 236 E5
Champaubert France 48°50N 3°45E 173 D10
Champawat India 29°20N 80°6E 243 E9
Champdeniers-St-Denis France 46°29N 0°25W 174 B3
Champdoré, L. Canada 55°55N 65°49W 299 A6
Champeix France 45°37N 3°8E 174 C7
Champhai India 23°28N 93°20E 241 D4
Champigny-sur-Marne France 48°49N 2°30E 134 B4
Champion U.S.A. 41°19N 80°51W 312 E4
Champlain U.S.A. 44°59N 73°27W 313 B11
Champlain, L. U.S.A. 44°40N 73°20W 313 B11
Champlain, Pont Canada 45°28N 73°31W 130 B2
Champlitte France 47°32N 5°31E 173 E12
Champotón Mexico 19°21N 90°43W 319 D6
Champs Elysées, Avenue des Paris, France 134 b2
Champs-sur-Marne France 48°50N 2°34E 134 A4
Champua India 22°5N 85°40E 243 H11
Chamrail India 22°38N 88°17E 124 B1
Chamrajnagar India 11°52N 76°52E 245 J3
Chamusca Portugal 39°21N 8°29W 195 F2
Chan Chan Peru 8°7S 79°0W 330 B2
Chana Thailand 6°55N 100°44E 237 J3
Chanakyapuri India 28°35N 77°11E 120 B2
Chañaral Chile 26°23S 70°40W 334 B1
Chanārān Iran 36°39N 59°6E 247 B8
Chanasma India 23°44N 72°5E 242 H5
Chancay Peru 11°32S 77°25W 330 C2
Chancel, Î. Martinique 14°41N 60°53W 322 j
Chanchiang = Zhanjiang China 21°15N 110°20E 229 G8
Chanco Chile 35°44S 72°32W 334 D1
Chand India 21°57N 79°7E 243 J8
Chandalar → U.S.A. 66°37N 146°0W 303 C11
Chandan Chauki India 28°33N 80°47E 243 E9
Chandannagar India 22°52N 88°24E 243 H13
Chandausi India 28°27N 78°49E 243 E8
Chandeleur Is. U.S.A. 29°55N 88°57W 315 G10
Chandeleur Sd. U.S.A. 29°55N 89°0W 315 G10
Chandigarh India 30°43N 76°47E 242 D7
Chandil India 22°58N 86°3E 243 H12
Chanditala India 22°41N 88°15E 124 A1
Chandler S. Austral., Australia 27°0S 133°19E 281 D1
Chandler Qué., Canada 48°18N 64°46W 299 C7
Chandler Ariz., U.S.A. 33°18N 111°50W 305 K8
Chandler Okla., U.S.A. 35°42N 96°53W 314 D6
Chandless → Brazil 9°8S 69°51W 330 B4
Chandod India 21°59N 73°28E 242 J5
Chandpur Bangla. 23°8N 90°45E 241 D3
Chandra Greece 35°3N 26°8E 205 F8
Chandragiri India 13°35N 79°19E 245 H4
Chandrapur India 19°57N 79°25E 244 E4
Chandrupatla India 18°33N 80°24E 244 E5
Chānf Iran 26°38N 60°29E 247 E9
Chang Pakistan 26°59N 68°30E 242 F3
Chang, Ko Thailand 12°0N 102°23E 237 G4
Chang, Ko Thailand 9°50N 98°27E 237 H2
Ch'ang Chiang = Chang Jiang → China 31°48N 121°10E 229 B13
Chang Jiang → China 31°48N 121°10E 229 B13
Chang-won S. Korea 35°16N 128°37E 224 E4
Changan = Xi'an China 34°15N 109°0E 226 G5
Changan China 22°48N 113°48E 219 a
Changanacheri India 9°25N 76°31E 245 K3
Changanassery = Changanacheri India 9°25N 76°31E 245 K3
Changane → Mozam. 24°30S 33°30E 271 B5
Changbai China 41°25N 128°5E 224 B4
Changbai Shan China 42°20N 129°0E 224 A4
Changchiak'ou = Zhangjiakou China 40°48N 114°55E 226 D8
Changchih = Changzhi China 36°10N 113°6E 226 F7
Changchih Taiwan 22°41N 120°32E 225 D2
Ch'angchou = Changzhou China 31°47N 119°58E 229 B12
Changchow = Changzhou China 31°47N 119°58E 229 B12
Changchun China 43°57N 125°17E 227 C13
Changchunling China 45°18N 125°27E 227 B13
Changde China 29°4N 111°35E 229 C8
Changdo-ri N. Korea 38°30N 127°40E 224 C3
Changfeng China 32°28N 117°10E 229 A11
Changfeng Park China 31°14N 121°24E 138 B1
Changge China 34°13N 113°46E 226 G7
Changhai = Shanghai China 31°15N 121°26E 138 B2
Changhua Zhejiang, China 30°12N 119°12E 229 B12
Changhua Taiwan 24°2N 120°30E 225 B2
Changhua □ Taiwan 24°15N 120°55E 225 B2
Changhŭngni N. Korea 40°24N 128°19E 224 B4
Changi Singapore 1°23N 103°59E 138 A3
Changi, Singapore ✈ (SIN) Singapore 1°23N 103°59E 138 A3
Changji China 44°1N 87°19E 217 D11
Changjiang China 19°20N 108°55E 229 a
Changjiang Shuiku China 22°29N 113°27E 219 a
Changjin N. Korea 40°23N 127°15E 224 B3
Changjin-ho N. Korea 40°30N 127°15E 224 B3
Changle China 25°59N 119°27E 229 E12
Changli China 39°40N 119°13E 227 E10
Changling China 44°20N 123°58E 227 B12
Changlun Malaysia 6°25N 100°26E 237 J3
Changning Hunan, China 26°28N 112°22E 229 D9
Changning Shanghai, China 31°13N 121°24E 138 B1
Changning Sichuan, China 28°40N 104°56E 228 C5
Changning Yunnan, China 24°45N 99°30E 228 E2
Ch'angpin Taiwan 23°19N 121°27E 225 C3
Changping China 40°14N 116°12E 226 D9
Changsha China 28°12N 113°0E 229 C9
Changshan China 28°55N 118°27E 229 C12
Changshan Qundao China 39°11N 122°32E 227 E12
Changshou China 29°50N 107°4E 228 C6
Changshu China 31°38N 120°43E 229 B13
Changshun China 26°3N 106°25E 228 D6
Changtai China 24°35N 117°42E 229 E11
Changt'e = Chongde China 30°32N 120°26E 229 B13
Changting China 25°50N 116°22E 229 E11
Changtu China 42°46N 124°6E 227 C13
Changuinola Panama 9°26N 82°31W 320 E3
Changwu Guangxi Zhuangzu, China 23°25N 111°17E 229 F8
Changwu Shaanxi, China 35°10N 107°45E 226 G4
Changxing China 31°0N 119°55E 229 B12
Changyang China 30°30N 111°10E 229 B8
Changyi China 36°40N 119°30E 227 F10
Changyŏn N. Korea 38°15N 125°6E 224 C2
Changyuan Henan, China 35°15N 114°42E 226 G8
Changyuan Taiwan 23°25N 121°29E 225 C3
Changzhi = Changchih Taiwan 22°41N 120°32E 225 D2
Changzhi China 36°10N 113°6E 226 F7
Changzhou China 31°47N 119°58E 229 B12
Chanhanga Angola 16°0S 14°8E 265 F2
Chania Greece 35°30N 24°4E 207 E5
Chania ✈ (CHQ) Greece 35°30N 24°6E 207 E5
Chanion, Kolpos Greece 35°33N 23°55E 207 E4
Chanlar = Goygöl Azerbaijan 40°37N 46°12E 191 K8
Channagiri India 14°2N 75°56E 245 G2
Channapatna India 12°40N 77°15E 245 H3
Channel Is. U.K. 49°19N 2°24W 169 H5
Channel Is. Calif., U.S.A. 33°40N 119°15W 307 M7
Channel Islands △ U.S.A. 34°0N 119°24W 307 L7
Channel-Port aux Basques Canada 47°30N 59°9W 299 C8
Channel Tunnel Europe 51°0N 1°30E 169 F9
Channing U.S.A. 35°41N 102°20W 314 D3
Chantada Spain 42°36N 7°46W 194 C3
Chantereine France 48°53N 2°37E 134 A4
Chanthaburi Thailand 12°38N 102°12E 236 F4
Chantian China 23°12N 113°16E 121 A2
Chantilly France 49°12N 2°29E 173 C9
Chantonnay France 46°40N 1°3W 172 F5
Chantrey Inlet Canada 67°48N 96°20W 294 D12
Chanumla India 8°19N 93°5E 245 K11
Chanute U.S.A. 37°41N 95°27W 308 G6
Chany, Ozero Russia 54°49N 77°29E 217 B9
Chanza → Spain 37°32N 7°30W 195 H3
Chao Hu China 31°30N 117°30E 229 B11
Chao Phraya → Thailand 13°40N 100°31E 236 F3
Chao Phraya Lowlands Thailand 15°30N 100°0E 236 E3
Chaocheng China 36°4N 115°37E 226 F8
Ch'aochou Taiwan 22°33N 120°32E 225 D2
Chaohu China 31°38N 117°50E 229 B11
Chaouia-Ouardigha □ Morocco 33°0N 7°30W 260 B3
Chaoyang Beijing, China 39°53N 116°26E 114 B2
Chaoyang Guangdong, China 23°17N 116°30E 229 F11
Chaoyang Liaoning, China 41°35N 120°22E 227 D11
Chaoyangmen China 39°54N 116°23E 114 B2
Chaozhou = Ch'aochou Taiwan 22°33N 120°32E 225 D2
Chaozhou China 23°42N 116°32E 229 F11
Chapada Diamantina △ Brazil 12°52S 41°30W 333 D3
Chapada dos Guimarães Brazil 15°26S 55°45W 331 D6
Chapada dos Guimarães △ Brazil 15°18S 55°54W 331 D6
Chapada dos Veadeiros △ Brazil 14°0S 47°30W 333 D2
Chapaev Kazakhstan 50°25N 51°10E 190 E10
Chapais Canada 49°47N 74°51W 298 C5
Chapala Mozam. 15°50S 37°35E 269 F4
Chapala, L. de Mexico 20°15N 103°0W 318 C4
Chaparé → Bolivia 15°58S 64°42W 331 D5
Chaparmukh India 26°12N 92°31E 241 B4
Chaparral Colombia 3°43N 75°28W 328 C2
Chapayevsk Russia 53°0N 49°40E 190 D9
Chapecó Brazil 27°14S 52°41W 335 B5
Chapel Hill U.S.A. 35°55N 79°4W 315 D15
Chapelton Jamaica 18°5N 77°16W 320 a
Chapin = Edinburg U.S.A. 26°18N 98°10W 314 H5
Chapin U.S.A. 39°46N 90°24W 310 E6
Chapleau Canada 47°50N 83°24W 298 C3
Chaplin Canada 50°28N 106°40W 297 C7
Chaplin L. Canada 50°22N 106°36W 297 C7
Chaplino Ukraine 48°8N 36°15E 189 H9
Chaplygin Russia 53°15N 40°0E 188 F11
Chappell U.S.A. 41°6N 102°28W 308 E2
Chappells U.S.A. 34°11N 81°52W 316 A8
Chapra = Chhapra India 25°48N 84°44E 243 G11
Chapultepec, Bosque de Mexico 19°25N 99°11W 128 B1
Chapultepec, Castillo de Mexico 19°25N 99°10W 128 B1
Chaqābel Iran 33°16N 47°30E 213 F12
Châr Mauritania 21°32N 12°45W 260 D2
Chara Russia 56°54N 118°20E 215 D12
Charadai Argentina 27°35S 59°55W 334 B4
Charagato, Pta. Venezuela 10°50N 64°9W 329 a
Charagua Bolivia 19°45S 63°10W 331 D5
Charakas Greece 35°1N 25°7E 207 E6
Charalá Colombia 6°17N 73°10W 328 B3
Charambirá, Punta Colombia 4°16N 77°32W 328 C2
Charaña Bolivia 17°30S 69°25W 330 D4
Charantsavan Armenia 40°35N 44°41E 191 K7
Charanwala India 27°51N 72°10E 242 F5
Charapita Colombia 0°37S 74°21W 328 D3
Charata Argentina 27°13S 61°14W 334 B3
Charcas Mexico 23°8N 101°7W 318 C4
Charcot I. Antarctica 70°0S 70°0W 151 C17
Chard U.K. 50°52N 2°58W 169 G5
Chardon U.S.A. 41°35N 81°12W 312 E3
Charduar India 26°51N 92°46E 241 B4
Chardzhou = Türkmenabat Turkmenistan 39°6N 63°34E 247 B9
Charente □ France 45°50N 0°16E 174 C4
Charente → France 45°57N 1°5W 174 C2
Charente-Inférieure = Charente-Maritime □ France 45°45N 0°45W 174 C3
Charente-Maritime □ France 45°45N 0°45W 174 C3
Charenton-du-Cher France 46°44N 2°39E 173 F9
Charenton-le-Pont France 48°49N 2°25E 134 B3
Chari → Chad 12°58N 14°31E 259 F2
Chari-Baguirmi □ Chad 11°0N 17°0E 259 F3
Chārīkār Afghan. 35°0N 69°10E 240 B3
Charing U.S.A. 32°28N 84°22W 316 C5
Charing Cross London, U.K. 125 b4
Chariton U.S.A. 41°1N 93°19W 310 C3
Chariton → U.S.A. 39°19N 92°58W 310 E4
Charity Guyana 7°24N 58°36W 329 B6
Chärjew = Türkmenabat Turkmenistan 39°6N 63°34E 247 B9
Charkhari India 25°24N 79°45E 243 G8
Charkhi Dadri India 28°37N 76°17E 242 E7
Charleroi Belgium 50°24N 4°27E 170 D4
Charleroi Pa., U.S.A. 40°9N 79°57W 312 F5
Charleroi, Kanal de → Belgium 50°51N 4°19E 116 B1
Charles, C. U.S.A. 37°7N 75°58W 309 G16
Charles, I. = Santa María, I. Ecuador 1°17S 90°26W 330 a
Charles, Peak Australia 32°52S 121°11E 279 F3
Charles Bridge = Karlův most Prague, Czechia 135 b1
Charles City U.S.A. 43°4N 92°41W 310 A4
Charles de Gaulle, Paris ✈ (CDG) France 49°0N 2°32E 173 D9
Charles Gates Dawes House U.S.A. 42°2N 87°40W 119 A2
Charles I. Canada 62°39N 74°15W 295 E17
Charles L. Canada 59°50N 110°33W 297 B6
Charles Sound N.Z. 45°2S 167°4E 285 F2
Charles Square = Karlovo náměstí Prague, Czechia 135 c1
Charles Town U.S.A. 39°17N 77°52W 309 F15
Charlesbourg Canada 46°51N 71°16W 309 B18
Charleston Ill., U.S.A. 39°30N 88°10W 311 E8
Charleston Miss., U.S.A. 34°1N 90°4W 315 D9
Charleston Mo., U.S.A. 36°55N 89°21W 308 G9
Charleston S.C., U.S.A. 32°46N 79°56W 316 C10
Charleston W. Va., U.S.A. 38°21N 81°38W 309 F13
Charleston L. Canada 44°32N 76°0W 313 B9
Charleston Peak U.S.A. 36°16N 115°42W 307 J11
Charlestown Mayo, Ireland 53°58N 8°48W 166 C3
Charlestown St. Kitts & Nevis 17°8N 62°37W 322 d
Charlestown KwaZulu Natal, S. Africa 27°26S 29°53E 271 C4
Charlestown Ind., U.S.A. 38°27N 85°40W 311 F11
Charlestown Mass., U.S.A. 42°22N 71°4W 116 A2
Charlestown N.H., U.S.A. 43°14N 72°25W 313 C12
Charlestown Bridge Boston, U.S.A. 116 a2
Charlestown of Aberlour U.K. 57°28N 3°14W 167 D5
Charleville Queens., Australia 26°24S 146°15E 281 D4
Charleville Cork, Ireland 52°21N 8°40W 166 D3
Charleville-Mézières France 49°44N 4°40E 173 C11
Charlevoix U.S.A. 45°19N 85°16W 309 C11
Charlie Gibbs Fracture Zone Atl. Oc. 52°45N 35°30W 152 A8
Charlieu France 46°10N 4°10E 173 F11
Charlotte Mich., U.S.A. 42°34N 84°50W 311 B12
Charlotte N.C., U.S.A. 35°13N 80°50W 315 D14
Charlotte Vt., U.S.A. 44°19N 73°16W 313 B11
Charlotte Amalie U.S. Virgin Is. 18°21N 64°56W 321 C7
Charlotte-Douglas Int. ✈ (CLT) U.S.A. 35°12N 80°56W 315 D14
Charlotte Harbor U.S.A. 26°57N 82°4W 317 J7
Charlotte L. Canada 52°12N 125°19W 296 C3
Charlotte Ville Dominica 15°17N 61°24W 323 k
Charlottenberg Sweden 59°54N 12°17E 162 E6
Charlottenburg Germany 52°31N 13°14E 115 A2
Charlottenburg, Schloss Germany 52°31N 13°18E 115 A2
Charlottenlund Denmark 55°44N 12°35E 118 A3
Charlottesville U.S.A. 38°2N 78°30W 309 F14
Charlottetown Nfld. & L., Canada 52°46N 56°7W 299 B8
Charlottetown P.E.I., Canada 46°14N 63°8W 299 C7
Charlotteville Trin. & Tob. 11°20N 60°33W 323 s
Charlton Vic., Australia 36°16S 143°24E 282 D5
Charlton London, U.K. 51°29N 0°1E 125 B4
Charlton I. Canada 52°0N 79°20W 298 B4
Charmes France 48°22N 6°17E 173 D13
Charneca Lisboa, Portugal 38°47N 9°8W 126 A2
Charneca Setúbal, Portugal 38°37N 9°12W 126 B1
Charny Canada 46°43N 71°15W 299 C5
Charnyany Belarus 51°59N 24°12E 185 G11
Charolles France 46°27N 4°16E 173 F11
Chârost France 47°0N 2°7E 173 F9
Charouine Algeria 29°0N 0°15W 261 C4
Charre Mozam. 17°13S 35°10E 269 F4
Charroux France 46°9N 0°25E 174 B4
Charsadda Pakistan 34°7N 71°45E 242 B4
Charshanga = Köýtendag Turkmenistan 37°30N 66°1E 240 A2
Charters Towers Australia 20°5S 146°13E 280 C4
Chartres France 48°29N 1°30E 172 D8
Chartreuse ⌓ France 45°22N 5°42E 175 C9
Charuma Trin. & Tob. 10°24N 61°9W 323 t
Charysh → Russia 52°22N 83°45E 217 B10
Chascomús Argentina 35°30S 58°0W 334 D4
Chase Canada 50°50N 119°41W 296 C5
Chase, L. U.S.A. 28°28N 81°31W 133 B1
Chasefu Zambia 11°55S 33°8E 269 E3
Chashma Barrage Pakistan 32°27N 71°20E 242 C4
Chaslands Mistake N.Z. 46°38S 169°22E 285 G4
Chasong N. Korea 41°27N 126°38E 224 B3
Chasseneuil-sur-Bonnieure France 45°52N 0°29E 174 C4
Chastanet, Anse St. Lucia 13°52N 61°5W 323 m
Chāt Iran 37°59N 55°16E 247 B7
Chatal Balkan = Udvoy Balkan Bulgaria 42°50N 26°50E 203 D10
Chatanika U.S.A. 65°7N 147°28W 303 D11
Château-Arnoux-St-Auban France 44°6N 6°0E 175 D10
Château-Chinon France 47°4N 3°56E 173 E10
Château-d'Olonne France 46°30N 1°44W 174 B2
Château-du-Loir France 47°40N 0°25E 172 E7
Château Dubug Martinique 14°46N 60°55W 322 j
Château Gaillard Guadeloupe 16°18N 61°23W 322 e
Château-Gontier France 47°50N 0°48W 172 E6
Château-la-Vallière France 47°30N 0°20E 172 E7
Château-Landon France 48°8N 2°40E 173 D9
Château Murat Guadeloupe 15°52N 61°17W 322 e
Château-Renard France 47°56N 2°55E 173 E9
Château-Renault France 47°36N 0°56E 172 E7
Château-Salins France 48°50N 6°30E 173 D13
Château-Thierry France 49°3N 3°20E 173 C10
Chateaubelair St. Vincent 13°17N 61°15W 323 n
Châteaubourg France 48°7N 1°25W 172 D5
Châteaubriant France 47°43N 1°23W 172 E5
Châteaudun France 48°3N 1°20E 172 D8
Châteaufort France 48°44N 2°5E 134 B1
Chateaugay U.S.A. 44°56N 74°5W 313 B10
Châteaugiron France 48°3N 1°30W 172 D5
Châteauguay, L. Canada 56°26N 70°3W 299 A5
Châteaulin France 48°11N 4°8W 172 D2
Châteaumeillant France 46°35N 2°12E 173 F9
Châteauneuf-du-Faou France 48°11N 3°50W 172 D3
Châteauneuf-sur-Charente France 45°36N 0°3W 174 C3
Châteauneuf-sur-Cher France 46°52N 2°18E 173 F9
Châteauneuf-sur-Loire France 47°52N 2°13E 173 E9
Châteaurenard France 43°53N 4°51E 175 E8
Châteauroux France 46°50N 1°40E 173 F8
Châteauvillain France 48°2N 4°55E 173 D11
Châteaux, Pte. des Guadeloupe 16°15N 61°10W 322 e
Châtel-Guyon France 45°55N 3°4E 174 C7
Châtelaillon-Plage France 46°5N 1°5W 174 B2
Châtellerault France 46°50N 0°30E 172 F7
Châtelus-Malvaleix France 46°18N 2°1E 173 F9
Châtenay-Malabry France 48°46N 2°16E 134 B2
Chatham = Miramichi Canada 47°2N 65°28W 299 C6
Chatham Ont., Canada 42°24N 82°11W 312 D2
Chatham Medway, U.K. 51°22N 0°32E 169 F8
Chatham Ill., U.S.A. 41°45N 87°36W 119 C3
Chatham Ill., U.S.A. 39°40N 89°42W 310 E7
Chatham N.Y., U.S.A. 42°21N 73°36W 313 D11
Chatham, I. = San Cristóbal, I. Ecuador 0°50S 89°26W 330 a
Chatham, I. Chile 50°40S 74°25W 336 D2
Chatham I. N.Z. 43°50S 176°20W 285 a
Chatham Is. Pac. Oc. 44°0S 176°40W 285 a
Chatham Rise Pac. Oc. 43°30S 180°0E 288 M10
Châtillon Hauts-de-Seine, France 48°48N 2°17E 134 B2
Châtillon Italy 45°45N 7°37E 198 C4
Châtillon-Coligny France 47°50N 2°51E 173 E9
Châtillon-en-Diois France 44°41N 5°29E 175 D9
Châtillon-sur-Indre France 46°59N 1°10E 172 F8
Châtillon-sur-Loire France 47°35N 2°44E 173 E9
Châtillon-sur-Seine France 47°50N 4°33E 173 E11
Chatmohar Bangla. 24°15N 89°15E 243 G13
Chatou France 48°53N 2°9E 134 A1
Chatpur India 22°36N 88°22E 124 B2
Chatra India 24°12N 84°56E 243 G11
Chatrapur India 19°22N 85°2E 244 E7
Chats, L. des Canada 45°30N 76°20W 313 A8
Chatsu India 26°36N 75°57E 242 F6
Chatswood Australia 33°47S 151°11E 139 A2
Chatsworth Ont., Canada 44°27N 80°54W 312 B4
Chatsworth Ill., U.S.A. 40°45N 88°18W 311 D8
Chatsworth Zimbabwe 19°38S 31°13E 269 F3
Chatta-Hantō Japan 34°45N 136°55E 223 C8
Châttagâm = Chattogram Bangla. 22°19N 91°48E 241 D3
Chattahoochee U.S.A. 30°42N 84°51W 316 E5
Chattahoochee → U.S.A. 30°54N 84°57W 316 E5
Chattanooga U.S.A. 35°3N 85°19W 315 D12
Chatteris U.K. 52°28N 0°2E 169 E8
Chattogram Bangla. 22°19N 91°48E 241 D3
Chattogram □ Bangla. 24°5N 91°0E 241 C3
Chatturat Thailand 15°40N 101°51E 236 E3
Chatuchak Thailand 13°48N 100°33E 113 B2
Chatuchak Park Thailand 13°48N 100°32E 113 B2
Chau Doc Vietnam 10°42N 105°7E 237 G5
Chaubourg, Mt. St. Lucia 14°2N 60°57W 323 m
Chaudes-Aigues France 44°51N 3°1E 174 D7
Chauffailles France 46°13N 4°20E 173 F11
Chauk Myanmar 20°53N 94°49E 241 E5
Chaukan Pass Myanmar 27°8N 97°10E 241 B6
Chauki Pakistan 24°55N 66°56E 123 A1
Chaumont Haute-Marne, France 48°7N 5°8E 173 D12
Chaumont N.Y., U.S.A. 44°4N 76°8W 313 B8
Chaumont-en-Vexin France 49°16N 1°53E 173 C8
Chaumont-sur-Loire France 47°29N 1°11E 172 E8
Chaunay France 46°13N 0°9E 174 B4
Chaung-u Myanmar 21°57N 95°16E 241 E5
Chaungtha Myanmar 16°58N 94°27E 241 G5
Chaunskaya G. Russia 69°0N 169°0E 215 C17
Chauny France 49°37N 3°12E 173 C10
Chaura India 8°27N 93°2E 245 K11
Chausey, Îs. France 48°52N 1°49W 172 D5
Chaussin France 46°59N 5°22E 173 F12
Chautara Nepal 27°46N 85°42E 243 F11
Chautauqua L. U.S.A. 42°10N 79°24W 312 D5
Chauvigny France 46°34N 0°39E 172 F7
Chauvin Canada 52°45N 110°10W 297 C6
Chavakachcheri Sri Lanka 9°39N 80°9E 245 K5
Chavanges France 48°30N 4°35E 173 D11
Chavantina Brazil 14°40S 52°21W 331 C7
Chavarria Peru 12°0S 77°7W 124 B2
Chavash Varmane △ Russia 54°50N 47°10E 190 C8
Chavdata Greece 38°12N 20°23E 207 C1
Chaves Brazil 0°15S 49°55W 332 B2
Chaves Portugal 41°45N 7°32W 194 D3
Chaville France 48°48N 2°11E 134 B2
Chavín de Huantar Peru 9°35S 77°10W 330 B2
Chavuma Zambia 13°4S 22°40E 265 E4
Chawang Thailand 8°25N 99°30E 237 H2
Chayang S. Korea 37°32N 127°3E 137 B2
Chaykovskiy Russia 56°47N 54°9E 186 C9
Chazelles-sur-Lyon France 45°39N 4°22E 175 C8
Chazuta Peru 6°30S 76°0W 330 B2
Chazy U.S.A. 44°53N 73°26W 313 B11
Cheaha Mt. U.S.A. 33°29N 85°49W 316 B4
Cheb Czechia 50°9N 12°28E 180 A5
Chebanse U.S.A. 41°0N 87°54W 311 D9
Chebbi, Erg Africa 31°12N 3°58W 260 B4
Cheboksarskoye Vdkhr. Russia 56°13N 46°58E 190 B8
Cheboksary Russia 56°8N 47°12E 190 B8
Cheboygan U.S.A. 45°39N 84°29W 309 C11
Chebsara Russia 59°10N 38°59E 188 C10
Chech, Erg Africa 25°0N 2°15W 260 D4
Chechelnyk Ukraine 48°13N 29°22E 183 B14
Chechen, Ostrov Russia 43°59N 47°40E 191 H8
Ch'ech'eng Taiwan 22°5N 120°42E 225 D2
Chechenia □ Russia 43°30N 45°29E 191 J7
Checheno-Ingush Republic = Chechenia □ Russia 43°30N 45°29E 191 J7
Chechnya = Chechenia □ Russia 43°30N 45°29E 191 J7
Chęciny Poland 50°46N 20°28E 185 H7
Checotah U.S.A. 35°28N 95°31W 314 D7
Chedabucto B. Canada 45°25N 61°8W 299 C7
Cheduba I. Myanmar 18°45N 93°40E 241 F4
Cheektowaga U.S.A. 42°54N 78°45W 312 D6
Cheepie Australia 26°33S 145°0E 281 D4
Cheeyou Trin. & Tob. 10°33N 61°8W 323 t
Chef-Boutonne France 46°7N 0°4W 174 B3
Chefchaouen Morocco 35°9N 5°15W 260 A3
Cheffadine Niger 19°57N 12°11E 259 D2
Chefoo = Yantai China 37°34N 121°22E 227 F11
Chefornak U.S.A. 60°13N 164°12W 303 F6
Chegdomyn Russia 51°7N 133°1E 215 D14
Chegga Mauritania 25°27N 5°40W 260 C3
Chegutu Zimbabwe 18°10S 30°14E 269 F3
Chehalis U.S.A. 46°40N 122°58W 306 D4
Chehalis → U.S.A. 46°57N 123°50W 306 D3
Cheile Bicazului-Hăşmaş △ Romania 46°55N 25°50E 183 D10
Cheile Nerei-Beusnita △ Romania 44°56N 21°52E 182 F6
Cheiron, Mt. du France 43°49N 6°58E 175 E10
Cheju = Jeju S. Korea 33°31N 126°32E 224 a
Cheju-do = Jeju-do S. Korea 33°29N 126°34E 224 a
Cheju Str. = Jeju Haehyop S. Korea 33°50N 126°30E 227 H14
Chek Lap Kok Hong Kong, China 22°18N 113°56E 122 B1
Chek Lap Kok ✈ (HKG) Hong Kong, China 22°19N 113°57E 122 B1
Chekalin Russia 54°10N 36°10E 188 E9
Chekhovo Russia 54°33N 20°43E 184 D7
Chekiang = Zhejiang □ China 29°0N 120°0E 229 C13
Chel = Kuru, Bahr el → South Sudan 8°10N 26°50E 257 F2
Chela, Sa. da Angola 16°20S 13°20E 265 F2
Chelan U.S.A. 47°51N 120°1W 304 C3
Chelan, L. U.S.A. 48°11N 120°30W 304 B3
Cheleken = Hazar Turkmenistan 39°34N 53°16E 187 G9
Cheleken Yarymadasy Turkmenistan 39°30N 53°15E 247 B7
Chelforó Argentina 39°0S 66°33W 336 A3
Chéliff, O. → Algeria 36°0N 0°8E 261 A5
Chelkar = Shalqar Kazakhstan 47°48N 59°39E 216 C5
Chella Ethiopia 5°0N 37°26E 257 F4
Chellala Dahrania Algeria 33°2N 0°1E 261 B5
Chelles France 48°53N 2°35E 134 A4
Chelles, Canal de France 48°51N 2°35E 134 A4
Chelles-le-Pin ✈ France 48°53N 2°36E 134 A4
Chełm Poland 51°8N 23°30E 185 G10
Chełmno Poland 53°20N 18°30E 185 E5
Chelmsford U.K. 51°44N 0°29E 169 F8
Chełmża Poland 53°10N 18°39E 185 E5
Chelny = Naberezhnyye Chelny Russia 55°42N 52°19E 190 C11
Chelsea Vic., Australia 38°5S 145°8E 283 E6
Chelsea London, U.K. 51°29N 0°10W 125 B2
Chelsea Mass., U.S.A. 42°23N 71°1W 116 A2
Chelsea Mich., U.S.A. 42°19N 84°1W 311 B12
Chelsea New York, U.S.A. 132 c1
Chelsea Vt., U.S.A. 43°59N 72°27W 313 C12
Cheltenham U.K. 51°54N 2°4W 169 F5
Chelva Spain 39°45N 1°0W 196 F4
Chelyabinsk Russia 55°10N 61°24E 216 A6
Chelyakobi = Kopeysk Russia 55°7N 61°37E 216 A6
Chelyuskin, C. = Chelyuskin, Mys Russia 77°30N 103°0E 215 B11
Chelyuskin, Mys Russia 77°30N 103°0E 215 B11
Chemainus Canada 48°55N 123°42W 306 B3
Chembar = Belinskiy Russia 53°0N 43°25E 190 D6
Chembur India 19°3N 72°53E 130 A2
Chemchâm, Sebkhet Mauritania 21°2N 12°4W 260 D2
Chemillé France 47°14N 0°45W 172 E6
Chemin Grenier Mauritius 20°29S 57°28E 272 e
Chemnitz Germany 50°51N 12°54E 178 E8
Chemulpho = Incheon S. Korea 37°27N 126°40E 224 D3
Chemult U.S.A. 43°14N 121°47W 304 E3
Chen, Gora Russia 65°16N 141°50E 215 C15
Chenab → Pakistan 30°23N 71°2E 242 D4
Chenab Nagar Pakistan 31°45N 72°55E 242 D5
Chenachane Algeria 26°0N 4°15W 260 C4
Chenachane, O. → Algeria 25°20N 3°20W 260 C4
Chenango Forks U.S.A. 42°15N 75°51W 313 D9
Chencha Ethiopia 6°15N 37°32E 257 F4
Chenchiang = Zhenjiang China 32°11N 119°26E 229 A12
Cheney U.S.A. 47°30N 117°35W 304 C5
Cheng Xian China 33°43N 105°42E 226 H3
Chengalpattu India 12°42N 79°58E 245 H4
Chengbu China 26°18N 110°16E 229 D8
Chengcheng China 35°8N 109°56E 226 G5
Chengchou = Zhengzhou China 34°45N 113°34E 226 G7
Chengde China 40°59N 117°58E 227 D9
Chengdong Hu China 32°15N 116°20E 229 A11
Chengdu China 30°38N 104°2E 228 B5
Chengdu Shuangliu Int. ✈ (CTU) China 30°35N 103°57E 228 B4
Chengele India 28°47N 96°16E 241 A6
Chenggong = Ch'engkung Taiwan 23°6N 121°22E 225 C3
Chenggong China 24°52N 102°56E 228 E4
Chenggu China 33°10N 107°21E 228 A6
Chenghai China 23°30N 116°42E 229 F11
Chengjiang China 24°39N 103°0E 228 E4
Chengkou China 31°54N 108°31E 228 B7
Ch'engkung Taiwan 23°6N 121°22E 225 C3
Chengmai China 19°50N 109°58E 229 a
Chengnan Taiwan 23°3N 120°7E 225 C2
Chengshan Jiao China 37°25N 122°44E 227 F12
Chengshousi China 39°49N 116°24E 114 C2
Chengteh = Chengde China 40°59N 117°58E 227 D9
Ch'engtu = Chengdu China 30°38N 104°2E 228 B5
Chengwu China 34°58N 115°50E 226 G8
Chengxi Hu China 32°15N 116°10E 229 A11
Chengyang China 36°18N 120°21E 227 F11
Chenjiagang China 34°23N 119°47E 227 G10
Chenkaladi Sri Lanka 7°47N 81°35E 245 L5
Chennai India 13°8N 80°19E 245 H5
Chennevières-sur-Marne France 48°47N 2°31E 134 B4
Chenoa U.S.A. 40°45N 88°43W 311 D8
Chenôve France 47°16N 5°1E 173 E12
Chenxi China 28°2N 110°12E 229 C8
Chenzhou China 25°47N 113°1E 229 E9
Cheò, Eilean a' = Skye U.K. 57°15N 6°10W 167 D2
Cheo Reo Vietnam 13°20N 108°25E 236 F7
Cheom Ksan Cambodia 14°13N 104°56E 236 E5
Cheonan S. Korea 36°48N 127°9E 224 D3
Cheongdam S. Korea 37°31N 127°2E 137 B2
Cheongdo S. Korea 35°38N 128°42E 224 E4

Cheongju S. Korea 36°39N 127°27E 224 D3
Cheongsando S. Korea 34°11N 126°53E 224 E3
Cheongsong S. Korea 36°25N 129°3E 224 D4
Cheonho S. Korea 37°32N 127°6E 137 B2
Cheonsumman S. Korea 36°33N 126°25E 224 D3
Cheops Egypt 29°58N 31°8E 117 B1
Cheorwon S. Korea 38°15N 127°10E 224 C3
Chepelare Bulgaria 41°44N 24°40E 203 E8
Chepelarska ➜ Bulgaria 42°9N 24°54E 203 D8
Chepén Peru 7°15S 79°23W 330 B2
Chépénéhé N. Cal. 20°47S 167°9E 288 d
Chepes Argentina 31°20S 66°35W 334 C2
Chepo Panama 9°10N 79°6W 320 E4
Chepstow U.K. 51°38N 2°41W 169 F5
Chequamegon B. U.S.A. 46°39N 90°51W 308 B8
Cher □ France 47°10N 2°30E 173 E9
Cher ➜ France 47°21N 0°29E 172 E7
Chéradi Italy 40°27N 17°10E 201 B10
Cheran India 25°45N 90°44E 241 C3
Cherasco Italy 44°39N 7°51E 198 D4
Cherating Malaysia 3°35N 103°5E 234 B2
Cheraw U.S.A. 34°42N 79°53W 315 D15
Cherbourg-Octeville
France 49°39N 1°40W 172 C5
Cherchell Algeria 36°35N 2°12E 261 A5
Cherdakly Russia 54°25N 48°50E 190 C9
Cherdyn Russia 60°24N 56°29E 186 B10
Cheremkhovo Russia 53°8N 103°1E 218 A9
Cherepanovo Russia 54°15N 83°30E 217 B10
Cherepovets Russia 59°5N 37°55E 188 C9
Chergui, Chott ech Algeria 34°21N 0°25E 261 B5
Chergui, Zahrez Algeria 35°11N 3°31E 261 A5
Cherial India 17°55N 78°59E 244 F4
Cheribon = Cirebon
Indonesia 6°45S 108°32E 235 D3
Cherikov = Cherykaw
Belarus 53°32N 31°20E 177 B16
Cheriyam I. India 10°9N 73°40E 245 J1
Cherkasy Ukraine 49°27N 32°4E 189 H7
Cherkasy □ Ukraine 48°55N 30°50E 189 H6
Cherkessk Russia 44°15N 42°5E 191 H6
Cherla India 18°5N 80°49E 244 E5
Cherlak Russia 54°15N 74°55E 217 B8
Chernaya Russia 70°30N 89°10E 215 B9
Chernelytsya Ukraine 48°49N 25°26E 183 B10
Cherni Bulgaria 42°35N 23°18E 202 D7
Chernigov = Chernihiv
Ukraine 51°28N 31°20E 189 G6
Chernigovka Russia 44°19N 132°34E 220 B6
Chernihiv Ukraine 51°28N 31°20E 189 G6
Chernihiv □ Ukraine 51°10N 32°5E 189 G7
Chernivtsi Chernivtsi, Ukraine 48°15N 25°52E 183 B10
Chernivtsi Vinnyts'ka, Ukraine 48°32N 28°9E 183 B13
Chernivtsi □ Ukraine 48°5N 25°30E 183 B10
Chernobyl = Chornobyl
Ukraine 51°20N 30°15E 177 C16
Chernogorsk Russia 53°49N 91°18E 217 B12
Chernomorskoye = Chornomorske
Ukraine 45°31N 32°40E 189 K7
Chernorechye = Dzerzhinsk
Russia 56°14N 43°30E 190 B6
Chernovtsy = Chernivtsi
Ukraine 48°15N 25°52E 183 B10
Chernyakhovsk Russia 54°36N 21°48E 184 D8
Chernyanka Russia 50°56N 37°49E 189 G9
Chernysheyskiy Russia 63°0N 112°30E 215 C12
Chernyye Zemli Russia 46°10N 46°0E 191 H8
Cherokee Iowa, U.S.A. 42°45N 95°33W 308 D6
Cherokee Okla., U.S.A. 36°45N 98°21W 314 C5
Cherokee Village U.S.A. 36°18N 91°31W 314 C9
Cherokees, Grand Lake O' The
U.S.A. 36°28N 94°55W 314 C7
Cherquenco Chile 38°35S 72°0W 336 A2
Cherrapunji India 25°17N 91°47E 241 C3
Cherry Valley U.S.A. 42°48N 74°45W 313 D10
Cherryville U.S.A. 37°51N 91°16W 310 G5
Cherskiy Russia 68°45N 161°18E 215 C17
Cherskogo Khrebet
Russia 65°0N 143°0E 215 C15
Cherso Greece 41°5N 22°47E 202 E6
Chersonesus Ukraine 44°37N 33°30E 189 K7
Chersonisos Akrotiri
Greece 35°30N 24°10E 207 E5
Chertanovka ➜ Russia 55°38N 37°48E 129 C2
Chertanovo Russia 55°38N 37°36E 129 C2
Cherthala India 9°42N 76°20E 245 K3
Chertkov = Chortkiv
Ukraine 49°2N 25°46E 177 D13
Chertkovo Russia 49°25N 40°19E 189 H11
Cherven Belarus 53°45N 28°28E 177 B15
Cherven-Bryag Bulgaria 43°17N 24°7E 203 C8
Chervonoarmiyske
Ukraine 45°47N 28°44E 183 E13
Chervonohrad Ukraine 50°25N 24°10E 177 C13
Cherwell ➜ U.K. 51°44N 1°14W 169 F6
Cherykaw Belarus 53°32N 31°20E 177 B16
Cheryomushki Russia 55°40N 37°35E 129 B2
Chesapeake U.S.A. 36°49N 76°16W 309 G15
Chesapeake B. U.S.A. 38°0N 76°10W 309 F14
Cheshire East □ U.K. 53°15N 2°15W 168 D5
Cheshire West and Chester □
U.K. 53°15N 2°40W 168 D5
Cheshskaya Guba Russia 67°20N 47°0E 186 A8
Cheshunt U.K. 51°43N 0°1W 169 F7
Chesil Beach U.K. 50°37N 2°33W 169 G5
Chesley Canada 44°17N 81°5W 312 B3
Chesnokovka = Novoaltaysk
Russia 53°30N 84°0E 217 B10
Cheste Spain 39°30N 0°41W 197 F4
Chester Ches., U.K. 53°12N 2°53W 168 D5
Chester Calif., U.S.A. 40°19N 121°14W 304 F3
Chester Ga., U.S.A. 32°24N 83°9W 316 C6
Chester Ill., U.S.A. 37°55N 89°49W 310 G7
Chester Mont., U.S.A. 48°31N 110°58W 304 B8
Chester Pa., U.S.A. 39°51N 75°22W 309 F16
Chester S.C., U.S.A. 34°43N 81°12W 315 D14
Chester Vt., U.S.A. 43°16N 72°36W 313 C12
Chester W. Va., U.S.A. 40°37N 80°34W 312 F4
Chester-le-Street U.K. 54°51N 1°34W 168 C6
Chesterfield Derby, U.K. 53°15N 1°25W 168 D6
Chesterfield Mo., U.S.A. 38°40N 90°35W 310 F6
Chesterfield, Îs. N. Cal. 19°52S 158°15E 277 D10
Chesterfield Inlet Canada 63°30N 90°45W 294 E13
Chesterton Ra. Australia 25°30S 147°27E 281 D4
Chesterton Range △
Australia 26°16S 147°22E 281 D4
Chestertown U.S.A. 43°40N 73°48W 313 C11
Chesterville Canada 45°6N 75°14W 313 A9
Chestnut Hill U.S.A. 42°19N 71°10W 116 B1
Chesuncook L. U.S.A. 46°0N 69°21W 309 C19
Chetamale India 10°43N 92°33E 245 J11
Chéticamp Canada 46°37N 60°59W 299 C7
Chetlat I. India 11°42N 72°42E 245 J1
Chetrosu Moldova 48°5N 27°54E 183 B12
Chetumal Mexico 18°30N 88°20W 319 D7
Chetumal, B. de
Cent. Amer. 18°40N 88°10W 319 D7
Chetwynd Canada 55°45N 121°36W 296 B4
Cheung Chau
Hong Kong, China 22°13N 114°1E 122 B2
Cheung Sha
Hong Kong, China 22°14N 113°57E 122 B1
Cheung Sha Wan
Hong Kong, China 22°20N 114°8E 122 B1
Cheung Shue Tan
Hong Kong, China 22°26N 114°11E 122 A3
Chevak U.S.A. 61°32N 165°35W 303 F6
Chevalier, Î. de Martinique 14°25N 60°50W 322 j
Chevanceaux France 45°18N 0°14W 174 C3
Cheverly U.S.A. 38°55N 76°54W 143 B3
Chevilly-Larue France 48°46N 2°21E 134 B3
Cheviot U.S.A. 39°9N 84°36W 311 E12
Cheviot, The U.K. 55°29N 2°9W 168 B5
Cheviot Hills Northumberland,
U.K. 55°20N 2°30W 168 B5
Cheviot Hills Calif., U.S.A. 34°2N 118°24W 126 B2
Cheviot Ra. Australia 25°20S 143°45E 280 D3
Chevreau, Île St. Barts 17°56N 62°51W 322 a
Chevy Chase U.S.A. 38°59N 77°4W 143 B2
Chew Bahir Ethiopia 4°40N 36°50E 257 G4
Chewelah U.S.A. 48°17N 117°43W 304 B5
Chewore ⌓ Zimbabwe 16°0S 29°52E 269 F2
Cheyenne Okla., U.S.A. 35°37N 99°40W 314 D5
Cheyenne Wyo., U.S.A. 41°8N 104°49W 304 F11
Cheyenne ➜ U.S.A. 44°41N 101°18W 308 C3
Cheyenne Wells U.S.A. 38°49N 102°21W 304 G12
Cheyne B. Australia 34°35S 118°50E 279 F2
Cheyur India 12°21N 80°0E 245 H5
Chhabra India 24°40N 76°54E 242 G7
Chhaktala India 22°6N 74°11E 242 H6
Chhapra India 25°48N 84°44E 243 G11
Chhata India 27°42N 77°30E 242 F7
Chhatak Bangla. 25°5N 91°37E 241 C3
Chhatarpur Jharkhand,
India 24°23N 84°11E 243 G11
Chhatarpur Mad. P., India 24°55N 79°35E 243 G8
Chhati India 20°47N 81°40E 244 D5
Chhatrapati Shivaji Int., Mumbai ✈
(BOM) India 19°5N 72°51E 130 A2
Chhatrapati Shivaji Terminus
India 18°56N 72°50E 130 B2
Chhattisgarh □ India 22°0N 82°0E 243 J10
Chhaygaon India 26°3N 91°24E 241 B3
Chhep Cambodia 13°45N 105°24E 236 F5
Chhindwara Mad. P., India 23°3N 79°29E 243 H8
Chhindwara Mad. P., India 22°2N 78°59E 243 H8
Chhinhdipada India 21°6N 84°52E 244 D7
Chhlong Cambodia 12°15N 105°58E 237 F5
Chhota Tawa ➜ India 22°14N 76°36E 242 H7
Chhoti Kali Sindh ➜ India 24°2N 75°31E 242 G6
Chhuikhadan India 21°32N 80°59E 243 J9
Chhuk Cambodia 10°46N 104°28E 237 G5
Chi ➜ Thailand 15°11N 104°43E 236 E5
Chi Ma Wan Pen.
Hong Kong, China 22°14N 114°0E 122 B1
Chi Thanh Vietnam 13°17N 109°16E 236 F7
Chia Keng Singapore 1°21N 103°52E 138 A3
Chiahsien Taiwan 23°5N 120°35E 225 C2
Chiai Taiwan 23°29N 120°25E 225 C2
Chiai □ Taiwan 23°30N 120°30E 225 C2
Chiaksan △ S. Korea 37°15N 128°0E 224 D4
Chiali Taiwan 23°9N 120°10E 225 C2
Chialulantsun Taiwan 22°49N 121°11E 225 D3
Chiamboni Somalia 1°39S 41°35E 267 E5
Chiamussu = Jiamusi
China 46°40N 130°26E 219 B15
Chian Taiwan 23°59N 121°33E 225 C3
Chianapu Taiwan 22°47N 120°36E 225 D2
Chianciano Terme Italy 43°2N 11°49E 199 E8
Chiang Dao Thailand 19°22N 98°58E 236 C2
Chiang Dao, Doi Thailand 19°23N 98°54E 236 C2
Chiang Kham Thailand 19°32N 100°18E 236 C3
Chiang Khan Thailand 17°52N 101°36E 236 D3
Chiang Khong Thailand 20°17N 100°24E 228 G3
Chiang Mai Thailand 18°47N 98°59E 236 C2
Chiang Rai Thailand 19°52N 99°50E 228 H2
Chiang Saen Thailand 20°16N 100°5E 228 G3
Chiangchun Taiwan 23°12N 120°5E 225 C2
Chiange Angola 15°35S 13°40E 265 F2
Chianti Italy 43°32N 11°25E 199 E8
Chiaohsi Taiwan 24°49N 121°46E 225 B3
Chiaotou Taiwan 22°45N 120°18E 225 D2
Chiapa de Corzo Mexico 16°42N 93°0W 319 D6
Chiapas □ Mexico 16°30N 92°30W 319 D6
Chiapas, Sa. Madre de
Mexico 15°40N 93°0W 319 D6
Chiaramonte Gulfi Italy 37°2N 14°42E 201 E7
Chiaravalle Italy 43°36N 13°19E 199 E10
Chiaravalle Centrale Italy 38°41N 16°25E 201 D9
Chiaravalle Milanese Italy 45°24N 9°16E 128 B2
Chiari Italy 45°32N 9°56E 198 C6
Chiatung Taiwan 22°25N 120°32E 225 D2
Chiatura Georgia 42°15N 43°17E 191 J6
Chiautla de Tapia Mexico 18°18N 98°36W 319 D5
Chiávari Italy 44°19N 9°19E 198 D6
Chiavenna Italy 46°19N 9°24E 198 B6
Chiayi = Chiai Taiwan 23°29N 120°25E 225 C2
Chiba Japan 35°30N 140°7E 223 B12
Chiba □ Japan 35°30N 140°20E 223 B12
Chibabava Mozam. 20°17S 33°35E 271 B5
Chibango Angola 13°38S 21°56E 265 E4
Chibemba Cunene, Angola 15°48S 14°8E 265 F2
Chibemba Huíla, Angola 16°20S 15°20E 265 F3
Chibi Zimbabwe 20°18S 30°25E 271 B5
Chibia Angola 15°10S 13°42E 265 F2
Chibizovka = Zherdevka
Russia 51°56N 41°29E 190 E5
Chibougamau Canada 49°56N 74°24W 298 C5
Chibougamau, L. Canada 49°50N 74°20W 298 C5
Chibuk Nigeria 10°52N 12°50E 263 C7
Chibuto Mozam. 24°40S 33°33E 271 B5
Chibyu = Ukhta Russia 63°34N 53°41E 186 B9
Chic-Chocs, Mts. Canada 48°55N 66°0W 299 C6
Chicacole = Srikakulam
India 18°14N 83°58E 244 E6
Chicago U.S.A. 41°52N 87°38W 119 B3
Chicago, Univ. of U.S.A. 41°47N 87°35W 119 C3
Chicago Harbor Chicago, U.S.A. 119 d3
Chicago Heights U.S.A. 41°30N 87°38W 311 C9
Chicago Lawn U.S.A. 41°47N 87°40W 119 C2
Chicago-Midway ✈ (MDW)
U.S.A. 41°47N 87°45W 311 C9
Chicago O'Hare Int. ✈ (ORD)
U.S.A. 41°59N 87°54W 311 C9
Chicago Ridge U.S.A. 41°41N 87°46W 119 C2
Chicago River ➜ Chicago, U.S.A. 119 b2
Chicago River, North Branch ➜
U.S.A. 41°53N 87°42W 119 B2
Chicago Sanitary and Ship Canal
U.S.A. 41°49N 87°45W 119 C2
Chicago State Univ.
U.S.A. 41°43N 87°36W 119 C3
Chicapa ➜
Dem. Rep. of the Congo 6°25S 20°48E 265 D4
Chicha Chad 16°57N 18°34E 259 E3
Chichagof I. U.S.A. 57°30N 135°30W 303 H14
Chichaoua Morocco 31°32N 8°44W 260 B3
Chichawatni Pakistan 30°32N 72°42E 242 D5
Chichén-Itzá Mexico 20°37N 88°35W 319 C7
Chicheng China 40°55N 115°55E 226 D8
Chichester U.K. 50°50N 0°47W 169 G7
Chichester Ra. Australia 22°12S 119°15E 278 D2
Chichi Hualien, Taiwan 23°44N 121°33E 225 C3
Chichi Nant'ou, Taiwan 23°49N 120°47E 225 C2
Chichibu Japan 35°59N 139°10E 223 A11
Chichibu-Tama-Kai △
Japan 35°52N 138°42E 223 B10
Ch'ich'ihaerh = Qiqihar
China 47°26N 124°0E 219 B13
Chicholi India 22°1N 77°40E 242 H8
Ch'ich'ou Taiwan 23°45N 120°33E 225 C2
Chickasaw ⌓ U.S.A. 34°26N 97°0W 314 D6
Chickasha U.S.A. 35°3N 97°58W 314 D6
Chicken U.S.A. 64°5N 141°56W 303 D12
Chiclana de la Frontera
Spain 36°26N 6°9W 195 J4
Chiclayo Peru 6°42S 79°50W 330 B2
Chico U.S.A. 39°44N 121°50W 306 F5
Chico ➜ Chubut, Argentina 44°0S 67°0W 336 B3
Chico ➜ Santa Cruz,
Argentina 50°0S 68°30W 336 D3
Chico ➜ Phil. 17°57N 121°36E 232 C3
Chicoa Mozam. 15°36S 32°20E 269 F3
Chicomba Angola 14°10S 14°52E 265 E2
Chicomo Mozam. 24°31S 34°6E 271 B5
Chicomostoc Mexico 22°28N 102°46W 318 C4
Chiconi Mayotte 12°50S 45°7E 272 b
Chicontepec Mexico 20°58N 98°10W 319 C5
Chicopee U.S.A. 42°9N 72°37W 313 D12
Chicoutimi Canada 48°28N 71°5W 299 C5
Chicualacuala Mozam. 22°6S 31°42E 271 B5
Chicuma Angola 13°26S 14°50E 265 E2
Chidambaram India 11°20N 79°45E 245 J4
Chidenguele Mozam. 24°55S 34°11E 271 B5
Chidley, C. Canada 60°23N 64°26W 295 E19
Chiducuane Mozam. 24°35S 34°25E 271 B5
Chiede Angola 17°15S 16°22E 265 F3
Chiefland U.S.A. 29°29N 82°52W 317 F7
Chiefs Pt. Canada 44°41N 81°18W 312 B3
Chiehting Taiwan 22°54N 120°11E 225 D2
Chiem Hoa Vietnam 22°12N 105°17E 236 A5
Chiemsee Germany 47°53N 12°28E 179 H8
Chienchen Taiwan 22°35N 120°18E 225 D2
Chiengi Zambia 8°45S 29°10E 269 D2
Chiengmai = Chiang Mai
Thailand 18°47N 98°59E 236 C2
Chiengo Angola 13°20S 21°55E 265 E4
Chienti ➜ Italy 43°18N 13°45E 199 E10
Chienzui China 23°12N 113°22E 121 A3
Chieri Italy 45°1N 7°49E 198 C4
Chiers ➜ France 49°39N 4°59E 173 C11
Chiesa in Valmalenco Italy 46°16N 9°51E 198 B6
Chiese ➜ Italy 45°8N 10°25E 198 C7
Chieti Italy 42°21N 14°10E 199 F11
Chifeng China 42°18N 118°58E 227 C10
Chigasaki Japan 35°19N 139°24E 223 B11
Chigirin Ukraine 49°4N 32°38E 189 H7
Chignecto B. Canada 45°30N 64°40W 299 C7
Chignik U.S.A. 56°18N 158°24W 303 H8
Chigorodó Colombia 7°41N 76°42W 328 B2
Chiguana Bolivia 21°0S 67°58W 334 A2
Chigwell U.K. 51°37N 0°5E 169 F8
Chihli, G. of = Bo Hai
China 39°0N 119°0E 227 E10
Ch'ihpen Taiwan 22°42N 121°2E 225 D3
Ch'ihshang Taiwan 23°7N 121°12E 225 C3
Chihsi = Jixi China 45°20N 130°50E 227 B16
Chihu Taiwan 23°54N 120°24E 225 C2
Chihuahua Mexico 28°38N 106°5W 318 B3
Chihuahua □ Mexico 28°30N 106°0W 318 B3
Chiili = Shīeli Kazakhstan 44°20N 66°15E 217 D7
Chik Bollapur India 13°25N 77°45E 245 H3
Chik Sha
Hong Kong, China 22°17N 114°16E 122 B3
Chikalda India 21°24N 77°19E 244 D3
Chikhli Ahmadabad, India 20°45N 73°4E 244 D1
Chikhli Maharashtra, India 20°20N 76°18E 244 D3
Chikkamagaluru India 13°15N 75°45E 245 H2
Chiknayakanhalli India 13°26N 76°37E 245 H3
Chikodi India 16°26N 74°38E 245 F2
Chiku Taiwan 23°8N 120°7E 225 C2
Chikugo Japan 33°14N 130°28E 222 D2
Chikuma-Gawa ➜
Japan 36°59N 138°35E 223 A10
Chikura Japan 34°55N 139°57E 223 C11
Chikushino Japan 33°30N 130°30E 222 D2
Chikwawa Malawi 16°2S 34°50E 269 F3
Chila Angola 12°3S 14°29E 265 E2
Ch'ilaichu Shan Taiwan 24°5N 121°20E 225 B3
Chilanga Zambia 15°33S 28°16E 269 F2
Chilapa Mexico 17°36N 99°10W 319 D5
Chilas Pakistan 35°25N 74°5E 243 B6
Chilaw Sri Lanka 7°30N 79°50E 245 L4
Chilcotin ➜ Canada 51°44N 122°23W 296 C4
Childers Australia 25°15S 152°17E 281 D5
Childersburg U.S.A. 33°16N 86°21W 316 B3
Children's Museum Boston, U.S.A. 116 c3
Children's Palace Beijing, China 114 b2
Childress U.S.A. 34°25N 100°13W 314 D4
Child's Hill U.K. 51°33N 0°12W 125 A2
Chile ■ S. Amer. 35°0S 72°0W 327 G3
Chile Chico Chile 46°33S 71°44W 336 C2
Chile Basin Pac. Oc. 33°0S 80°0W 289 L20
Chile Rise Pac. Oc. 38°0S 92°0W 289 L18
Chilecito Argentina 29°10S 67°30W 334 B2
Chilengue, Serra do
Angola 13°18S 15°22E 265 E2
Chilesso Angola 11°35S 16°34E 265 E3
Chilete Peru 7°10S 78°50W 330 B2
Chilhowee U.S.A. 38°36N 93°51W 310 F3
Chilia, Braţul ➜
Romania 45°14N 29°42E 183 E14
Chilibre Panama 9°9N 79°37W 320 c
Chilik = Shelek
Kazakhstan 43°33N 78°17E 217 D9
Chililabombwe Zambia 12°18S 27°43E 269 E2
Chilim Pakistan 35°5N 75°5E 243 B6
Chilin = Jilin China 43°44N 126°30E 227 C14
Chiliomodi Greece 37°48N 22°51E 204 D4
Chilka L. India 19°40N 85°25E 244 E7
Chilko ➜ Canada 52°0N 123°40W 296 C4
Chilko L. Canada 51°20N 124°10W 296 C4
Chilla Saroda India 28°35N 77°18E 120 B2
Chillagoe Australia 17°7S 144°33E 280 B3
Chillán Chile 36°40S 72°10W 334 D1
Chillicothe Ill., U.S.A. 40°55N 89°29W 310 D7
Chillicothe Mo., U.S.A. 39°48N 93°33W 310 E3
Chillicothe Ohio, U.S.A. 39°20N 82°59W 309 F12
Chilliwack Canada 49°10N 121°54W 296 D4
Chillum U.S.A. 38°56N 76°58W 143 B3
Chilly-Mazarin France 48°42N 2°17E 134 B2
Chilmari Bangla. 25°33N 89°43E 241 C2
Chilo India 27°25N 73°32E 242 F5
Chiloane, I. Mozam. 20°40S 34°55E 271 B5
Chiloé, I. de Chile 42°30S 73°50W 336 B2
Chiloé △ Chile 42°11S 73°59W 336 B2
Chilonda Angola 11°19S 16°12E 265 E3
Chilongo Angola 13°55S 16°35E 265 E3
Chilpancingo Mexico 17°33N 99°30W 319 D5
Chiltern Australia 36°10S 146°36E 283 D7
Chiltern Hills U.K. 51°40N 0°53W 169 F7
Chilton U.S.A. 44°2N 88°10W 308 C9
Chiluage Angola 9°30S 21°50E 265 D4
Chilubi Zambia 11°5S 29°58E 269 E2
Chilubula Zambia 10°14S 30°51E 269 E3
Chilumba Malawi 10°28S 34°12E 269 E3
Chilung Taiwan 25°3N 121°45E 225 A3
Chilwa, L. Malawi 15°15S 35°40E 269 F4
Chimakela Angola 15°24S 16°58E 265 F3
Chimakudi India 25°47N 93°48E 241 C4
Chimaltitán Mexico 21°35N 103°50W 318 C4
Chimán Panama 8°45N 78°40W 320 E4
Chimanimani Zimbabwe 19°48S 32°52E 271 A5
Chimanimani △ Zimbabwe 19°48S 33°0E 271 A5
Chimay Belgium 50°3N 4°20E 170 D4
Chimayo U.S.A. 36°0N 105°56W 305 J11
Chimba Zambia 9°54S 31°28E 269 D3
Chimborazo Ecuador 1°29S 78°55W 328 D2
Chimborazo □ Ecuador 1°0S 78°40W 328 D2
Chimbote Peru 9°0S 78°35W 330 B2
Chimboy Uzbekistan 42°57N 59°47E 216 D5
Chimbu □ Papua N. G. 6°15S 144°50E 286 D3
Ch'imei Taiwan 23°12N 119°25E 225 C1
Ch'imei Yü Taiwan 23°13N 119°26E 225 C1
Chimichagua Colombia 9°15N 73°49W 328 B3
Chimkent = Shymkent
Kazakhstan 42°18N 69°36E 217 D7
Chimoio Mozam. 19°4S 33°30E 269 F3
Chimpembe Zambia 9°31S 29°33E 269 D2
Chimur India 20°30N 79°23E 244 D4
Chin □ Myanmar 22°0N 93°0E 241 E4
Chin Hills Myanmar 22°30N 93°30E 241 D4
Chin Ling Shan = Qinling Shandi
China 33°50N 108°10E 226 H5
China Mexico 25°42N 99°14W 319 B5
China ■ Asia 30°0N 110°0E 219 E11
China, Great Plain of Asia 35°0N 115°0E 210 E13
China Basin San Francisco, U.S.A. 136 c3
China Lake U.S.A. 35°44N 117°37W 307 K9
China Town Toronto, Canada 141 b1
Chinacota Colombia 7°37N 72°36W 328 B3
Chinan = Jinan China 36°38N 117°1E 226 F9
Chinandega Nic. 12°35N 87°12W 320 D2
Chinati Peak U.S.A. 29°57N 104°29W 314 G2
Chinatown Singapore 138 c2
Chinatown Boston, U.S.A. 116 c2
Chinatown Los Angeles, U.S.A. 127 a3
Chinatown New York, U.S.A. 132 e2
Chinatown San Francisco, U.S.A. 136 b2
Chincha Alta Peru 13°25S 76°7W 330 C2
Chinchaga ➜ Canada 58°53N 118°20W 296 B5
Chincheros Peru 13°30S 73°44W 330 C3
Chinchilla Australia 26°45S 150°38E 281 D5
Chinchilla de Monte Aragón
Spain 38°53N 1°40W 197 G3
Chincholi India 17°28N 77°26E 244 E3
Chinchorro, Banco
Mexico 18°35N 87°22W 319 D7
Chinchou = Jinzhou
China 41°5N 121°3E 227 D11
Chinchoua Gabon 0°1N 9°48E 264 B1
Chincoteague U.S.A. 37°56N 75°23W 309 G16
Chinde Mozam. 18°35S 36°30E 269 F4
Chindwin ➜ Myanmar 21°26N 95°15E 241 E5
Chineni India 33°2N 75°15E 243 C6
Chinese Theatre
Los Angeles, U.S.A. 34°6N 118°20W 126 B2
Chinga Mozam. 15°13S 38°35E 269 F4
Chingaza △ Colombia 4°30N 73°40W 328 C3
Chingola Zambia 12°31S 27°53E 269 E2
Chingole Malawi 13°4S 34°17E 269 E3
Chingoni Mayotte 12°48S 45°8E 272 b
Chingpu Taiwan 23°28N 121°29E 225 C3
Ch'ingshui Changhua,
Taiwan 24°16N 120°34E 225 B2
Chingshui Hualien,
Taiwan 24°13N 121°41E 225 B3
Chingshui Ilan, Taiwan 24°39N 121°35E 225 B3
Ch'ingtao = Qingdao
China 36°5N 120°20E 227 F11
Chinguar Angola 12°25S 16°45E 265 E3
Chinguetti Mauritania 20°25N 12°24W 260 D2
Chingune Mozam. 20°33S 34°58E 271 B5
Chingupota India 22°29N 88°14E 124 C1
Chinhanguanine Mozam. 25°21S 32°30E 271 C5
Chinhoyi Zimbabwe 17°20S 30°8E 269 F3
Chinhsien = Jinxian
China 28°26N 116°17E 229 C11
Chiniot Pakistan 31°45N 73°0E 242 D5
Chinipas Mexico 27°23N 108°32W 318 B3
Chinji Pakistan 32°42N 72°22E 242 C5
Chinju = Jinju S. Korea 35°12N 128°2E 224 E4
Chinkai Afghan. 31°57N 67°26E 240 C2
Chinkapook Australia 35°11S 142°57E 282 C5
Chinkiang = Zhenjiang
China 32°11N 119°26E 229 A12
Chinko ➜ C.A.R. 4°50N 23°53E 264 B4
Chinle U.S.A. 36°9N 109°33W 305 H9
Ch'inlun Taiwan 22°32N 120°57E 225 D2
Chinmen Taiwan 24°26N 118°19E 225 a
Chinmen Tao Taiwan 24°26N 118°22E 225 a
Chinna Cr. ➜ Pakistan 24°50N 67°0E 123 B2
Chinnamanur India 9°50N 77°24E 245 K3
Chinnampo = Namp'o
N. Korea 38°52N 125°10E 224 C2
Chino Japan 35°59N 138°9E 223 B10
Chino Calif., U.S.A. 34°1N 117°41W 307 L9
Chino Valley U.S.A. 34°45N 112°27W 305 J7
Chinois, Quartier Montréal, Canada 130 b2
Chinon France 47°10N 0°15E 172 E7
Chinook U.S.A. 48°35N 109°14W 304 B9
Chinook Trough Pac. Oc. 44°0N 175°0W 288 C10
Chinoya Zambia 13°55S 23°16E 265 E4
Chinsali Zambia 10°30S 32°2E 269 E3
Chinshan Taiwan 25°13N 121°38E 225 A3
Chinsura = Chunchura
India 22°53N 88°27E 243 H13
Chintalapudi India 17°4N 80°59E 244 F5
Chintamani India 13°26N 78°3E 245 H4
Chinwangtao = Qinhuangdao
China 39°56N 119°30E 227 E10
Chióggia Italy 45°13N 12°17E 199 C9
Chios Greece 38°27N 26°9E 205 C8
Chipata Zambia 13°38S 32°28E 269 E3
Chipei Tao Taiwan 23°45N 119°37E 225 C1
Chiperceni Moldova 47°31N 28°50E 183 C13
Chipindo Angola 13°49S 15°48E 265 E3
Chipinge Zimbabwe 20°13S 32°28E 269 G3
Chipinge ⌓ Zimbabwe 20°14S 33°0E 269 G3
Chipiona Spain 36°44N 6°26W 195 J4
Chipley U.S.A. 30°47N 85°32W 316 E4
Chiplun India 17°31N 73°34E 244 F1
Chipman Canada 46°6N 65°53W 299 C6
Chipoka Malawi 13°57S 34°28E 269 E3
Chippenham U.K. 51°27N 2°6W 169 F5
Chippewa ➜ U.S.A. 44°25N 92°5W 308 C7
Chippewa Falls U.S.A. 44°56N 91°24W 308 C8
Chipping Norton U.K. 51°56N 1°32W 169 F6
Chiprovtsi Bulgaria 43°24N 22°52E 202 C6
Chiputneticook Lakes
N. Amer. 45°35N 67°35W 309 C20
Chiputo = Vila Vasco da Gama
Mozam. 14°54S 32°14E 269 E3
Chipwi Myanmar 25°53N 98°8E 241 C7
Chiquelequele Angola 16°44S 19°5E 265 F3
Chiquián Peru 10°10S 77°0W 330 C2
Chiquibul ⌓ Belize 16°49N 88°52W 320 C2
Chiquihuite, Cerro Mexico 19°32N 99°8W 128 A2
Chiquimula Guatemala 14°51N 89°37W 320 D2
Chiquinquira Colombia 5°37N 73°50W 328 B3
Chiquitos, Llanos de
Bolivia 18°0S 61°30W 331 D5
Chir ➜ Russia 48°30N 43°0E 191 F6
Chira ➜ Peru 4°54S 81°8W 328 D1
Chirala India 15°50N 80°26E 245 G5
Chiramba Mozam. 16°55S 34°39E 269 F3
Chirawa India 28°14N 75°42E 242 E6
Chirchiq Uzbekistan 41°29N 69°35E 217 D7
Chiredzi Zimbabwe 21°0S 31°38E 271 B5
Chirfa Niger 20°55N 12°22E 259 D2
Chirgua ➜ Venezuela 8°54N 67°58W 328 B4
Chiribiquete △ Colombia 0°31N 72°50W 328 C3
Chiricahua ⌓ U.S.A. 32°0N 109°20W 305 K9
Chiricahua Peak U.S.A. 31°51N 109°18W 305 L9
Chirikof I. U.S.A. 55°50N 155°40W 300 D8
Chiriquí, G. de Panama 8°0N 82°10W 320 E3
Chiriquí, L. de Panama 9°10N 82°0W 320 E3
Chirisa ⌓ Zimbabwe 17°53S 28°15E 269 F2
Chirivira Falls Zimbabwe 21°10S 32°12E 269 G3
Chirmiri India 23°15N 82°20E 243 H10
Chirnogi Romania 44°7N 26°32E 183 F11
Chirongui Mayotte 12°55S 45°9E 272 b
Chirpan Bulgaria 42°10N 25°19E 203 D9
Chirripó Grande, Cerro
Costa Rica 9°29N 83°29W 320 E3
Chirundu Zimbabwe 16°3S 28°50E 271 A4
Chisamba Zambia 14°55S 28°20E 269 E2
Chisapani Nepal 28°37N 81°16E 243 E9
Chisasa Zambia 12°6S 25°30E 265 E5
Chisasibi Canada 53°50N 79°0W 298 B4
Ch'ishan Taiwan 22°44N 120°31E 225 D2
Ch'ishan Hsi ➜ Taiwan 22°51N 120°28E 225 C2
Chisholm Alta., Canada 54°55N 114°10W 296 C6
Chisholm Minn., U.S.A. 47°29N 92°53W 308 B7
Chishtian Mandi Pakistan 29°50N 72°55E 242 E5
Chishui China 28°30N 105°42E 228 C5
Chishui He ➜ China 28°49N 105°50E 228 C5
Chisimaio = Kismaayo
Somalia 0°22S 42°32E 267 E5
Chisimba Falls Zambia 10°12S 30°56E 269 E3
Chişinău Moldova 47°2N 28°50E 183 C13
Chişinău ✈ (KIV) Moldova 47°3N 28°46E 183 C13
Chişineu Criş Romania 46°32N 21°37E 182 D6
Chislehurst U.K. 51°24N 0°6E 125 B4
Chisone ➜ Italy 44°49N 7°25E 198 D4
Chisos Mts. U.S.A. 29°5N 103°15W 314 G3
Chissengue Angola 9°13S 20°34E 265 D4
Chissilo Angola 13°48S 16°31E 265 E3
Chistochina U.S.A. 62°34N 144°40W 303 E11
Chistopol Russia 55°25N 50°38E 190 C10
Chiswick U.K. 51°29N 0°16W 125 B2
Chiswick House U.K. 51°28N 0°15W 125 B2
Chita Colombia 6°11N 72°28W 328 B3
Chita Russia 52°0N 113°35E 219 A11
Chitado Angola 17°10S 14°8E 265 F2
Chitaldrug = Chitradurga
India 14°14N 76°24E 245 G3
Chitan Taiwan 24°35N 121°29E 225 B3
Chitanda ➜ Angola 16°1S 15°12E 265 F3
Chitapur India 17°10N 77°5E 244 F3
Chitembo Angola 13°30S 16°50E 265 E3
Chitina U.S.A. 61°31N 144°26W 303 F11
Chitipa Malawi 9°41S 33°19E 269 D3
Chitose Hokkaidō, Japan 42°49N 141°39E 220 C10
Chitose Kanagawa, Japan 35°33N 139°37E 140 B2
Chitradurga India 14°14N 76°24E 245 G3
Chitrakot India 19°10N 81°40E 244 E5
Chitral Pakistan 35°50N 71°56E 240 B3
Chitralada Palace
Thailand 13°45N 100°31E 113 B2
Chitravati ➜ India 14°45N 78°15E 245 G4
Chitré Panama 7°59N 80°27W 320 E3
Chittagong = Chattogram
Bangla. 22°19N 91°48E 241 D3
Chittaurgarh India 24°52N 74°38E 242 G6
Chittoor India 13°15N 79°5E 245 H4
Chittur India 10°40N 76°45E 245 J3
Chitungwiza Zimbabwe 18°0S 31°6E 269 F3
Chiuju Taiwan 22°44N 120°29E 225 D2
Chiumbe ➜
Dem. Rep. of the Congo 6°59S 21°12E 265 D4
Chiumbo Angola 12°29S 16°8E 265 E3
Chiume Angola 15°3S 21°14E 265 F4
Chiusi Italy 43°1N 11°57E 199 E8
Chiva Spain 39°27N 0°41W 197 F4
Chivacoa Venezuela 10°10N 68°54W 328 A4
Chivasso Italy 45°11N 7°53E 198 C4
Chivay Peru 15°40S 71°35W 330 D3
Chive Bolivia 12°23S 68°35W 330 C4
Chivhu Zimbabwe 19°2S 30°52E 269 F3
Chivilcoy Argentina 34°55S 60°0W 334 C4
Chiwanda Tanzania 11°23S 34°55E 269 E3
Chixi China 22°0N 112°58E 229 G9
Chiyoda Tokyo, Japan 140 b4
Chizarira △ Zimbabwe 17°44S 27°52E 269 F2
Chizarira Ra. Zimbabwe 17°36S 27°45E 269 F2
Chizela Zambia 13°8S 25°0E 265 E4
Chizu Japan 35°16N 134°14E 222 B6
Chkalov = Orenburg
Russia 51°45N 55°6E 186 D10
Chkolovsk Russia 56°50N 43°10E 190 B6
Chloride U.S.A. 35°25N 114°12W 307 K12
Chlumec nad Cidlinou
Czechia 50°9N 15°29E 180 A8
Chmielnik Poland 50°37N 20°43E 185 H7
Cho-do N. Korea 38°30N 124°40E 224 C2
Cho Phuoc Hai Vietnam 10°26N 107°18E 237 G6
Choa Chu Kang Singapore 1°22N 103°41E 138 A2
Choba Kenya 2°30N 38°5E 266 D4
Chobe △ Botswana 18°37S 24°23E 270 A4
Choc B. St. Lucia 14°3N 60°59W 323 m
Choch'i Taiwan 23°20N 121°16E 225 C3
Chocianów Poland 51°27N 15°55E 185 G2
Chociwel Poland 53°29N 15°21E 184 E2
Chocó □ Colombia 6°0N 77°0W 328 B2
Chocolate Hills Phil. 9°55N 124°10E 233 G5
Chocolate Mts. U.S.A. 33°15N 115°15W 307 M11
Chocontá Colombia 5°9N 73°41W 328 B3
Choctawhatchee ➜
U.S.A. 30°25N 86°8W 316 E3
Choctawhatchee B.
U.S.A. 30°20N 86°20W 317 E3
Chodavaram Andhra Pradesh,
India 17°50N 82°57E 244 F6
Chodavaram Andhra Pradesh,
India 17°27N 81°46E 244 F5
Chodecz Poland 52°24N 19°2E 185 F6
Chodov Czechia 50°15N 12°45E 180 A5
Chodov u Prahy Czechia 50°1N 14°30E 135 B3
Chodziez Poland 52°58N 16°58E 185 F3
Choele Choel Argentina 39°11S 65°40W 336 A3
Chōfu Japan 35°38N 139°32E 140 B2
Choghā Zanbīl Iran 32°1N 48°32E 247 C6
Choirokoitia Cyprus 34°47N 33°20E 207 F9
Choiseul St. Lucia 13°47N 61°3W 323 m
Choiseul Solomon Is. 7°0S 156°40E 287 L9
Choix Mexico 26°43N 108°17W 318 B3
Chojna Poland 52°58N 14°25E 185 F1
Chojnice Poland 53°42N 17°32E 184 E4
Chojnów Poland 51°18N 15°58E 185 G2
Chok Chai Thailand 14°44N 102°10E 236 E4
Chōkai-San Japan 39°6N 140°3E 220 E10
Choke Canyon Res.
U.S.A. 28°30N 98°20W 314 G5
Choke Mts. Ethiopia 11°18N 37°15E 257 E4
Chokurdakh Russia 70°38N 147°55E 215 B15
Chokwé Mozam. 24°32S 32°59E 271 B5
Cholame U.S.A. 35°44N 120°18W 306 K6
Cholan Taiwan 24°18N 120°49E 225 B2
Cholargos Greece 37°59N 23°48E 112 B2
Cholet France 47°4N 0°52W 172 E6
Cholguan Chile 37°10S 72°3W 334 D1
Choloma Honduras 15°37N 87°57W 320 C2
Cholpon-Ata Kyrgyzstan 42°40N 77°6E 217 D9
Cholupice Czechia 49°59N 14°27E 135 C2
Choluteca Honduras 13°20N 87°14W 320 D2
Choluteca ➜ Honduras 13°0N 87°20W 320 D2
Chom Bung Thailand 13°37N 99°36E 236 F2
Chom Thong Bangkok,
Thailand 13°41N 100°29E 113 B1
Chom Thong Chiang Mai,
Thailand 18°25N 98°41E 236 C2
Choma Zambia 16°48S 26°59E 269 F2
Chomo Lhari Asia 27°49N 89°16E 241 B2
Chomolungma = Everest, Mt.
Nepal 28°5N 86°58E 243 E12
Chomun India 27°15N 75°40E 242 F6
Chomutov Czechia 50°28N 13°23E 180 A6
Chon Buri Thailand 13°21N 101°1E 236 F3
Chon Thanh Vietnam 11°24N 106°36E 237 G6
Chone Ecuador 0°40S 80°0W 328 D2
Chong Kai Cambodia 13°57N 103°35E 236 F4
Chong Mek Thailand 15°10N 105°27E 236 E5
Chong Pang Singapore 1°26N 103°49E 138 A2
Chong Phangan Thailand 9°39N 100°0E 237 b
Chong Samui Thailand 9°21N 99°50E 237 b
Chongde China 30°32N 120°26E 229 B13
Ch'ŏngjin N. Korea 41°47N 129°50E 224 B4
Chŏngju N. Korea 39°40N 125°5E 224 C2
Chongli China 40°58N 115°15E 226 D8
Chongming China 31°38N 121°23E 229 B13
Chongming Dao China 31°40N 121°30E 229 B13
Chongoni Rock Art
Malawi 14°17S 34°16E 269 E3
Chongoroi Angola 13°37S 14°1E 265 E2
Chongoyape Peru 6°35S 79°25W 330 B2
Chŏngp'yŏng N. Korea 39°47N 127°23E 224 C3
Chongqing Chongqing,
China 29°35N 106°25E 228 C6
Chongqing Sichuan,
China 30°38N 103°40E 228 B4
Chongqing Jiangbei Int. ✈ (CKG)
China 29°43N 106°38E 228 C6
Chongqing Shi □ China 30°0N 108°0E 228 C6
Chongren China 27°46N 116°3E 229 D11
Chonguene Mozam. 25°3S 33°49E 271 C5
Chongwe Zambia 15°21S 28°42E 269 F2
Chongwen Beijing, China 114 c2
Chongyi China 25°45N 114°29E 229 E10
Chongzuo China 22°23N 107°20E 228 F6
Chonogol Mongolia 45°54N 115°22E 226 B8
Chonos, Arch. de los Chile 45°0S 75°0W 336 C2
Chop Ukraine 48°26N 22°12E 182 B7
Chopda India 21°20N 75°15E 244 D2
Chopim ➜ Brazil 25°35S 53°5W 335 B5
Chopin Museum Warsaw, Poland 143 b2
Chor Pakistan 25°31N 69°46E 242 G3
Chora Greece 37°3N 21°42E 204 D3
Chora Sfakion Greece 35°15N 24°9E 207 E5
Chorbat La India 34°42N 76°37E 243 B7
Chorley U.K. 53°39N 2°38W 168 D5
Chorna Ukraine 47°36N 29°20E 183 C14
Chornobyl Ukraine 51°20N 30°15E 177 C16
Chornomorske Ukraine 45°31N 32°40E 189 K7
Chorolque, Cerro Bolivia 20°59S 66°5W 334 A2
Choroszcz Poland 53°10N 22°59E 185 E9
Chorregon Australia 22°40S 143°32E 280 C3
Chorrillos Peru 12°10S 77°1W 124 C2
Chortkiv Ukraine 49°2N 25°46E 177 D13
Chorzele Poland 53°15N 20°55E 185 E7
Chorzów Poland 50°18N 18°57E 185 H5
Chos-Malal Argentina 37°20S 70°15W 334 D1
Ch'osan N. Korea 40°50N 125°47E 224 B2
Chosheta Shan Taiwan 23°50N 121°6E 225 C3
Chōshi Japan 35°45N 140°51E 223 B12
Choshui Hsi ➜ Taiwan 23°50N 120°15E 225 C2
Choszczno Poland 53°7N 15°25E 185 E2
Chota Peru 6°33S 78°39W 330 B2
Choteau U.S.A. 47°49N 112°11W 304 C7
Chotěboř Czechia 49°43N 15°40E 180 B8
Chotila India 22°23N 71°15E 242 H4
Chotta Udepur India 22°19N 74°1E 242 H6
Choûm Mauritania 21°11N 13°3W 260 D2
Choungui Mayotte 12°57S 45°8E 272 b
Chowchilla U.S.A. 37°7N 120°16W 306 H6
Chowpatty Beach Mumbai, India 130 b1
Choybalsan Mongolia 48°4N 114°30E 219 B11
Choyr Mongolia 46°24N 108°30E 219 B10
Chrisman U.S.A. 39°48N 87°41W 311 E9
Chrisoupoli Greece 40°58N 24°42E 203 F8
Chrissi = Gaidouronisi
Greece 34°53N 25°41E 207 F6
Christ Church Cathedral
Montréal, Canada 130 c2
Christburg = Dzierzgoń
Poland 53°58N 19°20E 184 E6
Christchurch N.Z. 43°33S 172°47E 285 D7
Christchurch Dorset, U.K. 50°44N 1°47W 169 G6
Christian I. Canada 44°50N 80°12W 312 B4
Christian Quarter Jerusalem 123 b3
Christian Sd. U.S.A. 55°56N 134°40W 303 J14
Christiana Greece 36°14N 25°13E 205 E7
Christiana Jamaica 18°10N 77°29W 320 a
Christiana North West,
S. Africa 27°52S 25°8E 270 C4
Christiansborg Slot
Copenhagen, Denmark 118 c2
Christiansfeld Denmark 55°21N 9°29E 163 J3
Christianshåb = Qasigiannguit
Greenland 68°50N 51°18W 154 D5
Christianshavn Denmark 55°40N 12°35E 118 A3
Christiansted
U.S. Virgin Is. 17°45N 64°42W 321 C7
Christie B. Canada 62°32N 111°10W 297 A6
Christina ➜ Canada 56°40N 111°3W 297 B6
Christmas Cr. ➜
Australia 18°29S 125°23E 278 C4
Christmas I. = Kiritimati
Kiribati 1°58N 157°27W 289 G12
Christmas I. Ind. Oc. 10°30S 105°40E 273 F9
Christoffel △ Curaçao 12°21N 69°8W 322 g
Christopher U.S.A. 37°59N 89°3W 310 G7
Christopher, L. Australia 24°49S 127°42E 279 D4
Christyakovo = Thorez
Ukraine 48°4N 38°34E 189 H10
Chrudim Czechia 49°58N 15°43E 180 B8
Chrysler Building New York, U.S.A. 132 c2
Chrzanów Małopolskie,
Poland 50°10N 19°21E 185 H6
Chrzanów Warszawa,
Poland 52°13N 20°53E 143 B1
Chtimba Malawi 10°35S 34°13E 269 E3
Chū = Shū Kazakhstan 43°36N 73°42E 217 D8
Chū = Shū ➜ Kazakhstan 45°0N 67°44E 217 D7
Chu ➜ Vietnam 19°53N 105°45E 236 C5
Chu Lai Vietnam 15°28N 108°45E 236 E7
Chu Mom Ray △
Vietnam 14°29N 107°38E 236 E6
Chu Se Vietnam 13°40N 108°8E 236 F7
Chuadanga Bangla. 23°38N 88°51E 241 D2
Chuak, Ko Thailand 9°28N 99°41E 237 b
Ch'uanchou = Quanzhou
China 24°55N 118°34E 229 E12
Chüanchow = Quanzhou
China 24°55N 118°34E 229 E12
Chuangwei Taiwan 24°45N 121°47E 225 B3
Chuankou China 34°20N 110°59E 226 G6
Chuathbaluk U.S.A. 61°40N 159°15W 303 F8
Chubarovka = Pology
Ukraine 47°29N 36°15E 189 J9
Chubbuck U.S.A. 42°55N 112°28W 304 E7
Chūbu □ Japan 36°45N 137°30E 223 A9
Chūbu-Sangaku △ Japan 36°30N 137°40E 223 A9
Chubut □ Argentina 43°30S 69°0W 336 B3
Chubut ➜ Argentina 43°20S 65°5W 336 B3
Chuçand = Khŭjand
Tajikistan 40°17N 69°37E 217 D7
Chuch'i Taiwan 23°31N 120°33E 225 C2
Chuchi L. Canada 55°12N 124°30W 296 B4
Chuchow = Zhuzhou
China 27°49N 113°12E 229 D9
Chuda India 22°29N 71°41E 242 H4
Chudovo Russia 59°10N 31°41E 188 C6
Chudskoye, Ozero Russia 58°13N 27°30E 188 C4
Chuen Lung
Hong Kong, China 22°23N 114°6E 122 A2
Chugach Mts. U.S.A. 60°45N 147°0W 303 F11
Chuginadak I. U.S.A. 52°50N 169°45W 303 K5
Chūgoku □ Japan 35°0N 133°0E 222 C5
Chūgoku-Sanchi Japan 35°0N 133°0E 222 B5

Chuguyev = Chuhuyiv
Ukraine 49°55N 36°45E 189 H9
Chugwater U.S.A. 41°46N 104°50W 304 F11
Chuhuyiv Ukraine 49°55N 36°45E 189 H9
Chuk Kok
Hong Kong, China 22°20N 114°15E 122 A3
Chuka Kenya 0°20S 37°39E 268 C4
Chukchi Plateau Arctic 78°0N 165°0W 150 B17
Chukchi Sea Russia 68°0N 175°0W 215 C19
Chukotskiy, Mys Russia 64°14N 173°8W 300 C5
Chukotskiy Poluostrov
Russia 66°0N 174°0W 300 B5
Chukotskoye Nagorye
Russia 68°0N 175°0E 215 C18
Chula U.S.A. 31°33N 83°32W 316 D6
Chula Vista U.S.A. 32°38N 117°5W 307 N9
Chulalongkom Univ.
Thailand 13°44N 100°31E 113 B2
Chulband → India 20°40N 79°54E 244 D4
Ch'ulin Taiwan 22°8N 120°42E 225 D2
Chulucanas Peru 5°8S 80°10W 330 B1
Chulumani Bolivia 16°24S 67°31W 330 D4
Chulym → Russia 57°43N 83°51E 214 D9
Chum Phae Thailand 16°40N 102°6E 236 D4
Chum Saeng Thailand 15°55N 100°15E 236 E3
Chuma Bolivia 15°24S 68°56W 330 D4
Chumar India 32°40N 78°35E 243 C8
Chumbicha Argentina 29°0S 66°10W 334 B2
Chumerna Bulgaria 42°45N 25°55E 203 D9
Chumikan Russia 54°40N 135°10E 215 D14
Chumphon Thailand 10°35N 99°14E 237 G2
Chumpi Peru 15°4S 73°46W 330 D3
Chumuare Mozam. 14°31S 31°50E 269 E3
Chuna → Russia 57°47N 94°37E 215 D10
Chun'an Zhejiang, China 29°35N 119°3E 229 C12
Chunan Taiwan 24°41N 120°52E 225 B2
Chuncheon S. Korea 37°58N 127°44E 224 D4
Chunchura India 22°53N 88°27E 243 H13
Chung Hau
Hong Kong, China 22°14N 114°0E 122 B2
Chunga Zambia 15°0S 26°2E 269 F2
Chungcheongbuk-do □
S. Korea 36°45N 128°0E 224 D4
Chungcheonnam-do □
S. Korea 36°30N 127°0E 224 D3
Ch'ungch'ing = Chongqing
China 29°35N 106°25E 228 C6
Chunggang-ŭp N. Korea 41°48N 126°48E 224 B3
Chungho Taiwan 25°0N 121°28E 225 A3
Chunghwa N. Korea 38°52N 125°47E 224 C2
Chungju S. Korea 36°58N 127°58E 224 D3
Chungjuho S. Korea 36°57N 128°3E 224 D4
Chungking = Chongqing
China 29°35N 106°25E 228 C6
Chungli Taiwan 24°57N 121°13E 225 B3
Chungpu Taiwan 23°26N 120°31E 225 C2
Chungt'iaoshan = Zhongtiao Shan
China 35°0N 111°10E 226 G6
Chungtungwan Taiwan 24°31N 120°40E 225 B2
Chungyang Shanmo
Taiwan 23°10N 121°0E 225 C3
Chunian Pakistan 30°57N 74°0E 242 D6
Chunya Tanzania 8°30S 33°27E 269 D3
Chunyang China 43°38N 129°23E 227 C15
Chuō Tokyo, Japan 140 b5
Chupara B. Trin. & Tob. 10°48N 61°22W 323 t
Chupara Pt. Trin. & Tob. 10°49N 61°22W 323 t
Chupei Taiwan 24°50N 121°0E 225 B3
Chuquibamba Peru 15°47S 72°44W 330 D3
Chuquibambilla Peru 14°7S 72°41W 330 C3
Chuquicamata Chile 22°15S 69°0W 334 A2
Chuquisaca □ Bolivia 20°30S 63°30W 331 E5
Chur Switz. 46°52N 9°32E 179 J5
Churachandpur India 24°20N 93°40E 241 C4
Church End U.K. 51°35N 0°11W 125 A2
Church of our Lady = Frauenkirche
Munich, Germany 131 b2
Church Stretton U.K. 52°32N 2°48W 169 E5
Churchill Vic., Australia 38°19S 146°25E 283 E7
Churchill Man., Canada 58°47N 94°11W 297 B10
Churchill → Man.,
Canada 58°47N 94°12W 297 B10
Churchill → Nfld. & L.,
Canada 53°19N 60°10W 299 B7
Churchill, C. Canada 58°46N 93°12W 297 B10
Churchill Falls Canada 53°36N 64°19W 299 B7
Churchill L. Canada 55°55N 108°20W 297 B7
Churchill Pk. Canada 58°10N 125°10W 296 B3
Churdan U.S.A. 42°9N 94°29W 310 B2
Churki India 23°50N 83°12E 243 H10
Churu India 28°20N 74°50E 242 E6
Churubusco U.S.A. 41°14N 85°19W 311 C11
Churún Merú = Angel Falls
Venezuela 5°57N 62°30W 329 B5
Chushal India 33°40N 78°40E 243 C8
Chushan Taiwan 23°45N 120°40E 225 C2
Chuska Mts. U.S.A. 36°15N 108°50W 305 H9
Chusovoy Russia 58°22N 57°50E 186 C10
Chusovskoy Zavod = Chusovoy
Russia 58°22N 57°50E 186 C10
Chuspipata Bolivia 16°18S 67°48W 330 D4
Chust = Khust Ukraine 48°10N 23°18E 183 B8
Chust Uzbekistan 41°0N 71°13E 217 D8
Chute-aux-Outardes
Canada 49°7N 68°24W 299 C6
Chutung Taiwan 24°44N 121°5E 225 B3
Chuuk = Truk
Micronesia 7°25N 151°46E 287 T17
Chuuk Lagoon
Micronesia 7°24N 151°45E 287 T18
Chuvash Republic = Chuvashia □
Russia 55°30N 47°0E 190 C8
Chuvashia □ Russia 55°30N 47°0E 190 C8
Chuwārtah Iraq 35°43N 45°34E 213 E11
Chuwei Taiwan 25°6N 121°14E 225 A3
Chuxiong China 25°2N 101°28E 228 E3
Chüy Kyrgyzstan 42°55N 75°15E 217 D9
Chuy Uruguay 33°41S 53°27W 335 C5
Chüy □ Kyrgyzstan 42°25N 75°16E 217 D9
Chuzenji-Ko Japan 36°44N 139°27E 223 A11
Chuzhou China 32°19N 118°20E 229 A12
Chynadiyeve Ukraine 48°29N 22°50E 182 B7
Chyulu Hills Kenya 2°35S 37°50E 268 C4
Ci Xian China 36°20N 114°25E 226 F8
Ciacova Romania 45°35N 21°10E 182 E6
Ciales Puerto Rico 18°20N 66°28W 321 b
Ciamis Indonesia 7°20S 108°21E 235 D3
Ciampino Italy 41°47N 12°36E 136 C2
Ciampino ✈ (CIA) Italy 41°47N 12°35E 136 C2
Cianjur Indonesia 6°49S 107°8E 234 D3
Cianorte Brazil 23°37S 52°37W 335 A5
Cibola U.S.A. 33°17N 114°42W 307 M12
Çiçekdağı Turkey 39°36N 34°24E 212 C6
Cicero U.S.A. 41°51N 87°44W 119 B2
Cicero Dantas Brazil 10°36S 38°23W 332 D4
Ciceron St. Lucia 13°59N 61°1W 322 n
Cicia Fiji 17°45S 179°18W 287 A3
Cicilia Turkey 36°30N 34°0E 212 D5
Cidacos → Spain 42°21N 1°38W 196 C3
Cidade de Minas = Belo Horizonte
Brazil 19°55S 43°56W 333 E3
Cide Turkey 41°53N 33°1E 212 B5
Cidra Puerto Rico 18°11N 66°10W 321 b
Ciechanów Poland 52°52N 20°38E 185 F7
Ciechanowiec Poland 52°40N 22°31E 185 F9
Ciechocinek Poland 52°53N 18°45E 185 F5
Ciego de Ávila Cuba 21°50N 78°50W 320 B4
Ciénaga Colombia 11°1N 74°15W 328 A3
Ciénaga de Oro Colombia 8°53N 75°37W 328 B2
Ciénagas del Catatumbo △
Venezuela 9°26N 72°8W 328 B3
Cienfuegos Cuba 22°10N 80°30W 320 B3
Cierp-Gaud France 42°55N 0°40E 174 F4
Cies, Is. Spain 42°12N 8°55W 194 C2
Cieszanów Poland 50°14N 23°8E 185 H10
Cieszyn Poland 49°45N 18°35E 185 J5
Cieza Spain 38°17N 1°23W 197 G3
Çifteler Turkey 39°22N 31°2E 212 C4
Cifuentes Spain 40°47N 2°37W 196 E2
Cihanbeyli Turkey 38°40N 32°55E 212 C5
Cihuatlán Mexico 19°14N 104°35W 318 D4
Cijara, Embalse de Spain 39°18N 4°52W 195 F6
Cijara △ Spain 39°18N 4°35W 195 F6
Cijulang Indonesia 7°42S 108°27E 235 D3
Cilacap Indonesia 7°43S 109°0E 235 D3
Cilandak Indonesia 6°17S 106°47E 122 B1
Cilaos, Cirque de Réunion 21°7S 55°28E 272 f
Cilaos Réunion 21°8S 55°27E 272 f
Çıldır Turkey 41°7N 43°8E 213 B10
Çıldır Gölü Turkey 41°5N 43°15E 213 B10
Cilento e Vallo di Diano △
Italy 40°15N 15°20E 201 B8
Cili China 29°30N 111°8E 229 C8
Cilibia Romania 45°4N 27°4E 183 E12
Cilicia Turkey 36°30N 35°0E 250 B5
Cilincing Indonesia 6°6S 106°54E 122 A2
Ciliwung → Indonesia 6°6S 106°47E 122 B2
Cill Airne = Killarney
Ireland 52°4N 9°30W 166 D2
Cill Chainnigh = Kilkenny
Ireland 52°39N 7°15W 166 D4
Cill Dara = Kildare Ireland 53°9N 6°55W 166 C5
Cill Droichid = Celbridge
Ireland 53°20N 6°32W 166 C5
Cill Mhantáin = Wicklow
Ireland 52°59N 6°3W 166 D5
Cilo Dağı Turkey 37°28N 43°55E 213 D10
Cima U.S.A. 35°14N 115°30W 307 K11
Cimarron Kans., U.S.A. 37°48N 100°21W 308 G3
Cimarron N. Mex.,
U.S.A. 36°31N 104°55W 305 H11
Cimarron → U.S.A. 36°10N 96°16W 308 G6
Čimice Czechia 50°8N 14°25E 135 B2
Cimişlia Moldova 46°34N 28°44E 183 D13
Cimone, Mte. Italy 44°12N 10°42E 198 D7
Cina, Tanjung Indonesia 5°55S 104°45E 234 D2
Çinar Turkey 37°46N 40°19E 213 D9
Çınarcık Turkey 40°38N 29°5E 203 F13
Cinaruco-Capanaparo △
Venezuela 6°51N 67°32W 328 B4
Cinca → Spain 41°26N 0°21E 196 D5
Cincar Bos.-H. 43°55N 17°5E 182 G2
Cincinnati Iowa, U.S.A. 40°38N 92°56W 310 D4
Cincinnati Ohio, U.S.A. 39°9N 84°27W 311 E12
Cincinnati-Northern Kentucky
Int. ✈ (CVG) U.S.A. 39°3N 84°40W 311 E12
Cincinnatus U.S.A. 42°33N 75°54W 313 D9
Çine Turkey 37°37N 28°2E 205 D10
Cinecittà Italy 41°51N 12°34E 136 B2
Ciney Belgium 50°18N 5°5E 170 D5
Cingoli Italy 43°23N 13°10E 199 E10
Cinigiano Italy 42°53N 11°24E 199 F8
Cinisello Bálsamo Italy 45°33N 9°13E 128 A2
Cinkota Hungary 47°31N 19°14E 117 A3
Cinque I. India 11°16N 92°42E 245 J11
Cinque Terre △ Italy 44°10N 9°45E 198 D6
Cinto, Mte. France 42°24N 8°54E 175 F12
Cintra, G. de W. Sahara 23°0N 16°15W 260 D1
Cintruénigo Spain 42°5N 1°49W 196 C3
Ciocile Romania 44°49N 27°14E 182 F12
Ciolăneşti din Deal
Romania 44°19N 25°5E 183 F10
Ciorani Romania 44°45N 26°25E 183 F11
Čiovo Croatia 43°30N 16°17E 199 E13
Cipero → Trin. & Tob. 10°16N 61°28W 323 t
Cipete Indonesia 6°15S 106°47E 122 B1
Cipó Brazil 11°6S 38°31W 332 D4
Cipolletti Argentina 38°56S 67°59W 336 A3
Circeo, Mte. Italy 41°14N 13°3E 200 A6
Çirçir Turkey 40°3N 36°47E 212 C7
Circle Alaska, U.S.A. 65°50N 144°4W 303 D11
Circle Mont., U.S.A. 47°25N 105°35W 304 C11
Circleville U.S.A. 39°36N 82°57W 309 F12
Circular Reef Papua N. G. 3°25S 147°47E 286 B4
Cirebon Indonesia 6°45S 108°32E 235 D3
Cirencester U.K. 51°43N 1°57W 169 F6
Cireşu Romania 44°47N 22°31E 182 F7
Cirey-sur-Vezouze France 48°35N 6°57E 173 D13
Ciriè Italy 45°14N 7°36E 198 C4
Cirium Cyprus 34°40N 32°53E 207 F8
Cirò Italy 39°23N 17°4E 201 C10
Cirò Marina Italy 39°22N 17°8E 201 C10
Ciron → France 44°36N 0°18W 174 D3
Cisco U.S.A. 32°23N 98°59W 314 E5
Cislău Romania 45°14N 26°20E 183 E11
Cisna Poland 49°12N 22°20E 185 J9
Cisnădie Romania 45°42N 24°9E 183 E9
Cisne U.S.A. 38°31N 88°26W 311 F8
Cisneros Colombia 6°33N 75°4W 328 B2
Cissna Park U.S.A. 40°34N 87°54W 311 D9
Cisterna di Latina Italy 41°35N 12°49E 200 A5
Cisternino Italy 40°44N 17°25E 201 B10
Cistierna Spain 42°48N 5°7W 194 C5
Citadel = Kastellet Copenhagen, Denmark 118 a3
Citadel Budapest, Hungary 117 c2
Citaré → Brazil 1°11N 54°41W 329 C7
Citeli-Ckaro = Dedopolis Tsqaro
Georgia 41°33N 46°0E 191 K8
Citi Performing Arts Center
Boston, U.S.A. 116 c2
Citlaltépetl = Orizaba, Pico de
Mexico 18°58N 97°15W 319 D5
Citra U.S.A. 29°25N 82°7W 317 F7
Citron Fr. Guiana 4°44N 53°57W 329 C7
Citrus Heights U.S.A. 38°42N 121°17W 306 G5
Citrus Springs U.S.A. 29°2N 82°27W 317 F7
Citrusdal S. Africa 32°35S 19°0E 270 D2
Città degli Studi Italy 45°28N 9°12E 128 B2
Città del Vaticano = Vatican City ■
Europe 41°54N 12°27E 136 B1
Città della Pieve Italy 42°57N 12°1E 199 F9
Città di Castello Italy 43°27N 12°14E 199 E9
Città Sant' Angelo Italy 42°32N 14°5E 199 F11
Cittadella Italy 45°39N 11°47E 199 C8
Cittaducale Italy 42°23N 12°57E 199 F9
Cittanova Italy 38°21N 16°5E 201 D9
City, The U.K. 51°30N 0°6W 125 A3
City Hall = Rådhus Oslo, Norway 133 b1
City Hall = Stadshuset
Stockholm, Sweden 139 b1
City of the Dead Egypt 30°0N 31°15E 117 A2
City Park U.S.A. 30°0N 90°5W 131 A2
City Terrace U.S.A. 34°3N 118°11W 126 B3
Ciuc, Munţii Romania 46°25N 26°5E 183 D11
Ciucaş, Vf. Romania 45°31N 25°56E 183 E10
Ciucea Romania 46°57N 22°49E 182 D7
Ciuciulea Moldova 47°40N 27°29E 183 C12
Ciucuieni Moldova 47°2N 28°25E 183 C13
Ciudad Acuña Mexico 29°18N 100°55W 318 B4
Ciudad Altamirano
Mexico 18°20N 100°40W 318 D4
Ciudad Anáhuac Mexico 27°14N 100°7W 318 B4
Ciudad Bolívar Venezuela 8°5N 63°36W 329 B5
Ciudad Bolivia Venezuela 8°21N 70°34W 328 B3
Ciudad Camargo Mexico 27°40N 105°10W 318 B3
Ciudad Cortés Costa Rica 8°55N 84°0W 320 E3
Ciudad de México Mexico 19°24N 99°9W 128 B2
Ciudad de Nutrias Venezuela 8°6N 69°18W 328 B4
Ciudad del Carmen
Mexico 18°38N 91°50W 319 D6
Ciudad del Este Paraguay 25°30S 54°50W 335 B5
Ciudad Delicias = Delicias
Mexico 28°13N 105°28W 318 B3
Ciudad Deportiva Mexico 19°24N 99°5W 128 B2
Ciudad Fin de Semana
Spain 40°26N 3°34W 127 B2
Ciudad Frontera Mexico 26°56N 101°27W 318 B4
Ciudad General Belgrano
Argentina 34°43S 58°33W 117 C1
Ciudad Guayana Venezuela 8°0N 62°30W 329 B5
Ciudad Guerrero Mexico 28°33N 107°30W 318 B3
Ciudad Guzmán Mexico 19°41N 103°29W 318 D4
Ciudad Juárez Mexico 31°44N 106°29W 318 A3
Ciudad Lerdo Mexico 25°32N 103°32W 318 B4
Ciudad Lineál Spain 40°26N 3°38W 127 B2
Ciudad Madero Mexico 22°19N 97°50W 319 C5
Ciudad Mante Mexico 22°44N 98°59W 319 C5
Ciudad Obregón Mexico 27°29N 109°56W 318 B3
Ciudad Ojeda Venezuela 10°12N 71°19W 328 A3
Ciudad Piar Venezuela 7°27N 63°19W 329 B5
Ciudad Porfirio Díaz = Piedras
Negras Mexico 28°42N 100°31W 318 B4
Ciudad Real Spain 38°59N 3°55W 195 G7
Ciudad Real □ Spain 38°50N 4°0W 195 G7
Ciudad Rodrigo Spain 40°35N 6°32W 194 E4
Ciudad Satélite Mexico 19°30N 99°13W 128 A1
Ciudad Trujillo = Santo Domingo
Dom. Rep. 18°30N 69°59W 321 C6
Ciudad Universitaria B. Aires,
Argentina 34°33S 58°27W 117 B2
Ciudad Universitaria México,
Mexico 19°20N 99°11W 128 C1
Ciudad Valles Mexico 21°59N 99°1W 319 C5
Ciudad Victoria Mexico 23°44N 99°8W 319 C5
Ciudadela Spain 40°0N 3°50E 206 B4
Ciulniţa Romania 44°26N 27°22E 183 F12
Ciumeghiu Romania 46°44N 21°35E 182 D6
Ciuperceni Romania 44°54N 23°4E 182 F8
Ciutadella, Parc de la Barcelona, Spain 114 b3
Civa Burnu Turkey 41°21N 36°38E 212 B7
Civic Center Los Angeles, U.S.A. 127 b2
Civico Correr, Museo Venice, Italy 142 b3
Cividale del Friuli Italy 46°6N 13°25E 199 B10
Civita Castellana Italy 42°18N 12°24E 199 F9
Civitanova Marche Italy 43°18N 13°44E 199 E10
Civitavécchia Italy 42°6N 11°48E 199 F8
Civray France 46°10N 0°17E 174 B4
Çivril Turkey 38°20N 29°43E 205 C11
Cixerri → Italy 39°17N 8°59E 200 C1
Cixi China 30°17N 121°9E 229 B13
Cizre Turkey 37°19N 42°10E 213 D10
Clackmannanshire □
U.K. 56°10N 3°43W 167 E5
Clacton-on-Sea U.K. 51°47N 1°11E 169 F9
Clain → France 46°47N 0°33E 172 F7
Claire, L. Canada 58°35N 112°5W 296 B6
Claireville Res. Canada 43°45N 79°38W 141 A1
Clairvaux-les-Lacs France 46°35N 5°45E 173 F12
Clairton U.S.A. 40°18N 79°53W 312 F5
Claise → France 46°56N 0°42E 174 B5
Clallam Bay U.S.A. 48°15N 124°16W 306 B2
Clam Gulch U.S.A. 60°15N 151°23W 303 F10
Clamart France 48°48N 2°15E 134 B2
Clamecy France 47°28N 3°30E 173 E10
Clanton U.S.A. 32°51N 86°38W 315 E11
Clanwilliam S. Africa 32°11S 18°52E 270 D2
Clapham U.K. 51°27N 0°8W 125 B3
Clapton U.K. 51°33N 0°3W 125 A3
Clara Ireland 53°21N 7°37W 166 C4
Claraville U.S.A. 35°24N 118°20W 307 K8
Clare S. Austral., Australia 33°50S 138°37E 282 B3
Clare Mich., U.S.A. 43°49N 84°46W 309 D11
Clare □ Ireland 52°45N 9°0W 166 D3
Clare → Ireland 53°20N 9°2W 166 C2
Clare I. Ireland 53°47N 10°0W 166 C1
Claremont Jamaica 18°19N 77°11W 320 a
Claremont Western Cape,
S. Africa 34°8S 18°28E 118 A1
Claremont Calif., U.S.A. 34°6N 117°43W 307 L9
Claremont N.H., U.S.A. 43°23N 72°20W 313 C12
Claremont Pt. Australia 14°1S 143°41E 280 A3
Claremore U.S.A. 36°19N 95°36W 314 C7
Claremorris Ireland 53°45N 9°0W 166 C3
Clarence → N.S.W.,
Australia 29°25S 153°22E 281 D5
Clarence → N.Z. 42°10S 173°56E 285 C8
Clarence, I. Chile 54°0S 72°0W 336 D2
Clarence, Port U.S.A. 65°15N 166°40W 303 D6
Clarence B. Ascension I. 7°55S 14°25W 153 g
Clarence I. Antarctica 61°10S 54°0W 151 C18
Clarence Str. Australia 12°0S 131°0E 278 B5
Clarence Town
The Bahamas 23°6N 74°59W 321 B5
Clarendon Pa., U.S.A. 41°47N 79°6W 312 E5
Clarendon Tex., U.S.A. 34°56N 100°53W 314 D4
Clarenville Canada 48°10N 54°1W 299 C9
Claresholm Canada 50°2N 113°33W 296 D6
Clarie Coast Antarctica 68°0S 135°0E 151 C9
Clarinda U.S.A. 40°44N 95°2W 308 E6
Clarington Canada 43°55N 78°41W 312 C6
Clarion Iowa, U.S.A. 42°44N 93°44W 310 B3
Clarion Pa., U.S.A. 41°13N 79°23W 312 E5
Clarion → U.S.A. 41°7N 79°41W 312 E5
Clarion Fracture Zone
Pac. Oc. 20°0N 120°0W 292 H7
Clark Mo., U.S.A. 39°17N 92°21W 310 E4
Clark S. Dak., U.S.A. 44°53N 97°44W 308 C5
Clark, Pt. Canada 44°4N 81°45W 312 B3
Clark Fork U.S.A. 48°9N 116°11W 304 B5
Clark Fork → U.S.A. 48°9N 116°15W 304 B5
Clarke City Canada 50°12N 66°38W 299 B6
Clarke I. Australia 40°32S 148°10E 281 G4
Clarke Ra. Australia 20°40S 148°30E 280 b
Clarks Fork Yellowstone →
U.S.A. 45°32N 108°50W 304 D9
Clark's Harbour Canada 43°25N 65°38W 299 D6
Clarks Hill L. = J. Strom Thurmond
L. U.S.A. 33°40N 82°12W 316 B7
Clarks Point U.S.A. 58°51N 158°33W 303 G8
Clarks Summit U.S.A. 41°30N 75°42W 313 E9
Clark's Town Jamaica 18°25N 77°33W 320 a
Clarksburg U.S.A. 39°17N 80°30W 309 F13
Clarksdale U.S.A. 34°12N 90°35W 315 D9
Clarkston U.S.A. 46°25N 117°3W 304 C5
Clarksville Ark., U.S.A. 35°28N 93°28W 314 D8
Clarksville Ind., U.S.A. 38°17N 85°45W 311 F11
Clarksville Iowa, U.S.A. 42°47N 92°40W 310 B4
Clarksville Mo., U.S.A. 39°22N 90°54W 310 E6
Clarksville Tenn., U.S.A. 36°32N 87°21W 315 C11
Clarksville Tex., U.S.A. 33°37N 95°3W 314 E7
Claro → Brazil 19°8S 50°40W 333 E1
Clatskanie U.S.A. 46°6N 123°12W 306 D3
Claude U.S.A. 35°7N 101°22W 314 D4
Claveria Cagayan, Phil. 18°37N 121°4E 232 B3
Claveria Masbate, Phil. 12°54N 123°15E 232 E4
Claveria Mis. Or., Phil. 8°38N 124°55E 233 G5
Clavering Ø Greenland 74°15N 21°0W 154 C8
Claxton U.S.A. 32°10N 81°55W 316 C8
Claxton B. Trin. & Tob. 10°21N 61°28W 323 t
Claxton Bay Trin. & Tob. 10°21N 61°28W 323 t
Clay U.S.A. 38°17N 121°10W 306 G5
Clay Center U.S.A. 39°23N 97°8W 308 F5
Clay City Ind., U.S.A. 39°17N 87°7W 311 E9
Clay City Ky., U.S.A. 37°52N 83°55W 311 G13
Clayhall U.K. 51°35N 0°3E 125 A4
Claypool U.S.A. 33°25N 110°51W 305 K8
Claysburg U.S.A. 40°17N 78°27W 312 F6
Claysville U.S.A. 40°7N 80°25W 312 F4
Clayton Ont., Canada 45°11N 76°19W 313 A8
Clayton Ala., U.S.A. 31°53N 85°27W 316 D4
Clayton Ind., U.S.A. 39°41N 86°31W 311 E10
Clayton N. Mex., U.S.A. 36°27N 103°11W 305 H12
Clayton N.Y., U.S.A. 44°14N 76°5W 313 B8
Clear, C. Ireland 51°25N 9°32W 166 E2
Clear, L. Ont., Canada 45°26N 77°12W 312 A7
Clear, L. Fla., U.S.A. 28°31N 81°24W 133 A2
Clear Hills Canada 56°40N 119°30W 296 B5
Clear I. Ireland 51°26N 9°30W 166 E2
Clear L. U.S.A. 39°2N 122°47W 306 F4
Clear Lake Iowa, U.S.A. 43°8N 93°23W 310 A3
Clear Lake S. Dak., U.S.A. 44°45N 96°41W 308 C5
Clear Lake Res. U.S.A. 41°56N 121°5W 304 F3
Clear Water B.
Hong Kong, China 22°17N 114°18E 122 B3
Clearfield Pa., U.S.A. 41°2N 78°27W 312 E6
Clearfield Utah, U.S.A. 41°7N 112°2W 304 F7
Clearlake U.S.A. 38°57N 122°38W 306 G4
Clearwater B.C., Canada 51°38N 120°2W 296 C4
Clearwater Fla., U.S.A. 27°59N 82°48W 317 H7
Clearwater → Alta.,
Canada 52°22N 114°57W 296 C6
Clearwater → Alta.,
Canada 56°44N 111°23W 297 B6
Clearwater L. Canada 53°34N 99°49W 297 C9
Clearwater Lake △ Canada 54°0N 101°0W 297 C8
Clearwater Mts. U.S.A. 46°5N 115°20W 304 C6
Clearwater River △
Canada 56°55N 109°10W 297 B7
Cleburne U.S.A. 32°21N 97°23W 314 E6
Clee Hills U.K. 52°26N 2°35W 169 E5
Cleethorpes U.K. 53°33N 0°3W 168 D7
Cleeve Cloud U.K. 51°56N 2°0W 169 F6
Clelles France 44°50N 5°38E 175 D9
Clemson U.S.A. 34°41N 82°50W 315 D13
Cleopatra Needle Phil. 10°7N 118°58E 233 F2
Clerke Reef Australia 17°22S 119°20E 278 C2
Clerkenwell London, U.K. 125 a4
Clermiston U.K. 55°57N 3°17W 121 B2
Clermont Queens.,
Australia 22°49S 147°39E 280 C4
Clermont Oise, France 49°23N 2°24E 173 C9
Clermont Fla., U.S.A. 28°33N 81°46W 317 G8
Clermont-en-Argonne
France 49°5N 5°4E 173 C12
Clermont-Ferrand France 45°46N 3°4E 174 C7
Clermont-l'Hérault France 43°38N 3°26E 174 E7
Clerval France 47°25N 6°30E 173 E13
Clervaux Lux. 50°4N 6°2E 170 D6
Cles Italy 46°22N 11°2E 198 B8
Cleve Australia 33°43S 136°30E 282 B2
Clevedon U.K. 51°26N 2°52W 169 F5
Cleveland Miss., U.S.A. 33°45N 90°43W 315 E9
Cleveland Ohio, U.S.A. 41°29N 81°41W 312 E3
Cleveland Okla., U.S.A. 36°19N 96°28W 314 C6
Cleveland Tenn., U.S.A. 35°10N 84°53W 315 D12
Cleveland Tex., U.S.A. 30°21N 95°5W 314 F7
Cleveland, C. Australia 19°11S 147°1E 280 B4
Cleveland, Mt. U.S.A. 48°56N 113°51W 304 B7
Cleveland Heights U.S.A. 41°31N 81°33W 312 E3
Clevelândia Brazil 26°24S 52°23W 335 B5
Clevelândia do Norte
Brazil 3°49N 51°52W 329 C7
Cleves U.S.A. 39°10N 84°45W 311 E12
Clew B. Ireland 53°50N 9°49W 166 C2
Clewiston U.S.A. 26°45N 80°56W 317 J9
Clichy France 48°54N 2°18E 134 A2
Clichy-sous-Bois France 48°54N 2°32E 134 A4
Clifden Galway, Ireland 53°29N 10°1W 166 C1
Clifden N.Z. 46°1S 167°42E 285 G2
Cliffdell U.S.A. 46°56N 121°5W 306 D5
Cliffside Canada 43°44N 79°14W 141 A3
Cliffside Park U.S.A. 40°49N 73°59W 132 B2
Cliffy Hd. Australia 35°1S 116°29E 279 G2
Clifton Queens., Australia 27°59S 151°53E 281 D5
Clifton Sindh, Pakistan 24°48N 67°1E 123 B2
Clifton Western Cape,
S. Africa 33°56S 18°22E 118 A1
Clifton Ariz., U.S.A. 33°3N 109°18W 305 K9
Clifton Colo., U.S.A. 39°7N 108°25W 304 G9
Clifton Ill., U.S.A. 40°56N 87°56W 311 D9
Clifton N.Y., U.S.A. 40°37N 74°4W 132 C1
Clifton Tex., U.S.A. 31°47N 97°35W 314 F6
Clifton Beach Queens.,
Australia 16°46S 145°39E 280 B4
Clifton Beach Sindh,
Pakistan 24°48N 67°2E 123 B2
Clifton Pt. The Bahamas 25°1N 77°34W 153 b
Cliftondale U.S.A. 42°26N 71°0W 116 A2
Climax U.S.A. 30°53N 84°26W 316 E5
Clinch → U.S.A. 35°53N 84°29W 315 D12
Clingmans Dome U.S.A. 35°34N 83°30W 315 D13
Clint U.S.A. 31°35N 106°14W 314 F1
Clinton B.C., Canada 51°6N 121°35W 296 C4
Clinton Ont., Canada 43°37N 81°32W 312 C3
Clinton N.Z. 46°12S 169°23E 285 G4
Clinton Ark., U.S.A. 35°36N 92°28W 314 D8
Clinton Conn., U.S.A. 41°17N 72°32W 313 E12
Clinton Ill., U.S.A. 40°9N 88°57W 310 D8
Clinton Ind., U.S.A. 39°40N 87°24W 311 E9
Clinton Iowa, U.S.A. 41°51N 90°12W 310 C6
Clinton Mass., U.S.A. 42°25N 71°41W 313 D13
Clinton Mich., U.S.A. 42°4N 83°58W 311 B13
Clinton Miss., U.S.A. 32°20N 90°20W 315 E9
Clinton Mo., U.S.A. 38°22N 93°46W 310 F3
Clinton N.C., U.S.A. 35°0N 78°22W 315 D15
Clinton Okla., U.S.A. 35°31N 98°58W 314 D5
Clinton S.C., U.S.A. 34°29N 81°53W 315 D14
Clinton Tenn., U.S.A. 36°6N 84°8W 315 C12
Clinton Wash., U.S.A. 47°59N 122°21W 306 C4
Clinton Wis., U.S.A. 42°34N 88°52W 311 B8
Clinton, C. Australia 22°30S 150°45E 280 C5
Clinton, L. U.S.A. 40°15N 88°45W 311 D8
Clinton Colden L.
Canada 63°58N 107°27W 294 E10
Clio U.S.A. 31°43N 85°37W 316 D4
Clipperton, Î. Pac. Oc. 10°18N 109°13W 289 F17
Clipperton Fracture Zone
Pac. Oc. 19°0N 122°0W 289 G16
Clisham U.K. 57°58N 6°49W 167 D2
Clisson France 47°5N 1°16W 172 E5
Clitheroe U.K. 53°53N 2°22W 168 D5
Clive N.Z. 39°36S 176°58E 284 F5
Clive Iowa, U.S.A. 41°36N 93°43W 310 C3
Cliza Bolivia 17°36S 65°56W 331 D4
Clo-oose Canada 48°39N 124°49W 306 B2
Cloates, Pt. Australia 22°43S 113°40E 278 D1
Clocolan S. Africa 28°55S 27°34E 271 C4
Clodomira Argentina 27°35S 64°14W 334 B3
Cloghaneely Ireland 55°8N 8°5W 166 A3
Clogher Hd. Ireland 53°48N 6°14W 166 C5
Clonakilty Ireland 51°37N 8°53W 166 E3
Clonakilty B. Ireland 51°35N 8°51W 166 E3
Cloncurry Queens.,
Australia 20°40S 140°28E 280 C3
Cloncurry Kildare, Ireland 53°25N 6°48W 166 C5
Cloncurry → Australia 18°37S 140°40E 280 B3
Clondalkin Ireland 53°19N 6°25W 166 C5
Clones Ireland 54°11N 7°15W 166 B4
Clonmel Ireland 52°21N 7°42W 166 D4
Clontarf Australia 33°48S 151°16E 139 A2
Cloppenburg Germany 52°51N 8°1E 178 C4
Cloquet U.S.A. 46°43N 92°28W 308 B7
Clorinda Argentina 25°16S 57°45W 334 B4
Cloud Peak U.S.A. 44°23N 107°11W 304 D10
Cloudcroft U.S.A. 32°58N 105°45W 305 K11
Cloudy B. N.Z. 41°25S 174°10E 285 B9
Clovelly Australia 33°54S 151°15E 139 B2
Cloverdale Calif., U.S.A. 38°48N 123°1W 306 G4
Cloverdale Ind., U.S.A. 39°31N 86°48W 311 E10
Cloverport U.S.A. 37°50N 86°38W 311 G10
Clovis Calif., U.S.A. 36°49N 119°42W 306 J7
Clovis N. Mex., U.S.A. 34°24N 103°12W 305 J12
Cloyes-sur-le-Loir France 48°0N 1°14E 172 E8
Cloyne Canada 44°49N 77°11W 312 B7
Cluain Meala = Clonmel
Ireland 52°21N 7°42W 166 D4
Club Terrace Australia 37°35S 148°58E 283 D8
Cluj □ Romania 46°45N 23°30E 183 D8
Cluj-Napoca Romania 46°47N 23°38E 183 D8
Clunes Australia 37°20S 143°45E 282 D5
Cluny France 46°26N 4°38E 173 F11
Cluses France 46°5N 6°35E 173 F13
Clusone Italy 45°53N 9°57E 198 C6
Clutha → N.Z. 46°20S 169°49E 285 G4
Clwyd → U.K. 53°19N 3°31W 168 D4
Clyattville U.S.A. 30°42N 83°19W 316 E6
Clyde Alta., Canada 54°9N 113°39W 296 C6
Clyde N.Z. 45°12S 169°20E 285 F4
Clyde N.Y., U.S.A. 43°5N 76°52W 312 C8
Clyde Ohio, U.S.A. 41°18N 82°59W 311 C14
Clyde → U.K. 55°55N 4°30W 167 F4
Clyde, Firth of U.K. 55°22N 5°1W 167 F3
Clyde River Canada 70°30N 68°30W 295 C18
Clydebank U.K. 55°54N 4°23W 167 F4
Clymer N.Y., U.S.A. 42°1N 79°37W 312 D5
Clymer Pa., U.S.A. 40°40N 79°1W 312 D5
Clyo U.S.A. 32°29N 81°16W 316 C8
Ćmielów Poland 50°53N 21°31E 185 H8
CNN Center U.S.A. 33°45N 84°23W 113 B2
Côa → Portugal 41°5N 7°6W 194 D3
Coachella U.S.A. 33°41N 116°10W 307 M10
Coachella Canal U.S.A. 32°43N 114°57W 307 N12
Coahoma U.S.A. 32°18N 101°18W 314 E4
Coahuayana → Mexico 18°41N 103°45W 318 D4
Coahuila □ Mexico 27°20N 102°0W 318 B4
Coal → Canada 59°39N 126°57W 296 B3
Coal City U.S.A. 41°17N 88°17W 311 C8
Coal I. N.Z. 46°8S 166°40E 285 G1
Coalane Mozam. 17°48S 37°2E 269 F4
Coalcomán Mexico 18°47N 103°9W 318 D4
Coaldale Canada 49°45N 112°35W 296 D6
Coalgate U.S.A. 34°32N 96°13W 314 D6
Coalinga U.S.A. 36°9N 120°21W 306 J6
Coalisland U.K. 54°33N 6°42W 166 B5
Coalville Leics., U.K. 52°44N 1°23W 168 E6
Coalville Utah, U.S.A. 40°55N 111°24W 304 F8
Coamo Puerto Rico 18°5N 66°22W 321 b
Coaraci Brazil 14°38S 39°32W 333 D4
Coari Brazil 4°8S 63°7W 329 D5
Coari → Brazil 4°30S 63°33W 329 D5
Coari, L. Brazil 4°15S 63°22W 329 D5
Coast Mts. Canada 55°0N 129°20W 296 C3
Coast Ranges U.S.A. 39°0N 123°0W 306 G4
Coatbridge U.K. 55°52N 4°6W 167 F4
Coatepec Mexico 19°27N 96°58W 319 D5
Coatepeque Guatemala 14°46N 91°55W 320 D1
Coatesville U.S.A. 39°59N 75°50W 309 F16
Coaticook Canada 45°10N 71°46W 313 A13
Coats I. Canada 62°30N 83°0W 295 E15
Coats Land Antarctica 77°0S 25°0W 151 D1
Coatzacoalcos Mexico 18°7N 94°25W 319 D6
Cobá Mexico 20°31N 87°45W 319 C7
Cobadin Romania 44°5N 28°13E 183 F13
Cobalt Canada 47°25N 79°42W 298 C4
Cobán Guatemala 15°30N 90°21W 320 C1
Çobanlar Turkey 38°41N 30°47E 205 C12
Cobar Australia 31°27S 145°48E 283 A6
Cobargo Australia 36°20S 149°55E 283 D8
Cobbannah Australia 37°37S 147°13E 283 D7
Cobberas, Mt. Australia 36°53S 148°12E 283 D8
Cobden Australia 38°20S 143°3E 282 E5
Cobh Ireland 51°51N 8°17W 166 E3
Cóbh, An = Cobh Ireland 51°51N 8°17W 166 E3
Cobija Bolivia 11°0S 68°50W 330 C4
Cobleskill U.S.A. 42°41N 74°29W 313 D10
Coboconk Canada 44°39N 78°48W 312 B6
Cobourg Canada 43°58N 78°10W 312 C6
Cobourg Pen. Australia 11°20S 132°15E 278 B5
Cobram Australia 35°54S 145°40E 283 C6
Cobras, I. das Brazil 22°53S 43°9W 135 B2
Cóbué Mozam. 12°0S 34°58E 269 E3
Coburg Vic., Australia 37°44S 144°56E 128 A1
Coburg Bayern, Germany 50°15N 10°58E 179 E6
Coburg I. Canada 75°57N 79°26W 295 B16
Coca Spain 41°13N 4°32W 194 D6
Coca → Ecuador 0°29S 76°58W 328 D2
Cocachacra Peru 17°5S 71°45W 330 D3
Cocal Brazil 3°28S 41°34W 332 B3
Cocanada = Kakinada
India 16°57N 82°11E 244 F6
Cocentaina Spain 38°45N 0°27W 197 G4
Cochabamba Bolivia 17°26S 66°10W 331 D4
Coche, I. Venezuela 10°47N 63°56W 329 A5
Cochem Germany 50°9N 7°9E 179 E3
Cochemane Mozam. 17°0S 32°54E 269 F3
Cochin = Kochi India 9°58N 76°20E 245 K3
Cochin China = Nam Phan
Vietnam 10°30N 106°0E 237 G6
Cochran U.S.A. 32°23N 83°21W 316 C6
Cochrane Alta., Canada 51°11N 114°30W 296 C6
Cochrane Ont., Canada 49°0N 81°0W 298 C3
Cochrane Chile 47°15S 72°33W 336 C2
Cochrane → Canada 59°0N 103°40W 297 B8
Cochrane, L. Chile 47°10S 72°0W 336 C2
Cochranton U.S.A. 41°31N 80°3W 312 E4
Cockburn Australia 32°5S 141°0E 282 B4
Cockburn, Canal Chile 54°30S 72°0W 336 D2
Cockburn I. Canada 45°55N 83°22W 298 C3
Cockburn Ra. Australia 15°46S 128°0E 278 C4
Cockermouth U.K. 54°40N 3°22W 168 C4
Cocklebiddy Australia 32°0S 126°3E 279 F4
Cockpit Jamaica 18°16N 77°39W 320 a
Cockpit Country, The
Jamaica 18°15N 77°45W 320 a
Cockrell Hill U.S.A. 32°44N 96°53W 120 B4
Côco → Brazil 9°27S 50°2W 332 C2
Coco → Cent. Amer. 15°0N 83°8W 320 D3
Coco, Cayo Cuba 22°29N 78°34W 320 B4
Coco, I. del Pac. Oc. 5°25N 87°55W 289 G19
Coco, Pta. Colombia 2°58N 77°43W 328 C2
Coco Channel Asia 13°45N 93°10E 245 H11
Cocoa U.S.A. 28°21N 80°44W 317 G9
Cocoa Beach U.S.A. 28°19N 80°37W 317 G9
Cocoa Point Antigua & B. 17°33N 61°46W 322 c
Cocobeach Gabon 0°59N 9°34E 264 B1
Coconut Grove U.S.A. 25°42N 80°15W 129 D2
Cocoparra △ Australia 34°10S 146°12E 283 C7
Cocora Romania 44°45N 27°3E 183 F12
Côcos Brazil 14°10S 44°33W 333 D3
Côcos → Brazil 12°44S 44°48W 333 D3
Cocos B. Trin. & Tob. 10°24N 61°2W 323 t
Cocos Basin Ind. Oc. 1°0N 94°0E 273 D8
Cocos I. = Coco, I. del
Pac. Oc. 5°25N 87°55W 289 G19
Cocos I. Guam 13°14N 144°39E 302 d
Cocos Is. Ind. Oc. 12°10S 96°55E 273 F8
Cocos Ridge Pac. Oc. 4°0N 88°0W 289 G19
Cocotá Brazil 22°48S 43°11W 135 A1
Cod, C. U.S.A. 42°5N 70°10W 309 D18
Codajás Brazil 3°55S 62°0W 329 D5
Codera, C. Venezuela 10°35N 66°4W 328 A4
Codfish I. N.Z. 46°47S 167°38E 285 G2
Codigoro Italy 44°49N 12°8E 199 D9
Codlea Romania 45°42N 25°27E 183 E10
Codó Brazil 4°30S 43°55W 332 B3
Codogno Italy 45°9N 9°42E 198 C6
Codpa Chile 18°50S 69°44W 330 D4
Codrington Antigua & B. 17°38N 61°50W 322 c
Codrington Lagoon
Antigua & B. 17°39N 61°50W 322 c
Codróipo Italy 45°58N 13°0E 199 C10
Codru, Munţii Romania 46°30N 22°15E 182 D7
Cody U.S.A. 44°32N 109°3W 304 D9
Coe Hill Canada 44°52N 77°50W 312 B7
Coelemu Chile 36°30S 72°48W 334 D1
Coelho Neto Brazil 4°15S 43°0W 332 B3
Coen Australia 13°52S 143°12E 280 A3
Coeroeni Suriname 3°22N 57°21W 329 C6
Coeroeni → Suriname 3°21N 57°31W 329 C6
Coesfeld Germany 51°56N 7°10E 178 D3
Coetivy I. Seychelles 7°8S 56°16E 273 E4
Cœuilly France 48°48N 2°32E 134 B4
Coeur d'Alene U.S.A. 47°41N 116°46W 304 C5
Coeur d'Alene L. U.S.A. 47°32N 116°49W 304 C5
Coevorden Neths. 52°40N 6°44E 170 B6
Cofete Canary Is. 28°6N 14°23W 153 e2
Coffeyville U.S.A. 37°2N 95°37W 308 G6
Coffin B. Australia 34°38S 135°28E 281 E2
Coffin Bay Australia 34°37S 135°29E 281 E2
Coffin Bay △ Australia 34°34S 135°19E 281 E2
Coffin Bay Peninsula
Australia 34°32S 135°15E 281 E2
Coffs Harbour Australia 30°16S 153°5E 283 A10
Cofrentes Spain 39°13N 1°5W 197 F3
Cogalnic = Kohylnyk →
Ukraine 45°49N 29°40E 183 E14
Cogealac Romania 44°36N 28°36E 183 F13
Coghinas → Italy 40°55N 8°48E 200 B1
Coghinas, L. del Italy 40°46N 9°3E 200 B2
Cognac France 45°41N 0°20W 174 C3
Cogne Italy 45°37N 7°21E 198 C4
Cogolin France 43°15N 6°32E 175 E10
Cogolludo Spain 40°59N 3°10W 196 E1
Cohocton U.S.A. 42°30N 77°30W 312 D7
Cohocton → U.S.A. 42°9N 77°6W 312 D7
Cohoes U.S.A. 42°46N 73°42W 313 D11
Cohuna Australia 35°45S 144°15E 282 C6
Coiba, I. de Panama 7°30N 81°40W 320 E3
Coig → Argentina 51°0S 69°10W 336 D3
Coigeach, Rubha U.K. 58°6N 5°26W 167 C3
Coihaique Chile 45°30S 71°45W 336 C2
Coimbatore India 11°2N 76°59E 245 J3
Coimbra Mato Grosso,
Brazil 19°55S 57°48W 331 D6
Coimbra Portugal 40°15N 8°27W 194 E2
Coimbra □ Portugal 40°12N 8°25W 194 E2
Coín Spain 36°40N 4°48W 195 J6
Coina Portugal 38°39N 9°5W 126 B2
Coipasa, L. de Bolivia 19°12S 68°7W 330 D4
Coipasa, Salar de Bolivia 19°26S 68°9W 330 D4
Coit Tower San Francisco, U.S.A. 136 a2
Cojata Peru 15°2S 69°25W 330 D4
Cojedes □ Venezuela 9°20N 68°20W 328 B4
Cojedes → Venezuela 8°34N 68°5W 328 B4
Cojimies Ecuador 0°20N 80°0W 328 C1
Cojocna Romania 46°45N 23°50E 183 D8
Cojutepequé El Salv. 13°41N 88°54W 320 D2
Čoka Serbia 45°57N 20°12E 182 E5
Coker Nigeria 6°28N 3°20E 124 B2
Cokeville U.S.A. 42°5N 110°57W 304 E8
Colaba India 18°53N 72°48E 130 B1
Colaba Pt. India 18°53N 72°48E 130 B1
Colac Australia 38°21S 143°35E 282 E5
Colachel = Kolachel India 8°10N 77°15E 245 K3
Colán Peru 5°0S 81°0W 330 B1
Colatina Brazil 19°32S 40°37W 333 E3
Colbeck, C. Antarctica 77°6S 157°48W 151 D13
Colbert U.S.A. 34°2N 83°13W 316 A6
Colborne Canada 44°0N 77°53W 312 C7
Colby U.S.A. 39°24N 101°3W 308 F3
Colca = Majes → Peru 16°40S 72°44W 330 D3
Colca, Cañón del Peru 15°50S 72°0W 330 D3
Colchester Essex, U.K. 51°54N 0°55E 169 F8
Colchester Conn., U.S.A. 41°35N 72°20W 313 E12
Cold Bay U.S.A. 55°12N 162°42W 303 J7
Cold L. Canada 54°33N 110°5W 297 C7
Cold Lake Canada 54°27N 110°10W 297 C6
Coldstream B.C., Canada 50°13N 119°11W 296 C5
Coldstream Borders, U.K. 55°39N 2°15W 167 F6
Coldwater Ont., Canada 44°42N 79°40W 312 B5
Coldwater Kans., U.S.A. 37°16N 99°20W 308 G4
Coldwater Mich., U.S.A. 41°57N 85°0W 311 C11
Coldwater Ohio, U.S.A. 40°29N 84°38W 311 D12
Coldwater, L. U.S.A. 41°48N 84°59W 311 C12
Cole Camp U.S.A. 38°28N 93°12W 310 F3
Coleambally Australia 34°49S 145°52E 283 C6
Colebrook U.S.A. 44°54N 71°30W 313 B13
Colegiales Argentina 34°34S 58°27W 117 B2
Coleman Alta., Canada 49°40N 114°30W 296 D6
Coleman Fla., U.S.A. 28°48N 82°4W 317 G7
Coleman Tex., U.S.A. 31°50N 99°26W 314 F5
Coleman → Australia 15°6S 141°38E 280 B3
Colenso S. Africa 28°44S 29°50E 271 C4
Coleraine Vic., Australia 37°36S 141°40E 282 D4
Coleraine L'derry., U.K. 55°8N 6°41W 166 A5
Coleridge, L. N.Z. 43°17S 171°30E 285 D6
Coleroon → India 11°25N 79°50E 245 J4
Colesberg S. Africa 30°45S 25°5E 270 D4
Coleville U.S.A. 38°34N 119°30W 306 G7
Colfax Calif., U.S.A. 39°6N 120°57W 306 F6
Colfax Ill., U.S.A. 40°34N 88°37W 311 D8
Colfax Ind., U.S.A. 40°12N 86°40W 311 D10
Colfax Iowa, U.S.A. 41°41N 93°14W 310 C3
Colfax La., U.S.A. 31°31N 92°42W 314 F8
Colfax Wash., U.S.A. 46°53N 117°22W 304 C5
Colhué Huapi, L. Argentina 45°30S 69°0W 336 C3
Colibaşi = Mioveni
Romania 44°56N 24°54E 183 F9
Colibaşi Moldova 45°43N 28°11E 183 E13
Colibris, Pte. des Guadeloupe 16°17N 61°5W 322 e
Colico Italy 46°8N 9°22E 198 B6
Colider Brazil 10°45S 55°25W 331 C6
Coligny Ain, France 46°23N 5°21E 173 F12
Coligny North West,
S. Africa 26°17S 26°15E 271 C4
Colihaut Dominica 15°29N 61°29W 323 k
Colima Mexico 19°14N 103°43W 318 D4
Colima □ Mexico 19°10N 104°0W 318 D4
Colima, Nevado de
Mexico 19°33N 103°38W 318 D4
Colina Chile 33°13S 70°45W 334 C1
Colina do Norte
Guinea-Biss. 12°28N 15°0W 262 C2
Colinas Goiás, Brazil 14°15S 48°2W 333 D2
Colinas Maranhão, Brazil 6°0S 44°10W 332 C3
Colindale U.K. 51°35N 0°15W 125 A2
Colindres Spain 43°24N 3°27W 194 B7
Colinton U.K. 55°55N 3°14W 121 B2
Coll U.K. 56°39N 6°34W 167 E2
Collahuasi Chile 21°5S 68°45W 334 A2
Collarada, Peña Spain 42°43N 0°29W 196 C4
Collarenebri Australia 29°33S 148°34E 281 D4
Colle di Val d'Elsa Italy 43°25N 11°7E 198 E8
Collécchio Italy 44°45N 10°13E 198 D7
Colleen Bawn Zimbabwe 21°0S 29°12E 269 G2
College U.S.A. 64°52N 147°49W 303 D11
College Park Ga., U.S.A. 33°39N 84°27W 113 C2
College Park Md., U.S.A. 38°59N 76°55W 143 B3
College Point U.S.A. 40°47N 73°50W 132 B2
College Station U.S.A. 30°37N 96°21W 314 F6
Collégien France 48°50N 2°41E 134 B4
Collesalvetti Italy 43°34N 10°27E 198 E7

Colleyville *U.S.A.* 32°52N 97°9W **120** A3
Colli Euganei ⌓ *Italy* 45°18N 11°43E **199** C8
Collie *N.S.W., Australia* 31°41S 148°18E **283** A8
Collie *W. Austral., Australia* 33°22S 116°8E **279** F2
Collier B. *Australia* 16°10S 124°15E **278** C3
Collier Ra. *Australia* 24°45S 119°10E **279** D2
Collier Range △ *Australia* 24°39S 119°7E **279** D2
Collier Row *U.K.* 51°35N 0°9E **125** A4
Colliers Wood *U.K.* 51°24N 0°10W **125** B2
Collierville *U.S.A.* 35°3N 89°40W **315** D10
Collina, Passo di *Italy* 44°2N 10°56E **198** D7
Collingwood *Ont., Canada* 44°29N 80°13W **312** B4
Collingwood *N.Z.* 40°41S 172°40E **285** A7
Collins *Ont., Canada* 50°17N 89°27W **298** B2
Collins *Ga., U.S.A.* 32°11N 82°7W **316** C7
Collins *Mo., U.S.A.* 37°54N 93°37W **310** G3
Collins Bay *Canada* 44°14N 76°36W **313** B8
Collinson Pen. *Canada* 69°58N 101°24W **294** D11
Collinsville *Queens., Australia* 20°30S 147°56E **280** C4
Collinsville *Ill., U.S.A.* 38°40N 89°59W **310** F7
Collipulli *Chile* 37°55S 72°30W **334** D1
Collo *Algeria* 36°58N 6°37E **261** A6
Collooney *Ireland* 54°11N 8°29W **166** B3
Colma *U.S.A.* 37°40N 122°27W **136** B2
Colmar *France* 48°5N 7°20E **173** D14
Colmars *France* 44°11N 6°39E **175** D10
Colmenar *Spain* 36°54N 4°20W **195** J6
Colmenar de Oreja *Spain* 40°6N 3°25W **194** E7
Colmenar Viejo *Spain* 40°39N 3°47W **194** E7
Colney Hatch *U.K.* 51°36N 0°9W **125** A3
Colo → *Australia* 33°25S 150°52E **283** B9
Cologne = Köln *Germany* 50°56N 6°57E **178** E2
Cologno Monzese *Italy* 45°31N 9°16E **128** A2
Colom, I. d'en *Spain* 39°58N 4°16E **206** B5
Coloma *Calif., U.S.A.* 38°48N 120°53W **306** G6
Coloma *Mich., U.S.A.* 42°11N 86°19W **311** B10
Colomb-Béchar = Béchar *Algeria* 31°38N 2°18W **261** B4
Colombes *France* 48°55N 2°15E **134** A2
Colombey-les-Belles *France* 48°32N 5°54E **173** D12
Colombey-les-Deux-Églises *France* 48°13N 4°50E **173** D11
Colômbia *Brazil* 20°10S 48°40W **333** F2
Colombia ■ *S. Amer.* 3°45N 73°0W **328** C3
Colombian Basin *Caribbean* 14°0N 76°0W **321** D5
Colombier *St.-Martin* 18°5N 63°5W **322** a
Colombo *Sri Lanka* 6°56N 79°58E **245** L4
Colomiers *France* 43°36N 1°21E **174** E5
Colón *B. Aires, Argentina* 33°53S 61°7W **334** C3
Colón *Entre Ríos, Argentina* 32°12S 58°10W **334** C4
Colón *Cuba* 22°42N 80°54W **320** B3
Colón *Panama* 9°20N 79°54W **320** c
Colón, Arch. de *Ecuador* 0°0 91°0W **330** a
Colón, Monumente a *Barcelona, Spain* **114** c3
Colón, Plaza de *Madrid, Spain* **127** a3
Colonarie *St. Vincent* 13°14N 61°8W **323** n
Colonia *Micronesia* 9°30N 138°10E **287** R16
Colonia 25 de Mayo *Argentina* 37°48S 67°41W **336** A3
Colònia de Sant Jordi *Spain* 39°19N 2°59E **206** B3
Colonia del Sacramento *Uruguay* 34°25S 57°50W **334** C4
Colonia Dora *Argentina* 28°34S 62°59W **334** B3
Colonia Güell *Spain* 41°21N 2°2E **114** A1
Colonial Beach *U.S.A.* 38°15N 76°58W **309** F15
Colonie *U.S.A.* 42°43N 73°50W **313** D11
Colonna, C. *Italy* 39°2N 17°12E **201** C10
Colonsay *Sask., Canada* 51°59N 105°52W **297** C7
Colonsay *Argyll & Bute, U.K.* 56°5N 6°12W **167** E2
Colorado □ *U.S.A.* 39°30N 105°30W **304** G11
Colorado → *Argentina* 39°50S 62°8W **336** A4
Colorado → *N. Amer.* 31°45N 114°40W **305** L6
Colorado → *Tex., U.S.A.* 28°36N 95°59W **314** G7
Colorado City *U.S.A.* 32°24N 100°52W **314** E4
Colorado Plateau *U.S.A.* 37°0N 111°0W **305** H8
Colorado River Aqueduct *U.S.A.* 33°50N 117°23W **307** L12
Colorado Springs *U.S.A.* 38°50N 104°49W **304** G11
Colorno *Italy* 44°56N 10°23E **198** D7
Colosseo *Rome, Italy* **136** c3
Colosseum = Colosseo *Rome, Italy* **136** c3
Colotlán *Mexico* 22°6N 103°16W **318** C4
Colquechaca *Bolivia* 18°40S 66°1W **331** D4
Colquitt *U.S.A.* 31°10N 84°44W **316** D5
Colstrip *U.S.A.* 45°53N 106°38W **304** D10
Colton *U.S.A.* 44°33N 74°56W **313** B10
Columbia *Ala., U.S.A.* 31°18N 85°7W **316** D4
Columbia *Ill., U.S.A.* 38°27N 90°12W **310** F6
Columbia *Ky., U.S.A.* 37°6N 85°18W **309** G11
Columbia *La., U.S.A.* 32°6N 92°5W **314** E8
Columbia *Miss., U.S.A.* 31°15N 89°50W **315** F10
Columbia *Mo., U.S.A.* 38°57N 92°20W **310** F4
Columbia *Pa., U.S.A.* 40°2N 76°30W **313** F8
Columbia *S.C., U.S.A.* 34°0N 81°2W **316** A8
Columbia *Tenn., U.S.A.* 35°37N 87°2W **315** D11
Columbia → *N. Amer.* 46°15N 124°5W **306** D2
Columbia, C. *Canada* 83°6N 69°57W **295** A18
Columbia, District of □ *U.S.A.* 38°55N 77°0W **309** F15
Columbia, Mt. *Canada* 52°8N 117°20W **296** C5
Columbia Basin *U.S.A.* 46°45N 119°5W **304** C4
Columbia City *U.S.A.* 41°10N 85°29W **311** C11
Columbia Falls *U.S.A.* 48°23N 114°11W **304** B6
Columbia Mts. *Canada* 52°0N 119°0W **296** C5
Columbia Plateau *U.S.A.* 44°0N 117°30W **304** E5
Columbiana *U.S.A.* 40°53N 80°42W **312** F4
Columbretes, Is. *Spain* 39°50N 0°50E **196** F5
Columbus *Ga., U.S.A.* 32°28N 84°59W **316** C5
Columbus *Ind., U.S.A.* 39°13N 85°55W **311** E11
Columbus *Kans., U.S.A.* 37°10N 94°50W **308** G6
Columbus *Miss., U.S.A.* 33°30N 88°25W **315** E10
Columbus *Mont., U.S.A.* 45°38N 109°15W **304** D9
Columbus *N. Mex., U.S.A.* 31°50N 107°38W **305** L10
Columbus *Nebr., U.S.A.* 41°26N 97°22W **308** E5
Columbus *Ohio, U.S.A.* 39°58N 83°0W **311** E13
Columbus *Tex., U.S.A.* 29°42N 96°33W **314** G6
Columbus Circle *New York, U.S.A.* **132** b2
Columbus Circle *Washington, D.C., U.S.A.* **143** b3
Columbus Grove *U.S.A.* 40°55N 84°4W **311** D12
Columbus Junction *U.S.A.* 41°17N 91°22W **310** C5
Columbus Monument = Colón, Monumente a *Barcelona, Spain* **114** c3
Columbus Park *Jamaica* 18°28N 77°25W **320** a
Columbus Park *Boston, U.S.A.* **116** b3
Colunga *Spain* 43°29N 5°16W **194** B5
Colusa *U.S.A.* 39°13N 122°1W **306** F4
Colville *U.S.A.* 48°33N 117°54W **304** B5
Colville → *U.S.A.* 70°25N 150°30W **303** A10
Colville, C. *N.Z.* 36°29S 175°21E **284** C4
Colville Channel *N.Z.* 36°25S 175°27E **284** C4
Colville Ridge *Pac. Oc.* 30°0S 180°0E **277** G15
Colwood *Canada* 48°26N 123°29W **306** B3
Colwyn Bay *U.K.* 53°18N 3°44W **168** D4
Coma *Ethiopia* 8°29N 36°53E **257** F4
Comácchio *Italy* 44°42N 12°11E **199** D9
Comalcalco *Mexico* 18°16N 93°13W **319** D6
Comallo *Argentina* 41°0S 70°5W **336** B2
Comana *Romania* 44°10N 26°10E **183** F11
Comanche *U.S.A.* 31°54N 98°36W **314** F5
Comandante Arbues = Mirandópolis *Brazil* 21°9S 51°6W **335** A5
Comandante Ferraz *Antarctica* 62°30S 58°0W **151** C18
Comandante Luis Piedrabuena *Argentina* 49°59S 68°54W **336** C3
Comăneşti *Romania* 46°25N 26°26E **183** D11
Comarapa *Bolivia* 17°54S 64°29W **331** D5
Comarnic *Romania* 45°15N 25°38E **183** E10
Comayagua *Honduras* 14°25N 87°37W **320** D2
Combahee → *U.S.A.* 32°31N 80°31W **316** C9
Combara *Australia* 31°10S 148°22E **283** A8
Combarbalá *Chile* 31°11S 71°2W **334** C1
Combault *France* 48°48N 2°37E **134** B4
Combe Martin *U.K.* 51°12N 4°3W **169** F3
Combeaufontaine *France* 47°38N 5°54E **173** E12
Comber *Ont., Canada* 42°14N 82°33W **312** D2
Comber *Down, U.K.* 54°33N 5°45W **166** B6
Combermere *Canada* 45°22N 77°37W **312** A7
Combermere Bay *Myanmar* 19°37N 93°34E **241** F4
Comblain-au-Pont *Belgium* 50°29N 5°35E **170** D5
Combourg *France* 48°25N 1°46W **172** D5
Comboyne *Australia* 31°34S 152°27E **283** A10
Combrailles *France* 46°8N 2°8E **173** F9
Combronde *France* 45°58N 3°5E **174** C7
Comer *Ala., U.S.A.* 32°2N 85°23W **316** C4
Comer *Ga., U.S.A.* 34°4N 83°8W **316** A6
Comeragh Mts. *Ireland* 52°18N 7°34W **166** D4
Comércio, Praça do *Portugal* 38°41N 9°9W **126** A2
Comerio *Puerto Rico* 18°12N 66°12W **321** b
Comet *Australia* 23°36S 148°38E **280** C4
Comilla = Cumilla *Bangla.* 23°28N 91°10E **241** D3
Comino *Malta* 36°1N 14°20E **206** E7
Comino, C. *Italy* 40°32N 9°49E **200** B2
Cómiso *Italy* 36°56N 14°36E **201** F7
Comitán de Domínguez *Mexico* 16°15N 92°8W **319** D6
Commentry *France* 46°20N 2°46E **173** F9
Commerce *Calif., U.S.A.* 34°0N 118°9W **126** B4
Commerce *Ga., U.S.A.* 34°12N 83°28W **316** A6
Commerce *Tex., U.S.A.* 33°15N 95°54W **314** E7
Commercy *France* 48°43N 5°34E **173** D12
Commissioner's Pt. *Bermuda* 32°19N 64°49W **153** a
Committee B. *Canada* 68°30N 86°30W **295** D14
Commodore, C. *Canada* 44°47N 80°54W **312** B4
Commonwealth B. *Antarctica* 67°0S 144°0E **151** C10
Commoron Cr. → *Australia* 28°22S 150°8E **281** D5
Communism Pk. = imeni Ismail Samani, Pik *Tajikistan* 39°0N 72°2E **217** E8
Como *Italy* 45°47N 9°5E **198** C6
Como, L. di *Italy* 46°0N 9°11E **198** B6
Comodoro Rivadavia *Argentina* 45°50S 67°40W **336** C3
Comoé □ *Côte d'Ivoire* 6°48N 3°30W **262** D4
Comoé → *Côte d'Ivoire* 5°12N 3°44W **262** D4
Comoé △ *Côte d'Ivoire* 9°0N 3°35W **262** D4
Comorâşte *Romania* 45°10N 21°35E **182** E6
Comorin, C. = Kannyakumari *India* 8°3N 77°40E **245** K3
Comoros ■ *Ind. Oc.* 12°10S 44°15E **272** a
Comox *Canada* 49°42N 124°55W **296** D4
Company's Gardens *Cape Town, S. Africa* **118** c2
Compass Lake *U.S.A.* 30°36N 85°24W **316** E4
Compiègne *France* 49°24N 2°50E **173** C9
Comporta *Portugal* 38°22N 8°46W **195** G2
Compostela *Nayarit, Mexico* 21°14N 104°55W **318** C4
Compostela *Phil.* 7°40N 126°2E **233** H6
Compostela Valley □ *Phil.* 7°50N 126°0E **233** H5
Comprida, I. *Brazil* 24°50S 47°42W **335** A6
Compton *Qué., Canada* 45°14N 71°49W **313** A13
Compton *Calif., U.S.A.* 33°53N 118°13W **307** M8
Comrat *Moldova* 46°18N 28°40E **183** D13
Comunidad *Peru* 13°59S 69°20W **330** C4
Con Cuong *Vietnam* 19°2N 104°54E **236** C5
Con Dao △ *Vietnam* 8°42N 106°35E **237** H6
Con Son, Dao *Vietnam* 8°41N 106°37E **237** H6
Cona Niyeu *Argentina* 41°58S 67°0W **336** B3
Conakry *Guinea* 9°29N 13°49W **262** D2
Conara *Australia* 41°50S 147°26E **281** G4
Concarneau *France* 47°52N 3°56W **172** E3
Conceição *Paraiba, Brazil* 7°33S 38°31W **332** C4
Conceição *Mozam.* 18°47S 36°7E **269** B4
Conceição, I. da *Brazil* 22°52S 43°6W **135** B2
Conceição da Barra *Brazil* 18°35S 39°45W **333** E4
Conceição do Araguaia *Brazil* 8°0S 49°2W **332** C2
Conceição do Canindé *Brazil* 7°54S 41°34W **332** C3
Conceição do Maú *Brazil* 3°35N 59°53W **329** C6
Conceição do Paraíba = Capela *Brazil* 10°30S 37°0W **332** D4
Concepción *Argentina* 27°20S 65°35W **334** B2
Concepción *Bolivia* 16°15S 62°8W **331** D5
Concepción *Chile* 36°50S 73°0W **334** D1
Concepción *Paraguay* 23°22S 57°26W **334** A4
Concepción *Peru* 11°54S 75°19W **330** C2
Concepcion *Tarlac, Phil.* 15°27N 120°47E **232** D3
Concepción □ *Chile* 37°0S 72°30W **334** D1
Concepción, Est. de *Chile* 50°30S 74°55W **336** D2
Concepción, L. *Bolivia* 17°20S 61°20W **331** D5
Concepción, Pta. *Mexico* 26°53N 111°50W **318** B2
Concepción del Oro *Mexico* 24°38N 101°25W **318** C4
Concepción del Uruguay *Argentina* 32°35S 58°20W **334** C4
Conception, Pt. *U.S.A.* 34°27N 120°28W **307** L6
Conception B. *Nfld. & L., Canada* 47°45N 53°0W **299** C9
Conception B. *Namibia* 23°55S 14°22E **270** B1
Conception I. *The Bahamas* 23°52N 75°9W **321** B4
Concession *Zimbabwe* 17°27S 30°56E **269** F3
Conchalí *Chile* 33°22S 70°39W **137** B2
Conchas Dam *U.S.A.* 35°22N 104°11W **305** J11
Conches-en-Ouche *France* 48°58N 0°56E **172** D7
Concho *U.S.A.* 34°28N 109°36W **305** J9
Concho → *U.S.A.* 31°34N 99°43W **314** F5
Conchos → *Chihuahua, Mexico* 29°35N 104°25W **318** B4
Conchos → *Tamaulipas, Mexico* 24°55N 97°38W **319** B5
Concord *N.S.W., Australia* 33°52S 151°6E **139** B1
Concord *Ont., Canada* 43°48N 79°29W **141** A2
Concord *Grenada* 12°7N 61°44W **323** q
Concord *Calif., U.S.A.* 37°59N 122°2W **306** H4
Concord *Ga., U.S.A.* 33°5N 84°27W **316** B5
Concord *Mich., U.S.A.* 42°11N 84°38W **311** B12
Concord *Mo., U.S.A.* 38°32N 90°23W **310** F6
Concord *N.C., U.S.A.* 35°25N 80°35W **315** D14
Concord *N.H., U.S.A.* 43°12N 71°32W **313** C13
Concorde, Place de la *Paris, France* **134** b3
Concordia *Antarctica* 75°6S 123°23E **151** D9
Concordia *Argentina* 31°20S 58°2W **334** C4
Concórdia *Amazonas, Brazil* 4°36S 66°36W **328** D4
Concórdia *Sta. Catarina, Brazil* 27°14S 52°1W **335** B5
Concordia *Sinaloa, Mexico* 23°17N 106°4W **318** C3
Concordia *Kans., U.S.A.* 39°34N 97°40W **308** F5
Concordia *Mo., U.S.A.* 38°59N 93°34W **310** F3
Concordia Univ. *Montréal, Canada* **130** c1
Concorezzo *Italy* 45°35N 9°19E **128** A2
Concrete *U.S.A.* 48°32N 121°45W **304** B3
Conda *Angola* 11°9S 14°20E **265** E2
Condah *Australia* 37°57S 141°44E **282** D4
Condamine *Australia* 26°56S 150°9E **281** D5
Condat *France* 45°21N 2°46E **174** C6
Condé *Angola* 10°50S 14°37E **265** E2
Conde *Brazil* 11°49S 37°37W **333** D4
Conde *S. Dak., U.S.A.* 45°9N 98°6W **308** C4
Condé-sur-Noireau *France* 48°51N 0°33W **172** D6
Condet *Indonesia* 6°17S 106°51E **122** A2
Condeúba *Brazil* 14°52S 42°0W **333** D3
Condobolin *Australia* 33°4S 147°6E **283** B7
Condom *France* 43°57N 0°22E **174** E4
Condon *U.S.A.* 45°14N 120°11W **304** D3
Conegliano *Italy* 45°53N 12°18E **199** C9
Conejera, I. = Conills, I. des *Spain* 39°11N 2°58E **206** B3
Conejos *Mexico* 26°14N 103°53W **318** B4
Conemaugh → *U.S.A.* 40°28N 79°19W **312** F5
Conero ⌓ *Italy* 43°32N 13°35E **199** E10
Coney I. = Serangoon, Pulau *Singapore* 1°23N 103°55E **138** A3
Coney Island *U.S.A.* 40°34N 74°0W **132** C2
Conflict Group *Papua N. G.* 10°47S 151°45E **286** F6
Confolens *France* 46°2N 0°40E **174** B4
Confuso → *Paraguay* 25°9S 57°34W **334** B4
Congaree → *U.S.A.* 33°44N 80°38W **316** B9
Congaree △ *U.S.A.* 33°47N 80°47W **316** B9
Congaz *Moldova* 46°7N 28°36E **183** D13
Congerville *U.S.A.* 40°38N 89°11W **310** D7
Conghua *China* 23°36N 113°31E **229** F9
Congjiang *China* 25°43N 108°52E **228** E7
Congleton *U.K.* 53°10N 2°13W **168** D5
Congo *Brazil* 7°48S 36°40W **332** C4
Congo (Brazzaville) = Congo ■ *Africa* 1°0S 16°0E **264** C3
Congo (Kinshasa) = Congo, Dem. Rep. of the ■ *Africa* 3°0S 23°0E **265** C4
Congo ■ *Africa* 1°0S 16°0E **264** C3
Congo → *Africa* 6°4S 12°24E **265** D2
Congo, Dem. Rep. of the ■ *Africa* 3°0S 23°0E **265** C4
Congo Basin *Africa* 0°10S 24°30E **254** G6
Congo Free State = Congo, Dem. Rep. of the ■ *Africa* 3°0S 23°0E **265** C4
Congonhas *Brazil* 20°30S 43°52W **333** F3
Congonhas, São Paulo ✕ **(CGH)** *Brazil* 23°38S 46°39W **137** B2
Congress *U.S.A.* 34°9N 112°51W **305** J7
Conguillio △ *Chile* 38°40S 71°42W **336** A2
Conil de la Frontera *Spain* 36°17N 6°10W **195** J4
Conills, I. des *Spain* 39°11N 2°58E **206** B3
Conimbla △ *Australia* 33°45S 148°28E **283** B8
Coniston *Canada* 46°29N 80°51W **298** C3
Conjeeveram = Kanchipuram *India* 12°52N 79°45E **245** H4
Conklin *Alta., Canada* 55°38N 111°5W **297** B6
Conklin *N.Y., U.S.A.* 42°2N 75°49W **313** D9
Conkouati ⌓ *Congo* 3°50S 11°28E **264** C2
Conlendas, Pta. das *Azores* 38°38N 27°14W **153** d1
Conley → *U.S.A.* 33°40N 84°17W **113** C3
Conn, L. *Ireland* 54°3N 9°15W **166** B2
Connaught □ *Ireland* 53°43N 9°12W **166** C2
Connaught Place *Delhi, India* **120** b2
Conneaut *U.S.A.* 41°57N 80°34W **312** E4
Conneautville *U.S.A.* 41°45N 80°22W **312** E4
Connecticut □ *U.S.A.* 41°30N 72°45W **313** E12
Connecticut → *U.S.A.* 41°16N 72°20W **313** E12
Connell *U.S.A.* 46°40N 118°52W **304** C4
Connellsville *U.S.A.* 40°1N 79°35W **312** F5
Connemara *Ireland* 53°29N 9°45W **166** C2
Connemara △ *Ireland* 53°32N 9°52W **166** C2
Conner *Phil.* 17°48N 121°19E **232** C3
Connerré *France* 48°3N 0°30E **172** D7
Connersville *U.S.A.* 39°39N 85°8W **311** E11
Connors Ra. *Australia* 21°40S 149°10E **280** C4
Conoble *Australia* 32°55S 144°33E **283** B6
Conococha *Peru* 10°7S 77°18W **330** C2
Cononaco → *Ecuador* 1°32S 75°35W **328** D2
Conques *France* 44°36N 2°23E **174** D6
Conquest *Canada* 51°32N 107°14W **297** C7
Conquista = Vitória da Conquista *Brazil* 14°51S 40°51W **333** D3
Conrad *Iowa, U.S.A.* 42°14N 92°52W **310** B4
Conrad *Mont., U.S.A.* 48°10N 111°57W **304** B8
Conrad Rise *S. Ocean* 53°0S 41°0E **151** B5
Conran, C. *Australia* 37°49S 148°44E **283** D8
Conroe *U.S.A.* 30°19N 95°27W **314** F7
Consecon *Canada* 44°0N 77°31W **312** C7
Conselheiro Lafaiete *Brazil* 20°40S 43°48W **333** F3
Conselheiro Pena *Brazil* 19°10S 41°30W **333** E3
Consell *Spain* 39°40N 2°49E **206** B3
Conselve *Italy* 45°14N 11°52E **199** C8
Conservatori, Palazzo dei *Rome, Italy* **136** c3
Consett *U.K.* 54°51N 1°50W **168** C6
Consolação *Brazil* 23°32S 46°38W **137** B2
Consort *Canada* 52°1N 110°46W **297** C6
Constance = Konstanz *Germany* 47°40N 9°10E **179** H5
Constance, L. = Bodensee *Europe* 47°35N 9°25E **179** H5
Constanţa *Romania* 44°14N 28°38E **183** F13
Constanţa □ *Romania* 44°15N 28°15E **183** F13
Constantia *S. Africa* 34°2S 18°26E **118** B1
Constantina *Spain* 37°51N 5°40W **195** H5
Constantine *Algeria* 36°25N 6°42E **261** A6
Constantine *Mich., U.S.A.* 41°50N 85°40W **311** C11
Constantine □ *Algeria* 36°30N 6°40E **261** A6
Constantine, Arch of = Costantino, Arco di *Rome, Italy* **136** c3
Constantine, C. *U.S.A.* 58°24N 158°54W **303** G8
Constantinople = İstanbul *Turkey* 41°0N 28°58E **122** C1
Constitución *B. Aires, Argentina* 34°38S 58°23W **117** B2
Constitución *Chile* 35°20S 72°30W **334** D1
Constitución *Uruguay* 31°0S 57°50W **334** C4
Constitución de 1857 △ *Mexico* 32°4N 115°55W **318** A1
Constitution *U.S.A.* 33°42N 84°20W **113** B2
Constitution Avenue *Washington, D.C., U.S.A.* **143** b2
Constitution Square = Syntagma Square *Athens, Greece* **112** b2
Consuegra *Spain* 39°28N 3°36W **195** F7
Consul *Canada* 49°20N 109°30W **297** D7
Contact *U.S.A.* 41°46N 114°45W **304** F6
Contagem *Brazil* 19°55S 44°6W **333** E3
Contai *India* 21°54N 87°46E **243** J12
Contamana *Peru* 7°19S 74°55W **330** B3
Contarini Dal Zaffo, Palazzo *Venice, Italy* **142** c2
Contas → *Brazil* 14°17S 39°1W **333** D4
Contes *France* 43°49N 7°19E **175** E11
Continental *U.S.A.* 41°6N 84°16W **311** C12
Contoocook *U.S.A.* 43°13N 71°45W **313** C13
Contra Costa *Mozam.* 25°9S 33°30E **271** C5
Contres *France* 47°24N 1°26E **172** E8
Contrexéville *France* 48°10N 5°53E **173** D12
Controller B. *U.S.A.* 60°7N 144°15W **303** F11
Contumaza *Peru* 7°23S 78°57W **330** B2
Contwoyto L. *Canada* 65°42N 110°50W **294** D9
Convención *Colombia* 8°28N 73°21W **328** B3
Conversano *Italy* 40°58N 17°7E **201** B10
Converse *U.S.A.* 40°35N 85°52W **311** D11
Convoy *U.S.A.* 40°55N 84°43W **311** D12
Conway = Conwy *U.K.* 53°17N 3°50W **168** D4
Conway = Conwy → *U.K.* 53°17N 3°50W **168** D4
Conway *Australia* 20°24S 148°41E **280** b
Conway *Ont., Canada* 44°6N 76°54W **312** B8
Conway *Ark., U.S.A.* 35°5N 92°26W **314** D8
Conway *Fla., U.S.A.* 28°30N 81°19W **133** B2
Conway *N.H., U.S.A.* 43°59N 71°7W **313** C13
Conway *S.C., U.S.A.* 33°51N 79°3W **315** E15
Conway, C. *Australia* 20°34S 148°46E **280** b
Conway, L. *S. Austral., Australia* 28°17S 135°35E **281** D2
Conway, L. *Fla., U.S.A.* 28°28N 81°21W **133** B2
Conwy *U.K.* 53°17N 3°50W **168** D4
Conwy □ *U.K.* 53°10N 3°44W **168** D4
Conwy → *U.K.* 53°17N 3°50W **168** D4
Conyers *U.S.A.* 33°40N 84°1W **316** B5
Coober Pedy *Australia* 29°1S 134°43E **281** D1
Cooch Behar = Koch Bihar *India* 26°22N 89°29E **241** B2
Coogee *Australia* 33°55S 151°16E **139** B2
Cooinda *Australia* 13°15S 130°5E **278** B5
Cook *S. Austral., Australia* 30°37S 130°25E **279** F5
Cook *Minn., U.S.A.* 47°51N 92°41W **308** B7
Cook, B. *Chile* 55°10S 70°0W **336** E3
Cook, C. *Canada* 50°8N 127°55W **296** C3
Cook, Mt. = Aoraki Mount Cook *N.Z.* 43°36S 170°9E **285** D5
Cook, Récif de *N. Cal.* 19°25S 163°50E **288** d
Cook B. *Vanuatu* 18°46S 169°15E **287** H7
Cook Inlet *U.S.A.* 60°0N 152°0W **303** G10
Cook Is. ☐ *Pac. Oc.* 17°0S 160°0W **289** J12
Cook Strait *N.Z.* 41°15S 174°29E **284** H3
Cooke Plains *Australia* 35°23S 139°34E **282** C3
Cookeville *U.S.A.* 36°10N 85°30W **315** C12
Cookhouse *S. Africa* 32°44S 25°47E **270** D4
Cooks Hammock *U.S.A.* 29°56N 83°17W **316** F6
Cooks Harbour *Canada* 51°36N 55°52W **299** B8
Cookshire *Canada* 45°25N 71°38W **313** A13
Cookstown *Ont., Canada* 44°11N 79°42W **312** B5
Cookstown *Tyrone, U.K.* 54°38N 6°45W **166** B5
Cooksville *Canada* 43°35N 79°38W **141** B1
Cooktown *Australia* 15°30S 145°16E **280** B4
Coolabah *Australia* 31°1S 146°43E **283** A7
Cooladdi *Australia* 26°37S 145°23E **281** D4
Coolah *Australia* 31°48S 149°41E **283** A8
Coolah Tops △ *Australia* 31°52S 150°0E **283** A9
Coolamon *Australia* 34°46S 147°8E **283** C7
Coolgardie *Australia* 30°55S 121°8E **279** F3
Coolidge *Ariz., U.S.A.* 32°59N 111°31W **305** K8
Coolidge *Ga., U.S.A.* 31°1N 83°52W **316** D6
Coolidge Dam *U.S.A.* 33°10N 110°32W **305** K8
Cooma *Australia* 36°12S 149°8E **283** D8
Coon Rapids *Iowa, U.S.A.* 41°53N 94°41W **310** C2
Coon Rapids *Minn., U.S.A.* 45°9N 93°19W **308** C7
Coonabarabran *Australia* 31°14S 149°18E **283** A8
Coonalpyn *Australia* 35°43S 139°52E **282** C3
Coonamble *Australia* 30°56S 148°27E **283** A8
Coonana *Australia* 31°0S 123°0E **279** F3
Coonana ☼ *Australia* 30°51S 122°53E **279** F3
Coondapoor *India* 13°42N 74°40E **245** H2
Cooninnie, L. *Australia* 26°4S 139°59E **281** D2
Coonoor *India* 11°21N 76°45E **245** J3
Cooper *U.S.A.* 33°23N 95°42W **314** E7
Cooper → *U.S.A.* 32°50N 79°56W **316** C10
Cooper City *U.S.A.* 26°3N 80°16W **129** B1
Cooper Cr. → *Australia* 28°29S 137°46E **281** D2
Cooper Ridge *Pac. Oc.* 10°0N 150°30W **289** G12
Cooper's Hill *Jamaica* 18°4N 76°51W **320** a
Cooperstown *N. Dak., U.S.A.* 47°27N 98°8W **308** B4
Cooperstown *N.Y., U.S.A.* 42°42N 74°56W **313** D10
Coopersville *U.S.A.* 43°4N 85°57W **311** A11
Coopracambra △ *Australia* 37°20S 149°20E **283** D8
Coora → *Trin. & Tob.* 10°10N 61°28W **323** t
Coorabie *Australia* 31°54S 132°18E **279** F5
Coorong, The *Australia* 35°50S 139°20E **282** C3
Coorong △ *Australia* 36°0S 139°29E **282** D3
Coorow *Australia* 29°53S 116°2E **279** E2
Cooroy *Australia* 26°22S 152°54E **281** D5
Coos Bay *U.S.A.* 43°22N 124°13W **304** E1
Coosa → *U.S.A.* 32°30N 86°16W **315** E11
Cootamundra *Australia* 34°36S 148°1E **283** C8
Cootehill *Ireland* 54°4N 7°5W **166** B4
Copacabana *Brazil* 22°58S 43°11W **135** B1
Copahue Paso *Argentina* 37°49S 71°8W **334** D1
Copainalá *Mexico* 17°4N 93°18W **319** D6
Copake *U.S.A.* 42°7N 73°31W **313** D11
Copalnic Mănăştur *Romania* 47°30N 23°41E **183** C8
Copán *Honduras* 14°50N 89°9W **320** D2
Copatana *Brazil* 2°48S 67°4W **328** D4
Copceac *Moldova* 45°51N 28°42E **183** E13
Cope *Colo., U.S.A.* 39°40N 102°51W **304** G12
Cope *S.C., U.S.A.* 33°23N 81°0W **316** B8
Cope, C. *Spain* 37°26N 1°28W **197** H3
Copeland *U.S.A.* 26°1N 81°22W **317** K8
Copenhagen = København *Denmark* 55°40N 12°26E **118** A2
Copenhagen *U.S.A.* 43°54N 75°41W **313** C9
Copertino *Italy* 40°16N 18°3E **201** B11
Copiapó *Chile* 27°30S 70°20W **334** B1
Copiapó → *Chile* 27°19S 70°56W **334** B1
Coplay *U.S.A.* 40°44N 75°29W **313** F9
Copley *Australia* 30°36S 138°26E **282** A3
Copo △ *Argentina* 25°53S 61°41W **334** B3
Copp L. *Canada* 60°14N 114°40W **296** A6
Copparo *Italy* 44°54N 11°49E **199** D8
Coppell *U.S.A.* 32°57N 96°59W **120** A4
Coppename → *Suriname* 5°48N 55°55W **329** B6
Copper → *U.S.A.* 60°18N 145°3W **303** F11
Copper Canyon = Barranca del Cobre ⌓ *Mexico* 27°18N 107°40W **318** B3
Copper Center *U.S.A.* 61°58N 145°18W **303** F11
Copper City = Invermere *Canada* 50°30N 116°2W **296** C5
Copper Harbor *U.S.A.* 47°28N 87°53W **308** B10
Copper Queen *Zimbabwe* 17°29S 29°18E **269** F2
Copperas Cove *U.S.A.* 31°8N 97°54W **314** F6
Copperbelt □ *Zambia* 13°15S 27°30E **269** E2
Coppermine = Kugluktuk *Canada* 67°50N 115°5W **294** D8
Coppermine → *Canada* 67°49N 116°4W **294** D8
Copperopolis *U.S.A.* 37°58N 120°38W **306** H6
Copşa Mică *Romania* 46°7N 24°15E **183** D9
Coquet → *U.K.* 55°20N 1°32W **168** B6
Coquilhatville = Mbandaka *Dem. Rep. of the Congo* 0°1N 18°18E **264** B3
Coquille *U.S.A.* 43°11N 124°11W **304** E1
Coquimbo *Chile* 30°0S 71°20W **334** C1
Coquimbo □ *Chile* 31°0S 71°0W **334** C1
Coquitlam *Canada* 49°17N 122°45W **296** D4
Corabia *Romania* 43°48N 24°30E **183** G9
Coração de Jesus *Brazil* 16°43S 44°22W **333** E3
Coracora *Peru* 15°5S 73°45W **330** D3
Coraki *Australia* 28°59S 153°17E **281** D5
Coral *U.S.A.* 40°29N 79°10W **312** F5
Coral B. *Phil.* 8°25N 117°20E **233** G1
Coral Bay *Australia* 23°8S 113°46E **278** D1
Coral Gables *U.S.A.* 25°43N 80°16W **129** D1
Coral Harbour *Nunavut, Canada* 64°8N 83°10W **295** E15
Coral Harbour *The Bahamas* 24°58N 77°28W **153** b
Coral Heights *The Bahamas* 25°0N 77°27W **153** b
Coral Hills *U.S.A.* 38°51N 76°55W **143** B3
Coral Sea *Pac. Oc.* 15°0S 150°0E **276** C9
Coral Sea Basin *Pac. Oc.* 14°0S 152°0E **288** J7
Coral Sea Islands Terr. □ *Australia* 20°0S 155°0E **276** D9
Coral Springs *U.S.A.* 26°16N 80°17W **317** J9
Corales del Rosario △ *Colombia* 10°8N 75°46W **328** A2
Coralville *U.S.A.* 41°40N 91°35W **310** C5
Coralville L. *U.S.A.* 41°42N 91°33W **310** C5
Corangamite, L. *Australia* 38°5S 143°30E **282** E5
Corantijn = Courantyne → *S. Amer.* 5°50N 57°8W **329** B6
Coraopolis *U.S.A.* 40°31N 80°10W **312** F4
Corato *Italy* 41°9N 16°25E **201** A9
Corbeil-Essonnes *France* 48°36N 2°26E **173** D9
Corbeiro, C. *W. Sahara* 21°50N 17°0W **260** D1
Corbett △ *India* 29°20N 79°0E **243** E8
Corbie *France* 49°54N 2°30E **173** C9
Corbières *France* 42°55N 2°35E **174** F6
Corbigny *France* 47°16N 3°40E **173** E10
Corbin *U.S.A.* 36°57N 84°6W **309** G11
Corbones → *Spain* 37°36N 5°39W **195** H5
Corbu *Romania* 44°25N 28°39E **183** F13
Corby *U.K.* 52°30N 0°41W **169** E7
Corcaigh = Cork *Ireland* 51°54N 8°29W **166** E3
Corcoran *U.S.A.* 36°6N 119°33W **306** J7
Corcovado, Cristo Redentor *Brazil* 22°57S 43°12W **135** B1
Corcovado △ *Chile* 43°25S 72°45W **336** B2
Corcovado △ *Costa Rica* 8°33N 83°35W **320** E3
Cordele *U.S.A.* 31°58N 83°47W **316** D6
Cordell *U.S.A.* 35°17N 98°59W **314** D5
Cordenòns *Italy* 45°59N 12°42E **199** C9
Cordes-sur-Ciel *France* 44°5N 1°57E **174** D5
Cordillera Azul △ *Peru* 7°30S 76°30W **330** B2
Cordillera de los Picachos △ *Colombia* 2°39N 74°30W **328** C3
Cordisburgo *Brazil* 19°7S 44°21W **333** E3
Córdoba *Argentina* 31°20S 64°10W **334** C3
Córdoba *Veracruz, Mexico* 18°53N 96°56W **319** D5
Córdoba *Spain* 37°50N 4°50W **195** H6
Córdoba □ *Argentina* 31°22S 64°15W **334** C3
Córdoba □ *Colombia* 8°20N 75°40W **328** B2
Córdoba □ *Spain* 38°5N 5°0W **195** G6
Córdoba, Sierra de *Argentina* 31°10S 64°25W **334** C3
Cordon *Phil.* 16°42N 121°32E **232** C3
Cordova *U.S.A.* 60°33N 145°45W **303** F11
Corella *Spain* 42°7N 1°48W **196** C3
Corella → *Australia* 19°34S 140°47E **280** B3
Coremas *Brazil* 7°1S 37°58W **332** C4
Corentyne = Courantyne → *S. Amer.* 5°50N 57°8W **329** B6
Corfield *Australia* 21°40S 143°21E **280** C3
Corfu = Kerkyra *Greece* 39°38N 19°50E **206** B9
Corfu *U.S.A.* 42°57N 78°24W **312** D6
Corfu ✕ **(CFU)** *Greece* 39°35N 19°54E **204** B1
Corfu, Str. of = Kerkyras, Notio Steno *Greece* 39°34N 20°0E **206** B10
Corgo = O Corgo *Spain* 42°56N 7°25W **194** C3
Corguinho *Brazil* 19°53S 54°52W **331** D7
Cori *Italy* 41°39N 12°55E **200** A5
Coria *Spain* 39°58N 6°33W **194** F4
Coria del Río *Spain* 37°16N 6°3W **195** H4
Coricudgy *Australia* 32°51S 150°24E **283** B9
Corigliano Cálabro *Italy* 39°36N 16°31E **201** C9
Corimba, Barra de *Angola* 8°52S 13°9E **265** D2
Coringa Is. *Australia* 16°58S 149°58E **280** B4
Corinth = Korinthos *Greece* 37°56N 22°55E **204** D4
Corinth *Grenada* 12°2N 61°40W **323** q
Corinth *Ky., U.S.A.* 38°30N 84°34W **311** F12
Corinth *Miss., U.S.A.* 34°56N 88°31W **315** D10
Corinth *N.Y., U.S.A.* 43°15N 73°49W **313** C11
Corinth, G. of = Korinthiakos Kolpos *Greece* 38°16N 22°30E **204** C4
Corinth Canal *Greece* 37°58N 23°0E **204** D4
Corinto *Brazil* 18°20S 44°30W **333** E3
Corinto *Nic.* 12°30N 87°10W **320** D2
Coriole *Somalia* 1°47N 44°32E **267** D5
Corisco *Eq. Guin.* 0°55N 9°18E **264** B1
Cork *Ireland* 51°54N 8°29W **166** E3
Cork □ *Ireland* 51°57N 8°40W **166** E3
Cork Harbour *Ireland* 51°47N 8°16W **166** E3
Corlay *France* 48°20N 3°5W **172** D3
Corleone *Italy* 37°49N 13°18E **200** E6
Corleto Perticara *Italy* 40°23N 16°2E **201** B9
Çorlu *Turkey* 41°11N 27°49E **203** E11
Cormack L. *Canada* 60°56N 121°37W **296** A4
Cormano *Italy* 45°32N 9°10E **128** A2
Cormòns *Italy* 45°58N 13°28E **199** C10
Cormorant *Canada* 54°14N 100°35W **297** C8
Cormorant L. *Canada* 54°15N 100°50W **297** C8
Corn Is. = Maíz, Is. del *Nic.* 12°15N 83°4W **320** D3
Cornalvo ⌓ *Spain* 39°1N 6°13W **195** F4
Cornaredo *Italy* 45°30N 9°1E **128** A1
Cornélio Procópio *Brazil* 23°7S 50°40W **335** A5
Cornell *U.S.A.* 41°0N 88°44W **311** D8
Corner Brook *Canada* 48°57N 57°58W **299** C8
Corner della Regina, Palazzo *Venice, Italy* **142** b2
Corner Inlet *Australia* 38°45S 146°20E **283** E7
Corner Seamounts *Atl. Oc.* 35°0N 52°0W **152** C6
Corner Spinelli, Palazzo *Venice, Italy* **142** b2
Corneşti *Moldova* 47°21N 28°1E **183** C13
Corneto = Tarquínia *Italy* 42°15N 11°45E **199** F8
Cornigliano *Italy* 44°29N 10°5E **198** D7
Corning *Ark., U.S.A.* 36°25N 90°35W **315** C9
Corning *Calif., U.S.A.* 39°56N 122°11W **304** G2
Corning *Iowa, U.S.A.* 40°59N 94°44W **310** C2
Corning *N.Y., U.S.A.* 42°9N 77°3W **312** D7
Corno Grande *Italy* 42°28N 13°34E **199** F10
Cornwall *Ont., Canada* 45°2N 74°44W **313** A10
Cornwall *Pa., U.S.A.* 40°17N 76°25W **313** F8
Cornwall *Jamaica* 18°15N 77°54W **320** a
Cornwall □ *Jamaica* 50°26N 4°40W **169** G3
Cornwall □ *U.K.* 77°37N 94°38W **295** B13
Cornwall I. *Canada* 75°8N 95°0W **295** B13
Cornwallis I. *Canada* 27°23N 81°6W **317** H8
Cornwell *U.S.A.* 34°55S 137°0E **282** C2
Corny Pt. *Australia* 11°25N 69°41W **328** A4
Coro *Venezuela* 18°35S 42°17W **333** E3
Coroaci *Brazil* 4°8S 44°0W **332** B3
Coroatá *Brazil* 17°15S 68°28W **330** D4
Corocoro *Bolivia* 8°30N 60°10W **329** B5
Corocoro, I. *Venezuela* 16°0S 67°50W **330** D4
Coroico *Bolivia* 18°28S 47°13W **333** E2
Coromandel *Brazil* 36°45S 175°31E **284** C4
Coromandel *N.Z.* 12°30N 81°0E **245** H5
Coromandel Coast *India* 37°0S 175°45E **284** D4
Coromandel Pen. *N.Z.* 37°0S 175°40E **284** D4
Coromandel Ra. *N.Z.* 12°1N 120°12E **232** E3
Coron *Phil.* 11°54N 120°8E **233** F3
Coron B. *Phil.* 11°55N 120°14E **233** F3
Coron I. *Phil.* 33°53N 117°34W **307** M9
Corona *Calif., U.S.A.* 34°15N 105°36W **305** J11
Corona *N. Mex., U.S.A.* 32°41N 117°10W **307** N9
Coronado *U.S.A.* 9°0N 83°40W **320** E3
Coronado, B. de *Costa Rica* 41°40S 74°0W **336** B2
Coronados, G. de los *Chile*
Coronados, Is. Los *Mexico* 32°26N 117°19W **307** N9
Coronation *Canada* 52°5N 111°27W **296** C6
Coronation Gulf *Canada* 68°25N 110°0W **294** D10
Coronation I. *Antarctica* 60°45S 46°0W **151** C18
Coronation Is. *Australia* 14°57S 124°55E **278** B3
Coronda *Argentina* 31°58S 60°56W **334** C3
Coronel *Chile* 37°0S 73°10W **334** D1
Coronel Bogado *Paraguay* 27°11S 56°18W **334** B4
Coronel Dorrego *Argentina* 38°40S 61°10W **334** D3
Coronel Fabriciano *Brazil* 19°31S 42°38W **333** E3
Coronel Murta *Brazil* 16°37S 42°11W **333** E3
Coronel Oviedo *Paraguay* 25°24S 56°30W **334** B4
Coronel Ponce *Brazil* 15°34S 55°1W **331** D6
Coronel Pringles *Argentina* 38°0S 61°30W **334** D3
Coronel Suárez *Argentina* 37°30S 61°52W **334** D3
Coronel Vidal *Argentina* 37°28S 57°45W **334** D4
Corongo *Peru* 8°30S 77°53W **330** B2
Coropuna, Nevado *Peru* 15°30S 72°41W **330** D3
Corossol *St. Barts* 17°54N 62°51W **322** a
Çorovodë *Albania* 40°31N 20°14E **202** F4
Corowa *Australia* 35°58S 146°21E **283** C7
Corozal *Colombia* 9°19N 75°18W **328** B2
Corozal □ *Belize* 18°23N 88°23W **319** D7
Corozal Pt. *Trin. & Tob.* 10°45N 61°37W **323** t
Corps *France* 44°50N 5°56E **175** D9
Corpus *Argentina* 27°10S 55°30W **335** B4
Corpus Christi *U.S.A.* 27°47N 97°24W **314** H6
Corpus Christi, L. *U.S.A.* 28°2N 97°52W **314** G6
Corque *Bolivia* 18°20S 67°41W **330** D4
Corral *Chile* 39°52S 73°26W **336** A2
Corral de Almaguer *Spain* 39°45N 3°10W **194** F7
Corralejo *Canary Is.* 28°43N 13°53W **153** e2
Corraun Pen. *Ireland* 53°54N 9°54W **166** C2
Corréggio *Italy* 44°46N 10°47E **198** D7
Corregidor *Phil.* 14°23N 120°35E **232** D3
Corrente *Brazil* 10°27S 45°10W **332** D2
Corrente → *Brazil* 13°8S 43°28W **333** D3
Correntes → *Brazil* 17°38S 55°8W **331** D6
Correntes, C. das *Mozam.* 24°6S 35°34E **271** B6
Correntina *Brazil* 13°20S 44°39W **333** D3
Corrèze □ *France* 45°20N 1°45E **174** C5
Corrèze → *France* 45°10N 1°28E **174** C5
Corrib, L. *Ireland* 53°27N 9°16W **166** C2
Corridònia *Italy* 43°15N 13°30E **199** E10
Corrientes *Argentina* 27°30S 58°45W **334** B4
Corrientes □ *Argentina* 28°0S 57°0W **334** B4
Corrientes → *Argentina* 30°42S 59°38W **334** C4
Corrientes → *Peru* 3°43S 74°35W **328** D3
Corrientes, C. *Colombia* 5°30N 77°34W **328** B2
Corrientes, C. *Cuba* 21°43N 84°30W **320** B3
Corrientes, C. *Jalisco, Mexico* 20°25N 105°42W **318** C3
Corrigan *U.S.A.* 31°0N 94°52W **314** F7
Corrigin *Australia* 32°20S 117°53E **279** F2
Corriverton *Guyana* 5°55N 57°20W **329** B6
Corry *U.S.A.* 41°55N 79°39W **312** E5
Corryong *Australia* 36°12S 147°53E **283** D7
Corse □ *France* 42°0N 9°0E **175** G13
Corse, C. *France* 43°1N 9°25E **175** E13
Corse ⌓ *France* 42°14N 9°10E **175** F13
Corse-du-Sud □ *France* 41°45N 9°0E **175** G13
Corsica = Corse □ *France* 42°0N 9°0E **175** G13
Corsicana *U.S.A.* 32°6N 96°28W **314** E6
Córsico *Italy* 45°25N 9°6E **128** B1
Corsini, Palazzo *Rome, Italy* **136** c1
Corstorphine *U.K.* 55°56N 3°17W **121** B2
Corte *France* 42°19N 9°11E **175** F13
Corte Pinto *Portugal* 37°42N 7°29W **195** H3
Cortegana *Spain* 37°52N 6°49W **195** H4
Cortes *Phil.* 9°17N 126°11E **233** G6
Cortés, Mar de = California, G. de *Mexico* 27°0N 111°0W **318** B2
Cortez *U.S.A.* 37°21N 108°35W **305** H9
Córthaidh, Inis = Enniscorthy *Ireland* 52°30N 6°34W **166** D5
Cortina d'Ampezzo *Italy* 46°32N 12°8E **199** B9
Cortland *N.Y., U.S.A.* 42°36N 76°11W **313** D8
Cortland *Ohio, U.S.A.* 41°20N 80°44W **312** E4
Cortona *Italy* 43°16N 11°59E **199** E8
Corubal → *Guinea-Biss.* 11°57N 15°5W **262** C2
Coruche *Portugal* 38°57N 8°30W **195** G2
Çoruh → *Turkey* 41°38N 41°38E **191** K5
Çorum *Turkey* 40°30N 34°57E **212** B6
Çorum □ *Turkey* 40°40N 35°0E **212** B6
Corumbá *Brazil* 19°0S 57°30W **331** D6
Corumbá → *Brazil* 18°19S 48°55W **333** E2
Corumbá de Goiás *Brazil* 16°0S 48°50W **333** E2
Corumbaíba *Brazil* 18°9S 48°34W **333** E2
Corund *Romania* 46°30N 25°13E **183** D10
Corunna = A Coruña *Spain* 43°20N 8°25W **194** B2
Corunna *U.S.A.* 42°59N 84°7W **311** B12
Corvallis *U.S.A.* 44°34N 123°16W **304** D2
Corvette, L. de la *Canada* 53°25N 74°3W **298** B5
Corviale *Italy* 41°51N 12°25E **136** B1
Corvo *Azores* 39°42N 31°6W **153** d2
Coryal *Trin. & Tob.* 10°30N 61°11W **323** t
Corydon *Ind., U.S.A.* 38°13N 86°7W **311** F10
Corydon *Iowa, U.S.A.* 40°46N 93°19W **310** D3
Corydon *Ky., U.S.A.* 37°44N 87°43W **311** G9
Cosalá *Mexico* 24°23N 106°41W **318** C3
Cosamaloapan de Carpio *Mexico* 18°22N 95°48W **319** D5
Cosenza *Italy* 39°18N 16°15E **201** C9
Coşereni *Romania* 44°38N 26°35E **183** F11
Coshocton *U.S.A.* 40°16N 81°51W **312** F3
Coslada *Spain* 40°25N 3°35W **127** B2
Cosmo Newberry *Australia* 28°0S 122°54E **279** E3
Cosmo Newberry ☼ *Australia* 27°59S 122°53E **279** E3
Cosmonaut Sea *S. Ocean* 66°30S 40°0E **151** C5
Cosmonautics Museum *Russia* 55°49N 37°38E **129** B2
Cosne-Cours-sur-Loire *France* 47°24N 2°54E **173** E9
Coso Junction *U.S.A.* 36°3N 117°57W **307** J9
Coso Pk. *U.S.A.* 36°13N 117°44W **307** J9
Cospeito = A Feira do Monte *Spain* 43°12N 7°34W **194** B3
Cosquín *Argentina* 31°15S 64°30W **334** C3
Cossato *Italy* 45°34N 8°10E **198** C5
Cossé-le-Vivien *France* 47°57N 0°54W **172** E6
Cossigny *France* 48°43N 2°40E **134** B4
Cosson → *France* 47°30N 1°15E **172** E8
Costa Calma *Canary Is.* 28°6N 14°16W **153** e2
Costa del Pins *Spain* 39°38N 3°26E **206** B4
Costa Mesa *U.S.A.* 33°38N 117°55W **307** M9
Costa Rica ■ *Cent. Amer.* 10°0N 84°0W **320** E3
Costa Teguise *Canary Is.* 29°0N 13°31W **153** e2
Costantino, Arco di *Rome, Italy* **136** c3
Costermansville = Bukavu *Dem. Rep. of the Congo* 2°20S 28°52E **268** C2
Costeşti *Romania* 44°40N 24°53E **183** F9
Costigliole d'Asti *Italy* 44°47N 8°11E **198** D5
Cosumnes → *U.S.A.* 38°16N 121°26W **306** G5
Coswig *Sachsen, Germany* 51°7N 13°34E **178** D9
Coswig *Sachsen-Anhalt, Germany* 51°53N 12°27E **178** D8
Cotabato *Phil.* 7°14N 124°15E **233** H5
Cotacajes → *Bolivia* 16°0S 67°1W **330** D4
Cotagaita *Bolivia* 20°45S 65°40W **334** A2
Cotahuasi *Peru* 15°12S 72°50W **330** D3
Cotao *Portugal* 38°45N 9°17W **126** A1
Côte d'Ivoire ■ *Africa* 7°30N 5°0W **262** D4
Côte-d'Or □ *France* 47°30N 4°50E **173** E11
Côte-St-Luc *Canada* 45°28N 73°39W **130** B2
Coteau des Prairies *U.S.A.* 45°20N 97°50W **308** C5
Coteau du Missouri *U.S.A.* 47°0N 100°0W **308** B4
Cotegipe *Brazil* 12°2S 44°15W **333** D3
Cotentin *France* 49°15N 1°30W **172** C5
Côtes-d'Armor □ *France* 48°25N 2°40W **172** D4
Côtes de Meuse *France* 49°15N 5°22E **173** C12
Côtes-du-Nord = Côtes-d'Armor □ *France* 48°25N 2°40W **172** D4
Cotiella *Spain* 42°31N 0°19E **196** C5
Cotiujeni *Moldova* 47°51N 28°33E **183** C13
Cotoca *Bolivia* 17°49S 63°3W **331** D5
Cotonou *Benin* 6°20N 2°25E **263** D5
Cotopaxi *Ecuador* 0°40S 78°30W **328** D2
Cotopaxi □ *Ecuador* 0°5S 78°55W **328** D2

Cotopaxi △ Ecuador 0°39S 78°24W 328 D2
Cotronei Italy 39°9N 16°47E 201 C9
Cotswold Hills U.K. 51°42N 2°10W 169 F5
Cottage Grove U.S.A. 43°48N 123°3W 304 E2
Cottageville U.S.A. 32°56N 80°29W 316 C9
Cottam Canada 42°8N 82°45W 312 D2
Cottbus Germany 51°45N 14°20E 178 D10
Cottingham U.K. 53°48N 0°25W 168 D7
Cotton Ground
St. Kitts & Nevis 17°11N 62°36W 322 d
Cottondale U.S.A. 30°48N 85°23W 316 E4
Cottonwood Ala., U.S.A. 31°3N 85°18W 316 D4
Cottonwood Ariz., U.S.A. 34°45N 112°1W 305 J7
Cotulla U.S.A. 28°26N 99°14W 314 G5
Cotunduba, I. de Brazil 22°57S 43°8W 135 B2
Coubre, Pte. de la France 45°42N 1°15W 174 C2
Coubron France 48°54N 2°34E 134 A4
Couches France 46°53N 4°30E 173 F11
Couço Portugal 38°59N 8°17W 195 G2
Coudersport U.S.A. 41°46N 78°1W 312 E6
Couedic, C. du Australia 36°5S 136°40E 282 D2
Couëron France 47°13N 1°44W 172 E5
Couesnon ➜ France 48°38N 1°32W 172 D5
Couhé France 46°17N 0°11E 174 B4
Coulanges-sur-Yonne
France 47°31N 3°33E 173 E10
Coulee City U.S.A. 47°37N 119°17W 304 C4
Coulee Dam Nat. Recr. Area = Lake
Roosevelt ⌓ U.S.A. 48°5N 118°14W 304 B4
Coulibistrie Dominica 15°27N 61°28W 323 k
Coulman I. Antarctica 73°35S 170°0E 151 D11
Coulommiers France 48°50N 3°3E 173 D10
Coulon ➜ France 43°51N 5°6E 175 E9
Coulonge ➜ Canada 45°52N 76°46W 298 C4
Coulonges-sur-l'Autize
France 46°29N 0°36W 174 B3
Coulounieix-Chamiers
France 45°11N 0°42E 174 C4
Coulterville Calif., U.S.A. 37°43N 120°12W 306 H6
Coulterville Ill., U.S.A. 38°11N 89°36W 310 F7
Council Alaska, U.S.A. 64°53N 163°41W 303 D7
Council Ga., U.S.A. 30°37N 82°31W 316 E7
Council Idaho, U.S.A. 44°44N 116°26W 304 D5
Council Bluffs U.S.A. 41°16N 95°52W 308 E6
Council Grove U.S.A. 38°40N 96°29W 308 F5
Coupeville U.S.A. 48°13N 122°41W 306 B4
Courantyne ➜ S. Amer. 5°50N 57°8W 329 B6
Courbevoie France 48°53N 2°14E 134 A2
Courcelles Belgium 50°28N 4°22E 170 D4
Courchevel France 45°25N 6°36E 175 C10
Courçon France 46°15N 0°50W 174 B3
Courland ➜ Trin. & Tob. 11°13N 60°47W 323 s
Courmayeur Italy 45°47N 6°58E 198 C3
Couronne, C. France 43°19N 5°3E 175 E9
Cours-la-Ville France 46°7N 4°19E 173 F11
Coursan France 43°14N 3°4E 174 E7
Courseulles-sur-Mer
France 49°20N 0°29W 172 C6
Courtenay B.C., Canada 49°45N 125°0W 296 D4
Courtenay Loiret, France 48°2N 3°3E 173 D10
Courtland Ont., Canada 42°51N 80°38W 312 D4
Courtland Calif., U.S.A. 38°20N 121°34W 306 G5
Courtrai = Kortrijk
Belgium 50°50N 3°17E 170 D3
Courtright Canada 42°49N 82°28W 312 D2
Courtry France 48°55N 2°35E 134 A4
Coushatta U.S.A. 32°1N 93°21W 314 E8
Coutances France 49°3N 1°28W 172 C5
Coutras France 45°3N 0°8W 174 C3
Coutts Crossing Australia 29°49S 152°55E 281 D5
Couva Trin. & Tob. 10°25N 61°27W 323 t
Couva/Tabaquite/Talparo □
Trin. & Tob. 10°28N 61°18W 323 t
Couvin Belgium 50°3N 4°29E 170 D4
Covarrubias Spain 42°4N 3°31W 194 C7
Covasna Romania 45°50N 26°10E 183 E11
Covasna □ Romania 45°50N 26°0E 183 E10
Cove I. Canada 45°17N 81°44W 312 A3
Coveñas Colombia 9°24N 75°44W 328 B2
Covent Garden London, U.K. 125 b4
Coventry U.K. 52°25N 1°28W 169 E6
Coverdale U.S.A. 31°38N 83°58W 316 D6
Covilhã Portugal 40°17N 7°31W 194 E3
Covington Ga., U.S.A. 33°36N 83°51W 316 B6
Covington Ind., U.S.A. 40°9N 87°24W 311 D9
Covington Ky., U.S.A. 39°5N 84°30W 311 E12
Covington Ohio, U.S.A. 40°7N 84°21W 311 D12
Covington Tenn., U.S.A. 35°34N 89°39W 315 D10
Covington Va., U.S.A. 37°47N 79°59W 309 G14
Cowal, L. Australia 33°40S 147°25E 283 B7
Cowan, Cerro Ecuador 0°12S 90°48W 330 a
Cowan, L. Australia 31°45S 121°45E 279 F3
Cowan L. Canada 54°0N 107°15W 297 C7
Cowangie Australia 35°12S 141°26E 282 C4
Cowansville Canada 45°14N 72°46W 313 A12
Coward Springs Australia 29°24S 136°49E 281 D2
Cowcowing Lakes
Australia 30°55S 117°20E 279 F2
Cowden U.S.A. 39°15N 88°52W 311 E8
Cowdenbeath U.K. 56°7N 3°21W 167 E5
Cowell Australia 33°39S 136°56E 282 B2
Cowes Vic., Australia 38°28S 145°14E 283 E6
Cowes I. of W., U.K. 50°45N 1°18W 169 G6
Cowgate Edinburgh, U.K. 121 b3
Cowichan L. Canada 48°53N 124°17W 306 B2
Cowley U.K. 51°31N 0°28W 125 A1
Cowlitz ➜ U.S.A. 46°6N 122°55W 306 D4
Cowra Australia 33°49S 148°42E 283 B8
Cox Spain 38°8N 0°53W 197 G4
Coxilha Grande Brazil 28°18S 51°30W 335 B5
Coxim Brazil 18°30S 54°55W 331 D7
Coxim ➜ Brazil 18°34S 54°46W 331 D7
Cox's Bazar Bangla. 21°26N 91°59E 241 E3
Coyah Guinea 9°42N 13°22W 262 D2
Coyoacán Mexico 19°21N 99°9W 128 B2
Coyote Wells U.S.A. 32°44N 115°58W 307 N11
Coyuca de Benítez Mexico 17°2N 100°4W 319 D4
Coyuca de Catalán
Mexico 18°20N 100°39W 318 D4
Cozad U.S.A. 40°52N 99°59W 308 E4
Cozes France 45°34N 0°49W 174 C3
Cozia △ Romania 45°25N 24°16E 183 E9
Cozumel Mexico 20°31N 86°55W 319 C7
Cozumel, Isla Mexico 20°30N 86°40W 319 C7
Crab Hill Antigua & B. 17°2N 61°53W 322 b
Crab Hill Barbados 13°19N 59°38W 323 r
Crabs Pen. Antigua & B. 17°7N 61°45W 322 b
Crac des Chevaliers Syria 34°47N 36°18E 250 D7
Cracow = Kraków Poland 50°4N 19°57E 185 H6
Cracow Australia 25°17S 150°17E 281 D5
Craddock Channel N.Z. 36°10S 175°13E 284 C4
Cradle Mt.-Lake St. Clair △
Australia 41°49S 147°56E 281 G4
Cradock S. Austral.,
Australia 32°6S 138°31E 281 E2
Cradock Eastern Cape,
S. Africa 32°8S 25°36E 270 D4
Crafers Australia 35°0S 138°42E 282 C3
Craig Alaska, U.S.A. 55°29N 133°9W 303 J14
Craig Colo., U.S.A. 40°31N 107°33W 304 F10
Craigavon U.K. 54°27N 6°23W 166 B5
Craighall Park S. Africa 26°7S 28°1E 123 A2
Craigieburn Australia 37°36S 144°56E 283 D6
Craiglockhart U.K. 55°55N 3°14W 121 B2
Craigmillar U.K. 55°56N 3°9W 121 B3
Craigmore Zimbabwe 20°28S 32°50E 269 G3
Craik Canada 51°3N 105°49W 297 C7
Crailsheim Germany 49°8N 10°5E 179 F6
Craiova Romania 44°21N 23°48E 183 F8
Cramond U.K. 55°58N 3°18W 121 B2
Cramond Bridge U.K. 55°57N 3°19W 121 B1
Cramond I. U.K. 55°59N 3°17W 121 B2
Cramsie Australia 23°20S 144°15E 280 C3
Cranberry L. U.S.A. 44°11N 74°50W 313 B10
Cranberry Portage
Canada 54°35N 101°23W 297 C8
Cranbrook W. Austral.,
Australia 34°18S 117°33E 279 F2
Cranbrook B.C., Canada 49°30N 115°46W 296 D5
Crandon U.S.A. 45°34N 88°54W 308 C9
Crandon Park U.S.A. 25°42N 80°9W 129 D3
Crane Oreg., U.S.A. 43°25N 118°35W 304 E4
Crane Tex., U.S.A. 31°24N 102°21W 314 F3
Crane, The Barbados 13°6N 59°27W 323 r
Cranford U.K. 51°29N 0°25W 125 B1
Cranganore India 10°13N 76°13E 245 J3
Cranston U.S.A. 41°47N 71°26W 313 E13
Craon France 47°50N 0°58W 172 E6
Craonne France 49°27N 3°46E 173 C10
Craponne-sur-Arzon
France 45°19N 3°51E 174 C7
Crasna Romania 46°32N 27°51E 183 D12
Crasna ➜ Romania 47°44N 22°35E 182 C7
Crasnei, Munții Romania 47°0N 23°20E 183 C8
Crater L. U.S.A. 42°56N 122°6W 304 E2
Crater Lake △ U.S.A. 42°55N 122°10W 304 E2
Crater Mt. Papua N. G. 6°37S 145°7E 286 D3
Crater Pt. Papua N. G. 5°25S 152°9E 286 C7
Craters of the Moon ⌓
U.S.A. 43°25N 113°30W 304 E7
Crateús Brazil 5°10S 40°39W 332 C3
Crati ➜ Italy 39°43N 16°31E 201 C9
Crato Brazil 7°10S 39°25W 332 C4
Crato Portugal 39°16N 7°39W 195 F3
Craven, L. Canada 54°20N 76°56W 298 B4
Cravo Norte Colombia 6°18N 70°12W 328 B3
Cravo Norte ➜ Colombia 6°18N 70°12W 328 B3
Crawford Western Cape,
S. Africa 33°59S 18°30E 118 A2
Crawford Ala., U.S.A. 32°27N 85°11W 316 C4
Crawford Nebr., U.S.A. 42°41N 103°25W 308 D2
Crawfordsville Ind.,
U.S.A. 40°2N 86°54W 311 D10
Crawfordsville Iowa,
U.S.A. 41°12N 91°32W 310 C5
Crawfordville Fla., U.S.A. 30°11N 84°23W 316 E5
Crawfordville Ga., U.S.A. 33°33N 82°54W 316 B7
Crawley U.K. 51°7N 0°11W 169 F7
Crayford U.K. 51°27N 0°11E 125 B5
Crazy Mts. U.S.A. 46°12N 110°20W 304 C8
Crean L. Canada 54°5N 106°9W 297 C7
Crécy-en-Ponthieu France 50°15N 1°53E 173 B8
Crediton Ont., Canada 43°17N 81°33W 312 C3
Crediton Devon, U.K. 50°47N 3°40W 169 G4
Cree ➜ Sask., Canada 58°57N 105°47W 297 B7
Cree ➜ Dumf. & Gall., U.K. 54°55N 4°25W 167 G4
Cree L. Canada 57°30N 106°30W 297 B7
Creede U.S.A. 37°51N 106°56W 305 H10
Creekmouth U.K. 51°30N 0°6E 125 A4
Creekside U.S.A. 40°40N 79°11W 312 F5
Creel Mexico 27°45N 107°38W 318 B3
Creemore Canada 44°19N 80°6W 312 B4
Creighton Sask., Canada 54°45N 101°54W 297 C8
Creighton Nebr., U.S.A. 42°28N 97°54W 308 D5
Creil France 49°15N 2°29E 173 C9
Crema Italy 45°22N 9°41E 198 C6
Cremona Italy 45°7N 10°2E 198 C7
Crepaja Serbia 45°1N 20°38E 182 E5
Crepori ➜ Brazil 5°42S 57°8W 331 B6
Crépy France 49°35N 3°32E 173 C10
Crépy-en-Valois France 49°14N 2°54E 173 C9
Cres Croatia 44°58N 14°25E 199 D11
Crescent, L. U.S.A. 28°30N 81°33W 133 A1
Crescent Beach U.S.A. 29°46N 81°15W 316 F8
Crescent City Calif.,
U.S.A. 41°45N 124°12W 304 F1
Crescent City Fla., U.S.A. 29°26N 81°31W 317 F8
Crescent Group
S. China Sea 16°30N 111°40E 230 A4
Crescent Hd. Australia 31°11S 152°59E 283 A10
Crescent L. U.S.A. 29°28N 81°30W 317 F8
Crescentino Italy 45°11N 8°6E 198 C5
Crescenzago Italy 45°30N 9°13E 128 A2
Crespi d'Adda Italy 45°35N 9°32E 198 C6
Crespo Argentina 32°2S 60°19W 334 C3
Cressely France 48°44N 2°6E 134 B1
Cresskill U.S.A. 40°56N 73°57W 132 A2
Cresson U.S.A. 40°28N 78°36W 312 F6
Cressy Australia 38°2S 143°40E 282 E5
Crest France 44°44N 5°2E 175 D9
Cresta, Mt. Phil. 17°17N 122°6E 232 C4
Crestline Calif., U.S.A. 34°14N 117°18W 307 L9
Crestline Ohio, U.S.A. 40°47N 82°44W 312 F2
Creston B.C., Canada 49°10N 116°31W 296 D5
Creston Calif., U.S.A. 35°32N 120°33W 306 K6
Creston Iowa, U.S.A. 41°4N 94°22W 310 C2
Crestview Calif., U.S.A. 37°46N 118°58W 306 H8
Crestview Fla., U.S.A. 30°46N 86°34W 317 E3
Crestwood U.S.A. 41°38N 87°46W 119 D2
Creswick Australia 37°25S 143°58E 282 D5
Crêt de la Neige France 46°16N 5°58E 173 F12
Crete = Kriti Greece 35°15N 25°0E 207 E6
Crete Ill., U.S.A. 41°27N 87°38W 311 C9
Crete Nebr., U.S.A. 40°38N 96°58W 308 E5
Crete, Sea of Greece 36°0N 25°0E 205 E7
Créteil France 48°47N 2°27E 134 B3
Cretin, C. Papua N. G. 6°40S 147°53E 286 D4
Creus, C. de Spain 42°20N 3°19E 196 C8
Creuse □ France 46°10N 2°0E 173 F9
Creuse ➜ France 47°0N 0°34E 174 B4
Creutzwald France 49°12N 6°42E 173 C13
Creuzburg Germany 51°3N 10°14E 178 D6
Crèvecœur-le-Grand France 49°37N 2°5E 173 C9
Crevillent Spain 38°12N 0°48W 197 G4
Crewe U.K. 53°6N 2°26W 168 D5
Crewkerne U.K. 50°53N 2°48W 169 G5
Crianlarich U.K. 56°24N 4°37W 167 E4
Criciúma Brazil 28°40S 49°23W 335 B6
Cricklewood U.K. 51°33N 0°13W 125 A2
Cricova Moldova 47°8N 28°52E 183 C13
Cridersville U.S.A. 40°39N 84°9W 311 D12
Crieff U.K. 56°22N 3°50W 167 E5
Crikvenica Croatia 45°11N 14°40E 199 C11
Crimea □ Ukraine 45°30N 33°10E 189 K8
Crimean Pen. = Krymskyy Pivostriv
Ukraine 45°0N 34°0E 189 K8
Crimmitschau Germany 50°48N 12°24E 178 E8
Cristal, Mts. de Gabon 0°30N 10°30E 264 B2
Cristalândia Brazil 10°36S 49°11W 332 D1
Cristino Castro Brazil 8°49S 44°13W 332 C3
Cristo Redentor, Corcovado
Brazil 22°56S 43°12W 135 B1
Cristobal Panama 9°19N 79°54W 320 c
Cristóbal, Pta. Ecuador 0°54S 91°31W 330 a
Cristuru Secuiesc
Romania 46°17N 25°2E 183 D10
Crișul Alb ➜ Romania 46°42N 21°17E 182 D6
Crișul Negru ➜ Romania 46°42N 21°16E 182 D6
Crișul Repede ➜ Romania 46°55N 20°59E 182 D5
Crittenden U.S.A. 38°47N 84°36W 311 F12
Criuleni Moldova 47°13N 29°10E 183 C14
Crivitz Germany 53°34N 11°39E 178 B7
Crixás Brazil 14°27S 49°58W 333 D2
Crkvice Montenegro 42°34N 18°38E 202 D2
Crna ➜ N. Macedonia 41°33N 21°59E 202 E5
Crna Gora = Montenegro ■
Europe 42°40N 19°20E 202 D3
Crna Gora N. Macedonia 42°10N 21°30E 202 D5
Crna Reka = Crna ➜
N. Macedonia 41°33N 21°59E 202 E5
Crna Trava Serbia 42°49N 22°19E 202 D6
Crni Drim ➜
N. Macedonia 41°17N 20°40E 202 E4
Crni Timok ➜ Serbia 43°53N 22°15E 202 C6
Crnoljeva Planina = Zhar, Mali
Kosovo 42°20N 21°0E 202 D5
Črnomelj Slovenia 45°33N 15°10E 199 C12
Croagh Patrick Ireland 53°46N 9°40W 166 C2
Croajingolong △
Australia 37°45S 149°26E 283 D8
Croatia ■ Europe 45°20N 16°0E 199 C13
Croce, Ex Chiesa della Venice, Italy 142 c3
Crockenhill U.K. 51°22N 0°9E 125 B4
Crocker U.S.A. 37°57N 92°16W 310 G4
Crocker, Banjaran
Malaysia 5°40N 116°30E 235 A5
Crocker, Cerro Ecuador 0°36S 90°21W 330 a
Crocker Range △ Malaysia 5°33N 116°8E 235 A5
Crockett U.S.A. 31°19N 95°27W 314 F7
Crocodile = Umgwenya ➜
Mozam. 25°14S 32°18E 271 C5
Crocodile ➜ S. Africa 24°12S 26°53E 270 B4
Crocodile Is. Australia 12°3S 134°58E 280 A1
Crocq France 45°52N 2°21E 174 C6
Crocus B. Anguilla 18°13N 63°5W 322 a
Crohy Hd. Ireland 54°55N 8°26W 166 B3
Croisette, C. France 43°14N 5°22E 175 E9
Croisic, Pte. du France 47°19N 2°31W 172 E4
Croissy-Beaubourg France 48°49N 2°39E 134 B4
Croissy-sur-Seine France 48°52N 2°8E 134 A1
Croix, L. la Canada 48°20N 92°15W 298 C1
Croker, C. N. Terr.,
Australia 10°58S 132°35E 278 B5
Croker, C. Ont., Canada 44°58N 80°59W 312 B4
Croker I. Australia 11°12S 132°32E 278 B5
Croker Islands Seas ◎
Australia 11°20S 132°30E 278 B5
Cromarty U.K. 57°40N 4°2W 167 D4
Cromer U.K. 52°56N 1°17E 168 E9
Crompton Pt. Dominica 15°35N 61°19W 323 k
Cromwell N.Z. 45°3S 169°14E 285 F4
Cromwell Conn., U.S.A. 41°36N 72°39W 313 E12
Cronat France 46°43N 3°40E 173 F10
Crook U.K. 54°43N 1°45W 168 C6
Crooked ➜ B.C., Canada 54°50N 122°54W 296 C4
Crooked ➜ Oreg.,
U.S.A. 44°32N 121°16W 304 D3
Crooked Creek U.S.A. 61°52N 158°7W 303 F8
Crooked I. The Bahamas 22°50N 74°10W 321 B5
Crooked Island Passage
The Bahamas 22°55N 74°35W 321 B5
Crookston Minn., U.S.A. 47°47N 96°37W 308 B5
Crookston Nebr., U.S.A. 42°56N 100°45W 308 D3
Crookwell Australia 34°28S 149°24E 283 C8
Crosby U.K. 53°30N 3°3W 168 D4
Crosby N. Dak., U.S.A. 48°55N 103°18W 308 A2
Crosby Pa., U.S.A. 41°45N 78°23W 312 E6
Crosbyton U.S.A. 33°40N 101°14W 314 E4
Crosia Italy 39°35N 16°45E 201 C9
Crosne France 48°43N 2°27E 134 B3
Cross ➜ Nigeria 4°42N 8°21E 263 E6
Cross City U.S.A. 29°38N 83°7W 317 F6
Cross Fell U.K. 54°43N 2°28W 168 C5
Cross I. India 18°56N 72°51E 130 B2
Cross L. Canada 54°45N 97°30W 297 C9
Cross Lake Canada 54°37N 97°47W 297 C9
Cross River □ Nigeria 6°0N 8°0E 263 D6
Cross River △ Nigeria 5°50N 9°55E 263 D6
Cross Sound U.S.A. 58°0N 135°0W 303 G14
Cross Timbers U.S.A. 38°1N 93°14W 310 F3
Crossen = Krosno Odrzańskie
Poland 52°3N 15°7E 185 F2
Crossett U.S.A. 33°8N 91°58W 314 E9
Crosshaven Ireland 51°47N 8°17W 166 E3
Crossley, Mt. N.Z. 42°50S 172°5E 285 C7
Crossmaglen U.K. 54°5N 6°36W 166 B5
Crossmolina Ireland 54°6N 9°20W 166 B2
Crossville Ill., U.S.A. 38°10N 88°4W 311 F8
Crossville Tenn., U.S.A. 35°57N 85°2W 315 D12
Croswell U.S.A. 43°16N 82°37W 312 C2
Croton-on-Hudson
U.S.A. 41°12N 73°55W 313 E11
Crotone Italy 39°5N 17°8E 201 C10
Crouch End U.K. 51°34N 0°7W 125 A3
Crow ➜ Canada 59°41N 124°20W 296 B4
Crow Agency U.S.A. 45°36N 107°28W 304 D10
Crow Hd. Ireland 51°35N 10°9W 166 E1
Crowdy Bay △ Australia 31°45S 152°45E 283 A10
Crowell U.S.A. 33°59N 99°43W 314 E5
Crowl Cr. ➜ Australia 32°0S 145°30E 283 B6
Crowley La., U.S.A. 30°13N 92°22W 314 F8
Crowley Tex., U.S.A. 32°34N 97°21W 120 C1
Crowley, L. U.S.A. 37°35N 118°42W 306 H8
Crown I. Papua N. G. 5°7S 146°58E 286 C4
Crown Mine S. Africa 26°12S 27°57E 123 B1
Crown Point Ind., U.S.A. 41°25N 87°22W 311 C9
Crown Point N.Y.,
U.S.A. 43°57N 73°26W 313 C11
Crown Pt. Trin. & Tob. 11°18N 60°51W 323 s
Crownpoint U.S.A. 35°41N 108°9W 305 J9
Crows Landing U.S.A. 37°23N 121°6W 306 H5
Crows Nest N.S.W.,
Australia 33°49S 151°12E 139 A2
Crows Nest Queens.,
Australia 27°16S 152°4E 281 D5
Crowsnest Pass Canada 49°40N 114°40W 296 D6
Croydon Queens.,
Australia 18°13S 142°14E 280 B3
Croydon London, U.K. 51°22N 0°5W 125 B3
Croydon □ U.K. 51°22N 0°5W 169 F7
Croydon Park Australia 33°55S 151°7E 139 B1
Crozet, Îs. Ind. Oc. 46°27S 52°0E 273 J4
Crozet Basin Ind. Oc. 39°0S 60°0E 273 H5
Crozon France 48°15N 4°30W 172 D2
Cruce de Sardina
Canary Is. 27°52N 15°22W 153 e1
Cruces, Punta Colombia 6°39N 77°32W 328 B2
Crusheen Ireland 52°57N 8°53W 166 D3
Cruz, C. Cuba 19°50N 77°50W 320 C4
Cruz Alta Brazil 28°45S 53°40W 335 B5
Cruz Bay U.S. Virgin Is. 18°20N 64°48W 321 b
Cruz das Almas Brazil 12°0S 39°6W 333 D4
Cruz de Pau Portugal 38°37N 9°7W 126 B2
Cruz del Eje Argentina 30°45S 64°50W 334 C3
Cruzeiro Brazil 22°33S 45°0W 333 F3
Cruzeiro do Oeste Brazil 23°46S 53°4W 335 A5
Cruzeiro do Sul = Joaçaba
Brazil 27°5S 51°31W 335 B5
Cruzeiro do Sul Brazil 7°35S 72°35W 330 B3
Cry L. Canada 58°45N 129°0W 296 B3
Crystal B. U.S.A. 28°50N 82°45W 317 G7
Crystal Bay U.S.A. 39°15N 120°0W 306 F7
Crystal Brook Australia 33°21S 138°12E 282 B3
Crystal City Mo., U.S.A. 38°13N 90°23W 310 F6
Crystal City Tex., U.S.A. 28°41N 99°50W 314 G5
Crystal Falls U.S.A. 46°5N 88°20W 308 B9
Crystal Lake Fla., U.S.A. 30°26N 85°42W 316 E4
Crystal Lake Ill., U.S.A. 42°14N 88°19W 311 B8
Crystal Palace U.K. 51°25N 0°4W 125 B3
Crystal River U.S.A. 28°54N 82°35W 317 G7
Crystal Springs U.S.A. 31°59N 90°21W 315 F9
Csenger Hungary 47°50N 22°41E 182 C7
Csepel Hungary 47°25N 19°4E 117 B2
Csepelsziget Hungary 47°25N 19°4E 117 B2
Csillaghegy Hungary 47°35N 19°2E 117 A2
Csillagtelep Hungary 47°24N 19°5E 117 B2
Csömör Hungary 47°33N 19°14E 117 A3
Csömöri-patak ➜ Hungary 47°35N 19°5E 117 A3
Csongrád Hungary 46°43N 20°12E 182 D5
Csongrád □ Hungary 46°32N 20°15E 182 D5
Csorna Hungary 47°38N 17°18E 182 C2
Csurgo Hungary 46°16N 17°9E 182 D2
Cu Lao Hon Vietnam 10°54N 108°18E 237 G7
Cua Rao Vietnam 19°16N 104°27E 236 C5
Cuácua ➜ Mozam. 17°54S 37°0E 269 F4
Cuále Angola 8°22S 16°10E 265 D3
Cuále ➜ Angola 8°29S 15°1E 265 D3
Cuamato Angola 17°2S 15°7E 265 F3
Cuamba Mozam. 14°45S 36°22E 269 E4
Cuando Angola 14°34S 19°1E 265 E3
Cuando ➜ Angola 17°30S 23°15E 265 F4
Cuangar Angola 17°36S 18°39E 265 F3
Cuango = Kwango ➜
Dem. Rep. of the Congo 3°14S 17°22E 264 C3
Cuango Lunda Norte, Angola 9°8S 18°3E 265 D3
Cuango Moxico, Angola 14°30S 19°0E 265 E3
Cuango Uíge, Angola 6°15S 16°42E 265 D3
Cuanza ➜ Angola 9°21S 13°9E 265 D2
Cuao ➜ Venezuela 4°55N 67°40W 328 C4
Cuare ➜ Trin. & Tob. 10°36N 61°6W 323 t
Cuarto ➜ Argentina 33°25S 63°2W 334 C3
Cuatir ➜ Angola 17°1S 18°9E 265 F3
Cuatro Vientos Spain 40°22N 3°47W 127 B1
Cuatrociénegas Mexico 26°59N 102°5W 318 B4
Cuauhtémoc Chihuahua,
Mexico 28°25N 106°52W 318 B3
Cuauhtémoc México,
Mexico 19°25N 99°9W 128 B2
Cuba Portugal 38°10N 7°54W 195 G3
Cuba Mo., U.S.A. 38°4N 91°24W 310 F5
Cuba N. Mex., U.S.A. 36°1N 107°4W 305 H10
Cuba N.Y., U.S.A. 42°13N 78°17W 312 D6
Cuba ■ W. Indies 22°0N 79°0W 320 B4
Cuba City U.S.A. 42°36N 90°26W 310 B6
Cubagua, I. Venezuela 10°49N 64°11W 329 a
Cubal Angola 12°26S 14°3E 265 E2
Cubal ➜ Angola 15°9S 12°9E 265 F2
Cuban Museum U.S.A. 25°45N 80°13W 129 D1
Cubango ➜ Africa 18°50S 22°25E 265 F4
Cubanja Angola 14°49S 21°20E 265 E4
Cubao Phil. 14°37N 121°3E 127 B2
Cubia Angola 15°58S 21°42E 265 F4
Çubuk Turkey 40°14N 33°3E 212 B5
Çubuklu Turkey 41°5N 29°4E 122 B2
Cuc Phuong △ Vietnam 20°17N 105°38E 236 B5
Cuche Trin. & Tob. 10°22N 61°10W 323 t
Cuchi Angola 14°37S 16°58E 265 E3
Cuchi ➜ Angola 15°13S 17°20E 265 F3
Cuchillo-Co Argentina 38°20S 64°37W 336 A4
Cuchivero ➜ Venezuela 7°40N 65°57W 328 B4
Cuchumatanes, Sierra de los
Guatemala 15°35N 91°25W 320 C1
Cuckfield U.K. 51°1N 0°8W 169 F7
Cucuí Brazil 1°12N 66°50W 328 C4
Cucumbi Angola 10°17S 19°5E 265 E3
Cucurpé Mexico 30°20N 110°43W 318 A2
Cucurrupí Colombia 4°23N 76°56W 328 C2
Cúcuta Colombia 7°54N 72°31W 328 B3
Cudahy Calif., U.S.A. 33°57N 118°11W 126 C3
Cudahy Wis., U.S.A. 42°57N 87°51W 311 B9
Cudalbi Romania 45°46N 27°41E 183 E12
Cudarebe = Kudarebe
Aruba 12°37N 70°4W 322 f
Cuddalore India 11°46N 79°45E 245 J4
Cuddapah = Kadapa
India 14°30N 78°47E 245 G4
Cuddapan, L. Australia 25°45S 141°26E 280 D3
Cudgewa Australia 36°10S 147°42E 283 D7
Cudillero Spain 43°33N 6°9W 194 B4
Cudjoehead Montserrat 16°47N 62°12W 323 p
Cue Australia 27°25S 117°54E 279 E2
Cuebe ➜ Angola 15°46S 17°32E 265 F3
Cuéllar Spain 41°23N 4°21W 194 D6
Cuemba Angola 11°50S 17°42E 265 E3
Cuenca Ecuador 2°50S 79°9W 328 D2
Cuenca Spain 40°5N 2°10W 196 E2
Cuenca □ Spain 40°0N 2°0W 196 F3
Cuenca, Serranía de Spain 39°55N 1°50W 196 F3
Cuenca Alta del Manzanares △
Spain 40°40N 3°55W 194 E7
Cuerda del Pozo, Embalse de la
Spain 41°51N 2°44W 196 D2
Cuernavaca Mexico 18°55N 99°15W 319 D5
Cuero U.S.A. 29°6N 97°17W 314 G6
Cuers France 43°14N 6°5E 175 E10
Cueva de la Quebrada del Toro △
Venezuela 10°46N 69°3W 328 A4
Cueva de los Guácharos △
Colombia 1°35N 76°1W 328 C2
Cuevas, Cerro Bolivia 22°0S 65°12W 331 E4
Cuevas de Vera = Cuevas del
Almanzora Spain 37°18N 1°58W 197 H3
Cuevas del Almanzora
Spain 37°18N 1°58W 197 H3
Cuevo Bolivia 20°15S 63°30W 331 E5
Cugir Romania 45°48N 23°25E 183 E8
Cuglieri Italy 40°11N 8°34E 200 B1
Cugnaux France 43°32N 1°20E 174 E5
Cuhai-Bakony ➜
Hungary 47°35N 17°54E 182 C2
Cuiabá Brazil 15°30S 56°0W 333 D6
Cuiabá ➜ Brazil 17°5S 56°36W 331 D6
Cuicuilco, Pirámide de
Mexico 19°18N 99°11W 128 C1
Cuihangcun China 22°27N 113°32E 219 a
Cuijk Neths. 51°44N 5°50E 170 C5
Cuilco Guatemala 15°24N 91°58W 320 C1
Cuillin Hills U.K. 57°13N 6°15W 167 D2
Cuillin Sd. U.K. 57°4N 6°20W 167 D2
Cuilo = Kwilu ➜
Dem. Rep. of the Congo 3°22S 17°22E 265 C3
Cuilo Angola 8°12S 19°28E 265 D3
Cuilo-Futa Angola 6°28S 15°51E 265 D3
Cuima Angola 13°25S 15°45E 265 E3
Cuimba Angola 6°10S 14°41E 265 D2
Cuiseaux France 46°30N 5°22E 173 F12
Cuité Brazil 6°29S 36°9W 332 C4
Cuito ➜ Angola 18°1S 20°48E 265 F4
Cuito Cuanavale Angola 15°10S 19°10E 265 F3
Cuitzeo, L. de Mexico 19°55N 101°5W 318 D4
Cuiuni ➜ Brazil 0°45S 63°7W 329 D5
Cuivre ➜ U.S.A. 38°56N 90°41W 310 F6
Cujmir Romania 44°13N 22°57E 182 F7
Cukai Malaysia 4°13N 103°25E 237 K4
Çukurca Turkey 37°14N 43°37E 213 D10
Çukurova = Cicilia Turkey 36°30N 34°0E 212 D5
Cul-de-Sac St.-Maarten 18°2N 63°5W 322 a
Cul de Sac St.-Martin 18°6N 63°2W 322 a
Culasi Phil. 11°26N 122°3E 233 F4
Culbertson U.S.A. 48°9N 104°31W 304 B11
Culburra N.S.W.,
Australia 34°56S 150°46E 283 C9
Culburra S. Austral.,
Australia 35°50S 139°58E 282 C3
Culcairn Australia 35°41S 147°3E 283 C7
Culebra Puerto Rico 18°19N 65°18W 321 b
Culebra, Sierra de la Spain 41°55N 6°20W 194 D4
Culfa Azerbaijan 38°57N 45°38E 213 C11
Culgoa Australia 35°44S 143°6E 282 C5
Culgoa ➜ Australia 29°56S 146°20E 281 D4
Culgoa Flood Plain △
Australia 28°58S 147°5E 281 D4
Culiacán Mexico 24°50N 107°23W 318 C3
Culiacán ➜ Mexico 24°30N 107°42W 318 C3
Culik Indonesia 8°21S 115°37E 231 J18
Culion Phil. 11°54N 119°58E 233 F3
Culion I. Phil. 11°50N 120°0E 233 F2
Culiseu ➜ Brazil 12°14S 53°17W 331 C7
Cúllar Spain 37°35N 2°34W 195 H8
Cullarin Ra. Australia 34°30S 149°30E 283 C8
Cullen U.K. 57°42N 2°49W 167 D6
Cullen Bullen Australia 33°18S 150°2E 283 B9
Cullen Pt. Australia 11°57S 141°54E 286 F1
Cullera Spain 39°9N 0°17W 197 F4
Cullman U.S.A. 34°11N 86°51W 315 D11
Culloden U.S.A. 32°52N 84°6W 316 C5
Cullom U.S.A. 40°53N 88°16W 311 D8
Cullompton U.K. 50°51N 3°24W 169 G4
Culmore U.S.A. 38°51N 77°8W 143 B2
Culo ➜ Angola 6°13S 15°34E 265 D3
Culoz France 45°47N 5°46E 175 C9
Culpeper U.S.A. 38°30N 78°0W 309 F14
Culuene ➜ Brazil 12°56S 52°51W 331 C7
Culver U.S.A. 41°13N 86°25W 311 C10
Culver, Pt. Australia 32°54S 124°43E 279 F3
Culver City U.S.A. 34°1N 118°24W 126 B2
Culverden N.Z. 42°47S 172°49E 285 C7
Culverton U.S.A. 33°19N 82°54W 316 B7
Cuma Angola 12°52S 15°5E 265 E3
Cumanà Venezuela 10°30N 64°5W 329 A5
Cumana B. Trin. & Tob. 10°48N 60°56W 323 t
Cumaovası Turkey 38°15N 27°9E 205 C9
Cumari Brazil 18°16S 48°11W 333 E2
Cumballa Hill Mumbai, India 130 a1
Cumbe = Euclides da Cunha
Brazil 10°31S 39°1W 332 D4
Cumberland B.C., Canada 49°40N 125°0W 296 D4
Cumberland Ont., Canada 45°29N 75°24W 313 A9
Cumberland St. Vincent 13°16N 61°16W 323 n
Cumberland Iowa, U.S.A. 41°16N 94°52W 310 C2
Cumberland Md., U.S.A. 39°39N 78°46W 309 F14
Cumberland ➜ U.S.A. 37°9N 88°25W 308 G9
Cumberland, B. Chile 33°37S 78°49W 330 c
Cumberland, C. Vanuatu 14°39S 166°37E 287 D4
Cumberland, L. U.S.A. 36°52N 85°9W 309 G11
Cumberland Gap ⌓
U.S.A. 36°36N 83°40W 309 G12
Cumberland I. U.S.A. 30°50N 81°25W 316 E8
Cumberland Is. Australia 20°35S 149°10E 280 b
Cumberland Island ⌓
U.S.A. 30°12N 81°24W 316 E8
Cumberland L. Canada 54°3N 102°18W 297 C8
Cumberland Pen. Canada 67°0N 64°0W 295 D19
Cumberland Plateau
U.S.A. 36°0N 85°0W 315 D12
Cumberland Sd. Canada 65°30N 66°0W 295 D18
Cumbernauld U.K. 55°57N 3°58W 167 F5
Cumbira Angola 12°11S 15°8E 265 E3
Cumborah Australia 29°40S 147°45E 281 D4
Cumbres de Majalca △
Mexico 28°48N 106°30W 318 B3
Cumbres de Monterrey △
Mexico 25°26N 100°25W 318 B4
Cumbres Mayores Spain 38°4N 6°39W 195 G4
Cumbria □ U.K. 54°42N 2°52W 168 C5
Cumbrian Mts. U.K. 54°30N 3°0W 168 C5
Cumbum India 15°40N 79°10E 245 G4
Cumilla Bangla. 23°28N 91°10E 241 D3
Cuminá Brazil 1°57S 56°2W 329 D6
Cuminá ➜ Brazil 1°30S 56°0W 329 D6
Cuminapanema ➜ Brazil 1°9S 54°54W 329 D7
Cumming, C. Chile 27°6S 109°14W 330 b
Cummings Mt. U.S.A. 35°2N 118°34W 307 K8
Cummins Australia 34°16S 135°43E 281 E2
Cumnock N.S.W.,
Australia 32°59S 148°46E 283 B8
Cumnock E. Ayrs., U.K. 55°28N 4°17W 167 F4
Cumpas Mexico 30°2N 109°48W 318 B3
Cumplida, Pta. Canary Is. 28°50N 17°48W 153 e1
Çumra Turkey 37°34N 32°45E 212 D5
Cumuto Trin. & Tob. 10°35N 61°12W 323 t
Cunapo ➜ Trin. & Tob. 10°35N 61°8W 323 t
Cuñare Colombia 0°49N 72°32W 328 C3
Cunaripa Trin. & Tob. 10°33N 61°10W 323 t
Cuncumén Chile 31°53S 70°38W 334 C1
Cundeelee ◎ Australia 30°43S 123°25E 279 F3
Cunderdin Australia 31°37S 117°12E 279 F2
Cundinamarca □ Colombia 5°0N 74°0W 328 C3
Cunene □ Angola 16°30S 15°0E 265 F3
Cunene ➜ Angola 17°20S 11°50E 265 F2
Cúneo Italy 44°23N 7°32E 198 D4
Cung Son Vietnam 13°2N 108°58E 236 F7
Çüngüş Turkey 38°13N 39°17E 246 B3
Cunhinga Angola 12°11S 16°47E 265 E3
Cunhinga ➜ Angola 10°42S 16°41E 265 E3
Cunillera, I. = Sa Conillera
Spain 38°59N 1°13E 206 D1
Cunjamba Angola 15°27S 20°10E 265 F4
Cunlhat France 45°38N 3°32E 174 C7
Cunnamulla Australia 28°2S 145°38E 281 D4
Cunningham The Bahamas 25°5N 77°26W 153 b
Cunupia Trin. & Tob. 10°32N 61°22W 323 t
Cuorgnè Italy 45°23N 7°39E 198 C4
Cupar Sask., Canada 50°57N 104°10W 297 C8
Cupar Fife, U.K. 56°19N 3°1W 167 E5
Cupcini Moldova 48°6N 27°23E 183 B12
Cupecé ➜ Brazil 23°39S 46°40W 137 B1
Cupertino U.S.A. 37°19N 122°2W 306 H4
Cupica, G. de Colombia 6°25N 77°30W 328 B2
Ćuprija Serbia 43°57N 21°26E 202 C5
Curaçá Brazil 8°59S 39°54W 332 C4
Curaçao W. Indies 12°10N 69°0W 322 g
Curaçao Int. ✕ (CUR)
Curaçao 12°11N 68°57W 322 g
Curacautín Chile 38°26S 71°53W 336 A2
Curador = Presidente Dutra
Brazil 5°15S 44°30W 332 C3
Curahuara de Carangas
Bolivia 17°52S 68°26W 330 D4
Curalhinho = Coelho Neto
Brazil 4°15S 43°0W 332 B3
Curamata ➜ Trin. & Tob. 10°11N 61°28W 323 t
Curanilahue Chile 37°29S 73°28W 334 D1
Curaray ➜ Peru 2°20S 74°5W 328 D3
Curatabaca Venezuela 6°19N 62°51W 329 B5
Cure ➜ France 47°40N 3°41E 173 E10
Curepipe Mauritius 20°19S 57°31E 272 e
Curepipe Point Mauritius 20°21S 57°31E 272 e
Curepto Chile 35°8S 72°1W 334 D1
Curia Portugal 40°22N 8°22W 194 E2
Curiapo Venezuela 8°33N 61°5W 329 B5
Curicó Chile 34°55S 71°20W 334 C1
Curicuriari ➜ Brazil 0°14S 66°48W 328 D4
Curieuse Seychelles 4°15S 55°44E 272 c
Curimatá Brazil 10°2S 44°17W 332 D3
Curinga Italy 38°49N 16°19E 201 D9
Curiplaya Colombia 0°16N 74°52W 328 C3
Curitiba Brazil 25°20S 49°10W 335 B6
Curitibanos Brazil 27°18S 50°36W 335 B5
Curlewis Australia 31°7S 150°16E 283 A9
Curoca ➜ Angola 15°43S 11°55E 265 F2
Curonian Lagoon = Kurshskiy Zaliv
Russia 55°9N 21°6E 184 C8
Curonian Spit Europe 55°20N 20°55E 184 C7
Currabubula Australia 31°16S 150°44E 283 A9
Currais Novos Brazil 6°13S 36°30W 332 C4
Curral Velho Cabo Verde 16°8N 22°48W 153 j
Curralinho Brazil 1°45S 49°46W 332 B2
Currane, L. Ireland 51°49N 10°4W 166 E1
Currant U.S.A. 38°44N 115°28W 304 G6
Curraweena Australia 30°47S 145°54E 283 A6
Currawinya △ Australia 28°55S 144°27E 281 D3
Current ➜ U.S.A. 36°15N 90°55W 314 C9
Currie Tas., Australia 39°56S 143°53E 281 F3
Currie Edinburgh, U.K. 55°54N 3°17W 121 B2
Currie Nev., U.S.A. 40°16N 114°45W 304 F6
Curt-Bunar = Tervel
Bulgaria 43°45N 27°28E 203 C11
Curtea de Argeș Romania 45°12N 24°42E 183 E9
Curtici Romania 46°21N 21°18E 182 D6
Curtin Springs Australia 25°20S 131°45E 279 E5
Curtis U.S.A. 40°38N 100°31W 308 E3
Curtis Group Australia 39°30S 146°37E 281 F4
Curtis I. Queens., Australia 23°35S 151°10E 280 C5
Curtis I. N.Z. Pac. Oc. 30°30S 178°34W 277 G15
Curuá ➜ Pará, Brazil 2°24S 54°5W 329 D7
Curuá ➜ Pará, Brazil 5°23S 54°22W 331 B7
Curuá, I. Brazil 0°48N 50°10W 332 A1
Curuaés ➜ Brazil 7°30S 54°45W 331 B7
Curuaí Brazil 2°17S 55°29W 329 D6
Curuápanema ➜ Brazil 2°25S 55°2W 329 D6
Curuçá Brazil 0°43S 47°50W 332 B2
Curuçá ➜ Brazil 4°27S 71°23W 330 A3
Curuguaty Paraguay 24°31S 55°42W 335 A4
Çürüksu Çayi = Büyük
Menderes ➜ Turkey 37°28N 27°11E 205 D9
Curup Indonesia 3°26S 102°13E 234 C2
Curupira, Serra S. Amer. 1°25N 64°30W 329 C5
Cururu ➜ Brazil 7°12S 58°3W 331 B6
Cururupu Brazil 1°50S 44°50W 332 B3
Curuzú Cuatiá Argentina 29°50S 58°5W 334 B4
Curvelo Brazil 18°45S 44°27W 333 E3
Cusago Italy 45°26N 9°1E 128 B1
Cusano Milanino Italy 45°33N 9°11E 128 A2
Cusco Peru 13°32S 72°0W 330 C3
Cusco □ Peru 13°31S 71°59W 330 C3
Cushendall U.K. 55°5N 6°4W 166 A5
Cushing U.S.A. 35°59N 96°46W 314 D6
Cushing, Mt. Canada 57°35N 126°57W 296 B3
Cusihuiriáchic Mexico 28°14N 106°50W 318 B3
Cusna, Mte. Italy 44°17N 10°23E 198 D7
Cussabat = Al Qaşabāt
Libya 32°39N 14°1E 258 B2
Cusset France 46°8N 3°28E 173 F10
Cusseta U.S.A. 32°18N 84°47W 316 C5
Cusso, Sa. do Angola 6°30S 14°58E 265 D2
Custer U.S.A. 43°46N 103°36W 308 D2
Cut Bank U.S.A. 48°38N 112°20W 304 B7
Cutchogue U.S.A. 41°1N 72°30W 313 E12
Cutervo Peru 6°25S 78°55W 330 B2
Cuthbert U.S.A. 31°46N 84°48W 316 D5
Cutler U.S.A. 36°31N 119°17W 306 J7
Cutler Park U.S.A. 42°17N 71°12W 116 B1
Cutler Ridge U.S.A. 25°35N 80°20W 317 K9
Cutlerville U.S.A. 42°50N 85°40W 311 B11
Cutral-Có Argentina 38°58S 69°15W 336 A3
Cutro Italy 39°2N 16°59E 201 C9
Cuttaburra ➜ Australia 29°43S 144°22E 281 D3
Cuttack India 20°25N 85°57E 244 D7
Cuva ➜ Angola 11°42S 14°52E 265 E2
Cuvelai Angola 15°44S 15°50E 265 F3
Cuvette □ Congo 0°30S 16°0E 264 C3
Cuvette-Ouest □ Congo 0°10N 14°30E 264 B2
Cuvier, C. Australia 23°14S 113°22E 279 D1
Cuvier I. N.Z. 36°27S 175°50E 284 C4
Çuvuşabaşi ➜ Turkey 40°58N 28°51E 122 B1
Cuwei China 39°54N 116°15E 114 B1
Cuxhaven Germany 53°51N 8°41E 178 B4
Cuyabeno Ecuador 0°16S 75°53W 328 D2
Cuyahoga Falls U.S.A. 41°8N 81°29W 312 E3
Cuyahoga Valley △
U.S.A. 41°24N 81°33W 312 E3
Cuyapo Phil. 15°46N 120°40E 232 D3
Cuyo Phil. 10°51N 121°2E 233 F3
Cuyo East Pass. Phil. 11°0N 121°28E 233 F3
Cuyo Islands Phil. 11°4N 120°57E 233 F3
Cuyo West Pass. Phil. 11°0N 120°30E 233 F3
Cuyuni ➜ Guyana 6°23N 58°41W 329 B6
Cuyuni-Mazaruni □
Guyana 6°5N 59°46W 329 B5
Cuzco = Cusco Peru 13°32S 72°0W 330 C3
Cuzco Bolivia 20°0S 66°50W 330 E4
Črvsnica Bos.-H. 43°36N 17°35E 182 G2
Cwmbran U.K. 51°39N 3°2W 169 F4
Cyangugu Rwanda 2°29S 28°54E 268 C2
Cybinka Poland 52°12N 14°46E 185 F1
Cyclades = Kyklades
Greece 37°0N 24°30E 204 E6
Cygnet Australia 43°8S 147°1E 281 G4
Cynthiana U.S.A. 38°23N 84°18W 311 F12
Cypress Hills Sask.,
Canada 49°40N 109°30W 297 D7
Cypress Hills N.Y., U.S.A. 40°41N 73°53W 132 B2
Cypress Hills ⌓ Canada 49°40N 109°30W 297 D7
Cypress Park U.S.A. 34°6N 118°13W 126 B3
Cyprus ■ Asia 35°0N 33°0E 207 F9
Cyrenaica = Barqa Libya 27°0N 23°0E 258 B4
Cyrene Libya 32°53N 21°52E 258 B4
Czaplinek Poland 53°34N 16°14E 184 E3
Czar Canada 52°27N 110°50W 297 C6
Czarna ➜ Łódzkie, Poland 51°18N 19°55E 185 G6
Czarna ➜ Świętokrzyskie,
Poland 50°28N 21°21E 185 H8
Czarna Białostocka
Poland 53°18N 23°17E 185 E10
Czarna Woda Poland 53°51N 18°6E 184 E5
Czarne Poland 53°42N 16°58E 184 E3
Czarnków Poland 52°55N 16°38E 185 F3
Czaslau = Čáslav Czechia 49°54N 15°22E 180 B8
Czech Rep. = Czechia ■
Europe 50°0N 15°0E 180 B8
Czechia ■ Europe 50°0N 15°0E 180 B8
Czechowice-Dziedzice
Poland 49°54N 18°59E 185 J5
Czempiń Poland 52°9N 16°43E 185 F3
Czeremcha Poland 52°31N 23°21E 185 F10
Czerniejewo Poland 52°26N 17°30E 185 F4
Czernowitz = Chernivtsi
Ukraine 48°15N 25°52E 183 B10
Czerniaków Poland 52°11N 21°3E 143 B2
Czersk Poland 53°46N 17°58E 184 E4
Czerwieńsk Poland 52°1N 15°23E 185 F2
Czerwionka-Leszczyny
Poland 50°7N 18°37E 185 H5
Częstochowa Poland 50°49N 19°7E 185 H6
Człopa Poland 53°6N 16°6E 185 E3
Człuchów Poland 53°41N 17°22E 184 E4
Czortów = Chortkiv
Ukraine 49°2N 25°46E 177 D13
Czyste Poland 52°13N 20°57E 143 B1
Czyżew-Osada Poland 52°48N 22°19E 185 F9

D

D.C. War Memorial
Washington, D.C., U.S.A. 143 b1
D.H.A. Phase VIII Pakistan 24°47N 67°2E 123 B2
Da ➜ Vietnam 21°15N 105°20E 228 G5
Da Hinggan Ling China 48°0N 121°0E 219 B13
Da Lat Vietnam 11°56N 108°25E 237 G7
Da Moóca ➜ Brazil 23°35S 46°35W 137 B2
Da Nang Vietnam 16°4N 108°13E 236 D7
Da Qaidam China 37°50N 95°15E 218 D8
Da Yunhe ➜ Hopei,
China 39°10N 117°10E 227 E9
Da Yunhe ➜ Jiangsu,
China 34°25N 120°5E 227 H10
Da'an China 45°30N 124°7E 227 B13
Daan Viljoen ⌓ Namibia 22°2S 16°45E 270 B2
Daanbantayan Phil. 11°17N 124°2E 233 F5
Dab'a, Ras el Egypt 31°3N 28°31E 256 H6

Daba Shan China 32°0N 109°0E 228 B7
Dabai Nigeria 11°25N 5°15E 263 C6
Dabajuro Venezuela 11°2N 70°40W 328 A3
Dabakala Côte d'Ivoire 8°15N 4°20W 262 D4
Dabaka India 26°7N 92°52E 241 B4
Dabaro Somalia 6°21N 48°43E 267 C6
Dabas Hungary 47°11N 19°19E 182 C4
Dabat Ethiopia 12°58N 37°41E 257 E4
Dabbagh, Jabal Si. Arabia 27°52N 35°45E 246 E2
Dabeiba Colombia 7°1N 76°16W 328 B2
Daber = Dobra Poland 53°34N 15°20E 184 E2
Dabhoi India 22°10N 73°20E 242 H5
Dąbie Poland 52°5N 18°50E 185 F5
Dabie Shan China 31°20N 115°20E 229 B10
Dabilda Cameroon 12°45N 14°35E 259 F2
Dabl, W. ➜ Si. Arabia 29°5N 36°16E 251 J7
Ďáblice Czechia 50°8N 14°29E 135 B2
Dabnou Niger 14°10N 5°22E 263 C6
Dabo Indonesia 0°30S 104°33E 234 C2
Dabola Guinea 10°50N 11°5W 262 C2
Dabou Côte d'Ivoire 5°20N 4°23W 262 D4
Daboya Ghana 9°30N 1°20W 263 D4
Dabravolya Belarus 52°55N 23°59E 185 F10
Dąbrowa Poland 52°19N 20°52E 143 B1
Dąbrowa Białostocka Poland 53°40N 23°21E 184 E10
Dąbrowa Górnicza Poland 50°15N 19°10E 185 H6
Dąbrowa Tarnowska Poland 50°10N 20°59E 185 H7
Dabu China 24°22N 116°41E 229 E11
Dabugam India 19°27N 82°26E 244 E6
Dabung Malaysia 5°23N 102°1E 237 K4
Dabus ➜ Ethiopia 10°48N 35°10E 257 E4
Dacato ➜ Ethiopia 7°25N 42°40E 257 F5
Dacca = Dhaka Bangla. 23°43N 90°26E 241 D3
Dachang Jiangsu, China 32°13N 118°45E 229 A12
Dachang Shanghai, China 31°17N 121°24E 138 B1
Dachang ➜ China 31°18N 121°25E 138 B1
Dachaoshan Dam China 24°1N 100°22E 228 E3
Dachau Germany 48°15N 11°26E 131 A1
Dachau-Ost Germany 48°15N 11°27E 131 A1
Dachauer Moos Germany 48°13N 11°27E 131 A1
Dacheng = Tacheng Taiwan 23°51N 120°19E 225 C2
Dachigam △ India 34°10N 75°0E 242 B6
Dachstein, Hoher Austria 47°28N 13°35E 180 D6
Dačice Czechia 49°5N 15°26E 180 B8
Dacre Canada 45°22N 76°57W 312 A8
Dacula U.S.A. 33°59N 83°54W 316 B6
Dadanawa Guyana 2°50N 59°30W 329 C6
Dadar India 19°0N 72°49E 130 A1
Daday Turkey 41°28N 33°27E 212 B5
Dade City U.S.A. 28°22N 82°11W 317 G7
Dadès, Oued ➜ Morocco 30°58N 6°44W 260 B3
Dadeville U.S.A. 32°50N 85°46W 316 C4
Dadhar Pakistan 29°28N 67°39E 242 E2
Dadiya Nigeria 9°35N 11°24E 263 D7
Ḑadnah U.A.E. 25°32N 56°22E 247 E8
Dadohae △ S. Korea 34°0N 126°0E 224 E3
Dadra = Achalpur India 21°22N 77°32E 244 D3
Dadra & Nagar Haveli □ India 20°5N 73°0E 244 D1
Dadri = Charkhi Dadri India 28°37N 76°17E 242 E7
Dadu Pakistan 26°45N 67°45E 242 F2
Dadu He ➜ China 29°31N 103°46E 228 C4
Daebang S. Korea 37°30N 126°55E 137 B1
Daebudo S. Korea 37°14N 126°35E 224 D3
Daecheongdo S. Korea 37°49N 124°42E 224 D2
Daechi S. Korea 37°30N 127°2E 137 B2
Daegu S. Korea 35°50N 128°37E 224 E4
Daejeon S. Korea 36°20N 127°28E 224 D3
Daejeon □ S. Korea 36°20N 127°25E 224 D3
Daejeong S. Korea 33°8N 126°17E 224 a
Daemodo S. Korea 34°11N 126°45E 224 E3
Daet Phil. 14°2N 122°55E 232 D4
Daeyeonpyeong = Yeonpyeongdo S. Korea 37°40N 125°45E 224 D2
Dafang China 27°9N 105°39E 228 D5
Dafdaf, J. Si. Arabia 28°16N 35°35E 251 K6
Dafeng China 33°3N 120°45E 227 H11
Dafnes Greece 35°13N 25°3E 207 E6
Dafni Athina, Greece 37°55N 23°44E 112 B2
Dafni Peloponnese, Greece 37°48N 22°1E 204 D4
Dafnoudi, Akra Greece 38°28N 20°32E 207 C2
Dağ Turkey 37°12N 30°31E 205 D12
Daga Post South Sudan 9°13N 33°58E 266 C3
Dagali Norway 60°25N 8°28E 164 F5
Dagana Senegal 16°30N 15°35W 262 B1
Dagash Sudan 19°19N 33°25E 256 D3
Dagenham U.K. 51°32N 0°8E 125 A4
Dagestan □ Russia 42°30N 47°0E 191 J8
Dagestanskiye Ogni Russia 42°6N 48°12E 191 J9
Dagg Sd. N.Z. 45°23S 166°45E 285 F1
Daggett U.S.A. 34°52N 116°52W 307 L10
Daghestan Republic = Dagestan □ Russia 42°30N 47°0E 191 J8
Daghfeli Sudan 19°18N 32°40E 256 D3
Daglfing Germany 48°8N 11°39E 131 B2
Dağlıq Qarabağ = Nagorno-Karabakh □ Azerbaijan 39°55N 46°45E 213 C12
Dagö = Hiiumaa Estonia 58°50N 22°45E 188 C2
Dagu China 38°59N 117°40E 227 E9
Dagua Papua N. G. 3°27S 143°20E 286 B2
Daguan China 27°43N 103°56E 228 D4
D'Aguilar Pen. Hong Kong, China 22°13N 114°5E 122 B2
Dagupan Phil. 16°3N 120°20E 232 C3
Daguragu Australia 17°33S 130°30E 278 C5
Daguragu ◎ Australia 17°24S 130°48E 278 C5
Dahab Egypt 28°31N 34°31E 251 K5
Dahab, Gezîret el Egypt 29°59N 31°13E 117 B2
Dahanu India 19°58N 72°44E 244 E1
Daheisha West Bank 31°42N 35°11E 123 B2
Dahivadi India 17°43N 74°33E 244 F2
Dahlak Kebir Eritrea 15°50N 40°10E 257 D5
Dahlak Marine △ Eritrea 15°35N 40°1E 257 D5
Dahlem Germany 52°27N 13°16E 115 B2
Dahlenburg Germany 53°11N 10°44E 178 B6
Dahlonega U.S.A. 34°32N 83°59W 315 D13
Dahlwitz-Hoppegarten Germany 52°30N 13°41E 115 A5
Dahme Germany 51°52N 13°25E 178 D9
Dahod India 22°50N 74°15E 242 H6
Dahomey = Benin ■ Africa 10°0N 2°0E 263 D5
Dahong Shan China 31°25N 113°0E 229 B9
Dahongliutan China 35°45N 79°20E 243 B8
Dahongmen China 39°48N 116°21E 114 C2
Dahra Libya 29°30N 17°50E 258 C3
Dahra Senegal 15°22N 15°30W 262 B1
Dahra, Massif de Algeria 36°7N 1°21E 261 A5
Dahshûr Egypt 29°45N 31°14E 256 J7
Dahu = Tahu Taiwan 24°26N 120°52E 225 B2
Dahūk Iraq 36°50N 43°1E 213 D10
Dahūk □ Iraq 36°50N 42°50E 213 D10
Dahuofan Shuiku China 41°52N 124°12E 224 B2
Dahy, Nafūd ad Si. Arabia 22°0N 45°25E 248 B4
Dai Solomon Is. 7°54S 160°40E 287 L11
Dai Hao Vietnam 18°1N 106°25E 236 C6
Dai-Sen Japan 35°22N 133°32E 222 B5
Dai Shan China 30°25N 122°10E 229 B14
Dai Xian China 39°4N 112°58E 226 E7
Daiba = Odaiba Japan 35°38N 139°47E 140 B3
Daicheng China 38°42N 116°38E 226 E9
Daigo Japan 36°46N 140°21E 223 A12
Daik-u Myanmar 17°47N 96°40E 241 G6
Daikondi = Dāykondī □ Afghan. 34°0N 66°0E 240 B2
Dailekh Nepal 28°50N 81°44E 243 E9
Daimanji-San Japan 36°14N 133°20E 222 A5
Daimiel Spain 39°5N 3°35W 195 F7
Daingean Ireland 53°18N 7°17W 166 C4
Daingean, An = Dingle Ireland 52°9N 10°17W 166 D1
Dainkog China 32°30N 97°58E 228 A1
Daintree Australia 16°20S 145°20E 280 B4
Daintree △ Australia 16°8S 145°2E 280 B4
Daiō-Misaki Japan 34°15N 136°45E 223 C8
Dair, J. ed Sudan 12°27N 30°42E 257 E3
Dairen = Dalian China 38°50N 121°40E 227 E11
Dairût Egypt 27°34N 30°43E 256 B3
Daisen Japan 39°27N 140°29E 220 E10
Daisen-Oki △ Japan 35°23N 133°34E 222 B5
Daisetsu-Zan Japan 43°30N 142°57E 220 C11
Daisetsu-Zan △ Japan 43°30N 142°55E 220 C11
Daitari India 21°10N 85°46E 244 D7
Daitō Japan 35°19N 132°58E 222 B4
Daiyun Shan China 25°50N 118°15E 229 E12
Dajarra Australia 21°42S 139°30E 280 C2
Dajia = Tachia Taiwan 24°25N 120°28E 225 B2
Dajiaoting China 39°51N 116°27E 114 B2
Dajiawa China 37°9N 119°0E 227 F10
Dajin Chuan ➜ China 31°16N 101°59E 228 B3
Dajti △ Albania 41°22N 19°56E 202 E3
Dak Dam Cambodia 12°20N 107°21E 236 F6
Dak Nhe Vietnam 15°28N 107°48E 236 E6
Dak Pek Vietnam 15°4N 107°44E 236 E6
Dak Song Vietnam 12°19N 107°35E 237 F6
Dak Sui Vietnam 14°55N 107°43E 236 E6
Dakar Senegal 14°34N 17°29W 262 C1
Dakar □ Senegal 14°45N 17°20W 262 C1
Dakhal, W. el ➜ Egypt 28°48N 32°47E 251 K3
Dakhin Bangla. 22°30N 90°45E 241 D3
Dakhla W. Sahara 23°50N 15°53W 260 D1
Dakhla, El Wâhât el Egypt 25°30N 28°50E 256 B2
Dakhnoye Russia 59°49N 30°15E 137 C1
Dakingari Nigeria 11°37N 4°1E 263 C5
Dakoank India 7°2N 93°43E 245 L11
Dakor India 22°45N 73°11E 242 H5
Dakoro Niger 14°31N 6°46E 263 C6
Dakota City Iowa, U.S.A. 42°43N 94°12W 310 B2
Dakota City Nebr., U.S.A. 42°25N 96°25W 308 D5
Ðakovica = Gjakovë Kosovo 42°22N 20°26E 202 D4
Ðakovo Croatia 45°19N 18°24E 182 E3
Dal Norway 59°53N 8°40E 164 E5
Dala Lunda Sul, Angola 11°3S 20°17E 265 E4
Dala Uíge, Angola 8°5S 15°49E 265 D3
Dala Solomon Is. 8°30S 160°41E 287 M11
Dala-Cachibo Angola 10°30S 14°41E 265 E2
Dala-Järna Sweden 60°33N 14°26E 162 D8
Dalaba Guinea 10°47N 12°12W 262 C2
Dalachi China 36°48N 105°0E 226 F3
Dalagan = San Antonio Phil. 14°57N 120°5E 232 D3
Dalaguete Phil. 9°46N 123°32E 233 G4
Dalai Nur China 43°20N 116°45E 226 C9
Dālakī Iran 29°26N 51°17E 247 D6
Dalälven ➜ Sweden 60°12N 16°43E 162 D10
Dalaman Turkey 36°48N 28°47E 205 E10
Dalaman ➜ Turkey 36°41N 28°43E 205 E10
Dalandzadgad Mongolia 43°27N 104°30E 226 C3
Dalanganem Is. Phil. 10°40N 120°17E 233 F3
Dalap-Uliga-Darrit = Majuro Marshall Is. 7°9N 171°12E 288 G9
Dalarna Sweden 61°0N 14°0E 162 D8
Dalarna □ Sweden 61°0N 14°15E 162 C8
Dalasýsla Iceland 65°15N 22°0W 155 B4
Dalat Malaysia 2°44N 111°56E 235 B4
Dalay Mongolia 43°28N 103°30E 226 C2
Dālbandīn Pakistan 29°0N 64°23E 240 C2
Dalbeattie U.K. 54°56N 3°50W 167 G5
Dalbeg Australia 20°16S 147°18E 280 C4
Dalbosjön Sweden 58°40N 12°45E 163 F6
Dalby Queens., Australia 27°10S 151°17E 281 D5
Dalby Skåne, Sweden 55°40N 13°22E 163 J7
Dalby Söderskog △ Sweden 55°41N 13°21E 163 J7
Dale Sogn og Fjordane, Norway 61°22N 5°23E 164 C2
Dale Ind., U.S.A. 38°10N 86°59W 311 F10
Dale City U.S.A. 38°38N 77°19W 309 F15
Dale Hollow L. U.S.A. 36°32N 85°27W 315 C12
Dalejsky potok ➜ Czechia 50°2N 14°24E 135 B2
Dalen Norway 59°26N 8°0E 164 E4
Dalet Myanmar 19°59N 93°51E 241 F4
Daletme Myanmar 21°36N 92°46E 241 E4
Daleville Ala., U.S.A. 31°19N 85°43W 316 D4
Daleville Ind., U.S.A. 40°7N 85°33W 311 D11
Dalga Egypt 27°39N 30°41E 256 B3
Dalgān Iran 27°31N 59°19E 247 E8
Dalgety Bay U.K. 56°2N 3°20W 121 A1
Dalgopol Bulgaria 43°3N 27°22E 203 C11
Dalhart U.S.A. 36°4N 102°31W 314 C3
Dalhousie N.B., Canada 48°5N 66°26W 299 C6
Dalhousie India 32°38N 75°58E 242 C6
Dali Shaanxi, China 34°48N 109°58E 226 G5
Dali Yunnan, China 25°40N 100°10E 228 E3
Dalian China 38°50N 121°40E 227 E11
Daliang Shan China 28°0N 102°45E 228 D4
Daliao = Taliao Taiwan 22°36N 120°23E 225 D2
Dalin = Talin Taiwan 23°36N 120°27E 225 C2
Daling He ➜ China 40°55N 121°40E 227 D11
Dalj Croatia 45°29N 18°59E 182 E3
Dalkeith Midloth., U.K. 55°54N 3°4W 121 B3
Dalkeith Fla., U.S.A. 30°0N 85°9W 316 E4
Dalkey Ireland 53°16N 6°6W 166 C5
Dallas Ga., U.S.A. 33°55N 84°51W 316 B5
Dallas Oreg., U.S.A. 44°55N 123°19W 304 D2
Dallas Tex., U.S.A. 32°47N 96°48W 120 B4
Dallas City U.S.A. 40°38N 91°10W 310 D5
Dallas-Fort Worth Int. ✈ (DFW) U.S.A. 32°54N 97°2W 314 E6
Dallas-Fort Worth Int. ✈ (DFW) Tex., U.S.A. 32°53N 97°2W 120 A3
Dallas-Fort Worth Meacham Int. ✈ (FTW) U.S.A. 32°49N 97°21W 120 B1
Dalle = Yirga Alem Ethiopia 6°48N 38°22E 257 F4
Dalles, The U.S.A. 45°36N 121°10W 304 D3
Dallgow Germany 52°32N 13°5E 115 A1
Dallol Ethiopia 14°14N 40°17E 257 E5
Dalmā U.A.E. 24°30N 52°20E 247 E7
Dalmacija Croatia 43°20N 17°0E 199 E13
Dalmas, L. Canada 53°30N 71°50W 299 B5
Dalmatia = Dalmacija Croatia 43°20N 17°0E 199 E13
Dalmau India 26°4N 81°2E 243 F9
Dalmellington U.K. 55°19N 4°23W 167 F4
Dalmeny N.S.W., Australia 36°10S 150°8E 283 D9
Dalmeny Edinburgh, U.K. 55°59N 3°22W 121 B1
Dalnegorsk Russia 44°32N 135°33E 220 B7
Dalnerechensk Russia 45°50N 133°40E 220 B6
Dalnevostochnyy □ Russia 67°0N 140°0E 215 C14
Dalny = Dalian China 38°50N 121°40E 227 E11
Daloa Côte d'Ivoire 7°0N 6°30W 262 D3
Dalou Shan China 28°15N 107°0E 228 C6
Dalry U.K. 55°42N 4°43W 167 F4
Dalrymple, L. Australia 20°40S 147°0E 280 C4
Dalrymple, Mt. Australia 21°1S 148°39E 280 b
Dals Långed Sweden 58°56N 12°18E 163 F6
Dalsetra Norway 61°28N 9°26E 164 C6
Dalsjöfors Sweden 57°46N 13°5E 163 G7
Dalsland Sweden 58°50N 12°15E 163 F6
Dalsmynni Iceland 64°48N 21°29W 155 C5
Dalston U.K. 51°32N 0°4W 125 A3
Daltenganj India 24°0N 84°4E 243 H11
Dalton Ga., U.S.A. 34°46N 84°58W 315 D12
Dalton Mass., U.S.A. 42°28N 73°11W 313 D11
Dalton Nebr., U.S.A. 41°25N 102°58W 308 E2
Dalton, Kap Greenland 69°25N 24°3W 154 D8
Dalton-in-Furness U.K. 54°10N 3°11W 168 C4
Daludalu Indonesia 1°4N 100°15E 234 B2
Dalupiri I. Cagayan, Phil. 19°5N 121°12E 232 B3
Dalupiri I. N. Samar, Phil. 12°25N 124°16E 232 E5
Dalvík Iceland 65°58N 18°32W 155 B8
Dálvvadis = Jokkmokk Sweden 66°35N 19°50E 160 C18
Dalwallinu Australia 30°17S 116°40E 279 F2
Dalworthington Gardens U.S.A. 32°42N 97°9W 120 B3
Daly ➜ Australia 13°35S 130°19E 278 B5
Daly City U.S.A. 37°42N 122°27W 136 B2
Daly L. Canada 56°32N 105°39W 297 B7
Daly River Australia 13°46S 130°42E 278 B5
Daly River-Port Keats ◎ Australia 14°13S 129°36E 278 B4
Daly Waters Australia 16°15S 133°24E 280 B1
Dalyan Turkey 36°50N 28°39E 205 E10
Dam Amsterdam, Neths. 112 a2
Dam Doi Vietnam 8°50N 105°12E 237 H5
Dam Ha Vietnam 21°21N 107°36E 236 B6
Damachova Belarus 51°45N 23°36E 185 G10
Damaia Portugal 38°44N 9°12W 126 A1
Daman India 20°25N 72°57E 244 D1
Daman & Diu □ India 20°25N 72°58E 244 D1
Dāmaneh Iran 33°1N 50°29E 247 C6
Damanganga ➜ India 20°25N 72°56E 244 D1
Damanhûr Egypt 31°0N 30°30E 256 H7
Damant L. Canada 61°45N 105°5W 297 A7
Damaq Iran 35°25N 48°49E 213 E13
Damar Indonesia 7°7S 128°40E 231 F7
Damara C.A.R. 4°58N 18°42E 264 B3
Damarakia Greece 37°58N 23°39E 112 B1
Damaraland Namibia 20°0S 15°0E 270 B2
Damascus = Dimashq Syria 33°30N 36°18E 250 E7
Damascus U.S.A. 31°18N 84°43W 316 D5
Damasi Greece 39°43N 22°11E 204 B4
Damaturu Nigeria 11°45N 11°55E 263 C7
Damāvand Iran 35°47N 52°0E 247 C7
Damāvand, Qolleh-ye Iran 35°57N 52°7E 247 C7
Damba Angola 6°44S 15°20E 265 D3
Damboa Nigeria 11°15N 12°55E 259 F2
Dâmboviţa □ Romania 45°0N 25°30E 183 F10
Dâmboviţa ➜ Romania 44°12N 26°26E 183 F11
Dâmbovnic ➜ Romania 44°28N 25°18E 183 F10
Dambrowica = Dubrovytsya Ukraine 51°31N 26°35E 177 C14
Dambulla Sri Lanka 7°51N 80°39E 245 L5
Dame Marie Haiti 18°34N 74°26W 321 C5
Dämeritzsee Germany 52°25N 13°43E 115 B5
Dāmghān Iran 36°10N 54°17E 247 B7
Dămieneşti Romania 46°44N 26°59E 183 D11
Damietta = Dumyât Egypt 31°24N 31°48E 251 G2
Daming China 36°15N 115°6E 226 F8
Damīr Qābū Syria 36°58N 41°51E 246 B4
Dammai I. Phil. 5°47N 120°25E 233 J3
Dammam = Ad Dammām Si. Arabia 26°20N 50°5E 247 E6
Dammarie-les-Lys France 48°31N 2°39E 173 D9
Dammartin-en-Goële France 49°3N 2°41E 173 C9
Damme Germany 52°32N 8°11E 178 C4
Damodar ➜ India 23°17N 87°35E 243 H12
Damoh India 23°50N 79°28E 243 H8
Damous Algeria 36°31N 1°42E 261 A5
Dampier Australia 20°41S 116°42E 278 D2
Dampier, Selat Indonesia 0°40S 131°0E 231 E8
Dampier Arch. Australia 20°38S 116°32E 278 D2
Dampier Str. Papua N. G. 5°50S 148°0E 286 C5
Damqawt Yemen 16°34N 52°50E 249 D5
Damrak Amsterdam, Neths. 112 a2
Damrani Algeria 27°45N 2°56W 260 C4
Damrei, Chuor Phnum Cambodia 11°30N 103°0E 237 G4
Damroh India 28°26N 95°14E 241 A5
Damvillers France 49°20N 5°21E 173 C12
Damyang S. Korea 35°19N 126°59E 224 E3
Dan Gorayo Somalia 8°43N 49°20E 267 C6
Dan-Gulbi Nigeria 11°40N 6°15E 263 C6
Dan Ryan Woods U.S.A. 41°44N 87°40W 119 C2
Dan-Sadau Nigeria 11°17N 6°29E 263 C6
Dana Indonesia 11°0S 121°15E 231 F6
Dana Jordan 30°41N 35°37E 251 H6
Dana Nepal 28°32N 83°37E 243 E10
Dana, L. Canada 50°53N 77°20W 298 B4
Dana, Mt. U.S.A. 37°54N 119°12W 306 H7
Danakil Depression Ethiopia 13°10N 41°0E 267 B5
Danakil Desert Ethiopia 12°45N 41°0E 257 E5
Danan Ethiopia 6°31N 43°30E 267 C5
Danané Côte d'Ivoire 7°16N 8°9W 262 D3
Danao Phil. 10°31N 124°1E 233 F5
Danau Sentarum △ Indonesia 0°51N 112°6E 235 B4
Danba China 30°54N 101°48E 228 B3
Danbury U.S.A. 41°24N 73°28W 313 E11
Danby L. U.S.A. 34°13N 115°5W 307 L11
Dand Afghan. 31°28N 65°32E 242 D1
Dande ➜ Angola 8°28S 13°21E 265 D2
Dande △ Zimbabwe 15°56S 30°16E 269 F3
Dandeldhura Nepal 29°20N 80°35E 243 E9
Dandeli India 15°5N 74°30E 245 G2
Dandenong Australia 38°0S 145°15E 283 E6
Danderhall U.K. 55°55N 3°7W 121 B3
Danderyd Sweden 59°24N 18°1E 139 A2
Dandī Iran 36°32N 47°37E 213 D12
Dandîl Egypt 29°10N 31°2E 256 J7
Dandong China 40°10N 124°20E 224 B2
Daneborg Greenland 74°18N 20°14W 154 C8
Danfeng China 33°45N 110°25E 226 H6
Danforth Canada 43°43N 79°16W 141 A3
Dangan Liedao China 22°2N 114°8E 229 F10
Dangcagan Phil. 7°36N 125°0E 233 H5
Dange Angola 7°56S 15°3E 265 D3
Dangé-St-Romain France 46°56N 0°36E 174 B4
Dângeni Romania 47°51N 26°58E 183 C11
Danger Is. = Pukapuka Cook Is. 10°53S 165°49W 289 J11
Danger Pt. S. Africa 34°40S 19°17E 270 D2
Dangjin S. Korea 36°53N 126°37E 224 D3
Dangla Ethiopia 11°18N 36°56E 257 E4
Dangla Shan = Tanggula Shan China 32°40N 92°10E 218 E7
Dangora Nigeria 11°30N 8°7E 263 C6
Dangouadougou Burkina Faso 10°9N 4°56W 262 D4
Dangrek, Mts. = Dangrek, Phnom Thailand 14°20N 104°0E 236 E5
Dangrek, Phnom Thailand 14°20N 104°0E 236 E5
Dangriga Belize 17°0N 88°13W 320 C2
Dangshan China 34°27N 116°22E 226 G9
Dangtu China 31°32N 118°25E 229 B12
Dangyang China 30°52N 111°44E 229 B8
Dania Beach U.S.A. 26°3N 80°8W 129 B3
Daniel U.S.A. 42°52N 110°4W 304 E8
Daniel's Harbour Canada 50°13N 57°35W 299 B8
Danielskuil S. Africa 28°11S 23°33E 270 C3
Danielson U.S.A. 41°48N 71°53W 313 E13
Danielsville U.S.A. 34°8N 83°13W 316 A6
Danilov Russia 58°16N 40°13E 188 C11
Danilovgrad Montenegro 42°38N 19°4E 202 D3
Danilovka Russia 50°25N 44°12E 190 E7
Daning China 36°28N 110°45E 226 F6
Danish West Indies = Virgin Is. (U.S.) □ W. Indies 18°20N 65°0W 321 C7
Danissa Kenya 3°17N 40°59E 267 D5
Danja Nigeria 11°21N 7°30E 263 C6
Danje-la-Menha Angola 9°32S 14°39E 265 D2
Danjiangkou China 32°31N 111°30E 229 A8
Danjiangkou Shuiku China 32°37N 111°30E 229 A8
Dank Oman 23°33N 56°16E 247 F8
Dankalwa Nigeria 11°52N 12°12E 263 C7
Dankama Nigeria 13°20N 7°44E 263 C6
Dankhar Gompa India 32°10N 78°10E 242 C8
Dankov Russia 53°20N 39°5E 188 F10
Danleng China 30°1N 103°31E 228 B4
Danlí Honduras 14°4N 86°35W 320 D2
Danmark = Denmark ■ Europe 55°45N 10°0E 163 J3
Danmark Fjord Greenland 81°30N 22°0W 154 A8
Danmarkshavn Greenland 76°45N 18°50W 154 B9
Dannemora U.S.A. 44°43N 73°44W 313 B11
Dannenberg Germany 53°6N 11°5E 178 B7
Dannevirke N.Z. 40°12S 176°8E 284 G5
Dannhauser S. Africa 28°0S 30°3E 271 C5
Danot Ethiopia 7°33N 45°17E 267 C6
Dansalan = Marawi City Phil. 8°0N 124°21E 233 G5
Danshuei = Tanshui Taiwan 25°10N 121°28E 225 A3
Dansville U.S.A. 42°34N 77°42W 312 D7
Danta India 24°11N 72°46E 242 G5
Dantan India 21°57N 87°20E 243 J12
Dantewara India 18°54N 81°21E 244 E5
Danube = Dunărea ➜ Europe 45°20N 29°40E 183 E14
Danubyu Myanmar 17°15N 95°35E 241 G5
Danvers U.S.A. 42°34N 70°56W 313 D14
Danville Ga., U.S.A. 32°37N 83°15W 316 C6
Danville Ill., U.S.A. 40°8N 87°37W 311 D9
Danville Ind., U.S.A. 39°46N 86°32W 311 E10
Danville Ky., U.S.A. 37°39N 84°46W 311 G12
Danville Pa., U.S.A. 40°58N 76°37W 313 F8
Danville Va., U.S.A. 36°36N 79°23W 309 G14
Danville Vt., U.S.A. 44°25N 72°9W 313 B12
Danyang China 32°0N 119°31E 229 B12
Danzhai China 26°11N 107°48E 228 D6
Danzhou China 19°31N 109°33E 229 a
Danzig = Gdańsk Poland 54°22N 18°40E 184 D5
Dao Antique, Phil. 10°30N 121°57E 233 F3
Dao Capiz, Phil. 11°24N 122°41E 233 F4
Dão ➜ Portugal 40°20N 8°11W 194 E2
Dao Xian China 25°36N 111°31E 229 E8
Daocheng China 29°0N 100°10E 228 C3
Daora W. Sahara 27°25N 12°59W 260 C2
Daoud = Aïn Beïda Algeria 35°50N 7°29E 261 A6
Daoukro Côte d'Ivoire 7°10N 3°58W 262 D4
Dapa Phil. 9°46N 126°3E 233 G6
Dapaong Togo 10°55N 0°16E 263 C5
Dapchi Nigeria 12°32N 11°31E 263 C7
Dapiak, Mt. Phil. 8°15N 123°28E 233 G4
Dapitan Phil. 8°39N 123°25E 233 G4
Dapoli India 17°46N 73°11E 244 F1
Daporijo India 27°59N 94°13E 241 B5
Daqahlîya □ Egypt 30°55N 31°30E 251 H2
Daqing China 46°35N 125°0E 219 B13
Daqing Shan China 40°40N 111°0E 226 D6
Daqq-e Sorkh, Kavīr Iran 33°45N 52°50E 247 C7
Daqu Shan China 30°25N 122°20E 229 B14
Dar Banda Africa 8°0N 23°0E 254 F6
Dar el Beida = Casablanca Morocco 33°36N 7°36W 260 B3
Dar es Salaam Tanzania 6°50S 39°12E 268 D4
Dar Mazār Iran 29°14N 57°20E 247 D8
Dar Rounga C.A.R. 0°45N 22°20E 264 A4
Dār Ta'izzah Syria 36°20N 36°52E 250 B7
Dar'ā Syria 32°36N 36°7E 250 F7
Dar'ā □ Syria 32°55N 36°10E 250 F7
Dara Dere = Zlatograd Bulgaria 41°22N 25°7E 203 E9
Dārāb Iran 28°50N 54°30E 247 D7
Daraban Pakistan 31°44N 70°20E 242 D4
Darabani Romania 48°10N 26°39E 183 B11
Darai Hills Papua N. G. 7°8S 143°33E 286 D2
Daraina Madag. 13°12S 49°40E 272 A2
Daraj Libya 30°10N 10°28E 258 B2
Darakeh Iran 35°49N 51°22E 141 A2
Daram Phil. 11°38N 124°48E 233 F5
Dārān Iran 32°59N 50°24E 247 C6
Daravica = Gjeravicë Kosovo 42°32N 20°8E 202 D4
Daraw Egypt 24°22N 32°51E 256 C3
Dārayyā Syria 33°28N 36°15E 250 E7
Darazo Nigeria 11°1N 10°24E 263 C7
Darband Tehrān, Iran 35°49N 51°27E 141 A2
Darband Pakistan 34°20N 72°50E 242 B5
Darband, Kūh-e Iran 31°34N 57°8E 247 D8
Darbhanga India 26°15N 85°55E 243 F11
Darburruk Somalia 9°44N 44°31E 267 C5
Darby, C. U.S.A. 64°19N 162°47W 303 D7
D'Arcy Canada 50°33N 122°29W 296 C4
Darda Croatia 45°40N 18°41E 182 E3
Dardanë Kosovo 42°35N 21°35E 202 D5
Dardanelle Ark., U.S.A. 35°13N 93°9W 314 D8
Dardanelle Calif., U.S.A. 38°20N 119°50W 306 G7
Dardanelles = Çanakkale Boğazı Turkey 40°17N 26°32E 203 F10
Dare ➜ Ethiopia 7°20N 42°11E 257 F5
Darende Turkey 38°31N 37°30E 212 C7
Dārestān Iran 29°9N 58°42E 247 D8
Darfield N.Z. 43°29S 172°7E 285 D7
Darfo-Boario Terme Italy 45°53N 10°11E 198 C7
Dârfûr Sudan 13°40N 24°0E 259 F4
Dargai Pakistan 34°25N 71°55E 242 B4
Dargaville N.Z. 35°57S 173°52E 284 B2
Dargol Niger 13°54N 1°22E 263 C5
Darhan Mongolia 49°37N 106°21E 218 B10
Darhan Muminggan China 41°40N 110°28E 226 D6
Dari South Sudan 5°48N 30°26E 257 F3
Darica Turkey 40°45N 29°23E 212 B3
Darien U.S.A. 31°23N 81°26W 316 D8
Darién, G. del Caribbean 9°0N 77°0W 320 E4
Darién, Serranía del Cent. Amer. 8°30N 77°30W 320 E4
Darién △ Panama 7°36N 77°57W 320 E4
Dariganga = Ovoot Mongolia 45°21N 113°45E 226 B7
Daringbadi India 19°54N 84°8E 244 E7
Dario, Palazzo Venice, Italy 142 c2
Darjeeling = Darjiling India 27°3N 88°18E 241 B2
Darjiling India 27°3N 88°18E 241 B2
Darkan Australia 33°20S 116°43E 279 F2
Darke Peak Australia 33°27S 136°12E 282 B2
Darkhana Pakistan 30°39N 72°11E 242 D5
Darkhazīneh Iran 31°54N 48°39E 247 D6
Darkot Pass Pakistan 36°45N 73°26E 243 A5
Darling ➜ Australia 34°4S 141°54E 282 C4
Darling Downs Australia 27°30S 150°30E 281 D5
Darling Harbour Sydney, Australia 139 b1
Darling Point Australia 33°52S 151°15E 139 B2
Darling Ra. Australia 32°30S 116°20E 279 F2
Darlington Durham, U.K. 54°32N 1°33W 168 C6
Darlington Fla., U.S.A. 30°57N 86°3W 316 E3
Darlington S.C., U.S.A. 34°18N 79°52W 315 D15
Darlington Wis., U.S.A. 42°41N 90°7W 310 B6
Darlington □ U.K. 54°32N 1°33W 168 C6
Darlington, L. S. Africa 33°10S 25°9E 270 D4
Darlington Point Australia 34°37S 146°1E 283 C7
Darlot, L. Australia 27°48S 121°35E 279 E3
Darłowo Poland 54°25N 16°25E 184 D3
Dărmăneşti Bacău, Romania 46°21N 26°33E 183 D11
Dărmăneşti Suceava, Romania 47°44N 26°9E 183 C11
Darmstadt Germany 49°51N 8°39E 179 F4
Darnah Libya 32°45N 22°45E 258 B4
Darnah □ Libya 31°0N 23°40E 258 B4
Darnall S. Africa 29°23S 31°18E 271 C5
Darney France 48°5N 6°2E 173 D13
Darnick Australia 32°48S 143°38E 282 B5
Darnley Australia 9°35S 143°46E 280 a
Darnley, C. Antarctica 68°0S 69°0E 151 C6
Darnley B. Canada 69°30N 123°30W 294 D7
Daroca Spain 41°9N 1°25W 196 D3
Daror Ethiopia 8°14N 44°42E 267 C5
Darou-Mousti Senegal 15°3N 16°3W 262 B1
Darr ➜ Australia 23°39S 143°50E 280 C3
Darra Pezu Pakistan 32°19N 70°44E 242 C4
Darran Mts. N.Z. 44°37S 167°59E 285 E2
Darreh Shahr Iran 33°7N 47°22E 213 F12
Darrequeira Argentina 37°42S 63°10W 334 D3
Darrington U.S.A. 48°15N 121°36W 304 B3
Darrūs Iran 35°46N 51°27E 141 A2
Darsah Yemen 12°6N 53°16E 249 D6
Darsana Bangla. 23°35N 88°48E 241 D2
Darsi India 15°46N 79°44E 245 G4
Darsser Ort Germany 54°28N 12°32E 178 A8
Dart ➜ U.K. 50°24N 3°39W 169 G4
Dartford U.K. 51°26N 0°13E 125 B5
Dartmoor Vic., Australia 37°56S 141°19E 282 D4
Dartmoor Devon, U.K. 50°38N 3°57W 169 G4
Dartmoor △ U.K. 50°37N 3°59W 169 G4
Dartmouth N.S., Canada 44°40N 63°30W 299 D7
Dartmouth Devon, U.K. 50°21N 3°36W 169 G4
Dartmouth, L. Queens., Australia 26°4S 145°18E 281 D4
Dartmouth, L. Vic., Australia 36°34S 147°32E 283 D7
Dartuch, C. = Artrutx, C. de Spain 39°55N 3°49E 206 B4
Daru Papua N. G. 9°3S 143°13E 286 E2
Daruvar Croatia 45°35N 17°14E 182 E2
Darvaza = Içoguz Turkmenistan 40°11N 58°24E 216 D5
Darvel, Teluk = Lahad Datu, Telok Malaysia 4°50N 118°20E 235 B5
Darvi Mongolia 46°27N 94°7E 217 C12
Darwen U.K. 53°42N 2°29W 168 D5
Darwendale Zimbabwe 17°41S 30°33E 271 A5
Darwha India 20°15N 77°45E 244 D3
Darwin N. Terr., Australia 12°25S 130°51E 278 B5
Darwin Calif., U.S.A. 36°15N 117°35W 307 J9
Darwin, Mt. Chile 54°47S 69°55W 336 D3
Darwin, Volcán Ecuador 0°10S 91°18W 330 a
Darya Ganj Delhi, India 120 a3
Darya Khan Pakistan 31°48N 71°6E 242 D4
Daryapur India 20°55N 77°20E 244 D3
Daryoi Amu = Amudarya ➜ Uzbekistan 43°58N 59°34E 216 D5
Dās U.A.E. 25°20N 53°30E 247 E7
Dashahe China 42°44N 128°10E 224 A4
Dashen, Ras Ethiopia 13°8N 38°26E 257 E4
Dasher U.S.A. 30°45N 83°13W 316 E6
Dashetai China 41°0N 109°5E 226 D5
Dashi China 23°1N 113°17E 121 B2
Dashiqiao China 40°38N 122°30E 227 D12
Dashkesan = Daşkəsən Azerbaijan 40°25N 46°0E 191 K7
Dashköpri Turkmenistan 36°16N 62°8E 247 B9
Dasht ➜ Pakistan 25°10N 61°40E 240 D1
Dasht-i-Tahlab Pakistan 28°40N 62°25E 240 C1
Dashu = Tashu Taiwan 22°41N 120°25E 225 D2
Daska Pakistan 32°20N 74°20E 242 C6
Daşkəsən Azerbaijan 40°25N 46°0E 191 K7
Dasmariñas Phil. 14°20N 120°56E 232 D3
Daşoguz Turkmenistan 41°49N 59°58E 216 D5
Dasol B. Phil. 15°52N 119°50E 232 D2
Dassa Benin 7°46N 2°14E 263 D5
Dasuya India 31°49N 75°38E 242 D6
Datadian Indonesia 2°1N 115°13E 235 B5
Datansha China 23°8N 113°12E 121 B2
Datça Turkey 36°46N 27°40E 205 E9
Date Japan 42°28N 140°52E 220 C10
Datia India 25°39N 78°27E 243 G8
Datian China 25°40N 117°50E 229 E11
Datong Anhui, China 30°48N 117°44E 229 B11
Datong Qinghai, China 36°20N 102°50E 218 D9
Datong Shanxi, China 40°6N 113°18E 226 D7
Dattakhel Pakistan 32°54N 69°46E 242 C3
Dattapur = Dhamangaon India 20°48N 78°9E 244 D4
Datteln Germany 51°39N 7°21E 178 D3
Datu, Tanjung Indonesia 2°5N 109°39E 235 B3
Datu Piang Phil. 7°2N 124°30E 233 H5
Datuk, Tanjong = Datu, Tanjung Indonesia 2°5N 109°39E 235 B3
Datun China 40°0N 116°23E 114 B2
Daua = Dawa ➜ Africa 4°11N 42°6E 257 G5
Daud Khel Pakistan 32°53N 71°34E 242 C4
Daudnagar India 25°2N 84°24E 243 G11
Daugava ➜ Latvia 57°4N 24°3E 188 D3
Daugavpils Latvia 55°53N 26°32E 188 E4
Daulatabad India 19°57N 75°15E 244 E2
Daulatpur India 28°44N 77°6E 120 A1
Daule Ecuador 1°56S 79°56W 328 D2
Daule ➜ Ecuador 2°10S 79°52W 328 D2
Daule-Peripa, Presa Ecuador 1°0S 79°35W 328 D2
Daulpur India 26°45N 77°59E 242 F7
Daun Germany 50°11N 6°49E 179 E2
Daund India 18°26N 74°40E 244 E2
Daung Kyun Myanmar 12°13N 98°4E 237 F1
Dauphin Man., Canada 51°9N 100°5W 297 C8
Dauphin Pa., U.S.A. 40°22N 76°56W 312 F8
Dauphin L. Canada 51°20N 99°45W 297 C9
Dauphiné France 45°15N 5°25E 175 C9
Daura Borno, Nigeria 11°31N 11°24E 263 C7
Daura Katsina, Nigeria 13°2N 8°21E 263 C6
Daurada, Costa Spain 41°12N 1°15E 196 D6
Dausa India 26°52N 76°20E 242 F7
Däväçi Azerbaijan 41°15N 48°57E 191 K9
Davangere India 14°25N 75°55E 245 G2
Davao Phil. 7°0N 125°40E 233 H5
Davao □ Phil. 7°50N 125°55E 233 H5
Davao del Sur □ Phil. 7°0N 125°30E 233 H5
Davao G. Phil. 6°30N 125°48E 233 H5
Davao Occidental □ Phil. 6°0N 125°30E 233 H5
Davao Oriental □ Phil. 7°10N 126°30E 233 H6
Dāvar Panāh = Sarāvān Iran 27°25N 62°15E 247 E9
Davenport Calif., U.S.A. 37°1N 122°12W 306 H4
Davenport Fla., U.S.A. 28°10N 81°36W 317 G8
Davenport Iowa, U.S.A. 41°32N 90°35W 310 C6
Davenport Wash., U.S.A. 47°39N 118°9W 304 C4
Davenport Ra. Australia 20°28S 134°0E 280 C1
Davenport Range △ Australia 20°36S 134°22E 280 C1
Daventry U.K. 52°16N 1°10W 169 E6
David Panama 8°30N 82°30W 320 E3
David City U.S.A. 41°15N 97°8W 308 E5
David Glacier Antarctica 75°20S 162°0E 151 D11
David Gorodok = Davyd Haradok Belarus 52°4N 27°8E 177 B14
David's Citadel Jerusalem 123 b3
David's Tomb Jerusalem 123 b3
Davidson Canada 51°16N 105°59W 297 C7
Davidson, Mt. U.S.A. 37°44N 122°27W 136 B2
Davidson Mts. U.S.A. 68°41N 142°22W 303 B12
Davidson's Mains U.K. 55°58N 3°16W 121 B2
Davie U.S.A. 26°3N 80°14W 129 B2
Davis Antarctica 68°34S 77°55E 151 C6
Davis Calif., U.S.A. 38°33N 121°44W 306 G5
Davis Dam U.S.A. 35°12N 114°34W 307 K12
Davis Mts. U.S.A. 30°50N 103°55W 314 F3
Davis Sea Antarctica 66°0S 92°0E 151 C7
Davis Str. N. Amer. 65°0N 58°0W 295 D19
Davisboro U.S.A. 32°59N 82°36W 316 C7
Davison U.S.A. 43°2N 83°31W 311 A13
Davlos Cyprus 35°25N 33°54E 207 E9
Davo ➜ Côte d'Ivoire 5°0N 6°10W 262 D3
Davos Switz. 46°48N 9°49E 179 J5
Dāvūdiyeh Iran 35°45N 51°25E 141 A2
Davutlar Turkey 37°43N 27°17E 205 D9
Davy L. Canada 58°53N 108°18W 297 B7
Davyd Haradok Belarus 52°4N 27°8E 177 B14
Davydkovo Russia 55°43N 37°29E 129 B1
Dawa ➜ Africa 4°11N 42°6E 257 G5
Dawaki Bauchi, Nigeria 9°25N 9°33E 263 D6
Dawaki Kano, Nigeria 12°5N 8°23E 263 C6
Dawei Myanmar 14°2N 98°12E 236 E2
Dawes Ra. Australia 24°40S 150°40E 280 C5
Dawidy Poland 52°8N 20°58E 143 C1
Dawkah Oman 18°39N 54°5E 249 C6
Dawley = Telford U.K. 52°40N 2°27W 169 E5
Dawlish U.K. 50°35N 3°28W 169 G4
Dawmat al Jandal Si. Arabia 29°55N 39°40E 246 D3
Dawna Ra. Myanmar 16°30N 98°30E 236 D2
Dawnyein Myanmar 15°54N 95°36E 241 G5
Dawqah Si. Arabia 19°36N 40°54E 248 C3
Dawrān Yemen 14°45N 44°12E 248 D4
Dawros Hd. Ireland 54°50N 8°33W 166 B3
Dawson U.S.A. 31°46N 84°27W 316 D5
Dawson, I. Chile 53°50S 70°50W 336 D2
Dawson B. Canada 52°53N 100°49W 297 C8
Dawson City Canada 64°10N 139°30W 294 E4
Dawson Creek Canada 55°45N 120°15W 296 B4
Dawson Inlet Canada 61°50N 93°25W 297 A10
Dawson Ra. Australia 24°30S 149°48E 280 C4
Dawu Hubei, China 31°34N 114°7E 229 B10
Dawu Sichuan, China 30°55N 101°10E 228 B3
Dawwah Oman 20°33N 58°48E 249 B7
Dawwara, Ras id- Malta 35°52N 14°21E 206 F7
Dax France 43°44N 1°3W 174 E2
Daxi = Tach'i Taiwan 24°53N 121°17E 225 B3
Daxian China 31°15N 107°23E 228 B6
Daxin China 22°50N 107°11E 228 F6
Daxindian China 37°30N 120°50E 227 F11
Daxing China 39°47N 116°24E 114 C2
Daxinggou China 43°25N 129°40E 227 C15
Daxue Shan Sichuan, China 30°30N 101°30E 228 B3
Daxue Shan Yunnan, China 23°42N 99°48E 228 F2
Day U.S.A. 30°12N 83°17W 316 E6
Daya el Khadra Mauritania 25°14N 6°2W 260 C3
Dayang He ➜ China 39°51N 123°38E 224 C1
Dayao China 25°43N 101°20E 228 E3
Daye China 30°6N 114°58E 229 B10
Dayet en Naharat Mali 17°39N 3°10W 262 B4
Dayi China 30°41N 103°29E 228 B4
Dāykondī □ Afghan. 34°0N 66°0E 240 B2
Daylesford Australia 37°21S 144°9E 282 D6
Dayong = Zhangjiajie China 29°11N 110°30E 229 C8
Dayr az Zawr Syria 35°20N 40°5E 213 E9
Dayr az Zawr □ Syria 34°50N 40°10E 213 E9
Daysland Canada 52°50N 112°20W 296 C6
Dayton Iowa, U.S.A. 42°16N 94°4W 310 B2
Dayton Nev., U.S.A. 39°14N 119°36W 306 F7
Dayton Ohio, U.S.A. 39°45N 84°12W 311 E12
Dayton Pa., U.S.A. 40°53N 79°15W 312 F5
Dayton Tenn., U.S.A. 35°30N 85°1W 315 D12
Dayton Wash., U.S.A. 46°19N 117°59W 304 C5
Dayton Wyo., U.S.A. 44°53N 107°16W 304 D10
Daytona Beach U.S.A. 29°13N 81°1W 317 F8
Dayu China 25°24N 114°22E 229 E10
Dayuan = Tayuan Taiwan 25°3N 121°11E 225 A3
Dayville U.S.A. 44°28N 119°32W 304 D4
Dazaifu Japan 33°30N 130°32E 222 D2
Dazhu China 30°41N 107°15E 228 B6
Dazkırı Turkey 37°57N 29°52E 205 D11
Dazu China 29°40N 105°42E 228 C5
De Aar S. Africa 30°39S 24°0E 270 D3
De Armanville U.S.A. 33°38N 85°45W 316 B4
De Bary U.S.A. 28°54N 81°18W 317 G8
De Forest U.S.A. 43°15N 89°20W 310 A7
De Funiak Springs U.S.A. 30°43N 86°7W 316 E3
De Grey ➜ Australia 20°12S 119°13E 278 D2
De Haan Belgium 51°16N 3°2E 170 C3
De Hoop △ S. Africa 34°30S 20°28E 270 D3
De Kalb Junction U.S.A. 44°30N 75°16W 313 B9
De Land U.S.A. 29°2N 81°18W 317 F8
De Leon U.S.A. 32°7N 98°32W 314 E5
De Leon Springs U.S.A. 29°7N 81°21W 317 F8
De Long Mts. U.S.A. 68°10N 163°0W 303 B7
De Panne Belgium 51°6N 2°34E 170 C2
De Pere U.S.A. 44°27N 88°4W 308 C9
De Queen U.S.A. 34°2N 94°21W 314 D7
De Quincy U.S.A. 30°27N 93°26W 314 F8
De Ruyters U.S.A. 42°45N 75°53W 313 D9
De Smet U.S.A. 44°23N 97°33W 308 C5
De Soto Mo., U.S.A. 38°8N 90°34W 310 F6
De Soto Tex., U.S.A. 32°35N 96°51W 120 C5
De Soto City U.S.A. 27°27N 81°24W 317 H8
De Tour Village U.S.A. 46°0N 83°56W 309 B12
De Witt Ark., U.S.A. 34°18N 91°20W 314 D9
De Witt Iowa, U.S.A. 41°49N 90°33W 310 C6
De Witt Mich., U.S.A. 42°51N 84°34W 311 B12
Dead L. U.S.A. 30°10N 85°10W 316 E4
Dead Sea Asia 31°30N 35°30E 251 G6
Deadhorse U.S.A. 70°11N 148°27W 303 A10
Deadman B. U.S.A. 29°30N 83°30W 317 F6
Deadwood U.S.A. 44°23N 103°44W 308 C2
Deadwood L. Canada 59°10N 128°30W 296 B3
Deal U.K. 51°13N 1°25E 169 F9
Deal I. Australia 39°30S 147°20E 281 F4
Dealesville S. Africa 28°41S 25°44E 270 C4
De'an China 29°21N 115°46E 229 C10
Dean ➜ Canada 52°49N 126°58W 296 C3
Dean, Forest of U.K. 51°45N 2°33W 169 F5
Dean Chan. Canada 52°30N 127°15W 296 C3
Deán Funes Argentina 30°20S 64°20W 334 C3
Dearborn Mich., U.S.A. 42°19N 83°10W 311 B13
Dearborn Mo., U.S.A. 39°32N 94°46W 310 E2
Dease ➜ Canada 59°56N 128°32W 296 B3
Dease Inlet U.S.A. 71°2N 155°26W 303 A9
Dease L. Canada 58°40N 130°5W 296 B2
Dease Lake Canada 58°25N 130°6W 296 B2
Death Valley U.S.A. 36°15N 116°50W 307 J10
Death Valley △ U.S.A. 36°29N 117°6W 307 J9
Death Valley Junction U.S.A. 36°20N 116°25W 307 J10
Deatnu = Tana ➜ Norway 70°30N 28°14E 160 A23
Deauville France 49°23N 0°2E 172 C7
Deba Spain 43°18N 2°21W 196 B2
Deba Habe Nigeria 10°14N 11°20E 263 C7
Debagram India 23°41N 88°18E 243 H13
Debak Malaysia 1°34N 111°29E 235 B4
Debaltsevo Ukraine 48°22N 38°26E 189 H10
Debao China 23°21N 106°46E 228 F6
Debar N. Macedonia 41°31N 20°30E 202 E4
Debark Ethiopia 13°1N 37°48E 257 E4

Debden *Canada* 53°30N 106°50W **297** C7
Debdou *Morocco* 33°59N 3°0W **261** B4
Debe *Trin. & Tob.* 10°12N 61°27W **323** t
Dębica *Poland* 50°2N 21°25E **185** H8
Dęblin *Poland* 51°34N 21°50E **185** G8
Dębno *Poland* 52°44N 14°41E **185** F1
Débo, L. *Mali* 15°14N 4°15W **262** B4
DeBolt *Canada* 55°12N 118°1W **296** B5
Deborah East, L. *Australia* 30°45S 119°30E **279** F2
Deborah West, L. *Australia* 30°45S 119°5E **279** F2
Deboyne Is. *Papua N. G.* 10°43S 152°22E **286** F7
Debrc *Serbia* 44°38N 19°53E **202** B3
Debre Birhan *Ethiopia* 9°41N 39°31E **257** F4
Debre Markos *Ethiopia* 10°20N 37°40E **257** E4
Debre May *Ethiopia* 11°20N 37°25E **257** E4
Debre Sina *Ethiopia* 9°51N 39°50E **257** F4
Debre Tabor *Ethiopia* 11°50N 38°26E **257** E4
Debre Zebit *Ethiopia* 11°48N 38°30E **257** E4
Debre Zeyit *Ethiopia* 8°50N 39°0E **257** F4
Debrecen *Hungary* 47°33N 21°42E **182** C6
Debrzno *Poland* 53°31N 17°14E **184** E4
Debub □ *Eritrea* 14°45N 39°0E **257** E4
Debubawī K'eyih Bahrī □ *Eritrea* 13°30N 41°45E **257** E5
Debundscha *Cameroon* 4°7N 8°59E **263** E6
Deçan *Kosovo* 42°30N 20°18E **202** D4
Decatur *Ala., U.S.A.* 34°36N 86°59W **315** D11
Decatur *Ga., U.S.A.* 33°46N 84°16W **113** B3
Decatur *Ill., U.S.A.* 39°51N 88°57W **310** E8
Decatur *Ind., U.S.A.* 40°50N 84°56W **311** D12
Decatur *Mich., U.S.A.* 42°7N 85°58W **311** B11
Decatur *Tex., U.S.A.* 33°14N 97°35W **314** E6
Decazeville *France* 44°34N 2°15E **174** D6
Deccan *India* 18°0N 79°0E **244** F4
Deception, Mt. *Australia* 30°42S 138°16E **282** A3
Deception B. *Papua N. G.* 7°45S 144°40E **286** D3
Deception Bay *Australia* 27°10S 153°5E **281** D5
Deception I. *Antarctica* 63°0S 60°15W **151** C17
Deception L. *Canada* 56°33N 104°13W **297** B8
Dechang *China* 27°25N 102°11E **228** D4
Dechhu *India* 26°46N 72°20E **242** F5
Decimomannu *Italy* 39°19N 8°58E **200** C1
Děčín *Czechia* 50°47N 14°12E **180** A7
Decize *France* 46°50N 3°28E **173** F10
Deckerville *U.S.A.* 43°32N 82°44W **312** C2
Decollatura *Italy* 39°3N 16°21E **201** C9
Decorah *U.S.A.* 43°18N 91°48W **308** D8
Deda *Romania* 46°56N 24°50E **183** D9
Dedaye *Myanmar* 16°24N 95°53E **241** G5
Dedéagach = Alexandroupoli *Greece* 40°50N 25°54E **203** F9
Dededo *Guam* 13°31N 144°50E **302** d
Deder *Ethiopia* 9°19N 41°27E **257** F5
Dedham *U.S.A.* 42°15N 71°10W **116** B1
Dedopolis Tsqaro *Georgia* 41°33N 46°0E **219** K8
Dédougou *Burkina Faso* 12°30N 3°25W **262** C4
Dedovichi *Russia* 57°32N 29°56E **188** D5
Dedza *Malawi* 14°20S 34°20E **269** E3
Dee → *Aberds., U.K.* 57°9N 2°5W **167** D6
Dee → *Dumf. & Gall., U.K.* 54°51N 4°3W **167** G4
Dee → *Wales, U.K.* 53°22N 3°17W **168** D4
Deep B. *Canada* 61°15N 116°35W **296** A5
Deep Bay = Chilumba *Malawi* 10°28S 34°12E **269** E3
Deep Bay = Shenzhen Wan *China* 22°27N 113°55E **219** a
Deep Lead *Australia* 37°0S 142°43E **282** D5
Deep Water B. *Hong Kong, China* 22°14N 114°11E **122** B3
Deepwater *N.S.W., Australia* 29°25S 151°51E **281** D5
Deepwater *Mo., U.S.A.* 38°16N 93°47W **310** F3
Deer → *Canada* 58°23N 94°13W **297** B10
Deer I. *U.S.A.* 54°55N 162°18W **303** J7
Deer L. *Canada* 52°40N 94°20W **297** C10
Deer Lake *Nfld. & L., Canada* 49°11N 57°27W **299** C8
Deer Lake *Ont., Canada* 52°36N 94°20W **297** C10
Deer Lodge *U.S.A.* 46°24N 112°44W **304** C7
Deer Park *Fla., U.S.A.* 28°6N 80°54W **317** G9
Deer Park *Ohio, U.S.A.* 39°12N 84°23W **311** E12
Deer Park *Wash., U.S.A.* 47°57N 117°28W **304** C5
Deer River *U.S.A.* 47°20N 93°48W **308** B7
Deeragun *Australia* 19°16S 146°33E **280** B4
Deerfield *Ill., U.S.A.* 42°10N 87°51W **311** B9
Deerfield *Mo., U.S.A.* 37°50N 94°30W **310** G2
Deerfield Beach *U.S.A.* 26°19N 80°6W **317** J9
Deering *U.S.A.* 66°4N 162°42W **303** C7
Defensores del Chaco △ *Paraguay* 20°13S 60°27W **331** E5
Defiance *U.S.A.* 41°17N 84°22W **311** C12
Dega Medo *Ethiopia* 7°59N 43°1E **267** C5
Degana *India* 26°50N 74°20E **242** F6
Dêgê *China* 31°44N 98°39E **228** B2
Degebe → *Portugal* 38°13N 7°29W **195** G3
Degeberga *Sweden* 55°51N 14°5E **163** J8
Degeh Bur *Ethiopia* 8°11N 43°31E **267** C5
Dégelis *Canada* 47°30N 68°35W **299** C6
Degema *Nigeria* 4°50N 6°48E **263** E6
Degerfors *Sweden* 59°15N 14°27E **162** E8
Degerhamn *Sweden* 56°20N 16°24E **163** H10
Deggendorf *Germany* 48°50N 12°57E **179** G8
Degh → *Pakistan* 31°3N 73°21E **242** D5
Değirmendere *Turkey* 40°42N 29°47E **203** F13
Degirmenlik = Kythréa *Cyprus* 35°15N 33°29E **207** E9
Degunino *Russia* 55°52N 37°33E **129** A2
Deh Bīd *Iran* 30°39N 53°11E **247** D7
Deh Dasht *Iran* 30°47N 50°33E **247** D6
Deh-e Shīr *Iran* 31°29N 53°45E **247** D7
Deh Nugaleed, Dooxo *Somalia* 8°35N 48°35E **267** C6
Dehaj *Iran* 30°42N 54°53E **247** D7
Dehak *Iran* 27°11N 62°37E **240** D1
Déhane *Cameroon* 3°30N 10°5E **264** B2
Dehdez *Iran* 31°43N 50°17E **247** D6
Dehej *India* 21°44N 72°40E **242** J5
Dehestān *Iran* 28°30N 55°35E **247** D7
Dehgolān *Iran* 35°17N 47°25E **213** E12
Dehibat *Tunisia* 32°0N 10°47E **258** B2
Dehiwala *Sri Lanka* 6°50N 79°51E **245** L4
Dehlorān *Iran* 32°41N 47°16E **213** F12
Dehnow-e Kūhestān *Iran* 27°58N 58°32E **247** E8
Dehqonobod *Uzbekistan* 38°21N 66°30E **240** A2
Dehra Dun *India* 30°20N 78°4E **242** D8
Dehri *India* 24°50N 84°15E **243** G11
Dehua *China* 25°26N 118°14E **229** E12
Dehui *China* 44°30N 125°40E **227** B13
Deim Zubeir *South Sudan* 7°49N 26°16E **257** F2
Deinze *Belgium* 50°59N 3°32E **170** D3
Deir al Balah *Gaza Strip* 31°25N 34°21E **251** G5
Deir Dibwan *West Bank* 31°55N 35°16E **123** A2
Deir Ibzi'e *West Bank* 31°55N 35°7E **123** A1
Deira *U.A.E.* 25°16N 55°18E **119** A2
Deira Is. *U.A.E.* 25°17N 55°15E **119** A2
Dej *Romania* 47°10N 23°52E **183** C8
Deje *Sweden* 59°35N 13°29E **162** E7
Dejiang *China* 28°18N 108°7E **228** C7
Dejvice *Czechia* 50°6N 14°23E **135** B2
Deka → *Zimbabwe* 18°4S 26°42E **270** A4
Dekabristov, Ostrov *Russia* 59°56N 30°15E **137** B1
DeKalb *U.S.A.* 41°56N 88°46W **311** C8
Dekemhare *Eritrea* 15°6N 39°0E **257** D4
Dekese *Dem. Rep. of the Congo* 3°24S 21°24E **264** C4
Dekoa *C.A.R.* 6°19N 19°4E **264** A3
Del Caño Rise *Ind. Oc.* 45°15S 44°15E **273** J3
Del Carmen *Phil.* 9°50N 126°0E **233** G6
Del Mar *U.S.A.* 32°58N 117°16W **307** N9
Del Norte *U.S.A.* 37°41N 106°21W **305** H10
Del Rey *U.S.A.* 33°59N 118°25W **126** C2
Del Rio *U.S.A.* 29°22N 100°54W **314** G4
Delai *Sudan* 17°21N 36°6E **256** D4
Delambre I. *Australia* 20°26S 117°5E **278** D2
Delami *Sudan* 11°38N 30°23E **257** E3
Delano *U.S.A.* 35°46N 119°15W **307** K7
Delano Peak *U.S.A.* 38°22N 112°22W **304** G7
Delārām *Afghan.* 32°9N 63°25E **240** B1
Delareyville *S. Africa* 26°41S 25°26E **270** C4
Delaronde L. *Canada* 54°3N 107°3W **297** C7
Delavan *Ill., U.S.A.* 40°22N 89°33W **310** D7
Delavan *Wis., U.S.A.* 42°38N 88°39W **311** B8
Delaware *U.S.A.* 40°18N 83°4W **311** D13
Delaware □ *U.S.A.* 39°0N 75°20W **309** F16
Delaware B. *U.S.A.* 39°0N 75°10W **309** F16
Delaware Water Gap △ *U.S.A.* 41°10N 74°55W **313** E10
Delay → *Canada* 56°56N 71°28W **299** A5
Delbrück *Germany* 51°46N 8°34E **178** D4
Delčevo *N. Macedonia* 41°58N 22°46E **202** E6
Delegate *Australia* 37°4S 148°56E **283** D8
Delémont *Switz.* 47°22N 7°20E **179** H3
Delevan *U.S.A.* 42°29N 78°29W **312** D6
Delft *Neths.* 52°1N 4°22E **170** B4
Delft I. *Sri Lanka* 9°30N 79°40E **245** K4
Delfzijl *Neths.* 53°20N 6°55E **170** A6
Delgada, Punta *Chile* 52°28S 69°32W **336** D3
Delgado, C. *Mozam.* 10°45S 40°40E **269** E5
Delgerhet *Mongolia* 45°50N 110°30E **226** B6
Delgo *Sudan* 20°6N 30°40E **256** C3
Delhi *Ont., Canada* 42°51N 80°30W **312** D4
Delhi *India* 28°39N 77°13E **120** B2
Delhi *La., U.S.A.* 32°28N 91°30W **314** E9
Delhi *N.Y., U.S.A.* 42°17N 74°55W **313** D10
Delhi Gate *Delhi, India* **120** b3
Delhi Indira Gandhi Int. ✕ **(DEL)** *India* 28°34N 77°5E **120** B1
Deli Jovan *Serbia* 44°13N 22°9E **202** B6
Delia *Canada* 51°38N 112°23W **296** C6
Delice *Turkey* 39°54N 34°2E **212** C6
Delice → *Turkey* 40°45N 34°15E **212** B6
Délices *Dominica* 15°17N 61°17W **323** k
Delicias *Mexico* 28°13N 105°28W **318** B3
Delījān *Iran* 33°59N 50°40E **247** C6
Delimara Point *Malta* 35°49N 14°34E **206** F8
Déline *Canada* 65°11N 123°25W **294** D7
Delingha *China* 37°23N 97°23E **218** D8
Delisle *Canada* 51°55N 107°8W **297** C7
Delitzsch *Germany* 51°31N 12°20E **178** D8
Deliverance I. *Australia* 9°31S 141°34E **280** a
Dell City *U.S.A.* 31°56N 105°12W **314** F2
Dell Rapids *U.S.A.* 43°50N 96°43W **308** D5
Delle *France* 47°30N 7°2E **173** E14
Dellys *Algeria* 36°57N 3°57E **261** A5
Delmar *Iowa, U.S.A.* 42°0N 90°37W **310** C6
Delmar *N.Y., U.S.A.* 42°37N 73°47W **313** D11
Delmenhorst *Germany* 53°3N 8°37E **178** B4
Delmiro Gouveia *Brazil* 9°24S 38°6W **332** C4
Delnice *Croatia* 45°23N 14°50E **199** C11
Delonga, Ostrova *Russia* 76°40N 149°20E **215** B15
Deloraine *Tas., Australia* 41°30S 146°40E **281** G4
Deloraine *Man., Canada* 49°15N 100°29W **297** D8
Delos = Dilos *Greece* 37°23N 25°15E **205** D7
Delphi *Greece* 38°28N 22°30E **204** C4
Delphi *Ind., U.S.A.* 40°36N 86°41W **311** D10
Delphos *U.S.A.* 40°51N 84°21W **311** D12
Delportshoop *S. Africa* 28°22S 24°20E **270** C3
Delray Beach *U.S.A.* 26°28N 80°4W **317** J9
Delsbo *Sweden* 61°48N 16°32E **162** C10
Delta *Ala., U.S.A.* 33°26N 85°42W **316** B4
Delta *Colo., U.S.A.* 38°44N 108°4W **304** G9
Delta *Utah, U.S.A.* 39°21N 112°35W **304** G7
Delta □ *Nigeria* 5°30N 6°0E **263** D6
Delta Amacuro □ *Venezuela* 8°30N 61°30W **329** B5
Delta del Ebre △ *Spain* 40°43N 0°43E **196** E5
Delta del Po △ *Italy* 44°50N 12°15E **199** D9
Delta du Saloum △ *Senegal* 13°42N 16°43W **262** C1
Delta Dunărea △ *Romania* 45°15N 29°25E **183** E14
Delta Junction *U.S.A.* 64°2N 145°44W **303** D11
Deltebre *Spain* 40°43N 0°43E **196** E5
Deltona *U.S.A.* 28°54N 81°16W **317** G8
Delungra *Australia* 29°39S 150°51E **281** D5
Delvada *India* 20°46N 71°2E **242** J4
Delvinaki *Greece* 39°57N 20°32E **204** B2
Delvinë *Albania* 39°59N 20°6E **202** G4
Delyatyn *Ukraine* 48°32N 24°38E **183** B9
Demagiri *India* 22°55N 92°28E **241** D4
Demak *Indonesia* 6°53S 110°38E **233** G14
Demanda, Sierra de la *Spain* 42°15N 3°0W **196** C2
Demarcation Pt. *U.S.A.* 69°41N 141°18W **303** B12
Demarest *U.S.A.* 40°57N 73°57W **132** A2
Demavend = Damāvand, Qolleh-ye *Iran* 35°57N 52°7E **247** C7
Demba *Dem. Rep. of the Congo* 5°28S 22°15E **265** D4
Demba Chio *Angola* 9°41S 13°41E **265** D1
Dembecha *Ethiopia* 10°32N 37°30E **257** E4
Dembéni *Comoros Is.* 11°52S 43°23E **272** a
Dembéni *Mayotte* 12°50S 45°11E **272** b
Dembi *Ethiopia* 8°5N 36°25E **257** F4
Dembia *C.A.R.* 4°56N 23°53E **264** B4
Dembia *Dem. Rep. of the Congo* 3°33N 25°48E **268** B2
Dembica = Dębica *Poland* 50°2N 21°25E **185** H8
Dembidolo *Ethiopia* 8°34N 34°50E **257** F3
Demchok *India* 32°42N 79°29E **243** C8
Demer → *Belgium* 50°57N 4°42E **170** D4
Demerara Abyssal Plain *Atl. Oc.* 10°0N 48°0W **152** F7
Demerara-Mahaica □ *Guyana* 6°30N 58°8W **329** B6
Demetrias *Greece* 39°22N 23°1E **204** B5
Demidov *Russia* 55°16N 31°30E **188** E6
Deming *N. Mex., U.S.A.* 32°16N 107°46W **305** K10
Deming *Wash., U.S.A.* 48°50N 122°13W **306** B4
Demini → *Brazil* 0°46S 62°56W **329** D5
Demirci *Turkey* 39°2N 28°38E **205** B10
Demirköprü Barajı *Turkey* 38°42N 28°25E **205** C10
Demirköy *Turkey* 41°49N 27°45E **203** E11
Demirtas *Turkey* 36°25N 32°11E **250** B3
Demmin *Germany* 53°54N 13°2E **178** B9
Demnate *Morocco* 31°44N 6°59W **260** B3
Democracia *Brazil* 5°48S 61°26W **331** B5
Demonte *Italy* 44°19N 7°17E **198** D4
Demopolis *U.S.A.* 32°31N 87°50W **315** E11
Dempo *Indonesia* 4°2S 103°15E **234** C2
Demyansk *Russia* 57°40N 32°27E **188** D7
Den Bosch = 's-Hertogenbosch *Neths.* 51°42N 5°17E **170** C5
Den Burg *Neths.* 53°3N 4°47E **170** A4
Den Chai *Thailand* 17°59N 100°4E **236** D3
Den Haag = 's-Gravenhage *Neths.* 52°7N 4°17E **170** B4
Den Helder *Neths.* 52°57N 4°45E **170** B4
Den Ilp *Neths.* 52°27N 4°55E **112** A2
Den Lille Havfrue *Copenhagen, Denmark* **118** a3
Den Oever *Neths.* 52°56N 5°2E **170** B5
Denain *France* 50°20N 3°22E **173** B10
Denair *U.S.A.* 37°32N 120°48W **306** H6
Denali *U.S.A.* 63°4N 151°0W **303** E10
Denali △ *U.S.A.* 63°30N 152°0W **303** E10
Denau = Denov *Uzbekistan* 38°16N 67°54E **217** E7
Denbigh *Ont., Canada* 45°8N 77°15W **312** A7
Denbigh *Denbs., U.K.* 53°12N 3°25W **168** D4
Denbigh, C. *U.S.A.* 64°23N 161°32W **303** D7
Denbighshire □ *U.K.* 53°8N 3°22W **168** D4
Dendang *Indonesia* 3°7S 107°56E **235** C3
Dendé = Ndindi *Gabon* 3°46S 11°9E **264** C2
Dendermonde *Belgium* 51°2N 4°5E **170** C4
Deneba *Ethiopia* 9°47N 39°10E **257** F4
Deng Deng *Cameroon* 5°12N 13°31E **264** A2
Dengchuan *China* 25°59N 100°3E **228** E3
Denge *Nigeria* 12°52N 5°21E **263** C6
Dengfeng *China* 34°25N 113°2E **226** G7
Dengi *Nigeria* 9°25N 9°55E **263** D6
Dengkou *China* 40°18N 106°55E **226** D4
Denguélé □ *Côte d'Ivoire* 9°45N 7°30W **262** D3
Dengzhou *China* 32°34N 112°4E **229** A9
Denham *Australia* 25°56S 113°31E **279** E1
Denham, Mt. *Jamaica* 18°13N 77°32W **320** a
Denham Ra. *Australia* 21°55S 147°46E **280** C4
Denham Sd. *Australia* 25°45S 113°15E **279** E1
Denholm *Canada* 52°39N 108°1W **297** C7
Denia *Spain* 38°49N 0°8E **197** G5
Denial B. *Australia* 32°14S 133°32E **281** E1
Deniliquin *Australia* 35°30S 144°58E **283** C6
Denimoo = Fort Resolution *Canada* 61°10N 113°40W **296** A6
Denis *Gabon* 0°19N 9°22E **264** B1
Denison *Iowa, U.S.A.* 42°1N 95°21W **308** D6
Denison *Tex., U.S.A.* 33°45N 96°33W **314** E6
Denison, C. *Antarctica* 67°0S 142°40E **151** C10
Denison Plains *Australia* 18°35S 128°0E **278** C4
Denisovka *Kazakhstan* 52°27N 61°39E **216** B6
Denistone Heights *Australia* 33°48S 151°8E **139** A1
Deniyaya *Sri Lanka* 6°21N 80°33E **245** L5
Denizli *Turkey* 37°42N 29°2E **205** D11
Denizli □ *Turkey* 37°45N 29°5E **205** D11
Denman *Australia* 32°24S 150°42E **283** B9
Denman Glacier *Antarctica* 66°45S 100°0E **151** C8
Denmark *W. Austral., Australia* 34°59S 117°25E **279** F2
Denmark *S.C., U.S.A.* 33°19N 81°9W **316** B8
Denmark ■ *Europe* 55°45N 10°0E **163** J3
Denmark Str. *Atl. Oc.* 66°0N 30°0W **154** D8
Dennery *St. Lucia* 13°55N 60°54W **323** m
Dennison *U.S.A.* 40°24N 81°19W **312** F3
Denny *U.K.* 56°1N 3°55W **167** E5
Denov *Uzbekistan* 38°16N 67°54E **217** E7
Denpasar *Indonesia* 8°39S 115°13E **231** K18
Denpasar ✕ **(DPS)** *Indonesia* 8°44S 115°10E **231** K18
Denton *Ga., U.S.A.* 31°44N 82°42W **316** D7
Denton *Mont., U.S.A.* 47°19N 109°57W **304** C9
Denton *Tex., U.S.A.* 33°13N 97°8W **314** E6
Dentonia Park *Canada* 43°42N 79°17W **141** A3
D'Entrecasteaux, Îs. *N. Cal.* 18°0S 163°0E **277** D11
D'Entrecasteaux, Pt. *Australia* 34°50S 115°57E **279** F2
D'Entrecasteaux △ *Australia* 34°20S 115°33E **279** F2
D'Entrecasteaux Is. *Papua N. G.* 9°0S 151°0E **286** E6
Dentsville *U.S.A.* 34°4N 80°58W **316** B8
Denu *Ghana* 6°4N 1°8E **263** D5
Denver *Colo., U.S.A.* 39°42N 104°59W **304** G11
Denver *Ind., U.S.A.* 40°52N 86°5W **311** D10
Denver *Iowa, U.S.A.* 42°40N 92°20W **310** B4
Denver *Pa., U.S.A.* 40°14N 76°8W **313** F8
Denver City *U.S.A.* 32°58N 102°50W **314** E3
Denver Int. ✕ **(DEN)** *U.S.A.* 39°52N 104°40W **304** G11
Denwood = Wainwright *Canada* 52°50N 110°50W **297** C6
Deoband *India* 29°42N 77°43E **242** E7
Deobhog *India* 19°53N 82°44E **245** E6
Deodrug *India* 16°26N 76°55E **245** F3
Deogarh *Odisha, India* 21°32N 84°45E **244** D7
Deogarh *Raj., India* 25°32N 73°54E **242** G5
Deoghar *India* 24°30N 86°42E **243** G12
Deogyusan △ *S. Korea* 35°45N 127°40E **224** E3
Deokjeokdo *S. Korea* 37°13N 126°7E **224** D3
Deolali *India* 19°58N 73°50E **244** E1
Deoli = Devli *India* 25°50N 75°20E **242** G6
Déols *France* 46°50N 1°43E **173** F8
Deora *India* 26°22N 70°55E **242** F4
Deorha = Jubbal *India* 31°5N 77°40E **242** D7
Deori *India* 23°24N 79°1E **243** H8
Deoria *India* 26°31N 83°48E **243** F10
Deosai Mts. *Pakistan* 35°40N 75°0E **243** B6
Deosri *India* 26°46N 90°29E **241** B3
Depalpur *India* 22°51N 75°33E **242** H6
DePaul Univ. *U.S.A.* 41°55N 87°39W **119** B3
Deposit *U.S.A.* 42°4N 75°25W **313** D9
Deptford *U.K.* 51°28N 0°1W **125** B3
Depuch I. *Australia* 20°37S 117°44E **278** D2
Deputati, Camera dei *Rome, Italy* **136** b2
Deputatskiy *Russia* 69°18N 139°54E **215** C14
Dêqên *China* 28°34N 98°51E **228** C2
Deqing *China* 23°8N 111°42E **229** F8
Der-Chantecoq, L. du *France* 48°35N 4°40E **173** D11
Dera, Lach → *Somalia* 0°15N 42°17E **267** D5
Dera Ghazi Khan *Pakistan* 30°5N 70°43E **242** D4
Dera Ismail Khan *Pakistan* 31°50N 70°50E **242** D4
Derabugti *Pakistan* 29°2N 69°9E **242** E3
Derawar Fort *Pakistan* 28°46N 71°20E **242** E4
Derbent *Russia* 42°5N 48°15E **191** J9
Derbent *Turkey* 38°11N 28°33E **205** C10
Derby *W. Austral., Australia* 17°18S 123°38E **278** C3
Derby *Derby City, U.K.* 52°56N 1°28W **168** E6
Derby *Conn., U.S.A.* 41°19N 73°5W **313** E11
Derby *Kans., U.S.A.* 37°33N 97°16W **308** G5
Derby *N.Y., U.S.A.* 42°41N 78°58W **312** D6
Derby City □ *U.K.* 52°56N 1°28W **168** E6
Derby Line *U.S.A.* 45°0N 72°6W **313** B12
Derbyshire □ *U.K.* 53°11N 1°38W **168** D6
Derdap △ *Serbia* 44°40N 22°23E **202** B6
Derdepoort *S. Africa* 24°38S 26°24E **270** B4
Derecske *Hungary* 47°20N 21°33E **182** C6
Dereham *U.K.* 52°41N 0°57E **169** E8
Dereköy *Turkey* 41°55N 27°21E **203** E11
Dereli *Turkey* 40°44N 38°26E **213** B8
Derg → *U.K.* 54°44N 7°26W **166** B4
Derg, L. *Ireland* 53°0N 8°20W **166** D3
Dergachi = Derhaci *Ukraine* 50°9N 36°11E **189** G9
Derhaci *Ukraine* 50°9N 36°11E **189** G9
Derider *U.S.A.* 30°51N 93°17W **314** F8
Derik *Turkey* 37°21N 40°18E **213** D9
Derinkuyu *Turkey* 38°22N 34°45E **212** C6
Dermantsi *Bulgaria* 43°8N 24°17E **203** C8
Dermott *U.S.A.* 33°32N 91°26W **314** E9
Dernière Rivière *St. Lucia* 13°57N 60°55W **323** m
Dêrong *China* 28°44N 99°9E **228** C2
Derrinallum *Australia* 37°57S 143°15E **282** D5
Derry = Londonderry *U.K.* 55°0N 7°20W **166** B4
Derry *N.H., U.S.A.* 42°53N 71°19W **313** D13
Derry *Pa., U.S.A.* 40°20N 79°18W **312** F5
Derry City & Strabane □ *U.K.* 54°47N 7°22W **166** B3
Derryveagh Mts. *Ireland* 54°56N 8°11W **166** B3
Derudub *Sudan* 17°31N 36°7E **256** D4
Derval *France* 47°40N 1°41W **172** E5
Derveni *Greece* 38°8N 22°25E **204** C4
Derventa *Bos.-H.* 44°59N 17°55E **182** F2
Derwent → *Cumb., U.K.* 54°39N 3°33W **168** C4
Derwent → *Derby, U.K.* 52°57N 1°28W **168** E6
Derwent → *N. Yorks., U.K.* 53°45N 0°58W **168** D7
Derwent Water *U.K.* 54°35N 3°9W **168** C4
Derzhavīnsk *Kazakhstan* 51°6N 66°19E **217** B7
Des Moines *Iowa, U.S.A.* 41°35N 93°37W **310** C3
Des Moines *N. Mex., U.S.A.* 36°46N 103°50W **305** H12
Des Moines *Wash., U.S.A.* 47°24N 122°19W **306** C4
Des Moines → *U.S.A.* 40°23N 91°25W **310** D5
Des Moines ✕ **(DSM)** *U.S.A.* 41°32N 93°40W **310** C3
Des Plaines *U.S.A.* 42°2N 87°54W **311** B9
Des Plaines → *U.S.A.* 41°23N 88°15W **311** C8
Desa *Romania* 43°52N 23°2E **182** G8
Desaguadero *Peru* 16°34S 69°3W **330** D4
Desaguadero → *Argentina* 34°30S 66°46W **334** C2
Desaguadero → *Bolivia* 16°35S 69°5W **330** D4
Desantne *Ukraine* 45°34N 29°32E **183** E14
Désappointement, Is. du *French Polynesia* 14°10S 141°20W **289** f
Desaru *Malaysia* 1°31N 104°17E **237** d
Descanso, Pta. *Mexico* 32°21N 117°3W **307** N9
Descartes *France* 46°59N 0°42E **174** B4
Deschaillons-sur-St-Laurent *Canada* 46°32N 72°7W **299** C5
Deschambault L. *Canada* 54°50N 103°30W **297** C8
Deschutes → *U.S.A.* 45°38N 120°55W **304** D3
Descobrimento △ *Brazil* 16°53S 39°21W **333** E4
Dese *Ethiopia* 11°5N 39°40E **257** E4
Deseado, C. *Chile* 52°45S 74°42W **336** D2
Desenzano del Garda *Italy* 45°28N 10°32E **198** C7
Deseronto *Canada* 44°12N 77°3W **312** B7
Desert Center *U.S.A.* 33°43N 115°24W **307** M11
Desert Hot Springs *U.S.A.* 33°58N 116°30W **307** M10
Desert Wetlands Park *U.S.A.* 36°7N 115°2W **124** B2
Desertas, Ilhas *Madeira* 32°30N 16°30W **260** B1
Deset *Norway* 61°20N 11°26E **164** C8
Desfina *Greece* 38°25N 22°31E **204** C4
Deshaies *Guadeloupe* 16°18N 61°47W **322** e
Deshauteur *Guadeloupe* 16°15N 61°25W **322** e
Deshnok *India* 27°48N 73°21E **242** F5
Desierto Central de Baja California △ *Mexico* 29°40N 114°50W **318** B2
Desjardins, Complexe *Montréal, Canada* **130** b2
Deskati *Greece* 39°55N 21°49E **202** G5
Desna → *Ukraine* 50°33N 30°32E **177** C16
Desnătui → *Romania* 43°53N 23°35E **183** G8
Desnogorsk *Russia* 54°9N 33°17E **188** E7
Desolación, I. *Chile* 53°0S 74°0W **336** D2
Despeñaperros, Paso *Spain* 38°24N 3°30W **195** G7
Despeñaperros △ *Spain* 38°23N 3°32W **195** G7
Despotiko *Greece* 36°57N 24°58E **204** E6
Despotovac *Serbia* 44°6N 21°30E **202** B5
Dessau *Germany* 51°51N 12°14E **178** D8
Dessye = Dese *Ethiopia* 11°5N 39°40E **257** E4
Destin *U.S.A.* 30°24N 86°30W **317** E3
D'Estrees B. *Australia* 35°55S 137°45E **282** C2
Desuri *India* 25°18N 73°35E **242** G5
Desvres *France* 50°40N 1°48E **173** B8
Det Udom *Thailand* 14°54N 105°5E **236** E5
Deta *Romania* 45°24N 21°13E **182** E6
Dete *Zimbabwe* 18°38S 26°50E **270** A4
Detinja → *Serbia* 43°51N 20°5E **202** C4
Detmold *Germany* 51°56N 8°52E **178** D4
Detour, Pt. *U.S.A.* 45°40N 86°40W **308** C10
Detroit *U.S.A.* 42°19N 83°12W **312** D1
Detroit Lakes *U.S.A.* 46°49N 95°51W **308** B6
Detroit Metropolitan Wayne County ✕ **(DTW)** *U.S.A.* 42°13N 83°21W **311** B13
Detskoye Selo = Pushkin *Russia* 59°45N 30°25E **188** C6
Dettifoss *Iceland* 65°48N 16°24W **155** B10
Detva *Slovakia* 48°34N 19°25E **181** C12
Deua △ *Australia* 35°32S 149°46E **283** C8
Deurne *Neths.* 51°27N 5°49E **170** C5
Deutsch = Przemyśl *Poland* 49°50N 22°45E **185** J9
Deutsch Brod = Havlíčkův Brod *Czechia* 49°36N 15°33E **180** B8
Deutsch-Eylau = Iława *Poland* 53°36N 19°34E **184** E6
Deutsch Krone = Wałcz *Poland* 53°17N 16°27E **185** E3
Deutsch-Luxemburgischer △ *Germany* 49°58N 6°12E **179** F2
Deutsche Bucht *Germany* 54°15N 8°0E **178** A4
Deutsche Oper *Germany* 52°30N 13°19E **115** A2
Deutsches Museum *Germany* 48°7N 11°35E **131** B2
Deutschland = Germany ■ *Europe* 51°0N 10°0E **178** E6
Deutschlandsberg *Austria* 46°49N 15°14E **180** E8
Deux-Sèvres □ *France* 46°35N 0°20W **172** F6
Deva *Romania* 45°53N 22°55E **182** E7
Devakottai *India* 9°55N 78°45E **245** K4
Devaprayag *India* 30°13N 78°35E **243** D8
Devarkonda *India* 16°42N 78°56E **244** F4
Dévaványa *Hungary* 47°2N 20°59E **182** C5
Deveci Dağları *Turkey* 40°6N 36°15E **212** B7
Devecser *Hungary* 47°6N 17°26E **182** C2
Develi *Turkey* 38°23N 35°29E **212** C6
Deventer *Neths.* 52°15N 6°10E **170** B6
Devereux *U.S.A.* 33°13N 83°5W **316** B6
Deveron → *U.K.* 57°41N 2°32W **167** D6
Devesel *Romania* 44°28N 22°41E **182** F7
Devgad I. *India* 14°48N 74°5E **245** G2
Devgadh Bariya *India* 22°40N 73°55E **242** H5
Devgarh *India* 16°23N 73°23E **245** F1
Devi → *India* 19°59N 86°24E **244** E8
Devikot *India* 26°42N 71°12E **242** F4
Devil River Pk. *N.Z.* 40°56S 172°37E **285** A7
Devil's Bridge *Antigua & B.* 17°6N 61°41W **322** b
Devils Den *U.S.A.* 35°46N 119°58W **306** K7
Devils Hole = Death Valley △ *U.S.A.* 36°29N 117°6W **307** J9
Devils Island, I. = Diable, Île du *Fr. Guiana* 5°16N 52°34W **329** B7
Devils Lake *U.S.A.* 48°7N 98°52W **308** A4
Devils Paw *Canada* 58°47N 134°0W **296** B2
Devil's Peak *S. Africa* 33°57S 18°27E **118** A1
Devils Postpile △ *U.S.A.* 37°37N 119°5W **306** H7
Devil's Pt. *Sri Lanka* 9°26N 80°6E **245** K5
Devils Tower *U.S.A.* 44°35N 104°42W **304** D11
Devils Tower △ *U.S.A.* 44°48N 104°55W **304** D11
Devil's Woodyard Mud Volcanoe *Trin. & Tob.* 10°16N 61°22W **323** t
Devin *Bulgaria* 41°44N 24°24E **203** E8
Devine *U.S.A.* 29°8N 98°54W **314** G5
Devipattinam *India* 9°29N 78°54E **245** K4
Devizes *U.K.* 51°22N 1°58W **169** F6
Devli *India* 25°50N 75°20E **242** G6
Devnya *Bulgaria* 43°13N 27°33E **203** C11
Devoll → *Albania* 40°57N 20°15E **202** F4
Devon *Canada* 53°24N 113°44W **296** C6
Devon □ *U.K.* 50°50N 3°40W **169** G4
Devon I. *Canada* 75°10N 85°0W **295** B15
Devonport *Australia* 41°10S 146°22E **281** G4
Devrek *Turkey* 41°13N 31°57E **212** B4
Devrekâni *Turkey* 41°36N 33°50E **212** B5
Devrez → *Turkey* 41°6N 34°25E **212** B6
Devrukh *India* 17°3N 73°37E **244** F1
Dewas *India* 22°59N 76°3E **242** H7
Dewetsdorp *S. Africa* 29°33S 26°39E **270** C4
Dewey *Puerto Rico* 18°18N 65°18W **321** b
Dexing *China* 28°46N 117°30E **229** C11
Dexter *Maine, U.S.A.* 45°1N 69°18W **309** C19
Dexter *Mich., U.S.A.* 42°20N 83°53W **311** B13
Dexter *Mo., U.S.A.* 36°48N 89°57W **308** G9
Dexter *N. Mex., U.S.A.* 33°12N 104°22W **305** K11
Dey-Dey, L. *Australia* 29°12S 131°4E **279** E5
Deyang *China* 31°3N 104°27E **228** B5
Deyhūk *Iran* 33°15N 57°30E **247** C8
Deyyer *Iran* 27°55N 51°55E **247** E6
Dez → *Iran* 31°39N 48°52E **213** F13
Dezadeash L. *Canada* 60°28N 136°58W **296** A1
Dezfūl *Iran* 32°20N 48°30E **213** F13
Dezhneva, Mys *Russia* 66°5N 169°40W **215** C19
Dezhou *China* 37°26N 116°18E **226** F9
Dhadhar → *India* 24°56N 85°24E **243** G11
Dhahabān *Si. Arabia* 21°58N 39°3E **248** B2
Dhahiriya = Az Zāhirīyah *West Bank* 31°25N 34°58E **251** G5
Dhahran = Aẓ Ẓahrān *Si. Arabia* 26°10N 50°7E **247** E6
Dhak *Pakistan* 32°25N 72°33E **242** C5
Dhaka *Bangla.* 23°43N 90°26E **241** D3
Dhaka □ *Bangla.* 23°30N 90°0E **241** D2
Dhakuria *India* 22°30N 88°22E **124** B2
Dhali *Cyprus* 35°1N 33°25E **207** E9
Dhamangaon *India* 20°48N 78°9E **244** D4
Dhamār *Yemen* 14°30N 44°20E **248** D4
Dhamār □ *Yemen* 14°30N 44°20E **248** D4
Dhampur *India* 29°19N 78°33E **243** E8
Dhamra → *India* 20°47N 86°58E **244** D8
Dhamtari *India* 20°42N 81°35E **244** D5
Dhanbad *India* 23°50N 86°30E **243** H12
Dhangarhi *Nepal* 28°55N 80°40E **243** E9
Dhankuta *Nepal* 26°55N 87°40E **243** F12
Dhanora *India* 20°20N 80°22E **244** D5
Dhanpuri *India* 23°13N 81°30E **244** C5
Dhanushkodi *India* 9°11N 79°24E **245** K4
Dhar *India* 22°35N 75°26E **242** H6
Dharampur *India* 22°13N 75°18E **242** H6
Dharamsala = Dharmsala *India* 32°16N 76°23E **242** C7
Dharan *Nepal* 26°49N 87°17E **243** F12
Dharangaon *India* 21°1N 75°16E **244** D2
Dharapuram *India* 10°45N 77°34E **245** J3
Dharavi *India* 19°1N 72°51E **130** A2
Dharawal △ *Australia* 34°12S 150°52E **283** C9
Dhariwal *India* 31°57N 75°19E **242** D6
Dharla → *Bangla.* 25°46N 89°42E **243** G13
Dharmanagar *India* 24°22N 92°10E **241** C4
Dharmapuri *India* 12°10N 78°10E **245** H4
Dharmavaram *India* 14°29N 77°44E **245** G3
Dharmjaygarh *India* 22°28N 83°13E **243** H10
Dharmsala *India* 32°16N 76°23E **242** C7
Dharni *India* 21°33N 76°53E **242** J7
Dharug △ *Australia* 33°20S 151°2E **283** B9
Dharur *India* 18°3N 76°8E **244** E3
Dharwad *India* 15°30N 75°4E **245** G2
Dhasan → *India* 25°48N 79°24E **243** G8
Dhaulagiri *Nepal* 28°39N 83°28E **243** E10
Dhebar, L. *India* 24°10N 74°0E **242** G6
Dheftera *Cyprus* 35°5N 33°16E **207** D12
Dhemaji *India* 27°29N 94°35E **241** B5
Dhenkanal *India* 20°45N 85°35E **244** D7
Dherinia *Cyprus* 35°3N 33°57E **207** E9
Dheskáti = Deskati *Greece* 39°55N 21°49E **202** G5
Dhī Qār □ *Iraq* 31°0N 46°15E **246** D5
Dhiarrizos → *Cyprus* 34°41N 32°34E **207** E11
Dhībān *Jordan* 31°30N 35°46E **251** G6
Dhilwan *India* 31°31N 75°21E **242** D6
Dhimarkhera *India* 23°28N 80°22E **243** H9
Dholka *India* 22°44N 72°29E **242** H5
Dhomokós = Domokos *Greece* 39°10N 22°18E **204** B4
Dhond = Daund *India* 18°26N 74°40E **244** E2
Dhone *India* 15°25N 77°53E **245** G3
Dhoraji *India* 21°45N 70°37E **242** J4
Dhorpatan *Nepal* 28°29N 83°4E **243** E10
Dhragonisi = Tragonhsi *Greece* 37°27N 25°29E **205** D7
Dhrangadhra *India* 22°59N 71°31E **242** H4
Dhrol *India* 22°33N 70°25E **242** H4
Dhubāb *Yemen* 12°56N 43°25E **248** D3
Dhuburi *India* 26°2N 89°59E **241** B2
Dhulasar *Bangla.* 21°52N 90°14E **241** E3
Dhule *India* 20°58N 74°50E **244** D2
Dhupdhara *India* 26°10N 91°4E **241** B3
Dhurbo *Somalia* 11°37N 50°20E **267** B7
Dhusamarreeb *Somalia* 5°30N 46°15E **267** C6
Di-ib, W. → *Sudan* 22°38N 36°6E **256** C4
Di Linh *Vietnam* 11°35N 108°4E **237** G7
Di Linh, Cao Nguyen *Vietnam* 11°30N 108°0E **237** G7
Dia *Greece* 35°28N 25°14E **207** D7
Dia Deva = Butcher I. *India* 18°57N 72°53E **130** B2
Diabakania *Guinea* 10°38N 10°58W **262** C2
Diable, Île du *Fr. Guiana* 5°16N 52°34W **329** B7
Diable, Pt. du *Martinique* 14°46N 60°53W **322** j
Diables, Morne aux *Dominica* 15°37N 61°27W **323** k
Diablo Pt. *N. Marianas* 15°0N 145°35E **302** e
Diablo Range *U.S.A.* 37°20N 121°25W **306** J5
Diablotins, Morne *Dominica* 15°30N 61°24W **323** k
Diadema *Brazil* 23°41S 46°37W **137** C2
Diafarabé *Mali* 14°9N 4°57W **262** C4
Diala *Mali* 14°10N 9°58W **262** C3
Dialakoro *Mali* 12°18N 7°54W **262** C3
Dialakoto *Senegal* 13°21N 13°19W **262** C2
Diallassagou *Mali* 13°47N 3°41W **262** C4
Diamant, Pte. du *Martinique* 14°27N 61°3W **322** j
Diamant, Rocher du *Martinique* 14°27N 61°2W **322** j
Diamante *Argentina* 32°5S 60°40W **334** C3
Diamante *Italy* 39°41N 15°49E **201** C8
Diamante → *Argentina* 34°30S 66°46W **334** C2
Diamantina *Brazil* 18°17S 43°40W **333** E3
Diamantina → *Australia* 26°45S 139°10E **281** D2
Diamantina △ *Australia* 23°33S 141°23E **280** C3
Diamantino *Brazil* 14°30S 56°30W **331** C6
Diamond Bar *U.S.A.* 34°1N 117°48W **307** L9
Diamond Harbour *India* 22°11N 88°14E **243** H13
Diamond Head *U.S.A.* 21°16N 157°49W **302** K14
Diamond Is. *Australia* 17°25S 151°5E **280** B5
Diamond Mts. *U.S.A.* 39°40N 115°50W **304** G6
Diamond Springs *U.S.A.* 38°42N 120°49W **306** G6
Diamou *Mali* 14°5N 11°16W **262** C2
Dian Chi *China* 24°50N 102°43E **228** E4
Diana □ *Madag.* 12°15S 49°15E **272** A2
Dianalund *Denmark* 55°32N 11°30E **163** J5
Diana's Peak *St. Helena* 15°58S 5°42W **153** H6
Dianbai *China* 21°33N 111°0E **229** G8
Diancheng *China* 21°30N 111°4E **229** G8
Dianjiang *China* 30°24N 107°20E **228** B6
Diano Marina *Italy* 43°54N 8°5E **198** E5
Dianópolis *Brazil* 11°38S 46°50W **333** D2
Dianra *Côte d'Ivoire* 8°45N 6°14W **262** D3
Diaoyu Dao = Senkaku-Shotō *E. China Sea* 25°45N 123°30E **221** M1
Diaoyu Tai = Senkaku-Shotō *E. China Sea* 25°45N 123°30E **221** M1
Diapaga *Burkina Faso* 12°5N 1°46E **263** C5
Diapangou *Burkina Faso* 12°5N 0°10E **263** C5
Diariguila *Guinea* 10°35N 10°2W **262** C2
Diavolo, Mt. *India* 12°40N 92°56E **245** H11
Diba = Dibbā al Ḥiṣn *U.A.E.* 25°45N 56°16E **247** E8
Dibagah *Iraq* 35°52N 43°48E **213** E10
Dibai *India* 28°13N 78°15E **242** E8
Dibaya *Dem. Rep. of the Congo* 6°30S 22°57E **265** D4
Dibaya-Lubue *Dem. Rep. of the Congo* 4°12S 19°54E **265** C3
Dibbā al Ḥiṣn *U.A.E.* 25°45N 56°16E **247** E8
Dibbeen △ *Jordan* 32°20N 35°45E **251** F6
Dibella *Niger* 17°32N 13°6E **259** E2
Dibër □ *Albania* 41°30N 20°20E **202** E4
D'Iberville, Lac *Canada* 55°55N 73°15W **298** A5
Dibete *Botswana* 23°45S 26°32E **270** B4
Dibi *Cameroon* 7°8N 13°43E **264** A2
Dibru-Saikhowa △ *India* 27°40N 95°25E **241** B5
Dibrugarh *India* 27°29N 94°55E **241** B5
Diciosânmartin = Târnăveni *Romania* 46°19N 24°13E **183** D9
Dickens *U.S.A.* 33°37N 100°50W **314** E4
Dickenson B. *Antigua & B.* 17°10N 61°51W **322** b
Dickeyville *U.S.A.* 42°38N 90°36W **310** B6
Dickinson *U.S.A.* 46°53N 102°47W **308** B2
Dick's Pt. *The Bahamas* 25°4N 77°18W **153** b
Dickson = Dikson *Russia* 73°40N 80°5E **214** B9
Dickson *U.S.A.* 36°5N 87°23W **315** C11
Dickson City *U.S.A.* 41°28N 75°36W **313** E9
Dicle Barajı *Turkey* 38°20N 40°11E **213** C9
Dicle Nehri → *Turkey* 37°44N 41°10E **213** D9
Dicomano *Italy* 43°53N 11°31E **199** E8
Didesa, W. → *Ethiopia* 10°2N 35°32E **257** E4
Didiéni *Mali* 13°53N 8°6W **262** C3
Didim *Turkey* 37°22N 27°16E **205** D9
Didimbo *Angola* 17°30S 21°45E **265** F4
Didimotiho *Greece* 41°22N 26°29E **203** E10
Didsbury *Canada* 51°35N 114°10W **296** C6
Didwana *India* 27°23N 74°36E **242** F6
Die *France* 44°47N 5°22E **175** D9
Diébougou *Burkina Faso* 11°0N 3°15W **262** C4
Diecke *Guinea* 7°27N 8°54W **262** D3
Diedenhofen = Thionville *France* 49°20N 6°10E **173** C13
Diefenbaker, L. *Canada* 51°0N 106°55W **297** C7
Diegem *Belgium* 50°53N 4°26E **116** A2
Diego de Almagro *Chile* 26°22S 70°3W **334** B1
Diego Garcia *Ind. Oc.* 7°50S 72°50E **273** E6
Diego Martin *Trin. & Tob.* 10°43N 61°34W **323** t
Diego Ramírez, Islas *Chile* 56°30S 68°44W **336** E3
Diego Suarez = Antsiranana *Madag.* 12°25S 49°20E **272** A2
Diekirch *Lux.* 49°52N 6°10E **170** E6
Diéma *Mali* 14°32N 9°12W **262** C3
Diembéring *Senegal* 12°29N 16°47W **262** C1
Diemelsee △ *Germany* 51°20N 8°40E **178** D4
Diemen *Neths.* 52°21N 4°58E **112** A2
Dien Ban *Vietnam* 15°53N 108°16E **236** E7
Dien Bien Phu *Vietnam* 21°20N 103°0E **228** G4
Dien Chau, Vinh *Vietnam* 19°0N 105°55E **236** C5
Dien Khanh *Vietnam* 12°15N 109°6E **237** F7
Diepholz *Germany* 52°37N 8°22E **178** C4
Diepkloof *S. Africa* 26°14S 27°57E **123** B1
Dieppe *France* 49°54N 1°4E **172** C8
Dieppe Bay Town *St. Kitts & Nevis* 17°25N 62°48W **322** d
Dieprivier *S. Africa* 34°2S 18°27E **118** B1
Dierks *U.S.A.* 34°7N 94°1W **314** D7
Diest *Belgium* 50°58N 5°4E **170** D5
Dieterich *U.S.A.* 39°4N 88°23W **311** E8
Dietikon *Switz.* 47°24N 8°24E **179** H4
Dieulefit *France* 44°32N 5°4E **175** D9
Dieuze *France* 48°49N 6°43E **173** D13
Dievenow = Dziwnów *Poland* 54°2N 14°45E **184** D1
Dif *Somalia* 0°59N 40°58E **267** D5
Diffa *Niger* 13°18N 12°36E **263** C7
Diffa □ *Niger* 14°0N 12°30E **263** C7
Differdange *Lux.* 49°31N 5°54E **170** E5
Diffun *Phil.* 16°36N 121°33E **232** C3
Dig *India* 27°28N 77°20E **242** F7
Digba *Dem. Rep. of the Congo* 4°25N 25°48E **268** B2
Digboi *India* 27°23N 95°38E **241** B5
Digby *Canada* 44°38N 65°50W **299** D6
Digges Is. *Canada* 62°40N 77°50W **295** E16
Diggi *India* 26°22N 75°26E **242** F6
Dighinala *Bangla.* 23°15N 92°5E **241** D4
Dighton *U.S.A.* 38°29N 100°28W **308** F3
Digity Mud Volcanoes *Trin. & Tob.* 10°12N 61°25W **323** t
Diglur *India* 18°34N 77°33E **244** E3
Digna *Mali* 14°48N 8°10W **262** C3
Digne-les-Bains *France* 44°5N 6°12E **175** D10
Digoin *France* 46°29N 4°1E **173** F11
Digor *Turkey* 40°22N 43°25E **213** B10
Digos *Phil.* 6°45N 125°20E **233** H5
Digranes *Iceland* 66°4N 14°44W **155** A12
Digras *India* 20°6N 77°45E **244** D3
Digul → *Indonesia* 7°7S 138°42E **231** F9
Digya △ *Ghana* 7°15N 0°5E **263** D5
Dihang = Brahmaputra → *Asia* 23°40N 90°35E **241** D3
Diinsoor *Somalia* 2°24N 42°59E **267** D5
Dijlah, Nahr → *Asia* 31°0N 47°25E **246** D5
Dijon *France* 47°20N 5°3E **173** E12
Dikhil *Djibouti* 11°8N 42°20E **257** E5
Dikili *Turkey* 39°4N 26°53E **205** B8
Dikirnis *Egypt* 31°6N 31°35E **256** H7
Dikodougou *Côte d'Ivoire* 9°4N 5°45W **262** D3
Diksmuide *Belgium* 51°2N 2°52E **170** C2
Dikson *Russia* 73°40N 80°5E **214** B9
Dikti Oros *Greece* 35°8N 25°30E **207** E6
Dikwa *Nigeria* 12°4N 13°30E **263** C7
Dila *Ethiopia* 6°21N 38°22E **257** F4
Dilasag *Phil.* 16°25N 122°11E **232** C4
Dilbeek *Belgium* 50°51N 4°17E **116** A1
Dilek Yarimadisi △ *Turkey* 37°40N 27°10E **205** D9
Dili *Timor-Leste* 8°39S 125°34E **233** F7
Diligent Strait *India* 12°11N 92°57E **245** H11
Dilijan *Armenia* 40°46N 44°57E **191** K7
Dilinata *Greece* 38°13N 20°31E **207** C2
Dilj *Croatia* 45°29N 18°1E **182** E3
Dillenburg *Germany* 50°43N 8°17E **178** E4
Dilley *U.S.A.* 28°40N 99°10W **314** G5
Dilli = Delhi *India* 28°39N 77°13E **120** B2
Dilli *Mali* 15°1N 7°40W **262** B3
Dillia → *Niger* 14°9N 12°50E **259** F2
Dilling *Sudan* 12°3N 29°35E **257** E2
Dillingen *Bayern, Germany* 48°36N 10°30E **179** G6
Dillingen *Saarland, Germany* 49°22N 6°43E **179** F2
Dillingham *U.S.A.* 59°3N 158°28W **303** G8
Dillon *Sask., Canada* 55°56N 108°35W **297** B7
Dillon *Mont., U.S.A.* 45°13N 112°38W **304** D7
Dillon *S.C., U.S.A.* 34°25N 79°22W **315** D15
Dillon → *Canada* 55°56N 108°56W **297** B7
Dillsboro *U.S.A.* 39°1N 85°4W **311** E11
Dillsburg *U.S.A.* 40°7N 77°2W **312** F7
Dilolo *Dem. Rep. of the Congo* 10°28S 22°18E **265** E4
Dilos *Greece* 37°23N 25°15E **205** D7
Dilove *Ukraine* 47°56N 24°11E **183** C9
Dimapur *India* 25°54N 93°45E **241** C4
Dimas *Mexico* 23°43N 106°47W **318** C3
Dimasalang *Phil.* 12°12N 123°51E **232** E4

Dimashq *Syria* 33°30N 36°18E **250** E7
Dimashq □ *Syria* 33°30N 36°30E **250** E7
Dimbaza *S. Africa* 32°50S 27°14E **271** D4
Dimbelenge
Dem. Rep. of the Congo 5°33S 23°7E **265** D4
Dimbokro *Côte d'Ivoire* 6°45N 4°46W **262** D4
Dimboola *Australia* 36°28S 142°7E **282** D5
Dîmbovița = Dâmbovița ➝
Romania 44°12N 26°26E **183** F11
Dimbulah *Australia* 17°8S 145°4E **280** B4
Dimitrovgrad *Bulgaria* 42°5N 25°35E **203** D9
Dimitrovgrad *Russia* 54°14N 49°39E **190** C9
Dimitrovgrad *Serbia* 43°2N 22°48E **202** C6
Dimitrovo = Pernik
Bulgaria 42°35N 23°2E **202** D7
Dimitsana *Greece* 37°36N 22°3E **204** D4
Dimmitt *U.S.A.* 34°33N 102°19W **314** D3
Dimo *South Sudan* 5°19N 29°10E **257** F2
Dimona *Israel* 31°2N 35°1E **251** G6
Dimonika ⌓ *Congo* 4°13S 12°21E **264** C2
Dimovo *Bulgaria* 43°43N 22°50E **202** C6
Dinagat I. *Phil.* 10°10N 125°40E **233** F5
Dinagat Islands □ *Phil.* 10°0N 125°35E **233** F5
Dinaig *Phil.* 7°11N 124°10E **233** H5
Dinajpur *Bangla.* 25°33N 88°43E **241** G2
Dinalupihan *Phil.* 14°52N 120°28E **232** D3
Dinan *France* 48°28N 2°2W **172** D4
Dīnān Āb *Iran* 32°4N 56°49E **247** C8
Dinant *Belgium* 50°16N 4°55E **170** D4
Dinapur *India* 25°38N 85°5E **243** G11
Dinar *Turkey* 38°5N 30°10E **205** C12
Dīnār, Kūh-e *Iran* 30°42N 51°46E **247** D6
Dinara Planina *Croatia* 44°0N 16°30E **199** D13
Dinard *France* 48°38N 2°6W **172** D4
Dinaric Alps = Dinara Planina
Croatia 44°0N 16°30E **199** D13
Dinas *Phil.* 7°38N 123°20E **233** H4
Dinbych-y-Pysgod = Tenby
U.K. 51°40N 4°42W **169** F3
Dindanko *Mali* 14°8N 9°30W **262** C3
Dinde *Angola* 14°17S 13°42E **265** E2
Dinder, Nahr ed ➝ *Sudan* 14°6N 33°40E **257** E3
Dinder △ *Sudan* 12°30N 35°10E **257** E4
Dindi ➝ *India* 16°24N 78°15E **245** F4
Dindigul *India* 10°25N 78°0E **245** J4
Dindori *India* 22°57N 81°5E **243** H9
Ding Xian = Dingzhou
China 38°30N 114°59E **226** E8
Dinga *Dem. Rep. of the Congo* 5°17S 16°42E **265** D3
Dinga *Pakistan* 25°26N 67°10E **242** G2
Dingalan *Phil.* 15°18N 121°25E **232** D3
Dingalan B. *Phil.* 15°18N 121°25E **232** D3
Ding'an *China* 19°42N 110°19E **229** a
Dingbian *China* 37°35N 107°32E **226** F4
Dingelstädt *Germany* 51°18N 10°19E **178** D6
Dingle *Kerry, Ireland* 52°9N 10°17W **166** D1
Dingle *Sweden* 58°32N 11°35E **163** F5
Dingle B. *Ireland* 52°3N 10°20W **166** D1
Dingle Pen. *Ireland* 52°12N 10°5W **166** D1
Dingli *Malta* 35°52N 14°23E **206** F7
Dingmans Ferry *U.S.A.* 41°13N 74°55W **313** E10
Dingnan *China* 24°45N 115°0E **229** E10
Dingo *Australia* 23°38S 149°19E **280** C4
Dingolfing *Germany* 48°37N 12°30E **179** G8
Dingras *Phil.* 18°6N 120°42E **232** B3
Dingtao *China* 35°5N 115°35E **226** G8
Dinguiraye *Guinea* 11°18N 10°49W **262** C2
Dingwall *U.K.* 57°36N 4°26W **167** D4
Dingxi *China* 35°30N 104°33E **226** G3
Dingxiang *China* 38°30N 112°58E **226** E7
Dingyuan *China* 32°32N 117°41E **229** A11
Dingzhou *China* 38°30N 114°59E **226** E8
Dinh, Mui *Vietnam* 11°22N 109°1E **237** G7
Dinh Lap *Vietnam* 21°33N 107°6E **228** G6
Dinhata *India* 26°8N 89°27E **241** B2
Dinin ➝ *Ireland* 52°43N 7°18W **166** D4
Dinira △ *Venezuela* 9°57N 70°6W **328** B3
Dinokwe *Botswana* 23°29S 26°37E **270** B4
Dinorwic *Canada* 49°41N 92°30W **297** D10
Dinosaur ⌓ *Alta.,*
Canada 50°47N 111°30W **296** C6
Dinosaur ⌓ *Colo., U.S.A.* 40°30N 108°45W **304** F9
Dinuba *U.S.A.* 36°32N 119°23W **306** J7
Diö *Sweden* 56°37N 14°15E **163** H8
Dioïla *Mali* 12°23N 6°50W **262** C3
Dioka *Mali* 14°57N 10°4W **262** C2
Diomede *U.S.A.* 65°47N 169°0W **303** D5
Diona *Chad* 17°51N 22°36E **259** E4
Diongoï *Mali* 14°38N 8°34W **262** C3
Dionisades *Greece* 35°20N 26°10E **207** E7
Dionysos, Theatro *Athens, Greece* **112** c2
Diósgyör *Hungary* 48°7N 20°43E **182** B5
Diosig *Romania* 47°18N 22°2E **182** C7
Diougani *Mali* 14°19N 2°44W **262** C4
Diouloulou *Senegal* 13°5N 16°38W **262** C1
Dioura *Mali* 14°59N 5°12W **262** C3
Diourbel *Senegal* 14°39N 16°12W **262** C1
Diourbel □ *Senegal* 14°45N 16°15W **262** C1
Dipaculao *Phil.* 15°51N 121°32E **232** D3
Dipalpur *Pakistan* 30°40N 73°39E **242** D5
Diphu *India* 25°50N 93°26E **241** C4
Dipkarpaz = Rizokarpaso
Cyprus 35°36N 34°23E **207** E10
Diplo *Pakistan* 24°35N 69°35E **242** G3
Dipolog *Phil.* 8°36N 123°20E **233** G4
Dipperu △ *Australia* 21°56S 148°42E **280** C4
Dipton *N.Z.* 45°54S 168°22E **285** F3
Dir *Pakistan* 35°8N 71°59E **240** B3
Dirē *Mali* 16°20N 3°25W **262** B4
Dire Dawa *Ethiopia* 9°35N 41°45E **257** F5
Dirfis Oros *Greece* 38°40N 23°54E **204** C5
Diriamba *Nic.* 11°51N 86°19W **320** D2
Dirico *Angola* 17°50S 20°42E **265** F4
Dirk Hartog I. *Australia* 25°50S 113°5E **279** E1
Dirkou *Niger* 19°1N 12°53E **259** E2
Dirnismaning *Germany* 48°13N 11°38E **131** A2
Dirranbandi *Australia* 28°33S 148°17E **281** D4
Dirs *Si. Arabia* 18°32N 42°5E **248** C3
Dirschau = Tczew *Poland* 54°8N 18°50E **184** D5
Disa *India* 24°18N 72°10E **242** G5
Disa *Sudan* 12°5N 34°15E **257** E3
Disappointment, C.
U.S.A. 46°18N 124°5W **306** D2
Disappointment, L.
Australia 23°20S 122°40E **278** D3
Disaster B. *Australia* 37°15S 149°58E **283** D8
Discovery B. *Vic.,*
Australia 38°10S 140°40E **282** E4
Discovery B.
Hong Kong, China 22°18N 114°1E **122** B2
Discovery Bay △ *Australia* 38°9S 141°16E **282** E4
Discovery Seamount
Atl. Oc. 42°0S 0°10E **152** L12
Disentis Muster *Switz.* 46°42N 8°50E **179** J4
Dishna *Egypt* 26°9N 32°32E **256** B3
Disina *Nigeria* 11°35N 9°50E **263** C6
Disko = Qeqertarsuaq
Greenland 69°45N 53°30W **154** D5
Disko Bugt *Greenland* 69°10N 52°0W **154** D5
Disna = Dzisna ➝
Belarus 55°34N 28°12E **188** E5
Disney-M.G.M. Studios
U.S.A. 28°21N 81°33W **133** B1
Disney Reef *Tonga* 19°17S 174°7W **287** P13
Disney Studios *U.S.A.* 34°9N 118°19W **126** B3
Disneyland Hong Kong
China 22°19N 114°2E **122** B2
Disneyland Tōkyō
Tokyo, Japan 35°37N 139°53E **140** B4
Dispur *India* 26°3N 91°52E **241** B3
Diss *U.K.* 52°23N 1°7E **169** E9
Disteghil Sar *Pakistan* 36°20N 75°12E **243** A6
Distrito de Columbia □
U.S.A. 38°55N 77°0W **309** F15
Distrito Federal □ *Brazil* 15°45S 47°45W **333** E2
Distrito Federal □ *Mexico* 19°15N 99°10W **319** D5
Distrito Federal □
Venezuela 10°30N 66°55W **328** A4
Disûq *Egypt* 31°8N 30°35E **256** H7
Ditan Park *Beijing, China* **114** a2
Diu *India* 20°45N 70°58E **242** J4
Diuata Mts. *Phil.* 9°0N 125°50E **233** G5
Dīvāndarreh *Iran* 35°55N 47°2E **213** E12
Divarata *Greece* 38°20N 20°33E **207** C2
Divenié *Congo* 2°43S 12°1E **264** C2
Dives ➝ *France* 49°18N 0°7W **172** C6
Dives-sur-Mer *France* 49°18N 0°8W **172** C6
Divi Pt. *India* 15°59N 81°9E **245** G5
Divichi = Däväçi
Azerbaijan 41°15N 48°57E **191** K9
Divide *U.S.A.* 45°45N 112°45W **304** D7
Dividing Ra. *Australia* 27°45S 116°0E **279** E2
Divilacan B. *Phil.* 17°21N 122°19E **232** C4
Divinópolis *Brazil* 20°10S 44°54W **333** F3
Divisões, Serra dos *Brazil* 17°0S 51°0W **333** E1
Divjake *Albania* 41°0N 19°32E **202** F3
Divnoye *Russia* 45°55N 43°21E **191** H6
Divo *Côte d'Ivoire* 5°48N 5°15W **262** D3
Divriği *Turkey* 39°22N 38°7E **213** C8
Dīwāl Kol *Afghan.* 34°23N 67°52E **242** B2
Dix ➝ *U.S.A.* 37°49N 84°43W **311** G12
Dixie Mt. *U.S.A.* 39°55N 120°16W **306** F6
Dixie Union *U.S.A.* 31°20N 82°28W **316** D7
Dixmoor *U.S.A.* 41°37N 87°41W **119** D2
Dixon *Calif., U.S.A.* 38°27N 121°49W **306** G5
Dixon *Ill., U.S.A.* 41°50N 89°29W **310** C7
Dixon *Mo., U.S.A.* 37°59N 92°6W **310** G4
Dixon Entrance *U.S.A.* 54°30N 132°0W **303** J14
Dixville *Canada* 45°4N 71°46W **313** A13
Diyadin *Turkey* 39°33N 43°40E **213** C10
Diyālá □ *Iraq* 33°45N 44°50E **246** C5
Diyālá ➝ *Iraq* 33°13N 44°30E **213** F11
Diyarb Nigm *Egypt* 30°45N 31°26E **251** H2
Diyarbakır *Turkey* 37°55N 40°18E **213** D9
Diyarbakır □ *Turkey* 38°0N 40°10E **213** D9
Diyodar *India* 24°8N 71°50E **242** G4
Dizangué *Cameroon* 3°46N 9°59E **264** B1
Dja ⌓ *Cameroon* 3°10N 12°58E **264** B2
Djadié ➝ *Gabon* 0°46N 12°58E **264** B2
Djado *Niger* 21°4N 12°14E **259** D2
Djado, Plateau du *Niger* 21°29N 12°21E **259** D2
Djakarta = Jakarta
Indonesia 6°9S 106°52E **122** A2
Djalma Dutra = Miguel Calmon
Brazil 11°26S 40°36W **332** D3
Djalma Dutra = Poções
Brazil 14°31S 40°21W **333** D3
Djamâa *Algeria* 33°32N 5°59E **261** B6
Djamba *Angola* 16°45S 13°58E **265** F2
Djambala *Congo* 2°32S 14°30E **264** C2
Djanet *Algeria* 24°35N 9°32E **261** D6
Djanet □ *Algeria* 24°0N 9°0E **261** D6
Djaul I. *Papua N. G.* 2°58S 150°57E **286** B6
Djawa = Jawa *Indonesia* 7°0S 110°0E **235** D4
Djebel Tazzeka △ *Morocco* 34°6N 4°11W **260** B4
Djebiniana *Tunisia* 35°1N 11°0E **258** A2
Djédaa *Chad* 13°31N 18°34E **259** F3
Djelfa *Algeria* 34°40N 3°15E **261** B5
Djelfa □ *Algeria* 34°20N 3°40E **261** B5
Djema *C.A.R.* 6°3N 25°15E **264** A5
Djember *Chad* 10°25N 17°50E **259** F3
Djembo
Dem. Rep. of the Congo 9°54S 22°18E **265** D4
Djémila *Algeria* 36°19N 5°44E **261** A6
Djendel *Algeria* 36°15N 2°25E **261** A5
Djenné *Mali* 14°0N 4°30W **262** C4
Djenoun, Garet el *Algeria* 25°4N 5°31E **261** C6
Djerba *Tunisia* 33°48N 10°54E **258** B2
Djerba, Î. de *Tunisia* 33°50N 10°48E **258** B2
Djerém ➝ *Cameroon* 5°20N 13°24E **264** A2
Djerid, Chott *Tunisia* 33°42N 8°30E **258** B1
Djermaya *Chad* 12°24N 15°3E **259** F3
Djibo *Burkina Faso* 14°9N 1°35W **263** C4
Djibouti *Djibouti* 11°30N 43°5E **257** E5
Djibouti ■ *Africa* 12°0N 43°0E **257** E5
Djohong *Cameroon* 6°47N 14°20E **264** A2
Djolu *Dem. Rep. of the Congo* 0°35N 22°5E **264** B4
Djouab ➝ *Gabon* 1°13N 13°12E **264** B2
Djoudj △ *Senegal* 16°24N 16°14W **262** B1
Djougou *Benin* 9°40N 1°45E **263** D5
Djoum *Cameroon* 2°41N 12°35E **264** B2
Djouna *Chad* 10°27N 20°4E **259** F4
Djugu *Dem. Rep. of the Congo* 1°55N 30°35E **268** B3
Djúkbinj △ *Australia* 12°11S 131°2E **278** B5
Djúpavík *Iceland* 65°57N 21°34W **155** B5
Djúpivogur *Iceland* 64°39N 14°17W **155** C12
Djupvasshytta *Norway* 62°2N 7°16E **164** B4
Djurås *Sweden* 60°34N 15°8E **162** D9
Djurdjura △ *Algeria* 36°20N 4°15E **261** A5
Djurö △ *Sweden* 58°52N 13°28E **163** F7
Djursholm *Sweden* 59°24N 18°5E **139** A2
Djursland *Denmark* 56°27N 10°45E **163** H4
Dmitriya Lapteva, Proliv
Russia 73°0N 140°0E **215** B15
Dmitriyev Lgovskiy *Russia* 52°10N 35°0E **189** F8
Dmitriyevsk = Makiyivka
Ukraine 48°0N 38°0E **189** H9
Dmitriyevskoye = Talas
Kyrgyzstan 42°30N 72°13E **217** D8
Dmitrov *Russia* 56°25N 37°32E **188** D9
Dmitrovsk-Orlovskiy
Russia 52°29N 35°10E **189** F8
Dnepr = Dnipro ➝
Ukraine 46°30N 32°18E **189** J7
Dneprodzerzhinsk = Kamyanske
Ukraine 48°32N 34°37E **189** H8
Dneprodzerzhinskoye Vdkhr. = Dniprodzerzhynske Vdskh.
Ukraine 48°49N 34°8E **189** H8
Dnepropetrovsk = Dnipro
Ukraine 48°30N 35°0E **189** H8
Dneprorudnoye = Dniprorudne
Ukraine 47°21N 34°58E **189** J8
Dnestr = Dnister ➝
Europe 46°18N 30°17E **177** E16
Dnestrovski = Belgorod
Russia 50°35N 36°35E **189** G9
Dnieper = Dnipro ➝
Ukraine 46°30N 32°18E **189** J7
Dniester = Dnister ➝
Europe 46°18N 30°17E **177** E16
Dnipro *Ukraine* 48°30N 35°0E **189** H8
Dnipro ➝ *Ukraine* 46°30N 32°18E **189** J7
Dniprodzerzhynsk = Kamyanske
Ukraine 48°32N 34°37E **189** H8
Dniprodzerzhynske Vdskh.
Ukraine 48°49N 34°8E **189** H8
Dnipropetrovsk = Dnipro
Ukraine 48°30N 35°0E **189** H8
Dnipropetrovsk □
Ukraine 48°15N 34°50E **189** H8
Dniprorudne *Ukraine* 47°21N 34°58E **189** J8
Dnister ➝ *Europe* 46°18N 30°17E **177** E16
Dnistrovskyy Lyman
Ukraine 46°15N 30°17E **189** J6
Dno *Russia* 57°50N 29°58E **188** D5
Dnyapro = Dnipro ➝
Ukraine 46°30N 32°18E **189** J7
Do Gonbadān = Gachsārān
Iran 30°15N 50°45E **247** D6
Doabi *Afghan.* 36°1N 69°32E **240** A3
Doaktown *Canada* 46°33N 66°8W **299** C6
Doan Hung *Vietnam* 21°30N 105°10E **228** G5
Doany *Madag.* 14°21S 49°30E **272** A2
Doba *Chad* 8°40N 16°50E **259** G3
Dobandi *Pakistan* 31°13N 66°50E **242** D2
Dobbiaco *Italy* 46°44N 12°14E **199** B9
Dobbyn *Australia* 19°44S 140°2E **280** B3
Dobczyce *Poland* 49°52N 20°5E **185** J7
Dobele *Latvia* 56°37N 23°16E **184** B10
Döbeln *Germany* 51°6N 13°7E **178** D9
Doberai, Jazirah *Indonesia* 1°25S 133°0E **231** E8
Döberitz *Germany* 52°32N 13°3E **115** A1
Dobiegniew *Poland* 52°59N 15°45E **185** F2
Doblas *Argentina* 37°5S 64°0W **334** D3
Döbling *Austria* 48°14N 16°20E **142** A2
Dobo *Dem. Rep. of the Congo* 2°20N 22°11E **264** B4
Dobo *Indonesia* 5°45S 134°15E **231** F8
Doboj *Bos.-H.* 44°46N 18°4E **182** F3
Dobong *S. Korea* 37°39N 127°2E **137** B2
Dobongsan *S. Korea* 37°40N 127°0E **137** A2
Dobra *Wielkopolskie, Poland* 51°55N 18°37E **185** G5
Dobra *Zachodnio-Pomorskie,*
Poland 53°34N 15°20E **184** E2
Dobra *Dâmbovita,*
Romania 44°52N 25°40E **183** F10
Dobra *Hunedoara, Romania* 45°54N 22°36E **182** E7
Dobre Miasto *Poland* 53°58N 20°26E **184** E7
Dobreşti *Romania* 46°51N 22°18E **182** D7
Dobrich *Bulgaria* 43°37N 27°49E **203** C11
Dobrich □ *Bulgaria* 43°37N 27°49E **203** C11
Dobrinishte *Bulgaria* 41°49N 23°34E **202** E7
Dobřiš *Czechia* 49°46N 14°10E **180** B7
Dobrodzień *Poland* 50°45N 18°25E **185** H5
Dobromyl *Ukraine* 49°34N 22°46E **185** J9
Dobron *Ukraine* 48°25N 22°23E **182** B7
Dobropole *Ukraine* 48°25N 37°2E **189** H9
Dobrovolsk *Russia* 54°46N 22°31E **184** D9
Dobruja *Europe* 44°30N 28°15E **183** F13
Dobrush *Belarus* 52°25N 31°22E **177** B16
Dobrzany *Poland* 53°22N 15°25E **184** E2
Dobrzyń nad Wisłą *Poland* 52°39N 19°22E **185** F6
Doc, Mui *Vietnam* 17°58N 106°30E **236** D6
Doc Can I. *Phil.* 5°55N 119°56E **233** J2
Doce ➝ *Brazil* 19°37S 39°49W **333** E4
Docker River = Kaltukatjara
Australia 24°52S 129°5E **279** D4
Docklands *U.K.* 51°30N 0°1W **125** A3
Docksta *Sweden* 63°3N 18°18E **162** A12
Doctor Arroyo *Mexico* 23°40N 100°11W **318** C4
Doctor Pedro P. Peña
Paraguay 22°27S 62°21W **331** E5
Doctor Phillips *U.S.A.* 28°26N 81°29W **133** B2
Doctors Inlet *U.S.A.* 30°6N 81°47W **316** E8
Doda *India* 33°10N 75°34E **243** C6
Doda, L. *Canada* 49°25N 75°13W **298** C4
Doda Betta *India* 11°24N 76°44E **245** J3
Dodballapur *India* 13°18N 77°32E **245** H3
Dodecanese = Dodekanisa
Greece 36°35N 27°0E **205** E8
Dodekanisa *Greece* 36°35N 27°0E **205** E8
Dodge City *U.S.A.* 37°45N 100°1W **308** G3
Dodge L. *Canada* 59°50N 105°36W **297** B7
Dodger Stadium
Los Angeles, U.S.A. 34°4N 118°14W **126** B3
Dodgeville *U.S.A.* 42°58N 90°8W **310** B6
Dodo *Cameroon* 7°30N 12°3E **263** D7
Dodo *South Sudan* 5°10N 29°57E **257** F2
Dodola *Ethiopia* 6°59N 39°11E **257** F4
Dodoma *Tanzania* 6°8S 35°45E **268** D4
Dodoma □ *Tanzania* 6°0S 36°0E **268** D4
Dodoni *Greece* 39°40N 20°46E **204** B2
Dodori ⌓ *Kenya* 1°55S 41°7E **268** C5
Dodsland *Canada* 51°50N 108°45W **297** C7
Dodson *U.S.A.* 48°24N 108°15W **304** B9
Dodurga *Turkey* 39°49N 29°57E **205** B11
Doerun *U.S.A.* 31°19N 83°55W **316** D6
Doesburg *Neths.* 52°1N 6°9E **170** B6
Doetinchem *Neths.* 51°59N 6°18E **170** C6
Dog Creek *Canada* 51°35N 122°14W **296** C4
Dog I. *U.S.A.* 29°48N 84°36W **316** F5
Dog L. *Man., Canada* 51°2N 98°31W **297** C9
Dog L. *Ont., Canada* 48°48N 89°30W **298** C2
Dogana di Mare, Palazzo *Venice, Italy* **142** c3
Doğankent *Turkey* 36°52N 35°18E **250** B6
Doğanşehir *Turkey* 38°5N 37°53E **212** C7
Dogliani *Italy* 44°32N 7°56E **198** D4
Dōgo *Japan* 36°15N 133°16E **222** A5
Dōgo-San *Japan* 35°2N 133°12E **222** B5
Dogondoutchi *Niger* 13°38N 4°2E **263** C5
Dogons, Land of the = Bandiagara, Falaise de *Mali* 14°14N 3°29W **262** D4
Dogran *Pakistan* 31°48N 73°35E **242** D5
Dogs, Isle of *U.K.* 51°29N 0°1W **125** B3
Doğubayazıt *Turkey* 39°31N 44°5E **213** C11
Doguéraoua *Niger* 14°0N 5°31E **263** C6
Dogura *Papua N. G.* 10°6S 150°5E **286** F6
Doha = Ad Dawḥah
Qatar 25°15N 51°35E **247** E6
Doha Int. ✈ (DOH) *Qatar* 25°16N 51°34E **247** E6
Dohazari *Bangla.* 22°10N 92°5E **241** D4
Dohinog = Manukan
Phil. 8°32N 123°12E **233** G4
Dohrighat *India* 26°16N 83°31E **243** F10
Doi *Indonesia* 2°14N 127°49E **231** D7
Doi Inthanon *Thailand* 18°35N 98°29E **236** C2
Doi Inthanon △ *Thailand* 18°33N 98°34E **236** C2
Doi Khuntan △ *Thailand* 18°33N 99°14E **236** C2
Doi Luang *Thailand* 18°30N 101°0E **236** C3
Doi Luang △ *Thailand* 19°22N 99°35E **236** C2
Doi Phukha △ *Thailand* 19°8N 101°9E **236** C3
Doi Saket *Thailand* 18°52N 99°9E **236** C2
Doi Suthep Pui △ *Thailand* 18°49N 98°53E **236** C2
Doi Toa *Thailand* 17°55N 98°30E **236** D2
Dois Irmãos, Sa. *Brazil* 9°0S 42°30W **332** C3
Dojransko Jezero
N. Macedonia 41°13N 22°44E **202** E6
Doka *Sudan* 13°31N 35°46E **257** E4
Dokdo = Liancourt Rocks
Asia 37°15N 131°52E **221** F5
Dokka *Norway* 60°49N 10°7E **164** D7
Dokka ➝ *Norway* 60°49N 10°7E **164** D7
Dokkum *Neths.* 53°20N 5°59E **170** A5
Dokos *Greece* 37°20N 23°20E **204** D5
Dokri *Pakistan* 27°25N 68°7E **242** F3
Dokshukino = Nartkala
Russia 43°33N 43°51E **191** J6
Dokuchayevsk *Ukraine* 47°44N 37°40E **189** J9
Dol-de-Bretagne *France* 48°34N 1°47W **172** D5
Dolak, Pulau *Indonesia* 8°0S 138°30E **231** F9
Dolban = Līman *Russia* 45°45N 47°12E **191** H8
Dolbeau-Mistassini
Canada 48°53N 72°14W **299** C5
Dole *France* 47°7N 5°31E **173** E12
Doleib, Wadi ➝ *Sudan* 12°10N 33°15E **257** E3
Dolenji Logatec = Logatec
Slovenia 45°56N 14°15E **199** C11
Dolgellau *U.K.* 52°45N 3°53W **168** E4
Dolgelley = Dolgellau
U.K. 52°45N 3°53W **168** E4
Dolgoe Ozero *Russia* 60°0N 30°15E **137** A1
Dolhasca *Romania* 47°26N 26°36E **183** C11
Doliana *Greece* 39°54N 20°32E **204** B2
Dolianova *Italy* 39°22N 9°10E **200** C2
Dolinsk *Russia* 47°21N 142°48E **215** E15
Dolinskaya = Dolynska
Ukraine 48°6N 32°46E **189** H7
Dolj □ *Romania* 44°10N 23°30E **183** F8
Doll Museum *Delhi, India* **120** b3
Dollard *Neths.* 53°20N 7°10E **170** A7
Dollis Hill *U.K.* 51°33N 0°13W **125** A2
Dolna Banya *Bulgaria* 42°18N 23°44E **202** D7
Dolni Chiflik *Bulgaria* 42°59N 27°43E **203** D11
Dolní Chabry *Czechia* 50°8N 14°26E **135** B2
Dolni Chiflik *Bulgaria* 42°59N 27°43E **203** D11
Dolni Dabnik *Bulgaria* 43°24N 24°26E **203** C8
Dolni Dŭbnik = Dolni Dabnik
Bulgaria 43°24N 24°26E **203** C8
Dolní Počernice *Czechia* 50°5N 14°34E **135** B3
Dolnośląskie □ *Poland* 51°10N 16°30E **185** G3
Dolný Kubín *Slovakia* 49°12N 19°18E **181** B12
Dolo *Ethiopia* 4°11N 42°3E **257** G5
Dolo *Italy* 45°25N 12°5E **199** C9
Dolomites = Dolomiti
Italy 46°23N 11°51E **199** B8
Dolomiti *Italy* 46°23N 11°51E **199** B8
Dolomiti Bellunesi △ *Italy* 46°10N 12°5E **199** B9
Dolores *Argentina* 36°20S 57°40W **334** D4
Dolores *Phil.* 12°2N 125°29E **232** E5
Dolores *Uruguay* 33°34S 58°15W **334** C4
Dolores *Colo., U.S.A.* 37°28N 108°30W **305** H9
Dolores ➝ *U.S.A.* 38°49N 109°17W **304** G9
Dolovo *Serbia* 44°55N 20°52E **182** F5
Dolphin, C. *Falk. Is.* 51°10S 59°0W **153** f
Dolphin and Union Str.
Canada 69°5N 114°45W **294** D9
Dolphin Head *Jamaica* 18°22N 78°10W **320** a
Dolphin I. *Jamaica* 17°48N 77°10W **320** a
Dolsk *Poland* 51°59N 17°3E **185** G4
Dolton *U.S.A.* 41°38N 87°36W **119** D3
Dolungmukh *India* 27°30N 94°18E **241** B5
Dolyna *Ukraine* 48°58N 24°1E **183** B9
Dolynska *Ukraine* 48°6N 32°46E **189** H7
Dolynske *Ukraine* 47°32N 29°55E **183** C14
Dolzhanskaya *Russia* 46°37N 37°48E **189** J9
Dom Joaquim *Brazil* 18°57S 43°16W **333** E3
Dom Pedrito *Brazil* 31°0S 54°40W **335** C5
Dom Pedro *Brazil* 4°59S 44°27W **332** B3
Dom Pedro II, Parque
Brazil 23°33S 46°36W **137** B2
Doma = Gombe *Nigeria* 10°19N 11°2E **263** C7
Doma *Nigeria* 8°25N 8°18E **263** D6
Doma ⌓ *Zimbabwe* 16°28S 30°12E **269** F3
Domadare *Somalia* 1°52N 41°15E **267** D5
Domain, The *Sydney, Australia* **139** b2
Domaniç *Turkey* 39°48N 29°36E **205** B11
Domar, Enneri ➝ *Chad* 18°11N 18°4E **259** E3
Domariaganj ➝ *India* 26°17N 83°44E **243** F10
Domasi *Malawi* 15°15S 35°22E **269** F4
Domažlice *Czechia* 49°28N 12°58E **180** B5
Dombarovka = Dombarovskiy
Russia 50°46N 59°32E **214** D6
Dombarovskiy *Russia* 50°46N 59°32E **214** D6
Dombås *Norway* 62°4N 9°8E **164** B6
Dombasle-sur-Meurthe
France 48°38N 6°21E **173** D13
Dombe Grande *Angola* 12°57S 13°6E **265** E2
Dombes *France* 45°58N 5°0E **175** C9
Dombóvár *Hungary* 46°21N 18°9E **182** D3
Dombrád *Hungary* 48°13N 21°54E **182** B6
Dombrova = Dąbrowa Górnicza
Poland 50°15N 19°10E **185** H6
Dombrowitsa = Dubrovytsya
Ukraine 51°31N 26°35E **177** C14
Dome Argus *Antarctica* 80°50S 76°30E **151** E6
Dome C. *Antarctica* 75°12S 123°37E **151** D9
Dome of the Rock *Jerusalem* **123** b3
Domel I. = Letsôk-aw Kyun
Myanmar 11°30N 98°25E **237** G2
Domérat *France* 46°21N 2°32E **173** F9
Domett *N.Z.* 42°53S 173°12E **285** C8
Domeyko *Chile* 29°0S 71°0W **334** B1
Domeyko, Cordillera *Chile* 24°30S 69°0W **334** A2
Domfront *France* 48°37N 0°40W **172** D6
Dominador *Chile* 24°21S 69°20W **334** A2
Dominica ■ *W. Indies* 15°20N 61°20W **323** k
Dominica Passage
W. Indies 15°10N 61°20W **321** C7
Dominican Rep. ■
W. Indies 19°0N 70°30W **321** C5
Dominion Centre *Toronto, Canada* **141** b2
Domiongo
Dem. Rep. of the Congo 4°37S 21°15E **265** C4
Dömitz *Germany* 53°8N 11°15E **178** B7
Domme *France* 44°48N 1°12E **174** D5
Domnești *Romania* 45°12N 24°50E **183** E9
Domo *Ethiopia* 7°50N 47°10E **267** C6
Domodedovo *Russia* 55°26N 37°46E **188** E9
Domodedovo Int., Moscow ✈ (DME) *Russia* 55°24N 37°54E **188** E9
Domodóssola *Italy* 46°7N 8°17E **198** B5
Domogled-Valea Cernei △
Romania 44°52N 22°27E **182** F7
Domokos *Greece* 39°10N 22°18E **204** B4
Domoni *Comoros Is.* 12°15S 44°32E **272** a
Dompaire *France* 48°14N 6°14E **173** D13
Dompierre-sur-Besbre
France 46°31N 3°41E **173** F10
Dompim *Ghana* 5°10N 2°5W **262** D4
Dompu *Indonesia* 8°32S 118°28E **235** D5
Domrémy-la-Pucelle
France 48°26N 5°40E **173** D12
Domvena *Greece* 38°15N 22°59E **204** C4
Domville, Mt. *Australia* 28°1S 151°15E **281** D5
Domžale *Slovenia* 46°9N 14°35E **199** B11
Don ➝ *India* 16°20N 76°15E **245** F3
Don ➝ *Russia* 47°4N 39°18E **189** J10
Don ➝ *Aberds., U.K.* 57°11N 2°5W **167** D6
Don ➝ *S. Yorks., U.K.* 53°41N 0°52W **168** D7
Don, C. *Australia* 11°18S 131°46E **278** B5
Don Benito *Spain* 38°53N 5°51W **195** G5
Don Figuereroa Mts.
Jamaica 18°5N 77°36W **320** a
Don Mills *Canada* 43°44N 79°21W **141** A2
Don Muang Int. ✈ (BKK)
Thailand 13°53N 100°36E **113** A2
Don Sak *Thailand* 9°18N 99°41E **237** b
Dona Ana = Nhamaabué
Mozam. 17°25S 35°5E **269** F4
Doña Mencía *Spain* 37°33N 4°21W **195** H6
Donaghadee *U.K.* 54°39N 5°33W **166** B6
Donaghmore *Ireland* 52°52N 7°36W **166** D4
Donald *Australia* 36°23S 143°0E **282** D5
Donaldsonville *U.S.A.* 30°6N 90°59W **314** F9
Donalsonville *U.S.A.* 31°3N 84°53W **316** D5
Doñana △ *Spain* 36°59N 6°23W **195** J4
Donau = Dunărea ➝
Europe 45°20N 29°40E **183** E14
Donau ➝ *Austria* 48°10N 17°0E **181** C10
Donau Auen △ *Austria* 48°8N 16°44E **181** C9
Donau-Oder Kanal
Austria 48°12N 16°32E **142** A3
Donaueschingen *Germany* 47°56N 8°29E **179** H4
Donaufeld *Austria* 48°15N 16°24E **142** A2
Donaupark *Austria* 48°14N 16°24E **142** A2
Donaustadt *Austria* 48°13N 16°29E **142** A3
Donauwörth *Germany* 48°43N 10°47E **179** G6
Doncaster *U.K.* 53°32N 1°6W **168** D6
Dondo *Angola* 9°45S 14°25E **265** D2
Dondo
Dem. Rep. of the Congo 4°11N 21°39E **264** B4
Dondo *Mozam.* 19°33S 34°46E **269** F3
Dondo, Teluk *Indonesia* 0°50N 120°30E **231** D6
Dondra Head *Sri Lanka* 5°55N 80°40E **245** M5
Donduşeni *Moldova* 48°14N 27°36E **183** B12
Donegal *Ireland* 54°39N 8°5W **166** B3
Donegal □ *Ireland* 54°53N 8°0W **166** B4
Donegal B. *Ireland* 54°31N 8°49W **166** B3
Donets ➝ *Russia* 47°33N 40°55E **191** G5
Donets Basin *Ukraine* 49°0N 38°0E **158** F13
Donetsk *Ukraine* 48°0N 37°45E **189** J9
Donetsk □ *Ukraine* 47°30N 37°50E **189** J9
Dong Ba Thin *Vietnam* 12°8N 109°13E **237** F7
Dong Dang *Vietnam* 21°54N 106°42E **228** G6
Dong Giam *Vietnam* 19°25N 105°31E **236** C5
Dong Ha *Vietnam* 16°55N 107°8E **236** D6
Dong Hene *Laos* 16°40N 105°18E **236** D5
Dong Hoi *Vietnam* 17°29N 106°36E **236** D6
Dong Jiang ➝ *China* 23°6N 114°0E **229** F10
Dong Khe *Vietnam* 22°26N 106°27E **236** A6
Dong Phayayen *Thailand* 14°20N 101°22E **236** E3
Dong Ujimqin Qi *China* 45°32N 116°55E **226** B9
Dong Van *Vietnam* 23°16N 105°22E **236** A5
Dong Xoai *Vietnam* 11°32N 106°55E **237** G6
Donga *Nigeria* 7°45N 10°2E **263** D7
Donga ➝ *Nigeria* 8°20N 9°58E **263** D7
Dong'an *China* 26°23N 111°12E **229** D8
Dongan Hills *U.S.A.* 40°35N 74°5W **132** C1
Dongara *Australia* 29°14S 114°57E **279** E1
Dongargarh *India* 21°10N 80°40E **244** D5
Dongbei *China* 45°0N 125°0E **227** D13
Dongcheng *Beijing, China* **114** b2
Dongchuan *China* 26°8N 103°1E **228** D4
Dongdaemung *S. Korea* 37°34N 127°2E **137** B2
Dongducheon *S. Korea* 37°54N 127°3E **224** D3
Donges *France* 47°18N 2°4W **172** E4
Dongfang *China* 18°50N 108°33E **229** a
Dongfeng *China* 42°40N 125°34E **224** A2
Donggala *Indonesia* 0°30S 119°40E **235** C5
Donggan *China* 23°22N 105°9E **228** F5
Donggang = Tungkang
Taiwan 22°27N 120°26E **225** D2
Donggang *China* 39°52N 124°10E **224** C2
Donggou *China* 31°17N 121°33E **138** B2
Dongguan *China* 22°58N 113°44E **229** F9
Dongguang *China* 37°50N 116°30E **226** F9
Donghae *S. Korea* 37°29N 129°7E **224** D4
Donghai Dao *China* 21°0N 110°15E **229** G8
Dongjak *S. Korea* 37°30N 126°56E **137** B1
Dongjiao *China* 23°5N 113°12E **121** B2
Dongjingcheng *China* 44°5N 129°10E **227** B15
Dongkou *China* 27°6N 110°35E **229** D8
Donglan *China* 24°30N 107°21E **228** E6
Dongliao He ➝ *China* 42°58N 123°32E **227** C12
Dongliu *China* 30°13N 116°55E **229** B11
Dongmen *China* 22°20N 107°48E **228** F6
Dongnae *S. Korea* 35°12N 129°5E **224** G4
Dongning *China* 44°2N 131°5E **227** B16
Dongnyi *China* 28°3N 100°15E **228** C3
Dongo *Angola* 14°36S 15°48E **265** E3
Dongobe
Dem. Rep. of the Congo 4°35N 23°13E **264** B4
Dongola *Sudan* 19°9N 30°22E **256** D3
Dongou *Congo* 2°0N 18°5E **264** B3
Dongping *China* 35°55N 116°20E **226** G9
Dongri *India* 18°53N 72°57E **130** B2
Dongsha Dao
S. China Sea 20°45N 116°43E **219** G12
Dongshan = Tungshan
Taiwan 24°38N 121°47E **225** B3
Dongshan *China* 23°43N 117°30E **229** F11
Dongshanhu Park *China* 23°7N 113°17E **121** B2
Dongsheng = Ordos
China 39°50N 110°0E **226** E6
Dongshi = Tungshih *Changhua,*
Taiwan 24°12N 120°43E **225** B2
Dongshi = Tungshih *Chiai,*
Taiwan 23°27N 120°8E **225** C2
Dongsi Mosque *Beijing, China* **114** b2
Dongtai *China* 32°51N 120°21E **229** A13
Dongting Hu *China* 29°18N 112°45E **229** C9
Dongtou *China* 27°51N 121°10E **229** D13
Dongwe ➝ *Zambia* 13°59S 23°53E **265** E4
Dongxiang *China* 28°11N 116°34E **229** C11
Dongxing *China* 21°34N 108°0E **228** G7
Dongyang *China* 29°13N 120°15E **229** C13
Dongying *China* 37°37N 118°37E **227** F10
Dongyinggang *China* 37°55N 118°58E **227** F10
Dongzhi *China* 30°9N 117°0E **229** B11
Dongzhimen *China* 39°55N 116°24E **114** B2
Donington, C. *Australia* 34°45S 136°0E **282** C2
Doniphan *U.S.A.* 36°37N 90°50W **308** G8
Donja Stubica *Croatia* 45°59N 15°59E **199** C12
Donji Dušnik *Serbia* 43°12N 22°5E **202** C6
Donji Miholjac *Croatia* 45°45N 18°10E **182** E3
Donji Milanovac *Serbia* 44°28N 22°6E **202** B6
Donji Vakuf *Bos.-H.* 44°8N 17°24E **182** F2
Dønna *Nordland, Norway* 66°6N 12°30E **160** C15
Donna *Tex., U.S.A.* 26°9N 98°4W **314** H5
Donnacona *Canada* 46°41N 71°41W **299** C5
Donnelly's Crossing *N.Z.* 35°42S 173°38E **284** B2
Donner Pass *U.S.A.* 39°19N 120°20W **306** F6
Donnybrook *W. Austral.,*
Australia 33°34S 115°48E **279** F2
Donnybrook *KwaZulu Natal,*
S. Africa 29°59S 29°48E **271** C4
Donora *U.S.A.* 40°11N 79°52W **312** F5
Donostia = Donostia-San Sebastián
Spain 43°17N 1°58W **196** B3
Donostia-San Sebastián
Spain 43°17N 1°58W **196** B3
Donousa *Greece* 37°8N 25°48E **205** D7
Donovan *U.S.A.* 40°53N 87°37W **311** D9
Donque *Angola* 15°28S 14°6E **265** F2
Donskoy *Russia* 53°55N 38°15E **188** F10
Donsol *Phil.* 12°54N 123°36E **232** E4
Donwood *Canada* 44°19N 78°16W **312** B6
Donzère *France* 44°28N 4°43E **175** D8
Donzy *France* 47°20N 3°6E **173** E10
Dookie *Australia* 36°20S 145°41E **283** D6
Doomadgee *Australia* 17°56S 138°49E **280** B2
Doomadgee ◎ *Australia* 17°56S 138°49E **280** B2
Doon ➝ *U.K.* 55°27N 4°39W **167** F4
Doon Doon ◎ *Australia* 16°18S 128°14E **278** C4
Doornfontein *S. Africa* 26°11S 28°3E **123** B2
Doornik = Tournai
Belgium 50°35N 3°25E **170** D3
Dora *Iraq* 33°15N 44°23E **113** A2
Dora, L. *Australia* 22°0S 123°0E **278** D3
Dora Báltea ➝ *Italy* 45°11N 8°3E **198** C5
Dora Ripária ➝ *Italy* 45°5N 7°44E **198** C4
Doran L. *Canada* 61°13N 108°6W **297** A7
Doraville *U.S.A.* 33°54N 84°17W **316** B5
Dorchester *Dorset, U.K.* 50°42N 2°27W **169** G5
Dorchester *Mass., U.S.A.* 42°17N 71°4W **116** B2
Dorchester, C. *Canada* 65°27N 77°27W **295** D16
Dorchester B. *U.S.A.* 42°18N 71°1W **116** B2
Dorchester Heights Nat. Historical Site ⌂ *U.S.A.* 42°20N 71°2W **116** B2
Dordabis *Namibia* 22°52S 17°38E **270** B2
Dordogne □ *France* 45°5N 0°40E **174** C4
Dordogne ➝ *France* 45°2N 0°36W **174** C3
Dordrecht *Neths.* 51°48N 4°39E **170** C4
Dordrecht *Eastern Cape,*
S. Africa 31°20S 27°3E **270** D4
Dore ➝ *France* 45°50N 3°35E **174** C7
Dore, Mts. *France* 45°32N 2°50E **174** C6
Doré L. *Canada* 54°46N 107°17W **297** C7
Dorée ➝ *St. Lucia* 13°46N 61°3W **323** m
Dores da Boa Esperança = Boa Esperança *Brazil* 3°21N 61°23W **329** C5
Dores do Indaiá *Brazil* 19°27S 45°36W **333** E2
Dorfen *Germany* 48°15N 12°8E **179** G8
Dorgali *Italy* 40°17N 9°35E **200** B2
Dori *Burkina Faso* 14°3N 0°2W **263** C4
Doring ➝ *S. Africa* 31°54S 18°39E **270** D2
Doringbos *S. Africa* 31°59S 19°16E **270** D2
Dorking *U.K.* 51°14N 0°19W **169** F7
Dormaa-Ahenkro *Ghana* 7°15N 2°52W **262** D4
Dormans *France* 49°4N 3°38E **173** C10
Dormo, Ras *Eritrea* 13°14N 42°35E **257** E5
Dornach *Germany* 48°9N 11°41E **131** B3
Dornakal *India* 17°27N 80°10E **244** F5
Dornbirn *Austria* 47°25N 9°45E **180** D2
Dornes *France* 46°48N 3°18E **173** F10
Dornești *Romania* 47°52N 26°1E **183** C11
Dornie *U.K.* 57°17N 5°31W **167** D3
Dornoch *Ont., Canada* 44°18N 80°51W **312** B4
Dornoch *Highl., U.K.* 57°53N 4°2W **167** D4
Dornoch Firth *U.K.* 57°51N 4°4W **167** D4
Dornogovĭ □ *Mongolia* 44°0N 110°0E **226** C6
Doro *Mali* 16°9N 0°51W **263** B4
Doro, Kavo *Greece* 38°9N 24°38E **204** C6
Dorog *Hungary* 47°42N 18°45E **182** C3
Dorogobuzh *Russia* 54°50N 33°18E **188** E7
Dorohoi *Romania* 47°56N 26°23E **183** C11
Döröö Nuur *Mongolia* 48°0N 93°0E **217** C12
Dorpat = Tartu *Estonia* 58°20N 26°44E **188** C4
Dorr *Iran* 33°17N 50°38E **247** C6
Dorre I. *Australia* 25°13S 113°12E **279** E1
Dorrigo *Australia* 30°20S 152°44E **283** A10
Dorrigo △ *Australia* 30°22S 152°47E **283** A10
Dorris *U.S.A.* 41°58N 121°55W **304** F3
Dorset *Ont., Canada* 45°14N 78°54W **312** A6
Dorset *Ohio, U.S.A.* 41°40N 80°40W **312** E4
Dorset *Vt., U.S.A.* 43°15N 73°5W **313** C11
Dorset □ *U.K.* 50°45N 2°26W **169** G5
Dorsoduro *Venice, Italy* **142** b1
Dorsten *Germany* 51°40N 6°58E **178** D2
Dortmund *Germany* 51°30N 7°28E **178** D3
Dortmund-Ems-Kanal ➝
Germany 51°50N 7°26E **178** D3
Dörtyol *Turkey* 36°50N 36°13E **250** B7
Doruk *Turkey* 36°53N 35°45E **250** B6
Dorum *Germany* 53°41N 8°34E **178** B4
Doruma
Dem. Rep. of the Congo 4°42N 27°33E **268** B2
Dorūneh *Iran* 35°10N 57°18E **247** C8
Dorval Int., Montréal ✈ (YUL)
Canada 45°28N 73°44W **130** B1
Dos Bahías, C. *Argentina* 44°58S 65°32W **336** B3
Dos d'Âne *Réunion* 20°58S 55°23E **272** f
Dos Hermanas *Spain* 37°16N 5°55W **195** H5
Dos Moninos ➝ *Brazil* 23°40S 46°33W **137** B2
Dos Palos *U.S.A.* 36°59N 120°37W **306** J6
Döşemealtı *Turkey* 37°4N 30°36E **205** D12
Dosso *Niger* 13°0N 3°13E **263** C5
Dosso □ *Niger* 13°30N 3°30E **263** C5
Dosso ⌓ *Niger* 12°36N 2°36E **263** C5
Dostyq *Kazakhstan* 45°15N 82°29E **217** C10
Dot Lake *U.S.A.* 63°40N 144°4W **303** E11
Dothan *U.S.A.* 31°13N 85°24W **316** D4
Doty *U.S.A.* 46°38N 123°17W **306** D3
Douai *France* 50°21N 3°4E **173** B10
Douako *Guinea* 9°45N 10°8W **262** D2
Douala *Cameroon* 4°0N 9°45E **263** E6
Douala-Édéa ⌓ *Cameroon* 3°20N 9°41E **264** B1
Douamounou, C. *Mayotte* 12°38S 45°8E **272** b
Douaouir *Mali* 20°45N 3°0W **260** D4
Douarnenez *France* 48°6N 4°21W **172** D2
Doubabougou *Mali* 14°13N 7°59W **262** C3
Double Cone *N.Z.* 45°4S 168°49E **285** F3
Double Island Pt.
Australia 25°56S 153°11E **281** D5
Double Mountain Fork ➝
U.S.A. 33°16N 100°0W **314** E4
Doubrava ➝ *Czechia* 50°2N 15°20E **180** A8
Doubs □ *France* 47°10N 6°20E **173** E13
Doubs ➝ *France* 46°53N 5°1E **173** F12
Doubtful Sd. *N.Z.* 45°20S 166°49E **285** F1
Doubtless B. *N.Z.* 34°55S 173°26E **284** A2
Doudeville *France* 49°43N 0°47E **172** C7
Doué-la-Fontaine *France* 47°11N 0°16W **172** E6
Douentza *Mali* 14°58N 2°48W **262** C4
Douentza ⌓ *Mali* 15°40N 2°25W **262** B4
Dougga *Tunisia* 36°25N 9°13E **258** A1
Doughboy B. *N.Z.* 47°2S 167°40E **285** H2
Douglas *Ont., Canada* 45°31N 76°56W **312** A8
Douglas *I. of Man* 54°10N 4°28W **168** C3
Douglas *Northern Cape,*
S. Africa 29°4S 23°46E **270** C3
Douglas *Alaska, U.S.A.* 58°17N 134°24W **303** G14
Douglas *Ariz., U.S.A.* 31°21N 109°33W **305** L9
Douglas *Ga., U.S.A.* 31°31N 82°51W **316** D7
Douglas *Mich., U.S.A.* 42°39N 86°14W **311** B10
Douglas *Wyo., U.S.A.* 42°45N 105°24W **304** E11
Douglas Apsley △
Australia 41°45S 148°11E **281** G4
Douglas B. *Dominica* 15°36N 61°29W **323** k
Douglas C. *U.S.A.* 58°51N 153°15W **303** G9
Douglas Chan. *Canada* 53°40N 129°20W **296** C3
Douglas Park *U.S.A.* 41°51N 87°42W **119** B2
Douglas Pt. *Canada* 44°19N 81°37W **312** B3
Douglasville *U.S.A.* 33°45N 84°45W **316** B5
Douirat *Morocco* 33°2N 4°11W **260** B4
Doukaton, Akra *Greece* 38°34N 20°33E **207** B2
Doukoula *Cameroon* 10°10N 15°0E **259** F2
Doulevant-le-Château
France 48°23N 4°55E **173** D11
Douliou = Touliu *Taiwan* 23°42N 120°31E **225** C2
Doullens *France* 50°10N 2°20E **173** B9
Doumé *Cameroon* 4°15N 13°25E **264** B2
Doumen *China* 22°10N 113°18E **229** F9
Douna *Mali* 13°13N 6°0W **262** C3
Dounan = Tounan
Taiwan 23°41N 120°28E **225** C2
Dounreay *U.K.* 58°35N 3°44W **167** C5
Dourada, Serra *Brazil* 13°10S 48°45W **333** D2
Dourados *Brazil* 22°9S 54°50W **335** A5
Dourados ➝ *Brazil* 21°58S 54°18W **335** A5
Dourados, Serra dos
Brazil 23°30S 53°30W **335** A5
Dourbali *Chad* 11°49N 15°52E **259** F3
Dourdan *France* 48°30N 2°1E **173** D9
Douro ➝ *Europe* 41°8N 8°40W **194** D2
Douvaine *France* 46°19N 6°16E **173** F13
Douville *Guadeloupe* 16°15N 61°22W **322** e
Douz *Tunisia* 33°25N 9°0E **258** B1
Douze ➝ *France* 43°54N 0°30W **174** E3
Dove ➝ *U.K.* 52°51N 1°36W **168** E6
Dove Creek *U.S.A.* 37°46N 108°54W **305** H9
Dover *Tas., Australia* 43°18S 147°2E **281** G4
Dover *Kent, U.K.* 51°7N 1°19E **169** F9
Dover *Del., U.S.A.* 39°10N 75°32W **309** F16
Dover *Ky., U.S.A.* 38°43N 83°52W **311** F13
Dover *N.H., U.S.A.* 43°12N 70°56W **313** C14
Dover *N.J., U.S.A.* 40°53N 74°34W **313** F10
Dover *Ohio, U.S.A.* 40°32N 81°29W **312** F3
Dover, Pt. *Australia* 32°32S 125°32E **279** F4
Dover, Str. of *Europe* 51°0N 1°30E **169** G9
Dover-Foxcroft *U.S.A.* 45°11N 69°13W **309** C19
Dover Heights *Australia* 33°52S 151°16E **139** B2
Dover Plains *U.S.A.* 41°43N 73°35W **313** E11
Dovey = Dyfi ➝ *U.K.* 52°32N 4°3W **169** E3
Dovhe *Ukraine* 48°22N 23°17E **183** B8
Dovlen = Devin *Bulgaria* 41°44N 24°24E **203** E8
Dovre *Norway* 61°58N 9°15E **164** C6
Dovre △ *Norway* 62°10N 9°30E **164** B6
Dovrefjell *Norway* 62°15N 9°33E **164** B6
Dovrefjell-Sunndalsfjella △
Norway 62°23N 9°11E **164** B6
Dow Rūd *Iran* 33°28N 49°4E **247** C6
Dowa *Malawi* 13°38S 33°58E **269** E3
Dowagiac *U.S.A.* 41°59N 86°6W **311** C10
Dowerin *Australia* 31°12S 117°2E **279** F2
Dowgha'i *Iran* 36°54N 58°32E **247** B8

Dowlat Yār *Afghan.* 34°30N 65°45E **240** B2
Dowlatābād *Farāh, Afghan.* 32°47N 62°40E **240** B1
Dowlatābād *Fāryāb, Afghan.* 36°26N 64°55E **240** A2
Dowlatābād *Kermān, Iran* 28°20N 56°40E **247** D8
Dowlatābād *Khorāsān, Iran* 35°16N 59°29E **247** C8
Dowlatābād *Tehrān, Iran* 35°38N 51°27E **141** B2
Dowling Park *U.S.A.* 30°15N 83°15W **316** E6
Down, L. *U.S.A.* 28°30N 81°31W **133** A1
Downers Grove *U.S.A.* 41°48N 88°1W **311** C8
Downey *Calif., U.S.A.* 33°56N 118°9W **126** C4
Downey *Idaho, U.S.A.* 42°26N 112°7W **304** E7
Downham Market *U.K.* 52°37N 0°23E **169** E8
Downieville *U.S.A.* 39°34N 120°50W **306** F6
Downing *U.S.A.* 40°29N 92°22W **310** D4
Downpatrick *U.K.* 54°20N 5°43W **166** B6
Downpatrick Hd. *Ireland* 54°20N 9°21W **166** B2
Downsview *Canada* 43°43N 79°30W **141** A2
Downsview Park *Canada* 43°45N 79°29W **141** A2
Downsville *U.S.A.* 42°5N 75°0W **313** D10
Downton, Mt. *Canada* 52°42N 124°52W **296** C4
Dowsārī *Iran* 28°25N 57°59E **247** D8
Dowshī *Afghan.* 35°35N 68°43E **240** B3
Doxato *Greece* 41°9N 24°16E **203** E8
Doyle *U.S.A.* 40°2N 120°6W **306** E6
Doylestown *U.S.A.* 40°21N 75°10W **313** F9
Dōzen *Japan* 36°5N 133°5E **222** A5
Dozois, Rés. *Canada* 47°30N 77°5W **298** C4
Dra Khel *Pakistan* 27°58N 66°45E **242** F2
Drâa, C. *Morocco* 28°47N 11°0W **260** C2
Drâa, Hamada du *Algeria* 28°0N 7°0W **260** C3
Drâa, Oued → *Morocco* 28°40N 11°10W **260** C2
Draa-Tafilalet ☐ *Morocco* 31°0N 5°0W **260** B3
Drac → *France* 45°12N 5°42E **175** C9
Drac, Coves del *Spain* 39°31N 3°19E **206** B4
Dračevo *N. Macedonia* 41°56N 21°31E **202** E5
Drachten *Neths.* 53°7N 6°5E **170** A6
Drăgănești *Moldova* 47°43N 28°15E **183** C13
Drăgănești-Olt *Romania* 44°9N 24°32E **183** F9
Drăgănești-Vlașca *Romania* 44°5N 25°33E **183** F10
Dragaš = Sharr *Kosovo* 42°5N 20°41E **202** D4
Drăgășani *Romania* 44°39N 24°17E **183** F9
Dragichyn *Belarus* 52°15N 25°8E **177** B13
Dragocvet *Serbia* 43°58N 21°15E **202** C5
Dragon's Mouths *Trin. & Tob.* 11°0N 61°50W **323** t
Dragør *Denmark* 55°35N 12°38E **118** B3
Dragovishtitsa *Bulgaria* 42°22N 22°39E **202** D6
Draguignan *France* 43°32N 6°27E **175** E10
Drahove *Ukraine* 48°14N 23°33E **183** B8
Drain *U.S.A.* 43°40N 123°19W **304** E2
Drake *U.S.A.* 47°55N 100°23W **308** B3
Drake Passage *S. Ocean* 58°0S 68°0W **151** B17
Drakensberg *S. Africa* 31°0S 28°0E **271** D4
Drama *Greece* 41°9N 24°10E **203** E8
Dramburg = Drawsko Pomorskie *Poland* 53°35N 15°50E **184** E2
Drammen *Norway* 59°42N 10°12E **164** F7
Drancy *France* 48°55N 2°26E **134** A3
Drangajökull *Iceland* 66°9N 22°15W **155** A4
Drangedal *Norway* 59°6N 9°3E **164** E6
Drangsnes *Iceland* 65°41N 21°27W **155** B5
Dranov, Ostrovul *Romania* 44°55N 29°30E **183** F14
Drapetsona *Greece* 37°56N 23°37E **112** B1
Dras *India* 34°25N 75°48E **243** B6
Drastis, Akra *Greece* 39°48N 19°40E **206** B9
Drau = Drava → *Croatia* 45°33N 18°55E **182** E3
Drava → *Croatia* 45°33N 18°55E **182** E3
Dravograd *Slovenia* 46°36N 15°5E **199** B12
Drawa → *Poland* 52°52N 15°59E **185** F2
Drawieński △ *Poland* 53°6N 15°58E **185** E2
Drawno *Poland* 53°13N 15°46E **185** E2
Drawsko Pomorskie *Poland* 53°35N 15°50E **184** E2
Drayton *Canada* 43°46N 80°40W **312** C4
Drayton Plains *U.S.A.* 42°41N 83°23W **311** B13
Drayton Valley *Canada* 53°12N 114°58W **296** C6
Dreieich *Germany* 50°1N 8°41E **179** E4
Dreikikir *Papua N. G.* 3°35S 142°46E **286** B2
Dreilinden *Germany* 52°24N 13°10E **115** B2
Drenthe ☐ *Neths.* 52°52N 6°40E **170** B6
Drepano, Akra *Greece* 35°28N 24°14E **207** E5
Drepanum, C. *Cyprus* 34°54N 32°19E **207** F8
Dresden *Ont., Canada* 42°35N 82°11W **312** D2
Dresden *Sachsen, Germany* 51°3N 13°44E **178** D9
Dresden *N.Y., U.S.A.* 42°41N 76°57W **312** D8
Dreux *France* 48°44N 1°23E **172** D8
Drevsjø *Norway* 61°53N 12°1E **164** C9
Drewnica *Poland* 52°18N 21°6E **143** B2
Drexel *U.S.A.* 39°45N 84°18W **311** E12
Drezdenko *Poland* 52°50N 15°49E **185** F2
Driesen = Drezdenko *Poland* 52°50N 15°49E **185** F2
Driffield *U.K.* 54°0N 0°26W **168** C7
Driftwood *U.S.A.* 41°20N 78°8W **312** E6
Driggs *U.S.A.* 43°44N 111°6W **304** E8
Drigh Road *Pakistan* 24°52N 67°7E **123** A2
Drin → *Albania* 42°1N 19°38E **202** D3
Drin i Zi → *Albania* 41°37N 20°28E **202** E4
Drina → *Bos.-H.* 44°53N 19°21E **202** B3
Drincea → *Romania* 44°20N 22°55E **182** F7
Drinjača → *Bos.-H.* 44°15N 19°8E **182** F4
Driopida *Greece* 37°25N 24°26E **204** D6
Drissa = Vyerkhnyadzvinsk *Belarus* 55°45N 27°58E **188** E4
Driva → *Norway* 62°41N 9°31E **164** B6
Drivstoggo *Norway* 62°26N 9°47E **164** B6
Drniš *Croatia* 43°51N 16°10E **199** E13
Drøbak *Norway* 59°39N 10°39E **164** E7
Drobeta-Turnu Severin *Romania* 44°39N 22°41E **182** F7
Drobin *Poland* 52°42N 19°58E **185** F6
Drochia *Moldova* 48°2N 27°48E **183** B12
Drogenbos *Belgium* 50°47N 4°19E **116** B1
Drogheda *Ireland* 53°43N 6°22W **166** C5
Drogichin = Dragichyn *Belarus* 52°15N 25°8E **177** B13
Drogobych = Drohobych *Ukraine* 49°20N 23°30E **185** J10
Drohiczyn *Poland* 52°24N 22°39E **185** F9
Drohobych *Ukraine* 49°20N 23°30E **185** J10
Droichead Átha = Drogheda *Ireland* 53°43N 6°22W **166** C5
Droichead na Bandan = Bandon *Ireland* 51°44N 8°44W **166** E3
Droichead Nua = Newbridge *Ireland* 53°11N 6°48W **166** C5
Droitwich *U.K.* 52°16N 2°8W **169** E5
Drôme ☐ *France* 44°38N 5°15E **175** D9
Drôme → *France* 44°46N 4°46E **175** D8
Dromedary, C. *Australia* 36°17S 150°10E **283** D9
Drömling ⌓ *Germany* 52°29N 11°5E **178** C7
Dromore *Armagh B. & C., U.K.* 54°25N 6°9W **166** B5
Dromore *Ferman. & O., U.K.* 54°31N 7°28W **166** B4
Dromore West *Ireland* 54°15N 8°52W **166** B3
Dronero *Italy* 44°28N 7°22E **198** D4
Dronfield *U.K.* 53°19N 1°27W **168** D6
Dronne → *France* 45°2N 0°9W **174** C3
Dronning Ingrid Land *Greenland* 64°25N 52°5W **154** E5
Dronning Maud Land *Antarctica* 72°30S 12°0E **151** D3
Dronninglund *Denmark* 57°10N 10°19E **163** G4
Dronten *Neths.* 52°32N 5°43E **170** B5
Dropt → *France* 44°35N 0°6W **174** D3
Drosendorf *Austria* 48°52N 15°37E **180** C8
Drosh *Pakistan* 35°33N 71°48E **240** B3
Drottningholm *Sweden* 59°19N 17°53E **139** B1
Droué *France* 48°3N 1°6E **172** D8
Drouin *Australia* 38°10S 145°53E **283** E6
Druid Hills *U.S.A.* 33°47N 84°21W **113** B2
Druk Yul = Bhutan ■ *Asia* 27°25N 90°30E **241** B3
Drum Tower *Beijing, China* **114** a3
Drumbo *Canada* 43°16N 80°35W **312** C4
Drumcliff *Ireland* 54°20N 8°29W **166** B3
Drumheller *Canada* 51°25N 112°40W **296** C6
Drummond *U.S.A.* 46°40N 113°9W **304** C7
Drummond I. *U.S.A.* 46°1N 83°39W **309** B12
Drummond Pt. *Australia* 34°9S 135°16E **281** E2
Drummond Ra. *Australia* 23°45S 147°10E **280** C4
Drummondville *Canada* 45°55N 72°25W **298** C5
Drummoyne *Australia* 33°51S 151°8E **139** B1
Drumright *U.S.A.* 35°59N 96°36W **314** D6
Druskeniki = Druskininkai *Lithuania* 54°3N 23°58E **188** E2
Druskininkai *Lithuania* 54°3N 23°58E **188** E2
Drut → *Belarus* 53°8N 30°5E **177** B16
Druya *Belarus* 55°45N 27°28E **188** E4
Druzhba *Bulgaria* 43°15N 28°1E **203** C12
Druzhina *Russia* 68°14N 145°18E **215** C15
Druzhkivka *Ukraine* 48°38N 37°32E **189** H9
Drvar *Bos.-H.* 44°21N 16°23E **199** D13
Drvenik *Croatia* 43°27N 16°3E **199** E13
Drwęca → *Poland* 53°0N 18°42E **185** E5
Dry Harbour Mts. *Jamaica* 18°19N 77°24W **320** a
Dry Tortugas *U.S.A.* 24°38N 82°55W **315** J13
Dryander △ *Australia* 20°13S 148°34E **280** b
Dryanovo *Bulgaria* 42°59N 25°28E **203** D9
Dryden *Ont., Canada* 49°47N 92°50W **297** D10
Dryden *N.Y., U.S.A.* 42°30N 76°18W **313** D8
Drygalski I. *Antarctica* 66°0S 92°0E **151** C7
Drygalski Ice Tongue *Antarctica* 75°24S 163°30E **151** D11
Drylaw *U.K.* 55°58N 3°15W **121** B2
Drysdale → *Australia* 13°59S 126°51E **278** B4
Drysdale I. *Australia* 11°41S 136°0E **280** A2
Drysdale River △ *Australia* 14°56S 127°2E **278** B4
Drzewica *Poland* 51°27N 20°29E **185** G7
Drzewiczka → *Poland* 51°36N 20°36E **185** G7
Dschang *Cameroon* 5°32N 10°3E **263** D7
Du Gué → *Canada* 57°21N 70°45W **298** A5
Du He → *China* 32°48N 110°40E **229** A8
Du Quoin *U.S.A.* 38°1N 89°14W **310** G7
Du'an *China* 23°59N 108°3E **228** F7
Duanesburg *U.S.A.* 42°45N 74°11W **313** D10
Duaringa *Australia* 23°42S 149°42E **280** C4
Duarte, Pico *Dom. Rep.* 19°2N 70°59W **321** C5
Dubai = Dubayy *U.A.E.* 25°18N 55°20E **119** A2
Dubai Creek *U.A.E.* 25°15N 55°19E **119** A2
Dubai Int. ✕ (DXB) *U.A.E.* 25°15N 55°21E **119** A2
Dubai Int. Financial Centre *U.A.E.* 25°12N 55°17E **119** B2
Dubai Internet City *U.A.E.* 25°11N 55°10E **119** B1
Dubai Marina *U.A.E.* 25°11N 55°10E **119** B1
Dubai Maritime City *U.A.E.* 25°16N 55°16E **119** A2
Dubăsari *Moldova* 47°15N 29°10E **183** C14
Dubăsari Vdkhr. *Moldova* 47°30N 29°0E **183** C13
Dubawnt → *Canada* 64°33N 100°6W **297** A8
Dubawnt L. *Canada* 63°8N 101°28W **297** A8
Dubayy *U.A.E.* 25°18N 55°20E **119** A2
Dubbo *Australia* 32°11S 148°35E **283** B8
Dube → *Liberia* 5°16N 7°29W **262** D3
Dubeč *Czechia* 50°3N 14°35E **135** B3
Dubele *Dem. Rep. of the Congo* 2°56N 29°35E **268** B2
Dübendorf *Switz.* 47°24N 8°37E **179** H4
Dubica *Bos.-H.* 45°10N 16°50E **199** C13
Dubica *Croatia* 45°11N 16°48E **199** C13
Dublanc *Dominica* 15°31N 61°28W **323** k
Dublin *Dublin, Ireland* 53°21N 6°15W **166** C5
Dublin *Ga., U.S.A.* 32°32N 82°54W **316** C7
Dublin *Ohio, U.S.A.* 40°5N 83°7W **311** D13
Dublin *Tex., U.S.A.* 32°5N 98°21W **314** E5
Dublin ☐ *Ireland* 53°24N 6°20W **166** C5
Dublin ✕ (DUB) *Ireland* 53°26N 6°15W **166** C5
Dubna *Russia* 56°44N 37°10E **188** D9
Dubnica nad Váhom *Slovakia* 48°58N 18°11E **181** C11
Dubno *Ukraine* 50°25N 25°45E **177** C13
Dubois *Idaho, U.S.A.* 44°10N 112°14W **304** D7
Dubois *Ind., U.S.A.* 38°27N 86°48W **310** F10
DuBois *Pa., U.S.A.* 41°7N 78°46W **312** E6
Dubossary = Dubăsari *Moldova* 47°15N 29°10E **183** C14
Dubove *Ukraine* 48°10N 23°53E **183** B8
Dubovka *Russia* 49°5N 44°50E **191** F7
Dubovskoye *Russia* 47°28N 42°46E **191** G6
Dubrajpur *India* 23°48N 87°25E **243** H12
Dubréka *Guinea* 9°46N 13°31W **262** D2
Dubrovitsa = Dubrovytsya *Ukraine* 51°31N 26°35E **177** C14
Dubrovnik *Croatia* 42°39N 18°6E **202** D2
Dubrovytsya *Ukraine* 51°31N 26°35E **177** C14
Dubulu *Dem. Rep. of the Congo* 4°18N 20°16E **264** B4
Dubuque *U.S.A.* 42°30N 90°41W **310** B6
Dubysa → *Lithuania* 55°5N 23°26E **184** C10
Duc de Gloucester, Îs. *French Polynesia* 20°38S 143°20W **289** f
Duc Tho *Vietnam* 18°32N 105°35E **236** C5
Ducale, Palazzo *Venice, Italy* **142** b3
Ducassous, Pte. *Martinique* 14°32N 60°50W **322** j
Duchang *China* 29°18N 116°12E **229** C11
Duchesne *U.S.A.* 40°10N 110°24W **304** F8
Duchess *Australia* 21°20S 139°50E **280** C2
Ducie I. *Pac. Oc.* 24°40S 124°48W **289** K15
Duck → *U.S.A.* 36°2N 87°52W **315** C11
Duck Cr. → *Australia* 22°37S 116°53E **278** D2
Duck Lake *Canada* 52°50N 106°16W **297** C7
Duck Mountain ⌓ *Canada* 51°45N 101°0W **297** C8
Duckwall, Mt. *U.S.A.* 37°58N 120°7W **306** H6
Ducos *Martinique* 14°33N 60°59W **322** j
Duda → *Colombia* 2°34N 74°3W **328** C3
Duddington *U.K.* 55°56N 3°8W **121** B3
Duderstadt *Germany* 51°31N 10°15E **178** D6
Dudhi *India* 24°15N 83°10E **243** G10
Dudhnoi *India* 25°59N 90°47E **241** C3
Dudinka *Russia* 69°30N 86°13E **215** C9
Dudley *W. Mids., U.K.* 52°31N 2°5W **169** E5
Dudley *Ga., U.S.A.* 32°32N 83°5W **316** C6
Dudna → *India* 19°17N 76°54E **244** E3
Dudo *Somalia* 9°20N 50°12E **267** C7
Dudo, W. → *Somalia* 9°14N 50°40E **267** C7
Dudub *Ethiopia* 6°55N 46°43E **267** C6
Dudwa *India* 28°30N 80°41E **243** E9
Dudwa △ *India* 28°30N 80°40E **243** E9
Duékoué *Côte d'Ivoire* 6°40N 7°15W **262** D3
Duenas *Phil.* 11°4N 122°37E **233** F4
Dueñas *Spain* 41°52N 4°33W **194** D6
Duerê *Brazil* 11°20S 49°17W **333** D2
Duero = Douro → *Europe* 41°8N 8°40W **194** D2
Duff Is. *Pac. Oc.* 9°50S 167°10E **277** B12
Dufftown *U.K.* 57°27N 3°8W **167** D5
Dufourspitz *Switz.* 45°56N 7°52E **179** K3
Dugger *U.S.A.* 39°4N 87°18W **311** E9
Dugi Otok *Croatia* 44°0N 15°3E **199** D11
Dugiuma *Somalia* 1°15N 42°34E **267** D5
Dugnano *Italy* 45°33N 9°11E **128** A2
Dugo Selo *Croatia* 45°51N 16°18E **199** C13
Duida-Marahuaca △ *Venezuela* 3°33N 65°33W **328** C4
Duisburg *Germany* 51°26N 6°45E **178** D2
Duitama *Colombia* 5°50N 73°2W **328** B3
Duivendrecht *Neths.* 52°20N 4°55E **112** B2
Duiwelskloof = Modjadjiskloof *S. Africa* 23°42S 30°10E **271** B5
Dujiangyan *China* 31°2N 103°38E **228** B4
Duk Fadiat *South Sudan* 7°45N 31°25E **257** F3
Duk Faiwil *South Sudan* 7°30N 31°29E **257** F3
Dukat *Albania* 40°16N 19°32E **202** F3
Dūkdamīn *Iran* 35°59N 57°43E **247** C8
Dukelský Průsmyk *Slovakia* 49°25N 21°42E **181** B14
Dukhān *Qatar* 25°25N 50°50E **247** E6
Dukhovshchina *Russia* 55°15N 32°27E **188** E7
Duki *Pakistan* 30°14N 68°25E **240** C3
Dukla *Poland* 49°30N 21°35E **185** J8
Duku *Bauchi, Nigeria* 10°43N 10°43E **263** C7
Duku *Sokoto, Nigeria* 11°11N 4°55E **263** C5
Dukuza = Stanger *S. Africa* 29°27S 31°14E **271** C5
Dula *Dem. Rep. of the Congo* 4°40N 20°21E **264** B4
Dūlāb *Iran* 35°39N 51°27E **141** B2
Dulag *Phil.* 10°57N 125°2E **233** F5
Dulan *China* 36°0N 97°11E **218** D8
Dulawan = Datu Piang *Phil.* 7°2N 124°30E **233** H5
Dulce *U.S.A.* 36°56N 107°0W **305** H10
Dulce → *Argentina* 30°32S 62°33W **334** C3
Dulce, G. *Costa Rica* 8°40N 83°20W **320** E3
Dulcina *Antigua & B.* 17°35N 61°49W **322** c
Dulf *Iraq* 35°7N 45°51E **246** C5
Dŭlgopol = Dalgopol *Bulgaria* 43°3N 27°22E **203** C11
Duliu *China* 39°2N 116°55E **226** E9
Dullabchara *India* 24°30N 92°26E **241** C4
Dulles Int. ✕ (IAD) *U.S.A.* 38°57N 77°27W **309** F15
Dullewala *Pakistan* 31°50N 71°25E **242** D4
Dullstroom *S. Africa* 25°27S 30°7E **271** C5
Dülmen *Germany* 51°49N 7°17E **178** D3
Dulovo *Bulgaria* 43°48N 27°9E **203** C11
Dulpetorpet *Norway* 60°34N 12°19E **164** D9
Dulq Maghār *Syria* 36°22N 38°39E **213** D8
Duluth *Ga., U.S.A.* 34°0N 84°9W **316** A5
Duluth *Minn., U.S.A.* 46°47N 92°6W **308** B7
Dulwich *U.K.* 51°27N 0°5W **125** B3
Dum Dum *India* 22°39N 88°26E **124** B2
Dum Duma *India* 27°40N 95°40E **241** B5
Dūmā *Syria* 33°34N 36°24E **250** E7
Dumaguete *Phil.* 9°17N 123°15E **233** G4
Dumai *Indonesia* 1°35N 101°28E **234** B2
Dumalinao *Phil.* 7°49N 123°23E **233** H4
Dumanjug *Phil.* 10°4N 123°26E **233** F4
Dumanquilas B. *Phil.* 7°34N 123°4E **233** H4
Dumaran *Phil.* 10°33N 119°50E **233** F2
Dumaran I. *Phil.* 10°33N 119°51E **233** F2
Dumarao *Phil.* 11°16N 122°41E **233** F4
Dumas *Ark., U.S.A.* 33°53N 91°29W **314** E9
Dumas *Tex., U.S.A.* 35°52N 101°58W **314** D4
Dumayr *Syria* 33°39N 36°42E **250** E7
Dumbarton *U.K.* 55°57N 4°33W **167** F4
Dumbéa *N. Cal.* 22°10S 166°27E **288** d
Ďumbier *Slovakia* 48°56N 19°38E **181** C12
Dumbleyung *Australia* 33°17S 117°42E **279** F2
Dumbo *Angola* 14°6S 17°24E **265** E3
Dumbrăveni *Romania* 46°14N 24°34E **183** D9
Dumfries *U.K.* 55°4N 3°37W **167** F5
Dumfries & Galloway ☐ *U.K.* 55°9N 3°58W **167** F5
Dumingag *Phil.* 8°20N 123°20E **233** G4
Dumitrești *Romania* 45°33N 26°55E **183** E11
Dumka *India* 24°12N 87°15E **243** G12
Dumlupınar *Turkey* 38°53N 30°0E **205** C12
Dümmer *Germany* 52°31N 8°20E **178** C4
Dümmer ⌓ *Germany* 52°31N 8°21E **178** C4
Dumoine → *Canada* 46°13N 77°51W **298** C4
Dumoine, L. *Canada* 46°55N 77°55W **298** C4
Dumont *U.S.A.* 40°56N 73°59W **132** A2
Dumont d'Urville *Antarctica* 66°40S 140°0E **151** C10
Dumont d'Urville Sea *S. Ocean* 63°30S 138°0E **151** C9
Dumoulin Is. *Papua N. G.* 10°54S 150°46E **286** F6
Dumpu *Papua N. G.* 5°53S 145°44E **286** C3
Dumyât *Egypt* 31°24N 31°48E **251** G2
Dumyât, Far → *Egypt* 31°32N 31°51E **251** G2
Dumyât, Masabb *Egypt* 31°28N 31°51E **251** G2
Dún Dealgan = Dundalk *Ireland* 54°1N 6°24W **166** B5
Dún Garbhán = Dungarvan *Ireland* 52°5N 7°37W **166** D4
Dún Laoghaire *Ireland* 53°17N 6°8W **166** C5
Dún Laoghaire-Rathdown ☐ *Ireland* 53°14N 6°11W **166** C5
Dun-le-Palestel *France* 46°18N 1°39E **173** F8
Dun-sur-Auron *France* 46°53N 2°33E **173** F9
Dun-sur-Meuse *France* 49°23N 5°11E **173** C12
Duna = Dunărea → *Europe* 45°20N 29°40E **183** E14
Duna-Drava △ *Hungary* 46°15N 18°50E **182** D3
Duna Dzong *Bhutan* 27°2N 89°24E **241** B2
Duna-völgyi-főcsatorna *Hungary* 46°40N 19°14E **182** D4
Dünaburg = Daugavpils *Latvia* 55°53N 26°32E **188** E4
Dunaföldvár *Hungary* 46°50N 18°57E **182** D3
Dunagiri *India* 30°31N 79°52E **243** D8
Dunaj = Dunărea → *Europe* 45°20N 29°40E **183** E14
Dunajec → *Poland* 50°15N 20°44E **185** H7
Dunajská Streda *Slovakia* 48°0N 17°37E **181** C10
Dunakeszi *Hungary* 47°37N 19°8E **182** C4
Dunapataj *Hungary* 46°39N 19°4E **182** D4
Dunaszekcső *Hungary* 46°6N 18°45E **182** D3
Dunaújváros *Hungary* 46°58N 18°57E **182** D3
Dunav = Dunărea → *Europe* 45°20N 29°40E **183** E14
Dunavațu de Jos *Romania* 44°59N 29°13E **183** F14
Dunavtsi *Bulgaria* 43°57N 22°53E **202** C6
Dunay *Russia* 42°52N 132°22E **220** C6
Dunayivtsi *Ukraine* 48°54N 26°50E **183** B11
Dunback *N.Z.* 45°23S 170°36E **285** F5
Dunbar *U.K.* 56°0N 2°31W **167** E6
Dunblane *U.K.* 56°11N 3°58W **167** E5
Duncan *B.C., Canada* 48°45N 123°40W **306** B3
Duncan *Ariz., U.S.A.* 32°43N 109°6W **305** K9
Duncan *Okla., U.S.A.* 34°30N 97°57W **314** D6
Duncan, L. *Canada* 53°29N 77°58W **298** B4
Duncan Dock *Cape Town, S. Africa* **118** a3
Duncan L. *Canada* 62°51N 113°58W **296** A6
Duncan Passage *India* 11°0N 92°0E **245** J11
Duncan Town *The Bahamas* 22°15N 75°45W **320** B4
Duncannon *U.S.A.* 40°23N 77°2W **312** F7
Duncans *Jamaica* 18°28N 77°32W **320** a
Duncansby Head *U.K.* 58°38N 3°1W **167** C5
Duncansville *U.S.A.* 40°25N 78°26W **312** F6
Duncanville *U.S.A.* 32°39N 96°54W **120** C4
Dund-Us *Mongolia* 48°1N 91°38E **217** C12
Dundaga *Latvia* 57°31N 22°21E **184** A9
Dundalk *Ont., Canada* 44°10N 80°24W **312** B4
Dundalk *Louth, Ireland* 54°1N 6°24W **166** B5
Dundalk *Md., U.S.A.* 39°15N 76°31W **309** F15
Dundalk Bay *Ireland* 53°55N 6°15W **166** C5
Dundas = Uummannaq *Greenland* 77°33N 68°52W **154** B4
Dundas *Canada* 43°17N 79°59W **312** C5
Dundas, L. *Australia* 32°35S 121°50E **279** F3
Dundas I. *Canada* 54°30N 130°50W **296** C2
Dundas Str. *Australia* 11°15S 131°35E **278** B5
Dundee *KwaZulu Natal, S. Africa* 28°11S 30°15E **271** C5
Dundee *Dundee C., U.K.* 56°28N 2°59W **167** E6
Dundee *Mich., U.S.A.* 41°57N 83°40W **311** C13
Dundee *N.Y., U.S.A.* 42°32N 76°59W **312** D8
Dundee City ☐ *U.K.* 56°30N 2°58W **167** E6
Dundgovĭ ☐ *Mongolia* 45°10N 106°0E **226** B4
Dundrum *U.K.* 54°16N 5°52W **166** B6
Dundrum B. *U.K.* 54°13N 5°47W **166** B6
Dunearn *Singapore* 1°19N 103°49E **138** B2
Dunedin *N.Z.* 45°50S 170°33E **285** F5
Dunedin *Fla., U.S.A.* 28°1N 82°46W **317** G7
Dunedoo *Australia* 32°0S 149°25E **283** A8
Dunfanaghy *Ireland* 55°11N 7°58W **166** A4
Dunfermline *U.K.* 56°5N 3°27W **167** E5
Dungannon *Ont., Canada* 43°51N 81°36W **312** C3
Dungannon *Tyrone, U.K.* 54°31N 6°46W **166** B5
Dungarpur *India* 23°52N 73°45E **242** H5
Dungarvan *Ireland* 52°5N 7°37W **166** D4
Dungarvan Harbour *Ireland* 52°4N 7°35W **166** D4
Dungeness *U.K.* 50°54N 0°59E **169** G8
Dungiven *U.K.* 54°56N 6°56W **166** B5
Dunglow *Ireland* 54°57N 8°21W **166** B3
Dungo, L. do *Angola* 17°15S 19°0E **265** F3
Dungog *Australia* 32°22S 151°46E **283** B9
Dungu *Dem. Rep. of the Congo* 3°40N 28°32E **268** B2
Dungun *Malaysia* 4°45N 103°25E **237** K4
Dungunâb *Sudan* 21°10N 37°9E **256** C4
Dungunâb, Khalîg *Sudan* 21°5N 37°12E **256** C4
Dunhua *China* 43°20N 128°14E **227** C15
Dunhuang *China* 40°8N 94°36E **218** C7
Duni I. *Australia* 17°59S 146°29E **280** B4
Dunkassa *Benin* 10°21N 3°10E **263** C5
Dunkeld *Queens., Australia* 33°25S 149°29E **281** E4
Dunkeld *Vic., Australia* 37°40S 142°22E **282** D5
Dunkeld *Perth & Kinr., U.K.* 56°34N 3°35W **167** E5
Dunkerque *France* 51°2N 2°20E **173** A9
Dunkery Beacon *U.K.* 51°9N 3°36W **169** F4
Dunkirk = Dunkerque *France* 51°2N 2°20E **173** A9
Dunkirk *U.S.A.* 42°29N 79°20W **312** D5
Dunkuj *Sudan* 12°50N 32°49E **257** E3
Dunkwa *Central, Ghana* 6°0N 1°47W **262** D4
Dunkwa *Central, Ghana* 5°30N 1°0W **263** D4
Dunleary = Dún Laoghaire *Ireland* 53°17N 6°8W **166** C5
Dunleer *Ireland* 53°50N 6°24W **166** C5
Dunmanus B. *Ireland* 51°31N 9°50W **166** E2
Dunmanway *Ireland* 51°43N 9°6W **166** E2
Dunmarra *Australia* 16°42S 133°25E **280** B1
Dunmore *U.S.A.* 41°25N 75°38W **313** E9
Dunmore East *Ireland* 52°9N 7°0W **166** D5
Dunmore Town *The Bahamas* 25°30N 76°39W **320** A4
Dunn *U.S.A.* 35°19N 78°37W **315** D15
Dunnellon *U.S.A.* 29°3N 82°28W **317** F7
Dunnet Hd. *U.K.* 58°40N 3°21W **167** C5
Dunning *Ill., U.S.A.* 41°56N 87°48W **119** B2
Dunning *Nebr., U.S.A.* 41°50N 100°6W **308** E3
Dunn's River Falls *Jamaica* 18°25N 77°8W **320** a
Dunnville *Canada* 42°54N 79°36W **312** D5
Dunolly *Australia* 36°51S 143°44E **282** D5
Dunoon *U.K.* 55°57N 4°56W **167** F4
Dunqul *Egypt* 23°26N 31°37E **256** C3
Duns *U.K.* 55°47N 2°20W **167** F6
Dunseith *U.S.A.* 48°50N 100°3W **308** A3
Dunshaughlin *Ireland* 53°31N 6°33W **166** C5
Dunsmuir *U.S.A.* 41°13N 122°16W **304** F2
Dunstable *U.K.* 51°53N 0°32W **169** F7
Dunstan Mts. *N.Z.* 44°53S 169°35E **285** E4
Dunster *Canada* 53°8N 119°50W **296** C5
Duntroon *N.Z.* 44°51S 170°40E **285** E5
Dunvegan *Gauteng, S. Africa* 26°9S 28°8E **123** A2
Dunvegan *Highl., U.K.* 57°27N 6°35W **167** D2
Dunvegan L. *Canada* 60°8N 107°10W **297** A7
Duolun *China* 42°12N 116°28E **226** C9
Duomo *Italy* 45°28N 9°11E **128** B2
Duomula *China* 34°8N 82°29E **217** F10
Duong Dong *Vietnam* 10°13N 103°58E **237** G4
Dupax del Norte *Phil.* 16°17N 121°5E **232** C3
Dupree *U.S.A.* 45°4N 101°35W **308** C3
Dupuyer *U.S.A.* 48°13N 112°30W **304** B7
Duque de Caxias *Brazil* 22°46S 43°18W **135** A1
Duque de York, I. *Chile* 50°37S 75°25W **336** D1
Durack → *Australia* 15°33S 127°52E **278** C4
Durack Ra. *Australia* 16°50S 127°40E **278** C4
Durack River *Australia* 15°32S 127°39E **278** C4
Durağan *Turkey* 41°25N 35°3E **212** B6
Durak *Turkey* 39°42N 28°17E **205** B10
Durakovac = Gjurakoc *Kosovo* 42°43N 20°29E **202** D4
Durance → *France* 43°55N 4°45E **175** E8
Durand *Ga., U.S.A.* 32°55N 84°46W **316** C5
Durand *Ill., U.S.A.* 42°26N 89°20W **310** B7
Durand *Mich., U.S.A.* 42°55N 83°59W **311** B13
Durand *Wis., U.S.A.* 44°38N 91°58W **308** C8
Durandeau *St. Lucia* 13°56N 60°59W **323** m
Durango *Mexico* 24°3N 104°39W **318** C4
Durango *Colo., U.S.A.* 37°16N 107°53W **305** H10
Durango ☐ *Mexico* 24°50N 105°20W **318** C4
Durankulak *Bulgaria* 43°41N 28°32E **203** C12
Durant *Iowa, U.S.A.* 41°36N 90°54W **310** C6
Durant *Miss., U.S.A.* 33°4N 89°51W **315** E10
Durant *Okla., U.S.A.* 33°59N 96°25W **314** E6
Duratón → *Spain* 41°37N 4°7W **194** D6
Durazno *Uruguay* 33°25S 56°31W **334** C4
Durazzo = Durrës *Albania* 41°19N 19°28E **202** E3
Durban *Aude, France* 42°59N 2°49E **174** F6
Durban *KwaZulu Natal, S. Africa* 29°49S 31°1E **271** C5
Durban ✕ (DUR) *S. Africa* 29°37S 31°7E **271** C5
Durbuy *Belgium* 50°21N 5°28E **170** D5
Dúrcal *Spain* 36°59N 3°34W **195** J7
Durdevac *Croatia* 46°2N 17°3E **182** D2
Düren *Germany* 50°48N 6°29E **178** E2
Duren Sawit *Indonesia* 6°13S 106°54E **122** B2
Durg = Bhilainagar-Durg *India* 21°13N 81°26E **244** D5
Durgapur *India* 23°30N 87°20E **243** H12
Durham *Ont., Canada* 44°10N 80°49W **312** B4
Durham *Darlington, U.K.* 54°47N 1°34W **168** C6
Durham *Calif., U.S.A.* 39°39N 121°48W **306** F5
Durham *N.C., U.S.A.* 35°59N 78°54W **315** D15
Durham *N.H., U.S.A.* 43°8N 70°56W **313** C14
Durham ☐ *U.K.* 54°42N 1°45W **168** C6
Duri *Indonesia* 1°27N 101°15E **234** B2
Durlas = Thurles *Ireland* 52°41N 7°49W **166** D4
Durlești *Moldova* 47°1N 28°46E **183** C13
Ḑurmā *Si. Arabia* 24°37N 46°8E **246** E5
Durmitor *Montenegro* 43°10N 19°0E **202** C2
Durmitor △ *Montenegro* 43°15N 19°5E **202** C3
Durness *U.K.* 58°34N 4°45W **167** C4
Durnford, Pta. *W. Sahara* 23°37N 16°0W **260** D1
Durrës *Albania* 41°19N 19°28E **202** E3
Durrow *Ireland* 52°51N 7°24W **166** D4
Dursey I. *Ireland* 51°36N 10°12W **166** E1
Dursley *U.K.* 51°40N 2°21W **169** F5
Dursunbey *Turkey* 39°35N 28°37E **205** B10
Durtal *France* 47°40N 0°18W **172** E6
Duru *Dem. Rep. of the Congo* 4°14N 28°50E **268** B2
Duru Gölü *Turkey* 41°20N 28°35E **203** E12
Durukhsi *Ethiopia* 8°31N 45°28E **267** C6
Durusu *Turkey* 41°17N 28°41E **203** E12
Durūz, Jabal ad *Jordan* 32°35N 36°40E **250** F7
D'Urville, Tanjung *Indonesia* 1°28S 137°54E **231** E9
D'Urville I. *N.Z.* 40°50S 173°55E **285** A8
Duryea *U.S.A.* 41°20N 75°45W **313** E9
Dusa Mareb = Dhuusamarreeb *Somalia* 5°30N 46°15E **267** C6
Dûsh *Egypt* 24°35N 30°41E **256** C3
Dushak *Turkmenistan* 37°13N 60°1E **247** B9
Dushan *China* 25°48N 107°30E **228** E6
Dushanbe *Tajikistan* 38°33N 68°48E **217** E7
Dusheti *Georgia* 42°10N 44°42E **191** J7
Dushore *U.S.A.* 41°31N 76°24W **313** E8
Dusit *Bangkok, Thailand* **113** a2
Dusit Zoo *Bangkok, Thailand* **113** a2
Dusky Sd. *N.Z.* 45°47S 166°30E **285** F1
Dussejour, C. *Australia* 14°45S 128°13E **278** B4
Düsseldorf *Germany* 51°14N 6°47E **178** D2
Düsseldorf Rhein-Ruhr ✕ (DUS) *Germany* 51°17N 6°46E **178** D2
Dusti *Tajikistan* 37°20N 68°40E **217** E7
Duszniki-Zdrój *Poland* 50°24N 16°24E **185** H3
Dutch East Indies = Indonesia ■ *Asia* 5°0S 115°0E **235** C4
Dutch Guiana = Suriname ■ *S. Amer.* 4°0N 56°0W **329** C6
Dutch Harbor *U.S.A.* 53°53N 166°32W **303** K6
Dutlwe *Botswana* 23°58S 23°46E **270** B3
Dutsan Wai *Nigeria* 10°50N 8°10E **263** C6
Dutse *Nigeria* 11°46N 9°20E **263** C6
Dutton *Canada* 42°39N 81°30W **312** D3
Dutton → *Australia* 20°44S 143°10E **280** C3
Dutywa *S. Africa* 32°8S 28°18E **271** D4
Duved *Sweden* 63°23N 12°55E **162** A6
Düvertepe *Turkey* 39°14N 28°27E **205** B10
Dúvida = Roosevelt → *Brazil* 7°35S 60°20W **331** B5
Duwayhin, Khawr *U.A.E.* 24°20N 51°25E **247** E6
Duyfken Pt. *Australia* 12°33S 141°38E **280** A3
Duyun *China* 26°18N 107°29E **228** D6
Düzağac *Turkey* 38°48N 30°10E **205** C12
Düzce = Akhna *Cyprus* 35°3N 33°47E **207** E9
Düzce *Turkey* 40°50N 31°10E **212** B4
Düzce ☐ *Turkey* 40°50N 31°10E **212** B4
Duzdab = Zāhedān *Iran* 29°30N 60°50E **247** D9
Duzer *Guadeloupe* 16°20N 61°44W **322** e
Düziçi *Turkey* 37°15N 36°28E **212** D7
Dve Mogili *Bulgaria* 43°35N 25°55E **203** C9
Dvigatelstroy = Kaspiysk *Russia* 42°52N 47°40E **191** J8
Dvina, Severnaya → *Russia* 64°32N 40°30E **186** B7
Dvinsk = Daugavpils *Latvia* 55°53N 26°32E **188** E4
Dvinskaya Guba *Russia* 65°0N 39°0E **186** B6
Dvor *Croatia* 45°4N 16°22E **199** C13
Dvůr Králové nad Labem *Czechia* 50°27N 15°50E **180** A8
Dwarka *India* 22°18N 69°8E **242** H3
Dwellingup *Australia* 32°43S 116°4E **279** F2
Dwight *Ont., Canada* 45°20N 79°1W **312** A5
Dwight *Ill., U.S.A.* 41°5N 88°26W **311** C8
Dworp *Belgium* 50°44N 4°18E **116** B1
Dyakove *Ukraine* 48°1N 23°0E **182** B7
Dyakovo *Russia* 55°40N 37°39E **129** B2
Dyatkovo *Russia* 53°40N 34°27E **188** F8
Dyatlovo = Dzyatlava *Belarus* 53°28N 25°28E **177** B13
Dyce *U.K.* 57°13N 2°12W **167** D6
Dyer, C. *Canada* 66°37N 61°16W **295** D19
Dyer Bay *Canada* 45°10N 81°20W **312** A3
Dyer Plateau *Antarctica* 70°45S 65°30W **151** D17
Dyersburg *U.S.A.* 36°3N 89°23W **315** C10
Dyersville *U.S.A.* 42°29N 91°8W **310** B5
Dyfi → *U.K.* 52°32N 4°3W **169** E3
Dyhernfurth = Brzeg Dolny *Poland* 51°16N 16°41E **185** G3
Dyje → *Czechia* 48°37N 16°56E **181** C9
Dyke Ackland B. *Papua N. G.* 9°0S 148°45E **286** E5
Dyker Beach Park *U.S.A.* 40°36N 74°1W **132** C1
Dykh Tau *Russia* 43°3N 43°8E **191** J6
Dymer *Ukraine* 50°47N 30°18E **177** C16
Dynów *Poland* 49°50N 22°11E **185** J9
Dyranut *Norway* 60°22N 7°31E **164** D4
Dyrhólaey *Iceland* 63°24N 19°8W **155** D7
Dyrnes *Norway* 63°25N 7°52E **164** A4
Dysart *Queens., Australia* 22°32S 148°23E **280** C4
Dysart *Iowa, U.S.A.* 42°10N 92°18W **310** B4
Dytiki Ellas ☐ *Greece* 38°20N 21°30E **204** C3
Dyushambe = Dushanbe *Tajikistan* 38°33N 68°48E **217** E7
Dyviziya *Ukraine* 45°55N 29°59E **183** E14
Dzamin Üüd = Borhoyn Tal *Mongolia* 43°50N 111°58E **226** C6
Dzaoudzi *Mayotte* 12°47S 45°16E **272** b
Dzaoudzi ✕ (DZA) *Mayotte* 12°48S 45°18E **272** b
Dzaudzhikau = Vladikavkaz *Russia* 43°0N 44°35E **191** J7
Dzavhan ☐ *Mongolia* 48°0N 96°0E **217** C13
Dzavhan Gol → *Mongolia* 48°54N 93°23E **218** B7
Dzerzhinsk *Russia* 56°14N 43°30E **190** B6
Dzerzhinskiy *Russia* 55°37N 37°52E **129** B2
Dzerzhinskiy Park *Russia* 55°50N 37°37E **129** B2
Dzhalal-Abad = Jalal-Abad *Kyrgyzstan* 40°56N 73°0E **217** D8
Dzhalal-Ogly = Stepanavan *Armenia* 41°1N 44°23E **191** K7
Dzhalinda *Russia* 53°26N 124°0E **215** D13
Dzhambeyty = Zhympity *Kazakhstan* 50°16N 52°35E **216** B4
Dzhambul = Taraz *Kazakhstan* 42°54N 71°22E **217** D8
Dzhankoy *Ukraine* 45°40N 34°20E **189** K8
Dzhanybek = Zhānibek *Kazakhstan* 49°25N 46°50E **190** F8
Dzhargalantu = Hovd ☐ *Mongolia* 48°2N 91°37E **217** C12
Dzharkent = Zharkent *Kazakhstan* 44°10N 80°0E **217** D10
Dzharkurgan = Jarqo'rg'on *Uzbekistan* 37°31N 67°25E **240** A2
Dzharylhach, Ostriv *Ukraine* 46°2N 32°55E **189** J7
Dzhezkazgan = Zhezqazghan *Kazakhstan* 47°44N 67°40E **217** C7
Dzhibkhalantu = Uliastay *Mongolia* 47°56N 97°28E **218** B8
Dzhizak = Jizzax *Uzbekistan* 40°6N 67°50E **217** D7
Dzhugba *Russia* 44°19N 38°48E **191** H4
Dzhugdzur, Khrebet *Russia* 57°30N 138°0E **215** D14
Dzhulynk *Ukraine* 48°26N 29°45E **183** B14
Dzhumgoltau, Khrebet *Kyrgyzstan* 42°15N 74°30E **217** D8
Dzhungarskiye Vorota = Dzungarian Gate *Asia* 45°10N 82°0E **217** C10
Dzhuryn *Ukraine* 48°41N 28°18E **183** B13
Dzhvari = Jvari *Georgia* 42°42N 42°4E **191** J6
Działdowo *Poland* 53°15N 20°15E **185** E7
Działoszyce *Poland* 50°22N 20°20E **185** H7
Działoszyn *Poland* 51°6N 18°50E **185** G5
Dzibilchaltún *Mexico* 21°10N 89°35W **319** C7
Dzierzgoń *Poland* 53°58N 19°20E **184** E6
Dzierżoniów *Poland* 50°45N 16°39E **185** H3
Dzilam de Bravo *Mexico* 21°24N 88°53W **319** C7
Dzioua *Algeria* 33°14N 5°14E **261** B6
Dzisna *Belarus* 55°34N 28°12E **188** E5
Dzisna → *Belarus* 55°34N 28°12E **188** E5
Dziwnów *Poland* 54°2N 14°45E **184** D1
Dzūkija △ *Lithuania* 54°10N 24°30E **161** J21
Dzungarian Basin = Junggar Pendi *China* 44°30N 86°0E **217** D11
Dzungarian Gate *Asia* 45°10N 82°0E **217** C10
Dzur *Mongolia* 49°39N 95°46E **217** C13
Dzüünbayan *Mongolia* 44°29N 110°2E **226** B6
Dzüünharaa *Mongolia* 48°52N 106°28E **218** B10
Dzüünmod *Mongolia* 47°45N 106°58E **218** B10
Dzyarzhynsk *Belarus* 53°40N 27°1E **177** B14
Dzyatlava *Belarus* 53°28N 25°28E **177** B13

E

E.C. Manning ⌓ *Canada* 49°5N 120°45W **296** D4
E.U.R. = Esposizione Universale di Roma *Italy* 41°49N 12°28E **136** C1
Eabamet L. *Canada* 51°30N 87°46W **298** B2
Eabametoong *Canada* 51°30N 88°0W **298** B2
Éadan Doire = Edenderry *Ireland* 53°21N 7°4W **166** C4
Eads *U.S.A.* 38°29N 102°47W **304** G12
Eagar *U.S.A.* 34°6N 109°17W **305** J9
Eagle *Alaska, U.S.A.* 64°47N 141°12W **303** D12
Eagle *Colo., U.S.A.* 39°39N 106°50W **304** G10
Eagle → *Canada* 53°36N 57°26W **299** B8
Eagle, Mt. *U.S. Virgin Is.* 17°46N 64°49W **321** b
Eagle Beach *Aruba* 12°32N 70°3W **322** f
Eagle Butte *U.S.A.* 45°0N 101°10W **308** C3
Eagle Cr. → *U.S.A.* 38°36N 85°4W **311** F11
Eagle Grove *U.S.A.* 42°40N 93°54W **310** B3
Eagle L. *Ont., Canada* 49°42N 93°13W **297** D10
Eagle L. *Calif., U.S.A.* 40°39N 120°45W **304** F3
Eagle L. *Maine, U.S.A.* 46°20N 69°22W **309** B19
Eagle Lake *Ont., Canada* 45°8N 78°29W **312** A6
Eagle Lake *Maine, U.S.A.* 47°3N 68°36W **309** B19
Eagle Lake *Tex., U.S.A.* 29°35N 96°20W **314** G6
Eagle Mountain *U.S.A.* 33°49N 115°27W **307** M11
Eagle Nest *U.S.A.* 36°33N 105°16W **305** H11
Eagle Pass *U.S.A.* 28°43N 100°30W **314** G4
Eagle Pk. *U.S.A.* 38°10N 119°25W **306** G7
Eagle Pt. *Australia* 16°11S 124°23E **278** C3
Eagle River *Mich., U.S.A.* 47°25N 88°18W **308** B9
Eagle River *Wis., U.S.A.* 45°55N 89°15W **308** C9
Eagle Rock *U.S.A.* 34°8N 118°12W **126** B3
Eaglehawk *Australia* 36°44S 144°15E **282** D6
Eagles Mere *U.S.A.* 41°25N 76°33W **313** E8
Eagleville *U.S.A.* 40°28N 93°59W **310** D3
Ealing ☐ *U.K.* 51°31N 0°20W **125** A2
Ear Falls *Canada* 50°38N 93°13W **297** C10
Earlimart *U.S.A.* 35°53N 119°16W **307** K7
Earl's Court *London, U.K.* **125** c1
Earlsfield *U.K.* 51°26N 0°10W **125** B2
Earlville *Ill., U.S.A.* 41°35N 88°55W **311** C8
Earlville *N.Y., U.S.A.* 42°44N 75°32W **313** D9
Earlwood *Australia* 33°55S 151°8E **139** B1
Early Branch *U.S.A.* 32°45N 80°55W **316** C9
Earn → *U.K.* 56°21N 3°18W **167** E5
Earn, L. *U.K.* 56°23N 4°13W **167** E4
Earnslaw, Mt. *N.Z.* 44°32S 168°27E **285** E3
Earth *U.S.A.* 34°14N 102°24W **314** D3
Eas *Vanuatu* 16°20S 168°15E **287** F6
Easley *U.S.A.* 34°50N 82°36W **315** D13
East Anglia *U.K.* 52°50N 1°0E **168** E9
East Angus *Canada* 45°30N 71°40W **299** C5
East Antarctica *Antarctica* 80°0S 90°0E **151** D7
East Arlington *Mass., U.S.A.* 42°24N 71°8W **116** A2
East Arlington *Va., U.S.A.* 38°51N 77°4W **143** B2
East Aurora *U.S.A.* 42°46N 78°37W **312** D6
East Ayrshire ☐ *U.K.* 55°26N 4°11W **167** F4
East Bedfont *U.K.* 51°26N 0°28W **125** B1
East Berbice-Corentyne ☐ *Guyana* 4°11N 58°11W **329** C6
East Beskids = Vychodné Beskydy *Europe* 49°20N 22°0E **181** B15
East Boston *U.S.A.* 42°22N 71°1W **116** A2
East Brady *U.S.A.* 40°59N 79°37W **312** F5
East Branch Clarion River L. *U.S.A.* 41°35N 78°35W **312** E6
East C. = Dezhneva, Mys *Russia* 66°5N 169°40W **215** C19
East C. *N.Z.* 37°42S 178°35E **284** D7
East C. *Papua N. G.* 10°13S 150°53E **286** F6
East Caroline Basin *Pac. Oc.* 4°0N 146°45E **288** G6
East Chicago *U.S.A.* 41°38N 87°27W **311** C9
East China Sea *Asia* 30°0N 126°0E **219** F14
East Coulee *Canada* 51°23N 112°27W **296** C6
East Dereham = Dereham *U.K.* 52°41N 0°57E **169** E8
East Don → *Canada* 43°48N 79°25W **141** A2
East Don Parkland *Canada* 43°47N 79°22W **141** A2
East Dublin *U.S.A.* 32°32N 82°52W **316** C7
East Dubuque *U.S.A.* 42°30N 90°39W **310** B6
East Dunbartonshire ☐ *U.K.* 55°57N 4°13W **167** F4
East Elmhurst *U.S.A.* 40°45N 73°52W **132** B2
East End Pt. *The Bahamas* 25°3N 77°16W **153** b
East Falkland *Falk. Is.* 51°30S 58°30W **153** f
East Falls Church *U.S.A.* 38°53N 77°9W **143** B2
East Finchley *U.K.* 51°35N 0°10W **125** A2
East Flatbush *U.S.A.* 40°39N 73°55W **132** C2
East Fork White → *U.S.A.* 38°33N 87°14W **311** F9
East Grand Forks *U.S.A.* 47°56N 97°1W **308** B5
East Grand Rapids *U.S.A.* 42°58N 85°37W **311** B11
East Greenwich *U.S.A.* 41°40N 71°27W **313** E13
East Grinstead *U.K.* 51°7N 0°0 **169** F8
East Ham *U.K.* 51°32N 0°3E **125** A4
East Hartford *U.S.A.* 41°46N 72°39W **313** E12
East Haydon *Australia* 18°0S 141°30E **280** B3
East Helena *U.S.A.* 46°35N 111°56W **304** C8
East Humber → *Canada* 43°47N 79°35W **141** A1
East Indies *Asia* 0°0 120°0E **210** J14
East Kavango ☐ *Namibia* 18°0S 20°15E **270** A3
East Kilbride *U.K.* 55°47N 4°11W **167** F4
East Lamma Channel *Hong Kong, China* 22°14N 114°9E **122** B2
East Lansing *U.S.A.* 42°44N 84°29W **311** B12
East Las Vegas = Whitney *U.S.A.* 36°4N 115°5W **124** B2
East Lexington *U.S.A.* 42°25N 71°12W **116** A1
East Livermore = Livermore Falls *U.S.A.* 44°29N 70°11W **309** C18
East Liverpool *U.S.A.* 40°37N 80°35W **312** F4
East London *S. Africa* 33°0S 27°55E **271** D4
East Los Angeles *U.S.A.* 34°1N 118°10W **126** B3
East Lothian ☐ *U.K.* 55°58N 2°44W **167** F6
East Main = Eastmain *Canada* 52°10N 78°30W **298** B4
East Mariana Basin *Pac. Oc.* 12°0N 153°0E **288** F7
East Milwaukee = Shorewood *U.S.A.* 43°5N 87°53W **311** A9
East Molesey *U.K.* 51°24N 0°21W **125** B1
East Moline *U.S.A.* 41°32N 90°26W **310** C6
East Naples *U.S.A.* 26°8N 81°46W **317** J8
East New Britain ☐ *Papua N. G.* 6°30S 152°30E **286** D7

East New York U.S.A. 40°40N 73°53W 132 B2
East Northport U.S.A. 40°53N 73°19W 313 F11
East Orange U.S.A. 40°46N 74°12W 313 F10
East Pacific Rise Pac. Oc. 15°0S 110°0W 289 J17
East Pakistan = Bangladesh ■ Asia 24°0N 90°0E 241 D3
East Palatka U.S.A. 29°39N 81°36W 316 F8
East Palestine U.S.A. 40°50N 80°33W 312 F4
East Peoria U.S.A. 40°40N 89°34W 310 D7
East Pine Canada 55°48N 120°12W 296 B4
East Pines U.S.A. 38°57N 76°54W 143 B3
East Point U.S.A. 33°41N 84°25W 113 B2
East Potomac Park Washington, D.C., U.S.A. 143 c1
East Providence U.S.A. 41°49N 71°23W 313 E13
East Pt. Br. Virgin Is. 18°40N 64°18W 321 b
East Pt. N.S., Canada 46°27N 61°58W 299 C7
East Pt. U.S. Virgin Is. 17°45N 64°34W 321 b
East Renfrewshire □ U.K. 55°46N 4°21W 167 F4
East Retford = Retford U.K. 53°19N 0°56W 168 D7
East Riding of Yorkshire □ U.K. 53°55N 0°30W 168 D7
East River ➝ New York, U.S.A. 132 e3
East Rochester U.S.A. 43°7N 77°29W 312 C7
East Rutherford U.S.A. 40°50N 74°5W 132 A1
East St. Louis U.S.A. 38°37N 90°9W 310 F6
East Schelde = Oosterschelde ➝ Neths. 51°33N 4°0E 170 C4
East Sea = Japan, Sea of Asia 40°0N 135°0E 220 E7
East Sepik □ Papua N. G. 4°0S 143°45E 286 C2
East Sheen U.K. 51°27N 0°16W 125 B2
East Siberian Sea Russia 73°0N 160°0E 215 B17
East Stroudsburg U.S.A. 41°1N 75°11W 313 E9
East Sussex □ U.K. 50°56N 0°19E 169 G8
East Talpiyot West Bank 31°45N 35°13E 123 B2
East Tasman Plateau Pac. Oc. 43°30S 152°0E 288 M7
East Tawas U.S.A. 44°17N 83°29W 309 C12
East Timor = Timor-Leste ■ Asia 8°50S 126°0E 231 F7
East Toorale Australia 30°27S 145°28E 281 E4
East Troy U.S.A. 42°47N 88°24W 311 B8
East Village New York, U.S.A. 132 e2
East Walker ➝ U.S.A. 38°52N 119°10W 306 G7
East Wickham U.K. 51°28N 0°5E 125 B4
East Windsor U.S.A. 40°17N 74°34W 313 F10
East York Canada 43°40N 79°22W 141 A2
East Youngstown = Campbell U.S.A. 41°5N 80°37W 312 E4
Eastbourne N.Z. 41°19S 174°55E 284 H3
Eastbourne E. Sussex, U.K. 50°46N 0°18E 169 G8
Eastcote U.K. 51°34N 0°23W 125 A1
Eastend Canada 49°32N 108°50W 297 D7
Easter Fracture Zone Pac. Oc. 25°0S 115°0W 289 K16
Easter Howgate U.K. 55°52N 3°12W 121 B2
Easter I. = Pascua, I. de Chile 27°7S 109°23W 330 b
Eastern □ Ghana 6°30N 0°30W 263 D4
Eastern □ S. Leone 8°15N 11°0W 262 D2
Eastern Cape □ S. Africa 32°0S 26°0E 270 D4
Eastern Cr. ➝ Australia 20°40S 141°35E 280 C3
Eastern Desert = Sharqîya, Es Sahrâ esh Egypt 27°30N 32°30E 256 B3
Eastern Equatoria □ South Sudan 5°0N 33°0E 257 G3
Eastern Ghats India 14°0N 78°50E 245 H4
Eastern Group = Lau Group Fiji 17°0S 178°30W 287 A3
Eastern Group Australia 33°30S 124°30E 279 F3
Eastern Guruma ◎ Australia 22°0S 117°30E 278 D2
Eastern Highlands □ Papua N. G. 6°30S 145°35E 286 D3
Eastern I. Midway Is. 28°12N 177°19W 302 c
Eastern Samar □ Phil. 11°40N 125°40E 233 F5
Eastern Transvaal = Mpumalanga □ S. Africa 26°0S 30°0E 271 C5
Easterville Canada 53°8N 99°49W 297 C9
Easthampton U.S.A. 42°16N 72°40W 313 D12
Eastlake U.S.A. 41°40N 81°26W 312 E3
Eastland U.S.A. 32°24N 98°49W 314 E5
Eastleigh U.K. 50°58N 1°21W 169 G6
Eastmain Canada 52°10N 78°30W 298 B4
Eastmain ➝ Canada 52°27N 78°26W 298 B4
Eastman Qué., Canada 45°18N 72°19W 313 A12
Eastman Ga., U.S.A. 32°12N 83°11W 316 C6
Eastman Wis., U.S.A. 43°10N 91°1W 310 A5
Easton Md., U.S.A. 38°47N 76°5W 309 F15
Easton Pa., U.S.A. 40°41N 75°13W 313 F9
Easton Wash., U.S.A. 47°14N 121°11W 306 C5
Eastover U.S.A. 33°52N 80°41W 316 B9
Eastpoint U.S.A. 29°44N 84°53W 316 F5
Eastpoint Park Canada 43°46N 79°10W 141 A4
Eastport U.S.A. 44°56N 67°0W 309 C20
Eastsound U.S.A. 48°42N 122°55W 306 B4
Eastwood Australia 33°47S 151°4E 139 A1
Eaton Colo., U.S.A. 40°32N 104°42W 304 F11
Eaton Ohio, U.S.A. 39°45N 84°38W 311 E12
Eaton Canyon Park U.S.A. 34°10N 118°7W 126 A4
Eaton Centre Toronto, Canada 141 a2
Eaton Rapids U.S.A. 42°31N 84°39W 311 B12
Eatonia Canada 51°13N 109°25W 297 C7
Eatonton U.S.A. 33°20N 83°23W 316 B6
Eatontown U.S.A. 40°19N 74°4W 313 F10
Eatonville U.S.A. 46°52N 122°16W 306 D4
Eau Claire U.S.A. 44°49N 91°30W 308 C8
Eau Claire, L. à l' Canada 56°10N 74°25W 298 A5
Eauripik Rise Pac. Oc. 2°0N 142°0E 288 G6
Eauze France 43°53N 0°7E 174 E4
Eban Nigeria 9°40N 4°50E 263 D5
Ebanga Angola 12°45S 14°45E 265 E2
Ebangalakata Dem. Rep. of the Congo 0°29S 21°29E 264 C4
Ebano Mexico 22°13N 98°24W 319 C5
Ebara Japan 35°35N 139°42E 140 B3
Ebbegebirge ⌂ Germany 51°10N 7°55E 178 D3
Ebbw Vale U.K. 51°46N 3°12W 169 F4
Ebebiyín Eq. Guin. 2°9N 11°20E 264 B2
Ebel Gabon 0°7N 11°5E 264 B2
Ebeltoft Denmark 56°12N 10°41E 163 H4
Ebeltoft Vig Denmark 56°10N 10°35E 163 H4
Ebensburg U.S.A. 40°29N 78°44W 312 F6
Ebensee Austria 47°48N 13°46E 180 D6
Eber Gölü Turkey 38°38N 31°11E 212 C4
Eberbach Germany 49°28N 8°59E 179 F4
Eberswalde-Finow Germany 52°50N 13°49E 178 C9
Ebetsu Japan 43°7N 141°34E 220 C10
Ebey's Landing ⌂ U.S.A. 48°12N 122°41W 306 B4
Ebian China 29°11N 103°13E 228 C4
Ebingen = Albstadt Germany 48°13N 9°1E 179 G5
Ebino Japan 32°2N 130°48E 222 E2
Ebinur Hu China 44°55N 82°55E 217 D10
Ebisu Japan 35°38N 139°42E 140 B3
Ebla Syria 35°50N 36°48E 250 C7
Ebo Angola 11°40S 14°40E 265 E2
Ebola ➝ Dem. Rep. of the Congo 3°20N 20°57E 264 B4
Éboli Italy 40°39N 15°2E 201 B8
Ebolowa Cameroon 2°55N 11°10E 263 E7
Ebonda Dem. Rep. of the Congo 2°12N 22°21E 264 B4
Ebonyi □ Nigeria 6°20N 8°0E 263 D6
Eboy Dem. Rep. of the Congo 2°50N 23°11E 264 B4
Ebrach Germany 49°51N 10°29E 179 F6
Ebre = Ebro ➝ Spain 40°43N 0°54E 196 E5
Ébrié, Lagune Côte d'Ivoire 5°12N 4°26W 262 D4
Ebro ➝ Spain 40°43N 0°54E 196 E5
Ebro, Embalse del Spain 43°0N 3°58W 194 C7
Ebstorf Germany 53°2N 10°24E 178 B6
Ebute-Metta Nigeria 6°28N 3°23E 124 B2
Ecatepec de Morelos Mexico 19°36N 99°3W 319 D5
Ecbatana = Hamadān Iran 34°52N 48°32E 213 E13
Ecclesville Trin. & Tob. 10°19N 61°8W 323 t
Eceabat Turkey 40°11N 26°21E 203 F10
Ech Chéliff Algeria 36°10N 1°20E 261 A5
Ech Chéliff □ Algeria 36°15N 1°30E 261 A5
Echague Phil. 16°42N 121°38E 232 C3
Echechonnee ➝ U.S.A. 32°39N 83°36W 316 C6
Echigo-Sammyaku Japan 36°50N 139°50E 221 F9
Echinades Greece 38°25N 21°2E 207 C3
Echinos Greece 41°16N 25°1E 203 E9
Échirolles France 45°8N 5°44E 175 C9
Echizen Japan 35°50N 136°10E 223 B8
Echizen-Misaki Japan 35°59N 135°57E 223 B7
Echmiadzin = Ejmiatsin Armenia 40°12N 44°19E 191 K7
Echo U.S.A. 31°29N 85°28W 316 D4
Echo Bay N.W.T., Canada 66°5N 117°55W 294 D8
Echo Bay Ont., Canada 46°29N 84°4W 298 C3
Echo Park Los Angeles, U.S.A. 127 a1
Echoing ➝ Canada 55°51N 92°5W 298 B1
Echterdingen, Stuttgart ✈ (STR) Germany 48°42N 9°11E 179 G5
Echternach Lux. 49°49N 6°25E 170 E6
Echuca Australia 36°10S 144°45E 283 D6
Écija Spain 37°30N 5°10W 195 H5
Eckental Germany 49°35N 11°12E 179 F7
Eckernförde Germany 54°28N 9°50E 178 A5
Eclectic U.S.A. 32°38N 86°2W 316 C3
Eclipse I. Australia 35°5S 117°58E 279 G2
Eclipse Is. Australia 13°54S 126°19E 278 B4
Eclipse Sd. Canada 72°38N 79°0W 295 C16
Écommoy France 47°50N 0°17E 172 E7
Economy = Ambridge U.S.A. 40°36N 80°14W 312 F4
Ecoporanga Brazil 18°23S 40°50W 333 E3
Écouché France 48°42N 0°10W 172 D6
Ecrins △ France 44°54N 6°18E 175 D10
Ecuador ■ S. Amer. 2°0S 78°0W 328 D2
Ecuador, Volcán Ecuador 1°1S 91°32W 330 a
Écueillé France 47°5N 1°21E 172 E8
Ed Sweden 58°55N 11°55E 163 F5
Ed Dabbura Sudan 17°40N 34°15E 256 D3
Ed Da'ein Sudan 11°26N 26°9E 257 E2
Ed Damazin Sudan 11°46N 34°21E 266 B3
Ed Dâmer Sudan 17°27N 34°0E 256 D3
Ed Dar el Beida = Casablanca Morocco 33°36N 7°36W 260 B3
Ed Debba Sudan 18°0N 30°51E 256 D3
Ed Déffa Egypt 30°40N 26°30E 256 A2
Ed Deim Sudan 10°10N 28°20E 257 E2
Ed Dibeikir Sudan 10°23N 29°9E 266 B2
Ed Dueim Sudan 14°0N 32°10E 257 E3
Eda Japan 35°33N 139°33E 140 B2
Edam Sask., Canada 53°11N 108°46W 297 C7
Edam Neths. 52°31N 5°3E 170 B5
Edane Sweden 59°38N 12°49E 162 E6
Edapally India 11°19N 78°3E 245 J4
Eday U.K. 59°11N 2°47W 167 B6
Edchera W. Sahara 27°2N 13°4W 260 C2
Edd Eritrea 14°0N 41°38E 257 E5
Eddrachillis B. U.K. 58°17N 5°14W 167 C3
Eddystone U.K. 50°11N 4°16W 169 G3
Eddystone Pt. Australia 40°59S 148°20E 281 G4
Eddyville U.S.A. 41°9N 92°38W 310 C4
Ede Neths. 52°4N 5°40E 170 B5
Ede Nigeria 7°45N 4°29E 263 D5
Édéa Cameroon 3°51N 10°9E 263 E7
Edebäck Sweden 60°4N 13°32E 162 D7
Edehon L. Canada 60°25N 97°15W 297 A9
Edelény Hungary 48°18N 20°44E 182 B5
Eden = Bar Harbor U.S.A. 44°23N 68°13W 309 C19
Eden N.S.W., Australia 37°3S 149°55E 283 D8
Eden N.C., U.S.A. 36°29N 79°53W 315 C15
Eden N.Y., U.S.A. 42°39N 78°55W 312 D6
Eden Tex., U.S.A. 31°13N 99°51W 314 F5
Eden ➝ U.K. 54°57N 3°1W 168 C4
Eden Gardens Kolkata, India 22°34N 88°20E 124 B2
Edenburg S. Africa 29°43S 25°58E 270 C4
Edendale N.Z. 46°19S 168°48E 285 G3
Edendale Gauteng, S. Africa 26°8S 28°9E 123 A2
Edendale KwaZulu Natal, S. Africa 29°39S 30°18E 271 C5
Edenderry Ireland 53°21N 7°4W 166 C4
Edenhope Australia 37°4S 141°19E 282 D4
Edenton U.S.A. 36°4N 76°39W 315 C16
Edenville S. Africa 27°37S 27°34E 271 C4
Eder ➝ Germany 51°12N 9°28E 178 D5
Eder-Stausee Germany 51°10N 8°57E 178 D4
Edessa Greece 40°48N 22°5E 202 F6
Edewecht Germany 53°8N 7°58E 178 B3
Edfu = Idfû Egypt 24°55N 32°49E 256 C3
Edgar U.S.A. 40°22N 97°58W 308 E5
Edgars Cr. ➝ Australia 37°43S 144°58E 128 A1
Edgartown U.S.A. 41°23N 70°31W 313 E14
Edge Hill U.K. 52°8N 1°26W 169 E6
Edgecliff U.S.A. 32°39N 97°20W 120 C1
Edgecumbe N.Z. 37°59S 176°47E 284 D5
Edgefield U.S.A. 33°47N 81°56W 316 B8
Edgeley Ont., Canada 43°47N 79°31W 141 A1
Edgeley N. Dak., U.S.A. 46°22N 98°43W 308 B4
Edgemar U.S.A. 37°39N 122°29W 136 C2
Edgemont U.S.A. 43°18N 103°50W 308 D2
Edgeøya Svalbard 77°45N 22°30E 150 B9
Edgerton Ohio, U.S.A. 41°27N 84°45W 311 C12
Edgerton Wis., U.S.A. 42°50N 89°4W 310 B7
Edgewater Fla., U.S.A. 28°59N 80°54W 317 G9
Edgewater N.J., U.S.A. 40°49N 73°58W 132 B2
Edgewood Fla., U.S.A. 28°29N 81°22W 133 B2
Edgewood Ill., U.S.A. 38°55N 88°40W 311 F8
Édhessa = Edessa Greece 40°48N 22°5E 202 F6
Edievale N.Z. 45°49S 169°22E 285 F4
Edina Liberia 6°0N 10°10W 262 D2
Edina Mo., U.S.A. 40°10N 92°11W 310 D4
Edinboro U.S.A. 41°52N 80°8W 312 E4
Edinburg Ill., U.S.A. 39°39N 89°23W 310 E7
Edinburg Tex., U.S.A. 26°18N 98°10W 314 H5
Edinburgh U.K. 55°57N 3°13W 121 B2
Edinburgh Ind., U.S.A. 39°21N 85°58W 311 E11
Edinburgh ✈ (EDI) U.K. 55°54N 3°22W 121 B1
Edinburgh, City of □ U.K. 55°57N 3°17W 167 F5
Edinburgh Castle Edinburgh, U.K. 121 b2
Edineț Moldova 48°9N 27°18E 183 B12
Edirne Turkey 41°40N 26°34E 203 E10
Edirne □ Turkey 41°12N 26°30E 203 E10
Edison Ga., U.S.A. 31°34N 84°44W 316 D5
Edison Wash., U.S.A. 48°33N 122°27W 306 B4
Edison Park U.S.A. 42°1N 87°48W 119 A2
Edisto ➝ U.S.A. 32°29N 80°20W 316 C9
Edisto Beach U.S.A. 32°29N 80°20W 316 C9
Edisto I. U.S.A. 32°35N 80°20W 316 C9
Edithburgh Australia 35°5S 137°43E 282 C2
Edjeleh Algeria 28°38N 9°50E 261 C6
Edmeston U.S.A. 42°42N 75°15W 313 D9
Edmond U.S.A. 35°39N 97°29W 314 D6
Edmonds U.S.A. 47°48N 122°22W 306 C4
Edmondston U.S.A. 38°56N 76°54W 143 B3
Edmonton Queens., Australia 17°2S 145°46E 280 B4
Edmonton Alta., Canada 53°30N 113°30W 296 C6
Edmund L. Canada 54°45N 93°17W 298 B1
Edmundston Canada 47°23N 68°20W 299 C6
Edna U.S.A. 28°59N 96°39W 314 G6
Edo □ Nigeria 6°30N 6°0E 263 D6
Edo ➝ Japan 35°38N 139°52E 140 B4
Edogawa Japan 35°43N 139°52E 140 A4
Edolo Italy 46°10N 10°21E 198 B7
Edøya Norway 63°18N 8°10E 164 A5
Edremit Turkey 39°34N 27°0E 205 B9
Edremit Körfezi Turkey 39°30N 26°45E 205 B8
Edsberg Sweden 59°26N 17°57E 139 A1
Edsbro Sweden 59°54N 18°29E 162 E12
Edsbruk Sweden 58°1N 16°29E 163 F10
Edsbyn Sweden 61°23N 15°49E 162 C9
Edson Canada 53°35N 116°28W 296 C5
Eduardo Castex Argentina 35°50S 64°18W 334 D3
Edward ➝ Australia 35°5S 143°30E 282 C5
Edward, L. Africa 0°25S 29°40E 268 C2
Edward VII Land Antarctica 80°0S 150°0W 151 E13
Edwardesabad = Bannu Pakistan 33°0N 70°18E 240 B3
Edwards Calif., U.S.A. 34°50N 117°40W 307 L9
Edwards N.Y., U.S.A. 44°20N 75°15W 313 B9
Edwards ➝ U.S.A. 41°9N 90°59W 310 C6
Edwards L. Australia 37°42S 144°59E 128 A1
Edwards Plateau U.S.A. 30°45N 101°20W 314 F4
Edwardsburg U.S.A. 41°48N 86°6W 311 C10
Edwardsville Ill., U.S.A. 38°49N 89°58W 310 F7
Edwardsville Pa., U.S.A. 41°15N 75°56W 313 E9
Edzná Mexico 19°39N 90°19W 319 D6
Edzo = Behchoko Canada 62°50N 116°3W 296 A5
Eek U.S.A. 60°14N 162°2W 303 F7
Eeklo Belgium 51°11N 3°33E 170 C3
Eel ➝ Ind., U.S.A. 39°7N 86°57W 311 E10
Eel ➝ Ind., U.S.A. 40°45N 86°22W 311 D10
Eenhana Namibia 17°30S 16°23E 270 A2
Eesti = Estonia ■ Europe 58°30N 25°30E 188 C3
Efate, I. Vanuatu 17°40S 168°25E 287 G6
Eferding Austria 48°18N 14°1E 180 C7
Effigy Mounds ⌂ U.S.A. 43°5N 91°11W 310 A5
Effingham U.S.A. 39°7N 88°33W 311 E8
Eforie Romania 44°1N 28°37E 183 F13
Efoulen Cameroon 2°46N 10°43E 264 B2
Eftelot Norway 59°33N 9°49E 164 E6
Efxinoupoli Greece 39°12N 22°42E 204 B4
Efzonos Greece 37°55N 23°59E 112 B2
Ega ➝ Spain 42°19N 1°55W 196 C3
Égadi, Ísole Italy 37°55N 12°16E 200 E5
Egaleo Greece 37°59N 23°40E 112 B2
Egaleo, Oros Greece 38°0N 23°36E 112 B1
Egan Range U.S.A. 39°35N 114°55W 304 G6
Eganville Canada 45°32N 77°5W 312 A7
Egedesminde = Aasiaat Greenland 68°43N 52°56W 154 D5
Egegik U.S.A. 58°13N 157°22W 303 G8
Eger = Cheb Czechia 50°9N 12°28E 180 A5
Eger Hungary 47°53N 20°27E 182 C5
Eger ➝ Hungary 47°38N 20°50E 182 C5
Egersund Norway 58°26N 6°1E 164 F3
Egg I. St. Helena 15°58S 5°47W 153 h
Egg L. Canada 55°5N 105°30W 297 B7
Eggedal Norway 60°14N 9°22E 164 D6
Eggegebirge Südlicher Teutoburger Wald ⌂ Germany 51°40N 8°59E 178 D4
Eggenburg Austria 48°38N 15°50E 180 C8
Eggenfelden Germany 48°23N 12°46E 179 G8
Egherta Somalia 2°4N 43°11E 267 D5
Éghezée Belgium 50°35N 4°55E 170 D4
Egholo Solomon Is. 8°25S 157°25E 287 M9
Egilsstaðir Iceland 65°16N 14°25W 155 B12
Egina Greece 37°45N 23°26E 204 D5
Eginio Greece 40°28N 22°28E 202 F6
Egio Greece 38°15N 22°5E 204 C4
Egito Angola 12°4S 13°58E 265 E2
Égletons France 45°24N 2°3E 174 C6
Eglinton I. Canada 75°48N 118°30W 295 B8
Egmont Canada 49°45N 123°56W 296 D4
Egmont, C. N.Z. 39°16S 173°45E 284 F2
Egmont, Mt. = Taranaki, Mt. N.Z. 39°17S 174°5E 284 F3
Egmont △ N.Z. 39°17S 174°4E 284 F3
Egra India 21°54N 87°32E 243 J12
Eğridir Turkey 37°52N 30°51E 212 D4
Eğridir Gölü Turkey 37°53N 30°50E 212 D4
Egtved Denmark 55°38N 9°18E 163 J3
Éguas ➝ Brazil 13°26S 44°14W 333 D3
Egum Atoll Papua N. G. 9°25S 152°0E 286 E7
Éguzon-Chantôme France 46°27N 1°33E 173 F8
Egvekinot Russia 66°19N 179°50W 215 C19
Egyek Hungary 47°39N 20°52E 182 C5
Egypt ■ Africa 28°0N 31°0E 256 B3
Eha Amufu Nigeria 6°30N 7°46E 263 D6
Eheli Algeria 22°26N 4°40E 261 D5
Ehime □ Japan 33°30N 132°40E 222 D4
Ehingen Germany 48°16N 9°43E 179 G5
Ehrenberg U.S.A. 33°36N 114°31W 307 M12
Ehrhardt U.S.A. 33°6N 81°1W 316 B8
Ehrwald Austria 47°24N 10°56E 180 D3
Eiao French Polynesia 8°0S 140°40W 289 f
Eibar Spain 43°11N 2°28W 196 B2
Eibenschitz = Ivančice Czechia 49°6N 16°23E 181 B9
Eiche Germany 52°33N 13°35E 115 A4
Eiche Süd Germany 52°33N 13°35E 115 A4
Eichstätt Germany 48°54N 11°11E 179 G7
Eide Hordaland, Norway 60°31N 6°44E 164 D3
Eide Møre og Romsdal, Norway 62°55N 7°27E 164 B4
Eider ➝ Germany 54°19N 8°57E 178 A4
Eidsbugarden Norway 61°23N 8°16E 164 C5
Eidsbygda Norway 62°36N 7°30E 164 B4
Eidsdalen Norway 62°16N 7°10E 164 B4
Eidsvåg Norway 62°46N 8°2E 164 B5
Eidsvold Australia 25°25S 151°12E 281 D5
Eidsvoll Norway 60°19N 11°14E 164 D8
Eielson U.S.A. 64°40N 147°4W 303 D11
Eifel Germany 50°15N 6°50E 179 E2
Eiffel, Tour Paris, France 134 c2
Eiffel Flats Zimbabwe 18°20S 30°0E 269 F3
Eiger Switz. 46°34N 8°1E 198 B5
Eigg U.K. 56°54N 6°10W 167 E2
Eighty Mile Beach Australia 19°30S 120°40E 278 C3
Eikefjord Norway 61°35N 5°27E 164 C2
Eikelandsosen Norway 60°15N 5°34E 164 D2
Eiken Norway 58°29N 7°14E 164 F4
Eikeren Norway 59°38N 9°56E 164 E6
Eikesdalen Norway 62°28N 8°12E 164 B5
Eil, L. U.K. 56°51N 5°16W 167 E3
Eil Malk Palau 7°10N 134°23E 288 c
Eilat = Elat Israel 29°30N 34°56E 251 J5
Eildon Australia 37°14S 145°55E 283 D6
Eildon, L. Australia 37°10S 146°0E 283 D7
Eilean Siar □ U.K. 57°30N 7°10W 167 D1
Eilenburg Germany 51°27N 12°36E 178 D8
Ein Arik West Bank 31°54N 35°8E 123 A1
Ein el Luweiqa Sudan 14°5N 33°50E 257 E3
Ein Naquba Israel 31°47N 35°7E 123 B1
Ein Rafa Israel 31°47N 35°7E 123 B1
Eina Norway 60°38N 10°35E 164 D7
Einarsstaðir Iceland 65°44N 17°24W 155 B9
Einasleigh Australia 18°32S 144°5E 280 B3
Einasleigh ➝ Australia 17°30S 142°17E 280 B3
Einbeck Germany 51°49N 9°53E 178 D5
Eindhoven Neths. 51°26N 5°28E 170 C5
Einsiedeln Switz. 47°7N 8°46E 179 H4
Eire = Ireland ■ Europe 53°50N 7°52W 166 C4
Eiríksjökull Iceland 64°46N 20°24W 155 C6
Eiríksstaðir Iceland 65°7N 15°25W 155 B11
Eiriosgaigh = Eriskay U.K. 57°4N 7°18W 167 D1
Eirunepé Brazil 6°35S 69°53W 330 B4
Eiseb ➝ Namibia 20°33S 20°59E 270 B2
Eisenach Germany 50°58N 10°19E 178 E6
Eisenberg Germany 50°58N 11°54E 178 E7
Eisenerz Austria 47°32N 14°54E 180 D7
Eisenhüttenstadt Germany 52°9N 14°38E 178 C10
Eisenkappel Austria 46°29N 14°36E 180 E7
Eisenstadt Austria 47°51N 16°31E 181 D9
Eisenstein = Železná Ruda Czechia 49°8N 13°15E 180 B6
Eisleben Germany 51°32N 11°32E 178 D7
Eislingen Germany 48°41N 9°42E 179 G5
Eivindvik Norway 60°59N 5°5E 164 D2
Eivissa Spain 38°54N 1°26E 206 D1
Eixe, Serra do Spain 42°24N 6°54W 194 C4
Eizariya West Bank 31°46N 35°16E 123 B2
Ejby Denmark 55°41N 12°24E 118 A2
Ejea de los Caballeros Spain 42°7N 1°9W 196 C3
Ejeda Madag. 24°20S 44°31E 272 C1
Ejigbo Nigeria 6°33N 3°18E 124 A1
Ejmiatsin Armenia 40°12N 44°19E 191 K7
Ejura Ghana 7°23N 1°15W 263 D4
Ejutla Mexico 16°34N 96°44W 319 D5
Ekalaka U.S.A. 45°53N 104°33W 304 D11
Ekalla Gabon 1°27S 14°0E 264 C2
Ekanga Dem. Rep. of the Congo 2°23S 23°14E 264 C4
Ekaterinburg = Yekaterinburg Russia 56°50N 60°30E 214 D7
Ekeberg Norway 59°53N 10°46E 133 A3
Ekenäs = Raasepori Finland 60°0N 23°26E 188 B2
Ekenässjön Sweden 57°28N 15°1E 163 G9
Ekerö Sweden 59°16N 17°45E 162 E11
Eket Nigeria 4°38N 7°56E 263 E6
Eketahuna N.Z. 40°38S 175°43E 284 G4
Ekibastuz Kazakhstan 51°50N 75°10E 217 B9
Ekiti □ Nigeria 7°25N 5°20E 263 D6
Eklutna U.S.A. 61°27N 149°22W 303 F10
Eknäs Sweden 59°18N 18°13E 139 B3
Ekoli Dem. Rep. of the Congo 0°23S 24°13E 264 C4
Ekoln Sweden 59°45N 17°37E 162 E11
Ekouamou Congo 0°8N 16°31E 264 B3
Ekoungounou Congo 1°10S 15°52E 264 C3
Ekshärad Sweden 60°10N 13°30E 162 D7
Eksjö Sweden 57°40N 14°58E 163 G8
Ekukola Dem. Rep. of the Congo 0°31S 18°56E 264 C3
Ekuku Dem. Rep. of the Congo 0°41S 21°42E 264 C4
Ekukula Dem. Rep. of the Congo 0°15N 21°30E 264 B4
Ekuma ➝ Namibia 18°40S 16°2E 270 A2
Ekuta Dem. Rep. of the Congo 3°0N 18°50E 264 B3
Ekwan ➝ Canada 53°12N 82°15W 298 B3
Ekwan Pt. Canada 53°16N 82°7W 298 B3
Ekwok U.S.A. 59°22N 157°30W 303 G8
El Aaiún W. Sahara 27°9N 13°12W 260 C2
El Aargub Mauritania 23°37N 15°52W 260 D1
El Abanico Chile 37°20S 71°31W 334 D1
El 'Abbasiya El Qâhira, Egypt 30°3N 31°16E 117 A2
El Abbasiya Sudan 12°10N 31°18E 257 E3
El Abiodh-Sidi-Cheikh Algeria 32°53N 0°31E 261 B5
El Adde Somalia 2°35N 46°9E 267 D6
El Adeb Larache Algeria 27°22N 8°52E 261 C6
El 'Agrûd Egypt 30°14N 34°24E 251 H5
El Agua Venezuela 11°8N 63°52W 329 a
El Agustino Peru 12°2S 77°0W 124 B2
El Agustino, Cerro Peru 12°3S 76°59W 124 B3
El Aïoun Morocco 34°33N 2°30W 261 B4
El Ait Sudan 12°22N 27°27E 257 E2
El 'Aiyat Egypt 29°36N 31°15E 256 J7
El Alamein Egypt 30°48N 28°58E 256 A2
El Alto La Paz, Bolivia 16°30S 68°10W 330 D4
El Alto Peru 4°15S 81°14W 330 A1
El Aouj Mauritania 22°53N 12°49W 260 D2
El 'Aqaba, W. ➝ Egypt 30°7N 33°54E 251 H4
El 'Arag Egypt 28°40N 26°20E 256 B2
El Aricha Algeria 34°13N 1°10W 261 B4
El Arîḥâ West Bank 31°52N 35°27E 251 G6
El 'Arîsh Egypt 31°8N 33°50E 251 G4
El 'Arîsh, W. ➝ Egypt 31°8N 33°47E 251 G4
El Arrouch Algeria 36°37N 6°53E 261 A6
El Asnam = Ech Chéliff Algeria 36°10N 1°20E 261 A5
El Astillero Spain 43°24N 3°49W 194 B7
El Avagi Somalia 3°36N 46°57E 267 D6
El Badâri Egypt 27°4N 31°25E 256 B3
El Badrshein Egypt 29°51N 31°16E 251 J2
El Bagur Egypt 30°25N 31°2E 251 H2
El Bahr el Ahmar □ Egypt 28°15N 32°50E 251 K3
El Bahrein Egypt 28°30N 26°25E 256 B2
El Ballâs Egypt 26°2N 32°43E 256 B3
El Balyana Egypt 26°10N 32°3E 256 B3
El Banco Colombia 9°0N 73°58W 328 B3
El Baqeir Sudan 18°40N 33°40E 256 D3
El Baragil Egypt 30°4N 31°9E 117 A1
El Barco de Ávila Spain 40°21N 5°31W 194 E5
El Barco de Valdeorras = O Barco Spain 42°23N 6°58W 194 C4
El Basâlîn Egypt 29°58N 31°16E 117 B2
El Bauga Sudan 18°18N 33°52E 256 D3
El Baúl Venezuela 8°57N 68°17W 328 B4
El Bawiti Egypt 28°25N 28°45E 256 B2
El Bayadh Algeria 33°40N 1°1E 261 B5
El Bayadh □ Algeria 32°30N 1°10E 261 B5
El Bichar Venezuela 10°46N 63°58W 329 a
El Bierzo Spain 42°45N 6°30W 194 C4
El Bira West Bank 31°54N 35°13E 123 A2
El Bluff Nic. 11°59N 83°40W 320 D3
El Bolsón Argentina 41°55S 71°30W 336 B2
El Bonillo Spain 38°57N 2°35W 197 G2
El Bosque Chile 33°32S 70°40W 137 C2
El Buheirat = Lakes □ South Sudan 7°0N 30°0E 257 F3
El Bur Somalia 4°40N 46°37E 267 D6
El Burgo de Osma Spain 41°35N 3°4W 196 D1
El Cain Argentina 41°38S 68°19W 336 B3
El Cajon U.S.A. 32°48N 116°58W 307 N10
El Calafate Argentina 50°19S 72°15W 336 D2
El Callao Venezuela 7°18N 61°50W 329 B5
El Campello Spain 38°26N 0°24W 197 G4
El Campo U.S.A. 29°12N 96°16W 314 G6
El Capitan U.S.A. 37°44N 119°38W 306 H7
El Carbón Honduras 15°25N 85°32W 320 C2
El Cardón Venezuela 11°6N 63°51W 329 a
El Carmen Bolivia 13°40S 63°55W 331 C5
El Carmen Santiago, Chile 33°22S 70°43W 137 B1
El Carmen Colombia 9°43N 75°8W 328 B2
El Centro U.S.A. 32°48N 115°34W 307 N11
El Cerro Bolivia 17°30S 61°40W 331 D5
El Cerro de Andévalo Spain 37°45N 6°57W 195 H4
El Chaltén Argentina 49°19S 72°56W 336 C2
El Cocuy Colombia 6°25N 72°27W 328 B3
El Cocuy △ Colombia 6°33N 72°5W 328 B3
El Compadre Mexico 32°20N 116°14W 307 N10
El Copey, Cerro Venezuela 11°1N 63°55W 329 a
El Corcovado Argentina 43°25S 71°35W 336 B2
El Coronil Spain 37°5N 5°38W 195 H5
El Cortijo Chile 33°22S 70°42W 137 B1
El Cotillo Canary Is. 28°41N 14°1W 153 e2
El Cristo, Vaso Regulador Mexico 19°30N 99°5W 128 B1
El Cuy Argentina 39°55S 68°25W 336 A3
El Cuyo Mexico 21°31N 87°41W 319 C7
El Dab'a Egypt 31°0N 28°27E 256 H6
El Daheir Egypt 31°13N 34°10E 251 G5
El Dambahaddo Somalia 3°17N 46°40E 267 D6
El Deir Egypt 25°25N 32°20E 256 B3
El Dere = Ceeldheere Somalia 5°22N 46°11E 267 C6
El Dere Ethiopia 5°6N 43°5E 267 C5
El Descanso Mexico 32°12N 116°58W 307 N10
El Desemboque Mexico 30°33N 113°1W 318 A2
El Dilingat Egypt 30°50N 30°31E 256 H7
El Diviso Colombia 1°22N 78°14W 328 C2
El Djouf Mauritania 21°25N 6°40W 260 D3
El Dorado Sinaloa, Mexico 24°17N 107°21W 318 C3
El Dorado Ark., U.S.A. 33°12N 92°40W 314 E8
El Dorado Kans., U.S.A. 37°49N 96°52W 308 G5
El Dorado Venezuela 6°55N 61°37W 329 B5
El Dorado Int. ✈ (BOG) Colombia 4°42N 74°9W 328 C3
El Dorado Springs U.S.A. 37°52N 94°1W 310 G2
El Duqqi Egypt 30°1N 31°12E 117 A2
El Eglab Algeria 26°20N 4°30W 260 C4
El 'Ein Sudan 16°35N 29°22E 257 D2
El Ejido Spain 36°47N 2°49W 195 J8
El Encinar de los Reyes Spain 40°30N 3°39W 127 A2
El Escorial Spain 40°35N 4°7W 194 E6
El Espinal Venezuela 10°58N 63°59W 329 a
El Espinar Spain 41°43N 4°15W 194 D6
El Eulma Algeria 36°9N 5°42E 261 A6
El Faiyûm Egypt 29°19N 30°50E 256 J7
El Faourar Tunisia 33°22N 8°45E 258 B1
El Fâsher Sudan 13°33N 25°26E 257 E2
El Fashn Egypt 28°50N 30°54E 256 J7
El Ferrol = Ferrol Spain 43°29N 8°15W 194 B2
El Fifi Sudan 10°4N 25°0E 257 F2
El Fud Ethiopia 7°15N 42°52E 267 C5
El Fuerte Mexico 26°25N 108°39W 318 B3
El Ga'a Sudan 14°16N 29°59E 257 E2
El Gamâlîya Egypt 31°10N 31°52E 251 G2
El Garef Sudan 12°3N 34°19E 257 E3
El Gebir Sudan 13°40N 29°40E 257 E2
El Gedida Egypt 25°40N 28°30E 256 B2
El Geneina = Al Junaynah Sudan 13°27N 22°45E 259 F4
El Geteina Sudan 14°50N 32°27E 257 E3
El Gezira Egypt 30°2N 31°13E 117 A2
El Gezira □ Sudan 15°0N 33°0E 257 E3
El Gharbîya □ Egypt 30°50N 31°0E 251 H2
El Ghuriya Egypt 30°2N 31°15E 117 A2
El Gir Sudan 19°50N 28°18E 256 D2
El Gîza Egypt 30°1N 31°12E 117 A2
El Gogorrón △ Mexico 21°49N 100°57W 318 C4
El Goléa Algeria 30°30N 2°50E 261 B5
El Gouna Egypt 27°5N 33°47E 256 B3
El Guamache Nueva Esparta, Venezuela 10°44N 63°54W 329 a
El Guamache Nueva Esparta, Venezuela 10°54N 64°3W 329 a
El Hadjira Algeria 32°36N 5°30E 261 B6
El Hagiz Sudan 15°15N 35°50E 257 D4
El Hâi Egypt 29°39N 31°18E 256 J7
El Hajeb Morocco 33°43N 5°13W 260 B3
El Hamma Tunisia 33°54N 9°48E 258 B1
El Hammam Egypt 30°52N 29°25E 256 A2
El Hammâmi Mauritania 23°3N 11°30W 260 D2
El Hâmûl Egypt 31°18N 31°9E 251 G2
El Hamurre Somalia 7°13N 48°54E 267 C6
El Hank Mauritania 24°30N 7°0W 260 D3
El Hasian W. Sahara 26°20N 14°0W 260 C2
El Hawata Sudan 13°25N 34°42E 257 E3
El Hideib Sudan 13°0N 32°50E 257 E3
El Hilla Sudan 13°24N 27°2E 257 E2
El Homr Algeria 29°43N 1°45E 261 C5
El 'Idisât Egypt 25°30N 32°35E 256 B3
El Iskandarîya Egypt 31°13N 29°58E 256 H6
El Jadida Morocco 33°11N 8°17W 260 B3
El Jardal Honduras 14°54N 88°50W 320 D2
El Jebelein Sudan 12°40N 32°55E 257 E3
El Jebha Morocco 35°11N 4°43W 260 A4
El Jem Tunisia 35°19N 10°41E 258 A2
El Kab Sudan 19°27N 32°46E 256 D3
El Kafr el Sharqi Egypt 31°16N 31°10E 256 H7
El Kala Algeria 36°53N 8°26E 261 A6
El Kamlin Sudan 15°3N 33°11E 257 D3
El Kantara Algeria 35°14N 5°45E 261 A6
El Kantara Tunisia 33°45N 10°58E 258 B2
El Karaba Sudan 18°32N 33°41E 256 D3
El Kef Tunisia 36°12N 8°47E 258 A1
El Kef □ Tunisia 36°0N 9°0E 261 A6
El Kelaâ de Srahna Morocco 32°2N 7°27W 260 B3
El Kelaâ M'Gouna Morocco 31°14N 6°7W 260 B3
El Kere Ethiopia 5°50N 42°5E 257 F5
El Khadr West Bank 31°42N 35°10E 123 B1
El Khalifa Egypt 30°0N 31°15E 117 A2
El Khandaq Sudan 18°30N 30°30E 256 D3
El Khanka Egypt 30°13N 31°21E 251 H2
El Khârga Egypt 25°30N 30°33E 256 B3
El Khartûm Sudan 15°31N 32°35E 257 D3
El Khartûm □ Sudan 16°0N 33°0E 257 D3
El Khartûm Bahri Sudan 15°40N 32°31E 257 D3
El Khroub Algeria 36°10N 6°55E 261 A6
El Kôm el Ahmar Egypt 30°6N 31°10E 117 A2
El Kseur Algeria 36°46N 4°49E 261 A5
El Ksiba Morocco 32°45N 6°1W 260 B3
El Kuntilla Egypt 30°1N 34°45E 251 H5
El Laqâwa Sudan 11°25N 29°1E 257 E2
El Leh Ethiopia 3°46N 39°13E 257 G4
El Leiya Sudan 16°15N 35°28E 257 D4
El Leoncito △ Argentina 31°58S 69°10W 334 C2
El Limón Panama 9°15N 79°49W 320 c
El Lucero Mexico 30°37N 106°31W 318 A3
El Ma'âdi Egypt 29°57N 31°15E 117 B2
El Maestrazgo Spain 40°30N 0°25W 196 E4
El Mafâza Sudan 13°38N 34°30E 257 E3
El Maghra Egypt 30°15N 28°55E 256 A2
El Mahalla el Kubra Egypt 31°0N 31°0E 256 H7
El Mahârîq Egypt 25°35N 30°35E 256 B3
El Maîmûn Egypt 29°14N 31°12E 256 J7
El Maitén Argentina 42°3S 71°10W 336 B2
El Maiz Algeria 28°19N 0°9W 261 C4
El Maks el Bahari Egypt 24°30N 30°40E 256 C3
El Malpais ⌂ U.S.A. 34°53N 108°0W 305 J10
El Manshâh Egypt 26°26N 31°50E 256 B3
El Mansour Algeria 27°47N 0°14W 261 C4
El Mansûra Egypt 31°0N 31°19E 256 H7
El Manteco Venezuela 7°38N 62°45W 329 B5
El Manzala Egypt 31°10N 31°50E 256 H7
El Marâgha Egypt 26°35N 31°10E 256 B3
El Masid Sudan 15°15N 33°0E 257 D3
El Masnou Spain 41°28N 2°20E 196 D7
El Matarîya El Mansûra, Egypt 31°15N 32°0E 256 H8
El Matarîya El Qâhira, Egypt 30°7N 31°18E 117 A2
El Meda Ethiopia 5°39N 41°47E 257 F5
El Medano Canary Is. 28°3N 16°32W 153 e1
El Meghaier Algeria 33°55N 5°58E 261 B6
El Ménia = El Goléa Algeria 30°30N 2°50E 261 B5
El Menia □ Algeria 31°0N 2°30E 261 B5
El Meraguen Algeria 28°0N 0°7W 261 C4
El Metemma Sudan 16°50N 33°10E 257 D3
El M'Ghair □ Algeria 34°0N 6°0E 261 B6
El Miamo Venezuela 7°39N 61°46W 329 B5
El Milagro Argentina 30°59S 65°59W 334 C2
El Milia Algeria 36°51N 6°13E 261 A6
El Minufiya □ Egypt 30°30N 31°0E 251 H2
El Minyâ Egypt 28°7N 30°33E 256 B3
El Mohandessin Egypt 30°2N 31°11E 117 A2
El Monte U.S.A. 34°4N 118°1W 126 B4
El Montseny Spain 41°55N 2°25E 196 D7
El Mreiti Mauritania 23°29N 7°51W 260 D3
El Mreyye Mauritania 18°0N 6°0W 262 B3
El Muqattam Egypt 30°1N 31°17E 117 A2
El Mûskî Egypt 30°3N 31°15E 117 A2
El Nido Phil. 11°10N 119°25E 233 F2
El Niybo Ethiopia 4°40N 39°55E 257 G4
El Obeid Sudan 13°8N 30°10E 257 E3
El Odaiya Sudan 12°8N 28°12E 257 E2
El Oro Mexico 19°51N 100°7W 319 D4
El Oro □ Ecuador 3°30S 79°50W 328 D2
El Oued Algeria 33°20N 6°58E 261 B6
El Oued □ Algeria 33°10N 7°15E 261 B6
El Palmar Bolivia 17°50S 63°9W 331 D5
El Palmar Venezuela 7°58N 61°53W 329 B5
El Palmar △ Argentina 32°10S 58°31W 334 C4
El Pardo Spain 40°30N 3°46W 127 A1
El Paso = Derby U.S.A. 37°33N 97°16W 308 G5
El Paso Ill., U.S.A. 40°44N 89°1W 310 D7
El Paso Tex., U.S.A. 31°45N 106°29W 314 F1
El Paso de Robles = Paso Robles U.S.A. 35°38N 120°41W 306 K6
El Pedernoso Spain 39°29N 2°45W 197 F2
El Pedroso Spain 37°51N 5°45W 195 H5
El Pilar Venezuela 10°32N 63°9W 329 A5
El Pinacate y Gran Desierto de Altar = Gran Desierto del Pinacate ⌂ Mexico 31°51N 113°32W 318 A2
El Pobleneu Spain 41°23N 2°11E 114 A2
El Pobo de Dueñas Spain 40°46N 1°39W 196 E3
El Portal Calif., U.S.A. 37°41N 119°47W 306 H7
El Portal Fla., U.S.A. 25°51N 80°11W 129 C2
El Porvenir Mexico 31°15N 105°51W 318 A3
El Prat Barcelona ✈ (BCN) Spain 41°18N 2°5E 114 B1
El Prat de Llobregat Spain 41°19N 2°5E 114 B1
El Progreso Galápagos Is., Ecuador 0°54S 89°33W 330 a
El Progreso Honduras 15°26N 87°51W 320 C2
El Pueblo Canary Is. 28°36N 17°47W 153 e1
El Pueblo Historic Park ⌂ Los Angeles, U.S.A. 127 b2
El Puente del Arzobispo Spain 39°48N 5°10W 194 F5
El Puerto de Santa María Spain 36°36N 6°13W 195 J4
El Qâhira Egypt 30°2N 31°13E 117 A2
El Qâhira □ Egypt 29°30N 31°30E 251 J2
El Qanâyat Egypt 30°37N 31°27E 251 H2
El Qantara Egypt 30°51N 32°20E 251 H3
El Qasr Egypt 25°44N 28°42E 256 B2
El Qassâsîn Egypt 30°33N 31°55E 251 H2
El Qubâbât Egypt 29°28N 31°16E 256 J7
El Qubba Egypt 30°4N 31°16E 117 A2
El Quseima Egypt 30°40N 34°15E 251 H5
El Qusîya Egypt 27°29N 30°44E 256 B3
El Râshda Egypt 25°36N 28°57E 256 B2
El Reloj Mexico 19°19N 99°9W 128 C2
El Reno U.S.A. 35°32N 97°57W 301 H20
El Retiro Spain 40°25N 3°41W 127 B1
El Rey △ Argentina 24°40S 64°34W 334 A3
El Ridisiya Egypt 24°56N 32°51E 256 C3
El Rio U.S.A. 34°14N 119°10W 307 L7
El Ronquillo Spain 37°44N 6°10W 195 H4
El Roque, Pta. Canary Is. 28°10N 15°25W 153 e1
El Rosario Mexico 30°1N 115°45W 318 A1
El Rubio Spain 37°22N 5°0W 195 H5
El Saff Egypt 29°34N 31°16E 256 J7
El Salto Santiago, Chile 33°22S 70°38W 137 B2
El Salto Durango, Mexico 23°47N 105°22W 318 C3
El Salvador ■ Cent. Amer. 13°50N 89°0W 320 D2
El Sauce Nic. 13°0N 86°40W 320 D2
El Saucejo Spain 37°4N 5°6W 195 H5
El Sereno U.S.A. 34°4N 118°10W 126 B3
El Shallal Egypt 24°0N 32°53E 256 C3
El Sharqîya □ Egypt 30°48N 31°48E 251 H2
El Simbillawein Egypt 30°48N 31°25E 256 H7
El Sombrero Venezuela 9°23N 67°3W 328 B4
El Suweis Egypt 29°58N 32°31E 256 J8
El Suweis □ Egypt 29°30N 32°15E 251 J3
El Tabbîn Egypt 29°47N 31°18E 256 J7
El Talibîya Egypt 29°59N 31°10E 117 B2
El Tamá △ S. Amer. 7°25N 72°25W 328 B3
El Tamarâni, W. ➝ Egypt 30°7N 34°43E 251 H5
El Tarf Algeria 36°46N 8°19E 261 A6
El Tarf □ Algeria 36°45N 8°10E 261 A6
El Thamad Egypt 29°40N 34°28E 251 J5
El Tigre Venezuela 8°44N 64°15W 329 B5
El Tîh, Gebel Egypt 29°40N 33°50E 251 J4
El Tîna Egypt 31°3N 32°22E 256 H8
El Tirano Puerte Fermín Venezuela 11°7N 63°51W 329 a
El Tocuyo Venezuela 9°47N 69°48W 328 B4
El Tofo Chile 29°22S 71°18W 334 B1
El Tránsito Chile 28°52S 70°17W 334 B1
El Tucuche Trin. & Tob. 10°43N 61°25W 323 t
El Tuey Venezuela 11°1N 63°57W 329 a
El Tunal Venezuela 11°4N 64°18W 329 a
El Tuparro △ Colombia 5°19N 68°28W 328 B4
El Tûr Egypt 28°14N 33°36E 251 K4
El Turbio Argentina 51°45S 72°5W 336 D2
El Uarre Somalia 3°4N 45°20E 267 D6
El Uqsur Egypt 25°41N 32°38E 256 B3
El Valle ⌂ Spain 37°56N 1°6W 197 H3
El Valle del Espíritu Santo Venezuela 10°49N 63°53W 329 a
El Vendrell Spain 41°10N 1°30E 196 D6
El Vergel Chihuahua, Mexico 26°28N 106°22W 318 B3
El Vergel Distrito Federal, Mexico 19°18N 99°5W 128 C2
El Vigía Venezuela 8°38N 71°39W 328 B3
El Viso del Alcor Spain 37°23N 5°43W 195 H5
El Wabeira Egypt 29°34N 33°6E 251 J4
El Wâhli Egypt 30°3N 31°16E 117 A2
El Wak Somalia 2°44N 41°1E 267 D5
El Weguet Ethiopia 5°28N 42°17E 257 F5
El Wuz Sudan 15°5N 30°7E 257 D3
El Yaque Venezuela 10°54N 63°57W 329 a
El Yunque, Cerro Chile 33°39S 78°50W 330 c
El Yunque Puerto Rico 18°19N 65°48W 321 b
El Zamâlik Egypt 30°3N 31°12E 117 A2
El Zeitûn Egypt 30°6N 31°18E 117 A2
Elafonisos Greece 36°29N 22°56E 204 E4
Elamanchili India 17°33N 82°50E 244 F6
Élancourt France 48°47N 1°58E 173 D8
Elands Australia 31°37S 152°20E 283 A10
Elandsfontein Junc. = Germiston S. Africa 26°13S 28°10E 123 B2
Elasa Greece 35°18N 26°21E 205 F8
Elassona Greece 39°53N 22°12E 204 B4
Elat Israel 29°30N 34°56E 251 J5
Elati Oros Greece 38°43N 20°39E 207 B2
Elatia Greece 38°37N 22°46E 204 C4
Elâzığ Turkey 38°37N 39°14E 213 C8
Elâzığ □ Turkey 38°40N 39°15E 213 C8
Elba Italy 42°46N 10°17E 198 F7
Elba Ala., U.S.A. 31°25N 86°4W 316 D3
Elbasan Albania 41°9N 20°9E 202 E4
Elbe U.S.A. 46°45N 122°10W 306 D4
Elbe ➝ Europe 53°50N 9°0E 178 B4
Elbe-Seitenkanal Germany 52°45N 10°32E 178 C6
Elberfeld U.S.A. 38°10N 87°27W 310 F9
Elbert, Mt. U.S.A. 39°7N 106°27W 304 G10
Elberton U.S.A. 34°7N 82°52W 316 A7
Elbeuf France 49°17N 1°2E 172 C8
Elbeyli Turkey 36°40N 37°27E 250 B8

Elbing = Elbląg *Poland* 54°10N 19°25E **184** D6
Elbistan *Turkey* 38°13N 37°15E **212** C7
Elbląg *Poland* 54°10N 19°25E **184** D6
Elbow *Canada* 51°7N 106°35W **297** C7
Elbrus *Russia* 43°21N 42°30E **191** J6
Elbufer-Drawehn ⌓ *Germany* 53°8N 10°58E **178** B6
Elburn *U.S.A.* 41°54N 88°28W **311** C8
Elburz Mts. = Alborz, Reshteh-ye Kūhhā-ye *Iran* 36°0N 52°0E **247** C7
Elche *Spain* 38°15N 0°42W **197** G4
Elche de la Sierra *Spain* 38°27N 2°3W **197** G2
Elcho I. *Australia* 11°55S 135°45E **280** A2
Elda *Spain* 38°29N 0°47W **197** G4
Eldama Ravine *Kenya* 0°3N 35°43E **268** B4
Elde ➜ *Germany* 53°7N 11°15E **178** B7
Eldey *Iceland* 63°45N 22°55W **155** D4
Eldon *Iowa, U.S.A.* 40°55N 92°13W **310** D4
Eldon *Mo., U.S.A.* 38°21N 92°35W **310** F4
Eldon *Wash., U.S.A.* 47°33N 123°3W **306** C3
Eldora *U.S.A.* 42°22N 93°5W **310** B3
Eldorado = Echo Bay *Canada* 66°5N 117°55W **294** D8
Eldorado *Argentina* 26°28S 54°43W **335** B5
Eldorado *Ont., Canada* 44°35N 77°31W **312** B7
Eldorado *Ill., U.S.A.* 37°49N 88°26W **311** G8
Eldorado *Tex., U.S.A.* 30°52N 100°36W **314** F4
Eldorendo *U.S.A.* 31°3N 84°39W **316** D5
Eldoret *Kenya* 0°30N 35°17E **268** B4
Eldred *U.S.A.* 41°58N 78°23W **312** E6
Eldridge *U.S.A.* 41°39N 90°35W **310** C6
Elea, C. *Cyprus* 35°19N 34°4E **207** E10
Eleanora, Pk. *Australia* 32°57S 121°9E **279** F3
Eleao *U.S.A.* 21°27N 157°52W **302** K14
Elefantes ➜ *Africa* 24°10S 32°40E **271** B5
Elefantes, B. das *Angola* 13°13S 12°44E **265** E2
Elefantes, G. *Chile* 46°28S 73°49W **336** C2
Elefsina *Greece* 38°4N 23°26E **204** C5
Eleftherios Venizelos ✈ **(ATH)** *Greece* 37°56N 23°56E **112** A3
Elektrogorsk *Russia* 55°56N 38°50E **188** E10
Elektroperedacha = Elektrogorsk *Russia* 55°56N 38°50E **188** E10
Elektrostal *Russia* 55°41N 38°32E **188** E10
Elektrovoz = Stupino *Russia* 54°57N 38°2E **188** E10
Elele *Nigeria* 5°5N 6°50E **263** D6
Elemi Triangle = Ilemi Triangle *Africa* 5°0N 35°20E **257** G4
Elena *Bulgaria* 42°55N 25°53E **203** D9
Elephant Butte Res. *U.S.A.* 33°9N 107°11W **305** K10
Elephant I. *Antarctica* 61°0S 55°0W **151** C18
Elephant Pass *Sri Lanka* 9°35N 80°25E **245** K5
Elephanta Caves *India* 18°57N 72°57E **130** B2
Elephanta I. *India* 18°57N 72°56E **130** B2
Elesbão Veloso *Brazil* 6°13S 42°8W **332** C3
Eleshnitsa *Bulgaria* 41°52N 23°36E **202** E7
Eleşkirt *Turkey* 39°50N 42°50E **213** C10
Eleuthera *The Bahamas* 25°0N 76°20W **320** B4
Eleutheroupoli *Greece* 40°52N 24°20E **203** F8
Elfin Cove *U.S.A.* 58°12N 136°22W **303** G13
Elgå *Norway* 62°10N 11°56E **164** B8
Elgeyo-Marakwet □ *Kenya* 0°50N 35°35E **268** B4
Elgin *Ont., Canada* 44°36N 76°13W **313** B8
Elgin *Moray, U.K.* 57°39N 3°19W **167** D5
Elgin *Ill., U.S.A.* 42°2N 88°17W **311** B8
Elgin *N. Dak., U.S.A.* 46°24N 101°51W **308** B3
Elgin *Oreg., U.S.A.* 45°34N 117°55W **304** D5
Elgin *S.C., U.S.A.* 34°10N 80°48W **316** A9
Elgin *Tex., U.S.A.* 30°21N 97°22W **314** F6
Elgoibar *Spain* 43°13N 2°24W **196** B2
Elgon, Mt. *Africa* 1°10N 34°30E **268** B3
Elgspiggen *Norway* 62°10N 11°21E **164** B8
Elhovo *Bulgaria* 42°10N 26°35E **203** D10
Eliase *Indonesia* 8°21S 130°48E **231** F8
Elikonos Oros *Greece* 38°18N 22°45E **204** C4
Elim *Namibia* 17°48S 15°31E **270** A2
Elim *Western Cape, S. Africa* 34°35S 19°45E **270** D2
Elim *Alaska, U.S.A.* 64°37N 162°15W **303** D7
Elin Pelin *Bulgaria* 42°40N 23°36E **202** D7
Elingampangu *Dem. Rep. of the Congo* 2°0S 24°4E **264** C4
Elipa *Dem. Rep. of the Congo* 1°3S 24°20E **264** C4
Elis = Ilia *Greece* 37°45N 21°35E **204** D3
Eliseu Martins *Brazil* 8°13S 43°42W **332** C3
Elista *Russia* 46°16N 44°14E **191** G7
Eliza, L. *Australia* 37°15S 139°50E **282** D3
Elizabeth *S. Austral., Australia* 34°42S 138°41E **282** C3
Elizabeth *Ill., U.S.A.* 42°19N 90°13W **310** B6
Elizabeth *N.J., U.S.A.* 40°39N 74°12W **313** F10
Elizabeth, B. *Ecuador* 0°36S 91°12W **330** a
Elizabeth City *U.S.A.* 36°18N 76°14W **315** C16
Elizabethton *U.S.A.* 36°21N 82°13W **315** C13
Elizabethtown *Ky., U.S.A.* 37°42N 85°52W **311** G11
Elizabethtown *N.Y., U.S.A.* 44°13N 73°36W **313** B11
Elizabethtown *Pa., U.S.A.* 40°9N 76°36W **313** F8
Elizabethville = Lubumbashi *Dem. Rep. of the Congo* 11°40S 27°28E **269** E2
Elizondo *Spain* 43°12N 1°30W **196** B3
Ełk *Poland* 53°50N 22°21E **184** E9
Elk ➜ *B.C., Canada* 49°11N 115°14W **296** C5
Ełk ➜ *Poland* 53°41N 22°28E **184** E9
Elk ➜ *Ala., U.S.A.* 34°46N 87°16W **315** D11
Elk City *U.S.A.* 35°25N 99°25W **314** D5
Elk Creek *U.S.A.* 39°36N 122°32W **306** F4
Elk Grove *U.S.A.* 38°25N 121°22W **306** G5
Elk Island △ *Canada* 53°35N 112°59W **296** C6
Elk Lake *Canada* 47°40N 80°25W **298** C3
Elk Point *Canada* 53°54N 110°55W **297** C6
Elk River *Idaho, U.S.A.* 46°47N 116°11W **304** C5
Elk River *Minn., U.S.A.* 45°18N 93°35W **308** C7
Elkader *U.S.A.* 42°51N 91°24W **310** B5
Elkedra ➜ *Australia* 21°8S 136°22E **280** C2
Elkhart *Ind., U.S.A.* 41°41N 85°58W **311** C11
Elkhart *Kans., U.S.A.* 37°0N 101°54W **308** G3
Elkhart ➜ *U.S.A.* 41°41N 85°58W **311** C11
Elkhorn *Man., Canada* 49°59N 101°14W **297** D8
Elkhorn *Wis., U.S.A.* 42°40N 88°33W **311** B8
Elkhorn ➜ *U.S.A.* 41°8N 96°19W **308** E5
Elkhovo = Elhovo *Bulgaria* 42°10N 26°35E **203** D10
Elkin *U.S.A.* 36°15N 80°51W **315** C14
Elkins *U.S.A.* 38°55N 79°51W **309** F14
Elkland *U.S.A.* 41°59N 77°19W **312** E7
Elko *B.C., Canada* 49°20N 115°10W **296** D5
Elko *Nev., U.S.A.* 40°50N 115°46W **304** F6
Elkton *U.S.A.* 43°49N 83°11W **312** C1
Ellas = Greece ■ *Europe* 40°0N 23°0E **204** B3
Ellaville *Fla., U.S.A.* 30°23N 83°10W **316** E6
Ellaville *Ga., U.S.A.* 32°14N 84°19W **316** C5
Ellboda *Sweden* 59°24N 18°15E **139** A3
Ellef Ringnes I. *Canada* 78°30N 102°2W **295** B11
Ellen, Mt. *U.S.A.* 44°9N 72°56W **313** B12
Ellenburg *U.S.A.* 44°54N 73°48W **313** B11
Ellendale *U.S.A.* 46°0N 98°32W **308** B4
Ellenor, L. *U.S.A.* 28°28N 81°25W **133** B2
Ellensburg *U.S.A.* 46°59N 120°34W **304** C3
Ellenville *U.S.A.* 41°43N 74°24W **313** E10
Ellerton *Barbados* 13°7N 59°33W **323** r
Ellery, Mt. *Australia* 37°28S 148°47E **283** D8
Ellesmere = Scottsdale *Australia* 41°9S 147°31E **281** G4
Ellesmere, L. *N.Z.* 43°47S 172°28E **285** D7
Ellesmere I. *Canada* 79°30N 80°0W **295** B16
Ellesmere Port *U.K.* 53°17N 2°54W **168** D5
Ellettsville *U.S.A.* 39°14N 86°38W **311** E10
Ellice Is. = Tuvalu ■ *Pac. Oc.* 8°0S 178°0E **277** B14
Ellicottville *U.S.A.* 42°17N 78°40W **312** D6
Ellington *U.S.A.* 42°13N 79°6W **312** D5
Elliniko Olympic Complex *Greece* 37°50N 23°45E **112** B2
Elliot *N. Terr., Australia* 17°33S 133°32E **280** B1
Elliot *Eastern Cape, S. Africa* 31°22S 27°48E **271** D4
Elliot Lake *Canada* 46°25N 82°35W **298** C3
Elliotdale = Xhora *S. Africa* 31°55S 28°38E **271** D4
Elliott *U.S.A.* 34°6N 80°10W **316** A9
Elliott Key *U.S.A.* 25°27N 80°12W **317** K9
Ellipse, The *Washington, D.C., U.S.A.* **143** b1
Ellis *U.S.A.* 38°56N 99°34W **308** F4
Ellis I. *U.S.A.* 40°41N 74°2W **132** B1
Elliston *Australia* 33°39S 134°53E **281** E1
Ellisville *U.S.A.* 31°36N 89°12W **315** F10
Ellon *U.K.* 57°22N 2°4W **167** D6
Ellora *India* 20°1N 75°10E **244** D2
Ellore = Eluru *India* 16°48N 81°8E **244** F5
Elloree *U.S.A.* 33°32N 80°34W **316** B9
Ellsworth *Kans., U.S.A.* 38°44N 98°14W **308** F4
Ellsworth *Maine, U.S.A.* 44°33N 68°25W **309** C19
Ellsworth Land *Antarctica* 76°0S 89°0W **151** D16
Ellsworth Mts. *Antarctica* 78°30S 85°0W **151** D16
Ellwangen *Germany* 48°57N 10°8E **179** G6
Ellwood City *U.S.A.* 40°52N 80°17W **312** F4
Ellzey *U.S.A.* 29°19N 82°48W **317** F7
Elm *Switz.* 46°54N 9°10E **179** J5
Elm-Lappwald ⌓ *Germany* 52°15N 10°50E **178** C6
Elma *Man., Canada* 49°52N 95°55W **297** D9
Elma *Wash., U.S.A.* 47°0N 123°25W **306** D3
Elmadağ *Turkey* 39°55N 33°14E **212** C5
Elmalı *Turkey* 36°44N 29°56E **205** E11
Elmers End *U.K.* 51°23N 0°2W **125** B3
Elmhurst *Ill., U.S.A.* 41°53N 87°56W **311** C9
Elmhurst *N.Y., U.S.A.* 40°44N 73°53W **132** B2
Elmina *Ghana* 5°5N 1°21W **263** D4
Elmira *Ont., Canada* 43°36N 80°33W **312** C4
Elmira *N.Y., U.S.A.* 42°6N 76°48W **312** D8
Elmira Heights *U.S.A.* 42°8N 76°50W **312** D8
Elmodel *U.S.A.* 31°21N 84°29W **316** D5
Elmore *Vic., Australia* 36°30S 144°37E **282** D6
Elmore *Ala., U.S.A.* 32°32N 86°19W **316** C3
Elmore *Ohio, U.S.A.* 41°29N 83°18W **311** C13
Elmshorn *Germany* 53°43N 9°40E **178** B5
Elmstead *U.K.* 51°24N 0°2E **125** B4
Elmvale *Canada* 44°35N 79°52W **312** B5
Elmwood *Ill., U.S.A.* 40°47N 89°58W **310** D7
Elmwood *La., U.S.A.* 29°57N 90°11W **131** B1
Elmwood Park *Ill., U.S.A.* 41°55N 87°48W **119** B2
Elmwood Park *N.J., U.S.A.* 40°54N 74°7W **132** A1
Elne *France* 42°36N 2°58E **174** F6
Elnesvågen *Norway* 62°52N 7°10E **164** B4
Elnora *U.S.A.* 38°53N 87°5W **311** F9
Eloaua I. *Papua N. G.* 1°38S 149°40E **286** A5
Elobey, Is. *Eq. Guin.* 1°1N 9°29E **264** B1
Elongo *Dem. Rep. of the Congo* 0°19S 21°39E **264** C4
Elora *Canada* 43°41N 80°26W **312** C4
Elorza *Venezuela* 7°3N 69°31W **328** B4
Elos *Greece* 36°46N 22°43E **204** E4
Elounda *Greece* 35°16N 25°42E **207** E6
Eloy *U.S.A.* 32°45N 111°33W **305** K8
Éloyes *France* 48°6N 6°36E **173** D13
Elphin *Canada* 44°55N 76°37W **313** B8
Elpitiya *Sri Lanka* 6°17N 80°10E **245** L5
Elrose *Canada* 51°12N 108°0W **297** C7
Elsberry *U.S.A.* 39°10N 90°47W **310** E6
Elsby △ *Australia* 14°55S 133°10E **278** B5
Elsdorf *Germany* 50°55N 6°34E **178** E2
Elsie *Mich., U.S.A.* 43°5N 84°23W **311** A12
Elsie *Oreg., U.S.A.* 45°52N 123°36W **306** E3
Elsiesrivier *S. Africa* 33°55S 18°35E **118** A2
Elsinore = Helsingør *Denmark* 56°2N 12°35E **163** H6
Elster ➜ *Germany* 51°25N 11°57E **178** D7
Elsternwick *Australia* 37°52S 145°0E **128** B2
Elsterwerda *Germany* 51°27N 13°31E **178** D9
Eltanin Fracture Zone System *S. Ocean* 54°0S 130°0W **151** B14
Eltham *N.Z.* 39°26S 174°19E **284** F3
Eltham *London, U.K.* 51°27N 0°3E **125** B4
Elton *Russia* 49°5N 46°52E **191** F8
Elton, Ozero *Russia* 49°5N 46°42E **191** F8
Eltville *Germany* 50°2N 8°7E **179** E4
Eluanbi = Oluanpi *Taiwan* 21°54N 120°51E **225** E2
Eluru *India* 16°48N 81°8E **244** F5
Elvas *Portugal* 38°50N 7°10W **195** G3
Elven *France* 47°44N 2°36W **172** E4
Elverum *Norway* 60°53N 11°34E **164** D8
Elvire ➜ *Australia* 17°51S 128°11E **278** C4
Elvire, Mt. *Australia* 29°22S 119°36E **279** E2
Elvo ➜ *Italy* 45°23N 8°21E **198** C5
Elwell, L. = Tiber Res. *U.S.A.* 48°19N 111°6W **304** B8
Elwood *Vic., Australia* 37°53S 144°59E **128** B1
Elwood *Ill., U.S.A.* 41°24N 88°7W **311** C8
Elwood *Ind., U.S.A.* 40°17N 85°50W **311** D11
Elwood *Nebr., U.S.A.* 40°36N 99°52W **308** E4
Elx = Elche *Spain* 38°15N 0°42W **197** G4
Ely *Cambs., U.K.* 52°24N 0°16E **169** E8
Ely *Minn., U.S.A.* 47°55N 91°51W **308** B8
Ely *Nev., U.S.A.* 39°15N 114°54W **304** G6
Elyria *U.S.A.* 41°22N 82°7W **312** E2
Elyros *Greece* 35°15N 23°45E **204** F5
Élysée *France* 48°52N 2°19E **134** A2
Elysian Park *Los Angeles, U.S.A.* **127** a3
Elz ➜ *Germany* 48°18N 7°44E **179** G3
Émaé *Vanuatu* 17°4S 168°24E **287** G6
Emajõgi ➜ *Estonia* 58°25N 27°20E **188** C4
eMakhazeni *S. Africa* 25°42S 30°2E **271** C5
eMalahleni *S. Africa* 25°51S 29°14E **271** C4
Emāmrūd *Iran* 36°30N 55°0E **247** B7
Emāmzādeh Sāleh *Iran* 35°48N 51°26E **141** A2
Emån ➜ *Sweden* 57°8N 16°30E **163** G10
Emao *Vanuatu* 17°29S 168°30E **287** G6
Emas △ *Brazil* 18°2S 52°50W **331** D7
Emateloa *Dem. Rep. of the Congo* 1°16N 18°42E **264** B3
Embajadores *Madrid, Spain* **127** c2
eMbalenhle *S. Africa* 26°32S 29°4E **271** C4
Embarcación *Argentina* 23°10S 64°0W **334** A3
Embarcadero, The *San Francisco, U.S.A.* **136** b3
Embarras ➜ *U.S.A.* 38°39N 87°37W **311** F9
Embetsu *Japan* 44°44N 141°47E **220** B10
Embi *Kazakhstan* 48°50N 58°8E **216** C5
Embi ➜ *Kazakhstan* 46°55N 53°28E **187** E9
Embonas *Greece* 36°13N 27°51E **206** E11
Embro *Canada* 43°9N 80°54W **312** C4
Embrun *France* 44°34N 6°30E **175** D10
Embu *Kenya* 0°32S 37°38E **268** C4
Emden *Germany* 53°21N 7°12E **178** B3
Emecik *Turkey* 36°46N 27°49E **205** E9
Emei Shan *China* 29°32N 103°46E **228** C4
Emeishan *China* 29°31N 103°23E **228** C4
Emek Refa'im *Jerusalem* **123** c2
Émerainville *France* 48°48N 2°37E **134** B4
Emerald *Queens., Australia* 23°32S 148°10E **280** C4
Emerald *Vic., Australia* 37°56S 145°29E **276** E8
Emerald Buddha = Phra Kaeo *Bangkok, Thailand* **113** b1
Emerald I. *Canada* 76°48N 114°10W **295** B9
Émeraude, Côte d' *France* 48°45N 2°40W **172** D4
Emerson *Man., Canada* 49°0N 97°10W **297** D9
Emerson *Ga., U.S.A.* 34°8N 84°45W **316** A5
Emeryville *U.S.A.* 37°49N 122°17W **136** A3
Emet *Turkey* 39°20N 29°15E **205** B11
Emeti *Papua N. G.* 7°53S 143°15E **286** D2
Emgwenya *S. Africa* 25°40S 30°18E **271** C5
Emi Koussi *Chad* 19°45N 18°55E **259** E3
Emília-Romagna □ *Italy* 44°45N 11°0E **198** D8
Emilius, Mte. *Italy* 45°45N 7°20E **198** C4
Emin *China* 46°34N 83°36E **217** C10
Eminabad *Pakistan* 32°2N 74°8E **242** C6
Emine, Nos *Bulgaria* 42°40N 27°56E **203** D11
Eminence *U.S.A.* 38°22N 85°11W **311** F11
Eminönü *Turkey* 41°0N 28°57E **122** B1
Emirates, Mall of the *Dubai, U.A.E.* 25°7N 55°12E **119** B1
Emirau I. *Papua N. G.* 1°40S 150°0E **286** A6
Emirdağ *Turkey* 39°2N 31°8E **212** C4
Emirgan *Turkey* 41°6N 29°2E **122** B2
Emissi, Tarso *Chad* 21°27N 18°36E **259** D3
eMkhondo = Piet Retief *S. Africa* 27°1S 30°50E **271** C5
Emlenton *U.S.A.* 41°11N 79°43W **312** E5
Emlichheim *Germany* 52°37N 6°51E **178** C2
Emmaboda *Sweden* 56°37N 15°32E **163** H9
Emmalane *U.S.A.* 32°46N 82°0W **316** C7
Emmarentia *S. Africa* 26°9S 28°0E **123** A2
Emmastad *Curaçao* 12°8N 68°55W **322** g
Emmaus *S. Africa* 29°2S 25°15E **270** C4
Emmaus *Pa., U.S.A.* 40°32N 75°30W **313** F9
Emme ➜ *Switz.* 47°14N 7°32E **179** H3
Emmeloord *Neths.* 52°44N 5°46E **170** B5
Emmen *Neths.* 52°48N 6°57E **170** B6
Emmen *Switz.* 47°5N 8°18E **179** H4
Emmendingen *Germany* 48°6N 7°51E **179** G3
Emmental *Switz.* 46°55N 7°40E **179** J3
Emmerich *Germany* 51°50N 6°14E **178** D2
Emmet *Australia* 24°45S 144°30E **280** C3
Emmetsburg *U.S.A.* 43°7N 94°41W **310** A2
Emmett *Idaho, U.S.A.* 43°52N 116°30W **304** E5
Emmett *Mich., U.S.A.* 42°59N 82°46W **312** D2
Emmiganuru = Yemmiganur *India* 15°44N 77°29E **245** G3
Emmonak *U.S.A.* 62°47N 164°31W **303** E6
Emo *Canada* 48°38N 93°50W **297** D10
Emőd *Hungary* 47°57N 20°47E **182** C5
Emona *Bulgaria* 42°43N 27°53E **203** D11
Empalme *Mexico* 27°58N 110°51W **318** B2
Empangeni *S. Africa* 28°50S 31°52E **271** C5
Empedrado *Argentina* 28°0S 58°46W **334** B4
Emperor Seamount Chain *Pac. Oc.* 40°0N 170°0E **288** D9
Emperor Trough *Pac. Oc.* 43°0N 175°30E **288** C9
Empingham Res. = Rutland Water *U.K.* 52°39N 0°38W **169** E7
Empire *U.S.A.* 32°21N 83°18W **316** C6
Empire State Building *New York, U.S.A.* **132** c2
Empoli *Italy* 43°43N 10°57E **198** E7
Emporia *Kans., U.S.A.* 38°25N 96°11W **308** F5
Emporia *Va., U.S.A.* 36°42N 77°32W **309** G15
Emporium *U.S.A.* 41°31N 78°14W **312** E6
Empress *Canada* 50°57N 110°0W **297** C7
Empty Quarter = Rub' al Khālī *Si. Arabia* 19°0N 48°0E **249** C5
Ems ➜ *Germany* 53°20N 7°12E **178** B3
Emsdale *Canada* 45°32N 79°19W **312** A5
Emsdetten *Germany* 52°10N 7°32E **178** C3
Emu *China* 43°40N 128°6E **227** C15
Emu Park *Australia* 23°13S 150°50E **280** C5
eMuziwezinto *S. Africa* 30°15S 30°45E **271** D5
'En 'Avrona *Israel* 29°43N 35°0E **251** J6
'En Boqeq *Israel* 31°12N 35°21E **251** G6
'En Gannim = Ramat Gan *Israel* 32°4N 34°48E **251** F5
'En Gedi *Israel* 31°28N 35°25E **251** G6
En Na'am *Sudan* 10°21N 27°58E **266** B2
En Nahrat *Mali* 22°55N 3°36W **260** D4
En Nahud *Sudan* 12°45N 28°25E **257** E2
En Nofalab *Sudan* 15°52N 32°32E **257** D3
En Nuqra *Sudan* 10°4N 28°10E **266** B2
Ena *Japan* 35°25N 137°25E **223** B9
Ena-San *Japan* 35°26N 137°36E **223** B9
Enambú *Colombia* 1°1N 70°17W **328** C3
Enånger *Sweden* 61°30N 17°9E **162** C11
Enard B. *U.K.* 58°5N 5°20W **167** C3
Enare träsk = Inarijärvi *Finland* 69°0N 28°0E **160** B23
Enarotali *Indonesia* 3°55S 136°21E **231** E9
Encampment *U.S.A.* 41°12N 106°47W **304** F10
Encantadas, Serra *Brazil* 30°40S 53°0W **335** C5
Encantado *Brazil* 22°53S 43°19W **135** B1
Encarnación *Paraguay* 27°15S 55°50W **335** B4
Encarnación de Díaz *Mexico* 21°31N 102°14W **318** C4
Enchi *Ghana* 5°53N 2°48W **262** D4
Encinitas *U.S.A.* 33°3N 117°17W **307** M9
Encino *Calif., U.S.A.* 34°9N 118°28W **126** B2
Encino *N. Mex., U.S.A.* 34°39N 105°28W **305** J11
Encino Res. *U.S.A.* 34°8N 118°30W **126** B1
Encontrados *Venezuela* 9°3N 72°14W **328** B3
Encounter B. *Australia* 35°45S 138°45E **282** C3
Encruzilhada *Brazil* 15°31S 40°54W **333** E3
Encs *Hungary* 48°20N 21°8E **182** B6
Endako *Canada* 54°6N 125°2W **296** C3
Endau *Kenya* 1°18S 38°31E **268** C4
Endau Rompin △ *Malaysia* 2°27N 103°45E **237** L4
Ende *Indonesia* 8°45S 121°40E **231** F6
Endeavour Str. *Australia* 10°45S 142°0E **286** F2
Endelave *Denmark* 55°46N 10°18E **163** J4
Enden *Norway* 61°47N 10°15E **164** C7
Enderbury *Kiribati* 3°8S 171°5W **277** A16
Enderby *Canada* 50°35N 119°10W **296** C5
Enderby Abyssal Plain *S. Ocean* 60°0S 40°0E **151** C5
Enderby I. *Australia* 20°35S 116°30E **278** D2
Enderby Land *Antarctica* 66°0S 53°0E **151** C5
Enderlin *U.S.A.* 46°38N 97°36W **308** B5
Enderrocat, C. *Spain* 39°28N 2°43E **206** B3
Endicott *U.S.A.* 42°6N 76°4W **313** D8
Endicott Mts. *U.S.A.* 68°0N 152°0W **303** C9
Endimari ➜ *Brazil* 8°46S 66°7W **330** B4
Endwell *U.S.A.* 42°6N 76°2W **313** D8
Endyalgout I. *Australia* 11°40S 132°35E **278** B5
Ené ➜ *Peru* 11°10S 74°18W **330** C3
Eneabba *Australia* 29°49S 115°16E **279** E2
Enebyberg *Sweden* 59°25N 17°59E **139** A1
Enerhodar *Ukraine* 47°30N 34°28E **189** J8
Enewetak Atoll *Marshall Is.* 11°30N 162°15E **288** F8
Enez *Turkey* 40°45N 26°5E **203** F10
Enfer, Pte. d' *Martinique* 14°22N 60°54W **322** j
Enfield *N.S.W., Australia* 33°53S 151°6E **139** B1
Enfield *N.S., Canada* 44°56N 63°32W **299** D7
Enfield *Conn., U.S.A.* 41°58N 72°36W **313** E12
Enfield *Ill., U.S.A.* 38°6N 88°20W **311** F8
Enfield *N.C., U.S.A.* 36°11N 77°41W **315** C16
Enfield *N.H., U.S.A.* 43°39N 72°9W **313** C12
Enga □ *Papua N. G.* 5°30S 143°30E **286** C2
Engadin *Switz.* 46°45N 10°10E **179** J6
Engan *Norway* 63°8N 8°31E **164** A5
Engaño, C. *Dom. Rep.* 18°30N 68°20W **321** C6
Engaño, C. *Phil.* 18°35N 122°23E **232** B4
Engaru *Japan* 44°3N 143°31E **220** B11
Engcobo = Ngcobo *S. Africa* 31°37S 28°0E **271** D4
Engelberg *Switz.* 46°48N 8°26E **179** J4
Engels *Russia* 51°28N 46°6E **190** E8
Engelsberg = Ängelsberg *Sweden* 59°58N 16°0E **162** E10
Engemann L. *Canada* 58°0N 106°55W **297** B7
Engenho, I. do *Brazil* 22°50S 43°6W **135** B2
Engerdal *Norway* 61°45N 11°58E **164** C8
Engershatu *Eritrea* 16°7N 38°34E **257** D4
Enggano *Indonesia* 5°20S 102°40E **234** D2
Engineer Group *Papua N. G.* 10°35S 151°20E **286** F6
Engkilili *Malaysia* 1°3N 111°42E **235** B4
England *U.S.A.* 34°33N 91°58W **314** D9
England □ *U.K.* 53°0N 2°0W **169** E5
Englee *Canada* 50°45N 56°5W **299** B8
Englehart *Canada* 47°49N 79°52W **298** C4
Englewood *Fla., U.S.A.* 26°58N 82°21W **317** J7
Englewood *Ill., U.S.A.* 41°46N 87°38W **119** C3
Englewood *N.J., U.S.A.* 40°54N 73°58W **132** A2
Englewood *Ohio, U.S.A.* 39°53N 84°18W **311** E12
Englewood Cliffs *U.S.A.* 40°53N 73°59W **132** A2
English *U.S.A.* 38°20N 86°28W **311** F10
English ➜ *Ont., Canada* 49°12N 91°5W **297** C10
English ➜ *Iowa, U.S.A.* 41°29N 91°32W **310** C5
English B. *Ascension I.* 7°54S 14°23W **153** g
English Bazar = Ingraj Bazar *India* 24°58N 88°10E **243** G13
English Channel *Europe* 50°0N 2°0W **169** G6
English Company's Is., The *Australia* 11°50S 136°32E **280** A2
English Harbour Town *Antigua & B.* 17°1N 61°46W **322** b
English River *Canada* 49°14N 91°0W **298** C1
Engures ezers *Latvia* 57°16N 23°6E **184** A10
Enguri ➜ *Georgia* 42°27N 41°38E **191** J5
Enid *U.S.A.* 36°24N 97°53W **314** C6
Enipeas ➜ *Greece* 39°22N 22°17E **204** B4
Eniwa *Japan* 43°0N 141°30E **220** C10
Enkhuizen *Neths.* 52°42N 5°17E **170** B5
Enköping *Sweden* 59°37N 17°4E **162** E11
Enle *China* 24°0N 101°9E **228** F3
Enmore *Australia* 33°54S 151°10E **139** B2
Enna *Italy* 37°34N 14°16E **201** E7
Ennadai L. *Canada* 60°58N 101°20W **297** A8
Enné, O. ➜ *Chad* 14°24N 18°45E **259** F4
Ennedi *Chad* 17°15N 22°0E **259** E4
Ennedi Est □ *Chad* 18°5N 23°20E **259** E4
Ennedi Ouest □ *Chad* 18°41N 21°11E **259** E4
Enneri Achelouma ➜ *Niger* 21°55N 13°35E **261** D7
Enngonia *Australia* 29°21S 145°50E **281** D4
Ennigerloh *Germany* 51°50N 8°2E **178** D4
Ennis *Clare, Ireland* 52°51N 8°59W **166** D3
Ennis *Mont., U.S.A.* 45°21N 111°44W **304** D8
Ennis *Tex., U.S.A.* 32°20N 96°38W **314** E6
Enniscorthy *Ireland* 52°30N 6°34W **166** D5
Enniskillen *U.K.* 54°21N 7°39W **166** B4
Ennistymon *Ireland* 52°57N 9°17W **166** D2
Enns *Austria* 48°12N 14°28E **180** C7
Enns ➜ *Austria* 48°14N 14°32E **180** C7
Eno *Finland* 62°47N 30°10E **160** E24
Enosburg Falls *U.S.A.* 44°55N 72°48W **313** B12
Enping *China* 22°16N 112°21E **229** F9
Enrekang *Indonesia* 3°34S 119°47E **235** C5
Enrile *Phil.* 17°34N 121°42E **232** C3
Enriquillo, L. *Dom. Rep.* 18°20N 71°40W **321** C5
Enschede *Neths.* 52°13N 6°53E **170** B6
Ensenada *Argentina* 34°55S 57°55W **334** C4
Ensenada *Chile* 41°12S 72°33W **336** B2
Ensenada *Baja Calif., Mexico* 31°52N 116°37W **318** A1
Ensenada de los Muertos *Mexico* 23°59N 109°51W **318** C2
Ensenada La Guardia *Venezuela* 11°2N 64°5W **329** a
Enshi *China* 30°18N 109°29E **228** B7
Enshū-Nada *Japan* 34°27N 137°38E **223** C9
Ensiola, Pta. de n' *Spain* 39°7N 2°55E **206** B3
Ensisheim *France* 47°50N 7°20E **173** E14
Enskede *Sweden* 59°17N 18°4E **139** B2
Ensley *U.S.A.* 30°31N 87°16W **317** E2
Entebbe *Uganda* 0°4N 32°28E **268** B3
Enterprise *N.W.T., Canada* 60°47N 115°45W **296** A5
Enterprise *Ala., U.S.A.* 31°19N 85°51W **316** D4
Enterprise *Nev., U.S.A.* 36°13N 115°14W **124** B1
Enterprise *Oreg., U.S.A.* 45°25N 117°17W **304** D5
Entiako ⌓ *Canada* 53°15N 125°26W **296** C3
Entorno de Doñana ⌓ *Spain* 37°0N 6°26W **195** J4
Entrance, The *Australia* 33°21S 151°30E **283** B9
Entraygues-sur-Truyère *France* 44°38N 2°35E **174** D6
Entre-Deux *Réunion* 21°14S 55°28E **272** f
Entre Rios = Rio Brilhante *Brazil* 21°48S 54°33W **335** A5
Entre Rios = Três Rios *Brazil* 22°6S 43°15W **333** F3
Entre Ríos *Bolivia* 21°30S 64°25W **334** A3
Entre Rios *Bahia, Brazil* 11°56S 38°5W **333** D4
Entre Rios *Pará, Brazil* 5°24S 54°21W **331** B7
Entre Ríos □ *Argentina* 30°30S 58°30W **334** C4
Entrepeñas, Embalse de *Spain* 40°34N 2°42W **196** E2
Entrevias *Spain* 40°22N 3°40W **127** B1
Entroncamento *Portugal* 39°28N 8°28W **195** F2
Enugu *Nigeria* 6°30N 7°30E **263** D6
Enugu □ *Nigeria* 6°30N 7°45E **263** D6
Enugu Ezike *Nigeria* 7°0N 7°29E **263** D6
Enumclaw *U.S.A.* 47°12N 121°59W **306** C5
Envalira, Port d' *Europe* 42°33N 1°43E **196** C6
Envermeu *France* 49°53N 1°15E **172** C8
Envigado *Colombia* 6°10N 75°35W **328** B2
Enviken *Sweden* 60°49N 15°46E **162** D9
Envira *Brazil* 7°18S 70°13W **330** B3
Envira ➜ *Brazil* 7°19S 70°15W **330** B3
Enying *Hungary* 46°56N 18°15E **182** D3
Enyonga *Gabon* 0°59S 9°22E **264** C1
Enza ➜ *Italy* 44°54N 10°31E **198** D7
Enzan = Kōshū *Japan* 35°42N 138°44E **223** B10
Eochaill = Youghal *Ireland* 51°56N 7°52W **166** E4
Éolie, Ís. *Italy* 38°30N 14°57E **201** D7
Eot I. *Micronesia* 7°23N 151°44E **287** T17
Epanomi *Greece* 40°25N 22°59E **202** F6
Epcot *U.S.A.* 28°21N 81°32W **133** B1
Epe *Neths.* 52°21N 5°59E **170** B5
Epe *Nigeria* 6°36N 3°59E **263** D5
Epéna *Congo* 1°22N 17°29E **264** B3
Épernay *France* 49°3N 3°56E **173** C10
Épernon *France* 48°35N 1°40E **173** D8
Ephesus *Turkey* 37°55N 27°22E **205** D9
Ephraim *U.S.A.* 39°22N 111°35W **304** G8
Ephrata *Pa., U.S.A.* 40°11N 76°11W **313** F8
Ephrata *Wash., U.S.A.* 47°19N 119°33W **304** C4
Epi *Vanuatu* 16°43S 168°15E **287** F6
Epidaurus = Epidavros *Greece* 37°40N 23°7E **204** D5
Epidavros *Greece* 37°40N 23°7E **204** D5
Epidavros Limira *Greece* 36°46N 23°0E **204** E5
Épila *Spain* 41°36N 1°17W **196** D3
Épinac *France* 46°59N 4°31E **173** F11
Épinal *France* 48°10N 6°27E **173** D13
Epira *Guyana* 5°5N 57°20W **329** B6
Epiros □ *Greece* 39°30N 20°30E **204** B2
Episkopi *Cyprus* 34°40N 32°54E **207** F8
Episkopi *Kriti, Greece* 35°20N 24°20E **207** E5
Episkopi Bay *Cyprus* 34°35N 32°50E **207** F8
Epitalio *Greece* 37°37N 21°30E **204** D3
Eppalock, L. *Australia* 36°52S 144°34E **282** D6
Eppan = Appiano *Italy* 46°28N 11°15E **199** B8
Epping *Australia* 33°46S 151°5E **139** A1
Eppingen *Germany* 49°8N 8°53E **179** F4
Epsom *U.K.* 51°19N 0°16W **169** F7
Epukiro *Namibia* 21°40S 19°9E **270** B2
Equality *U.S.A.* 37°44N 88°20W **311** G8
Équateur □ *Dem. Rep. of the Congo* 1°0N 19°0E **264** B3
Equatorial Channel *Maldives* 0°0 73°10E **272** d
Equatorial Guinea ■ *Africa* 2°0N 8°0E **264** B1
Equeipa *Venezuela* 5°22N 62°43W **329** B5
Er Hai *China* 25°48N 100°11E **228** E3
Er Rachidia *Morocco* 31°58N 4°20W **260** B4
Er Rahad *Sudan* 12°45N 30°32E **257** E3
Er Rif *Morocco* 35°1N 4°1W **261** A4
Er Rogel *Sudan* 18°10N 35°25E **256** D4
Er Roseires *Sudan* 11°55N 34°30E **257** E3
Er Rua'at *Sudan* 12°21N 32°17E **257** E3
Eraclea *Italy* 45°35N 12°40E **199** C9
Eran *Phil.* 9°4N 117°42E **233** G1
Eran B. *Phil.* 9°5N 117°43E **233** G1
Erandol *India* 20°56N 75°20E **244** D2
Eranga *Dem. Rep. of the Congo* 1°52S 18°56E **264** C3
Erap *Papua N. G.* 6°37S 146°51E **286** D4
Erasmus = Bronkhorstspruit *S. Africa* 25°46S 28°45E **271** C4
Erave *Papua N. G.* 6°39S 144°0E **286** D2
Erave ➜ *Papua N. G.* 6°54S 144°47E **286** D3
Erāwadī Myit = Ayeyawadi ➜ *Myanmar* 15°50N 95°6E **241** G5
Erāwadī Myitwanya = Irrawaddy, Mouths of the *Myanmar* 15°30N 95°0E **241** H5
Erawan △ *Thailand* 14°25N 98°58E **236** E2
Erba *Italy* 45°48N 9°15E **198** C6
Erba *Sudan* 19°5N 36°51E **256** D4
Erba, J. *Sudan* 20°48N 36°47E **256** C4
Erbaa *Turkey* 40°42N 36°36E **212** B7
Erbeng Shan *China* 42°50N 84°59E **217** D10
Erbeskopf *Germany* 49°44N 7°2E **179** F3
Erbu *Ethiopia* 6°44N 34°53E **257** E3
Ercan, Nicosia ✈ **(ECN)** *Cyprus* 35°10N 33°30E **207** E9
Erçek *Turkey* 38°39N 43°36E **246** B4
Erçis *Turkey* 39°2N 43°21E **213** C10
Ercıyaş Dağı *Turkey* 38°30N 35°30E **246** B2
Érd *Hungary* 47°22N 18°56E **182** C3
Erdao Jiang ➜ *China* 42°37N 128°0E **224** A3
Erdek *Turkey* 40°23N 27°47E **203** F11
Erdély = Transilvania *Romania* 46°30N 24°0E **183** D9
Erdemli *Turkey* 36°36N 34°19E **250** B5
Erdene = Ulaan-Uul *Mongolia* 46°4N 100°49E **218** B9
Erdenet *Mongolia* 49°2N 104°5E **218** B9
Erdenetsogt *Mongolia* 42°55N 106°5E **226** C4
Erding *Germany* 48°18N 11°54E **179** G7
Erdre ➜ *France* 47°13N 1°32W **172** E5
Erebato ➜ *Venezuela* 5°54N 64°16W **329** B5
Erebus, Mt. *Antarctica* 77°35S 167°0E **151** D11
Erechim *Brazil* 27°35S 52°15W **335** B5
Ereğli *Konya, Turkey* 37°31N 34°4E **212** D6
Ereğli *Zonguldak, Turkey* 41°15N 31°24E **212** B4
Erei, Monti *Italy* 37°20N 14°20E **201** E7
Erenhot *China* 43°48N 112°2E **226** C7
Erenköy = Kokkina *Cyprus* 35°11N 32°36E **207** E8
Erenköy *Turkey* 40°58N 29°3E **122** C2
Eresfjord *Norway* 62°40N 8°8E **164** B5
Eresma ➜ *Spain* 41°26N 4°45W **194** D6
Eresos *Greece* 39°11N 25°57E **205** B7
Ereymentaū *Kazakhstan* 51°37N 73°6E **217** B8
Erfelek *Turkey* 41°53N 34°55E **212** B6
Erfenisdam *S. Africa* 28°30S 26°50E **270** C4
Erfjord *Norway* 59°20N 6°14E **164** E3
Erfoud *Morocco* 31°30N 4°15W **260** B4
Erfstadt *Germany* 50°50N 6°50E **178** E2
Erft ➜ *Germany* 51°11N 6°44E **178** D2
Erfurt *Germany* 50°58N 11°2E **178** E7
Ergani *Turkey* 38°17N 39°49E **213** C8
Ergel *Mongolia* 43°8N 109°5E **226** C5
Ergene ➜ *Turkey* 41°1N 26°22E **203** E10
Ergeni Vozvyshennost *Russia* 47°0N 44°0E **191** G7
Ērgli *Latvia* 56°54N 25°38E **188** D3
Ergun He = Argun ➜ *Russia* 53°20N 121°28E **219** A13
Ergun Youqi *China* 50°15N 120°11E **219** A13
Erhlin *Taiwan* 23°54N 120°22E **225** C2
Erhshui *Taiwan* 23°45N 120°37E **225** C2
Eria ➜ *Spain* 42°3N 5°44W **194** C5
Eriba *Sudan* 16°40N 36°10E **257** D4
Eriboll, L. *U.K.* 58°30N 4°42W **167** C4
Érice *Italy* 38°2N 12°35E **200** D5
Eridu *U.S.A.* 30°18N 83°45W **316** E6
Erie *Mich., U.S.A.* 41°47N 83°31W **311** C13
Erie *Pa., U.S.A.* 42°8N 80°5W **312** D4
Erie, L. *N. Amer.* 42°15N 81°0W **312** D4
Erie Canal *U.S.A.* 43°5N 78°43W **312** C7
Erieau *Canada* 42°16N 81°57W **312** D3
Erigavo = Ceerigaabo *Somalia* 10°35N 47°20E **267** B6
Erikoussa *Greece* 39°53N 19°34E **206** B9
Eriksdale *Canada* 50°52N 98°7W **297** C9
Erimanthos *Greece* 37°57N 21°50E **204** D3
Erimo-Misaki *Japan* 41°50N 143°15E **220** D11
Erin *Ont., Canada* 43°45N 80°7W **312** C4
Erin *Trin. & Tob.* 10°5N 61°39W **323** t
Erin B. *Trin. & Tob.* 10°4N 61°43W **323** t
Erin Pt. *Trin. & Tob.* 10°3N 61°39W **323** t
Erinpura *India* 25°9N 73°3E **242** G5
Eriskay *U.K.* 57°4N 7°18W **167** D1
Erith *U.K.* 51°28N 0°11E **125** B5
Erithres *Greece* 38°13N 23°20E **204** C5
Eritrea ■ *Africa* 14°0N 38°30E **257** E4
Erivan = Yerevan *Armenia* 40°10N 44°31E **191** K7
Erjas ➜ *Portugal* 39°40N 7°1W **194** F3
Erkech-Tam Pass *Asia* 39°46N 74°2E **217** E8
Erkelenz *Germany* 51°4N 6°19E **178** D2
Erkner *Germany* 52°25N 13°44E **178** C9
Erlaa *Austria* 48°9N 16°19E **142** B1
Erlangen *Germany* 49°36N 11°0E **179** F6
Erlanger *U.S.A.* 39°1N 84°36W **311** E12
Erldunda *Australia* 25°14S 133°12E **280** D1
Erlin = Erhlin *Taiwan* 23°54N 120°22E **225** C2
Ermelo *Neths.* 52°18N 5°35E **170** B5
Ermelo *Mpumalanga, S. Africa* 26°31S 29°59E **271** C4
Ermenek *Turkey* 36°38N 33°0E **250** B4
Ermenek ➜ *Turkey* 36°35N 33°23E **250** B4
Ermil *Sudan* 13°35N 27°40E **257** E2
Ermington *Australia* 33°48S 151°4E **139** A1
Ermioni *Greece* 37°23N 23°15E **204** D5
Ermita *Phil.* 14°35N 120°59E **127** B1
Ermones *Greece* 39°37N 19°46E **206** B9
Ermoupoli *Greece* 37°28N 24°57E **204** D6
Ernakulam *India* 9°59N 76°22E **245** K3
Erne ➜ *Ireland* 54°30N 8°16W **166** B3
Erne, Lower L. *U.K.* 54°28N 7°47W **166** B4
Erne, Upper L. *U.K.* 54°14N 7°32W **166** B4
Ernée *France* 48°18N 0°56W **172** D6
Ernest Giles Ra. *Australia* 27°0S 123°45E **279** E3
Ernest N. Morial Convention Center *New Orleans, U.S.A.* **131** c3
Ernstberg *Germany* 50°13N 6°47E **179** E2
Erode *India* 11°24N 77°45E **245** J3
Eromanga *Australia* 26°40S 143°11E **281** D3
Erongo *Namibia* 21°39S 15°58E **270** B2
Erongo □ *Namibia* 22°20S 15°0E **270** B2
Erquy *France* 48°38N 2°29W **172** D4
Erramala Hills *India* 15°30N 78°15E **245** G4
Errentería *Spain* 43°19N 1°54W **196** B3
Errer ➜ *Ethiopia* 7°32N 42°35E **257** F5
Errigal *Ireland* 55°2N 8°6W **166** A3
Errinundra △ *Australia* 37°20S 148°47E **283** D8
Erris Hd. *Ireland* 54°17N 10°0W **166** B1
Erromango *Vanuatu* 18°45S 169°5E **287** H7
Ersekë *Albania* 40°22N 20°40E **202** F4
Ersekújvár = Nové Zámky *Slovakia* 48°2N 18°8E **181** C11
Ershatou *China* 23°6N 113°18E **121** B2
Erskine *U.S.A.* 47°40N 96°0W **308** B6
Erskineville *Australia* 33°54S 151°12E **139** B2
Erstein *France* 48°25N 7°38E **173** D14
Erta Ale *Ethiopia* 13°36N 40°40E **257** E5
Ertai *China* 46°3N 90°5E **217** C12
Ertan Shuiku *China* 27°5N 101°52E **228** D3
Ertholmene *Denmark* 55°19N 15°11E **163** J9
Ertil *Russia* 51°55N 40°50E **190** E5
Ertis = Irtysh ➜ *Russia* 61°4N 68°52E **214** C7
Ertis *Kazakhstan* 53°20N 75°27E **217** B9
Ertis ➜ *Kazakhstan* 47°52N 84°16E **217** C10
Ertvågøy *Norway* 63°13N 8°26E **164** A5
Eruh *Turkey* 37°46N 42°13E **213** D10
Erunkan *Nigeria* 6°36N 3°23E **124** A2
Ervy-le-Châtel *France* 48°2N 3°55E **173** D10
Erwin *U.S.A.* 36°9N 82°25W **315** C13
Eryuan *China* 26°7N 99°57E **228** D2
Erzgebirge *Germany* 50°27N 12°55E **178** E8
Erzin *Russia* 50°15N 95°10E **217** B13
Erzin *Turkey* 36°57N 36°11E **250** B7
Erzincan *Turkey* 39°46N 39°30E **213** C8
Erzincan □ *Turkey* 39°45N 39°30E **213** C8
Erzsébet-Telep *Hungary* 47°27N 19°10E **117** B3
Erzurum *Turkey* 39°57N 41°15E **213** C9
Erzurum □ *Turkey* 39°55N 41°15E **213** C9
Es Caló *Spain* 38°40N 1°30E **206** D2
Es Canar *Spain* 39°2N 1°36E **206** C2
Es Mercadal *Spain* 39°59N 4°5E **206** B5
Es Migjorn Gran *Spain* 39°57N 4°3E **206** B5
Es Safiya *Sudan* 15°31N 30°7E **257** D3
Es Sînâ' *Egypt* 29°0N 34°0E **251** J4
Es Sûkî *Sudan* 13°20N 33°58E **257** E3
Es Vedrà *Spain* 38°52N 1°12E **206** D1
Esa'ala *Papua N. G.* 9°45S 150°49E **286** E6
Esambo *Dem. Rep. of the Congo* 3°48S 23°30E **264** C4
Esan-Misaki *Japan* 41°40N 141°10E **220** D10
Esashi *Hokkaidō, Japan* 44°56N 142°35E **220** B11
Esashi *Hokkaidō, Japan* 41°52N 140°7E **220** D10
Esbjerg *Denmark* 55°29N 8°29E **163** J2
Esbo = Espoo *Finland* 60°12N 24°40E **188** B3
Escada *Brazil* 8°22S 35°8W **332** C4
Escalante *Phil.* 10°50N 123°33E **233** F4
Escalante *Utah, U.S.A.* 37°47N 111°36W **305** H8
Escalante ➜ *U.S.A.* 37°24N 110°57W **305** H8
Escalón *Mexico* 26°45N 104°20W **318** B4
Escambia ➜ *U.S.A.* 30°32N 87°11W **317** E2
Escanaba *U.S.A.* 45°45N 87°4W **308** C10
Escárcega *Mexico* 18°37N 90°43W **319** D6
Escarparda Pt. *Phil.* 18°31N 122°13E **232** B4
Escarpé, C. *N. Cal.* 20°41S 167°13E **288** d
Escaut = Schelde ➜ *Belgium* 51°15N 4°16E **170** C4
Esch-sur-Alzette *Lux.* 49°32N 6°0E **170** E6
Eschede *Germany* 52°44N 10°14E **178** C6
Eschenried *Germany* 48°13N 11°24E **131** A1
Eschwege *Germany* 51°11N 10°2E **178** D6
Eschweiler *Germany* 50°49N 6°15E **178** E2
Escobal *Panama* 9°6N 80°1W **320** c
Escoma *Bolivia* 15°40S 69°8W **330** D4
Escondido *U.S.A.* 33°7N 117°5W **307** M9
Escravos ➜ *Nigeria* 5°35N 5°10E **263** D6
Escuinapa de Hidalgo *Mexico* 22°50N 105°50W **318** C3
Escuintla *Guatemala* 14°20N 90°48W **320** D1
Eséka *Cameroon* 3°41N 10°44E **263** E7
Eşen ➜ *Turkey* 36°27N 29°16E **205** E11
Esenguly *Turkmenistan* 37°37N 53°59E **216** E4
Esenler *Turkey* 41°1N 28°52E **122** B1
Esens *Germany* 53°38N 7°36E **178** B3
Esentepe = Áyios Amvrósios *Cyprus* 35°20N 33°35E **207** E9
Esenyurt *Turkey* 41°3N 28°48E **203** E12
Esera ➜ *Spain* 42°6N 0°15E **196** C5
Eşfahān *Iran* 32°39N 51°43E **247** C6
Eşfahān □ *Iran* 32°50N 51°50E **247** C6
Esfarāyen *Iran* 37°4N 57°30E **247** B8
Esfideh *Iran* 33°39N 59°46E **247** C8
Esgueva ➜ *Spain* 41°40N 4°43W **194** D6
Esh Sham = Dimashq *Syria* 33°30N 36°18E **250** E7
Esh Shamâlîya □ *Sudan* 19°0N 29°0E **256** D2
Esha Ness *U.K.* 60°29N 1°38W **167** A7
Eshan *China* 24°11N 102°24E **228** E4
Esher *U.K.* 51°21N 0°20W **125** B1
Eshkāshem = Ishkashim *Tajikistan* 36°44N 71°37E **217** E8
Eshkol △ *Israel* 31°20N 34°30E **251** G5
Eshowe *S. Africa* 28°50S 31°30E **271** C5
Esiama *Ghana* 4°56N 2°25W **262** E4
Esigodini *Zimbabwe* 20°18S 28°56E **271** B4
Esil = Ishim ➜ *Russia* 57°45N 71°10E **214** D8
Esil *Kazakhstan* 51°57N 66°24E **217** B7
Esino ➜ *Italy* 43°39N 13°22E **199** E10
Esira *Madag.* 24°20S 46°42E **272** C2
Esk ➜ *Dumf. & Gall., U.K.* 54°58N 3°2W **167** G5
Esk ➜ *N. Yorks., U.K.* 54°30N 0°37W **168** C7
Eskān *Iran* 26°48N 63°9E **240** D1
Eskbank *U.K.* 55°52N 3°4W **121** B3
Esker Siding *Canada* 53°53N 66°25W **299** B6
Eskifjörður *Iceland* 65°3N 13°55W **155** B13
Eskije = Xanthi *Greece* 41°10N 24°58E **203** E8
Eskilsäter *Sweden* 58°57N 13°10E **163** F7
Eskilstuna *Sweden* 59°22N 16°32E **162** E10
Eskimalatya *Turkey* 38°24N 38°22E **213** C8
Eskimo Point = Arviat *Canada* 61°6N 93°59W **297** A10
Eskişehir *Turkey* 39°50N 30°30E **205** B12
Eskişehir □ *Turkey* 39°40N 31°0E **205** B12
Esla ➜ *Spain* 41°29N 6°3W **194** D4
Eslāmābād-e Gharb *Iran* 34°10N 46°30E **213** E12
Eslāmshahr *Iran* 35°40N 51°10E **247** C6
Eslöv *Sweden* 55°50N 13°20E **163** J7
Eşme *Turkey* 38°23N 28°58E **205** C10
Esmeralda, I. *Chile* 48°55S 75°25W **336** C1
Esmeraldas *Ecuador* 1°0N 79°40W **328** C2
Esmeraldas □ *Ecuador* 0°40N 79°30W **328** C2
Esmeraldas ➜ *Ecuador* 0°58N 79°38W **328** C2
Esna = Isna *Egypt* 25°17N 32°30E **256** B3
Esnagi L. *Canada* 48°36N 84°33W **298** C3
Esom Hill *U.S.A.* 33°57N 85°23W **316** B4
Espa *Norway* 60°34N 11°16E **164** D8
Espada, Pta. *Colombia* 12°5N 71°7W **328** A3
Espalion *France* 44°32N 2°47E **174** D6
España = Spain ■ *Europe* 39°0N 4°0W **192** D3
Espanola *Ont., Canada* 46°15N 81°46W **298** C3
Espanola *N. Mex., U.S.A.* 35°59N 106°5W **305** J10
Española, I. *Ecuador* 1°23S 89°39W **330** a
Espanya, Plaça d' *Barcelona, Spain* **114** c1
Esparreguera *Spain* 41°33N 1°52E **196** D6
Esparza *Costa Rica* 9°59N 84°40W **320** E3
Espeland *Norway* 60°23N 5°28E **164** D2
Espelkamp *Germany* 52°24N 8°36E **178** C4
Espenberg, C. *U.S.A.* 66°33N 163°36W **303** C7
Esperança *Amazonas, Brazil* 4°24S 69°52W **328** D4
Esperança *Paraíba, Brazil* 7°1S 35°51W **332** C4
Esperance *Australia* 33°45S 121°55E **279** F3
Esperance, C. *Solomon Is.* 9°15S 159°43E **287** M10
Esperance B. *Australia* 33°48S 121°55E **279** F3
Esperantinópolis *Brazil* 4°53S 44°53W **332** B3
Esperanza *Antarctica* 65°0S 55°0W **151** C18

Esperanza Santa Cruz, Argentina 51°1S 70°49W 336 D2
Esperanza Santa Fe, Argentina 31°29S 61°3W 334 C3
Esperanza Mexico City, Mexico 128 c3
Esperanza Agusan del S., Phil. 8°43N 125°36E 233 G5
Esperanza Masbate, Phil. 11°45N 124°3E 233 F5
Esperanza Puerto Rico 18°6N 65°28W 321 b
Espéraza France 42°56N 2°14E 174 F6
Espevær Norway 59°35N 5°7E 164 E2
Espichel, C. Portugal 38°22N 9°16W 195 G1
Espiel Spain 38°11N 5°1W 195 G5
Espigão, Serra do Brazil 26°35S 50°30W 335 B5
Espinal Colombia 4°9N 74°53W 328 C3
Espinar Peru 14°51S 71°24W 330 C3
Espinazo, Sierra del = Espinhaço, Serra do Brazil 17°30S 43°30W 333 E3
Espinhaço, Serra do Brazil 17°30S 43°30W 333 E3
Espinho Portugal 41°1N 8°38W 194 D2
Espinilho, Serra do Brazil 28°30S 55°0W 335 B5
Espinosa de los Monteros Spain 43°5N 3°34W 194 B7
Espírito Santo □ Brazil 20°0S 40°45W 333 F3
Espírito Santo do Pinhal Brazil 22°10S 46°46W 335 A6
Espíritu Santo Vanuatu 15°15S 166°50E 287 E4
Espíritu Santo, B. del Mexico 19°20N 87°35W 319 D7
Espíritu Santo, I. Mexico 24°30N 110°22W 318 C2
Espita Mexico 21°1N 88°19W 319 C7
Espiye Turkey 40°56N 38°43E 213 B8
Esplanada Brazil 11°47S 37°57W 333 D4
Esplanade Singapore 138 c3
Esplugas Spain 41°22N 2°5E 114 A1
Espoo Finland 60°12N 24°40E 188 B3
Esposizione Universale di Roma Italy 41°49N 12°28E 136 C1
Espuña, Sierra de Spain 37°51N 1°35W 197 H3
Espungabera Mozam. 20°29S 32°45E 271 B5
Esquel Argentina 42°55S 71°20W 336 B2
Esquimalt Canada 48°26N 123°25W 306 B3
Esquina Argentina 30°0S 59°30W 334 C4
Essandsjøen Norway 63°0N 12°0E 164 A8
Essaouira Morocco 31°32N 9°42W 260 B3
Essen Belgium 51°28N 4°28E 170 C4
Essen Nordrhein-Westfalen, Germany 51°28N 7°2E 178 D3
Essendon Australia 37°44S 144°55E 128 A1
Essendon ✕ (MEB) Australia 37°43S 144°54E 128 A1
Essendon, Mt. Australia 25°0S 120°29E 279 E3
Essequibo → Guyana 6°50N 58°30W 329 B6
Essequibo Islands-West Demerara □ Guyana 6°33N 58°29W 329 B6
Essex Ont., Canada 42°10N 82°49W 312 D2
Essex Calif., U.S.A. 34°44N 115°15W 307 L11
Essex N.Y., U.S.A. 44°19N 73°21W 313 B11
Essex □ U.K. 51°54N 0°27E 169 F8
Essex Junction U.S.A. 44°29N 73°7W 313 B11
Essingen Sweden 59°19N 17°59E 139 B1
Essling Austria 48°12N 16°30E 142 A3
Esslingen Germany 48°44N 9°18E 179 G5
Essonne □ France 48°30N 2°20E 173 D9
Est, Gare de l' Paris, France 134 a5
Estaca de Bares, C. de Spain 43°46N 7°42W 194 B3
Estación Camacho Mexico 24°25N 102°18W 318 C4
Estación Simón Mexico 24°42N 102°35W 318 C4
Estadilla Spain 42°4N 0°16E 196 C5
Estado, Parque do Brazil 23°38S 46°38W 137 B2
Estados, I. de Los Argentina 54°40S 64°30W 336 D4
Estagel France 42°47N 2°40E 174 F6
Estagno Pt. Phil. 17°20N 122°24E 232 C4
Eşţahbānāt Iran 29°8N 54°4E 247 D7
Estância Brazil 11°16S 37°26W 332 D4
Estancia N. Mex., U.S.A. 34°46N 106°4W 305 J10
Estancia Monte León Argentina 50°14S 68°55W 336 D3
Estārm Iran 28°21N 58°21E 247 D8
Estarreja Portugal 40°45N 8°35W 194 E2
Estats, Pic d' Spain 42°40N 1°24E 196 C6
Estcourt S. Africa 29°0S 29°53E 271 C4
Este Italy 45°14N 11°39E 199 C8
Este △ Dom. Rep. 18°14N 68°42W 321 C6
Estefânia Lisbon, Portugal 126 a2
Estelí Nic. 13°9N 86°22W 320 D2
Estella Spain 42°40N 2°2W 196 C2
Estelle U.S.A. 29°50N 90°6W 131 B2
Estellencs Spain 39°39N 2°29E 206 B3
Estena → Spain 39°23N 4°44W 195 F6
Estepa Spain 37°17N 4°52W 195 H6
Estepona Spain 36°24N 5°7W 195 J5
Esterhazy Canada 50°37N 102°5W 297 C8
Esterias, C. Gabon 0°40N 9°20E 264 B1
Esternay France 48°44N 3°33E 173 D10
Esterri d'Aneu Spain 42°38N 1°5E 196 C6
Estevan Canada 49°10N 102°59W 297 D8
Estevan Group Canada 53°3N 129°38W 296 C3
Estherville U.S.A. 43°24N 94°50W 308 D6
Estill U.S.A. 32°45N 81°15W 316 C8
Estissac France 48°16N 3°48E 173 D10
Eston Canada 51°8N 108°40W 297 C7
Estonia ■ Europe 58°30N 25°30E 188 C3
Estoril Portugal 38°42N 9°23W 195 G1
Estouk Mali 18°14N 1°2E 263 B5
Estreito Brazil 6°34S 47°27W 332 C2
Estrela, Basilica da Portugal 38°42N 9°9W 126 A2
Estrela, Serra da Portugal 40°10N 7°45W 194 E3
Estrella Spain 38°25N 3°35W 195 G7
Estremoz Portugal 38°51N 7°39W 195 G3
Estrondo, Serra do Brazil 7°20S 48°0W 332 C2
Estuaire □ Gabon 0°30N 9°30E 264 B1
Esutoru = Uglegorsk Russia 49°5N 142°2E 215 E15
Eswatini ■ Africa 26°30S 31°30E 271 C5
Esztergom Hungary 47°47N 18°44E 182 C3
Et Tidra Mauritania 19°45N 16°20W 262 B1
Etah India 27°35N 78°40E 243 F8
Étain France 49°13N 5°38E 173 C12
Étampes France 48°26N 2°10E 173 D9
Étang-Salé-les-Bains Réunion 21°15S 55°20E 272 f
Etanga Namibia 17°55S 13°0E 270 A1
Étaples France 50°30N 1°39E 173 B8
Etawah India 26°48N 79°6E 243 F8
Etawney L. Canada 57°50N 96°50W 297 B9
Etchojoa Mexico 26°55N 109°38W 318 B3
Ete Nigeria 7°2N 7°28E 263 D6
Etéké Gabon 1°29S 11°35E 264 C2
Etelä-Konneveden △ Finland 62°34N 26°39E 160 E22
eThekwini = Durban S. Africa 29°49S 31°1E 271 C5
Ethel U.S.A. 46°32N 122°46W 306 D4
Ethelbert Canada 51°32N 100°25W 297 C8
Ethiopia ■ Africa 8°0N 40°0E 267 C4
Ethiopian Highlands Ethiopia 10°0N 37°0E 254 E7
Etili Turkey 39°59N 26°54E 203 G10
Etive, L. U.K. 56°29N 5°10W 167 E3
Etna Italy 37°50N 14°55E 201 E7
Etna → Norway 60°49N 10°7E 164 C6
Etne Norway 59°40N 5°58E 164 E2
Etobicoke Canada 43°39N 79°34W 141 B1
Etobicoke Cr. → Canada 43°35N 79°32W 141 B1
Etoile Dem. Rep. of the Congo 11°33S 27°30E 269 E2
Etoliko Greece 38°26N 21°21E 204 C3
Etolin Strait U.S.A. 60°20N 165°15W 303 F6
Etoloakarnania Greece 38°45N 21°18E 204 C3
Etosha △ Namibia 19°0S 16°0E 270 A2
Etosha Pan Namibia 18°40S 16°30E 270 A2
Etoumbi Congo 0°1S 14°57E 264 C2
Etowah U.S.A. 35°20N 84°32W 315 D12
Étréchy France 48°30N 2°12E 173 D9
Etrek Turkmenistan 37°36N 54°46E 247 B7
Étrépagny France 49°18N 1°36E 173 C8
Étretat France 49°42N 0°12E 172 C7
Etropole Bulgaria 42°50N 24°0E 203 D8
Ettelbruck Lux. 49°51N 6°5E 170 E6
Etterbeek Belgium 50°50N 4°23E 116 B2
Ettlingen Germany 48°56N 8°25E 179 G4
Ettrick Water → U.K. 55°31N 2°55W 167 F6
Etuku Dem. Rep. of the Congo 3°42S 25°45E 264 C5
Etulia Moldova 45°32N 28°27E 183 E13
Etzná-Tixmucuy = Edzná Mexico 19°39N 90°19W 319 D6
Eu France 50°3N 1°26E 172 B8
Eua Tonga 21°22S 174°56W 287 Q13
Euboea = Evia Greece 38°30N 24°0E 204 C6
Eucaliptus = Tomás Barrón Bolivia 17°35S 67°31W 330 D4
Eucareena Australia 32°57S 149°6E 283 B8
Eucla Australia 31°41S 128°52E 279 F4
Euclid U.S.A. 41°34N 81°32W 312 E3
Euclides da Cunha Brazil 10°31S 39°1W 332 D4
Eucumbene, L. Australia 36°2S 148°40E 283 D8
Eudora U.S.A. 33°7N 91°16W 314 E9
Eudunda Australia 34°12S 139°7E 282 C3
Eufaula Ala., U.S.A. 31°54N 85°9W 316 D4
Eufaula Okla., U.S.A. 35°17N 95°35W 314 D7
Eufaula L. U.S.A. 35°18N 95°21W 314 D7
Eugene U.S.A. 44°5N 123°4W 304 D2
Eugowra Australia 33°22S 148°24E 283 B8
Euless U.S.A. 32°50N 97°4W 120 A3
Eulo Australia 28°10S 145°3E 281 D4
Eulonia U.S.A. 31°32N 81°26W 316 D8
Eumungerie Australia 31°56S 148°36E 283 A8
Eung-am S. Korea 37°34N 126°55E 137 B1
Eungella △ Australia 20°57S 148°40E 280 b
Eunice La., U.S.A. 30°30N 92°25W 314 F8
Eunice N. Mex., U.S.A. 32°26N 103°10W 305 K12
Eunpyeong S. Korea 37°36N 126°56E 137 B1
Eupen Belgium 50°37N 6°3E 170 D6
Euphrates = Furāt, Nahr al → Asia 31°0N 47°25E 246 D5
Eure □ France 49°10N 1°0E 172 C8
Eure → France 49°18N 1°12E 172 C8
Eure-et-Loir □ France 48°22N 1°30E 172 D8
Eureka Nunavut, Canada 80°0N 85°56W 295 B14
Eureka Calif., U.S.A. 40°47N 124°9W 304 F1
Eureka Ill., U.S.A. 40°43N 89°16W 310 D7
Eureka Kans., U.S.A. 37°49N 96°17W 308 G5
Eureka Mo., U.S.A. 38°30N 90°38W 310 F6
Eureka Mont., U.S.A. 48°53N 115°3W 304 B6
Eureka Nev., U.S.A. 39°31N 115°58W 304 G6
Eureka S.C., U.S.A. 33°42N 81°46W 316 B8
Eureka S. Dak., U.S.A. 45°46N 99°38W 308 C4
Eureka, Mt. Australia 26°35S 121°35E 279 E3
Eureka Sd. Canada 79°0N 85°0W 295 B15
Eurelia Australia 32°33S 138°35E 282 B3
Eurinilla Cr. → Australia 30°53S 140°11E 282 A4
Euroa Australia 36°44S 145°35E 283 D6
Euroairport, Basle ✕ (BSL) France 47°36N 7°33E 173 E14
Europa, Île Ind. Oc. 22°20S 40°22E 271 B7
Europa, Picos de Spain 43°10N 4°49W 194 B6
Europa, Pt. Gib. 36°3N 5°21W 195 J5
Europe 50°0N 20°0E 158 E10
Europoort Neths. 51°57N 4°10E 170 C4
Euskadi = País Vasco □ Spain 42°50N 2°45W 196 C2
Euskirchen Germany 50°39N 6°48E 178 E2
Eustis U.S.A. 28°51N 81°41W 317 G8
Euston N.S.W., Australia 34°30S 142°46E 282 C5
Euston London, U.K. 125 a3
Eutawville U.S.A. 33°24N 80°21W 316 B9
Eutin Germany 54°8N 10°36E 178 A6
Eutsuk L. Canada 53°20N 126°45W 296 C3
Eva Perón = La Pampa □ Argentina 36°50S 66°0W 334 D2
Eva Perón = La Plata Argentina 35°0S 57°55W 334 C4
Evale Angola 16°33S 15°44E 265 F3
Evanger Norway 60°39N 6°7E 164 D3
Evanlı Turkey 36°46N 34°26E 250 B5
Evans U.S.A. 40°23N 104°41W 304 F11
Evans, L. Canada 50°50N 77°0W 298 B4
Evans City U.S.A. 40°46N 80°4W 312 F4
Evans Head Australia 29°7S 153°27E 281 D5
Evansburg Canada 53°36N 114°59W 296 C5
Evansdale U.S.A. 42°30N 92°17W 310 B4
Evanston Ill., U.S.A. 42°3N 87°40W 119 A2
Evanston Wyo., U.S.A. 41°16N 110°58W 304 F8
Evansville Ill., U.S.A. 38°5N 89°56W 310 F7
Evansville Ind., U.S.A. 37°58N 87°35W 311 G9
Evansville Wis., U.S.A. 42°47N 89°18W 310 B7
Évaux-les-Bains France 46°12N 2°29E 173 F9
Evaz Iran 27°46N 53°59E 247 E7
Evciler Afyon, Turkey 38°4N 29°54E 205 C11
Evciler Çanakkale, Turkey 39°47N 26°44E 205 B8
Eveleth U.S.A. 47°28N 92°32W 308 B7
Even Sapir Israel 31°46N 35°8E 123 B1
Evensk Russia 62°12N 159°30E 215 C16
Evenstad Norway 61°25N 11°7E 164 C8
Everard, L. Australia 31°30S 135°0E 281 E2
Everard Ranges Australia 27°5S 132°28E 279 E5
Evere Belgium 50°52N 4°25E 116 A2
Everest, Mt. Nepal 28°5N 86°58E 243 E12
Everett Ga., U.S.A. 31°24N 81°38W 316 D8
Everett Mass., U.S.A. 42°24N 71°3W 116 A2
Everett Pa., U.S.A. 40°1N 78°23W 312 F6
Everett Wash., U.S.A. 47°59N 122°12W 306 C4
Everglades, The U.S.A. 25°50N 81°0W 317 K9
Everglades △ U.S.A. 25°30N 81°0W 317 K9
Everglades City U.S.A. 25°52N 81°23W 317 K8
Evergreen Ala., U.S.A. 31°26N 86°57W 315 F11
Evergreen Mont., U.S.A. 48°14N 114°17W 304 B6
Evergreen Park U.S.A. 41°43N 87°42W 119 C2
Everman U.S.A. 32°37N 97°17W 120 C2
Everöd Sweden 55°53N 14°5E 163 J8
Everton Australia 36°25S 146°33E 283 D7
Evertsberg Sweden 61°8N 13°58E 162 C7
Evesham U.K. 52°6N 1°56W 169 E6
Evia Greece 38°30N 24°0E 204 C6
Évian-les-Bains France 46°24N 6°35E 173 F13
Evīn Iran 35°47N 51°23E 141 A2
Evinayong Eq. Guin. 1°26N 10°35E 264 B2
Evinos → Greece 38°27N 21°40E 204 C3
Évisa France 42°15N 8°48E 175 F12
Evje Norway 58°36N 7°51E 164 F4
Évora Portugal 38°33N 7°57W 195 G3
Évora □ Portugal 38°33N 7°50W 195 G3
Evowghlī Iran 38°43N 45°13E 213 C11
Évreux France 49°3N 1°8E 172 C8
Evritania Greece 39°5N 21°30E 204 B3
Évron France 48°10N 0°24W 172 D6
Evros → Greece 41°40N 26°34E 203 F10
Evrotas → Greece 36°50N 22°40E 204 E4
Évry France 48°38N 2°27E 173 D9
Évvoia = Evia Greece 38°30N 24°0E 204 C6
'Ewa Beach U.S.A. 21°19N 158°1W 302 K13
'Ewa District U.S.A. 21°25N 158°0W 302 K13
'Ewa Villages U.S.A. 21°20N 158°3W 302 K13
Ewarton Jamaica 18°11N 77°6W 320 a
Ewasse Papua N. G. 5°19S 151°1E 286 C6
Ewe, L. U.K. 57°49N 5°38W 167 D3
Ewing Mo., U.S.A. 40°6N 91°43W 310 E5
Ewing Nebr., U.S.A. 42°16N 98°21W 308 D4
Ewo Congo 0°48S 14°45E 264 C2
Ewu Nigeria 6°33N 3°19E 124 A1
Exaltación Bolivia 13°10S 65°20W 331 C4
Excelsior Springs U.S.A. 39°20N 94°13W 310 E2
Excideuil France 45°20N 1°4E 174 C5
Exe → U.K. 50°41N 3°29W 169 G4
Exeter Ont., Canada 43°21N 81°29W 312 C3
Exeter Devon, U.K. 50°43N 3°31W 169 G4
Exeter Calif., U.S.A. 36°18N 119°9W 306 J7
Exeter N.H., U.S.A. 42°59N 70°57W 313 D14
Exhibition Place Canada 43°38N 79°25W 141 B2
Exira U.S.A. 41°35N 94°52W 310 C2
Exmoor U.K. 51°12N 3°45W 169 F4
Exmoor △ U.K. 51°8N 3°42W 169 F4
Exmouth W. Austral., Australia 21°54S 114°10E 278 D1
Exmouth Devon, U.K. 50°37N 3°25W 169 G4
Exmouth G. Australia 22°15S 114°15E 278 D1
Exmouth Plateau Ind. Oc. 19°0S 114°0E 288 J3
Expedition △ Australia 25°41S 149°7E 281 D4
Expedition Ra. Australia 24°30S 149°12E 280 C4
Experiment = Highland Mills U.S.A. 33°17N 84°17W 316 B5
Experimentarium Denmark 55°43N 12°35E 118 A3
Expo Centre Shanghai, China 31°11N 121°29E 138 B1
Exposições, Palácio das Brazil 22°53S 43°13W 135 B1
Extremadura □ Spain 39°30N 6°5W 195 F4
Extrême-Nord □ Cameroon 11°0N 14°30E 259 F2
Exuma Sound The Bahamas 24°30N 76°20W 320 B4
Eyak U.S.A. 60°32N 145°36W 303 F11
Eyasi, L. Tanzania 3°30S 35°0E 268 C4
Eydehavn Norway 58°30N 8°53E 164 F5
Eydhafushi Maldives 5°7N 73°2E 272 d
Eye Pen. U.K. 58°13N 6°10W 167 C2
Eyemouth U.K. 55°52N 2°5W 167 F6
Eygues = Aigues → France 44°7N 4°43E 175 D8
Eygurande France 45°40N 2°26E 173 G9
Eyjafjallajökull Iceland 63°38N 19°36W 155 D7
Eyjafjarðarsýsla Iceland 65°30N 18°30W 155 B8
Eyjafjörður Iceland 66°15N 18°30W 155 A8
Eyl Somalia 8°0N 49°50E 267 C6
Eymet France 44°40N 0°25E 174 D4
Eymoutiers France 45°40N 1°45E 174 C5
Eynesil Turkey 41°4N 39°9E 213 B8
Eyrarbakki Iceland 63°52N 21°9W 155 D5
Eyre → France 44°39N 1°1W 174 D2
Eyre, L. = Kati Thanda-Lake Eyre Australia 29°30S 137°26E 276 F6
Eyre Mts. N.Z. 45°25S 168°25E 285 F3
Eyre Pen. Australia 33°30S 136°17E 282 C1
Eysturoy Færoe Is. 62°13N 6°54W 160 E9
Eyüp Turkey 41°2N 28°55E 122 B1
Eyvān = Jūy Zar Iran 33°50N 46°18E 213 F12
Eyvānkī Iran 35°24N 51°56E 247 C6
Ez Zeidab Sudan 17°25N 33°55E 256 D3
Ezcaray Spain 42°19N 3°0W 196 C1
Ezeiza ✕ (EZE) Argentina 34°49S 58°32W 117 C1
Ežerėlis Lithuania 54°53N 23°37E 184 D10
Ezhou China 30°23N 114°50E 229 B10
Ezhva Russia 61°48N 50°35E 186 B9
Ezine Turkey 39°48N 26°20E 205 B8
Ezouza → Cyprus 34°44N 32°27E 207 F8

F

F.Y.R.O.M. = North Macedonia ■ Europe 41°53N 21°40E 202 E5
Faaa Tahiti 17°34S 149°35W 289 e
Faaborg Denmark 55°6N 10°15E 163 J4
Faaone Tahiti 17°40S 149°21W 289 e
Fabala Guinea 9°44N 9°5W 262 D3
Fabbriche Nuove Venice, Italy 142 b2
Fabens U.S.A. 31°30N 106°10W 314 F1
Faber, Mt. Singapore 1°16N 103°49E 138 B2
Fåberg Norway 61°10N 10°25E 164 C7
Fabero Spain 42°46N 6°37W 194 C4
Fabius U.S.A. 42°50N 75°59W 313 D9
Fabriano Italy 43°20N 12°54E 199 E9
Făcăeni Romania 44°32N 27°53E 183 F12
Facatativá Colombia 4°49N 74°22W 328 C3
Faceville U.S.A. 30°45N 84°38W 316 E5
Fachi Niger 18°6N 11°34E 259 E2
Facundo Argentina 45°18S 69°58W 336 C3
Fada Chad 17°13N 21°34E 259 E4
Fada-n-Gourma Burkina Faso 12°10N 0°30E 263 C5
Fadd Hungary 46°28N 18°49E 182 D3
Faddeyevskiy, Ostrov Russia 76°0N 144°0E 215 B15
Faddor South Sudan 8°7N 32°17E 257 F3
Fadghāmī Syria 35°53N 40°52E 213 E9
Fadiffolu Atoll Maldives 5°23N 73°29E 272 d
Fadlab Sudan 17°42N 34°2E 256 D3
Fadwel South Sudan 8°11N 29°20E 266 C2
Fælledparken Denmark 55°42N 12°34E 118 A3
Faenza Italy 44°17N 11°53E 199 D8
Færingehavn = Kangerluarsoruseq Greenland 63°45N 51°27W 154 E5
Færoe Is. = Føroyar ☑ Atl. Oc. 62°0N 7°0W 160 F9
Fafa Mali 15°22N 0°48E 263 B5
Fafe Portugal 41°27N 8°11W 194 D2
Fafen → Ethiopia 5°59N 44°25E 267 C5
Fagam Nigeria 11°1N 10°1E 263 C7
Fagamalo Amer. Samoa 14°18S 170°48W 302 f
Făgăraş Romania 45°48N 24°58E 183 E9
Făgăraş, Munţii Romania 45°40N 24°40E 183 E9
Fagasa Amer. Samoa 14°17S 170°43W 302 f
Fagatele Bay △ Amer. Samoa 14°22S 170°46W 302 f
Fagatogo Amer. Samoa 14°16S 170°41W 302 f
Fågelfors Sweden 57°12N 15°51E 163 G9
Fågelmara Sweden 56°16N 15°58E 163 H9
Fågelön Sweden 59°18N 17°55E 139 B1
Fagerheim Norway 60°26N 7°46E 164 D4
Fagerhult Sweden 57°8N 15°40E 163 G9
Fagernes Norway 60°59N 9°14E 164 D6
Fagersjö Sweden 59°14N 18°4E 139 B2
Fagersta Sweden 60°1N 15°46E 162 D9
Făget Romania 45°52N 22°10E 182 E7
Făget, Munţii Romania 47°40N 23°10E 183 C8
Faggo Nigeria 11°21N 9°57E 263 C6
Faghmah Yemen 16°9N 49°26E 249 D5
Fagnano, L. Argentina 54°30S 68°0W 336 D3
Fagnières France 48°58N 4°20E 173 D11
Faguibine, L. Mali 16°45N 4°0W 262 B4
Fahlīān Iran 30°11N 51°28E 247 D6
Fahraj Kermān, Iran 29°0N 59°0E 247 D8
Fahraj Yazd, Iran 31°46N 54°36E 247 D7
Fai Tsi Long Vietnam 21°0N 107°30E 228 G6
Faial Azores 38°34N 28°42W 153 d1
Faial Madeira 32°47N 16°53W 153 c
Faial, Canal do Azores 38°33N 28°35W 153 d1
Faichan Kangri India 35°48N 76°34E 243 B7
Faichuk Micronesia 7°21N 151°38E 287 T17
Fair Haven N.Y., U.S.A. 43°18N 76°42W 313 C8
Fair Haven Vt., U.S.A. 43°36N 73°16W 313 C11
Fair Hd. U.K. 55°14N 6°9W 166 A5
Fair Isle U.K. 59°32N 1°38W 165 B6
Fair Oaks U.S.A. 38°39N 121°16W 306 G5
Fairbank U.S.A. 42°38N 92°3W 310 B4
Fairbanks Alaska, U.S.A. 64°51N 147°43W 303 D11
Fairbanks Fla., U.S.A. 29°44N 82°16W 316 F7
Fairborn U.S.A. 39°49N 84°2W 311 E12
Fairburn U.S.A. 33°34N 84°35W 316 B5
Fairbury Ill., U.S.A. 40°45N 88°31W 311 D8
Fairbury Nebr., U.S.A. 40°8N 97°11W 308 E5
Fairfax Ohio, U.S.A. 39°5N 83°37W 311 E13
Fairfax S.C., U.S.A. 32°59N 81°15W 316 C8
Fairfax Vt., U.S.A. 44°40N 73°1W 313 B11
Fairfield N.S.W., Australia 33°53S 150°57E 283 B9
Fairfield Calif., U.S.A. 38°15N 122°3W 306 G4
Fairfield Conn., U.S.A. 41°9N 73°16W 313 E11
Fairfield Idaho, U.S.A. 43°21N 114°44W 304 E6
Fairfield Ill., U.S.A. 38°23N 88°22W 311 F8
Fairfield Iowa, U.S.A. 40°56N 91°57W 310 D5
Fairfield Ohio, U.S.A. 39°20N 84°34W 311 E12
Fairfield Tex., U.S.A. 31°44N 96°10W 314 F6
Fairford Canada 51°37N 98°38W 297 C9
Fairhope U.S.A. 30°31N 87°54W 315 F11
Fairland S. Africa 26°8S 27°57E 123 A1
Fairlie N.Z. 44°5S 170°49E 285 E5
Fairmead U.S.A. 37°5N 120°10W 306 H6
Fairmilehead U.K. 55°54N 3°11W 121 B2
Fairmont Minn., U.S.A. 43°39N 94°28W 308 D6
Fairmont W. Va., U.S.A. 39°29N 80°9W 309 F13
Fairmount Calif., U.S.A. 34°45N 118°26W 307 L8
Fairmount N.Y., U.S.A. 43°5N 76°12W 313 C8
Fairplay U.S.A. 39°15N 106°2W 304 G10
Fairport Ont., Canada 43°49N 79°4W 141 A4
Fairport N.Y., U.S.A. 43°6N 77°27W 312 C7
Fairport Harbor U.S.A. 41°45N 81°17W 312 E3
Fairview Alta., Canada 56°5N 118°25W 296 B5
Fairview Mont., U.S.A. 47°51N 104°3W 304 C11
Fairview N.J., U.S.A. 40°48N 73°59W 132 B2
Fairview Okla., U.S.A. 36°16N 98°29W 314 C5
Fairview, L. U.S.A. 28°35N 81°24W 133 A2
Fairweather, Mt. U.S.A. 58°55N 137°32W 296 B1
Faisalabad Pakistan 31°30N 73°5E 242 D5
Faith U.S.A. 45°2N 102°2W 308 C2
Faizabad India 26°45N 82°10E 243 F10
Faizpur India 21°14N 75°49E 244 D2
Fajã Grande Azores 39°27N 31°16W 153 d2
Fajardo Puerto Rico 18°20N 65°39W 321 C6
Fajou, Îlet à Guadeloupe 16°21N 61°35W 322 e
Fajr, W. → Si. Arabia 29°10N 38°10E 246 D3
Fakaofo Pac. Oc. 9°23S 171°15W 277 B16
Fakarava French Polynesia 16°20S 145°37W 289 f
Fakenham U.K. 52°51N 0°51E 168 E8
Fåker Sweden 63°0N 14°34E 162 A8
Fakfak Indonesia 2°55S 132°18E 231 E8
Fakiya Bulgaria 42°10N 27°6E 203 D11
Fakobli Côte d'Ivoire 7°23N 7°23W 262 D3
Fakse Denmark 55°15N 12°8E 163 J6
Fakse Bugt Denmark 55°11N 12°15E 163 J6
Fakse Ladeplads Denmark 55°11N 12°9E 163 J6
Faku China 42°32N 123°21E 224 A1
Fala Beguets I. Micronesia 7°21N 151°41E 287 U17
Falaba S. Leone 9°54N 11°22W 262 D2
Falaise France 48°54N 0°12W 172 D6
Falakros Oros Greece 41°15N 23°58E 202 E7
Falam Myanmar 23°0N 93°45E 241 D4
Falas I. Micronesia 7°31N 151°44E 287 T18
Fălciu Romania 46°17N 28°7E 183 D13
Falcó, C. des Spain 38°50N 1°23E 206 D1
Falcón □ Venezuela 11°0N 69°50W 328 A4
Falcon, C. Algeria 35°50N 0°50W 261 A4
Falcón, Presa Mexico 26°35N 99°10W 319 B5
Falcon Lake Canada 49°42N 95°15W 297 D9
Falcon Res. U.S.A. 26°34N 99°10W 314 H5
Falconara Marittima Italy 43°37N 13°24E 199 E10
Falcone, C. del Italy 40°58N 8°12E 200 B1
Falconer U.S.A. 42°7N 79°12W 312 D5
Faléa Mali 12°16N 11°17W 262 C2
Falefa Samoa 13°54S 171°31W 287 V20
Falelatai Samoa 13°55S 171°59W 287 V20
Falelima Samoa 13°32S 172°41W 287 V19
Falémé → Senegal 14°46N 12°14W 262 C2
Faleniu Amer. Samoa 14°19S 170°44W 302 f
Falenty Poland 52°8N 20°55E 143 C1
Falerum Sweden 58°8N 16°13E 163 F10
Faleshty = Făleşti Moldova 47°32N 27°44E 183 C12
Făleşti Moldova 47°32N 27°44E 183 C12
Falfurrias U.S.A. 27°14N 98°9W 314 H5
Falher Canada 55°44N 117°15W 296 B5
Faliraki Greece 36°22N 28°12E 206 E12
Faliro Greece 37°55N 23°39E 112 B1
Faliro, Ormos Greece 37°54N 23°40E 112 B2
Falkenberg Brandenburg, Germany 51°35N 13°14E 178 D9
Falkenberg Sweden 56°54N 12°30E 163 H6
Falkenburg = Niemodlin Poland 50°38N 17°38E 185 H4
Falkenburg Germany 52°34N 13°32E 115 A4
Falkenhagen Germany 52°34N 13°5E 115 A1
Falkensee Germany 52°34N 13°4E 115 A1
Falkirk U.K. 56°0N 3°47W 167 F5
Falkirk □ U.K. 55°58N 3°49W 167 F5
Falkland U.K. 56°16N 3°12W 167 E5
Falkland, East, I. Falk. Is. 51°40S 58°30W 336 D5
Falkland, West, I. Falk. Is. 51°40S 60°0W 336 D5
Falkland Is. ☑ Atl. Oc. 51°30S 59°0W 153 f
Falkland Plateau Atl. Oc. 51°0S 50°0W 152 M7
Falkland Ridge Atl. Oc. 49°20S 40°0W 152 L8
Falkland Sd. Falk. Is. 52°0S 60°0W 153 f
Falknov nad Ohří = Sokolov Czechia 50°12N 12°40E 180 A5
Falkonera Greece 36°50N 23°52E 204 E5
Falköping Sweden 58°12N 13°33E 163 F7
Fall River U.S.A. 41°43N 71°10W 313 E13
Fallbrook U.S.A. 33°23N 117°15W 307 M9
Fallon U.S.A. 39°28N 118°47W 304 G4
Falls City U.S.A. 40°3N 95°36W 308 E6
Falls Creek U.S.A. 41°9N 78°48W 312 E6
Falmouth Jamaica 18°30N 77°40W 320 a
Falmouth U.K. 50°9N 5°5W 169 G2
Falmouth Ky., U.S.A. 38°41N 84°20W 311 F12
Falmouth Mass., U.S.A. 41°33N 70°37W 313 E14
Falo I. Micronesia 7°28N 151°52E 287 T18
Falomo Nigeria 6°26N 3°26E 124 B2
Falsa, Pta. Mexico 27°51N 115°3W 318 B1
False B. S. Africa 34°15S 18°40E 270 D2
False Bay S. Africa 34°6S 18°33E 118 B1
False Divi Pt. India 15°43N 80°50E 245 G5
False Pass U.S.A. 54°51N 163°25W 303 J7
False Pt. India 20°18N 86°48E 244 D8
Falso, C. Honduras 15°12N 83°21W 320 C3
Falster Denmark 54°45N 11°55E 163 K5
Fălticeni Romania 47°21N 26°20E 183 C11
Falun Sweden 60°37N 15°37E 162 D9
Famagusta Cyprus 35°8N 33°55E 207 E9
Famagusta Bay Cyprus 35°15N 34°0E 207 D10
Famatina, Sierra de Argentina 27°30S 68°0W 334 B2
Famenin Iran 35°5N 48°58E 213 E13
Family L. Canada 51°54N 95°27W 297 C9
Famões Portugal 38°47N 9°13W 126 A1
Famoso U.S.A. 35°37N 119°12W 307 K7
Fan Lau Hong Kong, China 22°12N 113°51E 122 B1
Fan Xian China 35°55N 115°38E 226 G8
Fana Mali 13°0N 6°56W 262 C3
Fanad Hd. Ireland 55°17N 7°38W 166 A4
Fanahammaren Norway 60°16N 5°20E 164 D2
Fanari Greece 39°24N 21°47E 204 B3
Fandriana Madag. 20°14S 47°21E 272 C2
Fânes-Sénnes-Braies △ Italy 46°38N 12°4E 199 B9
Faneuil Hall Marketplace Boston, U.S.A. 116 b3
Fang Thailand 19°55N 99°13E 236 C2
Fang Xian China 32°3N 110°40E 229 A8
Fangaga Sudan 17°40N 37°50E 256 D4
Fangak South Sudan 9°4N 30°53E 257 F3
Fangatau French Polynesia 15°22S 138°45W 289 f
Fangataufa French Polynesia 15°50S 140°52W 289 f
Fangchang China 31°5N 118°4E 229 B12
Fangcheng China 33°18N 112°59E 226 H7
Fangchenggang China 21°42N 108°21E 228 G7
Fangcun China 23°6N 113°13E 121 B2
Fangliao Taiwan 22°22N 120°38E 225 D2
Fangshan Beijing, China 39°41N 116°0E 226 E9
Fangshan Shanxi, China 38°3N 111°25E 226 E6
Fangshan Taiwan 22°15N 120°39E 225 D2
Fangyüan Taiwan 23°56N 120°19E 225 C2
Fangzi China 36°33N 119°10E 227 F10
Fani i Madh → Albania 41°56N 20°16E 202 E4
Fanjakana Madag. 21°10S 46°53E 272 C2
Fanjiatun China 43°40N 125°15E 227 C13
Fanling China 22°30N 114°8E 219 a
Fannich, L. U.K. 57°38N 4°59W 167 D4
Fannrem Norway 63°16N 9°50E 164 A6
Fannūj Iran 26°35N 59°38E 247 E8
Fanø Denmark 55°25N 8°25E 163 J2
Fano Italy 43°50N 13°1E 199 E10
Fanshi China 39°12N 113°20E 226 E7
Fantzuliao Hsi → Taiwan 22°42N 120°28E 225 D2
Fanuet I. Micronesia 7°32N 151°48E 287 T18
Fao = Al Fāw Iraq 30°0N 48°30E 247 D6
Faqirwali Pakistan 29°27N 73°0E 242 E5
Fâqûs Egypt 30°44N 31°47E 256 H7
Far East = Dalnevostochnyy □ Russia 67°0N 140°0E 215 C14
Far East Asia 40°0N 130°0E 210 E14
Fara in Sabina Italy 42°12N 12°43E 199 F9
Faradje Dem. Rep. of the Congo 3°50N 29°45E 268 B2
Farafangana Madag. 22°49S 47°50E 272 C2
Farafenni Gambia 13°34N 15°36W 262 C1
Farâfra, El Wâhât el Egypt 27°15N 28°20E 256 B2
Farāh Afghan. 32°20N 62°7E 240 B1
Farāh □ Afghan. 32°25N 62°10E 240 B1
Farāh → Afghan. 31°27N 61°28E 240 C1
Farahābād Iran 35°41N 51°30E 141 A2
Farahalana Madag. 14°26S 50°10E 272 A3
Faraid, Gebel Egypt 23°33N 35°19E 256 C4
Farako Côte d'Ivoire 10°45N 6°50W 262 D3
Farallon de Medinilla N. Marianas 16°1N 146°4E 302 a
Farallon de Pajaros N. Marianas 20°32N 144°54E 302 a
Farallones de Calí △ Colombia 3°13N 76°46W 328 C2
Faramana Burkina Faso 11°56N 4°45W 262 C4
Faranah Guinea 10°3N 10°45W 262 C2
Farap Turkmenistan 39°9N 63°36E 216 E6
Fararah Oman 17°55N 55°38E 249 C6
Farasān, Jazā'ir Si. Arabia 16°45N 41°55E 248 C3
Farasan Is. = Farasān, Jazā'ir Si. Arabia 16°45N 41°55E 248 C3
Faratsiho Madag. 19°24S 46°57E 272 B2
Farbaraki Somalia 2°30N 45°30E 267 D6
Fardes → Spain 37°35N 3°0W 195 H7
Fareham U.K. 50°51N 1°11W 169 G6
Farewell U.S.A. 62°31N 153°54W 303 E9
Farewell, C. = Nunap Isua Greenland 59°48N 43°55W 154 F6
Farewell, C. N.Z. 40°29S 172°43E 285 A7
Farewell Spit N.Z. 40°35S 173°0E 285 A8
Farforovskaya Russia 59°52N 30°27E 137 B2
Färgelanda Sweden 58°34N 12°0E 163 F5
Fargo Ga., U.S.A. 30°41N 82°34W 316 E7
Fargo N. Dak., U.S.A. 46°53N 96°48W 308 B5
Farg'ona Uzbekistan 40°23N 71°19E 217 D8
Farg'ona □ Uzbekistan 40°30N 71°15E 217 D8
Farg'ona vodiysi Asia 40°46N 71°30E 217 D8
Fār'iah, W. al → West Bank 32°12N 35°27E 251 F6
Faribault U.S.A. 44°18N 93°16W 308 C7
Faridabad India 28°26N 77°19E 242 E6
Faridkot India 30°44N 74°45E 242 D6
Faridpur Bangla. 23°15N 89°55E 241 D2
Faridpur India 28°13N 79°33E 243 E8
Fārigh, W. al → Libya 30°10N 20°44E 258 B3
Färila Sweden 61°48N 15°50E 162 C9
Farim Guinea-Biss. 12°27N 15°9W 262 C1
Farīmān Iran 35°40N 59°49E 247 C8
Farinha → Brazil 6°51S 47°30W 332 C2
Fariones, Pta. Canary Is. 29°13N 13°28W 153 e2
Fâriskûr Egypt 31°20N 31°43E 256 H7
Färjestaden Sweden 56°39N 16°27E 163 H10
Farkadona Greece 39°36N 22°4E 204 B4
Farleigh Australia 21°4S 149°8E 280 b
Farley U.S.A. 42°27N 91°0W 310 B6
Farmakonisi Greece 37°17N 27°5E 205 D9
Farmer City U.S.A. 40°15N 88°39W 311 D8
Farmers Branch U.S.A. 32°55N 96°53W 120 A4
Farmersburg U.S.A. 39°15N 87°23W 311 E9
Farmerville U.S.A. 32°47N 92°24W 314 E8
Farmingdale U.S.A. 40°12N 74°10W 313 F10
Farmington B.C., Canada 55°54N 120°30W 296 B4
Farmington Calif., U.S.A. 37°55N 120°59W 306 H6
Farmington Ga., U.S.A. 33°47N 83°26W 316 B6
Farmington Ill., U.S.A. 40°42N 90°0W 310 D7
Farmington Iowa, U.S.A. 40°38N 91°44W 310 D5
Farmington Maine, U.S.A. 44°40N 70°9W 309 C18
Farmington Mo., U.S.A. 37°47N 90°25W 310 G6
Farmington N.H., U.S.A. 43°24N 71°4W 313 C13
Farmington N. Mex., U.S.A. 36°44N 108°12W 305 H9
Farmington Utah, U.S.A. 40°59N 111°53W 304 F8
Farmington → U.S.A. 41°51N 72°38W 313 E12
Farmland U.S.A. 40°15N 85°5W 311 D11
Farmville U.S.A. 37°18N 78°24W 309 G14
Färnäs Sweden 61°0N 14°39E 162 D8
Farne Is. U.K. 55°38N 1°37W 168 B6
Färnebofjärden △ Sweden 60°10N 16°48E 162 D10
Farnham Canada 45°17N 72°59W 313 A12
Farnham, Mt. Canada 50°29N 116°30W 296 C5
Farningham U.K. 51°23N 0°12E 125 B5
Faro Brazil 2°10S 56°39W 329 D6
Faro Yukon, Canada 62°11N 133°22W 294 E5
Faro Portugal 37°2N 7°55W 195 H3
Fårö Gotland, Sweden 57°55N 19°5E 163 G13
Faro □ Portugal 37°12N 8°10W 195 H2
Faro ✕ (FAO) Portugal 37°1N 7°55W 195 H3
Faro △ Cameroon 8°15N 12°37E 264 A2
Fårösund Sweden 57°52N 19°2E 163 G13
Farquhar, C. Australia 23°50S 113°36E 279 D1
Farquhar Is. Seychelles 11°0S 52°0E 273 F4
Farrars Cr. → Australia 25°35S 140°43E 280 D3
Farrāshband Iran 28°57N 52°5E 247 D7
Farrell U.S.A. 41°13N 80°30W 312 E4
Farrell Flat Australia 33°48S 138°48E 282 B3
Farrokhī Iran 33°50N 59°31E 247 C8
Farruch, C. = Ferrutx, C. de Spain 39°47N 3°21E 206 B4
Farrukhabad India 27°24N 79°34E 244 A4
Fārs □ Iran 29°30N 55°0E 247 D7
Farsala Greece 39°17N 22°23E 204 B4
Fārsī Afghan. 33°47N 63°15E 240 B1
Fārsī Iran 27°58N 50°11E 247 E6
Farsø Denmark 56°46N 9°19E 163 H3
Farson U.S.A. 42°7N 109°26W 304 E9
Farsta Sweden 59°14N 18°5E 139 B2
Farsund Norway 58°5N 6°55E 164 F3
Fartak, Râs Si. Arabia 28°5N 34°34E 246 D2
Fartak, Ra's Yemen 15°38N 52°15E 249 D6
Fărțănești Romania 45°49N 27°59E 183 E12
Fartura, Serra da Brazil 26°21S 52°52W 335 B5
Faru Nigeria 12°48N 6°12E 263 C6
Fārūj Iran 37°14N 58°14E 247 B8
Fårup Denmark 56°33N 9°51E 163 H3
Farvel, Kap = Nunap Isua Greenland 59°48N 43°55W 154 F6
Farwell U.S.A. 34°23N 103°2W 314 D3
Fāryāb □ Afghan. 36°0N 65°0E 240 B2
Fasā Iran 29°0N 53°39E 247 D7
Fasanerie-Nord Germany 48°11N 11°32E 131 A2
Fasangarten Germany 48°5N 11°36E 131 B2
Fasano Italy 40°50N 17°22E 201 B10
Fashoda South Sudan 9°50N 32°2E 257 F3
Fasil Ghebbi Ethiopia 12°36N 37°28E 266 B4
Fáskrúðsfjörður Iceland 64°56N 14°1W 155 C12
Fassa Mali 13°26N 8°15W 262 C3
Fassalé Mauritania 15°33N 5°31W 262 B3
Fastiv Ukraine 50°7N 29°57E 177 C15
Fastnet Rock Ireland 51°22N 9°37W 166 E2
Fastov = Fastiv Ukraine 50°7N 29°57E 177 C15
Fatagartuting, Tanjung Indonesia 2°46S 131°57E 231 E8
Fataka Solomon Is. 11°55S 170°12E 277 C12
Fatatsu Ne Iwo Jima 24°45N 141°18E 288 b
Fatehabad Haryana, India 29°31N 75°27E 242 E6
Fatehabad Ut. P., India 27°1N 78°19E 242 F8
Fatehgarh India 27°25N 79°35E 243 F8
Fatehpur Bihar, India 24°38N 85°14E 243 G11
Fatehpur Raj., India 28°0N 74°40E 242 F6
Fatehpur Ut. P., India 25°56N 81°13E 243 G9
Fatehpur Ut. P., India 27°10N 81°13E 243 F9
Fatehpur Sikri India 27°6N 77°40E 242 F6
Fatesh Russia 52°8N 35°57E 189 F8
Fathai South Sudan 8°5N 31°48E 257 F3
Fathom Five △ Canada 45°17N 81°40W 312 A3
Fatick Senegal 14°19N 16°27W 262 C1
Fatick □ Senegal 14°15N 16°30W 262 C1
Fatih Turkey 41°0N 28°56E 122 B1
Fatima Qué., Canada 47°24N 61°53W 299 C7
Fátima Portugal 39°37N 8°39W 195 F2
Fatoya Guinea 11°37N 9°10W 262 C3
Fatsa Turkey 41°2N 37°31E 212 B7
Fatshan = Foshan China 23°3N 113°9E 121 B1
Faucille, Col de la France 46°22N 6°2E 173 F13
Faulkton U.S.A. 45°2N 99°8W 308 C4
Faulquemont France 49°3N 6°36E 173 C13
Faure I. Australia 25°52S 113°50E 279 E1
Făurei Romania 45°6N 27°19E 183 E12
Fauresmith S. Africa 29°44S 25°17E 270 C4
Fauro Solomon Is. 6°55S 156°7E 287 L9
Fauske Norway 67°17N 15°25E 160 C16
Fåvang Norway 61°27N 10°11E 164 C7
Favânia Brazil 3°7S 51°48W 329 D7
Favara Italy 37°19N 13°39E 200 E6
Faváritx, C. de Spain 40°0N 4°15E 206 B5
Faverges France 45°45N 6°17E 175 C10
Favignana Italy 37°56N 12°19E 200 E5
Favignana, I. Italy 37°56N 12°19E 200 E5
Favoriten Austria 48°9N 16°23E 142 B2
Fawcett, Pt. Australia 11°46S 130°2E 278 B5
Fawkner Australia 37°42S 144°56E 128 A1
Fawkner Park Australia 37°50S 144°58E 128 B1
Fawn → Canada 55°20N 87°35W 298 A2
Fawnskin U.S.A. 34°16N 116°56W 307 L10
Faxaflói Iceland 64°29N 23°0W 155 C3
Faxälven → Sweden 63°13N 17°13E 162 A10
Faya-Largeau Chad 17°58N 19°6E 259 E3
Fayaoué N. Cal. 20°38S 166°33E 288 d
Fayd Si. Arabia 27°1N 42°52E 246 E4
Fayence France 43°38N 6°42E 175 E10
Fayette Ala., U.S.A. 33°41N 87°50W 315 E11
Fayette Iowa, U.S.A. 42°51N 91°48W 310 B5
Fayette Mo., U.S.A. 39°9N 92°41W 310 E4
Fayette N.Y., U.S.A. 42°48N 76°48W 313 D8
Fayette Ohio, U.S.A. 41°40N 84°20W 311 C12
Fayetteville Ark., U.S.A. 36°4N 94°10W 314 C7
Fayetteville Ga., U.S.A. 33°27N 84°27W 316 B5
Fayetteville N.C., U.S.A. 35°3N 78°53W 315 D15
Fayetteville N.Y., U.S.A. 43°1N 76°0W 313 C9
Fayetteville Tenn., U.S.A. 35°9N 86°34W 315 D11
Fayied Egypt 30°18N 32°16E 256 H8
Faylakah Kuwait 29°27N 48°20E 247 D6
Fayón Spain 41°15N 0°20E 196 D5
Fazao-Malfakassa △ Togo 8°45N 0°50E 263 D5
Fazenda Libongo Angola 8°24S 13°24E 265 D2
Fazenda Nova Brazil 16°11S 50°48W 333 E1
Fazilka India 30°27N 74°2E 242 D6
Fazilpur Pakistan 29°18N 70°29E 242 E4
Fdérik Mauritania 22°40N 12°45W 260 D2
Feakle Ireland 52°56N 8°40W 166 D3
Feale → Ireland 52°27N 9°37W 166 D2
Fear, C. U.S.A. 33°50N 77°58W 315 E16
Feather → U.S.A. 38°47N 121°36W 306 G5
Feather Falls U.S.A. 39°36N 121°16W 306 F5
Featherston N.Z. 41°6S 175°20E 284 H4
Featherstone Zimbabwe 18°42S 30°55E 269 F3
Fécamp France 49°45N 0°22E 172 C7
Feda Norway 58°17N 6°50E 164 F3
Fedala = Mohammedia Morocco 33°44N 7°21W 260 B3
Federación Argentina 31°0S 57°55W 334 C4
Federal Argentina 30°57S 58°48W 334 C4
Federal Capital Terr. □ Nigeria 9°0N 7°10E 263 D6
Federal Way U.S.A. 47°18N 122°19W 306 C4
Fedeshkūh Iran 28°49N 53°50E 247 D7
Fedje Norway 60°47N 4°43E 164 D1
Fedorovka Kazakhstan 53°37N 62°42E 216 B6
Fefan I. Pac. Oc. 7°21N 151°51E 287 T18
Fehérgyarmat Hungary 47°58N 22°30E 182 C7
Fehmarn Germany 54°27N 11°7E 178 A7
Fehmarn Bælt Europe 54°35N 11°20E 163 K5
Fehmarn Belt = Fehmarn Bælt Europe 54°35N 11°20E 163 K5
Fei Xian China 35°18N 117°59E 227 G9
Feicheng China 36°14N 116°45E 226 F9
Feidong China 32°0N 117°35E 229 B11
Feijó Brazil 8°9S 70°21W 330 B3
Feilding N.Z. 40°13S 175°35E 284 G4
Feira de Santana Brazil 12°15S 38°57W 333 D4
Feirân, W. → Egypt 28°39N 33°12E 251 K4
Feirân, G. Egypt 28°31N 33°41E 251 K5
Feiring Norway 60°30N 11°10E 164 D8
Feixi China 31°43N 117°59E 229 B11
Feixiang China 36°30N 114°45E 226 F8
Fejér □ Hungary 47°9N 18°30E 182 C3
Fejø Denmark 54°55N 11°30E 163 K5
Feke Turkey 37°48N 35°56E 212 D6
Fekete → Hungary 45°47N 18°15E 182 E3
Felanitx Spain 39°28N 3°9E 206 B4
Felda U.S.A. 26°34N 81°26W 317 J8
Feldbach Austria 46°57N 15°52E 180 E8
Feldberg Baden-W., Germany 47°52N 8°0E 179 H3
Feldberg Mecklenburg-Vorpommern, Germany 53°20N 13°25E 178 B9
Feldkirch Austria 47°15N 9°37E 180 D2
Feldkirchen Austria 46°44N 14°6E 180 E7
Feldkirchen Oberbayern, Germany 48°8N 11°43E 131 B3
Feldmoching Germany 48°14N 11°32E 131 A2

Félicité Seychelles 4°19S 55°52E 272 c
Felicity U.S.A. 38°51N 84°6W 311 F12
Felidhoo Maldives 3°29N 73°32E 272 d
Felidu Atoll Maldives 3°29N 73°29E 272 d
Felipe Carrillo Puerto Mexico 19°38N 88°3W 319 D7
Felixburg Zimbabwe 19°29S 30°51E 271 A5
Felixlândia Brazil 18°47S 44°55W 333 E3
Felixstowe U.K. 51°58N 1°23E 169 F9
Felletin France 45°53N 2°11E 174 C6
Fellingsbro Sweden 59°26N 15°37E 162 E9
Fellsmere U.S.A. 27°46N 80°36W 317 H9
Felshtin = Gvardeyskoye Ukraine 45°7N 34°1E 189 K8
Felsogalla = Tatabánya Hungary 47°32N 18°25E 182 C3
Feltham U.K. 51°26N 0°24W 125 B1
Felton U.S.A. 37°3N 122°4W 306 H4
Feltre Italy 46°1N 11°54E 199 B8
Femer Bælt = Fehmarn Bælt Europe 54°35N 11°20E 163 K5
Femø Denmark 54°58N 11°35E 163 K5
Femunden Norway 62°10N 11°53E 164 B8
Femundsmarka △ Norway 62°18N 12°6E 164 B9
Fen He → China 35°36N 110°42E 226 G6
Fenchih Taiwan 23°30N 120°40E 225 C2
Fene Spain 43°27N 8°9W 194 B2
Fenelon Falls Canada 44°32N 78°45W 312 B6
Fener Turkey 41°1N 28°56E 122 B1
Fener Burnu Turkey 36°58N 27°18E 205 E9
Fenerbahçe Turkey 40°58N 29°2E 122 C2
Feneroa Ethiopia 13°5N 39°3E 257 E4
Feng Xian Jiangsu, China 34°43N 116°35E 226 G9
Feng Xian Shaanxi, China 33°54N 106°40E 226 H4
Fengari Greece 40°25N 25°32E 203 F9
Fengcheng Jiangxi, China 28°12N 115°48E 229 C10
Fengcheng Liaoning, China 40°28N 124°5E 224 B2
Fengdu China 29°55N 107°48E 228 C6
Fengfeng China 36°28N 114°8E 226 F8
Fenggang China 27°57N 107°47E 228 D6
Fenghua China 29°40N 121°25E 229 C13
Fenghuang China 27°57N 109°29E 228 D7
Fengjie China 31°3N 109°31E 228 B7
Fengkai China 23°24N 111°30E 229 F8
Fengkang Taiwan 22°12N 120°41E 225 D2
Fengle China 31°29N 112°29E 229 B9
Fenglin Taiwan 23°45N 121°26E 225 C3
Fengning China 41°10N 116°33E 226 D9
Fengpin Taiwan 23°36N 121°31E 225 C3
Fengqing China 24°38N 99°55E 228 E2
Fengqiu China 35°2N 114°25E 226 G8
Fengrun China 39°48N 118°8E 227 E10
Fengshan Guangxi Zhuangzu, China 24°39N 109°15E 228 E7
Fengshan Guangxi Zhuangzu, China 24°31N 107°3E 228 E6
Fengshan Taiwan 22°38N 120°21E 225 D2
Fengshun China 23°46N 116°10E 229 F11
Fengtai Anhui, China 32°50N 116°40E 229 A11
Fengtai Beijing, China 39°49N 116°14E 114 C1
Fengtai Stadium China 39°51N 116°15E 114 B1
Fengtongzhai △ China 30°32N 102°54E 228 B4
Fengxiang China 34°29N 107°25E 226 G4
Fengxin China 28°41N 115°18E 229 C10
Fengyang China 32°51N 117°29E 229 A11
Fengyi China 25°37N 100°20E 228 E3
Fengyüan Taiwan 24°15N 120°35E 225 B2
Fengzhen China 40°25N 113°2E 226 D7
Feni Bangla. 22°55N 91°32E 241 D3
Feni Is. Papua N. G. 4°0S 153°40E 286 C7
Fennimore U.S.A. 42°59N 90°39W 310 B6
Feno, C. de France 41°58N 8°33E 175 G12
Fenoarivo Amoron'i Mania, Madag. 20°52S 46°53E 272 C2
Fenoarivo Haute Matsiatra, Madag. 21°43S 46°24E 272 C2
Fenoarivo Afovoany Madag. 18°26S 46°34E 272 B2
Fenoarivo Atsinanana Madag. 17°22S 49°25E 272 B2
Fens, The U.K. 52°38N 0°2W 168 E7
Fensmark Denmark 55°17N 11°48E 163 J5
Fenton U.S.A. 42°48N 83°42W 311 B13
Fenxi China 36°40N 111°31E 226 F6
Fenyang China 37°18N 111°48E 226 F6
Fenyi China 27°45N 114°47E 229 D10
Fenyuan Taiwan 24°1N 120°37E 225 B2
Feodosiya Ukraine 45°2N 35°16E 189 K8
Fer, C. de Algeria 37°3N 7°10E 261 A6
Fera Solomon Is. 8°6S 159°37E 287 M10
Ferbane Ireland 53°16N 7°50W 166 C4
Ferdows Iran 33°58N 58°2E 247 C8
Fère-Champenoise France 48°45N 3°59E 173 D10
Fère-en-Tardenois France 49°10N 3°30E 173 C10
Ferenc Liszt, Budapest ✈ (BUD) Hungary 47°26N 19°14E 117 B3
Ferencváros Hungary 47°29N 19°5E 117 B2
Ferentino Italy 41°42N 13°15E 199 G10
Feres Greece 40°53N 26°10E 203 F10
Ferfer Somalia 5°4N 45°9E 267 C6
Fergana = Farg'ona Uzbekistan 40°23N 71°19E 217 D8
Fergana Range Asia 41°0N 73°50E 217 D8
Fergus Canada 43°43N 80°24W 312 C4
Fergus Falls U.S.A. 46°17N 96°4W 308 B5
Ferguson U.S.A. 38°44N 90°18W 310 F6
Fergusson I. Papua N. G. 9°30S 150°45E 286 E6
Fériana Tunisia 34°59N 8°33E 258 B1
Feričanci Croatia 45°32N 18°0E 182 E2
Ferizaj Kosovo 42°23N 21°10E 202 D5
Ferkane Algeria 34°37N 7°26E 261 B6
Ferkéssédougou Côte d'Ivoire 9°35N 5°6W 262 D3
Ferlach Austria 46°32N 14°18E 180 E7
Ferland Canada 50°19N 88°27W 298 B2
Ferlo, Vallée du Senegal 15°15N 14°15W 262 B2
Ferlo-Nord ⌓ Senegal 15°43N 14°0W 262 B2
Ferlo-Sud ⌓ Senegal 15°43N 14°0W 262 B2
Fermanagh & Omagh □ U.K. 54°34N 7°24W 166 B4
Fermo Italy 43°9N 13°43E 199 E10
Fermont Canada 52°47N 67°5W 299 B6
Fermoselle Spain 41°19N 6°27W 194 D4
Fermoy Ireland 52°9N 8°16W 166 D3
Fern Creek U.S.A. 38°9N 85°36W 311 G11
Fern Gully Jamaica 18°22N 77°5W 320 a
Fernán Núñez Spain 37°40N 4°44W 195 H6
Fernández Argentina 27°55S 63°50W 334 B3
Fernandina, I. Ecuador 0°25S 91°30W 330 a
Fernandina Beach U.S.A. 30°40N 81°27W 316 E8
Fernando de Noronha Brazil 4°0S 33°10W 152 G8
Fernando Póo = Bioko Eq. Guin. 3°30N 8°40E 263 E6
Fernandópolis Brazil 20°16S 50°14W 333 F1
Ferndale Ont., Canada 44°58N 81°17W 312 B3
Ferndale Gauteng, S. Africa 26°5S 28°0E 123 A2
Ferndale Wash., U.S.A. 48°51N 122°36W 306 B4
Fernie Canada 49°30N 115°5W 296 D5
Fernlees Australia 23°51S 148°7E 280 C4
Fernley U.S.A. 39°36N 119°15W 304 G4
Fernwood U.S.A. 43°16N 73°38W 313 C11
Feroke India 11°9N 75°46E 245 J2
Feroz Shah Kotla Cricket Stadium Delhi, India 120 b3
Ferozepore = Firozpur India 30°55N 74°40E 242 D6
Ferrandina Italy 40°29N 16°27E 201 B9
Ferrara Italy 44°50N 11°35E 199 D8
Ferrato, C. Italy 39°18N 9°38E 200 C2
Ferré, C. Martinique 14°27N 60°49W 322 j
Ferreira do Alentejo Portugal 38°4N 8°6W 195 G2
Ferreira Gomes Brazil 0°48N 51°8W 329 C7
Ferreñafe Peru 6°42S 79°50W 330 B2
Ferrerías Spain 39°59N 4°1E 206 B5
Ferret, C. France 44°38N 1°15W 174 D2
Ferrette France 47°30N 7°20E 173 E14
Ferriday U.S.A. 31°38N 91°33W 314 F9
Ferriere Italy 44°40N 9°30E 198 D6
Ferrières France 48°5N 2°48E 173 D9
Ferro, Capo Italy 41°9N 9°31E 200 A2
Ferrol Spain 43°29N 8°15W 194 B2
Ferrol, Pen. de Peru 9°10S 78°35W 330 B2
Ferron U.S.A. 39°5N 111°8W 304 G8
Ferros Brazil 19°14S 43°2W 333 E3
Ferrutx, C. de Spain 39°47N 3°21E 206 B4
Ferry Pass U.S.A. 30°31N 87°13W 317 E2
Ferryland Canada 47°2N 52°53W 299 C9
Ferrysburg U.S.A. 43°5N 86°13W 311 A10
Ferryville = Menzel-Bourguiba Tunisia 37°9N 9°49E 258 A1
Fertile U.S.A. 47°32N 96°17W 308 B5
Fertő-Hanság △ Hungary 47°25N 16°50E 182 C1
Fertőszentmiklós Hungary 47°35N 16°53E 182 C1
Fès Morocco 34°0N 5°0W 260 B4
Fès-Meknès □ Morocco 34°0N 4°30W 260 B4
Feshi Dem. Rep. of the Congo 6°8S 18°10E 265 D3
Fessenden U.S.A. 47°39N 99°38W 308 B4
Festenberg = Twardogóra Poland 51°23N 17°28E 185 G4
Festøya Norway 62°22N 6°19E 164 B3
Festus U.S.A. 38°13N 90°24W 310 F6
Feté Bowé Senegal 14°56N 13°30W 262 C2
Fetești Romania 44°22N 27°51E 183 F12
Fethiye Turkey 36°36N 29°6E 205 E11
Fethiye Körfezi Turkey 36°40N 28°50E 205 E10
Fetlar U.K. 60°36N 0°52W 167 A8
Fetsund Norway 59°56N 11°10E 164 E8
Feuilles → Canada 58°47N 70°4W 295 F17
Feurs France 45°45N 4°13E 175 C8
Fevik Norway 58°22N 8°39E 164 F5
Fevzipaşa Turkey 37°6N 36°37E 250 A7
Feyẕābād Badākhshān, Afghan. 37°7N 70°33E 240 A3
Feyẕābād Fāryāb, Afghan. 36°17N 64°52E 240 A2
Fez = Fès Morocco 34°0N 5°0W 260 B4
Fezzan Libya 27°0N 13°0E 258 C2
Fia Congo 3°25S 14°49E 264 C2
Fiambalá Argentina 27°45S 67°37W 334 B2
Fianarantsoa Madag. 21°26S 47°5E 272 C2
Fianga Cameroon 9°55N 15°9E 259 G3
Fiche Ethiopia 9°50N 38°46E 257 F4
Fichtelgebirge Germany 50°2N 11°55E 179 E7
Fichtelgebirge ⌓ Germany 50°8N 12°0E 179 E8
Fichtenau Germany 52°27N 13°42E 115 B5
Ficksburg S. Africa 28°51S 27°53E 271 C4
Fidenza Italy 44°52N 10°3E 198 D7
Fiditi Nigeria 7°45N 3°53E 263 D5
Fidjeland Norway 58°57N 6°56E 164 F3
Field → Australia 23°48S 138°0E 280 C2
Field I. Australia 12°5S 132°23E 278 B5
Field Museum of Natural History Chicago, U.S.A. 41°51N 87°37W 119 B3
Fields Corner U.S.A. 42°18N 71°3W 116 B2
Fieni Romania 45°8N 25°25E 183 E10
Fier Albania 40°43N 19°33E 202 F3
Fiera Camp Italy 45°28N 9°9E 128 B1
Fierzë Albania 42°15N 20°1E 202 D4
Fife □ U.K. 56°16N 3°1W 167 E5
Fife Ness U.K. 56°17N 2°35W 167 E6
Fifth Cataract Sudan 18°22N 33°50E 256 D3
Fig Tree St. Kitts & Nevis 17°8N 62°35W 322 d
Figari France 41°29N 9°7E 175 G13
Figeac France 44°37N 2°2E 174 D6
Figeholm Sweden 57°22N 16°33E 163 G10
Figino Italy 45°29N 9°4E 128 B1
Figline Valdarno Italy 43°37N 11°28E 199 E8
Figtree Zimbabwe 20°22S 28°20E 269 G2
Figueira = Governador Valadares Brazil 18°15S 41°57W 333 E3
Figueira Castelo Rodrigo Portugal 40°57N 6°58W 194 E4
Figueira da Foz Portugal 40°7N 8°54W 194 E2
Figueiró dos Vinhos Portugal 39°55N 8°16W 194 F2
Figueres Spain 42°18N 2°58E 196 C7
Figuig Morocco 32°5N 1°11W 261 B4
Fihaonana Madag. 18°36S 47°12E 272 B2
Fiherenana Madag. 18°29S 48°24E 272 B2
Fiherenana → Madag. 23°19S 43°37E 272 C1
Fiji ■ Pac. Oc. 17°20S 179°0E 287 A2
Fijir Iraq 33°21N 44°21E 113 A2
Fik Ethiopia 8°10N 42°19E 257 F5
Fika Nigeria 11°15N 11°13E 263 C7
Filabres, Sierra de los Spain 37°13N 2°20W 195 H8
Filabusi Zimbabwe 20°34S 29°20E 271 B4
Filadelfia Bolivia 11°20S 68°46W 330 C4
Filadélfia Brazil 7°21S 47°30W 332 C2
Filadelfia Athina, Greece 38°2N 23°43E 112 A2
Filadélfia Italy 38°47N 16°17E 201 D9
Filadelfia Paraguay 22°21S 60°2W 334 A3
Fil'akovo Slovakia 48°17N 19°50E 181 C12
Filchner Ice Shelf Antarctica 79°0S 40°0W 151 D1
Filefjell Norway 61°8N 8°10E 164 C5
Filey U.K. 54°12N 0°18W 168 C7
Filey B. U.K. 54°12N 0°15W 168 C7
Filfla Malta 35°47N 14°24E 206 F7
Fili-Mazilovo Russia 55°44N 37°29E 129 B1
Filiași Romania 44°32N 23°31E 183 F8
Filiates Greece 39°38N 20°16E 206 B10
Filiatra Greece 37°9N 21°35E 204 D3
Filicudi Italy 38°35N 14°33E 201 D7
Filim Oman 20°37N 58°12E 249 B7
Filingué Niger 14°21N 3°22E 263 C5
Filiourí = Lissos → Greece 41°15N 25°40E 203 E9
Filipiada Greece 39°12N 20°53E 204 B2
Filipstad Sweden 59°43N 14°9E 162 E8
Filisur Switz. 46°41N 9°40E 179 J5
Filitosa France 41°45N 8°52E 175 G12
Fillmore Calif., U.S.A. 34°24N 118°55W 307 L8
Fillmore Utah, U.S.A. 38°58N 112°20W 304 G7
Filothei Greece 38°2N 23°46E 112 A2
Filotio Greece 37°3N 25°30E 205 D7
Filottrano Italy 43°26N 13°21E 199 E10
Filtu Ethiopia 5°8N 40°35E 257 F5
Filyos Cayı → Turkey 41°35N 32°10E 212 B5
Fimbul Ice Shelf S. Ocean 69°30S 1°0W 151 C2
Fimi → Dem. Rep. of the Congo 3°1S 16°58E 264 C3
Fina ⌓ Mali 13°15N 8°46W 262 C3
Finale Emília Italy 44°50N 11°18E 199 D8
Finale Lígure Italy 44°10N 8°20E 198 D5
Finalmarina = Finale Lígure Italy 44°10N 8°20E 198 D5
Fiñana Spain 37°10N 2°50W 195 H8
Financial District San Francisco, U.S.A. 136 b3
Finch Canada 45°11N 75°7W 313 A9
Finch Hatton Australia 20°25S 148°39E 280 b
Finchaa, L. Ethiopia 9°35N 37°20E 266 C4
Finchley U.K. 51°36N 0°11W 125 A2
Findhorn → U.K. 57°38N 3°38W 167 D5
Fındıklı Turkey 41°16N 41°9E 213 B9
Findlay U.S.A. 41°2N 83°39W 311 C13
Fine U.S.A. 44°14N 75°8W 313 B9
Fine Art, Museum of = Kunsthistorischesmuseum Vienna, Austria 142 b1
Fine Arts, Museum of Boston, U.S.A. 42°20N 71°5W 116 A2
Fingal □ Ireland 53°29N 6°14W 166 C5
Finger L. Canada 53°33N 93°30W 298 B1
Finger Lakes U.S.A. 42°40N 76°30W 313 D8
Fíngoè Mozam. 15°55S 31°50E 269 F3
Finike Turkey 36°21N 30°10E 205 E12
Finike Körfezi Turkey 36°17N 30°16E 205 E12
Finiq Albania 39°54N 20°3E 202 G4
Finistère □ France 48°20N 4°0W 172 D3
Finisterre = Fisterra Spain 42°54N 9°16W 194 C1
Finisterre, C. = Fisterra, C. Spain 42°50N 9°19W 194 C1
Finisterre Ra. Papua N. G. 6°0S 146°30E 286 D4
Finke Australia 25°34S 134°35E 280 D1
Finke Gorge △ Australia 24°8S 132°49E 278 D5
Finland ■ Europe 63°0N 27°0E 160 E22
Finland, G. of Europe 60°0N 26°0E 188 C3
Finlay → Canada 57°0N 125°10W 296 B3
Finley N.S.W., Australia 35°38S 145°35E 283 C6
Finley N. Dak., U.S.A. 47°31N 97°50W 308 B5
Finn → Ireland 54°51N 7°28W 166 B4
Finnerödja Sweden 58°57N 14°24E 163 F8
Finnigan, Mt. Australia 15°49S 145°17E 280 B4
Finniss, C. Australia 33°8S 134°51E 281 E1
Finnmark Norway 69°37N 23°57E 160 B20
Finnsnes Norway 69°14N 18°0E 160 B18
Finsbury U.K. 51°31N 0°6W 125 A3
Finsbury Park U.K. 51°34N 0°6W 125 A3
Finschhafen Papua N. G. 6°33S 147°50E 286 D4
Finse Norway 60°36N 7°30E 164 D4
Finspång Sweden 58°43N 15°47E 163 F9
Finsteraarhorn Switz. 46°31N 8°10E 179 J4
Finsterwalde Germany 51°37N 13°42E 178 D9
Fiora → Italy 42°20N 11°34E 199 F8
Fiordland △ N.Z. 45°46S 167°0E 285 F2
Fiorenzuola d'Arda Italy 44°56N 9°55E 198 D6
Fiorito Argentina 34°42S 58°26W 117 C2
Fīq Syria 32°46N 35°41E 250 F6
Firat = Furāt, Nahr al → Asia 31°0N 47°25E 246 D5
Fire Island ⌓ U.S.A. 40°38N 73°8W 313 F11
Firebag → Canada 57°45N 111°21W 297 B6
Firebaugh U.S.A. 36°52N 120°27W 306 J6
Firedrake L. Canada 61°25N 104°30W 297 A8
Firenze Italy 43°46N 11°15E 199 E8
Firenze Amerigo Vespucci ✈ (FLR) Italy 43°49N 11°13E 199 E8
Firenze Pisa ✈ (PSA) Italy 43°40N 10°22E 198 E7
Firenzuola Italy 44°7N 11°23E 199 D8
Firk, Sha'ib → Iraq 30°59N 44°34E 246 D5
Firkachi Niger 15°40N 14°20E 259 E2
Firmi France 44°33N 2°19E 174 D6
Firminy France 45°23N 4°18E 175 C8
Firozabad India 27°10N 78°25E 243 F8
Firozpur India 30°55N 74°40E 242 D6
Firozpur-Jhirka India 27°48N 76°57E 242 F7
Fīrūzābād Iran 28°52N 52°35E 247 D7
Fīrūzkūh Iran 35°50N 52°50E 247 C7
Firvale Canada 52°27N 126°13W 296 C3
Fischerhäuser Germany 48°14N 11°41E 131 A3
Fish → Namibia 28°7S 17°10E 270 C2
Fish → Northern Cape, S. Africa 31°30S 20°16E 270 D3
Fish River Canyon Namibia 27°40S 17°35E 270 C2
Fisheating Cr. → U.S.A. 26°57N 81°7W 317 J8
Fisher B. Canada 51°35N 97°13W 297 C9
Fisher I. U.S.A. 25°45N 80°8W 129 D3
Fishermans Bend Australia 37°49S 144°55E 128 A1
Fisherman's Village U.S.A. 33°58N 118°27W 126 C2
Fisherman's Wharf San Francisco, U.S.A. 136 a1
Fishers U.S.A. 39°57N 86°0W 311 E11
Fishers I. U.S.A. 41°15N 72°0W 313 E13
Fisherville Canada 43°46N 79°28W 141 A2
Fishguard U.K. 52°0N 4°58W 169 E3
Fishing L. Canada 52°10N 95°24W 297 C9
Fishkill U.S.A. 41°32N 73°54W 313 E11
Fiskardo Greece 38°28N 20°35E 207 C2
Fiskenæsset = Qeqertarsuatsiaat Greenland 63°5N 50°45W 154 E5
Fisksätra Sweden 59°17N 18°13E 139 B3
Fismes France 49°20N 3°40E 173 C10
Fisterra Spain 42°54N 9°16W 194 C1
Fisterra, C. Spain 42°50N 9°19W 194 C1
Fitchburg Mass., U.S.A. 42°35N 71°48W 313 D13
Fitchburg Wis., U.S.A. 42°58N 89°28W 310 B7
Fitjar Iceland 64°28N 21°18W 155 C5
Fitjar Hordaland, Norway 59°55N 5°17E 164 E2
Fitri, L. Chad 12°50N 17°28E 259 F3
Fitz Roy Argentina 47°0S 67°0W 336 C3
Fitz Roy, Cerro Argentina 49°17S 73°5W 336 C2
Fitzgerald Alta., Canada 59°51N 111°36W 296 B6
Fitzgerald Ga., U.S.A. 31°43N 83°15W 316 D6
Fitzgerald River △ Australia 33°53S 119°55E 279 F3
Fitzmaurice → Australia 14°45S 130°5E 278 B5
Fitzroy → Queens., Australia 23°32S 150°52E 280 C5
Fitzroy → W. Austral., Australia 17°31S 123°35E 278 C3
Fitzroy Crossing Australia 18°9S 125°38E 278 C4
Fitzroy Gardens Australia 37°48S 144°58E 128 A1
Fitzwilliam I. Canada 45°30N 81°45W 312 A3
Fiuggi Italy 41°48N 13°13E 199 G10
Fiume = Rijeka Croatia 45°20N 14°21E 199 C11
Fiumicino Italy 41°46N 12°14E 200 A5
Fiumicino, Roma ✈ (FCO) Italy 41°48N 12°15E 199 G9
Five Cowrie Cr. → Nigeria 6°26N 3°24E 124 B2
Five Dock Australia 33°52S 151°8E 139 B1
Five Island Harbour Antigua & B. 17°6N 61°54W 322 b
Five Points U.S.A. 36°26N 120°6W 306 J6
Fivizzano Italy 44°14N 10°8E 198 D7
Fizi Dem. Rep. of the Congo 4°17S 28°55E 268 C2
Fjæra Norway 59°52N 6°22E 164 E3
Fjærland Norway 61°24N 6°43E 164 C3
Fjærlandsfjorden Norway 61°17N 6°40E 164 C3
Fjällbacka Sweden 58°36N 11°17E 163 F5
Fjällnäs Sweden 62°36N 12°11E 162 B6
Fjärdhundra Sweden 59°47N 16°56E 162 E10
Fjellerup Denmark 56°29N 10°34E 163 H4
Fjellstrand Norway 59°47N 10°36E 133 B2
Fjerritslev Denmark 57°5N 9°15E 163 G3
Fjugesta Sweden 59°11N 14°52E 162 E8
Fkih ben Salah Morocco 32°32N 6°45W 260 B3
Flå Norway 60°25N 9°28E 164 D6
Flacq Plain Mauritius 20°13S 57°43E 272 e
Flagler Beach U.S.A. 29°29N 81°8W 317 F8
Flagstaff U.S.A. 35°12N 111°39W 305 J8
Flagstaff B. St. Helena 15°54S 5°41W 153 h
Flagstaff L. U.S.A. 45°12N 70°18W 313 A14
Flaherty I. Canada 56°15N 79°15W 298 A4
Flåm Norway 60°50N 7°7E 164 D4
Flamands St. Barts 17°55N 62°51W 322 a
Flambeau → U.S.A. 45°18N 91°14W 308 C8
Flamborough Hd. U.K. 54°7N 0°5W 168 C7
Flamengo Brazil 22°56S 43°11W 135 B1
Flamengos Azores 38°33N 28°39W 153 d1
Fläming Germany 52°6N 12°23E 178 C8
Flaming Gorge ⌓ U.S.A. 41°10N 109°25W 304 F9
Flaming Gorge Res. U.S.A. 41°10N 109°25W 304 F9
Flamingo Fla., U.S.A. 28°22N 81°22W 133 B2
Flamingo Fla., U.S.A. 25°8N 80°57W 317 K9
Flamingo, Teluk Indonesia 5°30S 138°0E 231 F9
Flaminio Italy 41°55N 12°28E 136 B1
Flanagan U.S.A. 40°53N 88°52W 311 D8
Flanagin Town Trin. & Tob. 10°25N 61°19W 323 t
Flanders = Flandre Europe 50°50N 2°30E 173 B9
Flandre Europe 50°50N 2°30E 173 B9
Flandre-Occidentale = West-Vlaanderen □ Belgium 51°0N 3°0E 170 D2
Flandre-Orientale = Oost-Vlaanderen □ Belgium 51°5N 3°50E 170 C3
Flandreau U.S.A. 44°3N 96°36W 308 C5
Flanigan U.S.A. 40°10N 119°53W 306 E7
Flannan Is. U.K. 58°17N 7°36W 167 C1
Flåsjön Sweden 64°5N 15°40E 160 D16
Flaskebekk Norway 59°51N 10°39E 133 A2
Flat U.S.A. 62°28N 158°1W 303 E8
Flat → N.W.T., Canada 61°33N 125°18W 296 A3
Flat → Mich., U.S.A. 42°56N 85°20W 311 B11
Flat I. S. China Sea 10°49N 115°49E 230 B5
Flat Pt. N.Z. 41°14S 175°57E 284 H4
Flat Rock U.S.A. 42°6N 83°17W 311 B13
Flatbush U.S.A. 40°39N 73°56W 132 C2
Flateby Norway 59°50N 11°10E 164 E8
Flaten Sweden 59°15N 18°9E 139 B2
Flatey Iceland 66°10N 17°52W 155 A9
Flateyri Iceland 66°3N 23°31W 155 A3
Flathead L. U.S.A. 47°51N 114°8W 304 C6
Flatiron Building New York, U.S.A. 132 d2
Flatlands U.S.A. 40°37N 73°56W 132 C2
Flatow = Złotów Poland 53°22N 17°2E 184 E4
Flatrock → U.S.A. 39°12N 85°56W 311 F10
Flattery, C. Queens., Australia 14°58S 145°21E 280 A4
Flattery, C. Wash., U.S.A. 48°23N 124°29W 306 B2
Flatts Village Bermuda 32°18N 64°43W 153 a
Flatwoods U.S.A. 38°31N 82°43W 309 F12
Flecha Pt. Phil. 7°22N 123°24E 233 H4
Flechas Pt. Phil. 10°22N 119°34E 233 F2
Fleetwood Lancs., U.K. 53°55N 3°1W 168 D4
Fleetwood Pa., U.S.A. 40°27N 75°49W 313 F9
Flekke Norway 61°19N 5°20E 164 C2
Flekkefjord Norway 58°18N 6°39E 164 F3
Flemingsburg U.S.A. 38°25N 83°45W 311 F13
Flemington U.S.A. 41°7N 77°28W 312 E7
Flemington Racecourse Australia 37°47S 144°54E 128 A1
Flemish Cap Atl. Oc. 47°0N 45°0W 152 B7
Flen Sweden 59°4N 16°35E 162 E10
Flensburg Germany 54°47N 9°27E 178 A5
Flers France 48°47N 0°33W 172 D6
Flesberg Norway 59°51N 9°27E 164 E6
Flesherton Canada 44°16N 80°33W 312 B4
Flesko, Tanjung Indonesia 0°29N 124°30E 231 D6
Fletcher = Aurora U.S.A. 39°43N 104°49W 304 G11
Fleurance France 43°52N 0°40E 174 E4
Fleurie, Côte France 49°25N 0°40W 172 C6
Fleurier Switz. 46°54N 6°35E 179 J2
Fleurieu Pen. Australia 35°40S 138°5E 282 C3
Flevoland □ Neths. 52°30N 5°30E 170 B5
Flic en Flac Mauritius 20°17S 57°22E 272 e
Flin Flon Canada 54°46N 101°53W 297 C8
Flinders → Australia 17°36S 140°36E 280 B3
Flinders B. Australia 34°19S 115°19E 279 F2
Flinders Chase △ Australia 35°50S 136°42E 282 C2
Flinders Group Australia 14°11S 144°15E 280 A3
Flinders I. S. Austral., Australia 33°44S 134°41E 281 E1
Flinders I. Tas., Australia 40°0S 148°0E 281 G4
Flinders Ranges Australia 31°30S 138°30E 282 A3
Flinders Ranges △ Australia 31°30S 138°40E 282 A3
Flinders Reefs Australia 17°37S 148°31E 280 B4
Flint Flints., U.K. 53°15N 3°8W 168 D4
Flint Mich., U.S.A. 43°1N 83°41W 311 A13
Flint → U.S.A. 30°57N 84°34W 316 E5
Flint I. Kiribati 11°26S 151°48W 289 f
Flint Pk. U.S.A. 34°9N 118°11W 126 B3
Flintshire □ U.K. 53°17N 3°17W 168 D4
Flipper Pt. Wake I. 19°18N 166°37E 302 b
Flisa Norway 60°37N 12°0E 164 D9
Flisa → Norway 60°37N 12°0E 164 D9
Fliseryd Sweden 57°6N 16°15E 163 G10
Flix Spain 41°14N 0°32E 196 D5
Flixecourt France 50°1N 2°5E 173 B9
Floby Sweden 58°8N 13°20E 163 F7
Floda Sweden 57°49N 12°22E 163 G6
Flodden U.K. 55°37N 2°8W 168 B5
Flogny-la-Chapelle France 47°57N 3°57E 173 E10
Floodplains △ Sri Lanka 8°10N 81°10E 245 K5
Floodwood U.S.A. 46°56N 92°55W 308 B7
Flora Apayao, Phil. 18°14N 121°5E 232 B3
Flora Ill., U.S.A. 38°40N 88°29W 311 F8
Flora Ind., U.S.A. 40°33N 86°31W 311 D10
Florac France 44°20N 3°37E 174 D7
Florahome U.S.A. 29°44N 81°54W 316 F8
Floral City U.S.A. 28°45N 82°17W 317 G7
Florala U.S.A. 31°0N 86°20W 315 F11
Florânia Brazil 6°8S 36°49W 332 C4
Floreal Mauritius 20°19S 57°30E 272 e
Floreana, I. = Santa María, I. Ecuador 1°17S 90°26W 330 a
Florence = Firenze Italy 43°46N 11°15E 199 E8
Florence Ala., U.S.A. 34°48N 87°41W 315 D11
Florence Ariz., U.S.A. 33°2N 111°23W 305 K8
Florence Calif., U.S.A. 33°57N 118°13W 126 C3
Florence Colo., U.S.A. 38°23N 105°8W 304 G11
Florence Oreg., U.S.A. 43°58N 124°7W 304 D1
Florence S.C., U.S.A. 34°12N 79°46W 315 D15
Florence, L. Australia 28°53S 138°9E 281 D2
Florence Bay = Chtimba Malawi 10°35S 34°13E 269 E3
Florence Bloom Bird Sanctuary ⌓ S. Africa 26°7S 28°0E 123 A2
Florencia Colombia 1°36N 75°36W 328 C2
Florennes Belgium 50°15N 4°35E 170 D4
Florensac France 43°23N 3°28E 174 E7
Florentia S. Africa 26°16S 28°8E 123 B2
Florenville Belgium 49°40N 5°19E 170 E5
Flores = Florânia Brazil 6°8S 36°49W 332 C4
Flores = Timon Brazil 5°8S 42°52W 332 C3
Flores B. Aires, Argentina 34°38S 58°27W 117 B2
Flores Azores 39°26N 31°13W 153 d2
Flores Brazil 7°51S 37°59W 332 C4
Flores Guatemala 16°59N 89°50W 320 C2
Flores Indonesia 8°35S 121°0E 231 F6
Flores, Mercado de Mexico 19°19N 99°5W 128 C2
Flores I. Canada 49°20N 126°10W 296 D3
Flores Sea Indonesia 6°30S 120°0E 231 F6
Floresta B. Aires, Argentina 34°37S 58°27W 117 B2
Floresta Brazil 8°40S 37°26W 332 C4
Florești Moldova 47°53N 28°17E 183 C13
Floresville U.S.A. 29°8N 98°10W 314 G5
Floriano Brazil 6°50S 43°0W 332 C3
Florianópolis Brazil 27°30S 48°30W 335 B6
Florida B. Aires, Argentina 34°31S 58°28W 117 B2
Florida Cuba 21°32N 78°14W 320 B4
Florida Puerto Rico 18°22N 66°34W 321 b
Florida Gauteng, S. Africa 26°10S 27°55E 123 B1
Florida Uruguay 34°7S 56°10W 335 C4
Florida □ U.S.A. 28°0N 82°0W 317 H8
Florida, Straits of U.S.A. 25°0N 80°0W 320 B4
Florida B. U.S.A. 25°0N 80°45W 320 B3
Florida City U.S.A. 25°27N 80°29W 317 K9
Florida Is. Solomon Is. 9°55S 160°15E 287 M11
Florida Keys U.S.A. 24°40N 81°0W 317 L8
Floridablanca Phil. 14°59N 120°31E 232 D3
Florídia Italy 37°5N 15°9E 201 E8
Floridsdorf Austria 48°15N 16°26E 142 A2
Florin U.S.A. 38°30N 121°24W 306 G5
Florina Greece 40°48N 21°26E 202 F5
Florissant U.S.A. 38°47N 90°19W 310 F6
Florø Norway 61°35N 5°1E 164 C2
Flotte, C. de N. Cal. 21°10S 167°25E 288 d
Flower Station Canada 45°10N 76°41W 313 A8
Flowerpot I. Canada 45°18N 81°38W 312 A3
Floydada U.S.A. 33°59N 101°20W 314 E4
Fludir Iceland 64°7N 20°6W 155 C6
Flugumyri Iceland 65°34N 19°19W 155 B7
Fluk Indonesia 1°42S 127°44E 231 E7
Flúmen → Spain 41°43N 0°9W 196 D4
Flumendosa → Italy 39°26N 9°37E 200 C2
Fluminimaggiore Italy 39°26N 8°30E 200 C1
Flushing = Vlissingen Neths. 51°26N 3°34E 170 C3
Flushing Mich., U.S.A. 43°4N 83°51W 311 A13
Flushing N.Y., U.S.A. 40°45N 73°49W 132 B3
Flushing Meadows Corona Park U.S.A. 40°44N 73°50W 132 B2
Fluvià → Spain 42°12N 3°7E 196 C8
Fly → Papua N. G. 8°25S 143°0E 286 E2
Flying Fish, C. Antarctica 72°6S 102°29W 151 D15
Flysta Sweden 59°22N 17°54E 139 A1
Fo Tan Hong Kong, China 22°23N 114°11E 122 A3
Foa Tonga 19°45S 174°18W 287 P13
Foam Lake Canada 51°40N 103°32W 297 C8
Foča Bos.-H. 43°31N 18°47E 202 C2
Foça Turkey 38°39N 26°46E 205 C8
Fochabers U.K. 57°37N 3°6W 167 D5
Focșani Romania 45°41N 27°15E 183 E12
Fodé C.A.R. 5°29N 23°18E 264 A4
Fodécontéa Guinea 10°50N 14°22W 262 C2
Fogang China 23°52N 113°30E 229 F9
Foggaret el Arab Algeria 27°13N 2°49E 261 C5
Foggaret ez Zoua Algeria 27°20N 2°53E 261 C5
Fóggia Italy 41°27N 15°34E 201 A8
Foggy Bottom U.S.A. 38°54N 77°3W 143 B2
Foglia → Italy 43°55N 12°54E 199 E9
Fogo Cabo Verde 15°5N 24°20W 153 j
Fogo Nfld. & L., Canada 49°43N 54°17W 299 C9
Fogo I. Canada 49°40N 54°5W 299 C9
Fohnsdorf Austria 47°12N 14°40E 180 D7
Föhr Germany 54°43N 8°30E 178 A4
Föhrenhain Austria 48°19N 16°26E 142 A2
Fóia Portugal 37°19N 8°37W 195 H2
Foix France 42°58N 1°38E 174 E5
Fojnica Bos.-H. 43°59N 17°51E 182 G2
Fokida Greece 38°30N 22°15E 204 C4
Fokino Russia 53°30N 34°22E 188 F8
Fokku Nigeria 11°36N 4°32E 263 C5
Fokstugu Norway 62°7N 9°17E 164 B6
Folda Nord-Trøndelag, Norway 64°32N 10°30E 160 D14
Folda Nordland, Norway 67°38N 14°50E 160 C16
Főldeák Hungary 46°19N 20°30E 182 D5
Folegandros Greece 36°40N 24°55E 204 E6
Foley Botswana 21°34S 27°21E 270 B4
Foley Ala., U.S.A. 30°24N 87°41W 315 F11
Foley Fla., U.S.A. 30°4N 83°32W 316 E6
Foleyet Canada 48°15N 82°25W 298 C3
Folgefonna Norway 60°3N 6°23E 164 D3
Folgefonna △ Norway 60°5N 6°15E 164 D3
Foligno Italy 42°57N 12°42E 199 F9
Folkestad Norway 62°7N 6°1E 164 B3
Folkestone U.K. 51°5N 1°12E 169 F9
Folkestone Marine Park △ Barbados 13°11N 59°38W 323 r
Folkston U.S.A. 30°50N 82°0W 316 E7
Folla → Norway 62°7N 10°37E 164 B7
Follansbee U.S.A. 40°19N 80°35W 312 F4
Folldal Norway 62°8N 10°0E 164 B6
Folle Anse, Pte. de Guadeloupe 15°56N 61°19W 322 e
Follebu Norway 61°13N 10°16E 164 C7
Follónica Italy 42°55N 10°45E 198 F7
Follónica, G. di Italy 42°54N 10°43E 198 F7
Folsom U.S.A. 38°40N 121°9W 306 G5
Folsom L. U.S.A. 38°42N 121°9W 306 G5
Foltești Romania 45°45N 28°3E 183 E13
Fomboni Comoros Is. 12°18S 43°46E 272 a
Fomm ir-Rih Bay Malta 35°54N 14°20E 206 F7
Fond-du-Lac Sask., Canada 59°19N 107°12W 297 B7
Fond du Lac Wis., U.S.A. 43°47N 88°27W 308 D9
Fond-du-Lac → Canada 59°17N 106°0W 297 B7
Fond Rousseau Martinique 14°38N 61°6W 322 j
Fond St. Jacques St. Lucia 13°50N 61°1W 323 m
Fonda Iowa, U.S.A. 42°35N 94°51W 310 B2
Fonda N.Y., U.S.A. 42°57N 74°22W 313 D10
Fondamenta Nuove Venice, Italy 142 a3
Fondi Italy 41°21N 13°25E 200 A6
Fonds-St-Denis Martinique 14°44N 61°8W 322 j
Fonfría Spain 41°37N 6°9W 194 D4
Fongafale Tuvalu 8°31S 179°13E 277 B14
Fongen Norway 63°11N 11°38E 164 A8
Fongshan = Fengshan Taiwan 22°38N 120°21E 225 D2
Fongyuan = Fengyüan Taiwan 24°15N 120°35E 225 B2
Fonni Italy 40°7N 9°15E 200 B2
Fonsagrada = A Fonsagrada Spain 43°8N 7°4W 194 B3
Fonseca, G. de Cent. Amer. 13°10N 87°40W 320 D2
Font-Romeu-Odeillo-Via France 42°31N 2°3E 174 F5
Fontaine-Française France 47°32N 5°21E 173 E12
Fontainebleau Seine-et-Marne, France 48°24N 2°40E 173 D9
Fontainebleau Gauteng, S. Africa 26°6S 27°57E 123 A1
Fontana U.S.A. 34°6N 117°26W 307 L9
Fontana, L. Argentina 44°55S 71°30W 336 B2
Fontas → Canada 58°14N 121°48W 296 B4
Fonte Boa Brazil 2°33S 66°0W 328 D4
Fontem Cameroon 5°32N 9°52E 263 D6
Fontenay-aux-Roses France 48°47N 2°17E 134 B2
Fontenay-le-Comte France 46°28N 0°48W 174 B3
Fontenay-le-Fleury France 48°48N 2°2E 134 B1
Fontenay-sous-Bois France 48°51N 2°28E 134 A3
Fontenelle Res. U.S.A. 42°1N 110°3W 304 E8
Fontur Iceland 66°23N 14°32W 155 A12
Fonuafo'ou Tonga 20°19S 175°25W 287 Q13
Fonuakula Cook Is. 19°2S 169°55W 289 g
Fonualei Tonga 18°1S 174°19W 287 P13
Fonyód Hungary 46°44N 17°33E 182 D2
Foochow = Fuzhou China 26°5N 119°16E 229 D12
Foots Cray U.K. 51°24N 0°7E 125 B4
Footscray Australia 37°48S 144°56E 128 A1
Foping China 33°41N 108°0E 226 H5
Foraker, Mt. U.S.A. 62°58N 151°24W 303 E10
Forari Vanuatu 17°40S 168°31E 287 G6
Forbach France 49°10N 6°52E 173 C13
Forbes Australia 33°22S 148°5E 283 B8
Forbesganj India 26°17N 87°18E 243 F12
Forbidden City = Imperial Palace Museum Beijing, China 114 b3
Forcados Nigeria 5°26N 5°26E 263 D6
Forcados → Nigeria 5°25N 5°19E 263 D6
Forcalquier France 43°58N 5°47E 175 E9
Forchheim Germany 49°43N 11°2E 179 F7
Ford City Calif., U.S.A. 35°9N 119°27W 307 K7
Ford City Pa., U.S.A. 40°46N 79°32W 312 F5
Ford d'Or B. St. Lucia 13°56N 60°54W 323 m
Ford I. U.S.A. 21°22N 157°58W 302 K14
Forda → Norway 62°57N 10°40E 164 B7
Førde Rogaland, Norway 59°26N 5°23E 164 E2
Førde Sogn og Fjordane, Norway 61°27N 5°53E 164 C2
Førdefjorden Norway 61°29N 5°18E 164 C2
Fords Bridge Australia 29°41S 145°29E 281 D4
Ford's Theater Washington, D.C., U.S.A. 143 b2
Fordyce U.S.A. 33°49N 92°25W 314 E8
Forécariah Guinea 9°28N 13°10W 262 D2
Forel, Mt. Greenland 66°52N 36°55W 154 D7
Foremost Canada 49°26N 111°34W 296 D6
Foreshore Cape Town, S. Africa 118 a3
Forest Belgium 50°49N 4°20E 116 B1
Forest Ont., Canada 43°6N 82°0W 312 C3
Forest Miss., U.S.A. 32°22N 89°29W 315 E10
Forest Acres U.S.A. 34°1N 80°58W 316 A9
Forest City Iowa, U.S.A. 43°16N 93°39W 308 D7
Forest City N.C., U.S.A. 35°20N 81°52W 315 D14
Forest City Pa., U.S.A. 41°39N 75°28W 313 E9
Forest Gate U.K. 51°32N 0°1E 125 A4
Forest Grove U.S.A. 45°31N 123°7W 306 E3
Forest Heights U.S.A. 38°48N 77°0W 143 C2
Forest Hill Ont., Canada 43°41N 79°25W 141 A2
Forest Hill London, U.K. 51°26N 0°2W 125 B3
Forest Hill Tex., U.S.A. 32°40N 97°16W 120 B2
Forest Hills U.S.A. 40°42N 73°51W 132 B2
Forest Park Ga., U.S.A. 33°37N 84°22W 316 B5
Forest Park Ill., U.S.A. 41°51N 87°47W 119 B2
Forest Park N.Y., U.S.A. 40°42N 73°51W 132 B2
Forest Park Ohio, U.S.A. 39°17N 84°30W 311 E12
Forest View U.S.A. 41°48N 87°47W 119 C2
Forestburg Canada 52°35N 112°1W 296 C6
Foreste Casentinesi-Monte Falterona-Campigna △ Italy 43°50N 11°48E 199 E8
Foresthill U.S.A. 39°1N 120°49W 306 F6
Forestier Pen. Australia 43°0S 148°0E 281 G4
Forestville Qué., Canada 48°48N 69°2W 299 C6
Forestville Calif., U.S.A. 38°28N 122°54W 306 G4
Forestville N.Y., U.S.A. 42°28N 79°10W 312 D5
Forêt d'Orient ⌓ France 48°16N 4°25E 173 D11
Forêt du Day △ Djibouti 11°56N 42°40E 267 B5
Forez, Mts. du France 45°40N 3°50E 174 C7
Forfar U.K. 56°39N 2°53W 167 E6
Forillon △ Canada 48°46N 64°12W 299 C7
Forks U.S.A. 47°57N 124°23W 306 C2
Forks, The = Merritt Canada 50°10N 120°45W 296 C4
Forksville U.S.A. 41°29N 76°35W 313 E8
Forlì Italy 44°13N 12°3E 199 D9
Forlí-Cesena □ Italy 44°10N 12°20E 199 D9
Forman U.S.A. 46°7N 97°38W 308 B5
Formazza Italy 46°22N 8°26E 198 B5
Formby Pt. U.K. 53°33N 3°6W 168 D4
Formentera Spain 38°43N 1°27E 206 D1
Formentor, C. de Spain 39°58N 3°13E 206 B4
Formentor, Pen. de Spain 39°56N 3°11E 206 B4
Former Yugoslav Republic of Macedonia = North Macedonia ■ Europe 41°53N 21°40E 202 E5
Fórmia Italy 41°15N 13°37E 200 A6
Formiga Brazil 20°27S 45°25W 333 F2
Formígine Italy 44°37N 10°51E 198 D7
Formosa = Taiwan ■ Asia 23°30N 121°0E 225 C3
Formosa Argentina 26°15S 58°10W 334 B4
Formosa Brazil 15°32S 47°20W 333 E2
Formosa □ Argentina 25°0S 60°0W 334 B4
Formosa, Serra Brazil 12°0S 55°0W 331 C7
Formosa B. = Ungwana B. Kenya 2°45S 40°20E 268 C5
Formosa do Rio Prêto Brazil 11°2S 45°3W 332 D2
Formosa Strait = Taiwan Strait Asia 24°40N 120°0E 229 E12
Formoso → Brazil 10°34S 49°56W 333 D2
Fornebu Norway 59°53N 10°36E 133 A2
Fornells Spain 40°3N 4°7E 206 A5
Fornos de Algodres Portugal 40°38N 7°32W 194 E3
Fornovo di Taro Italy 44°42N 10°6E 198 D7
Foro Romano Rome, Italy 136 c3
Forollhogna △ Norway 62°39N 10°41E 164 B7
Føroyar ☒ Atl. Oc. 62°0N 7°0W 160 F9
Forres U.K. 57°37N 3°37W 167 D5
Forrest Vic., Australia 38°33S 143°47E 282 E5
Forrest W. Austral., Australia 30°51S 128°6E 279 F4
Forrest, Mt. Australia 24°48S 127°45E 279 D4
Forrest City U.S.A. 35°1N 90°47W 315 D9
Forreston U.S.A. 42°8N 89°35W 310 B7
Fors Sweden 60°14N 16°20E 162 D10
Forsand Norway 58°54N 6°5E 164 F3
Forsayth Australia 18°33S 143°34E 280 B3
Forserum Sweden 57°42N 14°30E 163 G8
Forshaga Sweden 59°33N 13°29E 162 E7
Förslöv Sweden 56°21N 12°48E 163 H6
Forsmo Sweden 63°16N 17°11E 162 A11
Forssa Finland 60°49N 23°38E 188 B2
Forst Germany 51°45N 14°37E 178 D10
Forstenried Germany 48°5N 11°29E 131 B1
Forstenrieder Park Germany 48°3N 11°27E 131 B1
Forster Australia 32°12S 152°31E 283 B10
Forsvik Sweden 58°35N 14°26E 163 F8
Forsyth Ga., U.S.A. 33°2N 83°56W 316 B6
Forsyth Mont., U.S.A. 46°16N 106°41W 304 C10
Forsyth I. N.Z. 40°58S 174°5E 285 A9
Fort Mumbai, India 130 c2
Fort Abbas Pakistan 29°12N 72°52E 242 E5
Fort Albany Canada 52°15N 81°35W 298 B3
Fort-Aleksandrovsky = Fort Shevchenko Kazakhstan 44°35N 50°23E 191 H10
Fort Archambault = Sarh Chad 9°5N 18°23E 259 G3
Fort Assiniboine Canada 54°20N 114°45W 296 C6
Fort Atkinson U.S.A. 42°56N 88°50W 311 B8
Fort Augustus U.K. 57°9N 4°42W 167 D4
Fort Bay Saba 17°37N 63°15W 322 a
Fort Bayard = Zhanjiang China 21°15N 110°20E 229 G8
Fort Beaufort S. Africa 32°46S 26°40E 270 D4
Fort Benton U.S.A. 47°49N 110°40W 304 C8
Fort Bragg U.S.A. 39°26N 123°48W 304 G2
Fort Bridger U.S.A. 41°19N 110°23W 304 F8
Fort Canning Park Singapore 138 b2
Fort Caroline ⌓ U.S.A. 30°23N 81°30W 316 E8
Fort Charles Jamaica 17°55N 76°50W 320 a
Fort Charlotte St. Lucia 13°59N 61°0W 323 m
Fort Chipewyan Canada 58°42N 111°8W 297 B6
Fort Clatsop = Lewis and Clark ⌓ U.S.A. 46°8N 123°53W 306 D3
Fort Collins U.S.A. 40°35N 105°5W 304 F11
Fort-Coulonge Canada 45°50N 76°45W 298 C4
Fort Covington U.S.A. 44°59N 74°29W 313 B10
Fort Dauphin = Taolanaro Madag. 25°2S 47°0E 272 D2
Fort Davis Ala., U.S.A. 32°15N 85°43W 316 C4
Fort Davis Tex., U.S.A. 30°35N 103°54W 314 F3
Fort-de-France Martinique 14°36N 61°5W 322 j
Fort-de-France, B. de Martinique 14°34N 61°4W 322 j
Fort de Kock = Bukittinggi Indonesia 0°20S 100°20E 234 C2
Fort de Polignac = Illizi Algeria 26°31N 8°32E 261 C6

Fort de Possel = Possel C.A.R. 5°5N 19°10E 264 A3
Fort Defiance U.S.A. 35°45N 109°5W 305 J9
Fort Dodge U.S.A. 42°30N 94°11W 310 B2
Fort Drum U.S.A. 27°32N 80°48W 317 H9
Fort Dupont Park U.S.A. 38°52N 76°56W 143 B3
Fort Edward U.S.A. 43°16N 73°35W 313 C11
Fort Erie Canada 42°54N 78°56W 312 D6
Fort Fairfield U.S.A. 46°46N 67°50W 309 B20
Fort Flatters = Bordj Omar Driss Algeria 28°10N 6°40E 261 C6
Fort Foote Village U.S.A. 38°46N 77°1W 143 C2
Fort Foureau = Kousseri Cameroon 12°0N 14°55E 259 F2
Fort Frances Canada 48°36N 93°24W 297 D10
Fort Franklin = Déline Canada 65°11N 123°25W 294 D7
Fort Frederica ⌂ U.S.A. 31°13N 81°23W 316 D8
Fort Gaines U.S.A. 31°36N 85°3W 316 D4
Fort Garland U.S.A. 37°26N 105°26W 305 H11
Fort George = Chisasibi Canada 53°50N 79°0W 298 B4
Fort George = Prince George Canada 53°55N 122°50W 296 C4
Fort George Grenada 12°3N 61°45W 323 q
Fort Good Hope Canada 66°14N 128°40W 294 D6
Fort Gouraud = Fdérik Mauritania 22°40N 12°45W 260 D2
Fort Hancock U.S.A. 31°18N 105°51W 314 F2
Fort Hertz = Putao Myanmar 27°28N 97°30E 241 B6
Fort Hill = Chitipa Malawi 9°41S 33°19E 269 D3
Fort Hope = Eabametoong Canada 51°30N 88°0W 298 B2
Fort Irwin U.S.A. 35°16N 116°41W 307 K10
Fort Jameson = Chipata Zambia 13°38S 32°28E 269 E3
Fort Jeudy, Pt. of Grenada 11°59N 61°42W 323 q
Fort Johnston = Mangoche Malawi 14°25S 35°16E 269 E4
Fort Kent U.S.A. 47°15N 68°36W 309 B19
Fort Klamath U.S.A. 42°42N 122°0W 304 D3
Fort Lamy = Ndjamena Chad 12°10N 15°0E 259 F3
Fort Laperrine = Tamanrasset Algeria 22°50N 5°30E 261 D6
Fort Laramie U.S.A. 42°13N 104°31W 304 E11
Fort Lauderdale U.S.A. 26°7N 80°8W 129 B3
Fort Lauderdale Executive ✈ (FXE) U.S.A. 26°11N 80°10W 129 A2
Fort Lauderdale-Hollywood Int. ✈ (FLL) U.S.A. 26°4N 80°10W 129 B3
Fort Lee U.S.A. 40°50N 73°58W 132 A2
Fort Liard Canada 60°14N 123°30W 296 A4
Fort Liberté Haiti 19°42N 71°51W 321 C5
Fort Lupton U.S.A. 40°5N 104°49W 304 F11
Fort MacKay Canada 57°12N 111°41W 296 B6
Fort Macleod Canada 49°45N 113°30W 296 D6
Fort MacMahon = El Homr Algeria 29°43N 1°45E 261 C5
Fort McMurray Canada 56°44N 111°7W 296 B6
Fort McPherson Canada 67°30N 134°55W 294 D5
Fort Madison U.S.A. 40°38N 91°27W 310 D5
Fort Manning = Mchinji Malawi 13°47S 32°58E 269 E3
Fort Marlborough Indonesia 3°48S 102°15E 234 C2
Fort Mason Center San Francisco, U.S.A. 136 a1
Fort Matanzas ⌂ U.S.A. 29°43N 81°14W 316 F8
Fort Meade U.S.A. 27°45N 81°48W 317 H8
Fort Mitchell U.S.A. 32°20N 85°1W 316 C4
Fort Morgan U.S.A. 40°15N 103°48W 304 F12
Fort Myers U.S.A. 26°39N 81°52W 317 J8
Fort Myers Beach U.S.A. 26°26N 81°52W 317 J8
Fort Myers Villas U.S.A. 26°33N 81°52W 317 J8
Fort Napoléon Guadeloupe 15°52N 61°35W 322 e
Fort Nelson Canada 58°50N 122°44W 296 B4
Fort Nelson → Canada 59°32N 124°0W 296 B4
Fort Norman = Tulita Canada 64°57N 125°30W 294 E6
Fort Ogden U.S.A. 27°5N 81°57W 317 H8
Fort Payne U.S.A. 34°26N 85°43W 315 D12
Fort Peck U.S.A. 48°1N 106°27W 304 B10
Fort Peck Dam U.S.A. 48°0N 106°26W 304 C10
Fort Peck L. U.S.A. 48°0N 106°26W 304 C10
Fort Pierce U.S.A. 27°27N 80°20W 317 H9
Fort Pierre U.S.A. 44°21N 100°22W 308 C3
Fort Pierre Bordes = Ti-n-Zaouatene Algeria 19°55N 2°55E 261 E5
Fort Plain U.S.A. 42°56N 74°37W 313 D10
Fort Portal Uganda 0°40N 30°20E 268 B3
Fort Providence Canada 61°3N 117°40W 296 A5
Fort Pulaski ⌂ U.S.A. 32°2N 80°56W 316 C9
Fort Qu'Appelle Canada 50°45N 103°50W 297 C8
Fort Recovery U.S.A. 40°25N 84°47W 311 D12
Fort Resolution Canada 61°10N 113°40W 296 A6
Fort Rixon Zimbabwe 20°2S 29°17E 269 G2
Fort Rosebery = Mansa Zambia 11°13S 28°55E 269 E2
Fort Ross U.S.A. 38°32N 123°13W 306 G3
Fort-Rousset = Owando Congo 0°29S 15°55E 264 C3
Fort Rupert = Waskaganish Canada 51°30N 78°40W 298 B4
Fort St. James Canada 54°30N 124°10W 296 C4
Fort St. John Canada 56°15N 120°50W 296 B4
Fort Sandeman = Zhob Pakistan 31°20N 69°31E 242 D3
Fort Saskatchewan Canada 53°40N 113°15W 296 C6
Fort Scott U.S.A. 37°50N 94°42W 308 G6
Fort Severn Canada 56°0N 87°40W 298 A2
Fort Shevchenko Kazakhstan 44°35N 50°23E 191 H10
Fort Simpson Canada 61°45N 121°15W 296 A4
Fort Smith Alta., Canada 60°0N 111°51W 296 B6
Fort Smith Ark., U.S.A. 35°23N 94°25W 314 D7
Fort Stockton U.S.A. 30°53N 102°53W 314 F3
Fort Sumner U.S.A. 34°28N 104°15W 305 J11
Fort Thomas U.S.A. 39°4N 84°26W 311 E12
Fort Thompson U.S.A. 44°3N 99°26W 308 C4
Fort Trinquet = Bîr Mogreïn Mauritania 25°10N 11°25W 260 C2
Fort Union ⌂ U.S.A. 35°54N 105°1W 305 J11
Fort Uritskogo = Fort Shevchenko Kazakhstan 44°35N 50°23E 191 H10
Fort Valley U.S.A. 32°33N 83°53W 316 C6
Fort Vermilion Canada 58°24N 116°0W 296 B5
Fort Walton Beach U.S.A. 30°25N 86°36W 317 E3
Fort Ware Canada 57°26N 125°41W 296 B3
Fort Wayne U.S.A. 41°4N 85°9W 311 C11
Fort White U.S.A. 29°55N 82°43W 316 F7
Fort William U.K. 56°49N 5°7W 167 E3
Fort Worth U.S.A. 32°43N 97°19W 120 B2
Fort Yates U.S.A. 46°5N 100°38W 308 B3
Fort Yukon U.S.A. 66°34N 145°16W 303 C11
Fortaleza = Pedra Azul Brazil 16°2S 41°17W 333 E3
Fortaleza Bolivia 12°6S 66°49W 330 C4
Fortaleza Brazil 3°45S 38°35W 332 B4
Forteau Canada 51°28N 56°58W 299 B8
Fortescue → Australia 21°0S 116°4E 278 D2
Fortescue River Roadhouse Australia 21°17S 116°8E 278 D2
Forth → U.K. 56°9N 3°50W 167 E5
Forth, Firth of U.K. 56°5N 2°55W 121 A3
Forth Rail Bridge U.K. 56°0N 3°23W 121 A1
Forth Road Bridge U.K. 56°0N 3°24W 121 A1
Forthassa Rharbia Algeria 32°52N 1°18W 261 B4
Fortín General Pando Paraguay 19°45S 59°47W 331 D6
Fortín Madrejón Paraguay 20°45S 59°52W 331 E6
Fortín Teniente Primero Ramiro Espínola Paraguay 21°27S 61°30W 331 E5
Fortín Uno Argentina 38°50S 65°18W 336 A3
Fortore → Italy 41°55N 15°17E 199 G12
Fortrose N.Z. 46°38S 168°45E 285 G3
Fortrose Highl., U.K. 57°35N 4°9W 167 D4
Fortuna Spain 38°11N 1°7W 197 G3
Fortuna Calif., U.S.A. 40°36N 124°9W 304 F1
Fortuna N. Dak., U.S.A. 48°55N 103°47W 308 A2
Fortuna Ledge = Marshall U.S.A. 61°53N 162°5W 303 F7
Fortune Canada 47°4N 55°50W 299 C8
Fortune B. Canada 47°30N 55°22W 299 C8
Forum, The Los Angeles, U.S.A. 33°57N 118°20W 126 C2
Forūr Iran 26°17N 54°32E 247 E7
Fos-sur-Mer France 43°26N 4°56E 175 E8
Fosen Norway 63°50N 10°20E 160 E14
Foshan China 23°3N 113°9E 121 B1
Fosnavåg Norway 62°22N 5°38E 164 B2
Foso Ghana 5°43N 1°15W 263 D4
Foss Iceland 63°51N 17°52W 155 D9
Fossano Italy 44°33N 7°43E 198 D4
Fossil U.S.A. 45°0N 120°9W 304 D3
Fossil Butte ⌂ U.S.A. 41°50N 110°27W 304 F8
Fossombrone Italy 43°41N 12°48E 199 E9
Fossvellir Iceland 65°27N 14°37W 155 B12
Foster Vic., Australia 38°40S 146°15E 283 E7
Foster Qué., Canada 45°17N 72°30W 313 A12
Foster Ky., U.S.A. 38°48N 84°13W 311 F12
Foster → Canada 55°47N 105°49W 297 B7
Foster Village U.S.A. 21°21N 157°55W 302 K14
Fosters Ra. Australia 21°35S 133°48E 280 C1
Fostoria U.S.A. 41°10N 83°25W 311 C13
Fót Hungary 47°35N 19°11E 117 A3
Fotadrevo Madag. 24°3S 45°1E 272 C2
Fouesnant France 47°53N 4°1W 172 E2
Fougamou Gabon 1°16S 10°30E 264 C2
Fougères France 48°21N 1°14W 172 D5
Foul Pt. Sri Lanka 8°35N 81°18E 245 K5
Foula U.K. 60°10N 2°5W 167 A6
Foulalaba Mali 10°40N 7°20W 262 C3
Foulness I. U.K. 51°36N 0°55E 169 F8
Foulpointe Madag. 17°41S 49°31E 272 B2
Foulwind, C. N.Z. 41°45S 171°28E 285 B6
Foum Assaka Morocco 29°8N 10°24W 260 C2
Foum Zguid Morocco 30°2N 6°59W 260 B3
Foumban Cameroon 5°45N 10°50E 263 D7
Foumbot Cameroon 5°31N 10°28E 263 D7
Foumbouni Comoros Is. 11°51S 43°29E 272 a
Fountain Colo., U.S.A. 38°41N 104°42W 304 G11
Fountain Fla., U.S.A. 30°29N 85°25W 316 E4
Fountain Hills U.S.A. 33°37N 111°43W 305 K8
Fountain Springs U.S.A. 35°54N 118°51W 307 K8
Four Mountains, Is. of U.S.A. 53°0N 170°0W 303 K5
Four Roads Trin. & Tob. 10°41N 61°33W 323 t
Fourchambault France 47°2N 3°3E 173 E10
Fourchue, Île St. Barts 17°58N 62°54W 322 a
Fouriesburg S. Africa 28°38S 28°14E 271 C4
Fourmies France 50°1N 4°2E 173 B11
Fourna Greece 39°3N 21°52E 204 B3
Fournaise, Piton de la Réunion 21°14S 55°43E 272 f
Fourni Greece 37°36N 26°32E 205 D8
Fourqueux France 48°53N 2°3E 134 A1
Fours France 46°50N 3°42E 173 F10
Fous, Pte. des Dominica 15°12N 61°20W 323 k
Fousinshin = Fuxin China 42°5N 121°48E 227 C11
Fouta Djallon Guinea 11°20N 12°10W 262 C2
Foux, Cap-à- Haiti 19°43N 73°27W 321 C5
Foveaux Str. N.Z. 46°42S 168°10E 285 G3
Fowey U.K. 50°20N 4°39W 169 G3
Fowler Calif., U.S.A. 36°38N 119°41W 306 J7
Fowler Colo., U.S.A. 38°8N 104°2W 304 G11
Fowler Ind., U.S.A. 40°37N 87°19W 311 D9
Fowler Mich., U.S.A. 43°0N 84°45W 311 B11
Fowler, Pt. Australia 32°2S 132°3E 279 F5
Fowlers B. Australia 31°59S 132°34E 279 F5
Fowlerville U.S.A. 42°40N 84°4W 311 B12
Fowman Iran 37°13N 49°19E 213 D13
Fox → Canada 56°3N 93°18W 297 B10
Fox Creek Canada 54°24N 116°48W 296 C5
Fox Is. U.S.A. 53°0N 168°0W 303 K6
Fox Lake Alta., Canada 58°28N 114°31W 296 B6
Fox Lake Ill., U.S.A. 42°24N 88°11W 311 B8
Fox Studios Australia 33°55S 151°13E 139 B2
Fox Valley Canada 50°30N 109°25W 297 C7
Foxboro Ont., Canada 44°14N 77°26W 312 B7
Foxboro Mass., U.S.A. 42°4N 71°16W 313 D13
Foxdale Australia 20°22S 148°35E 280 b
Foxe Basin Canada 66°0N 77°0W 295 D16
Foxe Chan. Canada 65°0N 80°0W 295 E16
Foxe Pen. Canada 65°0N 76°0W 295 E16
Foxen Sweden 59°25N 11°55E 162 E5
Foxford Ireland 53°59N 9°7W 166 C2
Foxton N.Z. 40°29S 175°18E 284 G4
Foyle, Lough U.K. 55°7N 7°4W 166 A4
Foynes Ireland 52°37N 9°7W 166 D2
Foz Spain 43°33N 7°20W 194 B3
Foz do Copeá Brazil 3°52S 63°19W 329 D5
Foz do Cunene Angola 17°15S 11°48E 265 F2
Foz do Gregório Brazil 6°47S 70°44W 330 B3
Foz do Iguaçu Brazil 25°30S 54°30W 335 B5
Foz do Mamoriá Brazil 2°27S 66°32W 328 D4
Frackville U.S.A. 40°47N 76°14W 313 F8
Fraga Spain 41°32N 0°21E 196 D5
Fraile Muerto Uruguay 32°31S 54°32W 335 C5
Fram Museum Norway 59°54N 10°42E 133 A3
Framingham U.S.A. 42°18N 71°24W 313 D13
Framnes Iceland 66°1N 20°26W 155 A6
Frampol Poland 50°41N 22°40E 185 H9
Franca Brazil 20°33S 47°30W 333 F2
Francavilla al Mare Italy 42°25N 14°17E 199 F11
Francavilla Fontana Italy 40°32N 17°35E 201 B10
France ■ Europe 47°0N 3°0E 171 C5
Frances Australia 36°41S 140°55E 282 D4
Frances → Canada 60°16N 129°10W 296 A3
Frances L. Canada 61°23N 129°30W 296 A3
Francesville U.S.A. 40°59N 86°53W 311 D10
Franceville Gabon 1°40S 13°32E 264 C2
Franche-Comté France 46°50N 5°55E 171 C6
Francis Case, L. U.S.A. 43°4N 98°34W 308 D4
Francisco Beltrão Brazil 26°5S 53°4W 335 B5
Francisco de Orellana Ecuador 0°28S 76°58W 328 D2
Francisco Ignacio Madero Coahuila, Mexico 25°48N 103°18W 318 B4
Francisco Ignacio Madero Durango, Mexico 24°26N 104°18W 318 C4
Francisco Ignacio Madero, Presa Mexico 28°10N 105°37W 318 B3
Francisco Sá Brazil 16°28S 43°30W 333 E3
Francistown Botswana 21°7S 27°33E 271 B4
Francofonte Italy 37°14N 14°53E 201 E7
François Canada 47°35N 56°45W 299 C8
François, B. du Martinique 14°38N 60°54W 322 j
François-Joseph, Chutes Dem. Rep. of the Congo 7°37S 17°17E 265 D3
François L. Canada 54°0N 125°30W 296 C3
Francois Peron △ Australia 25°42S 113°33E 279 E1
Franconia U.S.A. 38°47N 77°7W 143 C2
Francs Pk. U.S.A. 43°58N 109°20W 304 E9
Franeker Neths. 53°12N 5°33E 170 A5
Frank Hann △ Australia 32°52S 120°19E 279 F3
Frank Lloyd Wright Home Chicago, U.S.A. 41°53N 87°47W 119 B2
Frankel Singapore 1°18N 103°55E 138 B3
Frankenberg Germany 51°3N 8°48E 178 D4
Frankenhöhe ⌂ Germany 49°20N 10°25E 179 F6
Frankenstein = Ząbkowice Śląskie Poland 50°35N 16°50E 185 H3
Frankenwald Germany 50°20N 11°30E 179 E7
Frankenwald ⌂ Germany 50°15N 11°30E 179 E7
Frankfield Jamaica 18°8N 77°22W 320 a
Frankford Ont., Canada 44°12N 77°36W 312 B7
Frankford Mo., U.S.A. 39°29N 91°19W 310 E5
Frankfort Free State, S. Africa 27°17S 28°30E 271 C4
Frankfort Ind., U.S.A. 40°17N 86°31W 311 D10
Frankfort Kans., U.S.A. 39°42N 96°25W 308 F5
Frankfort Ky., U.S.A. 38°12N 84°52W 311 F12
Frankfort N.Y., U.S.A. 43°2N 75°4W 313 C9
Frankfort Ohio, U.S.A. 39°24N 83°11W 311 E13
Frankfurt Brandenburg, Germany 52°20N 14°32E 178 C10
Frankfurt Hessen, Germany 50°7N 8°41E 179 E4
Frankfurt ✈ (FRA) Germany 50°1N 8°34E 179 E4
Fränkische Alb Germany 49°10N 11°23E 179 F7
Fränkische Rezat → Germany 49°11N 11°1E 179 F7
Fränkische Saale → Germany 50°3N 9°42E 179 E5
Fränkische Schweiz Germany 49°50N 11°16E 179 F7
Fränkische Schweiz-Veldensteiner Forst ⌂ Germany 49°45N 11°22E 179 F7
Frankland → Australia 35°0S 116°48E 279 G2
Franklin Ga., U.S.A. 33°17N 85°6W 316 B4
Franklin Ind., U.S.A. 39°29N 86°3W 311 E10
Franklin Ky., U.S.A. 36°43N 86°35W 308 G10
Franklin La., U.S.A. 29°48N 91°30W 314 G9
Franklin Mass., U.S.A. 42°5N 71°24W 313 D13
Franklin N.H., U.S.A. 43°27N 71°39W 313 C13
Franklin N.Y., U.S.A. 42°20N 75°9W 313 D9
Franklin Nebr., U.S.A. 40°6N 98°57W 308 E4
Franklin Ohio, U.S.A. 39°34N 84°18W 311 E12
Franklin Pa., U.S.A. 41°24N 79°50W 312 E5
Franklin Va., U.S.A. 36°41N 76°56W 309 G15
Franklin W. Va., U.S.A. 38°39N 79°20W 309 F14
Franklin, Pt. U.S.A. 70°55N 158°48W 303 A8
Franklin B. Canada 69°45N 126°0W 294 D6
Franklin D. Roosevelt L. U.S.A. 48°18N 118°9W 304 B4
Franklin-Gordon Wild Rivers △ Australia 42°19S 145°51E 281 G4
Franklin Harb. Australia 33°43S 136°55E 282 B2
Franklin I. Antarctica 76°10S 168°30E 151 D11
Franklin I. Ont., Canada 45°24N 80°20W 312 A4
Franklin L. U.S.A. 40°25N 115°22W 304 F6
Franklin Mts. N.W.T., Canada 65°0N 125°0W 294 D6
Franklin Mts. N.Z. 44°55S 167°45E 285 E2
Franklin Park Mass., U.S.A. 42°18N 71°5W 116 B2
Franklin Park Va., U.S.A. 38°55N 77°9W 143 B2
Franklin Res. U.S.A. 34°5N 118°24W 126 B2
Franklin Str. Canada 72°0N 96°0W 294 C12
Franklinton U.S.A. 30°51N 90°9W 315 F9
Franklinville U.S.A. 42°20N 78°27W 312 D6
Franklyn Mt. N.Z. 42°4S 172°42E 285 C7
Frankston Australia 38°8S 145°8E 283 E6
Frånö Sweden 62°55N 17°50E 162 B11
Fransfontein Namibia 20°12S 15°1E 270 B2
Fränsta Sweden 62°30N 16°11E 162 B10
Frantsa Iosifa, Zemlya Arctic 82°0N 55°0E 214 A6
Franz Canada 48°25N 84°30W 298 C3
Franz Josef Land = Frantsa Iosifa, Zemlya Arctic 82°0N 55°0E 214 A6
Franz Josef Strauss ✈ (MUC) Germany 48°21N 11°47E 131 A2
Franzburg Germany 54°11N 12°51E 178 A8
Frascati Italy 41°48N 12°41E 199 G9
Fraser U.S.A. 42°32N 82°57W 312 D2
Fraser → B.C., Canada 49°7N 123°11W 306 A3
Fraser → Nfld. & L., Canada 56°39N 62°10W 299 A7
Fraser, Mt. Australia 25°35S 118°20E 279 E2
Fraser I. Australia 25°15S 153°10E 281 D5
Fraser Lake Canada 54°0N 124°50W 296 C4
Fraserburg S. Africa 31°55S 21°30E 270 D3
Fraserburg Road = Leeu Gamka S. Africa 32°47S 21°59E 270 D3
Fraserburgh U.K. 57°42N 2°1W 167 D6
Fraserdale Canada 49°55N 81°37W 298 C3
Fraserpet = Kushalnagar India 12°14N 75°57E 245 H2
Frasertown N.Z. 38°58S 177°28E 284 E6
Fraserville = Rivière-du-Loup Canada 47°50N 69°30W 299 C6
Frashër Albania 40°23N 20°30E 202 F4
Frasne France 46°50N 6°10E 173 F13
Frătești Romania 43°58N 25°58E 183 G10
Frauenfeld Switz. 47°34N 8°54E 179 H4
Frauenkirche Munich, Germany 131 b2
Frauenstadt = Wadowice Poland 49°52N 19°30E 185 J6
Fraustadt = Wschowa Poland 51°48N 16°20E 185 G3
Fray Bentos Uruguay 33°10S 58°15W 334 C4
Fray Jorge △ Chile 30°42S 71°40W 334 C1
Frazier Downs ☼ Australia 18°48S 121°42E 278 C3
Frechilla Spain 42°8N 4°50W 194 C6
Fredericia Denmark 55°34N 9°45E 163 J3
Frederick Md., U.S.A. 39°25N 77°25W 309 F15
Frederick Okla., U.S.A. 34°23N 99°1W 314 D5
Frederick S. Dak., U.S.A. 45°50N 98°31W 308 C4
Frederick E. Hyde Fjord Greenland 83°25N 29°0W 154 A8
Fredericksburg Pa., U.S.A. 40°27N 76°26W 313 F8
Fredericksburg Tex., U.S.A. 30°16N 98°52W 314 F5
Fredericksburg Va., U.S.A. 38°18N 77°28W 309 F15
Fredericktown Mo., U.S.A. 37°34N 90°18W 308 G8
Fredericktown Ohio, U.S.A. 40°29N 82°33W 312 F2
Frederico Westphalen Brazil 27°22S 53°24W 335 B5
Fredericton Canada 45°57N 66°40W 299 C6
Fredericton Junction Canada 45°41N 66°40W 299 C6
Frederiksberg Denmark 55°40N 12°32E 118 A3
Frederiksdal Denmark 55°46N 12°25E 118 A2
Frederikshåb = Paamiut Greenland 62°0N 49°43W 154 E6
Frederikshald = Halden Norway 59°9N 11°23E 164 E8
Frederikshamn = Hamina Finland 60°34N 27°12E 188 B4
Frederikshavn Denmark 57°28N 10°31E 163 G4
Frederikssund Denmark 55°50N 12°3E 163 J6
Frederiksted U.S. Virgin Is. 17°43N 64°53W 321 C7
Frederiksværk Denmark 55°58N 12°4E 163 J6
Fredersdorf Germany 52°31N 13°45E 115 A5
Fredonia Ariz., U.S.A. 36°57N 112°32W 305 H7
Fredonia Kans., U.S.A. 37°32N 95°49W 308 G6
Fredonia N.Y., U.S.A. 42°26N 79°20W 312 D5
Fredriksberg Sweden 60°8N 14°23E 162 D8
Fredrikstad Norway 59°13N 10°57E 164 E7
Fredriksvern = Stavern Norway 59°0N 10°1E 164 F7
Free State □ S. Africa 28°30S 27°0E 270 C4
Freeburg U.S.A. 38°19N 91°56W 310 F5
Freehold U.S.A. 40°16N 74°17W 313 F10
Freeland U.S.A. 41°1N 75°54W 313 E9
Freels, C. Nfld. & L., Canada 49°15N 53°30W 299 C9
Freels, C. Nfld. & L., Canada 46°37N 53°32W 299 C9
Freeman Calif., U.S.A. 35°35N 117°53W 307 K9
Freeman Mo., U.S.A. 38°37N 94°30W 310 F2
Freeman S. Dak., U.S.A. 43°21N 97°26W 308 D5
Freeport The Bahamas 26°30N 78°47W 320 A4
Freeport Trin. & Tob. 10°27N 61°25W 323 t
Freeport Fla., U.S.A. 30°30N 86°8W 316 E3
Freeport Ill., U.S.A. 42°17N 89°36W 310 B7
Freeport N.Y., U.S.A. 40°39N 73°35W 313 F11
Freeport Ohio, U.S.A. 40°12N 81°15W 312 F3
Freeport Pa., U.S.A. 40°41N 79°41W 312 F5
Freeport Tex., U.S.A. 28°57N 95°21W 314 G7
Freetown Antigua & B. 17°3N 61°42W 322 b
Freetown S. Leone 8°30N 13°17W 262 D2
Freeville U.S.A. 42°30N 76°20W 313 D8
Frégate, L. de la Canada 53°15N 74°45W 298 B5
Frigate Island Nature Reserve St. Lucia 13°52N 60°53W 323 m
Fregenal de la Sierra Spain 38°10N 6°39W 195 G4
Fregene Italy 41°51N 12°12E 199 G9
Fregon Australia 26°45S 132°1E 279 E5
Freguesia Brazil 22°48S 43°10W 135 A1
Fréhel, C. France 48°40N 2°20W 172 D4
Freiberg Germany 50°55N 13°20E 178 E9
Freibourg = Fribourg Switz. 46°49N 7°9E 179 J3
Freiburg Baden-W., Germany 47°59N 7°51E 179 H3
Freiburg Niedersachsen, Germany 53°49N 9°16E 178 B5
Freiburg in Schlesien = Świebodzice Poland 50°51N 16°20E 185 H3
Freidrichshain, Volkspark Germany 52°31N 13°25E 115 A3
Freienwalde = Chociwel Poland 53°29N 15°21E 184 E2
Freiham Germany 48°8N 11°25E 131 B1
Freilassing Germany 47°50N 12°58E 179 H8
Freimann Germany 48°11N 11°37E 131 A2
Freire Chile 38°54S 72°38W 336 A2
Freirina Chile 28°30S 71°10W 334 B1
Freising Germany 48°24N 11°45E 179 G7
Freistadt Austria 48°30N 14°30E 180 C7
Freital Germany 51°1N 13°39E 178 D9
Freiwaldau = Jeseník Czechia 50°14N 17°8E 181 A10
Fréjus France 43°25N 6°44E 175 E10
Fremantle Australia 32°7S 115°47E 279 F2
Fremont Calif., U.S.A. 37°32N 121°57W 306 H4
Fremont Ind., U.S.A. 41°44N 84°56W 311 C12
Fremont Iowa, U.S.A. 41°13N 92°26W 310 C4
Fremont Mich., U.S.A. 43°28N 85°57W 309 D11
Fremont Nebr., U.S.A. 41°26N 96°30W 308 E5
Fremont Ohio, U.S.A. 41°21N 83°7W 311 C13
Fremont → U.S.A. 38°24N 110°42W 304 G8
French Camp U.S.A. 37°53N 121°16W 306 H5
French Cays = Plana Cays The Bahamas 22°38N 73°30W 321 B5
French Creek → U.S.A. 41°24N 79°50W 312 E5
French Frigate Shoals U.S.A. 23°45N 166°10W 302 G10
French Guiana ☐ S. Amer. 4°0N 53°0W 329 C7
French Guinea = Guinea ■ W. Afr. 10°20N 11°30W 262 C2
French I. Australia 38°20S 145°22E 283 E6
French Island △ Australia 38°20S 145°22E 283 E6
French Lick U.S.A. 38°33N 86°37W 311 F10
French Market New Orleans, U.S.A. 131 a3
French Pass N.Z. 40°55S 173°55E 285 A8
French Polynesia ☐ Pac. Oc. 20°0S 145°0W 289 f
French Quarter New Orleans, U.S.A. 131 a2
French Riviera = Azur, Côte d' France 43°25N 7°10E 175 E11
French Sudan = Mali ■ Africa 17°0N 3°0W 262 B4
French Territory of the Afars and Issas = Djibouti ■ Africa 12°0N 43°0E 257 E5
French Togoland = Togo ■ W. Afr. 8°30N 1°35E 263 D5
Frenchburg U.S.A. 37°57N 83°38W 311 G13
Frenchman Cr. → N. Amer. 48°31N 107°10W 304 B10
Frenchman Cr. → Nebr., U.S.A. 40°14N 100°50W 308 E3
Frenda Algeria 35°2N 1°1E 261 A5
Frenštát pod Radhoštěm Czechia 49°33N 18°13E 181 B11
Fresco Côte d'Ivoire 5°3N 5°31W 262 D3
Fresco → Brazil 7°15S 51°30W 331 B7
Fresh Pond U.S.A. 42°23N 71°8W 116 A2
Freshfield, C. Antarctica 68°25S 151°10E 151 C10
Fresnay-sur-Sarthe France 48°17N 0°1E 172 D7
Fresnes France 48°45N 2°18E 134 B2
Fresnillo Mexico 23°10N 102°53W 318 C4
Fresno U.S.A. 36°44N 119°47W 306 J7
Fresno Alhándiga Spain 40°42N 5°37W 194 E5
Fresno Res. U.S.A. 48°36N 109°57W 304 B9
Fresvik Norway 61°4N 6°55E 164 C3
Freudenau Austria 48°11N 16°25E 142 A2
Freudenstadt Germany 48°27N 8°24E 179 G4
Freudenthal = Bruntál Czechia 49°59N 17°27E 181 B10
Frévent France 50°15N 2°17E 173 B9
Frew → Australia 20°0S 135°38E 280 C2
Frewsburg U.S.A. 42°3N 79°10W 312 D5
Freycinet △ Australia 42°11S 148°19E 281 G4
Freycinet Pen. Australia 42°10S 148°25E 281 G4
Freyming-Merlebach France 49°8N 6°48E 173 C13
Freystadt = Kisielice Poland 53°36N 19°16E 184 E6
Freystadt = Kożuchów Poland 51°45N 15°31E 185 G2
Freyung Germany 48°48N 13°31E 179 G9
Fria Guinea 10°27N 13°38W 262 C2
Fria, C. Namibia 18°0S 12°0E 270 A1
Friant U.S.A. 36°59N 119°43W 306 J7
Friar's B. St. Kitts & Nevis 17°16N 62°40W 322 d
Frías Argentina 28°40S 65°5W 334 B2
Fribourg Switz. 46°49N 7°9E 179 J3
Fribourg □ Switz. 46°40N 7°0E 179 J3
Frick Collection New York, U.S.A. 132 b3
Fridafors Sweden 56°25N 14°39E 163 H8
Friday Harbor U.S.A. 48°32N 123°1W 306 B3
Friedberg Bayern, Germany 48°21N 10°59E 179 G6
Friedberg Hessen, Germany 50°19N 8°45E 179 E4
Friedeberg = Mirsk Poland 50°58N 15°23E 185 H2
Friedeberg in Neumark = Strzelce Krajeńskie Poland 52°52N 15°33E 185 F2
Friedenau Germany 52°28N 13°22E 115 B3
Friedens U.S.A. 40°3N 78°59W 312 F6
Friedland = Mieroszów Poland 50°40N 16°11E 185 H3
Friedland = Pravdinsk Russia 56°29N 43°28E 190 B6
Friedland Germany 53°40N 13°33E 178 B9
Friedrichsfelde Germany 52°29N 13°30E 115 B4
Friedrichshafen Germany 47°39N 9°30E 179 H5
Friedrichshagen Germany 52°27N 13°37E 115 B4
Friedrichshain Germany 52°31N 13°25E 115 A3
Friedrichskoog Germany 54°1N 8°53E 178 A4
Friedrichslust Germany 52°33N 13°43E 115 A5
Friedrichstadt Germany 54°23N 9°6E 178 A5
Friendly Is. = Tonga ■ Pac. Oc. 19°50S 174°30W 287 P13
Friends Arena Stockholm, Sweden 59°53N 18°0E 139 A2
Friendship U.S.A. 42°12N 78°8W 312 D6
Friesach Austria 46°57N 14°24E 180 E7
Friesack Germany 52°44N 12°34E 178 C8
Friesland □ Neths. 53°5N 5°50E 170 A5
Friesoythe Germany 53°1N 7°51E 178 B3
Frigate Seychelles 4°35S 55°56E 272 c
Frigate Bay St. Kitts & Nevis 17°16N 62°41W 322 d
Frigate I. Grenada 12°25N 61°29W 323 q
Friggesund Sweden 61°54N 16°33E 162 C10
Friherrs Finland 60°16N 24°49E 121 B1
Frillesås Sweden 57°20N 12°12E 163 G6
Frilufts Museum Finland 60°11N 24°52E 121 B2
Frinnaryd Sweden 57°55N 14°50E 163 G8
Frio → U.S.A. 28°26N 98°11W 314 G5
Frio, C. Brazil 22°50S 41°50W 326 F6
Friol Spain 43°2N 7°47W 194 B3
Friona U.S.A. 34°38N 102°43W 314 D3
Frisches Haff = Wiślany, Zalew Poland 54°20N 19°50E 184 D6
Frisco U.S.A. 33°8N 96°49W 314 E6
Fristad Sweden 57°50N 13°0E 163 G6
Fritch U.S.A. 35°38N 101°36W 314 D4
Fritsla Sweden 57°33N 12°47E 163 G6
Fritzlar Germany 51°7N 9°16E 178 D5
Friuli-Venézia Giulia □ Italy 46°0N 13°0E 199 B9
Friza, Proliv Russia 45°30N 149°0E 215 E15
Frobisher B. Canada 62°30N 66°0W 295 E18
Frobisher Bay = Iqaluit Canada 63°44N 68°31W 295 E18
Frobisher L. Canada 56°20N 108°15W 297 B7
Frohavet Norway 64°0N 9°30E 160 E13
Frohenbruck = Veseli nad Lužnicí Czechia 49°12N 14°43E 180 B7
Frohnleiten Austria 47°16N 15°19E 180 D8
Frolovo Russia 49°45N 43°40E 190 F6
Frombork Poland 54°21N 19°41E 184 D6
Frome U.K. 51°14N 2°19W 169 F5
Frome → U.K. 50°41N 2°6W 169 G5
Frome, L. Australia 30°45S 139°45E 282 A3
Frome Downs Australia 31°13S 139°45E 282 A3
Frómista Spain 42°16N 4°25W 194 C6
Front Range U.S.A. 40°25N 105°45W 304 F11
Front Royal U.S.A. 38°55N 78°12W 309 F14
Fronteira Portugal 39°3N 7°39W 195 F3
Fronteiras Brazil 7°5S 40°37W 332 C3
Frontenac ⌂ Canada 44°32N 76°30W 313 B8
Frontera Canary Is. 27°47N 17°59W 153 e1
Frontera Tabasco, Mexico 18°32N 92°38W 319 D6
Fronteras Mexico 30°56N 109°31W 318 A3
Frontignan France 43°27N 3°45E 174 E7
Frontón, I. Peru 12°7S 77°11W 124 B1
Frosinone Italy 41°38N 13°19E 200 A6
Frostburg U.S.A. 39°39N 78°56W 309 F14
Frostisen Norway 68°14N 17°10E 160 B17
Frostproof U.S.A. 27°45N 81°32W 317 H8
Frouard France 48°47N 6°8E 173 D13
Frövi Sweden 59°28N 15°24E 162 E9
Frøya Norway 63°43N 8°40E 160 E13
Fruita U.S.A. 39°9N 108°44W 304 G9
Fruithurst U.S.A. 33°44N 85°26W 316 B4
Fruitland Park U.S.A. 28°51N 81°54W 317 G8
Frumoasa Romania 46°28N 25°48E 183 D10
Frunze = Bishkek Kyrgyzstan 42°54N 74°46E 217 D8
Frunze Russia 55°47N 37°33E 129 B2
Frunzivka Ukraine 47°20N 29°45E 183 C14
Fruška Gora Serbia 45°7N 19°30E 182 E4
Fruška Gora ⌂ Serbia 45°8N 19°40E 202 A3
Frutal Brazil 20°0S 49°0W 333 F2
Frutigen Switz. 46°35N 7°38E 179 J3
Frýdek-Místek Czechia 49°40N 18°20E 181 B11
Frýdlant Czechia 50°56N 15°9E 180 A8
Fryeburg U.S.A. 44°1N 70°59W 313 B14
Fryvaldov = Jeseník Czechia 50°14N 17°8E 181 A10
Fthiotida Greece 38°50N 22°25E 204 C4
Fu Jiang → China 30°0N 106°16E 228 C6
Fu Xian = Wafangdian China 39°38N 121°58E 227 E11
Fu Xian China 36°0N 109°20E 226 G5
Fua Mulaku Maldives 0°17S 73°26E 272 d
Fu'an China 27°11N 119°36E 229 D12
Fubian China 31°17N 102°22E 228 B4
Fucécchio Italy 43°44N 10°48E 198 E7
Fucheng China 37°50N 116°10E 226 F9
Fuchou = Fuzhou China 26°5N 119°16E 229 D12
Fuchū Hiroshima, Japan 34°34N 133°14E 222 C5
Fuchū Tōkyō, Japan 35°40N 139°29E 140 A1
Fuchuan China 24°50N 111°5E 229 E8
Fuchun Jiang → China 30°5N 120°5E 229 B13
Fúcino, Piana del Italy 42°1N 13°31E 199 F10
Fuding China 27°20N 120°12E 229 D13
Fuencaliente Canary Is. 28°28N 17°50W 153 e1
Fuencaliente Spain 38°25N 4°18W 195 G6
Fuencaliente, Pta. Canary Is. 28°27N 17°51W 153 e1
Fuencarral Spain 40°29N 3°42W 127 B1
Fuengirola Spain 36°32N 4°41W 195 J6
Fuenlabrada Spain 40°17N 3°48W 127 C1
Fuensalida Spain 40°3N 4°12W 194 E6
Fuente-Álamo Spain 38°44N 1°24W 197 G3
Fuente Álamo de Murcia Spain 37°42N 1°6W 197 H3
Fuente de Cantos Spain 38°15N 6°18W 195 G4
Fuente del Maestre Spain 38°31N 6°28W 195 G4
Fuente el Fresno Spain 39°14N 3°46W 195 F7
Fuente Obejuna Spain 38°15N 5°25W 195 G5
Fuente Palmera Spain 37°42N 5°6W 195 H5
Fuentes de Andalucía Spain 37°28N 5°20W 195 H5
Fuentes de Ebro Spain 41°31N 0°38W 196 D4
Fuentes de León Spain 38°5N 6°32W 195 G4
Fuentes de Oñoro Spain 40°33N 6°52W 194 E4
Fuentesaúco Spain 41°15N 5°30W 194 D5
Fuerte → Mexico 25°54N 109°22W 318 B3
Fuerte Olimpo Paraguay 21°0S 57°51W 334 A4
Fuerteventura Canary Is. 28°30N 14°0W 153 e2
Fuerteventura ✈ (FUE) Canary Is. 28°24N 13°52W 153 e2
Fufeng China 34°22N 108°0E 226 G5
Fuga I. Phil. 18°52N 121°20E 232 B3
Fugong China 27°5N 98°47E 228 D2
Fugou China 34°3N 114°25E 226 G8
Fugu China 39°2N 111°3E 226 E6
Fuhai China 47°2N 87°25E 217 C11
Fuḩaymī Iraq 34°16N 42°10E 213 E10
Fuhlsbüttel, Hamburg ✈ (HAM) Germany 53°35N 9°59E 178 B5
Fuhsien = Fu Xian China 36°0N 109°20E 226 G5
Fuhsing Changhua, Taiwan 24°3N 120°28E 225 B2
Fuhsing Kaohsiung, Taiwan 23°13N 120°48E 225 C2
Fuhsing Taoyüan, Taiwan 24°49N 121°21E 225 B3
Fuidhaigh = Wiay U.K. 57°24N 7°13W 167 D1
Fuji Japan 35°9N 138°39E 223 B10
Fuji-Hakone-Izu △ Japan 35°15N 138°45E 223 B10
Fuji-San Japan 35°22N 138°44E 223 B10
Fuji-Yoshida Japan 35°30N 138°46E 223 B10
Fujian □ China 26°0N 118°0E 229 E12
Fujieda Japan 34°52N 138°16E 223 C10
Fujin China 47°16N 132°1E 219 B15
Fujinomiya Japan 35°10N 138°40E 223 B10
Fujioka Japan 36°15N 139°5E 223 A11
Fujisawa Japan 35°22N 139°29E 223 B11
Fujiyama, Mt. = Fuji-San Japan 35°22N 138°44E 223 B10
Fukagawa Hokkaidō, Japan 43°43N 142°2E 220 C11
Fukagawa Tōkyō, Japan 35°39N 139°48E 140 B3
Fukang China 44°10N 87°59E 217 D11
Fukaya Japan 36°12N 139°12E 223 A11
Fukiage Japan 31°27N 130°17E 222 F2
Fukiage Imperial Garden Tokyo, Japan 140 a4
Fukien = Fujian □ China 26°0N 118°0E 229 E12
Fukuchiyama Japan 35°19N 135°9E 223 B7
Fukue Japan 32°41N 128°51E 221 H4
Fukue-Shima Japan 32°40N 128°45E 221 H4
Fukuei Chiao Taiwan 25°17N 121°32E 225 A3
Fukui Japan 36°5N 136°10E 223 A8
Fukui □ Japan 36°0N 136°12E 223 B8
Fukuma Japan 33°46N 130°28E 222 D2
Fukuoka Japan 33°39N 130°21E 222 D2
Fukuoka □ Japan 33°30N 131°0E 222 D3
Fukuoka Int. ✈ (FUK) Japan 33°34N 130°28E 222 D2
Fukuroi Japan 34°45N 137°55E 223 C9
Fukushima Fukushima, Japan 37°44N 140°28E 220 F10
Fukushima Ōsaka, Japan 34°41N 135°28E 133 A1
Fukushima □ Japan 37°30N 140°15E 220 F10
Fukuyama Japan 34°35N 133°20E 222 C5
Ful Bura South Sudan 7°50N 31°50E 257 F3
Fulacunda Guinea-Biss. 11°44N 15°3W 262 C1
Fulaga Fiji 19°8S 178°33W 287 B3
Fulda Germany 50°32N 9°40E 178 E5
Fulda → Germany 51°25N 9°39E 178 D5
Fulford = North Miami Beach U.S.A. 25°55N 80°9W 129 C2
Fulford Harbour Canada 48°47N 123°27W 306 B3
Fulham U.K. 51°28N 0°12W 125 B2
Fuli Taiwan 23°11N 121°14E 225 C3
Fuling China 29°23N 117°14E 229 C11
Fuling China 29°39N 107°17E 228 C6
Fullarton Trin. & Tob. 10°5N 61°54W 323 t
Fullerton Calif., U.S.A. 33°53N 117°56W 307 M9
Fullerton Nebr., U.S.A. 41°22N 97°58W 308 E5
Fulongquan China 44°20N 124°42E 227 B13
Fülöpszállás Hungary 46°49N 19°15E 182 D4
Fulton Ill., U.S.A. 41°52N 90°11W 310 C6
Fulton Ind., U.S.A. 40°57N 86°16W 311 D10
Fulton Mo., U.S.A. 38°52N 91°57W 310 F5
Fulton N.Y., U.S.A. 43°19N 76°25W 313 C8
Fulufjället Sweden 61°32N 12°41E 162 C6
Fumay France 49°58N 4°40E 173 C11
Fumel France 44°30N 0°58E 174 D4
Fumin China 25°10N 102°20E 228 E4
Funabashi Japan 35°45N 140°0E 223 B12
Funabori Japan 35°41N 139°52E 140 A4
Funafuti Pac. Oc. 8°31S 179°13E 277 B14
Funan China 32°39N 115°42E 229 A10
Funäsdalen Sweden 62°33N 12°32E 162 B6
Funchal Madeira 32°38N 16°54W 153 c
Funchal ✈ (FNC) Madeira 32°42N 16°45W 153 c
Fundación Colombia 10°31N 74°11W 328 A3
Fundão Brazil 19°55S 40°24W 333 E3
Fundão Portugal 40°8N 7°30W 194 E3
Fundão, I. do Brazil 22°51S 43°13W 135 B1
Fundong Cameroon 6°15N 10°16E 264 A2
Fundu Moldovei Romania 47°32N 25°24E 183 C10
Fundulea Romania 44°28N 26°31E 183 F11
Fundy, B. of Canada 45°0N 66°0W 299 D6
Fundy △ Canada 45°35N 65°10W 299 C6
Fünfhaus Austria 48°11N 16°20E 142 A2
Fünfkirchen = Pécs Hungary 46°5N 18°15E 182 D3
Funhalouro Mozam. 23°3S 34°25E 271 B5
Funing Hebei, China 39°53N 119°12E 227 E10
Funing Jiangsu, China 33°45N 119°50E 227 H10
Funing Yunnan, China 23°35N 105°45E 228 F5
Funiu Shan China 33°30N 112°20E 226 H7
Funsi Ghana 10°21N 1°54W 262 C4
Funtua Nigeria 11°30N 7°18E 263 C6
Fuping Hebei, China 38°48N 114°12E 226 E8
Fuping Shaanxi, China 34°42N 109°10E 226 G5
Fuqing China 25°41N 119°21E 229 E12
Fuquan China 26°40N 107°27E 228 D6
Furano Japan 43°21N 142°23E 220 C11
Furāt, Nahr al → Asia 31°0N 47°25E 246 D5
Fureso Denmark 55°47N 12°25E 118 A2
Fürg Iran 28°18N 55°13E 247 D7
Furkating India 26°28N 93°59E 241 B4
Furman U.S.A. 32°41N 81°11W 316 C8
Furmanov Russia 57°10N 41°9E 190 B5
Furnas Azores 37°46N 25°19W 153 d3
Furnás Spain 39°3N 1°32E 206 C2
Furnas, Represa de Brazil 20°50S 45°30W 333 F2
Furneaux Group Australia 40°10S 147°50E 281 G4
Furqlus Syria 34°36N 37°8E 250 D8
Fürstenau Germany 52°31N 7°40E 178 C3
Fürstenberg = Eisenhüttenstadt Germany 52°9N 14°38E 178 C10
Fürstenberg Germany 53°10N 13°8E 178 B9
Fürstenfeld Austria 47°3N 16°3E 180 D9
Fürstenfeldbruck Germany 48°11N 11°15E 179 G7
Fürstenwalde Germany 52°22N 14°3E 178 C10
Fürth Mittelfranken, Germany 49°28N 10°59E 179 F6
Fürth Oberbayern, Germany 48°2N 11°35E 131 B2
Fürth im Wald Germany 49°18N 12°50E 179 F8
Furtwangen Germany 48°2N 8°12E 179 G4
Furudal Sweden 61°10N 15°11E 162 C9
Furukawa = Hida Japan 36°14N 137°11E 223 A9
Furukawa = Ōsaki Japan 38°34N 140°58E 220 E10
Furulund Sweden 55°46N 13°6E 163 J7
Furuvik Sweden 61°38N 17°20E 162 D11
Fury and Hecla Str. Canada 69°56N 84°0W 295 D15
Fusagasugá Colombia 4°21N 74°22W 328 C3
Fuscaldo Italy 39°25N 16°2E 201 C9
Fushan Shandong, China 37°30N 121°15E 227 F11
Fushan Shanxi, China 35°58N 111°51E 226 G6
Fushë Arrëz Albania 42°4N 20°2E 202 D4
Fushë Kosovë Kosovo 42°40N 21°5E 202 D5
Fushë Krujë Albania 41°29N 19°43E 202 E3
Fushun Liaoning, China 41°50N 123°56E 224 B1
Fushun Sichuan, China 29°13N 104°52E 228 C5
Fusong China 42°20N 127°15E 224 A3
Füssen Germany 47°34N 10°42E 179 H6
Fusui China 22°40N 107°56E 228 F6
Futago-tamagawaen Japan 35°36N 139°39E 140 B2
Futago-Yama Japan 33°35N 131°36E 222 D3
Futian China 22°32N 114°4E 219 a
Futiga Amer. Samoa 14°21S 170°45W 302 f
Futog Serbia 45°15N 19°42E 182 E4
Futrono Chile 40°8S 72°24W 336 B2

Futtsu Japan 35°13N 139°49E 223 B11
Fuwa Egypt 31°12N 30°33E 256 H7
Fuxian Hu China 24°30N 102°53E 228 E4
Fuxin China 42°5N 121°48E 227 C11
Fuxing Dao China 31°16N 121°33E 138 B2
Fuxing Park China 31°13N 121°27E 138 B1
Fuxinglu China 39°52N 116°16E 114 B1
Fuyang Anhui, China 33°0N 115°48E 229 A10
Fuyang Zhejiang, China 30°5N 119°57E 229 B12
Fuyang He → China 38°12N 117°0E 226 E9
Fuying Dao China 26°34N 120°9E 229 D13
Fuyong China 22°40N 113°49E 219 a
Fuyot Springs △ Phil. 17°1N 121°58E 232 C3
Fuyu Heilongjiang, China 47°49N 124°27E 219 B13
Fuyu Jilin, China 45°12N 124°43E 227 B13
Fuyuan China 25°40N 104°16E 228 E5
Fuyun China 47°0N 89°28E 217 C11
Füzesgyarmat Hungary 47°6N 21°14E 182 C6
Fuzhou = Linchuan China 27°57N 116°15E 229 D11
Fuzhou China 26°5N 119°16E 229 D12
Füzuli Azerbaijan 39°36N 47°8E 213 C12
Fyn Denmark 55°20N 10°30E 163 J4
Fyne, L. U.K. 55°59N 5°23W 167 F3
Fynshav Denmark 54°59N 9°59E 163 K3
Fyresdal Norway 59°11N 8°5E 164 E5
Fyresvatn Norway 59°6N 8°10E 164 E5
Fyzabad = Faizabad India 26°45N 82°10E 243 F10
Fyzabad Trin. & Tob. 10°12N 61°33W 323 t

G

G. Ross Lord Park Canada 43°47N 79°28W 141 A2
Ga Ghana 9°47N 2°30W 262 D4
Ga-eun S. Korea 36°38N 128°5E 224 D4
Gaa Faru Atoll Maldives 4°45N 73°26E 272 d
Gaalkacyo Somalia 6°30N 47°30E 267 C6
Gaanda Nigeria 10°10N 12°27E 263 C7
Gabaldon Phil. 15°37N 121°20E 232 D3
Gabas → France 43°46N 0°42W 174 E3
Gabba Australia 9°45S 142°38E 280 a
Gabela Angola 11°0S 14°24E 265 E2
Gaberones = Gaborone Botswana 24°45S 25°57E 270 B4
Gabès Tunisia 33°53N 10°2E 258 B2
Gabès □ Tunisia 33°35N 9°30E 261 B6
Gabès, G. de Tunisia 34°0N 10°30E 258 B2
Gabgaba, W. → Egypt 22°10N 33°5E 256 C3
Gabia Dem. Rep. of the Congo 4°37S 17°14E 265 C3
Gabia la Grande Spain 37°8N 3°40W 195 H7
Gąbin Poland 52°23N 19°41E 185 F6
Gablonz = Jablonec nad Nisou Czechia 50°43N 15°10E 180 A8
Gabon ■ Africa 0°10S 10°0E 264 C2
Gabon → Gabon 0°25N 9°20E 264 B1
Gaborone Botswana 24°45S 25°57E 270 B4
Gabrat Sai'd Sudan 16°6N 31°50E 266 A3
Gabriels U.S.A. 44°26N 74°12W 313 B10
Gābrīk Iran 25°44N 58°28E 247 E8
Gabro Ethiopia 6°18N 43°16E 267 C5
Gabrovo Bulgaria 42°52N 25°19E 203 D9
Gabú = Nova Lamego Guinea-Biss. 12°19N 14°11W 262 C2
Gacé France 48°49N 0°20E 172 D7
Gāch Sār Iran 36°7N 51°19E 247 B6
Gachsārān Iran 30°15N 50°45E 247 D6
Gacko Bos.-H. 43°10N 18°33E 202 C2
Gad Hinglaj India 16°14N 74°21E 245 F2
Gadag India 15°30N 75°45E 245 G2
Gadaisu Papua N. G. 10°22S 149°46E 286 F5
Gadamai Sudan 17°11N 36°10E 257 D4
Gadap Pakistan 25°5N 67°28E 242 G2
Gadarwara India 22°50N 78°50E 243 H8
Gadebusch Germany 53°42N 11°7E 178 B7
Gadein South Sudan 8°10N 28°45E 257 F2
Gadhada India 22°0N 71°35E 242 J4
Gadis → Indonesia 1°2N 98°55E 234 B1
Gádor, Sierra de Spain 36°57N 2°45W 195 J8
Gadra Pakistan 25°40N 70°38E 242 G4
Gadsden Ala., U.S.A. 34°1N 86°1W 316 A3
Gadsden S.C., U.S.A. 33°51N 80°46W 316 B9
Gadwal India 16°10N 77°50E 245 F3
Gadyach = Hadyach Ukraine 50°21N 34°0E 189 G8
Gadzi C.A.R. 4°47N 16°42E 264 B3
Gaebong S. Korea 37°29N 126°52E 137 C1
Găeşti Romania 44°48N 25°19E 183 F10
Gaeta Italy 41°12N 13°35E 200 A6
Gaeta, G. di Italy 41°6N 13°30E 200 A6
Gaffney U.S.A. 35°5N 81°39W 315 D14
Gafsa Tunisia 34°24N 8°43E 258 B1
Gafsa □ Tunisia 34°30N 8°48E 261 B6
Gagarawa Nigeria 12°25N 9°32E 263 C6
Gagaria India 25°43N 70°46E 242 G4
Gagarin Russia 55°38N 35°0E 188 E8
Găgăuzia □ Moldova 46°10N 28°40E 183 D13
Gage Park U.S.A. 41°47N 87°42W 119 C2
Gaggenau Germany 48°48N 8°18E 179 G4
Gaghamni Sudan 11°41N 28°19E 257 E2
Gagil-Tomil, I. Pac. Oc. 9°31N 138°12E 287 R16
Gagino Russia 55°15N 45°1E 190 C7
Gagliano del Capo Italy 39°50N 18°22E 201 C11
Gagnef Sweden 60°36N 15°5E 162 D9
Gagnoa Côte d'Ivoire 6°56N 6°16W 262 D3
Gagnon Canada 51°50N 68°5W 299 B6
Gagnon, L. Canada 62°3N 110°27W 297 A6
Gagny France 48°53N 2°32E 134 A4
Gago Coutinho São Tomé & Príncipe 0°1S 6°32E 265 a
Gagra Georgia 43°20N 40°10E 191 J5
Gahini Rwanda 1°50S 30°30E 268 C3
Gahmar India 25°27N 83°49E 243 G10
Gahnpa = Ganta Liberia 7°15N 8°59W 262 D3
Gai Xian = Gaizhou China 40°22N 122°20E 224 B1
Gaibandha Bangla. 25°20N 89°36E 241 C2
Gaidouronisi Greece 34°53N 25°41E 207 F6
Gail U.S.A. 32°46N 101°27W 314 E4
Gail → Austria 46°36N 13°53E 180 E6
Gaillac France 43°54N 1°54E 174 E5
Gaillard Cut Panama 9°3N 79°40W 320 c
Gaillimh = Galway Ireland 53°17N 9°3W 166 C2
Gaillon France 49°10N 1°20E 172 C8
Gaimán Argentina 43°10S 65°25W 336 B3
Gaines U.S.A. 41°46N 77°35W 312 E7
Gainesville Fla., U.S.A. 29°40N 82°20W 317 F7
Gainesville Ga., U.S.A. 34°18N 83°50W 315 D13
Gainesville Mo., U.S.A. 36°36N 92°26W 308 G7
Gainesville Tex., U.S.A. 33°38N 97°8W 314 E6
Gainsborough U.K. 53°24N 0°46W 168 D7
Gairdner, L. Australia 31°30S 136°0E 282 A2
Gairloch U.K. 57°43N 5°41W 167 D3
Gairloch, L. U.K. 57°43N 5°45W 167 D3
Gaizhou China 40°22N 122°20E 224 B1
Gaj Croatia 45°28N 17°3E 182 E2
Gaj → Pakistan 26°26N 67°21E 242 F2
Gajendragarh India 15°44N 75°59E 245 G2
Gakona U.S.A. 62°18N 145°18W 303 E11
Gakuch Pakistan 36°7N 73°45E 243 A5
Gal Oya △ Sri Lanka 7°0N 81°20E 245 L5
Gal Oya Res. Sri Lanka 7°5N 81°30E 245 L5
Gal Tardo Somalia 3°34N 45°58E 267 D6
Galabovo Bulgaria 42°8N 25°55E 203 D9
Galachipa Bangla. 22°8N 90°26E 241 D3
Galâla, Gebel el Egypt 29°21N 32°22E 256 J8
Galâla el Baharîya, G. el Egypt 29°22N 32°23E 251 J3
Galâla el Qiblîya, G. el Egypt 28°42N 32°22E 251 K3
Galán, Cerro Argentina 25°55S 66°52W 334 B2
Galana → Kenya 3°9S 40°8E 268 C5
Galangue Angola 13°42S 16°9E 265 E3
Galangue, Serra Angola 14°18S 15°52E 265 E3
Galanta Slovakia 48°11N 17°45E 181 C10
Galapagar Spain 40°36N 3°58W 194 E7
Galápagos = Colón, Arch. de Ecuador 0°0 91°0W 330 a
Galapagos Fracture Zone Pac. Oc. 3°0N 110°0W 289 G17
Galapagos Rise Pac. Oc. 15°0S 95°0W 289 J18
Galashiels U.K. 55°37N 2°49W 167 F6
Galata Turkey 41°1N 28°58E 122 B1
Galata Tower Turkey 41°1N 28°59E 122 B1
Galatas Greece 37°30N 23°26E 204 D5
Galatea N.Z. 38°24S 176°45E 284 E5
Galateia Cyprus 35°25N 34°4E 207 E10
Galaţi Romania 45°27N 28°2E 183 E13
Galaţi □ Romania 45°45N 27°30E 183 E12
Galatia Turkey 39°30N 33°0E 212 C5
Galatina Italy 40°10N 18°10E 201 B11
Galátone Italy 40°9N 18°4E 201 B11
Galatsi Greece 38°1N 23°45E 112 A2
Galax U.S.A. 36°40N 80°56W 309 G13
Galaxidi Greece 38°22N 22°23E 204 C4
Galbïn Govĭ Mongolia 43°0N 107°0E 226 C4
Galcaio = Gaalkacyo Somalia 6°30N 47°30E 267 C6
Gáldar Canary Is. 28°9N 15°39W 153 e1
Galdhøpiggen Norway 61°38N 8°18E 164 C5
Galeana Chihuahua, Mexico 30°7N 107°38W 318 A3
Galeana Nuevo León, Mexico 24°50N 100°4W 318 A3
Galeão Int. ✕ (GIG) Brazil 22°49S 43°15W 135 A1
Galegu Sudan 12°36N 35°2E 257 E4
Galela Indonesia 1°50N 127°49E 231 D7
Galena Alaska, U.S.A. 64°44N 156°56W 303 D8
Galena Ill., U.S.A. 42°25N 90°26W 310 B6
Galeota Pt. Trin. & Tob. 10°8N 60°59W 323 t
Galera Spain 37°45N 2°33W 197 H2
Galera, Pta. Chile 39°59S 73°43W 336 A2
Galera, Pta. da Azores 37°42N 25°30W 153 d3
Galera Pt. Trin. & Tob. 10°49N 60°54W 323 t
Galeras Colombia 1°13N 77°20W 328 C2
Galesburg Ill., U.S.A. 40°57N 90°22W 310 D6
Galesburg Mich., U.S.A. 42°17N 85°26W 311 B11
Galestan △ Iran 37°30N 56°0E 247 B8
Galeton U.S.A. 41°44N 77°39W 312 E7
Galets → Réunion 20°56S 55°17E 272 f
Galga Ethiopia 6°39N 37°47E 257 F4
Galgasc Somalia 0°11N 41°38E 267 D5
Galguduud □ Somalia 5°0N 47°0E 267 D6
Galheirão → Brazil 12°23S 45°5W 333 D2
Gali Georgia 42°37N 41°46E 191 J5
Galicea Mare Romania 44°4N 23°19E 183 F8
Galich Russia 58°22N 42°24E 190 A6
Galiche Bulgaria 43°34N 23°53E 202 C7
Galicia □ Spain 42°43N 7°45W 194 C3
Galičica △ N. Macedonia 41°2N 20°55E 202 E4
Galien U.S.A. 41°48N 86°30W 311 C10
Galilee = Hagalil Israel 32°53N 35°18E 250 F6
Galilee, L. Australia 22°20S 145°50E 280 C4
Galilee, Sea of = Yam Kinneret Israel 32°45N 35°35E 250 F6
Galim Cameroon 7°6N 12°25E 263 D7
Galina Pt. Jamaica 18°24N 76°58W 320 a
Galinoporni Cyprus 35°31N 34°18E 207 E10
Galion U.S.A. 40°44N 82°47W 312 F2
Galion, B. du Martinique 14°44N 60°56W 322 j
Galite, Îs. de la Tunisia 37°30N 8°59E 261 A6
Galiuro Mts. U.S.A. 32°30N 110°20W 305 K8
Galiwinku Australia 12°2S 135°34E 280 A2
Gallâbât Sudan 12°58N 36°11E 257 E4
Gallan Hd. U.K. 58°15N 7°2W 167 C1
Gallarate Italy 45°40N 8°48E 198 C5
Gallatin Mo., U.S.A. 39°55N 93°58W 310 E3
Gallatin Tenn., U.S.A. 36°24N 86°27W 315 C11
Galle Sri Lanka 6°5N 80°10E 245 L5
Gállego → Spain 41°39N 0°51W 196 D4
Gallegos → Argentina 51°35S 69°0W 336 D3
Gallery of Inuit Art = Dominion Centre Toronto, Canada 141 b2
Galletti → Ethiopia 8°46N 41°10E 257 F5
Galley Hd. Ireland 51°32N 8°55W 166 E3
Galliate Italy 45°29N 8°42E 198 C5
Gallinas, Pta. Colombia 12°28N 71°40W 328 A3
Gallipoli = Gelibolu Turkey 40°28N 26°43E 203 F10
Gallípoli Italy 40°3N 17°58E 201 B10
Gallipolis U.S.A. 38°49N 82°12W 309 F12
Gällivare Sweden 67°9N 20°40E 160 C19
Gallneukirchen Austria 48°21N 14°25E 180 C7
Gällö Sweden 62°55N 15°13E 162 B9
Gallo, C. Italy 38°13N 13°19E 200 D6
Gallocanta, L. de Spain 40°58N 1°30W 196 E3
Galloo I. U.S.A. 43°55N 76°25W 313 C8
Galloway U.K. 55°1N 4°29W 167 F4
Galloway, Mull of U.K. 54°39N 4°52W 167 G4
Gallup U.S.A. 35°32N 108°45W 305 J9
Gallur Spain 41°52N 1°19W 196 D3
Gallura Italy 41°5N 9°20E 200 A2
Galma Galla Kenya 1°11S 40°47E 267 E5
Galmudug Somalia 6°30N 48°0E 267 C6
Galong Australia 34°37S 148°34E 283 C8
Galool Somalia 3°38N 43°49E 267 D5
Galoya Sri Lanka 8°10N 80°55E 245 K5
Galt Calif., U.S.A. 38°15N 121°18W 306 G5
Galt Mo., U.S.A. 40°8N 93°23W 310 D3
Galten Denmark 56°9N 9°54E 163 H3
Galtür Austria 46°58N 10°11E 180 E3
Galty Mts. Ireland 52°22N 8°10W 166 D3
Galtymore Ireland 52°21N 8°11W 166 D3
Galugāh Iran 36°43N 53°48E 247 B7
Galva U.S.A. 41°10N 90°3W 310 C6
Galvarino Chile 38°24S 72°47W 336 A2
Galve de Sorbe Spain 41°13N 3°10W 196 D1
Galveston Ind., U.S.A. 40°35N 86°11W 311 D10
Galveston Tex., U.S.A. 29°18N 94°48W 314 G7
Galveston B. U.S.A. 29°36N 94°50W 314 G7
Gálvez Argentina 32°0S 61°14W 334 C3
Galway Ireland 53°17N 9°3W 166 C2
Galway □ Ireland 53°22N 9°1W 166 C2
Galway B. Ireland 53°13N 9°10W 166 C2
Galyanovo Russia 55°48N 37°47E 129 B3
Gam → Vietnam 21°55N 105°12E 236 B5
Gamagōri Japan 34°50N 137°14E 223 C9
Gamari, L. Ethiopia 11°32N 41°40E 257 E5
Gamawa Nigeria 12°10N 10°31E 263 C7
Gamay Phil. 12°23N 125°18E 232 E5
Gamay B. Phil. 12°21N 125°21E 232 E5
Gamba Angola 11°42S 17°14E 265 E3
Gambaga Ghana 10°30N 0°28W 263 C4
Gambat Pakistan 27°17N 68°26E 242 F3
Gambela Ethiopia 8°14N 34°38E 257 F3
Gambela △ Ethiopia 8°0N 34°0E 257 F3
Gambela Hizboch □ Ethiopia 8°0N 34°0E 257 F3
Gambell U.S.A. 63°47N 171°45W 303 E5
Gambhir → India 26°58N 77°27E 242 F6
Gambia ■ W. Afr. 13°25N 16°0W 262 C1
Gambia → W. Afr. 13°28N 16°34W 262 C1
Gambier U.S.A. 40°22N 82°23W 312 F2
Gambier, C. Australia 11°56S 130°57E 278 B5
Gambier, Îs. French Polynesia 23°8S 134°58W 289 f
Gambier Is. Australia 35°3S 136°30E 282 C2
Gambier Village The Bahamas 25°4N 77°30W 153 b
Gambir Indonesia 6°9S 106°48E 122 A1
Gambo C.A.R. 4°39N 22°16E 264 B4
Gambo Canada 48°47N 54°13W 299 C9
Gamboa Rio de J., Brazil 22°53S 43°11W 135 B1
Gamboa Panama 9°7N 79°42W 320 c
Gamboli Pakistan 29°53N 68°24E 242 E3
Gambolóita Italy 45°26N 9°13E 128 B2
Gamboma Congo 1°55S 15°52E 264 C3
Gamboula C.A.R. 4°8N 15°9E 264 B3
Gamka → S. Africa 33°18S 21°39E 270 D3
Gamkab → Namibia 28°4S 17°54E 270 C2
Gamla Stan Stockholm, Sweden 139 c2
Gamla Uppsala Sweden 59°54N 17°40E 162 E11
Gamlakarleby = Kokkola Finland 63°50N 23°8E 160 E20
Gamleby Sweden 57°54N 16°24E 163 G10
Gamlebyen Norway 59°54N 10°46E 133 A3
Gammon → Canada 51°24N 95°44W 297 C9
Gammon Ranges △ Australia 30°38S 139°8E 281 E2
Gamo-Gofa Ethiopia 5°40N 36°40E 257 F4
Gamoda-Saki Japan 33°50N 134°45E 222 D6
Gamou Niger 14°20N 9°55E 259 F1
Gampaha Sri Lanka 7°5N 79°59E 245 L4
Gampo S. Korea 35°48N 129°31E 224 E4
Gampola Sri Lanka 7°10N 80°34E 245 L5
Gamtoos → S. Africa 33°58S 25°1E 270 D4
Gamzigrad-Romuliana Serbia 43°53N 22°11E 202 C6
Gan France 43°12N 0°27W 174 E3
Gan Gan Argentina 42°30S 68°10W 336 B3
Gan Goriama, Mts. Cameroon 7°44N 12°45E 263 D7
Gan Int. ✕ (GAN) Maldives 0°41S 73°1E 272 d
Gan Jiang → China 29°15N 116°0E 229 C11
Ganado U.S.A. 35°43N 109°33W 305 J9
Gananita Sudan 18°22N 33°50E 256 D3
Gananoque Canada 44°20N 76°10W 313 B8
Ganassi Phil. 7°49N 124°6E 233 H5
Ganāveh Iran 29°35N 50°35E 247 D6
Gäncä Azerbaijan 40°45N 46°20E 191 K8
Gancheng China 18°51N 108°37E 229 a
Gand = Gent Belgium 51°2N 3°42E 170 C3
Ganda Angola 13°3S 14°35E 265 E2
Gandajika Dem. Rep. of the Congo 6°46S 23°58E 265 D4
Gandak → India 25°39N 85°13E 243 G11
Gandara Phil. 12°1N 124°49E 232 E5
Gandava Pakistan 28°32N 67°32E 242 E2
Gander Canada 48°58N 54°35W 299 C9
Gander L. Canada 48°58N 54°35W 299 C9
Ganderkesee Germany 53°2N 8°32E 178 B4
Ganderowe Falls Zimbabwe 17°20S 29°10E 269 F2
Gandesa Spain 41°3N 0°26E 196 D5
Gandhi Sagar India 24°40N 75°40E 242 G6
Gandhinagar India 23°15N 72°45E 242 H5
Gandi Nigeria 12°55N 5°49E 263 C6
Gandia Spain 38°58N 0°9W 197 G4
Gandino Italy 45°49N 9°54E 198 C6
Gando, Pta. Canary Is. 27°55N 15°22W 153 e1
Gandole Nigeria 8°28N 11°35E 263 D7
Gandou Congo 2°25N 17°25E 264 B3
Gandu Brazil 13°45S 39°30W 333 D4
Gâneb Mauritania 18°29N 10°8W 262 B2
Ganedidalem = Gani Indonesia 0°48S 128°14E 231 E7
Ganga → India 23°20N 90°30E 243 H14
Ganga Sagar India 21°38N 88°5E 243 J13
Gangafani Mali 14°20N 2°20W 262 C4
Gangakher India 18°57N 76°45E 244 E3
Gangan → India 28°38N 78°58E 243 E8
Ganganagar India 29°56N 73°56E 242 E5
Gangapur Maharashtra, India 19°41N 75°1E 244 E2
Gangapur Raj., India 26°32N 76°49E 242 F7
Gangara Niger 14°35N 8°29E 259 F1
Gangaw Myanmar 22°5N 94°5E 241 D5
Gangaw Taungdan Myanmar 24°55N 96°35E 241 C6
Gangawati India 15°30N 76°36E 245 G3
Gangdisê Shan China 31°20N 81°0E 243 D9
Gangdong S. Korea 37°30N 127°5E 137 B2
Ganges = Ganga → India 23°20N 90°30E 243 H14
Ganges Canada 48°51N 123°31W 296 D4
Ganges Hérault, France 43°56N 3°42E 174 E7
Ganges, Mouths of the India 21°30N 90°0E 241 E3
Ganggyeong S. Korea 36°10N 127°0E 224 D3
Gånghester Sweden 57°42N 13°1E 163 G7
Ganghwa S. Korea 37°45N 126°30E 224 D3
Gangi Italy 37°48N 14°12E 201 E7
Gângiova Romania 43°54N 23°50E 183 G8
Gangnam S. Korea 37°30N 126°59E 137 B1
Gangneung S. Korea 37°45N 128°54E 224 D4
Gangoh India 29°46N 77°18E 242 E7
Gangotri India 30°50N 79°10E 243 D8
Gangotri △ India 30°50N 79°10E 243 D8
Gangseo S. Korea 37°32N 126°51E 137 B1
Gangseong S. Korea 38°24N 128°30E 224 C4
Gangshan = Kangshan Taiwan 22°48N 120°17E 225 D2
Gangtok India 27°20N 88°37E 241 B2
Gangtou China 23°12N 113°8E 121 A1
Gangu China 34°40N 105°15E 226 G3
Gangwa Dem. Rep. of the Congo 3°30S 20°54E 264 C4
Gangwei China 23°4N 113°11E 121 B2
Gangwon-do □ S. Korea 37°45N 128°15E 224 D4
Gangyao China 44°12N 126°37E 227 B14
Gani Indonesia 0°48S 128°14E 231 E7
Ganj India 27°45N 78°57E 243 F8
Ganjam India 19°23N 85°4E 244 E7
Ganjiakou China 39°54N 116°16E 114 B1
Ganluo China 28°58N 102°59E 228 C4
Ganmain Australia 34°47S 147°1E 283 C7
Ganna South Sudan 7°30N 28°0E 266 C2
Gannat France 46°7N 3°11E 173 F10
Gannett Peak U.S.A. 43°11N 109°39W 304 E9
Ganquan China 36°20N 109°20E 226 F5
Gänserdorf Austria 48°20N 16°43E 181 C9
Ganshoren Belgium 50°52N 4°18E 116 A1
Ganshui China 28°40N 106°40E 228 C6
Gansu □ China 36°0N 104°0E 226 G3
Ganta Liberia 7°15N 8°59W 262 D3
Gantheaume, C. Australia 36°4S 137°32E 282 D2
Gantheaume B. Australia 27°40S 114°10E 279 E1
Gants Hill U.K. 51°34N 0°4E 125 A4
Gantsevichi = Hantsavichy Belarus 52°49N 26°30E 177 B14
Gantung Indonesia 2°58S 108°9E 235 C3
Ganvie Benin 6°28N 2°25E 263 D5
Ganye Nigeria 8°25N 12°4E 263 D7
Ganyem = Genyem Indonesia 2°46S 140°12E 231 E10
Ganyu China 34°50N 119°8E 227 G10
Ganyushkino Kazakhstan 46°35N 49°20E 191 G9
Ganzhou China 25°51N 114°56E 229 E10
Gao Mali 16°15N 0°5W 263 B4
Gao Xian China 28°21N 104°32E 228 C5
Gao'an China 28°26N 115°17E 229 C10
Gaobeidian China 39°19N 115°51E 226 E8
Gaocheng China 38°2N 114°49E 226 E8
Gaochun China 31°20N 118°49E 229 B12
Gaohang China 31°20N 121°36E 138 B2
Gaohebu China 30°43N 116°49E 229 B11
Gaokeng China 27°40N 113°58E 229 D9
Gaolan Dao China 21°55N 113°10E 229 G9
Gaoligong Shan China 24°45N 98°45E 228 E2
Gaomi China 36°20N 119°42E 227 F10
Gaoping China 35°45N 112°55E 226 G7
Gaoqiao China 31°21N 121°34E 138 A2
Gaoshu = Kaoshu Taiwan 22°49N 120°36E 225 D2
Gaotang China 36°50N 116°15E 226 F9
Gaoua Burkina Faso 10°20N 3°8W 262 C4
Gaoual Guinea 11°45N 13°25W 262 C2
Gaoxiong = Kaohsiung Taiwan 22°35N 120°16E 225 D2
Gaoyang China 38°40N 115°45E 226 E8
Gaoyao China 23°3N 112°27E 229 F9
Gaoyou China 32°47N 119°26E 229 A12
Gaoyou Hu China 32°45N 119°20E 229 A12
Gaoyuan China 37°8N 117°58E 227 F9
Gaozhou China 21°58N 110°50E 229 G8
Gap France 44°33N 6°5E 175 D10
Gapan Phil. 15°19N 120°57E 232 D3
Gapat → India 24°30N 82°28E 243 G10
Gapuwiyak Australia 12°25S 135°43E 280 A2
Gar China 32°10N 79°58E 218 E4
Gara, L. Ireland 53°57N 8°26W 166 C3
Garāb Iran 33°27N 47°16E 213 F12
Garabogazköl Aylagy Turkmenistan 41°0N 53°30E 187 F9
Garacad Somalia 6°57N 49°24E 267 C6
Garachico Canary Is. 28°22N 16°46W 153 e1
Garachiné Panama 8°0N 78°12W 320 E4
Garafia Canary Is. 28°48N 17°57W 153 e1
Garagum Turkmenistan 39°30N 60°0E 247 B8
Garah Australia 29°5S 149°38E 281 D4
Garaina Papua N. G. 7°53S 147°8E 286 D4
Garajonay Canary Is. 28°7N 17°14W 153 e1
Garajonay △ Canary Is. 28°7N 17°14W 153 e1
Garamba △ Dem. Rep. of the Congo 4°10N 29°40E 268 B2
Garango Burkina Faso 11°48N 0°34W 263 C4
Garanhuns Brazil 8°50S 36°30W 332 C4
Garapan N. Marianas 15°12N 145°43E 302 e
Garautha India 25°34N 79°18E 243 G8
Garawa ۞ Australia 16°43S 136°51E 280 B2
Garawe Liberia 4°35N 8°0W 262 E3
Garba Harre = Garbahaarrey → Somalia 3°19N 42°13E 267 D5
Garba Tula Kenya 0°30N 38°32E 268 B4
Garbagnate Milanese Italy 45°34N 9°4E 128 A1
Garbagududu Ethiopia 6°12N 43°50E 267 C5
Garbahaarrey → Somalia 3°19N 42°13E 267 D5
Garbatella Italy 41°51N 12°30E 136 B2
Garberville U.S.A. 40°6N 123°48W 304 F2
Garbiyang India 30°8N 80°54E 243 D9
Garbsen Germany 52°26N 9°31E 178 C5
Garça Brazil 22°14S 49°37W 333 F2
Garças → Mato Grosso, Brazil 15°54S 52°16W 331 D7
Garças → Pernambuco, Brazil 8°43S 39°41W 332 C4
Garches France 48°50N 2°11E 134 A2
Garching Germany 48°14N 11°39E 131 A3
Garchitorena Phil. 13°52N 123°40E 232 E4
Garcia Hernandez Phil. 9°37N 124°18E 233 G5
Garcias Brazil 20°34S 52°13W 331 E7
Gard □ France 44°2N 4°10E 175 D8
Gard → France 43°51N 4°37E 175 E8
Garda, L. di Italy 45°40N 10°41E 198 C7
Gardabani Georgia 41°27N 45°5E 191 K7
Gardanne France 43°27N 5°27E 175 E9
Gårdby Sweden 56°36N 16°38E 163 H10
Garde L. Canada 62°50N 106°13W 297 A7
Gardelegen Germany 52°32N 11°24E 178 C7
Garden City El Qâhira, Egypt 30°2N 31°14E 117 A2
Garden City Ga., U.S.A. 32°6N 81°9W 316 C8
Garden City Kans., U.S.A. 37°58N 100°53W 308 G3
Garden City Mo., U.S.A. 38°34N 94°12W 310 F2
Garden City Tex., U.S.A. 31°52N 101°29W 314 F4
Garden District U.S.A. 29°56N 90°5W 131 B2
Garden Grove U.S.A. 33°47N 117°55W 307 M9
Garden Reach India 22°33N 88°15E 124 B1
Gardens of Stone △ Australia 33°14S 150°11E 283 B9
Garder Norway 59°45N 10°38E 133 B2
Gardēz Afghan. 33°37N 69°9E 242 C3
Garðabær Iceland 64°5N 21°55W 155 C5
Garðskagi Iceland 64°5N 22°43W 155 C4
Garður Iceland 66°4N 16°46W 155 A10
Gardiki Greece 38°50N 21°55E 204 C3
Gardiner Maine, U.S.A. 44°14N 69°47W 309 C19
Gardiner Mont., U.S.A. 45°2N 110°22W 304 D8
Gardiners I. U.S.A. 41°6N 72°6W 313 E12
Gardner Fla., U.S.A. 27°21N 81°48W 317 H8
Gardner Ill., U.S.A. 41°12N 88°17W 311 C8
Gardner Mass., U.S.A. 42°34N 71°59W 313 D13
Gardner Canal Canada 53°27N 128°8W 296 C3
Gardner Pinnacles U.S.A. 25°0N 167°55W 302 F10
Gardnerville U.S.A. 38°56N 119°45W 306 G7
Gardno, Jezioro Poland 54°40N 17°7E 184 D4
Gardo = Qardho Somalia 9°30N 49°6E 267 C6
Gardone Riviera Italy 45°37N 10°34E 198 C7
Gardone Val Trómpia Italy 45°41N 10°11E 198 C7
Gárdony Hungary 47°12N 18°39E 182 C3
Gare Tigre Fr. Guiana 4°58N 53°9W 329 C7
Gareloi I. U.S.A. 51°48N 178°48W 303 L3
Gares = Puente la Reina Spain 42°40N 1°49W 196 C3
Garešnica Croatia 45°36N 16°56E 199 C13
Garéssio Italy 44°12N 8°2E 198 D5
Garey U.S.A. 34°53N 120°19W 307 L6
Garfield N.J., U.S.A. 40°52N 74°7W 132 A1
Garfield Wash., U.S.A. 47°1N 117°9W 304 C5
Garfield Park U.S.A. 41°52N 87°42W 119 B2
Garforth U.K. 53°47N 1°24W 168 D6
Gargaliani Greece 37°4N 21°38E 204 D3
Gargan, Mt. France 45°37N 1°39E 174 C5
Gargano △ Italy 41°43N 15°52E 199 G12
Gargantua, C. Canada 47°36N 85°2W 309 B11
Gargareta Greece 37°57N 23°43E 112 B2
Gargett Australia 21°9S 148°46E 280 b
Gargouna Mali 15°56N 0°13E 263 B5
Gargždai Lithuania 55°43N 21°24E 184 C8
Garhchiroli India 20°10N 80°0E 244 D5
Garibaldi ⌓ Canada 49°50N 122°40W 296 D4
Garibong S. Korea 37°29N 126°54E 137 C1
Gariep, L. S. Africa 30°40S 25°40E 270 D4
Garies S. Africa 30°32S 17°59E 270 D2
Garig Gunak Barlu △ Australia 11°26S 131°58E 278 B5
Garigliano → Italy 41°13N 13°45E 200 A6
Garissa Kenya 0°25S 39°40E 268 C4
Garissa □ Kenya 0°20S 40°10E 268 C5
Garkida Nigeria 10°27N 12°36E 263 C7
Garko Nigeria 11°45N 8°35E 263 C6
Garland Tex., U.S.A. 32°54N 96°38W 120 A6
Garland Utah, U.S.A. 41°45N 112°10W 304 F7
Garlasco Italy 45°12N 8°55E 198 C5
Garliava Lithuania 54°49N 23°52E 184 D10
Garlin France 43°33N 0°16W 174 E3
Garmāb Semnān, Iran 35°25N 56°45E 247 C8
Garmāb Zanjān, Iran 35°50N 48°11E 213 E13
Garmisch-Partenkirchen Germany 47°30N 11°6E 179 H7
Garmo, Qullai = imeni Ismail Samani, Pik Tajikistan 39°0N 72°2E 217 E8
Garmsār Iran 35°20N 52°25E 247 C7
Garner U.S.A. 43°6N 93°36W 310 A3
Garnett U.S.A. 38°17N 95°14W 308 F6
Garnpung L. Australia 33°25S 143°10E 282 B5
Garo Hills India 25°30N 90°30E 241 C3
Garoe = Garoowe Somalia 8°25N 48°33E 267 C6
Garonne → France 45°2N 0°36W 174 C3
Garonne, Canal Latéral à la France 44°15N 0°18E 174 D4
Garoowe Somalia 8°25N 48°33E 267 C6
Garorimman S. Korea 36°54N 126°21E 224 D3
Garot India 24°19N 75°41E 242 G6
Garou, L. Mali 16°2N 2°45W 262 B4
Garoua Cameroon 9°19N 13°21E 263 D7
Garoua Boulaï Cameroon 5°53N 14°33E 264 A2
Garove I. Papua N. G. 4°42S 149°30E 286 C5
Garpenberg Sweden 60°19N 16°12E 162 D10
Garphyttan Sweden 59°18N 14°56E 162 E8
Garrauli India 25°5N 79°22E 243 G8
Garrel Germany 52°57N 8°1E 178 C4
Garreru Palau 7°19N 134°32E 288 c
Garrett U.S.A. 41°21N 85°8W 311 C11
Garrison Ky., U.S.A. 38°36N 83°10W 311 F13
Garrison Mont., U.S.A. 46°31N 112°49W 304 C7
Garrison N. Dak., U.S.A. 47°40N 101°25W 308 B3
Garrison Res. = Sakakawea, L. U.S.A. 47°30N 101°25W 308 B3
Garron Pt. U.K. 55°3N 5°59W 166 A6
Garrovillas de Alconétar Spain 39°40N 6°33W 195 F4
Garrucha Spain 37°11N 1°49W 197 H3
Garry → U.K. 56°44N 3°47W 167 E5
Garry, L. Canada 65°58N 100°18W 294 D11
Garrygala Turkmenistan 38°31N 56°29E 247 B8
Garsen Kenya 2°20S 40°5E 268 C5
Gärsnäs Sweden 55°32N 14°10E 163 J8
Garson L. Canada 56°19N 110°2W 297 B6
Garstang U.K. 53°55N 2°46W 168 D5
Gartempe → France 46°47N 0°49E 174 B4
Gartz Germany 53°13N 14°22E 178 B10
Garu Ghana 10°55N 0°11W 263 C4
Garu India 23°40N 84°14E 243 H11
Garub Namibia 26°37S 16°0E 270 C2
Garusuun Palau 7°21N 134°31E 288 c
Garut Indonesia 7°14S 107°53E 235 D3
Garvanza U.S.A. 34°6N 118°11W 126 B3
Garvão Portugal 37°42N 8°21W 195 H2
Garvie Mts. N.Z. 45°30S 168°50E 285 F3
Garwa = Garoua Cameroon 9°19N 13°21E 263 D7
Garwa India 24°11N 83°47E 243 G10
Garwolin Poland 51°55N 21°38E 185 G8
Gary U.S.A. 41°36N 87°20W 311 C9
Garz Germany 54°19N 13°20E 178 A9
Garzê China 31°38N 100°1E 228 B3
Garzón Colombia 2°10N 75°40W 328 C2
Gas City U.S.A. 40°29N 85°37W 311 D11
Gas-San Japan 38°32N 140°1E 220 E10
Gasa Bhutan 27°55N 89°40E 241 B2
Gasan Phil. 13°19N 121°51E 232 E3
Gasan Kuli = Esenguly Turkmenistan 37°37N 53°59E 216 E4
Gascogne France 43°45N 0°20E 174 E4
Gascogne, G. de Europe 44°0N 2°0W 174 E2
Gasconade U.S.A. 38°40N 91°34W 310 F5
Gasconade → U.S.A. 38°41N 91°33W 310 F5
Gascony = Gascogne France 43°45N 0°20E 174 E4
Gascoyne → Australia 24°52S 113°37E 279 D1
Gascoyne Junction Australia 25°2S 115°17E 279 E2
Gascueña Spain 40°18N 2°31W 196 E2
Gash, Wadi → Africa 16°48N 35°51E 257 D4
Gash Barka □ Eritrea 15°0N 37°0E 257 D4
Gash Setit ⌓ Eritrea 15°12N 36°58E 257 D4
Gåshaga Sweden 59°21N 18°13E 139 A3
Gashagar Nigeria 13°22N 12°47E 263 C7
Gashaka Nigeria 7°20N 11°29E 263 D7
Gashaka-Gumti △ Nigeria 7°23N 11°34E 263 D7
Gasherbrum Pakistan 35°40N 76°40E 243 B7
Gashua Nigeria 12°54N 11°0E 263 C7
Gasmata Papua N. G. 6°17S 150°20E 286 D6
Gaspar Grande Trin. & Tob. 10°40N 61°39W 323 t
Gaspar Str. = Gelasa, Selat Indonesia 2°50S 107°0E 235 C3
Gasparilla I. U.S.A. 26°46N 82°16W 317 J7
Gasparillo Trin. & Tob. 10°18N 61°26W 323 t
Gasparito Curaçao 12°8N 68°56W 322 g
Gaspé Canada 48°52N 64°30W 299 C7
Gaspé, C. de Canada 48°48N 64°7W 299 C7
Gaspé Pen. = Gaspésie, Pén. de la Canada 48°45N 65°40W 299 C6
Gaspésie, Pén. de la Canada 48°45N 65°40W 299 C6
Gaspésie ⌓ Canada 48°55N 66°10W 299 C6
Gassan Burkina Faso 12°49N 3°12W 262 C4
Gassen = Jasień Poland 51°46N 15°0E 185 G2
Gassol Nigeria 8°34N 10°25E 263 D7
Gasteiz = Vitoria-Gasteiz Spain 42°50N 2°41W 196 C2
Gaston U.S.A. 33°49N 81°5W 316 B8
Gastonia U.S.A. 35°16N 81°11W 315 D14
Gastouni Greece 37°51N 21°15E 204 D3
Gastouri Greece 39°34N 19°54E 206 B9
Gastre Argentina 42°20S 69°15W 336 B3
Gästrikland Sweden 60°45N 16°40E 162 D10
Gata, C. Cyprus 34°34N 33°2E 207 F9
Gata, C. de Spain 36°41N 2°13W 197 J2
Gata, Sierra de Spain 40°20N 6°45W 194 E4
Gataga → Canada 58°35N 126°59W 296 B3
Gătaia Romania 45°26N 21°30E 182 E6
Gatchina Russia 59°35N 30°9E 188 C6
Gatehouse of Fleet U.K. 54°53N 4°12W 167 G4
Gates U.S.A. 43°9N 77°42W 312 C7
Gates of the Arctic ⌓ U.S.A. 67°45N 153°15W 303 C9
Gateshead U.K. 54°57N 1°35W 168 C6
Gateshead I. Canada 70°36N 100°26W 294 C11
Gatesville U.S.A. 31°26N 97°45W 314 F6
Gateway ⌓ U.S.A. 40°38N 73°51W 132 C2
Gateway of India India 18°55N 72°50E 130 B2
Gateway Park U.S.A. 32°43N 96°42W 120 B2
Gaths Zimbabwe 20°2S 30°32E 269 G3
Gâtinais France 48°5N 2°40E 173 D9
Gâtine, Hauteurs de France 46°35N 0°45W 174 B3
Gatineau Canada 45°29N 75°39W 313 A9
Gatineau → Canada 45°27N 75°42W 298 C4
Gatineau △ Canada 45°40N 76°0W 298 C4
Gatow Germany 52°29N 13°11E 115 B1
Gattaran Phil. 18°4N 121°38E 232 B3
Gattinara Italy 45°37N 8°22E 198 C5
Gatton Australia 27°32S 152°17E 281 D5
Gatún, L. Panama 9°7N 79°56W 320 c
Gatún Dam Panama 9°16N 79°55W 320 c
Gatún Locks Panama 9°16N 79°55W 320 c
Gatwick, London ✕ (LGW) U.K. 51°10N 0°11W 169 F7
Gatyana S. Africa 32°16S 28°31E 271 D4
Gau Fiji 18°2S 179°18E 287 B2
Gaua Vanuatu 14°15S 167°30E 287 D5
Gaucín Spain 36°31N 5°19W 195 J5
Gauer L. Canada 57°0N 97°50W 297 B9
Gauhati = Guwahati India 26°10N 91°45E 241 B3
Gauja → Latvia 57°10N 24°16E 188 D3
Gaujas △ Latvia 57°10N 24°50E 161 H21
Gaula → Norway 63°21N 10°14E 164 A7
Gaupne Norway 61°25N 7°18E 164 C4
Gaurdak = Gowurdak Turkmenistan 37°50N 66°4E 217 E7
Gauri Phanta India 28°41N 80°36E 243 E9
Gauribidanur India 13°37N 77°32E 245 H3
Gaustatoppen Norway 59°48N 8°40E 164 E5
Gauteng □ S. Africa 26°0S 28°0E 271 C4
Gāv Koshī Iran 28°38N 57°12E 247 D8
Gavà Spain 41°18N 2°1W 114 B1
Gāvakān Iran 29°37N 53°10E 247 D7
Gavamar Spain 41°15N 2°1E 114 B1
Gavar Armenia 40°21N 45°7E 191 K7
Gavarnie France 42°44N 0°1W 174 F3
Gavāter Iran 25°10N 61°31E 247 E9
Gāvbandī Iran 27°12N 53°4E 247 E7
Gavdopoula Greece 34°56N 24°0E 207 F5
Gavdos Greece 34°50N 24°5E 207 F5
Gávea Brazil 22°58S 43°13W 135 B1
Gávea, Pedra da Brazil 22°59S 43°18W 135 B1
Gavi Italy 44°41N 8°49E 198 D5
Gavião Portugal 39°28N 7°56W 195 F3
Gaviota U.S.A. 34°29N 120°13W 307 L6
Gāvkhūnī, Bāţlāq-e Iran 32°6N 52°52E 247 C7
Gävle Sweden 60°40N 17°9E 162 D11
Gävleborg □ Sweden 61°30N 16°15E 162 C10
Gävlebukten Sweden 60°40N 17°20E 162 D11
Gavorrano Italy 42°55N 10°54E 198 F7
Gavray France 48°55N 1°20W 172 D5
Gavrilov Yam Russia 57°18N 39°49E 188 D10
Gavrio Greece 37°54N 24°44E 204 D6
Gawachab Namibia 27°4S 17°55E 270 C2
Gawai Myanmar 27°56N 97°30E 241 B6
Gawilgarh Hills India 21°15N 76°45E 244 D3
Gawler Australia 34°30S 138°42E 282 C3
Gawler Ranges Australia 32°30S 135°45E 282 B2
Gawu Nigeria 9°14N 6°52E 263 D6
Gaxun Nur China 42°22N 100°30E 218 C9
Gay Russia 51°27N 58°27E 186 D10
Gay Ga., U.S.A. 33°6N 84°35W 316 B5
Gaya India 24°47N 85°4E 243 G11
Gaya Niger 11°52N 3°28E 263 C5
Gaya Nigeria 11°57N 9°0E 263 C6
Gayasan △ S. Korea 35°45N 128°10E 224 E4
Gayéri Burkina Faso 12°39N 0°29E 263 C5
Gaylord U.S.A. 45°2N 84°41W 309 C11
Gayndah Australia 25°35S 151°32E 281 D5
Gaysin = Haysyn Ukraine 48°57N 29°25E 183 B14
Gayvoron = Hayvoron Ukraine 48°22N 29°52E 183 B14
Gaza Gaza Strip 31°30N 34°28E 251 G5
Gaza □ Mozam. 23°10S 32°45E 271 B5
Gaza Strip □ Asia 31°29N 34°25E 251 G5
Gazanjyk = Bereket Turkmenistan 39°16N 55°32E 247 B7
Gazaoua Niger 13°32N 7°55E 263 C6
Gāzbor Iran 28°5N 58°51E 247 D8
Gazdagrét Hungary 47°29N 19°0E 117 B1
Gazelle Pen. Papua N. G. 4°40S 152°0E 286 C7
Gazi Dem. Rep. of the Congo 1°3N 24°30E 264 B4
Gaziantep Turkey 37°6N 37°23E 250 A8
Gaziantep □ Turkey 37°0N 37°0E 250 B8
Gazimağusa = Famagusta Cyprus 35°8N 33°55E 207 E9
Gaziosmanpaşa Turkey 41°5N 28°50E 122 B1
Gazipaşa Turkey 36°16N 32°18E 250 B3
Gazipur Bangla. 23°48N 90°39E 241 D3
Gazli Uzbekistan 40°8N 63°27E 216 D6
Gazojak Turkmenistan 41°11N 61°24E 216 D6
Gbadolite Dem. Rep. of the Congo 4°17N 21°1E 264 B4
Gbarnga Liberia 7°19N 9°13W 262 D3
Gboko Nigeria 7°17N 9°4E 263 D6
Gcoverega Botswana 19°8S 24°18E 270 A3
Gcuwa S. Africa 32°20S 28°11E 271 D4
Gdańsk Poland 54°22N 18°40E 184 D5
Gdańsk ✕ (GDN) Poland 54°22N 18°30E 184 D5
Gdansk B. = Gdańska, Zatoka Poland 54°30N 19°20E 184 D6
Gdańska, Zatoka Poland 54°30N 19°20E 184 D6
Gdingen = Gdynia Poland 54°35N 18°33E 184 D5
Gdov Russia 58°48N 27°55E 188 C4
Gdynia Poland 54°35N 18°33E 184 D5
Geba → Guinea-Biss. 11°46N 15°36W 262 C1
Gebe Indonesia 0°5N 129°25E 231 D7
Gebeciler Turkey 38°46N 30°46E 205 C12
Gebeit Mine Sudan 21°3N 36°29E 256 C4
Gebel Abyad Sudan 19°0N 28°0E 256 D2
Gebel el Ahmar Egypt 30°2N 31°21E 117 A3
Gebel el Muqattam Egypt 30°1N 31°17E 117 A2
Gebel el Tura Egypt 29°56N 31°15E 117 B2
Gebel Iweibid Egypt 30°8N 32°13E 256 H8
Gebiley Somalia 9°42N 43°37E 267 C5
Gebze Turkey 40°47N 29°25E 203 F13
Gecha Ethiopia 7°30N 35°18E 257 F4
Geçitkale = Lefkoniko Cyprus 35°18N 33°44E 207 E9
Gedaref Sudan 14°2N 35°28E 257 E4
Gedaref □ Sudan 14°0N 35°0E 257 E4
Gede, Tanjung Indonesia 6°46S 105°12E 234 D3
Gediz Turkey 39°1N 29°24E 205 B11
Gediz → Turkey 38°35N 26°48E 205 C8
Gedo Ethiopia 9°2N 37°25E 257 F4
Gedo □ Somalia 2°15N 42°10E 267 D5
Gèdre France 42°47N 0°2E 174 F4
Gedser Denmark 54°35N 11°55E 163 K5
Gedung, Pulau Malaysia 5°17N 100°23E 237 c
Geegully Cr. → Australia 18°32S 123°41E 278 C3
Geel Belgium 51°10N 4°59E 170 C4
Geelong Australia 38°10S 144°22E 282 E6
Geelvink B. = Cenderawasih, Teluk Indonesia 3°0S 135°20E 231 E9
Geelvink Chan. Australia 28°30S 114°0E 279 E1
Geesthacht Germany 53°26N 10°22E 178 B6
Geidam Nigeria 12°57N 11°57E 263 C7
Geikie → Canada 57°45N 103°52W 297 B8
Geikie Gorge △ Australia 18°3S 125°41E 278 C4
Geilenkirchen Germany 50°57N 6°8E 178 E2
Geili Sudan 16°1N 32°37E 257 D3
Geilo Norway 60°32N 8°14E 164 D5
Geirangerfjorden Norway 62°7N 7°10E 164 B4
Geiselgasteig Germany 48°3N 11°33E 131 B2
Geisingen Germany 47°54N 8°38E 179 H4
Geislingen Germany 48°37N 9°50E 179 G5
Geistown U.S.A. 40°18N 78°52W 312 F6
Geita Tanzania 2°48S 32°12E 268 C3
Geita □ Tanzania 2°50S 32°10E 268 C3
Geitastrand Norway 63°22N 9°56E 164 A6
Geithus Norway 59°57N 9°59E 164 E6
Gejiu China 23°20N 103°10E 228 F4
Gel → South Sudan 7°5N 29°10E 257 F2
Gel, Meydān-e Iran 29°4N 54°50E 247 D7
Gel River South Sudan 7°5N 29°10E 257 F2
Gela Italy 37°4N 14°15E 201 E7
Gela, G. di Italy 37°0N 14°20E 201 F7
Geladi Ethiopia 6°59N 46°30E 267 C6
Gelahun Liberia 7°55N 10°28W 262 D2
Gelam Indonesia 2°54S 110°11E 235 C4
Gelang Patah Malaysia 1°27N 103°35E 237 d
Gelasa, Selat Indonesia 2°50S 107°0E 235 C3
Gelderland □ Neths. 52°5N 6°10E 170 B6
Geldern Germany 51°31N 6°20E 178 D2
Geldrop Neths. 51°25N 5°32E 170 C5
Geleen Neths. 50°57N 5°49E 170 D5
Gelehun S. Leone 8°20N 11°40W 262 D2
Gelembe Turkey 39°10N 27°50E 205 B9
Gelemso Ethiopia 8°49N 40°31E 257 F5
Gelendost Turkey 38°7N 31°1E 212 C4
Gelendzhik Russia 44°33N 38°10E 189 K10
Gelib = Jilib Somalia 0°29N 42°46E 267 D5
Gelibolu Turkey 40°28N 26°43E 203 F10
Gelibolu Yarımadası Turkey 40°20N 26°30E 203 F10
Gelidonya Burnu Turkey 36°12N 30°24E 212 D4

Gellinsoor Somalia 6°28N 46°39E 267 C6
Gelnhausen Germany 50°11N 9°11E 179 E5
Gelnica Slovakia 48°51N 20°55E 181 C13
Gelora Bung Karno Stadium Jakarta, Indonesia 6°13S 106°47E 122 B1
Gelsenkirchen Germany 51°32N 7°6E 178 D3
Gelting Germany 54°45N 9°53E 178 A5
Gelugur Malaysia 5°22N 100°18E 237 c
Gemas Malaysia 2°37N 102°36E 237 L4
Gembloux Belgium 50°34N 4°43E 170 D4
Gembu Nigeria 6°42N 11°10E 263 D7
Gemena Dem. Rep. of the Congo 3°13N 19°48E 264 B3
Gemerek Turkey 39°15N 36°10E 212 C7
Gemikonagı = Karavostasi Cyprus 35°8N 32°50E 207 E8
Gemla Sweden 56°52N 14°39E 163 H8
Gemlik Turkey 40°26N 29°9E 203 F13
Gemlik Körfezi Turkey 40°25N 28°55E 203 F12
Gemona del Friuli Italy 46°16N 13°9E 199 B10
Gemsa Egypt 27°39N 33°35E 256 B3
Gemsbok △ Botswana 25°5S 21°1E 270 C3
Gemünden Germany 50°3N 9°42E 179 E5
Genadi Greece 36°2N 27°56E 206 E11
Genale ➔ Ethiopia 6°2N 39°1E 257 F4
Genç Turkey 38°44N 40°34E 213 C9
Gençay France 46°23N 0°23E 174 B4
General Acha Argentina 37°20S 64°38W 334 D3
General Alvear B. Aires, Argentina 36°0S 60°0W 334 D4
General Alvear Mendoza, Argentina 35°0S 67°40W 334 D2
General Artigas Paraguay 26°52S 56°16W 334 B4
General Belgrano Argentina 36°35S 58°47W 334 D4
General Bernardo O'Higgins Antarctica 63°0S 58°3W 151 C18
General Cabrera Argentina 32°53S 63°52W 334 C3
General Carrera, L. S. Amer. 46°35S 72°0W 336 C2
General Cepeda Mexico 25°21N 101°22W 318 B4
General Conesa Argentina 40°6S 64°25W 336 B4
General Eugenio A. Garay Paraguay 20°31S 62°8W 331 E5
General Germán Busch = Villa Abecia Bolivia 21°0S 68°18W 334 A2
General Guido Argentina 36°40S 57°50W 334 D4
General Juan Madariaga Argentina 37°0S 57°0W 334 D4
General La Madrid Argentina 37°17S 61°20W 334 D3
General Lorenzo Vintter Argentina 40°45S 64°26W 336 B4
General Luna Phil. 13°41N 122°10E 232 E4
General MacArthur Phil. 11°18N 125°28E 233 F5
General Martin Miguel de Güemes Argentina 24°50S 65°0W 334 A3
General Pico Argentina 35°45S 63°50W 334 D3
General Pinedo Argentina 27°15S 61°20W 334 B3
General Pinto Argentina 34°45S 61°50W 334 C3
General Roca Argentina 39°2S 67°35W 336 A3
General Sampaio Brazil 4°2S 39°29W 332 B4
General San Martín Argentina 34°35S 58°32W 117 B1
General Santos Phil. 6°5N 125°14E 233 H5
General Tinio Phil. 15°39N 121°10E 232 D3
General Toshevo Bulgaria 43°42N 28°6E 203 C12
General Treviño Mexico 26°14N 99°29W 319 B5
General Trías Mexico 28°21N 106°22W 318 B3
General Uriburu = Zárate Argentina 34°7S 59°0W 334 C4
General Viamonte Argentina 35°1S 61°3W 334 D3
General Villegas Argentina 35°5S 63°0W 334 D3
General Vintter, L. Argentina 43°55S 71°40W 336 B2
Generoso Ponce = Jaci-Paraná Brazil 9°15S 64°23W 331 B5
Genesee Idaho, U.S.A. 46°33N 116°56W 304 C5
Genesee Pa., U.S.A. 41°59N 77°54W 312 E7
Genesee ➔ U.S.A. 43°16N 77°36W 312 C7
Geneseo Ill., U.S.A. 41°27N 90°9W 310 C6
Geneseo N.Y., U.S.A. 42°48N 77°49W 312 D7
Geneva = Genève Switz. 46°12N 6°9E 179 J2
Geneva Ala., U.S.A. 31°2N 85°52W 316 D4
Geneva Ga., U.S.A. 32°35N 84°33W 316 C5
Geneva Ill., U.S.A. 41°53N 88°18W 311 C8
Geneva Ind., U.S.A. 40°36N 84°58W 311 D12
Geneva N.Y., U.S.A. 42°52N 76°59W 312 D8
Geneva Nebr., U.S.A. 40°32N 97°36W 308 E5
Geneva Ohio, U.S.A. 41°48N 80°57W 312 E4
Geneva, L. = Léman, L. Europe 46°26N 6°30E 173 F13
Geneva, L. U.S.A. 42°38N 88°30W 311 B8
Genève Switz. 46°12N 6°9E 179 J2
Geng Afghan. 31°22N 61°28E 240 C1
Gengenbach Germany 48°24N 8°1E 179 G4
Gengma China 23°32N 99°20E 228 F2
Genhe China 50°47N 121°31E 219 A13
Genichesk = Henichesk Ukraine 46°12N 34°50E 189 J8
Genil ➔ Spain 37°42N 5°19W 195 H5
Génipa, B. de Martinique 14°33N 61°0W 322 j
Genisea Greece 41°1N 24°57E 203 E8
Genk Belgium 50°58N 5°32E 170 D5
Genkai-Nada Japan 34°0N 130°0E 222 D2
Genlis France 47°11N 5°12E 173 E12
Gennargentu, Mti. del Italy 40°1N 9°19E 200 B2
Gennes France 47°20N 0°17W 172 E6
Gennevilliers France 48°56N 2°17E 134 A2
Genoa = Génova Italy 44°25N 8°57E 198 D5
Genoa Vic., Australia 37°29S 149°35E 283 D8
Genoa Ill., U.S.A. 42°6N 88°42W 311 B8
Genoa N.Y., U.S.A. 42°40N 76°32W 313 D8
Genoa Nebr., U.S.A. 41°27N 97°44W 308 E5
Genoa Nev., U.S.A. 39°2N 119°50W 306 F7
Genoa ➔ Argentina 44°55S 70°5W 336 B2
Genoa City U.S.A. 42°30N 88°20W 311 B8
Génova Italy 44°25N 8°57E 198 D5
Génova ✈ (GOA) Italy 44°25N 8°56E 198 D5
Génova, G. di Italy 44°0N 9°0E 198 E6
Genovesa, I. Ecuador 0°20N 89°58W 330 a
Genriyetty, Ostrov Russia 77°6N 156°30E 215 B16
Gent Belgium 51°2N 3°42E 170 C3
Genteng Jawa Barat, Indonesia 7°22S 106°24E 234 D3
Genteng Jawa Timur, Indonesia 8°22S 114°9E 231 J17
Genthin Germany 52°25N 12°9E 178 C8
Gentilly Val-de-Marne, France 48°48N 2°21E 134 B3
Gentilly La., U.S.A. 30°0N 90°2W 131 A2
Gentio do Ouro Brazil 11°25S 42°30W 332 D3
Gentofte Denmark 55°44N 12°32E 118 A3
Gentryville U.S.A. 38°6N 87°2W 311 F9
Genval Belgium 50°43N 4°29E 116 B2
Genyem Indonesia 2°46S 140°12E 231 E10
Genzano di Lucània Italy 40°51N 16°2E 201 B9
Genzano di Roma Italy 41°42N 12°41E 199 G9
Geoagiu Romania 45°55N 23°12E 183 E8
Geochang S. Korea 35°41N 127°55E 224 E3
Geogeumdo S. Korea 34°27N 127°10E 224 E3
Geographe B. Australia 33°30S 115°15E 279 F2
Geographe Chan. Australia 24°30S 113°0E 279 D1
Geographical Society Ø Greenland 72°57N 23°15W 154 C8
Geoje S. Korea 34°51N 128°35E 224 E4
Geojedo S. Korea 34°51N 128°38E 224 E4
Geokchay = Göyçay Azerbaijan 40°42N 47°43E 191 K8
Georga, Zemlya Russia 80°30N 49°0E 214 A5
George S. Africa 33°58S 22°29E 270 D3
George ➔ Canada 58°49N 66°10W 299 A6
George, L. N.S.W., Australia 35°10S 149°25E 283 C8
George, L. S. Austral., Australia 37°25S 140°0E 282 D4
George, L. W. Austral., Australia 22°45S 123°40E 278 D3
George, L. Uganda 0°5N 30°10E 268 B3
George, L. Fla., U.S.A. 29°17N 81°36W 317 F8
George, L. N.Y., U.S.A. 43°37N 73°33W 313 C11
George Bush Intercontinental, Houston ✈ (IAH) U.S.A. 29°59N 95°20W 314 G7
George Gill Ra. Australia 24°22S 131°45E 278 D5
George I. Hong Kong, China 22°13N 114°7E 122 B2
George I. St. Helena 15°58S 5°38W 153 h
George Pt. Australia 20°6S 148°36E 280 b
George River = Kangiqsualujjuaq Canada 58°30N 65°59W 295 F18
George Rogers Clark Nat. Memorial ⌂ U.S.A. 38°41N 87°32W 311 F9
George Sound N.Z. 44°52S 167°25E 285 E2
George Town Tas., Australia 41°6S 146°49E 281 G4
George Town Cayman Is. 19°20N 81°24W 320 C3
George Town Malaysia 5°25N 100°20E 237 c
George Town The Bahamas 23°33N 75°47W 320 B4
George V Land Antarctica 69°0S 148°0E 151 C10
George VI Sound Antarctica 71°0S 68°0W 151 D17
George West U.S.A. 28°20N 98°7W 314 G5
Georges River Bridge Australia 34°0S 151°6E 139 C1
Georgetown = Janjanbureh Gambia 13°30N 14°47W 262 C2
Georgetown Ascension I. 7°56S 14°25W 153 g
Georgetown Queens., Australia 18°17S 143°33E 280 B3
Georgetown Ont., Canada 43°40N 79°56W 312 C5
Georgetown P.E.I., Canada 46°13N 62°24W 299 C7
Georgetown Guyana 6°50N 58°12W 329 B6
Georgetown St. Vincent 13°16N 61°7W 323 n
Georgetown Calif., U.S.A. 38°54N 120°50W 306 G6
Georgetown Colo., U.S.A. 39°42N 105°42W 304 G11
Georgetown D.C., U.S.A. 38°54N 77°3W 143 B2
Georgetown Fla., U.S.A. 29°23N 81°38W 317 F8
Georgetown Ga., U.S.A. 31°53N 85°6W 316 D4
Georgetown Ill., U.S.A. 39°59N 87°38W 311 E9
Georgetown Ky., U.S.A. 38°13N 84°33W 311 F12
Georgetown N.Y., U.S.A. 42°46N 75°44W 313 D9
Georgetown Ohio, U.S.A. 38°52N 83°54W 311 F13
Georgetown S.C., U.S.A. 33°23N 79°17W 315 E15
Georgetown Tex., U.S.A. 30°38N 97°41W 314 F6
Georgia ☐ U.S.A. 32°50N 83°15W 316 C6
Georgia ■ Asia 42°0N 43°0E 191 J6
Georgia, Str. of N. Amer. 49°25N 124°0W 306 A3
Georgia Aquarium Atlanta, U.S.A. 33°46N 84°23W 113 B2
Georgia Basin S. Ocean 50°45S 35°30W 151 B1
Georgia Dome Atlanta, U.S.A. 33°45N 84°23W 113 B2
Georgian B. Canada 45°15N 81°0W 312 A4
Georgian Bay Islands △ Canada 44°53N 79°52W 312 B5
Georgievka Kazakhstan 49°19N 84°34E 217 C10
Georgina ➔ Australia 23°30S 139°47E 280 C2
Georgina I. Canada 44°22N 79°17W 312 B5
Georgioupoli Greece 35°20N 24°15E 207 E5
Georgiu-Dezh = Liski Russia 51°3N 39°30E 189 G10
Georgiyevsk Russia 44°12N 43°28E 191 H6
Georgsmarienhütte Germany 52°13N 8°3E 178 C4
Gera Germany 50°53N 12°4E 178 E8
Geraardsbergen Belgium 50°45N 3°53E 170 D3
Geraki Greece 37°0N 22°42E 204 D4
Geraki, Akra Greece 37°42N 20°59E 207 D2
Geral, Serra Bahia, Brazil 14°0S 41°0W 333 D3
Geral, Serra Goiás, Brazil 11°15S 46°30W 332 D2
Geral, Serra Sta. Catarina, Brazil 26°25S 50°0W 335 B6
Geral de Goiás, Serra Brazil 12°0S 46°0W 333 D2
Geral do Paraná, Serra Brazil 15°0S 47°30W 333 E2
Gerald U.S.A. 38°24N 91°20W 310 F5
Geraldine N.Z. 44°5S 171°15E 285 E6
Geraldine Mont., U.S.A. 47°36N 110°16W 304 C8
Geraldton = Innisfail Australia 17°33S 146°5E 280 B4
Geraldton W. Austral., Australia 28°48S 114°32E 279 E1
Geraldton Ont., Canada 49°44N 87°10W 298 C2
Geranium Australia 35°23S 140°11E 282 C4
Gérardmer France 48°3N 6°50E 173 D13
Gerasdorf bei Wien Austria 48°17N 16°28E 142 A2
Gerberau Germany 48°12N 11°27E 131 A1
Gercüş Turkey 37°34N 41°23E 213 D9
Gerdine, Mt. U.S.A. 61°35N 152°27W 303 F9
Gerede Turkey 40°45N 32°10E 212 B5
Gerês, Sierra do Portugal 41°48N 8°0W 194 D3
Gereshk Afghan. 31°47N 64°35E 240 C2
Geretsried Germany 47°51N 11°28E 179 H7
Gérgal Spain 37°7N 2°31W 197 H2
Gerik Malaysia 5°50N 101°15E 237 K3
Gering U.S.A. 41°50N 103°40W 308 E2
Geriş Turkey 36°57N 31°43E 250 B2
Gerlach U.S.A. 40°39N 119°21W 304 F4
Gerlachovský štít Slovakia 49°11N 20°7E 181 B13
Gerli Argentina 34°41S 58°22W 117 C2
Gerlogubi Ethiopia 6°53N 45°3E 267 C6
German Bight = Deutsche Bucht Germany 54°15N 8°0E 178 A4
German East Africa = Tanzania ■ Africa 6°0S 34°0E 268 D3
German Planina N. Macedonia 42°20N 22°0E 202 D6
German South West Africa = Namibia ■ Africa 22°0S 18°9E 270 B2
Germania Land Greenland 77°5N 19°30W 154 B9
Germansen Landing Canada 55°43N 124°40W 296 B4
Germantown Ohio, U.S.A. 39°38N 84°22W 311 E12
Germantown Tenn., U.S.A. 35°5N 89°49W 315 D10
Germantown Wis., U.S.A. 43°14N 88°6W 311 A8
Germany ■ Europe 51°0N 10°0E 178 E6
Germencik Turkey 37°52N 27°37E 205 D9
Germering Germany 48°8N 11°22E 179 G7
Germersheim Germany 49°12N 8°22E 179 F4
Germī Iran 39°1N 48°3E 213 C13
Germiston S. Africa 26°13S 28°10E 123 B2
Gern Germany 48°10N 11°32E 131 B2
Gernene Algeria 21°40N 2°24E 261 D5
Gernika-Lumo Spain 43°19N 2°40W 196 B2
Gernsheim Germany 49°45N 8°30E 179 F4
Gero Japan 35°48N 137°14E 223 B9
Gerogery Australia 35°50S 147°1E 283 C7
Gerokgak Indonesia 8°11S 114°27E 231 J17
Gerolzhofen Germany 49°54N 10°21E 179 F6
Gerona = Girona Spain 41°58N 2°46E 196 D7
Gerona Phil. 15°36N 120°36E 232 D3
Geropotamos ➔ Greece 35°3N 24°50E 207 E5
Gerrard Canada 50°30N 117°17W 296 C5
Gerringong Australia 34°46S 150°47E 283 C9
Gers ☐ France 43°35N 0°30E 174 E4
Gers ➔ France 44°9N 0°39E 174 D4
Gersfeld Germany 50°27N 9°56E 178 E5
Gersoppa Falls India 14°12N 74°46E 245 G2
Gersthofen Germany 48°25N 10°53E 179 G6
Gertak Sanggul Malaysia 5°17N 100°12E 237 c
Gertak Sanggul, Tanjung Malaysia 5°16N 100°11E 237 c
Gerung Indonesia 8°43S 116°7E 231 K19
Géryville = El Bayadh Algeria 33°40N 1°1E 261 B5
Gerzat France 45°48N 3°8E 174 C7
Gerze Turkey 41°48N 35°12E 212 B6
GES-2 Moscow, Russia 129 c2
Geseke Germany 51°38N 8°31E 178 D4
Geser Indonesia 3°50S 130°54E 231 E8
Gesira △ Somalia 1°58N 44°59E 267 D6
Gesso ➔ Italy 44°24N 7°33E 198 D4
Gestro, Wabi ➔ Ethiopia 4°12N 42°2E 257 G5
Gesuit, Ex Convento dei Venice, Italy 142 a3
Getafe Spain 40°18N 3°43W 127 C1
Getinge Sweden 56°49N 12°44E 163 H6
Getty Center, The U.S.A. 34°4N 118°29W 126 B2
Gettysburg Pa., U.S.A. 39°50N 77°14W 309 F15
Gettysburg S. Dak., U.S.A. 45°1N 99°57W 308 C4
Getxo = Algorta Spain 43°21N 2°59W 196 B2
Getz Ice Shelf Antarctica 75°0S 130°0W 151 D14
Geumodo S. Korea 34°31N 127°45E 224 E3
Geumpang Indonesia 4°52N 96°6E 234 B1
Geunjeong S. Korea 37°28N 126°54E 137 C1
Geureudong, Gunung Indonesia 4°13N 96°42E 234 B1
Geurie Australia 32°22S 148°50E 283 B8
Geva Binyamin West Bank 31°51N 35°17E 123 A2
Gevaş Turkey 38°15N 43°6E 213 C10
Gévaudan France 44°40N 3°40E 174 D7
Gevgelija N. Macedonia 41°9N 22°30E 202 E6
Gévora ➔ Spain 38°53N 6°57W 195 G4
Gevrai India 19°16N 75°45E 244 E2
Gewani Ethiopia 10°12N 40°40E 257 E5
Gex France 46°21N 6°3E 173 F13
Geyikli Turkey 39°48N 26°12E 205 B8
Geylang Serai Singapore 1°19N 103°53E 138 B3
Geyser U.S.A. 47°16N 110°30W 304 C8
Geyserville U.S.A. 38°42N 122°54W 306 G4
Geysir Iceland 64°19N 20°18W 155 C6
Geyve Turkey 40°30N 30°18E 212 B4
Gezhouba Dam China 30°40N 111°20E 229 B8
Ghâbat el Arab = Wang Kai South Sudan 9°3N 29°23E 257 F2
Ghabeish Sudan 12°9N 27°21E 257 E2
Ghadāf, W. al ➔ Iraq 32°56N 43°30E 213 F10
Ghadāmis Libya 30°11N 9°29E 258 B1
Ghaddūwah Libya 26°26N 14°19E 258 C2
Ghaggar ➔ India 29°30N 74°53E 242 E6
Ghaghara ➔ India 25°45N 84°40E 243 G11
Ghaghat ➔ Bangla. 25°19N 89°38E 241 C2
Ghaghe Solomon Is. 7°24S 158°15E 287 L10
Ghagra India 23°17N 84°33E 243 H11
Ghajn Tuffieha Bay Malta 35°56N 14°21E 206 F7
Ghajnsielem Malta 36°2N 14°17E 206 E7
Ghalla, Wadi el ➔ Sudan 10°25N 27°32E 257 E2
Ghallamane Mauritania 23°15N 10°0W 260 D3
Ghallamane, Sebkhet Mauritania 23°41N 9°50W 260 D3
Ghamid az Zenad Si. Arabia 19°35N 41°24E 248 C3
Ghana ■ W. Afr. 8°0N 1°0W 263 D4
Ghanpokhara Nepal 28°17N 84°14E 243 E11
Ghansor India 22°39N 80°1E 243 H9
Ghanzi Botswana 21°50S 21°34E 270 B3
Ghanzi ☐ Botswana 22°30S 22°30E 270 B3
Gharapuri = Elephanta I. India 18°57N 72°56E 130 B2
Gharb = Shahrak-e Qods Iran 35°47N 51°22E 141 A2
Gharb Malta 36°4N 14°13E 206 E6
Gharb Bahr el Ghazâl = Western Bahr el Ghazal ☐ South Sudan 7°30N 25°30E 257 F2
Gharb Dârfûr ☐ Sudan 13°0N 23°0E 259 E4
Gharb el Istiwa'iya = Western Equatoria ☐ South Sudan 5°0N 30°0E 257 G3
Gharb Kordofân ☐ Sudan 12°0N 28°0E 257 E2
Gharbîya, Es Sahrâ el Egypt 27°40N 26°30E 256 B2
Ghardaïa Algeria 32°20N 3°37E 261 B5
Ghardaïa ☐ Algeria 32°0N 3°40E 261 B5
Ghârib, G. Egypt 28°6N 32°54E 256 B3
Gharig Sudan 10°47N 27°33E 257 E2
Gharm Tajikistan 39°0N 70°20E 214 F8
Gharm, W. ➔ Oman 19°57N 57°38E 249 C7
Gharyān Libya 32°10N 13°0E 258 B2
Ghāt Libya 24°59N 10°11E 258 D2
Ghāt ☐ Libya 25°35N 10°15E 258 C2
Ghatal India 22°40N 87°46E 243 H12
Ghatampur India 26°8N 80°13E 243 F9
Ghatgaon India 21°24N 85°53E 244 D7
Ghatkopar India 19°4N 72°54E 130 A2
Ghatprabha ➔ India 16°15N 75°20E 245 F2
Ghats, Eastern India 14°0N 78°50E 245 H4
Ghats, Western India 14°0N 75°0E 245 H2
Ghatsila India 22°36N 86°29E 243 H12
Ghaṭṭī Si. Arabia 31°16N 37°31E 246 D3
Ghawdex = Gozo Malta 36°3N 14°15E 206 E7
Ghayl Si. Arabia 21°40N 46°20E 248 B4
Ghayl Bā Wazīr Yemen 14°46N 49°22E 249 D5
Ghazal, Bahr el ➔ Chad 13°0N 15°47E 259 F3
Ghazal, Bahr el ➔ South Sudan 9°31N 30°25E 257 F3
Ghazaouet Algeria 35°8N 1°50W 261 A4
Ghaziabad India 28°42N 77°26E 242 E7
Ghazipur Delhi, India 28°37N 77°19E 120 B2
Ghazipur Ut. P., India 25°38N 83°35E 243 G10
Ghaznī Afghan. 33°30N 68°28E 242 C3
Ghaznī ☐ Afghan. 32°10N 68°20E 240 B3
Ghedi Italy 45°24N 10°16E 198 C7
Ghelari Romania 45°38N 22°45E 182 E7
Ghent = Gent Belgium 51°2N 3°42E 170 C3
Gheorghe Gheorghiu-Dej = Oneşti Romania 46°17N 26°47E 183 D11
Gheorgheni Romania 46°43N 25°41E 183 D10
Gherla Romania 47°2N 23°57E 183 C8
Ghidigeni Romania 46°3N 27°30E 183 D12
Ghilarza Italy 40°7N 8°50E 200 B1
Ghimeş-Făget Romania 46°35N 26°2E 183 D11
Ghīnah, Wādī al ➔ Si. Arabia 30°27N 38°14E 246 D3
Ghirān, W. ➔ Si. Arabia 20°52N 47°10E 248 B4
Ghirardelli Square San Francisco, U.S.A. 136 a1
Ghisonaccia France 42°1N 9°26E 175 F13
Ghisoni France 42°7N 9°12E 175 F13
Ghizar ➔ Pakistan 36°15N 73°43E 243 A5
Ghizri Pakistan 24°49N 67°2E 123 B2
Ghizri Cr. ➔ Pakistan 24°47N 67°5E 123 B2
Ghod ➔ India 18°30N 74°35E 244 E2
Ghogha India 21°40N 72°20E 244 D1
Ghonda India 28°41N 77°16E 120 A2
Ghot Ogrein Egypt 31°10N 25°20E 256 A2
Ghotaru India 27°20N 70°1E 242 F4
Ghotki Pakistan 28°5N 69°21E 242 E3
Ghowr ☐ Afghan. 34°0N 64°20E 240 B2
Ghubbet el Bûs Egypt 29°35N 32°21E 251 J3
Ghughri India 22°39N 80°41E 243 H9
Ghugus India 19°58N 79°12E 244 E4
Ghulam Mohammad Barrage Pakistan 25°30N 68°20E 242 G3
Ghurayrah Si. Arabia 18°37N 42°41E 248 C3
Ghūriān Afghan. 34°17N 61°25E 240 B1
Ghusuri India 22°37N 88°21E 124 B2
Ghuzzayil, Sabkhat Libya 29°30N 19°30E 258 C3
Gia Dinh Vietnam 10°49N 106°42E 237 G6
Gia Lai = Plei Ku Vietnam 13°57N 108°0E 236 F7
Gia Nghia Vietnam 11°58N 107°42E 237 G6
Gia Ngoc Vietnam 14°50N 108°58E 236 E7
Gia Vuc Vietnam 14°42N 108°34E 236 E7
Giali Greece 36°41N 27°11E 205 E9
Gialtra Greece 38°51N 22°59E 204 C4
Giamama = Jamaame Somalia 0°4N 42°44E 267 D5
Gian Phil. 5°49N 125°12E 233 J5
Gianicolense Italy 41°53N 12°28E 136 B1
Gianicolense, Parco Italy 136 c1
Gianitsa Greece 40°46N 22°24E 202 F6
Giannutri Italy 42°15N 11°6E 198 F8
Giant Forest U.S.A. 36°36N 118°43W 306 J8
Giant Mts. = Krkonoše Czechia 50°50N 15°35E 180 A8
Giant Panda △ China 32°0N 104°0E 228 A5
Giant Sequoia ⌂ U.S.A. 36°10N 118°35W 306 K8
Giant Wheel = Riesenrad Austria 48°14N 16°23E 142 A2
Giant's Causeway U.K. 55°16N 6°29W 166 A5
Giant's Tank Sri Lanka 8°51N 80°2E 245 K5
Gianyar Indonesia 8°32S 115°20E 231 K18
Giarabub = Al Jaghbūb Libya 29°42N 24°38E 258 C4
Giaros Greece 37°32N 24°40E 204 D6
Giarre Italy 37°43N 15°11E 201 E8
Giaveno Italy 45°2N 7°21E 198 C4
Gibara Cuba 21°9N 76°11W 320 B4
Gibbon U.S.A. 40°45N 98°51W 308 E4
Gibe ➔ Ethiopia 7°20N 37°36E 257 F4
Gibe I Ethiopia 8°7N 37°0E 257 F4
Gibe II Ethiopia 8°0N 37°30E 257 F4
Gibe III Ethiopia 7°0N 37°30E 257 F4
Gibellina Nuova Italy 37°47N 12°58E 200 E5
Gibeon Namibia 25°9S 17°43E 270 C2
Gibraleón Spain 37°23N 6°58W 195 H4
Gibraltar ☑ Europe 36°7N 5°22W 195 J5
Gibraltar, Str. of Medit. S. 35°55N 5°40W 195 K5
Gibraltar Pt. Canada 43°36N 79°23W 141 B2
Gibraltar Range △ Australia 29°31S 152°19E 281 D5
Gibson U.S.A. 33°14N 82°36W 316 B7
Gibson City U.S.A. 40°28N 88°22W 311 D8
Gibson Desert Australia 24°0S 126°0E 278 D4
Gibsonburg U.S.A. 41°23N 83°19W 311 C13
Gibsons Canada 49°24N 123°32W 296 D4
Gibsonton U.S.A. 27°51N 82°23W 317 H7
Gibsonville U.S.A. 39°46N 120°54W 306 F6
Gidami Ethiopia 8°59N 34°37E 266 C3
Gidar Pakistan 28°16N 66°0E 242 E2
Giddalur India 15°20N 78°57E 245 G4
Giddings U.S.A. 30°11N 96°56W 314 F6
Gidea Park U.K. 51°35N 0°11E 125 A5
Gidole Ethiopia 5°40N 37°25E 257 F4
Giebnegáisi = Kebnekaise Sweden 67°53N 18°33E 160 C18
Gien France 47°40N 2°36E 173 E9
Giengen Germany 48°37N 10°14E 179 G6
Giesing Germany 48°6N 11°35E 131 B2
Giessen Germany 50°34N 8°41E 178 E4
Gīfān Iran 37°54N 57°28E 247 B8
Gifatin, Geziret Egypt 27°10N 33°50E 256 B3
Gifford U.S.A. 27°40N 80°25W 317 H9
Gifhorn Germany 52°30N 10°33E 178 C6
Gift Lake Canada 55°53N 115°49W 296 B5
Gifu Japan 35°30N 136°45E 223 B8
Gifu ☐ Japan 35°40N 137°0E 223 B9
Gigant Russia 46°28N 41°20E 191 G5
Giganta, Sa. de la Mexico 26°0N 111°39W 318 B2
Gigen Bulgaria 43°40N 24°28E 203 C8
Gigha U.K. 55°42N 5°44W 167 F3
Giglio Italy 42°20N 10°52E 198 F7
Gignac France 43°39N 3°32E 174 E7
Gigüela ➔ Spain 39°8N 3°44W 195 F7
Gijang S. Korea 35°14N 129°12E 224 E4
Gijón Spain 43°32N 5°42W 194 B5
Gikongoro Rwanda 2°28S 29°34E 268 C2
Gil I. Canada 53°12N 129°15W 296 C3
Gila ➔ U.S.A. 32°43N 114°33W 305 K6
Gila Bend U.S.A. 32°57N 112°43W 305 K7
Gila Bend Mts. U.S.A. 33°10N 113°0W 305 K7
Gila Cliff Dwellings ⌂ U.S.A. 33°12N 108°16W 305 K9
Gīlān ☐ Iran 37°0N 50°0E 247 B6
Gīlān-e Gharb Iran 34°8N 45°55E 213 E11
Gilău Romania 46°45N 23°23E 183 D8
Gilbert ➔ Australia 16°35S 141°15E 280 B3
Gilbert Is. Kiribati 1°0N 172°0E 277 A14
Gilbert River Australia 18°9S 142°52E 280 B3
Gilbert Seamounts Pac. Oc. 52°50N 150°10W 150 D18
Gilbués Brazil 9°50S 45°21W 332 C2
Gilead U.S.A. 44°24N 70°59W 313 B14
Gilf el Kebir, Hadabat el Egypt 23°50N 25°50E 256 C2
Gilford I. Canada 50°40N 126°30W 296 C3
Gilgandra Australia 31°43S 148°39E 283 A8
Gilgil Kenya 0°30S 36°20E 268 C4
Gilgit India 35°50N 74°15E 243 B6
Gilgit ➔ Pakistan 35°44N 74°37E 243 B6
Gilgit-Baltistan ☐ Pakistan 36°30N 73°0E 243 A5
Gilgunnia Australia 32°26S 146°2E 283 B7
Gili, Pulau 10°0S 115°0E 235 D5
Gili ⌂ Mozam. 16°39S 38°27E 269 F4
Gilimanuk Indonesia 8°10S 114°26E 231 J17
Giljeva Planina Europe 43°9N 20°0E 202 C4
Gill Pt. St. Helena 15°58S 5°38W 153 h
Gillam Canada 56°20N 94°40W 297 B10
Gilleleje Denmark 56°8N 12°19E 163 H6
Gillen, L. Australia 26°11S 124°38E 279 E3
Gilles, L. Australia 32°50S 136°45E 282 B2
Gillespie U.S.A. 39°8N 89°49W 310 E7
Gillespies Pt. N.Z. 43°24S 169°49E 285 D4
Gillette U.S.A. 44°18N 105°30W 304 D11
Gilliat Australia 20°40S 141°28E 280 C3
Gillingham U.K. 51°23N 0°33E 169 F8
Gilman U.S.A. 40°46N 88°0W 311 D9
Gilman City U.S.A. 40°8N 93°53W 310 D3
Gilmer U.S.A. 32°44N 94°57W 314 E7
Gilmerton U.K. 55°54N 3°7W 121 B2
Gilmore, L. Australia 32°29S 121°37E 279 F3
Gilmour Canada 44°48N 77°37W 312 B7
Gilo West Bank 31°44N 35°11E 123 B2
Gilo ➔ Ethiopia 8°10N 33°15E 257 F3
Gilort ➔ Romania 44°38N 23°32E 183 F8
Gilroy U.S.A. 37°1N 121°34W 306 H5
Giluwe, Mt. Papua N. G. 6°8S 143°52E 286 D2
Gimbi Ethiopia 9°3N 35°42E 257 F4
Gimcheon S. Korea 36°11N 128°4E 224 D4
Gimhae S. Korea 35°14N 128°53E 224 E4
Gimhwa S. Korea 38°17N 127°28E 224 C3
Gimie, Mt. St. Lucia 13°54N 61°0W 323 m
Gimje S. Korea 35°48N 126°45E 224 E3
Gimli Canada 50°40N 97°0W 297 C9
Gimmersta Sweden 59°14N 18°14E 139 B3
Gimo Sweden 60°11N 18°12E 162 D12
Gimone ➔ France 44°0N 1°6E 174 E5
Gimont France 43°38N 0°52E 174 E4
Gimpo Int. ✈ (GMP) S. Korea 37°33N 126°47E 224 D3
Gin ➔ Sri Lanka 6°5N 80°7E 245 L5
Gin Gin Australia 25°0S 151°58E 281 D5
Ginâh Egypt 25°21N 30°30E 256 B3
Ginatilan Phil. 9°34N 123°19E 233 G4
Gineifa Egypt 30°12N 32°25E 256 H8
Gingee India 12°15N 79°25E 245 H4
Gingin Australia 31°22S 115°54E 279 F2
Gingindlovu S. Africa 29°2S 31°30E 271 C5
Gingoog Phil. 8°50N 125°7E 233 G5
Gingoog B. Phil. 8°54N 125°7E 233 G5
Ginir Ethiopia 7°6N 40°40E 257 F5
Ginosa Italy 40°35N 16°45E 201 B9
Ginowan Japan 26°15N 127°45E 288 a
Ginza Tokyo, Japan 140 b5
Ginzo de Limia = Xinzo de Limia Spain 42°3N 7°47W 194 C3
Giofyros ➔ Greece 35°20N 25°6E 207 E6
Giohar = Jawhar Somalia 2°48N 45°30E 267 D6
Gióia, G. di Italy 38°30N 15°45E 201 D8
Gióia del Colle Italy 40°48N 16°55E 201 B9
Gióia Táuro Italy 38°25N 15°54E 201 D8
Gioiosa Iónica Italy 38°20N 16°18E 201 D9
Gioiosa Marea Italy 38°10N 14°54E 201 D7
Giona, Oros Greece 38°38N 22°14E 204 C4
Giovi, Passo dei Italy 44°33N 8°57E 198 D5
Giovinazzo Italy 41°11N 16°40E 201 A9
Gippsland Australia 37°52S 147°0E 283 D7
Gipuzkoa ☐ Spain 43°12N 2°15W 196 B2
Gir △ India 21°0N 71°0E 242 J4
Gir Hills India 21°0N 71°0E 242 J4
Girab India 26°2N 70°38E 242 F4
Girâfi, W. ➔ Egypt 29°58N 34°39E 251 J5
Giraltovce Slovakia 49°7N 21°32E 181 B14
Girapetra, Akra Greece 38°51N 20°41E 207 B2
Girard St. Lucia 13°59N 60°57W 323 m
Girard Ga., U.S.A. 33°3N 81°43W 316 B8
Girard Ill., U.S.A. 39°27N 89°47W 310 E7
Girard Kans., U.S.A. 37°31N 94°51W 308 G6
Girard Ohio, U.S.A. 41°9N 80°42W 312 E4
Girard Pa., U.S.A. 42°0N 80°19W 312 E4
Girardot Colombia 4°18N 74°48W 328 C3
Giraud, Pte. Dominica 15°20N 61°15W 323 k
Girdle Ness U.K. 57°9N 2°3W 167 D6
Giresun Turkey 40°55N 38°30E 213 B8
Giresun ☐ Turkey 40°30N 38°30E 213 B8
Girga Egypt 26°17N 31°55E 256 B3
Girgaum Mumbai, India 130 b2
Girgenti = Agrigento Italy 37°19N 13°34E 200 E6
Girgir, C. Papua N. G. 3°50S 144°35E 286 B3
Giri ➔ Dem. Rep. of the Congo 0°28N 17°59E 264 B3
Giri ➔ India 30°28N 77°41E 242 D7
Giridih India 24°10N 86°21E 243 G12
Girifalco Italy 38°49N 16°25E 201 D9
Giriftu Kenya 1°59N 39°46E 268 B4
Girilambone Australia 31°16S 146°57E 283 A7
Girne = Kyrenia Cyprus 35°20N 33°20E 207 E9
Giro Nigeria 11°7N 4°42E 263 C5
Giromagny France 47°45N 6°50E 173 E13
Giron = Kiruna Sweden 67°52N 20°15E 160 C19
Girona Spain 41°58N 2°46E 196 D7
Girona ☐ Spain 42°11N 2°30E 196 C7
Gironde ☐ France 44°45N 0°30W 174 D3
Gironde ➔ France 45°32N 1°7W 174 C2
Gironella Spain 42°2N 1°53E 196 C6
Girraween △ Australia 28°46S 151°54E 281 D5
Girringun △ Australia 18°15S 145°32E 280 B4
Giru Australia 19°30S 147°5E 280 B4
Girvan U.K. 55°14N 4°51W 167 F4
Gisborne Vic., Australia 37°29S 144°36E 282 D6
Gisborne N.Z. 38°39S 178°5E 284 E7
Gisborne ☐ N.Z. 38°30S 178°0E 284 E7
Gisenyi Rwanda 1°41S 29°15E 268 C2
Gislaved Sweden 57°19N 13°32E 163 G7
Gisors France 49°15N 1°47E 173 C8
Gitarama Rwanda 2°4S 29°45E 268 C2
Gitega Burundi 3°26S 29°56E 268 C2
Githio Greece 36°46N 22°34E 204 E4
Gitschin = Jičín Czechia 50°25N 15°28E 180 A8
Giuba = Juba ➔ Somalia 1°30N 42°35E 267 D5
Giudecca, Canale della Venice, Italy 142 c2
Giugliano in Campania Italy 40°56N 14°12E 201 B7
Giulianova Italy 42°45N 13°57E 199 F10
Giura Greece 39°23N 24°10E 204 B6
Giurgeni Romania 44°45N 27°48E 183 F12
Giurgiu Romania 43°52N 25°57E 183 G10
Giurgiu ☐ Romania 44°20N 26°0E 183 F10
Giurgiuleşti Moldova 45°29N 28°12E 183 E13
Giustinian, Palazzo Venice, Italy 142 b3
Giv'at Ram Israel 31°47N 35°12E 123 B2
Giv'at Ye'arim Israel 31°47N 35°5E 123 B1
Giv'at Ze'ev West Bank 31°52N 35°10E 123 A2
Give Denmark 55°51N 9°13E 163 J3
Givet France 50°8N 4°49E 173 B11
Giv'on West Bank 31°51N 35°10E 123 A1
Givors France 45°35N 4°45E 175 C8
Givry France 46°41N 4°46E 173 F11
Giyani S. Africa 23°19S 30°43E 271 B5
Giyon Ethiopia 8°33N 38°1E 257 F4
Giza = El Giza Egypt 30°0N 31°12E 117 A2
Giza Pyramids Egypt 29°58N 31°9E 117 B1
Gizab Afghan. 33°22N 66°17E 242 C1
Gizhiga Russia 62°3N 160°30E 215 C17
Gizhiginskaya Guba Russia 61°0N 158°0E 215 C16
Gizo Solomon Is. 8°7S 156°50E 287 M9
Giżycko Poland 54°2N 21°48E 184 D8
Gizzeria Italy 38°59N 16°12E 201 D9
Gjakovë Kosovo 42°22N 20°26E 202 D4
Gjalicë e Lumës, Mal. Albania 42°2N 20°25E 202 D4
Gjantija Malta 36°2N 14°16E 206 E7
Gjegjan Albania 41°58N 20°3E 202 E4
Gjendesheim Norway 61°30N 8°48E 164 C5
Gjeravicë Kosovo 42°32N 20°8E 202 D4
Gjermundshamn Norway 60°40N 5°55E 164 D2
Gjersjøen Norway 59°47N 10°47E 133 B3
Gjerstad Norway 58°54N 9°1E 164 E6
Gjevillvatnet Norway 62°43N 9°23E 164 B6
Gjilan Kosovo 42°28N 21°29E 202 D5
Gjirokastër Albania 40°7N 20°10E 202 F4
Gjoa Haven Canada 68°38N 95°53W 294 D12
Gjøra Norway 62°33N 9°4E 164 B6
Gjøvik Norway 60°47N 10°43E 164 D7
Gjuhës, Kep i Albania 40°28N 19°15E 202 F3
Gjurakoc Kosovo 42°43N 20°29E 202 D4
Glace Bay Canada 46°11N 59°58W 299 C8
Glacier △ B.C., Canada 51°15N 117°30W 296 C5
Glacier △ Mont., U.S.A. 48°42N 113°48W 304 B7
Glacier Bay U.S.A. 58°40N 136°0W 303 G14
Glacier Bay ⌂ U.S.A. 58°45N 136°30W 296 B1
Glacier Peak U.S.A. 48°7N 121°7W 304 B3
Gladewater U.S.A. 32°33N 94°56W 314 E7
Gladsakse Denmark 55°45N 12°25E 118 A2
Gladstone Queens., Australia 23°52S 151°16E 280 C5
Gladstone S. Austral., Australia 33°15S 138°22E 282 B3
Gladstone Man., Canada 50°13N 98°57W 297 C9
Gladstone Ill., U.S.A. 40°52N 90°57W 310 D6
Gladstone Mich., U.S.A. 45°51N 87°1W 308 C10
Gladstone Mo., U.S.A. 39°13N 94°35W 310 E2
Gladwin U.S.A. 43°59N 84°29W 309 D11
Glafsfjorden Sweden 59°30N 12°37E 162 E6
Glagah Indonesia 8°13S 114°18E 231 J17
Glagów Małopolski Poland 50°10N 21°56E 185 H8
Glåma = Glomma ➔ Norway 59°12N 10°57E 164 E7
Gláma Iceland 65°48N 23°0W 155 B4
Glamis U.S.A. 32°55N 115°5W 307 N11
Glamoč Bos.-H. 44°3N 16°51E 199 D13
Glamorgan, Vale of ☐ U.K. 51°28N 3°25W 169 F4
Glåmos Norway 62°41N 11°25E 164 B8
Glamsbjerg Denmark 55°17N 10°6E 163 J4
Glanvillia Dominica 15°34N 61°28W 323 k
Glarus Switz. 47°3N 9°4E 179 H5
Glarus ☐ Switz. 47°0N 9°5E 179 J5
Glasco Kans., U.S.A. 39°22N 97°50W 308 F5
Glasco N.Y., U.S.A. 42°3N 73°57W 313 D11
Glasgow Glasg. City, U.K. 55°51N 4°15W 167 F4
Glasgow Ky., U.S.A. 37°0N 85°55W 309 G11
Glasgow Mo., U.S.A. 39°14N 92°51W 310 E4
Glasgow Mont., U.S.A. 48°12N 106°38W 304 B10
Glasgow City ☐ U.K. 55°51N 4°12W 167 F4
Glasgow Int. ✈ (GLA) U.K. 55°51N 4°21W 167 F4
Glaslyn Canada 53°22N 108°21W 297 C7
Glassmanor U.S.A. 38°49N 77°0W 143 C3
Glastonbury Somst., U.K. 51°9N 2°43W 169 F5
Glastonbury Conn., U.S.A. 41°43N 72°37W 313 E12
Glatz = Kłodzko Poland 50°28N 16°38E 185 H3
Glauchau Germany 50°49N 12°31E 178 E8
Glava Sweden 59°33N 12°35E 162 E6
Glavice Croatia 43°43N 16°41E 199 E13
Glazov Russia 58°9N 52°40E 190 A11
Gleichen Canada 50°52N 113°3W 296 C6
Gleisdorf Austria 47°6N 15°44E 180 D8
Gleiwitz = Gliwice Poland 50°22N 18°41E 185 H5
Glen U.S.A. 44°7N 71°11W 313 B13
Glen Affric U.K. 57°17N 5°1W 167 D3
Glen Afton N.Z. 37°37S 175°4E 284 D4
Glen Canyon U.S.A. 37°30N 110°40W 305 H8
Glen Canyon ⌂ U.S.A. 37°15N 111°0W 305 H8
Glen Canyon Dam U.S.A. 36°57N 111°29W 305 H8
Glen Coe U.K. 56°40N 5°0W 167 E3
Glen Cove U.S.A. 40°52N 73°38W 313 F11
Glen Garry U.K. 57°3N 5°7W 167 D3
Glen Innes Australia 29°44S 151°44E 281 D5
Glen Iris Australia 37°51S 145°3E 128 B2
Glen Lyon U.S.A. 41°10N 76°5W 313 E8
Glen Mar Park U.S.A. 38°57N 77°7W 143 B2
Glen Massey N.Z. 37°38S 175°2E 284 D4
Glen Mor U.K. 57°9N 4°37W 167 D4
Glen Moriston U.K. 57°11N 4°52W 167 D4
Glen Robertson Canada 45°22N 74°30W 313 A10
Glen Rouge Park Canada 43°49N 79°10W 141 A4
Glen Spean U.K. 56°53N 4°40W 167 E4
Glen Ullin U.S.A. 46°49N 101°50W 308 B3
Glenamaddy Ireland 53°37N 8°33W 166 C3
Glénan, Îs. de France 47°42N 4°0W 172 E3
Glenavy N.Z. 44°54S 171°7E 285 E6
Glenbeigh Ireland 52°3N 9°58W 166 D2
Glenburn Australia 37°27S 145°26E 283 D6
Glencoe Ont., Canada 42°45N 81°43W 312 D3
Glencoe KwaZulu Natal, S. Africa 28°11S 30°11E 271 C5
Glencoe Ala., U.S.A. 33°57N 85°56W 316 B4
Glencoe Ill., U.S.A. 42°8N 87°45W 119 A2
Glencoe Minn., U.S.A. 44°46N 94°9W 308 C6
Glencolumbkille Ireland 54°43N 8°42W 166 B3
Glencorse Res. U.K. 55°51N 3°15W 121 B2
Glendale Ariz., U.S.A. 33°32N 112°11W 305 K7
Glendale Calif., U.S.A. 34°9N 118°15W 126 B3
Glendale Fla., U.S.A. 30°52N 86°7W 316 E3
Glendale Zimbabwe 17°22S 31°5E 269 F3
Glendive U.S.A. 47°7N 104°43W 304 C11
Glendo U.S.A. 42°30N 105°2W 304 E11
Glenelg Australia 34°58S 138°31E 282 C3
Glenelg ➔ Australia 38°4S 140°59E 282 E4
Glenfield U.S.A. 43°43N 75°24W 313 C9
Glengad Hd. Ireland 55°20N 7°10W 166 A4
Glengarriff Ireland 51°45N 9°34W 166 E2
Glengoffe Jamaica 18°10N 76°53W 320 a
Glenham N.Z. 46°26S 168°52E 285 G3
Glenhope N.Z. 41°40S 172°39E 285 B7
Glenhuntly Australia 37°52S 145°1E 128 B2
Glenmary, Mt. N.Z. 43°55S 169°55E 285 D4
Glenmont U.S.A. 40°31N 82°6W 312 F2
Glenmorgan Australia 27°14S 149°42E 281 D4
Glenn U.S.A. 39°31N 122°1W 306 F4
Glennallen U.S.A. 62°7N 145°33W 303 E11
Glenns Ferry U.S.A. 42°57N 115°18W 304 E6
Glennville U.S.A. 31°56N 81°56W 316 D8
Glenora Canada 44°2N 77°3W 312 B7
Glenorchy Tas., Australia 42°49S 147°18E 281 G4
Glenorchy Vic., Australia 36°55S 142°41E 282 D5
Glenorchy N.Z. 44°51S 168°24E 285 E3
Glenore Australia 17°50S 141°12E 280 B3
Glenreagh Australia 30°2S 153°1E 281 E5
Glenrock U.S.A. 42°52N 105°52W 304 E11
Glenrothes U.K. 56°12N 3°10W 167 E5
Glenrowan Australia 36°29S 146°13E 283 D7
Glens Falls U.S.A. 43°19N 73°39W 313 C11
Glenside U.S.A. 40°6N 75°9W 313 F9
Glenthompson Australia 37°38S 142°38E 282 D5
Glenties Ireland 54°48N 8°17W 166 B3
Glenveagh △ Ireland 55°3N 8°1W 166 A3
Glenview U.S.A. 42°3N 87°48W 119 A2
Glenview Countryside U.S.A. 42°3N 87°49W 119 A2
Glenville U.S.A. 38°56N 80°50W 309 F13
Glenvista S. Africa 26°17S 28°3E 123 B2
Glenwood Nfld. & L., Canada 49°0N 54°58W 299 C9
Glenwood Ark., U.S.A. 34°20N 93°33W 314 D8
Glenwood Ga., U.S.A. 32°11N 82°40W 316 C7
Glenwood Hawai'i, U.S.A. 19°29N 155°9W 302 D6
Glenwood Iowa, U.S.A. 41°3N 95°45W 308 E6
Glenwood Minn., U.S.A. 45°39N 95°23W 308 C6
Glenwood Wash., U.S.A. 46°1N 121°17W 306 D5
Glenwood Springs U.S.A. 39°33N 107°19W 304 G10
Glettinganes Iceland 65°30N 13°37W 155 B13
Glidden U.S.A. 42°4N 94°44W 310 B2
Glifada Athens, Greece 37°52N 23°45E 112 B2
Glimåkra Sweden 56°19N 14°7E 163 H8
Glin Ireland 52°34N 9°17W 166 D2
Glina Croatia 45°20N 16°6E 199 C13
Glinojeck Poland 52°49N 20°21E 185 F7
Glittertind Norway 61°40N 8°32E 164 C5
Gliwice Poland 50°22N 18°41E 185 H5
Globe U.S.A. 33°24N 110°47W 305 K8
Glodeanu Siliştea Romania 44°50N 26°48E 183 F11
Glodeni Moldova 47°45N 27°31E 183 C12
Glödnitz Austria 46°53N 14°7E 180 E7
Glogau = Głogów Poland 51°37N 16°5E 185 G3
Gloggnitz Austria 47°41N 15°56E 180 D8
Głogów Poland 51°37N 16°5E 185 G3
Głogówek Poland 50°21N 17°53E 185 H4
Glomma ➔ Norway 59°12N 10°57E 164 E7
Glorias Phil. 12°59N 121°30E 232 E3
Glorieuses, Îs. Ind. Oc. 11°30S 47°20E 272 A2
Glosa Greece 39°10N 23°45E 204 B5
Glossop U.K. 53°27N 1°56W 168 D6
Glostrup Denmark 55°39N 12°23E 118 B2
Gloucester N.S.W., Australia 32°0S 151°59E 283 B9
Gloucester Papua N. G. 5°31S 148°31E 286 C5
Gloucester Glouc., U.K. 51°53N 2°15W 169 F5
Gloucester Mass., U.S.A. 42°37N 70°40W 313 D14
Gloucester, C. Papua N. G. 5°26S 148°21E 286 C5

Gloucester I. *Australia* 20°0S 148°30E **280** b
Gloucester Island △ *Australia* 20°2S 148°30E **280** b
Gloucester Point *U.S.A.* 37°15N 76°30W **309** G15
Gloucestershire □ *U.K.* 51°46N 2°15W **169** F5
Glover I. *Grenada* 11°59N 61°47W **323** q
Gloversville *U.S.A.* 43°3N 74°21W **313** C10
Glovertown *Canada* 48°40N 54°3W **299** C9
Gloverville = Warrenville *U.S.A.* 33°33N 81°48W **316** B8
Głowno *Poland* 51°59N 19°42E **185** G6
Głubczyce *Poland* 50°13N 17°52E **185** H4
Glubokiy *Russia* 48°35N 40°25E **191** F5
Glubokoye *Kazakhstan* 50°8N 82°18E **217** B10
Glubokoye = Hlybokaye *Belarus* 55°10N 27°45E **188** E4
Głuchołazy *Poland* 50°19N 17°24E **185** H4
Glücksburg *Germany* 54°50N 9°33E **178** A5
Glückstadt *Germany* 53°45N 9°25E **178** B5
Glukhov = Hlukhiv *Ukraine* 51°40N 33°58E **189** G7
Glusk *Belarus* 52°53N 28°41E **177** B15
Głuszyca *Poland* 50°41N 16°23E **185** H3
Glyfada = Glifada *Athens, Greece* 37°52N 23°45E **112** B2
Glyn Ebwy = Ebbw Vale *U.K.* 51°46N 3°12W **169** F4
Glyngøre *Denmark* 56°46N 8°52E **163** H2
Gmünd *Kärnten, Austria* 46°54N 13°31E **180** E6
Gmünd *Niederösterreich, Austria* 48°45N 15°0E **180** C8
Gmunden *Austria* 47°55N 13°48E **180** D6
Gnali *Gabon* 2°34S 11°18E **264** C2
Gnarp *Sweden* 62°3N 17°16E **162** B11
Gnesen = Gniezno *Poland* 52°30N 17°35E **185** F4
Gnesta *Sweden* 59°3N 17°17E **162** E11
Gniew *Poland* 53°50N 18°50E **184** E5
Gniewkowo *Poland* 52°54N 18°25E **185** F5
Gniezno *Poland* 52°30N 17°35E **185** F4
Gnjilane = Gjilan *Kosovo* 42°28N 21°29E **202** D5
Gnoien *Germany* 53°58N 12°41E **178** B8
Gnosjö *Sweden* 57°22N 13°43E **163** G7
Gnowangerup *Australia* 33°58S 117°59E **279** F2
Go Cong *Vietnam* 10°22N 106°40E **237** G6
Gō-Gawa ➔ *Japan* 35°2N 132°13E **222** B4
Gō-no-ura *Japan* 33°44N 129°40E **222** D1
Goa *India* 15°33N 73°59E **245** G1
Goa *Phil.* 13°42N 123°29E **232** E4
Goa □ *India* 15°33N 73°59E **245** G1
Goalen Hd. *Australia* 36°33S 150°4E **283** D9
Goalpara *India* 26°10N 90°40E **241** B3
Goaltor *India* 22°43N 87°10E **243** H12
Goalundo Ghat *Bangla.* 23°50N 89°47E **243** H13
Goaso *Ghana* 6°48N 2°30W **262** D4
Goat Fell *U.K.* 55°38N 5°11W **167** F3
Goat I. *Antigua & B.* 17°43N 61°51W **322** c
Goat Pt. *Antigua & B.* 17°44N 61°51W **322** c
Goba *Ethiopia* 7°1N 39°59E **257** F4
Goba *Mozam.* 26°15S 32°13E **271** C5
Gobabis *Namibia* 22°30S 19°0E **270** B2
Gobe *Papua N. G.* 9°4S 149°0E **286** E5
Göbel *Turkey* 40°0N 28°9E **203** F12
Gobernador Gregores *Argentina* 48°46S 70°15W **336** C2
Gobi *Asia* 44°0N 110°0E **226** C6
Gobi Gurvan Saykhan △ *Mongolia* 43°24N 101°24E **226** C2
Gobichettipalayam *India* 11°31N 77°21E **245** J3
Gobles *U.S.A.* 42°22N 85°53W **311** B11
Gobō *Japan* 33°53N 135°10E **223** D7
Gobo *South Sudan* 5°40N 31°10E **257** F3
Gobustan *Azerbaijan* 40°7N 49°22E **213** B13
Göçbeyli *Turkey* 39°13N 27°25E **205** B9
Goch *Germany* 51°41N 6°9E **178** D2
Gochang *S. Korea* 35°26N 126°42E **224** E3
Gochas *Namibia* 24°59S 18°55E **270** B2
God Dere *Ethiopia* 5°12N 44°1E **267** C5
Godalming *U.K.* 51°11N 0°36W **169** F7
Godavari ➔ *India* 16°25N 82°18E **244** F6
Godavari Pt. *India* 17°0N 82°20E **244** F6
Godbout *Canada* 49°20N 67°38W **299** C6
Godda *India* 24°50N 87°13E **243** G12
Gode *Ethiopia* 5°53N 43°35E **267** C5
Godech *Bulgaria* 43°1N 23°4E **202** C7
Goderich *Canada* 43°45N 81°41W **312** C3
Goderville *France* 49°38N 0°22E **172** C7
Godfrey *U.S.A.* 38°58N 90°11W **310** F6
Godfrey Ra. *Australia* 24°0S 117°0E **279** D2
Goðafoss *Iceland* 65°41N 17°33W **155** B9
Godhavn = Qeqertarsuaq *Greenland* 69°15N 53°38W **154** D5
Goðdalir *Iceland* 65°20N 19°6W **155** B7
Godhra *India* 22°49N 73°40E **242** H5
Godinlabe *Somalia* 5°54N 46°38E **267** C6
Gödöllő *Hungary* 47°38N 19°25E **182** C4
Godoy Cruz *Argentina* 32°56S 68°52W **334** C2
Gods ➔ *Canada* 56°22N 92°51W **298** A1
Gods L. *Canada* 54°40N 94°15W **298** B1
Gods River *Canada* 54°50N 94°5W **297** C10
Godthåb = Nuuk *Greenland* 64°10N 51°35W **154** E5
Godwin Austen = K2 *Pakistan* 35°58N 76°32E **243** B7
Goeie Hoop, Kaap die = Good Hope, C. of *S. Africa* 34°24S 18°30E **270** D2
Goéland, L. au *Canada* 49°50N 76°48W **298** C4
Goélands, L. aux *Canada* 55°27N 64°17W **299** A7
Goeree *Neths.* 51°50N 4°0E **170** C3
Goes *Neths.* 51°30N 3°55E **170** D3
Gofca ➔ *Somalia* 1°10N 43°43E **267** D5
Goffstown *U.S.A.* 43°1N 71°36W **313** C13
Gogama *Canada* 47°35N 81°43W **298** C3
Gogar *U.K.* 55°56N 3°20W **121** B2
Gogebic, L. *U.S.A.* 46°30N 89°35W **308** B9
Goggetti *Ethiopia* 8°11N 38°35E **257** F4
Gogolin *Poland* 50°30N 18°0E **185** H5
Gogonou *Benin* 10°50N 2°50E **263** C5
Gogra = Ghaghara ➔ *India* 25°45N 84°40E **243** G11
Gogrial *South Sudan* 8°30N 28°8E **257** F2
Gogti *Ethiopia* 10°7N 42°51E **257** E5
Gogui *Mali* 15°32N 9°25W **262** B3
Gôh-Djiboua □ *Côte d'Ivoire* 6°2N 5°33W **262** D3
Gohana *India* 29°8N 76°42E **242** E7
Goharganj *India* 23°1N 77°41E **242** H7
Goheung *S. Korea* 34°36N 127°17E **224** E3
Goi ➔ *India* 22°4N 74°46E **242** H6
Goiana *Brazil* 7°33S 34°59W **332** C5
Goianésia *Brazil* 15°18S 49°7W **333** E2
Goiânia *Brazil* 16°43S 49°20W **333** E2
Goiás *Brazil* 15°55S 50°10W **333** E1
Goiás □ *Brazil* 12°10S 48°0W **332** D2
Goiatins *Brazil* 7°42S 47°10W **332** C2
Goiatuba *Brazil* 18°1S 49°23W **333** E2
Goidu Atoll *Maldives* 4°53N 72°54E **272** d
Goio-Erê *Brazil* 24°12S 53°1W **335** A5
Góis *Portugal* 40°10N 8°6W **194** E2
Gojam *Ethiopia* 10°55N 36°30E **257** E4
Gojeb, Wabi ➔ *Ethiopia* 7°12N 36°40E **257** F4
Gojō *Japan* 34°21N 135°42E **223** C7
Gojra *Pakistan* 31°10N 72°40E **242** D5
Gokak *India* 16°11N 74°52E **245** F2
Gokarn *India* 14°33N 74°17E **245** G2
Gökçe = Sevana Lich *Armenia* 40°30N 45°20E **191** K7
Gökçe *Turkey* 40°10N 25°55E **203** F9
Gökçeada *Turkey* 40°10N 25°50E **203** F9
Gökçedağ *Turkey* 39°33N 28°56E **205** B10
Gökçen *Turkey* 38°7N 27°53E **205** C9
Gökçeören *Turkey* 38°37N 28°35E **205** C10
Gökçeyazı *Turkey* 39°40N 27°40E **205** B9
Gökırmak ➔ *Turkey* 41°25N 35°8E **212** B6
Gökova *Turkey* 37°1N 28°17E **205** D10
Gökova Körfezi *Turkey* 36°55N 27°50E **205** E9
Göksu ➔ *Turkey* 36°19N 34°5E **250** B5
Göksun *Turkey* 38°2N 36°30E **212** C7
Gokteik *Myanmar* 22°26N 97°0E **241** D6
Göktepe *Karaman, Turkey* 36°37N 32°37E **250** B3
Göktepe *Muğla, Turkey* 37°25N 28°34E **205** D10
Göktürk *Turkey* 41°10N 28°53E **122** A1
Gokurt *Pakistan* 29°40N 67°26E **242** E2
Gokwe *Zimbabwe* 18°7S 28°58E **271** A4
Gol *Norway* 60°42N 8°55E **164** D5
Gol Gol *Australia* 34°12S 142°14E **282** C5
Gola *India* 28°3N 80°32E **243** E9
Golabari *India* 22°35N 88°20E **124** B2
Golabki *Poland* 52°12N 20°52E **143** B1
Golaghat *India* 26°30N 94°0E **241** B5
Golakganj *India* 26°8N 89°52E **241** B2
Golan Heights = Hagolan *Syria* 33°0N 35°45E **250** F6
Gołańcz *Poland* 52°57N 17°18E **185** F4
Golāshkerd *Iran* 27°59N 57°16E **247** E8
Golaya Pristen = Hola Prystan *Ukraine* 46°29N 32°32E **189** J7
Gölbaşı *Adıyaman, Turkey* 37°43N 37°25E **212** D7
Gölbaşı *Ankara, Turkey* 39°47N 32°49E **212** C5
Golconda *India* 17°24N 78°23E **244** F4
Golconda *Nev., U.S.A.* 40°58N 117°30W **304** F5
Gölcük *Kocaeli, Turkey* 40°42N 29°48E **203** F13
Gölcük *Niğde, Turkey* 38°14N 34°47E **212** C6
Gold *U.S.A.* 41°52N 77°50W **312** E7
Gold Beach *U.S.A.* 42°25N 124°25W **304** E1
Gold Coast = Ghana ■ *W. Afr.* 8°0N 1°0W **263** D4
Gold Coast *Queens., Australia* 28°0S 153°25E **276** F9
Gold Coast *Chicago, U.S.A.* **119** a2
Gold Coast *W. Afr.* 4°0N 1°40W **263** E4
Gold Creek *U.S.A.* 62°46N 149°41W **303** E10
Gold Hill *U.S.A.* 42°26N 123°3W **304** E2
Gold River *Canada* 49°46N 126°3W **296** D3
Gołdap *Poland* 54°19N 22°18E **184** D9
Goldberg = Złotoryja *Poland* 51°8N 15°55E **185** G2
Goldberg *Germany* 53°35N 12°4E **178** B8
Golden *B.C., Canada* 51°20N 116°59W **296** C5
Golden *Ill., U.S.A.* 40°7N 91°1W **310** D5
Golden B. *N.Z.* 40°40S 172°50E **285** A7
Golden Beach *U.S.A.* 25°57N 80°7W **129** C3
Golden Buddha = Traimit *Bangkok, Thailand* **113** c2
Golden Gate *U.S.A.* 37°48N 122°29W **136** B2
Golden Gate △ *U.S.A.* 37°49N 122°31W **136** A2
Golden Gate Bridge *U.S.A.* 37°49N 122°28W **136** B2
Golden Gate Highlands △ *S. Africa* 28°40S 28°40E **271** C4
Golden Gate Park *U.S.A.* 37°46N 122°28W **136** B2
Golden Grove *Middlesex, Jamaica* 18°19N 77°9W **320** a
Golden Grove *Surrey, Jamaica* 17°55N 76°16W **320** a
Golden Hinde *Canada* 49°40N 125°44W **296** D3
Golden Horn = Haliç *Turkey* 41°1N 28°57E **122** B1
Golden Lake *Canada* 45°34N 77°21W **312** A7
Golden Rock *India* 10°45N 78°48E **245** J4
Golden Spike △ *U.S.A.* 41°37N 112°33W **304** F7
Golden Vale *Ireland* 52°33N 8°17W **166** D3
Goldendale *U.S.A.* 45°49N 120°50W **304** D3
Golders Green *U.K.* 51°34N 0°11W **125** A2
Goldfield *U.S.A.* 37°42N 117°14W **305** H5
Goldingen = Kuldīga *Latvia* 56°58N 21°59E **184** B8
Goldoni, Casa *Venice, Italy* **142** b2
Goldoni, Teatro *Venice, Italy* **142** b3
Goldsand L. *Canada* 57°2N 101°8W **297** B8
Goldsboro *U.S.A.* 35°23N 77°59W **315** D16
Goldsmith *U.S.A.* 31°59N 102°37W **314** F3
Goldthwaite *U.S.A.* 31°27N 98°34W **314** F5
Golegã *Portugal* 39°24N 8°29W **195** F2
Goleniów *Poland* 53°35N 14°50E **184** E1
Golestān □ *Iran* 37°20N 55°25E **247** B7
Golestan Palace *Iran* 35°41N 51°25E **141** A2
Golestānak *Iran* 30°36N 54°14E **247** D7
Goleta *U.S.A.* 34°27N 119°50W **307** L7
Golf *U.S.A.* 42°3N 87°46W **119** A2
Golfito *Costa Rica* 8°41N 83°5W **320** E3
Golfo Aranci *Italy* 40°59N 9°38E **200** B2
Golfo de Santa Clara *Mexico* 31°42N 114°30W **318** A2
Golfo di Orosei e del Gennargentu △ *Italy* 40°5N 9°15E **200** B2
Gölgeli Dağları *Turkey* 37°10N 28°55E **205** D10
Gölhisar *Turkey* 37°8N 29°31E **205** D11
Goliad *U.S.A.* 28°40N 97°23W **314** G6
Golija *Montenegro* 43°5N 18°45E **202** C2
Golija *Serbia* 43°22N 20°15E **202** C4
Golina *Poland* 52°15N 18°4E **185** F5
Gölköy *Turkey* 40°41N 37°37E **212** B7
Gollel = Lavumisa *Eswatini* 27°20S 31°55E **271** C5
Göllersdorf *Austria* 48°29N 16°7E **180** C9
Golmo = Golenów *Poland* 53°35N 14°50E **184** E1
Gölmarmara *Turkey* 38°42N 27°55E **205** C9
Golmud *China* 36°25N 94°53E **218** D7
Golo ➔ *France* 42°31N 9°32E **175** F13
Golo I. *Phil.* 13°39N 120°22E **232** E3
Gölova *Turkey* 36°48N 30°5E **205** E12
Golovin *U.S.A.* 64°33N 163°2W **303** D7
Golpāyegān *Iran* 33°27N 50°18E **247** C6
Gölpazarı *Turkey* 40°16N 30°18E **212** B4
Golra *Pakistan* 33°37N 72°56E **242** C5
Golspie *U.K.* 57°58N 3°59W **167** D5
Golub-Dobrzyń *Poland* 53°7N 19°2E **185** E6
Golubac *Serbia* 44°38N 21°38E **202** B5
Golungo Alto *Angola* 9°8S 14°46E **265** D2
Golyam Bratan = Morozov *Bulgaria* 42°30N 25°10E **203** D9
Golyam Perelik = Perelik *Bulgaria* 41°36N 24°33E **203** E8
Golyama Kamchia ➔ *Bulgaria* 43°10N 27°55E **203** C11
Golyama Kamchiya = Golyama Kamchia ➔ *Bulgaria* 43°10N 27°55E **203** C11
Golyshi = Vetluzhskiy *Russia* 58°23N 45°26E **190** A7
Goma *Dem. Rep. of the Congo* 1°37S 29°10E **268** C2
Gomal Pass *Pakistan* 31°56N 69°20E **242** D3
Gomantong Caves *Malaysia* 5°40N 118°6E **235** A5
Gomati ➔ *India* 25°32N 83°11E **243** G10
Gombari *Dem. Rep. of the Congo* 2°45N 29°3E **268** B2
Gombe *Dem. Rep. of the Congo* 0°45S 17°36E **264** C3
Gombe *Nigeria* 10°19N 11°2E **263** C7
Gombe *Tanzania* 4°38S 31°40E **268** C3
Gombe □ *Nigeria* 10°0N 11°10E **263** C7
Gombe ➔ *Tanzania* 4°38S 31°40E **268** C3
Gombe Stream △ *Tanzania* 4°42S 29°37E **268** C2
Gombi *Nigeria* 10°12N 12°30E **263** C7
Gomel = Homyel *Belarus* 52°28N 31°0E **177** B16
Gomera *Canary Is.* 28°7N 17°14W **153** e1
Gómez Palacio *Mexico* 25°34N 103°30W **318** B4
Gomfi *Greece* 39°26N 21°36E **204** B3
Gomīshān *Iran* 37°4N 54°6E **247** B7
Gommern *Germany* 52°4N 11°50E **178** C7
Gomogomo *Indonesia* 6°39S 134°43E **231** F8
Gomoh *India* 23°52N 86°10E **243** H12
Gomotartsi *Bulgaria* 44°6N 22°57E **202** B6
Gompa = Ganta *Liberia* 7°15N 8°59W **262** D3
Gonābād *Iran* 34°15N 58°45E **247** C8
Gonaïves *Haiti* 19°20N 72°42W **321** C5
Gonarezhou △ *Zimbabwe* 21°32S 31°55E **269** G3
Gonâve, G. de la *Haiti* 19°29N 72°42W **321** C5
Gonâve, Île de la *Haiti* 18°51N 73°3W **321** C5
Gonbad-e Kāvūs *Iran* 37°20N 55°25E **247** B7
Gönc *Hungary* 48°28N 21°14E **182** B6
Gonda *India* 27°9N 81°58E **243** F9
Gondal *India* 21°58N 70°52E **242** J4
Gonder *Ethiopia* 12°39N 37°30E **257** E4
Gondia *India* 21°23N 80°10E **244** D5
Gondola *Mozam.* 19°10S 33°37E **269** F3
Gondomar *Portugal* 41°10N 8°35W **194** D2
Gondrecourt-le-Château *France* 48°31N 5°30E **173** D12
Gonen *Israel* 31°46N 35°13E **123** B2
Gönen *Balıkesir, Turkey* 40°6N 27°39E **203** F11
Gönen *Isparta, Turkey* 37°57N 30°31E **205** D12
Gönen ➔ *Turkey* 40°6N 27°39E **203** F11
Gong Xian *China* 28°23N 104°47E **228** C5
Gong'an *China* 30°7N 112°12E **229** B9
Gongbei *China* 22°12N 113°32E **219** a
Gongchangling *China* 41°7N 123°27E **224** B1
Gongcheng *China* 24°50N 110°49E **229** E8
Gongga Shan *China* 29°40N 101°55E **228** C3
Gonggar *China* 29°23N 91°7E **218** F7
Gongguan = Kungkuan *Taiwan* 24°35N 120°44E **225** B2
Gongguan *China* 21°48N 109°36E **228** G7
Gonghe *China* 36°18N 100°32E **218** D9
Gongju *S. Korea* 36°27N 127°7E **224** D3
Gongliu *China* 43°28N 82°8E **217** D10
Gongming *China* 22°47N 113°53E **219** a
Gongneung *S. Korea* 37°36N 127°3E **137** B2
Gongo Yembe *Dem. Rep. of the Congo* 1°58S 18°40E **264** C3
Gongola ➔ *Nigeria* 9°30N 12°4E **263** D7
Gongolgon *Australia* 30°21S 146°54E **281** E4
Gongoué *Gabon* 0°31S 9°13E **264** C1
Gongshan *China* 27°43N 98°29E **228** D2
Gongtan *China* 28°55N 108°20E **228** C7
Gongyi *China* 34°45N 112°58E **226** G7
Gongzhuling *China* 43°30N 124°40E **227** C13
Goni *Greece* 39°52N 22°29E **204** B4
Goniadz *Poland* 53°30N 22°44E **184** E9
Goniri *Nigeria* 11°30N 12°15E **263** C7
Gonjo *China* 30°52N 98°17E **228** B2
Gonnesa *Italy* 39°16N 8°28E **200** C1
Gonnosfanádiga *Italy* 39°29N 8°39E **200** C1
Gonzaga *Phil.* 18°16N 122°0E **232** B4
Gonzales *Calif., U.S.A.* 36°30N 121°26W **306** J5
Gonzales *Tex., U.S.A.* 29°30N 97°27W **314** G6
González *Mexico* 22°48N 98°25W **319** C5
Goobang △ *Australia* 33°0S 148°32E **283** B8
Good Hope, C. of *S. Africa* 34°24S 18°30E **270** D2
Good Hope Lake *Canada* 59°16N 129°18W **296** B3
Good Hope Plantation *Jamaica* 18°25N 77°41W **320** a
Goodenough I. *Papua N. G.* 9°20S 150°15E **286** E6
Gooderham *Canada* 44°54N 78°21W **312** B6
Goodhouse *S. Africa* 28°57S 18°13E **270** C2
Gooding *U.S.A.* 42°56N 114°43W **304** E6
Goodland *U.S.A.* 39°21N 101°43W **308** F3
Goodlands *Mauritius* 20°2S 57°39E **272** e
Goodlow *Canada* 56°20N 120°8W **296** B4
Goodmayes *U.K.* 51°33N 0°6E **125** A4
Goodnews Bay *U.S.A.* 59°7N 161°35W **303** G7
Goodooga *Australia* 29°3S 147°28E **281** D4
Goodsprings *U.S.A.* 35°49N 115°27W **307** K11
Goodwater *U.S.A.* 33°4N 86°3W **316** B3
Goodwood *S. Africa* 33°55S 18°32E **118** A2
Goole *U.K.* 53°42N 0°53W **168** D7
Goolgowi *Australia* 33°58S 145°41E **283** B6
Goolwa *Australia* 35°30S 138°47E **282** C3
Goomalling *Australia* 31°15S 116°49E **279** F2
Goomeri *Australia* 26°12S 152°6E **281** D5
Goonda *Mozam.* 19°48S 33°57E **269** F3
Goondiwindi *Australia* 28°30S 150°21E **281** D5
Goongarrie, L. *Australia* 30°3S 121°9E **279** F3
Goongarrie △ *Australia* 30°7S 121°30E **279** F3
Goonyella *Australia* 21°47S 147°58E **280** C4
Goose ➔ *Canada* 53°20N 60°35W **299** B7
Goose Creek *U.S.A.* 32°59N 80°2W **316** C9
Goose L. *Calif., U.S.A.* 41°56N 120°26W **304** F3
Goose L. *Ill., U.S.A.* 40°55N 89°27W **310** D7
Gooty *India* 15°7N 77°41E **245** G3
Gop *India* 22°5N 69°50E **242** H3
Gopalganj *Bangla.* 23°1N 89°50E **241** D2
Gopalganj *India* 26°28N 84°30E **243** F11
Gopalpur *India* 22°38N 88°26E **124** B2
Göppingen *Germany* 48°42N 9°39E **179** G5
Goqên *China* 29°7N 97°12E **241** A6
Gor *Spain* 37°23N 2°58W **195** H8
Góra *Dolnośląskie, Poland* 51°40N 16°31E **185** G3
Góra *Mazowieckie, Poland* 52°39N 20°6E **185** F7
Góra Kalwaria *Poland* 51°59N 21°14E **185** G8
Gorakhpur *India* 26°47N 83°23E **243** F10
Goražde *Bos.-H.* 43°38N 18°58E **182** G3
Gorbatov *Russia* 56°12N 43°2E **190** B6
Gorbea *Spain* 43°1N 2°50W **196** B2
Górce *Poland* 52°15N 20°55E **143** B1
Gorczański △ *Poland* 49°30N 20°10E **185** J7
Gorda, Banco *Caribbean* 15°40N 80°27W **320** C3
Gorda, Pta. *Canary Is.* 28°45N 18°0W **153** e1
Gorda, Pta. *Nic.* 14°20N 83°10W **320** D3
Gordan B. *Australia* 11°35S 130°10E **278** B5
Gördes *Turkey* 38°54N 28°17E **205** C10
Gordon *Ga., U.S.A.* 32°54N 83°20W **316** C6
Gordon *Nebr., U.S.A.* 42°48N 102°12W **308** D2
Gordon ➔ *Australia* 42°27S 145°30E **281** G4
Gordon, I. *Chile* 54°55S 69°30W **336** D3
Gordon Bay *Canada* 45°12N 79°47W **312** A5
Gordon L. *Alta., Canada* 56°30N 110°25W **297** B6
Gordon L. *N.W.T., Canada* 63°5N 113°11W **296** A6
Gordonvale *Australia* 17°5S 145°50E **280** B4
Goré *Chad* 7°59N 16°31E **259** G3
Gorē *Ethiopia* 8°12N 35°32E **257** F4
Gore *N.Z.* 46°5S 168°58E **285** G3
Gore Bay *Canada* 45°57N 82°28W **298** C3
Gore Hill *Australia* 33°49S 151°10E **139** A2
Gorée, Île de *Senegal* 14°40N 17°23W **262** C1
Görele *Turkey* 41°2N 39°0E **212** B8
Gorelyy ➔ *Russia* 60°1N 30°30E **137** A3
Göreme *Turkey* 38°35N 34°52E **212** C6
Gorey *Ireland* 52°41N 6°18W **166** D5
Gorg *Iran* 29°29N 59°43E **247** D8
Gorgān *Iran* 36°55N 54°30E **247** B7
Gorgie *U.K.* 55°56N 3°14W **121** B2
Gorgol □ *Mauritania* 15°45N 13°0W **262** B2
Gorgona *Italy* 43°26N 9°54E **198** E6
Gorgora *Ethiopia* 12°15N 37°17E **257** E4
Gorgoram *Nigeria* 12°40N 10°45E **263** C7
Gorham *U.S.A.* 44°23N 71°10W **313** B13
Gori *Georgia* 42°0N 44°7E **191** J7
Goribidnur = Gauribidanur *India* 13°37N 77°32E **245** H3
Goriganga ➔ *India* 29°45N 80°23E **243** E9
Gorinchem *Neths.* 51°50N 4°59E **170** C4
Goris *Armenia* 39°31N 46°22E **213** C12
Goritsy *Russia* 57°4N 36°43E **188** D9
Gorizia *Italy* 45°56N 13°37E **199** C10
Gorj □ *Romania* 45°5N 23°25E **183** E8
Gorki = Horki *Belarus* 54°17N 30°59E **188** E6
Gorkiy = Nizhniy Novgorod *Russia* 56°20N 44°0E **190** B7
Gorkovskoye Vdkhr. *Russia* 57°2N 43°4E **190** B6
Gorky Park *Russia* 55°43N 37°36E **129** B2
Gorleston-on-Sea *U.K.* 52°35N 1°44E **169** E9
Gorlice *Poland* 49°35N 21°11E **185** J8
Görlitz *Germany* 51°9N 14°58E **178** D10
Gorlovka = Horlivka *Ukraine* 48°19N 38°5E **189** H10
Gorman *U.S.A.* 34°47N 118°51W **307** L8
Gorna Djumaya = Blagoevgrad *Bulgaria* 42°2N 23°5E **202** D7
Gorna Dzhumayo = Blagoevgrad *Bulgaria* 42°2N 23°5E **202** D7
Gorna Oryahovitsa *Bulgaria* 43°7N 25°40E **203** C9
Gorna Oryakhovitsa = Gorna Oryahovitsa *Bulgaria* 43°7N 25°40E **203** C9
Gornja Radgona *Slovenia* 46°40N 16°2E **199** B13
Gornja Tuzla *Bos.-H.* 44°35N 18°46E **182** F3
Gornji Grad *Slovenia* 46°20N 14°52E **199** B11
Gornji Milanovac *Serbia* 44°3N 20°29E **202** B4
Gornji Vakuf *Bos.-H.* 43°57N 17°34E **182** G2
Gorno Ablanovo *Bulgaria* 43°37N 25°43E **203** C9
Gorno-Altay □ *Russia* 51°0N 86°0E **217** B11
Gorno-Altaysk *Russia* 51°50N 86°5E **217** B11
Gorno-Badakhshan = Kŭhiston-Badakhshon □ *Tajikistan* 38°30N 73°0E **217** E8
Gornozavodsk *Russia* 46°33N 141°50E **215** E15
Gornyak *Russia* 50°59N 81°27E **217** B10
Gornyatski *Russia* 67°32N 64°3E **186** A11
Gornyatskiy *Russia* 48°18N 40°56E **191** F5
Gornyy *Primorsk, Russia* 44°57N 133°59E **220** B6
Gornyy *Saratov, Russia* 51°50N 48°30E **190** E9
Goro ➔ *C.A.R.* 9°14N 21°16E **264** A4
Gorodenka = Horodenka *Ukraine* 48°41N 25°29E **183** B10
Gorodets *Russia* 56°38N 43°28E **190** B6
Gorodishche = Horodyshche *Ukraine* 49°17N 31°27E **189** H6
Gorodishche *Russia* 53°13N 45°40E **190** D7
Gorodnya = Horodnya *Ukraine* 51°55N 31°33E **189** G6
Gorodok = Haradok *Belarus* 55°30N 30°3E **188** E6
Gorodok = Horodok *Ukraine* 49°46N 23°32E **177** D12
Gorodok = Zakamensk *Russia* 50°23N 103°17E **215** D11
Gorodovikovsk *Russia* 46°8N 41°58E **191** G5
Goroka *Papua N. G.* 6°7S 145°25E **286** D3
Goroke *Australia* 36°43S 141°29E **282** D4
Gorokhov = Horokhiv *Ukraine* 50°30N 24°45E **177** C13
Gorokhovets *Russia* 56°13N 42°39E **190** B6
Gorom Gorom *Burkina Faso* 14°26N 0°14W **263** C4
Goromonzi *Zimbabwe* 17°52S 31°22E **269** F3
Gorong, Kepulauan *Indonesia* 3°59S 131°25E **231** E8
Gorongose ➔ *Mozam.* 20°30S 34°40E **271** B5
Gorongoza *Mozam.* 18°44S 34°2E **269** F3
Gorongoza, Sa. da *Mozam.* 18°27S 34°2E **269** F3
Gorongoza △ *Mozam.* 18°50S 34°29E **271** A5
Gorontalo *Indonesia* 0°35N 123°5E **231** D6
Gorontalo □ *Indonesia* 0°50N 122°20E **231** D6
Goronyo *Nigeria* 13°29N 5°39E **263** C6
Górowo Iławeckie *Poland* 54°17N 20°30E **184** D7
Gorron *France* 48°25N 0°50W **172** D6
Gorror *Micronesia* 9°26N 138°4E **287** S16
Gorshechnoye *Russia* 51°31N 38°2E **189** G10
Gort *Ireland* 53°3N 8°49W **166** C3
Gortis *Greece* 35°4N 24°58E **207** E5
Gorumahisani *India* 22°20N 86°24E **244** C8
Gorumara △ *India* 26°42N 88°55E **241** B2
Góry Bystrzyckie *Poland* 50°16N 16°33E **185** H3
Goryachiy Klyuch *Russia* 44°38N 39°8E **191** H4
Goryeong *S. Korea* 35°44N 128°15E **224** E4
Gorzkowice *Poland* 51°13N 19°36E **185** G6
Górzno *Poland* 53°12N 19°38E **185** E6
Gorzów Śląski *Poland* 51°3N 18°22E **185** G5
Gorzów Wielkopolski *Poland* 52°43N 15°15E **185** F2
Gose *Japan* 34°27N 135°44E **223** C7
Gosen *Germany* 52°23N 13°43E **115** B5
Gosener kanal *Germany* 52°24N 13°42E **115** B5
Goseong *S. Korea* 34°58N 128°19E **224** E4
Gosford *Australia* 33°23S 151°18E **283** B9
Goshen *Calif., U.S.A.* 36°21N 119°25W **306** J7
Goshen *Ind., U.S.A.* 41°35N 85°50W **311** C11
Goshen *N.Y., U.S.A.* 41°24N 74°20W **313** E10
Goshogawara *Japan* 40°48N 140°27E **220** D10
Goskopi = Kopeysk *Russia* 55°7N 61°37E **216** A6
Goslar *Germany* 51°54N 10°25E **178** D6
Gospel Oak *U.K.* 51°32N 0°9W **125** A3
Gospič *Croatia* 44°35N 15°23E **199** D12
Gosport *Hants., U.K.* 50°48N 1°9W **169** G6
Gosport *Ind., U.S.A.* 39°21N 86°40W **311** E10
Gossa *Norway* 62°52N 6°50E **164** B3
Gossas *Senegal* 14°28N 16°0W **262** C1
Gosse ➔ *Australia* 19°32S 134°37E **280** B1
Gossi *Mali* 15°48N 1°20W **263** B4
Gossinga *South Sudan* 8°36N 25°59E **257** F2
Gostingen = Gostyń *Poland* 51°50N 17°3E **185** G4
Gostinopolye = Volkhov *Russia* 59°55N 32°15E **188** C7
Gostivar *N. Macedonia* 41°48N 20°57E **202** E4
Gostyń *Poland* 51°50N 17°3E **185** G4
Gostynin *Poland* 52°26N 19°29E **185** F6
Göta älv ➔ *Sweden* 57°42N 11°54E **163** G5
Göta kanal *Sweden* 58°30N 15°58E **163** F10
Götaland *Sweden* 57°30N 14°30E **163** G8
Gotanda *Japan* 35°37N 139°43E **140** B3
Göteborg *Sweden* 57°43N 11°59E **163** G5
Gotemba *Japan* 35°18N 138°56E **223** B10
Götene *Sweden* 58°32N 13°30E **163** F7
Gotenhafen = Gdynia *Poland* 54°35N 18°33E **184** D5
Goteşti *Moldova* 46°9N 28°10E **183** D13
Goth Goli Mar *Pakistan* 24°53N 67°1E **123** A2
Goth Sher Shah *Pakistan* 24°53N 66°59E **123** A1
Gotha *Thüringen, Germany* 50°56N 10°42E **178** E6
Gotha *Fla., U.S.A.* 28°31N 81°31W **133** A1
Gothenburg = Göteborg *Sweden* 57°43N 11°59E **163** G5
Gothenburg *U.S.A.* 40°56N 100°10W **308** E3
Gothèye *Niger* 13°52N 1°34E **263** C5
Gotland *Sweden* 57°30N 18°33E **163** G12
Gotland □ *Sweden* 57°15N 18°30E **163** G12
Gotō = Fukue *Japan* 32°41N 128°51E **221** H4
Goto Meer *Bonaire* 12°14N 68°22W **322** h
Gotō-Rettō *Japan* 32°55N 129°5E **221** H4
Gotse Delchev *Bulgaria* 41°36N 23°46E **202** E7
Gotska Sandön *Sweden* 58°24N 19°15E **163** F13
Gōtsu *Japan* 35°0N 132°14E **222** C4
Göttero, Monte *Italy* 44°22N 9°42E **198** D6
Gottesberg = Boguszów-Gorce *Poland* 50°45N 16°12E **185** H3
Göttingen *Germany* 51°31N 9°55E **178** D5
Gottschee = Kočevje *Slovenia* 45°39N 14°50E **199** C11
Gottskär *Sweden* 57°25N 12°2E **163** G6
Gottwald = Zmiyev *Ukraine* 49°39N 36°27E **189** H9
Gottwaldov = Zlin *Czechia* 49°14N 17°40E **181** B10
Goubangzi *China* 41°20N 121°52E **227** D11
Gouda *Neths.* 52°1N 4°42E **170** B4
Goudiri *Senegal* 14°15N 12°45W **262** C2
Goudoumaria *Niger* 13°40N 11°10E **259** F2
Goudouras, Akra *Greece* 34°59N 26°6E **207** F7
Gouéké *Guinea* 8°2N 8°43W **262** D3
Gough I. *Atl. Oc.* 40°10S 9°45W **152** L11
Gouin, Rés. *Canada* 48°35N 74°40W **298** C5
Gouitafla *Côte d'Ivoire* 7°30N 5°53W **262** D3
Goulburn *Australia* 34°44S 149°44E **283** C8
Goulburn Is. *Australia* 11°40S 133°20E **280** A1
Goulburn River △ *Australia* 32°19S 150°10E **283** B9
Goulds *U.S.A.* 25°33N 80°23W **317** K9
Goulia *Côte d'Ivoire* 10°1N 7°11W **262** C3
Goulimima *Morocco* 31°41N 4°57W **260** B4
Goumbou *Mali* 15°2N 7°25W **262** B3
Goumenissa *Greece* 40°56N 22°37E **202** F6
Gounatolo *Solomon Is.* 8°25S 160°52E **287** M11
Goundam *Mali* 16°27N 3°40W **262** B4
Goundi *Chad* 9°22N 17°21E **259** G3
Gounou-Gaya *Chad* 9°38N 15°31E **259** G3
Goura *Greece* 37°56N 22°20E **204** D4
Gouraya *Algeria* 36°31N 1°56E **261** A5
Gourbassi *Mali* 13°24N 11°38W **262** C2
Gourbeyre *Guadeloupe* 16°0N 61°41W **322** e
Gourde, Pt. *Trin. & Tob.* 10°40N 61°38W **323** t
Gourdon *France* 44°44N 1°23E **174** D5
Gouré *Niger* 14°0N 10°10E **259** F2
Gouri *Chad* 18°50N 16°49E **259** E3
Gourin *France* 48°8N 3°37W **172** D3
Gourits ➔ *S. Africa* 34°21S 21°52E **270** D3
Gourma-Rharous *Mali* 16°55N 1°50W **263** B4
Gournay-en-Bray *France* 49°29N 1°44E **173** C8
Gournay-sur-Marne *France* 48°51N 2°34E **134** A4
Gournes *Greece* 35°19N 25°16E **207** E6
Gouro *Chad* 19°36N 19°36E **259** E3
Gourock *U.K.* 55°57N 4°49W **167** F4
Gourock Ra. *Australia* 36°0S 149°25E **283** D8
Goursi *Burkina Faso* 12°42N 2°37W **262** C4
Gouvea *Brazil* 18°27S 43°44W **333** E3
Gouverneur *U.S.A.* 44°20N 75°28W **313** B9
Gouvia *Greece* 39°39N 19°50E **206** B9
Gouyave *Grenada* 12°10N 61°44W **323** q
Gouzon *France* 46°12N 2°14E **173** F9
Gove, Barragem do *Angola* 13°26S 15°53E **265** E3
Gove Peninsula *Australia* 12°17S 136°49E **280** A2
Governador, I. do *Brazil* 22°48S 43°13W **135** A1
Governador Valadares *Brazil* 18°15S 41°57W **333** E3
Governor Generoso *Phil.* 6°39N 126°5E **233** H6
Governor's Harbour *The Bahamas* 25°10N 76°14W **320** A4
Governors I. *New York, U.S.A.* **132** f1
Govĭaltay □ *Mongolia* 45°30N 96°0E **217** C13
Govindgarh *India* 24°23N 81°18E **243** G9
Gowan Ra. *Australia* 25°0S 145°0E **280** D4
Gowanda *U.S.A.* 42°28N 78°56W **312** D6
Gower *U.K.* 51°35N 4°10W **169** F3
Gowers Corner *U.S.A.* 28°20N 82°30W **317** G7
Gowna, L. *Ireland* 53°51N 7°34W **166** C4
Gowrie *U.S.A.* 42°17N 94°17W **310** B2
Gowurdak *Turkmenistan* 37°50N 66°4E **217** E7
Goya *Argentina* 29°10S 59°10W **334** B4
Goyang *S. Korea* 37°39N 126°50E **224** D3
Goyave *Guadeloupe* 16°8N 61°34W **322** e
Goyaves, Grande Rivière ➔ *Guadeloupe* 16°18N 61°36W **322** e
Göyçay *Azerbaijan* 40°42N 47°43E **191** K8
Goyder Lagoon *Australia* 27°3S 138°58E **281** D2
Goygöl *Azerbaijan* 40°37N 46°12E **191** K8
Goyllarisquizga *Peru* 10°31S 76°24W **330** C2
Göynük *Antalya, Turkey* 36°41N 30°33E **205** E12
Göynük *Bolu, Turkey* 40°24N 30°48E **212** B4
Goz Beïda *Chad* 12°10N 21°20E **259** F4
Goz Regeb *Sudan* 16°3N 35°33E **257** D4
Gozdnica *Poland* 51°28N 15°4E **185** G2
Gözneköy *Turkey* 36°58N 34°33E **250** B5
Gozo *Malta* 36°3N 14°15E **206** E7
Gqeberha *S. Africa* 33°58S 25°40E **270** D4
Graaff-Reinet *S. Africa* 32°13S 24°32E **270** D3
Graben *Vienna, Austria* **142** b2
Grabill *U.S.A.* 41°13N 84°57W **311** C12
Grabo *Côte d'Ivoire* 4°57N 7°30W **262** D3
Grabow *Mecklenburg-Vorpommern, Germany* 53°17N 11°34E **178** B7
Grabów *Warszawa, Poland* 52°8N 20°59E **143** C1
Grabów nad Prosną *Poland* 51°31N 18°7E **185** G5
Graça *Lisbon, Portugal* **126** b3
Gračac *Croatia* 44°18N 15°57E **199** D12
Gračanica *Bos.-H.* 44°43N 18°18E **182** F3
Graçay *France* 47°10N 1°50E **173** E8
Grace Cathedral *San Francisco, U.S.A.* **136** b2
Graceville *U.S.A.* 30°58N 85°31W **316** E4
Gracewood *U.S.A.* 33°22N 82°2W **316** B7
Gracia *Spain* 41°24N 2°10E **114** A2
Gracias a Dios, C. *Honduras* 15°0N 83°10W **320** D3
Graciosa *Azores* 39°4N 28°0W **153** d1
Graciosa, I. *Canary Is.* 29°15N 13°32W **153** e4
Gradac *Montenegro* 43°23N 19°9E **202** C3
Gradačac *Bos.-H.* 44°52N 18°26E **182** F3
Gradaús *Brazil* 7°43S 51°11W **332** C1
Gradaús, Serra dos *Brazil* 8°0S 50°45W **332** C1
Gradeška Planina *N. Macedonia* 41°30N 22°15E **202** E6
Gradets *Bulgaria* 42°46N 26°30E **203** D10
Gradišče *Slovenia* 46°37N 15°50E **199** B12
Gradiška *Bos.-H.* 45°10N 17°15E **182** E2
Gradiştea de Munte *Romania* 45°37N 23°13E **183** E8
Grado *Italy* 45°40N 13°23E **199** C10
Grado *Spain* 43°23N 6°4W **194** B4
Grady *U.S.A.* 34°49N 103°19W **305** J12
Graeca, Lacul *Romania* 44°5N 26°10E **183** F11
Grafarnes *Iceland* 64°55N 23°15W **155** C3
Gräfelfing *Germany* 48°7N 11°25E **131** B1
Grafenau *Germany* 48°51N 13°22E **179** G9
Gräfenberg *Germany* 49°39N 11°14E **179** F7
Grafham Water *U.K.* 52°19N 0°18W **169** E7
Grafton *N.S.W., Australia* 29°38S 152°58E **281** D5
Grafton *Ill., U.S.A.* 38°58N 90°26W **310** F6
Grafton *N. Dak., U.S.A.* 48°25N 97°25W **308** A5
Grafton *W. Va., U.S.A.* 39°21N 80°2W **309** F13
Grafton Caledonia Wildlife Estate *Trin. & Tob.* 11°11N 60°47W **323** s
Grafton's Pt. *Anguilla* 18°20N 62°54W **322** a
Gragoatá *Brazil* 22°53S 43°8W **135** B2
Graham *Ont., Canada* 49°20N 90°30W **298** C1
Graham *Ga., U.S.A.* 31°50N 82°30W **316** D7
Graham *Tex., U.S.A.* 33°6N 98°35W **314** E5
Graham, Mt. *U.S.A.* 32°42N 109°52W **305** K9
Graham Bell, Ostrov = Greem-Bell, Ostrov *Russia* 81°0N 62°0E **214** A7
Graham I. *B.C., Canada* 53°40N 132°30W **296** C2
Graham I. *Nunavut, Canada* 77°25N 90°30W **295** B13
Graham Land *Antarctica* 65°0S 64°0W **151** C17
Grahamstown = Makhanda *S. Africa* 33°19S 26°31E **270** D4
Grahamsville *U.S.A.* 41°51N 74°33W **313** E10
Grahovo *Montenegro* 42°40N 18°40E **202** D2
Graiba *Tunisia* 34°30N 10°13E **258** B2
Graie, Alpi *Europe* 45°30N 7°10E **175** C11
Grain Coast *W. Afr.* 4°20N 10°0W **262** E3
Grajagan *Indonesia* 8°35S 114°13E **231** K17
Grajaú *Brazil* 5°50S 46°4W **332** C2
Grajaú ➔ *Brazil* 3°41S 44°48W **332** B3
Grajewo *Poland* 53°39N 22°30E **184** E9
Gramada *Bulgaria* 43°49N 22°39E **202** C6
Gramat *France* 44°48N 1°43E **174** D5
Grammichele *Italy* 37°13N 14°38E **201** E7
Grámmos, Óros *Greece* 40°18N 20°47E **202** F4
Grampian *U.S.A.* 40°58N 78°37W **312** F6
Grampian Highlands = Grampian Mts. *U.K.* 56°50N 4°0W **167** E5
Grampian Mts. *U.K.* 56°50N 4°0W **167** E5
Grampians, The *Australia* 37°15S 142°20E **282** D5
Grampians △ *Australia* 37°15S 142°28E **282** D5
Gramsh *Albania* 40°52N 20°12E **202** F4
Gran *Norway* 60°23N 10°31E **164** D7
Gran ➔ *Suriname* 4°1N 55°30W **329** C6
Gran Altiplanicie Central *Argentina* 49°0S 69°30W **336** C3
Gran Canaria *Canary Is.* 27°55N 15°35W **153** e1
Gran Chaco *S. Amer.* 25°0S 61°0W **334** B3
Gran Couva *Trin. & Tob.* 10°24N 61°22W **323** t
Gran Desierto del Pinacate ⌂ *Mexico* 31°51N 113°32W **318** A2
Gran Laguna Salada *Argentina* 44°24S 67°23W **336** B3
Gran Pajonal *Peru* 10°45S 74°30W **330** C3
Gran Paradiso *Italy* 45°33N 7°17E **198** C4
Gran Sasso d'Itália *Italy* 42°27N 13°42E **199** F10
Gran Sasso e Monti Della Laga △ *Italy* 42°32N 13°22E **199** F10
Gran Tarajal *Canary Is.* 28°13N 14°1W **153** e2
Granada *Nic.* 11°58N 86°0W **320** D2
Granada *Spain* 37°10N 3°35W **195** H7
Granada *Colo., U.S.A.* 38°4N 102°19W **304** G12
Granada □ *Spain* 37°18N 3°0W **195** H7
Granadilla de Abona *Canary Is.* 28°7N 16°33W **153** e1
Granard *Ireland* 53°47N 7°30W **166** C4
Granbury *U.S.A.* 32°27N 97°47W **314** E6
Granby *Qué., Canada* 45°25N 72°45W **313** A12
Granby *Colo., U.S.A.* 40°5N 105°56W **304** F11
Grand ➔ *Ont., Canada* 42°51N 79°34W **312** D5
Grand ➔ *Mich., U.S.A.* 43°4N 86°15W **311** A10
Grand ➔ *Mo., U.S.A.* 39°23N 93°7W **310** E3
Grand ➔ *S. Dak., U.S.A.* 45°40N 100°45W **308** C3
Grand Abaque, Pte.du *Guadeloupe* 16°21N 61°0W **322** e
Grand-Anse = Portsmouth *Dominica* 15°34N 61°27W **323** k
Grand Anse *Grenada* 12°1N 61°45W **323** q
Grand Anse B. *Grenada* 12°2N 61°45W **323** q
Grand B. *Dominica* 15°14N 61°18W **323** k
Grand Bahama *The Bahamas* 26°40N 78°30W **320** A4
Grand Baie *Mauritius* 20°0S 57°35E **272** e
Grand Bank *Canada* 47°6N 55°48W **299** C8
Grand Banks *Atl. Oc.* 45°0N 52°0W **152** B6
Grand Bassam *Côte d'Ivoire* 5°10N 3°49W **262** D4
Grand Bassin *Réunion* 21°10S 55°32E **272** f
Grand Batanga *Cameroon* 2°50N 9°55E **264** B1
Grand Bazaar = Kapali Carsi *Turkey* 41°1N 28°58E **122** B1
Grand Bénare *Réunion* 21°6S 55°25E **272** f
Grand Bend *Canada* 43°18N 81°45W **312** C3
Grand Béréby *Côte d'Ivoire* 4°38N 6°55W **262** E3
Grand Blanc *U.S.A.* 42°56N 83°38W **311** B13
Grand Bois *Mauritius* 20°25S 57°32E **272** e
Grand-Bourg *Guadeloupe* 15°53N 61°19W **322** e
Grand Canal = Canal Grande *Venice, Italy* **142** b2
Grand Canal = Da Yunhe ➔ *China* 34°25N 120°5E **227** H10
Grand Canyon *U.S.A.* 36°3N 112°9W **305** H7
Grand Canyon △ *U.S.A.* 36°15N 112°30W **305** H7
Grand Canyon-Parashant ⌂ *U.S.A.* 36°30N 113°45W **305** H7
Grand Case *St.-Martin* 18°6N 63°4W **322** a
Grand Cayman *Cayman Is.* 19°20N 81°20W **320** C3
Grand Central Station *New York, U.S.A.* **132** c2
Grand Cess *Liberia* 4°40N 8°12W **262** E3
Grand Coulee *U.S.A.* 47°57N 119°0W **304** C4
Grand Coulee Dam *U.S.A.* 47°57N 118°59W **304** C4
Grand Cul-de-Sac Marin *Guadeloupe* 16°20N 61°35W **322** e
Grand Est □ *France* 48°30N 5°0E **173** D12
Grand Étang △ *Grenada* 12°5N 61°42W **323** q
Grand Falls *Canada* 47°3N 67°44W **299** C6
Grand Falls-Windsor *Canada* 48°56N 55°40W **299** C8
Grand Fond *St. Barts* 17°53N 62°48W **322** a
Grand Forks *B.C., Canada* 49°0N 118°30W **296** D5
Grand Forks *N. Dak., U.S.A.* 47°55N 97°3W **308** B5
Grand Galet *Réunion* 21°17S 55°38E **272** f
Grand Gaube *Mauritius* 20°0S 57°39E **272** e
Grand Gorge *U.S.A.* 42°21N 74°29W **313** D10
Grand Haven *U.S.A.* 43°4N 86°13W **311** A10
Grand I. *Mich., U.S.A.* 46°31N 86°40W **308** B10
Grand I. *N.Y., U.S.A.* 43°0N 78°58W **312** D6
Grand Îlet *Guadeloupe* 15°50N 61°35W **322** e
Grand Îlet *Réunion* 21°1S 55°29E **272** f
Grand Island *U.S.A.* 40°55N 98°21W **308** E4
Grand Isle *La., U.S.A.* 29°14N 90°0W **315** G9
Grand Isle *Vt., U.S.A.* 44°43N 73°18W **313** B11
Grand Junction *Colo., U.S.A.* 39°4N 108°33W **304** G9
Grand Junction *Iowa, U.S.A.* 42°2N 94°14W **310** B2
Grand L. *N.B., Canada* 45°57N 66°7W **299** C6
Grand L. *Nfld. & L., Canada* 49°0N 57°30W **299** C8
Grand L. *Nfld. & L., Canada* 53°40N 60°30W **299** B7
Grand L. *La., U.S.A.* 29°55N 92°47W **314** G8
Grand L. *Ohio, U.S.A.* 40°32N 84°25W **311** D12
Grand Lahou *Côte d'Ivoire* 5°10N 5°5W **262** D3
Grand Lake *U.S.A.* 40°15N 105°49W **304** F11
Grand Ledge *U.S.A.* 42°45N 84°45W **311** B12
Grand-Lieu, L. de *France* 47°6N 1°40W **172** E5
Grand Mal B. *Grenada* 12°4N 61°45W **323** q
Grand Manan I. *Canada* 44°45N 66°52W **299** D6
Grand Marais *Mich., U.S.A.* 46°40N 85°59W **309** B11
Grand Marais *Minn., U.S.A.* 47°45N 90°25W **298** C1
Grand Marigot B. *Dominica* 15°25N 61°16W **323** k
Grand-Mère *Canada* 46°36N 72°40W **298** C5
Grand Palace *Bangkok, Thailand* **113** b1
Grand Place *Belgium* 50°50N 4°21E **116** A2
Grand Popo *Benin* 6°15N 1°57E **263** D5
Grand Portage *U.S.A.* 47°58N 89°41W **308** B9
Grand Prairie *U.S.A.* 32°46N 96°59W **120** B3
Grand Rapids = Wisconsin Rapids *U.S.A.* 44°23N 89°49W **308** C9
Grand Rapids *Man., Canada* 53°12N 99°19W **297** C9
Grand Rapids *Mich., U.S.A.* 42°58N 85°40W **311** B10
Grand Rapids *Minn., U.S.A.* 47°14N 93°31W **308** B7
Grand Rapids ✈ (GRR) *U.S.A.* 42°53N 85°31W **311** B11
Grand Récif Sud *N. Cal.* 22°47S 166°55E **288** d
Grand Ridge *U.S.A.* 30°43N 85°1W **316** E4
Grand River *U.S.A.* 40°49N 93°58W **310** D3
Grand River Bay *Mauritius* 20°9S 57°27E **272** e
Grand River South East ➔ *Mauritius* 20°17S 57°46E **272** e
Grand' Rivière *Martinique* 14°52N 61°11W **322** j
Grand Roy *Grenada* 12°8N 61°45W **323** q
Grand St-Bernard, Col du *Europe* 45°50N 7°10E **179** K3

Grand Santi Fr. Guiana 4°20N 54°24W 329 C7
Grand Staircase-Escalante ⌓ U.S.A. 37°25N 111°33W 305 H8
Grand Teton U.S.A. 43°54N 110°50W 304 E8
Grand Teton △ U.S.A. 43°50N 110°50W 304 E8
Grand Union Canal U.K. 52°7N 0°53W 169 E7
Grandas Spain 43°13N 6°53W 194 B4
Grande → Jujuy, Argentina 24°20S 65°2W 334 A2
Grande → Mendoza, Argentina 36°52S 69°45W 334 D2
Grande → Bolivia 15°51S 64°39W 331 D5
Grande → Bahia, Brazil 11°30S 44°30W 332 D3
Grande → Minas Gerais, Brazil 20°6S 51°4W 333 F1
Grande → Venezuela 8°36N 61°39W 329 B5
Grande, B. Argentina 50°30S 68°20W 336 D3
Grande, Darsena Venice, Italy 142 b4
Grande, I. Brazil 23°9S 44°14W 333 F3
Grande, Rio → N. Amer. 25°58N 97°9W 314 J6
Grande, Serra Piauí, Brazil 8°0S 45°10W 332 C2
Grande, Serra Tocantins, Brazil 11°15S 46°30W 332 D2
Grande Anse = Beauséjour Guadeloupe 16°18N 61°4W 322 e
Grande Anse Guadeloupe 16°19N 61°47W 322 e
Grande Anse Martinique 14°30N 61°5W 322 j
Grande Anse St. Lucia 14°1N 60°54W 323 m
Grande Anse Seychelles 4°18S 55°45E 272 c
Grande Baleine → Canada 55°16N 77°47W 298 A4
Grande Cache Canada 53°53N 119°8W 296 C5
Grande Casse, Pte. de la France 45°24N 6°49E 175 C10
Grande Comore Comoros Is. 11°35S 43°20E 272 a
Grande Cul de Sac B St. Lucia 13°59N 61°2W 323 m
Grande-Entrée Canada 47°30N 61°40W 299 C7
Grande Matelot Pt. Trin. & Tob. 10°49N 61°9W 323 t
Grande Place Brussels, Belgium 116 b2
Grande Prairie Canada 55°10N 118°50W 296 B5
Grande Pte. Guadeloupe 15°58N 61°37W 322 e
Grande-Rivière Qué., Canada 48°26N 64°30W 299 C7
Grande Riviere Trin. & Tob. 10°50N 61°3W 323 t
Grande Rivière, Pte. de la Guadeloupe 16°18N 61°36W 322 e
Grande Rivière Noire Mauritius 20°21S 57°21E 272 e
Grande Rivière Sud Est Mauritius 20°17S 57°46E 272 e
Grande Sertão Veredas △ Brazil 15°10S 45°40W 333 E2
Grande-Terre Guadeloupe 16°20N 61°25W 322 e
Grande Terre Mayotte 12°46S 45°7E 272 b
Grande-Vallée Canada 49°14N 65°8W 299 C6
Grande Vigie, Pte. de la Guadeloupe 16°32N 61°27W 322 e
Grandfalls U.S.A. 31°20N 102°51W 314 F3
Grândola Portugal 38°12N 8°35W 195 G2
Grandpré France 49°20N 4°50E 173 C11
Grands Causses ⌓ France 44°5N 2°58E 174 D6
Grands-Jardins ⌓ Canada 47°41N 70°51W 299 C5
Grandview Man., Canada 51°10N 100°42W 297 C8
Grandview Mo., U.S.A. 38°53N 94°32W 310 F2
Grandview Wash., U.S.A. 46°15N 119°54W 304 C4
Grandview Heights U.S.A. 39°58N 83°2W 311 E13
Grandvilliers France 49°40N 1°57E 173 C8
Graneros Chile 34°5S 70°45W 334 C1
Grange Hill Jamaica 18°18N 78°11W 320 a
Grangemouth U.K. 56°1N 3°42W 167 E5
Granger U.S.A. 41°35N 109°58W 304 F9
Grängesberg Sweden 60°6N 15°1E 162 D9
Grangeville U.S.A. 45°56N 116°7W 304 D5
Granisle Canada 54°53N 126°13W 296 C3
Granit Rose, Côte France 48°50N 4°10W 172 D2
Granite City U.S.A. 38°42N 90°8W 310 F6
Granite Falls U.S.A. 44°49N 95°33W 308 C6
Granite L. Canada 48°8N 57°5W 299 C8
Granite Mt. U.S.A. 33°5N 116°28W 307 M10
Granite Pk. U.S.A. 45°10N 109°48W 304 D9
Graniteville S.C., U.S.A. 33°34N 81°49W 316 B8
Graniteville Vt., U.S.A. 44°8N 72°29W 313 B12
Granitola, C. Italy 37°34N 12°39E 200 E5
Granity N.Z. 41°39S 171°51E 285 B6
Granja Brazil 3°7S 40°50W 332 B3
Granja de Moreruela Spain 41°48N 5°44W 194 D5
Granja de Torrehermosa Spain 38°19N 5°35W 195 G5
Grankulla = Kauniainen Finland 60°13N 24°44E 121 B1
Gränna Sweden 58°1N 14°28E 163 F8
Granollers Spain 41°39N 2°18E 196 D7
Gransee Germany 53°1N 13°8E 178 B9
Grant Fla., U.S.A. 27°56N 80°32W 317 H9
Grant Nebr., U.S.A. 40°50N 101°43W 308 E3
Grant, Mt. U.S.A. 38°34N 118°48W 304 G4
Grant City U.S.A. 40°29N 94°25W 310 D2
Grant I. Australia 11°10S 132°52E 278 B5
Grant Park Chicago, U.S.A. 119 c2
Grant Range U.S.A. 38°30N 115°25W 304 G6
Grantham U.K. 52°55N 0°38W 168 E7
Grantley Adams Int. ✈ (BGI) Barbados 13°4N 59°29W 323 r
Granton U.K. 55°58N 3°14W 121 B2
Grantown-on-Spey U.K. 57°20N 3°36W 167 D5
Grants U.S.A. 35°9N 107°52W 305 J10
Grants Pass U.S.A. 42°26N 123°19W 304 E2
Grantsville U.S.A. 40°36N 112°28W 304 F7
Grantville U.S.A. 33°14N 84°50W 316 B5
Granville Manche, France 48°50N 1°35W 172 D5
Granville Trin. & Tob. 10°7N 61°48W 323 t
Granville Ill., U.S.A. 41°16N 89°14W 310 C7
Granville N. Dak., U.S.A. 48°16N 100°47W 308 A3
Granville N.Y., U.S.A. 43°24N 73°16W 313 C11
Granville Ohio, U.S.A. 40°4N 82°31W 312 F2
Granville L. Canada 56°18N 100°30W 297 B8
Granvin Norway 60°33N 6°45E 164 D3
Grapevine U.S.A. 32°56N 97°4W 120 A3
Grapevine Recr. Area U.S.A. 32°58N 97°3W 120 A3
Graskop S. Africa 24°56S 30°49E 271 B5
Gräsö Sweden 60°28N 18°35E 162 D12
Grass → Canada 56°3N 96°33W 297 B9
Grass Range U.S.A. 47°2N 108°48W 304 C9
Grass River ⌓ Canada 54°40N 100°50W 297 C8
Grass Valley Calif., U.S.A. 39°13N 121°4W 306 F6
Grass Valley Oreg., U.S.A. 45°22N 120°47W 304 D3
Grassano Italy 40°38N 16°17E 201 B9
Grasse France 43°38N 6°56E 175 E10
Grassflat U.S.A. 41°0N 78°6W 312 E6
Grassi, Palazzo Venice, Italy 142 b2
Grasslands △ Canada 49°11N 107°38W 297 D7
Grassy Australia 40°3S 144°5E 281 G3
Grassy Park S. Africa 34°3S 18°30E 118 B2
Gråsten Denmark 54°55N 9°35E 163 K3
Grästorp Sweden 58°20N 12°40E 163 F6
Gratis U.S.A. 39°38N 84°32W 311 E12
Gratkorn Austria 47°8N 15°21E 180 D8
Gratosóglio Italy 45°24N 9°1E 128 B2
Gratz U.S.A. 38°28N 84°57W 311 F12
Gratzwalde Germany 52°28N 13°42E 115 B5
Graubünden □ Switz. 46°45N 9°30E 179 J5
Graudenz = Grudziądz Poland 53°30N 18°47E 184 E5
Graulhet France 43°45N 1°59E 174 E5
Graus Spain 42°11N 0°20E 196 C5
Gravberget Norway 60°53N 12°14E 164 D9
Grave, Pte. de France 45°34N 1°4W 174 C2
Gravelbourg Canada 49°50N 106°35W 297 D7
Gravelines France 51°1N 2°10E 173 A9
's-Gravenhage Neths. 52°7N 4°17E 170 B4
Gravenhurst Canada 44°52N 79°20W 312 B5
Gravesend N.S.W., Australia 29°35S 150°20E 281 D5
Gravesend Kent, U.K. 51°26N 0°22E 169 F8
Gravesend N.Y., U.S.A. 40°36N 73°56W 132 C2
Gravina in Púglia Italy 40°49N 16°25E 201 B9
Gravois, Pointe-à- Haiti 18°2N 73°56W 321 C5
Gravona → France 41°58N 8°45E 175 G12
Gray Haute-Saône, France 47°22N 5°35E 173 E12
Gray Ga., U.S.A. 33°1N 83°32W 316 B6
Grayling Alaska, U.S.A. 62°57N 160°3W 303 E7
Grayling Mich., U.S.A. 44°40N 84°43W 309 C11
Grays U.K. 51°28N 0°21E 169 F8
Grays Harbor U.S.A. 46°59N 124°1W 306 D2
Grays L. U.S.A. 43°4N 111°26W 304 E8
Grays River U.S.A. 46°21N 123°37W 306 D3
Grayson U.S.A. 38°16N 88°0W 311 F9
Grayvoron Russia 50°29N 35°41E 189 G8
Graz Austria 47°4N 15°27E 180 D8
Grazhdanka Russia 59°59N 30°24E 137 B2
Grdelica Serbia 42°55N 22°3E 202 D6
Greåker Norway 59°16N 11°12E 164 E8
Greasy L. Canada 62°55N 122°12W 296 A4
Great Abaco I. = Abaco The Bahamas 26°25N 77°10W 320 A4
Great Artesian Basin Australia 23°0S 144°0E 280 C3
Great Australian Bight Australia 33°30S 130°0E 279 F5
Great Bacolet Bay Grenada 12°4N 61°37W 323 q
Great Bahama Bank The Bahamas 23°15N 78°0W 320 B4
Great Barrier I. N.Z. 36°11S 175°25E 284 C4
Great Barrier Reef Australia 18°0S 146°50E 280 B4
Great Barrier Reef ⌓ Australia 20°0S 150°0E 280 B4
Great Barrington U.S.A. 42°12N 73°22W 313 D11
Great Basalt Wall △ Australia 19°52S 145°43E 280 B4
Great Basin U.S.A. 40°0N 117°0W 304 G5
Great Basin △ U.S.A. 38°56N 114°15W 304 G6
Great Basses Sri Lanka 6°11N 81°29E 245 L5
Great Bear → Canada 65°0N 126°0W 294 E7
Great Bear L. Canada 65°30N 120°0W 294 D8
Great Belt = Store Bælt Denmark 55°20N 11°0E 163 J4
Great Bend Kans., U.S.A. 38°22N 98°46W 308 F4
Great Bend Pa., U.S.A. 41°58N 75°45W 313 E9
Great Blasket I. Ireland 52°6N 10°32W 166 D1
Great Britain Europe 54°0N 2°15W 158 E5
Great Camanoe Br. Virgin Is. 18°30N 64°35W 321 b
Great Channel Asia 6°0N 94°0E 245 L11
Great Coco I. = Koko Kyunzu Myanmar 14°7N 93°22E 245 G11
Great Codroy Canada 47°51N 59°16W 299 C8
Great Divide, The = Great Dividing Ra. Australia 23°0S 146°0E 280 C4
Great Divide Basin U.S.A. 42°0N 108°0W 304 E9
Great Dividing Ra. Australia 23°0S 146°0E 280 C4
Great Driffield = Driffield U.K. 54°0N 0°26W 168 C7
Great Exuma The Bahamas 23°30N 75°50W 320 B4
Great Falls Guyana 5°35N 61°0W 329 B5
Great Falls Mont., U.S.A. 47°30N 111°17W 304 C8
Great Fish = Groot-Vis → S. Africa 33°28S 27°5E 270 D4
Great Goat I. Jamaica 17°52N 77°3W 320 a
Great Guana Cay The Bahamas 24°0N 76°20W 320 B4
Great Hall of the People Beijing, China 114 c3
Great Himalayan △ India 31°30N 77°30E 242 D7
Great Inagua The Bahamas 21°0N 73°20W 321 B5
Great Indian Desert = Thar Desert India 28°0N 72°0E 242 F5
Great Karoo S. Africa 31°55S 21°0E 270 D3
Great Khingan Mts. = Da Hinggan Ling China 48°0N 121°0E 219 B13
Great Lake Australia 41°50S 146°40E 281 G4
Great Lakes N. Amer. 46°0N 84°0W 292 E11
Great Limpopo Transfrontier △ Africa 23°0S 31°45E 271 B5
Great Malvern U.K. 52°7N 2°18W 169 E5
Great Miami → U.S.A. 39°7N 84°49W 311 E12
Great Nicobar India 7°0N 93°50E 245 L11
Great Ormes Head U.K. 53°20N 3°52W 168 D4
Great Otway △ Australia 38°50S 143°50E 282 E5
Great Ouse → U.K. 52°48N 0°21E 168 E8
Great Palm I. Australia 18°45S 146°40E 280 B4
Great Pedro Bluff Jamaica 17°51N 77°44W 320 a
Great Pee Dee → U.S.A. 33°21N 79°10W 315 E15
Great Plains N. Amer. 47°0N 105°0W 292 E9
Great Ruaha → Tanzania 7°56S 37°52E 268 D4
Great Sacandaga L. U.S.A. 43°6N 74°16W 313 C10
Great Saint Bernard Pass = Grand St-Bernard, Col du Europe 45°50N 7°10E 179 K3
Great Salt Desert = Kavīr, Dasht-e Iran 34°30N 55°0E 247 C7
Great Salt L. U.S.A. 41°15N 112°40W 304 F7
Great Salt Lake Desert U.S.A. 40°50N 113°30W 304 F7
Great Salt Plains L. U.S.A. 36°45N 98°8W 314 C5
Great Salt Pond St. Kitts & Nevis 17°14N 62°40W 322 d
Great Sand Dunes ⌓ U.S.A. 37°48N 105°45W 305 H11
Great Sand Sea N. Afr. 29°0N 24°0E 258 C4
Great Sandy △ Australia 26°13S 153°2E 281 D5
Great Sandy Desert Australia 21°0S 124°0E 278 D3
Great Sangi = Sangihe, Pulau Indonesia 3°35N 125°30E 231 D7
Great Scarcies → S. Leone 9°0N 13°0W 262 D2
Great Sd. Bermuda 32°17N 64°51W 153 a
Great Sea Reef Fiji 16°15S 179°0E 287 A2
Great Sitkin I. U.S.A. 52°3N 176°6W 303 K3
Great Skellig Ireland 51°47N 10°33W 166 E1
Great Slave L. Canada 61°23N 115°38W 296 A5
Great Smoky Mts. △ U.S.A. 35°40N 83°40W 315 D13
Great Stour = Stour → U.K. 51°18N 1°22E 169 F9
Great Victoria Desert Australia 29°30S 126°30E 279 E4
Great Wall Antarctica 62°30S 58°0W 151 C18
Great Wall China 38°30N 109°30E 226 E5
Great Whale River = Kuujjuarapik Canada 55°20N 77°35W 298 A4
Great Whernside U.K. 54°10N 1°58W 168 C6
Great Yarmouth U.K. 52°37N 1°44E 169 E9
Great Zab = Zāb al Kabīr → Iraq 36°1N 43°24E 213 D10
Great Zimbabwe Zimbabwe 20°16S 30°54E 269 G3
Greater Accra □ Ghana 5°30N 0°5E 263 D4
Greater Antilles W. Indies 17°40N 74°0W 321 C5
Greater London □ U.K. 51°31N 0°6W 169 F7
Greater Manchester □ U.K. 53°30N 2°15W 168 D5
Greater Sudbury Canada 46°30N 81°0W 298 C3
Greater Sunda Is. Indonesia 7°0S 112°0E 230 F4
Grebbestad Sweden 58°42N 11°15E 163 F5
Grebenka = Hrebenka Ukraine 50°9N 32°22E 189 G7
Greco Italy 45°30N 9°12E 128 A2
Greco, C. Cyprus 34°57N 34°5E 207 F10
Greco, Mte. Italy 41°48N 13°58E 199 G10
Gredos, Sierra de Spain 40°20N 5°0W 194 E6
Greece U.S.A. 43°13N 77°41W 312 C7
Greece ■ Europe 40°0N 23°0E 204 B3
Greeley Colo., U.S.A. 40°25N 104°42W 304 F11
Greeley Nebr., U.S.A. 41°33N 98°32W 308 E4
Greeleyville U.S.A. 33°40N 79°59W 316 B10
Greely Fd. Canada 80°30N 85°0W 295 A15
Green-Bell, Ostrov Russia 81°0N 62°0E 214 A7
Green → Ky., U.S.A. 37°54N 87°30W 308 G10
Green → Utah, U.S.A. 38°11N 109°53W 304 G9
Green B. U.S.A. 45°0N 87°30W 308 C10
Green Bay U.S.A. 44°31N 88°0W 308 C9
Green C. Australia 37°13S 150°1E 283 D9
Green City U.S.A. 40°16N 92°57W 310 D4
Green Cove Springs U.S.A. 29°59N 81°42W 316 F8
Green I. = Lüdao Taiwan 22°40N 121°30E 225 D3
Green I. Antigua & B. 17°2N 61°40W 322 b
Green I. Hong Kong, China 22°17N 114°6E 122 B2
Green I. Grenada 12°13N 61°35W 323 q
Green Is. Papua N. G. 4°35S 154°10E 286 C8
Green Island Jamaica 18°23N 78°17W 320 a
Green Island B. Phil. 10°12N 119°22E 233 F2
Green Lake Canada 54°17N 107°47W 297 C7
Green Mt. = Peak, The Ascension I. 7°57S 14°20W 153 g
Green Mts. U.S.A. 43°45N 72°45W 313 C12
Green Point S. Africa 33°54S 18°25E 118 A1
Green Pond U.S.A. 32°44N 80°37W 316 C9
Green River Papua N. G. 3°54S 141°11E 286 B1
Green River Utah, U.S.A. 38°59N 110°10W 304 G8
Green River Wyo., U.S.A. 41°32N 109°28W 304 F9
Green Valley U.S.A. 31°52N 110°56W 305 L8
Greenacres U.S.A. 26°38N 80°7W 317 J9
Greenbank U.S.A. 48°6N 122°34W 306 B4
Greenbush Mich., U.S.A. 44°35N 83°19W 312 B1
Greenbush Minn., U.S.A. 48°42N 96°11W 308 A5
Greencastle U.S.A. 39°38N 86°52W 311 E10
Greene Iowa, U.S.A. 42°54N 92°48W 310 B4
Greene N.Y., U.S.A. 42°20N 75°46W 313 D9
Greeneville U.S.A. 36°10N 82°50W 315 C13
Greenfield Calif., U.S.A. 36°19N 121°15W 306 J5
Greenfield Calif., U.S.A. 35°15N 119°0W 307 K8
Greenfield Ill., U.S.A. 39°21N 90°12W 310 E6
Greenfield Ind., U.S.A. 39°47N 85°46W 311 E11
Greenfield Iowa, U.S.A. 41°18N 94°28W 310 C2
Greenfield Mass., U.S.A. 42°35N 72°36W 313 D12
Greenfield Mo., U.S.A. 37°25N 93°51W 308 G7
Greenfield Ohio, U.S.A. 39°21N 83°23W 311 E13
Greenfield Park Canada 45°29N 73°28W 130 B3
Greenford U.K. 51°31N 0°21W 125 A1
Greenhill U.K. 51°34N 0°18W 125 A2
Greenland ☒ N. Amer. 66°0N 45°0W 154 D6
Greenland Sea Arctic 73°0N 10°0W 154 B10
Greenmarket Square Cape Town, S. Africa 118 c2
Greenock U.K. 55°57N 4°46W 167 F4
Greenore Ireland 54°1N 6°9W 166 B5
Greenore Pt. Ireland 52°14N 6°19W 166 D5
Greenough Australia 28°58S 114°43E 279 E1
Greenough → Australia 28°51S 114°38E 279 E1
Greenough Pt. Canada 44°58N 81°26W 312 B3
Greenpoint New York, U.S.A. 132 e3
Greenport U.S.A. 41°6N 72°22W 313 E12
Greensboro Fla., U.S.A. 30°34N 84°45W 316 E5
Greensboro Ga., U.S.A. 33°35N 83°11W 316 B6
Greensboro N.C., U.S.A. 36°4N 79°48W 315 C15
Greensboro Vt., U.S.A. 44°36N 72°18W 313 B12
Greensburg Ind., U.S.A. 39°20N 85°29W 311 E11
Greensburg Kans., U.S.A. 37°36N 99°18W 308 G4
Greensburg Pa., U.S.A. 40°18N 79°33W 312 F5
Greenstone = Geraldton Canada 49°44N 87°10W 298 C2
Greenstone Pt. U.K. 57°55N 5°37W 167 D3
Greentown U.S.A. 40°29N 85°58W 311 D11
Greenup U.S.A. 39°15N 88°10W 311 E8
Greenvale Australia 18°59S 145°7E 280 B4
Greenville Liberia 5°1N 9°6W 262 D3
Greenville Ala., U.S.A. 31°50N 86°38W 315 F11
Greenville Calif., U.S.A. 40°8N 120°57W 306 E6
Greenville Fla., U.S.A. 30°28N 83°38W 316 E6
Greenville Ga., U.S.A. 33°2N 84°43W 316 B5
Greenville Ill., U.S.A. 38°53N 89°25W 310 F7
Greenville Ind., U.S.A. 38°22N 85°59W 311 F11
Greenville Maine, U.S.A. 45°28N 69°35W 309 C19
Greenville Mich., U.S.A. 43°11N 85°15W 311 A11
Greenville Miss., U.S.A. 33°24N 91°4W 315 E9
Greenville Mo., U.S.A. 37°8N 90°27W 308 G8
Greenville N.C., U.S.A. 35°37N 77°23W 315 D16
Greenville N.H., U.S.A. 42°46N 71°49W 313 D13
Greenville N.Y., U.S.A. 42°25N 74°1W 313 D10
Greenville Ohio, U.S.A. 40°6N 84°38W 311 D12
Greenville Pa., U.S.A. 41°24N 80°23W 312 E4
Greenville S.C., U.S.A. 34°51N 82°24W 315 D13
Greenville Tex., U.S.A. 33°8N 96°7W 314 E6
Greenwater Lake ⌓ Canada 52°32N 103°30W 297 C8
Greenwich Conn., U.S.A. 41°2N 73°38W 313 E11
Greenwich N.Y., U.S.A. 43°5N 73°30W 313 C11
Greenwich Ohio, U.S.A. 41°2N 82°31W 312 E2
Greenwich □ U.K. 51°29N 0°1E 125 B3
Greenwich Observatory U.K. 51°28N 0°0 125 B3
Greenwich Village New York, U.S.A. 132 d1
Greenwood B.C., Canada 49°10N 118°40W 296 D5
Greenwood Ark., U.S.A. 35°13N 94°16W 314 D7
Greenwood Fla., U.S.A. 30°52N 85°10W 316 E4
Greenwood Ind., U.S.A. 39°37N 86°7W 311 E10
Greenwood Mass., U.S.A. 42°29N 71°2W 116 A2
Greenwood Miss., U.S.A. 33°31N 90°11W 315 E9
Greenwood S.C., U.S.A. 34°12N 82°10W 316 A7
Greenwood, Mt. Australia 13°48S 130°4E 278 B5
Greenwood Great House Jamaica 18°29N 77°44W 320 a
Grefsen Norway 59°56N 10°47E 133 A3
Gregbe Côte d'Ivoire 6°48N 6°43W 262 D3
Gregório → Brazil 6°50S 70°46W 330 B3
Gregory S. Dak., U.S.A. 43°14N 99°26W 308 D4
Gregory → Australia 17°53S 139°17E 280 B2
Gregory, L. S. Austral., Australia 28°55S 139°0E 281 D2
Gregory, L. W. Austral., Australia 20°0S 127°40E 278 D4
Gregory, L. W. Austral., Australia 25°38S 119°58E 279 E2
Gregory △ Australia 15°38S 131°15E 278 C5
Gregory Downs Australia 18°35S 138°45E 280 B2
Gregory Ra. Queens., Australia 19°30S 143°40E 280 B3
Gregory Ra. W. Austral., Australia 21°20S 121°12E 278 D3
Greifenberg = Gryfice Poland 53°55N 15°13E 184 E2
Greifenhagen = Gryfino Poland 53°16N 14°29E 185 E1
Greiffenberg = Gryfów Śląski Poland 51°2N 15°24E 185 G2
Greiffenberg Germany 53°5N 13°57E 178 B9
Greifswald Germany 54°5N 13°23E 178 A9
Greifswalder Bodden Germany 54°12N 13°35E 178 A9
Grein Austria 48°14N 14°51E 180 C7
Greiz Germany 50°39N 12°10E 178 E8
Gremikha Russia 67°59N 39°47E 186 A6
Grenaa Denmark 56°25N 10°53E 163 H4
Grenada U.S.A. 33°47N 89°49W 315 E10
Grenada ■ W. Indies 12°10N 61°40W 323 q
Grenade France 43°47N 1°17E 174 E5
Grenadier I. U.S.A. 44°3N 76°22W 313 B8
Grenadines, The St. Vincent 12°40N 61°20W 323 n
Grenchen Switz. 47°12N 7°24E 179 H3
Grenen Denmark 57°44N 10°40E 163 G4
Grenfell N.S.W., Australia 33°52S 148°8E 283 B8
Grenfell Sask., Canada 50°30N 102°56W 297 C8
Grenivík Iceland 65°57N 18°11W 155 B8
Grenjaðarstaður Iceland 65°49N 17°21W 155 B9
Grenoble France 45°12N 5°42E 175 C9
Grenville Grenada 12°7N 61°37W 323 q
Grenville, C. Australia 12°0S 143°13E 286 F2
Grenville Chan. Canada 53°40N 129°46W 296 C3
Gréoux-les-Bains France 43°45N 5°52E 175 E9
Gresham U.S.A. 45°30N 122°25W 306 E4
Gresham Park U.S.A. 33°43N 84°20W 113 B2
Gresik Indonesia 7°13S 112°38E 235 D4
Gretna Dumf. & Gall., U.K. 55°0N 3°3W 167 F5
Gretna Fla., U.S.A. 30°37N 84°40W 316 E5
Gretna La., U.S.A. 29°54N 90°3W 131 B2
Gretna City Park U.S.A. 29°54N 90°3W 131 B2
Greve Strand Denmark 55°34N 12°18E 118 B1
Greven Germany 52°6N 7°37E 178 C3
Grevena Greece 40°4N 21°25E 202 F5
Grevenbroich Germany 51°5N 6°35E 178 D2
Grevenmacher Lux. 49°41N 6°26E 170 E6
Grevesmühlen Germany 53°52N 11°12E 178 B7
Grey → Nfld. & L., Canada 47°34N 57°6W 299 C8
Grey → N.Z. 42°27S 171°12E 285 C6
Grey, C. Australia 13°0S 136°35E 280 A2
Grey Is. Canada 50°50N 55°35W 295 G20
Grey Ra. Australia 27°0S 143°30E 281 D3
Greybull U.S.A. 44°30N 108°3W 304 D9
Greyfriars Kirk Edinburgh, U.K. 121 c3
Greymouth N.Z. 42°29S 171°13E 285 C6
Greynolds Park U.S.A. 25°56N 80°9W 129 C3
Greystones Ireland 53°9N 6°5W 166 C5
Greytown N.Z. 41°5S 175°29E 284 H4
Greytown KwaZulu Natal, S. Africa 29°1S 30°36E 271 C5
Gribanovskiy Russia 51°28N 41°50E 190 E5
Gribbell I. Canada 53°23N 129°0W 296 C3
Gribës, Mal i Albania 40°17N 19°45E 202 F3
Gribingui → C.A.R. 8°33N 19°5E 264 A3
Gribingui-Bamingui ⌓ C.A.R. 7°45N 19°17E 264 A3
Gridley U.S.A. 39°22N 121°42W 306 F5
Griebeg, Ras il- Malta 35°58N 14°23E 206 F7
Griebnitzsee Germany 52°23N 13°8E 115 B1
Griekwastad S. Africa 28°49S 23°15E 270 C3
Griesheim Germany 49°51N 8°33E 179 F4
Grieskirchen Austria 48°16N 13°48E 180 C6
Griffin U.S.A. 33°15N 84°16W 316 B5
Griffin, L. U.S.A. 28°52N 81°51W 317 G8
Griffith N.S.W., Australia 34°18S 146°2E 283 C7
Griffith Ont., Canada 45°15N 77°10W 312 A7
Griffith Ind., U.S.A. 41°32N 87°25W 311 C9
Griffith I. Canada 44°50N 80°55W 312 B4
Griffith Park U.S.A. 34°8N 118°17W 126 B3
Griggsville U.S.A. 39°43N 90°43W 310 E6
Grignols France 44°23N 0°2W 174 D3
Grigoriopol Moldova 47°9N 29°18E 183 C14
Grimari C.A.R. 5°43N 20°6E 264 A4
Grimaylov = Hrymayliv Ukraine 49°20N 26°5E 177 D14
Grimbergen Belgium 50°56N 4°22E 116 A2
Grimes U.S.A. 39°4N 121°54W 306 F5
Grimm = Kamenskiy Russia 50°48N 45°25E 190 E7
Grimma Germany 51°14N 12°43E 178 D8
Grimmen Germany 54°7N 13°2E 178 A9
Grimsay U.K. 57°29N 7°14W 167 D1
Grimsby Canada 43°12N 79°34W 312 C5
Grimsby N.E. Lincs., U.K. 53°34N 0°5W 168 D7
Grimsey Iceland 66°33N 17°58W 155 A9
Grimshaw Canada 56°10N 117°40W 296 B5
Grimslöv Sweden 56°44N 14°34E 163 H8
Grímsstaðir Iceland 65°39N 16°7W 155 B10
Grimstad Norway 58°20N 8°35E 164 F5
Grímsvötn Iceland 64°26N 17°22W 155 C9
Grindavík Iceland 63°50N 22°26W 155 D4
Grindelwald Switz. 46°38N 8°2E 179 J4
Grindsted Denmark 55°46N 8°55E 163 J2
Grindstone I. U.S.A. 44°17N 76°27W 313 B8
Grindu Romania 44°44N 26°50E 183 F11
Grinnell U.S.A. 41°45N 92°43W 310 C4
Grinnell Pen. Canada 76°40N 95°0W 295 B13
Grintavec Slovenia 46°22N 14°32E 199 B11
Grinzing Austria 48°15N 16°20E 142 A2
Griomasaigh = Grimsay U.K. 57°29N 7°14W 167 D1
Gris-Nez, C. France 50°52N 1°35E 173 B8
Grise Fiord Canada 76°25N 82°57W 295 B15
Grishino = Krasnoarmeisk Ukraine 48°18N 37°11E 189 H9
Grisolles France 43°49N 1°19E 174 E5
Grisons = Graubünden □ Switz. 46°45N 9°30E 179 J5
Grisslehamn Sweden 60°5N 18°49E 162 D12
Grmeč Planina Bos.-H. 44°43N 16°16E 199 D13
Groais I. Canada 50°55N 55°35W 299 B8
Gröbenried Germany 48°13N 11°25E 131 A1
Grobiņa Latvia 56°33N 21°10E 184 B8
Groblersdal S. Africa 25°15S 29°25E 271 C4
Grobming Austria 47°27N 13°54E 180 D6
Grochów Poland 52°15N 21°5E 143 B2
Grocka Serbia 44°40N 20°42E 202 B4
Gródek Poland 53°6N 23°40E 185 E10
Gródek Tagiellonski = Horodok Ukraine 49°46N 23°32E 177 D12
Grodekovo = Pogranichnyy Russia 44°25N 131°24E 220 B5
Grodków Poland 50°43N 17°21E 185 H4
Grodno = Hrodna Belarus 53°42N 23°52E 184 E10
Grodzisk Poland 52°19N 21°4E 143 B2
Grodzisk Mazowiecki Poland 52°7N 20°37E 185 F7
Grodzisk Wielkopolski Poland 52°15N 16°22E 185 F3
Grodzyanka = Hrodzyanka Belarus 53°31N 28°42E 177 B15
Groenendaal Belgium 50°46N 4°26E 116 B2
Groesbeck U.S.A. 31°31N 96°32W 314 F6
Grogol Petamburin Indonesia 6°9S 106°46E 122 A1
Groix France 47°38N 3°29W 172 E3
Groix, Î. de France 47°38N 3°28W 172 E3
Grójec Poland 51°50N 20°58E 185 G7
Gronau Niedersachsen, Germany 52°5N 9°47E 178 C5
Gronau Nordrhein-Westfalen, Germany 52°12N 7°2E 178 C3
Grong Norway 64°25N 12°8E 160 D15
Grönhögen Sweden 56°16N 16°24E 163 H10
Groningen Neths. 53°15N 6°35E 170 A6
Groningen Suriname 5°48N 55°28W 329 B6
Groningen □ Neths. 53°16N 6°40E 170 A6
Gronlands ⌓ Greenland 75°0N 35°0W 154 C7
Grønnedal = Kangilinnguit Greenland 61°20N 47°57W 154 E6
Gronsdorf Germany 48°7N 11°42E 131 B3
Groom U.S.A. 35°12N 101°6W 314 D4
Groot → S. Africa 33°45S 24°36E 270 D3
Groot-Berg → S. Africa 32°47S 18°8E 270 D2
Groot-Brakrivier S. Africa 34°2S 22°18E 270 D3
Groot Karasberge Namibia 27°20S 18°40E 270 C2
Groot-Kei → S. Africa 32°41S 28°22E 271 D4
Groot-Vis → S. Africa 33°28S 27°5E 270 D4
Grootdrink S. Africa 28°33S 21°42E 270 C3
Groote Eylandt Australia 14°0S 136°40E 280 A2
Groote Peel △ Neths. 51°22N 5°49E 170 C5
Grootfontein Namibia 19°31S 18°6E 270 A2
Grootlaagte → Africa 20°55S 21°27E 270 B3
Grootvloer → S. Africa 30°0S 20°40E 270 D3
Grorud Norway 59°57N 10°52E 133 A4
Gros C. Canada 61°59N 113°32W 296 A6
Gros Cap Guadeloupe 16°24N 61°25W 322 e
Gros Islet St. Lucia 14°5N 60°58W 323 m
Gros-Morne Martinique 14°43N 61°2W 322 j
Gros Morne △ Canada 49°40N 57°50W 299 C8
Gros Piton St. Lucia 13°49N 61°5W 323 m
Grósio Italy 46°18N 10°16E 198 B7
Grosne → France 46°42N 4°56E 173 F11
Gross Glienicke Berlin, Germany 52°28N 13°6E 115 B1
Gross-Hadern Germany 48°6N 11°29E 131 B1
Gross-Lappen Germany 48°11N 11°35E 131 A2
Gross-Meseritsch = Velké Meziříčí Czechia 49°21N 16°1E 180 B9
Gross-Strehlitz = Strzelce Opolskie Poland 50°31N 18°18E 185 H5
Gross Wartenberg = Syców Poland 51°19N 17°40E 185 G4
Grossa, Pta. Spain 39°6N 1°36E 206 C2
Grosse I. U.S.A. 42°8N 83°9W 311 B13
Grosse Krampe Germany 52°23N 13°40E 115 B5
Grosse Müggelsee Germany 52°26N 13°38E 115 B4
Grosse Point U.S.A. 42°23N 82°54W 312 D2
Grosse Point Lighthouse U.S.A. 42°2N 87°41W 119 A2
Grosse Pte. Guadeloupe 16°1N 61°17W 322 e
Grossenbrode Germany 54°21N 11°4E 178 A7
Grossenhain Germany 51°17N 13°32E 178 D9
Grossenzersdorf Austria 48°12N 16°33E 142 A3
Grossenzersdorfer Arm → Austria 48°12N 16°31E 142 A3
Grosser Arber Germany 49°6N 13°8E 179 F9
Grosser Biberhaufen Austria 48°12N 16°28E 142 A2
Grosser Plöner See Germany 54°10N 10°22E 178 A6
Grosser Wannsee Germany 52°25N 13°10E 115 B2
Grosseto Italy 42°46N 11°8E 199 F8
Grossfeld-Siedlung Austria 48°16N 16°26E 142 A2
Grossgerungs Austria 48°34N 14°57E 180 C7
Grossglockner Austria 47°5N 12°40E 180 D5
Grosshesselohe Germany 48°3N 11°32E 131 B2
Grossjedlersdorf Austria 48°16N 16°23E 142 A2
Grosswardein = Oradea Romania 47°2N 21°58E 182 C6
Grossziethen Germany 52°23N 13°26E 115 B3
Groswater B. Canada 54°20N 57°40W 299 B8
Grotli Norway 62°2N 7°42E 164 B4
Groton Conn., U.S.A. 41°21N 72°5W 313 E12
Groton N.Y., U.S.A. 42°36N 76°22W 313 D8
Groton S. Dak., U.S.A. 45°27N 98°6W 308 C4
Grottáglie Italy 40°32N 17°26E 201 B10
Grottaminarda Italy 41°4N 15°2E 201 A8
Grottammare Italy 42°59N 13°52E 199 F10
Grotte Chauvet-Pont d'Arc France 44°23N 4°25E 175 D8
Grottkau = Grodków Poland 50°43N 17°21E 185 H4
Grouard Mission Canada 55°33N 116°9W 296 B5
Grouin, Pte. du France 48°43N 1°51W 172 D5
Groulx, Mts. Canada 51°27N 68°41W 299 B6
Ground Zero = National September 11 Memorial and Museum New York, U.S.A. 132 e1
Groundhog → Canada 48°45N 82°58W 298 C3
Grouw Neths. 53°5N 5°51E 170 A5
Grove City Fla., U.S.A. 26°56N 82°19W 317 J7
Grove City Ohio, U.S.A. 39°53N 83°6W 311 E13
Grove City Pa., U.S.A. 41°10N 80°5W 312 E4
Grove Hall U.S.A. 42°18N 71°4W 116 B2
Grove Hill U.S.A. 31°42N 87°47W 315 F11
Grove Park Hounslow, U.K. 51°28N 0°15W 125 B2
Grove Park Lewisham, U.K. 51°25N 0°1E 125 B4
Grove Park Georgia, U.S.A. 33°46N 84°26W 113 B2
Groveland Calif., U.S.A. 37°50N 120°14W 306 H6
Groveland Fla., U.S.A. 28°34N 81°51W 317 G8
Grover = Tiltonsville U.S.A. 40°10N 80°41W 312 F4
Grover Beach U.S.A. 35°7N 120°37W 307 K6
Groves U.S.A. 29°57N 93°54W 314 G8
Groveton N.H., U.S.A. 44°36N 71°31W 313 B13
Groveton Va., U.S.A. 38°46N 77°6W 143 C2
Grovetown U.S.A. 33°27N 82°12W 316 B7
Groznjan Croatia 45°22N 13°43E 199 C10
Groznyy Russia 43°20N 45°45E 191 J7
Grua Norway 60°16N 10°40E 164 D7
Grubišno Polje Croatia 45°44N 17°12E 182 E2
Grudovo Bulgaria 42°21N 27°10E 203 D11
Grudusk Poland 53°3N 20°38E 185 E7
Grudziądz Poland 53°30N 18°47E 184 E5
Gruinard B. U.K. 57°56N 5°35W 167 D3
Gruissan France 43°8N 3°7E 174 E7
Grumo Áppula Italy 41°1N 16°42E 201 A9
Grums Sweden 59°22N 13°5E 162 E7
Grünau Germany 52°25N 13°34E 115 B4
Grünberg Germany 50°35N 8°58E 178 E4
Grünberg in Schlesien = Zielona Góra Poland 51°57N 15°31E 185 G2
Grund Iceland 65°31N 18°9W 155 B8
Gründau Germany 50°10N 9°9E 179 E5
Grundy Center U.S.A. 42°22N 92°47W 310 B4
Grunewald Germany 52°28N 13°15E 115 B2
Grungedal Norway 59°44N 7°43E 164 E4
Grünstadt Germany 49°34N 8°9E 179 F4
Grünwald Germany 48°2N 11°31E 131 B2
Grünwalder Forst Germany 48°2N 11°33E 131 B2
Gruppo di Tessa △ Italy 46°47N 11°0E 198 B8
Gruvberget Sweden 61°6N 16°10E 162 C10
Gruver U.S.A. 36°16N 101°24W 314 C4
Gruyères Switz. 46°35N 7°4E 179 J3
Gruža Serbia 43°54N 20°46E 202 C4
Gryazi Russia 52°30N 39°58E 190 D4
Gryazliv = Borovichi Russia 58°25N 33°55E 188 C7
Gryazovets Russia 58°50N 40°10E 188 C11
Grybów Poland 49°36N 20°55E 185 J7
Grycksbo Sweden 60°40N 15°29E 162 D9
Gryfice Poland 53°55N 15°13E 184 E2
Gryfino Poland 53°16N 14°29E 185 E1
Gryfów Śląski Poland 51°2N 15°24E 185 G2
Grymes Hill U.S.A. 40°36N 74°6W 132 C1
Gryt Sweden 58°12N 16°48E 163 F10
Grythyttan Sweden 59°41N 14°32E 162 E8
Grytviken S. Georgia 54°19S 36°33W 152 M8
Gstaad Switz. 46°28N 7°18E 179 J3
Gua India 22°18N 85°20E 243 H11
Gua Musang Malaysia 4°53N 101°58E 237 K3
Guabún, Pta. Chile 41°48S 74°2W 336 B2
Guacanayabo, G. de Cuba 20°40N 77°20W 320 B4
Guacara Venezuela 10°14N 67°53W 328 A4
Guachípas → Argentina 25°40S 65°30W 334 B2
Guadajoz → Spain 37°50N 4°51W 195 H6
Guadalajara Jalisco, Mexico 20°40N 103°20W 318 C4
Guadalajara Spain 40°37N 3°12W 196 E1
Guadalajara □ Spain 40°47N 2°30W 196 E2
Guadalaviar = Turia → Spain 39°27N 0°19W 197 F4
Guadalcanal Solomon Is. 9°32S 160°12E 287 M11
Guadalcanal Spain 38°5N 5°52W 195 G5
Guadalén → Spain 38°5N 3°32W 195 G7
Guadales Argentina 34°30S 67°55W 334 C2
Guadalete → Spain 36°35N 6°13W 195 J4
Guadalimar → Spain 38°5N 3°28W 195 G7
Guadalmena → Spain 38°19N 2°56W 195 G8
Guadalmez → Spain 38°46N 5°4W 195 G5
Guadalope → Spain 41°15N 0°3W 196 D4
Guadalquivir → Spain 36°47N 6°22W 195 J4
Guadalupe = Guadeloupe ☒ W. Indies 16°15N 61°40W 322 e
Guadalupe Brazil 6°44S 43°47W 332 C3
Guadalupe Zacatecas, Mexico 22°45N 102°31W 318 C4
Guadalupe Manila, Phil. 14°34N 121°2E 127 B2
Guadalupe Spain 39°27N 5°17W 195 F5
Guadalupe Calif., U.S.A. 34°58N 120°34W 307 L6
Guadalupe → U.S.A. 28°27N 96°47W 314 G6
Guadalupe, Basilica de Mexico 19°29N 99°7W 128 B2
Guadalupe, Sierra de Spain 39°28N 5°30W 195 F5
Guadalupe de Bravo Mexico 31°23N 106°7W 318 A3
Guadalupe I. Pac. Oc. 29°0N 118°50W 292 G8
Guadalupe Mts. △ U.S.A. 31°40N 104°30W 314 F2
Guadalupe Peak U.S.A. 31°50N 104°52W 314 F2
Guadalupe y Calvo Mexico 26°6N 106°58W 318 B3
Guadarrama, Sierra de Spain 41°0N 4°0W 194 E7
Guadeloupe ☒ W. Indies 16°15N 61°40W 322 e
Guadeloupe △ Guadeloupe 16°10N 61°40W 322 e
Guadeloupe Passage W. Indies 16°50N 62°15W 322 e
Guadalupe Peru 7°15S 79°29W 330 B2
Guadiamar → Spain 36°55N 6°24W 195 J4
Guadiana → Portugal 37°14N 7°22W 195 H3
Guadiana Menor → Spain 37°56N 3°15W 195 H7
Guadiaro → Spain 36°17N 5°17W 195 J5
Guadiato → Spain 37°48N 5°5W 195 H5
Guadiela → Spain 40°22N 2°49W 196 E2
Guadix Spain 37°18N 3°11W 195 H7
Guafo, Boca del Chile 43°35S 74°0W 336 B2
Guafo, I. Chile 43°35S 74°50W 336 B2
Guåhån = Guam ☒ Pac. Oc. 13°27N 144°45E 302 d
Guaico Trin. & Tob. 10°35N 61°9W 323 t
Guainía □ Colombia 2°30N 69°0W 328 C4
Guainía → Colombia 2°1N 67°7W 328 C4
Guaíra Brazil 24°5S 54°10W 335 A5
Guairá □ Paraguay 25°45S 56°30W 334 B4
Guaire = Gorey Ireland 52°41N 6°18W 166 D5
Guaitecas, Is. Chile 44°0S 74°30W 336 B2
Guajará-Mirim Brazil 10°50S 65°20W 331 C4
Guajira □ Colombia 11°30N 72°30W 328 A3
Guajira, Pen. de la Colombia 12°0N 72°0W 328 A3
Gualaceo Ecuador 2°54S 78°47W 328 D2
Gualán Guatemala 15°8N 89°22W 320 C2
Gualdo Tadino Italy 43°14N 12°47E 199 E9
Gualeguay Argentina 33°10S 59°14W 334 C4
Gualeguaychú Argentina 33°3S 59°31W 334 C4
Gualequay → Argentina 33°19S 59°39W 334 C4
Gualicho, Salina Argentina 40°25S 65°20W 336 B3
Gualjaina Argentina 42°45S 70°30W 336 B2
Guam ☒ Pac. Oc. 13°27N 144°45E 302 d
Guamache, B. de Venezuela 10°53N 64°5W 329 a
Guamblin, I. Chile 44°50S 75°0W 336 B2
Guamini Argentina 37°1S 62°28W 334 D3
Guamote Ecuador 1°56S 78°43W 328 D2
Guampí, Sierra de Venezuela 6°0N 65°35W 329 B4
Guamúchil Mexico 25°28N 108°6W 318 B3
Guana I. Br. Virgin Is. 18°30N 64°30W 321 b
Guanabacoa Cuba 23°8N 82°18W 320 B3
Guanabara, B. de Brazil 22°52S 43°10W 135 B1
Guanabara, Jardim Brazil 22°48S 43°11W 135 A1
Guanabara, Palácio da Brazil 22°56S 43°11W 135 B1
Guanacaste Costa Rica 10°30N 85°30W 320 D2
Guanacaste, Cordillera de Costa Rica 10°40N 85°4W 320 D2
Guanacaste △ Costa Rica 10°57N 85°30W 320 D2
Guanaceví Mexico 25°56N 105°57W 318 B3
Guanahani = San Salvador The Bahamas 24°0N 74°30W 321 B5
Guanaja Honduras 16°30N 85°55W 320 C2
Guanajay Cuba 22°56N 82°42W 320 B3
Guanajuato Mexico 21°1N 101°15W 318 C4
Guanajuato □ Mexico 21°0N 101°0W 318 C4
Guanambi Brazil 14°13S 42°47W 333 D3
Guanapo Trin. & Tob. 10°36N 61°15W 323 t
Guanare Venezuela 8°42N 69°12W 328 B4
Guanare → Venezuela 8°13N 67°46W 328 B4
Guandacol Argentina 29°30S 68°40W 334 B2
Guandi Shan China 37°53N 111°29E 226 F6
Guane Cuba 22°10N 84°7W 320 B3
Guang'an China 30°28N 106°35E 228 B6
Guang'anmen China 39°51N 116°18E 114 B1
Guangchang China 26°50N 116°21E 229 D11
Guangde China 30°54N 119°25E 229 B12
Guangdong □ China 23°0N 113°0E 229 F9
Guangdong Olympic Stadium Guangzhou, China 23°9N 113°22E 121 B3
Guangfeng China 28°20N 118°15E 229 C12
Guangfu = Kuangfu Taiwan 23°40N 121°25E 225 C3
Guanghan China 30°58N 104°17E 228 B5
Guangling China 39°47N 114°22E 226 E8
Guangnan China 24°5N 105°4E 228 E5
Guangning China 23°40N 112°22E 229 F9
Guangqumen China 39°52N 116°25E 114 B2
Guangrao China 37°5N 118°25E 227 F10
Guangshui China 31°37N 114°0E 229 B10
Guangshun China 26°8N 106°21E 228 D6
Guangwu China 37°48N 105°57E 226 F3
Guangxi Zhuangzu Zizhiqu □ China 24°0N 109°0E 228 F7
Guangyuan China 32°26N 105°51E 226 H3
Guangze China 27°30N 117°12E 229 D11
Guangzhou China 23°6N 113°13E 121 B2
Guangzhou Baiyun Int. ✈ (CAN) China 23°24N 113°18E 229 F9
Guanhães Brazil 18°47S 42°57W 333 E3
Guanica Puerto Rico 17°58N 66°55W 321 b
Guanipa → Venezuela 9°56N 62°26W 329 B5
Guanling China 25°56N 105°35E 228 E5
Guanmiao = Kuanmiao Taiwan 22°58N 120°19E 225 D2
Guannan China 34°8N 119°21E 227 G10
Guanshuo China 23°4N 113°22E 121 B3
Guanta Venezuela 10°14N 64°36W 329 A5
Guantánamo Cuba 20°10N 75°14W 321 B4
Guantánamo B. Cuba 19°59N 75°10W 321 C4
Guantao China 36°42N 115°25E 226 F8
Guanting Shuiku China 40°14N 115°35E 226 D8
Guanxi = Kuanhsi Taiwan 24°48N 121°10E 225 B3
Guanyang China 25°30N 111°8E 229 E8
Guanyin = Kuanyin Taiwan 25°2N 121°4E 225 A3
Guanyun China 34°20N 119°18E 227 G10

Guapay = Grande → Bolivia 15°51S 64°39W 331 D5
Guapí Colombia 2°36N 77°54W 328 C2
Guápiles Costa Rica 10°10N 83°46W 320 D3
Guapo → Trin. & Tob. 10°11N 61°40W 323 t
Guapo B. Trin. & Tob. 10°12N 61°41W 323 t
Guaporé = Rondônia Brazil 10°52S 61°57W 331 C5
Guaporé Brazil 28°51S 51°54W 335 B5
Guaporé → Brazil 11°55S 65°4W 331 C4
Guaqui Bolivia 16°41S 68°54W 330 D4
Guara, Sierra de Spain 42°19N 0°15W 196 C4
Guarabira Brazil 6°51S 35°29W 332 C4
Guaracara → Trin. & Tob. 10°18N 61°28W 323 t
Guarachirá → Colombia 5°27N 70°36W 328 B3
Guaranda Ecuador 1°36S 79°0W 328 D2
Guarani = Pacajus Brazil 4°10S 38°31W 332 B4
Guarapari Brazil 20°40S 40°30W 333 F3
Guarapuava Brazil 25°20S 51°30W 333 G1
Guaratinguetá Brazil 22°49S 45°9W 335 A6
Guaratuba Brazil 25°53S 48°38W 335 B6
Guarda Portugal 40°32N 7°20W 194 E3
Guarda □ Portugal 40°40N 7°20W 194 E3
Guardafui, C. = Asir, Ras Somalia 11°55N 51°10E 267 B7
Guardamar del Segura Spain 38°5N 0°39W 197 G4
Guardavalle Italy 38°30N 16°30E 201 D9
Guárdia Sanframondi Italy 41°15N 14°36E 201 A7
Guardiagrele Italy 42°11N 14°13E 199 F11
Guardo Spain 42°47N 4°50W 194 C6
Guareña Spain 38°51N 6°6W 195 G4
Guareña → Spain 41°29N 5°23W 194 D5
Guari Papua N. G. 8°3S 146°52E 286 E4
Guárico □ Venezuela 8°40N 66°35W 328 B4
Guarrojo → Colombia 4°6N 70°42W 328 C3
Guarujá Brazil 24°2S 46°25W 335 A6
Guarulhos Brazil 23°29S 46°33W 335 A6
Guarulhos Int., São Paulo ✈ (GRU) Brazil 23°26S 46°28W 333 F2
Guasave Mexico 25°34N 108°27W 318 B3
Guascama, Pta. Colombia 2°32N 78°24W 328 C2
Guasdualito Venezuela 7°15N 70°44W 328 B3
Guasipati Venezuela 7°28N 61°54W 329 B5
Guasopa Papua N. G. 9°12S 152°56E 286 E7
Guastalla Italy 44°55N 10°39E 198 D7
Guatemala Guatemala 14°40N 90°22W 320 D1
Guatemala ■ Cent. Amer. 15°40N 90°30W 320 C1
Guatemala Basin Pac. Oc. 11°0N 95°0W 289 F18
Guatemala Trench Pac. Oc. 14°0N 95°0W 292 H10
Guatire Venezuela 10°28N 66°32W 328 A4
Guatopo △ Venezuela 10°5N 66°30W 328 A4
Guatuaro Pt. Trin. & Tob. 10°19N 60°59W 323 t
Guavi → Papua N. G. 7°48S 143°16E 286 D2
Guaviare □ Colombia 2°0N 72°30W 328 C3
Guaviare → Colombia 4°3N 67°44W 328 C4
Guaxupé Brazil 21°10S 47°5W 335 A6
Guayabero → Colombia 2°36N 72°47W 328 C3
Guayacán Venezuela 11°8N 63°55W 329 a
Guayacancito Venezuela 10°56N 64°13W 329 a
Guayaguayare Trin. & Tob. 10°8N 61°2W 323 t
Guayaguayare B. Trin. & Tob. 10°7N 61°2W 323 t
Guayama Puerto Rico 17°59N 66°7W 321 C6
Guayamuri, Cerro Venezuela 11°4N 63°51W 329 a
Guayaneco, Arch. Chile 47°45S 75°10W 336 C1
Guayanilla Puerto Rico 18°1N 66°47W 321 b
Guayaquil Ecuador 2°15S 79°52W 328 D2
Guayaquil Baja Calif., Mexico 29°59N 115°4W 318 B1
Guayaquil, G. de Ecuador 3°10S 81°0W 328 D1
Guayaramerín Bolivia 10°48S 65°23W 331 C4
Guayas → Ecuador 2°36S 79°52W 328 D2
Guaymas Mexico 27°56N 110°54W 318 B2
Guaynabo Puerto Rico 18°22N 66°7W 321 b
Guba Dem. Rep. of the Congo 10°38S 26°27E 269 E2
Guba Ethiopia 11°17N 35°20E 257 E4
Gûbâl, Madîq Egypt 27°30N 34°0E 251 L4
Gubam Papua N. G. 8°39S 141°53E 286 E1
Guban Somalia 10°30N 44°0E 267 B5
Gubat Phil. 12°55N 124°7E 232 E5
Gubbi India 13°19N 76°56E 245 H3
Gúbbio Italy 43°21N 12°35E 199 E9
Guben Germany 51°57N 14°42E 178 D10
Gubin Poland 51°57N 14°43E 185 G1
Gubio Nigeria 12°30N 12°42E 263 C7
Gubkin Russia 51°17N 37°32E 189 G9
Gubkinskiy Russia 64°27N 76°36E 214 C8
Guča Serbia 43°46N 20°15E 202 C4
Gucheng China 32°20N 111°30E 229 A8
Gucun China 31°21N 121°22E 138 A1
Gudå Norway 63°27N 11°36E 164 A8
Gudalur India 11°30N 76°29E 245 J3
Gudauta Georgia 43°7N 40°32E 191 J5
Gudbrandsdalen Norway 61°33N 10°10E 164 C7
Guddu Barrage Pakistan 28°30N 69°50E 242 E3
Gudenå → Denmark 56°29N 10°13E 163 H4
Gudermes Russia 43°24N 46°5E 191 J8
Gudhjem Denmark 55°12N 14°58E 163 J8
Gudivada India 16°30N 81°3E 245 F5
Gudiyattam India 12°57N 78°55E 245 H4
Gudö Sweden 59°12N 18°12E 139 B3
Gudur India 14°12N 79°55E 245 G4
Gudvangen Norway 60°52N 6°49E 164 D3
Guebwiller France 47°55N 7°12E 173 E14
Guecho = Algorta Spain 43°21N 2°59W 196 B2
Guékédou Guinea 8°40N 10°5W 262 D2
Guelb er Rîchât Mauritania 21°7N 11°24W 260 D2
Guéle Mendouka Cameroon 4°23N 12°55E 263 E7
Guélengdeng Chad 10°55N 15°31E 259 F3
Güell, Parque de Spain 41°24N 2°10E 114 A2
Guelma Algeria 36°25N 7°29E 261 A6
Guelma □ Algeria 36°25N 7°25E 261 A6
Guelmim Morocco 28°56N 10°0W 260 C3
Guelmim-Oued Noun □ Morocco 28°30N 10°0W 260 C2
Guelph Canada 43°35N 80°20W 312 C4
Guelta Zemmur W. Sahara 25°8N 12°22W 260 C2
Guemar Algeria 33°30N 6°49E 261 B6
Guéméné-Penfao France 47°38N 1°50W 172 E5
Guéméné-sur-Scorff France 48°4N 3°13W 172 D3
Guéné Benin 11°44N 3°16E 263 C5
Güeppí Peru 0°7S 75°15W 328 D2
Guer France 47°54N 2°8W 172 E4
Güer Aike Argentina 51°39S 69°35W 336 D3
Guera Chad 11°55N 18°12E 259 F3
Guéra □ Chad 11°30N 18°30E 259 F3
Guérande France 47°20N 2°26W 172 E4
Guercif Morocco 34°14N 3°21W 261 B4
Guéréda Chad 14°31N 22°5E 259 F4
Guéret France 46°11N 1°51E 173 F8
Guérigny France 47°6N 3°10E 173 E10
Guerneville U.S.A. 38°30N 123°0W 306 G4
Guernica = Gernika-Lumo Spain 43°19N 2°40W 196 B2
Guernsey Chan. Is., U.K. 49°26N 2°35W 169 H5
Guernsey Wyo., U.S.A. 42°16N 104°45W 304 E11
Guerrara Oasis, Algeria 32°51N 4°22E 261 B5
Guerrara Saoura, Algeria 28°5N 0°8W 261 C4
Guerrero Mexico City, Mexico 128 a1
Guerrero □ Mexico 17°40N 100°0W 319 D5
Guerzim Algeria 29°39N 1°40W 261 C4
Guessou-Sud Benin 10°3N 2°38E 263 C5
Gueugnon France 46°36N 4°4E 173 F11
Guéyo Côte d'Ivoire 5°25N 6°5W 262 D3
Gufuðalur Iceland 65°34N 22°25W 155 B4
Guggenheim Museum New York, U.S.A. 132 b3
Gughe Ethiopia 6°12N 37°30E 257 F4
Gūgher Iran 29°28N 56°27E 247 D8
Guglionesi Italy 41°55N 14°55E 199 G11
Guguan N. Marianas 17°18N 145°51E 302 a
Guhrau = Góra Poland 51°40N 16°31E 185 G3
Gui Jiang → China 23°30N 111°15E 229 F8
Guia Canary Is. 28°8N 15°38W 153 e1
Guia de Isora Canary Is. 28°12N 16°46W 153 e1
Guia Lopes da Laguna Brazil 21°26S 56°7W 335 A4
Guiana Venezuela 5°9N 63°36W 329 B5
Guiana Highlands S. Amer. 5°10N 60°40W 326 C4
Guiana I. Antigua & B. 17°6N 61°44W 322 b
Guibéroua Côte d'Ivoire 6°14N 6°10W 262 D3
Guichen B. Australia 37°10S 139°45E 282 D3
Guichi China 30°39N 117°27E 229 B11
Guider Cameroon 9°56N 13°57E 263 D7
Guidiguir Niger 13°40N 9°50E 259 F1
Guidimaka □ Mauritania 15°20N 12°0W 262 B2
Guidimouni Niger 13°42N 9°31E 259 F1
Guiding China 26°34N 107°11E 228 D6
Guidong China 26°7N 113°57E 229 D9
Guidónia-Montecélio Italy 42°1N 12°45E 199 F9
Guiers, L. de Senegal 16°10N 15°50W 262 B1
Guigang China 23°8N 109°35E 228 F7
Guiglo Côte d'Ivoire 6°45N 7°30W 262 D3
Guihulngan Phil. 10°7N 123°16E 233 F4
Guijá Mozam. 24°27S 33°0E 271 B5
Guijuelo Spain 40°33N 5°40W 194 E5
Guildford U.K. 51°14N 0°34W 169 F7
Guildwood Canada 43°45N 79°13W 141 A3
Guilford U.S.A. 41°17N 72°41W 313 E12
Guilin China 25°18N 110°15E 229 E8
Guillaume-Delisle, L. Canada 56°15N 76°17W 298 A4
Guillaumes France 44°5N 6°52E 175 D10
Guillestre France 44°39N 6°40E 175 D10
Guilvinec France 47°48N 4°17W 172 E2
Güimar Canary Is. 28°18N 16°24W 153 e1
Guimarães Brazil 2°9S 44°42W 332 B3
Guimarães Portugal 41°28N 8°24W 194 D2
Guimaras □ Phil. 10°35N 122°37E 233 F4
Guimaras Str. Phil. 10°38N 122°48E 233 F4
Guimba Phil. 15°40N 120°46E 232 D3
Guinardó Spain 41°24N 2°10E 114 A2
Guinayangan Phil. 13°54N 122°27E 232 E4
Guinda U.S.A. 38°50N 122°12W 306 G4
Guindulman Phil. 9°46N 124°29E 233 G5
Guinea Africa 8°0N 8°0E 254 F4
Guinea ■ W. Afr. 10°20N 11°30W 262 C2
Guinea, Gulf of Atl. Oc. 3°0N 2°30E 263 E5
Guinea Basin Atl. Oc. 0°0 5°0W 152 G11
Guinea-Bissau ■ Africa 12°0N 15°0W 262 C2
Güines Cuba 22°50N 82°0W 320 B3
Guingamp France 48°34N 3°10W 172 D3
Guinguinéo Senegal 14°20N 15°57W 262 C1
Güinima Venezuela 10°44N 63°55W 329 a
Guinobatan Phil. 13°11N 123°36E 232 E4
Guipavas France 48°26N 4°29W 172 D2
Guiping China 23°21N 110°2E 229 F8
Guir Mali 18°52N 2°52W 262 B4
Guir, O. → Algeria 31°29N 2°17W 261 B4
Guiratinga Brazil 16°21S 53°45W 331 D7
Guirel Mauritania 15°30N 7°3W 262 B3
Güiria Venezuela 10°32N 62°18W 329 F8
Guiscard France 49°40N 3°1E 173 C10
Guise France 49°52N 3°35E 173 C10
Guishan Dao = Kueishan Tao Taiwan 24°51N 121°57E 225 B3
Guissona Spain 41°47N 1°17E 196 D6
Guita-Koulouba C.A.R. 5°58N 23°21E 264 A4
Guitiriz Spain 43°11N 7°50W 194 B3
Guitri Côte d'Ivoire 5°30N 5°14W 262 D3
Guiuan Phil. 11°5N 125°55E 233 F5
Guixi China 28°16N 117°15E 229 C11
Guiyang Guizhou, China 26°32N 106°40E 228 D6
Guiyang Hunan, China 25°46N 112°42E 229 E9
Guizhou □ China 27°0N 107°0E 228 D6
Gujan-Mestras France 44°38N 1°4W 174 D2
Gujar Khan Pakistan 33°16N 73°19E 242 C5
Gujarat □ India 23°20N 71°0E 242 H4
Gujiang China 27°11N 114°47E 229 D10
Gujiao China 37°54N 112°8E 226 F7
Gujō Japan 35°45N 136°57E 223 B8
Gujranwala Pakistan 32°10N 74°12E 242 C6
Gujrat Pakistan 32°40N 74°2E 242 C6
Gukovo Russia 48°1N 39°58E 191 F5
Gulargambone Australia 31°20S 148°30E 283 A8
Gulbai Pakistan 24°52N 66°58E 123 A1
Gulbarga = Kalaburagi India 17°20N 76°50E 244 F3
Gulbene Latvia 57°8N 26°52E 188 D4
Gülchö Kyrgyzstan 40°19N 73°26E 217 D8
Guledagudda India 16°3N 75°48E 245 F2
Gülek Turkey 37°12N 34°48E 250 A5
Gulf □ Papua N. G. 8°0S 145°0E 286 D3
Gulf, The = Persian Gulf Asia 27°0N 50°0E 247 E6
Gulf Breeze U.S.A. 30°21N 87°9W 317 E2
Gulf Hammock U.S.A. 29°15N 82°43W 317 F7
Gulf Islands ⌓ U.S.A. 30°10N 87°10W 317 K2
Gulfport Fla., U.S.A. 27°44N 82°42W 317 H7
Gulfport Miss., U.S.A. 30°22N 89°6W 315 F10
Gulgong Australia 32°20S 149°49E 283 B8
Gulian China 52°56N 122°21E 219 A13
Gulin China 28°1N 105°50E 228 C5
Gulistan Pakistan 30°30N 66°35E 242 D2
Guliston Uzbekistan 40°29N 68°46E 217 D7
Gulja = Yining China 43°58N 81°10E 217 D10
Gulkana U.S.A. 62°16N 145°23W 303 E11
Gull Lake Canada 50°10N 108°29W 297 C7
Gullbrå Norway 60°50N 6°17E 164 D3
Gullbrandstorp Sweden 56°42N 12°43E 163 H6
Gullbringusýsla Iceland 64°0N 22°0W 155 D4
Gullfoss Iceland 64°20N 20°8W 155 C6
Gullhaug Norway 59°30N 10°15E 164 E7
Gullivan B. U.S.A. 25°45N 81°40W 317 K8
Gullspång Sweden 58°59N 14°6E 163 F8
Gullstein Norway 63°13N 8°9E 164 A5
Güllük Turkey 37°14N 27°35E 205 D9
Güllük Dağı △ Turkey 37°0N 30°30E 205 E12
Güllük Korfezi Turkey 37°12N 27°30E 205 D9
Gulma Nigeria 12°40N 4°23E 263 C5
Gulmarg India 34°3N 74°25E 243 B6
Gülnar Turkey 36°19N 33°24E 250 B4
Gulnare Australia 33°27S 138°27E 282 B3
Gülpınar Turkey 39°32N 26°7E 205 B8
Gülşehir Turkey 38°44N 34°37E 212 C6
Gulshan-e Iqbal Pakistan 24°54N 67°5E 123 A2
Gülshat Kazakhstan 46°38N 74°21E 217 C8
Gulsvik Norway 60°24N 9°38E 164 D6
Gulu Uganda 2°48N 32°17E 268 B3
Gŭlŭbovo = Galabovo Bulgaria 42°8N 25°55E 203 D9
Gulud, J. Sudan 11°41N 29°31E 257 E2
Gulwe Tanzania 6°30S 36°25E 268 D4
Gulyaypole = Hulyaypole Ukraine 47°45N 36°21E 189 J9
Gum Lake Australia 32°42S 143°9E 282 B5
Gumaca Phil. 13°55N 122°6E 232 E4
Gumal → Pakistan 31°40N 71°50E 242 D4
Gumbaz Pakistan 30°2N 69°0E 242 D3
Gumbinnen = Gusev Russia 54°35N 22°10E 184 D9
Gumdag Turkmenistan 39°9N 54°56E 216 E4
Gumel Nigeria 12°39N 9°22E 263 C6
Gumi S. Korea 36°10N 128°12E 224 D4
Gumiel de Izán Spain 41°46N 3°41W 194 D7
Gumla India 23°3N 84°33E 243 H11
Gumlu Australia 19°53S 147°41E 280 B4
Gummersbach Germany 51°1N 7°34E 178 D3
Gummi Nigeria 12°4N 5°9E 263 C6
Gümüldür Turkey 38°6N 27°0E 205 C9
Gumuljina = Komotini Greece 41°9N 25°26E 203 E9
Gümüşçay Turkey 40°16N 27°17E 203 F11
Gümüşhacıköy Turkey 40°50N 35°18E 212 B6
Gümüşhane Turkey 40°30N 39°30E 213 B8
Gümüşsu Turkey 38°14N 30°1E 205 C12
Gumzai Indonesia 5°28S 134°42E 231 F8
Gun Hill Tower Barbados 13°8N 59°33W 323 r
Gun Pt. Grenada 12°32N 61°37W 323 q
Guna Amara, Ethiopia 11°43N 38°14E 266 B4
Guna Oromiya, Ethiopia 8°18N 39°52E 257 F4
Guna India 24°40N 77°19E 242 G7
Gunbalanya Australia 12°20S 133°4E 278 B5
Gundabooka △ Australia 30°30S 145°20E 281 E4
Gundagai Australia 35°3S 148°6E 283 C8
Gundarehi India 20°57N 81°17E 244 D5
Gundelfingen Germany 48°34N 10°22E 179 G6
Gundji Dem. Rep. of the Congo 2°5N 21°27E 264 B4
Gundlakamma → India 15°30N 80°15E 245 G5
Gundlupet India 11°48N 76°41E 245 J3
Gündoğmuş Turkey 36°48N 32°0E 250 B3
Gunebang Australia 33°1S 146°38E 283 B7
Güney Burdur, Turkey 37°29N 29°34E 205 D11
Güney Denizli, Turkey 38°9N 29°4E 205 C11
Güneydoğu Toroslar Turkey 38°20N 40°30E 213 C9
Gungal Australia 32°17S 150°32E 283 B9
Gungo Angola 10°58S 15°30E 265 E2
Güngören Turkey 41°1N 28°52E 122 B1
Gungu Dem. Rep. of the Congo 5°43S 19°20E 265 D3
Gunisao → Canada 53°56N 97°53W 297 C9
Gunisao L. Canada 53°33N 96°15W 297 C9
Gunjur Gambia 13°12N 16°44W 262 C1
Gunjyal Pakistan 32°20N 71°55E 242 C4
Günlüce Turkey 36°50N 28°20E 205 E10
Gunma □ Japan 36°30N 138°20E 223 A10
Gunnarskog Sweden 59°49N 12°34E 162 E6
Gunnbjørn Fjeld Greenland 68°55N 29°47W 154 D8
Gunnebo Sweden 57°44N 16°32E 163 G10
Gunnedah Australia 30°59S 150°15E 283 A9
Gunnersbury U.K. 51°29N 0°17W 125 B2
Gunnewin Australia 25°59S 148°33E 281 D4
Gunningbar Cr. → Australia 31°14S 147°6E 283 A7
Gunnison Colo., U.S.A. 38°33N 106°56W 304 G10
Gunnison Utah, U.S.A. 39°9N 111°49W 304 G8
Gunnison → U.S.A. 39°4N 108°35W 304 G9
Gunsan S. Korea 35°59N 126°45E 224 E3
Guntakal India 15°11N 77°27E 245 G3
Gunter Canada 44°52N 77°32W 312 B7
Guntersville U.S.A. 34°21N 86°18W 315 D11
Guntong Malaysia 4°36N 101°3E 237 K3
Guntur India 16°23N 80°30E 245 F5
Gunung Buda △ Malaysia 4°12N 114°57E 235 B4
Gunung Ciremay △ Indonesia 6°53S 108°24E 235 D3
Gunung Gading △ Malaysia 2°2N 109°52E 235 B3
Gunung Leuser △ Indonesia 3°39N 97°32E 234 B1
Gunung Mulu △ Malaysia 4°6N 114°53E 235 B4
Gunung Palung △ Indonesia 1°9S 110°13E 235 C4
Gunungapi Indonesia 6°45S 126°30E 231 F7
Gunungsitoli Indonesia 1°15N 97°30E 234 B1
Gunungtua Indonesia 1°30N 99°37E 234 B1
Gunupur India 19°5N 83°50E 244 E6
Günz → Germany 48°27N 10°16E 179 G6
Gunza Angola 10°50S 13°50E 265 E2
Günzburg Germany 48°26N 10°17E 179 G6
Gunzenhausen Germany 49°7N 10°44E 179 F6
Guo He → China 32°59N 117°10E 229 A11
Guomao China 39°54N 116°26E 114 B2
Guoxing = Kuohsing Taiwan 24°2N 120°51E 225 B2
Guoyang China 33°32N 116°12E 226 H9
Gupis Pakistan 36°15N 73°20E 243 A5
Gura Humorului Romania 47°35N 25°53E 183 C10
Gura-Teghii Romania 45°30N 26°25E 183 E11
Gurabo Puerto Rico 18°16N 65°58W 321 b
Gurag Ethiopia 8°20N 38°20E 257 F4
Gurahonț Romania 46°16N 22°21E 182 D7
Gurbantünggüt Shamo China 45°8N 87°20E 217 C11
Gurdaspur India 32°5N 75°31E 242 C6
Gurdon U.S.A. 33°55N 93°9W 314 E8
Güre Balıkesir, Turkey 39°36N 26°54E 205 B8
Güre Uşak, Turkey 38°39N 29°10E 205 C11
Gurgaon = Gurugram India 28°27N 77°1E 242 E7
Gürgentepe Turkey 40°51N 37°50E 212 B7
Gurghiu, Munții Romania 46°41N 25°15E 183 D10
Gurgueia → Brazil 6°50S 43°24W 332 C3
Gurha India 25°12N 71°39E 242 G4
Guri, Embalse de Venezuela 7°50N 62°52W 329 B5
Gurimatu Papua N. G. 6°45S 144°45E 286 D3
Gurin Nigeria 9°5N 12°54E 263 D7
Gurinhatã Brazil 19°14S 49°48W 333 E2
Gurjaani Georgia 41°43N 45°52E 191 K7
Gurk → Austria 46°35N 14°31E 180 E7
Gurkfeld = Krško Slovenia 45°57N 15°30E 199 C12
Gurkha Nepal 28°5N 84°40E 243 E11
Gurla Mandhata = Naimona'nyi Feng China 30°26N 81°18E 243 D9
Gurley Australia 29°45S 149°48E 281 D4
Gurnee U.S.A. 42°22N 87°55W 311 B9
Gurnet Point U.S.A. 42°1N 70°34W 313 D14
Guro Mozam. 17°26S 32°30E 269 F3
Güroymak Turkey 38°35N 42°1E 213 C10
Gürpınar İstanbul, Turkey 40°59N 28°37E 203 F12
Gürpınar Van, Turkey 38°18N 43°25E 213 C10
Gürsu Turkey 40°13N 29°11E 203 F13
Gurué Mozam. 15°25S 36°58E 269 F4
Gurueragu Ethiopia 6°23N 45°31E 267 C6
Gurugram India 28°27N 77°1E 242 E7
Gurun Malaysia 5°49N 100°27E 237 K3
Gürün Turkey 38°43N 37°15E 212 C7
Gurupá Brazil 1°25S 51°35W 329 D7
Gurupá, I. Grande de Brazil 1°25S 51°45W 329 D7
Gurupi Brazil 11°43S 49°4W 333 D2
Gurupi → Brazil 1°13S 46°6W 332 B2
Gurupi, Serra do Brazil 5°0S 47°50W 332 C2
Guruwe Zimbabwe 16°40S 30°42E 271 A5
Gurvan Sayhan Uul Mongolia 43°50N 104°0E 226 C3
Guryev = Atyraū Kazakhstan 47°5N 52°0E 187 E9
Guryevsk Russia 54°47N 20°38E 184 D7
Gus-Khrustalnyy Russia 55°42N 40°44E 190 C5
Gusau Nigeria 12°12N 6°40E 263 C6
Gusev Russia 54°35N 22°10E 184 D9
Gushan China 39°50N 123°35E 224 C1
Gushgy = Serhetabat Turkmenistan 35°20N 62°18E 247 C9
Gushi China 32°11N 115°41E 229 A10
Gushiago Ghana 9°55N 0°15W 263 D4
Gushikami Japan 26°7N 127°44E 288 a
Gushikawa = Uruma Japan 26°21N 127°52E 288 a
Gusinje Montenegro 42°35N 19°50E 202 D3
Gusinoozersk Russia 51°16N 106°27E 215 D11
Gúspini Italy 39°32N 8°37E 200 C1
Güssing Austria 47°3N 16°20E 181 D9
Gustav Holm, Kap Greenland 66°36N 34°15W 154 D7
Gustavia St. Barts 17°53N 62°51W 322 a
Gustavo A. Madero Mexico 19°29N 99°8W 128 B2
Gustavus U.S.A. 58°25N 135°44W 296 B1
Gustine U.S.A. 37°16N 121°0W 306 H6
Güstrow Germany 53°47N 12°10E 178 B8
Gusum Sweden 58°16N 16°30E 163 F10
Guta = Kolárovo Slovakia 47°54N 18°0E 181 D10
Gütersloh Germany 51°54N 8°24E 178 D4
Gutha Australia 28°58S 115°55E 279 E2
Guthalungra Australia 19°52S 147°50E 280 B4
Guthrie Ont., Canada 44°28N 79°32W 312 B5
Guthrie Okla., U.S.A. 35°53N 97°25W 314 D6
Guthrie Tex., U.S.A. 33°37N 100°19W 314 E4
Guthrie Center U.S.A. 41°41N 94°30W 310 C2
Gutian China 26°32N 118°43E 229 D12
Gutiérrez Bolivia 19°25S 63°34W 331 D5
Guttenberg Iowa, U.S.A. 42°47N 91°6W 310 B5
Guttenberg New York, U.S.A. 132 a1
Guttentag = Dobrodzień Poland 50°45N 18°25E 185 H5
Guttstadt = Dobre Miasto Poland 53°58N 20°26E 184 E7
Gutu Zimbabwe 19°41S 31°9E 271 A5
Gutulia △ Norway 62°2N 12°11E 164 B9
Gutuyevskiy, Ostrov Russia 59°53N 30°15E 137 B1
Guwahati India 26°10N 91°45E 241 B3
Guy Fawkes River △ Australia 30°0S 152°20E 281 D5
Guy-Fayreau, Complexe Montréal, Canada 130 b2
Guyana ■ S. Amer. 5°0N 59°0W 329 C6
Guyancourt France 48°46N 2°4E 134 B1
Guyane française = French Guiana ☐ S. Amer. 4°0N 53°0W 329 C7
Guyang China 41°0N 110°5E 226 D6
Guyenne France 44°30N 0°40E 174 D4
Guymon U.S.A. 36°41N 101°29W 314 C4
Guyotville = Aïn Benian Algeria 36°48N 2°55E 261 A5
Guyra Australia 30°15S 151°40E 281 E5
Guyton U.S.A. 32°20N 81°24W 316 C8
Guyuan Hebei, China 41°37N 115°40E 226 D8
Guyuan Ningxia Huizu, China 36°0N 106°20E 226 F4
Güzelbağ Turkey 36°44N 31°53E 250 B2
Güzelbahçe Turkey 38°21N 26°54E 205 C8
Güzeloluk Turkey 36°47N 34°4E 250 B5
Güzelsu Turkey 36°53N 31°51E 250 B2
Güzelyurt = Morphou Cyprus 35°12N 32°59E 207 E8
Guzhang China 28°42N 109°58E 228 C7
Guzhen China 33°22N 117°18E 227 H9
Guzmán, L. de Mexico 31°20N 107°30W 318 A3
G'uzor Uzbekistan 38°36N 66°15E 217 E7
Gvardeysk Russia 54°39N 21°5E 184 D8
Gvardeyskoye Ukraine 45°7N 34°1E 189 K8
Gvarv Norway 59°23N 9°9E 164 E6
Gwa Myanmar 17°36N 94°34E 241 G5
Gwaai Zimbabwe 19°15S 27°45E 269 F2
Gwaai → Zimbabwe 17°59S 26°52E 269 F2
Gwabegar Australia 30°37S 148°59E 283 A8
Gwadabawa Nigeria 13°28N 5°15E 263 C6
Gwādar Pakistan 25°10N 62°18E 240 D1
Gwagwada Nigeria 10°15N 7°15E 263 C6
Gwaii Haanas △ Canada 52°21N 131°26W 296 C2
Gwalior India 26°12N 78°10E 242 F8
Gwanak S. Korea 37°29N 126°57E 137 C1
Gwanaksan S. Korea 37°27N 126°58E 137 C1
Gwanara Nigeria 8°55N 3°9E 263 D5
Gwanda Zimbabwe 20°55S 29°0E 269 G2
Gwandu Nigeria 12°30N 4°41E 263 C5
Gwane Dem. Rep. of the Congo 4°45N 25°48E 268 B2
Gwang-yang S. Korea 34°58N 127°35E 224 E3
Gwangju S. Korea 35°9N 126°54E 224 E3
Gwangju □ S. Korea 35°10N 126°45E 224 E3
Gwangyang S. Korea 34°56N 127°41E 222 E3
Gwanju = Gwangju S. Korea 35°9N 126°54E 224 E3
Gwaram Nigeria 10°15N 10°25E 263 C7
Gwarzo Nigeria 12°20N 8°55E 263 C6
Gwasero Nigeria 9°29N 3°30E 263 D5
Gwda → Poland 53°3N 16°44E 185 E3
Gweebarra B. Ireland 54°51N 8°23W 166 B3
Gweedore Ireland 55°3N 8°14W 166 A3
Gweru Zimbabwe 19°28S 29°45E 269 F2
Gwi Nigeria 9°0N 7°10E 263 D6
Gwinn U.S.A. 46°19N 87°27W 308 B10
Gwio Kura Nigeria 12°40N 11°2E 263 C7
Gwoza Nigeria 11°5N 13°40E 263 C7
Gwydir → Australia 29°27S 149°48E 281 D4
Gwynedd □ U.K. 52°52N 4°10W 168 E3
Gyál Hungary 47°23N 19°13E 117 B3
Gyáli-patak → Hungary 47°23N 19°7E 117 B2
Gyandzha = Gäncä Azerbaijan 40°45N 46°20E 191 K8
Gyangzê China 29°5N 89°47E 218 F6
Gyaring Hu China 34°50N 97°40E 218 E8
Gydanskiy Poluostrov Russia 70°0N 78°0E 214 C8
Gyeonggi-do □ S. Korea 36°37N 127°15E 224 D3
Gyeonggi-man S. Korea 37°0N 125°30E 224 D2
Gyeongju S. Korea 35°51N 129°14E 224 E4
Gyeongsan S. Korea 35°49N 128°44E 224 E4
Gyeongsangbuk-do □ S. Korea 36°20N 128°45E 224 D4
Gyeongsangnam-do □ S. Korea 35°15N 128°15E 224 E4
Gyeryongsan △ S. Korea 36°20N 127°15E 224 D3
Gyigang China 28°40N 97°31E 241 A6
Gyl Norway 62°57N 8°7E 164 B5
Gyldenløve Fjord Greenland 64°15N 40°30W 154 E6
Gympie Australia 26°11S 152°38E 281 D5
Gyobingauk Myanmar 18°13N 95°39E 241 F5
Gyōda Japan 36°10N 139°30E 223 A11
Gyodongdo S. Korea 37°47N 126°15E 224 D3
Gyomaendrőd Hungary 46°56N 20°50E 182 D5
Gyöngyös Hungary 47°48N 19°56E 182 C4
Győr Hungary 47°41N 17°40E 182 C2
Győr-Moson-Sopron □ Hungary 47°40N 17°20E 182 C2
Gypsum Pt. Canada 61°53N 114°35W 296 A6
Gypsumville Canada 51°45N 98°40W 297 C9
Gyueshevo Bulgaria 42°14N 22°28E 202 D6
Gyula Hungary 46°38N 21°17E 182 D6
Gyumri Armenia 40°47N 43°50E 191 K6
Gyzylarbat = Serdar Turkmenistan 39°4N 56°23E 247 B8
Gyzyletrek = Etrek Turkmenistan 37°36N 54°46E 247 B7
Gyzylgaya Turkmenistan 40°40N 55°30E 216 D5
Gzhatsk = Gagarin Russia 55°38N 35°0E 188 E8
Gzira Malta 35°54N 14°29E 206 F7

H

H. Neely Henry L. U.S.A. 33°55N 86°2W 316 B3
Ha 'Arava → Israel 30°50N 35°20E 251 H6
Ha Coi Vietnam 21°26N 107°46E 228 G6
Ha Dong Vietnam 20°58N 105°46E 228 G5
Ha Giang Vietnam 22°50N 104°59E 228 F5
Ha Karmel, Har Israel 32°44N 35°3E 250 F5
Ha Karmel △ Israel 32°45N 35°5E 250 F6
Ha Long = Hong Gai Vietnam 20°57N 107°5E 228 G6
Ha Long, Vinh Vietnam 20°56N 107°3E 236 B6
Ha Tien Vietnam 10°23N 104°29E 237 G5
Ha Tinh Vietnam 18°20N 105°54E 236 C5
Ha Trung Vietnam 19°58N 105°50E 236 C5
Haaga Finland 60°13N 24°53E 121 B2
Haakon VII Topp = Beerenberg Norway 71°0N 8°20W 154 C10
Haaksbergen Neths. 52°9N 6°45E 170 B6
Ha'ano Tonga 19°41S 174°18W 287 P13
Ha'apai Group Tonga 19°47S 174°27W 287 P13
Haapiti Moorea 17°34S 149°52W 289 e
Haapsalu Estonia 58°56N 23°30E 188 C2
Haar Germany 48°6N 11°43E 131 B3
Haarby Denmark 55°13N 10°7E 163 J4
Haarlem Neths. 52°23N 4°39E 170 B4
Haas-Lilienthal House San Francisco, U.S.A. 136 b1
Haast N.Z. 43°51S 169°1E 285 D4
Haast → N.Z. 43°50S 169°2E 285 D4
Haast Pass N.Z. 44°6S 169°21E 285 E4
Haasts Bluff Australia 23°22S 132°0E 278 D5
Haasts Bluff ☼ Australia 23°39S 130°34E 278 D5
Hab → Pakistan 24°53N 66°41E 242 G3
Hab Nadi Chauki Pakistan 25°0N 66°50E 242 G2
Habahe China 48°3N 86°23E 217 C11
Ḩabarūt Yemen 17°18N 52°44E 249 C6
Habaswein Kenya 1°2N 39°30E 268 B4
Ḩabawnah, W. → Si. Arabia 17°57N 44°58E 248 C4
Habay Alta., Canada 58°50N 118°44W 296 B5
Habay Manila, Phil. 14°27N 120°56E 127 C1
Ḩabbān Yemen 14°21N 47°5E 248 D4
Ḩabbānīyah Iraq 33°17N 43°29E 213 F10
Ḩabbānīyah, Hawr al Iraq 33°17N 43°29E 213 F10
Habelschwerdt = Bystrzyca Kłodzka Poland 50°19N 16°39E 185 H3
Habibas, Îles Algeria 35°44N 1°8W 197 K3
Habichtswald ⌓ Germany 51°15N 9°15E 178 D5
Habiganj Bangla. 24°24N 91°30E 241 C3
Habirag China 42°17N 115°42E 226 C8
Habisa Sudan 15°38N 31°18E 266 A3
Habo Sweden 57°55N 14°6E 163 G8
Haboro Japan 44°22N 141°42E 220 B10
Ḩabshān U.A.E. 23°50N 53°37E 247 F7
Hachenburg Germany 50°40N 7°49E 178 E3
Hachi India 27°48N 94°2E 241 B5
Hachijō-Jima Japan 33°5N 139°45E 223 D11
Hachiman = Gujō Japan 35°45N 136°57E 223 B8
Hachinohe Japan 40°30N 141°29E 220 D10
Hachiōji Japan 35°40N 139°20E 223 B11
Hacı Zeynalabdin Azerbaijan 40°37N 49°33E 191 K9
Hacıbektaş Turkey 38°56N 34°33E 212 C6
Hacılar Turkey 38°38N 35°26E 212 C6
Hack, Mt. Australia 30°45S 138°55E 282 A3
Hackås Sweden 62°56N 14°30E 162 B8
Hackbridge U.K. 51°23N 0°9W 125 B3
Hackensack U.S.A. 40°52N 74°4W 132 A1
Hackensack → U.S.A. 40°42N 74°7W 132 B1
Hackettstown U.S.A. 40°51N 74°50W 313 F10
Hackney □ U.K. 51°33N 0°3W 125 A3
Hackney Wick U.K. 51°32N 0°1W 125 A3
Håckrenmagasinet Sweden 63°15N 13°30E 162 C7
Haco Angola 10°15S 15°44E 265 E3
Hadali Pakistan 32°16N 72°11E 242 C5
Hadano Japan 35°22N 139°14E 223 B11
Hadarba, Ras Sudan 22°4N 36°51E 256 C4
Hadarom □ Israel 31°0N 35°0E 251 H6
Ḩadbaram Oman 17°27N 55°15E 249 C6
Ḩadd, Ra's al Oman 22°35N 59°50E 249 B7
Ḩaddā Si. Arabia 21°27N 39°34E 248 B2
Haddington U.K. 55°57N 2°47W 167 F6
Haddock U.S.A. 33°2N 83°26W 316 B6
Haddummati Atoll Maldives 2°0N 73°30E 272 d
Hadejia Nigeria 12°30N 10°5E 263 C7
Hadejia → Nigeria 12°50N 10°51E 263 C7
Ḩadera Israel 32°27N 34°55E 251 F5
Hadersleben = Haderslev Denmark 55°15N 9°30E 163 J3
Haderslev Denmark 55°15N 9°30E 163 J3
Hadgaon India 19°30N 77°40E 244 E3
Hadhramaut = Ḩaḑramawt □ Yemen 15°30N 49°30E 249 D5
Hadībоh Yemen 12°39N 54°2E 249 D6
Hadilik China 37°56N 86°6E 217 E11
Hadım Turkey 36°58N 32°26E 250 B3
Hādīshahr Iran 38°51N 45°40E 213 C11
Hadithah Si. Arabia 31°27N 37°9E 251 G8
Hadjadj, O. el → Algeria 28°18N 5°20E 261 C6
Hadjeb el Aïoun Tunisia 35°21N 9°32E 258 A1
Hadjer Kamaran Chad 12°41N 21°46E 259 F4
Hadjer-Lamis □ Chad 12°55N 16°0E 259 F3
Hadjer Mornou Chad 17°12N 23°8E 259 E4
Hadlaskar Norway 60°15N 7°9E 164 D4
Hadley B. Canada 72°31N 108°12W 294 C10
Hadong S. Korea 35°5N 127°44E 224 E3
Hadr, Warrâq el Egypt 30°5N 31°12E 117 A2
Ḩaḑramawt □ Yemen 15°30N 49°30E 249 D5
Ḩaḑramawt, W. → Yemen 15°10N 51°8E 249 D5
Ḩadrānīyah Iraq 35°38N 43°14E 246 C4
Hadrian's Wall U.K. 55°0N 2°30W 168 B5
Hadsten Denmark 56°19N 10°3E 163 H4
Hadsund Denmark 56°44N 10°8E 163 H4
Hadyach Ukraine 50°21N 34°0E 189 G8
Hae, Ko Thailand 7°44N 98°22E 237 a
Hægeland Norway 58°22N 7°45E 164 F4
Haeinsa △ S. Korea 35°47N 128°5E 224 E4
Haeju N. Korea 38°3N 125°45E 224 C2
Haeju-man N. Korea 37°54N 125°45E 224 D2
Hä'ena U.S.A. 22°14N 159°34W 302 A2
Haenam S. Korea 34°34N 126°35E 224 E3
Haenertsburg S. Africa 24°0S 29°50E 271 B4
Haerhpin = Harbin China 45°48N 126°40E 227 B14
Hafar al Bāţin Si. Arabia 28°32N 45°52E 246 D5
Hafik Turkey 39°51N 37°23E 212 C7
Ḩafirat al 'Aydā Si. Arabia 26°26N 39°12E 246 E3
Ḩafit Oman 23°59N 55°49E 247 F7
Hafizabad Pakistan 32°5N 73°40E 242 C5
Haflong India 25°10N 93°5E 241 C4
Hafnarfjörður Iceland 64°4N 21°57W 155 C5
Hafnir Iceland 63°56N 22°41W 155 D4
Hafslo Norway 61°19N 7°10E 164 C4
Haft Gel Iran 31°30N 49°32E 247 D6
Haga Sweden 59°21N 18°1E 139 A2
Hagalil Israel 32°53N 35°18E 250 F6
Hagari → India 15°40N 77°0E 245 G3
Hagåtña Guam 13°28N 144°45E 302 d
Hagby Sweden 56°34N 16°11E 163 H10
Hagemeister I. U.S.A. 58°39N 160°54W 303 G7
Hagen Germany 51°21N 7°27E 178 D3
Hagenbrunn Austria 48°19N 16°27E 142 A2
Hagenow Germany 53°26N 11°12E 178 B7
Hagere Hiywet Ethiopia 8°59N 37°51E 266 C4
Hagerman U.S.A. 33°7N 104°20W 305 K11
Hagerman Fossil Beds ⌓ U.S.A. 42°48N 114°57W 304 E6
Hägersten Sweden 59°18N 17°59E 139 B1
Hagerstown Ind., U.S.A. 39°55N 85°10W 311 E11
Hagerstown Md., U.S.A. 39°39N 77°43W 309 F15
Hagersville Canada 42°58N 80°3W 312 D4
Hagetmau France 43°39N 0°37W 174 E3
Hagfors Sweden 60°3N 13°45E 162 D7
Häggvik Sweden 59°26N 17°56E 139 A1
Hagi Iceland 65°28N 23°25W 155 B3
Hagi Japan 34°30N 131°22E 222 C3
Hagolan Syria 33°0N 35°45E 250 F6
Hagondange France 49°16N 6°11E 173 C13
Hágöngulón Iceland 64°35N 18°8W 155 C8
Hagonoy Bulacan, Phil. 14°50N 120°44E 232 D3
Hagonoy Manila, Phil. 14°31N 121°3E 127 B2
Hags Hd. Ireland 52°57N 9°28W 166 D2
Hague, C. de la France 49°44N 1°56W 172 C5
Hague, The = 's-Gravenhage Neths. 52°7N 4°17E 170 B4
Hague Park Canada 43°45N 79°14W 141 A3
Haguenau France 48°49N 7°47E 173 D14
Hagunía W. Sahara 27°26N 12°24W 260 C2
Hahira U.S.A. 30°59N 83°22W 316 E6
Hai Duong Vietnam 20°56N 106°19E 228 G6
Hai'an Guangdong, China 20°18N 110°11E 229 a
Hai'an Jiangsu, China 32°37N 120°27E 229 A13
Haian Shanmo Taiwan 23°25N 121°25E 225 C3
Haicheng China 40°50N 122°45E 224 B1
Haida Gwaii Canada 53°20N 132°10W 296 C2
Haidar Khel Afghan. 33°58N 68°38E 242 C3
Haidarâbâd = Hyderabad India 17°22N 78°29E 244 F4
Haidargarh India 26°37N 81°22E 243 F9
Haidari = Chaidari Greece 38°2N 23°38E 112 A1
Haidarpur India 28°43N 77°8E 120 A1
Haidhausen Germany 48°7N 11°36E 131 B2
Haidian China 39°59N 116°16E 114 B1
Haifa = Ḩefa Israel 32°46N 35°0E 250 F6
Haifeng China 22°58N 115°10E 229 F10
Haiger Germany 50°43N 8°12E 178 E4
Haight-Ashbury U.S.A. 37°46N 122°26W 136 B2
Haikou China 20°1N 110°16E 229 a
Haiku-Pauwela U.S.A. 20°56N 156°19W 302 C5
Ḩā'īl Si. Arabia 27°28N 41°45E 246 E4
Ḩā'īl □ Si. Arabia 26°40N 41°40E 246 E4
Hailakandi India 24°42N 92°34E 241 C4
Hailar China 49°10N 119°38E 219 B12
Hailey U.S.A. 43°31N 114°19W 304 E6
Haileybury Canada 47°30N 79°38W 298 C4
Hailin China 44°37N 129°30E 227 B15
Hailing Dao China 21°35N 111°47E 229 G8
Hailun China 47°28N 126°50E 219 B14
Hailuoto Finland 65°3N 24°45E 160 D21
Haimen Guangdong, China 23°15N 116°38E 229 F11
Haimen Jiangsu, China 31°52N 121°10E 229 B13
Hainan □ China 19°0N 109°30E 229 a
Hainan Dao China 19°0N 109°30E 229 a
Hainan Str. = Qiongzhou Haixia China 20°10N 110°15E 229 a
Hainault U.K. 51°36N 0°6E 125 A4
Hainaut □ Belgium 50°30N 4°0E 170 D4
Hainburg Austria 48°9N 16°56E 181 C9
Haines Alaska, U.S.A. 59°14N 135°26W 296 B1
Haines Oreg., U.S.A. 44°55N 117°56W 304 D5
Haines City U.S.A. 28°7N 81°38W 317 G8
Haines Junction Canada 60°45N 137°30W 296 A1
Hainfeld Austria 48°3N 15°48E 180 C8
Haining China 30°28N 120°40E 229 B13
Haiphong Vietnam 20°47N 106°41E 228 G6
Haitan Dao China 25°30N 119°45E 229 E12
Haiti ■ W. Indies 19°0N 72°30W 321 C5
Haiya Sudan 18°20N 36°21E 256 D4
Haiyan Qinghai, China 36°53N 100°59E 218 D9
Haiyan Zhejiang, China 30°28N 120°58E 229 B13
Haiyang China 36°47N 121°9E 227 F11
Haiyang Dao China 39°2N 123°10E 224 C1
Haiyuan Guangxi Zhuangzu, China 22°8N 107°35E 228 F6
Haiyuan Ningxia Huizu, China 36°35N 105°52E 226 F3
Haizhou Guangdong, China 23°5N 113°18E 121 B2
Haizhou Jiangsu, China 34°37N 119°7E 227 G10
Haizhou Wan China 34°50N 119°20E 227 G10
Haizhu Guangchang China 23°6N 113°14E 121 B2
Hajar Bangar Sudan 10°40N 22°45E 259 F4
Hajdú-Bihar □ Hungary 47°30N 21°30E 182 C6
Hajdúböszörmény Hungary 47°40N 21°30E 182 C6
Hajdúdorog Hungary 47°48N 21°30E 182 C6
Hajdúhadház Hungary 47°40N 21°40E 182 C6
Hajdúnánás Hungary 47°50N 21°26E 182 C6
Hajdúsámson Hungary 47°37N 21°42E 182 C6
Hajdúszoboszló Hungary 47°27N 21°22E 182 C6
Haji Ibrahim Iraq 36°40N 44°30E 213 D11
Hajipur India 25°45N 85°13E 243 G11
Ḩājj Ali Qolī, Kavīr-e Iran 35°55N 54°50E 247 C7
Ḩajjah Yemen 15°42N 43°36E 248 D3
Ḩajjah □ Yemen 15°42N 43°36E 248 D3
Ḩājjīābād Hormozgān, Iran 28°19N 55°55E 247 D7
Ḩājjīābād Khorāsān, Iran 33°37N 60°0E 247 C9
Ḩājjīābād-e Zarrīn Iran 33°9N 54°51E 247 C7
Hajnówka Poland 52°47N 23°35E 185 F10
Hajo India 26°15N 91°32E 241 B3
Hajodo S. Korea 34°17N 126°3E 224 E3
Ḩajrah Si. Arabia 20°14N 41°3E 248 B3
Haka Myanmar 22°39N 93°37E 241 D4
Hakansson, Mts. Dem. Rep. of the Congo 8°40S 25°45E 265 D5
Hakataramea N.Z. 44°43S 170°30E 285 E5
Hakkâri Turkey 37°34N 43°44E 213 D10
Hakkâri □ Turkey 37°30N 44°0E 213 D10
Hakkâri Dağları Turkey 38°2N 42°58E 213 C10
Hakken-Zan Japan 34°10N 135°54E 223 C7
Hakkōda San Japan 40°50N 141°0E 220 D10
Hakodate Japan 41°45N 140°44E 220 D10
Hakos Namibia 23°13S 16°21E 270 B2
Hakota Japan 36°5N 140°30E 223 A12
Håksberg Sweden 60°11N 15°12E 162 D9
Hakskeenpan S. Africa 26°48S 20°13E 270 C3
Haku-San Japan 36°9N 136°46E 223 A8
Haku-San △ Japan 36°15N 136°45E 223 A8
Hakuba Japan 36°42N 137°51E 223 A9
Hakui Japan 36°53N 136°47E 221 F8
Hakun Myanmar 26°46N 95°42E 241 B5
Hakunila Finland 60°16N 25°6E 121 B3
Hakupu Cook Is. 19°6S 169°50W 289 g
Hakusan Japan 36°31N 136°34E 223 A8
Hal Saflieni Malta 35°52N 14°30E 206 F8
Hala Pakistan 25°43N 68°20E 240 D3
Ḩalab Syria 36°10N 37°15E 250 B8
Ḩalab □ Syria 36°10N 37°10E 250 B8
Ḩalaban Si. Arabia 23°29N 44°23E 248 B4
Ḩalabjah Iraq 35°10N 45°58E 213 E11
Halaib Sudan 22°12N 36°30E 256 C4
Halaib Triangle Africa 22°30N 35°20E 256 C4
Halandri = Chalandri Greece 38°3N 23°48E 112 A2
Halangingie Pt. Cook Is. 19°2S 169°58W 289 g
Halasa Sudan 14°26N 30°39E 257 E3
Halásztelek Hungary 47°22N 19°0E 117 B1
Ḩālat 'Ammār Si. Arabia 29°10N 36°4E 251 J7
Hālawa, C. U.S.A. 21°10N 156°43W 302 B5
Hālawa Heights U.S.A. 21°23N 157°55W 302 K14
Halbā Lebanon 34°34N 36°6E 250 D7
Halberstadt Germany 51°54N 11°3E 178 D7
Halcombe N.Z. 40°8S 175°30E 284 G4
Halcon, Mt. Phil. 13°16N 121°0E 232 E3
Halde Fjäll = Haltiatunturi Finland 69°17N 21°18E 160 B19
Halden Norway 59°9N 11°23E 164 E8
Haldensleben Germany 52°17N 11°24E 178 C7
Haldia Bangla. 22°1N 88°3E 243 H13
Haldwani India 29°31N 79°30E 243 E8
Hale U.S.A. 39°36N 93°20W 310 E3
Hale → Australia 24°56S 135°53E 280 C2

Haleakalā △ U.S.A. 20°40N 156°15W 302 C5
Hale'iwa U.S.A. 21°36N 158°6W 302 J13
Halesowen U.K. 52°27N 2°3W 169 E5
Halesworth U.K. 52°20N 1°31E 169 E9
Haleyville U.S.A. 34°14N 87°37W 315 D11
Half Assini Ghana 5°1N 2°50W 262 D4
Half Dome U.S.A. 37°44N 119°32E 306 H7
Half Tree Hollow St. Helena 15°56S 5°42W 153 h
Half Way Tree Jamaica 18°0N 76°48W 320 a
Halfa al Jadidah Sudan 15°20N 35°36E 256 A4
Halfeti Turkey 37°15N 37°52E 212 D7
Halfmoon Bay N.Z. 46°50S 168°5E 285 G3
Halfway → Canada 56°12N 121°32W 296 B4
Halia India 24°50N 82°19E 243 G10
Haliburton Canada 45°3N 78°30W 312 A6
Haliç Turkey 41°1N 28°57E 122 B1
Halifax Queens., Australia 18°32S 146°22E 280 B4
Halifax N.S., Canada 44°38N 63°35W 299 D7
Halifax W. Yorks., U.K. 53°43N 1°52W 168 D6
Halifax Pa., U.S.A. 40°25N 76°55W 312 F8
Halifax B. Australia 18°50S 147°0E 280 B4
Halifax Harbour Grenada 12°6N 61°45W 323 q
Halifax I. Namibia 26°38S 15°4E 270 C2
Halik Shan China 42°20N 81°22E 217 D10
Halīl → Iran 27°40N 58°30E 247 E8
Halim Perdana Kusuma Int. ✈ (HLP) Indonesia 6°16S 106°53E 122 B2
Halimun △ Indonesia 6°42S 106°26E 234 D3
Halin Myanmar 22°27N 95°49E 241 D5
Halkett, C. U.S.A. 70°48N 152°11W 303 A9
Halki = Chalki Greece 36°17N 27°35E 205 E9
Halkida = Chalkida Greece 38°27N 23°42E 204 C5
Halkidiki = Chalkidiki Greece 40°25N 23°20E 202 F7
Halkirk U.K. 58°30N 3°29W 167 C5
Hall Beach Canada 68°46N 81°12W 295 D15
Hall I. U.S.A. 60°40N 173°6W 303 F4
Hall in Tirol Austria 47°17N 11°30E 180 D4
Hall Pen. Canada 63°30N 66°0W 295 E18
Hall Pt. Australia 15°40S 124°23E 278 C3
Hallabro Sweden 56°22N 15°5E 163 H9
Halland Sweden 57°8N 12°47E 161 H15
Halland □ Sweden 57°0N 12°40E 163 H6
Hallandale Beach U.S.A. 25°58N 80°8W 129 C3
Hallands Väderö Sweden 56°27N 12°34E 163 H6
Hallandsås Sweden 56°22N 13°0E 163 H7
Ḩallāniyat, Ghubbat al Oman 17°40N 55°45E 249 C6
Ḩallāniyat, Jazā'ir al Oman 17°30N 55°58E 249 C6
Hallasan S. Korea 33°22N 126°32E 224 a
Hallasan △ S. Korea 33°20N 126°30E 224 a
Hällbybrunn Sweden 59°24N 16°25E 162 E10
Halle Belgium 50°44N 4°13E 116 B1
Halle Nordrhein-Westfalen, Germany 52°3N 8°22E 178 C4
Halle Sachsen-Anhalt, Germany 51°30N 11°56E 178 D7
Hällefors Sweden 59°47N 14°31E 162 E8
Hälleforsnäs Sweden 59°10N 16°30E 162 E10
Hallein Austria 47°40N 13°5E 180 D6
Hällekis Sweden 58°38N 13°27E 163 F7
Hallen Sweden 63°11N 14°4E 162 A8
Hallett Australia 33°25S 138°55E 282 B3
Hallettsville U.S.A. 29°27N 96°57W 314 G6
Halley Antarctica 75°35S 26°39W 151 D1
Hallia → India 16°55N 79°20E 244 F4
Hallim S. Korea 33°24N 126°15E 224 a
Hallingby Norway 60°7N 10°10E 164 D7
Hallingdal Norway 60°40N 9°8E 164 D6
Hallingdalselva → Norway 60°23N 9°35E 164 D6
Hallingskarvet Norway 60°36N 7°47E 164 D4
Hallingskarvet △ Norway 60°37N 7°45E 164 D4
Hallingskeid Norway 60°40N 7°17E 164 D4
Hallock U.S.A. 48°47N 96°57W 308 A5
Hallormsstaður Iceland 65°6N 14°45W 155 B12
Halls Creek Australia 18°16S 127°38E 278 C4
Halls Gap Australia 37°8S 142°34E 281 F3
Halls Lake Canada 45°7N 78°45W 312 A6
Hallsberg Sweden 59°5N 15°7E 162 E9
Hallstahammar Sweden 59°38N 16°15E 162 E10
Hallstatt Austria 47°33N 13°38E 180 D6
Hallstavik Sweden 60°5N 18°37E 162 D12
Hallstead U.S.A. 41°58N 75°45W 313 E9
Hallyeo △ S. Korea 34°45N 128°25E 224 E4
Halmahera Indonesia 0°40N 128°0E 231 D7
Halmahera Sea Indonesia 2°0N 130°0E 231 D7
Halmeu Romania 47°57N 23°2E 182 C8
Halmstad Sweden 56°41N 12°52E 163 H6
Halong Bay = Ha Long, Vinh Vietnam 20°56N 107°3E 236 B6
Halq el Oued = La Goulette Tunisia 36°53N 10°18E 200 F3
Hals Denmark 57°0N 10°18E 163 H4
Halsa Norway 63°3N 8°14E 164 A5
Halsafjorden Norway 63°5N 8°10E 164 A5
Hälsingborg = Helsingborg Sweden 56°3N 12°42E 163 H6
Hälsingland Sweden 61°40N 16°5E 162 C10
Halstead U.K. 51°57N 0°40E 169 F8
Haltdalen Norway 62°56N 11°8E 164 B8
Haltern Germany 51°44N 7°11E 178 D3
Haltiala Finland 60°16N 24°57E 121 B2
Haltiatunturi Finland 69°17N 21°18E 160 B19
Haltiavuori Finland 60°16N 24°56E 121 B2
Haltom City U.S.A. 32°47N 97°16W 120 B2
Halton □ U.K. 53°22N 2°45W 168 D5
Haltwhistle U.K. 54°58N 2°26W 168 C5
Ḩālūl Qatar 25°40N 52°40E 247 E7
Halvad India 23°1N 71°11E 242 H4
Ḩalvān Iran 33°57N 56°15E 247 C8
Halve Dag, Pt. Curaçao 12°14N 69°7W 322 g
Ham Chad 10°1N 15°35E 259 F3
Ham Somme, France 49°45N 3°4E 173 C10
Ham London, U.K. 51°25N 0°18W 125 B2
Hamab Namibia 28°7S 19°16E 270 C2
Hamad Sudan 15°20N 33°32E 257 D3
Hamada Japan 34°56N 132°4E 222 C4
Hamadān Iran 34°52N 48°32E 213 E13
Hamadān □ Iran 35°0N 49°0E 247 C6
Hamadia Algeria 35°28N 1°57E 261 A5
Ḩamāh Syria 35°5N 36°40E 250 C7
Ḩamāh □ Syria 35°10N 37°0E 250 C8
Hamakita Japan 34°45N 137°47E 223 C9
Hamale Ghana 10°56N 2°45W 262 C4
Hamamatsu Japan 34°45N 137°45E 223 C9
Haman S. Korea 35°14N 128°28E 224 E4
Hamar Norway 60°48N 11°7E 164 D8
Hamâta, Gebel Egypt 24°17N 35°0E 246 E2
Hamatonbetsu Japan 45°10N 142°20E 220 B11
Hambantota Sri Lanka 6°10N 81°10E 245 L5
Hamber ⌂ Canada 52°20N 118°0W 296 C5
Hamburg Hamburg, Germany 53°33N 9°59E 178 B5
Hamburg Ark., U.S.A. 33°14N 91°48W 314 E9
Hamburg N.Y., U.S.A. 42°43N 78°50W 312 D6
Hamburg Pa., U.S.A. 40°33N 75°59W 313 F9
Hamburg □ Germany 53°30N 10°0E 178 B5
Hamburg Fuhlsbüttel ✈ (HAM) Germany 53°35N 9°59E 178 B5
Ḩamḑ, W. al → Si. Arabia 24°55N 36°20E 246 E3
Ḩamdah Si. Arabia 19°2N 43°36E 248 C3
Ḩamdānah Si. Arabia 19°59N 40°34E 248 C3
Hamden U.S.A. 41°23N 72°54W 313 E12
Hamdibey Turkey 39°50N 27°15E 205 B9
Häme Finland 61°38N 25°10E 160 F21
Hämeenkylä Finland 60°16N 24°48E 121 B1
Hämeenlinna Finland 61°0N 24°28E 188 B3
Hamelin Pool Australia 26°22S 114°20E 279 E1
Hameln Germany 52°6N 9°21E 178 C5
Hamerkaz □ Israel 32°15N 34°55E 251 F5
Hamero Hadad Ethiopia 7°27N 42°14E 267 C5
Hamersley Ra. Australia 22°0S 117°45E 278 D2
Hamgyŏng-sanmaek N. Korea 41°35N 129°15E 224 B4
Hamgyŏngbuk-do □ N. Korea 41°50N 129°25E 224 B4
Hamgyŏngnam-do □ N. Korea 40°0N 127°30E 224 C3
Hamhŭng N. Korea 39°54N 127°30E 224 C3
Hamhŭng-man N. Korea 39°48N 127°27E 224 C3
Hami China 42°55N 93°25E 218 C7
Hamilton = Churchill → Canada 53°19N 60°10W 299 B7
Hamilton Vic., Australia 37°45S 142°2E 282 D5
Hamilton Bermuda 32°17N 64°47W 153 a
Hamilton Ont., Canada 43°15N 79°50W 312 C5
Hamilton N.Z. 37°47S 175°19E 284 D4
Hamilton S. Lanarks., U.K. 55°46N 4°2W 167 F4
Hamilton Ala., U.S.A. 34°9N 87°59W 315 D11
Hamilton Alaska, U.S.A. 62°54N 163°53W 303 E7
Hamilton Ga., U.S.A. 32°45N 84°53W 316 C5
Hamilton Ill., U.S.A. 40°24N 91°21W 310 D5
Hamilton Ind., U.S.A. 41°33N 84°56W 311 C12
Hamilton Mo., U.S.A. 39°45N 94°0W 310 E2
Hamilton Mont., U.S.A. 46°15N 114°10W 304 C6
Hamilton N.Y., U.S.A. 42°50N 75°33W 313 D9
Hamilton Ohio, U.S.A. 39°24N 84°34W 311 E12
Hamilton Tex., U.S.A. 31°42N 98°7W 314 F5
Hamilton → Queens., Australia 23°30S 139°47E 280 C2
Hamilton → S. Austral., Australia 26°40S 135°19E 281 D2
Hamilton City U.S.A. 39°45N 122°1W 306 F4
Hamilton I. Australia 20°21S 148°56E 280 b
Hamilton Inlet Canada 54°0N 57°30W 299 B8
Hamilton Mt. U.S.A. 43°25N 74°22W 313 C10
Hamina Finland 60°34N 27°12E 188 B4
Hamirpur H.P., India 31°41N 76°31E 242 D7
Hamirpur Ut. P., India 25°57N 80°9E 243 G9
Hamitabat Turkey 41°30N 27°17E 203 E11
Hamju N. Korea 39°51N 127°26E 224 C3
Hamlet U.S.A. 34°53N 79°42W 315 D15
Hamley Bridge Australia 34°17S 138°35E 282 C3
Hamlin = Hameln Germany 52°6N 9°21E 178 C5
Hamlin N.Y., U.S.A. 43°17N 77°55W 312 C7
Hamlin Tex., U.S.A. 32°53N 100°8W 314 E4
Hamm Germany 51°40N 7°50E 178 D3
Ḩammām al Alī Iraq 36°9N 43°15E 213 D10
Hammam Bouhadjar Algeria 35°23N 0°58W 261 A4
Ḩammām Damt Yemen 14°5N 44°40E 248 D4
Ḩammamet Tunisia 36°24N 10°38E 258 A2
Ḩammamet, G. de Tunisia 36°10N 10°48E 258 A2
Ḩammār, Hawr al Iraq 30°50N 47°10E 246 D5
Hammarby Sweden 59°17N 18°5E 139 B2
Hammarstrand Sweden 63°7N 16°20E 162 A10
Hamme Belgium 50°55N 4°17E 116 A1
Hammelburg Germany 50°6N 9°53E 179 E5
Hammeren Denmark 55°18N 14°47E 163 J8
Hammerfest Norway 70°39N 23°41E 160 A20
Hammersmith U.K. 51°29N 0°14W 125 B2
Hammerstein = Czarne Poland 53°42N 16°58E 184 E3
Hammerum Denmark 56°8N 9°3E 163 H3
Hamminkeln Germany 51°43N 6°35E 178 D2
Hammond Ind., U.S.A. 41°38N 87°30W 311 C9
Hammond La., U.S.A. 30°30N 90°28W 315 F9
Hammond N.Y., U.S.A. 44°27N 75°42W 313 B9
Hammondsport U.S.A. 42°25N 77°13W 312 D7
Hammonton U.S.A. 39°39N 74°48W 309 F16
Hamoyet, Jebel Sudan 17°33N 38°2E 256 D4
Hampden N.Z. 45°18S 170°50E 285 F5
Hampi India 15°18N 76°28E 245 G3
Hampshire □ U.K. 51°7N 1°23W 169 F6
Hampshire Downs U.K. 51°15N 1°10W 169 F6
Hampstead Qué., Canada 45°28N 73°37W 130 B2
Hampstead Dominica 15°36N 61°23W 323 k
Hampstead London, U.K. 51°33N 0°10W 125 A2
Hampstead Garden Suburb U.K. 51°34N 0°11W 125 A2
Hampstead Heath U.K. 51°33N 0°10W 125 A2
Hampton N.B., Canada 45°32N 65°51W 299 C6
Hampton Ont., Canada 43°58N 78°45W 312 C6
Hampton London, U.K. 51°24N 0°21W 125 B2
Hampton Ark., U.S.A. 33°32N 92°28W 314 E8
Hampton Ga., U.S.A. 33°23N 84°17W 316 B5
Hampton Iowa, U.S.A. 42°45N 93°13W 310 B3
Hampton N.H., U.S.A. 42°57N 70°50W 313 D14
Hampton S.C., U.S.A. 32°52N 81°7W 316 C8
Hampton Va., U.S.A. 37°2N 76°21W 309 G15
Hampton Bays U.S.A. 40°53N 72°30W 313 F12
Hampton Court Palace U.K. 51°24N 0°20W 125 B1
Hampton Springs U.S.A. 30°5N 83°40W 316 E6
Hampton Tableland Australia 32°0S 127°0E 279 F4
Hampton Wick U.K. 51°24N 0°18W 125 B2
Hampyeong S. Korea 35°3N 126°31E 224 E3
Hampyeongman S. Korea 35°6N 126°23E 224 E3
Hamrā' Baghdād, Iraq 33°18N 44°18E 113 B1
Hamra Gävleborg, Sweden 61°39N 14°59E 162 C8
Hamrat → Chad 12°52N 21°15E 259 F4
Hamrat esh Sheykh Sudan 14°38N 27°55E 257 E2
Ḩamrin, Jabal Iraq 34°30N 44°30E 213 E11
Hamrun Malta 35°53N 14°29E 206 F8
Hamtik Phil. 10°42N 121°59E 233 F3
Hamur Turkey 39°37N 43°3E 213 C10
Hamyang S. Korea 35°32N 127°42E 224 E3
Hamzalar Turkey 37°7N 32°33E 250 A3
Han = Hangang → S. Korea 37°50N 126°30E 224 D3
Han i Hotit Albania 42°19N 19°27E 202 D3
Han Jiang → China 23°25N 116°40E 229 F11
Han Shui → China 30°34N 114°17E 229 B10
Hāna U.S.A. 20°45N 155°59W 302 C6
Hanahan U.S.A. 32°55N 80°0W 316 C10
Hanak Si. Arabia 25°32N 37°0E 246 E3
Hanak Turkey 41°14N 42°50E 213 B10
Hanala Finland 60°20N 25°4E 121 A3
Hanalei U.S.A. 22°12N 159°30W 302 A2
Hanamaki Japan 39°23N 141°7E 220 E10
Hanamaulu U.S.A. 21°59N 159°22W 302 B2
Hanang Tanzania 4°30S 35°25E 268 C4
Hanapēpē U.S.A. 21°55N 159°35W 302 B2
Hanare Iwa Iwo Jima 24°48N 141°21E 218 b
Hanau Germany 50°7N 8°56E 179 E4
Hanauma B. U.S.A. 21°15N 157°40W 302 K14
Hanbogd = Ihbulag Mongolia 43°11N 107°10E 226 C4
Hançalar Turkey 38°8N 29°24E 205 C11
Hănceşti Moldova 46°50N 28°36E 183 D13
Hancheng China 35°31N 110°25E 226 G6
Hanchuan China 30°40N 113°50E 229 B9
Hanchung = Hanzhong China 33°10N 107°1E 228 A6
Hancock Mich., U.S.A. 47°8N 88°35W 308 B9
Hancock N.Y., U.S.A. 41°57N 75°17W 313 E9
Hancock Vt., U.S.A. 43°55N 72°50W 313 C12
Handa Japan 34°53N 136°55E 223 C8
Handa I. U.K. 58°23N 5°11W 167 C3
Handan China 36°35N 114°28E 226 F8
Handeni Tanzania 5°25S 38°2E 268 D4
Handlová Slovakia 48°45N 18°35E 181 C11
Handub Sudan 19°15N 37°16E 256 D4
Handwara India 34°21N 74°20E 243 B6
Haneda Japan 35°32N 139°44E 140 B3
Haneda, Tōkyō ✈ (HND) Japan 35°33N 139°46E 140 B3
Hanegev Israel 30°50N 35°0E 251 H6
Hanford U.S.A. 36°20N 119°39W 306 J7
Hanford Reach ⌂ U.S.A. 46°40N 119°30W 304 C4
Hang Chat Thailand 18°20N 99°21E 236 C2
Hang Hau Hong Kong, China 22°19N 114°16E 122 B3
Hanga Roa Chile 27°8S 109°26W 330 b
Hangang → S. Korea 37°50N 126°30E 224 D3
Hangayn Nuruu Mongolia 47°30N 99°0E 218 B8
Hangchou = Hangzhou China 30°18N 120°11E 229 B13
Hanger Sweden 57°6N 13°58E 163 G7
Hanggin Houqi China 40°58N 107°4E 226 D4
Hanggin Qi China 39°52N 108°50E 226 E5
Hanging Gardens Mumbai, India 130 b1
Hangkow = Wuhan China 30°31N 114°18E 229 B10
Hangku = Hangu China 39°18N 117°53E 227 E9
Hangu China 39°18N 117°53E 227 E9
Hangzhou China 30°18N 120°11E 229 B13
Hangzhou Wan China 30°15N 120°45E 229 B13
Hangzhou Xiaoshan Int. ✈ (HGH) China 30°14N 120°26E 229 B13
Hanh Mongolia 51°32N 100°35E 218 A9
Hanhöhiy Uul Mongolia 49°30N 94°30E 217 C12
Hanhongor Mongolia 43°55N 104°28E 226 C3
Hani Turkey 38°24N 40°23E 213 C9
Hania = Chania Greece 35°30N 24°4E 207 E5
Ḩanīdh Si. Arabia 26°35N 48°38E 247 E6
Ḩanīsh Yemen 13°45N 42°46E 248 D3
Haniska Slovakia 48°37N 21°15E 181 C14
Hanjiang China 25°26N 119°6E 229 E12
Hankinson U.S.A. 46°4N 96°54W 308 B5
Hankö Finland 59°50N 22°57E 188 C2
Hankou China 30°35N 114°30E 229 B10
Hanksville U.S.A. 38°22N 110°43W 304 G8
Hanle India 32°42N 79°4E 243 C8
Hanlon Canada 43°38N 79°39W 141 B1
Hanmer Springs N.Z. 42°32S 172°50E 285 C7
Hann → Australia 17°26S 126°17E 278 C4
Hann, Mt. Australia 15°45S 126°0E 278 C4
Hanna Alta., Canada 51°40N 111°54W 296 C6
Hanna Wyo., U.S.A. 41°52N 106°34W 304 F10
Hannah B. Canada 51°40N 80°0W 298 B4
Hannibal Mo., U.S.A. 39°42N 91°22W 310 E5
Hannibal N.Y., U.S.A. 43°19N 76°35W 313 C8
Hannik Sudan 18°12N 32°20E 256 D3
Hannover Germany 52°22N 9°46E 178 C5
Hanö Sweden 56°1N 14°50E 163 H8
Hanöbukten Sweden 55°35N 14°30E 163 J8
Hanoi Vietnam 21°5N 105°55E 228 G5
Hanover = Hannover Germany 52°22N 9°46E 178 C5
Hanover Ont., Canada 44°9N 81°2W 312 B3
Hanover Northern Cape, S. Africa 31°4S 24°29E 270 D3
Hanover Ind., U.S.A. 38°43N 85°28W 311 F11
Hanover N.H., U.S.A. 43°42N 72°17W 313 C12
Hanover Ohio, U.S.A. 40°4N 82°16W 312 F2
Hanover Pa., U.S.A. 39°48N 76°59W 309 F15
Hanover, I. Chile 51°0S 74°50W 336 D2
Hanpan, C. Papua N. G. 5°0S 154°35E 286 C8
Hans Lollik I. U.S. Virgin Is. 18°24N 64°53W 321 b
Hans Meyer Ra. Papua N. G. 4°20S 152°55E 286 C7
Hansdiha India 24°36N 87°5E 243 G12
Hanshou China 28°56N 111°50E 229 C8
Hansi H.P., India 32°27N 77°50E 242 C7
Hansi Haryana, India 29°10N 75°57E 242 E6
Hanson, L. Australia 31°0S 136°15E 282 A2
Hanstholm Denmark 57°7N 8°36E 163 G2
Hantan = Handan China 36°35N 114°28E 226 F8
Hanting China 36°46N 119°12E 227 F10
Hantsavichy Belarus 52°49N 26°30E 177 B14
Hanumangarh India 29°35N 74°19E 242 E6
Hanwell U.K. 51°30N 0°20W 125 A1
Hanworth U.K. 51°26N 0°23W 125 B1
Hanyin China 32°54N 108°28E 226 H5
Hanyū Japan 36°10N 139°32E 223 A11
Hanyuan China 29°21N 102°40E 228 C4
Hanzhong China 33°10N 107°1E 228 A6
Hanzhuang China 34°33N 117°23E 227 G9
Hao French Polynesia 18°15S 140°54W 289 f
Haora India 22°34N 88°18E 124 B1
Haouach, O. → Chad 16°45N 19°35E 259 E4
Haoxue China 30°3N 112°24E 229 B9
Haparanda Sweden 65°52N 24°8E 160 D21
Haparanda Skärgård △ Sweden 65°35N 23°44E 160 D20
Hapdeok S. Korea 36°48N 126°46E 224 D3
Hapeville U.S.A. 33°39N 84°24W 113 C2
Happy U.S.A. 34°45N 101°52W 314 D4
Happy Camp U.S.A. 41°48N 123°23W 304 F2
Happy Valley Hong Kong, China 22°16N 114°10E 122 B3
Happy Valley-Goose Bay Canada 53°15N 60°20W 299 B7
Hapsu N. Korea 41°13N 128°51E 224 B4
Hapur India 28°45N 77°45E 242 E7
Ḩaql Si. Arabia 29°10N 34°58E 251 J5
Haquira Peru 14°14S 72°12W 330 C3
Har Indonesia 5°16S 133°14E 231 F8
Har Adar West Bank 31°49N 35°8E 123 B1
Har-Ayrag Mongolia 45°47N 109°16E 226 B5
Har Gilo West Bank 31°43N 35°10E 123 B2
Har Homa West Bank 31°44N 35°12E 123 B2
Har Hu China 38°20N 97°38E 218 D8
Har Nof Israel 31°47N 35°11E 123 B2
Har Tsiyon Jerusalem 123 b3
Har Us Nuur Mongolia 48°0N 92°0E 217 C12
Har Yehuda Israel 31°35N 34°57E 251 G5
Ḩaraḑ Si. Arabia 24°22N 49°0E 249 A5
Ḩaraḑ Yemen 16°26N 43°5E 248 C3
Haradok Belarus 55°30N 30°3E 188 E6
Häradsbäck Sweden 56°32N 14°26E 163 H8
Harahan U.S.A. 29°56N 90°12W 131 B1
Haraiki French Polynesia 17°38S 143°27W 289 f
Haramosh Pakistan 35°50N 74°54E 243 B6
Haranomachi = Minamisōma Japan 37°38N 140°58E 220 F10
Harar = Harer Ethiopia 9°20N 42°8E 257 F5
Harare Zimbabwe 17°43S 31°2E 269 F3
Ḩarāsīs, Jiddat al Oman 19°30N 56°0E 249 C7
Harat Eritrea 16°5N 39°26E 257 D4
Harau Indonesia 0°7S 100°35E 234 C2
Haraz-Djombo Chad 14°20N 19°12E 259 F3
Harazé Chad 9°57N 20°48E 259 G4
Harbel Liberia 6°16N 10°20W 262 D2
Harbhanga India 20°38N 84°36E 244 D7
Harbin China 45°48N 126°40E 227 B14
Harbiye Turkey 36°10N 36°8E 250 B7
Harbo Sweden 60°7N 17°12E 162 D11
Harboøre Denmark 56°38N 8°10E 163 H2
Harbor Beach U.S.A. 43°51N 82°39W 312 C2
Harborcreek U.S.A. 42°9N 79°57W 312 D5
Harbour Breton Canada 47°29N 55°50W 299 C8
Harbour Deep Canada 50°25N 56°32W 299 B8
Harbour Front Centre Singapore 1°16N 103°49E 138 B2
Harbour View Jamaica 17°59N 76°50W 320 a
Harburg Germany 53°27N 9°58E 178 B5
Harburger Berge ⌂ Germany 53°26N 9°51E 178 B5
Harda India 22°27N 77°5E 242 H7
Hardangerfjorden Norway 60°5N 6°0E 164 D3
Hardangerjøkulen Norway 60°30N 7°27E 164 D4
Hardangervidda Norway 60°7N 7°20E 164 D4
Hardangervidda △ Norway 60°10N 7°25E 164 D4
Hardap □ Namibia 24°0S 17°0E 270 B2
Hardap ⌂ Namibia 24°29S 17°45E 270 B2
Hardap Dam Namibia 24°32S 17°50E 270 B2
Hardeeville U.S.A. 32°17N 81°5W 316 C8
Harden Australia 34°32S 148°24E 283 C8
Hardenberg Neths. 52°34N 6°37E 170 B6
Harderwijk Neths. 52°21N 5°38E 170 B5
Hardey → Australia 22°45S 116°8E 278 D2
Hardin Ill., U.S.A. 39°10N 90°37W 310 E6
Hardin Mont., U.S.A. 45°44N 107°37W 304 D10
Harding S. Africa 30°35S 29°55E 271 D4
Harding, L. U.S.A. 32°40N 85°5W 316 C4
Harding Ra. Australia 16°17S 124°55E 278 C3
Hardinsburg U.S.A. 37°47N 86°28W 311 G10
Hardisty Canada 52°40N 111°18W 296 C6
Hardoi India 27°26N 80°6E 243 F9
Hardwar = Haridwar India 29°58N 78°9E 242 E8
Hardwick Ga., U.S.A. 33°4N 83°14W 316 B6
Hardwick Vt., U.S.A. 44°30N 72°22W 313 B12
Hardwicke B. Australia 34°55S 137°20E 282 C2
Hardwood Lake Canada 45°12N 77°26W 312 A7
Hardy, Pen. Chile 55°30S 68°20W 336 E3
Hardy, Pte. St. Lucia 14°6N 60°56W 323 m
Hare B. Canada 51°15N 55°45W 299 B8
Hareid Norway 62°22N 6°1E 164 B3
Haren Brussels, Belgium 50°53N 4°25E 116 A2
Haren Niedersachsen, Germany 52°47N 7°13E 178 C3
Harer Ethiopia 9°20N 42°8E 257 F5
Harerge Ethiopia 7°12N 42°0E 257 F5
Hareskovby Denmark 55°45N 12°23E 118 A2
Harestua Norway 60°11N 10°44E 164 D7
Hareto Ethiopia 9°23N 37°6E 257 F4
Harfleur France 49°30N 0°10E 172 C7
Hargeisa Somalia 9°30N 44°2E 267 C5
Hargeisa ⌂ Somalia 10°2N 44°2E 267 B5
Harghita □ Romania 46°30N 25°30E 183 D10
Harghita, Munţii Romania 46°25N 25°35E 183 D10
Hargshamn Sweden 60°12N 18°30E 162 D12
Hari → Indonesia 1°16S 104°5E 234 C2
Haria Canary Is. 29°8N 13°32W 153 e2
Ḩarīb Yemen 14°56N 45°30E 248 D4
Haricha, Hamada el Mali 22°40N 3°15W 260 D4
Haridwar India 29°58N 78°9E 242 E8
Harihar India 14°32N 75°44E 245 G2
Harihari N.Z. 43°9S 170°33E 285 D5
Hariharpur Garhi Nepal 27°19N 85°29E 243 F11
Ḩārim Syria 36°13N 36°29E 250 B7
Harim, Jabal al Oman 25°58N 56°14E 247 E8
Harima-Nada Japan 34°30N 134°35E 222 C6
Haringey □ U.K. 51°34N 0°5W 125 A3
Haringhata → Bangla. 22°0N 89°58E 241 E2
Haripad India 9°14N 76°28E 245 K3
Harīr, W. al → Syria 32°44N 35°59E 250 F6
Harīrūd → Asia 37°24N 60°38E 240 A1
Härjedalen Sweden 62°22N 13°5E 162 B7
Harjusuo Finland 60°19N 25°0E 121 B3
Harlaching Germany 48°5N 11°33E 118 B2
Harlan Iowa, U.S.A. 41°39N 95°19W 308 E6
Harlan Ky., U.S.A. 36°51N 83°19W 309 G12
Hârlău Romania 47°23N 26°55E 183 C11
Harlaw Res. U.K. 55°52N 3°18W 121 B2
Harlech U.K. 52°52N 4°6W 168 E3
Harlem Ga., U.S.A. 33°25N 82°19W 316 B7
Harlem Mont., U.S.A. 48°32N 108°47W 304 B9
Harlem New York, U.S.A. 132 a3
Harlesden U.K. 51°32N 0°14W 125 A2
Hårlev Denmark 55°21N 12°14E 163 J6
Harleyville U.S.A. 33°13N 80°27W 316 B9
Harlingen Neths. 53°11N 5°25E 170 A5
Harlingen Tex., U.S.A. 26°12N 97°42W 314 H6
Harlington U.K. 51°29N 0°25W 125 B1
Harlow U.K. 51°46N 0°8E 169 F8
Harlowton U.S.A. 46°26N 109°50W 304 C9
Harmaja Finland 60°6N 24°58E 121 C2
Harmancık Turkey 39°41N 29°9E 205 B11
Harmånger Sweden 61°55N 17°20E 162 C11
Harmanli Bulgaria 41°55N 25°55E 203 E9
Harmashatar hegy Hungary 47°33N 19°0E 117 A2
Harmil Eritrea 16°30N 40°10E 257 D5
Harnai India 17°48N 73°6E 244 F1
Harnai Pakistan 30°6N 67°56E 242 D2
Harney, L. U.S.A. 28°45N 81°3W 317 G8
Harney Basin U.S.A. 43°0N 119°30W 304 E4
Harney L. U.S.A. 43°14N 119°8W 304 E4
Harney Peak U.S.A. 43°52N 103°32W 308 D2
Härnön Sweden 62°36N 18°0E 162 B12
Härnösand Sweden 62°38N 17°55E 162 B11
Haro Spain 42°35N 2°55W 196 C2
Harold U.S.A. 30°40N 86°53W 317 E3
Harold Pond The Bahamas 25°2N 77°22W 153 b
Haroldswick U.K. 60°48N 0°50W 167 A8
Háros Hungary 47°23N 19°2E 117 B2
Harp L. Canada 55°5N 61°50W 299 A7
Harpanahalli India 14°47N 76°2E 245 G3
Harper = Costa Mesa U.S.A. 33°38N 117°55W 307 M9
Harper Liberia 4°25N 7°43W 262 E3
Harper, Mt. U.S.A. 64°14N 143°51W 303 D12
Harperrig Res. U.K. 55°50N 3°26W 121 B1
Harplinge Sweden 56°45N 12°45E 163 H6
Harrah's Casino New Orleans, U.S.A. 131 b2
Harrai India 22°37N 79°13E 243 H8
Harrand Pakistan 29°28N 70°3E 242 E4
Harricana → Canada 50°56N 79°32W 298 B4
Harriman U.S.A. 35°56N 84°33W 315 D12
Harrington Australia 31°52S 152°42E 283 A10
Harrington Harbour Canada 50°31N 59°30W 299 B8
Harrington Sd. Bermuda 32°20N 64°44W 153 a
Harris U.K. 57°50N 6°55W 167 D2
Harris, L. S. Austral., Australia 31°10S 135°10E 281 E2
Harris, L. Fla., U.S.A. 28°47N 81°49W 317 G8
Harris, Sd. of U.K. 57°44N 7°6W 167 D1
Harris Mts. N.Z. 44°49S 168°49E 285 E3
Harris Pt. Canada 43°6N 82°9W 312 C2
Harrisburg Ill., U.S.A. 37°44N 88°32W 311 G8
Harrisburg Nebr., U.S.A. 41°33N 103°44W 308 E2
Harrisburg Pa., U.S.A. 40°16N 76°53W 312 F8
Harrismith S. Africa 28°15S 29°8E 271 C4
Harrison Ark., U.S.A. 36°14N 93°7W 314 C8
Harrison Maine, U.S.A. 44°7N 70°39W 313 B14
Harrison Nebr., U.S.A. 42°41N 103°53W 308 D2
Harrison, C. Canada 54°55N 57°55W 299 B8
Harrison Bay U.S.A. 70°40N 151°0W 303 A10
Harrison L. Canada 49°33N 121°50W 296 D4
Harrisonburg U.S.A. 38°27N 78°52W 309 F14
Harrison's Cave Barbados 13°11N 59°34W 323 n
Harrisonville U.S.A. 38°39N 94°21W 310 F2
Harriston Canada 43°57N 80°53W 312 C4
Harrisville Mich., U.S.A. 44°39N 83°17W 312 B1
Harrisville N.Y., U.S.A. 44°9N 75°19W 313 B9
Harrisville Pa., U.S.A. 41°8N 80°0W 312 E5
Harrodsburg Ind., U.S.A. 39°1N 86°33W 311 E10
Harrodsburg Ky., U.S.A. 37°46N 84°51W 311 G12
Harrogate U.K. 54°0N 1°33W 168 C6
Harrow Vic., Australia 37°9S 141°35E 282 D4
Harrow Ont., Canada 42°2N 82°55W 312 D2
Harrow □ U.K. 51°35N 0°21W 125 A1
Harrow on the Hill U.K. 51°34N 0°20W 125 A1
Harrow School U.K. 51°34N 0°20W 125 A1
Harrow Weald U.K. 51°36N 0°20W 125 A1
Harrowsmith Canada 44°24N 76°40W 313 B8
Harry S. Moss Park U.S.A. 32°53N 96°44W 120 A5
Harry S. Truman Res. U.S.A. 38°16N 93°24W 310 F3
Harsefeld Germany 53°27N 9°30E 178 B5
Harsewinkel Germany 51°56N 8°14E 178 D4
Harsīn Iran 34°18N 47°33E 213 E12
Hârşova Romania 44°40N 27°59E 183 F12
Harstad Norway 68°48N 16°30E 160 B17
Harsud India 22°6N 76°44E 242 H7
Hart U.S.A. 43°42N 86°22W 308 D10
Hart, L. Australia 31°10S 136°25E 282 A2
Hartbees → S. Africa 28°45S 20°32E 270 C3
Hartberg Austria 47°17N 15°58E 180 D8
Harteigen Norway 60°11N 7°3E 164 D4
Hartford Ala., U.S.A. 31°6N 85°42W 316 D4
Hartford Conn., U.S.A. 41°46N 72°41W 313 E12
Hartford Ky., U.S.A. 37°27N 86°55W 308 G10
Hartford Mich., U.S.A. 42°13N 86°10W 311 B10
Hartford S. Dak., U.S.A. 43°38N 96°57W 308 D5
Hartford Vt., U.S.A. 43°40N 72°20W 313 C12
Hartford Wis., U.S.A. 43°19N 88°22W 308 D9
Hartford City U.S.A. 40°27N 85°22W 311 D11
Hartingsburg = Bela Bela S. Africa 24°51S 28°19E 271 B4
Hartland N.B., Canada 46°20N 67°32W 299 C6
Hartland Wis., U.S.A. 43°6N 88°21W 311 A8
Hartland Pt. U.K. 51°1N 4°32W 169 F3
Hartlepool U.K. 54°42N 1°13W 168 C6
Hartlepool □ U.K. 54°42N 1°17W 168 C6
Hartley Bay Canada 53°25N 129°15W 296 C3
Hartmannberge Namibia 17°0S 13°0E 270 A1
Hartney Canada 49°30N 100°35W 297 D8
Hărtop Moldova 46°39N 28°40E 183 D13
Harts → S. Africa 28°24S 24°17E 270 C3
Harts Range Australia 23°6S 134°55E 280 C1
Hartselle U.S.A. 34°27N 86°56W 315 D11
Hartsfield-Jackson Atlanta Int. ✈ (ATL) U.S.A. 33°38N 84°26W 113 C2
Hartshorne U.S.A. 34°51N 95°34W 314 D7
Hartstown U.S.A. 41°33N 80°23W 312 E4
Hartsville U.S.A. 34°23N 80°4W 315 D14
Hartswater S. Africa 27°34S 24°43E 270 C3
Hartwell U.S.A. 34°21N 82°56W 315 D13
Harumi Tokyo, Japan 140 c5
Harunabad Pakistan 29°35N 73°8E 242 E5
Harur India 12°3N 78°29E 245 H4
Harūt → Afghan. 31°29N 61°24E 240 C1
Harvand Iran 28°25N 55°43E 247 D7
Harvard U.S.A. 42°25N 88°37W 311 B8
Harvard Univ. U.S.A. 42°22N 71°7W 116 A2
Harvey W. Austral., Australia 33°5S 115°54E 279 F2
Harvey Ill., U.S.A. 41°36N 87°50W 119 D3
Harvey La., U.S.A. 29°54N 90°4W 131 B2
Harvey N. Dak., U.S.A. 47°47N 99°56W 308 B4
Harwich U.K. 51°56N 1°17E 169 F9
Harwood Heights U.S.A. 41°57N 87°46W 119 B2
Haryana □ India 29°0N 76°10E 242 E7
Haryn → Belarus 52°7N 27°17E 177 B14
Harz Germany 51°38N 10°44E 178 D6
Harz △ Germany 51°40N 10°18E 178 D6
Harzgerode Germany 51°38N 11°8E 178 D7
Hasa Si. Arabia 25°50N 49°0E 247 E6
Ḩasā, W. al → Jordan 31°4N 35°29E 251 G6
Hasaheisa Sudan 14°44N 33°20E 257 E3
Ḩasanābād Eşfahan, Iran 32°8N 52°44E 247 C7
Ḩasanābād Tehrān, Iran 35°44N 51°16E 141 A1
Hasankeyf Turkey 37°42N 41°24E 213 D9
Hasanparti India 18°4N 79°32E 244 E4
Hasawinah, Jabal al Libya 28°15N 14°0E 258 C2
Ḩasb, W. → Iraq 31°45N 44°17E 246 D5
Hasbrouck Heights U.S.A. 40°51N 74°6W 132 A1
Hasdo → India 21°44N 82°44E 243 J10
Haselhorst Germany 52°33N 13°14E 115 A2
Haselünne Germany 52°40N 7°29E 178 C3
Hashima Japan 35°20N 136°40E 223 B8
Hashimoto Japan 34°19N 135°37E 223 C7
Hashtjerd Iran 35°52N 50°40E 247 C6
Hashtpar = Tālesh Iran 37°58N 48°58E 213 D13
Hashtrud Iran 37°28N 47°4E 213 D12
Hasi Nueifed W. Sahara 24°54N 14°49W 260 D2
Ḩāsik Oman 17°22N 55°17E 249 C6
Haskell U.S.A. 33°10N 99°44W 314 E5
Haskovo Bulgaria 41°56N 25°30E 203 E9
Haskovo □ Bulgaria 42°0N 25°40E 203 E9
Hasköy Edirne, Turkey 41°38N 26°52E 203 E10
Hasköy İstanbul, Turkey 41°2N 28°57E 122 B1
Haslach Germany 48°16N 8°7E 179 G4
Hasle Denmark 55°11N 14°44E 163 J8
Hasle Oslo, Norway 59°46N 10°38E 133 B2
Haslemere U.K. 51°5N 0°43W 169 F7
Haslev Denmark 55°18N 11°57E 163 J5
Haslum Norway 59°55N 10°34E 133 A2
Hasparren France 43°24N 1°18W 174 E2
Hassa Turkey 36°48N 36°29E 250 B7
Hassan India 13°0N 76°5E 245 H3
Hassberge ⌂ Germany 50°8N 10°45E 179 E6
Hassela Sweden 62°7N 16°42E 162 B10
Hasselt Belgium 50°56N 5°21E 170 D5
Hassfurt Germany 50°2N 10°30E 179 E6
Hassi bel Guebbour Algeria 28°30N 6°41E 261 C6
Hassi bou Khelala Algeria 30°17N 0°18W 261 B4
Hassi Bourarchet Algeria 27°26N 9°19E 261 C6
Hassi Djafou Algeria 30°55N 3°35E 261 B5
Hassi el Hadjar Algeria 31°28N 4°45E 261 B5
Hassi Imoulaye Algeria 29°54N 9°10E 261 C6
Hassi Inifeg Algeria 28°15N 1°30W 261 C4
Hassi Inifel Algeria 29°50N 3°41E 261 C5
Hassi Mana Algeria 28°48N 2°37W 261 C4
Hassi Marroket Algeria 30°10N 3°0E 261 B5
Hassi Mengoub Algeria 29°49N 5°26W 260 C3
Hassi Messaoud Algeria 31°51N 6°1E 261 B6
Hassi Sougoued Algeria 26°50N 9°28E 261 C6
Hassi Tartrat Algeria 30°5N 6°28E 261 B6
Hassi Zerzour Morocco 30°51N 3°56W 260 B4
Hassi Zguilma Morocco 30°19N 6°10W 260 B3
Hässleholm Sweden 56°10N 13°46E 163 H7
Hasslö Sweden 56°7N 15°28E 163 H9
Hassloch Germany 49°22N 8°16E 179 F4
Hästhagen Sweden 59°18N 18°9E 139 B2
Hästholmen Sweden 58°17N 14°38E 163 F8
Hastings Vic., Australia 38°18S 145°12E 283 E6
Hastings Barbados 13°4N 59°36W 323 r
Hastings N.Z. 39°39S 176°52E 284 F5
Hastings E. Sussex, U.K. 50°51N 0°35E 169 G8
Hastings Fla., U.S.A. 29°43N 81°31W 316 F8
Hastings Mich., U.S.A. 42°39N 85°17W 311 B11
Hastings Minn., U.S.A. 44°44N 92°51W 308 C7
Hastings Nebr., U.S.A. 40°35N 98°23W 308 E4
Hastings Ra. Australia 31°15S 152°14E 283 A10
Hästveda Sweden 56°17N 13°55E 163 H7
Ḩaşwayn Yemen 15°35N 52°6E 249 D6
Hat Ukraine 48°19N 22°38E 182 B7
Hat Head △ Australia 31°3S 153°1E 283 A10
Hat Lot Vietnam 21°15N 104°7E 236 B5
Hat Yai Thailand 7°1N 100°27E 237 J3
Hatanbulag = Ergel Mongolia 43°8N 109°5E 226 C5
Hatay Turkey 36°14N 36°10E 250 B7
Hatay □ Turkey 36°25N 36°15E 250 B7
Hatch U.S.A. 32°40N 107°9W 305 K10
Hatch End U.K. 51°36N 0°22W 125 A1
Hatchet L. Canada 58°36N 103°40W 297 B8
Haţeg Romania 45°36N 22°55E 182 E7
Hateruma-Shima Japan 24°3N 123°47E 221 M1
Hatfield Australia 33°54S 143°49E 282 B5
Hatgal Mongolia 50°26N 100°9E 218 A9
Hathras India 27°36N 78°6E 242 F8
Hatia Bangla. 22°30N 91°5E 241 D3
Hatia Nepal 27°43N 87°21E 243 F12
Hatia Is. Bangla. 22°30N 91°0E 241 D3
Hatiara India 22°36N 88°26E 124 B2
Ḩāţibah, Ra's Si. Arabia 21°55N 38°57E 256 C4
Hatid India 17°17N 75°3E 244 F2
Hatillo Puerto Rico 18°29N 66°50W 321 b
Hato Bonaire 12°11N 68°17W 322 h
Hato Curaçao 12°11N 68°57W 322 g
Hato Caves Curaçao 12°11N 68°57W 322 g
Hato Corozal Colombia 6°11N 71°45W 328 B3
Hato Mayor Dom. Rep. 18°46N 69°15W 321 C6
Hatra = Al Ḩaḑr Iraq 35°35N 42°44E 213 E10
Hatsukaichi Japan 34°22N 132°22E 222 C4
Hatta India 24°7N 79°36E 243 G8
Hatta U.A.E. 24°45N 56°4E 247 E8
Hattah Australia 34°48S 142°17E 282 C5
Hattah Kulkyne △ Australia 34°16S 142°33E 282 C5
Hatteras, C. U.S.A. 35°14N 75°32W 315 D17
Hatteras Abyssal Plain Atl. Oc. 28°0N 72°0W 152 D4
Hattiesburg U.S.A. 31°20N 89°17W 315 F10
Hattusa Turkey 40°0N 34°37E 212 B6
Hatutu French Polynesia 7°56S 140°38W 289 f
Hatvan Hungary 47°40N 19°45E 182 C4
Hau → Vietnam 9°30N 106°13E 237 H6
Haubstadt U.S.A. 38°12N 87°34W 311 F9
Haud Ethiopia 8°0N 45°0E 267 C6
Hauganes Iceland 65°56N 18°27W 155 B8
Haugastøl Norway 60°30N 7°50E 164 D4
Hauge Norway 58°20N 6°15E 164 F3
Haugesund Norway 59°23N 5°13E 164 E2
Hauhui Solomon Is. 9°10S 160°59E 287 M11
Hauhungaroa Ra. N.Z. 38°42S 175°40E 284 E4
Haukeligrend Norway 59°44N 7°33E 164 E4
Hauketo Norway 59°50N 10°48E 133 A3
Haukipudas Finland 65°12N 25°20E 160 D21
Haultain → Canada 55°51N 106°46W 297 B7
Haungpa Myanmar 25°29N 96°7E 241 C6
Hauraha Solomon Is. 10°46S 161°59E 287 N11
Hauraki G. N.Z. 36°35S 175°5E 284 C4
Hauroko L. N.Z. 45°59S 167°21E 285 F2
Hausruck Austria 48°6N 13°30E 180 C6
Haut Atlas Morocco 32°30N 5°0W 260 B4
Haut de la Montagne Guadeloupe 16°26N 61°28W 322 e
Haut-Jura ⌂ France 46°23N 2°23E 173 F9
Haut-Katanga □ Dem. Rep. of the Congo 10°30S 27°30E 269 E2
Haut-Kotto □ C.A.R. 8°0N 23°30E 264 A4
Haut-Languedoc ⌂ France 43°30N 2°43E 174 E6
Haut-Lomami □ Dem. Rep. of the Congo 8°30S 25°0E 265 D4
Haut-Mbomou □ C.A.R. 5°30N 25°30E 264 A5
Haut-Niger △ Guinea 10°20N 10°20W 262 C2
Haut-Ogooué □ Gabon 2°0S 14°0E 264 C2
Haut-Rhin □ France 48°0N 7°15E 173 E14
Haut-Uélé □ Dem. Rep. of the Congo 3°0N 29°0E 266 D2
Haute-Corse □ France 42°30N 9°30E 175 F13
Haute-Garonne □ France 43°30N 1°30E 174 E5
Haute-Loire □ France 45°5N 3°50E 174 C7
Haute-Marne □ France 48°10N 5°20E 173 D12
Haute Matsiatra □ Madag. 21°45S 47°0E 272 C2
Haute-Saône □ France 47°45N 6°10E 173 E13
Haute-Savoie □ France 46°0N 6°20E 175 C10
Haute-Vienne □ France 45°50N 1°10E 174 C5
Hautes-Alpes □ France 44°42N 6°20E 175 D10
Hautes-Fagnes = Hohes Venn Belgium 50°30N 6°5E 170 D6
Hautes-Pyrénées □ France 43°0N 0°10E 174 F4
Hauteville-Lompnès France 45°58N 5°36E 175 C9
Hautmont France 50°15N 3°55E 173 B10
Hauts-de-France □ France 50°30N 3°0E 173 B9
Hauts-de-Seine □ France 48°52N 2°15E 173 D9
Hauts Plateaux Algeria 35°0N 1°0E 261 B5
Hau'ula U.S.A. 21°37N 157°55W 302 J14
Hauz Khas India 28°33N 77°11E 120 B2
Hauzenberg Germany 48°40N 13°37E 179 G9
Havana = La Habana Cuba 23°8N 82°22W 320 B3
Havana Fla., U.S.A. 30°37N 84°25W 316 E5
Havana Ill., U.S.A. 40°18N 90°4W 310 D6
Havant U.K. 50°51N 0°58W 169 G7
Havârna Romania 48°4N 26°43E 183 B11
Havasor = Kığzı Turkey 38°18N 43°25E 246 B4
Havasu, L. U.S.A. 34°18N 114°28W 307 L12
Havdhem Sweden 57°10N 18°20E 163 G12
Havel → Germany 52°50N 12°3E 115 A2
Havelian Pakistan 34°2N 73°10E 242 B5
Havelkanal Germany 52°36N 13°10E 115 A2
Havelock Ont., Canada 44°26N 77°53W 312 B7
Havelock N.Z. 41°17S 173°48E 285 B8
Havelock N.C., U.S.A. 34°53N 76°54W 315 D16
Havelock I. India 11°58N 93°0E 245 J11
Havelock North N.Z. 39°40S 176°53E 284 F5
Haverfordwest U.K. 51°48N 4°58W 169 F3
Haverhill Suffolk, U.K. 52°5N 0°28E 169 E8
Haverhill Fla., U.S.A. 26°42N 80°7W 317 J9
Haverhill Mass., U.S.A. 42°47N 71°5W 313 D13
Haveri India 14°53N 75°24E 245 G2
Havering □ U.K. 51°34N 0°13E 125 A5
Havering-atte-Bower U.K. 51°37N 0°11E 125 A5
Havern Sweden 62°18N 15°7E 162 B9
Haverstraw U.S.A. 41°12N 73°58W 313 E11
Håverud Sweden 58°50N 12°28E 163 F6
Havirga Mongolia 45°41N 113°5E 226 B7
Havířov Czechia 49°46N 18°20E 181 B11
Havlíčkův Brod Czechia 49°36N 15°33E 180 B8
Havneby Denmark 55°5N 8°34E 163 J2
Havran Turkey 39°33N 27°6E 205 B9
Havre U.S.A. 48°33N 109°41W 304 B9
Havre-Aubert Canada 47°12N 61°56W 299 C7
Havre-St.-Pierre Canada 50°18N 63°33W 299 B7
Havsa Turkey 41°31N 26°48E 203 E10
Havza Turkey 41°0N 35°35E 212 B6
Haw → U.S.A. 35°36N 79°3W 315 D15
Hawadax U.S.A. 51°48N 178°15E 303 L2
Hawai'i U.S.A. 19°30N 155°30W 302 D6
Hawai'i □ U.S.A. 19°30N 156°30W 302 D5
Hawai'i County U.S.A. 19°30N 155°30W 302 D6
Hawai'i Kai U.S.A. 21°16N 157°42W 302 K14
Hawai'i Volcanoes △ U.S.A. 19°25N 155°18W 302 D6
Hawaiian Is. Pac. Oc. 20°30N 156°0W 302 G12
Hawaiian Ridge Pac. Oc. 24°0N 165°0W 289 E11
Hawarden U.S.A. 43°0N 96°29W 308 D5
Hawashîyah, W. Egypt 28°31N 32°58E 251 K3
Hawea, L. N.Z. 44°28S 169°19E 285 E4
Hawea Flat N.Z. 44°40S 169°19E 285 E4
Hawera N.Z. 39°35S 174°19E 284 F3
Hawesville U.S.A. 37°54N 86°45W 311 G10
Ḩawf Yemen 16°38N 53°2E 249 C6
Hawi U.S.A. 20°14N 155°50W 302 C6
Hawick U.K. 55°26N 2°47W 167 F6
Hawk Junction Canada 48°5N 84°38W 298 C3
Hawk Point U.S.A. 38°58N 91°8W 310 F5
Hawkdun Ra. N.Z. 44°53S 170°5E 285 E5
Hawke B. N.Z. 39°25S 177°20E 284 F6
Hawker Australia 31°59S 138°22E 282 A3
Hawke's Bay Canada 50°36N 57°10W 299 B8
Hawke's Bay □ N.Z. 39°45S 176°35E 284 F5
Hawkesbury Canada 45°37N 74°37W 298 C5
Hawkesbury I. Canada 53°37N 129°3W 296 C3
Hawkesbury Pt. Australia 11°55S 134°5E 280 A1
Hawkinsville U.S.A. 32°17N 83°28W 316 C6
Hawks Nest Australia 32°41S 152°11E 283 B10

Hawley Minn., U.S.A. 46°53N 96°19W 308 B5
Hawley Pa., U.S.A. 41°28N 75°11W 313 E9
Haworth U.S.A. 40°57N 73°59W 132 A2
Ḩawrā' Yemen 15°42N 48°16E 249 D5
Ḩawrān, W. → Iraq 33°58N 42°34E 213 F10
Hawsh Mūssá Lebanon 33°45N 35°55E 250 E6
Hawthorne Fla., U.S.A. 29°36N 82°5W 317 F7
Hawthorne Nev., U.S.A. 38°32N 118°38W 304 G4
Hawthorne Racecourse U.S.A. 41°49N 87°44W 119 C2
Hay Australia 34°30S 144°51E 283 C6
Hay → N. Terr., Australia 24°50S 138°0E 280 C2
Hay → Alta., Canada 60°50N 116°26W 296 A5
Hay, C. Australia 14°5S 129°29E 278 B4
Hay I. Canada 44°53N 80°58W 312 B4
Hay L. Canada 58°50N 118°50W 296 B5
Hay-on-Wye U.K. 52°5N 3°8W 169 E4
Hay Point Australia 21°18S 149°17E 280 C4
Hay River Canada 60°51N 115°44W 296 A5
Hay Springs U.S.A. 42°41N 102°41W 308 D2
Hayachine-San Japan 39°34N 141°29E 220 E10
Hayange France 49°20N 6°2E 173 C13
Hayastan = Armenia ■ Asia 40°20N 45°0E 191 K7
Hayato Japan 31°40N 130°43E 222 F2
Haydān, W. al → Jordan 31°29N 35°34E 251 G6
Haydarlı Turkey 38°16N 30°23E 205 C12
Hayden U.S.A. 40°30N 107°16W 304 F10
Hayes Jamaica 17°52N 77°14W 320 a
Hayes Kent, U.K. 51°22N 0°0 125 B4
Hayes Middlesex, U.K. 51°30N 0°25W 125 A1
Hayes S. Dak., U.S.A. 44°23N 101°1W 308 C3
Hayes → Canada 57°3N 92°12W 298 A1
Hayes, Mt. U.S.A. 63°37N 146°43W 303 E11
Hayes Creek Australia 13°43S 131°22E 278 B5
Hayes End U.K. 51°31N 0°25W 125 A1
Hayford U.S.A. 41°45N 87°42W 119 C2
Hayle U.K. 50°11N 5°26W 169 G2
Hayling I. U.K. 50°48N 0°59W 169 G7
Haymā' Oman 19°56N 56°19E 249 C7
Hayman I. Australia 20°4S 148°53E 280 b
Haymana Turkey 39°26N 32°31E 212 C5
Haynan Yemen 15°50N 48°18E 249 D5
Haynau = Chojnów Poland 51°18N 15°58E 185 G2
Hayneville U.S.A. 32°23N 83°37W 316 C6
Hayrabolu Turkey 41°12N 27°5E 203 E11
Hays Alta., Canada 50°6N 111°48W 296 C6
Hays Kans., U.S.A. 38°53N 99°20W 308 F4
Ḩays Yemen 13°56N 43°29E 248 D3
Haysville U.S.A. 38°28N 86°55W 311 F10
Haysyn Ukraine 48°57N 29°25E 183 B14
Hayvoron Ukraine 48°22N 29°52E 183 B14
Hayward Calif., U.S.A. 37°40N 122°4W 306 H4
Hayward Wis., U.S.A. 46°1N 91°29W 308 B8
Haywards Heath U.K. 51°0N 0°5W 169 G7
Hazafon □ Israel 32°40N 35°20E 250 F6
Hazar Turkmenistan 39°34N 53°16E 187 G9
Hazārān, Kūh-e Iran 29°35N 57°20E 247 D8
Hazard U.S.A. 37°15N 83°12W 309 G12
Hazaribag India 23°58N 85°26E 243 H11
Hazaribag Road India 24°12N 85°57E 243 G11
Hazebrouck France 50°42N 2°31E 173 B9
Hazelton B.C., Canada 55°20N 127°42W 296 B3
Hazelton N. Dak., U.S.A. 46°29N 100°17W 308 B3
Hazen U.S.A. 47°18N 101°38W 308 B3
Hazen, L. Canada 81°47N 71°1W 154 A3
Hazlehurst Ga., U.S.A. 31°52N 82°36W 316 D7
Hazlehurst Miss., U.S.A. 31°52N 90°24W 315 F9
Hazlet U.S.A. 40°25N 74°12W 313 F10
Hazleton Ind., U.S.A. 38°29N 87°33W 311 F9
Hazleton Pa., U.S.A. 40°57N 75°59W 313 F9
Hazlett, L. Australia 21°30S 128°48E 278 D4
Hazro Turkey 38°15N 40°47E 246 B4
He Xian = Hezhou China 24°27N 111°30E 229 E8
He Xian China 31°45N 118°20E 229 B12
Head of Bight Australia 31°30S 131°25E 279 F5
Head-Smashed-In Buffalo Jump Canada 49°44N 113°37W 296 D6
Headland U.S.A. 31°21N 85°21W 316 D4
Headlands Zimbabwe 18°15S 32°2E 269 F3
Healdsburg U.S.A. 38°37N 122°52W 306 G4
Healdton U.S.A. 34°14N 97°29W 314 D6
Healesville Australia 37°35S 145°30E 283 D6
Healy U.S.A. 63°52N 148°58W 303 E10
Heany Junction Zimbabwe 20°6S 28°54E 271 B4
Heanza-shima Japan 26°20N 127°57E 288 a
Heard I. Ind. Oc. 53°6S 72°36E 273 K6
Hearne U.S.A. 30°53N 96°36W 314 F6
Hearst Canada 49°40N 83°41W 298 C3
Heart → U.S.A. 46°46N 100°50W 308 B3
Heart's Content Canada 47°54N 53°27W 299 C9
Heath → Bolivia 12°31S 68°38W 330 C4
Heath, Pte. Canada 49°8N 61°40W 299 C7
Heath Mts. N.Z. 45°39S 167°9E 285 F2
Heathcote Australia 36°56S 144°45E 283 D6
Heatherwood = Edson Canada 53°35N 116°28W 296 C5
Heathfield S. Africa 34°3S 18°27E 118 B1
Heathrow, London ✈ (LHR) U.K. 51°28N 0°27W 125 B1
Heavener U.S.A. 34°53N 94°36W 314 D7
Hebbronville U.S.A. 27°18N 98°41W 314 H5
Hebe Haven Hong Kong, China 22°21N 114°15E 122 A3
Hebei □ China 39°0N 116°0E 226 E9
Hebel Australia 28°58S 147°47E 281 D4
Heber U.S.A. 32°44N 115°32W 307 N11
Heber Springs U.S.A. 35°30N 92°2W 314 D8
Hebgen L. U.S.A. 44°52N 111°20W 304 D8
Hebi China 35°57N 114°7E 226 G8
Hebrides U.K. 57°30N 7°0W 158 D4
Hebrides, Sea of the U.K. 57°5N 7°0W 167 D2
Hebron = Al Khalīl West Bank 31°32N 35°6E 251 G6
Hebron Nfld. & L., Canada 58°5N 62°30W 295 F19
Hebron N. Dak., U.S.A. 46°54N 102°3W 308 B2
Hebron Nebr., U.S.A. 40°10N 97°35W 308 E5
Heby Sweden 59°56N 16°53E 162 E10
Hecate Str. Canada 53°10N 130°30W 296 C2
Heceta I. U.S.A. 55°46N 133°40W 296 B2
Hechi China 24°40N 108°2E 228 E7
Hechingen Germany 48°21N 8°57E 179 G4
Hechuan China 30°2N 106°12E 228 B6
Hecla U.S.A. 45°53N 98°9W 308 C4
Hecla I. Canada 51°10N 96°43W 297 C9
Hedal Norway 60°37N 9°41E 162 D3
Heddal Norway 59°36N 9°9E 164 E6
Hédé Ille-et-Vilaine, France 48°18N 1°49W 172 D5
Hede Jämtland, Sweden 62°23N 13°30E 162 B7
Hedemora Sweden 60°18N 15°58E 162 D9
Hedensted Denmark 55°46N 9°42E 163 J3
Hedesunda Sweden 60°24N 17°0E 162 D10
Hedgehope N.Z. 46°12S 168°34E 285 G3
Hedmark □ Norway 61°17N 11°40E 164 C8
Hedo Japan 26°52N 128°15E 288 a
Hedo-misaki Japan 26°52N 128°16E 288 a
Hedong China 23°5N 113°14E 121 B2
Hedrick U.S.A. 41°11N 92°19W 310 C4
He'eia U.S.A. 21°25N 157°48W 302 K14
Heel Pt. Wake I. 19°18N 166°38E 302 b
Heerde Neths. 52°24N 6°2E 170 B6
Heerenveen Neths. 52°57N 5°55E 170 B5
Heerhugowaard Neths. 52°40N 4°51E 170 B4
Heerlen Neths. 50°55N 5°58E 170 D5
Heerwegen = Polkowice Poland 51°29N 16°3E 185 G3
Ḩefa Israel 32°46N 35°0E 250 F6
Ḩefa □ Israel 32°40N 35°0E 250 F6
Hefei China 31°52N 117°18E 229 B11
Hefeng China 29°55N 109°52E 228 C7
Heflin U.S.A. 33°39N 85°35W 316 B4
Hegalig Sudan 14°36N 31°54E 257 E3
Hegang China 47°20N 130°19E 219 B15
Heggenes Norway 61°9N 9°4E 164 C6
Heglig Sudan 10°0N 29°24E 257 F2
Hegra Norway 63°27N 11°8E 164 A8
Hei Ling Chau Hong Kong, China 22°15N 114°2E 122 B2
Heiban Sudan 11°13N 30°31E 257 E3
Heichengzhen China 36°24N 106°3E 226 F4
Heidal Norway 61°45N 9°19E 164 C6
Heide Germany 54°11N 9°6E 178 A5
Heidelberg Baden-W., Germany 49°24N 8°42E 179 F4
Heidelberg Western Cape, S. Africa 34°6S 20°59E 270 D3
Heidelberg Heights Australia 37°45S 145°4E 128 A2
Heidelberg West Australia 37°43S 145°2E 128 A2
Heidelburg S. Africa 26°30S 28°21E 271 C4
Heidemühle Germany 52°29N 13°40E 115 B5
Heidenau Germany 50°57N 13°52E 178 E9
Heidenheim Germany 48°41N 10°9E 179 G6
Heideveld S. Africa 33°58S 18°32E 118 A2
Heigun-Tō Japan 33°47N 132°14E 222 D4
Heihe China 50°10N 127°30E 219 A14
Heijing China 25°22N 101°44E 228 E3
Heijo = P'yŏngyang N. Korea 39°0N 125°30E 224 C2
Heilbad Heiligenstadt Germany 51°22N 10°8E 178 D6
Heilbron S. Africa 27°16S 27°59E 271 C4
Heilbronn Germany 49°9N 9°13E 179 F5
Heiligenblut Austria 47°2N 12°51E 180 D5
Heiligenhafen Germany 54°22N 10°59E 178 A6
Heiligensee Germany 52°36N 13°13E 115 A2
Heiligenstadt Austria 48°14N 16°21E 142 A2
Heilongjiang □ China 48°0N 126°0E 219 B14
Heiloo Neths. 52°36N 4°42E 170 B4
Heilprin Land Greenland 82°5N 33°0W 154 A7
Heilsberg = Lidzbark Warmiński Poland 54°7N 20°34E 184 D7
Heilunkiang = Heilongjiang □ China 48°0N 126°0E 219 B14
Heim Norway 63°26N 9°5E 164 A6
Heimaey Iceland 63°26N 20°17W 155 D6
Heimdal Norway 63°21N 10°22E 164 A7
Heineken Experience Amsterdam, Neths. 112 c2
Heinersdorf Germany 52°34N 13°26E 115 A3
Heinola Finland 61°13N 26°2E 188 B4
Heinsberg Germany 51°3N 6°5E 178 D2
Heinsun Myanmar 25°52N 95°35E 241 C5
Heinze Chaung Myanmar 14°42N 97°52E 236 E1
Heinze Kyun Myanmar 14°25N 97°45E 236 E1
Heirnkut Myanmar 25°14N 94°44E 241 C5
Heishan China 41°40N 122°5E 227 D12
Heishui Liaoning, China 42°8N 119°30E 227 C10
Heishui Sichuan, China 32°4N 103°2E 228 A4
Hejaz = Ḩijāz Si. Arabia 24°0N 40°0E 246 E3
Hejian China 38°25N 116°5E 226 E9
Hejiang China 28°43N 105°46E 228 C5
Hejin China 35°35N 110°42E 226 G6
Hejing China 42°18N 86°22E 217 D11
Hekımhan Turkey 38°50N 37°55E 212 C7
Hekinan Japan 34°52N 137°0E 223 C9
Hekla Iceland 63°56N 19°35W 155 D7
Hekou Gansu, China 36°10N 103°26E 226 F2
Hekou Guangdong, China 23°13N 112°45E 229 F9
Hekou Yunnan, China 22°30N 103°59E 228 F4
Hel Poland 54°37N 18°47E 184 D5
Hela □ Papua N. G. 5°30S 142°30E 286 C2
Helagsfjället Sweden 62°54N 12°25E 162 B6
Helan Shan China 38°30N 105°55E 226 E3
Heldenplatz Vienna, Austria 142 b1
Helden's Pt. St. Kitts & Nevis 17°25N 62°51W 322 d
Helechosa de los Montes Spain 39°22N 4°53W 195 F6
Helemano → U.S.A. 21°35N 158°7W 302 J13
Helen Atoll Palau 2°40N 132°0E 231 D8
Helena Ga., U.S.A. 32°5N 82°55W 316 C7
Helena Mont., U.S.A. 46°36N 112°2W 304 C7
Helena -West Helena U.S.A. 34°32N 90°36W 315 D9
Helendale U.S.A. 34°44N 117°19W 307 L9
Hélène de Champlain, Parc ⌂ Canada 45°31N 73°32W 130 A2
Helenelund Sweden 59°24N 17°58E 139 A1
Helensburgh N.S.W., Australia 34°11S 151°1E 283 C9
Helensburgh Argyll & Bute, U.K. 56°1N 4°43W 167 E4
Helensville N.Z. 36°41S 174°29E 284 C3
Helenvale Australia 15°43S 145°14E 280 B4
Helgasjön Sweden 56°55N 14°50E 163 H8
Helgeland Norway 66°7N 13°29E 160 C15
Helgoland Germany 54°10N 7°53E 178 A3
Helheim Gletscher Greenland 66°24N 38°12W 154 D7
Heligoland = Helgoland Germany 54°10N 7°53E 178 A3
Heligoland B. = Deutsche Bucht Germany 54°15N 8°0E 178 A4
Heliopolis = Masr el Gedida Egypt 30°5N 31°21E 117 A2
Hell Norway 63°26N 10°54E 164 A7
Hell-Bourg Réunion 21°3S 55°32E 272 f
Hell Hole Gorge △ Australia 25°31S 144°12E 280 D3
Hella Iceland 63°50N 20°24W 155 D6
Hellas = Greece ■ Europe 40°0N 23°0E 204 B3
Helleland Norway 58°33N 6°7E 164 F3
Hellersdorf Germany 52°32N 13°35E 115 A4
Hellertown U.S.A. 40°35N 75°21W 313 F9
Hellerup Denmark 55°44N 12°33E 118 A3
Hellespont = Çanakkale Boğazı Turkey 40°17N 26°32E 203 F10
Hellesylt Norway 62°6N 6°51E 164 B3
Hellevoetsluis Neths. 51°50N 4°8E 170 C4
Hellín Spain 38°31N 1°40W 197 G3
Hellissandur Iceland 64°55N 23°54W 155 C3
Hells Canyon ⌂ U.S.A. 45°30N 117°45W 304 D5
Hells Gate Saba 17°39N 63°14W 322 a
Hell's Gate △ Kenya 0°54S 36°19E 268 C4
Hellvik Norway 58°29N 5°52E 164 F2
Helmand □ Afghan. 31°20N 64°0E 240 C2
Helmand → Afghan. 31°12N 61°34E 240 C1
Helme → Germany 51°20N 11°21E 178 D7
Helmeringhausen Namibia 25°54S 16°57E 270 C2
Helmond Neths. 51°29N 5°41E 170 C5
Helmsdale U.K. 58°7N 3°39W 167 C5
Helmsdale → U.K. 58°8N 3°43W 167 C5
Helmstedt Germany 52°12N 11°0E 178 C7
Helong China 42°40N 129°0E 224 A4
Helper U.S.A. 39°41N 110°51W 304 G8
Helsingborg Sweden 56°3N 12°42E 163 H6
Helsinge Denmark 56°2N 12°12E 163 H6
Helsingfors = Helsinki Finland 60°10N 24°55E 121 B2
Helsingør Denmark 56°2N 12°35E 163 H6
Helsinki Finland 60°10N 24°55E 121 B2
Helsinki-Vantaa ✈ (HEL) Finland 60°18N 24°58E 121 B2
Helska, Mierzeja Poland 54°45N 18°40E 184 D5
Helston U.K. 50°6N 5°17W 169 G2
Helvellyn U.K. 54°32N 3°1W 168 C4
Helvetinjärvi △ Finland 62°5N 23°47E 160 E20
Helwân Egypt 29°50N 31°20E 256 J7
Hemavati → India 12°30N 76°20E 245 H3
Hemei = Homei Taiwan 24°7N 120°29E 225 B2
Hemel Hempstead U.K. 51°44N 0°28W 169 F7
Hemet U.S.A. 33°45N 116°58W 307 M10
Hemingford U.S.A. 42°19N 103°4W 308 D2
Hemis △ India 34°10N 77°15E 242 B7
Hemmingford Canada 45°3N 73°35W 313 A11
Hempe Dem. Rep. of the Congo 1°54N 22°42E 264 B4
Hempstead N.Y., U.S.A. 40°42N 73°37W 313 F11
Hempstead Tex., U.S.A. 30°6N 96°5W 314 F6
Hemse Sweden 57°15N 18°22E 163 G12
Hemsedal Norway 60°53N 8°30E 164 D5
Hemsön Sweden 62°42N 18°5E 162 B12
Hen Norway 60°13N 10°14E 164 D7
Hen and Chicken B. Australia 33°50S 151°7E 139 B1
Hen and Chickens Is. N.Z. 35°58S 174°45E 284 B3
Henån Sweden 58°14N 11°40E 163 F5
Henan □ China 34°0N 114°0E 226 H8
Henares → Spain 40°24N 3°30W 194 E7
Henashi-Misaki Japan 40°37N 139°51E 220 D9
Hendaye France 43°23N 1°47W 174 E2
Hendek Turkey 40°48N 30°44E 212 B4
Henderson Argentina 36°18S 61°43W 334 D3
Henderson Ga., U.S.A. 32°21N 83°47W 316 C6
Henderson Ky., U.S.A. 37°50N 87°35W 311 G9
Henderson N.C., U.S.A. 36°20N 78°25W 315 C15
Henderson N.Y., U.S.A. 43°50N 76°10W 313 C8
Henderson Nev., U.S.A. 36°2N 114°58W 124 B2
Henderson Tenn., U.S.A. 35°26N 88°38W 315 D10
Henderson Tex., U.S.A. 32°9N 94°48W 314 E7
Henderson I. Pac. Oc. 24°22S 128°19W 289 K15
Hendersonville N.C., U.S.A. 35°19N 82°28W 315 D13
Hendersonville Tenn., U.S.A. 36°18N 86°37W 315 C11
Hendījān Iran 30°14N 49°43E 247 D6
Hendon U.K. 51°35N 0°14W 125 A2
Hendorābī Iran 26°40N 53°37E 247 E7
Heng Jiang → China 28°40N 104°25E 228 C5
Heng Xian China 22°40N 109°17E 228 F7
Hengām Iran 26°38N 55°53E 247 E7
Henganofi Papua N. G. 6°15S 145°38E 286 D3
Hengcheng China 38°18N 106°28E 226 E4
Hëngch'un Taiwan 22°0N 120°44E 225 D2
Hengdaohezi China 44°52N 129°0E 227 B15
Hengduan Shan China 28°30N 98°50E 228 C2
Hengelo Neths. 52°16N 6°48E 170 B6
Henggang China 22°39N 114°12E 219 a
Hengmen China 22°33N 113°35E 219 a
Hengsha China 23°9N 113°12E 121 B2
Hengshan Hunan, China 27°16N 112°45E 229 D9
Hengshan Shaanxi, China 37°58N 109°5E 226 F5
Hengshui China 37°41N 115°40E 226 F8
Hengyang China 26°59N 112°22E 229 D9
Henichesk Ukraine 46°12N 34°50E 189 J8
Henima India 25°22N 93°36E 241 C4
Hénin-Beaumont France 50°25N 2°58E 173 B9
Hénin-Liétard = Hénin-Beaumont France 50°25N 2°58E 173 B9
Henley-on-Thames U.K. 51°32N 0°54W 169 F7
Henlopen, C. U.S.A. 38°48N 75°6W 309 F16
Henna Japan 26°19N 127°53E 288 a
Hennan Sweden 62°2N 15°54E 162 B9
Hennebont France 47°49N 3°19W 172 E3
Hennenman S. Africa 27°59S 27°1E 270 C4
Hennepin U.S.A. 41°15N 89°21W 310 C7
Hennessey U.S.A. 36°6N 97°54W 314 C6
Hennigsdorf Germany 52°38N 13°12E 115 A2
Henrietta N.Y., U.S.A. 43°4N 77°37W 312 C7
Henrietta Tex., U.S.A. 33°49N 98°12W 314 E5
Henrietta, Ostrov = Genriyetty, Ostrov Russia 77°6N 156°30E 215 B16
Henrietta Maria, C. Canada 55°9N 82°20W 298 A3
Henry U.S.A. 41°7N 89°22W 310 C7
Henry Ice Rise Antarctica 80°35S 62°0W 151 E17
Henry Lawrence I. India 12°9N 93°5E 245 H11
Henryetta U.S.A. 35°27N 95°59W 314 D7
Henryków Poland 52°19N 20°58E 143 B1
Henryville Canada 45°8N 73°11W 313 A11
Hensall Canada 43°26N 81°30W 312 C3
Henson Cr. → U.S.A. 38°47N 76°58W 143 C3
Henstedt-Ulzburg Germany 53°47N 10°0E 178 B6
Hentiesbaai Namibia 22°8S 14°18E 270 B1
Hentiyn Nuruu Mongolia 48°30N 108°30E 219 B10
Henttaa Finland 60°11N 24°45E 121 B1
Henty Australia 35°30S 147°3E 283 C7
Henzada = Hinthada Myanmar 17°38N 95°26E 241 G5
Hephaestia Greece 39°55N 25°14E 205 B7
Hephzibah U.S.A. 33°19N 82°6W 316 B7
Heping China 24°29N 115°0E 229 E10
Heping Park China 31°16N 121°30E 138 B2
Hepingli China 39°57N 116°23E 114 B2
Heppner U.S.A. 45°21N 119°33W 304 D4
Hepu China 21°40N 109°12E 228 G7
Hepworth Canada 44°37N 81°9W 312 B3
Heqing China 26°37N 100°11E 228 D3
Hequ China 39°20N 111°15E 226 E6
Héraðsflói Iceland 65°42N 14°12W 155 B12
Héraðsvötn → Iceland 65°45N 19°25W 155 B7
Heradsbygd Norway 60°49N 11°39E 164 D8
Heraklion = Iraklio Greece 35°20N 25°12E 207 E6
Heraklion Int. ✈ (HER) Greece 35°20N 25°15E 207 E6
Herald Cays Australia 16°58S 149°9E 280 B4
Herand Norway 60°20N 6°22E 164 D3
Herangi Ra. N.Z. 38°33S 174°48E 284 E3
Herāt Afghan. 34°20N 62°7E 240 B1
Herāt □ Afghan. 35°0N 62°0E 240 B1
Hérault □ France 43°34N 3°15E 174 E7
Hérault → France 43°17N 3°26E 174 E7
Herbault France 47°36N 1°8E 172 E8
Herbert Canada 50°30N 107°10W 297 C7
Herbert → Australia 18°31S 146°17E 280 B4
Herbert Hoover Nat. Historic Site ⌂ U.S.A. 41°40N 91°21W 310 C5
Herbert I. U.S.A. 52°45N 170°7W 303 K5
Herbertabad India 11°43N 92°37E 245 J11
Herberton Australia 17°20S 145°25E 280 B4
Herbertsdale S. Africa 34°1S 21°46E 270 D3
Herbertville N.Z. 40°30S 176°33E 284 G5
Herbignac France 47°27N 2°18W 172 E4
Herborn Germany 50°40N 8°18E 178 E4
Herby Poland 50°45N 18°50E 185 H5
Herceg-Novi Montenegro 42°30N 18°33E 202 D2
Hercegfalva = Mezőfalva Hungary 46°55N 18°49E 182 D3
Herchmer Canada 57°22N 94°10W 297 B10
Herculânia = Coxim Brazil 18°30S 54°55W 331 D7
Herðubreið Iceland 65°11N 16°21W 155 B10
Hereford Hereford, U.K. 52°4N 2°43W 169 E5
Hereford Tex., U.S.A. 34°49N 102°24W 314 D3
Herefordshire □ U.K. 52°8N 2°40W 169 E5
Herefoss Norway 58°32N 8°23E 164 F5
Héréhérétué French Polynesia 19°45S 144°58W 289 f
Herehogna Sweden 61°44N 12°8E 164 C9
Herekino N.Z. 35°18S 173°11E 284 B2
Herencia Spain 39°21N 3°22W 195 F7
Herentals Belgium 51°12N 4°51E 170 C4
Herford Germany 52°7N 8°39E 178 C4
Héricourt France 47°32N 6°45E 173 E13
Herington U.S.A. 38°40N 96°57W 308 F5
Herīs Iran 38°14N 47°6E 213 C12
Herisau Switz. 47°22N 9°17E 179 H5
Hérisson France 46°32N 2°42E 173 F9
Herkimer U.S.A. 43°2N 74°59W 313 D10
Herlen → Asia 48°48N 117°0E 219 B12
Herlev Denmark 55°43N 12°27E 118 A2
Herlong U.S.A. 40°8N 120°8W 306 E6
Herm U.K. 49°30N 2°28W 169 H5
Hermakivka Ukraine 48°42N 26°11E 183 B11
Herman Eckstein Park S. Africa 26°9S 28°1E 123 A2
Hermana Mayor I. Phil. 15°47N 119°47E 232 D2
Hermann U.S.A. 38°42N 91°27W 310 F5
Hermannsbad = Ciechocinek Poland 52°53N 18°45E 185 F5
Hermannsburg N. Terr., Australia 23°57S 132°45E 278 D5
Hermannsburg Niedersachsen, Germany 52°50N 10°5E 178 C6
Hermannskogel Austria 48°16N 16°17E 142 A1
Hermannstadt = Sibiu Romania 45°45N 24°9E 183 E9
Hermansverk Norway 61°11N 6°52E 164 C3
Hermanus S. Africa 34°27S 19°12E 270 D2
Herment France 45°45N 2°24E 174 C6
Hermidale Australia 31°30S 146°42E 283 A7
Hermiston Edinburgh, U.K. 55°55N 3°19W 121 B2
Hermiston Oreg., U.S.A. 45°51N 119°17W 304 D4
Hermit Is. Papua N. G. 1°32S 145°5E 286 A3
Hermitage Grenada 12°27N 61°28W 323 q
Hermitage Mo., U.S.A. 37°56N 93°19W 310 G3
Hermitage and Winter Palace Russia 59°55N 30°19E 137 B2
Hermon Ont., Canada 45°6N 77°37W 312 A7
Hermon N.Y., U.S.A. 44°28N 75°14W 313 B9
Hermon, Mt. = Shaykh, J. ash Lebanon 33°25N 35°50E 250 E6
Hermosillo Mexico 29°10N 111°0W 318 B2
Hermsdorf Germany 52°37N 13°18E 115 A2
Hernád → Hungary 47°56N 21°8E 182 C6
Hernals Austria 48°13N 16°20E 142 A2
Hernandarias Paraguay 25°20S 54°40W 335 B5
Hernandez U.S.A. 36°24N 120°46W 306 J6
Hernando Argentina 32°28S 63°40W 334 C3
Hernando Fla., U.S.A. 28°54N 82°23W 317 G7
Hernando Miss., U.S.A. 34°50N 90°0W 315 D10
Hernando de Magallanes △ Chile 54°0S 72°40W 336 D2
Hernani Spain 43°16N 1°58W 196 B3
Herndon U.S.A. 40°43N 76°51W 312 F8
Herne Germany 51°32N 7°14E 178 D3
Herne Bay U.K. 51°21N 1°8E 169 F9
Herne Hill U.K. 51°27N 0°6W 125 B3
Herning Denmark 56°8N 8°58E 163 H2
Herod U.S.A. 31°42N 84°26W 316 D5
Héroes de Churubusco Mexico 19°21N 99°6W 128 B2
Heroica Caborca = Caborca Mexico 30°37N 112°6W 318 A2
Heroica Nogales = Nogales Mexico 31°19N 110°56W 318 A2
Heron Bay Canada 48°40N 86°25W 298 C2
Heron I. Australia 23°27S 151°55E 280 C5
Herons, Î. aux Canada 45°25N 73°34W 130 B2
Herradura, Pta. de la Canary Is. 28°26N 14°8W 153 e2
Herre Norway 59°6N 9°34E 164 E6
Herreid U.S.A. 45°50N 100°4W 308 C3
Herrenberg Germany 48°35N 8°52E 179 G4
Herrera Spain 37°26N 4°55W 195 H6
Herrera de Alcántara Spain 39°39N 7°25W 195 F3
Herrera de Pisuerga Spain 42°35N 4°20W 194 C6
Herrera del Duque Spain 39°10N 5°3W 195 F5
Herrestad Sweden 58°21N 11°50E 163 F5
Herrin U.S.A. 37°48N 89°2W 310 G7
Herriot Canada 56°22N 101°16W 297 B8
Herrljunga Sweden 58°5N 13°1E 163 F7
Hersbruck Germany 49°30N 11°26E 179 F7
Herschel I. Canada 69°35N 139°5W 150 C1
Hershey U.S.A. 40°17N 76°39W 313 F8
Herso = Cherso Greece 41°5N 22°47E 202 E6
Herstal Belgium 50°40N 5°38E 170 D5
Herstedøster Denmark 55°40N 12°22E 118 A2
Hertford U.K. 51°48N 0°4W 169 F7
Hertfordshire □ U.K. 51°51N 0°5W 169 F7
's-Hertogenbosch Neths. 51°42N 5°17E 170 C5
Hertsa Ukraine 48°9N 26°15E 183 B11
Herttoniemi Finland 60°12N 25°2E 121 B3
Hertzogville S. Africa 28°9S 25°30E 270 C4
Hervás Spain 40°16N 5°52W 194 E5
Hervey B. Australia 25°0S 152°52E 280 C5
Herzberg Brandenburg, Germany 51°41N 13°14E 178 D9
Herzberg Niedersachsen, Germany 51°38N 10°20E 178 D6
Herzliyya Israel 32°10N 34°50E 251 F5
Herzogenburg Austria 48°17N 15°41E 180 C8
Ḩeşār Fārs, Iran 29°52N 50°16E 247 D6
Ḩeşār Markazī, Iran 35°50N 49°12E 247 C6
Ḩeşārak Iran 35°47N 51°18E 141 A1
Hesdin France 50°21N 2°2E 173 B9
Heshan Guangdong, China 22°34N 113°4E 229 F9
Heshan Guangxi Zhuangzu, China 23°50N 108°53E 228 F7
Heshui China 35°48N 108°0E 226 G5
Heshun China 37°22N 113°32E 226 F7
Heskestad Norway 58°28N 6°22E 164 F3
Hesperia U.S.A. 34°25N 117°18W 307 L9
Hessdalen Norway 62°48N 11°10E 164 B8
Hesse = Hessen □ Germany 50°30N 9°0E 178 E4
Hessen □ Germany 50°30N 9°0E 178 E4
Hessenreuther und Manteler Wald ⌂ Germany 49°45N 12°1E 179 F8
Hessle U.K. 53°44N 0°24W 168 D7
Hesso Australia 32°8S 137°27E 282 B2
Hesteyri Iceland 66°20N 22°53W 155 A4
Heston U.K. 51°28N 0°22W 125 B1
Hestra Sweden 57°26N 13°35E 163 G7
Hetauda Nepal 27°25N 85°2E 243 F11
Hetch Hetchy Aqueduct U.S.A. 37°29N 122°19W 306 H5
Hetta Enontekiö Finland 68°23N 23°37E 160 B20
Hettinger U.S.A. 46°0N 102°42W 308 B2
Hettstedt Germany 51°39N 11°31E 178 D7
Hetzendorf Austria 48°9N 16°17E 142 B1
Heuksando S. Korea 34°40N 125°30E 224 E2
Heunghae S. Korea 36°12N 129°21E 224 D4
Heuvelton U.S.A. 44°37N 75°25W 313 B9
Hevelândia Brazil 5°12S 61°50W 329 E5
Heves Hungary 47°36N 20°17E 182 C5
Heves □ Hungary 47°50N 20°0E 182 C5
Hewitt U.S.A. 31°28N 97°12W 314 F6
Hexham U.K. 54°58N 2°4W 168 C5
Hexi Yunnan, China 24°9N 102°38E 228 E4
Hexi Zhejiang, China 27°58N 119°38E 229 D12
Hexigten Qi China 43°18N 117°30E 227 C9
Hextable U.K. 51°24N 0°10E 125 B5
Ḩeydarābād Iran 30°33N 55°38E 247 D7
Heydebreck = Kędzierzyn-Koźle Poland 50°20N 18°12E 185 H5
Heyfield Australia 37°59S 146°47E 283 D7
Heysham U.K. 54°3N 2°53W 168 C5
Heyuan China 23°39N 114°40E 229 F10
Heywood Australia 38°8S 141°37E 282 E4
Heyworth U.S.A. 40°19N 88°59W 310 D8
Heze China 35°14N 115°20E 226 G8
Hezhang China 27°8N 104°41E 228 D5
Hezhou China 24°27N 111°30E 229 E8
Hi-no-Misaki Japan 35°26N 132°38E 222 B4
Hi Vista U.S.A. 34°45N 117°46W 307 L9
Hialeah U.S.A. 25°51N 80°16W 129 C1
Hialeah Race Track U.S.A. 25°51N 80°16W 129 C1
Hiawassa, L. U.S.A. 28°33N 81°28W 133 A2
Hiawatha U.S.A. 39°51N 95°32W 308 F6
Hibbing U.S.A. 47°25N 92°56W 308 B7
Hibernia Reef Australia 12°0S 123°23E 278 B3
Hibiki-Nada Japan 34°0N 130°0E 222 D2
Hibok-Hibok, Mt. Phil. 9°12N 124°40E 233 G5
Hickam Housing U.S.A. 21°21N 157°57W 302 K14
Hickman U.S.A. 36°34N 89°11W 308 G9
Hickory U.S.A. 35°44N 81°21W 315 D14
Hickory Hills U.S.A. 41°43N 87°49W 119 C2
Hicks, Pt. Australia 37°49S 149°17E 283 D8
Hicks Bay N.Z. 37°34S 178°21E 284 D7
Hicks L. Canada 61°25N 100°0W 297 A9
Hicksville N.Y., U.S.A. 40°46N 73°32W 313 F11
Hicksville Ohio, U.S.A. 41°18N 84°46W 311 C12
Hicpochee, L. U.S.A. 26°48N 81°9W 317 J8
Hida Gifu, Japan 36°14N 137°11E 223 A9
Hida Romania 47°10N 23°19E 183 C8
Hida-Gawa → Japan 35°26N 137°3E 223 B9
Hida-Sammyaku Japan 36°30N 137°40E 223 A9
Hida-Sanchi Japan 36°10N 137°0E 223 A9
Hidaka Hokkaidō, Japan 42°30N 142°10E 220 C11
Hidaka Hyōgo, Japan 35°30N 134°44E 222 B6
Hidaka-Sammyaku Japan 42°35N 142°45E 220 C11
Hidalgo □ Mexico 20°30N 99°0W 319 C5
Hidalgo del Parral Mexico 26°56N 105°40W 318 B3
Hiddensee Germany 54°32N 13°6E 178 A9
Hidrolândia Brazil 17°0S 49°15W 333 E2
Hieflau Austria 47°36N 14°46E 180 D7
Hiekkaharju Finland 60°18N 25°2E 121 B3
Hiendelaencina Spain 41°5N 3°0W 196 D2
Hienghène N. Cal. 20°41S 164°56E 288 d
Hierapolis-Pamukkale Turkey 37°55N 29°7E 205 D11
Hierro Canary Is. 27°44N 18°0W 153 e1
Hietaniemi Finland 60°10N 24°54E 121 B2
Hietzing Austria 48°10N 16°17E 142 A1
Higashi Japan 34°41N 135°30E 133 A2
Higashi-Hiroshima Japan 34°25N 132°45E 222 C4
Higashi-Matsuyama Japan 36°2N 139°25E 223 A11
Higashi-Suidō Japan 34°0N 129°30E 222 D1
Higashiajima-San Japan 37°40N 140°10E 220 F10
Higashikagawa Japan 34°13N 134°24E 222 C6
Higashimurayama Japan 35°45N 139°26E 140 A1
Higashinari Japan 34°40N 135°32E 133 A2
Higashiōsaka Japan 34°39N 135°37E 223 C7
Higashisumiyoshi Japan 34°37N 135°31E 133 B2
Higashiyodogawa Japan 34°44N 135°28E 133 A1
Higbee U.S.A. 39°19N 92°31W 310 E4
Higgins U.S.A. 36°7N 100°2W 314 C4
Higgins Corner U.S.A. 39°2N 121°5W 306 F5
Higginsville U.S.A. 39°4N 93°43W 310 E3
High Bridge U.S.A. 40°40N 74°54W 313 F10
High Desert U.S.A. 43°40N 120°20W 304 E3
High Island Res. China 22°22N 114°21E 219 a
High Junk Pk. Hong Kong, China 22°18N 114°17E 122 B3
High Level Canada 58°31N 117°8W 296 B5
High Park Canada 43°38N 79°27W 141 B2
High Peak Phil. 15°29N 120°7E 232 D3
High Pk. St. Helena 15°58S 5°44W 153 h
High Point U.S.A. 35°57N 80°0W 315 D15
High Prairie Canada 55°30N 116°30W 296 B5
High River Canada 50°30N 113°50W 296 C6
High Springs U.S.A. 29°50N 82°36W 316 F7
High Tatra = Tatry Slovakia 49°20N 20°0E 181 B13
High Veld Africa 27°0S 27°0E 254 J6
High Wycombe U.K. 51°37N 0°45W 169 F7
Highbank N.Z. 43°37S 171°45E 285 D6
Highbury U.K. 51°33N 0°6W 125 A3
Highgate Jamaica 18°16N 76°57W 320 a
Highgate London, U.K. 51°34N 0°8W 125 A3
Highland Ill., U.S.A. 38°44N 89°41W 310 F7
Highland Ind., U.S.A. 41°33N 87°28W 311 C9
Highland Wis., U.S.A. 43°5N 90°22W 310 A6
Highland □ U.K. 57°17N 4°21W 167 D4
Highland City U.S.A. 27°58N 81°53W 317 H8
Highland Cr. → Canada 43°45N 79°13W 141 A3
Highland Creek Canada 43°46N 79°8W 141 A3
Highland Home U.S.A. 31°57N 86°19W 316 D3
Highland Mills U.S.A. 33°17N 84°17W 316 B5
Highland Park Calif., U.S.A. 34°7N 118°13W 126 B3
Highland Park Ill., U.S.A. 42°11N 87°48W 311 B9
Highland Park Tex., U.S.A. 32°50N 96°47W 120 B5
Highland View U.S.A. 29°50N 85°19W 316 F4
Highlands = Fort Thomas U.S.A. 39°4N 84°26W 311 E12
Highlands, The Antigua & B. 17°38N 61°47W 322 c
Highlands North S. Africa 26°8S 28°5E 123 A2
Highmore U.S.A. 44°31N 99°27W 308 C4
Highrock L. Canada 55°45N 100°30W 297 B8
Higuero, Pta. Puerto Rico 18°22N 67°16W 321 b
Higüey Dom. Rep. 18°37N 68°42W 321 C6
Hihya Egypt 30°40N 31°36E 256 H7
Hiidenportti △ Finland 63°53N 29°0E 160 E23
Hiiraan □ Somalia 4°0N 45°30E 267 D6
Hiiumaa Estonia 58°50N 22°45E 188 C2
Híjar Spain 41°10N 0°27W 196 D4
Ḩijārah, Şaḩrā' al Iraq 30°25N 44°30E 246 D5
Ḩijāz Si. Arabia 24°0N 40°0E 246 E3
Hiji Japan 33°22N 131°32E 222 D3
Hijo = Tagum Phil. 7°33N 125°53E 233 H5
Hikari Japan 33°58N 131°58E 222 D3
Hiketa = Higashikagawa Japan 34°13N 134°24E 222 C6
Hikkaduwa Sri Lanka 6°8N 80°6E 245 L5
Hikmak, Ras el Egypt 31°15N 27°51E 256 A2
Hiko U.S.A. 37°32N 115°14W 306 H11
Hikone Japan 35°15N 136°10E 223 B8
Hikurangi Gisborne, N.Z. 37°55S 178°4E 284 D7
Hikurangi Northland, N.Z. 35°36S 174°17E 284 B3
Hikutavake Niue 18°56S 169°53W 289 g
Hiland Park U.S.A. 30°12N 85°33W 316 E4
Hilawng Myanmar 21°23N 93°48E 241 E4
Hildburghausen Germany 50°25N 10°42E 178 E6
Hildesheim Germany 52°9N 9°56E 178 C5
Hilðarendi Iceland 63°44N 19°57W 155 D7
Hill → Australia 30°23S 115°3E 279 F2
Hill City Idaho, U.S.A. 43°18N 115°3W 304 E6
Hill City Kans., U.S.A. 39°22N 99°51W 308 F4
Hill City Minn., U.S.A. 46°59N 93°36W 308 B7
Hill City S. Dak., U.S.A. 43°56N 103°35W 308 D2
Hill Island L. Canada 60°30N 109°50W 297 A7
Hillaby, Mt. Barbados 13°12N 59°35W 323 r
Hillared Sweden 57°37N 13°10E 163 G7
Hillbrow Tower Johannesburg, S. Africa 26°11S 28°3E 123 B2
Hillcrest Heights U.S.A. 38°49N 76°57W 143 C3
Hillegom Neths. 52°18N 4°35E 170 B4
Hillend U.K. 56°2N 3°22W 121 A1
Hillerød Denmark 55°56N 12°19E 163 J6
Hillerstorp Sweden 57°20N 13°52E 163 G7
Hilli Bangla. 25°17N 89°1E 241 C2
Hilliard U.S.A. 30°41N 81°55W 316 E8
Hillingdon □ U.K. 51°32N 0°27W 125 A1
Hillsboro = Deerfield Beach U.S.A. 26°19N 80°6W 317 J9
Hillsboro Ga., U.S.A. 33°11N 83°38W 316 B6
Hillsboro Ill., U.S.A. 39°9N 89°29W 310 E7
Hillsboro Kans., U.S.A. 38°21N 97°12W 308 F5
Hillsboro Mo., U.S.A. 38°14N 90°34W 310 F6
Hillsboro N. Dak., U.S.A. 47°26N 97°3W 308 B5
Hillsboro Ohio, U.S.A. 39°12N 83°37W 311 E13
Hillsboro Oreg., U.S.A. 45°31N 122°59W 306 E4
Hillsboro Tex., U.S.A. 32°1N 97°8W 314 E6
Hillsboro Canal U.S.A. 26°30N 80°15W 317 J9
Hillsborough Grenada 12°28N 61°28W 323 q
Hillsborough N.H., U.S.A. 43°7N 71°54W 313 C13
Hillsborough Channel Australia 20°56S 149°15E 280 b
Hillsborough Dam Trin. & Tob. 11°13N 60°40W 323 s
Hillsborough Land = Belle Glade U.S.A. 26°41N 80°40W 317 J9
Hillsdale Mich., U.S.A. 41°56N 84°38W 311 C12
Hillsdale N.Y., U.S.A. 42°11N 73°32W 313 D11
Hillsport Canada 49°27N 85°34W 298 C2
Hillston Australia 33°30S 145°31E 283 B6
Hilltonia U.S.A. 32°53N 81°40W 316 C8
Hillwood U.S.A. 38°52N 77°9W 143 B2
Hilmîya Egypt 30°6N 31°19E 117 A2
Hilo U.S.A. 19°44N 155°5W 302 D6
Hilo ✈ (ITO) U.S.A. 19°43N 155°2W 302 D6
Hilo B. U.S.A. 19°45N 155°5W 302 D6
Hilongos Phil. 10°22N 124°44E 233 F5
Hilton U.S.A. 43°17N 77°48W 312 C7
Hilton Head Island U.S.A. 32°13N 80°45W 316 C9
Hilvan Turkey 37°34N 38°58E 213 D8
Hilversum Neths. 52°14N 5°10E 170 B5
Himachal Pradesh □ India 31°30N 77°0E 242 D7
Himalaya Asia 29°0N 84°0E 243 E11
Himalchuli Nepal 28°27N 84°38E 243 E11
Himamaylan Phil. 10°6N 122°52E 233 F4
Himarë Albania 40°8N 19°43E 202 F3
Himatnagar India 23°37N 72°57E 242 H5
Himchari △ Bangla. 21°28N 92°5E 241 E4
Hime-Jima Japan 33°43N 131°40E 222 D3
Himeji Japan 34°50N 134°40E 222 C6
Himi Japan 36°50N 136°55E 223 A8
Himmerland Denmark 56°45N 9°30E 163 H3
Ḩimş Syria 34°40N 36°45E 250 D7
Ḩimş □ Syria 34°30N 37°0E 250 D8
Hin Keng Hong Kong, China 22°22N 114°10E 122 A3
Hin Khom, Laem Thailand 9°25N 99°56E 237 b
Hinatuan Phil. 8°23N 126°20E 233 G6
Hinatuan Passage Phil. 9°45N 125°47E 233 G5
Hinche Haiti 19°9N 72°1W 321 C5
Hinchinbrook I. Australia 18°20S 146°15E 280 B4
Hinchinbrook Island △ Australia 18°14S 146°6E 280 B4
Hinckley Leics., U.K. 52°33N 1°22W 169 E6
Hinckley Minn., U.S.A. 46°1N 92°56W 308 B7
Hindaun India 26°44N 77°5E 242 F7
Hindenburg = Zabrze Poland 50°18N 18°50E 185 H5
Hindmarsh, L. Australia 36°5S 141°55E 282 D4
Hindol India 20°40N 85°10E 244 D7
Hinds N.Z. 43°59S 171°36E 285 D6
Hindsholm Denmark 55°30N 10°40E 163 J4
Hindu Bagh Pakistan 30°56N 67°50E 242 D2
Hindu Kush Asia 36°0N 71°0E 240 B3
Hindupur India 13°49N 77°32E 245 H3
Hines Creek Canada 56°20N 118°40W 296 B5
Hinesville U.S.A. 31°51N 81°36W 316 D8
Hinganghat India 20°30N 78°52E 244 D4
Hingham U.S.A. 48°33N 110°25W 304 B8
Hinghwa = Xinghua China 32°58N 119°48E 229 A12
Hingir India 21°57N 83°41E 243 J10
Hingoli India 19°41N 77°15E 244 E3
Hinigaran Phil. 10°16N 122°50E 233 F4
Hinis Turkey 39°22N 41°43E 213 C9
Hinna = Imi Ethiopia 6°28N 42°10E 257 F5
Hinna Nigeria 10°25N 11°35E 263 C7
Hinnerup Denmark 56°16N 10°4E 163 H4
Hinnøya Norway 68°35N 15°50E 160 B16
Hino Japan 35°0N 136°15E 223 C8
Hinoba-an Phil. 9°35N 122°28E 233 G4
Hinojosa del Duque Spain 38°30N 5°9W 195 G5
Hinokage Japan 32°39N 131°24E 222 E3
Hinsdale U.S.A. 42°47N 72°29W 313 D12
Hinterrhein → Switz. 46°40N 9°25E 179 J5
Hinthada Myanmar 17°38N 95°26E 241 G5
Hinton Alta., Canada 53°26N 117°34W 296 C5
Hinton W. Va., U.S.A. 37°40N 80°54W 309 G13
Hinubuan = Antipolo Phil. 14°35N 121°10E 232 D3
Hinunangan Phil. 10°25N 125°12E 233 F5
Hios = Chios Greece 38°27N 26°9E 205 C8
Hirado Japan 33°22N 129°33E 222 D1
Hirado-Shima Japan 33°20N 129°30E 222 D1
Hirakata Japan 34°48N 135°38E 223 C7
Hirakud Dam India 21°32N 83°45E 244 D6
Hiran → India 23°6N 79°21E 243 H8
Hirapur India 24°22N 79°13E 243 G8
Hirara = Miyakojima Japan 24°48N 125°17E 221 M2
Hirata Japan 35°24N 132°49E 222 B4
Hiratsuka Japan 35°19N 139°21E 223 B11
Hirekerur India 14°28N 75°23E 245 G2
Hirfanlı Barajı Turkey 39°18N 33°31E 212 C5
Hirhafok Algeria 23°49N 5°45E 261 D6
Hiromi = Kihoku Japan 33°13N 132°36E 222 D4
Hiroo Japan 42°17N 143°19E 220 C11
Hirosaki Japan 40°34N 140°28E 220 D10
Hiroshima Japan 34°24N 132°30E 222 C4
Hiroshima □ Japan 34°50N 133°0E 222 C5
Hiroshima-Wan Japan 34°5N 132°20E 222 C4
Hirota Japan 34°45N 135°20E 133 A1
Hirschberg = Jelenia Góra Poland 50°50N 15°45E 185 H2
Hirschstetten Austria 48°14N 16°27E 142 A2
Hirson France 49°55N 4°4E 173 C11
Hirtshals Denmark 57°36N 9°57E 163 G3
Hisai Japan 34°40N 136°28E 223 C8
Hisar India 29°12N 75°45E 242 E6
Hisarcık Turkey 39°15N 29°14E 205 B11
Hisaria Bulgaria 42°30N 24°44E 203 D8
Hisb, Sha'ib = Ḩasb, W. → Iraq 31°45N 44°17E 246 D5
Ḩismá Si. Arabia 28°30N 36°0E 251 K7
Ḩişn al 'Abr Yemen 16°8N 47°14E 248 C4
Hispaniola W. Indies 19°0N 71°0W 321 C5
Hīt Iraq 33°38N 42°49E 213 F10
Hita Japan 33°20N 130°58E 222 D2
Hitachi Japan 36°36N 140°39E 223 A12
Hitachi-Ōta Japan 36°30N 140°30E 223 A12
Hitan, W. el Egypt 29°19N 30°10E 256 J7
Hitchin U.K. 51°58N 0°16W 169 F7
Hithadhoo Maldives 0°36S 73°5E 272 d
Hither Green U.K. 51°26N 0°0 125 B3
Hitiaa Tahiti 17°36S 149°18W 289 e
Hitoyoshi Japan 32°13N 130°45E 222 E2
Hitra Norway 63°30N 8°45E 164 A5
Hitzacker Germany 53°9N 11°2E 178 B7
Hiu Vanuatu 13°10S 166°35E 287 C4
Hiuchi-Nada Japan 34°5N 133°20E 222 C5
Hiva Oa French Polynesia 9°45S 139°0W 289 f
Hixon Canada 53°25N 122°35W 296 C4

Hiyoshi *Japan* 35°32N 139°38E **140** B2
Ḩiyyon, N. → *Israel* 30°25N 35°10E **251** H6
Hizma *West Bank* 31°50N 35°16E **123** B2
Hjalmar L. *Canada* 61°33N 109°25W **297** A7
Hjälmaren *Sweden* 59°18N 15°40E **162** E9
Hjältevad *Sweden* 57°38N 15°20E **163** G9
Hjalteyri *Iceland* 65°55N 18°18W **155** B8
Hjartdal *Norway* 59°37N 8°41E **164** E5
Hjelmelandsvågen *Norway* 59°14N 6°10E **164** E3
Hjelset *Norway* 62°48N 7°30E **164** B4
Hjerkinn *Norway* 62°13N 9°33E **164** B6
Hjo *Sweden* 58°22N 14°17E **163** F8
Hjørring *Denmark* 57°29N 9°59E **163** G3
Hjörsey *Iceland* 64°32N 22°21W **155** C4
Hjort Trench *S. Ocean* 58°0S 157°30E **151** B10
Hjortekær *Denmark* 55°47N 12°32E **118** A3
Hjortespring *Denmark* 55°44N 12°25E **118** A2
Hjortkvarn *Sweden* 58°54N 15°26E **163** F9
Hjukse *Norway* 59°31N 9°19E **164** E6
Hkakabo Razi *Myanmar* 28°25N 97°23E **228** C1
Hkakabo Razi △ *Myanmar* 28°0N 97°55E **241** A6
Hkamti *Myanmar* 26°0N 95°39E **241** C5
Hko-lam *Myanmar* 21°7N 98°15E **241** E7
Hko-ut *Myanmar* 20°58N 98°2E **241** E7
Hkyenhpa *Myanmar* 27°43N 97°25E **241** B6
Hlaingbwe *Myanmar* 17°8N 97°50E **241** G6
Hlinsko *Czechia* 49°45N 15°54E **180** B8
Hlobane *S. Africa* 27°42S 31°0E **271** C5
Hlohovec *Slovakia* 48°26N 17°49E **181** C10
Hlubočepy *Czechia* 50°2N 14°23E **135** B2
Hlučín *Czechia* 49°54N 18°11E **181** B11
Hluhluwe *S. Africa* 28°1S 32°15E **271** D5
Hluhluwe △ *S. Africa* 22°10S 32°5E **271** B5
Hlukhiv *Ukraine* 51°40N 33°58E **189** G7
Hlwaze *Myanmar* 18°54N 96°37E **241** F6
Hlyboka *Ukraine* 48°5N 25°56E **183** B10
Hlybokaye *Belarus* 55°10N 27°45E **188** E4
Hnappadalssýsla *Iceland* 64°50N 22°30W **155** C4
Hnífsdalur *Iceland* 66°7N 23°8W **155** A3
Hnúšťa *Slovakia* 48°35N 19°58E **181** C12
Ho *Ghana* 6°37N 0°27E **263** D5
Ho Chi Minh City = Thanh Pho Ho Chi Minh *Vietnam* 10°58N 106°40E **237** G6
Ho Chung *Hong Kong, China* 22°21N 114°14E **122** A3
Ho Hoa Binh *Vietnam* 20°50N 105°0E **228** G5
Ho Thac Ba *Vietnam* 21°42N 105°1E **236** A5
Ho Thuong *Vietnam* 19°32N 105°48E **236** C5
Hoa Binh *Vietnam* 20°50N 105°20E **228** G5
Hoa Hiep *Vietnam* 11°34N 105°51E **237** G5
Hoai Nhon *Vietnam* 14°28N 109°1E **236** E7
Hoang Lien △ *Vietnam* 21°30N 105°32E **236** B5
Hoang Lien Son *Vietnam* 22°0N 104°0E **228** F4
Hoang Sa, Dao = Paracel Is. *S. China Sea* 15°50N 112°0E **230** A4
Hoanib → *Namibia* 19°27S 12°46E **270** A2
Hoare B. *Canada* 65°17N 62°30W **295** D19
Hoarusib → *Namibia* 19°3S 12°36E **270** A2
Hobart *Tas., Australia* 42°50S 147°21E **281** G4
Hobart *Ind., U.S.A.* 41°32N 87°15W **311** C9
Hobart *Okla., U.S.A.* 35°1N 99°6W **314** D5
Hobbs *U.S.A.* 32°42N 103°8W **305** K12
Hobbs Coast *Antarctica* 74°50S 131°0W **151** D14
Hobe Sound *U.S.A.* 27°4N 80°8W **317** H9
Hobo *Colombia* 2°35N 75°30W **328** C2
Hoboken *Ga., U.S.A.* 31°11N 82°8W **316** D7
Hoboken *New York, U.S.A.* **132** d1
Hobro *Denmark* 56°39N 9°46E **163** H3
Hobsons B. *Australia* 37°51S 144°55E **128** B1
Hoburgen *Sweden* 56°55N 18°7E **163** H12
Hobyo *Somalia* 5°25N 48°30E **267** C6
Hocalar *Turkey* 38°36N 30°0E **205** C11
Hochbrück *Germany* 48°14N 11°37E **131** A2
Hochelaga *Canada* 45°32N 73°33W **130** A2
Hochfeld *Namibia* 21°28S 17°58E **270** B2
Hochharz △ *Germany* 51°48N 10°38E **178** D6
Hochschwab *Austria* 47°35N 15°0E **180** D8
Höchstadt *Germany* 49°42N 10°47E **179** F6
Hochtaunus △ *Germany* 50°20N 8°30E **179** E4
Hoch'uan = Hechuan *China* 30°2N 106°12E **228** B6
Hochwan = Hechuan *China* 30°2N 106°12E **228** B6
Hockenheim *Germany* 49°19N 8°32E **179** F4
Hockley = Levelland *U.S.A.* 33°35N 102°23W **314** E3
Hodaka-Dake *Japan* 36°17N 137°39E **223** A9
Hodeida = Al Ḩudaydah *Yemen* 14°50N 43°0E **248** D3
Hodgeville *Canada* 50°7N 106°58W **297** C7
Hodgson *Canada* 51°13N 97°36W **297** C9
Hodh El Gharbi □ *Mauritania* 16°30N 10°0W **262** B3
Hódmezővásárhely *Hungary* 46°28N 20°22E **182** D5
Hodna, Chott el *Algeria* 35°26N 4°43E **261** A5
Hodo-dan *N. Korea* 39°23N 127°32E **224** C3
Hodonín *Czechia* 48°50N 17°10E **181** C10
Hœdic, Î. de *France* 47°20N 2°53W **172** E4
Hoegi *S. Korea* 37°35N 127°3E **137** B2
Hoeilaart *Belgium* 50°46N 4°28E **116** B2
Hoek van Holland *Neths.* 52°0N 4°7E **170** C4
Hoengseong *S. Korea* 37°29N 127°59E **224** D3
Hoeryong *N. Korea* 42°30N 129°45E **224** A4
Hoeyang *N. Korea* 38°43N 127°36E **224** C3
Hof *Bayern, Germany* 50°19N 11°55E **179** E7
Hof *Austurland Iceland* 65°39N 15°0W **155** B11
Hof *Austurland Iceland* 64°33N 14°40W **155** C12
Hof *Vestfold, Norway* 59°32N 10°5E **164** E7
Hofburg *Vienna, Austria* **142** b1
Hofei = Hefei *China* 31°52N 117°18E **229** B11
Hoffell *Iceland* 64°23N 15°20W **155** C11
Hoffman I. *U.S.A.* 40°34N 74°3W **132** C1
Hofgarten *Munich, Germany* **131** a3
Hofgeismar *Germany* 51°29N 9°23E **178** D5
Hofheim *Germany* 50°5N 8°26E **179** E4
Hofmeyr *S. Africa* 31°39S 25°50E **270** D4
Höfn *Iceland* 64°15N 15°13W **155** C11
Hofors *Sweden* 60°31N 16°15E **162** D10
Hofsjökull *Iceland* 64°49N 18°48W **155** C8
Hofsós *Iceland* 65°53N 19°26W **155** B7
Hōfu *Japan* 34°3N 131°34E **222** C3
Hog Harbour *Vanuatu* 15°8S 167°6E **287** E5
Hog I. = Paradise I. *The Bahamas* 25°6N 77°19W **153** b
Hog I. *Grenada* 12°0N 61°44W **323** q
Hog Pt. *Antigua & B.* 17°41N 61°47W **322** c
Hogan Group *Australia* 39°13S 147°1E **281** F4
Höganäs *Sweden* 56°12N 12°33E **163** H6
Hogansville *U.S.A.* 33°10N 84°55W **316** B5
Hogarth, Mt. *Australia* 21°48S 136°58E **280** C2
Hoge Kempen △ *Belgium* 51°6N 5°35E **170** C5
Hoge Veluwe △ *Neths.* 52°5N 5°46E **170** B5
Høgeloft *Norway* 61°3N 8°12E **164** C5
Hogenakai Falls *India* 12°6N 77°50E **245** H3
Hoggar = Ahaggar *Algeria* 23°0N 6°30E **261** D6
Högsäter *Sweden* 58°38N 12°5E **163** F6
Högsby *Sweden* 57°10N 16°1E **163** G10
Högsjö *Sweden* 59°4N 15°44E **162** E9
Hogsty Reef *The Bahamas* 21°41N 73°48W **321** B5
Hoh → *U.S.A.* 47°45N 124°29W **306** C2
Hoh Xil Shan *China* 36°30N 89°0E **218** D6
Hohd ech Chargui □ *Mauritania* 19°0N 7°15W **260** E3
Hohe Acht *Germany* 50°22N 7°0E **179** E3
Hohe Tauern *Austria* 47°11N 12°40E **180** D5
Hohe Tauern △ *Austria* 47°5N 12°20E **180** D5
Hohenau *Austria* 48°36N 16°55E **181** C9
Hohenbrunn *Germany* 48°2N 11°42E **131** B3
Hohenelbe = Vrchlabí *Czechia* 50°38N 15°37E **180** A8
Hohenems *Austria* 47°22N 9°42E **180** D2
Hohenloher Ebene *Germany* 49°14N 9°36E **179** F5
Hohenmauth = Vysoké Mýto *Czechia* 49°58N 16°10E **181** B9
Hohensalza = Inowrocław *Poland* 52°50N 18°12E **185** F5
Hohensalzburg = Lunino *Russia* 53°38N 45°18E **190** D7
Hohenschönhausen *Germany* 52°33N 13°30E **115** A4
Hohenstadt = Zábřeh *Czechia* 49°53N 16°52E **181** B9
Hohenstein = Olsztynek *Poland* 53°34N 20°19E **184** E7
Hohenwald *U.S.A.* 35°33N 87°33W **315** D11
Hohenwestedt *Germany* 54°5N 9°40E **178** A5
Hoher Rhön = Rhön *Germany* 50°24N 9°58E **178** E5
Hoher Vogelsberg ⌓ *Germany* 51°45N 9°35E **178** D5
Hohes Venn *Belgium* 50°30N 6°5E **170** D6
Hohes Venn-Eifel △ *Europe* 50°30N 6°10E **178** E2
Hohhot *China* 40°52N 111°40E **226** D6
Hohoe *Ghana* 7°8N 0°32E **263** D5
Hoi An *Vietnam* 15°53N 108°19E **236** E7
Hoi Xuan *Vietnam* 20°25N 105°9E **228** G5
Hoihow = Haikou *China* 20°1N 110°16E **229** a
Hoisington *U.S.A.* 38°31N 98°47W **308** F4
Hojai *India* 26°2N 92°54E **241** B4
Hojambaz *Turkmenistan* 38°7N 65°0E **216** E6
Højer *Denmark* 54°58N 8°42E **163** K2
Hōjō *Japan* 33°58N 132°46E **222** D4
Hok *Sweden* 57°31N 14°16E **163** G8
Hok Tsui *Hong Kong, China* 22°12N 114°14E **122** B3
Hokang = Hegang *China* 47°20N 130°19E **219** B15
Hökensås *Sweden* 58°0N 14°5E **163** G8
Hökerum *Sweden* 57°51N 13°16E **163** G7
Hokianga Harbour *N.Z.* 35°31S 173°22E **284** B2
Hokitika *N.Z.* 42°42S 171°0E **285** C6
Hokkaidō □ *Japan* 43°30N 143°0E **220** C11
Hokksund *Norway* 59°48N 9°54E **164** E6
Hokuto *Japan* 41°49N 140°39E **220** D10
Hol-Hol *Djibouti* 11°20N 42°50E **257** E5
Hola *Kenya* 1°29S 40°2E **268** B4
Hola Prystan *Ukraine* 46°29N 32°32E **189** J7
Holakas *Greece* 35°57N 27°53E **206** F11
Holalkere *India* 14°2N 76°11E **245** G3
Hólar *Iceland* 65°44N 19°8W **155** B7
Holargos = Cholargos *Greece* 37°59N 23°48E **112** B2
Holašovice *Czechia* 48°57N 14°15E **180** C7
Holbæk *Denmark* 55°43N 11°43E **163** J5
Holborn *London, U.K.* **125** a4
Holbrook *N.S.W., Australia* 35°42S 147°18E **283** C7
Holbrook *Ariz., U.S.A.* 34°54N 110°10W **305** J8
Holcomb *U.S.A.* 42°54N 77°25W **312** D7
Holden *Mo., U.S.A.* 38°43N 94°0W **310** F3
Holden *Utah, U.S.A.* 39°6N 112°16W **304** G7
Holden, L. *U.S.A.* 28°30N 81°23W **133** B2
Holdenville *U.S.A.* 35°5N 96°24W **314** D6
Holdich *Argentina* 45°57S 68°13W **336** C3
Holdrege *U.S.A.* 40°26N 99°23W **308** E4
Hole-Narsipur *India* 12°48N 76°16E **245** H3
Holešov *Czechia* 49°20N 17°35E **181** B10
Holešovice *Czechia* 50°6N 14°28E **135** B2
Holetown *Barbados* 13°11N 59°38W **323** r
Holgate *U.S.A.* 41°15N 84°8W **311** C12
Holguín *Cuba* 20°50N 76°20W **320** B4
Holíč *Slovakia* 48°49N 17°10E **181** C10
Holice *Czechia* 50°5N 16°0E **180** A8
Holiday *U.S.A.* 28°11N 82°44W **317** G7
Holiday Park *U.S.A.* 26°8N 80°7W **129** B3
Höljes *Sweden* 60°50N 12°35E **162** D6
Hollabrunn *Austria* 48°34N 16°5E **180** C9
Hollams Bird I. *Namibia* 24°40S 14°30E **270** B1
Holland = Netherlands ■ *Europe* 52°0N 5°30E **170** C5
Holland *Mich., U.S.A.* 42°47N 86°7W **311** B10
Holland *N.Y., U.S.A.* 42°38N 78°32W **312** D6
Holland B. *Jamaica* 17°57N 76°13W **320** a
Holland Centre *Canada* 44°23N 80°47W **312** B4
Holland Patent *U.S.A.* 43°14N 75°15W **313** C9
Holland Tunnel *New York, U.S.A.* **132** d1
Holland Village *Singapore* 1°18N 103°47E **138** B2
Hollandale *U.S.A.* 33°10N 90°51W **315** E9
Hollandia = Jayapura *Indonesia* 2°28S 140°38E **231** E10
Holley *U.S.A.* 43°14N 78°2W **312** C6
Hollfeld *Germany* 49°56N 11°18E **179** F7
Hollidaysburg *U.S.A.* 40°26N 78°24W **312** F6
Hollis *U.S.A.* 34°41N 99°55W **314** D5
Hollis Reservoir *Trin. & Tob.* 10°40N 61°10W **323** t
Hollister *Calif., U.S.A.* 36°51N 121°24W **306** J5
Hollister *Idaho, U.S.A.* 42°21N 114°35W **304** E6
Höllriegelskreuth *Germany* 48°2N 11°30E **131** B1
Höllviken *Sweden* 55°26N 12°58E **163** J6
Höllviksnäs = Höllviken *Sweden* 55°26N 12°58E **163** J6
Holly *U.S.A.* 42°48N 83°38W **311** B13
Holly Hill *Fla., U.S.A.* 29°16N 81°3W **317** F8
Holly Hill *S.C., U.S.A.* 33°19N 80°25W **316** B9
Holly Springs *Ga., U.S.A.* 34°10N 84°30W **316** A5
Holly Springs *Miss., U.S.A.* 34°46N 89°27W **315** D10
Hollywood *Wicklow, Ireland* 53°6N 6°35W **166** B6
Hollywood *Calif., U.S.A.* 34°5N 118°19W **126** B3
Hollywood *Fla., U.S.A.* 26°0N 80°8W **129** B3
Hollywood Bowl *U.S.A.* 34°7N 118°20W **126** B2
Holman = Ulukhaktok *Canada* 70°44N 117°44W **294** C8
Hólmavík *Iceland* 65°42N 21°40W **155** B5
Holmen *Oppland, Norway* 60°40N 10°22E **164** D7
Holmen *Wis., U.S.A.* 43°58N 91°15W **308** D8
Holmenkollen *Norway* 59°57N 10°41E **133** A3
Holmes Beach *U.S.A.* 27°31N 82°43W **317** H7
Holmes Cr. → *U.S.A.* 30°30N 85°50W **316** E4
Holmes Reefs *Australia* 16°27S 148°0E **280** B4
Holmestrand *Norway* 59°31N 10°14E **164** E7
Holmgård *Sweden* 59°14N 18°0E **139** B1
Holmlia *Norway* 59°49N 10°46E **133** B3
Holmsjö *Sweden* 56°25N 15°32E **163** H9
Holmsjön *Västernorrland, Sweden* 62°41N 16°33E **162** B10
Holmsjön *Västernorrland, Sweden* 62°26N 15°20E **162** B9
Holmsland Klit *Denmark* 56°0N 8°5E **163** J2
Holmsund *Sweden* 63°41N 20°20E **160** E19
Holocaust Memorial *Jerusalem* 31°47N 35°11E **123** B2
Holocaust Memorial Park *Boston, U.S.A.* **116** b2
Holod *Romania* 46°49N 22°8E **182** D7
Holon *Israel* 32°0N 34°46E **251** G5
Holopaw *U.S.A.* 28°8N 81°5W **317** G8
Holovne *Ukraine* 51°20N 24°5E **185** G11
Holøydal *Norway* 62°12N 11°27E **164** B8
Holozubyntsi *Ukraine* 48°50N 26°55E **183** B11
Holroyd → *Australia* 14°10S 141°36E **280** A3
Holstebro *Denmark* 56°22N 8°37E **163** H2
Holsteinische Schweiz ⌓ *Germany* 54°8N 10°30E **178** A6
Holsteinsborg = Sisimiut *Greenland* 66°40N 53°30W **154** D5
Holsworthy *U.K.* 50°48N 4°22W **169** G3
Holt *Iceland* 63°33N 19°48W **155** D7
Holt *Fla., U.S.A.* 30°43N 86°45W **317** E3
Holt *Mich., U.S.A.* 42°39N 84°31W **311** B12
Holton *Nfld. & L., Canada* 54°31N 57°12W **299** B8
Holton *Kans., U.S.A.* 39°28N 95°44W **308** F6
Holts Summit *U.S.A.* 38°38N 92°7W **310** F4
Holtville *U.S.A.* 32°49N 115°23W **307** N11
Holualoa *U.S.A.* 19°37N 155°57W **302** D6
Holum *Norway* 58°6N 7°32E **164** F4
Holwerd *Neths.* 53°22N 5°54E **170** A5
Holy Cross *U.S.A.* 62°12N 159°46W **303** E8
Holy I. *Anglesey, U.K.* 53°17N 4°37W **168** D3
Holy I. *Northumberland, U.K.* 55°40N 1°47W **168** B6
Holyhead *U.K.* 53°18N 4°38W **168** D3
Holyoke *Colo., U.S.A.* 40°35N 102°18W **304** F12
Holyoke *Mass., U.S.A.* 42°12N 72°37W **313** D12
Holyrood *Canada* 47°27N 53°8W **299** C9
Holyrood House, Palace of *U.K.* 55°57N 3°10W **121** B3
Holysloot *Neths.* 52°25N 5°2E **112** A3
Holzkirchen *Germany* 47°52N 11°42E **179** H7
Holzminden *Germany* 51°50N 9°28E **178** D5
Homa Bay *Kenya* 0°36S 34°30E **268** C3
Homalin *Myanmar* 24°55N 95°0E **241** C5
Homand *Iran* 32°28N 59°37E **247** C8
Homathko → *Canada* 51°0N 124°56W **296** C4
Homberg *Germany* 51°2N 9°25E **178** D5
Hombori *Mali* 15°20N 1°38W **263** B4
Hombori Tondo *Mali* 15°16N 1°40W **263** B4
Homburg *Germany* 49°28N 7°18E **179** F3
Home B. *Canada* 68°40N 67°10W **295** D18
Home Hill *Australia* 19°43S 147°25E **280** B4
Home Reef *Tonga* 18°59S 174°47W **287** P13
Homedale *U.S.A.* 43°37N 116°56W **304** E5
Homei *Taiwan* 24°7N 120°29E **225** B2
Homeland *U.S.A.* 30°51N 82°1W **316** E7
Homer *Alaska, U.S.A.* 59°39N 151°33W **303** G10
Homer *Ill., U.S.A.* 40°4N 87°57W **311** D9
Homer *La., U.S.A.* 32°48N 93°4W **314** E8
Homer *Mich., U.S.A.* 42°9N 84°49W **311** B12
Homer *N.Y., U.S.A.* 42°38N 76°10W **313** D8
Homer City *U.S.A.* 40°32N 79°10W **312** F5
Homert ⌓ *Germany* 51°15N 8°0E **178** D4
Homerton *U.K.* 51°32N 0°2W **125** A3
Homerville *U.S.A.* 31°2N 82°45W **316** D7
Homestead *Queens., Australia* 20°20S 145°40E **280** C4
Homestead *Fla., U.S.A.* 25°28N 80°29W **317** K9
Homestead △ *U.S.A.* 40°17N 96°50W **308** E5
Hometown *U.S.A.* 41°44N 87°42W **119** C2
Homewood *U.S.A.* 41°34N 87°40W **311** C9
Hommelvik *Norway* 63°25N 10°48E **164** A7
Hommersåk *Norway* 58°56N 5°50E **164** F2
Homnabad *India* 17°45N 77°11E **244** F3
Homoine *Mozam.* 23°55S 35°8E **271** B6
Homoljske Planina *Serbia* 44°10N 21°45E **202** B5
Homonhon I. *Phil.* 10°44N 125°43E **233** F5
Homorod *Romania* 46°5N 25°15E **183** D10
Homosassa Springs *U.S.A.* 28°48N 82°35W **317** G7
Homs = Al Khums *Libya* 32°40N 14°17E **258** B2
Homs = Ḩimş *Syria* 34°40N 36°45E **250** D7
Homyel *Belarus* 52°28N 31°0E **177** B16
Homyel □ *Belarus* 52°40N 30°10E **189** F6
Hon Chong *Vietnam* 10°25N 104°30E **237** G5
Hon Hai *Vietnam* 10°0N 109°0E **237** H7
Hon Me *Vietnam* 19°23N 105°56E **236** C5
Honan = Henan □ *China* 34°0N 114°0E **226** H8
Hōnanchō *Japan* 35°40N 139°39E **140** A2
Hōnaunau *U.S.A.* 19°26N 155°55W **302** D6
Honavar *India* 14°17N 74°27E **245** G2
Honaz *Turkey* 37°46N 29°18E **205** D11
Honbetsu *Japan* 43°7N 143°37E **220** C11
Honcho *Japan* 35°40N 139°41E **140** A3
Honcut *U.S.A.* 39°20N 121°32W **306** F5
Honda *Colombia* 5°12N 74°45W **328** B3
Honda B. *Phil.* 9°53N 118°49E **233** G2
Hondarribia *Spain* 43°22N 1°47W **196** B3
Hondeklipbaai *S. Africa* 30°19S 17°17E **270** D2
Honden *Japan* 35°43N 139°50E **140** A4
Hondo *Japan* 32°27N 130°12E **222** E2
Hondo *Tex., U.S.A.* 29°21N 99°9W **314** G5
Hondo, Río → *Belize* 18°25N 88°21W **319** D7
Hondo, Río → *Calif., U.S.A.* 34°2N 118°15W **126** B4
Honduras ■ *Cent. Amer.* 14°40N 86°30W **320** D2
Honduras, G. de *Caribbean* 16°50N 87°0W **320** C2
Hønefoss *Norway* 60°10N 10°18E **164** D7
Honesdale *U.S.A.* 41°34N 75°16W **313** E9
Honey Harbour *Canada* 44°52N 79°49W **312** B5
Honey L. *U.S.A.* 40°15N 120°19W **306** E6
Honfleur *France* 49°25N 0°13E **172** C7
Høng *Denmark* 55°31N 11°18E **163** J5
Hong → *Asia* 20°16N 106°34E **236** B5
Hong Gai *Vietnam* 20°57N 107°5E **228** G6
Hong He → *China* 32°25N 115°35E **229** A10
Hong Hu *China* 29°54N 113°24E **229** C9
Hong Kong □ *China* 22°11N 114°14E **219** a
Hong Kong I. *China* 22°16N 114°12E **122** B3
Hong Kong Int. ✈ (HKG) *Hong Kong, China* 22°19N 113°57E **122** B1
Hong Kong Univ. *China* 22°16N 114°8E **122** B2
Honga *Angola* 15°9S 15°12E **265** F3
Hong'an *China* 31°20N 114°40E **229** B10
Hongcheon *S. Korea* 37°44N 127°53E **224** D3
Hongdo *S. Korea* 34°41N 125°12E **224** E2
Honghai Wan *China* 22°40N 115°0E **229** F10
Honghe *China* 23°25N 102°25E **228** F4
Honghu *China* 29°50N 113°30E **229** C9
Hongje *S. Korea* 37°35N 126°56E **137** B1
Hongjiang *China* 27°7N 109°59E **228** D7
Hongjimun Tunnel *S. Korea* 37°37N 126°58E **137** B1
Hongkou *China* 31°16N 121°29E **138** B1
Hongliu He → *China* 38°0N 109°50E **226** F5
Hongor *Mongolia* 45°45N 112°50E **226** B7
Hongqiao *China* 31°11N 121°22E **138** B1
Hongseong *S. Korea* 36°37N 126°38E **224** D3
Hongshan *China* 36°38N 117°58E **227** F9
Hongshui He → *China* 23°48N 109°30E **228** F7
Hongtong *China* 36°16N 111°40E **226** F6
Honguedo, Détroit d' *Canada* 49°15N 64°0W **299** C7
Hongwon *N. Korea* 40°0N 127°56E **224** C3
Hongya *China* 29°57N 103°22E **228** C4
Hongyuan *China* 32°51N 102°40E **228** A4
Hongze Hu *China* 33°15N 118°35E **227** H10
Honiara *Solomon Is.* 9°27S 159°57E **287** M10
Honiton *U.K.* 50°47N 3°11W **169** G4
Honjō = Yurihonjō *Japan* 39°23N 140°3E **220** E10
Honjō *Japan* 36°14N 139°11E **223** A11
Honjyo *Japan* 35°41N 139°48E **140** A3
Honkawane *Japan* 35°5N 138°5E **223** B10
Honkorâb, Ras *Egypt* 24°35N 35°10E **256** C4
Honnali *India* 14°15N 75°40E **245** G2
Honningsvåg *Norway* 70°59N 25°59E **160** A21
Hönö *Sweden* 57°41N 11°39E **163** G5
Honoka'a *U.S.A.* 20°5N 155°28W **302** C6
Honokai Hale *U.S.A.* 21°20N 158°6W **302** K13
Honolulu *U.S.A.* 21°19N 157°52W **302** K14
Honolulu District *U.S.A.* 21°19N 157°46W **302** K14
Honolulu Int. ✈ (HNL) *U.S.A.* 21°19N 157°55W **302** K14
Honomu *U.S.A.* 19°52N 155°7W **302** D6
Honoré Mercier, Pont *Canada* 45°24N 73°39W **130** B1
Honouliuli *U.S.A.* 21°22N 158°2W **302** K13
Hönow *Germany* 52°32N 13°38E **115** A4
Honshū *Japan* 36°0N 138°0E **223** A8
Hontoria del Pinar *Spain* 41°50N 3°10W **196** D1
Honu'apo B. *U.S.A.* 19°5N 155°33W **302** D6
Hood, I. = Española, I. *Ecuador* 1°23S 89°39W **330** a
Hood, Mt. *U.S.A.* 45°23N 121°42W **304** D3
Hood, Pt. *Australia* 34°23S 119°34E **279** F2
Hood Pt. *Papua N. G.* 10°4S 147°45E **286** F4
Hood River *U.S.A.* 45°43N 121°31W **304** D3
Hoodsport *U.S.A.* 47°24N 123°9W **306** C3
Hooge *Germany* 54°34N 8°33E **178** A4
Hoogeveen *Neths.* 52°44N 6°28E **170** B6
Hoogezand-Sappemeer *Neths.* 53°9N 6°45E **170** A6
Hooghly = Hugli → *India* 21°56N 88°4E **243** J13
Hooghly-Chinsura = Chunchura *India* 22°53N 88°27E **243** H13
Hook *U.K.* 51°22N 0°17W **125** B2
Hook Hd. *Ireland* 52°7N 6°56W **166** D5
Hook I. *Australia* 20°4S 149°0E **280** b
Hook of Holland = Hoek van Holland *Neths.* 52°0N 4°7E **170** C4
Hooker *U.S.A.* 36°52N 101°13W **314** C4
Hooker Creek = Lajamanu *Australia* 18°23S 130°38E **278** C5
Hooker Creek ◎ *Australia* 18°6S 130°23E **278** C5
Ho'olehua *U.S.A.* 21°10N 157°5W **302** B4
Hoonah *U.S.A.* 58°7N 135°27W **296** B1
Hoop *Bonaire* 12°7N 68°17W **322** h
Hooper Bay *U.S.A.* 61°32N 166°6W **303** F6
Hoopeston *U.S.A.* 40°28N 87°40W **311** D9
Hoopstad *S. Africa* 27°50S 25°55E **270** C4
Höör *Sweden* 55°56N 13°33E **163** J7
Hoorn *Neths.* 52°38N 5°4E **170** B5
Hoover *U.S.A.* 33°24N 86°49W **315** E11
Hoover Dam *U.S.A.* 36°1N 114°44W **307** K12
Hooversville *U.S.A.* 40°9N 78°55W **312** F6
Hop Bottom *U.S.A.* 41°42N 75°46W **313** E9
Hopa *Turkey* 41°28N 41°30E **213** B9
Hope *B.C., Canada* 49°25N 121°25W **296** D4
Hope *Ariz., U.S.A.* 33°43N 113°42W **307** M13
Hope *Ark., U.S.A.* 33°40N 93°36W **314** E8
Hope *Ind., U.S.A.* 39°18N 85°46W **311** E11
Hope, L. *S. Austral., Australia* 28°24S 139°18E **281** D2
Hope, L. *W. Austral., Australia* 32°35S 120°15E **279** F3
Hope, Pt. *U.S.A.* 68°21N 166°47W **303** B6
Hope Bay *Jamaica* 18°12N 76°34W **320** a
Hope I. *Canada* 44°55N 80°11W **312** B4
Hope Town *The Bahamas* 26°35N 76°57W **320** A4
Hope Vale *Australia* 15°16S 145°20E **280** B4
Hope Vale ◎ *Australia* 15°8S 145°15E **280** B4
Hopedale *Nfld. & L., Canada* 55°28N 60°13W **299** A7
Hopedale *Mass., U.S.A.* 42°8N 71°33W **313** D13
Hopefield *S. Africa* 33°3S 18°22E **270** D2
Hopei = Hebei □ *China* 39°0N 116°0E **226** E9
Hopelchén *Mexico* 19°46N 89°51W **319** D7
Hopetoun *Vic., Australia* 35°42S 142°22E **282** C5
Hopetoun *W. Austral., Australia* 33°57S 120°7E **279** F3
Hopetown *S. Africa* 29°34S 24°3E **270** C3
Hopewell *U.S.A.* 37°18N 77°17W **309** G15
Hopfgarten *Austria* 47°27N 12°10E **180** D5
Hopin *Myanmar* 24°58N 96°30E **241** C6
Hoping *Changhua, Taiwan* 24°10N 120°56E **225** B2
Hoping *T'aitung, Taiwan* 23°4N 121°20E **225** C3
Hopkins *U.S.A.* 40°33N 94°49W **310** D2
Hopkins, L. *Australia* 24°15S 128°35E **278** D4
Hopkinsville *U.S.A.* 36°52N 87°29W **308** G10
Hopland *U.S.A.* 38°58N 123°7W **306** G3
Hopong *Myanmar* 20°47N 97°11E **241** E6
Hopwood's Ferry = Echuca *Australia* 36°10S 144°45E **283** D6
Hoque *Angola* 14°40S 13°55E **265** E2
Hoquiam *U.S.A.* 46°59N 123°53W **306** D3
Hora Hoverla *Ukraine* 48°7N 24°41E **183** B9
Hora Sfakion = Chora Sfakion *Greece* 35°15N 24°9E **207** E5
Hōrai *Japan* 34°58N 137°32E **223** C9
Horana *Sri Lanka* 6°43N 80°4E **245** L5
Horasan *Turkey* 40°3N 42°11E **213** B10
Horažďovice *Czechia* 49°19N 13°42E **180** B6
Horb *Germany* 48°26N 8°47E **179** G4
Hörby *Sweden* 55°51N 13°40E **163** J7
Horcajo de Santiago *Spain* 39°50N 3°1W **196** F1
Hordabø *Norway* 60°42N 4°54E **164** D1
Hordaland □ *Norway* 60°25N 6°15E **164** D3
Hordern Hills *Australia* 20°15S 130°0E **278** D5
Horezu *Romania* 45°6N 24°0E **183** E8
Horgen *Switz.* 47°15N 8°35E **179** H4
Horgos *China* 44°10N 80°25E **217** D10
Horgoš *Serbia* 46°10N 20°0E **182** D4
Horikiri *Japan* 35°44N 139°50E **140** A4
Horinchove *Ukraine* 48°16N 23°26E **183** B8
Horinger *China* 40°28N 111°48E **226** D6
Horizontina *Brazil* 27°37S 54°19W **335** B5
Horki *Belarus* 54°17N 30°59E **188** E6
Horlick Mts. *Antarctica* 84°0S 102°0W **151** E15
Horlivka *Ukraine* 48°19N 38°5E **189** H10
Hormak *Iran* 29°58N 60°51E **247** D9
Hormigueros *Puerto Rico* 18°8N 67°8W **321** b
Hormoz *Iran* 27°35N 55°0E **247** E7
Hormoz, Jaz.-ye *Iran* 27°8N 56°28E **247** E8
Hormozgān □ *Iran* 27°30N 56°0E **247** E8
Hormuz, Kūh-e *Iran* 27°27N 55°10E **247** E7
Hormuz, Str. of *The Gulf* 26°30N 56°30E **247** E8
Horn *Austria* 48°39N 15°40E **180** C8
Horn *Vestfirðir Iceland* 66°28N 22°25W **155** A4
Horn *Sweden* 57°54N 15°51E **163** G9
Horn → *Canada* 61°30N 118°1W **296** A5
Horn, Cape = Hornos, C. de *Chile* 55°50S 67°30W **336** E3
Horn, Is. *Wall. & F. Is.* 14°16S 178°6W **277** C15
Horn Head *Ireland* 55°14N 8°0W **166** A3
Horn I. *Australia* 10°37S 142°17E **286** F2
Horn Plateau *Canada* 62°15N 119°15W **296** A5
Horn Pond *U.S.A.* 42°28N 71°9W **116** A1
Hornachuelos *Spain* 37°50N 5°14W **195** H5
Hornavan *Sweden* 66°15N 17°30E **160** C17
Hornbeck *U.S.A.* 31°20N 93°24W **314** F8
Hornbrook *U.S.A.* 41°55N 122°33W **304** F2
Hornburg *Germany* 52°2N 10°37E **178** C6
Hornby *N.Z.* 43°33S 172°33E **285** D7
Horncastle *U.K.* 53°13N 0°7W **168** D7
Hornchurch *U.K.* 51°33N 0°14E **125** A5
Horndal *Sweden* 60°18N 16°23E **162** D10
Hornell *U.S.A.* 42°20N 77°40W **312** D7
Hornell L. *Canada* 62°20N 119°25W **296** A5
Hornepayne *Canada* 49°14N 84°48W **298** C3
Horni *Czechia* 50°2N 14°33E **135** B3
Horní Planá *Czechia* 48°46N 14°2E **180** C7
Horni Počernice *Czechia* 50°6N 14°36E **135** B3
Hornindal *Norway* 61°58N 6°30E **164** C3
Hornindalsvatnet *Norway* 61°55N 6°20E **164** C3
Hornings Mills *Canada* 44°9N 80°12W **312** B4
Hornitos *U.S.A.* 37°30N 120°14W **306** H6
Hornopirén △ *Chile* 41°58S 72°17W **336** B2
Hornos, C. de *Chile* 55°50S 67°30W **336** E3
Hornos Is. *Papua N. G.* 2°12S 147°45E **286** B4
Hornoy-le-Bourg *France* 49°50N 1°54E **173** C8
Hornsby *Australia* 33°42S 151°2E **283** B9
Hornsea *U.K.* 53°55N 0°11W **168** D7
Hornsey *U.K.* 51°35N 0°7W **125** A3
Hornsjø *Norway* 61°19N 10°38E **164** C7
Hornslandet *Sweden* 61°35N 17°37E **162** C11
Hornslet *Denmark* 56°19N 10°19E **163** H4
Hörnum *Germany* 54°45N 8°17E **178** A4
Horobetsu = Noboribetsu *Japan* 42°24N 141°6E **220** C10
Horodenka *Ukraine* 48°41N 25°29E **183** B10
Horodnya *Ukraine* 51°55N 31°33E **189** G6
Horodok *Khmelnytskyy, Ukraine* 49°10N 26°34E **177** D14
Horodok *Lviv, Ukraine* 49°46N 23°32E **177** D12
Horodyshche *Ukraine* 49°17N 31°27E **189** H6
Horokhiv *Ukraine* 50°30N 24°45E **177** C13
Horoměřice *Czechia* 50°8N 14°20E **135** B1
Horovice *Czechia* 49°48N 13°53E **180** B6
Horqin Youyi Qianqi *China* 46°5N 122°3E **227** A12
Horqin Zuoyi Zhongqi *China* 44°8N 123°18E **227** B12
Horqueta *Paraguay* 23°15S 56°55W **334** A4
Horred *Sweden* 57°22N 12°28E **163** G6
Horse Cr. → *U.S.A.* 41°57N 103°58W **304** F12
Horse I. *Canada* 53°20N 99°6W **297** C9
Horse Is. *Canada* 50°15N 55°50W **299** B8
Horsefly L. *Canada* 52°25N 121°0W **296** C4
Horseheads *U.S.A.* 42°10N 76°49W **312** D8
Horsens *Denmark* 55°52N 9°51E **163** J3
Horseshoe Bend △ *U.S.A.* 32°59N 85°44W **316** C4
Horseshoe Lake *Canada* 45°17N 79°51W **312** A5
Horsham *Vic., Australia* 36°44S 142°13E **282** D5
Horsham *W. Susx., U.K.* 51°4N 0°20W **169** F7
Horšovský Týn *Czechia* 49°31N 12°58E **180** B5
Horta *Azores* 38°32N 28°38W **153** d1
Hortaleza *Spain* 40°28N 3°38W **127** B2
Horten *Norway* 59°25N 10°32E **164** E7
Hortense *U.S.A.* 31°20N 81°57W **316** D8
Horti *India* 17°7N 75°47E **244** F2
Hortobágy → *Hungary* 47°30N 21°6E **182** C6
Hortobágyi △ *Hungary* 47°36N 21°10E **182** C6
Horton *Kans., U.S.A.* 39°40N 95°32W **308** F6
Horton *Mo., U.S.A.* 37°58N 94°22W **310** G2
Horton → *Canada* 69°56N 126°52W **294** D6
Hortus Botanicus *Amsterdam, Neths.* **112** b3
Horwood L. *Canada* 48°5N 82°20W **298** C3
Hosaina *Ethiopia* 7°30N 37°47E **257** F4
Hosapete *India* 15°15N 76°20E **245** G3
Hosdrug = Kanhangad *India* 12°21N 74°58E **245** H2
Hosdurga *India* 13°49N 76°17E **245** H3
Hosenofu *Libya* 23°41N 21°4E **258** D4
Ḩoseynābād *Khuzestān, Iran* 32°45N 48°20E **247** C6
Ḩoseynābād *Kordestān, Iran* 35°33N 47°8E **213** E12
Hosford *U.S.A.* 30°23N 84°48W **316** E5
Hôsh 'Îsa *Egypt* 30°55N 30°17E **256** H7
Hoshangabad *India* 22°45N 77°45E **242** H7
Hoshiarpur *India* 31°30N 75°58E **242** D6
Hoskins *Papua N. G.* 5°29S 150°27E **286** C6
Hoskote *India* 13°4N 77°48E **245** H3
Hosoyama *Japan* 35°36N 139°31E **140** B2
Hospet = Hosapete *India* 15°15N 76°20E **245** G3
Hossegor *France* 43°39N 1°25W **174** E2
Hostafrancs *Spain* 41°21N 2°8E **114** A1
Hoste, I. *Chile* 55°0S 69°0W **336** E3
Hostens *France* 44°30N 0°40W **174** D3
Hostivař *Czechia* 50°3N 14°31E **135** B3
Hosur *India* 12°43N 77°49E **245** H3
Hot *Thailand* 18°8N 98°29E **236** C2
Hot Creek Range *U.S.A.* 38°40N 116°20W **304** G5
Hot Springs = Truth or Consequences *U.S.A.* 33°8N 107°15W **305** K10
Hot Springs *Ark., U.S.A.* 34°31N 93°3W **314** D8
Hot Springs *S. Dak., U.S.A.* 43°26N 103°29W **308** D2
Hot Springs △ *U.S.A.* 34°31N 93°3W **314** D8
Hotagen *Sweden* 63°59N 14°12E **160** E16
Hotan *China* 37°25N 79°55E **217** E9
Hotan He → *China* 40°22N 80°56E **217** D10
Hotazel *S. Africa* 27°17S 22°58E **270** C3
Hotchkiss *U.S.A.* 38°48N 107°43W **304** G10
Hôtel des Invalides *Paris, France* **134** c2
Hotham, C. *Australia* 12°2S 131°18E **278** B5
Hoting *Sweden* 64°8N 16°15E **160** D17
Hotolisht *Albania* 41°10N 20°25E **202** E4
Hotspur Seamount *Atl. Oc.* 17°55S 35°55W **333** E4
Hotte, Massif de la *Haiti* 18°30N 73°45W **321** C5
Hottentotsbaai *Namibia* 26°8S 14°59E **270** C1
Hou Hai *China* 22°32N 113°56E **219** a
Houailou *N. Cal.* 21°17S 165°38E **288** d
Houat, Î. de *France* 47°24N 2°58W **172** E4
Houbětin *Czechia* 50°6N 14°33E **135** B3
Houbi = Houpi *Taiwan* 23°22N 120°21E **225** C2
Houdan *France* 48°48N 1°35E **173** D8
Houei Sai *Laos* 20°18N 100°26E **228** G3
Houeillès *France* 44°12N 0°2E **174** D4
Houffalize *Belgium* 50°8N 5°48E **170** D5
Hougang *Singapore* 1°22N 103°53E **138** A3
Houghton *Gauteng, S. Africa* 26°10S 28°3E **123** B2
Houghton *Mich., U.S.A.* 47°7N 88°34W **308** B9
Houghton *N.Y., U.S.A.* 42°25N 78°10W **312** D6
Houghton L. *U.S.A.* 44°21N 84°44W **309** C11
Houghton-le-Spring *U.K.* 54°51N 1°28W **168** C6
Houhora Heads *N.Z.* 34°49S 173°9E **284** A2
Houilles *France* 48°56N 2°11E **134** A2
Houli *Taiwan* 24°19N 120°44E **225** B2
Houlton *U.S.A.* 46°8N 67°51W **309** B20
Houlung *Taiwan* 24°37N 120°47E **225** B2
Houma *China* 35°36N 111°20E **226** G6
Houma *La., U.S.A.* 29°36N 90°43W **315** G9
Houmt Souk = Djerba *Tunisia* 33°48N 10°54E **258** B2
Houndé *Burkina Faso* 11°34N 3°31W **262** C4
Hounslow □ *U.K.* 51°28N 0°21W **125** B1
Houpi *Taiwan* 23°22N 120°21E **225** C2
Hourtin *France* 45°11N 1°4W **174** C2
Hourtin-Carcans, L. d' *France* 45°10N 1°6W **174** C2
Housatonic → *U.S.A.* 41°10N 73°7W **313** E11
House of Nobility = Riddarhuset *Stockholm, Sweden* **139** c2
House of Parliament = Riksdagshuset *Stockholm, Sweden* **139** b2
Houses of Parliament *London, U.K.* **125** c3
Houston *B.C., Canada* 54°25N 126°39W **296** C3
Houston *Fla., U.S.A.* 30°15N 82°54W **316** E7
Houston *Mo., U.S.A.* 37°22N 91°58W **308** G8
Houston *Tex., U.S.A.* 29°45N 95°21W **314** G7
Houston George Bush Intercontinental ✈ (IAH) *U.S.A.* 29°59N 95°20W **314** G7
Hout = Mogwadi → *S. Africa* 23°4S 29°36E **271** B4
Hout Bay *S. Africa* 34°2S 18°23E **118** B1
Houtkraal *S. Africa* 30°23S 24°5E **270** D3
Houtman Abrolhos *Australia* 28°43S 113°48E **279** E1
Hov *Norway* 60°42N 10°20E **164** D7
Hovd = Dund-Us *Mongolia* 48°1N 91°38E **217** C12
Hovd □ *Mongolia* 48°2N 91°37E **217** C12
Hovda *Norway* 60°53N 9°11E **164** D6
Hovden *Aust-Agder, Norway* 59°33N 7°22E **164** E4
Hovden *Sogn og Fjordane, Norway* 61°41N 4°52E **164** C1
Hove *U.K.* 50°50N 0°10W **169** G7
Hove Å → *Denmark* 55°36N 12°23E **118** B2
Hovedøya *Norway* 59°53N 10°43E **133** A3
Hovenweep △ *U.S.A.* 37°20N 109°0W **305** H9
Hovet *Norway* 60°38N 8°8E **164** D5
Hoveyzeh *Iran* 31°27N 48°4E **247** D6
Hovgaard Ø *Greenland* 79°55N 18°50W **154** B9
Høvik *Norway* 59°54N 10°34E **133** A2
Hovin *Norway* 59°51N 9°10E **164** E6
Hovmantorp *Sweden* 56°47N 15°7E **163** H9
Hovorčovice *Czechia* 50°10N 14°31E **135** A3
Hövsgöl *Mongolia* 43°37N 109°39E **226** C5
Hövsgöl Nuur *Mongolia* 51°0N 100°30E **218** A9
Hovsta *Sweden* 59°22N 15°15E **162** E9
Howakil *Eritrea* 15°10N 40°16E **257** D5
Howar, Wadi → *Sudan* 17°30N 27°8E **257** D2
Howard *Queens., Australia* 25°16S 152°32E **281** D5
Howard *Pa., U.S.A.* 41°1N 77°40W **312** F7
Howard *S. Dak., U.S.A.* 44°1N 97°32W **308** C5
Howard Beach *U.S.A.* 40°39N 73°50W **132** C2
Howe *U.S.A.* 43°48N 113°0W **304** E7
Howe, C. *Australia* 37°30S 150°0E **283** D9
Howe, West Cape *Australia* 35°8S 117°36E **279** G2
Howe I. *Canada* 44°16N 76°17W **313** B8
Howell *U.S.A.* 42°36N 83°56W **311** B13
Howick *Qué., Canada* 45°11N 73°51W **313** A11
Howick *N.Z.* 36°54S 174°56E **284** C3
Howick *KwaZulu Natal, S. Africa* 29°28S 30°14E **271** C5
Howick Group *Australia* 14°20S 145°30E **280** A4
Howitt, L. *Australia* 27°40S 138°40E **281** D2
Howland I. *Pac. Oc.* 0°48N 176°38W **288** G10
Howlong *Australia* 35°59S 146°38E **283** C7
Howrah = Haora *India* 22°34N 88°18E **124** B1
Howth *Ireland* 53°23N 6°7W **166** C5
Howth Hd. *Ireland* 53°22N 6°4W **166** C5
Höxter *Germany* 51°46N 9°22E **178** D5
Hoxtolgay *China* 46°35N 85°59E **217** C11
Hoxton *London, U.K.* **125** a5
Hoxud *China* 42°15N 86°51E **217** D11
Hoy *U.K.* 58°50N 3°15W **167** C5
Hoya *Niedersachsen, Germany* 52°49N 9°8E **178** C5
Hōya *Tōkyō, Japan* 35°44N 139°34E **140** A2
Høyanger *Norway* 61°13N 6°4E **164** C3
Hoyerswerda *Germany* 51°26N 14°14E **178** D10
Hōyo-Kaikyō *Japan* 33°20N 131°58E **222** D3
Hoyos *Spain* 40°9N 6°45W **194** E4
Hpa-an = Pa-an *Myanmar* 16°51N 97°40E **241** G6
Hpakant *Myanmar* 25°37N 96°20E **241** C6
Hpawlum *Myanmar* 27°12N 98°12E **241** B7
Hpettintha *Myanmar* 24°14N 95°23E **241** C5
Hpizow *Myanmar* 26°57N 98°24E **241** B7
Hpunan Pass *Asia* 27°30N 96°55E **241** A6
Hpyu = Pyu *Myanmar* 18°30N 96°28E **241** F6
Hradčany *Czechia* 50°5N 14°24E **135** B2
Hradec Králové *Czechia* 50°15N 15°50E **180** A8
Hrádek *Czechia* 48°46N 16°16E **181** C9
Hrafnseyri *Iceland* 65°46N 23°28W **155** B3
Hranice *Czechia* 49°34N 17°45E **181** B10
Hrazdan *Armenia* 40°30N 44°46E **191** K7
Hrebenka *Ukraine* 50°9N 32°22E **189** G7
Hrífunes *Iceland* 63°38N 18°30W **155** D8
Hrísey *Iceland* 66°0N 18°23W **155** B8
Hrisoupoli = Chrisoupoli *Greece* 40°58N 24°42E **203** F8
Hrodna *Belarus* 53°42N 23°52E **184** E10
Hrodna □ *Belarus* 53°20N 24°45E **188** F3
Hrodzyanka *Belarus* 53°31N 28°42E **177** B15
Hron → *Slovakia* 47°49N 18°45E **181** D11
Hrubieszów *Poland* 50°49N 23°51E **185** H10
Hrubý Jeseník *Czechia* 50°5N 17°10E **181** A10
Hrvatska = Croatia ■ *Europe* 45°20N 16°0E **199** C13
Hrymayliv *Ukraine* 49°20N 26°5E **177** D14
Hrynyava *Ukraine* 47°59N 24°53E **183** C9
Hsa-paw *Myanmar* 19°1N 97°30E **241** F6
Hsenwi *Myanmar* 23°22N 97°55E **241** D6
Hsi-hkip *Myanmar* 20°25N 96°42E **241** E6
Hsiafu *Taiwan* 25°7N 121°17E **225** A3
Hsiamen = Xiamen *China* 24°25N 118°4E **229** E12
Hsian = Xi'an *China* 34°15N 109°0E **226** G5
Hsiangshan *Taiwan* 24°48N 120°54E **225** B2
Hsiaochinmen Tao *Taiwan* 24°26N 118°14E **225** a
Hsiaohungt'ou Hsü *Taiwan* 21°57N 121°36E **225** E3
Hsiaokang *Taiwan* 22°34N 120°20E **225** D2
Hsiatahsi *Taiwan* 22°28N 120°56E **225** D2
Hsiaying *Taiwan* 23°14N 120°15E **225** C2
Hsichih *Taiwan* 25°4N 121°39E **225** A3
Hsikang *Taiwan* 23°7N 120°12E **225** C2
Hsilo *Taiwan* 23°48N 120°27E **225** C2
Hsinche *Taiwan* 24°10N 120°50E **225** B2
Hsinch'eng *Taiwan* 24°8N 121°39E **225** B3
Hsinchu *Taiwan* 24°48N 120°58E **225** B2
Hsinchu □ *Taiwan* 24°45N 121°10E **225** B3
Hsinchuang *Kaohsiung, Taiwan* 22°34N 120°29E **225** D2
Hsinchuang *T'aipei, Taiwan* 25°2N 121°27E **225** A3
Hsinfa *Taiwan* 23°1N 120°39E **225** C2
Hsinfeng *Taiwan* 24°54N 120°59E **225** B2
Hsinhailien = Lianyungang *China* 34°40N 119°11E **227** G10
Hsinhua *Taiwan* 23°2N 120°18E **225** C2
Hsini *Taiwan* 23°41N 120°51E **225** C2
Hsinkai = Bhamo *Myanmar* 24°15N 97°15E **241** C6
Hsinking = Changchun *China* 43°57N 125°17E **227** C13
Hsinpi *Taiwan* 22°28N 120°33E **225** D2
Hsinshih *Taiwan* 23°4N 120°17E **225** C2
Hsintien *Taiwan* 24°57N 121°32E **225** B3
Hsinwu *Taiwan* 24°59N 121°6E **225** B3
Hsinying *Taiwan* 23°21N 120°17E **225** C2
Hsinyuan *Taiwan* 22°32N 120°23E **225** D2
Hsipaw *Myanmar* 22°37N 97°18E **241** D6
Hsiukuluan Hsi → *Taiwan* 23°28N 121°30E **225** C3
Hsiushui *Taiwan* 24°3N 120°29E **225** B2
Hsiyu *Taiwan* 23°36N 119°30E **225** C1
Hsopket *Myanmar* 23°11N 98°26E **228** F2
Hsüchou = Xuzhou *China* 34°18N 117°10E **227** G9
Hsüeh Shan *China* 24°24N 121°12E **225** B3
Hsüehchia *Taiwan* 23°14N 120°10E **225** C2
Hsühaitsun *Taiwan* 22°12N 120°52E **225** D2
Htawei = Dawei *Myanmar* 14°2N 98°12E **236** E2
Hu Xian *China* 34°8N 108°42E **226** G5
Hua Hin *Thailand* 12°34N 99°58E **236** F2
Hua Lamphong Railway Station *Bangkok, Thailand* **113** c2
Hua Muang *Laos* 20°13N 103°52E **236** B4
Hua Shan *China* 34°28N 110°4E **226** G6
Hua Xian *Henan, China* 35°30N 114°30E **226** G8
Hua Xian *Shaanxi, China* 34°30N 109°48E **226** G5
Hua Yü *Taiwan* 23°24N 119°19E **225** C1
Hua'an *China* 25°1N 117°32E **229** E11
Huab → *Namibia* 20°52S 13°25E **270** A2
Huacaya *Bolivia* 20°45S 63°43W **331** E5
Huachacalla *Bolivia* 18°45S 68°17W **330** D4
Huacheng *China* 24°4N 115°37E **229** E10
Huachinera *Mexico* 30°9N 108°55W **318** A3
Huacho *Peru* 11°10S 77°35W **330** C2
Huachón *Peru* 10°35S 76°0W **330** C2
Huade *China* 41°55N 113°59E **226** D7
Huadian *China* 43°0N 126°40E **227** C14
Huadu *China* 23°22N 113°12E **229** F9
Huahine, Î. *French Polynesia* 16°46S 150°58W **289** f
Huai Hat △ *Thailand* 16°52N 104°17E **236** D5
Huai He → *China* 33°0N 118°30E **229** A12

Huai Kha Khaeng ⌓ *Thailand* 15°20N 98°55E **236** E2
Huai Nam Dang △ *Thailand* 19°30N 98°30E **236** C2
Huai Yot *Thailand* 7°45N 99°37E **237** J2
Huai'an *Hebei, China* 40°30N 114°20E **226** D8
Huai'an *Jiangsu, China* 33°30N 119°10E **227** H10
Huaibei *China* 34°0N 116°48E **226** G9
Huaibin *China* 32°32N 115°27E **229** A10
Huaicho = Puerto Acosta *Bolivia* 15°32S 69°15W **330** D4
Huaide = Gongzhuling *China* 43°30N 124°40E **227** C13
Huaidezhen *China* 43°48N 124°50E **227** C13
Huaihua *China* 27°32N 109°57E **228** D7
Huaiji *China* 23°55N 112°12E **229** F9
Huainan *China* 32°38N 116°58E **229** A11
Huaining *China* 30°24N 116°40E **229** B11
Huairen *China* 39°48N 113°20E **226** E7
Huairou *China* 40°20N 116°35E **226** D9
Huaiyang *China* 33°40N 114°52E **226** H8
Huaiyin *China* 33°30N 119°2E **227** H10
Huaiyuan *Anhui, China* 32°55N 117°10E **229** A11
Huaiyuan *Guangxi Zhuangzu, China* 24°31N 108°22E **228** E7
Huajuapán de León *Mexico* 17°48N 97°46W **319** D5
Hualālai *U.S.A.* 19°42N 155°52W **302** D6
Hualapai Peak *U.S.A.* 35°5N 113°54W **307** K13
Hualian = Hualien *Taiwan* 23°59N 121°36E **225** C3
Hualien *Taiwan* 23°59N 121°36E **225** C3
Hualien □ *Taiwan* 23°45N 121°25E **225** C3
Huallaga → *Peru* 5°15S 75°30W **330** B2
Huallanca *Peru* 8°50S 77°56W **330** B2
Huamachuco *Peru* 7°50S 78°5W **330** B2
Huambo *Angola* 12°42S 15°54E **265** E3
Huambo □ *Angola* 13°0S 16°0E **265** E3
Huan Jiang → *China* 34°28N 109°0E **226** G5
Huan Xian *China* 36°33N 107°7E **226** F4
Huancabamba *Peru* 5°10S 79°15W **330** B2
Huancane *Peru* 15°10S 69°44W **330** D4
Huancapi *Peru* 13°40S 74°0W **330** C3
Huancavelica *Peru* 12°50S 75°5W **330** C2
Huancavelica □ *Peru* 13°0S 75°0W **330** C3
Huancayo *Peru* 12°5S 75°12W **330** C2
Huanchaca *Bolivia* 20°15S 66°40W **330** E4
Huanchaca, Serranía de *Bolivia* 14°30S 60°39W **331** C5
Huang Hai = Yellow Sea *China* 35°0N 123°0E **227** G12
Huang He → *China* 37°55N 118°50E **227** F10
Huang Xian *China* 37°38N 120°30E **227** F11
Huangchuan *China* 32°15N 115°10E **229** A10
Huangdao *China* 36°0N 120°7E **227** G11
Huanggang *China* 30°29N 114°52E **229** B10
Huangguoshu *China* 26°0N 105°40E **228** E5
Huanghua *China* 38°22N 117°20E **227** E9
Huanghuagang *China* 38°20N 117°54E **227** E9
Huanghuagang Mausoleum *China* 23°9N 113°17E **121** B2
Huangling *China* 35°34N 109°15E **226** G5
Huanglong *China* 35°30N 109°59E **226** G5
Huanglong ⌓ *China* 32°44N 103°50E **228** A4
Huanglongtan *China* 32°40N 110°33E **229** A8
Huangmei *China* 30°5N 115°56E **229** B10
Huangpi *China* 30°50N 114°22E **229** B10
Huangping *China* 26°52N 107°54E **228** D6
Huangpu *China* 31°14N 121°30E **138** B2
Huangpu Jiang → *China* 31°11N 121°29E **138** B1
Huangshan *Anhui, China* 30°8N 118°9E **229** B12
Huangshan *Anhui, China* 29°42N 118°25E **229** C12
Huangshi *China* 30°10N 115°3E **229** B10
Huangsongdian *China* 43°45N 127°25E **227** C14
Huangtugang *China* 39°49N 116°15E **114** C1
Huangyan *China* 28°38N 121°19E **229** C13
Huangyangsi *China* 26°33N 111°39E **229** D8
Huaning *China* 24°17N 102°56E **228** E4
Huanjiang *China* 24°50N 108°18E **228** E7
Huanren *China* 41°23N 125°20E **224** B2
Huanren Shuiku *China* 41°17N 125°34E **224** B2
Huanta *Peru* 12°55S 74°20W **330** C3
Huantai *China* 36°58N 117°56E **227** F9
Huánuco *Peru* 9°55S 76°15W **330** B2
Huánuco □ *Peru* 9°55S 76°14W **330** B2
Huanuni *Bolivia* 18°16S 66°51W **330** D4
Huanzo, Cordillera de *Peru* 14°35S 73°20W **330** C3
Huaping *China* 26°46N 101°25E **228** D3
Huara *Chile* 19°59S 69°47W **330** D4
Huaral *Peru* 11°32S 77°13W **330** C2
Huaraz *Peru* 9°30S 77°32W **330** B2
Huari *Peru* 9°14S 77°14W **330** B2
Huarmey *Peru* 10°5S 78°5W **330** C2
Huarochiri *Peru* 12°9S 76°15W **330** C2
Huarocondo *Peru* 13°26S 72°14W **330** C3
Huarong *China* 29°29N 112°30E **229** C9
Huascar *Peru* 11°59S 77°1W **124** A2
Huascarán, Nevado *Peru* 9°7S 77°37W **330** B2
Huasco *Chile* 28°30S 71°15W **334** B1
Huasco → *Chile* 28°27S 71°13W **334** B1
Huasna *U.S.A.* 35°6N 120°24W **307** K6
Huatabampo *Mexico* 26°50N 109°38W **318** B3
Huauchinango *Mexico* 20°12N 98°3W **319** C5
Huautla de Jiménez *Mexico* 18°8N 96°51W **319** D5
Huaxi *China* 26°25N 106°40E **228** D6
Huay Khwang *Thailand* 13°47N 100°33E **113** B2
Huayhuash, Cordillera *Peru* 10°30S 76°45W **330** B2
Huayin *China* 34°35N 110°5E **226** G6
Huaying *China* 30°8N 106°44E **228** B6
Huayllay *Peru* 11°3S 76°21W **330** C2
Huayuan *China* 28°37N 109°29E **228** C7
Huazhou *China* 21°33N 110°33E **229** G8
Hubballi *India* 15°22N 75°15E **245** G2
Hubbard *Iowa, U.S.A.* 42°18N 93°18W **310** B3
Hubbard *Ohio, U.S.A.* 41°9N 80°34W **312** E4
Hubbard *Tex., U.S.A.* 31°51N 96°48W **314** F6
Hubbard, Mt. *N. Amer.* 60°19N 139°4W **303** F13
Hubbard Glacier *Canada* 60°18N 139°22W **294** E4
Hubbart Pt. *Canada* 59°21N 94°41W **297** B10
Hubei □ *China* 31°0N 112°0E **229** B9
Hubli = Hubballi *India* 15°22N 75°15E **245** G2
Huch'ang *N. Korea* 41°25N 127°2E **224** B3
Huchow = Huzhou *China* 30°51N 120°8E **229** B13
Hucknall *U.K.* 53°3N 1°13W **168** D6
Huddersfield *U.K.* 53°39N 1°47W **168** D6
Huddinge *Sweden* 59°14N 18°0E **139** B2
Hude *Germany* 53°7N 8°26E **178** B4
Hudi *Sudan* 17°43N 34°18E **256** D3
Hudiksvall *Sweden* 61°43N 17°10E **162** C11
Hudson *Ont., Canada* 50°6N 92°9W **298** B1
Hudson *Fla., U.S.A.* 28°22N 82°42W **317** G7
Hudson *Mass., U.S.A.* 42°23N 71°34W **313** D13
Hudson *Mich., U.S.A.* 41°51N 84°21W **311** C12
Hudson *N.Y., U.S.A.* 42°15N 73°46W **313** D11
Hudson *Wis., U.S.A.* 44°58N 92°45W **308** C7
Hudson *Wyo., U.S.A.* 42°54N 108°35W **304** E9
Hudson → *U.S.A.* 40°42N 74°2W **313** F10
Hudson, C. *Antarctica* 68°21S 153°45E **151** C10
Hudson, Vol. *Chile* 46°4S 72°55W **336** C2
Hudson Bay *Nunavut, Canada* 60°0N 86°0W **295** F14
Hudson Bay *Sask., Canada* 52°51N 102°23W **297** C8
Hudson Falls *U.S.A.* 43°18N 73°35W **313** C11
Hudson Mts. *Antarctica* 74°32S 99°20W **151** D16
Hudson River Park *New York, U.S.A.* **132** e1
Hudson Str. *Canada* 62°0N 70°0W **295** E18
Hudson's Hope *Canada* 56°0N 121°54W **296** B4
Hudsonville *U.S.A.* 42°52N 85°52W **311** B11
Hue *Vietnam* 16°30N 107°35E **236** D6
Huebra → *Spain* 41°2N 6°48W **194** D4
Huechuraba *Chile* 33°22S 70°39W **137** B1
Huedin *Romania* 46°52N 23°2E **182** D8
Huehuetenango *Guatemala* 15°20N 91°28W **320** C1
Huejúcar *Mexico* 22°21N 103°13W **318** C4
Huélamo *Spain* 40°17N 1°48W **196** E3
Huelgoat *France* 48°22N 3°46W **174** D3
Huelma *Spain* 37°39N 3°28W **195** H7
Huelva *Spain* 37°18N 6°57W **195** H4
Huelva □ *Spain* 37°40N 7°0W **195** H4
Huelva → *Spain* 37°27N 6°0W **195** H5
Hueneme = Port Hueneme *U.S.A.* 34°7N 119°12W **307** L7
Huentelauquén *Chile* 31°38S 71°33W **334** C1
Huércal-Overa *Spain* 37°23N 1°57W **197** H3
Huerquehue △ *Chile* 39°6S 71°42W **336** A2
Huerta, Sa. de la *Argentina* 31°10S 67°30W **334** C2
Huertas, C. de las *Spain* 38°21N 0°24W **197** G4
Huerva → *Spain* 41°39N 0°52W **196** D4
Huesca *Spain* 42°8N 0°25W **196** C4
Huesca □ *Spain* 42°20N 0°1E **196** C5
Huéscar *Spain* 37°44N 2°35W **197** H2
Hueso Ballena, Pta. *Chile* 33°40S 78°46W **330** c
Huetamo *Mexico* 18°35N 100°53W **318** D4
Huete *Spain* 40°10N 2°43W **196** E2
Huevos I. *Trin. & Tob.* 10°42N 61°43W **323** t
Huger *U.S.A.* 33°6N 79°48W **316** B10
Hugh → *Australia* 25°1S 134°1E **280** D1
Hugh Taylor Birch State Recr. Area ⌓ *U.S.A.* 26°8N 80°6W **129** B3
Hughenden *Australia* 20°52S 144°10E **280** C3
Hughes *U.S.A.* 66°3N 154°15W **303** C9
Hughesville *U.S.A.* 41°14N 76°44W **313** E8
Hugli → *India* 21°56N 88°4E **243** J13
Hugo *Colo., U.S.A.* 39°8N 103°28W **304** G12
Hugo *Okla., U.S.A.* 34°1N 95°31W **314** D7
Hugoton *U.S.A.* 37°11N 101°21W **308** G3
Huguang Opera Museum *Beijing, China* **114** c2
Huhehaote = Hohhot *China* 40°52N 111°40E **226** D6
Huhsi *Taiwan* 23°35N 119°39E **225** C1
Hui Xian = Huixian *China* 35°27N 113°12E **226** G7
Hui Xian *China* 33°50N 106°4E **226** H4
Hui'an *China* 25°1N 118°43E **229** E12
Hui'anbu *China* 37°28N 106°38E **226** F4
Huiarau Ra. *N.Z.* 38°45S 176°55E **284** E5
Huichang *China* 25°32N 115°45E **229** E10
Huichapan *Mexico* 20°23N 99°39W **319** C5
Huichon *N. Korea* 40°10N 126°16E **224** D3
Huidong *Guangdong, China* 22°58N 114°43E **229** F10
Huidong *Sichuan, China* 26°34N 102°35E **228** D4
Huifa He → *China* 43°0N 127°50E **227** C14
Huíla *Angola* 15°4S 13°32E **265** F2
Huíla □ *Angola* 14°0S 15°0E **265** E2
Huila □ *Colombia* 2°30N 75°45W **328** C2
Huila, Nevado del *Colombia* 3°0N 76°0W **328** C2
Huilai *China* 23°0N 116°18E **229** F11
Huili *China* 26°35N 102°17E **228** D4
Huimin *China* 37°27N 117°28E **227** F9
Huinan *China* 42°40N 126°2E **224** A3
Huinca Renancó *Argentina* 34°51S 64°22W **334** C3
Huining *China* 35°38N 105°0E **226** G3
Huinong *China* 39°5N 106°35E **226** E4
Huiroa *N.Z.* 39°15S 174°30E **284** F3
Huishui *China* 26°7N 106°38E **228** D6
Huisne → *France* 47°59N 0°11E **172** E7
Huiting *China* 34°5N 116°5E **226** G9
Huitong *China* 26°51N 109°45E **228** D7
Huixian *China* 35°27N 113°12E **226** G7
Huixtla *Mexico* 15°9N 92°28W **319** D6
Huize *China* 26°24N 103°15E **228** D4
Huizhou *China* 23°0N 114°23E **229** F10
Huizingen *Belgium* 50°45N 4°17E **116** B1
Hukawng Valley *Myanmar* 26°30N 96°30E **241** B6
Hukeri *India* 16°14N 74°36E **245** F2
Hukou *Jiangxi, China* 29°45N 116°21E **229** C11
Huk'ou *Taiwan* 24°54N 121°2E **225** B3
Hukuntsi *Botswana* 23°58S 21°45E **270** B3
Hula *Papua N. G.* 10°5S 147°43E **286** F4
Ḩulayfā' *Si. Arabia* 25°58N 40°45E **246** E4
Huld = Ulaanjirem *Mongolia* 45°5N 105°30E **226** B3
Hulin *China* 45°48N 132°59E **219** B15
Hulin He → *China* 45°0N 122°10E **227** B12
Hull = Kingston upon Hull *U.K.* 53°45N 0°21W **168** D7
Hull *Canada* 45°26N 75°43W **313** A9
Hull → *U.K.* 53°44N 0°20W **168** D7
Hulst *Neths.* 51°17N 4°2E **170** C4
Hultschin = Hlučín *Czechia* 49°54N 18°11E **181** B11
Hultsfred *Sweden* 57°30N 15°52E **163** G9
Huludao *China* 40°45N 120°50E **227** D11
Hulun = Hailar *China* 49°10N 119°38E **219** B12
Hulun Nur *China* 49°0N 117°30E **219** B12
Hulunbuir = Hailar *China* 49°10N 119°38E **219** B12
Hulyaypole *Ukraine* 47°45N 36°21E **189** J9
Huma, Tanjung *Malaysia* 5°29N 100°16E **237** c
Humacao *Puerto Rico* 18°9N 65°50W **321** b
Humahuaca *Argentina* 23°10S 65°25W **334** A2
Humaitá = Porto Walter *Brazil* 8°15S 72°40W **330** B3
Humaitá *Brazil* 7°35S 63°1W **331** B5
Humaitá *Paraguay* 27°2S 58°31W **334** B4
Humansdorp *S. Africa* 34°2S 24°46E **270** D3
Humansville *U.S.A.* 37°48N 93°35W **310** G3
Humara, J. *Sudan* 16°16N 30°59E **257** D3
Humayun's Tomb *India* 28°35N 77°15E **120** B2
Humbe *Angola* 16°40S 14°55E **265** F2
Humbe, Serra do *Angola* 12°10S 15°25E **265** E2
Humber → *Ont., Canada* 43°47N 79°38W **141** A1
Humber → *England, U.K.* 53°42N 0°27W **168** D7
Humber B. *Canada* 43°37N 79°27W **141** B2
Humber Bay *Canada* 43°38N 79°29W **141** B2
Humber Bay Park *Canada* 43°37N 79°28W **141** B2
Humber College *Canada* 43°35N 79°30W **141** B1
Humber Summit *Canada* 43°45N 79°32W **141** B1
Humber Valley Village *Canada* 43°40N 79°31W **141** A1
Humberlea *Canada* 43°43N 79°31W **141** A1
Humberwood Park *Canada* 43°44N 79°37W **141** A1
Humboldt *Sask., Canada* 52°15N 105°9W **297** C7
Humboldt *Iowa, U.S.A.* 42°44N 94°13W **310** B3
Humboldt *Tenn., U.S.A.* 35°50N 88°55W **315** D10
Humboldt → *U.S.A.* 39°59N 118°36W **304** G4
Humboldt Forum *Berlin, Germany* **115** a5
Humboldt Gletscher = Sermersuaq *Greenland* 79°30N 62°0W **154** B4
Humboldt Mts. *N.Z.* 44°30S 168°15E **285** E3
Humboldt Park *U.S.A.* 41°54N 87°42W **119** B2
Humboldt, Mt. *N. Cal.* 21°53S 166°25E **288** d
Hume *U.S.A.* 36°48N 118°54W **306** J8
Hume, L. *Australia* 36°0S 147°5E **283** D7
Humen *China* 22°50N 113°40E **219** a
Humenné *Slovakia* 48°55N 21°50E **181** C14
Humera *Spain* 40°25N 3°46W **127** B1
Humeston *U.S.A.* 40°52N 93°30W **310** D3
Hummelsta *Sweden* 59°34N 16°58E **162** E10
Hummelvika *Norway* 63°29N 8°19E **164** A5
Hummingbird Centre *Toronto, Canada* **141** b3
Hummock Hill = Whyalla *Australia* 33°2S 137°30E **282** B2
Humpata *Angola* 15°2S 13°24E **265** F2
Humphreys, Mt. *U.S.A.* 37°17N 118°40W **306** H8
Humphreys Peak *U.S.A.* 35°21N 111°41W **305** J8
Humpolec *Czechia* 49°31N 15°20E **180** B8
Humptulips *U.S.A.* 47°14N 123°57W **306** C3
Humula *Australia* 35°30S 147°46E **283** C7
Hūn *Libya* 29°2N 16°0E **258** C3
Hun He → *China* 40°41N 122°8E **224** B1
Hun Jiang → *China* 40°50N 125°38E **227** D13
Húnaflói *Iceland* 65°50N 20°50W **155** B6
Hunan □ *China* 27°30N 112°0E **229** D9
Húnavatnssýsla *Iceland* 65°30N 20°25W **155** B6
Hunaydī *Iraq* 33°18N 44°29E **113** B2
Hunchun *China* 42°52N 130°28E **227** C16
Hundested *Denmark* 55°58N 11°52E **163** J5
Hundewali *Pakistan* 31°55N 72°38E **242** D5
Hundige *Denmark* 55°35N 12°18E **118** B1
Hundige Strand *Denmark* 55°35N 12°20E **118** B2
Hundorp *Norway* 61°33N 9°59E **164** C7
Hundred Islands △ *Phil.* 16°10N 120°2E **232** C3
Hundred Mile House *Canada* 51°38N 121°18W **296** C4
Hundvåg *Norway* 59°0N 5°43E **164** E2
Hunedoara *Romania* 45°40N 22°50E **182** E7
Hunedoara □ *Romania* 45°50N 22°54E **182** E7
Hunei *Taiwan* 22°53N 120°14E **225** D2
Hünfeld *Germany* 50°39N 9°46E **178** E5
Hung Hom *Hong Kong, China* 22°18N 114°11E **122** B3
Hung Yen *Vietnam* 20°39N 106°4E **228** G6
Hunga Ha'apai *Tonga* 20°41S 175°7W **287** Q13
Hungary ■ *Europe* 47°20N 19°20E **181** D12
Hungary, Plain of *Europe* 47°0N 20°0E **158** F10
Hungerford *Australia* 28°58S 144°24E **281** D3
Hŭngnam *N. Korea* 39°49N 127°45E **224** D3
Hungt'ou Hsü = Lan Yü *Taiwan* 22°4N 121°25E **225** D3
Huni Valley *Ghana* 5°33N 1°56W **262** D4
Hunjiang *China* 41°54N 126°26E **224** B3
Hunneberg *Sweden* 58°18N 12°30E **163** F6
Hunnebostrand *Sweden* 58°27N 11°18E **163** F5
Hunsberge *Namibia* 27°45S 17°12E **270** C2
Hunsrück *Germany* 49°56N 7°27E **179** F3
Hunstanton *U.K.* 52°56N 0°29E **168** E8
Hunsur *India* 12°16N 76°16E **245** H3
Hunte → *Germany* 53°14N 8°28E **178** B4
Hunter *N.Z.* 44°36S 171°2E **285** E6
Hunter *N.Y., U.S.A.* 42°13N 74°13W **313** D10
Hunter → *N.S.W., Australia* 32°52S 151°46E **283** B9
Hunter → *N.Z.* 44°21S 169°27E **285** E4
Hunter, C. *Solomon Is.* 9°48S 159°50E **287** M10
Hunter Hills, The *N.Z.* 44°26S 170°46E **285** E5
Hunter I. *Tas., Australia* 40°30S 144°45E **281** G3
Hunter I. *B.C., Canada* 51°55N 128°0W **296** C3
Hunter Mts. *N.Z.* 45°43S 167°25E **285** F2
Hunter Ra. *Australia* 32°45S 150°15E **283** B9
Hunters Hill *Australia* 33°50S 151°9E **139** B1
Hunters Pt. *U.S.A.* 37°43N 122°21W **136** B2
Hunters Road *Zimbabwe* 19°9S 29°49E **269** F2
Hunterville *N.Z.* 39°56S 175°35E **284** F4
Huntingburg *U.S.A.* 38°18N 86°57W **311** F10
Huntingdon *Cambs., U.K.* 52°20N 0°11W **169** E7
Huntingdon *Pa., U.S.A.* 40°30N 78°1W **312** F6
Huntington = Shelton *U.S.A.* 41°19N 73°5W **313** E11
Huntington *Ind., U.S.A.* 40°53N 85°30W **311** D11
Huntington *N.Y., U.S.A.* 40°52N 73°26W **313** F11
Huntington *Oreg., U.S.A.* 44°21N 117°16W **304** D5
Huntington *Utah, U.S.A.* 39°20N 110°58W **304** G8
Huntington *Va., U.S.A.* 38°47N 77°4W **143** C2
Huntington *W. Va., U.S.A.* 38°25N 82°27W **309** F12
Huntington Beach *U.S.A.* 33°40N 118°5W **307** M9
Huntington Park *U.S.A.* 33°58N 118°13W **126** C3
Huntley *Jamaica* 18°4N 77°35W **320** a
Huntley *Ill., U.S.A.* 42°10N 88°26W **311** B8
Huntly *N.Z.* 37°34S 175°11E **284** D4
Huntly *Aberds., U.K.* 57°27N 2°47W **167** D6
Huntsville *Ont., Canada* 45°20N 79°14W **312** A5
Huntsville *Ala., U.S.A.* 34°44N 86°35W **315** D11
Huntsville *Mo., U.S.A.* 39°26N 92°33W **310** E4
Huntsville *Tex., U.S.A.* 30°43N 95°33W **314** F7
Hunyani → *Zimbabwe* 15°57S 30°39E **269** F3
Hunyuan *China* 39°42N 113°42E **226** E7
Hunza → *India* 35°54N 74°20E **243** B6
Huo Shan *China* 36°26N 111°52E **226** F6
Huo Xian = Huozhou *China* 36°36N 111°42E **226** F6
Huocheng *China* 44°0N 80°48E **217** D10
Huolin Gol *China* 45°32N 119°38E **227** B10
Huon G. *Papua N. G.* 7°0S 147°30E **286** D4
Huon Pen. *Papua N. G.* 6°20S 147°30E **286** D4
Huong Khe *Vietnam* 18°13N 105°41E **236** C5
Huonville *Australia* 43°0S 147°5E **281** G4
Huoqiu *China* 32°20N 116°12E **229** A11
Huoshan *China* 31°25N 116°20E **229** B11
Huoshao Dao = Lütao *Taiwan* 22°40N 121°30E **225** D3
Huozhou *China* 36°36N 111°42E **226** F6
Hupeh = Hubei □ *China* 31°0N 112°0E **229** B9
Ḩūr *Iran* 30°50N 57°7E **247** D8
Hurānd *Iran* 38°51N 47°22E **213** C12
Ḩuraymila *Si. Arabia* 25°8N 46°8E **246** E5
Hurbanovo *Slovakia* 47°51N 18°11E **181** D11
Hurd, C. *Canada* 45°13N 81°44W **312** A3
Hurdiyo *Somalia* 10°33N 51°6E **267** B7
Hure Qi *China* 42°45N 121°45E **227** C11
Hurezani *Romania* 44°49N 23°40E **183** F8
Hurghada *Egypt* 27°15N 33°50E **256** B3
Hurīya *Iraq* 33°21N 44°19E **113** A1
Hurley *N. Mex., U.S.A.* 32°42N 108°8W **305** K9
Hurley *Wis., U.S.A.* 46°27N 90°11W **308** B8
Huron *Calif., U.S.A.* 36°12N 120°6W **306** J6
Huron *Ohio, U.S.A.* 41°24N 82°33W **312** E2
Huron *S. Dak., U.S.A.* 44°22N 98°13W **308** C4
Huron, L. *U.S.A.* 44°30N 82°40W **312** B2
Huron East *Canada* 43°37N 81°18W **312** C3
Hurricane *U.S.A.* 37°11N 113°17W **305** H7
Hurso *Ethiopia* 9°35N 41°33E **257** F5
Hurst *U.S.A.* 32°49N 97°10W **120** B3
Hurstville *Australia* 33°57S 151°6E **139** B1
Hurtsboro *U.S.A.* 32°15N 85°25W **316** C4
Hurungwe ⌓ *Zimbabwe* 16°7S 29°5E **269** F2
Hurunui → *N.Z.* 42°54S 173°18E **285** C8
Hurup *Denmark* 56°46N 8°25E **163** H2
Húsafell *Iceland* 64°42N 20°53W **155** C6
Husan *West Bank* 31°42N 35°8E **123** B1
Húsavík *Iceland* 66°3N 17°21W **155** A9
Husby *Sweden* 59°24N 17°56E **139** A1
Huşi *Romania* 46°41N 28°7E **183** D13
Huskisson *Australia* 35°2S 150°41E **283** C9
Huskvarna *Sweden* 57°47N 14°15E **163** G8
Huslia *U.S.A.* 65°41N 156°24W **303** D8
Husnes *Norway* 59°52N 5°45E **164** E2
Hustad *Norway* 62°57N 7°6E **164** B4
Hustadvika *Norway* 63°0N 7°0E **164** A3
Hustontown *U.S.A.* 40°3N 78°2W **312** F6
Hustopeče *Czechia* 48°57N 16°43E **181** C9
Husum *København, Denmark* 55°42N 12°27E **118** A2
Husum *Schleswig-Holstein, Germany* 54°28N 9°4E **178** A5
Husum *Sweden* 63°21N 19°12E **162** A13
Huszt = Khust *Ukraine* 48°10N 23°18E **183** B8
Hutanopan *Indonesia* 0°40N 99°42E **234** B1
Hutchins *U.S.A.* 32°38N 96°42W **120** C3
Hutchinson *Kans., U.S.A.* 38°5N 97°56W **308** F5
Hutchinson *Minn., U.S.A.* 44°54N 94°22W **308** C6
Ḩūth *Yemen* 16°14N 43°58E **248** C3
Hutiao Xia *China* 27°13N 100°9E **228** D3
Hutjena *Papua N. G.* 5°23S 154°42E **286** C8
Hutsonville *U.S.A.* 39°7N 87°40W **311** E9
Hutte Sauvage, L. de la *Canada* 56°15N 64°45W **299** A7
Hütteldorf *Austria* 48°12N 16°15E **142** A1
Hüttenberg *Austria* 46°56N 14°33E **180** E7
Hüttener Berge ⌓ *Germany* 54°24N 9°40E **178** A5
Hutton, Mt. *Australia* 25°51S 148°20E **281** D4
Huvadu Atoll *Maldives* 0°30N 73°15E **272** d
Hüvösvölgy *Hungary* 47°32N 19°0E **117** A2
Huwaki *Indonesia* 7°55S 126°30E **231** F7
Huwei *Taiwan* 23°42N 120°26E **225** C2
Huwei Hsi → *Taiwan* 23°37N 120°22E **225** C2
Huwon Secret Garden *S. Korea* 37°34N 126°59E **137** B1
Huwun *Ethiopia* 4°23N 40°6E **257** G5
Huy *Belgium* 50°31N 5°15E **170** D5
Huzhou *China* 30°51N 120°8E **229** B13
Huzurabad *India* 18°12N 79°25E **244** E4
Huzurnagar *India* 16°54N 79°53E **244** F4
Hvalfjörður *Iceland* 64°20N 21°40W **155** C5
Hvalpsund *Denmark* 56°42N 9°11E **163** H3
Hvalstad *Norway* 59°51N 10°27E **133** A1
Hvalstrand *Norway* 59°50N 10°30E **133** A2
Hvammsfjörður *Iceland* 65°4N 22°5W **155** B4
Hvammstangi *Iceland* 65°24N 20°57W **155** B6
Hvammur *Norðurland Vestra Iceland* 65°53N 19°51W **155** B7
Hvammur *Vesturland Iceland* 64°50N 21°21W **155** C5
Hvannadalshnúkur *Iceland* 64°1N 16°41W **155** C10
Hvanneyri *Iceland* 64°34N 21°36W **155** C5
Hvar *Croatia* 43°11N 16°28E **199** E13
Hvarski Kanal *Croatia* 43°15N 16°35E **199** E13
Hveragerði *Iceland* 64°0N 21°12W **155** C5
Hvidovre *Denmark* 55°38N 12°27E **118** B2
Hvítá → *Iceland* 64°30N 21°58W **155** C5
Hvítárvatn *Iceland* 64°37N 19°50W **155** C7
Hvittingfoss *Norway* 59°29N 10°0E **164** E7
Hvizdets *Ukraine* 48°35N 25°17E **183** B10
Hvolsvöllur *Iceland* 63°45N 20°14W **155** D6
Hwacheon-Cheosuji *S. Korea* 38°5N 127°50E **224** D3
Hwagok *S. Korea* 37°32N 126°51E **137** B1
Hwainan = Huainan *China* 32°38N 116°58E **229** A11
Hwaiyin = Huaiyin *China* 33°30N 119°2E **227** H10
Hwang Ho = Huang He → *China* 37°55N 118°50E **227** F10
Hwange *Zimbabwe* 18°18S 26°30E **269** F2
Hwange △ *Zimbabwe* 19°0S 26°30E **270** A4
Hwanghaebuk-do □ *N. Korea* 38°30N 126°25E **224** C3
Hwanghaenam-do □ *N. Korea* 38°15N 125°30E **224** C2
Hwangju *N. Korea* 38°40N 125°46E **224** C2
Hwangshih = Huangshi *China* 30°10N 115°3E **229** B10
Hwaseong *S. Korea* 37°12N 126°48E **224** D3
Hwasun *S. Korea* 35°3N 126°59E **224** E3
Hwekum *Myanmar* 26°7N 95°22E **241** B5
Hwlffordd = Haverfordwest *U.K.* 51°48N 4°58W **169** F3
Hyaing *Myanmar* 22°39N 94°44E **241** D5
Hyannis *Mass., U.S.A.* 41°39N 70°17W **309** E18
Hyannis *Nebr., U.S.A.* 42°0N 101°46W **308** E3
Hyargas Nuur *Mongolia* 49°0N 93°0E **217** C12
Hyattsville *U.S.A.* 38°57N 76°57W **143** B3
Hybo *Sweden* 61°49N 16°15E **162** C10
Hydaburg *U.S.A.* 55°15N 132°50W **296** B2
Hyde *N.Z.* 45°18S 170°16E **285** F5
Hyde Park *Sydney, Australia* **139** b2
Hyde Park *Guyana* 6°30N 58°16W **329** B6
Hyde Park *Gauteng, S. Africa* 26°6S 28°2E **123** A2
Hyde Park *London, U.K.* 51°30N 0°10W **125** A2
Hyde Park *Calif., U.S.A.* 33°58N 118°19W **126** C3
Hyde Park *Ill., U.S.A.* 41°47N 87°35W **119** C3
Hyde Park *Mass., U.S.A.* 42°15N 71°7W **116** B2
Hyde Park *N.Y., U.S.A.* 41°47N 73°56W **313** E11
Hyden *Australia* 32°24S 118°53E **279** F2
Hyder *U.S.A.* 55°55N 130°5W **296** B2
Hyderabad *India* 17°22N 78°29E **244** F4
Hyderabad *Pakistan* 25°23N 68°24E **242** G3
Hydra *Greece* 37°20N 23°28E **204** D5
Hyen *Norway* 61°44N 5°56E **164** C2
Hyères *France* 43°8N 6°9E **175** E10
Hyères, Îs. d' *France* 43°0N 6°20E **175** F10
Hyesan *N. Korea* 41°20N 128°10E **224** B4
Hyland → *Canada* 59°52N 128°12W **296** B3
Hyllestad *Norway* 59°6N 7°29E **164** E4
Hyllestad *Norway* 61°10N 5°17E **164** C2
Hyltebruk *Sweden* 56°59N 13°15E **163** H7
Hyndman Peak *U.S.A.* 43°45N 114°8W **304** E6
Hynnekleiv *Norway* 58°36N 8°25E **164** F5
Hyōgo □ *Japan* 35°15N 134°50E **222** B6
Hyrra Banda *C.A.R.* 5°58N 22°1E **264** A4
Hyrum *U.S.A.* 41°38N 111°51W **304** F8
Hysham *U.S.A.* 46°18N 107°14W **304** C10
Hythe *U.K.* 51°4N 1°5E **169** F9
Hyūga *Japan* 32°25N 131°35E **222** E3
Hyvinge = Hyvinkää *Finland* 60°38N 24°50E **188** B3
Hyvinkää *Finland* 60°38N 24°50E **188** B3

I

I-n-Akhmed *Mali* 19°49N 0°56W **261** E4
I-n-Azaoua *Illizi, Algeria* 25°42N 6°54E **261** C6
I-n-Azaoua *Tamanrasset, Algeria* 20°46N 7°32E **261** D6
I-n-Échaï *Mali* 20°10N 2°5W **260** D4
I-n-Ezzane *Algeria* 23°29N 11°15E **261** D7
I-n-Gall *Niger* 16°51N 7°1E **263** B6
I-n-Kelemet *Algeria* 26°57N 5°47E **261** C6
I-n-Oudad *Algeria* 20°17N 4°38E **261** D5
I-n-Ouzzal *Algeria* 20°41N 2°34E **261** D5
I-n-Tadreft *Niger* 19°5N 6°38E **263** B6
Iabès, Erg *Algeria* 27°30N 2°2W **261** C4
Iablaniţa *Romania* 44°57N 22°19E **182** F7
Iaco → *Brazil* 9°3S 68°34W **330** B4
Iacobeni *Romania* 47°25N 25°20E **183** C10
Iaçu *Brazil* 12°45S 40°13W **333** D3
Iakora *Madag.* 23°6S 46°40E **272** C2
Ialibu *Papua N. G.* 6°17S 143°59E **286** D2
Ialissos *Greece* 36°24N 28°10E **206** E12
Ialomiţa □ *Romania* 44°30N 27°30E **183** F12
Ialomiţa → *Romania* 44°42N 27°51E **183** F12
Ialoveni *Moldova* 46°56N 28°47E **183** D13
Ialpug → *Moldova* 45°41N 28°35E **183** E13
Iamonia L. *U.S.A.* 30°38N 84°14W **316** E5
Ianca *Romania* 45°6N 27°29E **183** E12
Iara *Romania* 46°31N 23°35E **183** D8
Iarda *Ethiopia* 11°9N 35°53E **257** E4
Iargara *Moldova* 46°24N 28°23E **183** D13
Iaşi *Romania* 47°10N 27°40E **183** C12
Iaşi □ *Romania* 47°20N 27°0E **183** C12
Iasmos *Greece* 41°8N 25°11E **203** E9
Iauaretê *Colombia* 0°36N 69°12W **328** C4
Ib → *India* 21°34N 83°48E **243** J10
Iba *Phil.* 15°22N 120°0E **232** D2
Ibadan *Nigeria* 7°22N 3°58E **263** D5
Ibagué *Colombia* 4°20N 75°20W **328** C2
Ibaiti *Brazil* 23°50S 50°10W **333** F1
Ibajay *Phil.* 11°49N 122°10E **233** F4
Iballë *Albania* 42°12N 20°2E **202** D4
Ibăneşti *Botoşani, Romania* 48°4N 26°22E **183** B11
Ibăneşti *Mureş, Romania* 46°45N 24°57E **183** D9
Ibanshe *Dem. Rep. of the Congo* 4°58S 21°30E **265** C4
Ibar → *Serbia* 43°43N 20°45E **202** C4
Ibara *Japan* 34°36N 133°28E **222** C5
Ibaraki *Ibaraki, Japan* 36°20N 140°30E **223** A12
Ibaraki *Ōsaka, Japan* 34°49N 135°34E **223** C7
Ibaraki □ *Japan* 36°10N 140°10E **223** A12
Ibarra *Ecuador* 0°21N 78°7W **328** C2
Ibb *Yemen* 14°2N 44°10E **248** D4
Ibb □ *Yemen* 14°2N 44°10E **248** D4
Ibba *South Sudan* 4°49N 29°2E **257** G2
Ibba, Bahr el → *South Sudan* 5°30N 28°55E **257** F2
Ibbenbüren *Germany* 52°16N 7°43E **178** C3
Ibeke Gembo *Dem. Rep. of the Congo* 1°24S 18°51E **264** C3
Ibembo *Dem. Rep. of the Congo* 2°35N 23°35E **264** B4
Ibenga → *Congo* 2°19N 18°9E **264** B3
Ibera, L. *Argentina* 28°30S 57°9W **334** B4
Iberia *Peru* 11°21S 69°35W **330** C4
Iberia *Mo., U.S.A.* 38°5N 92°18W **310** F4
Iberian Peninsula *Europe* 40°0N 5°0W **158** H5
Iberville *Canada* 45°19N 73°17W **313** A11
Iberville, Mt. d' *Canada* 58°50N 63°50W **295** F19
Ibese *Nigeria* 6°33N 3°28E **124** A2
Ibeto *Nigeria* 10°29N 5°8E **263** C6
Ibi *Nigeria* 8°15N 9°44E **263** D6
Ibi *Spain* 38°38N 0°34W **197** G4
Ibiá *Brazil* 19°30S 46°30W **333** E2
Ibiapaba, Sa. da *Brazil* 4°0S 41°30W **332** B3
Ibicaraí *Brazil* 14°51S 39°36W **333** D4
Ibicuí *Brazil* 14°51S 39°59W **333** D4
Ibicuí → *Brazil* 29°25S 56°47W **335** B4
Ibicuy *Argentina* 33°55S 59°10W **334** C4
Ibirapuera *Brazil* 23°36S 46°40W **137** B1
Ibirapuera, Parque do *Brazil* 23°35S 46°38W **137** B2
Ibitiara *Brazil* 12°39S 42°13W **333** D3
Ibiza = Eivissa *Spain* 38°54N 1°26E **206** D1
Ibiza ✕ (IBZ) *Spain* 38°53N 1°22E **197** G6
Îblei, Monti *Italy* 37°15N 14°45E **201** E7
Ibn Hāni', Ra's *Syria* 35°35N 35°43E **250** D6
Ibo *Mozam.* 12°22S 40°40E **269** E5
Ibonma *Indonesia* 3°29S 133°31E **231** E8
Ibotirama *Brazil* 12°13S 43°12W **333** D3
Iboundji *Gabon* 1°0S 11°51E **264** C2
Ibrā' *Oman* 22°41N 58°33E **249** B7
Ibradı *Turkey* 37°4N 31°35E **250** A2
Ibrāhīm → *Lebanon* 34°4N 35°38E **250** D6
'Ibrī *Oman* 23°14N 56°30E **249** B7
İbriktepe *Turkey* 41°0N 26°30E **203** E10
Ibshawâi *Egypt* 29°21N 30°40E **256** J7
Ibu *Indonesia* 1°35N 127°33E **231** D7
Ibuki-Sanchi *Japan* 35°25N 136°18E **223** B8
Ibusuki *Japan* 31°12N 130°40E **222** F2
Ica *Peru* 14°0S 75°48W **330** C2
Ica □ *Peru* 14°20S 75°30W **330** C3
Iça → *Brazil* 2°55S 67°58W **330** A4
Icabarú *Venezuela* 4°20N 61°45W **329** C5
Icabarú → *Venezuela* 4°45N 62°15W **329** C5
Icacos *Trin. & Tob.* 10°3N 61°54W **323** t
Icacos Pt. *Trin. & Tob.* 10°3N 61°57W **323** t
Içana *Brazil* 0°21N 67°19W **328** C4
Içana → *Brazil* 0°26N 67°19W **328** C4
Icaraí *Brazil* 22°54S 43°6W **139** B2
Icatu *Brazil* 2°46S 44°4W **332** B3
Icaturama = Santa Rosa de Viterbo *Colombia* 5°53N 72°59W **328** B3
İçel = Mersin *Turkey* 36°51N 34°36E **250** B5
Iceland ■ *Europe* 64°45N 19°0W **155** C8
Iceland Basin *Atl. Oc.* 61°0N 19°0W **150** C7
Icelandic Plateau *Arctic* 64°0N 10°0W **150** C7
İçerenköy *Turkey* 40°58N 29°6E **122** B2
İçeriçumra *Turkey* 37°34N 32°39E **212** D5
Ichalkaranji *India* 16°40N 74°33E **244** F2
Ich'ang = Yichang *China* 30°40N 111°20E **229** B8
Ichchapuram *India* 19°10N 84°40E **244** E7
Icheon *S. Korea* 37°17N 127°27E **224** D3
Ichgao *Japan* 35°32N 139°32E **140** B2
Ichhawar *India* 23°1N 77°1E **242** H7
Ichigat Mujica-Cordillera del Condor ⌓ *Peru* 4°20S 77°30W **330** A2
Ichigaya *Tokyo, Japan* **140** a3
Ichihara *Japan* 35°28N 140°5E **223** B12
Ichikawa *Japan* 35°43N 139°54E **140** A4
Ichilo → *Bolivia* 15°57S 64°50W **331** D5
Ichinohe *Japan* 40°13N 141°17E **220** D10
Ichinomiya *Gifu, Japan* 35°18N 136°48E **223** B8
Ichinomiya *Kumamoto, Japan* 32°58N 131°5E **222** E3
Ichinoseki *Japan* 38°55N 141°8E **220** E10
Ichkeul △ *Tunisia* 37°5N 9°37E **258** A1
Ichnya *Ukraine* 50°52N 32°24E **189** G7
Icht *Morocco* 29°6N 8°54W **260** C3
Ichu *Taiwan* 23°20N 120°14E **225** C2
Ichun = Yichun *China* 47°44N 128°52E **219** B14
Ickenham *U.K.* 51°33N 0°26W **125** A1
Icó *Brazil* 6°24S 38°51W **332** C4
Icoca *Angola* 6°12S 16°20E **265** D3
Icod *Canary Is.* 28°22N 16°43W **153** e1
İçoguz *Turkmenistan* 40°11N 58°24E **216** E5
Iconi *Comoros Is.* 12°21S 43°51E **272** a
Icy C. *U.S.A.* 70°20N 161°52W **303** A7
Ida Grove *U.S.A.* 42°21N 95°28W **308** D6
Idaan *Somalia* 6°10N 48°55E **267** C6
Idabel *U.S.A.* 33°54N 94°50W **314** E7
Idaga Hamus *Ethiopia* 14°13N 39°48E **257** E4
Idah *Nigeria* 7°5N 6°40E **263** D6
Idaho □ *U.S.A.* 45°0N 115°0W **304** D6
Idaho City *U.S.A.* 43°50N 115°50W **304** E6
Idaho Falls *U.S.A.* 43°30N 112°2W **304** E7
Idalia △ *Australia* 24°49S 144°36E **280** C3
Idanha-a-Nova *Portugal* 39°50N 7°15W **194** F3
Idar-Oberstein *Germany* 49°43N 7°16E **179** F3
Iday *Niger* 14°54N 11°33E **259** F2
'Idd el Ghanam *Sudan* 11°30N 24°19E **259** F4
Iddo *Nigeria* 6°28N 3°22E **124** B2
Idelès *Algeria* 23°50N 5°53E **261** D6
Idensalmi = Iisalmi *Finland* 63°32N 27°10E **160** E22
Idfû *Egypt* 24°55N 32°49E **256** C3
Idi *Indonesia* 5°2N 97°37E **234** A1
Idi, Oros = Psiloritis, Oros *Greece* 35°15N 24°45E **207** E5
Idi Amin Dada, L. = Edward, L. *Africa* 0°25S 29°40E **268** C2
Idi-Oro *Nigeria* 6°31N 3°21E **124** A2
Idil *Turkey* 37°20N 41°53E **213** D9
Idiofa *Dem. Rep. of the Congo* 4°55S 19°42E **265** C3
Idjil = Fdérik *Mauritania* 22°40N 12°45W **260** D2
Idkerberget *Sweden* 60°22N 15°15E **162** D9
Idku *Egypt* 31°18N 30°18E **256** H7
Idku, Bahra el *Egypt* 31°18N 30°18E **256** H7
Idlib *Syria* 35°55N 36°36E **250** C7
Idlib □ *Syria* 35°45N 36°45E **250** C7
Idomeni *Greece* 41°7N 22°31E **202** E6
Idra = Hydra *Greece* 37°20N 23°28E **204** D5
Idre *Sweden* 61°52N 12°42E **162** C6
Idria *U.S.A.* 36°25N 120°41W **306** J6
Idrija *Slovenia* 46°0N 14°5E **199** C11
Idritsa *Russia* 56°17N 28°53E **188** D5
Idutywa = Dutywa *S. Africa* 32°8S 28°18E **271** D4
Ie Shima *Japan* 26°43N 127°48E **288** a
Ie Suido *Japan* 26°42N 127°51E **288** a
Ieper *Belgium* 50°51N 2°53E **170** D2
Ierapetra *Greece* 35°1N 25°44E **207** F6
Ierissos *Greece* 40°22N 23°52E **202** F7
Ierissos Kolpos *Greece* 40°27N 23°57E **202** F7
Iernut *Romania* 46°27N 24°15E **183** D9
Ieshima-Shotō *Japan* 34°40N 134°32E **222** C6
Iesi *Italy* 43°31N 13°14E **199** E10
Iet *Ethiopia* 4°33N 43°1E **267** D5
Ifac, Penyal d' *Spain* 38°38N 0°5E **197** G5
'Ifāl, W. al → *Si. Arabia* 28°7N 35°3E **251** K6
Ifanadiana *Madag.* 21°19S 47°39E **272** C2
Ife *Nigeria* 7°30N 4°31E **263** D5
Iférouâne *Niger* 19°5N 8°24E **259** E1
Ifetesene *Algeria* 25°30N 4°33E **261** C5
Iffley *Australia* 18°53S 141°12E **280** B3
Ifon *Nigeria* 6°58N 5°40E **263** D6
Iforas, Adrar des *Africa* 19°40N 1°40E **261** D5
Ifould, L. *Australia* 30°52S 132°6E **279** F5
Ifrane *Morocco* 33°33N 5°7W **260** B3
Ifugao □ *Phil.* 16°40N 121°10E **232** C3
Iga *Japan* 34°45N 136°10E **223** C8
Igalo *Montenegro* 42°28N 18°30E **202** D2
Iganga *Uganda* 0°37N 33°28E **268** B3
Iganmu *Nigeria* 6°28N 3°22E **124** B2
Igara-Paraná → *Colombia* 2°9S 71°47W **328** D3
Igarapava *Brazil* 20°3S 47°47W **333** F2
Igarapé-Açu *Brazil* 1°4S 47°33W **332** B2
Igarapé-Miri *Brazil* 1°59S 48°58W **332** B2
Igarka *Russia* 67°30N 86°33E **214** C9
Igatpuri *India* 19°40N 73°35E **244** E1
Igbetti *Nigeria* 8°44N 4°8E **263** D5
Igbo-Ora *Nigeria* 7°29N 3°15E **263** D5
Igbobi *Nigeria* 6°31N 3°22E **124** A2
Igboho *Nigeria* 8°53N 3°50E **263** D5
Igbologun *Nigeria* 6°24N 3°19E **124** B1
Igbor *Nigeria* 7°27N 8°34E **263** D6
Iğdır *Turkey* 39°55N 44°2E **213** C11
Igelfors *Sweden* 58°52N 15°41E **163** F9
Iggesund *Sweden* 61°39N 17°10E **162** C11
Ighil Izane = Relizane *Algeria* 35°44N 0°31E **261** A5
Igiugig *U.S.A.* 59°20N 155°55W **303** G9
Iglau = Jihlava *Czechia* 49°28N 15°35E **180** B8
Iglésias *Italy* 39°19N 8°32E **200** C1
Igli *Algeria* 30°25N 2°19W **261** B4
Igloolik = Iglulik *Canada* 69°20N 81°49W **295** D15
Igluligaarjuk = Chesterfield Inlet *Canada* 63°30N 90°45W **294** E13
Iglulik *Canada* 69°20N 81°49W **295** D15
'Igma, G. el *Egypt* 29°10N 34°0E **251** J5
Ignace *Canada* 49°30N 91°40W **298** C1
İğneada *Turkey* 41°52N 27°59E **203** E11
İğneada Burnu *Turkey* 41°53N 28°2E **203** E12
Igny *France* 48°44N 2°13E **134** B2
Igoumenitsa *Greece* 39°32N 20°18E **206** B10
Igrim *Russia* 63°12N 64°30E **214** C7
Iguaçu → *Brazil* 25°36S 54°36W **335** B5
Iguaçu, Cat. del *Brazil* 25°41S 54°26W **335** B5
Iguaçu △ *Brazil* 25°30S 54°0W **335** B5
Iguaçu Falls = Iguaçu, Cat. del *Brazil* 25°41S 54°26W **335** B5
Iguala *Mexico* 18°21N 99°32W **319** D5
Igualada *Spain* 41°37N 1°37E **196** D6
Iguape *Brazil* 24°43S 47°33W **333** F2
Iguaratinga = São Francisco do Maranhão *Brazil* 6°15S 42°52W **332** C3
Iguassu = Iguaçu → *Brazil* 25°36S 54°36W **335** B5
Iguatu *Brazil* 6°20S 39°18W **332** C4
Iguazú △ *Argentina* 25°42S 54°22W **335** B5
Iguéla *Gabon* 2°0S 9°16E **264** C1
Iguéla, Lagune *Gabon* 1°48S 9°16E **264** C2
Iguidi, Erg *Africa* 27°0N 6°0W **260** C3
Iguig *Phil.* 17°45N 121°44E **232** C3
Igumen = Cherven *Belarus* 53°45N 28°28E **177** B15
Iharana *Madag.* 13°25S 50°0E **272** A3
Ihavandiffulu Atoll *Maldives* 7°0N 72°50E **272** d
Ihbulag *Mongolia* 43°11N 107°10E **226** C4
Iheya-Shima *Japan* 27°4N 127°58E **221** L3
Ihiala *Nigeria* 5°51N 6°55E **263** D6
Ihirene, O. → *Algeria* 20°28N 4°37E **261** D5
Ihorombe □ *Madag.* 22°25S 46°10E **272** C2
Ihosy *Madag.* 22°24S 46°8E **272** C2
Ihotry, Farihy *Madag.* 21°56S 43°41E **272** C1
Ihu *Papua N. G.* 7°55S 145°24E **286** D3
Ihugh *Nigeria* 7°2N 9°0E **263** D6
Ii *Finland* 65°19N 25°22E **160** D21
Ii-Shima *Japan* 26°43N 127°47E **221** L3
Iida *Japan* 35°35N 137°50E **223** B9
Iijoki → *Finland* 65°20N 25°20E **160** D21
Iisalmi *Finland* 63°32N 27°10E **160** E22
Iiyama *Japan* 36°51N 138°22E **221** F9
Iizuka *Japan* 33°38N 130°42E **222** D2
IJ, Het → *Neths.* 52°23N 4°54E **112** A2
IJ-meer *Neths.* 52°23N 4°54E **112** A3
Ijâfene *Mauritania* 20°40N 8°0W **260** D3
IJburg *Neths.* 52°22N 5°0E **112** A3
Ijebu-Igbo *Nigeria* 6°56N 4°1E **263** D5
Ijebu-Ode *Nigeria* 6°47N 3°58E **263** D5
Ijesa-Tedo *Nigeria* 6°29N 3°19E **124** B1
Ijevan *Armenia* 40°52N 45°8E **191** K7
Ijill, Sebkhet *Mauritania* 22°47N 12°53W **260** D2
IJmuiden *Neths.* 52°28N 4°35E **170** B4
Ijo älv = Iijoki → *Finland* 65°20N 25°20E **160** D21
Ijora *Nigeria* 6°27N 3°22E **124** B2
IJssel → *Neths.* 52°35N 5°50E **170** B5
IJsselmeer *Neths.* 52°45N 5°20E **170** B5
Ijuí *Brazil* 28°23S 53°55W **335** B5
Ijuí → *Brazil* 27°58S 55°20W **335** B4
Ijūin *Japan* 31°37N 130°24E **222** F2
Ikalamavony *Madag.* 21°9S 46°35E **272** C2
Ikali *Dem. Rep. of the Congo* 2°2S 21°4E **264** C4
Ikamatua *N.Z.* 42°16S 171°41E **285** C6
Ikang *Nigeria* 4°49N 8°30E **263** E6
Ikanga *Kenya* 1°42S 38°4E **268** C4
Ikara *Nigeria* 11°12N 8°15E **263** C6
Ikare *Nigeria* 7°32N 5°40E **263** D6
Ikaria *Greece* 37°35N 26°10E **205** D8
Ikast *Denmark* 56°8N 9°10E **163** H3
Ikebe *Japan* 35°31N 139°34E **140** B2
Ikebukuro *Japan* 35°43N 139°42E **140** A3
Ikeda *Japan* 34°1N 133°48E **222** C5
Ikegami *Japan* 35°33N 139°42E **140** B2
Ikei-shima *Japan* 26°23N 127°59E **288** a
Ikeja *Nigeria* 6°35N 3°20E **124** A2
Ikela *Dem. Rep. of the Congo* 1°6S 23°6E **264** C4
Ikélemba *Congo* 1°12N 16°38E **264** B3
Ikélemba → *Dem. Rep. of the Congo* 0°7N 18°17E **264** B3
Ikengo *Dem. Rep. of the Congo* 0°8S 18°8E **264** C3
Ikere *Nigeria* 7°25N 5°19E **263** D6
Ikeuchi *Japan* 34°35N 135°32E **133** B2
Ikhtiman *Bulgaria* 42°27N 23°48E **202** D7
Iki *Japan* 33°45N 129°42E **222** D1
Iki-Kaikyō *Japan* 33°40N 129°45E **222** D1
Ikimba L. *Tanzania* 1°30S 31°20E **268** C3
Ikire *Nigeria* 7°23N 4°15E **263** D5
Ikitsuki-Shima *Japan* 33°23N 129°26E **222** D1
İkizdere *Turkey* 40°46N 40°32E **213** B9

Iko Congo 0°35S 16°0E 264 C3
Ikom Nigeria 6°0N 8°42E 263 D6
Ikoma Japan 34°30N 135°40E 223 C7
Ikomu
Dem. Rep. of the Congo 1°54S 19°40E 264 C3
Ikongo Madag. 21°52S 47°27E 272 C2
Ikopa → Madag. 16°45S 46°40E 272 B2
Ikorodu Nigeria 6°35N 3°29E 124 C2
Ikorongo ⌂ Tanzania 1°50S 34°53E 268 C3
Ikot Ekpene Nigeria 5°12N 7°40E 263 D6
Ikoyi Nigeria 6°27N 3°26E 124 B2
Ikparjuk = Arctic Bay
Canada 73°1N 85°7W 295 C14
Iksan S. Korea 35°59N 127°0E 224 E3
Ikuata Nigeria 6°24N 3°21E 124 B2
Ikungu Tanzania 1°33S 33°42E 268 C3
Ikuno Hyōgo, Japan 35°10N 134°48E 222 B6
Ikuno Ōsaka, Japan 34°40N 135°30E 133 A2
Ikuntji = Haasts Bluff
Australia 23°22S 132°0E 278 D5
Ikurun Nigeria 7°54N 4°40E 263 D5
Ikuta Japan 35°36N 139°32E 140 B2
Il-Kullana Malta 35°50N 14°24E 206 F7
Il-Munxar Malta 35°51N 14°34E 206 F8
Ila Dem. Rep. of the Congo 2°53S 21°7E 264 C4
Ila Nigeria 8°0N 4°39E 263 D5
Ila Oslo, Norway 59°57N 10°35E 133 A2
Ilafer Algeria 21°40N 1°58E 261 D5
Ilagan Phil. 17°7N 121°53E 232 C3
Ilaka Madag. 19°33S 48°52E 272 B2
Īlām Iran 33°36N 46°36E 213 F12
Ilam Nepal 26°58N 87°58E 242 F9
Īlām □ Iran 33°0N 47°0E 246 C5
Ilan Taiwan 24°45N 121°44E 225 B3
Ilan □ Taiwan 24°30N 121°35E 225 B3
Ilan, Mt. Phil. 10°26N 119°33E 233 F2
Ilanskiy Russia 56°14N 96°3E 215 D10
Ilaro Nigeria 6°53N 3°3E 263 D5
Ilatane Niger 16°30N 4°45E 263 B5
Ilave Peru 16°5S 69°40W 330 D4
Iława Poland 53°36N 19°34E 184 E6
Ilayangudi India 9°34N 78°37E 245 K4
Ile → Kazakhstan 45°53N 77°10E 217 C9
Île-à-la-Crosse Canada 55°27N 107°53W 297 B7
Île-à-la-Crosse, Lac
Canada 55°40N 107°45W 297 B7
Ile-Alta Tau △ Kazakhstan 43°5N 77°5E 217 D9
Île-de-France □ France 49°0N 2°20E 173 D9
Ileanda Romania 47°20N 23°38E 183 C8
Ilebo Dem. Rep. of the Congo 4°17S 20°55E 265 C4
Ilek Russia 51°32N 53°21E 216 B4
Ilek → Russia 51°30N 53°22E 186 D9
Ilemi Triangle Africa 5°0N 35°20E 257 G4
Iler, O. → Algeria 20°59N 3°14E 261 D5
Ilero Nigeria 8°0N 3°20E 263 D5
Ilesha Kwara, Nigeria 8°57N 3°28E 263 D5
Ilesha Oyo, Nigeria 7°37N 4°40E 263 D5
Ilet = Krasnogorskiy
Russia 56°10N 48°28E 190 B9
Iletskaya = Sol Iletsk
Russia 51°10N 55°0E 186 D10
Iletsky Gorodok = Ilek
Russia 51°32N 53°21E 216 B4
Ilford Man., Canada 56°4N 95°35W 297 B9
Ilford London, U.K. 51°33N 0°4E 125 A4
Ilfov □ Romania 44°36N 26°7E 183 F11
Ilfracombe Queens.,
Australia 23°30S 144°30E 280 C3
Ilfracombe Devon, U.K. 51°12N 4°8W 169 F3
Ilgaz Turkey 40°55N 33°37E 212 B5
Ilgaz Dağları Turkey 41°10N 33°50E 212 B5
Ilgın Turkey 38°16N 31°55E 212 C4
Ilha, Pta. da Azores 38°25N 28°3W 153 d1
Ilha Grande Brazil 0°27S 65°2W 329 D4
Ilha Grande, B. da Brazil 23°9S 44°30W 333 F3
Ilha Grande, Represa
Brazil 23°10S 53°5W 335 A5
Ilha Grande △ Brazil 23°10S 53°20W 335 A5
Ílhavo Portugal 40°33N 8°43W 194 E2
Ilhéus Brazil 14°49S 39°2W 333 D4
Ili = Ile → Kazakhstan 45°53N 77°10E 217 C9
Ilia Greece 37°45N 21°35E 204 D3
Ilia Romania 45°57N 22°40E 182 E7
Iliamna U.S.A. 59°45N 154°55W 303 G9
Iliamna L. U.S.A. 59°30N 155°0W 303 G9
Ilias, Profitis Greece 36°17N 27°56E 206 E11
Iliç Turkey 39°27N 38°33E 213 C8
Ilıca Turkey 39°52N 27°46E 205 B9
Ilig, Ras Somalia 7°47N 49°50E 267 C6
Iligan Phil. 8°12N 124°13E 233 G5
Iligan B. Phil. 8°25N 124°5E 233 G5
Iligan Pt. Phil. 18°25N 122°25E 232 B4
Ilin I. Phil. 12°14N 121°5E 232 E3
'Īlio Pt. U.S.A. 21°13N 157°16W 302 B4
Ilion U.S.A. 43°1N 75°2W 313 D9
Ilioupoli Greece 37°54N 23°47E 112 B2
Ilirska-Bistrica Slovenia 45°34N 14°14E 199 C11
Ilium = Rewa → Guyana 3°19N 58°42W 329 C6
Iliysk = Qapshaghay
Kazakhstan 43°51N 77°14E 217 D9
Ilkal India 15°57N 76°8E 245 G3
Ilkenau = Olkusz Poland 50°18N 19°33E 185 H6
Ilkeston U.K. 52°58N 1°19W 168 E6
Ilkley U.K. 53°56N 1°48W 168 D6
Illampu = Ancohuma, Nevado
Bolivia 16°0S 68°50W 330 D4
Illana B. Phil. 7°35N 123°45E 233 H4
Illapel Chile 32°0S 71°10W 334 C1
Ille-et-Vilaine □ France 48°10N 1°30W 172 D5
Ille-sur-Têt France 42°40N 2°38E 174 F6
Illéla Niger 14°32N 5°20E 263 C6
Iller → Germany 48°23N 9°58E 179 G5
Illertissen Germany 48°12N 10°7E 179 G6
Illes Balears = Baleares, Is.
Spain 39°30N 3°0E 206 B4
Illescas Spain 40°8N 3°51W 194 E7
Illetas Spain 39°32N 2°35E 206 B3
Illichivsk Ukraine 46°20N 30°35E 189 J6
Illiers-Combray France 48°18N 1°15E 172 D8
Illimani, Nevado Bolivia 16°30S 67°50W 330 D4
Illinois □ U.S.A. 40°15N 89°30W 310 D7
Illinois → U.S.A. 38°58N 90°28W 310 F6
Illinois at Chicago, Univ. of
U.S.A. 41°52N 87°38W 119 B3
Illinois Institute of Technology
U.S.A. 41°50N 87°37W 119 B3
Illiopolis U.S.A. 39°51N 89°15W 310 E7
Illium = Troy Turkey 39°57N 26°12E 205 B8
Illizi Algeria 26°31N 8°32E 261 C6
Illizi □ Algeria 28°0N 8°10E 261 C6
Illkirch-Graffenstaden
France 48°34N 7°42E 173 D14
Íllora Spain 37°17N 3°53W 195 H7
Ilm → Germany 51°6N 11°40E 178 D7
Ilma, L. Australia 29°13S 127°46E 279 E4
Ilmajoki Finland 62°44N 22°34E 160 E20
Ilmen, Ozero Russia 58°15N 31°10E 188 C6
Ilmenau = Jordanów
Poland 49°41N 19°49E 185 J6
Ilmenau = Limanowa
Poland 49°42N 20°22E 185 J7
Ilmenau Germany 50°41N 10°54E 178 E6
Ilnytsya Ukraine 48°21N 23°5E 182 B8
Ilo Peru 17°40S 71°20W 330 D3
Ilobu Nigeria 7°45N 4°25E 263 D5
Iloc I. Phil. 11°17N 119°40E 232 F2
Ilocos Norte □ Phil. 18°10N 120°45E 232 B3
Ilocos Sur □ Phil. 17°20N 120°35E 232 C3
Iloilo Phil. 10°45N 122°33E 233 F4
Iloilo □ Phil. 11°0N 122°40E 233 F4
Ilomantsi Finland 62°38N 30°57E 160 E24
Ilora Nigeria 7°45N 3°50E 263 D5
Ilorin Nigeria 8°30N 4°35E 263 D5
Ilovatka Russia 50°30N 45°50E 190 E7
Ilovlya Russia 49°15N 44°2E 191 F7
Ilovlya → Russia 49°14N 44°2E 191 F7
Iłowa Poland 51°30N 15°10E 185 G2
Ilpendam Neths. 52°28N 4°57E 112 A2
Ilsos → Greece 37°55N 23°41E 112 B2
Ilubabor Ethiopia 7°25N 35°0E 257 F4
Ilulissat Greenland 69°12N 51°10W 154 D5
Ilva Mică Romania 47°17N 24°40E 183 C9
Ilwaco U.S.A. 46°19N 124°3W 306 D2
Ilyichevsk = Illichivsk
Ukraine 46°20N 30°35E 189 J6
Iłża Poland 51°10N 21°15E 185 G8
Iłżanka → Poland 51°14N 21°48E 185 G8
Imabari Japan 34°4N 133°0E 222 C5
Imagem e do Som, Museu da
Rio de J., Brazil 135 b3
Imaichi Japan 36°43N 139°46E 223 A11
Imaloto → Madag. 23°27S 45°13E 272 C2
İmamoğlu Turkey 37°15N 35°38E 212 D6
Iman = Dalnerechensk
Russia 45°50N 133°40E 220 B6
Imandra, Ozero Russia 67°30N 33°0E 160 C25
Imanombo Madag. 24°26S 45°49E 272 C2
Imari Japan 33°15N 129°52E 222 D1
Imasa Sudan 18°0N 36°12E 256 D4
Imatra Finland 61°12N 28°48E 188 B5
Imbâbah Egypt 30°3N 31°12E 117 A2
Imbabura □ Ecuador 0°30N 78°45W 328 C2
Imbaimadai Guyana 5°44N 60°17W 329 B5
Imbiah Lookout Singapore 1°16N 103°49E 138 B2
Imbonga
Dem. Rep. of the Congo 0°43S 19°44E 264 C3
Iménas Mali 16°20N 0°40E 263 B5
imeni 26 Bakinskikh Komissarov =
Neftçala Azerbaijan 39°19N 49°12E 213 C13
imeni 26 Bakinskikh Komissarov
Turkmenistan 39°22N 54°10E 247 B7
imeni Dvadtsati Shesti Bakinskikh
Komissarov = Neftçala
Azerbaijan 39°19N 49°12E 213 C13
imeni Dzerzhinskogo =
Naryan-Mar Russia 67°42N 53°12E 186 A9
imeni Ismail Samani, Pik
Tajikistan 39°0N 72°2E 217 E8
imeni Karl Libknekhta
Russia 51°40N 35°35E 189 G8
imeni Mikoyana = Kara-Balta
Kyrgyzstan 42°50N 73°49E 217 D8
imeni Petrovskogo G.I. =
Horodyshche Ukraine 49°17N 31°27E 189 H6
imeni Sverdlova = Sverdlovsk
Ukraine 48°5N 39°47E 189 H10
imeni Tovarishcha Khateyevicha =
Synelnykove Ukraine 48°25N 35°30E 189 H8
imeni Tretyego Internatsionala =
Novoshakhtinsk
Russia 47°46N 39°58E 189 J10
Imeri, Serra Brazil 0°50N 65°25W 328 C4
Imerimandroso Madag. 17°26S 48°35E 272 B2
Imese Dem. Rep. of the Congo 2°6N 18°9E 264 B3
Imfolozi ⌂ S. Africa 28°18S 31°50E 271 C5
Imi Ethiopia 6°28N 42°10E 257 F5
Imielin Poland 52°9N 21°0E 143 C2
Imirim Brazil 23°29S 46°39W 137 A2
Imişli Azerbaijan 39°55N 48°4E 191 L9
Imitek Morocco 29°43N 8°10W 260 C3
Imitos Greece 37°55N 23°45E 112 B2
Imitos, Oros Greece 37°53N 23°48E 112 B2
Imizu Japan 36°47N 137°4E 223 A9
Imjado S. Korea 35°5N 126°5E 224 E3
Imjin-gang → N. Korea 37°47N 126°39E 224 D3
Imlay U.S.A. 40°40N 118°9W 304 F4
Imlay City U.S.A. 43°2N 83°5W 312 D1
Immeseri Sudan 15°40N 25°31E 257 D2
Immenstadt Germany 47°33N 10°13E 179 H6
Immingham U.K. 53°37N 0°13W 168 D7
Immokalee U.S.A. 26°25N 81°25W 317 J8
Imo □ Nigeria 5°30N 7°10E 263 D6
Imo → Nigeria 4°36N 7°35E 263 E6
İmola Italy 44°20N 11°42E 199 D8
Imotski Croatia 43°27N 17°12E 199 E14
Impé Congo 2°45S 15°16E 264 C3
Imperatorskaya Gavan = Vanino
Russia 48°50N 140°5E 215 E15
Imperatriz Amazonas, Brazil 5°18S 67°11W 330 B4
Imperatriz Maranhão,
Brazil 5°30S 47°29W 332 C2
Impéria Italy 43°53N 8°3E 198 E5
Imperial Sask., Canada 51°21N 105°28W 297 C7
Imperial Peru 13°4S 76°21W 330 C2
Imperial Calif., U.S.A. 32°51N 115°34W 307 N11
Imperial Nebr., U.S.A. 40°31N 101°39W 308 E3
Imperial Beach U.S.A. 32°35N 117°6W 307 N9
Imperial Dam U.S.A. 32°55N 114°25W 307 N12
Imperial Palace = Paço Imperial
Rio de J., Brazil 135 a2
Imperial Palace Museum Beijing, China 114 b3
Imperial Res. U.S.A. 32°53N 114°28W 307 N12
Imperial Valley U.S.A. 33°0N 115°30W 307 N11
Imperieuse Reef Australia 17°36S 118°50E 278 C2
Impfondo Congo 1°40N 18°0E 264 B3
Imphal India 24°48N 93°56E 241 C4
Imphy France 46°55N 3°16E 173 F10
Impulo Angola 13°51S 13°39E 265 E2
Imranlı Turkey 39°54N 38°7E 213 C8
İmroz = Gökçeada Turkey 40°10N 25°50E 203 F9
Imst Austria 47°15N 10°44E 180 D3
Imuris Mexico 30°47N 110°52W 318 A2
Imuruan B. Phil. 10°40N 119°10E 233 F2
Imus Phil. 14°26N 120°56E 232 D3
In Aleï Mali 17°42N 2°30W 262 B4
In Amenas Algeria 28°5N 9°33E 261 C6
In Amguel Algeria 23°41N 5°9E 261 D6
In Atei Algeria 20°33N 6°4E 261 D6
In Belbel Algeria 27°55N 1°12E 261 C5
In Delimane Mali 15°52N 1°31E 263 B5
In Ghar Algeria 27°10N 1°59E 261 C5
In Guezzam Algeria 19°37N 5°52E 261 E6
In Guezzam □ Algeria 20°0N 4°0E 261 D5
In Koufi Mali 19°11N 1°25E 263 B5
In Salah Algeria 27°10N 2°32E 261 C5
In Salah □ Algeria 27°0N 2°30E 261 C5
In Tallak Mali 16°19N 3°15E 263 B5
In Tebezas Mali 17°49N 1°53E 263 B5
Ina Japan 35°50N 137°55E 223 B9
Ina Ill., U.S.A. 38°9N 88°54W 311 F8
Ina-Bonchi Japan 35°45N 137°58E 223 B9
Inabanga Phil. 10°2N 124°4E 233 F5
Inaccessible I. Atl. Oc. 37°18S 12°40W 152 K10
Inagauan Phil. 9°33N 118°39E 233 G2
Inagi Japan 35°38N 139°31E 140 B2
Inajá Brazil 8°54S 37°49W 332 C4
Inambari → Peru 12°41S 69°44W 330 C4
Inangahua N.Z. 41°52S 171°59E 285 B6
Inanwatan Indonesia 2°8S 132°10E 231 E8
Iñapari Peru 11°0S 69°40W 330 C4
Inarajan Guam 13°16N 144°45E 302 d
Inari Finland 68°54N 27°1E 160 B22
Inarijärvi Finland 69°0N 28°0E 160 B23
Inawashiro-Ko Japan 37°29N 140°6E 220 F10
Inazawa Japan 35°15N 136°47E 223 B8
tInbhear Mór, An = Arklow
Ireland 52°48N 6°10W 166 D5
Inbin Myanmar 18°6N 95°16E 241 F5
Inca Spain 39°43N 2°54E 206 B3
Inca de Oro Chile 26°45S 69°54W 334 B2
Incahuasi Argentina 27°2S 68°18W 334 B2
Incahuasi Chile 29°12S 71°5W 334 B1
İnce Burun Turkey 42°7N 34°56E 212 A6
İncekum Burnu Turkey 36°13N 33°57E 250 B4
İncesu Turkey 38°38N 35°11E 212 C6
Inchcolm U.K. 56°2N 3°18W 121 A2
Incheon S. Korea 37°27N 126°40E 224 D3
Incheon Int. ✈ (ICN)
S. Korea 37°28N 126°26E 224 D3
Inchiri □ Mauritania 20°0N 15°0W 260 E2
Inchkeith U.K. 56°2N 3°8W 121 A3
Inchmickery U.K. 56°0N 3°16W 121 B2
Incio = A Cruz do Incio
Spain 42°39N 7°21W 194 C3
Incirano Italy 45°34N 9°9E 128 A1
İncirliova Turkey 37°50N 27°41E 205 D9
Incline Village U.S.A. 39°10N 119°58W 306 F7
Incomáti → Mozam. 25°46S 32°43E 271 C5
Incudine, Mte. France 41°50N 9°12E 175 G13
Inda Silase Ethiopia 14°10N 38°15E 257 E4
Indal Sweden 62°35N 17°5E 162 B11
Indalsälven → Sweden 62°36N 17°30E 162 B11
Indaw Myanmar 24°15N 96°5E 241 C6
Indawgyi In Myanmar 25°8N 96°20E 241 C6
Indbir Ethiopia 8°7N 37°52E 257 F4
Indefatigable, I. = Santa Cruz, I.
Ecuador 0°38S 90°23W 330 a
Independence Calif.,
U.S.A. 36°48N 118°12W 306 J8
Independence Iowa,
U.S.A. 42°28N 91°54W 310 B5
Independence Kans.,
U.S.A. 37°14N 95°42W 308 G6
Independence Ky.,
U.S.A. 38°57N 84°33W 311 F12
Independence Mo., U.S.A. 39°6N 94°25W 310 E2
Independence Avenue
Washington, D.C., U.S.A. 143 c2
Independence Fjord
Greenland 82°10N 29°0W 154 A8
Independence Mts.
U.S.A. 41°20N 116°0W 304 F5
Independência Brazil 5°23S 40°19W 332 C3
Independencia Santiago,
Chile 33°25S 70°39W 137 B2
Independencia Lima, Peru 11°59S 77°3W 124 A2
Independencia, I. Peru 14°16S 76°12W 330 C2
Independența Romania 45°25N 27°42E 183 E12
Înderbor Kazakhstan 48°33N 51°47E 216 C4
Index U.S.A. 47°50N 121°33W 306 C5
Indi India 17°10N 75°58E 244 F2
India ■ Asia 20°0N 78°0E 239 F11
India Gate Delhi, India 120 c2
Indialantic U.S.A. 28°6N 80°34W 317 G9
Indian → U.S.A. 27°59N 80°34W 317 G9
Indian Cabins Canada 59°52N 117°40W 296 B5
Indian Creek Village
U.S.A. 25°52N 80°8W 129 C3
Indian Harbour Canada 54°27N 57°13W 299 B8
Indian Harbour Beach
U.S.A. 28°10N 80°35W 317 G9
Indian Head Canada 50°30N 103°41W 297 C8
Indian L. U.S.A. 43°46N 74°16W 313 C10
Indian Lake U.S.A. 43°47N 74°16W 313 C10
Indian Ocean 5°0S 75°0E 273 E6
Indian Rocks Beach
U.S.A. 27°52N 82°51W 317 H7
Indian Springs U.S.A. 36°35N 115°40W 307 J11
Indian Town Pt.
Antigua & B. 17°6N 61°40W 322 b
Indian Walk Trin. & Tob. 10°16N 61°20W 323 t
Indiana U.S.A. 40°37N 79°9W 312 F5
Indiana □ U.S.A. 40°0N 86°0W 311 E11
Indiana Dunes △ U.S.A. 41°40N 87°0W 311 C9
Indianapolis U.S.A. 39°46N 86°9W 311 E10
Indianapolis Int. ✈ (IND)
U.S.A. 39°43N 86°17W 311 E10
Indianola Iowa, U.S.A. 41°22N 93°34W 310 C3
Indianola Miss., U.S.A. 33°27N 90°39W 315 E9
Indianópolis Brazil 23°35S 46°38W 137 B2
Indiantown U.S.A. 27°1N 80°28W 317 H9
Indiapora Brazil 19°57S 50°17W 333 E1
Indiga Russia 67°38N 49°9E 186 A8
Indigirka → Russia 70°48N 148°54E 215 B15
Inđija Serbia 45°6N 20°7E 182 E5
Indio U.S.A. 33°43N 116°13W 307 M10
Indira Gandhi Canal India 28°0N 72°0E 242 F5
Indira Gandhi Int. ✈ (DEL)
India 28°34N 77°5E 120 B1
Indira Gandhi Memorial Museum
India 28°36N 77°12E 120 B2
Indira Pt. India 6°44N 93°49E 245 L11
Indira Sagar India 22°15N 76°40E 242 H7
Indispensable Str.
Solomon Is. 9°0S 160°30E 287 M11
Indo-China Asia 15°0N 102°0E 210 G12
Indonesia ■ Asia 5°0S 115°0E 235 C4
Indore India 22°42N 75°53E 242 H6
Indramayu Indonesia 6°20S 108°19E 235 D3
Indrapura = Kerinci
Indonesia 1°40S 101°15E 234 C2
Indravati → India 19°20N 80°20E 244 E5
Indre □ France 46°50N 1°39E 173 F8
Indre → France 47°16N 0°11E 172 E7
Indre Ålvik Norway 60°26N 6°26E 164 D3
Indre Arna Norway 60°26N 5°30E 164 D2
Indre-et-Loire □ France 47°20N 0°40E 172 E7
Indrio U.S.A. 27°31N 80°21W 317 H9
Indulkana Australia 26°58S 133°5E 281 D1
Indungo Angola 14°48S 16°17E 265 E3
Indura Belarus 53°26N 23°53E 184 E10
Indus → Pakistan 24°20N 67°47E 242 G2
Indus, Mouths of the
Pakistan 24°0N 68°0E 242 H3
Industria S. Africa 26°11S 27°58E 123 B1
Industrial Canal U.S.A. 30°4N 90°4W 131 A2
Industry U.S.A. 40°20N 90°36W 310 D6
İnebolu Turkey 41°55N 33°40E 212 B5
İnecik Turkey 40°56N 27°16E 203 F11
İnegöl Turkey 40°5N 29°31E 203 F13
Inés, Mt. Argentina 48°30S 69°40W 336 C3
Ineu Romania 46°26N 21°51E 182 D6
Inezgane Morocco 30°25N 9°29W 260 B3
Infanta Phil. 14°45N 121°39E 232 D3
Infantes = Villanueva de los
Infantes Spain 38°43N 3°1W 195 G7
Infiernillo, Presa del
Mexico 18°35N 101°50W 318 D4
Infiesto Spain 43°21N 5°21W 194 B5
Inga, Barrage d'
Dem. Rep. of the Congo 5°39S 13°39E 265 D2
Ingabu Myanmar 17°37N 95°20E 241 G5
Inganda
Dem. Rep. of the Congo 0°5S 20°57E 264 C4
Ingapirca Ecuador 2°38S 78°56W 328 D2
Ingarö Sweden 59°12N 18°45E 162 E12
Ingelstad Sweden 56°45N 14°56E 163 H8
Ingende
Dem. Rep. of the Congo 0°12S 18°57E 264 C3
Ingeniero Jacobacci
Argentina 41°20S 69°36W 336 B3
Ingenio Canary Is. 27°55N 15°26W 153 e1
Ingenio Santa Ana
Argentina 27°25S 65°40W 334 B2
Ingersoll Canada 43°4N 80°55W 312 C4
Ingham Australia 18°43S 146°10E 280 B4
Ingierstrand Norway 59°49N 10°46E 133 B3
Ingleborough U.K. 54°10N 2°22W 168 C5
Inglefield Land Greenland 78°30N 70°0W 154 B4
Inglewood Queens.,
Australia 28°25S 151°2E 281 D5
Inglewood Vic., Australia 36°29S 143°53E 282 D5
Inglewood N.Z. 39°9S 174°14E 284 F3
Inglewood Calif., U.S.A. 33°58N 118°21W 126 C3
Inglis U.S.A. 29°2N 82°40W 317 F7
Ingliston U.K. 55°56N 3°23W 121 B1
Ingolf Fjord Greenland 80°35N 17°30W 154 A9
Ingólfshöfði Iceland 63°48N 16°39W 155 D10
Ingolstadt Germany 48°46N 11°26E 179 G7
Ingomar U.S.A. 46°35N 107°23W 304 C10
Ingonish Canada 46°42N 60°18W 299 C7
Ingore Guinea-Biss. 12°24N 15°48W 262 C1
Ingraj Bazar India 24°58N 88°10E 243 G13
Ingrid Christensen Coast
Antarctica 69°30S 76°0E 151 C6
Ingul = Inhul → Ukraine 46°50N 32°0E 189 J7
Ingulec = Inhulec Ukraine 47°42N 33°14E 189 J7
Ingulets = Inhulets →
Ukraine 46°46N 32°47E 189 J7
Inguri = Enguri →
Georgia 42°27N 41°38E 191 J5
Ingushetia □ Russia 43°20N 44°50E 191 J7
Ingwavuma S. Africa 27°9S 31°59E 271 C5
Inhaca Mozam. 26°1S 32°57E 271 C5
Inhaca Pen. Mozam. 26°13S 32°55E 271 C5
Inhafenga Mozam. 20°36S 33°53E 271 B5
Inhambane Mozam. 23°54S 35°30E 271 B6
Inhambane □ Mozam. 22°30S 34°20E 271 B5
Inhambupe Brazil 11°47S 38°21W 333 D4
Inhaminga Mozam. 18°26S 35°0E 269 F4
Inharrime Mozam. 24°30S 35°0E 271 B6
Inharrime → Mozam. 24°30S 35°0E 271 B6
Inhaúma Brazil 22°51S 43°17W 135 B1
Inhisar Turkey 40°3N 30°23E 205 A12
Inhul → Ukraine 46°50N 32°0E 189 J7
Inhulec Ukraine 47°42N 33°14E 189 J7
Inhulets → Ukraine 46°46N 32°47E 189 J7
Inhuma Brazil 6°40S 41°42W 332 C3
Inhumas Brazil 16°22S 49°30W 333 E2
Iniesta Spain 39°27N 1°45W 197 F3
Ining = Yining China 43°58N 81°10E 217 D10
Inírida → Colombia 3°55N 67°52W 328 C4
Inis = Ennis Ireland 52°51N 8°59W 166 D3
Inishbofin Ireland 53°37N 10°13W 166 C1
Inisheer Ireland 53°3N 9°32W 166 C2
Inishfree B. Ireland 55°4N 8°23W 166 A3
Inishkea North Ireland 54°9N 10°11W 166 B1
Inishkea South Ireland 54°7N 10°12W 166 B1
Inishmaan Ireland 53°5N 9°35W 166 C2
Inishmore Ireland 53°8N 9°45W 166 C2
Inishmurray Ireland 54°26N 8°39W 166 B3
Inishowen Pen. Ireland 55°14N 7°15W 166 A4
Inishshark Ireland 53°37N 10°16W 166 C1
Inishturk Ireland 53°42N 10°7W 166 C1
Inishvickillane Ireland 52°3N 10°37W 166 D1
Initao Phil. 8°56N 124°20E 233 G5
Injibara Ethiopia 10°59N 37°0E 257 E4
Injinoo ✿ Australia 10°56S 142°15E 280 A3
Injune Australia 25°53S 148°32E 281 D4
Inkisi →
Dem. Rep. of the Congo 4°46S 14°52E 265 D3
Inklin → N. Amer. 58°50N 133°10W 296 B2
Inland Kaikoura Ra.
N.Z. 41°59S 173°41E 285 B8
Inland Sea = Setonaikai
Japan 34°20N 133°30E 222 C5
Inle L. Myanmar 20°30N 96°58E 241 E6
Inlet U.S.A. 43°45N 74°48W 313 C10
Inn → Austria 48°35N 13°28E 180 C6
Innamincka Australia 27°44S 140°46E 281 D3
Innbygda Norway 61°19N 12°17E 164 C9
Inner Hebrides U.K. 57°0N 6°30W 167 E2
Inner Mongolia = Nei Mongol
Zizhiqu □ China 42°0N 112°0E 226 D7
Inner Port Shelter
Hong Kong, China 22°22N 114°17E 122 A3
Inner Sound U.K. 57°30N 5°55W 167 D3
Innerkip Canada 43°13N 80°42W 312 C4
Innes △ Australia 35°52S 136°53E 282 C2
Innetalling I. Canada 56°0N 79°0W 298 A4
Innisfail Queens., Australia 17°33S 146°5E 280 B4
Innisfail Alta., Canada 52°2N 113°57W 296 C6
Innoko Nat. Wildlife Refuge ⌂
U.S.A. 63°20N 158°25W 303 E8
In'noshima Japan 34°19N 133°10E 222 C5
Innsbruck Austria 47°16N 11°23E 180 D4
Innviertel Austria 48°15N 13°15E 180 C6
Innvik Norway 61°51N 6°37E 164 C3
Inny → Ireland 53°32N 7°51W 166 C4
Ino Japan 33°33N 133°26E 222 D5
Inocência Brazil 19°47S 51°48W 333 E1
Inongo
Dem. Rep. of the Congo 1°55S 18°30E 264 C3
Inoni Congo 3°4S 15°39E 264 C3
İnönü Turkey 39°48N 30°9E 205 B12
Inoucdjouac = Inukjuak
Canada 58°25N 78°15W 295 F16
Inousses Greece 38°33N 26°14E 205 C8
Inowrocław Poland 52°50N 18°12E 185 F5
Inquisivi Bolivia 16°50S 67°10W 330 D4
Inscription, C. Australia 25°29S 112°59E 279 E1
Insein Myanmar 16°50N 96°5E 241 G6
Insjön Sweden 60°41N 15°6E 162 D9
Ińsko Poland 53°25N 15°32E 184 E2
Insterberg = Chernyakhovsk
Russia 54°36N 21°48E 184 D8
Însurăţei Romania 44°50N 27°40E 183 F12
Inta Russia 66°5N 60°8E 186 A11
Intendente Alvear
Argentina 35°12S 63°32W 334 D3
İntepe Turkey 40°1N 26°20E 205 A8
Interlachen U.S.A. 29°37N 81°53W 317 F8
Interlagos Brazil 23°41S 46°42W 137 C1
Interlaken Switz. 46°41N 7°50E 179 J3
Interlaken N.Y., U.S.A. 42°37N 76°44W 313 D8
International Falls U.S.A. 48°36N 93°25W 308 A7
Interview I. India 12°55N 92°43E 245 H11
Intiyaco Argentina 28°43S 60°5W 334 B3
Întorsura Buzăului
Romania 45°41N 26°2E 183 E11
Intramuros Phil. 14°35N 120°57E 127 B1
Intrepid Air and Space Museum
New York, U.S.A. 132 b1
Intutu Peru 3°32S 74°48W 328 D3
Inubō-Zaki Japan 35°42N 140°52E 223 B12
Inukjuak Canada 58°25N 78°15W 295 F16
Inútil, B. Chile 53°30S 70°15W 336 D2
Inuvik Canada 68°16N 133°40W 294 D5
Inuyama Japan 35°23N 136°56E 223 B8
Invalides France 48°51N 2°18E 134 A2
Inveraray U.K. 56°14N 5°5W 167 E3
Inverbervie U.K. 56°51N 2°17W 167 E6
Invercargill N.Z. 46°24S 168°24E 285 G3
Inverclyde □ U.K. 55°55N 4°49W 167 F4
Inverell Australia 29°45S 151°8E 281 D5
Invergordon U.K. 57°41N 4°10W 167 D4
Inverkeithing U.K. 56°2N 3°24W 121 A2
Inverleigh Australia 38°6S 144°3E 282 E6
Inverloch Australia 38°38S 145°45E 281 F4
Invermere Canada 50°30N 116°2W 296 C5
Inverness N.S., Canada 46°15N 61°19W 299 C7
Inverness Highl., U.K. 57°29N 4°13W 167 D4
Inverness Ala., U.S.A. 32°1N 85°45W 316 C4
Inverness Fla., U.S.A. 28°50N 82°20W 317 G7
Inverurie U.K. 57°17N 2°23W 167 D6
Investigator Group
Australia 34°45S 134°20E 281 E1
Investigator Ridge Ind. Oc. 11°30S 98°10E 273 F8
Investigator Str. Australia 35°30S 137°0E 282 C2
Inya Russia 50°28N 86°37E 217 B11
Inyanga Zimbabwe 18°12S 32°40E 269 F3
Inyangani Zimbabwe 18°5S 32°50E 269 F3
Inyantue Zimbabwe 18°33S 26°39E 270 A4
Inyo Mts. U.S.A. 36°40N 118°0W 306 J9
Inyokern U.S.A. 35°39N 117°49W 307 K9
Inyonga Tanzania 6°45S 32°5E 268 D3
Inywa Myanmar 23°56N 96°17E 241 D6
Inza Russia 53°55N 46°25E 190 D8
Inzersdorf Austria 48°8N 16°21E 142 B2
Inzhavino Russia 52°22N 42°30E 190 D6
Inzia →
Dem. Rep. of the Congo 3°45S 17°57E 265 C3
Iō-Jima Japan 30°48N 130°18E 221 J5
Ioannina Greece 39°42N 20°47E 204 B2
Iokea Papua N. G. 8°25S 146°16E 286 E4
Iola U.S.A. 37°55N 95°24W 308 G6
Iolani Palace U.S.A. 21°18N 157°51W 302 K14
Ioma Papua N. G. 8°19S 147°52E 286 E4
Ion Corvin Romania 44°7N 27°50E 183 F12
Iona Angola 16°54S 12°34E 265 F2
Iona Argyll & Bute, U.K. 56°20N 6°25W 167 E2
Iona △ Angola 16°47S 12°20E 265 F2
Ione U.S.A. 38°21N 120°56W 306 G6
Iongo Angola 9°11S 17°45E 265 D3
Ionia U.S.A. 42°59N 85°4W 311 B11
Ionian Is. = Ionioi Nisoi
Greece 38°40N 20°0E 204 C2
Ionian Sea Medit. S. 37°30N 17°30E 193 D7
Ionioi Nisoi Greece 38°40N 20°0E 204 C2
Ionioi Nisoi □ Greece 38°40N 20°0E 207 B2
Iony, Ostrov Russia 56°24N 143°22E 215 D15
Ios Greece 36°41N 25°20E 205 E7
Iowa □ U.S.A. 42°18N 93°30W 310 C3
Iowa → U.S.A. 41°10N 91°1W 310 C5
Iowa City U.S.A. 41°40N 91°32W 310 C5
Iowa Falls U.S.A. 42°31N 93°16W 310 B3
Iowa Park U.S.A. 33°57N 98°40W 314 E5
Ipala Tanzania 4°30S 32°52E 268 C3
Ipameri Brazil 17°44S 48°9W 333 E2
Ipanema Minas Gerais,
Brazil 19°47S 41°44W 333 E3
Ipanema Rio de J., Brazil 22°59S 43°12W 135 B1
Iparía Peru 9°17S 74°29W 330 B3
Ipati Greece 38°52N 22°14E 204 C4
Ipatinga Brazil 19°32S 42°30W 333 E3
Ipatovo Russia 45°45N 42°50E 191 H6
Ipek = Pejë Kosovo 42°40N 20°17E 202 D4
Ipel' → Europe 47°48N 18°53E 181 D11
Ipiales Colombia 0°50N 77°37W 328 C2
Ipiaú Brazil 14°8S 39°44W 333 D4
Ipil Phil. 7°47N 122°35E 233 H4
Ipin = Yibin China 28°45N 104°32E 228 C5
Ipirá Brazil 12°10S 39°44W 333 D4
Ipiranga Brazil 23°35S 46°36W 137 B2
Ipiranga → Brazil 23°37S 46°37W 137 B2
Ipixuna Brazil 7°0S 71°40W 330 B3
Ipixuna → Amazonas,
Brazil 7°11S 71°51W 330 B3
Ipixuna → Amazonas, Brazil 5°45S 63°2W 331 B5
Ipoh Malaysia 4°35N 101°5E 237 K3
Iponri Nigeria 6°28N 3°22E 124 B2
Iporá Brazil 16°28S 51°7W 331 D7
Ipota Vanuatu 18°52S 169°20E 287 H7
Ippy C.A.R. 6°5N 21°7E 264 A4
İpsala Turkey 40°55N 26°23E 203 F10
Ipsario, Oros Greece 40°40N 24°40E 203 F8
Ipsos Greece 39°43N 19°48E 206 B9
Ipswich Queens., Australia 27°35S 152°40E 281 D5
Ipswich Suffolk, U.K. 52°4N 1°10E 169 E9
Ipswich Mass., U.S.A. 42°41N 70°50W 313 D14
Ipswich S. Dak., U.S.A. 45°27N 99°2W 308 C4
Ipu Brazil 4°23S 40°44W 332 B3
Ipueiras Brazil 4°33S 40°43W 332 B3
Ipuh Indonesia 3°0S 101°30E 234 C2
Ipupiara Brazil 11°49S 42°37W 333 D3
Iqaluit Canada 63°44N 68°31W 295 E18
Iqaluktuutiaq = Cambridge Bay
Canada 69°10N 105°0W 294 D11
Iquique Chile 20°19S 70°5W 330 E3
Iquitos Peru 3°45S 73°10W 328 D3
Ir Gannim = Bat Yam
Israel 32°2N 34°44E 251 F5
Irabu-Jima Japan 24°50N 125°10E 221 M2
Iracoubo Fr. Guiana 5°30N 53°10W 329 B7
Īrafshān Iran 26°42N 61°56E 247 E9
Irago-Suidō Japan 34°35N 137°0E 223 C8
Irahuan Phil. 9°48N 118°41E 233 G2
Iraklia Cyclades, Greece 36°50N 25°28E 205 E7
Iraklia Serres, Greece 41°10N 23°16E 202 E7
Iraklio Greece 35°20N 25°12E 207 E6
Iráklion = Iraklio Greece 35°20N 25°12E 207 E6
Irakliou, Kolpos Greece 35°23N 25°8E 207 E6
Irako-Zaki Japan 34°35N 137°1E 223 C9
Irala Paraguay 25°55S 54°35W 335 B5
Iran ■ Asia 33°0N 53°0E 247 C7
Iran, Pegunungan
Malaysia 2°20N 114°50E 235 B4
Iran Ra. = Iran, Pegunungan
Malaysia 2°20N 114°50E 235 B4
Iranamadu Tank Sri Lanka 9°23N 80°29E 245 K5
Īrānshahr Iran 27°15N 60°40E 247 E9
Irapa Venezuela 10°34N 62°35W 329 A5
Irapuato Mexico 20°41N 101°28W 318 C4
Iraq ■ Asia 33°0N 44°0E 213 F10
Irarrar, O. → Mali 20°0N 1°30E 261 E5
Irati Brazil 25°25S 50°38W 335 B5
Irazú, Volcan Costa Rica 9°59N 83°51W 320 D3
Irbes saurums Latvia 57°45N 22°5E 184 A9
Irbid Jordan 32°35N 35°48E 251 F6
Irbid □ Jordan 32°30N 35°50E 250 F6
Irbil = Arbīl Iraq 36°15N 44°5E 213 D11
Irebu Dem. Rep. of the Congo 0°40S 17°46E 264 C3
Irecê Brazil 11°18S 41°52W 332 D3
Iregua → Spain 42°27N 2°24E 196 C7
Ireland ■ Europe 53°50N 7°52W 166 C4
Ireland I. Bermuda 32°19N 64°50W 153 a
Ireland Island Bermuda 32°19N 64°50W 153 a
Irele Nigeria 7°40N 5°40E 263 D6
Ireng → Brazil 3°33N 59°51W 329 C6
Irerrer, O. → Algeria 19°25N 5°47E 261 E6
Irgiz = Yrghyz Kazakhstan 48°37N 61°16E 216 C6
Irgiz = Yrghyz →
Kazakhstan 48°6N 62°30E 216 C6
Irgiz, Bolshaya → Russia 52°10N 49°10E 190 D9
Irharrhar, O. → Algeria 28°3N 6°15E 261 C6
Irherm Morocco 30°7N 8°18W 260 B3
Irhil M'Goun Morocco 31°30N 6°28W 260 B3
Iri = Iksan S. Korea 35°59N 127°0E 224 E3
Irian Barat = Papua □
Indonesia 4°0S 137°0E 231 E9
Irian Jaya = Papua □
Indonesia 4°0S 137°0E 231 E9
Irian Jaya Barat □
Indonesia 2°5S 132°50E 231 E8
Iriba Chad 15°7N 22°15E 259 E4
Irié Guinea 8°15N 9°10W 262 D3
Iriga Phil. 13°25N 123°25E 232 E4
Irinklinskoye Vdkhr. Russia 52°0N 59°0E 216 B5
Iringa Tanzania 7°48S 35°43E 268 D4
Iringa □ Tanzania 7°48S 35°43E 268 D4
Irinjalakuda India 10°21N 76°14E 245 J3
Iriomote ⌂ Japan 24°29N 123°53E 221 M1
Iriomote-Jima Japan 24°19N 123°48E 221 M1
Iriona Honduras 15°57N 85°11W 320 C2
Iriri → Brazil 3°52S 52°37W 329 D7
Iriri Novo → Brazil 8°46S 53°22W 331 B7
Irish Sea Europe 53°38N 4°48W 168 D3
Irkeshtam Pass = Erkech-Tam Pass
Asia 39°46N 74°2E 217 E8
Irkutsk Russia 52°18N 104°20E 218 A9
Irlığanlı Turkey 37°53N 29°12E 205 D11
Irma Canada 52°55N 111°14W 297 C6
Irō-Zaki Japan 34°36N 138°51E 223 C10
Irois B. Trin. & Tob. 10°9N 61°45W 323 t
Iroise, Mer d' France 48°15N 4°45W 172 D2
Iron Baron Australia 32°58S 137°11E 282 B2
Iron Gate = Portile de Fier
Europe 44°44N 22°30E 182 F7
Iron Knob Australia 32°46S 137°8E 282 B2
Iron Mountain U.S.A. 45°49N 88°4W 308 C9
Iron Range △ Australia 12°34S 143°18E 280 A3
Iron River U.S.A. 46°6N 88°39W 308 B9
Irondequoit U.S.A. 43°13N 77°35W 312 C7
Ironton Mo., U.S.A. 37°36N 90°38W 308 G8
Ironton Ohio, U.S.A. 38°32N 82°41W 309 F12
Ironwood U.S.A. 46°27N 90°9W 308 B8
Ironwood Forest ⌂
U.S.A. 32°32N 111°28W 305 K8
Iroquois Canada 44°51N 75°19W 313 B9
Iroquois → U.S.A. 41°5N 87°49W 311 C9
Iroquois Falls Canada 48°46N 80°41W 298 C3
Iroquois Point U.S.A. 21°19N 157°58W 302 K14
Irosin Phil. 12°42N 124°2E 232 E5
Irpin Ukraine 50°30N 30°15E 177 C16
Irqieqa, Ras l- Malta 35°56N 14°29E 206 F7
Irrara Cr. → Australia 29°35S 145°31E 281 D4
Irrawaddy = Ayeyawadi →
Myanmar 15°50N 95°6E 241 G5
Irrawaddy □ Myanmar 17°0N 95°0E 241 G5
Irrawaddy, Mouths of the
Myanmar 15°30N 95°0E 241 H5
Irricana Canada 51°19N 113°37W 296 C6
Irrunytju Australia 26°3S 128°56E 279 E4
Irshava Ukraine 48°19N 23°3E 182 B8
Irsina Italy 40°45N 16°14E 201 B9
Irtysh → Russia 61°4N 68°52E 214 C7
Irumu Dem. Rep. of the Congo 1°32N 29°53E 268 B2
Irún Spain 43°20N 1°52W 196 B3
Irunea = Pamplona-Iruña
Spain 42°48N 1°38W 196 C3
Irurzun Spain 42°55N 1°50W 196 C3
Irvine Alta., Canada 49°57N 110°16W 297 D6
Irvine N. Ayrs., U.K. 55°37N 4°41W 167 F4
Irvine Calif., U.S.A. 33°41N 117°46W 307 M9
Irvine Ky., U.S.A. 37°42N 83°58W 311 G13
Irvinestown U.K. 54°28N 7°39W 166 B4
Irving U.S.A. 32°48N 96°56W 120 B4
Irving Park U.S.A. 41°57N 87°42W 119 B2
Irvington U.S.A. 37°53N 86°17W 311 G10
Irvona U.S.A. 40°46N 78°33W 312 F6
Irwin → Australia 29°15S 114°54E 279 E1
Irwinton U.S.A. 32°49N 83°10W 316 C6
Irwinville U.S.A. 31°39N 83°23W 316 D6
Irymple Australia 34°14S 142°8E 282 C5
Is, Jebel Sudan 22°3N 35°28E 256 C4
Is-sur-Tille France 47°30N 5°8E 173 E12
Isa Nigeria 13°14N 6°24E 263 C6
Isa Khel Pakistan 32°41N 71°17E 242 C4
Isaac → Australia 22°55S 149°20E 280 C4
Isabel Rio de J., Brazil 22°55S 43°14W 135 B1
Isabel S. Dak., U.S.A. 45°24N 101°26W 308 C3
Isabel, I. Mexico 21°51N 105°55W 318 C3
Isabel Segunda Puerto Rico 18°9N 65°27W 321 b
Isabela Basilan, Phil. 6°40N 121°59E 233 H3
Isabela Negros, Phil. 10°12N 122°59E 233 F4
Isabela Puerto Rico 18°30N 67°2W 321 b
Isabela □ Phil. 17°0N 122°0E 232 C4
Isabela, Canal Ecuador 0°20S 90°55W 330 a
Isabela, I. Ecuador 0°30S 91°4W 330 a
Isabella, Cord. Nic. 13°30N 85°25W 320 D2
Isabella Ra. Australia 21°0S 121°4E 278 D3
Isaccea Romania 45°16N 28°28E 183 E13
Isachsen, C. Canada 79°20N 105°28W 295 B10
Isachsen Mt. Antarctica 72°8S 26°5E 151 D4
Ísafjarðardjúp Iceland 66°10N 23°0W 155 A3
Ísafjarðarsýsla Iceland 66°5N 23°9W 155 A3
Ísafjörður Iceland 66°5N 23°9W 155 A3
Isagarh India 24°48N 77°51E 242 G7
Isagatedo Nigeria 6°31N 3°19E 124 A1
Isahaya Japan 32°52N 130°2E 222 E2
Isaka Dem. Rep. of the Congo 2°33S 18°54E 264 C3
Isaka Tanzania 3°56S 32°59E 268 C3
Işalniţa Romania 44°24N 23°44E 183 F8
Isalo, Tangorombohitr'
Madag. 22°45S 45°15E 272 C2
Isalo △ Madag. 22°23S 45°16E 272 C2
Isan → India 26°51N 80°7E 243 F9
Isana = Içana → Brazil 0°26N 67°19W 328 C4
Isandja
Dem. Rep. of the Congo 2°59S 21°59E 264 C4
Isangano △ Zambia 11°8S 30°35E 269 E3
Isangi Dem. Rep. of the Congo 0°52N 24°10E 264 B4
Isanlu Makutu Nigeria 8°20N 5°50E 263 D6
Isar → Bayern, Germany 48°48N 12°57E 179 G8
Isar → Oberbayern,
Germany 48°15N 11°41E 131 A3
Isarco → Italy 46°27N 11°18E 199 B8
Isaris Greece 37°22N 22°0E 204 D3
Isarog, Mt. Phil. 13°39N 123°23E 232 E4
Isawa Japan 35°40N 138°35E 223 B10
Íscar Spain 41°22N 4°32W 194 D6
Iscayachi Bolivia 21°31S 65°3W 331 E4
İscehisar Turkey 38°51N 30°45E 205 C12
Íschia Italy 40°44N 13°57E 200 B6
Ischigualasto △ Argentina 30°0S 68°0W 334 B2
Iscuandé Colombia 2°28N 77°59W 328 C2
Isdell → Australia 16°27S 124°51E 278 C3
Ise Japan 34°25N 136°45E 223 C8
Ise-Shima △ Japan 34°25N 136°48E 223 C8
Ise-Wan Japan 34°43N 136°43E 223 C8
Isefjord Denmark 55°53N 11°50E 163 J5
Isel → Austria 46°50N 12°47E 180 E5
Iseo Italy 45°39N 10°3E 198 C7
Iseo, L. d' Italy 45°43N 10°4E 198 C7
Iseramagazi Tanzania 4°37S 32°10E 268 C3
Isère □ France 45°15N 5°40E 175 C9
Isère → France 44°59N 4°51E 175 D8
Iserlohn Germany 51°22N 7°41E 178 D3
Isérnia Italy 41°36N 14°14E 201 A7
Isesaki Japan 36°19N 139°12E 223 A11
Iseyin Nigeria 8°0N 3°36E 263 D5
Isfahan = Eşfahān Iran 32°39N 51°43E 247 C6
Isfjorden Norway 62°35N 7°49E 164 B4
Ishbīlīya Iraq 33°21N 44°26E 113 A2
Ishëm Albania 41°33N 19°34E 202 E3
Ishenga Oshwe
Dem. Rep. of the Congo 3°57S 22°33E 264 C4
Isherton Guyana 2°20N 59°25W 329 C6
Ishigaki Japan 24°26N 124°10E 221 M2
Ishigaki-Shima Japan 24°20N 124°10E 221 M2
Ishikari Japan 43°20N 141°15E 220 C10
Ishikari-Gawa → Japan 43°15N 141°23E 220 C10
Ishikari-Sammyaku
Japan 43°30N 143°0E 220 C11
Ishikari-Wan Japan 43°25N 141°1E 220 C10
Ishikawa Japan 26°25N 127°49E 288 a
Ishikawa □ Japan 36°30N 136°30E 223 A8
Ishim Russia 56°10N 69°30E 214 D7
Ishim → Russia 57°45N 71°10E 214 D8
Ishimbay Russia 53°28N 56°2E 216 B5
Ishinomaki Japan 38°32N 141°20E 220 E10
Ishioka Japan 36°11N 140°16E 223 A12
Ishizuchi-Yama Japan 33°45N 133°6E 222 D5

Ishkashim Tajikistan 36°44N 71°37E 217 E8
Ishkoman Pakistan 36°30N 73°50E 243 A5
Ishøj Strand Denmark 55°36N 12°20E 118 B2
Ishpeming U.S.A. 46°29N 87°40W 308 B10
Ishurdi Bangla. 24°9N 89°3E 241 C2
Isiboro Sécure △ Bolivia 16°15S 65°50W 331 D4
Isigny-sur-Mer France 49°19N 1°6W 172 C5
Isıklar Dağı Turkey 40°45N 27°15E 203 F11
Işıklı Turkey 38°19N 29°51E 205 C11
Isil Kul Russia 54°55N 71°16E 217 B8
Ísili Italy 39°44N 9°6E 200 C2
iSimangaliso ⌓ S. Africa 27°50S 32°32E 271 C5
Isiolo Kenya 0°24N 37°33E 268 B4
Isiolo □ Kenya 1°0N 37°30E 268 B4
Isiro Dem. Rep. of the Congo 2°53N 27°40E 268 B2
Isisford Australia 24°15S 144°21E 280 C3
Iskar ➝ Bulgaria 43°45N 24°25E 203 C8
İskele = Trikomo Cyprus 35°17N 33°52E 207 E9
İskenderun Turkey 36°32N 36°10E 250 B7
İskenderun Körfezi
Turkey 36°40N 35°50E 250 B6
İskilip Turkey 40°45N 34°29E 212 B6
Iskitim Russia 54°38N 83°18E 217 B10
Iskŭr = Iskar ➝ Bulgaria 43°45N 24°25E 203 C8
Iskŭr, Yazovir Bulgaria 42°23N 23°30E 202 D7
Iskushuban Somalia 10°18N 50°12E 267 B7
Iskut ➝ Canada 56°45N 131°49W 296 B2
Isla ➝ U.K. 56°32N 3°20W 167 E5
Isla Coiba △ Panama 7°33N 81°36W 320 E4
Isla Cristina Spain 37°13N 7°17W 195 H3
Isla de Salamanca △
Colombia 10°59N 74°40W 328 A3
Isla Gorge △ Australia 25°10S 149°57E 280 D4
Isla Gorgona △ Colombia 2°59N 78°10W 328 C2
Isla Guamblin △ Chile 44°50S 75°4W 336 B1
Isla Isabel △ Mexico 21°54N 105°58W 318 C3
Isla Magdalena △ Chile 44°20S 73°13W 336 B2
Isla Tiburón y San Esteban ⌓
Mexico 29°0N 112°27W 318 B2
Isla Vista U.S.A. 34°25N 119°53W 307 L7
İslahiye Turkey 37°0N 36°35E 250 B7
Islam Headworks Pakistan 29°49N 72°33E 242 E5
Islamabad Pakistan 33°40N 73°10E 242 C5
Islamgarh Pakistan 27°51N 70°48E 242 F4
Islamkot Pakistan 24°42N 70°13E 242 G4
Islamorada U.S.A. 24°56N 80°37W 317 L9
Islampur Bihar, India 25°9N 85°12E 243 G11
Islampur Maharashtra, India 17°2N 74°20E 244 F2
Islampur Paschimbanga,
India 26°16N 88°12E 243 F13
Island = Iceland ■ Europe 64°45N 19°0W 155 C8
Island B. Phil. 9°6N 118°10E 233 G2
Island Harbour Anguilla 18°12N 63°0W 322 a
Island L. Canada 53°47N 94°25W 297 C10
Island Lagoon Australia 31°30S 136°40E 282 A2
Island Park Canada 43°37N 79°22W 141 B2
Island Pond U.S.A. 44°49N 71°53W 313 B13
Islands, B. of Nfld. & L.,
Canada 49°11N 58°15W 299 C8
Islands, B. of N.Z. 35°15S 174°6E 284 B3
Islas Atlánticas de Galicia △
Spain 42°23N 8°55W 194 C2
Islay U.K. 55°46N 6°10W 167 F2
Isle ➝ France 44°55N 0°15W 174 D3
Isle aux Morts Canada 47°35N 59°0W 299 C8
Isle of Hope U.S.A. 31°58N 81°5W 316 D8
Isle of Wight □ U.K. 50°41N 1°17W 169 G6
Isle Royale △ U.S.A. 48°0N 88°55W 308 B9
Isleton U.S.A. 38°10N 121°37W 306 G5
Islev Denmark 55°41N 12°27E 118 A2
Isleworth U.K. 51°28N 0°19W 125 B2
Islington Canada 43°38N 79°30W 141 B1
Islington □ U.K. 51°33N 0°5W 125 A3
Islote Pt. Trin. & Tob. 10°4N 61°47W 323 t
Ismail = Izmayil Ukraine 45°22N 28°46E 183 E13
Ismâ'ilîya Egypt 30°37N 32°18E 251 H3
Ismâ'ilîya □ Egypt 30°35N 32°16E 251 H3
Ismâ'ilîya, Qanâ el Egypt 30°7N 31°17E 117 A2
Ismâ'ilîya, Tir'at el ➝
Egypt 30°4N 31°16E 251 H2
Ismaning Germany 48°13N 11°40E 131 A3
Ismayloskiy Park Russia 55°46N 37°46E 129 B3
Isna Egypt 25°17N 32°30E 256 B3
Isoanala Madag. 23°50S 45°44E 272 C2
Isojärvi △ Finland 61°40N 25°0E 160 F21
Ísola del Liri Italy 41°41N 13°34E 199 G10
Ísola della Scala Italy 45°16N 11°0E 198 C7
Ísola di Capo Rizzuto Italy 38°58N 17°6E 201 D10
Isolo Nigeria 6°31N 3°19E 124 A1
Isparta Turkey 37°47N 30°30E 205 D12
Isparta □ Turkey 38°0N 31°0E 212 D4
Isperih Bulgaria 43°43N 26°50E 203 C10
Isperikh = Isperih
Bulgaria 43°43N 26°50E 203 C10
Íspica Italy 36°47N 14°55E 201 F7
İspir Turkey 40°28N 40°59E 213 B9
Israel ■ Asia 32°0N 34°50E 251 G5
Isratu Eritrea 16°20N 39°53E 257 D4
Issakly Russia 54°8N 51°32E 190 C10
Issano Guyana 5°49N 59°26W 329 B6
Issaouane, Erg Algeria 26°58N 8°42E 258 C1
Issia Côte d'Ivoire 6°33N 6°33W 262 D3
Issoire France 45°32N 3°15E 174 C7
Issoudun France 46°57N 1°59E 173 F8
Issy-les-Moulineaux
France 48°49N 2°15E 134 B2
Issyk-Kul = Balykchy
Kyrgyzstan 42°26N 76°12E 217 D9
Issyk-Kul, Ozero = Ysyk-Köl
Kyrgyzstan 42°25N 77°15E 217 D9
Ist Croatia 44°17N 14°47E 199 D11
Istállós-kő Hungary 48°4N 20°26E 182 B5
İstanbul Turkey 41°0N 28°58E 122 C1
İstanbul □ Turkey 41°0N 29°0E 203 E12
İstanbul ✕ (IST) Turkey 40°59N 28°49E 203 F12
İstanbul Boğazı Turkey 41°5N 29°3E 122 B2
Istaravshān Tajikistan 39°55N 69°1E 217 E7
Isteren Norway 61°58N 11°47E 164 B8
Istiea Greece 38°57N 23°9E 204 C5
İstinye Turkey 41°6N 29°3E 122 B2
Istmina Colombia 5°10N 76°39W 328 B2
Isto, Mt. U.S.A. 69°12N 143°48W 303 B12
Istok = Burim Kosovo 42°45N 20°24E 202 D4
Istokpoga, L. U.S.A. 27°23N 81°17W 317 H8
Istra Croatia 45°10N 14°0E 199 C10
Istres France 43°31N 4°59E 175 E8
Istria = Istra Croatia 45°10N 14°0E 199 C10
Isugod Phil. 9°19N 118°5E 233 G2
Isulan Phil. 6°30N 124°29E 233 H5
Isumrud Str. Papua N. G. 4°50S 145°50E 286 D3
Itá Paraguay 25°29S 57°21W 334 B4
Itä Hakkila Finland 60°17N 25°7E 121 B3
Itabaiana Paraíba, Brazil 7°18S 35°19W 332 C4
Itabaiana Sergipe, Brazil 10°41S 37°37W 332 D4
Itabaianinha Brazil 11°16S 37°47W 332 D4
Itaberaba Brazil 12°32S 40°18W 333 D3
Itaberaí Brazil 16°2S 49°48W 333 E2
Itabira Brazil 19°37S 43°13W 333 E3
Itabirito Brazil 20°15S 43°48W 333 F3
Itaboca Brazil 4°50S 62°40W 329 D5
Itabuna Brazil 14°48S 39°16W 333 D4
Itacajá Brazil 8°19S 47°46W 332 C2
Itacaunas ➝ Brazil 5°21S 49°8W 332 C2
Itacoatiara Brazil 2°58S 58°30W 329 D6
Itaewon S. Korea 37°32N 126°58E 137 B1
Itaguaí Brazil 22°15S 43°46W 335 A7
Itaguari ➝ Brazil 14°11S 44°40W 333 D3
Itaguatins Brazil 5°47S 47°29W 332 C2
Itaim ➝ Brazil 7°2S 42°2W 332 C3
Itainópolis Brazil 7°24S 41°31W 332 C3
Itaipú, Represa de Brazil 25°30S 54°30W 335 B5
Itäisen Suomenlahti △
Finland 60°25N 27°15E 160 F22
Itaituba Brazil 4°10S 55°50W 329 D6
Itajaí Brazil 27°50S 48°39W 335 B6
Itajany do Sul = Rio do Sul
Brazil 27°13S 49°37W 335 B6
Itajubá Brazil 22°24S 45°30W 333 F2
Itajuípe Brazil 14°41S 39°22W 333 D4
Itaka Tanzania 8°50S 32°49E 269 D3
Itako Japan 35°56N 140°33E 223 B12
Itala ⌓ S. Africa 27°30S 31°7E 271 C5
Italy ■ Europe 42°0N 13°0E 192 C6
Itamaraju Brazil 17°4S 39°32W 333 E4
Itamarati Brazil 6°24S 68°15W 330 B4
Itamataré Brazil 2°16S 46°24W 332 B2
Itambacuri Brazil 18°1S 41°42W 333 E3
Itambé Brazil 15°15S 40°37W 333 E3
Itami Japan 34°46N 135°24E 133 A1
Itampolo Madag. 24°41S 43°57E 272 C1
Itanagar India 27°6N 93°37E 241 B4
Itandrano Madag. 21°47S 45°17E 272 C2
Itanhaém Brazil 24°11S 46°47W 333 F2
Itanhanga Brazil 22°59S 43°19W 135 B1
Itanhauã ➝ Brazil 4°45S 63°48W 329 D5
Itanhém Brazil 17°9S 40°20W 333 E3
Itano Japan 34°7N 134°28E 222 C6
Itapaci Brazil 14°57S 49°34W 333 D2
Itapagé Brazil 3°41S 39°34W 332 B4
Itaparica = Petrolândia
Brazil 9°5S 38°20W 332 C4
Itaparica, I. de Brazil 12°54S 38°42W 333 D4
Itaparica, Represa de
Brazil 11°3S 42°47W 332 D3
Itapebi Brazil 15°56S 39°32W 333 E4
Itapecuru Mirim Brazil 3°24S 44°20W 332 B3
Itaperuna Brazil 21°10S 41°54W 333 F3
Itapetinga Brazil 15°15S 40°15W 333 E3
Itapetininga Brazil 23°36S 48°7W 335 A6
Itapeva Brazil 23°59S 48°59W 335 A6
Itapicuru ➝ Bahia, Brazil 11°47S 37°32W 332 D4
Itapicuru ➝ Maranhão,
Brazil 2°52S 44°12W 332 B3
Itapipoca Brazil 3°30S 39°35W 332 B4
Itapira = Ubaitaba Brazil 14°18S 39°20W 333 D4
Itapiranga Brazil 2°45S 58°1W 329 D6
Itapiúna Brazil 4°33S 38°57W 332 B4
Itaporanga Paraíba, Brazil 7°18S 38°0W 332 C4
Itaporanga São Paulo,
Brazil 23°42S 49°29W 333 F2
Itapuá □ Paraguay 26°40S 55°40W 335 B4
Itapuranga Brazil 15°40S 49°59W 333 E2
Itaquai ➝ Brazil 4°20S 70°12W 330 A3
Itaquí Maranhão, Brazil 2°34S 44°22W 332 B3
Itaquí Rio Grande do S.,
Brazil 29°8S 56°30W 334 B4
Itararé Brazil 24°6S 49°23W 335 A6
Itarsi India 22°36N 77°51E 242 H7
Itarumã Brazil 18°42S 51°25W 333 E1
Itasy □ Madag. 19°0S 46°45E 272 B2
Itatí Argentina 27°16S 58°15W 334 B4
Itatiaia △ Brazil 22°22S 44°38W 335 A7
Itatira Brazil 4°30S 39°37W 332 B4
Itatuba Brazil 5°46S 63°20W 331 B5
Itatupã Brazil 0°37S 51°12W 329 D7
Itaueira Brazil 7°36S 43°2W 332 C3
Itaueira ➝ Brazil 6°41S 42°55W 332 C3
Itaúna Brazil 20°4S 44°34W 333 F3
Itbayat Phil. 20°47N 121°51E 232 A3
Itbayat I. Phil. 20°45N 121°50E 232 A3
Itcha Ilgachuz ⌓ Canada 52°42N 124°58W 296 C3
Itchen ➝ U.K. 50°55N 1°22W 169 G6
Itchouma Niger 20°14N 13°32E 261 D7
Ite Peru 17°55S 70°57W 330 D3
Itea Greece 38°25N 22°25E 204 C4
Itezhi Tezhi, L. Zambia 15°30S 25°30E 269 F2
Ithaca = Ithaki Greece 38°25N 20°40E 207 C2
Ithaca U.S.A. 42°27N 76°30W 313 D8
Ithaki Greece 38°25N 20°40E 207 C2
Ithakis, Stenon Greece 38°22N 20°39E 207 C2
Iti △ Greece 38°50N 22°15E 204 C4
Itimbiri ➝
Dem. Rep. of the Congo 2°2N 22°44E 264 B4
Itinga Brazil 16°36S 41°47W 333 E3
Itiquira Brazil 17°12S 54°7W 331 D7
Itiquira ➝ Brazil 17°18S 56°44W 331 D6
Itiruçu Brazil 13°31S 40°9W 333 D3
Itiúba Brazil 10°43S 39°51W 332 D4
Itiyuro ➝ Argentina 22°40S 63°50W 334 A3
Itkilik ➝ U.S.A. 70°9N 150°56W 303 A10
Itō Japan 34°58N 139°5E 223 C11
Itogon Phil. 16°22N 120°41E 232 C3
Itoigawa Japan 37°2N 137°51E 221 F8
Itoko Dem. Rep. of the Congo 1°0S 21°48E 264 C4
Itoman Japan 26°7N 127°40E 288 a
Iton ➝ France 49°9N 1°12E 172 C8
Itonamas ➝ Bolivia 12°28S 64°24W 331 C5
Itri Italy 41°17N 13°32E 200 A6
Itsa Egypt 29°15N 30°47E 256 J7
Itsamia Comoros Is. 12°21S 43°52E 272 a
Itsandra Comoros Is. 11°40S 43°15E 272 a
Itsuki Japan 32°24N 130°50E 222 E2
Itsukushima Shrine
Japan 34°17N 132°19E 222 C4
Íttiri Italy 40°36N 8°34E 200 B1
Ittoqqortoormiit Greenland 70°20N 23°0W 154 C8
Itu Brazil 23°17S 47°15W 335 A6
Itu Nigeria 5°10N 7°58E 263 D6
Itu Aba I. S. China Sea 10°23N 114°21E 230 B4
Ituaçu Brazil 13°50S 41°18W 333 D3
Ituango Colombia 7°4N 75°45W 328 B2
Ituí ➝ Brazil 4°38S 70°19W 328 D3
Ituiutaba Brazil 19°0S 49°25W 333 E2
Itumbiara Brazil 18°20S 49°10W 333 E2
Ituna Canada 51°10N 103°24W 297 C8
Itunge Port Tanzania 9°40S 33°55E 269 D3
Ituni Guyana 5°28N 58°15W 329 B6
Itupiranga Brazil 5°9S 49°20W 332 C2
Iturama Brazil 19°44S 50°11W 333 E1
Iturbe Argentina 23°0S 65°25W 334 A2
Ituri Dem. Rep. of the Congo 2°30N 29°30E 268 B2
Ituri □ Dem. Rep. of the Congo 1°30N 29°0E 266 D2
Ituri ➝
Dem. Rep. of the Congo 1°40N 27°1E 268 B2
Iturup, Ostrov Russia 45°0N 148°0E 215 E15
Ituverava Brazil 20°20S 47°47W 333 F2
Ituxi ➝ Brazil 7°18S 64°51W 331 B5
Itzehoe Germany 53°55N 9°31E 178 B5
Iuka U.S.A. 38°37N 88°47W 311 F8
Iungsdalshytta Norway 60°49N 7°55E 164 D4
Ivahona Madag. 23°27S 46°10E 272 C2
Ivaí ➝ Brazil 23°18S 53°42W 335 A5
Ivalo Finland 68°38N 27°35E 160 B22
Ivalojoki ➝ Finland 68°40N 27°40E 160 B22
Ivanava Belarus 52°7N 25°29E 177 B13
Ivančice Czechia 49°6N 16°23E 181 B9
Ivane-Puste Ukraine 48°39N 26°10E 183 B11
Ivănești Romania 46°39N 27°27E 183 D12
Ivangorod = Dęblin
Poland 51°34N 21°50E 185 G8
Ivangorod Russia 59°27N 28°13E 188 C5
Ivanhoe N.S.W., Australia 32°56S 144°20E 282 B6
Ivanhoe Vic., Australia 37°45S 145°3E 128 A2
Ivanhoe Ont., Canada 44°23N 77°28W 312 B7
Ivanhoe Calif., U.S.A. 36°23N 119°13W 306 J7
Ivanhoe Minn., U.S.A. 44°28N 96°15W 308 C5
Ivanhorod Ukraine 48°48N 29°50E 183 B14
Ivanić Grad Croatia 45°41N 16°25E 199 C13
Ivanjica Serbia 43°35N 20°12E 202 C4
Ivanjska Bos.-H. 44°55N 17°4E 182 F2
Ivankoyskoye Vdkhr.
Russia 56°37N 36°32E 188 D9
Ivano-Frankivsk Ukraine 48°40N 24°40E 183 B9
Ivano-Frankivsk □
Ukraine 48°45N 24°30E 183 B9
Ivanof Bay U.S.A. 55°54N 159°29W 303 J8
Ivanovo = Ivanava
Belarus 52°7N 25°29E 177 B13
Ivanovo Bulgaria 43°43N 25°58E 203 C9
Ivanovo Russia 57°5N 41°0E 188 D11
Ivanovo □ Russia 57°10N 41°50E 190 B5
Ivanšćica Croatia 46°12N 16°13E 199 B13
Ivashchenkovo = Chapayevsk
Russia 53°0N 49°40E 190 D9
Ivato Madag. 20°37S 47°10E 272 C2
Ivatsevichy Belarus 52°43N 25°21E 177 B13
Ivaylovgrad Bulgaria 41°32N 26°8E 203 E10
Ivdel Russia 60°42N 60°24E 186 B11
Iveragh Pen. Ireland 51°52N 10°15W 166 E1
Ives Estates U.S.A. 25°58N 80°10W 129 C2
Ivgres = Komsomolsk
Russia 57°2N 40°20E 188 D11
Ivindo ➝ Gabon 0°9S 12°9E 264 C2
Ivinheima ➝ Brazil 23°14S 53°42W 335 A5
Ivinhema Brazil 22°10S 53°37W 335 A5
Ivittuut Greenland 61°14N 48°12W 154 E6
Iviza = Eivissa Spain 38°54N 1°26E 206 D1
Ivohibe Madag. 22°31S 46°57E 272 C2
Ivolândia Brazil 16°34S 50°51W 333 E1
Ivory Coast = Côte d'Ivoire ■
Africa 7°30N 5°0W 262 D4
Ivory Coast W. Afr. 4°20N 5°0W 262 E4
Ivösjön Sweden 56°8N 14°25E 163 H8
Ivrea Italy 45°28N 7°52E 198 C4
İvrindi Turkey 39°34N 27°30E 205 B9
Ivry-sur-Seine France 48°49N 2°22E 134 B3
Ivujivik Canada 62°24N 77°55W 295 E16
Ivvavik △ Canada 69°6N 139°30W 294 D4
Ivybridge U.K. 50°23N 3°56W 169 G4
Iwa Japan 36°5N 139°52E 223 A11
Iwai-Jima Japan 33°47N 131°58E 222 D3
Iwaizumi Japan 39°50N 141°45E 220 E10
Iwaki Japan 37°3N 140°55E 221 F10
Iwakuni Japan 34°15N 132°8E 222 C4
Iwami Japan 35°32N 134°15E 222 B6
Iwami Ginzan Japan 35°6N 132°26E 222 B4
Iwamizawa Japan 43°12N 141°46E 220 C10
Iwanai Japan 42°58N 140°30E 220 C10
Iwase Japan 36°21N 140°6E 223 A12
Iwata Japan 34°42N 137°51E 223 C9
Iwate □ Japan 39°30N 141°30E 220 E10
Iwate-San Japan 39°51N 141°0E 220 E10
Iwo Nigeria 7°39N 4°9E 263 D5
Iwo Jima Pac. Oc. 24°47N 141°20E 288 b
Iwŏn N. Korea 40°19N 128°39E 224 B4
Iwonicz-Zdrój Poland 49°37N 21°47E 185 J8
Iwungu
Dem. Rep. of the Congo 5°16S 19°17E 265 D3
Ixelles Belgium 50°50N 4°22E 116 B2
Ixiamas Bolivia 13°50S 68°5W 330 C4
Ixopo S. Africa 30°11S 30°5E 271 D5
Ixtepec Mexico 16°34N 95°6W 319 D5
Ixtlán del Río Mexico 21°2N 104°22W 318 C4
Iyal Bakhit Sudan 13°20N 28°39E 257 E2
Iyo Japan 33°45N 132°45E 222 D4
Iyo-Mishima Japan 33°58N 133°30E 222 D5
Iyo-Nada Japan 33°40N 132°20E 222 D4
Izabal, L. de Guatemala 15°30N 89°10W 320 C2
Izamal Mexico 20°56N 89°1W 319 C7
Izberbash Russia 42°35N 47°52E 191 J8
Izbica Poland 50°53N 23°10E 185 H10
Izbica Kujawska Poland 52°25N 18°40E 185 F5
Izbiceni Romania 43°45N 24°40E 183 G9
Izembek Nat. Wildlife Refuge ⌓
U.S.A. 55°15N 162°45W 303 J7
Izena-Shima Japan 26°56N 127°56E 221 L3
Izgrev Bulgaria 43°36N 26°58E 203 C10
Izhevsk Russia 56°51N 53°14E 186 C9
Izhma = Sosnogorsk
Russia 63°37N 53°51E 186 B9
Izhma ➝ Russia 65°19N 52°54E 186 A9
Izileg Algeria 20°20N 6°4E 261 D6
Izkī Oman 22°56N 57°46E 249 B7
Izmayil Ukraine 45°22N 28°46E 183 E13
Izmaylovo Russia 55°47N 37°47E 129 B3
İzmir Turkey 38°25N 27°8E 205 C9
İzmir □ Turkey 38°15N 27°40E 205 C9
İzmir Adnan Menderes ✕ (ADB)
Turkey 38°23N 27°6E 205 C9
İzmir Körfezi Turkey 38°30N 26°50E 205 C8
İzmit = Kocaeli Turkey 40°45N 29°50E 203 F13
Iznájar Spain 37°15N 4°19W 195 H6
Iznalloz Spain 37°24N 3°30W 195 H7
İznik Turkey 40°23N 29°46E 212 B3
İznik Gölü Turkey 40°27N 29°30E 203 F13
Izobilno-Tishchenskoye = Izobil'nyy
Russia 45°25N 41°44E 191 H5
Izobil'nyy Russia 45°25N 41°44E 191 H5
Izola Slovenia 45°32N 13°39E 199 C10
Izozog, Bañados de
Bolivia 18°48S 62°10W 331 D5
Izra Syria 32°51N 36°15E 250 F7
Iztacalco Mexico 19°23N 99°5W 128 B2
Iztapalapa Mexico 19°21N 99°6W 128 B2
Iztochni Rodopi Bulgaria 41°45N 25°30E 203 E9
Izu Japan 34°58N 138°56E 223 C10
Izu-Hantō Japan 34°45N 139°0E 223 C11
Izu-Shotō Japan 34°30N 140°0E 221 G10
Izúcar de Matamoros
Mexico 18°36N 98°28W 319 D5
Izuhara Japan 34°12N 129°17E 222 C1
Izumi Kagoshima, Japan 32°5N 130°22E 222 E2
Izumi Ōsaka, Japan 34°28N 135°24E 223 C7
Izumi-Sano Japan 34°23N 135°18E 223 C7
Izumo Japan 35°20N 132°46E 222 B4
Izunokuni Japan 35°2N 138°55E 223 B10
Izyaslav Ukraine 50°5N 26°50E 177 C14
Izyum Ukraine 49°12N 37°19E 189 H9

J

J.F.K. Int. ✕ (JFK)
U.S.A. 40°38N 73°47W 313 F11
J.F. Rodrigues Brazil 2°55S 50°20W 332 B1
J.P. Koch Fjord Greenland 82°45N 44°0W 154 A6
J. Strom Thurmond L.
U.S.A. 33°40N 82°12W 316 B7
Ja-ela Sri Lanka 7°5N 79°53E 245 L4
Ja-eundo S. Korea 34°53N 126°2E 224 E3
Ja'ār Yemen 13°13N 45°18E 248 D4
Jaba Ethiopia 6°20N 35°7E 257 F4
Jaba West Bank 31°51N 35°16E 123 A2
Jabal al Awliya' Sudan 15°14N 32°29E 266 A3
Jabal as Sirāj Afghan. 35°7N 69°16E 240 B3
Jabalón ➝ Spain 38°53N 4°5W 195 G6
Jabalpur India 23°9N 79°58E 243 H8
Jabālya Gaza Strip 31°32N 34°29E 251 G5
Jabbūl Syria 36°4N 37°30E 246 B3
Jabiru Australia 12°40S 132°53E 278 B5
Jablah Syria 35°20N 36°0E 250 C7
Jablanac Croatia 44°42N 14°56E 199 D11
Jablanica Bos.-H. 43°40N 17°45E 182 G2
Jablonec nad Nisou
Czechia 50°43N 15°10E 180 A8
Jablonica Slovakia 48°37N 17°26E 181 C10
Jabłonowo Pomorskie
Poland 53°23N 19°10E 184 E6
Jablunkov Czechia 49°35N 18°46E 181 B11
Jaboatão Brazil 8°7S 35°1W 332 C4
Jabonga Phil. 9°20N 125°32E 233 G5
Jabotabek = Jakarta
Indonesia 6°9S 106°52E 122 A2
Jaboticabal Brazil 21°15S 48°17W 335 A6
Jabukovac Serbia 44°22N 22°21E 202 B6
Jaburu Brazil 5°30S 64°0W 331 B5
Jaca Spain 42°35N 0°33W 196 C4
Jacaré Brazil 22°53S 43°14W 135 B1
Jacaré ➝ Brazil 10°3S 42°13W 332 D3
Jacareí Brazil 23°20S 46°0W 335 A6
Jacarèzinho Brazil 23°5S 49°58W 335 A6
Jaci-Paraná Brazil 9°15S 64°23W 331 B5
Jaciara Brazil 15°59S 54°57W 331 D7
Jacinto Brazil 16°10S 40°17W 333 E3
Jack River △ Australia 14°58S 144°19E 280 A3
Jackman U.S.A. 45°37N 70°15W 309 C18
Jacksboro U.S.A. 33°13N 98°10W 314 E5
Jackson Barbados 13°7N 59°36W 323 r
Jackson Ala., U.S.A. 31°31N 87°53W 315 F11
Jackson Calif., U.S.A. 38°21N 120°46W 306 G6
Jackson Ga., U.S.A. 33°20N 83°57W 316 B6
Jackson Ky., U.S.A. 37°33N 83°23W 309 G12
Jackson Mich., U.S.A. 42°15N 84°24W 311 B12
Jackson Minn., U.S.A. 43°37N 95°1W 308 D6
Jackson Miss., U.S.A. 32°18N 90°12W 315 E9
Jackson Mo., U.S.A. 37°23N 89°40W 308 G9
Jackson N.H., U.S.A. 44°10N 71°11W 313 B13
Jackson Ohio, U.S.A. 39°3N 82°39W 309 F12
Jackson S.C., U.S.A. 33°20N 81°47W 316 B8
Jackson Tenn., U.S.A. 35°37N 88°49W 315 D10
Jackson Wyo., U.S.A. 43°29N 110°46W 304 E8
Jackson, C. N.Z. 40°59S 174°20E 285 A9
Jackson B. N.Z. 43°58S 168°42E 285 D3
Jackson Center U.S.A. 40°27N 84°4W 311 D12
Jackson Hd. N.Z. 43°58S 168°37E 285 D3
Jackson Heights U.S.A. 40°44N 73°53W 132 B2
Jackson L. Fla., U.S.A. 30°30N 84°17W 316 E5
Jackson L. Ga., U.S.A. 33°19N 83°50W 316 B6
Jackson L. Wyo., U.S.A. 43°52N 110°36W 304 E8
Jackson Park U.S.A. 41°46N 87°34W 119 C3
Jacksons N.Z. 42°46S 171°32E 285 C6
Jackson's Arm Canada 49°52N 56°47W 299 C8
Jacksonville Ala., U.S.A. 33°49N 85°46W 316 B4
Jacksonville Ark., U.S.A. 34°52N 92°7W 314 D8
Jacksonville Calif.,
U.S.A. 37°52N 120°24W 306 H6
Jacksonville Fla., U.S.A. 30°20N 81°39W 316 E8
Jacksonville Ga., U.S.A. 31°49N 82°59W 316 D7
Jacksonville Ill., U.S.A. 39°44N 90°14W 310 E6
Jacksonville N.C., U.S.A. 34°45N 77°26W 315 D16
Jacksonville Tex., U.S.A. 31°58N 95°17W 314 F7
Jacksonville Beach
U.S.A. 30°17N 81°24W 316 E8
Jacksonville Int. ✕ (JAX)
U.S.A. 30°30N 81°41W 316 E8
Jacmel Haiti 18°14N 72°32W 321 C5
Jaco, Pte. Dominica 15°39N 61°24W 323 k
Jacob Lake U.S.A. 36°43N 112°13W 305 H7
Jacobabad Pakistan 28°20N 68°29E 242 E3
Jacobina Brazil 11°11S 40°30W 332 D3
Jacobshagen = Dobrzany
Poland 53°22N 15°25E 184 E2
Jacon Javits Convention Center
New York, U.S.A. 132 c1
Jacotet, B. Mauritius 20°30S 57°26E 272 e
Jacqueline Kennedy Onassis Res.
New York, U.S.A. 132 a3
Jacques-Cartier Canada 45°31N 73°27W 130 A3
Jacques-Cartier, Dét. de
Canada 50°0N 63°30W 299 C7
Jacques-Cartier, Mt.
Canada 48°57N 66°0W 299 C6
Jacques-Cartier, Pont
Canada 45°31N 73°32W 130 A2
Jacques-Cartier ⌓ Canada 47°15N 71°33W 299 C5
Jacqueville Côte d'Ivoire 5°12N 4°25W 262 D4
Jacuí ➝ Brazil 30°2S 51°15W 335 C5
Jacumba U.S.A. 32°37N 116°11W 307 N10
Jacundá ➝ Brazil 1°57S 50°26W 332 B1
Jadavpur India 22°28N 88°22E 124 C2
Jadcherla India 16°46N 78°9E 244 F4
Jade Germany 53°20N 8°14E 178 B4
Jade, Côte de France 46°40N 2°0W 172 F4
Jade Buddha Temple
China 31°15N 121°25E 138 B1
Jade City Canada 59°15N 129°37W 296 B3
Jade Dragon Snow Mt. = Yulong
Xueshan China 27°6N 100°10E 228 D3
Jade Island Beijing, China 114 b2
Jade Mt. = Yü Shan
Taiwan 23°25N 120°52E 225 C2
Jadebusen Germany 53°29N 8°12E 178 B4
Jadotville = Likasi
Dem. Rep. of the Congo 10°55S 26°48E 269 E2
Jadovnik Serbia 43°20N 19°45E 202 C3
Jadraque Spain 40°55N 2°55W 196 E2
Jādū Libya 32°0N 12°0E 258 B2
Jægersborg Denmark 55°45N 12°31E 118 A3
Jægersborg Dyrehave
Denmark 55°46N 12°33E 118 A3
Jaén Peru 5°25S 78°40W 330 B2
Jaén Spain 37°44N 3°43W 195 H7
Jaén □ Spain 37°50N 3°30W 195 H7
Jæren Norway 58°42N 5°47E 164 F2
Jærens Rev Norway 58°45N 5°45E 164 F2
Jafarabad India 20°52N 71°22E 242 J4
Jaffa = Tel Aviv-Yafo Israel 32°4N 34°48E 251 F5
Jaffa, C. Australia 36°58S 139°40E 282 D3
Jaffna Sri Lanka 9°45N 80°2E 245 K5
Jaffrey U.S.A. 42°49N 72°2W 313 D12
Jagadhri India 30°10N 77°20E 242 D7
Jagadishpur Bihar, India 25°30N 84°21E 243 G11
Jagadishpur Paschimbanga,
India 22°39N 88°17E 124 B1
Jagat Nepal 28°19N 84°53E 243 E11
Jagatpur India 28°44N 77°13E 120 A2
Jagdalpur India 19°3N 82°0E 244 E6
Jagdaqi China 50°25N 124°7E 219 A13
Jagersfontein S. Africa 29°44S 25°27E 270 C4
Jaghīn ➝ Iran 27°17N 57°13E 247 E8
Jagna Phil. 9°39N 124°22E 233 G5
Jagodina Serbia 44°5N 21°15E 202 B5
Jagraon India 30°50N 75°25E 242 D6
Jagst ➝ Germany 49°14N 9°10E 179 F5
Jagtial India 18°50N 79°0E 244 E4
Jaguaquara Brazil 13°32S 39°58W 333 D4
Jaguaré, Rib. do ➝ Brazil 23°32S 46°45W 137 B1
Jaguariaíva Brazil 24°10S 49°50W 335 A6
Jaguaribe Brazil 5°53S 38°37W 332 C4
Jaguaribe ➝ Brazil 4°25S 37°45W 332 B4
Jaguaruana Brazil 4°50S 37°47W 332 B4
Jagüey Grande Cuba 22°35N 81°7W 320 B3
Jagungal, Mt. Australia 36°8S 148°22E 283 D8
Jahanabad India 25°13N 84°59E 243 G11
Jahangirpur India 28°43N 77°12E 120 A2
Jahazpur India 25°37N 75°17E 242 G6
Jahrom Iran 28°30N 53°31E 247 D7
Jaicós Brazil 7°21S 41°8W 332 C3
Jaigarh India 17°17N 73°13E 244 F1
Jaijon India 31°21N 76°9E 242 D7
Jailolo Indonesia 1°5N 127°30E 231 D7
Jailolo, Selat Indonesia 0°5N 129°5E 231 D7
Jaintiapur Bangla. 25°8N 92°7E 241 C4
Jaipur Assam, India 27°16N 95°24E 241 B5
Jaipur Raj., India 27°0N 75°50E 242 F6
Jais India 26°15N 81°32E 243 F9
Jaisalmer India 26°55N 70°54E 242 F4
Jaisinghnagar India 23°38N 78°34E 243 H8
Jaitaran India 26°12N 73°56E 242 F5
Jaithari India 23°14N 78°37E 243 H8
Jajarkot Nepal 28°42N 82°14E 243 E10
Jājarm Iran 36°58N 56°27E 247 B8
Jajce Bos.-H. 44°19N 17°17E 182 F2
Jajpur India 20°53N 86°22E 244 D8
Jakam ➝ India 23°54N 74°13E 242 H6
Jakar Dzong Bhutan 27°33N 90°43E 241 B3
Jakarta Indonesia 6°9S 106°52E 122 A2
Jakarta, Teluk Indonesia 6°5S 106°50E 122 A1
Jakarta Halim Perdana Kusuma
Int. ✕ (HLP) Indonesia 6°16S 106°53E 122 B2
Jakarta Sukarno-Hatta Int. ✕
(CGK) Indonesia 6°7S 106°40E 231 G12
Jakhal India 29°48N 75°50E 242 E6
Jakharrah Libya 29°13N 21°34E 258 C4
Jakhau India 23°13N 68°43E 242 H3
Jakobshavn = Ilulissat
Greenland 69°12N 51°10W 154 D5
Jakobstad = Pietarsaari
Finland 63°40N 22°43E 160 E20
Jakupica N. Macedonia 41°45N 21°22E 202 E5
Jal U.S.A. 32°7N 103°12W 305 K12
Jalaihai Pt. Guam 13°18N 144°46E 302 d
Jalājil Si. Arabia 25°40N 45°27E 246 E5
Jalal-Abad Kyrgyzstan 40°56N 73°0E 217 D8
Jalal-Abad □ Kyrgyzstan 41°30N 72°30E 217 D8
Jalālābād Afghan. 34°30N 70°29E 242 B4
Jalalabad India 27°41N 79°42E 243 F8
Jalalpur Jattan Pakistan 32°38N 74°11E 242 C6
Jalama U.S.A. 34°29N 120°29W 307 L6
Jalan Kayu Singapore 1°24N 103°52E 138 A3
Jalandhar India 31°20N 75°40E 242 D6
Jalapa Guatemala 14°39N 89°59W 320 D2
Jalapa Enríquez = Xalapa
Mexico 19°32N 96°55W 319 D5
Jalasjärvi Finland 62°29N 22°47E 160 E20
Jalaun India 26°8N 79°25E 243 F8
Jalāzin Afghan. 37°2N 64°49E 240 A2
Jaldak Afghan. 31°58N 66°43E 240 C2
Jaldhaka ➝ Bangla. 26°16N 89°16E 241 B2
Jales Brazil 20°10S 50°33W 333 F1
Jalesar India 27°29N 78°19E 242 F8
Jaleswar Nepal 26°38N 85°48E 243 F11
Jalgaon India 21°0N 75°42E 244 D2
Jalībah Iraq 30°35N 46°32E 246 D5
Jalingo Nigeria 8°55N 11°25E 263 D7
Jalisco □ Mexico 20°20N 103°40W 318 D4
Jalkot Pakistan 35°14N 73°24E 243 B5
Jalna India 19°48N 75°38E 244 E2
Jalón ➝ Spain 41°47N 1°4W 196 D3
Jalor India 25°21N 72°37E 242 G5
Jalpa Mexico 21°38N 102°58W 318 C4
Jalpaiguri India 26°32N 88°46E 241 B2
Jalpan Mexico 21°14N 99°29W 319 C5
Jālq Iran 27°35N 62°46E 240 D1
Jālū Libya 29°2N 21°33E 258 C4
Jaluit I. Marshall Is. 6°0N 169°30E 288 G8
Jalūlā Iraq 34°16N 45°10E 213 E11
Jam, Minaret of Afghan. 34°23N 64°30E 240 B2
Jamaame Somalia 0°4N 42°44E 267 D5
Jamaari Nigeria 11°44N 9°53E 263 C6
Jamaica ■ W. Indies 18°10N 77°30W 320 a
Jamaica B. U.S.A. 40°36N 73°50W 132 C3
Jamaica Channel Jamaica 17°0N 76°0W 321 C4
Jamaica Plain U.S.A. 42°18N 71°6W 116 B2
Jamakpuri India 28°37N 77°5E 120 B1
Jamalpur Bangla. 24°52N 89°56E 241 C2
Jamalpur India 25°18N 86°28E 243 G12
Jamalpurganj India 23°2N 87°59E 243 H13
Jamanota Aruba 12°29N 69°57W 322 f
Jamanxim ➝ Brazil 4°43S 56°18W 331 A6
Jamari Brazil 8°45S 63°27W 331 B5
Jamari ➝ Brazil 8°27S 63°30W 331 B5
Jamba Angola 14°40S 16°2E 265 E3
Jambewangi Indonesia 8°17S 114°7E 231 J17
Jambi Indonesia 1°38S 103°30E 234 C2
Jambi □ Indonesia 1°30S 102°30E 234 C2
Jambongan, Pulau
Malaysia 6°45N 117°20E 235 A5
Jambusar India 22°3N 72°51E 242 H5
James U.S.A. 32°58N 83°29W 316 C6
James ➝ S. Dak., U.S.A. 42°52N 97°18W 308 D5
James ➝ Va., U.S.A. 36°56N 76°27W 309 G15
James, I. = San Salvador, I.
Ecuador 0°16S 90°42W 330 a
James B. Canada 54°0N 80°0W 298 B3
James I. Gambia 13°19N 16°21W 262 C1
James Island U.S.A. 32°45N 79°55W 316 C10
James Ranges Australia 24°10S 132°30E 278 D5
James Ross I. Antarctica 63°58S 57°50W 151 C18
James Ross Str. Canada 69°40N 96°10W 294 D12
James Shoal S. China Sea 3°47N 112°10E 235 B4
Jamesabad Pakistan 25°17N 69°15E 242 G3
Jameson Land Greenland 71°0N 23°30W 154 C8
Jamesport U.S.A. 39°58N 93°48W 310 E3
Jamestown = Wawa
Canada 47°59N 84°47W 298 C3
Jamestown S. Austral.,
Australia 33°10S 138°32E 282 B3
Jamestown St. Helena 15°55S 5°43W 153 h
Jamestown Eastern Cape,
S. Africa 31°6S 26°45E 270 D4
Jamestown Ind., U.S.A. 39°56N 86°38W 311 E10
Jamestown Mo., U.S.A. 38°48N 92°30W 310 F4
Jamestown N. Dak.,
U.S.A. 46°54N 98°42W 308 B4
Jamestown N.Y., U.S.A. 42°6N 79°14W 312 D5
Jamestown Ohio, U.S.A. 39°39N 83°33W 311 E13
Jamestown Pa., U.S.A. 41°29N 80°27W 312 E4
Jamestown S.C., U.S.A. 33°17N 79°42W 316 B10
Jamīlābād Iran 34°24N 48°28E 247 C6
Jamira ➝ India 21°35N 88°28E 243 J13
Jämjö Sweden 56°12N 15°49E 163 H9
Jamkhandi India 16°30N 75°15E 244 F2
Jamkhed India 18°43N 75°19E 244 E2
Jammalamadugu India 14°51N 78°25E 245 G4
Jammerbugten Denmark 57°15N 9°20E 163 G3
Jammu India 32°43N 74°54E 242 C6
Jammu & Kashmir □ India 33°45N 75°0E 243 C6
Jamnagar India 22°30N 70°6E 242 H4
Jamner India 20°45N 75°52E 244 D2
Jamni ➝ India 25°13N 78°35E 243 G8
Jampur Pakistan 29°39N 70°40E 242 E4
Jamrud Pakistan 33°59N 71°24E 242 C4
Jämsä Finland 61°53N 25°10E 188 B3
Jamshedpur India 22°44N 86°12E 243 H12
Jamshīdīyeh Iran 35°42N 51°22E 141 A2
Jamsil S. Korea 37°30N 127°4E 137 B2
Jamtara India 23°59N 86°49E 243 H12
Jämtland Sweden 63°31N 14°0E 160 E16
Jämtland □ Sweden 63°0N 14°40E 162 B7
Jamuna ➝ Bangla. 23°51N 89°45E 241 D2
Jamurki Bangla. 24°9N 90°2E 241 C3
Jamwon S. Korea 37°30N 127°0E 137 B2
Jan L. Canada 54°56N 102°55W 297 C8
Jan Mayen Arctic 71°0N 9°0W 150 B7
Janakkala Finland 60°54N 24°36E 188 B3
Janakpur Nepal 26°42N 85°55E 244 A7
Janaúba Brazil 15°48S 43°19W 333 E3
Janaucu, I. Brazil 0°30N 50°10W 332 A1
Jand Pakistan 33°30N 72°6E 242 C5
Jandaia Brazil 17°6S 50°7W 333 E1
Jandanku ✪ Australia 16°20S 135°45E 280 B2
Jandaq Iran 34°3N 54°22E 247 C7
Jandía Canary Is. 28°6N 14°21W 153 e2
Jandía, Pta. de Canary Is. 28°3N 14°31W 153 e2
Jandía △ Canary Is. 28°4N 14°19W 153 e2
Jandiatuba ➝ Brazil 3°28S 68°42W 328 D4
Jandola Pakistan 32°20N 70°9E 242 C4
Jandowae Australia 26°45S 151°7E 281 D5
Jándula ➝ Spain 38°3N 4°6W 195 G6
Jane Pk. N.Z. 45°15S 168°20E 285 F3
Janesville U.S.A. 42°41N 89°1W 310 B7
Jang Bogo Antarctica 74°37S 164°12E 151 D11
Janga Ghana 10°5N 1°0W 263 C4
Jangamo Mozam. 24°6S 35°21E 271 B6
Janghai India 25°33N 82°19E 243 G10
Jangheung S. Korea 34°41N 126°52E 224 E3
Janghowon S. Korea 37°7N 127°37E 224 D3
Jangipur India 24°28N 88°4E 243 G12
Jangoon India 17°44N 79°5E 244 F4
Jangsu S. Korea 35°38N 127°31E 224 E3
Janhtang Ga Myanmar 26°32N 96°38E 241 B6
Jani Khel Afghan. 32°46N 68°24E 240 B3
Janikowo Poland 52°45N 18°7E 185 F5
Janiuay Phil. 10°58N 122°30E 233 F4
Janja Bos.-H. 44°40N 19°14E 182 F4
Janjanbureh Gambia 13°30N 14°47W 262 C2
Janjevë Kosovo 42°35N 21°19E 202 D5
Janjgir India 22°1N 82°34E 243 J10
Janjina Croatia 42°58N 17°25E 199 F14
Janjina Madag. 20°30S 45°50E 272 C2
Jankau = Janikowo Poland 52°45N 18°7E 185 F5
Janki Poland 52°8N 20°52E 143 C1
Jannaale Somalia 1°48N 44°42E 267 D5
Janos Mexico 30°54N 108°10W 318 A3
Jánoshalma Hungary 46°18N 19°21E 182 D4
Jánosháza Hungary 47°8N 17°12E 182 C2
Jánossomorja Hungary 47°47N 17°11E 182 C2
Janów Poland 50°44N 19°27E 185 H6
Janów Lubelski Poland 50°48N 22°23E 185 H9
Janów Podlaski Poland 52°11N 23°11E 185 F10
Janowiec Wielkopolski
Poland 52°45N 17°30E 185 F4
Jantho Indonesia 5°17N 95°38E 234 A1
Januária Brazil 15°25S 44°25W 333 E3
Janub = Southern △
South Sudan 6°50N 28°45E 257 F2
Janub al Batinah □ Oman 23°25N 57°25E 249 B7
Janub ash Sharqīyah □
Oman 22°0N 59°30E 249 B7
Janub Dârfûr □ Sudan 11°0N 24°0E 259 F4
Janub Kordofân □ Sudan 11°0N 31°0E 257 E3
Janûb Sînî □ Egypt 29°30N 33°50E 251 J4
Janubio Canary Is. 28°56N 13°50W 153 e2
Janville France 48°10N 1°50E 173 D8
Janwada India 18°0N 77°29E 244 E3
Janzé France 47°55N 1°28W 172 E5
Jaora India 23°40N 75°10E 242 H6
Japan ■ Asia 36°0N 136°0E 221 G8
Japan, Sea of Asia 40°0N 135°0E 220 E7
Japan Center San Francisco, U.S.A. 136 c1
Japan Trench Pac. Oc. 32°0N 142°0E 288 D6
Japen = Yapen Indonesia 1°50S 136°0E 231 E9
Japiim Brazil 7°37S 72°54W 330 B3
Japla India 24°33N 84°1E 243 G11
Japurá Brazil 1°48S 66°34W 328 D4
Japura Indonesia 0°19S 102°21E 234 C2
Japurá ➝ Brazil 3°8S 65°46W 328 D4
Jaquarão Brazil 32°34S 53°23W 335 C5
Jaqué Panama 7°27N 78°8W 320 E4
Jarābulus Syria 36°49N 38°1E 213 D8
Jaraguá Goiás, Brazil 15°45S 49°20W 333 E2
Jaraguá São Paulo, Brazil 23°27S 46°44W 137 A1
Jaraguá, Pico de Brazil 23°27S 46°46W 137 A1
Jaraguá do Sul Brazil 26°29S 49°4W 335 B6
Jaraguari Brazil 20°9S 54°35W 331 E7
Jaraicejo Spain 39°40N 5°49W 195 F5
Jaraíz de la Vera Spain 40°4N 5°45W 194 E5
Jarama ➝ Spain 40°24N 3°32W 194 E7
Jaramānah Syria 33°29N 36°21E 250 E7
Jaramillo Argentina 47°10S 67°7W 336 C3
Jarandilla de la Vera Spain 40°8N 5°39W 194 E5
Jaranwala Pakistan 31°15N 73°26E 242 D5
Jarash Jordan 32°17N 35°54E 251 F6
Jarash □ Jordan 32°17N 35°54E 251 F6
Jarauçu ➝ Brazil 1°48S 52°22W 329 D7
Järbo Sweden 60°43N 16°36E 162 D10
Jarboesville = Lexington Park
U.S.A. 38°16N 76°27W 309 F15
Jardas al 'Abīd Libya 32°18N 20°59E 258 B4
Jardim Brazil 21°28S 56°2W 334 A4
Jardim Paulista Brazil 23°34S 46°41W 137 B1
Jardín ➝ Spain 38°50N 2°10W 197 G2
Jardín América Argentina 27°3S 55°14W 335 B4
Jardin Botanique Brussels, Belgium 116 a3
Jardine River △ Australia 11°9S 142°21E 280 A3
Jardines de la Reina, Arch. de los
Cuba 20°50N 78°50W 320 B4
Jargalang China 43°5N 122°55E 227 C12
Jargalant = Hovd □
Mongolia 48°2N 91°37E 217 C12
Jari ➝ Brazil 1°9S 51°54W 329 D7
Jaria Janjail Bangla. 25°0N 90°40E 241 C3
Jarīr, W. al ➝ Si. Arabia 25°38N 42°30E 246 E4
Järlåsa Sweden 59°53N 17°12E 162 E11
Jarlsberg og Larvik = Vestfold □
Norway 59°15N 10°0E 164 E7
Jarmen Germany 53°54N 13°20E 178 B9
Järna Sweden 59°6N 17°34E 162 E11
Jarnac France 45°40N 0°11W 174 C3
Jarny France 49°9N 5°53E 173 C12
Jaro Phil. 11°11N 124°47E 233 F5
Jarocin Poland 51°59N 17°29E 185 G4
Jaroměř Czechia 50°22N 15°52E 180 A8
Jarosław Poland 50°2N 22°42E 185 H9
Järpås Sweden 58°23N 12°57E 163 F6
Järpen Sweden 63°21N 13°26E 162 A7
Jarqo'rg'on Uzbekistan 37°31N 67°25E 240 A2
Jarrahdale Australia 32°24S 116°5E 279 F2
Jarrahi ➝ Iran 30°49N 48°48E 247 D6
Jarso Ethiopia 5°15N 37°30E 257 F4
Jartai China 39°45N 105°48E 226 E3
Jaru Brazil 10°26S 62°27W 331 C5
Jaru ➝ Brazil 10°5S 61°59W 331 C5
Jarud Qi China 44°28N 120°50E 227 B11
Järvatältet Sweden 59°25N 17°54E 139 A1
Järvenpää Finland 60°29N 25°5E 188 B3
Jarvis Canada 42°53N 80°6W 312 D4
Jarvis I. Pac. Oc. 0°15S 160°5W 289 H12
Jarvorník Czechia 50°23N 17°2E 181 A10
Järvsö Sweden 61°43N 16°10E 162 C10
Jarwa India 27°38N 82°30E 243 F10
Jaša Tomić Serbia 45°26N 20°50E 182 E5
Jasaan Phil. 8°39N 124°45E 233 G5
Jasdan India 22°2N 71°12E 242 H4
Jashore Bangla. 23°10N 89°10E 241 D2
Jashpurnagar India 22°54N 84°9E 243 H11
Jasidih India 24°31N 86°39E 243 G12
Jasień Poland 51°46N 15°0E 185 G2
Jāsimīyah Iraq 33°45N 44°41E 213 F11
Jasin Malaysia 2°20N 102°26E 237 L4
Jāsk Iran 25°38N 57°45E 247 E8
Jaskhar India 18°54N 72°58E 130 B2
Jasliq Uzbekistan 43°58N 57°10E 216 D5
Jasło Poland 49°45N 21°30E 185 J8
Jasmund Germany 54°32N 13°35E 178 A9
Jasmund △ Germany 54°31N 13°38E 178 A9
Jaso India 24°30N 80°29E 243 G9
Jason Is. Falk. Is. 51°0S 61°0W 153 f
Jasonville U.S.A. 39°10N 87°12W 311 E9
Jasper Alta., Canada 52°55N 118°5W 296 C5
Jasper Ont., Canada 44°52N 75°57W 313 B9
Jasper Ala., U.S.A. 33°50N 87°17W 315 E11
Jasper Fla., U.S.A. 30°31N 82°57W 316 E7
Jasper Ind., U.S.A. 38°24N 86°56W 311 F10

Jasper *Tex., U.S.A.* 30°56N 94°1W **314** F7
Jasper △ *Canada* 52°50N 118°8W **296** C5
Jasrasar *India* 27°43N 73°49E **242** F5
Jassān *Iraq* 32°58N 45°52E **213** G11
Jassey = Iaşi *Romania* 47°10N 27°40E **183** C12
Jastarnia *Poland* 54°42N 18°40E **184** D5
Jastrebarsko *Croatia* 45°41N 15°39E **199** C12
Jastrow = Jastrowie *Poland* 53°26N 16°49E **184** E3
Jastrowie *Poland* 53°26N 16°49E **184** E3
Jastrzębie Zdrój *Poland* 49°57N 18°35E **185** J5
Jász-Nagykun-Szolnok □ *Hungary* 47°15N 20°30E **182** C5
Jászapáti *Hungary* 47°32N 20°10E **182** C5
Jászárokszállás *Hungary* 47°39N 19°58E **182** C4
Jászberény *Hungary* 47°30N 19°55E **182** C4
Jászkisér *Hungary* 47°27N 20°20E **182** C5
Jászladány *Hungary* 47°23N 20°10E **182** C5
Jataí *Brazil* 17°58S 51°48W **333** E1
Jatapu → *Brazil* 2°13S 58°17W **329** D6
Jath *India* 17°3N 75°13E **244** F2
Jati *Pakistan* 24°20N 68°19E **242** G3
Jatibarang *Indonesia* 6°28S 108°18E **235** D3
Jatiluwih *Indonesia* 8°23S 115°8E **231** J18
Jatinegara *Indonesia* 6°13S 106°52E **122** B2
Játiva = Xátiva *Spain* 38°59N 0°32W **197** G4
Jatobá = Petrolândia *Brazil* 9°5S 38°20W **332** C4
Jättendal *Sweden* 61°58N 17°15E **162** C11
Jaú *Angola* 15°12S 13°31E **265** F2
Jaú *Brazil* 22°10S 48°30W **335** A6
Jaú → *Brazil* 1°54S 61°26W **329** D5
Jauaperi → *Brazil* 1°26S 61°35W **329** D5
Jauer = Jawor *Poland* 51°4N 16°11E **185** G3
Jauja *Peru* 11°45S 75°15W **330** C2
Jaunpur *India* 25°46N 82°44E **243** G10
Jauru → *Brazil* 16°22S 57°46W **331** D6
Java = Jawa *Indonesia* 7°0S 110°0E **235** D4
Java Sea *Indonesia* 4°35S 107°15E **235** C3
Java Trench *Ind. Oc.* 9°0S 105°0E **234** D2
Javadi Hills *India* 12°40N 78°40E **245** H4
Javādīyeh *Iran* 35°39N 51°22E **141** B2
Javalambre, Sa. de *Spain* 40°6N 1°0W **196** E4
Javānrud *Iran* 34°47N 46°31E **213** E12
Jávea *Spain* 38°48N 0°10E **197** G5
Javhlant = Uliastay *Mongolia* 47°56N 97°28E **218** B8
Javier, I. *Chile* 47°5S 74°25W **336** C2
Javla *India* 17°18N 75°9E **244** F2
Jawa *Indonesia* 7°0S 110°0E **235** D4
Jawa Barat □ *Indonesia* 7°0S 107°0E **231** G12
Jawa Tengah □ *Indonesia* 7°0S 110°0E **235** D3
Jawa Timur □ *Indonesia* 8°0S 113°0E **235** D4
Jawad *India* 24°36N 74°51E **242** G6
Jawaharlal Nehru Port = Nhava Sheva *India* 18°58N 72°55E **130** B2
Jawf, W. al → *Yemen* 15°50N 45°30E **248** D4
Jawhar *India* 19°55N 73°14E **244** E1
Jawhar *Somalia* 2°48N 45°30E **267** D6
Jawor *Poland* 51°4N 16°11E **185** G3
Jaworowa *Poland* 52°9N 20°56E **143** C1
Jaworzno *Poland* 50°13N 19°11E **185** H6
Jaworzyna Śląska *Poland* 50°55N 16°28E **185** H3
Jawoyn ☼ *Australia* 14°16S 132°28E **278** B5
Jay *U.S.A.* 30°57N 87°9W **317** E2
Jay Peak *U.S.A.* 44°55N 72°32W **313** B12
Jaya, Puncak *Indonesia* 3°57S 137°17E **231** E9
Jayanca *Peru* 6°24S 79°50W **330** B2
Jayanti *India* 26°45N 89°40E **241** B2
Jayapura *Indonesia* 2°28S 140°38E **231** E10
Jayawijaya, Pegunungan *Indonesia* 5°0S 139°0E **231** F9
Jaynagar *India* 26°43N 86°9E **243** F12
Jaypur = Jeypore *India* 18°50N 82°38E **244** E6
Jayrūd *Syria* 33°49N 36°44E **250** E7
Jayton *U.S.A.* 33°15N 100°34W **314** E4
Jāz Mūrīān, Hāmūn-e *Iran* 27°20N 58°55E **247** E8
Jazīreh-ye Shīf *Iran* 29°4N 50°54E **247** D6
Jazminal *Mexico* 24°52N 101°24W **318** C4
Jazzīn *Lebanon* 33°31N 35°35E **250** E6
Jean *U.S.A.* 35°47N 115°20W **307** K11
Jean Lafitte Nat. Historical Park ⌓ *U.S.A.* 29°51N 90°9W **131** B1
Jean Marie River *Canada* 61°32N 120°38W **296** A4
Jean-Rabel *Haiti* 19°50N 73°5W **321** C5
Jeanerette *U.S.A.* 29°55N 91°40W **314** G9
Jeanette, Ostrov = Zhannetty, Ostrov *Russia* 76°43N 158°0E **215** B16
Jeanne-Mance, Parc *Montréal, Canada* **130** b1
Jeanneton, Morne *Guadeloupe* 16°14N 61°43W **322** e
Jeannette *U.S.A.* 40°20N 79°36W **312** F5
Jebāl Bārez, Kūh-e *Iran* 28°30N 58°20E **247** D8
Jebba *Nigeria* 9°9N 4°48E **263** D5
Jebel, Bahr el → *South Sudan* 9°30N 30°25E **257** F3
Jebel Ali = Minā' Jabal 'Alī *U.A.E.* 25°2N 55°8E **247** E7
Jebel Dud *Sudan* 13°25N 33°9E **257** E3
Jebel Elba △ *Egypt* 22°11N 36°22E **256** C4
Jebel Qerri *Sudan* 16°16N 32°50E **257** D3
Jeberos *Peru* 5°15S 76°10W **330** B2
Jebus *Indonesia* 1°43S 105°28E **234** C3
Jecheon *S. Korea* 37°8N 128°12E **224** D4
Jedburgh *U.K.* 55°29N 2°33W **167** F6
Jedda = Jiddah *Si. Arabia* 21°29N 39°10E **248** B2
Jeddore L. *Canada* 48°3N 55°55W **299** C8
Jedlesee *Austria* 48°15N 16°23E **142** A2
Jedlicze *Poland* 49°43N 21°40E **185** J8
Jędrzejów *Poland* 50°35N 20°15E **185** H7
Jedwabne *Poland* 53°17N 22°18E **185** E9
Jeetzel → *Germany* 53°9N 11°3E **178** B7
Jefferson *Ga., U.S.A.* 34°7N 83°35W **316** A6
Jefferson *Iowa, U.S.A.* 42°1N 94°23W **310** B2
Jefferson *La., U.S.A.* 29°57N 90°9W **131** B2
Jefferson *Ohio, U.S.A.* 41°44N 80°46W **312** E4
Jefferson *Tex., U.S.A.* 32°46N 94°21W **314** E7
Jefferson *Wis., U.S.A.* 43°0N 88°48W **311** B8
Jefferson, Mt. *Nev., U.S.A.* 38°47N 116°56W **304** G5
Jefferson, Mt. *Oreg., U.S.A.* 44°41N 121°48W **304** D3
Jefferson City *Mo., U.S.A.* 38°34N 92°10W **310** F4
Jefferson City *Tenn., U.S.A.* 36°7N 83°30W **315** C13
Jefferson Memorial *Washington, D.C., U.S.A.* **143** c1
Jefferson Park *Calif., U.S.A.* 34°2N 118°19W **126** B3
Jefferson Park *Ill., U.S.A.* 41°58N 87°46W **119** B2
Jeffersontown *U.S.A.* 38°12N 85°35W **311** F11
Jeffersonville *Ga., U.S.A.* 32°41N 83°20W **316** C6
Jeffersonville *Ind., U.S.A.* 38°17N 85°44W **311** F11
Jeffersonville *Ohio, U.S.A.* 39°39N 83°34W **311** E13
Jeffrey City *U.S.A.* 42°30N 107°49W **304** E10
Jega *Nigeria* 12°15N 4°23E **263** C5
Jegi *S. Korea* 37°34N 127°1E **137** B2
Jejevo *Solomon Is.* 8°6S 159°8E **287** M10
Jeju *S. Korea* 33°31N 126°32E **224** a
Jeju-do *S. Korea* 33°29N 126°34E **224** a
Jeju-do □ *S. Korea* 33°25N 126°30E **224** a
Jeju Haehyop *S. Korea* 33°50N 126°30E **227** H14
Jeju Int. ✈ **(CJU)** *S. Korea* 33°30N 126°30E **224** a
Jēkabpils *Latvia* 56°29N 25°57E **188** D3
Jekyll I. *U.S.A.* 31°4N 81°25W **316** D8
Jelambar *Indonesia* 6°9S 106°47E **122** A1
Jelcz-Laskowice *Poland* 51°2N 17°19E **185** G4
Jelenia Góra *Poland* 50°50N 15°45E **185** H2
Jelgava *Latvia* 56°41N 23°49E **184** B10
Jelica *Serbia* 43°50N 20°17E **202** C4
Jelli *South Sudan* 5°25N 31°45E **257** F3
Jelonki *Poland* 52°14N 20°54E **143** B1
Jelšava *Slovakia* 48°37N 20°15E **181** C13
Jema'a Mallam = Kafanchan *Nigeria* 9°40N 8°20E **263** D6
Jemaja *Indonesia* 3°5N 105°45E **234** B3
Jemaluang *Malaysia* 2°16N 103°52E **237** L4
Jember *Indonesia* 8°11S 113°41E **235** D4
Jempang, Danau *Indonesia* 0°25S 116°12E **235** C5
Jena *Thüringen, Germany* 50°54N 11°35E **178** E7
Jena *La., U.S.A.* 31°41N 92°8W **314** F8
Jenai *Taiwan* 24°2N 121°8E **225** B3
Jenbach *Austria* 47°24N 11°47E **180** D4
Jendouba *Tunisia* 36°29N 8°47E **258** A1
Jendouba □ *Tunisia* 36°34N 8°52E **261** A6
Jeneponto *Indonesia* 5°40S 119°44E **235** D5
Jengish Chokusu = Pobedy, Pik *Asia* 42°0N 79°58E **217** D9
Jenho *Taiwan* 23°54N 121°36E **225** C3
Jenīn *West Bank* 32°28N 35°18E **251** F6
Jenison *U.S.A.* 42°54N 85°47W **311** B11
Jenkins *U.S.A.* 37°10N 82°38W **309** G12
Jenner *U.S.A.* 38°27N 123°7W **306** G3
Jennings *Fla., U.S.A.* 30°36N 83°6W **316** E6
Jennings *La., U.S.A.* 30°13N 92°40W **314** F8
Jennings *Mo., U.S.A.* 38°43N 90°15W **310** F6
Jenny Pt. *Dominica* 15°28N 61°15W **323** k
Jensen Beach *U.S.A.* 27°15N 80°14W **317** H9
Jente *Taiwan* 22°58N 120°16E **225** D2
Jenwu *Taiwan* 22°42N 120°20E **225** D2
Jeollabuk-do □ *S. Korea* 35°45N 127°15E **224** E3
Jeollanam-do □ *S. Korea* 34°45N 127°0E **224** E3
Jeong-eup *S. Korea* 35°35N 126°50E **224** E3
Jeongseon *S. Korea* 37°20N 128°45E **224** D4
Jeonju *S. Korea* 35°50N 127°4E **224** E3
Jepara *Indonesia* 7°40S 109°14E **235** D3
Jeparit *Australia* 36°8S 142°1E **282** D5
Jequié *Brazil* 13°51S 40°5W **333** D3
Jequitaí → *Brazil* 17°4S 44°50W **333** E3
Jequitinhonha *Brazil* 16°30S 41°0W **333** E3
Jequitinhonha → *Brazil* 15°51S 38°53W **333** E4
Jerada *Morocco* 34°17N 2°10W **261** B4
Jerantut *Malaysia* 3°56N 102°22E **237** L4
Jerejak, Pulau *Malaysia* 5°19N 100°19E **237** c
Jérémie *Haiti* 18°40N 74°10W **321** C5
Jeremoabo *Brazil* 10°4S 38°21W **332** D4
Jerez, Pta. *Mexico* 22°58N 97°40W **319** C5
Jerez de García Salinas *Mexico* 22°39N 103°0W **318** C4
Jerez de la Frontera *Spain* 36°41N 6°7W **195** J4
Jerez de los Caballeros *Spain* 38°20N 6°45W **195** G4
Jericho = El Arīḥā *West Bank* 31°52N 35°27E **251** G6
Jericho *Australia* 23°38S 146°6E **280** C4
Jerichow *Germany* 52°30N 12°1E **178** C8
Jerico Springs *U.S.A.* 37°37N 94°1W **310** G2
Jerid, Chott el = Djerid, Chott *Tunisia* 33°42N 8°30E **258** B1
Jerilderie *Australia* 35°20S 145°41E **283** C6
Jermyn *U.S.A.* 41°32N 75°33W **313** E9
Jerningham Junction *Trin. & Tob.* 10°33N 61°23W **323** t
Jerome *U.S.A.* 42°44N 114°31W **304** E6
Jerónimos, Mosteiro dos *Portugal* 38°41N 9°11W **126** A1
Jerramungup *Australia* 33°55S 118°55E **279** F2
Jersey *U.K.* 49°11N 2°7W **169** H5
Jersey City *U.S.A.* 40°42N 74°4W **132** B1
Jersey Shore *U.S.A.* 41°12N 77°15W **312** E7
Jerseyville *U.S.A.* 39°7N 90°20W **310** E6
Jerumenha *Brazil* 7°5S 43°30W **332** C3
Jerusalem *Israel/West Bank* 31°47N 35°10E **123** B2
Jervis B. *Australia* 35°8S 150°46E **283** C9
Jervis Bay △ *Australia* 35°9S 150°40E **283** C9
Jervis Inlet *Canada* 50°0N 123°57W **296** C4
Jerzu *Italy* 39°47N 9°31E **200** C2
Jesenice *Slovenia* 46°28N 14°3E **199** B11
Jeseník *Czechia* 50°14N 17°8E **181** A10
Jesenké *Slovakia* 48°20N 20°10E **181** C13
Jesi = Iesi *Italy* 43°31N 13°14E **199** E10
Jésolo *Italy* 45°32N 12°38E **199** C9
Jessamine, L. *U.S.A.* 28°28N 81°23W **133** B2
Jessel = Jasło *Poland* 49°45N 21°30E **185** J8
Jesselton = Kota Kinabalu *Malaysia* 6°0N 116°4E **235** A5
Jessheim *Norway* 60°9N 11°10E **164** D8
Jessnitz *Germany* 51°40N 12°18E **178** D8
Jessore = Jashore *Bangla.* 23°10N 89°10E **241** D2
Jesup *Ga., U.S.A.* 31°36N 81°53W **316** D8
Jesup *Iowa, U.S.A.* 42°29N 92°4W **310** B4
Jesup, L. *U.S.A.* 28°43N 81°14W **317** G8
Jesús *Peru* 7°15S 78°25W **330** B2
Jésus, Î. *Canada* 45°36N 73°44W **130** A1
Jesús Carranza *Mexico* 17°26N 95°2W **319** D5
Jesús María *Argentina* 30°59S 64°5W **334** C3
Jesús Maria *Lima, Peru* 12°4S 77°3W **124** B2
Jetmore *U.S.A.* 38°4N 99°54W **308** F4
Jetpur *India* 21°45N 70°10E **242** J4
Jette *Belgium* 50°53N 4°20E **116** A1
Jeumont *France* 50°18N 4°6E **173** B11
Jeungdo *S. Korea* 34°56N 126°9E **224** E3
Jeungpyeong *S. Korea* 36°47N 127°34E **224** D3
Jevnaker *Norway* 60°15N 10°26E **164** D7
Jewell *U.S.A.* 42°20N 93°39W **310** B3
Jewett *U.S.A.* 40°22N 81°2W **312** F3
Jewett City *U.S.A.* 41°36N 71°59W **313** E13
Jewish Quarter *Jerusalem* **123** b3
Jey *Iran* 35°41N 51°20E **141** B2
Jeyḩūnābād *Iran* 34°58N 48°59E **247** C6
Jeypore *India* 18°50N 82°38E **244** E6
Jeziorak, Jezioro *Poland* 53°40N 19°35E **184** E6
Jeziorany *Poland* 53°58N 20°46E **184** E7
Jeziorka → *Poland* 52°8N 21°9E **185** F8
Jha Jha *India* 24°46N 86°22E **243** G12
Jhaarkand = Jharkhand □ *India* 24°0N 85°50E **243** H11
Jhabua *India* 22°46N 74°36E **242** H6
Jhajjar *India* 28°37N 76°42E **242** E7
Jhal *Pakistan* 28°17N 67°27E **242** E2
Jhal Jhao *Pakistan* 26°20N 65°35E **240** D2
Jhalakati *Bangla.* 22°39N 90°12E **241** D3
Jhalawar *India* 24°40N 76°10E **242** G7
Jhalida *India* 23°22N 85°58E **243** H11
Jhalrapatan *India* 24°33N 76°10E **242** G7
Jhang Maghiana *Pakistan* 31°15N 72°22E **242** D5
Jhang Sadr = Jhang Maghiana *Pakistan* 31°15N 72°22E **242** D5
Jhansi *India* 25°30N 78°36E **243** G8
Jhargram *India* 22°27N 86°59E **243** H12
Jharia *India* 23°45N 86°26E **243** H12
Jharkhand □ *India* 24°0N 85°50E **243** H11
Jharsuguda *India* 21°56N 84°5E **244** D7
Jhelum *Pakistan* 33°0N 73°45E **242** C5
Jhelum → *Pakistan* 31°20N 72°10E **242** D5
Jhenaidah *Bangla.* 23°33N 89°10E **241** D2
Jhilmilli *India* 23°24N 82°51E **243** H10
Jhudo *Pakistan* 24°58N 69°18E **242** G3
Jhunjhunun *India* 28°10N 75°30E **242** E6
Ji-Paraná *Brazil* 10°50S 61°58W **331** C5
Ji Xian *China* 36°7N 110°40E **226** F6
Jia Xian *Henan, China* 33°59N 113°12E **226** H7
Jia Xian *Shaanxi, China* 38°12N 110°28E **226** E6
Jiading = Chiehting *Taiwan* 22°54N 120°11E **225** D2
Jiadong = Chiatung *Taiwan* 22°25N 120°32E **225** D2
Jiahe *China* 25°38N 112°19E **229** E9
Jiaji = Qionghai *China* 19°15N 110°26E **229** a
Jiali = Chiali *Taiwan* 23°9N 120°10E **225** C2
Jialing Jiang → *China* 29°30N 106°20E **228** C6
Jiamusi *China* 46°40N 130°26E **219** B15
Jian = Chian *Taiwan* 23°59N 121°33E **225** C3
Ji'an *Jiangxi, China* 27°6N 114°59E **229** D10
Ji'an *Jilin, China* 41°5N 126°10E **227** D14
Jianchang *China* 40°55N 120°35E **227** D11
Jianchuan *China* 26°38N 99°55E **228** D2
Jiande *China* 29°23N 119°15E **229** C12
Jiang'an *China* 28°40N 105°3E **228** C5
Jiangbei *China* 29°40N 106°34E **228** C6
Jiangcheng *China* 22°36N 101°52E **228** F3
Jiangchuan *China* 24°8N 102°39E **228** E4
Jiangdi *China* 26°57N 103°37E **228** D4
Jiangdu *China* 32°27N 119°36E **229** A12
Jiange *China* 32°4N 105°32E **228** A5
Jianggao *China* 23°13N 113°13E **121** A2
Jianghua *China* 25°0N 111°47E **229** E8
Jiangjin *China* 29°14N 106°14E **228** C6
Jiangjun = Chiangchun *Taiwan* 23°12N 120°9E **225** C2
Jiangkou *China* 27°40N 108°49E **228** D7
Jiangle *China* 26°42N 117°23E **229** D11
Jiangmen *China* 22°32N 113°0E **229** F9
Jiangning *China* 31°55N 118°50E **229** B12
Jiangshan *China* 28°40N 118°37E **229** C12
Jiangsu □ *China* 33°0N 120°0E **227** H11
Jiangwan *China* 31°18N 121°28E **138** B1
Jiangxi □ *China* 27°30N 116°0E **229** D11
Jiangyan *China* 32°30N 120°7E **229** A13
Jiangyin *China* 31°54N 120°17E **229** B13
Jiangyong *China* 25°20N 111°22E **229** E8
Jiangyou *China* 31°44N 104°43E **228** B5
Jiangyuan *China* 42°2N 126°34E **227** C14
Jianhe *China* 26°37N 108°31E **228** D7
Jianli *China* 29°46N 112°56E **229** C9
Jianning *China* 26°50N 116°50E **229** D11
Jian'ou *China* 27°3N 118°17E **229** D12
Jianping *China* 41°53N 119°42E **227** D10
Jianshi *China* 30°37N 109°38E **228** B7
Jianshui *China* 23°36N 102°43E **228** F4
Jianyang *Fujian, China* 27°20N 118°5E **229** D12
Jianyang *Sichuan, China* 30°24N 104°33E **228** B5
Jiao Xian = Jiaozhou *China* 36°18N 120°1E **227** F11
Jiaohe *Hebei, China* 38°2N 116°20E **226** E9
Jiaohe *Jilin, China* 43°40N 127°22E **227** C14
Jiaoling *China* 24°41N 116°12E **229** E11
Jiaonan *China* 35°52N 119°58E **227** G10
Jiaoxi = Chiaohsi *Taiwan* 24°49N 121°46E **225** B3
Jiaozhou *China* 36°18N 120°1E **227** F11
Jiaozhou Wan *China* 36°5N 120°10E **227** F11
Jiaozuo *China* 35°16N 113°12E **226** G7
Jiawang *China* 34°28N 117°26E **227** G9
Jiaxiang *China* 35°25N 116°20E **226** G9
Jiaxing *China* 30°49N 120°45E **229** B13
Jiayi = Chiai *Taiwan* 23°29N 120°25E **225** C2
Jiayu *China* 29°55N 113°55E **229** C9
Jiayuguan *China* 39°49N 98°18E **218** D8
Jib *West Bank* 31°51N 35°11E **123** A2
Jibão, Serra do *Brazil* 14°48S 45°0W **333** D3
Jibeiyu = Chipei Tao *Taiwan* 23°45N 119°37E **225** C1
Jibiya *Nigeria* 13°5N 7°12E **263** C6
Jiblah *Yemen* 13°55N 44°9E **248** D4
Jibou *Romania* 47°15N 23°17E **183** C8
Jibuti = Djibouti ■ *Africa* 12°0N 43°0E **257** E5
Jicarón, I. *Panama* 7°10N 81°50W **320** E3
Jičín *Czechia* 50°25N 15°28E **180** A8
Jiddah *Si. Arabia* 21°29N 39°10E **248** B2
Jido *India* 29°2N 94°58E **241** A5
Jido *S. Korea* 35°4N 126°14E **224** E3
Jieshou *China* 33°18N 115°22E **226** H8
Jiexiu *China* 37°2N 111°55E **226** F6
Jieyang *China* 23°35N 116°21E **229** F11
Jigalong *Australia* 23°21S 120°47E **278** D3
Jigalong ☼ *Australia* 23°21S 120°46E **278** D3
Jigawa □ *Nigeria* 12°0N 9°45E **263** C6
Jigme Dorje △ *Bhutan* 28°0N 89°40E **241** B2
Jigme Singye Wangchuck *Bhutan* 27°20N 90°25E **241** B3
Jigni *India* 25°45N 79°25E **243** G8
Jihād *Iraq* 33°17N 44°19E **113** B1
Jihlava *Czechia* 49°28N 15°35E **180** B8
Jihlava → *Czechia* 48°55N 16°36E **181** C9
Jihnan *Taiwan* 24°22N 120°39E **225** B2
Jihočeský □ *Czechia* 49°8N 14°35E **180** B7
Jihomoravský □ *Czechia* 49°5N 16°30E **181** B9
Jihu = Chihu *Taiwan* 23°54N 120°24E **225** C2
Jiigley *Somalia* 5°25N 45°20E **267** C6
Jijel *Algeria* 36°52N 5°50E **261** A6
Jijel □ *Algeria* 36°45N 6°0E **261** A6
Jijiga *Ethiopia* 9°20N 42°50E **267** C5
Jikamshi *Nigeria* 12°12N 7°45E **263** C6
Jikau *South Sudan* 8°28N 33°47E **257** F3
Jilib *Somalia* 0°29N 42°46E **267** D5
Jilin *China* 43°44N 126°30E **227** C14
Jilin □ *China* 44°0N 127°0E **227** C14
Jiloca → *Spain* 41°21N 1°39W **196** D3
Jilong = Chilung *Taiwan* 25°3N 121°45E **225** A3
Jim Thompson's House *Bangkok, Thailand* **113** b3
Jim Thorpe *U.S.A.* 40°52N 75°44W **313** F9
Jima *Ethiopia* 7°40N 36°47E **257** F4
Jimbaran, Teluk *Indonesia* 8°46S 115°9E **231** K18
Jimbōchō *Tokyo, Japan* **140** a4
Jimbolia *Romania* 45°47N 20°43E **182** E5
Jimena de la Frontera *Spain* 36°27N 5°24W **195** J5
Jiménez *Chihuahua, Mexico* 27°8N 104°54W **318** B4
Jimenez *Phil.* 8°20N 123°50E **233** G4
Jimeta *Nigeria* 9°17N 12°28E **263** D7
Jimo *China* 36°23N 120°30E **227** F11
Jimsar *China* 43°59N 89°4E **217** D11
Jin Jiang → *China* 28°24N 115°48E **229** C10
Jin Xian = Jinzhou *China* 38°55N 121°42E **227** E11
Jinan *China* 36°38N 117°1E **226** F9
Jinchang *China* 38°30N 102°10E **218** D9
Jincheng *China* 35°29N 112°50E **226** G7
Jinchuan *China* 31°30N 102°3E **228** B4
Jind *India* 29°19N 76°22E **242** E7
Jindabyne *Australia* 36°25S 148°35E **283** D8
Jinding *China* 22°22N 113°33E **219** a
Jindo *S. Korea* 34°28N 126°15E **224** E3
Jindřichův Hradec *Czechia* 49°10N 15°2E **180** B8
Jing He → *China* 34°27N 109°4E **226** G5
Jing Shan *China* 31°20N 111°35E **229** B8
Jing Xian *China* 30°38N 118°25E **229** B12
Jing'an *Jiangxi, China* 28°50N 115°17E **229** C10
Jingan *Shanghai, China* 31°14N 121°25E **138** B1
Jingbian *China* 37°20N 108°30E **226** F5
Jingchuan *China* 35°20N 107°20E **226** G4
Jingde *China* 30°15N 118°27E **229** B12
Jingdezhen *China* 29°20N 117°11E **229** C11
Jingdong *China* 24°23N 100°47E **228** E3
Jinggangshan *China* 26°58N 114°15E **229** D10
Jinggu *China* 23°35N 100°41E **228** F3
Jinghai *Guangdong, China* 22°59N 116°31E **229** F11
Jinghai *Tianjin, China* 38°55N 116°55E **226** E9
Jinghong *China* 22°0N 100°45E **228** G3
Jinghong Dam *China* 22°10N 100°46E **228** F3
Jingjiang *China* 32°2N 120°16E **229** A13
Jingle *China* 38°20N 111°55E **226** E6
Jingmen *China* 31°0N 112°10E **229** B9
Jingning *China* 35°30N 105°43E **226** G3
Jingpo Hu *China* 43°55N 128°55E **227** C15
Jingshan *China* 31°1N 113°7E **229** B9
Jingtai *China* 37°10N 104°6E **226** F3
Jingtang *China* 39°10N 119°5E **227** E10
Jingu Outer Garden *Tokyo, Japan* **140** b2
Jingxi *China* 23°8N 106°27E **228** F6
Jingyang *China* 34°30N 108°50E **226** G5
Jingyu *China* 42°25N 126°45E **224** A3
Jingyuan *China* 36°30N 104°40E **226** F3
Jingzhou *Hubei, China* 30°21N 112°11E **229** B9
Jingzhou *Hunan, China* 26°33N 109°40E **228** D7
Jingziguan *China* 33°15N 111°0E **226** H6
Jinhua *China* 29°8N 119°38E **229** C12
Jining *Nei Monggol Zizhiqu, China* 41°5N 113°0E **226** D7
Jining *Shandong, China* 35°22N 116°34E **226** G9
Jinja *Uganda* 0°25N 33°12E **268** B3
Jinjang *Malaysia* 3°13N 101°39E **237** L3
Jinji *China* 37°58N 106°8E **226** F4
Jinjiang *Fujian, China* 24°43N 118°33E **229** E12
Jinjiang *Yunnan, China* 26°14N 100°34E **228** D3
Jinjini *Ghana* 7°26N 2°42W **262** D4
Jinju *S. Korea* 35°12N 128°2E **224** E4
Jinkou *China* 30°20N 114°8E **229** B10
Jinkouhe *China* 29°18N 103°4E **228** C4
Jinmu Jiao *China* 18°9N 109°34E **229** a
Jinnah Barrage *Pakistan* 32°58N 71°33E **242** C4
Jinnah Int. ✈ **(KHI)** *Karachi, Pakistan* 24°53N 67°9E **123** A2
Jinning *China* 24°38N 102°38E **228** E4
Jinočany *Czechia* 50°2N 14°16E **135** B1
Jinonice *Czechia* 50°3N 14°22E **135** B2
Jinotega *Nic.* 13°6N 85°59W **320** D2
Jinotepe *Nic.* 11°50N 86°10W **320** D2
Jinping *Guizhou, China* 26°41N 109°10E **228** D7
Jinping *Yunnan, China* 22°45N 103°18E **228** F4
Jinping Bend Dams *China* 28°1N 101°39E **228** C3
Jinqiao *China* 31°15N 121°36E **138** B2
Jinsha *China* 27°29N 106°12E **228** D6
Jinsha Jiang → *China* 28°50N 104°36E **228** C5
Jinshi *China* 29°40N 111°50E **229** C8
Jintan *China* 31°42N 119°36E **229** B12
Jintotolo Channel *Phil.* 11°48N 123°5E **233** F4
Jintotolo I. *Phil.* 11°51N 123°7E **233** F4
Jintur *India* 19°37N 76°42E **244** E3
Jinxi *Jiangxi, China* 27°56N 116°45E **229** D11
Jinxi *Liaoning, China* 40°52N 120°50E **227** D11
Jinxian *China* 28°26N 116°17E **229** C11
Jinxiang *China* 35°5N 116°22E **226** G9
Jinyang *China* 27°28N 103°5E **228** D4
Jinyun *China* 28°35N 120°5E **229** C13
Jinzhai *China* 31°40N 115°53E **229** B10
Jinzhong *China* 37°42N 112°46E **226** F7
Jinzhou *Liaoning, China* 38°55N 121°42E **227** E11
Jinzhou *Liaoning, China* 41°5N 121°3E **227** D11
Jiparaná → *Brazil* 8°3S 62°52W **331** B5
Jipijapa *Ecuador* 1°0S 80°40W **328** D1
Jiquilpan *Mexico* 19°59N 102°43W **318** D4
Jirau *Brazil* 9°18S 64°38W **331** B5
Jirisan *S. Korea* 35°20N 127°44E **224** E3
Jirisan △ *S. Korea* 35°15N 127°30E **224** E3
Jiroft *Iran* 28°45N 57°50E **247** D8
Jishan *China* 35°34N 110°58E **226** G6
Jishou *China* 28°21N 109°43E **228** C7
Jishui *China* 27°12N 115°8E **229** D10
Jisr ash Shughūr *Syria* 35°49N 36°18E **250** C7
Jitarning *Australia* 32°48S 117°57E **279** F2
Jitra *Malaysia* 6°16N 100°25E **237** J3
Jiu → *Romania* 43°47N 23°48E **183** G8
Jiudengkou *China* 39°56N 106°40E **226** E4
Jiujiang *Guangdong, China* 22°50N 113°0E **229** F9
Jiujiang *Jiangxi, China* 29°42N 115°58E **229** C10
Jiuling Shan *China* 28°40N 114°40E **229** C10
Jiulong = Kowloon *Hong Kong, China* 22°19N 114°11E **122** B3
Jiulong *China* 28°57N 101°31E **228** C3
Jiuquan *China* 39°50N 98°20E **218** D8
Jiutai *China* 44°10N 125°50E **227** B13
Jiuxincheng *China* 39°17N 115°59E **226** E8
Jiuzhaigou ⌓ *China* 33°8N 103°52E **228** A4
Jiwaka □ *Papua N. G.* 5°50S 144°40E **286** C3
Jiwani *Pakistan* 25°1N 61°44E **240** D1
Jiwani, Ras *Pakistan* 25°1N 61°44E **240** D1
Jixi *Anhui, China* 30°5N 118°34E **229** B12
Jixi *Heilongjiang, China* 45°20N 130°50E **227** B16
Jiyang *China* 37°0N 117°12E **227** F9
Jiyuan *China* 35°7N 112°57E **226** G7
Jiyūgaoka *Japan* 35°35N 139°40E **140** B3
Jiz', W. → *Yemen* 16°12N 52°14E **249** C6
Jizā'ir *Iraq* 33°15N 44°23E **113** B2
Jīzān *Si. Arabia* 17°0N 42°20E **248** C3
Jize *China* 36°54N 114°56E **226** F8
Jizera → *Czechia* 50°10N 14°43E **180** A7
Jizhou *China* 37°35N 115°30E **226** F8
Jizīra *Iraq* 33°15N 44°25E **113** B2
Jizl, Wādī al → *Si. Arabia* 25°39N 38°25E **246** E3
Jizō-Zaki *Japan* 35°34N 133°20E **222** B5
Jizzax *Uzbekistan* 40°6N 67°50E **217** D7
Jizzax □ *Uzbekistan* 40°20N 67°40E **217** D7
Joaçaba *Brazil* 27°5S 51°31W **335** B5
Joaíma *Brazil* 16°39S 41°2W **333** E3
Joal Fadiout *Senegal* 14°9N 16°50W **262** C1
João Amaro *Brazil* 12°46S 40°22W **333** D3
João Belo = Xai-Xai *Mozam.* 25°6S 33°31E **271** C5
João Câmara *Brazil* 5°32S 35°48W **332** C4
João Neiva *Brazil* 19°45S 40°24W **333** E3
João Pessoa = Eirunepé *Brazil* 6°35S 69°53W **330** B4
João Pessoa = Porto *Brazil* 3°54S 42°42W **332** B3
João Pessoa *Brazil* 7°10S 34°52W **332** C5
João Pinheiro *Brazil* 17°45S 46°10W **333** E2
Joaquín V. González *Argentina* 25°10S 64°0W **334** B3
Jobat *India* 22°25N 74°34E **242** H6
Jobourg, Nez de *France* 49°41N 1°57W **172** C5
Jódar *Spain* 37°50N 3°21W **195** H7
Jodhpur *India* 26°23N 73°8E **242** F5
Jodiya *India* 22°42N 70°18E **242** H4
Joe Pool Lake *U.S.A.* 32°38N 96°59W **120** C4
Joensuu *Finland* 62°37N 29°49E **160** E23
Jōetsu *Japan* 37°12N 138°10E **221** F9
Jœuf *France* 49°12N 6°0E **173** C12
Jofane *Mozam.* 21°15S 34°18E **271** B5
Joffre, Morne = Moustique, Morne *Guadeloupe* 16°7N 61°44W **322** e
Jog Falls = Gersoppa Falls *India* 14°12N 74°46E **245** G2
Jogbani *India* 26°25N 87°15E **243** F12
Jõgeva *Estonia* 58°45N 26°24E **188** C4
Jogjakarta = Yogyakarta *Indonesia* 7°49S 110°22E **235** D4
Joglo *Indonesia* 6°13S 106°45E **122** B1
Jōhana *Japan* 36°30N 136°57E **223** A8
Johannesburg *Gauteng, S. Africa* 26°11S 28°2E **123** B2
Johannesburg *Calif., U.S.A.* 35°22N 117°38W **307** K9
Johannesburg, Univ. of *S. Africa* 26°11S 28°0E **123** B2
Johanneskirchen *Germany* 48°10N 11°38E **131** A2
Johannesstift *Germany* 52°34N 13°12E **115** A2
Johannisburg = Pisz *Poland* 53°38N 21°49E **184** E8
Johannisthal *Germany* 52°26N 13°30E **115** B4
Johansfors *Sweden* 56°42N 15°32E **163** H9
Johilla → *India* 23°37N 81°14E **243** H9
John Crow Mts. *Jamaica* 18°5N 76°25W **320** a
John Day *U.S.A.* 44°25N 118°57W **304** D4
John Day → *U.S.A.* 45°44N 120°39W **304** D3
John Day Fossil Beds ⌓ *U.S.A.* 44°33N 119°38W **304** D4
John D'or Prairie *Canada* 58°30N 115°8W **296** B5
John F. Kennedy Nat. Historic Site ⌓ *U.S.A.* 42°20N 71°7W **116** A2
John F. Kennedy Space Center *U.S.A.* 28°40N 80°42W **317** G9
John H. Kerr Res. *U.S.A.* 36°36N 78°18W **315** C15
John Hancock Center *Chicago, U.S.A.* **119** a2
John McLaren Park *U.S.A.* 37°43N 122°24W **136** B2
John o' Groats *U.K.* 58°38N 3°4W **167** C5
John U. Lloyd Beach ⌓ *U.S.A.* 26°4N 80°6W **129** B3
Johnnie *U.S.A.* 36°25N 116°5W **307** J10
Johns Creek *U.S.A.* 34°2N 84°12W **316** A5
Johns I. *U.S.A.* 32°47N 80°7W **316** C9
John's Ra. *Australia* 21°55S 133°23E **280** C1
Johnson *U.S.A.* 44°38N 72°41W **313** B12
Johnson City *Kans., U.S.A.* 37°34N 101°45W **308** G3
Johnson City *N.Y., U.S.A.* 42°7N 75°58W **313** D9
Johnson City *Tenn., U.S.A.* 36°19N 82°21W **315** C13
Johnson City *Tex., U.S.A.* 30°17N 98°25W **314** F5
Johnsonburg *U.S.A.* 41°29N 78°41W **312** E6
Johnsondale *U.S.A.* 35°58N 118°32W **307** K8
Johnsons Crossing *Canada* 60°29N 133°18W **296** A2
Johnsons Pt. *Antigua & B.* 17°2N 61°53W **322** b
Johnsonville *N.Z.* 41°13S 174°48E **284** H3
Johnston *Iowa, U.S.A.* 41°40N 93°42W **310** C3
Johnston *S.C., U.S.A.* 33°50N 81°48W **316** B8
Johnston, L. *Australia* 32°25S 120°30E **279** F3
Johnston Atoll *Pac. Oc.* 17°10N 169°8W **289** F11
Johnston City *U.S.A.* 37°49N 88°56W **310** G8
Johnston Falls = Mambilima Falls *Zambia* 10°31S 28°45E **269** E2
Johnstone Str. *Canada* 50°28N 126°0W **296** C3
Johnstown *Kilkenny, Ireland* 52°45N 7°33W **166** D4
Johnstown *N.Y., U.S.A.* 43°0N 74°22W **313** C10
Johnstown *Ohio, U.S.A.* 40°9N 82°41W **312** F2
Johnstown *Pa., U.S.A.* 40°20N 78°55W **312** F6
Johor □ *Malaysia* 2°5N 103°20E **237** M4
Johor, Selat *Asia* 1°28N 103°47E **237** d
Johor Bahru *Malaysia* 1°28N 103°46E **237** d
Johor Port *Malaysia* 1°26N 103°53E **237** d
Jõhvi *Estonia* 59°22N 27°27E **188** C4
Joigny *France* 47°58N 3°20E **173** E10
Joinville *Brazil* 26°15S 48°55W **335** B6
Joinville *Haute-Marne, France* 48°27N 5°10E **173** D12
Joinville I. *Antarctica* 65°0S 55°30W **151** C18
Joinville-le-Pont *France* 48°49N 2°27E **134** B3
Jojutla *Mexico* 18°37N 99°11W **319** D5
Jøkelbugten *Greenland* 78°25N 20°20W **154** B9
Jokkmokk *Sweden* 66°35N 19°50E **160** C18
Jökulsá á Bru → *Iceland* 65°40N 14°16W **155** B12
Jökulsá á Fjöllum → *Iceland* 66°10N 16°30W **155** A10
Jolfā *Āzarbājān-e Sharqī, Iran* 38°57N 45°38E **213** C11
Jolfā *Eşfahan, Iran* 32°58N 51°37E **247** C6
Joli-Bois *Belgium* 50°42N 4°24E **116** B2
Joliet *U.S.A.* 41°32N 88°5W **311** C8
Joliette *Canada* 46°3N 73°24W **298** C5
Jollas *Finland* 60°10N 25°5E **121** B3
Jolo *Phil.* 6°0N 121°0E **233** H3
Jolo Group *Phil.* 6°0N 121°9E **233** J3
Jolon *U.S.A.* 35°58N 121°9W **306** K5
Jølstravatnet *Norway* 61°32N 6°23E **164** C3
Jomalig I. *Phil.* 14°42N 122°22E **232** D4
Jombang *Indonesia* 7°33S 112°14E **235** D4
Jomda *China* 31°28N 98°12E **228** B2
Jonåker *Sweden* 58°45N 16°45E **163** F10
Jonava *Lithuania* 55°8N 24°12E **188** E3
Jondal *Norway* 60°16N 6°15E **164** D3
Jones *Phil.* 16°33N 121°42E **232** C3
Jones Sound *Canada* 76°0N 85°0W **295** B15
Jonesboro *Ark., U.S.A.* 35°50N 90°42W **315** D9
Jonesboro *Ga., U.S.A.* 33°31N 84°22W **316** B5
Jonesboro *La., U.S.A.* 32°15N 92°43W **314** E8
Jonesburg *U.S.A.* 38°51N 91°18W **310** F5
Jonesville *Ind., U.S.A.* 39°5N 85°54W **311** E11
Jonesville *Mich., U.S.A.* 41°59N 84°40W **311** C12
Jong → *S. Leone* 7°32N 12°23W **262** D2
Jonglei *South Sudan* 6°25N 31°30E **257** F3
Jonglei □ *South Sudan* 7°30N 32°30E **257** F3
Jonglei Canal *South Sudan* 9°20N 31°39E **266** C3
Jongmyo Royal Shrine *S. Korea* 37°34N 126°59E **137** B1
Jongno *S. Korea* 37°35N 126°59E **137** B1
Joniškis *Lithuania* 56°13N 23°35E **184** B10
Jönköping *Sweden* 57°45N 14°8E **163** G8
Jönköping □ *Sweden* 57°30N 14°30E **163** G8
Jonquière *Canada* 48°27N 71°14W **299** C5
Jonsered *Sweden* 57°45N 12°10E **163** G6
Jonstrup *Denmark* 55°45N 12°20E **118** A2
Jonzac *France* 45°27N 0°28W **174** C3
Joplin *U.S.A.* 37°6N 94°31W **308** G6
Joppa *U.K.* 55°57N 3°6W **121** B3
Jora *India* 26°20N 77°49E **242** F6
Jordan *Guimaras, Phil.* 10°40N 122°35E **233** F4
Jordan *Mont., U.S.A.* 47°19N 106°55W **304** C10
Jordan *N.Y., U.S.A.* 43°4N 76°29W **313** C8
Jordan ■ *Asia* 31°0N 36°0E **251** H7
Jordan → *Asia* 31°48N 35°32E **251** G6
Jordan Valley *U.S.A.* 42°59N 117°3W **304** E5
Jordânia *Brazil* 15°55S 40°11W **333** E3
Jordanów *Poland* 49°41N 19°49E **185** J6
Jordet *Norway* 61°25N 12°8E **164** C9
Jorge, C. *Chile* 51°40S 75°35W **336** D1
Jorge Chavez Int. ✈ **(LIM)** *Lima, Peru* 12°2S 77°8W **124** B2
Jorge Newbery ✈ **(AEP)** *Argentina* 34°34S 58°25W **117** B2
Jørgen Bronlund Fjord *Greenland* 82°30N 31°0W **154** A7
Jorhat *India* 26°45N 94°12E **241** B5
Jori → *Norway* 62°4N 9°5E **162** B3
Jorm *Afghan.* 36°50N 70°52E **240** A3
Jörn *Sweden* 65°4N 20°1E **160** D19
Jorong *Indonesia* 3°58S 114°56E **235** C4
Jørpeland *Norway* 59°3N 6°1E **164** E3
Jorquera → *Chile* 28°3S 69°58W **334** B2
Joru *S. Leone* 7°41N 11°3W **262** D2
Jos *Nigeria* 9°53N 8°51E **263** D6
Jos Plateau *Nigeria* 9°55N 9°0E **263** D6
Jošanička Banja *Serbia* 43°24N 20°47E **202** C4
Jose Abad Santos *Phil.* 5°55N 125°39E **233** J5
José Batlle y Ordóñez *Uruguay* 33°20S 55°10W **335** C4
José Bonifácio = Erechim *Brazil* 27°35S 52°15W **335** B5
José de San Martín *Argentina* 44°4S 70°26W **336** B2
Jose Panganiban *Phil.* 14°17N 122°41E **232** D4
Józefa Piłsudskiego Park *Poland* 52°15N 21°2E **143** B1
Joseni *Romania* 46°42N 25°29E **183** D10
Joseph, L. *Canada* 45°10N 79°44W **312** A5
Joseph Banks Group *Australia* 34°36S 136°16E **282** C2
Joseph Bonaparte G. *Australia* 14°35S 128°50E **278** B4
Joseph L. *Canada* 52°45N 65°18W **299** B6
Joshinath *India* 30°34N 79°34E **243** D8
Joshinetsu-Kōgen △ *Japan* 36°42N 138°32E **223** A10
Joshua Tree *U.S.A.* 34°8N 116°19W **307** L10
Joshua Tree △ *U.S.A.* 33°55N 116°0W **307** M10
Joss House B. *Hong Kong, China* 22°16N 114°17E **122** B3
Josselin *France* 47°57N 2°33W **172** E4
Jost Van Dyke I. *Br. Virgin Is.* 18°29N 64°47W **321** b
Jostedal *Norway* 61°35N 7°15E **164** C4
Jostedalsbreen *Norway* 61°40N 6°59E **164** C3
Jōtō *Japan* 34°42N 135°33E **133** A2
Jotunheimen *Norway* 61°35N 8°25E **164** C5
Jotunheimen △ *Norway* 61°32N 8°25E **164** C5
Joubertberge *Namibia* 18°30S 14°0E **270** A1
Joué-lès-Tours *France* 47°21N 0°40E **172** E7
Jourdanton *U.S.A.* 28°55N 98°33W **314** G5
Joutseno *Finland* 61°7N 28°31E **188** B5
Jouy-en-Josas *France* 48°46N 2°10E **134** B2
Jovellanos *Cuba* 22°40N 81°10W **320** B3
Jovellar *Phil.* 13°4N 123°36E **232** E4
Jowai *India* 25°26N 92°12E **241** C4
Jowkār *Iran* 34°25N 48°40E **213** E13
Jowzjān □ *Afghan.* 36°10N 66°0E **240** A2
Joya de Cerén *El Salv.* 13°49N 89°22W **320** D2
Joyeuse *France* 44°29N 4°16E **175** D8
Jōyō *Japan* 34°50N 135°47E **223** C7
Józefów *Lubelskie, Poland* 50°28N 23°2E **185** H10
Józefów *Mazowieckie, Poland* 52°10N 21°11E **185** F8
Ju Xian *China* 35°35N 118°20E **227** G10
Juan Aldama *Mexico* 24°19N 103°21W **318** C4
Juan Anchorena *Argentina* 34°30S 58°29W **117** A2
Juan Bautista Alberdi *Argentina* 34°26S 61°48W **334** C3
Juan de Bolas *Jamaica* 18°5N 77°9W **320** a
Juan de Fuca, Str of. *N. Amer.* 48°15N 124°0W **306** B3
Juan de Nova *Ind. Oc.* 17°3S 43°45E **271** A7
Juan Fernández, Arch. de *Pac. Oc.* 33°50S 80°0W **326** G2
Juan Fernández △ *Chile* 33°38S 78°52W **330** c
Juan González Romero *Mexico* 19°30N 99°3W **128** A2
Juan José Castelli *Argentina* 25°27S 60°57W **334** B3
Juan L. Lacaze *Uruguay* 34°26S 57°25W **334** C4
Juana Días *Puerto Rico* 18°3N 66°31W **321** b
Juangriego *Venezuela* 11°5N 63°58W **329** a
Juangriego, B. de *Venezuela* 11°5N 63°59W **329** a
Juanjuí *Peru* 7°10S 76°45W **330** B2
Juankoski *Finland* 63°3N 28°19E **160** E23
Juara *Brazil* 11°20S 57°25W **331** C6
Juárez *Mexico* 27°37N 100°44W **318** B4
Juárez, Sa. de *Mexico* 32°0N 115°50W **318** A1
Juárez Int. ✈ **(MEX)** *Mexico* 19°25N 99°5W **128** B2
Juatinga, Pta. da *Brazil* 23°17S 44°30W **333** F3
Juàzeiro *Brazil* 9°30S 40°30W **332** C3
Juàzeiro do Norte *Brazil* 7°10S 39°18W **332** C4
Juazohn *Liberia* 5°22N 8°50W **262** D3
Juba *South Sudan* 4°50N 31°35E **257** G3
Juba → *Somalia* 1°30N 42°35E **267** D5
Jubail = Al Jubayl *Si. Arabia* 27°0N 49°50E **247** E6
Jubany = Carlini Base *Antarctica* 62°30S 58°0W **151** C18
Jubayl *Lebanon* 34°5N 35°39E **250** D6
Jubbada Dhexe □ *Somalia* 2°0N 41°30E **267** D5
Jubbada Hoose □ *Somalia* 0°0 42°0E **267** E5
Jubbah *Si. Arabia* 28°2N 40°56E **246** D4
Jubbal *India* 31°5N 77°40E **242** D7
Jubbulpore = Jabalpur *India* 23°9N 79°58E **243** H8
Jübek *Germany* 54°33N 9°22E **178** A5
Jubilee L. *Australia* 29°0S 126°50E **279** E4
Juby, C. *Morocco* 28°0N 12°59W **260** C2
Júcar = Xúquer → *Spain* 39°5N 0°10W **197** F4
Júcaro *Cuba* 21°37N 78°51W **320** B4
Juchitán de Zaragoza *Mexico* 16°26N 95°1W **319** D5
Judaberg *Norway* 59°10N 5°51E **164** E2
Judea = Har Yehuda *Israel* 31°35N 34°57E **251** G5
Judeira *West Bank* 31°52N 35°12E **123** A2
Judenburg *Austria* 47°12N 14°38E **180** D7
Judith → *U.S.A.* 47°44N 109°39W **304** C9
Judith, Pt. *U.S.A.* 41°22N 71°29W **313** E13
Judith Gap *U.S.A.* 46°41N 109°45W **304** C9
Juelsminde *Denmark* 55°43N 10°1E **163** J4
Jufari → *Brazil* 1°13S 62°0W **329** D5
Juhdum *West Bank* 31°42N 35°15E **123** B2
Juhu *India* 19°5N 73°0E **130** A2
Juifang *Taiwan* 25°7N 121°48E **225** A3
Juigalpa *Nic.* 12°6N 85°26W **320** D2
Juillac *France* 45°20N 1°19E **174** C5
Juist *Germany* 53°40N 6°59E **178** B2
Juisui *Taiwan* 23°30N 121°22E **225** C3
Juiz de Fora *Brazil* 21°43S 43°19W **333** F3
Jūjā *Japan* 35°45N 139°43E **140** A3
Jujuy □ *Argentina* 23°20S 65°40W **334** A2
Jukao = Rugao *China* 32°23N 120°31E **229** A13
Jukskeirivier → *S. Africa* 26°5S 28°6E **123** A2
Julesburg *U.S.A.* 40°59N 102°16W **304** F12
Juli *Peru* 16°10S 69°25W **330** D4
Julia Cr. → *Australia* 20°0S 141°11E **280** C3
Julia Creek *Australia* 20°39S 141°44E **280** C3
Juliaca *Peru* 15°25S 70°10W **330** D3
Julian *U.S.A.* 33°4N 116°38W **307** M10
Julian, L. *Canada* 54°25N 77°57W **298** B4
Julian Alps = Julijske Alpe *Slovenia* 46°15N 14°1E **199** B11
Juliana Top = Mandala, Puncak *Indonesia* 4°44S 140°20E **231** E10
Julianadorp *Curaçao* 12°9N 68°57W **322** g
Julianatop *Suriname* 3°40N 56°30W **329** C6
Julianehåb = Qaqortoq *Greenland* 60°43N 46°0W **154** E6
Julianów *Poland* 52°10N 21°9E **143** B2
Jülich *Germany* 50°55N 6°22E **178** E2
Juliette, L. *U.S.A.* 33°2N 83°50W **316** B6
Julijske Alpe *Slovenia* 46°15N 14°1E **199** B11
Julimes *Mexico* 28°25N 105°27W **318** B3
Jullundur = Jalandhar *India* 31°20N 75°40E **242** D6
Julu *China* 37°15N 115°2E **226** F8
Jumbo *Zimbabwe* 17°30S 30°58E **269** F3
Jumbo Pk. *U.S.A.* 36°12N 114°11W **307** J12
Jumeirah *U.A.E.* 25°11N 55°14E **119** B1
Jumentos Cays *The Bahamas* 23°0N 75°40W **320** B4
Jumilla *Spain* 38°28N 1°19W **197** G3
Jumla *Nepal* 29°15N 82°13E **243** E10
Jumna = Yamuna → *India* 25°30N 81°53E **243** G9
Jumunjin *S. Korea* 37°55N 128°54E **224** D4
Junagadh *India* 21°30N 70°30E **242** J4
Junan *China* 35°12N 118°53E **227** G10
Juncos *Puerto Rico* 18°14N 65°55W **321** b
Junction *Tex., U.S.A.* 30°29N 99°46W **314** F5
Junction *Utah, U.S.A.* 38°14N 112°13W **305** G7
Junction B. *Australia* 11°52S 133°55E **280** A1
Junction City *Ga., U.S.A.* 32°36N 84°28W **316** C5
Junction City *Kans., U.S.A.* 39°2N 96°50W **308** F5
Junction City *Oreg., U.S.A.* 44°13N 123°12W **304** D2
Junction Pt. *Australia* 11°45S 133°50E **280** A1

Jundah *Australia* 24°46S 143°2E **280** C3
Jundiaí *Brazil* 24°30S 47°0W **335** A6
Juneau *U.S.A.* 58°18N 134°25W **296** B2
Junee *Australia* 34°53S 147°35E **283** C7
Jung *S. Korea* 37°33N 126°59E **137** B1
Jungar Qi *China* 39°49N 110°57E **226** E6
Jungbunzlau = Mladá Boleslav *Czechia* 50°27N 14°53E **180** A7
Jungfernheide, Volkspark *Germany* 52°32N 13°18E **115** A2
Jungfernsee *Germany* 52°25N 13°6E **115** B1
Jungfrau *Switz.* 46°32N 7°58E **179** J3
Junggar Pendi *China* 44°30N 86°0E **217** D11
Junghans, Teatro *Venice, Italy* **142** c2
Junghwa *S. Korea* 37°35N 127°3E **137** B2
Jungkat *Indonesia* 0°4N 109°13E **235** B3
Jungnang *S. Korea* 37°36N 127°5E **137** B2
Jungnangcheon → *S. Korea* 37°32N 126°55E **137** B1
Jungsdalshytta = Iungsdalshytta *Norway* 60°49N 7°55E **164** D4
Jungshahi *Pakistan* 24°52N 67°44E **242** G2
Juniata → *U.S.A.* 40°24N 77°1W **312** F7
Junín *Argentina* 34°33S 60°57W **334** C3
Junín *Peru* 11°12S 76°0W **330** C2
Junín □ *Peru* 11°30S 75°0W **330** C3
Junín, L. de *Peru* 11°2S 76°6W **330** C2
Junín de los Andes *Argentina* 39°45S 71°0W **336** A2
Juniper Green *U.K.* 55°54N 3°16W **121** B2
Jūniyah *Lebanon* 33°59N 35°38E **250** E6
Junk B. *Hong Kong, China* 22°17N 114°15E **122** B3
Junkerdal △ *Norway* 66°50N 15°50E **160** C16
Junlian *China* 28°8N 104°29E **228** C5
Junnar *India* 19°12N 73°58E **244** E1
Juno Beach *U.S.A.* 26°52N 80°3W **317** J9
Juntas *Chile* 28°24S 69°58W **334** B2
Juntura *U.S.A.* 43°45N 118°5W **304** E4
Juparanã, L. *Brazil* 19°16S 40°8W **333** E3
Jupiter *U.S.A.* 26°57N 80°6W **317** J9
Juquiá *Brazil* 24°19S 47°38W **333** F2
Jur → *South Sudan* 8°45N 29°15E **257** F2
Jura = Jura, Mts. du *Europe* 46°40N 6°5E **173** F13
Jura = Schwäbische Alb *Germany* 48°20N 9°30E **179** G5
Jura *U.K.* 56°0N 5°50W **167** F3
Jura □ *France* 46°47N 5°45E **173** F12
Jura □ *Switz.* 47°20N 7°20E **179** H3
Jūra → *Lithuania* 55°3N 22°9E **184** C9
Jura, Mts. du *Europe* 46°40N 6°5E **173** F13
Jura, Sd. of *U.K.* 55°57N 5°45W **167** F3
Juradó *Colombia* 7°7N 77°46W **328** B2
Jurassic Coast *U.K.* 50°42N 2°50W **169** G5
Jurbarkas *Lithuania* 55°4N 22°46E **184** C9
Jurien Bay *Australia* 30°18S 115°2E **279** F2
Jurilovca *Romania* 44°46N 28°52E **183** F13
Jūrmala *Latvia* 56°58N 23°34E **184** B10
Jurong *Jiangsu, China* 31°57N 119°9E **229** B12
Jurong *Singapore* 1°19N 103°42E **138** B2
Jurong, Selat *Singapore* 1°17N 103°42E **138** B2
Jurong Industrial Estate *Singapore* 1°19N 103°40E **138** B1
Juruá *Brazil* 3°27S 66°3W **328** D4
Juruá → *Brazil* 2°37S 65°44W **328** D4
Juruena *Brazil* 13°0S 58°10W **331** C6
Juruena → *Brazil* 7°20S 58°3W **331** B6
Juruena △ *Brazil* 8°30S 58°0W **331** B6
Jurujuba, Enseada de *Brazil* 22°54S 43°6W **135** B2
Juruti *Brazil* 2°9S 56°4W **329** D6
Jūsō *Japan* 34°42N 135°27E **133** A1
Jussey *France* 47°50N 5°55E **173** E12
Justice *U.S.A.* 41°44N 87°49W **119** C2
Justicia *Madrid, Spain* **127** a3
Justo Daract *Argentina* 33°52S 65°12W **334** C2
Jutaí *Amazonas, Brazil* 2°44S 66°57W **328** D4
Jutaí *Amazonas, Brazil* 5°11S 68°54W **330** B4
Jutaí → *Brazil* 2°43S 66°57W **328** D4
Jüterbog *Germany* 51°59N 13°5E **178** D9
Juticalpa *Honduras* 14°40N 86°12W **320** D2
Jutland = Jylland *Denmark* 56°25N 9°30E **163** H3
Juuka *Finland* 63°13N 29°17E **160** E23
Juventud, I. de la *Cuba* 21°40N 82°40W **320** B3
Juvigny-sous-Andaine *France* 48°32N 0°30W **172** D6
Juwangsan △ *S. Korea* 36°20N 129°15E **224** D4
Jūy Zar *Iran* 33°50N 46°18E **213** F12
Juye *China* 35°22N 116°5E **226** G9
Juzennecourt *France* 48°10N 4°58E **173** D11
Južni Brod = Brod *N. Macedonia* 41°32N 21°17E **202** E5
Jvari *Georgia* 42°42N 42°4E **191** J6
Jwalahari *India* 28°40N 77°6E **120** B1
Jyderup *Denmark* 55°40N 11°26E **163** J5
Jylland *Denmark* 56°25N 9°30E **163** H3
Jyväskylä *Finland* 62°14N 25°50E **188** A3

K

K2 *Pakistan* 35°58N 76°32E **243** B7
Ka → *Nigeria* 11°40N 4°10E **263** C5
Kaa-Iya △ *Bolivia* 18°35S 61°40W **331** D5
Ka'a'awa *U.S.A.* 21°33N 157°51W **302** J14
Kaakha = Kaka *Turkmenistan* 37°21N 59°36E **247** B8
Ka'ala *U.S.A.* 21°31N 158°9W **302** J13
Kaala-Gomén *N. Cal.* 20°40S 164°25E **288** d
Ka'alu'alu B. *U.S.A.* 18°58N 155°37W **302** E6
Kaap Plateau *S. Africa* 28°30S 24°0E **270** C3
Kaapkruis *Namibia* 21°55S 13°57E **270** B1
Kaapstad = Cape Town *S. Africa* 33°55S 18°22E **118** A1
Kaashidhoo Atoll *Maldives* 4°58N 73°28E **272** d
Kaashidhoo Channel *Maldives* 5°1N 73°28E **272** d
Kaataon, Mt. *Phil.* 8°10N 124°52E **233** G5
Kaba *Guinea* 10°9N 11°40W **262** C2
Kabacan *Phil.* 7°8N 124°49E **233** H5
Kabachishche = Zelenodolsk *Russia* 55°55N 48°30E **190** C9
Kabaena *Indonesia* 5°15S 122°0E **231** F6
Kabala *S. Leone* 9°38N 11°37W **262** D2
Kabale *Uganda* 1°15S 30°0E **268** C3
Kabalo *Dem. Rep. of the Congo* 6°0S 27°0E **265** D5
Kabambare *Dem. Rep. of the Congo* 4°41S 27°39E **268** C2
Kabango *Dem. Rep. of the Congo* 8°35S 28°30E **269** D2
Kabanjahe *Indonesia* 3°6N 98°30E **234** B1
Kabankalan *Phil.* 9°59N 122°49E **233** G4
Kabara *Fiji* 18°59S 178°56W **287** B3
Kabara *Mali* 16°40N 2°50W **262** B4
Kabardinka *Russia* 44°40N 37°57E **189** K10
Kabardino-Balkaria □ *Russia* 43°30N 43°30E **191** J6
Kabarega Falls = Murchison Falls *Uganda* 2°15N 31°30E **268** B3
Kabarnet *Kenya* 0°30N 35°45E **268** B4
Kabasalan *Phil.* 7°47N 122°44E **233** H4
Kabat *Indonesia* 8°16S 114°19E **231** J17
Kabaty *Poland* 52°8N 21°4E **143** C2
Kabba *Nigeria* 7°50N 6°3E **263** D6
Kabbani → *India* 12°13N 76°54E **245** H3
Kabi *Niger* 13°30N 12°35E **259** F2
Kabin Buri *Thailand* 13°57N 101°43E **236** F3
Kabinakagami L. *Canada* 48°54N 84°25W **298** C3
Kabinda *Dem. Rep. of the Congo* 6°10S 24°29E **265** D4
Kabkabīyah *Sudan* 13°50N 24°0E **259** F4
Kablungu, C. *Papua N. G.* 6°20S 150°1E **286** D6
Kabna *Sudan* 19°6N 32°40E **256** D3
Kabo *C.A.R.* 7°35N 18°38E **264** A3
Kabompo *Zambia* 13°36S 24°14E **265** E4
Kabompo → *Zambia* 14°11S 23°11E **265** E4
Kabondo *Dem. Rep. of the Congo* 8°58S 25°40E **265** D5
Kabongo *Dem. Rep. of the Congo* 7°22S 25°33E **265** D5
Kabot *Guinea* 10°48N 14°57W **262** C2
Kabou *Togo* 9°28N 0°55E **263** D5
Kaboudia, Rass *Tunisia* 35°13N 11°10E **258** A2
Kabr *Sudan* 10°54N 26°50E **257** E2
Kabrît, G. el *Egypt* 29°42N 33°16E **251** J4
Kabrousse *Senegal* 12°25N 16°45W **262** C1
Kabubu *Dem. Rep. of the Congo* 9°42S 24°40E **265** D4
Kabūd Gonbad *Iran* 37°5N 59°45E **247** B8
Kabudar Ahang *Iran* 35°11N 48°43E **213** E13
Kabugao *Phil.* 18°2N 121°11E **232** B3
Kābul *Afghan.* 34°28N 69°11E **242** B3
Kābul □ *Afghan.* 34°30N 69°0E **240** B3
Kābul → *Pakistan* 33°55N 72°14E **242** C5
Kabuli *Papua N. G.* 2°7S 146°40E **286** B4
Kabunga *Dem. Rep. of the Congo* 1°38S 28°3E **268** C2
Kaburuang *Indonesia* 3°50N 126°30E **231** D7
Kabushiya *Sudan* 16°54N 33°41E **257** D3
Kabwanga *Dem. Rep. of the Congo* 7°2S 22°36E **265** D4
Kabwe *Zambia* 14°30S 28°29E **269** E2
Kabwum *Papua N. G.* 6°11S 147°15E **286** D4
Kaçanik *Kosovo* 42°13N 21°12E **202** D5
Kačerginė *Lithuania* 54°56N 23°42E **184** D10
Kachar *Kazakhstan* 53°23N 62°55E **216** B6
Kachchh, Gulf of *India* 22°50N 69°15E **242** H3
Kachchh, Rann of *India* 24°0N 70°0E **242** H4
Kachchhidhana *India* 21°44N 78°46E **243** J8
Kachebera *Zambia* 13°50S 32°50E **269** E3
Kachia *Nigeria* 9°50N 7°55E **263** D6
Kachikau *Botswana* 18°8S 24°26E **270** A3
Kachin □ *Myanmar* 26°0N 97°30E **228** D1
Kachira, L. *Uganda* 0°40S 31°7E **268** C3
Kachīry *Kazakhstan* 53°10N 75°50E **217** B9
Kachisi *Ethiopia* 9°40N 37°50E **257** F4
Kachnara *India* 23°50N 75°6E **242** H6
Kachot *Cambodia* 11°30N 103°3E **237** G4
Kaçkar *Turkey* 40°45N 41°10E **213** B9
Kada *Chad* 19°20N 19°39E **259** E3
Kadaingti *Myanmar* 17°37N 97°32E **241** G6
Kadaiyanallur *India* 9°3N 77°22E **245** K3
Kadam, Mt. *Uganda* 1°45N 34°45E **268** B3
Kadan *Czechia* 50°23N 13°16E **180** A6
Kadan Kyun *Myanmar* 12°30N 98°20E **236** F2
Kadanai → *Afghan.* 31°22N 65°45E **242** D1
Kadapa *India* 14°30N 78°47E **245** G4
Kadarkút *Hungary* 46°13N 17°39E **182** D2
Kadavu *Fiji* 19°0S 178°15E **287** B2
Kadavu Passage *Fiji* 18°45S 178°0E **287** B2
Kade *Ghana* 6°7N 0°56W **263** D4
Kadéï → *C.A.R.* 3°31N 16°3E **264** B3
Kademlija = Triglav *Slovenia* 46°21N 13°50E **199** B10
Kadena *Japan* 26°22N 127°45E **288** a
Kadhimain = Al Kāẓimīyah *Iraq* 33°22N 44°18E **213** F11
Kadi *India* 23°18N 72°23E **242** H5
Kadiak I. = Kodiak I. *U.S.A.* 57°30N 152°45W **303** H9
Kadiana *Mali* 10°45N 6°30W **262** C3
Kadıköy *Turkey* 40°59N 29°1E **122** C2
Kadina *Australia* 33°55S 137°43E **282** B2
Kadınhanı *Turkey* 38°14N 32°13E **212** C5
Kadiolo *Mali* 10°35N 7°41W **262** C3
Kadipur *India* 26°10N 82°23E **243** F10
Kadirabad *India* 19°51N 75°54E **244** E2
Kadiri *India* 14°12N 78°13E **245** G4
Kadirli *Turkey* 37°23N 36°5E **212** D7
Kadiyevka = Stakhanov *Ukraine* 48°35N 38°40E **189** H10
Kadja, O. → *Chad* 12°2N 22°28E **259** F4
Kadmat I. *India* 11°14N 72°47E **245** J1
Kadodo *Sudan* 11°4N 29°31E **257** E2
Kadoka *U.S.A.* 43°50N 101°31W **308** D3
Kadom *Russia* 54°37N 42°30E **190** C6
Kadoma *Ōsaka, Japan* 34°44N 135°35E **133** A2
Kadoma *Zimbabwe* 18°20S 29°52E **269** F2
Kâdugli *Sudan* 11°0N 29°45E **257** E2
Kaduna *Nigeria* 10°30N 7°21E **263** C6
Kaduna □ *Nigeria* 11°0N 7°30E **263** C6
Kaduna → *Nigeria* 8°45N 5°48E **263** D6
Kadur *India* 13°34N 76°1E **245** H3
Kaduy *Russia* 59°12N 37°9E **188** C9
Kaédi *Mauritania* 16°9N 13°28W **262** B2
Kaélé *Cameroon* 10°7N 14°27E **259** F2
Ka'ena *U.S.A.* 21°34N 158°14W **302** J13
Ka'ena Pt. *U.S.A.* 21°35N 158°17W **302** J13
Kaeng Khoi *Thailand* 14°35N 101°0E **236** E3
Kaeng Krachan △ *Thailand* 12°57N 99°23E **236** F2
Kaeng Krung △ *Thailand* 9°30N 98°50E **237** H2
Kaeng Tana △ *Thailand* 15°25N 105°32E **236** E5
Kaeo *N.Z.* 35°6S 173°49E **284** B2
Kaesŏng *N. Korea* 37°58N 126°35E **224** D3
Kaesŏng □ *N. Korea* 38°0N 126°37E **224** D3
Kāf *Si. Arabia* 31°25N 37°29E **246** D3
Kafakumba *Dem. Rep. of the Congo* 9°38S 23°46E **265** D4
Kafan = Kapan *Armenia* 39°18N 46°27E **213** C12
Kafanchan *Nigeria* 9°40N 8°20E **263** D6
Kafareti *Nigeria* 10°25N 11°12E **263** C7
Kaffrine *Senegal* 14°8N 15°36W **262** C1
Kafia Kingi *Sudan* 9°20N 24°25E **264** A4
Kafin *Nigeria* 9°30N 7°4E **263** D6
Kafin Madaki *Nigeria* 10°41N 9°46E **263** C6
Kafinda *Zambia* 12°32S 30°20E **269** E3
Kafireos, Stenon *Greece* 37°55N 24°35E **204** D6
Kafr 'Aqab *West Bank* 31°52N 35°13E **123** A2
Kafr el Battikh *Egypt* 31°25N 31°44E **256** H7
Kafr el Dauwâr *Egypt* 31°8N 30°8E **256** H7
Kafr el Sheikh *Egypt* 31°15N 30°50E **251** G1
Kafr el Sheikh □ *Egypt* 31°15N 30°55E **251** G1
Kafr el Zaiyât *Egypt* 30°49N 30°48E **256** H7
Kafue *Zambia* 15°46S 28°9E **269** F2
Kafue △ *Zambia* 15°12S 25°38E **269** F2
Kafue Flats *Zambia* 15°40S 27°25E **269** F2
Kafulwe *Zambia* 9°0S 29°1E **269** D2
Kafumba *Dem. Rep. of the Congo* 5°23S 18°55E **265** D3
Kaga *Afghan.* 34°14N 70°10E **242** B4
Kaga *Japan* 36°16N 136°15E **223** A8
Kaga Bandoro *C.A.R.* 7°0N 19°10E **264** A3
Kagamil I. *U.S.A.* 53°0N 169°43W **303** K5
Kaganovich = Tovarkovskiy *Russia* 53°40N 38°14E **188** F10
Kagarko *Nigeria* 9°28N 7°36E **263** D6
Kagawa □ *Japan* 34°15N 134°0E **222** C6
Kagera □ *Tanzania* 2°0S 31°30E **268** C3
Kagera → *Uganda* 0°57S 31°47E **268** C3
Kâğıthane *Turkey* 41°4N 28°58E **122** B1
Kâğıthane → *Turkey* 41°9N 28°56E **122** B1
Kağızman *Turkey* 40°5N 43°10E **213** B10
Kagmar *Sudan* 14°24N 30°25E **257** E3
Kagologolo *Indonesia* 1°9S 98°37E **234** C1
Kagopal *Chad* 8°16N 16°23E **259** G3
Kagoro *Nigeria* 9°36N 8°23E **263** D6
Kagoshima *Japan* 31°35N 130°33E **222** F2
Kagoshima □ *Japan* 31°30N 130°30E **222** F2
Kagoshima-Wan *Japan* 31°25N 130°40E **222** F2
Kagran *Austria* 48°14N 16°26E **142** A2
Kagua *Papua N. G.* 6°26S 143°48E **286** D2
Kagul = Cahul *Moldova* 45°50N 28°15E **183** E13
Kahak *Iran* 36°6N 49°46E **247** B6
Kāhala *U.S.A.* 21°16N 157°47W **302** K14
Kahalu'u *U.S.A.* 21°27N 157°50W **302** K14
Kahama *Tanzania* 4°8S 32°30E **268** C3
Kahan *Pakistan* 29°18N 68°54E **242** E3
Kahana *U.S.A.* 21°34N 157°53W **302** J14
Kahana B. *U.S.A.* 21°35N 157°50W **302** J14
Kahana Valley State Park ⌓ *U.S.A.* 21°32N 157°53W **302** J14
Kahang *Malaysia* 2°12N 103°32E **237** L4
Kahayan → *Indonesia* 3°40S 114°0E **235** C4
Kahe *Tanzania* 3°30S 37°25E **268** C4
Kahemba *Dem. Rep. of the Congo* 7°18S 18°55E **265** D3
Kaherekoau Mts. *N.Z.* 45°45S 167°15E **285** F2
Kahil, Djebel bou *Algeria* 34°26N 4°0E **261** B5
Kahnawake *Canada* 45°24N 73°40W **130** B1
Kahnūj *Iran* 27°55N 57°40E **247** E8
Kahoka *U.S.A.* 40°25N 91°44W **310** D5
Kaho'olawe *U.S.A.* 20°33N 156°37W **302** C5
Kahouanne *Guadeloupe* 16°15N 61°12W **322** e
Kahouanne, Îlet à *Guadeloupe* 16°22N 61°46W **322** e
Kahramanmaraş *Turkey* 37°37N 36°53E **212** D7
Kahramanmaraş □ *Turkey* 37°35N 36°33E **212** D7
Kâhta *Turkey* 37°46N 38°36E **213** D8
Kahuku *U.S.A.* 21°41N 157°57W **302** J14
Kahuku Pt. *U.S.A.* 21°43N 157°59W **302** J14
Kahul, Ozero *Ukraine* 45°24N 28°24E **183** E13
Kahului *U.S.A.* 20°54N 156°28W **302** C5
Kahului ✈ **(OGG)** *U.S.A.* 20°54N 156°26W **302** C5
Kahurangi △ *N.Z.* 41°10S 172°32E **285** B7
Kahurangi Pt. *N.Z.* 40°50S 172°10E **285** A7
Kahuta *Pakistan* 33°35N 73°24E **242** C5
Kahuzi-Biega △ *Dem. Rep. of the Congo* 1°50S 27°55E **268** C2
Kai *Japan* 35°42N 138°30E **223** B10
Kai, Kepulauan *Indonesia* 5°55S 132°45E **231** F8
Kai Besar *Indonesia* 5°35S 133°0E **231** F8
Kai Is. = Kai, Kepulauan *Indonesia* 5°55S 132°45E **231** F8
Kai Kecil *Indonesia* 5°45S 132°40E **231** F8
Kai Xian *China* 31°11N 108°21E **228** B7
Kaiama *Nigeria* 9°36N 4°1E **263** D5
Kaiapit *Papua N. G.* 6°18S 146°18E **286** D4
Kaiapoi *N.Z.* 43°24S 172°40E **285** D7
Kaidu He → *China* 41°46N 86°31E **218** C6
Kaieteur Falls *Guyana* 5°1N 59°10W **329** B6
Kaifeng *China* 34°48N 114°21E **226** G8
Kaihua *China* 29°12N 118°20E **229** C12
Kaijiang *China* 31°7N 107°55E **228** B6
Kaikohe *N.Z.* 35°25S 173°49E **284** B2
Kaikoura *N.Z.* 42°25S 173°43E **285** C8
Kaikoura Pen. *N.Z.* 42°25S 173°43E **285** C8
Kailahun *S. Leone* 8°18N 10°39W **262** D2
Kailash = Kangrinboqe Feng *China* 31°0N 81°25E **243** D9
Kailashahar *India* 24°19N 92°0E **241** C4
Kaileuna I. *Papua N. G.* 8°32S 150°57E **286** E6
Kaili *China* 26°33N 107°59E **228** D6
Kailu *China* 43°38N 121°18E **227** C11
Kailua *U.S.A.* 21°24N 157°44W **302** K14
Kailua B. *U.S.A.* 21°25N 157°40W **302** K14
Kailua Kona *U.S.A.* 19°39N 155°59W **302** D6
Kaim → *Papua N. G.* 6°55S 141°33E **286** D1
Kaimaktsalan Oros = Voras Oros *Greece* 40°57N 21°45E **202** F5
Kaimana *Indonesia* 3°39S 133°45E **231** E8
Kaimanawa Mts. *N.Z.* 39°15S 175°56E **284** F4
Kaimata *N.Z.* 42°34S 171°28E **285** C6
Kaimes *U.K.* 55°54N 3°10W **121** B2
Kaimganj *India* 27°33N 79°24E **243** F8
Kaimon-Dake *Japan* 31°11N 130°32E **222** F2
Kaimur Hills *India* 24°30N 82°0E **243** G10
Kainab → *Namibia* 28°32S 19°34E **270** C2
Kainan *Japan* 34°9N 135°12E **223** C7
Kainantu *Papua N. G.* 6°18S 145°52E **286** D3
Kainji Dam *Nigeria* 9°55N 4°35E **263** D5
Kainji Lake △ *Nigeria* 10°5N 4°6E **263** C5
Kainji Res. *Nigeria* 10°1N 4°40E **263** C5
Kainsk = Samara *Russia* 53°8N 50°6E **190** D10
Kainuu □ *Finland* 64°30N 29°7E **160** D23
Kaipara Harbour *N.Z.* 36°25S 174°14E **284** C3
Kaiping *China* 22°23N 112°42E **229** F9
Kaipokok B. *Canada* 54°54N 59°47W **299** B8
Kaira *India* 22°45N 72°50E **242** H5
Kairana *India* 29°24N 77°15E **242** E7
Kairiru I. *Papua N. G.* 3°21S 143°34E **286** B2
Kaironi *Indonesia* 0°47S 133°40E **231** E8
Kairouan *Tunisia* 35°45N 10°5E **258** A2
Kairouan □ *Tunisia* 35°30N 9°46E **261** A6
Kairuku *Papua N. G.* 8°51S 146°35E **286** E4
Kaiser Wilhelm Gedächtniskirche *Berlin, Germany* **115** b2
Kaiser Wilhelm Kanal = Nord-Ostsee-Kanal *Germany* 54°12N 9°32E **178** A5
Kaiser-Wilhelmsland = Papua □ *Indonesia* 4°0S 137°0E **231** E9
Kaiserebersdorf *Austria* 48°9N 16°26E **142** B2
Kaiserslautern *Germany* 49°26N 7°45E **179** F3
Kaiserstuhl *Germany* 48°4N 7°40E **179** G3
Kaita *Japan* 34°22N 132°32E **222** C4
Kaitaia *N.Z.* 35°8S 173°17E **284** B2
Kaitangata *N.Z.* 46°17S 169°51E **285** G4
Kaithal *India* 29°48N 76°26E **242** E7
Kaitu → *Pakistan* 33°10N 70°30E **242** C4
Kaivoksela *Finland* 60°15N 24°53E **121** B2
Kaiwi Channel *U.S.A.* 21°15N 157°30W **302** K14
Kaiyang *China* 27°4N 106°59E **228** D6
Kaiyuan *Liaoning, China* 42°28N 124°1E **224** A2
Kaiyuan *Yunnan, China* 23°40N 103°12E **228** F4
Kaiyuh Mts. *U.S.A.* 64°30N 158°0W **303** D8
Kajaani *Finland* 64°17N 27°46E **160** D22
Kajabbi *Australia* 20°0S 140°1E **280** C3
Kajaki *Afghan.* 32°18N 65°5E **240** B2
Kajana = Kajaani *Finland* 64°17N 27°46E **160** D22
Kajang *Malaysia* 2°59N 101°48E **237** L3
Kajaran *Armenia* 39°10N 46°7E **213** C12
Kajiado *Kenya* 1°53S 36°48E **268** C4
Kajiado □ *Kenya* 2°0S 36°50E **268** C4
Kajo Kaji *South Sudan* 3°58N 31°40E **257** G3
Kajok *South Sudan* 8°19N 28°0E **257** F2
Kajuru *Nigeria* 10°15N 7°34E **263** C6
Kaka *South Sudan* 10°38N 32°10E **257** E3
Kaka *Turkmenistan* 37°21N 59°36E **247** B8
Kakabeka Falls *Canada* 48°24N 89°37W **298** C2
Kakadu △ *Australia* 12°0S 132°3E **278** B5
Kakamas *S. Africa* 28°45S 20°33E **270** C3
Kakamega *Kenya* 0°20N 34°46E **268** B3
Kakamigahara *Japan* 35°28N 136°48E **223** B8
Kakana *India* 9°7N 92°48E **245** K11
Kakanj *Bos.-H.* 44°4N 18°4E **182** F3
Kakanui Mts. *N.Z.* 45°10S 170°30E **285** F5
Kakata *Liberia* 6°35N 10°20W **262** D2
Kakching *India* 24°29N 94°0E **241** C5
Kakdwip *India* 21°53N 88°11E **243** J13
Kake = Akiōta *Japan* 34°36N 132°19E **222** C4
Kake *U.S.A.* 56°59N 133°57W **296** B2
Kakegawa *Japan* 34°45N 138°1E **223** C10
Kakeroma-Jima *Japan* 28°8N 129°14E **221** K4
Kākhak *Iran* 34°9N 58°38E **247** C8
Kakhib *Russia* 42°28N 46°34E **191** J8
Kakhonak *U.S.A.* 59°26N 154°51W **303** G9
Kakhovka *Ukraine* 46°45N 33°30E **189** J7
Kakhovske Vdskh. *Ukraine* 47°5N 34°0E **189** J7
Kakinada *India* 16°57N 82°11E **244** F6
Kakisa *Canada* 60°56N 117°25W **296** A5
Kakisa → *Canada* 61°3N 118°10W **296** A5
Kakisa L. *Canada* 60°56N 117°43W **296** A5
Käkisalmi = Priozersk *Russia* 61°2N 30°7E **188** B6
Kakogawa *Japan* 34°46N 134°51E **222** C6
Kaktovik *U.S.A.* 70°8N 143°38W **303** A12
Kakum △ *Ghana* 5°24N 1°20W **263** D4
Kakuma *Kenya* 3°43N 34°52E **268** B3
Kakwa → *Canada* 54°37N 118°28W **296** C5
Kāl Gūsheh *Iran* 30°59N 58°12E **247** D8
Kal Sefīd *Iran* 34°52N 47°23E **213** E12
Kala *Nigeria* 12°2N 14°40E **263** C7
Kala Oya → *Sri Lanka* 8°20N 79°45E **245** K4
Kalaa-Kebira *Tunisia* 35°59N 10°32E **258** A2
Kalaallit Nunaat = Greenland ◪ *N. Amer.* 66°0N 45°0W **154** D6
Kalabagh *Pakistan* 33°0N 71°28E **242** C4
Kalabahi *Indonesia* 8°13S 124°31E **231** F6
Kalabak = Radomir *Bulgaria* 42°37N 22°59E **202** D6
Kalabakan *Malaysia* 4°25N 117°29E **235** B5
Kalabana *Mali* 14°10N 8°35W **262** C3
Kalabo *Zambia* 14°58S 22°40E **265** E4
Kalaburagi *India* 17°20N 76°50E **244** F3
Kalach *Russia* 50°22N 41°0E **190** E5
Kalach na Donu *Russia* 48°43N 43°32E **191** F6
Kalachinsk *Russia* 55°3N 74°33E **217** A8
Kaladan → *Myanmar* 20°20N 93°5E **241** E4
Kaladar *Canada* 44°37N 77°5W **312** B7
Kalae *U.S.A.* 18°55N 155°41W **302** E6
Kalahari *Africa* 24°0S 21°30E **270** B3
Kalahari Gemsbok △ *S. Africa* 25°30S 20°30E **270** C3
Kalaheo *U.S.A.* 21°56N 159°32W **302** B2
Kalaikhum *Tajikistan* 38°28N 70°46E **217** E8
Kalajoki *Finland* 64°12N 24°10E **160** D21
Kalajun-Ku'erdening ⌓ *China* 43°10N 81°50E **217** D10
Kalakamati *Botswana* 20°40S 27°25E **271** B4
Kalakan *Russia* 55°15N 116°45E **215** D12
Kalakol *Kenya* 3°33N 35°54E **266** D4
K'alak'unlun Shank'ou = Karakoram Pass *Asia* 35°33N 77°50E **243** B7
Kalam *Pakistan* 35°34N 72°30E **243** B5
Kalama *Dem. Rep. of the Congo* 2°52S 28°35E **268** C2
Kalama *Wash., U.S.A.* 46°1N 122°51W **306** E4
Kalamaki *Greece* 37°52N 23°43E **112** B2
Kalamaloué △ *Cameroon* 12°9N 14°58E **259** F2
Kalamansig *Phil.* 6°33N 124°3E **233** H5
Kalamaria *Greece* 40°33N 22°55E **202** F6
Kalamata *Greece* 37°3N 22°10E **204** D4
Kalamazoo *U.S.A.* 42°17N 85°35W **311** B11
Kalamazoo → *U.S.A.* 42°40N 86°10W **311** B10
Kalamb *India* 18°3N 74°48E **244** E2
Kalambaka *Greece* 39°42N 21°39E **204** B3
Kalambo Falls *Tanzania* 8°37S 31°35E **269** D3
Kalamitsi *Greece* 38°45N 20°36E **207** B2
Kalamnuri *India* 19°40N 77°20E **244** E3
Kalamos *Attiki, Greece* 38°17N 23°52E **204** C5
Kalamos *Lefkada, Greece* 38°37N 20°55E **207** B2
Kalan = Tunceli *Turkey* 39°6N 39°31E **213** C8
Kalangadoo *Australia* 37°34S 140°41E **282** D4
Kalankalan *Guinea* 10°7N 8°54W **262** C3
Kalannie *Australia* 30°22S 117°5E **279** F2
Kalāntarī *Iran* 32°10N 54°8E **247** C7
Kalao *Indonesia* 7°21S 121°0E **231** F6
Kalaoa *U.S.A.* 19°43N 155°58W **302** D6
Kalaotoa *Indonesia* 7°20S 121°50E **231** F6
Kalapana *U.S.A.* 19°21N 154°59W **302** D7
Kälarne *Sweden* 62°59N 16°5E **162** B10
Kalasin *Thailand* 16°26N 103°30E **236** D4
Kālat *Iran* 25°29N 59°22E **247** E8
Kalat *Pakistan* 29°8N 66°31E **240** C2
Kalāteh *Iran* 36°33N 55°41E **247** B7
Kalāteh-ye Ganj *Iran* 27°31N 57°55E **247** E8
Kalathos *Greece* 36°9N 28°8E **206** E12
Kalatungan, Mt. *Phil.* 7°54N 124°50E **233** H5
Kalaupapa *U.S.A.* 21°12N 156°59W **302** B5
Kalaupapa ⌓ *U.S.A.* 21°10N 156°59W **302** B5
Kalaus → *Russia* 45°40N 44°7E **191** H7
Kalavrita *Greece* 38°3N 22°8E **204** C4
Kalaw *Myanmar* 20°38N 96°34E **241** E6
Kalawao County *U.S.A.* 21°11N 156°58W **302** B5
Kalbā *U.A.E.* 25°5N 56°22E **247** E8
Kalbadevi *Mumbai, India* **130** b2
Kalbān *Oman* 20°18N 58°38E **249** B7
Kalbarri *Australia* 27°40S 114°10E **279** E1
Kalbarri △ *Australia* 27°51S 114°30E **279** E1
Kalce *Slovenia* 45°54N 14°13E **176** F8
Kaldrananes *Iceland* 65°45N 21°25W **155** B5
Kale *Antalya, Turkey* 36°14N 30°0E **205** E12
Kale *Denizli, Turkey* 37°27N 28°49E **205** D10
Kaleburnu = Galinoporni *Cyprus* 35°31N 34°18E **207** E10
Kalecik *Turkey* 40°4N 33°26E **212** B5
Kalegauk Kyun *Myanmar* 15°33N 97°35E **236** E1
Kalehe *Dem. Rep. of the Congo* 2°6S 28°50E **268** C2
Kalema *Tanzania* 1°12S 31°55E **268** C3
Kalemie *Dem. Rep. of the Congo* 5°55S 29°9E **268** D2
Kalemyo *Myanmar* 23°11N 94°4E **241** D5
Kalety *Poland* 50°35N 18°52E **185** H5
Kalewa *Myanmar* 23°10N 94°15E **241** D5
Kaleybar *Iran* 38°47N 47°2E **213** C12
Kálfafell *Iceland* 63°57N 17°41W **155** D9
Kalgan = Zhangjiakou *China* 40°48N 114°55E **226** D8
Kalghatgi *India* 15°11N 74°58E **245** G2
Kalgoorlie-Boulder *Australia* 30°40S 121°22E **279** F3
Kalhovd *Norway* 60°4N 8°21E **164** D5
Kali → *India* 27°6N 79°55E **243** F8
Kali Sindh → *India* 25°32N 76°17E **242** G6
Kaliakra, Nos *Bulgaria* 43°21N 28°30E **203** C12
Kalianda *Indonesia* 5°50S 105°45E **234** D3
Kalibo *Phil.* 11°43N 122°22E **233** F4
Kaliganj *Bangla.* 22°25N 89°8E **241** D2
Kalihi *U.S.A.* 21°20N 157°53W **302** K14
Kalihi Valley *U.S.A.* 21°20N 157°52W **302** K14
Kalima *Dem. Rep. of the Congo* 2°33S 26°32E **268** C2
Kalimantan *Indonesia* 0°0 114°0E **235** C4
Kalimantan Barat □ *Indonesia* 0°0 110°30E **235** C4
Kalimantan Selatan □ *Indonesia* 2°30S 115°30E **235** C5
Kalimantan Tengah □ *Indonesia* 2°0S 113°30E **235** C4
Kalimantan Timur □ *Indonesia* 1°30N 116°30E **235** B5
Kalimantan Utara □ *Indonesia* 3°30N 117°0E **235** B5
Kálimnos *Greece* 37°0N 27°0E **205** D8
Kalimpong *India* 27°4N 88°35E **241** B2
Kalinadi → *India* 14°50N 74°7E **245** G2
Kalinga □ *Phil.* 17°30N 121°20E **232** C3
Kalinikinsk *Russia* 51°29N 44°28E **216** B2
Kalinin = Tver *Russia* 56°55N 35°59E **188** D8
Kaliningrad *Russia* 54°42N 20°32E **184** D7
Kaliningrad ✈ **(KGD)** *Russia* 54°45N 20°33E **184** D7
Kalininsk = Petrozavodsk *Russia* 61°41N 34°20E **188** B8
Kalininsk *Russia* 51°30N 44°40E **190** E7
Kalinkavichy *Belarus* 52°12N 29°20E **177** B15
Kalinkovichi = Kalinkavichy *Belarus* 52°12N 29°20E **177** B15
Kalinovik *Bos.-H.* 43°31N 18°25E **202** C2
Kalipetrovo *Bulgaria* 44°5N 27°14E **203** B11
Kalipur *India* 22°40N 88°17E **124** A1
Kalirachi *Greece* 40°40N 24°35E **203** F8
Kaliro *Uganda* 0°56N 33°30E **268** B3
Kalispell *U.S.A.* 48°12N 114°19W **304** B6
Kalisz *Poland* 51°45N 18°8E **185** G5
Kalisz Pomorski *Poland* 53°17N 15°55E **185** E2
Kalithea *Greece* 37°56N 23°43E **112** B2
Kaliua *Tanzania* 5°5S 31°48E **268** D3
Kaliveli Tank *India* 12°5N 79°50E **245** H4
Kalivia Thorikou *Greece* 37°50N 23°55E **204** D5
Kalix *Sweden* 65°53N 23°12E **160** D20
Kalixälven → *Sweden* 65°50N 23°11E **160** D20
Kalka *India* 30°46N 76°57E **242** D7
Kalkaji *India* 28°32N 77°12E **120** B2
Kalkali Ghat *India* 24°36N 92°20E **241** C4
Kalkan *Turkey* 36°15N 29°23E **205** E11
Kalkarindji *Australia* 17°30S 130°47E **278** C5
Kalkaska *U.S.A.* 44°44N 85°11W **309** C11
Kalkfeld *Namibia* 20°57S 16°14E **270** B2
Kalkfontein *Botswana* 22°4S 20°57E **270** B3
Kalkım *Turkey* 39°48N 27°13E **205** B9
Kalkrand *Namibia* 24°1S 17°35E **270** B2
Kallakkurichchi *India* 11°44N 79°1E **245** J4
Kallam *India* 18°36N 76°2E **244** E3
Kållandsö *Sweden* 58°40N 13°5E **163** F7
Kallavesi *Finland* 62°58N 27°30E **160** E22
Källby *Sweden* 58°30N 13°8E **163** F7
Kållered *Sweden* 57°32N 12°4E **163** G6
Kallidaikurichi *India* 8°38N 77°31E **245** K3
Kallies = Kalisz Pomorski *Poland* 53°17N 15°55E **185** E2
Kallimasia *Greece* 38°18N 26°6E **205** C8
Kallinge *Sweden* 56°15N 15°18E **163** H9
Kallmet *Albania* 41°51N 19°41E **202** E3
Kallsjön *Sweden* 63°38N 13°0E **160** E15
Kalmalo *Nigeria* 13°40N 5°20E **263** C6
Kalmanstunga *Iceland* 64°44N 20°48W **155** C6
Kalmar *Sweden* 56°40N 16°20E **163** H10
Kalmar □ *Sweden* 57°25N 16°0E **163** G10
Kalmar sund *Sweden* 56°40N 16°25E **163** H10
Kalmunai *Sri Lanka* 7°25N 81°49E **245** L5
Kalmykia □ *Russia* 46°5N 46°1E **191** G8
Kalna *India* 23°13N 88°25E **243** H13
Kalnai *India* 22°46N 83°30E **243** H10
Kalni → *Bangla.* 24°21N 91°13E **241** C3
Kalo *Papua N. G.* 10°1S 147°48E **286** F4
Kalo Nero *Greece* 37°20N 21°38E **204** D3
Kalocsa *Hungary* 46°32N 19°0E **182** D4
Kalofer *Bulgaria* 42°37N 24°59E **203** D8
Kalohi Channel *U.S.A.* 21°0N 157°0W **302** C5
Kalokhorio *Cyprus* 34°51N 33°2E **207** F9
Kaloko *Dem. Rep. of the Congo* 6°47S 25°48E **265** D5
Kaloko-Honokōhau ⌓ *U.S.A.* 19°40N 156°1W **302** D5
Kalol *Gujarat, India* 22°37N 73°31E **242** H5
Kalol *Gujarat, India* 23°15N 72°33E **242** H5
Kalolimnos *Greece* 37°4N 27°5E **205** D9
Kalomo *Zambia* 17°0S 26°30E **269** F2
Kalona *U.S.A.* 41°29N 91°43W **310** C5
Kaloni *Greece* 39°14N 26°12E **205** B8
Kaloni, Kolpos *Greece* 39°10N 26°10E **205** B8
Kalookan = Caloocan *Phil.* 14°39N 120°58E **127** B1
Kalpeni I. *India* 10°5N 73°38E **245** J1
Kalpi *India* 26°8N 79°47E **243** F8
Kalpitiya *Sri Lanka* 8°14N 79°46E **245** K4
Kalputhi I. *India* 10°49N 72°10E **245** J1
Kalrayan Hills *India* 11°45N 78°40E **245** J4
Kalsubai *India* 19°35N 73°45E **244** E1
Kaltag *U.S.A.* 64°20N 158°43W **303** D8
Kaltern = Caldaro *Italy* 46°25N 11°14E **199** B8
Kaltukatjara *Australia* 24°52S 129°5E **279** D4
Kaltungo *Nigeria* 9°48N 11°19E **263** D7
Kalu *Pakistan* 25°5N 67°39E **242** G2
Kaluga *Russia* 54°35N 36°10E **188** E9
Kaluga □ *Russia* 54°15N 34°50E **188** E8
Kalulong, Bukit *Malaysia* 3°14N 114°39E **235** B4
Kalulushi *Zambia* 12°50S 28°3E **269** E2
Kalumburu *Australia* 13°55S 126°35E **278** B4
Kalumburu ۞ *Australia* 14°17S 126°38E **278** B4
Kalundborg *Denmark* 55°41N 11°5E **163** J5
Kalush *Ukraine* 49°3N 24°23E **177** D13
Kałuszyn *Poland* 52°13N 21°52E **185** F8
Kalutara *Sri Lanka* 6°35N 80°0E **245** L5
Kalvåg *Norway* 61°46N 4°51E **164** C1
Kalvarija *Lithuania* 54°24N 23°14E **184** D10
Kalvebod Fælled *Denmark* 55°35N 12°33E **118** B3
Kalveboderne *Denmark* 55°37N 12°31E **118** B3
Kalwakurti *India* 16°41N 78°30E **244** F4
Kalya *Russia* 60°15N 59°59E **186** B10
Kalyan = Basavakalyan *India* 17°52N 76°57E **244** F3
Kalyan *Maharashtra, India* 20°30N 74°3E **244** D2
Kalyan *Maharashtra, India* 19°15N 73°9E **244** E1
Kalyandurg *India* 14°33N 77°6E **245** G3
Kalyansingapuram *India* 19°30N 83°19E **244** E6
Kalyazin *Russia* 57°15N 37°55E **188** D9
Kam *Albania* 42°17N 20°18E **202** D4
Kam → *Nigeria* 8°15N 1°10E **263** D7
Kam Shan Country Park ⌓ *Hong Kong, China* 22°21N 114°9E **122** A2
Kama *Dem. Rep. of the Congo* 3°30S 27°5E **268** C2
Kama *Fukuoka, Japan* 33°33N 130°49E **222** D2
Kama *Myanmar* 19°1N 95°4E **241** F5
Kama → *Russia* 55°45N 52°0E **186** C9
Kama Iwa *Iwo Jima* 24°47N 141°17E **288** b
Kamachumu *Tanzania* 1°37S 31°37E **268** C3
Kamae *Japan* 32°48N 131°56E **222** E3
Kamaing *Myanmar* 25°26N 96°35E **241** C6
Kamaishi *Japan* 39°16N 141°53E **220** E10
Kamakou *U.S.A.* 21°7N 156°52W **302** B5
Kamakura *Japan* 35°19N 139°33E **223** B11
Kamalapurum *India* 14°35N 78°39E **245** G4
Kamaléte *Gabon* 0°43S 11°49E **264** C2
Kamalia *Pakistan* 30°44N 72°42E **242** D5
Kamamaung *Myanmar* 17°21N 97°40E **241** G6
Kaman *India* 27°39N 77°16E **242** F6
Kaman *Turkey* 39°22N 33°44E **212** C5
Kamana *Dem. Rep. of the Congo* 5°59S 24°58E **265** D4
Kamananui → *U.S.A.* 21°38N 158°4W **302** J13
Kamanjab *Namibia* 19°35S 14°51E **270** A2
Kamapanda *Zambia* 12°5S 24°0E **269** E1
Kamara *Mali* 14°38N 9°23W **262** C3
Kamarān *Yemen* 15°21N 42°35E **248** D3
Kamareddi *India* 18°19N 78°21E **244** E4
Kamarhati *India* 22°40N 88°23E **124** A2
Kamata *Japan* 35°33N 139°43E **140** B3
Kamativi *Zimbabwe* 18°20S 27°6E **270** A4
Kamba *Dem. Rep. of the Congo* 4°0S 22°22E **265** C4
Kamba *Nigeria* 11°50N 3°45E **263** C5
Kambalda West *Australia* 31°10S 121°37E **279** F3
Kambam *India* 9°45N 77°16E **245** K3
Kambangan, Nusa *Indonesia* 7°40S 108°10E **235** D3
Kambar *Pakistan* 27°37N 68°1E **242** F3
Kambarka *Russia* 56°15N 54°11E **186** C9
Kambia *S. Leone* 9°3N 12°53W **262** D2
Kambolé *Togo* 8°43N 1°39E **263** D5
Kambolé *Zambia* 8°47S 30°48E **269** D3
Kambos *Cyprus* 35°2N 32°44E **207** E8
Kambove *Dem. Rep. of the Congo* 10°51S 26°33E **269** E2
Kambuie *Dem. Rep. of the Congo* 6°59S 22°19E **265** D4
Kambwata *Zambia* 14°3S 23°43E **265** E4
Kamchatka, Poluostrov *Russia* 57°0N 160°0E **215** D17
Kamchatka Pen. = Kamchatka, Poluostrov *Russia* 57°0N 160°0E **215** D17
Kamchia → *Bulgaria* 43°4N 27°44E **203** C11
Kamchiya = Kamchia → *Bulgaria* 43°4N 27°44E **203** C11
Kame Ruins *Zimbabwe* 20°7S 28°25E **269** G2
Kameari *Japan* 35°45N 139°50E **140** A4
Kameda-Hantō *Japan* 41°50N 141°0E **220** D10
Kameido *Japan* 35°42N 139°50E **140** A4
Kamen *Russia* 53°50N 81°30E **217** B10
Kamen-Rybolov *Russia* 44°46N 132°2E **220** B5
Kamende *Dem. Rep. of the Congo* 6°26S 24°35E **265** D4
Kamenica *Serbia* 43°27N 22°27E **202** C6
Kamenica *Serbia* 44°25N 19°45E **202** B3
Kamenice nad Lipou *Czechia* 49°18N 15°2E **180** B8
Kamenjak, Rt *Croatia* 44°47N 13°55E **199** D10
Kamenka = Kamyanka *Ukraine* 49°3N 32°6E **189** H7
Kamenka *Kazakhstan* 51°7N 50°19E **190** E10
Kamenka *Arkhangelsk, Russia* 65°58N 44°0E **186** A7
Kamenka *Penza, Russia* 53°10N 44°5E **190** D6
Kamenka *Voronezh, Russia* 50°47N 39°20E **189** G10
Kamenka Bugskaya = Kamyanka-Buzka *Ukraine* 50°8N 24°16E **177** C13
Kamenka Dneprovskaya = Kamyanka-Dniprovska *Ukraine* 47°29N 34°28E **189** J8
Kamenka-Shevchenkovskaya = Kamyanka-Buzka *Ukraine* 50°8N 24°16E **177** C13
Kamennomostskiy *Russia* 44°18N 40°13E **191** H5
Kameno *Bulgaria* 42°34N 27°18E **203** D11
Kamenolomini *Russia* 47°40N 40°14E **191** G5
Kamensk-Shakhtinskiy *Russia* 48°23N 40°20E **191** F5
Kamensk Uralskiy *Russia* 56°25N 62°2E **214** D7
Kamenskaya = Kamensk-Shakhtinskiy *Russia* 48°23N 40°20E **191** F5
Kamenskiy *Russia* 50°48N 45°25E **190** E7
Kamenskoye = Kamyanske *Ukraine* 48°32N 34°37E **189** H8
Kamenskoye *Russia* 62°45N 165°30E **215** C17
Kamenyak *Bulgaria* 43°24N 26°57E **203** C10
Kamenz *Germany* 51°15N 14°5E **178** D10
Kameoka *Japan* 35°0N 135°35E **223** C7
Kamet *India* 30°55N 79°35E **243** D8
Kameyama *Japan* 34°51N 136°27E **223** C8
Kami *Japan* 33°36N 133°38E **222** D5
Kami-Itabashi *Japan* 35°45N 139°40E **140** A3
Kami-Jima *Japan* 32°27N 130°20E **222** E2
Kami-Koshiki-Jima *Japan* 31°50N 129°52E **222** F1
Kamiagata *Japan* 34°47N 129°24E **222** C1
Kamiah *U.S.A.* 46°14N 116°2W **304** C5
Kamień Krajeński *Poland* 53°32N 17°32E **184** E4
Kamień Pomorski *Poland* 53°57N 14°43E **184** E1
Kamienna → *Poland* 51°6N 21°47E **185** G8
Kamienna Góra *Poland* 50°47N 16°2E **185** H3
Kamieńsk *Poland* 51°12N 19°29E **185** G6
Kamieskroon *S. Africa* 30°9S 17°56E **270** D2
Kamikitazawa *Japan* 35°39N 139°36E **140** B2
Kamilukuak L. *Canada* 62°22N 101°40W **297** A8
Kamin-Kashyrskyy *Ukraine* 51°39N 24°56E **177** C13
Kamina *Dem. Rep. of the Congo* 8°45S 25°0E **265** D5
Kaminak L. *Canada* 62°10N 95°0W **297** A10
Kaminoyama *Japan* 38°9N 140°17E **220** E10
Kamioka *Japan* 36°25N 137°15E **223** A9
Kamiros *Greece* 36°20N 27°56E **206** E11
Kamishak Bay *U.S.A.* 59°15N 153°45W **303** G9
Kamisu *Japan* 35°50N 140°45E **223** B12
Kamitsuruma *Japan* 35°30N 139°26E **140** B1
Kamitsushima *Japan* 34°50N 129°28E **222** C1
Kamituga *Dem. Rep. of the Congo* 3°2S 28°10E **268** C2
Kamla → *India* 25°35N 86°36E **243** G12
Kamloops *Canada* 50°40N 120°20W **296** C4
Kamnik *Slovenia* 46°14N 14°37E **199** B11
Kamo *Japan* 37°39N 139°3E **220** F9
Kamo *N.Z.* 35°42S 174°20E **284** B3
Kamoa Mts. *Guyana* 1°30N 59°0W **329** C6
Kamogawa *Japan* 35°5N 140°5E **223** B12
Kamojima = Yoshinogawa *Japan* 34°4N 134°21E **222** C6
Kamoke *Pakistan* 32°4N 74°4E **242** C6
Kamo'oloa *U.S.A.* 21°34N 158°7W **302** J13
Kamoshida *Japan* 35°33N 139°31E **140** B2
Kamp → *Austria* 48°23N 15°42E **180** C8
Kampala *Uganda* 0°20N 32°32E **268** B3
Kampar *Malaysia* 4°18N 101°9E **237** K3
Kampar → *Indonesia* 0°30N 103°8E **234** B2
Kampen *Neths.* 52°33N 5°53E **170** B5
Kamphaeng Phet *Thailand* 16°28N 99°30E **236** D2
Kampinoski △ *Poland* 52°21N 20°40E **185** F7
Kampolombo, L. *Zambia* 11°37S 29°42E **269** E2
Kampong Cham *Cambodia* 12°0N 105°30E **237** G5
Kampong Chhnang *Cambodia* 12°20N 104°35E **237** F5
Kampong Landang *Singapore* 1°20N 103°55E **138** A3
Kampong Pengerang *Malaysia* 1°22N 104°7E **237** d
Kampong Punggai *Malaysia* 1°27N 104°18E **237** d
Kampong Saom *Cambodia* 10°38N 103°30E **237** G4
Kampong Saom, Chaak *Cambodia* 10°50N 103°32E **237** G4
Kampong Tanjong Langsat *Malaysia* 1°28N 104°1E **237** d
Kampong Tanjong Penjuru *Singapore* 1°18N 103°45E **138** B2
Kampong Telok Ramunia *Malaysia* 1°22N 104°15E **237** d
Kampot *Cambodia* 10°36N 104°10E **237** G5
Kampsville *U.S.A.* 39°18N 90°37W **310** E6
Kampti *Burkina Faso* 10°7N 3°25W **262** C4
Kampuchea = Cambodia ■ *Asia* 12°15N 105°0E **236** F5
Kampung Air Putih *Malaysia* 4°15N 103°10E **237** K4
Kampung Bali *Indonesia* 6°11S 106°48E **122** B1
Kampung Jerangau *Malaysia* 4°50N 103°10E **237** K4
Kampung Raja *Malaysia* 5°45N 102°35E **237** K4
Kampungbaru = Tolitoli *Indonesia* 1°5N 120°50E **231** D6
Kamrau, Teluk *Indonesia* 3°30S 133°36E **231** E8
Kamsack *Canada* 51°34N 101°54W **297** C8
Kamsar *Guinea* 10°40N 14°36W **262** C2
Kamskoye Ustye *Russia* 55°10N 49°20E **190** C9
Kamskoye Vdkhr. *Russia* 58°41N 56°7E **186** C10
Kamsuuma *Somalia* 0°15N 42°46E **267** D5
Kamthi *India* 21°9N 79°19E **244** D4
Kamuchawie L. *Canada* 56°18N 101°59W **297** B8
Kamuela *U.S.A.* 20°1N 155°41W **302** C6
Kamui-Misaki *Japan* 43°20N 140°21E **220** C10
Kamyanets-Podilskyy *Ukraine* 48°45N 26°40E **183** B11

Kamyanka Ukraine 49°3N 32°6E 189 H7
Kamyanka-Buzka Ukraine 50°8N 24°16E 177 C13
Kamyanka-Dniprovska Ukraine 47°29N 34°28E 189 J8
Kamyanske Ukraine 48°32N 34°37E 189 H8
Kamyanyets Belarus 52°23N 23°49E 185 F10
Kamyanyuki Belarus 52°32N 23°49E 185 F10
Kāmyārān Iran 34°47N 46°56E 213 E12
Kamyshin Russia 50°10N 45°24E 190 E7
Kamyzyak Russia 46°4N 48°10E 191 G9
Kan = Gan Jiang → China 29°15N 116°0E 229 C11
Kan Myanmar 22°25N 94°5E 241 D5
Kan South Sudan 9°1N 31°47E 257 F3
Kanaaupscow → Canada 54°2N 76°30W 298 B4
Kanab U.S.A. 37°3N 112°32W 305 H7
Kanab Cr. → U.S.A. 36°24N 112°38W 305 H7
Kanacea Lau Group, Fiji 17°15S 179°6W 287 A3
Kanacea Taveuni, Fiji 16°59S 179°56E 287 A2
Kanaga I. U.S.A. 51°45N 177°22W 303 L3
Kanagawa □ Japan 35°20N 139°20E 223 B11
Kanagi Japan 40°54N 140°27E 220 D10
Kanairiktok → Canada 55°2N 60°18W 299 A7
Kanakanak U.S.A. 59°0N 158°32W 303 G8
Kanakapura India 12°33N 77°28E 245 H3
Kanalia Greece 39°30N 22°53E 204 B4
Kanamori Japan 35°31N 139°27E 140 B1
Kananga Dem. Rep. of the Congo 5°55S 22°18E 265 D4
Kanangra-Boyd △ Australia 33°57S 150°15E 283 B9
Kanash Russia 55°30N 47°32E 190 C8
Kanaskat U.S.A. 47°19N 121°54W 306 C5
Kanastraíon, Ákra = Palioúri, Ákra Greece 39°57N 23°45E 202 G7
Kanawha → U.S.A. 38°50N 82°9W 309 F12
Kanazawa Japan 36°30N 136°38E 223 A8
Kanbalu Myanmar 23°12N 95°31E 241 D5
Kanchanaburi Thailand 14°2N 99°31E 236 E2
Kanchenjunga Nepal 27°50N 88°10E 243 F13
Kanchenjunga △ India 27°42N 88°8E 241 B2
Kanchipuram India 12°52N 79°45E 245 H4
Kanchow = Ganzhou China 25°51N 114°56E 229 E10
Kańczuga Poland 49°59N 22°25E 185 J9
Kanda Tokyo, Japan 140 a5
Kanda Kanda Dem. Rep. of the Congo 6°52S 23°48E 265 D4
Kandagach = Qandyaghash Kazakhstan 49°28N 57°25E 187 E10
Kandaghat India 30°59N 77°7E 242 D7
Kandahār Kandahār, Afghan. 31°32N 65°43E 240 C2
Kandahar India 18°52N 77°12E 244 E3
Kandahār □ Afghan. 31°0N 65°0E 240 C2
Kandala Dem. Rep. of the Congo 6°20S 19°40E 265 D3
Kandalaksha Russia 67°9N 32°30E 160 C25
Kandalakshskiy Zaliv Russia 66°0N 35°0E 186 A6
Kandang Indonesia 3°3N 97°19E 234 B1
Kandangan Indonesia 2°50S 115°20E 235 C5
Kandanos Greece 35°19N 23°44E 207 E5
Kandava Latvia 57°2N 22°46E 184 A9
Kandavu = Kadavu Fiji 19°0S 178°15E 287 B2
Kandavu Passage = Kadavu Passage Fiji 18°45S 178°0E 287 B2
Kandé = Kanté Togo 9°57N 1°3E 263 D5
Kandep Papua N. G. 5°54S 143°32E 286 C2
Kandhkot Pakistan 28°16N 69°8E 242 E3
Kandhla India 29°18N 77°19E 242 E7
Kandi Benin 11°7N 2°55E 263 C5
Kandi India 23°58N 88°5E 243 H13
Kandiaro Pakistan 27°4N 68°13E 242 F3
Kandila Arkadia, Greece 37°46N 22°22E 204 D4
Kandila Etoloakarnania, Greece 38°42N 20°56E 207 B2
Kandilli Turkey 41°4N 29°3E 122 B2
Kandira Turkey 41°4N 30°9E 212 B4
Kandla India 23°0N 70°10E 242 H4
Kandor, O. → Chad 17°13N 20°52E 259 E4
Kandos Australia 32°45S 149°58E 283 B8
Kandreho Madag. 17°29S 46°6E 272 B2
Kandrian Papua N. G. 6°14S 149°37E 286 C5
Kandy Sri Lanka 7°18N 80°43E 245 L5
Kane U.S.A. 41°40N 78°49W 312 E6
Kane Basin Greenland 79°1N 70°0W 154 B4
Kaneilio Pt. U.S.A. 21°27N 158°12W 302 K13
Kanel Senegal 15°30N 13°18W 262 B2
Kanem □ Chad 15°0N 15°0E 259 F3
Kāne'ohe U.S.A. 21°25N 157°48W 302 K14
Kāne'ohe B. U.S.A. 21°30N 157°50W 302 K14
Kaneohe Station U.S.A. 21°27N 157°46W 302 K14
Kanevskaya Russia 46°3N 38°57E 191 G4
Kanfanar Croatia 45°7N 13°50E 199 C10
Kang Botswana 23°41S 22°50E 270 B3
Kangaamiut Greenland 65°50N 53°20W 154 D5
Kangaatsiaq Greenland 68°18N 53°28W 154 D5
Kangaba Mali 11°56N 8°25W 262 C3
Kangal Turkey 39°14N 37°23E 212 C7
Kangān Fārs, Iran 27°50N 52°3E 247 E7
Kangān Hormozgān, Iran 25°48N 57°28E 247 E8
Kangar Malaysia 6°27N 100°12E 237 J3
Kangaré Mali 11°36N 8°4W 262 C3
Kangaroo I. Australia 35°45S 137°0E 282 C2
Kangaroo Mts. Australia 23°29S 141°51E 280 C3
Kangasala Finland 61°28N 24°4E 188 B3
Kangāvar Iran 34°40N 48°0E 213 E12
Kangding China 30°2N 101°57E 228 B3
Kangdong N. Korea 39°9N 126°5E 224 C3
Kangean, Kepulauan Indonesia 6°55S 115°23E 235 D5
Kangean Is. = Kangean, Kepulauan Indonesia 6°55S 115°23E 235 D5
Kangen → South Sudan 6°47N 33°9E 257 F3
Kangerdlugssuak Greenland 68°10N 32°20W 154 D7
Kangerluarsoruseq Greenland 63°45N 51°27W 154 E5
Kangerluarsoruset = Kangerluarsoruseq Greenland 63°45N 51°27W 154 E5
Kangerlussuaq Greenland 66°59N 50°40W 154 D5
Kangertittivaq = Scoresby Sund Greenland 70°28N 21°46W 154 C8
Kanggye N. Korea 41°0N 126°35E 224 B3
Kanghsi Taiwan 23°34N 120°8E 225 C2
Kangikajik Greenland 70°7N 22°0W 154 C8
Kangilinnguit Greenland 61°20N 47°57W 154 E6
Kangiqliniq = Rankin Inlet Canada 62°30N 93°0W 294 E13
Kangiqsualujjuaq Canada 58°30N 65°59W 295 F18
Kangiqsujuaq Canada 61°30N 72°0W 295 E17
Kangiqtugaapik = Clyde River Canada 70°30N 68°30W 295 C18
Kangirsuk Canada 60°0N 70°0W 295 F18
Kangkar Chemaran Malaysia 1°34N 104°12E 237 d
Kangkar Sungai Tiram Malaysia 1°35N 103°55E 237 d
Kangkar Teberau Malaysia 1°32N 103°51E 237 d
Kango Gabon 0°11N 10°5E 264 B2
Kangoku Iwa Iwo Jima 24°48N 141°17E 288 b
Kangoya Dem. Rep. of the Congo 9°55S 22°48E 265 D4
Kangping China 42°43N 123°18E 227 C12
Kangpokpi India 25°8N 93°58E 241 C4
Kangra India 32°6N 76°16E 242 C7
Kangrinboqe Feng China 31°0N 81°25E 243 D9
Kangshan Taiwan 22°48N 120°17E 225 D2
Kangto China 27°50N 92°35E 241 B4
Kangtzu Taiwan 22°8N 120°52E 225 D2
Kangwon-do □ N. Korea 38°47N 127°35E 224 C3
Kangyidaung Myanmar 16°56N 94°54E 241 G5
Kanha △ India 22°15N 80°40E 243 H9
Kanhan → India 21°4N 79°34E 244 D4
Kanhangad India 12°21N 74°58E 245 H2
Kanhar → India 24°28N 83°8E 243 G10
Kani Côte d'Ivoire 8°29N 6°36W 262 D3
Kani Japan 35°25N 137°7E 223 B9
Kani Sagaing, Myanmar 23°52N 95°22E 241 D5
Kani Sagaing, Myanmar 22°26N 94°51E 241 D5
Kani-Keli Mayotte 12°57S 45°6E 272 b
Kaniama Dem. Rep. of the Congo 7°30S 24°12E 265 D4
Kaniapiskau = Caniapiscau → Canada 56°40N 69°30W 299 A6
Kaniapiskau, L. = Caniapiscau, L. Canada 54°10N 69°55W 299 B6
Kaniere, L. N.Z. 42°50S 171°10E 285 C6
Kanif Micronesia 9°31N 138°5E 287 R16
Kanigiri India 15°24N 79°31E 245 G4
Kanin, Poluostrov Russia 68°0N 45°0E 186 A8
Kanin Nos, Mys Russia 68°39N 43°32E 186 A7
Kanin Pen. = Kanin, Poluostrov Russia 68°0N 45°0E 186 A8
Kaninë Albania 40°23N 19°30E 202 F3
Kaniva Australia 36°22S 141°18E 282 D4
Kanjiža Serbia 46°3N 20°4E 182 D5
Kanjut Sar Pakistan 36°7N 75°25E 243 A6
Kankaanpää Finland 61°44N 22°50E 188 B2
Kankakee U.S.A. 41°7N 87°52W 311 C9
Kankakee → U.S.A. 41°23N 88°15W 311 C8
Kankan Guinea 10°23N 9°15W 262 C3
Kankendy = Xankändi Azerbaijan 39°52N 46°49E 213 C12
Kanker India 20°10N 81°40E 244 D5
Kankesanturai Sri Lanka 9°49N 80°2E 245 K5
Kankossa Mauritania 15°54N 11°31W 262 B2
Kankroli India 25°4N 73°53E 242 G5
Kankurgachi India 22°34N 88°23E 124 B2
Kanlıca Turkey 41°5N 29°3E 122 B2
Kanmaw Kyun Myanmar 11°40N 98°28E 237 G2
Kanmuri-Yama Japan 34°30N 132°4E 222 C4
Kannabe Japan 34°32N 133°23E 222 C5
Kannapolis U.S.A. 35°30N 80°37W 315 D14
Kannauj India 27°3N 79°56E 243 F8
Kanniyakumari India 8°5N 77°34E 245 K3
Kannur India 11°53N 75°27E 245 J2
Kannyakumari India 8°3N 77°40E 245 K3
Kano Nigeria 12°2N 8°30E 263 C6
Kano □ Nigeria 11°30N 8°30E 263 C6
Kanonerskiy, Ostrov Russia 59°53N 30°13E 137 B1
Kan'onji Japan 34°7N 133°39E 222 C5
Kanoroba Côte d'Ivoire 9°7N 6°8W 262 D3
Kanowha U.S.A. 42°57N 93°47W 310 B3
Kanowit Malaysia 2°14N 112°20E 235 B4
Kanoya Japan 31°25N 130°50E 222 F2
Kanpetlet Myanmar 21°10N 93°59E 241 E4
Kanpur India 26°28N 80°20E 243 F9
Kansai Int. ✈ (KIX) Japan 34°27N 135°12E 133 B2
Kansas U.S.A. 39°33N 87°56W 311 E9
Kansas □ U.S.A. 38°30N 99°0W 308 F4
Kansas → U.S.A. 39°7N 94°37W 308 F6
Kansas City Kans., U.S.A. 39°7N 94°38W 310 E2
Kansas City Mo., U.S.A. 39°6N 94°35W 310 E2
Kansas City Int. ✈ (MCI) U.S.A. 39°18N 94°43W 310 E2
Kansenia Dem. Rep. of the Congo 10°20S 26°0E 269 E2
Kansk Russia 56°20N 95°37E 215 D10
Kansu = Gansu □ China 36°0N 104°0E 226 G3
Kantaphor India 22°35N 76°34E 242 H7
Kantchari Burkina Faso 12°37N 1°37E 263 C5
Kantché Niger 13°31N 8°30E 259 F1
Kanté Togo 9°57N 1°3E 263 D5
Kantemirovka Russia 49°43N 39°55E 189 H10
Kanth = Kąty Wrocławskie Poland 51°2N 16°45E 185 G3
Kantharalak Thailand 14°39N 104°39E 236 E5
Kanthi = Contai India 21°54N 87°46E 243 J12
Kantishna U.S.A. 63°31N 150°57W 303 E10
Kantishna → U.S.A. 64°45N 149°58W 303 D10
Kantli → India 28°20N 75°30E 242 E6
Kantō □ Japan 36°15N 139°30E 223 A11
Kantō-Sanchi Japan 35°59N 138°50E 223 B10
Kantu-long Myanmar 19°57N 97°36E 241 F6
Kanturk Ireland 52°11N 8°54W 166 D3
Kanuma Japan 36°34N 139°42E 223 A11
Kanus Namibia 27°50S 18°39E 270 C2
Kanuti Nat. Wildlife Refuge ⌂ U.S.A. 66°25N 151°50W 303 C10
Kanye Botswana 24°55S 25°28E 270 B4
Kanzaki → Japan 34°41N 135°24E 133 A1
Kanzenze Dem. Rep. of the Congo 10°30S 25°12E 265 E5
Kanzi, Ras Tanzania 7°1S 39°33E 268 D4
Kanzoni, Chissioua Comoros Is. 12°23S 43°40E 272 a
Kao Tonga 19°40S 175°1W 287 P13
Kao Phara Thailand 8°3N 98°22E 237 a
Kaohsiung Taiwan 22°35N 120°16E 225 D2
Kaohsung □ Taiwan 23°0N 120°35E 225 D2
Kaoka Solomon Is. 9°42S 160°43E 287 M11
Kaokaona = Kirakira Solomon Is. 10°27S 161°56E 287 N11
Kaokoveld Namibia 19°15S 14°30E 270 A1
Kaolack Senegal 14°5N 16°8W 262 C1
Kaolack □ Senegal 14°10N 15°15W 262 B1
Kaolan = Lanzhou China 36°1N 103°52E 226 F2
Kaolo Solomon Is. 8°24S 159°38E 287 M10
Kaoma Zambia 14°47S 24°48E 265 E4
Kaoshan China 44°38N 124°50E 227 B13
Kaoshu Taiwan 22°49N 120°36E 225 D2
Kaouar Niger 19°15N 12°52E 259 E2
Kaoyao = Zhaoqing China 23°0N 112°20E 229 F9
Kapa'a U.S.A. 22°5N 159°19W 302 A2
Kapadvanj India 23°5N 73°0E 242 H5
Kapagere Papua N. G. 9°46S 147°42E 286 E4
Kapahulu U.S.A. 21°16N 157°49W 302 K14
Kapakli Turkey 41°19N 27°59E 203 E11
Kapali Carsi Turkey 41°1N 28°58E 122 B1
Kapalua U.S.A. 20°59N 156°39W 302 C5
Kapan Armenia 39°18N 46°27E 213 C12
Kapanga Bandundu, Dem. Rep. of the Congo 5°4S 16°58E 265 D3
Kapanga Katanga, Dem. Rep. of the Congo 8°30S 22°40E 265 D4
Kapapa I. U.S.A. 21°29N 157°48W 302 K14
Kapatagan Phil. 7°52N 123°44E 233 H4
Kapchagai = Qapshaghay Kazakhstan 43°51N 77°14E 217 D9
Kapchagaiskoye Vdkhr. = Qapshaghay Bögeni Kazakhstan 43°45N 77°50E 217 D9
Kapedo Kenya 1°10N 36°6E 268 B4
Kapela = Velika Kapela Croatia 45°10N 15°5E 199 C12
Kapellerfeld Austria 48°18N 16°29E 142 A2
Kapellskär Sweden 59°44N 19°2E 162 E13
Kapelo, Akra Greece 36°9N 23°3E 204 E5
Kapema Dem. Rep. of the Congo 10°45S 28°22E 269 E2
Kapenguria Kenya 1°14N 35°7E 268 B4
Kapfenberg Austria 47°26N 15°18E 180 D8
Kapı Dağı Turkey 40°28N 27°50E 203 F11
Kapia Dem. Rep. of the Congo 4°17S 19°46E 265 C3
Kapiri Mposhi Zambia 13°59S 28°43E 269 E2
Kāpīsā □ Afghan. 35°0N 69°20E 240 B3
Kapiskau → Canada 52°47N 81°55W 298 B3
Kapit Malaysia 2°0N 112°55E 235 B4
Kapiti I. N.Z. 40°50S 174°56E 284 G3
Kapka, Massif du Chad 15°7N 21°45E 259 E4
Kaplan U.S.A. 30°0N 92°17W 314 F8
Kaplice Czechia 48°42N 14°30E 180 C7
Kapoe Thailand 9°34N 98°32E 237 H2
Kapoeta South Sudan 4°50N 33°35E 257 G3
Kapoho U.S.A. 19°30N 154°50W 302 D7
Kapolei U.S.A. 21°19N 158°5W 302 K13
Kápolnásnyék Hungary 47°16N 18°41E 182 C3
Kapombo Dem. Rep. of the Congo 10°40S 23°30E 265 E4
Kaponga N.Z. 39°29S 174°9E 284 F3
Kapos → Hungary 46°44N 18°30E 182 D3
Kaposvár Hungary 46°25N 17°47E 182 D2
Kapósztásmegyer Hungary 47°35N 19°6E 117 A2
Kapotnya Russia 55°39N 37°48E 129 C3
Kapowsin U.S.A. 46°59N 122°13W 306 D4
Kapp Norway 60°43N 10°52E 164 D7
Käppala Sweden 59°21N 18°13E 139 A3
Kappeln Germany 54°40N 9°55E 178 A5
Kappelshamn Sweden 57°52N 18°47E 163 G12
Kapps Namibia 22°32S 17°18E 270 B2
Kaprije Croatia 43°42N 15°43E 199 E12
Kapsabet Kenya 0°12N 35°6E 268 B4
Kapsan N. Korea 41°4N 128°19E 224 B4
Kapsukas = Marijampolė Lithuania 54°33N 23°19E 184 D10
Kaptai Bangla. 22°21N 92°17E 241 D4
Kaptai L. Bangla. 22°40N 92°20E 241 D4
Kapuas → Kalimantan Barat, Indonesia 0°25S 109°20E 235 C3
Kapuas → Kalimantan Tengah, Indonesia 3°1S 114°19E 235 C4
Kapuas Hulu, Pegunungan Malaysia 1°30N 113°30E 235 B4
Kapuas Hulu Ra. = Kapuas Hulu, Pegunungan Malaysia 1°30N 113°30E 235 B4
Kapuk Indonesia 6°7S 106°44E 122 A1
Kapulo Dem. Rep. of the Congo 8°18S 29°15E 269 D2
Kapunda Australia 34°20S 138°56E 282 C3
Kapuni N.Z. 39°29S 174°8E 284 F3
Kapurthala India 31°23N 75°25E 242 D6
Kapuskasing Canada 49°25N 82°30W 298 C3
Kapuskasing → Canada 49°49N 82°0W 298 C3
Kapustin Yar Russia 48°37N 45°40E 191 F7
Kaputar, Mt. Australia 30°15S 150°10E 281 E5
Kaputir Kenya 2°5N 35°28E 268 B4
Kapuvár Hungary 47°36N 17°1E 182 C2
Käpylä Finland 60°13N 24°57E 121 B2
Kara Russia 69°10N 65°0E 214 C7
Karā, W. → Si. Arabia 20°45N 41°42E 256 C5
Kara Ada Turkey 36°58N 27°28E 205 E9
Kara-Balta Kyrgyzstan 42°50N 73°49E 217 D8
Kara Bogaz Gol, Zaliv = Garabogazköl Aylagy Turkmenistan 41°0N 53°30E 187 F9
Kara Burun Turkey 36°32N 27°58E 205 E9
Kara Kala = Garrygala Turkmenistan 38°31N 56°29E 247 B8
Kara Kalpak Republic = Qoraqalpog'iston □ Uzbekistan 43°0N 58°0E 216 D5
Kara-Köl Kyrgyzstan 41°40N 72°43E 217 D8
Kara Kum = Garagum Turkmenistan 39°30N 60°0E 247 B8
Kara-Saki Japan 34°41N 129°30E 222 C1
Kara Sea Russia 75°0N 70°0E 214 B8
Karaadilli Turkey 38°18N 30°37E 205 C12
Karabiğa Turkey 40°23N 27°17E 203 F11
Karabük Turkey 41°12N 32°37E 212 B5
Karabük □ Turkey 41°10N 32°30E 212 B5
Karaburun Albania 40°25N 19°20E 202 F3
Karaburun Turkey 38°41N 26°28E 205 C8
Karaburun-Sazan △ Albania 40°30N 19°21E 202 F3
Karabutak = Qarabutaq Kazakhstan 50°0N 60°14E 216 C6
Karacabey Turkey 40°12N 28°21E 203 F12
Karacakılavuz Turkey 41°8N 27°21E 203 E11
Karacaköy Turkey 41°24N 28°22E 203 E12
Karaçal Tepesi Turkey 36°21N 32°38E 250 B3
Karacasu Turkey 37°43N 28°35E 205 D10
Karachala = Qaraçala Azerbaijan 39°45N 48°53E 191 L9
Karachayevsk Russia 43°50N 41°55E 191 J5
Karachev Russia 53°10N 35°5E 189 F8
Karachey-Cherkessia □ Russia 43°40N 41°30E 191 J5
Karachi Pakistan 24°50N 67°0E 123 A2
Karad India 17°15N 74°10E 244 F2
Karadirek Turkey 38°34N 30°11E 205 C12
Karaga Ghana 9°58N 0°28W 263 D4
Karaganda = Qaraghandy Kazakhstan 49°50N 73°10E 217 C8
Karagayly = Qaraghayly Kazakhstan 49°26N 76°0E 214 E8
Karaginskiy, Ostrov Russia 58°45N 164°0E 215 D17
Karagiye, Vpadina Kazakhstan 43°27N 51°45E 187 F9
Karagiye Depression = Karagiye, Vpadina Kazakhstan 43°27N 51°45E 187 F9
Karagola Road India 25°29N 87°23E 243 G12
Karagüney Dağları Turkey 40°30N 34°40E 212 B6
Karahallı Turkey 38°21N 29°33E 205 C11
Kárahnjúkar Iceland 64°57N 15°46W 155 C11
Karaikal India 10°59N 79°50E 245 J4
Karaikkudi India 10°5N 78°45E 245 J4
Karaisali Turkey 37°16N 35°2E 212 D6
Karaiskakis Greece 38°35N 21°4E 207 B3
Karaitivu I. Sri Lanka 9°45N 79°52E 245 K4
Karaj Iran 35°48N 51°0E 247 C6
Karajarri ⊙ Australia 19°0S 122°30E 278 C3
Karak Malaysia 3°25N 102°2E 237 L4
Karakalpakstan = Qoraqalpog'iston □ Uzbekistan 43°0N 58°0E 216 D5
Karakaya Barajı Turkey 38°31N 38°23E 213 C8
Karakelong Indonesia 4°35N 126°50E 231 D7
Karakitang Indonesia 3°14N 125°28E 231 D7
Karaklis = Vanadzor Armenia 40°48N 44°30E 191 K7
Karakoçan Turkey 38°57N 40°2E 213 C9
Karakol Kyrgyzstan 42°30N 78°20E 217 D9
Karakoram Pass Asia 35°33N 77°50E 243 B7
Karakoram Ra. Pakistan 35°30N 77°0E 243 B7
Karakul = Qorako'l Uzbekistan 39°32N 63°50E 216 E6
Karakul Tajikistan 39°2N 73°33E 217 E8
Karakul', Ozero Tajikistan 39°5N 73°25E 217 E8
Karakurt Turkey 40°10N 42°37E 213 B10
Karakuwisa Namibia 18°56S 19°40E 270 A2
Karal Chad 12°50N 14°46E 259 F2
Karalon Russia 57°5N 115°50E 215 D12
Karama Jordan 31°57N 35°35E 251 G6
Karaman Balıkesir, Turkey 39°39N 28°0E 205 B9
Karaman Konya, Turkey 37°14N 33°13E 212 D5
Karaman □ Turkey 37°5N 33°15E 250 A4
Karamanlı Turkey 37°23N 29°47E 205 D11
Karamay China 45°30N 84°58E 217 C10
Karambu Indonesia 3°53S 116°6E 235 C5
Karamea N.Z. 41°14S 172°6E 285 B7
Karamea → N.Z. 41°13S 172°26E 285 B7
Karamea Bight N.Z. 41°22S 171°40E 285 B6
Karamian Indonesia 5°5S 114°40E 235 D4
Karamnasa → India 25°31N 83°52E 243 G10
Karamürsel Turkey 40°41N 29°36E 203 F13
Karān Si. Arabia 27°43N 49°49E 247 E6
Karand Iran 34°16N 46°15E 213 E12
Karangana Mali 12°15N 5°4W 262 C3
Karanganyar Indonesia 7°38S 109°37E 235 D3
Karangasem = Amlapura Indonesia 8°27S 115°37E 231 J18
Karanja Maharashtra, India 21°11N 78°24E 244 D4
Karanja Maharashtra, India 20°29N 77°31E 244 D3
Karanjia India 21°47N 85°58E 243 J11
Karankasso Burkina Faso 10°50N 3°53W 262 C4
Karaova Turkey 37°5N 27°40E 205 D9
Karapınar Turkey 37°41N 33°30E 212 D5
Karapiro N.Z. 37°53S 175°32E 284 D4
Karas □ Namibia 27°0S 17°30E 270 C2
Karasburg Namibia 28°0S 18°44E 270 C2
Karasino Russia 66°50N 86°50E 214 C9
Karasjok Norway 69°27N 25°30E 160 B21
Karasu Turkey 41°4N 30°46E 212 B4
Karasu → Antalya, Turkey 36°18N 30°10E 205 E12
Karasu → Hatay, Turkey 36°20N 36°20E 250 B7
Karasubazar = Bilohirsk Ukraine 45°3N 34°35E 189 K8
Karasuk Russia 53°44N 78°2E 217 B9
Karasuyama Japan 36°39N 140°9E 223 A12
Karataş Adana, Turkey 36°36N 35°21E 250 B6
Karataş Manisa, Turkey 38°35N 28°16E 205 C10
Karataş Burnu Turkey 36°31N 35°24E 250 B6
Karatau, Khrebet = Qarataū Kazakhstan 43°30N 69°30E 217 D7
Karatax Shan China 35°57N 81°0E 217 E10
Karateki Shan China 40°40N 77°50E 217 D9
Karativu Sri Lanka 8°22N 79°47E 245 K4
Karatoprak = Turgutreis Turkey 37°2N 27°15E 205 D9
Karatoya → India 24°7N 89°36E 241 C2
Karatsu Japan 33°26N 129°58E 222 D1
Karaul Russia 70°6N 82°15E 214 B9
Karauli India 26°30N 77°4E 242 F7
Karavasta △ Albania 40°55N 19°29E 202 F3
Karavastasë, L. e Albania 40°55N 19°30E 202 F3
Karavia Greece 36°49N 23°37E 204 E5
Karavostasi Cyprus 35°8N 32°50E 207 E8
Karawa Dem. Rep. of the Congo 3°18N 20°17E 264 B4
Karawang Indonesia 6°30S 107°15E 235 D3
Karawanken Europe 46°30N 14°40E 180 E7
Karayazı Turkey 39°41N 42°9E 213 C10
Karazhal = Qarazhal Kazakhstan 48°2N 70°49E 214 E8
Karbalā' Iraq 32°36N 44°3E 213 F11
Karbalā' □ Iraq 32°30N 43°50E 213 F10
Kårböle Sweden 61°59N 15°22E 162 C9
Karcag Hungary 47°19N 20°57E 182 C5
Karcha → Pakistan 34°45N 76°10E 243 B7
Karchana India 25°17N 81°56E 243 G9
Karczew Poland 52°5N 21°15E 185 F8
Kardakata Greece 38°17N 20°28E 207 C1
Kardam Bulgaria 43°45N 28°6E 203 C12
Kardamila Greece 38°35N 26°5E 205 C8
Kardamili Greece 36°53N 22°13E 204 E4
Kardeljovo = Ploče Croatia 43°4N 17°26E 199 E14
Karditsa Greece 39°23N 21°54E 204 B3
Kärdla Estonia 59°0N 22°45E 188 C2
Kardzhali Bulgaria 41°38N 25°21E 203 E9
Kardzhali □ Bulgaria 41°38N 25°21E 203 E9
Kareeberge S. Africa 30°59S 21°50E 270 D3
Kareha → India 25°44N 86°21E 243 G12
Kareima Sudan 18°30N 31°49E 256 D3
Karelia □ Russia 65°30N 32°30E 186 A5
Karelian Republic = Karelia □ Russia 65°30N 32°30E 186 A5
Karelo-Finnish S.S.R. = Karelia □ Russia 65°30N 32°30E 186 A5
Karema Papua N. G. 9°12S 147°18E 286 E4
Karen = Kayin □ Myanmar 18°0N 97°30E 241 G6
Karenni = Kayah □ Myanmar 19°15N 97°15E 241 F6
Karera India 25°32N 78°9E 242 G8
Karevāndar Iran 27°53N 60°44E 247 E9
Kargasok Russia 59°3N 80°53E 214 D9
Kargat Russia 55°10N 80°15E 214 D9
Kargi Kenya 2°31N 37°34E 268 B4
Kargı Turkey 41°11N 34°30E 212 B6
Kargil India 34°32N 76°12E 243 B7
Kargopol Russia 61°30N 38°58E 188 B10
Kargowa Poland 52°5N 15°51E 185 F2
Karguéri Niger 13°27N 10°30E 259 F2
Karia Greece 38°45N 20°39E 207 B2
Karia ba Mohammed Morocco 34°22N 5°12W 260 B3
Kariān Iran 26°57N 57°14E 247 E8
Karianga Madag. 22°25S 47°22E 272 C2
Kariba Zimbabwe 16°28S 28°50E 269 F2
Kariba, L. Zimbabwe 16°40S 28°25E 269 F2
Kariba Dam Zimbabwe 16°30S 28°35E 269 F2
Kariba Gorge Zambia 16°30S 28°50E 269 F2
Karibib Namibia 22°0S 15°56E 270 B2
Kariega S. Africa 33°40S 25°28E 270 D4
Karies Greece 40°14N 24°19E 203 F8
Karijini △ Australia 23°8S 118°15E 278 D2
Karikari, C. N.Z. 34°46S 173°24E 284 A2
Karimata, Kepulauan Indonesia 1°25S 109°0E 235 C3
Karimata, Selat Indonesia 2°0S 108°40E 235 C3
Karimata Is. = Karimata, Kepulauan Indonesia 1°25S 109°0E 235 C3
Karimganj India 24°52N 92°20E 241 C4
Karimnagar India 18°26N 79°10E 244 E4
Karimun, Pulau Indonesia 1°3N 103°22E 237 d
Karimun Kecil, Pulau Indonesia 1°8N 103°22E 237 d
Karimunjawa, Kepulauan Indonesia 5°50S 110°30E 235 D4
Karin Bari, Somalia 10°59N 49°13E 267 B6
Karin Woqooyi Galbeed, Somalia 10°50N 45°52E 267 B6
Karistos Greece 38°1N 24°29E 204 C6
Karīt Iran 33°29N 56°55E 247 C8
Kariya Japan 34°58N 137°1E 223 C8
Kariyangwe Zimbabwe 18°0S 27°38E 271 A4
Karjala Finland 62°0N 30°25E 188 A5
Karjat India 18°33N 75°0E 244 E2
Karkal India 13°15N 74°56E 245 H2
Karkar Papua N. G. 4°32S 145°57E 286 C3
Karkar I. Papua N. G. 4°40S 146°0E 286 C4
Karkaralinsk = Qarqaraly Kazakhstan 49°26N 75°30E 217 C9
Karkh Iraq 33°20N 44°22E 113 A2
Karkheh → Iran 31°2N 47°29E 246 D5
Karki Azerbaijan 39°47N 44°57E 213 C11
Karkinitska Zatoka Ukraine 45°56N 33°0E 189 K7
Karkinitskiy Zaliv = Karkinitska Zatoka Ukraine 45°56N 33°0E 189 K7
Karkuk = Kirkūk Iraq 35°30N 44°21E 213 E11
Karkur Tohl Egypt 22°5N 25°5E 256 C2
Karl Liebknecht = imeni Karl Libknekhta Russia 51°40N 35°35E 189 G8
Karl-Marx-Stadt = Chemnitz Germany 50°51N 12°54E 178 E8
Karla, L. = Volvi, L. Greece 40°40N 23°34E 202 F7
Karlantijpa North ⊙ Australia 19°27S 133°33E 278 C5
Karlantijpa South ⊙ Australia 20°31S 133°9E 278 D5
Karleby = Kokkola Finland 63°50N 23°8E 160 E20
Karlholmsbruk Sweden 60°31N 17°37E 162 D11
Karlin Czechia 50°5N 14°26E 135 B2
Karlino Poland 54°3N 15°53E 184 D2
Karlıova Turkey 39°17N 41°0E 213 C9
Karlivka Ukraine 49°29N 35°8E 189 H8
Karlobag Croatia 44°32N 15°5E 199 D12
Karlovac Croatia 45°31N 15°36E 199 C12
Karlovarský □ Czechia 50°10N 12°50E 180 A5
Karlovasi Greece 37°45N 26°42E 205 D8
Karlovka = Karlivka Ukraine 49°29N 35°8E 189 H8
Karlovo Bulgaria 42°38N 24°47E 203 D8
Karlovo náměstí Prague, Czechia 135 c1
Karlovy Vary Czechia 50°13N 12°51E 180 A5
Karlowitz = Sremski Karlovci Serbia 45°12N 19°56E 182 E4
Karlowitz = Velké Karlovice Czechia 49°20N 18°17E 181 B11
Karlsbad = Karlovy Vary Czechia 50°13N 12°51E 180 A5
Karlsborg Sweden 58°33N 14°33E 163 F8
Karlsburg = Alba-Iulia Romania 46°8N 23°39E 183 D8
Karlsena, Mys Russia 77°0N 67°42E 214 B7
Karlsfeld Germany 48°13N 11°28E 131 A1
Karlshamn Sweden 56°10N 14°51E 163 H8
Karlshorst Germany 52°29N 13°31E 115 B4
Karlshus Norway 59°21N 10°52E 164 E7
Karlskoga Sweden 59°28N 14°33E 162 E8
Karlskrona Sweden 56°10N 15°35E 163 H9
Karlsplatz Munich, Germany 131 b1
Karlsruhe Germany 49°0N 8°23E 179 F4
Karlstad = Karlovac Croatia 45°31N 15°36E 199 C12
Karlstad Sweden 59°23N 13°30E 162 E7
Karlstad Minn., U.S.A. 48°35N 96°31W 308 A5
Karlstadt Germany 49°57N 9°47E 179 F5
Karluk U.S.A. 57°34N 154°28W 303 H9
Karlův most Prague, Czechia 135 b1
Karma Niger 13°38N 1°52E 263 C5
Karmala India 18°25N 75°12E 244 E2
Karmi'el Israel 32°55N 35°18E 250 F6
Karmøy Norway 59°15N 5°15E 164 E2
Karnak Egypt 25°43N 32°39E 256 B3
Karnal India 29°42N 77°2E 242 E7
Karnali = Ghaghara → India 25°45N 84°40E 243 G11
Karnali → Nepal 28°45N 81°16E 243 E9
Karnaphuli Res. = Kaptai L. Bangla. 22°40N 92°20E 241 D4
Karnaprayag India 30°16N 79°15E 243 D8
Karnataka □ India 13°15N 77°0E 245 H3
Karnes City U.S.A. 28°53N 97°54W 314 G6
Karnische Alpen Europe 46°36N 13°0E 180 E6
Karnobat Bulgaria 42°39N 26°59E 203 D10
Kärnten □ Austria 46°52N 13°30E 180 E6
Karntner Strasse Vienna, Austria 142 b2
Karo Mali 12°16N 3°18W 262 C4
Karoi Zimbabwe 16°48S 29°45E 269 F2
Karol Bagh India 28°39N 77°11E 120 B2
Karolinenhof Germany 52°23N 13°38E 115 B4
Karon, Ao Thailand 7°51N 98°17E 237 a
Karonga Malawi 9°57S 33°55E 269 D3
Karoo △ S. Africa 32°18S 22°27E 270 D3
Karoonda Australia 35°1S 139°59E 282 C3
Karor Pakistan 31°15N 70°59E 242 D4
Karora Sudan 17°44N 38°15E 256 D4
Karosa Indonesia 1°48S 119°20E 235 C5
Karounga Mali 15°20N 7°35W 262 B3
Karousades Greece 39°47N 19°45E 206 B9
Karow Germany 52°36N 13°29E 115 A3
Karpacz Poland 50°46N 15°46E 185 H2
Karpasia Cyprus 35°32N 34°15E 207 E10
Karpathos Greece 35°37N 27°10E 205 F9
Karpathou, Stenon Greece 36°0N 27°30E 205 F9
Karpatsky △ Ukraine 48°20N 24°35E 183 B9
Karpenisi Greece 38°55N 21°40E 204 C3
Karpilovka = Aktsyabrski Belarus 52°38N 28°53E 177 B15
Karpinsk Russia 59°45N 60°1E 186 C11
Karpogory Russia 64°0N 44°27E 186 B7
Karpuz Burnu = Apostolos Andreas, C. Cyprus 35°42N 34°35E 207 E10
Karpuzlu Turkey 37°33N 27°51E 205 D9
Karrādah Iraq 33°17N 44°23E 113 B2
Karratha Australia 20°44S 116°52E 278 D2
Kars Turkey 40°40N 43°5E 213 B10
Kars □ Turkey 40°40N 43°0E 213 B10
Karsakpay Kazakhstan 47°55N 66°40E 217 C7
Karsha Kazakhstan 49°45N 51°35E 190 F10
Karshi = Qarshi Uzbekistan 38°53N 65°48E 217 E7
Karsiyang India 26°56N 88°18E 241 B2
Karsog India 31°23N 77°12E 242 D7
Karsön Sweden 59°19N 17°54E 139 B1
Karst = Kras Slovenia 45°35N 14°0E 199 C10
Kartal Turkey 40°53N 29°11E 203 F13
Kartal Dağları Turkey 37°4N 36°55E 250 A7
Kartala Comoros Is. 11°45S 43°21E 272 a
Kartaly Russia 53°3N 60°40E 216 B6
Kartapur India 31°27N 75°32E 242 D6
Karthaus U.S.A. 41°8N 78°9W 312 E6
Kartuzy Poland 54°22N 18°10E 184 D5
Karuah Australia 32°37S 151°56E 283 B9
Karufa Indonesia 3°50S 133°20E 231 E8
Karula △ Estonia 57°43N 26°30E 188 D4
Karuma ⌂ Uganda 2°5N 32°15E 268 B3
Karumba Australia 17°31S 140°50E 280 B3
Karumo Tanzania 2°25S 32°50E 268 C3
Karumwa Tanzania 3°12S 32°38E 268 C3
Kārūn → Iran 30°26N 48°10E 247 D6
Karungu Kenya 0°50S 34°10E 268 C3
Karup Denmark 56°19N 9°10E 163 H3
Karur India 10°59N 78°2E 245 J4
Karviná Czechia 49°53N 18°31E 181 B11
Karwan → India 27°26N 78°4E 242 F8
Karwar India 14°55N 74°13E 245 G2
Karwendel ⌂ Austria 47°25N 11°30E 180 D4
Karwi India 25°12N 80°57E 243 G9
Karymskoye Russia 51°36N 114°21E 215 D12
Kas Sudan 12°30N 24°17E 259 F4
Kaş Turkey 36°11N 29°37E 205 E11
Kasaan U.S.A. 55°32N 132°24W 303 J14
Kasaba Turkey 36°18N 29°44E 205 E11
Kasabi Zambia 14°52S 23°45E 265 E4
Kasache Malawi 13°25S 34°20E 269 E3
Kasai Hyōgo, Japan 34°55N 134°52E 222 C6
Kasai Tōkyō, Japan 35°39N 139°52E 140 B4
Kasaï □ Dem. Rep. of the Congo 6°0S 21°0E 265 D4
Kasai → Dem. Rep. of the Congo 3°30S 16°10E 265 C3
Kasaï Central □ Dem. Rep. of the Congo 6°30S 22°30E 265 D4
Kasaï-Oriental □ Dem. Rep. of the Congo 6°20S 23°20E 265 D4
Kasaji Dem. Rep. of the Congo 10°25S 23°27E 265 E4
Kasama Japan 36°23N 140°16E 223 A12
Kasama Zambia 10°16S 31°9E 269 E3
Kasan-dong N. Korea 41°18N 126°55E 224 B3
Kasane Namibia 17°34S 24°50E 270 A3
Kasanga Tanzania 8°30S 31°10E 269 D3
Kasangaie Dem. Rep. of the Congo 6°20S 22°42E 265 D4
Kasangulu Dem. Rep. of the Congo 4°33S 15°15E 265 C3
Kasanka △ Zambia 11°34S 30°15E 269 E3
Kasaoka Japan 34°30N 133°30E 222 C5
Kasar, Ras Sudan 18°2N 38°35E 256 D4
Kasaragod India 12°30N 74°58E 245 H2
Kasat Myanmar 15°56N 98°13E 241 G7
Kasba L. Canada 60°20N 102°10W 297 A8
Kasba Tadla Morocco 32°36N 6°17W 260 B3
Kaschau = Košice Slovakia 48°42N 21°15E 181 C14
Kaseda Japan 31°25N 130°19E 222 F2
Kāseh Garān Iran 34°5N 46°2E 246 C5
Kasempa Zambia 13°30S 25°44E 269 E2
Kasenga Dem. Rep. of the Congo 10°20S 28°45E 269 E2
Kasese Uganda 0°13N 30°3E 268 B3
Kasganj India 27°48N 78°42E 243 F8
Kashabowie Canada 48°40N 90°26W 298 C1
Kashaf Iran 35°58N 61°7E 247 C9
Kāshān Iran 34°5N 51°30E 247 C6
Kashechewan Canada 52°18N 81°37W 298 B3
Kashgar = Kashi China 39°30N 76°2E 217 E9
Kashi China 39°30N 76°2E 217 E9
Kashihara Japan 34°27N 135°46E 223 C7
Kashiji Plain Zambia 13°12S 22°20E 265 E4
Kashima Ibaraki, Japan 35°58N 140°38E 223 B12
Kashima Saga, Japan 33°7N 130°6E 222 D2
Kashima-Nada Japan 36°0N 140°45E 223 B12
Kashimbo Dem. Rep. of the Congo 11°12S 26°19E 269 E2
Kashin Russia 57°20N 37°36E 188 D9
Kashing = Jiaxing China 30°49N 120°45E 229 B13
Kashipur Odisha, India 19°16N 83°3E 244 E6
Kashipur Uttarakhand, India 29°15N 79°0E 243 E8
Kashira Russia 54°45N 38°10E 188 E10
Kashiwa Japan 35°52N 139°59E 223 B11
Kashiwabara = Severo-Kurilsk Russia 50°40N 156°8E 215 D16
Kashiwazaki Japan 37°22N 138°33E 221 F9
Kashk-e Kohneh Afghan. 34°55N 62°30E 240 B1
Kashksaray Iran 38°27N 45°32E 213 C11
Kashkū'īyeh Iran 30°31N 55°40E 247 D7
Kāshmar Iran 35°16N 58°26E 247 C8
Kashmir Asia 34°0N 76°0E 243 C7
Kashmor Pakistan 28°28N 69°32E 242 E3
Kashpirovka Russia 53°0N 48°30E 190 D9
Kashun Noerh = Gaxun Nur China 42°22N 100°30E 218 C9
Kasiari India 22°8N 87°14E 243 H12
Kasilof U.S.A. 60°23N 151°18W 303 F10
Kasimov Russia 54°55N 41°20E 190 C5
Kasinge Dem. Rep. of the Congo 6°15S 26°58E 268 D2
Kasipur India 22°37N 88°22E 124 B2
Kasiruta Indonesia 0°25S 127°12E 231 E7
Kaskaskia → U.S.A. 37°58N 89°57W 310 G7
Kaskattama → Canada 57°3N 90°4W 297 B10
Kaskinen Finland 62°22N 21°15E 160 E19
Kaskö = Kaskinen Finland 62°22N 21°15E 160 E19
Kaslo Canada 49°55N 116°55W 296 D5
Kasmere L. Canada 59°34N 101°10W 297 B8
Kasongan Indonesia 2°0S 113°23E 235 C4
Kasongo Dem. Rep. of the Congo 4°30S 26°33E 268 C2
Kasongo Lunda Dem. Rep. of the Congo 6°35S 16°49E 265 D3
Kasos Greece 35°20N 26°55E 205 F8
Kasou, Stenon Greece 35°30N 26°30E 205 F8
Kaspi Georgia 41°59N 44°26E 191 K7
Kaspichan Bulgaria 43°18N 27°11E 203 C11
Kaspiysk Russia 42°52N 47°40E 191 J8
Kaspiyskiy Russia 45°22N 47°23E 191 H8
Kassab Syria 35°55N 35°59E 250 C6
Kassab ed Doleib Sudan 13°30N 33°35E 257 E3
Kassaba Egypt 22°40N 29°55E 256 C2
Kassalâ Sudan 15°30N 36°0E 257 D4
Kassalâ □ Sudan 15°20N 36°26E 257 D4
Kassandra Greece 40°0N 23°30E 202 F7
Kassandra Kolpos Greece 40°5N 23°30E 202 F7
Kassandras, Akra Greece 39°57N 23°30E 202 G7
Kassandria Greece 40°1N 23°27E 202 F7
Kassel Germany 51°18N 9°26E 178 D5
Kasserine Tunisia 35°10N 8°50E 258 A1
Kasserine □ Tunisia 35°15N 9°0E 258 A1
Kassinger Sudan 18°46N 31°51E 256 D3
Kassiopi Greece 39°48N 19°53E 206 B9
Kasson U.S.A. 44°2N 92°45W 308 C7
Kastamonu Turkey 41°25N 33°43E 212 B5
Kastamonu □ Turkey 41°20N 34°0E 212 B5
Kastav Croatia 45°22N 14°20E 199 C11
Kasteli = Kissamos Greece 35°29N 23°38E 207 E4
Kastellet Copenhagen, Denmark 118 a3
Kastelli Greece 35°12N 25°20E 207 E6
Kastellorizo = Megisti Greece 36°8N 29°34E 205 E11
Kastelo, Akra Greece 35°30N 27°15E 205 F9
Kasterlee Belgium 51°15N 4°59E 170 C4
Kastlösa Sweden 56°26N 16°25E 163 H10
Kastoria Greece 40°30N 21°19E 202 F5
Kastorias, L. Greece 40°30N 21°20E 202 F5
Kastorio Greece 37°10N 22°17E 204 D4
Kastornoye Russia 51°55N 38°2E 189 G10
Kastos Greece 38°35N 20°55E 207 B2
Kastro = Myrina Greece 39°52N 25°4E 205 B7
Kastrom Mefa'a = Umm al Rasas Jordan 31°30N 35°55E 251 G6
Kastrosikia Greece 39°6N 20°38E 207 A2
Kastrup Denmark 55°38N 12°39E 118 B3
Kastrup, København ✈ (CPH) Denmark 55°37N 12°39E 118 B3
Kastsyukovichy Belarus 53°20N 32°4E 189 F7
Kasubi Tombs Uganda 0°20N 32°30E 268 B3
Kasuga Fukuoka, Japan 33°32N 130°26E 222 D2
Kasuga Tōkyō, Japan 35°45N 139°38E 140 A2
Kasugai Japan 35°12N 136°59E 223 B8
Kasuge Japan 35°45N 139°49E 140 A3
Kasukabe Japan 35°58N 139°49E 223 B11
Kasulu Tanzania 4°37S 30°5E 268 C3
Kasumi Japan 35°38N 134°38E 222 B6
Kasumiga-Ura Japan 36°0N 140°25E 223 B12
Kasumigaseki Tokyo, Japan 140 b4
Kasumkent Russia 41°47N 48°15E 191 K9
Kasungu Malawi 13°0S 33°29E 269 E3
Kasungu △ Malawi 12°53S 33°9E 269 E3
Kasur Pakistan 31°5N 74°25E 242 D6
Kata, Ao Thailand 7°48N 98°18E 237 J2
Kata Archanes Greece 35°15N 25°10E 207 E6
Kata Tjuta Australia 25°20S 130°50E 279 E5
Kataba Zambia 16°5S 25°10E 269 F2
Katagum Nigeria 12°18N 10°21E 263 C7
Katahdin, Mt. U.S.A. 45°54N 68°56W 309 C19
Kataka = Cuttack India 20°25N 85°57E 244 D7
Katako Kombe Dem. Rep. of the Congo 3°25S 24°20E 264 C4
Katakolo Greece 37°38N 21°19E 204 D3
Katale Tanzania 4°52S 31°7E 268 C3
Katalla U.S.A. 60°12N 144°31W 303 F11
Katamatite Australia 36°6S 145°41E 283 D6

Katanda *Katanga, Dem. Rep. of the Congo* 7°52S 24°13E **265** D4
Katanda *Nord-Kivu, Dem. Rep. of the Congo* 0°55S 29°21E **268** C2
Katanga *Dem. Rep. of the Congo* 8°0S 25°0E **254** G6
Katangi *India* 21°56N 79°50E **244** D4
Katanning *Australia* 33°40S 117°33E **279** F2
Katapakishi *Dem. Rep. of the Congo* 8°15S 22°49E **265** D4
Katastari *Greece* 37°50N 20°45E **207** D2
Katavi □ *Tanzania* 6°0S 31°0E **268** D3
Katavi △ *Tanzania* 6°51S 31°3E **268** D3
Katavi Swamp *Tanzania* 6°50S 31°10E **268** D3
Katchall *India* 7°57N 93°22E **245** L11
Katchiungo *Angola* 12°35S 16°13E **265** E3
Katerini *Greece* 40°18N 22°37E **202** F6
Katghora *India* 22°30N 82°33E **243** H10
Katha *Myanmar* 24°10N 96°30E **241** C6
Katherîna, Gebel *Egypt* 28°30N 33°57E **251** K4
Katherine *Australia* 14°27S 132°20E **278** B5
Katherine Gorge = Nitmiluk △ *Australia* 14°6S 132°15E **278** B5
Kathi *India* 21°47N 74°3E **242** J6
Kathiawar *India* 22°20N 71°0E **242** H4
Kathikas *Cyprus* 34°55N 32°25E **207** F8
Kathleen *U.S.A.* 28°7N 82°2W **317** G7
Kathmandu *Nepal* 27°45N 85°20E **243** F11
Kathua *India* 32°23N 75°34E **242** C6
Kati *Mali* 12°41N 8°4W **262** C3
Kati Thanda-Lake Eyre *Australia* 29°30S 137°26E **276** F6
Kati Thanda-Lake Eyre (North) *Australia* 28°30S 137°20E **281** D2
Kati Thanda-Lake Eyre (South) *Australia* 29°18S 137°25E **281** D2
Katihar *India* 25°34N 87°36E **243** G12
Katikati *N.Z.* 37°32S 175°57E **284** D4
Katima Mulilo *Namibia* 17°28S 24°13E **270** A3
Katimbira *Malawi* 12°40S 34°0E **269** E3
Katingan = Mendawai → *Indonesia* 3°30S 113°0E **235** C4
Katiola *Côte d'Ivoire* 8°10N 5°10W **262** D3
Katipunan *Phil.* 8°31N 123°17E **233** G4
Katiti ☼ *Australia* 25°1S 131°11E **279** E5
Katla *Iceland* 63°36N 19°7W **155** D7
Katlabukh, Ozero *Ukraine* 45°28N 29°0E **183** E14
Katlanovo *N. Macedonia* 41°52N 21°40E **202** E5
Katmai △ *U.S.A.* 58°20N 155°0W **303** G9
Katmandu = Kathmandu *Nepal* 27°45N 85°20E **243** F11
Katni *India* 23°51N 80°24E **243** H9
Kato Achaia *Greece* 38°8N 21°33E **204** C3
Kato Chorio *Greece* 35°3N 25°47E **207** E6
Kato Korakiana *Greece* 39°42N 19°45E **206** B9
Kato Pyrgos *Cyprus* 35°11N 32°41E **207** E8
Katochi *Greece* 38°26N 21°15E **204** C3
Katol *India* 21°17N 78°38E **244** D4
Katompe *Dem. Rep. of the Congo* 6°2S 26°23E **265** D5
Katong *Singapore* 1°18N 103°53E **138** B3
Katonga → *Uganda* 0°34N 31°50E **268** B3
Katoomba *Australia* 33°41S 150°19E **283** B9
Katouna *Greece* 38°47N 21°7E **204** C3
Katowice *Poland* 50°17N 19°5E **185** H6
Katrancı Dağı *Turkey* 37°27N 30°25E **205** D12
Katrine, L. *U.K.* 56°15N 4°30W **167** E4
Katrineholm *Sweden* 59°0N 16°12E **162** E10
Katsepe *Madag.* 15°45S 46°15E **272** B2
Katsina *Nigeria* 13°0N 7°32E **263** C6
Katsina □ *Nigeria* 12°30N 7°30E **263** C6
Katsina Ala *Nigeria* 7°10N 9°30E **263** D6
Katsina Ala → *Nigeria* 7°10N 9°20E **263** D6
Katsumoto *Japan* 33°51N 129°42E **222** D1
Katsushika *Japan* 35°44N 139°51E **140** A4
Katsuta *Japan* 36°25N 140°31E **223** A12
Katsuura *Japan* 35°10N 140°20E **223** B12
Katsuyama *Fukui, Japan* 36°3N 136°30E **223** A8
Katsuyama *Okayama, Japan* 35°5N 133°41E **222** B5
Kattaqo'rg'on *Uzbekistan* 39°55N 66°15E **217** E7
Kattavia *Greece* 35°57N 27°46E **206** F11
Kattegat *Denmark* 56°40N 11°20E **163** H5
Katthammarsvik *Sweden* 57°26N 18°51E **163** G12
Kattowitz = Katowice *Poland* 50°17N 19°5E **185** H6
Katul, J. *Sudan* 14°12N 29°25E **257** E2
Katumba *Dem. Rep. of the Congo* 7°40S 25°17E **265** D5
Katun → *Russia* 52°25N 85°1E **217** B11
Katwa *India* 23°30N 88°5E **243** H13
Katwijk *Neths.* 52°12N 4°24E **170** B4
Kąty Wrocławskie *Poland* 51°2N 16°45E **185** G3
Ka'ū Desert *U.S.A.* 19°21N 155°19W **302** D6
Kau Pai Chau *Hong Kong, China* 22°12N 114°15E **122** B3
Kau Sai Chau *Hong Kong, China* 22°22N 114°19E **122** A3
Kau-Ye Kyun *Myanmar* 11°1N 98°32E **237** G2
Kau Yi Chau *Hong Kong, China* 22°17N 114°4E **122** B2
Kaua'i *U.S.A.* 22°3N 159°30W **302** A2
Kauai Channel *U.S.A.* 21°45N 158°50W **302** B3
Kauai Island Lihue Municipal ✈ **(LIH)** *U.S.A.* 21°58N 159°20W **302** B2
Kaub *Germany* 50°5N 7°46E **179** E3
Kaudom ⌓ *Namibia* 18°45S 20°51E **270** A3
Kauehi *French Polynesia* 15°49S 145°10W **289** f
Kaufbeuren *Germany* 47°53N 10°37E **179** H6
Kaufman *U.S.A.* 32°35N 96°19W **314** E6
Kauhajoki *Finland* 62°25N 22°10E **160** E20
Kauhaneva-Pohjankangas △ *Finland* 62°13N 22°20E **160** E20
Kaukauna *U.S.A.* 44°17N 88°17W **308** C9
Kaukauveld *Namibia* 20°0S 20°15E **270** B3
Kaukonahua → *U.S.A.* 21°35N 158°7W **302** J13
Ka'ula I. *U.S.A.* 21°40N 160°33W **302** B1
Kaulakahi Channel *U.S.A.* 22°0N 159°55W **302** B2
Kaulsdorf *Germany* 52°29N 13°34E **115** B4
Kaunā Pt. *U.S.A.* 19°2N 155°53W **302** D6
Kaunakakai *U.S.A.* 21°6N 157°1W **302** B4
Kaunas *Lithuania* 54°54N 23°54E **184** D10
Kaunas ✈ **(KUN)** *Lithuania* 54°57N 24°3E **184** D11
Kaunchi = Yangiyŭl *Uzbekistan* 41°0N 69°3E **217** D7
Kaunghein *Myanmar* 25°41N 95°26E **241** C5
Kaunia *Bangla.* 25°46N 89°26E **241** C2
Kauniainen *Finland* 60°13N 24°44E **121** B1
Kaunos *Turkey* 36°49N 28°39E **205** E10
Kaupangur *Iceland* 65°38N 18°2W **155** B8
Kaura Namoda *Nigeria* 12°37N 6°33E **263** C6
Kauru *Nigeria* 10°33N 8°12E **263** C6
Kautokeino *Norway* 69°0N 23°4E **160** B20
Kauwapur *India* 27°31N 82°18E **243** F10
Kavacha *Russia* 60°16N 169°51E **215** C17
Kavadarci *N. Macedonia* 41°26N 22°3E **202** E6
Kavajë *Albania* 41°11N 19°33E **202** E3
Kavak *Turkey* 41°4N 36°3E **212** B7
Kavak Dağı *Turkey* 37°10N 28°2E **205** D10
Kavaklı *Turkey* 41°39N 27°10E **203** E11
Kavaklıdere *Turkey* 37°27N 28°21E **205** D10
Kavaklii = Topolovgrad *Bulgaria* 42°5N 26°20E **203** D10
Kavala *Greece* 40°57N 24°28E **203** F8
Kavala Kolpos *Greece* 40°50N 24°25E **203** F8
Kavalerovo *Russia* 44°15N 135°4E **220** B7
Kavali *India* 14°55N 80°1E **245** G5
Kavango = Cubango → *Africa* 18°50S 22°25E **265** F4
Kavār *Iran* 29°11N 52°44E **247** D7
Kavaratti *India* 10°34N 72°37E **245** J1
Kavaratti I. *India* 10°33N 72°38E **245** J1
Kavarna *Bulgaria* 43°26N 28°22E **203** C12
Kavava *Dem. Rep. of the Congo* 8°52S 22°19E **265** D4
Kaveri = Cauvery → *India* 11°9N 78°52E **245** J4
Kavi *India* 22°12N 72°38E **242** H5
Kavieng *Papua N. G.* 2°36S 150°51E **286** B6
Kavimba *Botswana* 18°2S 24°38E **270** A3
Kavīr, Dasht-e *Iran* 34°30N 55°0E **247** C7
Kavīr △ *Iran* 34°40N 52°0E **247** C7
Kavirondo G. = Winam G. *Kenya* 0°20S 34°15E **268** C3
Kävlinge *Sweden* 55°47N 13°9E **163** J7
Kavos *Greece* 39°23N 20°3E **206** C10
Kavousi *Greece* 35°7N 25°51E **207** E6
Kavungo *Angola* 11°31S 23°3E **265** E4
Kaw *Fr. Guiana* 4°30N 52°15W **329** C7
Kawa *Sudan* 13°42N 32°34E **257** E3
Kawachi-Nagano *Japan* 34°28N 135°31E **223** C7
Kawagama L. *Canada* 45°18N 78°45W **312** A6
Kawagoe *Japan* 35°55N 139°29E **223** B11
Kawaguchi *Japan* 35°52N 139°45E **223** B11
Kawah Ijen △ *Indonesia* 8°3S 114°14E **235** D4
Kawaihae B. *U.S.A.* 20°0N 155°50W **302** C6
Kawaihoa Pt. *U.S.A.* 21°47N 160°12W **302** B1
Kawaikini *U.S.A.* 22°5N 159°29W **302** A2
Kawailoa *U.S.A.* 21°36N 158°3W **302** J13
Kawailoa Beach *U.S.A.* 21°37N 158°5W **302** J13
Kawakawa *N.Z.* 35°23S 174°6E **284** B3
Kawambwa *Zambia* 9°48S 29°3E **269** D2
Kawana *Zambia* 13°5S 25°58E **265** E5
Kawanabe *Japan* 31°23N 130°24E **222** F2
Kawanoe = Shikokochūō *Japan* 34°1N 133°34E **222** C5
Kawardha *India* 22°0N 81°17E **243** J9
Kawasaki *Japan* 35°31N 139°43E **140** B3
Kawasi *Indonesia* 1°38S 127°28E **231** E7
Kawau I. *N.Z.* 36°25S 174°52E **284** C3
Kawawa *Japan* 35°31N 139°33E **140** B2
Kawawachikamach *Canada* 54°48N 66°50W **299** B6
Kawęczyn *Poland* 52°16N 21°5E **143** B2
Kaweka Ra. *N.Z.* 39°17S 176°19E **284** F5
Kawela *U.S.A.* 21°42N 158°1W **302** J13
Kawerau *N.Z.* 38°7S 176°42E **284** E5
Kawhia *N.Z.* 38°4S 174°49E **284** E3
Kawhia Harbour *N.Z.* 38°5S 174°51E **284** E3
Kawio, Kepulauan *Indonesia* 4°30N 125°30E **231** D7
Kawkareik *Myanmar* 16°33N 98°14E **241** G7
Kawlin *Myanmar* 23°47N 95°41E **241** D5
Kawthaung *Myanmar* 10°5N 98°36E **237** H2
Kawthoolei = Kayin □ *Myanmar* 18°0N 97°30E **241** G6
Kawthule = Kayin □ *Myanmar* 18°0N 97°30E **241** G6
Kawya *Myanmar* 24°50N 94°58E **241** C5
Kaxgar He → *China* 39°45N 78°24E **217** E9
Kaxholmen *Sweden* 57°51N 14°19E **163** G8
Kaya *Burkina Faso* 13°4N 1°10W **263** C4
Kayah □ *Myanmar* 19°15N 97°15E **241** F6
Kayak I. *U.S.A.* 59°56N 144°23W **303** G11
Kayalıköy Barajı *Turkey* 41°50N 27°5E **203** E11
Kayamkulam *India* 9°10N 76°33E **245** K3
Kayan *Myanmar* 16°54N 96°34E **241** G6
Kayan → *Indonesia* 2°55N 117°35E **235** B5
Kayan Mentarang △ *Indonesia* 2°25N 115°30E **235** B5
Kaycee *U.S.A.* 43°43N 106°38W **304** E10
Kayeli *Indonesia* 3°20S 127°10E **231** E7
Kayenda *Dem. Rep. of the Congo* 10°48S 23°6E **265** E4
Kayenta *U.S.A.* 36°44N 110°15W **305** H8
Kayes *Congo* 4°25S 11°41E **265** C2
Kayes *Mali* 14°25N 11°30W **262** C2
Kayes □ *Mali* 14°0N 11°0W **262** C2
Kayı *Turkey* 39°12N 30°46E **205** B12
Kayima *S. Leone* 8°54N 11°15W **262** D2
Kayin □ *Myanmar* 18°0N 97°30E **241** G6
Kaymakçı *Turkey* 38°10N 28°8E **205** C10
Kayoa *Indonesia* 0°1N 127°28E **231** D7
Kayombo *Zambia* 13°3S 23°51E **265** E4
Kaysatskoye *Russia* 49°47N 46°49E **190** F8
Kayseri *Turkey* 38°45N 35°30E **212** C6
Kayseri □ *Turkey* 38°40N 36°0E **212** C7
Kaysville *U.S.A.* 41°2N 111°56W **304** F8
Kayts *Sri Lanka* 9°42N 79°51E **245** K4
Kayu Putih *Indonesia* 6°10S 106°53E **122** B2
Kayuagung *Indonesia* 3°24S 104°50E **234** C2
Kaz Dağı *Turkey* 39°42N 26°50E **205** B8
Kazachye *Russia* 70°52N 135°58E **215** B14
Kazakhstan ■ *Asia* 50°0N 70°0E **217** C8
Kazaly = Qazaly *Kazakhstan* 45°45N 62°6E **216** C6
Kazan *Russia* 55°50N 49°10E **190** C9
Kazan *Turkey* 40°14N 32°41E **212** B5
Kazan → *Canada* 64°2N 95°29W **297** A9
Kazan-Rettō *Pac. Oc.* 25°0N 141°0E **288** E6
Kazancı *Turkey* 36°29N 32°51E **250** B3
Kazanlak *Bulgaria* 42°38N 25°20E **203** D9
Kazanlı *Turkey* 36°49N 34°43E **250** B5
Kazanskaya *Russia* 49°50N 41°10E **190** F5
Kazatin = Kozyatyn *Ukraine* 49°45N 28°50E **177** D15
Kazaure *Nigeria* 12°42N 8°28E **263** C6
Kazbek *Russia* 42°42N 44°30E **191** J7
Kāzerūn *Iran* 29°38N 51°40E **247** D6
Kazi Magomed = Qazımämmäd *Azerbaijan* 40°3N 49°0E **191** K9
Kazimierz Dolny *Poland* 51°19N 21°57E **185** G8
Kazimierza Wielka *Poland* 50°15N 20°30E **185** H7
Kazincbarcika *Hungary* 48°17N 20°36E **182** B5
Kazipet *India* 17°58N 79°30E **244** F4
Kaziranga △ *India* 26°40N 93°30E **241** B4
Kaziza *Dem. Rep. of the Congo* 10°42S 23°52E **265** E4
Kazlų Rūda *Lithuania* 54°46N 23°30E **184** D10
Kazo *Japan* 36°7N 139°36E **223** A11
Kaztalovka *Kazakhstan* 49°47N 48°43E **190** F9
Kazu *Myanmar* 25°27N 97°46E **241** C6
Kazuma Pan △ *Zimbabwe* 18°20S 25°48E **269** F2
Kazumba *Dem. Rep. of the Congo* 6°25S 22°5E **265** D4
Kazungula *Zambia* 17°35S 25°15E **265** F5
Kazuno *Japan* 40°10N 140°45E **220** D10
Kazym → *Russia* 63°54N 65°50E **214** C7
Kbely *Czechia* 50°8N 14°32E **135** B3
Kcynia *Poland* 53°0N 17°30E **185** F4
Ke-hsi Mansam *Myanmar* 21°56N 97°50E **241** E6
Ké-Macina *Mali* 13°58N 5°22W **262** C3
Kea *Greece* 37°35N 24°22E **204** D6
Kea'au *U.S.A.* 19°37N 155°2W **302** D6
Keady *U.K.* 54°15N 6°42W **166** B5
Keahi Pt. *U.S.A.* 21°19N 157°59W **302** K14
Keahole Pt. *U.S.A.* 19°44N 156°4W **302** D5
Kealaikahiki Channel *U.S.A.* 20°35N 156°50W **302** C5
Kealakekua *U.S.A.* 19°31N 155°55W **302** D6
Kearney *Mo., U.S.A.* 39°22N 94°22W **310** E2
Kearney *Nebr., U.S.A.* 40°42N 99°5W **308** E4
Kearney ☼ *Australia* 20°10S 128°4E **278** D4
Kearny *U.S.A.* 33°3N 110°55W **305** K8
Kearsarge, Mt. *U.S.A.* 43°22N 71°50W **313** C13
Keban *Turkey* 38°50N 38°50E **213** C8
Keban Barajı *Turkey* 38°41N 38°33E **213** C8
Kebara *Congo* 2°27S 14°25E **264** C2
Kebayoran Baru *Indonesia* 6°14S 106°47E **122** B1
Kebayoran Lama *Indonesia* 6°13S 106°46E **122** B1
Kebbi □ *Nigeria* 11°35N 4°0E **263** C5
Kébémèr *Senegal* 15°23N 16°34W **262** B1
Kébi *Côte d'Ivoire* 9°18N 6°37W **262** D3
Kebi, Mayo → *Cameroon* 9°18N 13°33E **264** A2
Kébili *Tunisia* 33°47N 9°0E **258** B1
Kébili □ *Tunisia* 33°30N 8°50E **261** B6
Kebnekaise *Sweden* 67°53N 18°33E **160** C18
Kebon Jeruk *Indonesia* 6°11S 106°46E **122** B1
Kebri Dehar *Ethiopia* 6°45N 44°17E **267** C5
Kebumen *Indonesia* 7°42S 109°40E **235** D3
Kecel *Hungary* 46°31N 19°16E **182** D4
Kechika → *Canada* 59°41N 127°12W **296** B3
Keçiborlu *Turkey* 37°57N 30°18E **205** D12
Kecskemét *Hungary* 46°57N 19°42E **182** D4
Kedada *Ethiopia* 5°25N 35°58E **257** F4
Kedah □ *Malaysia* 5°50N 100°40E **237** K3
Kėdainiai *Lithuania* 55°15N 24°2E **184** C11
Kedar *West Bank* 31°44N 35°18E **123** B2
Kedarnath *India* 30°44N 79°4E **243** D8
Kedgwick *Canada* 47°40N 67°20W **299** C6
Kediet Ijill *Mauritania* 22°38N 12°33W **260** D2
Kediri *Indonesia* 7°51S 112°1E **235** D4
Kedja *Dem. Rep. of the Congo* 4°50N 19°16E **264** B3
Kedjebi *Ghana* 8°12N 0°25E **263** D5
Kédougou *Senegal* 12°35N 12°10W **262** C2
Kedoya *Indonesia* 6°10S 106°45E **122** B1
Kedros Oros *Greece* 35°11N 24°37E **207** E5
Kędzierzyn-Koźle *Poland* 50°20N 18°12E **185** H5
Ke'ehi Lagoon *U.S.A.* 21°20N 157°54W **302** K14
Keeler *U.S.A.* 36°29N 117°52W **306** J9
Keeley L. *Canada* 54°54N 108°8W **297** C7
Keeling Is. = Cocos Is. *Ind. Oc.* 12°10S 96°55E **273** F8
Keelung = Chilung *Taiwan* 25°3N 121°45E **225** A3
Keenapusan *Phil.* 6°50N 118°50E **233** H2
Keene *Ont., Canada* 44°15N 78°10W **312** B6
Keene *Calif., U.S.A.* 35°13N 118°33W **307** K8
Keene *N.H., U.S.A.* 42°56N 72°17W **313** D12
Keene *N.Y., U.S.A.* 44°16N 73°46W **313** B11
Keep River △ *Australia* 15°49S 129°8E **278** C4
Keeper Hill *Ireland* 52°45N 8°16W **166** D3
Keepit, L. *Australia* 30°50S 150°30E **283** A9
Keerweer, C. *Australia* 14°0S 141°32E **280** A3
Keeseville *U.S.A.* 44°29N 73°30W **313** B11
Keetmanshoop *Namibia* 26°35S 18°8E **270** C2
Keewatin *Canada* 49°46N 94°34W **297** D10
Keewatin → *Canada* 56°29N 100°46W **297** B8
Kefa *Ethiopia* 6°55N 36°30E **257** F4
Kefalonia *Greece* 38°15N 20°30E **207** C2
Kefalonia ✈ **(EFL)** *Greece* 38°10N 20°30E **207** C1
Kefalos *Greece* 36°45N 26°59E **205** E8
Kefamenanu *Indonesia* 9°28S 124°29E **231** F6
Kefar Sava *Israel* 32°11N 34°54E **251** F5
Keffi *Nigeria* 8°55N 7°43E **263** D6
Keffin Hausa *Nigeria* 12°13N 9°59E **263** C6
Keflavík *Iceland* 64°2N 22°35W **155** C4
Keflavík ✈ **(KEF)** *Iceland* 64°0N 22°45W **155** C4
Keftya *Ethiopia* 13°54N 37°7E **257** E4
Keg River *Canada* 57°54N 117°55W **296** B5
Kegalla *Sri Lanka* 7°15N 80°21E **245** L5
Kegaska *Canada* 50°9N 61°18W **299** B7
Kehancha *Kenya* 1°11S 34°37E **268** C3
Keheili *Sudan* 19°25N 32°50E **256** D3
Kehena *U.S.A.* 19°23N 154°55W **302** D7
Kehl *Germany* 48°34N 7°50E **179** G3
Kei Ling Ha *Hong Kong, China* 22°25N 114°16E **122** A3
Keibul Lamjao △ *India* 24°30N 93°55E **241** C4
Keighley *U.K.* 53°52N 1°54W **168** D6
Keijo = Seoul *S. Korea* 37°31N 126°58E **137** B2
Keila *Estonia* 59°18N 24°25E **188** C3
Keilor *Australia* 37°42S 144°50E **128** A1
Keilor North *Australia* 37°44S 144°51E **128** A1
Keimoes *S. Africa* 28°41S 20°59E **270** C3
Keimola *Finland* 60°20N 24°49E **121** A1
Keita *Niger* 14°46N 5°56E **263** C6
Keïta, B. → *Chad* 9°14N 18°21E **259** G3
Keitele *Finland* 63°10N 26°20E **160** E22
Keith *S. Austral., Australia* 36°6S 140°20E **282** D4
Keith *Moray, U.K.* 57°32N 2°57W **167** D6
Keithsburg *U.S.A.* 41°6N 90°56W **310** C6
Keiyasi *Fiji* 17°53S 177°46E **287** A1
Keizer *U.S.A.* 44°57N 123°1W **304** D2
Kejimkujik △ *Canada* 44°25N 65°25W **299** D6
Kejserr Franz Joseph Fd. *Greenland* 73°30N 24°30W **154** C8
Kekaha *U.S.A.* 21°58N 159°43W **302** B2
Kekri *India* 26°0N 75°10E **242** G6
Keksgolm = Priozersk *Russia* 61°2N 30°7E **188** B6
Kelafo *Ethiopia* 5°37N 44°8E **267** C5
Kelam *Ethiopia* 4°48N 35°58E **257** G4
Kelamet *Eritrea* 16°0N 38°30E **257** D4
Kelan *China* 38°43N 111°31E **226** E6
Kelang = Klang *Malaysia* 3°2N 101°26E **237** L3
Kelani Ganga → *Sri Lanka* 6°58N 79°50E **245** L4
Kelantan □ *Malaysia* 5°10N 102°0E **237** K3
Kelantan → *Malaysia* 6°13N 102°14E **237** J4
Kelapa Gading *Indonesia* 6°9S 106°52E **122** A2
Kelberg *U.S.A.* 32°42N 96°36W **120** B6
Këlcyrë *Albania* 40°20N 20°12E **202** F4
Kelekçi *Turkey* 37°15N 29°20E **205** D11
Kelenföld *Hungary* 47°27N 19°2E **117** B2
Keles *Turkey* 39°54N 29°14E **203** G13
Keleti-főcsatorna *Hungary* 47°45N 21°20E **182** C6
Kelheim *Germany* 48°54N 11°52E **179** G7
Kelibia *Tunisia* 36°50N 11°3E **258** A2
Kelkit *Turkey* 40°7N 39°16E **213** B8
Kelkit → *Turkey* 40°45N 36°32E **212** B7
Kellé *Congo* 0°8S 14°38E **264** C2
Kellé *Niger* 14°16N 10°7E **263** C7
Keller *Ga., U.S.A.* 31°50N 81°15W **316** D8
Keller *Tex., U.S.A.* 32°56N 97°15W **120** A2
Kellerberrin *Australia* 31°36S 117°38E **279** F2
Kellett, C. *Canada* 72°0N 126°0W **150** B1
Kelleys I. *U.S.A.* 41°36N 82°42W **312** E2
Kellogg *U.S.A.* 47°32N 116°7W **304** C5
Kells *Ireland* 53°44N 6°53W **166** C5
Kelmė *Lithuania* 55°38N 22°56E **184** C9
Kelmentsi *Ukraine* 48°28N 26°50E **183** B11
Kélo *Chad* 9°10N 15°45E **259** G3
Kelokedhara *Cyprus* 34°48N 32°39E **207** F8
Kelowna *Canada* 49°50N 119°25W **296** D5
Kelsey Creek *Australia* 20°26S 148°31E **280** b
Kelseyville *U.S.A.* 38°59N 122°50W **306** G4
Kelso *N.Z.* 45°54S 169°15E **285** F4
Kelso *Borders, U.K.* 55°36N 2°26W **167** F6
Kelso *Wash., U.S.A.* 46°9N 122°54W **306** D4
Keluang = Kluang *Malaysia* 2°3N 103°18E **237** L4
Kelud *Indonesia* 7°56N 112°18E **231** H15
Kelvin *S. Africa* 26°4S 28°5E **123** A2
Kelvington *Canada* 52°10N 103°30W **297** C8
Kem *Russia* 65°0N 34°38E **186** B5
Kem → *Russia* 64°57N 34°41E **186** B5
Kem-Kem *Morocco* 30°40N 4°30W **260** B4
Kema *Indonesia* 1°22N 125°8E **231** D7
Kemah *Turkey* 39°32N 39°5E **213** C8
Kemaliye *Erzincan, Turkey* 39°16N 38°29E **213** C8
Kemaliye *Manisa, Turkey* 38°27N 28°25E **205** C10
Kemalpaşa *Turkey* 38°25N 27°27E **205** C9
Kemaman *Malaysia* 4°12N 103°18E **237** K4
Kemang *Indonesia* 6°15S 106°48E **122** B1
Kemano *Canada* 53°35N 128°0W **296** C3
Kemapyu *Myanmar* 18°49N 97°19E **241** F6
Kemasik *Malaysia* 4°25N 103°27E **237** K4
Kemayoran *Indonesia* 6°10S 106°51E **122** B2
Kembé *C.A.R.* 4°36N 21°54E **264** B4
Kembolcha *Ethiopia* 11°2N 39°42E **257** E4
Kemer *Antalya, Turkey* 36°36N 30°34E **205** E12
Kemer *Burdur, Turkey* 37°21N 30°4E **205** D12
Kemer *Muğla, Turkey* 36°40N 29°22E **205** E11
Kemer Barajı *Turkey* 37°30N 28°37E **205** D10
Kemerburgaz *Turkey* 41°9N 28°54E **122** B1
Kemerovo *Russia* 55°20N 86°5E **214** D9
Kemerovo □ *Russia* 55°0N 86°0E **217** B11
Ķemeru △ *Latvia* 56°58N 23°25E **184** B10
Kemi *Finland* 65°44N 24°34E **160** D21
Kemi älv = Kemijoki → *Finland* 65°47N 24°32E **160** D21
Kemi träsk = Kemijärvi *Finland* 66°43N 27°22E **160** C22
Kemijärvi *Finland* 66°43N 27°22E **160** C22
Kemijoki → *Finland* 65°47N 24°32E **160** D21
Kemmerer *U.S.A.* 41°48N 110°32W **304** F8
Kemmuna = Comino *Malta* 36°1N 14°20E **206** E7
Kémo □ *C.A.R.* 6°0N 19°0E **264** A3
Kemp, L. *U.S.A.* 33°46N 99°9W **314** E5
Kemp Land *Antarctica* 69°0S 55°0E **151** C5
Kempas *Malaysia* 1°33N 103°42E **237** d
Kempen = Kępno *Poland* 51°18N 17°58E **185** G4
Kempsey *Australia* 31°1S 152°50E **283** A10
Kempt, L. *Canada* 47°25N 74°22W **298** C5
Kempten *Germany* 47°45N 10°17E **179** H6
Kempton *Tas., Australia* 42°31S 147°12E **281** G4
Kempton *Ind., U.S.A.* 40°17N 86°14W **311** D10
Kempton Park Races *U.K.* 51°24N 0°23W **125** B1
Kemptville *Canada* 45°0N 75°38W **313** B9
Ken → *India* 25°13N 80°27E **243** G9
Kenadsa *Algeria* 31°48N 2°26W **261** B4
Kenai *U.S.A.* 60°33N 151°16W **303** F10
Kenai Fjords △ *U.S.A.* 59°40N 149°50W **303** G10
Kenai Mts. *U.S.A.* 60°0N 150°0W **303** G10
Kenai Nat. Wildlife Refuge ⌓ *U.S.A.* 60°20N 150°30W **303** F10
Kenamuke Swamp *South Sudan* 5°55N 33°48E **257** F3
Kenansville *U.S.A.* 27°53N 80°59W **317** H9
Kendai *India* 22°45N 82°37E **243** H10
Kendal *Indonesia* 6°56S 110°14E **235** D4
Kendal *Cumb., U.K.* 54°20N 2°44W **168** C5
Kendall *N.S.W., Australia* 31°35S 152°44E **283** A10
Kendall *Fla., U.S.A.* 25°40N 80°19W **129** D1
Kendall → *Australia* 14°4S 141°35E **280** A3
Kendallville *U.S.A.* 41°27N 85°16W **311** C11
Kendari *Indonesia* 3°50S 122°30E **231** E6
Kendawangan *Indonesia* 2°32S 110°17E **235** C4
Kende *Nigeria* 11°30N 4°12E **263** C5
Kendégué *Chad* 10°0N 18°36E **259** F3
Kendi, Pulau *Malaysia* 5°13N 100°11E **237** c
Kendrapara *India* 20°35N 86°30E **244** D8
Këndrevicës, Maja e *Albania* 40°15N 19°52E **202** F3
Kendrew *S. Africa* 32°32S 24°30E **270** D3
Kendrick *U.S.A.* 29°15N 82°10W **317** F7
Kene Thao *Laos* 17°44N 101°10E **236** D3
Kenedy *U.S.A.* 28°49N 97°51W **314** G6
Kenema *S. Leone* 7°50N 11°14W **262** D2
Keng Kok *Laos* 16°26N 105°12E **236** D5
Keng Tawng *Myanmar* 20°45N 98°18E **241** E7
Keng Tung *Myanmar* 21°18N 99°39E **236** B2
Kengani *Dem. Rep. of the Congo* 2°59S 17°36E **264** C3
Kenge *Dem. Rep. of the Congo* 4°50S 17°4E **265** C3
Kengeja *Tanzania* 5°26S 39°45E **268** D4
Kenhardt *S. Africa* 29°19S 21°12E **270** C3
Kéniéba *Mali* 12°54N 11°17W **262** C2
Kenilworth *Western Cape, S. Africa* 33°59S 18°27E **118** A1
Kenilworth *Ill., U.S.A.* 42°5N 87°43W **119** A2
Keningau *Malaysia* 5°20N 116°10E **235** A5
Kenitra *Morocco* 34°15N 6°40W **260** B3
Kenli *China* 37°30N 118°20E **227** F10
Kenmare *Kerry, Ireland* 51°53N 9°36W **166** E2
Kenmare *N. Dak., U.S.A.* 48°41N 102°5W **308** A2
Kenmare River → *Ireland* 51°48N 9°51W **166** E2
Kennebago Lake *U.S.A.* 45°4N 70°40W **313** A14
Kennebec *U.S.A.* 43°54N 99°52W **308** D4
Kennebec → *U.S.A.* 43°45N 69°46W **309** D19
Kennebunk *U.S.A.* 43°23N 70°33W **313** C14
Kennedale *U.S.A.* 32°38N 97°13W **120** C2
Kennedy *Zimbabwe* 18°52S 27°10E **270** A4
Kennedy, C. = Canaveral, C. *U.S.A.* 28°27N 80°32W **317** G9
Kennedy Channel *Arctic* 80°50N 66°0W **154** A4
Kennedy Entrance *U.S.A.* 59°1N 152°0W **303** G10
Kennedy Ra. *Australia* 24°45S 115°10E **279** D2
Kennedy Range △ *Australia* 24°34S 115°2E **279** D2
Kennedy Space Center *U.S.A.* 28°40N 80°42W **317** G9
Kennedy Town *Hong Kong, China* 22°16N 114°6E **122** B2
Kennemerduinen △ *Neths.* 52°27N 4°33E **170** B4
Kenner *U.S.A.* 29°59N 90°14W **131** A1
Kennesaw *U.S.A.* 34°1N 84°37W **316** A5
Kennet → *U.K.* 51°27N 0°57W **169** F7
Kenneth Hahn State Recreation Area ⌓ *Los Angeles, U.S.A.* 34°1N 118°21W **126** B2
Kenneth Ra. *Australia* 23°50S 117°8E **279** D2
Kennett *U.S.A.* 36°14N 90°3W **308** G8
Kennewick *U.S.A.* 46°12N 119°7W **304** C4
Kennington *London, U.K.* **125** c4
Kennisis Lake *Canada* 45°13N 78°36W **312** A6
Kenogami → *Canada* 51°6N 84°28W **298** B3
Kenora *Canada* 49°47N 94°29W **297** D10
Kenosha *U.S.A.* 42°35N 87°49W **311** B9
Kenozersky △ *Russia* 62°5N 38°10E **214** C1
Kensal Green *U.K.* 51°32N 0°13W **125** A2
Kensal Rise *London, U.K.* **125** a1
Kensington *N.S.W., Australia* 33°54S 151°13E **139** B2
Kensington *P.E.I., Canada* 46°28N 63°34W **299** C7
Kensington *Gauteng, S. Africa* 26°11S 28°6E **123** B2
Kensington *London, U.K.* 51°29N 0°10W **125** B2
Kensington *N.Y., U.S.A.* 40°38N 73°57W **132** C2
Kensington Palace *U.K.* 51°30N 0°11W **125** A2
Kent *Ohio, U.S.A.* 41°9N 81°22W **312** E3
Kent *Tex., U.S.A.* 31°4N 104°13W **314** F2
Kent *Wash., U.S.A.* 47°22N 122°14W **306** C4
Kent □ *U.K.* 51°12N 0°40E **169** F8
Kent Group *Australia* 39°30S 147°20E **281** F4
Kent Pen. *Canada* 68°30N 107°0W **294** D10
Kentaū *Kazakhstan* 43°32N 68°36E **217** D7
K'enting △ *Taiwan* 21°57N 120°48E **225** E2
Kentish Town *U.K.* 51°32N 0°8W **125** A3
Kentland *U.S.A.* 40°46N 87°27W **311** D9
Kenton *London, U.K.* 51°34N 0°17W **125** A2
Kenton *Ohio, U.S.A.* 40°39N 83°37W **311** D13
Kentucky □ *U.S.A.* 37°0N 84°0W **309** G11
Kentucky → *U.S.A.* 38°41N 85°11W **311** F11
Kentucky L. *U.S.A.* 37°1N 88°16W **308** G9
Kentville *Canada* 45°6N 64°29W **299** C7
Kentwood *La., U.S.A.* 30°56N 90°31W **315** F9
Kentwood *Mich., U.S.A.* 42°52N 85°39W **311** B11
Kenwood House *U.K.* 51°34N 0°9W **125** A3
Kenya ■ *Africa* 1°0N 38°0E **268** B4
Kenya, Mt. *Kenya* 0°10S 37°18E **268** C4
Kenyir, Tasik *Malaysia* 5°1N 102°54E **237** K4
Kenzou *Cameroon* 4°10N 15°2E **264** B3
Keo Neua, Deo *Vietnam* 18°23N 105°10E **236** C5
Keokuk *U.S.A.* 40°24N 91°24W **310** D5
Keoladeo △ *India* 27°0N 77°20E **242** F7
Keonjhargarh *India* 21°28N 85°35E **243** J11
Keosauqua *U.S.A.* 40°44N 91°58W **310** D5
Keota *U.S.A.* 41°22N 91°57W **310** C5
Kep *Cambodia* 10°29N 104°19E **237** G5
Kep *Vietnam* 21°24N 106°16E **236** B6
Kep △ *Cambodia* 10°30N 104°18E **237** G5
Kepa *Poland* 52°13N 21°3E **143** B2
Kepala Batas *Malaysia* 5°31N 100°26E **237** c
Kepez *Turkey* 40°5N 26°24E **203** F10
Kepi *Indonesia* 6°32S 139°19E **231** F9
Kępice *Poland* 54°16N 16°51E **184** D3
Kepler Mts. *N.Z.* 45°25S 167°20E **285** F2
Kępno *Poland* 51°18N 17°58E **185** G4
Keppel Harbour *Singapore* 1°15N 103°49E **138** B2
Keppel Pt. *Papua N. G.* 10°10S 147°58E **286** F4
Kepsut *Turkey* 39°40N 28°9E **205** B10
Kepuhi Pt. *U.S.A.* 21°29N 158°14W **302** K13
Kepulauan Karimunjawa △ *Indonesia* 5°50S 110°25E **235** D4
Kerala □ *India* 11°0N 76°15E **245** J3
Keram → *Papua N. G.* 4°7S 144°5E **286** C3
Kerama-Rettō *Japan* 26°5N 127°15E **221** L3
Keramikos *Athens, Greece* **112** b1
Keramoti *Greece* 40°52N 24°42E **203** F8
Keran *Pakistan* 34°35N 73°59E **243** B5
Keran △ *Togo* 10°9N 0°41E **263** C5
Kerang *Vic., Australia* 35°40S 143°55E **282** C5
Kerang *Indonesia* 2°15S 116°3E **235** C5
Keranyo *Ethiopia* 5°3N 38°18E **257** F4
Kerao → *South Sudan* 11°0N 32°41E **257** E3
Keratea *Greece* 37°48N 23°58E **204** D5
Keraudren, C. *Australia* 19°58S 119°45E **278** C2
Kerava *Finland* 60°25N 25°5E **188** B3
Keravat *Papua N. G.* 4°17S 152°2E **286** C7
Kerch *Ukraine* 45°20N 36°20E **189** K9
Kerchenskiy Proliv *Black Sea* 45°10N 36°30E **189** K9
Kerchoual *Mali* 17°12N 0°20E **263** B5
Kerema *Papua N. G.* 7°58S 145°50E **286** D3
Kerempe Burnu *Turkey* 42°2N 33°20E **212** A5
Keren *Eritrea* 15°45N 38°28E **257** D4
Kerepakupai-Meru = Angel Falls *Venezuela* 5°57N 62°30W **329** B5
Kerewan *Gambia* 13°29N 16°10W **262** C1
Kerguelen *Ind. Oc.* 49°15S 69°10E **273** J5
Kerguelen Plateau *S. Ocean* 55°0S 75°0E **273** K6
Keri *Greece* 37°40N 20°49E **207** D2
Keri Kera *Sudan* 12°21N 32°42E **257** E3
Kerian, Kuala *Malaysia* 5°10N 100°25E **237** c
Kericho *Kenya* 0°22S 35°15E **268** C4
Kerikeri *N.Z.* 35°12S 173°59E **284** B2
Kerinci *Indonesia* 1°40S 101°15E **234** C2
Kerinci Seblat △ *Indonesia* 2°30S 101°30E **234** C1
Kerintji = Kerinci *Indonesia* 1°40S 101°15E **234** C2
Keriya He → *China* 38°30N 82°10E **217** E10
Kerkenna, Îs. *Tunisia* 34°48N 11°11E **258** B2
Kerki = Atamyrat *Turkmenistan* 37°50N 65°12E **217** E7
Kerkini, L. *Greece* 41°12N 23°10E **202** E7
Kerkouane *Tunisia* 36°58N 11°2E **200** F4
Kerkrade *Neths.* 50°53N 6°4E **170** D6
Kerkyra *Greece* 39°38N 19°50E **206** B9
Kerkyra ✈ **(CFU)** *Greece* 39°35N 19°54E **204** B1
Kerkyras, Notio Steno *Greece* 39°34N 20°0E **206** B10
Kerma *Sudan* 19°33N 30°32E **256** D3
Kermadec Is. *Pac. Oc.* 30°0S 178°15W **277** G15
Kermadec Trench *Pac. Oc.* 30°30S 176°0W **277** G15
Kermān *Iran* 30°15N 57°1E **247** D8
Kerman *Calif., U.S.A.* 36°43N 120°4W **306** J6
Kermān □ *Iran* 30°0N 57°0E **247** D8
Kermān, Bīābān-e *Iran* 28°45N 59°45E **247** D8
Kermānshāh *Iran* 34°23N 47°0E **213** E12
Kermānshāh □ *Iran* 34°0N 46°30E **246** C5
Kermen *Bulgaria* 42°30N 26°16E **203** D10
Kermine = Navoiy *Uzbekistan* 40°9N 65°22E **216** D7
Kermit *U.S.A.* 31°52N 103°6W **314** F3
Kern → *U.S.A.* 35°16N 119°18W **307** K7
Kernavė *Lithuania* 54°53N 24°49E **188** E3
Kernhof *Austria* 47°49N 15°32E **180** D8
Kernow = Cornwall □ *U.K.* 50°26N 4°40W **169** G3
Kernville *U.S.A.* 35°45N 118°26W **307** K8
Keroh *Malaysia* 5°43N 101°1E **237** K3
Keros *Greece* 36°54N 25°40E **205** E7
Kérou *Benin* 10°50N 2°5E **263** C5
Kérouane *Guinea* 9°15N 9°0W **262** D3
Kerowagi *Papua N. G.* 5°51S 144°51E **286** C3
Kerpen *Germany* 50°51N 6°41E **178** E2
Kerrera *U.K.* 56°24N 5°33W **167** E3
Kerrobert *Canada* 51°56N 109°8W **297** C7
Kerrville *U.S.A.* 30°3N 99°8W **314** F5
Kerry □ *Ireland* 52°7N 9°35W **166** D2
Kerry Hd. *Ireland* 52°25N 9°56W **166** D2
Kersa *Ethiopia* 9°28N 41°48E **257** F5
Kertosono *Indonesia* 7°38S 112°9E **235** D4
Kerulen = Herlen → *Asia* 48°48N 117°0E **219** B12
Kervo = Kerava *Finland* 60°25N 25°5E **188** B3
Kerzaz *Algeria* 29°29N 1°37W **261** C4
Kesagami → *Canada* 51°40N 79°45W **298** B4
Kesagami L. *Canada* 50°23N 80°15W **298** B3
Keşan *Turkey* 40°49N 26°38E **203** F10
Kesariani *Greece* 37°57N 23°46E **112** B2
Kesennuma *Japan* 38°54N 141°35E **220** E10
Keshāvar *Iran* 36°50N 46°22E **213** D12
Keshit *Iran* 29°43N 58°17E **247** D8
Kesigi = Kosgi *India* 15°51N 77°16E **245** G3
Keşiş Dağ *Turkey* 39°47N 39°46E **213** C8
Keskal *India* 20°5N 81°35E **244** D5
Keskin *Turkey* 39°40N 33°36E **212** C5
Kestenga *Russia* 65°50N 31°45E **160** D24
Keswick *U.K.* 54°36N 3°8W **168** C4
Keszthely *Hungary* 46°50N 17°15E **182** D2
Ket → *Russia* 58°55N 81°32E **214** D9
Keta *Ghana* 5°49N 1°0E **263** D5
Keta Lagoon *Ghana* 5°55N 1°0E **263** D5
Ketapang *Jawa Timur, Indonesia* 8°9S 114°23E **231** J17
Ketapang *Kalimantan Barat, Indonesia* 1°55S 110°0E **235** C4
Ketchenery *Russia* 47°18N 44°32E **191** G7
Ketchikan *U.S.A.* 55°21N 131°39W **296** B2
Ketchum *U.S.A.* 43°41N 114°22W **304** E6
Kete Krachi *Ghana* 7°46N 0°1W **263** D4
Keti Bandar *Pakistan* 24°8N 67°27E **242** G2
Kétou *Benin* 7°25N 2°45E **263** D5
Ketri *India* 28°1N 75°50E **242** E6
Kętrzyn *Poland* 54°7N 21°22E **184** D8
Ketta *Congo* 1°28N 15°54E **264** B3
Kettering *Northants., U.K.* 52°24N 0°43W **169** E7
Kettering *Ohio, U.S.A.* 39°41N 84°10W **311** E12
Kettle → *Canada* 56°40N 89°34W **297** B11
Kettle Falls *U.S.A.* 48°37N 118°3W **304** B4
Kettle Point *Canada* 43°10N 82°1W **312** C2
Kettle Pt. *Canada* 43°13N 82°1W **312** C2
Kettleman City *U.S.A.* 36°1N 119°58W **306** J7
Kęty *Poland* 49°51N 19°16E **185** J6
Keuka L. *U.S.A.* 42°30N 77°9W **312** D7
Keung Shan *Hong Kong, China* 22°15N 113°53E **122** B1
Keuruu *Finland* 62°16N 24°41E **188** A3
Kevelaer *Germany* 51°36N 6°15E **178** D2
Kew *Vic., Australia* 37°48S 145°2E **128** A2
Kew *London, U.K.* 51°28N 0°17W **125** B2
Kew Gardens *Ont., Canada* 43°39N 79°18W **141** A3
Kew Gardens *London, U.K.* 51°28N 0°17W **125** B2
Kewanee *U.S.A.* 41°14N 89°56W **310** C7
Kewanna *U.S.A.* 41°1N 86°25W **311** C10
Keware *Nepal* 27°57N 83°47E **243** F10
Kewaunee *U.S.A.* 44°27N 87°31W **308** C10
Keweenaw B. *U.S.A.* 47°0N 88°15W **308** B9
Keweenaw Pen. *U.S.A.* 47°15N 88°15W **308** B9
Keweenaw Pt. *U.S.A.* 47°25N 87°43W **308** B10
Kexholm = Priozersk *Russia* 61°2N 30°7E **188** B6
Key, L. *Ireland* 54°0N 8°15W **166** C3
Key Biscayne *U.S.A.* 25°41N 80°9W **129** D3
Key Colony Beach *U.S.A.* 24°45N 80°57W **317** L9
Key Lake Mine *Canada* 57°5N 105°32W **297** B7
Key Largo *U.S.A.* 25°5N 80°27W **317** K9
Key West *U.S.A.* 24°33N 81°48W **317** L8
Keyala *South Sudan* 4°27N 32°52E **257** G3
Keynsham *U.K.* 51°24N 2°29W **169** F5
Keyser *U.S.A.* 39°26N 78°59W **309** F14
Keystone Heights *U.S.A.* 29°47N 82°2W **316** F7
Keytesville *U.S.A.* 39°26N 92°56W **310** E4
Kezhma *Russia* 58°59N 101°9E **215** D11
Kezi *Zimbabwe* 20°58S 28°32E **271** B4
Kežmarok *Slovakia* 49°10N 20°28E **181** B13
Kgalagadi □ *Botswana* 24°30S 22°0E **270** B3
Kgalagadi Transfrontier ⌓ *Africa* 25°10S 21°0E **270** C3
Khabarovsk *Russia* 48°30N 135°5E **219** B16
Khabr △ *Iran* 28°51N 56°22E **247** D8
Khābūr → *Syria* 35°17N 40°35E **213** E9
Khachmas = Xaçmaz *Azerbaijan* 41°31N 48°42E **191** K9
Khachrod *India* 23°25N 75°20E **242** H6
Khadari, W. el → *Sudan* 10°29N 27°15E **257** E2
Khadro *Pakistan* 26°11N 68°50E **242** F3
Khadyzhensk *Russia* 44°26N 39°32E **191** H4
Khadzhilyangar = Dahongliutan *China* 35°45N 79°20E **243** B8
Khaga *India* 25°47N 81°7E **243** G9
Khagaria *India* 25°30N 86°32E **243** G12
Khagrachari *Bangla.* 23°6N 91°58E **241** D3
Khaipur *Pakistan* 29°34N 72°17E **242** E5
Khair *India* 27°57N 77°46E **242** F7
Khairabad *India* 27°33N 80°47E **243** F9
Khairagarh *India* 21°27N 81°2E **243** J9
Khairpur *Pakistan* 27°32N 68°49E **242** F3
Khairpur Nathan Shah *Pakistan* 27°6N 67°44E **242** F2
Khairwara *India* 23°58N 73°38E **242** H5
Khaisor → *Pakistan* 31°17N 68°59E **242** D3
Khajuraho *India* 24°51N 79°55E **243** G8
Khajuri Kach *Pakistan* 32°4N 69°51E **242** C3
Khāk Dow *Afghan.* 34°57N 67°16E **240** B2
Khakassia □ *Russia* 53°0N 90°0E **217** B12
Khakhea *Botswana* 24°48S 23°22E **270** B3
Khalafābād *Iran* 30°54N 49°24E **247** D6
Khalīj *Iraq* 33°18N 44°28E **113** B2
Khalilabad *India* 26°48N 83°5E **243** F10
Khalīlī *Iran* 27°38N 53°17E **247** E7
Khalkhāl *Iran* 37°37N 48°32E **213** D13
Khalkís = Chalkida *Greece* 38°27N 23°42E **204** C5
Khalmer-Sede = Tazovskiy *Russia* 67°30N 78°44E **214** C8
Khalmer Yu *Russia* 67°58N 65°1E **214** C7
Khalturin *Russia* 58°40N 48°50E **186** C8
Kham Keut *Laos* 18°15N 104°43E **236** C5
Khamaria *India* 23°5N 80°48E **243** H9
Khambhaliya *India* 22°14N 69°41E **242** H3
Khambhat *India* 22°23N 72°33E **242** H5
Khambhat, G. of *India* 20°45N 72°30E **239** E10
Khamgaon *India* 20°42N 76°37E **244** D3
Khami Ruins = Kame Ruins *Zimbabwe* 20°7S 28°25E **269** G2
Khamīr *Iran* 26°57N 55°36E **247** E7
Khamir *Yemen* 16°2N 44°0E **248** C4
Khamīs Mushayţ *Si. Arabia* 18°18N 42°44E **248** C3
Khammam *India* 17°11N 80°6E **244** F5
Khamsa *Egypt* 30°27N 32°23E **251** H3
Khan → *Namibia* 22°37S 14°56E **270** B2
Khān Abū Shāmat *Syria* 33°39N 36°53E **250** E7
Khān al Baghdādī *Iraq* 33°51N 42°32E **213** G10
Khān al Ḩammād *Iraq* 32°19N 44°16E **213** G11
Khān Azād *Iraq* 33°7N 44°22E **246** C5
Khān Mujiddah *Iraq* 32°21N 43°48E **246** C4
Khān Shaykhūn *Syria* 35°26N 36°38E **212** E7
Khan Tengri, Pik *Asia* 42°12N 80°10E **217** D10
Khān Yūnis *Gaza Strip* 31°21N 34°18E **251** G5
Khānābād *Afghan.* 36°45N 69°5E **240** A3
Khanai *Pakistan* 30°30N 67°8E **242** D2
Khānaqīn *Iraq* 34°23N 45°25E **213** E11
Khanāşir *Syria* 35°45N 37°30E **250** C8
Khānbāghī *Iran* 36°10N 55°25E **247** B7
Khandwa *India* 21°49N 76°22E **244** D3
Khandyga *Russia* 62°42N 135°35E **215** C14
Khanewal *Pakistan* 30°20N 71°55E **242** D4
Khangah Dogran *Pakistan* 31°50N 73°37E **242** D5
Khangchendzonga = Kanchenjunga △ *India* 27°42N 88°8E **241** B2
Khanh Duong *Vietnam* 12°44N 108°44E **236** F7
Khaniá = Chania *Greece* 35°30N 24°4E **207** E5
Khaniadhana *India* 25°1N 78°8E **242** G8
Khanka, L. *Asia* 45°0N 132°24E **220** B6
Khankendy = Xankändi *Azerbaijan* 39°52N 46°49E **213** C12
Khanna *India* 30°42N 76°16E **242** D7
Khanozai *Pakistan* 30°37N 67°19E **242** D2
Khanpur *Pakistan* 28°42N 70°35E **242** E4
Khansā' *Iraq* 33°21N 44°28E **113** A2
Khanty-Mansiysk *Russia* 61°0N 69°0E **214** C7
Khanzira, Ras *Somalia* 10°52N 45°48E **267** B6
Khao Khitchakut △ *Thailand* 12°50N 102°10E **236** F4
Khao Laem △ *Thailand* 14°56N 98°31E **236** E2
Khao Laem Res. *Thailand* 14°50N 98°30E **236** E2
Khao Lak △ *Malaysia* 8°38N 98°18E **237** H2
Khao Luang △ *Thailand* 8°34N 99°42E **237** H2
Khao Nam Khang △ *Thailand* 6°32N 100°35E **237** J3
Khao Phlu *Thailand* 9°29N 99°59E **237** b
Khao Pu -Khao Ya △ *Thailand* 7°26N 99°57E **237** J2
Khao Sam Roi Yot △ *Thailand* 12°13N 99°57E **237** F2
Khao Sok △ *Thailand* 8°55N 98°38E **237** H2
Khao Yai △ *Thailand* 14°21N 101°29E **236** E3
Khaoen Si Nakarin △ *Thailand* 14°47N 99°0E **236** E2
Khapalu *Pakistan* 35°10N 76°20E **243** B7
Khapcheranga *Russia* 49°42N 112°24E **215** E12
Khaptao △ *Nepal* 29°20N 81°10E **243** E9
Kharabali *Russia* 47°25N 47°15E **191** G8
Kharagauli *Georgia* 42°1N 43°12E **191** J6
Kharaghoda *India* 23°11N 71°46E **242** H4
Kharagpur *India* 22°20N 87°25E **243** H12
Kharan Kalat *Pakistan* 28°34N 65°21E **240** C2
Kharānaq *Iran* 32°20N 54°45E **247** C7
Kharavli *India* 18°54N 72°55E **130** B2
Kharda *India* 18°40N 75°34E **244** E2
Khardung La *India* 34°20N 77°43E **243** B7
Kharg = Khārk, Jazīreh-ye *Iran* 29°15N 50°28E **247** D6

Khârga, El Wâhât el
Egypt 25°10N 30°35E 256 B3
Khargon India 21°45N 75°40E 244 D2
Khari ➜ India 25°54N 74°31E 242 G6
Kharian Pakistan 32°49N 73°52E 242 C5
Khariar India 20°17N 82°46E 244 D6
Kharit, Wadi el ➜ Egypt 24°26N 33°3E 256 C3
Khārk, Jazīreh-ye Iran 29°15N 50°28E 247 D6
Kharkiv Ukraine 49°58N 36°20E 189 H9
Kharkiv □ Ukraine 48°20N 36°20E 189 H9
Kharkov = Kharkiv
Ukraine 49°58N 36°20E 189 H9
Kharmanli = Harmanli
Bulgaria 41°55N 25°55E 203 E9
Kharovsk Russia 59°56N 40°13E 188 C11
Kharsawangarh India 22°48N 85°50E 243 H11
Kharta Turkey 40°55N 29°7E 212 B3
Khartoum = El Khartûm
Sudan 15°31N 32°35E 257 D3
Khartum Canada 45°15N 77°5W 312 A7
Khasan Russia 42°25N 130°40E 220 C5
Khasavyurt Russia 43°16N 46°40E 191 J8
Khāsh Iran 28°15N 61°15E 240 C1
Khāsh, Dasht-e Afghan. 31°50N 62°30E 240 C1
Khashm el Girba Sudan 14°59N 35°58E 257 E4
Khashum Sudan 12°27N 28°2E 257 E2
Khashuri Georgia 42°3N 43°35E 191 J6
Khasi Hills India 25°30N 91°30E 241 C3
Khaskovo = Haskovo
Bulgaria 41°56N 25°30E 203 E9
Khat, Laem Thailand 8°6N 98°26E 237 a
Khatanga Russia 72°0N 102°20E 215 B11
Khatanga ➜ Russia 72°55N 106°0E 215 B11
Khatauli India 29°17N 77°43E 242 E7
Khatlon □ Tajikistan 37°50N 69°0E 217 E7
Khatra India 22°59N 86°51E 243 H12
Khātūnābād Iran 30°1N 55°25E 247 D7
Khatyrka Russia 62°3N 175°15E 215 C18
Khavda India 23°51N 69°43E 242 H3
Khawlaf, Ra's Yemen 12°40N 54°7E 249 D6
Khawr Fakkān U.A.E. 25°21N 56°22E 247 E8
Khay' Si. Arabia 18°45N 41°24E 248 C3
Khaybar, Ḥarrat
Si. Arabia 25°30N 39°45E 246 E4
Khāzimiyah Iraq 34°46N 43°37E 246 C4
Khazzān Jabal al Awliyā
Sudan 15°24N 32°20E 257 D3
Khe Bo Vietnam 19°8N 104°41E 236 C5
Khe Long Vietnam 21°29N 104°46E 236 B5
Khe Sanh Vietnam 16°37N 106°45E 236 D6
Khed Maharashtra, India 17°43N 73°27E 244 F1
Khed Maharashtra, India 18°51N 73°56E 244 E1
Khed Brahma India 24°7N 73°5E 242 G5
Khefren Egypt 29°58N 31°8E 117 B1
Khekra India 28°52N 77°20E 242 E7
Khem-Beldyr = Kyzyl
Russia 51°50N 94°30E 217 B12
Khemarak Phouminville = Krong
Kaoh Kong Cambodia 11°37N 102°59E 237 G4
Khemisset Morocco 33°50N 6°1W 260 B3
Khemmarat Thailand 16°10N 105°15E 236 D5
Khenāmān Iran 30°27N 56°29E 247 D8
Khenchela Algeria 35°28N 7°11E 261 A6
Khenchela □ Algeria 35°0N 7°0E 261 B6
Khenifra Morocco 32°58N 5°46W 260 B3
Kherrata Algeria 36°27N 5°13E 261 A5
Khersān ➜ Iran 31°33N 50°22E 247 D6
Kherson Ukraine 46°35N 32°35E 189 J7
Kherson □ Ukraine 46°15N 33°10E 189 J7
Kheta ➜ Russia 71°54N 102°6E 215 B11
Khewari Pakistan 26°36N 68°52E 242 F3
Khibinogorsk = Kirovsk
Russia 67°32N 33°41E 186 A5
Khichipur India 28°37N 77°18E 120 B2
Khidirpur India 22°32N 88°19E 124 B1
Khilchipur India 24°2N 76°34E 242 G7
Khilok Russia 51°30N 110°45E 215 D12
Khimki Russia 55°50N 37°20E 188 E9
Khimki-Khovrino Russia 55°51N 37°31E 129 A2
Khios = Chios Greece 38°27N 26°9E 205 C8
Khirbet Batin Abu Lihyah
West Bank 31°50N 35°6E 123 A1
Khirbet el-Misbah
West Bank 31°53N 35°4E 123 A1
Khirbet Jub e-Rum
West Bank 31°44N 35°16E 123 B2
Khirsadoh India 22°11N 78°47E 243 H8
Khiuma = Hiiumaa
Estonia 58°50N 22°45E 188 C2
Khiva = Xiva Uzbekistan 41°30N 60°18E 216 D6
Khiwa = Xiva Uzbekistan 41°30N 60°18E 216 D6
Khlebarovo Bulgaria 43°37N 26°15E 203 C10
Khlong Khlung Thailand 16°12N 99°43E 236 D2
Khlong Lan △ Thailand 16°12N 99°13E 236 D2
Khlong Phanom △
Thailand 8°45N 98°38E 237 H2
Khlong San Thailand 13°43N 100°29E 113 B2
Khlong Toey Thailand 13°43N 100°36E 113 B2
Khmelnik Ukraine 49°33N 27°58E 177 D14
Khmelnytskyy Ukraine 49°23N 27°0E 177 D14
Khmelnytskyy □
Ukraine 49°50N 26°40E 177 D14
Khmer Rep. = Cambodia ■
Asia 12°15N 105°0E 236 F5
Khoai, Hon Vietnam 8°26N 104°50E 237 H5
Khobar = Al Khubar
Si. Arabia 26°17N 50°12E 247 E6
Khodoriv Ukraine 49°24N 24°19E 177 D13
Khodzent = Khŭjand
Tajikistan 40°17N 69°37E 217 D7
Khojak Pass Afghan. 30°51N 66°34E 242 D2
Khojayli = Xo'jayli
Uzbekistan 42°29N 59°31E 216 D5
Khok Kloi Thailand 8°17N 98°19E 237 a
Khok Pho Thailand 6°43N 101°6E 237 J3
Khok Samrong Thailand 15°3N 100°43E 236 E3
Khokhropār Pakistan 25°42N 70°12E 240 D3
Kholm Afghan. 36°45N 67°40E 240 A2
Kholm Russia 57°10N 31°15E 188 D6
Kholmsk Russia 47°40N 142°5E 215 E15
Khomārlu Iran 39°6N 47°3E 213 C12
Khomas □ Namibia 23°30S 17°0E 270 B2
Khomas Hochland Namibia 22°40S 16°0E 270 B2
Khombole Senegal 14°43N 16°42W 262 C1
Khomeyn Iran 33°40N 50°7E 247 C6
Khomeynī Shahr Iran 32°41N 51°31E 247 C6
Khomodino Botswana 22°46S 23°52E 270 B3
Khon Kaen Thailand 16°30N 102°47E 236 D4
Khong ➜ Cambodia 13°32N 105°58E 236 F5
Khong Sedone Laos 15°34N 105°49E 236 E5
Khonsa India 26°57N 95°33E 241 B5
Khonuu Russia 66°30N 143°12E 215 C15
Khoper ➜ Russia 49°30N 42°20E 190 F6
Khor el 'Atash Sudan 13°20N 34°15E 257 E3
Khorāsān-e Janūb □ Iran 32°0N 59°0E 247 C8
Khorāsān-e Razavī □ Iran 35°0N 59°0E 247 C8
Khorāsān-e Shemālī □ Iran 37°0N 57°0E 247 B8
Khorat = Nakhon Ratchasima
Thailand 14°59N 102°12E 236 E4
Khorat, Cao Nguyen
Thailand 15°30N 102°50E 236 E4
Khorazm = Xorazm □
Uzbekistan 43°0N 60°0E 216 D6
Khorb el Ethel Algeria 28°30N 6°17W 260 C3
Khorel India 22°41N 88°18E 124 A1
Khorixas Namibia 20°16S 14°59E 270 B1
Khorol Ukraine 49°48N 33°15E 189 H7
Khorosovo Russia 55°46N 37°27E 129 B1
Khorramābād Khorāsān,
Iran 35°6N 57°57E 247 C8
Khorramābād Lorestān,
Iran 33°30N 48°25E 213 F13
Khorramdarreh Iran 36°11N 49°11E 213 D13
Khorramshahr Iran 30°29N 48°15E 247 D6
Khorugh Tajikistan 37°30N 71°36E 217 E8
Khosravī Iran 30°48N 51°28E 247 D6
Khosrowābād Khuzestān,
Iran 30°10N 48°25E 247 D6
Khosrowābād Kordestān,
Iran 35°31N 47°38E 213 E12
Khost Pakistan 30°13N 67°35E 242 D2
Khosūyeh Iran 28°32N 54°26E 247 D7
Khotan = Hotan China 37°25N 79°55E 217 E9
Khotang Nepal 27°1N 86°51E 243 F12
Khotyn Ukraine 48°31N 26°27E 183 B11
Khouribga Morocco 32°58N 6°57W 260 B3
Khowai Bangla. 24°5N 91°40E 241 C3
Khowst Afghan. 33°22N 69°58E 242 C3
Khowst □ Afghan. 33°20N 70°0E 240 B3
Khoyniki Belarus 51°54N 29°55E 177 C15
Khram, Ko Thailand 12°42N 100°47E 236 F3
Khrami ➜ Georgia 41°25N 45°0E 191 K7
Khrenovoye Russia 51°4N 40°16E 190 E5
Khromtaū Kazakhstan 50°17N 58°27E 216 B5
Khrysokhou B. Cyprus 35°6N 32°25E 207 E8
Khuan Wa Thailand 7°53N 98°17E 237 a
Khudrah, W. ➜ Yemen 18°10N 50°20E 249 C5
Khudzhand = Khŭjand
Tajikistan 40°17N 69°37E 217 D7
Khuff Si. Arabia 24°55N 44°53E 246 E5
Khūgīānī Afghan. 31°34N 66°32E 242 D2
Khuis Botswana 26°40S 21°49E 270 C3
Khuiyala India 27°9N 70°25E 242 F4
Khŭjand Tajikistan 40°17N 69°37E 217 D7
Khujner India 23°47N 76°36E 242 H7
Khukhan Thailand 14°42N 104°12E 236 E5
Khulayṣ Si. Arabia 22°9N 39°19E 248 B2
Khulna Bangla. 22°45N 89°34E 241 D2
Khulna □ Bangla. 22°25N 89°35E 241 D2
Khulo Georgia 41°33N 42°19E 191 K6
Khumago Botswana 20°26S 24°32E 270 B3
Khumrah Si. Arabia 21°22N 39°13E 248 B2
Khunjerab △ Pakistan 36°40N 75°30E 243 A6
Khunjerab Pass = Kinjirap Daban
Asia 36°40N 75°25E 240 A4
Khūnsorkh Iran 27°9N 56°7E 247 E8
Khunti India 23°5N 85°17E 243 H11
Khūr Iran 32°55N 58°18E 247 C8
Khurai India 24°3N 78°23E 242 G8
Khuraydah Yemen 15°33N 48°18E 249 D5
Khurayṣ Si. Arabia 25°6N 48°2E 247 E6
Khurda India 20°11N 85°37E 244 D7
Khureit Sudan 13°59N 26°3E 257 E2
Khurja India 28°15N 77°58E 242 E7
Khūrmāl Iraq 35°18N 46°2E 213 E12
Khurr, Wādī al Iraq 32°3N 43°52E 246 C4
Khūsf Iran 32°46N 58°53E 247 C8
Khushab Pakistan 32°20N 72°20E 242 C5
Khust Ukraine 48°10N 23°18E 183 B8
Khutse △ Botswana 23°31S 24°12E 270 B3
Khuwei Sudan 13°5N 29°14E 257 E2
Khuzdar Pakistan 27°52N 66°30E 242 F2
Khūzestān □ Iran 31°0N 49°0E 247 D6
Khvāf Iran 34°33N 60°8E 247 C9
Khvājeh Iran 38°9N 46°35E 246 B5
Khvājeh Moḥammad, Kūh-e
Afghan. 36°22N 70°17E 240 A3
Khvalynsk Russia 52°30N 48°2E 190 D9
Khvalynsky △ Russia 52°30N 48°0E 190 D9
Khvānsār Iran 29°56N 54°8E 247 D7
Khvatovka Russia 52°24N 46°32E 190 D8
Khvor Iran 33°45N 55°0E 247 C7
Khvorgū Iran 27°34N 56°27E 247 E8
Khvormūj Iran 28°40N 51°30E 247 D6
Khvoy Iran 38°35N 45°0E 213 C11
Khvoynaya Russia 58°58N 34°28E 188 C8
Khwae Noi ➜ Thailand 14°1N 99°32E 236 E2
Khyber Pakhtunkhwa □
Pakistan 33°0N 71°0E 242 C4
Khyber Pass Afghan. 34°10N 71°8E 242 B4
Khyriv Ukraine 49°32N 22°50E 185 J9
Kia Fiji 16°16S 179°8E 287 A2
Kia Solomon Is. 7°32S 158°26E 287 L10
Kiabukwa
Dem. Rep. of the Congo 8°40S 24°48E 265 D4
Kiadho ➜ India 19°37N 77°40E 244 E3
Kiama N.S.W., Australia 34°40S 150°50E 283 C9
Kiama
Dem. Rep. of the Congo 7°19S 17°49E 265 D3
Kiamari Pakistan 24°49N 66°58E 123 B1
Kiamba Phil. 6°2N 124°46E 233 H5
Kiambi Dem. Rep. of the Congo 7°15S 28°0E 268 D2
Kiambu □ Kenya 1°10S 36°50E 268 C4
Kiamusze = Jiamusi
China 46°40N 130°26E 219 B15
Kian = Ji'an China 41°5N 126°10E 227 D14
Kiana U.S.A. 66°58N 160°26W 303 C7
Kiang West △ Gambia 13°25N 15°50W 262 C1
Kiangara Madag. 17°58S 47°2E 272 B2
Kiangsi = Jiangxi □
China 27°30N 116°0E 229 D11
Kiangsu = Jiangsu □
China 33°0N 120°0E 227 H11
Kiato Greece 38°1N 22°45E 204 C4
Kibæk Denmark 56°2N 8°51E 163 H2
Kibale △ Uganda 0°16N 30°18E 268 B3
Kibanga Port Uganda 0°10N 32°58E 268 B3
Kibangou Congo 3°26S 12°22E 264 C2
Kibara Tanzania 2°8S 33°30E 268 C3
Kibare, Mts.
Dem. Rep. of the Congo 8°25S 27°10E 268 D2
Kibawe Phil. 7°34N 125°0E 233 H5
Kibenga
Dem. Rep. of the Congo 7°56S 17°30E 265 D3
Kibira △ Burundi 3°6S 30°24E 268 C3
Kiboga Uganda 0°58N 31°45E 268 B3
Kibombo
Dem. Rep. of the Congo 3°57S 25°53E 265 C5
Kibondo Tanzania 3°35S 30°45E 268 C3
Kibre Mengist Ethiopia 5°54N 38°59E 257 F4
Kıbrıs = Cyprus ■ Asia 35°0N 33°0E 207 F9
Kibumbu Burundi 3°32S 29°45E 268 C2
Kibungo Rwanda 2°10S 30°32E 268 C3
Kibuye Burundi 3°39S 29°59E 268 C2
Kibuye Rwanda 2°3S 29°21E 268 C2
Kibwesa Tanzania 6°30S 29°58E 268 D2
Kibwezi Kenya 2°27S 37°57E 268 C4
Kicasalih Turkey 41°23N 26°48E 203 E10
Kičevo N. Macedonia 41°34N 20°59E 202 E4
Kichha ➜ India 28°41N 79°18E 243 E8
Kichmengskiy Gorodok
Russia 59°59N 45°48E 186 B8
Kicking Horse Pass
Canada 51°28N 116°16W 296 C5
Kīd, W. ➜ Egypt 28°9N 34°27E 251 K5
Kid I. Antigua & B. 17°42N 61°49W 322 b
Kidal Mali 18°26N 1°22E 263 B5
Kidal □ Mali 19°55N 1°5E 261 E5
Kidapawan Phil. 7°1N 125°3E 233 H5
Kidderminster U.K. 52°24N 2°15W 169 E5
Kidepo Valley △ Uganda 3°52N 33°50E 268 B3
Kidete Tanzania 6°25S 37°17E 268 D4
Kidira Senegal 14°28N 12°13W 262 C2
Kidnappers, C. N.Z. 39°38S 177°5E 284 F6
Kidsgrove U.K. 53°5N 2°14W 168 D5
Kidston Australia 18°52S 144°8E 280 B3
Kidugallo Tanzania 6°49S 38°15E 268 D4
Kidurong, Tanjong
Malaysia 3°16N 113°3E 235 B4
Kiel Germany 54°19N 10°8E 178 A6
Kiel Canal = Nord-Ostsee-Kanal
Germany 54°12N 9°32E 178 A5
Kiel-Kanal = Nord-Ostsee-Kanal
Germany 54°12N 9°32E 178 A5
Kielce Poland 50°52N 20°42E 185 H7
Kielder Water U.K. 55°11N 2°31W 168 B5
Kieler Bucht Germany 54°35N 10°25E 178 A6
Kiembara Burkina Faso 13°15N 2°44W 262 C4
Kienge
Dem. Rep. of the Congo 10°30S 27°30E 269 E2
Kierling Austria 48°18N 16°16E 142 A1
Kierlingbach ➜ Austria 48°18N 16°19E 142 A1
Kiessé Niger 13°29N 4°1E 263 C5
Kieta Papua N. G. 6°12S 155°36E 286 D8
Kiev = Kyiv Ukraine 50°30N 30°28E 189 G6
Kifaya Guinea 12°10N 13°4W 262 C2
Kiffa Mauritania 16°37N 11°24W 262 B2
Kifisos ➜ Athina, Greece 37°58N 23°42E 112 B2
Kifisos ➜ Voiotia, Greece 38°35N 23°20E 204 C5
Kifissia Greece 38°4N 23°49E 204 C5
Kifrī Iraq 34°45N 45°0E 213 E11
Kigali Rwanda 1°59S 30°4E 268 C3
Kigarama Tanzania 1°1S 31°50E 268 C3
Kigelle South Sudan 8°40N 34°2E 257 F3
Kigezi △ Uganda 0°34S 29°55E 268 C2
Kiğı Turkey 39°18N 40°21E 213 C9
Kigoma □ Tanzania 5°0S 30°0E 268 D3
Kigoma-Ujiji Tanzania 4°55S 29°36E 268 C2
Kigomasha, Ras Tanzania 4°58S 38°58E 268 C4
Kigosi △ Tanzania 4°10S 31°45E 268 C3
Kığzı Turkey 38°18N 43°25E 246 B4
Kīhei U.S.A. 20°47N 156°28W 302 C5
Kihikihi N.Z. 38°2S 175°22E 284 E4
Kihnu Estonia 58°9N 24°1E 188 C3
Kihoku Japan 33°13N 132°36E 222 D4
Kīholo B. U.S.A. 19°50N 155°55W 302 D6
Kii-Hantō Japan 34°0N 135°45E 223 D7
Kii-Nagashima Japan 34°12N 136°20E 223 C8
Kii-Sanchi Japan 34°20N 136°0E 223 C8
Kii-Suidō Japan 33°40N 134°45E 222 D6
Kiira Dam Uganda 0°25N 33°0E 268 B3
Kiire Japan 31°22N 130°33E 222 F2
Kijik U.S.A. 60°20N 154°20W 303 F9
Kikaiga-Shima Japan 28°19N 129°59E 221 K4
Kikiak = Rigolet Canada 54°10N 58°23W 299 B8
Kikinda Serbia 45°50N 20°30E 182 E5
Kikládhes = Kyklades
Greece 37°0N 24°30E 204 E6
Kikoira Australia 33°39S 146°40E 283 B7
Kikombo Bandundu,
Dem. Rep. of the Congo 5°37S 18°50E 265 D3
Kikombo Bandundu,
Dem. Rep. of the Congo 5°49S 17°45E 265 D3
Kikongo
Dem. Rep. of the Congo 4°16S 17°17E 265 C3
Kikori Papua N. G. 7°25S 144°15E 286 D3
Kikori ➜ Papua N. G. 7°38S 144°20E 286 D3
Kikuchi Japan 32°59N 130°47E 222 E2
Kikuna Japan 35°30N 139°37E 140 B2
Kikuyu Kenya 1°15S 36°40E 268 C4
Kikwit Dem. Rep. of the Congo 5°0S 18°45E 265 D3
Kil Sweden 59°30N 13°20E 162 E7
Kilafors Sweden 61°14N 16°36E 162 C10
Kilakkarai India 9°12N 78°47E 245 K4
Kilar India 33°6N 76°25E 242 C7
Kilauea U.S.A. 22°13N 159°25W 302 A2
Kīlauea Caldera U.S.A. 19°25N 155°17W 302 D6
Kilbeggan Ireland 53°22N 7°30W 166 C4
Kilbrannan Sd. U.K. 55°37N 5°26W 167 F3
Kilbuck Mts. U.S.A. 60°36N 159°53W 303 F8
Kilburn U.K. 51°32N 0°11W 125 A2
Kilchu N. Korea 40°57N 129°25E 224 B4
Kilcoy Australia 26°59S 152°30E 281 D5
Kildare Ireland 53°9N 6°55W 166 C5
Kildare □ Ireland 53°10N 6°50W 166 C5
Kildinstroy Russia 68°48N 33°6E 160 B25
Kileikli Sudan 11°25N 25°31E 257 E2
Kilembe
Dem. Rep. of the Congo 5°42S 19°55E 265 D3
Kilen Norway 59°20N 8°49E 164 E5
Kilfinnane Ireland 52°21N 8°28W 166 D3
Kilgarvan Ireland 51°54N 9°27W 166 E2
Kilgore U.S.A. 32°23N 94°53W 314 E7
Kilgoris Kenya 1°0S 34°53E 268 C3
Kilibo Benin 8°32N 2°38E 263 D5
Kilifi Kenya 3°40S 39°48E 268 C4
Kilimanjaro Tanzania 3°7S 37°20E 268 C4
Kilimanjaro □ Tanzania 4°0S 38°0E 268 C4
Kilimanjaro △ Tanzania 3°2S 37°19E 268 C4
Kilimli Turkey 41°28N 31°50E 212 B4
Kilinailau Is. Papua N. G. 4°45S 155°20E 286 C8
Kilindini Kenya 4°4S 39°40E 268 C4
Kilinochchi Sri Lanka 9°24N 80°25E 245 K5
Kilis Turkey 36°42N 37°6E 250 B8
Kilis □ Turkey 36°50N 37°10E 212 D7
Kiliya Ukraine 45°28N 29°16E 183 E14
Kilkee Ireland 52°41N 9°39W 166 D2
Kilkeel U.K. 54°7N 5°55W 166 B5
Kilkenny Ireland 52°39N 7°15W 166 D4
Kilkenny □ Ireland 52°35N 7°15W 166 D4
Kilkieran B. Ireland 53°20N 9°41W 166 C2
Kilkis Greece 40°58N 22°57E 202 F6
Killala Ireland 54°13N 9°13W 166 B2
Killala B. Ireland 54°16N 9°8W 166 B2
Killaloe Ont., Canada 45°33N 77°25W 312 A7
Killaloe Clare, Ireland 52°48N 8°28W 166 D3
Killarney Queens.,
Australia 28°20S 152°18E 281 D5
Killarney Man., Canada 49°10N 99°40W 297 D9
Killarney Kerry, Ireland 52°4N 9°30W 166 D2
Killarney, L. The Bahamas 25°3N 77°27W 153 b
Killarney △ Canada 46°2N 81°35W 298 C3
Killarney △ Ireland 52°0N 9°33W 166 D2
Killary Harbour Ireland 53°38N 9°52W 166 C2
Killdeer U.S.A. 47°22N 102°45W 308 B2
Killeberg Sweden 56°29N 14°5E 163 H8
Killeen U.S.A. 31°7N 97°44W 314 F6
Killin U.K. 56°28N 4°19W 167 E4
Killiney Ireland 53°15N 6°7W 166 C5
Killington Pk. U.S.A. 43°36N 72°49W 313 C12
Killini = Kyllini Greece 37°55N 21°8E 207 D3
Killini Greece 37°54N 22°25E 204 D4
Killiniq I. Canada 60°24N 64°37W 295 E19
Killorglin Ireland 52°6N 9°47W 166 D2
Killybegs Ireland 54°38N 8°26W 166 B3
Kilmarnock U.K. 55°37N 4°29W 167 F4
Kilmez Russia 56°58N 50°55E 190 B10
Kilmez ➜ Russia 56°58N 50°28E 190 B10
Kilmore Australia 37°25S 144°53E 283 D6
Kilmore Quay Ireland 52°10N 6°36W 166 D5
Kilo Finland 60°13N 24°47E 121 B1
Kilokri India 28°34N 77°15E 120 B2
Kilómetro 1082 = Joaquín V.
González Argentina 25°10S 64°0W 334 B3
Kilondo Tanzania 9°45S 34°20E 269 D3
Kilosa Tanzania 6°48S 37°0E 268 D4
Kilrush Ireland 52°38N 9°29W 166 D2
Kiltan I. India 11°29N 73°0E 245 J1
Kilwa Kisiwani Tanzania 8°58S 39°32E 269 D4
Kilwa Kivinje Tanzania 8°45S 39°25E 269 D4
Kilwa Masoko Tanzania 8°55S 39°30E 269 D4
Kilwinning U.K. 55°39N 4°43W 167 F4
Kim U.S.A. 37°15N 103°21W 305 H12
Kim ➜ Cameroon 5°28N 11°7E 263 D7
Kimaam Indonesia 7°58S 138°53E 231 F9
Kimamba Tanzania 6°45S 37°10E 268 D4
Kimba Australia 33°8S 136°23E 282 B2
Kimball Nebr., U.S.A. 41°14N 103°40W 308 E2
Kimball S. Dak., U.S.A. 43°45N 98°57W 308 D4
Kimbanda
Dem. Rep. of the Congo 4°16S 18°30E 265 C3
Kimbe Papua N. G. 5°33S 150°11E 286 C6
Kimbe B. Papua N. G. 5°15S 150°30E 286 C6
Kimberley W. Austral.,
Australia 16°20S 127°0E 278 C4
Kimberley B.C., Canada 49°40N 115°59W 296 D5
Kimberley Ont., Canada 44°23N 80°32W 312 B4
Kimberley Northern Cape,
S. Africa 28°43S 24°46E 270 C3
Kimberly U.S.A. 42°32N 114°22W 306 E6
Kimbongo
Dem. Rep. of the Congo 6°8S 18°1E 265 D3
Kimch'aek N. Korea 40°40N 129°10E 224 B4
Kimhae = Gimhae
S. Korea 35°14N 128°53E 224 E4
Kimhwa N. Korea 38°25N 127°36E 224 C3
Kimi Greece 38°38N 24°6E 204 C6
Kimitsu Japan 35°19N 139°54E 223 B11
Kimjŏngsugŭp N. Korea 41°24N 127°45E 224 B3
Kimmirut Canada 62°50N 69°50W 295 E18
Kimolos Greece 36°48N 24°37E 204 E6
Kimongo Congo 4°27S 12°53E 265 C2
Kimovsk Russia 54°0N 38°29E 188 E10
Kimpangu
Dem. Rep. of the Congo 5°52S 15°22E 265 D3
Kimparana Mali 12°48N 5°0W 262 C4
Kimpese
Dem. Rep. of the Congo 5°33S 14°26E 265 D2
Kimry Russia 56°55N 37°15E 188 D9
Kimstad Sweden 58°35N 15°58E 163 F9
Kimvula
Dem. Rep. of the Congo 5°44S 15°58E 265 D3
Kin Myanmar 22°46N 94°42E 241 D5
Kin-u Myanmar 22°46N 95°37E 241 D5
Kin-wan Japan 26°23N 127°55E 288 a
Kinabalian, Mt. Phil. 8°12N 125°26E 233 G5
Kinabalu, Gunung
Malaysia 6°3N 116°14E 235 A5
Kinabalu △ Malaysia 6°0N 116°30E 235 A5
Kinango Kenya 4°8S 39°19E 268 C4
Kinard U.S.A. 30°16N 85°15W 316 E4
Kinaros Greece 36°59N 26°15E 205 E8
Kinaskan L. Canada 57°38N 130°8W 296 B2
Kinbasket L. Canada 52°0N 118°10W 296 C5
Kincaid U.S.A. 39°35N 89°25W 310 F7
Kincardine Canada 44°10N 81°40W 312 B3
Kinchafoonee Cr. ➜
U.S.A. 31°38N 84°10W 316 D5
Kinchega △ Australia 32°27S 142°15E 282 B5
Kincolith Canada 55°0N 129°57W 296 C3
Kincsem Park
Budapest, Hungary 47°30N 19°8E 117 B2
Kinda Kasai-Or.,
Dem. Rep. of the Congo 9°18S 25°4E 265 D5
Kinda Katanga,
Dem. Rep. of the Congo 4°47S 21°48E 265 C4
Kindambi
Dem. Rep. of the Congo 5°6S 18°14E 265 D4
Kindberg Austria 47°30N 15°27E 180 D8
Kinde U.S.A. 43°56N 83°0W 312 C2
Kindele
Dem. Rep. of the Congo 8°39S 24°10E 265 D4
Kinder Scout U.K. 53°24N 1°52W 168 D6
Kinderhook U.S.A. 39°42N 91°10W 310 E5
Kindersley Canada 51°30N 109°10W 297 C7
Kindi Iraq 33°18N 44°22E 113 B2
Kindia Guinea 10°0N 12°52W 262 D2
Kindongo
Dem. Rep. of the Congo 3°58S 17°30E 264 C3
Kindu Dem. Rep. of the Congo 2°55S 25°50E 264 C5
Kinel Russia 53°15N 50°40E 190 D10
Kineshma Russia 57°30N 42°5E 190 B6
Kinesi Tanzania 1°25S 33°50E 268 C3
King, L. Australia 33°10S 119°35E 279 F2
King, Mt. Australia 25°10S 147°30E 280 D4
King Abdulaziz Int. ✈ (JED)
Si. Arabia 21°41N 39°9E 248 B2
King Abdullah Economic City
Si. Arabia 22°24N 39°5E 248 B2
King Christian I.
Canada 77°48N 101°40W 295 B11
King City Calif., U.S.A. 36°13N 121°8W 306 J5
King City Mo., U.S.A. 40°3N 94°31W 310 D2
King Cove U.S.A. 55°3N 162°19W 303 J7
King Cr. ➜ Australia 24°35S 139°30E 280 C2
King Edward ➜
Australia 14°14S 126°35E 278 B4
King Edward Point
S. Georgia 54°17S 36°30W 151 B1
King Frederick VI Land = Kong
Frederik VI.s Kyst
Greenland 63°0N 43°0W 154 E6
King George B. Falk. Is. 51°30S 60°30W 153 f
King George I. Antarctica 60°0S 60°0W 151 C18
King George Is. Canada 57°20N 80°30W 295 F15
King George Sd. Australia 35°5S 118°0E 279 G2
King George VI Falls
Guyana 5°42N 61°5W 329 B5
King I. = Kadan Kyun
Myanmar 12°30N 98°20E 236 F2
King I. Tas., Australia 39°50S 144°0E 281 F3
King I. B.C., Canada 52°10N 127°40W 296 C3
King Khalid Int. ✈ (RUH)
Si. Arabia 24°57N 46°42E 246 E4
King Khalid Military City =
Madinat al Malik Khālid al
Askarīyah Si. Arabia 27°54N 45°31E 246 E5
King Leopold Ranges
Australia 17°30S 125°45E 278 C4
King of Prussia U.S.A. 40°5N 75°23W 313 F9
King Salmon U.S.A. 58°42N 156°40W 303 G8
King Sd. Australia 16°50S 123°20E 278 C3
King Sejong Antarctica 62°30S 58°0W 151 C18
King Shaka Int. ✈ (DUR)
S. Africa 29°37S 31°7E 271 C5
King William I. Canada 69°10N 97°25W 294 D12
King William's Town = Qonce
S. Africa 32°51S 27°22E 270 D4
Kingaok = Bathurst Inlet
Canada 66°50N 108°1W 294 D10
Kingaroy Australia 26°32S 151°51E 281 D5
Kingdom City U.S.A. 38°56N 91°56W 310 F5
Kingfisher U.S.A. 35°52N 97°56W 314 D6
Kinghorn U.K. 56°5N 3°10W 121 A2
Kingirbān Iraq 34°40N 44°54E 246 C5
Kingisepp = Kuressaare
Estonia 58°15N 22°30E 188 C2
Kingisepp Russia 59°25N 28°40E 188 C5
Kingking = Pantukan
Phil. 7°9N 125°54E 233 H5
Kinglake △ Australia 37°30S 145°22E 283 D6
Kingman Ariz., U.S.A. 35°12N 114°4W 307 K12
Kingman Ind., U.S.A. 39°58N 87°18W 311 E9
Kingman Kans., U.S.A. 37°39N 98°7W 308 G4
Kingoonya Australia 30°55S 135°19E 281 E2
Kingri Pakistan 30°27N 69°49E 242 D3
Kings ➜ U.S.A. 36°3N 119°50W 306 J7
Kings Canyon Australia 24°15S 131°34E 278 D5
Kings Canyon △ U.S.A. 36°50N 118°40W 306 J8
Kings County □
Ireland 53°15N 7°30W 166 C4
Kings Cross Sydney, Australia 139 c3
King's Cross London, U.K. 125 a4
Kings Domain Australia 37°49S 144°58E 128 A1
Kings Forest = Kongelunden
Denmark 55°34N 12°34E 118 B3
King's Lynn U.K. 52°45N 0°24E 168 E8
Kings Park U.S.A. 40°53N 73°16W 313 F11
Kings Peak U.S.A. 40°46N 110°23W 304 F8
King's Trough Atl. Oc. 43°48N 22°0W 152 B9
Kingsbridge U.K. 50°17N 3°47W 169 G4
Kingsburg U.S.A. 36°31N 119°33W 306 J7
Kingsbury Vic., Australia 37°43S 145°2E 128 A2
Kingsbury London, U.K. 51°34N 0°15W 125 A2
Kingscote Australia 35°40S 137°38E 282 C2
Kingscourt Ireland 53°54N 6°48W 166 C5
Kingsford N.S.W.,
Australia 33°56S 151°14E 139 B2
Kingsford Mich., U.S.A. 45°48N 88°4W 308 C9
Kingsford Smith, Sydney ✈ (SYD)
Australia 33°57S 151°11E 139 B2
Kingsland U.S.A. 30°48N 81°41W 316 E8
Kingsport U.S.A. 36°33N 82°33W 315 C13
Kingston Ont., Canada 44°14N 76°30W 313 B8
Kingston Jamaica 17°55N 76°50W 320 a
Kingston N.Z. 45°20S 168°43E 285 F3
Kingston N.H., U.S.A. 42°56N 71°3W 313 D13
Kingston N.Y., U.S.A. 41°56N 73°59W 313 E11
Kingston Pa., U.S.A. 41°16N 75°54W 313 E9
Kingston R.I., U.S.A. 41°29N 71°30W 313 E13
Kingston Pk. U.S.A. 35°44N 115°55W 307 K11
Kingston South East
Australia 36°51S 139°55E 282 D3
Kingston upon Hull U.K. 53°45N 0°21W 168 D7
Kingston upon Hull □
U.K. 53°45N 0°21W 168 D7
Kingston-upon-Thames □
U.K. 51°24N 0°17W 125 B2
Kingston Vale U.K. 51°25N 0°25W 125 B2
Kingstown = Dún Laoghaire
Ireland 53°17N 6°8W 166 C5
Kingstown N.S.W.,
Australia 30°29S 151°6E 283 A9
Kingstown St. Vincent 13°10N 61°10W 323 n
Kingstree U.S.A. 33°40N 79°50W 316 B10
Kingsville Ont., Canada 42°2N 82°45W 312 D2
Kingsville Tex., U.S.A. 27°31N 97°52W 314 H6
Kingsway Canada 43°38N 79°32W 141 B1
Kingtechen = Jingdezhen
China 29°20N 117°11E 229 C11
Kingunda
Dem. Rep. of the Congo 6°36S 16°58E 265 D3
Kingussie U.K. 57°6N 4°2W 167 D4
Kingwood U.S.A. 30°2N 95°16W 314 G7
Kinhwa = Jinhua China 29°8N 119°38E 229 C12
Kınık Antalya, Turkey 36°20N 29°20E 205 E11
Kınık İzmir, Turkey 39°6N 27°24E 205 B9
Kinistino Canada 52°57N 105°2W 297 C7
Kinjirap Daban Asia 36°40N 75°25E 240 A4
Kinkala Congo 4°18S 14°49E 265 C2
Kinki □ Japan 33°45N 136°0E 223 D8
Kinkony, Farihin' Madag. 16°8S 45°50E 272 B2
Kinleith N.Z. 38°20S 175°56E 284 E4
Kinlochleven U.K. 56°43N 5°0W 167 E4
Kinmen = Chinmen
Taiwan 24°26N 118°19E 225 a
Kinmount Canada 44°48N 78°45W 312 B6
Kinmundy U.S.A. 38°46N 88°51W 311 F8
Kinn Norway 61°34N 4°45E 164 C1
Kinna Sweden 57°32N 12°42E 163 G6
Kinnairds Hd. U.K. 57°43N 2°1W 167 D6
Kinnared Sweden 57°2N 13°7E 163 G7
Kinnarodden = Nordkinn
Norway 71°8N 27°40E 160 A22
Kinnarp Sweden 58°5N 13°32E 163 F7
Kinneviken Sweden 58°35N 13°15E 163 F7
Kinngait Canada 64°14N 76°32W 295 E16
Kinniyai Sri Lanka 8°29N 81°11E 245 K5
Kino Nuevo Mexico 28°52N 112°3W 318 B2
Kinogitan Phil. 9°0N 124°48E 233 G5
Kinoje ➜ Canada 52°8N 81°25W 298 B3
Kinokawa Japan 34°15N 135°20E 223 C7
Kinomoto Japan 35°30N 136°13E 223 B8
Kinoni Uganda 0°41S 30°28E 268 C3
Kinoosao Canada 57°5N 102°1W 297 B8
Kinross U.K. 56°13N 3°25W 167 E5
Kinsale Ireland 51°42N 8°31W 166 E3
Kinsale, Old Hd. of Ireland 51°37N 8°33W 166 E3
Kinsarvik Norway 60°22N 6°43E 164 D3
Kinsha = Chang Jiang ➜
China 31°48N 121°10E 229 B13
Kinshasa
Dem. Rep. of the Congo 4°20S 15°15E 265 C3
Kinsley U.S.A. 37°55N 99°25W 308 G4
Kinsman U.S.A. 41°26N 80°35W 312 E4
Kinston Ala., U.S.A. 31°13N 86°10W 316 D3
Kinston N.C., U.S.A. 35°16N 77°35W 315 D16
Kintamani Indonesia 8°14S 115°19E 231 J18
Kintampo Ghana 8°5N 1°41W 263 D4
Kintap Indonesia 3°51S 115°13E 235 C5
Kintore U.K. 57°14N 2°20W 167 D6
Kintore Ra. Australia 23°15S 128°47E 278 D4
Kintshua
Dem. Rep. of the Congo 4°27S 19°38E 265 C3
Kintyre U.K. 55°30N 5°35W 167 F3
Kintyre, Mull of U.K. 55°17N 5°47W 167 F3
Kinu-Gawa ➜ Japan 35°36N 139°57E 223 B11
Kinushseo ➜ Canada 55°15N 83°45W 298 A3
Kinuso Canada 55°20N 115°25W 296 B5
Kinvarra Ireland 53°8N 8°56W 166 C3
Kinwat India 19°38N 78°12E 244 E4
Kinyangiri Tanzania 4°25S 34°37E 268 C3
Kinyeti South Sudan 3°57N 32°54E 257 G3
Kinzia Dem. Rep. of the Congo 3°36S 18°26E 264 C3
Kinzig ➜ Germany 48°36N 7°49E 179 G3
Kinzua U.S.A. 41°52N 78°58W 312 E6
Kioni Greece 38°27N 20°41E 207 C2
Kiosk Canada 46°6N 78°53W 298 C4
Kiowa Kans., U.S.A. 37°1N 98°29W 308 G4
Kiowa Okla., U.S.A. 34°43N 95°54W 314 D7
Kipahigan L. Canada 55°20N 101°55W 297 B8
Kipanga Tanzania 6°15S 35°20E 268 D4
Kipapa ➜ U.S.A. 21°24N 158°1W 302 K13
Kiparissia Greece 37°15N 21°40E 204 D3
Kiparissiakos Kolpos
Greece 37°25N 21°25E 204 D3
Kipawa, L. Canada 46°50N 79°0W 298 C4
Kipembawe Tanzania 7°38S 33°27E 268 D3
Kipengere Ra. Tanzania 9°12S 34°15E 269 D3
Kipili Tanzania 7°28S 30°32E 268 D3
Kipini Kenya 2°30S 40°32E 268 C5
Kipling Canada 50°6N 102°38W 297 C8
Kipling Heights Canada 43°43N 79°34W 141 A1
Kipnuk U.S.A. 59°56N 164°3W 303 G6
Kippure Ireland 53°11N 6°21W 166 C5
Kipseli Athens, Greece 112 a3
Kipushi
Dem. Rep. of the Congo 11°48S 27°12E 269 E2
Kira Uganda 0°24N 32°38E 268 B3
Kira Panagia Greece 39°17N 24°4E 204 B6
Kirakira Solomon Is. 10°27S 161°56E 287 N11
Kirandul India 18°33N 81°10E 244 E5
Kirane Mali 15°20N 10°20W 262 B2
Kiranomena Madag. 18°17S 46°2E 272 B2
Kiraz Turkey 38°14N 28°13E 205 C10
Kirazlı Turkey 40°2N 26°41E 203 F10
Kirchhain Germany 50°47N 8°56E 178 E4
Kirchheim Germany 48°39N 9°27E 179 G5
Kirchheimbolanden
Germany 49°40N 8°0E 179 F3
Kirchschlag Austria 47°30N 16°19E 181 D9
Kirchstockbach Germany 48°1N 11°40E 131 B3
Kirchtrudering Germany 48°7N 11°40E 131 B3
Kirdâsa Egypt 30°2N 31°6E 251 H2
Kirdimi Chad 18°11N 18°31E 259 C2
Kireç Turkey 39°33N 28°22E 205 B10
Kirensk Russia 57°50N 107°55E 215 D11
Kirghiz Range Asia 42°40N 73°40E 217 D8
Kirghizia = Kyrgyzstan ■
Asia 42°0N 75°0E 217 D9
Kirgiz-Kulak = Chirchiq
Uzbekistan 41°29N 69°35E 217 D7
Kirgiziya Steppe Eurasia 50°0N 55°0E 187 E10
Kiri Dem. Rep. of the Congo 1°29S 19°0E 264 C3
Kiri Buru India 22°0N 85°0E 244 D7
Kiribati ■ Pac. Oc. 3°0S 180°0E 277 A15
Kırıkhan Turkey 36°31N 36°21E 250 B7
Kirikiri Nigeria 6°26N 3°18E 124 B1
Kırıkkale Turkey 39°51N 33°32E 212 C5
Kirikopuni N.Z. 35°50S 174°1E 284 B3
Kirillov Russia 59°49N 38°24E 188 C10
Kirin = Jilin China 43°44N 126°30E 227 C14
Kirindi Oya ➜ Sri Lanka 6°15N 81°20E 245 L5
Kirindy Mitea △ Madag. 20°44S 44°10E 272 C1
Kirinyaga = Kenya, Mt.
Kenya 0°10S 37°18E 268 C4
Kirinyaga □ Kenya 0°30S 37°20E 268 C4
Kirirom △ Cambodia 11°18N 104°5E 237 G5
Kirishi Russia 59°28N 32°0E 188 C7
Kirishima Japan 31°44N 130°46E 222 F2
Kirishima Yaku △ Japan 31°24N 130°50E 221 J5
Kirishima-Yama Japan 31°58N 130°55E 222 F2
Kiritimati Kiribati 1°58N 157°27W 289 G12
Kiriwina I. Papua N. G. 8°40S 151°6E 286 E6
Kirka Turkey 39°17N 30°33E 205 B12
Kırkağaç Turkey 39°8N 27°40E 205 B9
Kirkby U.K. 53°30N 2°54W 168 D5
Kirkby-in-Ashfield U.K. 53°6N 1°14W 168 D6
Kirkby Lonsdale U.K. 54°12N 2°36W 168 C5
Kirkby Stephen U.K. 54°29N 2°21W 168 C5
Kirkcaldy U.K. 56°7N 3°9W 167 E5
Kirkcudbright U.K. 54°50N 4°2W 167 G4
Kirke Værløse Denmark 55°47N 12°19E 118 A1
Kirkehamn Norway 58°14N 6°31E 164 F3
Kirkenær Norway 60°27N 12°3E 164 D9
Kirkenes Norway 69°40N 30°5E 160 B24
Kirkfield Canada 44°34N 78°59W 312 B6
Kirkhill U.K. 55°50N 3°13W 121 B2
Kirkintilloch U.K. 55°56N 4°8W 167 F4
Kirkjubæjarklaustur
Iceland 63°47N 18°4W 155 D8
Kirkkonummi Finland 60°8N 24°26E 188 B3
Kirkland Ill., U.S.A. 42°6N 88°51W 311 B8
Kirkland Wash., U.S.A. 47°40N 122°12W 306 C4
Kirkland Lake Canada 48°9N 80°2W 298 C3
Kırklareli Turkey 41°44N 27°15E 203 E11
Kırklareli □ Turkey 41°45N 27°15E 203 E11
Kirklin U.S.A. 40°12N 86°22W 311 D10
Kirkliston U.K. 55°57N 3°24W 121 B1
Kirkliston Ra. N.Z. 44°25S 170°34E 285 E5
Kirknewton U.K. 55°53N 3°25W 121 B1
Kirknitz = Cerknica
Slovenia 45°48N 14°21E 199 C11
Kirkpatrick, Mt.
Antarctica 84°20S 166°25E 151 E11
Kirksville U.S.A. 40°12N 92°35W 310 D4
Kirkūk Iraq 35°30N 44°21E 213 E11
Kirkwall U.K. 58°59N 2°58W 167 C6
Kirkwood Eastern Cape,
S. Africa 33°22S 25°15E 270 D4
Kirkwood Mo., U.S.A. 38°35N 90°24W 310 F6
Kirlampudi India 17°12N 82°12E 244 F6
Kirmasti = Mustafakemalpaşa
Turkey 40°2N 28°24E 203 F12
Kirn Germany 49°47N 7°26E 179 F3
Kirobası Turkey 36°43N 33°52E 250 B4
Kirov Kaluga, Russia 54°3N 34°20E 188 E8
Kirov Kirov, Russia 58°35N 49°40E 186 C8
Kirov Palace of Culture
Russia 59°55N 30°16E 137 B1
Kirovabad = Gäncä
Azerbaijan 40°45N 46°20E 191 K8
Kirovakan = Vanadzor
Armenia 40°48N 44°30E 191 K7
Kirovo = Kropyvnytskyy
Ukraine 48°35N 32°20E 189 H7
Kirovo-Chepetsk Russia 58°28N 50°0E 186 C9
Kirovograd = Kropyvnytskyy
Ukraine 48°35N 32°20E 189 H7
Kirovohrad = Kropyvnytskyy
Ukraine 48°35N 32°20E 189 H7
Kirovohrad □ Ukraine 48°30N 31°30E 189 H6
Kirovsk Russia 67°32N 33°41E 186 A5
Kirovskiy = Balpyq Bī
Kazakhstan 44°52N 78°12E 217 D9
Kirovskiy Astrakhan,
Russia 45°51N 48°11E 191 H9
Kirovskiy Kamchatka,
Russia 54°27N 155°42E 215 D16
Kirovskiy Primorsk, Russia 45°7N 133°30E 220 B6
Kirriemuir U.K. 56°41N 3°1W 167 E5
Kirsanov Russia 52°35N 42°40E 190 D6
Kırşehir Turkey 39°14N 34°5E 212 C6
Kirtachi Niger 12°52N 2°30E 263 C5
Kirteh Afghan. 32°15N 63°0E 240 B1
Kirthar △ Pakistan 25°45N 67°30E 242 F2
Kirthar Range Pakistan 27°0N 67°0E 242 F2
Kirtland U.S.A. 36°44N 108°21W 307 H15
Kiruna Sweden 67°52N 20°15E 160 C19
Kirundu
Dem. Rep. of the Congo 0°50S 25°35E 264 C5
Kirya Russia 55°8N 46°52E 190 C8
Kiryat Anavim Israel 31°49N 35°6E 123 B1
Kiryat Ha Yovel Israel 31°46N 35°10E 123 B1
Kiryū Japan 36°24N 139°20E 223 A11
Kisa Sweden 58°0N 15°39E 163 G9
Kisaga Tanzania 4°30S 34°23E 268 C3
Kisalföld Hungary 47°30N 17°0E 182 C2
Kisambo
Dem. Rep. of the Congo 6°25S 18°14E 265 D3
Kisandji
Dem. Rep. of the Congo 6°18S 19°16E 265 D3
Kisanga
Dem. Rep. of the Congo 2°30N 26°35E 268 B2
Kisangani
Dem. Rep. of the Congo 0°35N 25°15E 268 B2
Kisantu Dem. Rep. of the Congo 5°7S 15°5E 265 D3
Kisar Indonesia 8°5S 127°10E 231 F7
Kisaran Indonesia 3°0N 99°37E 234 B1
Kisarawe Tanzania 6°53S 39°0E 268 D4
Kisarazu Japan 35°23N 139°55E 223 B11
Kisbér Hungary 47°30N 18°2E 182 C3
Kiselevsk Russia 54°5N 86°39E 217 B11
Kish = Qeys Iran 26°32N 53°58E 249 A6
Kishanganga ➜ Pakistan 34°18N 73°28E 243 B5
Kishanganj India 26°3N 88°14E 241 B2
Kishangarh Raj., India 26°34N 74°52E 242 F6
Kishangarh Raj., India 27°50N 70°30E 242 F4
Kishb, Ḥarrat al Si. Arabia 22°30N 40°15E 248 B3
Kishi Nigeria 9°1N 3°52E 263 D5
Kishinev = Chişinău
Moldova 47°2N 28°50E 183 C13
Kishiwada Japan 34°28N 135°22E 223 C7
Kishkareny = Lazo
Moldova 47°33N 28°2E 183 C13
Kishkenekōl Kazakhstan 53°38N 72°20E 217 B8
Kishorganj Bangla. 24°26N 90°40E 241 C3
Kishtwar India 33°20N 75°48E 242 C6
Kishwaukee ➜ U.S.A. 42°12N 89°8W 310 B7
Kisielice Poland 53°36N 19°16E 184 E6
Kisigo △ Tanzania 6°27S 34°17E 268 D3
Kisii Kenya 0°40S 34°45E 268 C3
Kisiju Tanzania 7°23S 39°19E 268 D4
Kısıklı Turkey 38°11N 29°2E 212 C2
Kisir Turkey 41°0N 43°5E 213 B10

Kisizi Uganda 1°0S 29°58E 268 C2
Kiska I. U.S.A. 51°59N 177°30E 303 L2
Kiskomárom = Zalakomár Hungary 46°33N 17°10E 182 D2
Kiskörei-víztároló Hungary 47°31N 20°36E 182 C5
Kiskőrös Hungary 46°37N 19°20E 182 D4
Kiskundorozsma Hungary 46°16N 20°5E 182 D5
Kiskunfélegyháza Hungary 46°42N 19°53E 182 D4
Kiskunhalas Hungary 46°28N 19°37E 182 D4
Kiskunmajsa Hungary 46°30N 19°48E 182 D4
Kiskunsági △ Hungary 46°39N 19°30E 182 D4
Kislovodsk Russia 43°50N 42°45E 191 J6
Kismaayo Somalia 0°22S 42°32E 267 E5
Kismayu △ Somalia 1°25N 41°30E 267 D5
Kiso-Gawa → Japan 35°20N 136°45E 223 B8
Kiso-Sammyaku Japan 35°45N 137°45E 223 B9
Kisofukushima Japan 35°52N 137°43E 223 B9
Kisoro Uganda 1°17S 29°48E 268 C2
Kispest Hungary 47°27N 19°8E 117 B2
Kissamos Greece 35°29N 23°38E 207 E4
Kissamou, Kolpos Greece 35°30N 23°38E 207 E4
Kissidougou Guinea 9°5N 10°5W 262 D2
Kissimmee U.S.A. 28°18N 81°24W 317 G8
Kissimmee → U.S.A. 27°9N 80°52W 317 H8
Kissimmee, L. U.S.A. 27°55N 81°17W 317 H8
Kississing L. Canada 55°10N 101°20W 297 B8
Kissónerga Cyprus 34°49N 32°24E 207 F8
Kissu, J. Sudan 21°37N 25°10E 256 C2
Kista Sweden 59°24N 17°57E 139 A1
Kistanje Croatia 43°58N 15°55E 199 E12
Kistna = Krishna → India 15°57N 80°59E 245 G5
Kisújszállás Hungary 47°12N 20°50E 182 C5
Kisuki Japan 35°17N 132°54E 222 B4
Kisumu Kenya 0°3S 34°45E 268 C3
Kisvárda Hungary 48°14N 22°4E 182 B7
Kiswani Tanzania 4°5S 37°57E 268 C4
Kiswere Tanzania 9°27S 39°30E 269 D4
Kit Carson U.S.A. 38°46N 102°48W 304 G12
Kita Ōsaka, Japan 34°41N 135°30E 133 A2
Kita Tōkyō, Japan 35°44N 139°44E 140 A3
Kita Mali 13°5N 9°25W 262 C3
Kita-Ura Japan 36°0N 140°34E 223 B12
Kitaibaraki Japan 36°50N 140°45E 221 F10
Kitakami Japan 39°20N 141°10E 220 E10
Kitakami-Gawa → Japan 38°25N 141°19E 220 E10
Kitakami-Sammyaku Japan 39°30N 141°30E 220 E10
Kitakata Japan 37°39N 139°52E 220 F9
Kitakyūshū Japan 33°50N 130°50E 222 D2
Kitale Kenya 1°0N 35°0E 268 B4
Kitami Japan 43°48N 143°54E 220 C11
Kitami-Sammyaku Japan 44°22N 142°43E 220 B11
Kitangiri, L. Tanzania 4°5S 34°20E 268 C3
Kitanglad △ Phil. 8°57N 124°21E 233 G5
Kitano Hana Iwo Jima 24°49N 141°20E 288 b
Kitano-Kaikyō Japan 34°17N 134°58E 222 C6
Kitaotao Phil. 7°40N 125°1E 233 H5
Kitava I. Papua N. G. 8°40S 151°20E 286 E6
Kitaya Tanzania 10°38S 40°8E 269 E5
Kitazawa Japan 35°39N 139°40E 140 B3
Kitcharao Phil. 9°27N 125°36E 233 G5
Kitchener Canada 43°27N 80°29W 312 C4
Kitee Finland 62°5N 30°8E 188 A6
Kitega = Gitega Burundi 3°26S 29°56E 268 C2
Kitengo Dem. Rep. of the Congo 7°26S 24°8E 265 D4
Kitgum Uganda 3°17N 32°52E 268 B3
Kíthira = Kythira Greece 36°8N 23°0E 204 E5
Kíthnos = Kythnos Greece 37°26N 24°27E 204 D6
Kiti Cyprus 34°50N 33°34E 207 F9
Kiti, C. Cyprus 34°48N 33°36E 207 F9
Kitikmeot Canada 67°0N 110°0W 294 D9
Kitimat Canada 54°3N 128°38W 296 C3
Kitinen → Finland 67°14N 27°27E 160 C22
Kitiyab Sudan 17°13N 33°35E 257 D3
Kitombe Dem. Rep. of the Congo 5°22S 18°59E 265 D3
Kitridge Pt. Barbados 13°9N 59°25W 323 r
Kitros Greece 40°22N 22°34E 202 F6
Kitsman Ukraine 48°26N 25°46E 183 B10
Kitsuki Japan 33°25N 131°37E 222 D3
Kittakittaooloo, L. Australia 28°3S 138°14E 281 D2
Kittanning U.S.A. 40°49N 79°31W 312 F5
Kittatinny Mt. U.S.A. 41°19N 74°39W 313 F10
Kittery U.S.A. 43°5N 70°45W 313 C14
Kittilä Finland 67°40N 24°51E 160 C21
Kitui Kenya 1°17S 38°0E 268 C4
Kitui □ Kenya 1°30S 38°25E 268 C4
Kitwanga Canada 55°6N 128°4W 296 B3
Kitwe Zambia 12°54S 28°13E 269 E2
Kityang = Jieyang China 23°35N 116°21E 229 F11
Kitzbühel Austria 47°27N 12°24E 180 D5
Kitzbühler Alpen Austria 47°20N 12°20E 180 D5
Kitzingen Germany 49°44N 10°9E 179 F6
Kiukiang = Jiujiang China 29°42N 115°58E 229 C10
Kiunga Papua N. G. 6°7S 141°18E 286 D1
Kiunga Marine ⌂ Kenya 2°1S 41°14E 268 C5
Kivalina U.S.A. 67°44N 164°33W 303 C6
Kivalliq Canada 62°0N 97°30W 294 E12
Kivarli India 24°33N 72°46E 242 G5
Kivertsi Ukraine 50°50N 25°28E 177 C13
Kividhes Cyprus 34°46N 32°51E 207 F8
Kivik Sweden 55°41N 14°13E 163 J8
Kivistö Finland 60°18N 24°50E 121 B2
Kivotos Greece 40°13N 21°26E 202 F5
Kivu, L. Dem. Rep. of the Congo 1°48S 29°0E 268 C2
Kiwai I. Papua N. G. 8°35S 143°30E 286 E2
Kiwirrkurra Australia 22°49S 127°45E 278 D4
Kiwirrkurra ⊙ Australia 22°49S 127°45E 278 D4
Kiyev = Kyiv Ukraine 50°30N 30°28E 189 G6
Kiyevskoye Vdkhr. = Kyyivske Vdskh. Ukraine 51°0N 30°25E 177 C16
Kıyıköy Turkey 41°38N 28°5E 203 E12
Kiza → Japan 34°37N 135°27E 133 B1
Kizel Russia 59°3N 57°40E 186 C10
Kizhi, Ostrov Russia 62°4N 35°13E 188 B8
Kiziba-Baluba ⌂ Dem. Rep. of the Congo 11°50S 28°0E 269 E2
Kiziguru Rwanda 1°46S 30°23E 268 C3
Kızıl Adalar Turkey 40°52N 29°5E 203 F13
Kızıl Dağ Turkey 36°19N 35°57E 250 B6
Kızıl Irmak → Turkey 41°44N 35°58E 212 B6
Kizil Jilga China 35°26N 78°50E 243 B8
Kizil Yurt Russia 43°13N 46°54E 191 J8
Kızılcabölük Turkey 37°37N 29°1E 205 D11
Kızılcadağ Turkey 37°1N 29°58E 205 D11
Kızılcahamam Turkey 40°30N 32°30E 212 B5
Kızıldağ △ Turkey 38°5N 31°20E 246 B1
Kızılhisar Turkey 37°32N 29°17E 212 D3
Kızılırmak Turkey 40°21N 33°59E 212 B5
Kızılkaya Turkey 37°18N 30°27E 205 D12
Kızılören Turkey 38°15N 30°10E 205 C12
Kızıltepe Turkey 37°12N 40°35E 213 D9
Kızıltoprak Turkey 40°58N 29°3E 122 C2
Kizimkazi Tanzania 6°28S 39°30E 268 D4
Kizlyar Russia 43°51N 46°40E 191 J8
Kizuri Japan 34°38N 135°34E 133 B2
Kizyl-Arvat = Serdar Turkmenistan 39°4N 56°23E 247 B8
Kjellerup Denmark 56°17N 9°25E 163 H3
Kjellmyra Norway 60°39N 12°1E 164 D9
Kjelsås Norway 59°57N 10°47E 133 A3
Kjølen Norway 62°3N 8°45E 164 C5
Kjölur Iceland 64°50N 19°25W 155 C7
Kjósarsýsla Iceland 64°15N 21°30W 155 C5
Kladanj Bos.-H. 44°14N 18°42E 182 F3
Kladnica Serbia 43°23N 20°2E 202 C4
Kladno Czechia 50°10N 14°7E 180 A7
Kladovo Serbia 44°36N 22°33E 202 B6
Kladow Germany 52°27N 13°9E 115 B1
Klæbu Norway 63°18N 10°29E 164 A7
Klaeng Thailand 12°47N 101°39E 236 F3
Klagan Malaysia 5°58N 117°27E 235 A5
Klagenfurt Austria 46°38N 14°20E 180 E7
Klaipėda Lithuania 55°43N 21°10E 184 C8
Klaipėda □ Lithuania 55°43N 21°7E 184 C8
Klaksvík Færoe Is. 62°14N 6°35W 160 E9
Klamath → U.S.A. 41°33N 124°5W 304 F1
Klamath Falls U.S.A. 42°13N 121°46W 304 E3
Klamath Mts. U.S.A. 41°50N 123°20W 304 F2
Klamono Indonesia 1°8S 131°30E 231 E8
Klampenborg Denmark 55°46N 12°35E 118 A3
Klampo Indonesia 0°7N 116°58E 235 B5
Klang Malaysia 3°2N 101°26E 237 L3
Klangklang Myanmar 22°41N 93°26E 241 D4
Klanjec Croatia 46°3N 15°45E 199 B12
Klappan → Canada 58°0N 129°43W 296 B3
Klara = Trysilelva → Norway 61°2N 12°35E 164 C9
Klarälven → Sweden 59°23N 13°32E 162 E7
Klässbol Sweden 59°33N 12°45E 162 E6
Klaten Indonesia 7°43S 110°36E 235 D4
Klatovy Czechia 49°23N 13°18E 180 B6
Klausenburg = Cluj-Napoca Romania 46°47N 23°38E 183 D8
Klawer S. Africa 31°44S 18°36E 270 D2
Klawock U.S.A. 55°33N 133°6W 303 J14
Klazienaveen Neths. 52°44N 7°0E 170 B6
Klé Mali 12°0N 6°28W 262 C3
Klečany Czechia 50°10N 14°24E 135 A2
Klecko Poland 52°38N 17°25E 185 F4
Kleczew Poland 52°22N 18°9E 185 F5
Kledering Austria 48°8N 16°26E 142 B2
Kleena Kleene Canada 52°0N 124°59W 296 C4
Klein Bonaire Bonaire 12°9N 68°18W 322 h
Klein Jukskei → S. Africa 26°6S 27°57E 123 A1
Klein-Karas Namibia 27°33S 18°7E 270 C2
Klein-Schlatten = Zlatna Romania 46°8N 23°11E 183 D8
Kleinbegin S. Africa 28°54S 21°40E 270 C3
Kleinmachnow Germany 52°24N 13°14E 115 B2
Kleinschönebeck Germany 52°29N 13°42E 115 B5
Klekovača Bos.-H. 44°25N 16°32E 199 D13
Klembivka Ukraine 48°23N 28°25E 183 B13
Klemetsrud Norway 59°50N 10°51E 133 A4
Klender Indonesia 6°12S 106°54E 122 A2
Klenoec N. Macedonia 41°32N 20°49E 202 E4
Klenovec Slovakia 48°36N 19°54E 181 C12
Klerksdorp S. Africa 26°53S 26°38E 270 C4
Kleszczele Poland 52°35N 23°19E 185 F10
Kletnya Russia 53°23N 33°12E 188 F7
Kletsk = Klyetsk Belarus 53°5N 26°45E 177 B14
Kletskiy Russia 49°16N 43°11E 191 F6
Kleve Germany 51°47N 6°7E 178 D2
Kličany Czechia 50°11N 14°25E 135 A2
Klickitat U.S.A. 45°49N 121°9W 304 D3
Klickitat → U.S.A. 45°42N 121°17W 306 E5
Klidhes Cyprus 35°42N 34°36E 207 E10
Klimovichi Belarus 53°36N 32°0E 188 F6
Klimovsk Russia 55°21N 37°28E 188 E9
Klin Russia 56°20N 36°48E 188 D9
Klinaklini → Canada 51°21N 125°40W 296 C3
Klinë Kosovo 42°37N 20°35E 202 D4
Klintehamn Sweden 57°24N 18°12E 163 G12
Klintsy Russia 52°50N 32°10E 189 F7
Klip → S. Africa 27°3S 29°3E 271 C4
Klipdale S. Africa 34°19S 19°57E 270 D2
Klippan Sweden 56°8N 13°10E 163 H7
Klipplaat S. Africa 33°1S 24°22E 270 D3
Klipriviersberg Nature Reserve ⌂ S. Africa 26°16S 28°2E 123 B2
Klishkivtsi Ukraine 48°26N 26°16E 183 B11
Klisura Bulgaria 42°40N 24°28E 203 D8
Kljajićevo Serbia 45°45N 19°17E 182 E4
Ključ Bos.-H. 44°32N 16°48E 199 D13
Kłobuck Poland 50°55N 18°55E 185 H5
Klockestrand Sweden 62°53N 17°55E 162 B11
Kłodawa Poland 52°15N 18°55E 185 F5
Kłodzko Poland 50°28N 16°38E 185 H3
Kløfta Norway 60°4N 11°6E 164 D8
Klondike Canada 64°0N 139°26W 294 E4
Klondike Goldrush ⌂ U.S.A. 59°27N 135°19W 303 G14
Klong Wang Chao △ Thailand 16°20N 99°9E 236 D2
Klos Albania 41°28N 20°10E 202 E4
Klosterneuburg Austria 48°18N 16°19E 142 A1
Klosters Switz. 46°52N 9°52E 179 J5
Klötze Germany 52°37N 11°10E 178 C7
Klouto Togo 6°57N 0°44E 263 D5
Klövsjö Sweden 62°32N 14°11E 162 B8
Kluane △ Canada 60°45N 139°30W 296 A1
Kluane L. Canada 61°15N 138°40W 294 E4
Kluang Malaysia 2°3N 103°18E 237 L4
Kluczbork Poland 50°58N 18°12E 185 H5
Klukhori = Karachayevsk Russia 43°50N 41°55E 191 J5
Klukwan U.S.A. 59°24N 135°54W 296 B1
Klungkung Indonesia 8°32S 115°24E 231 K18
Klyetsk Belarus 53°5N 26°45E 177 B14
Klyuchevskaya, Sopka Russia 55°50N 160°30E 215 D17
Klyuchi Russia 56°18N 160°51E 215 D17
Knaben Norway 58°40N 7°4E 164 F4
Knappavellir Iceland 63°54N 16°36W 155 D10
Knäred Sweden 56°31N 13°19E 163 H7
Knaresborough U.K. 54°1N 1°28W 168 C6
Knarvik Norway 60°32N 5°19E 164 D2
Knee L. Man., Canada 55°3N 94°45W 298 A1
Knee L. Sask., Canada 55°51N 107°0W 297 B7
Kneïss, Îs. Tunisia 34°22N 10°18E 258 B2
Knesset Jerusalem 123 b1
Knezha Bulgaria 43°30N 24°5E 203 C8
Knight I. U.S.A. 60°21N 147°45W 303 F11
Knight Inlet Canada 50°45N 125°40W 296 C3
Knighton U.K. 52°21N 3°3W 169 E4
Knights Ferry U.S.A. 37°50N 120°40W 306 H6
Knights Landing U.S.A. 38°48N 121°43W 306 G5
Knightsbridge London, U.K. 125 c2
Knightstown U.S.A. 39°48N 85°32W 311 E11
Knin Croatia 44°3N 16°17E 199 D13
Knislinge Sweden 56°12N 14°5E 163 H8
Knittelfeld Austria 47°13N 14°51E 180 D7
Knivsta Sweden 59°43N 17°48E 162 E11
Knjaževac Serbia 43°35N 22°18E 202 C6
Knob, C. Australia 34°32S 119°16E 279 F2
Knob Lake = Kawawachikamach Canada 54°48N 66°50W 299 B6
Knob Noster U.S.A. 38°46N 93°33W 310 F3
Knock Ireland 53°48N 8°55W 166 C3
Knockmealdown Mts. Ireland 52°14N 7°56W 166 D4
Knokke-Heist Belgium 51°21N 3°17E 170 C3
Knossos Greece 35°16N 25°10E 207 E6
Knowlton Canada 45°13N 72°31W 313 A12
Knox U.S.A. 41°18N 86°37W 311 C10
Knox Coast Antarctica 66°30S 108°0E 151 C8
Knoxville Ga., U.S.A. 32°47N 83°59W 316 C6
Knoxville Ill., U.S.A. 40°55N 90°17W 310 D6
Knoxville Iowa, U.S.A. 41°19N 93°6W 310 C4
Knoxville Pa., U.S.A. 41°57N 77°27W 312 E7
Knoxville Tenn., U.S.A. 35°58N 83°55W 315 D13
Knud Rasmussen Land Greenland 78°0N 60°0W 154 B4
Knysna S. Africa 34°2S 23°2E 270 D3
Knyszyn Poland 53°20N 22°56E 184 E9
Ko Kha Thailand 18°11N 99°24E 236 C2
Kō-Saki Japan 34°5N 129°13E 222 C1
Ko Tarutao △ Thailand 6°31N 99°26E 237 J2
Ko Yao Thailand 8°7N 98°35E 237 a
Koani Tanzania 6°8S 39°17E 268 D4
Koartac = Quaqtaq Canada 60°55N 69°40W 295 E18
Koba Aru, Indonesia 6°37S 134°37E 231 F8
Koba Bangka, Indonesia 2°26S 106°14E 234 C3
Kőbánya Hungary 47°28N 19°9E 117 B2
Kobarid Slovenia 46°15N 13°30E 199 B10
Kobayashi Japan 31°56N 130°59E 222 F2
Kobbegem Belgium 50°55N 4°15E 116 A1
Kobdo = Hovd □ Mongolia 48°2N 91°37E 217 C12
Kōbe Japan 34°41N 135°13E 223 C7
Kobelyaky Ukraine 49°11N 34°9E 189 H8
København Denmark 55°40N 12°26E 118 A2
København ✈ (CPH) Denmark 55°37N 12°39E 118 B3
Kobenni Mauritania 15°58N 9°24W 262 B3
Kōbi-Sho E. China Sea 25°56N 123°41E 221 M1
Koblenz Germany 50°21N 7°36E 179 E3
Kobo Dem. Rep. of the Congo 4°54S 17°9E 265 C3
Kobo Ethiopia 12°2N 39°56E 257 E4
Kobryn Belarus 52°15N 24°22E 177 B13
Kobuchizawa Japan 35°52N 138°19E 223 B10
Kobuk U.S.A. 66°55N 156°52W 303 C8
Kobuk → U.S.A. 66°54N 160°38W 303 C7
Kobuk Valley △ U.S.A. 67°0N 160°0W 303 C7
Kobuleti Georgia 41°55N 41°45E 191 K5
Kobyletska Polyana Ukraine 48°3N 24°4E 183 B9
Kobylin Poland 51°43N 17°12E 185 G4
Kobylisy Czechia 50°7N 14°26E 135 B2
Kobyłka Poland 52°20N 21°10E 143 A3
Kobylkino Russia 54°8N 43°56E 190 C6
Koca → Turkey 40°8N 27°57E 203 F11
Kocabaş Turkey 37°49N 29°20E 205 D11
Kocaeli Turkey 40°45N 29°50E 203 F13
Kocaeli □ Turkey 40°45N 29°55E 203 F13
Kočane Serbia 43°12N 21°52E 202 C5
Kočani N. Macedonia 41°55N 22°25E 202 E6
Koçarlı Turkey 37°45N 27°43E 205 D9
Koceljevo Serbia 44°28N 19°50E 202 B3
Kočevje Slovenia 45°39N 14°50E 199 C11
Kocgiri = Zara Turkey 39°58N 37°43E 212 C7
Koch Bihar India 26°22N 89°29E 241 B2
Kochas India 25°15N 83°56E 243 G10
Kocher → Germany 49°13N 9°12E 179 F5
Kochi India 9°58N 76°20E 245 K3
Kōchi Japan 33°30N 133°35E 222 D5
Kōchi □ Japan 33°40N 133°30E 222 D5
Kochiu = Gejiu China 23°20N 103°10E 228 F4
Kochkor Kyrgyzstan 42°13N 75°46E 217 D9
Kochubey Russia 44°23N 46°32E 191 H8
Kock Poland 51°38N 22°27E 185 G9
Kodaira Japan 35°43N 139°28E 140 A1
Kodala India 19°38N 84°57E 244 E7
Kodanaka Japan 35°34N 139°37E 140 B2
Kodarma India 24°28N 85°36E 243 G11
Koddiyar B. Sri Lanka 8°33N 81°15E 245 K5
Kode Sweden 57°57N 11°51E 163 G5
Kodenmacho Tokyo, Japan 140 a5
Kodi Dem. Rep. of the Congo 3°34S 22°12E 264 C4
Kodiak U.S.A. 57°47N 152°24W 303 H9
Kodiak I. U.S.A. 57°30N 152°45W 303 H9
Kodikkarai = Point Calimere India 10°17N 79°49E 245 J4
Kodinar India 20°46N 70°46E 242 J4
Kodinsk Russia 58°40N 99°10E 215 D10
Kodlipet India 12°48N 75°53E 245 H2
Kodok South Sudan 9°53N 32°7E 257 F3
Kodori → Georgia 42°47N 41°10E 191 J5
Kodoro Dem. Rep. of the Congo 1°16N 20°6E 264 B4
Kodungallur = Cranganore India 10°13N 76°13E 245 J3
Kodyma Ukraine 48°6N 29°7E 183 B14
Koedoesberge S. Africa 32°40S 20°11E 270 D3
Koekelberg Belgium 50°52N 4°20E 116 A1
Koes Namibia 26°0S 19°15E 270 C2
Kofarnihon Tajikistan 38°33N 69°1E 217 E7
Kofçaz Turkey 41°58N 27°12E 203 E11
Koffiefontein S. Africa 29°30S 25°0E 270 C4
Kofiau Indonesia 1°11S 129°50E 231 E7
Köflach Austria 47°4N 15°5E 180 D8
Koforidua Ghana 6°3N 0°17W 263 D4
Kōfu Japan 35°40N 138°30E 223 B10
Koga Fukuoka, Japan 33°45N 130°25E 222 D2
Koga Ibaraki, Japan 36°11N 139°43E 223 A11
Kogaluc → Canada 56°12N 61°44W 299 A7
Koganei Japan 35°42N 139°31E 140 A2
Kogarah Australia 33°57S 151°8E 139 B1
Køge Denmark 55°27N 12°11E 163 J6
Køge Bugt Denmark 55°34N 12°24E 163 J6
Kogi □ Nigeria 7°45N 6°45E 263 D6
Kogin Baba Nigeria 7°55N 11°35E 263 D7
Kogo Eq. Guin. 1°5N 9°42E 264 B1
Kogon Uzbekistan 39°43N 64°33E 216 E6
Koh-i-Khurd Afghan. 33°30N 65°59E 242 C1
Koh-i-Maran Pakistan 29°18N 66°50E 242 E2
Koh Ker Cambodia 13°47N 104°32E 236 F5
Koh Wai Thailand 11°54N 102°25E 237 H4
Kohala Mts. U.S.A. 20°5N 155°45W 302 C6
Kohat Pakistan 33°40N 71°29E 242 C4
Kohima India 25°35N 94°10E 241 C5
Kohkīlūyeh va Būyer Aḩmadi □ Iran 31°30N 50°30E 247 D6
Kohler Ra. Antarctica 77°0S 110°0W 151 D15
Kohlfurt = Węgliniec Poland 51°18N 15°10E 185 G2
Kohlu Pakistan 29°54N 69°15E 242 E3
Kohtla-Järve Estonia 59°20N 27°20E 188 C4
Kohukohu N.Z. 35°22S 173°38E 284 B2
Kohylnyk → Ukraine 45°49N 29°40E 183 E14
Koi Sanjaq Iraq 36°5N 44°38E 213 D11
Koidu S. Leone 8°38N 10°59W 262 D2
Koihoa India 8°12N 93°29E 245 K11
Koilkuntla India 15°14N 78°19E 245 G4
Koillismaa Finland 65°44N 28°36E 160 D23
Koimbani Comoros Is. 11°37S 43°21E 272 a
Koin N. Korea 40°28N 126°18E 224 B3
Koinare Bulgaria 43°21N 24°8E 203 C8
Koindu S. Leone 8°26N 10°19W 262 D2
Koivisto = Primorsk Russia 60°22N 28°37E 188 B5
Koivupää Finland 60°18N 24°53E 121 B2
Koja Indonesia 6°8S 106°52E 122 A2
Koja Utara Indonesia 6°5S 106°53E 122 A2
Kojetín Czechia 49°21N 17°20E 181 B10
Kojō N. Korea 38°58N 127°58E 224 C3
Kojonup Australia 33°48S 117°10E 279 F2
Kojūr Iran 36°23N 51°43E 247 B6
Kokand = Qo'qon Uzbekistan 40°31N 70°56E 217 D8
Kokang Myanmar 23°45N 98°30E 228 F2
Kokas Indonesia 2°42S 132°26E 231 E8
Kokava Slovakia 48°35N 19°50E 181 C12
Kokcha → Afghan. 37°9N 69°24E 240 A3
Kokchetav = Kökshetaū Kazakhstan 53°20N 69°25E 217 B7
Koke'e State Park ⌂ U.S.A. 22°6N 159°40W 302 A2
Kokemäenjoki → Finland 61°32N 21°44E 188 B1
Kokerite Guyana 7°12N 59°35W 329 B6
Kokhav Ya'akov West Bank 31°53N 35°14E 123 A2
Kokhma Russia 56°57N 41°8E 190 B5
Koki Senegal 15°30N 15°59W 262 B1
Kokiu = Gejiu China 23°20N 103°10E 228 F4
Kokkilai Sri Lanka 9°0N 80°57E 245 K5
Kokkina Cyprus 35°11N 32°36E 207 E8
Kokkola Finland 63°50N 23°8E 160 E20
Koko Nigeria 11°28N 4°29E 263 C5
Koko Head U.S.A. 21°16N 157°43W 302 K14
Koko Kyunzu Myanmar 14°7N 93°22E 245 G11
Koko Nur = Qinghai Hu China 36°40N 100°10E 218 D9
Kokobunji Japan 35°42N 139°27E 140 A1
Kokobunji-Temple Japan 35°44N 139°55E 140 A4
Kokoda Papua N. G. 8°54S 147°47E 286 E4
Kokologo Burkina Faso 12°11N 1°53W 262 C4
Kokolopozo Côte d'Ivoire 5°8N 6°5W 262 D3
Kokomo U.S.A. 40°29N 86°8W 311 D10
Kokopo Papua N. G. 4°22S 152°19E 286 C7
Kokoro Niger 14°12N 0°55E 263 C5
Koksan N. Korea 38°46N 126°40E 224 C3
Kökshetaū Kazakhstan 53°20N 69°25E 217 B7
Koksoak → Canada 58°30N 68°10W 295 F18
Kokstad S. Africa 30°32S 29°29E 271 D4
Köktal Kazakhstan 44°8N 79°48E 217 D9
Kokubu = Kirishima Japan 31°44N 130°46E 222 F2
Kokyar China 37°23N 77°10E 217 E9
Kola Indonesia 5°35S 134°30E 231 F8
Kola Russia 68°45N 33°8E 160 B25
Kola Pen. = Kolskiy Poluostrov Russia 67°30N 38°0E 186 A6
Kolachel India 8°10N 77°15E 245 K3
Kolachi → Pakistan 27°8N 67°2E 242 F2
Kolahoi India 34°12N 75°22E 243 B6
Kolahun Liberia 8°15N 10°4W 262 D2
Kolaka Indonesia 4°3S 121°46E 231 E6
Kolar India 13°12N 78°15E 245 H4
Kolar Gold Fields India 12°58N 78°16E 245 H4
Kolarängen Sweden 59°16N 18°10E 139 B3
Kolaras India 25°14N 77°36E 242 G6
Kolari Finland 67°20N 23°48E 160 C20
Kolarovgrad = Shumen Bulgaria 43°18N 26°55E 203 C10
Kolárovo Slovakia 47°54N 18°0E 181 D10
Kolasib India 24°15N 92°45E 241 C4
Kolašin Montenegro 42°50N 19°31E 202 D3
Kolayat India 27°50N 72°50E 242 F5
Kolbäck Sweden 59°34N 16°15E 162 E10
Kolbäcksån → Sweden 59°36N 16°16E 162 E10
Kolbeinsstaðir Iceland 64°59N 22°16W 155 C4
Kolberg = Kołobrzeg Poland 54°10N 15°35E 184 D2
Kolbermoor Germany 47°51N 12°4E 179 H8
Kolbio Kenya 1°8S 41°12E 267 E5
Kolbotn Norway 59°48N 10°48E 133 B3
Kolbu Norway 60°39N 10°45E 164 D7
Kolbuszowa Poland 50°15N 21°46E 185 H8
Kolchugino = Leninsk-Kuznetskiy Russia 54°44N 86°10E 217 B11
Kolchugino Russia 56°17N 39°22E 188 D10
Kolda Senegal 12°55N 14°57W 262 C2
Kolda □ Senegal 13°5N 14°50W 262 C2
Koldegi Sudan 12°3N 30°16E 257 E3
Kolding Denmark 55°30N 9°29E 163 J3
Kole Dem. Rep. of the Congo 3°16S 22°42E 264 C4
Koléa Algeria 36°38N 2°46E 261 A5
Kolepom = Dolak, Pulau Indonesia 8°0S 138°30E 231 F9
Kolguyev, Ostrov Russia 69°20N 48°30E 186 A8
Kolhapur India 16°43N 74°15E 244 F2
Kolia Côte d'Ivoire 9°46N 6°28W 262 D3
Koliganek U.S.A. 59°48N 157°25W 303 G8
Kolimbia Greece 36°15N 28°10E 206 E12
Kolín Czechia 50°2N 15°9E 180 A8
Kolind Denmark 56°21N 10°34E 163 H4
Kolkas rags Latvia 57°46N 22°37E 184 A9
Kolkata India 22°34N 88°21E 124 B1
Kolkata Maidan India 22°33N 88°21E 124 B1
Kolkata Netaji Subhash Chandra Bose Int. ✈ (CCU) India 22°38N 88°26E 124 B2
Kollam India 8°50N 76°38E 245 K3
Kölleda Germany 51°11N 11°15E 178 D7
Kollegal India 12°9N 77°9E 245 H3
Kolleru L. India 16°40N 81°10E 244 F5
Kollum Neths. 53°17N 6°10E 170 A6
Kolmanskop Namibia 26°45S 15°14E 270 C2
Köln Germany 50°56N 6°57E 178 E2
Kolno Poland 53°25N 21°56E 184 E8
Koło Warszawa, Poland 52°14N 20°56E 143 B1
Koło Wielkopolskie, Poland 52°14N 18°40E 185 F5
Kołobrzeg Poland 54°10N 15°35E 184 D2
Kolochava Ukraine 48°26N 23°41E 183 B8
Kologi Sudan 10°51N 30°58E 257 E3
Kolokani Mali 13°35N 7°45W 262 C3
Kolokinthou Greece 38°0N 23°42E 112 B2
Koloko Burkina Faso 11°5N 5°19W 262 C3
Kololo Ethiopia 7°29N 41°58E 257 F5
Kolombangara Solomon Is. 8°0S 157°5E 287 M9
Kolomna Russia 55°8N 38°45E 188 E10
Kolomyagi Russia 60°0N 30°19E 137 A1
Kolomyya Ukraine 48°31N 25°2E 183 B10
Kolondiéba Mali 11°5N 6°54W 262 C3
Kolonodale Indonesia 2°0S 121°19E 231 E6
Kolonos Greece 37°59N 23°43E 112 B2
Kolonowskie Poland 50°39N 18°22E 185 H5
Kolpashevo Russia 58°20N 83°5E 214 D9
Kolpino Russia 59°44N 30°39E 188 C6
Kolpny Russia 52°17N 37°1E 189 F9
Kolsås Norway 59°55N 10°30E 133 A2
Kolskiy Poluostrov Russia 67°30N 38°0E 186 A6
Kolskiy Zaliv Russia 69°23N 34°0E 160 B26
Kolsva Sweden 59°36N 15°51E 162 E9
Kolubara → Serbia 44°35N 20°15E 202 B4
Kolumadulu Atoll Maldives 2°22N 73°7E 272 d
Koluszki Poland 51°45N 19°46E 185 G6
Kolwezi Dem. Rep. of the Congo 10°40S 25°25E 269 E2
Kolyma → Russia 69°30N 161°0E 215 C17
Kolymskoye Nagorye Russia 63°0N 157°0E 215 C16
Kôm Hamâda Egypt 30°46N 30°41E 256 H7
Kôm Ombo Egypt 24°25N 32°52E 256 C3
Koma Tou Yialou Cyprus 35°25N 34°8E 207 E10
Komadugu Gana → Nigeria 13°5N 12°24E 263 C7
Komae Japan 35°37N 139°34E 140 B2
Komagane Japan 35°44N 137°58E 223 B9
Komagome Japan 35°43N 139°45E 140 A3
Komaki Japan 35°17N 136°55E 223 B8
Komandorskiye Is. = Komandorskiye Ostrova Russia 55°0N 167°0E 215 D17
Komandorskiye Ostrova Russia 55°0N 167°0E 215 D17
Komárno Slovakia 47°49N 18°5E 181 D11
Komarnyky Ukraine 48°59N 23°3E 182 B8
Komárom Hungary 47°43N 18°7E 182 C3
Komárom-Esztergom □ Hungary 47°35N 18°20E 182 C3
Komáromújváros = Komárom Hungary 47°43N 18°7E 182 C3
Komatipoort S. Africa 25°25S 31°55E 271 C5
Komatsu Japan 36°25N 136°30E 223 A8
Komatsushima Japan 34°0N 134°35E 222 D6
Komavangard = Sobinka Russia 56°0N 40°0E 188 E11
Komazawa Japan 35°37N 139°40E 140 B3
Komba Dem. Rep. of the Congo 2°52N 24°3E 264 B4
Kombissiri Burkina Faso 12°4N 1°20W 263 C4
Kombo Gabon 0°20S 12°22E 264 C2
Kombong India 28°7N 94°51E 241 A5
Kombori Burkina Faso 13°26N 3°56W 262 C4
Komboti Greece 39°6N 21°5E 204 B3
Kome Channel Uganda 0°10S 32°35E 268 C3
Komebail Lagoon Palau 7°25N 134°25E 288 c
Komen Slovenia 45°49N 13°45E 199 C10
Komenda Ghana 5°4N 1°28W 263 D4
Komi Cyprus 35°24N 34°0E 207 E10
Komi □ Russia 64°0N 55°0E 186 B10
Kominter = Novoshakhtinsk Russia 47°46N 39°58E 189 J10
Komintern = Marhanets Ukraine 47°40N 34°40E 189 J8
Komiža Croatia 43°3N 16°11E 199 E13
Komló Hungary 46°15N 18°16E 182 D3
Kommamur Canal India 16°0N 80°25E 245 G5
Kommunarsk = Alchevsk Ukraine 48°30N 38°45E 189 H10
Kommunizma, Pik = imeni Ismail Samani, Pik Tajikistan 39°0N 72°2E 217 E8
Komodo Indonesia 8°37S 119°20E 235 D5
Komodo △ Indonesia 8°36S 119°34E 235 D5
Komono Congo 3°10S 13°20E 264 C2
Komoran, Pulau Indonesia 8°18S 138°45E 231 F9
Komoro Japan 36°19N 138°26E 223 A10
Komotau = Chomutov Czechia 50°28N 13°23E 180 A6
Komotini Greece 41°9N 25°26E 203 E9
Komovi Montenegro 42°41N 19°39E 202 D3
Kompasberg S. Africa 31°45S 24°32E 270 D3
Kompong Chhnang = Kampong Chhnang Cambodia 12°20N 104°35E 237 F5
Kompong Chikreng Cambodia 13°5N 104°18E 236 F5
Kompong Kleang Cambodia 13°6N 104°8E 236 F5
Kompong Luong Cambodia 11°49N 104°48E 237 G5
Kompong Pranak Cambodia 13°35N 104°55E 236 F5
Kompong Som = Kampong Saom Cambodia 10°38N 103°30E 237 G4
Kompong Som, Chhung = Kampong Saom, Chaak Cambodia 10°50N 103°32E 237 G4
Kompong Speu Cambodia 11°26N 104°32E 237 G5
Kompong Sralau Cambodia 14°5N 105°46E 236 E5
Kompong Thom Cambodia 12°35N 104°51E 236 F5
Kompong Trabeck Cambodia 13°6N 105°14E 236 F5
Kompong Trach Cambodia 11°25N 105°48E 237 G5
Kompong Tralach Cambodia 11°54N 104°47E 237 G5
Komrat = Comrat Moldova 46°18N 28°40E 183 D13
Komsberg S. Africa 32°40S 20°45E 270 D3
Komsomolets = Qarabalyq Kazakhstan 53°45N 62°2E 216 B6
Komsomolets, Ostrov Russia 80°30N 95°0E 215 A10
Komsomolsk Ivanovo, Russia 57°2N 40°20E 188 D11
Komsomolsk Ukraine 49°1N 33°38E 189 H7
Komsomolsk-na-Amur Russia 50°30N 137°0E 219 A16
Komsomolskiy Russia 54°27N 45°33E 190 C7
Komsomolskoe Kazakhstan 50°25N 60°5E 216 B6
Komsomolsky = Chirchiq Uzbekistan 41°29N 69°35E 217 D7
Kömür Burnu Turkey 38°39N 26°12E 205 C8
Kon Ka Kinh △ Vietnam 14°19N 107°23E 236 E6
Kon Tum Vietnam 14°24N 108°0E 236 E7
Kon Tum, Plateau du Vietnam 14°30N 108°30E 236 E7
Kona Paschimbanga, India 22°37N 88°18E 124 B1
Kona Mali 14°57N 3°53W 262 C4
Kona Nigeria 8°57N 11°21E 263 D7
Kona ✈ (KOA) U.S.A. 19°44N 156°3W 302 D5
Könähuanui U.S.A. 21°21N 157°47W 302 K14
Konakovo Russia 56°40N 36°51E 188 D9
Konala Finland 60°14N 24°52E 121 B2
Konar □ Afghan. 34°30N 71°3E 240 B3
Konarak India 19°54N 86°7E 244 E8
Konārak Iran 25°21N 60°23E 247 E9
Konārī Iran 28°13N 51°36E 247 D6
Konch India 26°0N 79°10E 243 G8
Kondagaon India 19°35N 81°35E 244 E5
Konde Tanzania 4°57S 39°45E 268 C4
Kondias Greece 39°49N 25°10E 205 B7
Kondinin Australia 32°34S 118°8E 279 F2
Kondli India 28°36N 77°19E 120 B2
Kondo Dem. Rep. of the Congo 5°35S 13°0E 265 D2
Kondoa Tanzania 4°55S 35°50E 268 C4
Kondopoga Russia 62°12N 34°17E 188 A8
Kondoz Afghan. 36°50N 68°50E 240 A3
Kondoz → Afghan. 37°0N 68°16E 240 A3
Kondratyevo Russia 57°22N 98°15E 215 D10
Kondrovo Russia 54°48N 35°56E 188 E8
Konduga Nigeria 11°35N 13°26E 263 C7
Kondukur India 15°12N 79°57E 245 G4
Kondūz □ Afghan. 36°50N 68°50E 240 A3
Koné Cameroon 8°50N 13°17E 259 G2
Koné N. Cal. 21°4S 164°52E 288 d
Köneürgench Turkmenistan 42°19N 59°10E 216 D5
Konevo Russia 62°8N 39°20E 188 A10
Kong = Khong → Cambodia 13°32N 105°58E 236 F5
Kong Côte d'Ivoire 8°54N 4°36W 262 D4
Kong, Koh Cambodia 11°20N 103°0E 237 G4
Kong Christian IX.s Land Greenland 68°0N 36°0W 154 D7
Kong Christian X.s Land Greenland 74°0N 29°0W 154 C8
Kong Frederik IX.s Land Greenland 67°0N 52°0W 154 D5
Kong Frederik VI.s Kyst Greenland 63°0N 43°0W 154 E6
Kong Frederik VIII.s Land Greenland 78°30N 26°0W 154 B8
Kong Karls Land Svalbard 79°0N 28°0E 154 B13
Kong Oscar Fjord Greenland 72°20N 24°0W 154 C8
Kongauru I. Palau 7°3N 134°16E 288 c
Kongbo C.A.R. 4°44N 21°23E 264 B4
Kongeå → Denmark 55°23N 8°39E 163 J2
Kongelunden Denmark 55°34N 12°34E 118 B3
Kongens Lyngby Denmark 55°47N 12°30E 118 A2
Kongernes Nordsjælland △ Denmark 56°5N 12°15E 163 H6
Kongerslev Denmark 56°54N 10°6E 163 H4
Kongkemul Indonesia 1°52N 116°10E 235 B5
Konglu Myanmar 27°13N 97°57E 241 B6
Kongmoon = Jiangmen China 22°32N 113°0E 229 F9
Kongo Helsinki, Finland 60°20N 24°47E 121 A1
Kongo Liberia 7°20N 11°6W 262 D2
Kongo Central □ Dem. Rep. of the Congo 5°0S 15°0E 265 D2
Kongola Namibia 17°45S 23°20E 270 A3
Kongolo Kasai-Or., Dem. Rep. of the Congo 5°26S 24°49E 265 D4
Kongolo Katanga, Dem. Rep. of the Congo 5°22S 27°0E 268 D2
Kongor South Sudan 7°1N 31°27E 257 F3
Kongossambougou ⌂ Mali 14°0N 8°30W 262 C3
Kongoulou Cameroon 2°59N 11°7E 264 B2
Kongoussi Burkina Faso 13°19N 1°32W 263 C4
Kongsberg Norway 59°39N 9°39E 164 E6
Kongsvinger Norway 60°12N 12°2E 164 D9
Kongur Shan China 38°34N 75°18E 217 E9
Kongwa Tanzania 6°11S 36°26E 268 D4
Koni Dem. Rep. of the Congo 10°40S 27°11E 269 E2
Koniakari Mali 14°35N 10°50W 262 C2
Koniecpol Poland 50°46N 19°40E 185 H6
Königgrätz = Hradec Králové Czechia 50°15N 15°50E 180 A8
Königs Wusterhausen Germany 52°19N 13°38E 178 C9
Königsberg = Chojna Poland 52°58N 14°25E 185 F1
Königsberg = Kaliningrad Russia 54°42N 20°32E 184 D7
Königsbrunn Germany 48°16N 10°54E 179 G6
Königshütte = Chorzów Poland 50°18N 18°57E 185 H5
Königslutter Germany 52°15N 10°49E 178 C6
Konin Poland 52°12N 18°15E 185 F5
Köninginhof an der Elbe = Dvůr Králové nad Labem Czechia 50°27N 15°50E 180 A8
Koninklijk Paleis Amsterdam, Neths. 112 a2
Konispol Albania 39°42N 20°10E 206 B10
Konitsa Greece 40°5N 20°48E 204 A2
Köniz Switz. 46°56N 7°25E 179 J3
Konjic Bos.-H. 43°42N 17°58E 182 G2
Konkiep Namibia 26°49S 17°15E 270 C2
Konkō Japan 34°33N 133°36E 222 C4
Konkouré → Guinea 9°50N 13°42W 262 D2
Konnagar India 22°42N 88°21E 124 A2
Könnern Germany 51°41N 11°47E 178 D7
Konnur India 16°14N 74°49E 245 F2
Kono S. Leone 8°30N 11°5W 262 D2
Konogogo Papua N. G. 3°29S 152°10E 286 B7
Konohana Japan 34°40N 135°26E 133 A1
Konongo Ghana 6°40N 1°15W 263 D4
Konos Papua N. G. 3°10S 151°44E 286 B6
Konosha Russia 61°0N 40°5E 188 B11
Kōnosu Japan 36°3N 139°31E 223 A11
Konotop Ukraine 51°12N 33°7E 189 G7
Konqi He → China 40°45N 90°10E 217 D11
Konradshof = Skawina Poland 49°59N 19°50E 185 J6
Konradshöhe Germany 52°35N 13°13E 115 A2
Konrei Palau 7°43N 134°36E 288 c
Konsankoro Guinea 9°2N 9°0W 262 D3
Końskie Poland 51°15N 20°23E 185 G7
Konsmo Norway 58°16N 7°23E 164 F4
Konstadt = Wołczyn Poland 51°1N 18°3E 185 G5
Konstancin-Jeziorna Poland 52°5N 21°7E 185 F8
Konstantinograd = Krasnohrad Ukraine 49°27N 35°27E 189 H8
Konstantinovka = Kostyantynivka Ukraine 48°32N 37°39E 189 H9
Konstantinovsk Russia 47°33N 41°10E 191 G5
Konstantynów Łódzki Poland 51°45N 19°20E 185 G6
Konstanz Germany 47°40N 9°10E 179 H5
Kont Iran 26°55N 61°50E 247 E9
Konta India 17°48N 81°23E 244 F5
Kontagora Nigeria 10°23N 5°27E 263 C6
Kontcha Cameroon 7°59N 12°15E 263 D7
Kontiolahti Finland 62°46N 29°50E 160 E23
Kontokali Greece 39°38N 19°51E 206 B9
Konya Turkey 37°52N 32°35E 212 D5
Konya □ Turkey 37°46N 32°20E 212 D5
Konya Ovası Turkey 38°9N 33°5E 212 C5
Konyin Myanmar 22°58N 94°42E 241 D5
Konz Germany 49°42N 6°34E 179 F2
Konza Kenya 1°45S 37°7E 268 C4
Koo-wee-rup Australia 38°13S 145°28E 283 E6
Koocanusa, L. Canada 49°20N 115°15W 304 B6
Kookynie Australia 29°17S 121°22E 279 E3
Ko'olau Range U.S.A. 21°35N 157°50W 302 J14
Ko'olauloa District U.S.A. 21°35N 157°55W 302 J14
Ko'olaupoko District U.S.A. 21°25N 157°50W 302 K14
Kö'Ölina U.S.A. 21°19N 158°7W 302 K13
Koolyanobbing Australia 30°48S 119°36E 279 F2
Koondrook Australia 35°33S 144°8E 282 C6
Koonibba Australia 31°54S 133°25E 281 E1
Koorawatha Australia 34°2S 148°33E 283 C8
Koorda Australia 30°48S 117°35E 279 F2
Kooskia U.S.A. 46°9N 115°59W 304 C6
Kootenay → U.S.A. 49°19N 117°39W 296 D5
Kootenay △ Canada 51°0N 116°0W 296 C5
Kootenay L. Canada 49°45N 116°50W 304 B5
Kootingal Australia 31°3S 151°4E 283 A9
Kootjieskolk S. Africa 31°15S 20°21E 270 D3
Kopanina Czechia 50°3N 14°17E 135 B1
Kopanovka Russia 47°28N 46°50E 191 G8
Kopaonik Serbia 43°10N 20°50E 202 C4
Kopaonik △ Serbia 43°20N 20°50E 202 C4
Kopargaon India 19°51N 74°28E 244 E2
Koparkhairna India 19°6N 72°59E 130 A2
Kópasker Iceland 66°18N 16°27W 155 A10
Kópavogur Iceland 64°6N 21°55W 155 C5
Kopayhorod Ukraine 48°52N 27°53E 183 B12
Köpenick Germany 52°26N 13°35E 115 B4
Koper Slovenia 45°31N 13°44E 199 C10
Kopervik Norway 59°17N 5°17E 164 E2
Kopet Dagh Asia 38°0N 58°0E 247 B8
Kopeysk Russia 55°7N 61°37E 216 A6
Kopi Australia 33°24S 135°40E 281 E2
Köping Sweden 59°31N 16°3E 162 E10
Köpingsvik Sweden 56°53N 16°43E 163 H10
Kopište Croatia 42°48N 16°42E 199 F13
Koplik Albania 42°15N 19°25E 202 D3
Köpmanholmen Sweden 63°10N 18°35E 162 A12
Koppa India 13°33N 75°21E 245 H2
Koppal India 15°23N 76°5E 245 G3
Koppang Norway 61°34N 11°3E 164 C8
Kopparberg Sweden 59°52N 15°0E 162 E9
Koppeh Dāgh = Kopet Dagh Asia 38°0N 58°0E 247 B8
Kopperå Norway 63°24N 11°50E 164 A8
Koppies S. Africa 27°20S 27°30E 271 C4
Koppom Sweden 59°43N 12°10E 162 E6
Koprivlen Bulgaria 41°31N 23°53E 202 E7
Koprivnica Croatia 46°12N 16°45E 199 B13
Kopřivnice Czechia 49°36N 18°9E 181 B11
Koprivshtitsa Bulgaria 42°40N 24°19E 203 D8
Köprü → Turkey 36°48N 31°11E 250 B2
Köprübaşı Turkey 38°43N 28°23E 205 C10
Köprülü Turkey 36°43N 32°10E 250 B3
Köprülü △ Turkey 37°20N 31°5E 246 B1
Kopychyntsi Ukraine 49°7N 25°58E 177 D13
Kor Aban Somalia 3°58N 42°44E 267 D5
Kora △ Kenya 0°14S 38°44E 268 C4
Koraa Shiir Somalia 3°16N 46°16E 267 D6
Korab N. Macedonia 41°44N 20°40E 202 E4
Korahe Ethiopia 6°39N 44°29E 267 C5
Korai India 21°20N 73°12E 242 J5
Korangal India 17°6N 77°38E 244 E3
Korangi Pakistan 24°47N 67°8E 123 B2
Koraput India 18°50N 82°40E 244 E6
Korarou, L. Mali 15°15N 3°15W 262 B4
Korba India 22°20N 82°45E 243 H10
Korbach Germany 51°16N 8°52E 178 D4
Korbu, Gunung Malaysia 4°41N 101°18E 237 K3
Korçë Albania 40°37N 20°50E 202 F4
Korčula Croatia 42°56N 16°57E 199 F13

Korčulanski Kanal Croatia 43°3N 16°40E 199 E13
Kord Küy Iran 36°48N 54°7E 247 B7
Kord Sheykh Iran 28°31N 52°53E 247 D7
Kordestān = Kurdistan Asia 37°20N 43°30E 213 D10
Kordestān □ Iran 36°0N 47°0E 246 C5
Kordié Burkina Faso 12°36N 2°22W 262 C4
Koré Mayroua Niger 13°18N 3°55E 263 C5
Korea, North ■ Asia 40°0N 127°0E 224 C3
Korea, South ■ Asia 36°0N 128°0E 224 D4
Korea Bay Korea 39°0N 124°0E 224 C2
Korea Strait Asia 34°0N 129°30E 227 H15
Koregaon India 17°40N 74°10E 244 F2
Korem Ethiopia 12°30N 39°32E 257 E4
Koremasa Japan 35°39N 139°29E 140 B1
Korenevo Russia 51°27N 34°55E 189 G8
Korenica = Titova Korenica Croatia 44°45N 15°41E 199 D12
Korenovsk Russia 45°30N 39°22E 191 H4
Korets Ukraine 50°40N 27°5E 177 C14
Korfantów Poland 50°29N 17°36E 185 H4
Körfez Turkey 40°47N 29°44E 203 F13
Korff Ice Rise Antarctica 79°0S 69°30W 151 D17
Korgalzhyn = Qorghalzhyn Kazakhstan 50°25N 69°11E 217 B7
Korgan Turkey 40°44N 37°13E 212 B7
Korgus Sudan 19°16N 33°29E 256 D3
Korhogo Côte d'Ivoire 9°29N 5°28W 262 D3
Koribundu S. Leone 7°41N 11°46W 262 D2
Koridalos Greece 37°59N 23°39E 112 B1
Korienzé Mali 15°22N 3°50W 262 B4
Korinthiakos Kolpos Greece 38°16N 22°30E 204 C4
Korinthos Greece 37°56N 22°55E 204 D4
Korioumé Mali 16°35N 3°0W 262 B4
Korissia, L. Greece 39°27N 19°53E 206 C9
Korithi Greece 37°55N 20°42E 207 D2
Kōriyama Japan 37°24N 140°23E 220 F10
Korkino Russia 54°54N 61°23E 216 B6
Korkuteli Turkey 37°4N 30°13E 205 D12
Korla China 41°45N 86°4E 217 D11
Kormakiti, C. Cyprus 35°23N 32°56E 207 E8
Körmend Hungary 47°5N 16°35E 182 C1
Kormor Iraq 35°8N 44°50E 213 E11
Kornat Croatia 43°50N 15°20E 199 E12
Kornat △ Croatia 43°50N 15°12E 199 E12
Korneshty = Corneşti Moldova 47°21N 28°1E 183 C13
Korneuburg Austria 48°20N 16°20E 181 C9
Kórnik Poland 52°15N 17°6E 185 F4
Kornsjø Norway 58°57N 11°39E 164 F8
Koro Côte d'Ivoire 8°32N 7°30W 262 D3
Koro Fiji 17°19S 179°23E 287 A2
Koro Mali 14°1N 2°58W 262 C4
Koro Sea Fiji 17°30S 179°45W 287 A3
Koro Toro Chad 16°5N 18°30E 259 E3
Koroba Papua N. G. 5°44S 142°47E 286 C2
Korobkovo = Gubkin Russia 51°17N 37°32E 189 G9
Korocha Russia 50°54N 37°19E 189 G9
Köroğlu Dağları Turkey 40°38N 33°0E 212 B5
Korogwe Tanzania 5°5S 38°25E 268 D4
Koroit Australia 38°18S 142°24E 282 E5
Koroleve Ukraine 48°9N 23°8E 183 B8
Korolevu Fiji 18°12S 177°46E 287 B1
Koromiri Cook Is. 21°15S 159°43W 289 h
Korona U.S.A. 29°25N 81°12W 317 F8
Koronadal Phil. 6°12N 124°51E 233 H5
Korong Vale Australia 36°22S 143°45E 282 D5
Koroni Greece 36°48N 21°57E 204 E3
Koronia, L. Greece 40°47N 23°10E 202 F7
Koronos Greece 37°12N 25°35E 205 D7
Koronowo Poland 53°19N 17°55E 185 E4
Koropelé C.A.R. 4°44N 17°11E 264 B3
Koropets Ukraine 48°56N 25°10E 183 B10
Koror Palau 7°20N 134°28E 288 c
Koror I. Palau 7°20N 134°29E 288 c
Körös → Hungary 46°43N 20°12E 182 D5
Körös Maros △ Hungary 47°8N 20°52E 182 C5
Köröstarcsa Hungary 46°53N 21°3E 182 D6
Korosten Ukraine 50°54N 28°36E 177 C15
Korostyshev Ukraine 50°19N 29°4E 177 C15
Korotoyak Russia 51°1N 39°2E 189 G10
Korovou Fiji 17°47S 178°32E 287 A2
Koroyanitu △ Fiji 17°40S 177°35E 287 A1
Korraraika, Helodranon' i Madag. 17°45S 43°57E 272 B1
Korsakov Russia 46°36N 142°42E 215 E15
Korsberga Sweden 57°19N 15°7E 163 G9
Korshiv Ukraine 48°39N 25°1E 183 B10
Korshunovo Russia 58°37N 110°10E 215 D12
Korsør Denmark 55°20N 11°9E 163 J5
Korsun Shevchenkovskiy Ukraine 49°26N 31°16E 189 H6
Korsze Poland 54°11N 21°9E 184 D8
Korti Sudan 18°6N 31°33E 256 D3
Kortrijk Belgium 50°50N 3°17E 170 D3
Korucu Turkey 39°28N 27°22E 205 B9
Korumburra Australia 38°26S 145°50E 283 E6
Korup △ Cameroon 5°15N 9°2E 264 A1
Korwai India 24°7N 78°5E 242 G8
Koryakskoye Nagorye Russia 61°0N 171°0E 215 C18
Koryukovka Ukraine 51°46N 32°16E 189 G7
Kos Greece 36°50N 27°15E 205 E9
Kosa Ethiopia 7°50N 36°50E 257 F4
Kosai Japan 34°42N 137°32E 223 C9
Kosan N. Korea 38°52N 127°25E 224 C3
Kosaya Gora Russia 54°10N 37°30E 188 E9
Kościan Poland 52°5N 16°40E 185 F3
Kościerzyna Poland 54°8N 17°59E 184 D4
Kosciusko U.S.A. 33°4N 89°35W 315 E10
Kosciuszko, Mt. Australia 36°27S 148°16E 283 D8
Kosciuszko △ Australia 36°30S 148°20E 283 D8
Kosély → Hungary 47°25N 21°5E 182 C6
Kosgi Andhra Pradesh, India 16°58N 77°43E 244 F3
Kosgi Andhra Pradesh, India 15°51N 77°16E 245 G3
Kosha Sudan 20°50N 30°30E 256 C3
Koshava Bulgaria 44°4N 23°2E 202 B7
Kōshi Japan 32°53N 130°48E 222 E2
Koshigaya Japan 35°54N 139°48E 223 B11
K'oshih = Kashi China 39°30N 76°2E 217 E9
Koshiki-Kaikyō Japan 31°30N 130°0E 222 F1
Koshiki-Rettō Japan 31°45N 129°49E 222 F1
Koshim → Kazakhstan 49°20N 50°30E 190 F10
Koshkonong L. U.S.A. 42°52N 88°58W 311 B8
Kōshoku Japan 36°38N 138°6E 223 A10
Kōshū Japan 35°42N 138°44E 223 B10
Koshu-Kavak = Krumovgrad Bulgaria 41°29N 25°38E 203 E9
Kosi India 27°48N 77°29E 242 F7
Kosi → India 28°41N 78°57E 243 E8
Košice Slovakia 48°42N 21°15E 181 C14
Košický □ Slovakia 48°45N 21°0E 181 C14
Kosino Russia 55°43N 37°50E 129 B4
Kosiv Ukraine 48°19N 25°6E 183 B10
Kosjerić Serbia 44°0N 19°55E 202 B3
Köşk Turkey 37°50N 28°3E 205 D10
Koskinou Greece 36°23N 28°13E 206 E12
Koslan Russia 63°34N 49°14E 186 B8
Köslin = Koszalin Poland 54°11N 16°8E 184 D3
Kosmach Ukraine 48°20N 24°50E 183 B9
Kosŏng N. Korea 38°40N 128°22E 224 C4
Kosovo ■ Europe 42°30N 21°0E 202 D4
Kosovo Polje = Fushë Kosovë Kosovo 42°40N 21°5E 202 D5
Kosovska Kamenica = Dardanë Kosovo 42°35N 21°35E 202 D5
Kosovska Mitrovica = Mitrovicë Kosovo 42°54N 20°52E 202 D4
Kossou, L. de Côte d'Ivoire 6°59N 5°31W 262 D3
Kosta Sweden 56°50N 15°24E 163 H9
Kostajnica Bos.-H. 45°11N 16°33E 199 C13
Kostajnica Croatia 45°17N 16°30E 199 C13
Kostanjevica Slovenia 45°51N 15°27E 199 C12
Kostenets = Pernik Bulgaria 42°35N 23°2E 202 D7
Kostenets Bulgaria 42°15N 23°52E 202 D7
Koster S. Africa 25°52S 26°54E 270 C4
Kosterhavet △ Sweden 58°44N 10°56E 164 F7
Kôstî Sudan 13°8N 32°43E 257 E3
Kostinbrod Bulgaria 42°49N 23°13E 202 D7
Kostolac Serbia 44°37N 21°15E 202 B5
Kostomuksha Russia 64°41N 30°49E 160 D24
Kostopil Ukraine 50°51N 26°22E 177 C14
Kostroma Russia 57°50N 40°58E 188 D11
Kostromo □ Russia 58°10N 42°50E 190 A6
Kostromskoye Vdkhr. Russia 57°52N 40°49E 188 D11
Kostryzhivka Ukraine 48°39N 25°43E 183 B10
Kostrzyn Lubuskie, Poland 52°35N 14°39E 185 F1
Kostrzyn Wielkopolskie, Poland 52°24N 17°14E 185 F4
Kostyantynivka Ukraine 48°32N 37°39E 189 H9
Kostyukovichi = Kastsyukovichy Belarus 53°20N 32°4E 189 F7
Kosugi Japan 35°34N 139°39E 140 B2
Koszalin Poland 54°11N 16°8E 184 D3
Kőszeg Hungary 47°23N 16°33E 182 C1
Kot Addu Pakistan 30°30N 71°0E 242 D4
Kot Kapura India 30°35N 74°50E 242 D6
Kot Moman Pakistan 32°13N 73°0E 242 C5
Kot Sultan Pakistan 30°46N 70°56E 242 D4
Kota India 25°14N 75°49E 242 G6
Kota Jakarta, Indonesia 6°7S 106°48E 122 A1
Kota Barrage India 25°6N 75°51E 242 G6
Kota Belud Malaysia 6°21N 116°26E 235 A5
Kota Bharu Malaysia 6°7N 102°14E 237 J4
Kota I. = Loaita I. S. China Sea 10°41N 114°25E 230 B4
Kota Kinabalu Malaysia 6°0N 116°4E 235 A5
Kota Tinggi Malaysia 1°44N 103°53E 237 M4
Kotaagung Indonesia 5°38S 104°29E 234 D2
Kotabaru Kalimantan Barat, Indonesia 0°49S 111°31E 235 C4
Kotabaru Kalimantan Selatan, Indonesia 3°20S 116°20E 235 C5
Kotabaru Sumatera Barat, Indonesia 1°7S 101°43E 234 C2
Kotabesi Indonesia 2°45S 112°58E 235 C4
Kotabumi Indonesia 4°49S 104°54E 234 C2
Kotajawa Indonesia 5°37S 104°19E 234 D2
Kotamobagu Indonesia 0°57N 124°31E 231 D6
Kotapad India 19°9N 82°21E 244 E6
Kotapinang Indonesia 1°53N 100°5E 237 M3
Kotawaringin Indonesia 2°28S 111°27E 235 C4
Kotcho L. Canada 59°7N 121°12W 296 B4
Kotdwara India 29°45N 78°32E 243 E8
Kotel Bulgaria 42°52N 26°26E 203 D10
Kotelnich Russia 58°22N 48°24E 190 A9
Kotelnikovo Russia 47°38N 43°8E 191 G6
Kotelnyy, Ostrov Russia 75°10N 139°0E 215 B14
Kothapet India 19°21N 79°28E 244 E4
Kothari → India 25°20N 75°4E 242 G6
Köthen Germany 51°45N 11°59E 178 D7
Kothi Chhattisgarh, India 23°21N 82°3E 243 H10
Kothi Mad. P., India 24°45N 80°40E 243 G9
Kotiro Pakistan 26°17N 67°13E 242 F2
Kotka Finland 60°28N 26°58E 188 B4
Kotlas Russia 61°17N 46°43E 186 B8
Kotlenska Planina Bulgaria 42°56N 26°30E 203 D10
Kotli Pakistan 33°30N 73°55E 242 C5
Kotlik U.S.A. 63°2N 163°33W 303 E7
Kotma India 23°12N 81°58E 243 H9
Kōtō Japan 35°40N 139°48E 140 A3
Kotohira Japan 34°11N 133°49E 222 C5
Koton-Karifi Nigeria 8°0N 6°48E 263 D6
Kotonkoro Nigeria 11°3N 5°58E 263 C6
Kotor Montenegro 42°25N 18°47E 202 D2
Kotor Varoš Bos.-H. 44°38N 17°22E 182 F2
Kotoriba Croatia 46°23N 16°48E 199 B13
Kotovo Russia 50°22N 44°45E 190 E7
Kotovsk Russia 52°36N 41°32E 190 D5
Kotovsk Ukraine 47°45N 29°35E 177 E15
Kotputli India 27°43N 76°12E 242 F7
Kotri Pakistan 25°22N 68°22E 242 G3
Kotri → India 19°15N 80°35E 244 E5
Kotronas Greece 36°38N 22°29E 204 E4
Kotrung India 22°41N 88°20E 124 A2
Kötschach-Mauthen Austria 46°41N 13°1E 180 E6
Kottagudem India 17°30N 80°40E 244 F5
Kottayam India 9°35N 76°33E 245 K3
Kotto C.A.R. 4°14N 22°2E 264 B4
Kotto → C.A.R. 4°14N 22°2E 264 B4
Kotturu India 14°45N 76°10E 245 G3
Kottur India 10°34N 76°56E 245 J3
Kotu Group Tonga 20°0S 174°45W 287 G13
Kotuy → Russia 71°54N 102°6E 215 B11
Kotyuzhany Ukraine 48°48N 27°42E 183 B12
Kotzebue U.S.A. 66°53N 162°39W 303 C7
Kotzebue Sound U.S.A. 66°20N 163°0W 303 C7
Kotzenau = Chocianów Poland 51°27N 15°55E 185 G2
Kouango C.A.R. 5°0N 20°10E 264 B4
Kouchibouguac △ Canada 46°50N 65°0W 299 C6
Koudougou Burkina Faso 12°10N 2°20W 262 C4
Koufey Niger 13°57N 7°56E 259 F1
Koufonisi Iraklio, Greece 34°56N 26°8E 207 F7
Koufonisi Notio Aigaio, Greece 36°57N 25°35E 205 E7
Kougaberge S. Africa 33°48S 23°50E 270 D3
K'ouhu Taiwan 23°35N 120°11E 225 C2
Kouibli Côte d'Ivoire 7°15N 7°14W 262 D3
Kouilou □ Congo 4°30S 12°0E 264 C2
Kouilou → Congo 4°10S 12°5E 265 C2
Koukdjuak → Canada 66°43N 73°0W 295 D17
Kouki C.A.R. 7°22N 17°3E 264 A3
Koukoulé, Mt. Comoros Is. 12°18S 43°41E 272 a
Koukourou C.A.R. 7°12N 20°2E 264 A4
Koula Greece 41°23N 24°44E 203 E8
Koula Moutou Gabon 1°15S 12°25E 264 C2
Koulen = Kulen Cambodia 13°50N 104°40E 236 F5
Koulikoro Mali 12°40N 7°50W 262 C3
Koulikoro □ Mali 14°0N 7°45W 262 C3
Kouloura Greece 39°42N 19°54E 206 B9
Koumac N. Cal. 20°33S 164°17E 288 d
Koumala Australia 21°38S 149°15E 280 C4
Koumameyeng Gabon 0°11N 11°51E 264 B2
Koumankou Mali 11°58N 6°6W 262 C3
Koumbia Burkina Faso 11°10N 3°50W 262 C4
Koumbia Guinea 11°48N 13°29W 262 C2
Koumboum Guinea 10°25N 13°0W 262 C2
Koumpenntoum Senegal 13°59N 14°34W 262 C2
Koumra Chad 8°50N 17°35E 259 G3
Koun-Fao Côte d'Ivoire 7°30N 3°15W 262 D4
Koundara Guinea 12°29N 13°18W 262 C2
Koundé C.A.R. 6°7N 14°38E 264 A2
Koungheul Senegal 14°0N 14°50W 262 C2
Koungou Mayotte 12°43S 45°12E 272 b
Kounguolou Congo 3°31S 13°20E 264 C2
Kountze U.S.A. 30°22N 94°19W 314 F7
Koupéla Burkina Faso 12°11N 0°21W 263 C4
Kouponia Greece 37°57N 23°47E 112 B2
Kourémalé Mali 11°59N 8°42W 262 C3
Kouri-shima Japan 26°42N 128°1E 288 a
Kouris → Cyprus 34°38N 32°54E 207 F8
Kourizo, P. de Chad 22°28N 15°27E 258 D3
Kourou Fr. Guiana 5°9N 52°39W 329 B7
Kourouba Mali 13°22N 10°57W 262 C2
Koûroudjél Mauritania 16°12N 11°30W 262 B2
Kouroukoto Mali 12°35N 10°5W 262 C2
Kourouma Burkina Faso 11°35N 4°50W 262 C4
Kourouninkoto Mali 13°52N 9°35W 262 C3
Kouroussa Guinea 10°45N 9°45W 262 C3
Koussanar Senegal 13°52N 14°5W 262 C2
Koussané Mali 14°53N 11°14W 262 C2
Koussané Senegal 14°10N 12°22W 262 C2
Kousseri Cameroon 12°0N 14°55E 259 F2
Koutiala Mali 12°25N 5°23W 262 C3
Kouto Côte d'Ivoire 9°53N 6°25W 262 D3
Kouts U.S.A. 41°19N 87°2W 311 C9
Kouvé Togo 6°25N 1°25E 263 D5
Kouvola Finland 60°52N 26°43E 188 B4
Kouyi Congo 2°29S 12°25E 264 C2
Kouyou → Congo 0°44S 16°38E 264 C3
Kovačica Serbia 45°5N 20°38E 182 E5
Kovdor Russia 67°34N 30°24E 160 C24
Kovel Ukraine 51°11N 24°38E 177 C13
Kovilpatti India 9°10N 77°50E 245 K3
Kovin Serbia 44°44N 20°59E 182 F5
Kovno = Kaunas Lithuania 54°54N 23°54E 184 D10
Kovrov Russia 56°25N 41°25E 190 B5
Kovur Andhra Pradesh, India 17°3N 81°39E 244 F5
Kovur Andhra Pradesh, India 14°30N 80°1E 245 G5
Kowal Poland 52°32N 19°7E 185 F6
Kowalewo Pomorskie Poland 53°10N 18°52E 185 E5
Kowanyama Australia 15°29S 141°44E 280 B3
Kowanyama ✪ Australia 15°20S 141°47E 280 B3
Kowlīnī Afghan. 37°39N 65°58E 240 A2
Kowloon Hong Kong, China 22°19N 114°11E 122 B3
Kowloon Peak Hong Kong, China 22°20N 114°13E 122 A3
Kowloon Tong Hong Kong, China 22°20N 114°10E 122 B3
Kowŏn N. Korea 39°26N 127°14E 224 C3
Kōyama Japan 31°20N 130°56E 222 F2
Koyampattur = Coimbatore India 11°2N 76°59E 245 J3
Köyceğiz Turkey 36°57N 28°40E 205 E10
Köyceğiz Gölü Turkey 36°56N 28°42E 205 E10
Köytendag Turkmenistan 37°30N 66°1E 240 A2
Koyuk U.S.A. 64°56N 161°9W 303 D7
Koyukuk U.S.A. 64°53N 157°42W 303 D8
Koyukuk → U.S.A. 64°55N 157°32W 303 D8
Koyukuk Nat. Wildlife Refuge ⌓ U.S.A. 65°35N 156°30W 303 D8
Koyulhisar Turkey 40°20N 37°52E 212 B7
Koyunyeri Turkey 40°50N 26°26E 203 F10
Koza = Okinawa Japan 26°19N 127°46E 288 a
Kozak Turkey 39°15N 27°6E 205 B9
Kozaklı Turkey 39°13N 34°49E 212 C6
Kozan Turkey 37°26N 35°50E 212 D6
Kozani Greece 40°19N 21°47E 202 F5
Kozara Bos.-H. 45°0N 17°0E 199 D14
Kozara △ Bos.-H. 45°0N 17°0E 182 F2
Kozarac Bos.-H. 44°58N 16°48E 199 D13
Kozelets Ukraine 50°55N 31°7E 189 G6
Kozelsk Russia 54°2N 35°48E 188 E8
Kozhikode India 11°15N 75°43E 245 J2
Kozhva Russia 65°10N 57°0E 186 A10
Koziegłowy Poland 50°37N 19°8E 185 H6
Kozienice Poland 51°35N 21°34E 185 G8
Kozje Slovenia 46°5N 15°35E 199 B12
Kozloduy Bulgaria 43°45N 23°42E 202 C7
Kozlov = Michurinsk Russia 52°58N 40°27E 190 D5
Kozlovets Bulgaria 43°30N 25°20E 203 C9
Kozlovka Russia 55°52N 48°14E 190 C9
Kozlu Turkey 41°26N 31°45E 212 B4
Kozluk Turkey 38°11N 41°31E 213 C9
Koźmin Poland 51°48N 17°27E 185 G4
Kozmodemyansk Russia 56°20N 46°36E 190 B8
Kōzu-Shima Japan 34°13N 139°10E 223 C11
Kożuchów Poland 51°45N 15°31E 185 G2
Kozyatyn Ukraine 49°45N 28°50E 177 D15
Kozyrevsk Russia 56°3N 159°51E 215 D16
Kpabia Ghana 9°10N 0°20W 263 D4
Kpalimé Togo 6°57N 0°44E 263 D5
Kpandae Ghana 8°30N 0°2W 263 D4
Kpessi Togo 8°4N 1°16E 263 D5
Kra, Isthmus of = Kra, Kho Khot Thailand 10°15N 99°30E 237 G2
Kra, Kho Khot Thailand 10°15N 99°30E 237 G2
Kra Buri Thailand 10°22N 98°46E 237 G2
Kraai → S. Africa 30°40S 26°45E 270 D4
Kraainem Belgium 50°52N 4°28E 116 A2
Krabi Thailand 8°4N 98°55E 237 H2
Kracheh = Kratie Cambodia 12°32N 106°10E 236 F6
Kragan Indonesia 6°43S 111°38E 235 D4
Kragerø Norway 58°52N 9°25E 164 F6
Kragujevac Serbia 44°2N 20°56E 202 B4
Krailling Germany 48°5N 11°25E 131 B1
Krainburg = Kranj Slovenia 46°16N 14°22E 199 B11
Krajenka Poland 53°18N 16°59E 185 E3
Krak Castle = Crac des Chevaliers Syria 34°47N 36°18E 250 D7
Krakatau = Rakata, Pulau Indonesia 6°10S 105°20E 234 D3
Krakatoa = Rakata, Pulau Indonesia 6°10S 105°20E 234 D3
Krakau = Kraków Poland 50°4N 19°57E 185 H6
Krakor Cambodia 12°32N 104°12E 236 F5
Kraków Poland 50°4N 19°57E 185 H6
Kraków ✕ (KRK) Poland 50°5N 19°52E 185 H6
Kraksaan Indonesia 7°43S 113°23E 235 D4
Kralanh Cambodia 13°35N 103°25E 236 F4
Kralendijk Bonaire 12°9N 68°16W 322 h
Králiky Czechia 50°6N 16°45E 181 A9
Kraljevo Serbia 43°44N 20°41E 202 C4
Kralovéhradecký □ Czechia 50°25N 15°50E 180 A8
Královský Chlmec Slovakia 48°27N 22°0E 181 C14
Kralupy nad Vltavou Czechia 50°13N 14°20E 180 A7
Kramatorsk Ukraine 48°50N 37°30E 189 H9
Kramfors Sweden 62°55N 17°48E 162 B11
Kramis, C. Algeria 36°26N 0°45E 261 A5
Krampnitz Germany 52°27N 13°3E 115 B1
Krampnitzsee Germany 52°27N 13°3E 115 B1
Krania Greece 39°53N 21°18E 202 G5
Krania Elassonas Greece 39°57N 22°2E 204 B4
Kranidi Greece 37°20N 23°10E 204 D5
Kranj Slovenia 46°16N 14°22E 199 B11
Kranji Industrial Estate Singapore 1°26N 103°45E 138 A2
Kranji Res. Singapore 1°25N 103°44E 138 A2
Kranjska Gora Slovenia 46°29N 13°48E 199 B10
Krankskop S. Africa 28°0S 30°47E 271 C5
Kranz = Zelenogradsk Russia 54°53N 20°29E 184 D7
Krapina Croatia 46°10N 15°52E 199 B12
Krapina → Croatia 45°50N 15°50E 199 C12
Krapkowice Poland 50°29N 17°56E 185 H4
Krappitz = Krapkowice Poland 50°29N 17°56E 185 H4
Kras Slovenia 45°35N 14°0E 199 C10
Krasavino Russia 60°58N 46°29E 186 B8
Krasieo Res. Thailand 14°49N 99°30E 236 E2
Kraskino Russia 42°44N 130°48E 220 C5
Krāslava Latvia 55°54N 27°10E 188 E4
Kraslice Czechia 50°19N 12°31E 180 A5
Krasnaya Gorbatka Russia 55°52N 41°45E 190 C5
Krasnaya Polyana Russia 43°40N 40°13E 191 J5
Krasnaya Sloboda = Krasnoslobodsk Russia 48°42N 44°33E 191 F7
Krasne Ukraine 46°7N 29°15E 183 D14
Krasni Okny Ukraine 47°32N 29°27E 183 C14
Kraśnik Poland 50°55N 22°15E 185 H9
Krasno-Presnenskaya Russia 55°45N 37°32E 129 B2
Krasnoarmeisk Ukraine 48°18N 37°11E 189 H9
Krasnoarmeysk = Tayynsha Kazakhstan 53°50N 69°45E 217 B7
Krasnoarmeysk Russia 51°0N 45°42E 190 E7
Krasnoarmeyskiy Russia 47°0N 42°12E 191 G6
Krasnoarmeysky Rudnik = Dobropole Ukraine 48°25N 37°2E 189 H9
Krasnobrod Poland 50°33N 23°12E 185 H10
Krasnodar Russia 45°5N 39°0E 191 H4
Krasnodar □ Russia 46°30N 39°30E 191 G4
Krasnodarskoye Vdkhr. Russia 45°1N 39°23E 191 H4
Krasnodon Ukraine 48°17N 39°44E 189 H10
Krasnogorskiy Russia 56°10N 48°28E 190 B9
Krasnograd = Krasnohrad Ukraine 49°27N 35°27E 189 H8
Krasnogvardeysk = Gatchina Russia 59°35N 30°9E 188 C6
Krasnogvardeyskiy Ukraine 45°32N 34°16E 189 K8
Krasnogvardeyskoye Russia 45°52N 41°33E 191 H5
Krasnohrad Ukraine 49°27N 35°27E 189 H8
Krasnokamensk Russia 50°3N 118°0E 215 D12
Krasnokamsk Russia 58°4N 55°48E 186 C10
Krasnokokshaysk = Yoshkar Ola Russia 56°38N 47°55E 190 B8
Krasnokutsk Ukraine 50°10N 34°50E 189 G8
Krasnolesnyy Russia 51°53N 39°35E 189 G10
Krasnoperekopsk Ukraine 46°0N 33°54E 189 J7
Krasnorechenskiy Russia 44°41N 135°14E 220 B7
Krasnoselkup Russia 65°20N 82°10E 214 C9
Krasnoslobodsk Mordvinia, Russia 54°25N 43°45E 190 C6
Krasnoslobodsk Volgograd, Russia 48°42N 44°33E 191 F7
Krasnoturinsk Russia 59°46N 60°12E 186 C11
Krasnoufimsk Russia 56°36N 57°38E 186 C10
Krasnouralsk Russia 58°21N 60°3E 186 C11
Krasnovishersk Russia 60°23N 57°3E 186 B10
Krasnovodsk = Türkmenbashi Turkmenistan 40°5N 53°5E 247 A7
Krasnoyarsk Russia 56°8N 93°0E 215 D10
Krasnoyarskoye Russia 54°31N 21°56E 184 D8
Krasnoyarskoye Vdkhr. Russia 56°0N 92°30E 215 D10
Krasnoye = Krasnyy Russia 54°25N 31°30E 188 E6
Krasnoye = Ulan Erge Russia 46°19N 44°53E 191 G7
Krasnoyilsk Ukraine 47°59N 25°38E 183 C10
Krasnozavodsk Russia 56°27N 38°25E 188 D10
Krasnoznamensk Russia 54°57N 22°30E 184 D9
Krasny = Kyzyl Russia 51°50N 94°30E 217 B12
Krasny = Mozhga Russia 56°26N 52°15E 190 B11
Krasnystaw Poland 50°57N 23°5E 185 H10
Krasnyy Russia 54°25N 31°30E 188 E6
Krasnyy Boyevik = Kotovsk Russia 52°36N 41°32E 190 D5
Krasnyy Kholm Russia 58°10N 37°10E 188 C9
Krasnyy Kut Russia 50°50N 47°0E 190 E8
Krasnyy Liman Ukraine 48°58N 37°50E 189 H9
Krasnyy Luch Ukraine 48°13N 39°0E 189 H10
Krasnyy Profintern Russia 57°45N 40°27E 188 D11
Krasnyy Sulin Russia 47°52N 40°8E 191 G5
Krasnyy Yar Astrakhan, Russia 46°43N 48°23E 191 G9
Krasnyy Yar Samara, Russia 53°30N 50°22E 190 D10
Krasnyy Yar Volgograd, Russia 50°42N 44°45E 190 E7
Krasnyye Baki Russia 57°8N 45°10E 190 B7
Krasnyyoskolske Vdskh. Ukraine 49°27N 37°40E 189 H9
Kraszna → Hungary 48°4N 22°20E 182 B7
Kratie Cambodia 12°32N 106°10E 236 F6
Kratke Ra. Papua N. G. 6°45S 146°0E 286 D4
Kratovo N. Macedonia 42°6N 22°10E 202 D6
Krau Indonesia 3°19S 140°5E 231 E10
Kraulshavn = Nuussauq Greenland 74°8N 57°3W 154 C5
Kravanh, Chuor Phnum Cambodia 12°0N 103°32E 237 G4
Krč Czechia 50°2N 14°26E 135 B2
Krefeld Germany 51°20N 6°33E 178 D2
Kremaston, L. Greece 38°52N 21°30E 204 C3
Kremen Croatia 44°28N 15°53E 199 D12
Kremenchuk Ukraine 49°5N 33°25E 189 H7
Kremenchuksk Vdskh. Ukraine 49°20N 32°30E 189 H7
Kremenets Ukraine 50°8N 25°43E 177 C13
Kremennaya Ukraine 49°1N 38°10E 189 H10
Kremges = Svitlovodsk Ukraine 49°2N 33°13E 189 H7
Kremlin Moscow, Russia 129 c2
Kremmen Germany 52°45N 13°1E 178 C9
Kremmling U.S.A. 40°4N 106°24W 304 F10
Kremnica Slovakia 48°45N 18°50E 181 C11
Krems an der Donau Austria 48°25N 15°36E 180 C8
Kremsmünster Austria 48°3N 14°8E 180 C7
Krenau = Chrzanów Poland 50°10N 19°21E 185 H6
Krestena Greece 37°35N 21°37E 204 D3
Krestovskiye, Ostrov Russia 59°57N 30°14E 137 B1
Kretinga Lithuania 55°53N 21°15E 184 C8
Krettamia Algeria 28°47N 3°27W 260 C4
Krettsy Russia 58°15N 32°30E 188 C7
Kreuzberg Bayern, Germany 50°22N 9°58E 179 E5
Kreuzberg Berlin, Germany 52°30N 13°24E 115 A3
Kreuzburg = Kluczbork Poland 50°58N 18°12E 185 H5
Kreuztal Germany 50°57N 8°0E 178 E4
Kria Vrisi Greece 40°41N 22°18E 202 F6
Kribi Cameroon 2°57N 9°56E 263 E6
Krichem Bulgaria 42°8N 24°28E 203 D8
Krichev = Krychaw Belarus 53°40N 31°41E 177 B16
Kril'on, Mys Russia 45°53N 142°5E 220 B11
Krim Slovenia 45°53N 14°30E 199 C11
Krim-Krim Chad 9°0N 15°24E 259 G3
Krindachyovka = Krasnyy Luch Ukraine 48°13N 39°0E 189 H10
Krios, Akra Greece 35°13N 23°34E 207 E4
Krishna → India 15°57N 80°59E 245 G5
Krishnagiri India 12°32N 78°16E 245 H4
Krishnanagar India 23°24N 88°33E 243 H13
Krishnaraja Sagar India 12°20N 76°30E 245 H3
Kristdala Sweden 57°24N 16°13E 163 G10
Kristians = Oppland □ Norway 61°15N 9°40E 164 C6
Kristiansand Norway 58°8N 8°1E 164 F5
Kristianstad Sweden 56°2N 14°9E 163 H8
Kristiansund Norway 63°7N 7°45E 164 A4
Kristiinankaupunki Finland 62°16N 21°21E 160 E19
Kristinehamn Sweden 59°18N 14°7E 162 E8
Kristinestad = Kristiinankaupunki Finland 62°16N 21°21E 160 E19
Kristinopol = Chervonohrad Ukraine 50°25N 24°10E 177 C13
Krithoti, Akra Greece 38°30N 21°2E 207 B3
Kriti Greece 35°15N 25°0E 207 E6
Kritsa Greece 35°10N 25°41E 207 E6
Kritzendorf Austria 48°19N 16°18E 142 A1
Kriva → N. Macedonia 42°5N 21°47E 202 D5
Kriva Palanka N. Macedonia 42°11N 22°19E 202 D6
Krivaja → Bos.-H. 44°27N 18°9E 182 F3
Krivelj Serbia 44°10N 22°5E 202 B6
Křivoklátsko ⌓ Czechia 50°1N 13°51E 180 A6
Krivoy Rog = Kryvyy Rih Ukraine 47°51N 33°20E 189 J7
Križevci Croatia 46°3N 16°32E 199 B13
Krk Croatia 45°8N 14°40E 199 C11
Krka → Slovenia 45°50N 15°30E 199 C12
Krka △ Croatia 43°53N 15°56E 199 E12
Krkonoše Czechia 50°50N 15°35E 180 A8
Krkonoše △ Czechia 50°43N 15°39E 180 A8
Krnjaja = Kljajićevo Serbia 45°45N 19°17E 182 E4
Krnov Czechia 50°5N 17°40E 181 A10
Krobia Poland 51°47N 16°59E 185 G3
Krøderen Norway 60°9N 9°49E 164 D6
Krokees Greece 36°53N 22°32E 204 E4
Krokek Sweden 58°40N 16°24E 163 F10
Krokodil = Umgwenya → Mozam. 25°14S 32°18E 271 C5
Krokom Sweden 63°20N 14°30E 162 A8
Krokowa Poland 54°47N 18°9E 184 D5
Króksfjarðarnes Iceland 65°27N 21°56W 155 B5
Krokstadelva Norway 59°56N 10°1E 164 E7
Krolevets Ukraine 51°35N 33°20E 189 G7
Królewska Huta = Chorzów Poland 50°18N 18°57E 185 H5
Kroměříž Czechia 49°18N 17°21E 181 B10
Krompachy Slovakia 48°54N 20°52E 181 C13
Kromy Russia 52°48N 35°48E 189 F8
Kronach Germany 50°14N 11°19E 179 E7
Kronau = Kranjska Gora Slovenia 46°29N 13°48E 199 B10
Krong Kaoh Kong Cambodia 11°37N 102°59E 237 G4
Kronoberg □ Sweden 56°45N 14°30E 163 H8
Kronprins Christian Land Greenland 80°30N 22°0W 154 A8
Kronprins Frederik Land Greenland 81°0N 45°0W 154 A6
Kronprins Olav Kyst Antarctica 69°0S 42°0E 151 C5
Kronprinsesse Märtha Kyst Antarctica 73°30S 10°0W 151 D2
Kronshtadt Russia 59°57N 29°51E 188 C5
Kronstadt = Braşov Romania 45°38N 25°35E 183 E10
Kroonstad S. Africa 27°43S 27°19E 270 C4
Kröpelin Germany 54°4N 11°47E 178 A7
Kropotkin Russia 45°28N 40°28E 191 H5
Kropp Germany 54°24N 9°31E 178 A5
Kropyvnytskyy Ukraine 48°35N 32°20E 189 H7
Krosna Lithuania 54°23N 23°33E 184 D10
Krośniewice Poland 52°15N 19°11E 185 F6
Krosno Poland 49°42N 21°46E 185 J8
Krosno Odrzańskie Poland 52°3N 15°7E 185 F2
Krotoszyn Poland 51°42N 17°23E 185 G4
Krotovka Russia 53°18N 51°10E 190 D10
Krousonas Greece 35°13N 24°59E 207 E5
Krrabë Albania 41°13N 20°0E 202 E3
Krško Slovenia 45°57N 15°30E 199 C12
Krstača Serbia 42°57N 20°8E 202 D4
Kruger △ S. Africa 24°50S 26°10E 271 B4
Krugersdorp S. Africa 26°5S 27°46E 271 C4
Krui Indonesia 5°10S 103°55E 234 D2
Kruisfontein S. Africa 33°59S 24°43E 270 D3
Krujë Albania 41°32N 19°46E 202 E3
Krulevshchina = Krulyewshchyna Belarus 55°5N 27°45E 188 E4
Krulyewshchyna Belarus 55°5N 27°45E 188 E4
Krumbach Germany 48°13N 10°22E 179 G6
Krumë Albania 42°14N 20°28E 202 D4
Krummau = Český Krumlov Czechia 48°43N 14°21E 180 C7
Krumme Lanke Germany 52°27N 13°14E 115 B2
Krummensee Germany 52°35N 13°41E 115 A5
Krummhübel = Karpacz Poland 50°46N 15°46E 185 H2
Krumovgrad Bulgaria 41°29N 25°38E 203 E9
Krung Thep = Bangkok Thailand 13°45N 100°35E 113 B2
Krupanj Serbia 44°25N 19°22E 202 B3
Krupina Slovakia 48°22N 19°5E 181 C12
Krupinica → Slovakia 48°4N 18°55E 181 C11
Krupki Belarus 54°19N 29°8E 177 A15
Krusboda Sweden 59°13N 18°14E 139 B3
Krusenstern, C. U.S.A. 67°8N 163°45W 303 C7
Kruševac Serbia 43°35N 21°28E 202 C5
Kruševo N. Macedonia 41°23N 21°19E 202 E5
Krushchyov = Svitlovodsk Ukraine 49°2N 33°13E 189 H7
Krushë e Madhe Kosovo 42°19N 20°39E 202 D4
Krushelnytsya Ukraine 49°7N 23°29E 185 J10
Kruszwica Poland 52°40N 18°20E 185 F5
Kruzenshterna, Proliv Russia 48°0N 154°0E 215 E16
Krychaw Belarus 53°40N 31°41E 177 B16
Krymsk Russia 44°50N 38°0E 189 K10
Krymskyy Poluostrov = Krymskyy Pivostriv Ukraine 45°0N 34°0E 189 K8
Krymskyy Pivostriv Ukraine 45°0N 34°0E 189 K8
Krynica Poland 49°25N 20°57E 185 J7
Krynica Morska Poland 54°23N 19°28E 184 D6
Krynki Poland 53°17N 23°43E 185 E10
Krynychne Ukraine 45°32N 28°40E 183 E13
Kryvyy Rih Ukraine 47°51N 33°20E 189 J7
Kryzhopil Ukraine 48°23N 28°53E 183 B13
Krzemieniec = Kremenets Ukraine 50°8N 25°43E 177 C13
Krzepice Poland 50°58N 18°50E 185 H5
Krzeszów Poland 50°24N 22°21E 185 H9
Krzna → Poland 52°8N 23°32E 185 F10
Krzywiń Poland 51°58N 16°50E 185 G3
Krzyż Wielkopolski Poland 52°52N 16°0E 185 F2
Ksabi Morocco 32°51N 4°13W 260 B4
Ksar Chellala Algeria 35°13N 2°19E 261 A5
Ksar el Boukhari Algeria 35°51N 2°52E 261 A5
Ksar el Kebir Morocco 35°0N 6°0W 260 B3
Ksar es Souk = Er Rachidia Morocco 31°58N 4°20W 260 B4
Ksar es Srhir Morocco 35°51N 5°34W 195 E3
Ksar Rhilane Tunisia 33°0N 9°39E 258 B1
Ksiąz Wielkopolski Poland 52°4N 17°14E 185 F4
Ksour, Mts. des Algeria 32°45N 0°30W 261 B4
Kstovo Russia 56°12N 44°13E 190 B7
Ku, W. el → Sudan 13°37N 25°15E 257 E2
Ku-Ring-Gai Chase △ Australia 33°39S 151°14E 283 B9
Ku Tree Res. U.S.A. 21°30N 157°59W 302 J14
Kuah Malaysia 6°19N 99°51E 237 J2
Kuala Indonesia 2°55N 105°47E 234 B3
Kuala Belait Malaysia 4°35N 114°11E 235 B4
Kuala Berang Malaysia 5°5N 103°1E 237 K4
Kuala Dungun = Dungun Malaysia 4°45N 103°25E 237 K4
Kuala Kangsar Malaysia 4°46N 100°56E 237 K3
Kuala Kelawang Malaysia 2°56N 102°5E 237 L4
Kuala Kerai Malaysia 5°30N 102°12E 237 K4
Kuala Kubu Bharu Malaysia 3°34N 101°39E 237 L3
Kuala Lipis Malaysia 4°10N 102°3E 237 K4
Kuala Lumpur Malaysia 3°9N 101°41E 237 L3
Kuala Lumpur Int. ✕ (KUL) Malaysia 2°44N 101°42E 237 L3
Kuala Nerang Malaysia 6°16N 100°37E 237 J3
Kuala Pilah Malaysia 2°45N 102°15E 237 L4
Kuala Rompin Malaysia 2°49N 103°29E 237 L4
Kuala Selangor Malaysia 3°20N 101°15E 237 L3
Kuala Sepetang Malaysia 4°49N 100°28E 237 K3
Kuala Terengganu Malaysia 5°20N 103°8E 237 K4
Kualajelai Indonesia 2°58S 110°46E 235 C4
Kualakapuas Indonesia 2°55S 114°20E 235 C4
Kualakurun Indonesia 1°10S 113°50E 235 C4
Kualapembuang Indonesia 3°14S 112°38E 235 C4
Kualapesaguan Indonesia 2°1S 110°7E 235 C4
Kualapu'u U.S.A. 21°9N 157°2W 302 B4
Kualasimpang Indonesia 4°17N 98°3E 234 B1
Kualatungkal Indonesia 0°49S 103°28E 234 C2
Kualoa Pt. U.S.A. 21°31N 157°50W 302 J14
Kuamat Malaysia 5°13N 117°30E 235 A5
Kuan Shan Taiwan 23°14N 120°54E 225 C2
Kuanao Taiwan 24°31N 118°24E 225 a
Kuancheng China 40°37N 118°30E 227 D10
Kuandang Indonesia 0°56N 123°1E 231 D6
Kuandian China 40°45N 124°45E 224 B2
Kuando Kubango □ Angola 16°25S 20°0E 265 F4
Kuangchou = Guangzhou China 23°6N 113°13E 121 B2
Kuangfu Taiwan 23°40N 121°25E 225 C3
Kuanhsi Taiwan 24°48N 121°10E 225 B3
Kuanmiao Taiwan 22°58N 120°19E 225 D2
Kuanshan Taiwan 23°3N 121°9E 225 C3
Kuantan Malaysia 3°49N 103°20E 237 L4
Kuanyin Ilan, Taiwan 24°23N 121°46E 225 B3
Kuanyin Taoyüan, Taiwan 25°2N 121°4E 225 A3
Kuapā Pond U.S.A. 21°17N 157°43W 302 K14
Kuapnit Balinsasayao △ Phil. 10°53N 124°55E 233 F5
Kuba = Quba Azerbaijan 41°21N 48°32E 191 K9
Kubah △ Malaysia 1°35N 110°9E 235 B4
Kuban → Russia 45°20N 37°30E 189 K9
Kuban Depression = Prikubanskaya Nizmennost Russia 45°39N 38°33E 191 H4
Kubaysah Iraq 33°35N 42°37E 213 G10
Kubenskoye, Ozero Russia 59°40N 39°25E 188 C10
Kuberle = Krasnoarmeyskiy Russia 47°0N 42°12E 191 G6
Kubokawa = Shimanto Japan 33°12N 133°8E 222 D5
Kubor, Mt. Papua N. G. 6°10S 144°44E 286 D3
Kubrat Bulgaria 43°49N 26°31E 203 C10
Kubu Indonesia 8°16S 115°35E 231 J18
Kubumesaai Indonesia 1°31N 115°6E 235 B5
Kubutambahan Indonesia 8°5S 115°10E 231 J18
Kucar, Tanjung Indonesia 8°39S 114°34E 231 K18
Kučevo Serbia 44°30N 21°40E 202 B5
Kuchaman India 27°13N 74°47E 242 F6
Kuchchaveli Sri Lanka 8°49N 81°6E 245 K5
Kuchenspitze Austria 47°7N 10°12E 180 D3
Kuchinda India 21°44N 84°21E 243 J11
Kuching Malaysia 1°33N 110°25E 235 B4
Kuchino-eruba-Jima Japan 30°28N 130°12E 221 J5
Kuchino-Shima Japan 29°57N 129°55E 221 K4
Kuchinotsu Japan 32°36N 130°11E 222 E2
Kuchl Austria 47°37N 13°9E 180 D6
Kūchnay Darvīshān Afghan. 30°59N 64°10E 240 C2
Kuchurhan → Ukraine 46°33N 29°57E 183 D14
Kucing = Kuching Malaysia 1°33N 110°25E 235 B4
Kuçovë Albania 40°47N 19°57E 202 F3
Küçükbahçe Turkey 38°33N 26°24E 205 C8
Küçükköy Balıkesir, Turkey 39°16N 26°42E 205 B8
Küçükköy İstanbul, Turkey 41°3N 28°52E 122 B1
Küçükkuyu Turkey 39°32N 26°36E 205 B8
Küçükmenderes → Turkey 37°57N 27°16E 205 D9
Küçüksu Turkey 41°5N 29°5E 122 B2
Kud → Pakistan 26°5N 66°20E 242 F2
Kuda India 23°10N 71°15E 242 H4
Kuda Indonesia 1°1N 112°58E 235 B4
Kudahuvadhoo Maldives 2°40N 72°54E 272 d
Kudahuvadhoo Channel Maldives 2°40N 73°0E 272 d
Kudaka-shima Japan 26°9N 127°53E 288 a
Kudal India 16°2N 73°41E 245 F1
Kudalier → India 18°35N 79°48E 244 E4
Kudamatsu Japan 34°0N 131°52E 222 D3
Kudankita Tokyo, Japan 140 a3
Kudarebe Aruba 12°37N 70°4W 322 f
Kudat Malaysia 6°55N 116°55E 235 A5
Kudirkos Naumiestis Lithuania 54°46N 22°53E 184 D9
Kudowa-Zdrój Poland 50°27N 16°15E 185 H3
Kudremukh India 13°15N 75°20E 245 H2
Kudrovo Russia 59°54N 30°30E 137 B3
Kudus Indonesia 6°48S 110°51E 235 D4
Kudymkar Russia 59°1N 54°39E 186 C9
Kueishan Tao Taiwan 24°51N 121°57E 225 B3
Kueiyang = Guiyang China 26°32N 106°40E 228 D6
Kufra Oasis = Al Kufrah Libya 24°17N 23°15E 258 D4
Kufstein Austria 47°35N 12°11E 180 D5
Kugaaruk = Pelly Bay Canada 68°38N 89°50W 295 D14
Kugluktuk Canada 67°50N 115°5W 294 D8
Kugong I. Canada 56°18N 79°50W 298 A4
Kūh Dasht Iran 33°32N 47°36E 213 F12
Kūh-e Sorkh Iran 35°30N 58°45E 216 E5
Kūhak Iran 27°12N 63°10E 240 D1
Kuhan Pakistan 28°19N 67°14E 242 E2
Kūhbonān Iran 31°23N 56°19E 247 D8
Kūhestak Iran 26°47N 57°2E 247 E8
Kūhestān Afghan. 34°39N 61°12E 240 B1
Kūhīn Iran 36°22N 49°40E 247 B6
Kūhīrī Iran 26°55N 61°2E 247 E9
Kūhiston-Badakhshon □ Tajikistan 38°30N 73°0E 217 E8
Kuhmo Finland 64°7N 29°31E 160 D23
Kuhn Chae △ Thailand 19°8N 99°24E 236 C2
Kuhnsdorf Austria 46°37N 14°38E 180 E7
Kūhpāyeh Eşfahan, Iran 32°44N 52°20E 247 C7
Kūhpāyeh Kermān, Iran 30°35N 57°15E 247 D8
Kūhrān, Kūh-e Iran 26°46N 58°12E 247 E8
Kui Buri Thailand 12°3N 99°52E 237 F2
Kuiburi △ Thailand 12°10N 99°37E 237 F2
Kuichong China 22°38N 114°25E 219 a
Kuiseb → Namibia 22°59S 14°31E 270 B1
Kuito Angola 12°22S 16°55E 265 E3
Kuiu I. U.S.A. 57°45N 134°10W 296 B2
Kujalleq □ Greenland 60°40N 45°0W 154 E6
Kujang N. Korea 39°57N 126°1E 224 C3
Kujawsko-Pomorskie □ Poland 53°20N 18°30E 184 E5
Kuji Japan 40°11N 141°46E 220 D10
Kujū-San Japan 33°5N 131°15E 222 D3

Kuk Papua N. G. 5°47S 144°19E 286 C3
Kukarka = Sovetsk Russia 57°38N 48°53E 190 B9
Kukava Ukraine 48°37N 27°43E 183 B12
Kukavica Serbia 42°48N 21°57E 202 D5
Kukawa Nigeria 12°58N 13°27E 263 C7
Kuk'eng Taiwan 23°38N 120°33E 225 C2
Kukës Albania 42°5N 20°27E 202 D4
Kuki Japan 36°4N 139°40E 223 A11
Kukipi Papua N. G. 8°10S 146°6E 286 E4
Kukmor Russia 56°11N 50°54E 190 B10
Kükong = Shaoguan China 24°48N 113°35E 229 E9
Kuku Pt. Wake I. 19°18N 166°34E 302 b
Kukuan Taiwan 24°17N 121°2E 225 B3
Kukuihaele U.S.A. 20°5N 155°35W 302 C6
Kukup Malaysia 1°20N 103°27E 237 d
Kukup, Pulau Malaysia 1°18N 103°25E 237 d
Kukvidze Russia 50°40N 43°0E 190 E6
Kula Bulgaria 43°52N 22°36E 202 C6
Kula Serbia 45°37N 19°32E 182 E4
Kula Turkey 38°32N 28°40E 205 C10
Kula Gulf Solomon Is. 8°5S 157°18E 287 M9
K'ula Kangri Asia 28°14N 90°36E 241 A3
K'ula Shan Bhutan 28°14N 90°36E 241 A3
Kulachi Pakistan 31°56N 70°27E 242 D4
Kulai Malaysia 1°44N 103°35E 237 M4
Kulal, Mt. Kenya 2°43N 36°56E 266 D4
Kulaly Aral Kazakhstan 45°0N 50°5E 191 H10
Kulasekarappattinam India 8°20N 78°5E 245 K4
Kulassein I. Phil. 6°25N 120°41E 233 H3
Kulaura Bangla. 24°32N 92°3E 241 C4
Kulautuva Lithuania 54°56N 23°36E 184 D10
Kuldīga Latvia 56°58N 21°59E 184 B8
Kuldja = Yining China 43°58N 81°10E 217 D10
Kuldu Sudan 12°50N 28°30E 257 E2
Kulebaki Russia 55°22N 42°25E 190 C6
Kulen Cambodia 13°50N 104°40E 236 F5
Kulen Vakuf Bos.-H. 44°35N 16°2E 199 D13
Kulgam India 33°36N 75°2E 243 C6
Kulgera Australia 25°50S 133°18E 280 D1
Kulhudhuffushi Maldives 6°37N 73°3E 272 d
Kulim Malaysia 5°22N 100°34E 237 K3
Kulin Australia 32°40S 118°2E 279 F2
Kulittalai India 10°55N 78°25E 245 J4
Kulkayu = Hartley Bay Canada 53°25N 129°15W 296 C3
Kullen Sweden 56°18N 12°26E 163 H6
Kullu India 31°58N 77°6E 242 D7
Kulmbach Germany 50°6N 11°26E 179 E7
Kŭlob Tajikistan 37°55N 69°50E 217 E7
Kulosaari Finland 60°11N 25°0E 121 B3
Kulp Turkey 38°29N 41°2E 213 C9
Kulpawn → Ghana 10°20N 1°5W 263 D4
Kulsary = Qulsary Kazakhstan 46°59N 54°1E 187 E9
Kulti India 23°43N 86°50E 243 H12
Kulu Turkey 39°5N 33°4E 212 C5
Kulumadau Papua N. G. 9°3S 152°43E 286 E7
Kulunda Russia 52°35N 78°57E 217 B9
Kulundinskoye, Ozero Russia 53°0N 79°36E 217 B9
Kulungar Afghan. 34°0N 69°2E 242 C3
Kūlvand Iran 31°21N 54°35E 247 D7
Kulwin Australia 35°2S 142°42E 282 C5
Kulyab = Kŭlob Tajikistan 37°55N 69°50E 217 E7
Kuma Japan 33°39N 132°54E 222 D4
Kuma → Russia 44°55N 47°0E 191 H8
Kumafşarı Turkey 37°19N 29°32E 205 D11
Kumaganum Nigeria 13°8N 10°38E 263 C7
Kumagaya Japan 36°9N 139°22E 223 A11
Kumai Indonesia 2°44S 111°43E 235 C4
Kumai, Teluk Indonesia 3°0S 111°43E 235 C4
Kumalar Dağı Turkey 38°15N 30°20E 205 C12
Kumamba, Kepulauan Indonesia 1°36S 138°45E 231 E9
Kumamoto Japan 32°45N 130°45E 222 E2
Kumamoto □ Japan 32°55N 130°55E 222 E2
Kumano Japan 33°54N 136°5E 223 D8
Kumano-Nada Japan 33°47N 136°20E 223 D8
Kumanovo N. Macedonia 42°9N 21°42E 202 D5
Kumar → Afghan. 34°30N 70°28E 240 B3
Kumara N.Z. 42°37S 171°12E 285 C6
Kumarina Roadhouse Australia 24°41S 119°32E 279 D2
Kumarkhali Bangla. 23°51N 89°15E 241 D2
Kumasi Ghana 6°41N 1°38W 262 D4
Kumba Cameroon 4°36N 9°24E 263 E6
Kumbağ Turkey 40°51N 27°27E 203 F11
Kumbakonam India 10°58N 79°25E 245 J4
Kumbarilla Australia 27°15S 150°55E 281 D5
Kumbatine △ Australia 31°8S 152°35E 283 A10
Kumbhalgarh △ India 25°10N 73°35E 242 G5
Kumbhraj India 24°22N 77°3E 242 G7
Kumbia Australia 26°41S 151°39E 281 D5
Kumbo Cameroon 6°15N 10°36E 263 D7
Kumbukkan Oya → Sri Lanka 6°35N 81°40E 245 L5
Kŭmch'on N. Korea 38°10N 126°29E 224 C3
Kumdah Si. Arabia 20°23N 45°5E 248 B4
Kume-Shima Japan 26°20N 126°47E 221 L3
Kumeny Russia 58°10N 49°47E 190 A9
Kumertau Russia 52°45N 55°57E 186 D10
Kumharsain India 31°19N 77°27E 242 D7
Kumi Uganda 1°30N 33°58E 268 B3
Kumkale Turkey 39°59N 26°11E 203 G10
Kumkurgan = Qumqo'rgo'n Uzbekistan 37°49N 67°35E 240 A2
Kumla Örebro, Sweden 59°8N 15°10E 162 E9
Kumla Stockholm, Sweden 59°13N 18°11E 139 B3
Kumlu Turkey 36°21N 36°27E 250 B7
Kumluca Turkey 36°22N 30°20E 205 E12
Kummerower See Germany 53°49N 12°51E 178 B8
Kumo Nigeria 10°1N 11°12E 263 C7
Kumo älv = Kokemäenjoki → Finland 61°32N 21°44E 188 B1
Kumon Bum Myanmar 26°30N 97°15E 241 B6
Kumotori-Yama Japan 35°51N 138°57E 223 B10
Kumta India 14°29N 74°25E 245 G2
Kumtag Shamo China 39°40N 92°0E 218 D7
Kumukahi, C. U.S.A. 19°31N 154°49W 302 D7
Kumul = Hami China 42°55N 93°25E 218 C7
Kumusi → Papua N. G. 8°16S 148°13E 286 E5
Kumyalı = Koma Tou Yialou Cyprus 35°25N 34°8E 207 E10
Kumylzhenskaya Russia 49°51N 42°38E 190 F6
Kuna U.S.A. 43°30N 116°25W 304 E5
Kunágota Hungary 46°26N 21°3E 182 D6
Kunak Malaysia 4°41N 118°15E 235 B5
Kunashir, Ostrov Russia 44°0N 146°0E 215 E15
Kunchaung Myanmar 23°50N 96°35E 241 D6
Kunchha Nepal 28°8N 84°20E 243 E11
Kunda Estonia 59°30N 26°34E 188 C4
Kunda India 25°43N 81°31E 243 G9
Kundar → Pakistan 31°56N 69°19E 242 D3
Kundelungu △ Dem. Rep. of the Congo 10°30S 27°40E 269 E2
Kundelungu Ouest △ Dem. Rep. of the Congo 9°55S 27°17E 269 D2
Kundian Pakistan 32°27N 71°28E 242 C4
Kundiawa Papua N. G. 6°2S 145°1E 286 D3
Kundla India 21°21N 71°25E 242 J4
Kundur Indonesia 0°45N 103°25E 234 B2
Kunene □ Namibia 20°0S 14°0E 270 A1
Kung, Ao Thailand 8°5N 98°24E 237 a
Kunga → Bangla. 21°46N 89°30E 241 E2
Kungälv Sweden 57°53N 11°59E 163 G5
Kungens kurva Sweden 59°15N 17°53E 139 B1
Kunghit I. Canada 52°6N 131°3W 296 C2
Kungkuan Taiwan 24°35N 120°44E 225 B2
Kungliao Taiwan 25°1N 121°54E 225 A3
Kungliga Slottet Stockholm, Sweden 139 b2
Kungrad = Qŭnghirot Uzbekistan 43°2N 58°50E 216 D5
Kungsängen Sweden 59°29N 17°45E 162 E11
Kungsbacka Sweden 57°30N 12°5E 163 G6
Kungsgården Sweden 60°37N 16°35E 162 D10
Kungshamn Sweden 58°22N 11°15E 163 F5
Kungshatt Sweden 59°17N 17°53E 139 B1
Kungsholmen Sweden 59°20N 18°2E 139 A2
Kungsör Sweden 59°25N 16°5E 162 E10
Kungssuliao Taiwan 24°37N 120°45E 225 B2
Kungu Dem. Rep. of the Congo 2°47N 19°12E 264 B3
Kungur Russia 57°25N 56°57E 186 C10
Kungurri Australia 21°4S 148°45E 280 b
Kungyangon Myanmar 16°27N 96°20E 241 G6
Kunhar → Pakistan 34°20N 73°30E 243 B5
Kunhegyes Hungary 47°22N 20°36E 182 C5
Kunia U.S.A. 21°28N 158°4W 302 K13
Kunigami Japan 26°46N 128°12E 288 a
Kunimi-Dake Japan 32°33N 131°1E 222 E3
Kuningan Jakarta, Indonesia 6°13S 106°49E 122 B1
Kuningan Jawa Barat, Indonesia 6°59S 108°29E 235 D3
Kunisaki Japan 33°33N 131°45E 222 D3
Kunitachi Japan 35°41N 139°27E 140 A1
Kunjirap Daban Pakistan 36°52N 75°27E 240 A4
Kunlara Australia 34°54S 139°55E 282 C3
Kunlong Myanmar 23°20N 98°50E 228 F2
Kunlun Antarctica 80°25S 77°7E 151 E6
Kunlun Shan Asia 36°0N 86°30E 217 E11
Kunlun Shankou China 35°38N 94°4E 218 D7
Kunmadaras Hungary 47°28N 20°45E 182 C5
Kunming China 25°1N 102°41E 228 E4
Kunming Changshui Int. ✈ (KMG) China 24°59N 102°45E 228 E4
Kunming Hu China 39°59N 116°13E 114 B1
Kunmunya ❂ Australia 15°26S 124°42E 278 C3
Kunnamkulam India 10°38N 76°7E 245 J3
Kunów Poland 50°57N 21°17E 185 H8
Kunratice Czechia 50°0N 14°28E 135 B2
Kunshan China 31°22N 120°58E 229 B13
Kunsthistorischesmuseum Vienna, Austria 142 b1
Kunszentmárton Hungary 46°50N 20°20E 182 D5
Kunszentmiklós Hungary 47°2N 19°8E 182 C4
Kuntaur Senegal 13°40N 14°48W 262 C2
Kunua Papua N. G. 5°46S 154°43E 286 C8
Kununurra Australia 15°40S 128°50E 278 C4
Kunwari → India 26°26N 79°11E 243 F8
Kunya-Urgench = Köneürgench Turkmenistan 42°19N 59°10E 216 D5
Künzelsau Germany 49°17N 9°42E 179 F5
Kunzulu Dem. Rep. of the Congo 3°28S 16°12E 264 C3
Kuohsing Taiwan 24°2N 120°51E 225 B2
Kuopio Finland 62°53N 27°35E 160 E22
Kupa → Croatia 45°28N 16°24E 199 C13
Kupang Indonesia 10°19S 123°39E 231 F6
Kupchino Russia 59°50N 30°23E 137 B2
Kupiano Papua N. G. 10°4S 148°14E 286 F5
Küpikipiki'ö Pt. U.S.A. 21°15N 157°47W 302 K14
Kupino Russia 54°21N 77°16E 217 B9
Kupreanof I. U.S.A. 56°50N 133°30W 296 B2
Kupres Bos.-H. 43°56N 17°15E 182 G2
Kupyansk Ukraine 49°52N 37°35E 189 H9
Kupyansk-Uzlovoi Ukraine 49°40N 37°43E 189 H9
Kuqa China 41°35N 82°30E 217 D10
Kür → Azerbaijan 39°29N 49°15E 213 C13
Kur → Bhutan 26°50N 91°0E 241 B3
Kür Dili Azerbaijan 39°3N 49°13E 213 C13
Kura = Kür → Azerbaijan 39°29N 49°15E 213 C13
Kurahashi-Jima Japan 34°8N 132°31E 222 C4
Kuramo Waters Nigeria 6°25N 3°26E 124 B2
Kuranda Australia 16°48S 145°35E 280 B4
Kuranga India 22°4N 69°10E 242 H3
Kurashiki Japan 34°40N 133°50E 222 C5
Kurayn Si. Arabia 27°39N 49°50E 247 E6
Kurayoshi Japan 35°26N 133°50E 222 B5
Kurbağalı → Turkey 40°58N 29°1E 122 C2
Kürchatov Kazakhstan 50°45N 78°32E 217 B9
Kurchatov Russia 51°40N 35°39E 189 G8
Kürdämir Azerbaijan 40°25N 48°3E 191 K9
Kurdistan Asia 37°20N 43°30E 213 D10
Kurduvadi India 18°8N 75°29E 244 E2
Kŭrdzhali = Kardzhali Bulgaria 41°38N 25°21E 203 E9
Kure Japan 34°14N 132°32E 222 C4
Küre Turkey 41°48N 33°43E 212 B5
Küre Dağları Turkey 41°50N 34°10E 212 B6
Kure I. U.S.A. 28°25N 178°25W 302 F8
Kuressaare Estonia 58°15N 22°30E 188 C2
Kurgan Russia 55°26N 65°18E 216 A7
Kurgan-Tyube = Qŭrghonteppa Tajikistan 37°50N 68°47E 217 E7
Kurganinsk Russia 44°54N 40°34E 191 H5
Kurgannaya = Kurganinsk Russia 44°54N 40°34E 191 H5
Kuri India 26°37N 70°43E 242 F4
Kuria Maria Is. = Ḩallāniyat, Jazā'ir al Oman 17°30N 55°58E 249 C6
Kurichchi India 11°36N 77°35E 245 J3
Kuridala Australia 21°16S 140°29E 280 C3
Kurigram Bangla. 25°49N 89°39E 241 C2
Kurihara Japan 35°45N 139°34E 140 A2
Kurikka Finland 62°36N 22°24E 160 E20
Kuril Basin Pac. Oc. 47°0N 150°0E 150 E15
Kuril Is. = Kurilskiye Ostrova Russia 45°0N 150°0E 215 E16
Kuril-Kamchatka Trench Pac. Oc. 44°0N 153°0E 288 C7
Kurilsk Russia 45°14N 147°53E 215 E15
Kurilskiye Ostrova Russia 45°0N 150°0E 215 E16
Kurino Japan 31°57N 130°43E 222 F2
Kurinskaya Kosa = Kür Dili Azerbaijan 39°3N 49°13E 213 C13
Kurisches Haff = Kurshskiy Zaliv Russia 55°9N 21°6E 184 C8
Kürkçü Turkey 36°34N 33°39E 250 B4
Kurkheda India 20°37N 80°12E 244 D5
Kurkur Egypt 23°50N 32°0E 256 C3
Kurla India 19°4N 72°52E 130 A2
Kurlkuta ❂ Australia 24°0S 127°5E 278 D4
Kurlovskiy Russia 55°25N 40°40E 190 C5
Kurmuk Sudan 10°33N 34°21E 257 E3
Kurmuri India 19°4N 72°53E 130 A2
Kurnool India 15°45N 78°0E 245 G4
Kuro-Shima Kagoshima, Japan 30°50N 129°57E 221 J4
Kuro-Shima Okinawa, Japan 24°14N 124°1E 221 M2
Kurobe-Gawe → Japan 36°55N 137°25E 223 A9
Kurogi Japan 33°12N 130°40E 222 D2
Kuror, J. Sudan 20°27N 31°30E 256 C3
Kurow N.Z. 44°44S 170°29E 285 E5
Kurów Poland 51°23N 22°12E 185 G9
Kurrajong Australia 33°33S 150°42E 283 B9
Kurram → Pakistan 32°36N 71°20E 242 C4
Kurri Kurri Australia 32°50S 151°28E 283 B9
Kurrimine Australia 17°47S 146°6E 280 B4
Kursavka Russia 44°29N 42°32E 191 H6
Kurse Korhi India 20°14N 80°46E 244 D5
Kurseong = Karsiyang India 26°56N 88°18E 241 B2
Kürshim Kazakhstan 48°34N 83°39E 217 C10
Kurshskaya Kosa ⌓ Russia 55°7N 20°45E 184 C7
Kurshskiy Zaliv Russia 55°9N 21°6E 184 C8
Kuršiu Nerijos △ Lithuania 55°30N 21°6E 184 C8
Kursk Russia 51°42N 36°11E 189 G9
Kursk □ Russia 51°50N 36°10E 189 G9
Kursu = Salla Finland 66°50N 28°49E 160 C23
Kuršumlija Serbia 43°9N 21°19E 202 C5
Kuršumlijska Banja Serbia 43°3N 21°11E 202 C5
Kurşunlu Bursa, Turkey 40°3N 29°40E 203 F13
Kurşunlu Çankırı, Turkey 40°51N 33°15E 212 B5
Kurtalan Turkey 37°56N 41°44E 213 D9
Kurtbey Turkey 41°9N 26°35E 203 E10
Kurtistown U.S.A. 19°36N 155°4W 302 D6
Kuru South Sudan 7°43N 26°31E 257 F2
Kuru, Bahr el → South Sudan 8°10N 26°50E 257 F2
Kurucaşile Turkey 41°49N 32°42E 212 B5
Kuruçay Turkey 39°39N 38°29E 246 B3
Kurukshetra = Thanesar India 30°1N 76°52E 242 D7
Kuruktag China 41°0N 89°0E 217 D11
Kuruman S. Africa 27°28S 23°28E 270 C3
Kuruman → S. Africa 26°56S 20°39E 270 C3
Kurume Fukuoka, Japan 33°15N 130°30E 222 D2
Kurume Tōkyō, Japan 35°45N 139°31E 140 A2
Kurun → South Sudan 5°30N 34°17E 257 F3
Kurunegala Sri Lanka 7°30N 80°23E 245 L5
Kurupukari Guyana 4°43N 58°37W 329 C6
Kurya Russia 61°42N 57°9E 186 B10
Kuryanovo Russia 55°39N 37°42E 129 C3
Kus Gölü Turkey 40°10N 27°55E 203 F11
Kuşadası Turkey 37°52N 27°15E 212 D2
Kuşadası Körfezı Turkey 37°56N 27°0E 205 D8
Kusamba Indonesia 8°34S 115°27E 231 K18
Kusatsu Gumma, Japan 36°37N 138°36E 223 A10
Kusatsu Shiga, Japan 34°58N 135°57E 223 C7
Kusawa L. Canada 60°20N 136°13W 296 A1
Kusel Germany 49°32N 7°24E 179 F3
Kushaka Nigeria 10°32N 6°48E 263 C6
Kushalgarh India 23°10N 74°27E 242 H6
Kushalnagar India 12°14N 75°57E 245 H2
Kushchevskaya Russia 46°33N 39°35E 191 G4
Kusheriki Nigeria 10°33N 6°28E 263 C6
Kushikino Japan 31°44N 130°16E 222 F2
Kushima Japan 31°29N 131°14E 222 F3
Kushimoto Japan 33°28N 135°47E 223 D7
Kushiro Japan 43°0N 144°25E 220 C12
Kushiro-Gawa → Japan 42°59N 144°23E 220 C12
Kushiro Shitsugen △ Japan 43°9N 144°26E 220 C12
Kūshk Iran 28°46N 56°51E 247 D8
Kushka = Serhetabat Turkmenistan 35°20N 62°18E 247 C9
Kushmurun = Qusmuryn Kazakhstan 52°27N 64°36E 216 B6
Kushnytsya Ukraine 48°27N 23°15E 183 B8
Kushol India 33°40N 76°36E 243 C7
Kushtia Bangla. 23°55N 89°5E 241 D2
Kushva Russia 58°18N 59°45E 186 C10
Kuskan Turkey 36°29N 33°17E 250 B4
Kuskokwim → U.S.A. 60°5N 162°25W 303 F7
Kuskokwim B. U.S.A. 59°45N 162°25W 303 G7
Kuskokwim Mts. U.S.A. 62°30N 156°0W 303 E9
Kuskovo Russia 55°44N 37°48E 129 B3
Kusmi India 23°17N 83°55E 243 H10
Kusŏng N. Korea 39°59N 125°15E 224 C2
Kussharo-Ko Japan 43°38N 144°21E 220 C12
Kustanay = Qostanay Kazakhstan 53°10N 63°35E 216 B6
Küstenje = Constanţa Romania 44°14N 28°38E 183 F13
Kustia India 22°31N 88°23E 124 B2
Küstrin = Kostrzyn Poland 52°35N 14°39E 185 F1
Kusu Japan 33°16N 131°9E 222 D3
Kut, Ko Thailand 11°40N 102°35E 237 G4
Kuta Indonesia 8°43S 115°11E 231 K18
Kutacane Indonesia 3°50N 97°50E 234 B1
Kütahya Turkey 39°30N 30°2E 205 B12
Kütahya □ Turkey 39°10N 29°30E 205 B11
Kutai △ Indonesia 0°23N 117°16E 235 B5
Kutaisi Georgia 42°19N 42°40E 191 J6
Kutaraja = Banda Aceh Indonesia 5°35N 95°20E 234 A1
Kutch, Gulf of = Kachchh, Gulf of India 22°50N 69°15E 242 H3
Kutch, Rann of = Kachchh, Rann of India 24°0N 70°0E 242 H4
Kutina Croatia 45°29N 16°48E 199 C13
Kutiyana India 21°36N 70°2E 242 J4
Kutjevo Croatia 45°23N 17°55E 182 E2
Kutkai Myanmar 23°27N 97°56E 241 D6
Kutkashen = Qäbälä Azerbaijan 40°58N 47°47E 191 K8
Kutná Hora Czechia 49°57N 15°16E 180 B8
Kutno Poland 52°15N 19°23E 185 F6
Kutru India 19°5N 80°46E 244 E5
Kutse Botswana 21°7S 22°16E 270 B3
Kuttabul Australia 21°1S 148°54E 280 b
Kutu Dem. Rep. of the Congo 2°40S 18°11E 264 C3
Kutu Moke Dem. Rep. of the Congo 3°12S 17°21E 264 C3
Kutum Sudan 14°10N 24°40E 257 E1
Kúty Slovakia 48°40N 17°3E 181 C10
Kuty Ukraine 48°16N 25°11E 183 B10
Kuujjuaq Canada 58°6N 68°15W 295 F18
Kuujjuarapik Canada 55°20N 77°35W 298 A4
Kuusamo Finland 65°57N 29°8E 160 D23
Kuusankoski Finland 60°55N 26°38E 188 B4
Kuvango Angola 14°28S 16°20E 265 E3
Kuvshinovo Russia 57°2N 34°11E 188 D8
Kuwait = Al Kuwayt Kuwait 29°30N 48°0E 246 D5
Kuwait ■ Asia 29°30N 47°30E 246 D5
Kuwana Japan 35°5N 136°43E 223 B8
Kuwana → India 26°25N 83°15E 243 F10
Kuwol-san N. Korea 38°30N 125°15E 224 C2
Kuybyshev = Samara Russia 53°8N 50°6E 190 D10
Kuybyshev Russia 55°27N 78°19E 214 D8
Kuybyshevka-Vostochnaya = Belogorsk Russia 51°0N 128°20E 215 D13
Kuybyshevo Ukraine 47°25N 36°40E 189 J9
Kuybyshevskoye Vdkhr. Russia 55°2N 49°30E 190 C9
Kuye He → China 38°23N 110°46E 226 E6
Kūyeh Iran 38°45N 47°57E 246 B5
Kuyto, Ozero Russia 65°6N 31°20E 160 D24
Kuytun China 44°25N 85°0E 217 D11
Kuyucak Turkey 37°55N 28°28E 205 D10
Kuyumba Russia 60°58N 96°59E 215 C10
Kuzey Anadolu Dağları Turkey 41°0N 36°45E 212 B7
Kuzguncuk Turkey 41°2N 29°2E 122 B2
Kuzhitturai India 8°18N 77°11E 245 K3
Kuzitrin → U.S.A. 65°10N 165°25W 303 D6
Kuzmin Serbia 45°2N 19°25E 182 E4
Kuznetsk Russia 53°12N 46°40E 190 D8
Kuznetsovo = Konakovo Russia 56°40N 36°51E 188 D9
Kuzomen Russia 66°22N 36°50E 186 A6
Kuzucubelen Turkey 36°51N 34°27E 250 B5
Kuzyminki Russia 55°42N 37°46E 129 B3
Kvænangen Norway 70°5N 21°15E 160 A19
Kværndrup Denmark 55°10N 10°31E 163 J4
Kvaløya Norway 69°40N 18°30E 160 B18
Kvam Norway 61°40N 9°42E 164 C6
Kvänum Sweden 58°18N 13°11E 163 F7
Kvareli = Qvareli Georgia 41°57N 45°47E 191 K7
Kvarner Croatia 44°50N 14°10E 199 D11
Kvarnerič Croatia 44°43N 14°37E 199 D11
Kvås Norway 58°16N 7°14E 164 F4
Kvernaland Norway 58°47N 5°45E 164 F2
Kvichak B. U.S.A. 58°48N 157°30W 303 G8
Kvicksund Sweden 59°27N 16°19E 162 E10
Kvikne Norway 62°35N 10°16E 164 B7
Kvillsfors Sweden 57°24N 15°29E 163 G9
Kvina → Norway 58°19N 6°55E 164 F3
Kvinlog Norway 58°31N 6°55E 164 F3
Kvirily = Zestaponi Georgia 42°6N 43°0E 191 J6
Kvismare kanal Sweden 59°11N 15°35E 162 E9
Kvissleby Sweden 62°18N 17°22E 162 B11
Kviteseid Norway 59°24N 8°29E 164 E5
Kvitøya Svalbard 80°8N 32°35E 154 A14
Kwabhaca S. Africa 30°51S 29°0E 271 D4
Kwai = Khwae Noi → Thailand 14°1N 99°32E 236 E2
Kwai Chung Hong Kong, China 22°22N 114°7E 122 A2
Kwajalein Marshall Is. 9°5N 167°20E 288 G8
Kwakhanai Botswana 21°39S 21°16E 270 B3
Kwakoegron Suriname 5°12N 55°25W 329 B6
Kwale Coast, Kenya 4°15S 39°31E 268 C4
Kwale Nigeria 5°46N 6°26E 263 D6
Kwamalasamutu Suriname 2°20N 56°47W 329 C6
KwaMashu S. Africa 29°45S 30°58E 271 C5
Kwamouth Dem. Rep. of the Congo 3°9S 16°12E 264 C3
Kwando → Africa 18°27S 23°32E 265 F4
Kwangchow = Guangzhou China 23°6N 113°13E 121 B2
Kwangdaeri N. Korea 40°34N 127°33E 227 D14
Kwango □ Dem. Rep. of the Congo 7°0S 18°0E 265 D3
Kwango → Dem. Rep. of the Congo 3°14S 17°22E 264 C3
Kwangsi-Chuang = Guangxi Zhuangzu Zizhiqu □ China 24°0N 109°0E 228 F7
Kwangtung = Guangdong □ China 23°0N 113°0E 229 F9
Kwanza Norte □ Angola 8°50S 14°30E 265 D2
Kwanza Sul □ Angola 10°50S 14°50E 265 E2
Kwara □ Nigeria 8°45N 4°30E 263 D6
Kwataboahegan → Canada 51°9N 80°50W 298 B3
Kwatisore Indonesia 3°18S 134°50E 231 E8
KwaZulu Natal □ S. Africa 29°0S 30°0E 271 C5
Kweichow = Guizhou □ China 27°0N 107°0E 228 D6
Kweilin = Guilin China 25°18N 110°15E 229 E8
Kweisui = Hohhot China 40°52N 111°40E 226 D6
Kweiyang = Guiyang China 26°32N 106°40E 228 D6
Kwekwe Zimbabwe 18°58S 29°48E 269 F2
Kweneng □ Botswana 24°0S 25°0E 270 B3
Kwenge → Dem. Rep. of the Congo 4°50S 18°44E 265 C3
Kwethluk U.S.A. 60°49N 161°26W 303 F7
Kwidzyn Poland 53°44N 18°55E 184 E5
Kwigillingok U.S.A. 59°51N 163°8W 303 G7
Kwiha Ethiopia 13°29N 39°32E 257 E4
Kwikila Papua N. G. 9°49S 147°38E 286 E4
Kwilu □ Dem. Rep. of the Congo 5°30S 19°0E 265 C3
Kwilu → Dem. Rep. of the Congo 3°22S 17°22E 265 C3
Kwinana Australia 32°15S 115°47E 279 F2
Kwinbet Myanmar 16°20N 94°14E 241 G5
Kwisa → Poland 51°34N 15°24E 185 G2
Kwoka Indonesia 0°31S 132°27E 231 E8
Kwolla Nigeria 9°0N 9°15E 263 D6
Kwun Tong Hong Kong, China 22°19N 114°13E 122 B3
Kya-in-Seikkyi Myanmar 16°2N 98°8E 241 G7
Kyabé Chad 9°30N 19°0E 259 G3
Kyabra Cr. → Australia 25°36S 142°55E 281 D3
Kyabram Australia 36°19S 145°4E 283 D6
Kyaikkami Myanmar 16°4N 97°34E 241 G6
Kyaiklat Myanmar 16°25N 95°40E 241 G5
Kyaikmaraw Myanmar 16°23N 97°44E 241 G6
Kyaikthin Myanmar 23°32N 95°40E 241 D5
Kyaikto Myanmar 17°20N 97°3E 236 D1
Kyaing Tong = Keng Tung Myanmar 21°18N 99°39E 236 B2
Kyakhta Russia 50°30N 106°25E 215 D11
Kyambura ⌓ Uganda 0°7S 30°9E 268 C3
Kyan-zaki Japan 26°5N 127°39E 288 a
Kyancutta Australia 33°8S 135°33E 281 E2
Kyangin Myanmar 18°20N 95°20E 241 F5
Kyaukhnyat Myanmar 18°15N 97°31E 241 F6
Kyaukki Myanmar 18°27N 96°56E 241 F6
Kyaukkyi Myanmar 18°15N 94°29E 241 F5
Kyaukme Myanmar 22°32N 97°2E 241 D6
Kyaukpadaung Myanmar 20°52N 95°8E 241 E5
Kyaukpyu Myanmar 19°28N 93°30E 241 F4
Kyaukse Myanmar 21°36N 96°10E 241 E6
Kyauktaga Myanmar 18°10N 96°37E 241 F6
Kyauktan Myanmar 16°38N 96°19E 241 G6
Kyauktaw Myanmar 20°51N 92°59E 241 E4
Kyaunggon Myanmar 17°6N 95°11E 241 G5
Kyawkku Myanmar 21°48N 96°56E 241 E6
Kybartai Lithuania 54°39N 22°45E 184 D9
Kyburz U.S.A. 38°47N 120°18W 306 G6
Kyeintali Myanmar 18°0N 94°29E 241 G5
Kyelang India 32°35N 77°2E 242 C7
Kyenjojo Uganda 0°40N 30°37E 268 B3
Kyidaunggan Myanmar 19°53N 96°12E 241 F6
Kyiv Ukraine 50°30N 30°28E 189 G6
Kyiv □ Ukraine 50°5N 30°45E 189 G6
Kyje Czechia 50°6N 14°33E 135 B3
Kyjov Czechia 49°1N 17°7E 181 B10
Kyklades Greece 37°0N 24°30E 204 E6
Kyle Sask., Canada 50°50N 108°2W 297 C7
Kyle Tex., U.S.A. 29°59N 97°53W 314 F6
Kyle Dam = Mutirikwe Dam Zimbabwe 20°15S 31°0E 269 G3
Kyle of Lochalsh U.K. 57°17N 5°44W 167 D3
Kyll → Germany 49°48N 6°41E 179 F2
Kyllburg Germany 50°2N 6°34E 179 E2
Kyllini Greece 37°55N 21°8E 207 D3
Kyllini, Akra Greece 37°57N 21°8E 207 D3
Kymijoki → Finland 60°30N 26°55E 188 B4
Kymmene älv = Kymijoki → Finland 60°30N 26°55E 188 B4
Kyneton Australia 37°10S 144°29E 282 D6
Kynuna Australia 21°37S 141°55E 280 C3
Kyō-ga-Saki Japan 35°45N 135°15E 223 B7
Kyoga, L. Uganda 1°35N 33°0E 268 B3
Kyogle Australia 28°40S 153°0E 281 D5
Kyom → South Sudan 8°58N 28°13E 257 F2
Kyŏngju = Gyeongju S. Korea 35°51N 129°14E 224 E4
Kyŏngsŏng N. Korea 41°35N 129°36E 224 B4
Kyōtamba Japan 35°6N 135°17E 223 B7
Kyōto Japan 35°0N 135°45E 223 C7
Kyōto □ Japan 35°15N 135°45E 223 B7
Kyparissovouno Cyprus 35°19N 33°10E 207 E9
Kyperounda Cyprus 34°56N 32°58E 207 F8
Kypros = Cyprus ■ Asia 35°0N 33°0E 207 F9
Kyrenia Cyprus 35°20N 33°20E 207 E9
Kyrgyzstan ■ Asia 42°0N 75°0E 217 D9
Kyritz Germany 52°56N 12°24E 178 C8
Kyrkhult Sweden 56°22N 14°34E 163 H8
Kyrksæterøra Norway 63°18N 9°5E 164 A6
Kyrnasivka Ukraine 48°35N 28°58E 183 B13
Kyrnychky Ukraine 45°42N 29°4E 183 E14
Kyro älv = Kyrönjoki → Finland 63°14N 21°45E 160 E19
Kyrönjoki → Finland 63°14N 21°45E 160 E19
Kystatyam Russia 67°20N 123°10E 215 C13
Kysucké Nové Mesto Slovakia 49°18N 18°47E 181 B11
Kytay, Ozero Ukraine 45°40N 29°13E 183 E14
Kythira Greece 36°8N 23°0E 204 E5
Kythnos Greece 37°26N 24°27E 204 D6
Kythréa Cyprus 35°15N 33°29E 207 E9
Kyu-hkok Myanmar 24°4N 98°4E 241 C7
Kyūhōji Japan 34°38N 135°33E 133 B2
Kyunhla Myanmar 23°25N 95°15E 241 D5
Kyuquot Sound Canada 50°2N 127°22W 296 D3
Kyurdamir = Kürdämir Azerbaijan 40°25N 48°3E 191 K9
Kyūshū Japan 33°0N 131°0E 222 E3
Kyūshū □ Japan 33°0N 131°0E 222 E3
Kyūshū-Palau Ridge Pac. Oc. 20°0N 136°0E 288 E5
Kyūshū-Sanchi Japan 32°35N 131°17E 222 E3
Kyūshū Trench Japan 31°35N 134°10E 222 F6
Kyustendil Bulgaria 42°16N 22°41E 202 D6
Kyustendil □ Bulgaria 42°16N 22°41E 202 D6
Kyusyur Russia 70°19N 127°30E 215 B13
Kywong Australia 34°58S 146°44E 283 C7
Kyyiv = Kyiv Ukraine 50°30N 30°28E 189 G6
Kyyivske Vdskh. Ukraine 51°0N 30°25E 177 C16
Kyzyl Russia 51°50N 94°30E 217 B12
Kyzyl-Adyr Kyrgyzstan 42°39N 71°35E 217 D8
Kyzyl-Burun = Siyäzän Azerbaijan 41°3N 49°10E 191 K9
Kyzyl-Khoto = Kyzyl Russia 51°50N 94°30E 217 B12
Kyzyl Kum Uzbekistan 42°30N 65°0E 217 D7
Kyzyl-Kyya Kyrgyzstan 40°16N 72°8E 217 D8
Kyzyl Orda = Qyzylorda Kazakhstan 44°48N 65°28E 216 D7
Kyzyl-Suu Kyrgyzstan 42°20N 78°0E 217 D9

L

L.A. County Art Museum U.S.A. 34°4N 118°21W 126 B2
L.F. Wade Int. ✈ (BDA) Bermuda 32°22N 64°41W 153 a
La Albuera Spain 38°45N 6°49W 195 G4
La Alcarria Spain 40°31N 2°45W 196 E2
La Almarcha Spain 39°41N 2°24W 196 F2
La Almunia de Doña Godina Spain 41°29N 1°23W 196 D3
La Amistad △ Cent. Amer. 9°28N 83°18W 320 E3
La Asunción Venezuela 11°2N 63°51W 329 a
La Baie Canada 48°19N 70°53W 299 C5
La Banda Argentina 27°45S 64°10W 334 B3
La Bañeza Spain 42°17N 5°54W 194 C5
La Barca Mexico 20°17N 102°34W 318 C4
La Barceloneta Spain 41°22N 2°11E 114 A2
La Barge U.S.A. 42°16N 110°12W 304 E8
La Barra Nic. 12°54N 83°33W 320 D3
La Bastide-Puylaurent France 44°35N 3°55E 174 D7
La Baule France 47°17N 2°24W 172 E4
La Belle Fla., U.S.A. 26°46N 81°26W 317 J8
La Belle Mo., U.S.A. 40°7N 91°55W 310 D5
La Biche → Canada 59°57N 123°50W 296 B4
La Biche, L. Canada 54°50N 112°3W 296 C6
La Bisbal d'Empordà Spain 41°58N 3°2E 196 D8
La Blanca Chile 33°30S 70°40W 137 C2
La Boca Argentina 34°38S 58°22W 117 B2
La Brea Peru 4°40S 81°7W 330 A1
La Brea Trin. & Tob. 10°15N 61°37W 323 t
La Brède France 44°41N 0°32W 174 D3
La Bresse France 48°2N 6°53E 173 D13
La Bretèche France 48°51N 2°1E 134 A1
La Bureba Spain 42°36N 3°24W 194 C7
La Cal → Bolivia 17°27S 58°15W 331 D6
La Calera Chile 32°50S 71°10W 334 C1
La Calle = El Kala Algeria 36°53N 8°26E 261 A6
La Campana △ Chile 32°58S 71°14W 334 C1
La Campiña Lima, Peru 12°11S 77°0W 124 C2
La Campiña Spain 37°45N 4°45W 195 H6
La Canal = Sa Canal Spain 38°51N 1°23E 206 D1
La Cañiza = A Cañiza Spain 42°13N 8°16W 194 C2
La Canourgue France 44°26N 3°13E 174 D7
La Capelle France 49°59N 3°50E 173 C10
La Carlota Argentina 33°30S 63°20W 334 C3
La Carlota Phil. 10°25N 122°55E 233 F4
La Carlota Spain 37°40N 4°56W 195 H6
La Carolina Spain 38°17N 3°38W 195 G7
La Castellana Phil. 10°20N 123°3E 233 F4
La Cavalerie France 44°1N 3°10E 174 D7
La Ceiba Honduras 15°40N 86°50W 320 C2
La Ceiba Venezuela 9°28N 71°4W 328 C3
La Celle-St-Cloud France 48°50N 2°9E 134 A1
La Certosa, Isole Venice, Italy 142 b5
La Chaise-Dieu France 45°18N 3°42E 174 C7
La Chapelle d'Angillon France 47°21N 2°25E 173 E9
La Chapelle-St-Luc France 48°20N 4°3E 173 D11
La Chapelle-sur-Erdre France 47°18N 1°34W 172 E5
La Charité-sur-Loire France 47°10N 3°1E 173 E10
La Chartre-sur-le-Loir France 47°44N 0°34E 172 E7
La Châtaigneraie France 46°39N 0°44W 174 B3
La Châtre France 46°35N 2°0E 173 F9
La Chaux → Mauritius 20°23S 57°41E 272 e
La Chaux-de-Fonds Switz. 47°7N 6°50E 179 H2
La Chorrera Colombia 0°44S 73°1W 328 D3
La Chorrera Panama 8°53N 79°47W 320 c
La Ciotat France 43°10N 5°37E 175 E9
La Cisterna Chile 33°32S 70°39W 137 C2
La Ciudadela Mexico City, Mexico 128 c2
La Clayette France 46°17N 4°19E 173 F11
La Cocha Argentina 27°50S 65°40W 334 B2
La Concepción = Ri-Aba Eq. Guin. 3°28N 8°40E 263 E6
La Concepción Panama 8°31N 82°37W 320 E3
La Concepción Venezuela 10°30N 71°50W 328 A3
La Concordia Mexico 16°5N 92°38W 319 D6
La Constitución, Plaza de = Zócalo Mexico City, Mexico 128 b3
La Coruña = A Coruña Spain 43°20N 8°25W 194 B2
La Côte-St-André France 45°24N 5°15E 175 C9
La Courneuve France 48°55N 2°22E 134 A3
La Courtine France 45°41N 2°15E 174 C6
La Crau Bouches-du-Rhône, France 43°32N 4°40E 175 E8
La Crau Var, France 43°9N 6°4E 175 E10
La Crescent U.S.A. 43°50N 91°18W 308 D8
La Crete Canada 58°11N 116°24W 296 B5
La Crosse Fla., U.S.A. 29°51N 82°24W 316 F7
La Crosse Kans., U.S.A. 38°32N 99°18W 308 F4
La Crosse Wis., U.S.A. 43°48N 91°15W 308 D8
La Cruz Costa Rica 11°4N 85°39W 320 D2
La Cruz Sinaloa, Mexico 23°55N 106°54W 318 C3
La Cumbre, Volcán Ecuador 0°21S 91°32W 330 a
La Dehesa Chile 33°21S 70°33W 137 B2
La Désirade Guadeloupe 16°18N 61°3W 322 e
La Digue Seychelles 4°20S 55°51E 272 c
La Dorada Colombia 5°30N 74°40W 328 B3
La Encantada Peru 12°13S 77°1W 124 C2
La Esperanza Argentina 40°26S 68°32W 336 B3
La Esperanza Cuba 22°46N 83°44W 320 B3
La Esperanza Honduras 14°15N 88°10W 320 D2
La Estación Spain 40°27N 3°48W 127 B1
La Estrada = A Estrada Spain 42°43N 8°27W 194 C2
La Falaise, Gorges de Martinique 14°49N 61°10W 322 j
La Faouët France 48°2N 3°30W 172 D3
La Fayette U.S.A. 34°42N 85°17W 315 D12
La Fé Cuba 22°2N 84°15W 320 B3
La Fenice, Teatro Venice, Italy 142 b2
La Fère France 49°39N 3°21E 173 C10
La Ferté-Bernard France 48°10N 0°40E 172 D7
La Ferté-Gaucher France 48°47N 3°19E 173 D10
La Ferté-Macé France 48°35N 0°22W 172 D6
La Ferté-St-Aubin France 47°42N 1°57E 173 E8
La Ferté-sous-Jouarre France 48°56N 3°8E 173 D10
La Ferté-Vidame France 48°37N 0°53E 172 D7
La Flèche France 47°42N 0°4W 172 E6
La Floresta Spain 41°26N 2°3E 114 A1
La Florida Chile 33°33S 70°34W 137 C2
La Foa N. Cal. 21°43S 165°50E 288 d
La Follette U.S.A. 36°23N 84°7W 315 C12
La Fontaine U.S.A. 40°40N 85°43W 311 D11
La Fortuna Spain 40°21N 3°46W 127 B1
La França Spain 41°22N 2°9E 114 A1
La Fregeneda Spain 40°58N 6°54W 194 E4
La Fría Venezuela 8°13N 72°15W 328 B3
La Fuente Venezuela 11°4N 63°52W 329 a
La Fuente de San Esteban Spain 40°49N 6°15W 194 E4
La Gacilly France 47°45N 2°8W 172 E4
La Garenne-Colombes France 48°54N 2°15E 134 A2
La Gi Vietnam 10°40N 107°45E 237 G6
La Gineta Spain 39°8N 2°1W 197 F2
La Giudecca Venice, Italy 142 c2
La Giustiniana Italy 41°59N 12°24E 136 B1
La Glória Colombia 8°37N 73°48W 328 B3
La Goulette Tunisia 36°53N 10°18E 200 F3
La Gran Sabana Venezuela 5°30N 61°30W 329 B5
La Grand'Combe France 44°13N 4°2E 175 D8
La Grande U.S.A. 45°20N 118°5W 304 D4
La Grande → Canada 53°50N 79°0W 298 B5
La Grande 3, Rés. Canada 53°40N 75°10W 298 B4
La Grande 4, Rés. Canada 54°0N 73°15W 298 B5
La Grande-Motte France 43°23N 4°5E 175 E8
La Grange Calif., U.S.A. 37°42N 120°27W 306 H6
La Grange Ga., U.S.A. 33°2N 85°2W 316 B4
La Grange Ky., U.S.A. 38°24N 85°22W 311 F11
La Grange Mo., U.S.A. 40°3N 91°35W 310 D5
La Grange Tex., U.S.A. 29°54N 96°52W 314 G6
La Granja Chile 33°31S 70°38W 137 C2
La Grave France 45°3N 6°18E 175 C10
La Grazia, Isola Venice, Italy 142 c3
La Grita Venezuela 8°8N 71°59W 328 B3
La Guaira Venezuela 10°36N 66°56W 328 A4
La Guarda △ Mexico 29°20N 113°27W 318 B2
La Guardia = A Guarda Spain 41°56N 8°52W 194 D2
La Guardia Venezuela 11°0N 64°1W 329 a
La Guardia, New York ✈ (LGA) U.S.A. 40°46N 73°52W 132 B2
La Gudiña = A Gudiña Spain 42°4N 7°8W 194 C3
La Güera Mauritania 20°51N 17°0W 260 D1
La Guerche-de-Bretagne France 47°57N 1°16W 172 E5
La Guerche-sur-l'Aubois France 46°58N 2°56E 173 F9
La Habana Cuba 23°8N 82°22W 320 B3
La Harpe U.S.A. 40°35N 90°58W 310 D6
La Haute Vallée de Chevreuse ⌓ France 48°35N 1°58E 173 D8
La Haye-du-Puits France 49°17N 1°33W 172 C5
La Horqueta Venezuela 7°55N 60°20W 329 B5
La Horquetta Trin. & Tob. 10°36N 61°16W 323 t
La Horra Spain 41°44N 3°53W 194 D7
La Hulpe Belgium 50°43N 4°30E 116 B2
La Independencia Mexico 16°15N 92°1W 319 D6
La Isabela Dom. Rep. 19°58N 71°2W 321 C5
La Isleta Venezuela 10°54N 63°56W 329 a
La Jonquera Spain 42°25N 2°53E 196 C7
La Joya Peru 16°43S 71°52W 330 D3
La Junta U.S.A. 37°59N 103°33W 304 H12
La Laguna = San Cristóbal de La Laguna Canary Is. 28°28N 16°18W 153 e1
La Lézarde → Martinique 14°35N 61°1W 322 j
La Libertad = Puerto Libertad Mexico 29°55N 112°43W 318 B2
La Libertad Guatemala 16°47N 90°7W 320 C1
La Libertad □ Peru 8°0S 78°30W 330 B2
La Ligua Chile 32°30S 71°16W 334 C1
La Línea de la Concepción Spain 36°15N 5°23W 195 J5
La Llacuna Spain 41°24N 2°12E 114 A2
La Loche Canada 56°29N 109°26W 297 B7
La Loma Mexico 19°31N 99°11W 128 A1
La Londe-les-Maures France 43°8N 6°14E 175 E10
La Lora Spain 42°45N 4°0W 194 C7
La Loupe France 48°29N 1°0E 172 D8
La Louvière Belgium 50°27N 4°10E 170 D4
La Lucila Argentina 34°30S 58°29W 117 B2
La Lune Trin. & Tob. 10°3N 61°22W 323 t
La Machine France 46°54N 3°27E 173 F10
La Maddalena Italy 41°13N 9°24E 200 A2
La Maladrerie France 48°54N 2°1E 134 A1
La Malbaie Canada 47°40N 70°10W 299 C5
La Malinche △ Mexico 19°15N 98°3W 319 D5
La Mancha Spain 39°10N 2°54W 197 F2
La Manche → Martinique 14°33N 61°0W 322 j
La Mariña Spain 43°30N 7°40W 194 B3
La Martre, L. Canada 63°15N 117°55W 296 A5
La Merced Peru 11°3S 75°19W 330 C2
La Mercy ✈ (DUR) S. Africa 29°37S 31°7E 271 C5
La Mesa Baja Calif., Mexico 32°30N 116°57W 307 N10
La Mesa Calif., U.S.A. 32°46N 117°1W 307 N9
La Mesilla U.S.A. 32°16N 106°48W 305 K10
La Milla, Cerro Peru 12°2S 77°5W 124 B2
La Moille U.S.A. 41°32N 89°17W 310 C7
La Moine → U.S.A. 39°59N 90°31W 310 E6
La Monachina Italy 41°53N 12°21E 136 B1
La Montagne Réunion 20°53S 55°26E 272 f
La Monte U.S.A. 38°46N 93°26W 310 F3
La Moraleja Spain 40°30N 3°38W 127 A2
La Mothe-Achard France 46°37N 1°40W 172 F5
La Motte-Chalançon France 44°30N 5°21E 175 D9
La Motte-du-Caire France 44°20N 6°3E 175 D10
La Motte-Servolex France 45°35N 5°53E 175 C9
La Moure U.S.A. 46°21N 98°18W 308 B4
La Moustique → Guadeloupe 16°10N 61°34W 322 e
La Muela Spain 41°36N 1°7W 196 D3
La Mure France 44°55N 5°48E 175 D9
La Negra Chile 23°46S 70°18W 334 A1
La Nopalera Mexico 19°18N 99°5W 128 C2
La Oliva Canary Is. 28°36N 13°57W 153 e2
La Oraya Peru 11°32S 75°54W 330 C2
La Orotava Canary Is. 28°22N 16°31W 153 e1
La Oroya Peru 11°32S 75°54W 330 C2
La Pacaudière France 46°11N 3°52E 173 F10
La Pagerie Martinique 14°32N 61°3W 322 j
La Palma Canary Is. 28°40N 17°50W 153 e1
La Palma Panama 8°15N 78°0W 320 E4
La Palma del Condado Spain 37°21N 6°38W 195 H4

La Palmyre France 45°43N 1°9W 174 C2
La Paloma Chile 30°35S 71°0W 334 C1
La Pampa □ Argentina 36°50S 66°0W 334 D2
La Paragua Venezuela 6°50N 63°20W 329 B5
La Pastora Trin. & Tob. 10°42N 61°19W 323 t
La Paternal Argentina 34°35S 58°26W 117 B2
La Paya △ Colombia 0°0 75°5W 328 C2
La Paz Entre Ríos, Argentina 30°50S 59°45W 334 C4
La Paz San Luis, Argentina 33°30S 67°20W 334 C2
La Paz Bolivia 16°20S 68°10W 330 D4
La Paz Honduras 14°20N 87°47W 320 D2
La Paz Baja Calif. S., Mexico 24°10N 110°18W 318 C2
La Paz Abra, Phil. 17°40N 120°41E 232 C3
La Paz Tarlac, Phil. 15°26N 120°45E 232 D3
La Paz □ Bolivia 15°30S 68°0W 330 D4
La Paz Centro Nic. 12°20N 86°41W 320 D2
La Pedrera Colombia 1°18S 69°43W 328 D4
La Pérade Canada 46°35N 72°12W 299 C5
La Perla Chihuahua, Mexico 28°18N 104°32W 318 B4
La Perla Lima, Peru 12°4S 77°7W 124 B2
La Perouse Australia 33°59S 151°14E 139 B2
La Perouse, Bahía Chile 27°55S 109°18W 330 b
La Perouse Str. Asia 45°40N 142°0E 220 B11
La Pesca Mexico 23°46N 97°47W 319 C5
La Piedad Mexico 20°21N 102°0W 318 C4
La Pine U.S.A. 43°40N 121°30W 304 E3
La Pisana Italy 41°51N 12°23E 136 B1
La Plaine Dominica 15°20N 61°15W 323 k
La Plaine des Cafres Réunion 21°13S 55°33E 272 f
La Plaine des Palmistes Réunion 21°7S 55°38E 272 f
La Plata Argentina 35°0S 57°55W 334 C4
La Plata Colombia 2°23N 75°53W 328 C2
La Plata Mo., U.S.A. 40°2N 92°29W 310 D4
La Plata, L. Argentina 44°55S 71°50W 336 B2
La Playa, Pta. Venezuela 10°48N 64°0W 329 a
La Plaza Venezuela 11°6N 63°52W 329 a
La Pobla de Lillet Spain 42°16N 1°59E 196 C6
La Pobla de Segur Spain 42°15N 0°58E 196 C5
La Pocatière Canada 47°22N 70°2W 299 C5
La Pola de Gordón Spain 42°51N 5°41W 194 C5
La Porta France 42°25N 9°21E 175 F13
La Porte U.S.A. 29°40N 95°1W 314 G7
La Porte City U.S.A. 42°19N 92°12W 310 B4
La Possession Réunion 20°55S 55°21E 272 f
La Prairie Canada 45°25N 73°29W 130 B3
La Presanella Italy 46°13N 10°40E 198 B7
La Puebla = Sa Pobla Spain 39°46N 3°1E 206 B4
La Puebla de Cazalla Spain 37°10N 5°20W 195 H5
La Puebla de los Infantes Spain 37°47N 5°24W 195 H5
La Puebla de Montalbán Spain 39°52N 4°22W 194 F6
La Puebla del Río Spain 37°16N 6°3W 195 H4
La Puerta de Segura Spain 38°22N 2°45W 195 G8
La Punta Peru 12°4S 77°10W 124 B1
La Puntigala Spain 41°27N 2°13E 114 A2
La Purísima Mexico 26°10N 112°4W 318 B2
La Push U.S.A. 47°55N 124°38W 306 C2
La Queue-en-Brie France 48°47N 2°34E 134 B4
La Quiaca Argentina 22°5S 65°35W 334 A2
La Rambla Barcelona, Spain 114 b2
La Reina Chile 33°26S 70°33W 137 B2
La Réole France 44°35N 0°1W 174 D3
La Republica, Plaza de Mexico City, Mexico 128 b1
La Restinga Canary Is. 27°38N 17°59W 153 e1
La Ribera Spain 41°21N 2°4E 114 A1
La Rinconada Peru 14°38S 69°27W 330 C4
La Rioja Argentina 29°20S 67°0W 334 B2
La Rioja □ Argentina 29°30S 67°0W 334 B2
La Rioja □ Spain 42°20N 2°20W 196 C2
La Rivière des Pluies Réunion 20°54S 55°31E 272 f
La Robla Spain 42°50N 5°41W 194 C5
La Roche N. Cal. 21°26S 168°2E 288 d
La Roche-Bernard France 47°31N 2°19W 172 E4
La Roche-Canillac France 45°12N 1°57E 174 C5
La Roche-en-Ardenne Belgium 50°11N 5°35E 170 D5
La Roche-sur-Foron France 46°4N 6°19E 173 F13
La Roche-sur-Yon France 46°40N 1°25W 172 F5
La Rochefoucauld France 45°44N 0°24E 174 C4
La Rochelle France 46°10N 1°9W 174 B2
La Roda Spain 39°13N 2°15W 197 F2
La Roda de Andalucía Spain 37°12N 4°46W 195 H6
La Romaine Trin. & Tob. 10°15N 61°29W 323 t
La Romaine Canada 50°13N 60°40W 299 B7
La Romana Dom. Rep. 18°27N 68°57W 321 C6
La Ronge Canada 55°5N 105°20W 297 B7
La Rue U.S.A. 40°35N 83°23W 311 D13
La Rumorosa Mexico 32°34N 116°6W 307 N10
La Sabina = Sa Savina Spain 38°44N 1°25E 206 D1
La Sagra Spain 37°57N 2°35W 197 H2
La Sagrera Spain 41°25N 2°11E 114 A2
La Salada Argentina 34°43S 58°28W 117 C2
La Saline Réunion 21°4S 55°16E 272 f
La Salle U.S.A. 41°20N 89°6W 310 C7
La Sanabria Spain 42°0N 6°30W 194 C4
La Santa Canary Is. 29°5N 13°40W 153 e2
La Sarre Canada 48°45N 79°15W 298 C4
La Scala Italy 45°28N 9°11E 128 B2
La Scie Canada 49°57N 55°36W 299 C8
La Selva Spain 42°0N 2°45E 196 C7
La Selva Beach U.S.A. 36°56N 121°51W 306 J5
La Selva del Camp Spain 41°13N 1°8E 196 D6
La Serena Chile 29°55S 71°10W 334 B1
La Serena Spain 38°45N 5°40W 195 G5
La Seu d'Urgell Spain 42°22N 1°23E 196 C6
La Seyne-sur-Mer France 43°7N 5°52E 175 E9
La Sila Italy 39°15N 16°35E 201 C9
La Solana Spain 38°59N 3°14W 195 G7
La Soufrière St. Vincent 13°20N 61°11W 323 n
La Souterraine France 46°15N 1°30E 173 F8
La Spézia Italy 44°7N 9°50E 198 D6
La Storta Italy 41°59N 12°20E 136 A1
La Suze-sur-Sarthe France 47°53N 0°2E 172 E7
La Tagua Colombia 0°3N 74°40W 328 C3
La Taxonera Spain 41°25N 2°9E 114 A2
La Teste-de-Buch France 44°37N 1°8W 174 D2
La Tortuga, I. Venezuela 11°0N 65°22W 321 D6
La Tour-du-Pin France 45°33N 5°27E 175 C9
La Tranche-sur-Mer France 46°20N 1°27W 172 F5
La Tremblade France 45°46N 1°8W 174 C2
La Trinidad Phil. 16°28N 120°35E 232 C3
La Trinité Martinique 14°45N 60°58W 322 j
La Tuque Canada 47°30N 72°50W 298 C5
La Unión Chile 40°10S 73°0W 336 B2
La Unión Colombia 1°35N 77°5W 328 C2
La Unión El Salv. 13°20N 87°50W 320 D2
La Unión Guerrero, Mexico 17°58N 101°49W 318 D4
La Unión Peru 9°43S 76°45W 330 B2
La Unión Spain 37°38N 0°53W 197 H4
La Union □ Phil. 16°30N 120°25E 232 C3
La Urbana Venezuela 7°8N 66°56W 328 B4
La Vache B. Trin. & Tob. 10°45N 61°29W 323 t
La Vache Pt. Trin. & Tob. 10°47N 61°28W 323 t
La Vall d'Uixó Spain 39°49N 0°15W 196 F4
La Vecilla Spain 42°51N 5°27W 194 C5
La Vecindad Venezuela 11°4N 63°56W 329 a
La Vega Dom. Rep. 19°20N 70°30W 321 C5
La Vega Peru 10°41S 77°44W 330 C2
La Vela de Coro Venezuela 11°27N 69°34W 328 A4
La Veleta Spain 37°1N 3°22W 195 H7
La Venta Mexico 18°5N 94°3W 319 D6
La Venturosa Colombia 6°8N 68°48W 328 B4
La Vergne U.S.A. 36°1N 86°35W 315 C11
La Veronica Trin. & Tob. 10°42N 61°21W 323 t
La Victoria Lima, Peru 12°3S 77°2W 124 B2
La Victoria Venezuela 10°14N 67°20W 328 A4
La Villa Joiosa = Villajoyosa Spain 38°30N 0°12W 197 G4
La Vista U.S.A. 33°48N 84°21W 113 B2
La Voulte-sur-Rhône France 44°48N 4°46E 175 D8
Laa an der Thaya Austria 48°43N 16°23E 181 C9
Laaber, Grosse → Germany 48°55N 12°30E 179 G8
Laage Germany 53°55N 12°21E 178 B8
Laajalahti Finland 60°11N 24°48E 121 B1
Laajasalo Finland 60°10N 25°1E 121 B3
Laaksolahti Finland 60°14N 24°45E 121 B1
Laas Dawaco Somalia 10°28N 49°0E 267 B6
Laascaanood = Las Anod Somalia 8°26N 47°19E 267 C6
Laasqoray Somalia 11°10N 48°20E 267 B6
Laatzen Germany 52°19N 9°48E 178 C5
Lā'au Pt. U.S.A. 21°6N 157°19W 302 B4
Laayoune-Sakia al Hamra □ Morocco 27°0N 11°30W 260 C2
Laba → Russia 45°11N 39°42E 191 H4
Labagou Nat. Forest Park ⌂ China 40°1N 116°22E 114 A2
Laban Myanmar 25°52N 96°40E 241 C6
Labasa Fiji 16°30S 179°27E 287 A2
Labason Phil. 8°4N 122°31E 233 G4
Labastide-Murat France 44°39N 1°33E 174 D5
Labastide-Rouairoux France 43°28N 2°39E 174 E6
Labbézenga Mali 15°2N 0°48E 263 B5
Labdah = Leptis Magna Libya 32°40N 14°12E 258 B2
Labe = Elbe → Europe 53°50N 9°0E 178 B4
Labé Guinea 11°24N 12°16W 262 C2
Laberge, L. Canada 61°11N 135°12W 296 A1
Labes = Łobez Poland 53°38N 15°39E 184 E2
Labia, Palazzo Venice, Italy 142 a2
Labian, Tanjong Malaysia 5°9N 119°13E 235 A5
Labiau = Polessk Russia 54°50N 21°8E 184 D8
Labig Pt. = Iligan Pt. Phil. 18°25N 122°25E 232 B4
Labin Croatia 45°5N 14°8E 199 C11
Labinsk Russia 44°40N 40°48E 191 H5
Labis Malaysia 2°22N 103°2E 237 L4
Łabiszyn Poland 52°57N 17°54E 185 F4
Lablâba, W. el → Egypt 30°1N 31°19E 117 A2
Labo Phil. 14°9N 122°51E 232 D4
Laboe Germany 54°24N 10°13E 178 A6
Laborec → Slovakia 48°37N 21°58E 181 C14
Laborie St. Lucia 13°45N 61°2W 323 m
Labouheyre France 44°13N 0°55W 174 D3
Laboulaye Argentina 34°10S 63°30W 334 C3
Labrador Canada 53°20N 61°0W 299 B7
Labrador City Canada 52°57N 66°55W 299 B6
Labrador Sea Atl. Oc. 57°0N 54°0W 295 F21
Lábrea Brazil 7°15S 64°51W 331 B5
Labruguière France 43°31N 2°16E 174 E6
Labuan □ Malaysia 5°20N 115°12E 235 A5
Labuan, Pulau Malaysia 5°21N 115°13E 235 A5
Labuha Indonesia 0°30S 127°30E 231 E7
Labuhan Indonesia 6°22S 105°50E 234 D3
Labuhanbajo Indonesia 8°28S 119°54E 235 D5
Labuhanbilik Indonesia 2°31N 100°10E 237 L3
Labuk, Telok Malaysia 6°10N 117°50E 235 A5
Labutta Myanmar 16°9N 94°46E 241 G5
Labyrinth, L. Australia 30°40S 135°11E 281 E2
Labytnangi Russia 66°39N 66°21E 186 A12
Laç Albania 41°38N 19°43E 202 E3
Lac □ Chad 13°30N 14°30E 259 F2
Lac Bay Bonaire 12°6N 68°13W 322 h
Lac-Bouchette Canada 48°16N 72°11W 299 C5
Lac-Édouard Canada 47°40N 72°16W 299 C5
Lac La Biche Canada 54°45N 111°58W 296 C6
Lac la Martre = Wha Ti Canada 63°8N 117°16W 294 E8
Lac La Ronge ⌂ Canada 55°9N 104°41W 297 B7
Lac-Mégantic Canada 45°35N 70°53W 299 C5
Lac Thien Vietnam 12°25N 108°11E 236 F7
Lacanau France 44°58N 1°5W 174 D2
Lacanau, L. de France 44°58N 1°7W 174 D2
Lacantún → Mexico 16°36N 90°39W 319 D6
Lácara → Spain 38°55N 6°25W 195 G4
Lacaune France 43°43N 2°40E 174 E6
Lacaune, Mts. de France 43°43N 2°50E 174 E6
Laccadive Is. = Lakshadweep Is. India 10°0N 72°30E 245 J1
Lacepede B. Australia 36°40S 139°40E 282 D3
Lacepede Is. Australia 16°55S 122°0E 278 C3
Lacerdónia Mozam. 18°3S 35°35E 269 F4
Lacey U.S.A. 47°7N 122°49W 306 C4
Lachania Greece 35°58N 27°54E 206 F11
Lachay, Pta. Peru 11°17S 77°44W 330 C2
Lachen India 27°46N 88°36E 241 B2
Lachhmangarh India 27°50N 75°4E 242 F6
Lachi Pakistan 33°25N 71°20E 242 C4
Lachia Taiwan 22°43N 120°53E 225 D2
Lachine Canada 45°26N 73°42W 130 B1
Lachine, Canal de Canada 45°26N 73°38W 130 B2
Lachlan → Australia 34°22S 143°55E 282 C5
Lachoc Peru 12°50S 75°6W 330 C2
Lachute Canada 45°39N 74°21W 298 C5
Laçın Azerbaijan 39°38N 46°33E 213 C12
Lackagh Hills Ireland 54°16N 8°10W 166 B3
Lackawanna U.S.A. 42°50N 78°50W 312 D6
Lackawaxen U.S.A. 41°29N 74°59W 313 E10
Lacolle Canada 45°5N 73°22W 313 A11
Lacombe Canada 52°30N 113°44W 296 C6
Lacon U.S.A. 41°2N 89°24W 310 C7
Lacona Iowa, U.S.A. 41°12N 93°23W 310 C3
Lacona N.Y., U.S.A. 43°39N 76°10W 313 C8
Láconi Italy 39°54N 9°4E 200 C2
Laconia = Lakonia Greece 36°55N 22°30E 204 E4
Laconia U.S.A. 43°32N 71°28W 313 C13
Lacoochee U.S.A. 28°28N 82°11W 317 G7
Lacq France 43°25N 0°35W 174 E3
Lacre Punt Bonaire 12°1N 68°14W 322 h
Lacs □ Côte d'Ivoire 7°1N 4°46W 262 D4
Lad Phrao Thailand 13°47N 100°35E 113 B2
Ladākh □ India 34°0N 77°35E 243 C7
Ladakh Ra. India 34°0N 78°0E 243 C8
Ladário Brazil 19°1S 57°35W 331 D6
Ladd U.S.A. 41°23N 89°13W 310 C7
Laddonia U.S.A. 39°15N 91°39W 310 E5
Lądek-Zdrój Poland 50°21N 16°53E 185 H3
Ladera Heights U.S.A. 33°59N 118°22W 126 C2
Lâdik Turkey 40°57N 35°58E 212 B6
Ladismith S. Africa 33°28S 21°15E 270 D3
Ladispoli Italy 41°56N 12°5E 199 G9
Lādīz Iran 28°55N 61°15E 247 D9
Ladnun India 27°38N 74°25E 242 F6
Ladoga, L. = Ladozhskoye Ozero Russia 61°15N 30°30E 188 B6
Ladonas → Greece 37°40N 21°50E 204 D3
Ladozhskoye Ozero Russia 61°15N 30°30E 188 B6
Ladrillero, G. Chile 49°20S 75°35W 336 C1
Ladson U.S.A. 32°59N 80°6W 316 C9
Ladushkin Russia 54°34N 20°10E 184 D7
Ládví Czechia 50°8N 14°27E 135 B2
Łady Poland 52°8N 20°57E 143 C1
Lady Elliott I. Australia 24°7S 152°42E 280 C5
Lady Frere S. Africa 31°42S 27°14E 270 D4
Lady Grey S. Africa 30°43S 27°13E 270 D4
Lady Lake U.S.A. 28°55N 81°55W 317 G8
Ladybrand S. Africa 29°9S 27°29E 270 C4
Ladysmith B.C., Canada 49°0N 123°49W 306 B3
Ladysmith KwaZulu Natal, S. Africa 28°32S 29°46E 271 C4
Ladysmith Wis., U.S.A. 45°28N 91°12W 308 C8
Ladyzhyn Ukraine 48°40N 29°15E 183 B14
Lae Papua N. G. 6°40S 147°2E 286 D4
Lae 'o Kealaikahiki U.S.A. 20°32N 156°42W 302 C5
Laem Chabang Thailand 13°5N 100°53E 236 F3
Laem Ngop Thailand 12°10N 102°26E 237 F4
Laem Son △ Thailand 9°29N 98°24E 237 H2
Lærdalsøyri Norway 61°6N 7°28E 164 C4
Laerma Greece 36°9N 27°57E 206 E11
Læsø Denmark 57°15N 11°5E 163 G5
Læsø Rende Denmark 57°20N 10°45E 163 G4
Lafayette Ala., U.S.A. 32°54N 85°24W 316 C4
Lafayette Ind., U.S.A. 40°25N 86°54W 311 D10
Lafayette La., U.S.A. 30°14N 92°1W 314 F8
Lafayette Tenn., U.S.A. 36°31N 86°2W 315 C11
Lafayette Park San Francisco, U.S.A. 136 b1
Lafayette Square New Orleans, U.S.A. 131 b2
Laferte → Canada 61°53N 117°44W 296 A5
Lafia Nigeria 8°30N 8°34E 263 D6
Lafiagi Nigeria 8°52N 5°20E 263 D6
Lafkos Greece 39°9N 23°14E 204 B5
Lafleche Canada 49°45N 106°40W 297 D7
Lafon South Sudan 5°5N 32°29E 257 F3
Lafontaine Montréal, Canada 130 a1
Lafontaine, Parc Canada 45°33N 73°34W 130 A2
Laful India 7°10N 93°52E 245 L11
Lagaip → Papua N. G. 5°4S 142°52E 286 C2
Lagan = Kaspiyskiy Russia 45°22N 47°23E 191 H8
Lagan Sweden 56°56N 13°58E 163 H7
Lagan → Sweden 56°30N 12°58E 163 H6
Lagan → Antrim, U.K. 54°36N 5°55W 166 B6
Lagana, Kolpos Greece 37°42N 20°53E 207 D2
Laganas Greece 37°44N 20°53E 207 D2
Lagangilang Phil. 17°37N 120°44E 232 C3
Lagarfljót → Iceland 65°40N 14°18W 155 B12
Lagarto Brazil 10°54S 37°41W 332 D4
Lagawe Phil. 16°49N 121°6E 232 C3
Lagdo Cameroon 9°3N 13°44E 259 G2
Lagdo, L. de Cameroon 8°40N 14°0E 264 A2
Lage Germany 51°59N 8°48E 178 D4
Lågen → Oppland, Norway 61°8N 10°25E 164 C7
Lågen → Vestfold, Norway 59°3N 10°3E 164 F7
Lägerdorf Germany 53°53N 9°34E 178 B5
Lages Brazil 27°48S 50°20W 335 B5
Laggan = Lake Louise Canada 51°30N 116°10W 296 C5
Lagh Badana △ Somalia 1°16S 41°49E 267 E5
Laghmān □ Afghan. 34°20N 70°0E 240 B3
Laghouat Algeria 33°50N 2°59E 261 B5
Laghouat □ Algeria 33°30N 2°40E 261 B5
Lagnieu France 45°55N 5°20E 175 C9
Lagny-sur-Marne France 48°52N 2°44E 173 D9
Lago = Niassa □ Mozam. 13°30S 36°0E 269 E4
Lago Italy 39°10N 16°9E 201 C9
Lago Agrio Ecuador 0°5N 76°52W 328 C2
Lago de Sanabria y Entorno ⌂ Spain 42°9N 6°45W 194 C4
Lago Posadas Argentina 47°30S 71°40W 336 C2
Lago Puelo △ Argentina 42°30S 71°55W 336 B2
Lago Ranco Chile 40°19S 72°30W 336 B2
Lagoa Azores 37°45N 25°20W 153 d3
Lagoa Rio de J., Brazil 22°58S 43°11W 135 B1
Lagôa Portugal 37°8N 8°27W 195 H2
Lagoa do Peixe △ Brazil 31°12S 50°55W 335 C5
Lagoa Vermelha Brazil 28°13S 51°32W 335 B5
Lagoaça Portugal 41°11N 6°44W 194 D4
Lagodekhi Georgia 41°50N 46°22E 191 K8
Lagona = Laguna Beach U.S.A. 33°33N 117°47W 307 M9
Lagónegro Italy 40°8N 15°45E 201 B8
Lagonoy G. Phil. 13°35N 123°50E 232 E4
Lagos Angola 16°3S 16°35E 265 F3
Lagos Greece 41°1N 25°6E 203 E9
Lagos Nigeria 6°25N 3°27E 124 B2
Lagos Portugal 37°5N 8°41W 195 H2
Lagos □ Nigeria 6°28N 3°25E 263 D5
Lagos de Moreno Mexico 21°21N 101°55W 318 C4
Lagos Harbour Nigeria 6°26N 3°23E 124 B2
Lagos-Ikeja ✈ (LOS) Nigeria 6°34N 3°19E 124 A1
Lagos Island Nigeria 6°26N 3°23E 124 B2
Lagos Lagoon Nigeria 6°30N 3°28E 124 B2
Lagrange = Bidyadanga Australia 18°45S 121°43E 278 C3
Lagrange U.S.A. 41°39N 85°25W 311 C11
Lagrange B. Australia 18°38S 121°42E 278 C3
Laguardia Spain 42°33N 2°35W 196 C2
Laguépie France 44°8N 1°57E 174 D5
Lagun Curaçao 12°19N 69°10W 322 g
Laguna = Padilla Bolivia 19°19S 64°20W 331 D5
Laguna Brazil 28°30S 48°50W 335 B6
Laguna N. Mex., U.S.A. 35°2N 107°25W 305 J10
Laguna □ Phil. 14°10N 121°20E 232 D3
Laguna, Sa. de la Mexico 23°35N 109°55W 318 C3
Laguna Beach U.S.A. 33°33N 117°47W 307 M9
Laguna Blanca △ Argentina 39°0S 70°5W 336 A2
Laguna de B. Phil. 14°29N 121°6E 127 C2
Laguna de Duero Spain 41°35N 4°43W 194 D6
Laguna de la Restinga △ Venezuela 11°0N 64°10W 329 a
Laguna de Lachuá △ Guatemala 15°55N 90°40W 320 C1
Laguna de Raya Venezuela 10°56N 64°7W 329 a
Laguna del Laja △ Chile 37°27S 71°20W 334 D1
Laguna del Tigre △ Guatemala 17°32N 90°56W 320 C1
Laguna Limpia Argentina 26°32S 59°45W 334 B4
Laguna San Rafael △ Chile 46°54S 73°31W 336 C2
Lagunas Chile 21°0S 69°45W 334 A2
Lagunas Peru 5°10S 75°35W 330 B2
Lagunas de Chacahua △ Mexico 16°0N 97°43W 319 D5
Lagunas de Montebello △ Mexico 16°4N 91°42W 319 D6
Lagunas de Ruidera ⌂ Spain 38°57N 2°52W 197 G2
Lagunes □ Côte d'Ivoire 5°47N 4°12W 262 D4
Lagunillas Bolivia 19°38S 63°43W 331 D5
Lahad Datu Malaysia 5°0N 118°20E 235 A5
Lahad Datu, Telok Malaysia 4°50N 118°20E 235 B5
Lahaina U.S.A. 20°53N 156°41W 302 C5
Lahan Sai Thailand 14°25N 102°52E 236 E4
Lahanam Laos 16°16N 105°16E 236 D5
Lahar India 26°12N 78°57E 243 F8
Laharpur India 27°43N 80°56E 243 F9
Lahat Indonesia 3°45S 103°30E 234 C2
Lahe Myanmar 26°20N 95°26E 241 B5
Lahewa Indonesia 1°22N 97°12E 234 B1
Laḥij Yemen 13°4N 44°53E 248 D4
Laḥij □ Yemen 13°0N 44°30E 248 D4
Lāhījān Iran 37°10N 50°6E 247 B6
Lahilahi Pt. U.S.A. 21°28N 158°13W 302 K13
Lahn → Germany 50°19N 7°37E 179 E3
Lahnstein Germany 50°19N 7°37E 179 E3
Laholm Sweden 56°30N 13°2E 163 H7
Laholmsbukten Sweden 56°30N 12°45E 163 H6
Lahore Pakistan 31°32N 74°22E 242 D6
Lahpongsel Myanmar 27°7N 98°25E 241 B7
Lahr Germany 48°20N 7°53E 179 G3
Lahri Pakistan 29°11N 68°13E 242 E3
Lāhrūd Iran 38°30N 47°52E 213 C12
Lahti Finland 60°58N 25°40E 188 B3
Lahtis = Lahti Finland 60°58N 25°40E 188 B3
Lahugala Kitulana △ Sri Lanka 6°50N 81°40E 245 L5
Laï Chad 9°25N 16°18E 259 G3
Lai Chau Vietnam 22°5N 103°3E 228 F4
Lai Chi Wo Hong Kong, China 22°32N 114°15E 122 B2
Lai-hka Myanmar 21°16N 97°40E 241 E6
Laiagam Papua N. G. 5°33S 143°30E 286 C2
Lai'an China 32°28N 118°30E 229 A12
Laibach = Ljubljana Slovenia 46°4N 14°33E 199 B11
Laibin China 23°42N 109°14E 228 F7
Lā'ie U.S.A. 21°39N 157°56W 302 J14
Laifeng China 29°27N 109°20E 228 C7
L'Aigle France 48°46N 0°38E 172 D7
Laignes France 47°50N 4°20E 173 E11
L'Aiguillon-sur-Mer France 46°20N 1°18W 174 B2
Laikipia □ Kenya 0°10N 36°40E 268 B4
Laila = Layla Si. Arabia 22°10N 46°40E 248 B4
Laim Germany 48°7N 11°30E 131 B2
Lainate Italy 45°34N 9°1E 128 A1
Laingsburg S. Africa 33°9S 20°52E 270 D3
Lainioälven → Sweden 67°35N 22°40E 160 C20
Lainz Austria 48°10N 16°16E 142 B1
Lairg U.K. 58°2N 4°24W 167 C4
Laïri, B. de Chad 12°28N 16°45E 259 F3
Lais Indonesia 3°31S 102°3E 234 C2
Lais Phil. 6°20N 125°39E 233 H5
Laisamis Kenya 1°36N 37°48E 268 B4
Laissac France 44°23N 2°50E 174 D6
Láives Italy 46°26N 11°20E 199 B8
Laiwu China 36°15N 117°40E 227 F9
Laixi China 36°50N 120°31E 227 F11
Laiyang China 36°59N 120°45E 227 F11
Laiyuan China 39°20N 114°40E 226 E8
Laizhou China 37°8N 119°57E 227 F10
Laizhou Wan China 37°30N 119°30E 227 F10
Lajamanu Australia 18°23S 130°38E 278 C5
Lajeado = Guiratinga Brazil 16°21S 53°45W 331 D7
Lajedo Azores 39°23N 31°15W 153 d2
Lajere Nigeria 12°10N 11°25E 263 C7
Lajes Azores 38°46N 27°6W 153 d1
Lajes Rio Grande do N., Brazil 5°41S 36°14W 332 C4
Lajes das Flores Azores 39°23N 31°10W 153 d2
Lajes do Pico Azores 38°23N 28°16W 153 d1
Lajinha Brazil 20°9S 41°37W 333 F3
Lajkovac Serbia 44°27N 20°14E 202 B4
Lajosmizse Hungary 47°3N 19°32E 182 C4
Lak Sao Laos 18°11N 104°59E 236 C5
Lakaband Pakistan 31°2N 69°15E 242 D3
Lakamané Mali 14°35N 9°44W 262 C3
Lakatoro Vanuatu 16°6S 167°25E 287 F5
Lake U.S.A. 44°33N 110°24W 304 D8
Lake Alfred U.S.A. 28°6N 81°44W 317 G8
Lake Alpine U.S.A. 38°29N 120°0W 306 G7
Lake Andes U.S.A. 43°9N 98°32W 308 D4
Lake Arthur U.S.A. 30°5N 92°41W 314 F8
Lake Bindegolly △ Australia 28°0S 144°12E 281 D3
Lake Boga Australia 35°26S 143°38E 282 C5
Lake Buena Vista U.S.A. 28°23N 81°32W 133 B1
Lake Butig △ Phil. 7°45N 124°16E 233 H5
Lake Butler U.S.A. 30°1N 82°21W 316 E7
Lake Cain Hills U.S.A. 28°29N 81°28W 133 B2
Lake Cargelligo Australia 33°15S 146°22E 283 B7
Lake Charles U.S.A. 30°14N 93°13W 314 F8
Lake City Colo., U.S.A. 38°2N 107°19W 304 G10
Lake City Fla., U.S.A. 30°11N 82°38W 316 E7
Lake City Iowa, U.S.A. 42°16N 94°44W 310 B2
Lake City Mich., U.S.A. 44°20N 85°13W 309 C11
Lake City Minn., U.S.A. 44°27N 92°16W 308 C7
Lake City Pa., U.S.A. 42°1N 80°21W 312 D4
Lake City S.C., U.S.A. 33°52N 79°45W 316 B10
Lake Clark △ U.S.A. 61°0N 154°0W 303 F9
Lake Coleridge N.Z. 43°17S 171°30E 285 D6
Lake Cowichan Canada 48°49N 124°3W 296 D4
Lake District △ U.K. 54°30N 3°21W 168 C4
Lake Eildon △ Australia 37°10S 145°56E 283 D6
Lake Elsinore U.S.A. 33°38N 117°20W 307 M9
Lake Eyre △ Australia 28°40S 137°31E 281 D2
Lake Forest U.S.A. 42°15N 87°50W 311 B9
Lake Gairdner △ Australia 31°41S 135°51E 281 E2
Lake Geneva U.S.A. 42°36N 88°26W 311 B8
Lake George U.S.A. 43°26N 73°43W 313 C11
Lake Grace Australia 33°7S 118°28E 279 F2
Lake Gregory ◎ Australia 20°12S 127°27E 278 D4
Lake Harbor U.S.A. 26°42N 80°48W 317 J9
Lake Harbour = Kimmirut Canada 62°50N 69°50W 295 E18
Lake Havasu City U.S.A. 34°27N 114°22W 307 L12
Lake Helen U.S.A. 28°59N 81°14W 317 G8
Lake Hughes U.S.A. 34°41N 118°26W 307 L8
Lake Isabella U.S.A. 35°38N 118°28W 307 K8
Lake Jackson U.S.A. 29°3N 95°27W 314 G7
Lake King Australia 33°5S 119°45E 279 F2
Lake Kopiago Papua N. G. 5°23S 142°31E 286 C2
Lake Kutubu Papua N. G. 6°20S 143°18E 286 D2
Lake Lenore Canada 52°24N 104°59W 297 C8
Lake Louise Canada 51°30N 116°10W 296 C5
Lake Mackay ◎ Australia 21°48S 129°46E 278 D4
Lake Mburo △ Uganda 0°33S 30°56E 268 C3
Lake Mead △ U.S.A. 36°30N 114°22W 307 K12
Lake Meredith △ U.S.A. 35°50N 101°50W 314 D4
Lake Mills Iowa, U.S.A. 43°25N 93°32W 308 D7
Lake Mills Wis., U.S.A. 43°5N 88°55W 311 A8
Lake Murray Papua N. G. 6°48S 141°29E 286 D1
Lake Nakura △ Kenya 0°21S 36°8E 268 C4
Lake Odessa U.S.A. 42°47N 85°8W 311 B11
Lake Orion U.S.A. 42°47N 83°14W 311 B13
Lake Park Fla., U.S.A. 26°48N 80°3W 317 J9
Lake Park Ga., U.S.A. 30°41N 83°11W 316 E6
Lake Placid Fla., U.S.A. 27°18N 81°22W 317 H8
Lake Placid N.Y., U.S.A. 44°17N 73°59W 313 B11
Lake Pleasant U.S.A. 43°28N 74°25W 313 C10
Lake Point Tower Chicago, U.S.A. 119 b3
Lake Providence U.S.A. 32°48N 91°10W 314 E9
Lake Pukaki N.Z. 44°11S 170°8E 285 E5
Lake Roosevelt ⌂ U.S.A. 48°5N 118°14W 304 B4
Lake St. Peter Canada 45°18N 78°2W 312 A6
Lake Shore Drive Chicago, U.S.A. 119 a2
Lake Shore Park Chicago, U.S.A. 119 a2
Lake Stevens U.S.A. 48°1N 122°4W 306 B4
Lake Superior ⌂ Canada 47°45N 84°45W 298 C3
Lake Tekapo N.Z. 44°0S 170°30E 285 E5
Lake Torrens △ Australia 30°55S 137°40E 281 E2
Lake View U.S.A. 42°18N 95°3W 310 B1
Lake Villa U.S.A. 42°25N 88°5W 311 B8
Lake Village U.S.A. 33°20N 91°17W 314 E9
Lake Wales U.S.A. 27°54N 81°35W 317 H8
Lake Worth U.S.A. 26°37N 80°3W 317 J9
Lake Zurich U.S.A. 42°12N 88°5W 311 B8
Lakeba Fiji 18°13S 178°47W 287 B3
Lakeba Passage Fiji 18°0S 178°45W 287 B3
Lakefield = Rinyirru △ Australia 15°24S 144°26E 280 B3
Lakefield Canada 44°25N 78°16W 312 B6
Lakehurst U.S.A. 40°1N 74°19W 313 F10
Lakeland Queens., Australia 15°49S 144°57E 280 B3
Lakeland Fla., U.S.A. 28°3N 81°57W 317 G8
Lakeland Ga., U.S.A. 31°2N 83°4W 316 D6
Lakemba = Lakeba Fiji 18°13S 178°47W 287 B3
Lakemba Australia 33°55S 151°5E 139 B1
Lakepa Cook Is. 18°59S 169°48W 289 g
Lakeport Calif., U.S.A. 39°3N 122°55W 306 F4
Lakeport Mich., U.S.A. 43°7N 82°30W 312 C2
Lakes □ South Sudan 7°0N 30°0E 257 F3
Lakes Entrance Australia 37°50S 148°0E 283 D8
Lakeside Gauteng, S. Africa 26°5S 28°8E 123 A2
Lakeside Western Cape, S. Africa 34°5S 18°27E 118 B1
Lakeside Calif., U.S.A. 32°52N 116°55W 307 N10
Lakeside Nebr., U.S.A. 42°3N 102°26W 308 D2
Lakeside Ohio, U.S.A. 41°32N 82°46W 312 E2
Lakeview Ill., U.S.A. 41°56N 87°38W 119 B3
Lakeview La., U.S.A. 30°0N 90°6W 131 A2
Lakeview Oreg., U.S.A. 42°11N 120°21W 304 E3
Lakeville U.S.A. 44°39N 93°14W 308 C7
Lakewood Colo., U.S.A. 39°42N 105°4W 304 G11
Lakewood N.J., U.S.A. 40°6N 74°13W 313 F10
Lakewood N.Y., U.S.A. 42°6N 79°19W 312 D5
Lakewood Ohio, U.S.A. 41°28N 81°47W 312 E3
Lakewood Wash., U.S.A. 47°11N 122°32W 306 C4
Lakewood Park Fla., U.S.A. 27°33N 80°24W 317 H9
Lakewood Park Georgia, U.S.A. 33°43N 84°24W 113 B2
Lakha India 26°9N 70°54E 242 F4
Lakhimpur India 27°57N 80°46E 243 F9
Lakhipur Assam, India 26°2N 90°18E 241 B3
Lakhipur Assam, India 24°48N 93°0E 241 C4
Lakhisarai India 25°11N 86°5E 243 G12
Lakhnadon India 22°36N 79°36E 243 H8
Lakhnau = Lucknow India 26°50N 81°0E 243 F9
Lakhonpheng Laos 15°54N 105°34E 236 E5
Lakhpat India 23°48N 68°47E 242 H3
Lakhtinskiy Russia 59°59N 30°9E 137 B1
Lakhtinskiy Razliv, Oz. Russia 59°59N 30°12E 137 B1
Läki Azerbaijan 40°34N 47°22E 191 K8
Laki Bulgaria 41°50N 24°43E 203 E8
Laki Iceland 64°4N 18°14W 155 C8
Lakin U.S.A. 37°57N 101°15W 308 G3
Lakitusaki → Canada 54°21N 82°25W 298 B3
Lakka Greece 39°17N 20°9E 206 C10
Lakki Greece 35°24N 23°57E 207 E4
Lakki Pakistan 32°36N 70°55E 242 C4
Lakonia Greece 36°55N 22°30E 204 E4
Lakonikos Kolpos Greece 36°40N 22°40E 204 E4
Lakor Indonesia 8°15S 128°17E 231 F7
Lakota Côte d'Ivoire 5°50N 5°30W 262 D3
Lakota N. Dak., U.S.A. 48°2N 98°21W 308 A4
Laksar India 29°46N 78°3E 242 E8
Laksefjorden Norway 70°45N 26°50E 160 A22
Lakselv Norway 70°2N 25°0E 160 A21
Laksettipet India 18°52N 79°13E 244 E4
Lakshadweep □ India 10°0N 72°30E 245 J1
Lakshadweep Is. India 10°0N 72°30E 245 J1
Laksham Bangla. 23°14N 91°8E 241 D3
Lakshimpur Bangla. 22°58N 90°50E 241 D3
Lakshmanpur Chhattisgarh, India 22°58N 83°3E 243 H10
Lakshmanpur Paschimbanga, India 22°38N 88°16E 124 B1
Lakshmeshwar India 15°9N 75°28E 245 G2
Lakshmikantapur India 22°5N 88°20E 243 H13
Laksi Thailand 13°53N 100°35E 113 A2
Lakuramau Papua N. G. 2°54S 151°15E 286 B6
Lal-lo Phil. 18°12N 121°40E 232 B3
Lal Qila Delhi, India 120 a3
Lala Dem. Rep. of the Congo 4°10S 20°30E 265 C4
Lala Phil. 7°59N 123°46E 233 H4
Lala Musa Pakistan 32°40N 73°57E 242 C5
Lalaghat India 24°30N 92°40E 241 C4
Lalago Tanzania 3°28S 33°58E 268 C3
Lalang → Indonesia 2°24S 104°39E 234 C2
Lalapanzi Zimbabwe 19°20S 30°15E 269 F3
Lalapaşa Turkey 41°49N 26°44E 203 E10
Lalara Gabon 0°19N 11°32E 264 B2
Lalbenque France 44°19N 1°34E 174 D5
Lalbert Australia 35°38S 143°20E 282 C5
L'Albufera Spain 39°20N 0°27W 197 F4
L'Alcora Spain 40°5N 0°14W 196 E4
L'Alfàs del Pi Spain 38°35N 0°5W 197 G4
Lalganj India 25°52N 85°13E 243 G11
Lalgola India 24°25N 88°15E 243 G13
Lālī Iran 32°21N 49°6E 247 C6
Lalibela Ethiopia 12°3N 39°0E 257 E4
Lalin Heilongjiang, China 45°12N 127°0E 227 B14
Lalín Spain 42°40N 8°5W 194 C2
Lalin He → China 45°32N 125°40E 227 B13
Lalinde France 44°50N 0°44E 174 D4
Lalitpur India 24°42N 78°28E 243 G8
Lalitpur Nepal 27°40N 85°20E 243 F11
Lalkua India 29°5N 79°31E 243 E8
Lalm Norway 61°50N 9°17E 164 C6
Lalmanir Hat Bangla. 25°54N 89°27E 241 C2
Lalsot India 26°34N 76°20E 242 F7
Lam Nam Nan △ Thailand 17°55N 100°28E 236 D3
Lam Pao Res. Thailand 16°50N 103°15E 236 D4
Lam Tin Hong Kong, China 22°18N 114°14E 122 B3
Lama Kara Togo 9°30N 1°15E 263 D5
Lamae Thailand 9°51N 99°5E 237 H2
Lamag Malaysia 5°29N 117°49E 235 A5
Lamaing Myanmar 15°25N 97°53E 236 E2
Lamaipum Myanmar 25°40N 97°57E 241 C6
Lamap Vanuatu 16°26S 167°43E 287 F5
Lamar Colo., U.S.A. 38°5N 102°37W 304 G12
Lamar Mo., U.S.A. 37°30N 94°16W 308 G6
Lamarque Argentina 39°24S 65°40W 336 A3
Lamas Peru 6°28S 76°31W 330 B2
Lamastre France 44°59N 4°35E 175 D8
Lamayuru India 34°25N 76°56E 243 B7
Lambach Austria 48°6N 13°51E 180 C6
Lamballe France 48°29N 2°31W 172 D4
Lambaréné Gabon 0°41S 10°12E 264 C2
Lambasa = Labasa Fiji 16°30S 179°27E 287 A2
Lambay I. Ireland 53°29N 6°1W 166 C5
Lambayeque □ Peru 6°45S 80°0W 330 B2
Lambert Norway 59°52N 10°48E 133 A3
Lambert, C. Papua N. G. 4°11S 151°31E 286 C6
Lambert-St. Louis Int. ✈ (STL) U.S.A. 38°45N 90°22W 310 F6
Lambert's Bay S. Africa 32°5S 18°17E 270 D2
Lambertville U.S.A. 41°46N 83°37W 311 C13
Lambesc France 43°39N 5°16E 175 E9
Lambèse = Tazoult Algeria 35°29N 6°11E 261 A6
Lambeth Canada 42°54N 81°18W 312 D3
Lambeth □ U.K. 51°28N 0°6W 125 B3
Lambi Solomon Is. 9°22S 159°39E 287 M10
Lambia Greece 37°52N 21°53E 204 D3
Lambir Hills △ Malaysia 4°12N 114°2E 235 B4
Lambomakondro Madag. 22°41S 44°44E 272 C1
Lambon Papua N. G. 4°45S 152°48E 286 C7
Lambrate Italy 45°28N 9°16E 128 B2
Lambro → Italy 45°8N 9°32E 198 C6
Lambro, Parco Italy 45°29N 9°14E 128 B2
Lambton Mills Canada 43°39N 79°30W 141 B1
Lambu Papua N. G. 3°18S 151°43E 286 B6
Lambunao Phil. 11°3N 122°29E 233 F4
Lamé Chad 9°15N 14°32E 259 G2
Lame Nigeria 10°30N 9°20E 263 C6
Lame Deer U.S.A. 45°37N 106°40W 304 D10
Lamego Portugal 41°5N 7°52W 194 D3
Lamentin Guadeloupe 16°16N 61°38W 322 e
Lamèque Canada 47°45N 64°38W 299 C7
Lameroo Australia 35°19S 140°33E 282 C4
Lamesa U.S.A. 32°44N 101°58W 314 E4
L'Ametlla de Mar Spain 40°53N 0°48E 196 E5
Lamezia Terme Italy 38°55N 16°16E 201 D9
Lami Fiji 18°7S 178°25E 287 B2
Lamia Greece 38°55N 22°26E 204 C4
Lamigan Pt. Phil. 6°48N 126°21E 233 H6
Lamine → U.S.A. 38°59N 92°51W 310 F4
Lamington, Mt. Papua N. G. 8°57S 148°9E 286 E5
Lamington △ Australia 28°13S 153°12E 281 D5
Lamitan Phil. 6°39N 122°8E 233 H4
Lamlam, Mt. Guam 13°22N 144°41E 302 d
Lamma I. Hong Kong, China 22°12N 114°7E 122 B2
Lammermuir Hills U.K. 55°50N 2°40W 167 F6
Lammeulo Indonesia 5°14N 95°56E 234 A1
Lammhult Sweden 57°10N 14°35E 163 G8
Lamoille → U.S.A. 44°38N 73°13W 313 B11
Lamon B. Phil. 14°30N 122°20E 232 D4
Lamongan Indonesia 7°7S 112°25E 235 D4
Lamoni U.S.A. 40°37N 93°56W 310 D3
Lamont Alta., Canada 53°46N 112°50W 296 C6
Lamont Calif., U.S.A. 35°15N 118°55W 307 K8
Lamont Fla., U.S.A. 30°23N 83°49W 316 E6
Lamont Iowa, U.S.A. 42°36N 91°39W 310 B5
Lamont Wyo., U.S.A. 42°13N 107°29W 304 E10
Lamotte-Beuvron France 47°36N 2°2E 173 E9
Lampa Peru 15°22S 70°22W 330 D3
Lampang Thailand 18°16N 99°32E 236 C2
Lampasas U.S.A. 31°4N 98°11W 314 F5
Lampazos de Naranjo Mexico 27°1N 100°31W 318 B4
Lampedusa Medit. S. 35°36N 12°40E 258 A2
Lampertheim Germany 49°35N 8°27E 179 F4
Lampeter U.K. 52°7N 4°4W 169 E3
Lamphun Thailand 18°40N 99°2E 236 C2
Lampione Medit. S. 35°33N 12°20E 258 A2
Lampman Canada 49°25N 102°50W 297 D8
Lamprechtshausen Austria 48°0N 12°58E 180 D5
Lampung □ Indonesia 5°30S 104°30E 234 D2
Lampung, Teluk Indonesia 5°40S 105°20E 234 D3
Lamta India 22°8N 80°7E 243 H9
Lamu Coast, Kenya 2°16S 40°55E 268 C5
Lamu Myanmar 19°14N 94°10E 241 F5
Lamud Peru 6°10S 77°57W 330 B2
Lamy U.S.A. 35°29N 105°53W 305 J11
Lan Xian China 38°15N 111°35E 226 E6
Lan Yü Taiwan 22°4N 121°25E 225 D3
Lāna'i U.S.A. 20°50N 156°55W 302 C5
Lāna'i City U.S.A. 20°50N 156°55W 302 C5
Lāna'ihale U.S.A. 20°49N 156°53W 302 C5
Lanak La China 34°27N 79°32E 243 B8
Lanak'o Shank'ou = Lanak La China 34°27N 79°32E 243 B8
Lanao, L. Phil. 7°52N 124°15E 233 H5
Lanao del Norte □ Phil. 8°0N 124°0E 233 H5
Lanao del Sur □ Phil. 7°40N 124°15E 233 H5
Lanark Ont., Canada 45°1N 76°22W 313 A8
Lanark S. Lanarks., U.K. 55°40N 3°47W 167 F5
Lanark Ill., U.S.A. 42°6N 89°50W 310 B7
Lanbi Kyun Myanmar 10°50N 98°20E 237 G2
Lancang China 22°36N 99°58E 228 F2
Lancang Jiang → China 21°40N 101°10E 228 G3
Lancashire □ U.K. 53°50N 2°48W 168 D5
Lancaster Ont., Canada 45°10N 74°30W 313 A10
Lancaster Lancs., U.K. 54°3N 2°48W 168 C5
Lancaster Calif., U.S.A. 34°42N 118°8W 307 L8
Lancaster Ky., U.S.A. 37°37N 84°35W 309 G11
Lancaster Mo., U.S.A. 40°31N 92°32W 310 D4
Lancaster N.H., U.S.A. 44°29N 71°34W 313 B13
Lancaster Ohio, U.S.A. 39°43N 82°36W 309 F12
Lancaster Pa., U.S.A. 40°2N 76°19W 313 F8
Lancaster S.C., U.S.A. 34°43N 80°46W 315 D14
Lancaster Tex., U.S.A. 32°35N 96°45W 120 C5
Lancaster Wis., U.S.A. 42°51N 90°43W 310 B6
Lancaster, Récif = Neilson, Récif Pac. Oc. 27°15S 146°2W 289 f
Lancaster Sd. Canada 74°13N 84°0W 295 C15
Lancelin Australia 31°0S 115°18E 279 F2
Lanchow = Lanzhou China 36°1N 103°52E 226 F2
Lanchyn Ukraine 48°33N 24°45E 183 B9
Lanciano Italy 42°14N 14°23E 199 F11
Lanco Chile 39°24S 72°46W 336 A2
Lancones Peru 4°30S 80°30W 330 A1
Lancun China 36°25N 120°10E 227 F11
Łańcut Poland 50°10N 22°13E 185 H9
Land Between the Lakes ⌂ U.S.A. 36°25N 88°0W 315 C11
Landau Bayern, Germany 48°40N 12°41E 179 G8
Landau Rhld-Pfz., Germany 49°12N 8°6E 179 F4
Landay Afghan. 30°31N 63°47E 240 C1
Landeck Austria 47°9N 10°34E 180 D3
Lander U.S.A. 42°50N 108°44W 304 E9
Lander → Australia 22°0S 132°0E 278 D5
Landerneau France 48°28N 4°17W 172 D2
Landeryd Sweden 57°7N 13°15E 163 G7
Landes France 44°0N 1°0W 174 D2
Landes □ France 43°57N 0°48W 174 E3
Landes de Gascogne ⌂ France 44°23N 0°50W 174 D3
Landeshut = Kamienna Góra Poland 50°47N 16°2E 185 H3
Landete Spain 39°56N 1°25W 196 F3
Landfall I. India 13°40N 93°2E 245 H11
Landi Kotal Pakistan 34°7N 71°6E 242 B4
Landianchang China 39°56N 116°17E 114 B1
Landisburg U.S.A. 40°21N 77°19W 312 F7
Landivisiau France 48°31N 4°6W 172 D2
Landmannalaugar Iceland 63°59N 19°4W 155 D7
Landquart Switz. 46°58N 9°32E 179 J5
Landrecies France 50°7N 3°40E 173 B10
Land's End U.K. 50°4N 5°44W 169 G2
Landsberg = Górowo Iławeckie Poland 54°17N 20°30E 184 D7
Landsberg Germany 48°2N 10°53E 179 G6
Landsberg an der Warthe = Gorzów Wielkopolski Poland 52°43N 15°15E 185 F2
Landsberg in Oberschlesien = Gorzów Śląski Poland 51°3N 18°22E 185 G5
Landsborough Cr. → Australia 22°28S 144°35E 280 C3
Landsbro Sweden 57°24N 14°56E 163 G8
Landshut Germany 48°34N 12°8E 179 G8
Landskrona Sweden 55°53N 12°50E 163 J6
Landsmeer Neths. 52°26N 4°55E 112 A2
Landstrasse Austria 48°12N 16°23E 142 A2
Landstuhl Germany 49°25N 7°34E 179 F3
Landvetter Sweden 57°41N 12°17E 163 G6
Landwehr kanal Germany 52°29N 13°24E 115 B3
Lane U.S.A. 33°32N 79°53W 316 B10
Lane Cove Australia 33°48S 151°9E 139 A1
Lane Cove Nat. Park △ Australia 33°47S 151°8E 139 A1
Lanesboro U.S.A. 41°57N 75°34W 313 E9
Lanester France 47°46N 3°22W 172 E3
Lanett U.S.A. 32°52N 85°12W 316 C4
Lang Shan China 41°0N 106°30E 226 D4
Lang Son Vietnam 21°52N 106°42E 228 G6
Lang Suan Thailand 9°57N 99°4E 237 H2
Langå Midtjylland, Denmark 56°23N 9°54E 163 H3
Langa Western Cape, S. Africa 33°57S 18°31E 118 A2
La'nga Co China 30°45N 81°15E 243 D9
Langa-Langa Dem. Rep. of the Congo 3°50S 15°59E 264 C3
Langadas Greece 40°46N 23°6E 202 F7
Langadia Greece 37°43N 22°1E 204 D4

Långan → *Sweden* 63°19N 14°44E **162** A8
Langanes *Iceland* 66°20N 14°53W **155** A12
Langano, L. *Ethiopia* 7°36N 38°43E **257** F4
Langar *Afghan.* 37°2N 73°47E **240** A4
Langar *Iran* 35°23N 60°25E **247** C9
Langara I. *Canada* 54°14N 133°1W **296** C2
Langarūd *Iran* 37°11N 50°8E **247** B6
Långås *Sweden* 56°58N 12°26E **163** H6
Langatabbetje *Suriname* 4°59N 54°28W **329** C7
Langdai *China* 26°6N 105°21E **228** D5
Langdon *U.S.A.* 48°45N 98°22W **308** A4
Långe Jan = Ölands södra udde *Sweden* 56°12N 16°23E **163** H10
Langeac *France* 45°7N 3°29E **174** C7
Langeais *France* 47°20N 0°24E **172** E7
Langeb Baraka → *Sudan* 17°28N 36°50E **256** D4
Langeberg *S. Africa* 33°55S 21°0E **270** D3
Langeberge *S. Africa* 28°15S 22°33E **270** C3
Langeland *Denmark* 54°56N 10°48E **163** K4
Langelands Bælt *Denmark* 54°50N 10°55E **163** K4
Langen *Hessen, Germany* 49°59N 8°40E **179** F4
Langen *Niedersachsen, Germany* 53°36N 8°36E **178** B4
Langenbielau = Bielawa *Poland* 50°43N 16°37E **185** H3
Langenburg *Canada* 50°51N 101°43W **297** C8
Langeneß *Germany* 54°38N 8°36E **178** A4
Langenlois *Austria* 48°29N 15°40E **180** C8
Langenzersdorf *Austria* 48°18N 16°21E **142** A2
Langeoog *Germany* 53°45N 7°32E **178** B3
Langer See *Germany* 52°24N 13°37E **115** B4
Langeskov *Denmark* 55°22N 10°35E **163** J4
Langesund *Norway* 59°0N 9°45E **164** F6
Langevåg *Norway* 62°26N 6°13E **164** B3
Langfang *China* 39°30N 116°41E **226** E9
Langfoss *Norway* 59°51N 6°20E **164** E3
Langgapayung *Indonesia* 1°43N 99°58E **234** B1
Långhem *Sweden* 57°36N 13°14E **163** G7
Langhirano *Italy* 44°37N 10°16E **198** D7
Langholm *U.K.* 55°9N 3°0W **167** F5
Langisjór *Iceland* 64°11N 18°15W **155** C8
Langjökull *Iceland* 64°39N 20°12W **155** C6
Langkawi, Pulau *Malaysia* 6°25N 99°45E **237** J2
Langklip *S. Africa* 28°12S 20°20E **270** C3
Langkon *Malaysia* 6°30N 116°40E **235** A5
Langley *B.C., Canada* 49°7N 122°39W **306** A4
Langley *Va., U.S.A.* 38°57N 77°11W **143** B1
Langley Park *U.S.A.* 38°59N 76°58W **143** B3
Langnau *Switz.* 46°56N 7°47E **179** J3
Langogne *France* 44°43N 3°50E **174** D7
Langon *France* 44°33N 0°16W **174** D3
Langøya *Norway* 68°45N 14°50E **160** B16
Langreo *Spain* 43°18N 5°40W **194** B5
Langres *France* 47°52N 5°20E **173** E12
Langres, Plateau de *France* 47°45N 5°3E **173** E12
Langsa *Indonesia* 4°30N 97°57E **234** B1
Långsele *Sweden* 63°12N 17°4E **162** A11
Långshyttan *Sweden* 60°27N 16°2E **162** D10
Langtang △ *Nepal* 28°10N 85°30E **243** E11
Langtao *Myanmar* 27°15N 97°34E **241** B6
Langting *India* 25°31N 93°7E **241** C4
Langtou *China* 40°1N 124°19E **227** D13
Langtry *U.S.A.* 29°49N 101°34W **314** G4
Langu *Thailand* 6°53N 99°47E **237** J2
Langue de Barbarie △ *Senegal* 14°54N 16°30W **262** C1
Languedoc *France* 43°58N 3°55E **174** E7
Langwald *Germany* 48°10N 11°25E **131** A1
Langwang *China* 22°38N 113°27E **219** a
Langxi *China* 31°10N 119°12E **229** B12
Langzhong *China* 31°38N 105°58E **228** B5
Lanigan *Canada* 51°51N 105°2W **297** C7
Lanikai *U.S.A.* 21°23N 157°42W **302** K14
Lanín △ *Argentina* 40°0S 71°58W **336** A2
Lanjigarh *India* 19°43N 83°23E **244** E6
Lankao *China* 34°48N 114°50E **226** G8
Länkäran *Azerbaijan* 38°48N 48°52E **213** C13
Lankwitz *Germany* 52°25N 13°21E **115** B3
Lanmeur *France* 48°39N 3°43W **172** D3
Lannemezan *France* 43°8N 0°23E **174** E4
Lannilis *France* 48°35N 4°32W **172** D2
Lannion *France* 48°46N 3°29W **172** D3
L'Annonciation *Canada* 46°25N 74°55W **298** C5
L'Annunziatella *Italy* 41°49N 12°33E **136** C2
Lanouaille *France* 45°24N 1°9E **174** C5
Lanping *China* 26°28N 99°15E **228** D2
Lansang △ *Thailand* 16°45N 99°0E **236** D2
Lansdale *U.S.A.* 40°14N 75°17W **313** F9
Lansdowne *N.S.W., Australia* 31°48S 152°30E **283** A10
Lansdowne *Ont., Canada* 44°24N 76°1W **313** B8
Lansdowne *India* 29°50N 78°41E **243** E8
Lansdowne *Western Cape, S. Africa* 33°59S 18°30E **118** A2
Lansdowne House = Neskantaga *Canada* 52°14N 87°53W **298** B2
L'Anse *U.S.A.* 46°45N 88°27W **308** B9
L'Anse à l'Âne *Martinique* 14°32N 61°4W **322** j
L'Anse au Loup *Canada* 51°32N 56°50W **299** B8
L'Anse Aux Epines *Grenada* 11°59N 61°45W **323** q
L'Anse aux Meadows *Canada* 51°36N 55°32W **299** B8
L'Anse Mitan *Martinique* 14°32N 61°3W **322** j
Lansford *U.S.A.* 40°50N 75°53W **313** F9
Lanshan *China* 25°24N 112°10E **229** E9
Lanshantou *China* 35°5N 119°20E **227** G10
Länsi-Turunmaa *Finland* 60°18N 22°18E **188** B2
Lansing *Ont., Canada* 43°45N 79°24W **141** A2
Lansing *Mich., U.S.A.* 42°44N 84°33W **311** B12
Lanslebourg-Mont-Cenis *France* 45°17N 6°52E **175** C10
Lanta, Ko *Thailand* 7°35N 99°3E **237** J2
Lantana *U.S.A.* 26°35N 80°3W **317** J9
Lantau I. *Hong Kong, China* 22°15N 113°56E **122** B1
Lantau Pk. *Hong Kong, China* 22°15N 113°55E **122** B1
Lantewa *Nigeria* 12°16N 11°44E **263** C7
Lantian *China* 34°11N 109°20E **226** G5
Lanus *Argentina* 34°42S 58°23W **117** C2
Lanusei *Italy* 39°52N 9°34E **200** C2
Lanuza *Phil.* 9°14N 126°4E **233** G6
Lanxi *China* 29°13N 119°28E **229** C12
Lanyang Hsi → *Taiwan* 24°43N 121°49E **225** B3
Lanyü *Taiwan* 22°2N 121°33E **225** D3
Lanzarote *Canary Is.* 29°0N 13°40W **153** e2
Lanzarote ✈ **(ACE)** *Canary Is.* 28°57N 13°40W **153** e2
Lanzhou *China* 36°1N 103°52E **226** F2
Lanzo Torinese *Italy* 45°16N 7°28E **198** C4
Lao → *Italy* 39°47N 15°48E **201** C8
Lao Cai *Vietnam* 22°30N 103°57E **228** F4
Laoag *Phil.* 18°7N 120°34E **232** B3
Laoang *Phil.* 12°32N 125°8E **232** E5
Laoha He → *China* 43°25N 120°35E **227** C11
Laohekou *China* 32°22N 111°38E **229** A8
Laois □ *Ireland* 52°57N 7°27W **166** D4
Laon *France* 49°33N 3°35E **173** C10
Laona *U.S.A.* 45°34N 88°40W **308** C9
Laonung Hsi → *Taiwan* 22°47N 120°27E **225** D2
Laos ■ *Asia* 17°45N 105°0E **236** D5
Lapa *Paraná, Brazil* 25°46S 49°44W **335** B6
Lapa *Rio de J., Brazil* 22°54S 43°10W **135** B1
Lapac I. *Phil.* 5°32N 120°47E **233** J3
Lapai *Nigeria* 9°5N 6°32E **263** D6
Lapalisse *France* 46°15N 3°38E **173** F10
Laparan I. *Phil.* 5°57N 120°0E **233** J2
Lapeer *U.S.A.* 43°3N 83°19W **311** A13
Lapeyrade *France* 44°4N 0°3W **174** D3
Lapithos *Cyprus* 35°21N 33°11E **207** E9
Lapland = Lappland *Europe* 68°7N 24°0E **160** B21
LaPorte *Ind., U.S.A.* 41°36N 86°43W **311** C10
Laporte *Pa., U.S.A.* 41°25N 76°30W **313** E8
Lapovo *Serbia* 44°10N 21°7E **202** B5
Lappeenranta *Finland* 61°3N 28°12E **188** B5
Lappland *Europe* 68°7N 24°0E **160** B21
Lappo = Lapua *Finland* 62°58N 23°0E **160** E20
Laprida *Argentina* 37°34S 60°45W **334** D3
Lâpsekı *Turkey* 40°20N 26°41E **203** F10
Lapta = Lapithos *Cyprus* 35°21N 33°11E **207** E9
Laptev Sea *Russia* 76°0N 125°0E **215** B13
Lapu-Lapu *Phil.* 10°20N 123°55E **233** F4
Lapua *Finland* 62°58N 23°0E **160** E20
Lăpuş → *Romania* 47°25N 23°40E **183** C8
Lăpuş, Munţii *Romania* 47°20N 23°50E **183** C8
Lăpuşna *Moldova* 46°53N 28°25E **183** D13
Łapy *Poland* 52°59N 22°52E **185** F9
Laqiya Arba'in *Sudan* 20°1N 28°1E **256** C2
Laqiya Umran *Sudan* 19°55N 28°18E **256** D2
L'Àquila *Italy* 42°22N 13°22E **199** F10
Lār *Iran* 27°40N 54°14E **247** E7
Lara *Australia* 38°2S 144°26E **282** E6
Lara □ *Venezuela* 10°10N 69°50W **328** A4
Larabanga *Ghana* 9°16N 1°56W **262** D4
Larache *Morocco* 35°10N 6°5W **260** A3
Laragaran = Plaridel *Phil.* 8°37N 123°43E **233** G4
Laragne-Montéglin *France* 44°18N 5°49E **175** D9
Lārak *Iran* 26°51N 56°21E **247** E8
Laramie *U.S.A.* 41°19N 105°35W **304** F11
Laramie Mts. *U.S.A.* 42°0N 105°30W **304** F11
Laranda = Karaman *Turkey* 37°14N 33°13E **212** D5
Laranjal do Jari *Brazil* 0°51S 52°32W **329** D7
Laranjeiras *Brazil* 22°55S 43°10W **135** B1
Laranjeiras do Sul *Brazil* 25°23S 52°23W **335** B5
Larantuka *Indonesia* 8°21S 122°55E **231** F6
Larat *Indonesia* 7°0S 132°0E **231** F8
L'Arbresle *France* 45°50N 4°36E **175** C8
Lärbro *Sweden* 57°47N 18°50E **163** G12
Lårdal *Norway* 59°25N 8°10E **164** E5
Larde *Mozam.* 16°28S 39°43E **269** F4
Larder Lake *Canada* 48°5N 79°40W **298** C4
Lardos *Greece* 36°6N 28°1E **206** E12
Lardos, Akra = Lindos, Akra *Greece* 36°4N 28°10E **206** E12
Lardos, Ormos *Greece* 36°4N 28°2E **206** E12
Lare *Kenya* 0°20N 37°56E **268** C4
Laredo *Spain* 43°26N 3°28W **194** B7
Laredo *Tex., U.S.A.* 27°30N 99°30W **314** H5
Laredo Sd. *Canada* 52°30N 128°53W **296** C3
Larena *Phil.* 9°15N 123°35E **233** G4
Lares *Puerto Rico* 18°18N 66°53W **321** b
Large I. *Grenada* 12°24N 61°30W **323** q
Largentière *France* 44°34N 4°18E **175** D8
L'Argentière-la-Bessée *France* 44°47N 6°33E **175** D10
Largo *U.S.A.* 27°54N 82°47W **317** H7
Largo, Cayo *Cuba* 21°37N 81°28W **320** B3
Largo, Key *U.S.A.* 25°15N 80°15W **317** K9
Largs *U.K.* 55°47N 4°52W **167** F4
Lari *Italy* 43°34N 10°35E **198** E7
Lariang *Indonesia* 1°26S 119°17E **235** C5
Larimore *U.S.A.* 47°54N 97°38W **308** B5
Larino *Italy* 41°48N 14°54E **199** G11
Lario, Il = Como, L. di *Italy* 46°0N 9°11E **198** B6
Larisa *Greece* 39°36N 22°27E **204** B4
Larisis Station *Athens, Greece* **112** a1
Larissa = Larisa *Greece* 39°36N 22°27E **204** B4
Larkana *Pakistan* 27°32N 68°18E **242** F3
Larkins = South Miami *U.S.A.* 25°42N 80°17W **129** D1
Larnaca *Cyprus* 34°55N 33°38E **207** F9
Larnaca Bay *Cyprus* 34°53N 33°45E **207** F9
Larnaca Int. ✈ **(LCA)** *Cyprus* 34°50N 33°34E **207** F9
Larnare, Pte. *Martinique* 14°47N 61°13W **322** j
Larne *U.K.* 54°51N 5°51W **166** B6
Larned *U.S.A.* 38°11N 99°6W **308** F4
Laroquebrou *France* 44°58N 2°12E **174** D6
Larose *U.S.A.* 29°34N 90°23W **315** G9
Larose, Pte. *Martinique* 14°39N 60°53W **322** j
Larrimah *Australia* 15°35S 133°12E **278** C5
Larsen Bay *U.S.A.* 57°32N 153°59W **303** H9
Larsen Ice Shelf *Antarctica* 67°0S 62°0W **151** C17
Laruns *France* 43°0N 0°26W **174** F3
Larvik *Norway* 59°4N 10°2E **164** E7
Larzac, Causse du *France* 44°0N 3°17E **174** E7
Las *Poland* 52°13N 21°6E **143** B2
Las Alpujarras *Spain* 36°55N 3°20W **197** J1
Las Animas *U.S.A.* 38°4N 103°13W **304** G12
Las Anod *Somalia* 8°26N 47°19E **267** C6
Las Arenas *Spain* 43°17N 4°50W **194** B6
Las Batuecas △ *Spain* 40°32N 6°5W **194** E4
Las Bermúdez *Venezuela* 10°56N 64°1W **329** a
Las Bonitas *Venezuela* 7°52N 65°40W **328** B4
Las Brenãs *Argentina* 27°5S 61°7W **334** B3
Las Cabezas de San Juan *Spain* 36°57N 5°58W **195** J5
Las Cabreras *Venezuela* 11°3N 63°58W **329** a
Las Cañadas del Teide △ *Canary Is.* 28°15N 16°37W **153** e1
Las Cejas *Argentina* 26°53S 64°44W **334** B3
Las Chimeneas *Mexico* 32°8N 116°5W **307** N10
Las Coloradas *Argentina* 39°34S 70°36W **336** A2
Las Corts *Spain* 41°23N 2°9E **114** A1
Las Cruces *U.S.A.* 32°19N 106°47W **305** K10
Las Flores *Argentina* 36°10S 59°7W **334** D4
Las Gabias = Gabia la Grande *Spain* 37°8N 3°40W **195** H7
Las Heras *Mendoza, Argentina* 32°51S 68°49W **334** C2
Las Heras *Santa Cruz, Argentina* 46°33S 68°57W **336** C3
Las Hermosas △ *Colombia* 3°48N 75°51W **328** C2
Las Horquetas *Argentina* 48°14S 71°11W **336** C2
Las Kabacki *Poland* 52°7N 21°2E **143** C2
Las Khoreh = Laasqoray *Somalia* 11°10N 48°20E **267** B6
Las Lajas *Argentina* 38°30S 70°25W **336** A2
Las Lomas *Peru* 4°40S 80°10W **330** A1
Las Lomitas *Argentina* 24°43S 60°35W **334** A3
Las Manos, Cueva de *Argentina* 47°9S 70°40W **336** C2
Las Marismas *Spain* 37°5N 6°20W **195** H4
Las Médulas *Spain* 42°28N 6°46W **194** C4
Las Mercedes *Venezuela* 9°7N 66°24W **328** B4
Las Minas *Spain* 38°20N 1°41W **197** G3
Las Navas de la Concepción *Spain* 37°56N 5°30W **195** H5
Las Navas del Marqués *Spain* 40°36N 4°20W **194** E6
Las Nieves *Phil.* 8°46N 125°34E **233** G5
Las Orquideas △ *Colombia* 6°36N 76°16W **328** B2
Las Palmas *Argentina* 27°8S 58°45W **334** B4
Las Palmas → *Mexico* 32°31N 116°58W **307** N10
Las Palmas ✈ **(LPA)** *Canary Is.* 27°55N 15°25W **153** e1
Las Palmas de Gran Canaria *Canary Is.* 28°7N 15°26W **153** e1
Las Pedroñeras *Spain* 39°26N 2°40W **197** F2
Las Piedras *Puerto Rico* 18°11N 65°52W **321** b
Las Piedras *Uruguay* 34°44S 56°14W **335** C4
Las Pinas *Phil.* 14°29N 120°58E **127** C1
Las Pipinas *Argentina* 35°30S 57°19W **334** D4
Las Plumas *Argentina* 43°40S 67°15W **336** B3
Las Ramblas = La Rambla *Barcelona, Spain* **114** b2
Las Rejas *Chile* 33°27S 70°42W **137** B1
Las Rosas *Argentina* 32°30S 61°35W **334** C3
Las Rozas *Spain* 40°29N 3°52W **194** E7
Las Tablas *Panama* 7°49N 80°14W **320** E3
Las Toscas *Argentina* 28°21S 59°18W **334** B4
Las Tunas *Cuba* 20°58N 76°59W **320** B4
Las Varillas *Argentina* 31°50S 62°50W **334** C3
Las Vegas *N. Mex., U.S.A.* 35°36N 105°13W **305** J11
Las Vegas *Nev., U.S.A.* 36°10N 115°8W **124** A2
Las Vegas McCarran Int. ✈ **(LAS)** *U.S.A.* 36°5N 115°9W **124** B2
Lasa = Lhasa *China* 29°25N 90°58E **218** F7
LaSalle *Canada* 45°26N 73°38W **130** B2
LaSalle Street *Chicago, U.S.A.* **119** a1
LaSalle Street Station *Chicago, U.S.A.* **119** d1
Lasanga I. *Papua N. G.* 7°25S 147°15E **286** D4
Lasarte-Oria *Spain* 43°16N 2°1W **196** B2
Lascano *Uruguay* 33°35S 54°12W **335** C5
Lascelles *Australia* 35°34S 142°34E **282** C5
Lasek Bielański *Poland* 52°17N 20°57E **143** B1
Lasek Na Kole *Poland* 52°15N 20°56E **143** B1
Lash-e Joveyn *Afghan.* 31°45N 61°30E **240** C1
Lashburn *Canada* 53°10N 109°40W **297** C7
Lashio *Myanmar* 22°56N 97°45E **241** D6
Lashkar *India* 26°10N 78°10E **242** F8
Lashkar Gāh *Afghan.* 31°35N 64°21E **240** C2
Łasin *Poland* 53°30N 19°2E **184** E6
Lasithi *Greece* 35°11N 25°31E **207** E6
Lāsjerd *Iran* 35°24N 53°4E **247** C7
Lask *Poland* 51°34N 19°8E **185** G6
Łaskarzew *Poland* 51°48N 21°36E **185** G8
Laško *Slovenia* 46°10N 15°16E **199** B12
Lassance *Brazil* 17°54S 44°34W **333** E3
Lassay-les-Châteaux *France* 48°27N 0°30W **172** D6
Lassen Pk. *U.S.A.* 40°29N 121°30W **304** F3
Lassen Volcanic △ *U.S.A.* 40°30N 121°20W **304** F3
Lassongo *Angola* 12°5S 22°46E **265** E4
Last Mountain L. *Canada* 51°5N 105°14W **297** C7
Lastchance Cr. → *U.S.A.* 40°2N 121°15W **306** E5
Lastoursville *Gabon* 0°55S 12°38E **264** C2
Lastovo *Croatia* 42°46N 16°55E **199** F13
Lastovski Kanal *Croatia* 42°50N 17°0E **199** F14
Lat Yao *Thailand* 15°45N 99°48E **236** E2
Lata Mt. *Amer. Samoa* 14°14S 169°27W **302** f
Latacunga *Ecuador* 0°50S 78°35W **328** D2
Latady I. *Antarctica* 70°45S 74°35W **151** D17
Latakia = Al Lādhiqīyah *Syria* 35°30N 35°45E **250** C6
Latchford *Canada* 47°20N 79°50W **298** C4
Late *Tonga* 18°48S 174°39W **287** D13
Latehar *India* 23°45N 84°30E **243** H11
Laterza *Italy* 40°37N 16°48E **201** B9
Latham *Australia* 29°44S 116°20E **279** E2
Lathen *Germany* 52°52N 7°19E **178** C3
Lathi *India* 27°43N 71°23E **242** F4
Lathi *Vanuatu* 14°57S 167°8E **287** D5
Lathrop *U.S.A.* 39°33N 94°20W **310** E2
Lathrop Wells *U.S.A.* 36°39N 116°24W **307** J10
Latiano *Italy* 40°33N 17°43E **201** B10
Latin, Quartier *Montréal, Canada* **130** b2
Latina *Italy* 41°28N 12°52E **200** A5
Latina *Madrid, Spain* 40°24N 3°44W **127** B1
Latisana *Italy* 45°47N 13°0E **199** C10
Latium = Lazio □ *Italy* 42°10N 12°30E **199** F9
Laton *U.S.A.* 36°26N 119°41W **306** J7
Latorytsya → *Slovakia* 48°28N 21°50E **181** C14
Latouche Treville, C. *Australia* 18°27S 121°49E **278** C3
Latouma *Niger* 22°10N 14°50E **259** D2
Látrar *Iceland* 66°24N 23°2W **155** A3
Latrobe *Tas., Australia* 41°14S 146°30E **281** G4
Latrobe *Pa., U.S.A.* 40°19N 79°23W **312** F5
Latrónico *Italy* 40°5N 16°1E **201** B9
Latur *India* 18°25N 76°40E **244** E3
Latvia ■ *Europe* 56°50N 24°0E **188** D2
Lau *Nigeria* 9°11N 11°19E **263** D7
Lau Basin *Pac. Oc.* 20°0S 177°0W **277** E15
Lau Group *Fiji* 17°0S 178°30W **287** A3
Lau Ridge *Pac. Oc.* 21°0S 178°30W **277** E15
Lauban = Lubań *Poland* 51°5N 15°15E **185** G2
Lauca → *Bolivia* 19°9S 68°10W **330** D4
Lauchhammer *Germany* 51°29N 13°47E **178** D9
Lauda-Königshofen *Germany* 49°33N 9°42E **179** F5
Laudal *Norway* 58°15N 7°30E **164** F4
Laudat *Dominica* 15°20N 61°21W **323** k
Lauderdale Lakes *U.S.A.* 26°9N 80°12W **129** B1
Lauderhill *U.S.A.* 26°8N 80°12W **129** B2
Laudio = Llodio *Spain* 43°9N 2°58W **196** B2
Lauenburg = Lębork *Poland* 54°33N 17°46E **184** D4
Lauenburg *Germany* 53°22N 10°32E **178** B6
Lauenburgische Seen ⌂ *Germany* 53°38N 10°45E **178** B6
Lauf *Germany* 49°30N 11°16E **179** F7
Laufás *Iceland* 65°53N 18°4W **155** B8
Laugar *Iceland* 65°15N 21°48W **155** B5
Laugarás *Iceland* 64°7N 20°30W **155** C6
Laugarbakki *Iceland* 65°20N 20°55W **155** B6
Laugarvatn *Iceland* 64°13N 20°44W **155** C6
Lauge Koch Kyst *Greenland* 75°45N 57°45W **295** B20
Laughlin *U.S.A.* 35°10N 114°34W **307** K12
Lauhanvuori △ *Finland* 62°8N 22°4E **160** E20
Laujar de Andarax *Spain* 37°0N 2°54W **197** H2
Laukaa *Finland* 62°24N 25°56E **160** E21
Laukkaing *Myanmar* 23°52N 98°38E **241** D7
Laulau, Bahia *N. Marianas* 15°8N 145°45E **302** e
Launceston *Tas., Australia* 41°24S 147°8E **281** G4
Launceston *Corn., U.K.* 50°38N 4°22W **169** G3
Laune → *Ireland* 52°7N 9°47W **166** D2
Launglon Bok *Myanmar* 13°50N 97°54E **236** F1
Laupheim *Germany* 48°14N 9°52E **179** G5
Laura *Queens., Australia* 15°32S 144°32E **280** B3
Laura *S. Austral., Australia* 33°10S 138°18E **282** B3
Laureana di Borrello *Italy* 38°30N 16°5E **201** D9
Laurel *Fla., U.S.A.* 27°8N 82°27W **317** H7
Laurel *Ind., U.S.A.* 39°30N 85°11W **311** E11
Laurel *Miss., U.S.A.* 31°41N 89°8W **315** F10
Laurel *Mont., U.S.A.* 45°40N 108°46W **304** D9
Laurel Bay *U.S.A.* 32°27N 80°47W **316** C9
Laurel Hill *U.S.A.* 40°14N 79°6W **312** F5
Laurencekirk *U.K.* 56°50N 2°28W **167** E6
Laurens *Iowa, U.S.A.* 42°51N 94°51W **308** D6
Laurens *S.C., U.S.A.* 34°30N 82°1W **315** D13
Laurentian Plateau *Canada* 52°0N 70°0W **299** B6
Lauria *Italy* 40°2N 15°50E **201** B8
Laurie L. *Canada* 56°35N 101°57W **297** B8
Laurinburg *U.S.A.* 34°47N 79°28W **315** D15
Laurium *U.S.A.* 47°14N 88°27W **308** B9
Lausanne *Switz.* 46°32N 6°38E **179** J2
Laut *Indonesia* 4°45N 108°0E **235** B3
Laut, Pulau *Indonesia* 3°40S 116°10E **235** C5
Laut Kecil, Kepulauan *Indonesia* 4°45S 115°40E **235** C5
Lautaro *Chile* 38°31S 72°27W **336** A2
Lauterbach *Germany* 50°37N 9°24E **178** E5
Lauterecken *Germany* 49°38N 7°35E **179** F3
Lautoka *Fiji* 17°37S 177°27E **287** A1
L'Autre Bord *Guadeloupe* 16°20N 61°20W **322** e
Lauttasaari *Finland* 60°9N 24°53E **121** C2
Lauwersmeer △ *Neths.* 53°22N 6°11E **170** A6
Lauzès *France* 44°34N 1°35E **174** D5
Lava → *Russia* 54°37N 21°14E **184** D8
Lava, Nosy *Madag.* 14°33S 47°36E **272** A2
Lava Beds ⌂ *U.S.A.* 41°40N 121°30W **304** F3
Lavagh More *Ireland* 54°46N 8°6W **166** B3
Lavagna *Italy* 44°18N 9°20E **198** D6
Laval *France* 48°4N 0°48W **172** D6
Laval-des-Rapides *Canada* 45°33N 73°42W **130** A1
Lavalle *Argentina* 28°15S 65°15W **334** B2
Lāvān *Iran* 26°48N 53°22E **247** E7
Lavanggu *Solomon Is.* 11°36S 160°16E **287** N11
Lavant *Canada* 45°3N 76°42W **313** A8
Lāvar Meydān *Iran* 30°20N 54°30E **247** D7
Lavara *Greece* 41°19N 26°22E **203** E10
Lavardac *France* 44°12N 0°20E **174** D4
Lavaur *France* 43°40N 1°49E **174** E5
Lavelanet *France* 42°57N 1°51E **174** F5
Lavello *Italy* 41°3N 15°48E **201** A8
L'Averdy, C. *Papua N. G.* 5°33S 155°4E **286** C8
Lavers Hill *Australia* 38°40S 143°25E **282** E5
Laverton *Australia* 28°44S 122°29E **279** E3
Lavezzi, Îs. *France* 41°22N 9°16E **175** G13
Lavik *Norway* 61°6N 5°25E **164** C2
Lavìs *Italy* 46°8N 11°7E **198** B8
Lavīzān *Iran* 35°47N 51°30E **141** A2
Lavos *Portugal* 40°6N 8°49W **194** E2
Lavoutte, Anse *St. Lucia* 14°5N 60°55W **323** m
Lavradio *Portugal* 38°40N 9°2W **126** A2
Lavras *Brazil* 21°20S 45°0W **333** F3
Lavre *Portugal* 38°46N 8°22W **195** G2
Lavrio *Greece* 37°40N 24°4E **204** D6
Lavris *Greece* 35°25N 24°40E **207** E5
Lavumisa *Eswatini* 27°20S 31°55E **271** C5
Lavushi Manda △ *Zambia* 12°46S 31°0E **269** E3
Lawa *Phil.* 6°12N 125°41E **233** H5
Lawa-an *Phil.* 11°51N 125°5E **233** F5
Lawachara △ *Bangla.* 24°20N 91°43E **241** C3
Lawak I. = Nanshan I. *S. China Sea* 10°45N 115°49E **230** B5
Lawaki *Fiji* 17°40S 178°35E **287** A2
Lawas *Malaysia* 4°55N 115°25E **235** B5
Lawdar *Yemen* 13°53N 45°52E **248** D4
Lawele *Indonesia* 5°13S 122°57E **231** F6
Lawit *Indonesia* 1°23N 112°55E **235** B4
Lawksawk *Myanmar* 21°15N 96°52E **241** E6
Lawn Hill = Boodjamulla △ *Australia* 18°15S 138°6E **280** B2
Lawndale *U.S.A.* 41°50N 87°42W **119** B2
Lawne L. *U.S.A.* 28°33N 81°26W **133** A2
Lawqah *Si. Arabia* 29°49N 42°45E **246** D4
Lawra *Ghana* 10°39N 2°51W **262** C4
Lawrence *N.Z.* 45°55S 169°41E **285** F4
Lawrence *Ind., U.S.A.* 39°50N 86°2W **311** E10
Lawrence *Kans., U.S.A.* 38°58N 95°14W **308** F6
Lawrence *Mass., U.S.A.* 42°43N 71°10W **313** D13
Lawrence Heights *Canada* 43°43N 79°25W **141** A2
Lawrenceburg *Ind., U.S.A.* 39°6N 84°52W **311** E12
Lawrenceburg *Ky., U.S.A.* 38°2N 84°54W **311** F12
Lawrenceburg *Tenn., U.S.A.* 35°14N 87°20W **315** D11
Lawrenceville *Ga., U.S.A.* 33°57N 83°59W **316** B6
Lawrenceville *Ill., U.S.A.* 38°44N 87°41W **311** F9
Lawrenceville *Pa., U.S.A.* 41°59N 77°8W **312** E7
Laws *U.S.A.* 37°24N 118°20W **306** H8
Lawson *U.S.A.* 39°26N 94°12W **310** E2
Lawtey *U.S.A.* 30°3N 82°5W **316** E7
Lawton *Mich., U.S.A.* 42°10N 85°50W **311** B11
Lawton *Okla., U.S.A.* 34°37N 98°25W **314** D5
Lawu *Indonesia* 7°40S 111°13E **235** D4
Lawz, J. al *Si. Arabia* 28°39N 35°18E **251** K6
Laxå *Sweden* 58°59N 14°37E **163** F8
Laxamýri *Iceland* 65°58N 17°24W **155** B9
Laxford, L. *U.K.* 58°24N 5°6W **167** C3
Laxiwa Dam *China* 36°4N 101°11E **218** D9
Laxou *France* 48°41N 6°8E **173** D13
Lay → *France* 46°18N 1°17W **174** B2
Layari *Pakistan* 24°52N 67°0E **123** A2
Layari → *Pakistan* 24°52N 66°58E **123** A1
Layla *Si. Arabia* 22°10N 46°40E **248** B4
Laylān *Iraq* 35°18N 44°31E **246** C5
Layon → *France* 47°20N 0°45W **172** E6
Layou *St. Vincent* 13°12N 61°17W **323** n
Layou → *Dominica* 15°23N 61°21W **323** k
Laysan I. *U.S.A.* 25°50N 171°50W **302** F9
Layton *Fla., U.S.A.* 24°50N 80°47W **317** L9
Layton *Utah, U.S.A.* 41°4N 111°58W **304** F8
Laytonville *U.S.A.* 39°41N 123°29W **304** G2
Laza *Myanmar* 26°30N 97°38E **241** B6
Lazarata *Greece* 38°47N 20°40E **207** B2
Lazarev *Russia* 52°13N 141°30E **215** D15
Lazarev Sea *S. Ocean* 67°30S 3°0W **151** C2
Lazarevac *Serbia* 44°23N 20°17E **202** B4
Lazarevskoye *Russia* 43°55N 39°21E **191** J4
Lazarivo *Madag.* 23°54S 44°59E **272** C1
Lázaro Cárdenas *Mexico* 17°55N 102°11W **318** D4
Lazdijai *Lithuania* 54°14N 23°31E **184** D10
Lazhuglung *China* 34°52N 81°24E **217** F10
Lazi *Phil.* 9°8N 123°38E **233** G4
Lazienki Palace *Warsaw, Poland* **143** c3
Łazienkowski Park *Poland* 52°13N 21°1E **143** B2
Lazio □ *Italy* 42°10N 12°30E **199** F9
Lazo *Moldova* 47°33N 28°2E **183** C13
Lazo *Russia* 43°25N 133°55E **220** C6
Lazy Lake *U.S.A.* 26°9N 80°8W **129** B3
Lbishchensk = Chapaev *Kazakhstan* 50°25N 51°10E **190** E10
Le Beausset *France* 43°12N 5°48E **175** E9
Le Bélier *Réunion* 21°2S 55°28E **272** f
Le Bic *Canada* 48°20N 68°41W **299** C6
Le Blanc *France* 46°37N 1°3E **174** B5
Le Blanc-Mesnil *France* 48°56N 2°27E **134** A3
Le Bleymard *France* 44°30N 3°42E **174** D7
Le Bourget *France* 48°56N 2°25E **134** A3
Le Bourgneuf-la-Fôret *France* 48°10N 0°59W **172** D6
Le Bugue *France* 44°55N 0°56E **174** D4
Le Carbet *Martinique* 14°42N 61°11W **322** j
Le Cateau Cambrésis *France* 50°7N 3°32E **173** B10
Le Caylar *France* 43°51N 3°19E **174** E7
Le Chambon-Feugerolles *France* 45°24N 4°19E **175** C8
Le Chameau *Guadeloupe* 15°51N 61°35W **322** e
Le Châtelet *France* 46°38N 2°16E **173** F9
Le Chenoi *Belgium* 50°41N 4°18E **116** B2
Le Chesnay *France* 48°49N 2°8E **134** B1
Le Chesne *France* 49°30N 4°45E **173** C11
Le Cheylard *France* 44°55N 4°25E **175** D8
Le Christ de Saclay *France* 48°43N 1°59E **134** B2
Le Claire *U.S.A.* 41°36N 90°21W **310** C6
Le Conquet *France* 48°21N 4°46W **172** D2
Le Creusot *France* 46°48N 4°24E **173** F11
Le Croisic *France* 47°18N 2°30W **172** E4
Le Diamant *Martinique* 14°28N 61°2W **322** j
Le Donjon *France* 46°22N 3°48E **173** F10
Le Dorat *France* 46°14N 1°5E **174** B5
Le François *Martinique* 14°38N 60°57W **322** j
Le Gosier *Guadeloupe* 16°14N 61°29W **322** e
Le Grand Brûlé *Réunion* 21°14S 55°47E **272** f
Le Grand-Lucé *France* 47°52N 0°28E **172** E7
Le Grand-Pressigny *France* 46°55N 0°48E **172** F7
Le Grand-Quevilly *France* 49°24N 1°3E **172** C8
Le Gris Gris *Mauritius* 20°31S 57°32E **272** e
Le Gros Morne *Réunion* 21°5S 55°28E **272** f
Le Havre *France* 49°30N 0°5E **172** C7
Le Kremlin-Bicêtre *France* 48°48N 2°21E **134** B3
Le Lamentin *Martinique* 14°35N 61°2W **322** j
Le Lavandou *France* 43°8N 6°22E **175** E10
Le Lion-d'Angers *France* 47°37N 0°43W **172** E6
Le Lorrain *Martinique* 14°48N 61°3W **322** j
Le Louroux-Béconnais *France* 47°30N 0°55W **172** E6
Le Luc *France* 43°23N 6°21E **175** E10
Le Lude *France* 47°39N 0°9E **172** E7
Le Maire, Estr. de *Argentina* 54°50S 65°0W **336** D4
Le Mans *France* 48°0N 0°10E **172** E7
Le Marigot *Martinique* 14°50N 61°4W **322** j
Le Marin *Martinique* 14°27N 60°55W **322** j
Le Mars *U.S.A.* 42°47N 96°10W **308** D5
Le Mayet-de-Montagne *France* 46°4N 3°40E **173** F10
Le Mêle-sur-Sarthe *France* 48°31N 0°22E **172** D7
Le Mesnil-le-Roi *France* 48°56N 2°7E **134** A1
Le Monastier-sur-Gazeille *France* 44°57N 3°59E **174** D7
Le Monêtier-les-Bains *France* 44°58N 6°30E **175** D10
Le Mont-Dore *France* 45°35N 2°49E **174** C6
Le Mont-St-Michel *France* 48°40N 1°30W **172** D5
Le Morne Brabant *Mauritius* 20°27S 57°19E **272** e
Le Morne Rouge *Martinique* 14°47N 61°8W **322** j
Le Morne-Vert *Martinique* 14°42N 61°8W **322** j
Le Moule *Guadeloupe* 16°20N 61°22W **322** e
Le Moyne, L. *Canada* 56°45N 68°47W **299** A6
Le Muy *France* 43°28N 6°34E **175** E10
Le Palais *France* 47°20N 3°10W **172** E3
Le Pecq *France* 48°53N 2°6E **134** A1
Le Perreux *France* 48°50N 2°29E **134** A3
Le Perthus *France* 42°30N 2°53E **174** F6
Le Pin *France* 48°54N 2°37E **134** A4
Le Plessis-Robinson *France* 48°47N 2°15E **134** B2
Le Plessis-Trévise *France* 48°48N 2°34E **134** B4
Le Port *Réunion* 20°56S 55°18E **272** f
Le Port-Marly *France* 48°52N 2°6E **134** A1
Le Pré-St-Gervais *France* 48°53N 2°23E **134** A3
Le Prêcheur *Martinique* 14°50N 61°12W **322** j
Le Puy-en-Velay *France* 45°3N 3°52E **174** C7
Le Raincy *France* 48°53N 2°31E **134** A4
Le Raysville *U.S.A.* 41°50N 76°10W **313** E8
Le Robert *Martinique* 14°40N 60°56W **322** j
Le Roy *Ill., U.S.A.* 40°21N 88°46W **311** D8
Le Roy *N.Y., U.S.A.* 42°58N 77°59W **312** D7
Le St-Esprit *Martinique* 14°34N 60°56W **322** j
Le Souffleur *Guadeloupe* 16°19N 61°2W **322** e
Le Sueur *U.S.A.* 44°28N 93°55W **308** C7
Le Tampon *Réunion* 21°16S 55°32E **272** f
Le Teil *France* 44°33N 4°40E **175** D8
Le Teilleul *France* 48°32N 0°53W **172** D6
Le Theil *France* 48°16N 0°42E **172** D7
Le Thillot *France* 47°53N 6°46E **173** E13
Le Thuy *Vietnam* 17°14N 106°49E **236** D6
Le Touquet-Paris-Plage *France* 50°30N 1°36E **173** B8
Le Tréport *France* 50°3N 1°20E **172** B8
Le Trou à Diable *Guadeloupe* 15°57N 61°14W **322** e
Le Val-André *France* 48°35N 2°32W **172** D4
Le Val-d'Ajol *France* 47°55N 6°30E **173** E13
Le Val Nature Park *Mauritius* 20°22S 57°37E **272** e
Le Vauclin *Martinique* 14°33N 60°52W **322** j
Le Verdon-sur-Mer *France* 45°33N 1°4W **174** C2
Le Vésinet *France* 48°54N 2°8E **134** A1
Le Vigan *France* 43°59N 3°36E **174** E7
Le Vignoble, Isola *Venice, Italy* **142** a4
Lea → *U.K.* 51°31N 0°1E **169** F8
Lea Bridge *U.K.* 51°33N 0°2W **125** A3
Lea Lea *Papua N. G.* 9°17S 146°59E **286** E4
Leach *Cambodia* 12°21N 103°46E **237** F4
Lead *U.S.A.* 44°21N 103°46W **308** C2
Leader *Canada* 50°50N 109°30W **297** C7
Leadville *U.S.A.* 39°15N 106°18W **304** G10
Leaf → *U.S.A.* 30°59N 88°44W **315** F10
Leaf Rapids *Canada* 56°30N 99°59W **297** B9
Leaghur, L. *Australia* 33°35S 143°3E **282** B5
League City *U.S.A.* 29°31N 95°6W **314** C7
Leaksville = Eden *U.S.A.* 36°29N 79°53W **315** C15
Lealui *Zambia* 15°10S 23°2E **265** F4
Leamington *Ont., Canada* 42°3N 82°36W **312** D2
Leamington *N.Z.* 37°55S 175°30E **284** D4
Leamington *Utah, U.S.A.* 39°32N 112°17W **304** G7
Leamington Spa = Royal Leamington Spa *U.K.* 52°18N 1°31W **169** E6
Le'an *China* 27°22N 115°48E **229** D10
Leander *U.S.A.* 30°34N 97°52W **314** F5
Leandro Norte Alem *Argentina* 27°34S 55°15W **335** B4
Leane, L. *Ireland* 52°2N 9°32W **166** D2
Learmonth *Australia* 22°13S 114°10E **278** D1
Leary *U.S.A.* 31°29N 84°31W **316** D5
Leaside *Canada* 43°42N 79°22W **141** A2
Leask *Canada* 53°5N 106°45W **297** C7
Leatherhead *U.K.* 51°18N 0°20W **169** F7
Leavdnja = Lakselv *Norway* 70°2N 25°0E **160** A21
Leavenworth *Ind., U.S.A.* 38°12N 86°21W **311** F10
Leavenworth *Kans., U.S.A.* 39°19N 94°55W **308** F6
Leavenworth *Wash., U.S.A.* 47°36N 120°40W **304** C3
Leawood *U.S.A.* 38°58N 94°37W **310** F2
Łeba *Poland* 54°45N 17°32E **184** D4
Łeba → *Poland* 54°46N 17°33E **184** D4
Lebach *Germany* 49°25N 6°54E **179** F2
Lebak *Phil.* 6°32N 124°5E **233** H5
Lebam *U.S.A.* 46°34N 123°33W **306** D3
Lebane *Serbia* 42°56N 21°44E **202** D5
Lebango *Congo* 0°39N 14°21E **264** B2
Lebango → *Congo* 0°2N 14°52E **264** B2
Lebanon *Fla., U.S.A.* 29°10N 82°37W **317** F7
Lebanon *Ill., U.S.A.* 38°38N 89°49W **310** F7
Lebanon *Ind., U.S.A.* 40°3N 86°28W **311** D10
Lebanon *Kans., U.S.A.* 39°49N 98°33W **308** F4
Lebanon *Ky., U.S.A.* 37°34N 85°15W **309** G11
Lebanon *Mo., U.S.A.* 37°41N 92°40W **310** G4
Lebanon *N.H., U.S.A.* 43°39N 72°15W **313** C12
Lebanon *Ohio, U.S.A.* 39°26N 84°13W **311** E12
Lebanon *Oreg., U.S.A.* 44°32N 122°55W **304** D2
Lebanon *Pa., U.S.A.* 40°20N 76°26W **313** F8
Lebanon *Tenn., U.S.A.* 36°12N 86°18W **315** C11
Lebanon ■ *Asia* 34°0N 36°0E **250** E7
Lebanon Junction *U.S.A.* 37°50N 85°44W **311** G11
Lebap □ *Turkmenistan* 40°0N 63°0E **216** D6
Lebec *U.S.A.* 34°51N 118°52W **307** L8
Lebedyan *Russia* 53°0N 39°10E **189** F10
Lebedyn *Ukraine* 50°35N 34°30E **189** G8
Lebel-sur-Quévillon *Canada* 49°3N 76°59W **298** C4
Leblon *Brazil* 22°59S 43°14W **135** B1
Lebo *Dem. Rep. of the Congo* 4°30N 23°58E **264** B4
Lebomboberge *S. Africa* 24°30S 32°0E **271** B5
Lębork *Poland* 54°33N 17°46E **184** D4
Lebowakgomo *S. Africa* 24°12S 29°30E **271** B4
Lebrija *Spain* 36°53N 6°5W **195** J4
Łebsko, Jezioro *Poland* 54°40N 17°25E **184** D4
Lebu *Chile* 37°40S 73°47W **334** D1
Leça da Palmeira *Portugal* 41°12N 8°42W **194** D2
Lecce *Italy* 40°23N 18°11E **201** B11
Lecco *Italy* 45°51N 9°23E **198** C6
Lecco, L. di *Italy* 45°55N 9°19E **198** C6
Lécera *Spain* 41°13N 0°43W **196** D4
Lech *Austria* 47°13N 10°9E **180** D3
Lech → *Germany* 48°43N 10°56E **179** G6
Lechang *China* 25°10N 113°20E **229** E9
Lechena *Greece* 37°57N 21°16E **204** D3
Lechtaler Alpen *Austria* 47°15N 10°30E **180** D3
Lecontes Mills *U.S.A.* 41°5N 78°17W **312** E6
Lectoure *France* 43°56N 0°38E **174** E4
Łęczna *Poland* 51°18N 22°53E **185** G9
Łęczyca *Poland* 52°5N 19°15E **185** F6
Ledang, Gunung *Malaysia* 2°22N 102°37E **237** L4
Ledesma *Spain* 41°6N 5°59W **194** D5
Lediba *Dem. Rep. of the Congo* 3°1S 16°34E **264** C3
Lednice *Czechia* 48°46N 16°46E **181** C9
Ledo *India* 27°18N 95°44E **241** B5
Lédo, Cabo *Angola* 9°43S 13°12E **265** D2
Ledong *China* 18°41N 109°5E **229** a
Leduc *Canada* 53°15N 113°30W **296** C6
Lee *London, U.K.* 51°27N 0°0 **125** B4
Lee *Fla., U.S.A.* 30°25N 83°18W **316** E6
Lee *Mass., U.S.A.* 42°19N 73°15W **313** D11
Lee → *Ireland* 51°53N 8°56W **166** E3
Lee Vining *U.S.A.* 37°58N 119°7W **306** H7
Leech L. *U.S.A.* 47°10N 94°24W **308** B6
Leechburg *U.S.A.* 40°37N 79°36W **312** F5
Leeds *W. Yorks., U.K.* 53°48N 1°33W **168** D6
Leeds *Ala., U.S.A.* 33°33N 86°33W **315** E11
Leek *Neths.* 53°10N 6°24E **170** A6
Leek *Staffs., U.K.* 53°7N 2°1W **168** D5
Leeman *Australia* 29°57S 114°58E **279** E1
Leeper *U.S.A.* 41°22N 79°18W **312** E5
Leer *Germany* 53°13N 7°26E **178** B3
Lee's Summit *U.S.A.* 38°55N 94°23W **310** F2
Leesburg *Fla., U.S.A.* 28°49N 81°53W **317** G8
Leesburg *Ga., U.S.A.* 31°44N 84°10W **316** D5
Leesburg *Ohio, U.S.A.* 39°21N 83°33W **311** E13
Leeston *N.Z.* 43°45S 172°19E **285** D7
Leesville *U.S.A.* 31°8N 93°16W **314** F8
Leeton *Australia* 34°33S 146°23E **283** C7
Leetonia *U.S.A.* 40°53N 80°45W **312** F4
Leeu Gamka *S. Africa* 32°47S 21°59E **270** D3
Leeuwarden *Neths.* 53°15N 5°48E **170** A5
Leeuwin, C. *Australia* 34°20S 115°9E **279** F2
Leeuwin Naturaliste △ *Australia* 34°6S 115°3E **279** F2
Leeward Is. *Atl. Oc.* 16°30N 63°30W **321** C7
Léfini *Congo* 2°55S 15°39E **264** C3
Léfini → *Congo* 2°56S 16°9E **264** C3
Léfini ⌂ *Congo* 2°55S 15°20E **264** C3
Lefka *Cyprus* 35°6N 32°51E **207** E8
Lefkada *Greece* 38°40N 20°43E **207** B2
Lefkimi *Greece* 39°25N 20°3E **206** C10
Lefkimis, Akra *Greece* 39°29N 20°4E **206** C10
Lefkoniko *Cyprus* 35°18N 33°44E **207** E9
Lefkosia = Nicosia *Cyprus* 35°10N 33°25E **207** E9
Lefroy *Canada* 44°16N 79°34W **312** B5
Lefroy, L. *Australia* 31°21S 121°40E **279** F3
Łeg → *Poland* 50°42N 21°50E **185** H8
Leganés *Spain* 40°19N 3°45W **127** C1
Legazpi *Phil.* 13°10N 123°45E **232** E4
Legazpi *Madrid, Spain* 40°23N 3°41W **127** B1
Lège-Cap-Ferret *France* 44°48N 1°9W **174** D2
Lege Hida *Ethiopia* 7°56N 41°4E **257** F5
Legendre I. *Australia* 20°22S 116°55E **278** D2
Leghorn = Livorno *Italy* 43°33N 10°19E **198** E7
Legian *Indonesia* 8°42S 115°10E **231** K18
Legionowo *Poland* 52°25N 20°50E **185** F7
Legnago *Italy* 45°11N 11°18E **199** C8
Legnano *Italy* 45°36N 8°54E **198** C5
Legnica *Poland* 51°12N 16°10E **185** G3
Legrad *Croatia* 46°17N 16°51E **199** B13
Leh *India* 34°9N 77°35E **243** B7
Lehigh Acres *U.S.A.* 26°36N 81°39W **317** J8
Lehighton *U.S.A.* 40°50N 75°43W **313** F9
Lehliu *Romania* 44°29N 26°50E **183** F11
Leho *South Sudan* 7°7N 33°52E **257** F3
Lehrte *Germany* 52°22N 9°58E **178** C5
Lehtisaari *Finland* 60°10N 24°51E **121** B2
Lehua I. *U.S.A.* 22°1N 160°6W **302** A1
Lehututu *Botswana* 23°54S 21°55E **270** B3
Lei Shui → *China* 26°55N 112°35E **229** D9
Lei Yue Mun *Hong Kong, China* 22°17N 114°14E **122** B3
Leiah *Pakistan* 30°58N 70°58E **242** D4
Leião *Portugal* 38°43N 9°17W **126** A1
Leibnitz *Austria* 46°47N 15°34E **180** E8
Leibo *China* 28°11N 103°34E **228** C4
Leicester *U.K.* 52°38N 1°8W **169** E6
Leicester City □ *U.K.* 52°38N 1°8W **169** E6
Leicester Square *London, U.K.* **125** b3
Leicestershire □ *U.K.* 52°41N 1°17W **169** E6
Leichhardt *Australia* 33°53S 151°9E **139** B1
Leichhardt → *Australia* 17°35S 139°48E **280** B2
Leichhardt Ra. *Australia* 20°46S 147°40E **280** C4
Leiden *Neths.* 52°9N 4°30E **170** B4
Leie → *Belgium* 51°2N 3°45E **170** C3
Leifers = Láives *Italy* 46°26N 11°20E **199** B8
Leigh → *Australia* 38°18S 144°30E **282** E6
Leigh Creek *Australia* 30°38S 138°26E **282** A3
Leikang *Norway* 62°15N 5°47E **164** B2
Leikanger *Sogn og Fjordane, Norway* 62°8N 5°18E **164** B2
Leikanger *Sogn og Fjordane, Norway* 61°10N 6°51E **164** C3
Leiktho *Myanmar* 19°13N 96°35E **241** F6
Leimen *Germany* 49°21N 8°41E **179** F4
Leimus *Nic.* 14°40N 84°3W **320** D3
Leine → *Germany* 52°43N 9°36E **178** C5
Leinefelde-Worbris *Germany* 51°23N 10°19E **178** D6
Leinster *Australia* 27°51S 120°36E **279** E3
Leinster □ *Ireland* 53°3N 7°8W **166** C4
Leinster, Mt. *Ireland* 52°37N 6°46W **166** D5
Leipalingis *Lithuania* 54°5N 23°51E **184** D10
Leipe = Lipno *Poland* 52°49N 19°15E **185** F6
Leipzig *Germany* 51°18N 12°22E **178** D8
Leira *Norway* 60°58N 9°17E **164** D6
Leiria *Portugal* 39°46N 8°53W **194** F2
Leiria □ *Portugal* 39°46N 8°53W **194** F2
Leirvassbu *Norway* 61°33N 8°13E **164** C5
Leirvik *Norway* 59°47N 5°28E **164** E2
Leishan *China* 26°15N 108°20E **228** D7
Leisler, Mt. *Australia* 23°23S 129°20E **278** D4
Leisure City *U.S.A.* 25°30N 80°26W **317** K9
Leith *U.K.* 55°59N 3°11W **121** B3
Leith Hill *U.K.* 51°11N 0°22W **169** F7
Leitha → *Europe* 47°50N 17°15E **181** D10
Leitir Ceanainn = Letterkenny *Ireland* 54°57N 7°45W **166** B4
Leitrim *Ireland* 54°0N 8°5W **166** B3
Leitrim □ *Ireland* 54°8N 8°0W **166** B4
Leitza *Spain* 43°5N 1°55W **196** B3
Leixlip *Ireland* 53°22N 6°30W **166** C5
Leiyang *China* 26°27N 112°45E **229** D9
Leizhou *China* 20°52N 110°8E **229** G8
Leizhou Bandao *China* 21°0N 110°0E **228** G7
Leizhou Wan *China* 20°50N 110°20E **229** G8
Lek → *Neths.* 51°54N 4°35E **170** C4
Leka *Norway* 65°5N 11°35E **160** D14
Lekani *Greece* 41°10N 24°35E **203** E8
Lekbibaj *Albania* 42°17N 19°56E **202** D3
Lekeitio *Spain* 43°20N 2°32W **196** B2
Lékéti, Mt. *Congo* 2°34S 14°17E **264** C2
Lekki *Nigeria* 6°26N 3°28E **124** B2
Lekki Lagoon *Nigeria* 6°30N 4°7E **263** D5
Lekki Peninsula *Nigeria* 6°26N 3°29E **124** B2
Léko *Mali* 13°37N 9°2W **262** C3
Lékoli-Pandaka ⌂ *Congo* 0°41N 14°50E **264** B2
Lékoni *Gabon* 1°35S 14°14E **264** C2
Lékoni → *Gabon* 1°11S 13°16E **264** C2
Lekoui *Burkina Faso* 12°37N 3°40W **262** C4
Lékoumou □ *Congo* 2°0S 13°0E **264** C2
Leksand *Sweden* 60°44N 15°1E **162** D9
Leksura = Lentekhi *Georgia* 42°47N 42°45E **191** J6
Leland *Mich., U.S.A.* 45°1N 85°45W **309** C11

Leland Miss., U.S.A. 33°24N 90°54W 315 E9
Lelång Sweden 59°10N 12°5E 162 E6
Lelepa Vanuatu 17°35S 168°11E 287 G6
Leleque Argentina 42°28S 71°0W 336 B2
Leli Solomon Is. 8°42S 161°4E 287 M11
Leling China 37°44N 117°13E 227 F9
Lélouma Guinea 11°11N 12°56W 262 C2
Lelu Myanmar 19°4N 95°30E 241 F5
Lelydorp Suriname 5°42N 55°14W 329 B6
Lelystad Neths. 52°30N 5°25E 170 B5
Lem Denmark 56°1N 8°24E 163 H2
Lema Nigeria 12°58N 4°13E 263 C5
Lema Shilindi Ethiopia 4°50N 42°6E 257 G5
Léman, L. Europe 46°26N 6°30E 173 F13
Lemankoa Papua N. G. 5°3S 154°34E 286 C8
Lembar Indonesia 8°45S 116°4E 231 K19
Lemberg = Lviv Ukraine 49°50N 24°0E 177 D13
Lembongan, Nusa Indonesia 8°40S 115°27E 231 K18
Lembuak Indonesia 8°36S 116°11E 231 K19
Leme Brazil 22°58S 43°10W 135 B1
Lemera Dem. Rep. of the Congo 3°0S 28°55E 268 C2
Lemery Phil. 13°51N 120°56E 232 E3
Lemesós = Limassol Cyprus 34°42N 33°1E 207 F9
Lemfu Dem. Rep. of the Congo 5°18S 15°13E 265 D3
Lemhi Ra. U.S.A. 44°0N 113°0W 304 D7
Lemmenjoki △ Finland 68°40N 25°30E 160 B21
Lemmer Neths. 52°51N 5°43E 170 B5
Lemmon U.S.A. 45°57N 102°10W 308 C2
Lemmon, L. U.S.A. 32°41N 96°44W 120 B5
Lemon Grove U.S.A. 32°44N 117°1W 307 N9
Lemoore U.S.A. 36°18N 119°46W 306 J7
Lemotol B. Micronesia 7°21N 151°35E 287 T17
Lemoyne Canada 45°29N 73°29W 130 B3
Lempdes-sur-Allagnon France 45°22N 3°17E 174 C7
Lemsid W. Sahara 26°33N 13°51W 260 C2
Lemukutan Indonesia 0°45N 108°43E 235 B3
Lemvig Denmark 56°33N 8°20E 163 H2
Lemyethna Myanmar 17°36N 95°9E 241 G5
Lena U.S.A. 42°23N 89°49W 310 B7
Lena → Russia 72°52N 126°40E 215 B13
Lena Pillars = Lenskiy Stolby Russia 60°55N 126°0E 215 C13
Lenadoon Pt. Ireland 54°18N 9°3W 166 B2
Lenakel Vanuatu 19°38S 169°16E 287 J7
Lenart Slovenia 46°36N 15°48E 199 B12
Lenartovce Slovakia 48°18N 20°19E 181 C13
Lencloître France 46°50N 0°20E 172 F7
Lençóis Brazil 12°35S 41°24W 333 D3
Lençóis Maranhenses △ Brazil 2°30S 43°0W 332 B3
Lendava Slovenia 46°35N 16°25E 199 B13
Lendinara Italy 45°5N 11°36E 199 C8
Lenger Kazakhstan 42°12N 69°54E 217 D7
Lengerich Germany 52°11N 7°52E 178 C3
Lenggong Malaysia 5°6N 100°58E 237 K3
Lenggries Germany 47°41N 11°35E 179 H7
Léngoué Congo 1°15N 15°38E 264 B3
Lengshuijiang China 27°40N 111°26E 229 D8
Lengshuitan China 26°27N 111°35E 229 D8
Lengua de Vaca, Pta. Chile 30°14S 71°38W 334 C1
Lengwe △ Malawi 16°14S 34°45E 269 F3
Lengwethen = Lunino Russia 53°38N 45°18E 190 D7
Lengyeltóti Hungary 46°40N 17°40E 182 D2
Lengyeltótihács = Lengyeltóti Hungary 46°40N 17°40E 182 D2
Lenhovda Sweden 57°0N 15°16E 163 G9
Lenin Mausoleum Moscow, Russia 129 b2
Lenina, Kanal → Russia 43°44N 45°17E 191 J7
Leninabad = Khŭjand Tajikistan 40°17N 69°37E 217 D7
Leninakan = Gyumri Armenia 40°47N 43°50E 191 K6
Lenine Ukraine 45°17N 35°46E 189 K8
Leningrad = Sankt-Peterburg Russia 59°55N 30°20E 137 B1
Leningrad □ Russia 59°40N 32°0E 188 C7
Lenino = Leninsk-Kuznetskiy Russia 54°44N 86°10E 217 B11
Lenino Russia 55°38N 37°39E 129 C2
Leninogorsk = Ridder Kazakhstan 50°20N 83°30E 217 B10
Leninogorsk Russia 54°36N 52°30E 216 B4
Leninsk = Petrodvorets Russia 59°52N 29°54E 188 C5
Leninsk Russia 48°40N 45°15E 191 F7
Leninsk-Kuznetskiy Russia 54°44N 86°10E 217 B11
Leninsk-Turkmensky = Türkmenabat Turkmenistan 39°6N 63°34E 247 B9
Leninskiye Gory Russia 55°41N 37°32E 129 C2
Leninskoye Russia 58°23N 47°3E 190 A8
Lenk Switz. 46°27N 7°28E 179 J3
Lenkoran = Länkäran Azerbaijan 38°48N 48°52E 213 C13
Lenmalu Indonesia 1°45S 130°15E 231 E8
Lennartsfors Sweden 59°20N 11°55E 162 E5
Lenne → Germany 51°25N 7°29E 178 D3
Lennestadt Germany 51°8N 8°2E 178 D4
Lennox Calif., U.S.A. 33°56N 118°20W 126 C2
Lennox S. Dak., U.S.A. 43°21N 96°53W 308 D5
Lennox, I. Chile 55°18S 66°50W 336 E3
Lennoxville Canada 45°22N 71°51W 313 A13
Leno Italy 45°22N 10°13E 198 C7
Lenoir U.S.A. 35°55N 81°32W 315 D14
Lenoir City U.S.A. 35°48N 84°16W 315 D12
Lenore L. Canada 52°30N 104°59W 297 C8
Lenox Ga., U.S.A. 31°16N 83°28W 316 D6
Lenox Iowa, U.S.A. 40°53N 94°34W 310 D2
Lenox Mass., U.S.A. 42°22N 73°17W 313 D11
Lens France 50°26N 2°50E 173 B9
Lensahn Germany 54°13N 10°53E 178 A6
Lensk Russia 60°48N 114°55E 215 C12
Lenskiy Stolby Russia 60°55N 126°0E 215 C13
Lensvik Norway 63°31N 9°48E 164 A6
Lentas Greece 34°56N 24°56E 207 F5
Lentekhi Georgia 42°47N 42°45E 191 J6
Lenti Hungary 46°37N 16°33E 182 D1
Lentini Italy 37°17N 15°0E 201 E8
Lentschütz = Łęczyca Poland 52°5N 19°15E 185 F6
Lenwood U.S.A. 34°53N 117°7W 307 L9
Lenya Myanmar 11°33N 98°57E 237 G2
Lenzen Germany 53°5N 11°29E 178 B7
Léo Burkina Faso 11°3N 2°2W 262 C4
Leoben Austria 47°22N 15°5E 180 D8
Leobschütz = Głubczyce Poland 50°13N 17°52E 185 H4
Leodhais = Lewis U.K. 58°9N 6°40W 167 C2
Leola U.S.A. 45°43N 98°56W 308 C4
Leominster Hereford, U.K. 52°14N 2°43W 169 E5
Leominster Mass., U.S.A. 42°32N 71°46W 313 D13
León = Cotopaxi □ Ecuador 0°5S 78°55W 328 D2
Léon Landes, France 43°53N 1°18W 174 E2
León Guanajuato, Mexico 21°6N 101°41W 318 C4
León Nic. 12°27N 86°51W 320 D2
León Spain 42°38N 5°34W 194 C5
Leon Iowa, U.S.A. 40°44N 93°45W 310 D3
León □ Spain 42°40N 5°55W 194 C5
Leon → U.S.A. 31°14N 97°28W 314 F6
León, Montes de Spain 42°30N 6°18W 194 C4
Leonardo da Vinci, Roma ✕ (FCO) Italy 41°48N 12°15E 199 G9
Leonardtown U.S.A. 38°17N 76°38W 309 F15
Leonardville Namibia 23°29S 18°49E 270 B2
Leonárisso Cyprus 35°28N 34°8E 207 E10
Leonberg Germany 48°48N 9°1E 179 G5
Leonding Austria 48°16N 14°15E 180 C7
Leone Amer. Samoa 14°23S 170°48W 302 f
Leonessa Italy 42°34N 12°58E 199 F9
Leonforte Italy 37°38N 14°23E 201 E7
Leongatha Australia 38°30S 145°58E 283 E6
Leonia Fla., U.S.A. 30°55N 86°1W 316 E3
Leonia N.J., U.S.A. 40°51N 73°59W 132 A2
Leonidio Greece 37°9N 22°52E 204 D4
Leonora Australia 28°49S 121°19E 279 E3
Leopold II, L. = Mai-Ndombe, L. Dem. Rep. of the Congo 2°0S 18°20E 264 C3
Leopoldau Austria 48°15N 16°26E 142 A2
Leopoldina = Aruanã Brazil 14°54S 51°10W 333 D1
Leopoldina = Parnamirim Brazil 8°5S 39°34W 332 C4
Leopoldina Brazil 21°28S 42°40W 333 F3
Leopoldo Bulhões Brazil 16°37S 48°46W 333 E2
Leopoldsburg Belgium 51°7N 5°13E 170 C5
Leopoldsdorf Austria 48°7N 16°23E 142 B2
Leopoldstadt Austria 48°13N 16°22E 142 A2
Léopoldville = Kinshasa Dem. Rep. of the Congo 4°20S 15°15E 265 C3
Leoti U.S.A. 38°29N 101°21W 308 F3
Leova Moldova 46°28N 28°15E 183 D13
Leoville Canada 53°39N 107°33W 297 C7
Lepar Indonesia 2°57S 106°49E 234 C3
Lepe Spain 37°15N 7°12W 195 H3
Lepel = Lyepyel Belarus 54°50N 28°40E 188 E5
Lepenou Greece 38°42N 21°17E 204 C3
Leping China 28°47N 117°7E 229 C11
Lépo, L. do Angola 17°0S 19°0E 265 F3
Lepontine, Alpi Italy 46°22N 8°27E 198 B5
Leportovo Russia 55°46N 37°43E 129 B3
Leposavić Kosovo 43°6N 20°48E 202 C4
Leppävaara Finland 60°13N 24°49E 121 B1
Leppävirta Finland 62°29N 27°46E 160 E22
Lepsény Hungary 47°0N 18°15E 182 D3
Leptis Magna Libya 32°40N 14°12E 258 B2
Lequeitio = Lekeitio Spain 43°20N 2°32W 196 B2
Lercara Friddi Italy 37°45N 13°36E 200 E6
Léré C.A.R. 6°46N 17°25E 264 A3
Léré Chad 9°39N 14°13E 259 G2
Léré Mali 15°45N 4°55W 262 B4
Lere Bauchi, Nigeria 9°43N 9°18E 263 D6
Lere Kaduna, Nigeria 10°23N 8°35E 263 C6
Leribe Lesotho 28°51S 28°3E 271 C4
Lérici Italy 44°4N 9°55E 198 D6
Lérida = Lleida Spain 41°37N 0°39E 196 D5
Lérins, Îs. de France 43°31N 7°3E 175 E11
Lerma Spain 42°0N 3°47W 194 C7
Leros Greece 37°10N 26°50E 205 D8
Lérouville France 48°44N 5°30E 173 D12
Lerum Sweden 57°46N 12°16E 163 G6
Lerwick U.K. 60°9N 1°9W 167 A7
Leş Romania 46°58N 21°50E 182 D6
Les Abrets France 45°32N 5°35E 175 C9
Les Abymes Guadeloupe 16°17N 61°32W 322 e
Les Andelys France 49°15N 1°25E 172 C8
Les Anses-d'Arlets Martinique 14°28N 61°6W 322 j
Les Avirons Réunion 21°14S 55°20E 272 f
Les Borges Blanques Spain 41°31N 0°52E 196 D5
Les Cayes Haiti 18°15N 73°46W 321 C5
Les Coteaux Canada 45°15N 74°13W 313 A10
Les Escoumins Canada 48°21N 69°24W 299 C6
Les Essarts France 46°47N 1°12W 172 F5
Les Grands Fonds Guadeloupe 16°16N 61°26W 322 e
Les Herbiers France 46°52N 1°1W 172 F5
Les Lilas France 48°52N 2°25E 134 A3
Les Loges-en-Josas France 48°45N 2°8E 134 B1
Les Mangles Guadeloupe 16°23N 61°27W 322 e
Les Minquiers, Plateau des Chan. Is. 48°58N 2°8W 172 D4
Les Moroubas C.A.R. 6°11N 20°13E 264 A4
Les Pavillons-sous-Bois France 48°54N 2°30E 134 A4
Les Pieux France 49°30N 1°48W 172 C5
Les Ponts-de-Cé France 47°25N 0°30W 172 E6
Les Riceys France 47°59N 4°22E 173 E11
Les Sables-d'Olonne France 46°30N 1°45W 174 B2
Les Tantes Grenada 12°19N 61°33W 323 q
Les Trois-Bassins Réunion 21°5S 55°18E 272 f
Les Trois-Îlets Martinique 14°32N 61°2W 322 j
Les Vans France 44°25N 4°7E 175 D8
Lesbos Greece 39°10N 26°20E 205 B8
L'Escala Spain 42°7N 3°8E 196 C8
L'Escalier Mauritius 20°28S 57°36E 272 e
Leschnitz = Leśnica Poland 50°26N 18°11E 185 H5
Leshan China 29°33N 103°41E 228 C4
Leshukonskoye Russia 64°54N 45°46E 186 B8
Leshwe ⌂ Dem. Rep. of the Congo 12°45S 29°30E 269 E2
Lésigny France 48°44N 2°37E 134 B4
Lésina Italy 41°52N 15°21E 199 G12
Lésina, L. di Italy 41°53N 15°26E 199 G12
Lesjaskog Norway 62°14N 8°22E 164 B5
Lesjaverk Norway 62°12N 8°34E 164 B5
Lesjöfors Sweden 59°58N 14°11E 162 E8
Leskhimstroy = Syeverodonetsk Ukraine 48°58N 38°35E 189 H10
Lesko Poland 49°30N 22°23E 185 J9
Leskov I. Antarctica 56°0S 28°0W 151 B1
Leskovac Serbia 43°0N 21°58E 202 C5
Leskovik Albania 40°10N 20°34E 202 F4
Leslau = Włocławek Poland 52°40N 19°3E 185 F6
Leslie Ga., U.S.A. 31°57N 84°5W 316 D5
Leslie Mich., U.S.A. 42°27N 84°26W 311 B12
Lesna Poland 51°1N 15°15E 185 G2
Lesneven France 48°35N 4°20W 172 D2
Leśnica Poland 50°26N 18°11E 185 H5
Lešnica Serbia 44°39N 19°20E 202 B3
Lesnoi = Umba Russia 66°42N 34°11E 186 A5
Lesnoye Russia 58°15N 35°18E 188 C8
Lesnozavodskaya Russia 59°51N 30°29E 137 B2
Lesopilnoye Russia 46°44N 134°20E 220 A7
Lesotho ■ Africa 29°40S 28°0E 271 C4
Lesozavodsk Russia 45°30N 133°29E 220 B6
Lesparre-Médoc France 45°18N 0°57W 174 C3
L'Espluga de Francolí Spain 41°24N 1°7E 196 D6
Lessay France 49°14N 1°30W 172 C5
Lesse → Belgium 50°15N 4°54E 170 D4
Lesse et Lomme ⌂ Belgium 50°8N 5°9E 170 D5
Lessebo Sweden 56°45N 15°16E 163 H9
Lesser Antilles W. Indies 15°0N 61°0W 321 D7
Lesser Slave L. Canada 55°30N 115°25W 296 B5
Lesser Sunda Is. Indonesia 8°0S 120°0E 235 D5
Lessines Belgium 50°42N 3°50E 170 D3
Lester B. Pearson Int., Toronto ✕ (YYZ) Canada 43°46N 79°35W 141 A1
L'Esterre Grenada 12°28N 61°29W 323 q
Lestershire = Johnson City U.S.A. 42°7N 75°58W 313 D9
Lestock Canada 51°19N 103°59W 297 C8
Lesuer I. Australia 13°50S 127°17E 278 B4
Lesueur △ Australia 30°11S 115°10E 279 F2
Lesung Indonesia 0°42N 114°42E 235 B4
Lésvos = Lesbos Greece 39°10N 26°20E 205 B8
Leszno Poland 51°50N 16°30E 185 G3
Letaba S. Africa 23°59S 31°50E 271 B5
Letälven → Sweden 59°5N 14°20E 162 E8
L'Étang-la-Ville France 48°52N 2°4E 134 A1
L'Étang-Salé Réunion 21°15S 55°23E 272 f
Létavértes Hungary 47°23N 21°55E 182 C6
Letchworth Garden City U.K. 51°59N 0°13W 169 F7
Letea, Ostrovul Romania 45°18N 29°20E 183 E14
Lethbridge Canada 49°45N 112°45W 296 D6
Lethem Guyana 3°20N 59°50W 329 C6
Leti, Kepulauan Indonesia 8°10S 128°0E 231 F7
Leti Is. = Leti, Kepulauan Indonesia 8°10S 128°0E 231 F7
Letiahau → Botswana 21°16S 24°0E 270 B3
Leticia Colombia 4°9S 70°0W 328 D4
Leting China 39°23N 118°55E 227 E10
Letjiesbos S. Africa 32°34S 22°16E 270 D3
Letlhakane Botswana 21°27S 25°30E 270 B4
Letlhakeng Botswana 24°0S 24°59E 270 B3
Letná Prague, Czechia 135 a2
Letňany Czechia 50°8N 14°30E 135 B3
Letopolis = Ausîm Egypt 30°7N 31°8E 117 A1
Letpadan Myanmar 17°45N 95°45E 241 G5
Letpan Myanmar 19°28N 94°10E 241 F5
Letsôk-aw Kyun Myanmar 11°30N 98°25E 237 G2
Letterkenny Ireland 54°57N 7°45W 166 B4
Leu Romania 44°10N 24°0E 183 F9
Léua Angola 11°34S 20°32E 265 E4
Leucadia U.S.A. 33°4N 117°18W 307 M9
Leucate France 42°56N 3°3E 174 F7
Leucate, Étang de France 42°50N 3°0E 174 F7
Leuchars U.K. 56°24N 2°53W 167 E6
Leuk Switz. 46°19N 7°37E 179 J3
Leuşeni Moldova 46°49N 28°12E 183 D13
Leuser, Gunung Indonesia 3°46N 97°12E 234 B1
Leusoalii Amer. Samoa 14°14S 169°25W 302 f
Leutkirch Germany 47°49N 10°1E 179 H6
Leutschau = Levoča Slovakia 49°2N 20°35E 181 B13
Leuven Belgium 50°52N 4°42E 170 D4
Leuze-en-Hainaut Belgium 50°36N 3°37E 170 D3
Lev Tolstoy Russia 53°13N 39°29E 188 F10
Levallois-Perret France 48°53N 2°16E 134 A2
Levan Albania 40°40N 19°28E 202 F3
Levanger Norway 63°45N 11°19E 160 E14
Levant, Î. du France 43°3N 6°28E 175 E10
Lévanto Italy 44°10N 9°38E 198 D6
Lévanzo Italy 38°0N 12°20E 200 D5
Leveld Norway 60°44N 8°33E 164 D5
Levelland U.S.A. 33°35N 102°23W 314 E3
Levelock U.S.A. 59°7N 156°51W 303 G8
Leven U.K. 56°12N 3°0W 167 E6
Leven, L. U.K. 56°12N 3°22W 167 E5
Leven, Toraka Madag. 12°30S 47°45E 272 A2
Levent Turkey 41°5N 29°0E 122 B2
Leveque C. Australia 16°20S 123°0E 278 C3
Levera △ Grenada 12°13N 61°38W 323 q
Leverano Italy 40°17N 18°0E 201 B10
Leverger = Santo Antônio do Leverger Brazil 15°52S 56°5W 331 D6
Leverkusen Germany 51°1N 7°1E 178 D3
Levice Slovakia 48°13N 18°35E 181 C11
Lévico Terme Italy 46°0N 11°18E 199 C8
Levie France 41°40N 9°7E 175 G13
Levier France 46°58N 6°8E 173 F13
Levin N.Z. 40°37S 175°18E 284 G4
Lévis Canada 46°48N 71°9W 299 C5
Levis, L. Canada 62°37N 117°58W 296 A5
Levitha Greece 37°0N 26°28E 205 D8
Levittown N.Y., U.S.A. 40°44N 73°31W 313 F11
Levittown Pa., U.S.A. 40°9N 74°51W 313 F10
Levka Bulgaria 41°52N 26°15E 203 E10
Levka Oros Greece 35°18N 24°3E 207 E5
Levkás = Lefkada Greece 38°40N 20°43E 207 B2
Levoča Slovakia 49°2N 20°35E 181 B13
Levroux France 46°59N 1°38E 173 F8
Levski Bulgaria 43°21N 25°10E 203 C9
Levskigrad = Karlovo Bulgaria 42°38N 24°47E 203 D8
Levuka Fiji 17°34S 179°0E 287 A2
Lewe Myanmar 19°38N 96°7E 241 F6
Lewes E. Sussex, U.K. 50°52N 0°1E 169 G8
Lewes Del., U.S.A. 38°46N 75°9W 309 F16
Lewin Brzeski Poland 50°45N 17°37E 185 H4
Lewis U.K. 58°9N 6°40W 167 C2
Lewis → U.S.A. 45°51N 122°48W 306 E4
Lewis, Butt of U.K. 58°31N 6°16W 167 C2
Lewis and Clark ⌂ U.S.A. 46°8N 123°53W 306 D3
Lewis Pass N.Z. 42°31S 172°11E 285 C7
Lewis Ra. Australia 20°3S 128°50E 278 D4
Lewis Range U.S.A. 48°5N 113°5W 304 B7
Lewis Run U.S.A. 41°52N 78°40W 312 E6
Lewisburg Ohio, U.S.A. 39°51N 84°33W 311 E12
Lewisburg Pa., U.S.A. 40°58N 76°54W 312 F8
Lewisburg Tenn., U.S.A. 35°27N 86°48W 315 D11
Lewisburg W. Va., U.S.A. 37°48N 80°27W 309 G13
Lewisdale U.S.A. 38°58N 76°59W 143 B3
Lewisham □ U.K. 51°27N 0°1W 125 B3
Lewisport U.S.A. 37°56N 86°54W 311 G10
Lewisporte Canada 49°15N 55°3W 299 C8
Lewiston Idaho, U.S.A. 46°25N 117°1W 304 C5
Lewiston Maine, U.S.A. 44°6N 70°13W 309 C18
Lewiston N.Y., U.S.A. 43°11N 79°3W 312 C5
Lewistown Ill., U.S.A. 40°24N 90°9W 310 D6
Lewistown Mo., U.S.A. 40°5N 91°49W 310 D5
Lewistown Mont., U.S.A. 47°4N 109°26W 304 C9
Lewistown Pa., U.S.A. 40°36N 77°34W 312 F7
Lexington Ga., U.S.A. 33°52N 83°7W 316 B6
Lexington Ill., U.S.A. 40°39N 88°47W 311 D8
Lexington Ky., U.S.A. 38°3N 84°30W 311 F12
Lexington Mass., U.S.A. 42°25N 71°12W 116 A1
Lexington Mich., U.S.A. 43°16N 82°32W 312 C2
Lexington Mo., U.S.A. 39°11N 93°52W 310 E3
Lexington N.C., U.S.A. 35°49N 80°15W 315 D14
Lexington N.Y., U.S.A. 42°15N 74°22W 313 D10
Lexington Nebr., U.S.A. 40°47N 99°45W 308 E4
Lexington Ohio, U.S.A. 40°41N 82°35W 312 F2
Lexington S.C., U.S.A. 33°59N 81°11W 316 B8
Lexington Tenn., U.S.A. 35°39N 88°24W 315 D10
Lexington Va., U.S.A. 37°47N 79°27W 309 G14
Lexington Park U.S.A. 38°16N 76°27W 309 F15
Leyburn U.K. 54°19N 1°48W 168 C6
Leye China 24°48N 106°29E 228 E6
Leyeh Taiwan 23°28N 120°42E 225 C2
Leyland U.K. 53°42N 2°43W 168 D5
Leyte Phil. 10°30N 125°0E 233 F5
Leyte □ Phil. 11°0N 125°0E 233 F5
Leyte Gulf Phil. 10°50N 125°25E 233 F5
Leyton U.K. 51°33N 0°1W 125 A3
Leytonstone U.K. 51°34N 0°0 125 A3
Leżajsk Poland 50°16N 22°25E 185 H9
Lezay France 46°15N 0°1W 174 B3
Lezhë Albania 41°47N 19°39E 202 E3
Lezhi China 30°19N 104°58E 228 B5
Lézignan-Corbières France 43°13N 2°43E 174 E6
Lezoux France 45°49N 3°21E 174 C7
Lgov Russia 51°42N 35°16E 188 G8
Lhasa China 29°25N 90°58E 218 F7
L'Haÿ-les-Roses France 48°46N 2°20E 134 B3
Lhazê China 29°5N 87°38E 218 F6
L'Hermite, I. Chile 55°50S 68°0W 336 E3
Lhokkruet Indonesia 4°55N 95°24E 234 B1
Lhokseumawe Indonesia 5°10N 97°10E 234 A1
Lhoksukon Indonesia 5°2N 97°19E 234 A1
L'Hospitalet de Llobregat Spain 41°21N 2°6E 114 A1
Lhotka Czechia 50°1N 14°26E 135 B2
Lhuntsi Dzong Bhutan 27°39N 91°10E 241 B3
Lhut, W. → Somalia 10°17N 50°9E 267 B7
Li Thailand 17°48N 98°57E 236 D2
Li Jiang → China 24°40N 110°40E 229 E8
Li Jiang △ China 24°38N 110°38E 229 E8
Li Shan China 35°30N 111°56E 226 G6
Li Shui → China 29°24N 112°1E 229 C9
Li Xian Gansu, China 34°10N 105°5E 226 G3
Li Xian Hebei, China 38°30N 115°35E 226 E8
Li Xian Hunan, China 29°36N 111°42E 229 C8
Li Yuba South Sudan 5°23N 27°25E 266 C2
Lia-Moya C.A.R. 6°54N 16°17E 264 A3
Liadi Greece 36°50N 26°11E 205 E8
Liamuiga, Mt. St. Kitts & Nevis 17°22N 62°48W 322 d
Lian Phil. 14°3N 120°39E 232 D3
Liancheng China 25°42N 116°40E 229 E11
Liancourt Rocks Asia 37°15N 131°52E 221 F5
Liang Tao Taiwan 26°23N 128°28E 225 b
Lianga Phil. 8°38N 126°6E 233 G6
Lianga B. Phil. 8°37N 126°12E 233 G6
Liangcheng Nei Monggol Zizhiqu, China 40°28N 112°25E 226 D7
Liangcheng Shandong, China 35°32N 119°37E 227 G10
Liangdang China 33°56N 106°18E 226 H4
Lianghe China 24°50N 98°20E 228 E2
Lianghekou China 29°11N 108°44E 228 C7
Liangping China 30°38N 107°47E 228 B6
Liangpran Indonesia 1°4N 114°23E 235 B4
Liangshui He → China 39°48N 116°23E 114 C2
Lianhua China 27°3N 113°54E 229 D9
Lianhua Chi China 39°52N 116°16E 114 B1
Lianhua He → China 39°52N 116°23E 114 B1
Lianhua Shan China 23°40N 115°48E 229 F10
Lianjiang Fujian, China 26°12N 119°27E 229 D12
Lianjiang Guangdong, China 21°40N 110°20E 229 G8
Lianping China 24°26N 114°30E 229 E10
Lianshan China 24°38N 112°8E 229 E9
Lianshanguan China 40°53N 123°43E 224 B1
Lianshui China 33°42N 119°20E 227 H10
Lianyuan China 27°40N 111°38E 229 D8
Lianyungang China 34°40N 119°11E 227 G10
Lianzhou China 24°51N 112°22E 229 E9
Liao He → China 41°0N 121°50E 227 D11
Liaocheng China 36°28N 115°58E 226 F8
Liaodong Bandao China 40°0N 122°30E 227 E12
Liaodong Wan China 40°20N 121°10E 227 D11
Liaoning □ China 41°40N 122°30E 224 B1
Liaotung, G. of = Liaodong Wan China 40°20N 121°10E 227 D11
Liaoyang China 41°15N 122°58E 224 B1
Liaoyuan China 42°58N 125°2E 227 C13
Liaozhong China 41°23N 122°50E 224 B1
Liapades Greece 39°42N 19°40E 206 B9
Liard → Canada 61°51N 121°18W 296 A4
Liard River Canada 59°25N 126°5W 296 B3
Liari Pakistan 25°37N 66°30E 242 G2
Liat Indonesia 2°53S 107°5E 234 C3
Libanggaon Nepal 28°18N 82°38E 243 E10
Libano Colombia 4°55N 75°4W 328 C2
Libau = Liepāja Latvia 56°30N 21°0E 184 B8
Libby U.S.A. 48°23N 115°33W 304 B6
Libčice nad Vltavou Czechia 50°11N 14°22E 135 A2
Liběň Czechia 50°6N 14°27E 135 B2
Libenge Dem. Rep. of the Congo 3°40N 18°55E 264 B3
Liberal U.S.A. 37°3N 100°55W 308 G3
Liberdade Acre, Brazil 10°5S 70°20W 330 C3
Liberdade São Paulo, Brazil 23°33S 46°37W 137 B2
Liberdade → Brazil 9°40S 52°17W 331 B7
Liberdade, Avenida da Lisbon, Portugal 126 b1
Liberec Czechia 50°47N 15°7E 180 A8
Liberecký □ Czechia 50°45N 15°0E 180 A8
Liberia Costa Rica 10°40N 85°30W 320 D2
Liberia ■ W. Afr. 6°30N 9°30W 262 D3
Libertà, Ponte della Venice, Italy 142 a1
Libertad Antique, Phil. 11°46N 121°55E 233 E4
Libertad Venezuela 8°20N 69°37W 328 B4
Libertador □ Chile 34°15S 70°45W 334 C1
Liberton U.K. 55°54N 3°9W 121 B3
Liberty Ind., U.S.A. 39°38N 84°56W 311 E12
Liberty Mo., U.S.A. 39°15N 94°25W 310 E2
Liberty N.Y., U.S.A. 41°48N 74°45W 313 E10
Liberty Pa., U.S.A. 41°34N 77°6W 312 E7
Liberty Tex., U.S.A. 30°3N 94°48W 314 F7
Liberty Center U.S.A. 41°27N 84°1W 311 C12
Liberty I. U.S.A. 40°41N 74°2W 132 B1
Liberty-Newark Int. ✕ (EWR) U.S.A. 40°42N 74°10W 313 F10
Liberty Ōsaka Museum Japan 34°38N 135°29E 133 B1
Liberty State Park ⌂ U.S.A. 40°42N 74°2W 132 B1
Libertyville U.S.A. 42°18N 87°57W 311 B9
Libeznice Czechia 50°11N 14°29E 135 A2
Libiąż Poland 50°7N 19°21E 185 H6
Libili Angola 14°42S 17°44E 265 E3
Lībīya, Sahrā' Africa 25°0N 25°0E 258 C4
Libjo Phil. 10°12N 125°32E 233 F5
Libmanan Phil. 13°42N 123°4E 232 E4
Libo China 25°22N 107°53E 228 E6
Libobo, Tanjung Indonesia 0°54S 128°28E 231 E7
Libode S. Africa 31°33S 29°2E 271 D4
Libohovë Albania 40°3N 20°10E 202 F4
Liboi Kenya 0°24N 40°57E 267 D5
Libona Phil. 8°20N 124°44E 233 G5
Libonda Zambia 14°28S 23°12E 265 E4
Libong, Ko Thailand 7°15N 99°23E 237 J2
Libourne France 44°55N 0°14W 174 D3
Libramont Belgium 49°55N 5°23E 170 E5
Library of Congress Washington, D.C., U.S.A. 143 b3
Librazhd Albania 41°12N 20°22E 202 E4
Libreville Gabon 0°25N 9°26E 264 B1
Librio Pt. Phil. 11°25N 119°28E 233 F2
Libuš Czechia 50°0N 14°27E 135 B2
Libya ■ N. Afr. 27°0N 17°0E 258 C3
Libyan Desert = Lībīya, Sahrā' Africa 25°0N 25°0E 258 C4
Libyan Plateau = Ed Déffa Egypt 30°40N 26°30E 256 A2
Licantén Chile 35°55S 72°0W 334 D1
Licata Italy 37°6N 13°56E 200 E6
Lice Turkey 38°27N 40°39E 213 C9
Licheng China 36°28N 113°20E 226 F7
Lichfield U.K. 52°41N 1°49W 169 E6
Lichia Taiwan 22°47N 121°3E 225 D3
Lichiao China 23°23N 113°18E 121 B2
Lichinga Mozam. 13°13S 35°11E 269 E4
Lichtenburg Berlin, Germany 52°31N 13°30E 115 A4
Lichtenburg North West, S. Africa 26°8S 26°8E 270 C4
Lichtenfels Germany 50°8N 11°4E 179 E7
Lichterfelde Germany 52°25N 13°19E 115 B2
Lichuan Hubei, China 30°18N 108°57E 228 B7
Lichuan Jiangxi, China 27°18N 116°55E 229 D11
Licking → U.S.A. 39°6N 84°30W 311 F12
Licosa, Punta Italy 40°15N 14°54E 201 B7
Licungo → Mozam. 17°40S 37°15E 269 F4
Lida Belarus 53°53N 25°15E 188 F3
Liden Sweden 62°42N 16°48E 162 B10
Lidhult Sweden 56°50N 13°27E 163 H7
Lidingö Sweden 59°21N 18°8E 139 A2
Lidköping Sweden 58°31N 13°7E 163 F7
Lido Niger 12°54N 3°44E 263 C5
Lido di Roma = Ostia, Lido di Italy 41°43N 12°17E 199 G9
Lidoriki Greece 38°32N 22°12E 204 C4
Lidzbark Poland 53°15N 19°49E 185 E6
Lidzbark Warmiński Poland 54°7N 20°34E 184 D7
Liebenthal = Lubomierz Poland 51°1N 15°31E 185 G2
Liebenwalde Germany 52°52N 13°24E 178 C9
Lieberose Germany 51°59N 14°17E 178 D10
Liebig, Mt. Australia 23°18S 131°22E 278 D5
Liebling Romania 45°36N 21°20E 182 E6
Liechtenstein ■ Europe 47°8N 9°35E 179 H5
Liège Belgium 50°38N 5°35E 170 D5
Liège □ Belgium 50°32N 5°35E 170 D5
Liegnitz = Legnica Poland 51°12N 16°10E 185 G3
Lieksa Finland 63°18N 30°2E 160 E24
Lienart Dem. Rep. of the Congo 3°3N 25°31E 268 B2
Lienyünchianghsih = Lianyungang China 34°40N 119°11E 227 G10
Lienz Austria 46°50N 12°46E 180 E5
Liepāja Latvia 56°30N 21°0E 184 B8
Liepājas ezers Latvia 56°27N 21°3E 184 B8
Lier Belgium 51°7N 4°34E 170 C4
Liernais France 47°13N 4°16E 173 E11
Lierne △ Norway 64°20N 13°50E 160 D15
Lieshi Lingyuan China 23°7N 113°16E 121 B2
Liesing Austria 48°8N 16°17E 142 B1
Liesing → Austria 48°8N 16°22E 142 B2
Liești Romania 45°38N 27°34E 183 E12
Lietuva = Lithuania ■ Europe 55°30N 24°0E 188 E2
Liévin France 50°24N 2°47E 173 B9
Lièvre → Canada 45°31N 75°26W 298 C4
Liezen Austria 47°34N 14°15E 180 D7
Liffey → Ireland 53°21N 6°13W 166 C5
Lifford Ireland 54°51N 7°29W 166 B4
Liffré France 48°12N 1°30W 172 D5
Lifjell Norway 59°27N 8°45E 164 E5
Lifou, Î. N. Cal. 20°53S 167°13E 288 d
Lifudzin Russia 44°21N 134°58E 220 B7
Lifuka Tonga 19°48S 174°21W 287 P13
Ligang = Likang Taiwan 22°47N 120°29E 225 D2
Ligao Phil. 13°14N 123°32E 232 E4
Ligasa Dem. Rep. of the Congo 0°44N 23°49E 264 B4
Lighthouse Point U.S.A. 26°15N 80°7W 317 J9
Lighthouse Pt. U.S.A. 29°54N 84°21W 316 F5
Lightning Ridge Australia 29°22S 148°0E 281 D4
Lignano Sabbiadoro Italy 45°42N 13°9E 199 C10
Ligny-en-Barrois France 48°36N 5°20E 173 D12
Ligonha → Mozam. 16°54S 39°9E 269 F4
Ligonier Ind., U.S.A. 41°28N 85°35W 311 C11
Ligonier Pa., U.S.A. 40°15N 79°14W 312 F5
Ligourio Greece 37°37N 23°2E 204 D5
Ligovo Russia 59°49N 30°10E 137 C1
Ligueil France 47°2N 0°49E 172 E7
Liguria □ Italy 44°30N 8°50E 198 D5
Ligurian Sea Medit. S. 43°20N 9°0E 198 E5
Lihir Group Papua N. G. 3°0S 152°35E 286 B7
Lihir I. Papua N. G. 3°5S 152°35E 286 B7
Lihou Reefs and Cays Australia 17°25S 151°40E 280 B5
Lihu'e U.S.A. 21°59N 159°23W 302 B2
Lihué Calel △ Argentina 38°0S 65°10W 334 D2
Lijiang China 26°55N 100°20E 228 D3
Lijordet Norway 59°56N 10°36E 133 A2
Lik → Laos 18°31N 102°30E 236 C4
Likala Dem. Rep. of the Congo 0°9N 19°12E 264 B3
Likang Taiwan 22°47N 120°29E 225 D2
Likasi Dem. Rep. of the Congo 10°55S 26°48E 269 E2
Likati Dem. Rep. of the Congo 3°20N 24°0E 264 B4
Likati → Dem. Rep. of the Congo 2°53N 24°3E 264 B4
Likenäs Sweden 60°37N 13°3E 162 D7
Likete Dem. Rep. of the Congo 0°48S 21°31E 264 C4
Likhaya = Likhovskoy Russia 48°10N 40°10E 191 F5
Likhoborka → Russia 55°50N 37°37E 129 A2
Likhoslavl Russia 57°12N 35°30E 188 D8
Likhovskoy Russia 48°10N 40°10E 191 F5
Likhvin = Chekalin Russia 54°10N 36°10E 188 E9
Likimi Dem. Rep. of the Congo 2°44N 20°47E 264 B4
Likita Dem. Rep. of the Congo 4°15N 23°36E 264 B4
Liknes Norway 58°19N 6°59E 164 F3
Likokou Gabon 0°12S 12°48E 264 C2
Likoma I. Malawi 12°3S 34°45E 269 E3
Likouala □ Congo 2°0N 17°30E 264 B3
Likouala → Congo 0°2N 14°53E 264 C3
Likouala aux Herbes → Congo 0°52S 17°8E 264 C3
Liku Cook Is. 19°2S 168°47W 289 g
Likumburu Tanzania 9°43S 35°8E 269 D4
Lilanga Dem. Rep. of the Congo 0°34S 23°56E 264 C4
L'Île-Bouchard France 47°7N 0°26E 172 E7
L'Île-Rousse France 42°38N 8°57E 175 F12
Lilenga Dem. Rep. of the Congo 1°4N 22°2E 264 B4
Liling China 27°42N 113°29E 229 D9
Lilla Edet Sweden 58°9N 12°8E 163 F6
Lilla Värtan Sweden 59°20N 18°11E 139 A3
Lille France 50°38N 3°3E 173 B10
Lille Bælt Denmark 55°20N 9°45E 163 J3
Lille Værløse Denmark 55°47N 12°22E 118 A2
Lillebonne France 49°30N 0°32E 172 C7
Lillehammer Norway 61°8N 10°30E 164 C7
Lillesand Norway 58°15N 8°23E 164 F5
Lillestrøm Norway 59°58N 11°5E 164 E8
Lillhärdal Sweden 61°51N 14°5E 162 C8
Lillian Pt. Australia 27°40S 126°6E 279 E4
Lillo Spain 39°45N 3°20W 194 F7
Lillooet Canada 50°44N 121°57W 296 C4
Lillooet → Canada 49°15N 121°57W 296 D4
Lilongwe Malawi 14°0S 33°48E 269 E3
Liloy Phil. 8°4N 122°39E 233 G4
Liluah India 22°37N 88°19E 124 B1
Lim → Europe 43°45N 19°15E 202 C3
Lim Chu Kang Singapore 1°26N 103°43E 138 A2
Lima Brazil 4°36S 63°40W 329 D5
Lima Indonesia 3°39S 127°58E 231 E7
Lima Peru 12°3S 77°2W 124 B2
Lima Ill., U.S.A. 40°11N 91°23W 310 D5
Lima Mont., U.S.A. 44°38N 112°36W 304 D7
Lima N.Y., U.S.A. 42°54N 77°36W 312 D7
Lima Ohio, U.S.A. 40°44N 84°6W 311 D12
Lima □ Peru 12°3S 77°3W 330 C2
Lima → Portugal 41°41N 8°50W 194 D2
Lima Jorge Chavez Int. ✕ (LIM) Lima, Peru 12°2S 77°8W 124 B2
Liman = Krasnyy Liman Ukraine 48°58N 37°50E 189 H9
Liman Azerbaijan 38°53N 48°47E 213 C13
Liman Russia 45°45N 47°12E 191 H8
Limanowa Poland 49°42N 20°22E 185 J7
Limassol Cyprus 34°42N 33°1E 207 F9
Limavady U.K. 55°3N 6°56W 166 A5
Limay → Argentina 39°0S 68°0W 336 A3
Limay Mahuida Argentina 37°10S 66°45W 334 D2
Limbach-Oberfrohna Germany 50°52N 12°43E 178 E8
Limbang Malaysia 4°42N 115°6E 235 B5
Limbara, Mte. Italy 40°51N 9°10E 200 B2
Limbaži Latvia 57°31N 24°42E 188 D3
Limbdi India 22°34N 71°51E 242 H4
Limbe Cameroon 4°1N 9°10E 263 E6
Limbiate Italy 45°35N 9°7E 128 A1
Limbueta Angola 12°30S 18°42E 265 E3
Limbuhan = Pio V. Corpuz Phil. 11°55N 124°2E 233 F5
Limburg Germany 50°22N 8°4E 179 E4
Limburg □ Belgium 51°2N 5°25E 170 C5
Limburg □ Neths. 51°20N 5°55E 170 C5
Lime Village U.S.A. 61°21N 155°28W 303 F9
Limedsforsen Sweden 60°52N 13°25E 162 D7
Limehouse U.K. 51°30N 0°1W 125 A3
Limeil-Brévannes France 48°44N 2°29E 134 B3
Limeira = Joaçaba Brazil 27°5S 51°31W 335 B5
Limeira Brazil 22°35S 47°28W 335 A6
Limenaria Greece 40°38N 24°32E 203 F8
Limenas = Thasos Greece 40°40N 24°40E 203 F8
Limenas Chersonisou Greece 35°18N 25°21E 207 E6
Limerick Limerick, Ireland 52°40N 8°37W 166 D3
Limerick Maine, U.S.A. 43°41N 70°48W 313 C14
Limerick □ Ireland 52°30N 8°50W 166 D3
Limestone U.S.A. 42°2N 78°38W 312 D6
Limestone → Canada 56°31N 94°7W 297 B10
Limestone Hill = Lackawanna U.S.A. 42°50N 78°50W 312 D6
Limfjorden Denmark 56°55N 9°0E 163 H3
Limia = Lima → Portugal 41°41N 8°50W 194 D2
Limingen Norway 64°48N 13°35E 160 D15
Limmared Sweden 57°34N 13°20E 163 G7
Limmen ◎ Australia 15°15S 135°30E 280 B2
Limmen Bight Australia 14°40S 135°35E 280 A2
Limmen Bight → Australia 15°7S 135°44E 280 B2
Limni Greece 38°43N 23°18E 204 C5
Limnos Greece 39°50N 25°5E 205 B7
Limoeiro Brazil 7°52S 35°27W 332 C4
Limoeiro do Norte Brazil 5°5S 38°0W 332 C4
Limoges Ont., Canada 45°20N 75°16W 313 A9
Limoges Haute-Vienne, France 45°50N 1°15E 174 C5
Limón Costa Rica 10°0N 83°2W 320 E3
Limon Colo., U.S.A. 39°16N 103°41W 304 G12
Limone Italy 45°48N 10°47E 198 C7
Limone Piemonte Italy 44°12N 7°34E 198 D4
Limonlu Turkey 36°34N 34°15E 250 B5
Limousin France 45°30N 1°30E 171 D4
Limousin, Plateaux du France 45°45N 1°15E 174 C5
Limoux France 43°4N 2°12E 174 E6
Limpopo □ S. Africa 24°5S 29°0E 271 B4
Limpopo → Africa 25°5S 33°30E 271 C5
Lin Xian China 37°57N 110°58E 226 F6
Lin'an China 30°15N 119°42E 229 B12
Linao Pt. Phil. 6°46N 123°58E 233 H4
Linapacan Phil. 11°30N 119°52E 233 F2
Linapacan I. Phil. 11°27N 119°49E 233 F2
Linapacan Str. Phil. 11°37N 119°56E 233 F2
Linares Chile 35°50S 71°40W 334 D1
Linares Colombia 1°23N 77°31W 328 C2
Linares Nuevo León, Mexico 24°52N 99°34W 319 C5
Linares Spain 38°10N 3°40W 195 G7
Linaria Greece 38°52N 24°31E 204 C6
Linaro, Capo Italy 42°2N 11°50E 199 F8
Linas Mte. Italy 39°25N 8°38E 200 C1
Linate, Milano ✕ (LIN) Italy 45°27N 9°16E 128 B2
Linbian = Linpien Taiwan 22°26N 120°30E 225 D2
Linbropark S. Africa 26°5S 28°7E 123 A2
Lincang China 23°58N 100°1E 228 F3
Lincheng China 37°25N 114°30E 226 F8
Linchuan China 27°57N 116°15E 229 D11
Lincoln = Beamsville Canada 43°12N 79°28W 312 C5
Lincoln Argentina 34°55S 61°30W 334 C3
Lincoln N.Z. 43°38S 172°30E 285 D7
Lincoln Lincs., U.K. 53°14N 0°32W 168 D7
Lincoln Calif., U.S.A. 38°54N 121°17W 306 G5
Lincoln Ill., U.S.A. 40°9N 89°22W 310 D7
Lincoln Kans., U.S.A. 39°3N 98°9W 308 F4
Lincoln Maine, U.S.A. 45°22N 68°30W 309 C19
Lincoln N.H., U.S.A. 44°3N 71°40W 313 B13
Lincoln N. Mex., U.S.A. 33°30N 105°23W 305 K11
Lincoln Nebr., U.S.A. 40°49N 96°41W 308 E5
Lincoln Boyhood ⌂ U.S.A. 38°7N 86°59W 311 F10
Lincoln Center for Performing Arts New York, U.S.A. 132 b2
Lincoln City U.S.A. 44°57N 124°1W 304 D1
Lincoln Hav = Lincoln Sea Arctic 84°0N 55°0W 154 A5
Lincoln Heights U.S.A. 34°4N 118°12W 126 B3
Lincoln Memorial U.S.A. 38°52N 77°4W 143 B2
Lincoln Park Calif., U.S.A. 37°47N 122°30W 136 B1
Lincoln Park Ga., U.S.A. 32°52N 84°20W 316 C5
Lincoln Park Ill., U.S.A. 41°57N 87°38W 119 B3
Lincoln Park Mich., U.S.A. 42°15N 83°11W 311 B13
Lincoln Park N.J., U.S.A. 40°55N 74°18W 132 B1
Lincoln Park Zoo U.S.A. 41°55N 87°38W 119 B3
Lincoln Sea Arctic 84°0N 55°0W 154 A5
Lincoln Tunnel New York, U.S.A. 132 c1
Lincolnshire □ U.K. 53°14N 0°32W 168 D7
Lincolnshire Wolds U.K. 53°26N 0°13W 168 D7
Lincolnton Ga., U.S.A. 33°48N 82°29W 316 B7
Lincolnton N.C., U.S.A. 35°29N 81°16W 315 D14
Lincolnwood U.S.A. 42°1N 87°43W 119 A2
Lind U.S.A. 46°58N 118°37W 304 C4
Linda U.S.A. 39°8N 121°34W 306 F5
Linda-a-Pastora Portugal 38°42N 9°15W 126 A1
Lindale U.S.A. 34°11N 85°11W 316 A4
Lindås Norway 60°44N 5°9E 164 D2
Lindau Germany 47°33N 9°42E 179 H5
Lindeman I. Australia 20°27S 149°3E 280 b
Lindeman Islands △ Australia 20°28S 149°5E 280 b
Linden = Gladstone U.S.A. 39°13N 94°35W 310 E2
Linden Guyana 6°0N 58°10W 329 B6
Linden Gauteng, S. Africa 26°8S 28°0E 123 A2
Linden Ala., U.S.A. 32°18N 87°48W 315 E11
Linden Calif., U.S.A. 38°1N 121°5W 306 G5
Linden Ind., U.S.A. 40°11N 86°54W 311 D10
Linden Mich., U.S.A. 42°49N 83°47W 311 B13
Linden Tex., U.S.A. 33°1N 94°22W 314 E7
Lindenberg Germany 52°36N 13°31E 115 A4
Lindenhurst U.S.A. 40°41N 73°23W 313 F11
Lindenow Fjord Greenland 60°30N 43°25W 154 E6
Lindesberg Sweden 59°36N 15°15E 162 E9
Lindesnes Norway 57°58N 7°3E 164 G4
Lindi Tanzania 9°58S 39°38E 269 D4
Lindi □ Tanzania 9°40S 38°30E 269 D4
Lindi → Dem. Rep. of the Congo 0°33N 25°5E 268 B2
Lindley U.S.A. 42°1N 77°8W 312 D7
Lindö Sweden 58°37N 16°15E 163 F10
Lindome Sweden 57°35N 12°5E 163 G6
Lindos Greece 36°6N 28°4E 206 E12
Lindos, Akra Greece 36°4N 28°10E 206 E12
Lindoso Portugal 41°52N 8°11W 194 D2
Lindow Germany 52°58N 12°58E 178 C8
Lindøya Norway 59°53N 10°42E 133 A3
Lindsay Ont., Canada 44°22N 78°43W 312 B6
Lindsay Calif., U.S.A. 36°12N 119°5W 306 J7
Lindsay Okla., U.S.A. 34°50N 97°38W 314 D6
Lindsborg U.S.A. 38°35N 97°40W 308 F5
Lindsdal Sweden 56°44N 16°18E 163 H10
Line Islands Pac. Oc. 7°0N 160°0W 289 H12
Linesville U.S.A. 41°39N 80°26W 312 E4
Lineville Ala., U.S.A. 33°19N 85°45W 316 B4
Lineville Iowa, U.S.A. 40°35N 93°32W 310 D3
Linfen China 36°3N 111°30E 226 F6
Ling Xian Hunan, China 26°29N 113°48E 229 D9

Ling Xian *Shandong, China* 37°22N 116°30E **226** F9
Lingal *India* 16°17N 78°31E **245** F4
Linganamakki Res. *India* 14°6N 74°52E **245** G2
Lingao *China* 19°56N 109°42E **229** a
Lingayen *Phil.* 16°1N 120°14E **232** C3
Lingayen G. *Phil.* 16°10N 120°15E **232** C3
Lingbao *China* 34°31N 110°51E **226** G6
Lingbi *China* 33°33N 117°33E **227** H9
Lingbo *Sweden* 61°3N 16°41E **162** C10
Lingchuan *Guangxi Zhuangzu, China* 25°26N 110°21E **229** E8
Lingchuan *Shanxi, China* 35°45N 113°12E **226** G7
Lingding Yang *China* 22°25N 113°44E **219** a
Lingen *Germany* 52°31N 7°19E **178** C3
Lingga *Indonesia* 0°12S 104°37E **234** C2
Lingga, Kepulauan *Indonesia* 0°10S 104°30E **234** C2
Lingga Arch. = Lingga, Kepulauan *Indonesia* 0°10S 104°30E **234** C2
Linghai *China* 41°11N 121°22E **227** D11
Linghed *Sweden* 60°48N 15°55E **162** D9
Linghem *Sweden* 58°26N 15°47E **163** F9
Lingig *Phil.* 8°2N 126°24E **233** G6
Lingle *U.S.A.* 42°8N 104°21W **304** E11
Lingomo *Dem. Rep. of the Congo* 0°38N 22°3E **264** B4
Lingqiu *China* 39°28N 114°22E **226** E8
Lingshan *China* 22°25N 109°18E **228** F7
Lingshi *China* 36°48N 111°48E **226** F6
Lingshou *China* 38°20N 114°20E **226** E8
Lingshui *China* 18°27N 110°0E **229** a
Lingsugur *India* 16°10N 76°31E **245** F3
Lingtai *China* 35°0N 107°40E **226** G4
Linguère *Senegal* 15°25N 15°5W **262** B1
Lingui *China* 25°12N 110°2E **229** E8
Lingunda *Dem. Rep. of the Congo* 0°49N 21°8E **264** C3
Lingwu *China* 38°6N 106°20E **226** E4
Lingyuan *China* 41°10N 119°15E **227** D10
Lingyun *China* 25°2N 106°35E **228** E6
Linhai *China* 28°50N 121°8E **229** C13
Linhares *Brazil* 19°25S 40°4W **333** E3
Linhe *China* 40°48N 107°20E **226** D4
Liniers *Argentina* 34°39S 58°30W **117** B1
Linjiang *China* 41°50N 127°0E **224** B3
Linkebeek *Belgium* 50°46N 4°20E **116** B2
Linköping *Sweden* 58°28N 15°36E **163** F9
Linkou *China* 45°15N 130°18E **227** B16
Linksfield *S. Africa* 26°9S 28°6E **123** A2
Linli *China* 29°27N 111°30E **229** C8
Linlithgow = West Lothian ☐ *U.K.* 55°54N 3°36W **167** F5
Linmeyer *S. Africa* 26°15S 28°4E **123** B2
Linn *U.S.A.* 38°29N 91°51W **310** F5
Linna *Finland* 60°20N 24°50E **121** A2
Linnansaari △ *Finland* 62°3N 28°40E **160** E23
Linnei *Taiwan* 23°45N 120°36E **225** C2
Linneus *U.S.A.* 39°53N 93°11W **310** E3
Linnhe, L. *U.K.* 56°36N 5°25W **167** E3
Linosa *Medit. S.* 35°51N 12°50E **258** A2
Linpien *Taiwan* 22°26N 120°30E **225** D2
Linqi *China* 35°45N 113°52E **226** G7
Linqing *China* 36°50N 115°42E **226** F8
Linqu *China* 36°25N 118°30E **227** F10
Linquan *China* 33°5N 115°17E **229** A10
Lins *Brazil* 21°40S 49°44W **335** A6
Linshu *China* 34°53N 118°38E **227** G10
Linshui *China* 30°21N 106°57E **228** B6
Linsia = Linxia *China* 35°36N 103°10E **218** D9
Linstead *Jamaica* 18°8N 77°2W **320** a
Linta ➔ *Madag.* 25°2S 44°5E **272** D1
Lintao *China* 35°26N 103°58E **226** G2
Linth ➔ *Switz.* 47°7N 9°7E **179** H5
Linthal *Switz.* 46°54N 9°0E **179** J5
Linton *Ind., U.S.A.* 39°2N 87°10W **311** F9
Linton *N. Dak., U.S.A.* 46°16N 100°14W **308** B3
Lintong *China* 34°20N 109°10E **226** G5
Lintuvaara *Finland* 60°14N 24°49E **121** B1
Linwood *Canada* 43°35N 80°43W **312** C4
Linwu *China* 25°19N 112°31E **229** E9
Linxi *Hebei, China* 39°42N 118°26E **227** E10
Linxi *Liaoning, China* 43°36N 118°2E **227** C10
Linxia *China* 35°36N 103°10E **218** D9
Linxiang *China* 29°28N 113°23E **229** C9
Linyanti ➔ *Africa* 17°50S 25°5E **270** A4
Linyi *Shandong, China* 37°13N 116°54E **226** F9
Linyi *Shandong, China* 35°5N 118°21E **227** G10
Linying *China* 33°48N 113°56E **226** H7
Linyuan *Taiwan* 22°30N 120°23E **225** D2
Linz *Austria* 48°18N 14°18E **180** C7
Linz *Rhld-Pfz., Germany* 50°34N 7°17E **178** E3
Linzhenzhen *China* 36°30N 109°59E **226** F5
Linzhou *China* 36°4N 113°49E **226** F7
Linzi *China* 36°50N 118°20E **227** F10
Lioko *Equateur, Dem. Rep. of the Congo* 0°2N 22°4E **264** B4
Lioko *Orientale, Dem. Rep. of the Congo* 1°25N 23°7E **264** B4
Liomseter *Norway* 61°15N 9°35E **164** C6
Lion, G. du *France* 43°10N 4°0E **174** E7
Lion Rock Country Park ⌓ *Hong Kong, China* 22°21N 114°11E **122** A3
Lionel Town *Jamaica* 17°50N 77°15W **320** a
Lioni *Italy* 40°52N 15°11E **201** B8
Lions, G. of = Lion, G. du *France* 43°10N 4°0E **174** E7
Lion's Den *Zimbabwe* 17°15S 30°5E **269** F3
Lion's Head *Ont., Canada* 44°58N 81°15W **312** B3
Lion's Head *Western Cape, S. Africa* 33°56S 18°23E **118** A1
Liouesso *Congo* 1°2N 15°43E **264** B3
Lioumi *Greece* 38°0N 23°40E **112** B2
Liozno = Lyozna *Belarus* 55°0N 30°50E **188** E6
Lipa *Phil.* 13°57N 121°10E **232** E3
Lipali *Mozam.* 15°50S 35°50E **269** F4
Lipany *Slovakia* 49°9N 20°58E **181** B13
Lipari *Italy* 38°26N 14°58E **201** D7
Lipari, I. *Italy* 38°29N 14°56E **201** D7
Lipari, Is. = Eòlie, Ís. *Italy* 38°30N 14°57E **201** D7
Lipatkain *Indonesia* 0°1N 101°12E **234** B2
Lipcani *Moldova* 48°14N 26°48E **183** B11
Liperi *Finland* 62°31N 29°24E **160** E23
Lipetsk *Russia* 52°37N 39°35E **189** F10
Lipetsk ☐ *Russia* 52°50N 38°50E **190** D4
Lipiany *Poland* 53°2N 14°58E **185** E1
Liping *China* 26°15N 109°7E **228** D7
Lipisi *Greece* 37°19N 26°50E **205** D8
Lipjan *Kosovo* 42°31N 21°7E **202** D5
Lipkany = Lipcani *Moldova* 48°14N 26°48E **183** B11
Lipník nad Bečvou *Czechia* 49°32N 17°36E **181** B10
Lipno *Poland* 52°49N 19°15E **185** F6
Lipova *Romania* 46°8N 21°42E **182** D6
Lipovets *Ukraine* 49°12N 29°1E **177** D15
Lippe ➔ *Germany* 51°39N 6°36E **178** D2
Lippehne = Lipiany *Poland* 53°2N 14°58E **185** E1
Lippstadt *Germany* 51°41N 8°22E **178** D4
Lipscomb *U.S.A.* 36°14N 100°16W **314** C4
Lipsk *Poland* 53°44N 23°24E **184** E10
Lipsko *Poland* 51°9N 21°40E **185** G8
Liptovský Hrádok *Slovakia* 49°2N 19°44E **181** B12
Liptovský Mikuláš *Slovakia* 49°6N 19°35E **181** B12
Liptrap, C. *Australia* 38°50S 145°55E **283** E6
Lipu *China* 24°30N 110°22E **229** E8
Lira *Uganda* 2°17N 32°57E **268** B3
Liranga *Congo* 0°43S 17°32E **264** C3
Liri ➔ *Italy* 41°25N 13°52E **200** A6
Liria = Llíria *Spain* 39°37N 0°35W **197** F4
Lisakovsk *Kazakhstan* 52°33N 62°37E **216** B6
Lisala *Dem. Rep. of the Congo* 2°12N 21°38E **264** B4
Lisboa *Portugal* 38°42N 9°8W **126** A2
Lisboa ☐ *Portugal* 39°0N 9°12W **195** F1
Lisboa ✕ **(LIS)** *Portugal* 38°46N 9°8W **126** A2
Lisbon = Lisboa *Portugal* 38°42N 9°8W **126** A2
Lisbon *N. Dak., U.S.A.* 46°27N 97°41W **308** B5
Lisbon *N.H., U.S.A.* 44°13N 71°55W **313** B13
Lisbon *N.Y., U.S.A.* 44°43N 75°19W **313** B9
Lisbon *Ohio, U.S.A.* 40°46N 80°46W **312** F4
Lisbon Falls *U.S.A.* 44°0N 70°4W **309** D18
Lisburn *U.K.* 54°31N 6°3W **166** B5
Lisburn, C. *Vanuatu* 15°39S 166°46E **287** E4
Lisburn & Castlereagh ☐ *U.K.* 54°30N 6°4W **166** B5
Lisburne, C. *U.S.A.* 68°53N 166°13W **303** B6
Liscannor B. *Ireland* 52°55N 9°24W **166** D2
Liscia ➔ *Italy* 41°11N 9°9E **200** A2
Lisdoonvarna *Ireland* 53°2N 9°18W **166** C2
Lishan *Taiwan* 24°16N 121°14E **225** B3
Lishe Jiang ➔ *China* 24°15N 101°35E **228** E3
Lishi *China* 37°31N 111°8E **226** F6
Lishu *China* 43°20N 124°18E **227** C13
Lishui *Guangdong, China* 23°12N 113°9E **121** A1
Lishui *Jiangsu, China* 31°38N 119°2E **229** B12
Lishui *Zhejiang, China* 28°28N 119°54E **229** C12
Lisianski I. *U.S.A.* 26°2N 174°0W **302** F9
Lisichansk = Lysychansk *Ukraine* 48°55N 38°30E **189** H10
Lisieux *France* 49°10N 0°12E **172** C7
Liski *Russia* 51°3N 39°30E **189** G10
L'Isle-Jourdain *Gers, France* 43°36N 1°5E **174** E5
L'Isle-Jourdain *Vienne, France* 46°13N 0°31E **174** B4
L'Isle-sur-la-Sorgue *France* 43°54N 5°2E **175** E9
Lisle-sur-Tarn *France* 43°52N 1°49E **174** E5
Lismore *N.S.W., Australia* 28°44S 153°21E **281** D5
Lismore *Waterford, Ireland* 52°8N 7°55W **166** D4
Lissa = Leszno *Poland* 51°50N 16°30E **185** G3
Lissos ➔ *Greece* 41°15N 25°40E **203** E9
Lista *Norway* 58°7N 6°39E **164** F3
Lister, Mt. *Antarctica* 78°0S 162°0E **151** D11
Lister og Mandals = Vest-Agder ☐ *Norway* 58°30N 7°15E **164** F4
Liston *Australia* 28°39S 152°6E **281** D5
Listowel *Ont., Canada* 43°44N 80°58W **312** C4
Listowel *Kerry, Ireland* 52°27N 9°29W **166** D2
Lit *Sweden* 63°19N 14°51E **162** A8
Lit-et-Mixe *France* 44°2N 1°15W **174** D2
Litang *Guangxi Zhuangzu, China* 23°12N 109°8E **228** F7
Litang *Sichuan, China* 30°1N 100°17E **228** B3
Litang *Malaysia* 5°27N 118°31E **235** A5
Litang Qu ➔ *China* 28°4N 101°32E **228** C3
Litani ➔ *Lebanon* 33°20N 35°15E **250** E6
Litchfield *Vic., Australia* 36°18S 142°52E **282** D5
Litchfield *Calif., U.S.A.* 40°24N 120°23W **306** E6
Litchfield *Conn., U.S.A.* 41°45N 73°11W **313** E11
Litchfield *Ill., U.S.A.* 39°11N 89°39W **310** E7
Litchfield *Minn., U.S.A.* 45°8N 94°32W **308** C6
Litchfield △ *Australia* 13°14S 131°1E **278** B5
Liteni *Romania* 47°32N 26°32E **183** C11
Lithakia *Greece* 37°43N 20°50E **207** D2
Lithgow *Australia* 33°25S 150°8E **283** B9
Lithino, Akra *Greece* 34°55N 24°44E **207** F5
Lithuania ■ *Europe* 55°30N 24°0E **188** E2
Litija *Slovenia* 46°3N 14°50E **199** B11
Lititz *U.S.A.* 40°9N 76°18W **313** F8
Litochoro *Greece* 40°8N 22°34E **202** F6
Litoko *Dem. Rep. of the Congo* 1°13S 24°47E **264** C4
Litoměřice *Czechia* 50°33N 14°10E **180** A7
Litomyšl *Czechia* 49°52N 16°20E **181** B9
Litschau *Austria* 48°58N 15°4E **180** C8
Little Abaco *The Bahamas* 26°50N 77°30W **320** A4
Little Andaman I. *India* 10°45N 92°30E **245** J11
Little Aral Sea = Northern Aral Sea *Kazakhstan* 46°20N 60°30E **216** C6
Little B. *N.S.W., Australia* 33°58S 151°15E **139** B2
Little B. *Montserrat* 16°43N 62°11W **323** p
Little Barrier I. *N.Z.* 36°12S 175°8E **284** C4
Little Basses *Sri Lanka* 6°24N 81°43E **245** L5
Little Belt Mts. *U.S.A.* 46°40N 110°45W **304** C8
Little Bighorn Battlefield ⌓ *U.S.A.* 45°34N 107°25W **304** D10
Little Blue ➔ *U.S.A.* 39°42N 96°41W **308** F5
Little Buffalo ➔ *Canada* 61°0N 113°46W **296** A6
Little Calumet ➔ *U.S.A.* 41°39N 87°34W **119** D3
Little Cayman *Cayman Is.* 19°41N 80°3W **320** C3
Little Churchill ➔ *Canada* 57°30N 95°22W **297** B9
Little Coco I. *Myanmar* 14°0N 93°13E **245** H11
Little Colorado ➔ *U.S.A.* 36°12N 111°48W **305** H8
Little Current *Canada* 45°55N 82°0W **298** C3
Little Current ➔ *Canada* 50°57N 84°36W **298** B3
Little Desert △ *Australia* 37°25S 141°30E **282** D4
Little Diomede I. *U.S.A.* 65°45N 168°56W **303** D5
Little Falls *Minn., U.S.A.* 45°59N 94°22W **308** C6
Little Falls *N.Y., U.S.A.* 43°3N 74°51W **313** C10
Little Ferry *U.S.A.* 40°50N 74°2W **132** A1
Little Fork ➔ *U.S.A.* 48°31N 93°35W **308** A7
Little Grand Rapids *Canada* 52°0N 95°29W **297** C9
Little Haiti *U.S.A.* 25°50N 80°11W **129** C2
Little Havana *U.S.A.* 25°47N 80°15W **129** D1
Little Humboldt ➔ *U.S.A.* 41°1N 117°43W **304** F5
Little Inagua *The Bahamas* 21°40N 73°50W **321** B5
Little India *Singapore* 1°19N 103°51E **138** B3
Little Italy *New York, U.S.A.* **132** e2
Little Karoo *S. Africa* 33°45S 21°0E **270** D3
Little Khingan Mts. = Xiao Hinggan Ling *China* 49°0N 127°0E **219** B14
Little Lake *U.S.A.* 35°56N 117°55W **307** K9
Little Lake Conway *U.S.A.* 28°29N 81°21W **133** B2
Little Laut Is. = Laut Kecil, Kepulauan *Indonesia* 4°45S 115°40E **235** C5
Little London *Jamaica* 18°15N 78°13W **320** a
Little Mecatina = Petit-Mécatina ➔ *Canada* 50°40N 59°30W **299** B8
Little Mermaid = Den Lille Havfrue *Copenhagen, Denmark* **118** a3
Little Minch *U.K.* 57°35N 6°45W **167** D2
Little Missouri ➔ *U.S.A.* 47°36N 102°25W **308** B2
Little Nicobar *India* 7°20N 93°40E **245** L11
Little Ouse ➔ *U.K.* 52°22N 1°12E **169** E9
Little Rann *India* 23°25N 71°25E **242** H4
Little Red ➔ *U.S.A.* 35°11N 91°27W **314** D9
Little River *N.Z.* 43°45S 172°49E **285** D7
Little Rock *U.S.A.* 34°45N 92°17W **314** D8
Little Rouge ➔ *Canada* 43°45N 79°11W **141** A4
Little Ruaha ➔ *Tanzania* 7°57S 37°53E **268** D4
Little Sable Pt. *U.S.A.* 43°38N 86°33W **308** D10
Little Scarcies ➔ *S. Leone* 8°50N 13°10W **262** D2
Little Sioux ➔ *U.S.A.* 41°48N 96°4W **308** E5
Little Sitkin I. *U.S.A.* 51°57N 178°31E **303** L2
Little Smoky ➔ *Canada* 54°44N 117°11W **296** C5
Little Snake ➔ *U.S.A.* 40°27N 108°26W **304** F9
Little Sound *Bermuda* 32°15N 64°50W **153** a
Little Tokyo *Los Angeles, U.S.A.* **127** c2
Little Valley *U.S.A.* 42°15N 78°48W **312** D6
Little Wabash ➔ *U.S.A.* 37°55N 88°5W **311** G8
Little White ➔ *U.S.A.* 43°40N 100°40W **308** D3
Little York *U.S.A.* 41°1N 90°45W **310** C6
Little Zab = Zāb aş Şaghīr ➔ *Iraq* 35°17N 43°29E **213** E10
Littlefield *U.S.A.* 33°55N 102°20W **314** E3
Littlehampton *U.K.* 50°49N 0°32W **169** G7
Littleton *U.S.A.* 44°18N 71°46W **313** B13
Littoral ☐ *Cameroon* 4°0N 10°0E **263** E7
Littoria = Latina *Italy* 41°28N 12°52E **200** A5
Litunga *Angola* 13°19S 16°48E **265** E3
Litvínov *Czechia* 50°36N 13°37E **180** A6
Liu He ➔ *Jilin, China* 42°46N 126°13E **224** A3
Liu He ➔ *Liaoning, China* 40°55N 121°35E **227** D11
Liu Jiang ➔ *China* 23°55N 109°30E **228** F7
Liuba *China* 33°38N 106°55E **226** H4
Liucheng *China* 24°38N 109°14E **228** E7
Liuchiu *Taiwan* 22°13N 120°21E **225** C2
Liuch'iu *Taiwan* 22°21N 120°23E **225** D2
Liuch'iu Yü *Taiwan* 22°21N 120°22E **225** D2
Liugou *China* 40°57N 118°15E **227** D10
Liuhang *China* 31°21N 121°21E **138** A1
Liuhe *China* 42°17N 125°43E **224** A2
Liuheng Dao *China* 29°40N 122°5E **229** C14
Liujiang *China* 24°26N 109°11E **228** E7
Liukang Tenggaja = Sabalana, Kepulauan *Indonesia* 6°45S 118°50E **231** F5
Liuli *Tanzania* 11°3S 34°38E **269** E3
Liupan Shan *China* 35°39N 106°12E **226** G4
Liupanshui *China* 26°38N 104°48E **228** D5
Liuqiu = Liuch'iu *Taiwan* 22°21N 120°23E **225** D2
Liurong Temple *China* 23°8N 113°15E **121** B2
Liuwa Plain *Zambia* 14°20S 22°30E **265** E4
Liuwa Plain △ *Zambia* 14°45S 22°35E **265** E4
Liuyang *China* 28°10N 113°37E **229** C9
Liuying *Taiwan* 23°17N 120°18E **225** C2
Liuzhou *China* 24°22N 109°22E **228** E7
Liuzhuang *China* 33°12N 120°18E **227** H11
Livada *Romania* 47°52N 23°5E **182** C8
Livadero *Greece* 40°2N 21°57E **202** F5
Livadhia *Cyprus* 34°57N 33°38E **207** E12
Livadhje *Albania* 39°47N 20°7E **206** B10
Livadi *Greece* 40°8N 22°9E **204** A4
Livadia *Greece* 38°27N 22°54E **204** C4
Livarot *France* 48°58N 0°9E **172** D7
Live Oak *Calif., U.S.A.* 39°17N 121°40W **306** F5
Live Oak *Fla., U.S.A.* 30°18N 82°59W **316** E7
Live Oak Manor *U.S.A.* 29°57N 90°14W **131** B1
Lively *Canada* 46°26N 81°9W **309** B13
Livengood *U.S.A.* 65°32N 148°33W **303** D10
Liveras *Cyprus* 35°23N 32°57E **207** E8
Livermore *U.S.A.* 37°41N 121°47W **306** H5
Livermore, Mt. *U.S.A.* 30°38N 104°11W **314** F2
Livermore Falls *U.S.A.* 44°29N 70°11W **309** C18
Liverpool *N.S.W., Australia* 33°54S 150°58E **283** B9
Liverpool *N.S., Canada* 44°5N 64°41W **299** D7
Liverpool *Mersey., U.K.* 53°25N 3°0W **168** D4
Liverpool *N.Y., U.S.A.* 43°6N 76°13W **313** C8
Liverpool Bay *U.K.* 53°30N 3°20W **168** D4
Liverpool Plains *Australia* 31°15S 150°15E **283** A9
Liverpool Ra. *Australia* 31°50S 150°30E **283** A9
Liverpool Street *London, U.K.* **125** a5
Livigno *Italy* 46°35N 10°10E **198** B7
Livingston *Guatemala* 15°50N 88°50W **320** C2
Livingston *W. Loth., U.K.* 55°54N 3°30W **167** F5
Livingston *Ala., U.S.A.* 32°35N 88°11W **315** E10
Livingston *Calif., U.S.A.* 37°23N 120°43W **306** H6
Livingston *Mont., U.S.A.* 45°40N 110°34W **304** D8
Livingston *S.C., U.S.A.* 33°38N 81°7W **316** B8
Livingston *Tenn., U.S.A.* 36°23N 85°19W **315** C12
Livingston *Tex., U.S.A.* 30°43N 94°56W **314** F7
Livingston *Wis., U.S.A.* 42°54N 90°26W **310** B6
Livingston, L. *U.S.A.* 30°50N 95°10W **314** F7
Livingston Manor *U.S.A.* 41°54N 74°50W **313** E10
Livingstone *Zambia* 17°46S 25°52E **269** F2
Livingstone △ *Australia* 35°22S 147°22E **283** C7
Livingstone Mts. *N.Z.* 45°15S 168°9E **285** F3
Livingstone Mts. *Tanzania* 9°40S 34°20E **269** D3
Livingstonia *Malawi* 10°38S 34°5E **269** E3
Livno *Bos.-H.* 43°50N 17°1E **182** G2
Livny *Russia* 52°30N 37°30E **189** F9
Livonia *Mich., U.S.A.* 42°23N 83°23W **311** B13
Livonia *N.Y., U.S.A.* 42°49N 77°40W **312** D7
Livorno *Italy* 43°33N 10°19E **198** E7
Livradois-Forez ⌓ *France* 44°0N 3°0E **174** E7
Livramento = Nossa Senhora do Livramento *Brazil* 15°48S 56°22W **331** D6
Livramento *Brazil* 30°55S 55°30W **335** C4
Livramento do Brumado *Brazil* 13°39S 41°50W **333** D3
Livron-sur-Drôme *France* 44°46N 4°51E **175** D8
Livry-Gargan *France* 48°55N 2°31E **134** A4
Livyntsi *Ukraine* 48°25N 26°37E **183** B11
Liwā' *U.A.E.* 23°0N 54°10E **249** B6
Liwale *Tanzania* 9°48S 37°58E **269** D4
Liwan *China* 23°3N 113°12E **121** B2
Liwiec ➔ *Poland* 52°36N 21°34E **185** F8
Liwonde *Malawi* 15°4S 35°13E **269** F4
Liwonde △ *Malawi* 14°48S 35°20E **269** E4
Lixi *China* 26°23N 101°59E **228** D3
Lixian *China* 31°23N 103°13E **228** B4
Lixin *China* 33°8N 116°13E **229** A11
Lixouri *Greece* 38°12N 20°26E **207** C2
Liyang *China* 31°26N 119°28E **229** B12
Lizard ➔ *Trin. & Tob.* 10°9N 61°1W **323** t
Lizard I. *Australia* 14°42S 145°30E **280** A4
Lizard Pt. *U.K.* 49°57N 5°13W **169** H2
Lizarda *Brazil* 9°36S 46°41W **332** C2
Lizarra = Estella *Spain* 42°40N 2°2W **196** C2
Lizella *U.S.A.* 32°48N 83°49W **316** C6
Lizzano *Italy* 40°23N 17°27E **201** B10
Ljan *Norway* 59°50N 10°46E **130** B3
Ljig *Serbia* 44°13N 20°18E **202** B4
Ljøra ➔ *Norway* 61°24N 12°35E **164** C8
Ljørdalen *Norway* 61°23N 12°41E **164** C9
Ljosland *Norway* 58°47N 7°22E **164** F4
Ljubija *Bos.-H.* 44°55N 16°35E **199** D13
Ljubinje *Bos.-H.* 42°58N 18°5E **202** D2
Ljubišnja *Europe* 43°18N 19°6E **202** C3
Ljubljana *Slovenia* 46°4N 14°33E **199** B11
Ljubljana ✕ **(LJU)** *Slovenia* 46°14N 14°33E **199** B11
Ljubno *Slovenia* 46°25N 14°46E **199** B11
Ljubovija *Serbia* 44°11N 19°22E **202** B3
Ljugarn *Sweden* 57°20N 18°43E **163** G12
Ljung *Sweden* 57°59N 13°3E **163** G7
Ljungan ➔ *Sweden* 62°18N 17°23E **162** B11
Ljungaverk *Sweden* 62°30N 16°5E **162** B10
Ljungby *Sweden* 56°49N 13°55E **163** H7
Ljungbyholm *Sweden* 56°39N 16°5E **163** H10
Ljungdalen *Sweden* 62°51N 12°47E **162** B6
Ljungsbro *Sweden* 58°31N 15°30E **163** F9
Ljungskile *Sweden* 58°14N 11°55E **163** F5
Ljusdal *Sweden* 61°46N 16°3E **162** C10
Ljusfallshammar *Sweden* 58°48N 15°30E **163** F9
Ljusnan ➔ *Sweden* 61°12N 17°8E **162** C11
Ljusne *Sweden* 61°13N 17°7E **162** C11
Ljusterö *Sweden* 59°31N 18°37E **162** E12
Ljustorp *Sweden* 62°38N 17°19E **162** B11
Ljutomer *Slovenia* 46°31N 16°11E **199** B13
Llagostera *Spain* 41°50N 2°54E **196** D7
Llamellin *Peru* 9°0S 76°54W **330** B2
Llançà *Spain* 42°22N 3°9E **196** C8
Llancanelo, Salina *Argentina* 35°40S 69°8W **334** D2
Llandeilo *U.K.* 51°53N 3°59W **169** F4
Llandovery *U.K.* 51°59N 3°48W **169** F4
Llandrindod Wells *U.K.* 52°14N 3°22W **169** E4
Llandudno *U.K.* 53°19N 3°50W **168** D4
Llanelli *U.K.* 51°41N 4°10W **169** F3
Llanes *Spain* 43°25N 4°50W **194** B6
Llanfair-ym-Muallt = Builth Wells *U.K.* 52°9N 3°25W **169** E4
Llanganates △ *Ecuador* 0°51S 72°20W **328** D3
Llangollen *U.K.* 52°58N 3°11W **168** E4
Llanidloes *U.K.* 52°27N 3°31W **169** E4
Llano *U.S.A.* 30°45N 98°41W **314** F5
Llano ➔ *U.S.A.* 30°39N 98°26W **314** F5
Llano de Can Gineu *Spain* 41°27N 2°10E **114** A2
Llano Estacado *U.S.A.* 33°30N 103°0W **314** E3
Llanos *S. Amer.* 5°0N 71°35W **326** C3
Llanos de Challe △ *Chile* 28°8S 71°1W **334** B1
Llanquihue, L. *Chile* 41°10S 72°50W **336** B1
Llanwrtyd Wells *U.K.* 52°7N 3°38W **169** E4
Llata *Peru* 9°25S 76°47W **330** B2
Llebeig, C. des *Spain* 39°33N 2°18E **206** B3
Lleida *Spain* 41°37N 0°39E **196** D5
Lleida ☐ *Spain* 42°6N 1°0E **196** C6
Llentrisca, C. *Spain* 38°52N 1°15E **206** D1
Llera de Canales *Mexico* 23°19N 99°1W **319** C5
Llerena *Spain* 38°17N 6°0W **195** G5
Llevant, Sa. de *Spain* 39°35N 3°17E **206** B4
Lleyn Peninsula *U.K.* 52°51N 4°36W **168** E3
Llica *Bolivia* 19°52S 68°16W **330** D4
Llico *Chile* 34°46S 72°5W **334** C1
Llíria *Spain* 39°37N 0°35W **197** F4
Llivia *Spain* 42°28N 1°59E **174** F5
Llobregat ➔ *Spain* 41°19N 2°5E **196** D7
Llodio *Spain* 43°9N 2°58W **196** B2
Llogara △ *Albania* 40°13N 19°35E **202** F3
Llorente *Phil.* 11°25N 125°33E **233** F5
Lloret de Mar *Spain* 41°41N 2°53E **196** D7
Lloseta *Spain* 39°43N 2°52E **206** B3
Lloyd B. *Australia* 12°45S 143°27E **280** A3
Lloyd L. *Canada* 57°22N 108°57W **297** B7
Lloydminster *Canada* 53°17N 110°0W **297** C7
Llubi *Spain* 39°42N 3°0E **206** B4
Llucena del Cid *Spain* 40°9N 0°17W **196** E4
Llucmajor *Spain* 39°29N 2°53E **206** B3
Lluidas Vale *Jamaica* 18°6N 77°5W **320** a
Llullaillaco, Volcán *S. Amer.* 24°43S 68°30W **334** A2
Llullaillaco △ *Chile* 24°50S 68°51W **334** A2
Lo ➔ *Vietnam* 21°18N 105°25E **236** B5
Lo Aranguiz *Chile* 33°23S 70°40W **137** B2
Lo Boza *Chile* 33°23S 70°43W **137** B1
Lo Espejo *Chile* 33°31S 70°42W **137** C1
Lo Hermida *Chile* 33°28S 70°33W **137** B2
Lo Prado *Chile* 33°26S 70°42W **137** B1
Lo So Shing *Hong Kong, China* 22°12N 114°7E **122** B2
Lo Wai *Hong Kong, China* 22°22N 114°8E **122** A2
Loa *U.S.A.* 38°24N 111°39W **304** G8
Loa ➔ *Chile* 21°26S 70°41W **334** A1
Loagan Bunut △ *Malaysia* 3°32N 114°40E **235** B4
Loaita I. *S. China Sea* 10°41N 114°25E **230** B4
Loakulu *Indonesia* 0°31S 117°1E **235** C5
Loange ➔ *Dem. Rep. of the Congo* 4°17S 20°2E **265** C4
Loango *Congo* 4°38S 11°50E **265** C2
Loanhead *U.K.* 55°53N 3°9W **121** B3
Loano *Italy* 44°8N 8°15E **198** D5
Loay *Phil.* 9°36N 124°1E **233** G5
Lobamba *Eswatini* 26°28S 31°12E **271** C5
Lobatse *Botswana* 25°12S 25°40E **270** C4
Lobau *Wien, Austria* 48°10N 16°31E **142** A3
Löbau *Sachsen, Germany* 51°5N 14°40E **178** D10
Lobaye ☐ *C.A.R.* 4°0N 17°30E **264** B3
Lobaye ➔ *C.A.R.* 3°41N 18°35E **264** B3
Loben = Lubliniec *Poland* 50°43N 18°45E **185** H5
Lobenstein *Germany* 50°25N 11°39E **178** E7
Lobería *Argentina* 38°10S 58°40W **334** D4
Löberöd *Sweden* 55°47N 13°31E **163** J7
Łobez *Poland* 53°38N 15°39E **184** E2
Lobito *Angola* 12°18S 13°35E **265** E2
Lobo *Phil.* 13°39N 121°13E **232** E3
Lobo ➔ *Côte d'Ivoire* 6°2N 6°45W **262** D3
Lobos *Argentina* 35°10S 59°0W **334** D4
Lobos, I. *Mexico* 27°20N 110°36W **318** B2
Lobos, I. de *Canary Is.* 28°45N 13°50W **153** e2
Lobos, Pt. *U.S.A.* 37°46N 122°30W **136** B1
Lobos de Afuera, Islas *Peru* 6°57S 80°42W **330** B1
Lobos de Tierra, I. *Peru* 6°27S 80°52W **330** B1
Łobżenica *Poland* 53°18N 17°15E **185** E4
Loc Binh *Vietnam* 21°46N 106°54E **236** B6
Loc Ninh *Vietnam* 11°50N 106°34E **237** G6
Locarno *Switz.* 46°10N 8°47E **179** J4
Loch Garman = Wexford *Ireland* 52°20N 6°28W **166** D5
Loch Lomond and the Trossachs △ *U.K.* 56°10N 4°40W **167** E4
Lochaber *U.K.* 56°59N 5°1W **167** E3
Locham *Germany* 48°7N 11°26E **131** B1
Locharbriggs *U.K.* 55°7N 3°35W **167** F5
Lochboisdale *U.K.* 57°9N 7°20W **167** D1
Loche, L. La *Canada* 56°30N 109°30W **297** B7
Lochem *Neths.* 52°9N 6°26E **170** B6
Loches *France* 47°7N 1°0E **172** E7
Lochgilphead *U.K.* 56°2N 5°26W **167** E3
Lochinvar △ *Zambia* 15°55S 27°15E **269** F2
Lochinver *U.K.* 58°9N 5°14W **167** C3
Lochkov *Czechia* 50°0N 14°21E **135** B2
Lochloosa L. *U.S.A.* 29°30N 82°7W **317** F7
Lochmaddy *U.K.* 57°36N 7°10W **167** D1
Lochnagar *Queens., Australia* 23°33S 145°38E **280** C4
Lochnagar *Aberds., U.K.* 56°57N 3°15W **167** E5
Lochów *Poland* 52°33N 21°42E **185** F8
Lochy, L. *U.K.* 57°0N 4°53W **167** E4
Lock *Australia* 33°34S 135°46E **281** E2
Lock Haven *U.S.A.* 41°8N 77°28W **312** E7
Lockeford *U.S.A.* 38°10N 121°9W **306** G5
Lockeport *Canada* 43°47N 65°4W **299** D6
Lockerbie *U.K.* 55°7N 3°21W **167** F5
Lockhart *N.S.W., Australia* 35°14S 146°40E **283** C7
Lockhart *Tex., U.S.A.* 29°53N 97°40W **314** G6
Lockhart, L. *Australia* 33°15S 119°3E **279** F2
Lockhart River *Australia* 12°58S 143°30E **280** A3
Lockhart River ◎ *Australia* 12°47S 143°20E **280** A3
Lockhausen *Germany* 48°10N 11°24E **131** A1
Lockney *U.S.A.* 34°7N 101°27W **314** D4
Lockport *Ill., U.S.A.* 41°35N 88°3W **311** C8
Lockport *N.Y., U.S.A.* 43°10N 78°42W **312** C6
Locminé *France* 47°54N 2°51W **172** E4
Locri *Italy* 38°14N 16°16E **201** D9
Locronan *France* 48°7N 4°15W **172** D2
Locust Cr. ➔ *U.S.A.* 39°40N 93°17W **310** E3
Locust Grove *U.S.A.* 33°21N 84°7W **316** B5
Lod *Israel* 31°57N 34°54E **251** G5
Lodalskåpa *Norway* 61°47N 7°13E **164** C4
Lodeinoye Pole *Russia* 60°44N 33°33E **188** B7
Lodève *France* 43°44N 3°19E **174** E7
Lodge Bay *Canada* 52°14N 55°51W **299** B8
Lodge Grass *U.S.A.* 45°19N 107°22W **304** D10
Lodhran *Pakistan* 29°32N 71°30E **242** E4
Lodi *Italy* 45°19N 9°30E **198** C6
Lodi *Calif., U.S.A.* 38°8N 121°16W **306** G5
Lodi *N.J., U.S.A.* 40°52N 74°5W **132** A1
Lodi *Ohio, U.S.A.* 41°2N 82°1W **312** E3
Lodi Estate *India* 28°36N 77°15E **120** B2
Lodja *Dem. Rep. of the Congo* 3°30S 23°23E **264** C4
Lodosa *Spain* 42°25N 2°4W **196** C2
Lödöse *Sweden* 58°2N 12°9E **163** F6
Lodwar *Kenya* 3°7N 35°36E **268** B4
Łódź *Poland* 51°45N 19°27E **185** G6
Łódzkie ☐ *Poland* 51°30N 19°30E **185** G6
Loei *Thailand* 17°29N 101°35E **236** D3
Loengo *Dem. Rep. of the Congo* 4°48S 26°30E **265** C5
Loeriesfontein *S. Africa* 31°0S 19°26E **270** D2
Lofa ➔ *Liberia* 6°35N 11°8W **262** D2
Lofa Mano △ *Liberia* 7°55N 10°25W **262** D2
Lofer *Austria* 47°35N 12°41E **180** D5
Lofoten *Norway* 68°30N 13°59E **160** B16
Lofsdalen *Sweden* 62°10N 13°20E **162** B7
Lofsen ➔ *Sweden* 62°7N 13°57E **162** B7
Loftahammar *Sweden* 57°54N 16°41E **163** G10
Loga *Niger* 13°40N 3°15E **263** C5
Logan *Iowa, U.S.A.* 41°39N 95°47W **308** E6
Logan *Ohio, U.S.A.* 39°32N 82°25W **309** F12
Logan *Utah, U.S.A.* 41°44N 111°50W **304** F8
Logan *W. Va., U.S.A.* 37°51N 81°59W **309** G13
Logan, Mt. *Canada* 60°34N 140°23W **294** E3
Logan Int., Boston ✕ **(BOS)** *U.S.A.* 42°22N 71°1W **116** A2
Logan Martin L. *U.S.A.* 33°26N 86°20W **316** B3
Logan Square *U.S.A.* 41°55N 87°42W **119** B2
Logandale *U.S.A.* 36°36N 114°29W **307** J12
Logansport *Ind., U.S.A.* 40°45N 86°22W **311** D10
Logansport *La., U.S.A.* 31°58N 94°0W **314** F8
Loganville *U.S.A.* 33°50N 83°54W **316** B6
Logatec *Slovenia* 45°56N 14°15E **199** C11
Logirim *South Sudan* 4°43N 33°14E **257** G3
Lognes-Émerainville ✕ **(XLG)** *France* 48°49N 2°37E **134** B4
Logo *South Sudan* 5°20N 30°18E **257** F3
Logodoro *Italy* 40°35N 8°45E **200** B1
Logone ➔ *Chad* 12°6N 15°2E **259** F3
Logone Gana *Chad* 11°36N 15°4E **259** F3
Logone Occidental ☐ *Chad* 8°40N 16°0E **259** G3
Logone Occidental ➔ *Chad* 8°50N 16°0E **259** G3
Logone Oriental ☐ *Chad* 8°30N 16°30E **259** G3
Logone Oriental ➔ *Chad* 9°7N 16°26E **259** G3
Logroño *Spain* 42°28N 2°27W **196** C2
Logrosán *Spain* 39°20N 5°32W **195** F5
Løgstør *Denmark* 56°58N 9°14E **163** H3
Logtak L. *India* 24°33N 93°50E **241** C4
Løgumkloster *Denmark* 55°4N 8°57E **163** J2
Loh *Vanuatu* 13°21S 166°38E **287** C4
Lohals *Denmark* 55°8N 10°55E **163** J4
Lohardaga *India* 23°27N 84°45E **243** H11
Loharia *India* 23°45N 74°14E **242** H6
Loharu *India* 28°27N 75°49E **242** E6
Lohja *Finland* 60°12N 24°5E **188** B3
Löhme *Germany* 52°37N 13°40E **115** A5
Löhne *Germany* 52°11N 8°40E **178** C4
Lohso = Luohe *China* 33°32N 114°2E **226** H8
Lohr *Germany* 49°59N 9°35E **179** F5
Lohri Wah ➔ *Pakistan* 27°27N 67°37E **242** F2
Loi-lem *Myanmar* 20°52N 97°22E **241** E6
Loikaw *Myanmar* 19°40N 97°17E **241** F6
Loimaa *Finland* 60°50N 23°5E **188** B2
Loir ➔ *France* 47°33N 0°32W **172** E6
Loir-et-Cher ☐ *France* 47°40N 1°20E **172** E8
Loire ☐ *France* 45°40N 4°5E **175** C8
Loire ➔ *France* 47°16N 2°10W **172** E4
Loire-Anjou-Touraine ⌓ *France* 47°14N 0°5W **172** E6
Loire-Atlantique ☐ *France* 47°25N 1°40W **172** E5
Loire Inférieure = Loire-Atlantique ☐ *France* 47°25N 1°40W **172** E5
Loiret ☐ *France* 47°55N 2°30E **173** E9
Loitz *Germany* 53°58N 13°8E **178** B9
Loja *Ecuador* 3°59S 79°16W **330** A2
Loja *Spain* 37°10N 4°10W **195** H6
Loja ☐ *Ecuador* 4°0S 79°13W **328** D2
Loje ➔ *Angola* 7°49S 13°6E **265** D2
Loji = Kawasi *Indonesia* 1°38S 127°28E **231** E7
Lojo = Lohja *Finland* 60°12N 24°5E **188** B3
Lojt Kirkeby *Denmark* 55°7N 9°26E **163** J3
Lojung *China* 24°27N 109°36E **228** E7
Loka *Dem. Rep. of the Congo* 0°22N 18°2E **264** B3
Loka *South Sudan* 4°13N 31°0E **257** G3
Lokako *Dem. Rep. of the Congo* 0°57S 18°55E **264** C4
Lokandu *Dem. Rep. of the Congo* 2°30S 25°45E **264** C5
Lokaw *Dem. Rep. of the Congo* 2°40S 20°12E **264** C4
Løken *Norway* 59°48N 11°29E **164** E8
Lokeren *Belgium* 51°6N 3°59E **170** C3
Lokgwabe *Botswana* 24°10S 21°50E **270** B3
Lokhvytsya *Ukraine* 50°25N 33°18E **189** G7
Lokichar *Kenya* 2°23N 35°39E **268** B4
Lokichokio *Kenya* 4°19N 34°13E **268** B3
Lokitaung *Kenya* 4°12N 35°48E **268** B4
Lokkan tekojärvi *Finland* 67°55N 27°35E **160** C22
Løkken *Denmark* 57°22N 9°41E **163** G3
Løkken *Sør-Trøndelag, Norway* 63°9N 9°41E **164** A6
Loknya *Russia* 56°49N 30°4E **188** D6
Loko *C.A.R.* 3°38N 18°2E **264** B3
Loko *Nigeria* 8°1N 7°53E **263** D6
Lokoja *Nigeria* 7°47N 6°45E **263** D6
Lokolama *Dem. Rep. of the Congo* 2°35S 19°50E **264** C3
Lokolenge *Dem. Rep. of the Congo* 1°12N 22°38E **264** B4
Lokolo ➔ *Dem. Rep. of the Congo* 1°43S 18°23E **264** C3
Lokot *Russia* 52°34N 34°36E **189** F8
Loktak L. = Logtak L. *India* 24°33N 93°50E **241** C4
Lokuru *Solomon Is.* 8°20S 157°0E **287** M9
Lol *South Sudan* 6°26N 29°37E **257** F2
Lol ➔ *South Sudan* 9°13N 26°30E **257** F2
Lola *Angola* 14°19S 13°37E **265** E2
Lola *Greece* 36°53N 21°55E **204** E3
Lola *Guinea* 7°52N 8°29W **262** D3
Lola, Mt. *U.S.A.* 39°26N 120°22W **306** F6
Lolgorien *Kenya* 1°14S 34°48E **268** C3
Lolibai, Gebel *South Sudan* 3°50N 33°0E **257** G3
Lolimi *South Sudan* 4°35N 34°0E **257** G3
Loliondo *Tanzania* 2°2S 35°39E **268** C4
Lolland *Denmark* 54°45N 11°30E **163** K5
Lollar *Germany* 50°37N 8°43E **178** E4
Lolo *U.S.A.* 46°45N 114°5W **304** C6
Lolo ➔ *Gabon* 0°18S 12°18E **264** C2
Lolobau I. *Papua N. G.* 4°55S 151°10E **286** C6
Lolodorf *Cameroon* 3°16N 10°49E **263** E7
Lolokhet *Pakistan* 24°54N 67°2E **123** A2
Loloma *Zambia* 13°24S 24°21E **265** E4
Loltong *Vanuatu* 15°32S 168°10E **287** E6
Lom *Bulgaria* 43°48N 23°12E **202** C7
Lom *Oppland, Norway* 61°50N 8°34E **164** C5
Lom ➔ *Bulgaria* 43°45N 23°15E **202** C7
Lom ➔ *Cameroon* 5°20N 13°24E **264** A2
Lom Kao *Thailand* 16°53N 101°14E **236** D3
Lom Sak *Thailand* 16°47N 101°15E **236** D3
Loma *U.S.A.* 47°56N 110°30W **304** C8
Loma Linda *U.S.A.* 34°3N 117°16W **307** L9
Loma Mansa *S. Leone* 9°13N 11°7W **262** D2
Loma Mts. *S. Leone* 9°10N 11°7W **262** D2
Lomako ➔ *Dem. Rep. of the Congo* 0°50N 20°50E **264** B4
Lomaloma *Fiji* 17°17S 178°59W **287** A3
Lomami ☐ *Dem. Rep. of the Congo* 6°0S 25°0E **265** D4
Lomami ➔ *Dem. Rep. of the Congo* 0°46N 24°16E **264** B4
Lomas Chapultepec *Mexico* 19°25N 99°12W **128** B1
Lomas de San Angel Inn *Mexico* 19°20N 99°13W **128** B1
Lomas de Zamora *Argentina* 34°45S 58°24W **334** C4
Lombadina *Australia* 16°31S 122°54E **278** C3
Lombard *U.S.A.* 41°53N 88°1W **311** C8
Lombárdia ☐ *Italy* 45°40N 9°30E **198** C6
Lombardy = Lombárdia ☐ *Italy* 45°40N 9°30E **198** C6
Lombardy East *S. Africa* 26°6S 28°7E **123** A2
Lombe *Angola* 9°27S 16°13E **265** D3
Lombez *France* 43°29N 0°55E **174** E4
Lomblen *Indonesia* 8°30S 123°32E **231** F6
Lombok *Indonesia* 8°45S 116°30E **235** D5
Lombok, Selat *Indonesia* 8°30S 115°50E **231** K18
Lomé *Togo* 6°9N 1°20E **263** D5
Lomela *Dem. Rep. of the Congo* 2°19S 23°15E **264** C4
Lomela ➔ *Dem. Rep. of the Congo* 0°15S 20°40E **264** C4
Łomianki *Poland* 52°21N 20°54E **143** A1
Lomié *Cameroon* 3°13N 13°38E **264** B2
Lomma *Sweden* 55°43N 13°6E **163** J7
Lommel *Belgium* 51°14N 5°19E **170** C5
Lomond *Canada* 50°24N 112°36W **296** C6
Lomond, L. *U.K.* 56°8N 4°38W **167** E4
Lomonosov Ridge *Arctic* 88°0N 140°0E **150** A
Lomphat *Cambodia* 13°30N 106°59E **236** F6
Lompobatang *Indonesia* 5°24S 119°56E **231** F5
Lompoc *U.S.A.* 34°38N 120°28W **307** L6
Lomsegga *Norway* 61°49N 8°21E **164** C5
Lomus Reforma *Mexico* 19°24N 99°14W **128** B1
Łomża *Poland* 53°10N 22°2E **185** E9
Lon, Ko *Thailand* 7°47N 98°23E **237** a
Lonavale *India* 18°46N 73°29E **244** E1
Loncoche *Chile* 39°20S 72°50W **336** A2
Loncopué *Argentina* 38°4S 70°37W **336** A2
Londa *India* 15°30N 74°30E **245** G2
Londiani *Kenya* 0°10S 35°33E **268** C4
Londinières *France* 49°50N 1°25E **172** C8
London *Ont., Canada* 42°59N 81°15W **312** D3
London *U.K.* 51°30N 0°3W **125** B3
London *Ky., U.S.A.* 37°8N 84°5W **309** G11
London *Ohio, U.S.A.* 39°53N 83°27W **311** E13
London, Greater ☐ *U.K.* 51°36N 0°5W **169** F7
London Avenue Canal *U.S.A.* 30°3N 90°6W **131** A2
London Bridge *Grenada* 12°15N 61°35W **323** q
London Bridge *London, U.K.* **125** b5
London City ✕ **(LCY)** *U.K.* 51°30N 0°3E **125** A4
London Gateway *U.K.* 51°31N 0°29E **169** F8
London Gatwick ✕ **(LGW)** *U.K.* 51°10N 0°11W **169** F7
London Heathrow ✕ **(LHR)** *U.K.* 51°28N 0°27W **125** B1
London Mills *U.S.A.* 40°43N 90°11W **310** D6
London Stansted ✕ **(STN)** *U.K.* 51°54N 0°14E **169** F8
London Zoo *U.K.* 51°31N 0°9W **125** A3
Londonderry *U.K.* 55°0N 7°20W **166** B4
Londonderry, C. *Australia* 13°45S 126°55E **278** B4
Londonderry, I. *Chile* 55°0S 71°0W **336** E2
Londres *Argentina* 27°46S 67°7W **334** B2
Londrina *Brazil* 23°18S 51°10W **335** A5
Londuimbale *Angola* 12°15S 15°19E **265** E3
Lone Pine *U.S.A.* 36°36N 118°4W **306** J8
Lonely Mine *Zimbabwe* 19°30S 28°49E **271** A4
Long, Î. *Martinique* 14°36N 60°51W **322** j
Long Akah *Malaysia* 3°19N 114°47E **235** B4
Long B. *N.S.W., Australia* 33°59S 151°15E **139** B2
Long B. *Cornwall, Jamaica* 18°20N 78°20W **320** a
Long B. *S.C., U.S.A.* 33°35N 78°45W **315** E15
Long Beach *Calif., U.S.A.* 33°46N 118°11W **307** M8
Long Beach *N.Y., U.S.A.* 40°35N 73°39W **313** F11
Long Beach *Wash., U.S.A.* 46°21N 124°3W **306** D2
Long Branch *Ont., Canada* 43°35N 79°31W **141** B1
Long Branch *N.J., U.S.A.* 40°18N 74°0W **313** F11
Long Cay *The Bahamas* 25°6N 77°22W **153** b
Long Creek *U.S.A.* 44°43N 119°6W **304** D4
Long Ditton *U.K.* 51°22N 0°19W **125** B2
Long Eaton *U.K.* 52°53N 1°15W **168** E6
Long I. *Antigua & B.* 17°8N 61°45W **322** b
Long I. *Queens., Australia* 20°22S 148°51E **280** b
Long I. *Nunavut, Canada* 54°50N 79°20W **298** B4
Long I. *Cork, Ireland* 51°30N 9°34W **166** E2
Long I. *Papua N. G.* 5°20S 147°5E **286** C4
Long I. *The Bahamas* 23°20N 75°10W **321** B4
Long I. *N.Y., U.S.A.* 40°45N 73°30W **313** F11
Long Island City *U.S.A.* 40°45N 73°56W **132** B2
Long Island Sd. *U.S.A.* 41°10N 73°0W **313** E12
Long L. *Ont., Canada* 49°30N 86°50W **298** C2
Long L. *N.Y., U.S.A.* 44°0N 74°23W **313** C10
Long Lake *U.S.A.* 43°58N 74°25W **313** C10
Long Mountain *Mauritius* 20°8S 57°33E **272** e
Long Point *Canada* 42°34N 80°25W **312** D4
Long Point B. *Canada* 42°40N 80°10W **312** D4
Long Prairie *U.S.A.* 45°59N 94°52W **308** C6
Long Prairie ➔ *U.S.A.* 46°20N 94°36W **308** B6
Long Pt. *Ont., Canada* 42°35N 80°2W **312** D4
Long Pt. *Ont., Canada* 43°56N 76°53W **313** C8
Long Pt. *Otago, N.Z.* 46°34S 169°36E **285** G4
Long Pt. *The Bahamas* 25°1N 77°20W **153** b
Long Range Mts. *Canada* 49°30N 57°30W **299** C8
Long Reef *Australia* 14°1S 125°48E **278** B4
Long Sault *Canada* 45°2N 74°53W **313** A10
Long Str. = Longa, Proliv *Russia* 70°0N 175°0E **215** C18
Long Street *Cape Town, S. Africa* **118** c2
Long Thanh *Vietnam* 10°47N 106°57E **237** G6
Long Xian *China* 34°55N 106°55E **226** G4
Long Xuyen *Vietnam* 10°19N 105°28E **237** G5
Longa *Angola* 14°42S 18°32E **265** E3
Longa *Greece* 36°53N 21°55E **204** E3
Longa ➔ *Angola* 10°14S 13°29E **265** E2
Longa, Proliv *Russia* 70°0N 175°0E **215** C18
Longa Mavinga △ *Angola* 16°20S 20°15E **265** F4
Longagung *Indonesia* 2°16N 115°16E **235** B5
Long'an *China* 23°10N 107°40E **228** F6
Longana *Vanuatu* 15°18S 168°0E **287** E5
Longarone *Italy* 46°16N 12°18E **199** B9
Longbenton *U.K.* 55°1N 1°31W **168** B6
Longberang *Indonesia* 3°43N 116°7E **235** B5
Longbia *Indonesia* 2°37N 116°42E **235** B5
Longboat Key *U.S.A.* 27°23N 82°39W **317** H7
Longboh *Indonesia* 0°52N 115°1E **235** B5
Longburn *N.Z.* 40°23S 175°35E **284** G4
Longchamp, Hippodrome de *France* 48°51N 2°13E **134** A2
Longchang *China* 29°18N 105°15E **228** C5
Longchuan *Guangdong, China* 24°5N 115°17E **229** E10
Longchuan *Yunnan, China* 24°23N 97°58E **228** E1
Longde *China* 35°30N 106°20E **226** G4
Longdenville *Trin. & Tob.* 10°31N 61°23W **323** t
Longeau-Percey *France* 47°47N 5°20E **173** E12
Longford *Tas., Australia* 41°32S 147°3E **281** G4
Longford *Longf., Ireland* 53°43N 7°49W **166** C4
Longford ☐ *Ireland* 53°42N 7°45W **166** C4
Longfort, An = Longford *Ireland* 53°43N 7°49W **166** C4
Longgan Shan *China* 42°19N 126°30E **224** A3
Longhai *China* 24°25N 117°46E **229** E11
Longhua *Guangdong, China* 22°39N 114°0E **219** a
Longhua *Hebei, China* 41°18N 117°45E **227** D9
Longhua Pagoda *China* 31°10N 121°26E **138** B1
Longhua Park *China* 31°10N 121°26E **138** B1
Longhui *China* 27°7N 111°2E **229** D8
Longido *Tanzania* 2°43S 36°42E **268** C4
Longiram *Indonesia* 0°5S 115°45E **235** C5

Longjela Indonesia 2°28N 115°28E 235 B5
Longjing China 42°46N 129°25E 227 C15
Longkou Jiangxi, China 26°N 115°10E 229 D10
Longkou Shandong, China 37°40N 120°18E 227 F11
Longlac Canada 49°45N 86°25W 298 C2
Longli China 26°25N 106°58E 228 D6
Longlin China 24°47N 105°20E 228 E5
Longling China 24°37N 98°39E 228 E2
Longmeadow U.S.A. 42°3N 72°34W 313 D12
Longmen China 23°40N 114°18E 229 F10
Longmen Shiku China 34°28N 112°28E 226 G7
Longming China 22°59N 107°7E 228 F6
Longmont U.S.A. 40°10N 105°6W 304 F11
Longnan China 24°55N 114°47E 229 E10
Longnawan Indonesia 1°51N 114°55E 235 B4
Longobucco Italy 39°27N 16°37E 201 C9
Longoni, B. de Mayotte 12°41S 45°8E 272 b
Longonot △ Kenya 0°55S 36°28E 266 E4
Longos Greece 39°16N 20°7E 206 C10
Longquan China 28°7N 119°10E 229 C12
Longreach Australia 23°28S 144°14E 280 C3
Longshan China 29°29N 109°25E 228 C7
Longsheng China 25°48N 110°0E 229 E8
Longtan = Lung'tan Taiwan 24°52N 121°12E 225 B3
Longtan Dam China 25°5N 107°0E 228 E6
Longtan Hu → China 39°51N 116°24E 114 B2
Longtan Shuiku China 25°10N 106°50E 228 E6
Longué-Jumelles France 47°22N 0°8W 172 E6
Longue-Pointe Canada 45°35N 73°31W 130 A2
Longueau France 49°52N 2°21E 173 C9
Longueuil Canada 45°31N 73°29W 130 A3
Longuy Cameroon 3°5N 9°58E 264 B1
Longuyon France 49°27N 5°35E 173 C12
Longvic France 47°17N 5°4E 173 E12
Longview Tex., U.S.A. 32°30N 94°44W 314 E7
Longview Wash., U.S.A. 46°8N 122°57W 306 D4
Longwood St. Helena 15°57S 5°41W 153 h
Longwood Fla., U.S.A. 28°42N 81°21W 317 G8
Longwy France 49°30N 5°46E 173 C12
Longxi China 34°53N 104°40E 226 G3
Longxue Dao China 22°41N 113°38E 219 a
Longyan China 25°10N 117°0E 229 E11
Longyearbyen Svalbard 78°13N 15°40E 150 B8
Longyou China 29°1N 119°8E 229 C12
Longzhou China 22°22N 106°50E 228 F6
Loni India 28°45N 77°17E 120 A2
Lonigo Italy 45°23N 11°23E 199 C8
Löningen Germany 52°44N 7°46E 178 C3
Lonja → Croatia 45°22N 16°40E 199 C13
Lonkala Dem. Rep. of the Congo 4°37S 23°14E 265 C4
Lonkin Myanmar 25°39N 96°22E 241 C6
Lonoke U.S.A. 34°47N 91°54W 314 D9
Lonquimay Chile 38°26S 71°14W 336 A2
Lons-le-Saunier France 46°40N 5°31E 173 F12
Lönsboda Sweden 56°24N 14°20E 163 H8
Lønset Norway 62°46N 7°24E 164 B4
Lonton Myanmar 25°6N 96°17E 241 C6
Looc Phil. 12°15N 121°59E 232 E3
Looe U.K. 50°22N 4°28W 169 G3
Loogootee U.S.A. 38°41N 86°55W 311 F10
Lookout, C. Canada 55°18N 83°56W 298 A3
Lookout, C. N.C., U.S.A. 34°35N 76°32W 315 D16
Loolmalasin Tanzania 3°0S 35°53E 268 C4
Loon → Alta., Canada 57°8N 115°3W 296 B5
Loon → Man., Canada 55°53N 101°59W 297 B8
Loon Lake Canada 54°2N 109°10W 297 C7
Loongana Australia 30°52S 127°5E 279 F4
Loop, The Chicago, U.S.A. 119 c1
Loop Hd. Ireland 52°34N 9°56W 166 D2
Lop China 37°3N 80°11E 217 E10
Lop Nor = Lop Nur China 40°20N 90°10E 217 D12
Lop Nur China 40°20N 90°10E 217 D12
Lopare Bos.-H. 44°39N 18°46E 182 F3
Lopatin Russia 43°50N 47°35E 191 J8
Lopatina, Gora Russia 50°47N 143°10E 215 D15
Lopatino = Volzhsk Russia 55°57N 48°23E 190 C9
Lopatka, Mys Russia 50°52N 156°40E 215 D16
Lopaye South Sudan 6°37N 33°40E 257 F3
Lopburi Thailand 14°48N 100°37E 236 E3
Lopé-Okanda ⌂ Gabon 0°45S 11°34E 264 C2
Lopevi Vanuatu 16°30S 168°21E 287 E6
Lopez Phil. 13°53N 122°15E 232 E4
Lopez Pa., U.S.A. 41°27N 76°20W 313 E8
Lopez, C. Gabon 0°47S 8°40E 264 C1
López de Filippis = Mariscal Estigarribia Paraguay 22°3S 60°40W 334 A3
Lopinot Trin. & Tob. 10°41N 61°19W 323 t
Lopori → Dem. Rep. of the Congo 1°14N 19°49E 264 B3
Lopphavet Norway 70°27N 21°15E 160 A19
Lora Norway 62°8N 8°45E 164 B5
Lora → Afghan. 31°35N 66°32E 240 C2
Lora → Oppland, Norway 62°8N 8°42E 164 B5
Lora, Hāmūn-i- Pakistan 29°38N 64°58E 240 C2
Lora Cr. → Australia 28°10S 135°22E 281 D2
Lora del Río Spain 37°39N 5°33W 195 H5
Lorain U.S.A. 41°28N 82°11W 312 E2
Loraine U.S.A. 40°9N 91°13W 310 D5
Loralai Pakistan 30°20N 68°41E 242 D3
Lorca Spain 37°41N 1°42W 197 H3
Lord Howe I. Pac. Oc. 31°33S 159°6E 277 G10
Lord Howe Rise Pac. Oc. 30°0S 162°30E 277 H12
Lord Howe Seamount Chain Pac. Oc. 28°0S 159°0E 277 F10
Lord Loughborough I. Myanmar 10°25N 97°54E 237 G1
Lord's Cricket Ground U.K. 51°31N 0°10W 125 A2
Lordsburg U.S.A. 32°21N 108°43W 305 K9
Lorengau Papua N. G. 2°1S 147°15E 286 B4
Lorestān □ Iran 33°30N 48°40E 247 C6
Loreto Bolivia 15°13S 64°40W 331 D5
Loreto Brazil 7°5S 45°10W 332 C2
Loreto Marche, Italy 43°26N 13°36E 199 E10
Loreto Piemonte, Italy 45°3N 7°30E 125 B2
Loreto Baja Calif. S., Mexico 26°0N 111°21W 318 B2
Loreto Surigao N., Phil. 10°21N 125°34E 233 F5
Loreto □ Peru 5°0S 75°0W 328 E3
Lorgues France 43°28N 6°22E 175 E10
Lorhosso = Loropéni Burkina Faso 10°17N 3°38W 262 C4
Lorian Swamp Kenya 0°40N 39°35E 267 D4
Lorica Colombia 9°14N 75°49W 328 B2
Lorient Morbihan, France 47°45N 3°23W 172 E3
Lorient St. Barts 17°54N 62°49W 322 a
Lorimor U.S.A. 41°8N 94°3W 310 C2
Lőrinci Hungary 47°44N 19°41E 182 C4
Lormi India 22°17N 81°41E 243 H9
Lorn U.K. 56°26N 5°10W 167 E3
Lorn, Firth of U.K. 56°20N 5°40W 167 E3
Lorne Australia 38°33S 143°59E 282 E5
Loronyo South Sudan 4°38N 32°38E 257 G3
Loropéni Burkina Faso 10°17N 3°38W 262 C4
Lorovouno Cyprus 35°8N 32°36E 207 E8
Lörrach Germany 47°36N 7°40E 179 H3
Lorrain → Martinique 14°50N 61°3W 322 j
Lorraine = Baker U.S.A. 46°22N 104°17W 304 C11
Lorraine France 48°53N 6°0E 171 B7
Lorraine ⌂ France 48°55N 5°50E 173 D12
Los Sweden 61°45N 15°10E 162 C9
Los, Îles de Guinea 9°30N 13°50W 262 D2
Los Alamos Calif., U.S.A. 34°44N 120°17W 307 L6
Los Alamos N. Mex., U.S.A. 35°53N 106°19W 305 J10
Los Alcornocales ⌂ Spain 36°21N 5°32W 195 J5
Los Alerces △ Argentina 42°55S 71°55W 336 B2
Los Altos U.S.A. 37°23N 122°7W 306 H4
Los Andes Chile 32°50S 70°40W 334 C1
Los Angeles Chile 37°28S 72°23W 334 D1
Los Angeles Calif., U.S.A. 34°4N 118°15W 126 B3
Los Angeles Aqueduct U.S.A. 35°22N 118°5W 307 K9
Los Angeles Int. ✈ (LAX) U.S.A. 33°57N 118°25W 126 C2
Los Angeles Museum of the Holocaust U.S.A. 34°4N 118°21W 126 B2
Los Antiguos Argentina 46°35S 71°40W 336 C2
Los Bagres Venezuela 10°57N 63°58W 329 a
Los Banos U.S.A. 37°4N 120°51W 306 H6
Los Barrios Spain 36°11N 5°30W 195 J5
Los Blancos Argentina 23°40S 62°30W 334 A3
Los Cabos Int. ✈ (SJD) Mexico 23°9N 109°43W 318 C3
Los Cardones △ Argentina 25°8S 65°55W 334 B2
Los Cerrillos ✈ (ULC) Chile 33°29S 70°42W 137 B1
Los Chiles Costa Rica 11°2N 84°43W 320 D3
Los Corrales de Buelna Spain 43°16N 4°4W 194 B6
Los Cristianos Canary Is. 28°3N 16°42W 153 e1
Los Frailes, I. Venezuela 11°11N 63°44W 329 a
Los Gallardos Spain 37°10N 1°57W 197 H3
Los Gallos Pt. Trin. & Tob. 10°5N 61°55W 323 t
Los Gatos U.S.A. 37°14N 121°59W 306 H5
Los Glaciares △ Argentina 50°0S 73°55W 336 C2
Los Gómez Venezuela 10°57N 64°4W 329 a
Los Haïtises △ Dom. Rep. 19°4N 69°36W 321 C6
Los Hermanos, Is. Venezuela 11°45N 64°25W 321 D7
Los Huemules △ Chile 46°10S 73°23W 336 C2
Los Islotes Canary Is. 29°4N 13°44W 153 e2
Los Katios △ Colombia 7°50N 77°10W 328 B2
Los Lagos Chile 39°51S 72°50W 336 A2
Los Llanos de Aridane Canary Is. 28°38N 17°54W 153 e1
Los Loros Chile 27°50S 70°6W 334 B1
Los Lunas U.S.A. 34°48N 106°44W 305 J10
Los Menucos Argentina 40°50S 68°10W 336 B3
Los Mochis Mexico 25°45N 108°57W 318 B3
Los Monegros Spain 41°29N 0°13W 196 D4
Los Monos Argentina 46°1S 69°36W 336 C3
Los Muermos Chile 41°24S 73°29W 336 B2
Los Nevados △ Colombia 4°41N 75°21W 328 C2
Los Nietos Spain 37°39N 0°47W 197 H4
Los Nietos Calif., U.S.A. 33°57N 118°4W 126 C4
Los Olivos Lima, Peru 11°59S 77°5W 124 A2
Los Olivos Calif., U.S.A. 34°40N 120°7W 307 L6
Los Palacios Cuba 22°35N 83°15W 320 B3
Los Palacios y Villafranca Spain 37°10N 5°55W 195 H5
Los Queñes Chile 35°1S 70°48W 334 D1
Los Remedios △ Mexico 19°28N 99°17W 128 B1
Los Reyes Mexico 19°21N 99°6W 128 B2
Los Reyes de Salgado Mexico 19°35N 102°29W 318 D4
Los Ríos □ Ecuador 1°30S 79°25W 328 D2
Los Roques, Is. Venezuela 11°50N 66°45W 321 D6
Los Santos de Maimona Spain 38°27N 6°22W 195 G4
Los Teques Venezuela 10°21N 67°2W 328 A4
Los Testigos, Is. Venezuela 11°23N 63°6W 329 A5
Los Vilos Chile 32°10S 71°30W 334 C1
Los Yébenes Spain 39°36N 3°55W 195 F7
Loshan = Leshan China 29°33N 103°41E 228 C4
Łosice Poland 52°13N 22°43E 185 F9
Lošinj Croatia 44°30N 14°30E 199 D11
Losiny Ostrov △ Russia 55°50N 37°45E 129 A3
Loskop Dam S. Africa 25°23S 29°20E 271 C4
Løsning Denmark 55°48N 9°42E 163 J3
Losombo Dem. Rep. of the Congo 1°2N 19°4E 264 B3
Lossiemouth U.K. 57°42N 3°17W 167 D5
Lossnen Sweden 62°26N 12°45E 162 B6
Lostwithiel U.K. 50°24N 4°41W 169 G3
Losuia Papua N. G. 8°30S 151°4E 286 E6
Lot Belgium 50°46N 4°16E 116 B1
Lot □ France 44°39N 1°40E 174 D5
Lot → France 44°18N 0°20E 174 D4
Lot-et-Garonne □ France 44°22N 0°30E 174 D4
Lota Chile 37°5S 73°10W 334 D1
Lotagipi Swamp Kenya 4°36N 34°55E 268 B3
Løten Norway 60°51N 11°21E 164 D8
Lotfābād Iran 37°32N 59°20E 247 B8
Lothair S. Africa 26°22S 30°27E 271 C5
Loto Dem. Rep. of the Congo 2°48S 22°3E 264 C4
Lotoi → Dem. Rep. of the Congo 1°35S 18°30E 264 C3
Lotorp Sweden 58°44N 15°50E 163 F9
Lötschbergtunnel Switz. 46°26N 7°43E 179 J3
Lotta → Europe 68°42N 31°6E 160 B24
Lottefors Sweden 61°25N 16°24E 162 C10
Löttorp Sweden 57°10N 17°0E 163 G11
Lotung Taiwan 24°41N 121°46E 225 B3
Lotus River S. Africa 34°4S 18°31E 118 B2
Lotus Temple India 28°33N 77°15E 120 B2
Lötzen = Giżycko Poland 54°2N 21°48E 184 D8
Lou I. Papua N. G. 2°25S 147°22E 286 B4
Loubière Dominica 15°16N 61°23W 323 k
Loubomo Congo 4°9S 12°47E 264 C2
Loudéac France 48°11N 2°47W 172 D4
Loudi China 27°42N 111°59E 229 D8
Loudima Congo 4°6S 13°5E 264 C2
Loudonville U.S.A. 40°38N 82°14W 312 F2
Loudun France 47°3N 0°5E 172 E7
Loue → France 47°1N 5°28E 173 E12
Louga Senegal 15°45N 16°5W 262 B1
Louga □ Senegal 15°20N 15°35W 262 B1
Loughborough U.K. 52°47N 1°11W 168 E6
Lougheed I. Canada 77°26N 105°6W 295 B10
Loughman U.S.A. 28°14N 81°34W 317 G8
Loughrea Ireland 53°12N 8°33W 166 C3
Loughros More B. Ireland 54°48N 8°32W 166 B3
Louhans France 46°38N 5°12E 173 F12
Louis Armstrong New Orleans Int. ✈ (MSY) U.S.A. 30°0N 90°15W 131 B1
Louis Armstrong Park New Orleans, U.S.A. 131 a2
Louis-Gentil = Youssoufia Morocco 32°16N 8°31W 260 B3
Louis Trichardt S. Africa 23°1S 29°43E 271 B4
Louis XIV, Pte. Canada 54°37N 79°45W 298 B4
Louisa U.S.A. 38°7N 82°36W 309 F12
Louisbourg Canada 45°55N 60°0W 299 C8
Louisburg U.S.A. 38°37N 94°41W 310 F2
Louisburgh Ireland 53°46N 9°49W 166 C2
Louise, L. U.S.A. 28°28N 81°32W 133 B1
Louise I. Canada 52°55N 131°50W 296 C2
Louiseville Canada 46°20N 72°56W 298 C5
Louisiade Arch. Papua N. G. 11°10S 153°0E 286 F7
Louisiana U.S.A. 39°27N 91°3W 310 E6
Louisiana □ U.S.A. 30°50N 92°0W 314 F9
Louisiana Superdome = Mercedes-Benz Superdome U.S.A. 29°56N 90°5W 131 b1
Louisville Ala., U.S.A. 31°47N 85°33W 316 D4
Louisville Ga., U.S.A. 33°0N 82°25W 316 B7
Louisville Ky., U.S.A. 38°15N 85°46W 311 F11
Louisville Miss., U.S.A. 33°7N 89°3W 315 E10
Louisville Ohio, U.S.A. 40°50N 81°16W 312 F3
Louisville Ridge Pac. Oc. 31°0S 172°30W 288 L10
Loukoléla Congo 1°4S 17°10E 264 C3
Loukouo Congo 3°38S 14°39E 264 C2
Loulay France 46°3N 0°30W 174 B3
Loulé Portugal 37°9N 8°0W 195 H3
Loulouni Mali 10°54N 5°36W 262 C3
Loum Cameroon 4°42N 9°44E 264 B1
Louny Czechia 50°20N 13°48E 180 A6
Loup City U.S.A. 41°17N 98°58W 308 E4
Loups Marins, Lacs des Canada 56°30N 73°45W 298 A5
Lourdes France 43°6N 0°3W 174 E3
Lourdes-de-Blanc-Sablon Canada 51°24N 57°12W 299 B8
Lourenço Brazil 2°30N 51°40W 329 C7
Lourenço Marques = Maputo Mozam. 25°58S 32°32E 271 C5
Loures Portugal 38°49N 9°10W 126 A1
Lourinhã Portugal 39°14N 9°17W 195 F1
Louros Greece 39°3N 20°47E 207 A2
Louroujina Cyprus 35°0N 33°28E 207 F9
Lousã Portugal 40°7N 8°14W 194 E2
Louta Burkina Faso 13°30N 3°10W 262 C4
Louth N.S.W., Australia 30°30S 145°8E 283 A6
Louth Louth, Ireland 53°58N 6°32W 166 C5
Louth Lincs., U.K. 53°22N 0°1W 168 D7
Louth □ Ireland 53°56N 6°34W 166 C5
Louth B. Australia 34°33S 135°56E 282 C1
Loutra Edipsou Greece 38°54N 23°2E 204 C5
Loutra Kyllinis Greece 37°52N 21°7E 207 D3
Loutraki Greece 37°58N 22°57E 204 D4
Loutropoli Thermis Greece 39°11N 26°29E 205 B8
Louvain = Leuven Belgium 50°52N 4°42E 170 D4
Louvale U.S.A. 32°10N 84°50W 316 C5
Louveciennes France 48°51N 2°8E 134 A1
Louviers France 49°12N 1°10E 172 C8
Louvre, Musée du Paris, France 134 b4
Louvre, Palais du Paris, France 134 b4
Louwsburg S. Africa 27°37S 31°7E 271 C5
Lovat → Russia 58°14N 31°28E 188 C6
Lovćen Montenegro 42°23N 18°51E 202 D2
Lovćen △ Montenegro 42°20N 18°50E 202 D2
Lovech Bulgaria 43°8N 24°42E 203 C8
Lovech □ Bulgaria 43°0N 24°45E 203 D8
Loveland Colo., U.S.A. 40°24N 105°5W 304 F11
Loveland Ohio, U.S.A. 39°16N 84°16W 311 E12
Lovell U.S.A. 44°50N 108°24W 304 D9
Lovelock U.S.A. 40°11N 118°28W 304 F4
Lóvere Italy 45°49N 10°4E 198 C7
Lovers Leap Jamaica 17°52N 77°39W 320 a
Loves Park U.S.A. 42°19N 89°3W 310 B7
Lövestad Sweden 55°40N 13°54E 163 J7
Loviisa Finland 60°28N 26°12E 188 B4
Lovilia U.S.A. 41°8N 92°55W 310 C4
Lovina Indonesia 8°9S 115°1E 231 J18
Loving U.S.A. 32°17N 104°6W 305 K11
Lovington Ill., U.S.A. 39°43N 88°38W 311 E8
Lovington N. Mex., U.S.A. 32°57N 103°21W 305 K12
Lovisa = Loviisa Finland 60°28N 26°12E 188 B4
Lovosice Czechia 50°30N 14°2E 180 A7
Lovran Croatia 45°18N 14°15E 199 C11
Lovrin Romania 45°58N 20°48E 182 E5
Lövstabruk Sweden 60°25N 17°53E 162 D11
Lövstabukten Sweden 60°35N 17°45E 162 D11
Lóvua Lunda Norte, Angola 7°19S 20°12E 265 D4
Lóvua Moxico, Angola 11°33S 23°33E 265 E4
Lóvua → Dem. Rep. of the Congo 6°6S 20°37E 265 D4
Low, L. Canada 52°29N 76°17W 298 B4
Low B. Antigua & B. 17°39N 61°51W 322 b
Low Pt. Australia 32°25S 127°25E 279 F4
Low Tatra = Nízké Tatry Slovakia 48°55N 19°30E 181 C12
Lowa Dem. Rep. of the Congo 1°25S 25°47E 268 C2
Lowa → Dem. Rep. of the Congo 1°24S 25°51E 268 C2
Lowden U.S.A. 41°52N 90°56W 310 C6
Lowell Ind., U.S.A. 41°18N 87°25W 311 C9
Lowell Mass., U.S.A. 42°38N 71°19W 313 D13
Lowell Mich., U.S.A. 42°56N 85°20W 311 B11
Lowellville U.S.A. 41°2N 80°32W 312 E4
Löwen = Lewin Brzeski Poland 50°45N 17°37E 185 H4
Löwen → Namibia 26°51S 18°17E 270 C2
Löwenberg = Lwówek Śląski Poland 51°7N 15°38E 185 G2
Löwenstadt = Brzeziny Poland 51°49N 19°42E 185 G6
Lower Alkali L. U.S.A. 41°16N 120°2W 304 F3
Lower Arrow L. Canada 49°40N 118°5W 296 D5
Lower Austria = Niederösterreich □ Austria 48°25N 15°40E 180 C8
Lower B. U.S.A. 40°32N 74°5W 132 C1
Lower California = Baja California Mexico 31°10N 115°12W 318 A1
Lower Don Lands Canada 43°38N 79°21W 141 B2
Lower East Side New York, U.S.A. 132 e2
Lower Glenelg △ Australia 38°4S 141°41E 282 E4
Lower Hutt N.Z. 41°10S 174°55E 284 H3
Lower Kalskag U.S.A. 61°31N 160°22W 303 F7
Lower Lake U.S.A. 38°55N 122°37W 306 G4
Lower Manhattan New York, U.S.A. 132 e1
Lower Manitou L. Canada 49°15N 93°0W 297 D10
Lower Manzanilla Trin. & Tob. 10°31N 61°3W 323 t
Lower New York B. = Lower B. U.S.A. 40°32N 74°5W 132 C1
Lower Paia U.S.A. 20°55N 156°23W 302 C5
Lower Peirce Res. Singapore 1°22N 103°49E 138 A2
Lower Post Canada 59°58N 128°30W 296 B3
Lower Red L. U.S.A. 47°58N 95°0W 308 B6
Lower Saxony = Niedersachsen □ Germany 52°50N 9°0E 178 C4
Lower Tunguska = Tunguska, Nizhnyaya → Russia 65°48N 88°4E 215 C9
Lower Zambezi △ Zambia 15°25S 29°40E 269 F2
Lowestoft U.K. 52°29N 1°45E 169 E9
Lowgar □ Afghan. 34°0N 69°0E 240 B3
Łowicz Poland 52°6N 19°55E 185 F6
Lowly, Pt. Australia 33°0S 137°46E 282 B2
Lowry City U.S.A. 38°8N 93°44W 310 F3
Lowther I. Canada 74°33N 97°30W 295 C12
Lowville U.S.A. 43°47N 75°29W 313 C9
Loxton S. Austral., Australia 34°28S 140°31E 282 C4
Loxton Northern Cape, S. Africa 31°30S 22°22E 270 D3
Loyalton U.S.A. 39°41N 120°14W 306 F6
Loyalty Is. = Loyauté, Îs. N. Cal. 20°50S 166°30E 288 d
Loyang = Luoyang China 34°40N 112°26E 226 G7
Loyauté, Îs. N. Cal. 20°50S 166°30E 288 d
Loyev = Loyew Belarus 51°56N 30°46E 177 C16
Loyew Belarus 51°56N 30°46E 177 C16
Loyola Univ. U.S.A. 42°0N 87°39W 119 B3
Loyoro Uganda 3°22N 34°14E 268 B3
Lož Slovenia 45°43N 14°30E 199 C11
Lozère □ France 44°35N 3°30E 174 D7
Loznica Serbia 44°32N 19°14E 202 B3
Lozova Ukraine 49°0N 36°20E 189 H9
Ltalaltuma ⚙ Australia 23°57S 132°25E 278 D5
Lu India 26°58N 95°14E 241 B5
Lü Shan China 29°30N 115°55E 229 C10
Lü Shan △ China 29°26N 115°52E 229 C10
Lu Verne U.S.A. 42°55N 94°5W 310 B2
Lu Wo China 22°33N 114°6E 219 a
Lu Xun, Tomb of China 31°17N 121°29E 138 B1
Lu Xun Museum Beijing, China 114 b1
Lu Xun Park China 31°17N 121°28E 138 B1
Lua → Dem. Rep. of the Congo 2°46N 18°26E 264 B3
Lua Makiki U.S.A. 20°33N 156°37W 302 C5
Luachimo Angola 7°23S 20°48E 265 D4
Luacono Angola 11°15S 21°37E 265 E4
Luajan → India 24°44N 85°1E 243 G11
Lualaba □ Dem. Rep. of the Congo 9°30S 23°0E 265 D4
Lualaba → Dem. Rep. of the Congo 0°26N 25°20E 264 B5
Luale Dem. Rep. of the Congo 1°9N 23°5E 264 B4
Luambe △ Zambia 12°30S 32°15E 269 E3
Luampa Zambia 15°4S 24°20E 265 F4
Lu'an China 31°45N 116°29E 229 B11
Luan Chau Vietnam 21°38N 103°24E 228 G4
Luan He → China 39°20N 119°5E 227 E10
Luan Xian China 39°40N 118°40E 227 E10
Luancheng Guangxi Zhuangzu, China 22°48N 108°55E 228 F7
Luancheng Hebei, China 37°53N 114°40E 226 F8
Luanco Spain 43°37N 5°48W 194 B5
Luanda Angola 8°50S 13°15E 265 D2
Luando → Angola 10°21S 16°27E 265 E3
Luando ⌂ Angola 11°0S 17°32E 265 E3
Luang, Doi Thailand 18°30N 101°15E 236 C3
Luang, Thale Thailand 7°30N 100°15E 237 J3
Luang Nam Tha Laos 20°58N 101°30E 228 G3
Luang Prabang Laos 19°52N 102°10E 228 H4
Luanginga → Zambia 15°11S 22°55E 265 F4
Luangwa Zambia 15°35S 30°16E 269 F3
Luangwa → Zambia 14°25S 30°25E 269 E3
Luangwa Valley Zambia 13°30S 31°30E 269 E3
Luangwe = Loange → Dem. Rep. of the Congo 4°17S 20°2E 265 C4
Luania-Bubi Dem. Rep. of the Congo 7°28S 24°49E 265 D4
Luanne China 40°55N 117°40E 227 D9
Luanping China 40°53N 117°23E 227 D9
Luanshya Zambia 13°3S 28°28E 269 E2
Luapula □ Zambia 11°0S 29°0E 269 E2
Luapula → Africa 9°26S 28°33E 269 D2
Luar, Danau Indonesia 0°55N 112°15E 234 B3
Luarca Spain 43°32N 6°32W 194 B4
Luashi Dem. Rep. of the Congo 10°50S 23°36E 265 E4
Luatamba Angola 12°6S 20°19E 265 E4
Luatira Angola 12°52S 17°14E 265 E3
Luau Angola 10°40S 22°10E 265 E4
Luba Phil. 17°19N 120°42E 232 C3
Lubaczów Poland 50°10N 23°8E 185 H10
Lubalo Angola 9°10S 19°15E 265 D3
Lubamiti Dem. Rep. of the Congo 2°28S 17°47E 264 C3
Lubań Poland 51°5N 15°15E 185 G2
Lubana, Ozero = Lubānas Ezers Latvia 56°45N 27°0E 188 D4
Lubānas Ezers Latvia 56°45N 27°0E 188 D4
Lubang Phil. 13°52N 120°7E 232 E3
Lubang Is. Phil. 13°50N 120°12E 232 E3
Lubango Angola 14°55S 13°30E 265 E2
Lubao Dem. Rep. of the Congo 5°17S 25°42E 265 D5
Lubao Phil. 14°56N 120°36E 232 D3
Lübars Germany 52°37N 13°21E 115 A3
Lubartów Poland 51°28N 22°42E 185 G9
Lubawa Poland 53°30N 19°48E 184 E6
Lübbecke Germany 52°18N 8°37E 178 C4
Lübben Germany 51°56N 13°54E 178 D9
Lübbenau Germany 51°52N 13°57E 178 D9
Lubbock U.S.A. 33°35N 101°51W 314 E4
Lübeck Germany 53°52N 10°40E 178 B6
Lübecker Bucht Germany 54°3N 10°54E 178 A6
Lubefu Dem. Rep. of the Congo 4°47S 24°27E 265 C4
Lubefu → Dem. Rep. of the Congo 4°10S 23°0E 265 C4
Lubelskie □ Poland 51°20N 22°50E 185 G9
Lüben = Lubin Poland 51°24N 16°11E 185 G3
Lubero = Luofu Dem. Rep. of the Congo 0°10S 29°15E 268 C2
Luberon ⌂ France 43°52N 5°25E 175 E9
Lubersac France 45°26N 1°23E 174 C5
Lubicon L. Canada 56°23N 115°56W 296 B5
Lubień Kujawski Poland 52°23N 19°9E 185 F6
Lubilash → Dem. Rep. of the Congo 6°2S 23°45E 265 D4
Lubin Poland 51°24N 16°11E 185 G3
Lublin Poland 51°12N 22°38E 185 G9
Lubliniec Poland 50°43N 18°45E 185 H5
Lubnān = Lebanon ■ Asia 34°0N 36°0E 250 E7
Lubnān, Jabal Lebanon 33°45N 35°40E 250 E6
Lubniewice Poland 52°31N 15°15E 185 F2
Lubny Ukraine 50°3N 32°58E 189 G7
Lubomierz Poland 51°1N 15°31E 185 G2
Luboń Poland 52°21N 16°51E 185 F3
Lubondaie Dem. Rep. of the Congo 8°1S 26°32E 265 D4
Lubongola Dem. Rep. of the Congo 2°35S 27°50E 268 C2
L'ubotín Slovakia 49°17N 20°53E 181 B13
Lubraniec Poland 52°33N 18°50E 185 F5
Lubsko Poland 51°45N 14°57E 185 G1
Lübtheen Germany 53°18N 11°5E 178 B7
Lubuagan Phil. 17°21N 121°10E 232 C3
Lubudi Dem. Rep. of the Congo 6°51S 21°18E 265 D4
Lubudi → Kasai-Occ., Dem. Rep. of the Congo 4°19S 20°23E 265 C4
Lubudi → Katanga, Dem. Rep. of the Congo 9°0S 25°35E 265 D5
Lubuklinggau Indonesia 3°15S 102°55E 234 C2
Lubukpakam Indonesia 3°33N 98°52E 234 B1
Lubuksikaping Indonesia 0°10N 100°15E 234 B2
Lubumbashi Dem. Rep. of the Congo 11°40S 27°28E 269 E2
Lubunda Dem. Rep. of the Congo 5°12S 26°41E 265 D5
Lubungu Zambia 14°35S 26°24E 269 E2
Lubuskie □ Poland 52°10N 15°20E 185 F2
Lubutu Dem. Rep. of the Congo 0°45S 26°30E 268 C2
Lubyanka Moscow, Russia 129 a2
Luc-en-Diois France 44°36N 5°28E 175 D9
Lucala Angola 9°7S 15°58E 265 D3
Lucala → Angola 9°38S 14°14E 265 D3
Lucan Ont., Canada 43°11N 81°24W 312 C3
Lucan Dublin, Ireland 53°22N 6°28W 166 C5
Lucania, Mt. Canada 61°1N 140°27W 294 E3
Lucapa Angola 8°25S 20°45E 265 D4
Lucas U.S.A. 41°2N 93°29W 310 D3
Lucas Channel = Main Channel Canada 45°21N 81°45W 312 A3
Lucban Phil. 14°6N 121°33E 232 D3
Lucca Italy 43°50N 10°29E 198 E7
Lucé France 48°26N 1°27E 172 D8
Luce Bay U.K. 54°45N 4°48W 167 G4
Lucea Jamaica 18°27N 78°10W 320 a
Lucedale U.S.A. 30°56N 88°35W 315 F10
Lucena Phil. 13°56N 121°37E 232 E3
Lucena Spain 37°27N 4°31W 195 H6
Lučenec Slovakia 48°18N 19°42E 181 C12
Lucera Italy 41°30N 15°20E 201 A8
Lucerne = Lake Worth U.S.A. 26°37N 80°3W 317 J9
Lucerne = Luzern Switz. 47°3N 8°18E 179 H4
Lucerne U.S.A. 39°6N 122°48W 306 F4
Lucerne Valley U.S.A. 34°27N 116°57W 307 L10
Luchena → Spain 37°44N 1°50W 197 H3
Lucheng China 36°20N 113°11E 226 F7
Lucheringo → Mozam. 11°43S 36°17E 269 E4
Luchow = Luzhou China 28°52N 105°20E 228 C5
Lüchow Germany 52°58N 11°8E 178 C7
Luchu Taiwan 22°52N 120°15E 225 D2
Luchuan China 22°21N 110°12E 229 F8
Lucia U.S.A. 36°2N 121°33W 306 J5
Luciara Brazil 10°45S 50°34W 333 D1
Lucie → Suriname 3°35N 57°38W 329 C6
Lucinda Australia 18°32S 146°20E 280 B4
Lucindale Australia 36°58S 140°26E 282 D4
Lucira Angola 14°0S 12°35E 265 E2
Luciras, B. das Angola 13°52S 12°31E 265 E2
Luckau Germany 51°50N 13°42E 178 D9
Luckenwalde Germany 52°5N 13°10E 178 C9
Luckey U.S.A. 41°27N 83°29W 311 C13
Luckhoff S. Africa 29°44S 24°43E 270 C3
Lucknow Ont., Canada 43°57N 81°31W 312 C3
Lucknow India 26°50N 81°0E 243 F9
Luçon France 46°28N 1°10W 174 B2
Lucusse Angola 12°32S 20°48E 265 E4
Lucy, L. U.S.A. 28°34N 81°39W 133 A2
Lüda = Dalian China 38°50N 121°40E 227 E11
Luda Kamchia → Bulgaria 43°3N 27°29E 203 C11
Luda Kamchiya = Luda Kamchia → Bulgaria 43°3N 27°29E 203 C11
Ludbreg Croatia 46°15N 16°38E 199 B13
Lüdenscheid Germany 51°13N 7°37E 178 D3
Lüderitz Namibia 26°41S 15°8E 270 C2
Lüderitzbaai Namibia 26°36S 15°8E 270 C2
Ludhiana India 30°57N 75°56E 242 D6
Ludian China 27°10N 103°33E 228 D4
Luding Qiao China 29°53N 102°12E 228 C4
Lüdinghausen Germany 51°46N 7°27E 178 D3
Ludington U.S.A. 43°57N 86°27W 308 D10
Ludlow Shrops., U.K. 52°22N 2°42W 169 E5
Ludlow Calif., U.S.A. 34°43N 116°10W 307 L10
Ludlow Pa., U.S.A. 41°43N 78°56W 312 E6
Ludlow Vt., U.S.A. 43°24N 72°42W 313 C12
Ludowici U.S.A. 31°43N 81°45W 316 D8
Luduș Romania 46°29N 24°5E 183 D9
Ludvika Sweden 60°8N 15°14E 162 D9
Ludwigsburg Germany 48°53N 9°11E 179 G5
Ludwigsfeld Germany 48°12N 11°27E 131 A1
Ludwigsfelde Germany 52°17N 13°17E 178 C9
Ludwigshafen Germany 49°29N 8°26E 179 F4
Ludwigslust Germany 53°19N 11°30E 178 B7
Ludza Latvia 56°32N 27°43E 188 D4
Lue Australia 32°38S 149°50E 283 B8
Luebo Dem. Rep. of the Congo 5°21S 21°23E 265 D4
Lueki Dem. Rep. of the Congo 3°20S 25°48E 264 C5
Luena Angola 12°13S 19°51E 265 E3
Luena Dem. Rep. of the Congo 9°28S 25°43E 269 D2
Luena Zambia 10°40S 30°25E 269 E3
Luena → Angola 12°30S 22°34E 265 E4
Luena → Zambia 14°46S 23°30E 265 E4
Luena Flats Zambia 14°47S 23°17E 265 E4
Luenguè ⌂ Angola 16°55S 19°55E 265 F3
Luenha = Ruenya → Africa 16°24S 33°48E 269 F3
Luepa Venezuela 5°43N 61°31W 329 B5
Lueta → Dem. Rep. of the Congo 7°4S 21°40E 265 D4
Luete → Zambia 15°46S 23°10E 265 F4
Lüeyang China 33°22N 106°10E 228 A6
Lufeng Guangdong, China 22°57N 115°38E 229 F10
Lufeng Yunnan, China 25°0N 102°5E 228 E4
Lufico Angola 6°24S 13°23E 265 D2
Lufira → Dem. Rep. of the Congo 9°30S 27°0E 269 D2
Lufkin U.S.A. 31°21N 94°44W 314 F7
Lufupa Dem. Rep. of the Congo 10°37S 24°56E 265 E4
Luga Russia 58°40N 29°55E 188 C5
Luga → Russia 59°40N 28°18E 188 C5
Lugang = Lukang Taiwan 24°1N 120°22E 225 B2
Lugano Switz. 46°1N 8°57E 179 J4
Lugano, L. di Switz. 46°0N 9°0E 198 C6
Lugansk = Luhansk Ukraine 48°38N 39°15E 189 H10
Luganville Vanuatu 15°27S 167°10E 287 E5
Lugard's Falls Kenya 3°6S 38°41E 268 C4
Lugela Mozam. 16°25S 36°43E 269 F4
Lugenda → Mozam. 11°25S 38°33E 269 E4
Lugh = Luuq Somalia 3°48N 42°34E 267 D5
Lugina e Valbonës △ Albania 42°27N 19°53E 202 D3
Lugnaquilla Ireland 52°58N 6°28W 166 D5
Lugnvik Sweden 62°56N 17°55E 162 B11
Lugo Italy 44°25N 11°54E 199 D8
Lugo Spain 43°2N 7°35W 194 B3
Lugo □ Spain 43°0N 7°30W 194 C3
Lugoj Romania 45°42N 21°57E 182 E6
Lugovoy = Qulan Kazakhstan 42°55N 72°43E 214 E8
Lugu = Luku Taiwan 23°44N 120°45E 225 C2
Lugus I. Phil. 5°41N 120°50E 233 J3
Luhansk Ukraine 48°38N 39°15E 189 H10
Luhansk □ Ukraine 49°10N 38°40E 189 H10
Luhe China 32°19N 118°50E 229 A12
Luhe → Germany 53°23N 10°13E 178 B6
Luhit → India 27°48N 95°28E 241 B5
Luhu China 23°9N 113°16E 121 B2
Luhuo China 31°21N 100°48E 228 B3
Lui → Angola 8°21S 17°33E 265 D3
Lui → Zambia 16°18S 23°17E 265 F4
Luia Angola 8°10S 21°32E 265 D4
Luia → Angola 8°32S 21°47E 265 D4
Luiana Angola 17°25S 22°59E 265 F4
Luiana → Angola 17°24S 23°3E 265 F4
Luiana ⌂ Angola 16°55S 22°20E 265 F4
Luichow Pen. = Leizhou Bandao China 21°0N 110°0E 228 G7
Luikuei Taiwan 23°0N 120°38E 225 D2
Luilaka → Dem. Rep. of the Congo 0°52S 20°12E 264 C4
Luimneach = Limerick Ireland 52°40N 8°37W 166 D3
Luing U.K. 56°14N 5°39W 167 E3
Luino Italy 45°59N 8°44E 198 C5
Luio → Angola 13°17S 21°37E 265 E4
Luís Correia Brazil 3°0S 41°35W 332 B3
Luís Gonçalves Brazil 5°37S 50°25W 332 C1
Luitpold Coast Antarctica 78°30S 32°0W 151 D1
Luiza Dem. Rep. of the Congo 7°40S 22°30E 265 D4
Luizi Dem. Rep. of the Congo 6°0S 27°25E 268 D2
Luján Argentina 34°45S 59°5W 334 C4
Lujiang China 31°20N 117°15E 229 B11
Luk Chau = George I. Hong Kong, China 22°13N 114°7E 122 B2
Lukang Taiwan 24°1N 120°22E 225 B2
Lukanga Bandundu, Dem. Rep. of the Congo 1°41S 18°9E 264 C3
Lukanga Équateur, Dem. Rep. of the Congo 1°0S 18°8E 264 C3
Lukanga Swamp Zambia 14°30S 27°40E 269 E2
Lukavac Bos.-H. 44°33N 18°32E 182 F3
Lukenie → Dem. Rep. of the Congo 3°0S 18°50E 264 C3
Lŭki = Laki Bulgaria 41°50N 24°43E 203 E8
Lukk Libya 32°1N 24°46E 258 B4
Lukla Nepal 27°42N 86°43E 243 F12
Lukolela Équateur, Dem. Rep. of the Congo 1°10S 17°12E 264 C3
Lukolela Kasai-Or., Dem. Rep. of the Congo 5°23S 24°32E 265 D4
Lukosi Zimbabwe 18°30S 26°30E 269 F2
Lukovë Albania 39°59N 19°54E 202 G3
Lukovit Bulgaria 43°13N 24°11E 203 C8
Łuków Poland 51°55N 22°23E 185 G9
Lukoyanov Russia 55°2N 44°29E 190 C7
Luksefjell Norway 59°23N 9°34E 164 E6
Luku Taiwan 23°44N 120°45E 225 C2
Lukula Dem. Rep. of the Congo 5°31S 14°32E 265 D2
Lukulu Zambia 14°23S 23°15E 265 E4
Lukuni Dem. Rep. of the Congo 5°50S 17°16E 265 D3
Lukusuzi △ Zambia 12°43S 32°36E 269 E3
Lula Dem. Rep. of the Congo 5°22S 16°2E 265 D3
Lülang Shan China 38°0N 111°15E 226 F6
Luleå Sweden 65°35N 22°10E 160 D20
Luleälven → Sweden 65°35N 22°10E 160 D20
Lüleburgaz Turkey 41°23N 27°22E 203 E11
Luliang China 25°0N 103°40E 228 E4
Lulima Dem. Rep. of the Congo 4°12S 25°36E 268 C2
Luling U.S.A. 29°41N 97°39W 314 G6
Lulong China 39°53N 118°51E 227 E10
Lulonga → Dem. Rep. of the Congo 1°0N 18°10E 264 B3
Lulu U.S.A. 30°7N 82°29W 316 E7
Lulu → Dem. Rep. of the Congo 1°18N 23°42E 264 B4
Lulua → Dem. Rep. of the Congo 4°30S 20°30E 265 C4
Luluabourg = Kananga Dem. Rep. of the Congo 5°55S 22°18E 265 D4
Luma Amer. Samoa 14°16S 169°33W 302 f
Lumai Angola 13°13S 21°25E 265 E4
Lumajang Indonesia 8°8S 113°13E 235 D4
Lumaku, Gunong Malaysia 4°52N 115°38E 235 B5
Lumār Iran 33°33N 46°49E 213 F12
Lumbala → Angola 12°39S 22°35E 265 E4
Lumbala Kaquengue Angola 12°39S 22°34E 265 E4
Lumbala N'guimbo Angola 14°18S 21°18E 265 E4
Lumbe → Zambia 16°42S 23°41E 265 F4
Lumber City U.S.A. 31°56N 82°41W 316 D7
Lumberton N.C., U.S.A. 34°37N 79°0W 315 D15
Lumberton Tex., U.S.A. 30°16N 94°12W 314 F7
Lumbis Indonesia 4°18N 116°15E 235 B5
Lumding India 25°46N 93°10E 241 C4
Lumi Papua N. G. 3°30S 142°2E 286 B2
Lumiar Portugal 38°46N 9°10W 126 A2
Lumière, Côte de France 46°50N 2°10W 172 F4
Lumpkin U.S.A. 32°3N 84°48W 316 C5
Lumsden Sask., Canada 50°39N 104°52W 297 C8
Lumsden N.Z. 45°44S 168°27E 285 F3
Lumut Malaysia 4°13N 100°37E 237 K3
Lumut, Tanjung Indonesia 3°50S 105°58E 234 C3
Lumwana Zambia 11°50S 25°8E 269 E2
Luna India 23°43N 69°16E 242 H3
Luna Apayao, Phil. 18°18N 121°21E 232 B3
Lunan China 24°40N 103°18E 228 E4
Lunavada India 23°8N 73°37E 242 H5
Lunbei = Lunpei Taiwan 24°45N 120°21E 225 C2
Lunca Romania 47°22N 25°1E 183 C10
Lunca Corbului Romania 44°42N 24°45E 183 F9
Lund Sweden 55°44N 13°12E 163 J7
Lunda Norte □ Angola 8°0S 20°0E 265 D4
Lunda Sul □ Angola 10°0S 20°0E 265 E4
Lundamo Norway 63°9N 10°19E 164 A7
Lundazi Zambia 12°20S 33°7E 269 E3
Lunde Sweden 62°53N 17°51E 162 B11
Lundenburg = Břeclav Czechia 48°46N 16°53E 181 C9
Lunderskov Denmark 55°29N 9°19E 163 J3
Lundi → Zimbabwe 21°43S 32°34E 269 G3
Lundtofte Denmark 55°47N 12°32E 118 A3
Lundu Malaysia 1°40N 109°50E 235 B3
Lundy U.K. 51°10N 4°41W 169 F3
Lune → U.K. 54°0N 2°51W 168 C5
Lüneburg Germany 53°15N 10°24E 178 B6
Lüneburg Heath = Lüneburger Heide Germany 53°10N 10°12E 178 B6
Lüneburger Heide Germany 53°10N 10°12E 178 B6
Lunel France 43°39N 4°9E 175 E8
Lünen Germany 51°37N 7°32E 178 D3
Lunenburg Canada 44°22N 64°18W 299 D7
Lunéville France 48°36N 6°30E 173 D13
Lung Kwu Chau Hong Kong, China 22°23N 113°53E 122 A1
Lung Kwu Tan Hong Kong, China 22°23N 113°55E 122 A1
Lung Mei Hong Kong, China 22°23N 114°15E 122 A3
Lunga Dem. Rep. of the Congo 5°46S 12°14E 265 C4
Lunga → Zambia 14°34S 26°25E 269 E2
Lunga Lunga Kenya 4°33S 39°7E 268 C4
Lungchin Taiwan 24°12N 120°31E 225 B2
Lunge Angola 12°13S 16°7E 265 E3
Lungga Solomon Is. 9°25S 160°3E 287 M11
Lungi S. Leone 8°40N 13°17W 262 D2
Lunglei India 22°55N 92°45E 241 D4
Lungngo Myanmar 21°57N 93°36E 241 E4
Lung'tan Taiwan 24°52N 121°12E 225 B3
Lungwebungu → Zambia 14°19S 23°14E 265 E4
Luni India 26°0N 73°6E 242 G5
Luni → India 24°41N 71°14E 242 G4
Luninets = Luninyets Belarus 52°15N 26°50E 177 B14
Luning U.S.A. 38°30N 118°11W 304 G4
Lunino Russia 53°38N 45°18E 190 D8
Luninyets Belarus 52°15N 26°50E 177 B14
Lunkaransar India 28°29N 73°44E 242 E5
Lunner Norway 60°19N 10°35E 164 D7
Lunpei Taiwan 24°45N 120°21E 225 C2
Lunsar S. Leone 8°41N 12°32W 262 D2
Lunsemfwa → Zambia 14°54S 30°12E 269 E3
Lunsemfwa Falls Zambia 14°30S 29°6E 269 E2
Luntai China 41°46N 84°14E 217 D10
Luo He → China 34°35N 110°20E 226 G6
Luocheng China 24°48N 108°53E 228 E7
Luochuan China 35°45N 109°26E 226 G5
Luoci China 25°19N 102°18E 228 E4
Luodian China 25°24N 106°43E 228 E6
Luoding China 22°45N 111°40E 229 F8
Luodong = Lotung Taiwan 24°41N 121°46E 225 B3
Luofu Dem. Rep. of the Congo 0°10S 29°15E 268 C2
Luohe China 33°32N 114°2E 226 H8
Luojiang Guangdong, China 23°5N 113°17E 121 B2
Luojiang Sichuan, China 31°18N 104°33E 228 B5
Luonan China 34°5N 110°10E 226 G6
Luoning China 34°35N 111°40E 226 G6
Luoshan China 32°13N 114°30E 229 A10
Luotian China 30°46N 115°22E 229 B10
Luoxiao Shan China 26°30N 114°1E 229 D10
Luoyang China 34°40N 112°26E 226 G7
Luoyuan China 26°28N 119°30E 229 D12
Luozi Dem. Rep. of the Congo 4°54S 14°0E 265 C2
Luozigou China 43°42N 130°18E 227 C16
Lupeni Romania 45°21N 23°13E 183 E8
Lupilichi Mozam. 11°47S 35°13E 269 E4
Lupire Angola 14°36S 19°29E 265 E3
Lupków Poland 49°15N 22°4E 185 J9
Lupoing China 24°53N 104°21E 228 E5
Lupon Phil. 6°54N 126°0E 233 H6
Luputa Dem. Rep. of the Congo 7°2S 23°43E 265 D4
Luqa Malta 35°52N 14°29E 206 F7
Luquan Hebei, China 38°4N 114°17E 226 E8
Luquan Yunnan, China 25°35N 102°25E 228 E4
Luque Paraguay 25°19S 57°25W 334 B4

Luquembo *Angola* 10°44S 17°43E **265** E3
Luquillo *Puerto Rico* 18°23N 65°43W **321** b
Luquillo, Sierra de *Puerto Rico* 18°20N 65°47W **321** b
Lúras *Italy* 40°56N 9°10E **200** B2
Luray *U.S.A.* 38°40N 78°28W **309** F14
Lure *France* 47°40N 6°30E **173** E13
Luremo *Angola* 8°30S 17°50E **265** D3
Lurës △ *Albania* 41°47N 20°11E **202** E4
Lurgan *U.K.* 54°27N 6°20W **166** B5
Luribay *Bolivia* 17°6S 67°39W **330** D4
Lurín *Peru* 12°17S 76°52W **330** C2
Lúrio *Mozam.* 13°32S 40°30E **269** E5
Lusaka *Zambia* 15°28S 28°16E **269** F2
Lusaka □ *Zambia* 15°30S 29°0E **269** F2
Lusambo *Dem. Rep. of the Congo* 4°58S 23°28E **265** C4
Lusancay Is. and Reefs *Papua N. G.* 8°30S 150°30E **286** E6
Lusangaye *Dem. Rep. of the Congo* 4°54S 26°0E **265** C5
Luseland *Canada* 52°5N 109°24W **297** C7
Lusenga Plain △ *Zambia* 9°22S 29°14E **269** D2
Lusengo *Dem. Rep. of the Congo* 1°47N 19°31E **264** B3
Lushan *Henan, China* 33°45N 112°55E **226** H7
Lushan *Sichuan, China* 30°12N 102°52E **228** B4
Lushi *China* 34°3N 111°3E **226** G6
Lushnjë *Albania* 40°55N 19°41E **202** F3
Lushoto *Tanzania* 4°47S 38°20E **268** C4
Lushui *China* 25°58N 98°44E **228** E2
Lushuihe *China* 42°31N 127°47E **224** A3
Lüshun *China* 38°45N 121°15E **227** E11
Lusignan *France* 46°26N 0°8E **174** B4
Lusigny-sur-Barse *France* 48°16N 4°15E **173** D11
Lusiye *Zambia* 15°30S 23°57E **265** F4
Lusk *U.S.A.* 42°46N 104°27W **304** E11
Luso *Portugal* 40°23N 8°23W **194** E2
Lussac-les-Châteaux *France* 46°24N 0°43E **174** B4
Lustenau *Austria* 47°26N 9°39E **180** D2
Lustheim *Germany* 48°14N 11°34E **131** A2
Lustrafjorden *Norway* 61°23N 7°25E **164** C4
Lūt, Dasht-e *Iran* 31°30N 58°0E **247** D8
Luta = Dalian *China* 38°50N 121°40E **227** E11
Lütao *Taiwan* 22°40N 121°30E **225** D3
Lutembo *Angola* 13°26S 21°16E **265** E4
Lutherstadt Wittenberg *Germany* 51°53N 12°39E **178** D8
Luthersville *U.S.A.* 33°13N 84°45W **316** B5
Luti *Solomon Is.* 7°14S 157°0E **287** L9
Luton *U.K.* 51°53N 0°24W **169** F7
Luton □ *U.K.* 51°53N 0°24W **169** F7
Lutong *Malaysia* 4°28N 114°0E **235** B4
Łutsel K'e *Canada* 62°24N 110°44W **297** A6
Lutshima → *Dem. Rep. of the Congo* 5°22S 18°59E **265** D3
Lutsk *Ukraine* 50°50N 25°15E **177** C13
Luttenberg = Ljutomer *Slovenia* 46°31N 16°11E **199** B13
Lutto = Lotta → *Europe* 68°42N 31°6E **160** B24
Lutuai *Angola* 12°41S 20°7E **265** E4
Lutz *U.S.A.* 28°9N 82°28W **317** G7
Lützow Holmbukta *Antarctica* 69°10S 37°30E **151** C4
Lutzputs *S. Africa* 28°3S 20°40E **270** C3
Luuk *Phil.* 5°58N 121°18E **233** J3
Luuq *Somalia* 3°48N 42°34E **267** D5
Luverne *Ala., U.S.A.* 31°43N 86°16W **316** D3
Luverne *Minn., U.S.A.* 43°39N 96°13W **308** D5
Luvo *Angola* 5°51S 14°5E **265** D2
Luvua *Dem. Rep. of the Congo* 8°48S 25°17E **265** D5
Luvua → *Dem. Rep. of the Congo* 6°50S 27°30E **268** D2
Luvuvhu → *S. Africa* 22°25S 31°18E **271** B5
Luwan *China* 31°12N 121°27E **138** B1
Luwegu → *Tanzania* 8°31S 37°23E **269** D4
Luwero *Uganda* 0°50N 32°28E **268** B3
Luwuk *Indonesia* 0°56S 122°47E **231** E6
Luxembourg *Lux.* 49°37N 6°9E **170** E6
Luxembourg □ *Belgium* 49°58N 5°30E **170** E5
Luxembourg ■ *Europe* 49°45N 6°0E **170** E5
Luxembourg ✕ **(LUX)** *Lux.* 49°37N 6°10E **170** E6
Luxembourg, Palais du *Paris, France* **134** c4
Luxemburg *U.S.A.* 42°36N 91°5W **310** B5
Luxeuil-les-Bains *France* 47°49N 6°24E **173** E13
Luxi *Hunan, China* 28°20N 110°7E **229** C8
Luxi *Yunnan, China* 24°40N 103°55E **228** E4
Luxi *Yunnan, China* 24°27N 98°36E **228** E2
Luxian *China* 29°9N 105°24E **228** C5
Luxor = El Uqsur *Egypt* 25°41N 32°38E **256** B3
Luy-de-Béarn → *France* 43°39N 0°48W **174** E3
Luy-de-France → *France* 43°39N 0°48W **174** E3
Luyeh *Hualien, Taiwan* 23°35N 121°32E **225** C3
Luyeh *T'aitung, Taiwan* 22°55N 121°8E **225** D3
Luyi *China* 33°50N 115°35E **226** H8
Luykau = Loikaw *Myanmar* 19°40N 97°17E **241** F6
Luz *Azores* 39°1N 28°0W **153** d1
Luz, Estádio da *Lisbon, Portugal* 38°45N 9°11W **126** A1
Luz-St-Sauveur *France* 42°53N 0°0 **174** F4
Luza *Russia* 60°39N 47°10E **186** B8
Luzern *Switz.* 47°3N 8°18E **179** H4
Luzern □ *Switz.* 47°2N 7°55E **179** H3
Luzhai *China* 24°29N 109°42E **228** E7
Luzhany *Ukraine* 48°22N 25°47E **183** B10
Luzhi *China* 26°21N 105°16E **228** D5
Luzhniki Sports Centre *Russia* 55°43N 37°31E **129** B2
Luzhou *China* 28°52N 105°20E **228** C5
Luzhu = Luchu *Taiwan* 22°52N 120°15E **225** D2
Luziânia *Brazil* 16°20S 48°0W **333** E2
Luzilândia *Brazil* 3°28S 42°22W **332** B3
Lužnice → *Czechia* 49°14N 14°23E **180** B7
Luzon *Phil.* 16°0N 121°0E **232** C3
Luzon Strait *Asia* 21°0N 120°40E **229** G13
Luzy *France* 46°47N 3°58E **173** F10
Luzzi *Italy* 39°27N 16°17E **201** C9
Lviv *Ukraine* 49°50N 24°0E **177** D13
Lviv □ *Ukraine* 49°30N 23°45E **177** D12
Lvov = Lviv *Ukraine* 49°50N 24°0E **177** D13
Lwówek *Poland* 52°28N 16°10E **185** F3
Lwówek Śląski *Poland* 51°7N 15°38E **185** G2
Lyakhavichy *Belarus* 53°2N 26°32E **177** B14
Lyakhovskiye, Ostrova *Russia* 73°40N 141°0E **215** B15
Lyaki = Läki *Azerbaijan* 40°34N 47°22E **191** K8
Lyal I. *Canada* 44°57N 81°24W **312** B3
Lyall Mt. *N.Z.* 45°16S 167°32E **285** F2
Lyallpur = Faisalabad *Pakistan* 31°30N 73°5E **242** D5
Lyaskovets *Bulgaria* 43°6N 25°44E **203** C9
Lyasnaya → *Belarus* 52°9N 23°31E **185** F10
Lybster *U.K.* 58°18N 3°15W **167** C5
Lycabettus *Athens, Greece* **112** b3
Lycaonia *Turkey* 38°0N 33°0E **212** D5
Lychen *Germany* 53°12N 13°18E **178** B9
Lychkova *Russia* 57°55N 32°24E **188** D7
Lycia *Turkey* 36°30N 29°30E **205** E11
Lyck = Ełk *Poland* 53°50N 22°21E **184** E9
Lyckebyån → *Sweden* 56°12N 15°39E **163** H9
Lycksele *Sweden* 64°38N 18°40E **160** D18
Lycosura *Greece* 37°20N 22°3E **204** D4
Lydda = Lod *Israel* 31°57N 34°54E **251** G5
Lyddan I. *Antarctica* 74°0S 21°0W **151** D2
Lydenburg *S. Africa* 25°10S 30°29E **271** C5
Lydia *Turkey* 38°48N 28°19E **205** C10
Łydynia → *Poland* 52°43N 20°26E **185** F7
Lyell *N.Z.* 41°48S 172°4E **285** B7
Lyell I. *Canada* 52°40N 131°35W **296** C2
Lyepyel *Belarus* 54°50N 28°40E **188** E5
Lyford Cay *The Bahamas* 25°2N 77°33W **153** b
Lygnern *Sweden* 57°30N 12°15E **163** G6
Lykavittos Hill = Lycabettus *Athens, Greece* **112** b3
Lykens *U.S.A.* 40°34N 76°42W **313** F8
Lyman *Ukraine* 45°41N 29°45E **183** E14
Lyman *Wyo., U.S.A.* 41°20N 110°18W **304** F8
Lymanske *Ukraine* 46°40N 29°58E **183** D14
Lyme B. *U.K.* 50°42N 2°53W **169** G4
Lyme Regis *U.K.* 50°43N 2°57W **169** G5
Lymington *U.K.* 50°45N 1°32W **169** G6
Łyna → *Poland* 54°37N 21°14E **184** D8
Lynchburg *Ohio, U.S.A.* 39°15N 83°48W **311** E13
Lynchburg *S.C., U.S.A.* 34°3N 80°4W **316** A9
Lynchburg *Va., U.S.A.* 37°25N 79°9W **309** G14
Lynd → *Australia* 16°28S 143°18E **280** B3
Lynd Ra. *Australia* 25°30S 149°20E **281** D4
Lynden *Ont., Canada* 43°14N 80°9W **312** C4
Lynden *Wash., U.S.A.* 48°57N 122°27W **306** B4
Lynden Pindling Int. ✕ **(NAS)** *The Bahamas* 25°3N 77°28W **153** b
Lyndhurst *S. Austral., Australia* 30°15S 138°18E **281** E2
Lyndhurst *N.J., U.S.A.* 40°49N 74°7W **132** B1
Lyndon → *Australia* 23°29S 114°6E **279** D1
Lyndonville *N.Y., U.S.A.* 43°20N 78°23W **312** C6
Lyndonville *Vt., U.S.A.* 44°31N 72°1W **313** B12
Lyngdal *Buskerud, Norway* 59°54N 9°32E **164** E6
Lyngdal *Vest-Agder, Norway* 58°8N 7°7E **164** F4
Lyngen *Norway* 69°45N 20°30E **160** B19
Lyngør *Norway* 58°38N 9°8E **164** F6
Lynher Reef *Australia* 15°27S 121°55E **278** C3
Lynn *Ind., U.S.A.* 40°3N 84°56W **311** D12
Lynn *Mass., U.S.A.* 42°28N 70°57W **313** D14
Lynn Canal *U.S.A.* 58°50N 135°15W **303** G14
Lynn Haven *U.S.A.* 30°15N 85°39W **316** E4
Lynn Lake *Canada* 56°51N 101°3W **297** B8
Lynn Woods Res. *U.S.A.* 42°29N 71°0W **116** A2
Lynne *U.S.A.* 29°12N 81°55W **317** F8
Lynnville *U.S.A.* 38°12N 87°18W **311** F9
Lynnwood *U.S.A.* 47°49N 122°18W **306** C4
Lynton *U.K.* 51°13N 3°50W **169** F4
Lyntupy *Belarus* 55°4N 26°23E **188** E4
Lynx L. *Canada* 62°25N 106°15W **297** A7
Lyon *France* 45°46N 4°50E **175** C8
Lyon, Gare de *Paris, France* **134** c5
Lyon St-Exupery ✕ **(LYS)** *France* 45°44N 5°2E **175** C9
Lyonnais *France* 45°45N 4°15E **175** C8
Lyons = Lyon *France* 45°46N 4°50E **175** C8
Lyons *Ga., U.S.A.* 32°12N 82°19W **316** C7
Lyons *Ill., U.S.A.* 41°48N 87°49W **119** C2
Lyons *Kans., U.S.A.* 38°21N 98°12W **308** F4
Lyons *N.Y., U.S.A.* 43°5N 77°0W **312** C8
Lyons → *Australia* 25°2S 115°9E **279** E2
Lyons Falls *U.S.A.* 43°37N 75°22W **313** C9
Lyozna *Belarus* 55°0N 30°50E **188** E6
Lyra Reef *Papua N. G.* 1°50S 153°35E **286** A7
Lys = Leie → *Belgium* 51°2N 3°45E **170** C3
Lysá nad Labem *Czechia* 50°11N 14°51E **180** A7
Lysaker *Norway* 59°54N 10°38E **133** A2
Lysakerselva → *Norway* 59°54N 10°38E **133** A2
Lysebotn *Norway* 59°3N 6°37E **164** E3
Lysefjorden *Norway* 59°0N 6°23E **164** E3
Lysekil *Sweden* 58°17N 11°26E **163** F5
Lysi *Cyprus* 35°6N 33°41E **207** E9
Lyskovo *Russia* 56°0N 45°3E **190** B7
Lysolaje *Czechia* 50°8N 14°22E **135** B2
Lystrup *Denmark* 56°14N 10°14E **163** H4
Lysva *Russia* 58°7N 57°49E **186** C10
Lysvik *Sweden* 60°1N 13°9E **162** D7
Lysychansk *Ukraine* 48°55N 38°30E **189** H10
Lytham St. Anne's *U.K.* 53°45N 3°0W **168** D4
Lyttelton *N.Z.* 43°35S 172°44E **285** D7
Lytton *Canada* 50°13N 121°31W **296** C4
Lyuban *Russia* 59°16N 31°18E **188** C6
Lyubertsy *Russia* 55°40N 37°51E **188** E9
Lyubim *Russia* 58°20N 40°39E **188** C11
Lyubimets *Bulgaria* 41°50N 26°5E **203** E10
Lyublino *Russia* 55°41N 37°44E **129** B3
Lyuboml *Ukraine* 51°11N 24°4E **185** G11
Lyubotyn *Ukraine* 50°0N 36°0E **189** H8
Lyubytino *Russia* 58°50N 33°16E **188** C7
Lyudao = Lütao *Taiwan* 22°40N 121°30E **225** D3
Lyudinovo *Russia* 53°52N 34°28E **188** F8

M

M.R. Štefánik, Bratislava ✕ **(BTS)** *Slovakia* 48°11N 17°9E **181** C10
Ma → *Vietnam* 19°47N 105°56E **228** H5
Ma, O. el → *Algeria* 27°45N 7°52W **260** C3
Ma Nam Wat *Hong Kong, China* 22°21N 114°16E **122** A3
Ma On Shan *Hong Kong, China* 22°23N 114°12E **122** A3
Ma On Shan Country Park ⌂ *Hong Kong, China* 22°22N 114°14E **122** A3
Ma Wan *Hong Kong, China* 22°21N 114°3E **122** A2
Ma Wan Channel *Hong Kong, China* 22°21N 114°4E **122** A2
Ma'adaba *Jordan* 31°43N 35°47E **251** H6
Maafushi *Maldives* 3°59N 73°27E **272** d
Maakhir *Somalia* 10°30N 47°30E **267** B6
Ma'ale Adumim *West Bank* 31°49N 35°17E **123** B2
Ma'ale Ha Khamisha *Israel* 31°49N 35°7E **123** B1
Ma'ale Mikhmas *West Bank* 31°52N 35°18E **123** A2
Ma'alot-Tarshiha *Israel* 33°1N 35°17E **250** E6
Maamba *Zambia* 17°17S 26°28E **270** A4
Ma'ān *Jordan* 30°12N 35°44E **251** H6
Ma'ān □ *Jordan* 30°0N 36°0E **251** J7
Maana'oba *Solomon Is.* 8°17S 160°50E **287** M11
Maanselkä *Finland* 63°52N 28°32E **160** C23
Ma'anshan *China* 31°44N 118°29E **229** B12
Maantiekylä *Finland* 60°20N 25°0E **121** A3
Maarianhamina = Mariehamn *Finland* 60°5N 19°55E **161** F18
Maarifa *Iraq* 33°15N 44°21E **113** B2
Maarmorilik *Greenland* 71°3N 51°0W **154** C5
Ma'arrat an Nu'mān *Syria* 35°43N 36°43E **250** C7
Maas → *Neths.* 51°45N 4°32E **170** C4
Maaseik *Belgium* 51°6N 5°45E **170** C5
Maasim *Phil.* 5°52N 125°0E **233** J5
Maasin *Phil.* 10°8N 124°50E **233** F5
Maastricht *Neths.* 50°50N 5°40E **170** D5
Maasupa *Solomon Is.* 9°16S 161°17E **287** M11
Maave *Mozam.* 21°4S 34°47E **271** B5
Mababe Depression *Botswana* 18°50S 24°15E **270** A3
Mabaia *Angola* 7°12S 14°2E **265** D2
Mabalane *Mozam.* 23°37S 32°31E **271** B5
Mabanga *Dem. Rep. of the Congo* 1°30N 19°6E **264** B3
Ma'bar *Yemen* 14°48N 44°17E **248** D4
Mabaruma *Guyana* 8°10N 59°50W **329** B6
Mabato Pt. *Phil.* 14°29N 121°3E **127** C2
Mabein *Myanmar* 23°29N 96°37E **241** D6
Mabel, L. *U.S.A.* 28°25N 81°32W **133** B1
Mabel L. *Canada* 50°35N 118°43W **296** C5
Mabenga *Dem. Rep. of the Congo* 3°39S 18°40E **264** C3
Mabenge *Dem. Rep. of the Congo* 4°15N 24°12E **264** B4
Maberly *Canada* 44°50N 76°32W **313** B8
Mabesi, L. *S. Leone* 7°10N 11°42W **262** D2
Mabian *China* 28°47N 103°37E **228** C4
Mabil *Ethiopia* 10°26N 36°52E **257** E4
Mabinay *Phil.* 9°48N 122°54E **233** G4
Mabirou *Congo* 1°3S 15°42E **264** C3
Mablethorpe *U.K.* 53°20N 0°15E **168** D8
Mableton *U.S.A.* 33°49N 84°35W **316** B5
Mably *France* 46°5N 4°4E **173** F11
Maboma *Dem. Rep. of the Congo* 2°30N 28°10E **268** B2
Mabonto *S. Leone* 8°53N 11°50W **262** D2
Maboukou *Congo* 3°39S 12°31E **264** C2
Mabouya I. *Grenada* 12°29N 61°30W **323** q
Mabroûk *Mali* 19°29N 1°15W **261** E4
Mabrous *Niger* 21°14N 13°35E **259** D2
Mabuasehube ⌂ *Botswana* 25°5S 21°10E **270** C3
Mabudis *Phil.* 20°55N 121°55E **232** A3
Mabuiag *Australia* 9°57S 142°11E **280** a
Mac Bac *Vietnam* 9°46N 106°7E **237** H6
Macachín *Argentina* 37°10S 63°43W **334** D3
Macaco, Morro do *Brazil* 22°56S 43°6W **135** B2
Macaé *Brazil* 22°20S 41°43W **333** F3
Macael *Spain* 37°20N 2°18W **197** H2
Macaíba *Brazil* 5°51S 35°21W **332** C4
Macajalar B. *Phil.* 8°55N 124°39E **233** G5
Macajuba *Brazil* 12°9S 40°22W **333** D3
McAlester *U.S.A.* 34°56N 95°46W **314** D7
McAllen *U.S.A.* 26°12N 98°14W **314** H5
McAlpin *U.S.A.* 30°8N 82°57W **316** E7
MacAlpine L. *Canada* 66°32N 102°45W **294** D11
Macamic *Canada* 48°45N 79°0W **298** C4
Macanao, B. de *Venezuela* 11°2N 64°23W **329** a
Macanao, Pen. de *Venezuela* 11°0N 64°18W **329** a
Macao = Macau *China* 22°12N 113°33E **229** F9
Macão *Portugal* 39°35N 7°59W **195** F3
Macapá *Brazil* 0°5N 51°4W **329** C7
Macaque, Morne *Dominica* 15°20N 61°20W **323** k
Macará *Ecuador* 4°23S 79°57W **328** D2
Macarani *Brazil* 15°33S 40°24W **333** E3
Macarena, Serranía de la *Colombia* 2°45N 73°55W **328** C3
Macareo, Caño → *Venezuela* 9°47N 61°36W **329** B5
Macarthur *Australia* 38°5S 142°0E **282** E5
McArthur → *Australia* 15°54S 136°40E **280** B2
McArthur, Port *Australia* 16°4S 136°23E **280** B2
Macas *Ecuador* 2°19S 78°7W **328** D2
Macate *Peru* 8°48S 78°7W **330** B2
Macau *Brazil* 5°15S 36°40W **332** C4
Macau *China* 22°12N 113°33E **229** F9
Macaúbas *Brazil* 13°2S 42°42W **333** D3
Macauley I. *Pac. Oc.* 30°12S 178°28W **277** G15
Macaya → *Colombia* 0°59N 72°20W **328** C3
McBride *Canada* 53°20N 120°19W **296** C4
McCall *U.S.A.* 44°55N 116°6W **304** D5
McCamey *U.S.A.* 31°8N 102°14W **314** F3
McCammon *U.S.A.* 42°39N 112°12W **304** E7
McCarran Int., Las Vegas ✕ **(LAS)** *U.S.A.* 36°5N 115°9W **124** B2
McCarthy *U.S.A.* 61°26N 142°56W **303** F12
McCauley I. *Canada* 53°40N 130°15W **296** C2
McCleary *U.S.A.* 47°3N 123°16W **306** C3
Macclenny *U.S.A.* 30°17N 82°7W **316** E7
Macclesfield *U.K.* 53°15N 2°8W **168** D5
Macclesfield Bank *S. China Sea* 16°0N 114°30E **230** A4
M'Clintock Chan. *Canada* 72°0N 102°0W **294** C11
McClintock Ra. *Australia* 18°44S 127°38E **278** C4
McCloud *U.S.A.* 41°15N 122°8W **304** F2
McCluer I. *Australia* 11°5S 133°0E **278** B5
McClure *U.S.A.* 40°42N 77°19W **312** F7
McClure, L. *U.S.A.* 37°35N 120°16W **306** H6
M'Clure Str. *Canada* 75°0N 119°0W **295** C8
McClusky *U.S.A.* 47°29N 100°27W **308** B3
McComb *U.S.A.* 31°15N 90°27W **315** F9
McCook *Ill., U.S.A.* 41°47N 87°49W **119** C2
McCook *Nebr., U.S.A.* 40°12N 100°38W **308** E3
McCormick *U.S.A.* 33°55N 82°17W **316** B7
McCreary *Canada* 50°47N 99°29W **297** C9
McCullough Mt. *U.S.A.* 35°35N 115°13W **307** K11
McCusker → *Canada* 55°32N 108°39W **297** B7
McDavid *U.S.A.* 30°52N 87°19W **317** E2
McDermitt *U.S.A.* 41°59N 117°43W **304** F5
McDonald *U.S.A.* 40°22N 80°14W **312** F4
Macdonald, L. *Australia* 23°30S 129°0E **278** D4
Macdonald, Mt. *Vanuatu* 17°36S 168°23E **287** G6
McDonald Is. *Ind. Oc.* 53°0S 73°0E **273** K6
MacDonnell Ranges *Australia* 23°40S 133°0E **278** D5
McDonough *U.S.A.* 33°27N 84°9W **316** B5
McDougalls Well *Australia* 31°8S 141°15E **282** A4
MacDowell L. *Canada* 52°15N 92°45W **298** B1
Macduff *U.K.* 57°40N 2°31W **167** D6
Maceda *Spain* 42°16N 7°39W **194** C3
Macedonia *U.S.A.* 41°19N 81°31W **312** E3
Macedonia, North ■ *Europe* 41°53N 21°40E **202** E5
Maceió *Brazil* 9°40S 35°41W **332** C4
Maceira *Portugal* 39°41N 8°55W **194** F2
Macenta *Guinea* 8°35N 9°32W **262** D3
Macerata *Italy* 43°18N 13°27E **199** E10
McFarland *U.S.A.* 35°41N 119°14W **307** K7
McFarlane → *Canada* 59°12N 107°58W **297** B7
Macfarlane, L. *Australia* 32°0S 136°40E **282** B2
McGehee *U.S.A.* 33°38N 91°24W **314** E9
McGill *U.S.A.* 39°23N 114°47W **304** G6
McGill Univ. *Montréal, Canada* **130** b1
Macgillycuddy's Reeks *Ireland* 51°58N 9°45W **166** E2
McGrath *U.S.A.* 62°58N 155°36W **303** E9
McGraw *U.S.A.* 42°36N 76°8W **313** D8
McGregor *U.S.A.* 43°1N 91°11W **310** A5
McGregor Ra. *Australia* 27°0S 142°45E **281** D3
McGuire, Mt. *Australia* 20°18S 148°23E **280** b
Mach *Pakistan* 29°50N 67°20E **242** E2
Māch Kowr *Iran* 25°48N 61°28E **247** E9
Machacalis *Brazil* 17°5S 40°45W **333** E3
Machado = Jiparaná → *Brazil* 8°3S 62°52W **331** B5
Machagai *Argentina* 26°56S 60°2W **334** B3
Machakos *Kenya* 1°30S 37°15E **268** C4
Machakos □ *Kenya* 1°15S 34°35E **268** C4
Machala *Ecuador* 3°20S 79°57W **328** D2
Machalilla △ *Ecuador* 1°24S 80°42W **328** D1
Machanbaw *Myanmar* 27°16N 97°36E **241** B6
Machanga *Mozam.* 20°59S 35°0E **271** B6
Machar Marshes *South Sudan* 9°0N 33°30E **266** C3
Machattie, L. *Australia* 24°50S 139°48E **280** C2
Machault *France* 49°21N 4°29E **173** C11
Machava *Mozam.* 25°54S 32°28E **271** C5
Machecoul *France* 47°0N 1°49W **172** F5
Macheke *Zimbabwe* 18°5S 31°51E **271** A5
Machelen *Belgium* 50°55N 4°26E **116** A2
Macheng *China* 31°12N 115°2E **229** B10
McHenry *U.S.A.* 42°21N 88°16W **311** B8
Macherado *Greece* 37°46N 20°49E **207** D2
Macherla *India* 16°29N 79°26E **244** F4
Machero *Spain* 39°21N 4°20W **195** F6
Machgaon *India* 20°5N 86°17E **244** D8
Machhu → *India* 23°6N 70°46E **242** H4
Machiara △ *Pakistan* 34°40N 73°30E **242** B5
Machias *Maine, U.S.A.* 44°43N 67°28W **309** C20
Machias *N.Y., U.S.A.* 42°25N 78°29W **312** D6
Machichi → *Canada* 57°3N 92°6W **297** B10
Machico *Madeira* 32°43N 16°44W **153** c
Machida *Japan* 35°32N 139°26E **140** B1
Machilipatnam *India* 16°12N 81°8E **245** F5
Machiques *Venezuela* 10°4N 72°34W **328** A3
Machu Picchu *Peru* 13°8S 72°30W **330** C3
Machynlleth *U.K.* 52°35N 3°50W **169** E4
Macia *Mozam.* 25°2S 33°8E **271** C5
Macias Nguema Biyoga = Bioko *Eq. Guin.* 3°30N 8°40E **263** E6
Maciejowice *Poland* 51°36N 21°26E **185** G8
McIlwraith Ra. *Australia* 13°50S 143°20E **280** A3
Măcin *Romania* 45°16N 28°8E **183** E13
Macina *Mali* 14°50N 5°0W **262** C4
McInnes L. *Canada* 52°13N 93°45W **297** C10
McIntosh *U.S.A.* 45°55N 101°21W **308** C3
McIntosh L. *Canada* 55°45N 105°0W **297** B8
Macintosh Ra. *Australia* 27°39S 125°32E **279** E4
Macintyre → *Australia* 28°37S 150°47E **281** D5
Maciołki *Poland* 52°19N 21°9E **143** B2
Macizo Galaico *Spain* 42°30N 7°30W **194** C3
Maçka *Turkey* 40°49N 39°36E **213** B8
Mackay *Queens., Australia* 21°8S 149°11E **280** K7
Mackay *Idaho, U.S.A.* 43°55N 113°37W **304** E7
MacKay → *Canada* 57°10N 111°38W **296** B6
Mackay, L. *Australia* 22°30S 129°0E **278** D4
McKay Ra. *Australia* 23°0S 122°30E **278** D3
McKean *Kiribati* 3°36S 174°8W **277** A16
McKeesport *U.S.A.* 40°20N 79°51W **312** F5
McKellar *Canada* 45°30N 79°55W **312** A5
McKenna *U.S.A.* 46°56N 122°33W **306** D4
Mackenzie = Linden *Guyana* 6°0N 58°10W **329** B6
Mackenzie *Canada* 55°20N 123°5W **296** B4
McKenzie *U.S.A.* 36°8N 88°31W **315** C10
Mackenzie → *Queens., Australia* 23°38S 149°46E **280** C4
Mackenzie → *N.W.T., Canada* 69°10N 134°20W **294** D5
McKenzie → *U.S.A.* 44°7N 123°6W **304** D2
Mackenzie Bay *Canada* 69°0N 137°30W **292** C6
Mackenzie King I. *Canada* 77°45N 111°0W **295** B9
Mackenzie Mts. *Canada* 64°0N 130°0W **292** C6
Mackenzie Plains *N.Z.* 44°10S 170°25E **285** E5
McKerrow, L. *N.Z.* 44°25S 168°5E **285** E3
Mackheim = Maków Mazowiecki *Poland* 52°52N 21°6E **185** F8
Mackinac, Straits of *U.S.A.* 45°50N 84°40W **309** C11
Mackinaw *U.S.A.* 40°32N 89°21W **310** D7
Mackinaw → *U.S.A.* 40°33N 89°44W **310** D7
Mackinaw City *U.S.A.* 45°47N 84°44W **309** C11
McKinlay *Australia* 21°16S 141°18E **280** C3
McKinlay → *Australia* 20°50S 141°28E **280** C3
McKinley, Mt. = Denali *U.S.A.* 63°4N 151°0W **303** E10
McKinley Park *Alaska, U.S.A.* 63°44N 148°55W **303** E10
McKinley Park *Ill., U.S.A.* 41°49N 87°40W **119** C2
McKinley Sea *Arctic* 82°0N 0°0 **154** A11
McKinney *U.S.A.* 33°12N 96°37W **314** E6
Mackinnon Road *Kenya* 3°40S 39°1E **268** C4
McKittrick *Calif., U.S.A.* 35°18N 119°37W **307** K7
McKittrick *Mo., U.S.A.* 38°44N 91°27W **310** F5
Macklin *Canada* 52°20N 109°56W **297** C7
Macksville *Australia* 30°40S 152°56E **283** A10
McLaren Vale *Australia* 35°13S 138°31E **282** C3
McLaughlin *U.S.A.* 45°49N 100°49W **308** C3
Maclean *Australia* 29°26S 153°16E **281** D5
McLean *Ill., U.S.A.* 40°19N 89°10W **310** D7
McLean *Tex., U.S.A.* 35°14N 100°36W **314** D4
McLean *Va., U.S.A.* 38°56N 77°10W **143** B1
McLeansboro *U.S.A.* 38°6N 88°32W **311** F8
Maclear = Nqanqarhu *S. Africa* 31°2S 28°23E **271** D4
Maclear, C. *Malawi* 13°58S 34°49E **269** E3
Macleay → *Australia* 30°56S 153°0E **283** A10
McLennan *Canada* 55°42N 116°50W **296** B5
MacLeod = Fort Macleod *Canada* 49°45N 113°30W **296** D6
McLeod → *Canada* 54°9N 115°44W **296** C5
MacLeod, L. *Australia* 24°9S 113°47E **279** D1
MacLeod B. *Canada* 62°53N 110°0W **297** A7
MacLeod Lake *Canada* 54°58N 123°0W **296** C4
McLoughlin, Mt. *U.S.A.* 42°27N 122°19W **304** E2
MacMahon = Aïn Touta *Algeria* 35°26N 5°54E **261** A6
McMechen *U.S.A.* 39°57N 80°44W **312** G4
McMinnville *Oreg., U.S.A.* 45°13N 123°12W **304** D2
McMinnville *Tenn., U.S.A.* 35°41N 85°46W **315** D12
McMurdo *Antarctica* 77°51S 166°37E **151** D11
McMurdo Sd. *Antarctica* 77°0S 170°0E **151** D11
McMurray = Fort McMurray *Canada* 56°44N 111°7W **296** B6
McMurray *U.S.A.* 48°19N 122°14W **306** B4
Maco *Phil.* 7°20N 125°50E **233** H5
Maçobere *Mozam.* 21°13S 32°47E **269** G3
Macocolo *Angola* 6°47S 16°8E **265** D3
Macodoene *Mozam.* 23°32S 35°5E **271** B6
Macolo *Angola* 7°5S 16°42E **265** D3
Macomb *U.S.A.* 40°27N 90°40W **310** D6
Macomer *Italy* 40°16N 8°47E **200** B1
Mâcon *Saône-et-Loire, France* 46°19N 4°50E **173** F11
Macon *Ga., U.S.A.* 32°51N 83°38W **316** C6
Macon *Ill., U.S.A.* 39°43N 89°0W **310** E8
Macon *Miss., U.S.A.* 33°7N 88°34W **315** E10
Macon *Mo., U.S.A.* 39°44N 92°28W **310** E4
Macondo *Angola* 12°37S 23°46E **265** E4
Macopocho → *Chile* 33°24S 70°40W **137** B1
Macossa *Mozam.* 17°55S 33°56E **269** F3
Macou → *Dominica* 15°25N 61°27W **323** k
Macou, Pte. *Guadeloupe* 16°21N 61°31W **322** e
Macouba *Martinique* 14°52N 61°9W **322** j
Macoun L. *Canada* 56°32N 103°40W **297** B8
Macoupin Cr. → *U.S.A.* 39°11N 90°38W **310** E6
Macovane *Mozam.* 21°30S 35°2E **271** B6
MacPherson = Kapuskasing *Canada* 49°25N 82°30W **298** C3
McPherson *U.S.A.* 38°22N 97°40W **308** F5
McPherson Pk. *U.S.A.* 34°53N 119°53W **307** L7
McPherson Ra. *Australia* 28°15S 153°15E **281** D5
Macquarie → *Australia* 30°7S 147°24E **283** A7
Macquarie Harbour *Australia* 42°15S 145°23E **281** G4
Macquarie I. *Pac. Oc.* 54°36S 158°55E **288** N7
Macquarie Ridge *S. Ocean* 57°0S 159°0E **151** B10
Macqueripe B. *Trin. & Tob.* 10°44N 61°37W **323** t
McRae *U.S.A.* 32°4N 82°54W **316** C7
MacRitchie Res. *Singapore* 1°20N 103°49E **138** A2
MacRobertson Land *Antarctica* 71°0S 64°0E **151** D6
Macrohon *Phil.* 10°4N 124°56E **233** F5
Macroom *Ireland* 51°54N 8°57W **166** E3
MacTier *Canada* 45°8N 79°47W **312** A5
Macubela *Mozam.* 16°53S 37°49E **269** F4
Macugnaga *Italy* 45°58N 7°58E **198** C4
Macuira △ *Colombia* 12°9N 71°21W **328** A3
Macuje *Colombia* 0°24N 73°10W **328** C3
Macul *Chile* 33°30S 70°35W **137** C2
Macumba → *Australia* 27°52S 137°12E **281** D2
Macuro *Venezuela* 10°42N 61°55W **329** F9
Macusani *Peru* 14°4S 70°29W **330** C3
Macuse *Mozam.* 17°45S 37°10E **269** F4
Macuspana *Mexico* 17°46N 92°36W **319** D6
Macusse *Angola* 17°48S 20°23E **265** F4
Macy's on State Street *Chicago, U.S.A.* **119** c2
Mada → *Nigeria* 7°59N 7°55E **263** D6
Ma'dabā □ *Jordan* 31°43N 35°47E **251** G6
Madadeni *S. Africa* 27°43S 30°3E **271** C5
Madadi *Chad* 18°28N 20°45E **259** E4
Madagali *Nigeria* 10°56N 13°33E **263** C7
Madagascar ■ *Africa* 20°0S 47°0E **272** B2
Madagoi → *Somalia* 0°49N 42°58E **267** D5
Madā'in Sālih *Si. Arabia* 26°46N 37°57E **246** E3
Madakasira *India* 13°56N 77°16E **245** H3
Madalena *Azores* 38°32N 28°32W **153** d1
Madama *Niger* 22°0N 13°40E **259** D2
Madame, I. *Canada* 45°30N 60°58W **299** C7
Madame Tussaud's *London, U.K.* **125** a3
Madan *Bulgaria* 41°30N 24°57E **203** E8
Madanapalle *India* 13°33N 78°28E **245** H4
Madang *Papua N. G.* 5°12S 145°49E **286** C3
Madang □ *Papua N. G.* 5°0S 145°30E **286** C3
Madaoua *Niger* 14°5N 6°27E **263** C6
Madara *Bulgaria* 43°17N 27°8E **203** C11
Madara *Nigeria* 11°45N 10°35E **263** C7
Madaripur *Bangla.* 23°19N 90°15E **241** D3
Madau I. *Papua N. G.* 8°58S 152°28E **286** E7
Madauk *Myanmar* 17°56N 96°52E **241** G6
Madawaska *Canada* 45°30N 78°0W **312** A7
Madawaska → *Canada* 45°27N 76°21W **312** A7
Madaxmaroodi *Somalia* 2°39N 44°36E **267** D5
Madaya *Myanmar* 22°12N 96°10E **241** D6
Madbar *South Sudan* 6°17N 30°45E **257** F3
Maddalena *Italy* 41°16N 9°23E **200** A2
Maddalena, Ex Monastero della *Venice, Italy* **142** c2
Maddaloni *Italy* 41°2N 14°23E **201** A7
Maddela *Phil.* 16°21N 121°41E **232** C3
Maddur *India* 12°36N 77°4E **245** H3
Madeira *Atl. Oc.* 32°50N 17°0W **153** c
Madeira *Ohio, U.S.A.* 39°11N 84°21W **311** E12
Madeira → *Brazil* 3°22S 58°45W **329** D6
Madeleine, Îs. de la *Canada* 47°30N 61°40W **299** C7
Maden *Turkey* 38°23N 39°40E **213** C8
Madera *Chihuahua, Mexico* 29°12N 108°7W **318** B3
Madera *Calif., U.S.A.* 36°57N 120°3W **306** J6
Madera *Pa., U.S.A.* 40°49N 78°26W **312** F6
Madgaon *India* 15°12N 73°58E **245** G1
Madha *India* 18°0N 75°30E **244** F2
Madhavpur *India* 21°15N 69°58E **242** J3
Madhepura *India* 26°11N 86°23E **243** F12
Madhira *India* 16°55N 80°22E **244** F5
Madhubani *India* 26°21N 86°7E **243** F12
Madhudaha *India* 22°30N 88°24E **124** B2
Madhugiri *India* 13°40N 77°12E **245** H3
Madhumati → *Bangla.* 22°53N 89°52E **241** D2
Madhupur *Bangla.* 24°37N 90°2E **241** C3
Madhupur *India* 24°16N 86°39E **243** G12
Madhupur △ *Bangla.* 24°43N 90°4E **241** C3
Madhya Pradesh □ *India* 22°50N 78°0E **242** J8
Madhyamgram *India* 22°41N 88°26E **124** A2
Madidi → *Bolivia* 12°32S 66°52W **330** C4
Madikeri *India* 12°30N 75°45E **245** H2
Madikwe ⌂ *S. Africa* 27°38S 32°15E **271** C5
Madill *U.S.A.* 34°6N 96°46W **314** D6
Madimba *Angola* 6°36S 14°23E **265** D2
Madimba *Dem. Rep. of the Congo* 4°58S 15°5E **265** C3
Madín *México, Mexico* 19°32N 99°16W **128** A1
Ma'din *Syria* 35°45N 39°36E **213** E8
Madín, L. *Mexico* 19°31N 99°16W **128** A1
Madina *Mali* 13°25N 8°50W **262** C3
Madīnah Al Mansūr *Iraq* 33°18N 44°20E **113** B2
Madinani *Côte d'Ivoire* 9°37N 6°57W **262** D3
Madinat al Malik Khālid al Askarīyah *Si. Arabia* 27°54N 45°31E **246** E5
Madīnat ash Sha'b *Yemen* 12°50N 45°0E **248** D4
Madīnat ath Thawrah *Syria* 35°50N 38°32E **213** E8
Madīnat Masdar *U.A.E.* 24°26N 54°37E **247** E7
Mâdinet Nasr *Egypt* 30°4N 31°18E **117** A2
Madingo *Congo* 4°5S 11°24E **264** C2
Madingou *Congo* 4°10S 13°33E **264** C2
Madirovalo *Madag.* 16°26S 46°32E **272** B2
Madison *Calif., U.S.A.* 38°41N 121°59W **306** G5
Madison *Fla., U.S.A.* 30°28N 83°25W **316** E6
Madison *Ga., U.S.A.* 33°36N 83°28W **316** B6
Madison *Ind., U.S.A.* 38°44N 85°23W **311** F11
Madison *Mo., U.S.A.* 39°28N 92°13W **310** E4
Madison *Nebr., U.S.A.* 41°50N 97°27W **308** E5
Madison *Ohio, U.S.A.* 41°46N 81°3W **312** E3
Madison *S. Dak., U.S.A.* 44°0N 97°7W **308** C5
Madison *Wis., U.S.A.* 43°4N 89°24W **310** A7
Madison → *U.S.A.* 45°56N 111°31W **304** D8
Madison Avenue *New York, U.S.A.* **132** c2
Madison Heights *U.S.A.* 37°25N 79°8W **309** G14
Madison Square *New York, U.S.A.* **132** d2
Madison Square Garden *New York, U.S.A.* **132** c2
Madisonville *Ky., U.S.A.* 37°20N 87°30W **308** G10
Madisonville *Tex., U.S.A.* 30°57N 95°55W **314** F7
Madista *Botswana* 21°15S 25°6E **270** B4
Madiun *Indonesia* 7°38S 111°32E **235** D4
Madjingo *Gabon* 1°20N 14°4E **264** B2
Mado Gashi *Kenya* 0°44N 39°10E **268** B4
Madoc *Canada* 44°30N 77°28W **312** B7
Madoi *China* 34°46N 98°18E **218** E8
Madon → *France* 48°36N 6°6E **173** D13
Madona *Latvia* 56°53N 26°5E **188** D4
Madonie *Italy* 37°50N 13°50E **200** E6
Madonna dell' Orto *Venice, Italy* **142** a2
Madonna di Campíglio *Italy* 46°14N 10°49E **198** B7
Madou = Matou *Taiwan* 23°11N 120°15E **225** C2
Madra Dağı *Turkey* 39°23N 27°12E **205** B9
Madrakah, Ra's al *Oman* 19°0N 57°50E **249** C7
Madras = Chennai *India* 13°8N 80°19E **245** H5
Madras = Tamil Nadu □ *India* 11°0N 77°0E **245** J3
Madras *U.S.A.* 44°38N 121°8W **304** D3
Madre, L. *U.S.A.* 26°50N 97°30W **314** J6
Madre, Sierra *Phil.* 17°0N 122°0E **232** C4
Madre de Dios □ *Peru* 12°0S 70°15W **330** C3
Madre de Dios → *Bolivia* 10°59S 66°8W **330** C4
Madre de Dios, I. *Chile* 50°20S 75°10W **336** D1
Madre del Sur, Sierra *Mexico* 17°30N 100°0W **319** D5
Madre Occidental, Sierra *Mexico* 27°0N 107°0W **318** B3
Madre Oriental, Sierra *Mexico* 25°0N 100°0W **318** C5
Madri *India* 24°16N 73°32E **242** G5
Madrid *Spain* 40°24N 3°42W **127** B1
Madrid *Ala., U.S.A.* 31°2N 85°24W **316** D4
Madrid *Iowa, U.S.A.* 41°53N 93°49W **310** C3
Madrid *N.Y., U.S.A.* 44°45N 75°8W **313** B9
Madrid □ *Spain* 40°30N 3°45W **194** E7
Madrid Barajas ✕ **(MAD)** *Spain* 40°26N 3°34W **127** B2
Madridejos *Spain* 39°28N 3°33W **195** F7
Madrigal de las Altas Torres *Spain* 41°5N 5°0W **194** D6
Madrona *Spain* 41°27N 2°1E **114** A1
Madrona, Sierra *Spain* 38°27N 4°16W **195** G6
Madroñera *Spain* 39°26N 5°42W **195** F5
Madrusah *Libya* 24°48N 14°58E **258** D2
Madu *Sudan* 14°37N 26°4E **257** E2
Madula *Dem. Rep. of the Congo* 0°27N 25°22E **264** B5
Maduo *Dem. Rep. of the Congo* 1°24S 20°44E **264** C4
Madupi *Myanmar* 21°36N 93°27E **241** E4
Madura *W. Austral., Australia* 31°55S 127°0E **279** F4
Madura *Indonesia* 7°30S 114°0E **231** G15
Madura, Selat *Indonesia* 7°30S 113°20E **235** D4
Madura Oya △ *Sri Lanka* 7°20N 81°10E **245** L5
Madurai *India* 9°55N 78°10E **245** K4
Madurantakam *India* 12°30N 79°50E **245** H4
Madzhalis *Russia* 42°9N 47°47E **191** J8
Mae Chan *Thailand* 20°9N 99°52E **236** B2
Mae Charim △ *Thailand* 18°17N 100°59E **236** C3
Mae Hong Son *Thailand* 19°16N 97°56E **236** C2
Mae Khlong → *Thailand* 13°24N 100°0E **236** F3
Mae Moei △ *Thailand* 17°26N 98°7E **236** D2
Mae Phang △ *Thailand* 19°7N 99°13E **236** C2
Mae Phrik *Thailand* 17°27N 99°7E **236** D2
Mae Ping △ *Thailand* 17°37N 98°51E **236** D2
Mae Ramat *Thailand* 16°58N 98°31E **236** D2
Mae Rim *Thailand* 18°54N 98°57E **236** C2
Mae Sai *Thailand* 20°20N 99°55E **228** G2
Mae Sot *Thailand* 16°43N 98°34E **236** D2
Mae Suai *Thailand* 19°39N 99°33E **228** H2
Mae Tha *Thailand* 18°28N 99°8E **236** C2
Mae Tup Res. *Thailand* 17°52N 98°45E **236** D2
Mae Wa △ *Thailand* 17°23N 99°16E **236** D2
Mae Wong △ *Thailand* 15°54N 99°12E **236** E2
Mae Yom △ *Thailand* 18°43N 100°15E **236** C3
Maebaru *Japan* 33°33N 130°12E **222** D2
Maebashi *Japan* 36°24N 139°4E **223** A11
Maekel □ *Eritrea* 15°20N 38°50E **257** D4
Maella *Spain* 41°8N 0°7E **196** D5
Maelpaeg L. *Canada* 48°20N 56°30W **299** C8
Maesawa *Japan* 35°44N 139°31E **140** A2
Maestra, Sierra *Cuba* 20°15N 77°0W **320** B4
Maestre de Campo I. *Phil.* 12°56N 121°42E **232** E3
Maetambe, Mt. *Solomon Is.* 7°3S 157°1E **287** L9
Maevatanana *Madag.* 16°56S 46°49E **272** B2
Maéwo *Vanuatu* 15°10S 168°10E **287** E6
Mafadi *S. Africa* 29°12S 29°21E **271** C4
Mafate, Cirque de *Réunion* 21°3S 55°25E **272** f
Mafeking = Mafikeng *S. Africa* 25°50S 25°38E **270** C4
Mafeking *Canada* 52°40N 101°10W **297** C8
Maféré *Côte d'Ivoire* 5°30N 3°2W **262** D4
Mafeteng *Lesotho* 29°51S 27°15E **270** C4
Maffra *Australia* 37°53S 146°58E **283** D7
Mafia I. *Tanzania* 7°45S 39°50E **268** D4
Mafikeng *S. Africa* 25°50S 25°38E **270** C4
Mafra *Brazil* 26°10S 49°55W **335** B6
Mafra *Portugal* 38°55N 9°20W **195** G1
Mafungabusi Plateau *Zimbabwe* 18°30S 29°8E **269** F2
Magadan *Russia* 59°38N 150°50E **215** D16
Magadi *India* 12°58N 77°14E **245** H3
Magadi *Rift Valley, Kenya* 1°54S 36°19E **268** C4
Magadi, L. *Kenya* 1°54S 36°19E **268** C4
Magaliesburg *S. Africa* 26°0S 27°32E **271** C4
Magallanes = Punta Arenas *Chile* 53°10S 71°0W **336** D2
Magallanes □ *Chile* 52°0S 72°0W **336** D2
Magallanes, Estrecho de *Chile* 52°30S 75°0W **336** D2
Magallanes y Antártica Chilena □ *Chile* 12°50N 123°50E **232** E4
Magaluf *Spain* 39°29N 2°32E **206** B3
Magangué *Colombia* 9°14N 74°45W **328** B3
Maganoy = Shariff Aguak *Phil.* 6°51N 124°31E **233** H5
Magaria *Niger* 13°4N 9°5E **259** F1
Magarida *Papua N. G.* 10°18S 149°20E **286** F5
Magburaka *S. Leone* 8°47N 12°0W **262** D2
Magdagachi *Russia* 53°27N 125°48E **215** D13
Magdalen Is. = Madeleine, Îs. de la *Canada* 47°30N 61°40W **299** C7
Magdalena *Argentina* 35°5S 57°30W **334** D4
Magdalena *Bolivia* 13°13S 63°57W **331** C5
Magdalena *Lima, Peru* 12°5S 77°5W **124** B2
Magdalena *N. Mex., U.S.A.* 34°7N 107°15W **305** J10
Magdalena □ *Colombia* 10°0N 74°0W **328** B3
Magdalena → *Colombia* 11°6N 74°51W **328** A3
Magdalena, B. *Mexico* 24°35N 112°0W **318** C2
Magdalena, I. *Chile* 44°40S 73°0W **336** B2
Magdalena, I. *Mexico* 24°40N 112°15W **318** C2
Magdalena, Llano de *Mexico* 25°0N 111°25W **318** C2
Magdalena Contreras *Mexico* 19°20N 99°13W **128** C1
Magdalena de Kino *Mexico* 30°38N 110°57W **318** A2
Magdeburg *Germany* 52°7N 11°38E **178** C7
Magdelaine Cays *Australia* 16°33S 150°18E **280** B5
Magdub *Sudan* 13°42N 25°5E **257** E2
Magee *U.S.A.* 31°52N 89°44W **315** F10
Magelang *Indonesia* 7°29S 110°13E **235** D4
Magellan's Str. = Magallanes, Estrecho de *Chile* 52°30S 75°0W **336** D2
Magelungen *Sweden* 59°13N 18°4E **139** B2
Magenta *Italy* 45°28N 8°53E **198** C5
Magenta, L. *Australia* 33°30S 119°2E **279** F2
Magerøya *Norway* 71°3N 25°40E **160** A21
Maggea *Australia* 34°28S 140°2E **282** C4
Maggia → *Switz.* 46°18N 8°36E **179** J4
Maggiorasca, Mte. *Italy* 44°33N 9°29E **198** D6
Maggiore, L. *Italy* 45°57N 8°39E **198** B5
Maggotty *Jamaica* 18°9N 77°46W **320** a
Maghâgha *Egypt* 28°38N 30°50E **256** B3
Maghama *Mauritania* 15°32N 12°57W **262** B2
Maghera *U.K.* 54°51N 6°41W **166** B5
Magherafelt *U.K.* 54°45N 6°37W **166** B5
Maghnia *Algeria* 34°50N 1°43W **261** B4
Maghreb *Baghdād, Iraq* 33°23N 44°22E **113** A2
Maghreb *N. Afr.* 32°0N 4°0W **254** C3
Maginu *Japan* 35°34N 139°34E **140** B2
Magione *Italy* 43°8N 12°12E **199** E9
Magistralnyy *Russia* 56°16N 107°36E **215** D11
Maglaj *Bos.-H.* 44°33N 18°7E **182** F3
Magliana *Italy* 41°50N 12°26E **136** B1
Magliano in Toscana *Italy* 42°36N 11°17E **199** F8
Máglie *Italy* 40°7N 18°18E **201** B11
Maglizh *Bulgaria* 42°37N 25°32E **203** D9
Magnac-Laval *France* 46°13N 1°11E **174** B5
Magnesia = Magnisia *Greece* 39°15N 23°0E **204** B5
Magnetic Pole (North) *Arctic* 86°25N 157°41W **150** A17
Magnetic Pole (South) *Antarctica* 64°2S 135°43E **151** C9
Magnisia *Greece* 39°15N 23°0E **204** B5
Magnitogorsk *Russia* 53°27N 59°4E **186** D10
Magnolia *Ark., U.S.A.* 33°16N 93°14W **314** E8
Magnolia *Miss., U.S.A.* 31°9N 90°28W **315** F9
Magnor *Norway* 59°56N 12°15E **164** E9
Magny-en-Vexin *France* 49°9N 1°47E **173** C8
Magny-les-Hameaux *France* 48°44N 2°3E **134** B1
Mago *Fiji* 17°26S 179°8W **287** A3
Mago △ *Ethiopia* 5°40N 36°18E **257** F4
Magog *Canada* 45°18N 72°9W **313** A12
Magong = Makung *Taiwan* 23°34N 119°34E **225** C1
Magoro *Uganda* 1°45N 34°12E **268** B3
Magoye *Zambia* 16°1S 27°30E **269** F2
Magpet *Phil.* 7°6N 125°6E **233** H5
Magpie, L. *Canada* 51°0N 64°41W **299** B7
Magrath *Canada* 49°25N 112°50W **296** D6
Magre → *Spain* 39°11N 0°25W **197** F4

Magrur *Sudan* 14°1N 30°27E **257** E3
Magrur, Wadi → *Sudan* 16°5N 26°30E **257** D2
Magsingal *Phil.* 17°41N 120°25E **232** C3
Magta Lahjar *Mauritania* 17°28N 13°17W **262** B2
Magu *Tanzania* 2°30S 33°30E **268** C3
Maguan *China* 23°0N 104°21E **228** F5
Maguarinho, C. *Brazil* 0°15S 48°30W **332** B2
Magude *Mozam.* 25°2S 32°40E **271** C5
Maguindanao □ *Phil.* 7°5N 124°40E **233** H5
Magura *Bangla.* 23°26N 89°26E **241** D2
Magurski △ *Poland* 49°30N 21°30E **185** J8
Maǧusa = Famagusta
Cyprus 35°8N 33°55E **207** E9
Maguse L. *Canada* 61°37N 95°10W **297** A9
Maguse Pt. *Canada* 61°20N 93°50W **297** A10
Magvana *India* 23°13N 69°22E **242** H3
Magway *Myanmar* 20°10N 95°0E **241** E5
Magway □ *Myanmar* 20°0N 95°0E **241** E5
Magwe *South Sudan* 4°8N 32°17E **257** G3
Magyarorszag = Hungary ■
Europe 47°20N 19°20E **181** D12
Maha Oya *Sri Lanka* 7°31N 81°22E **245** L5
Maha Sarakham
Thailand 16°12N 103°16E **236** D4
Mahābād *Iran* 36°50N 45°45E **211** D11
Mahabaleshwar *India* 17°58N 73°43E **244** F1
Mahabalipuram *India* 12°37N 80°11E **245** H5
Mahabharat Lekh *Nepal* 28°30N 82°0E **243** E10
Mahabo *Madag.* 20°23S 44°40E **272** C1
Mahad *India* 18°6N 73°29E **244** E1
Mahaddayweyne *Somalia* 2°58N 45°32E **267** D6
Mahadeo Hills *India* 22°20N 78°30E **243** H8
Mahadeopur *India* 18°48N 80°0E **244** E5
Mahaffey *U.S.A.* 40°53N 78°44W **312** F6
Mahagi
Dem. Rep. of the Congo 2°20N 31°0E **268** B3
Mahagnao Volcano △
Phil. 10°52N 124°51E **233** F5
Mahaica-Berbice □
Guyana 6°13N 57°51W **329** B6
Mahaicony *Guyana* 6°36N 57°48W **329** B6
Mahajamba → *Madag.* 15°33S 47°8E **272** B2
Mahajamba, Helodranon' i
Madag. 15°24S 47°5E **272** B2
Mahajan *India* 28°48N 73°56E **242** E5
Mahajanga *Madag.* 15°40S 46°25E **272** B2
Mahajilo → *Madag.* 19°42S 45°22E **272** B2
Mahakam → *Indonesia* 0°35S 117°17E **235** C5
Mahalapye *Botswana* 23°1S 26°51E **270** B4
Mahalaxmi *Mumbai, India* **130** a1
Mahalchhar *Bangla.* 22°55N 92°2E **241** D4
Mahale Mts. *Tanzania* 6°20S 30°0E **268** D3
Mahale Mts. △ *Tanzania* 6°10S 29°50E **268** D2
Maḩallāt *Iran* 33°55N 50°30E **247** C6
Māhān *Iran* 30°5N 57°18E **247** D8
Mahan → *India* 23°30N 82°50E **243** H10
Mahanadi → *India* 20°20N 86°25E **244** D8
Mahananda → *India* 25°12N 87°52E **243** G12
Mahanoro *Madag.* 19°54S 48°48E **272** B2
Mahanoy City *U.S.A.* 40°49N 76°9W **313** F8
Mahaplag *Phil.* 10°35N 124°57E **233** F5
Mahar, L. *U.S.A.* 25°46N 80°18W **129** D1
Maharashtra □ *India* 20°30N 75°30E **244** D2
Maharès *Tunisia* 34°32N 10°29E **258** B2
Maharivo → *Madag.* 20°26S 44°10E **272** C1
Mahasamund *India* 21°6N 82°6E **244** D6
Mahasham, W. → *Egypt* 30°15N 34°10E **251** H5
Mahasoa *Madag.* 22°12S 46°6E **272** C2
Mahasolo *Madag.* 19°7S 46°22E **272** B2
Mahattat ash Shīdīyah
Jordan 29°55N 35°55E **251** J6
Mahattat 'Unayzah
Jordan 30°30N 35°47E **251** H6
Mahaut *Dominica* 15°21N 61°24W **323** k
Mahaut *Guadeloupe* 16°11N 61°46W **322** e
Mahavavy → *Madag.* 15°57S 45°54E **272** B2
Mahaweli Ganga →
Sri Lanka 8°27N 81°13E **245** K5
Mahaxay *Laos* 17°22N 105°12E **236** D5
Mahbubabad *India* 17°42N 80°2E **244** F5
Mahbubnagar *India* 16°45N 77°59E **244** F3
Mahd adh Dhahab
Si. Arabia 23°30N 40°52E **248** B3
Mahda *U.A.E.* 25°20N 56°15E **247** E8
Maḩḑah *Oman* 24°24N 55°59E **247** E7
Mahdia *Guyana* 5°13N 59°8W **329** B6
Mahdia *Tunisia* 35°28N 11°0E **258** A2
Mahdia □ *Tunisia* 35°20N 10°35E **261** A7
Mahe *Ladākh, India* 33°10N 78°32E **242** C8
Mahé *Puducherry, India* 11°42N 75°34E **245** J2
Mahé *Seychelles* 5°0S 55°30E **272** c
Mahé ✕ (SEZ) *Seychelles* 4°40S 55°31E **272** c
Mahébourg *Mauritius* 20°24S 57°42E **272** e
Mahendra Giri *India* 8°20N 77°30E **245** K3
Mahendragarh *India* 28°17N 76°14E **242** E7
Mahendranagar *Nepal* 28°55N 80°20E **243** E9
Mahenge *Tanzania* 8°45S 36°41E **269** D4
Maheno *N.Z.* 45°10S 170°50E **285** F5
Mahesana *India* 23°39N 72°26E **242** H5
Maheshtala *India* 22°29N 88°15E **124** C1
Maheshwar *India* 22°11N 75°35E **242** H6
Maheskhali I. *Bangla.* 21°36N 91°56E **241** E3
Mahgawan *India* 26°29N 78°37E **243** F8
Mahi → *India* 22°15N 72°55E **242** H5
Mahia Pen. *N.Z.* 39°9S 177°55E **284** F6
Mahibadhoo *Maldives* 3°47N 72°58E **272** d
Mahighe *Solomon Is.* 8°30S 159°58E **287** M10
Mahikeng = Mafikeng
S. Africa 25°50S 25°38E **270** C4
Mahilyow *Belarus* 53°55N 30°18E **177** B16
Mahilyow □ *Belarus* 54°10N 30°50E **188** E6
Mahim *Maharashtra, India* 19°2N 72°50E **130** A2
Mahim *Maharashtra, India* 19°39N 72°44E **244** E1
Mahim B. *India* 19°2N 72°49E **130** A1
Mahina *Tahiti* 17°30S 149°27W **289** e
Mahipalpur *India* 28°32N 77°7E **120** B1
Mahirija *Morocco* 34°0N 3°16W **261** B4
Mahlaing *Myanmar* 21°6N 95°39E **241** E5
Mahlsdorf *Germany* 52°30N 13°37E **115** A4
Mahmiya *Sudan* 17°12N 33°43E **257** D3
Mahmoodabad *Pakistan* 24°51N 67°4E **123** A2
Mahmud Kot *Pakistan* 30°16N 71°0E **242** D4
Mahmudia *Romania* 45°5N 29°5E **183** E14
Mahmudiye *Turkey* 39°48N 30°15E **205** B12
Mahmutbey *Turkey* 41°3N 28°49E **203** E12
Mahmutlar *Turkey* 36°29N 32°5E **250** B3
Māhneshān *Iran* 36°44N 47°39E **213** D12
Mahnomen *U.S.A.* 47°19N 95°58W **308** B6
Maho *Sri Lanka* 7°49N 80°16E **245** L5
Mahoba *India* 25°15N 79°55E **243** G8
Mahomet *U.S.A.* 40°12N 88°24W **311** D8
Mahón = Maó *Spain* 39°53N 4°16E **206** B5
Mahon, Menorca ✕ (MAH)
Spain 39°50N 4°16E **196** F9
Mahone Bay *Canada* 44°27N 64°23W **299** D7
Mahongo ⌓ *Namibia* 18°0S 23°15E **270** B3
Mahopac *U.S.A.* 41°22N 73°45W **313** E11
Mahoua *Chad* 11°49N 18°26E **259** F3
Mahrāt, Jabal *Yemen* 17°0N 51°0E **249** C5
Mahrauli *India* 28°31N 77°10E **120** B2
Mährisch-Budwitz = Moravské
Budějovice *Czechia* 49°4N 15°49E **180** B8
Mährisch-Schönberg = Šumperk
Czechia 49°59N 16°59E **181** B9
Mährisch-Trubau = Moravská
Třebová *Czechia* 49°45N 16°40E **181** B9
Mahul *India* 19°0N 72°53E **130** A2
Mahuta *Nigeria* 11°32N 4°58E **263** C5
Mahuva *India* 21°5N 71°48E **242** J4
Mahya Daği *Turkey* 41°47N 27°36E **203** E11
Mai-Ndombe □
Dem. Rep. of the Congo 2°30S 19°0E **264** C3
Mai-Ndombe, L.
Dem. Rep. of the Congo 2°0S 18°20E **264** C3
Mai Thon, Ko *Thailand* 7°40N 98°28E **237** a
Maia *Amer. Samoa* 14°13S 169°25W **302** g
Maia *Azores* 36°56N 25°1W **153** d4
Maia *Portugal* 41°14N 8°37W **194** D2
Maials *Spain* 41°22N 0°30E **196** D5
Maibong *India* 25°18N 93°10E **241** C4
Maicao *Colombia* 11°23N 72°13W **328** A3
Maîche *France* 47°16N 6°48E **173** E13
Maici → *Brazil* 6°30S 61°43W **331** B5
Maicuru → *Brazil* 2°14S 54°17W **329** D7
Màida *Italy* 38°51N 16°22E **201** D9
Maida Vale *London, U.K.* **125** a1
Maidan Khula *Afghan.* 33°36N 69°50E **242** C3
Maidenhead *U.K.* 51°31N 0°42W **169** F7
Maidstone *Vic., Australia* 37°47S 144°52E **128** A1
Maidstone *Sask., Canada* 53°5N 109°20W **297** C7
Maidstone *Kent, U.K.* 51°16N 0°32E **169** F8
Maiduguri *Nigeria* 12°0N 13°20E **263** C7
Maiella △ *Italy* 42°5N 14°5E **199** F11
Măieruş *Romania* 45°53N 25°31E **183** E10
Maigatari *Nigeria* 12°46N 9°27E **263** C6
Maigh Nuad = Maynooth
Ireland 53°23N 6°34W **166** C5
Maignelay Montigny
France 49°32N 2°30E **173** C9
Maigo *Phil.* 8°10N 123°57E **233** G4
Maigualida, Sierra
Venezuela 5°30N 65°10W **329** B4
Maigudo *Ethiopia* 7°30N 37°8E **257** F4
Maihar *India* 24°16N 80°45E **243** G9
Maihara *Japan* 35°19N 136°17E **223** B8
Maikala Ra. *India* 22°0N 81°0E **244** D5
Maiko △
Dem. Rep. of the Congo 0°30S 27°50E **268** C2
Mailani *India* 28°17N 80°21E **243** E9
Mā'ili *U.S.A.* 21°25N 158°11W **302** K13
Mā'ili Pt. *U.S.A.* 21°24N 158°11W **302** K13
Mailiao *Taiwan* 23°48N 120°13E **225** C2
Maillezais *France* 46°22N 0°45W **174** B3
Mailsi *Pakistan* 29°48N 72°15E **242** E5
Maimbung *Phil.* 5°56N 121°2E **233** J3
Main → *Bayern, Germany* 50°0N 8°18E **179** F4
Main → *Antrim, U.K.* 54°48N 6°18W **166** B5
Main Channel *Canada* 45°21N 81°45W **312** A3
Main Range △ *Australia* 28°11S 152°27E **281** D5
Main Ridge *Trin. & Tob.* 11°16N 60°40W **323** s
Mainburg *Germany* 48°38N 11°47E **179** G7
Maindargi *India* 17°28N 76°18E **244** F3
Maine *France* 48°20N 0°15W **172** D6
Maine □ *U.S.A.* 45°20N 69°0W **309** C19
Maine → *Ireland* 52°9N 9°45W **166** D2
Maine, G. of *U.S.A.* 43°0N 68°30W **301** G26
Maine-et-Loire □ *France* 47°31N 0°30W **172** E6
Maïne-Soroa *Niger* 13°13N 12°2E **263** C7
Maingkaing *Myanmar* 24°48N 95°16E **241** C5
Maingkwan *Myanmar* 26°15N 96°37E **241** B6
Mainistir na Corann = Midleton
Ireland 51°55N 8°10W **166** E3
Mainit *Phil.* 9°32N 125°32E **233** G5
Mainit, L. *Phil.* 9°31N 125°32E **233** G5
Mainland *Orkney, U.K.* 58°59N 3°8W **167** C5
Mainland *Shet., U.K.* 60°15N 1°22W **167** A7
Mainpuri *India* 27°18N 79°4E **243** F8
Maintal *Germany* 50°7N 8°52E **179** E4
Maintenon *France* 48°35N 1°35E **173** D8
Maintirano *Madag.* 18°3S 44°1E **272** B1
Mainz *Germany* 50°1N 8°14E **179** E4
Maio *Cabo Verde* 15°10N 23°10W **153** j
Maipú *Argentina* 36°52S 57°50W **334** D4
Maipú *Santiago, Chile* 33°30S 70°45W **137** C1
Maiquetía *Venezuela* 10°36N 66°57W **328** A4
Màira → *Italy* 44°49N 7°38E **198** D4
Mairabari *India* 26°30N 92°22E **241** B4
Mairena del Aljarafe *Spain* 37°20N 6°6W **195** H4
Mairipotaba *Brazil* 17°18S 49°28W **333** E2
Maisi *Cuba* 20°17N 74°9W **321** B5
Maisí, Pta. de *Cuba* 20°10N 74°10W **321** B5
Maiskhal I. *Bangla.* 21°36N 91°56E **241** E3
Maison Coloniale
Guadeloupe 16°18N 61°16W **322** e
Maisonneuve, Parc
Canada 45°32N 73°33W **130** A2
Maisons-Alfort *France* 48°48N 2°26E **134** B3
Maisons-Laffitte *France* 48°57N 2°8E **134** A1
Maissoneuve *Canada* 45°32N 73°33W **130** A2
Maitland *N.S.W.,*
Australia 32°33S 151°36E **283** B9
Maitland *S. Austral.,*
Australia 34°23S 137°40E **282** C2
Maitland *Western Cape,*
S. Africa 33°53S 18°29E **118** A1
Maitland → *Canada* 43°45N 81°43W **312** C3
Maitland, Banjaran
Malaysia 4°55N 116°37E **235** B5
Maitri *Antarctica* 70°0S 3°0W **151** D3
Maitum *Phil.* 6°2N 124°30E **233** H5
Maiyema *Nigeria* 12°5N 4°25E **263** C5
Maiyuan *China* 25°34N 117°28E **229** E11
Maiz, Is. del *Nic.* 12°15N 83°4W **320** D3
Maizuru *Japan* 35°25N 135°22E **223** B7
Majagual *Colombia* 8°33N 74°38W **328** B3
Majalengka *Indonesia* 6°50S 108°13E **235** D3
Majanji *Uganda* 0°16N 34°0E **268** B3
Majari → *Brazil* 3°29N 60°58W **329** C5
Majdūl *Libya* 25°51N 15°7E **258** C3
Majella = Maiella △ *Italy* 42°5N 14°5E **199** F11
Majene *Indonesia* 3°38S 118°57E **235** C5
Majeng *Peru* 16°40S 72°44W **330** D3
Majete ⌓ *Malawi* 15°54S 34°34E **269** F3
Majevica *Bos.-H.* 44°45N 18°50E **182** F3
Maji *Ethiopia* 6°12N 35°30E **257** F4
Majiang *China* 26°28N 107°32E **228** D6
Majorca = Mallorca *Spain* 39°30N 3°0E **206** B4
Major's B. *St. Kitts & Nevis* 17°14N 62°38W **322** d
Majors Creek *Australia* 35°33S 149°45E **283** C8
Majuli I. *India* 26°58N 94°14E **241** B5
Majuriã *Brazil* 7°30S 64°55W **331** B5
Majuro *Marshall Is.* 7°9N 171°12E **288** G9
Mak, Ko *Thailand* 11°49N 102°29E **237** G4
Maka *Senegal* 13°40N 14°10W **262** C2
Mākaha *Hawai'i, U.S.A.* 21°29N 158°13W **302** K13
Makalamabedi *Botswana* 17°20S 32°39E **271** A5
Makahoa Pt. *U.S.A.* 21°41N 157°56W **302** J14
Makak *Cameroon* 3°36N 11°0E **263** E7
Makaka *Congo* 1°33S 13°39E **264** C2
Makakilo City *U.S.A.* 21°22N 158°5W **302** K13
Makakou *Gabon* 0°11S 12°12E **264** C2
Makalamabedi *Botswana* 20°19S 23°51E **270** B3
Makale *Indonesia* 3°6S 119°51E **235** C5
Makalu *Nepal* 27°55N 87°8E **243** F12
Makalu-Barun △ *Nepal* 27°45N 87°10E **243** F12
Makamba *Burundi* 4°8S 29°49E **268** C2
Makapu'u Pt. *U.S.A.* 21°19N 157°39W **302** K14
Makarewa Junction *N.Z.* 46°20S 168°21E **285** G3
Makari *Cameroon* 12°35N 10°27E **259** F2
Makarikari = Makgadikgadi Salt
Pans *Botswana* 20°40S 25°45E **270** B4
Makarov Basin *Arctic* 87°0N 150°0W **150** A
Makarovo *Russia* 57°40N 107°45E **215** D11
Makarska *Croatia* 43°20N 17°2E **199** E14
Makaryev *Russia* 57°52N 43°50E **190** B6
Makasar *Indonesia* 5°10S 119°20E **235** D5
Makassar, Selat *Indonesia* 1°0S 118°20E **235** C5
Makassar, Str. of = Makassar, Selat
Indonesia 1°0S 118°20E **235** C5
Makat = Maqat
Kazakhstan 47°39N 53°19E **187** E9
Makati *Phil.* 14°33N 121°7E **127** B2
Makaw
Dem. Rep. of the Congo 3°29S 18°20E **264** C3
Makawao *U.S.A.* 20°52N 156°17W **302** C5
Makaya
Dem. Rep. of the Congo 3°21S 18°1E **264** C3
Makedonija = North Macedonia ■
Europe 41°53N 21°40E **202** E5
Makefu *Cook Is.* 18°59S 169°55W **289** g
Makemo *French Polynesia* 16°35S 143°40W **289** f
Makeni *S. Leone* 8°55N 12°5W **262** D2
Makeyevka = Makiyivka
Ukraine 48°0N 38°0E **189** H9
Makgadikgadi △
Botswana 20°27S 24°47E **270** B3
Makgadikgadi Salt Pans
Botswana 20°40S 25°45E **270** B4
Makhachkala *Russia* 43°0N 47°30E **191** J8
Makhado = Louis Trichardt
S. Africa 23°1S 29°43E **271** B4
Makham, Ao *Thailand* 7°51N 98°25E **237** a
Makhanda *S. Africa* 33°19S 26°31E **270** D4
Makharadze = Ozurgeti
Georgia 41°55N 42°0E **191** K5
Makhfar al Buşayyah *Iraq* 30°0N 46°10E **246** D5
Makhmūr *Iraq* 35°46N 43°35E **213** E10
Makhtal *India* 16°30N 77°31E **245** E3
Makhyah, W. → *Yemen* 17°40N 49°1E **249** C5
Makian *Indonesia* 0°20N 127°20E **231** D7
Makina *Solomon Is.* 9°50S 160°50E **287** M11
Makindu *Kenya* 2°18S 37°50E **268** C4
Mäkiniitty *Finland* 60°20N 24°58E **121** A2
Makinka = Makinsk
Kazakhstan 52°37N 70°26E **217** B8
Makinsk *Kazakhstan* 52°37N 70°26E **217** B8
Makira = San Cristóbal
Solomon Is. 10°30S 161°0E **287** N11
Makiyivka *Ukraine* 48°0N 38°0E **189** H9
Makkah *Si. Arabia* 21°30N 39°54E **248** B2
Makkah □ *Si. Arabia* 21°30N 42°30E **248** B3
Makkovik *Canada* 55°10N 59°10W **299** A8
Makó *Hungary* 46°14N 20°33E **182** D5
Mako *Senegal* 12°52N 12°20W **262** C2
Makogai *Fiji* 17°28S 179°0E **287** A2
Makok *Gabon* 0°1S 9°35E **264** C1
Makokou *Gabon* 0°40N 12°50E **264** B2
Makongo
Dem. Rep. of the Congo 3°25N 26°17E **268** B2
Makoro
Dem. Rep. of the Congo 3°10N 29°59E **268** B2
Makoua *Congo* 0°5S 15°50E **264** C3
Maków Mazowiecki
Poland 52°52N 21°6E **185** F8
Maków Podhalański
Poland 49°43N 19°45E **185** J6
Makra *Greece* 36°15N 25°54E **205** E7
Makrai *India* 22°2N 77°0E **242** H7
Makran *Asia* 26°13N 61°30E **240** D1
Makran Coast Range
Pakistan 25°40N 64°0E **240** D2
Makrana *India* 27°2N 74°46E **242** F6
Makrany *Belarus* 51°48N 24°17E **185** G11
Makri *Greece* 40°52N 25°40E **203** F9
Makri *India* 19°46N 81°55E **244** E5
Makrigialos *Greece* 35°2N 25°59E **207** E6
Makthar *Tunisia* 35°48N 9°12E **258** A1
Mākū *Iran* 39°15N 44°31E **213** C11
Mākua *U.S.A.* 21°32N 158°13W **302** J13
Makueni □ *Kenya* 1°50S 37°40E **268** C4
Makum *India* 27°30N 95°23E **241** B5
Makumbi
Dem. Rep. of the Congo 5°50S 20°43E **265** D4
Makunda *Botswana* 22°30S 20°7E **270** B3
Makung *Taiwan* 23°34N 119°34E **225** C1
Makungo *Somalia* 0°49N 42°35E **267** D5
Makunudu Atoll *Maldives* 6°20N 72°35E **272** d
Makunza
Dem. Rep. of the Congo 8°52S 24°19E **265** D4
Makurazaki *Japan* 31°15N 130°20E **222** F2
Makurdi *Nigeria* 7°43N 8°35E **263** D6
Makushin Volcano
U.S.A. 53°53N 166°55W **303** K6
Makūyeh *Iran* 28°7N 53°9E **247** D7
Makwassie *S. Africa* 27°17S 26°0E **270** C4
Makwiro *Zimbabwe* 17°58S 30°25E **271** A5
Mal *India* 26°51N 88°45E **241** B2
Māl *Mauritania* 16°58N 13°23W **262** B2
Mal B. *Ireland* 52°50N 9°30W **166** D2
Mala = Mallow *Ireland* 52°8N 8°39W **166** D3
Mala *Peru* 12°40S 76°38W **330** C2
Mala ☼ *Australia* 21°39S 130°45E **278** D5
Mala, Pta. *Panama* 7°28N 80°2W **320** E3
Mala Belozërka *Ukraine* 47°12N 34°56E **189** J8
Malá Fatra △ *Slovakia* 49°10N 19°0E **181** B12
Mala Kapela *Croatia* 44°45N 15°30E **199** D12
Mala Panew → *Poland* 50°43N 17°54E **185** H4
Malá Strana *Czechia* 50°4N 14°24E **135** B2
Mala Vyska *Ukraine* 48°39N 31°36E **189** H6
Malabang *Phil.* 7°36N 124°3E **233** H5
Malabar *N.S.W., Australia* 33°58S 151°14E **139** B2
Malabar *Fla., U.S.A.* 28°0N 80°34W **317** H9
Malabar Coast *India* 11°0N 75°0E **245** J2
Malabar Hill *India* 18°57N 72°48E **130** B1
Malabar Pt. *India* 18°56N 72°48E **130** B1
Malabo = Rey Malabo
Eq. Guin. 3°45N 8°50E **263** E6
Malabon *Phil.* 14°39N 120°56E **127** B1
Malabrigo = Puerto Chicama
Peru 7°45S 79°20W **330** B2
Malabrigo Pt. *Phil.* 13°36N 121°15E **232** E3
Malabu *Nigeria* 9°32N 12°48E **263** D7
Malabuñgan *Phil.* 9°3N 117°38E **233** G1
Malacañang Palace *Phil.* 14°35N 120°59E **127** B1
Malacca, Straits of *Indonesia* 3°0N 101°0E **237** L3
Malacky *Slovakia* 48°27N 17°0E **181** C10
Malad City *U.S.A.* 42°12N 112°15W **304** E7
Maladeta *Spain* 42°39N 0°39E **196** C5
Maladzyechna *Belarus* 54°20N 26°50E **177** A14
Málaga *Colombia* 6°42N 72°44W **328** B3
Málaga *Spain* 36°43N 4°23W **195** J6
Málaga ✕ (AGP) *Spain* 36°38N 4°58W **195** J6
Málaga □ *Spain* 36°38N 4°58W **195** J6
Malagarasi *Tanzania* 5°5S 30°50E **268** D3
Malagarasi → *Tanzania* 5°12S 29°47E **268** D2
Malagasy Rep. = Madagascar ■
Africa 20°0S 47°0E **272** B2
Malagón *Spain* 39°11N 3°52W **195** F7
Malagón → *Spain* 37°35N 7°29W **195** H3
Malah *Syria* 32°33N 36°54E **251** F7
Malahide *Ireland* 53°26N 6°9W **166** C5
Malaimbandy *Madag.* 20°20S 45°36E **272** C2
Malaita *Solomon Is.* 9°0S 161°0E **287** M11
Malakal *South Sudan* 9°33N 31°40E **257** F3
Malakal Harb. *Palau* 7°19N 134°27E **288** c
Malakanagiri *India* 18°21N 81°54E **244** E5
Malakand *Pakistan* 34°40N 71°55E **242** B4
Malakoff *France* 48°49N 2°18E **134** B2
Malakula *Vanuatu* 16°15S 167°30E **287** F5
Malakwal *Pakistan* 32°34N 73°13E **242** C5
Malalag *Phil.* 6°36N 125°24E **233** H5
Malalaua *Papua N. G.* 8°4S 146°10E **286** E4
Malam *Chad* 11°27N 20°59E **259** F4
Malamala *Indonesia* 3°21S 120°55E **231** E6
Malanda *Australia* 17°22S 145°35E **280** B4
Malang *Indonesia* 7°59S 112°45E **235** D4
Malanga *Mozam.* 13°28S 36°7E **269** E4
Malangas *Phil.* 7°37N 123°1E **233** H4
Malangen *Norway* 69°24N 18°37E **160** B18
Malangwa *Nepal* 26°52N 85°34E **243** F11
Malanje *Angola* 9°36S 16°17E **265** D3
Malanje □ *Angola* 9°30S 16°0E **265** D3
Malanut B. *Phil.* 9°15N 117°59E **233** G1
Malapatan *Phil.* 5°59N 125°18E **233** J5
Malappuram *India* 11°7N 76°11E **245** J3
Mälaren *Sweden* 59°30N 17°10E **162** E11
Malargüe *Argentina* 35°32S 69°30W **334** D2
Malarhöjaen *Sweden* 59°18N 17°58E **139** B1
Malartic *Canada* 48°9N 78°9W **298** C4
Malaryta *Belarus* 51°50N 24°3E **185** G11
Malasiqui *Phil.* 15°55N 120°25E **232** D3
Malaspina Glacier
U.S.A. 59°50N 140°30W **303** G12
Malate *Phil.* 14°34N 120°59E **127** B1
Malatya *Turkey* 38°25N 38°20E **213** C8
Malatya □ *Turkey* 38°15N 38°0E **212** C7
Malawali, Pulau *Malaysia* 7°3N 117°18E **235** A5
Malawi ■ *Africa* 11°55S 34°0E **269** E3
Malawi, L. *Africa* 12°30S 34°30E **269** E3
Malay *Phil.* 11°54N 121°55E **233** F3
Malay Pen. *Asia* 7°25N 100°0E **237** J3
Malay Quarter *Cape Town, S. Africa* **118** c2
Malaya Belozërka = Mala Belozërka
Ukraine 47°12N 34°56E **189** J8
Malaya Neva *Russia* 59°56N 30°16E **137** B1
Malaya Okhta *Russia* 59°55N 30°25E **137** B2
Malaya Vishera *Russia* 58°55N 32°25E **188** C7
Malaya Viska = Mala Vyska
Ukraine 48°39N 31°36E **189** H6
Malaybalay *Phil.* 8°5N 125°7E **233** G5
Malāyer *Iran* 34°19N 48°51E **213** E13
Malaysia ■ *Asia* 5°0N 110°0E **235** B4
Malazgirt *Turkey* 39°10N 42°33E **213** C10
Malbaza *Niger* 13°59N 5°38E **263** C6
Malbon *Australia* 21°5S 140°17E **280** C3
Malbooma *Australia* 30°41S 134°11E **281** E1
Malbork *Poland* 54°3N 19°1E **184** D6
Malca Dube *Ethiopia* 6°47N 42°4E **267** C5
Malcésine *Italy* 45°46N 10°48E **198** C7
Malchin *Germany* 53°44N 12°44E **178** B8
Malchow *Berlin, Germany* 52°34N 13°29E **115** A3
Malchow *Mecklenburg-Vorpommern,*
Germany 53°28N 12°25E **178** B8
Malcolm *Australia* 28°51S 121°25E **279** E3
Malcolm, Pt. *Australia* 33°48S 123°45E **279** F3
Malczyce *Poland* 51°14N 16°29E **185** G3
Maldah *India* 25°2N 88°9E **243** G13
Maldegem *Belgium* 51°14N 3°26E **170** C3
Malden *London, U.K.* 51°23N 0°15W **125** B2
Malden *Mass., U.S.A.* 42°26N 71°3W **116** A2
Malden *Mo., U.S.A.* 36°34N 89°57W **308** G9
Malden I. *Kiribati* 4°3S 155°1W **289** H12
Maldives ■ *Ind. Oc.* 5°0N 73°0E **272** d
Maldon *Vic., Australia* 37°0S 144°6E **282** D6
Maldon *Essex, U.K.* 51°44N 0°42E **169** F8
Maldonado *Uruguay* 34°59S 55°0W **335** C5
Maldonado, Pta. *Mexico* 16°20N 98°33W **319** D5
Malè *Italy* 46°21N 10°55E **198** B7
Malé *Maldives* 4°10N 73°28E **272** d
Malé ✕ (MLE) *Maldives* 4°11N 73°28E **272** d
Malé Atoll *Maldives* 4°45N 73°15E **272** d
Malé Karpaty *Slovakia* 48°30N 17°20E **181** C10
Maleas, Akra *Greece* 36°28N 23°7E **204** E5
Malebo, Pool *Africa* 4°17S 15°20E **265** C3
Malegaon *India* 20°30N 74°38E **244** D2
Malei *Mozam.* 17°12S 36°58E **269** F4
Maleizen *Belgium* 50°45N 4°31E **116** B3
Malek *South Sudan* 6°4N 31°36E **257** F3
Malek Kandī *Iran* 37°9N 46°6E **213** D12
Malela *Bas-Congo,*
Dem. Rep. of the Congo 5°59S 12°37E **265** D2
Malela *Maniema,*
Dem. Rep. of the Congo 4°22S 26°8E **265** C5
Malema *Mozam.* 14°57S 37°20E **269** E4
Maleme *Greece* 35°31N 23°49E **207** E4
Malendok I. *Papua N. G.* 3°28S 153°13E **286** B7
Maler Kotla *India* 30°32N 75°58E **242** D6
Målerås *Sweden* 56°54N 15°34E **163** H9
Males *Greece* 35°6N 25°35E **207** E6
Malesherbes *France* 48°15N 2°24E **173** D9
Maleshevska Planina
Europe 41°38N 23°7E **202** E7
Malešice *Czechia* 50°5N 14°30E **135** B3
Malesina *Greece* 38°37N 23°14E **204** C5
Malestroit *France* 47°49N 2°25W **172** E4
Malfa *Italy* 38°35N 14°50E **201** D7
Malgobek *Russia* 43°30N 44°34E **191** J7
Malgomaj *Sweden* 64°40N 16°30E **160** D17
Malgrat de Mar *Spain* 41°39N 2°46E **196** D7
Malha *Sudan* 15°8N 25°10E **257** D2
Malhada *Brazil* 14°21S 43°47W **333** D3
Malhargarh *India* 24°17N 74°59E **242** G6
Malheur → *U.S.A.* 44°4N 116°59W **304** D5
Malheur L. *U.S.A.* 43°20N 118°48W **304** E4
Mali *Guinea* 12°10N 12°20W **262** C2
Mali ■ *Africa* 17°0N 3°0W **262** B4
Mali → *Myanmar* 25°42N 97°30E **241** C6
Mali Kanal *Serbia* 45°36N 19°24E **182** E4
Mali Kyun *Myanmar* 13°0N 98°20E **236** F2
Malia *Greece* 35°17N 25°32E **207** E6
Malia, Kolpos *Greece* 35°19N 25°27E **207** E6
Malibran, Teatro *Venice, Italy* **142** b3
Malibu *U.S.A.* 34°2N 118°41W **307** L8
Maligaya = Gloria *Phil.* 12°59N 121°30E **232** E3
Maliku = Minicoy I. *India* 8°17N 73°2E **245** K1
Maliku *Indonesia* 0°39S 123°16E **231** E6
Malili *Indonesia* 2°42S 121°6E **231** E6
Mälilla *Sweden* 57°23N 15°48E **163** G9
Malimba, Mts.
Dem. Rep. of the Congo 7°30S 29°30E **268** D2
Malin Hd. *Ireland* 55°23N 7°23W **166** A4
Malin Pen. *Ireland* 55°20N 7°17W **166** A4
Malindang, Mt. *Phil.* 8°13N 123°38E **233** G4
Malindi *Kenya* 3°12S 40°5E **268** C5
Malindi Marine ⌓ *Kenya* 3°15S 40°7E **268** C5
Malines = Mechelen
Belgium 51°2N 4°29E **170** C4
Malino *Indonesia* 1°0N 121°0E **231** D6
Malinyi *Tanzania* 8°56S 36°0E **269** D4
Malipo *China* 23°7N 104°42E **228** F5
Maliq *Albania* 40°45N 20°48E **202** F4
Malir → *Pakistan* 24°49N 67°4E **123** B2
Malita *Phil.* 6°19N 125°39E **233** H5
Maliwun *Myanmar* 10°17N 98°40E **237** G2
Maliya *India* 23°5N 70°46E **242** H4
Maljenik *Serbia* 43°54N 21°43E **202** C5
Malka Mari △ *Kenya* 4°11N 40°46E **268** B5
Malkapur *India* 20°53N 76°12E **244** D3
Malkara *Turkey* 40°53N 26°53E **203** F10
Malkhangiri = Malakanagiri
India 18°21N 81°54E **244** E5
Malkinia Górna *Poland* 52°42N 22°5E **185** F9
Malko Tarnovo *Bulgaria* 41°59N 27°31E **203** E11
Malko Tŭrnovo = Malko Tarnovo
Bulgaria 41°59N 27°31E **203** E11
Mall, The *Washington, D.C., U.S.A.* **143** b2
Mallacoota *Australia* 37°40S 149°40E **283** D8
Mallacoota Inlet
Australia 37°34S 149°40E **283** D8
Mallaig *U.K.* 57°0N 5°50W **167** D3
Mallala *Australia* 34°26S 138°30E **282** C3
Mallaoua *Niger* 13°2N 9°36E **263** C6
Mallard *U.S.A.* 42°56N 94°41W **310** D2
Mallawan *India* 27°4N 80°12E **243** F9
Mallawi *Egypt* 27°44N 30°44E **256** B3
Mallee Cliffs △ *Australia* 34°16S 142°32E **282** C5
Mallembe *Gabon* 3°34S 10°53E **264** C2
Mallemort *France* 43°43N 5°11E **175** E9
Malleny Mills *U.K.* 55°52N 3°20W **121** B2
Mâlles Venosta *Italy* 46°41N 10°32E **198** B7
Mallicolo = Malakula
Vanuatu 16°15S 167°30E **287** F5
Mallorca *Spain* 39°30N 3°0E **206** B4
Mallorytown *Canada* 44°29N 75°53W **313** B9
Mallow *Ireland* 52°8N 8°39W **166** D3
Malmbäck *Sweden* 57°34N 14°28E **163** G8
Malmberget *Sweden* 67°11N 20°40E **160** C19
Malmédy *Belgium* 50°25N 6°2E **170** D6
Malmesbury *S. Africa* 33°28S 18°41E **270** D2
Malmi *Finland* 60°15N 24°59E **121** B2
Malmivaara = Malmberget
Sweden 67°11N 20°40E **160** C19
Malmköping *Sweden* 59°8N 16°44E **162** E10
Malmö *Sweden* 55°36N 12°59E **163** J7
Malmok *Aruba* 12°36N 70°4W **322** f
Malmøya *Norway* 59°52N 10°45E **133** A3
Malmslätt *Sweden* 58°27N 15°33E **163** F9
Malmyzh *Russia* 56°31N 50°41E **190** B10
Malnaş *Romania* 46°2N 25°49E **183** D10
Malo *Vanuatu* 15°40S 167°11E **287** E5
Malo Konare *Bulgaria* 42°12N 24°24E **203** D8
Maloarkhangelsk *Russia* 52°28N 36°30E **189** F9
Maloca *Brazil* 0°43N 55°57W **329** C6
Malolo *Fiji* 17°45S 177°11E **287** A1
Malolos *Phil.* 14°50N 120°49E **232** D3
Malolotja ⌓ *Eswatini* 26°4S 31°6E **271** C5
Malombe L. *Malawi* 14°40S 35°15E **269** E4
Malomice *Poland* 51°34N 15°29E **185** G2
Malomir *Bulgaria* 42°16N 26°30E **203** D10
Malone *Fla., U.S.A.* 30°57N 85°10W **316** E4
Malone *N.Y., U.S.A.* 44°51N 74°18W **313** B10
Malong *China* 25°24N 103°34E **228** E4
Malonga
Dem. Rep. of the Congo 10°24S 23°10E **265** E4
Małopolskie □ *Poland* 49°50N 20°20E **185** J7
Malorad *Bulgaria* 43°28N 23°41E **202** C7
Maloti Mts. = Drakensberg
S. Africa 31°0S 28°0E **271** D4
Måløv *Denmark* 55°44N 12°20E **118** A1
Måløy *Norway* 61°57N 5°6E **164** C2
Maloyaroslovets *Russia* 55°2N 36°20E **188** E9
Malpartida de Cáceres
Spain 39°26N 6°30W **195** F4
Malpaso *Canary Is.* 27°43N 18°3W **153** e1
Malpaso, Presa = Netzahualcóyotl,
Presa *Mexico* 17°8N 93°35W **319** D6
Malpelo, I. de *Colombia* 4°3N 81°35W **289** G19
Malpense, Milano ✕ (MXP)
Italy 45°38N 8°43E **128** A1
Malpica de Bergantiños
Spain 43°19N 8°50W **194** B2
Malprabha → *India* 16°20N 76°5E **245** F3
Malpur *India* 23°21N 73°27E **242** H5
Malpura *India* 26°17N 75°23E **242** F6
Mals = Málles Venosta
Italy 46°41N 10°32E **198** B7
Malsiras *India* 17°52N 74°55E **244** F2
Malta *Brazil* 6°54S 37°31W **332** C4
Malta *Idaho, U.S.A.* 42°18N 113°22W **304** E7
Malta *Mont., U.S.A.* 48°21N 107°52W **304** B10
Malta ■ *Europe* 35°55N 14°26E **206** F7
Malta ✕ (MLA) *Malta* 35°52N 14°29E **206** F7
Malta Freeport *Malta* 35°49N 14°32E **206** F8
Maltahöhe *Namibia* 24°55S 17°0E **270** B2
Maltepe *Turkey* 40°55N 29°8E **203** F13
Malton *Ont., Canada* 43°42N 79°38W **141** A1
Malton *N. Yorks., U.K.* 54°8N 0°49W **168** C7
Malu'a *Solomon Is.* 8°20S 160°38E **287** M11
Maludam △ *Malaysia* 1°39N 111°2E **235** B4
Maluko = Manolo Fortich
Phil. 8°28N 124°50E **233** G5
Maluku *Indonesia* 1°0S 127°0E **231** E7
Maluku □ *Indonesia* 3°0S 128°0E **231** E7
Maluku Sea = Molucca Sea
Indonesia 0°0 125°0E **231** E6
Malumfashi *Nigeria* 11°48N 7°39E **263** C6
Malunda *Indonesia* 3°0S 118°50E **235** C5
Malundo *Angola* 14°51S 22°0E **265** E4
Malung *Sweden* 60°42N 13°44E **162** D7
Malungon *Phil.* 6°16N 125°14E **233** H5
Malungsfors *Sweden* 60°44N 13°33E **162** D7
Malur *India* 13°0N 77°55E **245** H3
Maluso *Phil.* 6°33N 121°53E **233** H3
Maluwe *Ghana* 8°40N 2°17W **262** D4
Malvalli *India* 12°28N 77°8E **245** H3
Malvan *India* 16°2N 73°30E **245** F1
Malvern *Vic., Australia* 37°50S 145°2E **128** B2
Malvern *Ont., Canada* 43°47N 79°13W **141** A3
Malvern *Gauteng, S. Africa* 26°11S 28°5E **123** B2
Malvern *Ark., U.S.A.* 34°22N 92°49W **314** D8
Malvern Hills *U.K.* 52°0N 2°19W **169** E5
Malvik *Norway* 63°25N 10°40E **164** A7
Malvinas, Is. = Falkland Is. ∅
Atl. Oc. 51°30S 59°0W **153** f
Malwal *South Sudan* 9°19N 31°35E **257** F3
Malý Dunaj → *Slovakia* 47°45N 18°9E **181** D11
Malya *Tanzania* 3°5S 33°38E **268** C3
Malye Derbety *Russia* 47°57N 44°42E **191** G7
Malyn *Ukraine* 50°46N 29°3E **177** C15
Malyy Lyakhovskiy, Ostrov
Russia 74°7N 140°36E **215** B15
Malyy Taymyr, Ostrov
Russia 78°6N 107°15E **215** B11
Mama *Russia* 58°18N 112°54E **215** D12
Mamaku *N.Z.* 38°5S 176°8E **284** E5
Mamala B. *U.S.A.* 21°15N 157°55W **302** K14
Mamanguape *Brazil* 6°50S 35°4W **332** C4
Mamanuca Group *Fiji* 17°35S 177°5E **287** A1
Mamarr Mitlā *Egypt* 30°2N 32°54E **251** H3
Mamasa *Indonesia* 2°55S 119°20E **235** C5
Mambajao *Phil.* 9°15N 124°43E **233** G5
Mambasa
Dem. Rep. of the Congo 1°22N 29°3E **268** B2
Mamberamo → *Indonesia* 2°0S 137°50E **231** E9
Mambéré → *C.A.R.* 3°31N 16°3E **264** B3
Mambéré-Kadéï □ *C.A.R.* 4°30N 15°30E **264** B3
Mambili → *Congo* 0°6N 16°5E **264** B3
Mambilima Falls *Zambia* 10°31S 28°45E **269** E2
Mambirima
Dem. Rep. of the Congo 11°25S 27°33E **269** E2
Mambo *Tanzania* 4°52S 38°22E **268** C4
Mambrui *Kenya* 3°5S 40°5E **268** C5
Mamburao *Phil.* 13°13N 120°39E **232** E3
Mamedkala *Russia* 42°10N 48°7E **191** J9
Mameigwess L. *Canada* 52°35N 87°50W **298** B2
Mamers *France* 48°21N 0°22E **172** D7
Mamfé *Cameroon* 5°50N 9°15E **263** D6
Māmī, Ra's *Yemen* 12°32N 54°30E **249** D6
Mamili △ *Namibia* 18°2S 24°1E **270** A3
Mamiña *Chile* 20°5S 69°14W **330** E4
Mamlyutka *Kazakhstan* 54°56N 68°32E **217** B7
Mammoth *U.S.A.* 32°43N 110°39W **305** K8
Mammoth Cave △
U.S.A. 37°8N 86°13W **308** G10
Mammoth Lakes *U.S.A.* 37°39N 118°59W **306** H8
Mamonovo *Russia* 54°28N 19°55E **184** D6
Mamoré → *Bolivia* 10°23S 65°53W **331** C4
Mamou *Guinea* 10°15N 12°0W **262** C2
Mamoudzou *Mayotte* 12°48S 45°14E **272** b
Mampang Prapatan
Indonesia 6°15S 106°49E **122** B1
Mampikony *Madag.* 16°6S 47°38E **272** B2
Mampoko
Dem. Rep. of the Congo 0°51N 18°42E **264** B3
Mampong *Ghana* 7°6N 1°26W **263** D4
Mampukuji *Japan* 35°36N 139°31E **140** B2
Mamry, Jezioro *Poland* 54°5N 21°50E **184** D8
Mamuil Malal, Paso
S. Amer. 39°35S 71°28W **336** A2
Mamuju *Indonesia* 2°41S 118°50E **235** C5
Ma'mūl *Oman* 18°8N 55°16E **249** C6
Mamuno *Botswana* 22°16S 20°1E **270** B3
Mamuras *Albania* 41°34N 19°41E **202** E3
Man *Côte d'Ivoire* 7°30N 7°40W **262** D3
Man → *India* 17°31N 75°32E **244** F2
Man, I. of *India* 8°28N 93°36E **245** K11
Man, I. of *U.K.* 54°15N 4°30W **168** C3
Man-Bazar *India* 23°4N 86°39E **243** H12
Man Budrukh *India* 19°2N 72°55E **130** A2
Man Kat *Myanmar* 22°5N 98°1E **241** D7
Man Khurd *India* 19°3N 72°55E **130** A2
Man Na *Myanmar* 23°27N 97°19E **241** D6
Man of War B. *Trin. & Tob.* 11°19N 60°34W **323** s
Mana *Fr. Guiana* 5°45N 53°55W **329** B7
Mānā *Hawai'i, U.S.A.* 22°2N 159°47W **302** A2
Mana → *Fr. Guiana* 5°45N 53°55W **329** B7
Mana Pools △ *Zimbabwe* 15°56S 29°25E **269** F2
Manaar, G. of = Mannar, G. of
Asia 8°30N 79°0E **245** K4
Manabí □ *Ecuador* 0°40S 80°5W **328** D1
Manacacias → *Colombia* 4°23N 72°4W **328** C3
Manacapuru *Brazil* 3°16S 60°37W **329** D5
Manacapuru → *Brazil* 3°18S 60°37W **329** D5
Manacor *Spain* 39°34N 3°13E **206** B4
Manadas *Azores* 38°38N 28°5W **153** d1
Manado *Indonesia* 1°29N 124°51E **231** D6
Managua *Nic.* 12°6N 86°20W **320** D2
Managua, L. de *Nic.* 12°20N 86°30W **320** D2
Manaia *N.Z.* 39°33S 174°8E **284** F3
Manakara *Madag.* 22°8S 48°1E **272** C2
Manakau *N.Z.* 42°15S 173°42E **285** C8
Manākhah *Yemen* 15°5N 43°44E **248** D3
Manakhat *Israel* 31°45N 35°11E **123** B2
Manali *India* 32°16N 77°10E **242** C7
Manam I. *Papua N. G.* 4°5S 145°0E **286** C3
Manama = Al Manāmah
Bahrain 26°10N 50°30E **247** E6
Manambao → *Madag.* 17°35S 44°0E **272** B1
Manambato *Madag.* 13°43S 49°7E **272** A2
Manambolo → *Madag.* 19°18S 44°22E **272** B1
Manambolosy *Madag.* 16°2S 49°40E **272** B2
Mánamo, Caño →
Venezuela 9°55N 62°16W **329** B5
Mānana I. *U.S.A.* 21°20N 157°40W **302** K14
Mananara *Madag.* 16°10S 49°46E **272** B2
Mananara → *Madag.* 23°21S 47°42E **272** C2
Mananara ⌓ *Madag.* 16°14S 49°45E **272** B2
Manangatang *Australia* 35°5S 142°54E **282** C5
Mananjary *Madag.* 21°13S 48°20E **272** C2
Manankoro *Mali* 10°28N 7°25W **262** C3
Manantali, L. de *Mali* 13°12N 10°28W **262** C2
Manantavadi *India* 11°49N 76°1E **245** J3
Manantenina *Madag.* 24°17S 47°19E **272** C2
Manaos = Manaus *Brazil* 3°0S 60°0W **329** D6
Manapire → *Venezuela* 7°42N 66°7W **328** B4
Manapla *Phil.* 10°58N 123°5E **233** F4
Manapouri *N.Z.* 45°34S 167°39E **285** F2
Manapouri, L. *N.Z.* 45°32S 167°32E **285** F2
Manapparai *India* 10°36N 78°25E **245** J4
Manaqil *Sudan* 14°15N 32°59E **257** E3
Manar → *India* 18°50N 77°20E **244** E3
Manār, Jabal *Yemen* 14°2N 44°17E **248** D4
Manaravolo *Madag.* 23°59S 45°39E **272** C2
Manas *Xinjiang Uygur,*
China 44°17N 86°10E **217** D11
Manas *Somalia* 2°57N 43°28E **267** D5
Manas → *India* 26°12N 90°40E **241** B3
Manas △ *India* 26°40N 91°0E **241** B3
Manas He → *China* 45°38N 85°12E **218** B6
Manas Hu *China* 45°45N 85°55E **217** C11
Manaslu *Nepal* 28°33N 84°33E **243** E11
Manasquan *U.S.A.* 40°8N 74°3W **313** F10
Manassa *U.S.A.* 37°11N 105°56W **305** H11
Manatí *Puerto Rico* 18°26N 66°29W **321** b
Manati B. *St. Helena* 16°0S 5°46W **153** h
Manau *Papua N. G.* 8°4S 148°0E **286** E4
Manaus *Brazil* 3°0S 60°0W **329** D6
Manavgat *Turkey* 36°47N 31°26E **250** B2
Manavgat → *Turkey* 36°43N 31°27E **250** B2
Manawan = Rizal *Phil.* 17°51N 121°21E **232** C3
Manawan L. *Canada* 55°24N 103°14W **297** B8
Manawatu → *N.Z.* 40°28S 175°12E **284** G4
Manawatu-Wanganui □
N.Z. 39°50S 175°30E **284** F4
Manay *Phil.* 7°17N 126°33E **233** H6
Manbij *Syria* 36°31N 37°57E **212** D7
Mancha Real *Spain* 37°48N 3°39W **195** H7
Manche □ *France* 49°10N 1°20W **172** C5
Manchegorsk *Russia* 67°54N 32°58E **214** C4
Manchester *Gt. Man., U.K.* 53°29N 2°12W **168** D5
Manchester *Calif.,*
U.S.A. 38°58N 123°41W **306** G3
Manchester *Conn.,*
U.S.A. 41°47N 72°31W **313** E12
Manchester *Ga., U.S.A.* 32°51N 84°37W **316** C5
Manchester *Iowa, U.S.A.* 42°29N 91°27W **310** B5
Manchester *Ky., U.S.A.* 37°9N 83°46W **309** G12
Manchester *Mich., U.S.A.* 42°9N 84°2W **311** B12
Manchester *N.H., U.S.A.* 42°59N 71°28W **313** D13
Manchester *N.Y., U.S.A.* 42°56N 77°16W **312** D7
Manchester *Ohio, U.S.A.* 38°41N 83°36W **311** F13
Manchester *Pa., U.S.A.* 40°4N 76°43W **313** F8
Manchester *Tenn., U.S.A.* 35°29N 86°5W **315** D11
Manchester *Vt., U.S.A.* 43°10N 73°5W **313** C11
Manchester Int. ✕ (MAN)
U.K. 53°21N 2°17W **168** D5
Manchester L. *Canada* 61°28N 107°29W **297** A7
Manchhar L. *Pakistan* 26°25N 67°39E **242** F2
Manchineel Bay *Grenada* 12°26N 61°29W **323** q
Manchou *Taiwan* 22°1N 120°50E **225** D2
Manchuria = Dongbei
China 45°0N 125°0E **227** D13
Manchurian Plain *China* 47°0N 124°0E **210** D14
Manciano *Italy* 42°35N 11°31E **199** F8
Mancifa *Ethiopia* 6°53N 41°50E **257** F5
Máncora *Peru* 4°9S 81°1W **330** A1
Mand → *India* 21°42N 83°15E **243** J10
Mand → *Iran* 28°20N 52°30E **247** D7
Manda *Ludewe, Tanzania* 10°30S 34°40E **269** E3
Manda *Mbeya, Tanzania* 7°58S 32°29E **268** D3
Manda *Mbeya, Tanzania* 8°30S 32°49E **269** D3
Manda △ *Chad* 9°45N 17°52E **259** G3
Mandabé *Madag.* 21°0S 44°55E **272** C1
Mandaguari *Brazil* 23°32S 51°42W **335** A5
Mandah = Töhöm
Mongolia 44°27N 108°2E **226** B4
Mandai *Singapore* 1°24N 103°45E **138** A2
Mandal *Norway* 58°2N 7°25E **164** F4
Mandala, Puncak
Indonesia 4°44S 140°20E **231** E10
Mandalay *Myanmar* 22°0N 96°4E **241** E6
Mandalay □ *Myanmar* 22°0N 96°5E **241** E5
Mandale = Mandalay
Myanmar 22°0N 96°4E **241** E6
Mandalgarh *India* 25°12N 75°6E **242** G6
Mandalgovĭ *Mongolia* 45°45N 106°10E **226** B4
Mandalī *Iraq* 33°43N 45°28E **213** F11
Mandalselva → *Norway* 58°2N 7°28E **164** F4
Mandaluyong *Phil.* 14°35N 121°1E **127** B2
Mandan *U.S.A.* 46°50N 100°54W **308** B3
Mandaoli *India* 28°37N 77°17E **120** B2
Mandaon *Phil.* 12°13N 123°17E **232** E4
Mandaqui → *Brazil* 23°30S 46°40W **137** A2
Mandar, Teluk *Indonesia* 3°32S 119°21E **235** C5

Mandara Mts. W. Afr. 10°40N 13°40E 259 F2
Mándas Italy 39°40N 9°8E 200 C2
Mandasor = Mandsaur India 24°3N 75°8E 242 G6
Mandaue Phil. 10°20N 123°56E 233 F4
Mandel Afghan. 33°17N 61°53E 240 B1
Mandelieu-la-Napoule France 43°34N 6°57E 175 E10
Mandera Kenya 3°55N 41°53E 268 B5
Mandera □ Kenya 3°20N 40°40E 268 B5
Mandeville Jamaica 18°2N 77°31W 320 a
Mandi India 31°39N 76°58E 242 D7
Mandi Burewala Pakistan 30°9N 72°41E 242 D5
Mandi Dabwali India 29°58N 74°42E 242 E6
Mandiana Guinea 10°37N 8°39W 262 C3
Mandigos = Manica Mozam. 18°58S 32°59E 271 A5
Mandimba Mozam. 14°20S 35°40E 269 E4
Mandioli Indonesia 0°40S 127°20E 231 E7
Mandioré, L. S. Amer. 18°8S 57°33W 331 D6
Mandla India 22°39N 80°30E 243 H9
Mandø Denmark 55°18N 8°33E 163 J2
Mandoli India 28°41N 77°18E 120 A2
Mandorah Australia 12°32S 130°42E 278 B5
Mandoto Madag. 19°34S 46°17E 272 B2
Mandoudi Greece 38°48N 23°29E 204 C5
Mandoul Chad 9°40N 15°30E 259 G3
Mandra Greece 38°4N 23°30E 204 C5
Mandra Pakistan 33°23N 73°12E 242 C5
Mandraki Greece 36°36N 27°11E 205 E9
Mandrare → Madag. 25°10S 46°30E 272 D2
Mandritsara Madag. 15°50S 48°49E 272 B2
Mandronarivo Madag. 21°7S 45°38E 272 C2
Mandsaur India 24°3N 75°8E 242 G6
Mandurah Australia 32°36S 115°48E 279 F2
Mandúria Italy 40°24N 17°38E 201 B10
Mandvi Gujarat, India 22°51N 69°22E 242 H3
Mandvi Maharashtra, India 18°56N 72°50E 130 B2
Mandya India 12°30N 77°0E 245 H3
Mandzai Pakistan 30°55N 67°6E 242 D2
Mané Burkina Faso 12°59N 1°21W 263 C4
Maneh Iran 37°39N 57°7E 247 B8
Manenberg S. Africa 33°58S 18°33E 118 A2
Manengouba, Mts. Cameroon 5°0N 9°50E 263 E6
Maner → India 18°30N 79°40E 244 E4
Manera Madag. 22°55S 44°20E 272 C1
Manérbio Italy 45°21N 10°8E 198 C7
Maneroo Cr. → Australia 23°21S 143°53E 280 C3
Manfalût Egypt 27°20N 30°52E 256 B3
Manfred Australia 33°19S 143°45E 282 B5
Manfredónia Italy 41°38N 15°55E 199 G12
Manfredónia, G. di Italy 41°35N 16°5E 199 G13
Mang Kung Uk Hong Kong, China 22°18N 114°16E 122 B3
Mang-won S. Korea 37°33N 126°55E 137 B1
Manga Brazil 14°46S 43°56W 333 D3
Manga Burkina Faso 11°40N 1°4W 263 C4
Manga Congo 0°13S 16°5E 264 C3
Manga Niger 15°0N 14°0E 259 F2
Mangabeiras, Chapada das Brazil 10°0S 46°30W 332 D2
Mangai Dem. Rep. of the Congo 4°2S 19°33E 265 C3
Mangaia Cook Is. 21°55S 157°55W 289 K12
Mangakino N.Z. 38°22S 175°47E 284 E4
Mangal Phil. 6°25N 121°58E 233 H3
Mangalagiri India 16°26N 80°36E 245 F5
Mangaldai India 26°26N 92°2E 241 B4
Mangaldan Phil. 16°4N 120°24E 232 C3
Mangalia Romania 43°50N 28°35E 183 G13
Mangalmé Chad 12°26N 19°37E 259 F3
Mangalore = Mangaluru India 12°55N 74°47E 245 H2
Mangaluru India 12°55N 74°47E 245 H2
Mangalvedha India 17°31N 75°28E 244 F2
Mangan India 27°31N 88°32E 241 B2
Mangaon India 18°15N 73°20E 244 E1
Mangarrayi ✪ Australia 15°5S 133°10E 280 B1
Mangawan India 24°41N 81°33E 243 G9
Mangaweka N.Z. 39°48S 175°47E 284 F4
Mangaweka, Mt. N.Z. 39°49S 176°5E 284 F5
Mange Dem. Rep. of the Congo 0°54N 20°30E 264 B4
Manger Norway 60°38N 5°3E 164 D2
Mangetti △ Namibia 18°43S 19°8E 270 A2
Manggar Indonesia 2°50S 108°10E 235 C3
Manggawitu Indonesia 4°8S 133°32E 231 E8
Mangghystaū Kazakhstan 43°40N 51°13E 216 D4
Mangghystaū □ Kazakhstan 45°0N 53°0E 216 D4
Mangghystaū Tübegi Kazakhstan 44°30N 52°30E 216 D4
Manggis Indonesia 8°29S 115°31E 231 J18
Mangin Taungdan Myanmar 24°15N 95°45E 241 C5
Mangindrano Madag. 14°17S 48°58E 272 A2
Mangkalihat, Tanjung Indonesia 1°2N 118°59E 235 B5
Mangkururrpa ✪ Australia 20°35S 129°43E 278 D4
Mangla Pakistan 33°7N 73°39E 242 C5
Mangla Dam Pakistan 33°9N 73°44E 243 C5
Manglares, C. Colombia 1°36N 79°2W 328 C2
Manglaur India 29°44N 77°49E 242 E7
Mangle, B. de Venezuela 10°57N 64°10W 329 a
Mangle, Pta. Venezuela 10°52N 64°3W 329 a
Manglillo Venezuela 10°57N 64°19W 329 a
Manglisi Georgia 41°41N 44°22E 191 K7
Mangnai China 37°52N 91°43E 218 D7
Mangnai Zhen China 38°24N 90°14E 217 E12
Mango Togo 10°20N 0°30E 263 C5
Mango Tonga 20°17S 174°29W 287 Q13
Mangoche Malawi 14°25S 35°16E 269 E4
Mangoky → Madag. 21°29S 43°41E 272 C1
Mangole Indonesia 1°50S 125°55E 231 E6
Mangolpuri India 28°41N 77°6E 120 A1
Mangombe Dem. Rep. of the Congo 1°20S 26°48E 268 C2
Mangonui N.Z. 35°1S 173°32E 284 B2
Mangoro → Madag. 20°0S 48°45E 272 C2
Mangrol Mad. P., India 21°7N 70°7E 242 J4
Mangrol Raj., India 25°20N 76°31E 242 G6
Mangrul Pir India 20°19N 77°21E 244 D3
Mangshi = Luxi China 24°27N 98°36E 228 E2
Manguaba = Pilar Brazil 9°36S 35°56W 332 C4
Mangualde Portugal 40°38N 7°48W 194 E3
Mangueigne Chad 10°30N 21°15E 259 F4
Mangueira, L. da Brazil 33°0S 52°50W 335 C5
Manguéni, Hamada Niger 22°35N 12°40E 258 D2
Mangui China 52°3N 122°3E 219 A13
Mangum U.S.A. 34°53N 99°30W 314 D5
Mangungu Dem. Rep. of the Congo 5°16S 19°36E 265 D3
Manguri Australia 28°58S 134°22E 281 A1
Mangyshlak, Poluostrov = Mangghystaū Tübegi Kazakhstan 44°30N 52°30E 216 D4
Manhattan Kans., U.S.A. 39°11N 96°35W 308 F5
Manhattan New York, U.S.A. 132 d2
Manhattan Beach U.S.A. 40°34N 73°56W 132 C2
Manhattan Bridge New York, U.S.A. 132 f2
Manhatten U.S.A. 41°26N 87°59W 311 C9
Manhiça Mozam. 25°23S 32°49E 271 C5
Manhuaçu Brazil 20°15S 42°2W 333 F3
Manhumirim Brazil 20°22S 41°57W 333 F3
Maní Colombia 4°49N 72°17W 328 C3
Mania → Madag. 19°42S 45°22E 272 B2
Maniago Italy 46°10N 12°43E 199 B9
Manica Mozam. 18°58S 32°59E 271 A5
Manica □ Mozam. 19°10S 33°45E 271 A5
Manicahan Phil. 7°1N 122°12E 233 H4
Manicaland □ Zimbabwe 19°0S 32°30E 269 F3
Manicoré Brazil 5°48S 61°16W 331 B5
Manicoré → Brazil 5°51S 61°19W 331 B5
Manicouagan → Canada 49°30N 68°30W 299 C6
Manicouagan, Rés. Canada 51°5N 68°40W 299 B6
Maniema □ Dem. Rep. of the Congo 3°0S 26°0E 268 C2
Manīfah Si. Arabia 27°44N 49°0E 247 E6
Manifold, C. Australia 22°41S 150°50E 280 C5
Maniganggo China 31°56N 99°10E 228 B2
Manigotagan Canada 51°6N 96°18W 297 C9
Manigotagan → Canada 51°7N 96°20W 297 C9
Manihari India 25°21N 87°38E 243 G12
Manihi French Polynesia 14°24S 145°56W 289 f
Manihiki Cook Is. 10°24S 161°1W 289 J11
Manihiki Plateau Pac. Oc. 11°0S 164°0W 289 J11
Maniitsoq Greenland 65°26N 52°55W 154 D5
Manika, Plateau de la Dem. Rep. of the Congo 10°0S 25°5E 269 E2
Manikchhari Bangla. 22°51N 91°50E 241 D3
Manikganj Bangla. 23°52N 90°0E 241 D3
Manikpur India 25°4N 81°7E 243 G9
Manila Phil. 14°35N 120°58E 127 B1
Manila Utah, U.S.A. 40°59N 109°43W 304 F9
Manila B. Phil. 14°40N 120°35E 232 D3
Manila Ninoy Aquino Int. ✈ (MNL) Phil. 14°31N 121°0E 127 B2
Manildra Australia 33°11S 148°41E 283 B8
Manilla Australia 30°45S 150°43E 283 A9
Manilva Spain 36°23N 5°15W 195 J5
Manimpé Mali 14°11N 5°28W 262 C3
Maningrida Australia 12°3S 134°13E 280 A1
Maninian Côte d'Ivoire 10°3N 7°52W 262 C3
Maninjau, Danau Indonesia 0°19S 100°11E 234 C2
Manipa, Selat Indonesia 3°20S 127°25E 231 E7
Manipur □ India 25°0N 94°0E 241 C5
Manipur → Myanmar 23°45N 94°20E 241 D5
Manisa Turkey 38°38N 27°30E 205 C9
Manisa □ Turkey 38°40N 28°0E 205 C9
Manistee U.S.A. 44°15N 86°19W 308 C10
Manistee → U.S.A. 44°15N 86°21W 308 C10
Manistique U.S.A. 45°57N 86°15W 308 C10
Manito U.S.A. 40°26N 89°47W 310 D7
Manitoba □ Canada 53°30N 97°0W 297 B9
Manitoba, L. Canada 51°0N 98°45W 297 C9
Manitou Canada 49°15N 98°32W 297 D9
Manitou, L. Canada 50°55N 65°17W 299 B6
Manitou Beach U.S.A. 41°58N 84°19W 311 C12
Manitou Is. U.S.A. 45°8N 86°0W 308 C10
Manitou L. Canada 52°43N 109°43W 297 C7
Manitou Springs U.S.A. 38°52N 104°55W 304 G11
Manitoulin I. Canada 45°40N 82°30W 298 C3
Manitouwadge Canada 49°8N 85°48W 298 C2
Manitowoc U.S.A. 44°5N 87°40W 308 C10
Manitsauá-Missu → Brazil 10°58S 53°20W 331 C7
Maniyachi India 8°51N 77°55E 245 K3
Manizales Colombia 5°5N 75°32W 328 B2
Manja Madag. 21°26S 44°20E 272 C1
Manjacaze Mozam. 24°45S 34°0E 271 B5
Manjakandriana Madag. 18°55S 47°47E 272 B2
Manjhand Pakistan 25°50N 68°10E 242 G3
Manjiang China 41°56N 127°35E 224 B3
Manjimup Australia 34°15S 116°6E 279 F2
Manjlegaon India 19°9N 76°14E 244 E3
Manjo Cameroon 4°50N 9°49E 264 B1
Manjra → India 18°49N 77°52E 244 E3
Mankato Kans., U.S.A. 39°47N 98°13W 308 F4
Mankato Minn., U.S.A. 44°10N 94°0W 308 C6
Mankayan Phil. 16°52N 120°47E 232 C3
Mankayane Eswatini 26°40S 31°4E 271 C5
Mankera Pakistan 31°23N 71°26E 242 D4
Mankim Cameroon 5°6N 12°3E 263 D7
Mankkaa Finland 60°11N 24°47E 121 B1
Mankono Côte d'Ivoire 8°1N 6°10W 262 D3
Mankota Canada 49°25N 107°5W 297 D7
Mankulam Sri Lanka 9°8N 80°26E 245 K5
Manlay = Üydzin Mongolia 44°9N 107°0E 226 B4
Manleluag △ Phil. 15°4N 120°17E 232 D3
Manley Hot Springs U.S.A. 65°0N 150°38W 303 D10
Manlleu Spain 42°2N 2°17E 196 C7
Manly Australia 33°47S 151°17E 139 A2
Manmad India 20°18N 74°28E 244 D2
Mann, L. U.S.A. 28°32N 81°35W 133 A2
Mann Ranges Australia 26°6S 130°5E 279 E5
Manna Indonesia 4°25S 102°55E 234 C2
Mannahill Australia 32°25S 140°0E 282 B4
Mannar Sri Lanka 9°1N 79°54E 245 K4
Mannar, G. of Asia 8°30N 79°0E 245 K4
Mannar I. Sri Lanka 9°5N 79°45E 245 K4
Mannargudi India 10°45N 79°51E 245 J4
Mannheim Germany 49°29N 8°29E 179 F4
Manning Alta., Canada 56°53N 117°39W 296 B5
Manning Oreg., U.S.A. 45°45N 123°13W 306 E3
Manning S.C., U.S.A. 33°42N 80°13W 316 B9
Manning → Australia 31°52S 152°43E 283 A10
Manning Str. Solomon Is. 7°30S 158°0E 287 L10
Mannswörth Austria 48°8N 16°30E 142 B3
Mannu → Italy 39°16N 9°0E 200 C2
Mannu, C. Italy 40°3N 8°21E 200 B1
Mannum Australia 34°50S 139°20E 282 C3
Mano S. Leone 8°3N 12°2W 262 D2
Mano → Liberia 6°56N 11°30W 262 D2
Manoa Bolivia 9°40S 65°27W 331 B4
Manoharpur India 22°23N 85°12E 243 H11
Manokotak U.S.A. 58°58N 159°3W 303 G8
Manokwari Indonesia 0°54S 134°0E 231 E8
Manolada Greece 38°4N 21°21E 204 C3
Manolo Fortich Phil. 8°28N 124°50E 233 G5
Manombo Madag. 22°57S 43°28E 272 C1
Manono Dem. Rep. of the Congo 7°15S 27°25E 268 D2
Manono Samoa 13°50S 172°5W 287 V19
Manoppello Italy 42°15N 14°3E 199 F11
Manor Park U.K. 51°32N 0°1E 125 A4
Manora Pakistan 24°47N 66°58E 123 B1
Manora Pt. Pakistan 24°47N 66°58E 123 B1
Manorhamilton Ireland 54°18N 8°11W 166 B3
Manosque France 43°49N 5°47E 175 E9
Manotick Canada 45°13N 75°41W 313 A9
Manouane → Canada 49°30N 71°10W 299 C5
Manouane, L. Canada 50°45N 70°45W 299 B5
Manovo-Gounda Saint Floris △ C.A.R. 9°30N 21°25E 264 A4
Manp'o N. Korea 41°6N 126°24E 224 B3
Manpojin = Manp'o N. Korea 41°6N 126°24E 224 B3
Manpur Chhattisgarh, India 23°17N 83°35E 243 H10
Manpur Chhattisgarh, India 20°22N 80°43E 244 D5
Manpur Mad. P., India 22°26N 75°37E 242 H6
Manquehue, Cerro Chile 33°21S 70°35W 137 B2
Manra Kiribati 4°27S 171°15W 277 A16
Manresa Spain 41°48N 1°50E 196 D6
Mansa Gujarat, India 23°27N 72°45E 242 H5
Mansa Punjab, India 30°0N 75°27E 242 E6
Mansa Zambia 11°13S 28°55E 269 E2
Mansa Konko Gambia 13°28N 15°33W 262 C1
Mansalay Phil. 12°31N 121°26E 232 E3
Månsåsen Sweden 63°5N 14°18E 162 A8
Mansehra Pakistan 34°20N 73°15E 242 B5
Mansel I. Canada 62°0N 80°0W 295 E15
Mansfield Vic., Australia 37°4S 146°6E 283 D7
Mansfield Notts., U.K. 53°9N 1°11W 168 D6
Mansfield Ga., U.S.A. 33°31N 83°44W 316 B6
Mansfield La., U.S.A. 32°2N 93°43W 314 E8
Mansfield Mass., U.S.A. 42°2N 71°13W 313 D13
Mansfield Ohio, U.S.A. 40°45N 82°31W 312 F2
Mansfield Pa., U.S.A. 41°48N 77°5W 312 E7
Mansfield Tex., U.S.A. 32°33N 97°8W 120 C3
Mansfield, Mt. U.S.A. 44°33N 72°49W 313 B12
Mansi Myanmar 24°48N 95°52E 241 C5
Mansidão Brazil 10°43S 44°2W 332 D3
Mansilla de las Mulas Spain 42°30N 5°25W 194 C5
Mansle France 45°52N 0°12E 174 C4
Manso → Brazil 13°50S 47°0W 333 D2
Mansôa Guinea-Biss. 12°0N 15°20W 262 C1
Manson U.S.A. 42°32N 94°32W 310 B2
Manson Creek Canada 55°37N 124°32W 296 B4
Mansoura Algeria 36°1N 4°31E 261 A5
Manta Ecuador 1°0S 80°40W 328 D1
Manta, B. de Ecuador 0°54S 80°44W 328 D1
Mantalingajan, Mt. Phil. 8°55N 117°45E 233 G1
Mantantale Dem. Rep. of the Congo 2°10S 20°11E 264 C4
Mantare Tanzania 2°42S 33°13E 268 C3
Mantaro → Peru 12°16S 73°57W 330 C3
Manteca U.S.A. 37°48N 121°13W 306 H5
Mantecal Venezuela 7°34N 69°17W 328 B4
Mantena Brazil 18°47S 40°59W 333 E3
Manteno U.S.A. 41°15N 87°50W 311 C9
Manteo U.S.A. 35°55N 75°40W 315 D17
Mantes-la-Jolie France 48°58N 1°41E 173 D8
Mantha India 19°40N 76°23E 244 E3
Manthani India 18°40N 79°35E 244 E4
Manti U.S.A. 39°16N 111°38W 304 G8
Mantiqueira, Serra da Brazil 22°0S 44°0W 333 F3
Manton U.S.A. 44°25N 85°24W 309 C11
Mantorp Sweden 58°21N 15°20E 163 F9
Mántova Italy 45°9N 10°48E 198 C7
Mänttä Vilppula Finland 62°3N 24°40E 188 A3
Mantua = Mántova Italy 45°9N 10°48E 198 C7
Mantung Australia 34°35S 140°3E 282 C4
Manturovo Russia 58°23N 44°45E 190 A7
Manú Peru 12°10S 70°51W 330 C3
Manú → Peru 12°16S 70°55W 330 C3
Manu'a Is. Amer. Samoa 14°13S 169°35W 302 g
Manuel Alves → Brazil 11°19S 48°28W 333 D2
Manuel Alves Grande → Brazil 7°27S 47°35W 332 C2
Manuel Urbano Brazil 8°53S 69°18W 330 B4
Manui Indonesia 3°35S 123°5E 231 E6
Manukan Phil. 8°32N 123°12E 233 G4
Manukau N.Z. 37°0S 174°52E 284 D3
Manukau Harbour N.Z. 37°3S 174°45E 284 D3
Manunui N.Z. 38°54S 175°21E 284 E4
Manuoha N.Z. 38°39S 177°7E 284 E6
Manuripi → Bolivia 11°6S 67°36W 330 C4
Manus □ Papua N. G. 2°0S 147°0E 286 B4
Manus I. Papua N. G. 2°0S 147°0E 286 B4
Manvi India 15°57N 76°59E 245 G3
Manwan Dam China 24°44N 100°20E 228 E3
Manwath India 19°19N 76°32E 244 E3
Many U.S.A. 31°34N 93°29W 314 F8
Manyallaluk ✪ Australia 14°16S 132°49E 278 B5
Manyani Kenya 3°5S 38°30E 268 C4
Manyara □ Tanzania 4°30S 37°10E 268 C4
Manyara, L. Tanzania 3°40S 35°50E 268 C4
Manyara △ Tanzania 3°35S 35°50E 268 C4
Manyas Turkey 40°2N 27°59E 203 F11
Manyas Gölü = Kus Gölü Turkey 40°10N 27°55E 203 F11
Manyava Ukraine 48°39N 24°21E 183 B9
Manych → Russia 47°13N 40°40E 191 G5
Manych-Gudilo, Ozero Russia 46°24N 42°38E 191 G6
Manyonga → Tanzania 4°10S 34°15E 268 C3
Manyoni Tanzania 5°45S 34°55E 268 D3
Manzai Pakistan 32°12N 70°15E 242 C4
Manzala, Bahra el Egypt 31°10N 31°56E 256 H7
Manzanar ⌓ U.S.A. 36°44N 118°9W 306 J7
Manzanares Spain 39°2N 3°22W 195 F7
Manzanares, Canal de Spain 40°19N 3°38W 127 C2
Manzaneda Spain 42°12N 7°15W 194 C3
Manzanilla Pt. Trin. & Tob. 10°31N 61°1W 323 t
Manzanillo Cuba 20°20N 77°31W 320 B4
Manzanillo Colima, Mexico 19°3N 104°20W 318 D4
Manzanillo Venezuela 11°9N 63°54W 329 a
Manzanillo, Pta. Panama 9°30N 79°40W 320 E4
Manzano Mts. U.S.A. 34°40N 106°20W 305 J10
Manzarīyeh Iran 34°53N 50°50E 247 C6
Manzhouli China 49°35N 117°25E 219 B12
Manzini Eswatini 26°30S 31°25E 271 C5
Manzouli = Manzhouli China 49°35N 117°25E 219 B12
Manzur Vadisi △ Turkey 39°10N 39°30E 246 B3
Mao Chad 14°4N 15°19E 259 F3
Maó Spain 39°53N 4°16E 206 B5
Mao Mausoleum Beijing, China 114 c3
Maoka = Kholmsk Russia 47°40N 142°5E 215 E15
Maoke, Pegunungan Indonesia 3°40S 137°30E 231 E9
Maolin China 43°58N 123°30E 227 C12
Maoming China 21°50N 110°54E 229 G8
Maopi T'ou China 21°56N 120°43E 225 E2
Maouri, Dallol → Niger 12°5N 3°30E 263 C5
Maoxian China 31°41N 103°49E 228 B4
Maoxing China 45°28N 124°40E 227 B13
Map Micronesia 9°35N 138°10E 287 R16
Mapalma Dem. Rep. of the Congo 2°3N 24°30E 264 B4
Mapam Yumco China 30°45N 81°28E 243 D9
Mapastepec Mexico 15°26N 92°54W 319 D6
Mapfongui Gabon 1°15S 12°59E 264 C2
Maphrao, Ko Thailand 7°56N 98°26E 237 a
Mapia, Kepulauan Indonesia 0°50N 134°20E 231 D8
Mapimí Mexico 25°49N 103°51W 318 B4
Mapimí, Bolsón de Mexico 27°0N 104°15W 318 B4
Maping China 31°34N 113°32E 229 B9
Mapinga Tanzania 6°40S 39°12E 268 D4
Mapinhane Mozam. 22°20S 35°0E 271 B6
Mapire Venezuela 7°45N 64°42W 329 B5
Maple → U.S.A. 42°59N 84°57W 311 B12
Maple Creek Canada 49°55N 109°29W 297 D7
Maple Valley U.S.A. 47°25N 122°3W 306 C4
Mapleton U.S.A. 44°2N 123°52W 304 D2
Mapo S. Korea 37°32N 126°56E 137 B1
Mapoon ✪ Australia 11°44S 142°8E 280 A3
Mapourika, L. N.Z. 43°16S 170°12E 285 D5
Maprik Papua N. G. 3°44S 143°3E 286 B2
Mapuca India 15°36N 73°46E 245 G1
Mapuera → Brazil 1°5S 57°2W 329 D6
Mapulanguene Mozam. 24°29S 32°6E 271 B5
Mapungubwe △ S. Africa 22°12S 29°22E 271 B4
Maputo Mozam. 25°58S 32°32E 271 C5
Maputo □ Mozam. 26°0S 32°25E 271 C5
Maputo, B. de Mozam. 25°50S 32°45E 271 C5
Maputo ⌓ Mozam. 26°23S 32°48E 271 C5
Maqanshy Kazakhstan 46°47N 82°1E 217 C10
Maqat Kazakhstan 47°39N 53°19E 187 E9
Maqên China 34°24N 100°6E 218 E9
Maqên Gangri China 34°55N 99°18E 218 E8
Maqiaohe China 44°40N 130°30E 227 B16
Maqnā Si. Arabia 28°25N 34°50E 251 K5
Maqran, W. → Si. Arabia 20°55N 47°12E 248 B4
Maqteïr Mauritania 21°50N 11°40W 260 D2
Maqu China 33°52N 101°42E 218 E9
Maquan He = Brahmaputra → Asia 23°40N 90°35E 241 D3
Maqueda Spain 40°4N 4°22W 194 E6
Maqueda Channel Phil. 13°42N 124°1E 232 E5
Maquela do Zombo Angola 6°0S 15°15E 265 D3
Maquinchao Argentina 41°15S 68°50W 336 B3
Maquoketa U.S.A. 42°4N 90°40W 310 B6
Mar Canada 44°49N 81°12W 312 B3
Mar, Serra do Brazil 25°30S 49°0W 335 B6
Mar Chiquita, L. Argentina 30°40S 62°50W 334 C3
Mar del Plata Argentina 38°0S 57°30W 334 D4
Mar Menor Spain 37°40N 0°45W 197 H4
Mar Vista U.S.A. 34°0N 118°25W 126 B2
Mara Guyana 6°0N 57°36W 329 B6
Mara India 28°11N 94°14E 241 A5
Mara Tanzania 1°30S 34°32E 268 C3
Mara □ Tanzania 1°45S 34°20E 268 C3
Mara Rosa Brazil 13°58S 49°9W 333 D2
Maraã Brazil 1°52S 65°25W 328 D4
Maraa Tahiti 17°46S 149°34W 289 e
Marabá Brazil 5°20S 49°5W 332 C2
Marabahan Indonesia 3°0S 114°45E 235 C4
Maraboon, L. Australia 23°41S 148°0E 280 C4
Maracá, I. de Brazil 2°10N 50°30W 329 C7
Maracaibo Venezuela 10°40N 71°37W 328 A3
Maracaibo, L. de Venezuela 9°40N 71°30W 328 B3
Maracaju Brazil 21°38S 55°9W 335 A4
Maracajú, Serra de Brazil 20°57S 55°1W 331 E6
Maracanã Brazil 0°46S 47°27W 332 B2
Maracanã, Estádio Rio de J., Brazil 22°54S 43°13W 135 B1
Maracanaú Brazil 3°52S 38°38W 332 B4
Maracás Brazil 13°26S 40°18W 333 D3
Maracas Trin. & Tob. 10°41N 61°24W 323 t
Maracas → Trin. & Tob. 10°34N 61°25W 323 t
Maracas B. Trin. & Tob. 10°45N 61°26W 323 t
Maracas Bay Village Trin. & Tob. 10°46N 61°28W 323 t
Maracas Falls Trin. & Tob. 10°44N 61°24W 323 t
Maracay Venezuela 10°15N 67°28W 328 A4
Maracena Spain 37°12N 3°38W 195 H7
Marādah Libya 29°15N 19°15E 258 C3
Maradi Niger 13°29N 7°20E 263 C6
Maradi □ Niger 14°15N 7°15E 263 C6
Marāgheh Iran 37°30N 46°12E 213 D12
Maragogipe Brazil 12°46S 38°55W 333 D4
Marāh Si. Arabia 25°0N 45°35E 246 E5
Marahoué △ Côte d'Ivoire 8°0N 7°8W 262 D3
Marais du Cotentin et du Bessin ⌓ France 49°10N 1°30W 172 C5
Marais Poitevin, Val de Sèvre et Vendée ⌓ France 46°18N 0°35W 174 B3
Maraisburg = Hofmeyr S. Africa 31°39S 25°50E 270 D4
Marajó, B. de Brazil 1°0S 48°30W 332 B2
Marajo, I. de Brazil 1°0S 49°30W 332 B2
Marākand Iran 38°51N 45°16E 246 B5
Marakele △ S. Africa 24°30S 25°30E 271 D4
Maralal Kenya 1°0N 36°38E 268 B4
Maralinga Australia 30°13S 131°32E 279 F5
Maralinga Tjarutja ✪ Australia 29°30S 131°0E 279 E5
Maram India 25°25N 94°6E 241 C5
Marama Australia 35°10S 140°10E 282 C4
Maramag Phil. 7°46N 125°0E 233 H5
Maramaraereğlisi Turkey 40°57N 27°57E 203 F11
Maramasike Solomon Is. 9°30S 161°25E 287 M11
Marambio Antarctica 64°0S 56°0W 151 C18
Maramureş □ Romania 47°45N 24°0E 183 C9
Maran Malaysia 3°35N 102°45E 237 L4
Marana U.S.A. 32°27N 111°13W 305 K8
Maranboy Australia 14°40S 132°39E 278 B5
Maranchón Spain 41°6N 2°15W 196 D2
Marand Iran 38°30N 45°45E 213 C11
Marandochori Greece 38°38N 20°39E 207 B2
Maranello Italy 44°32N 10°52E 198 D7
Marang Malaysia 5°12N 103°13E 237 K4
Maranguape Brazil 3°55S 38°50W 332 B4
Maranhão = São Luís Brazil 2°39S 44°15W 332 B3
Maranhão □ Brazil 5°0S 46°0W 332 B2
Marano, L. di Italy 45°44N 13°10E 199 C10
Maranoa → Australia 27°50S 148°37E 281 D4
Marañón → Peru 4°30S 73°35W 330 A3
Marão Mozam. 24°18S 34°2E 271 B5
Maraoli India 19°2N 72°53E 130 A2
Marapi → Brazil 0°37N 55°58W 329 C6
Marari Brazil 5°43S 67°47W 330 B4
Maraş = Kahramanmaraş Turkey 37°37N 36°53E 212 D7
Mărăşeşti Romania 45°52N 27°14E 183 E12
Maratea Italy 39°59N 15°43E 201 C8
Marateca Portugal 38°34N 8°40W 195 G2
Marathasa Cyprus 34°59N 32°51E 207 F8
Marathia, Akra Greece 37°39N 20°50E 207 D2
Marathokambos Greece 37°43N 26°42E 205 D8
Marathon Queens., Australia 20°51S 143°32E 280 C3
Marathon Ont., Canada 48°44N 86°23W 298 C2
Marathon Fla., U.S.A. 24°43N 81°5W 317 L8
Marathon N.Y., U.S.A. 42°27N 76°2W 313 D8
Marathon Tex., U.S.A. 30°12N 103°15W 314 F3
Marathonas Greece 38°11N 23°58E 204 C5
Marathóvounos Cyprus 35°13N 33°37E 207 E9
Maratua Indonesia 2°10N 118°35E 235 B5
Maraú Brazil 14°6S 39°0W 333 D4
Marau Indonesia 2°9S 110°42E 235 C4
Marau Solomon Is. 10°31S 161°31E 287 N11
Maraval Trin. & Tob. 10°42N 61°31W 323 t
Maraval → Trin. & Tob. 10°39N 61°32W 323 t
Maravari Solomon Is. 7°50S 156°42E 287 L9
Maravatío Mexico 19°54N 100°27W 318 D4
Marawi City Phil. 8°0N 124°21E 233 G5
Marāwih U.A.E. 24°18N 53°18E 247 E7
Marazliyivka Ukraine 46°8N 30°3E 183 D15
Marbella Spain 36°30N 4°57W 195 J6
Marble Bar Australia 21°9S 119°44E 278 D2
Marblehead Mass., U.S.A. 42°29N 70°51W 313 D14
Marblehead Ohio, U.S.A. 41°32N 82°44W 312 E2
Mårbu Norway 60°11N 8°9E 164 D5
Marburg = Maribor Slovenia 46°36N 15°40E 199 B12
Marburg Germany 50°47N 8°46E 178 E4
Marca, Pta. do Angola 16°31S 11°43E 265 F2
Marcal → Hungary 47°41N 17°40E 182 C2
Marcali Hungary 46°35N 17°25E 182 D2
Marcapata Peru 13°31S 70°52W 330 C3
Marcaria Italy 45°7N 10°32E 198 C7
Mărcăuţi Moldova 48°20N 27°14E 183 B12
Marcelin Poland 52°19N 20°59E 143 B1
Marceline U.S.A. 39°43N 92°57W 310 E4
March U.K. 52°33N 0°5E 169 E8
Marchal Dem. Rep. of the Congo 5°16S 14°58E 265 D2
Marchand = Rommani Morocco 33°31N 6°40W 260 B3
Marche France 46°5N 1°20E 174 B5
Marche □ Italy 43°30N 13°15E 199 E10
Marché Bonsecours Montréal, Canada 130 b3
Marche-en-Famenne Belgium 50°14N 5°19E 170 D5
Marchena Spain 37°18N 5°23W 195 H5
Marchena, Canal de Ecuador 0°19N 90°12W 330 a
Marchena, I. Ecuador 0°19N 90°29W 330 a
Marches = Marche □ Italy 43°30N 13°15E 199 E10
Marchesale ⌓ Italy 38°32N 16°13E 201 D9
Marciana Marina Italy 42°48N 10°12E 198 F7
Marcianise Italy 41°2N 14°17E 201 A7
Marcigny France 46°17N 4°2E 173 F11
Marcillat-en-Combraille France 46°12N 2°38E 173 F9
Marck France 50°57N 1°57E 173 B8
Marckolsheim France 48°10N 7°30E 173 D14
Marco Island U.S.A. 25°58N 81°44W 317 K8
Marco Rondon Brazil 12°0S 60°56W 331 C5
Marcona Peru 15°10S 75°0W 330 D3
Marcos Juárez Argentina 32°42S 62°5W 334 C3
Mărculeşti Moldova 47°52N 28°14E 183 C13
Marcus Baker, Mt. U.S.A. 61°26N 147°45W 303 F11
Marcus I. = Minami-Tori-Shima Pac. Oc. 24°20N 153°58E 288 E7
Marcy, Mt. U.S.A. 44°7N 73°56W 313 B11
Mardan Pakistan 34°20N 72°0E 242 B5
Mardarivka Ukraine 47°32N 29°44E 183 C14
Mardie Australia 21°12S 115°59E 278 D2
Mardin Turkey 37°20N 40°43E 213 D9
Mårdsjö Sweden 63°18N 15°35E 162 A9
Maré, Î. N. Cal. 21°30S 168°0E 277 E12
Mare e Brăila, I. Romania 45°0N 28°5E 183 F13
Marécchia → Italy 44°4N 12°34E 199 D9
Marechal Deodoro Brazil 9°43S 35°54W 332 C4
Marechal Floriano = Piranhas Brazil 9°27S 37°46W 332 C4
Maree, L. U.K. 57°40N 5°26W 167 D3
Mareeba Australia 16°59S 145°28E 280 B4
Mareeg Somalia 3°46N 47°18E 267 D6
Mareetsane S. Africa 26°9S 25°25E 270 C4
Mareil-Marly France 48°52N 2°4E 134 A1
Maremma Italy 42°30N 11°30E 199 F8
Maremma ⌓ Italy 42°35N 11°8E 198 F8
Maréna Kayes, Mali 14°36N 10°45W 262 C2
Maréna Koulikouro, Mali 13°55N 7°20W 262 C3
Marengo Ind., U.S.A. 38°22N 86°21W 311 F10
Marengo Iowa, U.S.A. 41°48N 92°4W 310 C4
Marennes France 45°49N 1°7W 174 C2
Marerano Madag. 21°23S 44°52E 272 C1
Maréttimo Italy 37°58N 12°4E 200 E5
Mareuil France 45°26N 0°29E 174 C4
Marfa U.S.A. 30°19N 104°1W 314 F2
Marganets = Marhanets Ukraine 47°40N 34°40E 189 J8
Margao = Madgaon India 15°12N 73°58E 245 G1
Margaret → Australia 18°9S 125°41E 278 C4
Margaret Bay Canada 51°20N 127°35W 296 C3
Margaret I. = Margitsziget Hungary 47°32N 19°3E 117 A2
Margaret L. Canada 58°56N 115°25W 296 B5
Margaret River Australia 33°57S 115°4E 279 F2
Margareten Austria 48°11N 16°20E 142 A2
Margarita, I. de Venezuela 11°0N 64°0W 329 a
Margariti Greece 39°22N 20°26E 204 B2
Margaritovo Russia 43°25N 134°45E 220 C7
Margate KwaZulu Natal, S. Africa 30°50S 30°20E 271 D5
Margate Kent, U.K. 51°23N 1°23E 169 F9
Margate Fla., U.S.A. 26°15N 80°12W 317 J9
Margeride, Mts. de la France 44°43N 3°38E 174 D7
Marggrabowa = Olecko Poland 54°2N 22°31E 184 D9
Margherita India 27°16N 95°40E 241 B5
Margherita di Savóia Italy 41°22N 16°9E 201 A9
Margherita Pk. Uganda 0°22N 29°51E 268 B3
Marghita Romania 47°22N 22°22E 182 C7
Marg'ilon Uzbekistan 40°27N 71°42E 217 D8
Margitsziget Hungary 47°32N 19°3E 117 A2
Margonin Poland 52°58N 17°5E 185 F4
Margosatubig Phil. 7°34N 123°10E 233 H4
Māgow, Dasht-e Afghan. 30°40N 62°30E 240 C1
Marguerite Canada 52°30N 122°25W 296 C4
Marhanets Ukraine 47°40N 34°40E 189 J8
Marhoum Algeria 34°27N 0°11W 261 B4
Mari Papua N. G. 9°11S 141°42E 286 E1
Māri' Syria 36°29N 37°10E 250 B8
Mari El □ Russia 56°30N 48°0E 190 B8
Mari Indus Pakistan 32°57N 71°34E 242 C4
Mari Republic = Mari El □ Russia 56°30N 48°0E 190 B8
Maria Austria 48°11N 16°21E 142 A2
Maria, Îs. French Polynesia 21°48S 154°41W 289 f
María, Sa. de Spain 37°39N 2°14W 197 H2
Maria Aurora Phil. 15°48N 121°28E 232 D3
María de la Salut Spain 39°40N 3°5E 206 B4
María Elena Chile 22°18S 69°40W 334 A2
María Grande Argentina 31°45S 59°55W 334 C4
Maria I. N. Terr., Australia 14°52S 135°45E 280 A2
Maria I. Tas., Australia 42°35S 148°0E 281 G4
Maria Is. St. Lucia 13°44N 60°56W 323 m
Maria Island △ Australia 42°38S 148°5E 281 G4
Maria Pereira = Mombaça Brazil 5°43S 39°45W 332 C4
Maria Theresiopel = Subotica Serbia 46°6N 19°39E 182 D4
Maria van Diemen, C. N.Z. 34°29S 172°40E 284 A1
Mariager Denmark 56°40N 9°59E 163 H3
Mariager Fjord Denmark 56°42N 10°19E 163 H4
Mariahilferstrasse Vienna, Austria 142 b1
Mariakani Kenya 3°50S 39°27E 268 C4
Mariala △ Australia 25°57S 145°2E 281 D4
Marian Australia 21°9S 148°57E 280 b
Marian L. Canada 63°0N 116°15W 296 A5
Mariana Islands Pac. Oc. 15°15N 145°48E 302 a
Mariana Trench Pac. Oc. 13°0N 145°0E 302 a
Mariani India 26°39N 94°19E 241 B5
Marianica, Cord. = Morena, Sierra Spain 38°20N 4°0W 195 G7
Marianna Ark., U.S.A. 34°46N 90°46W 315 D9
Marianna Fla., U.S.A. 30°46N 85°14W 316 E4
Mariannelund Sweden 57°37N 15°35E 163 G9
Mariánské Lázně Czechia 49°58N 12°41E 180 B5
Marias → U.S.A. 47°56N 110°30W 304 C8
Marías, Is. Mexico 21°25N 106°28W 318 C3
Mariato, Punta Panama 7°12N 80°52W 320 E3
Mariazell Austria 47°47N 15°19E 180 D8
Ma'rib Yemen 15°25N 45°21E 248 D4
Ma'rib □ Yemen 15°25N 45°21E 248 D4
Maribo Denmark 54°48N 11°30E 163 K5
Maribor Slovenia 46°36N 15°40E 199 B12
Maricaban I. Phil. 13°39N 120°53E 232 E3
Maricao Puerto Rico 18°11N 66°59W 321 b
Marico → Africa 23°35S 26°57E 270 B4
Maricopa Ariz., U.S.A. 33°4N 112°3W 305 K7
Maricopa Calif., U.S.A. 35°4N 119°24W 307 K7
Maridalen Norway 59°59N 10°45E 133 A3
Maridalsvatnet Norway 59°59N 10°46E 133 A3
Maridi South Sudan 4°55N 29°25E 257 G2
Maridi, Wadi → South Sudan 6°15N 29°21E 257 F2
Marié → Brazil 0°27S 66°26W 328 D4
Marie Byrd Land Antarctica 79°30S 125°0W 151 D14
Marie-Galante Guadeloupe 15°56N 61°16W 322 e
Marie-Galante, Canal de Guadeloupe 16°0N 61°25W 322 e
Mariecourt = Kangiqsujuaq Canada 61°30N 72°0W 295 E17
Mariefred Sweden 59°15N 17°12E 162 E11
Mariehamn Finland 60°5N 19°55E 161 F18
Marieholm Sweden 55°53N 13°10E 163 J7
Mariembourg Belgium 50°6N 4°31E 170 D4
Marienbad = Mariánské Lázně Czechia 49°58N 12°41E 180 B5
Marienberg Germany 50°39N 13°9E 178 E9
Marienburg = Malbork Poland 54°3N 19°1E 184 D6
Mariendorf Germany 52°26N 13°23E 115 B3
Marienfelde Germany 52°24N 13°23E 115 B3
Marienplatz Munich, Germany 131 b2
Mariental Namibia 24°36S 18°0E 270 B2
Marienville U.S.A. 41°28N 79°8W 312 E5
Mariestad Sweden 58°43N 13°50E 163 F7
Marietta Ga., U.S.A. 33°57N 84°33W 316 B5
Marietta Ohio, U.S.A. 39°25N 81°27W 309 F13
Marieville Canada 45°26N 73°10W 313 A11
Mariga → Nigeria 9°40N 5°55E 263 C6
Marignane France 43°25N 5°13E 175 E9
Marigot Dominica 15°33N 61°18W 323 k
Marigot Guadeloupe 16°5N 61°46W 322 e
Marigot St.-Martin 18°4N 63°5W 322 a
Marigot Bay St. Lucia 13°58N 61°1W 323 m
Marihatag Phil. 8°48N 126°18E 233 G6
Mariinsk Russia 56°10N 87°20E 214 D9
Mariinsk Water = Volgo-Baltiyskiy Kanal Russia 60°0N 38°0E 188 B9
Mariinskiy Posad Russia 56°10N 47°45E 190 B8
Marijampolė Lithuania 54°33N 23°19E 184 D10
Marijampolė □ Lithuania 54°34N 23°21E 184 D10
Marikina Phil. 14°37N 121°5E 127 B2
Marikina → Phil. 14°33N 121°3E 127 B2
Marília Brazil 22°13S 50°0W 335 A6
Marimba Angola 8°28S 17°8E 265 D3
Marín Spain 42°23N 8°42W 194 C2
Marin, Cul-de-Sac du Martinique 14°27N 60°53W 322 j
Marin City U.S.A. 37°52N 122°30W 136 A1
Marin Pen. U.S.A. 37°50N 122°30W 136 A1
Marina U.S.A. 36°41N 121°48W 306 J5
Marina Bay Sands Singapore 1°17N 103°51E 138 B3
Marina del Rey U.S.A. 33°58N 118°27W 126 C2
Marinduque Phil. 13°25N 122°0E 231 B6
Marinduque □ Phil. 13°18N 122°0E 232 E4
Marine City U.S.A. 42°43N 82°30W 312 D2
Marine Drive Mumbai, India 130 b1
Marineland U.S.A. 29°40N 81°13W 316 F8
Marineo Italy 37°57N 13°25E 200 E6
Marinette U.S.A. 45°6N 87°38W 308 C10
Maringá Brazil 23°26S 52°2W 335 A5
Maringa → Dem. Rep. of the Congo 1°14N 19°48E 264 B3
Marinha Grande Portugal 39°45N 8°56W 194 F2
Marinho dos Abrolhos △ Brazil 17°50S 39°0W 333 E4
Marino Italy 41°46N 12°39E 199 G9
Marino di Campo Italy 42°46N 10°11E 198 F7
Marion Ala., U.S.A. 32°38N 87°19W 315 E11
Marion Ark., U.S.A. 35°13N 90°12W 308 H8
Marion Ill., U.S.A. 37°44N 88°56W 310 G8
Marion Ind., U.S.A. 40°32N 85°40W 311 D11
Marion Iowa, U.S.A. 42°2N 91°36W 310 B5
Marion Kans., U.S.A. 38°21N 97°1W 308 F5
Marion N.C., U.S.A. 35°41N 82°1W 315 D13
Marion Ohio, U.S.A. 40°35N 83°8W 311 D13
Marion S.C., U.S.A. 34°11N 79°24W 315 D15
Marion Va., U.S.A. 36°50N 81°31W 309 G13
Marion, L. U.S.A. 33°28N 80°10W 316 B9
Marion Bay Australia 35°12S 136°59E 282 C2
Marion I. Ind. Oc. 47°0S 38°0E 273 J2
Maripa Venezuela 7°26N 65°9W 329 B4
Maripasoula Fr. Guiana 3°40N 54°4W 329 C7
Maripipi I. Phil. 11°47N 124°19E 233 F5
Mariposa U.S.A. 37°29N 119°58W 306 H7
Mariscal Estigarribia Paraguay 22°3S 60°40W 334 A3
Marisco, Ponta do Brazil 23°1S 43°18W 135 C1
Maritas, Laguna de las Venezuela 10°55N 63°56W 329 a
Maritime Alps = Maritimes, Alpes Europe 44°10N 7°10E 175 D11
Maritimes, Alpes Europe 44°10N 7°10E 175 D11
Maritsa = Evros → Greece 41°40N 26°34E 203 F10
Maritsa Greece 36°22N 28°8E 206 E12
Marittima, Stazione Italy 142 b1
Mariupol Ukraine 47°5N 37°31E 189 J9
Marīvān Iran 35°30N 46°25E 213 E12
Mariveles Phil. 14°26N 120°29E 232 D3
Mariy Chodra △ Russia 56°10N 48°30E 190 B9
Marj 'Uyūn Lebanon 33°21N 35°34E 250 E6
Marjan = Wazikhwah Afghan. 32°11N 68°21E 240 B3
Mark Twain L. U.S.A. 39°28N 91°55W 310 E5
Marka Si. Arabia 18°14N 41°19E 256 D5
Marka Somalia 1°48N 44°50E 267 D5
Markam China 29°42N 98°38E 228 C2
Markapur India 15°44N 79°19E 245 G4
Markaryd Sweden 56°28N 13°35E 163 H7
Markat Albania 39°44N 20°12E 206 B10
Markazī □ Iran 34°0N 49°30E 247 C6
Markdale Canada 44°19N 80°39W 312 B4
Marked Tree U.S.A. 35°32N 90°25W 315 D9
Markelsdorfer Huk Germany 54°33N 11°4E 178 A7
Market Drayton U.K. 52°54N 2°29W 168 E5
Market Harborough U.K. 52°29N 0°55W 169 E7
Market Rasen U.K. 53°24N 0°20W 168 D7
Markham Ont., Canada 43°52N 79°16W 141 A2
Markham Ill., U.S.A. 41°36N 87°42W 119 D2
Markham → Papua N. G. 6°41S 147°2E 286 D4
Markham, Mt. Antarctica 83°0S 164°0E 151 E11
Marki Poland 52°19N 21°6E 143 B2
Märkisch Friedland = Mirosławiec Poland 53°20N 16°5E 184 E3
Märkische Schweiz ⌓ Germany 52°34N 14°2E 178 C10
Markit China 38°54N 77°40E 217 E9
Markkleeberg Germany 51°16N 12°23E 178 D8
Markland Wood Canada 43°38N 79°34W 141 B1
Markleeville U.S.A. 38°42N 119°47W 306 G7
Markopoulo Greece 37°53N 23°57E 204 D5
Markounda C.A.R. 7°39N 16°55E 264 A3
Markovac Serbia 44°14N 21°7E 202 B5
Markovo Russia 64°40N 170°24E 215 C17
Markoye Burkina Faso 14°39N 0°2E 263 C5
Marks Russia 51°45N 46°50E 190 E8
Marksshtadt = Marks Russia 51°45N 46°50E 190 E8
Marksville U.S.A. 31°8N 92°4W 314 F8
Markt Schwaben Germany 48°11N 11°52E 179 G7
Marktoberdorf Germany 47°45N 10°37E 179 H6
Marktredwitz Germany 50°1N 12°6E 179 E8
Marl Germany 51°39N 7°4E 178 D3
Marla Australia 27°19S 133°33E 281 D1
Marlbank Canada 44°26N 77°6W 312 B7
Marlboro U.S.A. 41°36N 73°59W 313 E11
Marlborough Queens., Australia 22°46S 149°52E 280 C4
Marlborough Wilts., U.K. 51°25N 1°43W 169 F6
Marlborough Mass., U.S.A. 42°21N 71°33W 313 D13
Marlborough □ N.Z. 41°40S 173°50E 285 B8
Marlborough Downs U.K. 51°27N 1°53W 169 F6
Marle France 49°43N 3°47E 173 C10
Marlin U.S.A. 31°18N 96°54W 314 F6
Marlow Mecklenburg-Vorpommern, Germany 54°9N 12°33E 178 A8
Marlow Bucks., U.K. 51°34N 0°46W 169 F7
Marlow Okla., U.S.A. 34°39N 97°58W 314 D6

Marly, Forêt de *France* 48°52N 2°2E **134** A1
Marly-le-Roi *France* 48°52N 2°5E **134** A1
Marmagao *India* 15°25N 73°56E **245** G1
Marmande *France* 44°30N 0°10E **174** D4
Marmara *Turkey* 40°35N 27°34E **203** F11
Marmara, Sea of = Marmara Denizi *Turkey* 40°45N 28°15E **203** F12
Marmara Denizi *Turkey* 40°45N 28°15E **203** F12
Marmara Gölü *Turkey* 38°37N 28°2E **205** C10
Marmaris *Turkey* 36°50N 28°14E **205** E10
Marmaris Limanı *Turkey* 36°50N 28°19E **205** E10
Marmelos → *Brazil* 6°6S 61°46W **331** B5
Marmion, Mt. *Australia* 29°16S 119°50E **279** E2
Marmion L. *Canada* 48°55N 91°20W **298** C1
Marmolada, Mte. *Italy* 46°26N 11°51E **199** B8
Marmolejo *Spain* 38°3N 4°13W **195** G6
Marmora *Canada* 44°28N 77°41W **312** B7
Mármora, La *Italy* 39°59N 9°20E **200** C2
Marnay *France* 47°16N 5°48E **173** E12
Marne *Germany* 53°56N 9°2E **178** B5
Marne □ *France* 48°50N 4°10E **173** D11
Marne → *France* 48°47N 2°29E **173** D9
Marne-la-Vallée *France* 48°50N 2°37E **134** A4
Marneuli *Georgia* 41°30N 44°48E **191** K7
Marnia = Maghnia *Algeria* 34°50N 1°43W **261** B4
Marnoo *Australia* 36°40S 142°52E **282** D5
Maro *Chad* 8°30N 19°0E **259** G3
Maro Reef *U.S.A.* 25°25N 170°35W **302** F9
Maroa *Ill., U.S.A.* 40°2N 88°57W **310** D8
Maroa *Venezuela* 2°43N 67°33W **328** C4
Maroala *Madag.* 15°23S 47°59E **272** B2
Maroantsetra *Madag.* 15°26S 49°44E **272** B2
Maroelaboom *Namibia* 19°15S 18°53E **270** A2
Marofandilia *Madag.* 20°7S 44°34E **272** C1
Marojejy ⌓ *Madag.* 14°26S 49°21E **272** A2
Marokau *French Polynesia* 18°2S 142°17W **289** f
Marolambo *Madag.* 20°2S 48°7E **272** C2
Marolles-en-Brie *France* 48°44N 2°33E **134** B4
Maromandia *Madag.* 14°13S 48°5E **272** A2
Maromokotro *Madag.* 14°0S 49°0E **272** A2
Marondera *Zimbabwe* 18°5S 31°42E **269** F3
Maroni → *Fr. Guiana* 5°30N 54°0W **329** B7
Maronia *Greece* 40°53N 25°30E **203** F9
Maronne → *France* 45°5N 1°56E **174** C5
Maroochydore *Australia* 26°29S 153°5E **281** D5
Maroon Town *Jamaica* 18°22N 77°48W **320** a
Maroona *Australia* 37°27S 142°54E **282** D5
Maros *Indonesia* 5°0S 119°34E **235** C5
Maros → *Hungary* 46°15N 20°13E **182** D5
Marosakoa *Madag.* 15°26S 46°38E **272** B2
Maroseranana *Madag.* 18°32S 48°51E **272** B2
Maróstica *Italy* 45°44N 11°40E **199** C8
Marotandrano *Madag.* 16°10S 48°50E **272** B2
Marotiri, Îs. = Bass, Îs. de *French Polynesia* 27°55S 143°26W **289** f
Maroua *Cameroon* 10°40N 14°20E **259** F2
Maroubra *Australia* 33°56S 151°16E **139** B2
Marovato *Madag.* 15°48S 48°5E **272** B2
Marovoay *Madag.* 16°6S 46°39E **272** B2
Marowijne □ *Suriname* 4°0N 55°0W **329** C7
Marowijne → *Suriname* 5°45N 53°58W **329** B7
Marqaköl *Kazakhstan* 48°45N 85°45E **217** C11
Marquard *S. Africa* 28°40S 27°28E **270** C4
Marquesas Fracture Zone *Pac. Oc.* 9°0S 125°0W **289** H15
Marquesas Is. = Marquises, Îs. *French Polynesia* 9°30S 140°0W **289** f
Marquesas Keys *U.S.A.* 24°35N 82°10W **317** L7
Marquette *U.S.A.* 46°33N 87°24W **308** B10
Marquette Park *U.S.A.* 41°46N 87°42W **119** C2
Marquis *St. Lucia* 14°2N 60°54W **323** m
Marquis, C. *St. Lucia* 14°3N 60°54W **323** m
Marquis I. *Grenada* 12°5N 61°37W **323** q
Marquise *France* 50°50N 1°40E **173** B8
Marquises, Îs. *French Polynesia* 9°30S 140°0W **289** f
Marra, Gebel *South Sudan* 7°20N 27°35E **257** F2
Marra, Pta. da *Angola* 16°31S 11°43E **265** F2
Marra Cr. → *Australia* 30°8S 147°15E **283** A7
Marra-Marra △ *Australia* 33°30S 151°4E **283** B9
Marracuene *Mozam.* 25°45S 32°35E **271** C5
Marradi *Italy* 44°4N 11°37E **199** D8
Marrakech *Morocco* 31°9N 8°0W **260** B3
Marrakech-Safi □ *Morocco* 31°10N 8°30W **260** B3
Marratxí *Spain* 39°39N 2°48E **206** B3
Marrawah *Australia* 40°55S 144°42E **281** G3
Marrecas, Serra das *Brazil* 9°0S 41°0W **332** C3
Marree *Australia* 29°39S 138°1E **281** D2
Marrero *U.S.A.* 29°53N 90°6W **131** B2
Marrickville *Australia* 33°54S 151°9E **139** B1
Marrimane *Mozam.* 22°58S 33°34E **271** B5
Marromeu *Mozam.* 18°15S 36°25E **271** A6
Marromeu ⌓ *Mozam.* 19°0S 36°0E **271** A6
Marroquí, Punta *Spain* 36°0N 5°37W **195** K5
Marrowie Cr. → *Australia* 33°23S 145°40E **283** B6
Marruás = Porto *Brazil* 3°54S 42°42W **332** B3
Marrubane *Mozam.* 18°0S 37°0E **269** F4
Marrúbiu *Italy* 39°40N 8°35E **200** C1
Marrupa *Mozam.* 13°8S 37°30E **269** E4
Mars B. *Ascension I.* 7°59S 14°24W **153** g
Mars Hill *U.S.A.* 46°31N 67°52W **309** B20
Marsa al Burayqah *Libya* 30°24N 19°37E **258** B3
Marsá 'Alam *Egypt* 25°5N 34°54E **256** B3
Marsá Matrûh *Egypt* 31°19N 27°9E **256** A2
Marsa Sha'b *Sudan* 22°52N 35°47E **256** C4
Marsabit *Kenya* 2°18N 38°0E **268** B4
Marsabit □ *Kenya* 3°0N 37°30E **268** B4
Marsabit △ *Kenya* 2°23N 37°56E **268** B4
Marsala *Italy* 37°48N 12°26E **200** E5
Marsalforn *Malta* 36°4N 14°16E **206** E7
Mârşani *Romania* 44°1N 24°1E **183** F9
Marsaskala *Malta* 35°52N 14°34E **206** F8
Marsaxlokk *Malta* 35°51N 14°33E **206** F8
Marsaxlokk Bay *Malta* 35°49N 14°33E **206** F8
Marsberg *Germany* 51°28N 8°52E **178** D4
Marsciano *Italy* 42°54N 12°20E **199** F9
Marsden *Australia* 33°47S 147°32E **283** B7
Marsden Point *N.Z.* 35°50S 174°31E **284** B3
Marseillan *France* 43°23N 3°31E **174** E7
Marseille *France* 43°18N 5°23E **175** E9
Marseille-Marignane ✈ (MRS) *France* 43°26N 5°14E **175** E9
Marseilles = Marseille *France* 43°18N 5°23E **175** E9
Marseilles *U.S.A.* 41°20N 88°43W **311** C8
Marsfield *Australia* 33°46S 151°7E **139** A1
Marsh Harbour *The Bahamas* 26°33N 77°3W **320** A4
Marsh I. *U.S.A.* 29°34N 91°53W **314** G9
Marsha, L. *U.S.A.* 28°29N 81°29W **133** B2
Marshall *Liberia* 6°8N 10°22W **262** D2
Marshall *Alaska, U.S.A.* 61°53N 162°5W **303** F7
Marshall *Ark., U.S.A.* 35°55N 92°38W **314** D8
Marshall *Ill., U.S.A.* 39°23N 87°42W **311** E9
Marshall *Mich., U.S.A.* 42°16N 84°58W **311** B12
Marshall *Minn., U.S.A.* 44°27N 95°47W **308** C6
Marshall *Mo., U.S.A.* 39°7N 93°12W **310** E3
Marshall *Tex., U.S.A.* 32°33N 94°23W **314** E7
Marshall → *Australia* 22°59S 136°59E **280** C2
Marshall, C. *Ecuador* 0°1S 91°12W **330** a
Marshall Bennett Is. *Papua N. G.* 8°50S 151°55E **286** E6
Marshall Is. ■ *Pac. Oc.* 9°0N 171°0E **288** G9
Marshalltown *U.S.A.* 42°3N 92°55W **310** B4
Marshallville = Lewisporte *Canada* 49°15N 55°3W **299** C8
Marshallville *U.S.A.* 32°27N 83°56W **316** C6
Marshbrook *Zimbabwe* 18°33S 31°9E **271** A5
Marshfield = Coos Bay *U.S.A.* 43°22N 124°13W **304** E1
Marshfield *Mo., U.S.A.* 37°15N 92°54W **308** G7
Marshfield *Vt., U.S.A.* 44°20N 72°20W **313** B12
Marshfield *Wis., U.S.A.* 44°40N 90°10W **308** C8
Marshūn *Iran* 36°19N 49°23E **247** B6
Mársico Nuovo *Italy* 40°25N 15°44E **201** B8
Marsouins, R. des → *Réunion* 21°1S 55°44E **272** f
Märsta *Sweden* 59°37N 17°52E **162** E11
Marstal *Denmark* 54°51N 10°30E **163** K4
Marstrand *Sweden* 57°53N 11°35E **163** G5
Mart *U.S.A.* 31°33N 96°50W **314** F6
Marta → *Italy* 42°14N 11°42E **199** F8
Martaban *Myanmar* 16°30N 97°35E **241** G6
Martaban, G. of = Mottama, G. of *Myanmar* 16°5N 96°30E **241** G6
Martano *Italy* 40°12N 18°18E **201** B11
Martapura *Kalimantan Selatan, Indonesia* 3°22S 114°47E **235** C4
Martapura *Sumatera Selatan, Indonesia* 4°19S 104°22E **234** C2
Marte *Nigeria* 12°23N 13°46E **263** C7
Marte, Campo de *Brazil* 23°30S 46°38W **137** B2
Marte R. Gómez, Presa *Mexico* 26°10N 99°0W **319** B5
Martel *France* 44°57N 1°37E **174** D5
Martelange *Belgium* 49°49N 5°43E **170** E5
Martellago *Italy* 45°33N 12°9E **199** C9
Martés, Sierra *Spain* 39°20N 1°0W **197** F4
Martesana, Navíglio della *Italy* 45°31N 9°17E **128** A2
Martfű *Hungary* 47°1N 20°17E **182** C5
Marthaguy Cr. → *Australia* 30°16S 147°35E **283** A7
Marthapal *India* 19°24N 81°37E **244** E5
Martha's Vineyard *U.S.A.* 41°25N 70°38W **313** E14
Martigné-Ferchaud *France* 47°50N 1°20W **172** E5
Martigny *Switz.* 46°6N 7°3E **179** J3
Martigues *France* 43°24N 5°4E **175** E9
Martil *Morocco* 35°36N 5°15W **260** A3
Martin *Slovakia* 49°6N 18°58E **181** B11
Martin *S. Dak., U.S.A.* 43°11N 101°44W **308** D3
Martin *Tenn., U.S.A.* 36°21N 88°51W **315** C10
Martín → *Spain* 41°18N 0°19W **196** D4
Martin L. *U.S.A.* 32°41N 85°55W **316** C4
Martin Luther King Nat. Historic Site ⌓ *U.S.A.* 33°45N 84°22W **113** B2
Martin Pt. *U.S.A.* 70°8N 143°16W **303** A12
Martin Vaz *Atl. Oc.* 20°30S 28°51W **152** J9
Martina Franca *Italy* 40°42N 17°20E **201** B10
Martinborough *N.Z.* 41°14S 175°29E **284** H4
Martinez *B. Aires, Argentina* 34°29S 58°31W **117** A1
Martinez *Calif., U.S.A.* 38°1N 122°8W **306** G4
Martinez *Ga., U.S.A.* 33°31N 82°5W **316** B7
Martinho Campos *Brazil* 19°20S 45°13W **333** E2
Martinique ⊠ *W. Indies* 14°40N 61°0W **322** j
Martinique Channel *St. Vincent* 12°34N 61°25W **323** n
Martinique Passage *W. Indies* 15°15N 61°0W **321** C7
Martinkylä *Finland* 60°17N 24°51E **121** B2
Martino *Greece* 38°35N 23°12E **204** C5
Martinópolis *Brazil* 22°11S 51°12W **335** A5
Martins Ferry *U.S.A.* 40°6N 80°44W **312** F4
Martinsberg *Austria* 48°22N 15°9E **180** C8
Martinsburg *Pa., U.S.A.* 40°19N 78°20W **312** F6
Martinsburg *W. Va., U.S.A.* 39°27N 77°58W **309** F15
Martinsicuro *Italy* 42°54N 13°54E **199** F10
Martinsried *Germany* 48°6N 11°27E **131** B1
Martinsville *Ill., U.S.A.* 39°20N 87°53W **311** E9
Martinsville *Ind., U.S.A.* 39°26N 86°25W **311** E10
Martinsville *Va., U.S.A.* 36°41N 79°52W **309** G14
Marton *N.Z.* 40°4S 175°23E **284** G4
Martorell *Spain* 41°28N 1°56E **196** D6
Martos *Spain* 37°44N 3°58W **195** H7
Martu ✿ *Australia* 22°30S 122°30E **278** D3
Martūbah *Libya* 32°35N 22°46E **258** B4
Martuni *Armenia* 40°8N 45°20E **191** K7
Maru *Nigeria* 12°22N 6°22E **263** C6
Marudi *Malaysia* 4°11N 114°19E **235** B4
Maruf *Afghan.* 31°30N 67°6E **240** C2
Marugame *Japan* 34°15N 133°40E **222** C5
Marui = Pagwi *Papua N. G.* 4°4S 143°2E **286** C2
Maruia → *N.Z.* 41°47S 172°13E **285** B7
Maruim *Brazil* 10°45S 37°5W **332** D4
Maruko *Japan* 35°33N 139°40E **140** B3
Marulan *Australia* 34°43S 150°3E **283** C9
Marum, Mt. *Vanuatu* 16°15S 168°7E **287** F6
Marunga *Angola* 17°28S 20°2E **265** F4
Marungu, Mts. *Dem. Rep. of the Congo* 7°30S 30°0E **268** D3
Marunouchi *Tokyo, Japan* **140** b4
Maruoka = Sakai *Japan* 36°9N 136°16E **223** A8
Maruwa ✿ *Australia* 22°30S 127°30E **278** D4
Marv Dasht *Iran* 29°50N 52°40E **247** D7
Marvão = Castelo do Piauí *Brazil* 5°20S 41°33W **332** C3
Marvão *Portugal* 39°24N 7°20W **195** F3
Marvast *Iran* 30°30N 54°15E **247** D7
Marvejols *France* 44°33N 3°19E **174** D7
Marvel Loch *Australia* 31°28S 119°29E **279** F2
Marwar *India* 25°43N 73°45E **242** G5
Mary *Turkmenistan* 37°40N 61°50E **247** B9
Mary Esther *U.S.A.* 30°25N 86°40W **317** E3
Maryborough = Portlaoise *Ireland* 53°2N 7°18W **166** C4
Maryborough *Queens., Australia* 25°31S 152°37E **281** D5
Maryborough *Vic., Australia* 37°3S 143°44E **282** D5
Maryfield *Canada* 49°50N 101°35W **297** D8
Maryino = Pristen *Russia* 51°15N 36°44E **189** G9
Maryino *Russia* 55°40N 37°45E **129** B3
Maryland *Singapore* 1°19N 103°47E **138** B2
Maryland □ *U.S.A.* 39°0N 76°30W **309** F15
Maryland Junction *Zimbabwe* 17°45S 30°31E **269** F3
Marylebone *London, U.K.* **125** a2
Marymont *Poland* 52°16N 20°58E **143** B1
Maryport *U.K.* 54°44N 3°28W **168** C4
Mary's Harbour *Canada* 52°18N 55°51W **299** B8
Marysin Wawerski *Poland* 52°14N 21°9E **143** B2
Marystown *Canada* 47°10N 55°10W **299** C8
Marysville *Calif., U.S.A.* 39°9N 121°35W **306** F5
Marysville *Kans., U.S.A.* 39°51N 96°39W **308** F5
Marysville *Mich., U.S.A.* 42°54N 82°29W **312** D2
Marysville *Ohio, U.S.A.* 40°14N 83°22W **311** D13
Marysville *Wash., U.S.A.* 48°3N 122°11W **306** B4
Maryville *Mo., U.S.A.* 40°21N 94°52W **310** D2
Maryville *Tenn., U.S.A.* 35°46N 83°58W **315** D13
Marzahn *Germany* 52°32N 13°34E **115** A4
Marzo, Punta *Colombia* 6°50N 77°42W **328** B2
Masada *Israel* 31°18N 35°21E **251** G6
Mas'ada *Syria* 33°13N 35°45E **250** E6
Masahunga *Tanzania* 2°6S 33°18E **268** C3
Masai *Malaysia* 1°29N 103°55E **237** d
Masai Mara △ *Kenya* 1°25S 35°5E **268** C4
Masai Steppe *Tanzania* 4°30S 36°30E **268** C4
Masaka *Uganda* 0°21S 31°45E **268** C3
Māsāl *Iran* 37°23N 49°8E **213** D12
Masalembo, Kepulauan *Indonesia* 5°35S 114°30E **235** D4
Masalima, Kepulauan *Indonesia* 5°4S 117°5E **235** D5
Masallı *Azerbaijan* 39°3N 48°40E **213** C13
Masalog Pt. *N. Marianas* 15°1N 145°40E **302** e
Masamba *Indonesia* 2°30S 120°15E **231** E6
Masan *S. Korea* 35°11N 128°32E **224** E4
Masandam, Ra's *Oman* 26°30N 56°30E **247** E8
Masasi *Tanzania* 10°45S 38°52E **269** E4
Masaya *Nic.* 12°0N 86°7W **320** D2
Masba *Nigeria* 11°35N 13°1E **263** C7
Masbate *Phil.* 12°21N 123°36E **232** E4
Masbate □ *Phil.* 12°20N 123°30E **232** E4
Masbate Pass. *Phil.* 12°30N 123°35E **232** E4
Máscali *Italy* 37°45N 15°12E **201** E8
Mascara *Algeria* 35°26N 0°6E **261** A5
Mascara □ *Algeria* 35°25N 0°10E **261** A5
Mascarene Is. *Ind. Oc.* 22°0S 55°0E **254** J9
Mascot *Australia* 33°55S 151°12E **139** B2
Mascota *Mexico* 20°32N 104°49W **318** C4
Mascoutah *U.S.A.* 38°29N 89°48W **310** F7
Masdar City = Madīnat Masdar *U.A.E.* 24°26N 54°37E **247** E7
Masefau B. *Amer. Samoa* 14°15S 170°37W **302** f
Masein *Myanmar* 23°22N 94°21E **241** D5
Masela *Indonesia* 8°9S 129°51E **231** F7
Maseru *Lesotho* 29°18S 27°30E **270** C4
Masfjorden *Norway* 60°48N 5°18E **164** D2
Mashaba *Zimbabwe* 20°2S 30°29E **269** G3
Mashābih *Si. Arabia* 25°35N 36°30E **246** E3
Mashan *China* 23°40N 108°11E **228** F7
Mashang *China* 36°48N 117°57E **227** F9
Mashar *South Sudan* 9°16N 26°51E **257** F2
Mashatu ⌓ *Botswana* 22°45S 29°5E **271** B4
Mashegu *Nigeria* 10°0N 5°35E **263** D6
Masherbrum *Pakistan* 35°38N 76°18E **243** B7
Mashhad *Iran* 36°20N 59°35E **247** B8
Mashi *Nigeria* 13°0N 7°54E **263** C6
Mashiki *Japan* 32°51N 130°53E **222** E2
Mashīz *Iran* 29°56N 56°37E **247** D8
Mashkal → *Pakistan* 26°2N 65°19E **240** D2
Māshkel, Hāmūn-i- *Pakistan* 28°20N 62°56E **240** C1
Mashki Chāh *Pakistan* 29°5N 62°30E **240** C1
Mashonaland Central □ *Zimbabwe* 17°30S 31°0E **271** A5
Mashonaland East □ *Zimbabwe* 18°0S 32°0E **271** A5
Mashonaland West □ *Zimbabwe* 17°30S 29°30E **271** A4
Mashrakh *India* 26°7N 84°48E **243** F11
Masi Manimba *Dem. Rep. of the Congo* 4°40S 17°54E **265** C3
Masibi *Angola* 11°6S 22°41E **265** E4
Masig *Australia* 9°45S 143°24E **280** a
Masindi *Uganda* 1°40N 31°43E **268** B3
Masindi Port *Uganda* 1°43N 32°2E **268** B3
Masinga Res. *Kenya* 0°58S 37°38E **268** C4
Masinloc *Phil.* 15°32N 119°57E **232** D2
Maşīrah, Jazīrat *Oman* 21°0N 58°50E **249** B7
Maşīrah, Khalīj *Oman* 20°10N 58°10E **249** B7
Maşīrah, Tur'at *Oman* 20°30N 58°40E **249** B7
Masisea *Peru* 8°35S 74°22W **330** B3
Masisi *Dem. Rep. of the Congo* 1°23S 28°49E **268** C2
Masjed Soleyman *Iran* 31°55N 49°18E **247** D6
Mask, L. *Ireland* 53°36N 9°22W **166** C2
Maskelyne Is. *Vanuatu* 16°32S 167°49E **287** F5
Maski *India* 15°56N 76°46E **245** G3
Maskin *Oman* 23°44N 56°52E **247** F8
Maslen Nos *Bulgaria* 42°18N 27°48E **203** D11
Maslinica *Croatia* 43°24N 16°13E **199** E13
Masmo *Sweden* 59°15N 17°53E **139** B1
Maşna'ah *Yemen* 14°27N 48°17E **249** D5
Masnou = El Masnou *Spain* 41°28N 2°20E **196** D7
Masoala, Saikanosy *Madag.* 15°45S 50°10E **272** B3
Masoala, Tanjon' i *Madag.* 15°59S 50°13E **272** B3
Masoala △ *Madag.* 15°30S 50°12E **272** B3
Masoarivo *Madag.* 19°3S 44°19E **272** B1
Masohi = Amahai *Indonesia* 3°20S 128°55E **231** E7
Masomeloka *Madag.* 20°17S 48°37E **272** C2
Mason *Mich., U.S.A.* 42°35N 84°27W **311** B12
Mason *Nev., U.S.A.* 38°56N 119°8W **306** G7
Mason *Ohio, U.S.A.* 39°22N 84°19W **311** E12
Mason *Tex., U.S.A.* 30°45N 99°14W **314** F5
Mason B. *N.Z.* 46°55S 167°45E **285** G2
Mason City *Ill., U.S.A.* 40°12N 89°42W **310** D7
Mason City *Iowa, U.S.A.* 43°9N 93°12W **310** A3
Mason Hall *Trin. & Tob.* 11°13N 60°43W **323** s
Maspalomas *Canary Is.* 27°46N 15°35W **153** e1
Maspalomas, Pta. *Canary Is.* 27°43N 15°36W **153** e1
Maspeth *U.S.A.* 40°43N 73°55W **132** B2
Masqat *Oman* 23°37N 58°36E **249** B7
Masr el Gedida *Egypt* 30°5N 31°21E **117** A2
Masr el Qadîma *Egypt* 30°0N 31°14E **117** A2
Massa *Congo* 3°45S 15°29E **264** C3
Massa *Italy* 44°1N 10°9E **198** D7
Massa, O. → *Morocco* 30°2N 9°40W **260** B3
Massa e Carrara □ *Italy* 44°10N 10°10E **198** D7
Massa Maríttima *Italy* 43°3N 10°52E **198** E7
Massachusetts □ *U.S.A.* 42°30N 72°0W **313** D13
Massachusetts Avenue *Washington, D.C., U.S.A.* **143** a2
Massachusetts B. *U.S.A.* 42°25N 70°50W **313** D14
Massachusetts Inst. of Tech. *Boston, U.S.A.* 42°21N 71°5W **116** A2
Massacre *Dominica* 15°20N 61°25W **323** k
Massafra *Italy* 40°35N 17°7E **201** B10
Massaguet *Chad* 12°28N 15°26E **259** F3
Massakory *Chad* 13°0N 15°49E **259** F3
Massamá *Portugal* 38°45N 9°16W **126** A1
Massamba *Mozam.* 15°58S 33°31E **269** F3
Massanella *Spain* 39°48N 2°51E **206** B3
Massangano *Angola* 9°40S 14°13E **265** D2
Massangena *Mozam.* 21°34S 33°0E **271** B5
Massango *Angola* 8°1S 16°10E **265** D3
Massapê *Brazil* 3°31S 40°19W **332** B3
Massat *France* 42°53N 1°21E **174** F5
Massawa = Mitsiwa *Eritrea* 15°35N 39°25E **257** D4
Massena *U.S.A.* 44°56N 74°54W **313** B10
Massenya *Chad* 11°21N 16°9E **259** F3
Masset *Canada* 54°2N 132°10W **296** C2
Masseube *France* 43°25N 0°34E **174** E4
Massey → *Canada* 43°42N 79°19W **141** A3
Massey Hall *Toronto, Canada* **141** a3
Massiac *France* 45°15N 3°11E **174** C7
Massif Central *France* 44°55N 3°0E **174** D7
Massif des Bauges ⌓ *France* 45°40N 6°10E **173** G13
Massigui *Mali* 11°48N 6°50W **262** C3
Massillon *U.S.A.* 40°48N 81°32W **312** F3
Massima *Gabon* 1°27S 11°33E **264** C2
Massine, O. → *Algeria* 36°13N 2°12E **261** A5
Massinga *Mozam.* 23°15S 35°22E **271** B6
Massingir *Mozam.* 23°51S 32°4E **271** B5
Masson-Angers *Canada* 45°32N 75°25W **313** A9
Masson I. *Antarctica* 66°10S 93°20E **151** C7
Massouka *Gabon* 1°37S 9°56E **264** C1
Massow = Maszewo *Poland* 53°29N 15°3E **184** E2
Massy *France* 48°43N 2°16E **134** B2
Mastābah *Si. Arabia* 20°49N 39°26E **248** B2
Maştağa *Azerbaijan* 40°35N 50°1E **191** K10
Mastanli = Momchilgrad *Bulgaria* 41°33N 25°23E **203** E9
Masterton *N.Z.* 40°56S 175°39E **284** G4
Mastic *U.S.A.* 40°47N 72°54W **313** F12
Mastuj *Pakistan* 36°20N 72°36E **243** A5
Mastung *Pakistan* 29°50N 66°56E **240** C2
Mastūrah *Si. Arabia* 23°7N 38°52E **248** B2
Masty *Belarus* 53°27N 24°38E **177** B13
Masuda *Japan* 34°40N 131°51E **222** C3
Masuika *Dem. Rep. of the Congo* 7°37S 22°32E **265** D4
Masuku = Franceville *Gabon* 1°40S 13°32E **264** C2
Masurai *Indonesia* 2°30S 101°51E **234** C2
Masurian Lakes = Mazurski, Pojezierze *Poland* 53°50N 21°0E **184** E7
Masvingo *Zimbabwe* 20°8S 30°49E **269** G3
Masvingo □ *Zimbabwe* 21°0S 31°30E **269** G3
Maswa ⌓ *Tanzania* 2°58S 34°19E **268** C3
Maşyāf *Syria* 35°4N 36°20E **250** C7
Maszewo *Poland* 53°29N 15°3E **184** E2
Mat → *Albania* 41°40N 19°35E **202** E3
Mât → *Réunion* 20°57S 55°42E **272** f
Mata *Israel* 31°43N 35°4E **123** B1
Mata-au = Clutha → *N.Z.* 46°20S 169°49E **285** G4
Mata de São João *Brazil* 12°31S 38°17W **333** D4
Mata Redonda *Venezuela* 10°57N 64°7W **329** a
Mata-Utu *Wall. & F. Is.* 13°17S 176°8W **277** C15
Matabele Plain *Zambia* 16°20S 23°10E **265** F4
Matabeleland North □ *Zimbabwe* 19°0S 28°0E **269** F2
Matabeleland South □ *Zimbabwe* 21°0S 29°0E **269** G2
Matachel → *Spain* 38°50N 6°17W **195** G4
Matachewan *Canada* 47°56N 80°39W **298** C3
Matacuni → *Venezuela* 3°2N 65°16W **329** C4
Matadi *Dem. Rep. of the Congo* 5°52S 13°31E **265** D2
Matafao, Mt. *Amer. Samoa* 14°17S 170°42W **302** f
Matagalpa *Nic.* 13°0N 85°58W **320** D2
Matagami *Canada* 49°45N 77°34W **298** C4
Matagami, L. *Canada* 49°50N 77°40W **298** C4
Matagorda B. *U.S.A.* 28°40N 96°12W **314** G6
Matagorda I. *U.S.A.* 28°15N 96°30W **314** G6
Matahiva *French Polynesia* 17°32S 149°20W **289** f
Mataiea *Tahiti* 17°46S 149°25W **289** e
Matak *Indonesia* 3°18N 106°16E **234** B3
Matakana *N.S.W., Australia* 32°59S 145°54E **283** B6
Matakana *N.Z.* 36°21S 174°43E **284** C3
Matala *Angola* 14°46S 15°4E **265** E3
Matala *Kriti, Greece* 34°59N 24°45E **207** F5
Matalam *Phil.* 7°5N 124°54E **233** H5
Matalaque *Peru* 16°26S 70°49W **330** D3
Matale *Sri Lanka* 7°30N 80°37E **245** L5
Matam *Senegal* 15°34N 13°17W **262** B2
Matam □ *Senegal* 15°37N 13°19W **262** B2
Matamata *N.Z.* 37°48S 175°47E **284** D4
Matameye *Niger* 13°26N 8°28E **259** F1
Matamoros *Coahuila, Mexico* 25°32N 103°15W **318** B4
Matamoros *Tamaulipas, Mexico* 25°53N 97°30W **319** B5
Ma'ţan as Sarra *Libya* 21°45N 22°0E **259** D4
Ma'ţan Bishārah *Libya* 23°0N 22°32E **258** D4
Matandu → *Tanzania* 8°45S 34°19E **269** D3
Matane *Canada* 48°50N 67°33W **299** C6
Matang *China* 23°30N 104°7E **228** F5
Matankari *Niger* 13°46N 4°1E **263** C5
Matanomadh *India* 23°33N 68°57E **242** H3
Matanzas *Cuba* 23°0N 81°40W **320** B3
Matapa *Botswana* 23°11S 24°39E **270** B3
Matapan, C. = Tenaro, Akra *Greece* 36°22N 22°27E **204** E4
Matapédia *Canada* 48°0N 66°59W **299** C6
Matapo △ *Zimbabwe* 20°30S 29°40E **269** G2
Mataporquera *Spain* 42°52N 4°10W **194** C6
Matara *Sri Lanka* 5°58N 80°30E **245** M5
Mataram *Indonesia* 8°35S 116°7E **231** K19
Matarani *Peru* 17°0S 72°10W **330** D3
Mataranka *Australia* 14°55S 133°4E **278** B5
Matarinao B. *Phil.* 11°12N 125°33E **233** F5
Matarma, Râs *Egypt* 30°27N 32°44E **251** H3
Mataró *Spain* 41°32N 2°29E **196** D7
Matarraña → *Spain* 41°14N 0°22E **196** D5
Mataruška Banja *Serbia* 43°40N 20°40E **202** C4
Matasiete, Cerro *Venezuela* 11°3N 63°51W **329** a
Mataso *Vanuatu* 17°14S 168°26E **287** G6
Matata *N.Z.* 37°54S 176°48E **284** D5
Matatiele *S. Africa* 30°20S 28°49E **271** D4
Matatila Dam *India* 25°0N 78°22E **244** B4
Matatula, C. *Amer. Samoa* 14°15S 170°33W **302** f
Mataura *N.Z.* 46°11S 168°51E **285** G3
Mataura → *N.Z.* 46°34S 168°44E **285** G3
Matavai, B. de *Tahiti* 17°30S 149°23W **289** e
Matavera *Cook Is.* 21°13S 159°44W **289** h
Mataveri *Chile* 27°9S 109°27W **330** b
Mategua *Bolivia* 13°1S 62°48W **331** C5
Matehuala *Mexico* 23°39N 100°39W **318** C4
Mateke *Dem. Rep. of the Congo* 4°52S 24°25E **264** C3
Mateke Hills *Zimbabwe* 21°48S 31°0E **269** G3
Matelot *Trin. & Tob.* 10°50N 61°7W **323** t
Matera *Italy* 40°40N 16°36E **201** B9
Matese, Monti del *Italy* 41°27N 14°22E **201** A7
Matese ⌓ *Italy* 41°24N 14°23E **201** A7
Mátészalka *Hungary* 47°58N 22°20E **182** C7
Matetsi *Zimbabwe* 18°12S 26°0E **269** F2
Mateur *Tunisia* 37°0N 9°40E **258** A1
Matfors *Sweden* 62°21N 17°2E **162** B11
Matha *France* 45°52N 0°20W **174** C3
Matheniko ⌓ *Uganda* 2°49N 34°27E **268** B3
Mathis *U.S.A.* 28°6N 97°50W **314** G6
Mathoura *Australia* 35°50S 144°55E **283** C6
Mathraki *Greece* 39°48N 19°31E **206** B9
Mathura *India* 27°30N 77°40E **242** F7
Mati *Phil.* 6°55N 126°15E **233** H6
Matiakoali *Burkina Faso* 12°28N 1°2E **263** C5
Matiali *India* 26°56N 88°49E **243** F13
Matías Romero *Mexico* 16°53N 95°2W **319** D5
Matibane *Mozam.* 14°49S 40°45E **269** E5
Matinha *Portugal* 38°45N 9°5W **126** A2
Matinhos *Brazil* 25°49S 48°32W **333** G2
Matiri Ra. *N.Z.* 41°38S 172°20E **285** B7
Matjiesfontein *S. Africa* 33°14S 20°35E **270** D3
Matla → *India* 21°40N 88°40E **243** J13
Matlab Bazar *Bangla.* 23°20N 90°43E **241** D3
Matlamanyane *Botswana* 19°33S 25°57E **270** A4
Matli *Pakistan* 25°2N 68°39E **242** G3
Matlock *U.K.* 53°9N 1°33W **168** D6
Matmata *Tunisia* 33°37N 9°59E **258** B1
Matna *Sudan* 13°49N 35°10E **257** E4
Matnog *Phil.* 12°35N 124°5E **232** E5
Mato *Dem. Rep. of the Congo* 8°1S 24°24E **265** D4
Mato → *Venezuela* 7°9N 65°7W **329** B4
Mato, Serrania de *Venezuela* 6°25N 65°25W **328** B4
Mato Grosso □ *Brazil* 14°0S 55°0W **331** C7
Mato Grosso, Planalto do *Brazil* 15°0S 55°0W **331** D7
Mato Grosso do Sul □ *Brazil* 18°0S 55°0W **331** D7
Matobo = Matapo △ *Zimbabwe* 20°30S 29°40E **269** G2
Matochkin Shar, Proliv *Russia* 73°23N 55°12E **214** B6
Matola *Mozam.* 25°57S 32°27E **271** C5
Matong *Papua N. G.* 5°36S 151°50E **286** C6
Matopo Hills *Zimbabwe* 20°36S 28°20E **269** G2
Matopos *Zimbabwe* 20°20S 28°29E **269** G2
Matosinhos *Portugal* 41°11N 8°42W **194** D2
Matou *Taiwan* 23°11N 120°15E **225** C2
Matouba *Guadeloupe* 16°2N 61°41W **322** e
Matour *France* 46°19N 4°29E **173** F11
Matramam *Indonesia* 6°12S 106°51E **122** B2
Matroosberg *S. Africa* 33°23S 19°40E **270** D2
Maţruḩ *Oman* 23°37N 58°30E **249** B7
Matsalu △ *Estonia* 58°45N 23°36E **188** C2
Matsena *Nigeria* 13°5N 10°5E **263** C7
Matsesta *Russia* 43°34N 39°51E **191** J4
Matsu Tao *Taiwan* 26°8N 119°56E **225** b
Matsubara = Takahagi *Japan* 36°43N 140°45E **221** F10
Matsubara *Japan* 34°34N 135°33E **133** B2
Matsubase *Japan* 32°40N 130°40E **222** E2
Matsudo *Japan* 35°47N 139°54E **223** B11
Matsue *Japan* 35°25N 133°10E **222** B5
Matsum, Ko *Thailand* 9°22N 99°59E **237** b
Matsumae *Japan* 41°26N 140°7E **220** D10
Matsumae-Hantō *Japan* 41°30N 140°15E **220** D10
Matsumoto *Japan* 36°15N 138°0E **223** A10
Matsusaka *Japan* 34°34N 136°32E **223** C8
Matsushima *Kumamoto, Japan* 32°30N 130°25E **222** E2
Matsushima *Miyagi, Japan* 38°20N 141°10E **220** E10
Matsuura *Japan* 33°20N 129°49E **222** D1
Matsuyama *Japan* 33°45N 132°45E **222** D4
Matsuzaki *Japan* 34°43N 138°50E **223** C10
Mattagami → *Canada* 50°43N 81°29W **298** B3
Mattancheri *India* 9°50N 76°15E **245** K3
Mattapan *U.S.A.* 42°16N 71°6W **116** B2
Mattawa *Canada* 46°20N 78°45W **298** C4
Matterhorn *Switz.* 45°58N 7°39E **179** K3
Mattersburg *Austria* 47°44N 16°24E **181** D9
Matteson *U.S.A.* 41°30N 87°42W **311** C9
Matthew, Î. *N. Cal.* 22°29S 171°15E **277** E13
Matthew Town *The Bahamas* 20°57N 73°40W **321** B5
Matthews *U.S.A.* 40°23N 85°30W **311** D11
Matthews Ridge *Guyana* 7°37N 60°10W **329** B5
Mattias Church *Budapest, Hungary* **117** b1
Mattice *Canada* 49°40N 83°20W **298** C3
Mattili *India* 18°33N 82°12E **244** E6
Mattituck *U.S.A.* 40°59N 72°32W **313** F12
Mattō = Hakusan *Japan* 36°31N 136°34E **223** A8
Mattoon *U.S.A.* 39°29N 88°23W **311** E8
Matuba *Mozam.* 24°28S 32°49E **271** B5
Matucana *Peru* 11°55S 76°25W **330** C2
Matugama *Sri Lanka* 6°31N 80°7E **245** L5
Matuguinao *Phil.* 12°5N 124°55E **232** E5
Matuka *Papua N. G.* 4°54S 145°47E **286** C3
Matuku *Fiji* 19°10S 179°44E **287** B2
Matūn = Khowst *Afghan.* 33°22N 69°58E **242** C3
Matura *Trin. & Tob.* 10°40N 61°4W **323** t
Matura B. *Trin. & Tob.* 10°39N 61°1W **323** t
Maturín *Venezuela* 9°45N 63°11W **329** B5
Matusadona △ *Zimbabwe* 16°58S 28°42E **269** F2
Matutum, Mt. *Phil.* 6°22N 125°5E **233** H5
Matveyev Kurgan *Russia* 47°35N 38°57E **189** J10
Matxitxako, C. *Spain* 43°28N 2°47W **196** B2
Mátyásföld *Hungary* 47°30N 19°12E **117** A3
Mau *Mad. P., India* 26°17N 78°41E **243** F8
Mau *Ut. P., India* 25°56N 83°33E **243** G10
Mau *Ut. P., India* 25°17N 81°23E **243** G9
Mau Escarpment *Kenya* 0°40S 36°0E **268** C4
Mau Ranipur *India* 25°16N 79°8E **243** G8
Mau Tso Ngam *Hong Kong, China* 22°22N 114°13E **122** A3
Maua *Eastern, Kenya* 0°14N 37°56E **268** C4
Maua *Mozam.* 13°53S 37°10E **269** E4
Mauban *Phil.* 14°12N 121°44E **232** D3
Maubeuge *France* 50°17N 3°57E **173** B10
Maubin *Myanmar* 16°44N 95°39E **241** G5
Maubourguet *France* 43°29N 0°1E **174** E4
Maud, Pt. *Australia* 23°6S 113°45E **278** D1
Maud Rise *S. Ocean* 66°0S 3°0E **151** C3
Maude *Australia* 34°29S 144°18E **282** C6
Maudin Sun *Myanmar* 16°0N 94°30E **241** G5
Mauer *Austria* 48°9N 16°16E **142** B1
Maués *Brazil* 3°20S 57°45W **329** D6
Maués-Acu → *Brazil* 3°22S 57°44W **329** D6
Maug Is. *N. Marianas* 20°1N 145°13E **302** a
Mauganj *India* 24°50N 81°55E **243** G9
Maughold Hd. *I. of Man* 54°18N 4°18W **168** C3
Mauguio *France* 43°37N 4°1E **174** E7
Maui *U.S.A.* 20°48N 156°20W **302** C5
Maulamyaing = Mawlamyine *Myanmar* 16°30N 97°40E **241** G6
Maule □ *Chile* 36°5S 72°30W **334** D1
Mauléon-Licharre *France* 43°14N 0°54W **174** E3
Maullín *Chile* 41°38S 73°37W **336** B2
Maulvi Bazar *Bangla.* 24°29N 91°42E **241** C3
Maumee *U.S.A.* 41°34N 83°39W **311** C13
Maumee → *U.S.A.* 41°42N 83°28W **311** C13
Maumere *Indonesia* 8°38S 122°13E **231** F6
Maumusson, Pertuis de *France* 45°48N 1°14W **174** C2
Maun *Botswana* 20°0S 23°26E **270** B3
Mauna Kea *U.S.A.* 19°50N 155°28W **302** D6
Mauna Loa *U.S.A.* 19°30N 155°35W **302** D6
Mauna Loa Forest Reserve *U.S.A.* 19°35N 155°33W **302** D6
Maunabo *Puerto Rico* 18°1N 65°54W **321** b
Maunaloa *U.S.A.* 21°8N 157°13W **302** B4
Maunalua B. *U.S.A.* 21°15N 157°45W **302** K14
Maunath Bhanjan = Mau *India* 25°56N 83°33E **243** G10
Maunawili *U.S.A.* 21°23N 157°46W **302** K14
Maunga Orito *Chile* 27°10S 109°25W **330** b
Maunga Puakatiki *Chile* 27°6S 109°15W **330** b
Maunga Terevaka *Chile* 27°5S 109°23W **330** b
Maungaroa *Cook Is.* 21°13S 159°48W **289** h
Maungatongaiti *Cook Is.* 21°14S 159°48W **289** h
Maungaturoto *N.Z.* 36°6S 174°23E **284** C3
Maungdaw *Myanmar* 20°50N 92°21E **241** E4
Maungmagan Kyunzu *Myanmar* 14°0N 97°48E **236** E1
Maungu *Kenya* 3°33S 38°45E **268** C4
Maupihaa *French Polynesia* 16°50S 153°55W **289** f
Maupin *U.S.A.* 45°11N 121°5W **304** D3
Maupiti *French Polynesia* 16°27S 152°15W **289** f
Maure-de-Bretagne *France* 47°59N 1°58W **172** E5
Maurepas, L. *U.S.A.* 30°15N 90°30W **315** F9
Maures *France* 43°15N 6°15E **175** E10
Mauriac *France* 45°13N 2°19E **174** C6
Maurice, L. *Australia* 29°30S 131°0E **279** E5
Maurice Bishop Int. ✈ (GND) *Grenada* 12°0N 61°46W **323** q
Mauriceville *N.Z.* 40°45S 175°42E **284** G4
Mauricie △ *Canada* 46°45N 73°0W **298** C5
Maurienne *France* 45°13N 6°30E **175** C10
Mauripur *Pakistan* 24°52N 66°55E **123** A1
Mauritania ■ *Africa* 20°50N 10°0W **260** D3
Mauritius ■ *Ind. Oc.* 20°0S 57°0E **272** e
Mauritius ✈ (MRU) *Mauritius* 20°25S 57°40E **272** e
Mauron *France* 48°9N 2°18W **172** D4
Maurs *France* 44°43N 2°12E **174** D6
Mauston *U.S.A.* 43°48N 90°5W **308** D8
Mauterndorf *Austria* 47°9N 13°40E **180** D6
Mauthen *Austria* 46°40N 13°0E **180** E6
Mauvezin *France* 43°44N 0°53E **174** E4
Mauzé-sur-le-Mignon *France* 46°12N 0°41W **174** B3
Mavaca → *Venezuela* 2°31N 65°11W **329** C4
Mavinga *Angola* 15°50S 20°21E **265** F4
Mavli *India* 24°45N 73°55E **242** G5
Mavoko = Athi River *Kenya* 1°28S 36°58E **268** C4
Mavrata *Greece* 38°4N 20°44E **207** C2
Mavrovë *Albania* 40°26N 19°32E **202** F3
Mavrovo △ *N. Macedonia* 41°36N 20°45E **202** E4
Mavuradonha Mts. *Zimbabwe* 16°30S 31°30E **269** F3
Mawa *Dem. Rep. of the Congo* 2°45N 26°40E **268** B2
Mawai *India* 22°30N 81°4E **243** H9
Mawana *India* 29°6N 77°58E **242** E7
Mawand *Pakistan* 29°33N 68°38E **242** E3
Mawat *Iraq* 35°54N 45°24E **213** E11
Mawjib, W. al → *Jordan* 31°28N 35°36E **251** G6
Mawkmai *Myanmar* 20°14N 97°37E **241** E6
Mawlaik *Myanmar* 23°40N 94°26E **241** D5
Mawlamyine *Myanmar* 16°30N 97°40E **241** G6
Mawlamyinegyun *Myanmar* 16°23N 95°16E **241** G5
Mawlawkho *Myanmar* 17°50N 97°38E **241** G6
Mawqaq *Si. Arabia* 27°25N 41°8E **246** E4
Mawson *Antarctica* 67°30S 62°53E **151** C6
Mawson Coast *Antarctica* 68°30S 63°0E **151** C6
Mawson Pk. *Heard I.* 53°6S 73°31E **273** K6
Mawsynram *India* 25°15N 91°30E **241** C3
Mawza' *Yemen* 13°16N 43°30E **248** D3
Max *U.S.A.* 47°49N 101°18W **308** B3
Maxambamba = Nova Iguaçu *Brazil* 22°45S 43°28W **333** F3
Maxcanú *Mexico* 20°35N 90°0W **319** C6
Maxesibeni *S. Africa* 30°49S 29°23E **271** D4
Maxeys *U.S.A.* 33°45N 83°11W **316** B6
Maxhamish L. *Canada* 59°50N 123°17W **296** B4
Maxhof *Germany* 48°4N 11°29E **131** B1
Maxixe *Mozam.* 23°54S 35°17E **271** B6
Maxville *Canada* 45°17N 74°51W **313** A10
Maxwell *N.Z.* 39°51S 174°49E **284** F3
Maxwell *Calif., U.S.A.* 39°17N 122°11W **306** F4
Maxwelton *Australia* 20°43S 142°41E **280** C3
MAXXI National Museum of 21st Century Arts *Italy* 41°56N 12°28E **136** B1
May, C. *U.S.A.* 38°56N 74°58W **309** F16
May Jirgui *Niger* 13°44N 8°8E **259** F1
May Pen *Jamaica* 17°58N 77°15W **320** a
May River *Papua N. G.* 4°19S 141°58E **286** C1
Maya *Indonesia* 1°10S 109°35E **235** C3
Maya → *Russia* 60°28N 134°28E **215** D14
Maya, Costa *Mexico* 18°44N 87°42W **319** D7
Maya Mts. *Belize* 16°30N 89°0W **320** C2
Mayabandar *India* 12°56N 92°56E **245** H11
Mayaguana *The Bahamas* 22°30N 72°44W **321** B5
Mayagüez *Puerto Rico* 18°12N 67°9W **321** C6
Mayahi *Niger* 13°58N 7°40E **263** C6
Mayaky *Ukraine* 47°26N 29°33E **183** C14
Mayals = Maials *Spain* 41°22N 0°30E **196** D5
Mayama *Congo* 3°51S 14°54E **264** C2
Mayāmey *Iran* 36°24N 55°42E **247** B7
Mayang *China* 27°53N 109°49E **228** D7
Mayanup *Australia* 33°57S 116°27E **279** F2
Mayapán *Mexico* 20°29N 89°11W **319** C7
Mayarí *Cuba* 20°40N 75°41W **321** B4
Mayaro *Trin. & Tob.* 10°17N 61°1W **323** t
Mayaro □ *Trin. & Tob.* 10°10N 61°5W **323** t
Mayaro B. *Trin. & Tob.* 10°14N 60°59W **323** t
Mayavaram = Mayiladuthurai *India* 11°3N 79°42E **245** J4
Maybell *U.S.A.* 40°31N 108°5W **304** F9
Maybio *Phil.* 5°50N 125°35E **233** J5
Maybole *U.K.* 55°21N 4°42W **167** F4
Maychew *Ethiopia* 12°50N 39°31E **257** E4
Maydān *Iraq* 34°55N 45°37E **213** E11
Maydan *Ukraine* 48°36N 23°29E **183** B8
Mayen *Germany* 50°19N 7°13E **179** E3
Mayenne *France* 48°20N 0°38W **172** D6
Mayenne □ *France* 48°10N 0°40W **172** D6
Mayenne → *France* 47°30N 0°32W **172** E6
Mayer *U.S.A.* 34°24N 112°14W **305** J7
Mayerthorpe *Canada* 53°57N 115°8W **296** C5
Mayesville *U.S.A.* 34°0N 80°12W **316** A9
Mayfair *Gauteng, S. Africa* 26°11S 28°0E **123** B2
Mayfair *London, U.K.* **125** b3
Mayfield *Ky., U.S.A.* 36°44N 88°38W **308** G9
Mayfield *N.Y., U.S.A.* 43°6N 74°16W **313** C10
Mayhill *U.S.A.* 32°53N 105°29W **305** K11
Mayiladuthurai *India* 11°3N 79°42E **245** J4
Maykop *Russia* 44°35N 40°10E **191** H5
Mayma *Russia* 52°3N 85°55E **217** B11
Maymyo = Pyin-U-Lwin *Myanmar* 22°2N 96°28E **236** A1
Maynard *Mass., U.S.A.* 42°26N 71°27W **313** D13
Maynard *Wash., U.S.A.* 47°59N 122°55W **306** C4
Maynard Hills *Australia* 28°28S 119°49E **279** E2
Mayne → *Australia* 23°40S 141°55E **280** C3
Maynooth *Ont., Canada* 45°13N 77°56W **312** A7
Maynooth *Kildare, Ireland* 53°23N 6°34W **166** C5
Mayo *Yukon, Canada* 63°38N 135°57W **294** E4
Mayo *Trin. & Tob.* 10°21N 61°23W **323** t
Mayo *Fla., U.S.A.* 30°3N 83°10W **316** E6
Mayo □ *Ireland* 53°53N 9°3W **166** C2
Mayo → *Argentina* 45°45S 69°45W **336** C3
Mayo → *Peru* 6°38S 76°15W **330** B2
Mayo B. *Phil.* 6°56N 126°22E **233** H6
Mayo Daga *Nigeria* 6°59N 11°25E **263** D7
Mayo Faran *Nigeria* 8°57N 12°4E **263** D7
Mayo-Kébbi Est □ *Chad* 10°20N 15°30E **259** F3
Mayo-Kébbi Ouest □ *Chad* 9°40N 17°50E **259** G3
Mayoko *Congo* 2°18S 12°49E **264** C2
Mayoko *Dem. Rep. of the Congo* 1°6S 23°50E **264** C4
Mayon Volcano *Phil.* 13°15N 123°41E **232** E4
Mayor Buratovich *Argentina* 39°15S 62°37W **336** A4
Mayor I. *N.Z.* 37°16S 176°17E **284** D5
Mayor Pablo Lagerenza *Paraguay* 19°55S 60°47W **331** D5
Mayorga *Spain* 42°10N 5°16W **194** C5
Mayoro/Rio Claro □ *Trin. & Tob.* 10°20N 61°10W **323** t
Mayotte ⊠ *Ind. Oc.* 12°50S 45°10E **272** b
Mayoyao *Phil.* 16°59N 121°14E **232** C3
Mayqayyng *Kazakhstan* 51°27N 75°47E **217** B9
Mayraira Pt. *Phil.* 18°39N 120°51E **232** B3
Mayreau *St. Vincent* 12°39N 61°23W **323** n
Maysān □ *Iraq* 31°55N 47°15E **246** D5
Mayskiy *Russia* 43°47N 44°2E **191** J7
Maysville *Ky., U.S.A.* 38°39N 83°46W **311** F13
Maysville *Mo., U.S.A.* 39°53N 94°22W **310** E2
Maytiguid I. *Phil.* 11°3N 119°36E **233** F2
Mayu *Indonesia* 1°30N 126°30E **231** D7
Mayumba *Gabon* 3°25S 10°39E **264** C2
Mayuram = Mayiladuthurai *India* 11°3N 79°42E **245** J4
Mayville *N. Dak., U.S.A.* 47°30N 97°20W **308** B5
Mayville *N.Y., U.S.A.* 42°15N 79°30W **312** D5
Maywood *Calif., U.S.A.* 33°59N 118°12W **126** C3
Maywood *Ill., U.S.A.* 41°52N 87°51W **119** B1
Maywood *N.J., U.S.A.* 40°53N 74°3W **132** A1
Maywood Park Race Track *U.S.A.* 41°54N 87°50W **119** B1
Mazabuka *Zambia* 15°52S 27°44E **269** F2
Mazagán = El Jadida *Morocco* 33°11N 8°17W **260** B3
Mazagão *Brazil* 0°7S 51°16W **329** D7
Mazagaon *Mumbai, India* **130** a2
Mazamet *France* 43°30N 2°20E **174** E6
Mazán *Peru* 3°30S 73°0W **328** D3
Māzandarān □ *Iran* 36°30N 52°0E **247** B7
Mazapil *Mexico* 24°39N 101°34W **318** C4
Mazar *China* 36°32N 77°1E **217** E9
Mazar, O. → *Algeria* 31°50N 1°36E **261** B5
Mazār-e Sharīf *Afghan.* 36°41N 67°0E **240** A2
Mazara del Vallo *Italy* 37°39N 12°35E **200** E5
Mazarredo *Argentina* 47°10S 66°50W **336** C3

Mazarrón Spain 37°38N 1°19W 197 H3
Mazarrón, G. de Spain 37°27N 1°19W 197 H3
Mazaruni → Guyana 6°25N 58°35W 329 B6
Mazatán Mexico 29°0N 110°8W 318 B2
Mazatenango Guatemala 14°35N 91°30W 320 D1
Mazatlán Mexico 23°13N 106°25W 318 C3
Mažeikiai Lithuania 56°20N 22°20E 184 B9
Mazhafa, J. Si. Arabia 28°52N 35°5E 251 K6
Māzhān Iran 32°30N 59°0E 247 C8
Mazıdağı Turkey 37°28N 40°29E 213 D9
Mazīnān Iran 36°19N 56°56E 247 B8
Mazo Cruz Peru 16°45S 69°44W 330 D4
Mazoe Mozam. 16°42S 33°7E 269 F3
Mazoe → Mozam. 16°20S 33°30E 269 F3
Mazomanie U.S.A. 43°11N 89°48W 310 A7
Mazon U.S.A. 41°14N 88°25W 311 C8
Mazowe Zimbabwe 17°28S 30°58E 269 F3
Mazowieckie □ Poland 52°40N 21°0E 185 F8
Mazrûb Sudan 14°0N 29°20E 257 E2
Mazurski, Pojezierze Poland 53°50N 21°0E 184 E7
Mazyr Belarus 51°59N 29°15E 177 B15
Mba Fiji 17°33S 177°41E 287 A1
Mbaba Senegal 14°59N 16°44W 262 C1
Mbabane Eswatini 26°18S 31°6E 271 C5
Mbaéré → C.A.R. 3°47N 17°31E 264 B3
Mbagne Mauritania 16°6N 14°47W 262 B2
M'bahiakro Côte d'Ivoire 7°33N 4°19W 262 D4
Mbaïki C.A.R. 3°53N 18°1E 264 B3
Mbakana, Mt. de Cameroon 7°57N 15°6E 264 A3
Mbala Zambia 8°46S 31°24E 269 D3
Mbalabala Zimbabwe 20°27S 29°3E 271 B4
Mbalam Cameroon 2°13N 13°49E 264 B2
Mbale Uganda 1°8N 34°12E 268 B3
Mbali → C.A.R. 4°27N 18°20E 264 B3
Mbalmayo Cameroon 3°33N 11°33E 263 E7
Mbam → Cameroon 4°24N 11°17E 263 E7
Mbamba Bay Tanzania 11°13S 34°49E 269 E3
Mbandaka Dem. Rep. of the Congo 0°1N 18°18E 264 B3
Mbandjok Cameroon 4°27N 11°54E 264 B2
Mbanga Cameroon 4°30N 9°33E 263 E6
Mbanika Solomon Is. 9°3S 159°13E 287 M10
M'Banio, Lagune Gabon 3°35S 11°0E 264 C2
Mbanza Congo Angola 6°18S 14°16E 265 D2
Mbanza Ngungu Dem. Rep. of the Congo 5°12S 14°53E 265 D2
Mbarangandu Tanzania 10°11S 36°48E 269 D4
Mbarara Uganda 0°35S 30°40E 268 C3
Mbari → C.A.R. 4°34N 22°43E 264 B4
Mbatto Côte d'Ivoire 6°28N 4°22W 262 D4
Mbava Solomon Is. 7°47S 156°33E 287 L9
Mbé Congo 3°14S 15°50E 264 C3
Mbe Eq. Guin. 1°47N 9°56E 264 B1
Mbengga = Beqa Fiji 18°23S 178°8E 287 B2
Mbengué Gabon 2°2S 11°7E 264 C2
Mbengui Gabon 2°3S 10°4E 264 C2
Mbéni Comoros Is. 11°30S 43°22E 272 a
Mbenkuru → Tanzania 9°25S 39°50E 269 D4
Mbéré → Cameroon 7°45N 15°36E 264 A3
Mberengwa Zimbabwe 20°29S 29°57E 269 G2
Mberengwa, Mt. Zimbabwe 20°37S 29°55E 269 G2
Mberubu Nigeria 6°10N 7°38E 263 D6
Mbesuma Zambia 10°0S 32°2E 269 E3
Mbeya Tanzania 8°54S 33°29E 269 D3
Mbeya □ Tanzania 8°15S 33°30E 268 D3
Mbhashe → S. Africa 32°15S 28°54E 271 D4
Mbigou Gabon 1°53S 11°56E 264 C2
M'bili South Sudan 7°35N 28°15E 257 F2
Mbinga Tanzania 10°50S 35°0E 269 E4
Mbini = Río Muni □ Eq. Guin. 1°30N 10°0E 264 B2
Mbini Eq. Guin. 1°35N 9°37E 264 B1
Mbini → Eq. Guin. 1°36N 9°37E 264 B1
Mbizi Zimbabwe 21°23S 31°1E 269 G3
Mboi Dem. Rep. of the Congo 6°57S 21°54E 265 D4
Mboki C.A.R. 5°19N 25°58E 257 F2
Mbokonimbeti Solomon Is. 8°57S 160°7E 287 M11
Mboli Dem. Rep. of the Congo 4°8N 23°9E 264 B4
Mbombela S. Africa 25°29S 30°59E 271 C5
Mbomo Congo 0°25N 14°42E 264 B2
Mbomou = Bomu → C.A.R. 4°40N 22°30E 264 B4
Mbomou □ C.A.R. 5°30N 23°30E 264 A4
M'bonge Cameroon 4°33N 9°5E 263 E6
Mboro Senegal 15°9N 16°54W 262 B1
Mboua Cameroon 4°25N 14°16E 264 A2
Mbouda Cameroon 5°38N 10°15E 264 A2
M'boukou, L. de Cameroon 6°23N 12°50E 263 D7
Mboune Senegal 14°42N 13°34W 262 C2
Mbouoma Congo 0°52S 15°4E 264 C3
Mbour Senegal 14°22N 16°54W 262 C1
Mbout Mauritania 16°1N 12°38W 262 B2
Mbrés C.A.R. 6°40N 19°48E 264 A3
M'Bridge → Angola 7°12S 12°51E 265 D2
Mbuji-Mayi Dem. Rep. of the Congo 6°9S 23°40E 265 D4
Mbulu Tanzania 3°45S 35°30E 268 C4
Mbuma Dem. Rep. of the Congo 3°32N 24°50E 264 B4
Mbuma Solomon Is. 8°59S 160°46E 287 M11
Mburucuyá Argentina 28°1S 58°14W 334 B4
Mburucuyá △ Argentina 28°1S 58°12W 334 B4
M'bwat Cameroon 6°29N 10°45E 264 A2
Mcherrah Algeria 27°0N 4°30W 260 C4
Mchinga Tanzania 9°44S 39°45E 269 D4
Mchinji Malawi 13°47S 32°58E 269 E3
Mdantsane S. Africa 32°56S 27°46E 271 D4
Mdennah Mauritania 24°37N 6°0W 260 D3
Me'a She' Arim Jerusalem 123 a2
Mead, L. U.S.A. 36°0N 114°44W 307 J12
Meade = Atqasuk → U.S.A. 70°52N 155°55W 303 A9
Meade U.S.A. 37°17N 100°20W 308 G3
Meade River = Atqasuk U.S.A. 70°28N 157°24W 303 A8
Meadow Lake Canada 54°10N 108°26W 297 C7
Meadow Lake ⌓ Canada 54°27N 109°0W 297 C7
Meadow Valley Wash → U.S.A. 36°40N 114°34W 307 J12
Meadowbank Park Australia 33°49S 151°6E 139 A1
Meadowlands Sports Complex New York, U.S.A. 40°49N 74°5W 132 B1
Meadville Mo., U.S.A. 39°47N 93°18W 310 E3
Meadville Pa., U.S.A. 41°39N 80°9W 312 E4
Meaford Canada 44°36N 80°35W 312 B4
Meakan Dake Japan 45°15N 144°0E 220 C11
Mealhada Portugal 40°22N 8°27W 194 E2
Mealy Mts. Canada 53°10N 58°0W 299 B8
Meander River Canada 59°2N 117°42W 296 B5
Meares, C. U.S.A. 45°37N 124°0W 304 D1
Mearim → Brazil 3°4S 44°35W 332 B3
Meath □ Ireland 53°40N 6°57W 166 C5
Meath Park Canada 53°27N 105°22W 297 C7
Meaulne France 46°36N 2°36E 173 F9
Meaux France 48°58N 2°50E 173 D9
Mebechi-Gawa → Japan 40°31N 141°31E 220 D10
Mebonden Norway 63°13N 11°2E 164 A8
Mebulu, Tanjung Indonesia 8°50S 115°5E 231 K18
Mecanhelas Mozam. 15°12S 35°54E 269 F4
Mecaya → Colombia 0°29N 75°11W 328 C2
Mecca = Makkah Si. Arabia 21°30N 39°54E 248 B2
Mecca U.S.A. 33°34N 116°5W 307 M10
Mechanicsburg Ohio, U.S.A. 40°4N 83°33W 311 D13
Mechanicsburg Pa., U.S.A. 40°13N 77°1W 312 F8
Mechanicsville U.S.A. 41°54N 91°16W 310 C5
Mechanicville U.S.A. 42°54N 73°41W 313 D11
Mechara Ethiopia 8°36N 40°20E 257 F5
Mechelen Belgium 51°2N 4°29E 170 C4
Mecherchar = Eil Malk Palau 7°10N 134°23E 288 c
Mecheria Algeria 33°35N 0°18W 261 B4
Mechernich Germany 50°35N 6°39E 178 E2
Mechetinskaya Russia 46°45N 40°32E 191 G5
Mechol Micronesia 9°37N 138°9E 287 R16
Měcholupy Czechia 50°3N 14°32E 135 B3
Mechra Bel Ksiri Morocco 34°34N 5°57W 260 B3
Mechra Benâbbou Morocco 32°39N 7°48W 260 B3
Měčice Czechia 50°11N 14°31E 135 A3
Mecidiye Turkey 40°38N 26°32E 203 F10
Mecidiyeköy Turkey 41°4N 29°0E 122 B2
Mecitözü Turkey 40°32N 35°17E 212 B6
Mecklenburg Germany 53°33N 11°40E 176 B7
Mecklenburg-Vorpommern □ Germany 53°45N 12°15E 178 B8
Mecklenburger Bucht Germany 54°20N 11°40E 178 A7
Meconta Mozam. 14°59S 39°50E 269 E4
Mecsek Hungary 46°10N 18°18E 182 D3
Mecubúri Mozam. 14°39S 38°54E 269 E4
Mecubúri → Mozam. 14°10S 40°30E 269 E5
Mecúfi Mozam. 13°20S 40°32E 269 E5
Mêda Portugal 40°57N 7°18W 194 E3
Medak India 18°1N 78°15E 244 E4
Medan Indonesia 3°40N 98°38E 234 B1
Medang Indonesia 8°9S 117°22E 235 D5
Médanos Argentina 38°50S 62°42W 336 A4
Médanos de Coro △ Venezuela 11°35N 69°44W 328 A4
Medanosa, Pta. Argentina 48°8S 66°0W 336 C3
Medart U.S.A. 30°5N 84°23W 316 E5
Medaryville U.S.A. 41°5N 86°55W 311 C10
Medawachchiya Sri Lanka 8°30N 80°30E 245 K5
Medchal India 17°37N 78°29E 244 F4
Mede Italy 45°6N 8°44E 198 C5
Médéa Algeria 36°12N 2°50E 261 A5
Médéa □ Algeria 36°0N 3°0E 261 A5
Mededa Bos.-H. 43°44N 19°10E 182 G4
Médégué Gabon 0°37N 10°8E 264 B2
Medeiros Neto Brazil 17°20S 40°14W 333 E3
Medellín Colombia 6°15N 75°35W 328 B2
Medelpad Sweden 62°33N 16°30E 162 B10
Medemblik Neths. 52°46N 5°8E 170 B5
Médenine Tunisia 33°21N 10°30E 258 B2
Médenine □ Tunisia 32°20N 10°0E 261 B7
Mederdra Mauritania 17°0N 15°38W 262 B1
Medford Mass., U.S.A. 42°25N 71°7W 116 A2
Medford Oreg., U.S.A. 42°19N 122°52W 304 E2
Medford Wis., U.S.A. 45°9N 90°20W 308 C8
Medgidia Romania 44°15N 28°19E 183 F13
Medi South Sudan 5°4N 30°42E 257 F3
Media Agua Argentina 31°58S 68°25W 334 C2
Media Luna Argentina 34°45S 66°44W 334 C2
Medianeira Brazil 25°17S 54°5W 335 B5
Mediapolis U.S.A. 41°0N 91°10W 310 D5
Mediaş Romania 46°9N 24°22E 183 D9
Medicilândia Brazil 3°33S 53°8W 329 D7
Medicina Italy 44°28N 11°38E 199 D8
Medicine Bow U.S.A. 41°54N 106°12W 304 F10
Medicine Bow Mts. U.S.A. 40°40N 106°0W 304 F10
Medicine Hat Canada 50°0N 110°45W 297 D6
Medicine Lake U.S.A. 48°30N 104°30W 304 B11
Medicine Lodge U.S.A. 37°17N 98°35W 308 G4
Medina = Al Madīnah Si. Arabia 24°35N 39°52E 246 E3
Medina Brazil 16°15S 41°29W 333 E3
Medina Colombia 4°30N 73°21W 328 C3
Medina Mis. Or., Phil. 8°55N 125°0E 233 G5
Medina N. Dak., U.S.A. 46°54N 99°18W 308 B4
Medina N.Y., U.S.A. 43°13N 78°23W 312 C6
Medina Ohio, U.S.A. 41°8N 81°52W 312 E3
Medina → U.S.A. 29°16N 98°29W 314 G5
Medina de Pomar Spain 42°56N 3°29W 194 C7
Medina de Rioseco Spain 41°53N 5°3W 194 D5
Medina del Campo Spain 41°18N 4°55W 194 D6
Médina Gounas Senegal 13°8N 13°45W 262 C2
Medina L. U.S.A. 29°32N 98°56W 314 G5
Medina Sidonia Spain 36°28N 5°57W 195 J5
Medinaceli Spain 41°12N 2°30W 196 D2
Medinipur India 22°25N 87°21E 243 H12
Medio-Campidano □ Italy 39°35N 8°30E 200 C1
Mediodia Spain 40°22N 3°39W 127 B2
Mediterranean Sea Europe 35°0N 15°0E 193 E8
Medjerda, O. → Tunisia 37°7N 10°13E 258 A2
Mednogorsk Russia 51°24N 57°37E 216 B5
Medny = Mednogorsk Russia 51°24N 57°37E 216 B5
Médoc France 45°10N 0°50W 174 C3
Medog China 29°19N 95°19E 241 A5
Medora U.S.A. 38°49N 86°10W 311 F10
Médouneu Gabon 0°57N 10°47E 264 B2
Medulin Croatia 44°49N 13°55E 199 D10
Medveđa Serbia 42°50N 21°32E 202 D5
Medvedevo Russia 56°37N 47°47E 190 B8
Medveditsa → Tver, Russia 57°5N 37°30E 188 D9
Medveditsa → Volgograd, Russia 49°35N 42°41E 190 F6
Medvedok Russia 57°20N 50°1E 190 B10
Medvezhi, Ostrava Russia 71°0N 161°0E 215 B17
Medvezhye = Krasnogvardeyskoye Russia 45°52N 41°33E 191 H5
Medvezhyegorsk Russia 63°0N 34°25E 186 B5
Medway □ U.K. 51°25N 0°32E 169 F8
Medway → U.K. 51°27N 0°46E 169 F8
Medzev Slovakia 48°43N 20°55E 181 C13
Medzilaborce Slovakia 49°17N 21°52E 181 B14
Medžitlija N. Macedonia 40°56N 21°26E 202 F5
Meekatharra Australia 26°32S 118°29E 279 E2
Meeker U.S.A. 40°2N 107°55W 304 F10
Meeniyan Australia 38°35S 146°3E 283 E7
Meersburg Germany 47°41N 9°16E 179 H5
Meerut India 29°1N 77°42E 242 E7
Meeteetse U.S.A. 44°9N 108°52W 304 D9
Mega Ethiopia 3°57N 38°19E 257 G4
Mega Sumatera Barat, Indonesia 4°0S 101°2E 234 C2
Megalo Ethiopia 6°51N 40°47E 267 C5
Megalo Chorio Greece 36°27N 27°24E 205 E9
Megalopoli Greece 37°25N 22°7E 204 D4
Meganisi Greece 38°38N 20°46E 207 B2
Megara Greece 37°58N 23°22E 204 D5
Megasini India 21°38N 86°21E 243 J12
Megdovas = Tavropos → Greece 39°10N 21°45E 204 B3
Megève France 45°51N 6°37E 175 C10
Meghalaya □ India 25°50N 91°0E 241 C3
Meghezez Ethiopia 9°18N 39°26E 257 F4
Meghna → Bangla. 22°50N 90°50E 241 D3
Megion Russia 61°3N 76°6E 214 C8
Mégiscane, L. Canada 48°35N 75°55W 298 C4
Megisti Greece 36°8N 29°34E 205 E11
Megra Russia 60°11N 37°14E 188 B9
Meguro Japan 35°37N 139°42E 140 B3
Meguro → Japan 35°37N 139°45E 140 B3
Mehadia Romania 44°56N 22°23E 182 F7
Mehaïguene, O. → Algeria 32°15N 2°59E 261 B5
Meharry, Mt. Australia 22°59S 118°35E 278 D2
Mehedeby Sweden 60°27N 17°25E 162 D11
Mehedinți □ Romania 44°40N 22°45E 182 F7
Meheisa Sudan 19°38N 32°57E 256 D3
Mehekar India 20°9N 76°34E 244 D3
Méhétia French Polynesia 17°52S 148°3W 289 f
Mehlville U.S.A. 38°31N 90°19W 308 F8
Mehmetçik = Galateia Cyprus 35°25N 34°4E 207 E10
Mehndawal India 26°58N 83°5E 243 F10
Mehr Jān Iran 33°50N 55°6E 247 C7
Mehrābād Iran 36°53N 47°55E 213 D12
Mehrābād ✈ (THR) Iran 35°41N 51°18E 141 A1
Mehrābān Iran 38°4N 47°7E 213 C12
Mehram Nagar India 28°34N 77°8E 120 B1
Mehrān Iran 33°7N 46°10E 213 F12
Mehrān → Iran 26°45N 55°26E 247 E7
Mehrgarh Pakistan 29°30N 67°30E 242 E2
Mehrīz Iran 31°35N 54°28E 247 D7
Mehrow Germany 52°34N 13°37E 115 A4
Mehtar Lam Afghan. 34°39N 70°11E 240 B3
Mehun-sur-Yèvre France 47°10N 2°13E 173 E9
Mei Jiang → China 24°25N 116°35E 229 E11
Mei Lanfang, Pantheon of Beijing, China 114 a2
Mei Xian China 34°18N 107°55E 226 G4
Meia Ponte → Brazil 18°32S 49°36W 333 E2
Meicheng China 29°29N 119°16E 229 C12
Meichengzhen China 28°9N 111°40E 229 C8
Meichuan China 30°8N 115°31E 229 B10
Meidling Austria 48°10N 16°20E 142 A2
Meidougou Cameroon 6°25N 14°13E 264 A2
Méier Brazil 22°52S 43°15W 135 B1
Meiganga Cameroon 6°30N 14°25E 264 A2
Meighen I. Canada 80°0N 99°30W 295 B12
Meigs U.S.A. 31°4N 84°6W 316 D5
Meigu China 28°16N 103°20E 228 C4
Meihekou China 42°32N 125°40E 224 A2
Meiji Shrine Tokyo, Japan 140 b1
Meiktila Myanmar 20°53N 95°54E 241 E5
Meili Xue Shan China 28°30N 98°39E 228 C2
Meimyu = Pyin-U-Lwin Myanmar 22°2N 96°28E 236 A1
Meinerzhagen Germany 51°6N 7°38E 178 D3
Meiningen Germany 50°34N 10°25E 178 E6
Meinung Taiwan 22°54N 120°32E 225 D2
Meio → Brazil 13°36S 44°7W 333 D3
Meira, Serra de Spain 43°15N 7°15W 194 B3
Meiringen Switz. 46°43N 8°12E 179 J4
Meise Belgium 50°56N 4°20E 116 A1
Meishan Sichuan, China 30°3N 103°23E 228 B4
Meishan Taiwan 23°35N 120°33E 225 C2
Meissen Germany 51°9N 13°29E 178 D9
Meissner Germany 51°14N 9°50E 178 D5
Meissner-Kaufunger Wald ⌓ Germany 51°16N 9°45E 178 D5
Meitan China 27°45N 107°29E 228 D6
Meizhou China 24°16N 116°6E 229 E11
Meja India 25°9N 82°7E 243 G10
Mejillones Chile 23°10S 70°30W 334 A1
Mejiro Japan 35°43N 139°43E 140 A3
Mékambo Gabon 1°2N 13°50E 264 B2
Mekdela Ethiopia 11°24N 39°10E 257 E4
Mekele Ethiopia 13°33N 39°30E 257 E4
Mekerghene, Sebkra Algeria 26°21N 1°30E 261 C5
Mékhé Senegal 15°7N 16°38W 262 B1
Mekhomiya = Razlog Bulgaria 41°53N 23°28E 202 E7
Mekhtar Pakistan 30°30N 69°15E 240 C3
Meknès Morocco 33°57N 5°33W 260 B3
Meko Nigeria 7°27N 2°52E 263 D5
Mekong → Asia 9°30N 106°15E 237 H6
Mekongga Indonesia 3°39S 121°15E 231 E6
Mekoryuk U.S.A. 60°23N 166°11W 303 F6
Mekrou → Benin 12°25N 2°50E 263 C5
Mekvari = Kür → Azerbaijan 39°29N 49°15E 213 C13
Mel Italy 46°4N 12°5E 199 B9
Melagiri Hills India 12°20N 77°30E 245 H3
Melah, Oued el → Algeria 32°20N 2°28E 261 B5
Melaka Malaysia 2°15N 102°15E 237 L4
Melaka □ Malaysia 2°15N 102°15E 237 L4
Melaky □ Madag. 18°10S 44°0E 272 B1
Melambes Greece 35°8N 24°40E 207 E5
Melanesia Pac. Oc. 4°0S 155°0E 277 A10
Melanesian Basin Pac. Oc. 0°5N 160°35E 288 G8
Melapalaiyam India 8°39N 77°44E 245 K3
Melawi → Indonesia 0°5N 111°29E 235 B4
Melaya Indonesia 8°17S 114°30E 231 J17
Melbourne Vic., Australia 37°48S 144°58E 128 A1
Melbourne Fla., U.S.A. 28°5N 80°37W 317 G9
Melbourne Iowa, U.S.A. 41°57N 93°6W 310 C3
Melbourne ✈ (MEL) Australia 37°40S 144°50E 128 A1
Melcher-Dallas U.S.A. 41°14N 93°15W 310 C3
Melchor Múzquiz Mexico 27°53N 101°31W 318 B4
Melchor Ocampo Mexico 24°51N 101°39W 318 C4
Meldal Norway 63°3N 9°44E 164 A6
Méldola Italy 44°7N 12°5E 199 D9
Meldorf Germany 54°5N 9°5E 178 A5
Mélé C.A.R. 9°46N 21°33E 264 A4
Mele B. Vanuatu 17°44S 168°14E 287 G6
Meleden Somalia 10°25N 49°51E 267 B6
Melegnano Italy 45°21N 9°19E 198 C6
Meleizem Mauritania 22°19N 11°24W 260 D2
Melekess = Dimitrovgrad Russia 54°14N 49°39E 190 C9
Melenci Serbia 45°32N 20°20E 182 E5
Melenki Russia 55°20N 41°37E 190 C5
Meleuz Russia 52°58N 55°55E 216 B5
Mélèzes → Canada 57°40N 69°29W 298 A5
Melfi Chad 11°0N 17°59E 259 F3
Melfi Italy 41°0N 15°39E 201 B8
Melfort Sask., Canada 52°50N 104°37W 297 C8
Melfort Zimbabwe 18°0S 31°25E 269 F3
Melgaço Portugal 42°7N 8°15W 194 C2
Melgar de Fernamental Spain 42°27N 4°17W 194 C6
Melgraseyri Iceland 66°1N 22°27W 155 A4
Melhus Norway 63°17N 10°18E 164 A7
Melide Spain 42°55N 8°1W 194 C2
Meligales Greece 37°15N 21°59E 204 D3
Melilla N. Afr. 35°21N 2°57W 261 A4
Melilli Italy 37°11N 15°7E 201 E8
Melintang, Danau Indonesia 0°18S 116°20E 235 C5
Melipilla Chile 33°42S 71°15W 334 C1
Melissa Canada 45°24N 79°14W 312 A5
Melissa, Akra Greece 35°6N 24°33E 207 E5
Melissa Oros Greece 37°32N 26°4E 205 D8
Melissani Cave Greece 38°15N 20°38E 207 C2
Melita Canada 49°15N 101°0W 297 D8
Mélito di Porto Salvo Italy 37°55N 15°47E 201 E8
Melitopol Ukraine 46°50N 35°22E 189 J8
Melk Austria 48°13N 15°20E 180 C8
Melkki Finland 60°8N 24°53E 121 C2
Mellan Fryken Sweden 59°45N 13°10E 162 E7
Mellansel Sweden 63°26N 18°19E 160 E18
Mellbystrand Sweden 56°30N 12°56E 163 H6
Melle Deux-Sèvres, France 46°14N 0°10W 174 B3
Melle Niedersachsen, Germany 52°12N 8°20E 178 C4
Mellègue, O. → Tunisia 36°36N 9°14E 258 A1
Mellen U.S.A. 46°20N 90°40W 308 B8
Mellerud Sweden 58°41N 12°28E 163 F6
Mellette U.S.A. 45°9N 98°30W 308 C4
Mellid = Melide Spain 42°55N 8°1W 194 C2
Mellieha Malta 35°57N 14°22E 206 F7
Mellieha Bay Malta 35°59N 14°22E 206 F7
Mellit Sudan 14°7N 25°34E 257 E2
Mellizo Sur, Cerro Chile 48°33S 73°10W 336 C2
Mellrichstadt Germany 50°25N 10°17E 178 E6
Mellunkylä Finland 60°14N 25°5E 121 B3
Mellunmäki Finland 60°14N 25°6E 121 B3
Melnik Bulgaria 41°30N 23°25E 202 E7
Mělník Czechia 50°22N 14°23E 180 A7
Melnytsya Podilska Ukraine 48°37N 26°10E 183 B11
Melo Uruguay 32°20S 54°10W 335 C5
Melolo Indonesia 9°53S 120°40E 231 F6
Melouprey Cambodia 13°48N 105°16E 236 F5
Melrhir, Chott Algeria 34°13N 6°30E 261 B6
Melrose N.S.W., Australia 32°42S 146°57E 283 B7
Melrose Borders, U.K. 55°36N 2°43W 167 F6
Melrose Mass., U.S.A. 42°27N 71°2W 116 A2
Melrose Minn., U.S.A. 45°40N 94°49W 308 C6
Melrose N. Mex., U.S.A. 34°26N 103°38W 305 J12
Melrose N.Y., U.S.A. 40°49N 73°55W 132 B2
Melrose Park U.S.A. 26°6N 80°11W 129 B3
Melsbroek Belgium 50°55N 4°29E 116 A2
Melsisi Vanuatu 15°46S 168°10E 287 E6
Melstone U.S.A. 46°36N 107°52W 304 C10
Melsungen Germany 51°7N 9°32E 178 D5
Melton Australia 37°41S 144°35E 282 D6
Melton Mowbray U.K. 52°47N 0°54W 168 E7
Melun France 48°32N 2°39E 173 D9
Melung Nepal 27°31N 86°3E 243 F12
Melur India 10°2N 78°23E 245 J4
Melut South Sudan 10°30N 32°13E 257 E3
Melville Sask., Canada 50°55N 102°50W 297 C8
Melville Gauteng, S. Africa 26°11S 28°1E 123 B2
Melville, C. Queens., Australia 14°11S 144°30E 280 A3
Melville, C. Phil. 7°49N 117°0E 233 H1
Melville, L. Canada 53°30N 60°0W 299 B8
Melville B. N. Terr., Australia 12°0S 136°45E 280 A2
Melville B. Greenland 75°30N 63°0W 154 B4
Melville I. N. Terr., Australia 11°30S 131°0E 278 B5
Melville I. Canada 75°30N 112°0W 295 B9
Melville Pen. Canada 68°0N 84°0W 295 D15
Melvin, Lough Ireland 54°26N 8°10W 166 B3
Mélykút Hungary 46°11N 19°25E 182 D4
Memaliaj Albania 40°25N 19°56E 202 F3
Memba Mozam. 14°11S 40°30E 269 E5
Membalong Indonesia 3°9S 107°37E 235 C3
Memboro Indonesia 9°30S 119°30E 278 A2
Membrilla Spain 38°59N 3°21W 195 G7
Memel = Klaipėda Lithuania 55°43N 21°10E 184 C8
Memel S. Africa 27°38S 29°36E 271 C4
Memmingen Germany 47°58N 10°10E 179 H6
Mempawah Indonesia 0°30N 109°5E 235 B3
Memphis Egypt 29°52N 31°12E 256 J7
Memphis Mich., U.S.A. 42°54N 82°46W 312 D2
Memphis Mo., U.S.A. 40°28N 92°10W 310 D4
Memphis Tenn., U.S.A. 35°8N 90°2W 315 D9
Memphis Tex., U.S.A. 34°44N 100°33W 314 D4
Memphrémagog, L. N. Amer. 45°8N 72°17W 313 B12
Mena Ukraine 51°31N 32°13E 189 G7
Mena Ark., U.S.A. 34°35N 94°15W 314 D7
Mena → Ethiopia 5°40N 40°50E 257 F5
Menabe □ Madag. 20°20S 44°20E 272 C1
Menado = Manado Indonesia 1°29N 124°51E 231 D6
Menai Strait U.K. 53°11N 4°13W 168 D3
Ménaka Mali 15°59N 2°18E 263 B5
Menan = Chao Phraya → Thailand 13°40N 100°31E 236 F3
Menarandra → Madag. 25°17S 44°30E 272 D1
Menard U.S.A. 30°55N 99°47W 314 F5
Menard Fracture Zone Pac. Oc. 43°0S 97°0W 289 M18
Menate Indonesia 0°12S 113°3E 235 C4
Menawashei Sudan 12°41N 24°59E 257 E1
Mendaña Fracture Zone Pac. Oc. 16°0S 91°0W 289 J18
Mendawai → Indonesia 3°30S 113°0E 235 C4
Mende France 44°31N 3°30E 174 D7
Mendebo Mts. Ethiopia 7°0N 39°22E 257 F4
Mendeleyev Ridge Arctic 80°0N 178°0W 150 B17
Menden Germany 51°26N 7°47E 178 D3
Mendenhall, C. U.S.A. 59°45N 166°10W 303 G6
Menderes Turkey 38°14N 27°8E 205 C9
Mendhar India 33°35N 74°10E 243 C6
Mendi Ethiopia 9°47N 35°4E 257 F4
Mendi Papua N. G. 6°11S 143°39E 286 D2
Mendip Hills U.K. 51°17N 2°40W 169 F5
Mendocino U.S.A. 39°19N 123°48W 304 G2
Mendocino, C. U.S.A. 40°26N 124°25W 304 F1
Mendocino Fracture Zone Pac. Oc. 40°0N 142°0W 289 D13
Mendol Indonesia 0°36N 103°13E 234 B2
Mendon U.S.A. 42°0N 85°27W 311 B11
Mendooran Australia 31°50S 149°6E 283 A8
Mendota Calif., U.S.A. 36°45N 120°23W 306 J6
Mendota Ill., U.S.A. 41°33N 89°7W 310 C7
Mendoyo Indonesia 8°23S 114°42E 231 J17
Mendoza Argentina 32°50S 68°52W 334 C2
Mendoza □ Argentina 33°0S 69°0W 334 C2
Mene Grande Venezuela 9°49N 70°56W 328 B3
Menemen Turkey 38°34N 27°3E 205 C9
Menen Belgium 50°47N 3°7E 170 D3
Menéndez, L. Argentina 42°40S 71°51W 336 B2
Menfi Italy 37°36N 12°58E 200 E5
Mengcheng China 33°12N 116°36E 226 H9
Mengdingjie China 23°31N 98°58E 228 F2
Mengeš Slovenia 46°10N 14°35E 199 B11
Menggala Indonesia 4°30S 105°15E 234 C3
Menghai China 21°49N 100°55E 228 G3
Mengíbar Spain 37°58N 3°48W 195 H7
Mengjin China 34°55N 112°45E 226 G7
Mengla China 21°20N 101°25E 228 G3
Menglian China 22°21N 99°27E 228 F2
Mengong Cameroon 2°56N 11°25E 264 B2
Mengshan China 24°14N 110°55E 229 E8
Mengyin China 35°40N 117°58E 227 G9
Mengzhe China 22°2N 100°15E 228 F3
Mengzi China 23°20N 103°22E 228 F4
Menifee U.S.A. 33°41N 117°10W 307 M9
Menihek Canada 54°28N 56°36W 299 B6
Menihek L. Canada 54°0N 67°0W 299 B6
Menin = Menen Belgium 50°47N 3°7E 170 D3
Menindee Australia 32°20S 142°25E 282 B5
Menindee L. Australia 32°20S 142°25E 282 B5
Meningie Australia 35°50S 139°18E 282 C3
Menjangan, Pulau Indonesia 8°7S 114°31E 231 J17
Menkrour Algeria 26°27N 8°9E 261 C6
Menlo Park U.S.A. 37°27N 122°12W 306 H4
Menngen ❂ Australia 15°21S 131°16E 278 C5
Menominee U.S.A. 45°6N 87°37W 308 C10
Menominee → U.S.A. 45°6N 87°35W 308 C10
Menomonee Falls U.S.A. 43°10N 88°7W 311 A8
Menomonie U.S.A. 44°53N 91°55W 308 C8
Menongue Angola 14°48S 17°52E 265 E3
Menorca Spain 40°0N 4°0E 206 B5
Menorca ✈ (MAH) Spain 39°50N 4°16E 196 F9
Mentakab Malaysia 3°29N 102°21E 237 L4
Mentasta Lake U.S.A. 62°55N 143°45W 303 E12
Mentawai, Kepulauan Indonesia 2°0S 99°0E 234 C1
Mentawai, Selat Indonesia 1°45S 100°0E 234 C2
Menteng Indonesia 6°11S 106°49E 122 B1
Menton France 43°50N 7°29E 175 E11
Mentone U.S.A. 41°10N 86°2W 311 C10
Mentor U.S.A. 41°40N 81°21W 312 E3
Menyamya Papua N. G. 7°10S 145°59E 286 D3
Menyapa Indonesia 1°4N 116°4E 235 B5
Menzel-Bourguiba Tunisia 37°9N 9°49E 258 A1
Menzel-Chaker Tunisia 35°0N 10°26E 258 B2
Menzel-Temime Tunisia 36°46N 11°0E 258 A2
Menzelinsk Russia 55°47N 53°11E 186 C9
Menzies Australia 29°40S 121°2E 279 E3
Meob B. Namibia 24°25S 14°34E 270 B1
Meoqui Mexico 28°17N 105°29W 318 B3
Mepaco Mozam. 15°57S 30°48E 269 F3
Meppel Neths. 52°42N 6°12E 170 B6
Meppen Germany 52°42N 7°17E 178 C3
Mequinenza Spain 41°22N 0°17E 196 D5
Mequinenza, Embalse de Spain 41°25N 0°15E 196 D5
Mequon U.S.A. 43°14N 87°59W 311 A9
Mer France 47°42N 1°30E 172 E8
Merai Papua N. G. 4°52S 152°19E 286 C7
Merak Indonesia 6°10N 106°26E 231 F12
Meråker Norway 63°25N 11°46E 164 A8
Meramangye, L. Australia 28°25S 132°13E 279 E5
Meramec → U.S.A. 38°24N 90°21W 310 F6
Meran = Merano Italy 46°40N 11°9E 199 B8
Merano Italy 46°40N 11°9E 199 B8
Mérantaise → France 48°42N 2°8E 134 B1
Merapi Indonesia 7°32S 110°26E 235 D4
Merate Italy 45°42N 9°25E 198 C6
Meratus, Pegunungan Indonesia 2°45S 115°40E 235 C5
Merauke Indonesia 8°29S 140°24E 231 F10
Merbein Australia 34°10S 142°2E 282 C5
Merca = Marka Somalia 1°48N 44°50E 267 D5
Mercamadrid Spain 40°21N 3°39W 127 B2
Mercantour △ France 44°16N 6°43E 175 D10
Mercato Saraceno Italy 43°57N 12°12E 199 E9
Merced U.S.A. 37°18N 120°29W 306 H6
Merced → U.S.A. 37°21N 120°59W 306 H6
Merced, L. U.S.A. 37°43N 122°29W 136 B2
Merced Pk. U.S.A. 37°36N 119°24W 306 H7
Mercedes B. Aires, Argentina 34°40S 59°30W 334 C4
Mercedes Corrientes, Argentina 29°10S 58°5W 334 B4
Mercedes San Luis, Argentina 33°40S 65°21W 334 C2
Mercedes Camarines N., Phil. 14°7N 123°1E 232 D4
Mercedes Uruguay 33°12S 58°0W 334 C4
Mercedes-Benz Superdome U.S.A. 29°56N 90°5W 131 b1
Merceditas Chile 28°20S 70°35W 334 B1
Mercer N.Z. 37°16S 175°5E 284 D4
Mercer Mo., U.S.A. 40°31N 93°32W 310 D3
Mercer Pa., U.S.A. 41°14N 80°15W 312 E4
Mercer Island U.S.A. 47°34N 122°13W 306 C4
Merchandise Mart Chicago, U.S.A. 119 b1
Mercier Bolivia 10°42S 68°5W 330 C4
Mercury U.S.A. 36°40N 115°59W 307 J11
Mercury B. N.Z. 36°48S 175°45E 284 C4
Mercury Is. N.Z. 36°37S 175°52E 284 C4
Mercy, C. Canada 65°0N 63°30W 295 E19
Merdrignac France 48°11N 2°27W 172 D4
Mere U.K. 51°6N 2°16W 169 F5
Mere Lava Vanuatu 14°25S 168°3E 287 D6
Merebuk, Gunung Indonesia 8°13S 114°39E 231 J17
Meredale S. Africa 26°16S 27°58E 123 B1
Meredith Australia 37°49S 144°5E 282 D6
Meredith, C. Falk. Is. 52°15S 60°40W 153 f
Meredith, L. U.S.A. 35°43N 101°33W 314 D4
Meredosia U.S.A. 39°50N 90°34W 310 E6
Merefa Ukraine 49°48N 36°3E 189 H9
Merei Romania 45°7N 26°43E 183 E11
Merga = Nukheila Sudan 19°1N 26°21E 256 D2
Mergui Myanmar 12°26N 98°34E 236 F2
Mergui Arch. = Myeik Kyunzu Myanmar 11°30N 97°30E 237 G1
Meribah Australia 34°43S 140°51E 282 C4
Méribel-les-Allues France 45°25N 6°34E 175 C10
Meriç Turkey 41°11N 26°25E 203 E10
Meriç → Turkey 40°52N 26°12E 203 F10
Mérida Yucatán, Mexico 20°58N 89°37W 319 C7
Merida Phil. 10°55N 124°32E 233 F5
Mérida Spain 38°55N 6°25W 195 G4
Mérida Venezuela 8°24N 71°8W 328 B3
Mérida □ Venezuela 8°30N 71°10W 328 B3
Mérida, Cord. de Venezuela 9°0N 71°0W 328 B3
Meriden W. Mids., U.K. 52°26N 1°38W 169 E6
Meriden Conn., U.S.A. 41°32N 72°48W 313 E12
Meridian Calif., U.S.A. 39°9N 121°55W 306 F5
Meridian Ga., U.S.A. 31°27N 81°23W 316 D8
Meridian Idaho, U.S.A. 43°37N 116°24W 304 E5
Meridian Miss., U.S.A. 32°22N 88°42W 315 E10
Mérignac France 44°51N 0°39W 174 D3
Merimbula Australia 36°53S 149°54E 283 D8
Merin Gubai Somalia 1°26N 44°20E 267 D5
Merinda Australia 20°2S 148°11E 280 C4
Mering Germany 48°16N 10°59E 179 G6
Meringa Nigeria 10°44N 12°9E 263 C7
Meringur Australia 34°20S 141°19E 282 C4
Merir Palau 4°10N 132°30E 231 D8
Merirumã Brazil 1°15N 54°50W 329 C7
Merizo Guam 13°16N 144°40E 302 d
Merkel U.S.A. 32°28N 100°1W 314 E4
Merlimau, Pulau Singapore 1°17N 103°42E 138 B2
Mermaid Reef Australia 17°6S 119°36E 278 C2
Mero Dominica 15°25N 61°26W 323 k
Meroe India 7°33N 93°33E 245 L11
Merowe Sudan 18°29N 31°46E 256 D3
Merowe Dam Sudan 18°35N 31°56E 256 D3
Merredin Australia 31°28S 118°18E 279 F2
Merri Cr. → Australia 37°47S 144°59E 128 A1
Merrick U.K. 55°8N 4°28W 167 F4
Merrickville Canada 44°55N 75°50W 313 B9
Merrill Oreg., U.S.A. 42°1N 121°36W 304 E3
Merrill Wis., U.S.A. 45°11N 89°41W 308 C9
Merrillville U.S.A. 41°29N 87°20W 311 C9
Merrimack → U.S.A. 42°49N 70°49W 313 D14
Merriman U.S.A. 42°55N 101°42W 308 D3
Merrionette Park U.S.A. 41°41N 87°40W 119 C2
Merritt Canada 50°10N 120°45W 296 C4
Merritt Island U.S.A. 28°21N 80°42W 317 G9
Merriwa Australia 32°6S 150°22E 283 B9
Merriwagga Australia 33°47S 145°43E 283 B6
Merry I. Canada 55°29N 77°31W 298 A4
Merrygoen Australia 31°51S 149°12E 283 A8
Merryville U.S.A. 30°45N 93°33W 314 F8
Mersa Fatma Eritrea 14°57N 40°17E 257 E5
Mersch Lux. 49°44N 6°7E 170 E6
Merse → Italy 43°5N 11°22E 199 E8
Mersea I. U.K. 51°47N 0°58E 169 F8
Merseburg Germany 51°22N 11°59E 178 D7
Mersey → U.K. 53°25N 3°1W 168 D4
Merseyside □ U.K. 53°31N 3°2W 168 D4
Mersin Turkey 36°51N 34°36E 250 B5
Mersin □ Turkey 36°45N 34°0E 250 B5
Mersing Malaysia 2°25N 103°50E 237 L4
Merta India 26°39N 74°4E 242 F6
Merta Road India 26°43N 73°55E 242 F5
Merthyr Tydfil U.K. 51°45N 3°22W 169 F4
Merthyr Tydfil □ U.K. 51°46N 3°21W 169 F4
Merti Kenya 1°4N 38°40E 268 B4
Mértola Portugal 37°40N 7°40W 195 H3
Merton □ U.K. 51°25N 0°11W 125 B2
Mertz Glacier Antarctica 67°30S 144°45E 151 C10
Mertzon U.S.A. 31°16N 100°49W 314 F4
Méru Oise, France 49°13N 2°8E 173 C9
Meru Eastern, Kenya 0°3N 37°40E 268 B4
Meru Tanzania 3°15S 36°46E 268 C4
Meru △ Kenya 0°5N 38°10E 268 B4
Meru Betiri △ Indonesia 8°27S 113°51E 235 D4
Merv = Mary Turkmenistan 37°40N 61°50E 247 B9
Merville France 50°38N 2°38E 173 B9
Méry-sur-Seine France 48°31N 3°54E 173 D10
Merzifon Turkey 40°53N 35°32E 212 B6
Merzig Germany 49°26N 6°38E 179 F2
Merzouga, Erg Tin Algeria 24°0N 11°4E 261 D7
Mesa U.S.A. 33°25N 111°50W 305 K8
Mesa Verde △ U.S.A. 37°11N 108°29W 305 H9
Mesach Mellet Libya 24°30N 11°30E 258 D2
Mesada = Masada Israel 31°18N 35°21E 251 G6
Mesagne Italy 40°34N 17°48E 201 B10
Mesanagros Greece 36°1N 27°49E 206 E11
Mesaoría Cyprus 35°12N 33°14E 207 E9
Meschede Germany 51°20N 8°18E 178 D4
Mescit Turkey 40°21N 41°11E 213 B9
Mesemvriya = Nesebŭr Bulgaria 42°41N 27°46E 203 D11
Mesfinto Ethiopia 13°20N 37°22E 257 E4
Mesgarābād Iran 35°27N 51°30E 141 B3
Mesgouez, L. Canada 51°20N 75°0W 298 B5
Meshchovsk Russia 54°22N 35°17E 188 E8
Meshchyora △ Russia 55°30N 40°20E 190 C5
Meshchyorsky △ Russia 54°50N 41°0E 190 C5
Meshed = Mashhad Iran 36°20N 59°35E 247 B8
Meshgīn Shahr Iran 38°30N 47°45E 213 C12
Meshkede-Ser = Bābol Sar Iran 36°45N 52°45E 247 B7
Meshoppen U.S.A. 41°36N 76°3W 313 E8
Meshra er Req South Sudan 8°25N 29°18E 257 F2
Mesilinka → Canada 56°6N 124°30W 296 B4
Meslay-du-Maine France 47°58N 0°33W 172 E6
Mesocco Switz. 46°23N 9°12E 179 J5
Mesolongi Greece 38°21N 21°28E 204 C3
Mesongi Greece 39°29N 19°56E 206 C9
Mesopotamia = Al Jazirah Iraq 33°30N 44°0E 213 E10
Mesopotamia U.S.A. 41°27N 80°57W 312 E4
Mesopotamo Greece 39°14N 20°32E 204 B2
Mesoraca Italy 39°5N 16°48E 201 C9
Mésou Volímais = Volimes Greece 37°52N 20°39E 207 D2
Mesquite Nev., U.S.A. 36°48N 114°4W 305 H6
Mesquite Tex., U.S.A. 32°47N 96°36W 314 E6
Messaad Algeria 34°8N 3°30E 261 B5
Messac France 47°49N 1°50W 172 E5
Messalo → Mozam. 12°25S 39°15E 269 E4
Messaména Cameroon 3°48N 12°49E 264 B2
Messara, Kolpos Greece 35°6N 24°47E 207 E5
Messe Austria 48°13N 16°24E 142 A2
Messene Greece 37°4N 22°1E 204 D4
Messier, Canal Chile 48°20S 74°33W 336 C2
Messina = Musina S. Africa 22°20S 30°5E 271 B5
Messina Italy 38°11N 15°34E 201 D8
Messina, Str. di Italy 38°15N 15°35E 201 D8
Messiniakos Kolpos Greece 36°45N 22°5E 204 E4
Messkirch Germany 47°59N 9°7E 179 H5
Messlingen Sweden 62°40N 12°50E 162 B6
Mesta = Nestos → Europe 40°54N 24°49E 203 F8
Mesta, Akra Greece 38°16N 25°53E 205 C7
Mestanza Spain 38°35N 4°4W 195 G6
Mestersvig Greenland 72°10N 23°40W 154 C8
Mestre Italy 45°29N 12°15E 199 C9
Mestre, Espigão Brazil 12°30S 46°10W 333 D2
Mesudiye Turkey 40°28N 37°46E 212 B7
Meta U.S.A. 38°19N 92°10W 310 F4
Meta □ Colombia 3°30N 73°0W 328 C3
Meta → S. Amer. 6°12N 67°28W 328 B4
Meta Incognita Pen. Canada 62°45N 68°30W 295 E18
Metabetchouan Canada 48°26N 71°52W 299 C5
Metairie U.S.A. 29°59N 90°9W 131 A2
Metalici, Munții Romania 46°15N 22°50E 182 D7
Metaline Falls U.S.A. 48°52N 117°22W 304 B5
Metallifere, Colline Italy 43°10N 11°0E 198 E8
Metamora U.S.A. 40°47N 89°22W 310 D7
Metán Argentina 25°30S 65°0W 334 B3
Metangula Mozam. 12°40S 34°50E 269 E3
Metanópoli Italy 45°24N 9°15E 128 B2
Metauro → Italy 43°50N 13°3E 199 E10
Metcalf U.S.A. 30°43N 83°59W 316 E6
Metcalfe Canada 45°14N 75°28W 313 A9
Metema Ethiopia 12°58N 36°12E 257 E4
Metengobalame Mozam. 14°49S 34°30E 269 E3
Meteora Greece 39°43N 21°37E 204 B3
Methana Greece 37°35N 23°23E 204 D5
Methoni Greece 36°49N 21°42E 204 E3
Methven N.Z. 43°38S 171°40E 285 D6
Metil Mozam. 16°24S 39°0E 269 F4
Metkovets Bulgaria 43°37N 23°10E 202 C7
Metković Croatia 43°6N 17°39E 199 E14
Metlakatla U.S.A. 55°8N 131°35W 303 J15
Metlaoui Tunisia 34°24N 8°24E 258 B1
MetLife Stadium New York, U.S.A. 40°48N 74°5W 132 B1
Metlik Papua N. G. 4°46S 152°55E 286 C7
Metlika Slovenia 45°40N 15°20E 199 C12
Metlili Chaamba Algeria 32°16N 3°38E 261 B5
Metro Indonesia 5°5S 105°20E 234 D3
Metro Toronto Zoo Canada 43°48N 79°10W 141 A3
Metropolis U.S.A. 37°9N 88°44W 308 G9
Metropolitan Museum of Art New York, U.S.A. 132 b3
Metropolitana □ Chile 33°30S 70°50W 334 C1
Metsovo Greece 39°48N 21°12E 204 B3
Metter U.S.A. 32°24N 82°3W 316 C7
Mettuppalaiyam India 11°18N 76°59E 245 J3
Mettur India 11°48N 77°47E 245 J3
Metu Ethiopia 8°18N 35°35E 257 F4
Metz France 49°8N 6°10E 173 C13
Metzingen Germany 48°31N 9°17E 179 G5
Meudon France 48°48N 2°14E 134 B2
Meulaboh Indonesia 4°11N 96°3E 234 B1
Meung-sur-Loire France 47°50N 1°40E 173 E8
Meureudu Indonesia 5°19N 96°10E 234 A1
Meurthe → France 48°47N 6°9E 173 D13
Meurthe-et-Moselle □ France 48°52N 6°0E 173 D13
Meuse □ France 49°8N 5°25E 173 C12
Meuse → Europe 50°45N 5°41E 170 D5
Meuselwitz Germany 51°2N 12°17E 178 D8
Meutapok, Mt. Malaysia 5°40N 117°0E 235 A5
Mevaseret Zion Israel 31°48N 35°9E 123 B1
Mevo Beitar Israel 31°43N 35°6E 123 B1
Mexia U.S.A. 31°41N 96°29W 314 F6
Mexiana, I. Brazil 0°0 49°30W 332 B2
Mexicali Mexico 32°40N 115°30W 307 N11
Mexican Plateau Mexico 25°0N 104°0W 292 G9
Mexican Water U.S.A. 36°57N 109°32W 305 H9
Mexico Maine, U.S.A. 44°34N 70°33W 313 B14
Mexico Mo., U.S.A. 39°10N 91°53W 310 E5
Mexico N.Y., U.S.A. 43°28N 76°14W 313 C8
México □ Mexico 19°20N 99°30W 319 D5
Mexico ■ Cent. Amer. 25°0N 105°0W 318 C4
México, Ciudad de Mexico 19°24N 99°9W 128 B2
Mexico, G. of Cent. Amer. 25°0N 90°0W 319 C7
Mexico B. U.S.A. 43°35N 76°20W 313 C8
Mexico Beach U.S.A. 29°57N 85°25W 316 F4
Mexico City Int. ✈ (MEX) Mexico 19°25N 99°5W 128 B2
Meydān-e Naftūn Iran 31°56N 49°18E 247 D6
Meydani, Ra's-e Iran 25°24N 59°6E 247 E8
Meyenburg Germany 53°18N 12°14E 178 B8

Meyers Chuck U.S.A. 55°45N 132°15W 296 B2
Meyersdal S. Africa 26°17S 28°5E 123 B2
Meymac France 45°32N 2°10E 174 C6
Meymaneh Afghan. 35°53N 64°38E 240 B2
Meyo Cameroon 2°50N 11°11E 264 B2
Meyrueis France 44°12N 3°27E 174 D7
Meyssac France 45°3N 1°40E 174 C5
Meyzieu France 45°46N 4°59E 175 C8
Mezdra Bulgaria 43°12N 23°42E 202 C7
Mèze France 43°27N 3°36E 174 E7
Mezen Russia 65°50N 44°20E 186 A7
Mezen → Russia 65°44N 44°22E 186 A7
Mézenc, Mt. France 44°54N 4°11E 175 D8
Mezeş, Munţii Romania 47°5N 23°5E 182 C8
Mezha → Russia 55°44N 31°33E 188 E6
Mezhdurechensk Russia 53°41N 88°3E 217 B11
Mezhdurechenskiy Russia 59°36N 65°56E 214 D7
Mezhdurechye = Shali Russia 43°9N 45°55E 191 J7
Mezhevaya Utka = Sinegorskiy Russia 47°55N 40°52E 191 G5
Mézidon-Canon France 49°5N 0°1W 172 C6
Mézières-en-Brenne France 46°49N 1°13E 174 B5
Mézilhac France 44°49N 4°21E 175 D8
Mézin France 44°4N 0°16E 174 D4
Mezitli Turkey 36°45N 34°29E 250 B5
Mezőberény Hungary 46°49N 21°3E 182 D6
Mezőfalva Hungary 46°55N 18°49E 182 D3
Mezőhegyes Hungary 46°19N 20°49E 182 D5
Mezőkövácsháza Hungary 46°25N 20°57E 182 D5
Mezőkövesd Hungary 47°49N 20°35E 182 C5
Mézos France 44°5N 1°10W 174 D2
Mezőtúr Hungary 47°1N 20°41E 182 C5
Mezquital Mexico 23°29N 104°23W 318 C4
Mezzate Italy 45°26N 9°17E 128 B2
Mezzolombardo Italy 46°13N 11°5E 198 B8
Mfolozi → S. Africa 28°25S 32°26E 271 C5
Mgarr Malta 35°55N 14°22E 206 F7
Mgarr Gozo, Malta 36°2N 14°18E 206 E7
Mgeta Tanzania 8°22S 36°6E 269 D4
Mglin Russia 53°2N 32°50E 189 F7
Mhamid Morocco 29°49N 5°43W 260 C3
Mhlaba Hills Zimbabwe 18°30S 30°30E 269 F3
Mhow India 22°33N 75°50E 242 H6
Mi-Shima Japan 34°46N 131°9E 222 C3
Miadong S. Korea 37°36N 127°0E 127 B2
Miagao Phil. 10°39N 122°14E 233 F4
Miahuatlán Mexico 16°20N 96°36W 319 D5
Miaich South Sudan 9°30N 30°30E 257 F3
Miajadas Spain 39°9N 5°54W 195 F5
Miami Fla., U.S.A. 25°46N 80°11W 129 D2
Miami Okla., U.S.A. 36°53N 94°53W 314 C7
Miami Tex., U.S.A. 35°42N 100°38W 314 D4
Miami → U.S.A. 25°46N 80°11W 129 D1
Miami Beach U.S.A. 25°47N 80°7W 129 D3
Miami Canal U.S.A. 25°45N 80°12W 317 K9
Miami Gardens U.S.A. 25°56N 80°15W 129 C1
Miami Int. ✈ (MIA) U.S.A. 25°48N 80°17W 129 D1
Miami Lakes U.S.A. 25°54N 80°18W 129 C1
Miami Shores U.S.A. 25°51N 80°11W 129 C2
Miami Springs U.S.A. 25°49N 80°17W 129 D1
Miamisburg U.S.A. 39°38N 84°17W 311 E12
Mian Xian China 33°10N 106°32E 228 A6
Mianchi China 34°48N 111°48E 226 G6
Mīāndarreh Iran 35°37N 53°39E 247 C7
Mīāndowāb Iran 37°0N 46°5E 213 D12
Miandrivazo Madag. 19°31S 45°29E 272 B2
Mīāneh Iran 37°30N 47°40E 213 D12
Miangas, Pulau Indonesia 5°35N 126°34E 233 J6
Mianning China 28°32N 102°9E 228 C4
Mianwali Pakistan 32°38N 71°28E 242 C4
Mianyang China 31°22N 104°47E 228 B5
Mianzhu China 31°22N 104°7E 228 B5
Miao Ling China 26°5N 107°30E 228 D6
Miaodao Qundao China 38°10N 120°45E 227 E11
Miaoli Taiwan 24°37N 120°49E 225 B2
Miaoli □ Taiwan 24°30N 120°55E 225 B2
Miarinarivo Alaotra-Mangoro, Madag. 16°38S 48°15E 272 B2
Miarinarivo Itasy, Madag. 18°57S 46°55E 272 B2
Miariravaratra Madag. 20°13S 47°31E 272 C2
Miass Russia 54°59N 60°6E 186 D11
Miasteczko Krajeńskie Poland 53°7N 17°1E 185 E4
Miastko Poland 54°0N 16°58E 184 E3
Miasto Poland 52°15N 21°0E 143 B2
Mica S. Africa 24°10S 30°48E 271 B5
Micanopy U.S.A. 29°30N 82°17W 317 F7
Micăsasa Romania 46°7N 24°7E 183 D9
Micco U.S.A. 27°53N 80°30W 317 H9
Miccosukee U.S.A. 30°36N 84°3W 316 E5
Miccosukee, L. U.S.A. 30°33N 83°53W 316 E6
Michael, Mt. Papua N. G. 6°27S 145°22E 286 D3
Michalovce Slovakia 48°47N 21°58E 181 C14
Michałowice Poland 52°10N 20°52E 143 B1
Michigan □ U.S.A. 44°0N 85°0W 309 C11
Michigan, L. U.S.A. 44°0N 87°0W 308 D10
Michigan Avenue Chicago, U.S.A. 119 b2
Michigan Center U.S.A. 42°14N 84°20W 311 B12
Michigan City U.S.A. 41°43N 86°54W 311 C10
Michika Nigeria 10°36N 13°23E 263 C7
Michipicoten I. Canada 47°40N 85°40W 298 C2
Michle Czechia 50°3N 14°28E 135 B2
Michoacán □ Mexico 19°10N 101°50W 318 D4
Michurin = Tsarevo Bulgaria 42°9N 27°51E 203 D11
Michurinsk Russia 52°58N 40°27E 190 D5
Miconje Angola 4°26S 12°48E 265 C2
Micoud St. Lucia 13°49N 60°54W 323 m
Micronesia Pac. Oc. 11°0N 160°0E 288 G7
Micronesia, Federated States of ■ Pac. Oc. 9°0N 150°0E 288 G7
Mid & East Antrim □ U.K. 54°52N 6°14W 166 B5
Mid-Atlantic Ridge Atl. Oc. 0°0 20°0W 152 J10
Mid-City Calif., U.S.A. 34°4N 118°20W 126 B2
Mid City La., U.S.A. 29°58N 90°6W 131 B2
Mid-Indian Ocean Basin Ind. Oc. 10°0S 80°0E 273 F7
Mid-Indian Ridge Ind. Oc. 30°0S 75°0E 273 H6
Mid-Pacific Seamounts Pac. Oc. 18°0N 177°0W 288 F10
Mid Ulster □ U.K. 54°36N 6°45W 166 B5
Midai Indonesia 3°0N 107°47E 235 B3
Midale Canada 49°25N 103°20W 297 D8
Middelburg Neths. 51°30N 3°36E 170 C3
Middelburg Eastern Cape, S. Africa 31°30S 25°0E 270 D4
Middelburg Mpumalanga, S. Africa 25°49S 29°28E 271 C4
Middelfart Denmark 55°30N 9°43E 163 J3
Middelpos S. Africa 31°55S 20°13E 270 D3
Middelwit S. Africa 24°51S 27°3E 270 B4
Middle → U.S.A. 41°26N 93°30W 310 C3
Middle Alkali L. U.S.A. 41°27N 120°5W 304 F3
Middle America Trench = Guatemala Trench Pac. Oc. 14°0N 95°0W 292 H10
Middle Andaman I. India 12°30N 92°50E 245 H11
Middle Bass I. U.S.A. 41°41N 82°48W 312 E2
Middle East Asia 35°0N 40°0E 210 E5
Middle Fork Feather → U.S.A. 38°33N 121°30W 306 F5
Middle Ground Midway Is. 28°14N 177°24W 302 c
Middle Harbour Australia 33°47S 151°14E 139 A2
Middle Hd. Australia 33°49S 151°16E 139 A2
Middle I. Australia 34°6S 123°11E 279 F3
Middle Island St. Kitts & Nevis 17°20N 62°48W 322 d
Middle Loup → U.S.A. 41°17N 98°24W 308 E4
Middle Park Australia 37°50S 144°57E 128 B1
Middle Raccoon → U.S.A. 41°35N 93°35W 310 C3
Middle Village U.S.A. 40°43N 73°52W 132 B2
Middleboro U.S.A. 41°54N 70°55W 313 E14
Middleburg Fla., U.S.A. 30°4N 81°52W 316 E8
Middleburg Pa., U.S.A. 40°47N 77°3W 312 F7
Middleburgh U.S.A. 42°36N 74°20W 313 D10
Middlebury Ind., U.S.A. 41°41N 85°42W 311 C11
Middlebury Vt., U.S.A. 44°1N 73°10W 313 B11
Middlefield U.S.A. 41°27N 81°4W 312 E3
Middlemarch N.Z. 45°30S 170°9E 285 F5
Middlemount Australia 22°50S 148°40E 280 C4
Middleport N.Y., U.S.A. 43°13N 78°29W 312 C6
Middleport Ohio, U.S.A. 39°0N 82°3W 309 F12
Middlesboro U.S.A. 36°36N 83°43W 309 G12
Middlesbrough U.K. 54°35N 1°13W 168 C6
Middlesbrough □ U.K. 54°28N 1°13W 168 C6
Middlesex Belize 17°2N 88°31W 320 C2
Middlesex N.J., U.S.A. 40°36N 74°30W 313 F10
Middlesex N.Y., U.S.A. 42°42N 77°16W 312 D7
Middlesex □ Jamaica 18°10N 77°59W 320 a
Middlesex Fells Reservation U.S.A. 42°27N 71°6W 116 A2
Middleton Queens., Australia 22°22S 141°32E 280 C3
Middleton N.S., Canada 44°57N 65°4W 299 D6
Middleton Wis., U.S.A. 43°6N 89°30W 310 A7
Middleton Cr. → Australia 22°35S 141°51E 280 C3
Middleton I. U.S.A. 59°26N 146°20W 303 G11
Middletown Armagh, U.K. 54°17N 6°51W 166 B5
Middletown Calif., U.S.A. 38°45N 122°37W 306 G4
Middletown Conn., U.S.A. 41°34N 72°39W 313 E12
Middletown Ky., U.S.A. 38°14N 85°32W 311 F11
Middletown N.Y., U.S.A. 41°27N 74°25W 313 E10
Middletown Ohio, U.S.A. 39°31N 84°24W 311 E12
Middletown Pa., U.S.A. 40°12N 76°44W 313 F8
Middleville U.S.A. 42°43N 85°28W 311 B11
Midelt Morocco 32°46N 4°44W 260 B4
Midge Point Australia 20°39S 148°43E 280 b
Midhirst N.Z. 39°17S 174°18E 284 F3
Miðsandur Iceland 64°24N 21°28W 155 C5
Midhurst Ont., Canada 44°26N 79°43W 312 B5
Midhurst W. Sussx., U.K. 50°59N 0°44W 169 G7
Mīdī Yemen 16°19N 42°48E 248 C3
Midi, Canal du → France 43°45N 1°21E 174 E5
Midi, Gare du Brussels, Belgium 116 c1
Midi d'Ossau, Pic du France 42°50N 0°26W 174 F3
Midland W. Austral., Australia 31°54S 116°1E 279 F2
Midland Ont., Canada 44°45N 79°50W 312 B5
Midland Calif., U.S.A. 33°52N 114°48W 307 M12
Midland Mich., U.S.A. 43°37N 84°14W 309 D11
Midland Pa., U.S.A. 40°39N 80°27W 312 F4
Midland Tex., U.S.A. 32°0N 102°3W 314 F3
Midland Beach U.S.A. 40°34N 74°6W 132 C1
Midlands □ Zimbabwe 19°40S 29°0E 269 F2
Midleton Ireland 51°55N 8°10W 166 E3
Midlothian U.S.A. 41°37N 87°45W 119 D2
Midlothian □ U.K. 55°51N 3°5W 167 F5
Midnapore = Medinipur India 22°25N 87°21E 243 H12
Midongy, Tangorombohitr' i Madag. 23°30S 47°0E 272 C2
Midongy Atsimo Madag. 23°35S 47°1E 272 C2
Midongy de Sud △ Madag. 23°42S 47°6E 272 C2
Midori Japan 36°30N 139°15E 223 A11
Midou → France 43°54N 0°30W 174 E3
Midouze → France 43°48N 0°51W 174 E3
Midsayap Phil. 7°12N 124°32E 233 H5
Midsund Norway 62°41N 6°40E 164 B3
Midtgulen Norway 61°44N 5°11E 164 C2
Midu China 25°18N 100°30E 228 E3
Midville U.S.A. 32°49N 82°14W 316 C7
Midway Ala., U.S.A. 32°5N 85°31W 316 C4
Midway Fla., U.S.A. 30°30N 84°27W 316 E5
Midway, Chicago ✈ (MDW) U.S.A. 41°47N 87°45W 311 C9
Midway Is. Pac. Oc. 28°13N 177°22W 302 c
Midway Wells U.S.A. 32°41N 115°7W 307 N11
Midwest U.S.A. 42°0N 90°0W 301 G22
Midwest Wyo., U.S.A. 43°25N 106°16W 304 E10
Midwest City U.S.A. 35°27N 97°24W 314 D6
Midwood U.S.A. 40°37N 73°57W 132 C2
Midyat Turkey 37°25N 41°23E 213 D9
Midžor Bulgaria 43°24N 22°40E 202 C6
Mie Japan 32°58N 131°35E 222 E3
Mie □ Japan 34°30N 136°10E 223 C8
Miechów Poland 50°21N 20°5E 185 H7
Miedwie, Jezioro Poland 53°17N 14°54E 185 E1
Miedzeszyn Poland 52°10N 21°11E 143 B3
Międzybórz Poland 51°25N 17°34E 185 G4
Międzychód Poland 52°35N 15°53E 185 F2
Międzylesie Dolnośląskie, Poland 50°8N 16°40E 185 H3
Międzylesie Warszawa, Poland 52°12N 21°10E 143 B3
Międzyrzec Podlaski Poland 51°58N 22°45E 185 G9
Międzyrzecz Poland 52°26N 15°35E 185 F2
Międzyzdroje Poland 53°56N 14°26E 184 E1
Miejska Górka Poland 51°39N 16°58E 185 G3
Miélan France 43°27N 0°19E 174 E4
Mielau = Mława Poland 53°9N 20°25E 185 E7
Mielec Poland 50°15N 21°25E 185 H8
Mienga Angola 17°12S 19°48E 265 F3
Miercurea-Ciuc Romania 46°21N 25°48E 183 D10
Miercurea Sibiului Romania 45°53N 23°48E 183 E8
Mieres Spain 43°18N 5°48W 194 B5
Mieroszów Poland 50°40N 16°11E 185 H3
Mies = Stříbro Czechia 49°44N 13°0E 180 A6
Mieso Ethiopia 9°15N 40°43E 257 F5
Miessaari Finland 60°8N 24°47E 121 C1
Mieszkowice Poland 52°47N 14°30E 185 F1
Mifflintown U.S.A. 40°34N 77°24W 312 F7
Mifraz Hefa Israel 32°52N 35°0E 250 F6
Migang Shan China 35°32N 106°13E 226 G4
Migennes France 47°58N 3°31E 173 E10
Migliarino Italy 44°46N 11°56E 199 D8
Migliarino-San Rossore-Massaciuccoli △ Italy 43°44N 10°20E 198 E7
Migori Kenya 1°4S 34°28E 268 C3
Migrash Harusim Jerusalem 123 b2
Miguasha △ Canada 48°5N 66°26W 299 C6
Miguel Alemán, Presa Mexico 18°15N 96°32W 319 D5
Miguel Alves Brazil 4°11S 42°55W 332 B3
Miguel Calmon Brazil 11°26S 40°36W 332 D3
Miguel Hidalgo Mexico 19°25N 99°12W 128 B1
Miguel Hidalgo, Presa Mexico 26°30N 108°34W 318 B3
Migueturra Spain 38°58N 3°53W 195 G7
Mihăileni Romania 47°58N 26°9E 183 C11
Mihăileşti Romania 44°20N 25°54E 183 F10
Mihailovca Moldova 46°33N 28°56E 183 D13
Mihalgazi Turkey 40°2N 30°34E 205 A12
Mihaliççık Turkey 39°53N 31°30E 212 C4
Mihara Japan 34°24N 133°5E 222 C5
Mihara-Yama Japan 34°43N 139°23E 223 C11
Mihesu de Câmpie Romania 46°41N 24°9E 183 D9
Mijas Spain 36°36N 4°40W 195 J6
Mikawa-Wan Japan 34°44N 137°13E 223 C9
Mikese Tanzania 6°48S 37°55E 268 D4
Mikha-Tskhakaya = Senaki Georgia 42°15N 42°1E 191 J6
Mikhailovka = Mykhaylivka Ukraine 47°12N 35°15E 189 J8
Mikhaylov Russia 54°14N 39°0E 188 E10
Mikhaylovgrad = Montana Bulgaria 43°27N 23°16E 202 C7
Mikhaylovka = Kimovsk Russia 54°0N 38°29E 188 E10
Mikhaylovka Russia 50°3N 43°5E 190 E6
Mikhaylovsk Russia 45°8N 42°0E 191 H5
Mikhnevo Russia 55°4N 37°59E 188 E9
Miki Hyōgo, Japan 34°48N 134°59E 222 C6
Miki Kagawa, Japan 34°12N 134°7E 222 C6
Mikir Hills India 26°10N 93°30E 241 B4
Mikkeli Finland 61°43N 27°15E 188 B4
Mikkwa → Canada 58°25N 114°46W 296 B6
Mikniya Sudan 17°0N 33°45E 257 D3
Mikołajki Poland 53°49N 21°37E 184 E8
Mikonos = Mykonos Greece 37°30N 25°25E 205 D7
Mikope Dem. Rep. of the Congo 4°58S 20°43E 265 C4
Mikoyan-Shakhar = Karachayevsk Russia 43°50N 41°55E 191 J5
Mikri Prespa, L. Greece 40°47N 21°3E 202 F5
Mikro Derio Greece 41°19N 26°6E 203 E10
Mikstat Poland 51°32N 17°59E 185 G4
Mikulov Czechia 48°48N 16°39E 181 C9
Mikumi Tanzania 7°26S 37°0E 268 D4
Mikumi △ Tanzania 7°35S 37°15E 268 D4
Mikun Russia 62°20N 50°0E 186 B9
Mikuni Japan 36°13N 136°9E 223 A8
Mikuni-Tōge Japan 36°50N 138°50E 223 A10
Mikura-Jima Japan 33°52N 139°36E 223 D11
Mila Algeria 36°27N 6°15E 261 A6
Mila □ Algeria 36°20N 6°10E 261 A6
Milaca U.S.A. 45°45N 93°39W 308 C7
Miladummadulu Atoll Maldives 5°50N 73°30E 272 d
Milagro Ecuador 2°11S 79°36W 328 D2
Milagros Phil. 12°13N 123°30E 232 E4
Milan = Milano Italy 45°28N 9°10E 128 B1
Milan Ga., U.S.A. 32°1N 83°4W 316 C6
Milan Ill., U.S.A. 41°27N 90°34W 310 C6
Milan Mich., U.S.A. 42°5N 83°41W 311 B13
Milan Mo., U.S.A. 40°12N 93°7W 310 D3
Milan Tenn., U.S.A. 35°55N 88°46W 315 D10
Miland Norway 59°54N 8°45E 164 E5
Milando Angola 8°45S 17°36E 265 D3
Milando △ Angola 8°45S 17°10E 265 D3
Milanese, Parco Regionale △ Italy 45°35N 9°5E 128 A1
Milang Australia 35°24S 138°58E 282 C3
Milange Mozam. 16°3S 35°45E 269 F4
Milano Italy 45°28N 9°10E 128 B1
Milano Due Italy 45°29N 9°16E 128 B2
Milano Linate ✈ (LIN) Italy 45°27N 9°16E 128 B2
Milano Malpense ✈ (MXP) Italy 45°38N 8°43E 128 A1
Milano San Felice Italy 45°28N 9°18E 128 B2
Milanoa Madag. 13°35S 49°47E 272 A2
Milâs Turkey 37°20N 27°50E 205 D9
Milatos Greece 35°18N 25°34E 207 E6
Milazzo Italy 38°13N 15°15E 201 D8
Milbank U.S.A. 45°13N 96°38W 308 C5
Milbanke Sd. Canada 52°19N 128°33W 296 C3
Milbertshofen Germany 48°10N 11°34E 131 A2
Milden Canada 51°29N 107°32W 297 C7
Mildenhall U.K. 52°21N 0°32E 169 E8
Mildmay Canada 44°3N 81°7W 312 B3
Mildura Australia 34°13S 142°9E 282 C5
Mile China 24°28N 103°20E 228 E4
Mile and a Quarter Barbados 13°16N 59°37W 323 r
Miles Australia 26°40S 150°9E 281 D5
Miles City U.S.A. 46°25N 105°51W 304 C11
Mileşti Moldova 47°13N 28°3E 183 C13
Milestone Canada 49°59N 104°31W 297 D8
Mileto Italy 38°36N 16°4E 201 D9
Miletto, Mte. Italy 41°27N 14°22E 201 A7
Miletus Turkey 37°30N 27°18E 205 D9
Milevsko Czechia 49°27N 14°21E 180 B7
Milford Calif., U.S.A. 40°10N 120°22W 306 E6
Milford Conn., U.S.A. 41°14N 73°3W 313 E11
Milford Del., U.S.A. 38°55N 75°26W 309 F16
Milford Ill., U.S.A. 40°38N 87°42W 311 D9
Milford Mass., U.S.A. 42°8N 71°31W 313 D13
Milford Mich., U.S.A. 42°35N 83°36W 311 B13
Milford N.H., U.S.A. 42°50N 71°39W 313 D13
Milford N.Y., U.S.A. 42°35N 74°56W 313 D10
Milford Pa., U.S.A. 41°19N 74°48W 313 E10
Milford Utah, U.S.A. 38°24N 113°1W 304 G7
Milford Haven U.K. 51°42N 5°7W 169 F2
Milford Sd. N.Z. 44°41S 167°47E 285 E2
Milḥ, Baḥr al = Razāzah, Buḥayrat ar Iraq 32°40N 43°35E 213 F10
Miliana Aïn Salah, Algeria 27°20N 2°32E 261 C5
Miliana Médéa, Algeria 36°20N 2°15E 261 A5
Milicz Poland 51°31N 17°19E 185 G4
Milies Greece 39°20N 23°9E 204 B5
Milikapiti Australia 11°26S 130°40E 278 B5
Mililani Town U.S.A. 21°28N 158°1W 302 K13
Miling Australia 30°30S 116°17E 279 F2
Militello in Val di Catánia Italy 37°16N 14°48E 201 E7
Militsch = Milicz Poland 51°31N 17°19E 185 G4
Milk, Wadi el → Sudan 17°55N 30°20E 256 D3
Milk River Canada 49°10N 112°5W 296 D6
Milk River Spa Jamaica 17°50N 77°22W 320 a
Mill → U.S.A. 42°57N 83°23W 312 D1
Mill Hill U.K. 51°37N 0°14W 125 A2
Mill I. Antarctica 66°0S 101°30E 151 C8
Mill I. Nunavut, Canada 63°58N 77°47W 295 E16
Mill Shoals U.S.A. 38°15N 88°21W 311 F8
Mill Valley U.S.A. 37°54N 122°32W 306 H4
Millárs → Spain 39°55N 0°1W 196 F4
Millau France 44°8N 3°4E 174 D7
Millbridge Canada 44°41N 77°36W 312 B7
Millbrook Ont., Canada 44°10N 78°29W 312 B6
Millbrook Ala., U.S.A. 32°29N 86°22W 315 E11
Millbrook N.Y., U.S.A. 41°47N 73°42W 313 E11
Mille Lacs, L. des Canada 48°45N 90°35W 298 C1
Mille Lacs L. U.S.A. 46°15N 93°39W 308 B7
Milledgeville Ga., U.S.A. 33°5N 83°14W 316 B6
Milledgeville Ill., U.S.A. 41°58N 89°46W 310 C7
Millen U.S.A. 32°48N 81°57W 316 C8
Millennium Dome U.K. 51°30N 0°0E 125 B3
Millennium I. = Caroline I. Kiribati 9°58S 150°13W 289 H12
Millennium Park Chicago, U.S.A. 119 c2
Miller U.S.A. 44°31N 98°59W 308 C4
Miller Lake Canada 45°6N 81°26W 312 A3
Miller Meadow U.S.A. 41°51N 87°49W 119 B2
Millerhill U.K. 55°55N 3°5W 121 B3
Millerovo Russia 48°57N 40°28E 191 F5
Miller's Flat N.Z. 45°39S 169°23E 285 F4
Millers Point Sydney, Australia 139 a1
Millersburg Ind., U.S.A. 41°32N 85°42W 311 C11
Millersburg Ohio, U.S.A. 40°33N 81°55W 312 F3
Millersburg Pa., U.S.A. 40°32N 76°58W 312 F8
Millerton N.Z. 41°39S 171°54E 285 B6
Millerton N.Y., U.S.A. 41°57N 73°31W 313 E11
Millerton L. U.S.A. 37°1N 119°41W 306 J7
Millet St. Lucia 13°55N 60°59W 323 m
Millevaches, Plateau de France 45°45N 2°0E 174 C6
Millheim U.S.A. 40°54N 77°29W 312 F7
Millicent Australia 37°34S 140°21E 282 D4
Milligan U.S.A. 30°45N 86°38W 317 E3
Millington U.S.A. 35°20N 89°53W 315 D10
Millinocket U.S.A. 45°39N 68°43W 309 C19
Millmerran Australia 27°53S 151°16E 281 D5
Millom U.K. 54°13N 3°16W 168 C4
Mills L. Canada 61°30N 118°20W 296 A5
Millsboro U.S.A. 40°0N 80°0W 312 G5
Millstream Chichester △ Australia 21°35S 117°6E 278 D2
Millstreet Ireland 52°4N 9°4W 166 D2
Millthorpe Australia 33°26S 149°12E 283 B8
Millville N.J., U.S.A. 39°24N 75°2W 309 F16
Millville Pa., U.S.A. 41°7N 76°32W 313 E8
Millwood L. U.S.A. 33°42N 93°58W 314 E8
Milna Croatia 43°20N 16°28E 199 E13
Milne → Australia 21°10S 137°33E 280 C2
Milne Bay □ Papua N. G. 10°0S 152°30E 286 E7
Milne Land Greenland 70°40N 26°30W 154 C8
Milnerton S. Africa 33°53S 18°29E 118 A1
Milo U.S.A. 45°15N 68°59W 309 C19
Milo → Guinea 8°52N 9°0W 262 D3
Milolii U.S.A. 19°11N 155°55W 302 D6
Milon, Akra Greece 36°15N 28°11E 206 E12
Milon-la-Chapelle France 48°43N 2°3E 134 B1
Milos Greece 36°44N 24°25E 204 E6
Miłosław Poland 52°12N 17°32E 185 F4
Milot Albania 41°41N 19°43E 202 E3
Milparinka Australia 29°46S 141°57E 281 D3
Milpitas U.S.A. 37°26N 121°55W 306 H5
Milroy U.S.A. 39°30N 85°28W 311 E11
Miltenberg Germany 49°41N 9°16E 179 G5
Milton N.S.W., Australia 35°20S 150°27E 283 C9
Milton N.S., Canada 44°4N 64°45W 299 D7
Milton Ont., Canada 43°31N 79°53W 312 C5
Milton N.Z. 46°7S 169°59E 285 G4
Milton Calif., U.S.A. 38°3N 120°51W 306 G6
Milton Fla., U.S.A. 30°38N 87°3W 317 E2
Milton Iowa, U.S.A. 40°41N 92°10W 310 D4
Milton Mass., U.S.A. 42°14N 71°2W 116 B2
Milton Pa., U.S.A. 41°1N 76°51W 312 F8
Milton Vt., U.S.A. 44°38N 73°7W 313 B11
Milton Wis., U.S.A. 42°47N 88°56W 311 B8
Milton Bridge U.K. 55°51N 3°11W 121 B2
Milton-Freewater U.S.A. 45°56N 118°23W 304 D4
Milton Keynes U.K. 52°1N 0°44W 169 E7
Milton Keynes □ U.K. 52°1N 0°44W 169 E7
Milton Park Montréal, Canada 130 b1
Miltou Chad 10°14N 17°26E 259 F3
Miltown Malbay Ireland 52°52N 9°24W 166 D2
Miluo China 29°0N 112°59E 229 C9
Milverton Canada 43°34N 80°55W 312 C4
Milwaukee U.S.A. 43°2N 87°54W 311 A9
Milwaukee Deep Atl. Oc. 19°50N 68°0W 321 C6
Milwaukie U.S.A. 45°26N 122°38W 306 E4
Mim Ghana 6°57N 2°33W 262 D4
Mima Japan 34°4N 134°9E 222 C6
Mimarópa □ Phil. 11°30N 120°20E 233 F3
Mimico Canada 43°36N 79°29W 141 B2
Mimico Creek → Canada 43°37N 79°28W 141 B1
Mimili Australia 27°0S 132°42E 279 E5
Mimizan France 44°12N 1°13W 174 D2
Mimoň Czechia 50°38N 14°43E 180 A7
Mimongo Gabon 1°11S 11°36E 264 C2
Mimoso Brazil 15°10S 48°5W 333 E2
Mims U.S.A. 28°40N 80°51W 317 G9
Min Jiang → Fujian, China 26°0N 119°35E 229 E12
Min Jiang → Sichuan, China 28°45N 104°40E 228 C5
Min Xian China 34°25N 104°5E 226 G3
Mīnā' al Aḥmadī Kuwait 29°5N 48°10E 247 D6
Mīnā' Jabal 'Alī U.A.E. 25°2N 55°8E 247 E7
Mina Pirquitas Argentina 22°40S 66°30W 334 A2
Mīnā Raysūt = Raysūt Oman 16°56N 53°59E 249 C6
Mīnā Su'ud Si. Arabia 28°45N 48°28E 247 D6
Minago → Canada 54°33N 98°59W 297 C9
Minakami Japan 36°49N 138°59E 223 A10
Minaki Canada 49°59N 94°40W 297 D10
Minakuchi Japan 34°58N 136°10E 223 C8
Minalungao △ Phil. 15°2N 121°8E 232 D3
Minamata Japan 32°10N 130°30E 222 E2
Minami Japan 34°40N 135°30E 133 A2
Minami-Arapusa △ Japan 35°30N 138°9E 223 B10
Minami-Tori-Shima Pac. Oc. 24°20N 153°58E 288 E7
Minamiaizu Japan 37°12N 139°46E 221 F9
Minamiawaji Japan 34°10N 134°42E 222 C6
Minamisōma Japan 37°38N 140°58E 220 F10
Minamitsunashima Japan 35°32N 139°37E 140 B2
Minas Indonesia 0°50N 101°26E 234 B2
Minas Uruguay 34°20S 55°10W 335 C4
Minas, Sierra de las Guatemala 15°9N 89°31W 320 C2
Minas Basin Canada 45°20N 64°12W 299 C7
Minas de Riotinto Spain 37°42N 6°35W 195 H4
Minas Gerais □ Brazil 18°50S 46°0W 333 E2
Minas Novas Brazil 17°15S 42°36W 333 E3
Minatitlán Mexico 17°59N 94°31W 319 D6
Minato Ōsaka, Japan 34°39N 135°25E 133 B1
Minato Tokyo, Japan 140 c3
Minbu Myanmar 20°10N 94°52E 241 E5
Minbya Myanmar 20°22N 93°16E 241 E4
Minchinabad Pakistan 30°10N 73°34E 242 D5
Mincio → Italy 45°4N 10°59E 198 C7
Minčol Slovakia 49°15N 20°58E 181 B13
Mindanao Phil. 8°0N 125°0E 233 H6
Mindanao Sea = Bohol Sea Phil. 9°0N 124°0E 233 G5
Mindanao Trench Pac. Oc. 12°0N 126°6E 232 E5
Mindel → Germany 48°31N 10°23E 179 G6
Mindelheim Germany 48°2N 10°29E 179 G6
Mindelo Cabo Verde 16°24N 25°0W 153 j
Minden Ont., Canada 44°55N 78°43W 312 B6
Minden Nordrhein-Westfalen, Germany 52°17N 8°55E 178 C4
Minden La., U.S.A. 32°37N 93°17W 314 E8
Minden Nev., U.S.A. 38°57N 119°46W 306 G7
Mindibungu = Billiluna Australia 19°37S 127°41E 278 C4
Mindiptana Indonesia 5°55S 140°22E 231 F10
Mindon Myanmar 19°21N 94°44E 241 F5
Mindona L. Australia 33°6S 142°6E 282 B5
Mindoro Phil. 13°0N 121°0E 232 E3
Mindoro Occidental □ Phil. 13°0N 120°55E 232 E3
Mindoro Oriental □ Phil. 13°0N 121°5E 232 E3
Mindoro Str. Phil. 12°30N 120°30E 232 E3
Mindouli Congo 4°12S 14°28E 264 C2
Mindourou Cameroon 3°29N 13°26E 264 B2
Mine Japan 34°12N 131°7E 222 C3
Minehead U.K. 51°12N 3°29W 169 F4
Mineiros Brazil 17°34S 52°34W 331 D7
Mineola N.Y., U.S.A. 40°44N 73°38W 313 F11
Mineola Tex., U.S.A. 32°40N 95°29W 314 E7
Mineral Bath Jamaica 17°58N 76°2W 320 a
Mineral King U.S.A. 36°27N 118°36W 306 J8
Mineral Point U.S.A. 42°52N 90°11W 310 B6
Mineral Wells U.S.A. 32°48N 98°7W 314 E5
Mineralnyye Vody Russia 44°15N 43°8E 191 H6
Miners Bay Canada 44°49N 78°46W 312 B6
Minersville U.S.A. 40°41N 76°16W 313 F8
Minerva N.Y., U.S.A. 43°47N 73°59W 313 C11
Minerva Ohio, U.S.A. 40°44N 81°6W 312 F3
Minervino Murge Italy 41°5N 16°5E 201 A9
Minetto U.S.A. 43°24N 76°28W 313 C8
Minfeng China 37°4N 82°46E 217 E10
Ming-Kush Kyrgyzstan 41°40N 74°28E 217 D8
Mingäçevir Azerbaijan 40°45N 47°0E 191 K8
Mingäçevir Su Anbarı Azerbaijan 40°57N 46°50E 191 K8
Mingala C.A.R. 5°6N 21°49E 264 A4
Mingan Canada 50°20N 64°0W 299 B7
Mingary Australia 32°8S 140°45E 282 B4
Mingchien Taiwan 23°50N 120°42E 225 C2
Mingechaur = Mingäçevir Azerbaijan 40°45N 47°0E 191 K8
Mingechaurskoye Vdkhr. = Mingäçevir Su Anbarı Azerbaijan 40°57N 46°50E 191 K8
Mingela Australia 19°52S 146°38E 280 B4
Mingenew Australia 29°12S 115°21E 279 E2
Mingera Cr. → Australia 20°38S 137°45E 280 C2
Minggang China 32°24N 114°3E 229 A10
Mingguang China 32°46N 117°59E 229 A11
Mingin Myanmar 22°50N 94°30E 241 D5
Mingir Moldova 46°40N 28°20E 183 D13
Minglanilla Spain 39°34N 1°38W 197 F3
Minglun China 25°10N 108°21E 228 E7
Mingo Congo 1°55S 15°1E 264 C3
Mingo Junction U.S.A. 40°19N 80°37W 312 F4
Mingora Pakistan 34°48N 72°22E 243 B5
Mingorria Spain 40°45N 4°40W 194 E6
Mingshan China 30°6N 103°10E 228 B4
Mingteke Daban = Mintaka Pass Pakistan 37°0N 74°58E 243 A6
Mingxi China 26°18N 117°12E 229 D11
Mingyuegue China 43°2N 128°50E 227 C15
Minhe China 36°9N 102°45E 218 D9
Minhla Bago, Myanmar 17°59N 95°43E 241 G5
Minhla Magway, Myanmar 19°58N 95°3E 241 F5
Minho = Miño → Spain 41°52N 8°40W 194 D2
Minhou China 26°0N 119°15E 229 E12
Minhsiung Taiwan 23°33N 120°35E 225 C2
Miničevo Serbia 43°42N 22°18E 182 G7
Minicoy I. India 8°17N 73°2E 245 K1
Minidoka U.S.A. 42°45N 113°29W 304 E7
Minier U.S.A. 40°26N 89°19W 310 D7
Minigwal, L. Australia 29°31S 123°14E 279 E3
Minilya → Australia 23°45S 114°0E 279 D1
Minilya Roadhouse Australia 23°55S 114°0E 279 D1
Mininera Australia 37°37S 142°58E 282 D5
Minipi L. Canada 52°25N 60°45W 299 B7
Minj Papua N. G. 5°54S 144°37E 286 C3
Minjilang Australia 11°8S 132°33E 278 B5
Mink L. Canada 61°54N 117°40W 296 A5
Minkammen South Sudan 6°3N 31°32E 257 F3
Minkebé Gabon 1°56N 12°45E 264 B2
Minlaton Australia 34°45S 137°35E 282 C2
Minna Nigeria 9°37N 6°30E 263 D6
Minna-shima Japan 26°39N 127°49E 288 a
Minneapolis Kans., U.S.A. 39°8N 97°42W 308 F5
Minneapolis Minn., U.S.A. 44°57N 93°16W 308 C7
Minneapolis-St. Paul Int. ✈ (MSP) U.S.A. 44°53N 93°13W 308 C7
Minnedosa Canada 50°14N 99°50W 297 C9
Minnesota □ U.S.A. 46°0N 94°15W 308 B6
Minnesota → U.S.A. 44°54N 93°9W 308 C7
Minnesund Norway 60°23N 11°14E 164 D8
Minnewaukan U.S.A. 48°4N 99°15W 308 A4
Minnipa Australia 32°51S 135°9E 281 E2
Minnitaki L. Canada 49°57N 92°10W 298 C1
Miño = A Carreira Spain 43°21N 8°12W 194 B2
Mino Japan 35°32N 136°55E 223 B8
Miño → Spain 41°52N 8°40W 194 D2
Mino-Kamo Japan 35°23N 137°2E 223 B9
Mino-Mikawa-Kōgen Japan 35°10N 137°23E 223 B9
Minoa Greece 35°6N 25°45E 207 E6
Minobu Japan 35°22N 138°26E 223 B10
Minobu-Sanchi Japan 35°14N 138°20E 223 B10
Minonk U.S.A. 40°54N 89°2W 310 D7
Minooka U.S.A. 41°27N 88°16W 311 C8
Minorca = Menorca Spain 40°0N 4°0E 206 B5
Minore Australia 32°14S 148°27E 283 B8
Minot U.S.A. 48°14N 101°18W 308 A3
Minqin China 38°38N 103°20E 226 E2
Minqing China 26°15N 118°50E 229 D12
Minsen Germany 53°41N 7°58E 178 B3
Minshât el Bekkarî Egypt 30°0N 31°8E 117 A1
Minsk Belarus 53°52N 27°30E 177 B14
Minsk □ Belarus 53°15N 27°30E 188 F4
Mińsk Mazowiecki Poland 52°10N 21°33E 185 F8
Minster U.S.A. 40°24N 84°23W 311 D12
Mintabie Australia 27°15S 133°7E 281 D1
Mintaka Pass Pakistan 37°0N 74°58E 243 A6
Minthami Myanmar 23°55N 94°16E 241 D5
Minto N.B., Canada 46°5N 66°5W 299 C6
Minto Alaska, U.S.A. 64°53N 149°10W 303 D10
Minto, L. Canada 57°13N 75°0W 298 A5
Minton Canada 49°10N 104°35W 297 D8
Mintoum Gabon 0°27N 12°16E 264 B2
Minturn U.S.A. 39°35N 106°26W 304 G10
Minturno Italy 41°15N 13°45E 200 A6
Minudasht Iran 37°17N 56°7E 247 B8
Minûf Egypt 30°26N 30°52E 256 H7
Minusinsk Russia 53°43N 91°20E 217 B12
Minutang India 28°15N 96°30E 241 A6
Minvoul Gabon 2°9N 12°8E 264 B2
Minwakh Yemen 16°48N 48°6E 249 C5
Minxiong = Minhsiung Taiwan 23°33N 120°35E 225 C2
Minya el Qamh Egypt 30°31N 31°21E 256 H7
Minya Konka = Gongga Shan China 29°40N 101°55E 228 C3
Minyip Australia 36°29S 142°36E 282 D5
Minzhong China 22°37N 113°30E 219 a
Mionica Bos.-H. 44°51N 18°29E 182 F3
Mionica Serbia 44°14N 20°6E 202 B4
Mioveni Romania 44°56N 24°54E 183 F9
Miquan China 43°58N 87°42E 217 D11
Miquelon Qué., Canada 49°25N 76°27W 298 C4
Miquelon St-P. & M. 47°8N 56°22W 299 C8
Mir Belarus 53°27N 26°28E 177 B14
Mir Niger 14°5N 11°59E 259 F2
Mīr Kūh Iran 26°22N 58°55E 247 E8
Mīr Shahdād Iran 26°15N 58°29E 247 E8
Mira Italy 45°26N 12°8E 199 C9
Mira Portugal 40°26N 8°44W 194 E2
Mira → Colombia 1°36N 79°1W 328 C2
Mira → Portugal 37°43N 8°47W 195 H2
Mira por vos Cay The Bahamas 22°9N 74°30W 321 B5
Mirabad Afghan. 30°25N 61°50E 240 C1
Mirabella Eclano Italy 41°2N 14°59E 201 A7
Mirabello, Kolpos Greece 35°10N 25°50E 207 E6
Miracema do Norte Brazil 9°33S 48°24W 332 C2
Mirador Brazil 6°22S 44°22W 332 B3
Mirador-Río Azul △ Guatemala 17°45N 89°50W 320 C1
Miraflores = Rovira Colombia 4°15N 75°20W 328 C2
Miraflores Colombia 1°25N 72°13W 328 C3
Miraflores Lima, Peru 12°7S 77°2W 124 B2
Miraflores, L. Panama 9°1N 79°36W 320 c
Miraflores Locks Panama 9°0N 79°36W 320 c
Miraj India 16°50N 74°45E 244 F2
Miram Shah Pakistan 33°0N 70°2E 242 C4
Miramar Argentina 38°15S 57°50W 334 D4
Miramar Mozam. 23°50S 35°35E 271 B6
Miramar Fla., U.S.A. 25°59N 80°13W 129 C1
Miramas France 43°33N 4°59E 175 E8
Mirambeau France 45°23N 0°35W 174 C3
Miramichi Canada 47°2N 65°28W 299 C6
Miramichi B. Canada 47°15N 65°0W 299 C7
Miramont-de-Guyenne France 44°37N 0°21E 174 D4
Miranda Brazil 20°10S 56°15W 331 E6
Miranda □ Venezuela 10°15N 66°25W 328 A4
Miranda → Brazil 19°25S 57°20W 331 D6
Miranda de Ebro Spain 42°41N 2°57W 196 C2
Miranda do Corvo Portugal 40°6N 8°20W 194 E2
Miranda do Douro Portugal 41°30N 6°16W 194 D4
Mirande France 43°31N 0°25E 174 E4
Mirandela Portugal 41°32N 7°10W 194 D3
Mirándola Italy 44°53N 11°4E 198 D8
Mirandópolis Brazil 21°9S 51°6W 335 A5
Mirango Malawi 13°32S 34°58E 269 E3
Mirani Australia 21°8S 148°53E 280 b
Mirano Italy 45°30N 12°7E 199 C9
Miras Albania 40°30N 20°56E 202 F4
Mirassol Brazil 20°46S 49°28W 335 A6
Mirbāṭ Oman 17°0N 54°45E 249 C6
Mirboo North Australia 38°24S 146°10E 283 E7
Mirear Egypt 23°15N 35°41E 256 C4
Mirebeau France 46°49N 0°10E 172 F7
Mirebeau-sur-Bèze France 47°25N 5°20E 173 E12
Mirecourt France 48°20N 6°10E 173 D13
Mires Greece 35°4N 24°56E 207 E5
Mirgorod = Myrhorod Ukraine 49°58N 33°37E 189 H7
Miri Malaysia 4°23N 113°59E 235 B4
Mirialguda India 16°52N 79°35E 244 F4
Miriam Vale Australia 24°20S 151°33E 280 C5
Miribel France 45°50N 4°57E 173 G11
Mirigama Sri Lanka 7°15N 80°8E 245 L5
Mirim, L. S. Amer. 32°45S 52°50W 335 C5
Mirimire Venezuela 11°10N 68°43W 328 A4
Miringoni Comoros Is. 12°17S 43°38E 272 a
Miriti Brazil 6°15S 59°0W 331 B6
Miriuwung Gajerrong ✪ Australia 15°0S 128°45E 278 C4
Mīrjāveh Iran 29°1N 61°30E 247 D9
Mirny Antarctica 66°50S 92°30E 151 C14
Mirnyy Russia 62°33N 113°53E 215 C12
Miroč Serbia 44°32N 22°16E 202 B6
Mirokhan Pakistan 27°46N 68°6E 242 F3
Mirond L. Canada 55°6N 102°47W 297 B8
Mirosławiec Poland 53°20N 16°5E 184 E3
Mirpur Pakistan 33°32N 73°56E 243 C5
Mirpur Batoro Pakistan 24°44N 68°16E 242 G3
Mirpur Bibiwari Pakistan 28°33N 67°44E 242 E2
Mirpur Khas Pakistan 25°30N 69°0E 242 G3
Mirpur Sakro Pakistan 24°33N 67°41E 242 G2
Mirria Niger 13°43N 9°7E 259 F1
Mirrool Australia 34°19S 147°10E 283 C7
Mirs Bay = Tai Pang Wan China 22°33N 114°24E 219 a
Mirsale Somalia 5°57N 47°59E 267 C6
Mirsk Poland 50°58N 15°23E 185 H2
Mirtağ Turkey 38°23N 41°56E 246 B4
Mirtoo Sea Greece 37°0N 23°20E 204 D5
Mirtou, Kolpos Greece 38°20N 20°27E 207 C1
Miryang S. Korea 35°31N 128°44E 224 E4
Mirzaani Georgia 41°24N 46°5E 191 K8
Mirzachul = Guliston Uzbekistan 40°29N 68°46E 217 D7
Mirzapur India 25°10N 82°34E 243 G10
Mirzapur-cum-Vindhyachal = Mirzapur India 25°10N 82°34E 243 G10
Mirzoyan = Taraz Kazakhstan 42°54N 71°22E 217 D8
Misaki Japan 34°18N 135°9E 223 C7
Misamis = Ozamiz Phil. 8°15N 123°50E 233 G4
Misamis Occidental □ Phil. 8°20N 123°42E 233 G4
Misamis Oriental □ Phil. 8°45N 125°0E 233 G5
Misantla Mexico 19°56N 96°50W 319 D5
Misawa Japan 40°41N 141°24E 220 D10
Miscou I. Canada 47°57N 64°31W 299 C7
Misdroy = Międzyzdroje Poland 53°56N 14°26E 184 E1
Misericordia = Itaporanga Brazil 7°18S 38°0W 332 C4
Misericordia, Sa. da Brazil 22°51S 43°17W 135 B1
Misha India 7°59N 93°20E 245 L10
Mish'āb, Ra's al Si. Arabia 28°15N 48°43E 247 D6
Mishagua → Peru 11°12S 72°58W 330 C3
Mishamo Tanzania 5°41S 30°41E 268 D3
Mishan China 45°37N 131°48E 220 B5
Mishawaka U.S.A. 41°40N 86°11W 311 C10
Mishbih, Gebel Egypt 22°38N 34°44E 256 C3
Mishima Japan 35°10N 138°52E 223 B10
Mishmi Hills India 29°0N 96°0E 241 A6
Mishō Japan 32°57N 132°35E 222 E4
Misima I. Papua N. G. 10°40S 152°45E 286 F7
Misión Mexico 32°6N 116°53W 307 N10
Misión Fagnano Argentina 54°32S 67°17W 336 D3
Misiones □ Argentina 27°0S 55°0W 335 B5
Misiones □ Paraguay 27°0S 56°0W 334 B4
Miskah Si. Arabia 24°49N 42°56E 246 E4
Miski, E. → Chad 20°0N 17°55E 259 E3
Miskitos, Cayos Nic. 14°26N 82°50W 320 D3
Miskolc Hungary 48°7N 20°50E 182 B5
Misoke Dem. Rep. of the Congo 0°42S 28°2E 268 C2
Misool Indonesia 1°52S 130°10E 231 E8
Mişr = Egypt ■ Africa 28°0N 31°0E 256 B3
Mişrātah Libya 32°24N 15°3E 258 B3
Mişrātah □ Libya 33°30N 15°0E 258 B3
Missanabie Canada 48°20N 84°6W 298 C3
Missão Catrimani Brazil 2°48N 62°18W 329 C5
Missão Velha Brazil 7°15S 39°10W 332 C4
Missinaibi → Canada 50°43N 81°29W 298 B3
Missinaibi L. Canada 48°23N 83°40W 298 C3
Mission B.C., Canada 49°10N 122°15W 296 D4
Mission Calif., U.S.A. 37°44N 122°25W 306 H4
Mission S. Dak., U.S.A. 43°18N 100°39W 308 D3
Mission Tex., U.S.A. 26°13N 98°20W 314 H5
Mission Beach Australia 17°53S 146°6E 280 B4
Mission Viejo U.S.A. 33°36N 117°40W 307 M9
Missirah Senegal 13°40N 16°30W 262 C1
Missisa L. Canada 52°20N 85°7W 298 B2
Missisicabi → Canada 51°14N 79°31W 298 B4
Mississagi → Canada 46°15N 83°9W 298 C3
Mississauga Canada 43°32N 79°35W 141 B1
Mississinewa L. U.S.A. 40°42N 85°52W 311 D10
Mississippi □ U.S.A. 33°0N 90°0W 315 E10
Mississippi → U.S.A. 29°9N 89°15W 315 G10
Mississippi L. Canada 45°5N 76°10W 313 A8
Mississippi River Delta U.S.A. 29°10N 89°15W 315 G10
Mississippi Sd. U.S.A. 30°20N 89°0W 315 F10
Missoula U.S.A. 46°52N 114°1W 304 C6
Missour Morocco 33°3N 4°0W 260 B4
Missouri □ U.S.A. 38°25N 92°30W 310 F4
Missouri → U.S.A. 38°49N 90°7W 310 F6
Missouri City U.S.A. 29°37N 95°32W 314 G7
Missouri Valley U.S.A. 41°34N 95°53W 308 E6
Mist U.S.A. 45°59N 123°15W 306 E3
Mistassibi → Canada 48°53N 72°13W 299 B5
Mistassini Canada 48°53N 72°12W 299 C5
Mistassini → Canada 48°42N 72°20W 299 C5
Mistassini, L. Canada 51°0N 73°30W 298 B5
Mistastin L. Canada 55°57N 63°20W 299 A7
Mistelbach Austria 48°34N 16°34E 181 C9
Misterbianco Italy 37°31N 15°1E 201 E8
Misteriosa Bank Caribbean 18°50N 83°50W 320 C3

Misti, Volcán Peru 16°18S 71°24W 330 D3
Mistinibi, L. Canada 55°56N 64°17W 299 A7
Mistissini Canada 48°53N 72°12W 299 C5
Mistras = Mystras Greece 37°4N 22°22E 204 D4
Mistretta Italy 37°56N 14°22E 201 E7
Misty Fjords Nat. Monument △ U.S.A. 55°40N 130°40W 303 J15
Misty L. Canada 58°53N 101°40W 297 B8
Misugi Japan 34°31N 136°16E 223 C8
Misumi Japan 32°37N 130°27E 222 E2
Misurata = Mişrātah Libya 32°24N 15°3E 258 B3
Mît Ghamr Egypt 30°42N 31°12E 256 H7
Mitaka Japan 35°41N 139°34E 140 A2
Mitande Mozam. 14°6S 35°58E 269 E4
Mitatib Sudan 15°59N 36°12E 257 D4
Mitau = Jelgava Latvia 56°41N 23°49E 184 B10
Mitava = Jelgava Latvia 56°41N 23°49E 184 B10
Mitcham U.K. 51°23N 0°10W 125 B2
Mitcham Common U.K. 51°23N 0°8W 125 B3
Mitchell Queens., Australia 26°29S 147°58E 281 D4
Mitchell Ont., Canada 43°28N 81°12W 312 C3
Mitchell Ga., U.S.A. 33°13N 82°42W 316 B7
Mitchell Ind., U.S.A. 38°44N 86°28W 311 F10
Mitchell Nebr., U.S.A. 41°57N 103°49W 308 E2
Mitchell Oreg., U.S.A. 44°34N 120°9W 304 D3
Mitchell S. Dak., U.S.A. 43°43N 98°2W 308 D4
Mitchell → Australia 15°12S 141°35E 280 B3
Mitchell, Mt. U.S.A. 35°46N 82°16W 315 D13
Mitchell-Alice Rivers △ Australia 15°28S 142°5E 280 B3
Mitchell Museum of the American Indian Chicago, U.S.A. 42°4N 87°43W 119 A2
Mitchell Ra. Australia 12°49S 135°36E 280 A2
Mitchell River △ Australia 37°37S 147°22E 283 D7
Mitchell's Plain S. Africa 34°4S 18°35E 118 B2
Mitchelstown Ireland 52°15N 8°16W 166 D3
Mitha Tiwana Pakistan 32°13N 72°6E 242 C5
Mithi Pakistan 24°44N 69°48E 242 G3
Mithimna Greece 39°20N 26°12E 205 B8
Mithrao Pakistan 27°28N 69°40E 242 F3
Mitiamo Australia 36°12S 144°15E 282 D6
Mitikas Etoloakarnania, Greece 38°40N 20°56E 207 B2
Mitikas Preveza, Greece 39°0N 20°42E 207 B2
Mitilini Greece 39°6N 26°35E 205 B8
Mitilinii Greece 37°42N 26°56E 205 D8
Mitla Pass = Mamarr Mitlā Egypt 30°2N 32°54E 251 H3
Mito Japan 36°20N 140°30E 223 A12
Mitra, Mt. Eq. Guin. 1°23N 9°19E 264 B1
Mitre, Mt. N.Z. 40°50S 175°30E 284 G4
Mitrofanovka Russia 49°58N 39°42E 189 H10
Mitrovicë Kosovo 42°54N 20°52E 202 D4
Mitrowitz = Sremska Mitrovica Serbia 44°59N 19°38E 182 F4
Mitsamiouli Comoros Is. 11°20S 43°16E 272 a
Mitsang Gabon 0°42N 12°33E 264 B2
Mitsinjo Madag. 16°1S 45°52E 272 B2
Mitsio, Nosy Madag. 12°54S 48°36E 272 A2
Mitsiwa Eritrea 15°35N 39°25E 257 D4
Mitsiwa Channel Eritrea 15°30N 40°0E 257 D5
Mitsoudjé Comoros Is. 11°48S 43°16E 272 a
Mitsukaidō Japan 36°1N 139°59E 223 A11
Mitsushima Japan 34°15N 129°20E 222 C1
Mittagong Australia 34°28S 150°29E 283 C9
Mitte Germany 52°32N 13°24E 115 A3
Mittel Isarkanal → Germany 48°12N 11°40E 131 A3
Mittel Schreiberhau = Szklarska Poreba Poland 50°50N 15°33E 185 H2
Mittelberg Austria 47°20N 10°10E 180 D3
Mittelfranken □ Germany 49°25N 10°40E 179 F6
Mittellandkanal → Germany 52°20N 8°28E 178 C4
Mittelwalde = Międzylesie Poland 50°8N 16°40E 185 H3
Mittenwalde Germany 52°15N 13°31E 178 C9
Mittersill Austria 47°16N 12°29E 180 D5
Mitterteich Germany 49°57N 12°14E 179 F8
Mittimatalik = Pond Inlet Canada 72°40N 77°0W 295 C16
Mittweida Germany 50°59N 12°59E 178 E8
Mitú Colombia 1°15N 70°13W 328 C3
Mituas Colombia 3°52N 68°49W 328 C4
Mitumba Tanzania 7°8S 31°2E 268 D3
Mitumba, Mts. Dem. Rep. of the Congo 7°0S 27°30E 268 D2
Mitwaba Dem. Rep. of the Congo 8°2S 27°17E 269 D2
Mityana Uganda 0°23N 32°2E 268 B3
Mitzic Gabon 0°45N 11°40E 264 B2
Miura Japan 35°12N 139°40E 223 B11
Mixcoac Mexico 19°23N 99°11W 128 B1
Mixteco → Mexico 18°11N 98°30W 319 D5
Miyagi □ Japan 38°15N 140°45E 220 E10
Miyāh, W. el → Egypt 25°0N 33°23E 256 C3
Miyāh, W. el → Syria 34°44N 39°57E 246 C3
Miyake-Jima Japan 34°5N 139°30E 223 C11
Miyako Japan 39°40N 141°59E 220 E10
Miyako-Jima Japan 24°45N 125°20E 221 M2
Miyako-Rettō Japan 24°24N 125°0E 221 M2
Miyakojima Okinawa, Japan 24°48N 125°17E 221 M2
Miyakojima Ōsaka, Japan 34°42N 135°31E 133 A2
Miyakonojō Japan 31°40N 131°5E 222 F3
Miyān Rahan Iran 34°34N 47°26E 213 E12
Miyani India 21°50N 69°26E 242 J3
Miyanojō Japan 31°54N 130°27E 222 F2
Miyanoura-Dake Japan 30°20N 130°31E 221 J5
Miyata Japan 33°49N 130°42E 222 D2
Miyazaki Japan 31°56N 131°30E 222 F3
Miyazaki □ Japan 32°30N 131°30E 222 E3
Miyazu Japan 35°35N 135°10E 223 B7
Miyet, Bahr el = Dead Sea Asia 31°30N 35°30E 251 G6
Miyi China 26°47N 102°9E 228 D4
Miyoshi Japan 34°48N 132°51E 222 C4
Miyun China 40°28N 116°50E 226 D9
Miyun Shuiku China 40°30N 117°0E 227 D9
Mizan Teferi Ethiopia 6°57N 35°35E 257 F4
Mizdah Libya 31°30N 13°0E 258 B2
Mizen Hd. Cork, Ireland 51°27N 9°50W 166 E2
Mizen Hd. Wicklow, Ireland 52°51N 6°4W 166 D5
Mizhhirya Ukraine 48°32N 23°30E 183 B8
Mizhi China 37°47N 110°12E 226 F6
Mizil Romania 44°59N 26°29E 183 F11
Mizo Hills = Mizoram □ India 23°30N 92°40E 241 D4
Mizonokuchi Japan 35°35N 139°34E 140 B2
Mizoram □ India 23°30N 92°40E 241 D4
Mizpe Ramon Israel 30°34N 34°49E 251 H5
Mizue Japan 35°41N 139°54E 140 A4
Mizuho = Kyōtamba Japan 35°6N 135°17E 223 B7
Mizunami Japan 35°22N 137°15E 223 B9
Mizusawa = Ōshū Japan 39°8N 141°8E 220 E10
Mjällby Sweden 56°3N 14°40E 163 H8
Mjöbäck Sweden 57°28N 12°53E 163 G6
Mjölby Sweden 58°20N 15°10E 163 F9
Mjølfjell Norway 60°41N 6°55E 164 D3
Mjømna Norway 60°55N 4°55E 164 D1
Mjörn Sweden 57°55N 12°25E 163 G6
Mjøsa Norway 60°40N 11°0E 164 D8
Mkata Tanzania 5°45S 38°20E 268 D4
Mkhaya △ Eswatini 26°34S 31°45E 271 C5
Mkhuze △ S. Africa 29°27S 29°30E 271 C4
Mkoani Tanzania 5°22S 39°39E 268 D4
Mkokotoni Tanzania 5°55S 39°15E 268 D4
Mkomazi Tanzania 4°40S 38°7E 268 C4
Mkomazi → S. Africa 30°12S 30°50E 271 D5
Mkomazi △ Tanzania 4°4S 30°2E 268 C3
Mkulwe Tanzania 8°37S 32°20E 269 D3
Mkumbi, Ras Tanzania 7°38S 39°55E 268 D4
Mkushi Zambia 14°25S 29°15E 269 E2
Mkushi River Zambia 13°32S 29°45E 269 E2
Mkuze S. Africa 27°10S 32°0E 271 C5
Mladá Boleslav Czechia 50°27N 14°53E 180 A7
Mladenovac Serbia 44°28N 20°44E 202 B4
Mlala Hills Tanzania 6°50S 31°40E 268 D3
M'lang Phil. 6°56N 124°52E 233 H5
Mlange = Mulanje, Mt. Malawi 16°2S 35°33E 269 F4
Mlava → Serbia 44°45N 21°13E 202 B5
Mława Poland 53°9N 20°25E 185 E7
Mlawula △ Eswatini 26°12S 32°2E 271 C5
Mliniště Bos.-H. 44°15N 16°50E 199 D13
Mljet Croatia 42°43N 17°30E 199 F14
Mljet △ Croatia 42°45N 17°25E 199 F14
Mljetski Kanal Croatia 42°48N 17°35E 199 F14
Młocinski, Park Poland 52°19N 20°57E 143 B1
Młociny Poland 52°18N 20°55E 143 B1
Mlynary Poland 54°12N 19°46E 184 D6
Mmabatho S. Africa 25°49S 25°30E 270 C4
Mme Cameroon 6°18N 10°14E 263 D7
Mnevniki Russia 55°45N 37°28E 129 B1
Mnichovo Hradiště Czechia 50°32N 14°59E 180 A7
Mo Hordaland, Norway 60°49N 5°48E 164 D2
Mo Møre og Romsdal, Norway 63°0N 8°59E 164 A5
Mo Telemark, Norway 59°28N 7°50E 164 E4
Mo i Rana Norway 66°20N 14°7E 160 C16
Moa Queens., Australia 10°11S 142°16E 280 a
Moa Cuba 20°40N 74°56W 321 B4
Moa Indonesia 8°0S 128°0E 231 F7
Moa → S. Leone 6°59N 11°36W 262 D2
Moab U.S.A. 38°35N 109°33W 304 G9
Moabi Gabon 2°24S 10°59E 264 C2
Moaco → Brazil 7°41S 68°18W 330 B4
Moala Fiji 18°36S 179°53E 287 B2
Moama Australia 36°7S 144°46E 281 F3
Moamba Mozam. 25°36S 32°15E 271 C5
Moapa U.S.A. 36°40N 114°37W 307 J12
Moate Ireland 53°24N 7°44W 166 C4
Moba Dem. Rep. of the Congo 7°0S 29°48E 268 D2
Moba Lagos, Nigeria 6°26N 3°28E 124 B2
Mobara Japan 35°25N 140°18E 223 B12
Mobārakābād Iran 28°24N 53°20E 247 D7
Mobaye C.A.R. 4°25N 21°5E 264 B4
Mobayi Dem. Rep. of the Congo 4°15N 21°8E 264 B4
Mobeka Dem. Rep. of the Congo 1°52N 19°49E 264 B3
Mobenzélé Congo 0°56N 17°50E 264 B3
Moberly U.S.A. 39°25N 92°26W 310 E4
Moberly Lake Canada 55°50N 121°44W 296 B4
Mobile U.S.A. 30°41N 88°3W 315 F10
Mobile B. U.S.A. 30°30N 88°0W 315 F11
Mobridge U.S.A. 45°32N 100°26W 308 C3
Mobutu Sese Seko, L. = Albert, L. Africa 1°30N 31°0E 268 B3
Moc Chau Vietnam 20°50N 104°38E 236 B5
Moc Hoa Vietnam 10°46N 105°56E 237 G5
Moca Puerto Rico 18°24N 67°10W 321 b
Mocabe Kasari Dem. Rep. of the Congo 9°58S 26°12E 269 D2
Mocajuba Brazil 2°35S 49°30W 332 B2
Moçambique = Mozambique ■ Africa 19°0S 35°0E 269 F4
Moçambique Mozam. 15°3S 40°42E 269 F5
Moçâmedes = Namibe Angola 15°7S 12°11E 265 F2
Mocanaqua U.S.A. 41°9N 76°8W 313 E8
Mocapra → Venezuela 7°56N 66°46W 328 B4
Mocco, Morro de Angola 12°28S 15°11E 265 E3
Moce Fiji 18°40S 178°29W 287 B3
Mocenigo, Palazzo Venice, Italy 142 b2
Mocha = Al Mukhā Yemen 13°18N 43°15E 248 D3
Mocha, I. Chile 38°22S 73°56W 336 A2
Mochos Greece 35°16N 25°27E 207 E6
Mochudi Botswana 24°27S 26°7E 270 B4
Mocimboa da Praia Mozam. 11°25S 40°20E 269 E5
Mociu Romania 46°46N 24°3E 183 D9
Möckeln Sweden 56°40N 14°15E 163 H8
Mockfjärd Sweden 60°30N 14°57E 162 D8
Moclips U.S.A. 47°14N 124°13W 306 C2
Mocoa Colombia 1°7N 76°35W 328 C2
Mococa Brazil 21°28S 47°0W 335 A6
Mocorito Mexico 25°29N 107°55W 318 B3
Moctezuma Mexico 29°48N 109°42W 318 B3
Moctezuma → Mexico 21°59N 98°34W 319 C5
Mocuba Mozam. 16°54S 36°57E 269 F4
Moczydło Poland 52°8N 21°2E 143 C2
Moda Myanmar 24°22N 96°29E 241 C6
Modane France 45°12N 6°40E 175 C10
Modasa India 23°30N 73°21E 242 H5
Modder → S. Africa 29°2S 24°37E 270 C3
Modderfontein = Niekerkshoop S. Africa 29°19S 22°51E 270 C3
Modderfontein S. Africa 26°5S 28°10E 123 A2
Modderrivier S. Africa 29°2S 24°38E 270 C3
Módena Italy 44°40N 10°55E 198 D7
Modena Utah, U.S.A. 37°48N 113°56W 305 H7
Modernamuseet Stockholm, Sweden 139 b3
Modesto U.S.A. 37°39N 121°0W 306 H6
Möðrudalur Iceland 65°22N 15°53W 155 B11
Möðruvellir Iceland 65°46N 18°15W 155 B8
Módica Italy 36°52N 14°46E 201 F7
Modimolle S. Africa 24°42S 28°22E 271 B4
Modjadjiskloof S. Africa 23°42S 30°10E 271 B5
Modjamboli Dem. Rep. of the Congo 2°28N 22°6E 264 B4
Mödling Austria 48°5N 16°17E 181 C9
Modo South Sudan 5°31N 30°33E 257 F3
Modoc U.S.A. 33°44N 82°13W 316 B7
Modra Slovakia 48°19N 17°20E 181 C10
Modřany Czechia 50°0N 14°24E 135 B2
Modriča Bos.-H. 44°57N 18°17E 182 F3
Moe Australia 38°12S 146°19E 283 E7
Moebase Mozam. 17°3S 38°41E 269 F4
Moëlan-sur-Mer France 47°49N 3°38W 172 E3
Moelv Norway 60°56N 10°43E 164 D7
Moen I. = Weno Pac. Oc. 7°27N 151°52E 287 T18
Moengo Suriname 5°45N 54°20W 329 B7
Moenjodaro = Mohenjodaro Pakistan 27°19N 68°7E 242 F3
Moerewa N.Z. 35°8S 174°1E 284 B3
Moers Germany 51°27N 6°36E 178 D2
Moffat U.K. 55°21N 3°27W 167 F5
Moga India 30°48N 75°8E 242 D6
Mogadishu = Muqdisho Somalia 2°2N 45°25E 267 D6
Mogador = Essaouira Morocco 31°32N 9°42W 260 B3
Mogadouro Portugal 41°22N 6°47W 194 D4
Mogalakwena → S. Africa 22°38S 28°40E 271 B4
Mogami-Gawa → Japan 38°45N 140°0E 220 E10
Mogán Canary Is. 27°53N 15°43W 153 e1
Mogandjo Dem. Rep. of the Congo 1°23N 24°15E 264 B4
Mogaung Myanmar 25°20N 97°0E 241 C6
Mogen Norway 60°2N 7°52E 164 D4
Mogente = Moixent Spain 38°52N 0°45W 197 G4
Mogho Ethiopia 4°54N 40°16E 257 G5
Mogielnica Poland 51°42N 20°41E 185 G7
Mogige Ethiopia 5°24N 36°14E 257 F4
Mogilev = Mahilyow Belarus 53°55N 30°18E 177 B16
Mogilev-Podolskiy = Mohyliv-Podilskyy Ukraine 48°26N 27°48E 183 B12
Mogilno Poland 52°39N 17°55E 185 F4
Mogincual Mozam. 15°35S 40°25E 269 F5
Mogliano Véneto Italy 45°33N 12°14E 199 C9
Mogocha Russia 53°40N 119°50E 215 D12
Mogoditshane Botswana 24°37S 25°51E 270 B4
Mogok Myanmar 23°0N 96°40E 241 D6
Mogollon Rim U.S.A. 34°10N 110°50W 305 J8
Mŏgoro Italy 39°41N 8°47E 200 C1
Mograt Sudan 19°28N 33°16E 256 D3
Mogroum Chad 11°6N 15°25E 259 F3
Moguer Spain 37°15N 6°52W 195 H4
Mogumber Australia 31°2S 116°3E 279 F2
Mogwadi → S. Africa 23°4S 29°36E 271 B4
Mogyoród Hungary 47°35N 19°14E 117 A3
Mohács Hungary 45°58N 18°41E 182 E3
Mohaka → N.Z. 39°7S 177°12E 284 F6
Mohala India 20°35N 80°44E 244 D5
Mohales Hoek Lesotho 30°7S 27°26E 270 D4
Mohali = Ajitgarh India 30°47N 76°41E 242 D7
Mohali Congo 0°15N 15°29E 264 B3
Mohall U.S.A. 48°46N 101°31W 308 A3
Moḩammadābād Iran 37°52N 59°5E 247 B8
Mohammadia Algeria 35°33N 0°3E 261 A5
Mohammedia Morocco 33°44N 7°21W 260 B3
Mohammerah = Khorramshahr Iran 30°29N 48°15E 247 D6
Mohana India 19°27N 84°16E 244 E7
Mohana → India 24°43N 85°0E 243 G11
Mohanganj Bangla. 24°54N 90°59E 241 C3
Mohanlalganj India 26°41N 80°58E 243 F9
Mohave, L. U.S.A. 35°12N 114°34W 307 K12
Mohawk → U.S.A. 42°47N 73°41W 313 D11
Moheda Sweden 57°1N 14°35E 163 G8
Mohéli Comoros Is. 12°20S 43°40E 272 a
Mohéli ✕ (NWA) Comoros Is. 12°19S 43°47E 272 a
Mohenjodaro Pakistan 27°19N 68°7E 242 F3
Moher, Cliffs of Ireland 52°58N 9°27W 166 D2
Mohican, C. U.S.A. 60°12N 167°25W 303 F6
Mohicanville Res. U.S.A. 40°45N 82°9W 312 F2
Möhne → Germany 51°29N 7°57E 178 D3
Mohns Ridge Arctic 72°30N 5°0W 150 B7
Mohnyin Myanmar 24°47N 96°22E 241 C6
Mohoro Tanzania 8°6S 39°8E 268 D4
Mohrin = Moryń Poland 52°51N 14°22E 185 F1
Mohsenābād Iran 36°40N 59°35E 247 B8
Mohyliv-Podilskyy Ukraine 48°26N 27°48E 183 B12
Moi Norway 58°27N 6°32E 164 F3
Moia South Sudan 5°3N 28°2E 257 F2
Moidart, L. U.K. 56°47N 5°52W 167 E3
Moinabad India 17°44N 77°16E 244 F3
Moinești Romania 46°28N 26°31E 183 D11
Moinho Velho, Cor. → Brazil 23°55S 46°35W 137 B2
Moira → Canada 44°21N 77°24W 312 B7
Moirang India 24°30N 93°46E 241 C4
Moirans France 45°20N 5°33E 175 C9
Moirans-en-Montagne France 46°26N 5°43E 173 F12
Moisakūla Estonia 58°3N 25°12E 188 C3
Moisie Canada 50°12N 66°1W 299 B6
Moisie → Canada 50°14N 66°5W 299 B6
Moissac France 44°7N 1°5E 174 D5
Moïssala Chad 8°21N 17°46E 259 G3
Moita Portugal 38°38N 8°58W 195 G2
Moixent Spain 38°52N 0°45W 197 G4
Mōja Sweden 59°26N 18°55E 162 E12
Mojácar Spain 37°6N 1°55W 197 H3
Mojados Spain 41°26N 4°40W 194 D6
Mojave U.S.A. 35°3N 118°10W 307 K8
Mojave △ U.S.A. 35°7N 115°32W 307 K11
Mojave Desert U.S.A. 35°0N 116°30W 307 L10
Moji das Cruzes Brazil 23°31S 46°11W 335 A6
Moji-Guaçu Brazil 22°22S 46°57W 333 F2
Moji-Guaçu → Brazil 20°53S 48°10W 335 A6
Mojiang China 23°37N 101°35E 228 F3
Mojjo → Ethiopia 7°55N 42°0E 257 F5
Mojkovac Montenegro 42°58N 19°35E 202 D3
Mojo Bolivia 21°48S 65°33W 334 A2
Mojo Ethiopia 8°35N 39°5E 257 F4
Mojokerto Indonesia 7°28S 112°26E 235 D4
Mojos, Llanos de Bolivia 15°10S 65°0W 331 D5
Moju Brazil 1°53S 48°46W 332 B2
Moju → Brazil 1°40S 48°25W 332 B2
Mok S. Korea 37°32N 126°52E 137 B1
Moka Mauritius 20°13S 57°29E 272 e
Mokai N.Z. 38°32S 175°56E 284 E4
Mokala △ S. Africa 29°10S 24°10E 270 C3
Mokambo Dem. Rep. of the Congo 12°25S 28°20E 269 E2
Mokameh India 25°24N 85°55E 243 G11
Mokau N.Z. 38°41N 91°53W 310 F5
Mōkapu Peninsula U.S.A. 21°25N 157°45W 302 K14
Mokau N.Z. 38°42S 174°39E 284 E3
Mokau → N.Z. 38°35S 174°55E 284 E3
Mokelumne → U.S.A. 38°13N 121°28W 306 G5
Mokelumne Hill U.S.A. 38°18N 120°43W 306 G6
Mokhotlong Lesotho 29°22S 29°2E 271 C4
Mokihinui → N.Z. 41°33S 171°58E 285 B6
Möklinta Sweden 60°4N 16°33E 162 D10
Moknine Tunisia 35°35N 10°58E 258 A2
Mokoan, L. Australia 36°27S 146°5E 283 D7
Mokokchung India 26°15N 94°30E 241 B5
Mökölea Rock U.S.A. 21°27N 157°44W 302 K14
Mokolo Cameroon 10°49N 13°54E 259 F2
Mokolo Dem. Rep. of the Congo 1°55N 18°6E 264 B3
Mokolo → S. Africa 23°14S 27°43E 271 B4
Mokombe Dem. Rep. of the Congo 0°14S 23°48E 264 C4
Mokopane S. Africa 24°10S 28°55E 271 B4
Mokotów Poland 52°12N 21°0E 143 B2
Mokpalin Myanmar 17°26N 96°53E 241 G6
Mokp'o S. Korea 34°50N 126°25E 224 G4
Mokra Gora Europe 42°50N 20°30E 202 D4
Mokronog Slovenia 45°57N 15°9E 199 C12
Moksha → Russia 54°45N 41°53E 190 C6
Mokshan Russia 53°25N 44°35E 190 D7
Mokuauia I. U.S.A. 21°40N 157°56W 302 J14
Mokulē'ia U.S.A. 21°35N 158°9W 302 J13
Mokulua Is. U.S.A. 21°24N 157°42W 302 K14
Mokumanu U.S.A. 21°28N 157°43W 302 K14
Mokwa Nigeria 9°19N 5°0E 263 D6
Mol Belgium 51°11N 5°5E 170 C5
Mola di Bari Italy 41°4N 17°5E 201 A10
Molai Greece 36°49N 22°56E 204 E4
Molakalmuru India 14°55N 76°50E 245 G3
Molale Ethiopia 10°10N 39°41E 257 E4
Molaly Kazakhstan 45°27N 78°18E 217 C9
Molanda Dem. Rep. of the Congo 2°28N 20°48E 264 B4
Molara Italy 40°52N 9°43E 200 B2
Molat Croatia 44°15N 14°50E 199 D11
Molchanovo Russia 57°40N 83°50E 214 D9
Mold U.K. 53°9N 3°8W 168 D4
Moldava nad Bodvou Slovakia 48°38N 21°0E 181 C14
Moldavia = Moldova ■ Europe 47°0N 28°0E 183 C13
Moldavia Romania 46°30N 27°0E 183 D12
Molde Norway 62°45N 7°9E 164 B4
Moldova ■ Europe 47°0N 28°0E 183 C13
Moldova Nouă Romania 44°45N 21°41E 182 F6
Moldoveanu, Vf. Romania 45°36N 24°45E 183 E9
Moldovița Romania 47°41N 25°32E 183 C10
Mole → U.K. 51°24N 0°21W 169 F7
Mole △ Ghana 9°43N 1°44W 263 D4
Molegbwe Dem. Rep. of the Congo 4°12N 20°53E 264 B4
Molenbeek-St-Jean Belgium 50°51N 4°19E 116 A1
Molepolole Botswana 24°28S 25°28E 270 B4
Molesworth N.Z. 42°5S 173°16E 285 C8
Molfetta Italy 41°12N 16°36E 201 A9
Mōli'i Pond U.S.A. 21°31N 157°51W 302 J14
Molina de Aragón Spain 40°46N 1°52W 196 E3
Molina de Segura Spain 38°3N 1°12W 197 G3
Moline U.S.A. 41°30N 90°31W 310 C6
Molinella Italy 44°37N 11°40E 199 D8
Molino U.S.A. 30°43N 87°20W 317 E2
Molino de Rosas Mexico 19°21N 99°14W 128 B1
Molinos Argentina 25°28S 66°15W 334 B2
Moliro Dem. Rep. of the Congo 8°12S 30°30E 268 D3
Moliterno Italy 40°14N 15°52E 201 B8
Molivos = Mithimna Greece 39°20N 26°12E 205 B8
Molkom Sweden 59°37N 13°44E 162 E7
Mölle Sweden 56°17N 12°31E 163 H6
Molledo Spain 43°8N 4°6W 194 B6
Mollem Belgium 50°56N 4°13E 116 A1
Mollendo Peru 17°0S 72°0W 330 D3
Mollerin, L. Australia 30°30S 117°35E 279 F2
Mollerussa Spain 41°37N 0°54E 196 D5
Mollina Spain 37°8N 4°38W 195 H6
Mollins de Rey Spain 41°24N 2°1E 114 A1
Mölln Germany 53°39N 10°32E 178 B6
Mölltorp Sweden 58°30N 14°26E 163 F8
Mölndal Sweden 57°40N 12°3E 163 G5
Mölnlycke Sweden 57°40N 12°8E 163 G6
Molo Rift Valley, Kenya 0°15S 35°44E 268 C4
Molo Myanmar 23°22N 96°53E 241 D6
Molochansk Ukraine 47°15N 35°35E 189 J8
Molochnoye, Ozero Ukraine 46°30N 35°20E 189 J8
Molodechno = Maladzyechna Belarus 54°20N 26°50E 177 A14
Molodove Ukraine 46°13N 29°39E 183 D14
Moloka'i U.S.A. 21°8N 157°0W 302 B4
Molokai Fracture Zone Pac. Oc. 28°0N 125°0W 289 E15
Molokini I. U.S.A. 20°38N 156°30W 302 C5
Molong Australia 33°5S 148°54E 283 B8
Molopo → Africa 28°30S 20°12E 270 C3
Molos Greece 38°47N 22°37E 204 C4
Molotov = Perm Russia 58°0N 56°10E 186 C10
Molotov, Mys = Arkticheskiy, Mys Russia 81°10N 95°0E 215 A10
Molotovsk = Nolinsk Russia 57°28N 49°57E 190 B9
Molotovsk = Severodvinsk Russia 64°27N 39°58E 186 B6
Molotovskoye = Krasnogvardeyskoye Russia 45°52N 41°33E 191 H5
Moloundou Cameroon 2°8N 15°15E 264 B3
Molowaie Dem. Rep. of the Congo 5°47S 23°18E 265 D4
Molsheim France 48°33N 7°29E 173 D14
Molson L. Canada 54°22N 96°40W 297 C9
Molteno S. Africa 31°22S 26°22E 270 D4
Molu Indonesia 6°45S 131°40E 231 F8
Molucca Sea Indonesia 0°0 125°0E 231 E6
Moluccas = Maluku Indonesia 1°0S 127°0E 231 E7
Molundo Phil. 7°57N 124°23E 233 H5
Moma Dem. Rep. of the Congo 1°35S 23°52E 264 C4
Moma Mozam. 16°47S 39°4E 269 F4
Momba Australia 30°58S 143°30E 282 A5
Mombaça Brazil 5°43S 39°45W 332 C4
Mombango Dem. Rep. of the Congo 1°45N 24°26E 264 B4
Mombasa Kenya 4°3S 39°40E 268 C4
Mombetsu Japan 44°21N 143°22E 220 B11
Mombil Myanmar 27°46N 98°6E 241 B7
Momboyo → Dem. Rep. of the Congo 0°16S 19°0E 264 C3
Mombuey Spain 42°3N 6°20W 194 C4
Momchilgrad Bulgaria 41°33N 25°23E 203 E9
Momence U.S.A. 41°10N 87°40W 311 C9
Momi Dem. Rep. of the Congo 1°42S 27°0E 268 C2
Momote Papua N. G. 2°4S 147°27E 286 B4
Mompog Pass. Phil. 13°34N 122°13E 232 E4
Mompós Colombia 9°14N 74°26W 328 B3
Møn Denmark 54°57N 12°20E 163 K6
Mon India 26°45N 95°6E 241 B5
Mon Hordaland, Norway 60°37N 6°31E 164 D3
Mon □ Myanmar 16°0N 97°30E 241 G6
Mona, Canal de la = Mona Passage W. Indies 18°30N 67°45W 321 C6
Mona, Isla Puerto Rico 18°5N 67°54W 321 C6
Mona, Pta. Costa Rica 9°37N 82°36W 320 E3
Mona Passage W. Indies 18°30N 67°45W 321 C6
Mona Quimbundo Angola 9°55S 19°58E 265 D3
Monaca U.S.A. 40°41N 80°17W 312 F4
Monaco ■ Europe 43°46N 7°23E 175 E11
Monadhliath Mts. U.K. 57°10N 4°4W 167 D4
Monadnock, Mt. U.S.A. 42°52N 72°7W 313 D12
Monagas □ Venezuela 9°20N 63°0W 329 B5
Monaghan Ireland 54°15N 6°57W 166 B5
Monaghan □ Ireland 54°11N 6°56W 166 B5
Monahans U.S.A. 31°36N 102°54W 314 F3
Monapo Mozam. 14°56S 40°19E 269 E5
Monar, L. U.K. 57°26N 5°8W 167 D3
Monaragala Sri Lanka 6°52N 81°22E 245 L5
Monarch Mt. Canada 51°55N 125°57W 296 C3
Monashee Mts. Canada 51°0N 118°43W 296 C5
Monasterevin Ireland 53°8N 7°4W 166 C4
Monastir = Bitola N. Macedonia 41°1N 21°20E 202 E5
Monastir Tunisia 35°50N 10°49E 258 A2
Monastir □ Tunisia 35°37N 10°45E 261 A7
Monbetsu = Hidaka Japan 42°30N 142°10E 220 C11
Moncalieri Italy 45°0N 7°41E 198 D4
Moncalvo Italy 45°3N 8°16E 198 C5
Monção Portugal 42°4N 8°27W 194 C2
Moncarapacho Portugal 37°5N 7°46W 195 H3
Moncayo, Sierra del Spain 41°48N 1°50W 196 D3
Moncha-Guba = Monchegorsk Russia 67°54N 32°58E 160 C25
Monchegorsk Russia 67°54N 32°58E 160 C25
Mönchengladbach Germany 51°11N 6°27E 178 D2
Monchique Portugal 37°19N 8°38W 195 H2
Moncks Corner U.S.A. 33°12N 80°1W 316 B9
Monclova Mexico 26°54N 101°25W 318 B4
Moncontour France 48°22N 2°38W 172 D4
Moncton Canada 46°7N 64°51W 299 C7
Mondariz Spain 42°14N 8°27W 194 C2
Mondego → Portugal 40°9N 8°52W 194 E2
Mondego, C. Portugal 40°11N 8°54W 194 E2
Mondeodo Indonesia 3°34S 122°9E 231 E6
Mondeor S. Africa 26°16S 28°0E 123 B2
Mondeville France 49°10N 0°18W 172 C6
Mondimbi Dem. Rep. of the Congo 1°48N 22°46E 264 B4
Mondjuku Dem. Rep. of the Congo 1°41S 21°12E 264 C4
Mondlo S. Africa 27°59S 30°43E 271 C5
Mondo Chad 13°47N 15°32E 259 F3
Mondolfo Italy 43°45N 13°6E 199 E10
Mondoñedo Spain 43°25N 7°23W 194 B3
Mondovì Italy 44°23N 7°49E 198 D4
Mondragó Spain 39°21N 3°12E 206 B4
Mondragon = Arrasate Spain 43°4N 2°30W 196 B2
Mondragon Phil. 12°31N 124°45E 232 E5
Mondragone Italy 41°7N 13°53E 200 A6
Mondrain I. Australia 34°9S 122°14E 279 F3
Moneague Jamaica 18°16N 77°7W 320 a
Moneda, Palacio de la Chile 33°26S 70°39W 137 B2
Monemvasia Greece 36°41N 23°3E 204 E5
Monerō Brazil 22°48S 43°11W 135 A1
Moneron, Ostrov Russia 46°15N 141°16E 220 A10
Monessen U.S.A. 40°9N 79°54W 312 F5
Monesterio Spain 38°6N 6°15W 195 G4
Monestier-de-Clermont France 44°55N 5°38E 175 D9
Monett U.S.A. 36°55N 93°55W 308 G7
Moneymore U.K. 54°41N 6°40W 166 B5
Monfalcone Italy 45°49N 13°32E 199 C10
Monflanquin France 44°32N 0°47E 174 D4
Monforte Portugal 39°6N 7°25W 195 F3
Monforte de Lemos Spain 42°31N 7°33W 194 C3
Monfragüe △ Spain 39°48N 5°52W 194 F5
Mong Hpayak Myanmar 20°52N 99°55E 236 B2
Mong Hsat Shan, Myanmar 21°54N 98°30E 228 G2
Mong Hsat Shan, Myanmar 20°31N 99°15E 236 B2
Mong Hta Myanmar 19°50N 98°35E 241 F7
Mong Ket Myanmar 23°8N 98°22E 241 D7
Mong Kok Hong Kong, China 22°19N 114°10E 122 B3
Mong Kung Myanmar 21°35N 97°35E 241 E6
Mong Kyawt Myanmar 19°56N 98°45E 241 F7
Mong Long Myanmar 22°47N 96°36E 241 D6
Mong Mit Myanmar 23°7N 96°41E 241 D6
Mong Nai Myanmar 20°32N 97°46E 241 E6
Mong Pan Myanmar 20°19N 98°22E 241 E7
Mong Ping Myanmar 21°22N 99°2E 228 G2
Mong Pu Myanmar 20°55N 98°44E 241 E7
Mong Tai = Shan □ Myanmar 21°30N 98°30E 241 E7
Mong Ton Myanmar 20°17N 98°45E 241 E7
Mong Tung Myanmar 22°2N 97°41E 241 D6
Mong Yai Myanmar 22°21N 98°3E 241 D7
Mong Yang Myanmar 21°50N 99°41E 236 B2
Mong Yu Myanmar 23°30N 97°47E 241 D6
Monga Dem. Rep. of the Congo 4°12N 22°49E 264 B4
Mongala → Dem. Rep. of the Congo 1°53N 19°46E 264 B3
Mongalla South Sudan 5°8N 31°42E 257 F3
Mongandia Congo 0°45N 17°11E 264 B3
Mongers, L. Australia 29°25S 117°5E 279 E2
Mongga Solomon Is. 7°52S 157°0E 287 L9
Monghyr = Munger India 25°23N 86°30E 243 G12
Mongibello = Etna Italy 37°50N 14°55E 201 E7
Mongla Bangla. 22°8N 89°35E 241 D2
Mongmong Guam 13°28N 144°45E 302 d
Mongngaw Myanmar 22°47N 96°59E 241 D6
Mongo Chad 12°14N 18°43E 259 F3
Mongo Eq. Guin. 1°52N 10°10E 264 B2
Mongó → S. Leone 9°35N 12°10W 262 D2
Mongolia ■ Asia 47°0N 103°0E 218 B9
Mongolia, Plateau of Asia 45°0N 105°0E 210 D12
Mongomo Eq. Guin. 1°38N 11°19E 264 B2
Mongonu Nigeria 12°40N 13°32E 263 C7
Mongororo Chad 12°3N 22°26E 259 F4
Mongstad Norway 60°49N 5°2E 164 D2
Mongu Zambia 15°16S 23°12E 265 F4
Mônguà Angola 16°43S 15°20E 265 F3
Moniac U.S.A. 30°31N 82°14W 316 E7
Monifieth U.K. 56°30N 2°48W 167 E6
Monistrol-sur-Loire France 45°17N 4°11E 175 C8
Monkayo Phil. 7°50N 126°5E 233 H6
Monkey Bay Malawi 14°7S 35°1E 269 E4
Monkey Mia Australia 25°48S 113°43E 279 E1
Monkey River Belize 16°22N 88°29W 320 C2
Monkey Town Trin. & Tob. 10°12N 61°25W 323 t
Mońki Poland 53°23N 22°48E 184 E9
Monkland Canada 45°11N 74°52W 313 A10
Monkoto Dem. Rep. of the Congo 1°38S 20°35E 264 C4
Monkton Canada 43°35N 81°5W 312 C3
Monmouth Monmouths., U.K. 51°48N 2°42W 169 F5
Monmouth Ill., U.S.A. 40°55N 90°39W 310 D6
Monmouth Oreg., U.S.A. 44°51N 123°14W 304 D2
Monmouthshire □ U.K. 51°48N 2°54W 169 F5
Monnickendam Neths. 52°28N 5°2E 112 A3
Mono Solomon Is. 7°20S 155°35E 287 L8
Mono → Togo 6°17N 1°51E 263 D5
Mono, Pta. Nic. 12°0N 83°30W 320 D3
Mono L. U.S.A. 38°1N 119°1W 306 H7
Monolith U.S.A. 35°7N 118°22W 307 K8
Monolithos Greece 36°7N 27°45E 206 E11
Monon U.S.A. 40°52N 86°53W 311 D10
Monona Iowa, U.S.A. 43°3N 91°23W 310 A5
Monona Wis., U.S.A. 43°4N 89°20W 310 A7
Monongahela U.S.A. 40°12N 79°56W 312 F5
Monópoli Italy 40°57N 17°18E 201 B10
Monor Hungary 47°21N 19°27E 182 C4
Monos I. Trin. & Tob. 10°42N 61°44W 323 t
Monóvar Spain 38°28N 0°53W 197 G4
Monowai N.Z. 45°53S 167°31E 285 F2
Monowai, L. N.Z. 45°53S 167°25E 285 F2
Monqoumba C.A.R. 3°33N 18°40E 264 B3
Monreal del Campo Spain 40°47N 1°20W 196 E3
Monreale Italy 38°5N 13°17E 200 D6
Monroe Ga., U.S.A. 33°47N 83°43W 316 B6
Monroe Iowa, U.S.A. 41°31N 93°6W 310 C3
Monroe La., U.S.A. 32°30N 92°7W 314 E8
Monroe Mich., U.S.A. 41°55N 83°24W 311 C13
Monroe N.C., U.S.A. 34°59N 80°33W 315 D14
Monroe N.Y., U.S.A. 41°20N 74°11W 313 E10
Monroe Ohio, U.S.A. 39°27N 84°22W 311 E12
Monroe Utah, U.S.A. 38°38N 112°7W 304 G7
Monroe Wash., U.S.A. 47°51N 121°58W 306 C5
Monroe Wis., U.S.A. 42°36N 89°38W 310 B7
Monroe, L. U.S.A. 28°50N 81°19W 317 G8
Monroe City Ind., U.S.A. 38°37N 87°20W 311 F9
Monroe City Mo., U.S.A. 39°39N 91°44W 310 E5
Monroe L. U.S.A. 39°1N 86°31W 311 E10
Monroeton U.S.A. 41°43N 76°29W 313 E8
Monroeville Ala., U.S.A. 31°31N 87°20W 315 F11
Monroeville Ind., U.S.A. 40°59N 84°52W 311 D12
Monroeville Pa., U.S.A. 40°26N 79°45W 312 F5
Monrovia Liberia 6°18N 10°47W 262 D2
Monrovia Calif., U.S.A. 34°9N 118°1W 126 B4
Mons Belgium 50°27N 3°58E 170 D3
Møns Klint Denmark 54°57N 12°33E 163 K6
Monsanto Portugal 38°44N 9°12W 126 A1
Monsanto, Parque Florestal de Portugal 38°43N 9°11W 126 A1
Monsaraz Portugal 38°28N 7°22W 195 G3
Monse Indonesia 4°7S 123°15E 231 E6
Monsefú Peru 6°52S 79°52W 330 B2
Monségur France 44°38N 0°4E 174 D4
Monsélice Italy 45°14N 11°45E 199 C8
Mönsterås Sweden 57°3N 16°26E 163 G10
Mont Cenis, Col du France 45°15N 6°55E 175 C10
Mont-de-Marsan France 43°54N 0°31W 174 E3
Mont-Dore N. Cal. 22°16S 166°34E 288 d
Mont Fouari △ Congo 2°52S 11°32E 264 C2
Mont-Joli Canada 48°37N 68°10W 299 C6
Mont-Laurier Canada 46°35N 75°30W 298 C4
Mont-Louis Canada 49°15N 65°44W 299 C6
Mont Peko △ Côte d'Ivoire 9°5N 7°15W 262 D3
Mont-roig del Camp Spain 41°5N 0°58E 196 D5
Mont-Royal Canada 45°30N 73°38W 130 A2
Mont-Royal, Parc Canada 45°30N 73°36W 130 A2
Mont-St-Michel, Le France 48°40N 1°30W 172 D5
Mont Sangbé △ Côte d'Ivoire 8°0N 7°10W 262 D3
Mont-Tremblant △ Canada 46°30N 74°30W 298 C5
Montabaur Germany 50°25N 7°50E 178 E3
Montagnac = Remchi Algeria 35°2N 1°26W 261 A4
Montagnac France 43°29N 3°28E 174 E7
Montagnana Italy 45°14N 11°28E 199 C8
Montagne Blanche Mauritius 20°16S 57°39E 272 e
Montagne d'Ambre △ Madag. 12°37S 49°8E 272 A2
Montagne de Reims △ France 49°8N 4°0E 173 C11
Montagnes □ Côte d'Ivoire 6°54N 7°50W 262 D3
Montagu S. Africa 33°45S 20°8E 270 D3
Montagu I. Antarctica 58°25S 26°20W 151 B1
Montague Canada 46°10N 62°39W 299 C7
Montague, I. Mexico 31°45N 114°48W 318 A2
Montague I. N.S.W., Australia 36°16S 150°13E 283 D9
Montague I. Alaska, U.S.A. 60°0N 147°30W 303 G11
Montague Ra. Australia 27°15S 119°30E 279 E2
Montague Sd. Australia 14°28S 125°20E 278 B4
Montaigu France 46°59N 1°18W 172 F5
Montalbán Spain 40°50N 0°45W 196 E4
Montalbano Iónico Italy 40°17N 16°34E 201 B9
Montalbo Spain 39°53N 2°42W 196 F2
Montalcino Italy 43°3N 11°29E 199 E8
Montalegre Angola 8°45S 17°4E 265 D3
Montalegre Portugal 41°49N 7°47W 194 D3
Montalto Italy 38°10N 15°55E 201 D8
Montalto di Castro Italy 42°21N 11°37E 199 F8
Montalto Uffugo Italy 39°24N 16°9E 201 C9
Montalvo U.S.A. 34°15N 119°12W 307 L7
Montamarta Spain 41°39N 5°49W 194 D5
Montana Bulgaria 43°27N 23°16E 202 C7
Montaña Peru 6°0S 73°0W 330 B3
Montana □ Bulgaria 43°30N 23°10E 202 C7
Montana □ U.S.A. 47°0N 110°0W 304 C9
Montaña Clara, I. Canary Is. 29°17N 13°33W 153 e2
Montañas de Malaga △ Spain 36°48N 4°32W 195 J6
Montánchez Spain 39°15N 6°8W 195 F4
Montanhas do Tumucumaque △ Brazil 2°5N 53°0W 329 C7
Montañita Colombia 1°22N 75°28W 328 C2
Montargil Portugal 39°5N 8°10W 195 F2
Montargis France 47°59N 2°43E 173 E9
Montauban France 44°2N 1°21E 174 D5
Montauk U.S.A. 41°3N 71°57W 313 E13
Montauk Pt. U.S.A. 41°4N 71°51W 313 E13
Montbard France 47°38N 4°20E 173 E11
Montbarrey France 47°1N 5°39E 173 E12
Montbéliard France 47°31N 6°48E 173 E13
Montblanc Spain 41°23N 1°4E 196 D6
Montbrison France 45°36N 4°3E 175 C8
Montcada i Reixac Spain 41°29N 2°12W 114 A2
Montcalm, Pic de France 42°40N 1°25E 174 F5
Montceau-les-Mines France 46°40N 4°23E 173 F11
Montcenis France 46°47N 4°23E 175 B8
Montchanin France 46°45N 4°28E 175 B8
Montclair U.S.A. 40°49N 74°12W 313 F10
Montcornet France 49°40N 4°1E 173 C11
Montcuq France 44°21N 1°13E 174 D5
Montdidier France 49°38N 2°35E 173 C9
Monte Albán Mexico 17°2N 96°46W 319 D5
Monte Alegre Brazil 2°0S 54°0W 329 D7
Monte Alegre de Goiás Brazil 13°14S 47°10W 333 D2
Monte Alegre de Minas Brazil 18°52S 48°52W 333 E2
Monte Alegre do Piaui Brazil 9°46S 45°18W 332 C2
Monte Azul Brazil 15°9S 42°53W 333 E3
Monte-Carlo Monaco 43°44N 7°25E 175 E11
Monte Carmelo Brazil 18°43S 47°29W 333 E2
Monte Caseros Argentina 30°10S 57°50W 334 C4
Monte Chingolo Argentina 34°43S 58°22W 117 C2
Monte Comán Argentina 34°40S 67°53W 334 C2
Monte Cristi Dom. Rep. 19°52N 71°39W 321 C5
Monte Cucco △ Italy 43°22N 12°43E 199 E9
Monte Dinero Argentina 52°18S 68°33W 336 D3
Monte Dourado Brazil 0°52S 52°31W 329 D7
Monte Léon Argentina 50°15S 69°0W 336 D3
Monte Lindo → Paraguay 23°56S 57°12W 334 A4
Monte Palatino Rome, Italy 136 c3
Monte Pascoal △ Brazil 16°51S 39°21W 333 E4
Monte Patria Chile 30°42S 70°58W 334 C1
Monte Quemado Argentina 25°53S 62°41W 334 B3
Monte Redondo Portugal 39°53N 8°50W 194 F2
Monte Rio U.S.A. 38°28N 123°0W 306 G4
Monte San Giovanni Campano Italy 41°38N 13°31E 200 A6
Monte San Giuliano = Érice Italy 38°2N 12°35E 200 D5
Monte San Savino Italy 43°20N 11°43E 199 E8
Monte Sant' Ángelo Italy 41°42N 15°59E 199 G12
Monte Santu, C. di Italy 40°5N 9°44E 200 B2
Monte Subasio △ Italy 43°5N 12°40E 199 E9
Monte Vista U.S.A. 37°35N 106°9W 305 H10
Monteagudo Argentina 27°14S 54°8W 335 B5
Monteagudo Bolivia 19°49S 63°59W 331 D5
Montealegre del Castillo Spain 38°48N 1°17W 197 G3
Montebello Qué., Canada 45°40N 74°55W 298 C5
Montebello Guadeloupe 16°10N 61°36W 322 e
Montebello Calif., U.S.A. 34°1N 118°8W 126 B4
Montebello Iónico Italy 37°59N 15°45E 201 E8
Montebello Is. Australia 20°30S 115°45E 278 D2
Montebelluna Italy 45°47N 12°3E 199 C9
Montebourg France 49°30N 1°20W 172 C5
Montecarlo Argentina 26°34S 54°47W 335 B5
Montecastrilli Italy 42°39N 12°29E 199 F9
Montecatini Terme Italy 43°53N 10°46E 198 E7
Montecito U.S.A. 34°26N 119°40W 307 L7
Montecristi Ecuador 1°0S 80°40W 328 D1
Montecristo Italy 42°20N 10°19E 198 F7
Montefalco Italy 42°54N 12°39E 199 F9
Montefiascone Italy 42°32N 12°2E 199 F9
Montefrío Spain 37°20N 4°0W 195 H7
Montegiórgio Italy 43°8N 13°33E 199 E10
Montego B. Jamaica 18°28N 77°56W 320 a
Montego Bay Jamaica 18°28N 77°55W 320 a
Montehermoso Spain 40°5N 6°21W 194 E4
Monteiro Brazil 7°48S 37°2W 332 C4
Montejicar Spain 37°33N 3°30W 195 H7
Montelbaanstoren Amsterdam, Neths. 112 b3
Monteleone di Calabria = Vibo Valéntia Italy 38°40N 16°6E 201 D9
Montelíbano Colombia 8°5N 75°29W 328 B2
Montélimar France 44°33N 4°45E 175 D8
Montella Italy 40°51N 15°1E 201 B8

Montellano Spain 36°59N 5°29W 195 J5
Montello U.S.A. 43°48N 89°20W 308 D9
Montemayor, Meseta de
Argentina 44°20S 66°10W 336 B3
Montemor Portugal 38°49N 9°12W 126 A1
Montemor-o-Novo
Portugal 38°40N 8°12W 195 G2
Montemor-o-Velho
Portugal 40°11N 8°40W 194 E2
Montemorelos Mexico 25°12N 99°49W 319 B5
Montendre France 45°16N 0°26W 174 C3
Montenegro Brazil 29°39S 51°29W 335 B5
Montenegro ■ Europe 42°40N 19°20E 202 D3
Montenero di Bisáccia
Italy 41°57N 14°47E 199 G11
Montepuez Mozam. 13°8S 38°59E 269 E4
Montepuez ➝ Mozam. 12°32S 40°27E 269 E5
Montepulciano Italy 43°5N 11°47E 199 E8
Montereale Italy 42°31N 13°15E 199 F10
Montereau-Faut-Yonne
France 48°22N 2°57E 173 D9
Monterey Calif., U.S.A. 36°37N 121°55W 306 J5
Monterey Ind., U.S.A. 41°11N 86°30W 311 C10
Monterey B. U.S.A. 36°45N 122°0W 306 J5
Monterey Hills U.S.A. 34°6N 118°10W 126 B3
Monterey Park U.S.A. 34°3N 118°7W 126 B4
Montería Colombia 8°46N 75°53W 328 B2
Montero Bolivia 17°20S 63°15W 331 D5
Monteros Argentina 27°11S 65°30W 334 B2
Monterotondo Italy 42°3N 12°37E 199 F9
Monterrey Mexico 25°40N 100°19W 318 B4
Montes Altos Brazil 5°50S 47°4W 332 C2
Montes Azules ⌓ Mexico 16°21N 91°3W 319 D6
Montes Claros Brazil 16°30S 43°50W 333 E3
Montesano U.S.A. 46°59N 123°36W 306 D3
Montesano sulla Marcellana
Italy 40°16N 15°42E 201 B8
Montesárchio Italy 41°4N 14°38E 201 A7
Montescaglioso Italy 40°33N 16°40E 201 B9
Montesilvano Italy 42°29N 14°8E 199 F11
Montesinho ⌓ Portugal 41°54N 6°52W 194 D4
Montespaccato Italy 41°54N 12°23E 136 B1
Montesson France 48°54N 2°8E 134 A1
Montevarchi Italy 43°31N 11°34E 199 E8
Monteverde Nuovo Italy 41°52N 12°26E 136 B1
Montevideo Uruguay 34°50S 56°11W 335 C4
Montevideo Minn., U.S.A. 44°57N 95°43W 308 C6
Montezuma Ga., U.S.A. 32°18N 84°2W 316 C5
Montezuma Ind., U.S.A. 39°48N 87°22W 311 E9
Montezuma Iowa, U.S.A. 41°35N 92°32W 310 C4
Montezuma Castle ⌓
U.S.A. 34°39N 111°45W 305 J8
Montfaucon France 47°6N 1°7W 172 E5
Montfaucon-d'Argonne
France 49°16N 5°8E 173 C12
Montfaucon-en-Velay
France 45°11N 4°20E 175 C8
Montfermeil France 48°54N 2°33E 134 A4
Montfort-le-Gesnois France 48°3N 0°25E 172 D7
Montfort-sur-Meu France 48°9N 1°58W 172 D5
Montgenèvre France 44°56N 6°43E 175 D10
Montgó ⌓ Spain 38°48N 0°7W 197 G5
Montgomery = Sahiwal
Pakistan 30°45N 73°8E 242 D5
Montgomery Powys, U.K. 52°34N 3°8W 169 E4
Montgomery Ala., U.S.A. 32°23N 86°19W 316 C3
Montgomery Ill., U.S.A. 41°44N 88°21W 311 C8
Montgomery Pa., U.S.A. 41°10N 76°53W 312 E8
Montgomery W. Va.,
U.S.A. 38°11N 81°19W 309 F13
Montgomery City U.S.A. 38°59N 91°30W 310 F5
Montguyon France 45°12N 0°12W 174 C3
Monthermé France 49°52N 4°42E 173 C11
Monthey Switz. 46°15N 6°56E 179 J2
Monthois France 49°19N 4°43E 173 C11
Monti Italy 40°49N 9°19E 200 B2
Monti Lucrétili ⌓ Italy 42°5N 12°50E 199 F9
Monti Picentini ⌓ Italy 40°45N 15°2E 201 B8
Monti Sibillini △ Italy 42°55N 13°15E 199 F10
Monti Simbruini ⌓ Italy 41°55N 13°13E 199 G10
Monticelli d'Ongina Italy 45°5N 9°56E 198 C6
Monticello Ark., U.S.A. 33°38N 91°47W 314 E9
Monticello Fla., U.S.A. 30°33N 83°52W 316 E6
Monticello Ga., U.S.A. 33°18N 83°40W 316 B6
Monticello Ill., U.S.A. 40°1N 88°34W 311 D8
Monticello Ind., U.S.A. 40°45N 86°46W 311 D10
Monticello Iowa, U.S.A. 42°15N 91°12W 310 B5
Monticello Ky., U.S.A. 36°50N 84°51W 309 G11
Monticello Minn., U.S.A. 45°18N 93°48W 308 C7
Monticello Miss., U.S.A. 31°33N 90°7W 315 F9
Monticello Mo., U.S.A. 40°7N 91°43W 310 D5
Monticello N.Y., U.S.A. 41°39N 74°42W 313 E10
Monticello Utah, U.S.A. 37°52N 109°21W 305 H9
Montichiari Italy 45°25N 10°23E 198 C7
Montier-en-Der France 48°30N 4°45E 173 D11
Montignac France 45°4N 1°10E 174 C5
Montigny-le-Bretonneux
France 48°46N 2°1E 134 B1
Montigny-les-Metz France 49°7N 6°10E 173 C13
Montigny-sur-Aube
France 47°57N 4°45E 173 E11
Montijo Portugal 38°41N 8°54W 195 G2
Montijo Spain 38°52N 6°39W 195 G4
Montilla Spain 37°36N 4°40W 195 H6
Montivilliers France 49°33N 0°12E 172 C7
Montjay-la-Tour France 48°54N 2°40E 134 A4
Montjuïc Spain 41°22N 2°10E 114 A2
Montjuïc, Parc de Barcelona, Spain 114 c1
Montluçon France 46°22N 2°36E 173 F9
Montmagny Canada 46°58N 70°34W 299 C5
Montmarault France 46°19N 2°57E 173 F9
Montmartre Canada 50°14N 103°27W 297 C8
Montmédy France 49°30N 5°20E 173 C12
Montmélian France 45°30N 6°4E 175 C10
Montmirail France 48°51N 3°30E 173 D10
Montmoreau-St-Cybard
France 45°23N 0°8E 174 C4
Montmorillon France 46°26N 0°50E 174 B4
Montmort-Lucy France 48°55N 3°49E 173 D10
Monto Australia 24°52S 151°6E 280 C5
Montoire-sur-le-Loir
France 47°45N 0°52E 172 E7
Montongbuwoh Indonesia 8°33S 116°4E 231 K19
Montório al Vomano
Italy 42°35N 13°38E 199 F10
Montoro Spain 38°1N 4°27W 195 G6
Montour Falls U.S.A. 42°21N 76°51W 312 D8
Montoursville U.S.A. 41°15N 76°55W 312 E8
Montparnasse, Gare
Paris, France 48°50N 2°19E 134 A2
Montpelier Idaho, U.S.A. 42°19N 111°18W 304 E8
Montpelier Ind., U.S.A. 40°33N 85°17W 311 D11
Montpelier Ohio, U.S.A. 41°35N 84°37W 311 C12
Montpelier Vt., U.S.A. 44°16N 72°35W 313 B12
Montpellier France 43°37N 3°52E 174 E7
Montpezat-de-Quercy
France 44°15N 1°30E 174 D5
Montpon-Ménestérol
France 45°0N 0°11E 174 D4
Montréal Qué., Canada 45°30N 73°33W 130 A2
Montréal Aude, France 43°13N 2°8E 174 E6
Montréal Gers, France 43°56N 0°11E 174 E4
Montreal ➝ Canada 47°14N 84°39W 298 C3
Montréal, Î. de Canada 45°30N 73°40W 130 A2
Montréal, Univ. de
Canada 45°29N 73°37W 130 B2
Montréal Est Canada 45°37N 73°31W 130 A2
Montréal L. Canada 54°20N 105°45W 297 C7
Montreal Lake Canada 54°3N 105°46W 297 C7
Montréal Nord Canada 45°36N 73°36W 130 A2
Montréal Ouest Canada 45°27N 73°39W 130 B1
Montréal Trudeau Int. ✈ (YUL)
Canada 45°28N 73°44W 130 B1
Montredon-Labessonnié
France 43°45N 2°18E 174 E6
Montrésor France 47°10N 1°10E 172 E8
Montret France 46°40N 5°7E 173 F12
Montreuil Pas-de-Calais,
France 50°27N 1°45E 173 B8
Montreuil Seine-St-Denis,
France 48°51N 2°27E 134 A3
Montreuil-Bellay France 47°8N 0°9W 172 E6
Montreux Switz. 46°26N 6°55E 179 J2
Montrevel-en-Bresse
France 46°21N 5°8E 173 F12
Montrichard France 47°20N 1°10E 172 E8
Montrose Angus, U.K. 56°44N 2°27W 167 E6
Montrose Colo., U.S.A. 38°29N 107°53W 304 G10
Montrose Pa., U.S.A. 41°50N 75°53W 313 E9
Montrose, L. U.S.A. 38°18N 93°50W 310 F3
Montrouge France 48°48N 2°18E 134 B2
Monts, Pte. des Canada 49°20N 67°12W 299 C6
Montsalvy France 44°41N 2°30E 174 D6
Montsant, Serra de Spain 41°17N 1°0E 196 D6
Montsauche-les-Settons
France 47°13N 4°2E 173 E11
Montsec, Serra del Spain 42°5N 0°45E 196 C5
Montseny ⌓ Spain 41°43N 2°22W 196 D2
Montserrat B. Aires,
Argentina 34°37S 58°24W 117 B2
Montserrat Spain 41°36N 1°49E 196 D6
Montserrat ☒ W. Indies 16°40N 62°10W 323 p
Montserrat Hills
Trin. & Tob. 10°23N 61°21W 323 t
Montuenga Spain 41°3N 4°38W 194 D6
Montuiri Spain 39°34N 2°59E 206 B3
Montvert-les-Bas Réunion 21°19S 55°32E 272 f
Monveda
Dem. Rep. of the Congo 2°52N 21°30E 264 B4
Monyo Myanmar 17°59N 95°30E 241 G5
Monywa Myanmar 22°7N 95°11E 241 D5
Monza Italy 45°35N 9°16E 128 A2
Monza e Brianza □ Italy 45°30N 9°15E 198 C6
Monze Zambia 16°17S 27°29E 269 F2
Monze, C. Pakistan 24°47N 66°37E 242 G2
Monzón Spain 41°52N 0°10E 196 D5
Monzoro Italy 45°27N 9°2E 128 B1
Moóca Brazil 23°33S 46°35W 137 B2
Moodyville = North Vancouver
Canada 49°19N 123°4W 306 A3
Mooers U.S.A. 44°58N 73°35W 313 B11
Mooi ➝ S. Africa 28°45S 30°34E 271 C5
Mooi River S. Africa 29°13S 29°50E 271 C4
Mo'oka Japan 36°26N 140°1E 223 A12
Mookgopong S. Africa 24°31S 28°44E 271 B4
Moomba Australia 28°6S 140°12E 281 A3
Moonachie U.S.A. 40°50N 74°2W 132 B1
Moonah ➝ Australia 22°3S 138°33E 280 C2
Moonda, L. Australia 25°52S 140°25E 280 D3
Moonee Ponds Australia 37°45S 144°53E 128 A1
Moonee Valley Racecourse
Australia 37°45S 144°55E 128 A1
Moonie Australia 27°46S 150°20E 281 D5
Moonie ➝ Australia 29°19S 148°43E 281 D4
Moonta Australia 34°6S 137°32E 282 C2
Moora Australia 30°37S 115°58E 279 F2
Moorcroft U.S.A. 44°16N 104°57W 304 D11
Moore ➝ Australia 31°22S 115°30E 279 F2
Moore, L. Australia 29°50S 117°35E 279 E2
Moore Falls Canada 44°48N 78°48W 312 B6
Moore Haven U.S.A. 26°50N 81°6W 317 J8
Moore Park Australia 24°43S 152°17E 280 C5
Moore Res. U.S.A. 44°20N 71°53W 313 B13
Moore River △ Australia 31°7S 115°39E 279 F2
Moorea French Polynesia 17°30S 149°50W 289 e
Moorefield U.S.A. 39°4N 78°58W 309 F14
Mooresville U.S.A. 39°37N 86°22W 311 E10
Moorfoot Hills U.K. 55°44N 3°8W 167 F5
Moorhead U.S.A. 46°53N 96°45W 308 B5
Moorland U.S.A. 42°26N 94°18W 310 B2
Moormerland Germany 53°20N 7°20E 178 B3
Moornanyah L. Australia 33°15S 143°42E 282 B5
Mooroopna Australia 36°25S 145°22E 283 D6
Moorpark U.S.A. 34°17N 118°53W 307 L8
Moorreesburg S. Africa 33°6S 18°38E 270 D2
Moorrinya △ Australia 21°42S 144°58E 280 C3
Moosach Germany 48°10N 11°30E 131 A2
Moosburg Germany 48°27N 11°56E 179 G7
Moose ➝ Ont., Canada 51°20N 80°25W 298 B3
Moose ➝ N.Y., U.S.A. 43°38N 75°24W 313 C9
Moose Creek Canada 45°15N 74°58W 313 A10
Moose Factory Canada 51°16N 80°32W 298 B3
Moose Jaw Canada 50°24N 105°30W 297 C7
Moose Jaw ➝ Canada 50°34N 105°18W 297 C7
Moose Lake Man., Canada 53°46N 100°8W 297 C8
Moose Lake Minn., U.S.A. 46°27N 92°46W 308 B7
Moose Mountain ⌓
Canada 49°48N 102°25W 297 D8
Moose Pass U.S.A. 60°29N 149°22W 303 F10
Moosehead L. U.S.A. 45°38N 69°40W 309 C19
Mooselookmeguntic L.
U.S.A. 44°55N 70°49W 313 B14
Moosilauke, Mt. U.S.A. 44°3N 71°40W 313 B13
Moosomin Canada 50°9N 101°40W 297 C8
Moosonee Canada 51°17N 80°39W 298 B3
Moosup U.S.A. 41°43N 71°53W 313 E13
Mootwingee △ Australia 31°10S 142°30E 282 A5
Mopane S. Africa 22°37S 29°52E 271 B4
Mopeia Velha Mozam. 17°30S 35°40E 269 F4
Mopipi Botswana 21°6S 24°55E 270 B3
Mopoi C.A.R. 5°6N 26°54E 268 A2
Mopti Mali 14°30N 4°0W 262 C4
Mopti □ Mali 14°40N 4°0W 262 C4
Moqatta Sudan 14°38N 35°50E 257 E4
Moqor Afghan. 32°50N 67°42E 242 C2
Moquegua Peru 17°15S 70°46W 330 D3
Moquegua □ Peru 16°50S 70°55W 330 D3
Mór Hungary 47°25N 18°12E 182 C3
Mora Cameroon 11°2N 14°7E 259 F2
Mora Maharashtra, India 18°54N 72°55E 130 B2
Móra Portugal 38°55N 8°10W 195 G2
Mora Spain 39°41N 3°46W 195 F7
Mora Sweden 61°2N 14°38E 162 C8
Mora Minn., U.S.A. 45°53N 93°18W 308 C7
Mora N. Mex., U.S.A. 35°58N 105°20W 305 J11
Móra de Rubielos Spain 40°15N 0°45W 196 E4
Móra d'Ebre Spain 41°6N 0°38E 196 D5
Móra la Nova Spain 41°7N 0°39E 196 D5
Morača ➝ Montenegro 42°20N 19°9E 202 D3
Morada Nova Brazil 5°7S 38°23W 332 C4
Morada Nova de Minas
Brazil 18°37S 45°22W 333 E2
Moradabad India 28°50N 78°50E 243 E8
Morafenobe Madag. 17°50S 44°53E 272 B1
Morąg Poland 53°55N 19°56E 184 E6
Moral de Calatrava Spain 38°51N 3°33W 195 G7
Moraleda, Canal Chile 44°30S 73°30W 336 B2
Moraleja Spain 40°6N 6°43W 194 E4
Morales Bolívar, Colombia 8°16N 73°51W 328 B3
Morales Cauca, Colombia 2°45N 76°38W 328 C2
Moramanga Madag. 18°56S 48°12E 272 B2
Moran Kans., U.S.A. 37°55N 95°10W 308 G6
Moran Wyo., U.S.A. 43°50N 110°31W 304 E8
Moranbah Australia 22°1S 148°6E 280 C4
Morané French Polynesia 23°10S 137°7W 289 f
Morang = Biratnagar
Nepal 26°27N 87°17E 243 F12
Moranhat India 27°10N 94°50E 241 B5
Morano Cálabro Italy 39°50N 16°8E 201 C9
Morant Bay Jamaica 17°53N 76°25W 320 a
Morant Cays Jamaica 17°22N 76°0W 320 C4
Morant Pt. Jamaica 17°55N 76°12W 320 a
Morar India 26°14N 78°14E 242 F8
Morar, L. U.K. 56°57N 5°40W 167 E3
Moratalaz Spain 40°24N 3°39W 127 B2
Moratalla Spain 38°14N 1°49W 197 G3
Moratuwa Sri Lanka 6°45N 79°55E 245 L4
Morava ➝ Slovakia 48°10N 16°59E 181 C9
Moravia Iowa, U.S.A. 40°53N 92°49W 310 D4
Moravia N.Y., U.S.A. 42°43N 76°25W 313 D8
Moravian Hts. = Českomoravská
Vrchovina Czechia 49°30N 15°40E 180 B8
Moravica ➝ Serbia 43°52N 20°8E 202 C4
Moravița Romania 45°17N 21°14E 182 E6
Moravská Třebová
Czechia 49°45N 16°40E 181 B9
Moravské Budějovice
Czechia 49°4N 15°49E 180 B8
Moravskoslezský □
Czechia 49°55N 17°58E 181 B10
Morawa Australia 29°13S 116°0E 279 E2
Morawhanna Guyana 8°30N 59°40W 329 B6
Moray □ U.K. 57°31N 3°18W 167 D5
Moray Firth U.K. 57°40N 3°52W 167 D5
Morbach Germany 49°48N 7°6E 179 F3
Morbegno Italy 46°8N 9°34E 198 B6
Morbi India 22°50N 70°42E 242 H4
Morbihan □ France 47°55N 2°50W 172 E4
Mörby Sweden 59°23N 18°3E 139 A2
Mörbylånga Sweden 56°32N 16°22E 163 H10
Morcenx France 44°3N 0°55W 174 D3
Morcone Italy 41°20N 14°40E 201 A7
Mordelles France 48°5N 1°52W 172 D5
Morden Man., Canada 49°15N 98°10W 297 D9
Morden London, U.K. 51°24N 0°13W 125 B2
Mordoğan Turkey 38°30N 26°37E 205 C8
Mordovian Republic = Mordvinia □
Russia 54°20N 44°30E 190 C7
Mordovo Russia 52°6N 40°50E 190 D5
Mordvinia □ Russia 54°20N 44°30E 190 C7
Mordy Poland 52°13N 22°31E 185 F9
Møre og Romsdal □ Norway 62°30N 8°0E 164 B4
Moreau ➝ U.S.A. 45°18N 100°43W 308 C3
Morebeng S. Africa 23°30S 29°55E 271 B4
Morecambe U.K. 54°5N 2°52W 168 C5
Morecambe B. U.K. 54°7N 3°0W 168 C5
Moree Australia 29°28S 149°54E 281 D4
Morée ➝ France 48°57N 2°25E 134 A3
Morehead Papua N. G. 8°41S 141°41E 286 E1
Morehead Ky., U.S.A. 38°11N 83°26W 311 F13
Morehead City U.S.A. 34°43N 76°43W 315 D16
Morel ➝ India 26°13N 76°36E 242 F7
Moreland U.S.A. 33°17N 84°46W 316 B5
Morelia Mexico 19°42N 101°7W 318 D4
Morella Queens., Australia 23°0S 143°52E 280 C3
Morella Spain 40°35N 0°5W 196 E4
Morelos Mexico 26°42N 107°40W 318 B3
Morelos □ Mexico 18°45N 99°0W 319 D5
Moremi ⌓ Botswana 19°18S 23°10E 270 A3
Morena India 26°30N 78°4E 242 F8
Morena, Sierra Spain 38°20N 4°0W 195 G7
Morenci U.S.A. 41°43N 84°13W 311 C12
Moreni Romania 44°59N 25°36E 183 F10
Moreno Bolivia 11°9S 66°15W 330 C4
Moreno Valley U.S.A. 33°56N 117°14W 307 M10
Moreru ➝ Brazil 10°10S 59°15W 331 C6
Moresby I. Canada 52°30N 131°40W 296 C2
Morestel France 45°40N 5°28E 175 C9
Moreton I. Australia 27°10S 153°25E 281 D5
Moreton Island △
Australia 27°2S 153°24E 281 D5
Moreuil France 49°46N 2°30E 173 C9
Morez France 46°31N 6°2E 173 F13
Morgan S. Austral.,
Australia 34°2S 139°35E 282 C3
Morgan Ga., U.S.A. 31°32N 84°36W 316 D5
Morgan Utah, U.S.A. 41°2N 111°41W 304 F8
Morgan City U.S.A. 29°42N 91°12W 314 G9
Morgan Hill U.S.A. 37°8N 121°39W 306 H5
Morgan Park U.S.A. 41°41N 87°38W 119 C3
Morganfield U.S.A. 37°41N 87°55W 308 G10
Morgan's Port U.S.A. 29°40N 95°0W 314 G7
Morganton U.S.A. 35°45N 81°41W 315 D14
Morgantown Ind.,
U.S.A. 39°22N 86°16W 311 E10
Morgantown W. Va.,
U.S.A. 39°38N 79°57W 309 F14
Morgenzon S. Africa 26°45S 29°36E 271 C4
Morges Switz. 46°31N 6°29E 179 J2
Morghak Iran 29°7N 57°54E 247 D8
Morgongåva Sweden 59°57N 16°58E 162 E10
Morhange France 48°55N 6°38E 173 D13
Morhar ➝ India 25°29N 85°11E 243 G11
Mori China 43°49N 90°11E 217 D12
Mori Japan 42°6N 140°35E 220 C10
Moriah Trin. & Tob. 11°15N 60°43W 323 s
Moriarty U.S.A. 34°59N 106°3W 305 J10
Moribaya Guinea 9°53N 9°32W 262 D3
Morice L. Canada 53°50N 127°40W 296 C3
Morichal Largo ➝
Venezuela 9°27N 62°25W 329 B5
Morichal Viejo Colombia 2°13N 70°2W 328 C3
Moriguchi Japan 34°43N 135°34E 133 A2
Moriki Nigeria 12°52N 6°30E 263 C6
Morinville Canada 53°49N 113°41W 296 C6
Morioka Japan 39°45N 141°8E 220 E10
Moris Mexico 28°10N 108°32W 318 B3
Morisset Australia 33°6S 151°30E 283 B9
Morivione Italy 45°26N 9°12E 128 B2
Moriyama Japan 35°4N 135°59E 223 B7
Morlaàs France 43°21N 0°18W 174 E3
Morlaix France 48°36N 3°52W 172 D3
Mörlunda Sweden 57°19N 15°52E 163 G9
Mormanno Italy 39°53N 15°59E 201 C8
Mormant France 48°37N 2°52E 173 D9
Mormugao = Marmagao
India 15°25N 73°56E 245 G1
Morne-à-l'Eau Guadeloupe 16°20N 61°27W 322 e
Morne des Esses Martinique 14°44N 61°1W 322 j
Morne Diablotins
Dominica 15°30N 61°24W 323 k
Morne Fendue Grenada 12°12N 61°38W 323 q
Morne Raquette Dominica 15°27N 61°27W 323 k
Morne Trois Pitons △
Dominica 15°22N 61°20W 323 k
Morningside Gauteng,
S. Africa 26°4S 28°3E 123 A2
Morningside Edinburgh,
U.K. 55°56N 3°12W 121 B2
Morningside Park Ont.,
Canada 43°47N 79°12W 141 A3
Morningside Park Fla.,
U.S.A. 28°26N 81°24W 133 B2
Mornington Australia 38°15S 145°5E 283 E6
Mornington, I. Chile 49°50S 75°30W 336 C1
Mornington I. Australia 16°30S 139°30E 280 B2
Mornington Peninsula △
Australia 38°28S 144°53E 283 E6
Mornos ➝ Greece 38°25N 21°50E 204 C3
Moro Pakistan 26°40N 68°0E 242 F2
Moro Sudan 10°50N 30°9E 257 E3
Moro ➝ Pakistan 29°42N 67°22E 242 E2
Moro G. Phil. 6°30N 123°0E 233 H4
Morobe Papua N. G. 7°49S 147°38E 286 D4
Morobe □ Papua N. G. 7°0S 147°0E 286 D4
Morocco U.S.A. 40°57N 87°27W 311 D9
Morocco ■ N. Afr. 32°0N 5°50W 260 B3
Morococha Peru 11°40S 76°5W 330 C2
Morogoro Tanzania 6°50S 37°40E 268 D4
Morogoro □ Tanzania 8°0S 37°0E 268 D4
Moroleón Mexico 20°8N 101°32W 318 C4
Morombe Madag. 21°45S 43°22E 272 C1
Moron = Mörong Phil. 14°41N 120°16E 232 D3
Morón Argentina 34°39S 58°37W 334 C4
Morón Cuba 22°8N 78°39W 320 B4
Mörön Mongolia 49°38N 100°9E 218 B9
Morón de Almazán Spain 41°29N 2°27W 196 D2
Morón de la Frontera Spain 37°6N 5°28W 195 H5
Morona ➝ Peru 4°40S 77°10W 328 D2
Morona-Santiago □
Ecuador 2°30S 78°0W 328 D2
Morondava Madag. 20°17S 44°17E 272 C1
Morondo Côte d'Ivoire 8°57N 6°47W 262 D3
Morong Phil. 14°41N 120°16E 232 D3
Morongo Valley U.S.A. 34°3N 116°37W 307 L10
Moroni Comoros Is. 11°40S 43°16E 272 a
Moroni Utah, U.S.A. 39°32N 111°35W 304 G8
Moroni Iconi ✈ (YVA)
Comoros Is. 11°32S 43°15E 272 a
Moronou Côte d'Ivoire 6°16N 4°59W 262 D4
Morotai Indonesia 2°10N 128°30E 231 D7
Moroto Uganda 2°28N 34°42E 268 B3
Moroto, Mt. Uganda 2°30N 34°43E 268 B3
Morozov Bulgaria 42°30N 25°10E 203 D9
Morozovsk Russia 48°25N 41°50E 191 F5
Morpeth Ont., Canada 42°23N 81°50W 312 D3
Morpeth Northumberland,
U.K. 55°10N 1°41W 168 B6
Morphou Cyprus 35°12N 32°59E 207 E8
Morphou Bay Cyprus 35°15N 32°50E 207 E8
Morrelganj Bangla. 22°28N 89°51E 241 D2
Morrilton U.S.A. 35°9N 92°44W 314 D8
Morrinhos Ceará, Brazil 3°14S 40°7W 332 B3
Morrinhos Minas Gerais,
Brazil 17°45S 49°10W 333 E2
Morrinsville N.Z. 37°40S 175°32E 284 D4
Morris Man., Canada 49°25N 97°22W 297 D9
Morris Ill., U.S.A. 41°22N 88°26W 311 C8
Morris Minn., U.S.A. 45°35N 95°55W 308 C6
Morris N.Y., U.S.A. 42°33N 75°15W 313 D9
Morris Pa., U.S.A. 41°35N 77°17W 312 E7
Morris, Mt. Australia 26°9S 131°4E 279 E5
Morris Jesup, Kap
Greenland 83°40N 34°0W 154 A7
Morrisburg Canada 44°55N 75°7W 313 B9
Morrison U.S.A. 41°49N 89°58W 310 C7
Morrisonville U.S.A. 39°25N 89°27W 310 E7
Morristown Ariz., U.S.A. 33°51N 112°37W 305 K7
Morristown Ind., U.S.A. 39°40N 85°42W 311 E11
Morristown N.J., U.S.A. 40°48N 74°29W 313 F10
Morristown N.Y., U.S.A. 44°35N 75°39W 313 B9
Morristown Tenn.,
U.S.A. 36°13N 83°18W 315 C13
Morrisville N.Y., U.S.A. 42°53N 75°35W 313 D9
Morrisville Pa., U.S.A. 40°13N 74°47W 313 F10
Morrisville Vt., U.S.A. 44°34N 72°36W 313 B12
Morro, Pta. Chile 27°6S 71°0W 334 B1
Morro Bay U.S.A. 35°22N 120°51W 306 K6
Morro Chico Chile 52°2S 71°26W 336 D2
Morro del Jable Canary Is. 28°3N 14°23W 153 e2
Morro do Chapéu Brazil 11°33S 41°9W 333 D3
Morro Grande = Barão de Cocais
Brazil 19°56S 43°28W 333 E3
Morro Jable, Pta. de
Canary Is. 28°2N 14°20W 153 e2
Morro Solar, Cerro Peru 12°11S 77°1W 124 C2
Morrocoy △ Venezuela 10°48N 68°13W 328 A4
Morros Brazil 2°52S 44°3W 332 B3
Morrosquillo, G. de
Colombia 9°35N 75°40W 320 E4
Morrow U.S.A. 39°21N 84°8W 311 E12
Mörrum Sweden 56°12N 14°45E 163 H8
Morrumbene Mozam. 23°31S 35°16E 271 B6
Mörrumsån ➝ Sweden 56°10N 14°45E 163 H8
Mors Denmark 56°50N 8°45E 163 H2
Morshansk Russia 53°28N 41°50E 190 D5
Morsi India 21°21N 78°0E 244 D4
Mörsil Sweden 63°19N 13°40E 162 A7
Mortagne ➝ France 48°33N 6°27E 173 D13
Mortagne-au-Perche
France 48°31N 0°33E 172 D7
Mortagne-sur-Gironde
France 45°28N 0°47W 174 C3
Mortagne-sur-Sèvre France 47°0N 0°59W 172 F6
Mortain France 48°40N 0°57W 172 D6
Mortara Italy 45°15N 8°44E 198 C5
Morteau France 47°3N 6°35E 173 E13
Morteros Argentina 30°50S 62°0W 334 C3
Mortes, R. das ➝ Brazil 11°45S 50°44W 333 D1
Mortlach Canada 50°27N 106°4W 297 C7
Mortlake N.S.W., Australia 33°50S 151°6E 139 B1
Mortlake Vic., Australia 38°5S 142°50E 282 E5
Mortlake London, U.K. 51°27N 0°15W 125 B2
Morton Ill., U.S.A. 40°37N 89°28W 310 D7
Morton Tex., U.S.A. 33°44N 102°46W 314 E3
Morton Wash., U.S.A. 46°34N 122°17W 306 D4
Morton △ Australia 35°0S 150°12E 283 C9
Morton Grove U.S.A. 42°2N 87°46W 119 A2
Moruga Trin. & Tob. 10°4N 61°16W 323 t
Moruga ➝ Trin. & Tob. 10°5N 61°16W 323 t
Morumbi Brazil 23°35S 46°42W 137 B1
Morundah Australia 34°57S 146°19E 283 C7
Morungu Sudan 10°32N 31°3E 266 B3
Moruya Australia 35°58S 150°3E 283 C9
Morvan France 47°5N 4°3E 173 E11
Morvan ⌓ France 47°12N 4°3E 173 E11
Morvant Trin. & Tob. 10°40N 61°29W 323 t
Morven Queens., Australia 26°22S 147°5E 281 D4
Morven N.Z. 44°50S 171°6E 285 E6
Morven Ga., U.S.A. 30°57N 83°30W 316 E6
Morvern U.K. 56°38N 5°44W 167 E3
Morwell Australia 38°10S 146°22E 283 E7
Morwell △ Australia 38°14S 146°23E 283 E7
Moryń Poland 52°51N 14°22E 185 F1
Morzhovets, Ostrov
Russia 66°44N 42°35E 186 A7
Morzine France 46°11N 6°42E 173 F13
Mosakahiken = Moose Lake
Canada 53°46N 100°8W 297 C8
Mosalsk Russia 54°30N 34°55E 188 E8
Mosbach Germany 49°21N 9°9E 179 F5
Mosby Norway 58°12N 7°55E 164 F4
Moscavide Portugal 38°47N 9°6W 126 A2
Mošćenice Croatia 45°17N 14°16E 199 C11
Moschato Greece 37°55N 23°40E 112 B2
Mosciano Sant' Ángelo
Italy 42°42N 13°52E 199 F10
Moscone Convention Center
San Francisco, U.S.A. 136 c2
Moscos Is. Myanmar 14°0N 97°30E 236 F1
Moscow = Moskva Russia 55°45N 37°37E 129 B2
Moscow Idaho, U.S.A. 46°44N 117°0W 304 C5
Moscow Mich., U.S.A. 42°3N 84°30W 311 B12
Moscow Pa., U.S.A. 41°20N 75°31W 313 E9
Moscow Domodedovo Int. ✈ (DME)
Russia 55°24N 37°54E 188 E9
Moscow Mills U.S.A. 38°57N 90°55W 310 F6
Moscow Sheremetyevo Int. ✈ (SVO)
Russia 55°58N 37°25E 129 A1
Mosel ➝ Europe 50°22N 7°36E 173 B14
Moselle = Mosel ➝
Europe 50°22N 7°36E 173 B14
Moselle □ France 48°59N 6°33E 173 D13
Moses Lake U.S.A. 47°8N 119°17W 304 C4
Mosgiel N.Z. 45°53S 170°21E 285 F5
Moshaweng ➝ S. Africa 26°35S 22°50E 270 C3
Moshchnyy, Ostrov Russia 60°1N 27°50E 188 B4
Moshi Tanzania 3°22S 37°18E 268 C4
Moshi ➝ Nigeria 9°18N 4°20E 263 D5
Moshupa Botswana 24°46S 25°29E 270 B4
Mosi-oa-Tunya = Victoria Falls
Zimbabwe 17°58S 25°52E 269 F2
Mosina Poland 52°15N 16°50E 185 F3
Mosite
Dem. Rep. of the Congo 0°53N 23°40E 264 B4
Mosjøen Norway 65°51N 13°12E 160 D15
Moskenesøya Norway 67°58N 13°0E 160 C15
Moskenstraumen
Norway 67°47N 12°45E 160 C15
Moskog Norway 61°26N 6°0E 164 C2
Moskva Russia 55°45N 37°37E 129 B2
Moskva □ Russia 56°20N 37°20E 188 D9
Moskva ➝ Russia 55°5N 38°51E 188 E10
Moskvoretskiy Russia 55°42N 37°37E 129 B2
Moslavačka Gora
Croatia 45°40N 16°37E 199 C13
Mosman Australia 33°49S 151°15E 139 B2
Moso Vanuatu 17°30S 168°15E 287 G6
Mosomane Botswana 24°2S 26°19E 270 B4
Mosonmagyaróvár
Hungary 47°52N 17°18E 182 C2
Mošorin Serbia 45°19N 20°4E 182 E5
Mospyne Ukraine 47°52N 38°0E 189 J9
Mosqueiro Brazil 1°10S 48°28W 332 B2
Mosquera Colombia 2°35N 78°24W 328 C2
Mosquero U.S.A. 35°47N 103°58W 305 J12
Mosqueruela Spain 40°21N 0°27W 196 E4
Mosquitia Honduras 15°20N 84°10W 320 C3
Mosquito, Pta. Venezuela 10°53N 63°53W 329 a
Mosquito Coast = Mosquitos, Costa
de Nic. 13°20N 83°35W 320 D3
Mosquito Creek L. U.S.A. 41°18N 80°46W 312 E4
Mosquito L. Canada 62°35N 103°20W 297 A8
Mosquitos, Costa de Nic. 13°20N 83°35W 320 D3
Mosquitos, G. de los
Panama 9°15N 81°10W 320 E3
Moss Norway 59°27N 10°40E 164 E7
Moss Vale Australia 34°32S 150°25E 283 C9
Mossaka Congo 1°15S 16°45E 264 C3
Mossâmedes Brazil 16°7S 50°11W 333 E1
Mossbank Canada 49°56N 105°56W 297 D7
Mossburn N.Z. 45°41S 168°15E 285 F3
Mosselbaai S. Africa 34°11S 22°8E 270 D3
Mossendjo Congo 2°55S 12°42E 264 C2
Mossfellsbær Iceland 64°11N 21°45W 155 C5
Mossgiel Australia 33°15S 144°5E 282 B6
Mössingen Germany 48°24N 9°4E 179 G5
Mossman Australia 16°21S 145°15E 280 B4
Mossoró Brazil 5°10S 37°15W 332 C4
Mossuril Mozam. 14°58S 40°42E 269 E5
Mossy Head U.S.A. 30°45N 86°19W 317 E3
Mossy Point Australia 35°50S 150°11E 283 C9
Most Czechia 50°31N 13°38E 180 A6
Mosta Malta 35°55N 14°26E 206 F7
Mostaganem Algeria 35°54N 0°5E 261 A5
Mostaganem □ Algeria 35°40N 0°15E 261 A5
Mostar Bos.-H. 43°22N 17°50E 182 G2
Mostardas Brazil 31°2S 50°51W 335 C5
Mostefa, Rass Tunisia 36°55N 11°3E 258 A2
Mosteiros Azores 37°53N 25°49W 153 d3
Mosterhamn Norway 59°42N 5°21E 164 E2
Mostiska = Mostyska
Ukraine 49°48N 23°4E 185 J10
Móstoles Spain 40°19N 3°53W 194 E7
Mosty = Masty Belarus 53°27N 24°38E 177 B13
Mostyska Ukraine 49°48N 23°4E 185 J10
Mosul = Al Mawşil Iraq 36°15N 43°5E 213 D10
Møsvatnet Norway 59°52N 8°5E 164 E5
Mota Ethiopia 11°5N 37°52E 257 E4
Mota Vanuatu 13°49S 167°42E 287 C5
Mota del Cuervo Spain 39°30N 2°52W 197 F2
Mota del Marqués Spain 41°38N 5°11W 194 D5
Mota Lava Vanuatu 13°40S 167°40E 287 C5
Motaba Congo 2°6N 18°2E 264 B3
Motagua ➝ Guatemala 15°44N 88°14W 320 C2
Motala Sweden 58°32N 15°1E 163 F9
Motaze Mozam. 24°48S 32°52E 271 B5
Moţca Romania 47°15N 26°37E 183 C11
Motegi Japan 36°32N 140°11E 223 A12
Moth India 25°43N 78°57E 243 G8
Motherwell U.K. 55°47N 3°58W 167 F5
Moti Bagh India 28°33N 77°10E 120 B2
Motihari India 26°30N 84°55E 243 F11
Motilla del Palancar Spain 39°34N 1°55W 197 F3
Motiti I. N.Z. 37°38S 176°25E 284 D5
Motnik Slovenia 46°14N 14°54E 199 B11
Motobu Japan 26°39N 127°53E 288 a
Motocurunya Venezuela 4°24N 64°5W 329 C5
Motol Czechia 50°3N 14°21E 135 B2
Motovun Croatia 45°20N 13°50E 199 C10
Motozintla de Mendoza
Mexico 15°22N 92°14W 319 D6
Motril Spain 36°31N 3°37W 195 J7
Motru Romania 44°48N 22°59E 182 F7
Motru ➝ Romania 44°32N 23°31E 183 F8
Motsa Israel 31°47N 35°9E 123 B1
Motsa Ilit Israel 31°48N 35°9E 123 B1
Motspur Park U.K. 51°23N 0°14W 125 B2
Mott U.S.A. 46°23N 102°20W 308 B2
Mottama, G. of Myanmar 16°5N 96°30E 241 G6
Mottingham U.K. 51°26N 0°1E 125 B4
Möttling = Metlika
Slovenia 45°40N 15°20E 199 C12
Móttola Italy 40°38N 17°2E 201 B10
Motu ➝ N.Z. 37°52S 177°36E 284 D6
Motu Nui Chile 27°12S 109°28W 330 b
Motu Tapu Cook Is. 21°14S 159°43W 289 h
Motuba
Dem. Rep. of the Congo 2°20N 18°34E 264 B3
Motueka N.Z. 41°7S 173°1E 285 B8
Motueka ➝ N.Z. 41°5S 173°1E 285 B8
Motul Mexico 21°6N 89°17W 319 C7
Motupena Pt. Papua N. G. 6°30S 155°10E 286 D8
Mou N. Cal. 21°5S 167°26E 288 d
Mouanda Gabon 1°28S 13°7E 264 C2
Mouchalagane ➝
Canada 50°56N 68°41W 299 B6
Mouchoir Bank W. Indies 20°57N 70°47W 321 B5
Mouding China 25°20N 101°28E 228 E3
Moudjeria Mauritania 17°50N 12°28W 262 B2
Moudon Switz. 46°40N 6°49E 179 J2
Moudros Greece 39°50N 25°18E 205 B7
Mougins France 43°36N 7°0E 175 E10
Mougoundou Congo 2°40S 12°41E 264 C2
Mouhoun = Black Volta ➝
Africa 8°41N 1°33W 262 D4
Mouila Gabon 1°50S 11°0E 264 C2
Mouka C.A.R. 7°16N 21°52E 264 A4
Moukalaba ⌓ Gabon 2°50S 10°35E 264 C2
Moukambo Gabon 3°5S 11°38E 264 C2
Moul Niger 15°5N 13°11E 259 F2
Moulamein Australia 35°3S 144°1E 282 C6
Moule à Chique, C.
St. Lucia 13°43N 60°57W 323 m
Moulhoulé Djibouti 11°58N 42°58E 267 B5
Mouliana Greece 35°10N 25°59E 207 E6
Moulin Rouge Paris, France 134 a3
Moulins France 46°35N 3°19E 173 F10
Moulmein = Mawlamyine
Myanmar 16°30N 97°40E 241 G6
Moulouya, O. ➝ Morocco 35°5N 2°25W 261 A4
Moulton U.S.A. 40°41N 92°41W 310 D4
Moultrie U.S.A. 31°11N 83°47W 316 D6
Moultrie, L. U.S.A. 33°20N 80°5W 316 B9
Mounana Gabon 1°18S 13°13E 264 C2
Mound City Mo., U.S.A. 40°7N 95°14W 308 E6
Mound City S. Dak.,
U.S.A. 45°44N 100°4W 308 C3
Moundou Chad 8°40N 16°10E 259 G3
Moundsville U.S.A. 39°55N 80°44W 312 G4
Mounembé Congo 3°20S 12°32E 264 C2
Moung Cambodia 12°46N 103°27E 236 F4
Moungoudi Congo 2°45S 11°46E 264 C2
Mount Airy U.S.A. 36°31N 80°37W 315 C14
Mount Albert Canada 44°8N 79°19W 312 B5
Mount Apo △ Phil. 7°0N 125°10E 233 H5
Mount Arayat △ Phil. 15°39N 120°44E 232 D3
Mount Aspiring △ N.Z. 44°19S 168°47E 285 E3
Mount Ayliff = Maxesibeni
S. Africa 30°49S 29°23E 271 D4
Mount Ayr U.S.A. 40°43N 94°14W 310 D2
Mount Barker S. Austral.,
Australia 35°5S 138°52E 282 C3
Mount Barker W. Austral.,
Australia 34°38S 117°40E 279 F2
Mount Barnett Roadhouse
Australia 16°39S 125°57E 278 C4
Mount Beauty Australia 36°47S 147°10E 283 D7
Mount Brydges Canada 42°54N 81°29W 312 D3
Mount Buffalo △
Australia 36°43S 146°46E 283 D7
Mount Burr Australia 37°34S 140°26E 281 F3
Mount Carleton ⌓
Canada 47°25N 66°55W 299 C6
Mount Carmel = Ha Karmel △
Israel 32°45N 35°5E 250 F6
Mount Carmel Ill., U.S.A. 38°25N 87°46W 311 F9
Mount Carmel Pa., U.S.A. 40°47N 76°26W 313 F8
Mount Carroll U.S.A. 42°6N 89°59W 310 B7
Mount Clemens U.S.A. 42°35N 82°53W 312 D2
Mount Cook N.Z. 43°44S 170°5E 285 D5
Mount Cook △ N.Z. 43°35S 170°15E 285 D5
Mount Coolon Australia 21°25S 147°25E 280 C4
Mount Darwin Zimbabwe 16°47S 31°38E 269 F3
Mount Dennis Canada 43°40N 79°28W 141 A2
Mount Desert I. U.S.A. 44°21N 68°20W 309 C19
Mount Dora U.S.A. 28°48N 81°38W 317 G8
Mount Ebenezer Australia 25°6S 132°34E 279 E5
Mount Eccles △ Australia 38°5S 141°54E 282 E4
Mount Eden U.S.A. 38°3N 85°9W 311 F11
Mount Edziza ⌓ Canada 57°30N 130°45W 296 B2
Mount Elgon △ E. Afr. 1°4N 34°42E 268 B3
Mount Field △ Australia 42°39S 146°35E 281 G4
Mount Fletcher S. Africa 30°40S 28°30E 271 D4
Mount Forest Canada 43°59N 80°43W 312 C4
Mount Frankland △
Australia 31°47S 116°37E 279 F2
Mount Frederick ◎
Australia 19°39S 129°18E 278 C4
Mount Frere = Kwabhaca
S. Africa 30°51S 29°0E 271 D4
Mount Gambier
Australia 37°50S 140°46E 282 D4
Mount Garnet Australia 17°37S 145°6E 280 B4
Mount Greenwood
U.S.A. 41°42N 87°42W 119 C2
Mount Hagen Papua N. G. 5°52S 144°16E 286 C3
Mount Hamiguitan △
Phil. 6°44N 126°10E 233 H6
Mount Holly U.S.A. 39°59N 74°47W 313 G10
Mount Holly Springs
U.S.A. 40°7N 77°12W 312 F7
Mount Hood Memorial Park ⌓
U.S.A. 42°26N 71°1W 116 A2
Mount Hope N.S.W.,
Australia 32°51S 145°51E 283 B6
Mount Hope S. Austral.,
Australia 34°7S 135°23E 281 E2
Mount Horeb U.S.A. 43°1N 89°44W 310 B7
Mount Iglit-Mount Baco △
Phil. 12°45N 121°8E 232 E3
Mount Isa Australia 20°42S 139°26E 280 C2
Mount Isarog △ Phil. 13°38N 123°24E 232 E4
Mount James ◎ Australia 24°51S 116°54E 279 D2
Mount Jewett U.S.A. 41°44N 78°39W 312 E6
Mount Ka'ala Nat. Area Reserve ⌓
U.S.A. 21°31N 158°7W 302 J13
Mount Kaputar △
Australia 30°16S 150°10E 281 E5
Mount Kenya △ Kenya 0°7S 37°21E 268 C4
Mount Kisco U.S.A. 41°12N 73°44W 313 E11
Mount Laguna U.S.A. 32°52N 116°25W 307 N10
Mount Larcom Australia 23°48S 150°59E 280 C5
Mount Lofty Ranges
Australia 34°35S 139°5E 282 C3
Mount McKinley = Denali △
U.S.A. 63°30N 152°0W 303 E10
Mount Magnet Australia 28°2S 117°47E 279 E2
Mount Malindang △
Phil. 8°17N 123°32E 233 G4
Mount Manara Australia 32°29S 143°58E 282 B5
Mount Maunganui N.Z. 37°40S 176°14E 284 D5
Mount Molloy Australia 16°42S 145°20E 280 B4
Mount Morgan Australia 23°40S 150°25E 280 C5
Mount Morris Mich.,
U.S.A. 43°7N 83°42W 311 A13
Mount Morris N.Y.,
U.S.A. 42°44N 77°52W 312 D7
Mount Olive U.S.A. 39°4N 89°44W 310 E7
Mount Olivet U.S.A. 38°32N 84°2W 311 F12
Mount Olympus U.S.A. 34°7N 118°21W 126 B2
Mount Orab U.S.A. 39°2N 83°55W 311 E13
Mount Pearl Canada 47°31N 52°47W 299 C9
Mount Penn U.S.A. 40°20N 75°54W 313 F9
Mount Perry Australia 25°13S 151°42E 281 D5
Mount Pleasant Iowa,
U.S.A. 40°58N 91°33W 310 D5
Mount Pleasant Mich.,
U.S.A. 43°36N 84°46W 309 D11
Mount Pleasant Pa.,
U.S.A. 40°9N 79°33W 312 F5
Mount Pleasant S.C.,
U.S.A. 32°47N 79°52W 316 C10
Mount Pleasant Tenn.,
U.S.A. 35°32N 87°12W 315 D11
Mount Pleasant Tex.,
U.S.A. 33°9N 94°58W 314 E7
Mount Pleasant Utah,
U.S.A. 39°33N 111°27W 304 G8
Mount Pleasant ✈ (MPN)
Falk. Is. 51°49S 58°23W 153 f
Mount Pocono U.S.A. 41°7N 75°22W 313 E9
Mount Pulaski U.S.A. 40°1N 89°17W 310 D7
Mount Pulog △ Phil. 16°35N 120°57E 232 C3
Mount Rainier U.S.A. 38°56N 76°57W 143 B3
Mount Rainier △ U.S.A. 46°55N 121°50W 306 D5
Mount Remarkable △
Australia 32°47S 138°3E 282 B3
Mount Revelstoke △
Canada 51°5N 118°30W 296 C5
Mount Robson ⌓ Canada 53°0N 119°0W 296 C5
Mount St. Helens ⌓
U.S.A. 46°14N 122°11W 306 D4
Mount Selinda Zimbabwe 20°24S 32°43E 271 B5
Mount Shasta U.S.A. 41°19N 122°19W 304 F3
Mount Signal U.S.A. 32°39N 115°37W 307 N11
Mount Somers N.Z. 43°45S 171°27E 285 D6
Mount Sterling Ill.,
U.S.A. 39°59N 90°45W 310 E6
Mount Sterling Ky.,
U.S.A. 38°4N 83°56W 311 F13
Mount Sterling Ohio,
U.S.A. 39°43N 83°16W 311 E13
Mount Surprise Australia 18°10S 144°17E 280 B3

Mount Union U.S.A. 40°23N 77°53W 312 F7
Mount Upton U.S.A. 42°26N 75°23W 313 D9
Mount Vernon Ga., U.S.A. 32°11N 82°36W 316 C7
Mount Vernon Ill., U.S.A. 38°19N 88°55W 310 F8
Mount Vernon Ind., U.S.A. 37°56N 87°54W 311 G9
Mount Vernon Iowa, U.S.A. 41°55N 91°23W 310 C5
Mount Vernon N.Y., U.S.A. 40°54N 73°49W 132 A3
Mount Vernon Ohio, U.S.A. 40°23N 82°29W 312 F2
Mount Vernon Wash., U.S.A. 48°25N 122°20W 306 B4
Mount Vernon Square Washington, D.C., U.S.A. 143 a2
Mount Victor Australia 32°11S 139°44E 282 B3
Mount Washington U.S.A. 39°5N 84°24W 311 F11
Mount Wellington N.Z. 36°55S 174°52E 284 C3
Mount William △ Australia 40°56S 148°14E 281 G4
Mount Wynne St. Vincent 13°14N 61°16W 323 n
Mount Zion = Har Tsiyon Jerusalem 123 b3
Mount Zion U.S.A. 39°46N 88°53W 311 E8
Mounta, Akra Greece 38°3N 20°47E 207 C2
Mountain □ Phil. 17°20N 121°10E 232 C3
Mountain Ash U.K. 51°40N 3°23W 169 F4
Mountain Center U.S.A. 33°42N 116°44W 307 M10
Mountain City Nev., U.S.A. 41°50N 115°58W 304 F6
Mountain City Tenn., U.S.A. 36°29N 81°48W 315 C14
Mountain Creek L. U.S.A. 32°43N 96°56W 120 B4
Mountain Creek Lake Park U.S.A. 32°41N 96°58W 120 B4
Mountain Dale U.S.A. 41°41N 74°32W 313 E10
Mountain Grove U.S.A. 37°8N 92°16W 308 G7
Mountain Home Ark., U.S.A. 36°20N 92°23W 314 C8
Mountain Home Idaho, U.S.A. 43°8N 115°41W 304 E6
Mountain Iron U.S.A. 47°32N 92°37W 308 B7
Mountain Pass U.S.A. 35°29N 115°35W 307 K11
Mountain View Ark., U.S.A. 35°52N 92°7W 314 D8
Mountain View Calif., U.S.A. 37°23N 122°5W 306 H4
Mountain View Hawai'i, U.S.A. 19°33N 155°7W 302 D6
Mountain Village U.S.A. 62°5N 163°43W 303 E7
Mountain Zebra △ S. Africa 32°14S 25°27E 270 D4
Mountainair U.S.A. 34°31N 106°15W 305 J10
Mountbellew Ireland 53°28N 8°31W 166 C3
Mountlake Terrace U.S.A. 47°47N 122°18W 306 C4
Mountmellick Ireland 53°7N 7°20W 166 C4
Mountrath Ireland 53°0N 7°28W 166 D4
Moura Queens., Australia 24°35S 149°58E 280 C4
Moura Brazil 1°32S 61°38W 329 D5
Moura Portugal 38°7N 7°30W 195 G3
Mourão Portugal 38°22N 7°22W 195 G3
Mourdi, Dépression du Chad 18°10N 23°0E 259 E4
Mourdiah Mali 14°35N 7°25W 262 C3
Mourenx France 43°22N 0°38W 174 E3
Mouri Ghana 5°6N 1°14W 263 D4
Mourilyan Australia 17°35S 146°3E 280 B4
Mourmelon-le-Grand France 49°8N 4°22E 173 C11
Mourne → U.K. 54°52N 7°26W 166 B4
Mourne Mts. U.K. 54°10N 6°0W 166 B5
Mournies Greece 35°29N 24°1E 207 E5
Mouscron Belgium 50°45N 3°12E 170 D3
Mousgougou Chad 10°47N 16°9E 259 F3
Moussa 'Ali Djibouti 12°27N 42°24E 267 B5
Moussoro Chad 13°41N 16°35E 259 F3
Moustique, Morne Guadeloupe 16°7N 61°44W 322 e
Mouthe France 46°44N 6°12E 173 F13
Moutier Switz. 47°16N 7°21E 179 H3
Moûtiers France 45°29N 6°32E 175 C10
Moutong Indonesia 0°28N 121°13E 231 D6
Mouy France 49°18N 2°20E 173 C9
Mouydir, Monts du Algeria 25°30N 4°10E 261 C5
Mouyondzi Congo 4°1S 13°59E 264 C2
Mouzaki Greece 39°25N 21°37E 204 B3
Mouzarak Chad 13°17N 15°58E 259 F3
Mouzon France 49°36N 5°3E 173 C12
Movas Mexico 28°10N 109°25W 318 B3
Moville Ireland 55°11N 7°3W 166 A4
Mowandjum Australia 17°22S 123°40E 278 C3
Moweaqua U.S.A. 39°38N 89°1W 310 E7
Moxico □ Angola 12°0S 20°30E 265 E4
Moxotó → Brazil 9°19S 38°14W 332 C4
Moy → Ireland 54°8N 9°8W 166 B2
Moya Comoros Is. 12°18S 44°18E 272 a
Moyale Ethiopia 3°34N 39°5E 266 D4
Moyale Kenya 3°30N 39°4E 268 B4
Moyamba S. Leone 8°4N 12°30W 262 D2
Moyen Atlas Morocco 33°0N 5°0W 260 B4
Moyen-Chari □ Chad 9°0N 18°0E 259 G3
Moyen-Ogooué □ Gabon 0°30N 11°0E 264 C2
Moyo Indonesia 8°10S 117°40E 235 D5
Moyobamba Peru 6°0S 77°0W 330 B2
Moyowosi △ Tanzania 3°50S 31°0E 268 C3
Møysalen △ Norway 68°32N 15°29E 160 B16
Moyto Chad 12°35N 16°33E 259 F3
Moyu China 37°15N 79°44E 217 E9
Moyyero → Russia 68°44N 103°42E 215 C11
Moyynqum Zhambyl, Kazakhstan 44°17N 72°57E 217 D8
Moyynqum Zhambyl, Kazakhstan 44°12N 71°0E 217 D8
Moyynty Kazakhstan 47°10N 73°18E 217 C8
Mozambique = Moçambique Mozam. 15°3S 40°42E 269 F5
Mozambique ■ Africa 19°0S 35°0E 269 F4
Mozambique Basin Ind. Oc. 30°0S 40°0E 273 G2
Mozambique Chan. Africa 17°30S 42°30E 271 A7
Mozarthaus Vienna, Austria 142 b2
Mozdok Russia 43°45N 44°48E 191 J7
Mozdūrān Iran 36°9N 60°35E 247 B9
Mozhaysk Russia 55°30N 36°2E 188 E9
Mozhga Russia 56°26N 52°15E 190 B11
Mozhnābād Iran 34°7N 60°6E 247 C9
Mozirje Slovenia 46°22N 14°58E 199 B11
Mozyr = Mazyr Belarus 51°59N 29°15E 177 B15
Mpanda Tanzania 6°23S 31°1E 268 D3
Mpé Congo 2°58S 14°38E 264 C2
Mpese Dem. Rep. of the Congo 5°16S 15°30E 265 D3
Mpésoba Mali 12°31N 5°39W 262 C3
Mphoeng Zimbabwe 21°10S 27°51E 269 G2
Mpika Zambia 11°51S 31°25E 269 E3
Mpoko → C.A.R. 4°19N 18°33E 264 B3
Mpouya Congo 2°38S 16°13E 264 C3
Mpulungu Zambia 8°51S 31°5E 269 D3
Mpumalanga S. Africa 29°50S 30°33E 271 C5
Mpumalanga □ S. Africa 26°0S 30°0E 271 C5
Mpwapwa Tanzania 6°23S 36°30E 268 D4
Mqabba Malta 35°51N 14°28E 206 F7
Mqanduli S. Africa 31°49S 28°45E 271 D4
Mqinvartsveri = Kazbek Russia 42°42N 44°30E 191 J7
Mrągowo Poland 53°52N 21°18E 184 E8
M'ramani Comoros Is. 12°20S 44°31E 272 a
Mramor Serbia 43°20N 21°45E 202 C5
Mrauk-u = Myohaung Myanmar 20°35N 93°11E 241 E4
Mrimina Morocco 29°50N 7°9W 260 C3
Mrkonjić Grad Bos.-H. 44°26N 17°4E 182 F2
Mrkopalj Croatia 45°21N 14°52E 199 C11
Mrocza Poland 53°16N 17°35E 185 E4
Msaken Tunisia 35°49N 10°33E 258 A2
Msambansovu Zimbabwe 15°50S 30°3E 269 F3
Msida Malta 35°54N 14°29E 206 F7
M'sila Algeria 35°46N 4°30E 261 A5
M'sila □ Algeria 35°20N 4°20E 261 A5
Msoro Zambia 13°35S 31°50E 269 E3
Msta → Russia 58°25N 31°20E 188 C6
Mstislavl = Mstsislaw Belarus 54°0N 31°50E 177 A16
Mstsislaw Belarus 54°0N 31°50E 177 A16
Mszana Dolna Poland 49°41N 20°5E 185 J7
Mszczonów Poland 51°58N 20°33E 185 G7
Mtama Tanzania 10°17S 39°21E 269 E4
Mtamvuna = Mthamvuna → S. Africa 31°6S 30°12E 271 D5
Mthamvuna → S. Africa 31°6S 30°12E 271 D5
Mthatha S. Africa 31°36S 28°49E 271 D4
Mtilikwe → Zimbabwe 21°9S 31°30E 269 G3
Mtima Congo 3°49S 12°7E 264 C2
Mtirala △ Georgia 41°50N 42°2E 191 K6
Mtito Andei Kenya 2°41S 38°10E 268 C4
Mtsamboro Mayotte 12°42S 45°4E 272 b
Mtsamboro, Î. Mayotte 12°38S 45°2E 272 b
Mtsangamouji Mayotte 12°45S 45°5E 272 b
Mtsapéré Mayotte 12°46S 45°11E 272 b
Mtsensk Russia 53°17N 36°36E 188 F9
Mtskheta Georgia 41°52N 44°45E 191 K7
Mtubatuba S. Africa 28°30S 32°8E 271 C5
Mtwalume S. Africa 30°30S 30°38E 271 D5
Mtwara □ Tanzania 10°20S 39°0E 269 E4
Mtwara-Mikindani Tanzania 10°20S 40°20E 269 E5
Mu → Myanmar 21°56N 95°38E 241 E5
Mu Gia, Deo Vietnam 17°40N 105°47E 236 D5
Mu Ko Chang △ Thailand 11°59N 102°22E 237 G4
Mu Ko Surin Thailand 9°30N 97°55E 237 H1
Mu-se Myanmar 23°59N 97°54E 241 D6
Mu Us Shamo China 39°0N 109°0E 226 E5
Muacandala Angola 10°2S 19°40E 265 E3
Muan S. Korea 34°59N 126°28E 224 E3
Muaná Brazil 1°25S 49°15W 332 B2
Muanda Dem. Rep. of the Congo 6°0S 12°20E 265 D2
Muang Beng Laos 20°23N 101°46E 228 G3
Muang Chiang Rai = Chiang Rai Thailand 19°52N 99°50E 228 H2
Muang Et Laos 20°49N 104°1E 236 B5
Muang Hiam Laos 20°5N 103°22E 236 B4
Muang Hongsa Laos 19°43N 101°20E 236 C3
Muang Houn Laos 20°8N 101°23E 228 G3
Muang Kau Laos 15°6N 105°47E 236 E5
Muang Khao Laos 19°38N 103°32E 236 C4
Muang Khong Laos 14°7N 105°51E 236 E5
Muang Khoua Laos 21°5N 102°31E 228 G4
Muang Liap Laos 18°29N 101°40E 236 C3
Muang Mai Thailand 8°5N 98°21E 237 a
Muang May Laos 14°49N 106°56E 236 E6
Muang Na Mo Laos 21°3N 101°49E 228 G3
Muang Ngeun Laos 20°36N 101°3E 228 G3
Muang Ngoi Laos 20°43N 102°41E 228 G4
Muang Nong Laos 16°22N 106°30E 236 D6
Muang Ou Neua Laos 22°18N 101°48E 228 F3
Muang Ou Tay Laos 22°7N 101°48E 228 F3
Muang Pak Beng Laos 19°54N 101°8E 228 H3
Muang Phalane Laos 16°39N 105°34E 236 D5
Muang Phiang Laos 19°6N 101°32E 236 C3
Muang Phine Laos 16°32N 106°2E 236 D6
Muang Phonhong Laos 18°30N 102°25E 236 C4
Muang Saiapoun Laos 18°24N 101°31E 236 C3
Muang Sing Laos 21°11N 101°9E 228 G3
Muang Son Laos 20°27N 103°19E 236 B4
Muang Soui Laos 19°33N 102°52E 236 C4
Muang Va Laos 21°53N 102°19E 228 G4
Muang Va Laos 18°18N 101°20E 236 C3
Muang Xai Laos 20°42N 101°59E 228 G3
Muang Xamteu Laos 19°59N 104°38E 236 C5
Muangai Angola 12°32S 19°55E 265 E3
Muar Malaysia 2°3N 102°34E 237 L4
Muara Takus Indonesia 0°20N 100°39E 234 B2
Muaraaman Indonesia 3°7S 102°12E 234 C2
Muarabadak Indonesia 0°20S 117°26E 235 C5
Muarabeliti Indonesia 3°15S 103°1E 234 C2
Muarabungo Indonesia 1°28S 102°52E 234 C2
Muaradua Indonesia 4°31S 104°4E 234 C2
Muaraenim Indonesia 3°40S 103°50E 234 C2
Muarajambi Indonesia 1°28S 103°40E 234 C2
Muarajuloi Indonesia 0°12S 114°3E 235 C4
Muarakaman Indonesia 0°2S 116°45E 235 C5
Muararupit Indonesia 2°43S 102°54E 234 C2
Muarasabak Indonesia 1°7S 103°51E 234 C2
Muarasiberut Indonesia 1°35S 99°12E 234 C1
Muaratebo Indonesia 1°30S 102°26E 234 C2
Muaratembesi Indonesia 1°42S 103°8E 234 C2
Muaratewe Indonesia 0°58S 114°52E 235 C4
Muarawahau Indonesia 1°1N 116°52E 235 B5
Mubarakpur India 26°6N 83°18E 243 F10
Mubarraz = Al Mubarraz Si. Arabia 25°30N 49°40E 247 E6
Mubende Uganda 0°33N 31°22E 268 B3
Mubi Nigeria 10°18N 13°16E 263 C7
Mucaba, Sa. de Angola 7°12S 15°0E 265 D3
Mucajá Brazil 3°57S 57°32W 329 D6
Mucajai → Brazil 2°25N 60°52W 329 C5
Mucajai, Serra do Brazil 2°23N 61°10W 329 C5
Mucari Angola 9°30S 16°54E 265 D3
Muchachos, Roque de los Canary Is. 28°44N 17°52W 153 e1
Mücheln Germany 51°17N 11°47E 178 D7
Muchinga □ Zambia 12°0S 31°30E 269 E3
Muchinga Mts. Zambia 11°30S 31°30E 269 E3
Muchkapskiy Russia 51°52N 42°28E 190 E6
Muchuan China 28°57N 103°55E 228 C5
Muck U.K. 56°50N 6°15W 167 E2
Muckadilla Australia 26°35S 148°23E 281 D4
Muckalee Cr. → U.S.A. 31°38N 84°9W 316 D5
Muckaty ◎ Australia 18°37S 133°52E 280 B1
Muckle Flugga U.K. 60°51N 0°54W 167 A8
Muco → Colombia 4°15N 70°21W 328 C3
Mucoma Angola 15°18S 13°39E 265 F2
Muconda Angola 10°31S 21°15E 265 E4
Mucope Angola 16°24S 14°52E 265 F2
Mucugê Brazil 13°0S 41°23W 333 D3
Mucuim → Brazil 6°33S 64°18W 331 B5
Mucur Turkey 39°3N 34°22E 212 C6
Mucura Brazil 2°31S 62°43W 329 D5
Mucuri Brazil 18°0S 39°36W 333 E4
Mucurici Brazil 18°6S 40°31W 333 E3
Mucusso Angola 18°1S 21°25E 265 F4
Mucusso △ Angola 17°27S 21°0E 265 F4
Mucussueje Angola 11°1S 21°56E 265 E4
Muda Canary Is. 28°34N 13°57W 153 e2
Mudanjiang China 44°38N 129°30E 227 B15
Mudanya Turkey 40°25N 28°50E 203 F12
Muddebihal India 16°20N 76°8E 245 F3
Muddus △ Sweden 66°58N 20°15E 160 C19
Muddy Cr. → U.S.A. 38°24N 110°42W 304 G8
Mudeungsan S. Korea 35°7N 126°59E 224 F3
Mudgee Australia 32°32S 149°31E 283 B8
Mudhol Karnataka, India 16°21N 75°17E 245 F2
Mudhol Telangana, India 18°58N 77°55E 244 E3
Mudiata Dem. Rep. of the Congo 7°15S 22°1E 265 D4
Mudigere India 13°8N 75°38E 245 H2
Mūdiyah Yemen 13°56N 46°57E 248 D4
Mudjatik → Canada 56°1N 107°36W 297 B7
Mudon Myanmar 16°15N 97°44E 241 G6
Mudug □ Somalia 7°0N 48°0E 267 C6
Mudukulattur India 9°21N 78°31E 245 K4
Mudumu △ Namibia 18°5S 23°29E 270 A3
Mudurnu Turkey 40°27N 31°12E 212 B4
Muecate Mozam. 14°55S 39°40E 269 E4
Mueda Mozam. 11°36S 39°28E 269 E4
Mueller Ranges Australia 18°18S 126°46E 278 C4
Muende Mozam. 14°28S 33°0E 269 E3
Muerto, Mar Mexico 16°10N 94°10W 319 D6
Mufu Shan China 29°20N 114°30E 229 C10
Mufulira Zambia 12°32S 28°15E 269 E2
Mufumbwe Angola 9°12S 16°29E 265 D3
Mufumbiro Range Africa 1°25S 29°30E 268 C2
Mugardos Spain 43°27N 8°15W 194 B2
Muge → Portugal 39°8N 8°44W 195 F2
Müggelberge Germany 52°25N 13°37E 115 B4
Müggelheim Germany 52°24N 13°40E 115 B5
Múggia Italy 45°36N 13°46E 199 C10
Muggiò Italy 45°35N 9°13E 128 A2
Mughal Gardens Delhi, India 120 c1
Mughal Sarai India 25°18N 83°7E 243 G10
Mughalzhar Taūy Kazakhstan 49°0N 58°40E 216 C5
Mughayrā' Si. Arabia 29°17N 37°41E 246 D3
Mugi Japan 33°40N 134°25E 222 D6
Mugia = Muxía Spain 43°3N 9°10W 194 B1
Mugila, Mts. Dem. Rep. of the Congo 7°0S 28°50E 268 D2
Muginga Angola 8°21S 17°36E 265 D3
Muğla Turkey 37°15N 28°22E 205 D10
Muğla □ Turkey 37°15N 28°0E 205 D10
Muglad Sudan 11°1N 27°50E 257 E2
Müglizh = Maglizh Bulgaria 42°37N 25°32E 203 D9
Mugodzhary = Mughalzhar Taūy Kazakhstan 49°0N 58°40E 216 C5
Mugu Nepal 29°45N 82°30E 243 E10
Mugu Karnali → Nepal 29°38N 81°51E 243 E9
Muhagiriya Sudan 12°0N 25°38E 259 F5
Muhala Dem. Rep. of the Congo 5°40S 28°43E 268 D2
Muhammad, Râs Egypt 27°44N 34°16E 251 L5
Muhammad Qol Sudan 20°53N 37°9E 256 C4
Muhammadabad India 26°4N 83°25E 243 F10
Muḩāyil Si. Arabia 18°33N 42°3E 248 C3
Muḩayriqah Si. Arabia 23°59N 45°4E 248 B4
Muhesi → Tanzania 7°0S 35°20E 268 D4
Mühlacker Germany 48°57N 8°51E 179 G4
Mühldorf Germany 48°14N 12°32E 179 G8
Mühleiten Austria 48°10N 16°33E 142 A3
Mühlenfliess → Germany 52°32N 13°42E 115 A5
Mühlhausen = Milevsko Czechia 49°27N 14°21E 180 B7
Mühlhausen Germany 51°12N 10°27E 178 D6
Mühlig Hofmann fjell Antarctica 72°30S 5°0E 151 D3
Mühlviertel Austria 48°30N 14°10E 180 C7
Muhoro Kenya 1°1S 34°7E 266 E3
Muhos Finland 64°47N 25°59E 160 D21
Muḩradah Syria 35°15N 36°35E 250 C7
Muhu Estonia 58°36N 23°11E 188 C2
Muhutwe Tanzania 1°35S 31°45E 268 C3
Mui Wo Hong Kong, China 22°16N 114°0E 122 B1
Muiden Neths. 52°20N 5°4E 112 A3
Muie Angola 14°23S 20°25E 265 E4
Muileann gCearr, An = Mullingar Ireland 53°31N 7°21W 166 C4
Muine Bheag = Bagenalstown Ireland 52°42N 6°58W 166 D5
Muineachán = Monaghan Ireland 54°15N 6°57W 166 B5
Muir, L. Australia 34°30S 116°40E 279 F2
Muir of Ord U.K. 57°32N 4°28W 167 D4
Muisné Ecuador 0°36N 80°2W 328 C1
Muizenberg S. Africa 34°5S 18°27E 118 B1
Mujahidpur India 28°33N 77°14E 120 B2
Mujeres, I. Mexico 21°13N 86°43W 320 B2
Mujuí dos Campos Brazil 2°35S 54°41W 329 D7
Muka, Tanjung Malaysia 5°28N 100°11E 237 c
Mukacheve Ukraine 48°27N 22°45E 182 B7
Mukachevo = Mukacheve Ukraine 48°27N 22°45E 182 B7
Mukah Malaysia 2°55N 112°5E 235 B4
Mukandpur India 28°44N 77°11E 120 A2
Mukandwara India 24°49N 75°59E 242 G6
Mukawa Papua N. G. 9°38S 149°59E 286 E5
Mukawwa, Gezîret Egypt 23°55N 35°53E 256 C4
Mukawwar Sudan 20°50N 37°17E 256 C4
Mukaylah Si. Arabia 19°16N 41°48E 248 C3
Mukdahan Thailand 16°32N 104°43E 236 D5
Mukdahan △ Thailand 16°26N 104°45E 236 D5
Mukden = Shenyang China 41°48N 123°27E 224 B1
Mukerian India 31°57N 75°37E 242 D6
Mukhavyets → Belarus 52°5N 23°39E 185 F10
Mukher India 18°42N 77°22E 244 E3
Mukhmas West Bank 31°52N 35°17E 123 A2
Mukhtolovo Russia 55°29N 43°15E 190 C6
Mukhtuya = Lensk Russia 60°48N 114°55E 215 C12
Mukinbudin Australia 30°55S 118°5E 279 F2
Mukishi Kasai-Occ., Dem. Rep. of the Congo 5°39S 21°3E 265 D4
Mukishi Katanga, Dem. Rep. of the Congo 8°30S 24°44E 265 D4
Muko Japan 34°55N 135°40E 223 C7
Muko → Japan 34°48N 135°22E 133 A1
Muko Phetra △ Thailand 6°57N 99°33E 237 J2
Mukojima Japan 35°43N 139°49E 140 A3
Mukomuko Indonesia 2°30S 101°10E 234 C2
Mukomwenze Dem. Rep. of the Congo 6°49S 27°15E 268 D2
Mukono Uganda 0°21N 32°45E 268 B3
Muktinath Nepal 28°49N 83°53E 243 E10
Muktsar India 30°30N 74°30E 242 D6
Mukur = Moqor Afghan. 32°50N 67°42E 242 C2
Mukutuwa → Canada 53°10N 97°24W 297 C9
Mukwela Zambia 17°0S 26°40E 269 F2
Mukwonago U.S.A. 42°52N 88°20W 311 B8
Mul India 20°4N 79°40E 244 D4
Mula Spain 38°3N 1°33W 197 G3
Mula → India 18°34N 74°21E 244 E2
Mula → Pakistan 27°57N 67°36E 242 F2
Mulaku Atoll Maldives 3°0N 73°30E 272 d
Mulamba Dem. Rep. of the Congo 6°21S 21°13E 265 D4
Mulanay Phil. 13°31N 122°24E 232 E4
Mulange Dem. Rep. of the Congo 3°40S 27°10E 268 C2
Mulanje, Mt. Malawi 16°2S 35°33E 269 F4
Mulâtre, Pt. Dominica 15°17N 61°15W 323 k
Mulatupo Sasardi Panama 8°57N 77°45W 328 B2
Mulbagal India 13°10N 78°24E 245 H4
Mulbarton S. Africa 26°17S 28°3E 123 B2
Mulberry U.S.A. 27°54N 81°59W 317 H8
Mulberry Grove U.S.A. 38°56N 89°16W 310 F7
Mulchatna → U.S.A. 59°40N 157°7W 303 G8
Mulchén Chile 37°45S 72°20W 334 D1
Mulde → Germany 51°53N 12°15E 178 D8
Muldraugh U.S.A. 37°56N 85°59W 311 G11
Mule Creek Junction U.S.A. 43°23N 104°13W 304 E11
Muleba Tanzania 1°50S 31°37E 268 C3
Mulegé Mexico 26°53N 111°59W 318 B2
Muleshoe U.S.A. 34°13N 102°43W 314 D3
Muletta, Gara Ethiopia 9°15N 41°44E 257 F5
Mulgrave Canada 45°38N 61°31W 299 C7
Mulgrave I. = Badu Australia 10°7S 142°11E 280 a
Mulhacén Spain 37°4N 3°20W 195 H7
Mülheim Germany 51°25N 6°54E 178 D2
Mulhouse France 47°40N 7°20E 173 E14
Muli Sichuan, China 27°52N 101°8E 228 D3
Muli Maldives 2°55N 73°34E 272 d
Mulifanua Samoa 13°50S 171°59W 287 V20
Muling China 44°35N 130°10E 227 B16
Mulki India 13°6N 74°48E 245 H2
Mull U.K. 56°25N 5°56W 167 E3
Mull, Sound of U.K. 56°30N 5°50W 167 E3
Mullach Íde = Malahide Ireland 53°26N 6°9W 166 C5
Mullaittivu Sri Lanka 9°15N 80°49E 245 K5
Mullen U.S.A. 42°3N 101°1W 308 D3
Mullengudgery Australia 31°43S 147°23E 281 B4
Mullens U.S.A. 37°35N 81°23W 309 G13
Muller, Pegunungan Indonesia 0°30N 113°30E 235 B4
Muller Ra. Papua N. G. 5°35S 142°20E 286 C2
Mullet Pen. Ireland 54°13N 10°2W 166 B1
Mulletbaai St.-Maarten 18°4N 63°7W 322 a
Mullewa Australia 28°29S 115°30E 279 E2
Müllheim Germany 47°47N 7°36E 179 H3
Mulligan → Australia 25°0S 139°0E 280 D2
Mullingar Ireland 53°31N 7°21W 166 C4
Mullins U.S.A. 34°12N 79°15W 315 D15
Mullsjö Sweden 57°56N 13°55E 163 G7
Mullumbimby Australia 28°30S 153°30E 281 D5
Mulobezi Zambia 16°45S 25°7E 269 F2
Mulondo Angola 15°41S 15°12E 265 F3
Mulonga Plain Zambia 16°20S 22°40E 265 F4
Mulroy B. Ireland 55°15N 7°46W 166 A4
Mulshi L. India 18°30N 73°48E 244 E1
Multai India 21°50N 78°21E 244 D4
Multan Pakistan 30°15N 71°36E 242 D4
Mulu, Gunung Malaysia 4°3N 114°56E 235 B4
Mulug India 18°11N 79°57E 244 E4
Mulumbe, Mts. Dem. Rep. of the Congo 8°40S 27°30E 269 D2
Mulundu Dem. Rep. of the Congo 6°40S 20°33E 265 D4
Mulungushi Dam Zambia 14°48S 28°48E 269 E2
Mulurulu L. Australia 33°15S 143°20E 282 B5
Mulvane U.S.A. 37°29N 97°15W 308 G5
Mulwad Sudan 18°45N 30°39E 256 D3
Mulwala Australia 35°59S 146°0E 283 C7
Mulwala, L. Australia 35°59S 146°1E 281 C4
Muma Dem. Rep. of the Congo 3°25N 23°21E 264 B4
Mumbai India 18°56N 72°50E 130 B2
Mumbai Chhatrapati Shivaji Int. ✈ (BOM) India 19°5N 72°51E 130 A2
Mumbai Harbour India 18°58N 72°55E 130 B2
Mumbeji Zambia 13°51S 23°39E 265 E4
Mumbondo Angola 10°9S 14°15E 265 E2
Mumbwa Zambia 15°0S 27°0E 269 F2
Mumeng Papua N. G. 7°1S 146°37E 286 D4
Mumias Kenya 0°20N 34°29E 268 C4
Mummel Gulf △ Australia 31°17S 151°51E 283 A9
Mumra Russia 45°45N 47°41E 191 H8
Mun → Thailand 15°19N 105°30E 236 E5
Mun-gyeong S. Korea 36°35N 128°12E 224 D4
Muna Indonesia 5°0S 122°30E 231 F6
Munabao India 25°45N 70°17E 242 G4
Munakata Japan 33°48N 130°38E 222 D2
Munamagi Estonia 57°43N 27°4E 188 D4
Munaung Myanmar 18°45N 93°40E 241 F4
Munaung I. = Cheduba I. Myanmar 18°45N 93°40E 241 F4
Muncan Indonesia 8°34S 115°11E 231 K18
Muncar Indonesia 8°26S 114°20E 231 J17
Munch-museum Norway 59°55N 10°46E 133 A3
Münchberg Germany 50°11N 11°47E 179 E7
Müncheberg Germany 52°30N 14°9E 178 C10
Münchehofe Germany 52°29N 13°40E 115 B5
München Germany 48°8N 11°34E 131 B2
München Franz Josef Strauss ✈ (MUC) Germany 48°21N 11°47E 131 A2
Munchen-Gladbach = Mönchengladbach Germany 51°11N 6°27E 178 D2
Munchique △ Colombia 2°44N 77°1W 328 C2
Muncho Lake Canada 59°0N 125°50W 296 B3
Munch'ŏn N. Korea 39°14N 127°19E 224 C3
Muncie U.S.A. 40°12N 85°23W 311 D11
Muncoonie L. West Australia 25°12S 138°40E 280 D2
Munda Solomon Is. 8°20S 157°16E 287 M9
Mundabbera Australia 25°36S 151°18E 281 D5
Mundakayam India 9°30N 76°50E 245 K3
Mundal Sri Lanka 7°48N 79°48E 245 L4
Munday U.S.A. 33°27N 99°38W 314 E5
Mundelein U.S.A. 42°16N 88°0W 311 B8
Mundemba Cameroon 4°57N 8°52E 264 B1
Münden Germany 51°25N 9°38E 178 D5
Münden → Germany 51°28N 9°42E 178 D5
Mundiwindi Australia 23°47S 120°9E 278 D3
Mundo → Spain 38°30N 2°15W 197 G2
Mundo Novo Brazil 11°50S 40°29W 333 D3
Mundo Nuevo Trin. & Tob. 10°28N 61°15W 323 t
Mundra India 22°54N 69°48E 242 H3
Mundrabilla Australia 31°52S 127°51E 279 F4
Munenga Angola 10°2S 14°41E 265 E2
Munera Spain 39°2N 2°29W 197 F2
Muneru → India 16°45N 80°3E 244 F5
Mungallala Australia 26°28S 147°34E 281 D4
Mungallala Cr. → Australia 28°53S 147°5E 281 D4
Mungana Australia 17°8S 144°27E 280 B3
Mungaoli India 24°24N 78°7E 242 G8
Mungari Mozam. 17°12S 33°30E 269 F3
Mungbere Dem. Rep. of the Congo 2°36N 28°28E 268 B2
Mungeli India 22°4N 81°41E 243 H9
Munger India 25°23N 86°30E 243 G12
Mungerannie Australia 28°1S 138°39E 281 D2
Mungilli ◎ Australia 25°14S 124°17E 279 E3
Mungkan Kandju △ Australia 13°35S 142°52E 280 A3
Mungkarta ◎ Australia 20°22S 134°2E 280 C1
Mungo Angola 11°49S 16°16E 265 E3
Mungo, L. Australia 33°45S 143°0E 282 B5
Mungo △ Australia 33°44S 143°6E 282 B5
Munhango Angola 12°10S 18°38E 265 E3
Munhango → Angola 11°17S 19°20E 265 E3
Munich = München Germany 48°8N 11°34E 131 B2
Munising U.S.A. 46°25N 86°40W 308 B10
Munka-Ljungby Sweden 56°16N 12°58E 163 H6
Munkebo Denmark 55°27N 10°34E 163 J4
Munkedal Sweden 58°28N 11°40E 163 F5
Munkfors Sweden 59°47N 13°30E 162 E7
Munkkiniemi Finland 60°11N 24°52E 121 B2
Munku-Sardyk Russia 51°45N 100°20E 215 D11
Münnerstadt Germany 50°14N 10°12E 179 E6
Munnsville U.S.A. 42°58N 75°35W 313 D9
Munoz Phil. 15°43N 120°54E 232 D3
Muñoz Gamero, Pen. Chile 52°30S 73°5W 336 D2
Munro Argentina 34°31S 58°31W 117 B1
Munroe L. Canada 59°13N 98°35W 297 B9
Munsan S. Korea 37°51N 126°48E 224 D3
Munshiganj Bangla. 23°33N 90°32E 241 D3
Munson U.S.A. 30°52N 86°52W 317 E3
Münster Haut-Rhin, France 48°2N 7°8E 173 D14
Münster Niedersachsen, Germany 52°58N 10°5E 178 C6
Münster Nordrhein-Westfalen, Germany 51°58N 7°37E 178 D3
Munster □ Ireland 52°18N 8°44W 166 D3
Münsterberg = Ziębice Poland 50°37N 17°2E 185 H4
Muntadgin Australia 31°45S 118°33E 279 F2
Muntele Mare, Vf. Romania 46°30N 23°12E 183 D8
Muntinlupa Phil. 14°27N 121°2E 127 C2
Muntok Indonesia 2°5S 105°10E 234 C3
Munzur Dağları Turkey 39°30N 39°10E 213 C8
Muong Nhie Vietnam 22°12N 102°28E 228 F4
Muong Sen Vietnam 19°24N 104°8E 236 C5
Muong Te Vietnam 22°24N 102°49E 228 F4
Muong Xia Vietnam 20°19N 104°50E 236 B5
Muonio Finland 67°57N 23°40E 160 C20
Muonio älv = Muonionjoki → Finland 67°11N 23°34E 160 C20
Muonioälven = Muonionjoki → Finland 67°11N 23°34E 160 C20
Muonionjoki → Finland 67°11N 23°34E 160 C20
Mupa Angola 16°5S 15°50E 265 F3
Mupa → Mozam. 18°58S 35°54E 269 F4
Mupa △ Angola 15°55S 15°35E 265 F3
Muping China 37°22N 121°36E 227 F11
Mupoi South Sudan 5°28N 27°40E 257 F2
Muqaddam, Wadi → Sudan 18°4N 31°30E 256 D3
Muqaybirah Yemen 13°20N 46°5E 248 D4
Muqdisho Somalia 2°2N 45°25E 267 D6
Muqshin Oman 19°35N 54°55E 249 C6
Muqshin, W. → Oman 19°44N 55°14E 249 C6
Muquequete Angola 14°50S 14°16E 265 E2
Mur → Austria 46°18N 16°52E 181 E9
Mûr-de-Bretagne France 48°12N 3°0W 172 D4
Muradiye Manisa, Turkey 38°39N 27°21E 205 C9
Muradiye Van, Turkey 39°0N 43°44E 213 C10
Murai Res. Singapore 1°23N 103°40E 138 A2
Murakami Japan 38°14N 139°29E 220 E9
Muralag = Prince of Wales I. Australia 10°40S 142°10E 286 F2
Murallón, Cerro Chile 49°48S 73°30W 336 C2
Muranda Rwanda 1°52S 29°20E 268 C2
Murang'a Kenya 0°45S 37°9E 268 C4
Murano Venice, Italy 142 a4
Muranów Poland 52°14N 20°58E 143 B1
Murashi Russia 59°30N 49°0E 186 C8
Murat France 45°7N 2°53E 174 C6
Murat → Turkey 38°46N 40°0E 213 C9
Murat Bay = Ceduna Australia 32°7S 133°46E 281 E1
Murat Dağı Turkey 38°55N 29°43E 205 C11
Muratlı Turkey 41°10N 27°29E 203 E11
Murato France 42°35N 9°20E 175 F13
Murau Austria 47°6N 14°10E 180 D7
Murava Belarus 52°39N 24°15E 185 F11
Muravera Italy 39°25N 9°34E 200 C2
Muravyevo = Mažeikiai Lithuania 56°20N 22°20E 184 B9
Muravyovsky = Korsakov Russia 46°36N 142°42E 215 E15
Murayama Japan 38°30N 140°25E 220 E10
Murça Portugal 41°24N 7°28W 194 D3
Murcaayo Somalia 11°41N 50°34E 267 B7
Murchison N.Z. 41°49S 172°21E 285 B7
Murchison → Australia 27°45S 114°0E 279 E1
Murchison, Mt. Antarctica 73°25S 166°20E 151 D11
Murchison, Mt. N.Z. 43°0S 171°22E 285 D6
Murchison Falls Uganda 2°15N 31°30E 268 B3
Murchison Falls △ Uganda 2°17N 31°48E 268 B3
Murchison Mts. N.Z. 45°13S 167°23E 285 F2
Murchison Ra. Australia 20°0S 134°10E 280 C1
Murchison Rapids Malawi 15°55S 34°35E 269 F3
Murchison Roadhouse Australia 27°39S 116°14E 279 E2
Murcia Spain 38°5N 1°10W 197 G3
Murcia □ Spain 37°50N 1°30W 197 H3
Murdo U.S.A. 43°53N 100°43W 308 D3
Murdoch Pt. Australia 14°37S 144°55E 280 A3
Mürefte Turkey 40°40N 27°14E 203 F11
Mureş □ Romania 46°45N 24°40E 183 D9
Mureş → Romania 46°15N 20°13E 182 D5
Mureşul = Mureş → Romania 46°15N 20°13E 182 D5
Muret France 43°30N 1°20E 174 E5
Murewa Zimbabwe 17°39S 31°47E 271 A5
Murfreesboro N.C., U.S.A. 36°27N 77°6W 315 C16
Murfreesboro Tenn., U.S.A. 35°51N 86°24W 315 D11
Murgap Tajikistan 38°10N 74°2E 217 E8
Murgap → Turkmenistan 38°18N 61°12E 247 B9
Murgenella Australia 11°34S 132°56E 278 B5
Murgeni Romania 46°12N 28°1E 183 D13
Murgha Kibzai Pakistan 30°44N 69°25E 242 D3
Murghob = Murgap Tajikistan 38°10N 74°2E 217 E8
Murgon Australia 26°15S 151°54E 281 D5
Muri Cook Is. 21°15S 159°43W 289 h
Muri India 23°22N 85°52E 243 H11
Muria Indonesia 6°36S 110°53E 235 D4
Muriaé Brazil 21°8S 42°23W 333 F3
Murias de Paredes Spain 42°52N 6°11W 194 C4
Murici Brazil 9°19S 35°56W 332 C4
Muriége Angola 9°58S 21°11E 265 D4
Muriel Mine Zimbabwe 17°14S 30°40E 269 F3
Murilo △ India 23°45N 93°20E 241 C5
Murila Angola 10°44S 20°20E 265 E4
Müritz Germany 53°25N 12°42E 178 B8
Müritz △ Germany 53°22N 12°55E 178 B8
Muriwai Beach N.Z. 36°50S 174°26E 284 C3
Murkong Selek India 27°44N 95°18E 241 B5
Murliganj India 25°54N 86°59E 243 G12
Murmansk Russia 68°57N 33°10E 160 B25
Murmashi Russia 68°47N 32°42E 160 B25
Murnau Germany 47°40N 11°12E 179 H7
Muro Haute-Corse, France 42°34N 8°54E 175 F12
Muro Spain 39°44N 3°3E 206 B4
Muro, C. di France 41°44N 8°37E 175 G12
Muro de Alcoy Spain 38°46N 0°26W 197 G4
Muro Lucano Italy 40°45N 15°29E 201 B8
Murom Russia 55°35N 42°3E 190 C6
Muroran Japan 42°25N 141°0E 220 C10
Muros Spain 42°45N 9°5W 194 C1
Muros e Noya, Ría de → Spain 42°45N 9°0W 194 C1
Muroto Japan 33°18N 134°9E 222 D6
Muroto-Misaki Japan 33°15N 134°10E 222 D6
Murovani Kurylivtsi Ukraine 48°44N 27°31E 183 B12
Murowana Goślina Poland 52°35N 17°0E 185 F4
Murphy U.S.A. 43°13N 116°33W 304 E5
Murphys U.S.A. 38°8N 120°28W 306 G6
Murphy's Station = Sunnyvale U.S.A. 37°23N 122°2W 306 H4
Murphysboro U.S.A. 37°46N 89°20W 310 G7
Murrat Sudan 18°51N 29°33E 256 D2
Murrat Wells Sudan 21°3N 32°55E 256 C3
Murray Queens., Australia 9°56S 144°2E 280 a
Murray Iowa, U.S.A. 41°3N 93°57W 310 C3
Murray Ky., U.S.A. 36°37N 88°19W 308 G9
Murray Utah, U.S.A. 40°40N 111°53W 304 F8
Murray → Australia 35°20S 139°22E 282 C3
Murray, L. Papua N. G. 7°0S 141°35E 286 D1
Murray, L. S.C., U.S.A. 34°3N 81°13W 316 A8
Murray Bridge Australia 35°6S 139°14E 282 C3
Murray Fracture Zone Pac. Oc. 35°0N 130°0W 289 D14
Murray Harbour Canada 46°0N 62°28W 299 C7
Murray River △ Australia 34°23S 140°32E 281 E3
Murray-Sunset △ Australia 34°45S 141°30E 282 C4
Murrayfield U.K. 55°57N 3°15W 121 B2
Murraysburg S. Africa 31°58S 23°47E 270 D3
Murrayville U.S.A. 39°35N 90°15W 310 E6
Murree Pakistan 33°56N 73°28E 242 C5
Murrieta U.S.A. 33°33N 117°13W 307 M9
Murro di Porco, Capo Italy 37°0N 15°20E 201 F8
Murrumbateman Australia 34°58S 149°0E 283 C8
Murrumbidgee → Australia 34°43S 143°12E 282 C5
Murrumburrah Australia 34°32S 148°22E 283 C8
Murrurundi Australia 31°42S 150°51E 283 A9
Murshid Sudan 21°40N 31°10E 256 C3
Murshidabad India 24°11N 88°19E 243 G13
Murska Sobota Slovenia 46°39N 16°12E 199 B13
Murtala Mohammed Int. ✈ (LOS) Nigeria 6°34N 3°19E 124 A1
Murtazapur India 20°40N 77°25E 244 D3
Murtle L. Canada 52°8N 119°38W 296 C5
Murtoa Australia 36°35S 142°28E 282 D5
Murtosa Portugal 40°44N 8°40W 194 E2
Muru → Brazil 8°9S 70°45W 330 B3
Murud India 18°19N 72°58E 244 E1
Murung → Indonesia 0°12N 114°3E 235 B4
Murungu Tanzania 4°12S 31°10E 268 C3
Murupara N.Z. 38°28S 176°42E 284 E5
Mururoa French Polynesia 21°52S 138°55W 289 f
Murwara India 23°46N 80°28E 243 H9
Murwillumbah Australia 28°18S 153°27E 281 D5
Mürz → Austria 47°30N 15°25E 180 D8
Murzūq Libya 25°53N 13°57E 258 C2
Murzūq □ Libya 25°0N 16°0E 258 D3
Murzūq, Idehān Libya 24°50N 13°51E 258 D2
Mürzzuschlag Austria 47°36N 15°41E 180 D8
Mus India 9°14N 92°47E 245 K11
Muş Turkey 38°45N 41°30E 213 C9
Muş □ Turkey 38°45N 41°30E 213 C9
Musa Dem. Rep. of the Congo 2°40N 19°18E 264 B3
Musa → Papua N. G. 9°3S 148°55E 286 E5
Mûsa, Gebel Egypt 28°33N 33°59E 251 K4
Musa Khel Pakistan 30°59N 69°52E 242 D3
Mūsa Qal'eh Afghan. 32°20N 64°50E 240 B2
Musabeyli Turkey 36°53N 36°55E 250 B7
Musadi Dem. Rep. of the Congo 2°31S 22°50E 264 C4
Musafirkhana India 26°22N 81°48E 243 F9
Musala Bulgaria 42°13N 23°37E 202 D7
Musala Indonesia 1°41N 98°28E 234 B1
Musan N. Korea 42°12N 129°12E 224 A4
Musandam □ Oman 26°0N 56°20E 249 A7
Musandam, Ra's Oman 26°20N 56°20E 249 A7
Musangu Dem. Rep. of the Congo 10°28S 23°55E 265 E4
Musasa Tanzania 3°25S 31°30E 268 C3
Musashino Japan 35°42N 139°33E 140 A2
Musaymīr Yemen 13°27N 44°37E 248 D4
Muscat = Masqat Oman 23°37N 58°36E 249 B7
Muscat & Oman = Oman ■ Asia 23°0N 58°0E 249 B7
Muscatatuck → U.S.A. 38°46N 86°10W 311 F10
Muscatine U.S.A. 41°25N 91°3W 310 C5
Muschu I. Papua N. G. 3°25S 143°35E 286 B2
Muscle Shoals U.S.A. 34°45N 87°40W 315 D11
Muscoda U.S.A. 43°11N 90°27W 310 A6
Musengezi = Unsengedsi → Zimbabwe 15°43S 31°14E 269 F3
Museum of the Future Dubai, U.A.E. 25°13N 15°17E 119 B2
Museumquartier Vienna, Austria 142 c1
Museumsinsel Germany 52°30N 13°25E 115 A3
Musgrave Harbour Canada 49°27N 53°58W 299 C9
Musgrave Ranges Australia 26°0S 132°0E 279 E5
Mushie Dem. Rep. of the Congo 2°56S 16°55E 264 C3
Mushima Zambia 14°10S 24°56E 265 E4
Mushin Nigeria 6°31N 3°21E 124 A2
Musi → India 16°41N 79°40E 244 F4
Musi → Indonesia 2°20S 104°56E 234 C2
Musiektheater Amsterdam, Neths. 112 b3
Musina S. Africa 22°20S 30°5E 271 B5
Musiri India 10°56N 78°27E 245 J4
Muskauer Park Europe 51°34N 14°43E 178 D10
Muskeg → Canada 60°20N 123°20W 296 A4
Muskego U.S.A. 42°55N 88°8W 311 B8
Muskegon U.S.A. 43°14N 86°16W 311 A10
Muskegon → U.S.A. 43°14N 86°21W 308 D10
Muskegon Heights U.S.A. 43°12N 86°16W 311 A10
Muskogee U.S.A. 35°45N 95°22W 314 D7
Muskoka, L. Canada 45°0N 79°25W 312 B5
Muskoka Falls Canada 44°59N 79°17W 312 B5
Muskwa → Canada 58°47N 122°48W 296 B4
Muslim Mindanao = Bangsamoro □ Phil. 8°0N 123°0E 233 H3
Muslim Quarter Jerusalem 123 a3
Muslimiyah Syria 36°19N 37°12E 246 B3
Musmar Sudan 18°13N 35°40E 256 D4
Musocco Italy 45°29N 9°8E 128 B1
Musofu Zambia 13°30S 29°0E 269 E2
Musoma Tanzania 1°30S 33°48E 268 C3
Musquaro, L. Canada 50°38N 61°5W 299 B7
Musquodoboit Harbour Canada 44°50N 63°9W 299 D7
Mussau I. Papua N. G. 1°30S 149°40E 286 A5
Musselburgh U.K. 55°57N 3°2W 167 F5
Musselshell → U.S.A. 47°21N 107°57W 304 C10
Mussende Angola 10°32S 16°5E 265 E3
Musserra Angola 7°37S 13°2E 265 D2
Mussidan France 45°2N 0°22E 174 C4
Mussolinea di Sardegna = Arborea Italy 39°46N 8°35E 200 C1
Mussolo Angola 9°59S 17°19E 265 D3
Mussomeli Italy 37°35N 13°45E 200 E6
Mussoorie India 30°27N 78°6E 242 D8
Mussuco Angola 17°2S 19°3E 265 F3
Mustafakemalpaşa Turkey 40°2N 28°24E 203 F12
Mustahīl Ethiopia 5°16N 44°45E 267 C5
Mustang Nepal 29°10N 83°55E 243 E10
Mustansiriya Iraq 33°22N 44°24E 117 B3
Musters, L. Argentina 45°20S 69°25W 336 C3
Mustique I. St. Vincent 12°52N 61°11W 323 n
Musturud Egypt 30°8N 31°17E 117 A2
Musudan N. Korea 40°50N 129°43E 224 B4
Muswell Hill U.K. 51°35N 0°8W 125 A3
Muswellbrook Australia 32°16S 150°56E 283 B9
Muszyna Poland 49°22N 20°55E 185 J7
Mût Egypt 25°28N 28°58E 256 B2
Mut Turkey 36°40N 33°28E 250 B4
Mutalau Cook Is. 18°56S 169°50W 289 g
Mutanabi Iraq 33°19N 44°21E 113 B2
Mutanda Dem. Rep. of the Congo 5°17S 16°34E 265 D3
Mutanda Mozam. 21°0S 33°34E 271 B5
Mutanda Zambia 12°24S 26°13E 269 E2
Mutankiang = Mudanjiang China 44°38N 129°30E 227 B15
Mutanshe Taiwan 22°9N 120°48E 225 D2

Mutare Zimbabwe 18°58S 32°38E 269 F3
Mutawintji △ Australia 31°10S 142°30E 281 E3
Mutha Kenya 1°48S 38°26E 268 C4
Muthana Iraq 33°19N 44°27E 113 B2
Muting Indonesia 7°23S 140°20E 231 F10
Mutirikwe Dam Zimbabwe 20°15S 31°0E 269 G3
Mutki = Mirtağ Turkey 38°23N 41°56E 246 B4
Mutoko Zimbabwe 17°24S 32°13E 271 A5
Mutomo Kenya 1°51S 38°12E 268 C4
Mutoray Russia 60°56N 101°0E 215 C11
Mutoto Dem. Rep. of the Congo 5°42S 22°42E 265 D4
Mutoxo Angola 12°17S 21°40E 265 E4
Mutsamudu Comoros Is. 12°10S 44°25E 272 a
Mutshatsha Dem. Rep. of the Congo 10°35S 24°20E 265 E4
Mutsu Japan 41°5N 140°55E 220 D10
Mutsu-Wan Japan 41°5N 140°55E 220 D10
Muttaburra Australia 22°38S 144°29E 280 C3
Muttalip Turkey 39°50N 30°32E 205 B12
Mutton I. Ireland 52°49N 9°32W 166 D2
Muttra = Mathura India 27°30N 77°40E 242 F7
Muttukuru India 14°16N 80°6E 245 G5
Mutuáli Mozam. 14°55S 37°0E 269 E4
Mutum Biyu Nigeria 8°40N 10°50E 263 D7
Mutumba Burundi 3°25S 29°21E 268 C2
Mutunópolis Brazil 13°40S 49°15W 333 D2
Mutur Sri Lanka 8°27N 81°16E 245 K5
Muweilih Egypt 30°42N 34°19E 251 H5
Muxaluando Angola 8°8S 14°18E 265 D2
Muxía Spain 43°3N 9°10W 194 B1
Muxima Angola 9°33S 13°58E 265 D2
Muy Muy Nic. 12°39N 85°36W 320 D2
Muyinga Burundi 3°14S 30°33E 268 C3
Mŭynoq Uzbekistan 43°44N 59°10E 216 D5
Muyua = Woodlark I. Papua N. G. 9°10S 152°50E 286 E7
Muyunkum, Peski = Moyynqum Kazakhstan 44°12N 71°0E 217 D8
Muz Tag China 36°25N 87°25E 217 E11
Muzaffarabad Pakistan 34°25N 73°30E 243 B5
Muzaffargarh Pakistan 30°5N 71°14E 242 D4
Muzaffarnagar India 29°26N 77°40E 242 E7
Muzaffarpur India 26°7N 85°23E 243 F11
Muzafirpur Pakistan 30°58N 69°9E 242 D3
Mużakowski, Park = Muskauer Park Europe 51°34N 14°43E 178 D10
Muzeze Angola 15°3S 17°43E 265 F3
Muzhi Russia 65°25N 64°40E 186 A11
Muzillac France 47°35N 2°30W 172 E4
Muzon, C. U.S.A. 54°40N 132°42W 303 J14
Muztagh-Ata China 38°17N 75°7E 217 E9
Muztor = Toktogul Kyrgyzstan 41°50N 72°50E 217 D8
Muzūra Egypt 28°53N 30°48E 256 J7
Mvadhi-Ousyé Gabon 1°13N 13°12E 264 B2
Mvam Gabon 0°13S 9°39E 264 C1
Mvangan Cameroon 2°17N 11°43E 264 B2
Mvolo South Sudan 6°2N 29°53E 257 F2
Mvuma Zimbabwe 19°16S 30°30E 269 F3
Mvurwi Zimbabwe 17°0S 30°57E 269 F3
Mwabvi ⌂ Malawi 16°42S 35°0E 269 F3
Mwadi-Kalumbu Dem. Rep. of the Congo 7°53S 18°43E 265 D3
Mwadui Tanzania 3°26S 33°32E 268 C3
Mwali = Mohéli Comoros Is. 12°20S 43°40E 272 a
Mwambo Tanzania 10°30S 40°22E 269 E5
Mwandi Zambia 17°30S 24°51E 269 F1
Mwanza Katanga, Dem. Rep. of the Congo 7°55S 26°43E 265 D5
Mwanza Tanzania 2°30S 32°58E 268 C3
Mwanza Zambia 16°58S 24°28E 265 F4
Mwanza □ Tanzania 2°0S 33°0E 268 C3
Mwaya Tanzania 9°32S 33°55E 269 D3
Mweelrea Ireland 53°39N 9°49W 166 C2
Mweka Dem. Rep. of the Congo 4°50S 21°34E 265 C4
Mwendjila Dem. Rep. of the Congo 7°12S 18°51E 265 D3
Mwene-Ditu Dem. Rep. of the Congo 6°35S 22°27E 265 D4
Mwenezi Zimbabwe 21°15S 30°48E 269 G3
Mwenezi → Mozam. 22°40S 31°50E 269 G3
Mwenga Dem. Rep. of the Congo 3°1S 28°28E 268 C2
Mweru, L. Zambia 9°0S 28°40E 269 D2
Mweru Wantipa △ Zambia 8°39S 29°25E 269 D2
Mwetshi Dem. Rep. of the Congo 4°50S 22°38E 265 C4
Mweza Range Zimbabwe 21°0S 30°0E 269 G3
Mwilambwe Dem. Rep. of the Congo 8°7S 25°5E 265 D5
Mwimbi Tanzania 8°38S 31°39E 269 D3
Mwingi Kenya 0°56S 38°4E 268 C4
Mwinilunga Zambia 11°43S 24°25E 265 E4
My Son Vietnam 15°48N 108°7E 236 E7
My Tho Vietnam 10°29N 106°23E 237 G6
Mya, O. → Algeria 30°46N 4°54E 261 B5
Myajlar India 26°15N 70°20E 242 F4
Myakka → U.S.A. 26°56N 82°11W 317 J7
Myall Lakes △ Australia 32°25S 152°30E 283 B10
Myanaung Myanmar 18°18N 95°22E 241 F5
Myanmar ■ Asia 21°0N 96°30E 241 E6
Myaung Myanmar 21°50N 95°25E 241 E5
Myaungmya Myanmar 16°30N 94°40E 241 G5
Mycenæ = Mykenes Greece 37°43N 22°46E 204 D4
Myebon Myanmar 20°3N 93°22E 241 E4
Myedna Belarus 51°52N 23°42E 185 G10
Myeik = Mergui Myanmar 12°26N 98°34E 236 F2
Myeik Kyunzu Myanmar 11°30N 97°30E 237 G1
Myerstown U.S.A. 40°22N 76°19W 313 F8
Myingyan Myanmar 21°30N 95°20E 241 E5
Myitkyina Myanmar 25°24N 97°26E 241 C6
Myitson Myanmar 23°16N 96°34E 241 D6
Myittha Myanmar 21°25N 96°8E 241 E6
Myittha → Myanmar 23°12N 94°17E 241 D5
Myjava Slovakia 48°41N 17°37E 181 C10
Mykenes Greece 37°43N 22°46E 204 D4
Mykhaylivka Ukraine 47°12N 35°15E 189 J8
Mykines Færoe Is. 62°7N 7°35W 160 E9
Myking Norway 60°41N 5°19E 164 D2
Mykolayiv Ukraine 46°58N 32°0E 189 J7
Mykolayiv □ Ukraine 47°20N 31°50E 189 J6
Mykonos Greece 37°30N 25°25E 205 D7
Mylius Erichsen Land Greenland 81°30N 27°0W 154 A8
Myllypuro Finland 60°13N 25°3E 121 B3
Mymensingh Bangla. 24°45N 90°24E 241 C3
Mymensingh □ Bangla. 24°50N 90°30E 241 C3
Mynydd Du U.K. 51°52N 3°50W 169 F4
Myo-gyi Myanmar 21°27N 96°22E 241 E6
Myohaung Myanmar 20°35N 93°11E 241 E4
Myohla Myanmar 19°16N 95°25E 241 F5
Myotha Myanmar 21°41N 95°43E 241 E5
Myothit Kachin, Myanmar 24°24N 97°24E 241 C6
Myothit Magway, Myanmar 20°12N 95°27E 241 E5
Myrasýsla Iceland 64°45N 21°30W 155 C5
Mýrdalsjökull Iceland 63°40N 19°6W 155 D7
Myrhorod Ukraine 49°58N 33°37E 189 H7
Mýri Iceland 65°23N 17°23W 155 B9
Myrina Greece 39°53N 25°4E 205 B7
Myrtle Beach U.S.A. 33°42N 78°53W 315 E15
Myrtle Creek U.S.A. 43°1N 123°17W 304 E2
Myrtle Grove U.S.A. 30°23N 87°17W 317 E2
Myrtle Point U.S.A. 43°4N 124°8W 304 E1
Myrtleford Australia 36°34S 146°44E 283 D7
Myrtoan Sea = Mirtoo Sea Greece 37°0N 23°20E 204 D5
Myrtou Cyprus 35°18N 33°4E 207 E9
Myrviken Sweden 62°58N 14°20E 162 B8
Mysen Norway 59°33N 11°20E 164 E8
Mysia Turkey 39°50N 27°0E 203 G11
Myślenice Poland 49°51N 19°57E 185 J6
Myślibórz Poland 52°55N 14°50E 185 F1
Mysłowice Poland 50°15N 19°12E 185 H6
Myslowitz = Mysłowice Poland 50°15N 19°12E 185 H6
Mysore = Karnataka □ India 13°15N 77°0E 245 H3
Mysore = Mysuru India 12°17N 76°41E 245 H3
Mystic Conn., U.S.A. 41°21N 71°58W 313 E13
Mystic Iowa, U.S.A. 40°47N 92°57W 310 D4
Mystic → U.S.A. 42°22N 71°3W 116 A2
Mystras Greece 37°4N 22°22E 204 D4
Mysuru India 12°17N 76°41E 245 H3
Myszków Poland 50°45N 19°22E 185 H6
Myszyniec Poland 53°23N 21°21E 184 E8
Mytilene = Mitilini Greece 39°6N 26°35E 205 B8
Mytishchi Russia 55°50N 37°50E 188 E9
Mývatn Iceland 65°36N 17°0W 155 B10
M'zab, Oued → Algeria 32°15N 5°0E 261 B6
M'Zab Valley = M'zab, Oued → Algeria 32°15N 5°0E 261 B6
Mže → Czechia 49°46N 13°24E 180 B6
Mzimba Malawi 11°55S 33°39E 269 E3
Mzimkulu → S. Africa 30°44S 30°28E 271 D5
Mzimvubu → S. Africa 31°38S 29°33E 271 D4
Mzuzu Malawi 11°30S 33°55E 269 E3

N

N.S.C.B. Int. ✈ (CCU) India 22°38N 88°26E 124 B2
Na Clocha Liatha = Greystones Ireland 53°9N 6°5W 166 C5
Na Haeo △ Thailand 17°31N 100°58E 236 D3
Na Hearadh = Harris U.K. 57°50N 6°55W 167 D2
Na Hearadh, Caolas = Harris, Sd. of U.K. 57°44N 7°6W 167 D1
Na-lang Myanmar 22°42N 97°33E 241 D6
Na Noi Thailand 18°19N 100°43E 236 C3
Na Phao Laos 17°35N 105°44E 236 D5
Na Sam Vietnam 22°3N 106°37E 228 F6
Na Sceirí = Skerries Ireland 53°35N 6°8W 166 C5
Na Thon Thailand 9°32N 99°56E 237 b
Naab → Germany 49°1N 12°2E 179 F8
Nä'älehu U.S.A. 19°4N 155°35W 302 D6
Na'am Sudan 9°42N 28°27E 257 F2
Na'am → South Sudan 6°48N 29°57E 257 F2
Naama Algeria 33°16N 0°19E 261 B5
Naama □ Algeria 33°15N 0°45E 261 B5
Naantali Finland 60°29N 22°2E 188 B1
Naas Ireland 53°12N 6°40W 166 C5
Nababeep S. Africa 29°36S 17°46E 270 C2
Nabadwip = Navadwip India 23°34N 88°20E 243 H13
Nabari Japan 34°37N 136°5E 223 C8
Nabawa Australia 28°30S 114°48E 279 E1
Nabberu, L. Australia 25°50S 120°30E 279 E3
Nabburg Germany 49°27N 12°11E 179 F8
Naberezhnaya Tower Russia 55°45N 37°32E 129 B2
Naberezhnyye Chelny Russia 55°42N 52°19E 190 C11
Nabesna U.S.A. 62°22N 143°0W 303 E12
Nabeul Tunisia 36°30N 10°44E 258 A2
Nabeul □ Tunisia 36°30N 10°40E 261 A7
Nabha India 30°26N 76°14E 242 D7
Nabi Sâlih Egypt 28°37N 33°59E 251 K4
Nabīd Iran 29°40N 57°38E 247 D8
Nabire Indonesia 3°15S 135°26E 231 E9
Nabisar Pakistan 25°8N 69°40E 242 G3
Nabisipi → Canada 50°14N 62°13W 299 B7
Nabiswera Uganda 1°27N 32°15E 268 B3
Nāblus = Nābulus West Bank 32°14N 35°15E 251 F6
Naboomspruit S. Africa 24°32S 28°40E 271 B4
Nabou Burkina Faso 11°25N 2°50W 262 C4
Nabouwalu Fiji 17°0S 178°45E 287 A2
Nabq Egypt 28°6N 34°25E 251 K5
Nabua Phil. 13°24N 123°22E 232 E4
Nābulus West Bank 32°14N 35°15E 251 F6
Nabunturan Phil. 7°35N 125°58E 233 H5
Nacala Mozam. 14°32S 40°34E 269 E5
Nacaome Honduras 13°31N 87°30W 320 D2
Nacaroa Mozam. 14°22S 39°56E 269 E4
Naches U.S.A. 46°44N 120°42W 304 C3
Naches → U.S.A. 46°38N 120°31W 306 D6
Nachicapau, L. Canada 56°40N 68°5W 299 A6
Nachikatsuura Japan 33°33N 135°58E 223 D7
Nachingwea Tanzania 10°23S 38°49E 269 E4
Nachna India 27°34N 71°41E 242 F4
Náchod Czechia 50°25N 16°8E 180 A9
Nachuge India 10°47N 92°21E 245 J11
Nacimiento, L. U.S.A. 35°46N 120°53W 306 K6
Nacka Sweden 59°19N 18°10E 139 B3
Nackara Australia 32°48S 139°12E 282 B3
Naco Mexico 31°19N 109°56W 318 A3
Nacogdoches U.S.A. 31°36N 94°39W 314 F7
Nácori Chico Mexico 29°40N 108°57W 318 B3
Nacozari de García Mexico 30°25N 109°38W 318 A3
Nacula Fiji 16°54S 177°27E 287 A1
Nada = Danzhou China 19°31N 109°33E 229 a
Nådendal = Naantali Finland 60°29N 22°2E 188 B1
Nadezhdinsky = Serov Russia 59°29N 60°35E 186 C11
Nadi Fiji 17°42S 177°20E 287 A1
Nadi Sudan 18°40N 33°41E 256 D3
Nadiad India 22°41N 72°56E 242 H5
Nădlac Romania 46°10N 20°50E 182 D5
Nador Morocco 35°14N 2°58W 261 A4
Nadur Malta 35°54N 14°22E 206 F7
Nadur Gozo, Malta 36°2N 14°18E 206 E7
Nadūshan Iran 32°2N 53°35E 247 C7
Nadvirna Ukraine 48°37N 24°30E 183 B9
Nadvoitsy Russia 63°52N 34°14E 186 B5
Nadvornaya = Nadvirna Ukraine 48°37N 24°30E 183 B9
Nadym Russia 65°35N 72°42E 214 C8
Nadym → Russia 66°12N 72°0E 214 C8
Nærbø Norway 58°40N 5°39E 164 F2
Nærøyfjorden Norway 60°55N 6°55E 164 D3
Nærsnes Norway 59°45N 10°27E 133 B1
Næstved Denmark 55°13N 11°44E 163 J5
Nafada Nigeria 11°8N 11°20E 263 C7
Nafarroa = Navarra □ Spain 42°40N 1°40W 196 C3
Nafpaktos Greece 38°24N 21°50E 204 C3
Nafplio Greece 37°33N 22°50E 204 D4
Naft-e Safīd Iran 31°40N 49°17E 247 D6
Naftan Pt. N. Marianas 15°5N 145°45E 302 e
Naftshahr Iran 34°0N 45°30E 213 E11
Nafud Desert = An Nafūd Si. Arabia 28°15N 41°0E 246 D4
Nafūsah, Jabal Libya 32°12N 12°30E 258 B2
Nag Hammâdi Egypt 26°2N 32°18E 256 B3
Naga Japan 26°34N 127°43E 288 a
Naga Camarines S., Phil. 13°38N 123°15E 232 E4
Naga Cebu, Phil. 10°13N 123°45E 233 F4
Naga Zamboanga del S., Phil. 7°46N 122°45E 233 H4
Naga, Kreb en Africa 24°12N 6°0W 260 D3
Naga Hills = Nagaland □ India 26°0N 94°30E 241 C5
Naga-Shima Kagoshima, Japan 32°10N 130°9E 222 E2
Naga-Shima Yamaguchi, Japan 33°49N 132°5E 222 D4
Nagagami Canada 50°23N 84°20W 298 B3
Nagahama Ehime, Japan 33°36N 132°29E 222 D4
Nagahama Shiga, Japan 35°23N 136°16E 223 B8
Nagai Japan 38°6N 140°2E 220 E10
Nagai I. U.S.A. 55°5N 160°0W 303 J8
Nagaland □ India 26°0N 94°30E 241 C5
Nagambie Australia 36°47S 145°10E 283 D6
Nagano Japan 36°40N 138°10E 223 A10
Nagano □ Japan 36°15N 138°0E 223 A10
Nagaoka Japan 37°27N 138°51E 221 F9
Nagaon India 26°20N 92°50E 241 B4
Nagappattinam India 10°46N 79°51E 245 J4
Nagar → Bangla. 24°27N 89°12E 241 C2
Nagar Karnul India 16°29N 78°20E 245 F4
Nagar Parkar Pakistan 24°28N 70°46E 242 G4
Nagara-Gawa → Japan 35°40N 136°43E 223 B8
Nagaram India 18°21N 80°26E 244 E5
Nagarhole △ India 12°0N 76°10E 245 J3
Nagari Hills India 13°3N 79°45E 245 H4
Nagarjuna Sagar India 16°30N 79°13E 245 F4
Nagasaki Japan 32°47N 129°50E 222 E1
Nagasaki □ Japan 32°50N 129°40E 222 E1
Nagato Japan 34°19N 131°5E 222 C3
Nagatsuta Japan 35°32N 139°31E 140 B2
Nagaur India 27°15N 73°45E 242 F5
Nagayo Japan 32°48N 129°50E 222 E1
Nagbhir India 20°34N 79°55E 244 D4
Nagda India 23°27N 75°25E 242 H6
Nagercoil India 8°12N 77°26E 245 K3
Nagina India 29°30N 78°30E 243 E8
Nagīneh Iran 34°20N 57°15E 247 C8
Naginimara India 26°49N 94°50E 241 B5
Nagir Pakistan 36°12N 74°42E 243 A6
Naglarby Sweden 60°25N 15°34E 162 D9
Nagles Mts. Ireland 52°8N 8°30W 166 D3
Nago-wan Japan 26°34N 127°57E 288 a
Nagod India 24°34N 80°36E 243 G9
Nagold Germany 48°32N 8°43E 179 G4
Nagold → Germany 48°52N 8°42E 179 G4
Nagoorin Australia 24°17S 151°15E 280 C5
Nagorno-Karabakh □ Azerbaijan 39°55N 46°45E 213 C12
Nagornyy Russia 55°58N 124°57E 215 D13
Nagoya Indonesia 1°15N 104°5E 234 B2
Nagoya Japan 35°10N 136°50E 223 B8
Nagoya ✈ (NGO) Japan 34°53N 136°45E 223 C8
Nagpartian = Burgos Phil. 18°31N 120°39E 232 B3
Nagpur India 21°8N 79°10E 244 D4
Nagqu China 31°29N 92°3E 218 E7
Nags Head St. Kitts & Nevis 17°13N 62°38W 322 d
Nagua Dom. Rep. 19°23N 69°50W 321 C6
Naguabo Puerto Rico 18°13N 65°44W 321 b
Nagurunguru ☼ Australia 16°45S 129°45E 278 C4
Nagyatád Hungary 46°14N 17°22E 182 D2
Nagyecsed Hungary 47°53N 22°24E 182 C7
Nagykálló Hungary 47°53N 21°51E 182 C6
Nagykanizsa Hungary 46°28N 17°0E 182 D2
Nagykáta Hungary 47°25N 19°45E 182 C4
Nagykőrös Hungary 47°5N 19°48E 182 C4
Nagyszombat = Trnava Slovakia 48°23N 17°35E 181 C10
Nagytétény Hungary 47°23N 18°59E 117 B1
Nagyvárad = Oradea Romania 47°2N 21°58E 182 C6
Naha Japan 26°13N 127°42E 288 a
Nahabuan Indonesia 0°49N 114°4E 235 B4
Nahalin West Bank 31°41N 35°7E 123 B1
Nahan India 30°33N 77°18E 242 D7
Nahanni △ Canada 61°36N 125°41W 296 A4
Nahanni Butte Canada 61°2N 123°31W 296 A4
Nahargarh Mad. P., India 24°10N 75°14E 242 G6
Nahargarh Raj., India 24°55N 76°50E 242 G7
Nahariyya Israel 33°1N 35°5E 250 F6
Nahāvand Iran 34°10N 48°22E 213 E13
Nahe → Germany 49°58N 7°54E 179 F3
Nahirne Ukraine 45°26N 28°27E 183 E13
Nahîya, W. → Egypt 28°55N 31°0E 256 B3
Nahuel Huapi, L. Argentina 41°0S 71°32W 336 B2
Nahuel Huapi △ Argentina 41°3S 71°59W 336 B2
Nahuelbuta △ Chile 37°44S 72°57W 334 D1
Nahunta U.S.A. 31°12N 81°59W 316 D8
Nai Yong Thailand 8°14N 98°22E 237 a
Naic Phil. 14°19N 120°46E 232 D3
Naicá Mexico 27°53N 105°31W 318 B3
Naicam Canada 52°30N 104°30W 297 C8
Naifaru Maldives 5°26N 73°20E 272 d
Naikoon ⌂ Canada 53°55N 131°55W 296 C2
Naikul India 21°20N 84°58E 244 D7
Naila Germany 50°19N 11°42E 179 E7
Naimisharanya India 27°21N 80°30E 243 F9
Naimona'nyi Feng China 30°26N 81°18E 243 D9
Nain Nfld. & L., Canada 56°34N 61°40W 299 A7
Nā'īn Iran 32°54N 53°0E 247 C7
Nain Jamaica 17°57N 77°38W 320 a
Naini Tal India 29°30N 79°30E 243 E8
Nainpur India 22°30N 80°10E 243 H9
Naintré France 46°46N 0°29E 172 F7
Nainwa India 25°46N 75°51E 242 G6
Naipu Romania 44°12N 25°47E 183 F10
Nairai Fiji 17°49S 179°15E 287 A2
Nairn U.K. 57°35N 3°53W 167 D5
Nairobi Kenya 1°17S 36°48E 268 C4
Nairobi △ Kenya 1°22S 36°50E 268 C4
Naissaar Estonia 59°34N 24°29E 188 C3
Naita, Mt. Ethiopia 5°30N 35°18E 257 F4
Naitaba Fiji 17°0S 179°16W 287 A3
Naivasha Kenya 0°40S 36°30E 268 C4
Naivasha, L. Kenya 0°48S 36°20E 268 C4
Najac France 44°14N 1°58E 174 D5
Najaf = An Najaf Iraq 32°3N 44°15E 213 G11
Najafābād Iran 32°40N 51°15E 247 C6
Najafgarh Drain → India 28°39N 77°4E 120 B1
Najd Si. Arabia 26°30N 42°0E 248 A3
Nájera Spain 42°26N 2°48W 196 C2
Najerilla → Spain 42°32N 2°48W 196 C2
Najibabad India 29°40N 78°20E 242 E8
Najin N. Korea 42°12N 130°15E 224 A5
Najmah Si. Arabia 26°42N 50°6E 247 E6
Najrān Si. Arabia 17°34N 44°18E 248 C4
Najrān □ Si. Arabia 18°30N 45°50E 248 C4
Naju S. Korea 35°3N 126°43E 224 E3
Naka Japan 36°30N 140°35E 223 A12
Naka-Gawa → Japan 36°20N 140°36E 223 A12
Nakadōri-Shima Japan 32°57N 129°4E 221 H4
Nakagusuku-wan Japan 26°14N 127°53E 288 a
Nakahara Japan 35°33N 139°37E 140 B2
Nakal = Nakło nad Notecią Poland 53°9N 17°38E 185 E4
Nakalagba Dem. Rep. of the Congo 2°50N 27°58E 268 B2
Nakalele Pt. U.S.A. 21°2N 156°35W 302 B5
Nakama Japan 33°56N 130°43E 222 D2
Nakambé = White Volta → Ghana 9°10N 1°15W 263 D4
Nakaminato Japan 36°21N 140°36E 223 A12
Nakamura = Shimanto Japan 32°59N 132°56E 222 E4
Nakanai Mts. Papua N. G. 5°40S 151°0E 286 C6
Nakano Nagano, Japan 36°45N 138°22E 223 A10
Nakano Tōkyō, Japan 35°42N 139°39E 140 A2
Nakano-Shima Japan 29°51N 129°52E 221 K4
Nakanojō Japan 36°35N 138°51E 223 A10
Nakashibetsu Japan 43°33N 144°59E 220 C12
Nakatsu Japan 33°34N 131°15E 222 D3
Nakatsugawa Japan 35°29N 137°30E 223 B9
Nakfa Eritrea 16°40N 38°32E 257 D4
Nakfa ⌂ Eritrea 17°28N 38°55E 257 D4
Nakha Yai, Ko Thailand 8°3N 98°28E 237 a
Nakhichevan = Naxçıvan Azerbaijan 39°12N 45°15E 213 C11
Nakhichevan Rep. = Naxçıvan □ Azerbaijan 39°25N 45°26E 213 C11
Nakhl Egypt 29°55N 33°43E 251 J4
Nakhl-e Taqī Iran 27°28N 52°36E 247 E7
Nakhodka Russia 42°53N 132°54E 220 C6
Nakhon Nayok Thailand 14°12N 101°13E 236 E3
Nakhon Pathom Thailand 13°49N 100°3E 236 F3
Nakhon Phanom Thailand 17°23N 104°43E 236 D5
Nakhon Ratchasima Thailand 14°59N 102°12E 236 E4
Nakhon Sawan Thailand 15°35N 100°10E 236 E3
Nakhon Si Thammarat Thailand 8°29N 100°0E 237 H3
Nakhon Thai Thailand 17°5N 100°44E 236 D3
Nakhtarana India 23°20N 69°15E 242 H3
Nakijin Japan 26°40N 127°58E 288 a
Nakina Canada 50°10N 86°40W 298 B2
Nakło nad Notecią Poland 53°9N 17°38E 185 E4
Naknek U.S.A. 58°44N 157°1W 303 G8
Nako Burkina Faso 10°40N 3°4W 262 C4
Nakodar India 31°8N 75°31E 242 D6
Nakskov Denmark 54°50N 11°8E 163 K5
Naktong → S. Korea 35°7N 128°57E 224 E4
Nakuru Kenya 0°15S 36°4E 268 C4
Nakuru, L. Kenya 0°23S 36°5E 268 C4
Nakusp Canada 50°20N 117°45W 296 C5
Nal Pakistan 27°40N 66°12E 242 F2
Nal → Pakistan 25°20N 65°30E 242 G1
Nalázi Mozam. 24°3S 33°20E 271 B5
Nalchik Russia 43°30N 43°33E 191 J6
Nałęczów Poland 51°17N 22°9E 185 G9
Nalerigu Ghana 10°35N 0°25W 263 C4
Nalgonda India 17°6N 79°15E 244 F4
Nalhati India 24°17N 87°52E 243 G12
Naliya India 23°16N 68°50E 242 H3
Nallamalai Hills India 15°30N 78°50E 245 G4
Nallıhan Turkey 40°11N 31°20E 212 B4
Nalolo Zambia 15°33S 23°7E 265 F4
Nalón → Spain 43°32N 6°4W 194 B4
Nalong Myanmar 24°44N 97°28E 241 C6
Nalubaale Dam Uganda 0°30N 33°5E 268 B3
Nalumasortoq Greenland 60°23N 44°28W 154 E6
Nālūt Libya 31°54N 11°0E 258 B2
Nālūt □ Libya 31°52N 10°58E 258 B2
Nam Can Vietnam 8°46N 104°59E 237 H5
Nam-ch'on N. Korea 38°15N 126°26E 224 C3
Nam Co China 30°30N 90°45E 218 E7
Nam Dinh Vietnam 20°25N 106°5E 228 G6
Nam Du, Quan Dao Vietnam 9°41N 104°21E 237 H5
Nam Hka → Myanmar 21°34N 95°41E 228 G2
Nam Loi → Myanmar 21°3N 98°27E 228 G3
Nam Nao △ Thailand 16°44N 101°32E 236 D3
Nam Ngum Res. Laos 18°35N 102°34E 236 C4
Nam Phan Vietnam 10°30N 106°0E 237 G6
Nam Phong Thailand 16°42N 102°52E 236 D4
Nam Theun Res. Laos 17°51N 105°3E 236 D5
Nam Tok Thailand 14°21N 99°4E 236 E2
Nam Un Res. Thailand 17°13N 103°44E 236 D4
Namachire Angola 11°26S 22°43E 265 E4
Namacunde Angola 17°18S 15°50E 265 F3
Namacurra Mozam. 17°30S 36°50E 271 A6
Namadgi △ Australia 35°42S 149°0E 283 C8
Namai B. Palau 7°31N 134°38E 288 c
Namak, Daryācheh-ye Iran 34°30N 52°0E 247 C7
Namak, Kavir-e Iran 34°30N 57°30E 247 C8
Namakkal India 11°13N 78°13E 245 J4
Namakzār, Daryācheh-ye Iran 34°0N 60°30E 240 B1
Namaland Namibia 26°0S 17°0E 270 B2
Namanga Kenya 2°33S 36°47E 268 C4
Namangan Uzbekistan 41°0N 71°40E 217 D8
Namangan □ Uzbekistan 41°0N 71°15E 217 D8
Namapa Mozam. 13°43S 39°50E 269 E4
Namaqua △ S. Africa 30°0S 17°30E 270 D2
Namaqualand S. Africa 30°0S 17°25E 270 D2
Namasagali Uganda 1°2N 33°0E 268 B3
Namatanai Papua N. G. 3°40S 152°29E 286 B7
Namber Indonesia 1°2S 134°49E 231 E8
Nambour Australia 26°32S 152°58E 281 D5
Nambouwalu = Nabouwalu Fiji 17°0S 178°45E 287 A2
Nambuangongo Angola 8°1S 14°12E 265 D2
Nambucca Heads Australia 30°37S 153°0E 283 A10
Nambung △ Australia 30°30S 115°5E 279 F2
Namcha Barwa China 29°40N 95°10E 218 F8
Namche Bazar Nepal 27°51N 86°47E 243 F12
Namchonjŏm = Nam-ch'on N. Korea 38°15N 126°26E 224 C3
Namdapha △ India 27°30N 96°50E 241 B6
Namecunda Mozam. 14°54S 37°37E 269 E4
Nameh Indonesia 2°34N 116°21E 235 B5
Namen = Namur Belgium 50°27N 4°52E 170 D4
Namenalala Fiji 17°8S 179°9E 287 A2
Nameponda Mozam. 15°50S 39°50E 269 F4
Nameri △ India 26°55N 92°55E 241 B4
Namerikawa Japan 36°46N 137°20E 223 A9
Náměšť nad Oslavou Czechia 49°12N 16°10E 181 B9
Námestovo Slovakia 49°24N 19°25E 181 B12
Nametil Mozam. 15°40S 39°21E 269 F4
Namew L. Canada 54°14N 101°56W 297 C8
Namgia India 31°48N 78°40E 243 D8
Namhkam Myanmar 23°50N 97°41E 228 E1
Namhsan Myanmar 22°48N 97°2E 241 D6
Namialo Mozam. 14°55S 39°59E 269 E4
Namib Desert Namibia 22°30S 15°0E 270 B2
Namib-Naukluft ⌂ Namibia 24°40S 15°16E 270 B2
Namibe Angola 15°7S 12°11E 265 F2
Namibe □ Angola 16°35S 12°30E 265 F2
Namibe ⌂ Angola 16°35S 12°20E 265 F2
Namibia ■ Africa 22°0S 18°9E 270 B2
Namibia Abyssal Plain Atl. Oc. 30°0S 5°30E 152 J12
Namibwoestyn = Namib Desert Namibia 22°30S 15°0E 270 B2
Namīn Iran 38°25N 48°30E 213 C13
Naminüs = Lubango Angola 14°55S 13°30E 265 E2
Naminüs = Lüderitz Namibia 26°41S 15°8E 270 C2
Namjeju S. Korea 33°14N 126°33E 224 a
Namlan Myanmar 22°15N 97°24E 241 D6
Namlea Indonesia 3°18S 127°5E 231 E7
Namoi → Australia 30°12S 149°30E 283 A9
Namous, O. en → Algeria 31°0N 0°15W 261 B4
Nampa U.S.A. 43°34N 116°34W 304 E5
Nampala Mali 15°20N 5°30W 262 B3
Namp'o N. Korea 38°52N 125°10E 224 C2
Namp'o □ N. Korea 38°52N 125°25E 224 C2
Nampō-Shotō Japan 32°0N 140°0E 221 J10
Nampula Mozam. 15°6S 39°15E 269 F4
Namrole Indonesia 3°46S 126°46E 231 E7
Namsan Park S. Korea 37°32N 126°59E 137 B1
Namse Shankou China 30°0N 82°25E 243 E10
Namsen → Norway 64°28N 11°37E 160 D14
Namslau = Namysłów Poland 51°6N 17°42E 185 G4
Namsos Norway 64°29N 11°30E 160 D14
Namtok Chat Trakan △ Thailand 17°17N 100°40E 236 D3
Namtok Huay Yang △ Thailand 11°35N 99°30E 237 G2
Namtok Mae Surin △ Thailand 18°55N 98°2E 236 C2
Namtok Ngao △ Thailand 9°58N 98°46E 237 H2
Namtok Phlew △ Thailand 12°32N 102°13E 236 F4
Namtok Yong △ Thailand 8°15N 98°45E 237 H2
Namtsy Russia 62°43N 129°37E 215 C13
Namtu Myanmar 23°5N 97°28E 241 D6
Namtumbo Tanzania 10°30S 36°4E 269 E4
Namu Canada 51°52N 127°50W 296 C3
Namuka-i-Lau Fiji 18°53S 178°37W 287 B3
Namukulu Cook Is. 18°57S 169°54W 289 g
Namumea Tuvalu 5°41S 176°9E 277 B14
Namur Belgium 50°27N 4°52E 170 D4
Namur □ Belgium 50°17N 5°0E 170 D4
Namuruputh Kenya 4°34N 35°57E 268 B4
Namutoni Namibia 18°49S 16°55E 270 A2
Namwala Zambia 15°44S 26°30E 269 F2
Namwon Jeju-do, S. Korea 33°16N 126°43E 224 a
Namwon Jeollabuk-do, S. Korea 35°23N 127°23E 224 E3
Namyang N. Korea 42°57N 129°52E 224 A4
Namyangju S. Korea 37°38N 127°12E 224 D3
Namyeong S. Korea 37°32N 126°57E 137 B1
Namyit I. S. China Sea 10°11N 114°22E 230 C4
Namysłów Poland 51°6N 17°42E 185 G4
Nan Thailand 18°48N 100°46E 236 C3
Nan → Thailand 15°42N 100°9E 236 E3
Nan Ling China 25°0N 112°30E 229 E9
Nan Xian China 29°20N 112°22E 229 C9
Nana C.A.R. 5°0N 15°50E 264 A3
Nana Romania 44°17N 26°34E 183 F11
Nana-Barya ⌂ C.A.R. 7°40N 17°29E 264 A3
Nana-Grébizi □ C.A.R. 7°0N 19°0E 264 A3
Nana Kru Liberia 4°55N 8°45W 262 E3
Nana-Mambéré □ C.A.R. 5°30N 15°30E 264 A3
Nanaimo Canada 49°10N 124°0W 296 D4
Nänäkuli U.S.A. 21°24N 158°9W 302 K13
Nanam N. Korea 41°44N 129°40E 224 B4
Nan'an China 24°59N 118°21E 229 E12
Nanango Australia 26°40S 152°0E 281 D5
Nan'ao Guangdong, China 23°28N 117°5E 229 F11
Nanao Japan 37°0N 137°0E 221 F8
Nanao Taiwan 24°28N 121°48E 225 B3
Nanbiancun China 23°4N 113°10E 121 B1
Nanbu China 31°18N 106°3E 228 B6
Nanchang China 28°42N 115°55E 229 C10
Nanchang He → China 39°58N 116°14E 114 B1
Nancheng China 27°33N 116°35E 229 D11
Nanching = Nanjing China 32°2N 118°47E 229 A12
Nanchong China 30°43N 106°2E 228 B6
Nanchuan China 29°9N 107°6E 228 C6
Nanchung = Nanchong China 30°43N 106°2E 228 B6
Nancowry India 7°59N 93°32E 245 L11
Nancy France 48°42N 6°12E 173 D13
Nanda Devi India 30°23N 79°59E 243 D8
Nanda Devi △ India 30°30N 79°50E 243 D8
Nanda Kot India 30°17N 80°5E 243 D9
Nandan = Minamiawaji Japan 34°10N 134°42E 222 C6
Nandan China 24°58N 107°29E 228 E6
Nandang China 23°6N 113°12E 121 B2
Nanded India 19°10N 77°20E 244 E3
Nandewar Ra. Australia 30°15S 150°35E 281 E5
Nandgaon India 20°19N 74°39E 244 D2
Nandi = Nadi Fiji 17°42S 177°20E 287 A1
Nandi Zimbabwe 20°58S 31°44E 269 G3
Nandi □ Kenya 0°10N 35°10E 268 B4
Nandigama India 16°47N 80°18E 244 F5
Nandigram India 22°1N 87°58E 243 H12
Nandikotkur India 15°52N 78°18E 245 G4
Nandura India 20°52N 76°25E 244 D3
Nandurbar India 21°20N 74°15E 244 D2
Nandyal India 15°30N 78°30E 245 G4
Nanfeng Guangdong, China 23°45N 111°47E 229 F8
Nanfeng Jiangxi, China 27°12N 116°28E 229 D11
Nang Rong Thailand 14°38N 102°48E 236 E4
Nanga-Eboko Cameroon 4°41N 12°22E 263 E7
Nanga Parbat Pakistan 35°10N 74°35E 243 B6
Nangade Mozam. 11°5S 39°36E 269 E4
Nangal Dewat India 28°33N 77°5E 120 B1
Nangalao I. Phil. 11°26N 120°10E 233 F3
Nangamau Indonesia 0°6S 111°55E 235 C4
Nangamentebah Indonesia 0°33N 112°46E 235 B4
Nangapinoh Indonesia 0°20S 111°44E 235 C4
Nangar △ Australia 33°23S 148°3E 283 B8
Nangarhār □ Afghan. 34°20N 70°0E 240 B3
Nangatayap Indonesia 1°32S 110°34E 235 C4
Nangbéto, L. de Togo 7°26N 1°25E 263 D5
Nangeya Mts. Uganda 3°30N 33°30E 268 B3
Nangis France 48°33N 3°1E 173 D10
Nangnim-sanmaek N. Korea 40°13N 126°51E 224 B3
Nangong China 37°23N 115°22E 226 F8
Nangtud, Mt. Phil. 11°17N 122°11E 233 F4
Nanguneri India 8°29N 77°40E 245 K3
Nangwarry Australia 37°33S 140°48E 282 D4
Nanhua Yunnan, China 25°13N 101°21E 228 E3
Nanhua Taiwan 23°2N 120°28E 225 C2
Nanhuang China 36°58N 121°48E 227 F11
Nanhui China 31°5N 121°44E 229 B13
Nanhunan Shan Taiwan 24°21N 121°26E 225 B3
Nanisivik Canada 73°2N 84°33W 295 C15
Naniwa Japan 34°39N 135°29E 133 B1
Nanjangud India 12°6N 76°43E 245 H3
Nanji Shan China 27°27N 121°4E 229 D13
Nanjian China 25°2N 100°25E 228 E3
Nanjiang China 32°28N 106°51E 228 A6
Nanjing Fujian, China 24°25N 117°20E 229 E11
Nanjing Jiangsu, China 32°2N 118°47E 229 A12
Nanjirinji Tanzania 9°41S 39°5E 269 D4
Nankana Sahib Pakistan 31°27N 73°38E 242 D5
Nankang Jiangxi, China 25°40N 114°45E 229 E10
Nankang Taiwan 25°3N 121°35E 225 A3
Nanking = Nanjing China 32°2N 118°47E 229 A12
Nankoku Japan 33°39N 133°44E 222 D5
Nanlang China 22°30N 113°32E 219 a
Nanliao Taiwan 24°50N 120°55E 225 B2
Nanling China 30°55N 118°20E 229 B12
Nannial India 19°4N 79°38E 244 E4
Nanning China 22°48N 108°20E 228 F7
Nannup Australia 33°59S 115°48E 279 F2
Nanole India 19°0N 72°55E 130 A2
Nanortalik Greenland 60°10N 45°17W 154 E6
Nanpan Jiang → China 25°10N 106°5E 228 E6
Nanpara India 27°52N 81°33E 243 F9
Nanping Fujian, China 26°38N 118°10E 229 D12
Nanping Henan, China 29°55N 112°3E 229 C9
Nanpu Bridge China 31°12N 121°30E 138 B2
Nanri Dao China 25°15N 119°25E 229 E12
Nansang Myanmar 20°53N 97°43E 241 E6
Nansei-Shotō = Ryūkyū-Rettō Japan 26°0N 126°0E 221 M3
Nansen Basin Arctic 84°0N 50°0E 150 A10
Nansen Land Greenland 83°0N 43°0W 154 A6
Nansen Sd. Canada 81°0N 91°0W 295 A13
Nansha China 22°45N 113°34E 219 a
Nansha Port China 22°40N 113°40E 219 a
Nanshan China 18°19N 109°10E 229 a
Nanshan I. S. China Sea 10°45N 115°49E 230 B5
Nanshi China 31°12N 121°29E 138 B1
Nansio Tanzania 2°3S 33°4E 268 C3
Nant France 44°1N 3°18E 174 D7
Nantan Japan 35°6N 135°28E 223 B7
Nantawarrinna ☼ Australia 30°49S 138°58E 281 B2
Nanterre France 48°53N 2°12E 134 A2
Nantes France 47°12N 1°33W 172 E5
Nantiat France 46°1N 1°11E 174 B5
Nanticoke U.S.A. 41°12N 76°0W 313 E8
Nanton Canada 50°21N 113°46W 296 C6
Nanton Pt. Antigua & B. 17°0N 61°45W 322 b
Nantong China 32°1N 120°52E 229 A13
Nantou China 22°32N 113°55E 219 a
Nant'ou Taiwan 23°55N 120°41E 225 C2
Nant'ou □ Taiwan 23°50N 121°0E 225 C3
Nantua France 46°10N 5°35E 173 F12
Nantucket U.S.A. 41°17N 70°6W 309 E18
Nantucket I. U.S.A. 41°16N 70°5W 309 E18
Nantulo Mozam. 12°32S 38°45E 269 E4
Nantung = Nantong China 32°1N 120°52E 229 A13
Nantwich U.K. 53°4N 2°31W 168 D5
Nanty Glo U.S.A. 40°28N 78°50W 312 F6
Nantzu Taiwan 22°44N 120°19E 225 D2
Nanuku Passage Fiji 16°45S 179°15W 287 A3
Nanumanga Pac. Oc. 6°18S 176°20E 277 B14
Nanuque Brazil 17°50S 40°21W 333 E3
Nanusa, Kepulauan Indonesia 4°45N 127°1E 231 D7
Nanutarra Roadhouse Australia 22°32S 115°30E 278 D2
Nanwan Taiwan 21°57N 120°46E 225 E2
Nanxi China 28°54N 104°59E 228 C5
Nanxiong China 25°6N 114°15E 229 E10
Nanyang China 33°11N 112°30E 226 H7
Nanyi Hu China 31°5N 119°0E 229 B12
Nanyuan China 39°47N 116°24E 226 E9
Nanyuki Kenya 0°2N 37°4E 268 B4
Nanzhang China 31°45N 111°50E 229 B8
Nanzhao China 33°30N 112°20E 226 H7
Nanzi = Nantzu Taiwan 22°44N 120°19E 225 D2
Nao, C. de la Spain 38°44N 0°14E 197 G5
Naococane, L. Canada 52°50N 70°45W 299 B5
Naogaon Bangla. 24°52N 88°52E 241 C2
Naoné Vanuatu 15°0S 168°8E 287 E6
Naoussa Cyclades, Greece 37°7N 25°14E 205 D7
Naoussa Imathia, Greece 40°42N 22°9E 202 F6
Naozhou Dao China 20°55N 110°20E 229 G8
Napa U.S.A. 38°18N 122°17W 306 G4
Napa → U.S.A. 38°10N 122°19W 306 G4
Napaimiut U.S.A. 61°33N 158°42W 303 F8
Napakiak U.S.A. 60°42N 161°57W 303 F7
Näpali Coast U.S.A. 22°11N 159°39W 302 A2
Napanee Canada 44°15N 77°0W 312 B8
Napanoch U.S.A. 41°44N 74°22W 313 E10
Napaskiak U.S.A. 60°43N 161°55W 303 F7
Nape Laos 18°18N 105°6E 236 C5
Nape Pass = Keo Neua, Deo Vietnam 18°23N 105°10E 236 C5
Naperville U.S.A. 41°46N 88°9W 311 C8
Napier N.Z. 39°30S 176°56E 284 F5
Napier Broome B. Australia 14°2S 126°37E 278 B4
Napier Mole Pakistan 24°49N 66°58E 123 B1
Napier Pen. Australia 12°4S 135°43E 280 A2
Napierville Canada 45°11N 73°25W 313 A11
Napili-Honokowai U.S.A. 20°58N 156°39W 302 C5
Naples = Nápoli Italy 40°50N 14°15E 201 B7
Naples U.S.A. 26°8N 81°48W 317 J8
Naples Park U.S.A. 26°17N 81°46W 317 J8
Napo China 23°22N 105°50E 228 F5
Napo □ Ecuador 0°30S 77°0W 328 D2
Napo → Peru 3°20S 72°40W 328 D3
Napoleon N. Dak., U.S.A. 46°30N 99°46W 308 B4
Napoleon Ohio, U.S.A. 41°23N 84°8W 311 C12
Napoleon's Tomb St. Helena 15°56S 5°42W 153 h
Nápoli Italy 40°50N 14°15E 201 B7
Nápoli, G. di Italy 40°43N 14°10E 201 B7
Nápoli Capodichino ✈ (NAP) Italy 40°53N 14°16E 201 B7
Napopo Dem. Rep. of the Congo 4°15N 28°0E 268 B2
Nappanee U.S.A. 41°27N 86°0W 311 C11
Napperby Australia 33°9S 138°7E 282 B3
Naqadeh Iran 36°57N 45°23E 213 D11
Naqb, Ra's an Jordan 29°48N 35°44E 251 J6
Naqqāsh Iran 35°40N 49°6E 247 C6
När Sweden 57°15N 18°35E 163 G10
Nara Japan 34°40N 135°49E 223 C7
Nara Mali 15°10N 7°20W 262 B3
Nara □ Japan 34°30N 136°0E 223 C8
Nara Canal Pakistan 24°30N 69°20E 242 G3
Nara Visa U.S.A. 35°37N 103°6W 305 J12
Naracoorte Australia 36°58S 140°45E 282 D4
Naradhan Australia 33°34S 146°17E 283 B7
Naraina India 28°36N 77°8E 120 B1
Naraini India 25°11N 80°29E 243 G9
Naranjos Mexico 21°21N 97°41W 319 C5
Narasannapeta India 18°25N 84°3E 244 E7
Narasapur India 16°26N 81°40E 245 F5
Narasaraopet India 16°14N 80°4E 245 F5
Narathiwat Thailand 6°30N 101°48E 237 J3
Narayanapatnam India 18°53N 83°10E 244 E6
Narayangadh = Bharatpur Nepal 27°34N 84°10E 243 F11
Narayanganj Bangla. 23°40N 90°33E 241 D3
Narayanpet India 16°45N 77°30E 244 F3
Narbada = Narmada → India 21°38N 72°36E 242 J5
Narberth U.K. 51°47N 4°44W 169 F3
Narbonne France 43°11N 3°0E 174 E7
Narborough, I. = Fernandina, I. Ecuador 0°25S 91°30W 330 a
Narbuvoll Norway 62°21N 11°27E 164 B8
Narcea → Spain 43°33N 6°44W 194 B4
Narcondam I. India 13°20N 94°16E 245 H12
Nardīn Iran 37°3N 55°59E 247 B7
Nardò Italy 40°11N 18°2E 201 B11
Narembeen Australia 32°7S 118°24E 279 F2
Nares Abyssal Plain Atl. Oc. 22°0N 67°0W 152 D5
Nares Str. Arctic 80°0N 70°0W 154 B3
Naretha Australia 31°0S 124°45E 279 F3
Narew → Poland 52°26N 20°41E 185 F7
Nari → Pakistan 28°0N 67°40E 242 F2
Nariman Pt. Mumbai, India 130 c1
Narin Afghan. 36°5N 69°0E 240 A3
Narindra, Helodranon' i Madag. 14°55S 47°30E 272 A2
Narino □ Colombia 1°30N 78°0W 328 C2
Narita Japan 35°47N 140°19E 223 B12
Narita, Tōkyō ✈ (NRT) Japan 35°45N 140°25E 223 B12
Nariva → Trin. & Tob. 10°24N 61°4W 323 t
Nariva Swamp Trin. & Tob. 10°26N 61°4W 323 t
Närke Sweden 59°10N 15°0E 162 E8
Narmada → India 21°38N 72°36E 242 J5
Narmada Canal India 22°20N 73°45E 244 C1
Nārmak Iran 35°42N 51°28E 141 A2
Narman Turkey 40°26N 41°57E 213 B9
Narnaul India 28°5N 76°11E 242 E7
Narni Italy 42°30N 12°30E 199 F9
Naro Ghana 10°22N 2°27W 262 C4
Naro Fominsk Russia 55°23N 36°43E 188 E9
Narochanski △ Belarus 54°55N 26°50E 188 E4
Narodnaya Russia 65°5N 59°58E 186 A10
Narodowy, Stadion Warsaw, Poland 143 b3

Narok *Kenya* 1°55S 35°52E **268** C4
Narok ☐ *Kenya* 1°15S 35°40E **268** C4
Narón *Spain* 43°32N 8°9W **194** B2
Narooma *Australia* 36°14S 150°4E **283** D9
Narowal *Pakistan* 32°6N 74°52E **242** C6
Narrabri *Australia* 30°19S 149°46E **281** E4
Narran ➜ *Australia* 28°37S 148°12E **281** D4
Narrandera *Australia* 34°42S 146°31E **283** C7
Narrogin *Australia* 32°58S 117°14E **279** F2
Narromine *Australia* 32°12S 148°12E **283** B8
Narrow Hills ⌓ *Canada* 54°0N 104°37W **297** C8
Narrows, The
St. Kitts & Nevis 17°12N 62°40W **322** d
Narsampet *India* 17°57N 79°58E **244** F4
Narsaq *Greenland* 60°57N 46°4W **154** E6
Narsimhapur *India* 22°54N 79°14E **243** H8
Narsingdi *Bangla.* 23°55N 90°43E **241** D3
Narsinghgarh *India* 23°45N 76°40E **242** H7
Narsinghpur *India* 20°28N 85°5E **244** D7
Narsipatnam *India* 17°40N 82°37E **244** F6
Nartes, L. e *Albania* 40°32N 19°25E **202** F3
Nartkala *Russia* 43°33N 43°51E **191** J6
Naruo *Japan* 34°43N 135°22E **133** A1
Narutō = Sanmu *Kantō, Japan* 34°11N 134°37E **222** C6
Narutō = Sanmu *Shikoku, Japan* 35°36N 140°25E **223** B12
Naruto-Kaikyō *Japan* 34°14N 134°39E **222** C6
Narva *Estonia* 59°23N 28°12E **188** C5
Narva ➜ *Russia* 59°27N 28°2E **188** C4
Narva Bay = Narva Laht
Estonia 59°35N 27°35E **161** G22
Narva Laht *Estonia* 59°35N 27°35E **161** G22
Narvacan *Phil.* 17°25N 120°28E **232** C3
Narvik *Norway* 68°28N 17°26E **160** B17
Narvskoye Vdkhr. *Russia* 59°18N 28°14E **188** C5
Narwana *India* 29°39N 76°6E **242** E7
Narwiański △ *Poland* 52°5N 22°53E **185** F9
Narwinbi ◎ *Australia* 16°7S 136°17E **280** B2
Naryan-Mar *Russia* 67°42N 53°12E **186** A9
Narym *Russia* 59°0N 81°30E **214** D9
Naryn *Kyrgyzstan* 41°26N 75°58E **217** D9
Naryn ☐ *Kyrgyzstan* 41°26N 75°58E **217** D9
Naryn ➜ *Uzbekistan* 40°52N 71°36E **217** D8
Naryn Qum *Kazakhstan* 47°30N 49°0E **191** G9
Nás, An = Naas *Ireland* 53°12N 6°40W **166** C5
Nasa *Norway* 66°29N 15°23E **160** C16
Nasarawa *Nigeria* 8°32N 7°41E **263** D6
Nasarawa ☐ *Nigeria* 8°30N 8°20E **263** D6
Nasau *Fiji* 17°19S 179°27E **287** A2
Năsăud *Romania* 47°19N 24°29E **183** C9
Nasawa *Vanuatu* 15°12S 168°9E **287** E6
Naşb, W. ➜ *Egypt* 28°29N 34°31E **251** K5
Näsby *Sweden* 59°25N 18°5E **139** A2
Näsbypark *Sweden* 59°25N 18°5E **139** A2
Nasca *Peru* 14°50S 74°57W **330** C3
Nasca Ridge *Pac. Oc.* 20°0S 80°0W **289** K19
Nascentes do Rio Parnaíba △
Brazil 10°0S 47°0W **332** C2
Naseby *N.Z.* 45°1S 170°10E **285** F5
Naselle *U.S.A.* 46°22N 123°49W **306** D3
Naser, Buheirat en *Egypt* 23°0N 32°30E **256** C3
Nashik = Nasik *India* 19°58N 73°50E **244** E1
Nashua *Iowa, U.S.A.* 42°57N 92°32W **310** B4
Nashua *Mont., U.S.A.* 48°8N 106°22W **304** B10
Nashua *N.H., U.S.A.* 42°45N 71°28W **313** D13
Nashville *Ark., U.S.A.* 33°57N 93°51W **314** E8
Nashville *Ga., U.S.A.* 31°12N 83°15W **316** D6
Nashville *Ill., U.S.A.* 38°21N 89°23W **310** F7
Nashville *Ind., U.S.A.* 39°12N 86°15W **311** E10
Nashville *Mich., U.S.A.* 42°36N 85°5W **311** B11
Nashville *Tenn., U.S.A.* 36°10N 86°47W **315** C11
Našice *Croatia* 45°32N 18°4E **182** E3
Nasielsk *Poland* 52°35N 20°50E **185** F7
Nasik *India* 19°58N 73°50E **244** E1
Nasinu *Fiji* 18°4S 178°30E **287** A2
Nasipit *Phil.* 8°57N 125°19E **233** G5
Nasir *South Sudan* 8°36N 33°4E **257** F3
Nasirabad = Mymensingh
Bangla. 24°45N 90°24E **241** C3
Nasirabad *India* 26°15N 74°45E **242** F6
Nasirabad *Pakistan* 28°23N 68°24E **242** E3
Nasiri = Ahvāz *Iran* 31°20N 48°40E **247** D6
Nasiriyah = An Nāşiriyah
Iraq 31°0N 46°15E **246** D5
Naskaupi ➜ *Canada* 53°47N 60°51W **299** B7
Naso *Italy* 38°7N 14°47E **201** D7
Naso Pt. *Phil.* 10°25N 121°57E **233** F3
Naşrābād *Iran* 34°8N 51°26E **247** C6
Naşriān-e Pā'īn *Iran* 32°52N 46°52E **246** C5
Nass ➜ *Canada* 55°0N 129°40W **296** C3
Nassau *The Bahamas* 25°5N 77°20W **153** b
Nassau *N.Y., U.S.A.* 42°31N 73°37W **313** D11
Nassau, B. *Chile* 55°20S 68°0W **336** E3
Nassau Lynden Pindling Int. ✈
(NAS) *The Bahamas* 25°3N 77°28W **153** b
Nasser, L. = Naser, Buheirat en
Egypt 23°0N 32°30E **256** C3
Nasser City = Kôm Ombo
Egypt 24°25N 32°52E **256** C3
Nassian *Côte d'Ivoire* 8°28N 3°28W **262** D4
Nässjö *Sweden* 57°39N 14°42E **163** G8
Nastapoka ➜ *Canada* 56°55N 76°33W **298** A4
Nastapoka, Is. *Canada* 56°55N 76°50W **298** A4
Nasugbu *Phil.* 14°5N 120°38E **232** D3
Näsum *Sweden* 56°10N 14°29E **163** H8
Nasushiobara *Japan* 36°58N 140°3E **221** F10
Näsviken *Sweden* 61°46N 16°52E **162** C10
Nat Ma Taung △
Myanmar 21°30N 93°25E **241** E4
Nata *Botswana* 20°12S 26°12E **270** B4
Nata ➜ *Botswana* 20°14S 26°10E **270** B4
Natagaima *Colombia* 3°37N 75°6W **328** C2
Natal *Brazil* 5°47S 35°13W **332** C4
Natal *Indonesia* 0°35N 99°7E **234** B1
Natal Drakensberg = uKhahlamba Drakensberg ⌓
S. Africa 29°27S 29°30E **271** C4
Natalinci *Serbia* 44°15N 20°49E **182** F5
Naţanz *Iran* 33°30N 51°55E **247** C6
Natashquan *Canada* 50°14N 61°46W **299** B7
Natashquan ➜ *Canada* 50°7N 61°50W **299** B7
Natchez *U.S.A.* 31°34N 91°24W **314** F9
Natchitoches *U.S.A.* 31°46N 93°5W **314** F8
Natewa B. *Fiji* 16°35S 179°40E **287** A2
Nathalia *Australia* 36°1S 145°13E **283** D6
Nathan Philips Square *Toronto, Canada* **141** b2
Nathdwara *India* 24°55N 73°50E **242** G5
Nathu La *Asia* 27°24N 88°49E **241** B2
Nati, Pta. *Spain* 40°3N 3°50E **206** A4
Natimuk *Australia* 36°42S 142°0E **282** D5
Nation ➜ *Canada* 55°30N 123°32W **296** B4
National Arboretum
Washington, D.C., U.S.A. 38°54N 76°59W **143** B2
National Art Gallery *Beijing, China* **114** b2
National Atomic Testing Museum
U.S.A. 36°7N 115°9W **124** B2
National Capital District ☐
Papua N. G. 9°25S 147°10E **286** E4
National City *U.S.A.* 32°40N 117°5W **307** N9
National Grand Theatre *Beijing, China* **114** c2
National Maritime Museum
London, U.K. 51°29N 0°0 **125** B3
National September 11 Memorial and Museum *New York, U.S.A.* **132** e1
National University (N.U.S.)
Singapore 1°19N 103°46E **138** B2
National Zoological Park
Washington, D.C., U.S.A. 38°55N 77°4W **143** B2
Nationals Park *U.S.A.* 38°53N 77°1W **143** B2
Natitingou *Benin* 10°20N 1°26E **263** C5
Natividad, I. *Mexico* 27°52N 115°11W **318** B1
Natividade *Brazil* 11°43S 47°47W **333** D2
Nativity, Basilica of
West Bank 31°42N 35°12E **123** B2
Natkyizin *Myanmar* 14°57N 97°59E **236** E1
Natmauk *Myanmar* 20°20N 95°24E **241** E5
Natogyi *Myanmar* 21°25N 95°39E **241** E5
Natolin *Poland* 52°8N 21°4E **143** C2
Natonin *Phil.* 17°6N 121°18E **232** C3
Nator *Bangla.* 24°21N 89°5E **241** C2
Natron, L. *Tanzania* 2°20S 36°0E **268** C4
Natrona Heights *U.S.A.* 40°37N 79°44W **312** F5
Natrûn, W. el ➜ *Egypt* 30°25N 30°13E **256** H7
Nattai △ *Australia* 34°12S 150°22E **283** C9
Nättraby *Sweden* 56°13N 15°31E **163** H9
Natuashish *Canada* 55°55N 61°8W **299** A7
Natukanaoka Pan
Namibia 18°40S 15°45E **270** A2
Natuna Besar, Kepulauan
Indonesia 4°0N 108°15E **235** B3
Natuna Is. = Natuna Besar, Kepulauan *Indonesia* 4°0N 108°15E **235** B3
Natuna Selatan, Kepulauan
Indonesia 2°45N 109°0E **235** B3
Natural Bridge *U.S.A.* 44°5N 75°30W **313** B9
Natural Bridges ⌓ *U.S.A.* 37°36N 110°0W **305** H9
Naturaliste, C. *Tas., Australia* 40°50S 148°15E **281** G4
Naturaliste, C. *W. Austral., Australia* 33°32S 115°0E **279** F2
Naturaliste Plateau *Ind. Oc.* 34°0S 112°0E **276** G1
Nau Qala *Afghan.* 34°5N 68°5E **242** B3
Naucalpan de Juárez
Mexico 19°28N 99°14W **128** B1
Naucelle *France* 44°13N 2°20E **174** D6
Nauders *Austria* 46°54N 10°30E **180** E3
Nauen *Germany* 52°36N 12°52E **178** C8
Naugard = Nowogard
Poland 53°41N 15°10E **184** E2
Naugatuck *U.S.A.* 41°30N 73°3W **313** E11
Naujaat = Repulse Bay
Canada 66°30N 86°30W **295** D14
Naujan *Phil.* 13°20N 121°18E **232** E3
Naujan Lake △ *Phil.* 13°9N 121°20E **232** E3
Naujoji Akmenė *Lithuania* 56°19N 22°54E **184** B9
Naulila *Angola* 17°13S 14°39E **265** F2
Naumburg *Germany* 51°9N 11°47E **178** D7
Naumburg am Queis = Nowogrodziec *Poland* 51°12N 15°24E **185** G2
Naupada *Andhra Pradesh, India* 18°34N 84°18E **244** E7
Naupada *Maharashtra, India* 19°13N 72°50E **130** A2
Nā'ūr *Jordan* 31°53N 35°50E **251** D4
Nauru ■ *Pac. Oc.* 1°0S 166°0E **288** H8
Naushahra = Nowshera
Pakistan 34°0N 72°0E **240** B4
Naushahro *Pakistan* 26°50N 68°7E **242** F3
Naushon I. *U.S.A.* 41°29N 70°45W **313** E14
Nausori *Fiji* 18°2S 178°32E **287** B2
Naustdal *Norway* 61°31N 5°43E **164** C2
Nauta *Peru* 4°31S 73°35W **328** D3
Nautanwa *India* 27°20N 83°25E **243** F10
Naute ⌓ *Namibia* 26°55S 17°57E **270** C2
Nautla *Mexico* 20°13N 96°47W **319** C5
Nauvoo *U.S.A.* 40°33N 91°23W **310** D5
Nava *Coahuila, Mexico* 28°25N 100°45W **318** B4
Nava *Spain* 43°21N 5°31W **194** B5
Nava del Rey *Spain* 41°22N 5°6W **194** D5
Navadwip *India* 23°34N 88°20E **243** H13
Navahermosa *Spain* 39°41N 4°28W **195** F6
Navahrudak *Belarus* 53°40N 25°50E **177** B13
Navai *Fiji* 17°36S 177°57E **287** A1
Navajo Res. *U.S.A.* 36°48N 107°36W **305** H10
Naval *Phil.* 11°34N 124°23E **233** F5
Navalcarnero *Spain* 40°17N 4°5W **194** E6
Navalgund *India* 15°34N 75°22E **245** G2
Navalmoral de la Mata
Spain 39°52N 5°33W **194** F5
Navalvillar de Pela *Spain* 39°9N 5°24W **195** F5
Navan *Ireland* 53°39N 6°41W **166** C5
Navanagar = Jamnagar
India 22°30N 70°6E **242** H4
Navapolatsk *Belarus* 55°32N 28°37E **188** E5
Navarin, Mys *Russia* 62°15N 179°5E **215** C18
Navarino, I. *Chile* 55°0S 67°40W **336** E3
Navarra ☐ *Spain* 42°40N 1°40W **196** C3
Navarre *Fla., U.S.A.* 30°24N 86°52W **317** E3
Navarre *Ohio, U.S.A.* 40°43N 81°31W **312** F3
Navarro ➜ *U.S.A.* 39°11N 123°45W **306** G3
Navas de San Juan *Spain* 38°30N 3°19W **195** G7
Navasota *U.S.A.* 30°23N 96°5W **314** F6
Navassa I. *W. Indies* 18°30N 75°0W **321** C5
Nävekvarn *Sweden* 58°38N 16°49E **163** F10
Naver ➜ *U.K.* 58°32N 4°14W **167** C4
Navet *Trin. & Tob.* 10°21N 61°10W **323** t
Navet ➜ *Trin. & Tob.* 10°24N 61°3W **323** t
Navet Res. *Trin. & Tob.* 10°24N 61°15W **323** t
Navi Mumbai *India* 19°5N 73°0E **130** A2
Navia *Spain* 43°35N 6°42W **194** B4
Navia ➜ *Spain* 43°15N 6°50W **194** B4
Navia de Suarna = A Pobre
Spain 42°58N 7°3W **194** C3
Navibandar *India* 21°26N 69°48E **242** J3
Navidad *Chile* 33°57S 71°50W **334** C1
Navidad Bank *W. Indies* 20°0N 68°58W **321** B6
Navíglio di Pavia *Italy* 45°24N 9°9E **128** B1
Naviglio Grande *Italy* 45°25N 9°5E **128** B1
Navirai *Brazil* 23°8S 54°13W **335** A5
Naviti *Fiji* 17°7S 177°15E **287** A1
Navlakhi *India* 22°58N 70°28E **242** H4
Navlya *Russia* 52°53N 34°30E **189** F8
Năvodari *Romania* 44°19N 28°36E **183** F14
Navoiy *Uzbekistan* 40°9N 65°22E **216** D7
Navojoa *Mexico* 27°6N 109°26W **318** B3
Navolato *Mexico* 24°47N 107°42W **318** C3
Navona, Piazza *Rome, Italy* **136** b2
Navotas *Phil.* 14°39N 120°56E **127** B1
Navrongo *Ghana* 10°51N 1°3W **263** C4
Navsari *India* 20°57N 72°59E **244** D1
Navua *Fiji* 18°12S 178°11E **287** B2
Navy Pier *Chicago, U.S.A.* **119** b3
Nawa Kot *Pakistan* 28°21N 71°24E **242** E4
Nawab Khan *Pakistan* 30°17N 69°12E **242** D3
Nawabganj *Bangla.* 24°35N 88°14E **241** C2
Nawabganj *Ut. P., India* 26°56N 81°14E **243** F9
Nawabganj *Ut. P., India* 28°32N 79°40E **243** E8
Nawabshah *Pakistan* 26°15N 68°25E **242** F3
Nawada *India* 24°50N 85°33E **243** G11
Nāwah *Afghan.* 32°19N 67°53E **240** B2
Nawakot *Nepal* 27°55N 85°10E **243** F11
Nawalgarh *India* 27°50N 75°15E **242** F6
Nawanshahr *India* 32°33N 74°48E **243** C6
Nawapara *India* 20°46N 82°33E **244** D6
Nawar, Dasht-i- *Afghan.* 33°52N 68°0E **242** C3
Nawāşīf, Ḩarrat *Si. Arabia* 21°20N 42°10E **248** B3
Nawi *Sudan* 18°32N 30°50E **256** D3
Nawng Hpa *Myanmar* 22°30N 98°30E **241** D7
Nawoiy = Navoiy
Uzbekistan 40°9N 65°22E **216** D7
Nawş, Ra's *Oman* 17°15N 55°16E **249** C6
Naxçıvan *Azerbaijan* 39°12N 45°15E **213** C11
Naxçıvan ☐ *Azerbaijan* 39°25N 45°26E **213** C11
Naxos *Greece* 37°8N 25°25E **205** D7
Naxxar *Malta* 35°55N 14°27E **206** F7
Nay *France* 43°10N 0°18W **174** E3
Nay, Mui *Vietnam* 12°54N 109°26E **236** F7
Nāy Band *Būshehr, Iran* 27°20N 52°40E **247** E7
Nāy Band *Khorāsān, Iran* 32°20N 57°34E **247** C8
Nay Pyi Taw = Naypyidaw
Myanmar 19°44N 96°12E **241** F6
Naya ➜ *Colombia* 3°13N 77°22W **328** C2
Nayagarh *India* 20°8N 85°6E **244** D7
Nayakhan *Russia* 61°56N 159°0E **215** C16
Nayarit ☐ *Mexico* 22°0N 105°0W **318** C4
Nayé *Senegal* 14°28N 12°12W **262** C2
Nayong *China* 26°50N 105°20E **228** D5
Nayoro *Japan* 44°21N 142°28E **220** B11
Naypyidaw *Myanmar* 19°44N 96°12E **241** F6
Nayudupeta *India* 13°54N 79°54E **245** H4
Nayyāl, W. ➜ *Si. Arabia* 28°35N 39°4E **246** D3
Nazal Hikmat Beg *Iraq* 33°23N 44°25E **113** A2
Nazar Kahrīzī *Iran* 37°20N 46°45E **213** D12
Nazaré *Bahia, Brazil* 13°2S 39°0W **333** D4
Nazaré *Pará, Brazil* 6°25S 52°29W **331** B7
Nazaré *Tocantins, Brazil* 6°23S 47°40W **332** C2
Nazaré *Portugal* 39°36N 9°4W **195** F1
Nazareth = Naẓerat *Israel* 32°42N 35°17E **250** F6
Nazareth *U.S.A.* 40°44N 75°19W **313** F9
Nazarovo *Russia* 57°2N 90°40E **215** D10
Nazas *Mexico* 25°14N 104°8W **318** B4
Nazas ➜ *Mexico* 25°12N 104°12W **318** B4
Nazca = Nasca *Peru* 14°50S 74°57W **330** C3
Naze, The *U.K.* 51°53N 1°18E **169** F9
Naẓerat *Israel* 32°42N 35°17E **250** F6
Nāzīk *Iran* 39°1N 45°4E **213** C11
Nazilli *Turkey* 37°55N 28°15E **205** D10
Nazimabad *Pakistan* 24°54N 67°1E **123** A2
Nazinon = Red Volta ➜
Africa 10°34N 0°30W **263** C4
Nazir Hat *Bangla.* 22°35N 91°49E **241** D3
Nazko *Canada* 53°1N 123°37W **296** C4
Nazko ➜ *Canada* 53°7N 123°34W **296** C4
Nazlet el Simmân *Egypt* 29°59N 31°9E **117** B1
Năzlu *Iran* 37°41N 45°0E **213** D11
Nazret *Ethiopia* 8°32N 39°22E **257** F4
Ncama *Eq. Guin.* 1°55N 10°56E **264** B2
Nchanga *Zambia* 12°30S 27°49E **269** E2
Ncheu *Malawi* 14°50S 34°47E **269** E3
Ncue *Eq. Guin.* 2°1N 10°28E **264** B2
Ndala *Tanzania* 4°45S 33°15E **268** C3
Ndalatando *Angola* 9°12S 14°48E **265** D2
Ndali *Benin* 9°50N 2°46E **263** D5
Ndareda *Tanzania* 4°12S 35°30E **268** C4
Ndélé *C.A.R.* 8°25N 20°36E **264** A4
Ndendé *Gabon* 2°22S 11°23E **264** C2
Ndiael ⌓ *Senegal* 16°15N 16°0W **262** B1
Ndikinimeki *Cameroon* 4°46N 10°50E **263** E7
Ndim *Cameroon* 5°10N 10°41E **264** A2
Ndindi *Gabon* 3°46S 11°9E **264** C2
N'Dioum *Senegal* 16°31N 14°39W **262** B2
Ndjamena *Chad* 12°10N 15°0E **259** F3
Ndjolé *Gabon* 0°10S 10°45E **264** C2
Ndogo, Lagune *Gabon* 2°35S 10°0E **264** C2
Ndok *Cameroon* 7°57N 14°42E **264** A2
Ndola *Zambia* 13°0S 28°34E **269** E2
Ndomo ⌓ *S. Africa* 26°52S 32°15E **271** C5
Ndoto Mts. *Kenya* 2°0N 37°0E **268** B4
Ndoua, C. *N. Cal.* 22°24S 166°56E **288** d
Ndouba *Congo* 0°9S 14°4E **264** C2
Ndoukou *C.A.R.* 4°33N 20°39E **264** B4
Nduguti *Tanzania* 4°18S 34°41E **268** C3
Nea ➜ *Norway* 63°15N 11°0E **164** A8
Nea Alexandria *Greece* 37°52N 23°46E **112** B2
Nea Alikarnassos *Greece* 35°19N 25°11E **207** E6
Nea Anchialos *Greece* 39°16N 22°49E **204** B4
Nea Artaki *Greece* 38°31N 23°38E **204** C5
Nea Epidavros *Greece* 37°40N 23°7E **204** D5
Nea Flippias *Greece* 39°12N 20°53E **204** B2
Nea Ionia *Athina, Greece* 38°2N 23°45E **112** A2
Nea Ionia *Magnisia, Greece* 39°21N 22°56E **204** B4
Nea Kalikratia *Greece* 40°21N 23°3E **202** F7
Nea Liosia *Greece* 38°3N 23°43E **112** A2
Nea Makri *Greece* 38°5N 23°59E **204** C5
Nea Moudania *Greece* 40°15N 23°17E **202** F7
Nea Peramos *Attiki, Greece* 38°0N 23°26E **204** C5
Nea Peramos *Kavala, Greece* 40°50N 24°18E **203** F8
Nea Samsounda *Greece* 39°5N 20°45E **207** A2
Nea Smirni *Greece* 37°54N 23°43E **112** B2
Nea Visa *Greece* 41°34N 26°33E **203** E10
Nea Zichni *Greece* 41°2N 23°49E **202** E7
Neagari = Nomi *Japan* 36°26N 136°25E **223** A8
Neagh, Lough *U.K.* 54°37N 6°25W **166** B5
Neah Bay *U.S.A.* 48°22N 124°37W **306** B2
Neale, L. *Australia* 24°15S 130°0E **278** D5
Neales ➜ *Australia* 28°8S 136°47E **281** D2
Neamati *India* 26°50N 94°20E **241** B5
Neamţ ☐ *Romania* 47°0N 26°20E **183** C11
Neapoli *Athens, Greece* **112** a3
Neapoli *Kozani, Greece* 40°20N 21°24E **202** F5
Neapoli *Kriti, Greece* 35°15N 25°37E **207** E6
Neapoli *Lakonia, Greece* 36°27N 23°8E **204** E5
Near Is. *U.S.A.* 52°30N 174°0E **303** K1
Near North *Chicago, U.S.A.* **119** b1
Neath *U.K.* 51°39N 3°48W **169** F4
Neath Port Talbot ☐ *U.K.* 51°42N 3°45W **169** F4
Nebbi *Uganda* 2°28N 31°6E **268** B3
Nebbou *Burkina Faso* 11°9N 1°51W **263** C4
Nebelat el Hagana *Sudan* 13°13N 29°2E **257** E2
Nebine Cr. ➜ *Australia* 29°27S 146°56E **281** D4
Nebitdag = Balkanabat
Turkmenistan 39°30N 54°22E **247** B7
Nebka *Algeria* 27°28N 3°12W **260** C4
Neblina, Pico da *Brazil* 0°48N 66°0W **328** C4
Nebo *Australia* 21°42S 148°42E **280** C4
Nebolchy *Russia* 59°8N 33°18E **188** C7
Nebraska ☐ *U.S.A.* 41°30N 99°30W **308** E4
Nebraska City *U.S.A.* 40°41N 95°52W **308** E6
Nébrodi, Monti *Italy* 37°54N 14°35E **201** E7
Nebušice *Czechia* 50°6N 14°19E **135** B1
Necedah *U.S.A.* 44°2N 90°4W **308** C8
Nechako ➜ *Canada* 53°55N 122°42W **296** C4
Neches ➜ *U.S.A.* 29°58N 93°51W **314** G8
Nechisar △ *Ethiopia* 5°58N 37°56E **257** F4
Neckar ➜ *Germany* 49°27N 8°29E **179** F4
Neckartal-Odenwald ⌓
Germany 49°30N 9°5E **179** F5
Necker I. *U.S.A.* 23°35N 164°42W **302** G11
Necochea *Argentina* 38°30S 58°50W **334** D4
Nectar Brook *Australia* 32°43S 137°57E **282** B2
Neda *Spain* 43°30N 8°9W **194** B2
Neda ➜ *Greece* 37°25N 21°45E **204** D3
Nedalshytta *Norway* 62°59N 12°3E **164** B9
Nedelino *Bulgaria* 41°27N 25°5E **203** E9
Nedelišće *Croatia* 46°23N 16°22E **199** B13
Nederhorst *Neths.* 52°16N 5°3E **112** B3
Nederland = Netherlands ■
Europe 52°0N 5°30E **170** C5
Nedlitz *Germany* 52°25N 13°3E **115** B1
Nedoboyivtsi *Ukraine* 48°26N 26°21E **183** B11
Nedreberg *Norway* 60°59N 11°41E **164** D8
Nedroma *Algeria* 35°1N 1°45W **261** A4
Nedstrand *Norway* 59°21N 5°49E **164** E2
Nee Soon *Singapore* 1°24N 103°49E **138** A2
Needham *U.S.A.* 42°17N 71°14W **116** B1
Needham Heights *U.S.A.* 42°17N 71°14W **116** B1
Needles *B.C., Canada* 49°53N 118°7W **296** D5
Needles *Calif., U.S.A.* 34°51N 114°37W **307** L12
Needles, The *U.K.* 50°39N 1°35W **169** G6
Needles Pt. *N.Z.* 36°3S 175°25E **284** C4
Neembucú ☐ *Paraguay* 27°0S 58°0W **334** B4
Neemuch = Nimach *India* 24°30N 74°56E **242** G6
Neenah *U.S.A.* 44°11N 88°28W **308** C9
Neepawa *Canada* 50°15N 99°30W **297** C9
Neeses *U.S.A.* 33°33N 81°7W **316** B8
Nefta *Tunisia* 33°53N 7°50E **258** B1
Neftçala *Azerbaijan* 39°19N 49°12E **213** C13
Neftechala = Neftçala
Azerbaijan 39°19N 49°12E **213** C13
Neftegorsk *Krasnodar, Russia* 44°25N 39°45E **191** H4
Neftegorsk *Sakhalin, Russia* 53°1N 142°58E **215** D15
Neftekumsk *Russia* 44°46N 44°50E **191** H7
Nefteyugansk *Russia* 61°5N 72°42E **214** C8
Nefyn *U.K.* 52°56N 4°31W **168** E3
Négala *Mali* 12°52N 8°30W **262** C3
Negapatam = Nagappattinam
India 10°46N 79°51E **245** J4
Negara *Indonesia* 8°22S 114°37E **231** J17
Negaunee *U.S.A.* 46°30N 87°36W **308** B10
Negele *Oromiya, Ethiopia* 5°20N 39°36E **257** F4
Negele *Oromiya, Ethiopia* 7°21N 38°42E **266** C4
Negeri Sembilan ☐
Malaysia 2°45N 102°10E **237** L4
Negev Desert = Hanegev
Israel 30°50N 35°0E **251** H6
Negoiul, Vf. *Romania* 45°38N 24°35E **183** E9
Negombo *Sri Lanka* 7°12N 79°50E **245** L4
Negotin *Serbia* 44°16N 22°37E **202** B6
Negotino *N. Macedonia* 41°29N 22°7E **202** E6
Negra, Peña *Spain* 42°11N 6°30W **194** C4
Negra, Pta. *Mauritania* 22°54N 16°18W **260** D1
Negra, Pta. *Peru* 6°6S 81°10W **330** B1
Negra Pt. *Phil.* 18°40N 120°50E **232** B3
Negra Pt. *Trin. & Tob.* 10°4N 61°23W **323** t
Negrais, C. = Maudin Sun
Myanmar 16°0N 94°30E **241** G5
Nègres, Pte. des *Martinique* 14°35N 61°5W **322** j
Negreşti *Romania* 46°50N 27°30E **183** D12
Negreşti-Oaş *Romania* 47°52N 23°26E **183** C8
Negril *Jamaica* 18°22N 78°20W **320** a
Négrine *Algeria* 34°30N 7°30E **261** B6
Negro ➜ *Argentina* 41°2S 62°47W **336** B4
Negro ➜ *Bolivia* 14°11S 63°7W **331** C5
Negro ➜ *Brazil* 3°0S 60°0W **329** D6
Negro ➜ *Uruguay* 33°24S 58°22W **334** C4
Negro, C. = Tarf, Ras
Morocco 35°40N 5°11W **260** A3
Negro, C. *Venezuela* 11°11N 63°53W **329** a
Negros *Phil.* 9°30N 122°40E **233** G4
Negros Occidental ☐ *Phil.* 10°0N 122°55E **233** F4
Negros Oriental ☐ *Phil.* 9°45N 123°0E **233** G4
Negru Vodă *Romania* 43°47N 28°21E **183** G13
Neguac *Canada* 47°15N 65°5W **299** C6
Nehalem ➜ *U.S.A.* 45°40N 123°56W **306** E3
Nehāvand *Iran* 35°56N 49°31E **247** C6
Nehbandān *Iran* 31°35N 60°5E **247** D9
Nehe *China* 48°29N 124°50E **219** B13
Nehoiu *Romania* 45°24N 26°20E **183** E11
Nei Mongol Zizhiqu ☐
China 42°0N 112°0E **226** D7
Neiafu *Tonga* 18°39S 173°59W **287** P14
Neidenburg = Nidzica
Poland 53°25N 20°28E **185** E7
Neiges, Piton des *Réunion* 21°5S 55°29E **272** f
Neijiang *China* 29°35N 104°55E **228** C5
Neikiang = Neijiang
China 29°35N 104°55E **228** C5
Neilingding Dao *China* 22°25N 113°48E **219** a
Neill I. *India* 11°50N 93°3E **245** J11
Neillsville *U.S.A.* 44°34N 90°36W **308** C8
Neilson, Récif *Pac. Oc.* 27°1S 146°2W **289** f
Neilton *U.S.A.* 47°25N 123°53W **306** C3
Neipu *Taiwan* 22°37N 120°33E **225** D2
Neiqiu *China* 37°15N 114°30E **226** F8
Neisse = Nysa ➜ *Europe* 52°4N 14°46E **178** C10
Neiva *Colombia* 2°56N 75°18W **328** C2
Neiwan *Taiwan* 24°42N 121°10E **225** B3
Neixiang *China* 33°10N 111°52E **226** H6
Nejanilini L. *Canada* 59°33N 97°48W **297** B9
Nejd = Najd *Si. Arabia* 26°30N 42°0E **248** A3
Nejo *Ethiopia* 9°30N 35°28E **257** F4
Nejrab *Afghan.* 34°58N 69°34E **240** B3
Nekā *Iran* 36°39N 53°19E **247** B7
Nekemte *Ethiopia* 9°4N 36°30E **257** F4
Nêkheb *Egypt* 25°10N 32°48E **256** B3
Neksø *Denmark* 55°4N 15°8E **163** J9
Nelamangala *India* 13°6N 77°24E **245** H3
Nelas *Portugal* 40°32N 7°52W **194** E3
Nelaug *Norway* 58°39N 8°40E **164** F5
Nelia *Australia* 20°39S 142°12E **280** C3
Nelidovo *Russia* 56°13N 32°49E **188** D7
Neligh *U.S.A.* 42°8N 98°2W **308** D4
Nelkan *Russia* 57°40N 136°4E **215** D14
Nellikuppam *India* 11°46N 79°43E **245** J4
Nellis Air Force Base ✈ **(LSV)**
U.S.A. 36°14N 115°2W **124** A2
Nellore *India* 14°27N 79°59E **245** G4
Nelson *B.C., Canada* 49°30N 117°20W **296** D5
Nelson *N.Z.* 41°18S 173°16E **285** B8
Nelson *Lancs., U.K.* 53°50N 2°13W **168** D5
Nelson *Ariz., U.S.A.* 35°31N 113°19W **305** J7
Nelson *Nev., U.S.A.* 35°42N 114°49W **307** K12
Nelson ☐ *N.Z.* 41°20S 173°20E **285** B8
Nelson ➜ *Canada* 54°33N 98°2W **297** C9
Nelson, C. *Vic., Australia* 38°26S 141°32E **282** E4
Nelson, C. *Papua N. G.* 9°0S 149°20E **286** E5
Nelson, Estrecho *Chile* 51°30S 75°0W **336** D2
Nelson Bay *Australia* 32°43S 152°9E **283** B10
Nelson Forks *Canada* 59°30N 124°0W **296** B4
Nelson House *Canada* 55°47N 98°51W **297** B9
Nelson L. *Canada* 55°48N 100°7W **297** B8
Nelson Lakes △ *N.Z.* 41°55S 172°44E **285** B7
Nelson Mandela ✈ **(RAI)**
Cabo Verde 14°55N 23°30W **153** j
Nelson's Dockyard
Antigua & B. 17°1N 61°46W **322** b
Nelspoort *S. Africa* 32°7S 23°0E **270** D3
Nelspruit = Mbombela
S. Africa 25°29S 30°59E **271** C5
Néma *Mauritania* 16°40N 7°15W **262** B3
Neman = Nemunas ➜
Lithuania 55°25N 21°10E **184** C8
Neman *Russia* 55°2N 22°2E **184** C9
N'ematābād *Iran* 35°38N 51°21E **141** B2
Nembe *Nigeria* 4°32N 6°24E **263** E6
Nembrala *Indonesia* 10°53S 122°50E **278** B3
Nemea *Greece* 37°49N 22°40E **204** D4
Nemecký Brod = Havlíčkův Brod
Czechia 49°36N 15°33E **180** B8
Nemeiben L. *Canada* 55°20N 105°20W **297** B7
Nemërçkë, Mal *Albania* 40°15N 20°15E **202** F4
Nemira, Vf. *Romania* 46°17N 26°19E **183** D11
Nemiscau *Canada* 51°18N 76°54W **298** B4
Nemiscau, L. *Canada* 51°25N 76°40W **298** B4
Nemours = Ghazaouet
Algeria 35°8N 1°50W **261** A4
Nemours *France* 48°16N 2°40E **173** D9
Nemrut Dağı ⌓ *Turkey* 38°0N 38°55E **213** C8
Nemšová *Slovakia* 48°58N 18°7E **181** C11
Nemunas ➜ *Lithuania* 55°25N 21°10E **184** C8
Nemuro *Japan* 43°20N 145°35E **220** C12
Nemuro-Kaikyō *Japan* 43°30N 145°30E **220** C12
Nemyriv *Ukraine* 50°7N 23°27E **185** H10
Nen Jiang ➜ *China* 45°28N 124°30E **227** B13
Nenagh *Ireland* 52°52N 8°11W **166** D3
Nenana *U.S.A.* 64°34N 149°5W **303** D10
Nenasi *Malaysia* 3°9N 103°23E **237** L4
Nendo *Pac. Oc.* 10°45S 165°54E **277** C12
Nene ➜ *U.K.* 52°49N 0°11E **169** E8
Nengkao Shan *Taiwan* 23°58N 121°16E **225** C3
Nengonengo
French Polynesia 18°47S 141°48W **289** f
Nenita *Greece* 38°14N 26°6E **205** C8
Nenjiang *China* 49°10N 125°10E **219** B14
Neno *Malawi* 15°25S 34°40E **269** F3
Neo Chori *Greece* 38°25N 21°17E **204** C3
Neochori *Greece* 39°4N 21°0E **204** B2
Neodesha *U.S.A.* 37°25N 95°41W **308** G6
Neoga *U.S.A.* 39°19N 88°27W **311** E8
Neon Petritsi *Greece* 41°16N 23°15E **202** E7
Neópolis *Brazil* 10°18S 36°35W **332** D4
Neora Valley △ *India* 27°0N 88°45E **241** B2
Neos Marmaras *Greece* 40°6N 23°47E **202** F7
Neosho *U.S.A.* 36°52N 94°22W **308** G6
Neosho ➜ *U.S.A.* 36°48N 95°18W **314** C7
Nepal ■ *Asia* 28°0N 84°30E **243** F11
Nepalganj *Nepal* 28°5N 81°40E **243** E9
Nepalganj Road *India* 28°1N 81°41E **243** E9
Nepean B. *Australia* 35°42S 137°37E **282** C2
Nephi *U.S.A.* 39°43N 111°50W **304** G8
Nephin *Ireland* 54°1N 9°22W **166** B2
Nephin Beg Range *Ireland* 54°0N 9°40W **166** C2
Nepi *Italy* 42°14N 12°21E **199** F9
Nepomuk *Czechia* 49°29N 13°35E **180** B6
Neppel = Moses Lake
U.S.A. 47°8N 119°17W **304** C4
Neptune *U.S.A.* 40°13N 74°2W **313** F10
Neptune Is. *Australia* 35°17S 136°10E **282** C2
Neqāb *Iran* 36°42N 57°25E **247** B8
Nera ➜ *Italy* 42°26N 12°24E **199** F9
Nera ➜ *Romania* 44°48N 21°25E **182** F6
Nérac *France* 44°8N 0°21E **174** D4
Nerang *Australia* 27°58S 153°20E **281** D5
Nerastro, Sarīr *Libya* 24°20N 20°37E **258** D4
Neratovice *Czechia* 50°16N 14°31E **180** A7
Nerchinsk *Russia* 52°0N 116°39E **215** D12
Nereju *Romania* 45°43N 26°43E **183** E11
Nerekhta *Russia* 57°26N 40°38E **188** D11
Néret, L. *Canada* 54°45N 70°44W **299** B5
Neretvanski Kanal
Croatia 43°7N 17°10E **199** E14
Nerima *Japan* 35°44N 139°40E **140** A3
Neringa *Lithuania* 55°20N 21°5E **184** C8
Neris ➜ *Lithuania* 55°8N 24°16E **188** E3
Nerja *Spain* 36°43N 3°55W **195** J7
Nerl ➜ *Russia* 56°11N 40°34E **188** D11
Nerpio *Spain* 38°11N 2°16W **197** G2
Nerva *Spain* 37°42N 6°30W **195** H4
Nervi *Italy* 44°23N 9°2E **198** D6
Neryungri *Russia* 57°38N 124°28E **215** D13
Nes *Iceland* 65°53N 17°24W **155** B9
Nesbyen *Buskerud, Norway* 60°34N 9°59E **164** D6
Nesbyen *Norway* 60°34N 9°8E **164** D6
Nescopeck *U.S.A.* 41°3N 76°12W **313** E8
Nesebŭr *Bulgaria* 42°41N 27°46E **203** D11
Neset *Norway* 61°53N 10°7E **164** C7
Nesflaten *Norway* 59°38N 6°48E **164** E3
Nesjahverfi *Iceland* 64°20N 15°19W **155** C11
Neskantaga *Canada* 52°14N 87°53W **298** B2
Neskaupstaður *Iceland* 65°9N 13°42W **155** B13
Nesland *Norway* 59°31N 7°59E **164** E4
Neslandsvatn *Norway* 58°57N 9°10E **164** F6
Nesodden *Norway* 59°48N 10°41E **133** B3
Nesoddtangen *Norway* 59°48N 10°40E **133** A3
Nesøya *Norway* 59°52N 10°31E **133** A2
Ness, L. *U.K.* 57°15N 4°32W **167** D4
Ness City *U.S.A.* 38°27N 99°54W **308** F4
Nessebar = Nesebŭr
Bulgaria 42°41N 27°46E **203** D11
Nesterov = Zhovkva
Ukraine 50°4N 23°58E **177** C12
Nesterov *Russia* 54°38N 22°41E **184** D9
Nestorio *Greece* 40°24N 21°5E **202** F5
Nestos ➜ *Europe* 40°54N 24°49E **203** F8
Nesttun *Norway* 60°19N 5°20E **164** D2
Nesvady *Slovakia* 47°56N 18°7E **181** D11
Nesvizh = Nyasvizh
Belarus 53°14N 26°38E **177** B14
Netaji Subhash Chandra Bose Int. ✈
(CCU) *India* 22°38N 88°26E **124** B2
Netanya *Israel* 32°20N 34°51E **251** F5
Netarhat *India* 23°29N 84°16E **243** H11
Nete ➜ *Belgium* 51°7N 4°14E **170** C4
Netherdale *Australia* 21°10S 148°33E **280** b
Netherlands ■ *Europe* 52°0N 5°30E **170** C5
Netherlands Antilles = ABC Islands
W. Indies 12°15N 69°0W **322** g
Netherlands East Indies = Indonesia ■ *Asia* 5°0S 115°0E **235** C4
Netherlands Guiana = Suriname ■
S. Amer. 4°0N 56°0W **329** C6
Neto ➜ *Italy* 39°12N 17°9E **201** C10
Netrakona *Bangla.* 24°53N 90°47E **241** C3
Netrang *India* 21°39N 73°21E **242** J5
Nettancourt *France* 48°51N 4°57E **173** D11
Nettilling L. *Canada* 66°30N 71°0W **295** D17
Nettuno *Italy* 41°27N 12°39E **200** A5
Netzahualcóyotl, Presa
Mexico 17°8N 93°35W **319** D6
Neu Aubing *Germany* 48°8N 11°25E **131** B1
Neu-Bentschen = Zbąszynek
Poland 52°16N 15°51E **185** F2
Neu Buch *Germany* 52°37N 13°31E **115** A4
Neu Buchhorst *Germany* 52°24N 13°44E **115** B5
Neu Fahrland *Germany* 52°26N 13°3E **115** B1
Neu-Isenburg *Germany* 50°3N 8°42E **179** E4
Neu-Langenburg = Tukuyu
Tanzania 9°17S 33°35E **269** D3
Neu Lindenberg *Germany* 52°36N 13°33E **115** A4
Neu Mecklenberg = New Ireland
Papua N. G. 3°20S 151°50E **286** B6
Neu Pommern = New Britain
Papua N. G. 5°50S 150°20E **286** C6
Neu-Sandec = Nowy Sącz
Poland 49°40N 20°41E **185** J7
Neu Sandez = Nowy Sącz
Poland 49°40N 20°41E **185** J7
Neu-Ulm *Germany* 48°22N 10°0E **179** G6
Neubiberg *Germany* 48°4N 11°40E **131** B3
Neubrandenburg
Germany 53°33N 13°15E **178** B9
Neubukow *Germany* 54°2N 11°39E **178** A7
Neuburg *Germany* 48°44N 11°11E **179** G7
Neuchâtel *Switz.* 47°0N 6°55E **179** J2
Neuchâtel ☐ *Switz.* 47°0N 6°55E **179** J2
Neuchâtel, Lac de *Switz.* 46°53N 6°50E **179** J2
Neudau *Austria* 47°11N 16°6E **180** D9
Neuenberg an der Elbe = Nymburk
Czechia 50°10N 15°1E **180** A8
Neuenhagen *Germany* 52°32N 13°38E **115** A4
Neuenhaus *Germany* 52°30N 6°58E **178** C2
Neuessling *Austria* 48°15N 16°32E **142** A3
Neuf-Brisach *France* 48°1N 7°30E **173** D14
Neufahrn *Bayern, Germany* 48°41N 12°11E **179** G8
Neufahrn *Bayern, Germany* 48°18N 11°40E **179** G7
Neufchâteau *Belgium* 49°50N 5°25E **170** E5
Neufchâteau *Vosges, France* 48°21N 5°40E **173** D12
Neufchâtel-en-Bray *France* 49°44N 1°26E **172** C8
Neufchâtel-sur-Aisne
France 49°26N 4°1E **173** C11
Neuhaus = Jindřichův Hradec
Czechia 49°10N 15°2E **180** B8
Neuhaus *Germany* 53°17N 10°56E **178** B6
Neuhäusel = Nové Zámky
Slovakia 48°2N 18°8E **181** C11
Neuhausen *Germany* 48°9N 11°32E **131** B2
Neuherberg *Germany* 48°13N 11°35E **131** A2
Neuhönow *Germany* 52°33N 13°39E **115** A5
Neuillé-Pont-Pierre *France* 47°33N 0°33E **172** E7
Neuilly-Plaisance *France* 48°51N 2°30E **134** A4
Neuilly-St-Front *France* 49°10N 3°15E **173** C10
Neuilly-sur-Marne *France* 48°51N 2°31E **134** A4
Neuilly-sur-Seine *France* 48°53N 2°15E **134** A2
Neukagran *Austria* 48°14N 16°27E **142** A2
Neukalen *Germany* 53°49N 12°46E **178** B8
Neukettenhof *Austria* 48°7N 16°28E **142** B2
Neukölln *Germany* 52°28N 13°25E **115** B3
Neumarkt = Nowy Targ
Poland 49°29N 20°2E **185** J7
Neumarkt = Środa Śląska
Poland 51°10N 16°36E **185** G3
Neumarkt *Germany* 49°26N 11°27E **179** F7
Neumarktl = Tržič
Slovenia 46°22N 14°18E **199** B11
Neumayer III *Antarctica* 71°0S 68°30W **151** D2
Neumittelwalde = Międzybórz
Poland 51°25N 17°34E **185** G4
Neumünster *Germany* 54°4N 9°58E **178** A5
Neung-sur-Beuvron *France* 47°30N 1°50E **173** E8
Neunkirchen *Austria* 47°43N 16°4E **180** D9
Neunkirchen *Saarland, Germany* 49°20N 7°9E **179** F3
Neuperlach *Germany* 48°6N 11°37E **131** B2
Neuquén *Argentina* 38°55S 68°0W **336** A3
Neuquén ☐ *Argentina* 38°0S 69°50W **334** D2
Neuquén ➜ *Argentina* 38°59S 68°0W **336** A3
Neuried *Germany* 48°5N 11°27E **131** B1
Neuruppin *Germany* 52°55N 12°48E **178** C8
Neusalz an der Oder = Nowa Sól
Poland 51°48N 15°44E **185** G2
Neusäss *Germany* 48°24N 10°50E **179** G6
Neusatz = Novi Sad *Serbia* 45°18N 19°52E **182** E4
Neuse ➜ *U.S.A.* 35°6N 76°29W **315** D16
Neusiedl *Austria* 47°57N 16°50E **181** D9
Neusiedler See *Austria* 47°50N 16°47E **181** D9
Neusiedler See-Seewinkel △
Austria 47°50N 16°45E **181** D9
Neusohl = Banská Bystrica
Slovakia 48°46N 19°14E **181** C12
Neuss *Germany* 51°11N 6°42E **178** D2
Neussargues-Moissac *France* 45°9N 3°0E **174** C7
Neustadt = Lwówek
Poland 52°28N 16°10E **185** F3
Neustadt = Prudnik
Poland 50°20N 17°38E **185** H4
Neustadt = Wejherowo
Poland 54°35N 18°12E **184** D5
Neustadt *Bayern, Germany* 49°44N 12°10E **179** F8
Neustadt *Bayern, Germany* 49°48N 11°46E **179** G7
Neustadt *Bayern, Germany* 49°34N 10°37E **179** F6
Neustadt *Bayern, Germany* 50°19N 11°7E **179** E7
Neustadt *Brandenburg, Germany* 52°50N 12°27E **178** C8
Neustadt *Hessen, Germany* 50°51N 9°9E **178** E5
Neustadt *Sachsen, Germany* 51°2N 14°12E **178** D10
Neustadt *Schleswig-Holstein, Germany* 54°6N 10°49E **178** A6
Neustadt *Thüringen, Germany* 50°45N 11°43E **178** E7
Neustadt am Rübenberge
Germany 52°30N 9°30E **178** C5
Neustadt an der Weinstrasse
Germany 49°21N 8°10E **179** F4
Neustädtel = Nowe Miasteczko
Poland 51°42N 15°42E **185** G2
Neustädtl = Novo Mesto
Slovenia 45°47N 15°12E **199** C12
Neustettin = Szczecinek
Poland 53°43N 16°41E **184** E3
Neustift am Walde *Austria* 48°14N 16°17E **142** A1
Neustrelitz *Germany* 53°21N 13°4E **178** B9
Neusüssenbrunn *Austria* 48°16N 16°29E **142** A2
Neutitschein = Nový Jičín
Czechia 49°30N 18°2E **181** B11
Neuvic *France* 45°23N 2°16E **174** C6
Neuville-sur-Saône *France* 45°52N 4°51E **175** C8
Neuvy-le-Roi *France* 47°36N 0°36E **172** E7
Neuvy-St-Sépulchre *France* 46°35N 1°48E **173** F8
Neuvy-sur-Barangeon
France 47°20N 2°15E **173** E9
Neuwaldegg *Austria* 48°14N 16°17E **142** A1
Neuwedell = Drawno
Poland 53°13N 15°46E **185** E2
Neuwerk *Germany* 53°55N 8°30E **178** B4
Neuwied *Germany* 50°26N 7°29E **178** E3
Neva ➜ *Russia* 59°56N 30°20E **188** C6
Nevada *Iowa, U.S.A.* 42°1N 93°27W **310** B3
Nevada *Mo., U.S.A.* 37°51N 94°22W **308** G6
Nevada ☐ *U.S.A.* 39°0N 117°0W **304** G5
Nevada City *U.S.A.* 39°16N 121°1W **306** F6
Nevado, Cerro *Argentina* 35°30S 68°32W **334** D2
Nevado de Colima = Volcán de Colima △ *Mexico* 19°30N 103°40W **318** D4
Nevado de Tres Cruces △
Chile 27°13S 69°5W **334** B2
Nevado del Huila △
Colombia 3°5N 75°58W **328** C2
Nevasa *India* 19°34N 75°0E **244** E2
Neve, Sa. da *Angola* 13°43S 13°10E **265** E2
Neve Ya'akov *West Bank* 31°50N 35°14E **123** A2
Nevel *Russia* 56°0N 29°55E **188** D5
Nevelsk *Russia* 46°40N 141°51E **215** E15
Nevers *France* 47°0N 3°9E **173** F10
Nevertire *Australia* 31°50S 147°44E **283** A7
Neves *Brazil* 22°51S 43°5W **135** B2
Nevesinje *Bos.-H.* 43°14N 18°6E **202** C2
Neville *Canada* 49°58N 107°39W **297** D7
Nevinnomyssk *Russia* 44°40N 42°0E **191** H6
Nevis *St. Kitts & Nevis* 17°0N 62°30W **322** d
Nevis Pk. *St. Kitts & Nevis* 17°9N 62°34W **322** d
Nevlunghavn *Norway* 58°58N 9°53E **164** F6
Nevoso, Mte. = Snežnik
Slovenia 45°36N 14°35E **199** C11
Nevrokop = Gotse Delchev
Bulgaria 41°36N 23°46E **202** E7
Nevşehir *Turkey* 38°33N 34°40E **212** C6
Nevşehir ☐ *Turkey* 38°50N 34°40E **212** C6
Nevskoye *Russia* 54°32N 22°39E **184** D9
Nevyansk *Russia* 57°30N 60°13E **186** C11
New ➜ *Guyana* 3°20N 57°37W **329** C6
New ➜ *W. Va., U.S.A.* 38°10N 81°12W **309** F13
New Aiyansh *Canada* 55°12N 129°4W **296** B3
New Albany *Ind., U.S.A.* 38°18N 85°49W **311** F11
New Albany *Miss., U.S.A.* 34°29N 89°0W **315** D10
New Albany *Pa., U.S.A.* 41°36N 76°27W **313** E8
New Amsterdam *Guyana* 6°15N 57°36W **329** B6
New Athens *U.S.A.* 38°19N 89°53W **310** F7
New Atlas = Akhali Atoni
Georgia 43°7N 40°50E **191** J5
New Baghdād *Iraq* 33°18N 44°28E **113** B2
New Baltimore *U.S.A.* 42°41N 82°44W **312** D2
New Barrakpur *India* 22°40N 88°26E **124** A2
New Barbadoes = Hackensack
U.S.A. 40°52N 74°4W **132** A1
New Bedford *U.S.A.* 41°38N 70°56W **313** E14
New Berlin = North Canton
U.S.A. 40°53N 81°24W **312** F3
New Berlin *Ill., U.S.A.* 39°44N 89°55W **310** E7
New Berlin *N.Y., U.S.A.* 42°37N 75°20W **313** D9
New Berlin *Pa., U.S.A.* 40°50N 76°57W **312** F8
New Berlin *Wis., U.S.A.* 42°59N 88°6W **311** B8
New Bern *U.S.A.* 35°7N 77°3W **315** D16
New Bethlehem *U.S.A.* 41°0N 79°20W **312** F5
New Bight *The Bahamas* 24°19N 75°24W **321** B4
New Bloomfield *U.S.A.* 40°25N 77°11W **312** F7
New Boston *U.S.A.* 33°28N 94°25W **314** E7
New Braunfels *U.S.A.* 29°42N 98°8W **314** G5
New Brighton *N.Z.* 43°29S 172°43E **285** D7

New Brighton N.Y., U.S.A. 40°38N 74°5W 132 C1
New Brighton Pa., U.S.A. 40°42N 80°19W 312 F4
New Britain Papua N. G. 5°50S 150°20E 286 C6
New Britain Conn., U.S.A. 41°40N 72°47W 313 E12
New Britain Trench Pac. Oc. 6°0S 153°0E 276 J3
New Brockton U.S.A. 31°23N 85°56W 316 D4
New Brookland = West Columbia U.S.A. 33°59N 81°4W 316 B8
New Brunswick U.S.A. 40°30N 74°27W 313 F10
New Brunswick □ Canada 46°50N 66°30W 299 C6
New Buffalo U.S.A. 41°47N 86°45W 311 C10
New Bussa Nigeria 9°53N 4°31E 263 D5
New Caledonia ⊠ Pac. Oc. 21°0S 165°0E 288 d
New Caledonia Trough Pac. Oc. 30°0S 165°0E 288 L8
New Canada S. Africa 26°12S 27°56E 123 B1
New Canada Dam S. Africa 26°12S 27°56E 123 B1
New Carlisle Ind., U.S.A. 41°45N 86°32W 311 C10
New Carlisle Ohio, U.S.A. 39°56N 84°2W 311 E12
New Castile = Castilla-La Mancha □ Spain 39°30N 3°30W 195 F7
New Castle Ind., U.S.A. 39°55N 85°22W 311 E11
New Castle Ky., U.S.A. 38°26N 85°10W 311 F11
New Castle Pa., U.S.A. 41°0N 80°21W 312 F4
New Chitose ✈ (CTS) Japan 42°46N 141°41E 220 C10
New City U.S.A. 41°9N 73°59W 313 E11
New Concord U.S.A. 39°59N 81°54W 312 G3
New Cross U.K. 51°28N 0°1W 125 B3
New Cumberland U.S.A. 40°30N 80°36W 312 F4
New Cuyama U.S.A. 34°57N 119°38W 307 L7
New Delhi India 28°36N 77°11E 120 B2
New Denver Canada 50°0N 117°25W 296 D5
New Don Pedro Res. U.S.A. 37°43N 120°24W 306 H6
New Dorp U.S.A. 40°34N 74°7W 132 C1
New Dorp Beach U.S.A. 40°33N 74°6W 132 C1
New Ellenton U.S.A. 33°28N 81°41W 316 B8
New England U.S.A. 43°0N 71°0W 301 G25
New England N. Dak., U.S.A. 46°32N 102°52W 308 B2
New England △ Australia 30°25S 152°30E 283 A10
New England Aquarium Boston, U.S.A. 116 b3
New England Ra. Australia 30°20S 151°45E 281 E5
New England Seamounts Atl. Oc. 38°0N 63°0W 152 C5
New Forest △ U.K. 50°53N 1°34W 169 G6
New Franklin U.S.A. 39°1N 92°44W 310 E4
New Galloway U.K. 55°5N 4°9W 167 F4
New Georgia Is. Solomon Is. 8°15S 157°30E 287 M9
New Georgia Sound Solomon Is. 8°0S 158°20E 287 L9
New Glarus U.S.A. 42°49N 89°38W 310 B7
New Glasgow Canada 45°35N 62°36W 299 C7
New Grant Trin. & Tob. 10°17N 61°19W 323 t
New Guinea Oceania 4°0S 136°0E 276 B7
New Halfa = Halfa al Jadidah Sudan 15°20N 35°35E 266 A4
New Hamburg Canada 43°23N 80°42W 312 C4
New Hampshire □ U.S.A. 44°0N 71°30W 313 C13
New Hampton U.S.A. 43°3N 92°19W 310 A4
New Hanover Papua N. G. 2°30S 150°10E 286 B6
New Hanover KwaZulu Natal, S. Africa 29°22S 30°31E 271 C5
New Harmony U.S.A. 38°8N 87°56W 311 F9
New Hartford U.S.A. 43°4N 75°18W 313 C9
New Haven Conn., U.S.A. 41°18N 72°55W 313 E12
New Haven Ill., U.S.A. 37°55N 88°8W 311 G8
New Haven Ind., U.S.A. 41°4N 85°1W 311 C11
New Haven Mich., U.S.A. 42°44N 82°48W 312 D2
New Haven Mo., U.S.A. 38°37N 91°13W 310 F5
New Haven N.Y., U.S.A. 43°28N 76°18W 313 C8
New Hazelton Canada 55°20N 127°30W 296 B3
New Hebrides = Vanuatu ■ Pac. Oc. 15°0S 168°0E 287 E6
New Holland U.S.A. 40°6N 76°5W 313 F8
New Iberia U.S.A. 30°1N 91°49W 314 F9
New Ireland Papua N. G. 3°20S 151°50E 286 B6
New Ireland □ Papua N. G. 3°0S 151°30E 286 B6
New Jersey □ U.S.A. 40°0N 74°30W 309 F16
New Kensington U.S.A. 40°34N 79°46W 312 F5
New Lexington U.S.A. 39°43N 82°13W 309 F12
New Liskeard Canada 47°31N 79°41W 298 C4
New London Conn., U.S.A. 41°22N 72°6W 313 E12
New London Iowa, U.S.A. 40°55N 91°24W 310 D5
New London Mo., U.S.A. 39°35N 91°24W 310 E5
New London Ohio, U.S.A. 41°5N 82°24W 312 E2
New London Wis., U.S.A. 44°23N 88°45W 308 C9
New Madrid U.S.A. 36°36N 89°32W 308 G9
New Malden U.K. 51°24N 0°15W 125 B2
New Martinsville U.S.A. 39°39N 80°52W 309 F13
New Meadows U.S.A. 44°58N 116°18W 304 D5
New Melones L. U.S.A. 37°57N 120°31W 306 H6
New Mexico □ U.S.A. 34°30N 106°0W 305 J11
New Miami U.S.A. 39°26N 84°32W 311 E12
New Milford Conn., U.S.A. 41°35N 73°25W 313 E11
New Milford N.Y., U.S.A. 40°56N 74°0W 132 A1
New Milford Pa., U.S.A. 41°52N 75°44W 313 E9
New Mumbai = Navi Mumbai India 19°5N 73°0E 130 A2
New Norcia Australia 30°57S 116°13E 279 F2
New Norfolk Australia 42°46S 147°2E 281 G4
New Orleans U.S.A. 29°57N 90°4W 131 B2
New Orleans Int. ✈ (MSY) U.S.A. 30°0N 90°15W 131 B1
New Palestine U.S.A. 39°45N 85°52W 311 E11
New Paris U.S.A. 39°51N 84°48W 311 E12
New Pekin U.S.A. 38°30N 86°0W 311 F10
New Philadelphia U.S.A. 40°30N 81°27W 312 F3
New Plymouth N.Z. 39°4S 174°5E 284 F3
New Plymouth Idaho, U.S.A. 43°58N 116°49W 304 E5
New Pomerania = New Britain Papua N. G. 5°50S 150°20E 286 C6
New Port Richey U.S.A. 28°16N 82°43W 317 G7
New Providence The Bahamas 25°25N 77°35W 153 b
New Quay U.K. 52°13N 4°21W 169 E3
New Radnor U.K. 52°15N 3°9W 169 E4
New Richmond Qué., Canada 48°15N 65°45W 299 C6
New Richmond Ohio, U.S.A. 38°57N 84°17W 311 F12
New Richmond Wis., U.S.A. 45°7N 92°32W 308 C7
New River ➔ U.S.A. 26°6N 80°6W 129 B3
New River Gorge △ U.S.A. 37°53N 81°5W 309 G13
New Roads U.S.A. 30°42N 91°26W 314 F9
New Rochelle U.S.A. 40°55N 73°46W 313 F11
New Rockford U.S.A. 47°41N 99°8W 308 B4
New Romney U.K. 50°59N 0°57E 169 G8
New Ross Ireland 52°23N 6°57W 166 D5
New Salem U.S.A. 46°51N 101°25W 308 B3
New Scone = Scone U.K. 56°25N 3°24W 167 E5
New Sharon U.S.A. 41°28N 92°39W 310 C4
New Siberian I. = Novaya Sibir, Ostrov Russia 75°10N 150°0E 215 B16
New Siberian Is. = Novosibirskiye Ostrova Russia 75°0N 142°0E 215 B15
New Smyrna Beach U.S.A. 29°1N 80°56W 317 F9
New South Wales □ Australia 33°0S 146°0E 283 B7
New Stuyahok U.S.A. 59°29N 157°20W 303 G8
New Tecumseth = Alliston Canada 44°9N 79°52W 312 B5
New Territories Hong Kong, China 22°23N 114°5E 122 A2
New Toronto Canada 43°35N 79°30W 141 B1
New Town = Nowe Miasto Warsaw, Poland 143 a2
New Town Edinburgh, U.K. 121 a2
New Town N. Dak., U.S.A. 47°59N 102°30W 308 B2
New Ulm U.S.A. 44°19N 94°28W 308 C6
New Utrecht U.S.A. 40°36N 73°59W 132 C2
New Vienna U.S.A. 39°19N 83°42W 311 E13
New Washington Phil. 11°39N 122°26E 233 F4
New Waterford Canada 46°13N 60°4W 299 C7
New Westminster Canada 49°13N 122°55W 306 A4
New York U.S.A. 40°43N 74°0W 132 B2
New York □ U.S.A. 43°0N 75°0W 313 D9
New York Avenue Washington, D.C., U.S.A. 143 a2
New York J.F. Kennedy Int. ✈ (JFK) U.S.A. 40°38N 73°47W 313 F11
New York La Guardia ✈ (LGA) U.S.A. 40°46N 73°52W 132 B2
New York University New York, U.S.A. 132 d2
New Zealand ■ Oceania 40°0S 176°0E 284 G5
Newaj ➔ India 24°24N 76°49E 242 G7
Newala Tanzania 10°58S 39°18E 269 E4
Newark Del., U.S.A. 39°41N 75°46W 309 F16
Newark N.J., U.S.A. 40°44N 74°10W 313 F10
Newark N.Y., U.S.A. 43°3N 77°6W 312 C7
Newark Ohio, U.S.A. 40°3N 82°24W 312 F2
Newark B. U.S.A. 40°40N 74°8W 132 B1
Newark Liberty Int. ✈ (EWR) U.S.A. 40°42N 74°10W 313 F10
Newark-on-Trent U.K. 53°5N 0°48W 168 D7
Newark Valley U.S.A. 42°14N 76°11W 313 D8
Newbattle U.K. 55°53N 3°4W 121 B3
Newberg U.S.A. 45°18N 122°58W 304 D2
Newberry Fla., U.S.A. 29°39N 82°37W 317 F7
Newberry Mich., U.S.A. 46°21N 85°30W 309 B11
Newberry S.C., U.S.A. 34°17N 81°37W 315 D14
Newberry Springs U.S.A. 34°50N 116°41W 307 L10
Newboro L. Canada 44°38N 76°20W 313 B8
Newbridge Ireland 53°11N 6°48W 166 C5
Newburg U.S.A. 37°55N 91°54W 310 G5
Newburgh Ont., Canada 44°19N 76°52W 312 B8
Newburgh Ind., U.S.A. 37°57N 87°24W 311 G9
Newburgh N.Y., U.S.A. 41°30N 74°1W 313 E10
Newbury W. Berkshire, U.K. 51°24N 1°20W 169 F6
Newbury N.H., U.S.A. 43°19N 72°3W 313 B12
Newbury Vt., U.S.A. 44°5N 72°4W 313 B12
Newbury Park U.K. 51°34N 0°5E 125 A4
Newburyport U.S.A. 42°49N 70°53W 313 D14
Newcastle N.S.W., Australia 33°0S 151°46E 283 B9
Newcastle N.B., Canada 47°1N 65°38W 299 C6
Newcastle Ont., Canada 43°55N 78°35W 298 D4
Newcastle Limerick, Ireland 52°27N 9°3W 166 D2
Newcastle St. Kitts & Nevis 17°14N 62°42W 322 d
Newcastle KwaZulu Natal, S. Africa 27°45S 29°58E 271 C4
Newcastle Down, U.K. 54°13N 5°54W 166 B6
Newcastle Calif., U.S.A. 38°53N 121°8W 306 G5
Newcastle Wyo., U.S.A. 43°50N 104°11W 304 E11
Newcastle Emlyn U.K. 52°2N 4°28W 169 E3
Newcastle Ra. Australia 15°45S 130°15E 278 C5
Newcastle-under-Lyme U.K. 53°1N 2°14W 168 D5
Newcastle-upon-Tyne U.K. 54°58N 1°36W 168 C6
Newcastle Waters Australia 17°30S 133°28E 280 B1
Newcomb U.S.A. 43°58N 74°10W 313 C10
Newcomerstown U.S.A. 40°16N 81°36W 312 F3
Newcraighall U.K. 55°56N 3°5W 121 B3
Newdegate Australia 33°6S 119°0E 279 F2
Newell Queens., Australia 16°20S 145°16E 280 B4
Newell Iowa, U.S.A. 42°36N 95°0W 310 B1
Newell S. Dak., U.S.A. 44°43N 103°25W 308 C2
Newenham, C. U.S.A. 58°39N 162°11W 303 G7
Newfane U.S.A. 43°17N 78°43W 312 C6
Newfield U.S.A. 42°18N 76°33W 313 D8
Newfound L. U.S.A. 43°40N 71°47W 313 C13
Newfoundland Canada 49°0N 55°0W 299 C8
Newfoundland Pa., U.S.A. 41°18N 75°19W 313 E9
Newfoundland & Labrador □ Canada 52°0N 58°0W 299 B8
Newhalen U.S.A. 59°43N 154°54W 303 G9
Newham □ U.K. 51°31N 0°3E 125 A4
Newhaven E. Sussex, U.K. 50°47N 0°3E 169 G8
Newhaven Edinburgh, U.K. 55°59N 3°11W 121 B2
Newington Edinburgh, U.K. 55°56N 3°10W 121 B2
Newington London, U.K. 125 c5
Newington Ga., U.S.A. 32°35N 81°30W 316 C8
Newkirk U.S.A. 36°53N 97°3W 314 C6
Newlands S. Africa 26°10S 27°57E 123 B1
Newlyn U.K. 50°6N 5°34W 169 G2
Newman W. Austral., Australia 23°18S 119°45E 278 D2
Newman Calif., U.S.A. 37°19N 121°1W 306 H5
Newman Ill., U.S.A. 39°48N 87°59W 311 E9
Newmarket Ont., Canada 44°3N 79°28W 312 B5
Newmarket Cork, Ireland 52°13N 9°0W 166 D2
Newmarket Jamaica 18°9N 77°55W 320 a
Newmarket Suffolk, U.K. 52°15N 0°25E 169 E8
Newmarket N.H., U.S.A. 43°5N 70°56W 313 C14
Newnan U.S.A. 33°23N 84°48W 316 B5
Newport = Nieuwpoort Curaçao 12°3N 68°49W 322 g
Newport Vic., Australia 37°50S 144°51E 128 B1
Newport Mayo, Ireland 53°53N 9°33W 166 C2
Newport I. of W., U.K. 50°42N 1°17W 169 G6
Newport Newport, U.K. 51°35N 3°0W 169 F5
Newport Ark., U.S.A. 35°37N 91°16W 314 D9
Newport Fla., U.S.A. 30°11N 84°10W 316 E5
Newport Ind., U.S.A. 39°53N 87°25W 311 E9
Newport Ky., U.S.A. 39°5N 84°29W 311 E12
Newport N.H., U.S.A. 43°22N 72°10W 313 C12
Newport N.Y., U.S.A. 43°11N 75°1W 313 C9
Newport Oreg., U.S.A. 44°39N 124°3W 304 D1
Newport Pa., U.S.A. 40°29N 77°8W 312 F7
Newport R.I., U.S.A. 41°29N 71°19W 313 E13
Newport Tenn., U.S.A. 35°58N 83°11W 315 D13
Newport Vt., U.S.A. 44°56N 72°13W 313 B12
Newport Wash., U.S.A. 48°11N 117°3W 304 B5
Newport □ U.K. 51°33N 3°1W 169 F4
Newport Beach U.S.A. 33°37N 117°56W 307 M9
Newport News U.S.A. 36°58N 76°25W 309 G15
Newport Pagnell U.K. 52°5N 0°43W 169 E7
Newquay U.K. 50°25N 5°6W 169 G2
Newry U.K. 54°11N 6°21W 166 B5
Newry, Mourne & Down □ U.K. 54°8N 6°3W 166 B6
Newry Islands △ Australia 20°51S 148°56E 280 b
Newtok U.S.A. 60°56N 164°38W 303 F6
Newton Ga., U.S.A. 31°19N 84°20W 316 D5
Newton Ill., U.S.A. 38°59N 88°10W 311 F8
Newton Iowa, U.S.A. 41°42N 93°3W 310 C3
Newton Kans., U.S.A. 38°3N 97°21W 308 F5
Newton Mass., U.S.A. 42°21N 71°12W 116 B1
Newton Miss., U.S.A. 32°19N 89°10W 315 E10
Newton N.C., U.S.A. 35°40N 81°13W 315 D14
Newton N.J., U.S.A. 41°3N 74°45W 313 E10
Newton Tex., U.S.A. 30°51N 93°46W 314 F8
Newton Abbot U.K. 50°32N 3°37W 169 G4
Newton Aycliffe U.K. 54°37N 1°34W 168 C6
Newton Falls N.Y., U.S.A. 44°12N 74°59W 313 B10
Newton Falls Ohio, U.S.A. 41°11N 80°59W 312 E4
Newton L. U.S.A. 38°55N 88°15W 311 F8
Newton Stewart U.K. 54°57N 4°30W 167 G4
Newton Terrace Barbados 13°4N 59°32W 323 r
Newtonbrook Canada 43°47N 79°24W 141 A2
Newtongrange U.K. 55°53N 3°3W 121 B3
Newtonmore U.K. 57°4N 4°8W 167 D4
Newtontoppen Svalbard 79°0N 17°30E 154 B12
Newtonville U.S.A. 42°20N 71°11W 116 A1
Newtown N.S.W., Australia 33°54S 151°11E 139 B2
Newtown Powys, U.K. 52°31N 3°19W 169 E4
Newtown Ind., U.S.A. 40°13N 87°9W 311 D9
Newtown Mo., U.S.A. 40°22N 93°20W 310 D3
Newtownabbey U.K. 54°40N 5°56W 166 B6
Newtownards U.K. 54°36N 5°42W 166 B6
Newtownbarry = Bunclody Ireland 52°39N 6°40W 166 D5
Newtownstewart U.K. 54°43N 7°23W 166 B4
Newville U.S.A. 40°10N 77°24W 312 F7
Nexon France 45°41N 1°11E 174 C5
Neya Russia 58°21N 43°49E 190 A6
Neyrīz Iran 29°15N 54°19E 247 D7
Neyshābūr Iran 36°10N 58°50E 247 B8
Neyveli India 11°32N 79°29E 245 J4
Neyyattinkara India 8°26N 77°5E 245 K3
Nezametny = Aldan Russia 58°40N 125°30E 215 D13
Nezhin = Nizhyn Ukraine 51°5N 31°55E 189 G6
Nezperce U.S.A. 46°14N 116°14W 304 C5
Nezvysko Ukraine 48°46N 25°15E 183 B10
Nga, Laem Thailand 7°55N 98°27E 237 a
Ngaanyatjarra ◎ Australia 22°40S 127°0E 278 D4
Ngabang Indonesia 0°23N 109°55E 235 B3
Ngabe Congo 3°12S 16°12E 264 C3
Ngabordamlu, Tanjung Indonesia 6°56S 134°11E 231 F8
N'Gage Angola 7°46S 15°15E 265 D3
Ngaiphaipi Myanmar 22°14N 93°15E 241 D4
Ngala Nigeria 12°20N 14°11E 263 C7
Ngaliwurru Nungali ◎ Australia 15°42S 130°4E 278 C5
Ngalurrtju ◎ Australia 22°44S 132°5E 278 D5
Ngama Chad 11°45N 17°6E 259 F3
Ngambé Centre, Cameroon 5°48N 11°29E 263 D7
Ngambé Littoral, Cameroon 4°21N 10°40E 263 E7
Ngami Depression Botswana 20°30S 22°46E 270 B3
Ngamo Zimbabwe 19°3S 27°32E 269 F2
Ngamring China 29°14N 87°10E 218 F6
Nganbéto, L. de Togo 7°26N 1°25E 263 D5
Ngangala South Sudan 4°42N 31°55E 257 G3
Nganglong Kangri China 33°0N 81°0E 243 C9
Ngao Thailand 18°46N 99°59E 236 C2
Ngaoundéré Cameroon 7°15N 13°35E 264 A2
Ngapali Myanmar 18°26N 94°19E 241 F5
Ngapara N.Z. 44°57S 170°46E 285 E5
Ngape Myanmar 20°2N 94°28E 241 E5
Ngara Tanzania 2°29S 30°40E 268 C3
Ngardmau Palau 7°37N 134°34E 288 c
Ngardmau B. Palau 7°38N 134°34E 288 c
Ngardololok Palau 7°0N 134°14E 288 c
Ngaregur Palau 7°45N 134°37E 288 c
Ngarluma ◎ Australia 21°30S 118°30E 278 D2
Ngaruawahia N.Z. 37°42S 175°11E 284 D4
Ngaruroro ➔ N.Z. 39°34S 176°55E 284 F5
Ngatangiia Cook Is. 21°14S 159°43W 289 h
Ngatapa N.Z. 38°32S 177°45E 284 E6
Ngathainggyaung Myanmar 17°24N 95°5E 241 G5
Ngau Chi Wan Hong Kong, China 22°20N 114°12E 122 A3
Ngau Tau Kok Hong Kong, China 22°19N 114°12E 122 B3
Ngauruhoe, Mt. N.Z. 39°13S 175°45E 284 F4
Ngawi Indonesia 7°24S 111°26E 235 D4
Ngcobo S. Africa 31°37S 28°0E 271 D4
Ngele Dem. Rep. of the Congo 0°30S 20°22E 264 C4
Ngelebok Cameroon 4°16N 14°3E 264 B2
Ngeregong Palau 7°6N 134°21E 288 c
Ngergoi Palau 7°5N 134°15E 288 c
Ngerulmud Palau 7°27N 134°38E 288 c
Ngesebus I. Palau 7°3N 134°15E 288 c
Nggatokae Solomon Is. 8°45S 158°15E 287 M10
Nggela Pile Solomon Is. 9°5S 160°20E 287 M11
Nggela Sule Solomon Is. 9°2S 160°12E 287 M11
Nghia Lo Vietnam 21°33N 104°28E 228 G5
Ngidinga Dem. Rep. of the Congo 5°37S 15°17E 265 D3
Ngo Congo 2°29S 15°45E 264 C3
Ngoap Cameroon 4°9N 12°51E 264 B2
Ngobasangel Palau 7°16N 134°19E 288 c
Ngoboli South Sudan 4°57N 32°37E 257 G3
Ngol = Raqaba ez Zarqa ➔ South Sudan 9°14N 29°44E 257 F2
N'Gola Angola 14°10S 14°30E 265 E2
Ngoma Malawi 13°8S 33°45E 269 E3
Ngomahura Zimbabwe 20°26S 30°43E 269 G3
Ngomba Tanzania 8°20S 32°53E 269 D3
Ngomeni, Ras Kenya 2°59S 40°14E 268 C5
Ngong Kenya 1°22S 36°39E 268 C4
Ngong Ping Hong Kong, China 22°15N 113°54E 122 B1
Ngong Shuen Chau = Stonecutters I. Hong Kong, China 22°19N 114°8E 122 B2
Ngongotaha N.Z. 38°5S 176°12E 284 E5
Ngonye Falls Zambia 16°40S 23°25E 265 F4
Ngop South Sudan 6°17N 30°9E 257 F3
Ngoring Hu China 34°55N 97°5E 218 E8
Ngorkou Mali 15°40N 3°41W 262 B4
Ngorongoro Tanzania 3°11S 35°32E 268 C4
Ngorongoro ⌓ Tanzania 2°40S 35°30E 268 C4
Ngoto C.A.R. 3°59N 17°19E 264 B3
Ngounié □ Gabon 2°0S 11°0E 264 C2
Ngounie ➔ Gabon 0°37S 10°18E 264 C2
Ngouo, Dj. C.A.R. 7°55N 24°38E 264 A4
Ngoura Chad 12°44N 16°21E 259 F3
Ngouri Chad 13°38N 15°22E 259 F3
Ngourti Niger 15°19N 13°12E 259 E2
Ngoussou Gabon 3°0S 11°7E 264 C2
Ngozi Burundi 2°54S 29°50E 268 C2
Ngua Kok Wan Hong Kong, China 22°21N 114°5E 122 A2
Ngudu Tanzania 2°58S 33°25E 268 C3
Nguigmi Niger 14°20N 13°20E 259 F2
Nguila Cameroon 4°41N 11°43E 263 E7
Nguiu Australia 11°46S 130°38E 278 B5
Ngukurr Australia 14°44S 134°44E 280 A1
Ngum ➔ Laos 18°31N 102°32E 236 C4
Nguna Vanuatu 17°26S 168°22E 287 G6
Ngundu Zimbabwe 18°11S 31°15E 269 F3
Ngunga Tanzania 3°37S 33°37E 268 C3
Nguru Nigeria 12°56N 10°29E 263 C7
Nguru Mts. Tanzania 6°0S 37°30E 268 D4
Ngusi Malawi 14°0S 34°50E 269 E3
Nguyen Binh Vietnam 22°39N 105°56E 228 F5
Ngwaketse □ Botswana 25°0S 25°0E 270 C3
Ngwedaung Myanmar 19°31N 97°9E 241 F6
Ngwesaung Myanmar 16°52N 94°23E 241 G5
Nha Bang Vietnam 10°37N 105°0E 237 G5
Nha Trang Vietnam 12°16N 109°10E 237 F7
Nhacoongo Mozam. 24°18S 35°14E 271 B6
Nhamaabué Mozam. 17°25S 35°5E 269 F4
Nhambiquara Brazil 12°50S 59°49W 331 C6
Nhamundá Brazil 2°14S 56°43W 329 D6
Nhamundá ➔ Brazil 2°12S 56°41W 329 D6
Nhangulaze, L. Mozam. 24°0S 34°30E 271 B5
Nharêa Angola 11°38S 16°58E 265 E3
Nharnuwangga, Wajarri and Ngarlawangga ◎ Australia 24°50S 118°0E 279 D2
Nhava Sheva India 18°58N 72°55E 130 B2
Nhecolândia Brazil 19°17S 56°58W 331 D6
Nhill Australia 36°18S 141°40E 282 D4
Nho Quan Vietnam 20°18N 105°45E 228 G5
Nhulunbuy Australia 12°10S 137°20E 280 A2
Nhundo Angola 14°25S 21°23E 265 E4
Nia-nia Dem. Rep. of the Congo 1°30N 27°40E 268 B2
Niafounké Mali 16°0N 4°5W 262 B4
Niagara Falls Ont., Canada 43°7N 79°5W 312 C5
Niagara Falls N.Y., U.S.A. 43°5N 79°4W 312 C6
Niagara-on-the-Lake Canada 43°15N 79°4W 312 C5
Niah Malaysia 3°58N 113°46E 235 B4
Nialaha'u Pt. Solomon Is. 9°47S 161°34E 287 M11
Niamey Niger 13°27N 2°6E 263 C5
Niamtougou Togo 9°46N 1°6E 263 D5
Niandan-Koro Guinea 11°5N 9°15W 262 C3
Nianforando Guinea 9°37N 10°36W 262 D2
Niangara Dem. Rep. of the Congo 3°42N 27°50E 268 B2
Niangay, L. Mali 15°50N 3°0W 262 B4
Niangbo Côte d'Ivoire 8°49N 5°10W 262 D3
Niangoloko Burkina Faso 10°15N 4°55W 262 C4
Niangua ➔ U.S.A. 38°58N 92°48W 310 G4
Niantic U.S.A. 41°20N 72°11W 313 E12
Niari Congo 4°9S 14°9E 264 C2
Niari □ Congo 3°30S 12°0E 264 C2
Niaro Sudan 10°38N 31°31E 257 E3
Nias Indonesia 1°0N 97°30E 234 B1
Niassa □ Mozam. 13°30S 36°0E 269 E4
Niassa, L. = Malawi, L. Africa 12°30S 34°30E 269 E3
Niassa ⌓ Mozam. 12°4S 36°57E 269 E4
Nīāvarān Iran 35°47N 51°29E 141 A2
Nībāk Si. Arabia 24°25N 50°50E 247 E7
Nibe Denmark 56°59N 9°38E 163 H3
Nibra India 22°36N 88°15E 124 B1
Nicaragua ■ Cent. Amer. 11°40N 85°30W 320 D2
Nicaragua, L. de Nic. 12°0N 85°30W 320 D2
Nicastro Italy 38°59N 16°19E 201 D9
Nice France 43°42N 7°14E 175 E11
Nice-Côte-d'Azur ✈ (NCE) France 43°41N 7°12E 175 E11
Niceville U.S.A. 30°31N 86°30W 317 E3
Nichicun, L. Canada 53°5N 71°0W 299 B5
Nichinan Japan 31°38N 131°23E 222 F3
Nicholás, Canal Caribbean 23°30N 80°5W 320 B3
Nicholas Channel = Nicholás, Canal Caribbean 23°30N 80°5W 320 B3
Nicholasville U.S.A. 37°53N 84°34W 311 G12
Nicholls U.S.A. 31°31N 82°38W 316 D7
Nichols U.S.A. 42°1N 76°22W 313 D8
Nicholson W. Austral., Australia 18°2S 128°54E 278 C4
Nicholson Pa., U.S.A. 41°37N 75°47W 313 E9
Nicholson ➔ Australia 17°31S 139°36E 280 B2
Nicholson L. Canada 62°40N 102°40W 297 A8
Nicholson Ra. Australia 27°15S 116°45E 279 E2
Nicholville U.S.A. 44°41N 74°39W 313 B10
Nickerie ➔ Suriname 5°58N 57°0W 329 B6
Nico Pérez = José Batlle y Ordóñez Uruguay 33°20S 55°10W 335 C4
Nicobar Is. Ind. Oc. 8°0N 93°30E 245 L11
Nicola Canada 50°12N 120°40W 296 C4
Nicolls Town The Bahamas 25°8N 78°0W 320 A4
Nicosia Cyprus 35°10N 33°25E 207 E9
Nicosia Italy 37°45N 14°24E 201 E7
Nicótera Italy 38°33N 15°56E 201 D8
Nicoya Costa Rica 10°9N 85°27W 320 D2
Nicoya, G. de Costa Rica 10°0N 85°0W 320 E3
Nicoya, Pen. de Costa Rica 9°45N 85°40W 320 E2
Nictheroy = Niterói Brazil 22°53S 43°7W 135 B2
Nida Lithuania 55°20N 21°4E 184 C8
Nidāl Iraq 33°19N 44°25E 113 B2
Nidaros = Trondheim Norway 63°36N 10°25E 164 A7
Nidd ➔ U.K. 53°59N 1°23W 168 D6
Nidda Germany 50°23N 9°1E 179 E5
Nidda ➔ Germany 50°17N 8°48E 179 E4
Niddrie Vic., Australia 37°44S 144°51E 128 A1
Niddrie Edinburgh, U.K. 55°56N 3°7W 121 B3
Nidri Greece 38°43N 20°42E 207 B2
Nidwalden □ Switz. 46°50N 8°25E 179 J4
Nidzica Poland 53°25N 20°28E 185 E7
Niebüll Germany 54°46N 8°48E 178 A4
Nied ➔ Germany 49°23N 6°40E 173 C13
Nieder Neuendorf Germany 52°36N 13°12E 115 A2
Niederaula Germany 50°47N 9°36E 178 E5
Niederbayern □ Germany 48°40N 12°50E 179 G8
Niederbronn-les-Bains France 48°57N 7°39E 173 D14
Niedere Tauern Austria 47°20N 14°0E 180 D7
Niederlausitz Germany 51°42N 13°59E 178 D9
Niederösterreich □ Austria 48°25N 15°40E 180 C8
Niedersachsen □ Germany 52°50N 9°0E 178 C4
Niedersächsisches Wattenmeer △ Germany 53°45N 7°30E 178 B3
Niederschöneweide Germany 52°27N 13°30E 115 B3
Niederschönhausen Germany 52°35N 13°25E 115 A3
Niefang Eq. Guin. 1°50N 10°14E 264 B2
Niekerkshoop S. Africa 29°19S 22°51E 270 C3
Niellé Côte d'Ivoire 10°5N 5°38W 262 C3
Niellim Chad 9°42N 17°49E 259 G3
Niem C.A.R. 6°12N 15°14E 264 A3
Niemba Dem. Rep. of the Congo 5°58S 28°24E 268 D2
Niemen = Nemunas ➔ Lithuania 55°25N 21°10E 184 C8
Niemeyer Brazil 22°59S 43°16W 135 B1
Niemodlin Poland 50°38N 17°38E 185 H4
Niemur Australia 35°17S 144°9E 282 C6
Nienburg Germany 52°39N 9°13E 178 C5
Niepołomice Poland 50°3N 20°13E 185 H7
Niers ➔ Germany 51°43N 5°57E 178 D1
Niesky Germany 51°17N 14°49E 178 D10
Nieszawa Poland 52°52N 18°50E 185 F5
Nieu Bethesda S. Africa 31°51S 24°34E 270 D3
Nieuw Amsterdam Suriname 5°53N 55°5W 329 B6
Nieuw Nickerie Suriname 6°0N 56°59W 329 B6
Nieuwe Kerk Amsterdam, Neths. 112 a2
Nieuwendam Neths. 52°23N 4°57E 112 A2
Nieuwoudtville S. Africa 31°23S 19°7E 270 D2
Nieuwpoort Belgium 51°8N 2°45E 170 C2
Nieuwpoort Curaçao 12°3N 68°49W 322 g
Nieves, Pico de las Canary Is. 27°57N 15°35W 153 e1
Nièvre □ France 47°10N 3°40E 173 E10
Nif Micronesia 9°28N 138°4E 287 S16
Niga Mali 13°38N 5°27W 262 C3
Niğde Turkey 37°58N 34°40E 212 D6
Niğde □ Turkey 38°0N 34°30E 212 D6
Nigel S. Africa 26°27S 28°25E 271 C4
Niger □ Nigeria 10°0N 5°30E 263 D6
Niger ■ W. Afr. 17°30N 10°0E 259 E2
Niger ➔ W. Afr. 5°33N 6°33E 263 D6
Niger Delta Africa 5°0N 6°0E 263 E6
Nigeria ■ W. Afr. 8°30N 8°0E 263 D6
Nighasin India 28°14N 80°52E 243 E9
Nightcaps N.Z. 45°57S 168°2E 285 F3
Nightmute U.S.A. 60°29N 164°44W 303 F6
Nigrita Greece 40°56N 23°29E 202 F7
Nihoa U.S.A. 23°6N 161°58W 302 G11
Nihon = Japan ■ Asia 36°0N 136°0E 221 G8
Nihonbashi Tokyo, Japan 140 b5
Nii-Jima Japan 34°20N 139°15E 223 C11
Niigata Japan 37°58N 139°0E 220 F9
Niigata □ Japan 37°15N 138°45E 221 F9
Niihama Japan 33°55N 133°16E 222 D5
Ni'ihau U.S.A. 21°54N 160°9W 302 B1
Niimi Japan 34°59N 133°28E 222 C5
Niipperi Finland 60°18N 24°45E 121 B1
Niislel Khureheh = Ulaanbaatar Mongolia 47°55N 106°53E 218 B10
Niitsu Japan 37°48N 139°7E 220 F9
Nij Laluk India 27°7N 93°56E 241 B4
Níjar Spain 36°53N 2°15W 197 J2
Nijil Jordan 30°32N 35°33E 251 H6
Nijkerk Neths. 52°13N 5°30E 170 B5
Nijmegen Neths. 51°50N 5°52E 170 C5
Nijverdal Neths. 52°22N 6°28E 170 B6
Nīk Pey Iran 36°50N 48°10E 213 D13
Nikao Cook Is. 21°12S 159°48W 289 h
Nikaweratiya Sri Lanka 7°45N 80°7E 245 L5
Nike Nigeria 6°26N 7°29E 263 D6
Nikea Greece 37°57N 23°38E 112 B1
Nikel Russia 69°24N 30°13E 160 B24
Nikiboko Bonaire 12°9N 68°16W 322 h
Nikiniki Indonesia 9°49S 124°30E 278 A3
Nikisiani Greece 40°57N 24°9E 203 F8
Nikiski U.S.A. 61°41N 151°18W 303 F10
Nikiti Greece 40°13N 23°43E 202 F7
Nikitinskiye promysly = Kirovskiy Russia 45°51N 48°11E 191 H9
Nikki Benin 9°58N 3°12E 263 D5
Nikkō Japan 36°45N 139°35E 223 A11
Nikkō △ Japan 36°56N 139°37E 221 F9
Nikolai U.S.A. 62°58N 154°10W 303 E9
Nikolainkaupunki = Vaasa Finland 63°6N 21°38E 160 E19
Nikolaistad = Vaasa Finland 63°6N 21°38E 160 E19
Nikolassee Germany 52°25N 13°12E 115 B2
Nikolayev = Mykolayiv Ukraine 46°58N 32°0E 189 J7
Nikolayevsk Russia 50°0N 45°35E 190 E7
Nikolayevsk-na-Amur Russia 53°8N 140°44E 215 D15
Nikolsburg = Mikulov Czechia 48°48N 16°39E 181 C9
Nikolsk Russia 53°49N 46°4E 190 D8
Nikolsk-Ussuriysky = Ussuriysk Russia 43°48N 131°59E 220 C5
Nikolskaya Pestravka = Nikolsk Russia 53°49N 46°4E 190 D8
Nikolski U.S.A. 52°56N 168°52W 303 K5
Nikolskiy Russia 55°49N 37°29E 129 B1
Nikolskoye = Ussuriysk Russia 43°48N 131°59E 220 C5
Nikolskoye Russia 55°12N 166°0E 215 D17
Nikolsky Khutor = Sursk Russia 53°3N 45°40E 190 D7
Nikopol Bulgaria 43°43N 24°54E 203 C8
Nikopol Ukraine 47°35N 34°25E 189 J8
Nikopolis Greece 39°5N 20°43E 207 A2
Niksar Turkey 40°31N 37°2E 212 B7
Nīkshahr Iran 26°15N 60°10E 247 E9
Nikšić Montenegro 42°50N 18°57E 202 D2
Nikumaroro Kiribati 4°40S 174°32W 277 A16
Nikunau Kiribati 1°22S 176°28E 277 A14
Nîl, Nahr en ➔ Africa 30°10N 31°6E 256 H7
Nîl el Abyad ➔ Sudan 15°38N 32°31E 257 D3
Nîl el Azraq ➔ Sudan 15°38N 32°31E 257 D3
Nila Indonesia 6°44S 129°31E 231 F7
Nilakkottai India 10°10N 77°52E 245 J3
Niland U.S.A. 33°14N 115°31W 307 M11
Nilanga India 18°6N 76°46E 244 E3
Nile = Nîl, Nahr en ➔ Africa 30°10N 31°6E 256 H7
Nile Delta Egypt 31°40N 31°0E 256 H7
Niles Ill., U.S.A. 42°1N 87°48W 119 A2
Niles Mich., U.S.A. 41°50N 86°15W 311 C10
Niles Ohio, U.S.A. 41°11N 80°46W 312 E4
Niles Center = Skokie U.S.A. 42°2N 87°43W 119 A2
Nileshwar India 12°15N 75°6E 245 H2
Nilgiri Hills India 11°30N 76°30E 245 J3
Nilo Peçanha Brazil 13°37S 39°6W 333 D4
Nilsebu Norway 59°11N 6°39E 164 E3
Nilüfer ➔ Turkey 40°18N 28°27E 203 F12
Nim Ka Thana India 27°44N 75°48E 242 F6
Nimach India 24°30N 74°56E 242 G6
Nimba, Mt. Africa 7°37N 8°25W 262 D3
Nimbahera India 24°37N 74°45E 242 G6
Nîmes France 43°50N 4°23E 175 E8
Nimfaíon, Ákra = Pines, Akra Greece 40°5N 24°20E 203 F8
Nimmitabel Australia 36°29S 149°15E 283 D8
Nīmrūz □ Afghan. 30°0N 62°0E 240 C1
Nimta India 22°40N 88°24E 124 A2
Nimule South Sudan 3°32N 32°3E 257 G3
Nimule △ South Sudan 3°38N 32°2E 257 G3
Nin Croatia 44°16N 15°12E 199 D12
Nīnawá Iraq 36°25N 43°10E 213 D10
Nīnawá □ Iraq 36°15N 43°0E 246 B4
Ninda Angola 14°47S 21°24E 265 E4
Nindigully Australia 28°21S 148°50E 281 D4
Nine Degree Channel India 9°0N 73°0E 245 K1
Ninepin Group China 22°16N 114°21E 219 a
Ninety Mile Beach N.Z. 34°48S 173°0E 284 A2
Ninety Mile Beach, The Australia 38°15S 147°24E 283 E7
Ninety Six U.S.A. 34°11N 82°1W 316 A7
Ninetyeast Ridge Ind. Oc. 1°0S 90°0E 273 E7
Nineveh = Nīnawá Iraq 36°25N 43°10E 213 D10
Ning Xian China 35°30N 107°58E 226 G4
Ningaloo Marine ⌓ Australia 22°23S 113°32E 278 D1
Ning'an China 44°22N 129°20E 227 B15
Ningbo China 29°51N 121°28E 229 C13
Ningcheng China 41°32N 119°53E 227 D10
Ningde China 26°38N 119°23E 229 D12
Ningdu China 26°25N 115°59E 229 D10
Ningerum Papua N. G. 5°41S 141°8E 286 C1
Ninggang China 26°42N 113°55E 229 D9
Ningguo China 30°35N 119°0E 229 B12
Ninghai China 29°15N 121°27E 229 C13
Ninghua China 26°14N 116°45E 229 D11
Ningi Nigeria 10°55N 9°30E 263 C6
Ningjin China 37°35N 114°57E 226 F8
Ningjing Shan China 31°0N 98°20E 228 C2
Ninglang China 27°20N 100°55E 228 D3
Ningling China 34°25N 115°22E 226 G8
Ningming China 22°8N 107°4E 228 F6
Ningnan China 27°5N 102°36E 228 D4
Ningpo = Ningbo China 29°51N 121°28E 229 C13
Ningqiang China 32°47N 106°15E 226 H4
Ningshan China 33°21N 108°21E 228 A7
Ningsia Hui A.R. = Ningxia Huizu Zizhiqu □ China 38°0N 106°0E 226 F4
Ningwu China 39°0N 112°18E 226 E7
Ningxia Huizu Zizhiqu □ China 38°0N 106°0E 226 F4
Ningxiang China 28°15N 112°30E 229 C9
Ningyang China 35°47N 116°45E 226 G9
Ningyuan China 25°37N 111°57E 229 E8
Ninh Binh Vietnam 20°15N 105°55E 228 G5
Ninh Giang Vietnam 20°44N 106°24E 236 B6
Ninh Hoa Vietnam 12°30N 109°7E 236 F7
Ninh Ma Vietnam 12°48N 109°21E 236 F7
Nini-Suhien △ Ghana 5°20N 2°34W 262 D4
Ninigo Group Papua N. G. 1°22S 144°17E 286 A3
Ninove Belgium 50°51N 4°2E 170 D4
Ninoy Aquino Int. ✈ (MNL) Phil. 14°31N 121°0E 127 B2
Nioaque Brazil 21°5S 55°50W 335 A4
Niobrara U.S.A. 42°45N 98°2W 308 D4
Niobrara ➔ U.S.A. 42°46N 98°3W 308 D4
Nioki Dem. Rep. of the Congo 2°47S 17°40E 264 C3
Niokolo-Koba △ Senegal 13°3N 13°2W 262 C2
Niono Mali 14°15N 6°0W 262 C3
Nionsamoridougou Guinea 8°45N 8°50W 262 D3
Nioro du Rip Senegal 13°40N 15°50W 262 C1
Nioro du Sahel Mali 15°15N 9°30W 262 B3
Niort France 46°19N 0°29W 174 B3
Nioumachoua Comoros Is. 12°21S 43°42E 272 a
Nipa Papua N. G. 6°9S 143°29E 286 D2
Nipani India 16°20N 74°25E 245 F2
Nipawin Canada 53°20N 104°0W 297 C8
Nipfjället Sweden 61°59N 12°50E 162 C6
Nipigon Canada 49°0N 88°17W 298 C2
Nipigon, L. Canada 49°50N 88°30W 298 C2
Nipishish L. Canada 54°12N 60°45W 299 B7
Nipissing, L. Canada 46°20N 80°0W 298 C4
Nipomo U.S.A. 35°3N 120°29W 307 K6
Nippa Japan 35°31N 139°36E 140 B2
Nippon = Japan ■ Asia 36°0N 136°0E 221 G8
Nippori Japan 35°43N 139°45E 140 A3
Nipton U.S.A. 35°28N 115°16W 307 K11
Niquelândia Brazil 14°33S 48°23W 333 D2
Nīr Iran 38°2N 47°59E 213 C12
Nira ➔ India 17°58N 75°8E 244 F2
Nirasaki Japan 35°42N 138°27E 223 B10
Nirayama = Izunokuni Japan 35°2N 138°55E 223 B10
Nirmal India 19°3N 78°20E 244 E4
Nirmali India 26°20N 86°35E 243 F12
Niš Serbia 43°19N 21°58E 202 C5
Nisa = Nysa ➔ Europe 52°4N 14°46E 178 C10
Nisa Portugal 39°30N 7°41W 195 F3
Nisa Turkmenistan 37°59N 58°11E 247 B8
Nişāb Si. Arabia 29°11N 44°43E 246 D5
Nişāb Yemen 14°25N 46°29E 248 D4
Nišava ➔ Serbia 43°20N 21°46E 202 C5
Niscemi Italy 37°9N 14°23E 201 E7
Nishi Japan 34°40N 135°28E 133 A1
Nishi-Sonogi-Hantō Japan 32°55N 129°45E 222 E1
Nishi-Tosa Japan 33°13N 132°46E 222 D4
Nishinari Japan 34°37N 135°28E 133 B1
Nishinomiya Japan 34°45N 135°20E 133 A1
Nishino'omote Japan 30°43N 130°59E 221 J5
Nishio Japan 34°52N 137°3E 223 C9
Nishiwaki Japan 34°59N 134°58E 222 C6
Nishiyodogawa Japan 34°41N 135°24E 133 A1
Nishon Tumani Uzbekistan 38°49N 65°47E 240 A2
Nishtūn Yemen 15°49N 52°14E 249 D6
Nisibin = Nusaybin Turkey 37°3N 41°10E 213 D9
Niška Banja Serbia 43°18N 22°1E 202 C6
Niskibi ➔ Canada 56°29N 88°9W 298 A2
Nisko Poland 50°35N 22°7E 185 H9
Nisporeni Moldova 47°4N 28°10E 183 C13
Nisqually ➔ U.S.A. 47°7N 122°42W 306 C4
Nissaki Greece 39°43N 19°52E 206 B9
Nissan ➔ Sweden 56°40N 12°51E 163 H6
Nissedal Norway 59°10N 8°30E 164 E5
Nisser Norway 59°7N 8°28E 164 E5
Nissiros Greece 36°35N 27°12E 205 E9
Nissum Bredning Denmark 56°40N 8°20E 163 H2
Nissum Fjord Denmark 56°20N 8°11E 163 H2
Nistru = Dnister ➔ Europe 46°18N 30°17E 177 E16
Nisutlin ➔ Canada 60°14N 132°34W 296 A2
Nitchequon Canada 53°10N 70°58W 299 B5
Niterói Brazil 22°53S 43°7W 135 B2
Nith ➔ Ont., Canada 43°12N 80°23W 312 C4
Nith ➔ Dumf. & Gall., U.K. 55°14N 3°33W 167 F5
Nitmiluk △ Australia 14°6S 132°15E 278 B5
Nitra Slovakia 48°19N 18°4E 181 C11
Nitra ➔ Slovakia 47°46N 18°10E 181 D11
Nitriansky □ Slovakia 48°10N 18°30E 181 C11
Nittenau Germany 49°12N 12°16E 179 F8
Niu Valley U.S.A. 21°19N 157°44W 302 K14
Niua Group Tonga 15°57S 173°45W 277 D16
Niuafo'ou Tonga 15°30S 175°58W 277 D15
Niuatoputapu Tonga 15°57S 173°45W 277 D16
Niue ⊠ Pac. Oc. 19°2S 169°54W 289 g
Niulakita Pac. Oc. 10°45S 179°30E 277 C14
Niulan Jiang ➔ China 27°30N 103°5E 228 D4
Niulantsun Taiwan 25°1N 121°2E 225 A3
Niur Indonesia 0°26S 103°30E 234 C2
Niut Indonesia 0°55N 109°54E 235 B4
Niutao Pac. Oc. 6°7S 177°18E 277 B14
Niutou Shan China 29°5N 121°59E 229 C13
Niuzhuang China 40°58N 122°28E 224 B1
Nivala Finland 63°56N 24°57E 160 E21
Nivelles Belgium 50°35N 4°20E 170 D4
Nivernais France 47°15N 3°30E 173 E10
Niverville Canada 49°36N 97°3W 297 D9
Niwas India 23°3N 80°26E 243 H9
Nixa U.S.A. 37°3N 93°18W 308 G7
Nixon U.S.A. 29°16N 97°46W 314 G6
Nizam Sagar India 18°10N 77°58E 244 E3
Nizamabad India 18°45N 78°7E 244 E4
Nizamghat India 28°20N 95°45E 241 A5
Nizhne-Kolymsk Russia 68°34N 160°55E 215 C17
Nizhne-Svirskiy ⌓ Russia 60°30N 32°55E 188 B7
Nizhnegorskiy = Nyzhnohirskyy Ukraine 45°27N 34°38E 189 K8
Nizhnekamsk Russia 55°38N 51°49E 190 C10
Nizhneudinsk Russia 54°54N 99°3E 215 D10
Nizhnevartovsk Russia 60°56N 76°38E 214 C8
Nizhniy Bestyakh Russia 61°57N 129°54E 215 C13
Nizhniy Chir Russia 48°22N 43°5E 191 F6
Nizhniy Lomov Russia 53°34N 43°38E 190 D6
Nizhniy Novgorod Russia 56°20N 44°0E 190 B7
Nizhniy Novgorod □ Russia 56°30N 44°20E 190 B7
Nizhniy Tagil Russia 57°55N 59°57E 186 C10
Nizhniye Kresty = Cherskiy Russia 68°45N 161°18E 215 C17
Nizhyn Ukraine 51°5N 31°55E 189 G6
Nizina Mazowiecka Poland 52°30N 21°0E 185 F8
Nizip Turkey 37°5N 37°50E 212 D7
Nízké Tatry Slovakia 48°55N 19°30E 181 C12
Nízké Tatry △ Slovakia 48°55N 19°37E 181 C12
Nízký Jeseník Czechia 49°50N 17°30E 181 B10
Nizwá Oman 22°56N 57°32E 249 B7
Nizza Monferrato Italy 44°46N 8°21E 198 D5
Njakwa Malawi 11°1S 33°56E 269 E3
Njarðvíkur Iceland 63°59N 22°32W 155 D4
Njazidja = Grande Comore Comoros Is. 11°35S 43°20E 272 a
Njegoš Montenegro 42°53N 18°45E 202 D2
Njeru Uganda 0°27N 33°10E 268 B3
Njinjo Tanzania 8°48S 38°54E 269 D4
Njoko ➔ Zambia 17°8S 24°4E 265 F4
Njombe Tanzania 9°20S 34°50E 269 D3
Njombe □ Tanzania 9°10S 34°50E 269 D3
Njombe ➔ Tanzania 6°56S 35°6E 268 D4

Njurundabommen
Sweden 62°15N 17°25E 162 B11
Nkambe Cameroon 6°35N 10°40E 263 D7
Nkana Zambia 12°50S 28°8E 269 E2
Nkandla S. Africa 28°37S 31°5E 271 C5
Nkawkaw Ghana 6°36N 0°49W 263 D4
Nkayi Congo 4°9S 13°17E 264 C2
Nkayi Zimbabwe 19°41S 29°20E 269 F2
Nkhotakota Malawi 12°56S 34°15E 269 E3
Nkhotakota ⌓ Malawi 12°50S 34°0E 269 E3
Nkolabona Gabon 1°14N 11°43E 264 B2
Nkomi, Lagune Gabon 1°35S 9°17E 264 C1
Nkondwe Tanzania 5°51S 30°51E 268 D3
Nkone Dem. Rep. of the Congo 1°2S 22°20E 264 C4
Nkongsamba Cameroon 4°55N 9°55E 263 E6
Nkoteng Cameroon 4°31N 12°2E 264 B2
Nkunga
Dem. Rep. of the Congo 4°41S 18°34E 265 C3
Nkurenkuru Namibia 17°42S 18°32E 270 A2
Nkwanta Ghana 6°10N 2°10W 262 D4
Nmai ➜ Myanmar 25°30N 97°25E 228 F2
No, L. South Sudan 9°30N 30°28E 266 C3
Noakhali Bangla. 22°48N 91°10E 241 D3
Noatak U.S.A. 67°34N 162°58W 303 C7
Noatak ⌓ U.S.A. 68°10N 160°0W 303 B8
Nob Hill San Francisco, U.S.A. 136 b1
Nobel Canada 45°25N 80°6W 312 A4
Nobeoka Japan 32°36N 131°41E 222 E3
Noble U.S.A. 38°42N 88°14W 311 F8
Noblejas Spain 39°58N 3°26W 194 F7
Noblesville U.S.A. 40°3N 86°1W 311 D11
Noboribetsu Japan 42°24N 141°6E 220 C10
Nocatee U.S.A. 27°10N 81°53W 317 H8
Noccundra Australia 27°50S 142°36E 281 D3
Noce ➜ Italy 46°9N 11°4E 198 B8
Nocera Inferiore Italy 40°44N 14°38E 201 B7
Nocera Umbra Italy 43°5N 12°47E 199 E9
Noci Italy 40°48N 17°7E 201 B10
Nockeby Sweden 59°19N 17°56E 139 B1
Nocona U.S.A. 33°47N 97°44W 314 E6
Nocrich Romania 45°55N 24°26E 183 E9
Noda Japan 35°56N 139°52E 223 B11
Nodeland Norway 58°8N 7°51E 164 F4
Noel Kempff Mercado △
Bolivia 14°9S 60°49W 331 C5
Noel Park U.K. 51°35N 0°5W 125 A3
Nogal Valley = Nugaaleed, Dooxo
Somalia 8°35N 48°35E 267 C6
Nogales Sonora, Mexico 31°19N 110°56W 318 A2
Nogales Ariz., U.S.A. 31°21N 110°56W 305 L8
Nogaro France 43°45N 0°2W 174 E3
Nogat ➜ Poland 54°17N 19°17E 184 D6
Nōgata Japan 33°48N 130°44E 222 D2
Nogatino Russia 55°41N 37°41E 129 B3
Nogaysk = Prymorske
Ukraine 46°48N 36°20E 189 J9
Nogent France 48°1N 5°20E 173 D12
Nogent-le-Rotrou France 48°20N 0°50E 172 D7
Nogent-sur-Marne France 48°50N 2°28E 134 A3
Nogent-sur-Seine France 48°30N 3°30E 173 D10
Noggara Ethiopia 13°54N 36°35E 257 E4
Noggerup Australia 33°32S 116°5E 279 F2
Noginsk Russia 64°30N 90°50E 215 C10
Nogliki Russia 51°50N 143°10E 215 D15
Nogoa ➜ Australia 23°40S 147°55E 280 C4
Nogoyá Argentina 32°24S 59°48W 334 C4
Nógrád □ Hungary 48°0N 19°30E 182 C4
Noguera Pallaresa ➜
Spain 41°55N 0°55E 196 D5
Noguera Ribagorçana ➜
Spain 41°40N 0°43E 196 D5
Nohar India 29°11N 74°49E 242 E6
Nohfelden Germany 49°35N 7°7E 179 F3
Nohili Pt. U.S.A. 22°4N 159°47W 302 A2
Nohta India 23°40N 79°34E 243 H8
Nohwa S. Korea 34°10N 126°34E 224 E3
Nohwado S. Korea 34°12N 126°35E 224 E3
Noia Spain 42°48N 8°53W 194 C2
Noichi Japan 33°33N 133°42E 222 D5
Noida India 28°36N 77°19E 120 B2
Noipuos Papua N. G. 2°25S 150°7E 286 B6
Noire, Montagne France 43°28N 2°18E 174 E6
Noires, Mts. France 48°11N 3°40W 172 D3
Noirétable France 45°48N 3°46E 174 C7
Noirmoutier, Î. de France 46°58N 2°10W 172 F4
Noirmoutier-en-l'Île France 47°0N 2°14W 172 F4
Noiseau France 48°46N 2°32E 134 B4
Noisiel France 48°51N 2°37E 134 A4
Noisy-le-Grand France 48°50N 2°33E 134 A4
Noisy-le-Roi France 48°50N 2°3E 134 A1
Noisy-le-Sec France 48°53N 2°27E 134 A3
Nojane Botswana 23°15S 20°14E 270 B3
Nojima-Zaki Japan 34°54N 139°53E 223 C11
Nok Kundi Pakistan 28°50N 62°45E 240 C1
Nok Ta Phao, Ko Thailand 9°23N 99°40E 237 b
Nokaneng Botswana 19°40S 22°17E 270 A3
Nokia Finland 61°30N 23°30E 188 B2
Nokkala Finland 60°8N 24°45E 121 C1
Nokkeushi = Kitami
Japan 43°48N 143°54E 220 C11
Nokomis Sask., Canada 51°35N 105°0W 297 C8
Nokomis Fla., U.S.A. 27°7N 82°27W 317 H7
Nokomis Ill., U.S.A. 39°18N 89°18W 310 E7
Nokomis L. Canada 57°0N 103°0W 297 B8
Nokou Chad 14°35N 14°47E 259 F2
Nokuku Vanuatu 14°54S 166°35E 287 D4
Nola C.A.R. 3°35N 16°4E 264 B3
Nola Italy 40°55N 14°33E 201 B7
Nolay France 46°58N 4°35E 173 F11
Noli, C. di Italy 44°12N 8°25E 198 D5
Nolinsk Russia 57°28N 49°57E 190 B9
Noma U.S.A. 30°59N 85°37W 316 E4
Noma Omuramba ➜
Namibia 18°52S 20°53E 270 A3
Noma-Saki Japan 31°25N 130°7E 222 F2
Nomad Papua N. G. 6°19S 142°13E 286 D2
Nombre de Dios Panama 9°34N 79°28W 320 E4
Nome U.S.A. 64°30N 165°25W 303 D6
Nomentano Italy 41°55N 12°30E 136 B2
Nomgon Mongolia 42°50N 105°8E 226 C3
Nomi Japan 36°26N 136°25E 223 A8
Nomo-Zaki Japan 32°35N 129°44E 222 E1
Nomoneas Micronesia 7°24N 151°53E 287 T18
Nomuka Tonga 20°17S 174°48W 287 Q13
Nomuka Group Tonga 20°20S 174°48W 287 Q13
Nonacho L. Canada 61°42N 109°40W 297 A7
Nonakashinden Japan 35°44N 139°30E 140 A2
Nonancourt France 48°47N 1°11E 172 D8
Nonda Australia 20°40S 142°28E 280 C3
Nondalton U.S.A. 60°0N 154°51W 303 F9
None Italy 44°56N 7°32E 198 D4
Nong Chang Thailand 15°23N 99°51E 236 E2
Nong Han Res. Thailand 17°11N 104°9E 236 D5
Nong Het Laos 19°29N 103°59E 236 C4
Nong Khai Thailand 17°50N 102°46E 236 D4
Nong'an China 44°25N 125°5E 227 B13
Nongjrong India 25°29N 92°6E 241 C4
Nongminyundong Jiangxisuo
China 23°7N 113°15E 121 B2
Nongoma S. Africa 27°58S 31°35E 271 C5
Nongpoh India 25°54N 91°53E 241 C3
Nongsa Indonesia 1°11N 104°8E 237 d
Nongstoin India 25°31N 91°16E 241 C3
Nonhyeon S. Korea 37°30N 127°1E 137 B2
Nono Ethiopia 8°32N 37°26E 266 C4
Nonoava Mexico 27°28N 106°44W 318 B3
Nonoc I. Phil. 9°51N 125°37E 233 G5
Nonoichi Japan 36°35N 136°35E 223 A8
Nonsan S. Korea 36°12N 127°5E 224 D3
Nonsuch B. Antigua & B. 17°3N 61°42W 322 b
Nonthaburi Thailand 13°50N 100°29E 113 A1
Nontron France 45°31N 0°40E 174 C4
Nonza France 42°47N 9°21E 175 F13
Noon Gun Cape Town, S. Africa 118 b1
Noonamah Australia 12°40S 131°4E 278 B5
Noondie, L. Australia 28°30S 119°30E 279 E2
Noonkanbah ✪ Australia 18°30S 124°50E 278 C3
Noord Aruba 12°34N 70°1W 322 f
Noord Brabant □ Neths. 51°40N 5°0E 170 C5
Noord Holland □ Neths. 52°30N 4°45E 170 B4
Noord Saliña Bonaire 12°11N 68°16W 322 h
Noordbeveland Neths. 51°35N 3°50E 170 C3
Noorderkerk Amsterdam, Neths. 112 a1
Noordgesig S. Africa 26°13S 27°56E 123 B1
Noordkaap Aruba 12°34N 70°1W 322 f
Noordoostpolder Neths. 52°45N 5°45E 170 B5
Noordpunt Bonaire 12°18N 68°23W 322 h
Noordpunt Curaçao 12°24N 69°10W 322 g
Noordwijk Neths. 52°14N 4°26E 170 B4
Noordzeekanaal Neths. 52°28N 4°47E 112 A1
Noorvik U.S.A. 66°50N 161°3W 303 C7
Noosa Heads Australia 26°25S 153°6E 281 D5
Nootka I. Canada 49°32N 126°42W 296 D3
Nopiming ⌓ Canada 50°30N 95°37W 297 C9
Nóqui Angola 5°55S 13°30E 265 D2
Nor-Bayzzet = Gavar
Armenia 40°21N 45°7E 191 K7
Nora Eritrea 16°6N 40°4E 257 D5
Nora Sweden 59°32N 15°2E 162 E9
Nora Springs U.S.A. 43°9N 93°0W 310 A4
Norala Phil. 6°32N 124°40E 233 H5
Noralee Canada 53°59N 126°26W 296 C3
Noranda = Rouyn-Noranda
Canada 48°20N 79°0W 298 C4
Norberg Sweden 60°4N 15°56E 162 D9
Norborne U.S.A. 39°18N 93°40W 310 E3
Nórcia Italy 42°48N 13°5E 199 F10
Norco U.S.A. 33°56N 117°33W 307 M9
Norcross U.S.A. 33°56N 84°13W 316 B5
Nord □ Cameroon 8°30N 14°0E 263 D7
Nord □ France 50°15N 3°30E 173 B10
Nord, Gare du Paris, France 134 a4
Nord, Pt. Comoros Is. 11°22S 43°19E 272 a
Nord-Kivu □
Dem. Rep. of the Congo 1°0S 29°0E 268 C2
Nord-Ostsee-Kanal
Germany 54°12N 9°32E 178 A5
Nord-Ouest □ Cameroon 6°20N 10°30E 263 D7
Nord-Ubangi □
Dem. Rep. of the Congo 3°0N 21°0E 264 B4
Nordagutu Norway 59°25N 9°20E 164 E6
Nordaustlandet Svalbard 79°14N 23°0E 150 B9
Nordberg Norway 61°54N 8°10E 164 C5
Nordborg Denmark 55°5N 9°50E 163 J3
Nordby Denmark 55°27N 8°24E 163 J2
Norddeich Germany 53°36N 7°9E 178 B3
Nordegg Canada 52°29N 116°5W 296 C5
Norden Germany 53°35N 7°12E 178 B3
Nordenham Germany 53°30N 8°30E 178 B4
Nordenskjöld Sea = Laptev Sea
Russia 76°0N 125°0E 215 B13
Norderhov Norway 60°7N 10°17E 164 D7
Norderney Germany 53°42N 7°9E 178 B3
Norderstedt Germany 53°42N 10°1E 178 B6
Nordeste Azores 37°50N 25°10W 153 d3
Nordfjord Norway 61°55N 5°30E 164 C2
Nordfjordeid Norway 61°54N 6°0E 164 C2
Nordfriesische Inseln
Germany 54°40N 8°20E 178 A4
Nordhausen Germany 51°30N 10°47E 178 D6
Nordhorn Germany 52°26N 7°4E 178 C3
Norðoyar Færoe Is. 62°17N 6°35W 160 E9
Norðtunga Iceland 64°44N 21°24W 155 C5
Norður-múlasýsla Iceland 65°30N 15°0W 155 B11
Norðurbotn Iceland 65°36N 23°46W 155 B3
Norðurland Eystra □
Iceland 65°30N 17°0W 155 B9
Norðurland Vestra □
Iceland 65°30N 20°0W 155 B6
Nördinge-Nol Sweden 57°56N 12°5E 163 G6
Nordingrå Sweden 62°56N 18°17E 162 B12
Nordkapp Finnmark,
Norway 71°10N 25°50E 160 A21
Nordkapp Svalbard 80°31N 20°0E 150 A9
Nordkinn Norway 71°8N 27°40E 160 A22
Nordkinnhalvøya
Norway 70°55N 27°40E 160 A22
Nördlicher Teutoburger
Wald-Wiehengebirge ⌓
Germany 52°18N 8°10E 178 C4
Nördlingen Germany 48°48N 10°30E 179 G6
Nordmarka Norway 59°58N 10°41E 133 A3
Nordmøre Norway 63°6N 8°15E 164 B4
Nordostrundingen
Greenland 81°22N 11°40W 154 A9
Nordøyane Norway 62°40N 6°0E 164 B3
Nordrand-Siedlung
Austria 48°16N 16°26E 142 A2
Nordre Bergenhus = Sogn og
Fjordane □ Norway 61°40N 6°45E 164 C3
Nørdre Osa Norway 61°18N 11°45E 164 C8
Nordre Strømfjord
Greenland 67°10N 53°35W 154 D5
Nordrhein-Westfalen □
Germany 51°45N 7°30E 178 D3
Nordsinni Norway 60°50N 9°57E 164 D6
Nørdstedalssæter Norway 61°40N 7°48E 164 C4
Nordstrand Schleswig-Holstein,
Germany 54°30N 8°52E 178 A4
Nordstrand Oslo, Norway 59°52N 10°48E 133 A3
Nordvik Russia 74°2N 111°32E 215 B12
Nore ➜ Ireland 52°25N 6°58W 166 D4
Norefjell Norway 60°16N 9°29E 164 D6
Noreland Canada 44°43N 78°48W 312 B6
Noresund Norway 60°11N 9°37E 164 D6
Norfolk = Simcoe Canada 42°50N 80°23W 312 D4
Norfolk N.Y., U.S.A. 44°48N 74°59W 313 B10
Norfolk Nebr., U.S.A. 42°2N 97°25W 308 D5
Norfolk Va., U.S.A. 36°50N 76°17W 309 G15
Norfolk □ U.K. 52°39N 0°54E 169 E8
Norfolk Basin Pac. Oc. 32°0S 170°0E 277 G13
Norfolk Broads △ U.K. 52°45N 1°30E 169 E9
Norfolk I. Pac. Oc. 28°58S 168°3E 277 F12
Norfolk Ridge Pac. Oc. 29°0S 168°0E 288 K8
Norfork L. U.S.A. 36°15N 92°14W 314 C8
Norge = Norway ■ Europe 63°0N 11°0E 160 E14
Norheimsund Norway 60°23N 6°6E 164 D3
Norilsk Russia 69°20N 88°6E 215 C9
Norland U.S.A. 25°57N 80°12W 129 C2
Norma, Mt. Australia 20°55S 140°42E 280 C3
Normal U.S.A. 40°31N 88°59W 310 D8
Norman U.S.A. 35°13N 97°26W 314 D6
Norman ➜ Australia 19°18S 141°51E 280 B3
Norman Manley Int. ✈ (KIN)
Jamaica 17°56N 76°47W 320 a
Norman Park U.S.A. 31°16N 83°41W 316 D6
Norman Wells Canada 65°17N 126°51W 294 D6
Normanby N.Z. 39°32S 174°18E 284 F3
Normanby ➜ Australia 14°23S 144°10E 280 A3
Normanby I. Papua N. G. 10°5S 151°5E 286 F6
Normandie France 48°45N 0°10E 171 B4
Normandie □ France 49°0N 0°30E 172 D7
Normandie-Maine ⌓
France 48°30N 0°20W 172 D6
Normandin Canada 48°49N 72°31W 298 C5
Normandy = Normandie
France 48°45N 0°10E 171 B4
Normanhurst, Mt.
Australia 25°4S 122°30E 279 E3
Normanton Australia 17°40S 141°10E 280 B3
Normanville Australia 35°27S 138°18E 282 C3
Normétal Canada 49°0N 79°22W 298 C4
Norquay Canada 51°53N 102°5W 297 C8
Norquinco Argentina 41°51S 70°55W 336 B2
Norra Kvill △ Sweden 57°46N 15°35E 163 G9
Norra Ulvön Sweden 63°3N 18°40E 162 A12
Norrahammar Sweden 57°43N 14°7E 163 G8
Norrbottens län □ Sweden 66°50N 20°0E 160 C19
Norrdellen Sweden 61°53N 16°43E 162 C10
Nørre Aaby Denmark 55°27N 9°52E 163 J3
Nørre Alslev Denmark 54°54N 11°52E 163 K5
Nørrebro Copenhagen, Denmark 118 a1
Nørresundby Denmark 57°5N 9°52E 163 G3
Norrhult-Klavreström
Sweden 57°7N 15°10E 163 G9
Norridge U.S.A. 41°57N 87°49W 119 B2
Norris City U.S.A. 37°59N 88°20W 311 G8
Norris Point Canada 49°31N 57°53W 299 C8
Norristown Ga., U.S.A. 32°30N 82°30W 316 C7
Norristown Pa., U.S.A. 40°7N 75°21W 313 F9
Norrköping Sweden 58°37N 16°11E 163 F10
Norrland Sweden 62°15N 15°45E 160 E16
Norrmalm Stockholm, Sweden 139 a1
Norrsundet Sweden 60°56N 17°8E 162 D11
Norrtälje Sweden 59°46N 18°42E 162 E12
Norseman Australia 32°8S 121°43E 279 F3
Norsewood N.Z. 40°3S 176°13E 284 G5
Norsjø Norway 59°18N 9°20E 164 E6
Norsk Russia 52°30N 130°5E 215 D14
Norsup Vanuatu 16°3S 167°24E 287 F5
Norte, C. Chile 27°3S 109°24W 330 b
Norte, Canal do ➜ Brazil 0°40N 50°20W 329 C7
Norte, Pta. Argentina 42°5S 63°46W 336 B4
Norte, Pta. Chile 33°36S 78°54W 330 c
Norte, Pta. del Canary Is. 27°51N 17°57W 153 e1
Norte, Pta. do Azores 37°1N 25°4W 153 d4
Norte, Serra do Brazil 11°20S 59°0W 331 C6
Norte de Santander □
Colombia 8°0N 73°0W 328 B3
Norte Grande Azores 38°40N 28°4W 153 d1
Nortelândia Brazil 14°25S 56°48W 331 C6
North U.S.A. 33°37N 81°6W 316 B8
North, C. Canada 47°2N 60°20W 299 C7
North Adams U.S.A. 42°42N 73°7W 313 D11
North America 40°0N 100°0W 292 F10
North Andaman I. India 13°15N 92°55E 245 H11
North Arlington U.S.A. 40°47N 74°7W 132 B1
North Arm Canada 62°0N 114°30W 296 A5
North Atlanta U.S.A. 33°53N 84°19W 113 A3
North Augusta U.S.A. 33°30N 81°59W 316 B8
North Australian Basin
Ind. Oc. 14°30S 116°30E 276 C2
North Ayrshire □ U.K. 55°45N 4°44W 167 F4
North Balabac Str. Phil. 8°8N 117°4E 233 G1
North Baltimore U.S.A. 41°11N 83°41W 311 C13
North Bass I. U.S.A. 41°40N 82°56W 312 E2
North Battleford Canada 52°50N 108°17W 297 C7
North Bay Canada 46°20N 79°30W 298 C4
North Bay Village U.S.A. 25°50N 80°9W 129 C3
North Beach San Francisco, U.S.A. 136 a2
North Belcher Is. Canada 56°50N 79°50W 298 A4
North Bend Oreg., U.S.A. 43°24N 124°14W 304 E1
North Bend Pa., U.S.A. 41°20N 77°42W 312 E7
North Bend Wash.,
U.S.A. 47°30N 121°47W 306 C5
North Bennington
U.S.A. 42°56N 73°15W 313 D11
North Bergen U.S.A. 40°48N 74°0W 132 B1
North Berwick E. Loth.,
U.K. 56°4N 2°42W 167 E6
North Berwick Maine,
U.S.A. 43°18N 70°44W 313 C14
North Borneo = Sabah □
Malaysia 6°0N 117°0E 235 A5
North Breakers
Midway Is. 28°13N 177°24W 302 c
North Brother I. India 10°59N 92°40E 245 J11
North Bruce Canada 44°22N 81°26W 312 B3
North C. N.B., Canada 47°5N 64°0W 299 C7
North C. N.Z. 34°23S 173°4E 284 A2
North C. Papua N. G. 2°32S 150°50E 286 B6
North Canadian ➜
U.S.A. 35°22N 95°37W 314 D7
North Canton U.S.A. 40°53N 81°24W 312 F3
North Cape = Nordkapp
Norway 71°10N 25°50E 160 A21
North Caribou L. Canada 52°50N 90°40W 298 B1
North Carolina □ U.S.A. 35°30N 80°0W 315 D15
North Cascades △
U.S.A. 48°45N 121°10W 304 B3
North Cay The Bahamas 25°6N 77°26W 153 b
North Channel Ont., Canada 46°0N 83°0W 298 C3
North Channel U.K. 55°13N 5°52W 167 F3
North Charleston U.S.A. 32°53N 79°58W 316 C10
North Cheam U.K. 51°22N 0°11W 125 B2
North Chicago U.S.A. 42°19N 87°51W 311 B9
North College Hill
U.S.A. 39°13N 84°33W 311 E12
North Collins U.S.A. 42°35N 78°56W 312 D6
North Comino Channel
Malta 36°1N 14°20E 206 E7
North Cotabato □ Phil. 7°10N 125°0E 233 H5
North Cray U.K. 51°25N 0°8E 125 B4
North Creek U.S.A. 43°42N 73°59W 313 C11
North Dakota □ U.S.A. 47°30N 100°15W 308 B3
North Decatur U.S.A. 33°48N 84°17W 113 B3
North Downs U.K. 51°19N 0°21E 169 F8
North Druid Hills U.S.A. 33°49N 84°17W 113 B3
North East U.S.A. 42°13N 79°50W 312 D5
North East □ Botswana 20°45S 27°30E 271 B4
North East □ Ghana 10°20N 1°0W 263 C4
North East B. Ascension I. 7°55S 14°21W 153 g
North East Frontier Agency =
Arunachal Pradesh □
India 28°0N 95°0E 241 B5
North East Lincolnshire □
U.K. 53°34N 0°2W 168 D7
North End Boston, U.S.A. 116 a3
North Esk ➜ Angus, U.K. 56°46N 2°24W 167 E6
North Esk ➜ Midloth., U.K. 55°54N 3°4W 121 B2
North European Plain
Europe 55°0N 25°0E 158 E10
North Fabius ➜ U.S.A. 39°54N 91°30W 310 E5
North Foreland U.K. 51°22N 1°28E 169 F9
North Fork U.S.A. 37°14N 119°21W 306 H7
North Fork, Salt ➜
U.S.A. 39°26N 91°53W 310 E5
North Fork American ➜
U.S.A. 38°57N 120°59W 306 G5
North Fork Edisto ➜
U.S.A. 33°16N 80°54W 316 B9
North Fork Feather ➜
U.S.A. 38°33N 121°30W 306 F5
North Fork Grand ➜
U.S.A. 45°47N 102°16W 308 C2
North Fork Red ➜
U.S.A. 34°24N 99°14W 314 D5
North Fort Myers U.S.A. 26°41N 81°53W 317 J8
North Frisian Is. = Nordfriesische
Inseln Germany 54°40N 8°20E 178 A4
North Gower Canada 45°8N 75°43W 313 A9
North Greenfield = West Allis
U.S.A. 43°1N 88°0W 311 B8
North Gyle U.K. 55°57N 3°19W 121 B2
North Hackensack U.S.A. 40°54N 74°2W 132 A1
North Harbor Phil. 14°37N 120°57E 127 B1
North Hd. N.S.W.,
Australia 33°49S 151°18E 139 A2
North Hd. W. Austral.,
Australia 30°14S 114°59E 279 F1
North Henik L. Canada 61°45N 97°40W 297 A9
North Highlands U.S.A. 38°40N 121°23W 306 G5
North Hollywood U.S.A. 34°9N 118°22W 126 B2
North Horr Kenya 3°20N 37°8E 268 B4
North I. India 10°8N 72°20E 245 J1
North I. Rift Valley, Kenya 4°5N 36°5E 268 B4
North I. N.Z. 38°0S 175°0E 284 E4
North I. Seychelles 4°25S 55°13E 272 c
North Judson U.S.A. 41°13N 86°46W 311 C10
North Kingsville U.S.A. 41°54N 80°42W 312 E4
North Kitui ⌓ Kenya 0°15S 38°29E 268 C4
North Knife ➜ Canada 58°53N 94°45W 297 B10
North Koel ➜ India 24°45N 83°50E 243 G10
North Korea ■ Asia 40°0N 127°0E 224 C3
North L. N.S.W., Australia 32°30S 143°5E 282 B5
North L. Tex., U.S.A. 32°56N 96°58W 120 A4
North Lake Park U.S.A. 32°55N 96°58W 120 A4
North Lakhimpur India 27°14N 94°7E 241 B5
North Lanarkshire □ U.K. 55°52N 3°56W 167 F5
North Las Vegas U.S.A. 36°11N 115°7W 124 A1
North Las Vegas ✈ (VGT)
U.S.A. 36°12N 115°11W 124 A1
North Lexington U.S.A. 42°27N 71°14W 116 A1
North Liberty Ind.,
U.S.A. 41°32N 86°26W 311 C10
North Liberty Iowa,
U.S.A. 41°46N 91°35W 310 C5
North Lincolnshire □
U.K. 53°36N 0°30W 168 D7
North Little Rock U.S.A. 34°45N 92°16W 314 D8
North Loup ➜ U.S.A. 41°17N 98°24W 308 E4
North Luangwa △ Zambia 11°49S 32°9E 269 E3
North Macedonia ■
Europe 41°53N 21°40E 202 E5
North Magnetic Pole
Arctic 86°25N 157°41W 150 A17
North Malé Atoll Maldives 4°25N 73°30E 272 d
North Malosmadulu Atoll
Maldives 5°37N 72°55E 272 d
North Manchester U.S.A. 41°0N 85°46W 311 D11
North Mankato U.S.A. 44°10N 94°2W 308 C6
North Miami U.S.A. 25°53N 80°11W 129 C2
North Miami Beach
U.S.A. 25°55N 80°9W 129 C2
North Minch U.K. 58°5N 5°55W 167 C3
North Moose L. Canada 54°4N 100°12W 297 C8
North Myrtle Beach
U.S.A. 33°48N 78°42W 315 E15
North Nahanni ➜
Canada 62°15N 123°20W 296 A4
North Naples U.S.A. 26°12N 81°48W 317 J8
North Nazimabad Pakistan 24°55N 67°3E 123 A2
North New River Canal
U.S.A. 26°30N 80°30W 317 J9
North Nilandu Atoll
Maldives 3°14N 72°56E 272 d
North Northamptonshire □
U.K. 52°24N 0°43W 169 E7
North Olmsted U.S.A. 41°25N 81°56W 312 E3
North Ossetia-Alaniya □
Russia 43°30N 44°30E 191 J7
North Pagai, I. = Pagai Utara, Pulau
Indonesia 2°35S 100°0E 234 C2
North Palisade U.S.A. 37°6N 118°31W 306 H8
North Paravar India 10°13N 76°14E 245 J3
North Perry ✈ (HWO)
U.S.A. 26°0N 80°14W 129 B2
North Platte U.S.A. 41°8N 100°46W 308 E3
North Platte ➜ U.S.A. 41°7N 100°42W 308 E3
North Point
Hong Kong, China 22°17N 114°12E 122 B3
North Point Fla., U.S.A. 27°4N 82°10W 317 H7
North Point Park Boston, U.S.A. 116 a1
North Pole Arctic 90°0N 0°0 150 A
North Pole Alaska,
U.S.A. 64°45N 147°21W 303 D11
North Portal Canada 49°0N 102°33W 297 D8
North Powder U.S.A. 45°2N 117°55W 304 D5
North Pt. Ascension I. 7°53S 14°23W 153 g
North Pt. Barbados 13°20N 59°37W 323 r
North Pt. Mich., U.S.A. 45°2N 83°16W 312 A1
North Pt. Vanuatu 14°56S 168°6E 287 D6
North Queensferry U.K. 56°1N 3°24W 121 A1
North Quincy U.S.A. 42°16N 71°1W 116 B2
North Reef I. India 13°5N 92°43E 245 H11
North Res. U.S.A. 42°27N 71°6W 116 A2
North Rhine Westphalia =
Nordrhein-Westfalen □
Germany 51°45N 7°30E 178 D3
North Richland Hills
U.S.A. 32°50N 97°13W 120 A2
North River Canada 53°49N 57°6W 299 B8
North Riverside U.S.A. 41°50N 87°48W 119 B2
North Rona Atl. Oc. 59°7N 5°49W 165 B4
North Ronaldsay U.K. 59°22N 2°26W 167 B6
North Salem U.S.A. 39°52N 86°39W 311 E10
North Saskatchewan ➜
Canada 53°15N 105°5W 297 C7
North Saugus U.S.A. 42°29N 71°0W 116 A2
North Sea Europe 56°0N 4°0E 158 D6
North Seal ➜ Canada 58°50N 98°7W 297 B9
North Sentinel I. India 11°33N 92°15E 245 J11
North Shields Australia 34°38S 135°52E 282 C1
North Shore U.S.A. 21°39N 158°30W 302 J13
North Shore Channel ➜
U.S.A. 41°58N 87°42W 119 B2
North Slope U.S.A. 69°15N 152°0W 300 B9
North Somerset □ U.K. 51°24N 2°45W 169 F5
North Station Boston, U.S.A. 116 a2
North Sydney N.S.W.,
Australia 33°50S 151°13E 139 B2
North Sydney N.S.,
Canada 46°12N 60°15W 299 C7
North Syracuse U.S.A. 43°8N 76°7W 313 C8
North Taranaki Bight
N.Z. 38°50S 174°15E 284 E3
North Thompson ➜
Canada 50°40N 120°20W 296 C4
North Tonawanda U.S.A. 43°2N 78°53W 312 C6
North Troy U.S.A. 45°0N 72°24W 313 B12
North Twin I. Canada 53°20N 80°0W 298 B4
North Tyne ➜ U.K. 55°0N 2°8W 168 B5
North Ubian I. Phil. 6°9N 120°27E 233 H3
North Uist U.K. 57°40N 7°15W 167 D1
North Union = Shaker Heights
U.S.A. 41°28N 81°32W 312 E3
North Union St. Vincent 13°13N 61°8W 323 n
North Vancouver Canada 49°19N 123°4W 306 A3
North Vernon U.S.A. 39°0N 85°38W 311 F11
North Wabasca L. Canada 56°0N 113°55W 296 B6
North Walsham U.K. 52°50N 1°22E 168 E9
North Webster U.S.A. 41°25N 85°48W 311 C11
North West = Severo-Zapadnyy □
Russia 65°0N 40°0E 214 C4
North West □ Botswana 19°0S 22°30E 270 A3
North-West □ S. Africa 27°0S 25°0E 270 C4
North West Bluff
Montserrat 16°49N 62°12W 323 p
North West C. Australia 21°45S 114°9E 278 D1
North West Frontier = Khyber
Pakhtunkhwa □
Pakistan 33°0N 71°0E 242 C4
North West Highlands
U.K. 57°33N 4°58W 167 D4
North West Pt. Jamaica 18°27N 78°13W 320 a
North West River Canada 53°30N 60°10W 299 B7
North Western □ Zambia 13°30S 25°30E 269 E2
North-Western Provinces and Oudh
= Uttar Pradesh □ India 27°0N 80°0E 243 F9
North Wildwood U.S.A. 39°0N 74°48W 309 F16
North Woolwich U.K. 51°30N 0°3E 125 A4
North Yakima = Yakima
U.S.A. 46°36N 120°31W 304 C3
North York Canada 43°45N 79°27W 141 A2
North York Moors U.K. 54°23N 0°53W 168 C7
North York Moors △ U.K. 54°27N 0°51W 168 C7
North Yorkshire □ U.K. 54°15N 1°25W 168 C6
Northallerton U.K. 54°20N 1°26W 168 C6
Northam W. Austral.,
Australia 31°35S 116°42E 279 F2
Northam Limpopo, S. Africa 24°56S 27°18E 270 B4
Northampton W. Austral.,
Australia 28°27S 114°33E 279 E1
Northampton Northants.,
U.K. 52°15N 0°53W 169 E7
Northampton Mass.,
U.S.A. 42°19N 72°38W 313 D12
Northampton Pa., U.S.A. 40°41N 75°30W 313 F9
Northbridge N.S.W.,
Australia 33°49S 151°15E 139 A2
Northbridge Mass., U.S.A. 42°9N 71°39W 313 D13
Northbridge Park
Australia 33°49S 151°15E 139 A2
Northbrook Ont., Canada 44°44N 77°9W 312 B7
Northbrook Ill., U.S.A. 42°7N 87°50W 119 A2
Northcliff S. Africa 26°8S 27°58E 123 A1
Northcliffe Australia 34°39S 116°7E 279 F2
Northcote Australia 37°46S 145°0E 128 A2
Northeast C. U.S.A. 63°18N 168°42W 303 E5
Northeast Pacific Basin
Pac. Oc. 32°0N 145°0W 289 D13
Northeast Providence Channel
W. Indies 26°0N 76°0W 320 A4
Northeastern Univ. U.S.A. 42°20N 71°4W 116 A2
Northeim Germany 51°42N 10°0E 178 D6
Northern = Limpopo □
S. Africa 24°5S 29°0E 271 B4
Northern □ Ghana 9°30N 0°30W 263 D4
Northern □ Malawi 11°0S 34°0E 269 E3
Northern □ Papua N. G. 9°0S 148°30E 286 E5
Northern □ S. Leone 9°15N 11°30W 262 D2
Northern □ Zambia 10°30S 30°30E 269 E3
Northern Aral Sea
Kazakhstan 46°20N 60°30E 216 C6
Northern Areas = Gilgit-Baltistan □
Pakistan 36°30N 73°0E 243 A5
Northern Bahr el Ghazal □
South Sudan 8°0N 27°30E 257 F2
Northern Cape □ S. Africa 30°0S 20°0E 270 C3
Northern Circars India 17°30N 82°30E 244 F6
Northern Dvina = Dvina,
Severnaya ➜ Russia 64°32N 40°30E 186 B7
Northern Indian L.
Canada 57°20N 97°20W 297 B9
Northern Ireland □ U.K. 54°45N 7°0W 166 B5
Northern Lau Group
Fiji 17°30S 178°59W 287 A3
Northern Light L. Canada 48°15N 90°39W 298 C1
Northern Marianas ☑
Pac. Oc. 17°0N 145°0E 302 a
Northern Province □
S. Africa 24°0S 29°0E 271 B4
Northern Range
Trin. & Tob. 10°46N 61°15W 323 t
Northern Rhodesia = Zambia ■
Africa 15°0S 28°0E 269 F2
Northern Samar □ Phil. 12°30N 124°40E 232 E5
Northern Sporades = Voreios
Sporades Greece 39°15N 23°30E 204 B5
Northern Territory □
Australia 20°0S 133°0E 278 D5
Northfield Ill., U.S.A. 42°5N 87°47W 119 A2
Northfield Minn., U.S.A. 44°27N 93°9W 308 C7
Northfield Vt., U.S.A. 44°9N 72°40W 313 B12
Northgate Canada 49°0N 102°16W 297 D8
Northland □ N.Z. 35°30S 173°30E 284 B2
Northmount Canada 43°46N 79°23W 141 A2
Northolt U.K. 51°32N 0°22W 125 A1
Northome U.S.A. 47°52N 94°17W 308 B6
Northport Ala., U.S.A. 33°14N 87°35W 315 E11
Northport N.Y., U.S.A. 40°54N 73°21W 313 F11
Northport Wash., U.S.A. 48°55N 117°48W 304 B5
Northumberland □ U.K. 55°12N 2°0W 168 B6
Northumberland, C.
Australia 38°5S 140°40E 282 E4
Northumberland Heath
U.K. 51°28N 0°10E 125 B5
Northumberland Is.
Australia 21°30S 149°50E 280 C4
Northumberland Str.
Canada 46°20N 64°0W 299 C7
Northville Ont., Canada 43°10N 81°56W 312 C3
Northville N.Y., U.S.A. 43°13N 74°11W 313 C10
Northway U.S.A. 62°58N 141°56W 303 E12
Northwest Atlantic Mid-Ocean
Canyon Atl. Oc. 54°0N 48°0W 152 A7
Northwest Pacific Basin
Pac. Oc. 32°0N 165°0E 288 D8
Northwest Providence Channel
W. Indies 26°0N 78°0W 320 A4
Northwest Pt. The Bahamas 25°4N 77°31W 153 b
Northwest Territories □
Canada 63°0N 118°0W 294 E8
Northwestern Hawaiian Is. Marine
Nat. Monument =
Papahānaumokuākea Marine
Nat. Monument ⌓
U.S.A. 25°25N 170°35W 302 F9
Northwestern Univ.
U.S.A. 42°3N 87°40W 119 A2
Northwich U.K. 53°15N 2°31W 168 D5
Northwood London, U.K. 51°36N 0°25W 125 A1
Northwood Iowa, U.S.A. 43°27N 93°13W 308 D7
Northwood N. Dak.,
U.S.A. 47°44N 97°34W 308 B5
Northwood Park Canada 43°45N 79°30W 141 A1
Norton Kans., U.S.A. 39°50N 99°53W 308 F4
Norton Zimbabwe 17°52S 30°40E 269 F3
Norton B. U.S.A. 64°45N 161°15W 303 D7
Norton Sd. U.S.A. 63°50N 164°0W 303 E7
Norton Shores U.S.A. 43°10N 86°16W 311 A10
Nortorf Germany 54°10N 9°50E 178 A5
Norwalk Calif., U.S.A. 33°54N 118°4W 307 M8
Norwalk Conn., U.S.A. 41°7N 73°22W 313 E11
Norwalk Iowa, U.S.A. 41°29N 93°41W 310 C3
Norwalk Ohio, U.S.A. 41°15N 82°37W 312 E2
Norway Maine, U.S.A. 44°13N 70°32W 309 C18
Norway Mich., U.S.A. 45°47N 87°55W 308 C10
Norway ■ Europe 63°0N 11°0E 160 E14
Norway House Canada 53°59N 97°50W 297 C9
Norwegian B. Canada 77°30N 90°0W 295 B14
Norwegian Basin Atl. Oc. 68°0N 2°0W 150 C7
Norwegian Sea Atl. Oc. 66°0N 1°0E 158 B6
Norwich Ont., Canada 42°59N 80°36W 312 D4
Norwich Norfolk, U.K. 52°38N 1°18E 169 E9
Norwich Conn., U.S.A. 41°31N 72°5W 313 E12
Norwich N.Y., U.S.A. 42°32N 75°32W 313 D9
Norwood Ont., Canada 44°23N 77°59W 312 B7
Norwood Gauteng, S. Africa 26°9S 28°4E 123 A2
Norwood N.Y., U.S.A. 44°45N 75°0W 313 B10
Norwood Ohio, U.S.A. 39°9N 84°27W 311 E12
Norwood Park U.S.A. 41°59N 87°48W 119 B2
Noryangjin S. Korea 37°30N 126°56E 137 B1
Nosappu-Misaki Japan 45°26N 141°39E 220 C12
Noshaq Pakistan 36°24N 71°49E 240 A3
Noshiro Japan 40°12N 140°0E 220 D10
Nosivka Ukraine 50°50N 31°37E 189 G6
Nosovka = Nosivka
Ukraine 50°50N 31°37E 189 G6
Noşratābād Iran 29°55N 60°0E 247 D8
Noss Hd. U.K. 58°28N 3°3W 167 C5
Nossa Senhora da Glória
Brazil 10°14S 37°25W 332 D4
Nossa Senhora das Dores
Brazil 10°29S 37°13W 332 D4
Nossa Senhora de Candelária
Rio de J., Brazil 135 a2
Nossa Senhora do Livramento
Brazil 15°48S 56°22W 331 D6
Nossa Senhora do Ó
Brazil 23°30S 46°41W 137 B1
Nossa Senhora do Socorro
Brazil 10°52S 37°7W 332 D4
Nossebro Sweden 58°12N 12°43E 163 F6
Nossegem Belgium 50°53N 4°30E 116 A3
Nossob ➜ S. Africa 26°55S 20°45E 270 C3
Nossombougou Mali 13°5N 7°55W 262 C3
Nosy Varika Madag. 20°35S 48°32E 272 C2
Notasulga U.S.A. 32°34N 85°41W 316 C4
Noteć ➜ Poland 52°44N 15°26E 185 F2
Notikewin ➜ Canada 57°2N 117°38W 296 B5
Notio Aigaio □ Greece 36°52N 25°34E 205 E7
Notios Aiyaíon = Notio Aigaio □
Greece 36°52N 25°34E 205 E7
Notios Evvoikos Kolpos
Greece 38°20N 24°0E 204 C5
Noto Italy 36°53N 15°4E 201 F8
Noto, G. di Italy 36°50N 15°12E 201 F8
Noto, Val di Italy 37°14N 14°31E 201 E7
Noto-Hantō Japan 37°15N 136°40E 221 F8
Notodden Norway 59°35N 9°17E 164 E6
Notre-Dame Paris, France 134 c4
Notre-Dame, Basilique
Montréal, Canada 130 c3
Notre-Dame, Bois France 48°45N 2°34E 134 B4
Notre Dame B. Canada 49°45N 55°30W 299 C8
Notre-Dame-de-Grace
Canada 45°28N 73°38W 130 B2
Notre-Dame-de-Koartac = Quaqtaq
Canada 60°55N 69°40W 295 E18
Notre-Dame-des-Bois
Canada 45°24N 71°4W 313 A13
Notre-Dame-d'Ivugivic = Ivujivik
Canada 62°24N 77°55W 295 E16
Notre-Dame-du-Nord
Canada 47°36N 79°30W 298 C4
Notsé Togo 7°0N 1°17E 263 D5
Nottawasaga B. Canada 44°35N 80°15W 312 B4
Nottaway = Senneterre
Canada 48°25N 77°15W 298 C4
Nottaway ➜ Canada 51°22N 78°55W 298 B4
Notting Hill London, U.K. 125 b1
Nottingham U.K. 52°58N 1°10W 168 E6
Nottingham, City of □
U.K. 52°58N 1°10W 168 E6
Nottingham I. Canada 63°20N 77°55W 295 E16
Nottinghamshire □ U.K. 53°10N 1°3W 168 D6
Nottoway ➜ U.S.A. 36°33N 76°55W 309 G15
Notwane ➜ Botswana 23°35S 26°58E 270 B4
Nouabalé-Ndoki ⌓ Congo 2°32N 16°32E 264 B3
Nouâdhibou Mauritania 20°54N 17°0W 260 D1
Nouâdhibou, Dakhlet
Mauritania 20°55N 16°52W 260 D1
Nouâdhibou, Râs
Mauritania 20°50N 17°0W 260 D1
Nouakchott Mauritania 18°9N 15°58W 262 B1
Nouâmghâr Mauritania 19°20N 16°20W 262 B1
Nouméa N. Cal. 22°17S 166°30E 288 d
Nouna Burkina Faso 12°45N 3°52W 262 C4
Noupoort S. Africa 31°10S 24°57E 270 D3
Nouveau Comptoir = Wemindji
Canada 53°0N 78°49W 298 B4
Nouvelle Amsterdam, Î.
Ind. Oc. 38°30S 77°30E 273 H6
Nouvelle-Aquitaine □
France 45°0N 0°30E 174 C4
Nouvelle-Calédonie = New
Caledonia ☑ Pac. Oc. 21°0S 165°0E 288 d
Nouvelle France Mauritius 20°22S 57°33E 272 e
Nouzonville France 49°48N 4°44E 173 C11
Nová Baňa Slovakia 48°28N 18°39E 181 C11
Nová Bystřice Czechia 49°2N 15°8E 180 B8
Nova Cruz Brazil 6°28S 35°25W 332 C4
Nova Era Brazil 19°45S 43°3W 333 E3
Nova Esperança Brazil 23°8S 52°24W 335 A5
Nova Fontesvila = Vila Machado
Mozam. 19°15S 34°14E 269 F3
Nova-Freixo = Cuamba
Mozam. 14°45S 36°22E 269 E4
Nova Friburgo Brazil 22°16S 42°30W 333 F3
Nova Gaia = Cambundi-Catembo
Angola 10°10S 17°35E 265 E3
Nova Gorica Slovenia 45°57N 13°39E 199 C10
Nova Gradiška Croatia 45°17N 17°28E 182 E2
Nova Granada Brazil 20°30S 49°20W 333 F2
Nova Iguaçu Brazil 22°45S 43°28W 333 F3
Nova Iorque Brazil 7°0S 44°5W 332 C3
Nova Kakhovka Ukraine 46°42N 33°27E 189 J7
Nova Lamego
Guinea-Biss. 12°19N 14°11W 262 C2
Nova Lisboa = Huambo
Angola 12°42S 15°54E 265 E3
Nova Lusitânia Mozam. 19°50S 34°34E 269 F3
Nova Mambone Mozam. 21°0S 35°3E 271 B6
Nova Milanese Italy 45°35N 9°12E 128 A2
Nova Odesa Ukraine 47°19N 31°47E 189 J6
Nova Olinda do Norte
Brazil 3°45S 59°3W 329 D6
Nová Paka Czechia 50°29N 15°30E 180 A8
Nova Pavova Serbia 44°56N 20°14E 182 F5
Nova Ponte Brazil 19°8S 47°41W 333 E2
Nova Russas Brazil 4°42S 40°34W 332 B3
Nova Scotia □ Canada 45°10N 63°0W 299 C7
Nova Siri Italy 40°10N 16°35E 201 B9
Nova Sofala Mozam. 20°7S 34°42E 271 B5
Nova Ushytsya Ukraine 48°50N 27°17E 183 B12
Nova Varoš Serbia 43°29N 19°48E 202 C3
Nova Venécia Brazil 18°45S 40°24W 333 E3
Nova Vida Brazil 10°11S 62°47W 331 C5
Nova Zagora Bulgaria 42°32N 26°1E 203 D10
Novaci N. Macedonia 41°5N 21°29E 202 E5
Novaci Romania 45°10N 23°42E 183 E8
Novaféltria Italy 43°53N 12°17E 199 E9
Novar Canada 45°27N 79°15W 312 A5
Novara Italy 45°28N 8°38E 198 C5
Novate Milanese Italy 45°30N 9°8E 128 A1
Novato U.S.A. 38°6N 122°35W 306 G4
Novaya Aleksandriya = Puławy
Poland 51°23N 21°59E 185 G8
Novaya Bukhara = Kogon
Uzbekistan 39°43N 64°33E 216 E6
Novaya Derevnya Russia 60°0N 30°19E 137 A1
Novaya Kakhovka = Nova
Kakhovka Ukraine 46°42N 33°27E 189 J7
Novaya Kazanka = Zhangaqala
Kazakhstan 48°56N 49°36E 191 F9
Novaya Ladoga Russia 60°7N 32°16E 188 B7
Novaya Lyalya Russia 59°4N 60°45E 186 C11
Novaya Pismyanka = Ridder
Kazakhstan 50°20N 83°30E 217 B10
Novaya Sibir, Ostrov
Russia 75°10N 150°0E 215 B16
Novaya Zemlya Russia 75°0N 56°0E 214 B6
Nové Město Czechia 50°4N 14°25E 135 B2
Nové Město na Moravě
Czechia 49°34N 16°5E 180 B9

Nové Město nad Metují Czechia 50°20N 16°10E 181 A9
Nové Město nad Váhom Slovakia 48°45N 17°50E 181 C10
Nové Zámky Slovakia 48°2N 18°8E 181 C11
Novelda Spain 38°24N 0°45W 197 G4
Novellara Italy 44°51N 10°44E 198 D7
Novelty U.S.A. 40°1N 92°12W 310 D4
Noventa Vicentina Italy 45°17N 11°32E 199 C8
Novgorod = Velikiy Novgorod Russia 58°30N 31°25E 188 C6
Novgorod □ Russia 58°50N 32°30E 188 C7
Novgorod-Severskiy = Novhorod-Siverskyy Ukraine 52°2N 33°10E 189 G7
Novgradets = Suvorovo Bulgaria 43°20N 27°35E 203 C11
Novhorod-Siverskyy Ukraine 52°2N 33°10E 189 G7
Novi Bečej Serbia 45°36N 20°10E 182 E5
Novi Grad Bos.-H. 45°2N 16°22E 199 C13
Novi Iskar Bulgaria 42°48N 23°21E 202 D7
Novi Kneževac Serbia 46°4N 20°8E 182 D5
Novi Ligure Italy 44°46N 8°47E 198 D5
Novi Pazar Bulgaria 43°25N 27°15E 203 C11
Novi Pazar Serbia 43°12N 20°28E 202 C4
Novi Sad Serbia 45°18N 19°52E 182 E4
Novi Slankamen Serbia 45°8N 20°15E 182 E5
Novi Travnik Bos.-H. 44°10N 17°40E 182 F2
Novi Vinodolski Croatia 45°10N 14°48E 199 C11
Novigrad Istra, Croatia 45°19N 13°33E 199 C10
Novigrad Zadar, Croatia 44°10N 15°32E 199 D12
Novigradsko More Croatia 44°12N 15°33E 199 D12
Novinger U.S.A. 40°14N 92°43W 310 D4
Novo Acôrdo Brazil 10°10S 46°48W 332 D2
Novo Airão Brazil 2°40S 60°59W 329 D5
Novo Aripuanã Brazil 5°8S 60°22W 329 E5
Novo Cruzeiro Brazil 17°29S 41°53W 333 E3
Novo Hamburgo Brazil 29°37S 51°7W 335 B5
Novo Horizonte Brazil 21°25S 49°10W 333 F2
Novo Ivanivka Ukraine 45°55N 29°5E 183 E14
Novo-Mariinsk = Anadyr Russia 64°35N 177°20E 215 C18
Novo Mesto Slovenia 45°47N 15°12E 199 C12
Novo Miloševo Serbia 45°42N 20°20E 182 E5
Novo Nikolaevsk = Novosibirsk Russia 55°0N 83°5E 217 B10
Novo Paraiso Brazil 1°17N 60°28W 329 C5
Novo-Starobinsk = Salihorsk Belarus 52°51N 27°27E 177 B14
Novo Urgench = Urganch Uzbekistan 41°40N 60°41E 216 D6
Novoaleksandrovsk = Zarasai Lithuania 55°40N 26°20E 188 E4
Novoaleksandrovsk Russia 45°29N 41°17E 191 H5
Novoaleksandrovskaya = Novoaleksandrovsk Russia 45°29N 41°17E 191 H5
Novoaleksandrovskoye Russia 59°50N 30°31E 137 B2
Novoaltaysk Russia 53°30N 84°0E 217 B10
Novoannninskiy Russia 50°32N 42°39E 190 E6
Novoazovsk Ukraine 47°15N 38°4E 189 J10
Novocheboksarsk Russia 56°5N 47°27E 190 B8
Novocherkassk Russia 47°27N 40°15E 191 G5
Novodevichy Convent Russia 55°43N 37°34E 129 B2
Novodevichye Russia 53°37N 48°50E 190 D9
Novodvinsk Russia 64°25N 40°42E 186 B7
Novogireyevo Russia 55°45N 37°46E 129 B3
Novogrudok = Navahrudak Belarus 53°40N 25°50E 177 B13
Novohrad-Volynskyy Ukraine 50°34N 27°35E 177 C14
Novokachalinsk Russia 45°5N 132°0E 220 B5
Novokazalinsk = Ayteke Bi Kazakhstan 45°48N 62°6E 216 C6
Novokhopersk Russia 51°5N 41°39E 190 E5
Novokiyevskoye = Kraskino Russia 42°44N 130°48E 220 C5
Novokuybyshevsk Russia 53°7N 49°58E 190 D9
Novokuznetsk Russia 53°45N 87°10E 217 B11
Novolazarevskaya Antarctica 71°0S 12°0E 151 D3
Novolyalinsky = Novaya Lyalya Russia 59°4N 60°45E 186 C11
Novomoskovsk Russia 54°5N 38°15E 188 E10
Novomoskovsk Ukraine 48°33N 35°17E 189 H8
Novomyrhorod Ukraine 48°45N 31°33E 189 H6
Novonikolayevka = Novoazovsk Ukraine 47°15N 38°4E 189 J10
Novopolotsk = Navapolatsk Belarus 55°32N 28°37E 188 E5
Novorossiysk Russia 44°43N 37°46E 189 K9
Novorybnoye Russia 72°50N 105°50E 215 B11
Novorzhev Russia 57°3N 29°25E 188 D5
Novosaratovka Russia 59°50N 30°32E 137 B3
Novosej Albania 41°56N 20°35E 202 E4
Novoselytsya Ukraine 48°14N 26°15E 183 B11
Novoshakhtinsk Russia 47°46N 39°58E 189 J10
Novosibirsk Russia 55°0N 83°5E 217 B10
Novosibirskiye Ostrova Russia 75°0N 142°0E 215 B15
Novosibirskoye Vdkhr. Russia 54°35N 82°35E 217 B10
Novosil Russia 52°59N 37°2E 189 F9
Novosokolniki Russia 56°20N 30°2E 188 D6
Novotitarovskaya Russia 45°17N 39°2E 191 H4
Novotroitsk Russia 51°10N 58°15E 186 D10
Novotroitskoye = Tōle Bī Kazakhstan 43°42N 73°46E 217 D8
Novoukrayinka Ukraine 48°25N 31°30E 189 H6
Novoulyanovsk Russia 54°8N 48°24E 190 C9
Novouzensk Russia 50°32N 48°17E 190 E9
Novovolynsk Ukraine 50°45N 24°4E 185 H11
Novovoronezh Russia 51°19N 39°13E 189 G10
Novoyavoriske Ukraine 49°53N 23°33E 185 J10
Novozybkov Russia 52°30N 32°0E 189 F6
Novska Croatia 45°19N 17°0E 199 C14
Nový Bor Czechia 50°46N 14°35E 180 A7
Novy Bug = Novyy Buh Ukraine 47°34N 32°29E 189 J7
Nový Bydžov Czechia 50°14N 15°29E 180 A8
Novy Dvor Belarus 52°50N 24°21E 185 F11
Nowy Dwór Mazowiecki Poland 52°26N 20°44E 185 F7
Nový Jičín Czechia 49°30N 18°2E 181 B11
Novy Margelan = Farg'ona Uzbekistan 40°23N 71°19E 217 D8
Novyy Bor Russia 66°43N 52°19E 186 A9
Novyy Buh Ukraine 47°34N 32°29E 189 J7
Novyy Oskol Russia 50°44N 37°55E 189 G9
Novyy Port Russia 67°40N 72°30E 214 C8
Novyy Urengoy Russia 65°48N 76°52E 214 C8
Nowa Deba Poland 50°26N 21°41E 185 H8
Nowa Nowa Australia 37°44S 148°3E 283 D8
Nowa Ruda Poland 50°35N 16°30E 185 H3
Nowa Sarzyna Poland 50°21N 22°21E 185 H9
Nowa Sól Poland 51°48N 15°44E 185 G2
Nowata U.S.A. 36°42N 95°38W 314 C7
Nowbarān Iran 35°8N 49°42E 247 C6
Nowe Poland 53°41N 18°44E 184 E5
Nowe Brzesko Poland 50°13N 20°23E 185 H7
Nowe Miasteczko Poland 51°42N 15°42E 185 G2
Nowe Miasto Mazowieckie, Poland 51°38N 20°34E 185 G7
Nowe Miasto Warsaw, Poland 143 a2
Nowe Miasto Lubawskie Poland 53°27N 19°33E 184 E6
Nowe Skalmierzyce Poland 51°43N 18°0E 185 G4
Nowe Warpno Poland 53°42N 14°18E 184 E1
Nowendoc Australia 31°32S 151°44E 283 A9
Nowendoc △ Australia 31°33S 151°45E 283 A9
Nowghāb Iran 33°53N 59°4E 247 C8
Nowgong = Nagaon India 26°20N 92°50E 241 B4
Nowgong India 25°4N 79°27E 243 G8
Nowitna Nat. Wildlife Refuge ⊂ U.S.A. 64°40N 154°16W 303 D9
Nowogard Poland 53°41N 15°10E 184 E2
Nowogród Poland 53°14N 21°53E 185 E8
Nowogród Bobrzanski Poland 51°48N 15°15E 185 G2
Nowogrodziec Poland 51°12N 15°24E 185 G2
Noworadomsk = Radomsko Poland 51°5N 19°28E 185 G6
Nowra Australia 34°53S 150°35E 283 C9
Nowrangapur India 19°14N 82°33E 244 E6
Nowshāk = Noshaq Pakistan 36°24N 71°49E 240 A3
Nowshera Pakistan 34°0N 72°0E 240 B4
Nowy Dwór Gdański Poland 54°13N 19°7E 184 D6
Nowy Sącz Poland 49°40N 20°41E 185 J7
Nowy Staw Poland 54°13N 19°2E 184 D6
Nowy Targ Poland 49°29N 20°2E 185 J7
Nowy Tomyśl Poland 52°19N 16°10E 185 F3
Nowy Wiśnicz Poland 49°55N 20°28E 185 J7
Noxen U.S.A. 41°25N 76°4W 313 E8
Noyabr'sk Russia 64°34N 76°21E 214 C8
Noyant France 47°30N 0°6E 172 E7
Noyers France 47°40N 4°0E 173 E10
Nöykkiö Finland 60°10N 24°42E 121 B1
Noyon Oise, France 49°34N 2°59E 173 C9
Noyon Mongolia 43°2N 102°4E 226 C2
Nozay France 47°34N 1°38W 172 E5
Nqanqarhu S. Africa 31°2S 28°23E 271 D4
Nqutu S. Africa 28°13S 30°32E 271 C5
Nsa Congo 2°22S 15°19E 264 C3
Nsa, O. en → Algeria 32°28N 5°24E 261 B6
Nsa, Plateau de Congo 2°26S 15°20E 264 C3
Nsanje Malawi 16°55S 35°12E 269 F4
Nsawam Ghana 5°50N 0°24W 263 D4
Nseluka Zambia 9°58S 31°16E 269 D3
Nsok Eq. Guin. 1°10N 11°19E 264 B2
Nsomba Zambia 10°45S 29°51E 269 E2
Nsontin Dem. Rep. of the Congo 3°7S 17°56E 264 C3
Nsopzup Myanmar 25°51N 97°30E 241 C6
Nsukka Nigeria 6°51N 7°29E 263 D6
Ntaria ◎ Australia 24°0S 132°41E 278 D5
Ntem → Cameroon 2°21N 9°49E 264 B2
Ntingui, Mt. Comoros Is. 12°12S 44°25E 272 a
Ntoum Gabon 0°22N 9°47E 264 B1
N'Tsama Congo 0°53S 14°44E 264 C2
Ntsaouéni Comoros Is. 11°27S 43°15E 272 a
Ntsoudjini Comoros Is. 11°39S 43°15E 272 a
Ntui Cameroon 4°27N 11°38E 263 E7
Ntungamo Uganda 0°56S 30°17E 268 C3
Nu Jiang → China 29°58N 97°25E 228 E2
Nu Shan China 26°0N 99°20E 228 E2
Nuakata I. Papua N. G. 10°17S 151°2E 286 F6
Nuba Mts. = Nubah, Jibalan Sudan 12°0N 31°0E 257 E3
Nubah, Jibalan Sudan 12°0N 31°0E 257 E3
Nubia Africa 21°0N 32°0E 254 D7
Nubian Desert = Nûbîya, Es Sahrâ en Sudan 21°30N 33°30E 256 C3
Nûbîya, Es Sahrâ en Sudan 21°30N 33°30E 256 C3
Nubl Syria 36°22N 36°59E 250 B7
Ñuble □ Chile 36°40S 72°10W 334 D1
Nubledo Spain 43°31N 5°52W 194 B5
Nuboai Indonesia 2°10S 136°30E 231 E9
Nubra → India 34°35N 77°35E 243 B7
Nucet Romania 46°28N 22°35E 182 D7
Nueces → U.S.A. 27°51N 97°30W 314 H6
Nueltin L. Canada 60°30N 99°30W 297 A9
Nuestra Señora del Rosario de Caá-Catí Argentina 27°45S 57°36W 334 B4
Nueva, I. Chile 55°13S 66°30W 336 H3
Nueva Antioquia Colombia 6°5N 69°26W 328 B4
Nueva Atzacoalco Mexico 19°29N 99°4W 128 B2
Nueva Carteya Spain 37°35N 4°28W 195 H6
Nueva Ciudad Guerrero Mexico 26°34N 99°12W 319 B5
Nueva Ecija □ Phil. 15°35N 121°0E 232 D3
Nueva Esparta □ Venezuela 11°0N 64°0W 329 A5
Nueva Gerona Cuba 21°53N 82°49W 320 B3
Nueva Imperial Chile 38°45S 72°58W 336 A2
Nueva Loja = Lago Agrio Ecuador 0°5N 76°52W 328 C2
Nueva Palmira Uruguay 33°52S 58°20W 334 C4
Nueva Pompeya Argentina 34°40S 58°25W 117 C2
Nueva Rosita Mexico 27°57N 101°13W 318 B4
Nueva San Salvador El Salv. 13°40N 89°18W 320 D2
Nueva Tabarca Spain 38°17N 0°30W 197 G4
Nueva Tenochtitlán Mexico 19°27N 99°5W 128 B2
Nueva Vizcaya □ Phil. 16°20N 121°20E 232 C3
Nueve de Julio Argentina 35°30S 61°0W 334 D3
Nuevitas Cuba 21°30N 77°20W 320 B4
Nuevo, G. Argentina 43°0S 64°30W 336 B4
Nuevo Casas Grandes Mexico 30°25N 107°55W 318 A3
Nuevo Laredo Mexico 27°30N 99°31W 319 B5
Nuevo León □ Mexico 25°20N 100°0W 318 C5
Nuevo Mundo, Cerro Bolivia 21°55S 66°53W 330 E4
Nuevo Rocafuerte Ecuador 0°55S 75°27W 328 D2
Nugaal □ Somalia 8°10N 49°0E 267 C6
Nugaal → Somalia 8°0N 49°47E 267 C6
Nugaaleed, Dooxo Somalia 8°35N 48°35E 267 C6
Nugget Pt. N.Z. 46°27S 169°50E 285 G4
Nugrus, Gebel Egypt 24°47N 34°35E 256 C3
Nuguria Is. Papua N. G. 3°20S 154°45E 286 B8
Nuhaka N.Z. 39°3S 177°45E 284 F6
Nui Pac. Oc. 7°15S 177°10E 277 B14
Nuijala Finland 60°12N 24°46E 121 B1
Nuits-St-Georges France 47°10N 4°56E 173 E11
Nukey Bluff Australia 32°26S 135°29E 281 E2
Nukha = Şaki Azerbaijan 41°10N 47°5E 191 K8
Nukhayb Iraq 32°4N 42°3E 213 F10
Nukheila Sudan 19°1N 26°21E 256 D2
Nukiki Solomon Is. 6°46S 156°35E 287 L9
Nuku Papua N. G. 3°41S 142°28E 286 B2
Nuku Hiva French Polynesia 8°54S 140°6W 289 f
Nuku'alofa Tonga 21°10S 175°12W 287 Q13
Nukuhu Papua N. G. 5°34S 149°22E 286 C5
Nukulaelae Tuvalu 9°23S 179°52E 277 B14
Nukunonu Pac. Oc. 9°12S 171°54W 277 B16
Nukus Uzbekistan 42°27N 59°41E 216 D5
Nulato U.S.A. 64°43N 158°6W 303 D8
Nules Spain 39°51N 0°9W 196 F4
Nullagine Australia 21°53S 120°7E 278 D3
Nullagine → Australia 21°20S 120°20E 278 D3
Nullarbor Australia 31°28S 130°55E 279 F5
Nullarbor △ Australia 32°39S 130°0E 279 F5
Nullarbor Plain Australia 31°10S 129°0E 279 F4
Numabukuro Japan 35°43N 139°39E 140 A2
Numalla, L. Australia 28°43S 144°20E 281 D3
Numan Nigeria 9°29N 12°3E 263 D7
Numanuma Papua N. G. 9°41S 150°55E 286 E6
Numata Japan 36°45N 139°4E 223 A11
Numatinna → South Sudan 7°38N 27°20E 257 F2
Numaykoos Lake ⊂ Canada 57°52N 95°58W 297 B9
Numazu Japan 35°7N 138°51E 223 B10
Numbulwar Australia 14°15S 135°45E 280 A2
Numedal Norway 60°6N 9°6E 164 D6
Numfoor Indonesia 1°0S 134°50E 231 E8
Numurkah Australia 36°5S 145°26E 283 D6
Nunaksaluk I. Canada 55°49N 60°20W 299 A7
Nunap Isua Greenland 59°48N 43°55W 154 F6
Nunatsiavut Canada 55°30N 62°0W 299 A7
Nunavik Canada 56°30N 71°0W 295 F17
Nunavik Greenland 71°50N 54°25W 154 C5
Nunavut □ Canada 66°0N 85°0W 295 D15
Nunda U.S.A. 42°35N 77°56W 312 D7
Nuneaton U.K. 52°32N 1°27W 169 E6
Nuñez Argentina 34°32S 58°27W 117 B2
Nungarin Australia 31°12S 118°6E 279 F2
Nungo Mozam. 13°23S 37°43E 269 E4
Nungwe Tanzania 2°48S 32°2E 268 C3
Nunhead U.K. 51°27N 0°3W 125 B3
Nunivak I. U.S.A. 60°10N 166°30W 303 F6
Nunkun India 33°57N 76°2E 243 C7
Ñuñoa Chile 33°27S 70°35W 137 B2
Nunukan Indonesia 4°4N 117°40E 235 B5
Nùoro Italy 40°20N 9°20E 200 B2
Nuozhadu Dam China 22°39N 100°25E 228 F3
Núpur Iceland 65°56N 23°36W 155 B3
Nuqayy, Jabal Libya 23°11N 19°30E 258 D3
Nuqūb Yemen 14°59N 45°48E 248 D4
Nuquí Colombia 5°42N 77°17W 328 B2
Nūr Iran 36°33N 52°1E 247 B7
Nur Dağı Turkey 36°54N 35°39E 250 B6
Nur Dağları Turkey 36°50N 36°23E 250 B7
Nur-Sultan Kazakhstan 51°10N 71°30E 217 B8
Nura → Kazakhstan 50°30N 69°59E 217 B7
Nūrābād Hormozgān, Iran 27°47N 57°12E 247 E8
Nūrābād Lorestān, Iran 34°4N 47°58E 213 E12
Nure → Italy 45°3N 9°49E 198 C6
Nuremberg = Nürnberg Germany 49°27N 11°3E 179 F7
Nuri Sonora, Mexico 28°5N 109°22W 318 B3
Nuri Sudan 18°29N 31°59E 256 D3
Nuriootpa Australia 34°27S 139°0E 282 C3
Nuristān □ Afghan. 35°20N 71°0E 217 E8
Nurlat Russia 54°29N 50°45E 190 C10
Nurmes Finland 63°33N 29°10E 160 E23
Nürnberg Germany 49°27N 11°3E 179 F7
Nurpur Pakistan 31°53N 71°54E 242 D4
Nurra, La Italy 40°45N 8°15E 200 B1
Nurran, L. = Terewah, L. Australia 29°52S 147°35E 281 D4
Nurrari Lakes Australia 29°1S 130°5E 279 E5
Nurri Italy 39°43N 9°14E 200 C2
Nürtingen Germany 48°37N 9°19E 179 G5
Nus Italy 45°45N 7°28E 198 C4
Nusa Dua Indonesia 8°48S 115°14E 231 K18
Nusa Tenggara Barat □ Indonesia 8°50S 117°30E 235 D5
Nusa Tenggara Timur □ Indonesia 9°30S 122°0E 231 F6
Nusaybin Turkey 37°3N 41°10E 213 D9
Nuşayrīyah, J. an Syria 35°20N 36°13E 250 C7
Nuşeirat Gaza Strip 31°27N 34°24E 251 G5
Nushki Pakistan 29°35N 66°0E 242 E2
Nusle Czechia 50°3N 14°26E 135 B2
Nussdorf Austria 48°15N 16°21E 142 A2
Nuuk Greenland 64°10N 51°35W 154 E5
Nuupere, Pte. Moorea 17°36S 149°47W 289 e
Nuussauq Greenland 74°8N 57°3W 154 C5
Nu'uuli Amer. Samoa 14°19S 170°42W 302 f
Nuwakot Nepal 28°10N 83°55E 243 E10
Nuwara Eliya Sri Lanka 6°58N 80°48E 245 L5
Nuwayb'ī, W. an → Si. Arabia 29°18N 34°57E 251 J5
Nuweiba' Egypt 28°59N 34°39E 251 K5
Nuwerus S. Africa 31°8S 18°24E 270 D2
Nuweveldberge S. Africa 32°10S 21°45E 270 D3
Nuyts, Pt. Australia 35°4S 116°38E 279 G2
Nuyts Arch. Australia 32°35S 133°20E 281 E1
N'Vinda Angola 13°8S 19°2E 265 E3
Nxai Pan △ Botswana 19°50S 24°46E 270 A3
Nxaunxau Botswana 18°57S 21°4E 270 A3
Ny-Ålesund Svalbard 78°55N 11°56E 154 B12
Nyaake Liberia 4°52N 7°37W 262 E3
Nyabessan Cameroon 2°28N 10°24E 264 B2
Nyabing Australia 33°33S 118°9E 279 F2
Nyack U.S.A. 41°5N 73°55W 313 E11
Nyagan Russia 62°30N 65°38E 214 C7
Nyah West Australia 35°16S 143°21E 282 C5
Nyahanga Tanzania 2°20S 33°37E 268 C3
Nyahua Tanzania 5°25S 33°23E 268 D3
Nyahururu Kenya 0°2N 36°27E 268 B4
Nyainqêntanglha Shan China 30°0N 90°0E 218 F7
Nyakanazi Tanzania 3°2S 31°10E 268 C3
Nyakrom Ghana 5°40N 0°50W 263 D4
Nyâlâ Sudan 12°2N 24°58E 257 E1
Nyalam China 28°32N 86°4E 218 F6
Nyamandhlovu Zimbabwe 19°55S 28°16E 269 F2
Nyambiti Tanzania 2°48S 33°27E 268 C3
Nyamira Kenya 0°36S 34°52E 268 B4
Nyamlell South Sudan 9°7N 26°59E 257 F2
Nyamwaga Tanzania 1°27S 34°33E 268 C3
Nyandekwa Tanzania 3°57S 32°32E 268 C3
Nyanding → South Sudan 8°40N 32°41E 257 F3
Nyandoma Russia 61°40N 40°12E 188 B11
Nyandroa □ Kenya 0°30S 36°35E 268 C4
Nyanga Congo 2°52S 11°57E 264 C2
Nyanga Western Cape, S. Africa 33°59S 18°35E 118 A2
Nyanga → Gabon 2°58S 10°15E 264 C2
Nyanga △ Zimbabwe 18°17S 32°46E 269 F3
Nyangana Namibia 18°0S 20°40E 270 A3
Nyanguge Tanzania 2°30S 33°12E 268 C3
Nyanji Zambia 14°25S 31°46E 269 E3
Nyankpala Ghana 9°21N 0°58W 263 D4
Nyanza Rwanda 2°20S 29°42E 268 C2
Nyanza □ Kenya 0°30S 34°30E 268 C3
Nyanza-Lac Burundi 4°21S 29°36E 268 C2
Nyaponges South Sudan 8°30N 32°53E 257 F3
Nyasa, L. = Malawi, L. Africa 12°30S 34°30E 269 E3
Nyasaland = Malawi ■ Africa 11°55S 34°0E 269 E3
Nyasvizh Belarus 53°14N 26°38E 177 B14
Nyaungdon = Yandoon Myanmar 17°0N 95°40E 241 G5
Nyaunglebin Myanmar 17°52N 96°42E 241 G6
Nyazepetrovsk Russia 56°3N 59°36E 186 C10
Nyazura Zimbabwe 18°40S 32°16E 269 F3
Nyazwidzi → Zimbabwe 20°0S 31°17E 269 G3
Nybergsund Norway 61°15N 12°19E 164 C9
Nyborg Denmark 55°18N 10°47E 163 J4
Nybro Sweden 56°44N 15°55E 163 H9
Nyda Russia 66°40N 72°58E 214 C8
Nyeboe Land Greenland 82°0N 57°0W 154 A5
Nyengo Swamp Zambia 14°51S 22°7E 265 E4
Nyeri Kenya 0°23S 36°56E 268 C4
Nyerol South Sudan 8°41N 32°1E 257 F3
Nyhammar Sweden 60°17N 14°58E 162 D8
Nyika △ Malawi 10°30S 33°53E 269 E3
Nyimba Zambia 14°33S 30°50E 269 E3
Nyinahin Ghana 6°43N 2°3W 262 D4
Nyingchi China 29°32N 94°25E 218 F7
Nyirád Hungary 47°41N 21°55E 182 C6
Nyiragongo Dem. Rep. of the Congo 1°30S 29°15E 268 C2
Nyírbátor Hungary 47°49N 22°9E 182 C7
Nyíregyháza Hungary 47°58N 21°47E 182 C6
Nyiru, Mt. Kenya 2°8N 36°50E 268 B4
Nykarleby = Uusikaarlepyy Finland 63°32N 22°31E 160 E20
Nykirke Norway 60°54N 10°19E 164 D7
Nykøbing Nordjylland, Denmark 56°48N 8°51E 163 H2
Nykøbing Sjælland, Denmark 54°56N 11°52E 163 K5
Nykøbing Sjælland, Denmark 55°55N 11°40E 163 J5
Nyköping Sweden 58°45N 17°1E 163 F11
Nykroppa Sweden 59°37N 14°18E 162 E8
Nykvarn Sweden 59°11N 17°25E 162 E11
Nyland Sweden 63°1N 17°45E 162 A11
Nylstroom = Modimolle S. Africa 24°42S 28°22E 271 B4
Nymagee Australia 32°7S 146°20E 283 B7
Nymboida △ Australia 29°38S 152°26E 281 D5
Nymburk Czechia 50°10N 15°1E 180 A8
Nymphenburg Germany 48°9N 11°30E 131 B2
Nymphenburg, Schloss Germany 48°9N 11°30E 131 B2
Nynäshamn Sweden 58°54N 17°57E 163 F11
Nyngan Australia 31°30S 147°8E 283 A7
Nyoma Rap India 33°10N 78°40E 243 C8
Nyoman = Nemunas → Lithuania 55°25N 21°10E 184 C8
Nyon Switz. 46°23N 6°14E 179 J2
Nyong → Cameroon 3°17N 9°54E 263 E6
Nyons France 44°22N 5°10E 175 D9
Nyou Burkina Faso 12°42N 2°1W 263 C4
Nýrsko Czechia 49°18N 13°9E 180 B6
Nysa Poland 50°30N 17°22E 185 H4
Nysa → Europe 52°4N 14°46E 178 C10
Nysa Kłodzka → Poland 50°49N 17°40E 185 H4
Nysætre Norway 62°2N 8°20E 164 B5
Nysäter Sweden 59°17N 12°47E 162 E6
Nyslott = Savonlinna Finland 61°52N 28°53E 188 B5
Nyssa U.S.A. 43°53N 117°0W 304 E5
Nystad = Uusikaupunki Finland 60°47N 21°25E 188 B1
Nysted Denmark 54°40N 11°44E 163 K5
Nyunzu Dem. Rep. of the Congo 5°57S 27°58E 268 D2
Nyurba Russia 63°17N 118°28E 215 C12
Nyzhankovychi Ukraine 49°40N 22°49E 185 J9
Nyzhnohirskyy Ukraine 45°27N 34°38E 189 K8
Nyzhny Vorota Ukraine 48°46N 23°6E 182 B8
Nzébéla Guinea 8°9N 9°7W 262 D3
Nzega Tanzania 4°10S 33°12E 268 C3
Nzérékoré Guinea 7°49N 8°48W 262 D3
Nzeto Angola 7°10S 12°52E 265 D2
Nzilo, Chutes de Dem. Rep. of the Congo 10°18S 25°27E 265 E5
Nzilo, L. Dem. Rep. of the Congo 10°35S 25°39E 265 E5
N'zo → Côte d'Ivoire 6°15N 7°3W 262 D3
N'zo ⊂ Côte d'Ivoire 6°15N 7°15W 262 D3
Nzubuka Tanzania 4°45S 32°50E 268 C3
Nzwani = Anjouan Comoros Is. 12°15S 44°20E 272 a

O

O Barco Spain 42°23N 6°58W 194 C4
O Carballiño Spain 42°26N 8°5W 194 C2
O Castro de Ferreira Spain 42°31N 7°37W 194 C3
O Convento Spain 42°28N 8°41W 194 C2
O Corgo Spain 42°56N 7°25W 194 C3
O Le Pupū Pu'e △ Samoa 13°59S 171°43W 287 V20
O Pedrouzo Spain 42°56N 8°20W 194 C2
O Pino = O Pedrouzo Spain 42°56N 8°20W 194 C2
O Porriño Spain 42°10N 8°37W 194 C2
O Real Spain 43°20N 8°19W 194 B2
O Seixo Spain 41°59N 8°46W 194 D2
Ō-Shima Hokkaidō, Japan 41°30N 139°22E 220 D9
Ō-Shima Nagasaki, Japan 33°29N 129°33E 222 D1
Ō-Shima Shizuoka, Japan 34°44N 139°24E 223 C11
O.R. Tambo Int. ✈ (JNB) S. Africa 26°8S 28°15E 271 C4
Oa, Mull of U.K. 55°35N 6°20W 167 F2
Oacoma U.S.A. 43°48N 99°24W 308 D4
Oahe, L. U.S.A. 44°27N 100°24W 308 C3
Oahe Dam U.S.A. 44°27N 100°24W 308 C3
O'ahu U.S.A. 21°28N 157°58W 302 K14
Oak Creek U.S.A. 42°52N 87°55W 311 B9
Oak Forest U.S.A. 41°37N 87°47W 119 D2
Oak Grove U.S.A. 33°50N 84°18W 113 A3
Oak Harbor U.S.A. 48°18N 122°39W 306 B4
Oak Hill Fla., U.S.A. 28°52N 80°51W 317 G9
Oak Hill Mass., U.S.A. 42°18N 71°10W 116 B1
Oak Hill W. Va., U.S.A. 37°59N 81°9W 309 G13
Oak Island U.S.A. 33°55N 78°10W 315 E15
Oak Lawn U.S.A. 41°42N 87°45W 119 D2
Oak Park Ga., U.S.A. 32°22N 82°19W 316 C7
Oak Park Ill., U.S.A. 41°52N 87°47W 119 B2
Oak Ridge U.S.A. 36°1N 84°16W 315 C12
Oak Street Beach Chicago, U.S.A. 119 a2
Oak View Calif., U.S.A. 34°24N 119°18W 307 L7
Oak View Md., U.S.A. 39°1N 76°58W 143 A3
Oakan-Dake Japan 43°27N 144°10E 220 C12
Oakbank Australia 33°4S 140°33E 282 B4
Oakdale Calif., U.S.A. 37°46N 120°51W 306 H6
Oakdale Georgia, U.S.A. 33°51N 84°30W 113 A2
Oakdale La., U.S.A. 30°49N 92°40W 314 F8
Oakes U.S.A. 46°8N 98°6W 308 B4
Oakesdale U.S.A. 47°8N 117°15W 304 C5
Oakey Australia 27°25S 151°43E 281 D5
Oakfield Ga., U.S.A. 31°47N 83°58W 316 D6
Oakfield N.Y., U.S.A. 43°4N 78°16W 312 C6
Oakford U.S.A. 40°6N 89°58W 310 D7
Oakham U.K. 52°40N 0°43W 169 E7
Oakhurst U.S.A. 37°19N 119°40W 306 H7
Oakland Calif., U.S.A. 37°48N 122°18W 136 B3
Oakland Ill., U.S.A. 39°39N 88°2W 311 E8
Oakland Pa., U.S.A. 41°57N 75°36W 313 E9
Oakland City U.S.A. 38°20N 87°21W 311 F9
Oakland Park U.S.A. 26°10N 80°7W 129 A3
Oaklands Australia 35°34S 146°10E 283 C7
Oaklawn U.S.A. 38°46N 76°56W 143 C3
Oakleigh Australia 37°54S 145°5E 128 B2
Oakley Idaho, U.S.A. 42°15N 113°53W 304 E7
Oakley Kans., U.S.A. 39°8N 100°51W 308 F3
Oakover → Australia 21°0S 120°40E 278 D3
Oakridge U.S.A. 43°45N 122°28W 304 E2
Oaks, The Australia 34°3S 150°34E 283 C9
Oaktown U.S.A. 38°52N 87°27W 311 F9
Oakville Ont., Canada 43°27N 79°41W 312 C5
Oakville Wash., U.S.A. 46°51N 123°14W 306 D3
Oakwood U.S.A. 41°6N 84°23W 311 C12
Oakwood Beach U.S.A. 40°33N 74°7W 132 C1
Oamaru N.Z. 45°5S 170°59E 285 F5
Oamishirasato Japan 35°31N 140°18E 223 B12
Oancea Romania 45°21N 27°42E 183 E12
Oarai Japan 36°21N 140°34E 223 A12
Oasis Calif., U.S.A. 37°29N 117°55W 306 H9
Oasis Calif., U.S.A. 33°28N 116°6W 307 M10
Oates Land Antarctica 69°0S 160°0E 151 C11
Oatley Australia 33°59S 151°4E 139 B1
Oatman U.S.A. 35°1N 114°19W 307 K12
Oaxaca Mexico 17°3N 96°43W 319 D5
Oaxaca □ Mexico 17°0N 96°30W 319 D5
Ob → Russia 66°45N 69°30E 214 C7
Oba Canada 49°4N 84°7W 298 C3
Obala Cameroon 4°9N 11°32E 263 E7
Obalende Nigeria 6°26N 3°25E 124 B2
Obama Fukui, Japan 35°30N 135°45E 223 B7
Obama Nagasaki, Japan 32°43N 130°13E 222 E2
Obama, Mt. Antigua & B. 17°2N 61°52W 322 b
Oban Nigeria 5°17N 8°33E 263 D6
Oban Argyll & Bute, U.K. 56°25N 5°29W 167 E3
Oba's Palace Nigeria 6°26N 3°22E 124 B2
Obbia = Hobyo Somalia 5°25N 48°30E 267 C6
Obdorsk = Salekhard Russia 66°30N 66°35E 214 C7
Oberá Argentina 27°21S 55°2W 335 B4
Oberammergau Germany 47°36N 11°4E 179 H7
Oberasbach Germany 49°25N 10°57E 179 F6
Oberbayern □ Germany 48°5N 11°50E 179 G7
Oberburg = Gornji Grad Slovenia 46°20N 14°52E 199 B11
Oberdonau = Oberösterreich □ Austria 48°10N 14°0E 180 C7
Oberdrauburg Austria 46°44N 12°58E 180 E5
Obere Donau ⊂ Germany 48°5N 9°0E 179 G5
Oberer Bayerischer Wald ⊂ Germany 49°15N 12°40E 179 F8
Oberföhring Germany 48°10N 11°37E 131 B2
Oberfranken □ Germany 50°10N 11°20E 179 E7
Oberglogau = Głogówek Poland 50°21N 17°53E 185 H4
Oberhaching Germany 48°1N 11°35E 131 B2
Oberhausen Germany 51°28N 6°51E 178 D2
Oberkirch Germany 48°31N 8°4E 179 G4
Oberlaa Austria 48°8N 16°24E 142 B2
Oberlaibach = Vrhnika Slovenia 45°58N 14°15E 199 C11
Oberlausitz Germany 51°16N 14°18E 178 D10
Oberlin Kans., U.S.A. 39°49N 100°32W 308 F3
Oberlin La., U.S.A. 30°37N 92°46W 314 F8
Oberlin Ohio, U.S.A. 41°18N 82°13W 312 E2
Oberlisse Austria 48°17N 16°26E 142 A2
Obermenzing Germany 48°10N 11°28E 131 A1
Obermoos Schwaige Germany 48°14N 11°27E 131 A1
Obernai France 48°28N 7°30E 173 D14
Oberndorf Germany 48°17N 8°34E 179 G4
Obernigk = Oborniki Śląskie Poland 51°17N 16°53E 185 G3
Oberon Australia 33°45S 149°52E 283 B8
Oberösterreich □ Austria 48°10N 14°0E 180 C7
Oberpfalz □ Germany 49°20N 12°10E 179 F8
Oberpfälzer Wald Germany 49°30N 12°30E 179 F8
Oberpfälzer Wald ⊂ Germany 49°40N 12°20E 179 F8
Oberschleissheim Germany 48°15N 11°33E 131 A2
Oberschöneweide Germany 52°27N 13°31E 115 B4
Oberstdorf Germany 47°24N 10°15E 179 H6
Obertig Gabon 0°22S 9°46E 264 C1
Obertyn Ukraine 48°42N 25°10E 183 B10
Oberursel Germany 50°11N 8°35E 179 E4
Oberwart Austria 47°17N 16°12E 181 D9
Obi, Kepulauan Indonesia 1°23S 127°45E 231 E7
Obiaruku Nigeria 5°51N 6°9E 263 D6
Óbidos Brazil 1°50S 55°30W 329 D6
Óbidos Portugal 39°19N 9°10W 195 F1
Obihiro Japan 42°56N 143°12E 220 C11
Obilatu Indonesia 1°25S 127°20E 231 E7
Obilnoye Russia 47°32N 44°30E 191 G7
Obing Germany 48°0N 12°24E 179 G8
Objat France 45°16N 1°24E 174 C5
Oblong U.S.A. 39°0N 87°55W 311 F9
Obluchye Russia 49°1N 131°4E 215 E14
Obninsk Russia 55°8N 36°37E 188 E9
Obo C.A.R. 5°20N 26°32E 264 A5
Obock Djibouti 12°0N 43°20E 257 E5
Obodivka Ukraine 48°24N 29°15E 183 B14
Oborniki Poland 52°39N 16°50E 185 F3
Oborniki Śląskie Poland 51°17N 16°53E 185 G3
Obouya Congo 0°56S 15°43E 264 C3
Oboyan Russia 51°15N 36°21E 189 G9
Obozerskaya = Obozerskiy Russia 63°34N 40°21E 186 B7
Obozerskiy Russia 63°34N 40°21E 186 B7
Obrenovac Serbia 44°40N 20°11E 202 B4
O'Brien U.S.A. 30°2N 82°57W 316 E7
Obrovac Croatia 44°11N 15°41E 199 D12
Obruk Turkey 38°7N 33°12E 212 C5
Obrzycko Poland 52°42N 16°32E 185 F3
Observatory Sydney, Australia 139 a1
Observatory Gauteng, S. Africa 26°10S 28°4E 123 B2
Observatory Inlet Canada 55°10N 129°54W 296 B3
Obshchi Syrt Russia 52°0N 53°0E 158 E16
Obskaya Guba Russia 69°0N 73°0E 214 C8
Obu Japan 35°0N 136°58E 223 B8
Obuasi Ghana 6°17N 1°40W 263 D4
Obubra Nigeria 6°8N 8°20E 263 D6
Óbuda Hungary 47°33N 19°2E 117 A2
Obudu Nigeria 6°38N 9°5E 263 D6
Obukhovo Russia 59°53N 30°22E 137 B2
Obura Papua N. G. 6°33S 145°58E 286 D3
Obvodnyy Kanal Russia 59°54N 30°20E 137 B1
Obwalden □ Switz. 46°55N 8°15E 179 J4
Obzor Bulgaria 42°50N 27°52E 203 D11
Ocala U.S.A. 29°11N 82°8W 317 F7
Ocamo → Venezuela 2°48N 65°14W 329 C4
Ocampo Chihuahua, Mexico 28°11N 108°23W 318 B3
Ocampo Tamaulipas, Mexico 22°50N 99°20W 319 C5
Ocaña Colombia 8°15N 73°20W 328 B3
Ocaña Spain 39°55N 3°30W 194 F7
Occidental, Cordillera Colombia 5°0N 76°0W 328 C2
Occidental, Cordillera Peru 14°0S 74°0W 330 C3
Occidental, Grand Erg Algeria 30°20N 1°0E 261 B5
Occitanie □ France 44°0N 2°0E 174 E5
Ocean City Md., U.S.A. 38°20N 75°5W 309 F16
Ocean City N.J., U.S.A. 39°17N 74°35W 309 F16
Ocean City Wash., U.S.A. 47°4N 124°10W 306 C2
Ocean Falls Canada 52°18N 127°48W 296 C3
Ocean I. = Banaba Kiribati 0°45S 169°50E 288 H8
Ocean Park Hong Kong, China 22°13N 114°10E 122 B3
Ocean Park Wash., U.S.A. 46°30N 124°3W 306 D2
Oceano U.S.A. 35°6N 120°37W 307 K6
Oceanport U.S.A. 40°19N 74°3W 313 F10
Oceanside U.S.A. 33°12N 117°23W 307 M9
Ochagavía Spain 42°55N 1°5W 196 C3
Ochakiv Ukraine 46°37N 31°33E 189 J6
Ochamchire Georgia 42°46N 41°32E 191 J5
Ochi, Oros Greece 38°5N 24°25E 204 C6
Ochiai Japan 35°1N 133°45E 222 B5
Ochil Hills U.K. 56°14N 3°40W 167 E5
Ochlocknee U.S.A. 30°58N 84°3W 316 E5
Ochlockonee → U.S.A. 29°59N 84°26W 316 F5
Ocho Rios Jamaica 18°24N 77°6W 320 a
Ochopee U.S.A. 25°54N 81°18W 317 K8
Ochota Poland 52°13N 20°58E 143 B1
Ochsenfurt Germany 49°40N 10°4E 179 F6
Ochsenhausen Germany 48°4N 9°57E 179 G5
Ocilla U.S.A. 31°36N 83°15W 316 D6
Ockelbo Sweden 60°54N 16°45E 162 D10
Ocmulgee → U.S.A. 31°58N 82°33W 316 D7
Ocmulgee ⊂ U.S.A. 32°49N 83°37W 316 C6
Ocna Mureș Romania 46°23N 23°55E 183 D8
Ocna Sibiului Romania 45°52N 24°2E 183 E9
Ocnele Mari Romania 45°8N 24°18E 183 E9
Ocnița Moldova 48°25N 27°30E 183 B12
Ocoee U.S.A. 28°34N 81°32W 133 A1
Ocoña Peru 16°26S 73°8W 330 D3
Ocoña → Peru 16°28S 73°8W 330 D3
Oconee → U.S.A. 31°58N 82°33W 316 D7
Oconee, L. U.S.A. 33°28N 83°15W 316 B6
Oconomowoc U.S.A. 43°7N 88°30W 311 A8
Oconto U.S.A. 44°53N 87°52W 308 C10
Oconto Falls U.S.A. 44°52N 88°9W 308 C9
Ocosingo Mexico 16°53N 92°6W 319 D6
Ocotal Nic. 13°41N 86°31W 320 D2
Ocotlán Jalisco, Mexico 20°21N 102°46W 318 C4
Ocotlán Oaxaca, Mexico 16°48N 96°40W 319 D5
Ocreza → Portugal 39°32N 7°50W 195 F3
Öcsa Hungary 47°17N 19°15E 182 C4
Ocumare del Tuy Venezuela 10°7N 66°46W 328 A4
Ocuri Bolivia 18°45S 65°50W 331 D4
Oda Ghana 5°50N 0°51W 263 D4
Ōda Shimane, Japan 35°11N 132°30E 222 B4
Oda, J. Sudan 20°21N 36°39E 256 C4
Ódáðahraun Iceland 65°5N 17°0W 155 B9
Odaejin N. Korea 41°34N 129°40E 224 B4
Odaesan △ S. Korea 37°40N 128°30E 224 D4
Odaiba Japan 35°38N 139°47E 140 B3
Ödåkra Sweden 56°7N 12°45E 163 H6
Ōdana Japan 35°33N 139°35E 140 B1
Odate Japan 40°16N 140°34E 220 D10
Odawara Japan 35°20N 139°6E 223 B11
Odda Norway 60°3N 6°35E 164 D3
Odder = Xuddur Somalia 4°11N 43°52E 267 D5
Odder Denmark 55°58N 10°10E 163 J4
Odei → Canada 56°6N 96°54W 297 B9
Odell U.S.A. 41°0N 88°31W 311 C8
Odemira Portugal 37°35N 8°40W 195 H2
Ödemiş Turkey 38°15N 28°0E 205 C9
Öden-Stockach Germany 48°5N 11°41E 131 B3
Ödenburg = Sopron Hungary 47°45N 16°32E 182 C1
Odendaalsrus S. Africa 27°48S 26°45E 270 C4
Odensbacken Sweden 59°10N 15°32E 162 E9
Odense Denmark 55°22N 10°23E 163 J4
Odenwald Germany 49°35N 9°0E 179 F5
Oder → Europe 53°33N 14°38E 178 B10
Oder-Havel Kanal Germany 52°52N 14°2E 178 C10
Oderzo Italy 45°47N 12°29E 199 C9
Odesa Ukraine 46°30N 30°45E 189 J6
Odesa □ Ukraine 47°20N 29°55E 189 J5
Ödeshög Sweden 58°14N 14°39E 163 F8
Odessa = Odesa Ukraine 46°30N 30°45E 189 J6
Odessa Ont., Canada 44°17N 76°43W 313 B8
Odessa Mo., U.S.A. 39°0N 93°57W 310 F3
Odessa Tex., U.S.A. 31°52N 102°23W 314 F3
Odessa Wash., U.S.A. 47°20N 118°41W 304 C4
Odiakwe Botswana 20°12S 25°17E 270 B4
Odiel → Spain 37°10N 6°55W 195 H4
Odienné Côte d'Ivoire 9°30N 7°34W 262 D3
Odilampi Finland 60°18N 24°45E 121 B1
Odimba Gabon 2°2S 9°33E 264 C2
Odintsovo Russia 55°40N 37°16E 188 E9
Odiongan Phil. 12°24N 121°59E 232 E3
Odisha □ India 20°0N 84°0E 244 E7
Odivelas Portugal 38°47N 9°10W 126 A1
Odobești Romania 45°43N 27°4E 183 E12
Odolanów Poland 51°34N 17°40E 185 G4
Odolany Poland 52°13N 20°55E 143 B1
O'Donnell U.S.A. 32°58N 101°50W 314 E4
O'Donnell Pt. Canada 45°5N 80°5W 312 A4
Odorheiu Secuiesc Romania 46°21N 25°21E 183 D10
Odoyevo Russia 53°56N 36°42E 188 F9
Odra = Oder → Europe 53°33N 14°38E 178 B10
Odra → Spain 42°14N 4°17W 194 C6
Odum U.S.A. 31°40N 82°2W 316 D7
Odžaci Serbia 45°30N 19°17E 182 E4
Odžak Bos.-H. 45°3N 18°18E 182 E3
Odzala Congo 0°37N 14°37E 264 B2
Odzala △ Congo 0°55N 14°55E 264 B2
Odzi Zimbabwe 19°0S 32°20E 271 A5
Odzi → Zimbabwe 19°45S 32°23E 271 A5
Oebisfelde Germany 52°27N 10°57E 178 C6
Oecussi = Pante Macassar Timor-Leste 9°30S 123°58E 231 F6
Oedong S. Korea 35°42N 129°14E 224 E4
Oeiras Brazil 7°0S 42°8W 332 C3
Oeiras Portugal 38°41N 9°18W 126 A1
Oeiras do Para Brazil 1°58S 49°51W 329 D8
Oelrichs U.S.A. 43°11N 103°14W 308 D2
Oels in Schlesien = Oleśnica Poland 51°13N 17°22E 185 G4
Oelsnitz Germany 50°24N 12°10E 179 E8
Oelwein U.S.A. 42°41N 91°55W 310 B5
Oenarodo S. Korea 34°26N 127°26E 224 F3
Oeno I. Pac. Oc. 24°0S 131°0W 289 K14
Oenpelli = Gunbalanya Australia 12°20S 133°4E 278 B5
Oetz Austria 47°13N 10°53E 180 D3
Of Turkey 40°59N 40°23E 213 B9
O'Fallon U.S.A. 38°49N 90°42W 310 F6
Ofanto → Italy 41°22N 16°13E 201 A9
Offa Nigeria 8°13N 4°42E 263 D5
Offaly □ Ireland 53°15N 7°30W 166 C4
Offenbach Germany 50°6N 8°44E 179 E4
Offenburg Germany 48°28N 7°56E 179 G3
Officer Cr. → Australia 27°46S 132°30E 279 E5
Offida Italy 42°56N 13°41E 199 F10
Offoué → Gabon 0°4S 11°44E 264 C2
Ofidousa Greece 36°33N 26°8E 205 E8
Ofin Nigeria 6°32N 3°30E 124 A3
Ofolanga Tonga 19°38S 174°27W 287 P13
Ofotfjorden Norway 68°27N 17°0E 160 B17
Ofte Norway 59°30N 8°12E 164 E5
Ofu Amer. Samoa 14°11S 169°41W 302 g
Ōfunato Japan 39°4N 141°43E 220 E10
Oga Japan 39°55N 139°50E 220 E9
Oga-Hantō Japan 39°58N 139°47E 220 E9
Ogaden Ethiopia 7°30N 45°30E 267 C6
Ōgaki Japan 35°21N 136°37E 223 B8
Ogallala U.S.A. 41°8N 101°43W 308 E3
Ogan → Indonesia 3°1S 104°44E 234 C2
Ogasawara Gunto Pac. Oc. 27°0N 142°0E 288 E6
Ogawa Japan 35°44N 139°16E 140 A1
Ogbomosho Nigeria 8°1N 4°11E 263 D5
Ogden Iowa, U.S.A. 42°2N 94°2W 310 B2
Ogden Utah, U.S.A. 41°13N 111°58W 304 F8
Ogden Park U.S.A. 41°46N 87°39W 119 C2
Ogden Slip Chicago, U.S.A. 119 b3
Ogdensburg U.S.A. 44°42N 75°30W 313 B9
Ogea Driki Fiji 19°12S 178°27W 287 B3
Ogea Levu Fiji 19°8S 178°24W 287 B3
Ogeechee → U.S.A. 31°50N 81°3W 316 D8
Ogi Japan 33°20N 130°15E 222 D2
Ogikubo Japan 35°42N 139°37E 140 A2
Ogilby U.S.A. 32°49N 114°50W 307 N12
Ogilvie Transportation Center Chicago, U.S.A. 41°52N 87°38W 119 B3
Oglat Beraber Algeria 30°15N 3°34W 260 B4
Oglat el Khnâchich Mali 21°51N 3°58W 260 D4
Oglesby U.S.A. 41°18N 89°4W 310 C7
Oglethorpe U.S.A. 32°18N 84°4W 316 C5
Ogliastra □ Italy 39°50N 9°35E 200 C2
Oglio → Italy 45°2N 10°39E 198 C7
Oglio Nord ⊂ Italy 45°22N 9°54E 198 C6
Oglio Sud ⊂ Italy 45°7N 10°24E 198 C7
Ogmore Australia 22°37S 149°35E 280 C4
Ognon → France 47°16N 5°28E 173 E12
Ogogoro Nigeria 6°25N 3°24E 124 B2

Ogoja Nigeria 6°38N 8°39E 263 D6
Ogoki Canada 51°38N 85°58W 298 B2
Ogoki → Canada 51°38N 85°57W 298 B2
Ogoki L. Canada 50°50N 87°10W 298 B2
Ogoki Res. Canada 50°45N 88°15W 298 B2
Ogooué → Gabon 1°0S 9°0E 264 C1
Ogooué-Ivindo □ Gabon 1°0N 13°30E 264 B2
Ogooué-Lolo □ Gabon 1°0S 12°30E 264 C2
Ogooué-Maritime □ Gabon 1°0S 9°0E 264 C1
Ogōri Fukuoka, Japan 33°25N 130°30E 222 D2
Ogōri Yamaguchi, Japan 34°6N 131°24E 222 C3
Ogosta → Bulgaria 43°48N 23°55E 202 C7
Ogou → Togo 7°50N 1°19E 263 D5
Ogoueïleten Nmâdi Mauritania 19°46N 11°1W 260 E2
Ogowe = Ogooué → Gabon 1°0S 9°0E 264 C1
Ogoyo Nigeria 6°25N 3°29E 124 B2
Ogr = Sharafa Sudan 11°59N 27°7E 257 E2
Ograźden N. Macedonia 41°30N 22°50E 202 E6
Ogre Latvia 56°49N 24°36E 188 D3
Ogrein Sudan 17°55N 34°50E 256 D3
Ogudu Nigeria 6°34N 3°24E 124 A2
Ogulin Croatia 45°16N 15°16E 199 C12
Ogun □ Nigeria 7°0N 3°0E 263 D5
Oguni Japan 33°11N 131°8E 222 D3
Ögur Iceland 66°2N 22°44W 155 A4
Ogurja Ada Turkmenistan 38°55N 53°2E 247 B7
Oguta Nigeria 5°44N 6°44E 263 D6
Oğuzeli Turkey 36°57N 37°30E 250 B8
Ogwashi-Uku Nigeria 6°15N 6°30E 263 D6
Ogwe Nigeria 5°0N 7°14E 263 E6
Ohai N.Z. 45°55S 168°0E 285 F3
Ohakune N.Z. 39°24S 175°24E 284 F4
Ohanet Algeria 28°44N 8°46E 261 C6
Ohangwena □ Namibia 17°30S 17°0E 270 A2
Ōhara Japan 35°15N 140°23E 223 B12
O'Hare Int., Chicago ✈ (ORD) U.S.A. 41°59N 87°54W 311 C9
Ohata Japan 41°24N 141°10E 220 D10
Ohatchee U.S.A. 33°47N 86°0W 316 B4
Ohau, L. N.Z. 44°15S 169°53E 285 E4
Ohaupo N.Z. 37°56S 175°20E 284 D4
O'Higgins, C. Chile 27°5S 109°15W 330 b
O'Higgins, Parque Chile 33°27S 70°40W 137 B2
O'Higgins, Pta. Chile 33°41S 79°0W 330 c
Ohio □ U.S.A. 40°15N 82°45W 312 F2
Ohio → U.S.A. 36°59N 89°8W 308 G9
Ohio City U.S.A. 40°46N 84°37W 311 D12
Ohiwa Harbour N.Z. 37°59S 177°10E 284 D6
Ohlau = Oława Poland 50°57N 17°20E 185 H4
Ohře → Czechia 50°30N 14°10E 180 A7
Ohre → Sachsen-Anhalt, Germany 52°18N 11°46E 178 C7
Ohrid N. Macedonia 41°8N 20°52E 202 E4
Ohridsko Jezero N. Macedonia 41°8N 20°52E 202 E4
Ohrigstad S. Africa 24°39S 30°36E 271 B5
Öhringen Germany 49°12N 9°31E 179 F5
Ohura N.Z. 38°51S 174°59E 284 E3
Oi Qu → China 28°37N 98°16E 228 C2
Oiapoque Brazil 3°50N 51°50W 329 C7
Oiapoque → S. Amer. 4°8N 51°40W 329 C7
Oikou China 38°35N 117°42E 227 E9
Oil City U.S.A. 41°26N 79°42W 312 E5
Oil Springs Canada 42°47N 82°7W 312 D2
Oildale U.S.A. 35°25N 119°1W 307 K7
Ōimachi Japan 35°35N 139°43E 140 B3
Oinousa = Inousses Greece 38°33N 26°14E 205 C8
Oise □ France 49°28N 2°30E 173 C9
Oise → France 49°0N 2°4E 173 C9
Oistins Barbados 13°4N 59°33W 323 r
Ōita Japan 33°14N 131°36E 222 D3
Ōita □ Japan 33°15N 131°30E 222 D3
Oiticica Brazil 5°3S 41°5W 332 C3
Ojai U.S.A. 34°27N 119°15W 307 L7
Ojcowski △ Poland 50°15N 19°50E 185 H6
Ojhar India 20°6N 73°56E 244 D1
Ojinaga Mexico 29°34N 104°25W 318 B4
Ojiya Japan 37°18N 138°48E 221 F9
Ojo Caliente Mexico 22°34N 102°15W 318 C4
Ojo de Liebre, L. Mexico 27°45N 114°15W 318 B2
Ojos del Salado, Cerro Argentina 27°0S 68°40W 334 B2
Ojota Nigeria 6°35N 3°23E 124 A2
Ojus U.S.A. 25°26N 80°9W 129 C3
Oka Nigeria 7°9N 3°38E 263 D5
Oka → Russia 56°20N 43°59E 190 B7
Okaba Indonesia 8°6S 139°42E 231 F9
Okahandja Namibia 22°0S 16°59E 270 B2
Okahukura N.Z. 38°48S 175°14E 284 E4
Okaihau N.Z. 35°19S 173°47E 284 B2
Okakarara Namibia 20°35S 17°27E 270 B2
Okalataka Congo 0°18S 14°54E 264 C2
Okanagan L. Canada 50°0N 119°30W 296 D5
Okandja Gabon 0°35S 13°45E 264 C2
Okano → Gabon 0°5S 10°57E 264 C2
Okanogan U.S.A. 48°22N 119°35W 304 B4
Okanogan → U.S.A. 48°6N 119°44W 304 B4
Okanogan Range N. Amer. 49°0N 119°55W 296 D5
Okány Hungary 46°52N 21°21E 182 D6
Okapa Papua N. G. 6°38S 145°39E 286 D3
Okapi ⌓ Dem. Rep. of the Congo 2°30N 27°20E 268 B2
Okaputa Namibia 20°5S 17°0E 270 B2
Okara Pakistan 30°50N 73°31E 242 D5
Okarito N.Z. 43°15S 170°9E 285 D5
Okarukambe = Steinhausen Namibia 21°49S 18°20E 270 B2
Okato N.Z. 39°12S 173°53E 284 F2
Okau Micronesia 9°32N 138°6E 287 R16
Okaukuejo Namibia 19°10S 16°0E 270 A2
Okavango = Cubango → Africa 18°50S 22°25E 265 F4
Okavango Delta Botswana 18°45S 22°45E 270 A3
Okavango Swamp = Okavango Delta Botswana 18°45S 22°45E 270 A3
Ōkawa Japan 33°9N 130°21E 222 D2
Okawville U.S.A. 38°26N 89°33W 310 F7
Okaya Japan 36°5N 138°10E 223 A10
Okayama Japan 34°40N 133°54E 222 C5
Okayama □ Japan 35°0N 133°50E 222 C5
Okazaki Japan 34°57N 137°10E 223 C9
Oke-Iho Nigeria 8°1N 3°18E 263 D5
Oke-Ira Nigeria 6°29N 3°22E 124 B2
Okęcie Poland 52°11N 20°56E 143 B1
Okęcie, Warszawa ✈ (WAW) Poland 52°9N 20°59E 143 B1
Okeechobee U.S.A. 27°15N 80°50W 317 H9
Okeechobee, L. U.S.A. 27°0N 80°50W 317 J9
Okefenokee ⌓ U.S.A. 30°45N 82°18W 316 E7
Okefenokee Swamp U.S.A. 30°40N 82°20W 316 E7
Okehampton U.K. 50°44N 4°0W 169 G4
Okemos U.S.A. 42°43N 84°26W 311 B12
Okene Nigeria 7°32N 6°11E 263 D6
Okeogbe Nigeria 6°24N 3°23E 124 B2
Oker → Germany 52°32N 10°22E 178 C6
Okha Gujarat, India 22°27N 69°4E 242 H3
Okha Russia 53°40N 143°0E 215 D15
Okhla India 28°33N 77°16E 120 B2
Okhotsk Russia 59°20N 143°10E 215 D15
Okhotsk, Sea of Asia 55°0N 145°0E 215 D15
Okhotskiy Perevoz Russia 61°52N 135°35E 215 C14
Okhta → Russia 59°56N 30°25E 137 B2
Okhtyrka Ukraine 50°25N 35°0E 189 G8
Oki-no-Shima Japan 32°44N 132°33E 222 E4
Oki-Shotō Japan 36°5N 133°15E 222 A5
Okiep S. Africa 29°39S 17°53E 270 C2
Okigwi Nigeria 5°52N 7°20E 263 D6
Okija Nigeria 5°54N 6°55E 263 D6
Okinawa Japan 26°19N 127°46E 288 a
Okinawa □ Japan 26°40N 128°0E 288 a
Okinawa-Guntō Japan 26°40N 128°0E 221 L4
Okinawa-Jima Japan 26°32N 128°0E 221 L4
Okino-erabu-Shima Japan 27°21N 128°33E 221 L4
Okitipupa Nigeria 6°31N 4°50E 263 D5
Okkervil → Russia 59°56N 30°30E 137 B2
Oklahoma □ U.S.A. 35°20N 97°30W 314 D6
Oklahoma City U.S.A. 35°30N 97°30W 314 D6
Oklawaha → U.S.A. 29°28N 81°41W 317 F8
Okmulgee U.S.A. 35°37N 95°58W 314 D7
Oknitsa = Ocniţa Moldova 48°25N 27°30E 183 B12
Oko, W. → Sudan 21°15N 35°56E 256 C4
Okolo Uganda 2°37N 31°8E 268 B3
Okolona Ky., U.S.A. 38°8N 85°41W 311 F11
Okolona Miss., U.S.A. 34°0N 88°45W 315 E10
Okombahe Namibia 21°23S 15°22E 270 B2
Okonek Poland 53°32N 16°51E 184 E3
Okotoks Canada 50°43N 113°58W 296 C6
Okoyo Congo 1°28S 15°0E 264 C3
Okrika Nigeria 4°40N 7°10E 263 E6
Okrzeszyn Poland 52°8N 21°8E 143 C2
Oksapmin Papua N. G. 5°17S 142°15E 286 C2
Øksendalsøra Norway 62°42N 8°27E 164 B5
Oksovskiy Russia 62°33N 39°57E 186 B6
Oksval Norway 59°51N 10°40E 133 A3
Oktwin Myanmar 18°49N 96°26E 241 F6
Oktyabrsk = Qandyaghash Kazakhstan 49°28N 57°25E 187 E10
Oktyabrsk Russia 53°11N 48°40E 190 D9
Oktyabrskiy = Aktsyabrski Belarus 52°38N 28°53E 177 B15
Oktyabrskiy Bashkortostan, Russia 54°28N 53°28E 186 D9
Oktyabrskiy Kamchatka, Russia 52°39N 156°14E 215 D16
Oktyabrskiy Moskva, Russia 55°41N 37°35E 129 B2
Oktyabrskiy Rostov, Russia 47°30N 40°4E 191 G5
Oktyabrskoy Revolyutsii, Ostrov Russia 79°30N 97°0E 215 B10
Oktyabrskoye = Zhovtneve Ukraine 46°54N 32°3E 189 J7
Ōkubo Tokyo, Japan 140 a2
Ōkuchi Japan 32°4N 130°37E 222 E2
Okulovka Russia 58°25N 33°19E 188 C7
Ōkura Japan 35°35N 139°27E 140 B1
Okuru N.Z. 43°55S 168°55E 285 D3
Okushiri-Tō Japan 42°15N 139°30E 220 C9
Okuta Nigeria 9°14N 3°12E 263 D5
Okwa → Botswana 22°30S 23°0E 270 B3
Ola Russia 59°35N 151°17E 215 D16
Ola Ark., U.S.A. 35°2N 93°13W 314 D8
Ólafsfjörður Iceland 66°4N 18°39W 155 A8
Ólafsvík Iceland 64°53N 23°43W 155 C3
Olaine Latvia 56°48N 23°59E 184 B10
Olancha U.S.A. 36°17N 118°1W 307 J8
Olancha Pk. U.S.A. 36°16N 118°7W 307 J8
Olanchito Honduras 15°30N 86°30W 320 C2
Öland Sweden 56°45N 16°38E 163 H10
Ölands norra udde Sweden 57°22N 17°5E 163 G11
Ölands södra udde Sweden 56°12N 16°23E 163 H10
Olanta U.S.A. 33°56N 79°56W 316 B10
Olar U.S.A. 33°11N 81°11W 316 B8
Olargues France 43°34N 2°53E 174 E6
Olari Finland 60°10N 24°44E 121 B1
Olaria Brazil 22°50S 43°16W 135 B1
Olary Australia 32°18S 140°19E 282 B4
Olascoaga Argentina 35°15S 60°39W 334 D3
Olathe U.S.A. 38°53N 94°49W 308 F6
Olavarría Argentina 36°55S 60°20W 334 D3
Oława Poland 50°57N 17°20E 185 H4
Olbernhau Germany 50°40N 13°19E 178 E9
Ólbia Italy 40°55N 9°31E 200 B2
Ólbia, G. di Italy 40°55N 9°39E 200 B2
Olching Germany 48°12N 11°21E 179 G7
Olcott U.S.A. 43°20N 78°42W 312 C6
Old Admiralty Saint Petersburg, Russia 59°55N 30°20E 137 B1
Old Bahama Chan. = Bahama, Canal Viejo de W. Indies 22°10N 77°30W 320 B4
Old Baldy Pk. = San Antonio, Mt. U.S.A. 34°17N 117°38W 307 L9
Old Bar Australia 31°58S 152°35E 283 A10
Old Bridge U.S.A. 40°25N 74°22W 313 F10
Old Castile = Castilla y Leon □ Spain 42°0N 5°0W 194 D6
Old City Shanghai, China 31°13N 121°29E 138 B1
Old City Delhi, India 120 a3
Old City Jerusalem 123 b3
Old Crow Canada 67°30N 139°55W 294 D4
Old Dale U.S.A. 34°8N 115°47W 307 L11
Old Forge N.Y., U.S.A. 43°43N 74°58W 313 C10
Old Forge Pa., U.S.A. 41°22N 75°45W 313 E9
Old Fort = Purana Qila Delhi, India 120 c3
Old Fort B. The Bahamas 25°3N 77°32W 153 b
Old Fort Pt. Montserrat 16°40N 62°11W 323 p
Old Fort York Canada 43°39N 79°24W 141 B2
Old Harbor Alaska, U.S.A. 57°12N 153°18W 303 H9
Old Harbor Mass., U.S.A. 42°19N 71°1W 116 B2
Old Harbour Jamaica 17°56N 77°7W 320 a
Old Harbour Bay Jamaica 17°54N 77°6W 320 a
Old Ironsides = U.S.S. Constitution Boston, U.S.A. 116 a3
Old Mapoon ☼ Australia 11°5S 142°22E 280 A3
Old Panamao Phil. 5°59N 121°13E 233 J3
Old Perlican Canada 48°5N 53°1W 299 C9
Old Road Bluff Antigua & B. 16°59N 61°50W 322 b
Old Road Town St. Kitts & Nevis 17°17N 62°47W 322 d
Old Roundhouse Toronto, Canada 141 c2
Old Shinyanga Tanzania 3°33S 33°27E 268 C3
Old Speck Mt. U.S.A. 44°34N 70°57W 313 B14
Old Town = Stare Miasto Warsaw, Poland 143 a2
Old Town Edinburgh, U.K. 121 b2
Old Town Fla., U.S.A. 29°36N 82°59W 317 F7
Old Town Ill., U.S.A. 41°54N 87°37W 119 B3
Old Town Maine, U.S.A. 44°56N 68°39W 309 C19
Old Town Hall = Altes Rathaus Munich, Germany 131 b3
Old Town Square Warsaw, Poland 143 a2
Old U.S. Mint New Orleans, U.S.A. 131 a3
Old Washington U.S.A. 40°2N 81°27W 312 F3
Old Wives L. Canada 50°5N 106°0W 297 C7
Oldbury U.K. 51°38N 2°33W 169 F5
Oldcastle Ireland 53°46N 7°10W 166 C4
Oldeani Tanzania 3°22S 35°35E 268 C4
Olden Norway 61°49N 6°49E 164 C3
Oldenburg Niedersachsen, Germany 53°9N 8°13E 178 B4
Oldenburg Schleswig-Holstein, Germany 54°17N 10°52E 178 A6
Oldenzaal Neths. 52°19N 6°53E 170 B6
Oldham U.K. 53°33N 2°7W 168 D5
Oldman → Canada 49°57N 111°42W 296 D6
Oldmeldrum U.K. 57°20N 2°19W 167 D6
Olds Canada 51°50N 114°10W 296 C6
Oldsmar U.S.A. 28°2N 82°39W 317 G7
Olduvai Gorge Tanzania 2°57S 35°23E 268 C4
Öldziyt Mongolia 44°40N 109°1E 226 B5
Ole Rømer Land Greenland 74°10N 24°30W 154 C8
Olean U.S.A. 42°5N 78°26W 312 D6
Oleby Sweden 60°8N 13°2E 162 D7
Olecko Poland 54°2N 22°31E 184 D9
Oléggio Italy 45°36N 8°38E 198 C5
Oleiros = O Real Spain 43°20N 8°19W 194 B2
Oleiros Portugal 39°56N 7°56W 194 F3
Olekma → Russia 60°22N 120°42E 215 C13
Olekminsk Russia 60°25N 120°30E 215 C13
Oleksandrivka Ukraine 48°55N 32°20E 189 H7
Oleksandriya Kirovohrad, Ukraine 48°42N 33°3E 189 H7
Oleksandriya Rivne, Ukraine 50°37N 26°19E 177 C14
Olema U.S.A. 38°3N 122°47W 306 G4
Ølen Norway 59°36N 5°48E 164 E2
Olenegorsk Russia 68°9N 33°18E 160 B25
Olenek Russia 68°28N 112°18E 215 C12
Olenek → Russia 73°0N 120°10E 215 B13
Olenino Russia 56°15N 33°30E 188 D7
Olenya = Olenegorsk Russia 68°9N 33°18E 160 B25
Oléron, Î. d' France 45°55N 1°15W 174 C2
Olesk Ukraine 51°6N 24°11E 185 G11
Oleśnica Poland 51°13N 17°22E 185 G4
Olesno Poland 50°51N 18°26E 185 H5
Oleta River State Rec. Area U.S.A. 25°55N 80°8W 129 C3
Olevsk Ukraine 51°12N 27°39E 177 C14
Olga, L. Canada 49°47N 77°15W 298 C4
Olgas, The = Kata Tjuta Australia 25°20S 130°50E 279 E5
Olgino Russia 60°0N 30°10E 137 B1
Ölgiy Mongolia 48°56N 89°57E 217 C11
Ølgod Denmark 55°49N 8°36E 163 J2
Olhão Portugal 37°3N 7°48W 195 H3
Olhopil Ukraine 48°12N 29°30E 183 B14
Olhovatka Russia 54°30N 22°18E 184 D9
Olib Croatia 44°23N 14°44E 199 D11
Oliena Italy 40°16N 9°24E 200 B2
Oliete Spain 41°1N 0°41W 196 D4
Olifants = Elefantes → Africa 24°10S 32°40E 271 B5
Olifants → Namibia 25°30S 19°30E 270 B2
Olifantshoek S. Africa 27°57S 22°42E 270 C3
Olimbos Greece 35°44N 27°11E 205 F9
Ólimbos, Óros = Olymbos Oros Greece 40°6N 22°23E 202 F6
Olímpia Brazil 20°44S 48°54W 335 A6
Olimpico, Estadio Mexico 19°20N 99°11W 128 C1
Olimpos-Beydaglari △ Turkey 36°36N 30°30E 205 E12
Olin U.S.A. 42°0N 91°9W 310 B5
Olinda Brazil 8°1S 34°51W 332 C5
Olite Spain 42°29N 1°40W 196 C3
Oliva Argentina 32°0S 63°38W 334 C3
Oliva Spain 38°58N 0°9W 197 G4
Oliva de la Frontera Spain 38°17N 6°54W 195 G4
Olivais Portugal 38°45N 9°7W 126 A2
Olivar de los Padres Mexico 19°21N 99°14W 128 B1
Olivar del Conde Mexico 19°22N 99°12W 128 B1
Olivares, Cerro los Argentina 30°18S 69°55W 334 C2
Olivares de Júcar Spain 39°46N 2°20W 196 F2
Olive Branch U.S.A. 34°57N 89°49W 315 D10
Olive Hill U.S.A. 38°18N 83°13W 311 F13
Olive Park Chicago, U.S.A. 119 b3
Olivehurst U.S.A. 39°6N 121°34W 306 F5
Oliveira Brazil 20°39S 44°50W 333 F3
Oliveira de Azeméis Portugal 40°49N 8°29W 194 E2
Oliveira do Douro Portugal 41°5N 8°2W 194 D2
Oliveira dos Brejinhos Brazil 12°19S 42°54W 333 D3
Olivenza Spain 38°41N 7°9W 195 G3
Oliver Canada 49°13N 119°37W 296 D5
Oliver L. Canada 56°56N 103°22W 297 B8
Olives, Mt. of West Bank 31°46N 35°15E 123 B2
Olivet Loiret, France 47°51N 1°55E 173 E8
Olivet Mich., U.S.A. 42°27N 84°56W 311 B12
Olivia, L. U.S.A. 28°31N 81°31W 133 A1
Olivine Ra. N.Z. 44°15S 168°30E 285 E3
Olivos Argentina 34°30S 58°28W 117 B2
Olkhovka Russia 49°48N 44°32E 190 F7
Olkusz Poland 50°18N 19°33E 185 H6
Ollachea Peru 13°49S 70°29W 330 C3
Ollagüe Chile 21°15S 68°10W 334 A2
Ollombo Congo 1°18S 15°53E 264 C3
Olloua Congo 0°54S 14°34E 264 C2
Olmaliq Uzbekistan 40°50N 69°35E 217 D7
Olmedo Spain 41°20N 4°43W 194 D6
Olmeto France 41°43N 8°55E 175 G12
Olmos Peru 5°59S 79°46W 330 B2
Olmütz = Olomouc Czechia 49°38N 17°12E 181 B10
Olney Ill., U.S.A. 38°44N 88°5W 311 F8
Olney Tex., U.S.A. 33°22N 98°45W 314 E5
Olofström Sweden 56°17N 14°32E 163 H8
Oloitokitok Kenya 2°56S 37°30E 268 C4
Ololi Congo 0°15S 14°36E 264 C2
Oloma Cameroon 3°29N 11°19E 263 E7
Olomane → Canada 50°14N 60°37W 299 B7
Olomouc Czechia 49°38N 17°12E 181 B10
Olomoucký □ Czechia 49°45N 17°5E 181 B10
Olona → Italy 45°29N 9°6E 128 B1
Olonets Russia 61°0N 32°54E 188 B7
Olongapo Phil. 14°50N 120°18E 232 D3
Olonkinbyen Norway 70°55N 8°43W 154 C10
Olonne-sur-Mer France 46°32N 1°47W 174 B2
Oloron, Gave d' → France 43°33N 1°5W 174 E2
Oloron-Ste-Marie France 43°11N 0°38W 174 E3
Olosega Amer. Samoa 14°10S 169°37W 302 g
Olosenga = Swains I. Amer. Samoa 11°11S 171°4W 289 J11
Olot Spain 42°11N 2°30E 196 C7
Olovo Bos.-H. 44°8N 18°35E 182 F3
Olovyannaya Russia 50°58N 115°35E 215 D12
Oloy → Russia 66°29N 159°29E 215 C16
Olsberg Germany 51°21N 8°31E 178 D4
Olshammar Sweden 58°45N 14°48E 163 F8
Olshanka Ukraine 48°16N 30°58E 189 H6
Olshany Ukraine 50°3N 35°53E 189 G8
Olsztyn Poland 53°48N 20°29E 184 E7
Olsztynek Poland 53°34N 20°19E 184 E7
Olt □ Romania 44°20N 24°30E 183 F9
Olt → Romania 43°43N 24°51E 183 G9
Oltedal Norway 58°49N 6°2E 164 F3
Olten Switz. 47°21N 7°53E 179 H3
Olteniţa Romania 44°7N 26°42E 183 F11
Olton U.S.A. 34°11N 102°8W 314 D3
Oltu Turkey 40°35N 41°58E 213 B9
Oluan Pi Taiwan 21°53N 120°51E 225 E2
Oluanpi Taiwan 21°54N 120°51E 225 E2
Olula del Rio Spain 37°21N 2°18W 197 H2
Olur Turkey 40°49N 42°8E 213 B10
Olustee U.S.A. 30°12N 82°26W 316 E7
Olutanga Phil. 7°26N 122°54E 233 H4
Olutanga I. Phil. 7°22N 122°52E 233 H4
Olvega Spain 41°47N 2°0W 196 D2
Olvera Spain 36°55N 5°18W 195 J5
Olymbos Cyprus 35°21N 33°45E 207 E9
Olymbos Oros Greece 40°6N 22°23E 202 F6
Olympia Greece 37°39N 21°39E 204 D3
Olympia London, U.K. 125 c1
Olympia Wash., U.S.A. 47°3N 122°53W 306 D4
Olympia, L. U.S.A. 28°34N 81°31W 133 A1
Olympic △ U.S.A. 47°45N 123°43W 306 C3
Olympic Dam Australia 30°30S 136°55E 282 A2
Olympic Green China 39°59N 116°23E 114 B2
Olympic Mts. U.S.A. 47°55N 123°45W 306 C3
Olympic Stadium = Turner Field Atlanta, U.S.A. 33°44N 84°23W 113 B2
Olympic Stadium Beijing, China 39°59N 116°23E 114 B2
Olympic Stadium Helsinki, Finland 60°11N 24°55E 121 B2
Olympique, Stade Montréal, Canada 45°33N 73°33W 130 A2
Olympus Cyprus 34°56N 32°52E 207 F8
Olympus, Mt. = Olymbos Oros Greece 40°6N 22°23E 202 F6
Olympus, Mt. = Uludağ Turkey 40°4N 29°13E 203 F13
Olympus, Mt. U.S.A. 47°48N 123°43W 306 C3
Olyphant U.S.A. 41°27N 75°36W 313 E9
Olyutorskiy, Mys Russia 59°55N 170°27E 215 D18
Om → Russia 54°59N 73°22E 217 B8
Om Hajer Eritrea 14°20N 36°41E 257 E4
Om Koi Thailand 17°48N 98°22E 236 D2
Ōma Japan 41°45N 141°5E 220 D10
Ōmachi Japan 36°30N 137°50E 223 A9
Omae-Zaki Japan 34°36N 138°14E 223 C10
Ōmagari = Daisen Japan 39°27N 140°29E 220 E10
Omagh U.K. 54°36N 7°19W 166 B4
Omagh □ U.K. 54°35N 7°15W 166 B4
Omaha U.S.A. 41°17N 95°58W 308 E6
Omaheke □ Namibia 21°30S 19°0E 270 B2
Omak U.S.A. 48°25N 119°31W 304 B4
Omalos Greece 35°19N 23°55E 207 E4
Omalur India 11°44N 78°4E 245 J4
Oman ■ Asia 23°0N 58°0E 249 B7
Oman, G. of Asia 24°30N 58°30E 247 E8
Omapere N.Z. 35°37S 173°25E 284 B2
Omar Combon Somalia 3°10N 45°47E 267 D6
Omaruru Namibia 21°26S 16°0E 270 B2
Omaruru → Namibia 22°7S 14°15E 270 B1
Omate Peru 16°45S 71°0W 330 D3
Ombai, Selat Indonesia 8°30S 124°50E 231 F6
Ombella-Mpoko □ C.A.R. 5°30N 17°30E 264 A3
Omboué Gabon 1°35S 9°15E 264 C1
Ombrone → Italy 42°42N 11°5E 198 F8
Omchi Chad 21°22N 17°53E 259 D3
Omdurmân Sudan 15°40N 32°28E 257 D3
Ōme Japan 35°47N 139°15E 223 B11
Omega U.S.A. 31°21N 83°36W 316 D6
Omegna Italy 45°53N 8°24E 198 C5
Omemee Canada 44°18N 78°33W 312 B6
Omeo Australia 37°6S 147°36E 283 D7
Omeonga Dem. Rep. of the Congo 3°40S 24°22E 264 C4
Ometepe, I. de Nic. 11°32N 85°35W 320 D2
Ometepec Mexico 16°41N 98°25W 319 D5
Ōmi-Shima Ehime, Japan 34°15N 133°0E 222 C5
Ōmi-Shima Yamaguchi, Japan 34°25N 131°9E 222 C3
Omihachiman Japan 35°7N 136°3E 223 B8
Omin Micronesia 9°36N 138°9E 287 R16
Ominato Japan 41°17N 141°10E 220 D10
Omineca → Canada 56°3N 124°16W 296 B4
Omineca Mts. Canada 56°30N 125°30W 296 B3
Omiš Croatia 43°28N 16°40E 199 E13
Omišalj Croatia 45°13N 14°32E 199 C11
Omitara Namibia 22°16S 18°2E 270 B2
Ōmiya = Saitama Japan 35°54N 139°38E 223 B11
Ommaney, C. U.S.A. 56°10N 134°40W 303 H14
Omme Å → Denmark 55°56N 8°32E 163 J2
Ommen Neths. 52°31N 6°26E 170 B6
Ömnögovĭ □ Mongolia 43°15N 104°0E 226 C3
Omo → Ethiopia 6°25N 36°10E 257 F4
Omo △ Ethiopia 5°54N 35°55E 257 F4
Omo Valley Ethiopia 5°7N 36°0E 257 F4
Omodeo, L. Italy 40°8N 8°56E 200 B1
Omodhos Cyprus 34°51N 32°48E 207 F8
Omoï Congo 2°56S 13°13E 264 C2
Omoko Nigeria 5°19N 6°40E 263 D6
Omolon → Russia 68°42N 158°36E 215 C16
Omona Solomon Is. 7°30S 158°43E 287 L10
Omonia Square Athens, Greece 112 b1
Omono-Gawa → Japan 39°46N 140°3E 220 E10
Ōmori Japan 35°34N 139°43E 140 B3
Ompha Canada 45°0N 76°50W 313 B8
Omsk Russia 55°0N 73°12E 217 B8
Omsukchan Russia 62°32N 155°48E 215 C16
Ōmu Japan 44°34N 142°58E 220 B11
Omul, Vf. Romania 45°27N 25°29E 183 E10
Omulew → Poland 53°5N 21°33E 185 E8
Ōmura Japan 32°56N 129°57E 222 E1
Ōmura-Wan Japan 32°57N 129°52E 222 E1
Omuramba Omatako → Namibia 17°45S 20°25E 270 A2
Omuramba Ovambo → Namibia 18°45S 16°59E 270 A2
Omurtag Bulgaria 43°8N 26°26E 203 C10
Omusati □ Namibia 18°30S 15°0E 270 A1
Ōmuta Japan 33°5N 130°26E 222 D2
Omuthiya Namibia 17°43S 16°13E 270 A2
On-ma-thi Myanmar 22°17N 96°41E 241 D6
On-Take Japan 31°35N 130°39E 222 F2
Oña Spain 42°43N 3°25W 194 C7
Ona Fla., U.S.A. 27°29N 81°55W 317 H8
Ona Dikonde Dem. Rep. of the Congo 3°51S 24°11E 264 C4
Onaga U.S.A. 39°29N 96°10W 308 F5
Onalaska U.S.A. 43°53N 91°14W 308 D8
Onancock U.S.A. 37°43N 75°45W 309 G16
Onangue, L. Gabon 0°57S 10°4E 264 C1
Onaping L. Canada 47°3N 81°30W 298 C3
Onarga U.S.A. 40°43N 88°1W 311 D8
Oñati Spain 43°3N 2°25W 196 B2
Onavas Mexico 28°31N 109°35W 318 B3
Onawa U.S.A. 42°2N 96°6W 308 D5
Oncócua Angola 16°30S 13°25E 265 F2
Onda Spain 39°55N 0°17W 196 F4
Ondangwa Namibia 17°57S 16°4E 270 A2
Ondarroa Spain 43°19N 2°25W 196 B2
Ondas → Brazil 12°8S 44°55W 333 D3
Ondava → Slovakia 48°27N 21°48E 181 C14
Ondjiva Angola 16°48S 15°50E 265 F3
Ondo Japan 34°11N 132°32E 222 C4
Ondo Nigeria 7°4N 4°47E 263 D5
Ondo □ Nigeria 6°45N 5°0E 263 D6
Öndörhaan Mongolia 47°19N 110°39E 219 B11
Öndverðarnes Iceland 64°52N 24°0W 155 C2
One and a Half Degree Channel Maldives 1°30N 73°20E 272 d
One Arm Point Australia 16°26S 123°3E 278 C3
One Arm Point ☼ Australia 16°31S 122°53E 278 C3
One Prudential Plaza Chicago, U.S.A. 119 c2
One Tree Australia 34°11S 144°43E 281 E3
One World Trade Center New York, U.S.A. 40°43N 74°1W 132 e1
Oneata Fiji 18°26S 178°25W 287 B3
Oneco U.S.A. 27°25N 82°31W 317 H7
Onega Russia 64°0N 38°10E 186 B6
Onega → Russia 63°58N 38°2E 186 B6
Onega, G. of = Onezhskaya Guba Russia 64°24N 36°38E 186 B6
Onega, L. = Onezhskoye Ozero Russia 61°44N 35°22E 188 B8
Onehunga N.Z. 36°55S 174°48E 284 C3
Oneida Ill., U.S.A. 41°4N 90°13W 310 C6
Oneida N.Y., U.S.A. 43°6N 75°39W 313 C9
Oneida L. U.S.A. 43°12N 75°54W 313 C9
O'Neill U.S.A. 42°27N 98°39W 308 D4
Onekotan, Ostrov Russia 49°25N 154°45E 215 E16
Onema Dem. Rep. of the Congo 4°35S 24°30E 265 C4
Oneonta U.S.A. 42°27N 75°4W 313 D9
Onerahi N.Z. 35°45S 174°22E 284 B3
Oneroa Cook Is. 21°15S 159°43W 289 h
Oneşti Romania 46°17N 26°47E 183 D11
Onezhskaya Guba Russia 64°24N 36°38E 186 B6
Onezhskoye Ozero Russia 61°44N 35°22E 188 B8
Ongarue N.Z. 38°42S 175°19E 284 E4
Ongea Levu = Ogea Levu Fiji 19°8S 178°24W 287 B3
Ongers → S. Africa 31°4S 23°13E 270 D3
Ongerup Australia 33°58S 118°28E 279 F2
Ongi Mongolia 45°27N 103°54E 226 B2
Ongjin N. Korea 37°56N 125°21E 224 D2
Ongkharak Thailand 14°8N 101°1E 236 E3
Ongniud Qi China 43°0N 118°38E 227 C10
Ongoka Dem. Rep. of the Congo 1°20S 26°0E 268 C2
Ongole India 15°33N 80°2E 245 G5
Ongon = Havirga Mongolia 45°41N 113°5E 226 B7
Ongouendjo Gabon 1°23S 9°5E 264 C1
Ongoujou Comoros Is. 12°18S 44°30E 272 a
Ongtüstik Qazaqstan □ Kazakhstan 43°0N 68°0E 217 D7
Ongwediva Namibia 17°47S 15°46E 270 A2
Oni Georgia 42°33N 43°26E 191 J6
Onida U.S.A. 44°42N 100°4W 308 C3
Onilahy → Madag. 23°34S 43°45E 272 C1
Onima Bonaire 12°15N 68°19W 322 h
Onisigun Nigeria 6°35N 3°24E 124 A2
Onitsha Nigeria 6°6N 6°42E 263 D6
Onna Japan 26°29N 127°51E 288 a
Onne Nigeria 4°47N 7°9E 263 E6
Ono Fiji 18°55S 178°29E 287 B2
Ono Fukui, Japan 35°59N 136°29E 223 B8
Ono Hyōgo, Japan 34°51N 134°56E 222 C6
Onoda Japan 33°59N 131°11E 222 C3
Onohara Japan 34°5N 133°40E 222 C5
Onoke, L. N.Z. 41°22S 175°8E 284 H4
Onomichi Japan 34°25N 133°12E 222 C5
Onotoa Kiribati 1°52S 175°34E 277 A14
Ons, I. de Spain 42°23N 8°55W 194 C2
Onsala Sweden 57°26N 12°0E 163 G6
Onslow Australia 21°40S 115°12E 278 D2
Onslow B. U.S.A. 34°20N 77°15W 315 D16
Onsŏng N. Korea 42°57N 59°30E 224 A4
Ontake-San Japan 35°53N 137°29E 223 B9
Ontar Vanuatu 14°17S 167°27E 287 D5
Ontario Calif., U.S.A. 34°4N 117°39W 307 L9
Ontario Oreg., U.S.A. 44°2N 116°58W 304 D5
Ontario □ Canada 48°0N 83°0W 298 B2
Ontario, L. N. Amer. 43°20N 78°0W 312 C7
Ontario Science Centre Canada 43°43N 79°20W 141 A2
Ontinyent Spain 38°50N 0°35W 197 G4
Ontonagon U.S.A. 46°52N 89°19W 308 B9
Ontong Java Plateau Pac. Oc. 1°0N 157°0E 277 A10
Ontur Spain 38°38N 1°29W 197 G3
Onverwacht Suriname 5°35N 55°11W 329 B6
Onyx U.S.A. 35°41N 118°14W 307 K8
Oodaaq Greenland 83°40N 30°40W 154 A8
Oodnadatta Australia 27°33S 135°30E 281 D2
Oodweyne Somalia 9°25N 45°4E 267 C6
'Ō'ōkala U.S.A. 20°1N 155°17W 302 C6
Ōokayama Japan 35°36N 139°40E 140 B3
Ooku = Ōma Japan 41°45N 141°5E 220 D10
Ooldea Australia 30°27S 131°50E 279 F5
Oombulgurri Australia 15°15S 127°45E 278 C4
Oombulgurri ☼ Australia 15°10S 127°50E 278 C4
Oorindi Australia 20°40S 141°1E 280 C3
Oost-Vlaanderen □ Belgium 51°5N 3°50E 170 C3
Oostende Belgium 51°15N 2°54E 170 C2
Oosterhout Neths. 51°39N 4°47E 170 C4
Oosterschelde → Neths. 51°33N 4°0E 170 C4
Oosterwolde Neths. 53°0N 6°17E 170 B6
Oosteschelde △ Neths. 51°40N 3°40E 170 C3
Oostpunt Curaçao 12°2N 68°44W 322 g
Oostvaardersplassen ⌓ Neths. 52°27N 5°22E 170 B5
Oostzaan Tuindorp Neths. 52°25N 4°54E 112 A2
Ootacamund = Udagamandalam India 11°30N 76°44E 245 J3
Ootha Australia 33°6S 147°29E 283 B7
Ootsa L. Canada 53°50N 126°2W 296 C3
Ooty = Udagamandalam India 11°30N 76°44E 245 J3
Op Luang △ Thailand 18°12N 98°32E 236 C2
Opa-Locka U.S.A. 25°54N 80°15W 129 C1
Opa-Locka ✈ (OPF) U.S.A. 25°54N 80°16W 129 C1
Opacz Poland 52°10N 20°53E 143 B1
Opaka Bulgaria 43°28N 26°10E 203 C10
Opala Dem. Rep. of the Congo 0°40S 24°20E 264 C4
Opâle, Côte d' France 50°30N 1°30E 172 B8
Opalenica Poland 52°18N 16°24E 185 F3
Opan Bulgaria 42°13N 25°41E 203 D9
Opanake Sri Lanka 6°35N 80°40E 245 L5
Opapa N.Z. 39°47S 176°42E 284 F5
Opasatika Canada 49°30N 82°50W 298 C3
Opasquia ⌓ Canada 53°33N 93°5W 298 B1
Opatija Croatia 45°21N 14°17E 199 C11
Opatów Poland 50°50N 21°27E 185 H8
Opava Czechia 49°57N 17°58E 181 B10
Opelika U.S.A. 32°39N 85°23W 316 C4
Opelousas U.S.A. 30°32N 92°5W 314 F8
Opémisca, L. Canada 49°56N 74°52W 298 C5
Opera House Sydney, Australia 139 a2
Opheim U.S.A. 48°51N 106°24W 304 B10
Ophir U.S.A. 63°10N 156°31W 303 E8
Ophirton S. Africa 26°13S 28°1E 123 B2
Ophthalmia Ra. Australia 23°15S 119°30E 278 D2
Opi Nigeria 6°36N 7°28E 263 D6
Opihikao U.S.A. 19°26N 154°53W 302 D7
Opinaca → Canada 52°15N 78°2W 298 B4
Opinaca, Rés. Canada 52°39N 76°20W 298 B4
Opinnagau → Canada 54°12N 82°25W 298 B3
Opiscotéo, L. Canada 53°10N 68°10W 299 B6
Opobo Nigeria 4°35N 7°34E 263 E6
Opochka Russia 56°42N 28°45E 188 D5
Opoczno Poland 51°22N 20°18E 185 G7
Opol Phil. 8°31N 124°34E 233 G5
Opole Poland 50°42N 17°58E 185 H4
Opole Lubelskie Poland 51°9N 21°58E 185 G8
Opolskie □ Poland 50°30N 18°0E 185 H5
Opon = Lapu-Lapu Phil. 10°20N 123°55E 233 F4
 Opono L. Namibia 18°8S 15°45E 270 A2
Opornyy = Borankul Kazakhstan 46°11N 54°25E 216 C4
Oporto = Porto Portugal 41°8N 8°40W 194 D2
Opotiki N.Z. 38°1S 177°19E 284 E6
Opp U.S.A. 31°17N 86°16W 316 D3
Oppdal Norway 62°35N 9°41E 164 B6
Oppegård Norway 59°45N 10°49E 133 B3
Oppeln = Opole Poland 50°42N 17°58E 185 H4
Oppem Belgium 50°56N 4°18E 116 A1
Óppido Mamertina Italy 38°16N 15°59E 201 D8
Oppland □ Norway 61°15N 9°40E 164 C6
Opportunity U.S.A. 47°39N 117°15W 304 C5
Oppsal Norway 59°53N 10°50E 133 A4
Oprişor Romania 44°17N 23°5E 182 F8
Oprtalj Croatia 45°23N 13°50E 199 C10
Opua N.Z. 35°19S 174°9E 284 B3
Opunake N.Z. 39°26S 173°52E 284 F2
Opuwo Namibia 18°3S 13°45E 270 A1
Opuzen Croatia 43°1N 17°34E 199 E14
Oquawka U.S.A. 40°56N 90°57W 310 D6
Or → Kazakhstan 51°11N 58°32E 216 B5
Or, Côte d' France 47°10N 4°50E 173 E11
Ora Cyprus 34°51N 33°12E 207 F9
Ora Israel 31°45N 35°9E 123 B1
Oracabessa Jamaica 18°24N 76°57W 320 a
Oracle U.S.A. 32°37N 110°46W 305 K8
Oracuzar Peru 4°42S 78°6W 328 D2
Oradea Romania 47°2N 21°58E 182 C6
Oradell U.S.A. 40°57N 74°2W 132 A1
Oradell Res. U.S.A. 40°57N 74°1W 132 A1
Öræfajökull Iceland 64°2N 16°39W 155 C10
Orahovac = Rahovec Kosovo 42°24N 20°40E 202 D4
Orahovica Croatia 45°35N 17°52E 182 E2
Orai India 25°58N 79°30E 243 G8
Oraiokastro Greece 40°44N 22°55E 202 F6
Oraison France 43°55N 5°55E 175 E9
Oral = Zhayyq → Kazakhstan 47°0N 51°48E 187 E9
Oral Kazakhstan 51°20N 51°20E 190 E10
Oran Algeria 35°45N 0°39W 261 A4
Oran □ Algeria 35°0N 0°45W 261 A4
Orang △ India 26°37N 92°29E 241 B4
Orange N.S.W., Australia 33°15S 149°7E 283 B8
Orange Vaucluse, France 44°8N 4°47E 175 D8
Orange Calif., U.S.A. 33°47N 117°51W 307 M9
Orange Mass., U.S.A. 42°35N 72°19W 313 D12
Orange Tex., U.S.A. 30°6N 93°44W 314 F8
Orange Va., U.S.A. 38°15N 78°7W 309 F14
Orange → S. Africa 28°41S 16°28E 270 C2
Orange, C. Brazil 4°20N 51°30W 329 C7
Orange City U.S.A. 28°57N 81°18W 317 G8
Orange Cove U.S.A. 36°38N 119°19W 306 J7
Orange Free State = Free State □ S. Africa 28°30S 27°0E 270 C4
Orange Grove U.S.A. 27°58N 97°56W 314 H6
Orange Hill Barbados 13°12N 59°36W 323 r
Orange Hill Jamaica 18°16N 77°59W 320 a
Orange Hill St. Vincent 13°19N 61°7W 323 n
Orange L. U.S.A. 29°25N 82°13W 317 F7
Orange Park U.S.A. 30°10N 81°42W 316 E8
Orange River Colony = Free State □ S. Africa 28°30S 27°0E 270 C4
Orange Walk Belize 18°6N 88°33W 319 D7
Orangeburg U.S.A. 33°30N 80°52W 316 B9
Orangeville Ont., Canada 43°55N 80°5W 312 C4
Orangeville Ill., U.S.A. 42°28N 89°39W 310 B7
Orangi Pakistan 24°54N 67°0E 123 A2
Orango Guinea-Biss. 11°5N 16°0W 262 C1
Orani Italy 40°15N 9°11E 200 B2
Orani Phil. 14°49N 120°32E 232 D3
Oranienburg Germany 52°45N 13°14E 178 C9
Oranje = Orange → S. Africa 28°41S 16°28E 270 C2
Oranjemund Namibia 28°38S 16°29E 270 C2
Oranjerivier S. Africa 29°40S 24°12E 270 C3
Oranjestad Aruba 12°32N 70°2W 322 f
Oranjestad St. Eustatius 17°28N 62°59W 322 a
Orap Vanuatu 15°58S 167°20E 287 E5
Oras Phil. 12°9N 125°28E 232 E5
Orašje Bos.-H. 45°1N 18°42E 182 E3
Orăştie Romania 45°50N 23°10E 183 E8
Orava → Slovakia 49°9N 19°8E 181 B12
Orava, Vodna nádriž Slovakia 49°25N 19°35E 181 B12
Oraviţa Romania 45°2N 21°43E 182 E6
Orawia N.Z. 46°1S 167°50E 285 G2
Orb → France 43°15N 3°18E 174 E7
Orba → Italy 44°53N 8°37E 198 D5
Ørbæk Denmark 55°17N 10°39E 163 J4
Orbe Switz. 46°43N 6°32E 179 J2
Orbec France 49°1N 0°23E 172 C7
Orbetello Italy 42°27N 11°13E 199 F8
Órbigo → Spain 42°5N 5°42W 194 C5
Orbisonia U.S.A. 40°15N 77°54W 312 F7
Orbost Australia 37°40S 148°29E 283 D8
Örbyhus Sweden 60°15N 17°43E 162 D11
Orcadas Antarctica 60°44S 44°37W 151 C18
Orcas I. U.S.A. 48°42N 122°56W 306 B4
Orce Spain 37°44N 2°28W 197 H2
Orce → Spain 37°44N 2°28W 197 H2
Orchard City U.S.A. 38°50N 107°58W 304 G10
Orchard Homes U.S.A. 46°55N 114°4W 304 C6
Orchard Road Singapore 138 a1
Orchid I. = Lan Yü Taiwan 22°4N 121°25E 225 D3
Orchies France 50°28N 3°14E 173 B10
Orchila, I. Venezuela 11°48N 66°10W 321 D6
Orchilla, Pta. Canary Is. 27°42N 18°10W 153 e1
Órcia → Italy 42°58N 11°21E 199 F8
Orco → Italy 45°10N 7°52E 198 C4
Orcopampa Peru 15°20S 72°23W 330 D3
Orcutt U.S.A. 34°52N 120°27W 307 L6
Ord U.S.A. 41°36N 98°56W 308 E4
Ord → Australia 15°33S 128°15E 278 C4
Ord, Mt. Australia 17°20S 125°34E 278 C4
Ord Mts. U.S.A. 34°39N 116°45W 307 L10
Ordenes = Ordes Spain 43°5N 8°29W 194 B2
Orderville U.S.A. 37°17N 112°38W 305 H7
Ordes Spain 43°5N 8°29W 194 B2
Ordesa y Monte Perido △ Spain 42°40N 0°10W 196 C4
Ording = Sankt Peter-Ording Germany 54°20N 8°36E 178 A4
Ordos = Mu Us Shamo China 39°0N 109°0E 226 E5
Ordos China 39°50N 110°0E 226 E6
Ordrup Denmark 55°45N 12°34E 118 A3
Ordu Turkey 40°55N 37°53E 212 B7
Ordu □ Turkey 41°0N 37°50E 212 B7
Ordubad Azerbaijan 38°54N 46°1E 213 C12
Orduña Álava, Spain 42°58N 2°58W 196 C2
Orduña Granada, Spain 37°20N 3°30W 195 H7
Ordway U.S.A. 38°13N 103°46W 304 G12
Ordzhonīkīdze = Denīsovka Kazakhstan 52°27N 61°39E 216 B6
Ordzhonīkīdze = Vladikavkaz Russia 43°0N 44°35E 191 J7
Ordzhonīkīdze = Yenakiyeve Ukraine 48°15N 38°15E 189 H10
Ordzhonīkīdze Ukraine 47°39N 34°3E 189 J8
Ore Dem. Rep. of the Congo 3°17N 29°30E 268 B2
Ore Mts. = Erzgebirge Germany 50°27N 12°55E 178 E8
Orealla Guyana 5°15N 57°23W 329 B6
Orebić Croatia 43°0N 17°11E 199 F14
Örebro Sweden 59°20N 15°18E 162 E9
Örebro □ Sweden 59°27N 15°0E 162 E8
Orecchiella ⌓ Italy 44°16N 10°22E 198 D7
Ořech Czechia 50°1N 14°17E 135 B1
Oregon Ill., U.S.A. 42°1N 89°20W 310 B7
Oregon Ohio, U.S.A. 41°38N 83°25W 311 C13
Oregon Wis., U.S.A. 42°56N 89°23W 310 B7
Oregon □ U.S.A. 44°0N 121°0W 304 E3
Oregon City U.S.A. 45°21N 122°36W 306 E4
Oregon Dunes ⌓ U.S.A. 43°40N 124°10W 304 E1
Öregrund Sweden 60°21N 18°30E 162 D12
Öregrundsgrepen Sweden 60°25N 18°15E 162 D12
Oregun Nigeria 6°35N 3°22E 124 A2
Orekhov = Orikhiv Ukraine 47°30N 35°48E 189 J8

Orekhovo-Zuyevo *Russia* 55°50N 38°55E **188** E10
Orel *Russia* 52°57N 36°3E **189** F9
Orel □ *Russia* 52°30N 36°40E **189** F9
Orellana □ *Ecuador* 0°45S 76°25W **328** D2
Orellana, Canal de *Spain* 39°2N 6°0W **195** F5
Orellana, Embalse de *Spain* 39°5N 5°10W **195** F5
Orellana la Vieja *Spain* 39°1N 5°32W **195** F5
Orem *U.S.A.* 40°19N 111°42W **304** F8
Ören *Turkey* 37°3N 27°57E **205** D9
Orenburg *Russia* 51°45N 55°6E **186** D10
Örencik *Turkey* 39°16N 29°33E **205** B11
Orense = Ourense *Spain* 42°19N 7°55W **194** C3
Orepuki *N.Z.* 46°19S 167°46E **285** G2
Ørestad *Denmark* 55°38N 12°35E **118** B3
Orestes Pereyra *Mexico* 26°30N 105°39W **318** B3
Orestiada *Greece* 41°30N 26°33E **203** E10
Øresund *Europe* 55°45N 12°40E **163** J6
Oretana, Cordillera = Toledo, Montes de *Spain* 39°33N 4°20W **195** F6
Oreti → *N.Z.* 46°28S 168°14E **285** G3
Orfanos Kolpos *Greece* 40°33N 24°0E **202** F7
Orford Ness *U.K.* 52°5N 1°35E **169** E9
Organ Pipe Cactus ⌂ *U.S.A.* 32°0N 112°52W **305** K7
Organos, Pta. de los *Canary Is.* 28°12N 17°17W **153** e1
Organyà *Spain* 42°13N 1°20E **196** C6
Orgaz *Spain* 39°39N 3°53W **195** F7
Ørgenvika *Norway* 60°17N 9°42E **164** D6
Orgeyev = Orhei *Moldova* 47°24N 28°50E **183** C13
Orgiva *Spain* 36°53N 3°24W **195** J7
Orgūn *Afghan.* 32°55N 69°12E **240** B3
Orhaneli *Turkey* 39°54N 28°59E **203** G12
Orhaneli → *Turkey* 39°50N 28°55E **203** G12
Orhangazi *Turkey* 40°29N 29°18E **203** F13
Orhei *Moldova* 47°24N 28°50E **183** C13
Orhon Gol → *Mongolia* 50°21N 106°0E **218** A10
Ória *Italy* 40°30N 17°38E **201** B10
Orida *Niger* 21°20N 12°15E **261** D7
Orient Heights *U.S.A.* 42°23N 70°59W **116** A3
Oriental □ *Morocco* 33°0N 2°0W **261** B4
Oriental, Cordillera *Bolivia* 17°0S 66°0W **331** D4
Oriental, Cordillera *Colombia* 6°0N 73°0W **328** B3
Oriental, Grand Erg *Algeria* 30°0N 6°30E **261** B6
Oriental Pearl Tower *Shanghai, China* 31°14N 121°30E **138** B2
Oriente *Argentina* 38°44S 60°37W **334** D3
Orihuela *Spain* 38°7N 0°55W **197** G4
Orihuela del Tremedal *Spain* 40°33N 1°39W **196** E3
Orikhiv *Ukraine* 47°30N 35°48E **189** J8
Orikum *Albania* 40°20N 19°26E **202** F3
Oril → *Ukraine* 48°40N 34°39E **189** H8
Orillia *Canada* 44°40N 79°24W **312** B5
Orinduik *Guyana* 4°40N 60°3W **329** C5
Orinoco → *Venezuela* 9°15N 61°30W **329** B5
Orinoco, Delta del *Venezuela* 9°0N 61°30W **329** B5
Orion *Canada* 49°27N 110°49W **297** D6
Orion *Ala., U.S.A.* 31°58N 86°0W **316** D4
Orion *Ill., U.S.A.* 41°21N 90°23W **310** C6
Oriskany *U.S.A.* 43°10N 75°20W **313** C9
Orissa = Odisha □ *India* 20°0N 84°0E **244** E7
Orissaare *Estonia* 58°34N 23°5E **188** C2
Oristano *Italy* 39°54N 8°36E **200** C1
Oristano, G. di *Italy* 39°50N 8°29E **200** C1
Orituco → *Venezuela* 8°45N 67°27W **328** B4
Oriximina *Brazil* 1°45S 55°52W **329** D6
Orizaba *Mexico* 18°51N 97°6W **319** D5
Orizaba, Pico de *Mexico* 18°58N 97°15W **319** D5
Orizare *Bulgaria* 42°44N 27°39E **203** D11
Orizona *Brazil* 17°3S 48°18W **333** E2
Ørje *Norway* 59°29N 11°39E **164** E8
Orjen *Bos.-H.* 42°35N 18°34E **202** D2
Orjiva = Orgiva *Spain* 36°53N 3°24W **195** J7
Orkanger *Norway* 63°18N 9°52E **164** A6
Örkelljunga *Sweden* 56°17N 13°17E **163** H7
Örken *Sweden* 57°6N 15°1E **163** G9
Örkény *Hungary* 47°9N 19°26E **182** C4
Orkhaniye = Botevgrad *Bulgaria* 42°55N 23°47E **202** D7
Orkhon = Orhon Gol → *Mongolia* 50°21N 106°0E **218** A10
Orkla → *Norway* 63°18N 9°51E **164** A6
Orkney *S. Africa* 26°58S 26°40E **270** C4
Orkney □ *U.K.* 59°2N 3°13W **167** B5
Orkney Is. *U.K.* 59°0N 3°0W **167** B6
Orland *Calif., U.S.A.* 39°45N 122°12W **306** F4
Orland *Ind., U.S.A.* 41°47N 85°12W **311** C11
Orland Park *U.S.A.* 41°38N 87°52W **119** D2
Orlando *U.S.A.* 28°32N 81°22W **133** A2
Orlando, C. d' *Italy* 38°10N 14°43E **201** D7
Orlando Dam *S. Africa* 26°15S 27°55E **123** B1
Orlando East *S. Africa* 26°14S 27°55E **123** B1
Orlando Executive ✈ **(ORL)** *U.S.A.* 28°32N 81°20W **133** A2
Orlando Int. ✈ **(MCO)** *U.S.A.* 28°26N 81°19W **133** B3
Orléanais *France* 48°0N 2°0E **173** E9
Orléans *France* 47°54N 1°52E **173** E8
Orleans *Ind., U.S.A.* 38°40N 86°27W **311** F10
Orleans *Vt., U.S.A.* 44°49N 72°12W **313** B12
Orléans, Î. d' *Canada* 46°54N 70°58W **299** C5
Orléansville = Ech Chéliff *Algeria* 36°10N 1°20E **261** A5
Orlice → *Czechia* 50°13N 15°50E **180** A8
Orlivka *Ukraine* 45°19N 28°27E **183** E13
Orlov = Khalturin *Russia* 58°40N 48°50E **186** C8
Orlov *Slovakia* 49°17N 20°51E **181** B13
Orlov Gay *Russia* 50°56N 48°19E **190** E9
Orlová *Czechia* 49°51N 18°26E **181** B11
Orlovat *Serbia* 45°14N 20°33E **182** E5
Orlovista *U.S.A.* 28°32N 81°27W **133** A2
Orlovskoye Polesye △ *Russia* 58°30N 35°30E **188** F8
Orly *France* 48°45N 2°23E **134** B3
Orly, Paris ✈ **(ORY)** *France* 48°44N 2°23E **134** B3
Ormara *Pakistan* 25°16N 64°33E **240** D2
Ormea *Italy* 44°9N 7°54E **198** D4
Ormesson-sur-Marne *France* 48°47N 2°32E **134** B4
Ormília *Greece* 40°16N 23°39E **202** F7
Ormoc *Phil.* 11°0N 124°37E **233** F5
Ormond *Vic., Australia* 37°54S 145°1E **128** B2
Ormond *N.Z.* 38°33S 177°56E **284** E6
Ormond Beach *U.S.A.* 29°17N 81°3W **317** F8
Ormond-by-the-Sea *U.S.A.* 29°21N 81°4W **317** F8
Ormondville *N.Z.* 40°5S 176°19E **284** G5
Ormøya *Norway* 59°52N 10°45E **143** C3
Ormož *Slovenia* 46°25N 16°10E **199** B13
Ormskirk *U.K.* 53°35N 2°54W **168** D5
Ormstown *Canada* 45°8N 74°0W **313** A11
Ormtjernkampen △ *Norway* 61°12N 9°48E **164** C6
Ornans *France* 47°7N 6°10E **173** E13
Orne □ *France* 48°40N 0°5E **172** D7
Orne → *France* 49°18N 0°15W **172** C6
Orneta *Poland* 54°8N 20°9E **184** D7
Örnö *Sweden* 59°4N 18°24E **162** E12
Örnsköldsvik *Sweden* 63°17N 18°40E **162** A12
Oro = Northern □ *Papua N. G.* 9°0S 148°30E **286** E5
Oro *N. Korea* 40°1N 127°27E **224** B3
Oro → *Mexico* 25°35N 105°2W **318** B3
Oro Grande *U.S.A.* 34°36N 117°20W **307** L9
Oro Valley *U.S.A.* 32°26N 110°58W **305** K8
Orobie, Alpi *Italy* 46°7N 10°0E **198** B6
Orobie Bergamasche ⌂ *Italy* 46°0N 9°45E **198** C6
Orobie Valtellinesi ⌂ *Italy* 46°5N 9°45E **198** B6
Orocué *Colombia* 4°48N 71°20W **328** C3
Orodara *Burkina Faso* 11°0N 4°55W **262** C4
Orodo *Nigeria* 5°34N 7°4E **263** D6
Orofino *U.S.A.* 46°29N 116°15W **304** C5
Orohena, Mt. *Tahiti* 17°37S 149°28W **289** e
Orol Dengizi = Aral Sea *Asia* 45°0N 58°20E **216** C5
Oromiya □ *Ethiopia* 7°0N 40°0E **257** F5
Oromocto *Canada* 45°54N 66°29W **299** C6
Oron *Nigeria* 4°48N 8°14E **263** E6
Orona *Kiribati* 4°31S 172°11W **277** A16
Orongo *Chile* 27°11S 109°27W **330** b
Orono *Ont., Canada* 43°59N 78°37W **312** C6
Orono *Maine, U.S.A.* 44°53N 68°40W **309** C19
Oronsay *U.K.* 56°1N 6°15W **167** E2
Oropesa *Spain* 39°57N 5°10W **194** F5
Oropuche → *Trin. & Tob.* 10°36N 61°6W **323** t
Oropuche Lagoon *Trin. & Tob.* 10°14N 61°31W **323** t
Oroquieta *Phil.* 8°32N 123°44E **233** G4
Orós *Brazil* 6°15S 38°55W **332** C4
Orosei *Italy* 40°23N 9°42E **200** B2
Orosei, G. di *Italy* 40°15N 9°44E **200** B2
Orosháza *Hungary* 46°32N 20°42E **182** D5
Oroszlány *Hungary* 47°29N 18°19E **182** C3
Orote Pen. *Guam* 13°26N 144°38E **302** d
Orotukan *Russia* 62°16N 151°42E **215** C16
Oroville *Calif., U.S.A.* 39°31N 121°33W **306** F5
Oroville *Wash., U.S.A.* 48°56N 119°26W **304** B4
Oroville, L. *U.S.A.* 39°33N 121°29W **306** F5
Orpington *U.K.* 51°22N 0°6E **125** B4
Orrefors *Sweden* 56°50N 15°45E **163** H9
Orrick *U.S.A.* 39°13N 94°7W **310** E2
Orroroo *Australia* 32°43S 138°38E **282** B3
Orrviken *Sweden* 63°6N 14°26E **162** A8
Orrville *U.S.A.* 40°50N 81°46W **312** F3
Orsa *Sweden* 61°7N 14°37E **162** C8
Orsara di Púglia *Italy* 41°17N 15°16E **201** A8
Orsasjön *Sweden* 61°7N 14°37E **162** C8
Orsay, Musée d' *Paris, France* **134** b3
Orsha *Belarus* 54°30N 30°25E **188** E6
Örsjö *Sweden* 56°42N 15°45E **163** H9
Orsk *Russia* 51°12N 58°34E **216** B5
Orşova *Romania* 44°41N 22°25E **182** F7
Ørsta *Norway* 62°13N 6°8E **164** B3
Ørsted *Denmark* 56°30N 10°20E **163** H4
Örsundsbro *Sweden* 59°44N 17°18E **162** E11
Országos Levéltár *Budapest, Hungary* **117** b1
Orta *Turkey* 40°38N 33°6E **212** B5
Orta, L. d' *Italy* 45°49N 8°24E **198** C5
Orta Nova *Italy* 41°19N 15°42E **201** A8
Ortaca *Turkey* 36°49N 28°45E **205** E10
Ortakent *Turkey* 37°5N 27°21E **205** D9
Ortaklar *Turkey* 37°53N 27°30E **205** D9
Ortaköy *Çorum, Turkey* 40°16N 35°15E **212** B6
Ortaköy *İstanbul, Turkey* 41°3N 29°1E **122** B2
Ortaköy *Niğde, Turkey* 38°44N 34°3E **212** C6
Orte *Italy* 42°27N 12°23E **199** F9
Ortegal, C. *Spain* 43°43N 7°52W **194** B3
Orteguaza → *Colombia* 0°43N 75°16W **328** C2
Ortelsburg = Szczytno *Poland* 53°33N 21°0E **184** E7
Orthez *France* 43°29N 0°48W **174** E3
Ortica *Italy* 45°28N 9°16E **128** B2
Ortigueira *Spain* 43°40N 7°50W **194** B3
Ortigueira, Ría de *Spain* 43°44N 7°45W **194** B3
Orting *U.S.A.* 47°6N 122°12W **306** C4
Ortisei *Italy* 46°34N 11°40E **199** B8
Ortles *Italy* 46°31N 10°33E **198** B7
Ortnevik *Norway* 61°6N 6°7E **164** C3
Ortoire → *Trin. & Tob.* 10°20N 61°0W **323** t
Ortón → *Bolivia* 10°50S 67°0W **330** C4
Ortona *Italy* 42°21N 14°24E **199** F11
Ortonville *U.S.A.* 45°19N 96°27W **308** C5
Orūmīyeh *Iran* 37°40N 45°0E **213** D11
Orūmīyeh, Daryācheh-ye *Iran* 37°50N 45°30E **213** D11
Orune *Italy* 40°24N 9°22E **200** B2
Oruro *Bolivia* 18°0S 67°9W **330** D4
Oruro □ *Bolivia* 18°40S 67°30W **330** D4
Orust *Sweden* 58°10N 11°40E **163** F5
Oruzgān □ *Afghan.* 33°0N 66°0E **240** B2
Orvault *France* 47°17N 1°38W **172** E5
Orvieto *Italy* 42°43N 12°7E **199** F9
Orwell *N.Y., U.S.A.* 43°35N 75°50W **313** C9
Orwell *Ohio, U.S.A.* 41°32N 80°52W **312** E4
Orwell → *U.K.* 51°59N 1°18E **169** F9
Orwigsburg *U.S.A.* 40°38N 76°6W **313** F8
Oryakhovo *Bulgaria* 43°40N 23°57E **202** C7
Oryakhovo = Oryakhovo *Bulgaria* 43°40N 23°57E **202** C7
Orynyn *Ukraine* 48°46N 26°24E **183** B11
Oryol = Orel *Russia* 52°57N 36°3E **189** F9
Orzinuovi *Italy* 45°24N 9°55E **198** C6
Orzyc → *Poland* 52°46N 21°14E **185** F8
Orzysz *Poland* 53°50N 21°58E **184** E8
Os *Norway* 62°30N 11°14E **164** B8
Osa *Russia* 57°17N 55°26E **186** C10
Osa → *Poland* 53°33N 18°46E **184** E5
Osa, Pen. de *Costa Rica* 8°0N 84°0W **320** E3
Osage *U.S.A.* 43°17N 92°49W **308** D7
Osage → *U.S.A.* 38°36N 91°57W **310** F5
Osage City *U.S.A.* 38°38N 95°50W **308** F6
Ōsaka *Japan* 34°42N 135°30E **223** G7
Ōsaka □ *Japan* 34°30N 135°30E **223** C7
Ōsaka Castle *Japan* 34°41N 135°30E **133** A2
Ōsaka Harbour *Japan* 34°38N 135°25E **133** B1
Ōsaka Itami Int. ✈ **(ITM)** *Japan* 34°46N 135°26E **133** A1
Ōsaka Kansai Int. ✈ **(KIX)** *Japan* 34°27N 135°12E **133** B2
Ōsaka-Wan *Japan* 34°30N 135°18E **223** C7
Osakarovka *Kazakhstan* 50°33N 72°34E **217** B8
Osaki *Kagoshima, Japan* 31°25N 131°2E **222** F3
Ōsaki *Miyagi, Japan* 38°34N 140°58E **220** E10
Ōsaki *Tōkyō, Japan* 35°36N 139°42E **140** B3
Osam → *Bulgaria* 43°40N 24°50E **203** C8
Osan *S. Korea* 37°11N 127°4E **224** D3
Osasco *Brazil* 23°31S 46°46W **137** B1
Osawatomie *U.S.A.* 38°31N 94°57W **308** F6
Osborn Plateau *Ind. Oc.* 14°45S 87°0E **273** F7
Osborne *U.S.A.* 39°26N 98°42W **308** F4
Osby *Sweden* 56°23N 13°59E **163** H7
Osceola *Ark., U.S.A.* 35°42N 89°58W **315** D10
Osceola *Iowa, U.S.A.* 41°2N 93°46W **310** C3
Osceola *Mo., U.S.A.* 38°3N 93°42W **310** F3
Oschatz *Germany* 51°17N 13°6E **178** D9
Oschersleben *Germany* 52°2N 11°14E **178** C7
Óschiri *Italy* 40°43N 9°6E **200** B2
Oscoda *U.S.A.* 44°26N 83°20W **312** B1
Osdorf *Germany* 52°24N 13°10E **115** B2
Osdorp *Neths.* 52°22N 4°47E **112** A1
Osečina *Serbia* 44°23N 19°34E **202** B3
Ösel = Saaremaa *Estonia* 58°30N 22°30E **188** C2
Osensjøen *Norway* 61°13N 11°50E **164** C8
Osery *Russia* 54°52N 38°28E **188** E10
Osgood *U.S.A.* 39°8N 85°18W **311** E11
Osgoode *Canada* 45°8N 75°36W **313** A9
Osgoode Hall *Toronto, Canada* **141** b2
Osh *Kyrgyzstan* 40°37N 72°49E **217** D8
Osh □ *Kyrgyzstan* 40°0N 73°0E **217** E8
Oshana □ *Namibia* 17°50S 15°40E **270** A2
Oshawa *Canada* 43°50N 78°50W **312** C6
Oshigambo *Namibia* 17°45S 16°5E **270** A2
Oshika-Hantō *Japan* 38°20N 141°30E **220** E10
Oshikoto □ *Namibia* 18°30S 17°0E **270** A2
Oshivelo *Namibia* 18°37S 17°10E **270** A2
Oshkosh *Nebr., U.S.A.* 41°24N 102°21W **308** E2
Oshkosh *Wis., U.S.A.* 44°1N 88°33W **308** C9
Oshmyany = Ashmyany *Belarus* 54°26N 25°52E **177** A13
Oshnovīyeh *Iran* 37°2N 45°6E **213** D11
Oshodi *Nigeria* 6°33N 3°21E **124** A2
Oshogbo *Nigeria* 7°48N 4°37E **263** D5
Oshtorīnān *Iran* 34°1N 48°38E **213** E13
Ōshū *Japan* 39°8N 141°8E **220** E10
Oshwe *Dem. Rep. of the Congo* 3°25S 19°28E **264** C3
Osi *Nigeria* 8°8N 5°14E **263** D6
Osieczna *Poland* 51°55N 16°40E **185** G3
Osijek *Croatia* 45°34N 18°41E **182** E3
Ósilo *Italy* 40°45N 8°40E **200** B1
Ósimo *Italy* 43°28N 13°30E **199** E10
Osintorf *Belarus* 54°40N 30°39E **188** E6
Osipenko = Berdyansk *Ukraine* 46°45N 36°50E **189** J9
Osipovichi = Asipovichy *Belarus* 53°19N 28°33E **177** B15
Osiyan *India* 26°43N 72°55E **242** F5
Osizweni *S. Africa* 27°49S 30°7E **271** C5
Oskaloosa *U.S.A.* 41°18N 92°39W **310** C4
Oskarshamn *Sweden* 57°15N 16°27E **163** G10
Oskarström *Sweden* 56°48N 12°58E **163** H6
Oskélanéo *Canada* 48°5N 75°15W **298** C4
Öskemen *Kazakhstan* 50°0N 82°36E **217** C10
Oskol → *Ukraine* 49°6N 37°25E **189** H9
Oskū *Iran* 37°54N 46°8E **213** D12
Oslo *Norway* 59°54N 10°43E **133** A3
Oslo □ *Norway* 59°54N 10°43E **164** D7
Oslo ✈ **(OSL)** *Norway* 60°11N 11°6E **133** A4
Oslob *Phil.* 9°31N 123°26E **233** G4
Oslofjorden *Norway* 59°20N 10°35E **164** E7
Osmanabad *India* 18°5N 76°10E **244** E3
Osmancık *Turkey* 40°58N 34°47E **212** B6
Osmaniye *Turkey* 37°5N 36°10E **250** A7
Osmanlı *Turkey* 41°35N 26°51E **203** E10
Osmannagar *India* 18°32N 79°20E **244** E4
Ösmo *Sweden* 58°58N 17°55E **162** F11
Osnabrück *Germany* 52°17N 8°3E **178** C4
Ośno Lubuskie *Poland* 52°28N 14°51E **185** F1
Osoblaha *Czechia* 50°17N 17°44E **181** A10
Osogbo = Oshogbo *Nigeria* 7°48N 4°37E **263** D5
Osogovska Planina *N. Macedonia* 42°10N 22°30E **202** D6
Ōsone *Japan* 35°31N 139°37E **140** B2
Osor *Italy* 44°42N 14°24E **199** D11
Osório *Brazil* 29°53S 50°17W **335** B5
Osório da Fonseca *Brazil* 3°52S 58°14W **329** D6
Osorno *Chile* 40°25S 73°0W **336** B2
Osorno *Spain* 42°24N 4°22W **194** C6
Osorno □ *Chile* 40°34S 73°9W **336** B2
Osorno, Vol. *Chile* 41°0S 72°30W **336** B2
Osoro *Nigeria* 6°33N 3°29E **124** A2
Osoyoos *Canada* 49°0N 119°30W **296** D5
Osøyro *Norway* 60°9N 5°30E **164** D2
Óspakseyri *Iceland* 65°27N 21°26W **155** B5
Ospiate *Italy* 45°32N 9°6E **128** A1
Ospika → *Canada* 56°20N 124°0W **296** B4
Osprey *U.S.A.* 27°12N 82°29W **317** H7
Osprey Reef *Australia* 13°52S 146°36E **280** A4
Oss *Neths.* 51°46N 5°32E **170** C5
Ossa, Mt. *Australia* 41°52S 146°3E **281** G4
Ossa, Oros *Greece* 39°47N 22°42E **204** B4
Ossa de Montiel *Spain* 38°58N 2°45W **197** G2
Ossabaw I. *U.S.A.* 31°50N 81°5W **316** D8
Ossabaw Sd. *U.S.A.* 31°50N 81°6W **316** D8
Osse → *Lot-et-Garonne, France* 44°7N 0°17E **174** D4
Osse → *Nigeria* 6°10N 5°20E **263** D6
Ossersee = Zarasai *Lithuania* 55°40N 26°20E **188** E4
Ossi *Italy* 40°40N 8°35E **200** B1
Ossining *U.S.A.* 41°10N 73°55W **313** E11
Ossipee *U.S.A.* 43°41N 71°7W **313** C13
Ossokmanuan L. *Canada* 53°25N 65°0W **299** B7
Ossora *Russia* 59°20N 163°13E **215** D17
Ostankino *Russia* 55°49N 37°37E **129** B2
Ostashkov *Russia* 57°4N 33°2E **188** D7
Östavall *Sweden* 62°26N 15°29E **162** B9
Østby *Norway* 61°15N 12°33E **164** C9
Oste → *Germany* 53°49N 9°2E **178** B5
Ostenburg = Pultusk *Poland* 52°43N 21°6E **185** F8
Ostend = Oostende *Belgium* 51°15N 2°54E **170** C2
Ostend *N.Z.* 36°48S 175°2E **284** C4
Oster *Ukraine* 50°57N 30°53E **177** C16
Österbotten = Pohjanmaa □ *Finland* 62°58N 22°50E **160** E20
Østerbro *Copenhagen, Denmark* **118** a1
Osterburg *Sachsen-Anhalt, Germany* 52°47N 11°45E **178** C7
Osterburg *Pa., U.S.A.* 40°16N 78°31W **312** F6
Osterburken *Germany* 49°25N 9°26E **179** F5
Österbybruk *Sweden* 60°13N 17°55E **162** D11
Österbymo *Sweden* 57°49N 15°15E **163** G9
Österdalälven → *Sweden* 60°30N 15°7E **162** C7
Østerdalen *Norway* 61°40N 10°50E **162** C4
Österfärnebo *Sweden* 60°19N 16°48E **162** D10
Österforse *Sweden* 63°9N 17°3E **162** A11
Östergötland □ *Sweden* 58°35N 15°45E **163** F9
Osterholz-Scharmbeck *Germany* 53°13N 8°47E **178** B4
Østerild *Denmark* 57°2N 8°51E **163** G2
Osterley *U.K.* 51°29N 0°21W **125** B1
Osterley Park *U.K.* 51°29N 0°21W **125** B1
Östermalm *Stockholm, Sweden* **139** a3
Östermyra = Seinäjoki *Finland* 62°40N 22°51E **160** E20
Osterode *Germany* 51°43N 10°15E **178** D6
Osterode in Ostpreussen = Ostróda *Poland* 53°42N 19°58E **184** E6
Österreich = Austria ■ *Europe* 47°0N 14°0E **180** E7
Österreich ober der Ems = Oberösterreich □ *Austria* 48°10N 14°0E **180** C7
Österskär *Sweden* 59°26N 18°16E **139** A3
Östersund *Sweden* 63°10N 14°38E **162** A8
Östervåla *Sweden* 60°11N 17°11E **162** D11
Østfold □ *Norway* 59°25N 11°25E **164** E8
Ostfriesische Inseln *Germany* 53°42N 7°0E **178** B3
Ostfriesland *Germany* 53°20N 7°30E **178** B3
Östhammar *Sweden* 60°16N 18°22E **162** D12
Óstia, Lido di *Italy* 41°43N 12°17E **199** G9
Óstia Malpasso *Italy* 41°47N 12°26E **136** C1
Ostiense *Italy* 41°51N 12°29E **136** B1
Ostíglia *Italy* 45°4N 11°8E **199** C8
Östmark *Sweden* 60°17N 12°45E **162** D6
Østmarkkapellet *Norway* 59°52N 10°51E **133** A4
Østøya *Norway* 59°52N 10°34E **133** A2
Östra Husby *Sweden* 58°35N 16°33E **163** F10
Ostrava *Czechia* 49°51N 18°18E **181** B11
Ostróda *Poland* 53°42N 19°58E **184** E6
Ostrogozhsk *Russia* 50°55N 39°7E **189** G10
Ostroh *Ukraine* 50°20N 26°30E **177** C14
Ostrołęka *Poland* 53°4N 21°32E **185** E8
Ostrov *Bulgaria* 43°40N 24°9E **203** C8
Ostrov *Czechia* 50°18N 12°57E **180** A5
Ostrov *Romania* 44°6N 27°24E **183** F12
Ostrov *Russia* 57°25N 28°20E **188** D5
Ostrów Lubelski *Poland* 51°29N 22°51E **185** G9
Ostrów Mazowiecka *Poland* 52°50N 21°51E **185** F8
Ostrów Wielkopolski *Poland* 51°36N 17°44E **185** G4
Ostrowiec-Świętokrzyski *Poland* 50°55N 21°22E **185** H8
Ostrowo = Ostrów Wielkopolski *Poland* 51°36N 17°44E **185** G4
Ostrožac *Bos.-H.* 43°43N 17°49E **182** G2
Ostrzeszów *Poland* 51°25N 17°52E **185** G4
Ostseebad Kühlungsborn *Germany* 54°8N 11°44E **178** A7
Osttirol □ *Austria* 46°50N 12°30E **180** E5
Ostuni *Italy* 40°44N 17°35E **201** B10
Ostyako-Vogulsk = Khanty-Mansiysk *Russia* 61°0N 69°0E **214** C7
Osŭm = Osam → *Bulgaria* 43°40N 24°50E **203** C8
Osum → *Albania* 40°40N 20°10E **202** F4
Ōsumi-Hantō *Japan* 31°20N 130°55E **222** F2
Ōsumi-Kaikyō *Japan* 30°55N 131°0E **221** J5
Ōsumi-Shotō *Japan* 30°30N 130°0E **221** J5
Osun □ *Nigeria* 7°30N 4°30E **263** D5
Osuna *Spain* 37°14N 5°8W **195** H5
Oswegatchie → *U.S.A.* 44°42N 75°30W **313** B9
Oswego *Ill., U.S.A.* 41°41N 88°21W **311** C8
Oswego *N.Y., U.S.A.* 43°27N 76°31W **313** C8
Oswego → *U.S.A.* 43°27N 76°30W **313** C8
Oswestry *U.K.* 52°52N 3°3W **168** E4
Oświęcim *Poland* 50°2N 19°11E **185** H6
Ōta *Fukui, Japan* 35°57N 136°3E **223** B8
Ōta *Gumma, Japan* 36°18N 139°22E **223** A11
Ōta *Tōkyō, Japan* 35°34N 139°41E **140** B3
Ōta-Gawa → *Japan* 34°21N 132°18E **222** C4
Otaci *Moldova* 48°27N 27°47E **183** B12
Otago □ *N.Z.* 45°15S 170°0E **285** F5
Otago Harbour *N.Z.* 45°47S 170°42E **285** F5
Otago Pen. *N.Z.* 45°48S 170°39E **285** F5
Otaheite B. *Trin. & Tob.* 10°15N 61°30W **323** t
Otahuhu *N.Z.* 36°56S 174°51E **284** C3
Ōtake *Japan* 34°12N 132°13E **222** C4
Ōtaki *Japan* 35°17N 140°15E **223** B12
Otaki *N.Z.* 40°45S 175°10E **284** G4
Otane *N.Z.* 39°54S 176°39E **284** F5
Otaniemi *Finland* 60°11N 24°49E **121** B1
Otaru *Japan* 43°10N 141°0E **220** C10
Otaru-Wan = Ishikari-Wan *Japan* 43°25N 141°1E **220** C10
Otautau *N.Z.* 46°9S 168°1E **285** G3
Otava → *Czechia* 49°26N 14°12E **180** B7
Otavalo *Ecuador* 0°13N 78°20W **328** C2
Otavi *Namibia* 19°40S 17°24E **270** A2
Ōtawara *Japan* 36°50N 140°5E **221** F10
Otchinjau *Angola* 16°30S 13°56E **265** F2
Otego *U.S.A.* 42°23N 75°10W **313** D9
Oteiza = Marihatag *Phil.* 8°48N 126°18E **233** G6
Otelec *Romania* 45°36N 20°50E **182** E5
Otelnuk, L. *Canada* 56°9N 68°12W **299** A6
Oțelu Roșu *Romania* 45°32N 22°22E **182** E7
Otero de Rey = Outeiro de Rei *Spain* 43°6N 7°36W **194** B3
Othello *U.S.A.* 46°50N 119°10W **304** C4
Othoni *Greece* 39°52N 19°22E **206** B9
Othris, Oros *Greece* 39°2N 22°37E **204** B4
Oti □ *Ghana* 7°30N 0°20E **263** D5
Oti → *Africa* 7°48N 0°8E **263** D5
Oti ⌂ *Togo* 10°40N 0°35E **263** C5
Otira *N.Z.* 42°49S 171°35E **285** C6
Otira Gorge *N.Z.* 42°53S 171°33E **285** C6
Otish, Mts. *Canada* 52°22N 70°30W **299** B5
Otishi △ *Peru* 11°40S 73°5W **330** C3
Otjinene *Namibia* 21°8S 18°46E **270** B2
Otjiwarongo *Namibia* 20°30S 16°33E **270** B2
Otjozondjupa □ *Namibia* 21°0S 17°0E **270** B2
Otmuchów *Poland* 50°28N 17°10E **185** H4
Oto Tolu Group *Tonga* 20°21S 174°32W **287** Q13
Otočac *Croatia* 44°53N 15°12E **199** D12
Otoineppu *Japan* 44°44N 142°16E **220** B11
Otok *Croatia* 43°42N 16°44E **199** E13
Otomavi = Korsakov *Russia* 46°36N 142°42E **215** E15
Oton *Phil.* 10°42N 122°29E **233** F4
Otopeni, Bucureşti ✈ **(OTP)** *Romania* 44°30N 26°11E **183** F11
Otorohanga *N.Z.* 38°12S 175°14E **284** E4
Otoskwin → *Canada* 52°13N 88°6W **298** B2
Ōtoyo *Japan* 33°43N 133°45E **222** D5
Otpor = Zabaykalsk *Russia* 49°40N 117°25E **215** E12
Otra → *Norway* 58°9N 8°1E **164** F5
Otradnyy *Russia* 53°22N 51°21E **190** D10
Otranto *Italy* 40°9N 18°28E **201** B11
Otranto, C. d' *Italy* 40°7N 18°30E **201** B11
Otranto, Str. of *Italy* 40°15N 18°40E **201** B11
Otrobanda *Curaçao* 12°7N 68°57W **322** g
Otrokovice *Czechia* 49°12N 17°32E **181** B10
Otse *S. Africa* 25°2S 25°45E **270** C4
Otsego *U.S.A.* 42°27N 85°42W **311** B11
Otsego L. *U.S.A.* 42°45N 74°53W **313** D10
Ōtsu *Japan* 35°0N 135°50E **223** C7
Otsuka *Japan* 35°43N 139°44E **140** A3
Ōtsuki *Japan* 35°36N 138°57E **223** B10
Otta *Norway* 61°46N 9°32E **164** C6
Otta → *Norway* 61°46N 9°31E **164** C6
Ottakring *Austria* 48°12N 16°18E **142** A1
Ottapalam *India* 10°46N 76°23E **245** J3
Ottávia *Italy* 41°57N 12°24E **136** B1
Ottawa = Outaouais → *Canada* 45°27N 74°8W **298** C5
Ottawa *Ont., Canada* 45°26N 75°42W **313** A9
Ottawa *Ill., U.S.A.* 41°21N 88°51W **311** C8
Ottawa *Kans., U.S.A.* 38°37N 95°16W **308** F6
Ottawa *Ohio, U.S.A.* 41°1N 84°3W **311** C12
Ottawa Is. *Canada* 59°35N 80°10W **295** F15
Ottélé *Cameroon* 3°38N 11°19E **263** E7
Ottensheim *Austria* 48°21N 14°12E **180** C7
Otter Cr. → *U.S.A.* 44°13N 73°17W **313** B11
Otter Creek *U.S.A.* 29°19N 82°46W **317** F7
Otter Lake *Canada* 45°17N 79°56W **312** A5
Otterbäcken *Sweden* 58°57N 14°3E **163** F8
Otterbein *U.S.A.* 40°29N 87°6W **311** D9
Otterndorf *Germany* 53°48N 8°53E **178** B4
Otterøya *Norway* 62°45N 6°50E **164** B3
Otterup *Denmark* 55°30N 10°22E **163** J4
Otterville *Ont., Canada* 42°55N 80°36W **312** D4
Otterville *Mo., U.S.A.* 38°42N 93°0W **310** F4
Ottery *S. Africa* 34°1S 18°32E **118** B2
Ottery St. Mary *U.K.* 50°44N 3°17W **169** G4
Ottilien Reef *Papua N. G.* 4°33S 148°49E **286** C5
Ottmachau = Otmuchów *Poland* 50°28N 17°10E **185** H4
Otto Beit Bridge *Zimbabwe* 15°59S 28°56E **269** F2
Ottobrunn *Germany* 48°3N 11°40E **131** B3
Ottosdal *S. Africa* 26°46S 25°59E **270** C4
Ottoville *U.S.A.* 40°57N 84°22W **311** D12
Ottumwa *U.S.A.* 41°1N 92°25W **310** D4
Otukpa *Nigeria* 7°9N 7°41E **263** D6
Otuquis △ *Bolivia* 19°45S 58°44W **331** D6
Oturkpo *Nigeria* 7°16N 8°8E **263** D6
Otvazhnoye = Zhigulevsk *Russia* 53°28N 49°30E **190** D9
Otvazhny = Zhigulevsk *Russia* 53°28N 49°30E **190** D9
Otway, B. *Chile* 53°30S 74°0W **336** D2
Otway, C. *Australia* 38°52S 143°30E **282** E5
Otway, Seno de *Chile* 53°5S 71°30W **336** D2
Otway △ *Australia* 38°47S 143°34E **282** E5
Otwock *Poland* 52°5N 21°20E **185** F8
Otyniya *Ukraine* 48°44N 24°51E **183** B9
Ötztaler Ache → *Austria* 47°14N 10°50E **180** D3
Ötztaler Alpen *Austria* 46°56N 11°0E **180** E3
Ou → *Laos* 20°4N 102°13E **236** B4
Ou-Sammyaku *Japan* 39°20N 140°35E **220** E10
Ouachita → *U.S.A.* 31°38N 91°49W **314** F9
Ouachita, L. *U.S.A.* 34°34N 93°12W **314** D8
Ouachita Mts. *U.S.A.* 34°30N 94°30W **314** D7
Ouadâne *Mauritania* 20°50N 11°40W **260** D2
Ouadda *C.A.R.* 8°15N 22°20E **264** A4
Ouaddaï □ *Chad* 13°0N 21°0E **259** F4
Ouagadougou *Burkina Faso* 12°25N 1°30W **263** C4
Ouahigouya *Burkina Faso* 13°31N 2°25W **262** C4
Ouahran = Oran *Algeria* 35°45N 0°39W **261** A4
Ouaka □ *C.A.R.* 6°30N 21°0E **264** A4
Ouaka → *C.A.R.* 4°59N 19°56E **264** B3
Oualâta *Mauritania* 17°20N 6°55W **262** B3
Ouallah *Comoros Is.* 12°19S 43°39E **272** a
Ouallam *Niger* 14°23N 2°10E **263** C5
Ouallene *Algeria* 24°41N 1°11E **261** D5
Ouanary *Fr. Guiana* 4°13N 51°40W **329** C7
Ouanda Djallé *C.A.R.* 8°55N 22°53E **264** A4
Ouandago *C.A.R.* 7°13N 18°50E **264** A3
Ouandja *C.A.R.* 8°28N 23°17E **264** A4
Ouandjia, Bahr → *C.A.R.* 9°35N 21°43E **264** A4
Ouandjia-Vakaga ⌂ *C.A.R.* 9°2N 22°18E **264** A4
Ouangani *Mayotte* 12°50S 45°8E **272** b
Ouango *C.A.R.* 4°19N 22°30E **264** B4
Ouani *Comoros Is.* 12°9S 44°18E **272** a
Ouantonou *C.A.R.* 7°19N 15°18E **264** A3
Ouarâne *Mauritania* 21°0N 10°30W **260** D2
Ouargaye *Burkina Faso* 11°40N 0°5E **263** C5
Ouargla *Algeria* 31°59N 5°16E **261** B6
Ouargla □ *Algeria* 30°30N 6°10E **261** B6
Ouarkoye *Burkina Faso* 12°5N 3°40W **262** C4
Ouarkziz, Jebel *Algeria* 28°50N 8°0W **260** C3
Ouarra → *C.A.R.* 5°5N 24°26E **264** A4
Ouarzazate *Morocco* 30°55N 6°50W **260** B3
Ouassouas *Mali* 16°10N 1°23E **263** B5
Ouatagouna *Mali* 15°11N 0°43E **263** B5
Ouatere *C.A.R.* 5°30N 19°8E **264** A3
Oubangi → *Dem. Rep. of the Congo* 0°30S 17°50E **264** C3
Oubarakai, O. → *Algeria* 27°20N 9°0E **261** C6
Ouche → *France* 47°6N 5°16E **173** E12
Oud Zuid *Amsterdam, Neths.* **112** c1
Ouddorp *Neths.* 51°50N 3°57E **170** C3
Oude Kerk *Amsterdam, Neths.* **112** a2
Oude Rijn → *Neths.* 52°12N 4°24E **170** B4
Oudeïka *Mali* 17°30N 1°40W **263** B4
Oudenaarde *Belgium* 50°50N 3°37E **170** D3
Ouderkerk *Neths.* 52°18N 4°55E **112** B2
Oudon → *France* 47°41N 0°53W **172** E6
Oudtshoorn *S. Africa* 33°35S 22°14E **270** D3
Oued Zem *Morocco* 32°52N 6°34W **260** B3
Ouégoa *N. Cal.* 20°20S 164°26E **288** d
Oueita *Chad* 17°47N 20°39E **259** E4
Ouella *Niger* 14°48N 3°38E **263** C5
Ouellé *Côte d'Ivoire* 7°26N 4°1W **262** D4
Ouémé → *Benin* 6°30N 2°30E **263** D5
Ouenza *Algeria* 35°57N 8°4E **261** A6
Ouessa *Burkina Faso* 11°4N 2°47W **262** C4
Ouessant, Î. d' *France* 48°28N 5°6W **172** D1
Ouesso *Congo* 1°37N 16°5E **264** B3
Ouest □ *Cameroon* 5°30N 10°30E **263** D7
Ouest, Pte. de l' *Canada* 49°52N 64°40W **299** C7
Ouezzane *Morocco* 34°51N 5°35W **260** B3
Ougarou *Burkina Faso* 12°10N 0°58E **263** C5
Oughter, L. *Ireland* 54°1N 7°28W **166** B4
Oughterard *Ireland* 53°26N 9°18W **166** C2
Ouham □ *C.A.R.* 7°0N 17°30E **264** A3
Ouham → *C.A.R.* 6°35N 15°12E **264** A3
Ouham → *Chad* 9°18N 18°14E **259** G3
Ouham-Pendé □ *C.A.R.* 7°0N 16°0E **264** A3
Ouidah *Benin* 6°25N 2°0E **263** D5
Ouidi *Niger* 14°10N 13°0E **259** F2
Ouistreham *France* 49°17N 0°18W **172** C6
Oujda *Morocco* 34°41N 1°55W **261** B4
Oujeft *Mauritania* 20°2N 13°0W **260** D2
Oulad-Teïma *Morocco* 30°24N 9°12W **260** B3
Oulainen *Finland* 64°17N 24°47E **160** D21
Oulanka △ *Finland* 66°26N 29°25E **160** C23
Ould Yenjé *Mauritania* 15°38N 12°16W **262** B2
Ouled Djellal *Algeria* 34°28N 5°2E **261** B6
Ouled Djellal □ *Algeria* 34°0N 5°0E **261** B5
Ouled Naïl, Mts. des *Algeria* 34°30N 3°30E **261** B5
Ouli *Cameroon* 5°12N 14°33E **264** A2
Oullins *France* 45°43N 4°49E **175** C8
Oulmès *Morocco* 33°17N 6°0W **260** B3
Oulou, Bahr → *C.A.R.* 9°48N 21°32E **264** A4
Oulu *Finland* 65°1N 25°29E **160** D21
Oulujärvi *Finland* 64°25N 27°15E **160** D22
Oulujoki → *Finland* 65°1N 25°30E **160** D21
Oulunkylä *Finland* 60°13N 24°58E **121** B2
Oulx *Italy* 45°2N 6°50E **198** C3
Oum Chalouba *Chad* 15°48N 20°46E **259** E4
Oum-el-Bouaghi *Algeria* 35°55N 7°6E **261** A6
Oum-el-Bouaghi □ *Algeria* 35°50N 7°5E **261** A6
Oum el Ksi *Algeria* 29°4N 6°59W **260** C3
Oum-er-Rbia, O. → *Morocco* 33°19N 8°21W **260** B3
Oum Hadjer *Chad* 13°18N 19°41E **259** F3
Oum Hadjer, O. → *Chad* 16°38N 20°14E **259** E4
Oumé *Côte d'Ivoire* 6°21N 5°27W **262** D3
Oumm ed Droûs Guebli, Sebkhet *Mauritania* 24°3N 11°45W **260** D2
Oumm ed Droûs Telli, Sebkhet *Mauritania* 24°20N 11°30W **260** D2
Ounane, Dj. *Algeria* 25°4N 7°19E **261** C6
Ounasjoki → *Finland* 66°31N 25°40E **160** C21
Ounguati *Namibia* 22°0S 15°46E **270** B2
Ounianga Kébir *Chad* 19°4N 20°29E **259** E4
Ounianga Sérir *Chad* 18°54N 20°51E **259** E4
Ounissoui *Niger* 17°34N 12°13E **259** E2
Our → *Lux.* 49°55N 6°5E **170** E6
Oura, Akra *Greece* 38°10N 26°2E **205** C8
Oura-wan *Japan* 26°32N 128°4E **288** a
Ouranoupoli *Greece* 40°20N 23°59E **202** F7
Ourârene *Niger* 19°30N 7°10E **263** B6
Ourari, Tarso *Chad* 21°27N 17°27E **259** D3
Ouray *U.S.A.* 38°1N 107°40W **305** G10
Ourcq → *France* 49°1N 3°1E **173** C10
Ourcq, Canal de l' *France* 48°54N 2°28E **134** A3
Ourém *Brazil* 1°33S 47°6W **332** B2
Ourém *Portugal* 39°40N 8°35W **194** F2
Ourense *Spain* 42°19N 7°55W **194** C3
Ourense □ *Spain* 42°15N 7°51W **194** C3
Ouricuri *Brazil* 7°53S 40°5W **332** C3
Ourinhos *Brazil* 23°0S 49°54W **335** A6
Ourique *Portugal* 37°38N 8°16W **195** H2
Ouro Fino *Brazil* 22°16S 46°25W **335** A6
Ouro-Ndia *Mali* 15°8N 4°35W **262** B4
Ouro Prêto *Brazil* 20°20S 43°30W **333** F3
Ouro Prêto do Oeste *Brazil* 10°40S 62°18W **331** C5
Ouro Sogui *Senegal* 15°36N 13°19W **262** B2
Oursi *Burkina Faso* 14°41N 0°27W **263** C4
Ourthe → *Belgium* 50°29N 5°35E **170** D5
Ouse → *E. Sussex, U.K.* 50°47N 0°4E **169** G8
Ouse → *N. Yorks., U.K.* 53°44N 0°55W **168** D7
Oust *France* 42°52N 1°13E **174** F5
Oust → *France* 47°35N 2°6W **172** E4
Outamba-Kilimi △ *S. Leone* 9°50N 12°40W **262** D2
Outaouais → *Canada* 45°27N 74°8W **298** C5
Outapi *Namibia* 17°30S 15°0E **270** A2
Outardes → *Canada* 49°24N 69°30W **299** C6
Outat Oulad el Haj *Morocco* 33°22N 3°42W **261** B4
Outeiro de Rei *Spain* 43°6N 7°36W **194** B3
Outer Hebrides *U.K.* 57°30N 7°15W **167** D1
Outer Mission *U.S.A.* 37°43N 122°26W **136** B2
Outes = A Serra de Outes *Spain* 42°52N 8°55W **194** C2
Outjo *Namibia* 20°5S 16°7E **270** B2
Outlook *Canada* 51°30N 107°0W **297** C7
Outokumpu *Finland* 62°43N 29°1E **160** E23
Outreau *France* 50°40N 1°36E **173** B8
Outremont *Canada* 45°31N 73°36W **130** A2
Ouvéa, Î. *N. Cal.* 20°35S 166°35E **288** d
Ouvèze → *France* 43°59N 4°51E **175** E8
Ouyen *Australia* 35°1S 142°22E **282** C5
Ouzinkie *U.S.A.* 57°56N 152°30W **303** H9
Ouzouer-le-Marché *France* 47°54N 1°32E **173** E8
Ovacık *Turkey* 36°11N 33°40E **250** B4
Ovada *Italy* 44°38N 8°38E **198** D5
Ovahe *Chile* 27°5S 109°19W **330** b
Ovalau *Fiji* 17°40S 178°48E **287** A2
Ovalle *Chile* 30°33S 71°18W **334** C1
Ovamboland *Namibia* 18°30S 16°0E **270** A2
Ovan *Gabon* 0°19N 12°10E **264** B2
Ovanåker *Sweden* 61°22N 15°53E **162** C9
Ovar *Portugal* 40°51N 8°40W **194** E2
Ovau *Solomon Is.* 6°40S 156°8E **287** L9
Overath *Germany* 50°56N 7°17E **178** E3
Overflakkee *Neths.* 51°44N 4°10E **170** C4
Overijse *Belgium* 50°47N 4°32E **116** B3
Overijssel □ *Neths.* 52°25N 6°35E **170** B6
Overland *U.S.A.* 38°42N 90°21W **310** F6
Overland Park *U.S.A.* 38°58N 94°40W **308** F6
Overlander Roadhouse *Australia* 26°19S 114°28E **279** E1
Overton *U.S.A.* 36°33N 114°27W **307** J12
Övertorneå *Sweden* 66°23N 23°38E **160** C20
Överum *Sweden* 58°0N 16°20E **163** F10
Ovid *Mich., U.S.A.* 43°1N 84°22W **311** A12
Ovid *N.Y., U.S.A.* 42°41N 76°49W **313** D8
Ovidiopol *Ukraine* 46°15N 30°30E **189** J6
Ovidiu *Romania* 44°16N 28°34E **183** F13
Oviedo *Spain* 43°25N 5°50W **194** B5
Oviedo *Fla., U.S.A.* 28°40N 81°13W **317** G8
Oviksfjällen *Sweden* 63°0N 13°49E **162** A7
Ovišrags *Latvia* 57°33N 21°44E **184** A8
Ovoot *Mongolia* 45°21N 113°45E **226** B7
Övör Hangay □ *Mongolia* 45°0N 102°30E **226** B2
Ovoro *Nigeria* 5°26N 7°16E **263** D6
Øvre Anárjohka △ *Norway* 68°30N 24°40E **160** B21
Øvre Årdal *Norway* 61°19N 7°48E **164** C4
Øvre Dividal △ *Norway* 68°43N 19°50E **160** B18
Övre Fryken *Sweden* 60°0N 13°7E **162** E7
Øvre Pasvik △ *Norway* 69°6N 28°54E **160** B23
Øvre Rendal *Norway* 61°54N 11°4E **164** C8
Øvre Rindal *Norway* 63°6N 9°10E **164** A6
Øvre Sirdal *Norway* 58°48N 6°43E **164** F3
Ovruch *Ukraine* 51°25N 28°45E **177** C15
Owaka *N.Z.* 46°27S 169°40E **285** G4
Owambo = Ovamboland *Namibia* 18°30S 16°0E **270** A2
Owando *Congo* 0°29S 15°55E **264** C3
Owariasahi *Japan* 35°10N 137°5E **223** B9
Owasco L. *U.S.A.* 42°50N 76°31W **313** D8
Owase *Japan* 34°7N 136°12E **223** C8
Owatonna *U.S.A.* 44°5N 93°14W **308** C7
Owbeh *Afghan.* 34°28N 63°10E **240** B1
Owego *U.S.A.* 42°6N 76°16W **313** D8
Owen *Australia* 34°15S 138°32E **282** C3
Owen, Mt. *N.Z.* 41°35S 172°33E **285** B7
Owen Falls Dam = Nalubaale Dam *Uganda* 0°30N 33°5E **268** B3
Owen Sound *Canada* 44°35N 80°55W **312** B4
Owen Stanley Ra. *Papua N. G.* 8°30S 147°0E **286** E4
Owendo *Gabon* 0°17N 9°30E **264** B1
Oweniny → *Ireland* 54°8N 9°34W **166** B2
Owens → *U.S.A.* 36°32N 117°59W **306** J9
Owens L. *U.S.A.* 36°26N 117°57W **307** J9
Owensboro *U.S.A.* 37°46N 87°7W **311** G9
Owensville *Ind., U.S.A.* 38°16N 87°41W **311** F9
Owensville *Mo., U.S.A.* 38°21N 91°30W **310** F5
Owenteik *Guyana* 4°27N 59°35W **329** C6
Owenton *U.S.A.* 38°32N 84°50W **311** F12
Owerri *Nigeria* 5°29N 7°0E **263** D6
Owhango *N.Z.* 39°0S 175°23E **284** F4
Owingsville *U.S.A.* 38°9N 83°46W **311** F13
Owl → *Canada* 57°51N 92°44W **297** B10
Owo *Nigeria* 7°10N 5°39E **263** D6
Oworonsoki *Nigeria* 6°32N 3°24E **124** A2
Owosso *U.S.A.* 43°0N 84°10W **311** B12
Owyhee *U.S.A.* 41°57N 116°6W **304** F5
Owyhee → *U.S.A.* 43°49N 117°2W **304** E5
Owyhee, L. *U.S.A.* 43°38N 117°14W **304** E5
Ox Mts. = Slieve Gamph *Ireland* 54°6N 9°0W **166** B3
Oxapampa *Peru* 10°33S 75°26W **330** C2
Öxarfjörður *Iceland* 66°15N 16°45W **155** A10
Oxbow *Canada* 49°14N 102°10W **297** D8
Oxelösund *Sweden* 58°43N 17°5E **163** F11
Oxford *N.Z.* 43°18S 172°11E **285** D7
Oxford *Oxon., U.K.* 51°46N 1°15W **169** F6
Oxford *Ala., U.S.A.* 33°36N 85°51W **316** B4
Oxford *Iowa, U.S.A.* 41°43N 91°47W **310** C5
Oxford *Mass., U.S.A.* 42°7N 71°52W **313** D13
Oxford *Mich., U.S.A.* 42°49N 83°16W **311** B13
Oxford *Miss., U.S.A.* 34°22N 89°31W **315** D10
Oxford *N.C., U.S.A.* 36°19N 78°35W **315** C15
Oxford *N.Y., U.S.A.* 42°27N 75°36W **313** D9
Oxford *Ohio, U.S.A.* 39°31N 84°45W **311** E12
Oxford L. *Canada* 54°51N 95°37W **297** C9
Oxford Street *London, U.K.* **125** b3
Oxfordshire □ *U.K.* 51°48N 1°16W **169** F6
Oxgangs *U.K.* 55°54N 3°13W **121** B2
Oxia *Greece* 38°18N 21°6E **207** C3
Oxie *Sweden* 55°33N 13°6E **163** J7
Oxilithos *Greece* 38°35N 24°7E **204** C6
Oxley *Australia* 34°11S 144°6E **282** C6
Oxley Wild Rivers △ *Australia* 30°57S 152°12E **283** A10
Oxnard *U.S.A.* 34°12N 119°11W **307** L7
Oxon Hill *U.S.A.* 38°48N 76°59W **143** C3
Oxsjövålen *Sweden* 62°34N 13°57E **162** B7
Oxus = Amudarya → *Uzbekistan* 43°58N 59°34E **216** D5
Oya *Malaysia* 2°55N 111°55E **235** B4
Oyabe *Japan* 36°47N 136°56E **223** A8
Oyala *Eq. Guin.* 1°35N 10°49E **264** B2
Oyama *Japan* 36°18N 139°48E **223** A11
Oyambre ⌂ *Spain* 43°22N 4°21W **194** B6
Oyapock → *Fr. Guiana* 4°8N 51°40W **329** C7
Øye *Norway* 58°16N 6°49E **164** F3
Oyem *Gabon* 1°34N 11°31E **264** B2
Oyen *Canada* 51°22N 110°28W **297** C6
Øyer *Norway* 61°16N 10°25E **164** C7
Øyeren *Norway* 59°50N 11°15E **164** E8
Oykel → *U.K.* 57°56N 4°26W **167** D4
Oymyakon *Russia* 63°25N 142°44E **215** C15
Oyo *Congo* 0°0 15°51E **264** C3
Oyo *Nigeria* 7°46N 3°56E **263** D5
Oyo *Sudan* 21°58N 36°10E **256** C4
Oyo □ *Nigeria* 8°15N 3°30E **263** D5
Oyodo *Japan* 34°42N 135°29E **133** A1
Oyón *Peru* 10°37S 76°47W **330** C2
Oyonnax *France* 46°16N 5°40E **173** F12
Oyrot = Gorno-Altay □ *Russia* 51°0N 86°0E **217** B11
Oyrot-Tura = Gorno-Altaysk *Russia* 51°50N 86°5E **217** B11
Øyslebø *Norway* 58°9N 7°34E **164** F4

Oyster Harbour = Ladysmith
Canada 49°0N 123°49W 306 B3
Oyster Rock India 18°54N 72°49E 130 B1
Oyster Rocks Pakistan 24°48N 66°59E 123 B2
Øystese Norway 60°22N 6°9E 164 D3
Ōyūbari Japan 43°1N 142°5E 220 C11
Oyyl → Kazakhstan 49°4N 54°40E 216 C4
Özalp Turkey 38°39N 43°59E 213 C10
Ozamiz Phil. 8°15N 123°50E 233 G4
Ozar = Ojhar India 20°6N 73°56E 244 D1
Ozark Ala., U.S.A. 31°28N 85°39W 316 D4
Ozark Ark., U.S.A. 35°29N 93°50W 314 D8
Ozark Mo., U.S.A. 37°1N 93°12W 308 G7
Ozark Plateau U.S.A. 37°20N 91°40W 308 G8
Ozarks, L. of the U.S.A. 38°12N 92°38W 310 F4
Ożarów Poland 50°53N 21°40E 185 H8
Ózd Hungary 48°14N 20°15E 182 B5
Ozernovskiy Russia 51°30N 156°31E 215 D16
Ozernoye Russia 51°46N 51°28E 190 E10
Ozersk Russia 54°25N 22°0E 184 D8
Ozette, L. U.S.A. 48°6N 124°38W 306 B2
Ozieri Italy 40°35N 9°0E 200 B2
Ozimek Poland 50°41N 18°11E 185 H5
Ozinki Russia 51°12N 49°44E 190 E9
Ozoir-la-Ferrière France 48°46N 2°40E 134 B4
Ozona U.S.A. 30°43N 101°12W 314 F4
Ozone Park U.S.A. 40°40N 73°50W 132 B2
Ozorków Poland 51°57N 19°16E 185 G6
Ozren Bos.-H. 43°55N 18°29E 182 G3
Ōzu Ehime, Japan 33°30N 132°33E 222 D4
Ōzu Kumamoto, Japan 32°52N 130°52E 222 E2
Ozuluama Mexico 21°40N 97°51W 319 C5
Ozun Romania 45°47N 25°50E 183 E10
Ozurgeti Georgia 41°55N 42°0E 191 K5

P

Pa Burkina Faso 11°33N 3°19W 262 C4
Pa-an Myanmar 16°51N 97°40E 241 G6
Pa Mong Dam Thailand 18°0N 102°22E 236 D4
Pa Sak → Thailand 15°30N 101°0E 236 E3
Paama Vanuatu 16°28S 168°14E 287 F6
Paamiut Greenland 62°0N 49°43W 154 E6
Paanayarvi △ Russia 66°16N 30°10E 160 C24
Paar → Germany 48°46N 11°36E 179 G7
Paarl S. Africa 33°45S 18°56E 270 D2
Pa'auilo U.S.A. 20°2N 155°22W 302 C6
Pab Hills Pakistan 26°30N 66°45E 242 F2
Pabaidh = Pabbay U.K. 57°46N 7°14W 167 D1
Pabbay U.K. 57°46N 7°14W 167 D1
Pabean Indonesia 6°49S 115°19E 235 D5
Pabianice Poland 51°40N 19°20E 185 G6
Pabna Bangla. 24°1N 89°18E 241 C2
Pabo Uganda 3°1N 32°10E 268 B3
Pacaás Novos, Serra dos
Brazil 10°45S 64°15W 331 C5
Pacaás Novos △ Brazil 11°0S 63°0W 331 C5
Pacaipampa Peru 5°35S 79°39W 330 B2
Pacaja → Brazil 1°56S 50°50W 332 B1
Pacajus Brazil 4°10S 38°31W 332 B4
Pacaraima, Sa. S. Amer. 4°0N 62°30W 329 C5
Pacarán Peru 12°50S 76°3W 330 C2
Pacaraos Peru 11°12S 76°42W 330 C2
Pacasmayo Peru 7°20S 79°35W 330 B2
Pace U.S.A. 30°36N 87°10W 317 E2
Paceco Italy 37°59N 12°33E 200 E5
Pachacamac Peru 12°14S 77°53W 330 C2
Pachang Hsi → Taiwan 23°20N 120°7E 225 C2
Pachao Yü Taiwan 23°22N 119°29E 225 C1
Pachia Greece 36°17N 25°50E 205 E7
Pachino Italy 36°43N 15°5E 201 F8
Pachitea → Peru 8°46S 74°33W 330 B3
Pachiza Peru 7°16S 76°46W 330 B2
Pachmarhi India 22°28N 78°26E 243 H8
Pachnai India 26°57N 92°19E 241 B4
Pachnes Greece 35°16N 24°4E 207 E5
Pacho Colombia 5°8N 74°10W 328 B3
Pachora India 20°38N 75°29E 244 D2
Pachpadra India 25°58N 72°10E 242 G5
Pachuca Mexico 20°7N 98°44W 319 C5
Pacific U.S.A. 38°29N 90°45W 310 F6
Pacific Antarctic Ridge
Pac. Oc. 43°0S 115°0W 151 B13
Pacific City = Huntington Beach
U.S.A. 33°40N 118°5W 307 M9
Pacific Grove U.S.A. 36°38N 121°56W 306 J5
Pacific Heights U.S.A. 37°47N 122°26W 136 B2
Pacific Manor U.S.A. 37°38N 122°29W 136 C2
Pacific Ocean 10°0N 140°0W 289 G14
Pacific Palisades Calif.,
U.S.A. 34°2N 118°32W 126 B1
Pacific Palisades Hawai'i,
U.S.A. 21°25N 157°58W 302 K14
Pacific Rim △ Canada 48°40N 124°45W 306 B2
Pacifica U.S.A. 37°37N 122°27W 136 C2
Pacitan Indonesia 8°12S 111°7E 235 D4
Packsaddle Australia 30°36S 141°58E 282 A4
Packwood U.S.A. 46°36N 121°40W 306 D5
Paco Phil. 14°35N 120°59E 127 B1
Paco de Arcos Portugal 38°41N 9°17W 126 A1
Paço Imperial Rio de J., Brazil 135 a2
Pacov Czechia 49°27N 15°0E 180 B8
Pacoval Brazil 2°40S 54°11W 329 D7
Pacuí → Brazil 16°46S 45°1W 333 E2
Pacy-sur-Eure France 49°1N 1°23E 172 C8
Padaido, Kepulauan
Indonesia 1°15S 136°30E 231 E9
Padali = Amursk
Russia 50°14N 136°54E 215 D14
Padampur India 20°59N 83°4E 244 D6
Padang Kalimantan Barat,
Indonesia 1°39S 108°55E 235 C3
Padang Riau, Indonesia 1°30N 102°30E 237 M4
Padang Sumatera Barat,
Indonesia 1°0S 100°20E 234 C2
Padang Endau Malaysia 2°40N 103°38E 237 L4
Padang Lawas Indonesia 1°40N 99°56E 234 B1
Padangpanjang Indonesia 0°40S 100°20E 234 C2
Padangsidempuan
Indonesia 1°30N 99°15E 234 B1
Padangtikar Indonesia 0°44S 109°15E 235 C3
Padauari → Brazil 0°15S 64°5W 329 D5
Padaung Myanmar 18°43N 95°9E 241 F5
Padborg Denmark 54°49N 9°21E 163 K3
Padcaya Bolivia 21°52S 64°48W 331 E5
Paddington N.S.W.,
Australia 33°53S 151°14E 139 B2
Paddington London, U.K. 125 b2
Paddle Prairie Canada 57°57N 117°29W 296 B5
Paderborn Germany 51°42N 8°45E 178 D4
Paderno Italy 45°33N 9°9E 128 A1
Paderoo India 18°5N 82°40E 244 E6
Padeş, Vf. Romania 45°40N 22°22E 182 E7
Padilla Bolivia 19°19S 64°20W 331 D5
Padina Romania 44°50N 27°8E 183 F12
Padjelanta △ Sweden 67°20N 16°35E 160 C17
Padma India 24°12N 85°22E 243 G11
Padma → Bangla. 23°22N 90°32E 241 D3
Pádova Italy 45°25N 11°53E 199 C8
Padra India 22°15N 73°7E 242 H5
Padrão, Pta. Angola 6°5S 12°20E 265 D2
Padrauna India 26°54N 83°59E 243 F10
Padre I. U.S.A. 27°10N 97°25W 314 H6
Padre Island ⌓ U.S.A. 27°0N 97°25W 314 H6
Padrón Spain 42°41N 8°39W 194 C2
Padstow U.K. 50°33N 4°58W 169 G3
Padthaway Australia 36°36S 140°31E 282 D4
Padua = Pádova Italy 45°25N 11°53E 199 C8
Paducah Ky., U.S.A. 37°5N 88°37W 308 G9
Paducah Tex., U.S.A. 34°1N 100°18W 314 D4
Padukka Sri Lanka 6°50N 80°5E 245 L5
Padul Spain 37°1N 3°38W 195 H7
Padwa India 18°27N 82°47E 244 E6
Paea Tahiti 17°41S 149°35W 289 e
Paekakariki N.Z. 40°59S 174°58E 284 G3
Paektu-san N. Korea 41°59N 128°4E 224 B4
Paengaroa N.Z. 37°49S 176°29E 284 D5
Paeroa N.Z. 37°23S 175°41E 284 D4
Paesana Italy 44°41N 7°16E 198 D4
Paete Phil. 14°23N 121°29E 232 D3
Pafúri Mozam. 22°28S 31°17E 271 B5
Pag Croatia 44°25N 15°3E 199 D12
Paga Gabon 0°45S 10°21E 264 C2
Paga Ghana 11°1N 1°8W 263 C4
Pagadian Phil. 7°55N 123°30E 233 H4
Pagai Selatan, Pulau
Indonesia 3°0S 100°15E 234 C2
Pagai Utara, Pulau
Indonesia 2°35S 100°0E 234 C2
Pagalu = Annobón Atl. Oc. 1°25S 5°36E 255 G4
Pagalungan Phil. 7°4N 124°41E 233 H5
Pagan Myanmar 21°10N 94°52E 241 E5
Pagan N. Marianas 18°7N 145°46E 302 a
Pagara India 24°22N 80°1E 243 G9
Pagaralam Indonesia 4°1S 103°16E 234 C2
Pagasa I. = Thitu I.
S. China Sea 11°3N 114°17E 230 B4
Pagastikos Kolpos Greece 39°15N 23°0E 204 B5
Pagatan Indonesia 3°33S 115°59E 235 C5
Page U.S.A. 36°57N 111°27W 305 H8
Pagėgiai Lithuania 55°9N 21°54E 184 C8
Paget Papua N. G. 3°2S 141°10E 286 B2
Pageri South Sudan 4°0N 32°0E 257 G3
Paget, Mt. S. Georgia 54°26S 36°31W 326 H6
Paget I. India 13°26N 92°50E 245 H11
Pagewood Australia 33°56S 151°14E 139 B2
Pago B. Guam 13°25N 144°47E 302 d
Pago Pago Amer. Samoa 14°16S 170°43W 302 f
Pago Pago Harbor
Amer. Samoa 14°17S 170°40W 302 f
Pagosa Springs U.S.A. 37°16N 107°1W 305 H10
Pagote India 18°53N 72°59E 130 B2
Pagri China 27°45N 89°10E 218 F6
Pagsanjan Phil. 14°16N 121°27E 232 D3
Pagua B. Dominica 15°32N 61°17W 323 k
Pagudpud Phil. 18°34N 120°47E 232 B3
Pagwa River Canada 50°2N 85°14W 298 B2
Pagwi Papua N. G. 4°4S 143°2E 286 C2
Pāhala U.S.A. 19°12N 155°29W 302 D6
Pahang □ Malaysia 3°30N 102°45E 237 L4
Pahang → Malaysia 3°30N 103°9E 237 L4
Paharpur Bangla. 24°51N 88°44E 241 C2
Pahia Pt. N.Z. 46°20S 167°41E 285 G2
Pahiatua N.Z. 40°27S 175°50E 284 G4
Pāhoa U.S.A. 19°30N 154°57W 302 D7
Pahokee U.S.A. 26°50N 80°40W 317 J9
Pahrump U.S.A. 36°12N 115°59W 307 J11
Pahute Mesa U.S.A. 37°20N 116°45W 306 H10
Pai Thailand 19°19N 98°27E 236 C2
Pai, I. do Brazil 22°59S 43°5W 135 B2
Paia U.S.A. 20°54N 156°22W 302 C5
Paichuan Liehtao Taiwan 25°58N 119°57E 225 b
Paicines U.S.A. 36°44N 121°17W 306 J5
Paide Estonia 58°53N 25°33E 188 C3
Paignton U.K. 50°26N 3°35W 169 G4
Paihia N.Z. 35°17S 174°6E 284 B3
Paiho Taiwan 23°21N 120°25E 225 C2
Paiján Peru 7°42S 79°20W 330 B2
Päijänne Finland 61°30N 25°30E 188 B3
Pailani India 25°45N 80°26E 243 G9
Pailin Cambodia 12°46N 102°36E 236 F4
Pailolo Channel U.S.A. 21°0N 156°40W 302 B5
Paimpol France 48°48N 3°4W 172 D3
Painan Indonesia 1°21S 100°34E 234 C2
Paine Grande, Cerro Chile 50°59S 73°4W 336 D2
Painesville U.S.A. 41°43N 81°15W 312 E3
Paint Hills = Wemindji
Canada 53°0N 78°49W 298 B4
Paint L. Canada 55°28N 97°57W 297 B9
Painted Desert U.S.A. 36°0N 111°0W 305 H8
Paintsville U.S.A. 37°49N 82°48W 309 G12
País Vasco □ Spain 42°50N 2°45W 196 C2
Paisha Taiwan 23°40N 119°35E 225 C1
Paisley Ont., Canada 44°18N 81°16W 312 B3
Paisley Renf., U.K. 55°50N 4°25W 167 F4
Paisley Oreg., U.S.A. 42°42N 120°32W 304 E3
Païta N. Cal. 22°8S 166°22E 288 d
Paita Peru 5°11S 81°9W 330 B1
Paithan India 19°29N 75°23E 244 E2
Paiva → Portugal 41°4N 8°16W 194 D2
Paizhou China 30°12N 113°55E 229 B9
Paja, Cerro Ecuador 1°17S 90°26W 330 a
Pájara Canary Is. 28°21N 14°6W 153 e2
Pajares Spain 43°1N 5°46W 194 B5
Pajares, Puerto de Spain 42°58N 5°46W 194 C5
Pajarito Colombia 5°17N 72°43W 328 B3
Pajęczno Poland 51°10N 19°0E 185 G5
Paju S. Korea 37°45N 126°46E 224 D3
Pak Kok Hong Kong, China 22°14N 114°7E 122 B3
Pak Kong
Hong Kong, China 22°22N 114°15E 122 A3
Pak Lay Laos 18°15N 101°27E 236 C3
Pak Ou Laos 20°3N 102°12E 236 B4
Pak Phanang Thailand 8°21N 100°12E 237 H3
Pak Sane Laos 18°22N 103°39E 236 C4
Pak Song Laos 15°11N 106°14E 236 E6
Pak Suang Laos 19°58N 102°15E 228 H4
Pak Tam
Hong Kong, China 22°25N 114°19E 122 A3
Pak Tam Chung China 22°24N 114°19E 219 a
Pak Thong Chai Thailand 14°43N 102°1E 236 E4
Pakala India 13°29N 79°8E 245 H4
Pakaraima Mts. Guyana 5°15N 60°0W 329 B6
Pakaur India 24°38N 87°51E 243 G12
Pakch'ŏn N. Korea 39°44N 125°35E 224 C2
Pakenham Vic., Australia 38°6S 145°30E 283 E6
Pakenham Ont., Canada 45°18N 76°18W 313 A8
Pakhoi = Beihai China 21°28N 109°6E 228 G7
Pakhuis S. Africa 32°9S 19°5E 270 D2
Pakila Finland 60°15N 24°55E 121 B2
Pakistan ■ Asia 30°0N 70°0E 242 E4
Pakkading Laos 18°19N 103°59E 236 C4
Paklay = Sayaboury
Laos 19°15N 101°45E 236 C3
Paklenica △ Croatia 44°20N 15°39E 199 D12
Pakokku Myanmar 21°20N 95°0E 241 E5
Pakość Poland 52°48N 18°6E 185 F5
Pakowki L. Canada 49°20N 111°0W 297 D6
Pakpattan Pakistan 30°25N 73°27E 242 D5
Pakrac Croatia 45°27N 17°12E 182 E2
Pakruojis Lithuania 55°58N 23°52E 184 C10
Paks Hungary 46°38N 18°55E 182 D3
Paktīā □ Afghan. 33°30N 69°15E 240 B3
Paktīkā □ Afghan. 32°30N 69°0E 240 C3
Paku, Tanjung Indonesia 3°6S 106°31E 234 C3
Pakwach Uganda 2°28N 31°27E 268 B3
Pakxe Laos 15°5N 105°52E 236 E5
Pal Lahara India 21°27N 85°11E 243 J11
Pala Chad 9°25N 15°5E 259 G3
Pala Dem. Rep. of the Congo 6°45S 29°30E 268 D2
Pala Calif., U.S.A. 33°22N 117°5W 307 M9
Palabek Uganda 3°22N 32°33E 268 B3
Palacio Real Madrid, Spain 127 b1
Palacios U.S.A. 28°42N 96°13W 314 G6
Palafrugell Spain 41°55N 3°10E 196 D8
Palagiano Italy 40°35N 17°2E 201 B10
Palagonia Italy 37°19N 14°45E 201 E7
Palagruža Croatia 42°24N 16°15E 199 F13
Palais Royal Brussels, Belgium 116 b3
Palaiseau France 48°42N 2°14E 134 B2
Palakkad India 10°46N 76°42E 245 J3
Palakol India 16°31N 81°46E 245 F5
Palalankwe India 10°52N 92°29E 245 J11
Palam India 19°0N 77°0E 244 E3
Palamas Greece 39°26N 22°4E 204 B4
Palamós Spain 41°50N 3°10E 196 D8
Palampur India 32°10N 76°30E 242 C7
Palamut Turkey 38°59N 27°41E 205 C9
Palana Tas., Australia 39°45S 147°55E 281 F4
Palana Russia 59°10N 159°59E 215 D16
Palanan Phil. 17°8N 122°29E 232 C4
Palanan B. Phil. 17°9N 122°27E 232 C4
Palanan Pt. Phil. 17°17N 122°30E 232 C4
Palandri Pakistan 33°42N 73°40E 243 C5
Palanga Lithuania 55°58N 21°3E 184 C8
Palanganene
Dem. Rep. of the Congo 6°32S 18°52E 265 D3
Palangkaraya Indonesia 2°16S 113°56E 235 C4
Palani India 10°30N 77°30E 245 J3
Palani Hills India 10°14N 77°33E 245 J3
Palanpur India 24°10N 72°25E 242 G5
Palaoa Pt. U.S.A. 20°44N 156°58W 302 C5
Palapag Phil. 12°33N 125°7E 232 E5
Palapye Botswana 22°30S 27°7E 270 B4
Palar → India 12°27N 80°13E 245 H5
Palas Pakistan 35°4N 73°14E 243 B5
Palas de Rei Spain 42°52N 7°52W 194 C3
Palasan I. Phil. 14°51N 122°2E 232 D4
Palasponga India 21°47N 85°34E 243 J11
Palatine U.S.A. 42°7N 88°3W 311 B8
Palatka Russia 60°6N 150°54E 215 C16
Palatka Fla., U.S.A. 29°39N 81°38W 316 F8
Palau Italy 41°11N 9°23E 200 A2
Palau ■ Palau 7°30N 134°30E 288 c
Palauì I. Phil. 18°32N 122°8E 232 B4
Palauk Myanmar 13°10N 98°40E 236 F2
Palaw Myanmar 12°58N 98°39E 236 F2
Palawan Phil. 9°30N 118°30E 233 G2
Palawan □ Phil. 10°0N 119°0E 233 G2
Palawan Passage Phil. 10°0N 118°0E 233 G2
Palayan Phil. 15°36N 121°8E 232 D3
Palayankottai India 8°45N 77°45E 245 K3
Palazzo, Pte. France 42°28N 8°30E 175 F12
Palazzo San Gervásio
Italy 40°56N 15°59E 201 B8
Palazzolo Italy 45°34N 9°9E 128 A1
Palazzolo Acréide Italy 37°4N 14°54E 201 E7
Palca Chile 19°7S 69°9W 330 D4
Paldiski Estonia 59°23N 24°9E 188 C3
Pale Bos.-H. 43°50N 18°38E 182 G3
Palekastro Greece 35°12N 26°15E 207 E7
Paleleh Indonesia 1°10N 121°50E 231 D6
Palembang Indonesia 3°0S 104°50E 234 C2
Palena → Chile 43°50S 73°50W 336 B2
Palena, L. Chile 43°55S 71°40W 336 B2
Palencia Spain 42°1N 4°34W 194 C6
Palencia □ Spain 42°31N 4°33W 194 C6
Paleng Taiwan 24°41N 121°23E 225 B3
Palenque Mexico 17°29N 92°1W 319 D6
Paleo Faliro Greece 37°53N 23°42E 112 B2
Paleochora Greece 35°16N 23°39E 207 E4
Paleokastritsa Greece 39°40N 19°41E 206 B9
Paleometokho Cyprus 35°7N 33°11E 207 E9
Paleopoli Greece 37°49N 24°50E 204 D6
Palermo B. Aires,
Argentina 34°35S 58°24W 117 B2
Palermo Colombia 2°54N 75°26W 328 C2
Palermo Italy 38°7N 13°22E 200 D6
Palermo Calif., U.S.A. 39°26N 121°33W 306 F5
Palermo ✈ (PMO) Italy 38°11N 13°5E 200 D6
Paleros Greece 38°47N 20°53E 206 C2
Palestina = Jordânia
Brazil 15°55S 40°11W 333 E3
Palestina Chile 23°50S 69°47W 334 A2
Palestine Asia 32°0N 35°0E 251 G6
Palestine Ill., U.S.A. 39°0N 87°37W 311 F9
Palestine Tex., U.S.A. 31°46N 95°38W 314 F7
Palestrina Italy 41°50N 12°53E 199 G9
Paletwa Myanmar 21°10N 92°50E 241 E4
Palghat = Palakkad India 10°46N 76°42E 245 J3
Palgrave, Mt. Australia 23°22S 115°58E 278 D2
Palhais Portugal 38°37N 9°2W 126 B2
Palhoça Brazil 27°38S 48°40W 335 B6
Pali India 25°50N 73°20E 242 G5
Pali Taiwan 25°8N 121°23E 225 A3
Pali-Aike △ Chile 52°6S 69°44W 336 D3
Palikea U.S.A. 21°26N 158°6W 302 K13
Palikir Micronesia 6°55N 158°9E 288 G7
Palimbang Phil. 6°12N 124°12E 233 H5
Palin, Mt. Malaysia 6°10N 117°10E 235 A5
Palinuro Italy 40°2N 15°17E 201 B8
Palinuro, C. Italy 40°1N 15°16E 201 B8
Paliouri, Akra Greece 39°57N 23°45E 202 G7
Palisades Park U.S.A. 40°50N 74°1W 132 A1
Palisades Res. U.S.A. 43°20N 111°12W 304 E8
Palisadoes, The Jamaica 17°57N 76°48W 320 a
Paliseul Belgium 49°54N 5°8E 170 E5
Palitana India 21°32N 71°49E 242 J4
Palizada Mexico 18°15N 92°5W 319 D6
Palk Bay Asia 9°30N 79°15E 245 K4
Palk Strait Asia 10°0N 79°45E 245 K4
Palkānah Iraq 35°49N 44°26E 246 C5
Palkonda India 18°36N 83°48E 244 E6
Palkonda Ra. India 13°50N 79°20E 245 H4
Palkot India 22°53N 84°39E 243 H11
Palla Road = Dinokwe
Botswana 23°29S 26°37E 270 B4
Pallanza = Verbánia Italy 45°56N 8°33E 198 C5
Pallarenda Australia 19°12S 146°46E 280 B4
Pallas-Yllästunturi △
Finland 68°8N 24°15E 160 B21
Pallasovka Russia 50°4N 47°0E 190 E8
Palleru → India 16°45N 80°2E 244 F5
Pallës, Bishti i Albania 41°24N 19°24E 202 E3
Pallinup → Australia 34°27S 118°50E 279 F2
Pallisa Uganda 1°12N 33°43E 268 B3
Palliser, C. N.Z. 41°37S 175°14E 284 H4
Palliser, Îs.
French Polynesia 15°30S 146°30W 289 f
Palliser B. N.Z. 41°26S 175°5E 284 H4
Pallu India 28°59N 74°14E 242 E6
Palm Bay U.S.A. 28°2N 80°35W 317 G9
Palm Beach Aruba 12°34N 70°2W 322 f
Palm Beach Fla., U.S.A. 26°43N 80°2W 317 J9
Palm Coast U.S.A. 29°35N 81°12W 317 F8
Palm Desert U.S.A. 33°43N 116°22W 307 M10
Palm-Grove △ Australia 24°57S 149°21E 280 C4
Palm Harbor U.S.A. 28°5N 82°46W 317 G7
Palm Is. Australia 18°40S 146°35E 280 B4
Palm Jumeirah, The
U.A.E. 25°11N 55°11E 119 B1
Palm Springs U.S.A. 33°50N 116°33W 307 M10
Palm Valley U.S.A. 30°11N 81°23W 316 E8
Palma = Paraná Brazil 12°30S 47°48W 333 D2
Palma Mozam. 10°46S 40°29E 269 E5
Palma → Brazil 12°33S 47°52W 333 D2
Palma, B. de Spain 39°30N 2°39E 206 B3
Palma de Mallorca Spain 39°35N 2°39E 206 B3
Palma de Mallorca ✈ (PMI)
Spain 39°34N 2°43E 197 F7
Palma del Río Spain 37°43N 5°17W 195 H5
Palma di Montechiaro
Italy 37°11N 13°46E 200 E6
Palma Nova = Palmanova
Spain 39°32N 2°34E 206 B3
Palma Soriano Cuba 20°15N 76°0W 320 B4
Palmaner India 13°12N 78°45E 245 H4
Palmanova Spain 39°32N 2°34E 206 B3
Palmares Brazil 8°41S 35°28W 332 C4
Palmarito Venezuela 7°37N 70°10W 328 B3
Palmarola Italy 40°56N 12°51E 200 B5
Palmas Paraná, Brazil 26°29S 52°0W 335 B5
Palmas Tocantins, Brazil 10°13S 48°16W 332 D2
Palmas, C. Liberia 4°27N 7°46W 262 E3
Pálmas, G. di Italy 39°0N 8°30E 200 D1
Palmas de Monte Alto
Brazil 14°16S 43°10W 333 D3
Palmdale Calif., U.S.A. 34°35N 118°7W 307 L8
Palmdale Fla., U.S.A. 26°57N 81°19W 317 J8
Palmeira Brazil 25°25S 50°0W 333 G2
Palmeira das Missões
Brazil 27°55S 53°17W 335 B5
Palmeira dos Índios Brazil 9°25S 36°37W 332 C4
Palmeirais Brazil 6°0S 43°0W 332 C3
Palmeiras Brazil 12°31S 41°34W 333 D3
Palmeiras → Brazil 12°22S 47°8W 333 D2
Palmeirinhas, Pta. das
Angola 9°2S 12°57E 265 D2
Palmela Portugal 38°32N 8°57W 195 G2
Palmelo Brazil 17°20S 48°27W 333 E2
Palmer Antarctica 64°35S 65°0W 151 C17
Palmer Alaska, U.S.A. 61°36N 149°7W 303 F10
Palmer → Australia 16°0S 142°26E 280 B3
Palmer Arch. Antarctica 64°15S 65°0W 151 C17
Palmer Lake U.S.A. 39°7N 104°55W 304 G11
Palmer Land Antarctica 73°0S 63°0W 151 D18
Palmerston N. Terr.,
Australia 12°31S 130°59E 278 B5
Palmerston Ont., Canada 43°50N 80°51W 312 C4
Palmerston N.Z. 45°29S 170°43E 285 F5
Palmerston North N.Z. 40°21S 175°39E 284 G4
Palmerton U.S.A. 40°48N 75°37W 313 F9
Palmetto Fla., U.S.A. 27°31N 82°34W 317 H7
Palmetto Ga., U.S.A. 33°31N 84°40W 316 B5
Palmetto Pt. Antigua & B. 17°37N 61°51W 322 c
Palmetto Pt.
St. Kitts & Nevis 17°18N 62°46W 322 d
Palmi Italy 38°21N 15°51E 201 D8
Palmira Argentina 32°59S 68°34W 334 C2
Palmira Colombia 3°32N 76°16W 328 C2
Palms U.S.A. 34°1N 118°24W 126 B2
Palmyra = Tudmur Syria 34°36N 38°15E 213 E8
Palmyra Ill., U.S.A. 39°26N 90°0W 310 E7
Palmyra Mo., U.S.A. 39°48N 91°32W 310 E5
Palmyra N.J., U.S.A. 40°0N 75°1W 313 F9
Palmyra N.Y., U.S.A. 43°5N 77°18W 312 C7
Palmyra Pa., U.S.A. 40°18N 76°36W 313 F8
Palmyra Wis., U.S.A. 42°52N 88°36W 311 B8
Palmyra Is. Pac. Oc. 5°52N 162°5W 289 G11
Palmyras = Santos Dumont
Brazil 22°55S 43°10W 333 F3
Palmyras Pt. India 20°46N 87°1E 244 D8
Palo Phil. 11°10N 124°59E 233 F5
Palo Alto U.S.A. 37°27N 122°10W 306 H4
Palo Seco Trin. & Tob. 10°4N 61°36W 323 t
Palo Verde U.S.A. 33°26N 114°44W 307 M12
Palo Verde △ Costa Rica 10°21N 85°21W 320 D2
Paloh Indonesia 1°43N 109°18E 235 B3
Paloheinä Finland 60°15N 24°56E 121 B2
Paloich South Sudan 10°28N 32°32E 257 E3
Palomar Mt. U.S.A. 33°22N 116°50W 307 M10
Palomeras Spain 40°22N 3°39W 127 B2
Palompon Phil. 11°3N 124°23E 233 F5
Palopo Indonesia 3°0S 120°16E 231 E6
Palos, C. de Spain 37°38N 0°40W 197 H4
Palos de la Frontera Spain 37°14N 6°53W 195 H4
Palos Heights U.S.A. 41°39N 87°47W 119 D2
Palos Hills U.S.A. 41°42N 87°49W 119 C2
Palos Park U.S.A. 41°40N 87°50W 119 C1
Palos Verdes, Pt. U.S.A. 33°46N 118°25W 307 M8
Palos Verdes Estates
U.S.A. 33°48N 118°23W 307 M8
Palpa Peru 14°30S 75°15W 330 C2
Palpara India 22°38N 88°22E 124 B2
Pålsboda Sweden 59°3N 15°22E 162 E9
Palu Indonesia 1°0S 119°52E 235 C5
Palu Turkey 38°45N 40°0E 213 C9
Paluan Phil. 13°26N 120°29E 232 E3
Paluke Liberia 5°2N 8°5W 262 D3
Paluma Ra. Australia 19°9S 146°22E 280 B4
Paluzza Italy 46°32N 13°1E 199 B10
Palwal India 28°8N 77°19E 242 E7
Pama Burkina Faso 11°19N 0°44E 263 C5
Pama → C.A.R. 4°23N 18°43E 264 B3
Pama ⌓ Burkina Faso 11°27N 0°40E 263 C5
Pamandzi Mayotte 12°47S 45°16E 272 b
Pamanukan Indonesia 6°16S 107°49E 235 D3
Pamban I. India 9°15N 79°20E 245 K4
Pamekasan Indonesia 7°10S 113°28E 235 D4
Pamenang Indonesia 8°24S 116°6E 231 J19
Pameungpeuk Indonesia 7°37S 107°43E 235 D3
Pamiers France 43°7N 1°39E 174 E5
Pamir Tajikistan 37°40N 73°0E 217 E8
Pamirsky Post = Murgap
Tajikistan 38°10N 74°2E 217 E8
Pamlico → U.S.A. 35°20N 76°28W 315 D16
Pamlico Sd. U.S.A. 35°20N 76°0W 315 D17
Pampa U.S.A. 35°32N 100°58W 314 D4
Pampa de Agma
Argentina 43°45S 69°40W 336 B3
Pampa de las Salinas
Argentina 32°1S 66°58W 334 C2
Pampa Grande Bolivia 18°5S 64°6W 331 D5
Pampa Hermosa Peru 7°7S 75°4W 330 B2
Pampanga □ Phil. 15°4N 120°40E 232 D3
Pampanua Indonesia 4°16S 120°8E 231 E6
Pampas Argentina 35°0S 63°0W 334 D3
Pampas Peru 12°20S 74°50W 330 C3
Pampas → Peru 13°24S 73°12W 330 C3
Pampatar Venezuela 11°1N 63°48W 329 a
Pamphylia Turkey 37°0N 31°20E 250 B2
Pamplemousses Mauritius 20°6S 57°34E 272 e
Pamplona Colombia 7°23N 72°39W 328 B3
Pamplona Phil. 18°31N 121°20E 232 B3
Pamplona-Iruña Spain 42°48N 1°38W 196 C3
Pampoenpoort S. Africa 31°3S 22°40E 270 D3
Pamuk → Turkey 37°2N 34°49E 250 A5
Pamukçu Turkey 39°30N 27°54E 205 B9
Pamukkale Turkey 37°55N 29°8E 205 D11
Pan de Azúcar Chile 24°5S 68°10W 334 A2
Pan de Azúcar △ Chile 26°0S 70°40W 334 B1
Pan Xian China 25°46N 104°38E 228 E5
Pana U.S.A. 39°23N 89°5W 310 E7
Panabo Phil. 7°19N 125°42E 233 H5
Panaca U.S.A. 37°47N 114°23W 305 H6
Panacea U.S.A. 30°2N 84°23W 316 E5
Panadura Sri Lanka 6°47N 79°53E 245 L4
Panagyurishte Bulgaria 42°30N 24°15E 203 D8
Panaitan Indonesia 6°36S 105°12E 234 D3
Panajam Indonesia 1°15S 116°46E 235 C5
Panaji India 15°25N 73°50E 245 G1
Panamá Panama 9°0N 79°25W 320 E4
Panama Sri Lanka 6°45N 81°48E 245 L5
Panama ■ Cent. Amer. 8°48N 79°55W 320 E4
Panamá, G. de Panama 8°4N 79°20W 320 E4
Panama, Isthmus of
Cent. Amer. 9°0N 79°0W 292 J12
Panama Basin Pac. Oc. 5°0N 83°30W 289 G19
Panama Canal Panama 9°10N 79°37W 320 c
Panama City U.S.A. 30°10N 85°40W 316 E4
Panama City Beach
U.S.A. 30°11N 85°48W 316 E4
Panamint Range U.S.A. 36°20N 117°20W 307 J9
Panamint Springs
U.S.A. 36°20N 117°28W 307 J9
Panão Peru 9°55S 75°55W 330 B2
Panaon I. Phil. 9°50N 125°13E 233 G5
Panare Thailand 6°51N 101°30E 237 J3
Panarea Italy 38°38N 15°4E 201 D8
Panaro → Italy 44°55N 11°25E 199 D8
Panay Phil. 11°10N 122°30E 233 F4
Panay G. Phil. 11°0N 122°30E 233 F4
Pančevo Serbia 44°52N 20°41E 182 F5
Panch'iao Taiwan 25°1N 121°27E 225 A3
Panchur India 22°32N 88°16E 124 B1
Panciu Romania 45°54N 27°8E 183 E12
Pancol Phil. 10°52N 119°25E 233 F2
Pancorbo, Desfiladero
Spain 42°32N 3°5W 194 C7
Pâncota Romania 46°20N 21°45E 182 D6
Panda Mozam. 24°2S 34°45E 271 B5
Pandacan Phil. 14°35N 121°0E 127 B2
Pandan Malaysia 1°32N 103°46E 237 d
Pandan Antique, Phil. 11°45N 122°10E 233 F4
Pandan Catanduanes, Phil. 14°3N 124°10E 232 D5
Pandan, Selat Singapore 1°15N 103°44E 138 B2
Pandan B. Phil. 11°43N 122°0E 233 F4
Pandan Res. Singapore 1°18N 103°44E 138 B2
Pandan Tampoi = Tampoi
Malaysia 1°30N 103°39E 237 d
Pandanan I. Phil. 8°17N 117°13E 233 G1
Pandegelang Indonesia 6°25S 106°5E 234 D3
Pandhana India 21°42N 76°13E 242 J7
Pandharkawada India 20°1N 78°32E 244 D4
Pandharpur India 17°41N 75°20E 244 F2
Pandhurna India 21°36N 78°35E 244 D4
Pando Uruguay 34°44S 56°0W 335 C4
Pando □ Bolivia 11°20S 67°40W 330 C4
Pando, L. = Hope, L.
Australia 28°24S 139°18E 281 D2
Pandokratoras Greece 39°45N 19°50E 206 B9
Pandora Costa Rica 9°43N 83°3W 320 E3
Pandrup Denmark 57°14N 9°40E 163 G3
Pandu
Dem. Rep. of the Congo 4°59N 19°16E 264 B3
Panepistimio Athens, Greece 112 b2
Panevéggio-Pale di San Martino ⌓
Italy 46°14N 11°46E 199 B8
Panevėžys Lithuania 55°42N 24°25E 188 E3
Panfilov = Zharkent
Kazakhstan 44°10N 80°0E 217 D10
Panfilovo Russia 50°25N 42°46E 190 E6
Pang Sida △ Thailand 14°5N 102°17E 236 E4
Panga Dem. Rep. of the Congo 1°52N 26°18E 268 B2
Pangai Tonga 19°48S 174°21W 287 P13
Pangaion Oros Greece 40°50N 24°0E 203 F8
Pangala Congo 3°16S 14°34E 264 C2
Pangalanes, Canal des =
Ampangalana, Lakandranon'
Madag. 22°48S 47°50E 272 C2
Pangandaran Indonesia 7°40S 108°39E 235 D3
Pangandaran △ Indonesia 7°43S 108°42E 235 D3
Pangani Tanzania 5°25S 38°58E 268 D4
Pangani → Tanzania 5°26S 38°58E 268 D4
Pangantocan Phil. 7°50N 124°49E 233 H5
Pangar Djerème ⌓
Cameroon 5°50N 13°10E 263 D7
Pangasinan □ Phil. 15°55N 120°20E 232 D3
Pangfou = Bengbu
China 32°58N 117°20E 229 A11
Pangga, Tanjung
Indonesia 8°54S 116°2E 231 K19
Panghsang = Bangkang
Myanmar 22°4N 99°1E 228 F2
Pangil Dem. Rep. of the Congo 3°10S 26°35E 268 C2
Pangjiabu China 40°38N 115°26E 226 D8
Pangkah, Tanjung
Indonesia 6°51S 112°33E 235 D4
Pangkai Myanmar 22°49N 98°39E 228 F2
Pangkajene Indonesia 4°46S 119°34E 235 C5
Pangkalanbrandan
Indonesia 4°1N 98°20E 234 B1
Pangkalanbuun Indonesia 2°41S 111°37E 235 C4
Pangkalansusu Indonesia 4°2N 98°13E 234 B1
Pangkalpinang Indonesia 2°10S 106°10E 234 C3
Pangkoh Indonesia 3°5S 114°8E 235 C4
Pangkor, Pulau Malaysia 4°13N 100°34E 237 K3
Panglao Phil. 9°35N 123°45E 233 G4
Panglao I. Phil. 9°35N 123°48E 233 G4
Pangniqtuuq = Pangnirtung
Canada 66°8N 65°43W 295 D18
Pangnirtung Canada 66°8N 65°43W 295 D18
Pango Alucuem Angola 8°43S 14°33E 265 D2
Pangody Russia 65°52N 74°27E 214 C8
Pangong Tso = Bangong Co
China 33°45N 78°43E 243 C8
Pangrati Greece 37°56N 23°45E 112 B2
Pangsau Pass Asia 27°15N 96°10E 241 B6
Pangsua, Sungei →
Singapore 1°25N 103°45E 138 A2
Pangtara Myanmar 20°57N 96°40E 241 E6
Panguipulli Chile 39°38S 72°20W 336 A2
Panguitch U.S.A. 37°50N 112°26W 305 H7
Panguna Papua N. G. 6°21S 155°25E 286 D8
Pangururan Indonesia 2°37N 98°42E 234 B1
Pangutaran Phil. 6°18N 120°35E 233 H3
Pangutaran Group Phil. 6°18N 120°34E 233 H3
Panhala India 16°49N 74°7E 244 F2
Panhandle U.S.A. 35°21N 101°23W 314 D4
Pani Mines India 22°29N 73°50E 242 H5
Pania-Mutombo
Dem. Rep. of the Congo 5°11S 23°51E 265 D4
Pāni'au U.S.A. 21°56N 160°5W 302 B1
Panié, Mt. N. Cal. 20°36S 164°46E 288 d
Panihati India 22°41N 88°22E 124 A2
Panikota I. India 20°46N 71°21E 242 J4
Panipat India 29°25N 77°2E 242 E7
Paniqui Phil. 15°40N 120°34E 232 D3
Panitan Phil. 11°28N 122°46E 233 F4
Panj = Pyandzh → Asia 37°6N 68°20E 240 A2
Panjab Afghan. 34°23N 67°1E 240 B2
Panjakent Tajikistan 39°29N 67°37E 217 E7
Panjal Range = Pir Panjal Range
India 32°30N 76°50E 242 C7
Panjang Kepulauan Riau,
Indonesia 4°15N 108°12E 235 B3
Panjang Lampung,
Indonesia 5°25S 105°20E 234 D3
Panjang, Bukit Singapore 1°22N 103°45E 138 A2
Panjgur Pakistan 27°0N 64°5E 240 D2
Panjhra → India 21°13N 74°57E 244 D2
Panjim = Panaji India 15°25N 73°50E 245 G1
Panjin China 41°3N 122°2E 227 D12
Panjnad → Pakistan 28°57N 70°30E 242 E4
Panjnad Barrage Pakistan 29°22N 71°15E 242 E4
Panjshīr □ Afghan. 35°50N 69°45E 240 B3
Panjwai Afghan. 31°26N 65°27E 242 D1
Panke → Germany 52°31N 13°22E 115 A3
Pankisi Gorge = Pankisis Kheoba
Georgia 42°7N 45°15E 191 J7
Pankisis Kheoba Georgia 42°7N 45°15E 191 J7
Pankow Germany 52°34N 13°23E 115 A3
Pankshin Nigeria 9°16N 9°25E 263 D6
Panmunjŏm N. Korea 37°59N 126°38E 224 D3
Panna India 24°40N 80°15E 243 G9
Panna △ India 24°40N 80°0E 243 G8
Panna Hills India 24°40N 81°15E 243 G9
Pannawonica Australia 21°39S 116°19E 278 D2
Panngi Vanuatu 15°58S 168°12E 287 E6
Pano Akil Pakistan 27°51N 69°7E 242 F3
Pano Lefkara Cyprus 34°53N 33°20E 207 F9
Pano Panayia Cyprus 34°55N 32°38E 207 F8
Panopah Indonesia 1°55S 111°10E 235 C4
Panora U.S.A. 41°42N 94°22W 310 C2
Panorama Brazil 21°21S 51°51W 335 A5
Panormos Greece 35°25N 24°41E 207 E5
Panruti India 11°46N 79°35E 245 J4
Pansemal India 21°39N 74°42E 242 J6
Panshan = Panjin China 41°3N 122°2E 227 D12
Panshi China 42°58N 126°5E 227 C14
Pantabangan L. Phil. 15°50N 121°9E 232 D3
Pantanal Matogrossense △
Brazil 17°35S 57°27W 331 D6
Pantanaw Myanmar 16°59N 95°28E 241 G5
Pantanos de Centla ⌓
Mexico 18°25N 92°25W 319 D6
Pantar Indonesia 8°28S 124°10E 231 F6
Pante Macassar
Timor-Leste 9°30S 123°58E 231 F6
Pantego U.S.A. 32°42N 97°9W 120 B3
Pantelleria Italy 36°50N 11°57E 200 F4
Panthéon Paris, France 134 c4
Pantheon Rome, Italy 136 b2
Panthersville U.S.A. 33°43N 84°16W 113 B3
Panti Indonesia 0°22N 100°3E 234 B2
Pantin France 48°53N 2°24E 134 A3
Pantin Sakan Myanmar 18°38N 97°33E 241 F6
Pantitlán Mexico 19°24N 99°4W 128 B2
Pantoja Peru 0°58S 75°10W 328 D2
Pantón = O Castro de Ferreira
Spain 42°31N 7°37W 194 C3
Pantukan Phil. 7°9N 125°54E 233 H5
Panu Dem. Rep. of the Congo 3°50S 19°16E 264 C3
Pánuco Mexico 22°3N 98°10W 319 C5
Panuitan I. Phil. 19°26N 121°32E 232 B3
Panukulan Phil. 14°56N 121°49E 232 D3
Panvel India 18°59N 73°4E 244 E1
Panyabungan Indonesia 0°51N 99°33E 234 B1
Panyam Nigeria 9°27N 9°8E 263 D6
Panyu China 23°1N 113°21E 121 B2
Panzhihua China 26°33N 101°44E 228 D3
Panzi Dem. Rep. of the Congo 7°17S 18°1E 265 D3
Pao → Anzoátegui, Venezuela 8°6N 64°17W 329 B5
Pao → Apure, Venezuela 8°33N 68°1W 328 B4
Paoay Phil. 18°3N 120°30E 232 B3
Paochi = Baoji China 34°20N 107°5E 226 G4
Paoki = Baoji China 34°20N 107°5E 226 G4
Páola Italy 39°21N 16°2E 201 C9
Paola Malta 35°52N 14°30E 206 F8
Paola Kans., U.S.A. 38°35N 94°53W 308 F6
Paoli U.S.A. 38°33N 86°28W 311 F10
Paonia U.S.A. 38°52N 107°36W 304 G10
Paopao Moorea 17°30S 149°49W 289 e
Paoting = Baoding China 38°50N 115°28E 226 E8
Paot'ou = Baotou China 40°32N 110°2E 226 D6
Paoua C.A.R. 7°9N 16°20E 264 A3
Pápa Hungary 47°22N 17°30E 182 C2
Pāpā Hawai'i, U.S.A. 19°13N 155°52W 302 D6
Papa Stour U.K. 60°20N 1°42W 167 A7
Papa Westray U.K. 59°20N 2°55W 167 B6
Pāpa'aloa U.S.A. 19°59N 155°13W 302 D6
Papadopoli, Palazzo Venice, Italy 142 b2
Papagayo → Mexico 16°46N 99°43W 319 D5
Papagayo, G. de
Costa Rica 10°30N 85°50W 320 D2
Papagni → India 15°35N 77°45E 245 G3
Papahānaumokuākea Marine Nat.
Monument ⌓ U.S.A. 25°25N 170°35W 302 F9
Papaïchton Fr. Guiana 3°48N 54°10W 329 C7
Pāpa'ikou U.S.A. 19°47N 155°6W 302 D6
Papakura N.Z. 37°4S 174°59E 284 D3
Papantla Mexico 20°27N 97°19W 319 C5
Papar Malaysia 5°45N 116°0E 235 A5
Papara Tahiti 17°43S 149°31W 289 e
Paparoa N.Z. 36°6S 174°16E 284 C3
Paparoa △ N.Z. 42°7S 171°26E 285 C6
Paparoa Ra. N.Z. 42°5S 171°35E 285 C6
Papatoetoe N.Z. 36°59S 174°51E 284 C3
Papatura Solomon Is. 7°32S 158°47E 287 L10
Papeete Tahiti 17°32S 149°34W 289 e
Papenburg Germany 53°5N 7°23E 178 B3
Papenoo Tahiti 17°30S 149°25W 289 e
Papenoo → Tahiti 17°30S 149°25W 289 e
Papetoai Moorea 17°29S 149°52W 289 e
Paphlagonia Turkey 41°30N 33°0E 212 B5
Paphos Cyprus 34°46N 32°25E 207 F8
Paphos ✈ (PFO) Cyprus 34°43N 32°30E 207 F8
Papien Chiang = Da →
Vietnam 21°15N 105°20E 228 G5
Papikio Oros Greece 41°15N 25°13E 203 E9
Papiol Spain 41°25N 2°0E 114 A1
Paposo Chile 25°0S 70°30W 334 B1
Papoutsa Cyprus 34°54N 33°4E 207 F9
Papua □ Indonesia 4°0S 137°0E 231 E9
Papua, G. of Papua N. G. 9°0S 144°50E 286 E3
Papua New Guinea ■
Oceania 8°0S 145°0E 286 E3
Papudo Chile 32°29S 71°27W 334 C1
Papuk Croatia 45°30N 17°30E 182 E2
Papun Myanmar 18°2N 97°30E 241 F6
Papunya Australia 23°15S 131°54E 278 D5
Pará = Belém Brazil 1°20S 48°30W 332 B2
Pará □ Brazil 3°20S 52°0W 331 B7
Paraburdoo Australia 23°14S 117°32E 278 D2
Paracale Phil. 14°17N 122°48E 232 D4
Paracas, Pen. de Peru 13°53S 76°20W 330 C2
Paracatu Brazil 17°10S 46°50W 333 E2
Paracatu → Brazil 16°30S 45°4W 333 E2
Paracel Is. S. China Sea 15°50N 112°0E 230 A4
Parachilna Australia 31°10S 138°21E 282 A3
Parachinar Pakistan 33°55N 70°5E 242 C4
Paraćin Serbia 43°54N 21°27E 202 C5
Paracuru Brazil 3°24S 39°4W 332 B4
Parada, Punta Peru 15°22S 75°11W 330 D2
Paradas Spain 37°18N 5°29W 195 H5
Paradela Spain 42°44N 7°37W 194 C3
Paradera Aruba 12°32N 70°0W 322 f
Paradip India 20°15N 86°35E 244 D8
Paradise Calif., U.S.A. 39°46N 121°37W 306 F5
Paradise Nev., U.S.A. 36°5N 115°8W 124 B2
Paradise → Canada 53°27N 57°19W 299 B8
Paradise Hill Canada 53°32N 109°28W 297 C7
Paradise I. The Bahamas 25°6N 77°19W 153 b
Paradise River Canada 53°27N 57°17W 299 B8
Paradise Valley U.S.A. 41°30N 117°32W 304 F5
Paradisi Greece 36°18N 28°7E 206 E12
Paragould U.S.A. 36°3N 90°29W 315 C9
Paragua = Palawan Phil. 9°30N 118°30E 233 G2
Paragua → Bolivia 13°34S 61°53W 331 C5
Paragua → Venezuela 6°55N 62°55W 329 B5
Paraguaçu = Paraguaçu Paulista
Brazil 22°22S 50°35W 335 A5
Paraguaçu → Brazil 12°45S 38°54W 333 D4
Paraguaçu Paulista
Brazil 22°22S 50°35W 335 A5
Paraguaipoa Venezuela 11°21N 71°57W 328 A3
Paraguaná, Pen. de
Venezuela 12°0N 70°0W 328 A4
Paraguarí Paraguay 25°36S 57°0W 334 B4
Paraguarí □ Paraguay 26°0S 57°10W 334 B4
Paraguay ■ S. Amer. 23°0S 57°0W 334 A4
Paraguay → Paraguay 27°18S 58°38W 334 B4
Paraíba = João Pessoa
Brazil 7°10S 34°52W 332 C5
Paraíba □ Brazil 7°0S 36°0W 332 C4
Paraíba do Sul → Brazil 21°37S 41°3W 333 F3
Paraíso Brazil 19°3S 52°59W 331 D7
Paraíso Tabasco, Mexico 18°24N 93°14W 319 D6
Paraíso Panama 9°3N 79°38W 320 c
Parak Iran 27°38N 52°25E 247 E7
Parakhino Paddubye
Russia 58°26N 33°10E 188 C7
Parakou Benin 9°25N 2°40E 263 D5

Parakylia Australia 30°24S 136°25E 282 A2
Paralimni Cyprus 35°2N 33°58E 207 E9
Paralio Astros Greece 37°25N 22°45E 204 D4
Paralkote India 19°47N 80°41E 244 E5
Param I. Micronesia 7°21N 151°47E 287 T18
Parama I. Papua N. G. 9°0S 143°25E 286 E2
Paramaribo Suriname 5°50N 55°10W 329 B6
Parambu Brazil 6°13S 40°43W 332 C3
Paramillo, Cerro Colombia 7°4N 75°55W 328 B2
Paramillo △ Colombia 7°37N 76°13W 328 B2
Paramirim Brazil 13°26S 42°15W 333 D3
Paramirim ➝ Brazil 11°34S 43°18W 333 D3
Paramithia Greece 39°30N 20°35E 204 B2
Paramonga Peru 10°40S 77°50W 330 C2
Paramount Studios U.S.A. 34°5N 118°19W 126 B3
Paramus U.S.A. 40°56N 74°2W 132 A1
Paramushir, Ostrov Russia 50°24N 156°0E 215 D16
Paran ➝ Israel 30°20N 35°10E 251 H6
Paraná Argentina 31°45S 60°30W 334 C3
Paraná Brazil 12°30S 47°48W 333 D2
Paraná □ Brazil 24°30S 51°0W 335 A5
Paraná ➝ Argentina 33°43S 59°15W 334 C4
Paraná ➝ Brazil 12°30S 48°14W 333 D2
Paranaguá Brazil 25°30S 48°30W 335 B6
Paranaíba Brazil 19°40S 51°11W 331 D7
Paranaíba ➝ Brazil 20°6S 51°4W 333 F1
Paranal, Cerro Chile 24°38S 70°24W 334 A1
Paranapanema ➝ Brazil 22°40S 53°9W 335 A5
Paranapiacaba, Serra do Brazil 24°31S 48°35W 335 A6
Paranaque Phil. 14°30N 120°59E 127 B1
Paranas Phil. 11°42N 125°2E 233 F5
Paranavaí Brazil 23°4S 52°56W 335 A5
Parang Maguindanao, Phil. 7°23N 124°16E 233 H5
Parang Sulu, Phil. 5°55N 120°54E 233 J3
Parangippettai India 11°30N 79°38E 245 J4
Parângul Mare, Vf. Romania 45°20N 23°37E 183 E8
Paranthan Sri Lanka 9°26N 80°24E 245 K5
Paraoa French Polynesia 19°9S 140°43W 289 f
Paraparaumu N.Z. 40°57S 175°3E 284 G4
Parapetí ➝ Bolivia 18°58S 62°21W 331 D5
Paraspori, Akra Greece 35°55N 27°15E 205 F9
Parate Bueno Venezuela 10°59N 64°22W 329 a
Paratinga Brazil 12°40S 43°10W 333 D3
Paratoo Australia 32°42S 139°20E 282 B3
Parauapebas Brazil 6°4S 49°54W 332 C2
Paraúna Brazil 16°55S 50°26W 333 E1
Paray-le-Monial France 46°27N 4°7E 173 F11
Paray-Vieille-Poste France 48°42N 2°20E 134 B3
Parbati ➝ Mad. P., India 25°50N 76°30E 242 G7
Parbati ➝ Raj., India 26°54N 77°53E 242 F7
Parbatipur Bangla. 25°39N 88°55E 241 C2
Parbhani India 19°8N 76°52E 244 E3
Parc des Princes Paris, France 48°50N 2°15E 134 A2
Parchim Germany 53°26N 11°52E 178 B7
Parchwitz = Prochowice Poland 51°17N 16°20E 185 G3
Parco = Sinclair U.S.A. 41°47N 107°7W 304 F10
Parczew Poland 51°40N 22°52E 185 G9
Pardes Hanna-Karkur Israel 32°28N 34°57E 251 F5
Pardilla Spain 41°33N 3°43W 194 D7
Pardisān Nature Park Iran 35°44N 51°22E 141 A2
Pardo ➝ Bahia, Brazil 15°40S 39°0W 333 E4
Pardo ➝ Mato Grosso, Brazil 21°46S 52°9W 335 A5
Pardo ➝ Minas Gerais, Brazil 15°48S 44°48W 333 E3
Pardo ➝ São Paulo, Brazil 20°10S 48°38W 333 F2
Pardoo Roadhouse Australia 20°6S 119°3E 278 D2
Pardubice Czechia 50°3N 15°45E 180 A8
Pardubický □ Czechia 49°50N 16°0E 180 B8
Pardubitz = Pardubice Czechia 50°3N 15°45E 180 A8
Pare Indonesia 7°43S 112°12E 231 G15
Pare Mts. Tanzania 4°0S 37°45E 268 C4
Parecis, Serra dos Brazil 13°0S 60°0W 331 C6
Paredes de Nava Spain 42°9N 4°42W 194 C6
Parel India 18°59N 72°49E 130 B1
Parelhas Brazil 6°41S 36°39W 332 C4
Paren Russia 62°30N 163°15E 215 C17
Parenda India 18°16N 75°28E 244 E2
Parengarenga Harbour N.Z. 34°31S 173°0E 284 A2
Parent Canada 47°55N 74°35W 298 C5
Parent, L. Canada 48°31N 77°1W 298 C4
Parentis-en-Born France 44°21N 1°4W 174 D2
Parepare Indonesia 4°0S 119°40E 235 C5
Parfino Russia 57°59N 31°34E 188 D6
Parga Greece 39°15N 20°29E 204 B2
Pargas = Länsi-Turunmaa Finland 60°18N 22°18E 188 B2
Pargi India 17°11N 77°53E 244 E3
Pargo, Pta. do Madeira 32°49N 17°17W 153 c
Parguera Puerto Rico 17°59N 67°3W 321 b
Parham Canada 44°39N 76°43W 313 B8
Pari Brazil 23°32S 46°36W 137 B2
Paria ➝ U.S.A. 36°52N 111°36W 305 H8
Paria, G. de Venezuela 10°30N 61°40W 323 t
Paria, Pen. de Venezuela 10°50N 62°30W 329 A5
Pariaguán Venezuela 8°51N 64°34W 329 B5
Pariaman Indonesia 0°47S 100°11E 234 C2
Paricatuba Brazil 4°26S 61°53W 329 D5
Paricutín, Cerro Mexico 19°28N 102°15W 318 D4
Parigi Indonesia 0°50S 120°5E 231 E6
Parika Guyana 6°50N 58°20W 329 B6
Parikia Greece 37°6N 25°11E 205 D7
Parikkala Finland 61°33N 29°31E 188 B5
Parima, Serra Brazil 2°30N 64°0W 329 C5
Parinari Peru 4°35S 74°25W 330 A3
Pariñas, Pta. Peru 4°30S 82°0W 330 A1
Parincea Romania 46°27N 27°9E 183 D12
Paringa Australia 34°10S 140°46E 282 C4
Parintins Brazil 2°40S 56°50W 329 D6
Parioli Italy 41°55N 12°29E 136 B1
Pariparit Kyun Myanmar 14°52N 93°41E 245 G11
Paris Ont., Canada 43°12N 80°25W 312 C4
Paris France 48°53N 2°20E 134 A3
Paris Idaho, U.S.A. 42°14N 111°24W 304 E8
Paris Ill., U.S.A. 39°36N 87°42W 311 E9
Paris Ky., U.S.A. 38°13N 84°15W 311 F12
Paris Mo., U.S.A. 39°29N 92°0W 310 E5
Paris Tenn., U.S.A. 36°18N 88°19W 315 C10
Paris Tex., U.S.A. 33°40N 95°33W 314 E7
Paris, Ville de □ France 48°50N 2°20E 173 D9
Paris Charles de Gaulle ✈ (CDG) France 49°0N 2°32E 173 D9
Paris Orly ✈ (ORY) France 48°44N 2°23E 134 B3
Parish U.S.A. 43°25N 76°8W 313 C8
Parishville U.S.A. 44°38N 74°49W 313 B10
Pariti Indonesia 10°1S 123°45E 278 B3
Parje India 18°54N 72°57E 130 B2
Park U.S.A. 48°45N 122°18W 306 B4
Park City U.S.A. 37°48N 97°20W 308 G5
Pārk-e Āzādegān Iran 35°37N 51°28E 141 B2
Pārk-e Mellat Iran 35°47N 51°24E 141 A2
Park Falls U.S.A. 45°56N 90°27W 308 C8
Park Forest U.S.A. 41°29N 87°40W 311 C9
Park Head Canada 44°36N 81°9W 312 B3
Park Hills U.S.A. 37°51N 90°51W 310 G6
Park Range U.S.A. 40°41N 106°41W 304 F10
Park Rapids U.S.A. 46°55N 95°4W 308 B6
Park Ridge U.S.A. 42°2N 87°51W 119 A1
Park River U.S.A. 48°24N 97°45W 308 A5
Park Royal U.K. 51°31N 0°16W 125 A2
Park Rynie S. Africa 30°25S 30°45E 271 D5
Parkā Bandar Iran 25°55N 59°35E 247 E8
Parkán = Štúrovo Slovakia 47°48N 18°41E 181 D11
Parkano Finland 62°1N 23°0E 188 A2
Parkchester U.S.A. 40°49N 73°50W 132 B2
Parkdale Canada 43°38N 79°25W 141 B2
Parkent Uzbekistan 41°18N 69°40E 217 D7
Parker Ariz., U.S.A. 34°9N 114°17W 307 L12
Parker Pa., U.S.A. 41°5N 79°41W 312 E5
Parker Center Los Angeles, U.S.A. 127 b2
Parker Dam U.S.A. 34°18N 114°8W 307 L12
Parkersburg Iowa, U.S.A. 42°35N 92°47W 310 B4
Parkersburg W. Va., U.S.A. 39°16N 81°34W 309 F13
Parkes Australia 33°9S 148°11E 283 B8
Parkfield U.S.A. 35°54N 120°26W 306 K6
Parkhill Canada 43°15N 81°38W 312 C3
Parkhurst S. Africa 26°8S 28°1E 123 A2
Parkland U.S.A. 47°9N 122°26W 306 C4
Parklawn U.S.A. 38°50N 77°7W 143 B2
Parkmore S. Africa 26°5S 28°2E 123 A2
Parkside U.S.A. 37°44N 122°29W 136 B2
Parkston U.S.A. 43°24N 97°59W 308 D5
Parksville Canada 49°20N 124°21W 296 D4
Parktown S. Africa 26°10S 28°2E 123 B2
Parkview S. Africa 26°9S 28°1E 123 A2
Parkville U.S.A. 40°38N 73°57W 132 C2
Parkway U.S.A. 38°32N 121°26W 306 G5
Parkwood Gauteng, S. Africa 26°9S 28°2E 123 A2
Parkwood Western Cape, S. Africa 34°2S 18°30E 118 B1
Parla Spain 40°14N 3°46W 194 E7
Parlakimidi India 18°45N 84°5E 244 E7
Parlatuvier Trin. & Tob. 11°18N 60°39W 323 s
Parli India 18°50N 76°35E 244 E3
Parliament Budapest, Hungary 117 b2
Pârliţa Moldova 47°19N 27°52E 183 C12
Parma Italy 44°48N 10°20E 198 D7
Parma Idaho, U.S.A. 43°47N 116°57W 304 E5
Parma Ohio, U.S.A. 41°24N 81°43W 312 E3
Parma ➝ Italy 44°56N 10°26E 198 D7
Parnaguá Brazil 10°10S 44°38W 332 D3
Parnaíba Brazil 2°54S 41°47W 332 B3
Parnaíba ➝ Brazil 3°0S 41°50W 332 B3
Parnamirim Pernambuco, Brazil 8°5S 39°34W 332 C4
Parnamirim Rio Grande do N., Brazil 5°55S 35°15W 332 C4
Parnarama Brazil 5°31S 43°6W 332 C3
Parnassos Greece 38°35N 22°30E 204 C4
Parnassus N.Z. 42°42S 173°23E 285 C8
Parndana Australia 35°48S 137°12E 282 C2
Parner India 19°0N 74°26E 244 E2
Parnitha Greece 38°14N 23°45E 204 C5
Parnitha △ Greece 38°12N 23°44E 204 C5
Parnonas Oros Greece 37°15N 22°45E 204 D4
Pärnu Estonia 58°28N 24°33E 188 C3
Pärnu ➝ Estonia 58°28N 24°33E 188 C3
Paro Dzong Bhutan 27°32N 89°53E 241 B2
Parola India 20°47N 75°7E 244 D2
Paroo ➝ Australia 31°28S 143°32E 282 A5
Paros Greece 37°5N 25°12E 205 D7
Parow S. Africa 33°53S 18°37E 118 A2
Parowan U.S.A. 37°51N 112°50W 305 H7
Parpaillon France 44°30N 6°40E 175 D10
Parque Chacabuco Argentina 34°39S 58°26W 117 B2
Parque Patricios Argentina 34°39S 58°23W 117 B2
Parral Chile 36°10S 71°52W 334 D1
Parramatta Australia 33°48S 151°1E 283 B9
Parramatta ➝ Australia 33°49S 151°3E 139 A1
Parras Mexico 25°25N 102°11W 318 B4
Parrett ➝ U.K. 51°12N 3°1W 169 F4
Parris I. U.S.A. 32°20N 80°41W 316 C9
Parrish U.S.A. 27°35N 82°26W 317 H7
Parrott U.S.A. 31°54N 84°31W 316 D5
Parrsboro Canada 45°30N 64°25W 299 C7
Parry Channel Canada 74°15N 94°0W 295 C13
Parry I. Canada 45°18N 80°10W 312 A4
Parry Is. Canada 77°0N 110°0W 295 B10
Parry Sound Canada 45°20N 80°0W 312 A5
Parsābād Iran 39°39N 47°50E 213 C12
Parsaloi Kenya 1°16N 36°51E 268 B4
Parsberg Germany 49°10N 11°43E 179 F7
Parsęta ➝ Poland 54°11N 15°34E 184 D2
Parsnip ➝ Canada 55°10N 123°2W 296 B4
Parsons U.S.A. 37°20N 95°16W 308 G6
Parsons Ra. Australia 13°30S 135°15E 280 A2
Partabpur India 20°0N 80°42E 244 E5
Partanna Italy 37°43N 12°53E 200 E5
Partenio ⌂ Italy 40°56N 14°38E 201 B7
Parthenay France 46°38N 0°16W 172 F6
Parthenon Athens, Greece 112 c2
Partinico Italy 38°3N 13°7E 200 D6
Partizansk Russia 43°8N 133°9E 215 E14
Partizánske Slovakia 48°38N 18°23E 181 C11
Partridge I. Canada 55°59N 87°37W 298 A2
Partry Mts. Ireland 53°40N 9°28W 166 C2
Partur India 19°40N 76°14E 244 E3
Paru ➝ Brazil 1°33S 52°38W 329 D7
Parú ➝ Venezuela 4°20N 66°27W 328 C4
Paru de Oeste ➝ Brazil 1°30N 56°0W 329 C6
Parucito ➝ Venezuela 5°18N 65°59W 328 B4
Parur = North Paravar India 10°13N 76°14E 245 J3
Paruro Peru 13°45S 71°50W 330 C3
Parvān □ Afghan. 35°0N 69°0E 240 B3
Parvatipuram India 18°50N 83°25E 244 E6
Parvatsar India 26°52N 74°49E 242 F6
Parvomay Bulgaria 42°8N 25°17E 203 D9
Påryd Sweden 56°34N 15°55E 163 H9
Parys S. Africa 26°52S 27°29E 270 C4
Pas, Pta. des Spain 38°46N 1°26E 206 D1
Pas, The Canada 53°45N 101°15W 297 C8
Pas-de-Calais □ France 50°30N 2°10E 173 B9
Paşabahçe Turkey 41°6N 29°5E 122 B2
Pasada Spain 43°23N 5°40W 194 B5
Pasadena Nfld. & L., Canada 49°1N 57°36W 299 C8
Pasadena Calif., U.S.A. 34°9N 118°8W 126 B4
Pasadena Tex., U.S.A. 29°43N 95°13W 314 G7
Pasaje Ecuador 3°23S 79°50W 328 D2
Pasaje ➝ Argentina 25°39S 63°56W 334 B3
Paşalimanı Turkey 40°29N 27°36E 203 F11
Pasar Indonesia 8°27S 114°54E 231 J17
Pasar Minggu Indonesia 6°16S 106°49E 122 B1
Pasargadae Iran 30°11N 53°10E 247 D7
Pasarkuok Indonesia 1°27S 100°36E 234 C2
Pasarsibuhuan Indonesia 1°3N 99°43E 234 B1
Pasay Phil. 14°32N 120°59E 127 B1
Pascagoula U.S.A. 30°21N 88°33W 315 F10
Pascagoula ➝ U.S.A. 30°23N 88°37W 315 F10
Paşcani Romania 47°14N 26°45E 183 C11
Paschimbanga □ India 23°0N 88°0E 243 H13
Pasco U.S.A. 46°14N 119°6W 304 C4
Pasco □ Peru 10°40S 75°0W 330 C3
Pasco I. Australia 20°57S 115°20E 278 D2
Pascoag U.S.A. 41°57N 71°42W 313 E13
Pascoe Vale Australia 37°43S 144°55E 128 A1
Pascua, I. de Chile 27°7S 109°23W 330 b
Paseo de la Reforma Mexico City, Mexico 128 b2
Pasewalk Germany 53°30N 13°58E 178 B9
Pasfield L. Canada 58°24N 105°20W 297 B7
Pasha ➝ Russia 60°29N 32°55E 188 B7
Pashmakli = Smolyan Bulgaria 41°36N 24°38E 203 E8
Pasig Phil. 14°33N 121°4E 127 B2
Pasig ➝ Phil. 14°31N 121°6E 127 B2
Pasighat India 28°4N 95°21E 241 A5
Pasila Finland 60°12N 24°56E 121 B2
Pasing Germany 48°8N 11°28E 131 B1
Pasinler Turkey 39°59N 41°41E 213 C9
Pasir Mas Malaysia 6°2N 102°8E 237 J4
Pasir Panjang Singapore 1°18N 103°46E 138 B2
Pasir Putih Malaysia 5°50N 102°24E 237 K4
Pasir Ris Singapore 1°22N 103°56E 138 A3
Pasirian Indonesia 8°13S 113°8E 235 D4
Pasirkuning = Dabo Indonesia 0°30S 104°33E 234 C2
Pasirpengarayan Indonesia 0°51N 100°16E 234 B2
Påskallavik Sweden 57°10N 16°26E 163 G10
Paskūh Iran 27°34N 61°39E 247 E9
Pasłęk Poland 54°3N 19°41E 184 D6
Pasłęka ➝ Poland 54°26N 19°46E 184 D6
Pasley, C. Australia 33°52S 123°35E 279 F3
Pašman Croatia 43°58N 15°20E 199 E12
Pasmore ➝ Australia 31°5S 139°49E 282 A3
Pasni Pakistan 25°15N 63°27E 240 D1
Paso Bravo △ Paraguay 22°32S 57°5W 334 A4
Paso Cantinela Mexico 32°33N 115°47W 307 N11
Paso de Indios Argentina 43°55S 69°0W 336 B3
Paso de los Indios Argentina 38°32S 69°25W 336 A3
Paso de los Libres Argentina 29°44S 57°10W 334 B4
Paso de los Toros Uruguay 32°45S 56°30W 334 C4
Paso Flores Argentina 40°35S 70°38W 336 B2
Paso Robles U.S.A. 35°38N 120°41W 306 K6
Pasorapa Bolivia 18°16S 64°37W 331 D5
Paspébiac Canada 48°3N 65°17W 299 C6
Pasrur Pakistan 32°16N 74°43E 242 C6
Passage East Ireland 52°14N 7°0W 166 D5
Passage West Ireland 51°52N 8°21W 166 E3
Passaic U.S.A. 40°51N 74°7W 132 A1
Passaic ➝ U.S.A. 40°42N 74°10W 132 B1
Passam Papua N. G. 3°41S 143°38E 286 B2
Passau Germany 48°34N 13°28E 179 G9
Passenheim = Pasym Poland 53°48N 20°49E 184 E7
Passero, C. Italy 36°41N 15°10E 201 F8
Passi Phil. 11°6N 122°38E 233 F4
Passirana Italy 45°32N 9°2E 128 A1
Passo Fundo Brazil 28°10S 52°20W 335 B5
Passos Brazil 20°45S 46°37W 333 F2
Passow Germany 53°8N 14°6E 178 B10
Passy France 45°55N 6°41E 175 C10
Pastavy Belarus 55°4N 26°50E 188 E4
Pastaza □ Ecuador 2°0S 77°0W 328 D2
Pastaza ➝ Peru 4°50S 76°52W 328 D2
Pasto Colombia 1°13N 77°17W 328 C2
Pastol B. U.S.A. 63°7N 163°15W 303 E7
Pastos Bons Brazil 6°36S 44°5W 332 C3
Pastrana Spain 40°27N 2°53W 196 E2
Pasuquin Phil. 18°20N 120°37E 232 B3
Pasuruan Indonesia 7°40S 112°44E 235 D4
Pasym Poland 53°48N 20°49E 184 E7
Pásztó Hungary 47°52N 19°43E 182 C4
Pata Phil. 5°51N 121°10E 233 J3
Pata I. Phil. 5°49N 121°10E 233 J3
Patag I. = Flat I. S. China Sea 10°49N 115°49E 230 B5
Patagonia Argentina 45°0S 69°0W 336 C3
Patagonia Ariz., U.S.A. 31°33N 110°45W 305 L8
Patambar Iran 29°45N 60°17E 247 D9
Patan = Lalitpur Nepal 27°40N 85°20E 243 F11
Patan = Somnath India 20°53N 70°22E 242 J4
Patan Gujarat, India 23°54N 72°14E 242 H5
Patan Maharashtra, India 17°22N 73°57E 244 F1
Patani Indonesia 0°20N 128°50E 231 D7
Pătârlagele Romania 45°19N 26°21E 183 E11
Pataudi India 28°18N 76°48E 242 E7
Patchewollock Australia 35°22S 142°12E 282 C5
Patchogue U.S.A. 40°46N 73°1W 313 F11
Pate Coast, Kenya 2°10S 41°0E 268 C5
Pate Taiwan 24°56N 121°17E 225 B3
Patea N.Z. 39°45S 174°30E 284 F3
Pategi Nigeria 8°50N 5°45E 263 D6
Patel Nagar India 28°39N 77°10E 120 B1
Patensie S. Africa 33°46S 24°49E 270 D3
Paterna Spain 39°30N 0°26W 197 F4
Paternion Austria 46°43N 13°38E 180 E6
Paternò Italy 37°34N 14°54E 201 E7
Pateros Manila, Phil. 14°32N 121°3E 127 B2
Pateros Wash., U.S.A. 48°3N 119°54W 304 B4
Paterson N.S.W., Australia 32°35S 151°36E 283 B9
Paterson N.J., U.S.A. 40°54N 74°9W 313 F10
Paterson Inlet N.Z. 46°56S 168°12E 285 G3
Paterson Ra. Australia 21°45S 122°10E 278 D3
Pathankot India 32°18N 75°45E 242 C6
Pathardi India 19°10N 75°11E 244 E2
Patharghata Bangla. 22°2N 89°58E 241 D2
Pathein Myanmar 16°45N 94°30E 241 G5
Pathfinder Res. U.S.A. 42°28N 106°51W 304 E10
Pathiu Thailand 10°42N 99°19E 237 G2
Pathri India 19°15N 76°27E 244 E3
Pathum Thani Thailand 14°1N 100°32E 236 E3
Pathumwan Thailand 13°44N 100°31E 113 B2
Pati Indonesia 6°45S 111°1E 235 D4
Pati Pt. Guam 13°35N 144°57E 302 d
Patía Colombia 2°4N 77°4W 328 C2
Patía ➝ Colombia 2°13N 78°40W 328 C2
Patiala Punjab, India 30°23N 76°26E 242 D7
Patiala Ut. P., India 27°43N 79°1E 243 F8
Patine Kouka Senegal 12°45N 13°45W 262 C2
Patipukur India 22°36N 88°24E 124 B2
Patisia Greece 38°2N 23°45E 112 A2
Patitiri Greece 39°8N 23°50E 204 B5
Patkai Bum India 27°0N 95°30E 241 B5
Patmos Greece 37°21N 26°36E 205 D8
Patna India 25°35N 85°12E 243 G11
Patnagarh India 20°43N 83°9E 244 D6
Patnanongan I. Phil. 14°48N 122°11E 232 D4
Patnongon Phil. 10°55N 122°0E 233 F4
Patnos Turkey 39°13N 42°51E 213 C10
Pato Branco Brazil 26°13S 52°40W 335 B5
Patoka L. U.S.A. 38°20N 86°40W 311 F10
Patong, Ao Thailand 7°54N 98°17E 237 a
Patonga Uganda 2°45N 33°15E 268 B3
Patos Albania 40°42N 19°38E 202 F3
Patos Brazil 6°55S 37°16W 332 C4
Patos, L. dos Brazil 31°20S 51°0W 335 C5
Patos, Río de los ➝ Argentina 31°18S 69°25W 334 C2
Patos de Minas Brazil 18°35S 46°32W 333 E2
Patquía Argentina 30°2S 66°55W 334 C2
Patra Greece 38°14N 21°47E 204 C3
Patraikos Kolpos Greece 38°17N 21°30E 204 C3
Patras = Patra Greece 38°14N 21°47E 204 C3
Patreksfjörður Iceland 65°35N 24°0W 155 B2
Patriarsheye = Donskoy Russia 53°55N 38°15E 188 F10
Patricio Lynch, I. Chile 48°35S 75°30W 336 C1
Patrocínio Brazil 18°57S 47°0W 333 E2
Pattada Italy 40°35N 9°6E 200 B2
Pattadakal India 16°1N 75°42E 245 F2
Pattallassang Indonesia 5°26S 119°26E 235 D5
Pattani Thailand 6°48N 101°15E 237 J3
Pattaya Thailand 12°52N 100°55E 236 F3
Patten U.S.A. 46°0N 68°38W 309 B19
Patterson Calif., U.S.A. 37°28N 121°8W 306 H5
Patterson Ga., U.S.A. 31°23N 82°8W 316 D7
Patterson La., U.S.A. 29°42N 91°18W 314 G9
Patterson, Mt. U.S.A. 38°29N 119°20W 306 G7
Patteson, Passage Vanuatu 15°26S 168°12E 287 E6
Patti Punjab, India 31°17N 74°54E 242 D6
Patti Ut. P., India 25°55N 82°12E 243 G10
Patti Italy 38°8N 14°58E 201 D7
Pattoki Pakistan 31°5N 73°52E 242 D5
Patton = Monroeville U.S.A. 40°26N 79°45W 312 F5
Patton U.S.A. 40°38N 78°39W 312 F6
Pattonsburg U.S.A. 40°3N 94°8W 310 D2
Pattukkattai India 10°25N 79°20E 245 J4
Patu Brazil 6°6S 37°38W 332 C4
Patuakhali Bangla. 22°20N 90°25E 241 D3
Patuanak Canada 55°55N 107°43W 297 B7
Patuca ➝ Honduras 15°50N 84°18W 320 C3
Patuca, Punta Honduras 15°49N 84°14W 320 C3
Patuca △ Honduras 14°30N 85°30W 320 D2
Pătulele Romania 44°21N 22°47E 182 F7
Patur India 20°27N 76°56E 244 D3
Patvinsuo △ Finland 63°7N 30°45E 160 E24
Pátzcuaro Mexico 19°31N 101°38W 318 D4
Pau France 43°19N 0°25W 174 E3
Pau, Gave de ➝ France 43°33N 1°12W 174 E2
Pau d'Arco Brazil 7°30S 49°22W 332 C2
Pau dos Ferros Brazil 6°7S 38°10W 332 C4
Pauanui N.Z. 37°1S 175°52E 284 D4
Paucartambo Peru 13°19S 71°35W 330 C3
Paudash Canada 44°59N 77°58W 312 B7
Pauillac France 45°11N 0°46W 174 C3
Pauini Brazil 7°40S 66°58W 330 B4
Pauini ➝ Brazil 1°42S 62°50W 329 D5
Pauk Myanmar 21°27N 94°30E 241 E5
Paukkaung Myanmar 18°54N 95°33E 241 F5
Pauktaw Myanmar 20°11N 93°4E 241 E4
Paul I. Canada 56°30N 61°20W 299 A7
Paul Isnard Fr. Guiana 4°47N 54°1W 329 C7
Paul Revere Park Boston, U.S.A. 116 a2
Paul Smiths U.S.A. 44°26N 74°15W 313 B10
Paulatuk Canada 69°25N 124°0W 294 D7
Paulding U.S.A. 41°8N 84°35W 311 C12
Paulding Bay S. Ocean 66°0S 118°0E 151 C8
Paulhan France 43°33N 3°28E 174 E7
Paulis = Isiro Dem. Rep. of the Congo 2°53N 27°40E 268 B2
Paulista = Paulistana Brazil 8°9S 41°9W 332 C3
Paulista Brazil 7°57S 34°53W 332 C5
Paulistana Brazil 8°9S 41°9W 332 C3
Paulistrôm Sweden 57°28N 15°31E 163 G9
Paulo Afonso Brazil 9°21S 38°15W 332 C4
Paulo de Faria Brazil 20°2S 49°24W 333 F2
Paulo E. Virginia, Gruta Brazil 22°56S 43°16W 135 B1
Paulpietersburg S. Africa 27°23S 30°50E 271 C5
Pauls Valley U.S.A. 34°44N 97°13W 314 D6
Paulshof Germany 52°34N 13°42E 115 A5
Pauma Valley U.S.A. 33°16N 116°58W 307 M10
Paung Myanmar 16°37N 94°28E 241 G5
Paungde Myanmar 18°29N 95°30E 241 F5
Pauni India 20°48N 79°40E 244 D4
Pauri India 30°9N 78°47E 243 D8
Pausa Peru 15°16S 73°22W 330 D3
Pauto ➝ Colombia 5°9N 70°55W 328 B3
Pavagada India 14°6N 77°16E 245 G3
Pāveh Iran 35°3N 46°22E 213 E12
Pavelets Russia 53°49N 39°14E 188 F10
Pavia Italy 45°7N 9°8E 198 C6
Pavilion U.S.A. 42°52N 78°1W 312 D6
Pavilly France 49°34N 0°57E 172 C7
Pāvilosta Latvia 56°53N 21°14E 184 B8
Pavlikeni Bulgaria 43°14N 25°20E 203 C9
Pavlodar Kazakhstan 52°33N 77°0E 217 B9
Pavlograd = Pavlohrad Ukraine 48°30N 35°52E 189 H8
Pavlohrad Ukraine 48°30N 35°52E 189 H8
Pavlovo Russia 55°58N 43°5E 190 C6
Pavlovsk Russia 50°26N 40°5E 190 E5
Pavlovskaya Russia 46°17N 39°47E 191 G4
Pavlovskiy-Posad Russia 55°47N 38°42E 188 E10
Pavo U.S.A. 30°58N 83°45W 316 E6
Pavullo nel Frignano Italy 44°20N 10°50E 198 D7
Pavuvu Solomon Is. 9°4S 159°8E 287 M10
Paw Paw Ill., U.S.A. 41°41N 88°59W 310 C8
Paw Paw Mich., U.S.A. 42°13N 85°53W 311 B11
Pawahku Myanmar 26°11N 98°40E 241 B7
Pawai, Pulau Singapore 1°11N 103°44E 237 d
Pawan ➝ Indonesia 1°55S 110°0E 235 C4
Pawayan India 28°4N 80°6E 243 E9
Pawhuska U.S.A. 36°40N 96°20W 314 C6
Pawling U.S.A. 41°34N 73°36W 313 E11
Pawnee Ill., U.S.A. 39°36N 89°35W 310 E7
Pawnee Okla., U.S.A. 36°20N 96°48W 314 C6
Pawnee City U.S.A. 40°7N 96°9W 308 E5
Pawtucket U.S.A. 41°53N 71°23W 313 E13
Paxi Greece 39°14N 20°12E 206 C10
Paximadia Greece 35°0N 24°35E 207 F5
Paxson U.S.A. 63°2N 145°30W 303 E11
Paxton U.S.A. 40°27N 88°6W 311 D8
Paya Lebar Singapore 1°21N 103°52E 138 A3
Payagyi Myanmar 17°29N 96°32E 241 G6
Payakumbuh Indonesia 0°20S 100°35E 234 C2
Payapa = General Tinio Phil. 15°39N 121°10E 232 D3
Payas = Yakacık Turkey 36°46N 36°11E 250 B7
Payerne Switz. 46°49N 6°56E 179 J2
Payette U.S.A. 44°5N 116°56W 304 D5
Paymogo Spain 37°44N 7°21W 195 H3
Payne U.S.A. 41°5N 84°44W 311 C12
Payne Bay = Kangirsuk Canada 60°0N 70°0W 295 F18
Payne L. Canada 59°30N 74°30W 295 F17
Payne Pt. Ascension I. 7°57S 14°25W 153 g
Paynes Find Australia 29°15S 117°42E 279 E2
Paynesville Liberia 6°20N 10°45W 262 D2
Paynesville Minn., U.S.A. 45°23N 94°43W 308 C6
Payo Obispo = Chetumal Mexico 18°30N 88°20W 319 D7
Pays de la Loire □ France 47°45N 0°25W 172 E6
Paysandú Uruguay 32°19S 58°8W 334 C4
Payson Ariz., U.S.A. 34°14N 111°20W 305 J8
Payson Utah, U.S.A. 40°3N 111°44W 304 F8
Paz ➝ Guatemala 13°44N 90°10W 320 D1
Paz, B. de la Mexico 24°9N 110°25W 318 C2
Pāzanān Iran 30°35N 49°59E 247 D6
Pazar Turkey 41°10N 40°50E 213 B9
Pazarcık Turkey 37°30N 37°17E 212 D7
Pazardzhik Bulgaria 42°12N 24°20E 203 D8
Pazardzhik □ Bulgaria 42°12N 24°20E 203 D8
Pazarköy Turkey 39°51N 27°24E 205 B9
Pazarlar Turkey 39°0N 29°7E 205 C11
Pazaryeri Turkey 40°0N 29°56E 205 B11
Pazaryolu Turkey 40°21N 40°47E 213 B9
Pazin Croatia 45°14N 13°56E 199 C10
Pazña Bolivia 18°36S 66°55W 330 D4
Pčinja ➝ N. Macedonia 41°50N 21°45E 202 E5
Pe Ell U.S.A. 46°34N 123°18W 306 D3
Pea ➝ U.S.A. 31°1N 85°51W 316 D4
Peabody U.S.A. 42°31N 70°56W 313 D14
Peace ➝ Alta., Canada 59°0N 111°25W 296 B6
Peace ➝ Fla., U.S.A. 26°56N 82°6W 317 J7
Peace Point Canada 59°7N 112°27W 296 B6
Peace River Canada 56°15N 117°18W 296 B5
Peach Springs U.S.A. 35°32N 113°25W 305 J7
Peachland Canada 49°47N 119°45W 296 D5
Peachtree City U.S.A. 33°25N 84°35W 316 B5
Peacock Pt. Wake I. 19°16N 166°37E 302 b
Peak, The = Kinder Scout U.K. 53°24N 1°52W 168 D6
Peak, The Ascension I. 7°57S 14°20W 153 g
Peak Charles △ Australia 32°42S 121°10E 279 F3
Peak District △ U.K. 53°24N 1°46W 168 D6
Peak Hill Australia 32°47S 148°11E 283 B8
Peak Ra. Australia 22°50S 148°20E 280 C4
Peake Australia 35°25S 139°55E 282 C3
Peake Cr. ➝ Australia 28°2S 136°7E 281 D2
Peakhurst Australia 33°57S 151°3E 139 B1
Peal de Becerro Spain 37°55N 3°7W 195 H7
Peale, Mt. U.S.A. 38°26N 109°14W 304 G9
Peale I. Wake I. 19°18N 166°37E 302 b
Peania Greece 37°56N 23°50E 112 B3
Pearblossom U.S.A. 34°30N 117°55W 307 L9
Pearl U.S.A. 39°28N 90°38W 310 E6
Pearl ➝ U.S.A. 30°11N 89°32W 315 F10
Pearl and Hermes Reef U.S.A. 27°55N 175°45W 302 F8
Pearl Banks Sri Lanka 8°45N 79°45E 245 K4
Pearl City U.S.A. 21°24N 157°59W 302 K14
Pearl Harbor U.S.A. 21°21N 157°57W 302 K14
Pearl Harbor Nat. Wildlife Refuge ⌂ U.S.A. 21°23N 157°59W 302 K14
Pearl River = Zhu Jiang ➝ China 22°45N 113°37E 229 F9
Pearl River U.S.A. 41°4N 74°2W 313 E10
Pearl River Bridge China 22°15N 113°48E 219 a
Pearls Grenada 12°9N 61°37W 323 q
Pearls Rock Grenada 12°9N 61°36W 323 q
Pearsall U.S.A. 28°54N 99°6W 314 G5
Pearson U.S.A. 31°18N 82°51W 316 D7
Pearson Int. Toronto ✈ (YYZ) Canada 43°46N 79°35W 141 A1
Peary Chan. Canada 79°40N 101°30W 295 B11
Peary Land Greenland 82°40N 33°0W 154 A7
Pease ➝ U.S.A. 34°12N 99°2W 314 D5
Peawanuck Canada 55°15N 85°12W 298 A2
Pebane Mozam. 17°10S 38°8E 269 F4
Pebas Peru 3°10S 71°46W 328 D3
Pebble, I. Falk. Is. 51°20S 59°40W 153 f
Pebble Beach U.S.A. 36°34N 121°57W 306 J5
Peć = Pejë Kosovo 42°40N 20°17E 202 D4
Peçanha Brazil 18°33S 42°34W 333 E3
Pecatonica U.S.A. 42°19N 89°22W 310 B7
Pecatonica ➝ U.S.A. 42°26N 89°12W 310 B7
Péccioli Italy 43°33N 10°43E 198 E7
Pechea Romania 45°36N 27°49E 183 E12
Pechenga Russia 69°29N 31°4E 160 B24
Pechenizhyn Ukraine 48°30N 24°48E 183 B9
Pechiguera, Pta. Canary Is. 28°51N 13°53W 153 e2
Pechnezhskoye Vdkhr. Ukraine 50°5N 36°54E 189 G9
Pechora Russia 65°10N 57°11E 186 A10
Pechora ➝ Russia 68°13N 54°15E 186 A9
Pechorskaya Guba Russia 68°40N 54°0E 186 A9
Pechory Russia 57°48N 27°40E 188 D4
Pecica Romania 46°10N 21°3E 182 D6
Pecka Serbia 44°18N 19°33E 202 B3
Peckham U.K. 51°28N 0°3W 125 B3
Pécora, C. Italy 39°27N 8°23E 200 C1
Pecos N. Mex., U.S.A. 35°35N 105°41W 305 J11
Pecos Tex., U.S.A. 31°26N 103°30W 314 F3
Pecos ➝ U.S.A. 29°42N 101°22W 314 G4
Pécs Hungary 46°5N 18°15E 182 D3
Pedasí Panama 7°32N 80°2W 320 E3
Pedda Bellala India 19°4N 78°49E 244 E4
Peddapalli India 18°40N 79°24E 244 E4
Peddapuram India 17°6N 82°8E 244 F6
Pedder, L. Australia 42°55S 146°10E 281 G4
Peddie S. Africa 33°14S 27°7E 271 D4
Pedernales Dom. Rep. 18°2N 71°44W 321 C5
Pedernales Ecuador 0°5N 80°3W 328 C1
Pederstrup Denmark 55°44N 12°20E 118 A2
Pedieos ➝ Cyprus 35°10N 33°54E 207 E9
Pedirka Desert Australia 26°47S 134°11E 281 A1
Pedra Azul Brazil 16°2S 41°17W 333 E3
Pedra Branca Brazil 0°51N 51°58W 329 C7
Pedra Grande, Recifes de Brazil 17°45S 38°58W 333 E4
Pedra Lume Cabo Verde 16°40N 22°52W 153 j
Pedralbes Spain 41°23N 2°7E 114 A1
Pedras Negras Brazil 12°51S 62°54W 331 C5
Pedras Tinhosas, I. São Tomé & Príncipe 1°22N 7°17E 265 a
Pedregal de San Angel, Jardines del Mexico 19°19N 99°12W 128 C1
Pedreguer Spain 38°48N 0°3E 197 G5
Pedreiras Brazil 4°32S 44°40W 332 B3
Pedro Afonso Brazil 9°0S 48°10W 332 C2
Pedro Bank Caribbean 17°5N 78°20W 320 C4
Pedro Bay U.S.A. 59°47N 154°7W 303 G9
Pedro Cays Jamaica 17°5N 77°48W 320 C4
Pedro Chico Colombia 1°4N 70°25W 328 C3
Pedro de Valdivia Chile 22°55S 69°38W 334 A2
Pedro Dorado Colombia 1°0N 70°14W 328 C3
Pedro González Venezuela 11°7N 63°56W 329 a
Pedro Juan Caballero Paraguay 22°30S 55°40W 335 A4
Pedro Miguel Locks Panama 9°1N 79°36W 320 c
Pedro Muñoz Spain 39°25N 2°56W 195 F8
Pedro Pt. = North West Pt. Jamaica 18°27N 78°13W 320 a
Pedrógão Grande Portugal 39°55N 8°9W 194 F2
Pee Dee = Great Pee Dee ➝ U.S.A. 33°21N 79°10W 315 E15
Peebinga Australia 34°52S 140°57E 282 C4
Peebles Borders, U.K. 55°40N 3°11W 167 F5
Peebles Ohio, U.S.A. 38°57N 83°24W 311 F13
Peekskill U.S.A. 41°17N 73°55W 313 E11
Peel I. of Man 54°13N 4°40W 168 C3
Peel ➝ N.S.W., Australia 30°50S 150°29E 283 A9
Peel ➝ N.W.T., Canada 67°0N 135°0W 294 D5
Peel Sd. Canada 73°0N 96°0W 294 C12
Peene ➝ Germany 54°9N 13°46E 178 A9
Peera Peera Poolanna L. Australia 26°30S 138°0E 281 D2
Peerless Lake Canada 56°37N 114°40W 296 B6
Peers Canada 53°40N 116°0W 296 C5
Peery L. Australia 30°45S 143°35E 282 A5
Pegasus Bay N.Z. 43°20S 173°10E 285 D8
Peggau Austria 47°12N 15°21E 180 D8
Peggy Guggenheim, Collezione Venice, Italy 142 b2
Pegnitz Germany 49°44N 11°31E 179 F7
Pegnitz ➝ Germany 49°30N 10°59E 179 F6
Pego Spain 38°51N 0°8W 197 G4
Pegu = Bago Myanmar 17°20N 96°29E 241 G6
Pegu Yoma Myanmar 19°0N 96°0E 241 F6
Peguera Spain 39°32N 2°26E 206 B3
Pehčevo N. Macedonia 41°41N 22°55E 202 E6
Pehlıvanköy Turkey 41°20N 26°55E 203 E10
Pehuajó Argentina 35°45S 62°0W 334 D3
Pei Xian China 34°44N 116°55E 226 G9
Peian = Bei'an China 48°10N 126°20E 219 B14
Peihai = Beihai China 21°28N 109°6E 228 G7
Peikang Taiwan 23°34N 120°18E 225 C2
Peikang Hsi ➝ Taiwan 24°2N 120°50E 225 B2
Peikant'ang Taiwan 26°13N 120°0E 225 b
Peimen Taiwan 23°16N 120°7E 225 C2
Peinan Taiwan 22°47N 121°7E 225 D3
Peinan Hsi ➝ Taiwan 22°46N 121°10E 225 D3
Peinanchu Shan Taiwan 23°3N 120°52E 225 C2
Peine Chile 23°45S 68°8W 334 A2
Peine Niedersachsen, Germany 52°19N 10°14E 178 C6
Peip'ing = Beijing China 39°53N 116°21E 114 B1
Peipu Taiwan 24°2N 121°36E 225 B3
Peipus, L. = Chudskoye, Ozero Russia 58°13N 27°30E 188 C4
Peissenberg Germany 47°48N 11°4E 179 H7
Peitawu Shan Taiwan 22°38N 120°46E 225 D2
Peitou Changhua, Taiwan 23°52N 120°30E 225 C2
Peitou T'aipei, Taiwan 25°11N 121°27E 225 A3
Peitun Taiwan 24°10N 120°41E 225 B2
Peitz Germany 51°51N 14°24E 178 D10
Peixe Brazil 12°0S 48°40W 333 D2
Peixe ➝ Brazil 21°31S 51°58W 333 F1
Peixoto de Azeredo ➝ Brazil 10°6S 55°31W 331 C6
Pejantan, Pulau Indonesia 0°7N 107°13E 234 B3
Pejë Kosovo 42°40N 20°17E 202 D4
Pek ➝ Serbia 44°45N 21°29E 202 B5
Pekalongan Indonesia 6°53S 109°40E 235 D3
Pekan Malaysia 3°30N 103°25E 237 L4
Pekan Nenas Malaysia 1°31N 103°31E 237 d
Pekanbaru Indonesia 0°30N 101°15E 234 B2
Pekin U.S.A. 40°35N 89°40W 310 D7
Peking = Beijing China 39°53N 116°21E 114 B1
Pekutatan Indonesia 8°25S 114°49E 231 J17
Pela Greece 40°46N 22°23E 202 F6
Pelabuhan Ratu, Teluk Indonesia 7°5S 106°30E 234 D3
Pelabuhanratu Indonesia 7°0S 106°32E 234 D3
Pélagos = Kira Panagia Greece 39°17N 24°4E 204 B6
Pelaihari Indonesia 3°55S 114°45E 235 C4
Pelat, Mt. France 44°16N 6°42E 175 D10
Pelcowizna Poland 52°17N 21°0E 143 B2
Pełczyce Poland 53°3N 15°16E 185 E2
Peleaga, Vf. Romania 45°22N 22°55E 182 E7
Pelechuco Bolivia 14°48S 69°4W 330 C4
Pelée, Mt. Martinique 14°48N 61°10W 322 j
Pelee, Pt. Canada 41°54N 82°31W 298 D3
Pelee I. Canada 41°47N 82°40W 312 E2
Pelejo Peru 6°10S 75°49W 330 B2
Pelekech Kenya 3°52N 35°8E 268 B4
Peleliu I. Palau 7°1N 134°15E 288 c
Peleng Indonesia 1°20S 123°30E 231 E6
Pelenge Dem. Rep. of the Congo 2°44S 22°39E 264 C4
Pelentong Malaysia 1°32N 103°49E 237 d
Pélézi Côte d'Ivoire 7°17N 6°54W 262 D3
Pelham U.S.A. 31°8N 84°9W 316 D5
Pelhřimov Czechia 49°24N 15°12E 180 B8
Pelican U.S.A. 57°58N 136°14W 296 B1
Pelican L. Canada 52°28N 100°20W 297 C8
Pelican Narrows Canada 55°10N 102°56W 297 B8
Pelion U.S.A. 33°46N 81°15W 316 B8
Pelister △ N. Macedonia 41°0N 21°10E 202 F5
Pelješac Croatia 42°55N 17°25E 199 F14
Pelkosenniemi Finland 67°6N 27°28E 160 C22
Pell City U.S.A. 33°35N 86°17W 316 B3
Pella Greece 40°52N 22°0E 202 F6
Pella Northern Cape, S. Africa 29°1S 19°6E 270 C2
Pella Iowa, U.S.A. 41°25N 92°55W 310 C4
Pello Finland 66°47N 23°59E 160 C20
Pellworm Germany 54°31N 8°39E 178 A4
Pelly ➝ Canada 62°47N 137°19W 296 A1
Pelly Bay Canada 68°38N 89°50W 295 D14
Peloponnesos □ Greece 37°10N 22°0E 204 D4
Peloponnisos Station Athens, Greece 112 a1
Peloritani, Monti Italy 38°3N 15°20E 201 D8
Pelorus ➝ N.Z. 41°16S 173°45E 285 B8
Pelorus Sd. N.Z. 40°59S 173°59E 285 A8
Pelotas Brazil 31°42S 52°23W 335 C5
Pelotas ➝ Brazil 27°28S 51°55W 335 B5
Pelovo Bulgaria 43°26N 24°17E 203 C8
Pelplin Poland 53°55N 18°42E 184 E5
Pelvoux, Massif du France 44°52N 6°20E 175 D10
Pemalang Indonesia 6°53S 109°23E 235 D3
Pemanggil, Pulau Malaysia 2°37N 104°21E 237 L5
Pematangsiantar Indonesia 2°57N 99°5E 234 B1
Pemba Mozam. 12°58S 40°30E 269 E5
Pemba Zambia 16°30S 27°28E 269 F2
Pemba Channel Tanzania 5°0S 39°37E 268 D4
Pemba I. Tanzania 5°0S 39°45E 268 D4
Pemberton W. Austral., Australia 34°30S 116°0E 279 F2
Pemberton B.C., Canada 50°25N 122°50W 296 C4
Pembina ➝ Canada 54°45N 114°17W 296 C6
Pembroke Ont., Canada 45°50N 77°7W 298 C4
Pembroke Trin. & Tob. 11°13N 60°37W 323 s
Pembroke Pembs., U.K. 51°41N 4°55W 169 F3
Pembroke Ga., U.S.A. 32°8N 81°37W 316 C8
Pembroke Park U.S.A. 25°59N 80°10W 129 C2
Pembroke Pines U.S.A. 26°0N 80°13W 129 B1
Pembrokeshire □ U.K. 51°52N 4°56W 169 F3
Pembrokeshire Coast △ U.K. 51°50N 5°2W 169 F2
Pembuang ➝ Indonesia 3°24S 112°33E 235 C4
Pen India 18°45N 73°5E 244 E1
Pen-y-bont ar Ogwr = Bridgend U.K. 51°30N 3°34W 169 F4
Pen-y-Ghent U.K. 54°10N 2°14W 168 C5
Peña, Sierra de la Spain 42°32N 0°45W 196 C4
Peña de Francia, Sierra de la Spain 40°32N 6°10W 194 E4
Penafiel Portugal 41°12N 8°17W 194 D2
Peñafiel Spain 41°35N 4°7W 194 D6
Peñaflor Spain 37°43N 5°21W 195 H5
Penal Trin. & Tob. 10°9N 61°29W 323 t
Peñalara Spain 40°51N 3°57W 194 E7
Peñalolén Chile 33°28S 70°32W 137 B2
Penalva Brazil 3°18S 45°10W 332 B2
Penal/Debe □ Trin. & Tob. 10°14N 61°27W 323 t
Penamacôr Portugal 40°10N 7°10W 194 E3
Penang = Pinang Malaysia 5°25N 100°15E 237 c
Penápolis Brazil 21°30S 50°0W 335 A6
Peñaranda de Bracamonte Spain 40°53N 5°13W 194 E5
Peñarroya Spain 40°25N 0°40W 196 E4
Peñarroya-Pueblonuevo Spain 38°19N 5°16W 195 G5
Penarth U.K. 51°26N 3°11W 169 F4
Peñas, C. de Spain 43°42N 5°52W 194 B5
Peñas, G. de Chile 47°0S 75°0W 336 C2
Peñas, Pta. Venezuela 11°17N 62°0W 329 A5
Peñas de San Pedro Spain 38°44N 2°0W 197 G3
Peñas del Chache Canary Is. 29°6N 13°33W 153 e2
Peñausende Spain 41°17N 5°52W 194 D5
Pench ➝ India 21°17N 79°10E 244 D4
Pench △ India 21°45N 79°20E 243 J8
Pench'i = Benxi China 41°20N 123°48E 224 B1
Pend Oreille ➝ U.S.A. 49°4N 117°37W 304 B5
Pend Oreille, L. U.S.A. 48°10N 116°21W 304 B5
Pendalofos Greece 40°14N 21°12E 202 F5
Pendé ➝ C.A.R. 7°55N 16°36E 264 A3
Pendembu Eastern, S. Leone 8°10N 10°42W 262 D2
Pendembu Northern, S. Leone 9°7N 11°14W 262 D2
Pendências Brazil 5°15S 36°43W 332 C4
Pender B. Australia 16°45S 122°42E 278 C3
Pendik Turkey 40°53N 29°13E 203 F13
Pendjari ➝ Benin 10°55N 0°50E 263 C5
Pendjari △ Benin 11°15N 1°32E 263 C5
Pendleton Ind., U.S.A. 40°0N 85°45W 311 E11
Pendleton Oreg., U.S.A. 45°40N 118°47W 304 D4
Pendopo Indonesia 3°16S 103°52E 234 C2
Pendra India 22°46N 81°57E 243 H9
Pendzhikent = Panjakent Tajikistan 39°29N 67°37E 217 E7
Penebangan Indonesia 1°13S 109°15E 235 C3
Peneda-Gerês △ Portugal 41°57N 8°15W 194 D2
Penedo Brazil 10°15S 36°36W 332 D4
Penelokan Indonesia 8°17S 115°22E 231 J18

Penetanguishene *Canada* 44°50N 79°55W **312** B5
Penfield *U.S.A.* 41°13N 78°35W **312** E6
Penfro = Pembroke *U.K.* 51°41N 4°55W **169** F3
Peng Chau *Hong Kong, China* 22°17N 114°2E **122** B2
Peng Siang → *Singapore* 1°24N 103°43E **138** A2
Peng'an *China* 31°2N 106°22E **228** B6
Penganga → *India* 19°53N 79°9E **244** E4
Penge *Kasai-Or., Dem. Rep. of the Congo* 5°30S 24°33E **265** D4
Penge *Sud-Kivu, Dem. Rep. of the Congo* 4°27S 28°25E **268** C2
Penge *London, U.K.* 51°24N 0°3W **125** B3
P'enghu □ *Taiwan* 23°30N 119°30E **225** C1
P'enghu Ch'üntou *Taiwan* 23°34N 119°30E **225** C1
P'enghu Tao *Taiwan* 23°34N 119°37E **225** C1
Penglai *China* 37°48N 120°42E **227** F11
Pengshan *China* 30°14N 103°58E **228** B4
Pengshui *China* 29°17N 108°12E **228** C7
Penguin *Australia* 41°8S 146°6E **281** G4
Pengxi *China* 30°44N 105°45E **228** B5
Pengze *China* 29°52N 116°32E **229** C11
Pengzhou *China* 31°4N 103°32E **228** B4
Penha *Brazil* 22°49S 43°17W **135** A1
Penhalonga *Zimbabwe* 18°52S 32°40E **269** F3
Peniche *Portugal* 39°19N 9°22W **195** F1
Penicuik *U.K.* 55°50N 3°13W **121** B2
Penida, Nusa *Indonesia* 8°45S 115°30E **231** K18
Peninnes, Alpes = Pennine, Alpi *Alps* 46°4N 7°30E **179** J3
Peninsular Malaysia □ *Malaysia* 4°0N 102°0E **237** L4
Peñíscola *Spain* 40°22N 0°24E **196** E5
Penitente, Serra do *Brazil* 8°45S 46°20W **332** C2
Penjaringan *Indonesia* 6°7S 106°48E **122** A1
Pēnjwīn *Iraq* 35°37N 45°56E **213** E11
Penki = Benxi *China* 41°20N 123°48E **224** B1
Penkridge *U.K.* 52°44N 2°6W **168** E5
Penmarch *France* 47°49N 4°21W **172** E2
Penmarch, Pte. de *France* 47°48N 4°22W **172** E2
Penn = Penn Hills *U.S.A.* 40°28N 79°52W **312** F5
Penn Hills *U.S.A.* 40°28N 79°52W **312** F5
Penn Station *New York, U.S.A.* **132** c2
Penn Yan *U.S.A.* 42°40N 77°3W **312** D7
Penna, Punta della *Italy* 42°10N 14°43E **199** F11
Pennant *Canada* 50°32N 108°14W **297** C7
Penne *Italy* 42°27N 13°55E **199** F10
Penner → *India* 14°35N 80°10E **245** G5
Penneshaw *Australia* 35°44S 137°56E **282** C2
Pennine, Alpi *Alps* 46°4N 7°30E **179** J3
Pennines *U.K.* 54°45N 2°27W **168** C5
Pennington *U.S.A.* 39°15N 121°47W **306** F5
Pennington → *Nigeria* 4°45N 5°35E **263** E6
Pennino, Mte. *Italy* 43°6N 12°53E **199** E9
Pennsburg *U.S.A.* 40°23N 75°29W **313** F9
Pennsylvania □ *U.S.A.* 40°45N 77°30W **309** E15
Pennsylvania Avenue *Washington, D.C., U.S.A.* **143** b2
Pennville *U.S.A.* 40°30N 85°9W **311** D11
Penny *Canada* 53°51N 121°20W **296** C4
Peno *Russia* 57°2N 32°49E **188** D7
Penobscot → *U.S.A.* 44°30N 68°48W **309** C19
Penobscot B. *U.S.A.* 44°35N 68°50W **309** C19
Penola *Australia* 37°25S 140°48E **282** D4
Penong *Australia* 31°56S 133°1E **279** F5
Penonomé *Panama* 8°31N 80°21W **320** E3
Penot, Mt. *Vanuatu* 16°20S 167°31E **287** F5
Penrhyn *Cook Is.* 9°0S 158°0W **289** H12
Penrith *N.S.W., Australia* 33°43S 150°38E **283** B9
Penrith *Cumb., U.K.* 54°40N 2°45W **168** C5
Penryn *U.K.* 50°9N 5°7W **169** G2
Pensacola *U.S.A.* 30°25N 87°13W **317** E2
Pensacola B. *U.S.A.* 30°25N 87°5W **317** E2
Pensacola Mts. *Antarctica* 84°0S 40°0W **151** E1
Pense *Canada* 50°25N 104°59W **297** C8
Penshurst *Australia* 37°49S 142°20E **282** D5
Pensiangan *Malaysia* 4°33N 116°19E **235** B5
Pentadaktylos *Cyprus* 35°20N 33°20E **207** E9
Pentagon *U.S.A.* 38°53N 77°3W **143** B2
Pentecost *Vanuatu* 15°42S 168°10E **287** E6
Pentecostes *Brazil* 3°48S 39°17W **332** B4
Pentecôte = Pentecost *Vanuatu* 15°42S 168°10E **287** E6
Penticton *Canada* 49°30N 119°38W **296** D5
Pentland *Australia* 20°32S 145°25E **280** C4
Pentland Firth *U.K.* 58°43N 3°10W **167** C5
Pentland Hills *U.K.* 55°48N 3°25W **167** F5
Penukonda *India* 14°5N 77°38E **245** G3
Penza *Russia* 53°15N 45°5E **190** D7
Penza □ *Russia* 52°50N 44°50E **190** D7
Penzance *U.K.* 50°7N 5°33W **169** G2
Penzberg *Germany* 47°45N 11°22E **179** H7
Penzhino *Russia* 63°30N 167°55E **215** C17
Penzhinskaya Guba *Russia* 61°30N 163°0E **215** C17
Penzing *Austria* 48°11N 16°18E **142** A1
Penzlin *Germany* 53°30N 13°5E **178** B9
People's Park *China* 31°13N 121°28E **138** B1
People's Square *China* 31°13N 121°28E **138** B1
Peoria *Ariz., U.S.A.* 33°43N 112°14W **305** K7
Peoria *Ill., U.S.A.* 40°42N 89°36W **310** D7
Peoria Heights *U.S.A.* 40°45N 89°35W **310** D7
Peotone *U.S.A.* 41°20N 87°48W **311** C9
Pepacton Res. *U.S.A.* 42°5N 74°58W **313** D10
Pepani → *S. Africa* 25°49S 22°47E **270** C3
Pepeekeo *U.S.A.* 19°51N 155°6W **302** D6
Pepel *S. Leone* 8°40N 13°5W **262** D2
Peqin *Albania* 41°3N 19°44E **202** E3
Pera Hd. *Australia* 12°55S 141°37E **280** A3
Perabumulih *Indonesia* 3°27S 104°15E **234** C2
Perachora *Greece* 38°2N 22°56E **204** C4
Perachori *Greece* 38°21N 20°43E **207** C2
Perak □ *Malaysia* 5°0N 101°0E **237** K3
Perak → *Malaysia* 4°0N 100°50E **237** K3
Perales del Alfambra *Spain* 40°38N 1°0W **196** E4
Perales del Puerto *Spain* 40°10N 6°40W **194** E4
Perales del Rio *Spain* 40°18N 3°38W **127** C2
Peralta *Spain* 42°20N 1°48W **196** C3
Perama *Epiros, Greece* 39°42N 20°51E **204** B2
Perama *Kerkyra, Greece* 39°34N 19°54E **206** B9
Perama *Kriti, Greece* 35°20N 24°40E **207** E5
Perämeri △ *Finland* 65°35N 24°22E **160** D21
Perancak *Indonesia* 8°24S 114°37E **231** J17
Peräpohjola *Finland* 66°16N 26°10E **160** C22
Perast *Montenegro* 42°31N 18°47E **202** D2
Peratia *Greece* 38°49N 20°45E **207** B2
Peravillo *Mexico City, Mexico* **128** a3
Percé *Canada* 48°31N 64°13W **299** C7
Perche *France* 48°31N 1°1E **172** D8
Perche, Collines du *France* 48°30N 0°40E **171** B4
Perche ⌂ *France* 48°24N 0°46E **172** D7
Perchtoldsdorf *Austria* 48°7N 16°17E **142** B1
Percival Lakes *Australia* 21°25S 125°0E **278** D4
Percy *Manche, France* 48°55N 1°11W **172** D5
Percy *Ill., U.S.A.* 38°5N 89°41W **310** F7
Percy Is. *Australia* 21°39S 150°16E **280** C5
Perdido → *Argentina* 42°55S 67°0W **336** B3
Perdido, Mte. *Spain* 42°40N 0°5E **196** C5
Perdizes *Brazil* 23°32S 46°39W **137** B2
Perdu, Mt. = Perdido, Mte. *Spain* 42°40N 0°5E **196** C5
Perechyn *Ukraine* 48°44N 22°28E **182** B7
Perehinske *Ukraine* 48°49N 24°11E **183** B9
Pereira *Colombia* 4°49N 75°43W **328** C2
Perejil *Spain* 35°55N 5°25W **195** K5
Perelazovskiy *Russia* 49°8N 42°35E **191** F6
Perelik *Bulgaria* 41°36N 24°33E **203** E8
Peremul Par *India* 11°10N 72°4E **245** J1
Peremyshl = Przemyśl *Poland* 49°50N 22°45E **185** J9
Perené → *Peru* 11°9S 74°14W **330** C3
Perenjori *Australia* 29°26S 116°16E **279** E2
Peresecina *Moldova* 47°16N 28°46E **183** C13
Pereslavl-Zalesskiy *Russia* 56°45N 38°50E **188** D10
Peretu *Romania* 44°3N 25°5E **183** F10
Pereyaslav-Khmelnytskyy *Ukraine* 50°3N 31°28E **189** G6
Pereyma *Ukraine* 48°4N 29°30E **183** B14
Pérez, I. *Mexico* 22°24N 89°42W **319** C7
Perg *Austria* 48°15N 14°38E **180** C7
Pergamino *Argentina* 33°52S 60°30W **334** C3
Pergamon *Turkey* 39°8N 27°11E **205** B9
Pergamon Museum *Berlin, Germany* **115** a4
Pergau → *Malaysia* 5°23N 102°2E **237** K3
Perge *Turkey* 37°3N 30°56E **250** A1
Pérgine Valsugana *Italy* 46°4N 11°14E **199** B8
Pérgola *Italy* 43°34N 12°50E **199** E9
Perham *U.S.A.* 46°36N 95°34W **308** B6
Perhentian, Kepulauan *Malaysia* 5°54N 102°42E **237** K4
Peri → *Turkey* 38°53N 39°52E **213** C8
Periam *Romania* 46°2N 20°52E **182** D5
Péribonka → *Canada* 48°45N 72°5W **299** C5
Péribonka, L. *Canada* 50°1N 71°10W **299** B5
Péribonka, La Centrale de *Canada* 49°30N 71°10W **299** C5
Perico *Argentina* 24°20S 65°5W **334** A2
Pericos *Mexico* 25°3N 107°42W **318** B3
Périers *France* 49°11N 1°25W **172** C5
Périgord *France* 45°0N 0°40E **174** D4
Périgord-Limousin ⌂ *France* 45°40N 0°50E **174** C4
Périgueux *France* 45°10N 0°42E **174** C4
Perijá, Sierra de *Colombia* 9°30N 73°3W **328** B3
Perijá △ *Venezuela* 9°30N 72°55W **328** B3
Peringat *Malaysia* 6°2N 102°17E **237** J4
Perisher Valley *Australia* 36°27S 148°25E **283** D8
Peristera *Greece* 39°15N 23°58E **204** B5
Peristeri *Greece* 38°1N 23°42E **112** A2
Peristerona → *Cyprus* 35°8N 33°5E **207** E9
Perito Moreno *Argentina* 46°36S 70°56W **336** C2
Perito Moreno △ *Argentina* 47°49S 72°17W **336** C2
Peritoró *Brazil* 4°20S 44°18W **332** B3
Perivale *U.K.* 51°31N 0°18W **125** A2
Perivol = Dragovishtitsa *Bulgaria* 42°22N 22°39E **202** D6
Periyakulam *India* 10°5N 77°30E **245** J3
Periyar → *India* 10°15N 76°10E **245** J3
Periyar, L. *India* 9°25N 77°10E **245** K3
Periyar △ *India* 9°25N 77°10E **245** K3
Perk *Belgium* 50°56N 4°30E **116** A2
Perkasie *U.S.A.* 40°22N 75°18W **313** F9
Perković *Croatia* 43°41N 16°10E **199** E13
Perlach *Germany* 48°5N 11°37E **131** B2
Perlacher Forst *Germany* 48°4N 11°34E **131** B2
Perlas, Arch. de las *Panama* 8°41N 79°7W **320** E4
Perlas, Punta de *Nic.* 12°30N 83°30W **320** D3
Perleberg *Germany* 53°5N 11°52E **178** B7
Perlez *Serbia* 45°11N 20°22E **182** E5
Perlis □ *Malaysia* 6°30N 100°15E **237** J2
Perm *Russia* 58°0N 56°10E **186** C10
Përmet *Albania* 40°15N 20°21E **202** F4
Permskoye = Komsomolsk-na-Amur *Russia* 50°30N 137°0E **219** A16
Pernambuco = Recife *Brazil* 8°0S 35°0W **332** C5
Pernambuco □ *Brazil* 8°0S 37°0W **332** C4
Pernambuco Abyssal Plain *Atl. Oc.* 5°0S 24°0W **152** G9
Pernatty Lagoon *Australia* 31°30S 137°12E **282** A2
Pernik *Bulgaria* 42°35N 23°2E **202** D7
Pernik □ *Bulgaria* 42°35N 23°2E **202** D7
Pernov = Pärnu *Estonia* 58°28N 24°33E **188** C3
Pero *Italy* 45°30N 9°5E **128** A1
Peron Is. *Australia* 13°9S 130°4E **278** B5
Peron Pen. *Australia* 26°0S 113°10E **279** E1
Péronne *France* 49°55N 2°57E **173** C9
Peropok, Bukit *Singapore* 1°19N 103°42E **138** B2
Perosa Argentina *Italy* 44°58N 7°10E **198** D4
Perovo *Russia* 55°44N 37°45E **129** B3
Perovsk = Qyzylorda *Kazakhstan* 44°48N 65°28E **216** D7
Perow *Canada* 54°35N 126°10W **296** C3
Perparim = Pogradec *Albania* 40°54N 20°37E **202** F4
Perpignan *France* 42°42N 2°53E **174** F6
Perrégaux = Mohammadia *Algeria* 35°33N 0°3E **261** A5
Perrine *U.S.A.* 25°36N 80°21W **317** K9
Perris *U.S.A.* 33°47N 117°14W **307** M9
Perros-Guirec *France* 48°49N 3°28W **172** D3
Perry *Fla., U.S.A.* 30°7N 83°35W **316** E6
Perry *Ga., U.S.A.* 32°28N 83°44W **316** C6
Perry *Iowa, U.S.A.* 41°51N 94°6W **310** C2
Perry *Mich., U.S.A.* 42°50N 84°13W **311** B12
Perry *Mo., U.S.A.* 39°26N 91°40W **310** E5
Perry *N.Y., U.S.A.* 42°42N 78°0W **312** D7
Perry *Okla., U.S.A.* 36°17N 97°14W **314** C6
Perrysburg *U.S.A.* 41°34N 83°38W **311** C13
Perryton *U.S.A.* 36°24N 100°48W **314** C4
Perryville *Alaska, U.S.A.* 55°55N 159°9W **303** J8
Perryville *Mo., U.S.A.* 37°43N 89°52W **310** G7
Persan *France* 49°9N 2°16E **173** C9
Persberg *Sweden* 59°47N 14°15E **162** E8
Perşembe *Turkey* 41°5N 37°46E **212** B7
Persepolis *Iran* 29°55N 52°50E **247** D7
Perseverancia *Bolivia* 14°44S 62°48W **331** C5
Pershing Square *Los Angeles, U.S.A.* **127** c1
Pershotravensk *Ukraine* 50°13N 27°40E **177** C14
Pershotravnevoye = Pershotravensk *Ukraine* 50°13N 27°40E **177** C14
Persia = Iran ■ *Asia* 33°0N 53°0E **247** C7
Persian Gulf *Asia* 27°0N 50°0E **247** E6
Perstorp *Sweden* 56°10N 13°25E **163** H7
Pertek *Turkey* 38°51N 39°19E **213** C8
Perth *W. Austral., Australia* 31°57S 115°52E **279** F2
Perth *Ont., Canada* 44°55N 76°15W **313** B8
Perth *Perth & Kinr., U.K.* 56°24N 3°26W **167** E5
Perth & Kinross □ *U.K.* 56°45N 3°55W **167** E5
Perth Amboy *U.S.A.* 40°30N 74°15W **313** F10
Perth-Andover *Canada* 46°44N 67°42W **299** C6
Pertuis *France* 43°42N 5°30E **175** E9
Pertusato, C. *France* 41°21N 9°11E **175** G13
Pertusella *Italy* 45°35N 9°3E **128** A1
Peru *Ill., U.S.A.* 41°20N 89°8W **310** C7
Peru *Ind., U.S.A.* 40°45N 86°4W **311** D10
Peru *N.Y., U.S.A.* 44°35N 73°32W **313** B11
Peru ■ *S. Amer.* 4°0S 75°0W **328** D3
Peru Basin *Pac. Oc.* 20°0S 95°0W **289** J18
Peru-Chile Trench *Pac. Oc.* 20°0S 72°0W **326** E3
Perugia *Italy* 43°7N 12°23E **199** E9
Perušić *Croatia* 44°40N 15°22E **199** D12
Peruvian Vale *St. Vincent* 13°11N 61°12W **323** n
Pervomaysk *Russia* 54°56N 43°58E **190** C6
Pervomaysk *Ukraine* 48°10N 30°46E **189** H6
Pervomayskīy *Kazakhstan* 50°16N 82°0E **217** B10
Pervouralsk *Russia* 56°59N 59°59E **186** C10
Pervouralsky = Pervouralsk *Russia* 56°59N 59°59E **186** C10
Pesada *Greece* 38°7N 20°35E **207** C2
Pesagot *West Bank* 31°54N 35°13E **123** A2
Pesanggrahag, Kali → *Indonesia* 6°10S 106°44E **122** B1
Pésaro *Italy* 43°54N 12°55E **199** E9
Pésaro e Urbino □ *Italy* 43°45N 12°40E **199** E9
Pescadores = P'enghu Ch'üntou *Taiwan* 23°34N 119°30E **225** C1
Pescara *Italy* 42°28N 14°13E **199** F11
Pescara → *Italy* 42°28N 14°13E **199** F11
Peschanokopskoye *Russia* 46°14N 41°4E **191** G5
Peschanoye = Yashkul *Russia* 46°11N 45°21E **191** G7
Peschiera Borromeo *Italy* 45°26N 9°19E **128** B2
Péscia *Italy* 43°54N 10°41E **198** E7
Pescina *Italy* 42°2N 13°39E **199** F10
Pesek, Pulau *Singapore* 1°17N 103°41E **138** B2
Peshawar *Pakistan* 34°2N 71°37E **242** B4
Peshkopi *Albania* 41°41N 20°25E **202** E4
Peshtera *Bulgaria* 42°2N 24°18E **203** D8
Peshtigo *U.S.A.* 45°3N 87°45W **308** C10
Peski *Russia* 51°14N 42°29E **190** E6
Peski *Turkmenistan* 38°11N 62°59E **216** E6
Pêso da Régua *Portugal* 41°10N 7°47W **194** D3
Pesochnya = Kirov *Russia* 54°3N 34°20E **188** E8
Pesqueira *Brazil* 8°20S 36°42W **332** C4
Pessac *France* 44°48N 0°37W **174** D3
Pest *Hungary* 47°29N 19°4E **117** B2
Pest □ *Hungary* 47°29N 19°5E **182** C4
Pesterzsébet *Hungary* 47°26N 19°6E **117** B2
Pesthidegkút *Hungary* 47°33N 18°57E **117** A1
Pestimre *Hungary* 47°24N 19°11E **117** B3
Pestlörinc *Hungary* 47°26N 19°11E **117** B3
Pestovo = Zavolzhye *Russia* 56°37N 43°26E **190** B6
Pestovo *Russia* 58°33N 35°42E **188** C8
Pestravka *Russia* 52°28N 49°57E **190** D9
Pestújhely *Hungary* 47°32N 19°7E **117** A2
Petah Tiqwa *Israel* 32°6N 34°53E **251** F5
Petalas *Greece* 38°25N 21°5E **207** C3
Petalidi *Greece* 36°57N 21°55E **204** E3
Petalii *Greece* 38°0N 24°15E **204** D6
Petaling Jaya *Malaysia* 3°4N 101°42E **237** L3
Petaloudes *Greece* 36°18N 28°5E **206** E12
Petaluma *U.S.A.* 38°14N 122°39W **306** G4
Pétange *Lux.* 49°33N 5°55E **170** E5
Petare *Venezuela* 10°29N 66°49W **321** D6
Petaro *Pakistan* 25°31N 68°18E **242** G3
Petas *Helsinki, Finland* 60°15N 24°50E **121** B2
Petas *Greece* 39°10N 21°2E **204** B3
Petatlán *Mexico* 17°31N 101°16W **318** D4
Petauke *Zambia* 14°14S 31°20E **269** E3
Petawawa *Canada* 45°54N 77°17W **298** C4
Petén Itzá, L. *Guatemala* 16°58N 89°50W **320** C2
Peter I. *Br. Virgin Is.* 18°22N 64°35W **321** b
Peter I. Øy *Antarctica* 69°0S 91°0W **151** C16
Peter Pond L. *Canada* 55°55N 108°44W **297** B7
Peterbell *Canada* 48°36N 83°21W **298** C3
Peterborough *S. Austral., Australia* 32°58S 138°51E **282** B3
Peterborough *Ont., Canada* 44°20N 78°20W **312** B6
Peterborough *Peterborough, U.K.* 52°35N 0°15W **169** E7
Peterborough *N.H., U.S.A.* 42°53N 71°57W **313** D13
Peterborough □ *U.K.* 52°35N 0°15W **169** E7
Peterculter *U.K.* 57°6N 2°16W **167** D6
Peterhead *U.K.* 57°31N 1°48W **167** D7
Peterhof = Petrodvorets *Russia* 59°52N 29°54E **188** C5
Peterlee *U.K.* 54°47N 1°20W **168** C6
Petermann ✿ *Australia* 24°58S 130°0E **279** E4
Petermann Bjerg *Greenland* 73°7N 28°25W **154** C8
Petermann Gletscher *Greenland* 80°30N 60°0W **154** A4
Petermann Ranges *Australia* 26°0S 130°30E **279** E5
Peter's Mine *Guyana* 6°14N 59°20W **329** B6
Petersburg = Peterborough *Australia* 32°58S 138°51E **282** B3
Petersburg *Alaska, U.S.A.* 56°48N 132°58W **303** H14
Petersburg *Ill., U.S.A.* 40°1N 89°51W **310** D7
Petersburg *Ind., U.S.A.* 38°30N 87°17W **311** F9
Petersburg *Mich., U.S.A.* 41°54N 83°43W **311** C13
Petersburg *Pa., U.S.A.* 40°34N 78°3W **312** F6
Petersburg *Va., U.S.A.* 37°14N 77°24W **309** G15
Petersburg *W. Va., U.S.A.* 39°1N 79°5W **309** F14
Petersfield *U.K.* 51°1N 0°56W **169** F7
Petershagen *Germany* 52°23N 8°58E **178** C4
Petília Policastro *Italy* 39°7N 16°48E **201** C9
Petilla de Aragón *Spain* 42°28N 1°6W **196** C3
Petit Batanga *Cameroon* 3°15N 9°54E **264** B1
Petit-Bourg *Guadeloupe* 16°11N 61°37W **322** e
Petit-Canal *Guadeloupe* 16°25N 61°31W **322** e
Petit Cul-de-Sac Marin *Guadeloupe* 16°12N 61°33W **322** e
Petit Dominique *Grenada* 12°30N 61°24W **323** q
Petit-Goâve *Haiti* 18°27N 72°51W **321** C5
Petit Lac Manicouagan *Canada* 51°25N 67°40W **299** B6
Petit Loango ⌂ *Gabon* 2°20S 9°40E **264** C1
Petit-Mécatina → *Canada* 50°40N 59°30W **299** B8
Petit-Mécatina, Î. du *Canada* 50°30N 59°25W **299** B8
Petit Piton *St. Lucia* 13°51N 61°5W **323** m
Petit Raffray *Mauritius* 20°0S 57°36E **272** e
Petit-Saguenay *Canada* 48°15N 70°4W **299** C5
Petit Saint Bernard, Col du *Italy* 45°40N 6°52E **175** C10
Petit Soufrière B. *Dominica* 15°23N 61°15W **323** k
Petitcodiac *Canada* 45°57N 65°11W **299** C6
Petite Anse *Martinique* 14°28N 61°4W **322** j
Petite-Île *Réunion* 21°20S 55°35E **272** f
Petite Martinique *Grenada* 12°31N 61°23W **323** q
Petite Rivière *Mauritius* 20°11S 57°26E **272** e
Petite Savane *Dominica* 15°15N 61°17W **323** k
Petite Terre = Pamandzi *Mayotte* 12°47S 45°16E **272** b
Petite Terre, Îles de la *Guadeloupe* 16°13N 61°9W **322** e
Petites-Anses *Guadeloupe* 15°51N 61°38W **322** e
Petitjean = Sidi Kacem *Morocco* 34°12N 5°42W **260** B3
Petitot → *Canada* 60°14N 123°29W **296** A4
Petitsikapau L. *Canada* 54°37N 66°25W **299** B6
Petlad *India* 22°30N 72°45E **242** H5
Peto *Mexico* 20°8N 88°55W **319** C7
Petone *N.Z.* 41°13S 174°53E **284** H3
Petorca *Chile* 32°15S 70°56W **334** C1
Petoskey *U.S.A.* 45°22N 84°57W **309** C11
Petra *Jordan* 30°20N 35°22E **251** H6
Petra *Spain* 39°37N 3°6E **206** B4
Petra, Ostrov *Russia* 76°15N 118°30E **215** B12
Petra Velikogo, Zaliv *Russia* 42°40N 132°0E **220** C6
Petre, Pt. *Canada* 43°50N 77°9W **312** C7
Petrel = Petrer *Spain* 38°30N 0°46W **197** G4
Petrella, Monte *Italy* 41°18N 13°40E **200** A6
Petrer *Spain* 38°30N 0°46W **197** G4
Petreto-Bicchisano *France* 41°47N 8°58E **175** G12
Petrich *Bulgaria* 41°24N 23°13E **202** E7
Petrified Forest △ *U.S.A.* 35°0N 109°30W **305** J9
Petrijanec *Croatia* 46°23N 16°17E **199** B13
Petrikov = Pyetrikaw *Belarus* 52°11N 28°29E **177** B15
Petrila *Romania* 45°29N 23°29E **183** E8
Petrillo Music Shell *Chicago, U.S.A.* **119** c2
Petrinja *Croatia* 45°28N 16°18E **199** C13
Petrodvorets *Russia* 59°52N 29°54E **188** C5
Petrograd = Sankt-Peterburg *Russia* 59°55N 30°20E **137** B1
Petrogradskaya Storona *Russia* 59°56N 30°20E **137** B2
Petrolândia *Brazil* 9°5S 38°20W **332** C4
Petrolia *Canada* 42°54N 82°9W **312** D2
Petrolina *Brazil* 9°24S 40°30W **332** C3
Petromaryevka = Pervomaysk *Ukraine* 48°10N 30°46E **189** H6
Petropavl *Kazakhstan* 54°53N 69°13E **217** B7
Petropavlovsk = Petropavl *Kazakhstan* 54°53N 69°13E **217** B7
Petropavlovsk-Kamchatskiy *Russia* 53°3N 158°43E **215** D16
Petropavlovskiy = Akhtubinsk *Russia* 48°13N 46°7E **191** F8
Petropavlovsky = Severouralsk *Russia* 60°9N 59°57E **186** B10
Petrópolis *Brazil* 22°33S 43°9W **333** F3
Petroşani *Romania* 45°28N 23°20E **183** E8
Petroupoli *Greece* 38°3N 23°40E **112** A2
Petrova Gora *Croatia* 45°15N 15°45E **199** C12
Petrovac *Montenegro* 42°13N 18°57E **202** D2
Petrovac *Serbia* 44°22N 21°26E **202** B5
Petrovaradin *Serbia* 45°16N 19°55E **182** E4
Petrovgrad = Zrenjanin *Serbia* 45°22N 20°23E **182** E5
Petrovice *Czechia* 50°2N 14°33E **135** B3
Petrovsk *Russia* 52°22N 45°19E **190** D7
Petrovsk-Port = Makhachkala *Russia* 43°0N 47°30E **191** J8
Petrovsk-Zabaykalskiy *Russia* 51°20N 108°55E **215** D11
Petrovskaya *Russia* 45°25N 37°58E **189** K9
Petrovskiy Park *Russia* 55°47N 37°34E **129** B2
Petrovsko-Razumovskoye *Russia* 55°49N 37°34E **129** B2
Petrovskoye = Svetlograd *Russia* 45°25N 42°58E **191** H6
Petrovsky Stadium *Saint Petersburg, Russia* 59°57N 30°19E **137** B1
Petrovsky Zavod = Petrovsk-Zabaykalskiy *Russia* 51°20N 108°55E **215** D11
Petrozavodsk *Russia* 61°41N 34°20E **188** B8
Petrus Steyn *S. Africa* 27°38S 28°8E **271** C4
Petrusburg *S. Africa* 29°4S 25°26E **270** C4
Petsamo = Pechenga *Russia* 69°29N 31°4E **160** B24
Pettycur *U.K.* 56°4N 3°10W **121** A2
Petukhovo *Russia* 55°6N 67°58E **217** A7
Petuna = Fuyu *China* 45°12N 124°43E **227** B13
Petzeck *Austria* 46°57N 12°48E **180** E5
Peumo *Chile* 34°21S 71°12W **334** C1
Peureulak *Indonesia* 4°48N 97°45E **234** B1
Peusangan → *Indonesia* 5°16N 96°51E **234** A1
Peutie *Belgium* 50°56N 4°27E **116** A2
Pevek *Russia* 69°41N 171°19E **215** C18
Pevely *U.S.A.* 38°17N 90°24W **310** F6
Peveragno *Italy* 44°20N 7°37E **198** D4
Peyrehorade *France* 43°34N 1°7W **174** E2
Peyruis *France* 44°1N 5°56E **175** D9
Pézenas *France* 43°28N 3°24E **174** E7
Pezinok *Slovakia* 48°17N 17°17E **181** C10
Pfaffenhofen *Germany* 48°31N 11°31E **179** G7
Pfälzerwald ⌂ *Germany* 49°18N 9°55E **179** F5
Pfarrkirchen *Germany* 48°25N 12°56E **179** G8
Pfaueninsel *Germany* 52°26N 13°7E **115** B1
Pfeffenhausen *Germany* 48°39N 11°58E **179** G7
Pforzheim *Germany* 48°52N 8°41E **179** G4
Pfullendorf *Germany* 47°55N 9°15E **179** H5
Pfungstadt *Germany* 49°48N 8°35E **179** F4
Pha Taem △ *Thailand* 15°32N 105°30E **236** E5
Phaestos *Greece* 35°2N 24°50E **207** E5
Phagwara *India* 31°10N 75°40E **242** D6
Phala *Botswana* 23°45S 26°50E **270** B4
Phalaborwa *S. Africa* 23°57S 31°7E **271** B5
Phalera = Phulera *India* 26°52N 75°16E **242** F6
Phalodi *India* 27°12N 72°24E **242** F5
Phalsbourg *France* 48°46N 7°15E **173** D14
Phaltan *India* 17°59N 74°26E **244** F2
Phaluai, Ko *Thailand* 9°32N 99°41E **237** b
Phan *Thailand* 19°28N 99°43E **236** C2
Phan Rang -Thap Cham *Vietnam* 11°34N 109°0E **237** G7
Phan Ri Cua *Vietnam* 11°16N 108°40E **237** G7
Phan Si Pan *Vietnam* 22°18N 103°46E **236** A4
Phan Thiet *Vietnam* 11°1N 108°9E **237** G7
Phan Thiet, Vinh *Vietnam* 10°53N 108°5E **237** G7
Phan Wa, Laem *Thailand* 7°47N 98°25E **237** a
Phanae *Greece* 38°8N 25°57E **205** C7
Phanat Nikhom *Thailand* 13°27N 101°11E **236** F3
Phangan, Ko *Thailand* 9°45N 100°0E **237** H3
Phangnga *Thailand* 8°28N 98°30E **237** H2
Phangnga, Ao *Thailand* 8°16N 98°33E **237** a
Phanom Sarakham *Thailand* 13°45N 101°21E **236** F3
Phaphund *India* 26°36N 79°28E **243** F8
Pharenda *India* 27°5N 83°17E **243** F10
Pharr *U.S.A.* 26°12N 98°11W **314** H5
Phatthalung *Thailand* 7°39N 100°6E **237** J3
Phawngpui Blue Mountain △ *India* 22°45N 93°5E **241** D4
Phaya Thai *Thailand* 13°45N 100°37E **113** B2
Phayam, Ko *Thailand* 9°44N 98°25E **237** H2
Phayao *Thailand* 19°11N 99°55E **236** C2
Phelps *U.S.A.* 42°58N 77°3W **312** D7
Phelps L. *Canada* 59°15N 103°15W **297** B8
Phenix City *U.S.A.* 32°28N 85°1W **316** C4
Phet Buri = Phetchaburi *Thailand* 13°1N 99°55E **236** F2
Phetchabun *Thailand* 16°25N 101°8E **236** D3
Phetchabun, Thiu Khao *Thailand* 16°0N 101°20E **236** E3
Phetchaburi *Thailand* 13°1N 99°55E **236** F2
Phi Phi, Ko *Thailand* 7°45N 98°46E **237** J2
Phiafay *Laos* 14°48N 106°0E **236** E6
Phibun Mangsahan *Thailand* 15°14N 105°14E **236** E5
Phichai *Thailand* 17°22N 100°10E **236** D3
Phichit *Thailand* 16°26N 100°22E **236** D3
Phihai *Pakistan* 24°50N 67°8E **123** A2
Philadelphia *Miss., U.S.A.* 32°46N 89°7W **315** E10
Philadelphia *N.Y., U.S.A.* 44°9N 75°43W **313** B9
Philadelphia *Pa., U.S.A.* 39°57N 75°9W **313** G9
Philadelphia Int. ✈ **(PHL)** *U.S.A.* 39°51N 75°18W **313** G9
Philip *U.S.A.* 44°2N 101°40W **308** C3
Philip Smith Mts. *U.S.A.* 68°0N 148°0W **303** C10
Philipi *Greece* 41°1N 24°16E **203** E8
Philippeville = Skikda *Algeria* 36°50N 6°58E **261** A6
Philippeville *Belgium* 50°12N 4°33E **170** D4
Philippi *U.S.A.* 39°9N 80°3W **309** F13
Philippi L. *Australia* 24°20S 138°55E **280** C2
Philippine Basin *Pac. Oc.* 17°0N 132°0E **288** F5
Philippine Sea *Pac. Oc.* 18°0N 125°0E **288** F4
Philippine Trench = Mindanao Trench *Pac. Oc.* 12°0N 126°6E **232** E5
Philippines ■ *Asia* 12°0N 123°0E **232** E4
Philippolis *S. Africa* 30°15S 25°16E **270** D4
Philippopolis = Plovdiv *Bulgaria* 42°8N 24°44E **203** D8
Philipsburg *Qué., Canada* 45°2N 73°5W **313** A11
Philipsburg *St.-Maarten* 18°3N 63°5W **322** a
Philipsburg *Mont., U.S.A.* 46°20N 113°18W **304** C7
Philipsburg *Pa., U.S.A.* 40°54N 78°13W **312** F6
Philipstown = Daingean *Ireland* 53°18N 7°17W **166** C4
Philipstown *S. Africa* 30°28S 24°30E **270** D3
Phillip B. *Australia* 33°58S 151°14E **139** B2
Phillip I. *Australia* 38°30S 145°12E **283** E6
Phillips *U.S.A.* 45°42N 90°24W **308** C8
Phillipsburg *Ga., U.S.A.* 31°25N 83°30W **316** D6
Phillipsburg *Kans., U.S.A.* 39°45N 99°19W **308** F4
Phillipsburg *N.J., U.S.A.* 40°42N 75°12W **313** F9
Philmont *U.S.A.* 42°15N 73°39W **313** D11
Philomath *Ga., U.S.A.* 33°44N 82°59W **316** B7
Philomath *Oreg., U.S.A.* 44°32N 123°22W **304** D2
Phimai *Thailand* 15°13N 102°30E **236** E4
Phitsanulok *Thailand* 16°50N 100°12E **236** D3
Phnom Kulen △ *Cambodia* 13°38N 104°15E **236** F5
Phnom Penh *Cambodia* 11°33N 104°55E **237** G5
Phnum Penh = Phnom Penh *Cambodia* 11°33N 104°55E **237** G5
Pho, Laem *Thailand* 6°55N 101°19E **237** J3
Phocis = Fokida *Greece* 38°30N 22°15E **204** C4
Phoenicia *U.S.A.* 42°5N 74°14W **313** D10
Phoenix *Mauritius* 20°17S 57°30E **272** e
Phoenix *Ariz., U.S.A.* 33°26N 112°4W **305** K7
Phoenix *Ill., U.S.A.* 41°36N 87°37W **119** D3
Phoenix *N.Y., U.S.A.* 43°14N 76°18W **313** C8
Phoenix Is. *Kiribati* 3°30S 172°0W **277** A16
Phoenix Sky Harbour Int. ✈ **(PHX)** *U.S.A.* 33°26N 112°5W **305** K7
Phoenixville *U.S.A.* 40°8N 75°31W **313** F9
Phon *Thailand* 15°49N 102°36E **236** E4
Phong → *Thailand* 16°23N 102°56E **236** D4
Phong Nha -Ke Bang △ *Vietnam* 17°30N 106°10E **236** D6
Phong Saly *Laos* 21°42N 102°9E **228** G4
Phong Tho *Vietnam* 22°32N 103°21E **236** A4
Phonsavan *Laos* 19°27N 103°10E **236** C4
Phonum *Thailand* 8°49N 98°48E **237** H2
Phosphate Hill *Australia* 21°53S 139°58E **280** C2
Photharam *Thailand* 13°41N 99°51E **236** F2
Phra Kaeo *Bangkok, Thailand* **113** b1
Phra Khanong *Thailand* 13°40N 100°36E **113** B2
Phra Nakhon *Thailand* 13°45N 100°30E **113** B2
Phra Nakhon Si Ayutthaya *Thailand* 14°25N 100°30E **236** E3
Phra Pradaeng *Thailand* 13°39N 100°33E **113** C2
Phra Thong, Ko *Thailand* 9°5N 98°17E **237** H2
Phrae *Thailand* 18°7N 100°9E **236** C3
Phrom Phiram *Thailand* 17°2N 100°12E **236** D3
Phrom Thep, Laem *Thailand* 7°45N 98°19E **237** a
Phrygia *Turkey* 38°40N 30°0E **212** C4
Phthiotis = Fthiotida *Greece* 38°50N 22°25E **204** C4
Phu Bia *Laos* 19°10N 103°0E **236** C4
Phu Chong -Na Yoi △ *Thailand* 14°25N 105°30E **236** E5
Phu Hin Rong Kla △ *Thailand* 17°0N 100°59E **236** D3
Phu Kao -Phu Phan Kham △ *Thailand* 16°53N 102°31E **236** D4
Phu Kradung △ *Thailand* 17°2N 101°44E **236** D3
Phu Loi *Laos* 20°14N 103°14E **236** B4
Phu Luang △ *Thailand* 17°15N 101°29E **236** D3
Phu Ly *Vietnam* 20°35N 105°50E **228** G5
Phu My *Vietnam* 14°15N 109°5E **236** E7
Phu Pha Man △ *Thailand* 16°44N 101°50E **236** D3
Phu Phan △ *Thailand* 17°0N 103°56E **236** D4
Phu Quoc, Dao *Vietnam* 10°20N 104°0E **237** G4
Phu Sa Dok Bua △ *Thailand* 16°11N 104°45E **236** D5
Phu Sang △ *Thailand* 19°35N 100°19E **236** C3
Phu Tho *Vietnam* 21°24N 105°13E **228** G5
Phu Wiang △ *Thailand* 16°39N 102°23E **236** D4
Phuc Yen *Vietnam* 21°16N 105°45E **228** G5
Phuket *Thailand* 7°53N 98°24E **237** a
Phuket, Ko *Thailand* 8°0N 98°22E **237** a
Phul *India* 30°19N 75°14E **242** D6
Phulad *India* 25°38N 73°49E **242** G5
Phulbani *India* 20°28N 84°14E **244** D7
Phulbari *India* 25°55N 90°2E **241** C3
Phulchari *Bangla.* 25°11N 89°37E **241** C2
Phulera *India* 26°52N 75°16E **242** F6
Phulpur *India* 25°31N 82°49E **243** G10
Phunphin *Thailand* 9°7N 99°12E **237** H2
Phuntsholing *Bhutan* 26°51N 89°23E **243** F13
Phuphrabat *Thailand* 17°40N 102°45E **236** D4
Phuthaditjhaba *S. Africa* 28°29S 28°48E **271** C4
Phyu = Pyu *Myanmar* 18°30N 96°28E **241** F6
Pia ✿ *Australia* 27°7S 116°23E **279** E2
Piaçabuçu *Brazil* 10°24S 36°25W **332** D4
Piacenza *Italy* 45°1N 9°40E **198** C6
Piai, Tanjung *Malaysia* 1°17N 103°30E **237** d
Piako → *N.Z.* 37°12S 175°30E **284** D4
Pian Cr. → *Australia* 30°2S 148°12E **281** E4
Pian-Upe ⌂ *Uganda* 1°44N 34°20E **268** B3
Piana *France* 42°15N 8°34E **175** F12
Pianella *Italy* 42°24N 14°2E **199** F11
Piangil *Australia* 35°5S 143°20E **282** C5
Pianosa *Puglia, Italy* 42°12N 15°44E **199** F12
Pianosa *Toscana, Italy* 42°35N 10°5E **198** F7
Piao'ertun *China* 41°50N 123°47E **227** D12
Piapot *Canada* 49°59N 109°8W **297** D7
Piarco *Trin. & Tob.* 10°35N 61°20W **323** t
Piarco Int. ✈ **(POS)** *Trin. & Tob.* 10°36N 61°20W **323** t
Pias *Portugal* 38°1N 7°29W **195** G3
Piaseczno *Poland* 52°5N 21°2E **185** F8
Piaski *Poland* 51°8N 22°52E **185** G9
Piastów *Poland* 52°12N 20°48E **185** F7
Piatã *Brazil* 13°9S 41°48W **333** D3
Piatra *Romania* 43°51N 25°9E **183** G10
Piatra Craiului △ *Romania* 45°30N 25°12E **183** E10
Piatra Neamţ *Romania* 46°56N 26°21E **183** D11
Piatra Olt *Romania* 44°22N 24°16E **183** F9
Piauí □ *Brazil* 7°0S 43°0W **332** C3
Piauí → *Brazil* 6°38S 42°42W **332** C3
Piave → *Italy* 45°32N 12°44E **199** C9
Piazza Ármerina *Italy* 37°21N 14°20E **201** E7
Pibor → *South Sudan* 7°35N 33°0E **257** F3
Pibor Post *South Sudan* 6°47N 33°3E **257** F3
Pic St-Loup *France* 43°47N 3°48E **174** E7
Pica *Chile* 20°35S 69°25W **330** E4
Picardie *France* 49°50N 3°0E **171** B5
Picardie, Plaine de *France* 50°0N 2°0E **173** C9
Picardy = Picardie *France* 49°50N 3°0E **171** B5
Picasso, Museu *Barcelona, Spain* **114** c2
Picayune *U.S.A.* 30°32N 89°41W **315** F10
Piccadilly *London, U.K.* **125** b3
Picerno *Italy* 40°38N 15°38E **201** B8
Pichhor *India* 25°58N 78°20E **243** G8
Pichilemu *Chile* 34°22S 72°0W **334** C1
Pichincha, □ *Ecuador* 0°10S 78°40W **328** D2
Pichor *India* 25°11N 78°11E **242** G8
Pickerel L. *Canada* 48°40N 91°25W **298** C1
Pickering *U.K.* 54°15N 0°46W **168** C7
Pickering, Vale of *U.K.* 54°14N 0°45W **168** C7
Pickle Lake *Canada* 51°30N 90°12W **298** B1
Pickwick L. *U.S.A.* 35°4N 88°15W **315** D10
Picnic B. *Hong Kong, China* 22°13N 114°8E **122** B2
Pico *Azores* 38°28N 28°20W **153** d1
Pico, Ponta do *Azores* 38°28N 28°25W **153** d1
Pico Bonito △ *Honduras* 15°34N 86°48W **320** C2
Pico da Neblina △ *Brazil* 0°19N 66°28W **328** C4
Pico Rivera *U.S.A.* 33°59N 118°5W **126** C4
Pico Truncado *Argentina* 46°40S 68°0W **336** C3
Picos = Colinas *Brazil* 6°0S 44°10W **332** C3
Picos *Brazil* 7°5S 41°28W **332** C3
Picos, Pta. dos *Spain* 41°52N 8°53W **194** D2
Picos de Europa △ *Spain* 43°14N 4°59W **194** B6
Picota *Peru* 6°54S 76°24W **330** B2
Picton *N.S.W., Australia* 34°12S 150°34E **283** C9
Picton *Ont., Canada* 44°1N 77°9W **312** B7
Picton *N.Z.* 41°18S 174°3E **285** B9
Picton, I. *Chile* 55°2S 66°57W **336** E3
Pictou *Canada* 45°41N 62°42W **299** C7
Picture Butte *Canada* 49°55N 112°45W **296** D6
Pictured Rocks ⌂ *U.S.A.* 46°30N 86°30W **308** B10
Picuí *Brazil* 6°31S 36°21W **332** C4
Picún Leufú *Argentina* 39°30S 69°5W **336** A3
Pidbuzh *Ukraine* 49°19N 23°14E **185** J10
Pidurutalagala *Sri Lanka* 7°10N 80°50E **245** L5
Piechowice *Poland* 50°51N 15°36E **185** H2
Piedade *Rio de J., Brazil* 22°52S 43°18W **135** B1
Piedade *Lisboa, Portugal* 38°49N 9°16W **126** A1
Piedade, Cova da *Portugal* 38°40N 9°8W **126** A2
Piedecuesta *Colombia* 6°59N 73°3W **328** B3
Piedimonte Matese *Italy* 41°22N 14°22E **201** A7
Piedmont = Piemonte □ *Italy* 45°0N 8°0E **198** D5
Piedmont *Ala., U.S.A.* 33°55N 85°37W **316** B4
Piedmont *S.C., U.S.A.* 34°42N 82°28W **292** F11
Piedmont Park *U.S.A.* 33°47N 84°22W **113** B2
Piedra → *Spain* 41°18N 1°47W **196** D3
Piedra del Águila *Argentina* 40°2S 70°4W **336** B2
Piedra del Águila, Embalse *Argentina* 40°15S 70°4W **336** B2
Piedra Lais *Venezuela* 3°10N 65°50W **328** C4
Piedrabuena *Spain* 39°0N 4°10W **195** G6
Piedrahita *Spain* 40°28N 5°23W **194** E5
Piedralaves *Spain* 40°19N 4°42W **194** E6
Piedras, R. de las → *Peru* 12°30S 69°15W **330** C4
Piedras Blancas *Spain* 43°33N 5°58W **194** B5
Piedras Negras *Mexico* 28°42N 100°31W **318** B4
Piedras Pt. *Phil.* 10°11N 118°48E **233** F2
Piekar = Piekary Śląskie *Poland* 50°24N 18°57E **185** H5
Piekary Śląskie *Poland* 50°24N 18°57E **185** H5
Pieksämäki *Finland* 62°18N 27°10E **188** A4
Pielinen *Finland* 63°15N 29°40E **160** E23
Pieljekaise △ *Sweden* 66°20N 16°45E **160** C17
Piemonte □ *Italy* 45°0N 8°0E **198** D5
Pienaarsrivier *S. Africa* 25°15S 28°18E **271** C4
Pieniężno *Poland* 54°14N 20°8E **184** D7
Pieninský △ *Europe* 49°25N 20°28E **181** B13
Pieńsk *Poland* 51°16N 15°2E **185** G2
Pienza *Italy* 43°4N 11°40E **199** E8
Piercefield *U.S.A.* 44°13N 74°35W **313** B10
Pierceland *Canada* 54°20N 109°46W **297** C7
Pieria *Greece* 40°13N 22°25E **202** F6
Pierpont *U.S.A.* 41°45N 80°34W **312** E4
Pierre *U.S.A.* 44°22N 100°21W **308** C3
Pierre-Buffière *France* 45°41N 1°22E **174** C5
Pierre-de-Bresse *France* 46°54N 5°13E **173** F12
Pierre Elliott Trudeau Int. ✈ **(YUL)** *Canada* 45°28N 73°44W **130** B1
Pierrefonds *Canada* 45°29N 73°51W **313** A11
Pierrefontaine-les-Varans *France* 47°14N 6°32E **173** E13
Pierrefort *France* 44°55N 2°50E **174** D6
Pierrelatte *France* 44°23N 4°43E **175** D8
Pierson *U.S.A.* 29°14N 81°28W **317** F8
Piešt'any *Slovakia* 48°38N 17°55E **181** C10
Piesting → *Austria* 48°6N 16°40E **181** C9
Pieszyce *Poland* 50°43N 16°33E **185** H3
Piet Retief *S. Africa* 27°1S 30°50E **271** C5
Pietarsaari *Finland* 63°40N 22°43E **160** E20
Pieter Both *Mauritius* 20°11S 57°32E **272** e
Pietermaritzburg *S. Africa* 29°35S 30°25E **271** C5
Pietersburg = Polokwane *S. Africa* 23°54S 29°25E **271** B4
Pietragalla *Italy* 40°45N 15°53E **201** B8
Pietralata *Italy* 41°55N 12°33E **136** B2
Pietrasanta *Italy* 43°57N 10°14E **198** E7
Pietroşiţa *Romania* 45°11N 25°26E **183** E10
Pietrosul, Vf. *Maramureş, Romania* 47°35N 24°43E **183** C9
Pietrosul, Vf. *Suceava, Romania* 47°12N 25°18E **183** C10
Pieve di Cadore *Italy* 46°26N 12°22E **199** B9
Pieve di Teco *Italy* 44°3N 7°56E **198** D4
Pievepélago *Italy* 44°12N 10°37E **198** D7
Pigaditsa *Greece* 39°59N 21°23E **202** G5
Pigeon *Guadeloupe* 16°9N 61°46W **322** e
Pigeon I. *India* 14°2N 74°20E **245** G2
Pigeon I. *St. Lucia* 14°6N 60°58W **323** m
Pigeon L. *Canada* 44°27N 78°30W **312** B6
Piges *Greece* 39°17N 21°25E **204** B3
Piggott *U.S.A.* 36°23N 90°11W **315** C9
Pigna *Italy* 43°56N 7°40E **198** E4
Pigüe *Argentina* 37°36S 62°25W **334** D3
Piha *N.Z.* 36°57S 174°28E **284** C3
Pihani *India* 27°36N 80°15E **243** F9
Pihlajamäki *Finland* 60°14N 24°58E **121** B2
Pihlajasaari *Finland* 60°8N 24°55E **121** C2
Pihlajavesi *Finland* 61°45N 28°45E **188** B5
Pijijiapan *Mexico* 15°42N 93°14W **319** D6
Pikalevo *Russia* 59°37N 34°9E **188** C8
Pikangikum *Canada* 51°49N 94°0W **297** C10
Pikes Peak *U.S.A.* 38°50N 105°3W **304** G11
Piketberg *S. Africa* 32°55S 18°40E **270** D2
Pikeville *U.S.A.* 37°29N 82°31W **309** G12
Pikit *Phil.* 7°4N 124°41E **233** H5
Pikou *China* 39°18N 122°22E **227** E12
Pikounda *Congo* 0°30N 16°44E **264** B3
Pikwitonei *Canada* 55°35N 97°9W **297** B9
Piła *Poland* 53°10N 16°48E **185** E3
Pila *Spain* 38°16N 1°11W **197** G3
Pilanesberg △ *S. Africa* 25°15S 27°4E **270** C4
Pilani *India* 28°22N 75°33E **242** E6
Pilar *Brazil* 9°36S 35°56W **332** C4
Pilar *Paraguay* 26°50S 58°20W **334** B4
Pilar *Capiz, Phil.* 11°29N 123°0E **233** F4
Pilar *Sorsogon, Phil.* 12°56N 123°40E **232** E4
Pilar de la Horadada *Spain* 37°52N 0°47W **197** H4
Pilares *Brazil* 22°52S 43°18W **135** B1
Pilas Group *Phil.* 6°45N 121°35E **233** H3
Pilat, Dune du *France* 44°35N 1°13W **174** D2
Pilat ⌂ *France* 45°20N 4°30E **175** C8
Pilawa *Poland* 51°57N 21°32E **185** G8
Pilaya → *Bolivia* 20°55S 64°4W **331** E5
Pilbara *Australia* 21°15S 118°16E **278** D2
Pilcomaya → *Paraguay* 25°21S 57°42W **334** B4
Pilea *Greece* 40°32N 22°59E **202** F6
Pilgrim's Rest *S. Africa* 24°55S 30°44E **271** B5
Pilgrimstad *Sweden* 62°57N 15°2E **162** B9
Pili *Greece* 36°50N 27°15E **205** E9
Pili *Phil.* 13°33N 123°19E **232** E4
Pilibhit *India* 28°40N 79°50E **243** E8
Pilica → *Poland* 51°52N 21°17E **185** G8
Pilio, Oros *Greece* 39°27N 23°3E **204** B5
Pilipinas = Philippines ■ *Asia* 12°0N 123°0E **232** E4
Pilis *Hungary* 47°17N 19°35E **182** C4
Pilisvörösvár *Hungary* 47°38N 18°56E **182** C3
Pilkhawa *India* 28°43N 77°42E **242** E7
Pillar B. *Ascension I.* 7°59S 14°21W **153** g
Pillaro *Ecuador* 1°10S 78°32W **328** D2
Pillau = Baltiysk *Russia* 54°41N 19°58E **184** D6
Pilliga *Australia* 30°21S 148°54E **281** E4
Pilos *Greece* 36°55N 21°42E **204** E3
Pilot Grove *U.S.A.* 38°53N 92°55W **310** F4
Pilot Mound *Canada* 49°15N 98°54W **297** D9
Pilot Point *Alaska, U.S.A.* 57°34N 157°35W **303** H8
Pilot Point *Tex., U.S.A.* 33°24N 96°58W **314** E6
Pilot Rock *U.S.A.* 45°29N 118°50W **304** D4
Pilot Station *U.S.A.* 61°56N 162°53W **303** F7
Pilote → *Martinique* 14°28N 60°55W **322** j
Pilsen = Pilzno *Poland* 49°58N 21°16E **185** J8

Pilsen = Plzeň Czechia 49°45N 13°22E 180 B6
Pilštanj Slovenia 46°8N 15°39E 199 B12
Piltene Latvia 57°13N 21°40E 184 A8
Pilton U.K. 55°58N 3°13W 121 B2
Pilzno Poland 49°58N 21°16E 185 J8
Pima U.S.A. 32°54N 109°50W 305 K9
Pimba Australia 31°18S 136°46E 282 A2
Pimenta Bueno Brazil 11°35S 61°10W 331 C5
Pimenteiras Brazil 13°40S 60°58W 331 C5
Pimentel Peru 6°45S 79°55W 330 B2
Pimlico London, U.K. 125 c3
Pimpri Chinchwad India 18°37N 73°47E 244 E1
Pimu Dem. Rep. of the Congo 1°42N 20°58E 264 B4
Pin Valley △ India 31°50N 77°50E 242 D7
Pina de Ebro Spain 41°29N 0°33W 196 D4
Pinamalayan Phil. 13°2N 121°29E 232 E3
Pinang Malaysia 5°25N 100°15E 237 c
Pinang □ Malaysia 5°20N 100°20E 237 K3
Pinar, C. des Spain 39°53N 3°12E 206 B4
Pinar del Río Cuba 22°26N 83°40W 320 B3
Pınarbaşı Çanakkale, Turkey 39°53N 26°15E 205 B8
Pınarbaşı Kayseri, Turkey 38°43N 36°23E 212 C7
Pınarhisar Turkey 41°37N 27°30E 203 E11
Pinatubo, Mt. Phil. 15°8N 120°21E 232 D3
Pinawa Canada 50°9N 95°50W 297 C9
Pincehely Hungary 46°41N 18°27E 182 D3
Pinchang China 31°36N 107°3E 228 B6
Pincher Creek Canada 49°30N 113°57W 296 D6
Pinchi L. Canada 54°38N 124°30W 296 C4
Pinckard U.S.A. 31°19N 85°33W 316 D4
Pinckneyville U.S.A. 38°5N 89°23W 310 F7
Pińczów Poland 50°32N 20°32E 185 H7
Pind Dadan Khan Pakistan 32°36N 73°7E 217 F8
Pindar Australia 28°30S 115°47E 279 E2
Pindaré → Brazil 3°17S 44°47W 332 B3
Pindaré-Mirim Brazil 3°37S 45°21W 332 B2
Pindera Downs ✪ Australia 29°24S 142°37E 281 A3
Pindi Gheb Pakistan 33°14N 72°21E 242 C5
Pindiga Nigeria 9°58N 10°53E 263 D7
Pindobal Brazil 3°16S 48°25W 332 B2
Pindos △ Greece 39°52N 21°11E 204 B3
Pindos Oros Greece 40°0N 21°0E 204 B3
Pindus Mts. = Pindos Oros Greece 40°0N 21°0E 204 B3
Pine → B.C., Canada 56°8N 120°43W 296 B4
Pine → Sask., Canada 58°50N 105°38W 297 B7
Pine Bluff U.S.A. 34°13N 92°1W 314 D8
Pine Bluffs U.S.A. 41°11N 104°4W 304 F11
Pine Castle U.S.A. 28°28N 81°22W 133 B2
Pine City U.S.A. 45°50N 92°59W 308 C7
Pine Cr. → U.S.A. 41°10N 77°16W 312 E7
Pine Creek Australia 13°50S 131°50E 278 B5
Pine Falls Canada 50°34N 96°11W 297 C9
Pine Flat L. U.S.A. 36°50N 119°20W 306 J7
Pine Grove Ont., Canada 43°47N 79°34W 141 A1
Pine Grove Pa., U.S.A. 40°33N 76°23W 313 F8
Pine Hill Australia 23°38S 146°57E 280 C4
Pine Hills U.S.A. 28°33N 81°27W 133 A2
Pine I. U.S.A. 26°36N 82°7W 317 J7
Pine Island U.S.A. 26°5N 80°16W 129 B1
Pine Island Glacier Antarctica 76°0S 100°0W 151 D15
Pine Level U.S.A. 32°4N 86°4W 316 C3
Pine Mountain U.S.A. 32°49N 84°51W 316 C5
Pine Pass Canada 55°25N 122°42W 296 B4
Pine Ridge N.S.W., Australia 31°30S 150°28E 283 A9
Pine Ridge S. Dak., U.S.A. 43°2N 102°33W 308 D2
Pine River Man., Canada 51°45N 100°30W 297 C8
Pine River Minn., U.S.A. 46°43N 94°24W 308 B6
Pine Valley U.S.A. 32°50N 116°32W 307 N10
Pinecrest Calif., U.S.A. 38°12N 120°1W 306 G6
Pinecrest Fla., U.S.A. 25°40N 80°18W 129 D1
Pineda de Mar Spain 41°37N 2°42E 196 D7
Pinedale Calif., U.S.A. 36°50N 119°48W 306 J7
Pinedale Wyo., U.S.A. 42°52N 109°52W 304 E9
Pinega → Russia 64°30N 44°19E 186 B8
Pinehouse L. Canada 55°32N 106°35W 297 B7
Pineimuta → Canada 52°8N 88°33W 298 B1
Pinellas Park U.S.A. 27°50N 82°41W 317 H7
Pinerolo Italy 44°53N 7°21E 198 D4
Pines, Akra Greece 40°5N 24°20E 203 F8
Pineto Italy 42°36N 14°4E 199 F11
Pinetop-Lakeside U.S.A. 34°9N 109°58W 305 J9
Pinetown S. Africa 29°48S 30°54E 271 C5
Pinetta U.S.A. 30°36N 83°21W 316 E6
Pineview U.S.A. 32°7N 83°30W 316 C6
Pineville La., U.S.A. 31°19N 92°26W 314 F8
Pineville S.C., U.S.A. 33°26N 80°1W 316 B9
Pinewood U.S.A. 33°44N 80°27W 316 B9
Pinewood Park U.S.A. 25°52N 80°13W 129 C2
Piney France 48°22N 4°21E 173 D11
Ping → Thailand 15°42N 100°9E 236 E3
Pingaring Australia 32°40S 118°32E 279 F2
Pingba China 26°23N 106°12E 228 D6
Pingbian China 23°0N 103°45E 228 F4
Pingchuan China 27°35N 101°55E 228 D3
Pingding China 37°47N 113°38E 226 F7
Pingdingshan China 33°43N 113°27E 226 H7
Pingdong = P'ingtung Taiwan 22°38N 120°30E 225 D2
Pingdu China 36°42N 119°59E 227 F10
Pingelly Australia 32°32S 117°5E 279 F2
Pingguo China 23°19N 107°36E 228 F6
Pinghe China 24°17N 117°21E 229 E11
Pinghu China 30°40N 121°2E 229 B13
Pingjiang China 28°45N 113°36E 229 C9
Pingle China 24°40N 110°40E 229 E8
Pingli China 32°27N 109°22E 228 A7
Pingliang China 35°35N 106°31E 226 G4
Pinglin Taiwan 24°56N 121°42E 225 B3
Pinglu China 39°31N 112°30E 226 E7
Pingluo China 38°52N 106°30E 226 E4
Pingnan Fujian, China 26°55N 119°0E 229 D12
Pingnan Guangxi Zhuangzu, China 23°33N 110°22E 229 F8
Pingo Gabon 1°19S 10°55E 264 C2
Pingquan China 41°1N 118°37E 227 D10
Pingrup Australia 33°32S 118°29E 279 F2
Pingshan China 28°39N 104°3E 228 C5
Pingtan China 25°31N 119°47E 229 E12
Pingtang China 25°49N 107°17E 228 E6
P'ingtung Taiwan 22°38N 120°30E 225 D2
P'ingtung □ Taiwan 22°30N 120°40E 225 D2
Pingwu China 32°25N 104°30E 226 H3
Pingxiang Guangxi Zhuangzu, China 22°6N 106°46E 228 F6
Pingxiang Jiangxi, China 27°43N 113°48E 229 D9
Pingyao China 37°12N 112°10E 226 F7
Pingyi China 35°30N 117°35E 227 G9
Pingyin China 36°20N 116°25E 226 F9
Pingyuan Guangdong, China 24°37N 115°57E 229 E10
Pingyuan Shandong, China 37°10N 116°22E 226 F9
Pingyuanjie China 23°45N 103°48E 228 F4
Pingzhou China 23°1N 113°11E 121 B2
Pinhal Novo Portugal 38°38N 8°55W 195 G2
Pinheiro Brazil 2°31S 45°5W 332 B2
Pinheiro Machado Brazil 31°34S 53°23W 335 C5
Pinheiros → Brazil 23°37S 46°44W 137 B1
Pinhel Portugal 40°50N 7°1W 194 E3
Pinhuá → Brazil 6°21S 65°0W 331 B5
Pini Indonesia 0°10N 98°40E 234 B1
Pinios → Ilia, Greece 37°48N 21°20E 204 D3
Pinios → Trikala, Greece 39°55N 22°41E 204 B4
Pinjarra Australia 32°37S 115°52E 279 F2
Pinjrapur Pakistan 24°53N 67°4E 123 A2
Pink Beach Bonaire 12°5N 68°17W 322 h
Pink Mountain Canada 57°3N 122°52W 296 B4
Pinkafeld Austria 47°22N 16°9E 181 D9
Pinlaung Myanmar 20°8N 96°47E 241 E6
Pinlebu Myanmar 24°5N 95°22E 241 C5
Pinnacle Is. = Senkaku-Shotō E. China Sea 25°45N 123°30E 221 M1
Pinnacles △ U.S.A. 36°25N 121°12W 306 J5
Pinnaroo Australia 35°17S 140°53E 282 C4
Pinneberg Germany 53°40N 9°48E 178 B5
Pinner U.K. 51°35N 0°22W 125 A1
Pinner Green U.K. 51°35N 0°23W 125 A1
Pino Hachado, Paso S. Amer. 38°39S 70°54W 336 A2
Pinon Hills U.S.A. 34°26N 117°39W 307 L9
Pinos Mexico 22°18N 101°34W 318 C4
Pinos, Mt. U.S.A. 34°49N 119°8W 307 L7
Pinos Pt. U.S.A. 36°38N 121°57W 305 H3
Pinos Puente Spain 37°15N 3°45W 195 H7
Pinrang Indonesia 3°46S 119°41E 235 C5
Pins, Î. des N. Cal. 22°37S 167°30E 288 d
Pins, Pte. aux Canada 42°15N 81°51W 312 D3
Pinsk Belarus 52°10N 26°1E 177 B14
Pinta, Canal de Ecuador 0°27N 90°38W 330 a
Pinta, I. Ecuador 0°35N 90°44W 330 a
Pintados Chile 20°35S 69°40W 330 E4
Pinturas → Argentina 46°30S 70°20W 336 C2
Pintuyan Phil. 9°57N 125°15E 233 G5
Pinukpuk Phil. 17°35N 121°22E 232 C3
Pinyang China 27°42N 120°31E 229 D13
Pinyug Russia 60°5N 48°0E 186 B8
Pio Duran Phil. 13°2N 123°25E 232 E4
Pio V. Corpuz Phil. 11°55N 124°2E 233 F5
Pio XII Brazil 3°53S 45°17W 332 B2
Pioche U.S.A. 37°56N 114°27W 305 H6
Pioltello Italy 45°30N 9°19E 128 A2
Piombino Italy 42°55N 10°32E 198 F7
Piombino, Canale di Italy 42°53N 10°30E 198 F7
Pioner, Ostrov Russia 79°50N 92°0E 215 B10
Pionerskiy Russia 54°56N 20°14E 184 D7
Pionki Poland 51°29N 21°28E 185 G8
Piopiotaki = Milford Sd. N.Z. 44°41S 167°47E 285 E2
Piorini → Brazil 3°23S 63°30W 329 D5
Piorini, L. Brazil 3°15S 62°35W 329 D5
Piotrków Trybunalski Poland 51°23N 19°43E 185 G6
Piove di Sacco Italy 45°18N 12°2E 199 C9
Pīp Iran 26°45N 60°10E 247 E9
Pipar India 26°25N 73°31E 242 F5
Pipar Road India 26°27N 73°27E 242 F5
Piparia Mad. P., India 22°45N 78°23E 242 H8
Piparia Mad. P., India 21°49N 77°37E 242 J7
Piparo Trin. & Tob. 10°20N 61°20W 323 t
Pipas Angola 14°57S 12°11E 265 E2
Piperi Greece 39°20N 24°19E 204 B6
Piperno = Priverno Italy 41°28N 13°11E 200 A6
Pipestone U.S.A. 44°0N 96°19W 308 D5
Pipestone → Canada 52°53N 89°23W 298 B2
Pipestone Cr. → Canada 49°38N 100°15W 297 D8
Pipiriki N.Z. 39°28S 175°5E 284 F4
Piplan Pakistan 32°17N 71°21E 242 C4
Piploda India 23°37N 74°56E 242 H6
Pipmuacan, Rés. Canada 49°45N 70°30W 299 C5
Pippingarra Australia 20°27S 118°42E 278 D2
Pipriac France 47°59N 1°58W 172 E5
Piqua U.S.A. 40°9N 84°15W 311 D12
Piquet Carneiro Brazil 5°48S 39°25W 332 C4
Piquiri → Brazil 24°3S 54°14W 335 A5
Pir Panjal Range India 32°30N 76°50E 242 C7
Pīr Sohrāb Iran 25°44N 60°54E 247 E9
Pira Benin 8°28N 1°48E 263 D5
Piracanjuba Brazil 17°18S 49°1W 333 E2
Piracicaba Brazil 22°45S 47°40W 335 A6
Piracuruca Brazil 3°50S 41°50W 332 B3
Pirae Tahiti 17°31S 149°32W 289 e
Piræus = Pireas Greece 37°57N 23°42E 112 B1
Piraiévs = Pireas Greece 37°57N 23°42E 112 B1
Pirajuçara → Brazil 23°33S 46°42W 137 B1
Pirajuí Brazil 21°59S 49°29W 335 A6
Piram I. India 21°36N 72°21E 242 J5
Piran Slovenia 45°31N 13°33E 199 C10
Pirané Argentina 25°42S 59°6W 334 B4
Piranhas Brazil 9°27S 37°46W 332 C4
Pirano = Piran Slovenia 45°31N 13°33E 199 C10
Pīrānshahr Iran 36°41N 45°8E 213 D11
Pirapemas Brazil 3°43S 44°14W 332 B3
Pirapora Brazil 17°20S 44°56W 333 E3
Pirara Guyana 3°37N 59°40W 329 C6
Piravam India 24°10N 76°2E 242 G7
Piray → Bolivia 16°32S 63°45W 331 D5
Pirdop Bulgaria 42°40N 24°10E 203 D8
Pireas Greece 37°57N 23°42E 112 B1
Pires do Rio Brazil 17°18S 48°17W 333 E2
Pirganj Bangla. 25°51N 88°24E 241 C2
Pirgos Greece 38°13N 25°59E 205 C7
Pirgos Ilia, Greece 37°40N 21°27E 204 D3
Pirgos Kriti, Greece 35°0N 25°9E 207 E6
Pirgovo Bulgaria 43°44N 25°43E 203 C9
Piribebuy Paraguay 25°26S 57°2W 334 B4
Pirimapun Indonesia 6°20S 138°24E 231 F9
Pirin △ Bulgaria 41°48N 23°22E 202 E7
Pirin Planina Bulgaria 41°40N 23°30E 202 E7
Pirinçi Turkey 41°10N 28°52E 122 B1
Pirineos = Pyrénées Europe 42°45N 0°18E 174 F4
Piripiri Brazil 4°15S 41°46W 332 B3
Piritu Venezuela 9°23N 69°12W 328 B4
Pirituba Brazil 23°29S 46°44W 137 A1
Pirkkola Finland 60°14N 24°55E 121 B2
Pirlangimpi Australia 11°24S 130°26E 278 B5
Pirmasens Germany 49°12N 7°36E 179 F3
Pirna Germany 50°57N 13°56E 178 E9
Pirojpur Bangla. 22°35N 90°1E 241 D3
Pirot Serbia 43°9N 22°33E 202 C6
Piru Indonesia 3°4S 128°12E 231 E7
Piru Calif., U.S.A. 34°25N 118°48W 307 L8
Piryatin = Pyryatyn Ukraine 50°15N 32°25E 189 G7
Pisa Italy 43°43N 10°23E 198 E7
Pisa → Poland 53°14N 21°52E 185 E8
Pisa, Firenze ✈ (PSA) Italy 43°40N 10°22E 198 E7
Pisa Ra. N.Z. 44°52S 169°12E 285 E4
Pisac Peru 13°25S 71°50W 330 C3
Pisagua Chile 19°40S 70°15W 330 D3
Pisarovina Croatia 45°35N 15°50E 199 C12
Pisau, Tanjong Malaysia 6°4N 117°59E 235 A5
Pisba △ Colombia 10°39N 74°30W 328 A3
Pisco Peru 13°50S 76°12W 330 C2
Piscu Romania 45°30N 27°43E 183 E12
Písek Czechia 49°19N 14°10E 180 B7
Pisgat O'mer West Bank 31°49N 35°14E 123 B2
Pisgat Ze'ev West Bank 31°49N 35°15E 123 B2
Pishan China 37°30N 78°33E 217 E9
Pishcha Ukraine 51°35N 23°50E 185 G10
Pishchanka Ukraine 48°12N 28°54E 183 B13
Pīshīn Iran 26°6N 61°47E 247 E9
Pishin Pakistan 30°35N 67°0E 242 D2
Pishin Lora → Pakistan 29°9N 64°5E 242 E1
Pishpek = Bishkek Kyrgyzstan 42°54N 74°46E 217 D8
Pisidia Turkey 37°30N 31°40E 212 D4
Pising Indonesia 5°8S 121°53E 231 F6
Pismo Beach U.S.A. 35°9N 120°38W 307 K6
Piso, L. Liberia 6°50N 11°15W 262 D2
Pisogne Italy 45°45N 10°10E 198 C7
Pissila Burkina Faso 13°7N 0°50W 263 C4
Pissis, Cerro Argentina 27°45S 68°48W 334 B2
Pissos France 44°19N 0°49W 174 D3
Pissouri Cyprus 34°40N 32°42E 207 F8
Pisticci Italy 40°23N 16°33E 201 B9
Pistóia Italy 43°55N 10°54E 198 E7
Pistol B. Canada 62°25N 92°37W 297 A10
Pisuerga → Spain 41°33N 4°52W 194 D6
Pisz Poland 53°38N 21°49E 184 E8
Pit → U.S.A. 40°47N 122°6W 304 F2
Pita Guinea 11°5N 12°15W 262 C2
Pitalito Colombia 1°51N 76°2W 328 C2
Pitampura India 28°41N 77°7E 120 A1
Pitanga Brazil 24°46S 51°44W 333 F1
Pitangui Brazil 19°40S 44°54W 333 E3
Pitarpunga L. Australia 34°24S 143°30E 282 C5
Pitcairn I. Pac. Oc. 25°5S 130°5W 289 K14
Pitch Pt. Trin. & Tob. 10°15N 61°37W 323 t
Piteå Sweden 65°20N 21°25E 160 D19
Piteälven → Sweden 65°20N 21°25E 160 D19
Piterka Russia 50°41N 47°29E 190 E8
Piteşti Romania 44°52N 24°54E 183 F9
Pithapuram India 17°10N 82°15E 244 F6
Pithara Australia 30°20S 116°35E 279 F2
Pithio Greece 41°24N 26°40E 203 E10
Pithiviers France 48°10N 2°13E 173 D9
Pithora India 21°16N 82°31E 244 D6
Pithoragarh India 29°35N 80°13E 243 E9
Pithoro Pakistan 25°31N 69°23E 242 G3
Piti Guam 13°28N 144°41E 302 d
Pitigliano Italy 42°38N 11°40E 199 F8
Pitkäjärvi Finland 60°15N 24°45E 121 B1
Pitkyaranta Russia 61°34N 31°37E 188 B6
Pitlochry U.K. 56°42N 3°44W 167 E5
Pitoa Cameroon 9°23N 13°32E 264 A2
Pitogo Phil. 13°47N 122°5E 232 E4
Piton, Pte. du Guadeloupe 16°30N 61°26W 322 e
Piton de la Petite Rivière Noire Mauritius 20°24S 57°23E 272 e
Pitons, Anses des St. Lucia 13°49N 61°4W 323 m
Pitou Taiwan 23°53N 120°27E 225 C2
Pitou Chiao Taiwan 25°8N 121°55E 225 A3
Pitrufquén Chile 38°59S 72°39W 336 A2
Pitschen = Byczyna Poland 51°7N 18°12E 185 G5
Pitsilia Cyprus 34°55N 33°0E 207 F9
Pitsunda = Bichvinta Georgia 43°9N 40°21E 191 J5
Pitt, Pta. Ecuador 0°43S 89°14W 330 a
Pitt I. B.C., Canada 53°30N 129°50W 296 C3
Pitt I. N.Z. 44°15S 176°15W 285 c
Pitti I. India 10°50N 72°38E 245 J1
Pittsburg Calif., U.S.A. 38°2N 121°53W 306 G5
Pittsburg Kans., U.S.A. 37°25N 94°42W 308 G6
Pittsburg Tex., U.S.A. 33°0N 94°59W 314 E7
Pittsburgh U.S.A. 40°26N 79°58W 312 F5
Pittsfield Ill., U.S.A. 39°36N 90°49W 310 E6
Pittsfield Maine, U.S.A. 44°47N 69°23W 309 C19
Pittsfield Mass., U.S.A. 42°27N 73°15W 313 D11
Pittsfield N.H., U.S.A. 43°18N 71°20W 313 C13
Pittston U.S.A. 41°19N 75°47W 313 E9
Pittsview U.S.A. 32°11N 85°10W 316 C4
Pittsworth Australia 27°41S 151°37E 281 D5
Pituri → Australia 22°35S 138°30E 280 C2
Pium Brazil 10°27S 49°11W 332 D2
Piumafua Mt. Amer. Samoa 14°11S 169°37W 302 f
Piumhi Brazil 20°28S 45°58W 333 F2
Piura Peru 5°15S 80°38W 330 B1
Piura □ Peru 5°10S 80°0W 330 B2
Piuthan Nepal 28°7N 82°56E 243 E10
Piva → Montenegro 43°20N 18°50E 202 C2
Pivijay Colombia 10°28N 74°37W 328 A3
Piwniczna Poland 49°27N 20°42E 185 J7
Pixian China 30°48N 103°52E 228 B4
Pixley U.S.A. 35°58N 119°18W 306 K7
Pizarra Spain 36°36N 4°42W 195 J6
Pizarro Colombia 4°58N 77°22W 328 C2
Pizhou = Pei Xian China 34°44N 116°55E 226 G9
Pizhou China 34°18N 117°57E 227 G9
Pizzo Italy 38°44N 16°10E 201 D9
Placentia Canada 47°20N 54°0W 299 C9
Placentia B. Canada 47°0N 54°40W 299 C9
Placer Masbate, Phil. 11°52N 123°55E 233 F4
Placer Surigao N., Phil. 9°36N 125°38E 233 G5
Placerville U.S.A. 38°44N 120°48W 306 G6
Placetas Cuba 22°15N 79°44W 320 B4
Plácido de Castro Brazil 10°20S 67°11W 330 C4
Plačkovica N. Macedonia 41°45N 22°30E 202 E6
Plaine des Jarres Laos 19°27N 103°10E 236 C4
Plaine Magnien Mauritius 20°25S 57°39E 272 e
Plaines des Papayes Mauritius 20°3S 57°34E 272 e
Plainfield Ill., U.S.A. 41°37N 88°12W 311 C8
Plainfield Ind., U.S.A. 39°42N 86°24W 311 E10
Plainfield N.J., U.S.A. 40°37N 74°25W 313 F10
Plainfield Ohio, U.S.A. 40°13N 81°43W 312 F3
Plainfield Vt., U.S.A. 44°17N 72°26W 313 B12
Plains Ga., U.S.A. 32°2N 84°24W 316 C5
Plains Mont., U.S.A. 47°28N 114°53W 304 C6
Plains Tex., U.S.A. 33°11N 102°50W 314 E3
Plainview Nebr., U.S.A. 42°21N 97°47W 308 D5
Plainview Tex., U.S.A. 34°11N 101°43W 314 D4
Plainwell U.S.A. 42°27N 85°38W 311 B11
Plaisance France 43°36N 0°3E 174 E4
Plaistow U.S.A. 42°50N 71°6W 313 D13
Plaju Indonesia 2°58S 104°49E 234 C2
Plaka Greece 40°0N 25°24E 205 B7
Plaka, Akra Greece 35°11N 26°19E 207 E7
Plakenska Planina N. Macedonia 41°14N 21°2E 202 E5
Plampang Indonesia 8°47S 117°46E 235 D5
Planá Czechia 49°50N 12°44E 180 B5
Plana Cays The Bahamas 22°38N 73°30W 321 B5
Planada U.S.A. 37°16N 120°19W 306 H6
Planchón Peru 12°14S 69°11W 330 C4
Plancoët France 48°32N 2°13W 172 D4
Plandište Serbia 45°16N 21°10E 182 E6
Planegg Germany 48°6N 11°25E 131 B1
Planeta Rica Colombia 8°25N 75°36W 328 B2
Plano Ill., U.S.A. 41°40N 88°32W 311 C8
Plano Tex., U.S.A. 33°1N 96°42W 314 E6
Plant City U.S.A. 28°1N 82°7W 317 G7
Plantation U.S.A. 26°7N 80°14W 129 B2
Plantation Isles U.S.A. 26°6N 80°14W 129 B2
Plaquemine U.S.A. 30°17N 91°14W 314 F9
Plaridel Phil. 8°37N 123°43E 233 G4
Plasencia Spain 40°3N 6°8W 194 E4
Plaški Croatia 45°4N 15°22E 199 C12
Plassen Norway 61°9N 12°30E 164 C9
Plast Russia 54°22N 60°50E 216 B6
Plaster City U.S.A. 32°47N 115°51W 307 N11
Plaster Rock Canada 46°53N 67°22W 299 C6
Plastun Russia 44°45N 136°19E 222 B8
Plasy Czechia 49°56N 13°24E 180 B6
Plata, Río de la → S. Amer. 34°45S 57°30W 334 C4
Plátani → Italy 37°23N 13°16E 200 E6
Platanos Greece 35°28N 23°33E 207 E4
Plataria Greece 39°27N 20°16E 206 C10
Plateau □ Nigeria 8°30N 9°0E 263 D6
Plateau d'Ipassa ⌓ Gabon 0°26N 12°40E 264 B2
Plateaux □ Congo 2°30S 15°30E 264 C3
Plathe = Płoty Poland 53°48N 15°18E 184 E2
Platinum U.S.A. 59°1N 161°49W 303 G7
Platja d'Aro Spain 41°49N 3°4E 196 D8
Plato Colombia 9°47N 74°47W 328 B3
Platte → Mo., U.S.A. 39°16N 94°50W 310 E2
Platte → Nebr., U.S.A. 41°4N 95°53W 308 E6
Platte City U.S.A. 39°22N 94°47W 310 E2
Platteville U.S.A. 42°44N 90°29W 310 B6
Plattling Germany 48°46N 12°53E 179 G8
Plattsburg U.S.A. 39°34N 94°27W 310 E2
Plattsburgh U.S.A. 44°42N 73°28W 313 B11
Plattsmouth U.S.A. 41°1N 95°53W 308 E6
Plau Germany 53°27N 12°15E 178 B8
Plauen Germany 50°30N 12°8E 178 E8
Plauer See Germany 53°28N 12°17E 178 B8
Plav Montenegro 42°38N 19°57E 202 D3
Plavinas Latvia 56°35N 25°46E 188 D3
Plavnica Montenegro 42°20N 19°13E 202 D3
Plavno Croatia 44°9N 16°10E 199 D13
Plavsk Russia 53°40N 37°18E 188 F9
Playa Blanca Canary Is. 28°51N 13°50W 153 e2
Playa de las Americas Canary Is. 28°5N 16°43W 153 e1
Playa de Mogán Canary Is. 27°48N 15°47W 153 e1
Playa del Carmen Mexico 20°37N 87°4W 319 C7
Playa del Inglés Canary Is. 27°45N 15°33W 153 e1
Playas Ecuador 2°38S 80°23W 328 D1
Playgreen L. Canada 54°0N 98°15W 297 C9
Plaza Mayor Madrid, Spain 127 b2
Pleasant Bay Canada 46°51N 60°48W 299 C7
Pleasant Hill Calif., U.S.A. 37°57N 122°4W 306 H4
Pleasant Hill Ill., U.S.A. 39°27N 90°52W 310 E6
Pleasant Hill Mo., U.S.A. 38°47N 94°16W 310 F2
Pleasant Mount U.S.A. 41°44N 75°26W 313 E9
Pleasant Point N.Z. 44°16S 171°9E 285 c
Pleasant Prairie U.S.A. 42°33N 87°56W 311 B9
Pleasanton Calif., U.S.A. 37°39N 121°52W 306 H5
Pleasanton Tex., U.S.A. 28°58N 98°29W 314 G5
Pleasantville Iowa, U.S.A. 41°23N 93°18W 310 C3
Pleasantville N.J., U.S.A. 39°24N 74°32W 309 F16
Pleasantville Pa., U.S.A. 41°35N 79°34W 312 E5
Pleasure Island U.S.A. 28°21N 81°31W 133 B1
Pleasure Ridge Park U.S.A. 38°9N 85°50W 311 F11
Pléaux France 45°8N 2°13E 174 C6
Plei Ku Vietnam 13°57N 108°0E 236 F7
Plélan-le-Grand France 48°0N 2°7W 172 D4
Pleniţa Romania 44°14N 23°10E 183 F8
Plenty → Australia 23°25S 136°31E 280 C2
Plenty, B. of N.Z. 37°45S 177°0E 284 D6
Plentywood U.S.A. 48°47N 104°34W 304 B11
Plérin France 48°32N 2°46W 172 D4
Plesetsk Russia 62°43N 40°20E 186 B7
Pleshcheyevo Ozero △ Russia 56°45N 38°50E 188 D10
Pleskau = Pskov Russia 57°50N 28°25E 188 D5
Plessisville Canada 46°14N 71°47W 299 C5
Plestin-les-Grèves France 48°40N 3°39W 172 D3
Pleszew Poland 51°53N 17°47E 185 G4
Pleternica Croatia 45°17N 17°48E 182 E2
Plétipi, L. Canada 51°44N 70°6W 299 B5
Pleven Bulgaria 43°26N 24°37E 203 C8
Pleven □ Bulgaria 43°26N 24°37E 203 C8
Plevlja Montenegro 43°21N 19°21E 202 C3
Plevna Canada 44°58N 76°59W 312 B8
Plitvice Lakes = Plitvička Jezera △ Croatia 44°54N 15°35E 199 D12
Plitvička Jezera △ Croatia 44°54N 15°35E 199 D12
Plješevica Croatia 44°45N 15°45E 199 D12
Pljevlja Montenegro 43°21N 19°21E 202 C3
Ploaghe Italy 40°40N 8°45E 200 B1
Ploče Croatia 43°4N 17°26E 199 E14
Płock Poland 52°32N 19°40E 185 F6
Plöckenpass Italy 46°37N 12°57E 199 B9
Plöckenstein Germany 48°46N 13°51E 179 G9
Ploemeur France 47°44N 3°26W 172 E3
Ploërmel France 47°55N 2°26W 172 E4
Plöhnen = Płońsk Poland 52°37N 20°21E 185 F7
Ploieşti Romania 44°57N 26°5E 183 F11
Plomari Greece 38°59N 26°22E 205 C8
Plombières-les-Bains France 47°58N 6°27E 173 E13
Plomin Croatia 45°8N 14°10E 199 C11
Plön Germany 54°9N 10°24E 178 A6
Plonge, Lac la Canada 55°8N 107°20W 297 B7
Płońsk Poland 52°37N 20°21E 185 F7
Plopeni Romania 45°4N 25°59E 183 E10
Plopişului, Munţii Romania 47°5N 22°30E 182 C7
Plotsk = Płock Poland 52°32N 19°40E 185 F6
Płoty Poland 53°48N 15°18E 184 E2
Plouaret France 48°37N 3°28W 172 D3
Plouay France 47°55N 3°21W 172 E3
Ploučnice → Czechia 50°46N 14°13E 180 A7
Ploudalmézeau France 48°34N 4°41W 172 D2
Plouescat France 48°39N 4°10W 172 D2
Plougasnou France 48°42N 3°49W 172 D3
Plougastel-Daoulas France 48°22N 4°17W 172 D2
Plouguerneau France 48°36N 4°30W 172 D2
Plouha France 48°41N 2°57W 172 D4
Plouhinec France 48°0N 4°29W 172 E2
Plovdiv Bulgaria 42°8N 24°44E 203 D8
Plovdiv □ Bulgaria 42°15N 24°30E 203 D8
Plover Cove Res. China 22°28N 114°15E 219 a
Pluies, R. des → Réunion 20°52S 55°31E 272 f
Plum U.S.A. 40°29N 79°47W 312 F5
Plum I. U.S.A. 41°11N 72°12W 313 E12
Plumas U.S.A. 39°45N 120°4W 306 F6
Plummer U.S.A. 47°20N 116°53W 304 C5
Plumridge Lakes Australia 29°26S 125°16E 279 E4
Plumstead Western Cape, S. Africa 34°1S 18°28E 118 B1
Plumstead London, U.K. 51°29N 0°5E 125 B4
Plumtree Zimbabwe 20°27S 27°55E 269 G2
Plungė Lithuania 55°53N 21°59E 184 C8
Pluvigner France 47°46N 3°1W 172 E3
Plužine Montenegro 43°8N 18°51E 202 C2
Plymouth Montserrat 16°41N 62°12W 323 p
Plymouth Trin. & Tob. 11°14N 60°48W 323 s
Plymouth Plymouth, U.K. 50°22N 4°10W 169 G3
Plymouth Calif., U.S.A. 38°29N 120°51W 306 G6
Plymouth Ill., U.S.A. 40°18N 90°58W 310 D6
Plymouth Ind., U.S.A. 41°21N 86°19W 311 C10
Plymouth Mass., U.S.A. 41°57N 70°40W 313 E14
Plymouth N.C., U.S.A. 35°52N 76°43W 315 D16
Plymouth N.H., U.S.A. 43°46N 71°41W 313 C13
Plymouth Pa., U.S.A. 41°14N 75°57W 313 E9
Plymouth Wis., U.S.A. 43°45N 87°59W 308 D10
Plympton-Wyoming = Wyoming Canada 42°57N 82°7W 312 D2
Plynlimon = Pumlumon Fawr U.K. 52°28N 3°46W 169 E4
Plyusa Russia 58°28N 29°27E 188 C5
Plyussa → Russia 59°4N 28°6E 188 C5
Plyushchevo Russia 55°44N 37°45E 129 B3
Plzeň Czechia 49°45N 13°22E 180 B6
Plzeňský □ Czechia 49°35N 13°0E 180 B6
Pmere Nyente ✪ Australia 24°15S 136°10E 280 C2
Pniewy Poland 52°31N 16°16E 185 F3
Pnika Greece 112 c1
Pnyx = Pnika Greece 112 c1
Pô Burkina Faso 11°14N 1°5W 263 C4
Po → Italy 44°57N 12°4E 199 D9
Po, Delta del Italy 44°55N 12°30E 199 D9
Pô △ Burkina Faso 11°25N 1°5W 263 C4
Po Hai = Bo Hai China 39°0N 119°0E 227 E10
Po Toi China 22°10N 114°16E 219 a
Po Toi Is. Hong Kong, China 22°10N 114°16E 122 B3
Po Toi O Hong Kong, China 22°16N 114°17E 122 B3
Poasco Italy 45°24N 9°16E 128 B2
Pobé Benin 7°0N 2°56E 263 D5
Pobé Burkina Faso 13°53N 1°42W 263 C4
Pobeda Russia 65°12N 146°12E 215 C15
Pobedy, Pik Asia 42°0N 79°58E 217 D9
Pobiedziska Poland 52°29N 17°11E 185 F4
Pobladura del Valle Spain 42°6N 5°44W 194 C5
Poblet, Monasterio de Spain 41°22N 1°4E 196 D6
Pobra de Trives Spain 42°20N 7°10W 194 C3
Pocahontas Ark., U.S.A. 36°16N 90°58W 315 C9
Pocahontas Ill., U.S.A. 38°50N 89°33W 310 F7
Pocahontas Iowa, U.S.A. 42°44N 94°40W 310 B2
Pocatello U.S.A. 42°52N 112°27W 304 E7
Počátky Czechia 49°15N 15°14E 180 B8
Pocheon S. Korea 37°53N 127°13E 224 D3
Pochep Russia 52°58N 33°29E 189 F7
Pochinki Russia 54°41N 44°59E 190 C7
Pochinok Russia 54°28N 32°29E 188 E7
Pöchlarn Austria 48°12N 15°12E 180 C8
Poci Venezuela 5°57N 61°29W 329 B5
Pocinhos Brazil 7°4S 36°3W 332 C4
Pocking Germany 48°23N 13°19E 179 G9
Pocklington Reef Papua N. G. 10°51S 155°44E 286 F8
Poções Brazil 14°31S 40°21W 333 D3
Pocomoke City U.S.A. 38°5N 75°34W 309 F16
Poconé Brazil 16°15S 56°37W 331 D6
Poços de Caldas Brazil 21°50S 46°33W 335 A6
Podbaba Czechia 50°7N 14°22E 135 B2
Podbořany Czechia 50°14N 13°25E 180 A6
Poddębice Poland 51°54N 18°58E 185 G5
Poděbrady Czechia 50°9N 15°8E 180 A8
Podensac France 44°40N 0°22W 174 D3
Podenzano Italy 44°57N 9°41E 198 D6
Podgorač Croatia 45°27N 18°13E 182 E3
Podgorica Montenegro 42°30N 19°19E 202 D3
Podgorie Albania 40°49N 20°48E 202 F4
Podile India 15°37N 79°37E 245 G4
Podilska Vysochyna Ukraine 49°0N 28°0E 183 B13
Podkarpackie □ Poland 50°0N 22°10E 185 H9
Podkova Bulgaria 41°24N 25°24E 203 E9
Podlapača Croatia 44°37N 15°47E 199 D12
Podlaskie □ Poland 53°10N 23°0E 185 E10
Podocarpus △ Ecuador 4°13S 79°2W 328 D2
Podoleni Romania 46°46N 26°39E 183 D11
Podoli Czechia 50°2N 14°25E 135 B2
Podolínec Slovakia 49°16N 20°31E 181 B13
Podolsk Russia 55°25N 37°30E 188 E9
Podor Senegal 16°40N 15°2W 262 B1
Podporozhye Russia 60°55N 34°2E 188 B8
Podu Iloaiei Romania 47°13N 27°16E 183 C12
Podu Turcului Romania 46°11N 27°25E 183 D12
Podujevo = Besianë Kosovo 42°54N 21°10E 202 D5
Podyji △ Czechia 48°51N 15°57E 180 C8
Poechos Peru 4°41S 80°34W 328 D1
Poel Germany 54°0N 11°25E 178 B6
Pofadder S. Africa 29°10S 19°22E 270 C2
Poggiardo Italy 40°3N 18°23E 201 B11
Poggibonsi Italy 43°28N 11°9E 198 E8
Póggio Mirteto Italy 42°16N 12°41E 199 F9
Pogoanele Romania 44°55N 27°0E 183 F12
Pogorzela Poland 51°50N 17°12E 185 G4
Pogoso Dem. Rep. of the Congo 6°46S 17°12E 265 D3
Pogradec Albania 40°54N 20°37E 202 F4
Pogranichnyy Russia 44°25N 131°24E 220 B5
Poh Indonesia 0°46S 122°51E 231 E6
Pohang S. Korea 36°1N 129°23E 224 D4
Pohjanmaa □ Finland 62°58N 22°50E 160 E20
Pohjois-Pirkkala = Nokia Finland 61°30N 23°30E 188 B2
Pohnpei Micronesia 6°55N 158°10E 288 G7
Pohořelá Slovakia 48°50N 20°2E 181 C13
Pohořelice Czechia 48°59N 16°31E 181 C9
Pohorje Slovenia 46°30N 15°20E 199 B12
Pohri India 25°32N 77°22E 242 G6
Pōhue B. U.S.A. 19°0N 155°48W 302 E6
Poi Solomon Is. 10°9S 161°42E 287 N11
Poiana Mare Romania 43°57N 23°5E 182 G8
Poiana Ruscăi, Munţii Romania 45°45N 22°25E 182 E7
Poiana Stampei Romania 47°19N 25°8E 183 C10
Poie Dem. Rep. of the Congo 2°50S 23°14E 264 C4
Poike, Península Chile 27°6S 109°15W 330 b
Poindimié N. Cal. 20°56S 165°20E 288 d
Poinsett, C. Antarctica 65°42S 113°18E 151 C8
Point Arena U.S.A. 38°55N 123°41W 306 G3
Point Baker U.S.A. 56°21N 133°37W 296 B2
Point Calimere India 10°17N 79°49E 245 J4
Point Fortin Trin. & Tob. 10°10N 61°42W 323 t
Point Hope U.S.A. 68°21N 166°47W 303 B6
Point L. Canada 65°15N 113°4W 294 D9
Point Lay U.S.A. 69°46N 163°3W 303 B7
Point Lisas Trin. & Tob. 10°24N 61°29W 323 t
Point Pedro Sri Lanka 9°50N 80°15E 245 K5
Point Pelee △ Canada 41°57N 82°31W 312 E2
Point Pleasant N.J., U.S.A. 40°5N 74°4W 313 F10
Point Pleasant W. Va., U.S.A. 38°51N 82°8W 309 F12
Point Reyes ⌓ U.S.A. 38°10N 122°55W 306 G2
Pointe-à-Pierre Trin. & Tob. 10°19N 61°28W 323 t
Pointe-à-Pitre Guadeloupe 16°15N 61°32W 322 e
Pointe-au-Pic = La Malbaie Canada 47°40N 70°10W 299 C5
Pointe-Aux-Trembles Canada 45°38N 73°30W 130 A2
Pointe-Claire Canada 45°26N 73°50W 313 A11
Pointe-Gatineau Canada 45°27N 75°41W 313 A9
Pointe Michel Dominica 15°15N 61°23W 323 k
Pointe-Noire Congo 4°48S 11°53E 265 C2
Pointe-Noire Guadeloupe 16°14N 61°47W 322 e
Poio = O Convento Spain 42°28N 8°41W 194 C2
Poipet Cambodia 13°39N 102°33E 236 F4
Poirino Italy 44°56N 7°48E 198 D4
Poisonbush Ra. Australia 22°30S 121°30E 278 D3
Poissonnier Pt. Australia 19°57S 119°10E 278 C2
Poissy France 48°55N 2°2E 134 A1
Poitiers France 46°35N 0°20E 172 F7
Poitou France 46°40N 0°10W 174 B3
Poix-de-Picardie France 49°47N 1°58E 173 C8
Poix-Terron France 49°38N 4°38E 173 C11
Pojoaque U.S.A. 35°54N 106°1W 305 J10
Pok Fu Lam Hong Kong, China 22°16N 114°7E 122 B2
Pōka'ī B. U.S.A. 21°27N 158°12W 302 K13
Pokaran India 27°0N 71°50E 242 F4
Pokataroo Australia 29°30S 148°36E 281 D4
Pokcheong S. Korea 37°28N 127°8E 137 C2
Pokhara Nepal 28°14N 83°58E 243 E10
Pokhvistnevo Russia 53°36N 52°0E 190 D11
Pokigron Suriname 4°30N 55°22W 329 C6
Poko Dem. Rep. of the Congo 3°7N 26°52E 268 B2
Poko South Sudan 5°41N 31°55E 257 F3
Pokrov Russia 55°55N 39°7E 188 E10
Pokrovka = Kyzyl-Suu Kyrgyzstan 42°20N 78°0E 217 D9
Pokrovsk = Engels Russia 51°28N 46°6E 190 E8
Pokrovsk Russia 61°29N 129°0E 215 C13
Pokrovskoye = Priazovskoye Ukraine 46°44N 35°40E 189 J8
Pokrovskoye Russia 47°25N 38°54E 189 J10
Pol-e Dokhtar Iran 33°9N 47°42E 213 F12
Pol-e Khomri Afghan. 35°56N 68°42E 240 B3
Pol-e Zahāb Iran 34°27N 45°51E 213 E11
Pola = Pula Croatia 44°54N 13°57E 199 D10
Pola Russia 57°55N 32°0E 188 D7
Pola de Allande Spain 43°16N 6°37W 194 B4
Pola de Lena Spain 43°10N 5°49W 194 B5
Pola de Siero Spain 43°24N 5°39W 194 B5
Pola de Somiedo Spain 43°5N 6°15W 194 B4
Pola I. Amer. Samoa 14°14S 170°40W 302 f
Polacca U.S.A. 35°50N 110°23W 305 J8
Polan Iran 25°30N 61°10E 247 E9
Pol'ana Slovakia 48°38N 19°29E 181 C12
Poland U.S.A. 43°13N 75°3W 313 C9
Poland ■ Europe 52°0N 20°0E 185 G3
Polanica-Zdrój Poland 50°24N 16°32E 185 H3
Połaniec Poland 50°26N 21°17E 185 H8
Polanów Poland 54°7N 16°41E 184 D3
Polar Bear ⌓ Canada 55°0N 83°45W 298 A2
Polatlı Turkey 39°36N 32°9E 212 C5
Polatsk Belarus 55°30N 28°50E 188 E5
Polavaram India 17°15N 81°38E 244 F5
Polcura Chile 37°17S 71°43W 334 D1
Połczyn-Zdrój Poland 53°47N 16°5E 184 E3
Poldasht Iran 39°20N 45°4E 213 C11
Poleski △ Poland 51°29N 23°5E 185 G10
Polessk Russia 54°50N 21°8E 184 D7
Polesye = Pripet Marshes Europe 52°10N 27°10E 177 B15
Polevskoy Russia 56°26N 60°11E 186 C11
Polewali Indonesia 3°25S 119°20E 235 C5
Polgar Hungary 47°54N 21°6E 182 C6
Poli Cameroon 8°34N 13°15E 263 C7
Policastro, G. di Italy 40°0N 15°35E 201 C8
Police Poland 53°33N 14°33E 184 E1
Police, Pte. Seychelles 4°51S 55°32E 272 c
Polichnitos Greece 39°6N 26°10E 205 B8
Polička Czechia 49°43N 16°15E 181 B9
Policoro Italy 40°13N 16°41E 201 B9
Poliegos Greece 36°45N 24°38E 204 E6
Poligiros Greece 40°23N 23°25E 202 F7
Polignano a Mare Italy 41°0N 17°13E 201 A9
Poligny France 46°50N 5°42E 173 F12
Polillo Phil. 14°43N 121°56E 232 D3
Polillo Is. Phil. 14°56N 122°0E 232 D4
Polillo Str. Phil. 14°44N 121°51E 232 D3
Polis Cyprus 35°2N 32°26E 207 E8
Polistena Italy 38°24N 16°4E 201 D9
Pölitz = Police Poland 53°33N 14°33E 184 E1
Polk U.S.A. 41°22N 79°56W 312 E5
Polkowice Poland 51°29N 16°3E 185 G3
Polkwitz = Polkowice Poland 51°29N 16°3E 185 G3
Polla Italy 40°31N 15°29E 201 B8
Pollachi India 10°35N 77°0E 245 J3
Pollença Spain 39°54N 3°1E 206 B4
Pollença, B. de Spain 39°53N 3°8E 206 B4
Pollfoss Norway 61°58N 7°54E 164 C4
Póllica Italy 40°11N 15°3E 201 B8
Pollino, Mte. Italy 39°55N 16°11E 201 C9
Pollino △ Italy 40°0N 16°12E 201 C9
Polna Russia 58°31N 28°5E 188 C5
Polnovat Russia 63°50N 65°54E 214 C7
Polo Ill., U.S.A. 41°59N 89°35W 310 C7
Polo Mo., U.S.A. 39°33N 94°3W 310 E2
Pology Ukraine 47°29N 36°15E 189 J9
Polokwane S. Africa 23°54S 29°25E 271 B4
Polokwane → S. Africa 22°25S 30°5E 271 B5
Polomolok Phil. 6°13N 125°3E 233 H5
Polonnaruwa Sri Lanka 7°56N 81°0E 245 L5
Polonne Ukraine 50°6N 27°30E 177 C14
Polonnoye = Polonne Ukraine 50°6N 27°30E 177 C14
Polski Trambesh Bulgaria 43°20N 25°38E 203 C9
Polski Trŭmbesh = Polski Trambesh Bulgaria 43°20N 25°38E 203 C9
Polsko Kosovo Bulgaria 43°23N 25°38E 203 C9
Polson U.S.A. 47°41N 114°9W 304 C6
Poltár Slovakia 48°26N 19°48E 181 C12
Poltava Ukraine 49°35N 34°35E 189 H8
Poltava □ Ukraine 50°15N 33°15E 189 G7
Polton U.K. 55°52N 3°7W 121 B3
Poltoratsk = Ashgabat Turkmenistan 37°58N 58°24E 247 B8
Põltsamaa Estonia 58°39N 25°58E 188 C3
Polunochnoye Russia 60°52N 60°25E 214 C7
Polur India 12°32N 79°11E 245 H4
Põlva Estonia 58°3N 27°3E 188 C4
Polvoranca, Parque de Spain 40°19N 3°48W 127 C1
Polyana Ukraine 48°38N 22°58E 182 B7
Polyarny Russia 69°8N 33°20E 160 B25
Polyarnyye Zori Russia 67°22N 32°30E 160 C25
Polykastro Greece 41°0N 22°34E 202 E6
Polynesia Pac. Oc. 10°0S 162°0W 289 F11
Polynesian Cultural Center U.S.A. 21°38N 157°55W 302 J14
Polynésie française = French Polynesia ☑ Pac. Oc. 20°0S 145°0W 289 f
Polyustrovo Russia 59°57N 30°25E 137 B2
Pomabamba = Azurduy Bolivia 19°59S 64°29W 331 D5
Pomabamba Peru 8°50S 77°28W 330 B2
Pomarance Italy 43°18N 10°52E 198 E7
Pombal Brazil 6°45S 37°50W 332 C4
Pombal Portugal 39°55N 8°40W 194 F2
Pombia Greece 35°0N 24°51E 207 F5
Pombos, B. dos Angola 11°40S 13°47E 265 E2
Pomene Mozam. 22°53S 35°33E 271 B6
Pomeroon-Supenaam □ Guyana 7°5N 58°51W 329 B6
Pomeroy Ohio, U.S.A. 39°2N 82°2W 309 F12
Pomeroy Wash., U.S.A. 46°28N 117°36W 304 C5
Pomézia Italy 41°40N 12°30E 200 A5
Pomichna Ukraine 48°13N 31°36E 189 H6
Pomio Papua N. G. 5°32S 151°33E 286 C6
Pomme de Terre L. U.S.A. 37°54N 93°19W 310 G3
Pomme Rose Grenada 12°3N 61°39W 323 q
Pomona Queens., Australia 26°22S 152°52E 281 D5
Pomona Calif., U.S.A. 34°4N 117°45W 307 L9
Pomona Park U.S.A. 29°30N 81°36W 317 F8
Pomorie Bulgaria 42°32N 27°41E 203 D11
Pomorskie □ Poland 54°30N 18°0E 184 D5
Pomorskie, Pojezierze Poland 53°40N 16°37E 184 E3
Pomos Cyprus 35°9N 32°33E 207 E8
Pomos, C. Cyprus 35°10N 32°33E 207 E8
Pompano Beach U.S.A. 26°14N 80°7W 129 A3
Pompei Italy 40°45N 14°30E 201 B7
Pompey France 48°46N 6°6E 173 D13
Pompeys Pillar U.S.A. 45°59N 107°57W 304 D10
Pompeys Pillar ⌓ U.S.A. 46°0N 108°0W 304 D10
Pompidou, Centre Paris, France 134 b4
Pomprap Thailand 13°44N 100°30E 113 B2
Pompton Lakes U.S.A. 41°0N 74°17W 313 F10
Ponape = Pohnpei Micronesia 6°55N 158°10E 288 G7
Ponask L. Canada 54°0N 92°41W 298 B1
Ponca U.S.A. 42°34N 96°43W 308 D5
Ponca City U.S.A. 36°42N 97°5W 314 C6
Ponce Puerto Rico 18°1N 66°37W 321 C6
Ponce de Leon U.S.A. 30°44N 85°56W 316 E4
Ponce de Leon B. U.S.A. 25°15N 81°10W 317 K8
Ponchatoula U.S.A. 30°26N 90°26W 315 F9
Poncheville, L. Canada 50°10N 76°55W 298 B4
Pond U.S.A. 35°43N 119°20W 307 K7
Pond Inlet Canada 72°40N 77°0W 295 C16
Pondicherry = Puducherry India 11°59N 79°50E 245 J4
Pondo Papua N. G. 4°33S 151°38E 286 C6
Pondok Gede Indonesia 6°17S 106°55E 122 A2
Pondok Indah Indonesia 6°16S 106°46E 122 B1
Ponds, I. of Canada 53°27N 55°52W 299 B8
Ponérihouen N. Cal. 21°5S 165°24E 288 d

Ponferrada Spain 42°32N 6°35W 194 C4
Pongo, Wadi → South Sudan 8°42N 27°40E 257 F2
Poniatowa Poland 51°11N 22°3E 185 G9
Poniec Poland 51°48N 16°50E 185 G3
Ponikva Slovenia 46°16N 15°26E 199 B12
Ponizovkino = Krasnyy Profintern Russia 57°45N 40°27E 188 D11
Ponnaiyar → India 11°50N 79°45E 245 J4
Ponnani India 10°45N 75°59E 245 J2
Ponneri India 13°20N 80°15E 245 H5
Ponnuru India 16°5N 80°34E 245 F5
Ponoka Canada 52°42N 113°40W 296 C6
Ponorogo Indonesia 7°52S 111°27E 235 D4
Ponot Phil. 8°25N 123°0E 233 G4
Ponoy Russia 67°0N 41°13E 186 A7
Ponoy → Russia 66°59N 41°17E 186 A7
Pons = Ponts Spain 41°55N 1°12E 196 D6
Pons France 45°35N 0°34W 174 C3
Ponsul → Portugal 39°40N 7°31W 194 F3
Pont-à-Mousson France 48°54N 6°1E 173 D13
Pont-Audemer France 49°21N 0°30E 172 C7
Pont-Aven France 47°51N 3°47W 172 E3
Pont Canavese Italy 45°25N 7°36E 198 C4
Pont Casse Dominica 15°22N 61°21W 323 k
Pont-d'Ain France 46°3N 5°21E 173 F12
Pont-de-Roide France 47°23N 6°45E 173 E13
Pont-de-Salars France 44°18N 2°44E 174 D6
Pont-de-Vaux France 46°26N 4°56E 173 F11
Pont-de-Veyle France 46°17N 4°53E 173 F11
Pont-du-Château France 45°47N 3°15E 173 G10
Pont du Gard France 43°57N 4°32E 175 E8
Pont-l'Abbé France 47°52N 4°15W 172 E2
Pont-l'Évêque France 49°18N 0°11E 172 C7
Pont-St-Esprit France 44°16N 4°40E 175 D8
Pont-St-Martin Italy 45°36N 7°48E 198 C4
Pont-Ste-Maxence France 49°18N 2°36E 173 C9
Pont-sur-Yonne France 48°18N 3°10E 173 D10
Pont-Viau Canada 45°35N 73°41W 130 A1
Ponta de Pedras Brazil 1°23S 48°52W 332 B2
Ponta Delgada Flores, Azores 39°31N 31°13W 153 d2
Ponta Delgada São Miguel, Azores 37°44N 25°40W 153 d3
Ponta Delgada ✈ (PDL) Azores 37°44N 25°41W 153 d3
Ponta do Pargo Madeira 32°49N 17°15W 153 c
Ponta do Sol Madeira 32°42N 17°7W 153 c
Ponta Grossa Brazil 25°7S 50°10W 335 B5
Ponta Porã Brazil 22°20S 55°35W 335 A4
Pontacq France 43°11N 0°8W 174 E3
Pontailler-sur-Saône France 47°13N 5°25E 173 E12
Pontal → Brazil 9°8S 40°12W 332 C3
Pontalina Brazil 17°31S 49°27W 333 E2
Pontardawe U.K. 51°43N 3°51W 169 F3
Pontarlier France 46°54N 6°20E 173 F13
Pontassieve Italy 43°46N 11°26E 199 E8
Pontault-Combault France 48°47N 2°36E 134 B4
Pontaumur France 45°52N 2°40E 174 C6
Pontcharra France 45°26N 6°1E 175 C10
Pontchartrain, L. U.S.A. 30°5N 90°5W 315 F9
Pontchâteau France 47°25N 2°5W 172 E4
Ponte Alta, Serra do Brazil 19°42S 47°40W 333 E2
Ponte Alta do Norte Brazil 10°45S 47°34W 332 D2
Ponte Branca Brazil 16°27S 52°40W 331 D7
Ponte da Barca Portugal 41°48N 8°25W 194 D2
Ponte de Lima Portugal 41°46N 8°35W 194 D2
Ponte de Sor Portugal 39°17N 8°1W 195 F2
Ponte dell'Ólio Italy 44°52N 9°39E 198 D6
Ponte di Legno Italy 46°16N 10°31E 198 B7
Ponte do Pungué Mozam. 19°30S 34°33E 269 F3
Ponte-Leccia France 42°28N 9°13E 175 F13
Ponte nelle Alpi Italy 46°11N 12°16E 199 B9
Ponte Nova Brazil 20°25S 42°54W 333 F3
Ponte Vedra Beach U.S.A. 30°15N 81°23W 316 E8
Ponteareas Spain 42°10N 8°28W 194 C2
Pontebba Italy 46°30N 13°18E 199 B10
Ponteceso Spain 43°15N 8°54W 194 B2
Pontecorvo Italy 41°27N 13°40E 200 A6
Pontedeume Spain 43°24N 8°10W 194 B2
Ponteix Canada 49°46N 107°29W 297 D7
Pontes e Lacerda Brazil 15°12S 59°22W 331 D6
Pontevedra Capiz, Phil. 11°29N 122°50E 233 F4
Pontevedra Neg. Occ., Phil. 10°22N 122°52E 233 F4
Pontevedra Spain 42°26N 8°40W 194 C2
Pontevedra □ Spain 42°25N 8°39W 194 C2
Pontevedra, R. de → Spain 42°22N 8°45W 194 C2
Pontevico Italy 45°16N 10°5E 198 C7
Pontiac Ill., U.S.A. 40°53N 88°38W 311 D8
Pontiac Mich., U.S.A. 42°38N 83°18W 311 B13
Pontian Kechil Malaysia 1°29N 103°23E 237 d
Pontianak Indonesia 0°3S 109°15E 235 C3
Pontine Is. = Ponziane, Ísole Italy 40°55N 12°57E 200 B5
Pontine Mts. = Kuzey Anadolu Dağları Turkey 41°0N 36°45E 212 B7
Pontinha Portugal 38°45N 9°11W 126 A1
Pontínia Italy 41°25N 13°2E 200 A6
Pontivy France 48°5N 2°58W 172 D4
Pontoise France 49°3N 2°5E 173 C9
Ponton → Canada 58°27N 116°11W 296 B5
Pontorson France 48°34N 1°30W 172 D5
Pontrémoli Italy 44°22N 9°53E 198 D6
Pontrieux France 48°42N 3°10W 172 D3
Ponts Spain 41°55N 1°12E 196 D6
Pontypool Ont., Canada 44°6N 78°38W 312 B6
Pontypool Torf., U.K. 51°42N 3°2W 169 F4
Pontypridd U.K. 51°36N 3°20W 169 F4
Ponza Italy 40°54N 12°58E 200 B5
Ponziane, Ísole Italy 40°55N 12°57E 200 B5
Poochera Australia 32°43S 134°51E 281 E1
Pool □ Congo 3°30S 15°0E 264 C2
Poole Trin. & Tob. 10°17N 61°14W 323 t
Poole Poole, U.K. 50°43N 1°59W 169 G6
Poole → Trin. & Tob. 10°15N 61°5W 323 t
Pooler U.S.A. 32°7N 81°15W 316 C8
Poona = Pune India 18°29N 73°57E 244 E1
Poonamallee India 13°3N 80°10E 245 H5
Pooncarie Australia 33°22S 142°31E 282 B5
Poopelloe L. Australia 31°40S 144°0E 282 A6
Poopó Bolivia 18°23S 66°59W 330 D4
Poopó, L. de Bolivia 18°30S 67°35W 330 D4
Poor Knights Is. N.Z. 35°29S 174°43E 284 B3
Poorman U.S.A. 64°5N 155°33W 303 D9
Popa Gabon 1°35S 12°32E 264 C2
Popa, Mt. Myanmar 20°55N 95°15E 241 E5
Popayán Colombia 2°27N 76°36W 328 C2
Poperinge Belgium 50°51N 2°42E 170 D2
Popiltah L. Australia 33°10S 141°42E 282 B4
Popina Bulgaria 44°7N 26°57E 203 B10
Popio L. Australia 33°10S 141°52E 282 B4
Poplar London, U.K. 51°30N 0°0 125 A3
Poplar Mont., U.S.A. 48°7N 105°12W 304 B11
Poplar → Canada 53°0N 97°19W 297 C9
Poplar Bluff U.S.A. 36°46N 90°24W 308 G8
Poplar Head = Dothan U.S.A. 31°13N 85°24W 316 D4
Poplarville U.S.A. 30°51N 89°32W 315 F10
Popocatépetl, Volcán Mexico 19°2N 98°38W 319 D5
Popokabaka Dem. Rep. of the Congo 5°41S 16°40E 265 D3
Pópoli Italy 42°10N 13°50E 199 F10
Popolo Dem. Rep. of the Congo 2°22N 21°8E 264 B4
Popolo, Porta del Rome, Italy 136 a2
Popomanaseu, Mt. Solomon Is. 9°40S 160°1E 287 M11
Popondetta Papua N. G. 8°48S 148°17E 286 E5
Popovača Croatia 45°30N 16°41E 199 C13
Popovo Bulgaria 43°21N 26°18E 203 C10
Poppberg Germany 49°26N 11°37E 179 F7
Poppi Italy 43°43N 11°46E 199 E8
Poprad Slovakia 49°3N 20°18E 181 B13
Poprad → Slovakia 49°38N 20°42E 181 B13
Poradaha Bangla. 23°51N 89°1E 241 D2
Porali → Pakistan 25°58N 66°26E 242 G2
Porangaba Brazil 8°48S 70°36W 330 B3
Porangahau N.Z. 40°17S 176°37E 284 G5
Porangatu Brazil 13°26S 49°10W 333 D2
Porbandar India 21°44N 69°43E 242 J3
Porce → Colombia 7°28N 74°53W 328 B3
Porcher I. Canada 53°50N 130°30W 296 C2
Porco Bolivia 19°50S 65°59W 331 D4
Porcos → Brazil 12°42S 45°7W 333 D2
Porcuna Spain 37°52N 4°11W 195 H6
Porcupine → Sask., Canada 59°11N 104°46W 297 B8
Porcupine → Alaska, U.S.A. 66°34N 145°19W 303 C11
Porcupine Abyssal Plain Atl. Oc. 48°0N 8°0W 152 B10
Porcupine Gorge △ Australia 20°22S 144°26E 280 C3
Pordenone Italy 45°57N 12°39E 199 C9
Pordim Bulgaria 43°23N 24°51E 203 C8
Pore Colombia 5°43N 72°0W 328 B3
Poreč Croatia 45°14N 13°36E 199 C10
Porecatu Brazil 22°43S 51°24W 333 F1
Porechye = Demidov Russia 55°16N 31°30E 188 E6
Poretskoye Russia 55°9N 46°21E 190 C8
Porgera Papua N. G. 5°28S 143°12E 286 C2
Pori Finland 61°29N 21°48E 188 B1
Pori Greece 35°58N 23°13E 204 F5
Porkhov Russia 57°45N 29°38E 188 D5
Porlamar Venezuela 10°57N 63°51W 329 a
Porlezza Italy 46°2N 9°7E 198 B6
Porma → Spain 42°49N 5°28W 194 C5
Pormpuraaw Australia 14°59S 141°26E 280 A3
Pormpuraaw ☼ Australia 14°55S 141°47E 280 A3
Pornic France 47°7N 2°5W 172 E4
Poronaysk Russia 49°13N 143°0E 219 B17
Poros Attiki, Greece 37°30N 23°30E 204 D5
Poros Kefalonia, Greece 38°9N 20°47E 207 C2
Poros Lefkada, Greece 38°38N 20°43E 207 B2
Poroshiri-Dake Japan 42°41N 142°52E 220 C11
Poroszló Hungary 47°39N 20°40E 182 C5
Poroto Mts. Tanzania 9°0S 33°30E 269 D3
Porpoise B. Antarctica 66°0S 127°0E 151 C9
Porpoise Pt. Ascension I. 7°54S 14°21W 153 g
Porquerolles, Î. de France 43°0N 6°13E 175 F10
Porrentruy Switz. 47°25N 7°6E 179 H3
Porreres Spain 39°31N 3°2E 206 B4
Porsangerfjorden Norway 70°40N 25°40E 160 A21
Porsgrunn Norway 59°10N 9°40E 164 E6
Port Adelaide Australia 34°50S 138°30E 282 C3
Port Alberni Canada 49°14N 124°50W 296 D4
Port Albert Australia 38°42S 146°42E 283 E7
Port Alexander U.S.A. 56°15N 134°38W 303 H14
Port Alfred S. Africa 33°36S 26°55E 270 D4
Port Alice Canada 50°20N 127°25W 296 C3
Port Allegany U.S.A. 41°48N 78°17W 312 E6
Port Allen U.S.A. 30°27N 91°12W 314 F9
Port Alma Queens., Australia 23°38S 150°53E 280 C5
Port Alma Ont., Canada 42°10N 82°14W 312 D2
Port Angeles U.S.A. 48°7N 123°27W 306 B3
Port Antonio Jamaica 18°10N 76°26W 320 a
Port Aransas U.S.A. 27°50N 97°4W 314 H6
Port Arthur Tas., Australia 43°7S 147°50E 281 G4
Port Arthur Tex., U.S.A. 29°54N 93°56W 314 G8
Port au Choix Canada 50°43N 57°22W 299 B8
Port au Port B. Canada 48°40N 58°50W 299 C8
Port-au-Prince Haiti 18°40N 72°20W 321 C5
Port Augusta Australia 32°30S 137°50E 282 B2
Port Austin U.S.A. 44°3N 83°1W 312 B2
Port Authority Bus Terminal New York, U.S.A. 132 c2
Port-aux-Français Kerguelen 49°21S 70°13E 273 J6
Port Bergé Vaovao Madag. 15°33S 47°40E 272 B2
Port Blair India 11°40N 92°45E 245 J11
Port Blandford Canada 48°20N 54°10W 299 C9
Port Botany Australia 33°58S 151°13E 139 B2
Port-Bouët Côte d'Ivoire 5°16N 3°57W 262 D4
Port Bradshaw Australia 12°30S 137°20E 280 A2
Port Broughton Australia 33°37S 137°56E 282 B2
Port Bruce Canada 42°39N 81°0W 312 D4
Port Burwell Canada 42°40N 80°48W 312 D4
Port Byron U.S.A. 41°36N 90°20W 310 C6
Port Campbell Vic., Australia 38°37S 143°1E 282 E5
Port Campbell India 11°56N 92°37E 245 J11
Port Campbell △ Australia 38°8S 143°6E 282 E5
Port Canning India 22°23N 88°40E 243 H13
Port Carling Canada 45°7N 79°35W 312 A5
Port-Cartier Canada 50°2N 66°50W 299 B6
Port Chalmers N.Z. 45°49S 170°30E 285 F5
Port Charles N.Z. 36°33S 175°30E 284 C4
Port Charlotte U.S.A. 26°59N 82°6W 317 J7
Port Chester U.S.A. 41°0N 73°40W 313 F11
Port Clements Canada 53°40N 132°10W 296 C2
Port Clinton U.S.A. 41°31N 82°56W 311 C14
Port Colborne Canada 42°50N 79°10W 312 D5
Port Coquitlam Canada 49°15N 122°45W 306 A4
Port Cornwallis India 13°17N 93°5E 245 H11
Port Credit Canada 43°33N 79°35W 312 C5
Port-Cros △ France 43°0N 6°24E 175 F10
Port Curtis Australia 23°57S 151°20E 280 C5
Port d'Alcúdia Spain 39°50N 3°7E 206 B4
Port Dalhousie Canada 43°13N 79°16W 312 C5
Port d'Andratx Spain 39°32N 2°23E 206 B3
Port Darwin N. Terr., Australia 12°24S 130°45E 278 B5
Port Darwin Falk. Is. 51°50S 59°0W 153 f
Port Davey Australia 43°16S 145°55E 281 G4
Port-de-Bouc France 43°24N 4°59E 175 E8
Port-de-Paix Haiti 19°50N 72°50W 321 C5
Port de Pollença Spain 39°54N 3°4E 206 B4
Port de Sóller Spain 39°48N 2°42E 206 B3
Port Dickson Malaysia 2°30N 101°49E 237 L3
Port Douglas Australia 16°30S 145°30E 280 B4
Port Dover Canada 42°47N 80°12W 312 D4
Port Edward Canada 54°12N 130°10W 296 C2
Port Elgin Canada 44°25N 81°25W 312 B3
Port Elizabeth = Gqeberha S. Africa 33°58S 25°40E 270 D4
Port Ellen U.K. 55°38N 6°11W 167 F2
Port Elliot Australia 35°32S 138°41E 282 C3
Port-en-Bessin-Huppain France 49°21N 0°45W 172 C6
Port Erin I. of Man 54°5N 4°45W 168 C3
Port Essington Australia 11°15S 132°10E 278 B5
Port Etienne = Nouâdhibou Mauritania 20°54N 17°0W 260 D1
Port Ewen U.S.A. 41°54N 73°59W 313 E11
Port Fairy Australia 38°22S 142°12E 282 E5
Port Fitzroy N.Z. 36°8S 175°20E 284 C4
Port Florence = Kisumu Kenya 0°3S 34°45E 268 C3
Port Fouâd = Bûr Fuad Egypt 31°15N 32°20E 256 H8
Port Francqui = Ilebo Dem. Rep. of the Congo 4°17S 20°55E 265 C4
Port Gamble U.S.A. 47°51N 122°34W 306 C4
Port-Gentil Gabon 0°40S 8°50E 264 C1
Port Germein Australia 33°1S 138°1E 281 E2
Port Ghalib Egypt 25°20N 34°50E 246 E2
Port Gibson U.S.A. 31°58N 90°59W 314 F9
Port Glasgow U.K. 55°56N 4°41W 167 F4
Port-Gueydon = Azeffoun Algeria 36°51N 4°26E 261 A5
Port Harcourt Nigeria 4°40N 7°10E 263 E6
Port Hardy Canada 50°41N 127°30W 296 C3
Port Harrison = Inukjuak Canada 58°25N 78°15W 295 F16
Port Hawkesbury Canada 45°36N 61°22W 299 C7
Port Hedland Australia 20°25S 118°35E 278 D2
Port Heiden U.S.A. 56°55N 158°41W 303 H8
Port Henry U.S.A. 44°3N 73°28W 313 B11
Port Herald = Nsanje Malawi 16°55S 35°12E 269 F4
Port Hood Canada 46°0N 61°32W 299 C7
Port Hope Ont., Canada 43°56N 78°20W 312 C6
Port Hope Mich., U.S.A. 43°57N 82°43W 312 C2
Port Hope Simpson Canada 52°33N 56°18W 299 B8
Port Hueneme U.S.A. 34°7N 119°12W 307 L7
Port Huron U.S.A. 42°58N 82°26W 312 D2
Port Iliç = Liman Azerbaijan 38°53N 48°47E 213 C13
Port Jefferson U.S.A. 40°57N 73°3W 313 F11
Port Jervis U.S.A. 41°22N 74°41W 313 E10
Port-Joinville France 46°45N 2°23W 172 F4
Port Katon Russia 46°52N 38°46E 189 J10
Port Kavkaz Russia 45°20N 36°40E 189 K9
Port Kembla Australia 34°52S 150°49E 283 C9
Port Kenny Australia 33°10S 134°41E 281 E1
Port Klang Malaysia 3°0N 101°35E 237 L3
Port-la-Nouvelle France 43°1N 3°3E 174 E7
Port Láirge = Waterford Ireland 52°15N 7°8W 166 D4
Port Launay Seychelles 4°39S 55°24E 272 c
Port Lavaca U.S.A. 28°37N 96°38W 314 G6
Port Leyden U.S.A. 43°35N 75°21W 313 C9
Port Lincoln Australia 34°42S 135°52E 282 C1
Port Lions U.S.A. 57°52N 152°53W 303 H9
Port Loko S. Leone 8°48N 12°46W 262 D2
Port Louis Morbihan, France 47°42N 3°22W 172 E3
Port-Louis Guadeloupe 16°28N 61°32W 322 e
Port Louis Mauritius 20°10S 57°30E 272 e
Port Lyautey = Kenitra Morocco 34°15N 6°40W 260 B3
Port MacDonnell Australia 38°5S 140°48E 282 E4
Port McNeill Canada 50°35N 127°6W 296 C3
Port Macquarie Australia 31°25S 152°25E 283 A10
Port Maria Jamaica 18°22N 76°54W 320 a
Port Mathurin Rodrigues 19°41S 63°25E 273 F5
Port Matilda U.S.A. 40°48N 78°3W 312 F6
Port Mayaca U.S.A. 26°59N 80°36W 317 J9
Port McNicoll Canada 44°44N 79°48W 312 B5
Port Melbourne Australia 37°50S 144°54E 128 B1
Port Mellon Canada 49°32N 123°31W 296 D4
Port-Menier Canada 49°51N 64°15W 299 C7
Port Moller U.S.A. 55°59N 160°34W 303 J7
Port Moody Canada 49°17N 122°51W 306 A4
Port Morant Jamaica 17°54N 76°19W 320 a
Port Moresby Papua N. G. 9°24S 147°8E 286 E4
Port Mourant Guyana 6°15N 57°20W 329 B6
Port Muhammed Bin Qasim = Port Qasim Pakistan 24°46N 67°20E 242 G2
Port Musgrave Australia 11°55S 141°50E 280 A3
Port Narevin = Potnavin Vanuatu 18°45S 169°10E 287 H7
Port-Navalo France 47°34N 2°54W 172 E4
Port Neches U.S.A. 30°0N 93°59W 314 G8
Port Nicholson N.Z. 41°20S 174°52E 284 H3
Port Nolloth S. Africa 29°17S 16°52E 270 C2
Port Nouveau-Québec = Kangiqsualujjuaq Canada 58°30N 65°59W 295 F18
Port of Climax Canada 49°10N 108°20W 297 D7
Port of Coronach Canada 49°7N 105°31W 297 D7
Port of Spain Trin. & Tob. 10°40N 61°31W 323 t
Port Olry Vanuatu 15°1S 167°4E 287 E5
Port Orange U.S.A. 29°9N 80°59W 317 F9
Port Orchard U.S.A. 47°32N 122°38W 306 C4
Port Orford U.S.A. 42°45N 124°30W 304 E1
Port Pegasus N.Z. 47°12S 167°41E 285 H2
Port Perry Canada 44°6N 78°56W 312 B6
Port Phillip B. Australia 38°10S 144°50E 283 E6
Port Pirie Australia 33°10S 138°1E 282 B3
Port Qasim Pakistan 24°46N 67°20E 242 G2
Port Rashid U.A.E. 25°16N 55°17E 119 A2
Port Renfrew Canada 48°30N 124°20W 306 B2
Port Richmond U.S.A. 40°38N 74°7W 132 C1
Port Roper Australia 14°45S 135°25E 280 A2
Port Rowan Canada 42°40N 80°30W 312 D4
Port Royal Jamaica 17°56N 76°51W 320 a
Port Royal Sd. U.S.A. 32°15N 80°40W 316 C9
Port Saeed U.A.E. 25°15N 55°20E 119 B2
Port Safaga = Bûr Safâga Egypt 26°43N 33°57E 246 E2
Port Said = Bûr Sa'îd Egypt 31°16N 32°18E 256 H8
Port St. Joe U.S.A. 29°49N 85°18W 316 F4
Port St. John U.S.A. 28°29N 80°47W 317 G9
Port St. Johns = Umzimvubu S. Africa 31°38S 29°33E 271 D4
Port-St-Louis-du-Rhône France 43°23N 4°49E 175 E8
Port St. Lucie U.S.A. 27°18N 80°21W 317 H9
Port-Ste-Marie France 44°15N 0°25E 174 D4
Port Salerno U.S.A. 27°9N 80°12W 317 H9
Port Sanilac U.S.A. 43°26N 82°33W 312 C2
Port Severn Canada 44°48N 79°43W 312 B5
Port Shelter Hong Kong, China 22°20N 114°17E 122 A3
Port Shepstone S. Africa 30°44S 30°28E 271 D5
Port Simpson Canada 54°30N 130°20W 296 C2
Port Stanley = Stanley Falk. Is. 51°40S 59°51W 153 f
Port Stanley Canada 42°40N 81°10W 312 D3
Port Sudan = Bûr Sûdân Sudan 19°32N 37°9E 256 D4
Port Sulphur U.S.A. 29°29N 89°42W 315 G10
Port-sur-Saône France 47°42N 6°2E 173 E13
Port Talbot U.K. 51°35N 3°47W 169 F4
Port Taufiq = Bûr Taufiq Egypt 29°54N 32°32E 256 J8
Port Townsend U.S.A. 48°7N 122°45W 306 B4
Port Union Canada 43°47N 79°7W 141 A4
Port-Vato Vanuatu 16°20S 168°1E 287 F6
Port-Vendres France 42°32N 3°8E 174 F7
Port Victoria Australia 34°30S 137°29E 282 C2
Port Vila Vanuatu 17°45S 168°18E 287 G6
Port Vladimir Russia 69°25N 33°6E 160 B25
Port Wakefield Australia 34°12S 138°10E 282 C3
Port Washington U.S.A. 43°23N 87°53W 308 D10
Port Weld = Kuala Sepetang Malaysia 4°49N 100°28E 237 K3
Port Wentworth U.S.A. 32°9N 81°10W 316 C8
Porta Orientalis Romania 45°6N 22°18E 177 F12
Portachuelo Bolivia 17°10S 63°20W 331 D5
Portacloy Ireland 54°20N 9°46W 166 B2
Portadown U.K. 54°25N 6°27W 166 B5
Portaferry U.K. 54°23N 5°33W 166 B6
Portage Ind., U.S.A. 41°34N 87°11W 311 C10
Portage Mich., U.S.A. 42°12N 85°35W 311 B11
Portage Pa., U.S.A. 40°23N 78°41W 312 F6
Portage Wis., U.S.A. 43°33N 89°28W 308 D9
Portage → U.S.A. 41°31N 83°5W 311 C14
Portage la Prairie Canada 49°58N 98°18W 297 D9
Portage Park U.S.A. 41°56N 87°45W 119 B2
Portageville U.S.A. 36°26N 89°42W 308 G9
Portal U.S.A. 32°33N 81°56W 316 C8
Portal de la Pau, Plaza Barcelona, Spain 114 c2
Portalegre Portugal 39°19N 7°25W 195 F3
Portalegre □ Portugal 39°20N 7°40W 195 F3
Portales U.S.A. 34°11N 103°20W 305 J12
Portarlington Ireland 53°9N 7°14W 166 C4
Portbou Spain 42°25N 3°9E 196 C8
Porteira Brazil 1°5S 57°4W 329 D6
Porteirinha Brazil 15°44S 43°2W 333 E3
Portel Brazil 1°57S 50°49W 332 B1
Portel Portugal 38°19N 7°41W 195 G3
Portela, Lisboa ✈ (LIS) Portugal 38°46N 9°8W 126 A2
Porter U.S.A. 41°36N 87°4W 311 C9
Porter, L. U.S.A. 28°30N 81°19W 133 A3
Porter L. N.W.T., Canada 61°41N 108°5W 297 A7
Porter L. Sask., Canada 56°20N 107°20W 297 B7
Porterville Western Cape, S. Africa 33°0S 19°0E 270 D2
Porterville Calif., U.S.A. 36°4N 119°1W 306 J8
Portes-lès-Valence France 44°52N 4°54E 175 D8
Porth Tywyn = Burry Port U.K. 51°41N 4°15W 169 F3
Porthcawl U.K. 51°29N 3°42W 169 F4
Porthill U.S.A. 48°59N 116°30W 304 B5
Porthmadog U.K. 52°55N 4°8W 168 E3
Portile de Fier Europe 44°44N 22°30E 182 F7
Portimão Portugal 37°8N 8°32W 195 H2
Portishead U.K. 51°29N 2°46W 169 F5
Portiţei, Gura Romania 44°41N 29°0E 183 F14
Portknockie U.K. 57°42N 2°51W 167 D6
Portland N.S.W., Australia 33°20S 150°0E 283 B9
Portland Vic., Australia 38°20S 141°35E 282 E4
Portland Ont., Canada 44°42N 76°12W 313 B8
Portland Conn., U.S.A. 41°34N 72°38W 313 E12
Portland Fla., U.S.A. 30°31N 86°12W 316 E3
Portland Ind., U.S.A. 40°26N 84°59W 311 D12
Portland Maine, U.S.A. 43°39N 70°16W 309 D18
Portland Mich., U.S.A. 42°52N 84°54W 311 B12
Portland Oreg., U.S.A. 45°32N 122°37W 306 E4
Portland Pa., U.S.A. 40°55N 75°6W 313 F9
Portland Tex., U.S.A. 27°53N 97°20W 314 H6
Portland, I. of U.K. 50°33N 2°26W 169 G5
Portland, Récif French Polynesia 23°42S 134°30W 289 f
Portland B. Australia 38°15S 141°45E 282 E4
Portland Bight Jamaica 17°52N 77°5W 320 a
Portland Bill U.K. 50°31N 2°28W 169 G5
Portland Canal U.S.A. 55°56N 130°0W 296 B2
Portland I. N.Z. 39°20S 177°51E 284 F6
Portland Int. ✈ (PDX) U.S.A. 45°35N 122°36W 306 E4
Portland Pt. Ascension I. 7°59S 14°25W 153 g
Portland Pt. Jamaica 17°42N 77°11W 320 a
Portlaoise Ireland 53°2N 7°18W 166 C4
Portmadoc = Porthmadog U.K. 52°55N 4°8W 168 E3
Portmore Jamaica 17°53N 76°53W 320 a
Porto Brazil 3°54S 42°42W 332 B3
Porto Corse-du-Sud, France 42°16N 8°42E 175 F12
Porto Portugal 41°8N 8°40W 194 D2
Porto □ Portugal 41°8N 8°20W 194 D2
Porto, G. de France 42°17N 8°34E 175 F12
Porto Acre Brazil 9°34S 67°31W 330 B4
Pôrto Alegre = Luzilândia Brazil 3°28S 42°22W 332 B3
Pôrto Alegre Pará, Brazil 4°22S 52°44W 329 D7
Pôrto Alegre Rio Grande do S., Brazil 30°5S 51°10W 335 C5
Porto Alegre São Tomé & Príncipe 0°2N 6°32E 265 a
Porto Amboim = Gunza Angola 10°50S 13°50E 265 E2
Porto Amélia = Pemba Mozam. 12°58S 40°30E 269 E5
Porto Azzurro Italy 42°46N 10°24E 198 F7
Porto Brandão Portugal 38°40N 9°12W 126 A1
Pôrto Cajueiro Brazil 11°3S 55°53W 331 C6
Porto Cervo Italy 41°8N 9°33E 200 A2
Porto Colom Spain 39°26N 3°15E 206 B4
Porto Cristo Spain 39°33N 3°20E 206 B4
Pôrto da Fôlha Brazil 9°55S 37°17W 332 C4
Porto de Moz Brazil 1°41S 52°13W 329 D7
Porto de Pedras Brazil 9°10S 35°17W 332 C4
Pôrto des Meinacos Brazil 12°33S 53°7W 331 C7
Pôrto dos Gaúchos Brazil 11°32S 57°16W 331 C6
Porto Empédocle Italy 37°17N 13°32E 200 E6
Porto Esperança Brazil 19°37S 57°29W 331 D6
Porto Espirdão Brazil 15°51S 58°28W 331 D6
Porto Formoso Azores 37°49N 25°25W 153 d3
Porto Franco Brazil 6°20S 47°24W 332 C2
Porto Grande Brazil 0°42N 51°24W 329 C7
Porto Inglês = Vila do Maio Cabo Verde 15°21N 23°10W 153 j
Porto Jofre Brazil 17°20S 56°48W 331 D6
Porto Lengone = Porto Azzurro Italy 42°46N 10°24E 198 F7
Porto Maurizio = Impéria Italy 43°53N 8°3E 198 E5
Porto Mendes Brazil 24°30S 54°15W 335 A5
Porto Moniz Madeira 32°52N 17°11W 153 c
Porto Murtinho Brazil 21°45S 57°55W 331 E6
Porto Nacional Brazil 10°40S 48°30W 332 D2
Porto-Novo Benin 6°23N 2°42E 263 D5
Pôrto Novo Rio de J., Brazil 22°50S 43°7W 135 A2
Porto Novo Cr. → Nigeria 6°25N 3°22E 124 B2
Porto Primavera, Represa Brazil 22°10S 52°45W 335 A5
Porto San Giórgio Italy 43°11N 13°48E 199 E10
Porto Santana Brazil 0°3S 51°11W 329 D7
Porto Santo, I. de Madeira 33°45N 16°25W 260 B1
Porto Sant' Elpídio Italy 43°15N 13°43E 199 E10
Porto Santo Stéfano Italy 42°26N 11°7E 198 F8
Porto São José Brazil 22°43S 53°10W 335 A5
Porto Seguro = Guadalupe Brazil 6°44S 43°47W 332 C3
Porto Seguro Brazil 16°26S 39°5W 333 E4
Porto Tolle Italy 44°56N 12°22E 199 D9
Porto Tórres Italy 40°50N 8°24E 200 B1
Porto União Brazil 26°10S 51°10W 335 B5
Porto-Vecchio France 41°35N 9°16E 175 G13
Porto Velho Brazil 8°46S 63°54W 331 B5
Porto Viro Italy 45°1N 12°13E 199 C9
Porto Walter Brazil 8°15S 72°40W 330 B3
Portobello U.K. 55°57N 3°7W 121 B3
Portobelo Panama 9°35N 79°42W 320 E4
Portoferráio Italy 42°48N 10°20E 198 F7
Portofino Italy 44°18N 9°12E 198 D6
Portogruaro Italy 45°47N 12°50E 199 C9
Portola U.S.A. 39°49N 120°28W 306 F6
Portomaggiore Italy 44°42N 11°48E 199 D8
Portopetro Spain 39°22N 3°13E 206 B4
Portør Norway 58°48N 9°28E 164 F6
Portoscuso Italy 39°12N 8°24E 200 C1
Portovénere Italy 44°3N 9°51E 198 D6
Portoviejo Ecuador 1°7S 80°28W 328 D1
Portpatrick U.K. 54°51N 5°7W 167 G3
Portree U.K. 57°25N 6°12W 167 D2
Portrero U.S.A. 37°46N 122°25W 136 B3
Portrush U.K. 55°12N 6°40W 166 A5
Portsmouth Dominica 15°34N 61°27W 323 k
Portsmouth Portsmouth, U.K. 50°48N 1°6W 169 G6
Portsmouth N.H., U.S.A. 43°5N 70°45W 313 C14
Portsmouth Ohio, U.S.A. 38°44N 82°57W 309 F12
Portsmouth R.I., U.S.A. 41°36N 71°15W 313 E13
Portsmouth Va., U.S.A. 36°58N 76°23W 309 G15
Portsmouth □ U.K. 50°48N 1°6W 169 G6
Portsoy U.K. 57°41N 2°41W 167 D6
Portstewart U.K. 55°11N 6°43W 166 A5
Porttipahdan tekojärvi Finland 68°5N 26°40E 160 B22
Portugal ■ Europe 40°0N 8°0W 194 F3
Portugalete Spain 43°19N 3°4W 196 B1
Portuguesa □ Venezuela 9°10N 69°15W 328 B4
Portuguese East Africa = Mozambique ■ Africa 19°0S 35°0E 269 F4
Portuguese Guinea = Guinea-Bissau ■ Africa 12°0N 15°0W 262 C2
Portuguese Timor = Timor-Leste ■ Asia 8°50S 126°0E 231 F7
Portuguese West Africa = Angola ■ Africa 12°0S 18°0E 265 E3
Portumna Ireland 53°6N 8°14W 166 C3
Portville U.S.A. 42°3N 78°20W 312 D6
Poruma Australia 10°2S 143°4E 280 a
Porus Jamaica 18°2N 77°25W 320 a
Porvenir Bolivia 11°10S 68°50W 330 C4
Porvenir Chile 53°10S 70°16W 336 D2
Porvoo Finland 60°24N 25°40E 188 B3
Porzuna Spain 39°9N 4°9W 195 F6
Pos Chiquito Aruba 12°27N 69°57W 322 f
Posada Italy 40°38N 9°43E 200 B2
Posada → Italy 40°39N 9°45E 200 B2
Posadas Argentina 27°30S 55°50W 335 B4
Posadas Spain 37°47N 5°11W 195 H5
Poschiavo Switz. 46°19N 10°4E 179 J6
Posen = Poznań Poland 52°25N 16°55E 185 F3
Posen U.S.A. 41°38N 87°42W 119 D2
Posets Spain 42°39N 0°25E 196 C5
Poseyville U.S.A. 38°10N 87°47W 311 F9
Poshan = Boshan China 36°28N 117°49E 227 F9
Posht-e Badam Iran 33°2N 55°23E 247 C7
Posidium Greece 35°30N 27°10E 205 F9
Poso Indonesia 1°20S 120°55E 231 E6
Poso, Danau Indonesia 1°52S 120°35E 231 E6
Posoegroenoe Suriname 4°23N 55°43W 329 C6
Posof Turkey 41°30N 42°43E 213 B10
Pospelikha Russia 51°57N 81°46E 217 B10
Posse Brazil 14°4S 46°18W 333 D2
Possedimenti Italiani dell'Egeo = Dodekanisa Greece 36°35N 27°0E 205 E8
Possel C.A.R. 5°5N 19°10E 264 A3
Possession I. Antarctica 72°4S 172°0E 151 D11
Pössneck Germany 50°42N 11°35E 178 E7
Possum Kingdom L. U.S.A. 32°52N 98°26W 314 E5
Post U.S.A. 33°12N 101°23W 314 E4
Post Falls U.S.A. 47°43N 116°57W 304 C5
Postavy = Pastavy Belarus 55°4N 26°50E 188 E4
Poste, R. du Mauritius 20°29S 57°36E 272 e
Poste de Flacq Mauritius 20°9S 57°43E 272 e
Poste de Flacq → Mauritius 20°9S 57°44E 272 e
Poste-de-la-Baleine = Kuujjuarapik Canada 55°20N 77°35W 298 A4
Postmasburg S. Africa 28°18S 23°5E 270 C3
Postojna Slovenia 45°46N 14°12E 199 C11
Poston U.S.A. 34°0N 114°24W 307 M12
Postumia = Postojna Slovenia 45°46N 14°12E 199 C11
Postville Nfld. & L., Canada 54°54N 59°47W 299 B8
Postville Iowa, U.S.A. 43°5N 91°34W 310 A5
Posyet Russia 42°39N 130°48E 220 C5
Potamos Antikythira, Greece 35°52N 23°15E 204 F5
Potamos Kythira, Greece 36°15N 22°58E 204 E4
Potaro-Siparuni □ Guyana 4°50N 59°19W 329 C6
Potchefstroom S. Africa 26°41S 27°7E 270 C4
Potcoava Romania 44°30N 24°39E 183 F9
Poté Brazil 17°49S 41°49W 333 E3
Poteau U.S.A. 35°3N 94°37W 314 D7
Poteet U.S.A. 29°2N 98°35W 314 G5
Potenza Italy 40°38N 15°48E 201 B8
Potenza → Italy 43°25N 13°40E 199 E10
Potenza Picena Italy 43°22N 13°37E 199 E10
Poteriteri, L. N.Z. 46°5S 167°10E 285 G2
Potgietersrus = Mokopane S. Africa 24°10S 28°55E 271 B4
Poti Georgia 42°10N 41°38E 191 J5
Potiraguá Brazil 15°36S 39°53W 333 E4
Potiskum Nigeria 11°39N 11°2E 263 C7
Potlogi Romania 44°34N 25°34E 183 F10
Potnavin Vanuatu 18°45S 169°10E 287 H7
Potomac → U.S.A. 38°0N 76°23W 309 F14
Potomac Overlook Reg. Park ⌂ U.S.A. 38°55N 77°6W 143 B2
Potomac Park Washington, D.C., U.S.A. 143 c1
Potosí Bolivia 19°38S 65°50W 331 D4
Potosi Mo., U.S.A. 37°56N 90°47W 310 G6
Potosí □ Bolivia 20°31S 67°0W 330 E4
Potosi Mt. U.S.A. 35°57N 115°29W 307 K11
Pototan Phil. 10°54N 122°38E 233 F4
Potrerillos Chile 26°30S 69°30W 334 B2
Potrero Pt. U.S.A. 37°45N 122°22W 136 B2
Potsdam Brandenburg, Germany 52°23N 13°3E 115 B1
Potsdam N.Y., U.S.A. 44°40N 74°59W 313 B10
Potsdamer Platz Berlin, Germany 115 b3
Pottangi India 18°34N 82°58E 244 E6
Pottenstein Germany 49°46N 11°24E 179 F7
Potters Village Antigua & B. 17°5N 61°49W 322 b
Pottersville U.S.A. 43°43N 73°50W 313 C11
Pottery Hill = Abu Ballas Egypt 24°26N 27°36E 256 C2
Pottstown U.S.A. 40°15N 75°39W 313 F9
Pottsville U.S.A. 40°41N 76°12W 313 F8
Pottuvil Sri Lanka 6°55N 81°50E 245 L5
Potzham Germany 48°1N 11°36E 131 B2
Pötzleinsdorf Austria 48°14N 16°17E 142 A1
P'otzu Taiwan 23°28N 120°15E 225 C2
Pouancé France 47°44N 1°10W 172 E5
Pouce Coupé Canada 55°40N 120°10W 296 B4
Pouébo N. Cal. 20°24S 164°36E 288 d
Poughkeepsie U.S.A. 41°42N 73°56W 313 E11
Pouilly-sur-Loire France 47°17N 2°57E 173 E9
Poulan U.S.A. 31°31N 83°47W 316 D6
Poulaphouca Res. Ireland 53°8N 6°30W 166 C5
Poulata Greece 38°14N 20°36E 207 C2
Poulsbo U.S.A. 47°44N 122°38W 306 C4
Poultney U.S.A. 43°31N 73°14W 313 C11
Poulton-le-Fylde U.K. 53°51N 2°58W 168 D5
Poum N. Cal. 20°14S 164°2E 288 d
Pounga-Nganda Gabon 2°58S 10°51E 264 C2
Pouso Alegre Mato Grosso, Brazil 11°46S 57°16W 331 C6
Pouso Alegre Minas Gerais, Brazil 22°14S 45°57W 335 A6
Pouso Alto = Piracanjuba Brazil 17°18S 49°1W 333 E2
Pout Senegal 14°45N 17°0W 262 C1
Pouthisat Cambodia 12°34N 103°50E 236 F4
Pouytenga Burkina Faso 12°15N 0°25W 263 C4
Pouzauges France 46°47N 0°50W 172 F6
Považská Bystrica Slovakia 49°8N 18°27E 181 B11
Povenets Russia 62°50N 34°50E 186 B5
Poverty B. N.Z. 38°43S 178°2E 284 E7
Poverty Point Nat. Monument ⌂ U.S.A. 32°39N 91°24W 314 E9
Povlen Serbia 44°9N 19°44E 202 B3
Póvoa de Lanhosa Portugal 41°33N 8°15W 194 D2
Póvoa de Santa Iria Portugal 38°51N 9°4W 195 G1
Póvoa de Santo Adriao Portugal 38°47N 9°9W 126 A2
Póvoa de Varzim Portugal 41°25N 8°46W 194 D2
Povoação Azores 37°45N 25°15W 153 d3
Povorino Russia 51°12N 42°5E 190 E6
Povorotnyy, Mys Russia 42°40N 133°2E 220 C6
Povungnituk = Puvirnituq Canada 60°2N 77°10W 295 E16
Powassan Canada 46°5N 79°25W 298 C4
Poway U.S.A. 32°58N 117°2W 307 N9
Powązki Poland 52°15N 20°58E 143 B1
Powder → U.S.A. 46°45N 105°26W 304 C11
Powder River U.S.A. 43°2N 106°59W 304 E10
Powder Springs U.S.A. 33°52N 84°41W 316 B5
Powell U.S.A. 44°45N 108°46W 304 D9
Powell, L. U.S.A. 36°57N 111°29W 305 H8
Powell River Canada 49°50N 124°35W 296 D4
Powelton U.S.A. 33°26N 82°52W 316 B7
Power House = Drayton Valley Canada 53°12N 114°58W 296 C6
Powers U.S.A. 45°41N 87°32W 308 C10
Powiśle Poland 52°14N 21°1E 143 B2
Pownal U.S.A. 42°45N 73°14W 313 D11
Powsin Poland 52°8N 21°6E 143 C2
Powsinek Poland 52°9N 21°6E 143 C2
Powys □ U.K. 52°20N 3°20W 169 E4
Poxoréo Brazil 15°50S 54°23W 331 D7
Poya N. Cal. 21°19S 165°7E 288 d
Poyan Res. Singapore 1°22N 103°40E 138 A2
Poyang Hu China 29°5N 116°20E 229 C11
Poyarkovo Russia 49°36N 128°41E 215 E13
Poysdorf Austria 48°40N 16°37E 181 C9
Poza de la Sal Spain 42°35N 3°31W 194 C7
Poza Rica Mexico 20°33N 97°27W 319 C5
Pozantı Turkey 37°25N 34°50E 212 D6
Požarevac Serbia 44°35N 21°18E 202 B5
Pozazal, Puerto Spain 42°56N 4°10W 194 C6
Požega Croatia 45°20N 17°40E 182 E2
Požega Serbia 43°53N 20°2E 202 C4
Poznań Poland 52°25N 16°55E 185 F3
Poznań ✈ (POZ) Poland 52°26N 16°45E 185 F3
Pozo U.S.A. 35°20N 120°24W 307 K6
Pozo Alcón Spain 37°42N 2°56W 195 H8
Pozo Almonte Chile 20°10S 69°50W 330 E4
Pozo Colorado Paraguay 23°30S 58°45W 334 A4
Pozo Negro Canary Is. 28°19N 13°55W 153 e2
Pozoblanco Spain 38°23N 4°51W 195 G6
Pozorrubio Phil. 16°7N 120°33E 232 C3
Pozuelo de Alarcón Spain 40°24N 3°49W 127 B1
Pozuzo Peru 10°5S 75°35W 330 C2
Pozzallo Italy 36°43N 14°51E 201 F7
Pozzomaggiore Italy 40°24N 8°39E 200 B1
Pozzuoli Italy 40°49N 14°7E 201 B7
Pra → Ghana 5°1N 1°37W 263 D4
Prabuty Poland 53°47N 19°15E 184 E6
Prača Bos.-H. 43°47N 18°43E 182 G3
Prachatice Czechia 49°1N 14°0E 180 B6
Prachin Buri Thailand 14°0N 101°25E 236 F3
Prachuap Khirikhan Thailand 11°49N 99°48E 237 G2
Pradelles France 44°46N 3°52E 174 D7
Pradera Colombia 3°25N 76°15W 328 C2
Prades France 42°38N 2°23E 174 F6
Prado Brazil 17°20S 39°13W 333 E4
Prado, Museo del Madrid, Spain 127 b3
Prado Churubusco Mexico 19°20N 99°8W 128 B2
Prado del Rey Spain 36°48N 5°33W 195 J5
Præstø Denmark 55°8N 12°2E 163 J6
Praga Poland 52°15N 21°2E 143 B2
Pragersko Slovenia 46°27N 15°42E 199 B12
Prague = Praha Czechia 50°4N 14°25E 135 B2
Praha Czechia 50°4N 14°25E 135 B2
Praha ✈ (PRG) Czechia 50°6N 14°16E 135 B1
Prahecq France 46°19N 0°26W 174 B3
Prahita → India 19°0N 79°55E 244 E4
Prahova □ Romania 45°10N 26°0E 183 E10
Prahova → Romania 44°50N 25°50E 183 F10
Prahovo Serbia 44°18N 22°39E 202 B6
Praia Azores 39°3N 27°58W 153 d1
Praia Cabo Verde 15°2N 23°34W 153 j
Praia ✈ (RAI) Cabo Verde 14°55N 23°30W 153 j
Praia a Mare Italy 39°50N 15°45E 201 C8
Praia da Vitória Azores 38°44N 27°4W 153 d1
Praia do Norte Azores 38°36N 28°46W 153 d1
Praia Grande Brazil 24°0S 46°24W 333 F2
Praid Romania 46°32N 25°10E 183 D10
Prainha Azores 38°27N 28°12W 153 d1
Prainha Pará, Brazil 1°45S 53°30W 329 D7
Prainha Nova Brazil 7°10S 60°30W 331 B5
Praires, R. des → Canada 45°38N 73°36W 130 A2
Prairie Australia 20°50S 144°35E 280 C3
Prairie City U.S.A. 44°28N 118°43W 304 D4
Prairie Dog Town Fork Red → U.S.A. 34°34N 99°58W 314 D5
Prairie du Chien U.S.A. 43°3N 91°9W 310 A5
Prairie du Rocher U.S.A. 38°5N 90°6W 310 F6
Prairie Village U.S.A. 38°58N 94°38W 310 F2
Prairies, L. of the Canada 51°16N 101°32W 297 C8
Pramanda Greece 39°32N 21°8E 204 B3
Prambanan Indonesia 7°45S 110°29E 235 D4
Prambanan △ Indonesia 7°45S 110°28E 231 G14
Prampram Ghana 5°43N 0°8E 263 D5
Pran Buri Thailand 12°23N 99°55E 236 F2
Prándarjökull Iceland 64°40N 14°55W 155 C12
Prang Ghana 8°1N 0°56W 263 D4
Prapat Indonesia 2°41N 98°58E 234 B1
Praslin St. Lucia 13°52N 60°54W 323 m
Praslin Seychelles 4°18S 55°45E 272 c
Prasonisi, Akra Greece 35°42N 27°46E 206 F11
Prassberg = Mozirje Slovenia 46°22N 14°58E 199 B11
Praszka Poland 51°5N 18°31E 185 G5
Prata Brazil 19°25S 48°54W 333 E2
Pratabpur India 23°28N 83°15E 243 H10
Pratapgarh Raj., India 24°2N 74°40E 242 G6
Pratapgarh Ut. P., India 25°56N 81°59E 243 G9
Pratas I. = Dongsha Dao S. China Sea 20°45N 116°43E 219 G12
Prater Austria 48°12N 16°25E 142 A2
Prato Italy 43°53N 11°6E 198 E8
Prátola Peligna Italy 42°6N 13°52E 199 F10
Prats-de-Mollo-la-Preste France 42°25N 2°27E 174 F6
Pratt U.S.A. 37°39N 98°44W 308 G4
Prattville U.S.A. 32°28N 86°29W 315 E11
Praust = Pruszcz Gdański Poland 54°17N 18°40E 184 D5
Pravara → India 19°35N 74°45E 244 E2
Pravdinsk Kaliningrad, Russia 54°27N 21°1E 184 D8
Pravdinsk Nizhniy Novgorod, Russia 56°29N 43°28E 190 B6
Pravets Bulgaria 42°53N 23°55E 202 D7
Pravia Spain 43°30N 6°12W 194 B4
Praya Indonesia 8°39S 116°17E 235 D5
Prayagraj India 25°25N 81°58E 243 G9
Pre-delta △ Argentina 32°10S 60°40W 334 C3
Pré-en-Pail France 48°28N 0°12W 172 D6
Preah Seihanu = Kampong Saom Cambodia 10°38N 103°30E 237 G4
Preah Vihear Cambodia 14°23N 104°41E 236 E5
Preau Trin. & Tob. 10°12N 61°19W 323 t
Preble U.S.A. 42°44N 76°8W 313 D8
Prêcheur Martinique 14°48N 61°13W 322 j
Precipice △ Australia 25°18S 150°5E 281 D5
Precordillera Argentina 30°0S 69°1W 334 C2
Precotto Italy 45°30N 9°13E 128 A2

Predáppio *Italy* 44°6N 11°59E **199** D8
Predazzo *Italy* 46°19N 11°36E **199** B8
Predeal *Romania* 45°30N 25°34E **183** E10
Predejane *Serbia* 42°51N 22°9E **202** D6
Preeceville *Canada* 51°57N 102°40W **297** C8
Preetz *Germany* 54°14N 10°18E **178** A6
Pregolya → *Russia* 54°41N 20°22E **184** D7
Pregrada *Croatia* 46°11N 15°45E **199** B12
Preiļi *Latvia* 56°18N 26°43E **188** D4
Preko *Croatia* 44°7N 15°10E **199** D12
Prelog *Croatia* 46°18N 16°32E **199** B13
Premer *Australia* 31°29S 149°56E **283** A8
Prémery *France* 47°10N 3°18E **173** E10
Premià de Mar *Spain* 41°29N 2°22E **196** D7
Premont *U.S.A.* 27°22N 98°7W **314** H5
Premuda *Croatia* 44°20N 14°36E **199** D11
Prenestino Labicano *Italy* 41°53N 12°33E **136** B2
Prentice *U.S.A.* 45°33N 90°17W **308** C8
Prenzlau *Germany* 53°19N 13°50E **178** B9
Prenzlauerberg *Germany* 52°32N 13°24E **115** A3
Preobrazheniye *Russia* 42°54N 133°54E **220** C6
Preparis I. = Pariparit Kyun
Myanmar 14°52N 93°41E **245** G11
Preparis North Channel
Ind. Oc. 15°27N 94°5E **245** G11
Preparis South Channel
Ind. Oc. 14°33N 93°30E **245** G11
Přerov *Czechia* 49°28N 17°27E **181** B10
Prescott *Ont., Canada* 44°45N 75°30W **313** B9
Prescott *Ariz., U.S.A.* 34°33N 112°28W **305** J7
Prescott *Ark., U.S.A.* 33°48N 93°23W **314** E8
Prescott Valley *U.S.A.* 34°40N 112°18W **305** J7
Preservation Inlet *N.Z.* 46°8S 166°35E **285** G1
Preševo *Serbia* 42°19N 21°39E **202** D5
Presho *U.S.A.* 43°54N 100°3W **308** D3
Presicce *Italy* 39°54N 18°16E **201** C11
Presidencia de la Plaza
Argentina 27°0S 59°50W **334** B4
Presidencia Roque Saenz Peña
Argentina 26°45S 60°30W **334** B3
Président-Thiers, Récif
French Polynesia 24°30S 146°0W **289** f
Presidente Dutra *Brazil* 5°15S 44°30W **332** C3
Presidente Epitácio *Brazil* 21°56S 52°6W **333** F1
Presidente Figueiredo
Brazil 1°57S 60°2W **329** D5
Presidente Hayes □
Paraguay 24°0S 59°0W **334** A4
Presidente Juán Perón = Chaco □
Argentina 26°30S 61°0W **334** B3
Presidente Médici *Brazil* 11°17S 61°55W **331** C5
Presidente Prudente *Brazil* 22°5S 51°25W **335** A5
Presidente Ríos, L. *Chile* 46°28S 74°25W **336** C2
Presidente Vargas = Nova Era
Brazil 19°45S 43°3W **333** E3
Presidio *U.S.A.* 29°34N 104°22W **314** G2
Preslav *Bulgaria* 43°10N 26°52E **203** C10
Preslavska Planina
Bulgaria 43°10N 26°45E **203** C10
Prešov *Slovakia* 49°0N 21°15E **181** B14
Prešovský □ *Slovakia* 49°10N 21°0E **181** B13
Prespa *Bulgaria* 41°44N 24°55E **203** E8
Prespa, L. = Prespansko Jezero
N. Macedonia 40°55N 21°0E **202** F5
Prespa △ *Europe* 40°48N 21°4E **202** F4
Prespansko Jezero
N. Macedonia 40°55N 21°0E **202** F5
Presque I. *U.S.A.* 42°10N 80°6W **312** D4
Presque Isle *U.S.A.* 46°41N 68°1W **309** B19
Pressburg = Bratislava
Slovakia 48°10N 17°7E **181** C10
Prestatyn *U.K.* 53°20N 3°24W **168** D4
Prestea *Ghana* 5°22N 2°7W **262** D4
Presteigne *U.K.* 52°17N 3°0W **169** E5
Přeštice *Czechia* 49°34N 13°20E **180** B6
Presto *Bolivia* 18°55S 64°56W **331** D5
Preston *Vic., Australia* 37°44S 145°0E **128** A1
Preston *Ont., Canada* 43°23N 80°21W **312** C4
Preston *Lancs., U.K.* 53°46N 2°42W **168** D5
Preston *Ga., U.S.A.* 32°4N 84°32W **316** C5
Preston *Idaho, U.S.A.* 42°6N 111°53W **304** E8
Preston *Iowa, U.S.A.* 42°3N 90°24W **310** B6
Preston *Minn., U.S.A.* 43°40N 92°5W **308** D7
Preston *Mo., U.S.A.* 37°56N 93°13W **310** G3
Preston, C. *Australia* 20°51S 116°12E **278** D2
Prestonsburg *U.S.A.* 37°40N 82°47W **309** G12
Prestranda *Norway* 59°6N 9°4E **162** E3
Prestwick *U.K.* 55°29N 4°37W **167** F4
Prêto → *Amazonas, Brazil* 0°8S 64°6W **329** D5
Prêto → *Bahia, Brazil* 11°21S 43°52W **332** D3
Prêto do Igapó-Açu →
Brazil 4°26S 59°48W **329** D6
Pretoria *S. Africa* 25°44S 28°12E **271** C4
Pretos Forros, Sa. dos
Brazil 22°54S 43°17W **135** B1
Preuilly-sur-Claise *France* 46°51N 0°56E **172** F7
Preussisch-Eylau = Bagrationovsk
Russia 54°23N 20°39E **184** D7
Preussisch Friedland = Debrzno
Poland 53°31N 17°14E **184** E4
Preussisch Holland = Pasłęk
Poland 54°3N 19°41E **184** D6
Preussisch-Stargard = Starogard Gdański *Poland* 53°59N 18°30E **184** E5
Preveza *Greece* 38°57N 20°45E **207** B2
Preveza-Lefkada ✕ **(PVK)**
Greece 38°57N 20°45E **207** B2
Préville *Canada* 45°28N 73°29W **130** B3
Prey Veng *Cambodia* 11°35N 105°29E **237** G5
Přezletice *Czechia* 50°9N 14°34E **135** B3
Priazovskoye *Ukraine* 46°44N 35°40E **189** J8
Pribalkhash = Balqash
Kazakhstan 46°50N 74°50E **214** E8
Pribaykalsky △ *Russia* 52°30N 106°0E **215** D11
Pribilof Is. *U.S.A.* 57°0N 170°0W **303** H5
Priboj *Serbia* 43°35N 19°32E **202** C3
Příbram *Czechia* 49°41N 14°2E **180** B7
Price *U.S.A.* 39°36N 110°49W **304** G8
Price, C. *India* 13°34N 93°3E **245** H11
Price I. *Canada* 52°23N 128°41W **296** C3
Prichard *U.S.A.* 30°44N 88°5W **315** F10
Prickly Pear Cays *Anguilla* 18°16N 63°11W **322** a
Prickly Pt. *Grenada* 11°59N 61°45W **323** q
Priego *Spain* 40°26N 2°21W **196** E2
Priego de Córdoba *Spain* 37°27N 4°12W **195** H6
Priekule *Latvia* 56°26N 21°35E **184** B8
Priekule *Lithuania* 55°33N 21°19E **184** C8
Prielbrusye △ *Russia* 43°20N 42°37E **191** J6
Prien *Germany* 47°51N 12°20E **179** H8
Prienai *Lithuania* 54°38N 23°57E **184** D10
Prieska *S. Africa* 29°40S 22°42E **270** C3
Priest L. *U.S.A.* 48°35N 116°52W **304** B5
Priest River *U.S.A.* 48°11N 116°55W **304** B5
Priest Valley *U.S.A.* 36°10N 120°39W **306** J6
Prieto Diaz *Phil.* 13°2N 124°12E **232** E5
Prievidza *Slovakia* 48°46N 18°36E **181** C11
Prignitz *Germany* 53°6N 11°45E **178** B7
Prijedor *Bos.-H.* 44°58N 16°41E **199** D13
Prijepolje *Serbia* 43°27N 19°40E **202** C3
Prikaspiyskaya Nizmennost = Caspian Depression
Eurasia 47°0N 48°0E **191** G9
Prikro *Côte d'Ivoire* 7°40N 3°59W **262** D4
Prikubanskaya Nizmennost
Russia 45°39N 38°33E **191** H4
Prilep *N. Macedonia* 41°21N 21°32E **202** E5
Priluki = Pryluky *Ukraine* 50°30N 32°24E **189** G7
Prima Porta *Italy* 42°0N 12°30E **136** B1
Primavalle *Italy* 41°55N 12°25E **136** B1
Prime Hd. *Antarctica* 63°12S 48°57W **151** C18
Prime Seal I. *Australia* 40°3S 147°43E **281** G4
Primeira Cruz *Brazil* 2°30S 43°26W **332** B3
Primkenau = Przemków
Poland 51°31N 15°48E **185** G2
Primo Tapia *Mexico* 32°16N 116°54W **307** N10
Primorsk *Kaliningrad, Russia* 54°44N 20°0E **184** D6
Primorsk *St. Petersburg, Russia* 60°22N 28°37E **188** B5
Primorskiy Kray □ *Russia* 45°0N 135°0E **220** B7
Primorsko *Bulgaria* 42°15N 27°44E **203** D11
Primorsko-Akhtarsk
Russia 46°2N 38°10E **189** J10
Primrose *S. Africa* 26°11S 28°9E **123** B2
Primrose L. *Canada* 54°55N 109°45W **297** C7
Prince Albert *Sask., Canada* 53°15N 105°50W **297** C7
Prince Albert *Western Cape, S. Africa* 33°12S 22°2E **270** D3
Prince Albert △ *Canada* 54°0N 106°25W **297** C7
Prince Albert Mts.
Antarctica 76°0S 161°30E **151** D11
Prince Albert Pen.
Canada 72°30N 116°0W **294** C8
Prince Albert Sd. *Canada* 70°25N 115°0W **294** C9
Prince Alfred, C. *Canada* 74°20N 124°40W **150** B1
Prince Charles I. *Canada* 67°47N 76°12W **295** D16
Prince Charles Mts.
Antarctica 72°0S 67°0E **151** D6
Prince Edward Fracture Zone
Ind. Oc. 46°0S 35°0E **151** A4
Prince Edward I. □
Canada 46°20N 63°20W **299** C7
Prince Edward Is. *Ind. Oc.* 46°35S 38°0E **273** J2
Prince George *Canada* 53°55N 122°50W **296** C4
Prince of Wales, C.
U.S.A. 65°36N 168°5W **303** D5
Prince of Wales I. *Queens., Australia* 10°40S 142°10E **286** F2
Prince of Wales I. *Nunavut, Canada* 73°0N 99°0W **294** C12
Prince of Wales I. *Alaska, U.S.A.* 55°47N 132°50W **303** J14
Prince of Wales Icefield
Canada 78°15N 79°0W **295** B16
Prince of Wales Str.
Canada 73°0N 117°0W **294** C8
Prince Patrick I. *Canada* 77°0N 120°0W **295** B8
Prince Regent Inlet
Canada 73°0N 90°0W **295** C14
Prince Rupert *Canada* 54°20N 130°20W **296** C2
Prince Rupert B. *Dominica* 15°34N 61°29W **323** k
Prince Rupert Bluff Pt.
Dominica 15°35N 61°29W **323** k
Prince William Sd.
U.S.A. 60°40N 147°0W **303** F11
Princes Street *Edinburgh, U.K.* **121** b2
Princes Town *Trin. & Tob.* 10°16N 61°23W **323** t
Princesa Isabel *Brazil* 7°44S 38°0W **332** C4
Princess Charlotte B.
Australia 14°25S 144°0E **280** A3
Princess Elizabeth Trough
S. Ocean 64°10S 83°0E **151** C7
Princess May Ranges
Australia 15°30S 125°30E **278** C4
Princess Royal I. *Canada* 53°0N 128°40W **296** C3
Princeton *B.C., Canada* 49°27N 120°30W **296** D4
Princeton *Calif., U.S.A.* 39°24N 122°1W **306** F4
Princeton *Ill., U.S.A.* 41°23N 89°28W **310** C7
Princeton *Ind., U.S.A.* 38°21N 87°34W **311** F9
Princeton *Ky., U.S.A.* 37°7N 87°53W **308** G10
Princeton *Mo., U.S.A.* 40°24N 93°35W **310** D3
Princeton *N.J., U.S.A.* 40°21N 74°39W **313** F10
Princeton *W. Va., U.S.A.* 37°22N 81°6W **309** G13
Princeville *Hawai'i, U.S.A.* 22°13N 159°29W **302** A2
Princeville *Ill., U.S.A.* 40°56N 89°46W **310** D7
Principe *São Tomé & Príncipe* 1°37N 7°25E **265** a
Principe da Beira *Brazil* 12°20S 64°30W **331** C5
Prineville *U.S.A.* 44°18N 120°51W **304** D3
Pringles Bay *Dominica* 15°21N 61°25W **323** k
Pringsewu *Indonesia* 5°24S 104°55E **234** D2
Prins Christian Sund
Greenland 60°4N 43°10W **154** E6
Prins Harald Kyst *Antarctica* 70°0S 35°1E **151** D4
Prins Karls Forland
Svalbard 78°30N 11°0E **154** B12
Prinsesse Astrid Kyst
Antarctica 70°45S 12°30E **151** D3
Prinsesse Ragnhild Kyst
Antarctica 70°15S 27°30E **151** D4
Printer's Row *Chicago, U.S.A.* **119** d2
Prinzapolca *Nic.* 13°20N 83°35W **320** D3
Prior, C. *Spain* 43°34N 8°17W **194** B2
Priozersk *Russia* 61°2N 30°7E **188** B6
Pripet = Prypyat →
Europe 51°20N 30°15E **177** C16
Pripet Marshes *Europe* 52°10N 27°10E **177** B15
Pripyat Marshes = Pripet Marshes
Europe 52°10N 27°10E **177** B15
Pripyats = Prypyat →
Europe 51°20N 30°15E **177** C16
Prishib = Leninsk *Russia* 48°40N 45°15E **191** F7
Prishtinë *Kosovo* 42°40N 21°13E **202** D5
Prislop, Pasul *Romania* 47°37N 24°48E **183** C9
Pristen *Russia* 51°15N 36°44E **189** G9
Priština = Prishtinë
Kosovo 42°40N 21°13E **202** D5
Pritzwalk *Germany* 53°9N 12°10E **178** B8
Privas *France* 44°45N 4°37E **175** D8
Priverno *Italy* 41°28N 13°11E **200** A6
Privolzhsk *Russia* 57°23N 41°16E **190** B5
Privolzhskaya Vozvyshennost
Russia 51°0N 46°0E **190** E7
Privolzhskiy *Russia* 51°25N 46°3E **190** E8
Privolzhskiy □ *Russia* 56°0N 50°0E **214** D6
Privolzhye *Russia* 52°52N 48°33E **190** D9
Priyutnoye *Russia* 46°12N 43°40E **191** G6
Prizren *Kosovo* 42°13N 20°45E **202** D4
Prizzi *Italy* 37°43N 13°26E **200** E6
Prnjavor *Bos.-H.* 44°52N 17°43E **182** F2
Probolinggo *Indonesia* 7°46S 113°13E **235** D4
Prochowice *Poland* 51°17N 16°20E **185** G3
Proctor *U.S.A.* 43°40N 73°2W **313** C11
Proddatur *India* 14°45N 78°30E **245** G4
Prodhromos *Cyprus* 34°57N 32°50E **207** F8
Proença-a-Nova *Portugal* 39°45N 7°54W **194** F3
Professor Julio Escudero
Antarctica 62°30S 58°0W **151** C18
Profilia *Greece* 36°5N 27°51E **206** E11
Profondeville *Belgium* 50°23N 4°52E **170** D4
Progreso *Coahuila, Mexico* 27°28N 100°59W **318** B4
Progreso *Yucatán, Mexico* 21°20N 89°40W **319** C7
Progreso Nacional *Mexico* 19°30N 99°9W **128** A2
Progress *Antarctica* 66°22S 76°22E **151** C12
Progress *Russia* 49°45N 129°37E **215** E13
Prokhladnyy *Russia* 43°50N 44°2E **191** J7
Prokhorovka *Russia* 51°2N 36°44E **190** E3
Prokletije *Albania* 42°30N 19°45E **202** D3
Prokopyevsk *Russia* 54°0N 86°45E **217** B11
Prokuplje *Serbia* 43°16N 21°36E **202** C5
Proletarsk *Russia* 46°42N 41°50E **191** G5
Prome = Pye *Myanmar* 18°49N 95°13E **241** F5
Promise City *U.S.A.* 40°45N 93°9W **310** D3
Promzino = Surskoye
Russia 54°30N 46°44E **190** C8
Prophet → *Canada* 58°48N 122°40W **296** B4
Prophet River *Canada* 58°6N 122°43W **296** B4
Prophetstown *U.S.A.* 41°40N 89°56W **310** C7
Propriá *Brazil* 10°13S 36°51W **332** D4
Propriano *France* 41°41N 8°52E **175** G12
Proserpine *Australia* 20°21S 148°36E **280** b
Prosek *Czechia* 50°7N 14°30E **135** B3
Proskurov = Khmelnytskyy
Ukraine 49°23N 27°0E **177** D14
Prosna → *Poland* 52°6N 17°44E **185** F4
Prospect *N.Y., U.S.A.* 43°18N 75°9W **313** C9
Prospect *Ohio, U.S.A.* 40°27N 83°11W **311** D13
Prospect Hill Park *U.S.A.* 42°23N 71°13W **116** A1
Prosperidad *Phil.* 8°34N 125°52E **233** G5
Prosperity *U.S.A.* 30°51N 85°56W **316** E4
Prosperous B. *St. Helena* 15°56S 5°39W **153** h
Prosser *U.S.A.* 46°12N 119°46W **304** C4
Prossnitz = Prostějov
Czechia 49°30N 17°9E **181** B10
Prostějov *Czechia* 49°30N 17°9E **181** B10
Prostki *Poland* 53°42N 22°25E **184** E9
Proston *Australia* 26°8S 151°32E **281** D5
Proszowice *Poland* 50°13N 20°16E **185** H7
Proti *Greece* 37°5N 21°32E **204** D3
Provadiya *Bulgaria* 43°12N 27°30E **203** C11
Provadiyska → *Bulgaria* 43°12N 27°42E **203** C11
Provence *France* 43°40N 5°46E **175** E9
Provence-Alpes-Côte d'Azur □
France 44°0N 6°15E **175** D10
Providence *Ky., U.S.A.* 37°24N 87°46W **308** G10
Providence *R.I., U.S.A.* 41°49N 71°24W **313** E13
Providence, C. *N.Z.* 45°59S 166°29E **285** F1
Providence Bay *Canada* 45°41N 82°15W **298** C3
Providence Mts. *U.S.A.* 35°10N 115°15W **307** K11
Providencia *Chile* 33°25S 70°36W **137** B2
Providencia, I. de
Caribbean 13°25N 81°26W **320** D3
Providenciales
Turks & Caicos 21°48N 72°15W **321** B5
Provideniya *Russia* 64°23N 173°18W **215** C19
Provincetown *U.S.A.* 42°3N 70°11W **309** D18
Provins *France* 48°33N 3°15E **173** D10
Provo = Providenciales
Turks & Caicos 21°48N 72°15W **321** B5
Provo *U.S.A.* 40°14N 111°39W **304** F8
Provost *Canada* 52°25N 110°20W **297** C6
Prozor *Bos.-H.* 43°50N 17°34E **182** G2
Prrenjas *Albania* 41°4N 20°32E **202** E4
Prudentópolis *Brazil* 25°12S 50°57W **333** G1
Prudhoe Bay *U.S.A.* 70°18N 148°22W **303** A10
Prudhoe I. *Australia* 21°19S 149°41E **280** C4
Prud'homme *Canada* 52°20N 105°54W **297** C7
Prudnik *Poland* 50°20N 17°38E **185** H4
Průhonice *Czechia* 50°0N 14°33E **135** C3
Prüm *Germany* 50°12N 6°25E **179** E2
Prundu *Romania* 44°6N 26°14E **183** F11
Prundu Bârgăului
Romania 47°13N 24°46E **183** C9
Pruszcz Gdański *Poland* 54°17N 18°40E **184** D5
Pruszków *Poland* 52°9N 20°49E **185** F7
Prut → *Romania* 45°28N 28°10E **183** E13
Pruzhany *Belarus* 52°33N 24°28E **177** B13
Prvič *Croatia* 44°55N 14°47E **199** D11
Prydz B. *Antarctica* 69°0S 74°0E **151** C6
Pryluky *Ukraine* 50°30N 32°24E **189** G7
Prymorske *Ukraine* 46°48N 36°20E **189** J9
Pryor *U.S.A.* 36°19N 95°19W **314** C7
Prypyat → *Europe* 51°20N 30°15E **177** C16
Prypyatsky △ *Belarus* 52°0N 28°0E **177** C14
Przasnysz *Poland* 53°2N 20°54E **185** E7
Przedbórz *Poland* 51°6N 19°53E **185** G6
Przedecz *Poland* 52°20N 18°53E **185** F5
Przemków *Poland* 51°31N 15°48E **185** G2
Przemyśl *Poland* 49°50N 22°45E **185** J9
Przeworsk *Poland* 50°6N 22°32E **185** H9
Przewóz *Poland* 51°28N 14°57E **185** G1
Przhevalsk = Karakol
Kyrgyzstan 42°30N 78°20E **217** D9
Przysucha *Poland* 51°22N 20°38E **185** G7
Psachna *Greece* 38°34N 23°35E **204** C5
Psara *Greece* 38°37N 25°38E **205** C7
Psathoura *Greece* 39°30N 24°12E **204** B6
Pserimos *Greece* 36°56N 27°8E **205** E9
Psichiko *Greece* 38°1N 23°46E **112** A2
Psiloritis, Oros *Greece* 35°15N 24°45E **207** E5
Psira *Greece* 35°12N 25°52E **207** E6
Pskem → *Uzbekistan* 41°38N 70°1E **217** D7
Pskov *Russia* 57°50N 28°25E **188** D5
Pskov □ *Russia* 57°20N 29°0E **188** D5
Pskovskoye, Ozero *Russia* 58°0N 27°58E **188** D5
Psol → *Ukraine* 49°10N 33°37E **189** H7
Psunj *Croatia* 45°25N 17°19E **182** E2
Pteleos *Greece* 39°3N 22°57E **204** B4
Ptich = Ptsich → *Belarus* 52°9N 28°52E **177** B15
Ptichia = Vidos *Greece* 39°38N 19°55E **206** B9
Ptolemaida *Greece* 40°30N 21°43E **202** F5
Ptsich → *Belarus* 52°9N 28°52E **177** B15
Ptuj *Slovenia* 46°28N 15°50E **199** B12
Ptujska Gora *Slovenia* 46°23N 15°47E **199** B12
Pu Xian *China* 36°24N 111°6E **226** F6
Pua *Thailand* 19°11N 100°55E **236** C3
Pua'ena Pt. *U.S.A.* 21°36N 158°6W **302** J13
Puán *Argentina* 37°30S 62°45W **334** D3
Pu'an *Guizhou, China* 25°46N 104°57E **228** E5
Pu'apu'a *Samoa* 13°34S 172°9W **287** V19
Pubei *China* 22°16N 109°31E **228** F7
Pucacuro → *Peru* 3°20S 74°58W **328** D3
Pucallpa *Peru* 8°25S 74°30W **330** B3
Pucará *Bolivia* 18°43S 64°11W **331** D5
Pucará *Cajamarca, Peru* 6°0S 79°7W **330** B2
Pucará *Puno, Peru* 15°5S 70°24W **330** D3
Pucarani *Bolivia* 16°23S 68°30W **330** D4
Pucheng *China* 27°59N 118°31E **229** D12
Pucheni *Romania* 45°12N 25°17E **183** E10
Puchheim *Germany* 48°9N 11°21E **179** G7
Puch'on = Bucheon
S. Korea 37°28N 126°45E **224** D3
Púchov *Slovakia* 49°8N 18°20E **181** B11
Pucio Pt. *Phil.* 11°46N 121°51E **233** F3
Pucioasa *Romania* 45°5N 25°25E **183** E10
Pučišća *Croatia* 43°22N 16°43E **199** E13
Puck *Poland* 54°45N 18°23E **184** D5
Pucka, Zatoka *Poland* 54°30N 18°40E **184** D5
Puçol *Spain* 39°37N 0°18W **197** F4
Pudasjärvi *Finland* 65°23N 26°53E **160** D22
Puding *China* 26°18N 105°44E **228** D5
Pudong New Area *China* 31°13N 121°30E **138** B2
Pudozh *Russia* 61°48N 36°32E **188** B9
Pudu = Suizhou *China* 31°42N 113°24E **229** B9
Puducherry *India* 11°59N 79°50E **245** J4
Pudukkottai *India* 10°28N 78°47E **245** J4
Pue *Cook Is.* 21°12S 159°45W **289** h
Puebla *Mexico* 19°3N 98°12W **319** D5
Puebla □ *Mexico* 18°50N 98°0W **319** D5
Puebla de Alcocer *Spain* 38°59N 5°14W **195** G5
Puebla de Don Fadrique
Spain 37°58N 2°25W **197** H2
Puebla de Don Rodrigo
Spain 39°5N 4°37W **195** F6
Puebla de Guzmán *Spain* 37°37N 7°15W **195** H3
Puebla de la Calzada *Spain* 38°54N 6°37W **195** G4
Puebla de Sanabria *Spain* 42°4N 6°38W **194** C4
Puebla de Trives = Pobra de Trives
Spain 42°20N 7°10W **194** C3
Pueblo *U.S.A.* 38°16N 104°37W **304** G11
Pueblo Libre *Peru* 12°5S 77°4W **124** B2
Pueblo Nuevo = El Pobleneu
Spain 41°23N 2°11E **114** A2
Pueblo Nuevo *Spain* 40°25N 3°37W **127** B2
Puelches *Argentina* 38°5S 65°51W **334** D2
Puelén *Argentina* 37°32S 67°38W **334** D2
Puente Alto *Chile* 33°32S 70°35W **334** C1
Puente-Genil *Spain* 37°22N 4°47W **195** H6
Puente la Reina *Spain* 42°40N 1°49W **196** C3
Puente San Miguel *Spain* 43°21N 4°5W **194** B6
Puenteareas = Ponteareas
Spain 42°10N 8°28W **194** C2
Puentedeume = Pontedeume
Spain 43°24N 8°10W **194** B2
Puentes de Garcia Rodríguez = As Pontes de García Rodríguez
Spain 43°27N 7°50W **194** B3
Pu'er *China* 23°0N 101°15E **228** F3
Puerca, Pta. *Puerto Rico* 18°13N 65°36W **321** b
Puerco → *U.S.A.* 34°22N 107°50W **305** J10
Puerta del Sol, Plaza *Madrid, Spain* **127** b2
Puerto Acosta *Bolivia* 15°32S 69°15W **330** D4
Puerto Aisén *Chile* 45°27S 73°0W **336** C2
Puerto Ángel *Mexico* 15°40N 96°29W **319** D5
Puerto Arista *Mexico* 15°56N 93°48W **319** D6
Puerto Armuelles *Panama* 8°20N 82°51W **320** E3
Puerto Asis *Colombia* 0°30N 76°30W **328** C2
Puerto Ayacucho
Venezuela 5°40N 67°35W **328** B4
Puerto Ayora *Ecuador* 0°45S 90°19W **330** a
Puerto Baquerizo Moreno
Ecuador 0°54S 89°36W **330** a
Puerto Barrios *Guatemala* 15°40N 88°32W **320** C2
Puerto Bermejo *Argentina* 26°55S 58°34W **334** B4
Puerto Bermúdez *Peru* 10°20S 74°58W **330** C3
Puerto Bolívar *Colombia* 12°15N 71°59W **328** A3
Puerto Bolívar *Ecuador* 3°19S 79°55W **328** D2
Puerto Cabello *Venezuela* 10°28N 68°1W **328** A4
Puerto Cabezas *Nic.* 14°0N 83°30W **320** D3
Puerto Cabo Gracias á Dios
Nic. 15°0N 83°10W **320** D3
Puerto Capaz = El Jebha
Morocco 35°11N 4°43W **260** A4
Puerto Carreño *Colombia* 6°12N 67°22W **328** B4
Puerto Castilla *Honduras* 16°0N 86°0W **320** C2
Puerto Chicama *Peru* 7°45S 79°20W **330** B2
Puerto Cisnes *Chile* 44°45S 72°42W **336** B2
Puerto Coig *Argentina* 50°54S 69°15W **336** D3
Puerto Cortés *Honduras* 15°51N 88°0W **320** C2
Puerto Cumarebo
Venezuela 11°29N 69°30W **328** A4
Puerto de Alcudia = Port d'Alcúdia
Spain 39°50N 3°7E **206** B4
Puerto de Cabras = Puerto del Rosario *Canary Is.* 28°30N 13°52W **153** e2
Puerto de Cabrera *Spain* 39°8N 2°56E **206** B3
Puerto de la Cruz
Canary Is. 28°24N 16°32W **153** e1
Puerto de los Angeles ⌂
Mexico 23°39N 105°45W **318** C3
Puerto de Mazarrón *Spain* 37°34N 1°15W **197** H3
Puerto de Sóller = Port de Sóller
Spain 39°48N 2°42E **206** B3
Puerto de Somosierra *Spain* 41°9N 3°35W **194** D7
Puerto del Carmen
Canary Is. 28°55N 13°38W **153** e2
Puerto del Rosario
Canary Is. 28°30N 13°52W **153** e2
Puerto Deseado *Argentina* 47°55S 66°0W **336** C3
Puerto Escondido *Mexico* 15°50N 97°3W **319** D5
Puerto Gaitán *Colombia* 4°19N 72°4W **328** C3
Puerto Galera *Phil.* 13°30N 120°57E **232** E3
Puerto Guaraní *Paraguay* 21°18S 57°55W **331** E6
Puerto Heath *Bolivia* 12°34S 68°39W **330** C4
Puerto Huitoto *Colombia* 0°18N 74°3W **328** C3
Puerto Inca *Peru* 9°22S 74°54W **330** B3
Puerto Inírida *Colombia* 3°53N 67°52W **328** C4
Puerto Juárez *Mexico* 21°11N 86°49W **319** C7
Puerto La Cruz *Venezuela* 10°13N 64°38W **329** A5
Puerto Leguízamo
Colombia 0°12S 74°46W **328** D3
Puerto Lempira *Honduras* 15°16N 83°46W **320** C3
Puerto Libertad *Mexico* 29°55N 112°43W **318** B2
Puerto Limón *Colombia* 3°23N 73°30W **328** C3
Puerto Lobos *Argentina* 42°0S 65°3W **336** B3
Puerto López *Colombia* 4°5N 72°58W **328** C3
Puerto Lumbreras *Spain* 37°34N 1°48W **197** H3
Puerto Madero *Argentina* 34°37S 58°21W **117** B2
Puerto Madryn *Argentina* 42°48S 65°4W **336** B3
Puerto Maldonado *Peru* 12°30S 69°10W **330** C4
Puerto Manatí *Cuba* 21°22N 76°50W **320** B4
Puerto Mariti *Colombia* 1°10S 69°59W **328** D4
Puerto Mercedes *Colombia* 1°11N 72°53W **328** C3
Puerto Mexico = Coatzacoalcos
Mexico 18°7N 94°25W **319** D6
Puerto Miraña *Colombia* 1°20S 70°19W **328** D3
Puerto Montt *Chile* 41°28S 73°0W **336** B2
Puerto Morazán *Nic.* 12°51N 87°11W **320** D2
Puerto Morelos *Mexico* 20°50N 86°52W **319** C7
Puerto Nariño *Colombia* 4°56N 67°48W **328** C4
Puerto Natales *Chile* 51°45S 72°15W **336** D2
Puerto Nuevo *Colombia* 5°53N 69°56W **328** B4
Puerto Ordaz *Venezuela* 8°16N 62°44W **329** B5
Puerto Oscuro *Chile* 31°24S 71°35W **334** C1
Puerto Padre *Cuba* 21°13N 76°35W **320** B4
Puerto Páez *Venezuela* 6°13N 67°28W **328** B4
Puerto Peñasco *Mexico* 31°20N 113°33W **318** A2
Puerto Pinasco *Paraguay* 22°36S 57°50W **334** A4
Puerto Pirámides
Argentina 42°35S 64°20W **336** B4
Puerto Piritu *Venezuela* 10°4N 65°3W **329** A5
Puerto Plata *Dom. Rep.* 19°48N 70°45W **321** C5
Puerto Pollensa = Port de Pollença
Spain 39°54N 3°4E **206** B4
Puerto Portillo *Peru* 9°45S 72°42W **330** B3
Puerto Princesa *Phil.* 9°46N 118°45E **233** G2
Puerto Princesa Subterranean River △ *Phil.* 10°10N 118°55E **233** F2
Puerto Quepos *Costa Rica* 9°29N 84°6W **320** E3
Puerto Real *Spain* 36°33N 6°12W **195** J4
Puerto Rico *Bolivia* 11°5S 67°38W **330** C4
Puerto Rico *Canary Is.* 27°47N 15°42W **153** e1
Puerto Rico ☑ *W. Indies* 18°15N 66°45W **321** C6
Puerto Rico Trench
Atl. Oc. 19°50N 66°0W **321** C6
Puerto Rondón *Colombia* 6°17N 71°6W **328** B3
Puerto Saavedra *Chile* 38°47S 73°24W **336** A2
Puerto San Julián
Argentina 49°15S 67°45W **336** C3
Puerto Santa Cruz
Argentina 50°0S 68°32W **336** D3
Puerto Sastre *Paraguay* 22°2S 57°55W **334** A4
Puerto Serrano *Spain* 36°56N 5°33W **195** J5
Puerto Siles *Bolivia* 12°48S 65°5W **331** C4
Puerto Suárez *Bolivia* 18°58S 57°52W **331** D6
Puerto Supe *Peru* 11°0S 77°30W **330** C2
Puerto Tejada *Colombia* 3°14N 76°24W **328** C2
Puerto Umbría *Colombia* 0°52N 76°33W **328** C2
Puerto Vallarta *Mexico* 20°37N 105°15W **318** C3
Puerto Varas *Chile* 41°19S 72°59W **336** B2
Puerto Velasco Ibarra
Ecuador 1°17S 90°29W **330** a
Puerto Villamil *Ecuador* 0°56S 91°1W **330** a
Puerto Villazón *Bolivia* 13°32S 61°57W **331** C5
Puerto Wilches *Colombia* 7°21N 73°54W **328** B3
Puerto Williams *Chile* 54°56S 67°37W **336** D3
Puertollano *Spain* 38°43N 4°7W **195** G6
Puesto Cunambo *Peru* 2°10S 76°0W **328** D2
Pueu *Tahiti* 17°44S 149°13W **289** e
Pueyrredón, L. *Argentina* 47°20S 72°0W **336** C2
Püez Odle ⌂ *Italy* 46°37N 11°48E **199** B8
Puffin I. *Ireland* 51°50N 10°24W **166** E1
Pugachev *Russia* 52°0N 48°49E **190** D9
Pugal *India* 28°30N 72°48E **242** E5
Puge *Sichuan, China* 27°20N 102°31E **228** D4
Puge *Tanzania* 4°45S 33°11E **268** C3
Puget Sound *U.S.A.* 47°50N 122°30W **306** C4
Puget-Théniers *France* 43°58N 6°53E **175** E10
Púglia □ *Italy* 41°15N 16°15E **201** A9
Pugŏdong *N. Korea* 42°5N 130°0E **224** A5
Pugu *Guangdong, China* 23°10N 113°19E **121** A2
Pugu *Tanzania* 6°55S 39°4E **268** D4
Pūgūnzī *Iran* 25°49N 59°10E **247** E8
Puha *N.Z.* 38°30S 177°50E **284** E6
Puhuangyu *China* 39°50N 116°22E **114** B2
Pui *Romania* 45°30N 23°4E **182** E8
Pui O Wan
Hong Kong, China 22°15N 113°58E **122** B1
Puica *Peru* 15°0S 72°33W **330** D3
Puieşti *Romania* 46°25N 27°33E **183** D12
Puig Major *Spain* 39°48N 2°47E **206** B3
Puigcerdà *Spain* 42°24N 1°50E **196** C6
Puigmal *Spain* 42°23N 2°7E **196** C7
Puigpunyent *Spain* 39°38N 2°32E **206** B3
Puijiang *China* 30°14N 103°30E **228** B4
Puisaye, Collines de la
France 47°37N 3°20E **173** E10
Puiseaux *France* 48°11N 2°30E **173** D9
Puistola *Finland* 60°16N 25°2E **121** B3
Pujehun *S. Leone* 7°23N 11°45W **262** D2
Pujiang *China* 29°29N 119°54E **229** C12
Pujilí *Ecuador* 0°57S 78°41W **328** D2
Pujols *France* 44°48N 0°2W **174** D3
Pujon-ho *N. Korea* 40°35N 127°35E **224** B3
Puka Puka
French Polynesia 14°49S 138°48W **289** f
Puka Ruha
French Polynesia 18°20S 137°2W **289** f
Pukaki, L. *N.Z.* 44°4S 170°1E **285** E5
Pukalani *U.S.A.* 20°51N 156°20W **302** C5
Pukapuka *Cook Is.* 10°53S 165°49W **289** J11
Pukaskwa △ *Canada* 48°20N 86°0W **298** C2
Pukatawagan *Canada* 55°45N 101°20W **297** B8
Pukchin *N. Korea* 40°12N 125°45E **224** B2
Pukch'ŏng *N. Korea* 40°14N 128°19E **224** B4
Pukë *Albania* 42°2N 19°53E **202** D3
Pukearuhe *N.Z.* 38°55S 174°31E **284** E3
Pukekohe *N.Z.* 37°12S 174°55E **284** D3
Puketeraki Ra. *N.Z.* 42°58S 172°13E **285** C7
Puketoi Ra. *N.Z.* 40°30S 176°5E **284** G5
Pukeuri *N.Z.* 45°4S 171°2E **285** F6
Pukhrayan *India* 26°14N 79°51E **243** F8
Pukinmäki *Finland* 60°15N 24°57E **121** B2
Puksubaek-san *N. Korea* 40°42N 127°45E **224** B3
Pula *Croatia* 44°54N 13°57E **199** D10
Pula *Italy* 39°1N 9°0E **200** C1
Pulacayo *Bolivia* 20°25S 66°41W **330** E4
Pulandian *China* 39°25N 121°58E **227** E11
Pulandua Pt. *Phil.* 11°54N 123°9E **233** F4
Pulangpisau *Indonesia* 2°46S 114°13E **235** C4
Pulaski *N.Y., U.S.A.* 43°34N 76°8W **313** C8
Pulaski *Tenn., U.S.A.* 35°12N 87°2W **315** D11
Pulaski *Va., U.S.A.* 37°3N 80°47W **309** G13
Pulau → *Indonesia* 5°50S 138°15E **231** F9
Pulau Gili *Indonesia* 8°21S 116°1E **231** J19
Puławy *Poland* 51°23N 21°59E **185** G8
Pulga *U.S.A.* 39°48N 121°29W **306** F5
Pulgaon *India* 20°44N 78°21E **244** D4
Puli *Taiwan* 23°58N 120°57E **225** C2
Pulicat *India* 13°25N 80°19E **245** H5
Pulicat L. *India* 13°40N 80°15E **245** H5
Pulivendla *India* 14°25N 78°14E **245** G4
Puliyangudi *India* 9°11N 77°24E **245** K3
Pulkovo Int. ✕ **(LED)**
Russia 59°48N 30°18E **137** C1
Pullach *Germany* 48°3N 11°31E **131** B1
Pullman *U.S.A.* 46°44N 117°10W **304** C5
Pullman Historic District
U.S.A. 41°41N 87°36W **119** C3
Pulo Gadung *Indonesia* 6°11S 106°54E **122** B2
Pulog, Mt. *Phil.* 16°40N 120°50E **232** C3
Pulpí *Spain* 37°24N 1°44W **197** H3
Pułtusk *Poland* 52°43N 21°6E **185** F8
Pülümür *Turkey* 39°30N 39°51E **213** C8
Pumlumon Fawr *U.K.* 52°28N 3°46W **169** E4
Puna *Bolivia* 19°45S 65°28W **331** D4
Puná, I. *Ecuador* 2°55S 80°5W **328** D1
Punaauia *Tahiti* 17°37S 149°34W **289** e
Pūnak *Iran* 35°46N 51°20E **141** A2
Punakha Dzong *Bhutan* 27°42N 89°52E **241** B2
Punalur *India* 9°0N 76°56E **245** K3
Punalu'u *U.S.A.* 21°35N 157°53W **302** J14
Punasar *India* 27°6N 73°6E **242** F5
Punata *Bolivia* 17°32S 65°50W **331** D4
Punch *India* 33°48N 74°4E **243** C6
Punch → *Pakistan* 33°12N 73°40E **242** C5
Punchbowl *Australia* 33°55S 151°3E **139** B1
Punda *Curaçao* 12°6N 68°55W **322** g
Punda Maria *S. Africa* 22°40S 31°5E **271** B5
Punde *India* 18°53N 72°57E **130** B2
Pune *India* 18°29N 73°57E **244** E1
Punggol *Singapore* 1°23N 103°54E **138** A3
Punggol, Sungei →
Singapore 1°24N 103°54E **138** A3
Punggol Pt. *Singapore* 1°24N 103°54E **138** A3
Pungo Andongo *Angola* 9°44S 15°35E **265** D3
P'ungsan *N. Korea* 40°50N 128°9E **224** B4
Pungsan *S. Korea* 36°34N 128°34E **224** D4
Pungue, Ponte de *Mozam.* 19°0S 34°0E **269** F3
Puning *China* 23°20N 116°12E **229** F11
Punjab □ *India* 31°0N 76°0E **242** D7
Punjab □ *Pakistan* 32°0N 72°30E **242** E6
Punjabi Bagh *India* 28°40N 77°6E **120** A1
Puno *Peru* 15°55S 70°3W **330** D3
Puno □ *Peru* 15°0S 70°0W **330** C3
Punpun → *India* 25°31N 85°18E **243** G11
Punta, Cerro de
Puerto Rico 18°10N 66°37W **321** b
Punta Alta *Argentina* 38°53S 62°4W **336** A4
Punta Arenas *Chile* 53°10S 71°0W **336** D2
Punta Cana ✕ **(PUJ)**
Dom. Rep. 18°34N 68°21W **321** C6
Punta Cardón *Venezuela* 11°38N 70°14W **328** A3
Punta Coles *Peru* 17°43S 71°23W **330** D3
Punta de Bombón *Peru* 17°10S 71°48W **330** D3
Punta de Piedras *Venezuela* 10°54N 64°5W **329** a
Punta del Diaz *Chile* 28°0S 70°45W **334** B1
Punta del Hidalgo
Canary Is. 28°33N 16°19W **153** e1
Punta Delgado *Argentina* 42°43S 63°38W **336** B4
Punta Gorda *Belize* 16°10N 88°45W **320** C2
Punta Gorda *Fla., U.S.A.* 26°56N 82°3W **317** J7
Punta Prieta *Mexico* 28°58N 114°17W **318** B2
Punta Prima *Spain* 39°48N 4°16E **206** B5
Punta Umbría *Spain* 37°10N 6°56W **195** H4
Puntarenas *Costa Rica* 10°0N 84°50W **320** E3
Puntland *Somalia* 9°0N 50°0E **267** C6
Punto Fijo *Venezuela* 11°50N 70°13W **328** A3
Punxsutawney *U.S.A.* 40°57N 78°59W **312** F6
Punyu = Guangzhou
China 23°6N 113°13E **121** B2
Puolanka *Finland* 64°52N 27°42E **160** D22
Puolo Pt. *Kauai, U.S.A.* 21°53N 159°36W **302** A1
Puotila *Finland* 60°13N 25°5E **121** B3
Pupuan *Indonesia* 8°19S 115°0E **231** J18
Pŭpŭkea *U.S.A.* 21°40N 158°3W **302** J13
Puqi *China* 29°40N 113°50E **229** C9
Puquio *Peru* 14°45S 74°10W **330** C3
Pur → *Russia* 67°31N 77°55E **214** C8
Puracé, Vol. *Colombia* 2°21N 76°23W **328** C2
Puracé ⌂ *Colombia* 2°10N 76°21W **328** C2
Puračić *Bos.-H.* 44°33N 18°28E **182** F3
Puralia = Puruliya *India* 23°17N 86°24E **243** H12
Purana Qila *Delhi, India* **120** c3
Puranpur *India* 28°31N 80°9E **243** E9
Purari → *Papua N. G.* 7°49S 145°0E **286** D3
Purbalingga *Indonesia* 7°23S 109°21E **235** D3
Purbeck, Isle of *U.K.* 50°39N 1°59W **169** G5
Purcell *U.S.A.* 35°1N 97°22W **314** D6
Purcell Mts. *Canada* 49°55N 116°15W **296** D5
Purdy *Canada* 45°19N 77°44W **312** A7
Puri *India* 19°50N 85°58E **244** E7
Purificación *Colombia* 3°51N 74°55W **328** C3
Purmerend *Neths.* 52°32N 4°58E **170** B4
Purna → *India* 19°6N 77°2E **244** E3
Purnia *India* 25°45N 87°31E **243** G12
Purnululu △ *Australia* 17°20S 128°20E **278** C4
Pursat = Pouthisat
Cambodia 12°34N 103°50E **236** F4
Purukcahu *Indonesia* 0°35S 114°35E **235** C4
Puruliya *India* 23°17N 86°24E **243** H12
Purus → *Brazil* 3°42S 61°28W **329** D5
Purutu I. *Papua N. G.* 8°24S 143°27E **286** E2
Puruvesi *Finland* 61°50N 29°30E **188** B5
Purvis *U.S.A.* 31°9N 89°25W **315** F10
Pŭrvomay = Parvomay
Bulgaria 42°8N 25°17E **203** D9
Purwa *India* 26°28N 80°47E **243** F9
Purwakarta *Indonesia* 6°35S 107°29E **235** D3
Purwo, Tanjung
Indonesia 8°44S 114°21E **231** K18
Purwodadi *Indonesia* 7°7S 110°55E **235** D4
Purwokerto *Indonesia* 7°25S 109°14E **235** D3
Purworejo *Indonesia* 7°43S 110°2E **235** D3
Puryŏng *N. Korea* 42°5N 129°43E **224** A4
Pus → *India* 19°55N 77°55E **244** E3
Pusa *India* 25°59N 85°41E **243** G11
Pusad *India* 19°56N 77°36E **244** E3
Pusan = Busan *S. Korea* 35°5N 129°0E **224** E4
Pushkin *Russia* 59°45N 30°25E **188** C6
Pushkino *Moskva, Russia* 56°2N 37°49E **188** D9
Pushkino *Saratov, Russia* 51°16N 47°0E **190** E8
Püspökladány *Hungary* 47°19N 21°6E **182** C6
Pustoshka *Russia* 56°20N 29°30E **188** D5
Puszczykowo *Poland* 52°18N 16°49E **185** F3
Put-in-Bay *U.S.A.* 41°39N 82°49W **312** E2
Putahow L. *Canada* 59°54N 100°40W **297** B8
Putai *Taiwan* 23°23N 120°9E **225** C2
Putao *Myanmar* 27°28N 97°30E **241** B6
Putaruru *N.Z.* 38°2S 175°50E **284** E4
Putatan *Malaysia* 5°53N 116°3E **235** A5
Putbus *Germany* 54°22N 13°28E **178** A9
Puteaux *France* 48°53N 2°14E **134** A2
Puteran *Indonesia* 7°5S 114°0E **235** D4
Putian *China* 25°23N 119°0E **229** E12
Putignano *Italy* 40°51N 17°7E **201** B10
Putina *Peru* 14°55S 69°55W **330** C4
Puting, Tanjung *Indonesia* 3°31S 111°46E **235** C4
Putlitz *Germany* 53°15N 12°2E **178** B8
Putna *Romania* 47°50N 25°33E **183** C10
Putna → *Romania* 45°42N 27°26E **183** E12
Putnam *U.S.A.* 41°55N 71°55W **313** E13
Putney *London, U.K.* 51°27N 0°13W **125** B2
Putney *Ga., U.S.A.* 31°29N 84°8W **316** D5
Putnok *Hungary* 48°18N 20°26E **182** B5
Putorana, Gory *Russia* 69°0N 95°0E **215** C10
Putorino *N.Z.* 39°4S 176°58E **284** F5
Putrajaya *Malaysia* 2°55N 101°40E **237** L3
Putre *Chile* 18°12S 69°35W **330** D4
Puttalam *Sri Lanka* 8°1N 79°55E **245** K5
Puttalam Lagoon *Sri Lanka* 8°15N 79°45E **245** K4
Puttegga *Norway* 62°13N 7°42E **164** B4
Puttgarden *Germany* 54°30N 11°10E **178** A7
Püttlingen *Germany* 49°17N 6°53E **179** F2
Puttur *Andhra Pradesh, India* 13°27N 79°33E **245** H4
Puttur *Karnataka, India* 12°46N 75°12E **245** H2
Putty *Australia* 32°57S 150°42E **283** B9
Putumayo → *S. Amer.* 3°7S 67°58W **328** D4
Putuo *Shanghai, China* 31°15N 121°24E **138** B1
Putuo *Zhejiang, China* 29°56N 122°20E **229** C14
Putussibau *Indonesia* 0°50N 112°56E **235** B4
Pututahi *N.Z.* 38°39S 177°53E **284** E6
Putxet *Spain* 41°24N 2°8E **114** A1
Putyla *Ukraine* 48°0N 25°5E **183** B10
Pu'uanahulu *U.S.A.* 19°49N 155°51W **302** D6
Pu'uhonua o Hōnaunau ⌂
U.S.A. 19°25N 155°54W **302** D6
Pu'uka'aumakua
U.S.A. 21°30N 157°54W **302** J14
Pu'ukeahiakahoe
U.S.A. 21°23N 157°49W **302** K14
Pu'ukoholā Heiau ⌂
U.S.A. 20°1N 155°49W **302** C6
P'u'ula'ula *U.S.A.* 20°42N 156°15W **302** C5
Pu'u'oke'oke'o *U.S.A.* 19°13N 155°44W **302** D6
Pu'uwai *U.S.A.* 21°54N 160°12W **302** B1
Puvirnituq *Canada* 60°2N 77°10W **295** E16
Puxi *China* 31°12N 121°30E **138** B1
Puy-de-Dôme *France* 45°46N 2°57E **174** C6
Puy-de-Dôme □ *France* 45°40N 3°5E **174** C7
Puy-l'Évêque *France* 44°31N 1°9E **174** D5
Puyallup *U.S.A.* 47°12N 122°18W **306** C4
Puyang *China* 35°40N 115°1E **226** G8
Puyehue *Chile* 40°40S 72°37W **336** B2
Puyehue △ *Chile* 40°27S 72°6W **336** B2
Puylaurens *France* 43°35N 2°0E **174** E6
Puyo *Ecuador* 1°28S 77°59W **328** D2
Puysegur Pt. *N.Z.* 46°9S 166°37E **285** G1
Pūzeh Rīg *Iran* 27°20N 58°40E **247** E8
Puzhaykove *Ukraine* 48°7N 29°50E **183** B14
Puzi = P'otzu *Taiwan* 23°28N 120°15E **225** C2
Pwani □ *Tanzania* 7°0S 39°0E **268** D4
Pweto *Dem. Rep. of the Congo* 8°25S 28°51E **269** D2
Pwinbyu *Myanmar* 20°23N 94°40E **241** E5
Pwllheli *U.K.* 52°53N 4°25W **168** E3
Pyana → *Russia* 55°43N 46°1E **190** C8
Pyandzh → *Asia* 37°6N 68°20E **240** A2
Pyaozero, Ozero *Russia* 66°5N 30°58E **160** C24
Pyapon *Myanmar* 16°20N 95°40E **241** G5
Pyasina → *Russia* 73°30N 87°0E **215** B9
Pyatigorsk *Russia* 44°2N 43°6E **191** H6
Pyatykhatky *Ukraine* 48°28N 33°38E **189** H7
Pyawbwe *Myanmar* 20°35N 96°4E **241** E6
Pyay = Pye *Myanmar* 18°49N 95°13E **241** F5
Pyaye *Myanmar* 19°12N 95°10E **241** E5
Pydhuni *Mumbai, India* **130** b2
Pydna *Greece* 40°20N 22°34E **202** F6
Pye *Myanmar* 18°49N 95°13E **241** F5
Pyeongchang *S. Korea* 37°22N 128°23E **224** D4
Pyeonghae *S. Korea* 36°43N 129°26E **224** D5
Pyeongtaek *S. Korea* 37°1N 127°4E **224** D3
Pyetrikaw *Belarus* 52°11N 28°29E **177** B15
Pyhäjoki → *Finland* 64°28N 24°14E **160** D21
Pyhätunturi △ *Finland* 66°58N 27°5E **160** C22
Pyin-U-Lwin *Myanmar* 22°2N 96°28E **236** A1
Pyinbauk *Myanmar* 19°10N 95°12E **241** F5
Pyingaing *Myanmar* 23°9N 94°50E **241** D5
Pyinkayaing *Myanmar* 15°58N 94°24E **241** H5
Pyinmana *Myanmar* 19°45N 96°12E **241** E6
Pyinyaung *Myanmar* 20°49N 96°25E **241** E6
Pyla, C. *Cyprus* 34°56N 33°51E **207** F9
Pymatuning Res. *U.S.A.* 41°30N 80°28W **312** E4
Pyŏktong *N. Korea* 40°50N 125°50E **224** B2
P'yŏngan-bukto □
N. Korea 40°0N 125°15E **224** C2
P'yŏngannam-do □
N. Korea 39°30N 126°24E **224** C3
P'yŏnggang *N. Korea* 38°24N 127°17E **224** C3
P'yŏngsong *N. Korea* 39°14N 125°52E **224** C2
P'yŏngyang *N. Korea* 39°0N 125°30E **224** C2
P'yŏngyang □ *N. Korea* 39°4N 125°50E **224** C2
Pyote *U.S.A.* 31°32N 103°8W **314** F3

Pyramid L. *U.S.A.* 40°1N 119°35W **304** F4
Pyramid Pk. *U.S.A.* 36°25N 116°37W **307** J10
Pyramid Pt. *Ascension I.* 7°55S 14°24W **153** g
Pyramids *Egypt* 29°58N 31°9E **117** B1
Pyrénées *Europe* 42°45N 0°18E **174** F4
Pyrénées △ *France* 42°52N 0°10W **174** F3
Pyrénées-Atlantiques □ *France* 43°10N 0°50W **174** E3
Pyrénées-Orientales □ *France* 42°35N 2°26E **174** F6
Pyry *Poland* 52°8N 21°0E **143** C1
Pyryatyn *Ukraine* 50°15N 32°25E **189** G7
Pyrzyce *Poland* 53°10N 14°55E **185** E1
Pyskowice *Poland* 50°24N 18°38E **185** H5
Pytalovo *Russia* 57°5N 27°55E **188** D4
Pyttegga = Puttegga *Norway* 62°13N 7°42E **164** B4
Pyu *Myanmar* 18°30N 96°28E **241** F6
Pyzdry *Poland* 52°11N 17°42E **185** F4

Q

Qaanaaq *Greenland* 77°30N 69°10W **154** B4
Qäbälä *Azerbaijan* 40°58N 47°47E **191** K8
Qabanbay *Kazakhstan* 45°50N 80°37E **217** C10
Qabirri → *Azerbaijan* 41°3N 46°17E **191** K8
Qabr Hūd *Yemen* 16°9N 49°34E **249** C5
Qachasnek *S. Africa* 30°6S 28°42E **271** D4
Qādisiyah, Buhayrat al *Iraq* 34°20N 42°12E **213** E10
Qādub *Yemen* 12°37N 53°57E **249** D6
Qa'el Jafr *Jordan* 30°20N 36°25E **251** H7
Qa'emābād *Iran* 31°44N 60°2E **247** D9
Qā'emshahr *Iran* 36°30N 52°53E **247** B7
Qafë-Shtamë △ *Albania* 41°31N 19°54E **202** E3
Qagan Nur *Jilin, China* 45°15N 124°18E **227** B13
Qagan Nur *Nei Monggol Zizhiqu, China* 43°30N 114°55E **226** C8
Qahar Youyi Zhongqi *China* 41°12N 112°40E **226** D7
Qahremānshahr = Kermānshāh *Iran* 34°23N 47°0E **213** E12
Qaidam Pendi *China* 37°0N 95°0E **218** D8
Qaiyara *Iraq* 35°48N 43°17E **213** E10
Qajarīyeh *Iran* 31°1N 48°22E **247** D6
Qala *Malta* 36°2N 14°19E **206** E7
Qala, Ras il *Malta* 36°2N 14°20E **206** E7
Qala-i-Jadid = Spīn Būldak *Afghan.* 31°1N 66°25E **242** D2
Qala Point = Qala, Ras il *Malta* 36°2N 14°20E **206** E7
Qala Viala *Pakistan* 30°49N 67°17E **242** D2
Qala Yangi *Afghan.* 34°20N 66°30E **242** B2
Qalācheh *Afghan.* 35°30N 67°43E **240** B2
Qalaikhum = Kalaikhum *Tajikistan* 38°28N 70°46E **217** E8
Qalandiya *West Bank* 31°52N 35°12E **123** A2
Qalansīyah *Yemen* 12°41N 53°29E **249** D6
Qal'at al Akhḑar *Si. Arabia* 28°4N 37°9E **251** K8
Qal'at Bīshah *Si. Arabia* 20°0N 42°36E **248** C3
Qal'at Dīzah *Iraq* 36°11N 45°7E **213** D11
Qalāt-i-Ghilzai *Afghan.* 32°15N 66°58E **240** B2
Qal'at Salah el Din *Syria* 34°46N 36°15E **250** D7
Qal'at Şāliḩ *Iraq* 31°31N 47°16E **246** D5
Qal'at Sukkar *Iraq* 31°51N 46°5E **213** G12
Qal'eh Morghī *Iran* 35°38N 51°22E **141** B2
Qal'eh-ye Bost *Afghan.* 31°30N 64°21E **240** C2
Qal'eh-ye Now *Afghan.* 35°0N 63°5E **240** B1
Qal'eh-ye Panjeh *Afghan.* 37°0N 72°35E **240** A4
Qal'eh-ye Sarkari *Afghan.* 35°54N 67°17E **240** B2
Qal'eh-ye Valī *Afghan.* 35°46N 63°45E **240** B1
Qalyûb *Egypt* 30°12N 31°11E **251** H2
Qalyûbîya □ *Egypt* 30°18N 31°18E **251** H2
Qamani'tuaq = Baker Lake *Canada* 64°20N 96°3W **294** E12
Qamar, Ghubbat al *Yemen* 16°20N 52°30E **249** C6
Qamar, Jabal al *Oman* 16°48N 53°15E **249** C6
Qamdo *China* 31°15N 97°6E **228** B1
Qamea *Fiji* 16°45S 179°45W **287** A3
Qamīnis *Libya* 31°40N 20°1E **258** B4
Qammieh Point *Malta* 35°58N 14°19E **206** F7
Qamruddin Karez *Pakistan* 31°45N 68°20E **242** D3
Qandahār = Kandahār *Afghan.* 31°32N 65°43E **240** C2
Qandahār = Kandahār □ *Afghan.* 31°0N 65°0E **240** C2
Qandala *Somalia* 11°30N 49°58E **267** B6
Qandyaghash *Kazakhstan* 49°28N 57°25E **187** E10
Qapān *Iran* 37°40N 55°47E **247** B7
Qapqal *China* 43°48N 81°5E **217** D10
Qapshaghay *Kazakhstan* 43°51N 77°14E **217** D9
Qapshaghay Bögeni *Kazakhstan* 43°45N 77°50E **217** D9
Qaqortoq *Greenland* 60°43N 46°0W **154** E6
Qâra *Egypt* 29°38N 26°30E **256** B2
Qarā', Jabal al *Oman* 17°15N 54°15E **249** C6
Qara Dāgh *Iraq* 35°18N 45°18E **213** E11
Qara Qash → *China* 35°0N 78°30E **243** B8
Qarabalyq *Kazakhstan* 53°45N 62°2E **216** B6
Qarabutaq *Kazakhstan* 50°0N 60°14E **216** C6
Qaraçala *Azerbaijan* 39°45N 48°53E **191** L9
Qaraçuxar *Azerbaijan* 40°25N 50°1E **191** K10
Qaraghandy *Kazakhstan* 49°50N 73°10E **217** C8
Qaraghayly *Kazakhstan* 49°26N 76°0E **214** E8
Qārah *Si. Arabia* 29°55N 40°3E **246** D4
Qarah Āghāj *Iran* 37°8N 46°58E **213** D12
Qaraoba *Kazakhstan* 47°6N 56°15E **216** C5
Qaraqīya Oyysy *Kazakhstan* 43°27N 51°45E **216** D4
Qaraqosh *Iraq* 36°16N 43°22E **213** D10
Qarataū *Ongtüstik Qazaqstan, Kazakhstan* 43°30N 69°30E **217** D7
Qarataū *Zhambyl, Kazakhstan* 43°10N 70°28E **217** D8
Qarāvol *Afghan.* 37°14N 68°46E **240** A3
Qarazhal *Kazakhstan* 48°2N 70°49E **214** E8
Qarchak *Iran* 35°25N 51°34E **247** C6
Qardho *Somalia* 9°30N 49°6E **267** C6
Qardud *Sudan* 10°20N 29°56E **257** E2
Qareh → *Iran* 39°25N 47°22E **213** C12
Qareh Tekān *Iran* 36°38N 49°29E **247** B6
Qarnein *U.A.E.* 24°56N 52°52E **247** E7
Qarokŭl = Karakul, Ozero *Tajikistan* 39°5N 73°25E **217** E8
Qarqan He → *China* 39°30N 88°30E **217** E11
Qarqaraly *Kazakhstan* 49°26N 75°30E **217** C9
Qarqin *Afghan.* 37°24N 66°4E **240** A2
Qarrasa *Sudan* 14°38N 32°5E **257** E3
Qarshi *Uzbekistan* 38°53N 65°48E **217** E7
Qartabā *Lebanon* 34°4N 35°50E **250** D6
Qārūh *Kuwait* 28°49N 48°46E **247** D6
Qaryat al Gharab *Iraq* 31°27N 44°48E **246** D5
Qaryat al 'Ulyā *Si. Arabia* 27°33N 47°42E **246** E5
Qarynzharyq Oyysy *Kazakhstan* 42°55N 54°25E **216** D4
Qaşbah, Râs al *Si. Arabia* 28°2N 34°38E **251** K5
Qāsemābād *Iran* 35°46N 51°30E **141** A3
Qashqadaryo □ *Uzbekistan* 38°35N 66°0E **217** E7
Qasigiannguit *Greenland* 68°50N 51°18W **154** D5
Qasr 'Amra *Jordan* 31°48N 36°35E **246** D3
Qaşr Bū Hadi *Libya* 31°1N 16°45E **258** B3
Qasr-e Firūzeh *Iran* 35°29N 51°31E **141** B3
Qaşr-e Qand *Iran* 26°15N 60°45E **247** E9
Qaşr-e Shīrīn *Iran* 34°31N 45°35E **213** E11
Qasr Farâfra *Egypt* 27°0N 28°1E **256** B2
Qaşr Larocu *Libya* 26°32N 13°19E **258** C2
Qasuittuq = Resolute *Canada* 74°42N 94°54W **295** C13
Qa'ţabah *Yemen* 13°51N 44°42E **248** D4
Qatanā *Syria* 33°26N 36°4E **250** E7
Qaţānan, Ra's *Yemen* 12°21N 53°33E **249** D6
Qatane *West Bank* 31°50N 35°6E **123** B1
Qatar ■ *Asia* 25°30N 51°15E **247** E6
Qatlīsh *Iran* 37°50N 57°19E **247** B8
Qattâra *Egypt* 30°12N 27°3E **256** A2
Qattâra, Munkhafed el *Egypt* 29°30N 27°30E **256** B2
Qattâra Depression = Qattâra, Munkhafed el *Egypt* 29°30N 27°30E **256** B2
Qausuittuq △ *Canada* 76°0N 101°0W **295** B11
Qawām al Ḩamzah = Al Ḩamzah *Iraq* 31°43N 44°58E **246** D5
Qawra Point *Malta* 35°58N 14°26E **206** F7
Qāyen *Iran* 33°40N 59°10E **247** C8
Qaynar *Kazakhstan* 49°12N 77°22E **217** C9
Qazaly *Kazakhstan* 45°45N 62°6E **216** C6
Qazaqstan = Kazakhstan ■ *Asia* 50°0N 70°0E **217** C8
Qazaqtyng Usaqshogylyghy *Kazakhstan* 50°0N 72°0E **217** C8
Qazax *Azerbaijan* 41°5N 45°21E **191** K7
Qazımämmäd *Azerbaijan* 40°3N 49°0E **191** K9
Qazvīn *Iran* 36°15N 50°0E **247** B6
Qazvīn □ *Iran* 36°20N 50°0E **247** B6
Qazyghurt *Kazakhstan* 41°45N 69°23E **217** D7
Qeisari = Caesarea *Israel* 32°30N 34°53E **251** F5
Qeissan *Sudan* 11°4N 34°40E **257** E3
Qena *Egypt* 26°10N 32°43E **256** B3
Qena, W. → *Egypt* 26°12N 32°44E **256** B3
Qeqertalik □ *Greenland* 68°0N 48°0W **154** D6
Qeqertarsuaq *Qaasuitsup, Greenland* 69°45N 53°30W **154** D5
Qeqertarsuaq *Qaasuitsup, Greenland* 69°15N 53°38W **154** D5
Qeqertarsuatsiaat *Greenland* 63°5N 50°45W **154** E5
Qeqqata □ *Greenland* 66°30N 48°0W **154** D6
Qeshlāq *Iran* 34°55N 46°28E **213** E12
Qeshm *Iran* 26°55N 56°10E **247** E8
Qeydār *Iran* 36°6N 48°35E **213** D13
Qeys *Iran* 26°32N 53°58E **249** A6
Qezel Owzen → *Iran* 36°45N 49°22E **247** B6
Qezi'ot *Israel* 30°52N 34°26E **251** H5
Qi Xian *China* 34°40N 114°48E **226** G8
Qian Gorlos *China* 45°5N 124°42E **227** B13
Qian Hai *China* 22°32N 113°54E **219** a
Qian Xian *China* 34°31N 108°15E **226** G5
Qian'an *China* 40°0N 118°41E **227** E10
Qiancheng *China* 27°12N 109°50E **228** D7
Qianjiang *Guangxi Zhuangzu, China* 23°38N 108°58E **228** F7
Qianjiang *Hubei, China* 30°24N 112°55E **229** B9
Qianjiang *Sichuan, China* 29°33N 108°47E **228** C7
Qianjin *China* 47°34N 133°4E **219** B15
Qianmen *China* 39°51N 116°21E **114** B2
Qianshan *Anhui, China* 30°37N 116°35E **229** B11
Qianshan *Guangdong, China* 22°15N 113°31E **219** a
Qianwei *China* 29°13N 103°56E **228** C4
Qianxi *China* 27°3N 106°3E **228** D6
Qianyang *Hunan, China* 27°18N 110°10E **229** D8
Qianyang *Shaanxi, China* 34°40N 107°8E **226** G4
Qianyang *Zhejiang, China* 30°11N 119°25E **229** B12
Qi'ao *China* 22°25N 113°39E **219** a
Qi'ao Dao *China* 22°25N 113°38E **219** a
Qiaocun *China* 39°56N 112°55E **226** E7
Qiaojia *China* 26°56N 102°58E **228** D4
Qichun *China* 30°18N 115°25E **229** B10
Qidong *Hunan, China* 26°49N 112°7E **229** D9
Qidong *Jiangsu, China* 31°48N 121°38E **229** B13
Qiemo *China* 38°8N 85°32E **217** E11
Qijiang *China* 28°57N 106°35E **228** C6
Qijiaojing *China* 43°28N 91°36E **217** D12
Qikiqtaaluk = Baffin I. *Canada* 68°0N 75°0W **295** D17
Qikiqtarjuaq *Canada* 67°33N 63°0W **295** D19
Qila Saifullāh *Pakistan* 30°45N 68°17E **242** D3
Qilian Shan *China* 38°30N 96°0E **218** D8
Qimei = Ch'imei *Taiwan* 23°12N 119°25E **225** C1
Qimen *China* 29°50N 117°42E **229** C11
Qin He → *China* 35°1N 113°22E **226** G7
Qin Jiang → *Guangxi Zhuangzu, China* 21°53N 108°35E **228** F7
Qin Jiang → *Jiangxi, China* 26°15N 115°55E **229** D10
Qin Ling = Qinling Shandi *China* 33°50N 108°10E **226** H5
Qināb, W. → *Yemen* 17°55N 49°59E **249** C5
Qin'an *China* 34°48N 105°40E **226** G3
Qing Xian *China* 38°35N 116°45E **226** E9
Qingcheng *China* 37°15N 117°40E **227** F9
Qingcheng Shan *China* 30°58N 103°31E **228** B4
Qingchuan *China* 32°36N 105°9E **226** H3
Qingdao *China* 36°5N 120°20E **227** F11
Qingfeng *China* 35°52N 115°8E **226** G8
Qinghai □ *China* 36°0N 98°0E **218** D8
Qinghai Hu *China* 36°40N 100°10E **218** D9
Qinghe *China* 46°37N 90°25E **217** C12
Qinghecheng *China* 41°28N 124°15E **224** B2
Qinghemen *China* 41°48N 121°25E **227** D11
Qinghuayuan *China* 39°59N 116°19E **114** B1
Qingjian *China* 37°8N 110°8E **226** F6
Qingjiang = Huaiyin *China* 33°30N 119°2E **227** H10
Qingliu *China* 26°11N 116°48E **229** D11
Qinglong *China* 25°49N 105°12E **228** E5
Qingningsi *China* 31°16N 121°33E **138** B2
Qingping *China* 26°39N 107°47E **228** D6
Qingshui *China* 34°48N 106°8E **226** G4
Qingshuihe *China* 39°55N 111°35E **226** E6
Qingtian *China* 28°12N 120°15E **229** C13
Qingtongxia *China* 38°2N 106°3E **226** E4
Qingtongxia Shuiku *China* 37°50N 105°58E **226** F3
Qingxi *China* 27°8N 108°43E **228** D7
Qingxu *China* 37°34N 112°22E **226** F7
Qingyang *Anhui, China* 30°38N 117°50E **229** B11
Qingyang *Gansu, China* 36°2N 107°55E **226** F4
Qingyi Jiang → *China* 29°32N 103°44E **228** C4
Qingyuan *Guangdong, China* 23°40N 112°59E **229** F9
Qingyuan *Liaoning, China* 42°10N 124°55E **224** A2
Qingyuan *Zhejiang, China* 27°36N 119°3E **229** D12
Qingyun *China* 37°45N 117°20E **227** F9
Qingzhen *China* 26°31N 106°25E **228** D6
Qinhuangdao *China* 39°56N 119°30E **227** E10
Qinling Shandi *China* 33°50N 108°10E **226** H5
Qinshui = Ch'ingshui *Taiwan* 24°16N 120°34E **225** B2
Qinshui *China* 35°40N 112°8E **226** G7
Qinyang = Jiyuan *China* 35°7N 112°57E **226** G7
Qinyang *China* 35°5N 112°56E **226** G7
Qinyuan *China* 36°29N 112°20E **226** F7
Qinzhou *China* 21°58N 108°38E **228** G7
Qionghai *China* 19°15N 110°26E **229** a
Qionglai *China* 30°25N 103°31E **228** B4
Qionglai Shan *China* 31°0N 102°30E **228** B4
Qiongshan *China* 19°51N 110°26E **229** a
Qiongzhou Haixia *China* 20°10N 110°15E **229** a
Qiqihar *China* 47°26N 124°0E **219** B13
Qira *China* 37°0N 80°48E **217** E10
Qiraîya, W. → *Egypt* 30°27N 34°0E **251** H5
Qiryat Ata *Israel* 32°47N 35°6E **250** F6
Qiryat Gat *Israel* 31°32N 34°46E **251** G5
Qiryat Mal'akhi *Israel* 31°44N 34°44E **251** G5
Qiryat Shemona *Israel* 33°13N 35°35E **250** E6
Qiryat Yam *Israel* 32°51N 35°4E **250** F6
Qirzah, W. → *Libya* 30°56N 14°31E **258** B2
Qishan = Ch'ishan *Taiwan* 22°44N 120°31E **225** D2
Qishan *China* 34°25N 107°38E **226** G4
Qishn *Yemen* 15°26N 51°40E **249** D5
Qitai *China* 44°2N 89°35E **217** D11
Qitaihe *China* 45°48N 130°51E **220** B5
Qitbīt, W. → *Oman* 19°15N 54°23E **249** C6
Qiubei *China* 24°2N 104°12E **228** E5
Qixia *China* 37°17N 120°52E **227** F11
Qiyang *China* 26°35N 111°50E **229** D8
Qızılağac Körfäzi *Azerbaijan* 39°9N 49°0E **213** C13
Qobda *Kazakhstan* 50°55N 54°31E **216** B4
Qods *Iran* 35°45N 51°15E **247** C6
Qojūr *Iran* 36°12N 47°55E **246** B5
Qolhak *Iran* 35°45N 51°26E **141** A2
Qom *Iran* 34°40N 51°0E **247** C6
Qom □ *Iran* 34°40N 51°0E **247** C6
Qomolangma Feng = Everest, Mt. *Nepal* 28°5N 86°58E **243** E12
Qomsheh *Iran* 32°0N 51°55E **247** D6
Qonce *S. Africa* 32°51S 27°22E **270** D4
Qong Muztag *China* 35°42N 82°22E **217** E10
Qoqek = Tacheng *China* 46°40N 82°58E **217** C10
Qoqon = Qo'qon *Uzbekistan* 40°31N 70°56E **217** D8
Qo'qon *Uzbekistan* 40°31N 70°56E **217** D8
Qorako'l *Uzbekistan* 39°32N 63°50E **216** E6
Qoraqalpog'istan □ *Uzbekistan* 43°0N 58°0E **216** D5
Qorghalzhyn *Kazakhstan* 50°25N 69°11E **217** B7
Qormi *Malta* 35°53N 14°28E **206** F7
Qorveh *Iran* 35°10N 47°48E **213** E12
Qosshaghyl *Kazakhstan* 46°40N 54°0E **187** E9
Qostanay *Kazakhstan* 53°10N 63°35E **216** B6
Qotanqaraghay *Kazakhstan* 49°10N 85°36E **217** C11
Qoţūr *Iran* 38°28N 44°25E **213** C11
Qoz Salsilgo *C.A.R.* 10°45N 22°54E **264** A4
Qrejten Point *Malta* 35°57N 14°27E **206** F7
Qu Jiang → *China* 30°1N 106°24E **228** B6
Qu Xian *China* 30°48N 106°58E **228** B6
Quabbin Res. *U.S.A.* 42°20N 72°20W **313** D12
Quadraro *Italy* 41°51N 12°33E **136** B2
Quaid-i-Azam *Pakistan* 24°50N 66°59E **123** A1
Quairading *Australia* 32°0S 117°21E **279** F2
Quakenbrück *Germany* 52°41N 7°57E **178** C3
Quakertown *U.S.A.* 40°26N 75°21W **313** F9
Qualicum Beach *Canada* 49°22N 124°26W **296** D4
Quambatook *Australia* 35°49S 143°34E **282** C5
Quambone *Australia* 30°57S 147°53E **283** A7
Quamby *Australia* 20°22S 140°17E **280** C3
Quan Long = Ca Mau *Vietnam* 9°7N 105°8E **237** H5
Quanah *U.S.A.* 34°18N 99°44W **314** D5
Quandialla *Australia* 34°1S 147°47E **283** C7
Quang Ngai *Vietnam* 15°13N 108°58E **236** E7
Quang Tri *Vietnam* 16°45N 107°13E **236** D6
Quang Yen *Vietnam* 20°56N 106°52E **228** G6
Quannan *China* 24°45N 114°33E **229** E10
Quantock Hills *U.K.* 51°8N 3°10W **169** F4
Quanyang *China* 42°21N 127°32E **227** C14
Quanzhou *Fujian, China* 24°55N 118°34E **229** E12
Quanzhou *Guangxi Zhuangzu, China* 25°57N 111°5E **229** E8
Qu'Appelle → *Canada* 50°33N 103°53W **297** C8
Quaqtaq *Canada* 60°55N 69°40W **295** E18
Quaraí *Brazil* 30°15S 56°20W **334** C4
Quarré-les-Tombes *France* 47°21N 4°0E **173** E11
Quarteira *Portugal* 37°4N 8°6W **195** H2
Quarter, The *Anguilla* 18°13N 63°3W **322** a
Quartier D'Orléans *St.-Martin* 18°5N 63°2W **322** a
Quartier Militaire *Mauritius* 20°14S 57°35E **272** e
Quartiere Zingone *Italy* 45°25N 9°3E **128** B1
Quartu Sant'Élena *Italy* 39°15N 9°10E **200** C2
Quartzsite *U.S.A.* 33°40N 114°13W **307** M12
Quatre, I. à *St. Vincent* 12°59N 61°15W **323** n
Quatre Bornes *Mauritius* 20°15S 57°28E **272** e
Quatsino Sd. *Canada* 50°25N 127°58W **296** C3
Quba *Azerbaijan* 41°21N 48°32E **191** K9
Qubeiba *West Bank* 31°50N 35°8E **123** A1
Qūchān *Iran* 37°10N 58°27E **247** B8
Quds *Iraq* 33°23N 44°24E **113** A2
Queanbeyan *Australia* 35°17S 149°14E **283** C8
Québec *Canada* 46°52N 71°13W **299** C5
Québec □ *Canada* 48°0N 74°0W **298** B6
Quebo *Guinea-Biss.* 11°20N 14°56W **262** C2
Quebrada del Condorito △ *Argentina* 31°49S 64°40W **334** C3
Quebradillas *Puerto Rico* 18°29N 66°56W **321** b
Quedlinburg *Germany* 51°47N 11°8E **178** D7
Queen Alexandra Ra. *Antarctica* 85°0S 170°0E **151** E11
Queen Charlotte B. *Falk. Is.* 51°50S 60°40W **153** f
Queen Charlotte City *Canada* 53°15N 132°2W **296** C2
Queen Charlotte Is. = Haida Gwaii *Canada* 53°20N 132°10W **296** C2
Queen Charlotte Sd. *B.C., Canada* 51°0N 128°0W **296** C3
Queen Charlotte Sd. *N.Z.* 41°10S 174°15E **285** B9
Queen Charlotte Strait *Canada* 50°45N 127°10W **296** C3
Queen City *U.S.A.* 40°25N 92°34W **310** D4
Queen Elizabeth △ *Uganda* 0°0 30°0E **268** C3
Queen Elizabeth Is. *Canada* 76°0N 95°0W **295** B13
Queen Elizabeth Land *Antarctica* 85°0S 60°0W **151** E17
Queen Elizabeth Nat. Park = Ruwenzori △ *Uganda* 0°20N 30°0E **268** B2
Queen Elizabeth Olympic Park *London, U.K.* 51°33N 0°0 **125** A3
Queen Mary Land *Antarctica* 70°0S 95°0E **151** D7
Queen Mary Res. *U.K.* 51°24N 0°27W **125** B1
Queen Maud G. *Canada* 68°15N 102°30W **294** D11
Queen Maud Land = Dronning Maud Land *Antarctica* 72°30S 12°0E **151** D3
Queen Maud Mts. *Antarctica* 86°0S 160°0W **151** E12
Queen Street *Edinburgh, U.K.* **121** a1
Queen Victoria Market *Australia* 37°47S 144°57W **128** A1
Queens Channel *Australia* 15°0S 129°30E **278** C4
Queens-Midtown Tunnel *New York, U.S.A.* **132** d2
Queen's Quay Terminal *Toronto, Canada* **141** c2
Queensboro Bridge *New York, U.S.A.* **132** c3
Queensbury *U.K.* 51°35N 0°16W **125** A2
Queenscliff *Australia* 38°16S 144°39E **282** E6
Queenscliffe *Australia* 33°47S 151°17E **139** A2
Queensferry *U.K.* 55°59N 3°23W **121** B1
Queensland *U.S.A.* 31°46N 83°14W **316** D6
Queensland □ *Australia* 22°0S 142°0E **280** C3
Queensland Plateau *Pac. Oc.* 17°0S 150°0E **276** D8
Queenstown = Cobh *Ireland* 51°51N 8°17W **166** E3
Queenstown *Tas., Australia* 42°4S 145°35E **281** G4
Queenstown *N.Z.* 45°1S 168°40E **285** F3
Queenstown *Singapore* 1°18N 103°48E **138** B2
Queenstown *Eastern Cape, S. Africa* 31°52S 26°52E **270** D4
Queets *U.S.A.* 47°32N 124°19W **306** C2
Queguay Grande → *Uruguay* 32°9S 58°9W **334** C4
Queimada, Pta. da *Azores* 38°23N 28°14W **153** d1
Queimadas *Brazil* 11°0S 39°38W **332** D4
Queiros, C. *Vanuatu* 14°55S 167°1E **287** D5
Quela *Angola* 9°10S 16°56E **265** D3
Quelimane *Mozam.* 17°53S 36°58E **269** F4
Quellerina *S. Africa* 26°9S 27°56E **123** A1
Quellón *Chile* 43°7S 73°37W **336** B2
Quelo *Angola* 6°29S 12°36E **265** D2
Quelpart = Jeju-do *S. Korea* 33°29N 126°34E **224** a
Queluz *Portugal* 38°45N 9°14W **126** A1
Quemado *N. Mex., U.S.A.* 34°20N 108°30W **305** J9
Quemado *Tex., U.S.A.* 28°56N 100°37W **314** G4
Quemoy = Chinmen *Taiwan* 24°26N 118°19E **225** a
Quemú-Quemú *Argentina* 36°3S 63°36W **334** D3
Quepem *India* 15°13N 74°3E **245** G2
Quequén *Argentina* 38°30S 58°30W **334** D4
Querco *Peru* 13°50S 74°52W **330** C3
Querétaro *Mexico* 20°36N 100°23W **318** C4
Querétaro □ *Mexico* 21°0N 99°55W **318** C5
Querfurt *Germany* 51°23N 11°35E **178** D7
Quérigut *France* 42°42N 2°6E **174** F6
Querqueville *France* 49°40N 1°42W **172** C5
Quesada *Spain* 37°51N 3°4W **195** H7
Queshan *China* 32°55N 114°2E **229** A10
Quesnel *Canada* 53°0N 122°30W **296** C4
Quesnel → *Canada* 52°58N 122°29W **296** C4
Quesnel L. *Canada* 52°30N 121°20W **296** C4
Questa *U.S.A.* 36°42N 105°36W **305** H11
Questembert *France* 47°40N 2°28W **172** E4
Quetena *Bolivia* 22°10S 67°25W **330** E4
Quetico ⌓ *Canada* 48°30N 91°45W **298** C1
Quetrequile *Argentina* 41°33S 69°22W **336** B3
Quetta *Pakistan* 30°15N 66°55E **242** D2
Quetzaltenango *Guatemala* 14°50N 91°30W **320** D1
Queulat △ *Chile* 44°29S 72°24W **336** B2
Quevedo *Ecuador* 1°2S 79°29W **328** D2
Queyras ⌓ *France* 44°45N 6°50E **175** D10
Quezon *Phil.* 9°15N 117°59E **233** G1
Quezon □ *Phil.* 14°40N 121°30E **232** D3
Quezon △ *Phil.* 14°0N 121°55E **232** D3
Quezon City *Phil.* 14°37N 121°2E **127** B2
Qufār *Si. Arabia* 27°26N 41°37E **246** E4
Qufu *China* 35°36N 116°58E **226** G9
Qui Nhon *Vietnam* 13°40N 109°13E **236** F7
Quibala *Angola* 10°46S 14°59E **265** E2
Quibaxe *Angola* 8°24S 14°27E **265** D2
Quibdó *Colombia* 5°42N 76°40W **328** B2
Quiberon *France* 47°29N 3°9W **172** E3
Quiberon, Presqu'île de *France* 47°30N 3°8W **172** E3
Quiçama △ *Angola* 9°41S 13°35E **265** D2
Quickborn *Germany* 53°42N 9°52E **178** B5
Quiet L. *Canada* 61°5N 133°5W **296** A2
Quiindy *Paraguay* 25°58S 57°14W **334** B4
Quilá *Mexico* 24°23N 107°13W **318** C3
Quilán, C. *Chile* 43°15S 74°30W **336** B2
Quilcene *U.S.A.* 47°49N 122°53W **306** C4
Quilenda *Angola* 10°39S 14°23E **265** E2
Quilengues *Angola* 14°12S 14°12E **265** E2
Quilicura *Chile* 33°22S 70°43W **137** B1
Quilimarí *Chile* 32°5S 71°30W **334** C1
Quilino *Argentina* 30°14S 64°29W **334** C3
Quill, The *St. Eustatius* 17°28N 62°57W **322** a
Quillabamba *Peru* 12°50S 72°50W **330** C3
Quillacollo *Bolivia* 17°26S 66°17W **330** D4
Quillagua *Chile* 21°40S 69°40W **334** A2
Quillan *France* 42°53N 2°10E **174** F6
Quillota *Chile* 32°54S 71°16W **334** C1
Quilmes *Argentina* 34°43S 58°15W **334** C4
Quilon = Kollam *India* 8°50N 76°38E **245** K3
Quilpie *Australia* 26°35S 144°11E **281** D3
Quilpué *Chile* 33°5S 71°33W **334** C1
Quilua *Mozam.* 16°17S 39°54E **269** F4
Quimbele *Angola* 6°17S 16°41E **265** D3
Quimbo *Angola* 14°4S 16°11E **265** E3
Quimbonge *Angola* 8°36S 18°30E **265** D3
Quime *Bolivia* 17°2S 67°15W **330** D4
Quimilí *Argentina* 27°40S 62°30W **334** B3
Quimper *France* 48°0N 4°9W **172** E2
Quimperlé *France* 47°53N 3°33W **172** E3
Quinam B. *Trin. & Tob.* 10°4N 61°30W **323** t
Quinault → *U.S.A.* 47°21N 124°18W **306** C2
Quince Mil *Peru* 13°15S 70°40W **330** C3
Quincy *Calif., U.S.A.* 39°56N 120°57W **306** F6
Quincy *Fla., U.S.A.* 30°35N 84°34W **316** E5
Quincy *Ill., U.S.A.* 39°56N 91°23W **310** E5
Quincy *Mass., U.S.A.* 42°14N 71°0W **116** B2
Quincy *Mich., U.S.A.* 41°57N 84°53W **311** C12
Quincy *Wash., U.S.A.* 47°14N 119°51W **304** C4
Quincy B. *U.S.A.* 42°16N 70°59W **116** B3
Quines *Argentina* 32°13S 65°48W **334** C2
Quinga *Mozam.* 15°49S 40°15E **269** F5
Quingey *France* 47°7N 5°52E **173** E12
Quingombe *Angola* 6°38S 13°1E **265** D2
Quinhagak *U.S.A.* 59°45N 161°54W **303** G7
Quinhámel *Guinea-Biss.* 11°53N 15°51W **262** C1
Quiniluban Group *Phil.* 11°27N 120°48E **233** F3
Quinta Normal *Chile* 33°26S 70°42W **137** B1
Quintana de la Serena *Spain* 38°45N 5°40W **195** G5
Quintana Roo □ *Mexico* 19°40N 88°30W **319** D7
Quintana Roo △ *Quintana Roo, Mexico* 20°15N 87°45W **319** C7
Quintanar de la Orden *Spain* 39°36N 3°5W **195** F7
Quintanar de la Sierra *Spain* 41°57N 2°55W **196** D2
Quintanar del Rey *Spain* 39°21N 1°56W **197** F3
Quintero *Chile* 32°45S 71°30W **334** C1
Quintin *France* 48°26N 2°56W **172** D4
Quinto *Spain* 41°25N 0°32W **196** D4
Quinto de Stampi *Italy* 45°24N 9°10E **128** B2
Quinto Romano *Italy* 45°28N 9°7E **128** B1
Quinzáu *Angola* 6°51S 12°44E **265** D2
Quípar → *Spain* 38°15N 1°40W **197** G3
Quipeio *Angola* 12°27S 15°30E **265** E3
Quirihue *Chile* 36°15S 72°35W **334** D1
Quirima *Angola* 10°47S 18°6E **265** E3
Quirimbas △ *Mozam.* 12°30S 40°15E **269** E5
Quirimbo *Angola* 10°36S 14°12E **265** E2
Quirinale *Italy* 41°53N 12°29E **136** B1
Quirinale, Palazzo dei *Rome, Italy* **136** b3
Quirindi *Australia* 31°28S 150°40E **283** A9
Quirino □ *Phil.* 16°15N 121°40E **232** C3
Quirinópolis *Brazil* 18°32S 50°30W **333** E1
Quiroga *Spain* 42°28N 7°18W **194** C3
Quiruvilca *Peru* 8°1S 78°19W **330** B2
Quissac *France* 43°55N 4°0E **175** E8
Quissanga *Mozam.* 12°24S 40°28E **269** E5
Quissico *Mozam.* 24°42S 34°44E **271** B5
Quissongo *Angola* 10°2S 15°5E **265** E3
Quitapa *Angola* 10°20S 18°19E **265** E3
Quitilipi *Argentina* 26°50S 60°13W **334** B3
Quitman *U.S.A.* 30°47N 83°34W **316** E6
Quito *Ecuador* 0°15S 78°35W **328** D2
Quitralco △ *Chile* 45°43S 73°25W **336** C2
Quixadá *Brazil* 4°55S 39°0W **332** B4
Quixaxe *Mozam.* 15°17S 40°4E **269** F5
Quixeramobim *Brazil* 5°12S 39°17W **332** C4
Quixico *Angola* 7°59S 14°25E **265** D2
Quixinge *Angola* 9°52S 14°23E **265** D2
Quizenga *Angola* 9°21S 15°28E **265** D3
Qujing *China* 25°32N 103°41E **228** E4
Qulan *Kazakhstan* 42°55N 72°43E **214** E8
Qul'ân, Jazâ'ir *Egypt* 24°22N 35°31E **246** E2
Qulsary *Kazakhstan* 46°59N 54°1E **187** E9
Qumbu *S. Africa* 31°10S 28°48E **271** D4
Qumqo'rgo'n *Uzbekistan* 37°49N 67°35E **240** A2
Qunayyin, Sabkhat al *Libya* 30°10N 21°0E **258** B4
Quneitra = Al Qunayţirah *Syria* 33°5N 35°45E **250** F6
Qŭnghirot *Uzbekistan* 43°2N 58°50E **216** D5
Qu'nyido *China* 31°15N 98°6E **228** B2
Quoin I. *Australia* 14°54S 129°32E **278** B4
Quoin Pt. *S. Africa* 34°46S 19°37E **270** D2
Quorn *Australia* 32°25S 138°5E **282** B3
Qurein *Sudan* 13°30N 34°50E **257** E3
Qŭrghonteppa *Tajikistan* 37°50N 68°47E **217** E7
Qurimbas △ *Mozam.* 12°20S 40°10E **269** E5
Qurnat as Sawdā' *Lebanon* 34°18N 36°6E **250** D7
Quryq *Kazakhstan* 43°12N 51°39E **216** D4
Qûs *Egypt* 25°55N 32°50E **256** B3
Qusar *Azerbaijan* 41°25N 48°26E **191** K9
Quşaybā' *Si. Arabia* 26°53N 43°35E **246** E4
Qusaybah *Iraq* 34°24N 40°59E **213** E9
Quşay'ir *Yemen* 14°55N 50°20E **249** D5
Quseir *Egypt* 26°7N 34°16E **246** E2
Quseir Amra = Qasr 'Amra *Jordan* 31°48N 36°35E **246** D3
Qūshchī *Iran* 37°59N 45°3E **213** D11
Qusmuryn *Kazakhstan* 52°27N 64°36E **216** B6
Qusmuryn Köli *Kazakhstan* 52°41N 64°48E **216** B6
Qutang Gorge = Qutang Xia *China* 31°0N 109°40E **228** B7
Qutang Xia *China* 31°0N 109°40E **228** B7
Qutb Minar *India* 28°31N 77°11E **120** B2
Quthing *Lesotho* 30°25S 27°36E **271** D4
Qūţīābād *Iran* 35°47N 48°30E **213** E13
Quttinirpaaq = Ellesmere I. *Canada* 79°30N 80°0W **295** B16
Quttinirpaaq △ *Canada* 82°13N 72°13W **295** A17
Quwayq → *Syria* 36°20N 37°10E **250** B8
Quweisna *Egypt* 30°34N 31°9E **251** H2
Quwo *China* 35°38N 111°25E **226** G6
Quyang *China* 38°35N 114°40E **226** E8
Quynh Nhai *Vietnam* 21°49N 103°33E **236** B4
Quyon *Canada* 45°31N 76°14W **313** A8
Quzhou *China* 28°57N 118°54E **229** C12
Quzi *China* 36°20N 107°20E **226** F4
Qvareli *Georgia* 41°57N 45°47E **191** K7
Qytet Stalin = Kuçovë *Albania* 40°47N 19°57E **202** F3
Qyzylorda *Kazakhstan* 44°48N 65°28E **216** D7
Qyzylorda □ *Kazakhstan* 45°0N 65°0E **216** D6
Qyzylzhar *Kazakhstan* 48°17N 69°38E **217** C7

R

R.F.K. Memorial Stadium *U.S.A.* 38°52N 76°58W **143** B3
Ra, Ko *Thailand* 9°13N 98°16E **237** H2
Raab *Austria* 48°21N 13°39E **180** C6
Raahe *Finland* 64°40N 24°28E **160** D21
Raalte *Neths.* 52°23N 6°16E **170** B6
Ra'ananna *Israel* 32°10N 34°52E **251** F5
Raas *Indonesia* 7°8S 114°33E **235** D4
Raasay *U.K.* 57°25N 6°4W **167** D2
Raasay, Sd. of *U.K.* 57°30N 6°8W **167** D2
Raasdorf *Austria* 48°14N 16°33E **142** A3
Raasepori *Finland* 60°0N 23°26E **188** B2
Rab *Croatia* 44°45N 14°45E **199** D11
Raba *Indonesia* 8°36S 118°55E **235** D5
Rába → *Hungary* 47°38N 17°38E **182** C2
Raba → *Poland* 50°8N 20°30E **185** H7
Rabaçal → *Portugal* 41°30N 7°12W **194** D3
Rabah *Nigeria* 13°5N 5°30E **263** C6
Rabai *Kenya* 3°50S 39°31E **268** C4
Rabak *Sudan* 13°9N 32°44E **257** E3
Rabaraba *Papua N. G.* 9°58S 149°49E **286** E5
Rabastens *France* 43°50N 1°43E **174** E5
Rabastens-de-Bigorre *France* 43°23N 0°9E **174** E4
Rabat = Victoria *Malta* 36°3N 14°14E **206** E6
Rabat *Malta* 35°53N 14°24E **206** F7
Rabat *Morocco* 34°2N 6°48W **260** B3
Rabat-Sale-Kenitra □ *Morocco* 34°10N 6°20W **260** B3
Rabaul *Papua N. G.* 4°24S 152°18E **286** C7
Rabbit Flat *Australia* 20°11S 130°1E **278** D5
Rabbit Lake Mine *Canada* 58°4N 104°5W **297** B8
Rabi *Fiji* 16°30S 179°59W **287** A3
Rābigh *Si. Arabia* 22°50N 39°5E **248** B2
Rabka *Poland* 49°37N 19°59E **185** J6
Râbniţa = Rîbniţa *Moldova* 47°45N 29°0E **183** C14
Rābor *Iran* 29°17N 56°55E **247** D8
Rabwah = Chenab Nagar *Pakistan* 31°45N 72°55E **242** D5
Rača *Serbia* 44°14N 21°0E **202** B4
Răcăciuni *Romania* 46°20N 26°59E **183** D11
Răcăşdia *Romania* 44°59N 21°36E **182** F6
Racconigi *Italy* 44°46N 7°46E **198** D4
Raccoon → *U.S.A.* 41°35N 93°37W **310** C3
Raccoon Cr. → *U.S.A.* 39°47N 87°23W **311** E9
Race, C. *Canada* 46°40N 53°5W **299** C9
Race Course *Jamaica* 17°51N 77°20W **320** a
Race Pond *U.S.A.* 31°1N 82°8W **316** D7
Rach Gia *Vietnam* 10°5N 105°5E **237** G5
Rach Soi *Vietnam* 9°57N 105°7E **237** H5
Racha Noi, Ko *Thailand* 7°30N 98°19E **237** J2
Racha Yai, Ko *Thailand* 7°36N 98°21E **237** J2
Rachid *Mauritania* 18°45N 11°35W **262** B2
Raciąż *Poland* 52°46N 20°10E **185** F7
Racibórz *Poland* 50°7N 18°18E **185** H5
Racichy *Belarus* 53°44N 23°42E **184** E10
Racine *U.S.A.* 42°44N 87°47W **311** B9
Račisdorf = Rača *Serbia* 44°14N 21°0E **202** B4
Rackerby *U.S.A.* 39°26N 121°22W **306** F5
Råda *Sweden* 60°0N 13°36E **162** E7
Radama, Nosy *Madag.* 14°0S 47°47E **272** A2
Radama, Saikanosy *Madag.* 14°16S 47°53E **272** A2
Radan *Serbia* 42°59N 21°29E **202** D5
Rădăuţi *Romania* 47°50N 25°59E **183** C10
Rădăuţi-Prut *Romania* 48°14N 26°48E **183** B11
Radbuza → *Czechia* 49°45N 13°22E **180** B6
Radcliff *U.S.A.* 37°51N 85°57W **311** G11
Radcliffe College *U.S.A.* 42°22N 71°7W **116** A2
Radeberg *Germany* 51°7N 13°53E **178** D9
Radebeul *Germany* 51°6N 13°39E **178** D9
Radeče *Slovenia* 46°5N 15°14E **199** B12
Radekhiv *Ukraine* 50°25N 24°32E **177** C13
Radekhov = Radekhiv *Ukraine* 50°25N 24°32E **177** C13
Radenthein *Austria* 46°48N 13°43E **180** E6
Radew → *Poland* 54°2N 15°52E **184** D2
Radford *U.S.A.* 37°8N 80°34W **309** G13
Radhanpur *India* 23°50N 71°38E **242** H4
Rådhus *Oslo, Norway* **133** b1
Radhwa, Jabal *Si. Arabia* 24°34N 38°18E **246** E3
Radika → *N. Macedonia* 41°38N 20°37E **202** E4
Radisson *Qué., Canada* 53°47N 77°37W **298** B4
Radisson *Sask., Canada* 52°30N 107°20W **297** C7
Radium Hot Springs *Canada* 50°35N 116°2W **296** C5
Radlice *Czechia* 50°3N 14°23E **135** B2
Radlje ob Dravi *Slovenia* 46°38N 15°13E **199** B12
Radmannsdorf = Radovljica *Slovenia* 46°22N 14°12E **199** B11
Radnevo *Bulgaria* 42°17N 25°58E **203** D9
Radnice *Czechia* 49°51N 13°35E **180** B6
Radnor Forest *U.K.* 52°17N 3°10W **169** E4
Radolfzell *Germany* 47°39N 8°59E **179** H4
Radom *Poland* 51°23N 21°12E **185** G8
Radom △ *Sudan* 9°20N 23°50E **264** A4
Radomir *Bulgaria* 42°37N 22°59E **202** D6
Radomka → *Poland* 51°43N 21°28E **185** G8
Radomsko *Poland* 51°5N 19°28E **185** G6
Radomyshl *Ukraine* 50°30N 29°12E **177** C15
Radomyśl Wielki *Poland* 50°14N 21°15E **185** H8
Radość *Poland* 52°11N 21°11E **143** B3
Radoszyce *Poland* 51°4N 20°15E **185** G7
Radotin *Czechia* 49°59N 14°21E **135** C2
Radoviš *N. Macedonia* 41°38N 22°28E **202** E6
Radovljica *Slovenia* 46°22N 14°12E **199** B11
Radstadt *Austria* 47°24N 13°28E **180** D6
Radstock, C. *Australia* 33°12S 134°20E **281** E1
Răducăneni *Romania* 46°58N 27°54E **183** D12
Raduša *N. Macedonia* 42°7N 21°15E **202** D5
Raduzhnyy *Russia* 62°5N 77°28E **214** C8
Radvanichy *Belarus* 52°1N 24°0E **185** F11
Radviliškis *Lithuania* 55°49N 23°33E **184** C10
Radville *Canada* 49°30N 104°15W **297** D8
Raḑwá, J. *Si. Arabia* 24°34N 38°18E **256** C4
Radymno *Poland* 49°59N 22°52E **185** J9
Radzanów *Poland* 52°56N 20°8E **185** F7
Radziejów *Poland* 52°40N 18°30E **185** F5
Radzyń Chełmiński *Poland* 53°23N 18°55E **184** E5
Radzyń Podlaski *Poland* 51°47N 22°37E **185** G9
Rae = Behchoko *Canada* 62°50N 116°3W **296** A5
Rae Bareli *India* 26°18N 81°20E **243** F9
Rae Isthmus *Canada* 66°40N 87°30W **295** D14
Raeren *Belgium* 50°41N 6°7E **170** D6
Raeside, L. *Australia* 29°20S 122°0E **279** E3
Raetihi *N.Z.* 39°25S 175°17E **284** F4
Rafaela *Argentina* 31°10S 61°30W **334** C3
Rafah *Gaza Strip* 31°18N 34°14E **251** G5
Rafai *C.A.R.* 4°59N 23°58E **264** B4
Rafat *West Bank* 31°52N 35°11E **123** A2
Raffadali *Italy* 37°24N 13°32E **200** E6
Raffili *South Sudan* 6°50N 28°0E **257** F2
Raffles Hotel *Singapore* **138** b3
Raffles Park *Singapore* 1°19N 103°48E **138** B2
Rafḩā *Si. Arabia* 29°35N 43°35E **246** D4
Rafina *Greece* 38°2N 24°0E **204** C6
Rafsanjān *Iran* 30°30N 56°5E **247** D8
Raft Pt. *Australia* 16°4S 124°26E **278** C3
Raga *South Sudan* 8°28N 25°41E **257** F2
Raga → *South Sudan* 8°41N 25°52E **257** F2
Ragachow *Belarus* 53°8N 30°5E **177** B16
Ragag *Sudan* 10°59N 24°40E **257** E1
Ragang, Mt. *Phil.* 7°43N 124°32E **233** H5
Ragay *Phil.* 13°49N 122°47E **232** E4
Ragay G. *Phil.* 13°30N 122°45E **232** E4
Ragged, Mt. *Australia* 33°27S 123°25E **279** F3
Rāgh *Afghan.* 37°32N 70°27E **240** A3
Raghunathpalli *India* 22°14N 84°48E **243** H11
Raghunathpur *India* 23°33N 86°40E **243** H12
Raglan *N.Z.* 37°55S 174°55E **284** D3
Raglan Harbour *N.Z.* 37°47S 174°50E **284** D3
Ragland *U.S.A.* 33°45N 86°9W **316** B3
Ragnit = Neman *Russia* 55°2N 22°2E **184** C9
Raguda, Ghubbet *Somalia* 10°43N 46°22E **267** B6
Ragusa = Dubrovnik *Croatia* 42°39N 18°6E **202** D2
Ragusa *Italy* 36°55N 14°44E **201** F7
Raha *Indonesia* 4°55S 123°0E **231** E6
Rahad, Nahr ed → *Sudan* 14°28N 33°31E **257** E3
Rahad al Bardī *Sudan* 11°20N 23°40E **259** F4
Rahaeng = Tak *Thailand* 16°52N 99°8E **236** D2
Rahat *Israel* 31°24N 34°45E **251** G5
Rahat, Ḩarrat *Si. Arabia* 23°0N 40°5E **256** C5
Rahatgarh *India* 23°47N 78°22E **243** H8
Rahden *Germany* 52°26N 8°36E **178** C4
Raheb, Ras ir- *Malta* 35°54N 14°20E **206** F7
Raheita *Eritrea* 12°46N 43°4E **257** E5
Raheng = Tak *Thailand* 16°52N 99°8E **236** D2
Rahimyar Khan *Pakistan* 28°30N 70°25E **242** E4
Rāhjerd *Iran* 34°22N 50°22E **247** C6
Rahnsdorf *Germany* 52°25N 13°41E **115** B5
Rahole ⌓ *Kenya* 0°5N 38°57E **268** B4
Råholt *Norway* 60°16N 11°11E **164** D8
Rahon *India* 31°3N 76°7E **242** D7
Rahotu *N.Z.* 39°20S 173°49E **284** F2
Rahovec *Kosovo* 42°24N 20°40E **202** D4
Rahuri *India* 19°23N 74°39E **244** E2
Rai, Hon *Vietnam* 9°48N 104°38E **237** H5
Raiatéa, Î. *French Polynesia* 16°50S 151°25W **289** f
Raichur *India* 16°10N 77°20E **245** F3
Raiford *U.S.A.* 30°4N 82°14W **316** E7
Raiganj *India* 25°37N 88°10E **243** G13
Raigarh *India* 21°56N 83°25E **244** D6
Raighar *India* 19°51N 82°6E **244** E6
Raijua *Indonesia* 10°37S 121°36E **231** F6
Raikot *India* 30°41N 75°42E **242** D6
Railton *Australia* 41°25S 146°28E **281** G4
Rainbow Bridge ⌓ *U.S.A.* 37°5N 110°58W **305** H8
Rainbow City *U.S.A.* 33°57N 86°5W **316** B3
Rainbow Lake *Canada* 58°30N 119°23W **296** B5
Rainier *U.S.A.* 46°53N 122°41W **306** D4
Rainier, Mt. *U.S.A.* 46°52N 121°46W **306** D5
Rainy L. *Canada* 48°42N 93°10W **297** D10
Rainy River *Canada* 48°43N 94°29W **297** D10
Raippaluoto *Finland* 63°13N 21°14E **160** E19
Raipur *India* 21°17N 81°45E **244** D5
Rairakhol *India* 21°4N 84°21E **244** D7
Ra'is *Si. Arabia* 23°33N 38°43E **256** C4
Raisen *India* 23°20N 77°48E **242** H8
Raisio *Finland* 60°28N 22°11E **188** B2
Raivavae *French Polynesia* 23°52S 147°40W **289** f
Raj Ghat *Delhi, India* **120** b3
Raj Nandgaon *India* 21°5N 81°5E **244** D5
Raj Nilgiri *India* 21°28N 86°46E **243** J12
Raja, Ujung *Indonesia* 3°40N 96°25E **234** B1
Raja Ampat, Kepulauan *Indonesia* 0°30S 130°0E **231** E8
Rajah Sikatuna △ *Phil.* 9°40N 124°20E **233** G5
Rajahmahendravaram *India* 17°1N 81°48E **244** F5
Rajahmundry = Rajahmahendravaram *India* 17°1N 81°48E **244** F5
Rajaji △ *India* 30°10N 78°20E **242** D8
Rajakylä *Finland* 60°15N 25°5E **121** B3
Rajampet *India* 14°11N 79°10E **245** G4
Rajang → *Malaysia* 2°30N 112°0E **235** B4
Rajang Mangroves △ *Malaysia* 2°6N 111°16E **235** B4
Rajanpur *Pakistan* 29°6N 70°19E **242** E4
Rajapalaiyam *India* 9°25N 77°35E **245** K3
Rajapur *India* 16°40N 73°31E **244** F1
Rajasthan □ *India* 26°45N 73°30E **242** F5
Rajasthan Canal = Indira Gandhi Canal *India* 28°0N 72°0E **242** F5
Rajauri *India* 33°25N 74°21E **243** C6
Rajbari *Bangla.* 23°47N 89°41E **241** D2
Rajendranagar *India* 17°18N 78°27E **244** F4
Rajgarh *Mad. P., India* 24°2N 76°45E **242** G7
Rajgarh *Raj., India* 27°14N 76°38E **242** F7
Rajgarh *Raj., India* 28°40N 75°25E **242** E6
Rajghat Dam *India* 24°45N 78°20E **244** B4
Rajgir *India* 25°2N 85°25E **243** G11
Rajgród *Poland* 53°42N 22°42E **184** E9
Rajim *India* 20°58N 81°53E **244** D5
Rajkot *India* 22°15N 70°56E **242** H4
Rajmahal Hills *India* 24°30N 87°30E **243** G12
Rajpath *Delhi, India* **120** c2

Rajpipla *India* 21°50N 73°30E **244** D1
Rajpur *India* 22°18N 74°21E **242** H6
Rajpura *Delhi, India* 28°41N 77°12E **120** A2
Rajpura *Punjab, India* 30°25N 76°32E **242** D7
Rajputana = Rajasthan ☐ *India* 26°45N 73°30E **242** F5
Rajsamand = Kankroli *India* 25°4N 73°53E **242** G5
Rajshahi *Bangla.* 24°22N 88°39E **241** C2
Rajshahi ☐ *Bangla.* 25°0N 89°0E **241** C2
Rājū *Syria* 36°40N 36°40E **250** B7
Rajula *India* 21°3N 71°26E **242** J4
Rajur *India* 20°7N 78°55E **244** D4
Rajura *India* 19°47N 79°22E **244** E4
Rakaia *N.Z.* 43°45S 172°1E **285** D7
Rakaia → *N.Z.* 43°36S 172°15E **285** D7
Rakan, Ra's *Qatar* 26°10N 51°20E **247** E6
Rakaposhi *Pakistan* 36°10N 74°25E **243** A6
Rakata, Pulau *Indonesia* 6°10S 105°20E **234** D3
Rakbah, Sahl *Si. Arabia* 22°15N 41°0E **256** C5
Rakhine ☐ *Myanmar* 19°0N 94°15E **241** F5
Rakhiv *Ukraine* 48°3N 24°12E **183** B9
Rakhni *Pakistan* 30°4N 69°56E **242** D3
Rakhni → *Pakistan* 29°31N 69°36E **242** E3
Rakhny-Lisovi *Ukraine* 48°47N 28°29E **183** B13
Rakhyūt *Oman* 16°44N 53°20E **249** C6
Rakiraki *Fiji* 17°22S 178°11E **287** A2
Rakitnoye *Russia* 50°57N 35°56E **189** G8
Rakitnoye *Russia* 45°36N 134°17E **220** B7
Rakitovo *Bulgaria* 41°59N 24°5E **203** E8
Rakiura = Stewart I. *N.Z.* 46°58S 167°54E **285** G2
Rakkestad *Norway* 59°25N 11°21E **164** E8
Rakoniewice *Poland* 52°10N 16°16E **185** F3
Rakops *Botswana* 21°1S 24°28E **270** B3
Rákos-patak → *Hungary* 47°29N 19°12E **117** B3
Rákoshegy *Hungary* 47°27N 19°14E **117** B3
Rákoskeresztúr *Hungary* 47°29N 19°15E **117** B3
Rákoskert *Hungary* 47°27N 19°18E **117** B3
Rákosliget *Hungary* 47°29N 19°16E **117** B3
Rákospalota *Hungary* 47°34N 19°7E **117** A2
Rákosszentmihály *Hungary* 47°31N 19°8E **117** A2
Rakovica *Croatia* 44°59N 15°38E **199** D12
Rakovník *Czechia* 50°6N 13°42E **180** A6
Rakovski *Bulgaria* 42°21N 24°57E **203** D8
Raków *Poland* 52°11N 20°56E **143** B1
Rakshan → *Pakistan* 27°10N 63°25E **240** D1
Rakvere *Estonia* 59°20N 26°25E **188** C4
Raleigh *Fla., U.S.A.* 29°25N 82°32W **317** F7
Raleigh *N.C., U.S.A.* 35°47N 78°39W **315** D15
Ralik Chain *Pac. Oc.* 8°0N 168°0E **288** G8
Ralja *Serbia* 44°33N 20°34E **202** B4
Rälla *Sweden* 56°40N 16°30E **163** H10
Ralls *U.S.A.* 33°41N 101°24W **314** E4
Ralston *U.S.A.* 41°30N 76°57W **312** E8
Ram *West Bank* 31°51N 35°14E **123** A2
Ram → *Canada* 62°1N 123°41W **296** A4
Rām Allāh *West Bank* 31°55N 35°10E **123** A2
Rama *Nic.* 12°9N 84°15W **320** D3
Ramacca *Italy* 37°23N 14°42E **201** E7
Ramachandrapuram *India* 16°50N 82°4E **244** F6
Ramadān *Iraq* 33°19N 44°20E **113** B2
Ramagiri Udayagiri *India* 19°5N 84°18E **244** E7
Ramagundam *India* 18°55N 79°15E **244** E4
Ramakona *India* 21°43N 78°50E **243** J8
Ramakrishna Puram *India* 28°32N 77°10E **120** B1
Ramalho, Serra do *Brazil* 13°45S 44°0W **333** D3
Rāmallāh = Rām Allāh *West Bank* 31°55N 35°10E **123** A2
Raman *Thailand* 6°29N 101°18E **237** J3
Ramanathapuram *India* 9°25N 78°55E **245** K4
Ramanathpur *India* 22°41N 88°14E **124** A1
Ramanujganj *India* 23°48N 83°42E **243** H10
Ramas C. *India* 15°5N 73°55E **245** G1
Ramat Allon *West Bank* 31°49N 35°12E **123** B2
Ramat Eshkol *West Bank* 31°48N 35°13E **123** B2
Ramat Gan *Israel* 32°4N 34°48E **251** F5
Ramat Razi'el *Israel* 31°46N 35°4E **123** B1
Ramat Shafet *West Bank* 31°48N 35°12E **123** B2
Ramatlhabama *S. Africa* 25°37S 25°33E **270** C4
Ramban *India* 33°14N 75°12E **243** C6
Rambervillers *France* 48°20N 6°38E **173** D13
Rambi = Rabi *Fiji* 16°30S 179°59W **287** A3
Rambipuji *Indonesia* 8°12S 113°37E **235** D4
Rambler Channel *Hong Kong, China* 22°21N 114°6E **122** A2
Rambouillet *France* 48°39N 1°50E **173** D8
Rambrai *India* 25°40N 91°19E **241** C3
Rambutyo I. *Papua N. G.* 2°18S 147°49E **286** B4
Ramdurg *India* 15°58N 75°22E **245** G2
Rame Hd. *Australia* 37°47S 149°30E **283** D8
Ramechhap *Nepal* 27°25N 86°10E **243** F12
Ramelton *Ireland* 55°2N 7°39W **166** A4
Ramenki *Russia* 55°41N 37°28E **129** B1
Ramenskoye *Russia* 55°32N 38°15E **188** E10
Ramer *U.S.A.* 32°3N 86°13W **316** C3
Ramersdorf *Germany* 48°6N 11°35E **131** B2
Rameses Station *Egypt* 30°3N 31°15E **117** A2
Rameswaram *India* 9°17N 79°18E **245** K4
Ramganga → *India* 27°5N 79°58E **243** F8
Ramgarh *Bangla.* 22°59N 91°44E **241** D3
Ramgarh *Jharkhand, India* 23°40N 85°35E **243** H11
Ramgarh *Raj., India* 27°16N 75°14E **242** F6
Ramgarh *Raj., India* 27°30N 70°36E **242** F4
Rāmhormoz *Iran* 31°15N 49°35E **247** D6
Ramīān *Iran* 37°3N 55°16E **247** B7
Ramiers *Haiti* 19°34N 72°14W **321** C5
Ramingining *Australia* 12°19S 135°3E **280** A2
Ramla *Israel* 31°55N 34°52E **251** G5
Ramlat Zaltan *Libya* 28°30N 19°30E **258** C3
Ramlu *Eritrea* 13°32N 41°40E **257** E5
Ramm = Rum *Jordan* 29°39N 35°26E **251** J6
Râmna → *Romania* 45°36N 27°3E **183** E12
Ramnad = Ramanathapuram *India* 9°25N 78°55E **245** K4
Ramnagar *Jammu & Kashmir, India* 32°47N 75°18E **243** C6
Ramnagar *Uttarakhand, India* 29°24N 79°7E **243** E8
Ramnäs *Sweden* 59°46N 16°12E **162** E10
Râmnicu Sărat *Romania* 45°26N 27°3E **183** E12
Râmnicu Vâlcea *Romania* 45°9N 24°21E **183** E9
Ramnous *Greece* 38°12N 24°3E **204** C6
Ramon *Isabela, Phil.* 16°50N 121°31E **232** C3
Ramon *Russia* 51°55N 39°21E **189** G10
Ramona *U.S.A.* 33°2N 116°52W **307** M10
Ramonville-St-Agne *France* 43°33N 1°28E **174** E5
Ramore *Canada* 48°30N 80°25W **298** C3
Ramos *Brazil* 22°50S 43°14W **135** B1
Ramos → *Nigeria* 5°8N 5°22E **263** D6
Ramos I. *Phil.* 8°6N 117°1E **233** G1
Ramos Mejía *Argentina* 34°39S 58°33W **117** B1
Ramot *West Bank* 31°48N 35°13E **123** B2
Ramotswa *Botswana* 24°50S 25°52E **270** B4
Rampanalgas *Trin. & Tob.* 10°44N 60°59W **323** t
Rampart *U.S.A.* 65°30N 150°10W **303** D10
Rampur *H.P., India* 31°26N 77°43E **242** D7
Rampur *Mad. P., India* 23°25N 73°53E **242** H5
Rampur *Odisha, India* 21°48N 83°58E **244** D6
Rampur *Ut. P., India* 28°44N 77°18E **120** A2
Rampur *Ut. P., India* 28°50N 79°5E **243** E8
Rampur Hat *India* 24°10N 87°50E **243** G12
Rampura *India* 24°30N 75°27E **242** G6
Ramrama Tola *India* 21°52N 79°55E **243** J8
Ramree I. *Myanmar* 19°0N 93°40E **241** F5
Ramsagar △ *Bangla.* 25°33N 88°37E **241** C2
Rāmsar *Iran* 36°53N 50°41E **247** B6
Ramsey *I. of Man* 54°20N 4°22W **168** C3
Ramsey *Ill., U.S.A.* 39°8N 89°7W **310** E7
Ramsey *N.J., U.S.A.* 41°4N 74°9W **313** E10
Ramsey L. *Canada* 47°13N 82°15W **298** C3
Ramsgate *N.S.W., Australia* 33°58S 151°8E **139** B1
Ramsgate *Kent, U.K.* 51°20N 1°25E **169** F9
Ramshai *India* 26°44N 88°51E **241** B2
Ramsjö *Sweden* 62°11N 15°37E **162** B9
Ramstein *Germany* 49°27N 7°32E **179** F3
Ramtek *India* 21°20N 79°15E **244** D4
Ramu *Kenya* 3°55N 41°10E **268** B5
Ramu → *Papua N. G.* 4°0S 144°41E **286** C3
Ramvik *Sweden* 62°49N 17°51E **162** B11
Ramville, Î. = Chancel, Î. *Martinique* 14°41N 60°53W **322** j
Rana Pratap Sagar Dam *India* 24°58N 75°38E **242** G6
Ranaghat *India* 23°15N 88°35E **243** H13
Ranahu *Pakistan* 25°55N 69°45E **242** G3
Ranai *Indonesia* 3°55N 108°22E **235** B3
Ranau *Malaysia* 6°2N 116°40E **235** A5
Ranau, Danau *Indonesia* 4°49S 103°55E **234** C2
Rancagua *Chile* 34°10S 70°50W **334** C1
Rance → *France* 48°34N 1°59W **172** D5
Rancharia *Brazil* 22°15S 50°55W **333** F1
Rancheria → *Canada* 60°13N 129°7W **296** A3
Ranchester *U.S.A.* 44°54N 107°10W **304** D10
Ranchi *India* 23°19N 85°27E **243** H11
Rancho Cordova *U.S.A.* 38°36N 121°18W **306** G5
Rancho Cucamonga *U.S.A.* 34°10N 117°30W **307** L9
Rancho Park *U.S.A.* 34°3N 118°26W **126** B2
Ranco, L. *Chile* 40°15S 72°25W **336** B2
Rand *Australia* 35°33S 146°32E **283** C7
Rand ✕ **(QRA)** *S. Africa* 26°14S 28°8E **123** B2
Randaberg *Norway* 59°1N 5°36E **164** E2
Randabygda *Norway* 61°51N 6°20E **164** C3
Randalls I. *U.S.A.* 40°47N 73°55W **132** B2
Randalstown *U.K.* 54°45N 6°19W **166** B5
Randan *France* 46°2N 3°21E **173** F10
Randazzo *Italy* 37°53N 14°57E **201** E7
Randburg *S. Africa* 26°5S 27°57E **123** A1
Rander *India* 21°14N 72°47E **244** D1
Randers *Denmark* 56°29N 10°1E **163** H4
Randers Fjord *Denmark* 56°37N 10°20E **163** H4
Randfontein *S. Africa* 26°8S 27°45E **271** C4
Randhart *S. Africa* 26°16S 28°7E **123** B2
Randle *U.S.A.* 46°32N 121°57W **306** D5
Randolph *Mass., U.S.A.* 42°10N 71°2W **313** D13
Randolph *N.Y., U.S.A.* 42°10N 78°59W **312** D6
Randolph *Utah, U.S.A.* 41°40N 111°11W **304** F8
Randolph *Vt., U.S.A.* 43°55N 72°40W **313** C12
Randpark Ridge *S. Africa* 26°6S 27°58E **123** A1
Randsburg *U.S.A.* 35°22N 117°39W **307** K9
Randsfjorden *Norway* 60°25N 10°24E **164** D7
Randsverk *Norway* 61°44N 9°3E **164** C6
Randwick *Australia* 33°54S 151°14E **139** B2
Råneälven → *Sweden* 65°50N 22°20E **160** D20
Ranenburg = Chaplygin *Russia* 53°15N 40°0E **188** F11
Ranfurly *N.Z.* 45°7S 170°6E **285** F5
Rangae *Thailand* 6°19N 101°44E **237** J3
Rangamati *Bangla.* 22°38N 92°12E **241** D4
Rangapara *India* 26°49N 92°39E **241** B4
Rangárvallasýsla *Iceland* 63°55N 20°0W **155** D7
Rangataua *N.Z.* 39°26S 175°28E **284** F4
Rangaunu B. *N.Z.* 34°51S 173°15E **284** A2
Range, The *Zimbabwe* 19°2S 31°2E **269** F3
Rangeley *U.S.A.* 44°58N 70°39W **313** B14
Rangeley L. *U.S.A.* 44°55N 70°43W **313** B14
Rangely *U.S.A.* 40°5N 108°48W **304** F9
Ranger *U.S.A.* 32°28N 98°41W **314** E5
Rangia *India* 26°28N 91°38E **241** B3
Rangiora *N.Z.* 43°19S 172°36E **285** D7
Rangiroa *French Polynesia* 15°10S 147°35W **289** f
Rangitaiki *N.Z.* 38°52S 176°24E **284** E5
Rangitaiki → *N.Z.* 37°54S 176°49E **284** D5
Rangitata → *N.Z.* 43°45S 171°15E **285** D6
Rangitikei → *N.Z.* 40°17S 175°15E **284** G4
Rangitoto ke te tonga = D'Urville I. *N.Z.* 40°50S 173°55E **285** A8
Rangitoto Ra. *N.Z.* 38°25S 175°35E **284** E4
Rangkasbitung *Indonesia* 6°21S 106°15E **234** D3
Rangoon = Yangôn *Myanmar* 16°45N 96°20E **241** G6
Rangoon → *Myanmar* 16°28N 96°40E **241** G6
Rangpur *Bangla.* 25°42N 89°22E **241** C2
Rangpur ☐ *Bangla.* 26°0N 89°0E **241** C2
Rangpuri *India* 28°32N 77°8E **120** B1
Rangsang *Indonesia* 1°20N 103°5E **237** M4
Rangwe *Kenya* 0°36S 34°35E **266** E3
Rani-ki-Vav *India* 23°51N 72°6E **242** H4
Ranibennur *India* 14°35N 75°30E **245** G2
Raniganj *India* 23°40N 87°5E **243** H12
Ranikhet *India* 29°39N 79°25E **243** E8
Ranippettai *India* 12°56N 79°23E **245** H4
Raniwara *India* 24°50N 72°10E **242** G5
Rāniyah *Iraq* 36°15N 44°53E **213** D11
Ranka *India* 23°59N 83°47E **243** H10
Ranken → *Australia* 20°31S 137°36E **280** C2
Rankin *Ill., U.S.A.* 40°28N 87°54W **311** D9
Rankin *Tex., U.S.A.* 31°13N 101°56W **314** F4
Rankin Inlet *Canada* 62°30N 93°0W **294** E13
Rankins Springs *Australia* 33°49S 146°14E **283** B7
Rankovicevo = Kraljevo *Serbia* 43°44N 20°41E **202** C4
Rankweil *Austria* 47°17N 9°39E **180** D2
Rannersdorf *Austria* 48°7N 16°27E **142** B2
Rannoch, L. *U.K.* 56°41N 4°20W **167** E4
Rannoch Moor *U.K.* 56°38N 4°48W **167** E4
Rano Kau *Chile* 27°11S 109°26W **330** b
Rano Raraku, Volcán *Chile* 27°7S 109°17W **330** b
Ranobe → *Madag.* 17°10S 44°8E **272** B1
Ranobe, Helodranon' i *Madag.* 23°3S 43°33E **272** C1
Ranohira *Madag.* 22°29S 45°24E **272** C2
Ranomafana *Anosy, Madag.* 24°34S 47°0E **272** C2
Ranomafana *Atsinanana, Madag.* 18°57S 48°50E **272** B2
Ranomafana △ *Madag.* 21°16S 47°25E **272** C2
Ranomena *Madag.* 23°25S 47°17E **272** C2
Ranon *Vanuatu* 16°9S 168°7E **287** F6
Ranong *Thailand* 9°56N 98°40E **237** H2
Ranongga *Solomon Is.* 8°5S 156°35E **287** M9
Ranotsara Nord *Madag.* 22°48S 46°36E **272** C2
Ranpur *India* 20°5N 85°20E **244** D7
Rānsa *Iran* 33°39N 48°18E **247** C6
Ransbèche *Belgium* 50°56N 4°27E **116** B2
Ransdorp *Neths.* 52°24N 5°0E **112** A2
Ransiki *Indonesia* 1°30S 134°10E **231** E8
Ransom *U.S.A.* 41°9N 88°39W **311** C8
Rantabe *Madag.* 15°42S 49°39E **272** B2
Rantau *Indonesia* 2°56S 115°9E **235** C5
Rantau Abang *Malaysia* 4°52N 103°24E **237** K4
Rantauapanjang *Kalimantan Tengah, Indonesia* 1°22S 112°4E **235** C4
Rantauapanjang *Kalimantan Timur, Indonesia* 2°9N 117°25E **235** B5
Rantauprapat *Indonesia* 2°15N 99°50E **234** B1
Rantaupulut *Indonesia* 1°55S 112°12E **235** C4
Rantemario *Indonesia* 3°15S 119°57E **231** E5
Ranthambore △ *India* 26°10N 76°30E **242** F7
Rantoul *U.S.A.* 40°19N 88°9W **311** D8
Ranum *Denmark* 56°54N 9°14E **163** H3
Ranvad *India* 18°53N 72°55E **130** B2
Ranyah, W. → *Si. Arabia* 21°18N 43°20E **248** B3
Raohe *China* 46°47N 134°0E **220** A7
Raon l'Étape *France* 48°24N 6°50E **173** D13
Raoping *China* 23°42N 117°1E **229** F11
Raoui, Erg er *Algeria* 29°0N 2°0W **261** C4
Raoul I. *Pac. Oc.* 29°16S 177°54W **277** F15
Raoyang *China* 38°15N 115°45E **226** E8
Rap, Ko *Thailand* 9°19N 99°58E **237** b
Rapa *French Polynesia* 27°35S 144°20W **289** f
Rapa Nui = Pascua, I. de *Chile* 27°7S 109°23W **330** b
Rapallo *Italy* 44°21N 9°14E **198** D6
Rapar *India* 23°34N 70°38E **242** H4
Rāpch *Iran* 25°40N 59°15E **247** E8
Rapel, Lago *Chile* 34°20S 71°14W **334** C1
Raper, C. *Canada* 69°44N 67°6W **295** D18
Rapid City *U.S.A.* 44°5N 103°14W **308** C2
Rapid River *U.S.A.* 45°55N 86°58W **308** C10
Rapla *Estonia* 59°1N 24°52E **188** C3
Raposo *Portugal* 38°40N 9°11W **126** A1
Rapti → *India* 26°18N 83°41E **243** F10
Rapu Rapu I. *Phil.* 13°12N 124°9E **232** E5
Raqaba ez Zarqa → *South Sudan* 9°14N 29°44E **257** F2
Rāqūbah *Libya* 28°58N 19°2E **258** C3
Raquette → *U.S.A.* 45°0N 74°42W **313** B10
Raquette Lake *U.S.A.* 43°49N 74°40W **313** C10
Rara △ *Nepal* 29°30N 82°10E **243** E10
Raraka *French Polynesia* 16°10S 144°54W **289** f
Raroia *French Polynesia* 16°1S 142°27W **289** f
Rarotonga *Cook Is.* 21°30S 160°0W **289** h
Ra's al 'Ayn *Syria* 36°45N 40°12E **213** D9
Ras al Hadd *Oman* 22°30N 59°50E **249** B7
Ra's Al Khair *Si. Arabia* 27°27N 49°18E **247** E6
Ra's al Khaymah *U.A.E.* 25°50N 55°59E **247** E7
Ra's aṭ Tib *Tunisia* 37°1N 11°2E **258** A2
Râs el Ma *Algeria* 34°26N 0°50W **261** B4
Râs el Mâ *Mali* 16°35N 4°30W **262** B4
Râs el Oued *Algeria* 35°57N 5°2E **261** A6
Râs Ghârib *Egypt* 28°6N 33°18E **256** B3
Râs Kôh *Pakistan* 28°43N 64°55E **240** C2
Ra's Lānūf *Libya* 30°46N 18°11E **258** B3
Râs Muhammad △ *Egypt* 27°45N 34°16E **256** B3
Ra's Shamrah *Syria* 35°35N 35°45E **250** C6
Râs Sudr *Egypt* 29°40N 32°42E **256** B3
Rasa, Pta. *B. Aires, Argentina* 36°20S 56°41W **334** D4
Rasa, Pta. *Río Negro, Argentina* 40°50S 62°15W **336** B4
Rasa I. *Phil.* 9°13N 118°26E **233** G2
Rasca, Pta. de la *Canary Is.* 27°59N 16°41W **153** e1
Rășcani *Moldova* 47°58N 27°33E **183** C12
Rasdhoo *Maldives* 4°17N 72°58E **272** d
Rasdu Atoll *Maldives* 4°18N 72°58E **272** d
Raseiniai *Lithuania* 55°25N 23°5E **184** C10
Rashad *Sudan* 11°55N 31°0E **257** E3
Rashîd *Egypt* 31°21N 30°22E **256** H7
Rashîd, Masabb *Egypt* 31°22N 30°17E **256** H7
Rashin = Najin *N. Korea* 42°12N 130°15E **224** A5
Rashmi *India* 25°4N 74°22E **242** G6
Rasht *Iran* 37°20N 49°40E **213** D13
Rashtrapati Bhawan *Delhi, India* **120** c1
Rasi Salai *Thailand* 15°20N 104°9E **236** E5
Rasipuram *India* 11°30N 78°15E **245** J4
Raška *Serbia* 43°19N 20°39E **202** C4
Raskot *Nepal* 29°14N 81°39E **243** E9
Râșnov *Romania* 45°35N 25°27E **183** E10
Rasŏn ☐ *N. Korea* 42°21N 130°23E **224** A5
Rason L. *Australia* 28°45S 124°25E **279** E3
Rașova *Romania* 44°15N 27°55E **183** F12
Rasovo *Bulgaria* 43°42N 23°17E **202** C7
Rasra *India* 25°50N 83°50E **243** G10
Rasskazovo *Russia* 52°35N 41°50E **190** D5
Rast *Romania* 43°53N 23°16E **183** G8
Rastaala *Finland* 60°15N 24°47E **121** B1
Rastatt *Germany* 48°50N 8°11E **179** G4
Rastede *Germany* 53°15N 8°12E **178** B4
Rastenburg = Kętrzyn *Poland* 54°7N 21°22E **184** D8
Rastila *Finland* 60°12N 25°7E **121** B3
Răstolița *Romania* 46°59N 24°58E **183** D9
Rastyapino = Dzerzhinsk *Russia* 56°14N 43°30E **190** B6
Rasua Garhi *Nepal* 28°17N 85°23E **243** E11
Rasul *Pakistan* 32°42N 73°34E **242** C5
Raszków *Poland* 51°43N 17°40E **185** G4
Raszyn *Poland* 52°9N 20°54E **143** C1
Rat → *Canada* 49°35N 97°10W **297** D9
Rat Buri = Ratchaburi *Thailand* 13°30N 99°54E **236** F2
Rat I. = Hawadax *U.S.A.* 51°48N 178°15E **303** L2
Rat I. *St. Lucia* 14°2N 60°58W **323** m
Rat Islands *U.S.A.* 52°0N 178°0E **303** L2
Rat L. *Canada* 56°10N 99°40W **297** B9
Ratak Chain *Pac. Oc.* 10°0N 170°0E **288** G8
Rätan *Sweden* 62°29N 14°33E **162** B8
Ratangarh *India* 28°5N 74°35E **242** E6
Raṭāwī *Iraq* 30°38N 47°13E **246** D5
Ratcatchers L. *Australia* 32°30S 143°12E **282** B5
Ratchaburi *Thailand* 13°30N 99°54E **236** F2
Rath *India* 25°36N 79°37E **243** G8
Rath Luirc = Charleville *Ireland* 52°21N 8°40W **166** D3
Rathangan *Ireland* 53°14N 7°0W **166** C4
Rathbun L. *U.S.A.* 40°54N 93°5W **310** D4
Rathdrum *Ireland* 52°56N 6°14W **166** D5
Rathedaung *Myanmar* 20°29N 92°45E **241** E4
Rathenow *Germany* 52°37N 12°19E **178** C8
Rathkeale *Ireland* 52°32N 8°56W **166** D3
Rathlin I. *U.K.* 55°18N 6°14W **166** A5
Ratho *U.K.* 55°55N 3°23W **121** B1
Ratho Station *U.K.* 55°56N 3°23W **121** B1
Ratibor = Racibórz *Poland* 50°7N 18°18E **185** H5
Rätikon *Austria* 47°0N 9°55E **180** D2
Ratingen *Germany* 51°18N 6°52E **178** D2
Ratlam *India* 23°20N 75°0E **242** H6
Ratmanova, Ostrov *Russia* 65°46N 169°6W **300** B6
Ratnagiri *India* 16°57N 73°18E **244** F1
Ratnapura *Sri Lanka* 6°40N 80°20E **245** L5
Rato *Portugal* 38°43N 9°8W **126** A2
Ratodero *Pakistan* 27°48N 68°18E **242** F3
Raton *U.S.A.* 36°54N 104°24W **305** H11
Ratschach = Radeče *Slovenia* 46°5N 15°14E **199** B12
Rattaphum *Thailand* 7°8N 100°16E **237** J3
Ratten *Austria* 47°28N 15°44E **180** D8
Rattray Hd. *U.K.* 57°38N 1°50W **167** D7
Rättvik *Sweden* 60°52N 15°7E **162** D9
Ratz, Mt. *Canada* 57°23N 132°12W **296** B2
Ratzebuhr = Okonek *Poland* 53°32N 16°51E **184** E3
Ratzeburg *Germany* 53°40N 10°46E **178** B6
Rau *Indonesia* 0°34N 100°1E **234** B2
Raub *Malaysia* 3°47N 101°52E **237** L3
Rauch *Argentina* 36°45S 59°5W **334** D4
Raudales *Mexico* 17°27N 93°39W **319** D6
Raudeberg *Norway* 61°59N 5°7E **164** C2
Raufarhöfn *Iceland* 66°27N 15°57W **155** A11
Raufoss *Norway* 60°44N 10°37E **164** D7
Raukumara *N.Z.* 38°5S 177°55E **284** E6
Raukumara Ra. *N.Z.* 38°5S 177°55E **284** E6
Raul Soares *Brazil* 20°5S 42°22W **333** F3
Rauma *Finland* 61°10N 21°30E **188** B1
Rauma → *Norway* 62°34N 7°43E **164** B4
Raumo = Rauma *Finland* 61°10N 21°30E **188** B1
Raung, Gunung *Indonesia* 8°8S 114°3E **231** J17
Raurkela *India* 22°14N 84°50E **243** H11
Rausu-Dake *Japan* 44°4N 145°7E **220** B12
Răut → *Moldova* 47°15N 29°9E **183** C14
Rava-Ruska *Ukraine* 50°15N 23°42E **185** H10
Rava Russkaya = Rava-Ruska *Ukraine* 50°15N 23°42E **185** H10
Ravahere *French Polynesia* 18°14S 142°9W **289** f
Ravalli *U.S.A.* 47°17N 114°11W **304** C6
Ravānsar *Iran* 34°43N 46°40E **213** E12
Ravanusa *Italy* 37°16N 13°58E **200** E6
Rāvar *Iran* 31°20N 56°51E **247** D8
Ravelston *U.K.* 55°57N 3°14W **121** B2
Ravena *U.S.A.* 42°28N 73°49W **313** D11
Ravenel *U.S.A.* 32°46N 80°15W **316** C9
Ravenna *Italy* 44°25N 12°12E **199** D9
Ravenna *Ky., U.S.A.* 37°41N 83°57W **311** G13
Ravenna *Nebr., U.S.A.* 41°1N 98°55W **308** E4
Ravenna *Ohio, U.S.A.* 41°9N 81°15W **312** E3
Ravensburg *Germany* 47°46N 9°36E **179** H5
Ravenshoe *Australia* 17°37S 145°29E **280** B4
Ravensthorpe *Australia* 33°35S 120°2E **279** F3
Ravenswood *Queens., Australia* 20°6S 146°54E **280** C4
Ravenswood *W. Va., U.S.A.* 38°57N 81°46W **309** F13
Ravensworth *Australia* 32°26S 151°4E **283** B9
Ravenwood *U.S.A.* 40°22N 94°41W **310** D2
Raver *India* 21°15N 76°2E **244** D3
Ravi → *Pakistan* 30°35N 71°49E **242** D4
Ravine Chaude *Guadeloupe* 16°14N 61°40W **322** e
Ravna Gora *Croatia* 45°24N 14°50E **199** C11
Ravna Reka *Serbia* 44°1N 21°35E **202** B5
Ravne na Koroškem *Slovenia* 46°36N 14°59E **199** B11
Rawa Mazowiecka *Poland* 51°46N 20°12E **185** G7
Rawaki *Kiribati* 3°43S 170°43W **277** A16
Rawalpindi *Pakistan* 33°38N 73°8E **242** C5
Rawamangun *Indonesia* 6°11S 106°52E **122** B2
Rawang *Malaysia* 3°20N 101°35E **237** L3
Rawene *N.Z.* 35°25S 173°32E **284** B2
Rawi, Ko *Thailand* 6°33N 99°14E **237** J2
Rawicz *Poland* 51°36N 16°52E **185** G3
Rawitsch = Rawicz *Poland* 51°36N 16°52E **185** G3
Rawka → *Poland* 52°9N 20°8E **185** F7
Rawlinna *Australia* 30°58S 125°28E **279** F4
Rawlins *U.S.A.* 41°47N 107°14W **304** F10
Rawlinson Ra. *Australia* 24°40S 128°30E **279** D4
Rawson *Argentina* 43°15S 65°5W **336** B3
Raxaul *India* 26°59N 84°51E **243** F11
Ray *U.S.A.* 48°21N 103°10W **308** A2
Ray, C. *Canada* 47°33N 59°15W **299** C8
Ray City *U.S.A.* 31°5N 83°11W **316** D6
Ray Mts. *U.S.A.* 66°0N 152°0W **303** D10
Raya Ring, Ko *Thailand* 8°18N 98°29E **237** a
Rayachoti *India* 14°4N 78°50E **245** G4
Rayadurg *India* 14°40N 76°50E **245** G3
Rayagada *India* 19°15N 83°20E **244** E6
Raychikhinsk *Russia* 49°46N 129°25E **215** E13
Rāyen *Iran* 29°34N 57°26E **247** D8
Rayle *U.S.A.* 33°48N 82°54W **316** B7
Rayleigh *U.K.* 51°36N 0°37E **169** F8
Raymond *Alta., Canada* 49°30N 112°35W **296** D6
Raymond *Calif., U.S.A.* 37°13N 119°54W **306** H7
Raymond *Ill., U.S.A.* 39°19N 89°34W **310** E7
Raymond *N.H., U.S.A.* 43°2N 71°11W **313** C13
Raymond *Wash., U.S.A.* 46°41N 123°44W **306** D3
Raymond Terrace *Australia* 32°45S 151°44E **283** B9
Raymondville *U.S.A.* 26°29N 97°47W **314** H6
Raymore *Canada* 51°25N 104°31W **297** C8
Rayners Lane *U.K.* 51°34N 0°23W **125** A1
Raynes Park *U.K.* 51°24N 0°12W **125** B2
Rayón *Mexico* 29°43N 110°35W **318** B2
Rayong *Thailand* 12°40N 101°20E **236** F3
Raypur *India* 22°28N 88°22E **124** C2
Raystown L. *U.S.A.* 40°25N 78°5W **312** F6
Raysūt *Oman* 16°56N 53°59E **249** C6
Raytown *U.S.A.* 39°1N 94°28W **310** E2
Rayville *U.S.A.* 32°29N 91°46W **314** E9
Raz, Pte. du *France* 48°2N 4°47W **172** D2
Razan *Iran* 35°23N 49°2E **213** E13
Ražana *Serbia* 44°6N 19°55E **202** B3
Ražanj *Serbia* 43°40N 21°31E **202** C5
Razāzah, Buḩayrat ar *Iraq* 32°40N 43°35E **213** F10
Razdelna *Bulgaria* 43°13N 27°41E **203** C11
Razdel'naya = Rozdilna *Ukraine* 46°50N 30°2E **183** D15
Razdolnoye *Russia* 43°30N 131°52E **220** C5
Razdolnoye *Ukraine* 45°46N 33°29E **189** K7
Razeh *Iran* 32°47N 48°9E **247** C6
Razgrad *Bulgaria* 43°33N 26°34E **203** C10
Razgrad ☐ *Bulgaria* 43°33N 26°30E **203** C10
Razhevo Konare *Bulgaria* 42°23N 24°46E **203** D8
Razim, Lacul *Romania* 44°50N 29°0E **183** F14
Razlog *Bulgaria* 41°53N 23°28E **202** E7
Razmak *Pakistan* 32°45N 69°50E **242** C3
Răznas Ezers △ *Latvia* 56°30N 27°30E **188** D4
Razzaza, L. = Razāzah, Buḩayrat ar *Iraq* 32°40N 43°35E **213** F10
Re, Cu Lao *Vietnam* 15°22N 109°8E **236** E7
Ré, Î. de *France* 46°12N 1°30W **174** B2
Reach Falls *Jamaica* 18°2N 76°18W **320** a
Reading *Reading, U.K.* 51°27N 0°58W **169** F7
Reading *Mich., U.S.A.* 41°50N 84°45W **311** C12
Reading *Ohio, U.S.A.* 39°13N 84°26W **311** E12
Reading *Pa., U.S.A.* 40°20N 75°56W **313** F9
Reading ☐ *U.K.* 51°27N 0°58W **169** F7
Real, Cordillera *Bolivia* 17°0S 67°10W **330** D4
Real Felipe, Fuerte *Peru* 12°4S 77°9W **124** B2
Realejo Alto *Canary Is.* 28°22N 16°34W **153** e1
Realicó *Argentina* 35°0S 64°15W **334** D3
Réalmont *France* 43°48N 2°10E **174** E6
Ream *Cambodia* 10°34N 103°39E **237** G4
Ream △ *Cambodia* 10°30N 103°45E **237** G4
Reams, L. *U.S.A.* 28°26N 81°34W **133** B1
Réao *French Polynesia* 18°31S 136°23W **289** f
Reay Forest *U.K.* 58°22N 4°55W **167** C4
Rebais *France* 48°50N 3°10E **173** D10
Rebecca, L. *Australia* 30°0S 122°15E **279** F3
Rebi *Indonesia* 6°23S 134°7E **231** F8
Rebiana *Libya* 24°12N 22°10E **258** D4
Rebiana, Sahrâ' *Libya* 24°30N 21°0E **258** D3
Reboly *Russia* 63°49N 30°47E **160** E24
Rebun-Tō *Japan* 45°23N 141°2E **220** B10
Recanati *Italy* 43°24N 13°32E **199** E10
Recaş *Romania* 45°46N 21°30E **182** E6
Recco *Italy* 44°22N 9°9E **198** D6
Recherche, Arch. of the *Australia* 34°15S 122°50E **279** F3
Rechna Doab *Pakistan* 31°35N 73°30E **242** D5
Rechytsa *Belarus* 52°21N 30°24E **177** B16
Recife *Brazil* 8°0S 35°0W **332** C5
Recife *Seychelles* 4°36S 55°42E **272** c
Recklinghausen *Germany* 51°37N 7°12E **178** D3
Reckong Peo *India* 31°32N 78°16E **242** D8
Reclining Buddha = Wat Pho *Bangkok, Thailand* **113** b1
Recoleta *B. Aires, Argentina* 34°36S 58°24W **117** B2
Recoleta *Santiago, Chile* 33°25S 70°40W **137** B2
Reconquista *Argentina* 29°10S 59°45W **334** B4
Recreio *Brazil* 8°0S 58°25W **331** B6
Recreo *Argentina* 29°25S 65°10W **334** B2
Recuay *Peru* 9°43S 77°28W **330** B2
Recz *Poland* 53°16N 15°31E **185** E2
Red = **Hong** → *Asia* 20°16N 106°34E **236** B5
Red → *U.S.A.* 31°1N 91°45W **314** F9
Red Bank *U.S.A.* 40°21N 74°5W **313** F10
Red Bay *Canada* 51°44N 56°25W **299** B8
Red Bluff *U.S.A.* 40°11N 122°15W **304** F2
Red Bluff Res. *U.S.A.* 31°54N 103°55W **305** L12
Red Bud *U.S.A.* 38°13N 89°59W **310** F7
Red Cliffs *Australia* 34°19S 142°11E **282** C5
Red Cloud *U.S.A.* 40°5N 98°32W **308** E4
Red Creek *U.S.A.* 43°14N 76°45W **313** C8
Red Deer *Canada* 52°20N 113°50W **296** C6
Red Deer → *Alta., Canada* 50°58N 110°0W **297** C7
Red Deer → *Man., Canada* 52°53N 101°1W **297** C8
Red Deer L. *Canada* 52°55N 101°20W **297** C8
Red Devil *U.S.A.* 61°46N 157°19W **303** F8
Red Fort = Lal Qila *Delhi, India* **120** a3
Red Hook *U.S.A.* 41°55N 73°53W **313** E11
Red Indian L. *Canada* 48°35N 57°0W **299** C8
Red L. *Canada* 51°3N 93°49W **297** C10
Red Lake *Canada* 51°3N 93°49W **297** C10
Red Lake Falls *U.S.A.* 47°53N 96°16W **308** B5
Red Lake Road *Canada* 49°59N 93°25W **297** C10
Red Lodge *U.S.A.* 45°11N 109°15W **304** D9
Red Mountain *U.S.A.* 35°37N 117°38W **307** K9
Red Oak *U.S.A.* 41°1N 95°14W **308** E6
Red River of the North → *N. Amer.* 49°0N 97°15W **308** A5
Red Rock *Canada* 48°55N 88°15W **298** C2
Red Rock, L. *U.S.A.* 41°22N 92°59W **310** C3
Red Rocks Pt. *Australia* 32°13S 127°32E **279** F4
Red Sea *Asia* 25°0N 36°0E **238** E3
Red Slate Mt. *U.S.A.* 37°31N 118°52W **306** H8
Red Square *Moscow, Russia* **129** b2
Red Sucker L. *Canada* 54°9N 93°40W **298** B1
Red Tower Pass = Turnu Roşu, P. *Romania* 45°33N 24°17E **183** E9
Red Volta → *Africa* 10°34N 0°30W **263** C4
Red Wing *U.S.A.* 44°34N 92°31W **308** C7
Reda *Poland* 54°40N 18°19E **184** D5
Redang, Pulau *Malaysia* 5°49N 103°2E **237** K4
Redange *Lux.* 49°46N 5°52E **170** E5
Redbridge ☐ *U.K.* 51°35N 0°7E **125** A4
Redcar *U.K.* 54°37N 1°4W **168** C6
Redcar & Cleveland ☐ *U.K.* 54°29N 1°0W **168** C7
Redcliff *Canada* 50°10N 110°50W **304** A8
Redcliffe *Australia* 27°12S 153°6E **281** D5
Redcliffe, Mt. *Australia* 28°30S 121°30E **279** E3
Reddersburg *S. Africa* 29°41S 26°10E **270** C4
Reddick *Fla., U.S.A.* 29°22N 82°12W **317** F7
Reddick *Ill., U.S.A.* 41°6N 88°15W **311** C8
Redding *Calif., U.S.A.* 40°35N 122°24W **304** F2
Redding *Iowa, U.S.A.* 40°36N 94°23W **310** D2
Redditch *U.K.* 52°18N 1°55W **169** E6
Redenção *Brazil* 4°13S 38°43W **332** B4
Redentore, Chiesa del *Venice, Italy* **142** c2
Redfern *Australia* 33°54S 151°12E **139** B2
Redfield *U.S.A.* 44°53N 98°31W **308** C4
Redford *U.S.A.* 44°38N 73°48W **313** B11
Redhead *Trin. & Tob.* 10°44N 60°58W **323** t
Redkey *U.S.A.* 40°21N 85°9W **311** D11
Redkino *Russia* 56°39N 36°16E **188** D9
Redlands *U.S.A.* 34°4N 117°11W **307** M9
Redmond *Oreg., U.S.A.* 44°17N 121°11W **304** D3
Redmond *Wash., U.S.A.* 47°40N 122°7W **306** C4
Redon *France* 47°40N 2°6W **172** E4
Redonda *Antigua & B.* 16°58N 62°19W **321** C7
Redonda, Pta. *Chile* 27°10S 109°22W **330** b
Redondela *Spain* 42°15N 8°38W **194** C2
Redondo *Portugal* 38°39N 7°37W **195** G3
Redondo Beach *U.S.A.* 33°50N 118°23W **307** M8
Redoubt Volcano *U.S.A.* 60°29N 152°45W **303** F9
Redpath Sugar Museum *Toronto, Canada* **141** c3
Redruth *U.K.* 50°14N 5°14W **169** G2
Redvers *Canada* 49°35N 101°40W **297** D8
Redwater *Canada* 53°55N 113°6W **296** C6
Redwood *U.S.A.* 44°18N 75°48W **313** B9
Redwood △ *U.S.A.* 41°40N 124°5W **304** F1
Redwood City *U.S.A.* 37°30N 122°15W **306** H4
Redwood Falls *U.S.A.* 44°32N 95°7W **308** C6
Ree, L. *Ireland* 53°35N 8°0W **166** C3
Reed City *U.S.A.* 43°53N 85°31W **309** D11
Reed L. *Canada* 54°38N 100°30W **297** C8
Reedley *U.S.A.* 36°36N 119°27W **306** J7
Reedsburg *U.S.A.* 43°32N 90°0W **308** D8
Reedsport *U.S.A.* 43°42N 124°6W **304** E1
Reedsville *U.S.A.* 40°39N 77°35W **312** F7
Reedy Creek *Australia* 36°58S 140°2E **282** D4
Reef Is. *Pac. Oc.* 10°15S 166°10E **277** C12
Reefton *N.Z.* 42°6S 171°51E **285** C6
Rees *Germany* 51°46N 6°24E **178** D2
Reese → *U.S.A.* 40°48N 117°4W **304** F5
Reetz = Recz *Poland* 53°16N 15°31E **185** E2
Refahiye *Turkey* 39°54N 38°47E **213** C8
Reflecting Pool *Washington, D.C., U.S.A.* **143** b1
Refsfhaleøen *Denmark* 55°41N 12°36E **118** A3
Reftele *Sweden* 57°11N 13°35E **163** G7
Refugio *U.S.A.* 28°18N 97°17W **314** G6
Rega → *Poland* 54°10N 15°18E **184** D2
Regalbuto *Italy* 37°39N 14°38E **201** E7
Regana, C. de *Spain* 39°25N 2°43E **206** B3
Regar = Tursunzoda *Tajikistan* 38°30N 68°14E **217** E7
Regen *Germany* 48°58N 13°8E **179** G9
Regen → *Germany* 49°1N 12°6E **179** F8
Regeneração *Brazil* 6°15S 42°41W **332** C3
Regensburg *Germany* 49°1N 12°6E **179** F8
Regenstauf *Germany* 49°7N 12°8E **179** F8
Regents Park *Gauteng, S. Africa* 26°14S 28°3E **123** B2
Regent's Park *London, U.K.* **125** a2
Regenwalde = Resko *Poland* 53°47N 15°25E **184** E2
Reggâne = Zaouiet Reggâne *Algeria* 26°32N 0°3E **261** C5
Reggello *Italy* 43°41N 11°32E **199** E8
Réggio di Calàbria *Italy* 38°6N 15°39E **201** D8
Réggio nell'Emília *Italy* 44°43N 10°36E **198** D7
Reghin *Romania* 46°46N 24°42E **183** D9
Regina *Sask., Canada* 50°27N 104°35W **297** C8
Régina *Fr. Guiana* 4°19N 52°8W **329** C7
Regina Beach *Canada* 50°47N 105°0W **297** C8
Registro *U.S.A.* 32°22N 81°53W **316** C8
Registro *Brazil* 24°29S 47°49W **335** A6
Rego Park *U.S.A.* 40°43N 73°51W **132** B3
Reguengos de Monsaraz *Portugal* 38°25N 7°32W **195** G3
Rehar → *India* 23°55N 82°40E **243** H10
Rehli *India* 23°38N 79°5E **243** H8
Rehoboth *Namibia* 23°15S 17°4E **270** B2
Rehovot *Israel* 31°54N 34°48E **251** G5
Rei, Costa *Italy* 39°15N 9°40E **200** C2
Reibell = Ksar Chellala *Algeria* 35°13N 2°19E **261** A5
Reichenau = Rychnov nad Kněžnou *Czechia* 50°10N 16°17E **181** A9
Reichenbach = Dzierżoniów *Poland* 50°45N 16°39E **185** H3
Reichenbach *Germany* 50°37N 12°17E **178** E8
Reichenberg = Liberec *Czechia* 50°47N 15°7E **180** A8
Reichshof = Rzeszów *Poland* 50°5N 21°58E **185** H8
Reichstag *Berlin, Germany* **115** a3
Reid *Australia* 30°49S 128°26E **279** F4
Reidsville *Ga., U.S.A.* 32°6N 82°7W **316** C7
Reidsville *N.C., U.S.A.* 36°21N 79°40W **315** C15
Reifnig = Ribnica *Slovenia* 45°45N 14°45E **199** C11
Reigate *U.K.* 51°14N 0°12W **169** F7
Reillo *Spain* 39°54N 1°53W **196** F3
Reims *France* 49°15N 4°1E **173** C11
Reina Adelaida, Arch. *Chile* 52°20S 74°0W **336** D2
Reina Beatrix Int. ✕ **(AUA)** *Aruba* 12°30N 70°1W **322** f
Reina Sofía, Centro de Arte *Madrid, Spain* **127** c3
Reina Sofía, Tenerife ✕ **(TFS)** *Canary Is.* 28°3N 16°33W **153** e1
Reinbeck *U.S.A.* 42°19N 92°36W **310** B4
Reinbek *Germany* 53°30N 10°16E **178** B6
Reindeer → *Canada* 55°36N 103°11W **297** B8
Reindeer I. *Canada* 52°30N 98°0W **297** C9
Reindeer L. *Canada* 57°15N 102°15W **297** B8
Reinga, C. *N.Z.* 34°25S 172°43E **284** A1
Reinheimen △ *Norway* 62°10N 7°45E **164** B4
Reinickendorf *Germany* 52°34N 13°22E **115** A3
Reinosa *Spain* 43°2N 4°15W **194** B6
Reinsvoll *Norway* 60°40N 10°38E **164** D7
Reitan *Norway* 62°49N 11°22E **164** B8
Reitz *S. Africa* 27°48S 28°29E **271** C4
Reivilo *S. Africa* 27°36S 24°8E **270** C3
Rejaf *South Sudan* 4°45N 31°35E **257** G3
Rejmyre *Sweden* 58°50N 15°55E **163** F9
Rejowiec Fabryczny *Poland* 51°5N 23°17E **185** G10
Reka → *Slovenia* 45°40N 14°0E **199** C11
Rekohu = Chatham I. *N.Z.* 43°50S 176°20W **285** a
Rekola *Finland* 60°19N 25°4E **121** B3
Rekovac *Serbia* 43°51N 21°3E **202** C5
Relámpago, Pta. *Venezuela* 11°3N 64°23W **329** a
Reliance *Canada* 63°0N 109°20W **297** A7
Relizane *Algeria* 35°44N 0°31E **261** A5
Relizane ☐ *Algeria* 35°45N 0°55E **261** A5
Remad, Oued → *Algeria* 33°28N 1°20W **261** B4
Rémalard *France* 48°26N 0°47E **172** D7
Remanso *Brazil* 9°41S 42°4W **332** C3
Remarkable, Mt. *Australia* 32°48S 138°10E **282** B3
Remarkables, The *N.Z.* 45°10S 168°50E **285** F3
Rembang *Indonesia* 6°42S 111°21E **235** D4
Rembau *Malaysia* 2°35N 102°6E **237** L4
Rembert *U.S.A.* 34°6N 80°32W **316** A9
Rembertów *Poland* 52°15N 21°9E **143** B2
Rembrandthuis *Amsterdam, Neths.* **112** b3
Rembrandtpark *Neths.* 52°22N 4°51E **112** A2
Rembrandtplein *Amsterdam, Neths.* **112** b2
Remchi *Algeria* 35°2N 1°26W **261** A4
Remedios *Colombia* 7°2N 74°41W **328** B3
Remedios *Panama* 8°15N 81°50W **320** E3
Remedios de Escalada *Argentina* 34°43S 58°24W **117** C2
Remeshk *Iran* 26°55N 58°50E **247** E8
Remetea *Romania* 46°45N 25°29E **183** D10
Remich *Lux.* 49°32N 6°22E **170** E6
Remington *U.S.A.* 40°46N 87°9W **311** D9
Rémire *Fr. Guiana* 4°53N 52°17W **329** C7
Remiremont *France* 48°2N 6°36E **173** D13
Remo *Ethiopia* 6°48N 41°20E **257** F5
Rémola, Estany del *Spain* 41°16N 2°4E **114** B1
Remontnoye *Russia* 46°34N 43°37E **191** G6
Remoulins *France* 43°55N 4°35E **175** E8
Rempang *Indonesia* 0°51N 104°10E **234** B2
Rempart → *Mauritius* 20°19S 57°22E **272** e
Remparts → *Réunion* 21°22S 55°37E **272** f
Remscheid *Germany* 51°11N 7°12E **178** D3
Ren Xian *China* 37°8N 114°40E **226** F8
Rena *Norway* 61°8N 11°20E **164** C8
Rena → *Norway* 61°8N 11°23E **164** C8
Renascença *Brazil* 3°50S 66°21W **328** D4
Renca *Chile* 33°24S 70°42W **137** B1
Rend Lake *U.S.A.* 38°2N 88°58W **310** F8
Rendang *Indonesia* 8°26S 115°25E **231** J18
Rende *Italy* 39°20N 16°11E **201** C9
Rendezvous Barbados 13°4N 59°35W **323** r
Rendina *Greece* 39°4N 21°58E **204** B3
Rendova *Solomon Is.* 8°33S 157°17E **287** M9
Rendsburg *Germany* 54°17N 9°39E **178** A5
René-Levasseur, Î. *Canada* 51°20N 68°40W **299** B6
Renfrew *Canada* 45°30N 76°40W **313** A8
Renfrewshire ☐ *U.K.* 55°49N 4°38W **167** F4
Renfroe *U.S.A.* 32°14N 84°43W **316** C5
Rengat *Indonesia* 0°30S 102°45E **234** C2
Rengo *Chile* 34°24S 70°50W **334** C1
Renhua *China* 25°5N 113°40E **229** E9
Renhuai *China* 27°48N 106°24E **228** D6
Reni = Taranagar *India* 28°43N 74°50E **242** E6
Reni *Ukraine* 45°28N 28°15E **183** E13
Renigunta *India* 13°38N 79°30E **245** H4
Renk *South Sudan* 11°50N 32°50E **257** E3
Renland *Greenland* 71°10N 26°30W **154** C8
Renmark *Australia* 34°11S 140°43E **282** C4
Rennebu *Norway* 62°52N 9°49E **164** B6
Rennell *Solomon Is.* 11°40S 160°10E **287** N11
Rennell Sd. *Canada* 53°23N 132°35W **296** C2
Rennemoulin *France* 48°50N 2°2E **134** A1
Renner Springs *Australia* 18°20S 133°47E **280** B1
Rennes *France* 48°7N 1°41W **172** D5
Rennick Glacier *Antarctica* 70°30S 161°45E **151** D11
Rennie L. *Canada* 61°32N 105°35W **297** A7
Reno *U.S.A.* 39°31N 119°48W **306** F7
Reno → *Italy* 44°38N 12°16E **199** D9
Renovo *U.S.A.* 41°20N 77°45W **312** E7
Renqiu *China* 38°43N 116°5E **226** E9
Rens *Denmark* 54°54N 9°5E **163** K3
Renshou *China* 29°59N 104°9E **228** C5
Rensselaer *Ind., U.S.A.* 40°57N 87°9W **311** D9
Rensselaer *N.Y., U.S.A.* 42°38N 73°45W **313** D11
Renton *U.S.A.* 47°28N 122°12W **306** C4
Renukoot *India* 24°12N 83°2E **243** G10
Renwick *N.Z.* 41°30S 173°51E **285** B8
Renwick Gallery *Washington, D.C., U.S.A.* **143** a1
Renwu = Jenwu *Taiwan* 22°42N 120°20E **225** D2
Réo *Burkina Faso* 12°28N 2°35W **262** C4
Reocín = Puente San Miguel *Spain* 43°21N 4°5W **194** B6
Reotipur *India* 25°33N 83°45E **243** G10
Repalle *India* 16°2N 80°45E **245** F5
Répcelak *Hungary* 47°24N 17°1E **182** C2
Řeporyje *Czechia* 50°1N 14°18E **135** B1
Reppen = Rzepin *Poland* 52°20N 14°49E **185** F1
Republic *Mo., U.S.A.* 37°7N 93°29W **308** G7
Republic *Wash., U.S.A.* 48°39N 118°44W **304** B4
Republican → *U.S.A.* 39°4N 96°48W **308** F5
Republiek *Suriname* 5°30N 55°13W **329** B6
Republika Srpska ☐ *Bos.-H.* 44°56N 17°11E **199** D14
République, Place de la *Paris, France* **134** b5
Repulse B. *Australia* 20°35S 148°46E **280** b
Repulse Bay *Nunavut, Canada* 66°30N 86°30W **295** D14
Repulse Bay *Hong Kong, China* 22°13N 114°10E **122** B3
Repy *Czechia* 50°4N 14°17E **135** B1
Requena *Peru* 5°5S 73°52W **330** B3
Requena *Spain* 39°30N 1°4W **197** F3
Requin Bay *Grenada* 12°2N 61°39W **323** q
Réquista *France* 44°1N 2°32E **174** D6
Reşadiye *Muğla, Turkey* 36°45N 27°39E **205** E9
Reşadiye *Tokat, Turkey* 40°23N 37°20E **212** B7
Reşadiye Yarımadası *Turkey* 36°40N 27°45E **205** E9
Resavica *Serbia* 44°4N 21°31E **202** B5
Resen *N. Macedonia* 41°5N 21°0E **202** E5

Reserve U.S.A. 33°43N 108°45W 305 K9
Resht = Rasht Iran 37°20N 49°40E 213 D13
Residenz Germany 48°8N 11°34E 131 B2
Residenzmuseum Munich, Germany 131 b3
Resistencia Argentina 27°30S 59°0W 334 B4
Reşiţa Romania 45°18N 21°53E 182 E6
Resko Poland 53°47N 15°25E 184 E2
Reso = Raisio Finland 60°28N 22°11E 188 B2
Resolute Canada 74°42N 94°54W 295 C13
Resolution I. Nunavut, Canada 61°30N 65°0W 295 E19
Resolution I. N.Z. 45°40S 166°40E 285 F1
Resplandes Brazil 6°17S 45°13W 332 C2
Resplendor Brazil 19°20S 41°15W 333 E3
Ressano Garcia Mozam. 25°25S 32°0E 271 C5
Restinga, L. de la Venezuela 10°59N 64°48W 329 a
Restinga de Jurubatiba △ Brazil 22°5S 41°20W 333 F3
Reston Canada 49°33N 101°6W 297 D8
Resulayn = Ceylanpınar Turkey 36°50N 40°2E 213 D9
Reszel Poland 54°4N 21°10E 184 D8
Retalhuleu Guatemala 14°33N 91°46W 320 D1
Retenue, L. de Dem. Rep. of the Congo 11°0S 27°0E 269 E2
Retezat, Munţii Romania 45°25N 23°0E 182 E8
Retezat △ Romania 45°23N 22°56E 182 E7
Retford U.K. 53°19N 0°56W 168 D7
Rethel France 49°30N 4°20E 173 C11
Rethem Germany 52°47N 9°22E 178 C5
Rethimno Greece 35°18N 24°30E 207 E5
Reti Pakistan 28°5N 69°48E 242 E3
Retiche, Alpi Switz. 46°30N 10°0E 179 J6
Retiers France 47°55N 1°23W 172 E5
Retiro B. Aires, Argentina 34°35S 58°23W 117 B2
Retiro Madrid, Spain 40°24N 3°40W 127 B1
Retiro, Puerto Argentina 34°36S 58°21W 117 B2
Retortillo Spain 40°48N 6°21W 194 E4
Retreat S. Africa 34°4S 18°28E 118 B1
Rétság Hungary 47°58N 19°10E 182 C4
Réunion ☒ Ind. Oc. 21°0S 56°0E 272 f
Reus Spain 41°10N 1°5E 196 D6
Reusam Indonesia 2°11N 96°38E 234 B1
Reuterstadt Stavenhagen Germany 53°42N 12°54E 178 B8
Reutlingen Germany 48°29N 9°12E 179 G5
Reutov Russia 55°45N 37°50E 129 B4
Reutte Austria 47°29N 10°42E 180 D3
Reval = Tallinn Estonia 59°22N 24°48E 188 C3
Revda Russia 56°48N 59°57E 186 C10
Réveillon → France 48°42N 2°30E 134 B4
Revel = Tallinn Estonia 59°22N 24°48E 188 C3
Revel France 43°28N 2°1E 174 E6
Revelganj India 25°50N 84°40E 243 G11
Revelstoke Canada 51°0N 118°10W 296 C5
Reventazón Peru 6°10S 80°58W 330 B1
Revere U.S.A. 42°25N 71°0W 116 A2
Revere House Boston, U.S.A. 116 b3
Revigny-sur-Ornain France 48°49N 4°59E 173 D11
Revillagigedo, Is. de Pac. Oc. 18°40N 112°0W 318 D2
Revillagigedo Archipelago △ Mexico 19°0N 112°30W 318 D2
Revin France 49°55N 4°39E 173 C11
Revúca Slovakia 48°41N 20°7E 181 C13
Revuè → Mozam. 19°50S 34°0E 269 F3
Rewa India 24°33N 81°25E 243 G9
Rewa → Guyana 3°19N 58°42W 329 C6
Rewari India 28°15N 76°40E 242 E7
Rexburg U.S.A. 43°49N 111°47W 304 E8
Rexdale Canada 43°43N 79°35W 141 A1
Rey Iran 35°35N 51°25E 216 E4
Rey, I. del Panama 8°20N 78°30W 320 E4
Rey, L. del Mexico 27°1N 103°26W 318 B4
Rey, Mayo → Cameroon 8°47N 14°1E 264 A2
Rey, Rio-del- → Cameroon 4°31N 8°45E 264 B1
Rey Bouba Cameroon 8°40N 14°15E 264 A2
Rey Malabo Eq. Guin. 3°45N 8°50E 263 E6
Reyðarfjörður Iceland 65°2N 14°13W 155 B12
Reyes Bolivia 14°19S 67°23W 330 C4
Reyes, Pt. U.S.A. 38°0N 123°0W 306 H3
Reyhanlı Turkey 36°16N 36°35E 250 B7
Reykhólar Iceland 65°27N 22°12W 155 B4
Reykholt Suðurnes Iceland 64°40N 21°18W 155 C5
Reykholt Vesturland Iceland 64°10N 20°25W 155 C6
Reykjahlíð Iceland 65°40N 16°55W 155 B10
Reykjanes Iceland 63°48N 22°40W 155 D4
Reykjanes Ridge Atl. Oc. 59°0N 31°0W 152 A8
Reykjavík Iceland 64°10N 21°57W 155 C5
Reykjavík Keflavík ✈ (KEF) Iceland 64°0N 22°45W 155 C4
Reynolds Ga., U.S.A. 32°33N 84°6W 316 C5
Reynolds Ill., U.S.A. 41°20N 90°40W 310 C6
Reynolds Ra. Australia 22°30S 133°0E 278 D5
Reynoldsville Ga., U.S.A. 30°51N 84°47W 316 E5
Reynoldsville Pa., U.S.A. 41°6N 78°53W 312 E6
Reynosa Mexico 26°7N 98°18W 319 B5
Reynosa Tamaulipas Mexico 19°30N 99°10W 128 A1
Reza'iyeh = Orūmīyeh Iran 37°40N 45°0E 213 D11
Reza'iyeh, L. = Orūmīyeh, Daryācheh-ye Iran 37°50N 45°30E 213 D11
Rēzekne Latvia 56°30N 27°17E 188 D4
Rezhitsa = Rēzekne Latvia 56°30N 27°17E 188 D4
Rezina Moldova 47°45N 28°58E 183 C13
Rezovo Bulgaria 42°0N 28°0E 203 D12
Rezvān Iran 27°34N 56°6E 247 E8
Rezvānshahr Iran 37°32N 49°7E 213 D13
Rgotina Serbia 44°1N 22°17E 202 B6
Rharbi, Zahrez Algeria 34°50N 2°55E 261 B5
Rharis, O. → Algeria 26°0N 5°4E 261 C6
Rhayader U.K. 52°18N 3°29W 169 E4
Rheda-Wiedenbrück Germany 51°50N 8°20E 178 D4
Rhede Germany 51°50N 6°42E 178 D2
Rhein → Europe 51°52N 6°2E 170 C6
Rhein-Main-Donau-Kanal Germany 49°1N 11°27E 179 F7
Rhein-Ruhr, Düsseldorf ✈ (DUS) Germany 51°17N 6°46E 178 D2
Rhein-Taunus ⌂ Germany 50°10N 8°10E 179 E4
Rhein-Westerwald ⌂ Germany 50°32N 7°20E 178 E3
Rheinbach Germany 50°38N 6°57E 178 E2
Rheine Germany 52°17N 7°26E 178 C3
Rheinfelden Germany 47°33N 7°47E 179 H3
Rheinland-Pfalz □ Germany 50°0N 7°0E 179 E2
Rheinsberg Germany 53°6N 12°54E 178 B8
Rheris, Oued → Morocco 30°50N 4°34W 260 B4
Rhin = Rhein → Europe 51°52N 6°2E 170 C6
Rhine = Rhein → Europe 51°52N 6°2E 170 C6
Rhine U.S.A. 31°59N 83°12W 316 D6
Rhinebeck U.S.A. 41°56N 73°55W 313 E11
Rhineland-Palatinate = Rheinland-Pfalz □ Germany 50°0N 7°0E 179 E2
Rhinelander U.S.A. 45°38N 89°25W 308 C9
Rhinns Pt. U.K. 55°40N 6°29W 167 F2
Rhino Camp Uganda 3°0N 31°22E 268 B3
Rhir, Cap Morocco 30°38N 9°54W 260 B3
Rho Italy 45°31N 9°2E 128 A1
Rhode Island □ U.S.A. 41°40N 71°30W 313 E13
Rhodes N.S.W., Australia 33°49S 151°6E 139 A1
Rhodes Greece 36°15N 28°10E 206 E12
Rhodes ✈ (RHO) Greece 36°23N 28°12E 205 E10
Rhodesia = Zimbabwe ■ Africa 19°0S 30°0E 269 F3
Rhodon France 48°42N 2°3E 134 B1
Rhodon → France 48°42N 2°4E 134 B1
Rhodope Mts. = Rodopi Planina Bulgaria 41°40N 24°20E 203 E8
Rhön Germany 50°24N 9°58E 178 E5
Rhondda U.K. 51°39N 3°31W 169 F4
Rhondda Cynon Taff □ U.K. 51°42N 3°27W 169 F4
Rhône □ France 45°54N 4°35E 175 C8
Rhône → France 43°28N 4°42E 175 E8
Rhum = Rùm U.K. 57°0N 6°20W 167 E2
Rhydaman = Ammanford U.K. 51°48N 3°59W 169 F4
Rhyl U.K. 53°20N 3°29W 168 D4
Ri-Aba Eq. Guin. 3°28N 8°40E 263 E6
Ria Formosa ⌂ Portugal 37°1N 7°48W 195 H3
Riachão Brazil 7°20S 46°37W 332 C2
Riacho de Santana Brazil 13°37S 42°57W 333 D3
Rialma Brazil 15°18S 49°34W 333 E2
Rialto, Ponte di Venice, Italy 142 b3
Rialto Towers Australia 37°49S 144°57W 128 A1
Riam Indonesia 1°49S 111°54E 235 C4
Riang India 27°31N 92°56E 241 B4
Riang, Laem Thailand 8°7N 98°27E 237 a
Riangnom South Sudan 9°55N 30°1E 257 F3
Riaño Spain 42°59N 4°59W 194 C6
Rians France 43°37N 5°44E 175 E9
Riansáres → Spain 39°32N 3°18W 195 F7
Riasi India 33°10N 74°50E 243 C6
Riau □ Indonesia 0°0 102°35E 234 B2
Riau, Kepulauan □ Indonesia 0°30N 104°20E 234 B2
Riau Arch. = Riau, Kepulauan □ Indonesia 0°30N 104°20E 234 B2
Riaza Spain 41°18N 3°30W 194 D7
Riaza → Spain 41°42N 3°55W 194 D7
Riba de Saelices Spain 40°55N 2°17W 196 E2
Riba-roja de Túria Spain 39°33N 0°34W 197 F4
Ribadavia Spain 42°17N 8°8W 194 C2
Ribadeo Spain 43°35N 7°5W 194 B3
Ribadesella Spain 43°30N 5°7W 194 B5
Ribado Nigeria 9°16N 12°47E 263 D7
Ribamar Brazil 2°33S 44°3W 332 B3
Ribao Cameroon 6°32N 11°30E 263 D7
Ribas = Ribes de Freser Spain 42°19N 2°15E 196 C7
Ribas do Rio Pardo Brazil 20°27S 53°46W 331 E7
Ribauè Mozam. 14°57S 38°17E 269 E4
Ribble → U.K. 53°52N 2°25W 168 D5
Ribe Denmark 55°19N 8°44E 163 J2
Ribeauvillé France 48°10N 7°20E 173 D14
Ribécourt-Dreslincourt France 49°30N 2°55E 173 C9
Ribeira Rio de J., Brazil 22°49S 43°10W 135 A1
Ribeira Spain 42°36N 8°58W 194 C2
Ribeira Brava Madeira 32°41N 17°4W 153 c
Ribeira do Pombal Brazil 10°50S 38°32W 332 D4
Ribeira Grande Azores 37°49N 25°31W 153 d3
Ribeira Grande Cabo Verde 17°0N 25°4W 153 j
Ribeira Grande Cabo Verde 14°54N 23°36W 153 j
Ribeirão Prêto Brazil 21°10S 47°50W 335 A6
Ribeiro Gonçalves Brazil 7°32S 45°14W 332 C2
Ribemont France 49°47N 3°27E 173 C10
Ribera Italy 37°30N 13°16E 200 E6
Ribérac France 45°15N 0°20E 174 C4
Riberalta Bolivia 11°0S 66°0W 331 C4
Ribes de Freser Spain 42°19N 2°15E 196 C7
Ribnica Slovenia 45°45N 14°45E 199 C11
Ribnița Moldova 47°45N 29°0E 183 C14
Ribnitz-Damgarten Germany 54°15N 12°27E 178 A8
Říčany Czechia 50°0N 14°40E 180 B7
Ricarda, Estany de la Spain 41°17N 2°6E 114 B1
Riccarton N.Z. 43°32S 172°37E 285 D7
Riccia Italy 41°30N 14°50E 201 A7
Riccione Italy 43°59N 12°39E 199 E9
Rice U.S.A. 34°5N 114°51W 307 L12
Rice L. Canada 44°12N 78°10W 312 B6
Rice Lake U.S.A. 45°30N 91°44W 308 C8
Riceboro U.S.A. 31°44N 81°26W 316 D8
Rich, C. Canada 44°43N 80°38W 312 B4
Richard Toll Senegal 16°25N 15°42W 262 B1
Richards Bay S. Africa 28°48S 32°6E 271 D5
Richardson U.S.A. 32°56N 96°43W 120 A5
Richardson → Canada 58°25N 111°14W 297 B6
Richardson Lakes U.S.A. 44°46N 70°58W 309 C18
Richardson Mts. N.Z. 44°49S 168°34E 285 E3
Richardson Springs U.S.A. 39°51N 121°46W 306 F5
Riche, C. Australia 34°36S 118°47E 279 F2
Richelieu France 47°1N 0°20E 172 E7
Richey U.S.A. 47°39N 105°4W 304 C11
Richfield U.S.A. 38°46N 112°5W 304 G7
Richfield Springs U.S.A. 42°51N 74°59W 313 D10
Richford U.S.A. 45°0N 72°40W 313 B12
Richibucto Canada 46°42N 64°54W 299 C7
Richland Ga., U.S.A. 32°5N 84°40W 316 C5
Richland Iowa, U.S.A. 41°13N 92°0W 310 C5
Richland Mo., U.S.A. 37°51N 92°26W 310 G4
Richland Wash., U.S.A. 46°17N 119°18W 304 C4
Richland Center U.S.A. 43°21N 90°23W 308 D8
Richland Hills U.S.A. 32°48N 97°13W 120 B2
Richlands U.S.A. 37°6N 81°48W 309 G13
Richmond N.S.W., Australia 33°35S 150°42E 283 B9
Richmond Queens., Australia 20°43S 143°8E 280 C3
Richmond Vic., Australia 37°48S 145°0E 128 A2
Richmond Nelson-Marlborough, N.Z. 41°20S 173°12E 285 B8
Richmond N. Yorks., U.K. 54°25N 1°43W 168 C6
Richmond Calif., U.S.A. 37°46N 122°27W 136 B2
Richmond Calif., U.S.A. 37°56N 122°21W 306 H4
Richmond Ind., U.S.A. 39°50N 84°53W 311 E12
Richmond Ky., U.S.A. 37°45N 84°18W 311 G12
Richmond Mich., U.S.A. 42°49N 82°45W 312 D2
Richmond Mo., U.S.A. 39°17N 93°58W 310 E3
Richmond Tex., U.S.A. 29°35N 95°46W 314 G7
Richmond Utah, U.S.A. 41°56N 111°48W 304 F8
Richmond Va., U.S.A. 37°33N 77°27W 309 G15
Richmond Vt., U.S.A. 44°24N 72°59W 313 B12
Richmond, Mt. N.Z. 41°32S 173°22E 285 B8
Richmond Hill Ont., Canada 43°52N 79°27W 312 C5
Richmond Hill Ga., U.S.A. 31°56N 81°18W 316 D8
Richmond Hill N.Y., U.S.A. 40°41N 73°51W 132 B2
Richmond Park U.K. 51°26N 0°16W 125 B2
Richmond Peak St. Vincent 13°17N 61°13W 323 n
Richmond Ra. N.S.W., Australia 29°0S 152°45E 281 D5
Richmond Ra. N.Z. 41°32S 173°22E 285 B8
Richmond-upon-Thames □ U.K. 51°27N 0°17W 125 B2
Richmondville U.S.A. 42°38N 74°33W 313 D10
Richtersveld △ S. Africa 28°15S 17°10E 270 D2
Richville U.S.A. 44°25N 75°23W 313 B9
Richwood Ohio, U.S.A. 40°26N 83°18W 311 D13
Richwood W. Va., U.S.A. 38°14N 80°32W 309 F13
Ricla Spain 41°31N 1°24W 196 D3
Ricupe Angola 14°37S 21°25E 265 E4
Ridā' Yemen 14°25N 44°50E 248 D4
Riddarholmen Stockholm, Sweden 139 c1
Riddarhuset Stockholm, Sweden 139 c2
Ridder Kazakhstan 50°20N 83°30E 217 B10
Riddlesburg U.S.A. 40°9N 78°15W 312 F6
Rideau → Canada 45°27N 75°42W 313 A9
Ridge, The India 28°37N 77°10E 120 B2
Ridge Farm U.S.A. 39°54N 87°39W 311 E9
Ridge Spring U.S.A. 33°51N 81°40W 316 B8
Ridgecrest U.S.A. 35°38N 117°40W 307 K9
Ridgefield Conn., U.S.A. 41°17N 73°30W 313 E11
Ridgefield N.J., U.S.A. 40°49N 74°0W 132 B1
Ridgefield Wash., U.S.A. 45°49N 122°45W 306 E4
Ridgefield Park U.S.A. 40°52N 74°1W 132 A1
Ridgeland Miss., U.S.A. 32°26N 90°8W 315 E9
Ridgeland S.C., U.S.A. 32°29N 80°59W 316 C9
Ridgetown Canada 42°26N 81°52W 312 D3
Ridgeville Ind., U.S.A. 40°18N 85°2W 311 D11
Ridgeville S.C., U.S.A. 33°6N 80°19W 316 B9
Ridgewood N.J., U.S.A. 40°59N 74°7W 313 F10
Ridgewood N.Y., U.S.A. 40°42N 73°53W 132 B2
Ridgway Ill., U.S.A. 37°48N 88°16W 311 G8
Ridgway Pa., U.S.A. 41°25N 78°44W 312 E6
Riding Mountain △ Canada 50°50N 100°0W 297 C9
Ridley, Mt. Australia 33°12S 122°7E 279 F3
Riebeek-Oos S. Africa 33°10S 26°10E 270 D4
Ried Austria 48°14N 13°30E 180 C6
Riedlingen Germany 48°9N 9°28E 179 G5
Riedstadt Germany 49°45N 8°30E 179 F4
Riem Germany 48°8N 11°41E 131 B3
Rienza → Italy 46°49N 11°47E 199 B8
Riesa Germany 51°17N 13°17E 178 D9
Riesco, I. Chile 52°55S 72°40W 336 D2
Riesenburg = Prabuty Poland 53°47N 19°15E 184 E6
Riesenrad Austria 48°14N 16°23E 142 A2
Riesi Italy 37°17N 14°5E 201 E7
Riet → S. Africa 29°0S 23°54E 270 C3
Rietavas Lithuania 55°44N 21°56E 184 C8
Rietbron S. Africa 32°54S 23°10E 270 D3
Rietfontein Namibia 21°58S 20°58E 270 B3
Rieti Italy 42°24N 12°51E 199 F9
Rieupeyroux France 44°19N 2°12E 174 D6
Riez France 43°49N 6°6E 175 E10
Rif = Er Rif Morocco 35°1N 4°1W 261 A4
Rif Iceland 64°56N 23°49W 155 C3
Riffe L. U.S.A. 46°32N 122°26W 306 D4
Rifle U.S.A. 39°32N 107°47W 304 G10
Rifstangi Iceland 66°32N 16°12W 155 A10
Rift Valley Africa 7°0N 30°0E 254 G7
Rig Rig Chad 14°13N 14°25E 259 F2
Riga India 28°26N 95°2E 241 A5
Rīga Latvia 56°53N 24°8E 184 B11
Rīga ✈ (RIX) Latvia 56°54N 23°59E 184 B10
Riga, G. of Latvia 57°40N 23°45E 184 A10
Rigacikun Nigeria 10°40N 7°28E 263 C6
Rīgān Iran 28°37N 58°58E 247 D8
Rīgas Jūras Līcis = Riga, G. of Latvia 57°40N 23°45E 184 A10
Rigaud Canada 45°29N 74°18W 313 A10
Rigby U.S.A. 43°40N 111°55W 304 E8
Rīgestān Afghan. 30°15N 65°0E 240 C2
Riggins U.S.A. 45°25N 116°19W 304 D5
Rignac France 44°25N 2°16E 174 D6
Rigolet Canada 54°10N 58°23W 299 B8
Rigu Ghana 9°59N 0°48W 263 D4
Rihand Dam India 24°9N 83°2E 243 G10
Riihimäki Finland 60°45N 24°48E 188 B3
Riiser-Larsen-halvøya Antarctica 68°0S 35°0E 151 C4
Riiser-Larsen Ice Shelf S. Ocean 74°0S 19°0W 151 D2
Riiser-Larsen Sea S. Ocean 67°30S 22°0E 151 C4
Riisitunturi △ Finland 66°27N 28°27E 160 C23
Rijau Nigeria 11°8N 5°17E 263 C6
Rijeka Croatia 45°20N 14°21E 199 C11
Rijeka Crnojevića Montenegro 42°24N 19°1E 202 D3
Rijksmuseum Amsterdam, Neths. 112 c1
Rijssen Neths. 52°19N 6°31E 170 B6
Rika → Ukraine 48°11N 23°16E 183 B8
Rikā', W. ar → Si. Arabia 22°25N 44°50E 248 B4
Rike Ethiopia 10°50N 39°53E 257 E4
Rikers I. U.S.A. 40°47N 73°53W 132 B2
Riksdagshuset Stockholm, Sweden 139 b2
Rikuchū-Kaigan △ Japan 39°20N 142°0E 220 E11
Rikuzentakata Japan 39°0N 141°40E 220 E10
Rila Bulgaria 42°7N 23°7E 202 D7
Rila Planina Bulgaria 42°10N 23°20E 202 D7
Riley U.S.A. 43°32N 119°28W 304 E4
Rima → Nigeria 13°4N 5°10E 263 C6
Rimac Peru 12°2S 77°2W 124 B2
Rimāf Yemen 17°30N 50°35E 249 C5
Rimah, Wadi ar → Si. Arabia 26°5N 41°30E 246 E4
Rimatara French Polynesia 22°38S 152°51W 289 f
Rimau, Pulau Malaysia 5°15N 100°16E 237 c
Rimavská Sobota Slovakia 48°22N 20°2E 181 C13
Rimbey Canada 52°35N 114°15W 296 C6
Rimbo Sweden 59°44N 18°21E 162 E12
Rimé, O. → Chad 14°2N 18°3E 259 F3
Rimersburg U.S.A. 41°3N 79°30W 312 E5
Rimforsa Sweden 58°6N 15°43E 163 F9
Rimini Italy 44°3N 12°33E 199 D9
Rimouski Canada 48°27N 68°30W 299 C6
Rimrock U.S.A. 46°40N 121°7W 306 D5
Rinca Indonesia 8°45S 119°35E 235 D5
Rincon Bonaire 12°14N 68°20W 322 h
Rincon Puerto Rico 18°20N 67°15W 321 b
Rincon Ga., U.S.A. 32°18N 81°14W 316 C8
Rincón de Anchuras = Anchuras Spain 39°29N 4°50W 195 F6
Rincón de la Victoria Spain 36°43N 4°18W 195 J6
Rincón de Romos Mexico 22°14N 102°18W 318 C4
Rincon Falls Trin. & Tob. 10°46N 61°24W 323 t
Rinconada Argentina 22°26S 66°10W 334 A2
Rind → India 25°53N 80°33E 243 G9
Rindal Norway 63°3N 9°13E 164 A6
Ringarum Sweden 58°21N 16°26E 163 F10
Ringas India 27°21N 75°34E 242 F6
Ringdove Vanuatu 16°40S 168°10E 287 F6
Ringe Denmark 55°13N 10°28E 163 J4
Ringebu Norway 61°32N 10°7E 164 C7
Ringgi Solomon Is. 8°5S 157°10E 287 M9
Ringgold Is. Fiji 16°15S 179°25W 287 A3
Ringim Nigeria 12°13N 9°10E 263 C6
Ringkøbing Denmark 56°5N 8°15E 163 H2
Ringkøbing Fjord Denmark 56°0N 8°15E 163 H2
Ringoma Angola 12°5S 17°32E 265 E3
Ringsaker Norway 60°54N 10°45E 164 D7
Ringsjön Sweden 55°55N 13°30E 163 J7
Ringsted Denmark 55°25N 11°46E 163 J5
Ringvassøya Norway 69°56N 19°15E 160 B18
Ringwood U.S.A. 41°7N 74°15W 313 E10
Rinia Greece 37°23N 25°13E 205 D7
Rinjani, Gunung Indonesia 8°24S 116°28E 235 D5
Rinjani △ Indonesia 8°26S 116°23E 235 D5
Rinkeby Sweden 59°23N 17°55E 139 A1
Rinteln Germany 52°10N 9°5E 178 C5
Rinyirru △ Australia 15°24S 144°26E 280 B3
Rio, Punta del Spain 36°49N 2°24W 197 J2
Rio Bonito = Caiapônia Brazil 16°57S 51°49W 331 D7
Rio Branco = Arcoverde Brazil 8°25S 37°4W 332 C4
Rio Branco = Paratinga Brazil 12°40S 43°10W 333 D3
Rio Branco = Roraima □ Brazil 2°0N 61°30W 329 C5
Rio Branco Brazil 9°58S 67°49W 330 B4
Rio Branco Uruguay 32°40S 53°40W 335 C5
Rio Bravo Mexico 25°59N 98°6W 319 B5
Rio Bravo ⌂ N. Amer. 29°2N 102°45W 318 B4
Rio Bravo del Norte → Mexico 25°57N 97°9W 319 B5
Rio Brilhante Brazil 21°48S 54°33W 335 A5
Rio Bueno Chile 40°19S 72°58W 336 B2
Rio Bueno Jamaica 18°28N 77°28W 320 a
Rio Caribe Venezuela 10°42N 63°7W 329 A5
Rio Chico Venezuela 10°19N 65°59W 328 A4
Rio Claro Brazil 22°19S 47°35W 335 A6
Rio Claro Trin. & Tob. 10°20N 61°10W 323 t
Rio Cobre → Jamaica 17°59N 76°52W 320 a
Rio Colorado Argentina 39°0S 64°0W 336 A4
Rio Comprido Brazil 22°55S 43°13W 135 B1
Rio Cuarto Argentina 33°10S 64°25W 334 C3
Rio das Pedras Mozam. 23°8S 35°28E 271 B6
Rio de Contas Brazil 13°36S 41°48W 333 D3
Rio de Janeiro Brazil 22°54S 43°12W 135 B1
Rio de Janeiro □ Brazil 22°50S 43°0W 333 F3
Rio de Janeiro Galeão ✈ (GIG) Brazil 22°49S 43°15W 135 A1
Rio de Mouro Portugal 38°46N 9°15W 126 A1
Río de Oro, B. de W. Sahara 23°45N 15°50W 260 D1
Rio do Prado Brazil 16°35S 40°34W 333 E3
Rio do Sul Brazil 27°13S 49°37W 335 B6
Río Dulce △ Guatemala 15°43N 88°50W 320 C2
Río Gallegos Argentina 51°35S 69°15W 336 D3
Río Grande Argentina 53°50S 67°45W 336 D3
Río Grande Bolivia 20°51S 67°17W 330 E4
Rio Grande Brazil 32°0S 52°20W 335 C5
Río Grande Zacatecas, Mexico 23°50N 103°2W 318 C4
Río Grande Puerto Rico 18°23N 65°50W 321 b
Rio Grande → N. Amer. 25°58N 97°9W 314 J6
Rio Grande City U.S.A. 26°23N 98°49W 314 H5
Río Grande de Santiago → Mexico 21°36N 105°26W 318 C3
Rio Grande do Norte □ Brazil 5°40S 36°0W 332 C4
Rio Grande do Sul □ Brazil 30°0S 53°0W 335 C5
Rio Grande Rise Atl. Oc. 31°0S 35°0W 152 K8
Río Hato Panama 8°22N 80°10W 320 E3
Río Lagartos Mexico 21°36N 88°10W 319 C7
Rio Largo Brazil 9°28S 35°50W 332 C4
Rio Maior Portugal 39°19N 8°57W 195 F2
Rio Marina Italy 42°49N 10°25E 198 F7
Río Mayo Argentina 45°40S 70°15W 336 C2
Río Mulatos Bolivia 19°40S 66°50W 330 D4
Río Muni □ Eq. Guin. 1°30N 10°0E 264 B2
Rio Negro Brazil 26°0S 49°55W 335 B6
Río Negro Chile 40°47S 73°14W 336 B2
Rio Negro, Pantanal do Brazil 19°0S 56°0W 331 D6
Rio Novo = Ipiaú Brazil 14°8S 39°44W 333 D4
Rio Pardo = Ribas do Rio Pardo Brazil 20°27S 53°46W 331 E7
Rio Pardo Brazil 30°0S 52°30W 335 C5
Río Pico Argentina 44°0S 70°22W 336 B2
Río Pilcomayo △ Argentina 25°5S 58°5W 334 B4
Río Plátano Honduras 15°45N 84°40W 320 C3
Rio Prêto = Santa Rita de Cássia Brazil 11°0S 44°32W 332 D3
Rio Preto da Eva Brazil 2°46S 59°41W 329 D6
Rio Rancho U.S.A. 35°14N 106°41W 305 J10
Rio Real Brazil 11°28S 37°56W 333 D4
Rio Seco = Villa de María Argentina 29°55S 63°43W 334 B3
Río Segundo Argentina 31°40S 63°59W 334 C3
Río Simpson △ Chile 45°27S 73°30W 336 C2
Río Tercero Argentina 32°15S 64°8W 334 C3
Rio Tinto Brazil 6°48S 35°5W 332 C4
Rio Tinto Portugal 41°11N 8°34W 194 D2
Rio Tuba Phil. 8°31N 117°26E 233 G1
Río Turbio Argentina 51°32S 72°18W 336 D2
Rio Verde Brazil 17°50S 51°0W 333 E1
Río Verde San Luis Potosí, Mexico 21°56N 99°59W 319 C5
Rio Verde de Mato Grosso Brazil 18°56S 54°52W 331 D7
Río Viejo △ Venezuela 7°15N 71°20W 328 B3
Rio Vista U.S.A. 38°10N 121°42W 306 G5
Riobamba Ecuador 1°50S 78°45W 328 D2
Riohacha Colombia 11°33N 72°55W 328 A3
Rioja Peru 6°11S 77°5W 330 B2
Riom France 45°54N 3°7E 174 C7
Riom-ès-Montagnes France 45°17N 2°39E 174 C6
Rion-des-Landes France 43°55N 0°56W 174 E3
Rionegro Antioquia, Colombia 6°9N 75°22W 328 B2
Rionegro Santander, Colombia 7°15N 73°9W 328 B3
Rionero in Vúlture Italy 40°55N 15°40E 201 B8
Rioni → Georgia 42°14N 41°44E 191 J5
Riós Spain 41°58N 7°16W 194 D3
Riosinho → Brazil 7°7S 51°39W 331 B7
Riosucio Caldas, Colombia 5°30N 75°40W 328 B2
Riosucio Choco, Colombia 7°27N 77°7W 328 B2
Riou L. Canada 59°7N 106°25W 297 B7
Rioz France 47°26N 6°5E 173 E13
Riozinho → Brazil 2°55S 67°7W 328 D4
Ripatransone Italy 42°59N 13°46E 199 F10
Ripley Ont., Canada 44°4N 81°35W 312 B3
Ripley Calif., U.S.A. 33°32N 114°39W 307 M12
Ripley N.Y., U.S.A. 42°16N 79°43W 312 D5
Ripley Ohio, U.S.A. 38°45N 83°51W 311 F13
Ripley Tenn., U.S.A. 35°45N 89°32W 315 D10
Ripley W. Va., U.S.A. 38°49N 81°43W 309 F13
Ripoll Spain 42°15N 2°13E 196 C7
Ripollet Spain 41°26N 2°10E 114 A1
Ripon N. Yorks., U.K. 54°9N 1°31W 168 C6
Ripon Calif., U.S.A. 37°44N 121°7W 306 H5
Ripon Wis., U.S.A. 43°51N 88°50W 308 D9
Riposto Italy 37°44N 15°12E 201 E8
Rippin = Rypin Poland 53°3N 19°25E 185 E6
Ris Norway 59°56N 10°41E 133 A3
Risan Montenegro 42°32N 18°42E 202 D2
Risaralda □ Colombia 5°0N 76°10W 328 B2
Risby Denmark 55°41N 12°19E 118 A1
Risca U.K. 51°37N 3°5W 169 F4
Rishā', W. ar → Si. Arabia 25°33N 44°5E 246 E5
Rishikesh India 30°7N 78°19E 242 D8
Rishiri-Rebun-Sarobetsu △ Japan 45°26N 141°30E 220 B10
Rishiri-Tō Japan 45°11N 141°15E 220 B10
Rishon le Ziyyon Israel 31°58N 34°48E 251 G5
Rishra India 22°42N 88°20E 124 A2
Rising Sun U.S.A. 38°57N 84°51W 311 F12
Risle → France 49°26N 0°23E 172 C7
Risnjak △ Croatia 45°25N 14°36E 199 C11
Rison U.S.A. 33°58N 92°11W 314 E8
Risør Norway 58°43N 9°13E 164 F6
Rissani Morocco 31°18N 4°12W 260 B4
Rita Blanca Cr. → U.S.A. 35°40N 102°29W 314 D3
Ritchie's Arch. India 12°14N 93°10E 245 H11
Rithala India 28°43N 77°6E 120 A1
Riti Nigeria 7°57N 9°41E 263 D6
Ritidian Pt. Guam 13°39N 144°51E 302 d
Ritter, Mt. U.S.A. 37°41N 119°12W 306 H7
Rittman U.S.A. 40°58N 81°47W 312 F3
Ritzville U.S.A. 47°8N 118°23W 304 C4
Riu India 28°19N 95°3E 241 A5
Riva del Garda Italy 45°53N 10°50E 198 C7
Riva Ligure Italy 43°50N 7°50E 198 E4
Rivadavia B. Aires, Argentina 35°29S 62°59W 334 D3
Rivadavia Mendoza, Argentina 33°13S 68°30W 334 C2
Rivadavia Salta, Argentina 24°5S 62°54W 334 A3
Rivadavia Chile 29°57S 70°35W 334 B1
Rivarolo Canavese Italy 45°19N 7°43E 198 C4
Rivas Nic. 11°30N 85°50W 320 D2
Rivash Iran 35°28N 58°26E 247 C8
Rive-de-Gier France 45°32N 4°37E 175 C8
Rive Sud, Canal de la Canada 45°24N 73°31W 130 B2
River Cess Liberia 5°30N 9°32W 262 D3
River Edge U.S.A. 40°56N 74°1W 132 A1
River Estate & Waterwheel Trin. & Tob. 10°41N 61°33W 323 t
River Forest U.S.A. 41°53N 87°49W 119 B2
River Grove U.S.A. 41°55N 87°50W 119 B1
River Jordan Canada 48°26N 124°3W 306 B2
River North Chicago, U.S.A. 119 b1
River Ridge U.S.A. 29°57N 90°12W 131 B1
Rivera Argentina 37°12S 63°14W 334 D3
Rivera Uruguay 31°0S 55°50W 335 C4
Riverbank U.S.A. 37°44N 120°56W 306 H6
Riverdale Calif., U.S.A. 36°26N 119°52W 306 J7
Riverdale Ga., U.S.A. 33°34N 84°25W 316 B5
Riverdale Ill., U.S.A. 41°38N 87°37W 119 D3
Riverdale Md., U.S.A. 38°57N 76°54W 143 B3
Riverdale N.Y., U.S.A. 40°59N 74°17W 132 A2
Riverdale Park Canada 43°40N 79°21W 141 A2
Riverhead U.S.A. 40°55N 72°40W 313 F12
Riverhurst Canada 50°55N 106°50W 297 C7
Riverlea S. Africa 26°12S 27°58E 123 B1
Rivers Canada 50°2N 100°14W 297 C8
Rivers □ Nigeria 4°30N 7°10E 263 E6
Rivers Inlet Canada 51°42N 127°15W 296 C3
Riversdale Ont., Canada 44°5N 81°20W 312 B3
Riversdale N.Z. 45°54S 168°44E 285 F3
Riversdale Western Cape, S. Africa 34°7S 21°15E 270 D3
Riverside Calif., U.S.A. 33°59N 117°22W 307 M9
Riverside Ill., U.S.A. 41°49N 87°49W 119 C2
Riversleigh Australia 19°5S 138°40E 280 B2
Riverton S. Austral., Australia 34°10S 138°46E 282 C3
Riverton Man., Canada 51°1N 97°0W 297 C9
Riverton N.Z. 46°21S 168°0E 285 G3
Riverton Ill., U.S.A. 39°51N 89°33W 310 E7
Riverton Wyo., U.S.A. 43°2N 108°23W 304 E9
Riverview Fla., U.S.A. 27°52N 82°20W 317 H7
Riverview Fla., U.S.A. 30°32N 87°12W 317 E2
Riverwood Australia 33°57S 151°3E 139 B1
Rives France 45°21N 5°31E 175 C9
Rivesaltes France 42°47N 2°50E 174 F6
Riviera = Azur, Côte d' France 43°25N 7°10E 175 E11
Riviera U.S.A. 35°4N 114°35W 307 K12
Riviera Beach U.S.A. 26°47N 80°3W 317 J9
Riviera di Levante Italy 44°15N 9°30E 198 D6
Riviera di Ponente Italy 44°10N 8°20E 198 D5
Rivière-à-Goyave, Pte. de la Guadeloupe 16°8N 61°33W 322 e
Rivière-au-Renard Canada 48°59N 64°23W 299 C7
Rivière des Anguilles Mauritius 20°29S 57°33E 272 e
Rivière-des-Prairies Canada 45°38N 73°34W 130 A2
Rivière-du-Loup Canada 47°50N 69°30W 299 C6
Rivière du Rempart Mauritius 20°6S 57°41E 272 e
Rivière-Pentecôte Canada 49°57N 67°1W 299 C6
Rivière-Pilote Martinique 14°26N 60°53W 322 j
Rivière St-Paul Canada 51°28N 57°45W 299 B8
Rivière-Salée Martinique 14°31N 61°0W 322 j
Rivne Odesa, Ukraine 46°1N 29°10E 183 D14
Rivne Rivne, Ukraine 50°40N 26°10E 177 C14
Rivne □ Ukraine 51°15N 26°30E 177 C14
Rívoli Italy 45°3N 7°31E 198 C4
Rivoli B. Australia 37°32S 140°3E 282 D4
Riwaka N.Z. 41°5S 172°59E 285 B7
Rixensart Belgium 50°43N 4°32E 116 B3
Rixheim France 47°40N 7°24E 173 E14
Riyad Iraq 33°18N 44°27E 113 B2
Riyadh = Ar Riyāḍ Si. Arabia 24°41N 46°42E 246 E5
Riza Greece 40°31N 23°15E 202 F7
Rizal Cagayan, Phil. 17°51N 121°21E 232 C3
Rizal Nueva Ecija, Phil. 15°43N 121°6E 232 D3
Rizal Zamboanga del N., Phil. 8°35N 123°26E 233 G4
Rizal Park Phil. 14°35N 120°58E 127 B1
Rizal Stadium Phil. 14°34N 120°59E 127 B1
Rize Turkey 41°0N 40°30E 213 B9
Rize □ Turkey 41°0N 40°30E 213 B9
Rizhao China 35°25N 119°30E 227 G10
Rizokarpaso Cyprus 35°36N 34°23E 207 E10
Rizzuto, C. Italy 38°53N 17°5E 201 D10
Rjukan Norway 59°54N 8°33E 164 E5
Rjuven Norway 59°9N 7°8E 164 E4
Rkîz, L. Mauritania 16°50N 15°23W 262 B1
Ro Greece 36°9N 29°33E 205 E11
Roa Dem. Rep. of the Congo 3°49N 24°56E 264 B4
Roa Oppland, Norway 60°17N 10°37E 164 D7
Roa Oslo, Norway 59°57N 10°39E 133 A2
Roa Spain 41°41N 3°56W 194 D7
Roachdale U.S.A. 39°51N 86°48W 311 E10
Road Town Br. Virgin Is. 18°27N 64°37W 321 C7
Roan Plateau U.S.A. 39°20N 109°20W 304 G9
Roanne France 46°3N 4°4E 173 F11
Roanoke Ala., U.S.A. 33°9N 85°22W 316 B4
Roanoke Ind., U.S.A. 40°58N 85°22W 311 D11
Roanoke Va., U.S.A. 37°16N 79°56W 309 G14
Roanoke → U.S.A. 35°57N 76°42W 315 D16
Roanoke I. U.S.A. 35°55N 75°39W 315 D17
Roanoke Rapids U.S.A. 36°28N 77°40W 315 C16
Roatán Honduras 16°18N 86°35W 320 C2
Rob Roy Solomon Is. 7°23S 157°36E 287 L9
Robāt Iran 34°16N 46°47E 213 E12
Robāt Sang Iran 35°35N 59°10E 247 C8
Robāṭkarīm Iran 35°25N 50°59E 247 C6
Robben I. S. Africa 33°46S 18°22E 270 D2
Robbins U.S.A. 41°38N 87°42W 119 D2
Robbins I. Australia 40°42S 145°0E 281 G4
Róbbio Italy 45°17N 8°35E 198 C5
Robe Australia 37°11S 139°45E 282 D3
Robe → Australia 21°42S 116°15E 278 D2
Röbel Germany 53°22N 12°35E 178 B8
Robert, Havre du Martinique 14°40N 60°55W 322 j
Robert Bourassa, Rés. Canada 53°40N 76°55W 298 B4
Robert Lee U.S.A. 31°54N 100°29W 314 F4
Roberta U.S.A. 32°43N 84°1W 316 C5
Roberts U.S.A. 40°37N 88°11W 311 D8
Roberts, Mt. Trin. & Tob. 10°47N 61°10W 323 t
Roberts, Mt. Alaska, U.S.A. 60°2N 166°16W 303 F6
Robertsdale U.S.A. 40°11N 78°6W 312 F6
Robertsganj India 24°44N 83°4E 243 G10
Robertson S. Africa 33°46S 19°50E 270 D2
Robertson I. Antarctica 65°15S 59°30W 151 C18
Robertson Ra. Australia 23°15S 121°0E 278 D3
Robertsport Liberia 6°45N 11°26W 262 D2
Robertstown Australia 33°58S 139°5E 282 B3
Roberval Canada 48°32N 72°15W 299 C5
Robeson Chan. N. Amer. 82°0N 61°30W 154 A4
Robesonia U.S.A. 40°21N 76°8W 313 F8
Robi Ethiopia 7°52N 39°38E 257 F4
Robinson U.S.A. 39°0N 87°44W 311 F9
Robinson → Australia 16°3S 137°16E 280 B2
Robinson Crusoe I. Pac. Oc. 33°38S 78°52W 330 c
Robinson Ra. Australia 25°40S 119°0E 279 E2
Robinvale Australia 34°40S 142°45E 282 C5
Robledal Venezuela 11°2N 64°22W 329 a
Robledo Spain 38°46N 2°26W 197 G2
Roblin Canada 51°14N 101°21W 297 C8
Roboré Bolivia 18°10S 59°45W 331 D6
Robson, Mt. Canada 53°10N 119°10W 296 C5
Robstown U.S.A. 27°47N 97°40W 314 H6
Roca, C. da Portugal 38°40N 9°31W 195 G1
Roca Partida, I. Mexico 19°1N 112°2W 318 D2
Rocamadour France 44°48N 1°37E 174 D5
Rocas, Atol das Brazil 4°0S 34°1W 332 B5
Rocca San Casciano Italy 44°3N 11°50E 199 D8
Roccadáspide Italy 40°27N 15°10E 201 B8
Roccastrada Italy 43°0N 11°10E 199 F8
Roccella Iónica Italy 38°19N 16°24E 201 D9
Rocciamelone, Mte. Italy 45°12N 7°5E 175 C11
Rocha Uruguay 34°30S 54°25W 335 C5
Rochdale U.K. 53°38N 2°9W 168 D5
Roche Melon = Rocciamelone, Mte. Italy 45°12N 7°5E 175 C11
Rochechouart France 45°50N 0°49E 174 C4
Rochedo Brazil 19°57S 54°52W 331 D7
Rochefort Belgium 50°9N 5°12E 170 D5
Rochefort Charente-Maritime, France 45°56N 0°57W 174 C3
Rochefort-en-Terre France 47°42N 2°22W 172 E4
Rochelle Ga., U.S.A. 31°57N 83°27W 316 D6
Rochelle Ill., U.S.A. 41°56N 89°4W 310 C7
Rochelle Park U.S.A. 40°54N 74°4W 132 A1
Rocher River Canada 61°23N 112°44W 296 A6
Roches, R. des → Réunion 21°0S 55°42E 272 f
Roche's Bluff Montserrat 16°42N 62°9W 323 p
Roches Noires Mauritius 20°6S 57°42E 272 e
Rocheservière France 46°57N 1°30W 172 F5
Rochester Vic., Australia 36°22S 144°41E 282 D6
Rochester Medway, U.K. 51°23N 0°31E 169 F8
Rochester Ind., U.S.A. 41°4N 86°13W 311 C10
Rochester Minn., U.S.A. 44°1N 92°28W 308 C7
Rochester N.H., U.S.A. 43°18N 70°59W 313 C14
Rochester N.Y., U.S.A. 43°10N 77°37W 312 C7
Rochester Hills U.S.A. 42°41N 83°8W 311 B13
Rochester Park U.S.A. 32°43N 96°44W 120 B5
Rociu Romania 44°43N 25°2E 183 F10
Rock → Yukon, Canada 60°7N 127°7W 296 A3
Rock → Ill., U.S.A. 41°29N 90°37W 310 C6
Rock, The Australia 35°15S 147°2E 283 C7
Rock Cr. → U.S.A. 38°54N 77°3W 143 B2
Rock Creek U.S.A. 41°40N 80°52W 312 E4
Rock Creek Park U.S.A. 38°56N 77°2W 143 B2
Rock Falls U.S.A. 41°47N 89°41W 310 C7
Rock Flat Australia 36°21S 149°13E 283 D8
Rock Hall Barbados 13°11N 59°36W 323 r
Rock Hill U.S.A. 34°56N 81°1W 315 D14
Rock Island U.S.A. 41°30N 90°34W 310 C6
Rock Port U.S.A. 40°25N 95°31W 308 E6
Rock Rapids U.S.A. 43°26N 96°10W 308 D5
Rock Sound The Bahamas 24°54N 76°12W 320 B4
Rock Springs Mont., U.S.A. 46°49N 106°15W 304 C10
Rock Springs Wyo., U.S.A. 41°35N 109°14W 304 F9
Rock Valley U.S.A. 43°12N 96°18W 308 D5
Rockall Atl. Oc. 57°37N 13°42W 158 D3
Rockall Trough Atl. Oc. 57°0N 12°0W 152 A10
Rockaway Beach U.S.A. 40°34N 73°49W 132 C3
Rockaway Pt. U.S.A. 40°33N 73°54W 132 C2
Rockdale N.S.W., Australia 33°57S 151°8E 139 B1
Rockdale Tex., U.S.A. 30°39N 97°0W 314 F6
Rockdale Wash., U.S.A. 47°22N 121°28W 306 C5
Rockeby = Mungkan Kandju △ Australia 13°35S 142°52E 280 A3
Rockefeller Center New York, U.S.A. 132 c2
Rockefeller Plateau Antarctica 76°0S 130°0W 151 E14
Rockford Ala., U.S.A. 32°53N 86°13W 316 C3
Rockford Ill., U.S.A. 42°16N 89°6W 310 B7
Rockford Iowa, U.S.A. 43°3N 92°57W 310 A4
Rockford Mich., U.S.A. 43°7N 85°34W 311 A11
Rockford Ohio, U.S.A. 40°41N 84°39W 311 D12
Rockglen Canada 49°11N 105°57W 297 D7
Rockhampton Australia 23°22S 150°32E 280 C5
Rockingham W. Austral., Australia 32°15S 115°38E 279 F2
Rockingham N.C., U.S.A. 34°57N 79°46W 315 D15
Rockingham Vt., U.S.A. 43°11N 72°29W 313 C12
Rockingham B. Australia 18°5S 146°10E 280 B4
Rocklake U.S.A. 48°47N 99°15W 308 A4
Rockland Ont., Canada 45°33N 75°17W 313 A9
Rockland Idaho, U.S.A. 42°34N 112°53W 304 E7
Rockland Maine, U.S.A. 44°6N 69°7W 309 C19
Rockland Mich., U.S.A. 46°44N 89°11W 308 B9
Rocklands Bird Sanctuary Jamaica 18°24N 77°55W 320 a
Rocklands Reservoir Australia 37°15S 142°5E 282 D5
Rockledge U.S.A. 28°20N 80°43W 317 G9
Rocklin U.S.A. 38°48N 121°14W 306 G5
Rockly B. Trin. & Tob. 11°9N 60°46W 323 s
Rockmart U.S.A. 34°1N 85°3W 316 A4
Rockport Ind., U.S.A. 37°53N 87°3W 311 G9
Rockport Mass., U.S.A. 42°39N 70°37W 313 D14
Rockport Tex., U.S.A. 28°2N 97°3W 314 G6
Rocksprings U.S.A. 30°1N 100°13W 314 F4
Rockstone Guyana 5°59N 58°33W 329 B6
Rockville Conn., U.S.A. 41°52N 72°28W 313 E12
Rockville Ind., U.S.A. 39°46N 87°14W 311 E9
Rockville Md., U.S.A. 39°5N 77°9W 309 F15
Rockwall U.S.A. 32°56N 96°28W 314 E6
Rockwell City U.S.A. 42°24N 94°38W 310 B2
Rockwood Ont., Canada 43°37N 80°8W 312 C4
Rockwood Maine, U.S.A. 45°41N 69°45W 309 C19
Rockwood Tenn., U.S.A. 35°52N 84°41W 315 D12
Rocky Ford U.S.A. 38°3N 103°43W 304 G12
Rocky Fork L. U.S.A. 39°11N 83°26W 311 E13
Rocky Gully Australia 34°30S 116°57E 279 F2
Rocky Harbour Canada 49°36N 57°55W 299 C8
Rocky Island L. Canada 46°55N 83°0W 298 C3
Rocky Lane Canada 58°31N 116°22W 296 B5
Rocky Mount U.S.A. 35°57N 77°48W 315 D16
Rocky Mountain △ U.S.A. 40°25N 105°45W 304 F11
Rocky Mountain House Canada 52°22N 114°55W 296 C6
Rocky Mts. N. Amer. 49°0N 115°0W 304 B6
Rocky Point Namibia 19°3S 12°30E 270 A2
Rocroi France 49°55N 4°30E 173 C11
Rod Pakistan 28°10N 63°5E 240 C1
Roda = Stadtroda Germany 50°52N 11°44E 178 E7
Roda Greece 39°48N 19°46E 206 B9
Roda, Gezîret el Egypt 30°1N 31°13E 117 B2
Roda I. = Roda, Gezîret el Egypt 30°1N 31°13E 117 A2
Rodaun Austria 48°8N 16°12E 142 B1
Rødberg Norway 60°17N 8°56E 164 D5
Rødby Denmark 54°41N 11°23E 163 K5
Rødbyhavn Denmark 54°39N 11°22E 163 K5
Roddickton Canada 50°51N 56°8W 299 B8
Rødding Denmark 55°23N 9°3E 163 J3
Rödeby Sweden 56°15N 15°37E 163 H9
Rødekro Denmark 55°4N 9°20E 163 J3
Rodenkirchen Germany 53°23N 8°26E 178 B4
Rodez France 44°21N 2°33E 174 D6
Ródhos = Rhodes Greece 36°15N 28°10E 206 E12
Rodi Gargánico Italy 41°55N 15°53E 199 G12
Rodia Greece 35°22N 25°1E 207 E6
Rodīna Kazakhstan 50°16N 66°53E 217 B7

Rodna Romania 47°25N 24°50E 183 C9
Rodna ✪ Australia 23°45S 132°4E 278 D5
Rodnei, Munţii Romania 47°35N 24°35E 183 C9
Rodney Canada 42°34N 81°41W 312 D3
Rodney, C. N.Z. 36°17S 174°50E 284 C3
Rodney B. St. Lucia 14°5N 60°58W 323 m
Rodniki Russia 57°7N 41°47E 190 B5
Rodolivos Greece 40°55N 24°0E 202 F7
Rodonit, Kepi i Albania 41°35N 19°27E 202 E3
Rodopi Greece 41°5N 25°30E 203 E9
Rodopi Planina Bulgaria 41°40N 24°20E 203 E8
Rodopos Greece 35°34N 23°45E 207 E4
Rødovre Denmark 55°40N 12°26E 118 A2
Rodrigo de Freitas, L.
Brazil 22°58S 43°12W 135 B1
Rodrigues Ind. Oc. 19°45S 63°20E 273 F5
Roe → U.K. 55°6N 6°59W 166 A5
Roebling U.S.A. 40°7N 74°47W 313 F10
Roebourne Australia 20°44S 117°9E 278 D2
Roebuck B. Australia 18°5S 122°20E 278 C3
Roebuck Roadhouse
Australia 17°59S 122°36E 278 C3
Roehampton U.K. 51°27N 0°15W 125 B2
Roermond Neths. 51°12N 6°0E 170 C6
Roes Welcome Sd. Canada 65°0N 87°0W 295 E14
Roeselare Belgium 50°57N 3°7E 170 D3
Rogachev = Ragachow
Belarus 53°8N 30°5E 177 B16
Rogačica Serbia 44°4N 19°40E 202 B3
Rogagua, L. Bolivia 13°43S 66°50W 330 C4
Rogaland □ Norway 59°12N 6°20E 164 E3
Rogaška Slatina Slovenia 46°15N 15°42E 199 B12
Rogatec Slovenia 46°15N 15°46E 199 B12
Rogatica Bos.-H. 43°47N 19°0E 182 G4
Rogatyn Ukraine 49°24N 24°36E 177 D13
Rogen Sweden 62°20N 12°20E 162 B6
Rogers U.S.A. 36°20N 94°7W 314 C7
Rogers Centre Toronto, Canada 141 c1
Rogers City U.S.A. 45°25N 83°49W 309 C12
Rogers Park U.S.A. 42°0N 87°40W 119 A3
Rogersville Canada 46°44N 65°26W 299 C6
Roggan → Canada 54°24N 79°25W 298 B4
Roggan L. Canada 54°8N 77°50W 298 B4
Roggeveen Basin
Pac. Oc. 31°30S 95°30W 289 L18
Roggeveldberge S. Africa 32°10S 20°10E 270 D3
Roggiano Gravina Italy 39°37N 16°9E 201 C9
Rogliano Haute-Corse,
France 42°57N 9°30E 175 F13
Rogliano Italy 39°10N 16°19E 201 C9
Rogoaguado, L. Bolivia 13°0S 65°30W 330 C4
Rogojampi Indonesia 8°19S 114°17E 231 J17
Rogoźno Poland 52°45N 16°59E 185 F3
Rogue → U.S.A. 42°26N 124°26W 304 E1
Roha India 18°26N 73°7E 244 E1
Rohan France 48°4N 2°45W 172 D4
Rohnert Park U.S.A. 38°16N 122°40W 306 G4
Rohri Pakistan 27°45N 68°51E 242 F3
Rohri Canal Pakistan 26°15N 68°27E 242 F3
Rohtak India 28°55N 76°43E 242 E7
Rohtisch-Sauerbrunn = Rogaška
Slatina Slovenia 46°15N 15°42E 199 B12
Roi Et Thailand 16°4N 103°40E 236 D4
Roi-Georges, Îs. du
French Polynesia 14°32S 145°8W 289 f
Roihuvuori Finland 60°11N 25°2E 121 B3
Roing India 28°9N 95°51E 241 A5
Roissy-en-Brie France 48°48N 2°39E 134 B4
Roja Latvia 57°29N 22°43E 184 A9
Rojas Argentina 34°10S 60°45W 334 C3
Rojište Romania 44°4N 23°56E 183 F8
Rojo, C. Mexico 21°33N 97°20W 319 C5
Rokan → Indonesia 2°0N 100°50E 234 B2
Rokel → S. Leone 8°30N 12°48W 262 D2
Rokin Amsterdam, Neths. 112 b2
Rokiškis Lithuania 55°55N 25°35E 188 E3
Rokua △ Finland 64°30N 26°15E 160 D22
Rokycany Czechia 49°43N 13°35E 180 B6
Rokytka → Czechia 50°6N 14°27E 135 B3
Roland Garros Paris, France 48°51N 2°15E 134 A2
Rolândia Brazil 23°18S 51°23W 335 A5
Røldal Norway 59°47N 6°50E 164 E3
Rolfe U.S.A. 42°49N 94°31W 310 B2
Rolla Mo., U.S.A. 37°57N 91°46W 310 G5
Rolla N. Dak., U.S.A. 48°52N 99°37W 308 A4
Rolleston Queens.,
Australia 24°28S 148°35E 280 C4
Rolleston N.Z. 43°35S 172°24E 285 D7
Rolling Fork → U.S.A. 37°55N 85°50W 311 G11
Rollingstone Australia 19°2S 146°24E 280 B4
Rom Vest-Agder, Norway 58°8N 7°5E 164 F4
Rom South Sudan 9°54N 32°16E 257 F3
Roma Queens., Australia 26°32S 148°49E 281 D4
Roma Italy 41°54N 12°28E 136 B1
Roma Sweden 57°32N 18°26E 163 G12
Roma, Piazzale Venice, Italy 142 b2
Roma Fiumicino ✈ (FCO)
Italy 41°48N 12°15E 199 G9
Roma-Los Saenz U.S.A. 26°24N 99°1W 314 H5
Roma Urbe ✈ Italy 41°57N 12°30E 136 B2
Római-Fürdő Hungary 47°34N 19°4E 117 A2
Romain, C. U.S.A. 33°0N 79°22W 315 E15
Romaine → Canada 50°18N 63°47W 299 B7
Romainville France 48°52N 2°26E 134 A3
Roman Bulgaria 43°8N 23°57E 202 C7
Roman Romania 46°57N 26°55E 183 D11
Roman Forum = Foro Romano
Rome, Italy 136 c3
Roman-Kosh, Gora
Ukraine 44°37N 34°15E 189 K8
Romanche → France 45°5N 5°43E 175 C9
Romang Indonesia 7°30S 127°20E 231 F7
Români Egypt 30°59N 32°38E 251 H3
Romania ■ Europe 46°0N 25°0E 183 D10
Romanija Bos.-H. 43°50N 18°45E 182 G3
Romano, C. U.S.A. 25°51N 81°41W 317 K8
Romano, Cayo Cuba 22°0N 77°30W 320 B4
Romano Banco Italy 45°25N 9°6E 128 B1
Romanov-Borisoglebsk = Tutayev
Russia 57°53N 39°32E 188 D10
Romanovka = Basarabeasca
Moldova 46°21N 28°58E 183 D13
Romanovna-Murmane =
Murmansk Russia 68°57N 33°10E 160 B25
Romanovsk = Kropotkin
Russia 45°28N 40°28E 191 H5
Romanovskiy Khutor = Kropotkin
Russia 45°28N 40°28E 191 H5
Romans-sur-Isère France 45°3N 5°3E 175 C9
Romanshorn Switz. 47°33N 9°22E 179 H5
Romanzof C. U.S.A. 61°49N 166°6W 303 F6
Rombari South Sudan 4°33N 31°2E 257 G3
Romblon Phil. 12°33N 122°17E 232 E4
Romblon □ Phil. 12°30N 122°15E 232 E4
Romblon Pass. Phil. 12°27N 122°12E 232 E4
Rome = Roma Italy 41°54N 12°28E 136 B1
Rome Ga., U.S.A. 34°15N 85°10W 315 D12
Rome N.Y., U.S.A. 43°13N 75°27W 313 C9
Rome Pa., U.S.A. 41°51N 76°21W 313 E8
Romema Israel 31°48N 35°12E 123 B2
Romeoville U.S.A. 41°39N 88°3W 311 C8
Rometta Italy 38°10N 15°25E 201 D8
Romford U.K. 51°34N 0°11E 125 A5
Romilly-sur-Seine France 48°31N 3°44E 173 D10
Romiton Uzbekistan 39°56N 64°23E 216 E6
Rommani Morocco 33°31N 6°40W 260 B3
Romney U.S.A. 39°21N 78°45W 309 F14
Romney Marsh U.K. 51°2N 0°54E 169 F8
Romny Ukraine 50°48N 33°28E 189 G7
Rømø Denmark 55°10N 8°30E 163 J2
Romodan Ukraine 49°55N 33°15E 189 G7
Romodanovo Russia 54°26N 45°23E 190 C7
Romont Switz. 46°42N 6°54E 179 J2
Romorantin-Lanthenay
France 47°21N 1°45E 173 E8
Rompin → Malaysia 2°49N 103°29E 237 L4
Romsdalen Norway 62°25N 7°52E 164 B4
Romsdalsfjorden Norway 62°38N 7°20E 164 B4
Romsey U.K. 51°0N 1°29W 169 G6
Ron India 15°40N 75°44E 245 G2
Ron Vietnam 17°53N 106°27E 236 D6
Rona U.K. 57°34N 5°59W 167 D3
Ronald Reagan Nat. Washington ✈
(DCA) U.S.A. 38°51N 77°2W 143 B2
Ronan U.S.A. 47°32N 114°6W 304 C6
Roncador, Cayos
Caribbean 13°32N 80°4W 320 D3
Roncador, Serra do
Brazil 12°30S 52°30W 333 D1
Ronciglione Italy 42°17N 12°13E 199 F9
Ronco → Italy 44°24N 12°12E 199 D9
Ronda Spain 36°46N 5°12W 195 J5
Ronda, Serranía de Spain 36°44N 5°3W 195 J5
Rondane Norway 61°57N 9°50E 164 C6
Rondane △ Norway 61°55N 9°44E 164 C6
Ronde, Pt. Dominica 15°33N 61°29W 323 k
Ronde I. Grenada 12°29N 61°36W 323 q
Rondebosch S. Africa 33°58S 18°28E 118 A1
Rondón Colombia 6°17N 71°6W 328 B3
Rondônia Brazil 10°52S 61°57W 331 C5
Rondônia □ Brazil 11°0S 63°0W 331 C5
Rondonópolis Brazil 16°28S 54°38W 331 D7
Rondslottet Norway 61°55N 9°45E 164 C6
Rondu Pakistan 35°32N 75°10E 243 B6
Rong, Koh Cambodia 10°45N 103°15E 237 G4
Rong Jiang → China 24°35N 109°20E 228 E7
Rong Xian China 22°50N 110°31E 229 F8
Rong'an China 25°14N 109°22E 228 E7
Rongchang China 29°20N 105°32E 228 C5
Rongcheng China 37°9N 122°23E 227 F12
Ronge, L. la Canada 55°6N 105°17W 297 B7
Rongjiang China 25°57N 108°28E 228 E7
Rongotea N.Z. 40°19S 175°25E 284 G4
Rongshui China 25°5N 109°12E 228 E7
Rongxian China 29°23N 104°22E 228 C5
Rønne Denmark 55°6N 14°43E 163 J8
Ronne Ice Shelf
Antarctica 77°30S 60°0W 151 D18
Ronneby Sweden 56°12N 15°17E 163 H9
Ronnebyån → Sweden 56°11N 15°18E 163 H9
Rönneshytta Sweden 58°56N 15°2E 163 F9
Ronsard, C. Australia 24°46S 113°10E 279 D1
Ronse Belgium 50°45N 3°35E 170 D3
Ronuro → Brazil 11°56S 53°33W 331 C7
Roodepoort S. Africa 26°11S 27°54E 271 C4
Roodhouse U.S.A. 39°29N 90°24W 310 E6
Roof Butte U.S.A. 36°28N 109°5W 305 H9
Rooiboklaagte → Namibia 20°50S 21°0E 270 B3
Rooniu, Mt. Tahiti 17°49S 149°12W 289 e
Roopville U.S.A. 33°27N 85°8W 316 B4
Roorkee India 29°52N 77°59E 242 E7
Roosendaal Neths. 51°32N 4°29E 170 C4
Roosevelt U.S.A. 40°18N 109°59W 304 F9
Roosevelt → Brazil 7°35S 60°20W 331 B5
Roosevelt, Mt. Canada 58°26N 125°20W 296 B3
Roosevelt I. Antarctica 79°30S 162°0W 151 D12
Roosevelt I. New York, U.S.A. 132 c3
Ropczyce Poland 50°4N 21°38E 185 H8
Roper → Australia 14°43S 135°27E 280 A2
Roper Bar Australia 14°44S 134°44E 280 A1
Roper River = St. Vidgeon's ✪
Australia 14°47S 134°53E 280 A1
Roppongi Tokyo, Japan 140 c3
Roque Pérez Argentina 35°25S 59°24W 334 D4
Roquefort France 44°2N 0°20W 174 D3
Roquemaure France 44°3N 4°48E 175 D8
Roquetas de Mar Spain 36°46N 2°36W 197 J2
Roquetes Spain 40°50N 0°30E 196 E5
Roquevaire France 43°20N 5°36E 175 E9
Roraima □ Brazil 2°0N 61°30W 329 C5
Roraima, Mt. Venezuela 5°10N 60°40W 329 B5
Røros Norway 62°35N 11°23E 164 B8
Rorschach Switz. 47°28N 9°28E 179 H5
Ros Comáin = Roscommon
Ireland 53°38N 8°11W 166 C3
Ros Mhic Thriúin = New Ross
Ireland 52°23N 6°57W 166 D5
Rosa Zambia 9°33S 31°15E 269 D3
Rosa, C. Algeria 37°0N 8°16E 261 A6
Rosa, C. Galápagos Is., Ecuador 1°4S 91°10W 330 a
Rosa, Monte Europe 45°57N 7°53E 198 C4
Rosais, Pta. dos Azores 38°45N 28°19W 153 d1
Rosal de la Frontera Spain 37°59N 7°13W 195 H3
Rosales Phil. 15°54N 120°38E 232 D3
Rosalia U.S.A. 47°14N 117°22W 304 C5
Rosalie Dominica 15°22N 61°16W 323 k
Rosalie → Dominica 15°22N 61°15W 323 k
Rosalind Bank Caribbean 16°30N 80°30W 320 C3
Rosamond U.S.A. 34°52N 118°10W 307 L8
Rosans France 44°24N 5°29E 175 D9
Rosario Argentina 33°0S 60°40W 334 C3
Rosário Maranhão, Brazil 3°0S 44°15W 332 B3
Rosario Sinaloa, Mexico 22°58N 105°53W 318 C3
Rosario Paraguay 24°30S 57°35W 334 A4
Rosario Agusan del S., Phil. 8°24N 125°59E 233 G5
Rosario Batangas, Phil. 13°50N 121°12E 232 E3
Rosario, Villa del
Venezuela 10°19N 72°19W 328 A3
Rosario de la Frontera
Argentina 25°50S 65°0W 334 B3
Rosario de Lerma
Argentina 24°59S 65°35W 334 A2
Rosario del Tala
Argentina 32°20S 59°10W 334 C4
Rosário do Sul Brazil 30°15S 54°55W 335 C5
Rosário Oeste Brazil 14°50S 56°25W 331 C6
Rosarito Baja Calif.,
Mexico 32°20N 117°2W 307 N9
Rosarito Baja Calif.,
Mexico 28°38N 114°1W 318 B2
Rosarno Italy 38°29N 15°58E 201 D8
Rosas = Roses Spain 42°19N 3°10E 196 C8
Roscoe Mo., U.S.A. 37°58N 93°48W 310 G3
Roscoe N.Y., U.S.A. 41°56N 74°55W 313 E10
Roscoff France 48°44N 3°58W 172 D3
Roscommon Ireland 53°38N 8°11W 166 C3
Roscommon □ Ireland 53°49N 8°23W 166 C3
Roscrea Ireland 52°57N 7°49W 166 D4
Rose → Australia 14°16S 135°45E 280 A2
Rose, L. The Bahamas 21°0N 73°30W 321 B5
Rose, L. Fla., U.S.A. 28°32N 81°30W 133 A1
Rose Belle Mauritius 20°24S 57°36E 272 e
Rose Blanche Canada 47°38N 58°45W 299 C8
Rose Bowl U.S.A. 34°9N 118°10W 126 B4
Rose Hall Great House
Jamaica 18°31N 77°49W 320 a
Rose Hill = Port Mourant
Guyana 6°15N 57°20W 329 B6
Rose Hill Mauritius 20°14S 57°27E 272 e
Rose Hill Va., U.S.A. 38°47N 77°6W 143 C2
Rose Pt. Canada 54°11N 131°39W 296 C2
Rose Rock Grenada 12°24N 61°28W 323 q
Rose Valley Canada 52°19N 103°49W 297 C8
Roseau Dominica 15°17N 61°24W 323 k
Roseau Minn., U.S.A. 48°51N 95°46W 308 A6
Rosebank Gauteng, S. Africa 26°8S 28°2E 123 a2
Rosebank N.Y., U.S.A. 40°36N 74°4W 132 C1
Rosebery N.S.W.,
Australia 33°55S 151°12E 139 B2
Rosebery Tas., Australia 41°46S 145°33E 281 G4
Rosebud Vic., Australia 38°21S 144°54E 282 E6
Rosebud S. Dak., U.S.A. 43°14N 100°51W 308 D3
Rosebud Tex., U.S.A. 31°4N 96°59W 314 F6
Roseburg U.S.A. 43°13N 123°20W 304 E2
Rosedal La Candelaria
Mexico 19°20N 99°10W 128 B2
Rosedale U.S.A. 33°51N 91°2W 315 E9
Rosehearty U.K. 57°42N 2°7W 167 D6
Roseires Res. Sudan 11°51N 34°23E 256 B3
Roseland Calif., U.S.A. 38°25N 122°43W 306 G4
Roseland Ill., U.S.A. 41°42N 87°37W 119 C3
Rosemary Canada 50°46N 112°5W 296 C6
Rosemead U.S.A. 34°4N 118°4W 126 B4
Rosemont Qué., Canada 45°34N 73°33W 130 A2
Rosemont Ill., U.S.A. 41°59N 87°53W 119 B1
Rosenberg = Olesno
Poland 50°51N 18°26E 185 H5
Rosenberg = Susz Poland 53°44N 19°20E 184 E6
Rosenberg U.S.A. 29°34N 95°49W 314 G7
Rosenborg Slot Copenhagen, Denmark 118 b2
Rosendaël France 51°3N 2°24E 173 A9
Rosendal Norway 59°59N 6°0E 164 E3
Rosendale U.S.A. 40°4N 94°51W 310 D2
Rosenheim Germany 47°51N 12°7E 179 H8
Rosenthal Germany 52°35N 13°22E 115 A3
Roses Spain 42°19N 3°10E 196 C8
Roses, G. de Spain 42°10N 3°15E 196 C8
Roseto degli Abruzzi Italy 42°41N 14°1E 199 F11
Rosetown Canada 51°35N 107°59W 297 C7
Rosetta = Rashîd Egypt 31°21N 30°22E 256 H7
Rosettenville S. Africa 26°15S 28°3E 123 B2
Roseville Calif., U.S.A. 38°45N 121°17W 306 G5
Roseville Ill., U.S.A. 40°44N 90°40W 310 D6
Roseville Mich., U.S.A. 42°30N 82°56W 312 D2
Roseville Pa., U.S.A. 41°51N 76°57W 313 E8
Rosewell U.K. 55°51N 3°8W 121 B3
Rosewood Australia 27°38S 152°36E 281 D5
Rosherville Dam S. Africa 26°13S 28°6E 123 B2
Roshkhvär Iran 34°58N 59°37E 247 C8
Rosières-en-Santerre
France 49°49N 2°42E 173 C9
Rosignano Marittimo
Italy 43°24N 10°28E 198 E7
Rosignol Guyana 6°15N 57°30W 329 B6
Roşiori de Vede Romania 44°9N 25°0E 183 F10
Rositsa Bulgaria 43°57N 27°57E 203 C11
Rositsa → Bulgaria 43°10N 25°30E 203 C9
Röslön Sweden 59°26N 18°0E 139 A2
Roskilde Denmark 55°38N 12°3E 163 J6
Roskovec Albania 40°44N 19°43E 202 F3
Roslags-Näsby Sweden 59°25N 18°2E 139 A2
Roslavl Russia 53°57N 32°55E 188 F7
Roslin U.K. 55°51N 3°11W 121 B3
Roslindale U.S.A. 42°17N 71°7W 116 B2
Rosmaninhal Portugal 39°44N 7°5W 194 F3
Rosmead S. Africa 31°29S 25°8E 270 D4
Røsnæs Denmark 55°44N 10°55E 163 J4
Rosny-sous-Bois France 48°52N 2°30E 134 A4
Rosolini Italy 36°49N 14°57E 201 F7
Rosporden France 47°57N 3°50W 172 E3
Ross Tas., Australia 42°2S 147°30E 281 G4
Ross N.Z. 42°53S 170°49E 285 C5
Ross Béthio Mauritania 16°15N 16°8W 262 B1
Ross Dependency
Antarctica 76°0S 170°0W 151 D12
Ross I. Antarctica 77°30S 168°0E 151 D11
Ross Ice Shelf Antarctica 80°0S 180°0E 151 E12
Ross L. U.S.A. 48°44N 121°4W 304 B3
Ross-on-Wye U.K. 51°54N 2°34W 169 F5
Ross River N. Terr.,
Australia 23°44S 134°30E 280 C1
Ross River Yukon,
Canada 62°30N 131°30W 296 A2
Ross Sea Antarctica 74°0S 178°0E 151 D11
Rossall Pt. U.K. 53°55N 3°3W 168 D4
Rossan Pt. Ireland 54°42N 8°47W 166 B3
Rossano Italy 39°36N 16°39E 201 C9
Rossburn Canada 50°40N 100°49W 297 C8
Rosseau Canada 45°16N 79°39W 312 A5
Rosseau, L. Canada 45°10N 79°35W 312 A5
Rössel = Reszel Poland 54°4N 21°10E 184 D8
Rossel I. Papua N. G. 11°21S 154°9E 286 F8
Rosses, The Ireland 55°2N 8°20W 166 A3
Rossford U.S.A. 41°36N 83°34W 311 C13
Rossignol, L. Canada 52°43N 73°40W 298 B5
Rossignol L. Canada 44°12N 65°10W 299 D6
Rossiya = Russia ■
Eurasia 62°0N 105°0E 215 C11
Rosskreppfjorden Norway 59°4N 7°10E 164 E4
Rossland Canada 49°6N 117°50W 296 D5
Rosslare Ireland 52°17N 6°24W 166 D5
Rosslare Europort = Rosslare
Harbour Ireland 52°15N 6°20W 166 D5
Rosslare Harbour Ireland 52°15N 6°20W 166 D5
Rosslau Germany 51°52N 12°15E 178 D8
Rosslyn U.S.A. 38°53N 77°4W 143 B2
Rossmore Canada 44°8N 77°23W 312 B7
Rosso Mauritania 16°40N 15°45W 262 B1
Rosso, C. France 42°13N 8°32E 175 F12
Rossosh Russia 50°15N 39°28E 189 G10
Røssvatnet Norway 65°45N 14°5E 160 D16
Rossville Ill., U.S.A. 40°23N 87°40W 311 D9
Rossville Ind., U.S.A. 40°25N 86°36W 311 D10
Røst Norway 67°32N 12°10E 160 C15
Rostaq = Ar Rustāq Oman 23°23N 57°26E 249 B7
Rostāq Afghan. 37°7N 69°49E 240 A3
Rosthern Canada 52°40N 106°20W 297 C7
Rostock Germany 54°5N 12°8E 178 A8
Rostov Don, Russia 47°15N 39°45E 189 J10
Rostov Yaroslavl, Russia 57°14N 39°25E 188 D10
Rostov □ Russia 48°50N 41°0E 191 F5
Rostrenen France 48°14N 3°21W 172 D3
Roswell Ga., U.S.A. 34°2N 84°22W 316 A5
Roswell N. Mex., U.S.A. 33°24N 104°32W 305 K11
Rosyth U.K. 56°2N 3°25W 121 A1
Rot-Front = Dobropole
Ukraine 48°25N 37°2E 189 H9
Rota N. Marianas 14°9N 145°12E 302 a
Rota Spain 36°37N 6°20W 195 J4
Rotan U.S.A. 32°51N 100°28W 314 E4
Rote Indonesia 10°50S 123°0E 231 F6
Rotenburg Hessen, Germany 50°59N 9°44E 178 E5
Rotenburg Niedersachsen,
Germany 53°6N 9°25E 178 B5
Roth Germany 49°15N 11°5E 179 F7
Rothaargebirge Germany 51°2N 8°13E 178 D4
Rothaargebirge △ Germany 51°0N 8°15E 178 E4
Rothenburg ob der Tauber
Germany 49°23N 10°11E 179 F6
Rother → U.K. 50°59N 0°45E 169 G8
Rothera Antarctica 67°34S 68°8W 151 C17
Rotherham U.K. 53°26N 1°20W 168 D6
Rotherhithe U.K. 51°29N 0°2W 125 B3
Rothes U.K. 57°32N 3°13W 167 D5
Rothesay N.B., Canada 45°23N 66°0W 299 C6
Rothesay Argyll & Bute, U.K. 55°50N 5°3W 167 F3
Rothneusiedl Austria 48°8N 16°23E 142 B2
Rothschild Germany 48°14N 11°27E 131 A1
Roti = Rote Indonesia 10°50S 123°0E 231 F6
Rotja, Pta. Spain 38°38N 1°35E 206 D2
Rotnes Norway 60°3N 10°51E 164 D7
Roto Australia 33°0S 145°30E 283 B6
Rotoehu, L. N.Z. 38°1S 176°32E 284 E5
Rotoiti, L. Bay of Plenty,
N.Z. 38°2S 176°26E 284 E5
Rotoiti, L. W. Coast, N.Z. 41°51S 172°49E 285 B7
Rotoma, L. N.Z. 38°2S 176°35E 284 E5
Rotondo, Mte. France 42°14N 9°8E 175 F13
Rotoroa, L. N.Z. 41°55S 172°39E 285 B7
Rotorua N.Z. 38°9S 176°16E 284 E5
Rotorua, L. N.Z. 38°5S 176°18E 284 E5
Rott → Germany 48°27N 13°25E 179 G9
Rottenburg Germany 48°28N 8°55E 179 G4
Rottenmann Austria 47°31N 14°22E 180 D7
Rotterdam Neths. 51°55N 4°30E 170 C4
Rotterdam N.Y., U.S.A. 42°48N 74°1W 313 D10
Rottne Sweden 57°1N 14°54E 163 G8
Rottnest I. Australia 32°0S 115°27E 279 F2
Rottumeroog Neths. 53°33N 6°34E 170 A6
Rottweil Germany 48°9N 8°37E 179 G4
Rotuma Fiji 12°25S 177°5E 277 C14
Roubaix France 50°40N 3°10E 173 B10
Rouche Island St. Lucia 13°57N 60°52W 323 m
Roudnice nad Labem
Czechia 50°25N 14°15E 180 A7
Rouen France 49°27N 1°4E 172 C8
Rouergue France 44°15N 2°0E 174 D5
Rouge Hill Canada 43°48N 79°6W 141 A4
Rough Ridge N.Z. 45°10S 169°55E 285 F4
Rouillac France 45°47N 0°4W 174 C3
Rouissat Algeria 31°55N 5°20E 261 B6
Rouleau Canada 50°10N 104°56W 297 C8
Roulers = Roeselare
Belgium 50°57N 3°7E 170 D3
Roulpmaulpma ✪
Australia 23°52S 133°0E 278 D5
Round Hill Jamaica 17°50N 77°23W 320 a
Round Hill St. Kitts & Nevis 17°11N 62°36W 322 d
Round I.
Hong Kong, China 22°13N 114°11E 122 B3
Round Mountain U.S.A. 38°43N 117°4W 304 G5
Round Mt. Australia 30°26S 152°16E 283 A10
Round Rock U.S.A. 30°31N 97°41W 314 F6
Roundhouse Park Toronto, Canada 141 c2
Roundup U.S.A. 46°27N 108°33W 304 C9
Roura Fr. Guiana 4°44N 52°20W 329 C7
Rousay U.K. 59°10N 3°2W 167 B5
Rouses Point U.S.A. 44°59N 73°22W 313 B11
Rouseville U.S.A. 41°28N 79°42W 312 E5
Rousse = Ruse Bulgaria 43°48N 25°59E 203 C9
Roussenski Lom △
Bulgaria 43°40N 26°10E 203 C10
Roussillac Swamp
Trin. & Tob. 10°14N 61°35W 323 t
Roussillon Isère, France 45°24N 4°49E 175 C8
Roussillon Pyrénées-Or.,
France 42°30N 2°35E 174 F6
Rouxville S. Africa 30°25S 26°50E 270 D4
Rouyn-Noranda Canada 48°20N 79°0W 298 C4
Rovaniemi Finland 66°29N 25°41E 160 C21
Rovato Italy 45°34N 10°0E 198 C7
Rovenki Ukraine 48°5N 39°21E 189 H10
Rovereto Italy 45°53N 11°3E 198 C8
Roverud Norway 60°15N 12°3E 164 D9
Rovigno = Rovinj Croatia 45°5N 13°40E 199 C10
Rovigo Italy 45°4N 11°47E 199 C8
Rovinj Croatia 45°5N 13°40E 199 C10
Rovira Colombia 4°15N 75°20W 328 C2
Rovno = Rivne Ukraine 50°40N 26°10E 177 C14
Rovnoye Russia 50°52N 46°3E 190 E8
Rovuma = Ruvuma →
Tanzania 10°29S 40°28E 269 E5
Row'ān Iran 35°8N 48°51E 247 C6
Rowena Australia 29°48S 148°55E 281 D4
Rowley I. Canada 69°6N 77°52W 295 D16
Rowley Shoals Australia 17°30S 119°0E 278 C2
Roxa Guinea-Biss. 11°15N 15°45W 262 C1
Roxas Capiz, Phil. 11°36N 122°49E 233 F4
Roxas Isabela, Phil. 17°8N 121°36E 232 C3
Roxas Mind. Or., Phil. 12°35N 121°31E 232 E3
Roxas Palawan, Phil. 10°20N 119°21E 233 F2
Roxboro U.S.A. 36°24N 78°59W 315 C15
Roxborough Trin. & Tob. 11°15N 60°35W 323 s
Roxburgh N.Z. 45°33S 169°19E 285 F4
Roxbury Mass., U.S.A. 42°19N 71°5W 116 B2
Roxbury N.Y., U.S.A. 42°17N 74°33W 313 D10
Roxbury Pa., U.S.A. 40°6N 77°39W 312 F7
Roxby Downs Australia 30°43S 136°46E 281 E2
Roxen Sweden 58°30N 15°40E 163 F9
Roxeth U.K. 51°33N 0°20W 125 A1
Roy Mont., U.S.A. 47°20N 108°58W 304 C9
Roy N. Mex., U.S.A. 35°57N 104°12W 305 J11
Roy Utah, U.S.A. 41°10N 112°2W 304 F7
Roy Hill Australia 22°41S 119°57E 278 D3
Roy Thomson Hall Toronto, Canada 141 b2
Royal △ Australia 34°5S 151°5E 283 C9
Royal Bardia △ Nepal 28°20N 81°20E 243 E9
Royal Botanic Gardens
Sydney, Australia 139 b2
Royal Botanic Gardens Edinburgh,
U.K. 55°58N 3°12W 121 B2
Royal Canal Ireland 53°30N 7°13W 166 C4
Royal Center U.S.A. 40°52N 86°30W 311 D10
Royal Chitawan △ Nepal 26°30N 84°30E 243 F11
Royal Exhibition Building
Australia 37°48S 144°58E 128 A1
Royal Geographical Society Is.
Canada 68°56N 100°15W 294 D11
Royal Leamington Spa
U.K. 52°18N 1°31W 169 E6
Royal Manas △ Bhutan 26°45N 90°50E 241 B3
Royal Natal △ S. Africa 28°43S 28°51E 271 C4
Royal Oak U.S.A. 42°30N 83°9W 311 B13
Royal Observatory U.K. 55°55N 3°12W 121 B2
Royal Palace = Koninklijk Paleis
Amsterdam, Neths. 112 a2
Royal Palace = Kungliga Slottet
Stockholm, Sweden 139 b2
Royal Palace = Palacio Real
Madrid, Spain 127 b1
Royal Palace = Palais Royal
Brussels, Belgium 116 b3
Royal Palace = Slottet Oslo, Norway 133 a1
Royal Palm Beach U.S.A. 26°42N 80°14W 317 J9
Royal Park Australia 37°46S 144°57E 128 A1
Royal Tunbridge Wells U.K. 51°7N 0°16E 169 F8
Royal Turf Club Bangkok, Thailand 113 b2
Royale, Isle U.S.A. 48°0N 88°54W 308 B9
Royalla Australia 35°30S 149°9E 283 C8
Royan France 45°37N 1°2W 174 C2
Roye France 49°42N 2°48E 173 C9
Röylä Finland 60°18N 24°42E 121 B1
Royston U.K. 52°3N 0°0 169 E7
Rožaj Montenegro 42°50N 20°11E 202 D4
Różan Poland 52°52N 21°25E 185 F8
Rozas, Portilleros de las
Spain 40°29N 3°49W 127 B1
Rozay-en-Brie France 48°41N 2°58E 173 D9
Rozdilna Ukraine 46°50N 30°2E 183 D15
Rozhnyativ Ukraine 48°56N 24°9E 183 B9
Rozhyshche Ukraine 50°54N 25°15E 177 C13
Rožmitál pod Třemšínem
Czechia 49°36N 13°53E 180 B6
Rožňava Slovakia 48°37N 20°35E 181 C13
Rozogi Poland 53°28N 21°19E 184 E8
Rozoy-sur-Serre France 49°40N 4°8E 173 C11
Roztoczański △ Poland 50°37N 23°0E 185 H10
Roztoky Czechia 50°9N 14°23E 135 B2
Rozzano Italy 45°22N 9°10E 128 B1
Rrëshen Albania 41°47N 19°49E 202 E3
Rrogozhine Albania 41°4N 19°50E 202 E3
Rtanj Serbia 43°45N 21°50E 202 C5
Rtem, O. er → Algeria 33°29N 5°38E 261 B6
Rtishchevo Russia 52°18N 43°46E 190 D6
Rúa = A Rúa Spain 42°24N 7°6W 194 C3
Ruacaná Namibia 17°27S 14°21E 265 F2
Ruaha △ Tanzania 7°41S 34°30E 268 D3
Ruahine Ra. N.Z. 39°55S 176°2E 284 F5
Ruamahanga → N.Z. 41°24S 175°8E 284 H4
Ruapehu N.Z. 39°17S 175°35E 284 F4
Ruapuke I. N.Z. 46°46S 168°31E 285 G3
Ruâq, W. → Egypt 30°0N 33°49E 251 J4
Ruatoria N.Z. 37°55S 178°20E 284 D7
Ruavatu Solomon Is. 9°26S 160°26E 287 M11
Ruawai N.Z. 36°8S 173°59E 284 C2
Rub' al Khālī Si. Arabia 19°0N 48°0E 249 C5
Rubeho Mts. Tanzania 6°50S 36°25E 268 D4
Rubezhnoye = Rubizhne
Ukraine 49°6N 38°25E 189 H10
Rubh a' Mhail U.K. 55°56N 6°8W 167 F2
Rubha Hunish U.K. 57°42N 6°20W 167 D2
Rubha Robhanais = Lewis, Butt of
U.K. 58°31N 6°16W 167 C2
Rubí Spain 41°29N 2°2E 196 D7
Rubi →
Dem. Rep. of the Congo 2°48N 23°54E 264 B4
Rubí → Barcelona, Spain 41°26N 2°0E 114 A1
Rubiataba Brazil 15°8S 49°48W 333 E2
Rubicon → U.S.A. 38°53N 121°4W 306 G5
Rubicone → Italy 44°8N 12°28E 199 D9
Rubik Albania 41°46N 19°47E 202 E3
Rubinéia Brazil 20°13S 51°2W 333 F1
Rubino Côte d'Ivoire 6°4N 4°18W 262 D4
Rubio Venezuela 7°43N 72°22W 328 B3
Rubizhne Ukraine 49°6N 38°25E 189 H10
Rubondo △ Tanzania 2°18S 31°58E 268 C3
Rubtsovsk Russia 51°30N 81°10E 217 B10
Ruby U.S.A. 64°45N 155°30W 303 D9
Ruby Beach = Jacksonville Beach
U.S.A. 30°17N 81°24W 316 E8
Ruby L. U.S.A. 40°10N 115°28W 304 F6
Ruby Mts. U.S.A. 40°30N 115°20W 304 F6
Rubyvale Australia 23°25S 147°42E 280 C4
Rucheng China 25°33N 113°38E 229 E9
Ruciane-Nida Poland 53°40N 21°32E 184 E8
Rūd Sar Iran 37°8N 50°18E 247 B6
Ruda Sweden 57°6N 16°7E 163 G10
Ruda Śląska Poland 50°16N 18°50E 185 H5
Rudall Australia 33°43S 136°17E 282 B2
Rudall → Australia 22°34S 122°13E 278 D3
Rudall River △ Australia 22°38S 122°30E 278 D3
Rūdbār Afghan. 30°9N 62°36E 240 C1
Rudbar Iran 36°48N 49°23E 247 B6
Rüdersdorf Germany 52°27N 13°47E 178 C9
Rudewa Tanzania 10°7S 34°40E 269 E3
Rudkøbing Denmark 54°56N 10°41E 163 K4
Rudky Ukraine 49°38N 23°29E 185 J10
Rudna Poland 51°30N 16°17E 185 G3
Rudnik Bulgaria 42°36N 27°30E 203 D11
Rudnik Poland 50°26N 22°15E 185 H9
Rudnik Serbia 44°7N 20°35E 202 B4
Rudnya Russia 54°55N 31°7E 188 E6
Rudnytsa Ukraine 48°16N 28°54E 183 B13
Rudnyy Kazakhstan 52°57N 63°7E 216 B6
Rudo Bos.-H. 43°41N 19°23E 182 G4
Rudolfa, Ostrov Russia 81°45N 58°30E 214 A6
Rudolfsheim Austria 48°12N 16°20E 142 A2
Rudolfshöhe Germany 52°37N 13°44E 115 A5
Rudolstadt Germany 50°44N 11°19E 178 E7
Rudong China 32°20N 121°12E 229 A13
Rudow Germany 52°24N 13°29E 115 B3
Rudozem Bulgaria 41°29N 24°51E 203 E8
Rudrapur India 28°59N 79°24E 243 E8
Rudyard U.S.A. 46°14N 84°36W 309 B11
Rue France 50°15N 1°40E 173 B8
Rueil-Malmaison France 48°52N 2°11E 134 A2
Ruenya → Africa 16°24S 33°48E 269 F3
Rufa'a Sudan 14°44N 33°22E 257 E3
Ruffin U.S.A. 33°0N 80°49W 316 B9
Ruffling Pt. Br. Virgin Is. 18°44N 64°27W 321 b
Rufiji → Tanzania 7°50S 39°15E 268 D4
Rufino Argentina 34°20S 62°50W 334 C3
Rufisque Senegal 14°40N 17°15W 262 C1
Rufunsa Zambia 15°4S 29°34E 269 F2
Rugao China 32°23N 120°31E 229 A13
Rugby Warks., U.K. 52°23N 1°16W 169 E6
Rugby N. Dak., U.S.A. 48°22N 100°0W 308 A4
Rügen Germany 54°22N 13°24E 178 A9
Rügen △ Germany 54°25N 13°25E 178 A9
Rugles France 48°50N 0°40E 172 D7
Ruhea Bangla. 26°10N 88°25E 241 B2
Ruhengeri Rwanda 1°30S 29°36E 268 C2
Ruhla Germany 50°54N 10°23E 178 E6
Ruhland Germany 51°27N 13°51E 178 D9
Ruhnu Estonia 57°48N 23°15E 184 A10
Ruhr → Germany 51°27N 6°43E 178 D2
Ruhuhu → Tanzania 10°31S 34°34E 269 E3
Rui Barbosa Brazil 12°18S 40°27W 333 D3
Rui'an China 27°47N 120°40E 229 D13
Ruichang China 29°40N 115°39E 229 C10
Ruidoso U.S.A. 33°20N 105°41W 305 K11
Ruifang = Juifang Taiwan 25°7N 121°48E 229 E13
Ruijin China 25°48N 116°0E 229 E10
Ruili China 24°6N 97°46E 241 D4
Ruiru Kenya 1°9S 36°58E 268 C4
Ruisbroek Belgium 50°47N 4°18E 116 B1
Ruislip U.K. 51°34N 0°24W 125 A1
Ruivo, Pico Madeira 32°45N 16°56W 153 c
Ruj Bulgaria 42°52N 22°34E 202 D6
Rujen N. Macedonia 42°9N 22°30E 202 D6
Rujm Tal'at al Jamā'ah
Jordan 30°24N 35°30E 251 H6
Ruk Pakistan 27°50N 68°42E 242 F3
Rukan-sho Japan 26°6N 127°32E 218 a2
Rukhla Pakistan 32°27N 71°57E 242 C4
Rukumkot Nepal 28°37N 82°37E 243 E10
Rukwa □ Tanzania 7°0S 31°30E 268 D3
Rukwa, L. Tanzania 8°0S 32°20E 268 D3
Rulenge Burundi 2°43S 30°37E 268 C3
Rulhieres, C. Australia 13°56S 127°22E 278 B4
Rum Jordan 29°39N 35°26E 251 J6
Rum Highl., U.K. 57°0N 6°20W 167 E2
Rum Cay The Bahamas 23°40N 74°58W 321 B5
Rum Jungle Australia 13°0S 130°59E 278 B5
Ruma Serbia 45°0N 19°50E 182 E4
Ruma △ Kenya 0°39S 34°18E 268 C3
Rumāh Si. Arabia 25°29N 47°10E 246 E5
Rumah Kulit Malaysia 2°9N 114°4E 235 B4
Rumania = Romania ■
Europe 46°0N 25°0E 183 D10
Rumaylah Iraq 30°47N 47°37E 246 D5
Rumaylah, 'Urūq ar
Si. Arabia 22°0N 48°30E 249 B5
Rumbek South Sudan 6°54N 29°37E 257 F2
Rumburk Czechia 50°57N 14°32E 180 A7
Rumelihisarı Turkey 41°4N 29°1E 122 A2
Rumford U.S.A. 44°33N 70°33W 313 B14
Rumia Poland 54°37N 18°25E 184 D5
Rumilly France 45°53N 5°56E 175 C9
Rummelsburg = Miastko
Poland 54°0N 16°58E 184 E3
Rumoi Japan 43°56N 141°39E 220 C10
Rumonge Burundi 3°59S 29°26E 268 C2
Rumphi Malawi 11°1S 33°52E 269 E3
Rumson U.S.A. 40°23N 74°0W 313 F11
Rumung Micronesia 9°37N 138°9E 287 R16
Rumuruti Kenya 0°17N 36°32E 268 B4
Runan China 33°0N 114°30E 229 A10
Runanga N.Z. 42°25S 171°15E 285 C6
Runaway, C. N.Z. 37°32S 177°59E 284 D6
Runaway B. Antigua & B. 17°9N 61°51W 322 b
Runaway Bay Jamaica 18°27N 77°20W 320 a
Runcorn U.K. 53°21N 2°44W 168 D5
Rundu Namibia 17°52S 19°43E 270 A2
Rungis France 48°44N 2°20E 134 B3
Rungwa Tanzania 6°55S 33°32E 268 D3
Rungwa → Tanzania 7°36S 31°50E 268 D3
Rungwa ⌓ Tanzania 6°53S 34°2E 268 D3
Rungwe Tanzania 9°11S 33°32E 269 D3
Runka Nigeria 12°28N 7°20E 263 C6
Runn Sweden 60°30N 15°40E 162 D9
Runton Ra. Australia 23°31S 123°6E 278 D3
Runu Micronesia 9°35N 138°8E 287 R16
Ruo Shui → China 41°0N 100°16E 218 C9
Ruokolahti Finland 61°17N 28°50E 188 B5
Ruoqiang China 38°55N 88°10E 217 E11
Rupa India 27°15N 92°21E 241 B4
Rupar India 31°2N 76°38E 242 D7
Rupat Indonesia 1°45N 101°40E 234 B2
Rupea Romania 46°2N 25°13E 183 D10
Rupen → India 23°28N 71°31E 242 H4
Rupert U.S.A. 42°37N 113°41W 304 E7
Rupert → Canada 51°29N 78°45W 298 B4
Rupert B. Canada 51°35N 79°0W 298 B4
Rupert House = Waskaganish
Canada 51°30N 78°40W 298 B4
Rupnagar = Rupar India 31°2N 76°38E 242 D7
Rupsa India 21°37N 87°1E 243 J12
Rupununi → Guyana 4°3N 58°35W 329 C6
Rur → Germany 51°11N 5°59E 178 D1
Rurópolis Brazil 4°3S 54°59W 329 D7
Rurrenabaque Bolivia 14°30S 67°32W 330 C4
Rurutu French Polynesia 22°26S 151°20W 289 f
Rus → Spain 39°30N 2°30W 197 F2
Rusāfa Iraq 33°21N 44°23E 113 A2
Rusambo Zimbabwe 16°30S 32°4E 269 F3
Rusape Zimbabwe 18°35S 32°8E 269 F3
Ruschuk = Ruse Bulgaria 43°48N 25°59E 203 C9
Ruse Bulgaria 43°48N 25°59E 203 C9
Ruse □ Bulgaria 43°35N 25°40E 203 C9
Ruşeţu Romania 44°57N 27°14E 183 F12
Rush Ireland 53°31N 6°6W 166 C5
Rush Green U.K. 51°33N 0°10E 125 A5
Rushan China 36°56N 121°30E 227 F11
Rushden U.K. 52°18N 0°35W 169 E7
Rushikulya → India 19°23N 85°5E 244 E7
Rushmore, Mt. U.S.A. 43°53N 103°28W 308 D2
Rushville Ill., U.S.A. 40°7N 90°34W 310 D6
Rushville Ind., U.S.A. 39°37N 85°27W 311 E11
Rushville Nebr., U.S.A. 42°43N 102°28W 308 D2
Rushworth Australia 36°32S 145°1E 283 D6
Ruskin U.S.A. 27°43N 82°26W 317 H7
Russa India 22°29N 88°21E 124 B2
Russas Brazil 4°55S 37°50W 332 B4
Russell Man., Canada 50°50N 101°20W 297 C8
Russell N.Z. 35°16S 174°10E 284 B3
Russell Fla., U.S.A. 30°3N 81°45W 316 E8
Russell Kans., U.S.A. 38°54N 98°52W 308 F4
Russell N.Y., U.S.A. 44°27N 75°9W 313 B9
Russell Pa., U.S.A. 41°56N 79°8W 312 E5
Russell Cave ⌓ U.S.A. 34°59N 85°49W 315 D12
Russell I. Solomon Is. 9°4S 159°12E 287 M10
Russell L. Man., Canada 56°15N 101°30W 297 B8
Russell L. N.W.T., Canada 63°5N 115°44W 296 A5
Russellkonda India 19°57N 84°42E 244 E7
Russells Point U.S.A. 40°28N 83°54W 311 D13
Russellville Ala., U.S.A. 34°30N 87°44W 315 D11
Russellville Ark., U.S.A. 35°17N 93°8W 314 D8
Russellville Ky., U.S.A. 36°51N 86°53W 308 G10
Rüsselsheim Germany 49°59N 8°23E 179 F4
Russi Italy 44°22N 12°2E 199 D9
Russia ■ Eurasia 62°0N 105°0E 215 C11
Russian → U.S.A. 38°27N 123°8W 306 G3
Russian Hill San Francisco, U.S.A. 136 a1
Russian Mission U.S.A. 61°47N 161°19W 303 F7
Russiaville U.S.A. 40°25N 86°16W 311 D10
Russkaya Arktika △
Russia 73°40N 55°55E 214 B6
Russkiy, Ostrov Russia 43°0N 131°50E 220 C5
Russky Sever △ Russia 59°57N 38°34E 188 B10
Rust Austria 47°49N 16°42E 181 D9
Rustam Shahr Pakistan 26°58N 66°6E 242 F2
Rustavi Georgia 41°30N 45°0E 191 K7
Rustenburg S. Africa 25°41S 27°14E 270 C4
Ruston U.S.A. 32°32N 92°38W 314 E8
Rutana Burundi 3°55S 30°0E 268 C3
Rute Spain 37°19N 4°23W 195 H6
Ruteng Indonesia 8°35S 120°30E 231 F6
Rutenga Zimbabwe 21°15S 30°44E 269 G3
Ruth U.S.A. 43°42N 82°45W 312 C2
Rutherford Calif., U.S.A. 38°26N 122°24W 306 G4
Rutherford N.J., U.S.A. 40°49N 74°6W 132 B1
Rutherglen Australia 36°5S 146°29E 283 D7
Rutland U.S.A. 43°37N 72°58W 313 C12
Rutland □ U.K. 52°38N 0°40W 169 E7
Rutland I. India 11°25N 92°10E 245 J11
Rutland Water U.K. 52°39N 0°38W 169 E7
Rutledalen Norway 61°4N 5°10E 164 C2
Rutledge U.S.A. 33°38N 83°37W 316 B6
Rutledge → Canada 61°4N 112°0W 297 A6
Rutledge L. Canada 61°33N 110°47W 297 A6
Rutog China 33°27N 79°42E 217 F9
Rutqa, W. → Syria 34°30N 41°3E 213 E9
Rutshuru
Dem. Rep. of the Congo 1°13S 29°25E 268 C2
Ruvo di Púglia Italy 41°7N 16°29E 201 A9
Ruvu Tanzania 6°49S 38°43E 268 D4
Ruvu → Tanzania 6°23S 38°52E 268 D4
Ruvuba △ Burundi 3°3S 29°33E 268 C2
Ruvuma □ Tanzania 10°20S 36°0E 269 E4
Ruvuma → Tanzania 10°29S 40°28E 269 E5
Ruwais U.A.E. 24°5N 52°50E 247 E7
Ruwenzori Africa 0°30N 29°55E 268 B2
Ruwenzori △ Uganda 0°20N 30°0E 268 B2
Ruya → Zimbabwe 16°27S 32°5E 271 A5
Ruyang China 34°9N 112°27E 226 G7
Ruyigi Burundi 3°29S 30°15E 268 C3
Ruyuan China 24°46N 113°16E 229 E9
Rūzaevka Kazakhstan 52°49N 66°59E 217 B7
Ruzayevka Russia 54°4N 45°0E 190 C7
Růžhevo Konare = Razhevo Konare
Bulgaria 42°23N 24°46E 203 D8
Ruzhou China 34°11N 112°52E 226 G7
Ružomberok Slovakia 49°3N 19°17E 181 B12
Ruzyně, Praha ✈ (PRG)
Czechia 50°6N 14°16E 135 B1
Rwanda ■ Africa 2°0S 30°0E 268 C3
Ryakhovo Bulgaria 43°58N 26°18E 203 C10
Ryan, L. U.K. 55°0N 5°2W 167 G3
Ryazan Russia 54°40N 39°40E 188 E10
Ryazan □ Russia 54°5N 39°30E 190 C4
Ryazhsk Russia 53°45N 40°3E 188 F11
Rybachiy Russia 55°10N 20°50E 184 C7
Rybachiy Poluostrov
Russia 69°43N 32°0E 160 B25
Rybachye = Balykchy
Kyrgyzstan 42°26N 76°12E 217 D9
Rybatskaya Russia 59°50N 30°29E 137 B2
Rybinsk Russia 58°5N 38°50E 188 C10
Rybinskoye Vdkhr.
Russia 58°30N 38°25E 188 C10
Rybnik Poland 50°6N 18°32E 185 H5
Rybnitsa = Rîbnița
Moldova 47°45N 29°0E 183 C14
Rybnoye Russia 54°45N 39°30E 188 E10
Rychnov nad Kněžnou
Czechia 50°10N 16°17E 181 A9
Rychwał Poland 52°4N 18°10E 185 F5
Rycroft Canada 55°45N 118°40W 296 B5
Ryd Sweden 56°27N 14°42E 163 H8
Rydaholm Sweden 56°59N 14°18E 163 H8
Rydboholm Sweden 59°26N 18°12E 139 A3
Ryde N.S.W., Australia 33°48S 151°6E 139 A1

Ryde I. of W., U.K. 50°43N 1°9W 169 G6
Ryderwood U.S.A. 46°23N 123°3W 306 D3
Rydzyna Poland 51°47N 16°39E 185 G3
Rye U.K. 50°57N 0°45E 169 G8
Rye → U.K. 54°11N 0°44W 168 C7
Rye Bay U.K. 50°52N 0°49E 169 G8
Rye Patch Res. U.S.A. 40°28N 118°19W 304 F4
Ryegate U.S.A. 46°18N 109°15W 304 C9
Ryerson University Toronto, Canada 141 a3
Ryfylke Norway 59°25N 6°25E 164 E3
Rykene Norway 58°24N 8°37E 164 F5
Ryki Poland 51°38N 21°56E 185 G8
Rykovo = Yenakiyeve Ukraine 48°15N 38°15E 189 H10
Ryley Canada 53°17N 112°26W 296 C6
Rylsk Russia 51°36N 34°43E 189 G8
Rylstone Australia 32°46S 149°58E 283 B8
Rymanów Poland 49°35N 21°51E 185 J8
Ryn Poland 53°57N 21°34E 184 E8
Ryn Peski = Naryn Qum Kazakhstan 47°30N 49°0E 191 G9
Ryogoku Japan 35°40N 139°48E 140 A3
Ryōhaku-Sanchi Japan 36°9N 136°49E 223 A8
Ryojun = Lüshun China 38°45N 121°15E 227 E11
Ryōtsu Japan 38°5N 138°26E 220 E9
Rypin Poland 53°3N 19°25E 185 E6
Ryssby Sweden 56°52N 14°10E 163 H8
Rysy Europe 49°10N 20°4E 181 B13
Ryūgasaki Japan 35°54N 140°11E 223 B12
Ryukyu Is. = Ryūkyū-Rettō Japan 26°0N 126°0E 221 M3
Ryūkyū-Rettō Japan 26°0N 126°0E 221 M3
Ryūō = Kai Japan 35°42N 138°30E 223 B10
Rzepin Poland 52°20N 14°49E 185 F1
Rzeszów Poland 50°5N 21°58E 185 H8
Rzhev Russia 56°20N 34°20E 188 D8
Rzhevka Russia 59°59N 30°31E 137 B3

S

S.I.B.D. = Songdo S. Korea 37°23N 126°39E 224 D3
Sa Cabaneta Spain 39°37N 2°45E 206 B3
Sa Canal Spain 38°51N 1°23E 206 D1
Sa Conillera Spain 38°59N 1°13E 206 D1
Sa Dec Vietnam 10°20N 105°46E 237 G5
Sa Dragonera Spain 39°35N 2°19E 206 B3
Sa Kaeo Thailand 13°49N 102°4E 236 F4
Sa-koi Myanmar 19°54N 97°3E 241 F6
Sa Mesquida Spain 39°55N 4°16E 206 B5
Sa Pa Vietnam 22°20N 103°47E 236 A4
Sa Pobla Spain 39°46N 3°1E 206 B4
Sa Savina Spain 38°44N 1°25E 206 C1
Sa'a Solomon Is. 9°43S 161°35E 287 M11
Sa'ādat Shahr Iran 30°10N 53°5E 247 D7
Sa'ādatābād Hormozgān, Iran 28°3N 55°53E 247 D7
Sa'ādatābād Kermān, Iran 29°40N 55°51E 247 D7
Sa'ādatābād Tehrān, Iran 35°47N 51°22E 141 A2
Saadūn Iraq 33°19N 44°25E 113 B2
Saale → Germany 51°56N 11°54E 178 D7
Saaler Bodden Germany 54°20N 12°27E 178 A8
Saalfeld Germany 50°38N 11°21E 178 E7
Saalfelden Austria 47°25N 12°51E 180 D5
Saane → Switz. 47°8N 7°10E 179 H3
Saanich Canada 48°29N 123°26W 306 B3
Saar → Europe 49°41N 6°32E 170 E6
Saar-Hunsrück △ Germany 49°30N 6°50E 179 F2
Saar in Mähren = Žďár nad Sázavou Czechia 49°34N 15°57E 180 B8
Saarbrücken Germany 49°14N 6°59E 179 F2
Saarburg Germany 49°36N 6°32E 179 F2
Saaremaa Estonia 58°30N 22°30E 188 C2
Saarijärvi Finland 62°43N 25°16E 160 E21
Saarland □ Germany 49°20N 7°0E 179 F2
Saarlautern = Saarlouis Germany 49°18N 6°45E 179 F2
Saarlouis Germany 49°18N 6°45E 179 F2
Saatlı Azerbaijan 39°55N 48°22E 213 C13
Saavedra Argentina 37°45S 62°29W 117 B2
Saaz = Žatec Czechia 50°20N 13°32E 180 A6
Sab 'Ābar Syria 33°46N 37°41E 212 F7
Saba W. Indies 17°38N 63°14W 322 a
Šabac Serbia 44°48N 19°42E 202 B3
Sabadell Spain 41°28N 2°7E 196 D7
Sabae Japan 35°57N 136°11E 223 B8
Sabah □ Malaysia 6°0N 117°0E 235 A5
Şabāḩ, Wadi → Si. Arabia 23°50N 48°30E 249 B5
Sabak Bernam Malaysia 3°46N 100°58E 237 L3
Sabalān, Kūhhā-ye Iran 38°15N 47°45E 213 C12
Sabalana, Kepulauan Indonesia 6°45S 118°50E 231 F5
Sabalana, Kepuluauan Indonesia 6°45S 118°49E 235 D5
Sabana, Arch. de Cuba 23°0N 80°0W 320 B3
Sabana de la Mar Dom. Rep. 19°7N 69°24W 321 C6
Sabana Grande Puerto Rico 18°5N 66°58W 321 b
Sabana Westpunt = Westpunt Curaçao 12°22N 69°10W 322 g
Sábanalarga Colombia 10°38N 74°55W 328 A3
Sabaneta Pt. N. Marianas 15°17N 145°49E 302 e
Sabang Indonesia 5°50N 95°15E 234 A1
Şabanözü Turkey 40°28N 33°16E 212 B5
Săbăoani Romania 47°1N 26°51E 183 C11
Sabari → India 17°35N 81°16E 244 F5
Sabarmati → India 22°18N 72°22E 242 H5
Sab'atayn, Ramlat as Yemen 15°30N 46°10E 248 D4
Sabattis U.S.A. 44°6N 74°40W 313 B10
Sabáudia Italy 41°18N 13°1E 200 A6
Sabaya Bolivia 19°1S 68°23W 330 D4
Şābāyā, Jaza'ir Si. Arabia 18°35N 41°3E 248 C3
Saberania Indonesia 2°5S 138°18E 231 E9
Sabhā Libya 27°9N 14°29E 258 C2
Sabhar Bangla. 23°50N 90°15E 241 D3
Sabi → India 28°29N 76°44E 242 E7
Sabi Game Reserve = Kruger △ S. Africa 24°50S 26°10E 271 B4
Sabidana, J. Sudan 18°4N 36°50E 256 D4
Sabie S. Africa 25°10S 30°48E 271 C5
Sabina U.S.A. 39°29N 83°38W 311 E13
Sabinal U.S.A. 29°19N 99°28W 314 G5
Sabiñánigo Spain 42°31N 0°22W 196 C4
Sabinar, Punta del Spain 36°43N 2°44W 197 J2
Sabinas Mexico 27°51N 101°7W 318 B4
Sabinas → Mexico 27°37N 100°42W 318 B4
Sabinas Hidalgo Mexico 26°30N 100°10W 318 B4
Sabine → U.S.A. 29°59N 93°47W 314 G8
Sabine L. U.S.A. 29°53N 93°51W 314 G8
Sabine Pass U.S.A. 29°44N 93°54W 314 G8
Sabinópolis Brazil 18°40S 43°6W 333 E3
Sabinov Slovakia 49°6N 21°5E 181 B14
Sabirabad Azerbaijan 40°5N 48°30E 191 K9
Sabka Chad 19°15N 16°35E 259 E3
Sablayan Phil. 12°50N 120°50E 232 E3
Sable Canada 55°30N 68°21W 299 A6
Sable, C. N.S., Canada 43°29N 65°38W 299 D6
Sable, C. Fla., U.S.A. 25°9N 81°8W 317 K8
Sable I. N.S., Canada 44°0N 60°0W 299 D8
Sable I. Papua N. G. 3°38S 154°42E 286 B8
Sablé-sur-Sarthe France 47°50N 0°20W 172 E6
Saboeiro Brazil 6°32S 39°54W 332 C4
Saboli India 28°42N 77°18E 129 A2
Sabonkafi Niger 14°40N 8°45E 259 F1
Sabor → Portugal 41°10N 7°7W 194 D3
Sabou Burkina Faso 12°1N 2°15W 262 C4
Sabres France 44°9N 0°43W 174 D3
Sabrina Coast Antarctica 68°0S 120°0E 151 C9
Sabtang I. Phil. 20°19N 121°52E 232 A3
Sabugal Portugal 40°20N 7°5W 194 E3
Sabugo Portugal 38°49N 9°17W 126 A1
Sabula U.S.A. 42°4N 90°10W 310 B6
Sabulubek Indonesia 1°36S 98°40E 234 C1
Sabuncu Turkey 39°33N 30°12E 205 B12
Şabyā Si. Arabia 17°9N 42°37E 248 C3
Sabzevār Iran 36°15N 57°40E 247 B8
Sabzi Mand India 28°40N 77°12E 120 A2
Sabzvārān = Jiroft Iran 28°45N 57°50E 247 D8
Sac City U.S.A. 42°25N 95°0W 310 B2
Sacaba Bolivia 17°24S 66°2W 331 D4
Sacaolo Angola 12°58S 22°28E 265 E4
Sacatengo Angola 13°16S 21°20E 265 E4
Sacavém Portugal 38°47N 9°5W 126 A2
Sacca Fisola Venice, Italy 142 c1
Sacca San Biágio Venice, Italy 142 c1
Sacedón Spain 40°29N 2°41W 196 E2
Săcele Romania 45°37N 25°41E 183 E10
Sacheon S. Korea 35°0N 128°6E 224 E4
Sachigo → Canada 55°6N 88°58W 298 A2
Sachigo, L. Canada 53°50N 92°12W 298 B1
Sachimbo Angola 9°14S 20°16E 265 D4
Sachin India 21°5N 72°53E 244 D1
Sachkhere Georgia 42°25N 43°28E 191 J6
Sachsen □ Germany 50°55N 13°10E 178 E9
Sachsen-Anhalt □ Germany 52°0N 12°0E 178 D7
Sächsische Schweiz △ Germany 50°55N 14°10E 178 E10
Sacile Italy 45°57N 12°30E 199 C9
Sackets Harbor U.S.A. 43°57N 76°7W 313 C8
Sackville Canada 45°54N 64°22W 299 C7
Saclay France 48°43N 2°10E 134 B2
Saclay, Étang de France 48°44N 2°9E 134 B1
Saco Maine, U.S.A. 43°30N 70°27W 313 C14
Saco Mont., U.S.A. 48°28N 107°21W 304 B10
Sacol I. Phil. 6°58N 122°13E 233 H4
Sacomã Brazil 23°36S 46°35W 137 B2
Sacramento = Itatupã Brazil 0°37S 51°12W 329 D7
Sacramento Brazil 19°53S 47°27W 333 E2
Sacramento Calif., U.S.A. 38°35N 121°29W 306 G5
Sacramento → U.S.A. 38°3N 121°56W 306 G5
Sacramento Mts. U.S.A. 32°30N 105°30W 305 K11
Sacramento Valley U.S.A. 39°30N 122°0W 306 G5
Sacratif, C. Spain 36°42N 3°28W 195 J7
Sacré Cœur Paris, France 134 a4
Sacrow Germany 52°25N 13°6E 115 B1
Sacrower See Germany 52°26N 13°6E 115 B1
Săcueni Romania 47°20N 22°5E 182 C7
Sada Mayotte 12°51S 45°6E 272 b
Sada Spain 43°22N 8°15W 194 B2
Sada-Misaki Japan 33°20N 132°5E 222 D4
Sada-Misaki-Hantō Japan 33°22N 132°1E 222 D4
Sádaba Spain 42°19N 1°12W 196 C3
Sadabad India 27°27N 78°3E 242 F8
Şa'dah Yemen 16°15N 43°37E 248 C3
Şa'dah □ Yemen 16°15N 43°37E 248 C3
Sadang S. Korea 37°29N 126°58E 137 C1
Sadani Tanzania 5°58S 38°35E 268 D4
Sadani △ Tanzania 6°3S 38°47E 268 D4
Sadao Thailand 6°38N 100°26E 237 J3
Sadar Bazar Delhi, India 120 a1
Sadaseopet India 17°38N 77°59E 244 F3
Sadd el Aali Egypt 23°54N 32°54E 256 C3
Saddle → U.S.A. 40°51N 74°6W 132 A1
Saddle Brook U.S.A. 40°53N 74°5W 132 A1
Saddle Hill St. Kitts & Nevis 17°7N 62°33W 322 d
Saddle Mt. U.S.A. 45°58N 123°41W 306 E3
Saddle Pk. India 13°9N 93°1E 245 H11
Saddle Pt. St. Helena 15°57S 5°38W 153 h
Sade Nigeria 11°22N 10°45E 263 C7
Şadḩ Oman 17°3N 55°4E 249 C6
Sadhoowa Trin. & Tob. 10°8N 61°27W 323 t
Sadimi Dem. Rep. of the Congo 9°25S 23°32E 265 D4
Sadiola Mali 13°50N 11°40W 262 C2
Sadiya India 27°50N 95°40E 241 B5
Sa'dīyah, Hawr as Iraq 32°15N 46°30E 213 F12
Sadlers St. Kitts & Nevis 17°24N 62°47W 322 d
Sado Japan 38°0N 138°25E 220 F9
Sado → Portugal 38°29N 8°55W 195 G2
Sadon Russia 42°52N 43°58E 191 J6
Sadovoye Russia 47°47N 44°31E 191 G7
Sadowara Japan 32°2N 131°26E 222 E3
Sadr Pakistan 24°51N 67°2E 123 A2
Sadr City Iraq 33°23N 44°27E 113 A2
Sadra India 23°21N 72°43E 242 H5
Sadrazamköy = Liveras Cyprus 35°23N 32°57E 207 E8
Sadri India 25°11N 73°26E 242 G5
Sadyba Poland 52°11N 21°3E 143 B2
Sæbøvik Norway 59°47N 5°40E 164 E2
Sæby Denmark 57°21N 10°30E 163 G4
Saedinenie Bulgaria 42°16N 24°33E 203 D8
Saegertown U.S.A. 41°43N 80°9W 312 E4
Saelices Spain 39°55N 2°49W 196 F2
Sætre Norway 59°41N 10°33E 164 E7
Sævareid Norway 60°11N 5°46E 164 D2
Safaalan Turkey 41°26N 28°6E 203 E12
Şafājah Si. Arabia 26°25N 39°0E 246 E3
Šafárikovo = Tornal'a Slovakia 48°25N 20°20E 181 C13
Safata B. Samoa 14°0S 171°50W 287 W20
Safdar Jang's Tomb India 28°35N 77°12E 120 B2
Safed Koh Afghan. 34°0N 70°0E 240 B3
Säffle Sweden 59°8N 12°55E 162 E6
Safford U.S.A. 32°50N 109°43W 305 K9
Saffron Walden U.K. 52°1N 0°16E 169 E8
Safi Morocco 32°18N 9°20W 260 B3
Safia Papua N. G. 9°35S 148°38E 286 E5
Safia, Hamada Mali 23°10N 4°15W 260 D4
Şafīdābād Iran 36°45N 57°58E 247 B8
Safīd Dasht Iran 33°27N 48°11E 247 C6
Safīd Kūh Afghan. 34°45N 63°0E 240 B1
Safīd Rūd → Iran 37°23N 50°11E 247 B6
Safipur India 26°44N 80°21E 243 F9
Şāfītā Syria 34°48N 36°7E 250 D7
Safonovo Russia 55°4N 33°16E 188 E7
Safranbolu Turkey 41°15N 32°41E 212 B5
Saft el Laban Egypt 30°1N 31°10E 117 A2
Saft Rashîn Egypt 28°58N 30°55E 256 J7
Safune Samoa 13°25S 172°21W 287 V19
Safwān Iraq 30°7N 47°43E 246 D5
Sag Harbor U.S.A. 41°0N 72°18W 313 F12
Sag Sag Papua N. G. 5°32S 148°23E 286 C5
Saga Kōchi, Japan 33°5N 133°6E 222 D5
Saga Saga, Japan 33°15N 130°16E 222 D2
Saga □ Japan 33°15N 130°20E 222 D2
Sagae Japan 38°22N 140°17E 220 E10
Sagaing Myanmar 21°52N 95°59E 241 E5
Sagaing □ Myanmar 23°55N 95°56E 241 D5
Sagala Mali 14°9N 6°38W 262 C3
Sagami-Nada Japan 34°58N 139°30E 223 C11
Sagami-Wan Japan 35°15N 139°25E 223 B11
Sagamihara Japan 35°33N 139°25E 223 B11
Sagamore U.S.A. 40°46N 79°14W 312 F5
Sagan = Żagań Poland 51°39N 15°22E 185 G2
Saganaga L. Canada 48°14N 90°52W 308 A8
Saganoseki Japan 33°15N 131°53E 222 D3
Saganthit Kyun Myanmar 11°56N 98°29E 237 G2
Sagar Karnataka, India 16°38N 76°48E 244 F3
Sagar Karnataka, India 14°14N 75°6E 245 G2
Sagar Mad. P., India 23°50N 78°44E 243 H8
Sagara Japan 34°41N 138°12E 223 C10
Sagara, L. Tanzania 5°20S 31°0E 268 D3
Sagarejo Georgia 41°44N 45°19E 191 K7
Sagarmatha = Everest, Mt. Nepal 28°5N 86°58E 243 E12
Sagarmatha △ Nepal 27°55N 86°45E 243 F12
Sagavanirktok → U.S.A. 70°19N 147°53W 303 A11
Sagay Phil. 10°57N 123°25E 233 F4
Sagene Norway 59°55N 10°46E 133 A3
Saghîr, El Bahr el → Egypt 31°8N 31°54E 251 G2
Sagiada Greece 39°38N 20°12E 206 B10
Saginaw Mich., U.S.A. 43°26N 83°56W 309 D12
Saginaw Tex., U.S.A. 32°51N 97°21W 120 A1
Saginaw B. U.S.A. 43°50N 83°40W 309 D12
Sagleipie Liberia 7°0N 8°52W 262 D3
Saglouc = Salluit Canada 62°14N 75°38W 295 E16
Sagone France 42°7N 8°42E 175 F12
Sagone, G. de France 42°4N 8°40E 175 F12
Sagrada Família, Templo de Barcelona, Spain 114 a2
Sagres Portugal 37°0N 8°58W 195 J2
Sagu Myanmar 20°13N 94°46E 241 E5
Sagua la Grande Cuba 22°50N 80°10W 320 B3
Saguache U.S.A. 38°5N 106°8W 304 G10
Saguaro △ U.S.A. 32°12N 110°38W 305 K8
Saguenay → Canada 48°22N 71°0W 299 C5
Saguia el Hamra → W. Sahara 27°24N 13°49W 260 C2
Sagunt Spain 39°42N 0°18W 196 F4
Sagunto = Sagunt Spain 39°42N 0°18W 196 F4
Sagvåg Norway 59°46N 5°25E 164 E2
Sagwara India 23°41N 74°1E 242 H6
Sahaba Sudan 18°57N 30°25E 256 D3
Sahagún Colombia 8°57N 75°27W 328 B2
Sahagún Spain 42°18N 5°2W 194 C5
Saḩam al Jawlān Syria 32°45N 35°55E 250 F6
Sahamandrevo Madag. 23°15S 45°35E 272 C2
Sahand, Kūh-e Iran 37°44N 46°27E 213 D12
Sahar, Mumbai ✈ (BOM) India 19°5N 72°51E 130 A2
Sahara Africa 23°0N 5°0E 254 D4
Saḩara, G. Egypt 28°2N 34°8E 251 K5
Saharan Atlas = Saharien, Atlas Algeria 33°30N 1°0E 261 B5
Saharan Seamounts Atl. Oc. 25°30N 19°50W 152 D10
Saharanpur India 29°58N 77°33E 242 E7
Saharien, Atlas Algeria 33°30N 1°0E 261 B5
Saharsa India 25°53N 86°36E 243 G12
Sahasinaka Madag. 21°49S 47°49E 272 C2
Sahaswan India 28°5N 78°45E 243 E8
Saheira, W. el → Egypt 30°5N 33°25E 251 H4
Sahel Africa 16°0N 5°0E 254 E3
Sahel, Canal du Mali 14°20N 6°0W 262 C3
Sahibganj India 25°12N 87°40E 243 G12
Şāhilīyah Iraq 33°43N 42°42E 213 F10
Sahiwal Pakistan 30°45N 73°8E 242 D5
Şahneh Iran 34°29N 47°41E 213 E12
Sahrawi = Western Sahara ■ Africa 25°0N 13°0W 260 D2
Sahuaripa Mexico 29°3N 109°14W 318 B3
Sahuarita U.S.A. 31°57N 110°58W 305 L8
Sahuayo de Díaz Mexico 20°4N 102°43W 318 C4
Šahy Slovakia 48°4N 18°55E 181 C11
Sai → India 25°39N 82°47E 243 G10
Sai Buri Thailand 6°43N 101°45E 237 J3
Sai-Cinza Brazil 6°17S 57°42W 331 B6
Sai Kung Hong Kong, China 22°23N 114°16E 122 A3
Sai Thong △ Thailand 15°56N 101°10E 236 E3
Sai Tso Wan Hong Kong, China 22°16N 113°53E 122 B1
Sai Wan Ho Hong Kong, China 22°17N 114°12E 122 B3
Sai Ying Pun Hong Kong, China 22°17N 114°8E 122 B2
Sai Yok △ Thailand 14°25N 98°40E 236 E2
Saibai I. Australia 9°25S 142°40E 280 a
Sa'id Bundas South Sudan 8°24N 24°48E 259 G4
Saïda Algeria 34°50N 0°11E 261 B5
Saïda □ Algeria 34°40N 0°20E 261 B5
Sa'īdābād = Sīrjān Iran 29°30N 55°45E 247 D7
Sa'īdābād Iran 36°8N 54°11E 247 B7
Saidaiji Japan 34°39N 134°2E 222 C6
Saïdia Morocco 35°5N 2°14W 261 A4
Saidor Papua N. G. 5°40S 146°29E 286 C4
Saidpur Bangla. 25°48N 89°0E 241 C2
Saidpur India 25°33N 83°11E 243 G10
Saidu Sharif Pakistan 34°43N 72°24E 243 B5
Saignes France 45°20N 2°31E 174 C6
Saigō Japan 36°12N 133°20E 222 A5
Saigon = Thanh Pho Ho Chi Minh Vietnam 10°58N 106°40E 237 G6
Saiha India 22°29N 92°58E 241 D4
Saijō Japan 33°55N 133°11E 222 D5
Saikai △ Japan 33°12N 129°36E 222 D1
Saikhoa Ghat India 27°50N 95°40E 241 B5
Saiki Japan 32°58N 131°51E 222 E3
Sailana India 23°28N 74°55E 242 H6
Saillans France 44°42N 5°12E 175 D9
Sailolof Indonesia 1°15S 130°46E 231 E8
Sailu India 19°28N 76°28E 244 E3
Saimaa Finland 61°15N 28°15E 188 B5
Saimbeyli Turkey 37°59N 36°6E 212 D7
Saimen = Saimaa Finland 61°15N 28°15E 188 B5
Şa'in Dezh Iran 36°40N 46°25E 213 D12
St. Abb's Head U.K. 55°55N 2°8W 167 F6
St-Affrique France 43°57N 2°53E 174 E6
St-Agrève France 45°0N 4°23E 175 C8
St-Aignan France 47°16N 1°22E 172 E8
St. Alban's Nfld. & L., Canada 47°51N 55°50W 299 C8
St. Albans Herts., U.K. 51°45N 0°19W 169 F7
St. Albans Vt., U.S.A. 44°49N 73°5W 313 B11
St. Albans W. Va., U.S.A. 38°23N 81°50W 309 F13
St. Alban's Head U.K. 50°34N 2°4W 169 G5
St. Albert Canada 53°37N 113°32W 296 C6
St-Amand-en-Puisaye France 47°32N 3°5E 173 E10
St-Amand-les-Eaux France 50°27N 3°25E 173 B10
St-Amand-Montrond France 46°43N 2°30E 173 F9
St-Amarin France 47°54N 7°2E 173 E14
St-Amour France 46°26N 5°21E 173 F12
St-André Montréal, Canada 130 c1
St-André Réunion 20°57S 55°39E 272 f
St-André-de-Cubzac France 44°59N 0°26W 174 D3
St-André-les-Alpes France 43°58N 6°30E 175 E10
St. Andrew Sd. U.S.A. 30°58N 81°25W 316 E8
St. Andrew's Nfld. & L., Canada 47°45N 59°15W 299 C8
St. Andrews N.Z. 44°33S 171°10E 285 E6
St. Andrews Fife, U.K. 56°20N 2°47W 167 E6
St. Andrews S.C., U.S.A. 32°47N 80°0W 316 C9
St-Anicet Canada 45°8N 74°22W 313 A10
St. Anne U.S.A. 41°1N 87°43W 311 C9
St. Annes Canada 49°40N 96°39W 297 D9
St. Anns B. Canada 46°22N 60°25W 299 C7
St. Ann's Bay Jamaica 18°26N 77°12W 320 a
St. Anthony Nfld. & L., Canada 51°22N 55°35W 299 B8
St. Anthony Idaho, U.S.A. 43°58N 111°41W 304 E8
St-Antoine Canada 46°22N 64°45W 299 C7
St-Antonin-Noble-Val France 44°10N 1°45E 174 D5
St-Arnaud = El Eulma Algeria 36°9N 5°42E 261 A6
St. Arnaud Australia 36°40S 143°16E 282 D5
St. Arnaud Ra. N.Z. 42°1S 172°53E 285 C7
St-Astier France 45°8N 0°31E 174 C4
St-Aubin France 48°44N 2°8E 134 B1
St-Aubin-du-Cormier France 48°15N 1°26W 172 D5
St-Augustin Canada 51°13N 58°38W 299 B8
St-Augustin → Canada 51°16N 58°40W 299 B8
St. Augustine U.S.A. 29°54N 81°19W 316 F8
St. Augustine Beach U.S.A. 29°51N 81°16W 316 F8
St-Aulaye France 45°12N 0°9E 174 C4
St. Austell U.K. 50°20N 4°47W 169 G3
St-Avold France 49°6N 6°43E 173 C13
St. Barbe Canada 51°12N 56°46W 299 B8
St-Barthélemy ⊠ W. Indies 17°50N 62°50W 322 a
St-Barthélemy Channel St.-Martin 18°0N 63°0W 322 a
St. Barts = St-Barthélemy ⊠ W. Indies 17°50N 62°50W 322 a
St. Basil's Cathedral Moscow, Russia 129 b3
St. Bathans N.Z. 44°53S 169°50E 285 E4
St. Bathan's, Mt. N.Z. 44°45S 169°45E 285 E4
St-Béat France 42°55N 0°41E 174 F4
St. Bees Hd. U.K. 54°31N 3°38W 168 C4
St. Bees I. Australia 20°56S 149°26E 280 b
St-Benoît Réunion 21°2S 55°43E 272 f
St-Benoît-du-Sault France 46°26N 1°24E 174 B5
St-Bonnet-en-Champsaur France 44°40N 6°5E 175 D10
St-Brevin-les-Pins France 47°14N 2°10W 172 E4
St-Brice-en-Coglès France 48°25N 1°22W 172 D5
St. Bride's Canada 46°56N 54°10W 299 C9
St. Brides B. U.K. 51°49N 5°9W 169 F2
St-Brieuc France 48°30N 2°46W 172 D4
St-Calais France 47°55N 0°45E 172 E7
St-Cast-le-Guildo France 48°37N 2°18W 172 D4
St. Catharines Canada 43°10N 79°15W 312 C5
St. Catherine, Mt. Grenada 12°10N 61°40W 323 q
St. Catherine Pt. Bermuda 32°23N 64°40W 153 a
St. Catherines I. U.S.A. 31°40N 81°10W 316 D8
St. Catherine's Monastery Egypt 28°34N 33°58E 251 K4
St. Catherine's Pt. U.K. 50°34N 1°18W 169 G6
St-Céré France 44°51N 1°54E 174 D5
St-Cergue Switz. 46°27N 6°10E 179 J2
St-Cernin France 45°5N 2°25E 174 C6
St-Chamond France 45°28N 4°31E 175 C8
St. Charles Ill., U.S.A. 41°54N 88°19W 311 C8
St. Charles Md., U.S.A. 38°36N 76°56W 309 F15
St. Charles Mo., U.S.A. 38°47N 90°29W 310 F6
St. Charles Va., U.S.A. 36°48N 83°4W 309 G12
St-Chély-d'Apcher France 44°48N 3°17E 174 D7
St-Chinian France 43°25N 2°56E 174 E6
St. Christopher = St. Kitts W. Indies 17°20N 62°40W 322 d
St. Christopher-Nevis = St. Kitts & Nevis ■ W. Indies 17°20N 62°40W 322 d
St-Ciers-sur-Gironde France 45°17N 0°37W 174 C3
St. Clair Ga., U.S.A. 33°9N 82°13W 316 B7
St. Clair Mich., U.S.A. 42°50N 82°30W 312 D2
St. Clair Mo., U.S.A. 38°21N 90°59W 310 F6
St. Clair Pa., U.S.A. 40°43N 76°12W 313 F8
St. Clair → U.S.A. 42°38N 82°31W 312 D2
St. Clair, L. S. Austral., Australia 37°20S 139°55E 282 D3
St. Clair, L. N. Amer. 42°27N 82°39W 312 D2
St. Clair Shores U.S.A. 42°30N 82°53W 311 B14
St. Clairsville U.S.A. 40°5N 80°54W 312 F4
St-Claud France 45°54N 0°28E 174 C4
St. Claude Canada 49°40N 98°20W 297 D9
St-Claude Jura, France 46°22N 5°52E 173 F12
St-Claude Guadeloupe 16°3N 61°42W 322 e
St. Clears U.K. 51°49N 4°31W 169 F3
St-Clet Canada 45°21N 74°13W 313 A10
St-Cloud France 48°50N 2°12E 134 A2
St. Cloud Fla., U.S.A. 28°15N 81°17W 317 G8
St. Cloud Minn., U.S.A. 45°34N 94°10W 308 C6
St. Cricq, C. Australia 25°17S 113°6E 279 E1
St. Croix U.S. Virgin Is. 17°45N 64°45W 321 C7
St. Croix → U.S.A. 44°45N 92°48W 308 C7
St. Croix Falls U.S.A. 45°24N 92°38W 308 C7
St-Cyprien France 42°37N 3°2E 174 F7
St-Cyr-l'École France 48°47N 2°4E 134 B1
St-Cyr-l'École ✈ France 48°48N 2°4E 134 B1
St-Cyr-sur-Mer France 43°11N 5°43E 175 E9
St. David U.S.A. 40°30N 90°3W 310 D6
St. David's Nfld. & L., Canada 48°12N 58°52W 299 C8
St. David's Grenada 12°2N 61°40W 323 q
St. David's Pembs., U.K. 51°53N 5°16W 169 F2
St. David's Head U.K. 51°54N 5°19W 169 F2
St. David's I. Bermuda 32°21N 64°39W 153 a
St-Denis = Sig Algeria 35°32N 0°12W 261 A4
St-Denis Seine-St-Denis, France 48°56N 2°20E 134 A3
St-Denis Réunion 20°52S 55°27E 272 f
St-Denis → Réunion 20°52S 55°22E 272 f
St-Denis ✈ (RUN) Réunion 20°53S 55°32E 272 f
St-Dié-en-Vosges France 48°17N 6°56E 173 D13
St-Dizier France 48°38N 4°56E 173 D11
St-Égrève France 45°14N 5°41E 175 C9
St. Elias, Mt. U.S.A. 60°18N 140°56W 303 F12
St. Elias Mts. N. Amer. 60°33N 139°28W 296 A1
St-Élie Fr. Guiana 4°49N 53°17W 329 C7
St. Elmo U.S.A. 39°2N 88°51W 310 F8
St-Eloy-les-Mines France 46°10N 2°51E 173 F9
St-Émilion France 44°53N 0°9W 174 D3
St-Étienne France 45°27N 4°22E 175 C8
St-Étienne → Réunion 21°17S 55°25E 272 f
St-Étienne-de-Tinée France 44°16N 6°56E 175 D10
St-Étienne-du-Rouvray France 49°23N 1°6E 172 C8
St. Eugène Canada 45°30N 74°28W 313 A10
St. Eustatius W. Indies 17°20N 63°0W 322 a
St-Exupery, Lyon ✈ (LYS) France 45°44N 5°2E 175 C9
St-Fargeau France 47°39N 3°4E 173 E10
St-Félicien Canada 48°40N 72°25W 298 C5
St. Ferdinand = Florissant U.S.A. 38°47N 90°19W 310 F6
St-Florent France 42°41N 9°18E 175 F13
St-Florent, G. de France 42°47N 9°12E 175 F13
St-Florent-sur-Cher France 46°59N 2°15E 173 F9
St-Florentin France 48°0N 3°45E 173 E10
St-Flour France 45°2N 3°6E 174 C7
St. Francis U.S.A. 39°47N 101°48W 308 F3
St. Francis → U.S.A. 34°38N 90°36W 315 D9
St. Francis, C. S. Africa 34°14S 24°49E 270 D3
St. Francisville Ill., U.S.A. 38°36N 87°39W 311 F9
St. Francisville La., U.S.A. 30°47N 91°23W 314 F9
St-François Guadeloupe 16°16N 61°18W 322 e
St-François, L. Canada 45°10N 74°22W 313 A10
St-Fulgent France 46°50N 1°10W 172 F5
St-Gabriel Canada 46°17N 73°24W 298 C5
St. Gallen = Sankt Gallen Switz. 47°26N 9°22E 179 H5
St-Galmier France 45°35N 4°19E 173 G11
St-Gaudens France 43°6N 0°44E 174 E4
St-Gaultier France 46°39N 1°26E 172 F8
St-Gengoux-le-National France 46°37N 4°40E 173 F11
St-Geniez-d'Olt France 44°27N 2°58E 174 D6
St. George Queens., Australia 28°1S 148°30E 281 D4
St. George N.B., Canada 45°11N 66°50W 299 C6
St. George Ont., Canada 43°15N 80°15W 312 C4
St. George Ga., U.S.A. 30°31N 82°2W 316 E7
St. George S.C., U.S.A. 33°11N 80°35W 316 B9
St. George Utah, U.S.A. 37°6N 113°35W 305 H7
St. George, C. Nfld. & L., Canada 48°30N 59°16W 299 C8
St. George, C. Papua N. G. 4°49S 152°53E 286 C7
St. George, C. Fla., U.S.A. 29°40N 85°5W 316 F4
St. George I. Alaska, U.S.A. 56°35N 169°35W 303 H5
St. George I. Fla., U.S.A. 29°35N 84°55W 316 F5
St. George Ra. Australia 18°40S 125°0E 278 C4
St. George's Bermuda 32°22N 64°40W 153 a
St. George's Nfld. & L., Canada 48°26N 58°31W 299 C8
St-Georges Qué., Canada 46°8N 70°40W 299 C5
St-Georges Fr. Guiana 3°53N 51°50W 329 C7
St. George's Grenada 12°5N 61°43W 323 q
St. George's B. Canada 48°24N 58°53W 299 C8
St. Georges Basin N.S.W., Australia 35°7S 150°36E 283 C9
St. Georges Basin W. Austral., Australia 15°23S 125°2E 278 C4
St. George's Channel Europe 52°0N 6°0W 166 E6
St. George's Channel India 7°15N 93°43E 245 L11
St. George's Channel Papua N. G. 4°10S 152°20E 286 C7
St. George's Harbour Bermuda 32°23N 64°42W 153 a
St. Georges Hd. Australia 35°12S 150°42E 283 C9
St. George's I. Bermuda 32°23N 64°40W 153 a
St-Georges-lès-Baillargeaux France 46°41N 0°22E 174 B4
St-Germain, Forêt de France 48°57N 2°5E 134 A1
St-Germain-de-Calberte France 44°13N 3°48E 174 D7
St-Germain-en-Laye France 48°53N 2°4E 134 A1
St-Germain-Lembron France 45°27N 3°14E 174 C7
St-Gervais-d'Auvergne France 46°4N 2°50E 173 F9
St-Gervais-les-Bains France 45°53N 6°42E 175 C10
St-Gildas, Pte. de France 47°8N 2°14W 172 E4
St. Giles Cathedral Edinburgh, U.K. 121 b2
St-Gilles Brussels, Belgium 50°49N 4°20E 116 B2
St-Gilles Gard, France 43°40N 4°26E 175 E8
St-Gilles-les-Bains Réunion 21°2S 55°14E 272 f
St-Gilles-les-Hauts Réunion 21°2S 55°15E 272 f
St-Girons France 42°59N 1°8E 174 F5
St. Gotthard P. = San Gottardo, P. del Switz. 46°33N 8°33E 179 J4
St. Helena Atl. Oc. 15°58S 5°42W 153 h
St. Helena Calif., U.S.A. 38°30N 122°28W 306 G4
St. Helena, Mt. U.S.A. 38°40N 122°36W 306 G4
St. Helena B. S. Africa 32°40S 18°10E 270 D2
St. Helena Sd. U.S.A. 32°15N 80°25W 316 C9
St. Helens Tas., Australia 41°20S 148°15E 281 G4
St. Helens Mersey., U.K. 53°27N 2°44W 168 D5
St. Helens Oreg., U.S.A. 45°52N 122°48W 306 E4
St. Helens, Mt. U.S.A. 46°12N 122°12W 306 D4
St. Helier Chan. Is., U.K. 49°10N 2°7W 169 H5
St. Helier London, U.K. 51°23N 0°11W 125 B2
St-Herblain France 47°13N 1°40W 172 E5
St-Hilaire-du-Harcouët France 48°35N 1°5W 172 D5
St-Hillaire-de-Riez France 46°43N 1°57W 174 B2
St-Hippolyte France 47°19N 6°50E 173 E13
St-Hippolyte-du-Fort France 43°58N 3°52E 174 E7
St-Honoré-les-Bains France 46°54N 3°50E 173 F10
St-Hubert Canada 45°29N 73°25W 130 B3
St-Hubert, Galeries Royales Brussels, Belgium 116 b2
St-Hyacinthe Canada 45°40N 72°58W 298 C5
St. Ignace U.S.A. 45°52N 84°44W 309 C11
St. Ignace I. Canada 48°45N 88°0W 298 C2
St. Ignatius U.S.A. 47°19N 114°6W 304 C6
St-Imier Switz. 47°9N 6°58E 179 H2
St. Isaac's Cathedral Russia 59°55N 30°19E 137 B1
St. Ives Cambs., U.K. 52°20N 0°4W 169 E7
St. Ives Corn., U.K. 50°12N 5°30W 169 G2
St-Jacques Montréal, Canada 130 a2
St-Jacques → Canada 45°26N 73°29W 130 B3
St-James France 48°31N 1°20W 172 D5
St. James Minn., U.S.A. 43°59N 94°38W 308 D6
St. James Mo., U.S.A. 38°0N 91°37W 310 G5
St. James Cathedral Toronto, Canada 141 b3
St. James's London, U.K. 125 b3
St-Jean St. Barts 17°53N 62°50W 322 a
St-Jean → Canada 50°17N 64°20W 299 B7
St-Jean, L. Canada 48°40N 72°0W 299 C5
St-Jean Baptiste Montréal, Canada 130 a1
St-Jean-d'Angély France 45°57N 0°31W 174 C3
St-Jean-de-Braye France 47°53N 1°58E 173 E8
St-Jean-de-Luz France 43°23N 1°39W 174 E2
St-Jean-de-Maurienne France 45°16N 6°21E 175 C10
St-Jean-de-Monts France 46°47N 2°4W 172 F4
St-Jean-du-Gard France 44°7N 3°52E 174 D7
St-Jean-en-Royans France 45°1N 5°18E 175 C9
St-Jean-Pied-de-Port France 43°10N 1°14W 174 E2
St-Jean-Port-Joli Canada 47°15N 70°13W 299 C5
St-Jean-sur-Richelieu Canada 45°20N 73°20W 313 A11
St-Jérôme Canada 45°47N 74°0W 298 C5
St. Joe U.S.A. 41°19N 84°54W 311 C12
St. John N.B., Canada 45°20N 66°8W 299 C6
St. John Kans., U.S.A. 38°0N 98°46W 308 F4
St. John → Liberia 6°40N 9°10W 262 D2
St. John → N. Amer. 45°12N 66°5W 309 C20
St. John, C. Canada 50°0N 55°32W 299 C8
St. John I. U.S. Virgin Is. 18°20N 64°42W 321 b
St. John's Antigua & B. 17°6N 61°51W 322 b
St. John's Nfld. & L., Canada 47°35N 52°40W 299 C9
St. Johns Montserrat 16°46N 62°11W 323 p
St. Johns Ariz., U.S.A. 34°30N 109°22W 305 J9
St. Johns Mich., U.S.A. 43°0N 84°33W 311 B12
St. Johns → U.S.A. 30°24N 81°24W 316 E8
St. John's Pt. Ireland 54°34N 8°27W 166 B3
St. Johnsbury U.S.A. 44°25N 72°1W 313 B12
St. Johnston Village Antigua & B. 17°7N 61°50W 322 b
St. Johnsville U.S.A. 43°0N 74°43W 313 C10
St-Joost-Ten-Node Belgium 50°51N 4°21E 116 A2
St. Joseph Ont., Canada 43°24N 81°42W 312 C3
St-Joseph Dominica 15°24N 61°26W 323 k
St-Joseph Martinique 14°39N 61°4W 322 j
St-Joseph Réunion 21°22S 55°37E 272 f
St. Joseph Mayaro, Trin. & Tob. 10°18N 60°59W 323 t
St. Joseph Tunapuna, Trin. & Tob. 10°40N 61°25W 323 t
St. Joseph Ill., U.S.A. 40°7N 88°2W 311 D8
St. Joseph La., U.S.A. 31°55N 91°14W 314 F9
St. Joseph Mich., U.S.A. 42°6N 86°29W 311 B10
St. Joseph Mo., U.S.A. 39°46N 94°50W 310 E2
St. Joseph → U.S.A. 42°7N 86°29W 311 B10
St. Joseph, I. Canada 46°12N 83°58W 298 C3
St. Joseph, L. Canada 51°10N 90°35W 298 B1
St. Joseph Pt. U.S.A. 29°52N 85°24W 316 F4
St-Juéry France 43°57N 2°12E 174 E6
St. Julian's Malta 35°55N 14°29E 206 F7
St-Julien-Chapteuil France 45°2N 4°4E 175 C8
St-Julien-de-Vouvantes France 47°38N 1°13W 172 E5
St-Julien-en-Genevois France 46°9N 6°5E 173 F13
St-Junien France 45°53N 0°55E 174 C4
St-Just-en-Chaussée France 49°30N 2°25E 173 C9
St-Just-en-Chevalet France 45°55N 3°50E 174 C7
St. Kilda Vic., Australia 37°51S 144°58E 128 B1
St. Kilda N.Z. 45°53S 170°31E 285 F5
St. Kilda W. Isles, U.K. 57°49N 8°34W 165 C2
St. Kitts W. Indies 17°20N 62°40W 322 d
St. Kitts & Nevis ■ W. Indies 17°20N 62°40W 322 d
St-Lambert Qué., Canada 45°30N 73°29W 130 A3
St-Lambert Yvelines, France 48°43N 2°1E 134 B1
St. Laurent Canada 50°25N 97°58W 297 C9
St-Laurent Canada 45°30N 73°43W 130 A1
St-Laurent-de-la-Salanque France 42°46N 2°59E 174 F6
St-Laurent-du-Maroni Fr. Guiana 5°29N 54°3W 329 B7
St-Laurent-du-Maroni □ Fr. Guiana 4°0N 53°45W 329 C7
St-Laurent-du-Pont France 45°23N 5°45E 175 C9
St-Laurent-en-Grandvaux France 46°35N 5°58E 173 F12
St-Laurent-Médoc France 45°8N 0°49W 174 C3
St. Lawrence Queens., Australia 22°16S 149°31E 280 C4
St. Lawrence Nfld. & L., Canada 46°54N 55°23W 299 C8
St. Lawrence → Canada 49°30N 66°0W 299 C6
St. Lawrence, Gulf of Canada 48°25N 62°0W 299 C7
St. Lawrence I. U.S.A. 63°30N 170°30W 303 E5
St. Lawrence Islands △ Canada 44°27N 75°52W 313 B9
St. Lawrence Market Toronto, Canada 141 b3
St-Lazare, Gare Paris, France 134 a3
St. Léonard Canada 47°12N 67°58W 299 C6
St-Léonard Canada 45°35N 73°34W 130 A2
St-Léonard-de-Noblat France 45°49N 1°29E 174 C5
St-Leu Réunion 21°9S 55°18E 272 f
St. Lewis → Canada 52°26N 56°11W 299 B8
St-Lô France 49°7N 1°5W 172 C5
St-Louis Montréal, Canada 130 b2
St-Louis Haut-Rhin, France 47°30N 7°34E 173 E14
St-Louis Guadeloupe 15°56N 61°19W 322 e
St-Louis Réunion 21°16S 55°25E 272 f
St-Louis Senegal 16°8N 16°27W 262 B1
St. Louis U.S.A. 38°37N 90°11W 310 F6
St-Louis □ Senegal 16°20N 15°0W 262 B2
St. Louis → U.S.A. 46°44N 92°9W 308 B7
St. Louis Lambert Int. ✈ (STL) U.S.A. 38°45N 90°22W 310 F6
St-Loup-sur-Semouse France 47°53N 6°16E 173 E13
St-Luc Canada 45°22N 73°18W 313 A11
St. Lucia ■ W. Indies 14°0N 60°57W 323 m
St. Lucia, L. S. Africa 28°5S 32°30E 271 C5
St. Lucia △ S. Africa 28°6S 32°27E 271 C5
St. Lucia Channel W. Indies 14°15N 61°0W 321 D7
St. Lucie U.S.A. 27°29N 80°20W 317 H9
St. Lucie Canal U.S.A. 27°10N 80°18W 317 H9
St. Maarten ⊠ W. Indies 18°2N 63°5W 322 a
St. Magnus B. U.K. 60°25N 1°35W 167 A7
St-Maixent-l'École France 46°24N 0°12W 174 B3
St-Malo France 48°39N 2°1W 172 D4
St-Malo, G. de France 48°50N 2°30W 172 D4
St-Mandé France 48°50N 2°24E 134 A3
St-Mandrier-sur-Mer France 43°4N 5°57E 175 E9
St-Marc Haiti 19°10N 72°41W 321 C5
St-Marcellin France 45°9N 5°20E 175 C9
St-Marcouf, Îs. France 49°30N 1°10W 172 C5
St. Maries U.S.A. 47°19N 116°35W 304 C5
St. Mark B. Grenada 12°11N 61°42W 323 q
St. Marks U.S.A. 30°9N 84°12W 316 E5
St. Mark's Square = San Marco, Piazza Venice, Italy 142 b3
St-Martin ⊠ W. Indies 18°5N 63°5W 322 a
St-Martin, Bois France 48°48N 2°35E 134 B4
St-Martin, C. Martinique 14°52N 61°14W 322 j
St. Martin, L. Canada 51°40N 98°30W 297 C9
St-Martin-de-Crau France 43°38N 4°48E 175 E8
St-Martin-de-Ré France 46°12N 1°21W 174 B2
St-Martin-d'Hères France 45°9N 5°45E 175 C9
St-Martin-Vésubie France 44°4N 7°15E 175 D11
St. Martin's I. Bangla. 20°36N 92°20E 241 E4
St-Martory France 43°9N 0°56E 174 E4
St. Mary U.S.A. 37°53N 89°57W 310 G7
St. Mary, Mt. Papua N. G. 8°8S 147°2E 286 E4
St. Mary Cray U.K. 51°23N 0°7E 125 B4
St. Mary Is. India 13°20N 74°35E 245 H2
St. Mary Pk. Australia 31°32S 138°34E 282 A3
St. Marys Tas., Australia 41°35S 148°11E 281 G4
St. Marys Ont., Canada 43°20N 81°10W 312 C3
St. Mary's Trin. & Tob. 10°14N 61°33W 323 t
St. Mary's Corn., U.K. 49°55N 6°18W 169 H1
St. Mary's Orkney, U.K. 58°54N 2°54W 167 C6
St. Mary's Alaska, U.S.A. 62°4N 163°10W 303 E7
St. Marys Ga., U.S.A. 30°44N 81°33W 316 E8
St. Marys Ohio, U.S.A. 40°33N 84°24W 311 D12
St. Marys Pa., U.S.A. 41°26N 78°34W 312 E6
St. Marys → U.S.A. 30°43N 81°27W 316 E8
St. Mary's, C. Canada 46°50N 54°12W 299 C9
St. Mary's B. Canada 46°50N 53°50W 299 C9
St. Mary's Bay Canada 44°25N 66°10W 299 D6
St. Mary's Cathedral San Francisco, U.S.A. 136 c1
St-Mathieu, Pte. France 48°20N 4°45W 172 D2
St. Matthew I. U.S.A. 60°24N 172°42W 303 F4
St. Matthews Ky., U.S.A. 38°15N 85°39W 311 F11
St. Matthews S.C., U.S.A. 33°40N 80°46W 316 B9
St. Matthews, I. = Zadetkyi Kyun Myanmar 10°0N 98°25E 237 G2
St. Matthias Group Papua N. G. 1°30S 150°0E 286 A6
St-Maur-des-Fossés France 48°48N 2°29E 134 B3
St-Maurice France 48°49N 2°24E 134 B3
St-Maurice → Canada 46°21N 72°31W 298 C5
St. Mawes U.K. 50°10N 5°2W 169 G2
St-Maximin-la-Ste-Baume France 43°27N 5°52E 175 E9
St-Médard-en-Jalles France 44°53N 0°43W 174 D3
St-Méen-le-Grand France 48°11N 2°12W 172 D4
St. Meinrad U.S.A. 38°10N 86°49W 311 F10
St. Michael U.S.A. 63°29N 162°2W 303 E7
St. Michael's Cathedral Toronto, Canada 141 a3
St-Michel Canada 45°34N 73°37W 130 A2
St-Mihiel France 48°54N 5°32E 173 D12
St-Nazaire France 47°17N 2°12W 172 E4
St. Neots U.K. 52°14N 0°15W 169 E7
St-Nicolas-de-Port France 48°38N 6°18E 173 D13
St-Omer France 50°45N 2°15E 173 B9
St-Ouen France 48°56N 2°20E 134 A3
St-Palais-sur-Mer France 45°38N 1°5W 174 C2
St-Pamphile Canada 46°58N 69°48W 299 C6
St. Pancras International London, U.K. 125 a4
St-Pardoux-la-Rivière France 45°29N 0°45E 174 C4
St. Paris U.S.A. 40°8N 83°58W 311 D13
St-Pascal Canada 47°32N 69°48W 299 C6
St. Patricks Barbados 13°6N 59°30W 323 r
St. Patrick's Cathedral New York, U.S.A. 132 c2
St. Patrick's Church Toronto, Canada 141 a1
St. Paul Canada 54°0N 111°17W 296 C6
St-Paul Réunion 20°59S 55°17E 272 f
St. Paul Alaska, U.S.A. 57°7N 170°17W 303 H5

St. Paul *Ind., U.S.A.* 39°26N 85°38W **311** E11
St. Paul *Minn., U.S.A.* 44°56N 93°5W **308** C7
St. Paul *Nebr., U.S.A.* 41°13N 98°27W **308** E4
St-Paul → *Canada* 51°27N 57°42W **299** B8
St. Paul → *Liberia* 6°25N 10°48W **262** D2
St. Paul, Î. *Ind. Oc.* 38°55S 77°34E **273** H6
St-Paul-de-Fenouillet *France* 42°48N 2°30E **174** F6
St. Paul I. *N.S., Canada* 47°12N 60°9W **299** C7
St. Paul I. *Alaska, U.S.A.* 57°10N 170°15W **303** H5
St-Paul-lès-Dax *France* 43°44N 1°3W **174** E2
St-Paul-sur-Ubaye *France* 44°31N 6°45E **175** D10
St. Pauls *St. Helena* 15°57S 5°43W **153** h
St. Paul's Bay *Malta* 35°57N 14°24E **206** F7
St. Paul's Cathedral *London, U.K.* **125** b4
St. Paul's Cray *U.K.* 51°23N 0°6E **125** B4
St-Péray *France* 44°57N 4°50E **175** D8
St. Pete Beach *U.S.A.* 27°43N 82°44W **317** H7
St. Peter *U.S.A.* 44°20N 93°57W **308** C7
St. Peter & St. Paul *San Francisco, U.S.A.* **136** a2
St. Peter Port *U.K.* 49°26N 2°33W **169** H5
St. Peters *N.S.W., Australia* 33°55S 151°11E **139** B2
St. Peters *N.S., Canada* 45°40N 60°53W **299** C7
St. Peters *P.E.I., Canada* 46°25N 62°35W **299** C7
St. Peters *Montserrat* 16°43N 62°13W **323** p
St. Peters *Mo., U.S.A.* 38°48N 90°37W **310** F6
St. Peter's Square = San Pietro, Piazza *Rome, Italy* **136** b1
St. Petersburg = Sankt-Peterburg *Russia* 59°55N 30°20E **137** B1
St. Petersburg *U.S.A.* 27°46N 82°40W **317** H7
St. Petersburg Pulkovo Int. ✈ **(LED)** *Russia* 59°48N 30°18E **137** C1
St-Philbert-de-Grand-Lieu *France* 47°2N 1°39W **172** E5
St-Phillippe *Réunion* 21°21S 55°44E **272** f
St-Pie *Canada* 45°30N 72°54W **313** A12
St-Pierre *Qué., Canada* 45°27N 73°38W **130** B2
St-Pierre *Martinique* 14°45N 61°10W **322** j
St. Pierre *Mauritius* 20°13S 57°31E **272** e
St-Pierre *Réunion* 21°19S 55°28E **272** f
St-Pierre *St-P. & M.* 46°46N 56°12W **299** C8
St-Pierre, L. *Canada* 46°12N 72°52W **298** C5
St-Pierre, Rade de *Martinique* 14°44N 61°11W **322** j
St-Pierre-de-la-Pointe-aux-Esquimaux = Havre-St.-Pierre *Canada* 50°18N 63°33W **299** B7
St-Pierre-d'Oléron *France* 45°57N 1°19W **174** C2
St-Pierre-en-Port *France* 49°48N 0°30E **172** C7
St-Pierre-et-Miquelon ⊠ *N. Amer.* 46°55N 56°10W **299** C8
St-Pierre-le-Moûtier *France* 46°47N 3°7E **173** F10
St-Pierre-sur-Dives *France* 49°2N 0°1W **172** C6
St-Pieters Leew *Belgium* 50°47N 4°16E **116** B1
St-Pol-de-Léon *France* 48°41N 4°0W **172** D3
St-Pol-sur-Mer *France* 51°1N 2°20E **173** A9
St-Pol-sur-Ternoise *France* 50°23N 2°20E **173** B9
St-Pons *France* 43°30N 2°45E **174** E6
St-Pourçain-sur-Sioule *France* 46°18N 3°18E **173** F10
St-Priest *France* 45°42N 4°57E **175** C8
St-Quay-Portrieux *France* 48°39N 2°51W **172** D4
St-Quentin *N.B., Canada* 47°30N 67°23W **299** C6
St-Quentin *Aisne, France* 49°50N 3°16E **173** C10
St-Quentin, Étang de *France* 48°47N 2°0E **134** B1
St-Raphaël *France* 43°25N 6°46E **175** E10
St. Regis *U.S.A.* 47°18N 115°6W **304** C6
St. Regis Falls *U.S.A.* 44°40N 74°32W **313** B10
St-Renan *France* 48°26N 4°37W **172** D2
St. Robert *U.S.A.* 37°50N 92°11W **310** G4
St-Saëns *France* 49°41N 1°16E **172** C8
St-Savin *France* 46°34N 0°53E **174** B4
St-Savinien *France* 45°53N 0°42W **174** C3
St. Sebastien, Tanjon' i *Madag.* 12°26S 48°44E **272** A2
St-Seine-l'Abbaye *France* 47°26N 4°47E **173** E11
St-Sernin-sur-Rance *France* 43°54N 2°35E **174** E6
St-Sever *France* 43°45N 0°35W **174** E3
St-Siméon *Canada* 47°51N 69°54W **299** C6
St. Simons I. *U.S.A.* 31°12N 81°15W **316** D8
St. Simons Island *U.S.A.* 31°9N 81°22W **316** D8
St. Stephen *N.B., Canada* 45°16N 67°17W **299** C6
St. Stephen *S.C., U.S.A.* 33°24N 79°55W **316** B10
St. Stephen's Basilica *Budapest, Hungary* **117** b2
St. Stephen's Cathedral = Stephansdom *Vienna, Austria* **142** b2
St-Stevens-Woluwe *Belgium* 50°52N 4°26E **116** A2
St-Sulpice *France* 43°46N 1°41E **174** E5
St-Sulpice-Laurière *France* 46°3N 1°29E **174** B5
St-Sulpice-les-Feuilles *France* 46°19N 1°21E **174** B5
St-Syprien = St-Cyprien *France* 42°37N 3°2E **174** F7
St. Teresa *U.S.A.* 29°55N 84°27W **316** F5
St-Thégonnec *France* 48°31N 3°57W **172** D3
St. Thomas = Charlotte Amalie *U.S. Virgin Is.* 18°21N 64°56W **321** C7
St. Thomas *Canada* 42°45N 81°10W **312** D3
St. Thomas Bay *Malta* 35°51N 14°34E **206** F8
St. Thomas I. *U.S. Virgin Is.* 18°20N 64°55W **321** C7
St-Tite *Canada* 46°45N 72°34W **298** C5
St-Trond = Sint-Truiden *Belgium* 50°48N 5°10E **170** D5
St-Tropez *France* 43°17N 6°38E **175** E10
St-Vaast-la-Hougue *France* 49°35N 1°17W **172** C5
St-Valery-en-Caux *France* 49°52N 0°43E **172** C7
St-Valéry-sur-Somme *France* 50°11N 1°38E **173** B8
St-Vallier *France* 46°38N 4°22E **173** F11
St-Vallier-de-Thiey *France* 43°42N 6°51E **175** E10
St-Varent *France* 46°53N 0°13W **172** F6
St-Vaury *France* 46°12N 1°46E **174** B5
St. Vidgeon's ☼ *Australia* 14°47S 134°53E **280** A1
St. Vincent = São Vicente *Cabo Verde* 17°0N 25°0W **153** j
St. Vincent *Italy* 45°45N 7°39E **198** C4
St. Vincent *W. Indies* 13°15N 61°10W **323** n
St. Vincent, G. *Australia* 35°0S 138°0E **282** C3
St. Vincent & the Grenadines ■ *W. Indies* 13°0N 61°10W **323** n
St-Vincent-de-Paul *Canada* 45°36N 73°39W **130** A2
St-Vincent-de-Tyrosse *France* 43°39N 1°19W **174** E2
St. Vincent I. *U.S.A.* 29°42N 85°3W **317** F4
St. Vincent Passage *W. Indies* 13°30N 61°0W **321** D7
St-Vith *Belgium* 50°17N 6°9E **170** D6
St-Vivien-de-Médoc *France* 45°25N 1°2W **174** C2
St. Walburg *Canada* 53°39N 109°12W **297** C7
St. Xavier Univ. *U.S.A.* 41°42N 87°42W **119** C2
St-Yrieix-la-Perche *France* 45°31N 1°12E **174** C5
Saintala *India* 20°26N 83°20E **244** D6
Ste-Adresse *France* 49°31N 0°5E **172** C7
Ste-Agathe-des-Monts *Canada* 46°3N 74°17W **298** C5
Ste-Anne *Guadeloupe* 16°13N 61°24W **322** e
Ste-Anne *Martinique* 14°25N 60°54W **322** j
Ste-Anne *Réunion* 21°4S 55°45E **272** f
Ste-Anne *Seychelles* 4°36S 55°31E **272** c
Ste-Anne, L. *Canada* 50°0N 67°42W **299** B6
Ste-Anne-des-Monts *Canada* 49°8N 66°30W **299** C6
Ste-Catherine *Canada* 45°24N 73°34W **130** B2
Ste-Croix *Switz.* 46°49N 6°34E **179** J2
Ste-Enimie *France* 44°22N 3°26E **174** D7
Ste-Foy-la-Grande *France* 44°50N 0°13E **174** D4
Ste. Genevieve *U.S.A.* 37°59N 90°2W **310** G6
Ste-Hélène, Î. *Canada* 45°31N 73°32W **130** A2
Ste-Hermine *France* 46°32N 1°4W **174** B2
Ste-Livrade-sur-Lot *France* 44°24N 0°36E **174** D4
Ste-Luce *Martinique* 14°28N 60°55W **322** j
Ste. Madeleine *Trin. & Tob.* 10°16N 61°26W **323** t
Ste-Marguerite *Guadeloupe* 16°23N 61°24W **322** e
Ste-Marguerite → *Canada* 50°9N 66°36W **299** B6
Ste-Marie *Canada* 46°26N 71°0W **299** C5
Ste. Marie *Gabon* 3°48S 11°1E **264** C2
Ste-Marie *Guadeloupe* 16°6N 61°33W **322** e
Ste-Marie *Martinique* 14°48N 61°1W **322** j
Ste-Marie *Réunion* 20°53S 55°33E **272** f
Ste-Marie, Ile = Boraha, Nosy *Madag.* 16°50S 49°55E **272** B2
Ste-Marie-aux-Mines *France* 48°15N 7°12E **173** D14
Ste-Marthe *Guadeloupe* 16°15N 61°15W **322** e
Ste-Maure-de-Touraine *France* 47°7N 0°37E **172** E7
Ste-Maxime *France* 43°19N 6°39E **175** E10
Ste-Menehould *France* 49°5N 4°54E **173** C11
Ste-Mère-Église *France* 49°24N 1°19W **172** C5
Ste-Rose *Guadeloupe* 16°20N 61°45W **322** e
Ste-Rose *Réunion* 21°8S 55°45E **272** f
Ste. Rose du Lac *Canada* 51°4N 99°30W **297** C9
Ste-Savine *France* 48°18N 4°3E **173** D11
Ste-Sigolène *France* 45°15N 4°14E **175** C8
Ste-Suzanne *Réunion* 20°54S 55°36E **272** f
Saintes *France* 45°45N 0°37W **174** C3
Saintes, Canal des *Guadeloupe* 15°55N 61°40W **322** e
Saintes, Îs. des *Guadeloupe* 15°50N 61°35W **322** e
Stes-Maries-de-la-Mer *France* 43°26N 4°26E **175** E8
Saintfield *U.K.* 54°28N 5°49W **166** B6
Saintonge *France* 45°40N 0°50W **174** C3
Saipal *Nepal* 29°50N 81°40E **243** E9
Saipan *N. Marianas* 15°12N 145°45E **302** e
Saipan Channel *N. Marianas* 15°5N 145°41E **302** e
Sairang *India* 23°50N 92°45E **241** D4
Sairecábur, Cerro *Bolivia* 22°43S 67°54W **334** A2
Sāitah *Si. Arabia* 16°36N 42°56E **248** C3
Saitama *Japan* 35°54N 139°38E **223** B11
Saitama □ *Japan* 36°25N 139°30E **223** A11
Saiteli = Kadınhanı *Turkey* 38°14N 32°13E **212** C5
Saiţi *Moldova* 46°30N 29°24E **183** D14
Saito *Japan* 32°3N 131°24E **222** E3
Saiwai *Japan* 35°32N 139°41E **140** B3
Saiyid *Pakistan* 33°7N 73°2E **242** C5
Saja-Besaya ⌂ *Spain* 43°10N 4°9W **194** B6
Sajama *Bolivia* 18°7S 69°0W **330** D4
Sajama, Nevado *Bolivia* 18°6S 68°54W **330** D4
Sajan *Serbia* 45°50N 20°20E **182** E5
Sajó → *Hungary* 47°56N 21°7E **182** C6
Sajókazinc = Kazincbarcika *Hungary* 48°17N 20°36E **182** B5
Sajószentpéter *Hungary* 48°12N 20°44E **182** B5
Sajum *India* 33°20N 79°0E **243** C8
Sak → *S. Africa* 30°52S 20°25E **270** D3
Saka *Kenya* 0°9S 39°20E **268** B4
Saka Kalat *Pakistan* 27°3N 65°3E **240** D2
Sakaba *Nigeria* 11°4N 5°35E **263** C6
Sakai *Fukui, Japan* 36°9N 136°16E **223** A8
Sakai *Ōsaka, Japan* 34°34N 135°27E **133** B1
Sakai Harbour *Japan* 34°36N 135°26E **133** B1
Sakaide *Japan* 34°19N 133°50E **222** C5
Sakaiminato *Japan* 35°38N 133°11E **222** B5
Sakākah *Si. Arabia* 30°0N 40°8E **246** D4
Sakakawea, L. *U.S.A.* 47°30N 101°25W **308** B3
Sakami → *Canada* 53°40N 76°40W **298** B4
Sakami, L. *Canada* 53°15N 77°0W **298** B4
Sâkâne, 'Erg i-n *Mali* 20°30N 1°30W **260** D4
Sakania *Dem. Rep. of the Congo* 12°43S 28°30E **269** E2
Sakar I. *Papua N. G.* 5°25S 148°6E **286** C5
Sakaraha *Madag.* 22°55S 44°32E **272** C1
Sakartvelo = Georgia ■ *Asia* 42°0N 43°0E **191** J6
Sakarya *Turkey* 40°48N 30°25E **212** B4
Sakarya □ *Turkey* 40°45N 30°25E **212** B4
Sakarya → *Turkey* 41°7N 30°39E **212** B4
Sakashima-Guntō *Japan* 24°46N 124°0E **221** M2
Sakassou *Côte d'Ivoire* 7°29N 5°19W **262** D3
Sakata *Japan* 38°55N 139°50E **220** E9
Sakawa *Japan* 33°28N 133°11E **222** D5
Sakchu *N. Korea* 40°23N 125°2E **224** B2
Sakeny → *Madag.* 20°0S 45°25E **272** C2
Sakété *Benin* 6°40N 2°45E **263** D5
Sakha □ *Russia* 66°0N 130°0E **215** C14
Sakhalin *Russia* 51°0N 143°0E **215** D15
Sakhalinskiy Zaliv *Russia* 54°0N 141°0E **215** D15
Sakhi Gopal *India* 19°58N 85°50E **244** E7
Şaki *Azerbaijan* 41°10N 47°5E **191** K8
Šakiai *Lithuania* 54°59N 23°2E **184** D10
Sakiz-Adasi = Chios *Greece* 38°27N 26°9E **205** C8
Sakmara → *Russia* 51°46N 55°1E **216** B5
Sakoli *India* 21°5N 79°59E **244** D4
Sakon Nakhon *Thailand* 17°10N 104°9E **236** D5
Sakra, Pulau *Singapore* 1°15N 103°41E **138** B2
Sakrand *Pakistan* 26°10N 68°15E **242** F3
Sakri *Maharashtra, India* 26°13N 86°5E **243** F12
Sakri *Maharashtra, India* 21°2N 74°20E **244** D2
Sakrivier *S. Africa* 30°54S 20°28E **270** D3
Sakskøbing *Denmark* 54°49N 11°39E **163** K5
Sakti *India* 22°2N 82°58E **243** H10
Saku *Japan* 36°17N 138°31E **223** A10
Sakuma *Japan* 35°3N 137°49E **223** B9
Sakura *Japan* 35°43N 140°14E **223** B12
Sakurai *Japan* 34°30N 135°51E **223** C7
Sakurajima = On-Take *Japan* 31°35N 130°39E **222** F2
Saky *Ukraine* 45°9N 33°34E **189** K7
Sal → *Russia* 47°31N 40°45E **191** G5
Sal Rei *Cabo Verde* 16°11N 22°53W **153** j
Sala *Eritrea* 16°53N 37°36E **257** D4
Šal'a *Slovakia* 48°10N 17°50E **181** C10
Sala *Sweden* 59°58N 16°35E **162** E10
Sala → *Eritrea* 16°53N 37°36E **257** D4
Sala, O. → *Chad* 17°0N 20°53E **259** E4
Sala Consilina *Italy* 40°23N 15°36E **201** B8
Sala-y-Gómez *Pac. Oc.* 26°28S 105°28W **289** K17
Sala-y-Gómez Ridge *Pac. Oc.* 25°0S 98°0W **289** K18
Salaberry-de-Valleyfield *Canada* 45°15N 74°8W **313** A10
Salacgrīva *Latvia* 57°45N 24°21E **184** A11
Salada, L. *Mexico* 32°20N 115°40W **305** K6
Saladas *Argentina* 28°15S 58°40W **334** B4
Saladillo *Argentina* 35°40S 59°55W **334** D4
Saladin's Castle = Qal'at Salah el Din *Syria* 34°46N 36°15E **250** D7
Salado → *B. Aires, Argentina* 35°44S 57°22W **334** D4
Salado → *La Pampa, Argentina* 37°30S 67°0W **336** A3
Salado → *Río Negro, Argentina* 41°34S 65°3W **336** B3
Salado → *Santa Fe, Argentina* 31°40S 60°41W **334** C3
Salado → *Tamaulipas, Mexico* 26°52N 99°19W **314** H5
Salaga *Ghana* 8°31N 0°31W **263** D4
Sālah *Syria* 32°40N 36°45E **250** F7
Şalāḩ ad Dīn □ *Iraq* 34°35N 43°35E **246** C4
Salahin *Somalia* 2°57N 46°26E **267** D6
Sălaj □ *Romania* 47°15N 23°0E **182** C8
Salakos *Greece* 36°17N 27°57E **206** E11
Salal *Chad* 14°48N 17°12E **259** F3
Salala *Liberia* 6°42N 10°7W **262** D2
Salala *Sudan* 21°17N 36°16E **256** C4
Salālah *Oman* 16°56N 53°59E **249** C6
Salam *Iraq* 33°20N 44°20E **113** A2
Salamajärvi △ *Finland* 63°12N 24°50E **160** E21
Salamanca *Chile* 31°46S 70°59W **334** C1
Salamanca *Madrid, Spain* 40°25N 3°41W **127** B1
Salamanca *Salamanca, Spain* 40°58N 5°39W **194** E5
Salamanca *N.Y., U.S.A.* 42°10N 78°43W **312** D6
Salamanca □ *Spain* 40°57N 5°40W **194** E5
Salamat □ *Chad* 11°0N 20°30E **259** F4
Salamat, Bahr → *Chad* 9°20N 18°0E **259** G3
Salāmatābād *Iran* 35°39N 47°50E **246** C5
Salamina *Colombia* 5°25N 75°29W **328** B2
Salamina *Greece* 37°56N 23°30E **204** D5
Salamis *Cyprus* 35°11N 33°54E **207** E9
Salamonie L. *U.S.A.* 40°46N 85°37W **311** D11
Salar de Atacama *Chile* 23°30S 68°25W **334** A2
Salar de Uyuni *Bolivia* 20°30S 67°45W **330** E4
Sălard *Romania* 47°12N 22°3E **182** C7
Salas *Spain* 43°25N 6°15W **194** B4
Salas de los Infantes *Spain* 42°2N 3°17W **194** C7
Salatiga *Indonesia* 7°19S 110°30E **235** D4
Salavat *Russia* 53°21N 55°55E **186** D10
Salaverry *Peru* 8°15S 79°0W **330** B2
Salawati *Indonesia* 1°7S 130°52E **231** E8
Salawin △ *Thailand* 18°18N 97°40E **236** C1
Salay *Phil.* 8°52N 124°47E **233** G5
Salaya *India* 22°19N 69°35E **242** H3
Salayar *Indonesia* 6°7S 120°30E **231** F6
Salazar → *Spain* 42°40N 1°20W **196** C3
Salazie *Réunion* 21°2S 55°32E **272** f
Salazie, Cirque de *Réunion* 21°3S 55°30E **272** f
Salbris *France* 47°25N 2°3E **173** E9
S'Albufera *Spain* 39°47N 3°7E **206** B4
S'Albufera d'es Grau *Spain* 39°56N 4°16E **206** B5
Salcantay, Nevado *Peru* 13°19S 72°33W **330** C3
Salcedo *Phil.* 11°9N 125°40E **233** F5
Salcia *Romania* 43°56N 24°55E **183** G9
Sălciua *Romania* 46°24N 23°26E **183** D8
Salcombe *U.K.* 50°14N 3°47W **169** G4
Saldaña *Spain* 42°32N 4°48W **194** C6
Saldanha *S. Africa* 33°0S 17°58E **270** D2
Saldanha B. *S. Africa* 33°6S 18°0E **270** D2
Saldus *Latvia* 56°38N 22°30E **184** B9
Sale *Vic., Australia* 38°6S 147°6E **283** E7
Sale *Italy* 44°59N 8°48E **198** D5
Salé *Morocco* 34°3N 6°48W **260** B3
Sale *Myanmar* 20°50N 94°45E **241** E5
Sale *Gt. Man., U.K.* 53°26N 2°19W **168** D5
Sale City *U.S.A.* 31°16N 84°1W **316** D5
Salée, Rivière *Guadeloupe* 16°17N 61°33W **322** e
Salegard = Salekhard *Russia* 66°30N 66°35E **214** C7
Saleh, Teluk *Indonesia* 8°34S 117°57E **235** D5
Salekhard *Russia* 66°30N 66°35E **214** C7
Salelologa *Samoa* 13°41S 172°11W **287** V19
Salem *India* 11°40N 78°11E **245** J4
Salem *Montserrat* 16°45N 62°13W **323** p
Salem *Fla., U.S.A.* 29°53N 83°25W **316** F6
Salem *Ill., U.S.A.* 38°38N 88°57W **310** F8
Salem *Ind., U.S.A.* 38°36N 86°6W **311** F10
Salem *Mass., U.S.A.* 42°31N 70°53W **313** D14
Salem *Mo., U.S.A.* 37°39N 91°32W **308** G8
Salem *N.H., U.S.A.* 42°45N 71°12W **313** D13
Salem *N.J., U.S.A.* 39°34N 75°28W **309** F16
Salem *N.Y., U.S.A.* 43°10N 73°20W **313** C11
Salem *Ohio, U.S.A.* 40°54N 80°52W **312** F4
Salem *Oreg., U.S.A.* 44°56N 123°2W **304** D2
Salem *S. Dak., U.S.A.* 43°44N 97°23W **308** D5
Salem *Va., U.S.A.* 37°18N 80°3W **309** G13
Salemi *Italy* 37°49N 12°48E **200** E5
Sälen *Sweden* 61°20N 13°10E **162** C7
Salernes *France* 43°34N 6°15E **175** E10
Salerno *Italy* 40°41N 14°47E **201** B7
Salerno, G. di *Italy* 40°32N 14°42E **201** B7
Sales *Brazil* 4°2S 63°40W **329** D5
Salford *U.K.* 53°30N 2°18W **168** D5
Salgótarján *Hungary* 48°5N 19°47E **182** B4
Salgueiro *Brazil* 8°4S 39°6W **332** C4
Salher *India* 20°40N 73°55E **244** D1
Salhus *Norway* 60°30N 5°15E **164** D2
Salhyr → *Ukraine* 45°38N 35°1E **189** K8
Salibabu *Indonesia* 3°51N 126°40E **231** D7
Salibea = Salybia *Trin. & Tob.* 10°43N 61°2W **323** t
Salibia *Dominica* 15°30N 61°16W **323** k
Salida *U.S.A.* 38°32N 106°0W **304** G11
Salies-de-Béarn *France* 43°28N 0°56W **174** E3
Salihli *Turkey* 38°28N 28°8E **212** C3
Salihorsk *Belarus* 52°51N 27°27E **177** B14
Salin *Myanmar* 20°35N 94°40E **241** E5
Salina *Italy* 38°34N 14°50E **201** D7
Salina *Kans., U.S.A.* 38°50N 97°37W **308** F5
Salina *Utah, U.S.A.* 38°58N 111°51W **304** G8
Salina Cruz *Mexico* 16°10N 95°12W **319** D5
Salina di Margherita di Savóia ⌂ *Italy* 41°23N 16°4E **201** A9
Salinas = Salinópolis *Brazil* 0°40S 47°20W **332** B2
Salinas *Brazil* 16°10S 42°10W **333** E3
Salinas *Ecuador* 2°10S 80°58W **328** D1
Salinas *Calif., U.S.A.* 36°40N 121°39W **306** J5
Salinas → *Guatemala* 16°28N 90°31W **319** D6
Salinas → *Calif., U.S.A.* 36°45N 121°48W **306** J5
Salinas, B. das *Angola* 14°11S 12°21E **265** E2
Salinas, B. de *Nic.* 11°4N 85°45W **320** D2
Salinas, Pampa de las *Argentina* 31°58S 66°42W **334** C2
Salinas Ambargasta *Argentina* 29°0S 65°0W **334** B3
Salinas de Hidalgo *Mexico* 22°38N 101°43W **318** C4
Salinas Grandes *Argentina* 30°0S 65°0W **334** C3
Salinas Pueblo Missions ⌂ *U.S.A.* 34°6N 106°4W **305** J10
Salinas Valley *U.S.A.* 36°15N 121°15W **306** J5
Saline *U.S.A.* 42°10N 83°47W **311** B13
Saline → *Ark., U.S.A.* 33°10N 92°8W **314** E8
Saline → *Kans., U.S.A.* 38°52N 97°30W **308** F5
Saline B. *Trin. & Tob.* 10°42N 61°2W **323** t
Saline di Trapani e Paceco ⌂ *Italy* 37°59N 12°28E **200** E5
Saline I. *Grenada* 12°26N 61°28W **323** q
Salines, C. de ses *Spain* 39°16N 3°4E **206** B4
Salines, Étang des *Martinique* 14°24N 60°52W **322** j
Salines, Pt. *Grenada* 12°0N 61°48W **323** q
Salines, Pte. de *Martinique* 14°23N 60°53W **322** j
Salinópolis *Brazil* 0°40S 47°20W **332** B2
Salins-les-Bains *France* 46°58N 5°52E **173** F12
Salir *Portugal* 37°14N 8°2W **195** H2
Salisbury = Harare *Zimbabwe* 17°43S 31°2E **269** F3
Salisbury *S. Austral., Australia* 34°46S 138°38E **282** C3
Salisbury *Dominica* 15°26N 61°27W **323** k
Salisbury *Wilts., U.K.* 51°4N 1°47W **169** F6
Salisbury *Md., U.S.A.* 38°22N 75°36W **309** F16
Salisbury *Mo., U.S.A.* 39°25N 92°48W **310** E4
Salisbury *N.C., U.S.A.* 35°40N 80°29W **315** D14
Salisbury I. *Canada* 63°30N 77°0W **295** E16
Salisbury Plain *U.K.* 51°14N 1°55W **169** F6
Săliște *Romania* 45°45N 23°56E **183** E8
Salitre → *Brazil* 9°29S 40°39W **332** C3
Salkehatchie → *U.S.A.* 32°37N 80°53W **316** C9
Şalkhad *Syria* 32°29N 36°43E **251** F7
Salkove *Ukraine* 48°15N 29°59E **183** B14
Salla *Finland* 66°50N 28°49E **160** C23
Sallanches *France* 45°55N 6°38E **175** C10
Sallent *Spain* 41°49N 1°54E **196** D6
Salles *France* 44°33N 0°52W **174** D3
Salles-Curan *France* 44°11N 2°48E **174** D6
Salling *Denmark* 56°40N 8°55E **163** H2
Salliq = Coral Harbour *Canada* 64°8N 83°10W **295** E15
Sallisaw *U.S.A.* 35°28N 94°47W **314** D7
Sallom *Sudan* 19°17N 37°6E **256** D4
Salluit *Canada* 62°14N 75°38W **295** E16
Sallyana *Nepal* 28°22N 82°10E **243** E10
Salmān Pak *Iraq* 33°6N 44°34E **213** G11
Salmannsdorf *Austria* 48°14N 16°14E **142** A1
Salmās *Iran* 38°11N 44°47E **213** C11
Salmedina *Spain* 40°18N 3°35W **127** C2
Salmerón *Spain* 40°33N 2°29W **196** E2
Salmo *Canada* 49°10N 117°20W **296** D5
Salmon *U.S.A.* 45°11N 113°54W **304** D7
Salmon → *B.C., Canada* 54°3N 122°40W **296** C4
Salmon → *Idaho, U.S.A.* 45°51N 116°47W **304** D5
Salmon Arm *Canada* 50°40N 119°15W **296** C5
Salmon Gums *Australia* 32°59S 121°38E **279** F3
Salmon Pt. *Canada* 43°52N 77°15W **312** C7
Salmon River Mts. *U.S.A.* 44°50N 115°30W **304** D6
Salmon River Res. *U.S.A.* 43°32N 75°55W **313** C9
Salo *C.A.R.* 3°10N 16°8E **264** B3
Salo *Finland* 60°22N 23°10E **188** B2
Salò *Italy* 45°36N 10°31E **198** C7
Salobreña *Spain* 36°44N 3°35W **195** J7
Salome *U.S.A.* 33°47N 113°37W **307** M13
Salomea *Poland* 52°11N 20°55E **143** B1
Salomon, C. *Martinique* 14°30N 61°6W **322** j
Salon *India* 26°2N 81°27E **243** F9
Salon-de-Provence *France* 43°39N 5°6E **175** E9
Salonga → *Dem. Rep. of the Congo* 0°10S 19°50E **264** C4
Salonga-Nord △ *Dem. Rep. of the Congo* 1°55S 21°45E **264** C4
Salonga-Sud △ *Dem. Rep. of the Congo* 2°25S 21°0E **264** C4
Salonica = Thessaloniki *Greece* 40°38N 22°58E **202** F6
Salonta *Romania* 46°49N 21°42E **182** D6
Salop = Shropshire □ *U.K.* 52°36N 2°45W **169** E5
Salor → *Spain* 39°39N 7°3W **195** F3
Salou *Spain* 41°4N 1°8E **196** D6
Salou, C. de *Spain* 41°3N 1°10E **196** D6
Saloum → *Senegal* 13°50N 16°45W **262** C1
Salpausselkä *Finland* 61°3N 26°15E **188** B4
Salsacate *Argentina* 31°20S 65°5W **334** C2
Salses *France* 42°50N 2°55E **174** F6
Salsette I. *India* 19°2N 72°53E **130** A2
Salsk *Russia* 46°28N 41°30E **191** G5
Salso → *Italy* 37°6N 13°57E **200** E6
Salsomaggiore Terme *Italy* 44°49N 9°59E **198** D6
Salt *Spain* 41°59N 2°47E **196** D7
Salt → *Alta., Canada* 60°0N 112°25W **296** B6
Salt → *Ariz., U.S.A.* 33°23N 112°19W **305** K7
Salt → *Mo., U.S.A.* 39°28N 91°4W **310** E5
Salt Cay *The Bahamas* 25°6N 77°18W **153** b
Salt Flats = Witte Pan *Bonaire* 12°3N 68°17W **322** h
Salt Fork Red → *U.S.A.* 34°27N 99°21W **314** D5
Salt L. *N.S.W., Australia* 30°6S 142°8E **281** E3
Salt L. *Hawai'i, U.S.A.* 21°21N 157°55W **302** K14
Salt Lake City = Bidhan Nagar *India* 22°35N 88°25E **124** B2
Salt Lake City *U.S.A.* 40°45N 111°53W **304** F8
Salt Lake City Int. ✈ **(SLC)** *U.S.A.* 40°47N 111°58W **304** F7
Salt Lake Stadium *Kolkata, India* 22°34N 88°25E **124** B2
Salt Range *Pakistan* 32°30N 72°25E **242** C5
Salt River *S. Africa* 34°6S 18°28E **118** A1
Salt Springs *U.S.A.* 29°21N 81°44W **317** F8
Salt Water L. *India* 22°33N 88°26E **124** B2
Salta *Argentina* 24°57S 65°25W **334** A2
Salta □ *Argentina* 24°48S 65°30W **334** A2
Saltara *Italy* 43°45N 12°50E **199** E9
Saltash *U.K.* 50°24N 4°14W **169** G3
Saltburn-by-the-Sea *U.K.* 54°35N 0°58W **168** C7
Saltcoats *U.K.* 55°38N 4°47W **167** F4
Saltee Is. *Ireland* 52°7N 6°37W **166** D5
Salters *U.S.A.* 33°36N 79°51W **316** B10
Saltfjellet *Norway* 66°40N 15°15E **160** C16
Saltfjellet-Svartisen △ *Norway* 66°45N 15°10E **160** C16
Saltfjorden *Norway* 67°15N 14°10E **160** C16
Saltholm *Denmark* 55°38N 12°43E **163** J6
Salthólmavík *Iceland* 65°24N 21°57W **155** B5
Saltillo *Mexico* 25°25N 101°0W **318** B4
Salto *Argentina* 34°20S 60°15W **334** C3
Salto *Uruguay* 31°27S 57°50W **334** C4
Salto da Divisa *Brazil* 16°0S 39°57W **333** E4
Salto del Guaíra *Paraguay* 24°3S 54°17W **335** A5
Salton City *U.S.A.* 33°18N 115°57W **307** M11
Salton Sea *U.S.A.* 33°15N 115°45W **307** M11
Saltpond *Ghana* 5°15N 1°3W **263** D4
Saltrød *Norway* 58°30N 8°49E **164** F5
Saltsburg *U.S.A.* 40°29N 79°27W **312** F5
Saltsjö-Duvnäs *Sweden* 59°18N 18°12E **139** B3
Saltsjöbaden *Sweden* 59°15N 18°20E **162** E12
Saluda *U.S.A.* 34°0N 81°46W **316** A8
Saluda → *U.S.A.* 34°1N 81°4W **316** A8
Salue Timpaus, Selat *Indonesia* 1°50S 123°50E **231** E6
Salug *Phil.* 8°7N 122°47E **233** G4
Salûm *Egypt* 31°31N 25°7E **256** A2
Salûm, Khâlig el *Egypt* 31°35N 25°24E **256** A2
Salur *India* 18°27N 83°18E **244** E6
Salut, Is. du *Fr. Guiana* 5°15N 52°35W **329** B7
Saluzzo *Italy* 44°39N 7°29E **198** D4
Salvación, B. *Chile* 50°50S 75°10W **336** D1
Salvador *Brazil* 13°0S 38°30W **333** D4
Salvador *Sask., Canada* 52°10N 109°32W **297** C7
Salvador, El ■ *Cent. Amer.* 13°50N 89°0W **320** D2
Salvador, L. *U.S.A.* 29°43N 90°15W **315** G9
Salvaterra *Brazil* 0°46S 48°31W **332** B2
Salvaterra de Magos *Portugal* 39°1N 8°47W **195** F2
Salvisa *U.S.A.* 37°54N 84°51W **311** G12
Sálvora, I. de *Spain* 42°30N 8°58W **194** C2
Salween → *Myanmar* 16°31N 97°37E **241** G6
Salyan *Azerbaijan* 39°33N 48°59E **213** C13
Salybia *Trin. & Tob.* 10°43N 61°2W **323** t
Salza → *Austria* 47°40N 14°43E **180** D7
Salzach → *Austria* 48°12N 12°56E **180** C5
Salzburg *Austria* 47°48N 13°2E **180** D6
Salzburg □ *Austria* 47°15N 13°0E **180** D6
Salzburgen = Château-Salins *France* 48°50N 6°30E **173** D13
Salzgitter *Germany* 52°9N 10°19E **178** C6
Salzkotten *Germany* 51°40N 8°37E **178** D4
Salzwedel *Germany* 52°52N 11°10E **178** C7
Sam *Gabon* 0°58N 11°16E **264** B2
Sam *India* 26°50N 70°31E **242** F4
Sam Neua *Laos* 20°29N 104°5E **228** G5
Sam Ngao *Thailand* 17°18N 99°0E **236** D2
Sam Rayburn Res. *U.S.A.* 31°4N 94°5W **314** F7
Sam Rong, Laem *Thailand* 9°35N 100°4E **237** b
Sam Son *Vietnam* 19°44N 105°54E **236** C5
Sama de Langreo = Langreo *Spain* 43°18N 5°40W **194** B5
Šamac *Bos.-H.* 45°3N 18°29E **182** E3
Samacimbo *Angola* 13°33S 16°59E **265** E3
Şamad *Oman* 22°48N 58°9E **249** B7
Samagaltay *Russia* 50°36N 95°3E **217** B13
Samā'il *Oman* 23°40N 57°50E **249** B7
Samaipata *Bolivia* 18°9S 63°52W **331** D5
Samal *Phil.* 7°5N 125°42E **233** H5
Samal I. *Phil.* 7°3N 125°44E **233** H5
Samales Group *Phil.* 6°0N 122°0E **233** J3
Samalga Pass *U.S.A.* 52°50N 169°0W **300** E6
Samalkot *India* 17°3N 82°13E **244** F6
Samâlût *Egypt* 28°20N 30°42E **256** B3
Samana *India* 30°10N 76°13E **242** D7
Samana Cays *The Bahamas* 23°3N 73°45W **321** B5
Samandağ *Turkey* 36°5N 35°59E **250** B6
Samandıra *Turkey* 40°59N 29°13E **203** F13
Samanga *Tanzania* 8°20S 39°13E **269** D4
Samangān □ *Afghan.* 36°15N 68°3E **240** A3
Samangwa *Dem. Rep. of the Congo* 4°23S 24°10E **265** C4
Samani *Japan* 42°7N 142°56E **220** C11
Samanli Dağları *Turkey* 40°32N 29°10E **203** F13
Samannûd *Egypt* 30°57N 31°14E **251** H2
Samar *Phil.* 12°0N 125°0E **233** F5
Samar □ *Phil.* 11°50N 125°0E **233** F5
Samar Sea *Phil.* 12°0N 124°15E **232** E5
Samara *Russia* 53°8N 50°6E **190** D10
Samara → *Russia* 53°10N 50°4E **190** D10
Samara → *Ukraine* 48°28N 35°7E **189** H8
Samarai *Papua N. G.* 10°39S 150°41E **286** F6
Samaria *West Bank* 32°17N 35°12E **251** F6
Samaria △ *Greece* 35°17N 23°58E **207** E4
Samariapo *Venezuela* 5°15N 67°48W **328** B4
Samarinda *Indonesia* 0°30S 117°9E **235** C5
Samarkand = Samarqand *Uzbekistan* 39°40N 66°55E **217** E7
Samarkandsky = Temirtau *Kazakhstan* 50°5N 72°56E **217** B8
Samarqand *Uzbekistan* 39°40N 66°55E **217** E7
Samarqand □ *Uzbekistan* 39°35N 66°35E **217** E7
Sāmarrā' *Iraq* 34°12N 43°52E **213** E10
Samarskaya Luka △ *Russia* 53°30N 49°30E **190** D9
Samastipur *India* 25°50N 85°50E **243** G11
Samatya *Turkey* 40°59N 28°55E **122** C1
Samaúma *Brazil* 7°50S 60°2W **331** B5
Şamaxı *Azerbaijan* 40°38N 48°37E **191** K9
Samba *Équateur, Dem. Rep. of the Congo* 0°13N 21°25E **264** B4
Samba *Maniema, Dem. Rep. of the Congo* 4°38S 26°22E **265** C5
Samba *Jammu & Kashmir, India* 32°32N 75°10E **243** C6
Samba Caju *Angola* 8°46S 15°24E **265** D3
Sambaíba *Brazil* 7°8S 45°21W **332** C2
Sambalpur *India* 21°28N 84°4E **244** D7
Sambar, Tanjung *Indonesia* 2°59S 110°19E **235** C4
Sambas *Indonesia* 1°20N 109°20E **235** B3
Sambava *Madag.* 14°16S 50°10E **272** A3
Sambawizi *Zimbabwe* 18°24S 26°13E **269** F2
Sambhajinagar = Aurangabad *India* 19°50N 75°23E **244** E2
Sambhal *India* 28°35N 78°37E **243** E8
Sambhar *India* 26°52N 75°6E **242** F6
Sambhar L. *India* 26°55N 75°12E **242** F6
Sambir *Ukraine* 49°30N 23°10E **185** J10
Sambo *Angola* 13°3S 16°8E **265** E3
Sambo *Indonesia* 3°22S 118°52E **235** C5
Samboja *Indonesia* 1°1S 117°1E **235** C5
Sambor *Cambodia* 12°46N 106°0E **236** F6
Sambor Prei Kuk *Cambodia* 12°46N 105°58E **236** F5
Samborombón, B. *Argentina* 36°5S 57°20W **334** D4
Sambuca di Sicília *Italy* 37°39N 13°7E **200** E6
Samburu □ *Kenya* 1°10N 36°40E **268** B4
Samburu ⌂ *Kenya* 0°37N 37°31E **268** B4
Samcheok *S. Korea* 37°26N 129°10E **224** D4
Same *Tanzania* 4°2S 37°38E **268** C4
Samer *France* 50°38N 1°44E **173** B8
Samet, Ko *Thailand* 12°34N 101°27E **236** F3
Samfya *Zambia* 11°22S 29°31E **269** E2
Samḩah *Yemen* 12°15N 53°5E **249** D6
Samḩān, Jabal *Oman* 17°12N 54°55E **249** C6
Sami *Greece* 38°15N 20°39E **207** C2
Samka *Myanmar* 20°9N 96°57E **241** E6
Şämkir *Azerbaijan* 40°50N 46°0E **191** K8
Samland = Zemlandskiy Poluostrov *Russia* 54°50N 20°20E **184** D7
Şamlı *Turkey* 39°48N 27°51E **205** B9
Sammanturai *Sri Lanka* 7°36N 81°39E **245** L5
Samnah *Si. Arabia* 25°10N 37°15E **246** E3
Samnū *Libya* 27°15N 14°55E **258** C2
Samo Alto *Chile* 30°22S 71°0W **334** C1
Samoa ■ *Pac. Oc.* 14°0S 172°0W **287** V20
Samoan Is. *Pac. Oc.* 14°0S 171°0W **287** V20
Samobor *Croatia* 45°47N 15°44E **199** C12
Samoëns *France* 46°5N 6°45E **173** F13
Samokov *Bulgaria* 42°18N 23°35E **202** D7
Šamorín *Slovakia* 48°2N 17°19E **181** C10
Samorogouan *Burkina Faso* 11°21N 4°57W **262** C4
Samos *Greece* 37°45N 26°50E **205** D8
Samoš *Serbia* 45°13N 20°46E **182** E5
Samos *Spain* 42°44N 7°20W **194** C3
Samoset *U.S.A.* 27°28N 82°33W **317** H7
Samosir *Indonesia* 2°55N 98°50E **234** B1
Samothráki = Mathraki *Greece* 39°48N 19°31E **206** B9
Samothraki *Greece* 40°28N 25°28E **203** F9
Samoylovka *Russia* 51°12N 43°43E **190** E6
Sampa *Angola* 10°38S 18°56E **265** E3
Sampa *Ghana* 8°0N 2°36W **262** D4
Sampacho *Argentina* 33°20S 64°50W **334** C3
Sampalan *Indonesia* 8°41S 115°34E **231** K18
Sampaloc *Phil.* 14°36N 120°59E **127** B1
Sampang *Indonesia* 7°11S 113°13E **235** D4
Samper de Calanda *Spain* 41°11N 0°28W **196** D4
Sampéyre *Italy* 44°34N 7°11E **198** D4
Samphan Thawong *Thailand* 13°44N 100°31E **113** B2
Sampit *Indonesia* 2°34S 113°0E **235** C4
Sampit → *Indonesia* 2°44S 112°54E **235** C4
Sampit, Teluk *Indonesia* 3°5S 113°3E **235** C4
Sampun *Papua N. G.* 5°21S 152°8E **286** C7
Samrong *Cambodia* 14°15N 103°30E **236** E4
Samseon *S. Korea* 37°34N 127°0E **137** B2
Samseong *S. Korea* 37°31N 127°2E **137** B2
Samsø *Denmark* 55°50N 10°35E **163** J4
Samsø Bælt *Denmark* 55°45N 10°45E **163** J4
Samson *U.S.A.* 31°7N 86°3W **316** D3
Samsun *Turkey* 41°15N 36°22E **212** B7
Samsun □ *Turkey* 41°10N 36°10E **212** B7
Samtah *Si. Arabia* 16°36N 42°56E **248** C3
Samtredia *Georgia* 42°7N 42°24E **191** J6
Samuel Smith Park *Canada* 43°35N 79°30W **141** B1
Samui, Ko *Thailand* 9°30N 100°0E **237** b
Samur → *Russia* 41°53N 48°32E **191** K9
Samurskiy Khrebet *Russia* 41°55N 47°11E **191** K8
Samusole *Dem. Rep. of the Congo* 10°2S 24°0E **265** E4
Samut Prakan *Bangkok, Thailand* 13°40N 100°36E **113** B2
Samut Sakhon *Thailand* 13°32N 100°17E **236** F3
Samut Songkhram *Thailand* 13°24N 100°1E **236** F3
Samwari *Pakistan* 28°30N 66°46E **242** E2
San *Mali* 13°15N 4°57W **262** C4
San → *Cambodia* 13°32N 105°57E **236** F5
San → *Poland* 50°45N 21°51E **185** H8
San Adrián *Spain* 42°20N 1°56W **196** C3
San Adrián, C. de *Spain* 43°21N 8°50W **194** B2
San Agustín *Colombia* 1°53N 76°16W **328** C2
San Agustin *Romblon, Phil.* 12°34N 122°6E **232** E4
San Agustin, C. *Phil.* 6°20N 126°13E **233** H6
San Agustín de Valle Fértil *Argentina* 30°35S 67°30W **334** C2
San Ambrosio *Pac. Oc.* 26°28S 79°53W **326** F3
San Andreas *U.S.A.* 38°12N 120°41W **306** G6
San Andres *Catanduanes, Phil.* 13°36N 124°6E **232** E5
San Andres *Romblon, Phil.* 13°19N 122°41E **232** E4
San Andres *Romblon, Phil.* 12°31N 122°2E **232** E4
San Andrés *Barcelona, Spain* 41°26N 2°11E **114** A2
San Andrés, I. de *Caribbean* 12°42N 81°46W **320** D3
San Andrés del Rabanedo *Spain* 42°37N 5°36W **194** C5
San Andres Mts. *U.S.A.* 33°0N 106°30W **305** K10
San Andres Pt. *Phil.* 13°34N 121°52E **232** E3
San Andrés Tuxtla *Mexico* 18°27N 95°13W **319** D5
San Angel *Mexico* 19°20N 99°11W **128** B1
San Angelo *U.S.A.* 31°28N 100°26W **314** F4
San Angelo Raffaele *Venice, Italy* **142** b2
San Anselmo *U.S.A.* 37°59N 122°34W **306** H4
San Antonio *Belize* 16°15N 89°2W **320** C2
San Antonio *Chile* 33°40S 71°40W **334** C1
San Antonio *Phil.* 14°57N 120°5E **232** D3
San Antonio *N. Mex., U.S.A.* 33°55N 106°52W **305** K10
San Antonio *Tex., U.S.A.* 29°25N 98°29W **314** G5
San Antonio *Amazonas, Venezuela* 3°30N 66°44W **328** C4
San Antonio *Nueva Esparta, Venezuela* 10°57N 63°54W **329** a
San Antonio → *U.S.A.* 28°30N 96°54W **314** G6
San Antonio, C. *Argentina* 36°15S 56°40W **334** D4
San Antonio, C. de *Cuba* 21°50N 84°57W **320** B3
San Antonio, C. de *Spain* 38°48N 0°12E **197** G5
San Antonio, Mt. *U.S.A.* 34°17N 117°38W **307** L9
San Antonio B. *Phil.* 8°38N 117°35E **233** G1
San Antonio de los Baños *Cuba* 22°54N 82°31W **320** B3
San Antonio de los Cobres *Argentina* 24°10S 66°17W **334** A2
San Antonio Oeste *Argentina* 40°40S 65°0W **336** B4
San Arcángelo *Italy* 40°14N 16°14E **201** B9
San Ardo *U.S.A.* 36°1N 120°54W **306** J6
San Augustín *Canary Is.* 27°47N 15°32W **153** e1
San Augustine *U.S.A.* 31°32N 94°7W **314** F7
San Bartolomé *Canary Is.* 28°59N 13°37W **153** e2
San Bartolomé de Tirajana *Canary Is.* 27°54N 15°34W **153** e1
San Bartolomeo in Galdo *Italy* 41°24N 15°1E **201** A8
San Basilio *Italy* 41°56N 12°35E **136** B2
San Benedetto del Tronto *Italy* 42°57N 13°53E **199** F10
San Benedetto Po *Italy* 45°2N 10°55E **198** C7
San Benedicto, I. *Mexico* 19°18N 110°49W **318** D2
San Benito *U.S.A.* 26°8N 97°38W **314** H6
San Benito → *U.S.A.* 36°53N 121°34W **306** J5
San Benito Mt. *U.S.A.* 36°22N 120°37W **306** J6
San Bernardino *U.S.A.* 34°7N 117°19W **307** L9
San Bernardino Mts. *U.S.A.* 34°10N 116°45W **307** L10
San Bernardino Str. *Phil.* 12°30N 124°10E **232** E5
San Bernardo *Chile* 33°40S 70°50W **334** C1
San Bernardo, I. de *Colombia* 9°45N 75°50W **328** B2
San-Beyse = Choybalsan *Mongolia* 48°4N 114°30E **219** B11
San Biagio *Venice, Italy* **142** b4
San Blas *Mexico* 26°5N 108°46W **318** B3
San Blas, Arch. de *Panama* 9°50N 78°31W **320** E4
San Blas, C. *U.S.A.* 29°40N 85°21W **316** F4
San Bonifacio *Italy* 45°24N 11°16E **199** C8
San Borja *Bolivia* 14°50S 66°52W **330** C4
San Borja *Lima, Peru* 12°6S 76°59W **124** B3
San Bóvio *Italy* 45°27N 9°18E **128** B2
San Bruno, Pt. *U.S.A.* 37°39N 122°22W **136** C2
San Bruno Mountain State Park ⌂ *U.S.A.* 37°41N 122°26W **136** B2
San Buenaventura = Ventura *U.S.A.* 34°17N 119°18W **307** L7
San Buenaventura *Bolivia* 14°28S 67°35W **330** C4
San Buenaventura *Coahuila, Mexico* 27°5N 101°32W **318** B4
San Carlos = Butuku-Luba *Eq. Guin.* 3°29N 8°33E **263** E6
San Carlos = Sant Carles *Spain* 39°3N 1°34E **206** C2
San Carlos *Argentina* 33°50S 69°0W **334** C2
San Carlos *Bolivia* 17°24S 63°45W **331** D5
San Carlos *Chile* 36°10S 72°0W **334** D1
San Carlos *Baja Calif. S., Mexico* 24°47N 112°7W **318** C2
San Carlos *Coahuila, Mexico* 29°1N 100°51W **318** B4
San Carlos *Nic.* 11°12N 84°50W **320** D3
San Carlos *Neg. Occ., Phil.* 10°29N 123°25E **233** F4
San Carlos *Pangasinan, Phil.* 15°55N 120°20E **232** D3
San Carlos *Uruguay* 34°46S 54°58W **335** C5
San Carlos *Ariz., U.S.A.* 33°21N 110°27W **305** K8
San Carlos *Amazonas, Venezuela* 1°55N 67°4W **328** C4
San Carlos *Cojedes, Venezuela* 9°40N 68°36W **328** B4
San Carlos de Bariloche *Argentina* 41°10S 71°25W **336** B2
San Carlos de Bolívar *Argentina* 36°15S 61°6W **334** D3
San Carlos de la Rápita = Sant Carles de la Ràpita *Spain* 40°37N 0°35E **196** E5
San Carlos de Río Negro *Venezuela* 1°55N 67°4W **328** C4
San Carlos del Zulia *Venezuela* 9°1N 71°55W **328** B3
San Carlos L. *U.S.A.* 33°11N 110°32W **305** K8
San Carlos Park *U.S.A.* 26°28N 81°49W **317** J8
San Cataldo *Italy* 37°29N 13°59E **200** E6
San Celoni = Sant Celoni *Spain* 41°42N 2°30E **196** D7
San Clemente *Chile* 35°30S 71°29W **334** D1
San Clemente *Spain* 39°24N 2°25W **197** F2
San Clemente *Calif., U.S.A.* 33°26N 117°37W **307** M9
San Clemente I. *U.S.A.* 32°53N 118°29W **307** N8
San Cristóbal = Es Migjorn Gran *Spain* 39°57N 4°3E **206** B5
San Cristóbal *B. Aires, Argentina* 34°38S 58°23W **117** B2
San Cristóbal *Santa Fe, Argentina* 30°20S 61°10W **334** C3
San Cristóbal *Colombia* 2°18S 73°2W **328** D3
San Cristóbal *Dom. Rep.* 18°25N 70°6W **321** C5

San Cristóbal Solomon Is. 10°30S 161°0E 287 N11
San Cristóbal Madrid, Spain 40°25N 3°35W 127 B2
San Cristóbal Venezuela 7°46N 72°14W 328 B3
San Cristóbal, Cerro Chile 33°25S 70°38W 137 B2
San Cristóbal, I. Ecuador 0°50S 89°26W 330 a
San Cristóbal, Virgen del Chile 33°25S 70°38W 137 B2
San Cristóbal de La Laguna Canary Is. 28°28N 16°18W 153 e1
San Cristóbal de las Casas Mexico 16°45N 92°38W 319 D6
San Cristoforo Italy 45°26N 9°9E 128 B1
San Damiano d'Asti Italy 44°50N 8°4E 198 D5
San Daniele del Friuli Italy 46°9N 13°1E 199 B10
San Diego Calif., U.S.A. 32°42N 117°9W 307 N9
San Diego Tex., U.S.A. 27°46N 98°14W 314 H5
San Diego, C. Argentina 54°40S 65°10W 336 D3
San Diego de la Unión Mexico 21°28N 100°52W 318 C4
San Diego Int. ✈ (SAN) U.S.A. 32°44N 117°11W 307 N9
San Dimitri, Ras Malta 36°4N 14°11E 206 E6
San Dimitri Point = San Dimitri, Ras Malta 36°4N 14°11E 206 E6
San Donà di Piave Italy 45°38N 12°34E 199 C9
San Donato Milanese Italy 45°24N 9°16E 128 B2
San el Hagar Egypt 30°58N 31°52E 251 H2
San Estanislao Paraguay 24°39S 56°26W 334 A4
San Esteban △ Venezuela 10°24N 67°58W 328 A4
San Esteban de Gormaz Spain 41°34N 3°13W 196 D1
San Eugenio = Artigas Uruguay 30°20S 56°30W 334 C4
San Felice Circeo Italy 41°14N 13°5E 200 A6
San Felice sul Panaro Italy 44°50N 11°8E 199 D8
San Felipe Chile 32°43S 70°42W 334 C1
San Felipe Colombia 1°55N 67°6W 328 C4
San Felipe Baja Calif., Mexico 31°1N 114°52W 318 A2
San Felipe Phil. 15°4N 120°4E 232 D3
San Felipe Venezuela 10°20N 68°44W 328 A4
San Felipe → U.S.A. 33°10N 115°49W 307 M11
San Félix Chile 28°56S 70°28W 334 B1
San Félix Pac. Oc. 26°23S 80°0W 326 F2
San Fernando = Sant Ferran Spain 38°42N 1°28E 206 D1
San Fernando Chile 34°30S 71°0W 334 C1
San Fernando Tamaulipas, Mexico 24°51N 98°10W 319 C5
San Fernando Cebu, Phil. 10°10N 123°42E 233 F4
San Fernando La Union, Phil. 16°40N 120°23E 232 C3
San Fernando Pampanga, Phil. 15°5N 120°37E 232 D3
San Fernando Romblon, Phil. 12°18N 122°36E 232 E4
San Fernando Cádiz, Spain 36°28N 6°17W 195 J4
San Fernando Trin. & Tob. 10°16N 61°28W 323 t
San Fernando Calif., U.S.A. 34°17N 118°26W 307 L8
San Fernando de Apure Venezuela 7°54N 67°15W 328 B4
San Fernando de Atabapo Venezuela 4°3N 67°42W 328 C4
San Fernando di Púglia Italy 41°18N 16°5E 201 A9
San Francesco di Paola Venice, Italy 142 b4
San Francique = Erin Trin. & Tob. 10°5N 61°39W 323 t
San Francisco Córdoba, Argentina 31°30S 62°5W 334 C3
San Francisco Bolivia 15°16S 65°31W 331 D4
San Francisco Peru 12°36S 73°49W 330 C3
San Francisco Agusan del S., Phil. 8°30N 125°56E 233 G5
San Francisco Cebu, Phil. 10°39N 124°23E 233 F5
San Francisco Quezon, Phil. 13°21N 122°31E 232 E4
San Francisco S. Leyte, Phil. 10°4N 125°9E 233 F5
San Francisco Calif., U.S.A. 37°46N 122°23W 136 B2
San Francisco → U.S.A. 32°59N 109°22W 305 K9
San Francisco, C. de Colombia 6°18N 77°29W 328 B2
San Francisco, Paso de S. Amer. 27°0S 68°0W 334 B2
San Francisco B. U.S.A. 37°39N 122°14W 136 B3
San Francisco Culhuacán Mexico 19°19N 99°8W 128 C2
San Francisco de Macanao Venezuela 11°1N 64°17W 329 a
San Francisco de Macorís Dom. Rep. 19°19N 70°15W 321 C5
San Francisco del Monte de Oro Argentina 32°36S 66°8W 334 C2
San Francisco del Oro Mexico 26°52N 105°51W 318 B3
San Francisco della Vigna Venice, Italy 142 b3
San Francisco Int. ✈ (SFO) U.S.A. 37°37N 122°22W 306 H4
San Francisco Javier = Sant Francesc de Formentera Spain 38°42N 1°26E 206 D1
San Fratello Italy 38°1N 14°36E 201 D7
San Fruttuoso Italy 45°34N 9°14E 128 A2
San Gabriel Chile 33°47S 70°15W 334 C1
San Gabriel Ecuador 0°36N 77°49W 328 C2
San Gabriel Calif., U.S.A. 34°5N 118°5W 126 B4
San Gabriel → U.S.A. 33°58N 118°5W 126 C4
San Gabriel Chilac Mexico 18°19N 97°21W 319 D5
San Gabriel Mts. U.S.A. 34°17N 117°38W 307 L9
San Gavino Monreale Italy 39°33N 8°47E 200 C1
San Gerardo Venice, Italy 142 c1
San Geremia Venice, Italy 142 a2
San German Puerto Rico 18°4N 67°4W 321 b
San Giacomo dall'Orio Venice, Italy 142 b2
San Gil Colombia 6°33N 73°8W 328 B3
San Giljan = St. Julian's Malta 35°55N 14°29E 206 F7
San Gimignano Italy 43°28N 11°2E 198 E8
San Giobbe Venice, Italy 142 a2
San Giorgio degli Schiavoni, Scuola di Venice, Italy 142 b3
San Giórgio di Nogaro Italy 45°50N 13°13E 199 C10
San Giórgio Iónico Italy 40°27N 17°23E 201 B10
San Giorgio Maggiore Venice, Italy 142 c3
San Giorgio Maggiore, Isola di Venice, Italy 142 c3
San Giovani e Paolo Venice, Italy 142 b3
San Giovanni Bianco Italy 45°52N 9°39E 198 C6
San Giovanni in Bragora Venice, Italy 142 b3
San Giovanni in Fiore Italy 39°15N 16°42E 201 C9
San Giovanni in Persiceto Italy 44°38N 11°11E 199 D8
San Giovanni Rotondo Italy 41°42N 15°44E 199 G12
San Giovanni Valdarno Italy 43°34N 11°32E 199 E8
San Giuliano Milanese Italy 45°24N 9°17E 128 B2
San Giuliano Terme Italy 43°46N 10°26E 198 E7
San Gorgonio Mt. U.S.A. 34°6N 116°50W 307 L10
San Gottardo, P. del Switz. 46°33N 8°33E 179 J4
San Gregorio Uruguay 32°37S 55°40W 335 C4
San Gregorio Calif., U.S.A. 37°20N 122°23W 306 H4
San Guillermo △ Argentina 27°50S 69°45W 334 B2
San Guiseppe Jato Italy 37°57N 13°11E 200 E6
San Ignacio Belize 17°10N 89°5W 320 C2
San Ignacio Beni, Bolivia 14°53S 65°36W 331 C4
San Ignacio Santa Cruz, Bolivia 16°20S 60°55W 331 D5
San Ignacio Baja Calif. S., Mexico 27°27N 112°51W 318 B2
San Ignacio Paraguay 26°52S 57°3W 334 B4
San Ignacio Peru 5°8S 78°59W 330 B2
San Ignacio, L. Mexico 26°54N 113°13W 318 B2
San Ildefonso Phil. 15°4N 120°56E 232 D3
San Ildefonso, C. Phil. 16°0N 122°1E 232 C4
San Ildefonso Pen. Phil. 16°9N 122°5E 232 C4
San Isidro Argentina 34°29S 58°31W 334 C4
San Isidro Lima, Peru 12°5S 77°2W 124 B2
San Isidro Phil. 6°50N 126°5E 233 H6
San Isidro de Potot = Burgos Phil. 16°4N 119°52E 232 C2
San Jacinto Colombia 9°50N 75°8W 328 B2
San Jacinto Phil. 12°34N 123°44E 232 E4
San Jacinto Calif., U.S.A. 33°47N 116°57W 307 M10
San Jaime = Sant Jaume Spain 39°54N 4°4E 206 B5
San Javier Misiones, Argentina 27°55S 55°5W 335 B4
San Javier Santa Fe, Argentina 30°40S 59°55W 334 C4
San Javier Beni, Bolivia 14°34S 64°42W 331 C5
San Javier Santa Cruz, Bolivia 16°18S 62°30W 331 D5
San Javier Chile 35°40S 71°45W 334 D1
San Javier Spain 37°49N 0°50W 197 H4
San Jerónimo Lidice Mexico 19°19N 99°14W 128 C1
San Jerónimo Taviche Mexico 16°44N 96°35W 319 D5
San Joaquín Bolivia 13°4S 64°49W 331 C5
San Joaquín Santiago, Chile 33°29S 70°35W 137 B2
San Joaquin Phil. 10°35N 122°8E 233 F4
San Joaquin Calif., U.S.A. 36°36N 120°11W 306 J6
San Joaquín → Bolivia 13°8S 63°41W 331 C5
San Joaquin → Calif., U.S.A. 38°4N 121°51W 306 G5
San Joaquín, Cerro Ecuador 0°53S 89°30W 330 a
San Joaquin Valley U.S.A. 37°20N 121°0W 306 J6
San Jon U.S.A. 35°6N 103°20W 305 J12
San Jordi = Sant Jordi Spain 39°33N 2°46E 206 B3
San Jorge Argentina 31°54S 61°50W 334 C3
San Jorge Solomon Is. 8°28S 159°38E 287 M10
San Jorge, B. Mexico 31°20N 113°20W 318 A2
San Jorge, G. Argentina 46°0S 66°0W 336 C3
San José = San Josep Spain 38°55N 1°18E 206 D1
San José Argentina 32°12S 58°15W 334 C4
San José Costa Rica 9°55N 84°2W 320 E3
San José Guatemala 14°0N 90°50W 320 D1
San José Mind. Occ., Phil. 12°27N 121°4E 232 E3
San Jose Nueva Ecija, Phil. 15°45N 120°55E 232 D3
San Jose Calif., U.S.A. 37°20N 121°53W 306 H5
San Jose Ill., U.S.A. 40°18N 89°36W 310 D7
San Jose → U.S.A. 34°25N 106°45W 305 J10
San José, G. Argentina 42°20S 64°18W 336 B4
San José, I. Mexico 25°0N 110°38W 318 C2
San Jose de Buenavista Phil. 10°45N 121°56E 233 F3
San José de Chiquitos Bolivia 17°53S 60°50W 331 D5
San José de Feliciano Argentina 30°26S 58°46W 334 C4
San José de Guanipa Venezuela 8°53N 64°9W 329 B5
San José de Jáchal Argentina 30°15S 68°46W 334 C2
San José de Mayo Uruguay 34°27S 56°40W 334 C4
San José de Ocuné Colombia 4°15N 70°20W 328 C3
San José de Uchapiamonas Bolivia 14°13S 68°5W 330 C4
San José del Cabo Mexico 23°3N 109°41W 318 C3
San José del Guaviare Colombia 2°35N 72°38W 328 C3
San José del Monte Phil. 14°49N 121°3E 232 D3
San José do Anauá Brazil 0°58N 61°22W 329 C5
San José Rio Hondo Mexico 19°26N 99°14W 128 B1
San Josep Spain 38°55N 1°18E 206 D1
San Juan Argentina 31°30S 68°30W 334 C2
San Juan Antioquia, Colombia 8°46N 76°32W 328 B2
San Juan Curaçao 12°15N 69°6W 322 g
San Juan Ica, Peru 15°22S 75°7W 330 D2
San Juan Batangas, Phil. 13°50N 121°24E 232 E3
San Juan S. Leyte, Phil. 10°16N 125°10E 233 F5
San Juan Puerto Rico 18°28N 66°7W 321 C6
San Juan Trin. & Tob. 10°39N 61°29W 323 t
San Juan □ Argentina 31°9S 69°0W 334 C2
San Juan → Argentina 32°20S 67°25W 334 C2
San Juan → Bolivia 21°2S 65°19W 331 E4
San Juan → Colombia 4°3N 77°27W 328 C2
San Juan → Nic. 10°56N 83°42W 320 D3
San Juan → Manila, Phil. 14°35N 121°0E 127 B2
San Juan → Utah, U.S.A. 37°16N 110°26W 305 H8
San Juan → Nueva Esparta, Venezuela 10°56N 63°57W 329 a
San Juan → Sucre, Venezuela 10°14N 62°38W 329 A5
San Juan, C. Argentina 54°44S 63°44W 336 D4
San Juan, C. Eq. Guin. 1°5N 9°20E 264 B1
San Juan Bautista = Sant Joan de Labritja Spain 39°5N 1°31E 206 C2
San Juan Bautista = Villahermosa Mexico 17°59N 92°55W 319 D6
San Juan Bautista Chile 33°37S 78°50W 330 c
San Juan Bautista Paraguay 26°37S 57°6W 334 B4
San Juan Bautista Calif., U.S.A. 36°51N 121°32W 306 J5
San Juan Bautista Venezuela 11°1N 63°56W 329 a
San Juan Capistrano U.S.A. 33°30N 117°40W 307 M9
San Juan Cr. → U.S.A. 35°40N 120°22W 306 J5
San Juan de Aragón Mexico 19°28N 99°4W 128 B2
San Juan de Aragón, Parque Mexico 19°27N 99°4W 128 B2
San Juan de Guadelupe Mexico 24°38N 102°44W 318 C4
San Juan de Guía, Cabo de Colombia 11°21N 73°59W 328 A3
San Juan de la Costa Mexico 24°20N 110°41W 318 C2
San Juan de los Lagos Mexico 21°15N 102°18W 318 C4
San Juan de los Morros Venezuela 9°55N 67°21W 328 B4
San Juan de Lurigancho Peru 11°59S 77°0W 124 A2
San Juan de Manapiare Venezuela 5°15N 66°5W 328 B4
San Juan de Villa Hermosa = Villahermosa Mexico 17°59N 92°55W 319 D6
San Juan del César Colombia 10°46N 73°1W 328 A3
San Juan del Monte Phil. 14°36N 121°1E 127 B2
San Juan del Norte Nic. 10°58N 83°40W 320 D3
San Juan del Norte, B. de Nic. 11°0N 83°40W 320 D3
San Juan del Río Mexico 20°23N 100°0W 319 C5
San Juan del Sur Nic. 11°20N 85°51W 320 D2
San Juan I. U.S.A. 48°32N 123°5W 306 B3
San Juan Island △ U.S.A. 48°35N 123°8W 306 B4
San Juan Ixtacala Mexico 19°31N 99°10W 128 A1
San Juan Mts. U.S.A. 37°30N 107°0W 305 H10
San Juan/Laventille □ Trin. & Tob. 10°40N 61°28W 323 t
San Julián Phil. 11°45N 125°27E 233 F5
San Just, Sierra de Spain 40°45N 0°49W 196 E4
San Just Desvern Spain 41°22N 2°4E 114 A1
San Justo B. Aires, Argentina 34°40S 58°33W 117 C1
San Justo Santa Fe, Argentina 30°47S 60°30W 334 C3
San Kamphaeng Thailand 18°45N 99°8E 236 C2
San Lázaro, C. Mexico 24°50N 112°18W 318 C2
San Leandro U.S.A. 37°42N 122°9W 306 H4
San Leonardo de Yagüe Spain 41°51N 3°5W 196 D1
San Lorenzo = Sant Llorenç des Cardassar Spain 39°37N 3°17E 206 B4
San Lorenzo Argentina 32°45S 60°45W 334 C3
San Lorenzo Beni, Bolivia 15°22S 65°48W 331 D4
San Lorenzo Tarija, Bolivia 21°26S 64°47W 331 E5
San Lorenzo Ecuador 1°15N 78°50W 328 C2
San Lorenzo Venice, Italy 142 b3
San Lorenzo Paraguay 25°20S 57°32W 334 B4
San Lorenzo → Mexico 24°15N 107°24W 318 C3
San Lorenzo, I. Baja Calif., Mexico 28°38N 112°51W 318 B2
San Lorenzo, I. Peru 12°7S 77°15W 330 C2
San Lorenzo, Mte. Argentina 47°40S 72°20W 336 C2
San Lorenzo de la Parrilla Spain 39°51N 2°22W 196 F2
San Lorenzo de Morunys = Sant Llorenç de Morunys Spain 42°8N 1°35E 196 C6
San Lorenzo Tezonco Mexico 19°19N 99°3W 128 C2
San Lucas = Cabo San Lucas Mexico 22°53N 109°54W 318 C3
San Lucas Bolivia 20°5S 65°7W 331 E4
San Lucas Baja Calif. S., Mexico 27°10N 112°14W 318 B2
San Lucas Calif., U.S.A. 36°8N 121°1W 306 J5
San Lucas, C. Mexico 22°52N 109°53W 318 C3
San Lúcido Italy 39°18N 16°3E 201 C9
San Luis = Entre Ríos Bolivia 21°30S 64°25W 334 A3
San Luis = Sevilla Colombia 4°16N 75°57W 328 C2
San Luis Argentina 33°20S 66°20W 334 C2
San Luis Pinar del Río, Cuba 22°17N 83°46W 320 B3
San Luis Guatemala 16°14N 89°27W 320 C2
San Luis Lima, Peru 12°4S 77°0W 124 B2
San Luis Ariz., U.S.A. 32°29N 114°47W 305 K6
San Luis Colo., U.S.A. 37°12N 105°25W 305 H11
San Luis □ Argentina 34°0S 66°0W 334 C2
San Luis, I. Mexico 29°58N 114°26W 318 B2
San Luis, L. de Bolivia 13°45S 64°0W 331 C5
San Luis, Sierra de Argentina 32°30S 66°10W 334 C2
San Luis de la Paz Mexico 21°18N 100°31W 318 C4
San Luis Obispo U.S.A. 35°17N 120°40W 307 K6
San Luis Potosí Mexico 22°9N 100°59W 318 C4
San Luis Potosí □ Mexico 23°0N 101°0W 318 C4
San Luis Res. U.S.A. 37°4N 121°5W 306 H5
San Luis Rio Colorado Mexico 32°29N 114°58W 318 A2
San Manuel Phil. 16°4N 120°40E 232 C3
San Manuel Ariz., U.S.A. 32°36N 110°38W 305 K8
San Marco Venice, Italy 142 b2
San Marco, C. Italy 39°51N 8°26E 200 C1
San Marco, Canale di Venice, Italy 142 b3
San Marco, Piazza Venice, Italy 142 b2
San Marco Argentano Italy 39°33N 16°7E 201 C9
San Marco in Lámis Italy 41°43N 15°38E 199 G12
San Marcos Colombia 8°39N 75°8W 328 B2
San Marcos Calif., U.S.A. 33°9N 117°10W 307 M9
San Marcos Tex., U.S.A. 29°53N 97°56W 314 G6
San Marcos, I. Mexico 27°13N 112°6W 318 B2
San Mariano Phil. 17°0N 122°2E 232 C4
San Marino San Marino 43°55N 12°30E 199 E9
San Marino Calif., U.S.A. 34°7N 118°5W 126 B4
San Marino ■ Europe 43°56N 12°25E 199 E9
San Martín = Tarapoto Peru 6°30S 76°20W 330 B2
San Martín Antarctica 68°11S 67°0W 151 C17
San Martín Argentina 33°5S 68°28W 334 C2
San Martín Colombia 3°42N 73°42W 328 C3
San Martín Barcelona, Spain 41°24N 2°11E 114 A2
San Martín □ Peru 7°0S 76°50W 330 B2
San Martín → Bolivia 13°8S 63°43W 331 C5
San Martín, L. Argentina 48°50S 72°50W 336 C2
San Martín de la Vega Spain 40°13N 3°34W 194 E7
San Martín de los Andes Argentina 40°10S 71°20W 336 B2
San Martín de Porras Peru 12°1S 77°5W 124 B2
San Martín de Valdeiglesias Spain 40°21N 4°24W 194 E6
San Mateo = Sant Mateu Baleares, Spain 39°3N 1°23E 206 C1
San Mateo = Sant Mateu Valencia, Spain 40°28N 0°10E 196 E5
San Mateo Isabela, Phil. 16°54N 121°33E 232 C3
San Mateo Calif., U.S.A. 37°34N 122°19W 306 H4
San Mateo Tlaltenango Mexico 19°20N 99°16W 128 B1
San Matías Bolivia 16°25S 58°20W 331 D6
San Matías, G. Argentina 41°30S 64°0W 336 B4
San Michele, Isola di Venice, Italy 142 a3
San Miguel = Linapacan Phil. 11°30N 119°52E 233 F2
San Miguel = Sant Miquel Spain 39°3N 1°26E 206 C1
San Miguel = Sarrat Phil. 18°9N 120°39E 232 B3
San Miguel Bolivia 16°42S 61°1W 331 C5
San Miguel Brazil 28°35S 54°33W 335 B5
San Miguel Santiago, Chile 33°29S 70°39W 137 B2
San Miguel El Salv. 13°30N 88°12W 320 D2
San Miguel Panama 8°27N 78°55W 320 E4
San Miguel Lima, Peru 12°5S 77°6W 124 B2
San Miguel Bulacan, Phil. 15°9N 120°59E 232 D3
San Miguel Palawan, Phil. 11°30N 119°51E 233 F2
San Miguel Surigao S., Phil. 9°3N 125°59E 233 G5
San Miguel Calif., U.S.A. 35°45N 120°42W 306 K6
San Miguel → Bolivia 13°52S 63°56W 331 C5
San Miguel → Ecuador 0°25N 76°30W 328 C2
San Miguel, Golfo de Panama 8°22N 78°17W 328 B2
San Miguel B. Phil. 13°51N 123°11E 232 E4
San Miguel de Huachi Bolivia 15°40S 67°15W 330 D4
San Miguel de Tucumán Argentina 26°50S 65°20W 334 B2
San Miguel del Monte Argentina 35°23S 58°50W 334 D4
San Miguel I. U.S.A. 34°2N 120°23W 307 L6
San Miguel Is. Phil. 7°45N 118°28E 233 H2
San Miguelito Panama 9°2N 79°30W 320 c
San Millán de la Cogolla Spain 42°19N 2°51W 196 C2
San Miniato Italy 43°41N 10°51E 198 E7
San Narciso Phil. 13°34N 122°34E 232 E4
San Nicandro Gargánico Italy 41°50N 15°34E 199 G12
San Nicolas = Sint Nicolaas Curaçao 12°17N 69°8W 322 g
San Nicolás B. Aires, Argentina 34°36S 58°22W 117 B2
San Nicolás Canary Is. 27°58N 15°47W 153 e1
San Nicolas Phil. 18°10N 120°36E 232 B3
San Nicolás de los Arroyos Argentina 33°25S 60°10W 334 C3
San Nicolas I. U.S.A. 33°15N 119°30W 307 M7
San Nicolo dei Mendicoli Venice, Italy 142 b1
San Onofre Colombia 9°44N 75°32W 328 B2
San Onofre Calif., U.S.A. 33°22N 117°34W 307 M9
San Onófrio Italy 41°57N 12°25E 136 B1
San Pablo Bolivia 21°43S 66°38W 334 A2
San Pablo Isabela, Phil. 17°27N 121°48E 232 C3
San Pablo Laguna, Phil. 14°11N 121°31E 232 D3
San Pablo Calif., U.S.A. 37°58N 122°21W 306 H4
San Pablo de Manta = Manta Ecuador 1°0S 80°40W 328 D1
San Pantalon Venice, Italy 142 b2
San Páolo di Civitate Italy 41°44N 15°15E 199 G12
San Pascual Phil. 13°8N 122°59E 232 E4
San Pedro B. Aires, Argentina 33°40S 59°40W 334 C4
San Pedro Misiones, Argentina 26°30S 54°10W 335 B5
San Pedro Chile 33°54S 71°28W 334 C1
San Pedro Colombia 4°56N 71°53W 328 C3
San Pédro Côte d'Ivoire 4°50N 6°33W 262 E3
San Pedro Baja Calif. S., Mexico 23°55N 110°17W 318 C2
San Pedro Peru 14°49S 74°5W 330 C3
San Pedro □ Paraguay 24°0S 57°0W 334 A4
San Pedro → Chihuahua, Mexico 28°21N 105°25W 318 B3
San Pedro → Nayarit, Mexico 21°45N 105°30W 318 C3
San Pedro → Ariz., U.S.A. 32°59N 110°47W 305 K8
San Pedro, Pta. Chile 25°30S 70°38W 334 B1
San Pedro, Sierra de Spain 39°18N 6°40W 195 F4
San Pedro B. Phil. 11°10N 125°6E 233 F5
San Pedro Channel U.S.A. 33°30N 118°25W 307 M8
San Pedro de Arimena Colombia 4°37N 71°42W 328 C3
San Pedro de Atacama Chile 22°55S 68°15W 334 A2
San Pedro de Coche Venezuela 10°47N 64°0W 329 a
San Pedro de Jujuy Argentina 24°12S 64°55W 334 A3
San Pedro de las Colonias Mexico 25°45N 102°59W 318 B4
San Pedro de Lloc Peru 7°15S 79°28W 330 B2
San Pedro de Macorís Dom. Rep. 18°30N 69°18W 321 C6
San Pedro del Norte Nic. 13°4N 84°33W 320 D3
San Pedro del Paraná Paraguay 26°43S 56°13W 334 B4
San Pedro del Pinatar Spain 37°50N 0°50W 197 H4
San Pedro Mártir Spain 41°23N 2°6E 114 A1
San Pedro Mártir, Sa. de Mexico 30°45N 115°13W 318 A1
San Pedro Ocampo = Melchor Ocampo Mexico 24°51N 101°39W 318 C4
San Pedro Pochutla Mexico 15°44N 96°28W 319 D5
San Pedro Sula Honduras 15°30N 88°0W 320 C2
San Pedro Tututepec Mexico 16°9N 97°38W 319 D5
San Pedro Zacatenco Mexico 19°30N 99°6W 128 A2
San Pietro Italy 39°8N 8°17E 200 C1
San Pietro, Isola di Venice, Italy 142 b4
San Pietro, Piazza Rome, Italy 136 b1
San Pietro di Castello Venice, Italy 142 b4
San Pietro Vernótico Italy 40°29N 18°0E 201 B11
San Po Kong Hong Kong, China 22°20N 114°11E 122 B3
San Polo Venice, Italy 142 b2
San Rafael Argentina 34°40S 68°21W 334 C2
San Rafael Bolivia 16°45S 60°34W 331 D5
San Rafael Trin. & Tob. 10°34N 61°16W 323 t
San Rafael Calif., U.S.A. 37°58N 122°32W 306 H4
San Rafael N. Mex., U.S.A. 35°7N 107°53W 305 J10
San Rafael Venezuela 10°58N 71°46W 328 A3
San Rafael Chamapa Mexico 19°27N 99°15W 128 B1
San Rafael Hills U.S.A. 34°10N 118°12W 126 A3
San Rafael Mt. U.S.A. 34°41N 119°52W 307 L7
San Rafael Mts. U.S.A. 34°40N 119°50W 307 L7
San Ramón Bolivia 13°17S 64°43W 331 C5
San Ramón de la Nueva Orán Argentina 23°10S 64°20W 334 A3
San Remo Italy 43°49N 7°46E 198 E4
San Román, C. Venezuela 12°12N 70°0W 328 A4
San Roque Argentina 28°25S 58°45W 334 B4
San Roque Manila, Phil. 14°37N 121°5E 127 B2
San Roque N. Samar, Phil. 12°37N 124°52E 232 E5
San Roque Spain 36°17N 5°21W 195 J5
San Rosendo Chile 37°16S 72°43W 334 D1
San Saba U.S.A. 31°12N 98°43W 314 F5
San Salvador El Salv. 13°40N 89°10W 320 D2
San Salvador Venice, Italy 142 b3
San Salvador The Bahamas 24°0N 74°30W 321 B5
San Salvador, Canal de Ecuador 0°25S 90°30W 330 a
San Salvador, I. Ecuador 0°16S 90°42W 330 a
San Salvador de Jujuy Argentina 24°10S 64°48W 334 A3
San Salvo Italy 42°3N 14°44E 199 F11
San Sebastián = Donostia-San Sebastián Spain 43°17N 1°58W 196 B3
San Sebastián Argentina 53°10S 68°30W 336 D3
San Sebastián Puerto Rico 18°20N 66°59W 321 b
San Sebastián de la Gomera Canary Is. 28°5N 17°7W 153 e1
San Sebastiano Venice, Italy 142 b2
San Serra = Son Serra Spain 39°43N 3°13E 206 B4
San Serverino Marche Italy 43°13N 13°10E 199 E10
San Severo Italy 41°41N 15°23E 199 G12
San Simeon U.S.A. 35°39N 121°11W 306 K5
San Simeon Grande Venice, Italy 142 a2
San Simon U.S.A. 32°16N 109°14W 305 K9
San Siro Italy 45°28N 9°7E 128 B1
San Souci Australia 33°59S 151°8E 139 B1
San Stefano Venice, Italy 142 b2
San Stéfano di Cadore Italy 46°34N 12°33E 199 B9
San Stino di Livenza Italy 45°44N 12°41E 199 C9
San Tau Hong Kong, China 22°17N 113°55E 122 B1
San Telmo = Sant Elm Spain 39°35N 2°21E 206 B3
San Telmo B. Aires, Argentina 34°37S 58°23W 117 B2
San Telmo Baja Calif., Mexico 30°58N 116°6W 318 A1
San Teodoro Italy 40°46N 9°40E 200 B2
San Teodoro Phil. 13°26N 121°1E 232 E3
San Tiburcio Mexico 24°8N 101°32W 318 C4
San Trovaso Venice, Italy 142 c2
San Valentin, Mte. Chile 46°30S 73°30W 336 C2
San Vicenç dels Horts Spain 41°23N 2°0E 114 A1
San Vicente de Alcántara Spain 39°22N 7°8W 195 F3
San Vicente de Cañete Peru 13°8S 76°30W 330 C2
San Vicente de la Barquera Spain 43°23N 4°29W 194 B6
San Vicente del Caguán Colombia 2°7N 74°46W 328 C3
San Vicenzo Spain 42°58N 8°46W 194 C2
San Vincenzo Italy 43°6N 10°32E 198 E7
San Vito Costa Rica 8°50N 82°58W 320 E3
San Vito Italy 39°26N 9°32E 200 C2
San Vito, C. Italy 38°11N 12°41E 200 D5
San Vito al Tagliamento Italy 45°54N 12°52E 199 C9
San Vito Chietino Italy 42°18N 14°27E 199 F11
San Vito dei Normanni Italy 40°39N 17°42E 201 B10
San Yanaro Colombia 2°47N 69°42W 328 C4
San Zaccaria Venice, Italy 142 b3
Sana' = Ṣan'ā' Yemen 15°27N 44°12E 248 D4
Saña Peru 6°54S 79°36W 330 B2
Ṣan'ā' Yemen 15°27N 44°12E 248 D4
Ṣan'ā' □ Yemen 15°27N 44°12E 248 D4
Sana → Bos.-H. 45°3N 16°23E 199 C13
Sanaa = Ṣan'ā' Yemen 15°27N 44°12E 248 D4
Sanaag □ Somalia 10°30N 48°0E 267 B6
Sanaba Burkina Faso 12°25N 3°47W 262 C4
Sanae IV Antarctica 70°20S 9°0W 151 D2
Ṣanāfīr Si. Arabia 27°56N 34°42E 251 K5
Sanaga → Cameroon 3°35N 9°38E 263 E6
Sanak I. U.S.A. 54°25N 162°40W 303 J7
Sanalona, Presa Mexico 24°49N 107°7W 318 C3
Sanām Si. Arabia 23°40N 44°45E 248 B4
Sanana Indonesia 2°4S 125°58E 231 E7
Sanand India 22°59N 72°25E 242 H5
Sanandaj Iran 35°18N 47°1E 213 E12
Sanandita Bolivia 21°40S 63°45W 334 A3
Sanaroa I. Papua N. G. 9°37S 151°0E 286 E6
Sanary-sur-Mer France 43°7N 5°49E 175 E9
Sanāw Yemen 17°50N 51°5E 249 C5
Sanawad India 22°11N 76°5E 242 H7
Sanbancho Tokyo, Japan 140 a3
Sanbe-San Japan 35°6N 132°38E 222 B4
Sancellas = Sencelles Spain 39°39N 2°54E 206 B3
Sancergues France 47°10N 2°54E 173 E9
Sancerre France 47°20N 2°50E 173 E9
Sancerrois, Collines du France 47°20N 2°40E 173 E9
Sancha He → China 26°48N 106°7E 228 D6
Sanchahe China 44°50N 126°2E 227 B14
Sánchez Dom. Rep. 19°15N 69°36W 321 C6
Sanchez Mira Phil. 18°34N 121°14E 232 B3
Sanchi India 23°28N 77°44E 242 H7
Sanchih Taiwan 25°15N 121°30E 225 A3
Sanchor India 24°45N 71°55E 242 G4
Sanch'ung Taiwan 25°4N 121°30E 225 A3
Sanco Pt. Phil. 8°15N 126°27E 233 G6
Sancoins France 46°47N 2°55E 173 F9
Sancti Spíritus Cuba 21°52N 79°33W 320 B4
Sancy, Puy de France 45°32N 2°50E 174 C6
Sand = Polokwane → S. Africa 22°25S 30°5E 271 B5
Sand Norway 59°29N 6°16E 164 E3
Sand Bank B. St. Kitts & Nevis 17°15N 62°38W 322 d
Sand Cr. → U.S.A. 39°3N 85°51W 311 E11
Sand Hills Guyana 6°27N 58°19W 329 B6
Sand Hills Nebr., U.S.A. 42°10N 101°30W 308 D3
Sand I. Midway Is. 28°12N 177°23W 302 c
Sand I. Hawai'i, U.S.A. 21°19N 157°53W 302 K14
Sand Islet Midway Is. 28°16N 177°22W 302 c
Sand Lakes △ Canada 57°51N 98°32W 297 B9
Sand Point U.S.A. 55°20N 160°30W 303 J7
Sand Springs U.S.A. 36°9N 96°7W 314 C6
Sanda Japan 34°53N 135°14E 223 C7
Sandai Indonesia 1°15S 110°31E 235 C4
Sandakan Malaysia 5°53N 118°4E 235 A5
Sandalwood Australia 34°55S 140°9E 282 C4
Sandan = Sambor Cambodia 12°46N 106°0E 236 F6
Sandane Norway 61°46N 6°13E 164 C3
Sandanski Bulgaria 41°35N 23°16E 202 E7
Sandaré Mali 14°40N 10°15W 262 C2
Sandared Sweden 57°43N 12°47E 163 G6
Sandarne Sweden 61°16N 17°9E 162 C11
Sandaun □ Papua N. G. 3°30S 142°0E 286 B2
Sanday U.K. 59°16N 2°31W 167 B6
Sande Møre og Romsdal, Norway 62°15N 5°27E 164 B2
Sande Sogn og Fjordane, Norway 61°20N 5°47E 164 C2
Sande Vestfold, Norway 59°36N 10°12E 162 E4
Sandefjord Norway 59°10N 10°15E 164 E7
Sandeid Norway 59°33N 5°52E 164 E2
Sanders Ariz., U.S.A. 35°13N 109°20W 305 J9
Sanders Ky., U.S.A. 38°40N 84°56W 311 F12
Sanderson Fla., U.S.A. 30°15N 82°16W 316 E7
Sanderson Tex., U.S.A. 30°9N 102°24W 314 F3
Sandersville U.S.A. 32°59N 82°48W 316 C7
Sandfire Roadhouse Australia 19°45S 121°15E 278 C3
Sandfloegga Norway 59°58N 7°10E 164 E4
Sandfly L. Canada 55°43N 106°6W 297 B7
Sandfontein Namibia 23°48S 19°1E 270 B2
Sandhammaren Sweden 55°23N 14°14E 163 J8
Sandheads, The India 21°10N 88°20E 241 E2
Sandgerði Iceland 64°3N 22°42W 155 C4
Sandia Peru 14°10S 69°30W 330 C4
Sandıklı Turkey 38°28N 30°17E 205 C12
Sandila India 27°5N 80°31E 243 F9
Sandilands The Bahamas 25°3N 77°19W 153 b
Sanding Indonesia 3°28S 100°40E 234 C2
Sanding, Selat Indonesia 3°24S 100°34E 234 C2
Sandnes Aust-Agder, Norway 58°53N 7°45E 164 F4
Sandnes Rogaland, Norway 58°50N 5°45E 164 F2
Sandnessjøen Norway 66°2N 12°38E 160 C15
Sandoa Dem. Rep. of the Congo 9°41S 23°0E 265 D4
Sandomierz Poland 50°40N 21°43E 185 H8
Sândominic Romania 46°35N 25°47E 183 D10
Sandona Colombia 1°17N 77°28W 328 C2
Sandongo Angola 15°30S 21°28E 265 F4
Sandoval U.S.A. 38°37N 89°7W 310 F7
Sandover → Australia 21°43S 136°32E 280 C2
Sandoway = Thandwe Myanmar 18°20N 94°30E 241 F5
Sandown S. Africa 26°5S 28°4E 123 A2
Sandown Park Races U.K. 51°22N 0°21W 125 B1
Sandpoint U.S.A. 48°17N 116°33W 304 B5
Sandray U.K. 56°53N 7°31W 167 E1
Sandringham U.K. 52°51N 0°31E 168 E8
Sandstone Australia 27°59S 119°16E 279 E2
Sandton S. Africa 26°5S 28°4E 123 A2
Sandu China 26°0N 107°52E 228 E6
Sandumba Angola 13°45S 17°34E 265 E3
Sandur India 15°6N 76°33E 245 F3
Sandusky Mich., U.S.A. 43°25N 82°50W 312 C2
Sandusky Ohio, U.S.A. 41°27N 82°42W 312 E2
Sandusky → U.S.A. 41°27N 83°0W 311 C14
Sandveld Namibia 21°25S 20°0E 270 B3
Sandvig Denmark 55°18N 14°47E 163 J8
Sandvika Norway 59°54N 10°31E 133 A2
Sandviken Sweden 60°38N 16°46E 162 D10
Sandwich U.S.A. 41°39N 88°37W 311 C8
Sandwich, C. Australia 18°14S 146°18E 280 B4
Sandwich B. Nfld. & L., Canada 53°40N 57°15W 299 B8
Sandwich B. Namibia 23°25S 14°20E 270 B1
Sandwip I. Bangla. 22°30N 91°25E 241 D3
Sandy Oreg., U.S.A. 45°24N 122°16W 306 E4
Sandy Pa., U.S.A. 41°6N 78°46W 312 E6
Sandy Utah, U.S.A. 40°32N 111°50W 304 F8
Sandy B. St. Helena 16°0S 5°43W 153 h
Sandy Bay Canada 55°31N 102°19W 297 B8
Sandy Bight Australia 33°50S 123°20E 279 F3
Sandy C. Queens., Australia 24°42S 153°15E 280 C5
Sandy C. Tas., Australia 41°25S 144°45E 281 G3
Sandy Cay The Bahamas 23°13N 75°18W 321 B4
Sandy Cr. → N.S.W., Australia 31°54S 145°18E 281 B4
Sandy Cr. → Wyo., U.S.A. 41°51N 109°47W 304 F9
Sandy Creek U.S.A. 43°38N 76°5W 313 C8
Sandy Ground Village Anguilla 18°12N 63°6W 322 a
Sandy Hill B. Anguilla 18°13N 63°1W 322 a
Sandy I. Anguilla 18°13N 63°7W 322 a
Sandy I. Grenada 12°29N 61°29W 323 q
Sandy I. Grenada 12°13N 61°35W 323 q
Sandy L. Canada 53°2N 93°0W 298 B1
Sandy Lake Canada 53°0N 93°15W 298 B1
Sandy Point India 10°32N 92°22E 245 J11
Sandy Point Town St. Kitts & Nevis 17°22N 62°51W 322 d
Sandy Springs U.S.A. 33°56N 84°23W 316 B5
Sandy Valley U.S.A. 35°49N 115°38W 307 K11
Sånfjället △ Sweden 62°17N 13°35E 162 B7
Sanford Fla., U.S.A. 28°48N 81°16W 317 G8
Sanford Maine, U.S.A. 43°27N 70°47W 313 C14
Sanford N.C., U.S.A. 35°29N 79°10W 315 D15
Sanford → Australia 27°22S 115°53E 279 E2
Sanford, Mt. U.S.A. 62°13N 144°8W 303 E11
Sang-i-Masha Afghan. 33°8N 67°27E 242 C2
Sanga Angola 11°9S 15°21E 265 E3
Sanga Mozam. 12°22S 35°21E 269 E4
Sanga → Congo 1°5S 17°0E 264 C3
Sangaie Dem. Rep. of the Congo 6°48S 22°46E 265 D4
Sangamner India 19°37N 74°15E 244 E2
Sangamon → U.S.A. 40°1N 90°26W 310 D6
Sangān Iran 34°23N 60°15E 247 C9
Sanganeb Atoll △ Sudan 19°33N 37°11E 256 D4
Sangar Afghan. 32°56N 65°30E 242 C1
Sangar Russia 64°2N 127°31E 215 C13
Sangar Sarai Afghan. 34°27N 70°35E 242 B4
Sangareddi India 17°38N 78°7E 244 F4
Sangaredi Guinea 11°7N 13°52W 262 C2
Sangarh → Pakistan 30°43N 70°44E 242 D4
Sangasanga Indonesia 0°36S 117°13E 235 C5
Sangasso Mali 12°5N 5°35W 262 C3
Sangatte France 50°56N 1°44E 173 B8
Sangāw Iraq 35°17N 45°10E 213 E11
Sangay Ecuador 2°0S 78°20W 328 D2
Sangay △ Ecuador 2°15S 78°26W 328 D2
Sangbé Cameroon 6°3N 12°28E 264 A2
Sangchris L. U.S.A. 39°39N 89°29W 310 E7
Sangdong S. Korea 37°7N 128°49E 224 D4
Sange Dem. Rep. of the Congo 6°58S 28°21E 268 D2
Sangeang Indonesia 8°12S 119°6E 235 D5
Sangenjaya Japan 35°37N 139°39E 140 B2
Săngeorz-Băi Romania 47°22N 24°41E 183 C9
Sanger U.S.A. 36°42N 119°33W 306 J7
Săngera Moldova 46°55N 28°58E 183 D13
Sangerhausen Germany 51°28N 11°18E 178 D7
Sanggan He → China 38°12N 117°15E 226 E9
Sanggau Kalimantan Barat, Indonesia 0°5N 110°30E 235 B4
Sanggau Kalimantan Barat, Indonesia 1°7N 109°36E 235 B3
Sanggye S. Korea 37°38N 127°3E 137 B2
Sangha □ Congo 1°0N 15°30E 264 B3
Sangha-Mbaéré □ C.A.R. 4°30N 16°30E 264 B3
Sanghar Pakistan 26°2N 68°57E 242 F3
Sangihe, Kepulauan Indonesia 3°0N 125°30E 231 D7
Sangihe, Pulau Indonesia 3°35N 125°30E 231 D7
Sangin Afghan. 32°4N 64°50E 240 B2
Sangiran Indonesia 7°25S 110°50E 235 f
Sangiran △ Indonesia 7°27S 110°50E 231 G14
Sangju S. Korea 36°25N 128°10E 224 D4
Sangkapura Indonesia 5°52S 112°40E 235 D4
Sangkha Thailand 14°37N 103°52E 236 E4
Sangkhla Buri Thailand 14°57N 98°28E 236 E2
Sangkulirang Indonesia 0°59N 117°58E 235 B5
Sangla Pakistan 31°43N 73°23E 242 D5
Sangley Pt. Phil. 14°29N 120°54E 127 C1
Sangli India 16°55N 74°33E 244 F2
Sangmélima Cameroon 2°57N 12°1E 263 E7
Sango Angola 9°51S 15°44E 265 D2
Sango Zimbabwe 18°44S 31°44E 269 F3
Sangod India 24°55N 76°17E 242 G7
Sangole India 17°26N 75°12E 244 F2
Sangorodok = Ust-Vorkuta Russia 67°24N 64°0E 186 A11
Sangpang Bum Myanmar 26°30N 95°50E 241 B5
Sangre de Cristo Mts. U.S.A. 37°30N 105°20W 305 H11
Sangre Grande Trin. & Tob. 10°35N 61°8W 323 t
Sangro → Italy 42°14N 14°32E 199 F11
Sangrur India 30°14N 75°50E 242 D6
Sangudo Canada 53°50N 114°54W 296 C6
Sangue → Brazil 11°1S 58°39W 331 C6
Sangüesa Spain 42°37N 1°17W 196 C3
Sanguinaires, Îs. France 41°51N 8°36E 175 G12
Sangzhi China 29°25N 110°12E 229 C8
Sanhala Côte d'Ivoire 10°3N 6°51W 262 C3
Sanhsia Taiwan 24°56N 121°22E 225 B3
Sanhsien Hualien, Taiwan 23°8N 121°22E 225 C3
Sanhsien T'aitung, Taiwan 23°24N 121°19E 225 C3
Sanhsing Taiwan 24°40N 121°36E 225 B3
Sani Taiwan 24°24N 120°46E 225 B2
Sanibel U.S.A. 26°27N 82°1W 317 J7
Sanibel I. U.S.A. 26°26N 82°6W 317 J7
Sanikiluaq Canada 56°32N 79°14W 298 A4
Sanin-Kaigan △ Japan 35°39N 134°37E 222 B6
Sanirajak = Hall Beach Canada 68°46N 81°12W 295 D15
Sanjawi Pakistan 30°17N 68°21E 242 D3
Sanje Uganda 0°49S 31°30E 268 C3
Sanjiang China 25°48N 109°37E 228 E7
Sanjo Japan 37°37N 138°57E 220 F9
Sankarankovil India 9°10N 77°35E 245 K3
Sankeshwar India 16°23N 74°32E 245 F2
Sankh → India 22°15N 84°48E 243 H11
Sankosh → India 26°24N 89°47E 241 B2
Sankrail India 22°33N 88°13E 124 B1
Sankt Andrä Austria 46°46N 14°50E 180 E7
Sankt Anton Austria 47°8N 10°16E 179 H6
Sankt Augustin Germany 50°45N 7°10E 178 E3
Sankt Blasien Germany 47°47N 8°7E 179 H4
Sankt Gallen Switz. 47°26N 9°22E 179 H5
Sankt Gallen □ Switz. 47°25N 9°22E 179 H5
Sankt Goar Germany 50°12N 7°43E 179 E3
Sankt Ingbert Germany 49°16N 7°6E 179 F3
Sankt Johann im Pongau Austria 47°22N 13°12E 180 D6
Sankt Johann in Tirol Austria 47°30N 12°25E 180 D5

Sankt Marein = Smarje Slovenia 46°15N 15°34E 199 B12
Sankt Michel = Mikkeli Finland 61°43N 27°15E 188 B4
Sankt Moritz Switz. 46°30N 9°51E 179 J5
Sankt Peter-Ording Germany 54°20N 8°36E 178 A4
Sankt-Peterburg Russia 59°55N 30°20E 137 B1
Sankt Pölten Austria 48°12N 15°38E 180 C8
Sankt Ulrich = Ortisei Italy 46°34N 11°40E 199 B8
Sankt Valentin Austria 48°11N 14°33E 180 C7
Sankt Veit Austria 48°11N 16°16E 142 A1
Sankt Veit an der Glan Austria 46°47N 14°22E 180 E7
Sankt Wendel Germany 49°27N 7°9E 179 F3
Sankt Wolfgang Austria 47°43N 13°27E 180 D6
Sankuru □ Dem. Rep. of the Congo 5°0S 24°0E 265 C4
Sankuru → Dem. Rep. of the Congo 4°17S 20°25E 265 C4
Sanlihe China 39°53N 116°18E 114 B1
Sanlin China 31°9N 121°29E 138 C1
Sanlintang China 31°9N 121°29E 138 C1
Sanliurfa Turkey 37°12N 38°50E 213 D8
Sanliurfa □ Turkey 37°0N 39°0E 213 D8
Sanlúcar de Barrameda Spain 36°46N 6°21W 195 J4
Sanluri Italy 39°34N 8°54E 200 C1
Sânmartin Romania 46°19N 25°58E 183 D10
Sanmen China 29°5N 121°35E 229 C13
Sanmenxia China 34°47N 111°12E 226 G6
Sanming China 26°15N 117°40E 229 D11
Sanmu Kantō, Japan 34°11N 134°37E 222 C6
Sanmu Shikoku, Japan 35°36N 140°25E 223 B12
Sannan Japan 35°2N 135°1E 223 B7
Sannat Malta 36°1N 14°15E 206 E6
Sanndraigh = Sandray U.K. 56°53N 7°31W 167 E1
Sânnicolau Mare Romania 46°5N 20°39E 182 D5
Sannieshof S. Africa 26°30S 25°47E 270 C4
Sannīn, J. Lebanon 33°57N 35°52E 250 E6
Sanniquellie Liberia 7°19N 8°38W 262 D3
Sannûr Egypt 28°58N 31°3E 251 K2
Sannûr, W. → Egypt 28°59N 31°3E 251 K2
Sano Japan 36°19N 139°35E 223 A11
Sanok Poland 49°35N 22°10E 185 J9
Sanqingshan △ China 28°54N 118°3E 229 C12
Sanquhar U.K. 55°22N 3°54W 167 F5
Sanquianga △ Colombia 2°33N 78°14W 328 C2
Sanremo = San Remo Italy 43°49N 7°46E 198 E4
Sans Spain 41°22N 2°7E 114 A1
Sans Souci St. Vincent 13°13N 61°7W 323 n
Sans Souci Trin. & Tob. 10°50N 61°0W 323 t
Sansanding Mali 13°48N 6°0W 262 C3
Sansané Niger 13°50N 1°36E 263 C5
Sansepolcro Italy 43°34N 12°8E 199 E9
Sansha China 26°58N 120°12E 229 D13
Sanshui China 23°10N 112°56E 229 F9
Sanski Most Bos.-H. 44°46N 16°40E 199 D13
Sansom Park U.S.A. 32°48N 97°24W 120 B1
Sanssouci Germany 52°23N 13°2E 115 B1
Sansui China 26°58N 108°39E 228 D7
Sant Agusti Barcelona, Spain 114 c2
Sant Ambrogio, Basilica di Italy 45°27N 9°10E 128 B2
Sant Antoni de Portmany Spain 38°59N 1°19E 206 D1
Sant Boi de Llobregat Spain 41°20N 2°2E 114 A1
Sant Carles Spain 39°3N 1°34E 206 C2
Sant Carles de la Ràpita Spain 40°37N 0°35E 196 E5
Sant Celoni Spain 41°42N 2°30E 196 D7
Sant Cugat Spain 41°28N 2°5E 114 A1
Sant Elm Spain 39°35N 2°21E 206 B3
Sant Feliu de Guíxols Spain 41°45N 3°1E 196 D8
Sant Feliu de Llobregat Spain 41°22N 2°2E 114 A1
Sant Ferran Spain 38°42N 1°28E 206 D1
Sant Francesc de Formentera Spain 38°42N 1°26E 206 D1
Sant Jaume Spain 39°54N 4°4E 206 B5
Sant Joan Spain 39°36N 3°4E 206 B4
Sant Joan d'Alacant Spain 38°24N 0°26W 197 G4
Sant Joan de Labritja Spain 39°5N 1°31E 206 C2
Sant Joan Despi Spain 41°22N 2°2E 114 A1
Sant Jordi Ibiza, Spain 38°53N 1°24E 206 D1
Sant Jordi Mallorca, Spain 39°33N 2°46E 206 B3
Sant Jordi, G. de Spain 40°53N 1°2E 196 E6
Sant Llorenç de Morunys Spain 42°8N 1°35E 196 C6
Sant Llorenç del Munt y l'Obac ⌂ Spain 41°39N 1°55W 196 D3
Sant Llorenç des Cardassar Spain 39°37N 3°17E 206 B4
Sant Maria del Mar Barcelona, Spain 114 b3
Sant Mateu Baleares, Spain 39°3N 1°23E 206 C1
Sant Mateu Valencia, Spain 40°28N 0°10E 196 E5
Sant Miquel Spain 39°3N 1°26E 206 C1
Sant Pau del Camp Barcelona, Spain 114 c2
Sant Pere de Ribes Spain 41°16N 1°46E 196 D6
Sant Salvador Spain 39°27N 3°11E 206 B4
Sant Vicent del Raspeig Spain 38°24N 0°31W 197 G4
Santa Peru 8°59S 78°40W 330 B2
Sant' Ágata Militello Italy 38°2N 14°8E 201 D7
Santa Agnés Spain 39°3N 1°21E 206 C1
Santa Ana Beni, Bolivia 13°50S 65°40W 331 C4
Santa Ana La Paz, Bolivia 15°31S 67°30W 330 D4
Santa Ana Santa Cruz, Bolivia 18°43S 58°44W 331 D6
Santa Ana Santa Cruz, Bolivia 16°37S 60°43W 331 D5
Santa Ana Ecuador 1°16S 80°20W 328 D1
Santa Ana El Salv. 14°0N 89°31W 320 D2
Santa Ana Guam 13°32N 145°46E 302 d
Santa Ana Sonora, Mexico 30°33N 111°7W 318 A2
Santa Ana Cagayan, Phil. 18°28N 122°20E 232 B4
Santa Ana Manila, Phil. 14°34N 121°0E 127 B2
Santa Ana Solomon Is. 10°50S 162°30E 287 N12
Santa Ana Calif., U.S.A. 33°46N 117°52W 307 M9
Santa Ana → Venezuela 9°30N 71°57W 328 B3
Santa Ana de los Ríos de Cuenca = Cuenca Ecuador 2°50S 79°9W 328 D2
Sant' Andrea Venice, Italy 142 b1
Santa Anita Park U.S.A. 34°8N 118°5W 126 B4
Santa Bárbara Santa Maria, Azores 36°59N 25°4W 153 d4
Santa Bárbara Terciera, Azores 38°41N 27°20W 153 d1
Santa Bárbara Chile 37°40S 72°1W 334 D1
Santa Bárbara Colombia 5°53N 75°35W 328 B2
Santa Barbara Curaçao 12°5N 68°51W 322 g
Santa Bárbara Honduras 14°53N 88°14W 320 D2
Santa Bárbara Chihuahua, Mexico 26°48N 105°49W 318 B3
Santa Barbara Phil. 10°50N 122°32E 233 F4
Santa Bárbara Spain 40°42N 0°29E 196 E5
Santa Barbara Calif., U.S.A. 34°25N 119°42W 307 L7
Santa Bárbara Amazonas, Venezuela 3°57N 67°6W 328 C4
Santa Bárbara Barinas, Venezuela 7°47N 71°10W 328 B3
Santa Bárbara, Mt. Spain 37°23N 2°50W 197 H2
Santa Bárbara, Serra de Azores 38°44N 27°19W 153 d1
Santa Barbara Channel U.S.A. 34°15N 120°0W 307 L7
Santa Barbara I. U.S.A. 33°29N 119°2W 307 M7
Santa Catalina Colombia 10°36N 75°17W 328 A2
Santa Catalina Neg. Or., Phil. 9°20N 122°52E 233 G4
Santa Catalina Solomon Is. 10°53S 162°29E 287 N12
Santa Catalina, Gulf of U.S.A. 33°10N 117°50W 307 N9
Santa Catalina, I. Mexico 25°40N 110°47W 318 B2
Santa Cataliña de Armada Spain 43°2N 8°49W 194 B2
Santa Catalina I. U.S.A. 33°23N 118°25W 307 M8
Santa Catarina □ Brazil 27°25S 48°30W 335 B6
Santa Catarina, I. de Brazil 27°30S 48°40W 335 B6
Santa Caterina Venice, Italy 142 a3
Santa Caterina di Pittinuri Italy 40°6N 8°27E 200 B1
Santa Caterina Villarmosa Italy 37°35N 14°2E 201 E7
Santa Cecília Brazil 26°56S 50°18W 335 B5
Santa Clara Cuba 22°20N 80°0W 320 B4
Santa Clara Calif., U.S.A. 37°21N 121°57W 306 H5
Santa Clara N.Y., U.S.A. 44°38N 74°27W 313 B10
Santa Clara Utah, U.S.A. 37°8N 113°39W 305 H7
Santa Clara → Mexico 29°51N 107°6W 318 A3
Santa Clara, I. Chile 33°42S 79°0W 330 c
Santa Clara de Olimar Uruguay 32°50S 54°54W 335 C5
Santa Clara Valley U.S.A. 36°50N 121°30W 306 J5
Santa Clarita U.S.A. 34°24N 118°33W 307 L8
Santa Clotilde Peru 2°33S 73°45W 328 D3
Santa Coloma de Farners Spain 41°50N 2°39E 196 D7
Santa Coloma de Gramenet Spain 41°27N 2°13E 114 A2
Santa Comba = Santa Cataliña de Armada Spain 43°2N 8°49W 194 B2
Santa Croce Venice, Italy 142 b2
Santa Croce Camerina Italy 36°50N 14°31E 201 F7
Santa Croce di Magliano Italy 41°42N 14°59E 199 G11
Santa Cruz Aruba 12°30N 69°59W 322 f
Santa Cruz Bolivia 17°43S 63°10W 331 D5
Santa Cruz Brazil 6°13S 36°1W 332 C4
Santa Cruz Chile 34°38S 71°27W 334 C1
Santa Cruz Costa Rica 10°15N 85°35W 320 D2
Santa Cruz Curaçao 12°18N 69°7W 322 g
Santa Cruz Maharashtra, India 19°4N 72°51E 130 A1
Santa Cruz Jamaica 18°3N 77°43W 320 a
Santa Cruz Madeira 32°42N 16°46W 153 c
Santa Cruz Peru 5°40S 75°56W 330 B2
Santa Cruz Davao del S., Phil. 6°50N 125°25E 233 H5
Santa Cruz Laguna, Phil. 14°20N 121°24E 232 D3
Santa Cruz Manila, Phil. 14°36N 120°58E 127 B1
Santa Cruz Marinduque, Phil. 13°28N 122°2E 232 E4
Santa Cruz Mind. Occ., Phil. 13°4N 120°43E 232 E3
Santa Cruz Zambales, Phil. 15°46N 119°55E 232 D2
Santa Cruz Calif., U.S.A. 36°58N 122°1W 306 J4
Santa Cruz Venezuela 8°3N 64°27W 329 B5
Santa Cruz □ Argentina 49°0S 70°0W 336 C3
Santa Cruz □ Bolivia 17°43S 63°10W 331 D5
Santa Cruz → Argentina 50°10S 68°20W 336 D3
Santa Cruz, B. Curaçao 12°18N 69°10W 322 g
Santa Cruz, I. Ecuador 0°38S 90°23W 330 a
Santa Cruz, I. de Brazil 22°51S 43°7W 135 B2
Santa Cruz Cabrália Brazil 16°17S 39°2W 333 E4
Santa Cruz da Graciosa Azores 39°5N 28°1W 153 d1
Santa Cruz das Flores Azores 39°27N 31°7W 153 d2
Santa Cruz de Bravo = Felipe Carrillo Puerto Mexico 19°38N 88°3W 319 D7
Santa Cruz de la Palma Canary Is. 28°41N 17°46W 153 e1
Santa Cruz de la Palma ✈ (SPC) Canary Is. 28°40N 17°45W 153 e1
Santa Cruz de Mompox = Mompós Colombia 9°14N 74°26W 328 B3
Santa Cruz de Mudela Spain 38°39N 3°28W 195 G7
Santa Cruz de Olorde Spain 41°25N 2°3E 114 A1
Santa Cruz de Tenerife Canary Is. 28°28N 16°15W 153 e1
Santa Cruz del Norte Cuba 23°9N 81°55W 320 B3
Santa Cruz del Retamar Spain 40°8N 4°14W 194 E6
Santa Cruz del Sur Cuba 20°44N 78°0W 320 B4
Santa Cruz do Rio Pardo Brazil 22°54S 49°37W 335 A6
Santa Cruz do Sul Brazil 29°42S 52°25W 335 B5
Santa Cruz I. U.S.A. 34°1N 119°43W 307 M7
Santa Cruz Is. Solomon Is. 10°30S 166°0E 277 C12
Santa Cruz la Vieja △ Bolivia 17°55S 60°50W 331 D5
Santa Cruz Mts. Jamaica 17°58N 77°43W 320 a
Santa Efigénia Brazil 23°32S 46°38W 137 B2
Santa Elena Argentina 30°58S 59°47W 334 C4
Santa Elena Ecuador 2°16S 80°52W 328 D1
Sant' Elena Venice, Italy 142 c4
Santa Elena Camarines N., Phil. 14°12N 122°24E 232 D4
Santa Elena Manila, Phil. 14°38N 121°5E 127 B2
Santa Elena, C. Costa Rica 10°54N 85°56W 320 D2
Sant' Elena, Darsena di Venice, Italy 142 c4
Sant' Elena, Isola di Venice, Italy 142 c4
Santa Elena del Gomero Chile 33°28S 70°45W 137 B1
Sant' Eufémia, G. di Italy 38°51N 16°4E 201 D9
Santa Eulalia Spain 41°25N 2°10E 114 A2
Santa Eulària des Riu Spain 38°59N 1°32E 206 D2
Santa Fé Argentina 31°35S 60°41W 334 C3
Santa Fe Nueva Viscaya, Phil. 16°10N 120°57E 232 C3
Santa Fe Romblon, Phil. 12°10N 122°0E 232 E4
Santa Fé Spain 37°11N 3°43W 195 H7
Santa Fe N. Mex., U.S.A. 35°41N 105°57W 305 J11
Santa Fé □ Argentina 31°50S 60°55W 334 C3
Santa Fé, Canal de Ecuador 0°48S 89°55W 330 a
Santa Fé, I. Ecuador 0°49S 90°5W 330 a
Santa Fé do Sul Brazil 20°13S 50°56W 333 F1
Santa Fe Springs U.S.A. 33°56N 118°3W 126 C4
Santa Filomena Brazil 9°6S 45°50W 332 C2
Santa Fiora Italy 42°50N 11°35E 199 F8
Santa Gertrudis Spain 39°0N 1°26E 206 C1
Santa Giulia France 41°32N 9°17E 175 G13
Santa Giustina Italy 46°10N 12°5E 199 B9
Santa Helena Brazil 2°14S 45°18W 332 B2
Santa Helena de Goiás Brazil 17°53S 50°35W 333 E1
Santa Inês Bahia, Brazil 13°17S 39°48W 333 D4
Santa Inês Maranhão, Brazil 3°39S 45°20W 332 B2
Santa Inés Extremadura, Spain 38°32N 5°37W 195 G5
Santa Inés, I. Chile 54°0S 73°0W 336 D2
Santa Iria da Azóia Portugal 38°49N 9°5W 126 A2
Santa Isabel = Rey Malabo Eq. Guin. 3°45N 8°50E 263 E6
Santa Isabel Argentina 36°10S 66°54W 334 D2
Santa Isabel Puerto Rico 17°58N 66°24W 321 b
Santa Isabel Solomon Is. 8°0S 159°0E 287 M10
Santa Isabel do Araguaia Brazil 6°7S 48°19W 332 C2
Santa Isabel do Morro Brazil 11°34S 50°40W 333 D1
Santa Isabel do Río Negro Brazil 0°24S 65°2W 329 D4
Santa Julia Chile 33°30S 70°35W 137 C2
Santa Lucía Corrientes, Argentina 28°58S 59°5W 334 B4
Santa Lucía San Juan, Argentina 31°30S 68°30W 334 C2
Santa Lucia Phil. 17°7N 120°27E 232 C3
Santa Lucía Spain 37°35N 0°58W 197 H4
Santa Lucía Uruguay 34°27S 56°24W 334 C4
Santa Lucia, Stazione Venice, Italy 142 a2
Santa Lucía de Tirajana Canary Is. 27°55N 5°32W 153 e1
Santa Lucia Range U.S.A. 36°0N 121°20W 306 K5
Santa Luzia = Luziânia Brazil 16°20S 48°0W 333 E2
Santa Luzia Brazil 19°47S 43°52W 333 E3
Santa Luzia Cabo Verde 16°50N 24°35W 153 j
Santa Margalida Spain 39°42N 3°6E 206 B4
Santa Margarita Argentina 38°28S 61°35W 334 D3
Santa Margarita Calif., U.S.A. 35°23N 120°37W 306 K6
Santa Margarita → U.S.A. 33°13N 117°23W 307 M9
Santa Margarita, I. Mexico 24°27N 111°50W 318 C2
Santa Margherita Italy 38°58N 8°58E 200 D1
Santa Margherita Ligure Italy 44°20N 9°11E 198 D6
Santa María Argentina 26°40S 66°0W 334 B2
Santa Maria Azores 36°58N 25°6W 153 d4
Santa Maria Brazil 29°40S 53°48W 335 B5
Santa Maria Cabo Verde 16°31N 22°53W 153 j
Santa María Mexico City, Mexico 128 a1
Santa Maria Ilocos S., Phil. 17°22N 120°29E 232 C3
Santa Maria Isabela, Phil. 17°28N 121°45E 232 C3
Santa Maria Calif., U.S.A. 34°57N 120°26W 307 L6
Santa María → Mexico 31°0N 107°14W 318 A3
Santa María, B. de Mexico 25°4N 108°6W 318 B3
Santa Maria, C. de Portugal 36°58N 7°53W 195 J3
Santa María, I. Ecuador 1°17S 90°26W 330 a
Santa María, Vol. Guatemala 14°45N 91°33W 320 D1
Santa Maria Cápua Vétere Italy 41°5N 14°15E 201 A7
Santa Maria da Feira Portugal 40°55N 8°35W 194 E2
Santa Maria da Vitória Brazil 13°24S 44°12W 333 D3
Santa María de Guadalupe = Guadalupe Spain 39°27N 5°17W 195 F5
Santa María de Ipire Venezuela 8°49N 65°19W 329 B4
Santa Maria dei Frari Venice, Italy 142 b2
Santa Maria dei Miracoli Venice, Italy 142 b3
Santa María del Camí Spain 39°38N 2°47E 206 B3
Santa Maria della Misericórdia Venice, Italy 142 a3
Santa Maria della Pianto Venice, Italy 142 b3
Santa Maria della Salute Venice, Italy 142 c2
Santa Maria della Visitazione Venice, Italy 142 b3
Santa Maria delle Penitenti Venice, Italy 142 a2
Santa Maria di Léuca, C. Italy 39°47N 18°22E 201 C11
Santa Maria do Boiaçu Brazil 0°25S 61°48W 329 D5
Santa Maria do Suaçuí Brazil 18°12S 42°25W 333 E3
Santa Maria dos Marmelos Brazil 6°7S 61°51W 331 B5
Santa Maria Formosa Venice, Italy 142 b3
Santa María la Real de Nieva Spain 41°4N 4°24W 194 D6
Santa Maria Maggiore, Ex Chiesa di Venice, Italy 142 b1
Santa Marinella Italy 42°2N 11°52E 199 F8
Santa Marta Colombia 11°15N 74°13W 328 A3
Santa Marta, Sierra Nevada de Colombia 10°55N 73°50W 328 A3
Santa Marta de Tormes Spain 40°57N 5°38W 194 E5
Santa Marta Grande, C. Brazil 28°43S 48°50W 335 B6
Santa Martabaai = Sint Marthabaai Curaçao 12°17N 69°8W 322 g
Santa Maura = Lefkada Greece 38°40N 20°43E 207 B2
Santa Monica U.S.A. 34°1N 118°29W 126 B2
Santa Monica Mts. U.S.A. 34°6N 118°29W 126 B2
Santa Monica Mts. ⌂ U.S.A. 34°4N 118°44W 307 L8
Santa Olalla Spain 40°2N 4°25W 194 E6
Santa Olalla del Cala Spain 37°54N 6°14W 195 H4
Santa Paula U.S.A. 34°21N 119°4W 307 L7
Santa Pola Spain 38°13N 0°35W 197 G4
Santa Ponça Spain 39°30N 2°28E 206 B3
Santa Quitéria Brazil 4°20S 40°10W 332 B3
Santa Rita = Itumbiara Brazil 18°20S 49°10W 333 E2
Santa Rita Amazonas, Brazil 3°29S 69°19W 328 D4
Santa Rita Paraíba, Brazil 7°8S 34°58W 332 C5
Santa Rita Colombia 4°53N 68°24W 328 C4
Santa Rita Guam 13°23N 144°40E 302 d
Santa Rita Samar, Phil. 11°27N 124°56E 233 F5
Santa Rita Zulia, Venezuela 10°32N 71°32W 328 A3
Santa Rita de Cássia Brazil 11°0S 44°32W 332 D3
Santa Rita do Araguaia = Guiratinga Brazil 16°21S 53°45W 331 D7
Santa Rita do Araguaia Brazil 17°20S 53°12W 331 D7
Santa Rosa = Bella Unión Uruguay 30°15S 57°40W 334 C4
Santa Rosa La Pampa, Argentina 36°40S 64°17W 334 D3
Santa Rosa San Luis, Argentina 32°21S 65°10W 334 C2
Santa Rosa Beni, Bolivia 14°10S 66°53W 330 C4
Santa Rosa Pando, Bolivia 10°36S 67°20W 330 C4
Santa Rosa Santa Cruz, Bolivia 17°7S 63°35W 331 D5
Santa Rosa Brazil 27°52S 54°29W 335 B5
Santa Rosa Colombia 3°32N 69°48W 328 C4
Santa Rosa Curaçao 12°7N 68°53W 322 g
Santa Rosa El Oro, Ecuador 3°27S 79°58W 328 D2
Santa Rosa Galápagos Is., Ecuador 0°40S 90°25W 330 a
Santa Rosa Puno, Peru 14°30S 70°50W 330 C3
Santa Rosa San Martin, Peru 6°41S 76°37W 330 B2
Santa Rosa Phil. 15°25N 120°57E 232 D3
Santa Rosa Calif., U.S.A. 38°26N 122°43W 306 G4
Santa Rosa N. Mex., U.S.A. 34°57N 104°41W 305 J11
Santa Rosa Amazonas, Venezuela 1°29N 66°55W 328 C4
Santa Rosa, Mt. Guam 13°32N 144°55E 302 d
Santa Rosa and San Jacinto Mts. ⌂ U.S.A. 33°28N 116°20W 307 M10
Santa Rosa Beach U.S.A. 30°22N 86°14W 316 E3
Santa Rosa de Amanadona Venezuela 1°29N 66°55W 328 C4
Santa Rosa de Cabal Colombia 4°52N 75°38W 328 C2
Santa Rosa de Copán Honduras 14°47N 88°46W 320 D2
Santa Rosa de la Roca Bolivia 16°3S 61°34W 331 D5
Santa Rosa de Locobe Chile 33°25S 70°33W 137 B2
Santa Rosa de Osos Colombia 6°39N 75°28W 328 B2
Santa Rosa de Río Primero Argentina 31°8S 63°20W 334 C3
Santa Rosa de Viterbo Colombia 5°53N 72°59W 328 B3
Santa Rosa del Palmar Bolivia 16°54S 62°24W 331 D5
Santa Rosa I. Calif., U.S.A. 33°58N 120°6W 307 M6
Santa Rosa I. Fla., U.S.A. 30°20N 86°50W 317 E3
Santa Rosa Range U.S.A. 41°45N 117°40W 304 F5
Santa Rosalía Mexico 27°19N 112°17W 318 B2
Santa Stae Venice, Italy 142 b2
Santa Sylvina Argentina 27°50S 61°10W 334 B3
Santa Tecla = Nueva San Salvador El Salv. 13°40N 89°18W 320 D2
Santa Teresa Argentina 33°25S 60°47W 334 C3
Santa Teresa N. Terr., Australia 24°8S 134°22E 280 C1
Santa Teresa Brazil 19°55S 40°36W 333 E3
Santa Teresa Tamaulipas, Mexico 25°17N 97°51W 319 B5
Santa Teresa Venezuela 4°43N 61°4W 329 C5
Santa Teresa △ Uruguay 33°57S 53°31W 335 C5
Santa Teresa de la Ovalle Chile 33°22S 70°44W 137 B1
Santa Teresa di Riva Italy 37°57N 15°22E 201 E8
Santa Teresa Gallura Italy 41°14N 9°11E 200 A2
Santa Teresinha Brazil 10°28S 50°31W 332 D1
Santa Teresita Argentina 36°32S 56°41W 334 D4
Santa Uxía de Ribeira = Ribeira Spain 42°36N 8°58W 194 C2
Santa Vitória Brazil 18°50S 50°8W 333 E1
Santa Vitória do Palmar Brazil 33°32S 53°25W 335 C5
Santa Ynez → U.S.A. 34°41N 120°36W 307 L6
Santa Ynez Mts. U.S.A. 34°30N 120°0W 307 L6
Santa Ysabel U.S.A. 33°7N 116°40W 307 M10
Santadi Italy 39°5N 8°43E 200 C1
Santaella Spain 37°34N 4°51W 195 H6
Santahamina Finland 60°8N 25°2E 121 C3
Santahar Bangla. 24°48N 88°59E 241 C2
Santai China 31°5N 104°58E 228 B5
Santaluz Brazil 11°15S 39°22W 332 D4
Santan Indonesia 0°3S 117°28E 235 C5
Santana = Uruaçu Brazil 14°30S 49°10W 333 D2
Santana Bahia, Brazil 13°2S 44°5W 333 D3
Santana São Paulo, Brazil 23°29S 46°36W 137 A2
Santana Madeira 32°48N 16°52W 153 c
Sântana Romania 46°20N 21°30E 182 D6
Santana, Coxilha de Brazil 30°50S 55°35W 335 C4
Santana do Ipanema Brazil 9°22S 37°14W 332 C4
Santana do Livramento Brazil 30°55S 55°30W 335 C4
Santana do Paranaíba = Paranaíba Brazil 19°40S 51°11W 331 D7
Santander Colombia 3°1N 76°28W 328 C2
Santander Phil. 9°25N 123°20E 233 G4
Santander Spain 43°27N 3°51W 194 B7
Santander □ Colombia 7°0N 73°15W 328 B3
Santander Jiménez Mexico 24°13N 98°28W 319 C5
Santanilla, Is. Honduras 17°22N 83°57W 320 C3
Santanyí Spain 39°20N 3°5E 206 B4
Santaquin U.S.A. 39°59N 111°47W 304 G8
Santarcángelo di Romagna Italy 44°4N 12°26E 199 D9
Santarém Brazil 2°25S 54°42W 329 D7
Santarém Portugal 39°12N 8°42W 195 F2
Santarém □ Portugal 39°10N 8°40W 195 F2
Santaren Channel W. Indies 24°0N 79°30W 320 B4
Santee U.S.A. 32°50N 116°58W 307 N10
Santee → U.S.A. 33°7N 79°17W 315 E15
Santeny France 48°43N 2°34E 134 B4
Santéramo in Colle Italy 40°49N 16°45E 201 B9
Santerno → Italy 44°34N 11°58E 199 D8
Santhià Italy 45°22N 8°10E 198 C5
Santi Taiwan 22°43N 120°39E 225 D2
Santi-Quaranta = Sarandë Albania 39°52N 19°55E 206 B9
Santiago = Río Grande de Santiago → Mexico 21°36N 105°26W 318 C3
Santiago = São Tiago Cabo Verde 15°0N 23°40W 153 j
Santiago Brazil 29°11S 54°52W 335 B5
Santiago Canary Is. 28°2N 17°12W 153 e1
Santiago Chile 33°26S 70°40W 137 B2
Santiago Panama 8°0N 81°0W 320 E3
Santiago Peru 14°11S 75°43W 330 C2
Santiago Ilocos S., Phil. 17°18N 120°27E 232 C3
Santiago Isabela, Phil. 16°41N 121°33E 232 C3
Santiago → Peru 4°27S 77°38W 328 D2
Santiago, C. Chile 50°46S 75°27W 336 D1
Santiago, I. = San Salvador, I. Ecuador 0°16S 90°42W 330 a
Santiago, Punta de Eq. Guin. 3°12N 8°40E 263 E6
Santiago, Sierra de Bolivia 18°25S 59°25W 331 D6
Santiago Benítez Int. ✈ (SCL) Santiago, Chile 33°33S 70°42W 137 B1
Santiago de Chiquitos Bolivia 18°19S 59°34W 331 D6
Santiago de Chuco Peru 8°9S 78°11W 330 B2
Santiago de Compostela Spain 42°52N 8°37W 194 C2
Santiago de Cuba Cuba 20°0N 75°49W 320 C4
Santiago de los Caballeros Dom. Rep. 19°30N 70°40W 321 C5
Santiago de Surco Peru 12°9S 77°0W 124 B2
Santiago del Estero Argentina 27°50S 64°15W 334 B3
Santiago del Estero □ Argentina 27°40S 63°15W 334 B3
Santiago del Teide Canary Is. 28°17N 16°48W 153 e1
Santiago do Boqueirão = Santiago Brazil 29°11S 54°52W 335 B5
Santiago do Cacém Portugal 38°1N 8°42W 195 G2
Santiago I. Phil. 16°23N 119°56E 232 C2
Santiago Ixcuintla Mexico 21°49N 105°13W 318 C3
Santiago Jamiltepec Mexico 16°17N 97°49W 319 D5
Santiago Papasquiaro Mexico 25°3N 105°25W 318 C3
Santiago Pinotepa Nacional Mexico 16°19N 98°1W 319 D5
Santiaguillo, L. de Mexico 24°48N 104°48W 318 C4
Santialing Taiwan 25°5N 121°51E 225 A3
Santiao Chiao Taiwan 25°1N 122°0E 225 A3
Santiaolun Taiwan 23°39N 120°9E 225 C2
Santiguila Mali 12°42N 7°25W 262 C3
Santillana del Mar Spain 43°24N 4°6W 194 B6
Santisteban del Puerto Spain 38°17N 3°15W 195 G7
Santo → Peru 8°56S 78°37W 330 B2
Santo Amaro Bahia, Brazil 12°30S 38°43W 333 D4
Santo Amaro São Paulo, Brazil 23°39S 46°42W 137 B1
Santo Amaro Lisboa, Portugal 38°42N 9°11W 126 A1
Santo Anastácio Brazil 21°58S 51°39W 335 A5
Santo André Brazil 23°39S 46°29W 335 A6
Santo André Lisboa, Portugal 38°38N 9°3W 126 B2
Santo Ângelo Brazil 28°15S 54°15W 335 B5
Sant' Angelo, Castel Rome, Italy 136 b1
Sant' Ángelo Lodigiano Italy 45°14N 9°25E 198 C6
Santo Antão Cabo Verde 16°52N 25°10W 153 j
Santo Antão do Tojal Portugal 38°49N 9°9W 126 A2
Sant' Antíoco Italy 39°4N 8°27E 200 C1
Santo Antônia São Tomé & Príncipe 1°37N 7°27E 265 a
Santo Antônio Brazil 2°24S 60°58W 329 D5
Santo Antônio, Qta. de Portugal 38°39N 9°15W 126 B1
Santo Antônio da Cachoeira = Itaguatins Brazil 5°47S 47°29W 332 C2
Santo Antônio de Jesus Brazil 12°58S 39°16W 333 D4
Santo Antônio do Abaixo = Santo Antônio do Leverger Brazil 15°52S 56°5W 331 D6
Santo Antônio do Içá Brazil 3°5S 67°57W 328 D4
Santo Antônio do Leverger Brazil 15°52S 56°5W 331 D6
Santo Corazón Bolivia 18°0S 58°45W 331 D6
Santo Cosimo e Damiano, Ex Chiesa di Venice, Italy 142 c2
Santo Domingo Dom. Rep. 18°30N 69°59W 321 C6
Santo Domingo Baja Calif. S., Mexico 25°29N 111°55W 318 B2
Santo Domingo Nic. 12°14N 84°59W 320 D3
Santo Domingo, Cay The Bahamas 21°25N 75°45W 320 B4
Santo Domingo de la Calzada Spain 42°26N 2°57W 196 C2
Santo Domingo de los Colorados Ecuador 0°15S 79°9W 328 D2
Santo Domingo Pueblo U.S.A. 35°31N 106°22W 305 J10
Santo Domingo Tehuantepec = Tehuantepec Mexico 16°21N 95°13W 319 D5
Sant' Egídio alla Vibrata Italy 42°49N 13°42E 199 F10
Santo Nino I. Phil. 11°54N 124°26E 233 F5
Santo Stéfano di Camastro Italy 38°1N 14°22E 201 D7
Santo Tirso Portugal 41°21N 8°28W 194 D2
Santo Tomás Galápagos Is., Ecuador 0°51S 91°2W 330 a
Santo Tomás Baja Calif., Mexico 31°33N 116°24W 318 A1
Santo Tomás Peru 14°26S 72°8W 330 C3
Santo Tomas Phil. 7°32N 125°37E 233 H5
Santo Tomas, Univ. of Phil. 14°36N 120°59E 127 B1
Santo Tomás, Volcán Ecuador 0°48S 91°7W 330 a
Santo Tomé Argentina 28°40S 56°5W 335 B4
Santo Tomé de Guayana = Ciudad Guayana Venezuela 8°0N 62°30W 329 B5
Santomera Spain 38°4N 1°3W 197 G3
Santoña Spain 43°29N 3°27W 194 B7
Santorini Greece 36°23N 25°27E 205 E7
Santos Brazil 24°0S 46°20W 335 A6
Santos, Sierra de los Spain 38°7N 5°12W 195 G5
Santos Dumont Brazil 22°55S 43°10W 333 F3
Santos Dumont ✈ (SDU) Brazil 22°54S 43°9W 135 B2
Santoshpur India 22°31N 88°16E 124 B1
Santragachi India 22°35N 88°17E 124 B1
Santuario de Aves Laguna Colorada △ Bolivia 22°10S 67°45W 334 A2
Sanuki Japan 34°19N 134°10E 222 C6
Sanur Indonesia 8°41S 115°15E 231 K18
Sanwan Taiwan 24°39N 120°57E 225 B2
Sanwer India 22°59N 75°50E 242 H6
Sanxenxo Spain 42°24N 8°49W 194 C2
Sanxia = Sanhsia Taiwan 24°56N 121°22E 225 B3
Sanxia Shuiku China 30°3N 107°58E 228 B6
Sanxiang China 22°21N 113°25E 219 a
Sanxing = Sanhsing Taiwan 24°40N 121°36E 225 B3
Sanya China 18°14N 109°29E 229 a
San'yō Japan 34°2N 131°5E 222 C3
Sanyuan China 34°35N 108°58E 226 G5
Sanyuanli China 23°8N 113°14E 121 B2
Sanyuki-Sammyaku Japan 34°5N 134°0E 222 C6
Sanza Pombo Angola 7°18S 15°56E 265 D3
São Bartolomeu de Messines Portugal 37°15N 8°17W 195 H2
São Benedito = Beneditinos Brazil 5°27S 42°22W 332 C3
São Benedito Brazil 4°3S 40°53W 332 B3
São Benedito → Brazil 9°11S 57°2W 331 B6
São Bento Brazil 2°42S 44°50W 332 B3
São Bento do Norte Brazil 5°4S 36°2W 332 C4
São Bernardo do Campo Brazil 23°45S 46°34W 333 F2
São Borja Brazil 28°39S 56°0W 335 B4
São Brás de Alportel Portugal 37°8N 7°37W 195 H3
São Braz, C. de Angola 9°58S 13°19E 265 D2
São Caetano do Sul Brazil 23°37S 46°34W 137 B2
São Caitano Brazil 8°21S 36°6W 332 C4
São Carlos Brazil 22°0S 47°50W 335 A6
São Conrado Brazil 23°0S 43°17W 135 B1
São Cristóvão Rio de J., Brazil 22°53S 43°13W 135 B1
São Cristóvão Sergipe, Brazil 11°1S 37°15W 332 D4
São Domingos Brazil 13°25S 46°19W 333 D2
São Domingos Guinea-Biss. 12°19N 16°13W 262 C1
São Domingos da Boa Vista = São Domingos do Capim Brazil 1°41S 47°47W 332 B2
São Domingos do Capim Brazil 1°41S 47°47W 332 B2
São Domingos do Maranhão Brazil 5°42S 44°22W 332 C3
São Felipe = Eirunepé Brazil 6°35S 69°53W 330 B4
São Felipe = Içana Brazil 0°21N 67°19W 328 C4
São Félix Brazil 11°36S 50°39W 333 D1
São Félix do Xingu Brazil 6°38S 51°59W 331 B7
São Filipe Cabo Verde 15°2N 24°30W 153 j
São Francisco = Itapagé Brazil 3°41S 39°34W 332 B4
São Francisco Brazil 16°0S 44°50W 333 E3
São Francisco → Brazil 10°30S 36°24W 332 D4
São Francisco do Maranhão Brazil 6°15S 42°52W 332 C3
São Francisco do Sul Brazil 26°15S 48°36W 335 B6
São Francisco Penitência Rio de J., Brazil 135 b1
São Gabriel Brazil 30°20S 54°20W 335 C5
São Gabriel da Cachoeira Brazil 0°8S 67°5W 328 D4
São Gabriel da Palha Brazil 18°47S 40°39W 333 E3
São Gonçalo = Araripina Brazil 7°33S 40°34W 332 C3
São Gonçalo Brazil 22°48S 43°5W 333 F3
São Gotardo Brazil 19°19S 46°3W 333 E2
Sao Hill Tanzania 8°20S 35°12E 269 D4
São João Guinea-Biss. 11°32N 15°25W 262 C1
São João da Baliza Brazil 0°52N 59°52W 329 C6
São João da Barra Brazil 21°38S 41°3W 333 F3
São João da Boa Vista Brazil 22°0S 46°52W 335 A6
São João da Madeira Portugal 40°54N 8°30W 194 E2
São João da Pesqueira Portugal 41°8N 7°24W 194 D3
São João da Ponte Brazil 15°56S 44°1W 333 E3
São João de Meriti Brazil 22°48S 43°21W 333 F3
São João de Montenegro = Montenegro Brazil 29°39S 51°29W 335 B5
São João del Rei Brazil 21°8S 44°15W 333 F3
São João do Araguaia Brazil 5°23S 48°46W 332 C2
São João do Paraíso Brazil 15°19S 42°1W 333 E3
São João do Piauí Brazil 8°21S 42°15W 332 C3
São João do Sul Angola 15°46S 12°0E 265 F2
São João dos Patos Brazil 6°30S 43°42W 332 C3
São Joaquim Amazonas, Brazil 0°1S 67°16W 328 D4
São Joaquim Sta. Catarina, Brazil 28°18S 49°56W 335 B6
São Joaquim △ Brazil 28°12S 49°37W 335 B6
São Joaquim da Barra Brazil 20°35S 47°53W 333 F2
São Jorge Azores 38°38N 28°3W 153 d1
São Jorge, Canal de Azores 38°30N 28°0W 153 d1
São Jorge, Castelo de Portugal 38°42N 9°8W 126 A2
São Jorge, Pta. de Azores 38°42N 27°3W 153 d1
São Jorge, Pta. de Madeira 32°50N 16°53W 153 c
São José Brazil 27°38S 48°39W 335 B5
São José, B. de Brazil 2°38S 44°4W 332 B3
São José da Lagoa = Nova Era Brazil 19°45S 43°3W 333 E3
São José da Laje Brazil 9°1S 36°3W 332 C4
São José de Mipibu Brazil 6°5S 35°15W 332 C4
São José de Tocantins = Niquelândia Brazil 14°33S 48°23W 333 D2
São José do Norte Brazil 32°1S 52°3W 335 C5
São José do Peixe Brazil 7°24S 42°34W 332 C3
São José do Rio Preto Brazil 20°50S 49°20W 335 A6
São José dos Campos Brazil 23°7S 45°52W 335 A6
São José dos Cocais = Nossa Senhora do Livramento Brazil 15°48S 56°22W 331 D6
São José dos Matões = Parnarama Brazil 5°31S 43°6W 332 C3
São Juliao do Tojal Portugal 38°49N 9°8W 126 A2
São Leopoldo Brazil 29°50S 51°10W 335 B5
São Lourenço Brazil 22°7S 45°3W 333 F2
São Lourenço → Brazil 17°53S 57°27W 331 D6
São Lourenço, Pantanal do Brazil 17°30S 56°20W 331 D6
São Lourenço, Pta. de Madeira 32°44N 16°39W 153 c
São Lourenço do Sul Brazil 31°22S 51°58W 335 C5
São Luís Brazil 2°39S 44°15W 332 B3
São Luís do Curu Brazil 3°40S 39°14W 332 B4
São Luís do Tapajós Brazil 4°25S 56°12W 329 D6
São Luís Gonzaga = Ipixuna Brazil 7°0S 71°40W 330 B3
São Luís Gonzaga Brazil 28°25S 55°0W 335 B5
São Marcos → Brazil 18°15S 47°37W 333 E2
São Marcos, B. de Brazil 2°0S 44°0W 332 B3
São Martinho da Cortiça Portugal 40°18N 8°8W 194 E2
São Mateus Azores 38°26N 28°27W 153 d1
São Mateus Brazil 18°44S 39°50W 333 E4
São Mateus → Brazil 18°35S 39°44W 333 E4
São Mateus do Sul Brazil 25°52S 50°23W 335 B5
São Miguel Azores 37°47N 25°30W 153 d3
São Miguel do Araguaia Brazil 13°19S 50°13W 333 D1
São Miguel do Guamá Brazil 1°37S 47°29W 332 B2
São Miguel do Oeste Brazil 26°45S 53°34W 335 B5
São Miguel dos Campos Brazil 9°47S 36°5W 332 C4
São Nicolau Cabo Verde 16°20N 24°20W 153 j
São Nicolau → Angola 14°16S 12°22E 265 E2
São Nicolau → Brazil 5°45S 42°2W 332 C3
São Paulo Atl. Oc. 0°56N 29°22W 152 F9
São Paulo Brazil 23°32S 46°38W 137 B2
São Paulo □ Brazil 22°0S 49°0W 335 A6
São Paulo Congonhas ✈ (CGH) Brazil 23°38S 46°39W 137 B2
São Paulo de Olivença Brazil 3°27S 68°48W 328 D4
São Paulo-Guarulhos Int. ✈ (GRU) Brazil 23°26S 46°28W 333 F2
São Pedro Atl. Oc. 0°56N 29°22W 152 F9
São Pedro do Sul Portugal 40°46N 8°4W 194 E2
São Rafael Brazil 5°47S 36°55W 332 C4
São Raimundo das Mangabeiras Brazil 7°1S 45°29W 332 C2
São Raimundo Nonato Brazil 9°1S 42°42W 332 C3
São Romão Brazil 16°22S 45°4W 333 E2
São Roque Madeira 32°46N 16°48W 153 c
São Roque, C. de Brazil 5°30S 35°16W 332 C4
São Roque do Pico Azores 38°31N 28°19W 153 d1
São Salvador do Congo = Mbanza Congo Angola 6°18S 14°16E 265 D2
São Sebastião Azores 38°39N 27°6W 153 d1
São Sebastião, I. de Brazil 23°50S 45°18W 335 A6
São Sebastião do Paraíso Brazil 20°54S 46°59W 335 A6
São Simão Brazil 18°56S 50°30W 333 E1
São Teotónio Portugal 37°30N 8°42W 195 H2
São Tiago Cabo Verde 15°0N 23°40W 153 j
São Tomé Brazil 5°58S 36°4W 332 C4
São Tomé São Tomé & Príncipe 0°10N 6°39E 265 a
São Tomé, C. de Brazil 22°0S 40°59W 333 F3
São Tomé, Pico de São Tomé & Príncipe 0°16N 6°33E 265 a
São Tomé & Príncipe ■ Africa 0°12N 6°39E 265 a
São Vicente = Araguatins Brazil 5°38S 48°7W 332 C2
São Vicente Brazil 23°57S 46°23W 335 A6
São Vicente Cabo Verde 17°0N 25°0W 153 j
São Vicente Madeira 32°48N 17°3W 153 c
São Vicente, C. de Portugal 37°0N 9°0W 195 H1
Saona, I. Dom. Rep. 18°10N 68°40W 321 C6
Saône → France 45°44N 4°50E 173 G11

Saône-et-Loire □ France 46°30N 4°50E 173 F11
Saonek Indonesia 0°22S 130°55E 231 E8
Saoura, O. → Algeria 29°0N 0°55W 261 C4
Sapa India 22°30N 88°15E 124 B1
Sapam, Ao Thailand 8°0N 98°26E 237 a
Sapanca Turkey 40°41N 30°16E 212 B4
Sapanjang Indonesia 7°10S 115°50E 235 D5
Sapão → Brazil 11°1S 45°32W 332 D2
Saparua Indonesia 3°33S 128°40E 231 E7
Sapateiro, Cor. do → Brazil 23°35S 46°41W 137 B1
Sapé Brazil 7°6S 35°13W 332 C4
Sape Indonesia 8°34S 118°59E 235 D5
Sape, Teluk Indonesia 8°32S 119°4E 235 D5
Sapele Nigeria 5°50N 5°40E 263 D6
Sapelo I. U.S.A. 31°25N 81°12W 316 D8
Sapelo Sound U.S.A. 31°30N 81°10W 316 D8
Sapes Greece 41°2N 25°43E 203 E9
Şaphane Turkey 39°1N 29°13E 205 B11
Sapi ⌓ Zimbabwe 15°48S 29°42E 269 F2
Sapienza Greece 36°45N 21°43E 204 E3
Sapindji Dem. Rep. of the Congo 9°39S 23°12E 265 D4
Sapo △ Liberia 5°15N 8°30W 262 D3
Sapone Burkina Faso 12°3N 1°35W 263 C4
Saposoa Peru 6°55S 76°45W 330 B2
Sapotskina Belarus 53°49N 23°40E 184 E10
Sapouy Burkina Faso 11°34N 1°44W 263 C4
Sapozhok Russia 53°59N 40°41E 190 D5
Sapphire Australia 23°28S 147°43E 280 C4
Sappho U.S.A. 48°4N 124°16W 306 B2
Sapporo Japan 43°0N 141°21E 220 C10
Sapporo New Chitose ✈ (CTS) Japan 42°46N 141°41E 220 C10
Sapri Italy 40°4N 15°38E 201 B8
Sapt Kosi → Nepal 26°32N 86°56E 243 F12
Sapu Angola 12°28S 19°26E 265 E3
Sapudi Indonesia 7°6S 114°20E 235 D4
Sapulpa U.S.A. 35°59N 96°5W 314 D6
Sapulut Malaysia 4°42N 116°28E 235 B5
Saqqez Iran 36°15N 46°20E 213 D12
Sar Dasht Āzarbāyjān-e Gharbī, Iran 36°9N 45°28E 213 D11
Sar Dasht Khuzestān, Iran 32°32N 48°52E 247 C6
Sar-e Pol Afghan. 36°10N 66°0E 240 A2
Sar-e Pol □ Afghan. 36°20N 65°50E 240 A2
Sar Gachīneh = Yāsūj Iran 30°31N 51°31E 247 D6
Sar Passage Palau 7°12N 134°22E 288 c
Sar Planina N. Macedonia 42°0N 21°0E 202 E4
Sara Burkina Faso 11°40N 3°53W 262 C4
Sara Niger 20°46N 12°35E 259 D2
Sara Phil. 11°16N 123°1E 233 F4
Šara △ Serbia 42°12N 21°0E 202 D5
Sara Buri = Saraburi Thailand 14°30N 100°55E 236 E3
Sarāb Iran 37°55N 47°40E 213 D12
Sarābādī Iraq 33°1N 44°48E 246 C5
Sarabît el Khâdim Egypt 29°2N 33°25E 251 J4
Sarābleh Iran 33°44N 46°34E 213 F12
Saraburi Thailand 14°30N 100°55E 236 E3
Saradiya India 21°34N 70°2E 242 J4
Saraféré Mali 15°50N 3°40W 262 B4
Saragossa = Zaragoza Spain 41°39N 0°53W 196 D4
Saraguro Ecuador 3°35S 79°16W 328 D2
Sarahs Turkmenistan 36°32N 61°13E 247 B9
Sarai Naurang Pakistan 32°50N 70°47E 242 C4
Saraikela India 22°42N 85°56E 243 H11
Saraipali India 21°20N 82°59E 244 D6
Saraiu Romania 44°43N 28°10E 183 F13
Sarajevo Bos.-H. 43°52N 18°26E 182 G3
Sarakhs = Sarahs Turkmenistan 36°32N 61°13E 247 B9
Sarakhs Iran 36°32N 61°9E 216 E6
Saramacca → Suriname 5°50N 55°55W 329 B6
Saramati Myanmar 25°44N 95°2E 241 C5
Saran, Gunung Indonesia 0°30S 111°25E 235 C4
Saranac U.S.A. 42°56N 85°13W 311 B11
Saranac Lake U.S.A. 44°20N 74°10W 313 B10
Saranac Lakes U.S.A. 44°20N 74°28W 313 B10
Saranda Tanzania 5°45S 34°59E 268 D3
Sarandë Albania 39°52N 19°55E 206 B9
Sarandi Argentina 34°40S 58°20W 117 C2
Sarandí del Yí Uruguay 33°18S 55°38W 335 C4
Sarandí Grande Uruguay 33°44S 56°20W 334 C4
Sarangani □ Phil. 5°45N 125°20E 233 J5
Sarangani B. Phil. 6°0N 125°13E 233 J5
Sarangani I. Phil. 5°26N 125°28E 233 J5
Sarangani Is. Phil. 5°25N 125°25E 233 J5
Sarangarh India 21°30N 83°5E 244 D6
Saranovo = Septemvri Bulgaria 42°13N 24°6E 203 D8
Saransk Russia 54°10N 45°10E 190 C7
Sarapul Russia 56°28N 53°48E 186 C9
Sarāqib Syria 35°52N 36°47E 250 C7
Sarar Plain = Bannaanka Saraar Somalia 9°25N 46°17E 267 C6
Sarasota U.S.A. 27°20N 82°32W 317 H7
Saraswati → India 22°46N 88°15E 124 A1
Sarata Ukraine 46°1N 29°40E 183 D14
Sarata → Ukraine 45°51N 29°41E 183 E14
Saratoga Calif., U.S.A. 37°16N 122°2W 306 H4
Saratoga Wyo., U.S.A. 41°27N 106°49W 304 F10
Saratoga ⌓ U.S.A. 43°0N 73°38W 313 D11
Saratoga L. U.S.A. 43°1N 73°44W 313 C11
Saratoga Springs U.S.A. 43°5N 73°47W 313 C11
Saratok Malaysia 1°55N 111°17E 235 B4
Saratov Russia 51°30N 46°2E 190 E7
Saratov □ Russia 51°50N 46°20E 190 E8
Saratovskoye Vdkhr. Russia 53°10N 48°35E 190 D9
Sarāvān Iran 27°25N 62°15E 247 E9
Saravane Laos 15°43N 106°25E 236 E6
Sarawak □ Malaysia 2°0N 113°0E 235 B4
Saray Tekirdağ, Turkey 41°26N 27°55E 203 E11
Saray Van, Turkey 38°38N 44°9E 213 C11
Saraya Senegal 12°50N 11°45W 262 C2
Saraycık Turkey 39°1N 29°49E 205 B11
Sarayköy Turkey 37°55N 28°54E 205 D10
Saraylar Turkey 40°39N 27°40E 203 F11
Sarayönü Turkey 38°16N 32°24E 212 C5
Sarbāz Iran 26°38N 61°19E 247 E9
Sarbīsheh Iran 32°30N 59°40E 247 C8
Sárbogárd Hungary 46°50N 18°40E 182 D3
Sarca → Italy 45°52N 10°52E 198 C7
Sarcelles France 49°1N 2°23E 173 D9
Sarda → India 27°21N 81°23E 243 F9
Sardalas Libya 25°50N 10°34E 258 C2
Sardar Sarovar Dam India 21°50N 73°50E 244 D1
Sardarshahr India 28°30N 74°29E 242 E6
Sardegna □ Italy 40°0N 9°0E 200 B1
Sardhana India 29°9N 77°39E 242 E7
Sardina, Pta. Canary Is. 28°9N 15°44W 153 e1
Sardinata Colombia 8°5N 72°48W 328 B3
Sardinia = Sardegna □ Italy 40°0N 9°0E 200 B1
Sardinia U.S.A. 39°0N 83°49W 311 F13
Sardis Turkey 38°28N 27°58E 205 C10
Sardis Ga., U.S.A. 32°58N 81°46W 316 C8
Sārdūīyeh = Dar Mazār Iran 29°14N 57°20E 247 D8
Sarecky potok → Czechia 50°7N 14°23E 135 B2
Sarek △ Sweden 67°22N 17°35E 160 C17
Saren Indonesia 8°26S 115°34E 231 J18
S'Arenal Spain 39°30N 2°45E 206 B3
Sarentino Italy 46°38N 11°21E 199 B8
Saréyamou Mali 16°7N 3°10W 262 B4
Sargasso Sea Atl. Oc. 27°0N 72°0W 292 G13
Sargent U.S.A. 33°26N 84°52W 316 B5
Sargodha Pakistan 32°10N 72°40E 242 C5
Sarh Chad 9°5N 18°23E 259 G3
Sarhala Côte d'Ivoire 8°22N 6°8W 262 D3
Sarhro, Jebel Morocco 31°6N 5°0W 260 B4
Sārī Iran 36°30N 53°4E 247 B7
Sari d'Orcino France 42°3N 8°49E 175 F12
Saria Greece 35°54N 27°17E 205 F9
Saria India 21°38N 83°22E 243 J10
Sariab Pakistan 30°6N 66°59E 242 D2
Sarıbeyler Turkey 39°24N 27°35E 205 B9
Saricumbe Angola 12°12S 19°46E 265 E3
Sarigan N. Marianas 16°43N 145°47E 302 a
Sarıgöl Turkey 38°14N 28°41E 212 C3
Sarıkamiş Turkey 40°22N 42°35E 213 B10
Sarıkaya Turkey 39°29N 35°22E 212 C6
Sarikei Malaysia 2°8N 111°30E 235 B4
Sarıköy Turkey 40°12N 27°37E 203 F11
Sarila India 25°46N 79°41E 243 G8
Sarimbun Singapore 1°24N 103°40E 138 A2
Sarimbun Res. Singapore 1°25N 103°41E 138 A2
Sarina Australia 21°22S 149°13E 280 C4
Sariñena Spain 41°47N 0°10W 196 D4
Sarinleey Somalia 2°22N 42°17E 267 D5
Sarıoğlan Turkey 39°5N 35°59E 212 C6
Sariri Papua N. G. 9°11S 148°35E 286 E5
Sarita U.S.A. 27°13N 97°47W 314 H6
Sarıveliler Turkey 36°41N 32°37E 250 B3
Sariwŏn N. Korea 38°31N 125°46E 224 C2
Sariyar Barajı Turkey 40°2N 31°33E 212 B4
Sarıyer Turkey 41°10N 29°3E 122 A2
Sarız Turkey 38°28N 36°30E 212 C7
Sarju → India 27°21N 81°23E 243 F9
Sark U.K. 49°25N 2°22W 169 H5
Sarkad Hungary 46°47N 21°23E 182 D6
Sarkari Tala India 27°39N 70°52E 242 F4
Şarkışla Turkey 39°21N 36°25E 212 C7
Şarköy Turkey 40°36N 27°6E 203 F11
Sarlat-la-Canéda France 44°54N 1°13E 174 D5
Sărmăşag Romania 47°21N 22°50E 182 C7
Sărmaşu Romania 46°45N 24°13E 183 D9
Sarmi Indonesia 1°49S 138°44E 231 E9
Sarmiento Argentina 45°35S 69°5W 336 C3
Sarmiento, Mt. Chile 54°27S 70°50W 336 D2
Sarmizegetusa Romania 45°31N 22°47E 182 E7
Särna Sweden 61°41N 13°8E 162 C7
Sarnano Italy 43°2N 13°18E 199 E10
Sarnen Switz. 46°53N 8°13E 179 J4
Sarnia Canada 42°58N 82°23W 312 D2
Sarno Italy 40°49N 14°37E 201 B7
Sarnthein = Sarentino Italy 46°38N 11°21E 199 B8
Särö Sweden 57°31N 11°57E 163 G5
Sarolangun Indonesia 2°19S 102°42E 234 C2
Saronikos Kolpos Greece 37°45N 23°45E 204 D5
Saronno Italy 45°38N 9°2E 198 C6
Saros Körfezi Turkey 40°30N 26°15E 203 F10
Sárospatak Hungary 48°18N 21°33E 182 B6
Sarov Russia 54°56N 43°19E 190 C6
Sarowbī Afghan. 34°36N 69°44E 240 B3
Sarpsborg Norway 59°16N 11°7E 164 E8
Sarqan Kazakhstan 45°24N 79°55E 217 C9
Sarracín Spain 42°15N 3°45W 194 C7
Sarralbe France 49°0N 7°1E 173 D14
Sarrat Phil. 18°9N 120°39E 232 B3
Sarre = Saar → Europe 49°41N 6°32E 170 E6
Sarre Italy 45°40N 7°15E 198 C4
Sarre-Union France 48°57N 7°4E 173 D14
Sarrebourg France 48°43N 7°3E 173 D14
Sarreguemines France 49°5N 7°4E 173 C14
Sarriá Barcelona, Spain 41°22N 2°8E 114 A1
Sarria Galicia, Spain 42°49N 7°29W 194 C3
Sarrión Spain 40°9N 0°49W 196 E4
Sarro Mali 13°40N 5°15W 262 C3
Sarroch Italy 39°4N 9°1E 200 C2
Sarsing Iraq 37°2N 43°20E 213 D10
Sarstedt Germany 52°14N 9°52E 178 C5
Sarsuna India 22°28N 88°17E 124 C1
Sartell U.S.A. 45°37N 94°12W 308 C6
Sartène France 41°38N 8°58E 175 G12
Sarthe □ France 48°10N 0°10E 172 D7
Sarthe → France 47°33N 0°31W 172 E6
Sartilly France 48°45N 1°28W 172 D5
Sartrouville France 48°56N 2°10E 134 A2
Saruhanlı Turkey 38°44N 27°36E 205 C9
Sărulești Romania 44°25N 26°39E 183 F11
Saruna → Pakistan 26°31N 67°7E 242 F2
Sarupeta India 26°30N 91°5E 241 B3
Särur Azerbaijan 39°22N 45°5E 213 C11
Saruwaged Ra. Papua N. G. 6°13S 146°45E 286 D4
Sárvár Hungary 47°15N 16°56E 182 C1
Sarvar India 26°4N 75°0E 242 F6
Sarvestān Iran 29°20N 53°10E 247 D7
Särvfjället Sweden 62°42N 13°30E 162 B7
Sárviz → Hungary 46°24N 18°41E 182 D3
Sary-Tash Kyrgyzstan 39°44N 73°15E 217 E8
Sarych, Mys Ukraine 44°25N 33°45E 189 K7
Saryesik-Atyraū Qumy Kazakhstan 45°30N 76°0E 217 C9
Sarykamyshskoye, Ozero = Saryqamysh Köli Turkmenistan 41°56N 57°25E 216 D5
Sarykemer Kazakhstan 43°0N 71°30E 217 D8
Sarykenggir → Kazakhstan 48°22N 67°59E 217 C7
Saryköl Kazakhstan 53°20N 65°12E 216 B7
Sarykolskiy Khrebet Tajikistan 38°30N 74°30E 217 E8
Saryözek Kazakhstan 44°22N 77°59E 217 D9
Saryqamysh Köli Turkmenistan 41°56N 57°25E 216 D5
Saryshaghan Kazakhstan 46°12N 73°38E 217 C8
Sarysū → Kazakhstan 45°12N 66°36E 217 C7
Sarzana Italy 44°7N 9°58E 198 D6
Sarzeau France 47°31N 2°48W 172 E4
Sasabeneh Ethiopia 7°59N 44°43E 267 C5
Sasad Hungary 47°28N 19°0E 117 B2
Sasamungga Solomon Is. 7°0S 156°50E 287 L9
Sasan Gir India 21°10N 70°36E 242 J4
Sasaram India 24°57N 84°5E 243 G11
Sasari, Mt. Solomon Is. 8°10S 159°30E 287 M10
Sasayama Japan 35°4N 135°13E 223 B7
Sasebo Japan 33°10N 129°43E 222 D1
Saser Kangri India 34°50N 77°50E 243 B7
Sashalom Hungary 47°30N 19°10E 117 A3
Saska Poland 52°14N 21°3E 143 B2
Saskatchewan □ Canada 54°40N 106°0W 297 C7
Saskatchewan → Canada 53°37N 100°40W 297 C8
Saskatoon Canada 52°10N 106°38W 297 C7
Saskylakh Russia 71°55N 114°1E 215 B12
Sasolburg S. Africa 26°46S 27°49E 271 C4
Sason Turkey 38°19N 41°24E 213 C9
Sasovo Russia 54°25N 41°55E 190 C5
Sassandra Côte d'Ivoire 4°55N 6°8W 262 E3
Sassandra → Côte d'Ivoire 4°58N 6°5W 262 E3
Sassandra-Marahoué □ Côte d'Ivoire 6°58N 6°26W 262 D3
Sássari Italy 40°43N 8°34E 200 B1
Sassie Australia 10°2S 142°51E 280 a
Sassnitz Germany 54°29N 13°39E 178 A9
Sasso Marconi Italy 44°24N 11°15E 199 D8
Sassocorvaro Italy 43°47N 12°30E 199 E9
Sassoferrato Italy 43°26N 12°51E 199 E9
Sassuolo Italy 44°33N 10°47E 198 D7
Sástago Spain 41°19N 0°21W 196 D4
Sastamala Finland 61°20N 22°54E 188 B2
Sastown Liberia 4°45N 8°27W 262 E3
Sasvad India 18°20N 74°2E 244 E2
Sasyk, Ozero Ukraine 45°45N 29°40E 183 E14
Sasyqköl Kazakhstan 46°35N 81°0E 217 C10
Sata-Misaki Japan 31°0N 130°40E 222 F2
Satadougou Mali 12°25N 11°25W 262 C2
Satakunta □ Finland 61°45N 23°0E 160 F20
Satalice Czechia 50°7N 14°34E 135 B3
Satama-Soukoura Côte d'Ivoire 7°55N 4°27W 262 D4
Satara India 17°44N 73°58E 244 F1
Satara S. Africa 24°29S 31°47E 271 B5
Sätbaev Kazakhstan 48°10N 67°31E 217 C7
Satbarwa India 23°55N 84°16E 243 H11
Satellite Beach U.S.A. 28°10N 80°36W 317 G9
Säter Sweden 60°21N 15°45E 162 D9
Satevó Mexico 27°57N 106°7W 318 B3
Satgachi India 22°37N 88°25E 124 B2
Satilla → U.S.A. 30°59N 81°29W 316 E8
Satipo Peru 11°15S 74°25W 330 C3
Satka Russia 55°3N 59°1E 186 C10
Satkania Bangla. 22°4N 92°3E 241 D4
Satkhira Bangla. 22°43N 89°8E 241 D2
Satluj = Sutlej → Pakistan 29°23N 71°3E 242 E4
Satmala Hills Maharashtra, India 20°15N 74°40E 244 D2
Satmala Hills Telangana, India 19°45N 78°45E 244 E4
Satna India 24°35N 80°50E 243 G9
Šator Bos.-H. 44°11N 16°37E 199 D13
Sátoraljaújhely Hungary 48°25N 21°41E 182 B6
Satpukur India 22°37N 88°24E 124 B2
Satpura △ India 22°40N 78°15E 242 H8
Satpura Ra. India 21°25N 76°10E 244 D3
Sätra Sweden 59°17N 17°54E 139 B1
Satrup Germany 54°41N 9°36E 178 A5
Satsuma-Hantō Japan 31°25N 130°25E 222 F2
Satsuma-Sendai Japan 31°50N 130°20E 222 F2
Satsunan-Shotō Japan 30°0N 130°0E 221 K5
Sattahip Thailand 12°41N 100°54E 236 F3
Sattenapalle India 16°25N 80°6E 245 F5
Sattru Phai Bangkok, Thailand 113 b2
Satu Mare Romania 47°46N 22°55E 182 C7
Satu Mare □ Romania 47°45N 23°0E 182 C8
Satui Indonesia 3°50S 115°27E 235 C5
Satun Thailand 6°43N 100°2E 237 J3
Satupa'itea Samoa 13°45S 172°18W 287 V19
Saturnina → Brazil 12°15S 58°10W 331 C6
Sauce = Juan L. Lacaze Uruguay 34°26S 57°25W 334 C4
Sauce Argentina 30°5S 58°46W 334 C4
Sauceda Mexico 25°46N 101°19W 318 B4
Saucillo Mexico 28°1N 105°17W 318 B3
Sauda Norway 59°40N 6°20E 164 E3
Saudasjøen Norway 59°38N 6°17E 164 E3
Saúde Bahia, Brazil 10°56S 40°24W 332 D3
Saúde São Paulo, Brazil 23°36S 46°37W 137 B2
Sauðarkrókur Iceland 65°45N 19°40W 155 B7
Saudi Arabia ■ Asia 26°0N 44°0E 246 B3
Sauerland Germany 51°12N 7°59E 176 C4
Saugatuck U.S.A. 42°40N 86°12W 311 B10
Saugeen → Canada 44°30N 81°22W 312 B3
Saugerties U.S.A. 42°5N 73°57W 313 D11
Saugues France 44°58N 3°32E 174 D7
Saugus Calif., U.S.A. 34°25N 118°32W 307 L8
Saugus Mass., U.S.A. 42°28N 71°0W 116 A2
Saugus → U.S.A. 42°27N 70°58W 116 A2
Saujbulagh = Mahābād Iran 36°50N 45°45E 213 D11
Saujon France 45°41N 0°55W 174 C3
Sauk Centre U.S.A. 45°44N 94°57W 308 C6
Sauk City U.S.A. 43°17N 89°43W 310 A7
Sauk Rapids U.S.A. 45°35N 94°10W 308 C6
Saül Fr. Guiana 3°37N 53°12W 329 C7
Sauland Norway 59°37N 8°56E 164 E5
Saulgau Germany 48°1N 9°29E 179 G5
Saulieu France 47°17N 4°14E 173 E11
Sault France 44°6N 5°24E 175 D9
Sault-au-Récollet Canada 45°35N 73°39W 130 A2
Sault Ste. Marie Ont., Canada 46°30N 84°20W 298 C3
Sault Ste. Marie Mich., U.S.A. 46°30N 84°21W 309 B11
Saūmalkol Kazakhstan 53°17N 68°6E 217 B7
Saumlaki Indonesia 7°55S 131°20E 231 F8
Saumur France 47°15N 0°5W 172 E6
Saundatti India 15°47N 75°7E 245 G2
Saunders, C. N.Z. 45°53S 170°45E 285 F5
Saunders I. Antarctica 57°48S 26°28W 151 B1
Saunders Pt. Australia 27°52S 125°38E 279 E4
Saunemin U.S.A. 40°54N 88°24W 311 D8
Saupite Angola 13°54S 17°43E 265 E3
Saurbær Norðurland Eystra, Iceland 65°27N 18°13W 155 B8
Saurbær Vesturland, Iceland 64°24N 21°35W 155 C5
Sauri Nigeria 11°42N 6°44E 263 C6
Saurimo Angola 9°40S 20°12E 265 D4
Sausalito U.S.A. 37°51N 122°29W 136 A2
Sautatá Colombia 7°50N 77°4W 328 B2
Sauteurs Grenada 12°14N 61°38W 323 q
Sauvage, Côte France 45°50N 1°30W 174 C2
Sauveterre-de-Béarn France 43°24N 0°57W 174 E3
Sauzé-Vaussais France 46°8N 0°8E 174 B4
Savá Honduras 15°32N 86°15W 320 C2
Sava Italy 40°24N 17°33E 201 B10
Sava □ Madag. 14°15S 50°10E 272 A2
Sava → Serbia 44°50N 20°26E 182 F5
Savage U.S.A. 47°27N 104°21W 304 C11
Savage I. = Niue ⧄ Pac. Oc. 19°2S 169°54W 289 g
Savage River Australia 41°31S 145°14E 281 G4
Savai'i Samoa 13°28S 172°24W 287 V19
Savalou Benin 7°57N 1°58E 263 D5
Savane Mozam. 19°37S 35°8E 269 F4
Savanes □ Côte d'Ivoire 9°30N 6°0W 262 D3
Savaneta Aruba 12°27N 69°56W 322 f
Savanna U.S.A. 42°5N 90°8W 310 B6
Savanna-la-Mar Jamaica 18°10N 78°10W 320 a
Savannah Ga., U.S.A. 32°5N 81°6W 316 C8
Savannah Mo., U.S.A. 39°56N 94°50W 310 E2
Savannah Tenn., U.S.A. 35°14N 88°15W 315 D10
Savannah □ Ghana 9°0N 2°0W 262 D4
Savannah → U.S.A. 32°2N 80°53W 316 C9
Savannah Beach = Tybee Island U.S.A. 32°1N 80°51W 316 C9
Savannakhet Laos 16°30N 104°49E 236 D5
Savanne, Piton Mauritius 20°26S 57°29E 272 e
Savannes B. St. Lucia 13°45N 60°56W 323 m
Savant L. Canada 50°16N 90°44W 298 B1
Savant Lake Canada 50°14N 90°40W 298 B1
Savantvadi India 15°55N 73°54E 245 G1
Savanur India 14°59N 75°21E 245 G2
Savarkundla = Kundla India 21°21N 71°25E 242 J4
Săvârşin Romania 46°1N 22°14E 182 D7
Savaştepe Turkey 39°22N 27°42E 205 B9
Savda India 21°9N 75°56E 244 D2
Savé Benin 8°2N 2°29E 263 D5
Save → Haute-Garonne, France 43°47N 1°17E 174 E5
Save → Mozam. 21°16S 34°0E 271 B5
Sāveh Iran 35°2N 50°20E 247 C6
Savelugu Ghana 9°38N 0°54W 263 D4
Savenay France 47°20N 1°55W 172 E5
Săveni Romania 47°57N 26°52E 183 C11
Saverdun France 43°14N 1°34E 174 E5
Saverne France 48°43N 7°20E 173 D14
Savigliano Italy 44°38N 7°40E 198 D4
Savigny-sur-Braye France 47°53N 0°49E 172 E7
Sávio → Italy 44°19N 12°20E 199 D9
Šavnik Montenegro 42°59N 19°10E 202 D3
Savo Finland 62°45N 27°30E 160 E22
Savo Solomon Is. 9°8S 159°48E 287 M10
Savoie □ France 45°26N 6°25E 175 C10
Savolax = Savo Finland 62°45N 27°30E 160 E22
Savona Italy 44°17N 8°30E 198 D5
Savona N.Y., U.S.A. 42°17N 77°13W 312 D7
Savonet Curaçao 12°21N 69°7W 322 g
Savonlinna Finland 61°52N 28°53E 188 B5
Savoonga U.S.A. 63°42N 170°29W 303 E5
Savoy = Savoie □ France 45°26N 6°25E 175 C10
Şavşat Turkey 41°15N 42°20E 213 B10
Sävsjö Sweden 57°20N 14°40E 163 G8
Savur Turkey 37°34N 40°53E 246 B4
Savusavu Fiji 16°34S 179°15E 287 A2
Savusavu B. Fiji 16°45S 179°15E 287 A2
Savuti Botswana 18°37S 24°5E 270 A3
Sawah Besar Indonesia 6°8S 106°49E 122 A1
Sawahlunto Indonesia 0°40S 100°52E 234 C2
Sawai Indonesia 3°0S 129°5E 231 E7
Sawai Madhopur India 26°0N 76°25E 242 G7
Sawaleke Fiji 17°59S 179°18E 287 A2
Sawang Daen Din Thailand 17°28N 103°28E 236 D4
Sawankhalok Thailand 17°19N 99°50E 236 D2
Sawara Japan 35°55N 140°30E 223 B12
Sawatch Range U.S.A. 39°0N 106°30W 304 G10
Sawdā', Jabal as Libya 28°51N 15°12E 258 C3
Sawel Mt. U.K. 54°50N 7°2W 166 B4
Sawfajjin, W. → Libya 31°41N 14°44E 258 B2
Sawi Thailand 10°14N 99°5E 237 G2
Sawla Ghana 9°17N 2°25W 262 D4
Sawmills Zimbabwe 19°30S 28°2E 269 F2
Şawqirah Oman 18°7N 56°32E 249 C7
Şawqirah, Ghubbat Oman 18°35N 57°0E 249 C7
Sawtell Australia 30°19S 153°6E 283 A10
Sawtelle U.S.A. 34°2N 118°27W 126 B2
Sawtooth ⌓ U.S.A. 44°0N 114°50W 304 D6
Sawtooth Range U.S.A. 44°3N 114°58W 304 D6
Sawu Indonesia 10°35S 121°50E 231 F6
Sawu Sea Indonesia 9°30S 121°50E 231 F6
Saxby → Australia 18°25S 140°53E 280 B3
Saxmundham U.K. 52°13N 1°30E 169 E9
Saxon Switzerland = Sächsische Schweiz △ Germany 50°55N 14°10E 178 E10
Saxony = Sachsen □ Germany 50°55N 13°10E 178 E9
Saxony, Lower = Niedersachsen □ Germany 52°50N 9°0E 178 C4
Saxton U.S.A. 40°13N 78°15W 312 F6
Say Mali 13°50N 4°57W 262 C4
Say Niger 13°8N 2°22E 263 C5
Saya Nigeria 9°30N 3°18E 263 D5
Sayabec Canada 48°35N 67°41W 299 C6
Sayaboury Laos 19°15N 101°45E 236 C3
Sayán Peru 11°8S 77°12W 330 C2
Sayan, Vostochnyy Russia 54°0N 96°0E 215 D10
Sayan, Zapadnyy Russia 52°30N 94°0E 217 B12
Sayano-Shushenskoye Vdkhr. Russia 52°50N 91°22E 217 B12
Sayanogorsk Russia 53°5N 91°23E 215 D10
Saydā Lebanon 33°35N 35°25E 250 E6
Sayghān Afghan. 35°10N 67°55E 240 B2
Sayhandulaan = Öldziyt Mongolia 44°40N 109°1E 226 B5
Sayḩūt Yemen 15°12N 51°10E 249 D5
Saykhin Kazakhstan 48°50N 46°47E 191 F8
Saylac Somalia 11°21N 43°30E 267 B5
Saylorville L. U.S.A. 41°48N 93°46W 310 C3
Saynshand = Buyant-Uhaa Mongolia 44°55N 110°11E 226 B6
Sayō Japan 34°59N 134°22E 222 C6
Sayre Okla., U.S.A. 35°18N 99°38W 314 D5
Sayre Pa., U.S.A. 41°59N 76°32W 313 E8
Sayreville U.S.A. 40°28N 74°22W 313 F10
Sayula Mexico 19°52N 103°36W 318 D4
Say'ūn Yemen 15°56N 48°47E 249 D5
Sayward Canada 50°21N 125°55W 296 C3
Saza Japan 33°14N 129°39E 222 D1
Sazanit Albania 40°30N 19°20E 202 F3
Sázava → Czechia 49°53N 14°24E 180 B7
Sazin Pakistan 35°35N 73°30E 243 B5
Sazlika → Bulgaria 41°59N 25°50E 203 E9
Sbeïtla Tunisia 35°12N 9°7E 258 A1
Scaër France 48°2N 3°42W 172 D3
Scafell Pike U.K. 54°27N 3°14W 168 C4
Scald Law U.K. 55°50N 3°17W 121 B2
Scalea Italy 39°49N 15°47E 201 C8
Scalloway U.K. 60°9N 1°17W 167 A7
Scalpay U.K. 57°18N 6°0W 167 D3
Scalzi, Ponte degli Venice, Italy 142 b2
Scammon Bay U.S.A. 61°51N 165°35W 303 F6
Scandia Canada 50°20N 112°2W 296 C6
Scandiano Italy 44°36N 10°43E 198 D7
Scandicci Italy 43°45N 11°11E 199 E8
Scandinavia Europe 64°0N 12°0E 160 E15
Scansano Italy 42°41N 11°20E 199 F8
Scapa Flow U.K. 58°53N 3°3W 167 C5
Scappoose U.S.A. 45°45N 122°53W 306 E4
Scarámia, Capo Italy 36°47N 14°29E 201 F7
Scarba U.K. 56°11N 5°43W 167 E3
Scarborough Ont., Canada 43°44N 79°14W 141 A3
Scarborough Trin. & Tob. 11°11N 60°42W 323 s
Scarborough N. Yorks., U.K. 54°17N 0°24W 168 C7
Scarborough Bluffs Canada 43°42N 79°14W 141 A3
Scarborough Junction Canada 43°43N 79°15W 141 A3
Scarborough Shoal S. China Sea 15°0N 117°50E 232 D1
Scargill N.Z. 42°56S 172°58E 285 C7
Scariff I. Ireland 51°44N 10°15W 166 E1
Scarp U.K. 58°1N 7°8W 167 C1
Scarpanto = Karpathos Greece 35°37N 27°10E 205 F9
Scarpe-Escaut ⌓ France 50°26N 3°23E 173 B10
Scarsdale Australia 37°41S 143°39E 282 D5
Sceaux France 48°46N 2°17E 134 B2
Scebeli = Shabeelle → Somalia 2°0N 44°0E 267 D5
Šćedro Croatia 43°6N 16°43E 199 E13
Scenery, Mt. Saba 17°38N 63°14W 322 a
Schaal See Germany 53°36N 10°55E 178 B6
Schaalsee ⌓ Germany 53°40N 10°59E 178 B6
Schaerbeek Belgium 50°52N 4°22E 116 A2
Schaffhausen Switz. 47°42N 8°39E 179 H4
Schagen Neths. 52°49N 4°48E 170 B4
Schaghticoke U.S.A. 42°54N 73°35W 313 D11
Schärding Austria 48°27N 13°27E 180 C6
Scharfenberg Germany 52°35N 13°15E 115 A2
Scharfenwiese = Ostrołęka Poland 53°4N 21°32E 185 E8
Scharhörn Germany 53°57N 8°24E 178 B4
Schässburg = Sighişoara Romania 46°12N 24°50E 183 D9
Scheessel Germany 53°10N 9°29E 178 B5
Schefferville Canada 54°48N 66°50W 299 B6
Scheibbs Austria 48°1N 15°9E 180 C8
Scheidt = Schelde → Belgium 51°15N 4°16E 170 C4
Schelde → Belgium 51°15N 4°16E 170 C4
Schell City U.S.A. 38°1N 94°7W 310 F2
Schell Creek Ra. U.S.A. 39°25N 114°40W 304 G6
Schellsburg U.S.A. 40°3N 78°39W 312 F6
Schemnitz = Banská Štiavnica Slovakia 48°25N 18°55E 181 C11
Schenectady U.S.A. 42°49N 73°57W 313 D11
Schenevus U.S.A. 42°33N 74°50W 313 D10
Scherfede Germany 51°32N 9°2E 178 D5
Schesslitz Germany 49°58N 11°1E 179 F7
Schiavoni, Riva degli Venice, Italy 142 b3
Schiedam Neths. 51°55N 4°25E 170 C4
Schieratz = Sieradz Poland 51°37N 18°41E 185 G5
Schiermonnikoog Neths. 53°30N 6°15E 170 A6
Schiermonnikoog △ Neths. 53°30N 6°15E 170 A6
Schiller Woods U.S.A. 41°57N 87°51W 119 B1
Schiltigheim France 48°35N 7°45E 173 D14
Schinousa Greece 36°53N 25°31E 205 E7
Schio Italy 45°43N 11°21E 199 C8
Schiphol, Amsterdam ✈ (AMS) Neths. 52°18N 4°45E 112 B1
Schippenbeil = Sępopol Poland 54°16N 21°2E 184 D8
Schivelbein = Świdwin Poland 53°47N 15°49E 184 E2
Schiza Greece 36°41N 21°40E 204 E3
Schlachtensee Germany 52°26N 13°13E 115 B2
Schladming Austria 47°23N 13°41E 180 D6
Schlanders = Silandro Italy 46°38N 10°46E 198 B7
Schlawa = Sława Poland 51°52N 16°2E 185 G3
Schlei → Germany 54°40N 10°0E 178 A5
Schleiden Germany 50°31N 6°28E 178 E2
Schleinitz Ra. Papua N. G. 3°0S 151°30E 286 B6
Schleiz Germany 50°35N 11°49E 178 E7
Schlesiersee = Sława Poland 51°52N 16°2E 185 G3
Schleswig Germany 54°31N 9°34E 178 A5
Schleswig-Holstein □ Germany 54°30N 9°30E 178 A5
Schlettstadt = Sélestat France 48°16N 7°26E 173 D14
Schlichtingsheim = Szlichtyngowa Poland 51°42N 16°15E 185 G3
Schlochau = Człuchów Poland 53°41N 17°22E 184 E4
Schloppe = Człopa Poland 53°6N 16°6E 185 E3
Schlossgarten Germany 52°31N 13°18E 115 A2
Schlüchtern Germany 50°20N 9°32E 179 E5
Schmalkalden Germany 50°44N 10°26E 178 E6
Schmargendorf Germany 52°28N 13°17E 115 B2
Schmölln Germany 50°54N 12°19E 178 E8
Schneeberg Austria 47°47N 15°48E 180 D8
Schneeberg Sachsen, Germany 50°35N 12°38E 178 E8
Schneidemühl = Piła Poland 53°10N 16°48E 185 E3
Schneider U.S.A. 41°13N 87°28W 311 C9
Schneverdingen Germany 53°7N 9°48E 178 B5
Schœlcher Martinique 14°36N 61°7W 322 j
Schofield Barracks U.S.A. 21°29N 158°7W 302 K13
Schoharie U.S.A. 42°40N 74°19W 313 D10
Schoharie Cr. → U.S.A. 42°57N 74°18W 313 D10
Schokland Neths. 52°38N 5°46E 170 B5
Scholls U.S.A. 45°24N 122°56W 306 E4
Schönau = Świerzawa Poland 51°1N 15°54E 185 G2
Schönberg Mecklenburg-Vorpommern, Germany 53°52N 10°56E 178 B6
Schönberg Schleswig-Holstein, Germany 54°23N 10°21E 178 A6
Schönblick Germany 52°27N 13°43E 115 B5
Schönbrunn Austria 48°10N 16°19E 142 A1
Schönbuch ⌓ Germany 48°35N 9°2E 179 G5
Schönebeck Germany 52°2N 11°44E 178 C7
Schöneberg Germany 52°28N 13°20E 115 B3
Schönefeld Germany 52°22N 13°33E 115 B4
Schöneiche Germany 52°28N 13°41E 115 B5
Schöngau Germany 47°47N 10°53E 179 H6
Schöningen Germany 52°8N 10°56E 178 C6
Schönlanke = Trzcianka Poland 53°3N 16°25E 185 E3
Schönstein = Šoštanj Slovenia 46°23N 15°4E 199 B12
Schönwalde Germany 52°37N 13°7E 115 A1
Schoolcraft U.S.A. 42°7N 85°38W 311 B11
Schopfheim Germany 47°38N 7°50E 179 H3
Schorndorf Germany 48°47N 9°32E 179 G5
Schortens Germany 53°31N 7°56E 178 B3
Schotschekloof Cape Town, S. Africa 118 b1
Schottegat Curaçao 12°7N 68°55W 322 g
Schouten I. Australia 42°20S 148°20E 281 G4
Schouten Is. = Supiori Indonesia 1°0S 136°0E 231 E9
Schouten Is. Papua N. G. 3°30S 144°30E 286 B3
Schouwen Neths. 51°43N 3°45E 170 C3
Schramberg Germany 48°13N 8°22E 179 G4
Schrankogel Austria 47°3N 11°7E 180 D4
Schreiber Canada 48°45N 87°20W 298 C2
Schrems Austria 48°47N 15°4E 180 C8
Schrobenhausen Germany 48°34N 11°16E 179 G7
Schroffenstein Namibia 27°11S 18°42E 270 C2
Schroon Lake U.S.A. 43°50N 73°46W 313 C11
Schröttersberg = Płock Poland 52°32N 19°40E 185 F6
Schruns Austria 47°5N 9°56E 180 D2
Schuchye = Shchūchīnsk Kazakhstan 52°56N 70°12E 217 B8
Schuler Canada 50°20N 110°6W 297 C6
Schulzendorf Germany 52°36N 13°16E 115 A2
Schumacher Canada 48°30N 81°16W 298 C3
Schurz U.S.A. 38°57N 118°49W 304 G4
Schuyler U.S.A. 41°27N 97°4W 308 E5
Schuylerville U.S.A. 43°6N 73°35W 313 C11
Schuylkill → U.S.A. 39°53N 75°12W 313 G9
Schuylkill Haven U.S.A. 40°37N 76°11W 313 F8
Schwabach Germany 49°19N 11°2E 179 F7
Schwaben □ Germany 48°15N 10°30E 179 G6
Schwabing Germany 48°10N 11°35E 131 B2
Schwäbisch-Fränkischer Wald ⌓ Germany 49°0N 9°30E 179 G5
Schwäbisch Gmünd Germany 48°48N 9°47E 179 G5
Schwäbisch Hall Germany 49°6N 9°44E 179 F5
Schwäbische Alb Germany 48°20N 9°30E 179 G5
Schwabmünchen Germany 48°10N 10°46E 179 G6
Schwalmstadt Germany 50°55N 9°10E 178 E5
Schwandorf Germany 49°20N 12°7E 179 F8
Schwanebeck Germany 52°37N 13°32E 115 A4
Schwanenwerder Germany 52°26N 13°10E 115 B2
Schwaner, Pegunungan Indonesia 1°0S 112°30E 235 C4
Schwanewede Germany 53°14N 8°35E 178 B4
Schwarmstedt Germany 52°39N 9°38E 178 C5
Schwarze Elster → Germany 51°48N 12°50E 178 D8
Schwarzenberg Germany 50°32N 12°47E 178 E8
Schwarzlackenau Austria 48°16N 16°23E 142 A2
Schwarzrand Namibia 25°37S 16°50E 270 C2
Schwarzwald Germany 48°30N 8°20E 179 G4
Schwatka Mts. U.S.A. 67°20N 156°30W 303 C8
Schwaz Austria 47°20N 11°44E 180 D4
Schwechat Austria 48°8N 16°28E 142 B2
Schwechat, Wien ✈ (VIE) Austria 48°7N 16°35E 142 B3
Schwedt Germany 53°3N 14°16E 178 B10
Schweidnitz = Świdnica Poland 50°50N 16°30E 185 H3
Schweinfurt Germany 50°3N 10°14E 179 E6
Schweiz = Switzerland ■ Europe 46°30N 8°0E 179 J4
Schweizer-Reneke S. Africa 27°11S 25°18E 270 C4
Schwenningen = Villingen-Schwenningen Germany 48°3N 8°26E 179 G4
Schwerin = Skwierzyna Poland 52°33N 15°30E 185 F2
Schwerin Germany 53°36N 11°22E 178 B7
Schweriner See Germany 53°43N 11°28E 178 B7
Schwetzingen Germany 49°23N 8°35E 179 F4
Schwiebus = Świebodzin Poland 52°15N 15°31E 185 F2
Schwyz Switz. 47°2N 8°39E 179 H4
Schwyz □ Switz. 47°2N 8°39E 179 H4
Sciacca Italy 37°31N 13°3E 200 E6
Scicli Italy 36°47N 14°42E 201 F7
Science and Industry, Museum of U.S.A. 41°47N 87°34W 119 C3
Sciliar-Catinaccio ⌓ Italy 46°28N 11°35E 199 B8
Scilla Italy 38°15N 15°43E 201 D8
Scilly, Isles of U.K. 49°56N 6°22W 169 H1
Ścinawa Poland 51°25N 16°26E 185 G3
Scione Greece 39°57N 23°36E 202 G7
Scioto → U.S.A. 38°44N 83°1W 311 D13
Scituate U.S.A. 42°12N 70°44W 313 D14
Scobey U.S.A. 48°47N 105°25W 304 B11
Scomenzera, Canale Venice, Italy 142 b1
Scone N.S.W., Australia 32°5S 150°52E 283 B9
Scone Perth & Kinr., U.K. 56°25N 3°24W 167 E5
Scopus, Mt. West Bank 31°48N 35°14E 123 B2
Scordia Italy 37°18N 14°51E 201 E7
Scoresby Sund Greenland 70°28N 21°46W 154 C8
Scoresbysund = Ittoqqortoormiit Greenland 70°20N 23°0W 154 C8
Scornicești Romania 44°34N 24°33E 183 F9
Scotia Calif., U.S.A. 40°29N 124°6W 304 F1
Scotia N.Y., U.S.A. 42°50N 73°58W 313 D11
Scotia Sea Antarctica 56°5S 56°0W 151 B18
Scotland Canada 43°1N 80°22W 312 C4
Scotland □ U.K. 57°0N 4°0W 167 E5
Scott Antarctica 77°50S 166°45E 151 D11
Scott, C. Australia 13°30S 129°49E 278 B4
Scott Circle Washington, D.C., U.S.A. 143 a1
Scott City U.S.A. 38°29N 100°54W 308 F3
Scott Glacier Antarctica 66°15S 100°5E 151 C8
Scott I. Antarctica 67°0S 179°0E 151 C11
Scott Is. Canada 50°48N 128°40W 296 C3
Scott L. Canada 59°55N 106°18W 297 B7
Scott Monument Edinburgh, U.K. 121 b2
Scott Reef Australia 14°0S 121°50E 278 B3
Scottburgh S. Africa 30°15S 30°47E 271 D5
Scottdale Georgia, U.S.A. 33°47N 84°16W 113 B3
Scottdale Pa., U.S.A. 40°6N 79°35W 312 F5
Scottish Borders □ U.K. 55°35N 2°50W 167 F6
Scottish Parliament Edinburgh, U.K. 55°57N 3°10W 121 B2
Scotts Head N.S.W., Australia 30°45S 153°0E 283 A10
Scotts Head Dominica 15°13N 61°23W 323 k
Scotts Head Village Dominica 15°12N 61°22W 323 k
Scotts Valley U.S.A. 37°3N 122°1W 306 H4
Scottsbluff U.S.A. 41°52N 103°40W 308 E2
Scottsboro U.S.A. 34°40N 86°2W 315 D11
Scottsburg U.S.A. 38°41N 85°47W 311 F11
Scottsdale Tas., Australia 41°9S 147°31E 281 G4
Scottsdale Ariz., U.S.A. 33°40N 111°53W 305 K8
Scottsville Ky., U.S.A. 36°45N 86°11W 308 G10
Scottsville N.Y., U.S.A. 43°2N 77°47W 312 C7
Scottville U.S.A. 43°58N 86°17W 308 D10
Scranton U.S.A. 41°25N 75°40W 313 E9
Screven U.S.A. 31°29N 82°1W 316 D7
Scrub I. Anguilla 18°19N 62°55W 322 a
Scugog, L. Canada 44°10N 78°55W 312 B6
Sculeni Moldova 47°20N 27°37E 183 C12
Scunthorpe U.K. 53°36N 0°39W 168 D7
Scuol Schuls Switz. 46°48N 10°17E 179 J6
Scutari = Shkodër Albania 42°4N 19°32E 202 D3
Scutari = Üsküdar Turkey 41°1N 29°0E 122 B2
Sea Is. U.S.A. 31°30N 81°7W 316 D9
Sea Lake Australia 35°28S 142°55E 282 C5
Sea Point S. Africa 34°5S 18°23E 118 A1
Seabra = Tarauacá Brazil 8°6S 70°48W 330 B3
Seabra Brazil 12°25S 41°46W 333 D3
Seabrook, L. Australia 30°55S 119°40E 279 F2
Seacliff U.S.A. 37°47N 122°28W 136 B2
Seaford E. Sussex, U.K. 50°47N 0°7E 169 G8
Seaford Del., U.S.A. 38°39N 75°37W 309 F16
Seaforth N.S.W., Australia 33°48S 151°15E 139 A2
Seaforth Queens., Australia 20°55S 148°57E 280 b
Seaforth Ont., Canada 43°35N 81°25W 312 C3
Seaforth, L. U.K. 57°52N 6°36W 167 D2
Seagate U.S.A. 40°34N 74°0W 132 C1
Seagraves U.S.A. 32°57N 102°34W 314 E3
Seaham U.K. 54°50N 1°20W 168 C6
Seal → Canada 59°4N 94°48W 297 B10
Seal I. Anguilla 18°16N 63°9W 322 a
Seal L. Canada 54°20N 61°30W 299 B7
Seale U.S.A. 32°18N 85°10W 316 C4
Sealy U.S.A. 29°47N 96°9W 314 G6
Seaman U.S.A. 38°57N 83°34W 311 F13
Searchlight U.S.A. 35°28N 114°55W 307 K12
Searcy U.S.A. 35°15N 91°44W 314 D9
Searles L. U.S.A. 35°44N 117°21W 307 K9
Sears Tower = Willis Tower Chicago, U.S.A. 119 c1
Seascale U.K. 54°24N 3°29W 168 C4
Seaside Calif., U.S.A. 36°37N 121°50W 306 J5
Seaside Oreg., U.S.A. 46°0N 123°56W 306 E3
Seaspray Australia 38°25S 147°15E 283 E7
Seattle U.S.A. 47°36N 122°19W 306 C4
Seattle-Tacoma Int. ✈ (SEA) U.S.A. 47°27N 122°18W 306 C4
Seaward Kaikoura Ra. N.Z. 42°10S 173°44E 285 C8
SeaWorld U.S.A. 28°24N 81°28W 133 B2
Seba Indonesia 10°29S 121°50E 278 B3
Sebago L. U.S.A. 43°52N 70°34W 313 C14
Sebago Lake U.S.A. 43°51N 70°34W 313 C14
Sebakung Indonesia 1°37S 116°25E 235 C5
Sebangau △ Indonesia 2°34S 113°38E 235 C4
Sebangka Indonesia 0°7N 104°36E 234 B2
Sebastian U.S.A. 27°49N 80°28W 317 H9
Sebastián Vizcaíno, B. Mexico 28°0N 114°30W 318 B2
Sebastopol = Sevastopol Ukraine 44°35N 33°30E 189 K7
Sebastopol U.S.A. 38°24N 122°49W 306 G4
Sebatik Asia 4°10N 117°45E 235 B5
Sebba Burkina Faso 13°35N 0°32E 263 C5
Sebderat Eritrea 15°26N 36°42E 257 D4
Sebdou Algeria 34°38N 1°19W 261 B4
Sébé → Gabon 1°2S 13°6E 264 C2
Sébékoro Mali 12°58N 9°0W 262 C3
Seben Turkey 40°24N 31°34E 212 B4
Šeberov Czechia 50°0N 14°30E 135 B3
Sebeş Romania 45°58N 23°34E 183 E8
Sebeşului, Munţii Romania 45°36N 23°40E 183 E8
Sebewaing U.S.A. 43°44N 83°27W 309 D12
Sebezh Russia 56°14N 28°22E 188 D5
Sebezhsky △ Russia 56°16N 28°30E 188 D5
Sebha = Sabhā Libya 27°9N 14°29E 258 C2
Sébi Mali 15°50N 4°12W 262 B4
Şebinkarahisar Turkey 40°22N 38°28E 213 B8
Sebino, L. di = Iseo, L. d' Italy 45°43N 10°4E 198 C7
Sebiş Romania 46°23N 22°13E 182 D7
Seblat Indonesia 3°14S 101°38E 234 C2
Sebnitz Germany 50°58N 14°15E 178 E10

Sebou, Oued → Morocco 34°16N 6°40W 260 B3
Sebring Fla., U.S.A. 27°30N 81°27W 317 H8
Sebring Ohio, U.S.A. 40°55N 81°2W 312 F3
Sebringville Canada 43°24N 81°4W 312 C3
Sebta = Ceuta N. Afr. 35°52N 5°18W 260 A3
Sebuku Indonesia 3°30S 116°25E 235 C5
Sebuku, Teluk Indonesia 4°0N 118°10E 235 B5
Sečanj Serbia 45°25N 20°47E 182 E5
Secaucus U.S.A. 40°47N 74°3W 132 B1
Secchia → Italy 45°4N 11°0E 198 C8
Sechelt Canada 49°25N 123°42W 296 D4
Sechura Peru 5°39S 80°50W 330 B1
Sechura, Desierto de Peru 6°0S 80°30W 330 B1
Seclin France 50°33N 3°2E 173 B10
Second World War Memorial
Washington, D.C., U.S.A. 143 b1
Secondigny France 46°37N 0°26W 172 F6
Sečovce Slovakia 48°42N 21°40E 181 C14
Secretary I. N.Z. 45°15S 166°56E 285 F1
Secunderabad India 17°28N 78°30E 244 F4
Sécure → Bolivia 15°10S 64°52W 331 D5
Security U.S.A. 38°45N 104°45W 304 G11
Sedalia U.S.A. 38°42N 93°14W 310 F3
Sedam India 17°11N 77°17E 244 E3
Sedan S. Austral., Australia 34°34S 139°19E 282 C3
Sedan Ardennes, France 49°43N 4°57E 173 C11
Sedan Kans., U.S.A. 37°8N 96°11W 308 G5
Sedano Spain 42°43N 3°49W 194 C7
Sedaw Myanmar 22°19N 96°19E 241 D6
Sedbergh U.K. 54°20N 2°31W 168 C5
Seddinsee Germany 52°23N 13°41E 115 B5
Seddon N.Z. 41°40S 174°7E 285 B9
Seddonville N.Z. 41°33S 172°1E 285 B7
Sedé Boqér Israel 30°52N 34°47E 251 H5
Sedeh Fārs, Iran 30°45N 52°11E 247 D7
Sedeh Khorāsān, Iran 33°20N 59°14E 247 C8
Séderon France 44°12N 5°32E 175 D9
Sederot Israel 31°32N 34°37E 251 G5
Sédhiou Senegal 12°44N 15°30W 262 C1
Sedico Italy 46°8N 12°6E 199 B9
Sedlčany Czechia 49°40N 14°25E 180 B7
Sedley Canada 50°10N 104°0W 297 C8
Sedom Israel 31°5N 35°20E 251 G6
Sedona U.S.A. 34°52N 111°46W 305 J8
Sedova, Pik Russia 73°29N 54°58E 214 B6
Sedrata Algeria 36°7N 7°31E 261 A6
Sedro-Woolley U.S.A. 48°30N 122°14W 306 B4
Šeduva Lithuania 55°45N 23°45E 184 C10
Sędziszów Poland 50°35N 20°4E 185 H7
Sędziszów Małapolski Poland 50°5N 21°45E 185 H8
Seebad Ahlbeck Germany 53°56N 14°10E 178 B10
Seeberg Germany 52°33N 13°41E 115 A5
Seeburg = Jeziorany Poland 53°58N 20°46E 184 E7
Seeburg Germany 52°30N 13°7E 115 B1
Seefeld Germany 52°37N 13°40E 115 A5
Seefeld in Tirol Austria 47°19N 11°13E 180 D4
Seegefeld Germany 52°33N 13°5E 115 A1
Seehausen Germany 52°54N 11°45E 178 C7
Seeheim Namibia 26°50S 17°45E 270 C2
Seeheim-Jugenheim Germany 49°49N 8°40E 179 F4
Seehof Germany 52°24N 13°17E 115 B2
Seeis Namibia 22°29S 17°39E 270 B2
Seekoei → S. Africa 30°18S 25°1E 270 D4
Seeley's Bay Canada 44°29N 76°14W 313 B8
Seelow Germany 52°32N 14°23E 178 C10
Seemandhra = Andhra Pradesh □ India 18°0N 79°0E 244 F4
Sées France 48°38N 0°10E 172 D7
Seesen Germany 51°54N 10°10E 178 D6
Seevetal Germany 53°26N 10°1E 178 B6
Seewinkel = Neusiedler See-Seewinkel △ Austria 47°50N 16°45E 181 D9
Şefaatli Turkey 39°30N 34°45E 212 C6
Seferihisar Turkey 38°10N 26°50E 205 C8
Séféto Mali 14°8N 9°49W 262 C3
Sefophe Botswana 22°11S 27°58E 271 B4
Sefrou Morocco 33°52N 4°52W 260 B4
Sefton N.Z. 43°15S 172°41E 285 D7
Sefuri-San Japan 33°28N 130°18E 222 D2
Sefwi Bekwai Ghana 6°10N 2°25W 262 D4
Seg-ozero Russia 63°20N 33°46E 186 B5
Segag Ethiopia 7°39N 42°50E 267 C5
Segamat Malaysia 2°30N 102°50E 237 L4
Şegarcea Romania 44°6N 23°43E 183 F8
Ségbana Benin 10°55N 3°42E 263 C5
Segbwema S. Leone 8°0N 11°0W 262 D2
Segeltorp Sweden 59°16N 17°56E 139 B1
Segersta Sweden 61°16N 16°39E 162 C10
Segesta Italy 37°56N 12°50E 200 E5
Seget Indonesia 1°24S 130°58E 231 E8
Segewold = Sigulda Latvia 57°10N 24°55E 188 D3
Segezha Russia 63°44N 34°19E 186 B5
Seggueur, O. → Algeria 32°14N 1°48E 261 B5
Seghe Solomon Is. 8°32S 157°54E 287 M9
Segmon Sweden 59°17N 13°3E 162 E7
Segonzac France 45°36N 0°14W 174 C3
Segorbe Spain 39°50N 0°30W 196 F4
Ségou Mali 13°30N 6°16W 262 C3
Ségou □ Mali 14°0N 6°0W 262 C3
Segovia = Coco → Cent. Amer. 15°0N 83°8W 320 D3
Segovia Colombia 7°7N 74°42W 328 B3
Segovia Spain 40°57N 4°10W 194 E6
Segovia □ Spain 40°55N 4°10W 194 E6
Segrate Italy 45°29N 9°17E 128 B2
Segré France 47°40N 0°52W 172 E6
Segre → Spain 41°40N 0°43E 196 D5
Seguam I. U.S.A. 52°19N 172°30W 303 K4
Seguam Pass U.S.A. 52°0N 172°30W 303 K4
Séguédine Niger 20°9N 12°55E 259 D2
Séguéla Côte d'Ivoire 7°55N 6°40W 262 D3
Séguélon Côte d'Ivoire 9°13N 7°7W 262 D3
Séguénéga Burkina Faso 13°25N 1°58W 263 C4
Seguin U.S.A. 29°34N 97°58W 314 G6
Segundo → Argentina 30°53S 62°44W 334 C3
Segura → Spain 38°3N 0°44W 197 G4
Segura, Sierra de Spain 38°5N 2°45W 197 G2
Seguro Italy 45°28N 9°3E 128 B1
Seh Konj, Kūh-e Iran 30°6N 57°30E 247 D8
Seh Qal'eh Iran 33°40N 58°24E 247 C8
Sehitwa Botswana 20°30S 22°30E 270 B3
Sehlabathebe △ Lesotho 29°53S 29°7E 271 C4
Sehore India 23°10N 77°5E 242 H7
Sehulea Papua N. G. 9°58S 151°10E 286 E6
Sehwan Pakistan 26°28N 67°53E 242 F2
Seia Portugal 40°25N 7°42W 194 E3
Şeica Mare Romania 46°1N 24°7E 183 D9
Seikan Tunnel Japan 41°28N 140°10E 220 D10
Seikpyu Myanmar 20°54N 94°48E 241 E5
Seil U.K. 56°18N 5°38W 167 E3
Seiland Norway 70°25N 23°15E 160 A20
Seilhac France 45°22N 1°43E 174 C5
Seiling U.S.A. 36°9N 98°56W 314 C5
Seille → Moselle, France 49°7N 6°11E 173 C13
Seille → Saône-et-Loire, France 46°31N 4°57E 173 F11
Sein, Î. de France 48°2N 4°52W 172 D2
Seinäjoki Finland 62°40N 22°51E 160 E20
Seine → France 49°26N 0°26E 172 C7
Seine, B. de la France 49°40N 0°40W 172 C6
Seine-et-Marne □ France 48°45N 3°0E 173 D10
Seine-Inférieure = Seine-Maritime □ France 49°40N 1°0E 172 C7
Seine-Maritime □ France 49°40N 1°0E 172 C7
Seine-St-Denis □ France 48°58N 2°24E 173 D9
Seini Romania 47°44N 23°21E 183 C8
Seirijai Lithuania 54°14N 23°49E 184 D10
Seis de Septiembre = Moron Argentina 34°39S 58°37W 334 C4
Seistan = Sīstān Asia 30°50N 61°0E 247 D9
Seistan, Daryācheh-ye = Sīstān, Daryācheh-ye Iran 31°0N 61°0E 247 D9
Seitler = Nyzhnohirskyy Ukraine 45°27N 34°38E 189 K8
Seitseminen △ Finland 61°55N 23°25E 160 F20
Seixal Madeira 32°48N 17°7W 153 c
Seixal Lisboa, Portugal 38°38N 9°5W 126 B2
Sejerø Denmark 55°54N 11°9E 163 J5
Sejerø Bugt Denmark 55°53N 11°15E 163 J5
Sejny Poland 54°6N 23°21E 184 D10
Sejong S. Korea 36°35N 127°15E 224 D3
Sejong □ S. Korea 36°33N 127°16E 224 D3
Seka Ethiopia 8°10N 36°52E 257 F4
Sekadau Indonesia 0°1N 110°54E 235 C4
Sekayu Indonesia 2°51S 103°51E 234 C2
Seke Tanzania 3°20S 33°31E 268 C3
Seke-Banza Dem. Rep. of the Congo 5°20S 13°16E 265 D2
Sekenke Tanzania 4°18S 34°11E 268 C3
Sekhira Tunisia 34°20N 10°5E 258 B2
Seki Japan 35°29N 136°55E 223 B8
Seki Turkey 36°48N 29°33E 205 E11
Sekigahara Japan 35°22N 136°28E 223 B8
Sekondi-Takoradi Ghana 4°58N 1°45W 262 E4
Sekota Ethiopia 12°40N 39°2E 257 E4
Sekseūil Kazakhstan 47°5N 61°9E 216 C6
Seksna Russia 59°13N 38°30E 188 C10
Sekudai Malaysia 1°32N 103°39E 237 d
Sekuma Botswana 24°36S 23°50E 270 B3
Selah U.S.A. 46°39N 120°32W 304 C3
Selama Malaysia 5°12N 100°42E 237 K3
Selangor □ Malaysia 3°10N 101°30E 237 L3
Selárgius Italy 39°16N 9°10E 200 C2
Selaru Indonesia 8°9S 131°0E 231 F8
Selatan, Selat Malaysia 5°15N 100°20E 237 c
Selatpanjang Indonesia 1°0N 102°43E 234 B2
Selawik U.S.A. 66°36N 160°0W 303 C8
Selawik L. U.S.A. 66°30N 160°45W 303 C7
Selawik Nat. Wildlife Refuge ⌂ U.S.A. 66°35N 159°10W 303 C8
Selb Germany 50°10N 12°7E 179 E8
Selbusjøen Norway 63°15N 10°50E 164 A7
Selby Gauteng, S. Africa 26°12S 28°2E 123 B2
Selby N. Yorks., U.K. 53°47N 1°5W 168 D6
Selby S. Dak., U.S.A. 45°31N 100°2W 308 C3
Selca Croatia 43°20N 16°50E 199 E13
Selçuk Turkey 37°56N 27°22E 205 D9
Selden U.S.A. 39°33N 100°34W 308 F3
Seldovia U.S.A. 59°26N 151°43W 303 D10
Sele → Italy 40°29N 14°56E 201 B7
Selebi-Phikwe Botswana 21°58S 27°48E 271 B4
Selemdzha → Russia 51°42N 128°53E 215 D13
Selendi Manisa, Turkey 38°43N 28°50E 205 C10
Selendi Manisa, Turkey 38°46N 27°53E 205 C9
Selenga = Selenge Mörön → Asia 52°16N 106°16E 218 A10
Selenge Dem. Rep. of the Congo 1°58S 18°11E 264 C3
Selenge Mörön → Asia 52°16N 106°16E 218 A10
Selenicë Albania 40°33N 19°39E 202 F3
Selenter See Germany 54°18N 10°26E 178 A6
Sélestat France 48°16N 7°26E 173 D14
Seletan, Tanjung Indonesia 4°10S 114°40E 235 C4
Seletar Singapore 1°22N 103°53E 138 A3
Seletar, Pulau Singapore 1°26N 103°51E 138 A3
Seletar Hills Singapore 1°23N 103°52E 138 A3
Seletar Res. Singapore 1°24N 103°48E 138 A2
Selevac Serbia 44°28N 20°52E 202 B4
Selfoss Iceland 63°56N 21°0W 155 D6
Selhurst U.K. 51°23N 0°5W 125 B3
Sélibabi Mauritania 15°10N 12°15W 262 B2
Seliger, Ozero Russia 57°15N 33°0E 188 D7
Seligman U.S.A. 35°20N 112°53W 305 J7
Şelim Turkey 40°30N 42°46E 213 B10
Selima Sudan 21°22N 29°19E 256 C2
Selimiye Turkey 37°24N 27°40E 205 D9
Selinda Spillway → Botswana 18°35S 23°10E 270 A3
Selingué, L. de Mali 11°37N 8°14W 262 C3
Selinsgrove U.S.A. 40°48N 76°52W 312 F8
Selizharovo Russia 56°51N 33°27E 188 D7
Selje Norway 62°3N 5°22E 164 B2
Seljord Norway 59°30N 8°40E 164 E5
Selkirk Man., Canada 50°10N 96°55W 297 C9
Selkirk Ont., Canada 42°49N 79°56W 312 D5
Selkirk Borders, U.K. 55°33N 2°50W 167 F6
Selkirk I. = Horse I. Canada 53°20N 99°6W 297 C9
Selkirk Mts. Canada 51°15N 117°40W 294 G8
Sellafield U.K. 54°25N 3°29W 168 C4
Sellama Sudan 12°51N 29°46E 257 E2
Sellia Greece 35°12N 24°23E 207 E5
Sellières France 46°50N 5°32E 173 F12
Sells U.S.A. 31°55N 111°53W 305 L8
Sellye Hungary 45°52N 17°51E 182 E2
Selma Ala., U.S.A. 32°25N 87°1W 315 E11
Selma Calif., U.S.A. 36°34N 119°37W 306 J7
Selma N.C., U.S.A. 35°32N 78°17W 315 D15
Selmer U.S.A. 35°10N 88°36W 315 D10
Selong Indonesia 8°39S 116°32E 235 D5
Selongey France 47°36N 5°11E 173 E12
Selouane Morocco 35°7N 2°57W 261 A4
Selous △ Tanzania 8°37S 37°42E 269 D4
Selowandoma Falls Zimbabwe 21°15S 31°50E 269 G3
Selpele Indonesia 0°1S 130°5E 231 E8
Selsey Bill U.K. 50°43N 0°47W 169 G7
Seltso Russia 53°22N 34°4E 188 F8
Seltz France 48°54N 8°4E 173 D15
Selu Indonesia 7°32S 130°55E 231 F8
Sélune → France 48°38N 1°22W 172 D5
Selva = La Selva del Camp Spain 41°13N 1°8E 196 D6
Selva Argentina 29°50S 62°0W 334 B3
Selva Mallorca, Spain 39°46N 2°54E 206 B3
Selva Lancandona = Montes Azules ⌂ Mexico 16°21N 91°3W 319 D6
Selvagens, Ilhas Madeira 30°5N 15°55W 260 B1
Selvas Brazil 6°30S 67°0W 330 B4
Selwyn L. Canada 60°0N 104°30W 297 B8
Selwyn Mts. Canada 63°0N 130°0W 294 E5
Selwyn Passage Vanuatu 16°3S 168°12E 287 F6
Selwyn Ra. Australia 21°10S 140°0E 280 C3
Selyatyn Ukraine 47°50N 25°12E 183 C10
Sem Norway 59°14N 10°17E 164 E7
Sem Kolodezey = Lenine Ukraine 45°17N 35°46E 189 K8
Semadrek = Samothraki Greece 40°28N 25°28E 203 F9
Seman → Albania 40°47N 19°30E 202 F3
Semangka, Teluk Indonesia 5°36S 104°42E 234 D2
Semarang Indonesia 7°0S 110°26E 235 D4
Semarapura = Klungkung Indonesia 8°32S 115°24E 231 K18
Sematan Malaysia 1°48N 109°46E 235 B3
Semayang, Danau Indonesia 0°14S 116°28E 235 C5
Sembabule Uganda 0°4S 31°25E 268 C3
Sembawang Singapore 1°27N 103°50E 138 A2
Sembé Congo 1°39N 14°36E 264 B2
Sembilang △ Indonesia 1°59S 104°34E 234 C2
Sembung Indonesia 8°28S 115°11E 231 J18
Şemdinli Turkey 37°18N 44°35E 213 D11
Sémé Senegal 15°4N 13°41W 262 B2
Semeih Sudan 12°43N 30°53E 257 E3
Semēnawī K'eyih Bahrī □ Eritrea 16°30N 38°30E 257 D4
Semendua Dem. Rep. of the Congo 3°10S 18°6E 264 C3
Semenic-Cheile Caraşului △ Romania 45°8N 22°5E 182 E7
Semenivka Chernihiv, Ukraine 52°8N 32°36E 189 F7
Semenivka Kremenchuk, Ukraine 49°37N 33°10E 189 H7
Semenov Russia 56°43N 44°30E 190 B7
Semera Ethiopia 11°48N 41°1E 257 E5
Semeru Indonesia 8°4S 112°55E 235 D4
Semey Kazakhstan 50°30N 80°10E 217 B10
Semichi Is. U.S.A. 52°42N 174°0E 303 K1
Semikarakorsk Russia 47°31N 40°48E 191 G5
Semiluki Russia 51°41N 39°2E 189 G10
Seminoe Res. U.S.A. 42°9N 106°55W 304 E10
Seminole Fla., U.S.A. 27°50N 82°47W 317 H7
Seminole Okla., U.S.A. 35°14N 96°41W 314 D6
Seminole Tex., U.S.A. 32°43N 102°39W 314 E3
Seminole, L. U.S.A. 30°43N 84°52W 316 E5
Seminole Draw → U.S.A. 32°27N 102°20W 314 E3
Semipalatinsk = Semey Kazakhstan 50°30N 80°10E 217 B10
Semirara I. Phil. 12°4N 121°23E 232 E3
Semirara Is. Phil. 12°0N 121°20E 233 F3
Semisopochnoi I. U.S.A. 51°55N 179°36E 303 L2
Semitau Indonesia 0°29N 111°57E 235 B4
Semliki △ Uganda 0°49N 30°4E 268 B3
Semlin = Zemun Serbia 44°51N 20°25E 202 B4
Semmelweis Museum Budapest, Hungary 117 c2
Semmering P. Austria 47°41N 15°45E 180 D8
Semnān Iran 35°40N 53°23E 247 C7
Semnān □ Iran 36°0N 54°0E 247 C7
Sempang Mengayou, Tanjung Malaysia 7°0N 116°40E 235 A5
Semporna Malaysia 4°30N 118°33E 235 B5
Semuda Indonesia 2°51S 112°58E 235 C4
Semur-en-Auxois France 47°30N 4°20E 173 E11
Semyonovka = Arsenev Russia 44°10N 133°15E 220 B6
Semyonovskoye = Bereznik Russia 62°51N 42°40E 186 B7
Sen → Cambodia 12°32N 104°28E 236 F5
Sena Bolivia 11°32S 67°11W 330 C4
Senā Iran 28°27N 51°36E 247 D6
Sena Mozam. 17°25S 35°0E 269 F4
Sena → Bolivia 11°31S 67°11W 330 C4
Sena Madureira Brazil 9°5S 68°45W 330 B4
Senachwine L. U.S.A. 41°10N 89°18W 310 C7
Senador José Porfirio Brazil 2°35S 51°55W 329 D7
Senador Pompeu Brazil 5°40S 39°20W 332 C4
Senago Italy 45°34N 9°7E 128 A1
Senaja Malaysia 6°45N 117°3E 235 A5
Senaki Georgia 42°15N 42°1E 191 J6
Senang, Pulau Singapore 1°11N 103°52E 237 d
Senanga Zambia 16°7S 23°16E 265 F4
Senatobia U.S.A. 34°37N 89°58W 315 D10
Senayan Stadium = Gelora Bung Karno Stadium Jakarta, Indonesia 6°13S 106°47E 122 B1
Sencelles Spain 39°39N 2°54E 206 B3
Sendafa Ethiopia 9°11N 39°3E 257 F4
Sendai = Satsuma-Sendai Japan 31°50N 130°20E 222 F2
Sendai Japan 38°15N 140°53E 220 E10
Sendai-Wan Japan 38°15N 141°0E 220 E10
Senden Bayern, Germany 48°19N 10°4E 179 G6
Senden Nordrhein-Westfalen, Germany 51°52N 7°22E 178 D3
Sendhwa India 21°41N 75°6E 242 J6
Sendling Germany 48°7N 11°31E 131 B2
Sendlinger Tor Platz Munich, Germany 131 c1
Sendurjana India 21°32N 78°17E 244 D4
Sene → Ghana 7°30N 0°33W 263 D4
Senec Slovakia 48°12N 17°23E 181 C10
Seneca Ill., U.S.A. 41°19N 88°37W 311 C8
Seneca S.C., U.S.A. 34°41N 82°57W 315 D13
Seneca Falls U.S.A. 42°55N 76°48W 313 D8
Seneca L. U.S.A. 42°40N 76°54W 312 D8
Senecaville L. U.S.A. 39°55N 81°25W 312 G3
Senegal ■ W. Afr. 14°30N 14°30W 262 C2
Sénégal → W. Afr. 15°48N 16°32W 262 B1
Senegambia Africa 12°45N 12°0W 254 E2
Senegambia & Niger = Mali ■ Africa 17°0N 3°0W 262 B4
Senekal S. Africa 28°20S 27°36E 271 C4
Senftenberg Germany 51°32N 14°0E 178 D10
Senga Hill Zambia 9°19S 31°11E 269 D3
Senge Khambab = Indus → Pakistan 24°20N 67°47E 242 G2
Sengerema Tanzania 2°42S 32°35E 268 C3
Sengeti Indonesia 1°28S 103°31E 234 C2
Senggigi Indonesia 8°29S 116°2E 231 J19
Sengiley Russia 53°58N 48°46E 190 D9
Sengua → Zimbabwe 17°7S 28°5E 269 F2
Senguerr → Argentina 45°35S 68°50W 336 C3
Senhor-do-Bonfim Brazil 10°30S 40°10W 332 D3
Senica Slovakia 48°41N 17°25E 181 C10
Senigállia Italy 43°43N 13°13E 199 E10
Seniku Myanmar 25°32N 97°48E 241 C6
Senio → Italy 44°35N 12°15E 199 D9
Senirkent Turkey 38°6N 30°33E 205 C12
Senise Italy 40°9N 16°17E 201 B9
Senj Croatia 45°0N 14°58E 199 D11
Senja Norway 69°25N 17°30E 160 B17
Senju Japan 35°44N 139°48E 140 A3
Senkaku-Shotō E. China Sea 25°45N 123°30E 221 M1
Senkang Singapore 1°23N 103°53E 138 A3
Senlis France 49°13N 2°35E 173 C9
Senmonorom Cambodia 12°27N 107°12E 236 F6
Sennār Sudan 13°30N 33°35E 257 E3
Sennâr □ Sudan 13°0N 34°0E 257 E3
Senneterre Canada 48°25N 77°15W 298 C4
Senno Belarus 54°45N 29°43E 188 E5
Sénnori Italy 40°47N 8°35E 200 B1
Seno Laos 16°35N 104°50E 236 D5
Senoia U.S.A. 33°18N 84°33W 316 B5
Senonches France 48°34N 1°2E 172 D8
Senorbì Italy 39°32N 9°8E 200 C2
Senožeče Slovenia 45°43N 14°3E 199 C11
Senqu = Orange → S. Africa 28°41S 16°28E 270 C2
Senriyama Japan 34°47N 135°30E 133 A2
Sens France 48°11N 3°15E 173 D10
Senta Serbia 45°55N 20°3E 182 E5
Sentarum, Danau Indonesia 0°51N 112°6E 235 B4
Sentery = Lubao Dem. Rep. of the Congo 5°17S 25°42E 265 D5
Sentinel U.S.A. 32°52N 113°13W 305 K7
Šentjur Slovenia 46°14N 15°24E 199 B12
Sentolo Indonesia 7°55S 110°13E 235 G14
Sentosa Singapore 1°16N 103°50E 138 B2
Sentry Hill St.-Maarten 18°2N 63°4W 322 a
Senwabarana S. Africa 23°17S 29°7E 271 B4
Senya Beraku Ghana 5°28N 0°31W 263 D4
Seo de Urgel = La Seu d'Urgell Spain 42°22N 1°23E 196 C6
Seobinggo S. Korea 37°31N 126°58E 137 B1
Seocho S. Korea 37°28N 127°0E 137 C1
Seodaemun S. Korea 37°34N 126°55E 137 B1
Seogwipo S. Korea 33°13N 126°34E 224 a
Seohara India 29°15N 78°33E 243 E8
Seokguram Grotto S. Korea 35°46N 129°20E 224 E4
Seokkwan S. Korea 37°35N 127°2E 137 B2
Seonath → India 21°44N 82°28E 243 J10
Seondha India 26°9N 78°48E 243 F8
Seongbuk S. Korea 37°35N 127°0E 137 B2
Seongdong S. Korea 37°33N 127°2E 137 B2
Seongmodo S. Korea 37°41N 126°19E 224 D3
Seongnam S. Korea 37°26N 127°8E 224 D3
Seongsu S. Korea 37°32N 127°2E 137 B2
Seoni India 22°5N 79°30E 243 H8
Seoni Malwa India 22°27N 77°28E 242 H8
Seonsan S. Korea 36°14N 128°17E 224 D4
Seonyudo S. Korea 35°49N 126°24E 224 E3
Seoraksan S. Korea 38°7N 128°27E 224 C4
Seoraksan △ S. Korea 38°10N 128°25E 224 C4
Seoriuarayan India 21°45N 82°34E 244 D6
Seosan S. Korea 36°47N 126°27E 224 D3
Seoul S. Korea 37°31N 126°58E 137 B2
Seoul Nat. Univ. S. Korea 37°28N 126°57E 137 C1
Seoul Tower S. Korea 37°32N 126°59E 137 B1
Sepang Malaysia 2°49N 101°44E 237 L3
Separation Pt. N.Z. 40°47S 172°59E 285 A7
Sepasu Indonesia 0°43N 117°34E 235 B5
Sepatini → Brazil 7°36S 65°24W 330 B4
Sepi Solomon Is. 8°31S 159°52E 287 M10
Sepidān Iran 30°20N 52°5E 247 D7
Sepik → Papua N. G. 3°49S 144°30E 286 B3
Sepo-ri N. Korea 38°57N 127°25E 224 C3
Sepolia Greece 38°1N 23°42E 112 A2
Sępólno Krajeńskie Poland 53°26N 17°30E 184 E4
Sepone Laos 16°45N 106°13E 236 D6
Sepopol Poland 54°16N 21°2E 184 D8
Seppa India 27°16N 92°54E 241 B4
Sept-Îles Canada 50°13N 66°22W 299 B6
Septemvri Bulgaria 42°13N 24°6E 203 D8
Sepúlveda Spain 41°18N 3°45W 194 D7
Sepulveda Dam Rec. Area ⌂ U.S.A. 34°10N 118°28W 126 A2
Sequeros Spain 40°31N 6°2W 194 E4
Sequim U.S.A. 48°5N 123°6W 306 B3
Sequoia △ U.S.A. 36°30N 118°30W 306 J8
Serafimovich Russia 49°36N 42°43E 190 F6
Seraing Belgium 50°35N 5°32E 170 D5
Serakhis → Cyprus 35°13N 32°55E 207 E8
Seram Indonesia 3°10S 129°0E 231 E7
Seram Sea Indonesia 2°30S 128°30E 231 E7
Serampore = Shrirampur India 22°44N 88°21E 243 H13
Seranantsara Madag. 18°30S 49°5E 272 B2
Serang Indonesia 6°8S 106°10E 234 D3
Serangoon Singapore 1°23N 103°54E 138 A3
Serangoon, Pulau Singapore 1°23N 103°55E 138 A3
Serangoon, Sungei → Singapore 1°23N 103°55E 138 A3
Serangoon Harbour Singapore 1°23N 103°57E 138 A3
Serasan Indonesia 2°29N 109°4E 235 B3
Serasan, Selat Indonesia 2°20N 109°0E 235 B3
Seravezza Italy 43°59N 10°13E 198 E7
Seraya, Pulau Singapore 1°16N 103°43E 138 B2
Serbāl, G. Egypt 28°40N 33°39E 251 K4
Şerbettar Turkey 41°27N 26°46E 203 E10
Serbia ■ Europe 43°20N 20°0E 202 C4
Şercaia Romania 45°49N 25°9E 183 E10
Serchhip India 23°18N 92°51E 241 D4
Serdar Turkmenistan 39°4N 56°23E 247 B8
Serdo Ethiopia 11°56N 41°14E 257 E5
Serdobol = Sortavala Russia 61°42N 30°41E 188 B6
Serdobsk Russia 52°28N 44°10E 190 D7
Serebryanka → Russia 55°47N 37°44E 129 B3
Serebryansk Kazakhstan 49°41N 83°17E 217 C10
Sered' Slovakia 48°17N 17°44E 181 C10
Sereda = Furmanov Russia 57°10N 41°9E 190 B5
Seredka Russia 58°12N 28°10E 188 C5
Serednye Ukraine 48°32N 22°30E 182 B7
Şereflikoçhisar Turkey 38°56N 33°32E 212 C5
Seregno Italy 45°39N 9°12E 198 C6
Seremban Malaysia 2°43N 101°53E 237 L3
Serengeti △ Tanzania 2°11S 35°0E 268 C3
Serengeti Plain Tanzania 2°40S 35°0E 268 C4
Serenje Zambia 13°14S 30°15E 269 E3
Seret → Ukraine 48°37N 25°52E 183 B10
Sereth = Siret → Romania 45°24N 28°1E 183 E12
Sergach Russia 55°30N 45°30E 190 C7
Sergeevka Kazakhstan 53°52N 67°24E 217 B7
Sergen Turkey 41°41N 27°42E 203 E11
Sergeya Kirova, Ostrova Russia 77°30N 89°0E 215 B10
Sergino Russia 62°25N 65°12E 214 C7
Sergiopol = Ayaköz Kazakhstan 48°10N 80°10E 217 C10
Sergipe □ Brazil 10°30S 37°30W 332 D4
Sergiyev Posad Russia 56°20N 38°10E 188 D10
Sergo = Stakhanov Ukraine 48°35N 38°40E 189 H10
Serhetabat Turkmenistan 35°20N 62°18E 247 C9
Seria Brunei 4°37N 114°23E 235 B4
Serian Malaysia 1°10N 110°31E 235 B4
Seriate Italy 45°41N 9°43E 198 C6
Seribu △ Indonesia 5°32S 106°33E 234 D3
Seribudolok Indonesia 2°55N 98°37E 234 B1
Sericho Kenya 1°5N 39°5E 268 B4
Sérifontaine France 49°20N 1°45E 173 C8
Serifos Greece 37°9N 24°30E 204 D6
Sérignan France 43°17N 3°17E 174 E7
Sérigny → Canada 56°47N 66°0W 299 A6
Serik Turkey 36°55N 31°7E 250 B2
Seringapatam Reef Australia 13°38S 122°5E 278 B3
Serinhisar Turkey 37°36N 29°18E 205 D11
Seririt Indonesia 8°12S 114°56E 231 J17
Serishābād Iran 35°14N 47°36E 213 E12
Serkout Algeria 23°56N 6°47E 261 D6
Sermaize-les-Bains France 48°47N 4°54E 173 D11
Sermata Indonesia 8°15S 128°50E 231 F7
Sermersooq □ Greenland 68°0N 40°0W 154 D7
Sermersuaq Greenland 79°30N 62°0W 154 B4
Sérmide Italy 45°0N 11°18E 199 D8
Sernovodsk Russia 53°58N 51°16E 190 D10
Sernur Russia 56°52N 49°2E 190 B9
Serock Poland 52°31N 21°4E 185 F8
Seroe Colorado Aruba 12°25N 69°52W 322 f
Serón Spain 37°20N 2°29W 197 H2
Serós Spain 41°27N 0°24E 196 D5
Serouenout Algeria 24°18N 7°25E 261 D6
Serov Russia 59°29N 60°35E 186 C11
Serowe Botswana 22°25S 26°43E 270 B4
Serpa Portugal 37°57N 7°38W 195 H3
Serpeddi, Pta. Italy 39°22N 9°18E 200 C2
Serpentara Italy 39°8N 9°36E 200 C2
Serpentine Lakes Australia 28°30S 129°10E 279 E4
Serpent's Mouth = Sierpe, Bocas de la Venezuela 10°0N 61°30W 329 G9
Serpis → Spain 38°59N 0°9W 197 G4
Serpneve Ukraine 46°18N 29°1E 183 D14
Serpukhov Russia 54°55N 37°28E 188 E9
Serra Brazil 20°7S 40°18W 333 F3
Serra da Bocaina △ Brazil 23°0S 44°50W 333 F2
Serra da Canastra △ Brazil 20°3S 46°50W 333 F2
Serra da Capivara △ Brazil 8°42S 42°15W 332 C3
Serra da Estrela ⌂ Portugal 40°27N 7°33W 194 E3
Serra das Confusões △ Brazil 8°50S 43°50W 332 C3
Serra de Mesa, Barragem de Brazil 14°30S 49°50W 333 D2
Serra do Cipó △ Brazil 19°14S 43°23W 333 E3
Serra do Divisor △ Brazil 8°3S 73°29W 330 B3
Serra do Navio Brazil 0°59N 52°3W 329 C7
Serra do Salitre Brazil 19°6S 46°41W 333 E2
Serra dos Órgãos △ Brazil 22°25S 43°8W 333 F3
Serra San Bruno Italy 38°35N 16°20E 201 D9
Serra Talhada Brazil 7°59S 38°18W 332 C4
Serradilla Spain 39°50N 6°9W 194 F4
Serramanna Italy 39°25N 8°55E 200 C1
Serramonte U.S.A. 37°39N 122°28W 136 C2
Serranía de la Neblina △ Venezuela 1°5N 65°51W 328 C4
Serranía San Luís △ Paraguay 22°35S 57°22W 334 A4
Serranía San Rafael △ Paraguay 26°30S 56°0W 335 B4
Serranilla Bank Caribbean 15°50N 80°0W 320 C4
Serranópolis Brazil 18°16S 52°0W 331 D7
Serras d'Aire e Candeeiros ⌂ Portugal 39°31N 8°48W 195 F2
Serrat, C. Tunisia 37°14N 9°10E 261 A6
Serravalle Scrivia Italy 44°43N 8°51E 198 D5
Serre-Ponçon, L. de France 44°22N 6°20E 175 D10
Serrejón Spain 39°49N 5°48W 194 F5
Serres Hautes-Alpes, France 44°26N 5°43E 175 D9
Serres Greece 41°5N 23°31E 202 E7
Serrezuela Argentina 30°40S 65°20W 334 C2
Serrinha Brazil 11°39S 39°0W 333 D4
Serrita Brazil 7°56S 39°19W 332 C4
Sersale Italy 39°1N 16°43E 201 C9
Sertã Portugal 39°48N 8°6W 194 F2
Sertânia Brazil 8°5S 37°20W 332 C4
Sertanópolis Brazil 23°4S 51°2W 335 A5
Sêrtar China 32°20N 100°41E 228 A3
Serua Indonesia 6°18S 130°1E 231 F8
Serui Indonesia 1°53S 136°10E 231 E9
Serule Botswana 21°57S 27°20E 270 B4
Serutu Indonesia 1°42S 108°45E 235 C3
Servia Greece 40°11N 22°0E 202 F6
Serzedelo Portugal 41°24N 8°14W 194 D2
Ses Salines Spain 39°21N 3°3E 206 B4
Sesayap → Indonesia 3°36N 117°15E 235 B5
Sese Is. Uganda 0°20S 32°20E 268 C3
Seseko-shima Japan 26°39N 127°52E 288 a
Sesepe Indonesia 1°30S 127°59E 231 E7
Sesfontein Namibia 19°7S 13°39E 270 A1
Sesheke Zambia 17°29S 24°13E 270 A3
Sésia → Italy 45°5N 8°37E 198 C5
Sesimbra Portugal 38°28N 9°6W 195 G1
S'Espalmador Spain 38°47N 1°26E 206 D1
S'Espardell Spain 38°48N 1°29E 206 D1
Sessa Angola 13°56S 20°38E 265 E4
Sessa Aurunca Italy 41°14N 13°56E 200 A6
Sesser U.S.A. 38°5N 89°1W 310 F7
S'Estanyol Spain 39°22N 2°54E 206 B3
Sestao Spain 43°18N 3°0W 196 B2
Sesto Calende Italy 45°44N 8°37E 198 C5
Sesto San Giovanni Italy 45°31N 9°13E 128 A2
Sesto Ulteriano Italy 45°24N 9°16E 128 B2
Sestri Levante Italy 44°16N 9°24E 198 D6
Sestriere Italy 44°57N 6°53E 198 D3
Sestroretsk Russia 60°5N 29°58E 188 B6
Sestrunj Croatia 44°10N 15°0E 199 D11
Sestu Italy 39°18N 9°5E 200 C2
Setagaya Japan 35°37N 139°36E 140 B2
Setaka Japan 33°9N 130°28E 222 D2
Setana Japan 42°26N 139°51E 220 C9
Sète France 43°25N 3°42E 174 E7
Sete Cidades △ Brazil 4°0S 41°37W 332 B3
Sete Lagoas Brazil 19°27S 44°16W 333 E3
Seter Norway 59°52N 10°47E 133 A3
Setesdalsheiene = Suldalsheiene Norway 59°28N 7°10E 164 E3
Seti → Nepal 28°59N 81°8E 243 E9
Setia Budi Indonesia 6°12S 106°49E 122 B1
Sétif Algeria 36°9N 5°26E 261 A6
Sétif □ Algeria 36°10N 5°0E 261 A6
Setit → Sudan 14°20N 35°50E 257 E4
Seto Japan 35°14N 137°6E 223 B9
Setonaikai Japan 34°20N 133°30E 222 C5
Setonaikai △ Japan 34°15N 133°15E 222 C5
Setsan Myanmar 16°3N 95°23E 241 G5
Settat Morocco 33°0N 7°40W 260 B3
Setté-Cama Gabon 2°32S 9°45E 264 C1
Settebagni Italy 42°0N 12°31E 136 A2
Settecamini Italy 41°57N 12°38E 136 B2
Séttimo Milanese Italy 45°28N 9°3E 128 B1
Séttimo Torinese Italy 45°9N 7°46E 198 C4
Setting L. Canada 55°0N 98°38W 297 C9
Settle U.K. 54°5N 2°16W 168 C5
Settlement Wake I. 19°18N 166°38E 302 b
Settlement, The Br. Virgin Is. 18°43N 64°22W 321 b
Settlers S. Africa 25°2S 28°30E 271 C4
Settsu Japan 34°47N 135°33E 133 A2
Setúbal Portugal 38°30N 8°58W 195 G2
Setúbal □ Portugal 38°25N 8°35W 195 G2
Setúbal, B. de Portugal 38°40N 8°56W 195 G2
Seugne → France 45°42N 0°32W 174 C3
Seul, Lac Canada 50°20N 92°30W 298 B1
Seulimeum Indonesia 5°27N 95°15E 234 A1
Seurre France 47°0N 5°8E 173 F12
Seutula Finland 60°20N 24°52E 121 A2
Sevan Armenia 40°33N 44°56E 191 K7
Sevan, Ozero = Sevana Lich Armenia 40°30N 45°20E 191 K7
Sevana Lich Armenia 40°30N 45°20E 191 K7
Sevastopol Ukraine 44°35N 33°30E 189 K7
Seven Corners U.S.A. 38°53N 77°9W 143 B2
Seven Islands = Sept-Îles Canada 50°13N 66°22W 299 B6
Seven Kings U.K. 51°33N 0°5E 125 A4
Seven Sisters Canada 54°56N 128°10W 296 C3
Seventeenth Street Canal U.S.A. 30°30N 90°7W 131 A2
Sever → Spain 39°40N 7°32W 195 F3
Sévérac-le-Château France 44°20N 3°5E 174 D7
Severn → Ont., Canada 56°2N 87°36W 298 A2
Severn → U.K. 51°35N 2°40W 169 F5
Severnaya Zemlya Russia 79°0N 100°0E 215 B11
Severno Kosovo Kosovo 43°29N 21°27E 202 C4
Severnyye Uvaly Russia 60°0N 50°0E 186 C8
Severo-Kurilsk Russia 50°40N 156°8E 215 D16
Severo-Yeniseyskiy Russia 60°22N 93°1E 215 C10
Severo-Zapadnyy □ Russia 65°0N 40°0E 214 C4
Severobaykalsk Russia 55°39N 109°19E 215 D11
Severočeský □ Czechia 50°30N 14°0E 180 A7
Severodonetsk = Syeverodonetsk Ukraine 48°58N 38°35E 189 H10
Severodvinsk Russia 64°27N 39°58E 186 B6
Severomoravský □ Czechia 49°38N 17°40E 181 B10
Severomorsk Russia 69°5N 33°27E 160 B25
Severouralsk Russia 60°9N 59°57E 186 B10
Seversk Russia 56°36N 84°49E 214 D9
Séveso → Italy 45°35N 9°9E 128 A1
Sevier → U.S.A. 39°4N 113°6W 304 G7
Sevier Desert U.S.A. 39°40N 112°45W 304 G7
Sevier L. U.S.A. 38°54N 113°9W 304 G7
Sevilla Colombia 4°16N 75°57W 328 C2
Sevilla Spain 37°23N 5°58W 195 H5
Sevilla □ Spain 37°25N 5°30W 195 H5
Seville = Sevilla Spain 37°23N 5°58W 195 H5
Seville Fla., U.S.A. 29°19N 81°30W 317 F8
Seville Ga., U.S.A. 31°58N 83°36W 316 D6
Sevlievo Bulgaria 43°2N 25°6E 203 C9
Sevnica Slovenia 46°2N 15°19E 199 B12
Sevran France 48°56N 2°31E 134 A4
Sèvre-Nantaise → France 47°12N 1°33W 172 E5
Sèvre-Niortaise → France 46°28N 0°50W 174 B3
Sèvres Paris, France 48°49N 2°12E 134 B2
Sevsk Russia 52°10N 34°30E 189 F8
Sewa → S. Leone 7°20N 12°10W 262 D2
Sewani India 28°58N 75°39E 242 E6
Seward Alaska, U.S.A. 60°7N 149°27W 303 F10
Seward Nebr., U.S.A. 40°55N 97°6W 308 E5
Seward Pa., U.S.A. 40°25N 79°1W 312 F5
Seward Peninsula U.S.A. 65°30N 166°0W 303 D6
Sewell Chile 34°10S 70°23W 334 C1
Sewer Indonesia 5°53S 134°40E 231 F8
Sewickley U.S.A. 40°32N 80°12W 312 F4
Sewri India 18°59N 72°50E 130 B2
Sexsmith Canada 55°21N 118°47W 296 B5
Seychelles ■ Ind. Oc. 5°0S 56°0E 272 c
Seyðisfjörður Iceland 65°16N 13°57W 155 B13
Seydişehir Turkey 37°25N 31°51E 212 D4
Seydvān Iran 38°34N 45°2E 213 C11
Seyhan → Turkey 36°43N 34°53E 250 B5
Seyhan Barajı Turkey 37°2N 35°18E 212 D6
Seyitgazi Turkey 39°27N 30°43E 205 B12
Seyitömer Turkey 39°34N 29°52E 205 B11
Seym → Ukraine 51°27N 32°34E 189 G7
Seymen Turkey 41°6N 27°57E 203 E11
Seymour Vic., Australia 37°2S 145°10E 283 D6
Seymour Eastern Cape, S. Africa 32°33S 26°46E 271 D4
Seymour Conn., U.S.A. 41°24N 73°4W 313 E11
Seymour Ind., U.S.A. 38°58N 85°53W 311 F11
Seymour Tex., U.S.A. 33°35N 99°16W 314 E5
Seyne France 44°21N 6°22E 175 D10
Seyssel France 45°57N 5°50E 175 C9
Sežana Slovenia 45°43N 13°41E 199 C10
Sézanne France 48°40N 3°40E 173 D10
Sezze Italy 41°30N 13°3E 200 A6
Sfântu Gheorghe Covasna, Romania 45°52N 25°48E 183 E10
Sfântu Gheorghe Tulcea, Romania 44°53N 29°36E 183 F14
Sfântu Gheorghe, Braţul → Romania 44°51N 29°36E 183 F14
Sfax Tunisia 34°49N 10°48E 258 B2
Sfax □ Tunisia 34°40N 10°20E 261 B7
Sforzesco, Castello Italy 45°28N 9°10E 128 B2
Sha Chau Hong Kong, China 22°21N 113°53E 122 A1
Sha Kok Mei Hong Kong, China 22°23N 114°16E 122 A3
Sha Lo Wan Hong Kong, China 22°17N 113°54E 122 B1
Sha Tau Kok China 22°33N 114°13E 219 a
Sha Tin Hong Kong, China 22°23N 114°12E 122 A3
Sha Xi → China 26°35N 118°0E 229 D12
Sha Xian China 26°23N 117°45E 229 D11
Sha'ab Iraq 33°25N 44°26E 113 A2
Sha'ab North Iraq 33°25N 44°24E 113 A2
Shaanxi □ China 35°0N 109°0E 226 G5
Sha'ar Binyamin West Bank 31°52N 35°16E 123 A2
Shaba = Katanga Dem. Rep. of the Congo 8°0S 25°0E 254 G6
Shaba ⌂ Kenya 0°38N 37°48E 268 B4
Shabeellaha Dhexe □ Somalia 3°0N 46°0E 267 D6
Shabeellaha Hoose □ Somalia 1°0N 44°0E 267 D5
Shabeelle → Somalia 2°0N 44°0E 267 D5
Shabestar Iran 38°11N 45°41E 213 C11
Shabla Bulgaria 43°31N 28°32E 203 C12
Shabogamo L. Canada 53°15N 66°30W 299 B6
Shabrâmant Egypt 29°56N 31°11E 117 B2
Shabunda Dem. Rep. of the Congo 2°40S 27°16E 268 C2
Shabwah Yemen 15°22N 47°1E 248 D4
Shabwah □ Yemen 15°22N 47°1E 248 D4
Shache China 38°20N 77°10E 217 E9
Shackleton Fracture Zone S. Ocean 60°0S 60°0W 151 B18
Shackleton Ice Shelf Antarctica 66°0S 100°0E 151 C8
Shackleton Inlet Antarctica 83°0S 160°0E 151 E11
Shādegān Iran 30°40N 48°38E 247 D6
Shadi Jiangxi, China 26°7N 114°47E 229 D10
Shadi Jammu & Kashmir, India 33°24N 77°14E 243 C7
Shadrinsk Russia 56°5N 63°32E 214 D7
Shady Dale U.S.A. 33°24N 83°36W 316 B6
Shady Grove U.S.A. 30°17N 83°38W 316 E6
Shadyside U.S.A. 39°58N 80°45W 312 G4
Shafer, L. U.S.A. 40°46N 86°46W 311 D10
Shaffa Nigeria 10°30N 12°6E 263 C7
Shafter U.S.A. 35°30N 119°16W 307 K7
Shaftesbury U.K. 51°0N 2°11W 169 F5
Shaftsbury U.S.A. 43°0N 73°11W 313 D11
Shag Pt. N.Z. 45°29S 170°52E 285 F5
Shag Rocks Atl. Oc. 53°0S 41°0W 152 M7
Shagamu Nigeria 6°51N 3°39E 263 D5
Shageluk U.S.A. 62°41N 159°34W 303 E8
Shagram Pakistan 36°24N 72°20E 243 A5
Shah Alam Malaysia 3°5N 101°32E 237 L3
Shah Alizai Pakistan 29°25N 66°33E 242 E2
Shah Bunder Pakistan 24°13N 67°56E 242 G2
Shāh Jūy Afghan. 32°31N 67°25E 240 B2
Shah Mosque Iran 35°41N 51°25E 141 A2
Shahabad Karnataka, India 17°10N 76°54E 244 F3
Shahabad Punjab, India 30°10N 76°55E 242 D7
Shahabad Raj., India 25°15N 77°11E 242 G7
Shahabad Ut. P., India 27°36N 79°56E 243 F8
Shahada India 21°33N 74°30E 244 D2
Shahadpur Pakistan 25°55N 68°35E 242 G3
Shahapur India 15°50N 74°34E 245 G2
Shahbā' Syria 32°52N 36°38E 250 F7
Shahbazpur I. Bangla. 22°30N 90°45E 241 D3
Shahdād Iran 30°30N 57°40E 247 D8
Shahdād, Namakzār-e Iran 30°20N 58°20E 247 D8
Shahdadkot Pakistan 27°50N 67°55E 242 F2
Shahdara India 28°40N 77°18E 120 A2
Shahdol India 23°19N 81°26E 243 H9
Shahe Guangdong, China 23°9N 113°19E 121 B2
Shahe Hebei, China 37°0N 114°32E 226 F8
Shahganj India 26°3N 82°44E 243 F10
Shahgarh India 27°15N 69°50E 242 F3
Shaḥḥāt Libya 32°48N 21°54E 258 B4
Shahid Rajaee Port = Bandar Shahid Rajaee Iran 27°7N 56°4E 247 E8
Shahīdān Afghan. 36°42N 67°49E 240 A2
Shāhīn Shahr Iran 32°49N 51°32E 247 C6
Shahjahanpur India 27°54N 79°57E 243 F8
Shahpur = Salmās Iran 38°11N 44°47E 213 C11
Shahpur Karnataka, India 16°40N 76°48E 244 F3
Shahpur Mad. P., India 22°12N 77°58E 242 H7
Shahpur Baluchistan, Pakistan 28°46N 68°27E 242 E3
Shahpur Punjab, Pakistan 32°17N 72°26E 242 C5
Shahpur Chakar Pakistan 26°9N 68°39E 242 F3
Shahpura Mad. P., India 23°10N 80°45E 243 H9
Shahpura Raj., India 25°38N 74°56E 242 G6
Shahr-e Bābak Iran 30°7N 55°9E 247 D7
Shahr-e Kord Iran 32°15N 50°55E 247 C6
Shahr-e Rey Iran 35°36N 51°25E 141 B2

Shahr-I Sokhta *Iran* 30°34N 61°21E **247** D9
Shahrak-e Golshahr *Iran* 35°37N 51°18E **141** B1
Shahrak-e Qods *Iran* 35°47N 51°22E **141** A2
Shāhrakht *Iran* 33°38N 60°16E **247** C9
Shāhrezā = Qomsheh *Iran* 32°0N 51°55E **247** D6
Shahrig *Pakistan* 30°15N 67°40E **242** D2
Shahrisabz *Uzbekistan* 39°3N 66°50E **217** E7
Shāhrud = Emāmrūd *Iran* 36°30N 55°0E **247** B7
Shahukou *China* 40°20N 112°18E **226** D7
Shaikh Aomar *Iraq* 33°20N 44°23E **113** A2
Shaikhabad *Afghan.* 34°2N 68°45E **242** B3
Shajapur *India* 23°27N 76°21E **242** H7
Shajing *China* 22°44N 113°48E **219** a
Shajuwan *Taiwan* 23°13N 121°23E **225** C3
Shakargarh *Pakistan* 32°17N 75°10E **242** C6
Shakawe *Botswana* 18°28S 21°49E **270** A3
Shakenge *Dem. Rep. of the Congo* 6°14S 18°41E **265** D3
Shaker Heights *U.S.A.* 41°28N 81°32W **312** E3
Shakhrisyabz = Shahrisabz *Uzbekistan* 39°3N 66°50E **217** E7
Shakhtersk *Russia* 49°10N 142°8E **215** E15
Shakhtīnsk *Kazakhstan* 49°42N 72°35E **217** C8
Shakhty *Russia* 47°40N 40°16E **191** G5
Shakhtyorskoye = Pershotravensk *Ukraine* 50°13N 27°40E **177** C14
Shakhunya *Russia* 57°40N 46°46E **190** B8
Shaki *Nigeria* 8°41N 3°21E **263** D5
Shākir *Egypt* 27°30N 33°59E **256** B3
Shakotan-Hantō *Japan* 43°10N 140°30E **220** C10
Shaksam Valley *Asia* 36°0N 76°20E **243** A7
Shaktoolik *U.S.A.* 64°20N 161°9W **303** D7
Shakurbasti *India* 28°41N 77°6E **120** A1
Shala, L. *Ethiopia* 7°30N 38°30E **257** F4
Shali *Russia* 43°9N 45°55E **191** J7
Shalim *Oman* 18°7N 55°38E **249** C6
Shalkar Köli *Kazakhstan* 50°35N 51°47E **190** E10
Shalkiya *India* 22°36N 88°21E **124** B2
Shallow Lake *Canada* 44°36N 81°5W **312** B3
Shalqar *Kazakhstan* 47°48N 59°39E **216** C5
Shalqar Köli *Kazakhstan* 50°33N 51°40E **216** B4
Shalskiy *Russia* 61°48N 35°58E **188** B8
Shalu *Taiwan* 24°14N 120°34E **225** B2
Shaluli Shan *China* 30°40N 99°55E **228** B2
Shām *Iran* 26°39N 57°21E **247** E8
Shām, Bādiyat ash *Asia* 32°0N 40°0E **246** C3
Shām, J. ash *Oman* 23°14N 57°16E **249** B7
Sham Shui Po *Hong Kong, China* 22°19N 114°9E **122** B2
Sham Tseng *Hong Kong, China* 22°22N 114°3E **122** A2
Sham Wat *Hong Kong, China* 22°16N 113°53E **122** B1
Shamal al Batinah □ *Oman* 24°30N 56°20E **249** A7
Shamal ash Sharqīyah □ *Oman* 22°40N 58°30E **249** B7
Shamâl Bahr el Ghazal = Northern Bahr el Ghazal □ *South Sudan* 8°0N 27°30E **257** F2
Shamâl Dârfûr □ *Sudan* 15°0N 25°0E **257** E2
Shamâl Kordofân □ *Sudan* 15°0N 30°0E **257** E3
Shamâl Sînî □ *Egypt* 30°30N 33°30E **251** H4
Shamapur *India* 28°44N 77°8E **120** A1
Shamattawa *Canada* 55°51N 92°5W **298** A1
Shamattawa → *Canada* 55°1N 85°23W **298** A2
Shambe *South Sudan* 7°8N 30°46E **257** F3
Shambe △ *South Sudan* 6°57N 30°50E **257** F3
Shambu *Ethiopia* 9°32N 37°3E **257** F4
Shamgong Dzong *Bhutan* 27°13N 90°35E **241** B3
Shamian *China* 23°6N 113°13E **121** B2
Shamīl *Iran* 27°30N 56°55E **247** E8
Shamkhor = Şämkir *Azerbaijan* 40°50N 46°0E **191** K8
Shāmkūh *Iran* 35°47N 57°50E **247** C8
Shamli *India* 29°32N 77°18E **242** E7
Shammar, Jabal *Si. Arabia* 27°40N 41°0E **246** E4
Shamo = Gobi *Asia* 44°0N 110°0E **226** C6
Shamo, L. *Ethiopia* 5°45N 37°30E **257** F4
Shamokin *U.S.A.* 40°47N 76°34W **313** F8
Shamrock *Ont., Canada* 45°23N 76°50W **313** A8
Shamrock *Tex., U.S.A.* 35°13N 100°15W **314** D4
Shamva *Zimbabwe* 17°20S 31°32E **269** F3
Shan □ *Myanmar* 21°30N 98°30E **241** E7
Shan Mei *Hong Kong, China* 22°23N 114°11E **122** A3
Shan Xian *China* 34°50N 116°5E **226** G9
Shana = Kurilsk *Russia* 45°14N 147°53E **215** E15
Shanan → *Ethiopia* 8°0N 40°20E **257** F5
Shanchengzhen *China* 42°20N 125°20E **224** A2
Shāndak *Iran* 28°28N 60°27E **247** D9
Shandan *China* 38°45N 101°15E **218** D9
Shandon *U.S.A.* 35°39N 120°23W **306** K6
Shandong □ *China* 36°0N 118°0E **227** G10
Shandong Bandao *China* 37°0N 121°0E **227** F11
Shandur Pass *Pakistan* 36°4N 72°31E **243** A5
Shang Xian = Shangzhou *China* 33°50N 109°58E **226** H5
Shangalowe *Dem. Rep. of the Congo* 10°50S 26°30E **269** E2
Shangani *Zimbabwe* 19°41S 29°20E **271** A4
Shangani → *Zimbabwe* 18°41S 27°10E **269** F2
Shangbancheng *China* 40°50N 118°1E **227** D10
Shangcheng *China* 31°47N 115°26E **229** B10
Shangchuan Dao *China* 21°40N 112°50E **229** G9
Shangdu *China* 41°30N 113°30E **226** D7
Shanggao *China* 28°17N 114°55E **229** C10
Shanghai *China* 31°15N 121°26E **138** B2
Shanghai Hongqiao Int. ✈ **(SHA)** *China* 31°12N 121°20E **138** B1
Shanghai Pudong Int. ✈ **(PVG)** *China* 31°9N 121°47E **138** B2
Shanghai Shi □ *China* 31°0N 121°30E **229** B13
Shanghang *China* 25°2N 116°23E **229** E11
Shanghe *China* 37°20N 117°10E **227** F9
Shangjao = Shangrao *China* 28°25N 117°59E **229** C11
Shanglin *China* 23°27N 108°33E **228** F7
Shangnan *China* 33°32N 110°50E **226** H6
Shangqiu *China* 34°26N 115°36E **226** G8
Shangrao *China* 28°25N 117°59E **229** C11
Shangri-La = Zhongdian *China* 27°48N 99°42E **228** D2
Shangshui *China* 33°32N 114°35E **226** H8
Shangsi *China* 22°8N 107°58E **228** F6
Shangyi *China* 41°4N 113°57E **226** D7
Shangyou *China* 25°48N 114°32E **229** E10
Shangyu *China* 30°3N 120°52E **229** B13
Shangzhi *China* 45°22N 127°56E **227** B14
Shangzhou *China* 33°50N 109°58E **226** H5
Shanhetun *China* 44°33N 127°15E **227** B14
Shanhu Tan *Taiwan* 23°12N 120°23E **225** C2
Shanhua *Taiwan* 23°8N 120°17E **225** C2
Shani *Nigeria* 10°14N 12°2E **263** C7
Shānidar *Iraq* 36°48N 44°14E **213** D11
Shanklin *U.K.* 50°38N 1°11W **169** G6
Shanlin *Taiwan* 23°0N 120°32E **225** C2
Shannon *N.Z.* 40°33S 175°25E **284** G4
Shannon → *Ireland* 52°35N 9°30W **166** D2
Shannon ✈ **(SNN)** *Ireland* 52°42N 8°57W **166** D3
Shannon, Mouth of the *Ireland* 52°30N 9°55W **166** D2
Shannon △ *Australia* 34°35S 116°25E **279** F2
Shannon Ø *Greenland* 75°10N 18°30W **154** B9
Shannonbridge *Ireland* 53°17N 8°3W **166** C3
Shannontown *U.S.A.* 33°53N 80°21W **316** B9
Shanshan *China* 42°52N 90°10E **217** D12
Shanshang *Taiwan* 23°6N 120°21E **225** C2
Shansi = Shanxi □ *China* 37°0N 112°0E **226** F7
Shantar, Ostrov Bolshoy *Russia* 55°9N 137°40E **215** D14
Shantipur *India* 23°17N 88°25E **243** H13
Shantou *China* 23°18N 116°40E **229** F11
Shantung = Shandong □ *China* 36°0N 118°0E **227** G10
Shanwei *China* 22°48N 115°22E **229** F10
Shanxi □ *China* 37°0N 112°0E **226** F7
Shanyang *China* 33°31N 109°55E **226** H5
Shanyin *China* 39°25N 112°56E **226** E7
Shaodong *China* 27°15N 111°43E **229** D8
Shaoguan *China* 24°48N 113°35E **229** E9
Shaohing = Shaoxing *China* 30°0N 120°35E **229** C13
Shaoshan *China* 27°55N 112°33E **229** D9
Shaowu *China* 27°22N 117°28E **229** D11
Shaoxing *China* 30°0N 120°35E **229** C13
Shaoyang *China* 27°14N 111°25E **229** D8
Shap *U.K.* 54°32N 2°40W **168** C5
Shapinsay *U.K.* 59°3N 2°51W **167** B6
Shaqlāwah *Iraq* 36°23N 44°20E **213** D11
Shaqq el Gi'eifer → *Sudan* 15°16N 26°0E **257** D2
Shaqra' *Si. Arabia* 25°15N 45°16E **246** E5
Shar *Kazakhstan* 49°35N 81°2E **217** C10
Sharafa *Sudan* 11°59N 27°7E **257** E2
Sharafkhāneh *Iran* 38°11N 45°29E **213** C11
Sharashova *Belarus* 52°34N 24°12E **185** F11
Sharavati → *India* 14°20N 74°25E **245** G2
Sharbaqty *Kazakhstan* 51°23N 78°17E **217** B9
Sharbithāt, Ra's ash *Oman* 17°56N 56°21E **249** C7
Sharbot Lake *Canada* 44°46N 76°41W **313** B8
Shard Building *London, U.K.* **125** b5
Shardara, Step *Kazakhstan* 42°20N 68°0E **217** D7
Sharg'un *Uzbekistan* 38°35N 67°58E **240** A2
Sharhorod *Ukraine* 48°45N 28°5E **183** B13
Shari *Japan* 43°55N 144°40E **220** C12
Shariff Aguak *Phil.* 6°51N 124°31E **233** H5
Sharjah = Ash Shāriqah *U.A.E.* 25°23N 55°26E **247** E7
Shark B. *Australia* 25°30S 113°32E **279** E1
Shark Bay △ *Australia* 25°30S 113°30E **279** E1
Sharm el Sheikh *Egypt* 27°53N 34°18E **251** L5
Sharon *Ont., Canada* 44°6N 79°26W **312** B5
Sharon *Mass., U.S.A.* 42°7N 71°11W **313** D13
Sharon *Pa., U.S.A.* 41°14N 80°31W **312** E4
Sharon *Wis., U.S.A.* 42°30N 88°44W **311** B8
Sharon Springs *Kans., U.S.A.* 38°54N 101°45W **308** F3
Sharon Springs *N.Y., U.S.A.* 42°48N 74°37W **313** D10
Sharonville *U.S.A.* 39°16N 84°25W **311** E12
Sharp I. *Hong Kong, China* 22°21N 114°17E **122** A3
Sharp Pk. *Phil.* 5°58N 125°31E **233** J5
Sharp Pt. *Australia* 10°58S 142°43E **286** F2
Sharpe L. *Canada* 54°24N 93°40W **298** B1
Sharpes *U.S.A.* 28°26N 80°46W **317** G9
Sharpsville *U.S.A.* 41°15N 80°29W **312** E4
Sharq Dârfûr □ *Sudan* 11°0N 23°30E **267** E2
Sharq el Istiwa'iya = Eastern Equatoria □ *South Sudan* 5°0N 33°0E **257** G3
Sharqi, Al Jabal ash *Lebanon* 33°40N 36°10E **250** E7
Sharqîya, Es Sahrâ esh *Egypt* 27°30N 32°30E **256** B3
Sharr *Kosovo* 42°5N 20°41E **202** D4
Sharya *Russia* 58°22N 45°20E **190** A7
Shasha *Ethiopia* 6°29N 35°59E **257** F4
Shashemene *Ethiopia* 7°13N 38°33E **257** F4
Shashi *Botswana* 21°15S 27°27E **271** B4
Shashi → *Africa* 21°14S 29°20E **269** G2
Shasta, Mt. *U.S.A.* 41°25N 122°12W **304** F2
Shasta L. *U.S.A.* 40°43N 122°25W **304** F2
Shastrinagar *India* 28°40N 77°10E **120** A2
Shatawi *Sudan* 14°39N 32°6E **257** E3
Shāţi', Wādī ash → *Libya* 27°30N 15°0E **258** C3
Shatilki = Svyetlahorsk *Belarus* 52°38N 29°46E **177** B15
Shatsk *Russia* 54°5N 41°45E **190** C5
Shatsk *Ukraine* 51°29N 23°55E **185** G10
Shatsky Rise *Pac. Oc.* 34°0N 157°0E **288** D7
Shatskyy ⌓ *Ukraine* 51°30N 23°52E **185** G10
Shatt al Arab *Asia* 29°57N 48°34E **247** D6
Shatura *Russia* 55°33N 39°21E **188** E10
Shaturtof = Shatura *Russia* 55°33N 39°21E **188** E10
Shau Kei Wan *Hong Kong, China* 22°16N 114°13E **122** B3
Shaumyani = Shulaveri *Georgia* 41°22N 44°45E **191** K7
Shaunavon *Canada* 49°35N 108°25W **297** D7
Shaver L. *U.S.A.* 37°9N 119°18W **306** H7
Shavgar = Türkistan *Kazakhstan* 43°17N 68°16E **217** D7
Shavli = Šiauliai *Lithuania* 55°56N 23°15E **184** C10
Shaw → *Australia* 20°21S 119°17E **278** D2
Shaw I. *Australia* 20°30S 149°2E **280** b
Shawanaga *Canada* 45°31N 80°17W **312** A4
Shawangunk Mts. *U.S.A.* 41°35N 74°30W **313** E10
Shawano *U.S.A.* 44°47N 88°36W **308** C9
Shawinigan *Canada* 46°35N 72°50W **298** C5
Shawmari, J. ash *Jordan* 30°35N 36°35E **251** H7
Shawnee *Ga., U.S.A.* 32°29N 81°25W **316** C8
Shawnee *Kans., U.S.A.* 39°1N 94°43W **310** E2
Shawnee *Okla., U.S.A.* 35°20N 96°55W **314** D6
Shawocun *China* 39°53N 116°13E **114** B1
Shay Gap *Australia* 20°30S 120°10E **278** D3
Shayang *China* 30°42N 112°29E **229** B9
Shaybārā *Si. Arabia* 25°26N 36°47E **246** E3
Shayib el Banat, Gebel *Egypt* 26°59N 33°29E **256** B3
Shaykh, J. ash *Lebanon* 33°25N 35°50E **250** E6
Shaykh Miskīn *Syria* 32°49N 36°9E **250** F7
Shaykh Sa'd *Iraq* 32°34N 46°17E **213** F12
Shaykh 'Uthmān *Yemen* 12°52N 44°59E **248** D4
Shaytansky Zavod = Pervouralsk *Russia* 56°59N 59°59E **186** C10
Shayuan *China* 23°5N 113°15E **121** B2
Shāzand *Iran* 33°56N 49°24E **247** C6
Shazud *Tajikistan* 37°45N 72°25E **217** E8
Shcheglovo = Kemerovo *Russia* 55°20N 86°5E **214** D9
Shchekino *Russia* 54°1N 37°34E **188** E9
Shcherbakov = Rybinsk *Russia* 58°5N 38°50E **188** C10
Shchigry *Russia* 51°55N 36°58E **189** G9
Shchors *Ukraine* 51°48N 31°56E **189** G6
Shchūchīnsk *Kazakhstan* 52°56N 70°12E **217** B8
She Xian *Anhui, China* 29°50N 118°25E **229** C12
She Xian *Hebei, China* 36°30N 113°40E **226** F7
Shea *Guyana* 2°48N 59°4W **329** C6
Shebekino *Russia* 50°28N 36°54E **189** G9
Shebela → *Ethiopia* 7°32N 45°43E **267** C6
Shebele = Shabeelle → *Somalia* 2°0N 44°0E **267** D5
Shebele *Ethiopia* 8°8N 42°40E **267** C5
Shebenik-Jabllanicë △ *Albania* 41°12N 20°28E **202** E4
Sheberghān *Afghan.* 36°40N 65°45E **240** A2
Sheboygan *U.S.A.* 43°46N 87°45W **308** D10
Shebshi Mts. *Nigeria* 8°30N 12°0E **263** D7
Shediac *Canada* 46°14N 64°32W **299** C7
Sheelin, L. *Ireland* 53°48N 7°20W **166** C4
Sheen, L. *U.S.A.* 28°25N 81°31W **133** B1
Sheenjek → *U.S.A.* 66°45N 144°33W **303** C11
Sheep Haven *Ireland* 55°11N 7°52W **166** A4
Sheep Range *U.S.A.* 36°35N 115°15W **307** J11
Sheepshead Bay *U.S.A.* 40°35N 73°55W **132** C2
Sheerness *U.K.* 51°26N 0°47E **169** F8
Sheet Harbour *Canada* 44°56N 62°31W **299** D7
Sheffield *N.Z.* 43°23S 172°1E **285** D7
Sheffield *S. Yorks., U.K.* 53°23N 1°28W **168** D6
Sheffield *Ala., U.S.A.* 34°46N 87°41W **315** D11
Sheffield *Ill., U.S.A.* 41°21N 89°44W **310** C7
Sheffield *Iowa, U.S.A.* 42°54N 93°13W **310** B3
Sheffield *Mass., U.S.A.* 42°5N 73°21W **313** D11
Sheffield *Pa., U.S.A.* 41°42N 79°3W **312** E5
Shegaon *India* 20°48N 76°47E **244** D3
Shehojele *Ethiopia* 10°40N 35°9E **257** E4
Shehong *China* 30°54N 105°18E **228** B5
Shehuen → *Argentina* 49°35S 69°34W **336** C3
Shei-Pa △ *Taiwan* 24°36N 121°22E **225** B3
Shei Shan *Taiwan* 24°22N 121°15E **225** B3
Sheikh, W. el → *Egypt* 28°41N 33°41E **251** K4
Sheikh Zayed Canal *Egypt* 23°30N 30°15E **256** C3
Sheikh Zayed Road *Dubai, U.A.E.* 25°11N 55°15E **119** B2
Sheikhpura *India* 25°9N 85°53E **243** G11
Shek Hasan *Ethiopia* 12°5N 35°58E **257** E4
Shek Kong *Hong Kong, China* 22°26N 114°6E **122** A2
Shek Kwu Chau *Hong Kong, China* 22°12N 113°59E **122** B1
Shek O *Hong Kong, China* 22°13N 114°15E **122** B3
Shek O Country Park ⌓ *Hong Kong, China* 22°16N 114°14E **122** B3
Shek Pik *Hong Kong, China* 22°14N 113°53E **122** B1
Shek Pik Res. *Hong Kong, China* 22°14N 113°54E **122** B1
Shekhupura *Pakistan* 31°42N 73°58E **242** D5
Sheki = Şaki *Azerbaijan* 41°10N 47°5E **191** K8
Shekki = Zhongshan *China* 22°26N 113°20E **229** F9
Shekou *China* 22°30N 113°55E **219** a
Shelbina *U.S.A.* 39°47N 92°2W **310** E4
Shelburn *U.S.A.* 39°11N 87°24W **311** E9
Shelburne *N.S., Canada* 43°47N 65°20W **299** D6
Shelburne *Ont., Canada* 44°4N 80°15W **312** B4
Shelburne *Vt., U.S.A.* 44°23N 73°14W **313** B11
Shelburne B. *Australia* 11°50S 142°50E **286** F2
Shelburne Falls *U.S.A.* 42°36N 72°45W **313** D12
Shelby *Mich., U.S.A.* 43°37N 86°22W **308** D10
Shelby *Miss., U.S.A.* 33°57N 90°46W **315** E9
Shelby *Mont., U.S.A.* 48°30N 111°51W **304** B8
Shelby *N.C., U.S.A.* 35°17N 81°32W **315** D14
Shelby *Ohio, U.S.A.* 40°53N 82°40W **312** F2
Shelbyville *Ill., U.S.A.* 39°24N 88°48W **311** E8
Shelbyville *Ind., U.S.A.* 39°31N 85°47W **311** E11
Shelbyville *Ky., U.S.A.* 38°13N 85°14W **311** F11
Shelbyville *Mo., U.S.A.* 39°48N 92°2W **310** E4
Shelbyville *Tenn., U.S.A.* 35°29N 86°28W **315** D11
Shelbyville, L. *U.S.A.* 39°26N 88°46W **311** E8
Sheldon *Ill., U.S.A.* 40°46N 87°34W **311** D9
Sheldon *Iowa, U.S.A.* 43°11N 95°51W **308** D6
Sheldon *Mo., U.S.A.* 37°40N 94°18W **310** G2
Sheldon *S.C., U.S.A.* 32°36N 80°48W **316** C9
Sheldon Point *U.S.A.* 62°32N 164°52W **303** E6
Sheldrake *Canada* 50°20N 64°51W **299** B7
Shelek *Kazakhstan* 43°33N 78°17E **217** D9
Shelengo, Khawr → *Sudan* 10°33N 28°40E **257** E2
Shelikhova, Zaliv *Russia* 59°30N 157°0E **215** D16
Shelikof Strait *U.S.A.* 57°30N 155°0W **303** H9
Shell Beach = Huntington Beach *U.S.A.* 33°40N 118°5W **307** M9
Shell Lakes *Australia* 29°20S 127°30E **279** E4
Shellbrook *Canada* 53°13N 106°24W **297** C7
Shellharbour *Australia* 34°31S 150°51E **283** C9
Shellman *U.S.A.* 31°46N 84°37W **316** D5
Shellsburg *U.S.A.* 42°6N 91°52W **310** B5
Shelon → *Russia* 58°13N 30°47E **188** C6
Shelter Bay = Port-Cartier *Canada* 50°2N 66°50W **299** B6
Shelter I. *Hong Kong, China* 22°19N 114°17E **122** B3
Shelter I. *N.Y., U.S.A.* 41°4N 72°20W **313** E12
Shelton *Conn., U.S.A.* 41°19N 73°5W **313** E11
Shelton *Wash., U.S.A.* 47°13N 123°6W **306** C3
Shemakha = Şamaxı *Azerbaijan* 40°38N 48°37E **191** K9
Shemonaīkha *Kazakhstan* 50°37N 81°54E **217** B10
Shëmri *Albania* 42°7N 20°13E **202** D4
Shemsi *Sudan* 19°2N 29°57E **256** D2
Shen Xian *China* 36°15N 115°40E **226** F8
Shenandoah *Iowa, U.S.A.* 40°46N 95°22W **308** E6
Shenandoah *Pa., U.S.A.* 40°49N 76°12W **313** F8
Shenandoah *Va., U.S.A.* 38°29N 78°37W **309** F14
Shenandoah → *U.S.A.* 39°19N 77°44W **309** F15
Shenandoah △ *U.S.A.* 38°35N 78°22W **309** F14
Shenchi *China* 39°8N 112°10E **226** E7
Shencottah *India* 8°59N 77°18E **245** K3
Shendam *Nigeria* 8°49N 9°30E **263** D6
Shendî *Sudan* 16°46N 33°22E **257** D3
Shendurni *India* 20°39N 75°36E **244** D2
Shengang = Shenkang *Taiwan* 24°9N 120°39E **225** B2
Shenge *S. Leone* 7°54N 12°55W **262** D2
Shengfang *China* 39°3N 116°42E **226** E9
Shëngjergj *Albania* 41°17N 20°10E **202** E4
Shëngjin *Albania* 41°50N 19°35E **202** E3
Shengzhou *China* 29°35N 120°50E **229** C13
Shenjingzi *China* 44°40N 124°30E **227** B13
Shenkang *Taiwan* 24°9N 120°39E **225** B2
Shenmu *China* 38°50N 110°29E **226** E6
Shennongjia *China* 31°43N 110°44E **229** B8
Shenqiu *China* 33°25N 115°5E **226** H8
Shensi = Shaanxi □ *China* 35°0N 109°0E **226** G5
Shenyang *China* 41°48N 123°27E **224** B1
Shenzhen *China* 22°32N 114°5E **229** F10
Shenzhen Bao'an Int. ✈ **(SZX)** *China* 22°41N 113°49E **219** a
Shenzhen Shuiku *China* 22°34N 114°8E **219** a
Shenzhen Wan *China* 22°27N 113°55E **219** a
Sheo *India* 26°11N 71°15E **242** F4
Sheopur Kalan *India* 25°40N 76°40E **242** G7
Shepetivka *Ukraine* 50°10N 27°10E **177** C14
Shepherd Is. *Vanuatu* 16°55S 168°36E **287** F6
Shepherds Bush *U.K.* 51°30N 0°13W **125** A2
Shepherdsville *U.S.A.* 37°59N 85°43W **311** G11
Shepparton *Australia* 36°23S 145°26E **283** D6
Shepperton *U.K.* 51°23N 0°26W **125** B1
Sheppey, I. of *U.K.* 51°25N 0°48E **169** F8
Shepton Mallet *U.K.* 51°11N 2°33W **169** F5
Sheqi *China* 33°12N 112°57E **226** H7
Sher Khan Qala *Afghan.* 29°53N 66°13E **240** C2
Sher Qila *Pakistan* 36°7N 74°2E **243** A6
Sherab *Sudan* 10°44N 24°41E **257** E1
Sherborne *U.K.* 50°57N 2°31W **169** G5
Sherbro → *S. Leone* 7°45N 12°55W **262** D2
Sherbro I. *S. Leone* 7°30N 12°40W **262** D2
Sherbrooke *N.S., Canada* 45°8N 61°59W **299** C7
Sherbrooke *Qué., Canada* 45°28N 71°57W **313** A13
Sherburne *U.S.A.* 42°41N 75°30W **313** D9
Sherburne Reef *Papua N. G.* 3°20S 148°0E **286** B5
Sherda *Chad* 20°7N 16°46E **259** D3
Shereik *Sudan* 18°44N 33°47E **256** D3
Sheremetyevo Int., Moscow ✈ **(SVO)** *Russia* 55°58N 37°25E **129** A1
Shergaon *India* 27°7N 92°16E **241** B4
Shergarh *India* 26°20N 72°18E **242** F5
Sherghati *India* 24°34N 84°47E **243** G11
Sheridan *Ark., U.S.A.* 34°19N 92°24W **314** D8
Sheridan *Ill., U.S.A.* 41°32N 88°41W **311** C8
Sheridan *Ind., U.S.A.* 40°8N 86°13W **311** D10
Sheridan *Wyo., U.S.A.* 44°48N 106°58W **304** D10
Sheringham *U.K.* 52°56N 1°13E **168** E9
Sherkin I. *Ireland* 51°28N 9°26W **166** E2
Sherkot *India* 29°22N 78°35E **243** E8
Sherlovaya Gora *Russia* 50°34N 116°15E **215** D12
Sherman *N.Y., U.S.A.* 42°9N 79°35W **312** D5
Sherman *Tex., U.S.A.* 33°38N 96°36W **314** E6
Sherman Oaks *U.S.A.* 34°8N 118°29W **126** B2
Sherman Park *U.S.A.* 41°47N 87°39W **119** C2
Sherobod *Uzbekistan* 37°40N 67°1E **217** E7
Sherpur *Bangla.* 25°0N 90°0E **241** C3
Sherpur *India* 25°34N 83°47E **243** G10
Sherridon *Canada* 55°8N 101°5W **297** B8
Sherriffs *St. Kitts & Nevis* 17°10N 62°32W **322** d
Shertallai = Cherthala *India* 9°42N 76°20E **245** K3
Sherwood *U.S.A.* 41°17N 84°33W **311** C12
Sherwood, L. *U.S.A.* 28°33N 81°29W **133** A2
Sherwood Forest *U.K.* 53°6N 1°7W **168** D6
Sherwood Park *Canada* 53°31N 113°19W **296** C6
Sheslay → *Canada* 58°48N 132°5W **296** B2
Shet Bandar *India* 18°57N 72°55E **130** B2
Shete Boka △ *Curaçao* 12°22N 69°8W **322** g
Shethanei L. *Canada* 58°48N 97°50W **297** B9
Shetland □ *U.K.* 60°30N 1°30W **167** A7
Shetland Is. *U.K.* 60°30N 1°30W **167** A7
Shetou *Taiwan* 23°53N 120°35E **225** C2
Shetpe *Kazakhstan* 44°10N 52°7E **216** D4
Shetrunji → *India* 21°19N 72°7E **242** J5
Sheung Fa Shan *Hong Kong, China* 22°23N 114°5E **122** A2
Sheung Lau Wan *Hong Kong, China* 22°16N 114°16E **122** B3
Sheung Shui *China* 22°31N 114°7E **219** a
Sheung Wan *Hong Kong, China* 22°16N 114°9E **122** B2
Sheva *India* 18°56N 72°57E **130** B2
Sheva Nhava *India* 18°57N 72°57E **130** B2
Shevaroy Hills *India* 11°58N 78°12E **245** J4
Shevchenkovo = Dolynska *Ukraine* 48°6N 32°46E **189** H7
Shevchenkovo *Ukraine* 45°33N 29°20E **183** E14
Shevgaon *India* 19°21N 75°14E **244** E2
Shevisheh *Iran* 35°21N 46°40E **213** E12
Shewa *Ethiopia* 9°33N 38°10E **257** F4
Shewa Gimira *Ethiopia* 7°4N 35°51E **257** F4
Shey-Phoksundo △ *Nepal* 29°30N 82°45E **243** E10
Sheyang *China* 33°48N 120°29E **227** H11
Sheyenne → *U.S.A.* 47°2N 96°50W **308** B5
Shiashkotan, Ostrov *Russia* 48°49N 154°6E **215** E16
Shiba *Tokyo, Japan* **140** c4
Shibām *Yemen* 15°59N 48°36E **249** D5
Shibata *Japan* 37°57N 139°20E **220** F9
Shibecha *Japan* 43°17N 144°36E **220** C12
Shibetsu *Hokkaidō, Japan* 43°30N 145°10E **220** C12
Shibetsu *Hokkaidō, Japan* 44°10N 142°23E **220** B11
Shibîn el Kôm *Egypt* 30°31N 30°55E **256** H7
Shibîn el Qanâtir *Egypt* 30°19N 31°19E **256** H7
Shibing *China* 27°2N 108°7E **228** D7
Shibogama L. *Canada* 53°35N 88°15W **298** B2
Shibpur *India* 22°34N 88°19E **124** B1
Shibukawa *Japan* 36°29N 139°0E **223** A11
Shibushi *Japan* 31°25N 131°8E **222** F3
Shibushi-Wan *Japan* 31°24N 131°8E **222** F3
Shibuya *Tokyo, Japan* **140** c1
Shicheng *China* 26°22N 116°20E **229** D11
Shicheng Dao *China* 39°31N 122°59E **224** C1
Shickshinny *U.S.A.* 41°9N 76°9W **313** E8
Shickshock Mts. = Chic-Chocs, Mts. *Canada* 48°55N 66°0W **299** C6
Shidād *Si. Arabia* 21°19N 40°3E **248** B3
Shidao *China* 36°50N 122°25E **227** F12
Shiderti → *Kazakhstan* 52°32N 74°50E **217** B8
Shidian *China* 24°40N 99°5E **228** E2
Shido = Sanuki *Japan* 34°19N 134°10E **222** C6
Shiel, L. *U.K.* 56°48N 5°34W **167** E3
Shield, C. *Australia* 13°20S 136°20E **280** A2
Shīeli *Kazakhstan* 44°20N 66°15E **217** D7
Shifang *China* 31°8N 104°10E **228** B5
Shiga □ *Japan* 35°20N 136°0E **223** B8
Shigaib *Sudan* 15°5N 23°35E **259** E4
Shigu *China* 26°51N 99°56E **228** D2
Shiguaigou *China* 40°52N 110°15E **226** D6
Shihan *Yemen* 17°42N 52°27E **249** C6
Shihan, W. → *Yemen* 17°24N 51°26E **249** C5
Shihchiachuangi = Shijiazhuang *China* 38°2N 114°28E **226** E8
Shihezi *China* 44°15N 86°2E **217** D11
Shihiu *Taiwan* 24°38N 121°10E **225** B3
Shihkangkeng *Taiwan* 24°1N 120°57E **225** B2
Shihmen *Taiwan* 25°17N 121°33E **225** A3
Shihmen Shuiku *Taiwan* 24°49N 121°21E **225** B3
Shihtan *Taiwan* 24°32N 120°55E **225** B2
Shiiba *Japan* 32°29N 131°4E **222** E3
Shiikh *Somalia* 9°56N 45°13E **267** C6
Shijak *Albania* 41°21N 19°33E **202** E3
Shijiazhuang *China* 38°2N 114°28E **226** E8
Shijiu Hu *China* 31°25N 118°50E **229** B12
Shikarpur *India* 28°17N 78°7E **242** E8
Shikarpur *Pakistan* 27°57N 68°39E **242** F3
Shikhrany = Kanash *Russia* 55°30N 47°32E **190** C8
Shikine-Jima *Japan* 34°19N 139°13E **223** C11
Shikohabad *India* 27°6N 78°36E **243** F8
Shikokochūō *Japan* 34°1N 133°34E **222** C5
Shikoku *Japan* 33°30N 133°30E **222** D5
Shikoku □ *Japan* 33°30N 133°30E **222** D5
Shikoku-Sanchi *Japan* 33°30N 133°30E **222** D5
Shikotan, Ostrov *Asia* 43°47N 146°44E **215** E15
Shikotsu-Ko *Japan* 42°45N 141°25E **220** C10
Shikotsu-Tōya △ *Japan* 44°4N 145°8E **220** C10
Shikuka = Poronaysk *Russia* 49°13N 143°0E **219** B17
Shilabo *Ethiopia* 6°5N 44°46E **267** C5
Shiliguri *India* 26°45N 88°25E **241** B2
Shilihe *China* 39°50N 116°25E **114** B2
Shiliu = Changjiang *China* 19°20N 108°55E **229** a
Shilka *Russia* 52°0N 115°55E **215** D12
Shilka → *Russia* 53°20N 121°26E **215** D13
Shillelagh *Ireland* 52°45N 6°32W **166** D5
Shillington *U.S.A.* 40°18N 75°58W **313** F9
Shillong *India* 25°35N 91°53E **241** C3
Shilo *West Bank* 32°4N 35°18E **251** F6
Shilong *China* 23°5N 113°52E **229** F9
Shilou *China* 37°0N 110°48E **226** F6
Shilovo *Russia* 54°25N 40°57E **190** C5
Shima-Hantō *Japan* 34°22N 136°45E **223** C8
Shimabara *Japan* 32°48N 130°20E **222** E2
Shimada *Japan* 34°49N 138°10E **223** C10
Shimane □ *Japan* 35°0N 132°30E **222** C4
Shimane-Hantō *Japan* 35°30N 133°0E **222** B5
Shimanovsk *Russia* 52°15N 127°30E **215** D13
Shimanto *Kōchi, Japan* 33°12N 133°8E **222** D5
Shimanto *Kōchi, Japan* 32°59N 132°56E **222** E4
Shimba Hills ⌓ *Kenya* 4°14S 39°25E **268** C4
Shimbiris *Somalia* 10°44N 47°14E **267** B6
Shimen *China* 29°35N 111°20E **229** C8
Shimenjie *China* 29°29N 116°48E **229** C11
Shimian *China* 29°17N 102°23E **228** C4
Shimizu *Japan* 35°0N 138°30E **223** C10
Shimla *India* 31°2N 77°9E **242** D7
Shimo-Jima *Japan* 32°15N 130°7E **222** E2
Shimo-Koshiki-Jima *Japan* 31°40N 129°43E **222** F1
Shimoda *Japan* 34°40N 138°57E **223** C10
Shimodate *Japan* 36°20N 139°55E **223** A11
Shimoga = Shivamogga *India* 13°57N 75°32E **245** H2
Shimogawara *Japan* 35°39N 139°27E **140** B1
Shimokita-Hantō *Japan* 41°20N 141°0E **220** D10
Shimoni *Kenya* 4°38S 39°20E **268** C4
Shimonita *Japan* 36°13N 138°47E **223** A10
Shimonoseki *Japan* 33°58N 130°55E **222** D2
Shimosalo *Japan* 35°45N 139°31E **140** A2
Shimoshakujii *Japan* 35°43N 139°35E **140** A2
Shimotsuma *Japan* 36°11N 139°58E **223** A11
Shimpuru Rapids *Namibia* 17°45S 19°55E **265** F3
Shimsha → *India* 13°15N 77°10E **245** H3
Shimsk *Russia* 58°15N 30°50E **188** C6
Shin, L. *U.K.* 58°5N 4°30W **167** C4
Shin-Nan'yō *Japan* 34°3N 131°49E **222** C3
Shin-Tone-Gawa → *Japan* 35°44N 140°51E **223** B12
Shinagawa *Japan* 35°36N 139°44E **140** B3
Shinan *China* 22°44N 109°53E **228** F7
Shinano-Gawa → *Japan* 36°50N 138°30E **221** F9
Shināş *Oman* 24°46N 56°28E **247** E8
Shīndand *Afghan.* 33°12N 62°8E **240** B1
Shing Mun Country Park ⌓ *Hong Kong, China* 22°23N 114°8E **122** A2
Shing Mun Res. *Hong Kong, China* 22°23N 114°8E **122** A2
Shingbwiyang *Myanmar* 26°41N 96°13E **241** B6
Shinglehouse *U.S.A.* 41°58N 78°12W **312** E6
Shingū *Japan* 33°40N 135°55E **223** D7
Shingwidzi *S. Africa* 23°5S 31°25E **271** B5
Shinji *Japan* 35°24N 132°54E **222** B4
Shinji-Ko *Japan* 35°26N 132°57E **222** B4
Shinjō *Japan* 38°46N 140°18E **220** E10
Shinjuku *Tokyo, Japan* **140** a1
Shinjuku Nat. Garden *Tokyo, Japan* **140** a2
Shinkafe *Nigeria* 13°8N 6°29E **263** C6
Shinkoiwa *Japan* 35°43N 139°51E **140** A4
Shinminato = Imizu *Japan* 36°47N 137°4E **223** A9
Shinnakano *Japan* 35°41N 139°40E **140** A3
Shinshār *Syria* 34°36N 36°43E **250** D7
Shinshiro *Japan* 34°54N 137°30E **223** C9
Shintuya *Peru* 12°41S 71°15W **330** C3
Shinyanga *Tanzania* 3°45S 33°27E **268** C3
Shinyanga □ *Tanzania* 3°50S 33°30E **268** C3
Shio-no-Misaki *Japan* 33°25N 135°45E **223** D7
Shiogama *Japan* 38°19N 141°1E **220** E10
Shiojiri *Japan* 36°6N 137°58E **223** A9
Shipai *China* 23°8N 113°20E **121** B3
Shipchenski Prokhod *Bulgaria* 42°45N 25°15E **203** D9
Shiphoirt, L. = Seaforth, L. *U.K.* 57°52N 6°36W **167** D2
Shiping *China* 23°45N 102°23E **228** F4
Shippagan *Canada* 47°45N 64°45W **299** C7
Shippensburg *U.S.A.* 40°3N 77°31W **312** F7
Shippenville *U.S.A.* 41°15N 79°28W **312** E5
Shiprock *U.S.A.* 36°47N 108°41W **305** H9
Shiqian *China* 27°32N 108°13E **228** D7
Shiqma, N. → *Israel* 31°37N 34°30E **251** G5
Shiquan *China* 33°5N 108°15E **228** A7
Shiquan He = Indus → *Pakistan* 24°20N 67°47E **242** G2
Shīr Khān *Afghan.* 37°11N 68°36E **240** A3
Shīr Kūh *Iran* 31°39N 54°3E **247** D7
Shira'awh *Qatar* 25°2N 52°14E **247** E7
Shirabad = Sherobod *Uzbekistan* 37°40N 67°1E **217** E7
Shiragami-Misaki *Japan* 41°24N 140°12E **220** D10
Shirahama *Japan* 33°41N 135°20E **223** D7
Shirakawa *Fukushima, Japan* 37°7N 140°13E **221** F10
Shirakawa *Gifu, Japan* 36°17N 136°56E **223** A8
Shirane-San *Gumma, Japan* 36°48N 139°22E **223** A11
Shirane-San *Yamanashi, Japan* 35°42N 138°9E **223** B10
Shiraoi *Japan* 42°33N 141°21E **220** C10
Shirati *Tanzania* 1°8S 33°59E **266** E3
Shīrāz *Iran* 29°42N 52°30E **247** D7
Shirbīn *Egypt* 31°11N 31°32E **256** H7
Shire → *Africa* 17°42S 35°19E **269** F4
Shiren *China* 41°57N 126°34E **227** D14
Shiretoko △ *Japan* 44°15N 145°15E **220** B12
Shiretoko-Misaki *Japan* 44°21N 145°20E **220** B12
Shirinab → *Pakistan* 30°15N 66°28E **242** D2
Shirinashi → *Japan* 34°38N 135°27E **133** B1
Shiriya-Zaki *Japan* 41°25N 141°30E **220** D10
Shirley *U.S.A.* 39°53N 85°35W **311** E11
Shirogane *Japan* 35°37N 139°44E **140** B3
Shiroishi *Japan* 38°0N 140°37E **220** F10
Shirol *India* 16°47N 74°41E **244** F2
Shiroro Res. *Nigeria* 9°56N 6°54E **263** D6
Shirpur *India* 21°21N 74°57E **244** D2
Shirshov Ridge *Pac. Oc.* 58°0N 170°0E **288** B8
Shīrvān *Iran* 37°30N 57°50E **247** B8
Shirwa, L. = Chilwa, L. *Malawi* 15°15S 35°40E **269** F4
Shishaldin Volcano *U.S.A.* 54°45N 163°58W **303** J7
Shishi *China* 24°44N 118°37E **229** E12
Shishmaref *U.S.A.* 66°15N 166°4W **303** C6
Shishou *China* 29°38N 112°22E **229** C9
Shisur *Oman* 18°15N 53°39E **249** C6
Shitai *China* 30°12N 117°25E **229** B11
Shitata *South Sudan* 4°30N 30°10E **257** G3
Shitennoji Temple *Japan* 34°39N 135°31E **133** B2
Shithāthah *Iraq* 32°34N 43°28E **213** G10
Shivamogga *India* 13°57N 75°32E **245** H2
Shively *U.S.A.* 38°12N 85°49W **311** F11
Shivpuri *India* 25°26N 77°42E **242** G7
Shiweitang *China* 23°6N 113°12E **121** B2
Shixian *China* 43°5N 129°50E **227** C15
Shixing *China* 24°46N 114°5E **229** E10
Shiyan *Guangdong, China* 22°42N 113°56E **219** a
Shiyan *Hubei, China* 32°35N 110°45E **229** A8
Shiyan Shuiku *China* 22°42N 113°54E **219** a
Shiyata *Egypt* 29°25N 25°7E **256** B2
Shizhu *China* 29°58N 108°7E **228** C7
Shizong *China* 24°50N 104°0E **228** E5
Shizuishan *China* 39°15N 106°50E **226** E4
Shizuoka *Japan* 34°57N 138°24E **223** C10
Shizuoka □ *Japan* 35°15N 138°40E **223** B10
Shkhara *Georgia* 43°0N 43°8E **213** A10
Shklov = Shklow *Belarus* 54°16N 30°15E **177** A16
Shklow *Belarus* 54°16N 30°15E **177** A16
Shkodër *Albania* 42°4N 19°32E **202** D3
Shkodra = Shkodër *Albania* 42°4N 19°32E **202** D3
Shkumbini → *Albania* 41°2N 19°31E **202** E3
Shmidta, Ostrov *Russia* 81°0N 91°0E **215** A10
Shō-Gawa → *Japan* 36°47N 137°4E **223** A9
Shoal Cr. → *U.S.A.* 39°44N 93°32W **310** E3
Shoal L. *Canada* 49°33N 95°1W **297** D9
Shoal Lake *Canada* 50°30N 100°35W **297** C8
Shoalhaven → *Australia* 34°54S 150°42E **283** C9
Shoals *U.S.A.* 38°40N 86°47W **311** F10
Shōbara *Japan* 34°51N 133°1E **222** C5
Shōdo-Shima *Japan* 34°30N 134°15E **222** C6
Shogunle *Nigeria* 6°34N 3°20E **124** A2
Sholapur = Solapur *India* 17°43N 75°56E **244** F2
Shomolu *Nigeria* 6°32N 3°22E **124** A2
Shōmrōn *West Bank* 32°15N 35°13E **251** F6
Shonian Harb. *Palau* 7°10N 134°23E **288** c
Shonzhy *Kazakhstan* 43°32N 79°28E **217** D9
Shooters Hill *U.K.* 51°28N 0°4E **125** B4
Shoranur *India* 10°46N 76°19E **245** J3
Shorapur *India* 16°31N 76°48E **245** F3
Sho'rchi *Uzbekistan* 37°59N 67°47E **240** A2
Shoreditch *London, U.K.* **125** a5
Shoreham *U.S.A.* 43°53N 73°18W **313** C11
Shoreham-by-Sea *U.K.* 50°50N 0°16W **169** G7
Shorewood *U.S.A.* 43°5N 87°53W **311** A9
Shori → *Pakistan* 28°29N 69°44E **242** E3
Shorkot *Pakistan* 30°50N 72°0E **242** D4
Shorkot Road *Pakistan* 30°47N 72°15E **242** D5
Shorsky △ *Russia* 52°40N 88°0E **217** B11
Shorter *U.S.A.* 32°24N 85°57W **316** C4
Shorterville *U.S.A.* 31°34N 85°6W **316** D4
Shortland I. *Solomon Is.* 7°0S 155°45E **287** L8
Shortland Is. *Solomon Is.* 7°0S 156°0E **287** L8
Shortlands *U.K.* 51°23N 0°0 **125** B4
Shortt's I. *India* 20°47N 87°4E **244** D8
Shoshone *Calif., U.S.A.* 35°58N 116°16W **307** K10
Shoshone *Idaho, U.S.A.* 42°56N 114°25W **304** E6
Shoshone L. *U.S.A.* 44°22N 110°43W **304** D8
Shoshone Mts. *U.S.A.* 39°20N 117°25W **304** G5
Shoshong *Botswana* 22°56S 26°31E **270** B4
Shoshoni *U.S.A.* 43°14N 108°7W **304** E9
Shostka *Ukraine* 51°57N 33°32E **189** G7
Shotor Khūn *Afghan.* 34°19N 64°56E **240** B2
Shotover → *N.Z.* 44°59S 168°41E **285** E3
Shou Xian *China* 32°37N 116°42E **229** A11
Shouchang *China* 29°18N 119°12E **229** C12
Shouchia *Taiwan* 22°14N 120°50E **225** D2
Shoufeng *Taiwan* 23°52N 121°30E **225** C3
Shouguang *China* 37°52N 118°45E **227** F10
Shouning *China* 27°27N 119°31E **229** D12
Shouyang *China* 37°54N 113°8E **226** F7
Show Low *U.S.A.* 34°15N 110°2W **305** J8
Showa *Japan* 35°36N 138°29E **223** B10
Showak *Sudan* 14°23N 35°52E **257** E4
Showt *Iran* 39°12N 44°49E **213** C11
Shpola *Ukraine* 49°1N 31°30E **189** H6
Shpykiv *Ukraine* 48°47N 28°34E **183** B13
Shqipëria = Albania ■ *Europe* 41°0N 20°0E **202** E4
Shreveport *U.S.A.* 32°31N 93°45W **314** E8
Shrewsbury *U.K.* 52°43N 2°45W **169** E5
Shri Mohangarh *India* 27°17N 71°18E **242** F4
Shrigonda *India* 18°37N 74°41E **244** E2
Shrirampur *India* 22°44N 88°21E **243** H13
Shropshire □ *U.K.* 52°36N 2°45W **169** E5
Shtërpcë *Kosovo* 42°14N 21°1E **202** D5
Shū *Kazakhstan* 43°36N 73°42E **217** D8
Shū → *Kazakhstan* 45°0N 67°44E **217** D7
Shu'afat *West Bank* 31°49N 35°14E **123** B2
Shuangbai *China* 24°42N 101°38E **228** E3
Shuangcheng *China* 45°20N 126°15E **227** B14
Shuangfeng *China* 27°29N 112°11E **229** D9
Shuanggou *China* 34°2N 117°30E **227** G9
Shuangjiang *China* 23°26N 99°58E **228** F2
Shuangliao *China* 43°29N 123°30E **227** C12
Shuangshanzi *China* 40°20N 119°8E **227** D10
Shuangyang *China* 43°28N 125°40E **227** C13
Shuangyashan *China* 46°28N 131°5E **219** B15
Shu'b, Ra's *Yemen* 12°30N 53°25E **249** D6
Shubarqudyq *Kazakhstan* 49°13N 56°34E **216** C5
Shubarshī *Kazakhstan* 48°39N 57°11E **216** C5
Shubrâ *Egypt* 30°5N 31°14E **117** A2
Shubrâ el Kheima *Egypt* 30°4N 31°14E **117** A2
Shubrâ Khit *Egypt* 31°2N 30°42E **256** H7
Shucheng *China* 31°28N 116°57E **229** B11
Shugozero *Russia* 59°54N 34°10E **188** C8
Shuguri Falls *Tanzania* 8°33S 37°22E **269** D4
Shuḩayr *Yemen* 14°41N 49°23E **249** D5
Shui Hau *Hong Kong, China* 22°13N 113°55E **122** B1
Shuiding = Huocheng *China* 44°0N 80°48E **217** D10
Shuiji *China* 27°13N 118°20E **229** D12
Shuikuo *China* 23°10N 113°10E **121** A2
Shuili *Taiwan* 23°49N 120°51E **225** C2
Shuilien *Taiwan* 23°47N 121°34E **225** C3
Shuishang *Taiwan* 23°25N 120°23E **225** C2
Shuitiliao *Taiwan* 22°23N 120°35E **225** D2
Shujalpur *India* 23°18N 76°46E **242** H7
Shukpa Kunzang *India* 34°22N 78°22E **243** B8
Shulan *China* 44°28N 127°0E **227** B14
Shulaveri *Georgia* 41°22N 44°45E **191** K7
Shule *China* 39°25N 76°3E **217** E9
Shule He → *China* 40°20N 92°50E **218** C7
Shullsburg *U.S.A.* 42°35N 90°13W **310** B6
Shumagin Is. *U.S.A.* 55°7N 160°30W **303** J7
Shumanay *Uzbekistan* 42°38N 58°55E **216** D5
Shumen *Bulgaria* 43°18N 26°55E **203** C10
Shumerlya *Russia* 55°30N 46°25E **190** C8
Shumikha *Russia* 55°10N 63°15E **214** D7
Shûna, W. el → *Egypt* 29°38N 32°6E **251** J3
Shunān *Japan* 34°3N 131°50E **222** C3
Shunchang *China* 26°54N 117°48E **229** D11
Shunde *China* 22°42N 113°14E **229** F9
Shungay *Kazakhstan* 48°30N 46°45E **191** F8
Shungnak *U.S.A.* 66°52N 157°9W **303** C8
Shuo Xian = Shuozhou *China* 39°20N 112°33E **226** E7
Shuozhou *China* 39°20N 112°33E **226** E7
Shuqrā' *Yemen* 13°22N 45°44E **248** D4
Shūr → *Fārs, Iran* 28°30N 55°0E **247** D7
Shūr → *Kermān, Iran* 30°52N 57°37E **247** D8
Shūr → *Yazd, Iran* 31°45N 55°15E **247** D7
Shūr Āb *Iran* 34°23N 51°11E **247** C6
Shūr Gaz *Iran* 29°10N 59°20E **247** D8
Shūrāb *Iran* 33°43N 56°29E **247** C8
Shuri *Japan* 26°13N 127°43E **288** a
Shūrjestān *Iran* 31°24N 52°25E **247** D7
Shurkhua *Myanmar* 22°15N 93°38E **241** D4
Shurugwi *Zimbabwe* 19°40S 30°0E **269** F3
Shūsf *Iran* 31°50N 60°5E **247** D9
Shūsh *Iran* 32°11N 48°15E **213** F13
Shushenskoye *Russia* 53°19N 91°56E **217** B12
Shushensky Bor △ *Russia* 52°40N 91°15E **217** B12
Shūshtar *Iran* 32°0N 48°50E **247** D6
Shuswap L. *Canada* 50°55N 119°3W **296** C5
Shute Harbour △ *Australia* 20°17S 148°47E **280** b
Shuya *Russia* 56°50N 41°28E **190** B5
Shuyak I. *U.S.A.* 58°31N 152°30W **303** G9
Shuyang *China* 34°10N 118°42E **227** G10
Shuzenji = Izu *Japan* 34°58N 138°56E **223** C10
Shūzū *Iran* 29°52N 54°30E **247** D7
Shwangliao = Liaoyuan *China* 42°58N 125°2E **227** C13
Shwebo *Myanmar* 22°30N 95°45E **241** D5
Shwegu *Myanmar* 24°15N 96°26E **241** C6
Shwegun *Myanmar* 17°9N 97°39E **241** G6
Shwegyin *Myanmar* 17°55N 96°53E **241** G6
Shweli → *Myanmar* 23°45N 96°45E **241** D6
Shwenyaung *Myanmar* 20°46N 96°57E **241** E6
Shyamnagar *India* 13°21N 92°57E **245** H11
Shyghanaq *Kazakhstan* 45°6N 73°59E **217** C8
Shyghys Qazaqstan □ *Kazakhstan* 48°30N 82°0E **217** D10
Shymkent *Kazakhstan* 42°18N 69°36E **217** D7
Shyok *India* 34°13N 78°12E **243** B8
Shyok → *Pakistan* 35°13N 75°53E **243** B6
Shyroke *Odesa, Ukraine* 45°59N 30°5E **183** E15
Shyroke *Ternopil, Ukraine* 48°13N 23°6E **182** B8
Si Kiang = Xi Jiang → *China* 22°5N 113°20E **229** F9
Si Lanna △ *Thailand* 19°17N 99°12E **236** C2
Si-ngan = Xi'an *China* 34°15N 109°0E **226** G5
Si Phangnga *Thailand* 9°8N 98°29E **237** H2
Si Prachan *Thailand* 14°37N 100°9E **236** E3
Si Racha *Thailand* 13°10N 100°48E **236** F3
Si Sa Ket *Thailand* 15°8N 104°23E **236** E5
Siachen Glacier *Asia* 35°20N 77°30E **243** B7

Sīah Cheshmeh Iran 39°3N 44°25E 213 C11
Siahaf → Pakistan 29°3N 68°57E 242 E3
Siahan Range Pakistan 27°30N 64°40E 240 D2
Siak → Indonesia 1°13N 102°9E 234 B2
Siak Sri Indrapura Indonesia 0°51N 102°0E 234 B2
Sialkot Pakistan 32°32N 74°30E 242 C6
Sialum Papua N. G. 6°5S 147°36E 286 D4
Siam = Thailand ■ Asia 16°0N 102°0E 236 E4
Sian = Xi'an China 34°15N 109°0E 226 G5
Sian Ka'an ⌓ Mexico 19°35N 87°40W 319 D7
Siangtan = Xiangtan China 27°51N 112°54E 229 D9
Sianów Poland 54°13N 16°18E 184 D3
Siantan Indonesia 3°10N 106°15E 234 B3
Siaolanyu = Hsiaohungt'ou Hsü Taiwan 21°57N 121°36E 225 E3
Siàpo → Venezuela 2°7N 66°28W 328 C4
Sīāreh Iran 28°5N 60°14E 247 D9
Siargao I. Phil. 9°52N 126°3E 233 G6
Siasi Phil. 5°34N 120°50E 233 J3
Siasi I. Phil. 5°33N 120°51E 233 J3
Siassi Papua N. G. 5°40S 147°51E 286 C4
Siatista Greece 40°15N 21°33E 202 F5
Siaton Phil. 9°4N 123°2E 233 G4
Siau Indonesia 2°50N 125°25E 231 D7
Šiauliai Lithuania 55°56N 23°15E 184 C10
Šiauliai □ Lithuania 55°56N 23°19E 184 C10
Siavonga Zambia 16°33S 28°42E 271 A4
Siaya Kenya 0°4N 34°17E 268 B3
Siazan = Siyäzän Azerbaijan 41°3N 49°10E 191 K9
Sibâi, Gebel el Egypt 25°45N 34°10E 246 E2
Sibang Gabon 0°25N 9°31E 264 B1
Sibang Bali, Indonesia 8°34S 115°13E 231 K18
Sibay Russia 52°42N 58°39E 186 D10
Sibay I. Phil. 11°51N 121°29E 233 F3
Sibayi, L. S. Africa 27°20S 32°45E 271 C5
Sibdu Sudan 10°57N 26°17E 257 E2
Šibenik Croatia 43°48N 15°54E 199 E12
Siberia = Sibirskiy □ Russia 58°0N 90°0E 215 D10
Siberia Russia 60°0N 100°0E 210 B12
Siberië Curaçao 12°14N 69°3W 322 g
Siberut Indonesia 1°30S 99°0E 234 C1
Siberut, Selat Indonesia 0°42S 98°35E 234 C1
Siberut △ Indonesia 1°17S 98°45E 234 C1
Sibi Pakistan 29°30N 67°54E 242 E2
Sibigo Indonesia 2°50N 95°54E 234 B1
Sibiloi △ Kenya 4°0N 36°20E 268 B4
Sibirskiy □ Russia 58°0N 90°0E 215 D10
Sibirtsevo Russia 44°12N 132°26E 220 B5
Sibiti Congo 3°38S 13°19E 264 C2
Sibiu Romania 45°45N 24°9E 183 E9
Sibiu □ Romania 45°50N 24°15E 183 E9
Sibium Mts. Papua N. G. 9°19S 148°25E 286 E5
Sibley Ill., U.S.A. 40°35N 88°23W 311 D8
Sibley Iowa, U.S.A. 43°24N 95°45W 308 D6
Sibo Sweden 61°13N 16°37E 162 C10
Sibolga Indonesia 1°42N 98°45E 234 B1
Siborongborong Indonesia 2°13N 98°58E 237 L2
Sibsagar = Sivasagar India 27°0N 94°36E 241 B5
Sibu Malaysia 2°18N 111°49E 235 B4
Sibuco Phil. 7°20N 122°10E 233 H4
Sibuguey B. Phil. 7°50N 122°45E 233 H4
Sibut C.A.R. 5°46N 19°10E 264 A3
Sibutu Phil. 4°45N 119°30E 235 B5
Sibutu Group Phil. 4°45N 119°20E 233 J2
Sibutu I. Phil. 4°47N 119°29E 233 J2
Sibutu Passage E. Indies 4°50N 120°0E 233 J3
Sibuyan I. Phil. 12°25N 122°40E 232 E4
Sibuyan Sea Phil. 12°30N 122°20E 232 E4
Sic Romania 46°56N 23°53E 183 D8
Sicamous Canada 50°49N 119°0W 296 C5
Sicapoo, Mt. Phil. 18°1N 120°56E 232 B3
Sicasica Bolivia 17°22S 67°45W 330 D4
Siccus → Australia 31°55S 139°17E 282 A3
Sichelberg = Sierpc Poland 52°55N 19°43E 185 F6
Sichon Thailand 9°0N 99°54E 237 H2
Sichuan □ China 30°30N 103°0E 228 B5
Sichuan Pendi China 31°0N 105°0E 228 B5
Sicilia Italy 37°30N 14°30E 201 E7
Sicily = Sicilia Italy 37°30N 14°30E 201 E7
Sicily, Str. of Medit. S. 37°35N 11°56E 200 E4
Sico → Honduras 15°58N 84°58W 320 C3
Sicuani Peru 14°21S 71°10W 330 C3
Šid Serbia 45°8N 19°14E 182 E4
Sidamo Ethiopia 5°0N 37°50E 257 G4
Sidaouet Niger 18°34N 8°3E 259 E1
Sidari Greece 39°47N 19°41E 206 B9
Sidcup U.K. 51°25N 0°6E 125 B4
Siddapur India 14°20N 74°53E 245 G2
Siddhapur India 23°56N 72°25E 242 H5
Siddipet India 18°5N 78°51E 244 E4
Side Turkey 36°45N 31°23E 250 B2
Sidensjö Sweden 63°18N 18°17E 162 A12
Sidéradougou Burkina Faso 10°42N 4°12W 262 C4
Siderno Italy 38°16N 16°18E 201 D9
Sideros, Akra Greece 35°19N 26°19E 207 E7
Sidhauli India 27°17N 80°50E 243 F9
Sidhi India 24°25N 81°53E 243 G9
Sîdi Abd el Rahmân Egypt 30°55N 29°44E 256 A2
Sîdi Barrâni Egypt 31°38N 25°58E 256 A2
Sidi-bel-Abbès Algeria 35°13N 0°39W 261 A4
Sidi-bel-Abbès □ Algeria 34°50N 0°30W 261 B4
Sidi Bennour Morocco 32°40N 8°25W 260 B3
Sidi Boubekeur Algeria 35°1N 0°4E 261 A5
Sidi Bouzid Tunisia 35°1N 9°16E 258 B1
Sidi Bouzid □ Tunisia 35°0N 9°30E 258 B1
Sîdi Haneish Egypt 31°10N 27°35E 256 A2
Sidi Ifni Morocco 29°29N 10°12W 260 C2
Sidi Kacem Morocco 34°12N 5°42W 260 B3
Sîdi Omar Egypt 31°24N 24°57E 256 A1
Sidi Slimane Morocco 34°16N 5°56W 260 B3
Sidi Smaïl Morocco 32°50N 8°31W 260 B3
Sīdī 'Uzayz Libya 31°41N 24°55E 258 B4
Sidikalang Indonesia 2°45N 98°19E 237 L2
Sidimo Somalia 2°27N 41°58E 267 D5
Siding No 14 = Ponoka Canada 52°42N 113°40W 296 C6
Sidirokastro Greece 41°13N 23°24E 202 E7
Sidlaw Hills U.K. 56°32N 3°2W 167 E5
Sidley, Mt. Antarctica 77°2S 126°2W 151 D14
Sidmouth U.K. 50°40N 3°15W 169 G4
Sidmouth, C. Australia 13°25S 143°36E 280 A3
Sidney B.C., Canada 48°39N 123°24W 306 B3
Sidney Mont., U.S.A. 47°43N 104°9W 304 C11
Sidney N.Y., U.S.A. 42°19N 75°24W 313 D9
Sidney Nebr., U.S.A. 41°8N 102°59W 308 E2
Sidney Ohio, U.S.A. 40°17N 84°9W 311 D12
Sidney Lanier, L. U.S.A. 34°10N 84°4W 316 A5
Sido Mali 11°37N 7°29W 262 C3
Sidoarjo Indonesia 7°27S 112°43E 235 D4
Sidoktaya Myanmar 20°27N 94°15E 241 E5
Sidon = Saydā Lebanon 33°35N 35°25E 250 E6
Sidra = Surt Libya 31°11N 16°39E 258 B3
Sidra, G. of = Surt, Khalīj Libya 31°40N 18°30E 258 B3
Sidrolândia Brazil 20°55S 54°58W 331 E7
Siebenhirten Austria 48°8N 16°17E 142 B1
Siedlce Poland 52°10N 22°20E 185 F9
Siedlung Germany 52°35N 13°7E 115 A1
Sieg → Germany 50°46N 7°6E 178 E3
Siegburg Germany 50°47N 7°12E 178 E3
Siegen Germany 50°51N 8°0E 178 E4
Siekierki Poland 52°12N 21°4E 143 B2
Sielce Poland 52°12N 21°2E 143 B2
Siem Pang Cambodia 14°7N 106°23E 236 E6
Siem Reap = Siemreab Cambodia 13°20N 103°52E 236 F4
Siemensstadt Germany 52°32N 13°16E 115 A2
Siemiatycze Poland 52°27N 22°53E 185 F9
Siemreab Cambodia 13°20N 103°52E 236 F4
Siena Italy 43°19N 11°21E 199 E8
Sieniawa Poland 50°11N 22°38E 185 H9
Sienyang = Xianyang China 34°20N 108°40E 226 G5
Sieradz Poland 51°37N 18°41E 185 G5
Sieraków Poland 52°39N 16°2E 185 F3
Sierck-les-Bains France 49°26N 6°20E 173 C13
Sierning Austria 48°2N 14°18E 180 C7
Sierpc Poland 52°55N 19°43E 185 F6
Sierpe, Bocas de la Venezuela 10°0N 61°30W 329 G9
Sierra Blanca U.S.A. 31°11N 105°22W 314 F2
Sierra Blanca Peak U.S.A. 33°23N 105°49W 305 K11
Sierra City U.S.A. 39°34N 120°38W 306 F6
Sierra Colorada Argentina 40°35S 67°50W 336 B3
Sierra de Agalta △ Honduras 15°1N 85°48W 320 C2
Sierra de Andújar ⌓ Spain 38°20N 3°50W 195 G7
Sierra de Aracena y Picos de Aroche ⌓ Spain 37°53N 6°41W 195 H4
Sierra de Bahoruco △ Dom. Rep. 18°10N 71°25W 321 C5
Sierra de Baza ⌓ Spain 37°20N 2°48W 197 H2
Sierra de Castril ⌓ Spain 37°54N 2°50W 197 H2
Sierra de Espuña ⌓ Spain 37°50N 1°31W 197 H3
Sierra de Grazalema ⌓ Spain 36°31N 5°28W 195 J5
Sierra de Gredos ⌓ Spain 40°17N 5°17W 194 E5
Sierra de Guadarrama △ Spain 40°50N 4°0W 194 E6
Sierra de Hornachuelos ⌓ Spain 37°56N 5°14W 195 H5
Sierra de Huétor ⌓ Spain 37°14N 3°30W 195 H7
Sierra de la Culata △ Venezuela 8°48N 70°56W 328 B3
Sierra de la Macarena △ Colombia 11°19N 74°1W 328 A3
Sierra de las Nieves ⌓ Spain 36°42N 5°0W 195 J6
Sierra de las Quijadas △ Argentina 32°29S 67°5W 334 C2
Sierra de María-Los Vélez ⌓ Spain 37°41N 2°10W 197 H2
Sierra de San Luis △ Venezuela 11°11N 69°33W 328 A4
Sierra de San Pedro Mártir △ Mexico 31°10N 115°30W 318 A1
Sierra de Yeguas Spain 37°7N 4°52W 195 H6
Sierra del São Mamede ⌓ Portugal 39°17N 7°18W 195 F3
Sierra Gorda Chile 22°50S 69°15W 334 A2
Sierra Grande Argentina 41°36S 65°22W 336 B3
Sierra Leone ■ W. Afr. 9°0N 12°0W 262 D2
Sierra Leone Basin Atl. Oc. 5°0N 17°0W 152 F10
Sierra Leone Rise Atl. Oc. 7°0N 22°0W 152 F9
Sierra Madre Mexico 16°0N 93°0W 319 D6
Sierra Madre Calif., U.S.A. 34°9N 118°3W 126 B4
Sierra Madre Occidental Mexico 27°0N 107°0W 318 B3
Sierra Madre Oriental Mexico 25°0N 100°0W 318 C5
Sierra Mágina ⌓ Spain 37°44N 3°28W 195 H7
Sierra Mojada Mexico 27°18N 103°41W 318 B4
Sierra Nevada Spain 37°3N 3°15W 195 H7
Sierra Nevada Calif., U.S.A. 39°0N 120°30W 306 H8
Sierra Nevada ⌓ Spain 37°4N 3°7W 195 H7
Sierra Norte de Sevilla ⌓ Spain 37°55N 5°46W 195 H5
Sierra Subbéticas ⌓ Spain 37°26N 4°18W 195 H6
Sierra Vista U.S.A. 31°33N 110°18W 305 L8
Sierras de Cardeña y Montoro ⌓ Spain 38°13N 4°15W 195 G6
Sierras de Cazorla, Segura y las Villas ⌓ Spain 37°0N 2°45W 197 J2
Sierraville U.S.A. 39°36N 120°22W 306 F6
Sierre Switz. 46°17N 7°31E 179 J3
Sievering Austria 48°15N 16°20E 142 A2
Sīf Yemen 15°19N 48°20E 249 D5
Sifani Ethiopia 12°18N 40°19E 257 E5
Sifié Côte d'Ivoire 8°0N 7°5W 262 D3
Sifnos Greece 37°0N 24°45E 204 E6
Sifton Canada 51°21N 100°8W 297 C8
Sifton Pass Canada 57°52N 126°15W 296 B3
Sig Algeria 35°32N 0°12W 261 A4
Sigaboy = Governor Generoso Phil. 6°39N 126°5E 233 H6
Sigatoka Fiji 18°8S 177°32E 287 B1
Sigdal Norway 60°3N 9°38E 164 D6
Sigean France 43°2N 2°58E 174 E6
Siggiewi Malta 35°51N 14°26E 206 F7
Sighetu-Marmaţiei Romania 47°57N 23°52E 183 C8
Sighişoara Romania 46°12N 24°50E 183 D9
Sighthill U.K. 55°56N 3°17W 121 B2
Sigiriya Sri Lanka 7°57N 80°45E 245 L5
Sigli Indonesia 5°25N 96°0E 234 A1
Siglufjörður Iceland 66°12N 18°55W 155 A8
Siglunes Iceland 66°12N 18°50W 155 A8
Sigmaringen Germany 48°5N 9°12E 179 G5
Signa Italy 43°45N 11°10E 198 E8
Signakhi = Tsnori Georgia 41°40N 45°57E 191 K7
Signal de Botrang Belgium 50°29N 6°4E 170 D6
Signal Hill S. Africa 34°5S 18°24E 118 A1
Signal Pk. U.S.A. 33°20N 114°2W 307 M12
Signy I. Antarctica 60°43S 45°36W 151 C18
Signy-l'Abbaye France 49°40N 4°25E 173 C11
Sigourney U.S.A. 41°20N 92°12W 310 C4
Sigsbee U.S.A. 31°16N 83°52W 316 D6
Sigsbee Deep Gulf of Mexico 25°0N 92°0W 152 D1
Sígsig Ecuador 3°0S 78°50W 328 D2
Sigtuna Sweden 59°36N 17°44E 162 E11
Sigüenza Spain 41°3N 2°40W 196 D2
Siguiri Guinea 11°31N 9°10W 262 C3
Sigulda Latvia 57°10N 24°55E 188 D3
Siguniangshan China 31°15N 103°10E 228 B4
Sihanoukville = Kampong Saom Cambodia 10°38N 103°30E 237 G4
Sihawa India 20°19N 81°55E 244 D5
Siheung S. Korea 37°28N 126°54E 137 C1
Sihong China 33°27N 118°16E 227 H10
Sihora India 23°29N 80°6E 243 H9
Sihu = Ssuhu Taiwan 23°38N 120°13E 225 C2
Sihuas Peru 8°40S 77°40W 330 B2
Sihui China 23°20N 112°40E 229 F9
Siikajoki → Finland 64°50N 24°43E 160 D21
Siilinjärvi Finland 63°4N 27°39E 160 E22
Siirt Turkey 37°57N 41°55E 213 D9
Siirt □ Turkey 37°55N 41°55E 213 D9
Sijarira Ra. = Chizarira Ra. Zimbabwe 17°36S 27°45E 269 F2
Sijungjung Indonesia 0°42S 100°58E 234 C2
Sika India 22°26N 69°47E 242 H3
Sikanni Chief → Canada 57°47N 122°15W 296 B4
Sikao Thailand 7°34N 99°21E 237 J2
Sikar India 27°33N 75°10E 242 F6
Sikasso Mali 11°18N 5°35W 262 C3
Sikasso □ Mali 10°55N 7°0W 262 C3
Sikátorpuszta Hungary 47°34N 19°10E 117 A3
Sikelenge Zambia 14°53S 24°14E 265 E4
Sikeston U.S.A. 36°53N 89°35W 308 G9
Sikhote Alin, Khrebet Russia 45°0N 136°0E 220 B8
Sikhote Alin Ra. = Sikhote Alin, Khrebet Russia 45°0N 136°0E 220 B8
Sikia Greece 40°2N 23°56E 202 F7
Sikinos Greece 36°40N 25°8E 205 E7
Sikkim □ India 27°50N 88°30E 241 B2
Siklós Hungary 45°50N 18°19E 182 E3
Sil → Spain 42°27N 7°43W 194 C3
Sila □ Chad 12°20N 21°0E 259 F4
Silacayoapan Mexico 17°30N 98°9W 319 D5
Šilalė Lithuania 55°28N 22°12E 184 C9
Silampur India 28°39N 77°16E 120 B2
Silandro Italy 46°38N 10°46E 198 B7
Silang Phil. 14°14N 120°58E 232 D3
Silawad India 21°54N 74°54E 242 J6
Silay Phil. 10°47N 122°58E 233 F4
Silba Croatia 44°24N 14°41E 199 D11
Silchar India 24°49N 92°48E 241 C4
Sildegapet Norway 62°5N 5°0E 164 B2
Şile Turkey 41°10N 29°37E 203 E13
Silent Valley △ India 11°10N 76°20E 245 J3
Siler City U.S.A. 35°44N 79°28W 315 D15
Sileru → India 17°49N 81°24E 244 F5
Silesia = Śląsk Poland 51°0N 16°30E 176 C9
Silet Algeria 22°44N 4°37E 261 D5
Siletitengiz Köli Kazakhstan 53°20N 73°10E 217 B8
Silgarhi Doti Nepal 29°15N 81°0E 243 E9
Silghat India 26°35N 93°0E 241 B4
Silhouette Seychelles 4°29S 55°12E 272 c
Sili Burkina Faso 11°37N 2°30W 262 C4
Siliana Tunisia 36°5N 9°22E 261 A6
Siliana □ Tunisia 36°0N 9°20E 261 A6
Silicon Valley = Santa Clara Valley U.S.A. 36°50N 121°30W 306 J5
Silifke Turkey 36°22N 33°58E 250 B4
Siliguri = Shiliguri India 26°45N 88°25E 241 B2
Silil Somalia 11°0N 43°26E 267 B5
Siling Co China 31°50N 89°20E 218 E6
Silisili, Mt. Samoa 13°37S 172°29W 287 V19
Silistea Nouă Romania 44°23N 25°1E 183 F10
Silistra Bulgaria 44°6N 27°19E 203 B11
Silistra □ Bulgaria 44°6N 27°19E 203 B11
Silivri Turkey 41°4N 28°14E 203 E12
Siljan Telemark, Norway 59°18N 9°42E 164 E6
Siljan Sweden 60°55N 14°45E 162 D8
Siljansnäs Sweden 60°47N 14°52E 162 D8
Silkeborg Denmark 56°10N 9°32E 163 H3
Silkwood Australia 17°45S 146°2E 280 B4
Silla Spain 39°22N 0°25W 197 F4
Sillajhuay, Cordillera Chile 19°46S 68°40W 330 D4
Sillamäe Estonia 59°24N 27°45E 188 C4
Sillé-le-Guillaume France 48°10N 0°8W 172 D6
Silleda Spain 42°42N 8°14W 194 C2
Sillein = Žilina Slovakia 49°12N 18°42E 181 B11
Sillim S. Korea 37°28N 126°56E 137 C1
Sillod India 20°18N 75°39E 244 D2
Silloth U.K. 54°52N 3°23W 168 C4
Sillustani Peru 15°50S 70°7W 330 D3
Silo Greece 41°10N 25°53E 203 E9
Siloam Springs U.S.A. 36°11N 94°32W 314 C7
Silopi Turkey 37°15N 42°27E 213 D10
Siltou Chad 16°46N 15°33E 259 E3
Siluko Nigeria 6°35N 5°10E 263 D6
Siluo = Hsilo Taiwan 23°48N 120°27E 225 C2
Šilutė Lithuania 55°21N 21°33E 184 C8
Silva Porto = Kuito Angola 12°22S 16°55E 265 E3
Silvan Turkey 38°7N 41°2E 213 C9
Silvani India 23°18N 78°25E 243 H8
Silvassa India 20°16N 73°1E 244 D1
Silver, L. U.S.A. 28°35N 81°23W 133 A2
Silver Bank W. Indies 20°30N 69°45W 321 B6
Silver Bank Passage W. Indies 20°0N 70°0W 321 B5
Silver City U.S.A. 32°46N 108°17W 305 K9
Silver Cr. → U.S.A. 43°16N 119°13W 304 E4
Silver Creek U.S.A. 42°33N 79°10W 312 D5
Silver Grove U.S.A. 39°2N 84°23W 311 E12
Silver Hill Montserrat 16°49N 62°11W 323 p
Silver Hill Md., U.S.A. 38°49N 76°55W 143 B3
Silver L. U.S.A. 38°39N 120°6W 306 G6
Silver Lake Calif., U.S.A. 34°5N 118°15W 126 B3
Silver Lake Calif., U.S.A. 35°21N 116°7W 307 K10
Silver Lake Ind., U.S.A. 41°4N 85°53W 311 C11
Silver Lake Oreg., U.S.A. 43°8N 121°3W 304 E3
Silver Lake Wis., U.S.A. 42°33N 88°13W 311 B8
Silver Mine B. Hong Kong, China 22°16N 114°0E 122 B2
Silver Spring U.S.A. 38°59N 77°2W 143 A2
Silver Springs U.S.A. 29°13N 82°3W 317 F7
Silverdalen Sweden 57°32N 15°45E 163 G9
Silvermine Mts. Ireland 52°47N 8°15W 166 D3
Silvermine Nature Reserve S. Africa 34°6S 18°27E 118 B1
Silverstrand Hong Kong, China 22°19N 114°16E 122 B3
Silverton N.S.W., Australia 31°52S 141°10E 282 A4
Silverton Colo., U.S.A. 37°49N 107°40W 305 H10
Silverton Tex., U.S.A. 34°28N 101°19W 314 D4
Silves Brazil 2°54S 58°27W 329 D6
Silves Portugal 37°11N 8°26W 195 H2
Silvi Marina Italy 42°34N 14°5E 199 F11
Silvia Colombia 2°37N 76°21W 328 C2
Silvies → U.S.A. 43°34N 119°2W 304 E4
Silvolantekojärvi Finland 60°17N 24°54E 121 B2
Silvrettahorn Switz. 46°50N 10°6E 198 B7
Silwa Bahari Egypt 24°45N 32°55E 256 C3
Silz Austria 47°16N 10°56E 180 D3
Sim, C. Morocco 31°26N 9°51W 260 B3
Simakumba Zambia 14°12S 23°16E 265 E4
Simaltala India 24°43N 86°33E 243 G12
Simaluguri India 26°55N 94°46E 241 B5
Sim'ān, J. Syria 36°25N 36°53E 250 B7
Simanggang = Bandar Sri Aman Malaysia 1°15N 111°32E 235 B4
Simao China 22°47N 101°5E 228 F3
Simão Dias Brazil 10°44S 37°49W 332 D4
Simara I. Phil. 12°48N 122°3E 232 E4
Simard, L. Canada 47°40N 78°40W 298 C4
Şīmareh → Iran 33°9N 47°41E 213 F12
Simav Turkey 39°4N 28°58E 205 B10
Simav → Turkey 40°23N 28°31E 203 F12
Simav Dağları Turkey 39°10N 28°30E 205 B10
Simba Dem. Rep. of the Congo 0°38N 22°59E 264 B4
Simba Tanzania 2°10S 37°36E 268 C4
Simbach Germany 48°16N 13°2E 179 G9
Simberi I. Papua N. G. 2°38S 152°0E 286 B7
Simbirsk = Ulyanovsk Russia 54°20N 48°25E 190 C9
Simbo Solomon Is. 8°16S 156°33E 287 M9
Simbo Tanzania 4°51S 29°41E 268 C2
Simbu = Chimbu □ Papua N. G. 6°15S 144°50E 286 D3
Simcoe Canada 42°50N 80°23W 312 D4
Simcoe, L. Canada 44°25N 79°20W 312 B5
Simdega India 22°37N 84°31E 243 H11
Simei Singapore 1°20N 103°47E 138 A3
Simeonovgrad Bulgaria 42°1N 25°50E 203 D9
Simeria Romania 45°51N 23°1E 182 E8
Simeto → Italy 37°24N 15°6E 201 E8
Simeulue Indonesia 2°45N 95°45E 234 B1
Simferopol Ukraine 44°55N 34°3E 189 K8
Simi Greece 36°35N 27°50E 205 E9
Simi Valley U.S.A. 34°16N 118°47W 307 L8
Simien △ Ethiopia 13°19N 38°0E 257 E4
Simikot Nepal 30°0N 81°50E 243 E9
Similajau △ Malaysia 3°27N 113°15E 235 B4
Simineh → Iran 36°59N 45°54E 213 D11
Simití Colombia 7°58N 73°57W 328 B3
Simitli Bulgaria 41°52N 23°7E 202 E7
Simiyu □ Tanzania 2°55S 34°20E 268 C3
Simla = Shimla India 31°2N 77°9E 242 D7
Simla India 22°35N 88°22E 124 B2
Simlångsdalen Sweden 56°43N 13°6E 163 H7
Şimleu-Silvaniei Romania 47°17N 22°50E 182 C7
Simlipal △ India 21°45N 86°30E 243 J12
Simmering Austria 48°10N 16°24E 142 A2
Simmering Heide Austria 48°10N 16°26E 142 A2
Simmern Germany 49°58N 7°30E 179 F3
Simmie Canada 49°56N 108°6W 297 D7
Simmler U.S.A. 35°21N 119°59W 307 K7
Simnas Lithuania 54°24N 23°39E 184 D10
Simo älv = Simojoki → Finland 65°35N 25°1E 160 D21
Simões Brazil 7°36S 40°49W 332 C3
Simojoki → Finland 65°35N 25°1E 160 D21
Simojovel Mexico 17°12N 92°38W 319 D6
Simonette → Canada 55°9N 118°15W 296 B5
Simonière, Plaine de la Guadeloupe 16°16N 61°19W 322 e
Simonkylä Finland 60°18N 25°1E 121 B3
Šimonovany = Partizánske Slovakia 48°38N 18°23E 181 C11
Simonstown S. Africa 34°14S 18°26E 270 D2
Simontornya Hungary 46°45N 18°33E 182 D3
Simpang Indonesia 1°16S 104°4E 234 C2
Simpang Empat Malaysia 5°27N 100°29E 237 c
Simpangkiri → Indonesia 2°50N 97°40E 234 B1
Simplício Mendes Brazil 7°51S 41°54W 332 C3
Simplonpass Switz. 46°15N 8°3E 179 J4
Simplontunnel Switz. 46°15N 8°7E 179 J4
Simpson, Mt. Papua N. G. 10°2S 149°34E 286 F5
Simpson Bay Lagoon St.-Martin 18°3N 63°6W 322 a
Simpson Desert Australia 25°0S 137°0E 280 D2
Simpson Desert △ Australia 24°59S 138°21E 280 C2
Simpson Pen. Canada 68°34N 88°45W 295 D14
Simrishamn Sweden 55°33N 14°22E 163 J8
Simsbury U.S.A. 41°53N 72°48W 313 E12
Simsonbaai St.-Maarten 18°2N 63°7W 322 a
Simuk Indonesia 0°4S 97°52E 234 C1
Simunjan Malaysia 1°25N 110°45E 235 B4
Simunul Phil. 4°54N 119°51E 233 J2
Simushir, Ostrov Russia 46°50N 152°30E 215 E16
Sin Cowe I. S. China Sea 9°53N 114°19E 230 C4
Sin-do N. Korea 39°52N 124°14E 224 C2
Sina → India 17°30N 75°55E 244 F2
Sina Dhago Somalia 5°50N 47°0E 267 C6
Sinabang Indonesia 2°30N 96°24E 234 B1
Sinabung Indonesia 3°10N 98°23E 234 B1
Sinai = Es Sînâ' Egypt 29°0N 34°0E 251 J4
Sinai, Mt. = Mûsa, Gebel Egypt 28°33N 33°59E 251 K4
Sinai, Mt. Grenada 12°4N 61°42W 323 q
Sinai Peninsula Egypt 29°30N 34°0E 251 J5
Sinaia Romania 45°21N 25°38E 183 E10
Sinait Phil. 17°52N 120°27E 232 C3
Sinako, Mt. Phil. 7°30N 125°17E 233 H5
Sinaloa □ Mexico 25°0N 107°30W 318 C3
Sinaloa de Leyva Mexico 25°50N 108°14W 318 B3
Sinalunga Italy 43°12N 11°44E 199 E8
Sinan China 27°56N 108°13E 228 D7
Sînandrei Romania 45°52N 21°13E 182 E6
Sinarades Greece 39°34N 19°51E 206 B9
Sīnāwan Libya 31°0N 10°37E 258 B2
Sinbaungwe Myanmar 19°43N 95°10E 241 F5
Sinbo Myanmar 24°46N 97°3E 241 C6
Sincan Turkey 40°0N 32°36E 212 B5
Sincanlı Turkey 38°45N 30°15E 205 C12
Sincé Colombia 9°15N 75°9W 328 B2
Sincelejo Colombia 9°18N 75°24W 328 B2
Sinch'ang N. Korea 40°7N 128°28E 224 B4
Sincheorwon S. Korea 38°8N 127°18E 224 C3
Sinch'ŏn N. Korea 38°17N 125°21E 224 C2
Sinchon Seoul, S. Korea 37°34N 126°57E 137 B1
Sinclair U.S.A. 41°47N 107°7W 304 F10
Sinclair, L. U.S.A. 33°8N 83°12W 316 B6
Sinclair Mills Canada 54°5N 121°40W 296 C4
Sinclair's B. U.K. 58°31N 3°5W 167 C5
Sinclairville U.S.A. 42°16N 79°16W 312 D5
Sincorá, Serra do Brazil 13°10S 41°20W 333 D3
Sind = Sindh □ Pakistan 26°0N 69°0E 242 G3
Sind → Jammu & Kashmir, India 34°18N 74°45E 243 B6
Sind → Mad. P., India 26°26N 79°13E 243 F8
Sind Sagar Doab Pakistan 32°0N 71°30E 242 D4
Sindal Denmark 57°28N 10°10E 163 G4
Sindang S. Korea 37°35N 127°2E 137 B2
Sindangan Phil. 8°10N 123°5E 233 G4
Sindangan B. Phil. 8°11N 122°50E 233 G4
Sindangbarang Indonesia 7°27S 107°1E 234 D3
Sindara Gabon 1°7S 10°41E 264 C2
Sinde Zambia 17°28S 25°51E 269 F2
Sindelfingen Germany 48°42N 9°0E 179 G4
Sindewahi India 20°17N 79°39E 244 D4
Sindgi India 16°55N 76°14E 244 F3
Sindh = Indus → Pakistan 24°20N 67°47E 242 G2
Sindh □ Pakistan 26°0N 69°0E 242 G3
Sindhnur India 15°47N 76°46E 245 F3
Sindhuli Garhi Nepal 27°16N 85°58E 243 F11
Sindi India 20°48N 78°52E 244 D4
Sındırgı Turkey 39°13N 28°10E 205 B10
Sindou Burkina Faso 10°35N 5°4W 262 C3
Sindri India 23°45N 86°42E 243 H12
Sine → Senegal 14°10N 16°28W 262 C1
Sinegorskiy Russia 47°55N 40°52E 191 G5
Sinekli Turkey 41°14N 28°12E 203 E12
Sinelnikovo = Synelnykove Ukraine 48°25N 35°30E 189 H8
Sinendé Benin 10°20N 2°22E 263 C5
Sines Portugal 37°56N 8°51W 195 H2
Sines, C. de Portugal 37°58N 8°53W 195 H2
Sineu Spain 39°38N 3°1E 206 B4
Sinewit, Mt. Papua N. G. 4°44S 152°2E 286 C7
Sinfra Côte d'Ivoire 6°35N 5°56W 262 D3
Sing Buri Thailand 14°53N 100°25E 236 E3
Sing Sing = Ossining U.S.A. 41°10N 73°55W 313 E11
Singa Sudan 13°10N 33°57E 257 E3
Singako Chad 9°50N 19°24E 259 G3
Singalila △ India 27°10N 88°5E 241 B2
Singanallur India 11°2N 77°1E 245 J3
Singapore ■ Asia 1°17N 103°51E 138 B3
Singapore, Straits of Asia 1°15N 104°0E 237 d
Singapore Changi ✕ (SIN) Singapore 1°23N 103°59E 138 A3
Singaraja Indonesia 8°7S 115°6E 231 J18
Singatoka = Sigatoka Fiji 18°8S 177°32E 287 B1
Singen Germany 47°45N 8°50E 179 H4
Singida Tanzania 4°49S 34°48E 268 C3
Singida □ Tanzania 6°0S 34°30E 268 D3
Singkang Indonesia 4°8S 120°1E 231 E6
Singkarak, Danau Indonesia 0°36S 100°32E 234 C2
Singkawang Indonesia 1°0N 108°57E 235 B3
Singkep Indonesia 0°30S 104°25E 234 C2
Singkil Indonesia 2°17N 97°49E 237 L1
Singkuang Indonesia 1°3N 98°55E 237 L2
Singleton Australia 32°33S 151°10E 283 B9
Singleton, Mt. N. Terr., Australia 22°0S 130°46E 278 D5
Singleton, Mt. W. Austral., Australia 29°27S 117°15E 279 E2
Singö Sweden 60°12N 18°45E 162 D12
Singoli India 25°0N 75°22E 242 G6
Singora = Songkhla Thailand 7°13N 100°37E 237 J3
Singrauli India 24°7N 82°23E 243 G10
Singri India 26°36N 92°29E 241 B4
Singsås Norway 62°56N 10°37E 164 B7
Singu Myanmar 22°33N 96°0E 241 D6
Sinh Ton, Dao = Sin Cowe I. S. China Sea 9°53N 114°19E 230 C4
Sinharaja Sri Lanka 6°25N 80°30E 245 L5
Sinhgarh India 18°22N 73°45E 244 E1
Sinhŭng Hamgyŏngnam-do, N. Korea 40°11N 127°34E 224 B3
Sinhŭng Hamgyŏngnam-do, N. Korea 41°8N 127°31E 224 B3
Siniloan Phil. 14°25N 121°27E 232 D3
Sining = Xining China 36°34N 101°40E 218 D9
Sínis Italy 38°55N 8°25E 200 C1
Siniscóla Italy 40°34N 9°41E 200 B2
Sinj Croatia 43°42N 16°39E 199 E13
Sinjai Indonesia 5°7S 120°20E 231 F6
Sinjajevina Montenegro 42°57N 19°22E 202 D3
Sinjār Iraq 36°19N 41°52E 213 D9
Sinjār Syria 35°35N 37°0E 250 C8
Sinjār, Jabal Iraq 36°23N 41°47E 213 D9
Sinkat Sudan 18°55N 36°49E 256 D4
Sinki, Selat Singapore 1°15N 103°42E 138 B2
Sinkiang = Xinjiang Uygur Zizhiqu □ China 42°0N 86°0E 217 D11
Sinko Guinea 8°53N 8°16W 262 D3
Sinlumkaba Myanmar 24°16N 97°31E 241 C6
Sinmak N. Korea 38°25N 126°14E 224 C3
Sinmi-do N. Korea 39°33N 124°53E 224 C2
Sínnai Italy 39°18N 9°13E 200 C2
Sinnar India 19°48N 74°0E 244 E2
Sinni → Italy 40°8N 16°41E 201 B9
Sinnuris Egypt 29°26N 30°31E 256 J7
Sinoie, Lacul Romania 44°35N 28°50E 183 F13
Sinop Turkey 42°1N 35°11E 212 A6
Sinop □ Turkey 42°0N 35°0E 212 B6
Sinor India 21°55N 73°20E 242 J5
Sinp'o N. Korea 40°0N 128°13E 224 C4
Sinsa S. Korea 37°31N 127°0E 137 B2
Sinsang N. Korea 39°38N 127°24E 224 C3
Sinsheim Germany 49°15N 8°52E 179 F4
Sinsiang = Xinxiang China 35°18N 113°50E 226 G7
Sinsk Russia 61°8N 126°48E 215 C13
Sint Annabaai Curaçao 12°6N 68°55W 322 g
Sint Christoffelberg Curaçao 12°20N 69°8W 322 g
Sint-Genesius-Rode Belgium 50°45N 4°22E 116 B2
Sint-Hubert Belgium 50°2N 5°23E 170 D5
Sint Jorisbaai Curaçao 12°7N 68°48W 322 g
Sint Marie, K. Curaçao 12°11N 69°3W 322 g
Sint Marthabaai Curaçao 12°17N 69°8W 322 g
Sint Michiel Curaçao 12°8N 69°0W 322 g
Sint Nicolaas Aruba 12°27N 69°54W 322 f
Sint Nicolaas Curaçao 12°17N 69°8W 322 g
Sint-Niklaas Belgium 51°10N 4°8E 170 C4
Sint-Truiden Belgium 50°48N 5°10E 170 D5
Sint Willibrordus Curaçao 12°12N 69°4W 322 g
Sintang Indonesia 0°5N 111°35E 235 B4
Sinton U.S.A. 28°2N 97°31W 314 G6
Sintra Portugal 38°47N 9°25W 195 G1
Sintra-Cascais ⌓ Portugal 38°50N 9°25W 195 G1
Sinŭiju N. Korea 40°5N 124°24E 224 B2
Sinujif Somalia 8°33N 48°59E 267 C6
Sinyukha → Ukraine 48°3N 30°51E 189 H6
Sinzig Germany 50°32N 7°14E 178 E3
Sio → Hungary 46°20N 18°53E 182 D3
Siocon Phil. 7°40N 122°10E 233 H4
Siófok Hungary 46°54N 18°3E 182 D3
Sioma Zambia 16°40S 23°32E 265 F4
Sioma Ngwezi △ Zambia 17°14S 23°26E 265 F4
Sion Maharashtra, India 19°3N 72°52E 130 A2
Sion Switz. 46°14N 7°20E 179 J3
Sion Mills U.K. 54°48N 7°29W 166 B4
tSionainn, An = Shannon → Ireland 52°35N 9°30W 166 D2
Sioux Center U.S.A. 43°5N 96°11W 308 D5
Sioux City U.S.A. 42°30N 96°24W 308 D5
Sioux Falls U.S.A. 43°33N 96°44W 308 D5
Sioux Lookout Canada 50°10N 91°50W 298 B1
Sioux Narrows Canada 49°25N 94°10W 297 D10
Sipadan Malaysia 4°6N 118°38E 235 B5
Sipalay Phil. 9°45N 122°24E 233 G4
Šipan Croatia 42°45N 17°52E 202 D1
Sipang, Tanjong Malaysia 1°48N 110°20E 235 B4
Siparia Trin. & Tob. 10°8N 61°31W 323 t
Siparia □ Trin. & Tob. 10°9N 61°28W 323 t
Sipil Daği △ Turkey 38°35N 27°30E 205 C9
Siping China 43°8N 124°21E 227 C13
Sipitang Malaysia 5°5N 115°33E 235 A5
Sipiwesk L. Canada 55°5N 97°35W 297 B9
Siple I. Antarctica 73°40S 125°10W 151 D14
Sipocot Phil. 13°46N 122°58E 232 E4
Šipovo Bos.-H. 44°16N 17°6E 182 F2
Sipra → India 23°55N 75°28E 242 H6
Sipson U.K. 51°29N 0°26W 125 B1
Sipsongpanna = Xishuangbanna China 22°5N 101°1E 228 F3
Sipur India 21°11N 85°9E 244 D7
Sipura Indonesia 2°18S 99°40E 234 C1
Sipura, Selat Indonesia 2°27S 99°54E 234 C1
Siqeil Egypt 30°7N 31°10E 117 A1
Siqirah Yemen 12°37N 54°20E 249 D6
Siqueira Campos Brazil 23°42S 49°50W 333 F2
Siquia → Nic. 12°10N 84°20W 320 D3
Siquijor Phil. 9°12N 123°35E 233 G4
Siquijor □ Phil. 9°11N 123°35E 233 G4
Siquirres Costa Rica 10°6N 83°30W 320 D3
Siquisique Venezuela 10°34N 69°42W 328 A4
Şīr Abu Nu'ayr U.A.E. 25°20N 54°20E 247 E7
Şīr Banī Yās U.A.E. 24°19N 52°37E 247 E7
Sir Edward Pellew Group Australia 15°40S 137°10E 280 B2
Sir Graham Moore Is. Australia 13°53S 126°34E 278 B4
Sir James MacBrien, Mt. Canada 62°7N 127°41W 294 E6
Sira India 13°41N 76°49E 245 H3
Sira Vest-Agder, Norway 58°24N 6°40E 164 F3
Sira → Norway 58°23N 6°34E 164 F3
Siracusa Italy 37°4N 15°17E 201 E8
Sirajganj Bangla. 24°25N 89°47E 241 C2
Sirakoro Mali 12°41N 9°14W 262 C3
Şiran Turkey 40°11N 39°7E 213 B8
Sirasso Côte d'Ivoire 9°16N 6°6W 262 D3
Sirathu India 25°39N 81°19E 243 G9
Siraway Phil. 7°34N 122°8E 233 H4
Sirdalsvatnet Norway 58°34N 6°43E 164 F3
Sīrdān Iran 36°39N 49°12E 213 D13
Sirdaryo □ Uzbekistan 40°30N 68°45E 217 D7
Sire Ethiopia 6°55N 35°36E 257 F4
Siren U.S.A. 45°47N 92°24W 308 C7
Sirente-Velino ⌓ Italy 42°10N 13°32E 199 F10
Sirer Spain 38°56N 1°22E 206 D1
Siret Romania 47°55N 26°5E 183 C11
Siret → Romania 45°24N 28°1E 183 E12
Sirevåg Norway 58°30N 5°48E 164 F2
Sirghāyā Syria 33°51N 36°8E 250 E7
Şiria Romania 46°16N 21°38E 182 D6
Sirik, Tanjong Malaysia 2°47N 111°15E 235 B4
Sirikit Res. Thailand 17°45N 100°34E 236 C3
Sirinat △ Thailand 8°6N 98°17E 237 a
Sirino, Mte. Italy 40°7N 15°50E 201 B8
Sīrjān Iran 29°30N 55°45E 247 D7
Sirkali = Sirkazhi India 11°15N 79°41E 245 J4
Sirkazhi India 11°15N 79°41E 245 J4
Sirmans U.S.A. 30°21N 83°39W 316 E6
Sirmaur India 24°51N 81°23E 243 G9
Sirmilik △ Canada 72°50N 80°35W 295 C15
Sirmione Italy 45°30N 10°36E 198 C7
Sirna Greece 36°22N 26°42E 205 E8
Şirnak Turkey 37°32N 42°28E 213 D10
Sirohi India 24°52N 72°53E 242 G5
Sirombu Indonesia 0°57N 97°25E 234 B1
Sironj India 24°5N 77°39E 242 G7
Síros = Ermoupoli Greece 37°28N 24°57E 204 D6
Siroz = Serres Greece 41°5N 23°31E 202 E7
Sirpur India 19°29N 79°36E 244 E4
Sirr, Nafud as Si. Arabia 25°33N 44°35E 246 E5
Sirrayn Si. Arabia 19°38N 40°36E 248 C3
Sirretta Pk. U.S.A. 35°56N 118°19W 307 K8
Sīrrī Iran 25°55N 54°32E 247 E7
Sirsa India 29°33N 75°4E 242 E6
Sirsa → India 26°51N 79°4E 243 F8
Sirsi India 14°40N 74°49E 245 G2
Sirsilla India 18°23N 78°50E 244 E4
Sirte = Surt Libya 31°11N 16°39E 258 B3
Siruela Spain 38°58N 5°3W 195 G5
Siruguppa India 15°38N 76°54E 245 F3
Sirur India 18°50N 74°23E 244 E2
Şirvan Azerbaijan 39°59N 48°52E 191 L9
Sirvān → Iran 35°4N 46°50E 213 E12
Sisak Croatia 45°30N 16°21E 199 C13
Sisante Spain 39°25N 2°12W 197 F2
Sisargas, Is. Spain 43°21N 8°50W 194 B2
Sishen S. Africa 27°47S 22°59E 270 C3
Sishui China 35°42N 117°18E 227 G9
Sisian Armenia 39°31N 46°1E 213 C12
Sisiga Solomon Is. 7°54S 159°10E 287 L10
Sisimiut Greenland 66°40N 53°30W 154 D5
Sisipuk L. Canada 55°45N 101°50W 297 B8
Şişli Turkey 41°3N 28°58E 122 B1
Sisophon Cambodia 13°38N 102°59E 236 F4
Sissano Papua N. G. 3°0S 142°3E 286 B2
Sisseton U.S.A. 45°40N 97°3W 308 C5
Sisson = Mount Shasta U.S.A. 41°19N 122°19W 304 F2
Sissonne France 49°34N 3°51E 173 C10
Sīstān Asia 30°50N 61°0E 247 D9
Sīstān, Daryācheh-ye Iran 31°0N 61°0E 247 D9
Sīstān va Balūchestān □ Iran 27°0N 62°0E 247 E9
Sisteron France 44°12N 5°57E 175 D9
Sisters U.S.A. 44°18N 121°33W 304 D3
Sisters, The Grenada 12°18N 61°36W 323 q
Sisters, The Seychelles 4°16S 55°52E 272 c
Sisters Pk. Ascension I. 7°56S 14°22W 153 g
Sisters Rocks Trin. & Tob. 11°20N 60°39W 323 s
Siswa Bazar India 27°9N 83°46E 243 F10
Sitakili Mali 13°7N 11°14W 262 C2
Sitakunda Bangla. 22°37N 91°39E 241 D3
Sitamarhi India 26°37N 85°30E 243 F11
Sitampiky Madag. 16°41S 46°6E 272 B2
Sitangkai Phil. 4°40N 119°24E 233 J2
Sitapur India 27°38N 80°45E 243 F9
Siteki Eswatini 26°32S 31°58E 271 C5
Sitges Spain 41°17N 1°47E 196 D6
Sithonia Greece 40°0N 23°45E 202 F7
Sitia Greece 35°13N 26°6E 207 E7
Sitia ✕ (JSH) Greece 35°15N 26°5E 207 E7
Sítio da Abadia Brazil 14°48S 46°16W 333 D2
Sitito-Ozima Ridge Pac. Oc. 23°0N 143°0E 288 E6
Sitka U.S.A. 57°3N 135°20W 296 B1
Sitka ⌓ U.S.A. 57°3N 135°19W 303 H14
Sitkaing = Sagaing Myanmar 21°52N 95°59E 241 E5
Sitkinak I. U.S.A. 56°33N 154°10W 303 H9
Sitoti Botswana 23°15S 23°40E 270 B3
Sitra Egypt 28°40N 26°53E 256 B2
Sittang Myit → Myanmar 17°20N 96°45E 241 G6
Sittard Neths. 51°0N 5°52E 170 C5
Sittaung Myanmar 24°10N 94°35E 241 C5
Sittensen Germany 53°17N 9°32E 178 B5
Sittingbourne U.K. 51°21N 0°45E 169 F8
Sittona Eritrea 14°25N 37°23E 257 E4
Sittoung = Sittang Myit → Myanmar 17°20N 96°45E 241 G6
Sittwe Myanmar 20°18N 92°45E 241 E4
Situbondo Indonesia 7°42S 113°56E 235 D4
Siu Kau Yi Chau Hong Kong, China 22°17N 114°3E 122 B2
Siufaalete Pt. Amer. Samoa 14°17S 169°29W 302 f
Siulagi Pt. Amer. Samoa 14°13S 169°30W 302 g
Si'umu Samoa 14°1S 171°48W 287 W20
Siuna Nic. 13°37N 84°45W 320 D3
Siuri India 23°50N 87°34E 243 H12
Siutghiol, Lacul Romania 44°15N 28°35E 183 F13
Sivaganga India 9°50N 78°28E 245 K4
Sivagiri India 9°16N 77°26E 245 K3
Sivakasi India 9°24N 77°47E 245 K3
Sīvand Iran 30°5N 52°55E 247 D7
Sivas Turkey 39°43N 36°58E 212 C7
Sivas □ Turkey 39°45N 37°0E 212 C7
Sivasagar India 27°0N 94°36E 241 B5
Sivasamudram India 12°16N 77°10E 245 H3
Sivaslı Turkey 38°31N 29°42E 205 C11
Siverek Turkey 37°50N 39°19E 213 D8
Sivomaskinskiy Russia 66°40N 62°35E 186 A11
Sivota Greece 39°24N 20°13E 206 C10
Sivrihisar Turkey 39°30N 31°35E 212 C4
Sivros Greece 38°40N 20°39E 207 B2
Sîwa Egypt 29°11N 25°31E 256 B2
Sîwa, El Wâhât es Egypt 29°10N 25°30E 256 B2
Siwa Oasis = Sîwa, El Wâhât es Egypt 29°10N 25°30E 256 B2
Siwalik Range Nepal 28°0N 83°0E 243 F10
Siwan India 26°13N 84°21E 243 F11
Siwana India 25°38N 72°25E 242 G5
Six Cross Roads Barbados 13°7N 59°28W 323 r
Six-Fours-les-Plages France 43°6N 5°49E 175 E9
Sixian China 33°30N 117°50E 227 H9
Sixmilebridge Ireland 52°44N 8°46W 166 D3
Sixth Cataract Sudan 16°20N 32°42E 257 D3
Siyabuswa S. Africa 25°7S 29°3E 271 C4
Siyah Kuh, Kavīr-e Iran 32°55N 53°55E 247 C7
Siyâl, Jazâ'ir Egypt 22°49N 36°12E 256 C4
Siyang China 33°42N 118°40E 227 H10
Siyäzän Azerbaijan 41°3N 49°10E 191 K9
Siziwang Qi China 41°25N 111°40E 226 D6
Sjælland Denmark 55°30N 11°30E 163 J5
Sjællands Odde Denmark 55°58N 11°24E 163 J5
Sjenica Serbia 43°16N 20°0E 202 C3
Sjeverni Velebit △ Croatia 44°30N 15°15E 199 D12
Sjoa Norway 61°41N 9°33E 164 C6
Sjöbo Sweden 55°37N 13°45E 163 J7
Sjøholt Norway 62°27N 6°52E 164 B3
Sjølisand Norway 61°29N 11°18E 164 C8
Sjötofta Sweden 57°22N 13°17E 163 G7
Sjötorp Sweden 58°50N 14°0E 163 F8
Sjumen = Shumen Bulgaria 43°18N 26°55E 203 C10
Sjuntorp Sweden 58°12N 12°13E 163 F6
Skåbu Norway 61°32N 9°24E 164 C6
Skadarsko Jezero Europe 42°10N 19°20E 202 D3
Skadarsko Jezero △ Montenegro 42°10N 19°20E 202 D3
Skadovsk Ukraine 46°17N 32°52E 189 J7
Skælskør Denmark 55°15N 11°18E 163 J5
Skærbæk Denmark 55°9N 8°45E 163 J2
Skaftafell Iceland 64°1N 17°0W 155 C9
Skagafjarðarsýsla Iceland 65°30N 19°0W 155 B7
Skagafjörður Iceland 65°54N 19°35W 155 B7
Skagastølstindane Norway 61°28N 7°52E 164 C4
Skagaströnd Iceland 65°50N 20°19W 155 B6
Skagatá Iceland 66°7N 20°6W 155 A6
Skagen Denmark 57°43N 10°35E 163 G4

Skagern *Sweden* 59°0N 14°20E **162** E8
Skagerrak *Denmark* 57°30N 9°0E **163** G2
Skagit → *U.S.A.* 48°23N 122°22W **306** B4
Skagway *U.S.A.* 59°28N 135°19W **303** G14
Skala *Greece* 38°5N 20°47E **207** C2
Skala nad Zbruczem = Skala-Podilska *Ukraine* 48°50N 26°15E **183** B11
Skala-Podilska *Ukraine* 48°50N 26°15E **183** B11
Skalat *Ukraine* 49°23N 25°55E **177** D13
Skálavík *Iceland* 66°11N 23°29W **155** A3
Skalbmierz *Poland* 50°20N 20°25E **185** H7
Skälderviken *Sweden* 56°22N 12°30E **163** H6
Skålevik *Norway* 58°5N 8°1E **164** F5
Skalica *Slovakia* 48°50N 17°15E **181** C10
Skallingen *Denmark* 55°32N 8°13E **163** J2
Skalni Dol = Kamenyak *Bulgaria* 43°24N 26°57E **203** C10
Skanderborg *Denmark* 56°2N 9°55E **163** H3
Skåne *Sweden* 55°59N 13°30E **163** J7
Skåne ☐ *Sweden* 56°15N 14°0E **163** H7
Skaneateles *U.S.A.* 42°57N 76°26W **313** D8
Skaneateles L. *U.S.A.* 42°51N 76°22W **313** D8
Skånevik *Norway* 59°43N 5°53E **164** E2
Skänninge *Sweden* 58°24N 15°5E **163** F9
Skanör med Falsterbo *Sweden* 55°24N 12°50E **163** J6
Skansen *Sweden* 59°19N 18°7E **139** B2
Skantzoura *Greece* 39°5N 24°6E **204** B6
Skara *Sweden* 58°25N 13°30E **163** F7
Skärblacka *Sweden* 58°35N 15°54E **163** F9
Skarð *Iceland* 65°17N 22°19W **155** B4
Skardu *Pakistan* 35°20N 75°44E **243** B6
Skare *Hordaland, Norway* 59°55N 6°36E **164** E3
Skåre *Sweden* 59°26N 13°26E **162** E7
Skärhamn *Sweden* 57°59N 11°34E **163** G5
Skärholmen *Sweden* 59°16N 17°53E **139** B1
Skarnes *Norway* 60°15N 11°41E **164** D8
Skarpäng *Sweden* 59°26N 18°0E **139** A2
Skarpnäck *Sweden* 59°16N 18°7E **139** B2
Skarszewy *Poland* 54°4N 18°25E **184** D5
Skarvan og Roltdalen △ *Norway* 63°16N 11°31E **160** E14
Skaryszew *Poland* 51°19N 21°15E **185** G8
Skaryszewski, Park *Poland* 52°15N 21°3E **143** B2
Skarżysko-Kamienna *Poland* 51°7N 20°52E **185** G7
Skattkärr *Sweden* 59°25N 13°40E **162** E7
Skattungbyn *Sweden* 61°10N 14°56E **162** C8
Skawina *Poland* 49°59N 19°50E **185** J6
Skebobruk *Sweden* 59°58N 18°36E **162** E12
Skee *Sweden* 58°56N 11°19E **163** F5
Skeena → *Canada* 54°9N 130°5W **296** C2
Skeena Mts. *Canada* 56°40N 128°30W **296** B3
Skegness *U.K.* 53°9N 0°20E **168** D8
Skei *Norway* 61°34N 6°28E **164** C3
Skeiðarársandur *Iceland* 63°54N 17°14W **155** D9
Skeiðflötur *Iceland* 63°26N 19°11W **155** D7
Skeleton Coast ⌓ *Namibia* 20°0S 13°20E **270** B1
Skellefteå *Sweden* 64°45N 20°50E **160** D19
Skellefteälven → *Sweden* 64°45N 21°10E **160** D19
Skelleftehamn *Sweden* 64°40N 21°9E **160** D19
Skellig Michael = Great Skellig *Ireland* 51°47N 10°33W **166** E1
Skender Vakuf *Bos.-H.* 44°29N 17°22E **182** F2
Skënderaj *Kosovo* 42°45N 20°47E **202** D4
Skeppsholmen *Stockholm, Sweden* **139** c3
Skerries *Ireland* 53°35N 6°8W **166** C5
Skerries, The *U.K.* 53°25N 4°36W **168** D3
Skhidnytsya *Ukraine* 49°13N 23°20E **185** J10
Ski *Norway* 59°43N 10°52E **164** E7
Skiathos *Greece* 39°12N 23°30E **204** B5
Skibbereen *Ireland* 51°33N 9°16W **166** E2
Skiddaw *U.K.* 54°39N 3°9W **168** C4
Skidegate *Canada* 53°15N 132°1W **296** C2
Skidra *Greece* 40°46N 22°10E **202** F6
Skien *Norway* 59°12N 9°35E **164** E6
Skierniewice *Poland* 51°58N 20°10E **185** G7
Skihist, Mt. *Canada* 50°12N 121°54W **296** C4
Skikda *Algeria* 36°50N 6°58E **261** A6
Skikda ☐ *Algeria* 36°45N 6°50E **261** A6
Skillet Fork → *U.S.A.* 38°5N 88°5W **311** F8
Skillingaryd *Sweden* 57°27N 14°5E **163** G8
Skillinge *Sweden* 55°30N 14°16E **163** J8
Skilloura *Cyprus* 35°14N 33°10E **207** E9
Skinari, Akra *Greece* 37°56N 20°42E **207** D2
Skinnastaður *Iceland* 66°4N 16°27W **155** A10
Skinnskatteberg *Sweden* 59°50N 15°42E **162** E9
Skipton *Vic., Australia* 37°39S 143°40E **282** D5
Skipton *N. Yorks., U.K.* 53°58N 2°3W **168** D5
Skiptvet *Norway* 59°28N 11°11E **164** E8
Skiring, C. *Senegal* 12°26N 16°46W **262** C1
Skirmish Pt. *Australia* 11°59S 134°17E **280** A1
Skíros = Skyros *Greece* 38°55N 24°34E **204** C6
Skivarp *Sweden* 55°26N 13°34E **163** J7
Skive *Denmark* 56°33N 9°2E **163** H3
Skjærhalden *Norway* 59°2N 11°2E **164** E8
Skjálfandafljót → *Iceland* 65°59N 17°25W **155** B9
Skjálfandi *Iceland* 66°5N 17°30W **155** A9
Skjeberg *Norway* 59°12N 11°12E **164** E8
Skjern *Denmark* 55°57N 8°30E **163** J2
Skjern Å △ *Denmark* 55°50N 8°30E **163** H2
Skjold *Norway* 59°31N 5°34E **164** E2
Skjolden *Norway* 61°29N 7°36E **164** C4
Skjöldólfsstaðir *Iceland* 65°19N 15°7W **155** B11
Skjønhaug *Norway* 59°39N 11°19E **164** E8
Skobelev = Farg'ona *Uzbekistan* 40°23N 71°19E **217** D8
Škocjanskie Jame *Slovenia* 45°40N 14°0E **199** C10
Skoczów *Poland* 49°49N 18°45E **185** J5
Skodje *Norway* 62°30N 6°43E **164** B3
Škofja Loka *Slovenia* 46°9N 14°19E **199** B11
Skógar *Iceland* 63°32N 19°28W **155** D7
Skógarnes *Iceland* 64°46N 22°34W **155** C4
Skoghall *Sweden* 59°20N 13°30E **162** E7
Skogskyrkogården *Sweden* 59°16N 18°5E **139** B2
Skogstorp *Sweden* 59°19N 16°29E **162** E10
Skoki *Poland* 52°40N 17°11E **185** F4
Skokie *U.S.A.* 42°2N 87°43W **119** A2
Skokie → *U.S.A.* 42°3N 87°46W **119** A2
Skokie Heritage Museum *Chicago, U.S.A.* 42°2N 87°44W **119** A2
Skoklefall *Norway* 59°50N 10°40E **133** A3
Skole *Ukraine* 49°3N 23°30E **177** D12
Skollenborg *Norway* 59°38N 9°43E **164** E6
Sköndal *Sweden* 59°15N 18°6E **139** B2
Skopelos *Greece* 39°9N 23°47E **204** B5
Skopi *Greece* 35°11N 26°2E **207** E7
Skopin *Russia* 53°55N 39°32E **188** F10
Skopje *N. Macedonia* 42°1N 21°26E **202** D5
Skopje ✈ **(SKP)** *N. Macedonia* 41°59N 21°29E **202** E5
Skoppum *Norway* 59°23N 10°26E **164** E7
Skórcz *Poland* 53°47N 18°30E **184** E5
Skørping *Denmark* 56°50N 9°53E **163** H3
Skotfoss *Norway* 59°12N 9°30E **164** E6
Skotterud *Norway* 60°0N 12°7E **164** D9
Skövde *Sweden* 58°24N 13°50E **163** F7
Skovlunde *Denmark* 55°42N 12°25E **118** A2
Skovorodino *Russia* 54°0N 124°0E **215** D13
Skovshoved *Denmark* 55°45N 12°35E **118** A3
Skowhegan *U.S.A.* 44°46N 69°43W **309** C19
Skradin *Croatia* 43°52N 15°53E **199** E12
Skrea *Sweden* 56°53N 12°34E **163** H6
Skreia *Norway* 60°40N 10°56E **164** D7
Skrim *Norway* 59°31N 9°38E **164** E6
Skrunda *Latvia* 56°41N 22°1E **184** B9
Skrwa → *Poland* 52°35N 19°32E **185** F6
Skudeneshavn *Norway* 59°10N 5°10E **164** E2
Skuleskogen △ *Sweden* 63°6N 18°30E **162** A12
Skull *Ireland* 51°32N 9°34W **166** E2
Skultorp *Sweden* 58°24N 13°51E **163** F7
Skultuna *Sweden* 59°43N 16°25E **162** E10
Skunk → *U.S.A.* 40°42N 91°7W **310** D5
Skuodas *Lithuania* 56°16N 21°33E **184** B8
Skuru *Sweden* 59°18N 18°12E **139** B3
Skurup *Sweden* 55°28N 13°30E **163** J7
Skutskär *Sweden* 60°37N 17°25E **162** D11
Skútustaðir *Iceland* 65°34N 17°2W **155** B9
Skvyra *Ukraine* 49°44N 29°40E **177** D15
Skwierzyna *Poland* 52°33N 15°30E **185** F2
Sky Dome = Rogers Centre *Toronto, Canada* **141** c1
Sky Harbour Int., Phoenix ✈ **(PHX)** *U.S.A.* 33°26N 112°5W **305** K7
Sky Lake *U.S.A.* 28°27N 81°23W **133** B2
Skye *U.K.* 57°15N 6°10W **167** D2
Skykomish *U.S.A.* 47°42N 121°22W **304** C3
Skyring, Seno *Chile* 52°35S 72°0W **336** D3
Skyropoula *Greece* 38°50N 24°21E **204** C6
Skyros *Greece* 38°55N 24°34E **204** C6
Skyttorp *Sweden* 60°5N 17°44E **162** D11
Slade Green *U.K.* 51°27N 0°11E **125** B5
Slade Point *Australia* 21°4S 149°13E **280** b
Slade Pt. *Australia* 21°5S 149°13E **280** b
Slættaratindur *Færoe Is.* 62°18N 7°1W **160** E9
Slagelse *Denmark* 55°23N 11°19E **163** J5
Slamet *Indonesia* 7°16S 109°8E **235** D3
Slanchev Bryag *Bulgaria* 42°40N 27°41E **203** D11
Slane *Ireland* 53°42N 6°33W **166** C5
Slaney → *Ireland* 52°26N 6°33W **166** D5
Slangberge *S. Africa* 31°32S 20°48E **270** D3
Slănic *Romania* 45°14N 25°58E **183** E10
Slano *Croatia* 42°48N 17°53E **202** D1
Slantsy *Russia* 59°7N 28°5E **188** C5
Slaný *Czechia* 50°13N 14°6E **180** A7
Śląsk *Poland* 51°0N 16°30E **176** C9
Śląskie ☐ *Poland* 50°30N 19°0E **185** H6
Slätbaken *Sweden* 58°25N 16°45E **163** F10
Slate Is. *Canada* 48°40N 87°0W **298** C2
Slater *U.S.A.* 39°13N 93°4W **310** E3
Slatina *Croatia* 45°42N 17°45E **182** E2
Slatina *Romania* 44°28N 24°22E **183** F9
Slatina Timiş *Romania* 45°15N 22°17E **182** E7
Slatington *U.S.A.* 40°45N 75°37W **313** F9
Slaton *U.S.A.* 33°26N 101°39W **314** E4
Slave → *Canada* 61°18N 113°39W **296** A6
Slave Coast *W. Afr.* 6°0N 2°30E **263** D5
Slave Lake *Canada* 55°17N 114°43W **296** B6
Slave Pt. *Canada* 61°11N 115°56W **296** A5
Slavgorod *Russia* 53°1N 78°37E **217** B9
Slavinja *Serbia* 43°9N 22°50E **202** C6
Slavkov u Brna *Czechia* 49°10N 16°52E **181** B9
Slavkovský Les ⌓ *Czechia* 50°5N 12°44E **180** A5
Slavonija *Europe* 45°20N 17°40E **182** E2
Slavonski Brod *Croatia* 45°11N 18°1E **182** E3
Slavsk *Russia* 55°3N 21°41E **184** C8
Slavske *Ukraine* 48°51N 23°27E **183** B8
Slavskoye *Russia* 54°30N 20°27E **184** D7
Slavuta *Ukraine* 50°15N 27°2E **177** C14
Slavyanka *Russia* 42°53N 131°21E **220** C5
Slavyanovo *Bulgaria* 43°28N 24°52E **203** C8
Slavyansk = Slovyansk *Ukraine* 48°55N 37°36E **189** H9
Slavyansk-na-Kubani *Russia* 45°15N 38°11E **189** K10
Sława *Poland* 51°52N 16°2E **185** G3
Slawharad *Belarus* 53°27N 31°0E **177** B16
Sławno *Poland* 54°20N 16°41E **184** D3
Sławoborze *Poland* 53°55N 15°42E **184** E2
Slea Hd. *Ireland* 52°6N 10°27W **166** D1
Sleaford *U.K.* 53°0N 0°24W **168** D7
Sleaford B. *Australia* 34°55S 135°45E **281** E2
Sleat, Sd. of *U.K.* 57°5N 5°47W **167** D3
Sleðbrjótur *Iceland* 65°34N 14°30W **155** B12
Sleeper Is. *Canada* 58°30N 81°0W **295** F15
Sleeping Bear Dunes ⌓ *U.S.A.* 44°50N 86°5W **308** C10
Sleepy Eye *U.S.A.* 44°18N 94°43W **308** C6
Sleetmute *U.S.A.* 61°42N 157°10W **303** F8
Slemon L. *Canada* 63°13N 116°4W **296** A5
Slependen *Norway* 59°52N 10°30E **133** A2
Ślesin *Poland* 52°22N 18°14E **185** F5
Slide Mt. *U.S.A.* 42°0N 74°25W **313** E10
Slidell *U.S.A.* 30°17N 89°47W **315** F10
Slidre *Norway* 61°5N 8°58E **164** C5
Sliema *Malta* 35°55N 14°30E **206** F8
Slieve Aughty *Ireland* 53°4N 8°30W **166** C3
Slieve Bloom *Ireland* 53°4N 7°40W **166** C4
Slieve Donard *U.K.* 54°11N 5°55W **166** B6
Slieve Gamph *Ireland* 54°6N 9°0W **166** B3
Slieve Gullion *U.K.* 54°7N 6°26W **166** B5
Slieve League *Ireland* 54°40N 8°42W **166** B3
Slieve Mish *Ireland* 52°12N 9°50W **166** D2
Slievenamon *Ireland* 52°25N 7°34W **166** D4
Sligeach = Sligo *Ireland* 54°16N 8°28W **166** B3
Sligo *Sligo, Ireland* 54°16N 8°28W **166** B3
Sligo *Pa., U.S.A.* 41°6N 79°29W **312** E5
Sligo ☐ *Ireland* 54°8N 8°42W **166** B3
Sligo B. *Ireland* 54°18N 8°40W **166** B3
Slipi *Indonesia* 6°11S 106°47E **122** B1
Slippery Rock *U.S.A.* 41°4N 80°3W **312** E4
Slite *Sweden* 57°42N 18°48E **163** G12
Slīteres ⌓ *Latvia* 57°41N 22°21E **184** A9
Sliven *Bulgaria* 42°42N 26°19E **203** D10
Sliven ☐ *Bulgaria* 42°42N 26°19E **203** D10
Slivenec *Czechia* 50°1N 14°21E **135** B2
Slivnitsa *Bulgaria* 42°50N 23°2E **202** D7
Sljeme *Croatia* 45°57N 15°58E **199** C12
Sloan *U.S.A.* 35°57N 115°13W **307** K11
Sloansville *U.S.A.* 42°45N 74°22W **313** D10
Slobidka *Ukraine* 47°54N 29°21E **183** C14
Slobodskoy *Russia* 58°40N 50°6E **186** C9
Slobozia *Moldova* 46°45N 29°42E **183** D14
Slobozia *Argeş, Romania* 44°30N 25°14E **183** F10
Slobozia *Ialomiţa, Romania* 44°34N 27°23E **183** F12
Slocan *Canada* 49°48N 117°28W **296** D5
Slocomb *U.S.A.* 31°7N 85°36W **316** D4
Slomikhino = Zhalpaqtal *Kazakhstan* 49°42N 49°25E **190** F9
Słomniki *Poland* 50°16N 20°4E **185** H7
Slonim *Belarus* 53°4N 25°19E **177** B13
Slot, The = New Georgia Sound *Solomon Is.* 8°0S 158°20E **287** L9
Sloten *Neths.* 52°21N 4°48E **112** A1
Sloterdijk *Neths.* 52°23N 4°51E **112** A1
Sloterpark *Neths.* 52°22N 4°49E **112** A1
Slottet *Oslo, Norway* **133** a1
Slough *U.K.* 51°30N 0°36W **169** F7
Slough ☐ *U.K.* 51°30N 0°36W **169** F7
Sloughhouse *U.S.A.* 38°26N 121°12W **306** G5
Slovak Rep. = Slovakia ■ *Europe* 48°30N 20°0E **181** C13
Slovakia ■ *Europe* 48°30N 20°0E **181** C13
Slovakian Ore Mts. = Slovenské Rudohorie *Slovakia* 48°45N 20°0E **181** C12
Slovenia ■ *Europe* 45°58N 14°30E **199** C11
Slovenija = Slovenia ■ *Europe* 45°58N 14°30E **199** C11
Slovenj Gradec *Slovenia* 46°31N 15°5E **199** B12
Slovenska = Slovakia ■ *Europe* 48°30N 20°0E **181** C13
Slovenska Bistrica *Slovenia* 46°24N 15°35E **199** B12
Slovenské Konjice *Slovenia* 46°20N 15°28E **199** B12
Slovenské Rudohorie *Slovakia* 48°45N 20°0E **181** C12
Slovenský Raj △ *Slovakia* 48°53N 20°25E **181** C13
Slovyansk *Ukraine* 48°55N 37°36E **189** H9
Słowiński △ *Poland* 54°43N 17°26E **184** D4
Słubice *Poland* 52°22N 14°35E **185** F1
Sluch → *Ukraine* 51°37N 26°38E **177** C14
Sluhy *Czechia* 50°11N 14°33E **135** A3
Sluis *Neths.* 51°18N 3°23E **170** C3
Slŭnchev Bryag = Slanchev Bryag *Bulgaria* 42°40N 27°41E **203** D11
Slunj *Croatia* 45°6N 15°33E **199** C12
Słupca *Poland* 52°15N 17°52E **185** F4
Słupia → *Poland* 54°35N 16°51E **184** D3
Słupsk *Poland* 54°30N 17°3E **184** D4
Slurry *S. Africa* 25°49S 25°42E **270** C4
Slutsk = Pavlovsk *Russia* 50°26N 40°5E **190** E5
Slutsk *Belarus* 53°2N 27°31E **177** B14
Służew *Poland* 52°10N 21°1E **143** B2
Służewiec *Poland* 52°10N 21°0E **143** B2
Slyne Hd. *Ireland* 53°25N 10°10W **166** C1
Slyudyanka *Russia* 51°40N 103°40E **215** D11
Smaalenene = Østfold ☐ *Norway* 59°25N 11°25E **164** E8
Småland *Sweden* 57°15N 15°25E **163** G9
Smålandsfarvandet *Denmark* 55°10N 11°20E **163** J5
Smålandsstenar *Sweden* 57°10N 13°25E **163** G7
Smaldeel = Theunissen *S. Africa* 28°26S 26°43E **270** C4
Smalltree L. *Canada* 61°0N 105°0W **297** A8
Smallwood Res. *Canada* 54°5N 64°30W **299** B7
Smara *W. Sahara* 26°48N 11°41W **260** C2
Smarhon *Belarus* 54°20N 26°24E **177** A14
Smarje *Slovenia* 46°15N 15°34E **199** B12
Smartt Syndicate Dam *S. Africa* 30°45S 23°10E **270** D3
Smartville *U.S.A.* 39°13N 121°18W **306** F5
Smeaton *Canada* 53°30N 104°49W **297** C8
Smedby *Sweden* 56°41N 16°13E **163** H10
Smederevo *Serbia* 44°40N 20°57E **202** B4
Smederevska Palanka *Serbia* 44°22N 20°58E **202** B4
Smedjebacken *Sweden* 60°8N 15°25E **162** D9
Smela = Smila *Ukraine* 49°15N 31°58E **189** H6
Smeralda, Costa *Italy* 41°5N 9°35E **200** A2
Smerwick Harbour *Ireland* 52°12N 10°23W **166** D1
Smethport *U.S.A.* 41°49N 78°27W **312** E6
Smíchov *Czechia* 50°4N 14°23E **135** B2
Smidovich *Russia* 48°36N 133°49E **215** E14
Śmigiel *Poland* 52°1N 16°32E **185** F3
Smila *Ukraine* 49°15N 31°58E **189** H6
Smilyan *Bulgaria* 41°29N 24°46E **203** E8
Smith *Canada* 55°10N 114°0W **296** B6
Smith B. *U.S.A.* 70°30N 154°20W **303** A9
Smith Center *U.S.A.* 39°47N 98°47W **308** F4
Smith Forest Preserve *U.S.A.* 41°59N 87°45W **119** B2
Smith I. *Nunavut, Canada* 60°45N 78°25W **295** E16
Smith I. *India* 13°20N 93°4E **245** H11
Smith Islands △ *Australia* 20°40S 149°9E **280** b
Smith River ⌓ *U.S.A.* 41°55N 124°0W **304** F2
Smith Sd. *N. Amer.* 78°25N 74°0W **154** B3
Smithburne → *Australia* 17°3S 140°57E **280** B3
Smithers *Canada* 54°45N 127°10W **296** C3
Smithfield *Free State, S. Africa* 30°9S 26°30E **271** D4
Smithfield *N.C., U.S.A.* 35°31N 78°21W **315** D15
Smithfield *Utah, U.S.A.* 41°50N 111°50W **304** F8
Smiths *U.S.A.* 32°32N 85°6W **316** C4
Smiths Falls *Canada* 44°55N 76°0W **313** B9
Smithsonian Institution *Washington, D.C., U.S.A.* **143** b2
Smithton *Australia* 40°53S 145°6E **281** G4
Smithville *Ont., Canada* 43°6N 79°33W **312** C5
Smithville *Ga., U.S.A.* 31°54N 84°15W **316** D5
Smithville *Mo., U.S.A.* 39°23N 94°35W **310** E2
Smithville *Tex., U.S.A.* 30°1N 97°10W **314** F6
Smoke Creek Desert *U.S.A.* 40°30N 119°40W **304** F4
Smoky → *Canada* 56°10N 117°21W **296** B5
Smoky Bay *Australia* 32°22S 134°13E **281** E1
Smoky Hill → *U.S.A.* 39°4N 96°48W **308** F5
Smoky Hills *U.S.A.* 39°15N 99°30W **308** F4
Smoky Lake *Canada* 54°10N 112°30W **296** C6
Smøla *Norway* 63°23N 8°3E **164** A5
Smolensk *Russia* 54°45N 32°5E **188** E7
Smolensk ☐ *Russia* 55°20N 33°0E **188** E7
Smolenskoye Poozerye △ *Russia* 55°35N 31°50E **188** E6
Smolikas, Oros *Greece* 40°9N 20°58E **202** F4
Smolník *Slovakia* 48°43N 20°44E **181** C13
Smolny *Russia* 59°56N 30°25E **137** B2
Smolny △ *Russia* 54°50N 47°10E **190** C7
Smolny Cathedral *Russia* 59°56N 30°24E **137** B2
Smolyan *Bulgaria* 41°36N 24°38E **203** E8
Smolyan ☐ *Bulgaria* 41°36N 24°38E **203** E8
Smooth Rock Falls *Canada* 49°17N 81°37W **298** C3
Smoothstone L. *Canada* 54°40N 106°50W **297** C7
Smorgon = Smarhon *Belarus* 54°20N 26°24E **177** A14
Smotrych *Ukraine* 48°57N 26°33E **183** B11
Smotrych → *Ukraine* 48°34N 26°39E **183** B11
Smulţi *Romania* 45°57N 27°44E **183** E12
Smyadovo *Bulgaria* 43°2N 27°1E **203** C11
Smygehamn *Sweden* 55°21N 13°22E **163** J7
Smygehuk *Sweden* 55°20N 13°20E **163** J7
Smyley I. *Antarctica* 72°55S 78°0W **151** D17
Smyrna = İzmir *Turkey* 38°25N 27°8E **205** C9
Smyrna *Del., U.S.A.* 39°18N 75°36W **309** F16
Smyrna *Ga., U.S.A.* 33°53N 84°31W **316** B5
Snæfell *Iceland* 64°48N 15°34W **155** C11
Snaefell *I. of Man* 54°16N 4°27W **168** C3
Snæfellsjökull *Iceland* 64°49N 23°46W **155** C3
Snæfellsjökull △ *Iceland* 64°48N 23°47W **155** C3
Snæfellsnessýsla *Iceland* 65°0N 23°0W **155** C3
Snake → *U.S.A.* 46°12N 119°2W **304** C4
Snake Creek Canal *U.S.A.* 25°57N 80°19W **129** C2
Snake I. = Zmiinyi, Ostriv *Black Sea* 45°15N 30°12E **189** K6
Snake I. *Australia* 38°47S 146°33E **283** E7
Snake Pt. *Anguilla* 18°17N 62°58W **322** a
Snake Range *U.S.A.* 39°0N 114°20W **304** G6
Snake River Plain *U.S.A.* 42°50N 114°0W **304** E7
Snarøya *Norway* 59°52N 10°33E **133** A2
Snasahögarna *Sweden* 63°13N 12°21E **162** A6
Snåsavatnet *Norway* 64°12N 12°0E **160** D15
Snättringe *Sweden* 59°15N 17°58E **139** B1
Snedsted *Denmark* 56°55N 8°32E **163** H2
Sneek *Neths.* 53°2N 5°40E **170** A5
Sneem *Ireland* 51°50N 9°54W **166** E2
Sneeuberge *S. Africa* 31°46S 24°20E **270** D3
Snegurovka = Tetiyev *Ukraine* 49°22N 29°38E **177** D15
Snejbjerg *Denmark* 56°8N 8°54E **163** H2
Snelling *Calif., U.S.A.* 37°31N 120°26W **306** H6
Snelling *S.C., U.S.A.* 33°15N 81°27W **316** B8
Snells Beach *N.Z.* 36°25S 174°44E **284** C3
Snezhnoye *Ukraine* 48°0N 38°58E **189** J10
Sněžka *Europe* 50°41N 15°50E **185** A8
Snežnik *Slovenia* 45°36N 14°35E **199** C11
Śniadowo *Poland* 53°2N 22°0E **185** E8
Śniardwy, Jezioro *Poland* 53°48N 21°50E **184** E8
Śnieżka *Europe* 50°44N 15°44E **180** A8
Snigirevka = Snihurivka *Ukraine* 47°2N 32°49E **189** J7
Snihurivka *Ukraine* 47°2N 32°49E **189** J7
Snillfjord *Norway* 63°24N 9°30E **164** A6
Snina *Slovakia* 48°58N 22°9E **181** C15
Snizort, L. *U.K.* 57°33N 6°28W **167** D2
Snøhetta *Norway* 62°19N 9°16E **164** B6
Snohomish *U.S.A.* 47°55N 122°6W **306** C4
Snønuten *Norway* 59°31N 6°52E **164** E3
Snoqualmie *U.S.A.* 47°31N 121°49W **306** C5
Snoqualmie Pass *U.S.A.* 47°25N 121°25W **306** C5
Snoul *Cambodia* 12°4N 106°26E **237** F6
Snover *U.S.A.* 43°27N 82°58W **312** C2
Snovsk = Shchors *Ukraine* 51°48N 31°56E **189** G6
Snow Hill *U.S.A.* 38°11N 75°24W **309** F16
Snow Lake *Canada* 54°52N 100°3W **297** C8
Snow Mt. *Calif., U.S.A.* 39°23N 122°45W **306** F4
Snow Mt. *Maine, U.S.A.* 45°18N 70°48W **313** A14
Snow Shoe *U.S.A.* 41°2N 77°57W **312** E7
Snowbird L. *Canada* 60°45N 103°0W **297** A8
Snowdon *U.K.* 53°4N 4°5W **168** D3
Snowdonia △ *U.K.* 53°7N 3°59W **168** D4
Snowdoun *U.S.A.* 32°15N 86°18W **316** C3
Snowdrift = Łutsel K'e *Canada* 62°24N 110°44W **297** A6
Snowdrift → *Canada* 62°24N 110°44W **297** A6
Snowflake *U.S.A.* 34°30N 110°5W **305** J8
Snowshoe Pk. *U.S.A.* 48°13N 115°41W **304** B6
Snowtown *Australia* 33°46S 138°14E **282** B3
Snowville *U.S.A.* 41°58N 112°43W **304** F7
Snowy → *Australia* 37°46S 148°30E **283** D8
Snowy Mt. *U.S.A.* 43°42N 74°23W **313** C10
Snowy Mts. *Australia* 36°30S 148°20E **283** D8
Snowy River △ *Australia* 37°15S 147°29E **283** D7
Snug Corner *The Bahamas* 22°33N 73°52W **321** B5
Snug Harbour *Canada* 45°22N 80°17W **312** A4
Snyatyn *Ukraine* 48°27N 25°38E **183** B10
Snyder *Okla., U.S.A.* 34°40N 98°57W **314** D5
Snyder *Tex., U.S.A.* 32°44N 100°55W **314** E4
So Kwun Wat *Hong Kong, China* 22°23N 114°0E **122** A2
Soacha *Colombia* 4°35N 74°13W **328** C3
Soahanina *Madag.* 18°42S 44°13E **272** B1
Soalala *Madag.* 16°6S 45°20E **272** B2
Soaloka *Madag.* 18°32S 45°15E **272** B2
Soamanonga *Madag.* 23°52S 44°47E **272** C1
Soan → *Pakistan* 33°1N 71°44E **242** C4
Soanierana-Ivongo *Madag.* 16°55S 49°35E **272** B2
Soanindraniny *Madag.* 19°54S 47°14E **272** B2
Şoarş *Romania* 45°56N 24°55E **183** E9
Soavina *Madag.* 20°23S 46°56E **272** C2
Soavinandriana *Madag.* 19°9S 46°45E **272** B2
Soba *Nigeria* 10°58N 8°4E **263** C6
Sobaeksan △ *S. Korea* 36°50N 128°25E **224** D4
Sobat → *South Sudan* 9°22N 31°33E **257** F3
Soběslav *Czechia* 49°16N 14°45E **180** B7
Sobhapur *India* 22°47N 78°17E **242** H8
Sobinka *Russia* 56°0N 40°0E **188** E11
Sobo-Yama *Japan* 32°51N 131°22E **222** E3
Søborg *Denmark* 55°43N 12°29E **118** A2
Sobótka *Poland* 50°54N 16°44E **185** H3
Sobra *Croatia* 42°44N 17°34E **199** F14
Sobradinho, Represa de *Brazil* 9°30S 42°0W **332** C3
Sobral *Brazil* 3°50S 40°20W **332** B3
Sobrance *Slovakia* 48°45N 22°11E **181** C15
Sobreda *Portugal* 38°39N 9°11W **126** B1
Sobreira Formosa *Portugal* 39°46N 7°51W **194** F3
Soc Giang *Vietnam* 22°54N 106°1E **228** F6
Soc Trang *Vietnam* 9°37N 105°50E **237** H5
Soča → *Europe* 46°20N 13°40E **180** E6
Socastee *U.S.A.* 33°41N 78°59W **315** E15
Soccer City Stadium *Johannesburg, S. Africa* 26°14S 27°59E **123** B1
Soccsksargen ☐ *Phil.* 6°30N 125°0E **233** J5
Sochaczew *Poland* 52°15N 20°13E **185** F7
Soch'e = Shache *China* 38°20N 77°10E **217** E9
Sochi *Russia* 43°35N 39°40E **191** J4
Sochi ✈ **(AER)** *Russia* 43°27N 39°57E **191** J4
Sochi △ *Russia* 43°40N 39°35E **191** J4
Sochos *Greece* 40°48N 23°22E **202** F7
Social Circle *U.S.A.* 33°39N 83°43W **316** B6
Société, Îs. de la *French Polynesia* 17°0S 151°0W **289** f
Society Hill *U.S.A.* 32°26N 85°27W **316** C4
Society Is. = Société, Îs. de la *French Polynesia* 17°0S 151°0W **289** f
Socompa, Portezuelo de *Chile* 24°27S 68°18W **334** A2
Socorro = Fronteiras *Brazil* 7°5S 40°37W **332** C3
Socorro *Colombia* 6°29N 73°16W **328** B3
Socorro *Phil.* 9°37N 125°58E **233** G5
Socorro *N. Mex., U.S.A.* 34°4N 106°54W **305** J10
Socorro *Tex., U.S.A.* 31°39N 106°18W **314** F1
Socorro, I. *Mexico* 18°45N 110°58W **318** D2
Socotra *Yemen* 12°30N 54°0E **249** D6
Socovos *Spain* 38°20N 1°58W **197** G3
Socuéllamos *Spain* 39°16N 2°47W **197** F2
Soda L. *U.S.A.* 35°10N 116°4W **307** K10
Soda Plains *India* 35°30N 79°0E **243** B8
Soda Springs *U.S.A.* 42°39N 111°36W **304** E8
Sodankylä *Finland* 67°29N 26°40E **160** C22
Soddy-Daisy *U.S.A.* 35°17N 85°10W **315** D12
Söderala *Sweden* 61°17N 16°55E **162** C10
Söderåsen △ *Sweden* 56°2N 13°13E **163** H7
Söderbärke *Sweden* 60°5N 15°33E **162** D9
Söderby *Sweden* 59°24N 18°12E **139** A3
Söderfors *Sweden* 60°23N 17°25E **162** D11
Söderhamn *Sweden* 61°18N 17°10E **162** C11
Söderköping *Sweden* 58°31N 16°20E **163** F10
Södermalm *Sweden* 59°18N 18°4E **139** B2
Södermanland *Sweden* 58°56N 16°55E **161** G17
Södermanland ☐ *Sweden* 59°10N 16°30E **162** E10
Södertälje *Sweden* 59°12N 17°39E **162** E11
Sodiri *Sudan* 14°27N 29°0E **257** E2
Sodo *Ethiopia* 7°0N 37°41E **257** F4
Sodpur *India* 22°42N 88°24E **124** A2
Södra Finnskoga *Sweden* 60°42N 12°34E **162** D6
Södra Sandby *Sweden* 55°43N 13°21E **163** J7
Södra Ulvön *Sweden* 62°59N 18°38E **162** B12
Södra Vi *Sweden* 57°45N 15°45E **163** G9
Sodražica *Slovenia* 45°45N 14°39E **199** C11
Sodus *U.S.A.* 43°14N 77°4W **312** C7
Sodwana Bay △ *S. Africa* 27°35S 32°43E **271** C5
Soe *Indonesia* 9°52S 124°17E **278** A3
Soekmekaar = Morebeng *S. Africa* 23°30S 29°55E **271** B4
Soest *Nordrhein-Westfalen, Germany* 51°34N 8°7E **178** D4
Soest *Neths.* 52°9N 5°19E **170** B5
Soeurs, Î. des *Canada* 45°27N 73°32W **130** B2
Sofades *Greece* 39°20N 22°4E **204** B4
Sofaïa *Guadeloupe* 16°17N 61°43W **322** e
Sofala ☐ *Mozam.* 19°30S 34°30E **271** A5
Sofara *Mali* 13°59N 4°9W **262** C4
Sofia *Bulgaria* 42°45N 23°20E **202** D7
Sofia ☐ *Madag.* 14°50S 48°0E **272** A2
Sofia → *Madag.* 15°27S 47°23E **272** B2
Sofia ✈ **(SOF)** *Bulgaria* 42°46N 23°28E **202** D7
Sofia-Grad ☐ *Bulgaria* 42°35N 23°20E **202** D7
Sofievka *Ukraine* 48°6N 33°55E **189** H7
Sofiko *Greece* 37°47N 23°3E **204** D5
Sofiya = Sofia *Bulgaria* 42°45N 23°20E **202** D7
Sofiya = Sofia *Bulgaria* 42°45N 23°20E **202** D7
Sofrana *Greece* 36°5N 26°24E **205** E8
Sōfu-Gan *Japan* 29°49N 140°21E **221** K10
Sogakofe *Ghana* 6°2N 0°39E **263** D5
Sogamoso *Colombia* 5°43N 72°56W **328** B3
Sogār *Iran* 25°53N 58°6E **247** E8
Sögel *Germany* 52°50N 7°31E **178** C3
Sogeri *Papua N. G.* 9°26S 147°35E **286** E4
Sogn og Fjordane ☐ *Norway* 61°40N 6°45E **164** C3
Sogndalsfjøra *Norway* 61°14N 7°5E **164** C4
Søgne *Norway* 58°5N 7°48E **164** F4
Sognefjorden *Norway* 61°10N 5°50E **164** C2
Sognsvatn *Norway* 59°58N 10°43E **133** A3
Sogod *Phil.* 10°28N 124°59E **233** F5
Söğüt *Bilecik, Turkey* 40°2N 30°11E **205** A12
Söğüt *Burdur, Turkey* 37°2N 29°50E **205** D11
Söğüt Dağı *Turkey* 37°50N 29°55E **205** D11
Söğütköy *Turkey* 36°40N 28°8E **205** E10
Soh *Iran* 33°26N 51°27E **247** C6
Sohâg *Egypt* 26°33N 31°43E **256** B3
Sohagpur *India* 22°42N 78°12E **242** H8
Sohano *Papua N. G.* 5°22S 154°37E **286** C8
Sohar = Şuḩār *Oman* 24°20N 56°40E **247** E8
Sohela *India* 21°18N 83°24E **244** D6
Soheuksando *S. Korea* 34°4N 125°7E **224** E2
Sohm Abyssal Plain *Atl. Oc.* 36°0N 55°0W **152** C6
Soho *London, U.K.* **125** b3
Soho *New York, U.S.A.* **132** e1
Sohoton △ *Phil.* 11°22N 125°6E **233** F5
Soignes, Forêt de *Belgium* 50°47N 4°25E **116** B2
Soignies *Belgium* 50°35N 4°5E **170** D4
Soin *Burkina Faso* 12°47N 3°50W **262** C4
Soira *Eritrea* 14°45N 39°30E **257** E4
Soissons *France* 49°25N 3°19E **173** C10
Sōja *Japan* 34°40N 133°45E **222** C5
Sojat *India* 25°55N 73°45E **242** G5
Sok → *Russia* 53°24N 50°8E **190** D10
Sok Kwu Wan *Hong Kong, China* 22°12N 114°7E **122** B2
Sokal *Ukraine* 50°31N 24°15E **177** C13
Sokcho *S. Korea* 38°12N 128°36E **224** C4
Söke *Turkey* 37°48N 27°28E **205** D9
Sokelo *Dem. Rep. of the Congo* 9°55S 24°36E **265** D4
Sokhumi *Georgia* 43°0N 41°0E **191** J5
Sokki, Oued In → *Algeria* 29°30N 3°42E **261** C5
Sokna *Norway* 60°16N 9°58E **164** D6
Soknedal *Norway* 62°57N 10°13E **164** B7
Soko Banja *Serbia* 43°40N 21°51E **202** C5
Soko Is. *Hong Kong, China* 22°10N 113°54E **122** B1
Sokodé *Togo* 9°0N 1°11E **263** D5
Sokol *Russia* 59°30N 40°5E **188** C11
Sokolac *Bos.-H.* 43°56N 18°48E **182** G3
Sokółka *Poland* 53°25N 23°30E **184** E10
Sokolniki *Russia* 55°47N 37°40E **129** B3
Sokolniki Park *Russia* 55°48N 37°40E **129** B3
Sokolo *Ségou, Mali* 14°53N 6°8W **262** C3
Sokolo *Sikasso, Mali* 10°52N 6°59W **262** C3
Sokolov *Czechia* 50°12N 12°40E **180** A5
Sokołów *Poland* 52°9N 20°51E **143** C1
Sokołów Małpolski *Poland* 50°12N 22°7E **185** H9
Sokołów Podlaski *Poland* 52°25N 22°15E **185** F9
Sokoły *Poland* 52°59N 22°42E **185** F9
Sokoto *Nigeria* 13°2N 5°16E **263** C6
Sokoto ☐ *Nigeria* 12°30N 6°0E **263** C6
Sokoto → *Nigeria* 11°20N 4°10E **263** C5
Sokyrnytsya *Ukraine* 48°7N 23°23E **183** B8
Sokyryany *Ukraine* 48°27N 27°25E **183** B12
Sol, Costa del *Spain* 36°30N 4°30W **195** J6
Sol Iletsk *Russia* 51°10N 55°0E **186** D10
Sola *Rogaland, Norway* 58°53N 5°36E **164** F2
Sola *Vanuatu* 13°51S 167°33E **287** C5
Sola → *Poland* 50°4N 19°15E **185** H6
Solai *Kenya* 0°2N 36°12E **268** B4
Solalinden *Germany* 48°5N 11°42E **131** B3
Solan *India* 30°55N 77°7E **242** D7
Solana *Phil.* 17°39N 121°41E **232** C3
Solana Beach *U.S.A.* 32°58N 117°16W **307** N9
Solander I. *N.Z.* 46°34S 166°54E **285** G1
Solano *Phil.* 16°31N 121°15E **232** C3
Solapur *India* 17°43N 75°56E **244** F2
Solca *Romania* 47°40N 25°50E **183** C10
Solda Gölü *Turkey* 37°33N 29°42E **205** D11
Soldăneşti *Moldova* 47°49N 28°48E **183** C13
Soldeu *Andorra* 42°35N 1°40E **196** C6
Soldier Pt. *Antigua & B.* 17°2N 61°41W **322** b
Soldin = Myślibórz *Poland* 52°55N 14°50E **185** F1
Soldotna *U.S.A.* 60°29N 151°3W **303** F10
Soléa *Cyprus* 35°5N 33°4E **207** E9
Solec Kujawski *Poland* 53°5N 18°14E **185** E5
Soledad *Colombia* 10°55N 74°46W **328** A3
Soledad *Calif., U.S.A.* 36°26N 121°20W **306** J5
Soledad *Venezuela* 8°10N 63°34W **329** B5
Sølen *Norway* 61°53N 11°31E **164** C8
Solent, The *U.K.* 50°45N 1°25W **169** G6
Solenzara *France* 41°53N 9°23E **175** G13
Solesmes *France* 50°10N 3°30E **173** B10
Solferino *Italy* 45°22N 10°34E **198** C7
Solfonntaggen *Norway* 60°2N 6°57E **164** D3
Solhan *Turkey* 38°57N 41°3E **213** C9
Solheim *Norway* 60°53N 5°27E **164** D2
Soligalich *Russia* 59°5N 42°10E **186** C7
Soligorsk = Salihorsk *Belarus* 52°51N 27°27E **177** B14
Solihull *U.K.* 52°26N 1°47W **169** E6
Solikamsk *Russia* 59°38N 56°50E **186** C10
Solila *Madag.* 21°25S 46°37E **272** C2
Solimões = Amazonas → *S. Amer.* 0°5S 50°0W **329** D8
Solin *Croatia* 43°33N 16°30E **199** E13
Solingen *Germany* 51°10N 7°5E **178** D3
Söll *Austria* 47°30N 12°11E **179** H8
Sollebrunn *Sweden* 58°8N 12°32E **163** F6
Sollefteå *Sweden* 63°12N 17°20E **162** A11
Sollentuna *Sweden* 59°25N 17°56E **139** A1
Sóller *Spain* 39°46N 2°43E **206** B3
Sollerön *Sweden* 60°55N 14°37E **162** D8
Solling *Germany* 51°42N 9°38E **178** D5
Solling-Vogler ⌓ *Germany* 51°45N 9°32E **178** D5
Solln *Germany* 48°4N 11°31E **131** B2
Sollsvika *Norway* 60°26N 4°58E **164** D1
Solna *Sweden* 59°21N 17°59E **139** A1
Solnechnogorsk *Russia* 56°10N 36°57E **188** D9
Solo → *Indonesia* 6°47S 112°22E **231** G15
Solofra *Italy* 40°50N 14°51E **201** B7
Sologne *France* 47°40N 1°45E **173** E8
Solok *Indonesia* 0°45S 100°40E **234** C2
Sololá *Guatemala* 14°49N 91°10W **320** D1
Sololo *Kenya* 3°33N 38°39E **268** B4
Solomon, N. Fork → *U.S.A.* 39°29N 98°26W **308** F4
Solomon, S. Fork → *U.S.A.* 39°25N 99°12W **308** F4
Solomon Is. *Papua N. G.* 6°0S 155°0E **286** D8
Solomon Is. ■ *Pac. Oc.* 6°0S 155°0E **287** L8
Solomon Rise *Pac. Oc.* 1°0N 157°0E **288** G7
Solomon Sea *Papua N. G.* 7°0S 150°0E **286** D6
Solon *China* 46°32N 121°10E **219** B13
Solon Springs *U.S.A.* 46°22N 91°49W **308** B8
Solonópole *Brazil* 5°44S 39°1W **332** C4
Solor *Indonesia* 8°27S 123°0E **231** F6
Solotcha *Russia* 54°48N 39°53E **188** E10
Solothurn *Switz.* 47°13N 7°32E **179** H3
Solothurn ☐ *Switz.* 47°18N 7°40E **179** H3
Solotvyn *Ukraine* 48°42N 24°25E **183** B9
Solovetskiye Ostrova *Russia* 65°5N 35°40E **186** B6
Solsona *Phil.* 18°5N 120°46E **232** B3
Solsona *Spain* 42°0N 1°31E **196** C6
Solt *Hungary* 46°45N 19°1E **182** D4
Šolta *Croatia* 43°24N 16°15E **199** E13
Solţānābād *Khorāsān, Iran* 34°13N 59°58E **247** C8
Solţānābād *Khorāsān, Iran* 36°29N 58°5E **247** B8
Soltāniyeh *Iran* 36°26N 48°47E **213** D13
Soltau *Germany* 52°59N 9°50E **178** C5
Soltsy *Russia* 58°10N 30°30E **188** C6
Soltüstik Qazaqstan ☐ *Kazakhstan* 54°0N 70°0E **217** B8
Solund *Norway* 61°5N 4°50E **164** C1
Solunska Glava *N. Macedonia* 41°44N 21°31E **202** E5
Solvang *U.S.A.* 34°36N 120°8W **307** L6
Solvay *U.S.A.* 43°3N 76°13W **313** C8
Sölvesborg *Sweden* 56°5N 14°35E **163** H8
Solvychegodsk *Russia* 61°21N 46°56E **186** B8
Solway Firth *U.K.* 54°49N 3°35W **168** C4
Solwezi *Zambia* 12°11S 26°21E **269** E2
Sōma *Japan* 37°40N 140°50E **220** F10
Soma *Turkey* 39°10N 27°35E **205** B9
Somabhula *Zimbabwe* 19°42S 29°40E **271** A4
Somali = Sumale ☐ *Ethiopia* 7°0N 45°0E **267** C6
Somali Pen. *Africa* 7°0N 46°0E **254** F8
Somalia ■ *Africa* 7°0N 47°0E **267** C6
Somaliland ☐ *Somalia* 10°0N 46°0E **267** C6
Sombe Dzong *Bhutan* 27°13N 89°8E **241** B2
Sombernon *France* 47°20N 4°40E **173** E11
Sombo *Angola* 8°42S 20°59E **265** D4
Sombor *Serbia* 45°46N 19°9E **182** E4
Sombra *Canada* 42°43N 82°29W **312** D2
Sombrerete *Mexico* 23°38N 103°39W **318** C4
Sombrero *Anguilla* 18°37N 63°30W **321** C7
Sombrero Channel *India* 7°41N 93°35E **245** L11
Şomcuta Mare *Romania* 47°31N 23°28E **183** C8
Somdari *India* 25°47N 72°38E **242** G5
Someido ⌓ *Spain* 43°5N 6°11W **194** B4
Somers *U.S.A.* 48°5N 114°13W **304** B6
Somerset *Bermuda* 32°17N 64°52W **153** a
Somerset *Ky., U.S.A.* 37°5N 84°36W **309** G11
Somerset *Mass., U.S.A.* 41°47N 71°8W **313** E13
Somerset *Md., U.S.A.* 38°57N 77°5W **143** B2
Somerset *Pa., U.S.A.* 40°1N 79°5W **312** F5
Somerset ☐ *U.K.* 51°9N 3°0W **169** F5
Somerset East *S. Africa* 32°42S 25°35E **270** D4
Somerset I. *Bermuda* 32°17N 64°52W **153** a
Somerset I. *Nunavut, Canada* 73°30N 93°0W **294** C13
Somerset West *S. Africa* 34°8S 18°50E **270** D2
Somersworth *U.S.A.* 43°16N 70°52W **313** C14
Somerton *U.S.A.* 32°36N 114°43W **305** K6
Somerville *Mass., U.S.A.* 42°22N 71°5W **116** A2
Somerville *N.J., U.S.A.* 40°35N 74°38W **313** F10
Someş → *Romania* 47°49N 22°43E **182** C7
Someşul Mare → *Romania* 47°9N 23°55E **183** C8
Somme ☐ *France* 49°57N 2°20E **173** C9
Somme → *France* 50°11N 1°38E **173** B8
Somme, B. de la *France* 50°14N 1°33E **172** B8
Sommen *Jönköping, Sweden* 58°12N 14°58E **163** F8
Sommen *Östergötland, Sweden* 58°0N 15°15E **163** F9
Sommepy-Tahure *France* 49°15N 4°31E **173** C11
Sömmerda *Germany* 51°9N 11°7E **178** D7
Sommerfeld = Lubsko *Poland* 51°45N 14°57E **185** G1
Sommesous *France* 48°44N 4°12E **173** D11
Sommières *France* 43°47N 4°6E **175** E8
Somnath *India* 20°53N 70°22E **242** J4
Somogy ☐ *Hungary* 46°19N 17°30E **182** D2
Somogyszob *Hungary* 46°18N 17°20E **182** D2
Somosomo *Fiji* 16°47S 179°58W **287** A3
Somosomo Str. *Fiji* 16°0S 180°0E **287** A3
Somoto *Nic.* 13°28N 86°37W **320** D2
Sompolno *Poland* 52°26N 18°30E **185** F5
Somport, Túnel de *Spain* 42°48N 0°31W **196** C4
Somuncurá, Meseta de *Argentina* 41°30S 67°0W **336** B3
Somvarpet *India* 12°36N 75°52E **245** H2
Son *Norway* 59°32N 10°42E **164** E7
Son → *India* 25°42N 84°52E **243** G11
Son, Laem *Thailand* 7°59N 98°16E **237** a
Son Ha *Vietnam* 15°3N 108°34E **236** E7
Son La *Vietnam* 21°20N 103°50E **228** G4
Son Morrell *Spain* 39°44N 3°20E **206** B4
Son Rapinya *Spain* 39°35N 2°37E **206** B3
Son Sardina *Spain* 39°37N 2°40E **206** B3
Son Serra *Spain* 39°43N 3°13E **206** B4
Son Servera *Spain* 39°37N 3°21E **206** B4
Son Tay *Vietnam* 21°8N 105°30E **228** G5
Son Tinh *Vietnam* 15°10N 108°40E **236** E7
Soná *Panama* 8°0N 81°20W **320** E3
Sonamarg *India* 34°18N 75°21E **243** B6
Sonamukhi *India* 23°18N 87°27E **243** H12
Sonamura *India* 23°29N 91°15E **241** D3
Sonar → *India* 24°24N 79°56E **243** G8
Sonari *India* 18°54N 72°59E **130** B2
Sŏnch'ŏn *N. Korea* 39°48N 124°55E **224** C2
Sondags → *S. Africa* 33°44S 25°51E **270** D4
Sóndalo *Italy* 46°20N 10°19E **198** B7
Søndeled *Norway* 58°46N 9°3E **164** F6
Sønder Felding *Denmark* 55°57N 8°47E **163** J2
Sønder Omme *Denmark* 55°50N 8°54E **163** J2
Sønderborg *Denmark* 54°55N 9°49E **163** K3
Sondershausen *Germany* 51°22N 10°51E **178** D6
Søndersø *Denmark* 55°46N 12°21E **118** A2
Søndre Bergenhaus = Hordaland ☐ *Norway* 60°25N 6°15E **164** D3
Søndre Strømfjord = Kangerlussuaq *Greenland* 66°59N 50°40W **154** D5
Søndre Trøndhjem = Sør-Trøndelag ☐ *Norway* 63°0N 11°0E **164** A7
Sóndrio *Italy* 46°10N 9°52E **198** B6
Sondur → *India* 20°40N 82°1E **244** D6
Sone *Mozam.* 17°23S 34°55E **269** F3
Sonepur *India* 20°55N 83°50E **244** D6
Sonfim *Brazil* 6°0S 67°52W **330** B4
Song *Nigeria* 9°49N 12°39E **263** D7
Song *Thailand* 18°28N 100°11E **236** C3
Song Cau *Vietnam* 13°27N 109°18E **236** F7
Song-Köl *Kyrgyzstan* 41°50N 75°12E **217** D9
Song Ma *Vietnam* 20°56N 103°53E **228** G4
Song Qingling, Former Residence of *Beijing, China* **114** a2
Song Xian *China* 34°12N 112°8E **226** G7
Songadh *India* 21°9N 73°33E **244** D1
Songan *Indonesia* 8°13S 115°24E **231** J18
Songavatnet *Norway* 59°52N 7°32E **164** E4
Songdo *S. Korea* 37°23N 126°39E **224** D3
Songea *Tanzania* 10°40S 35°40E **269** E4
Songeons *France* 49°32N 1°50E **173** C8
Sŏnggan *N. Korea* 40°47N 126°34E **224** B3
Songgang *China* 22°46N 113°50E **219** a
Songhua Hu *China* 43°35N 126°50E **227** C14
Songhua Jiang → *China* 47°45N 132°30E **219** B15
Songimvelo ⌓ *S. Africa* 25°50S 31°2E **271** C5
Songjiang *Jilin, China* 42°34N 128°20E **224** A4
Songjiang *Shanghai, China* 31°1N 121°12E **229** B13
Songjianghe *China* 42°10N 127°29E **224** A3
Sŏngjin = Kimch'aek *N. Korea* 40°40N 129°10E **224** B4
Songkan *China* 28°35N 106°52E **228** C6
Songkhla *Thailand* 7°13N 100°37E **237** J3
Songming *China* 25°12N 103°2E **228** E4
Songnim *N. Korea* 38°45N 125°39E **224** C2
Songnisan △ *S. Korea* 36°28N 127°45E **224** D3
Songo *Angola* 7°22S 14°51E **265** D2
Songo *Mozam.* 15°34S 32°38E **271** A5
Songololo = Mbanza Ngungu *Dem. Rep. of the Congo* 5°12S 14°53E **265** D2
Songololo *Dem. Rep. of the Congo* 5°42S 14°2E **265** D2
Songpa *S. Korea* 37°30N 127°7E **137** B2
Songpan *China* 32°40N 103°30E **228** A4
Songtao *China* 28°11N 109°10E **228** C7
Songwe *Dem. Rep. of the Congo* 3°20S 26°16E **268** C2

Songwe → Africa 9°44S 33°58E 269 D3
Songxi China 27°31N 118°44E 229 D12
Songzi China 30°12N 111°45E 229 B8
Sonhat India 23°29N 82°31E 243 H10
Sonid Youqi China 42°45N 112°48E 226 C7
Sonid Zuoqi China 43°50N 113°42E 226 C7
Sonipat India 29°0N 77°5E 242 E7
Sonkach India 22°59N 76°21E 242 H7
Sonkovo Russia 57°50N 37°5E 188 D9
Sonmiani Pakistan 25°25N 66°40E 242 G2
Sonmiani B. Pakistan 25°15N 66°30E 242 G2
Sonneberg Germany 50°21N 11°10E 179 F7
Sonnino Italy 41°25N 13°14E 200 A6
Sono → Minas Gerais, Brazil 17°2S 45°32W 333 E2
Sono → Tocantins, Brazil 9°58S 48°11W 332 C2
Sonobe = Nantan Japan 35°6N 135°28E 223 B7
Sonoma U.S.A. 38°18N 122°28W 306 G4
Sonora Calif., U.S.A. 37°59N 120°23W 306 H6
Sonora Tex., U.S.A. 30°34N 100°39W 314 F4
Sonora □ Mexico 29°20N 110°40W 318 B2
Sonora → Mexico 29°5N 110°55W 318 B2
Sonoran Desert U.S.A. 33°40N 113°30W 307 L12
Sonoyta Mexico 31°51N 112°50W 318 A2
Sonqor Iran 34°47N 47°36E 213 E12
Sonseca Spain 39°42N 3°57W 195 F7
Sonsón Colombia 5°43N 75°18W 328 B2
Sonsonate El Salv. 13°43N 89°44W 320 D2
Sonstorp Sweden 58°44N 15°38E 163 F9
Sonthofen Germany 47°30N 10°16E 179 H6
Sony Picture Studio U.S.A. 34°1N 118°4W 126 B2
Soo Japan 31°40N 131°5E 222 F3
Soochow = Suzhou China 31°19N 120°38E 229 B13
Sooke Canada 48°13N 123°43W 306 B3
Sool □ Somalia 8°40N 47°30E 267 C6
Soomaa △ Estonia 58°30N 28°5E 188 C3
Soomaaliya = Somalia ■ Africa 7°0N 47°0E 267 C6
Sop Hao Laos 20°33N 104°27E 228 G5
Sop Prap Thailand 17°53N 99°20E 236 D2
Sopachuy Bolivia 19°29S 64°31W 331 D5
Sopchoppy U.S.A. 30°4N 84°29W 316 E5
Sopelana Spain 43°23N 2°58W 196 B2
Soperton U.S.A. 32°23N 82°35W 316 C7
Sopi Indonesia 2°34N 128°28E 231 D7
Sopo, Nahr → South Sudan 8°40N 26°30E 257 F2
Sopot Bulgaria 42°39N 24°45E 203 D8
Sopot Poland 54°27N 18°31E 184 D5
Sopot Serbia 44°29N 20°36E 202 B4
Sopotnica N. Macedonia 41°18N 21°13E 202 E5
Sopron Hungary 47°45N 16°32E 182 C1
Sopur India 34°18N 74°27E 243 B6
Sør-Rondane Antarctica 72°0S 25°0E 151 D4
Sør-Trøndelag □ Norway 63°0N 11°0E 164 A7
Sora Italy 41°43N 13°37E 199 G10
Sorab India 14°23N 75°6E 245 G2
Sorada India 19°45N 84°26E 244 E7
Sorah Pakistan 27°13N 68°56E 242 F3
Soråker Sweden 62°30N 17°32E 162 B11
Sorang Kazakhstan 49°46N 72°51E 217 C8
Sorano Italy 42°41N 11°43E 199 F8
Soraon India 25°37N 81°51E 243 G9
Sorata Bolivia 15°50S 68°40W 330 D4
Sorbas Spain 37°6N 2°7W 197 H2
Sörbygden Sweden 62°48N 16°12E 162 B10
Sord = Swords Ireland 53°28N 6°13W 166 C5
Sordellen Sweden 61°48N 16°43E 162 C10
Sore France 44°18N 0°35W 174 D3
Søre Osa → Norway 61°18N 11°46E 164 C8
Sorel-Tracy Canada 46°0N 73°10W 298 C5
Soresina Italy 45°17N 9°51E 198 C6
Sørfjorden Norway 60°20N 6°37E 164 D3
Sörforsa Sweden 61°43N 16°58E 162 C10
Sórgono Italy 40°1N 9°6E 200 B2
Sorgues France 44°1N 4°53E 175 D8
Sorgun Turkey 39°46N 35°11E 212 C6
Sorgun → Turkey 36°36N 34°20E 250 B5
Sori Papua N. G. 1°58S 146°42E 286 A4
Soria Spain 41°43N 2°32W 196 D2
Soria □ Spain 41°46N 2°28W 196 D2
Soriano Uruguay 33°24S 58°19W 334 C4
Soriano nel Cimino Italy 42°25N 12°14E 199 F9
Sorkh, Kuh-e Iran 35°40N 58°30E 247 C8
Sorø Denmark 55°26N 11°32E 163 J5
Soro Guinea 10°9N 9°48W 262 C3
Soroca Moldova 48°8N 28°12E 183 B13
Sorocaba Brazil 23°31S 47°27W 335 A6
Sorochinsk Russia 52°26N 53°10E 186 D9
Soroka = Belomorsk Russia 64°35N 34°54E 186 B5
Soroki = Soroca Moldova 48°8N 28°12E 183 B13
Sorokino = Krasnodon Ukraine 48°17N 39°44E 189 H10
Soroksár Hungary 47°24N 19°7E 117 B2
Soroksari Duna → Hungary 47°25N 19°5E 117 B2
Sorong Indonesia 0°55S 131°15E 231 E8
Soroni Greece 36°21N 28°1E 206 E12
Soroti Uganda 1°43N 33°35E 268 B3
Sørøya Norway 70°40N 22°30E 160 A20
Sørøyane Norway 62°25N 5°32E 164 B2
Sørøysundet Norway 70°25N 23°0E 160 A20
Sorraia → Portugal 38°55N 8°53W 195 G2
Sorrell Australia 42°47S 147°34E 281 G4
Sorrento Italy 40°37N 14°22E 201 B7
Sorsele Sweden 65°31N 17°30E 160 D17
Sörsjön Sweden 61°24N 13°5E 162 C7
Sorso Italy 40°48N 8°34E 200 B1
Sorsogon Phil. 13°0N 124°0E 232 E5
Sorsogon □ Phil. 12°50N 123°55E 232 E4
Sortavala Russia 61°42N 30°41E 188 B6
Sortino Italy 37°9N 15°2E 201 E8
Sortland Norway 68°42N 15°25E 160 B16
Sortot Sudan 19°30N 30°28E 256 D3
Sorum Norway 60°30N 10°17E 164 D7
Sorvågen Norway 67°53N 13°1E 160 C15
Sorvizhi Russia 57°52N 48°32E 190 B9
Sos del Rey Católico Spain 42°30N 1°13W 196 C3
Soscumica, L. Canada 50°15N 77°27W 298 B4
Sösdala Sweden 56°2N 13°41E 163 H7
Sosenka → Russia 55°46N 37°42E 129 B3
Sosna → Russia 52°42N 38°55E 189 F10
Sosnogorsk Russia 63°37N 53°51E 186 B9
Sosnovka Kirov, Russia 56°17N 51°17E 190 B10
Sosnovka St. Petersburg, Russia 60°0N 30°22E 137 B2
Sosnovka Tambov, Russia 53°13N 41°24E 190 D5
Sosnovyy Bor Russia 59°55N 29°6E 188 C5
Sosnowiec Poland 50°20N 19°10E 185 H6
Sosnowitz = Sosnowiec Poland 50°20N 19°10E 185 H6
Soso C.A.R. 3°55N 15°30E 264 B3
Sospel France 43°52N 7°27E 175 E11
Sospiri, Ponte dei Venice, Italy 142 b3
Sossus Vlei Namibia 24°40S 15°23E 270 B2
Šoštanj Slovenia 46°23N 15°4E 199 B12
Sŏsura N. Korea 42°16N 130°36E 224 A5
Sot → India 27°27N 79°37E 243 F8
Sotasæter Norway 61°49N 7°43E 164 C4
Sotavento Cabo Verde 15°0N 24°0W 153 j
Sotik Kenya 0°41S 35°7E 268 C4
Sotkamo Finland 64°8N 28°23E 160 D23
Soto Curaçao 12°16N 69°6W 322 g
Soto Spain 43°32N 6°4W 194 B4
Soto la Marina Mexico 23°46N 98°13W 319 C5
Soto la Marina → Mexico 23°45N 97°45W 319 C5
Soto y Amío Spain 42°46N 5°53W 194 C5
Sotouboua Togo 8°34N 0°59E 263 D5
Sotrondio Spain 43°17N 5°36W 194 B5
Sotuf, Adrar W. Sahara 21°42N 15°36W 260 D1
Sotuta Mexico 20°36N 89°1W 319 C7
Souanké Congo 2°10N 14°3E 264 B2
Soubré Côte d'Ivoire 5°50N 6°35W 262 D3
Souda Greece 35°29N 24°4E 207 E6
Soudas, Ormos Greece 35°25N 24°10E 207 E5
Souderton U.S.A. 40°19N 75°19W 313 F9
Soufflay Congo 2°1N 14°54E 264 B2
Soufli Greece 41°12N 26°18E 203 E10
Soufrière Dominica 15°13N 61°22W 323 k
Soufrière Guadeloupe 16°5N 61°40W 322 e
Soufrière St. Lucia 13°51N 61°3W 323 m
Soufrière Bay Dominica 15°13N 61°22W 323 k
Soufrière Bay St. Lucia 13°51N 61°4W 323 m
Soufrière Hills Volcano Montserrat 16°43N 62°10W 323 p
Souillac Lot, France 44°53N 1°29E 174 D5
Souillac Mauritius 20°31S 57°31E 272 e
Souilly France 49°3N 5°17E 173 C12
Souk-Ahras Algeria 36°23N 7°57E 261 A6
Souk-Ahras □ Algeria 36°10N 7°55E 261 A6
Souk el Arba du Rharb Morocco 34°43N 5°59W 260 B3
Soukhouma Laos 14°38N 105°48E 236 E5
Sŏul = Seoul S. Korea 37°31N 126°58E 137 B2
Soulac-sur-Mer France 45°30N 1°7W 174 C2
Soulougou Burkina Faso 13°1N 0°25E 263 C5
Soultz-sous-Forêts France 48°57N 7°52E 173 D14
Sound, The = Øresund Europe 55°45N 12°40E 163 J6
Sound, The U.K. 50°20N 4°10W 169 G3
Sound I. India 12°58N 92°59E 245 H11
Soundview U.S.A. 40°49N 73°53W 132 B2
Sounio, Akra Greece 37°37N 24°1E 204 D6
Sour el Ghozlane Algeria 36°10N 3°45E 261 A5
Sources, Mt. aux Lesotho 28°45S 28°50E 271 C4
Soure Brazil 0°35S 48°30W 332 B2
Soure Portugal 40°4N 8°38W 194 E2
Souris Man., Canada 49°40N 100°20W 297 D8
Souris P.E.I., Canada 46°21N 62°15W 299 C7
Souris → N. Amer. 49°40N 99°34W 308 A4
Sourou → Africa 12°45N 3°25W 262 C4
Sourpi Greece 39°6N 22°54E 204 B4
Sous, O. → Morocco 30°27N 9°31W 260 B3
Sous le Vent, Is. French Polynesia 16°30S 155°30W 289 f
Sous le Vent, Région Réunion 21°12S 55°20E 272 f
Sousa-Massa △ Morocco 30°26N 9°35W 260 B3
Sousa Brazil 6°45S 38°10W 332 C4
Sousel Brazil 2°38S 52°29W 332 B1
Sousel Portugal 38°57N 7°40W 195 G3
Sousse-Massa □ Morocco 30°0N 9°0W 260 C3
Sousse Tunisia 35°50N 10°38E 258 A2
Sousse □ Tunisia 35°40N 10°30E 261 A7
Soustons France 43°45N 1°19W 174 E2
Sout → S. Africa 31°35S 18°24E 270 D2
South Africa ■ Africa 32°0S 23°0E 270 D3
South African National Museum of Military History S. Africa 26°10S 28°2E 123 A2
South America 10°0S 60°0W 326 E5
South Andaman India 11°45N 92°10E 245 J11
South Aulatsivik I. Canada 56°45N 61°30W 299 A7
South Australia □ Australia 32°0S 139°0E 282 B3
South Australian Basin Ind. Oc. 38°0S 126°0E 288 L4
South Ayrshire □ U.K. 55°18N 4°41W 167 F4
South Baldy Pk. U.S.A. 34°6N 107°11W 305 J10
South Bass I. U.S.A. 41°39N 82°49W 312 E2
South Bay U.S.A. 26°40N 80°43W 317 J9
South Beach The Bahamas 25°1N 77°20W 153 b
South Beach Fla., U.S.A. 25°46N 80°7W 129 D3
South Beach N.Y., U.S.A. 40°35N 74°4W 132 C1
South Beach Harbor San Francisco, U.S.A. 136 c3
South Beloit U.S.A. 42°29N 89°2W 310 B7
South Bend Ind., U.S.A. 41°41N 86°15W 311 C10
South Bend Wash., U.S.A. 46°40N 123°48W 306 D3
South Bend Park U.S.A. 33°42N 84°23W 113 B2
South Boston Mass., U.S.A. 42°20N 71°2W 116 A2
South Boston Va., U.S.A. 36°42N 78°54W 309 G14
South Branch Canada 47°55N 59°2W 299 C8
South Branch Chicago River → Chicago, U.S.A. 119 d1
South Brook Canada 49°26N 56°5W 299 C8
South Brother I. India 10°56N 92°37E 245 J11
South Bruny I. Australia 43°20S 147°15E 281 G4
South C. = Kalae U.S.A. 18°55N 155°41W 302 E6
South Carolina □ U.S.A. 34°0N 81°0W 315 E14
South Channel Phil. 14°18N 120°37E 232 D3
South Charleston U.S.A. 38°22N 81°44W 309 F13
South China Sea Asia 10°0N 113°0E 230 C4
South Comino Channel Malta 36°0N 14°20E 206 F7
South Congaree U.S.A. 33°53N 81°9W 316 B8
South Cotabato □ Phil. 6°10N 125°0E 233 J5
South Cumberland Is. △ Australia 20°42S 149°11E 280 b
South Dakota □ U.S.A. 44°15N 100°0W 308 C4
South Dayton U.S.A. 42°21N 79°3W 312 D5
South Daytona U.S.A. 29°10N 81°0W 317 F8
South Decatur U.S.A. 33°44N 84°16W 113 B3
South Deerfield U.S.A. 42°29N 72°37W 313 D12
South Deering U.S.A. 41°42N 87°33W 119 C3
South Downs U.K. 50°52N 0°25W 169 G7
South Downs △ U.K. 50°50N 0°50W 169 G7
South Dublin □ Ireland 53°16N 6°24W 166 C5
South East □ Botswana 25°0S 25°40E 270 C4
South East B. Ascension I. 7°57S 14°18W 153 g
South East C. Australia 43°40S 146°50E 281 G4
South East Forest △ Australia 37°0S 149°30E 283 D8
South East Is. Australia 34°17S 123°30E 279 F3
South El Monte U.S.A. 34°3N 118°2W 126 B4
South Elgin U.S.A. 42°0N 88°18W 311 C8
South Esk → U.K. 56°43N 2°31W 167 E6
South Fiji Basin Pac. Oc. 26°0S 175°0E 288 K9
South Foreland U.K. 51°8N 1°24E 169 F9
South Fork American → U.S.A. 38°57N 120°59W 306 G5
South Fork Edisto → U.S.A. 33°16N 80°54W 316 B9
South Fork Feather → U.S.A. 39°17N 121°36W 306 F5
South Fork Grand → U.S.A. 45°43N 102°17W 308 C2
South Fork Licking → U.S.A. 38°40N 84°18W 311 F12
South Fork Milk → U.S.A. 48°4N 106°19W 304 B10
South Fork Republican → U.S.A. 40°3N 101°31W 308 E3
South Gate U.S.A. 33°56N 118°12W 126 C3
South Georgia Antarctica 54°30S 37°0W 151 B1
South Gloucestershire □ U.K. 51°32N 2°28W 169 F5
South Grand → U.S.A. 38°17N 93°25W 310 F3
South Hadley U.S.A. 42°16N 72°35W 313 D12
South Harbor Phil. 14°34N 120°58E 127 B1
South Harrow U.K. 51°33N 0°21W 125 A1
South Haven U.S.A. 42°24N 86°16W 311 B10
South Hd. Australia 33°50S 151°16E 139 B2
South Henik L. Canada 61°30N 97°20W 297 A9
South Hill Village Anguilla 18°11N 63°5W 322 a
South Hills S. Africa 26°14S 28°5E 123 B2
South Holland U.S.A. 41°36N 87°36W 119 D3
South Horr Kenya 2°12N 36°56E 268 B4
South I. India 10°3N 72°17E 245 J1
South I. Eastern, Kenya 2°35N 36°35E 268 B4
South I. N.Z. 44°0S 170°0E 285 E5
South Indian Lake Canada 56°47N 98°56W 297 B9
South Invercargill N.Z. 46°26S 168°23E 285 G3
South Island △ Kenya 2°39N 36°35E 268 B4
South Kensington London, U.K. 125 c2
South Kitui ⌓ Kenya 1°48S 38°46E 268 C4
South Knife → Canada 58°55N 94°37W 297 B10
South Koel → India 22°32N 85°14E 243 H11
South Korea ■ Asia 36°0N 128°0E 224 D4
South Lake Tahoe U.S.A. 38°57N 119°59W 306 G6
South Lanarkshire □ U.K. 55°37N 3°53W 167 F5
South Lawn U.S.A. 38°47N 77°0W 143 C2
South Loup → U.S.A. 41°4N 98°39W 308 E4
South Luangwa △ Zambia 13°0S 31°20E 269 E3
South Lyon U.S.A. 42°28N 83°39W 311 B13
South Magnetic Pole Antarctica 64°2S 135°43E 151 C9
South Malé Atoll Maldives 4°0N 73°25E 272 d
South Malosmadulu Atoll Maldives 5°12N 73°0E 272 d
South Miami U.S.A. 25°42N 80°17W 129 D1
South Milwaukee U.S.A. 42°55N 87°52W 311 B9
South Molton U.K. 51°1N 3°51W 169 F4
South Monroe U.S.A. 41°54N 83°26W 311 C13
South Moose L. Canada 53°49N 100°1W 297 C8
South Nahanni → Canada 61°3N 123°21W 296 A4
South Nation → Canada 45°34N 75°6W 313 A9
South Natuna Is. = Natuna Selatan, Kepulauan Indonesia 2°45N 109°0E 235 B3
South Negril Pt. Jamaica 18°16N 78°22W 320 a
South New Hebrides Trench Pac. Oc. 22°30S 170°0E 277 E13
South Newport U.S.A. 31°38N 81°24W 316 D8
South Nilandu Atoll Maldives 2°52N 72°57E 272 d
South Norwood U.K. 51°23N 0°3W 125 B3
South of Market San Francisco, U.S.A. 136 c2
South Orkney Is. Antarctica 63°0S 45°0W 151 C18
South Ossetia □ Georgia 42°21N 44°2E 191 J7
South Otselic U.S.A. 42°38N 75°46W 313 D9
South Ozone Park U.S.A. 40°41N 73°49W 132 B3
South Pagai, I. = Pagai Selatan, Pulau Indonesia 3°0S 100°15E 234 C2
South Paris U.S.A. 44°14N 70°31W 313 B14
South Pasadena U.S.A. 34°7N 118°8W 126 B4
South Pekin U.S.A. 40°30N 89°39W 310 D7
South Pittsburg U.S.A. 35°1N 85°42W 315 D12
South Platte → U.S.A. 41°7N 100°42W 308 E3
South Pole Antarctica 90°0S 0°0 151 E
South Ponte Vedra Beach U.S.A. 30°3N 81°20W 316 E8
South Porcupine Canada 48°30N 81°12W 298 C3
South Portland U.S.A. 43°38N 70°15W 309 D18
South Pt. Ascension I. 8°0S 14°24W 153 g
South Pt. Barbados 13°2N 59°32W 323 r
South Pt. Mich., U.S.A. 44°52N 83°19W 312 B1
South Res. U.S.A. 42°26N 71°6W 116 A2
South River Ont., Canada 45°52N 79°23W 298 C4
South River N.J., U.S.A. 40°27N 74°23W 313 F10
South Ronaldsay U.K. 58°48N 2°58W 167 C6
South Ruislip U.K. 51°33N 0°24W 125 A1
South Rukuru → Malawi 10°44S 34°14E 269 E3
South San Francisco U.S.A. 37°38N 122°26W 136 C2
South San Gabriel U.S.A. 34°3N 118°6W 126 B4
South Sandwich Is. Antarctica 57°0S 27°0W 151 B1
South Sandwich Trench Atl. Oc. 56°0S 24°0W 151 B1
South Saskatchewan → Canada 53°15N 105°5W 297 C7
South Seal → Canada 58°48N 98°8W 297 B9
South Sentinel I. India 10°59N 92°14E 245 J11
South Shetland Is. Antarctica 62°0S 59°0W 151 C18
South Shields U.K. 55°0N 1°25W 168 C6
South Shore U.S.A. 41°45N 87°34W 119 C3
South Sioux City U.S.A. 42°28N 96°24W 308 D5
South Sister U.S.A. 44°4N 121°51W 304 D3
South Solomon Trench Pac. Oc. 11°0S 164°30E 277 C11
South Soufrière Hills Montserrat 16°41N 62°10W 323 p
South Street Boston, U.S.A. 116 c2
South Sudan ■ Africa 8°0N 30°0E 257 F2
South Taranaki Bight N.Z. 39°40S 174°5E 284 F3
South Tasman Rise S. Ocean 48°0S 146°0E 151 A10
South Thompson → Canada 50°40N 120°20W 296 C4
South Twin I. Canada 53°7N 79°52W 298 B4
South Tyne → U.K. 54°59N 2°8W 168 C5
South Ubian Phil. 5°11N 120°30E 233 J3
South Uist U.K. 57°20N 7°15W 167 D1
South Valley U.S.A. 35°1N 106°41W 305 J10
South Venice U.S.A. 27°3N 82°25W 317 H7
South Verde I. Phil. 10°4N 119°13E 233 F2
South Wayne U.S.A. 42°34N 89°53W 310 B7
South Wellesley Is. Australia 16°58S 139°17E 280 B2
South West Africa = Namibia ■ Africa 22°0S 18°9E 270 B2
South West B. Ascension I. 7°58S 14°25W 153 g
South West B. The Bahamas 25°0N 77°32W 153 b
South West C. Tas., Australia 43°34S 146°3E 281 G4
South West C. N.Z. 47°17S 167°28E 285 H2
South West Pt. Papua N. G. 2°14S 146°34E 286 B4
South West Pt. St. Helena 15°59S 5°48W 153 h
South West Rocks Australia 30°52S 153°3E 283 A10
South Whitley U.S.A. 41°5N 85°38W 311 C11
South Williamsport U.S.A. 41°13N 77°0W 312 E8
South Yemen = Yemen ■ Asia 15°0N 44°0E 248 D4
South Yorkshire □ U.K. 53°27N 1°36W 168 D6
Southall U.K. 51°30N 0°22W 125 A1
Southampton Ont., Canada 44°30N 81°25W 312 B3
Southampton Southampton, U.K. 50°54N 1°23W 169 G6
Southampton N.Y., U.S.A. 40°53N 72°23W 313 F12
Southampton □ U.K. 50°54N 1°23W 169 G6
Southampton I. Canada 64°30N 84°0W 295 E15
Southaven U.S.A. 34°59N 90°0W 315 D9
Southbank Canada 54°2N 125°46W 296 C3
Southborough U.K. 51°23N 0°32E 125 B4
Southbridge N.Z. 43°48S 172°16E 285 D7
Southbridge Mass., U.S.A. 42°5N 72°2W 313 D12
Southeast C. U.S.A. 62°56N 169°39W 303 E5
Southeast Indian Ridge Ind. Oc. 43°0S 80°0E 273 J10
Southend Sask., Canada 56°19N 103°22W 297 B8
Southend London, U.K. 51°25N 0°0 125 B3
Southend-on-Sea U.K. 51°32N 0°44E 169 F8
Southend-on-Sea □ U.K. 51°32N 0°44E 169 F8
Southern = Yedebub Biheroch Bihereseboch na Hizboch □ Ethiopia 12°0N 36°0E 257 F4
Southern = Yuzhnyy □ Russia 44°0N 40°0E 214 E5
Southern □ Malawi 15°0S 35°0E 269 F4
Southern □ S. Leone 8°0N 12°30W 262 D2
Southern □ Zambia 16°20S 26°20E 269 F2
Southern △ South Sudan 6°50N 28°45E 257 F2
Southern Alps N.Z. 43°41S 170°11E 285 D5
Southern Aral Sea Asia 45°0N 58°0E 216 D5
Southern California, Univ. of U.S.A. 34°1N 118°17W 126 B3
Southern Cross Australia 31°12S 119°15E 279 F2
Southern Highlands □ Papua N. G. 6°30S 143°25E 286 D2
Southern Indian L. Canada 57°10N 98°30W 297 B9
Southern Lau Group Fiji 18°40S 178°40W 287 B3
Southern Leyte □ Phil. 10°30N 125°10E 233 F5
Southern Ocean 62°0S 60°0E 151 C6
Southern Pines U.S.A. 35°11N 79°24W 315 D15
Southern Rhodesia = Zimbabwe ■ Africa 19°0S 30°0E 269 F3
Southern Uplands U.K. 55°28N 3°52W 167 F5
Southfield U.S.A. 42°28N 83°15W 311 B13
Southfields U.K. 51°26N 0°11W 125 B2
Southington U.S.A. 41°36N 72°53W 313 E12
Southlake U.S.A. 32°56N 97°8W 120 A3
Southland □ N.Z. 45°30S 168°0E 285 F3
Southold U.S.A. 41°4N 72°26W 313 E12
Southport Queens., Australia 27°58S 153°25E 281 D5
Southport Mersey., U.K. 53°39N 3°0W 168 D4
Southport Fla., U.S.A. 30°17N 85°38W 316 E4
Southport La., U.S.A. 29°57N 90°8W 131 B2
Southport N.Y., U.S.A. 42°3N 76°49W 312 D8
Southwark □ U.K. 51°29N 0°6W 125 B3
Southwest △ Australia 43°8S 146°5E 281 G4
Southwest Museum Los Angeles, U.S.A. 34°6N 118°13W 126 B3
Southwest Pacific Basin Pac. Oc. 40°0S 140°0W 277 G17
Southwest Pt. U.S. Virgin Is. 17°40N 64°55W 321 b
Southwold U.K. 52°20N 1°41E 169 E9
Southwood △ Australia 27°48S 150°8E 281 D5
Soutpansberg S. Africa 23°0S 29°30E 271 B4
Souvigny France 46°33N 3°10E 173 F10
Søvang Denmark 55°34N 12°37E 118 B3
Sovata Romania 46°35N 25°3E 183 D10
Soverato Italy 38°41N 16°33E 201 D9
Sovetsk Kaliningrad, Russia 55°6N 21°50E 184 C8
Sovetsk Kirov, Russia 57°38N 48°53E 190 B9
Sovetskaya Gavan Russia 48°50N 140°18E 215 E15
Sovetskoye = Zelenokumsk Russia 44°24N 44°0E 191 H6
Sovicille Italy 43°17N 11°13E 199 E8
Søvik Norway 62°33N 6°17E 164 B3
Soweto S. Africa 26°14S 27°52E 123 B1
Sowhānak Iran 35°48N 51°31E 141 A3
Sowma'eh Sarā Iran 37°17N 49°18E 213 D13
Soya Japan 35°44N 139°55E 140 A4
Sōya-Kaikyō = La Perouse Str. Asia 45°40N 142°0E 220 B11
Sōya-Misaki Japan 45°30N 141°55E 220 B10
Soyang-ho S. Korea 37°57N 127°54E 224 D3
Soyaux France 45°39N 0°12E 174 C4
Søyland Norway 58°41N 5°36E 164 F2
Soyo Angola 6°13S 12°20E 265 D2
Sozaq Kazakhstan 44°8N 68°28E 217 D7
Sozh → Belarus 51°57N 30°48E 177 B16
Sozopol Bulgaria 42°23N 27°42E 203 D11
Spa Belgium 50°29N 5°53E 170 D5
Spaans Lagoen Aruba 12°28N 69°58W 322 f
Spaanse Water Curaçao 12°4N 68°51W 322 g
Spaatz I. Antarctica 73°10S 75°0W 151 D17
Spaccaforno = Ispica Italy 36°47N 14°55E 201 F7
Spagna, Piazza di Rome, Italy 136 b3
Spain ■ Europe 39°0N 4°0W 192 D3
Spalato = Split Croatia 43°31N 16°26E 199 E13
Spalding S. Austral., Australia 33°30S 138°37E 282 B3
Spalding Lincs., U.K. 52°48N 0°9W 168 E7
Spanaway U.S.A. 47°6N 122°26W 306 C4
Spandau Germany 52°33N 13°9E 115 A1
Spånga Sweden 59°23N 17°53E 139 A1
Spangler U.S.A. 40°39N 78°48W 312 F6
Spanische Reitschule Vienna, Austria 142 b1
Spanish Canada 46°12N 82°20W 298 C3
Spanish Fork U.S.A. 40°7N 111°39W 304 F8
Spanish Pt. Antigua & B. 17°33N 61°44W 322 c
Spanish Pt. Bermuda 32°18N 64°49W 153 a
Spanish Riding School = Spanische Reitschule Vienna, Austria 142 b1
Spanish Steps = Spagna, Piazza di Rome, Italy 136 b3
Spanish Town Br. Virgin Is. 18°26N 64°26W 321 b
Spanish Town Jamaica 18°0N 76°57W 320 a
Sparks Ga., U.S.A. 31°11N 83°26W 316 D6
Sparks Nev., U.S.A. 39°32N 119°45W 306 F7
Sparreholm Sweden 59°4N 16°49E 162 E10
Sparrow Bay Grenada 12°30N 61°27W 323 q
Sparta = Sparti Greece 37°5N 22°25E 204 D4
Sparta Ga., U.S.A. 33°17N 82°58W 316 B7
Sparta Ill., U.S.A. 38°8N 89°42W 310 F7
Sparta Mich., U.S.A. 43°10N 85°42W 311 A11
Sparta N.J., U.S.A. 41°2N 74°38W 313 E10
Sparta Wis., U.S.A. 43°56N 90°49W 308 D8
Spartanburg U.S.A. 34°56N 81°57W 315 D14
Spartel, C. Morocco 35°47N 5°56W 260 A3
Sparti Greece 37°5N 22°25E 204 D4
Spartivento, C. Calabria, Italy 37°55N 16°4E 201 E9
Spartivento, C. Sard., Italy 38°53N 8°50E 200 D1
Spartochori Greece 38°40N 20°46E 207 B2
Sparwood Canada 49°44N 114°53W 296 D6
Spas-Demensk Russia 54°20N 34°0E 188 E7
Spas-Klepiki Russia 55°10N 40°10E 188 E11
Spassk = Bednodemyanovsk Russia 53°55N 43°15E 190 D6
Spassk-Dalniy Russia 44°40N 132°48E 220 B6
Spassk-Ryazanskiy Russia 54°24N 40°25E 188 E11
Spatha, Akra Greece 35°42N 23°43E 207 E5
Spatsizi → Canada 57°42N 128°7W 296 B3
Spatsizi Plateau Wilderness ⌓ Canada 57°40N 128°0W 296 B3
Spean → U.K. 56°55N 4°59W 167 E4
Spearfish U.S.A. 44°30N 103°52W 308 C2
Spearman U.S.A. 36°12N 101°12W 314 C4
Spectacle I. U.S.A. 42°19N 70°59W 116 A3
Speculator U.S.A. 43°30N 74°22W 313 C10
Speed Australia 35°21S 142°27E 282 C5
Speedway U.S.A. 39°48N 86°16W 311 E10
Speery I. St. Helena 16°1S 5°46W 153 h
Speia Moldova 46°59N 29°19E 183 D14
Speicher-See Germany 48°12N 11°42E 131 A3
Speightstown Barbados 13°15N 59°39W 323 r
Speising Austria 48°10N 16°17E 142 B1
Speke Gulf Tanzania 2°20S 32°50E 268 C3
Spello Italy 42°59N 12°40E 199 F9
Spence Bay = Taloyoak Canada 69°32N 93°32W 294 D13
Spencer Idaho, U.S.A. 44°22N 112°11W 304 D7
Spencer Ind., U.S.A. 39°17N 86°46W 311 E10
Spencer Iowa, U.S.A. 43°9N 95°9W 308 D6
Spencer N.Y., U.S.A. 42°13N 76°30W 313 D8
Spencer Nebr., U.S.A. 42°53N 98°42W 308 D4
Spencer, C. Australia 35°20S 136°53E 282 C2
Spencer B. Namibia 25°30S 14°47E 270 C1
Spencer G. Australia 34°0S 137°20E 282 C2
Spencerville Ont., Canada 44°51N 75°33W 313 B9
Spencerville Ohio, U.S.A. 40°43N 84°21W 311 D12
Spences Bridge Canada 50°25N 121°20W 296 C4
Spennymoor U.K. 54°42N 1°36W 168 C6
Spenser Mts. N.Z. 42°15S 172°45E 285 C7
Spentrup Denmark 56°33N 10°2E 163 H4
Sperchios → Greece 38°57N 22°3E 204 C4
Sperillen Norway 60°28N 10°3E 164 D7
Sperrgebiet △ Namibia 27°38S 15°56E 270 C2
Sperrin Mts. U.K. 54°50N 7°0W 166 B5
Spessart Germany 49°56N 9°18E 179 F5
Spetalen Norway 59°18N 10°45E 164 E7
Spetses Greece 37°15N 23°10E 204 D5
Spey → U.K. 57°40N 3°6W 167 D5
Speyer Germany 49°29N 8°25E 179 F4
Speyside Trin. & Tob. 11°17N 60°32W 323 s
Spezand Pakistan 29°59N 67°0E 242 E2
Spezzano Albanese Italy 39°40N 16°19E 201 C9
Sphinx Egypt 29°58N 31°8E 117 B1
Spickard U.S.A. 40°14N 93°36W 310 D3
Spiddal Ireland 53°15N 9°18W 166 C2
Spiekeroog Germany 53°46N 7°42E 178 B3
Spiez Switz. 46°40N 7°40E 179 J3
Spili Greece 35°13N 24°31E 207 E5
Spilimbergo Italy 46°7N 12°54E 199 B9
Spīn Būldak Afghan. 31°1N 66°25E 242 D2
Spinaceto Italy 41°47N 12°27E 136 C1
Spinalonga Greece 35°18N 25°44E 207 E6
Spinazzola Italy 40°58N 16°5E 201 B9
Spineni Romania 44°43N 24°37E 183 F9
Spinifex ◎ Australia 28°30S 128°30E 279 E4
Spirding = Śniardwy, Jezioro Poland 53°48N 21°50E 184 E8
Spirit Lake U.S.A. 46°15N 122°9W 306 D4
Spirit River Canada 55°45N 118°50W 296 B5
Spiritwood Canada 53°24N 107°33W 297 C7
Spišská Nová Ves Slovakia 48°58N 20°34E 181 C13
Spišské Podhradie Slovakia 49°0N 20°48E 181 B13
Spit Junction Australia 33°49S 151°14E 139 A2
Spital Austria 47°42N 14°18E 180 D7
Spithead U.K. 50°45N 1°10W 169 G6
Spitsbergen = Svalbard Arctic 78°0N 17°0E 154 B12
Spittal an der Drau Austria 46°48N 13°31E 180 E6
Spjelkavik Norway 62°28N 6°22E 164 B3
Split Croatia 43°31N 16°26E 199 E13
Split ✈ (SPU) Croatia 43°33N 16°15E 199 E13
Split L. Canada 56°8N 96°15W 297 B9
Split Lake Canada 56°8N 96°15W 297 B9
Splitski Kanal Croatia 43°31N 16°20E 199 E13
Splügenpass Switz. 46°30N 9°20E 179 J5
Spofford U.S.A. 29°10N 100°25W 314 G4
Spokane U.S.A. 47°40N 117°24W 304 C5
Spoleto Italy 42°44N 12°44E 199 F9
Sponvika Norway 59°7N 11°15E 164 E8
Spoon → U.S.A. 40°19N 90°4W 310 D6
Spooner U.S.A. 45°50N 91°53W 308 C8
Spořilov Czechia 50°2N 14°29E 135 B3
Sporyy Navolok, Mys Russia 75°50N 68°40E 214 B7
Spot Pond U.S.A. 42°26N 71°4W 116 A2
Spotswood Australia 37°50S 144°52E 128 B1
Sprague U.S.A. 47°18N 117°59W 304 C5
Spratly I. S. China Sea 8°38N 111°55E 230 C4
Spratly Is. S. China Sea 8°20N 112°0E 230 C4
Spray U.S.A. 44°50N 119°48W 304 D4
Spreča → Bos.-H. 44°44N 18°6E 182 F3
Spree → Germany 52°32N 13°13E 178 C9
Spreewald Germany 51°58N 13°51E 178 D9
Spremberg Germany 51°34N 14°22E 178 D10
Sprengisandur Iceland 64°52N 18°7W 155 C8
Spring City U.S.A. 40°11N 75°33W 313 F9
Spring Cr. → U.S.A. 30°54N 84°45W 316 E5
Spring Creek U.S.A. 40°44N 115°35W 304 F6
Spring Garden Guyana 6°59N 58°31W 329 B6
Spring Garden Calif., U.S.A. 39°52N 120°47W 306 F6
Spring Green U.S.A. 43°11N 90°4W 310 A6
Spring Hill Ala., U.S.A. 31°42N 85°58W 316 D4
Spring Hill Fla., U.S.A. 28°27N 82°41W 317 G7
Spring Mts. U.S.A. 36°0N 115°45W 307 J11
Spring Temple Buddha China 33°46N 112°27E 226 H7
Spring Valley Calif., U.S.A. 32°44N 116°59W 307 N10
Spring Valley Ill., U.S.A. 41°20N 89°12W 310 C7
Spring Valley Nev., U.S.A. 36°6N 115°14W 124 B1
Springbok S. Africa 29°42S 17°54E 270 C2
Springboro U.S.A. 41°48N 80°22W 312 E4
Springdale Nfld. & L., Canada 49°30N 56°6W 299 C8
Springdale Ark., U.S.A. 36°11N 94°8W 314 C7
Springdale Ohio, U.S.A. 39°17N 84°29W 311 E12
Springe Germany 52°12N 9°33E 178 C5
Springeberg Germany 52°26N 13°43E 115 B5
Springer U.S.A. 36°22N 104°36W 305 H11
Springerville U.S.A. 34°8N 109°17W 305 J9
Springfield Ont., Canada 42°50N 80°56W 312 D4
Springfield Dominica 15°21N 61°23W 323 k
Springfield N.Z. 43°19S 171°56E 285 D6
Springfield Colo., U.S.A. 37°24N 102°37W 305 H12
Springfield Fla., U.S.A. 30°10N 85°37W 316 E4
Springfield Ga., U.S.A. 32°22N 81°18W 316 C8
Springfield Ill., U.S.A. 39°48N 89°39W 310 E7
Springfield Ky., U.S.A. 37°41N 85°13W 311 G11
Springfield Mass., U.S.A. 42°6N 72°35W 313 D12
Springfield Mo., U.S.A. 37°13N 93°17W 308 G7
Springfield Ohio, U.S.A. 39°55N 83°49W 311 E13
Springfield Oreg., U.S.A. 44°3N 123°1W 304 D2
Springfield S.C., U.S.A. 33°30N 81°17W 316 B8
Springfield Tenn., U.S.A. 36°31N 86°53W 315 C11
Springfield Va., U.S.A. 38°46N 77°10W 143 C1
Springfield Vt., U.S.A. 43°18N 72°29W 313 C12
Springfield, L. U.S.A. 39°46N 89°36W 310 E7
Springfontein S. Africa 30°15S 25°40E 270 D4
Springhill Canada 45°40N 64°4W 299 C7
Springhill La., U.S.A. 33°0N 93°28W 314 E8
Springhouse Canada 51°56N 122°7W 296 C4
Springlands = Corriverton Guyana 5°55N 57°20W 329 B6
Springs S. Africa 26°13S 28°25E 271 C4
Springsure Australia 24°8S 148°6E 280 C4
Springvale Ga., U.S.A. 31°50N 84°53W 316 D5
Springvale Maine, U.S.A. 43°28N 70°48W 313 C14
Springville Calif., U.S.A. 36°8N 118°49W 306 J8
Springville Iowa, U.S.A. 42°3N 91°27W 310 B5
Springville N.Y., U.S.A. 42°31N 78°40W 312 D6
Springville Utah, U.S.A. 40°10N 111°37W 304 F8
Springwater U.S.A. 42°38N 77°35W 312 D7
Sprottau = Szprotawa Poland 51°33N 15°35E 185 G2
Spruce-Creek U.S.A. 40°36N 78°9W 312 F6
Spruce Knob-Seneca Rocks ⌓ U.S.A. 38°50N 79°30W 309 F14
Spruce Mt. U.S.A. 44°12N 72°19W 313 B12
Sprucedale Canada 45°29N 79°28W 312 A5
Spur U.S.A. 33°28N 100°52W 314 E4
Spurn Hd. U.K. 53°35N 0°8E 168 D8
Spuž Montenegro 42°32N 19°10E 202 D3
Spuzzum Canada 49°37N 121°23W 296 D4
Spydeberg Norway 59°36N 11°5E 164 E8
Squam L. U.S.A. 43°45N 71°32W 313 C13
Squamish Canada 49°45N 123°10W 296 D4
Squantum U.S.A. 42°17N 71°0W 116 B2
Square Islands Canada 52°47N 55°47W 299 B8
Squillace, G. di Italy 38°45N 16°50E 201 D9
Squinzano Italy 40°26N 18°2E 201 B11
Squires, Mt. Australia 26°14S 127°28E 279 E4
Sragen Indonesia 7°26S 111°2E 235 D4
Srbac Bos.-H. 45°7N 17°30E 182 E2
Srbica = Skënderaj Kosovo 42°45N 20°47E 202 D4
Srbija = Serbia ■ Europe 43°20N 20°0E 202 C4
Srbobran Serbia 45°32N 19°48E 182 E4
Sre Ambel Cambodia 11°8N 103°46E 237 G4
Sre Khtum Cambodia 12°10N 106°52E 237 F6
Sre Umbell = Sre Ambel Cambodia 11°8N 103°46E 237 G4
Srebarna Bulgaria 44°6N 27°4E 203 B11
Srebrenica Bos.-H. 44°6N 19°18E 182 F4
Sredinnyy Khrebet Russia 57°0N 160°0E 215 D17
Sredinnyy Ra. = Sredinnyy Khrebet Russia 57°0N 160°0E 215 D17
Središče Slovenia 46°24N 16°17E 199 B13
Sredna Gora Bulgaria 42°40N 24°20E 203 D8
Srednaya Rogatka Russia 59°49N 30°22E 137 C2
Srednekolymsk Russia 67°27N 153°40E 215 C16
Sredni Rodopi Bulgaria 41°40N 24°45E 203 E8
Srednogorie Bulgaria 42°43N 24°10E 203 D8
Śrem Poland 52°6N 17°2E 185 F4
Sremska Mitrovica Serbia 44°59N 19°38E 182 F4
Sremski Karlovci Serbia 45°12N 19°56E 182 E4
Srepok → Cambodia 13°33N 106°16E 236 F6
Sretensk Russia 52°10N 117°40E 215 D12
Sri Aman = Bandar Sri Aman Malaysia 1°15N 111°32E 235 B4
Sri Jayewardenepura Kotte Sri Lanka 6°54N 79°55E 245 L4
Sri Kalahasti India 13°45N 79°44E 245 H4
Sri Ksetra Myanmar 18°48N 95°17E 241 F5
Sri Lanka ■ Asia 7°30N 80°50E 245 L5
Sri Nakarin Res. Thailand 14°35N 99°0E 236 E2
Sri Pada = Adam's Peak Sri Lanka 6°48N 80°30E 245 L5
Sriharikota I. India 13°40N 80°20E 245 H5
Srikakulam India 18°14N 83°58E 244 E6
Srinagar India 34°5N 74°50E 243 B6
Sripur Bangla. 24°14N 90°30E 241 C3
Srivardhan India 18°4N 73°3E 244 E1
Srivilliputtur India 9°31N 77°40E 245 K3
Środa Śląska Poland 51°10N 16°36E 185 G3
Środa Wielkopolski Poland 52°15N 17°19E 185 F4
Śródmieście Poland 52°13N 21°0E 143 B2
Srono Indonesia 8°24S 114°16E 231 J17
Srpska Crnja Serbia 45°38N 20°44E 182 E5
Srpski Itebej Serbia 45°35N 20°44E 182 E5
Srungavarapukota India 18°7N 83°10E 244 E6
Ssese Is. = Sese Is. Uganda 0°20S 32°20E 268 C3
Ssuhu Taiwan 23°38N 120°13E 225 C2
Staaken Germany 52°31N 13°8E 115 A1
Staaten → Australia 16°24S 141°17E 280 B3
Staaten River △ Australia 16°15S 142°40E 280 B3
Stabbursdalen △ Norway 70°5N 24°15E 160 A21
Stabekk Norway 59°54N 10°36E 133 A2
Staberhuk Germany 54°23N 11°18E 178 A7
Stade Germany 53°35N 9°29E 178 B5
Stade de France Paris, France 48°55N 2°22E 134 A3
Staðarfell Iceland 65°7N 22°12W 155 B4
Staðarhólskirkja Iceland 65°23N 21°58W 155 B5
Staðastaður Iceland 64°49N 23°1W 155 C3
Stadhavet Norway 62°13N 5°0E 164 B2
Stadhuis Amsterdam, Neths. 112 b3
Staður Norðurland Vestra, Iceland 65°9N 21°3W 155 B5
Staður Vestfirðir Iceland 66°15N 22°50W 155 A4
Stadlandet Norway 62°10N 5°10E 164 B2
Stadlau Austria 48°13N 16°27E 142 A2
Stadshuset Stockholm, Sweden 139 b1
Stadskanaal Neths. 53°4N 6°55E 170 A6
Stadsschouwburg Amsterdam, Neths. 112 c1
Stadtallendorf Germany 50°48N 9°1E 178 E5
Stadthagen Germany 52°19N 9°13E 178 C5
Stadtlohn Germany 51°59N 6°55E 178 D2
Stadtroda Germany 50°52N 11°44E 178 E7
Stafafell Iceland 64°25N 14°52W 155 C12
Staffa U.K. 56°27N 6°21W 167 E2
Staffanstorp Sweden 55°39N 13°13E 163 J7
Stafford U.K. 52°49N 2°7W 168 E5
Stafford Kans., U.S.A. 37°58N 98°36W 308 G4
Stafford Va., U.S.A. 38°25N 77°24W 309 F15
Stafford, L. U.S.A. 29°20N 82°29W 317 F7
Stafford Springs U.S.A. 41°57N 72°18W 313 E12
Staffordshire □ U.K. 52°53N 2°10W 168 E5
Stagnone Italy 37°53N 12°26E 200 E5
Stagnone di Marsala ⌓ Italy 37°52N 12°26E 200 E5
Staines-upon-Thames U.K. 51°26N 0°29W 169 F7
Stains France 48°57N 2°22E 134 A3
Stainz Austria 46°53N 15°17E 180 E8
Stakhanov Ukraine 48°35N 38°40E 189 H10
Stalać Serbia 43°43N 21°28E 202 C5
Stalin = Kuçovë Albania 40°47N 19°57E 202 F3
Stalin = Varna Bulgaria 43°13N 27°56E 203 C11
Stalin Pk. = Gerlachovský štít Slovakia 49°11N 20°7E 181 B13
Stalin Pk. = imeni Ismail Samani, Pik Tajikistan 39°0N 72°2E 217 E8
Stalin Pk. = Musala Bulgaria 42°13N 23°37E 202 D7
Stalinabad = Dushanbe Tajikistan 38°33N 68°48E 217 E7
Stalingrad = Volgograd Russia 48°40N 44°25E 191 F7
Staliniri = Tskhinvali Georgia 42°14N 44°1E 191 J7
Stalinogorsk = Novomoskovsk Russia 54°5N 38°15E 188 E10
Stalinogrod = Katowice Poland 50°17N 19°5E 185 H6
Stalinsk = Novokuznetsk Russia 53°45N 87°10E 217 B11
Stalinstadt = Eisenhüttenstadt Germany 52°9N 14°38E 178 C10
Stallarholmen Sweden 59°22N 17°12E 162 E11
Ställdalen Sweden 59°56N 14°56E 162 E8
Stalowa Wola Poland 50°34N 22°3E 185 H9
Stalybridge U.K. 53°28N 2°3W 168 D5
Stamford Queens., Australia 21°15S 143°46E 280 C3
Stamford Lincs., U.K. 52°39N 0°29W 169 E7
Stamford Conn., U.S.A. 41°3N 73°32W 313 E11
Stamford N.Y., U.S.A. 42°25N 74°38W 313 D10
Stamford Tex., U.S.A. 32°57N 99°48W 314 E5
Stamford Hill U.K. 51°34N 0°4W 125 A3
Stammersdorf Austria 48°18N 16°24E 142 A2
Stamnes Norway 60°40N 5°45E 164 D2
Stamping Ground U.S.A. 38°16N 84°41W 311 F12
Stampriet Namibia 24°20S 18°28E 270 B2
Stamps U.S.A. 33°22N 93°30W 314 E8
Stanberry U.S.A. 40°13N 94°35W 310 D2
Stančevo = Kalipetrovo Bulgaria 44°5N 27°14E 203 B11
Standerton S. Africa 26°55S 29°7E 271 C4
Standish U.S.A. 43°59N 83°57W 309 D12
Stanford S. Africa 34°26S 19°29E 270 E2
Stanford Mont., U.S.A. 47°9N 110°13W 304 C8

Stånga Sweden 57°17N 18°29E 163 G12
Stange Norway 60°43N 11°5E 164 D8
Stanger S. Africa 29°27S 31°14E 271 C5
Stängselåsen = Salpausselkä Finland 61°3N 26°15E 188 B4
Stangvik Norway 62°55N 8°28E 164 B5
Stanhope Vic., Australia 36°27S 144°59E 283 D6
Stanhope Iowa, U.S.A. 42°17N 93°48W 310 B3
Stanimaka = Asenovgrad Bulgaria 42°1N 24°51E 203 D8
Stanišić Serbia 45°56N 19°10E 182 E4
Stanislaus → U.S.A. 37°40N 121°14W 306 H5
Stanislav = Ivano-Frankivsk Ukraine 48°40N 24°40E 183 B9
Stanisławów = Ivano-Frankivsk Ukraine 48°40N 24°40E 183 B9
Stanisławów Poland 52°18N 21°33E 185 F8
Stanley Tas., Australia 40°46S 145°19E 281 G4
Stanley Hong Kong, China 22°13N 114°12E 122 B3
Stanley Falk. Is. 51°40S 59°51W 153 f
Stanley Durham, U.K. 54°53N 1°41W 168 C6
Stanley Idaho, U.S.A. 44°13N 114°56W 304 D6
Stanley N. Dak., U.S.A. 48°19N 102°23W 308 A2
Stanley N.Y., U.S.A. 42°48N 77°6W 312 D7
Stanley B. Hong Kong, China 22°13N 114°13E 122 B3
Stanley Falls = Boyoma, Chutes Dem. Rep. of the Congo 0°35N 25°23E 264 B5
Stanley Mission Canada 55°25N 104°33W 297 B8
Stanley Pen. Hong Kong, China 22°12N 114°12E 122 B3
Stanley Pool = Malebo, Pool Africa 4°17S 15°20E 265 C3
Stanley Res. India 11°50N 77°40E 245 J3
Stanleyville = Kisangani Dem. Rep. of the Congo 0°35N 25°15E 268 B2
Stanmore U.K. 51°37N 0°18W 125 A2
Stannards U.S.A. 42°5N 77°55W 312 D7
Stanovoy Khrebet Russia 55°0N 130°0E 215 D14
Stanovoy Ra. = Stanovoy Khrebet Russia 55°0N 130°0E 215 D14
Stansmore Ra. Australia 21°23S 128°33E 278 D4
Stansted, London ✈ (STN) U.K. 51°54N 0°14E 169 F8
Stanthorpe Australia 28°36S 151°59E 281 D5
Stanton Ky., U.S.A. 37°54N 83°52W 311 G13
Stanton Tex., U.S.A. 32°8N 101°48W 314 E4
Stantsiya Regar = Tursunzoda Tajikistan 38°30N 68°14E 217 E7
Stanwood U.S.A. 48°15N 122°23W 306 B4
Staples Ont., Canada 42°10N 82°35W 312 D2
Staples Minn., U.S.A. 46°21N 94°48W 308 B6
Stapleton N.Y., U.S.A. 40°36N 74°5W 132 C1
Stapleton Nebr., U.S.A. 41°29N 100°31W 308 E3
Stapodia Greece 37°24N 25°34E 205 D7
Stąporków Poland 51°9N 20°31E 185 G7
Star City Canada 52°50N 104°20W 297 C8
Star Harbour Solomon Is. 10°47S 162°19E 287 N12
Star Lake U.S.A. 44°10N 75°2W 313 B9
Stará Ďala = Hurbanovo Slovakia 47°51N 18°11E 181 D11
Stará L'ubovňa Slovakia 49°18N 20°42E 181 B13
Stara Moravica Serbia 45°50N 19°30E 182 E4
Stara Pazova Serbia 44°58N 20°10E 182 F5
Stara Planina Bulgaria 43°15N 23°0E 202 C7
Stara Sil Ukraine 49°29N 22°58E 185 J9
Stará Turá Slovakia 48°47N 17°42E 181 C10
Stara Ushytsya Ukraine 48°35N 27°8E 183 B12
Stara Zagora Bulgaria 42°26N 25°39E 203 D9
Stara Zagora □ Bulgaria 42°26N 25°39E 203 D9
Starachowice Poland 51°3N 21°2E 185 G8
Staraya Derevnya Russia 59°58N 30°15E 137 B1
Staraya Russa Russia 57°58N 31°23E 188 D6
Starbuck I. Kiribati 5°37S 155°55W 289 H12
Starchiojd Romania 45°19N 26°11E 183 E11
Starcke △ Australia 14°56S 145°2E 280 A4
Staré Město Czechia 50°5N 14°25E 135 B2
Stare Miasto Warsaw, Poland 143 a2
Stargard in Pommern = Stargard Szczeciński Poland 53°20N 15°0E 184 E2
Stargard Szczeciński Poland 53°20N 15°0E 184 E2
Stårheim Norway 61°56N 5°40E 164 C2
Stari Bar Montenegro 42°7N 19°10E 202 D3
Stari Bečej = Bečej Serbia 45°36N 20°3E 182 E5
Stari Grad Croatia 43°10N 16°38E 199 E13
Stari Trg Slovenia 45°29N 15°7E 199 C12
Staritsa Russia 56°33N 34°55E 188 D8
Starke U.S.A. 29°57N 82°7W 316 F7
Starke, L. U.S.A. 28°34N 81°32W 133 A1
Starkville U.S.A. 33°28N 88°49W 315 E10
Starnberg Germany 48°0N 11°21E 179 H7
Starnberger See Germany 47°54N 11°19E 179 H7
Staro Oryakhovo Bulgaria 42°59N 27°47E 203 D11
Starobilsk Ukraine 49°16N 39°0E 189 H10
Starodub Russia 52°30N 32°50E 189 F7
Starogard Gdański Poland 53°59N 18°30E 184 E5
Starokonstantinov = Starokonstyantyniv Ukraine 49°48N 27°10E 177 D14
Starokonstyantyniv Ukraine 49°48N 27°10E 177 D14
Starokozache Ukraine 46°20N 29°59E 183 D14
Starominskaya Russia 46°33N 39°0E 191 G4
Staroshcherbinovskaya Russia 46°40N 38°53E 191 G4
Starrs Mill U.S.A. 33°19N 84°31W 316 B5
Start Pt. U.K. 50°13N 3°39W 169 G4
Stary Sącz Poland 49°33N 20°35E 185 J7
Staryy Biryuzyak Russia 44°46N 46°50E 191 H8
Staryy Chartoriysk Ukraine 51°15N 25°54E 177 C13
Staryy Krym Ukraine 45°3N 35°8E 189 K8
Staryy Margilan = Marg'ilon Uzbekistan 40°27N 71°42E 217 D8
Staryy Oskol Russia 51°19N 37°55E 189 G9
Staryy Sambir Ukraine 49°27N 22°59E 185 J9
Stassfurt Germany 51°51N 11°35E 178 D7
Staszów Poland 50°33N 21°10E 185 H8
State Center U.S.A. 42°1N 93°10W 310 B3
State College U.S.A. 40°48N 77°52W 312 F7
State Street Chicago, U.S.A. 119 c2
Stateline U.S.A. 38°57N 119°56W 306 G7
Staten, I. = Estados, I. de Los Argentina 54°40S 64°30W 336 D4
Staten I. U.S.A. 40°35N 74°9W 313 F10
Staten Island Zoo U.S.A. 40°38N 74°6W 132 C1
Staten Islands Ferry Terminal U.S.A. 40°38N 74°4W 132 C1
Statenice Czechia 50°9N 14°19E 135 B1
Statenville U.S.A. 30°42N 83°2W 316 E6
Statesboro U.S.A. 32°27N 81°47W 316 C8
Statesville U.S.A. 35°47N 80°53W 315 D14
Statham U.S.A. 33°58N 83°35W 316 B6
Stathelle Norway 59°3N 9°41E 164 E6
Statia = St. Eustatius W. Indies 17°20N 63°0W 322 a
Stauffer U.S.A. 34°45N 119°3W 307 L7
Staunton Ill., U.S.A. 39°1N 89°47W 310 F7
Staunton Va., U.S.A. 38°9N 79°4W 309 F14
Stavanger = Rogaland □ Norway 59°12N 6°20E 164 E3
Stavanger Norway 58°57N 5°40E 164 F2
Stavelot Belgium 50°23N 5°55E 170 D5
Stavern Norway 59°0N 10°1E 164 F7
Stavoren Neths. 52°53N 5°22E 170 B5
Stavropol Russia 45°5N 42°0E 191 H6
Stavropol □ Russia 47°20N 42°50E 191 G6
Stavros Cyprus 35°1N 32°38E 207 E8
Stavros Ithaki, Greece 38°27N 20°39E 207 C2
Stavros Kriti, Greece 35°12N 24°45E 207 E5
Stavros Thessaloniki, Greece 40°39N 23°43E 202 F7
Stavros, Akra Greece 35°26N 24°58E 207 E5
Stavros Niarchos Cultural Centre Greece 37°56N 23°41E 112 B2
Stavroupoli Greece 41°12N 24°45E 203 E8
Stawell Australia 37°5S 142°47E 282 D5
Stawell → Australia 20°20S 142°55E 280 C3
Stawiski Poland 53°22N 22°9E 184 E9
Stawiszyn Poland 51°56N 18°4E 185 G5
Stayner Canada 44°25N 80°5W 312 B4
Stayton U.S.A. 44°48N 122°48W 304 D2
Steamboat Springs U.S.A. 40°29N 106°50W 304 F10
Stean Norway 59°16N 8°33E 164 E5
Stebbins U.S.A. 63°31N 162°17W 303 E7
Steblevë Albania 41°23N 20°33E 202 E4
Steele Ala., U.S.A. 33°56N 86°12W 316 B3
Steele N. Dak., U.S.A. 46°51N 99°55W 308 B4
Steele Creek Australia 37°44S 144°52E 128 A1
Steelton U.S.A. 40°14N 76°50W 312 F8
Steelville U.S.A. 37°58N 91°22W 310 G5
Steen River Canada 59°40N 117°12W 296 B5
Steenkool = Bintuni Indonesia 2°7S 133°32E 231 E8
Steenokkerzeel Belgium 50°55N 4°31E 116 A2
Steens Mt. U.S.A. 42°35N 118°40W 304 E4
Steenstrup Gletscher Greenland 75°15N 57°0W 154 B5
Steenwijk Neths. 52°47N 6°7E 170 B6
Steep Pt. Australia 26°8S 113°8E 279 E1
Steep Rock Canada 51°30N 98°48W 297 C9
Steer, L. U.S.A. 28°31N 81°30W 133 A2
Ştefan Vodă Moldova 46°27N 29°42E 183 D14
Ştefăneşti Romania 47°44N 27°15E 183 C12
Stefanie △ Ethiopia 4°55N 36°55E 257 G4
Stefanie L. = Chew Bahir Ethiopia 4°40N 36°50E 257 G4
Stefansson Bay Antarctica 67°20S 59°8E 151 C5
Stefansson I. Canada 73°20N 105°45W 295 C10
Stege Denmark 54°59N 12°18E 163 K6
Stegi = Siteki Eswatini 26°32S 31°58E 271 C5
Steglitz Germany 52°27N 13°19E 115 B2
Stegman = Artesia U.S.A. 32°51N 104°24W 305 K11
Ştei Romania 46°32N 22°27E 182 D7
Steiermark □ Austria 47°26N 15°0E 180 D8
Steigerwald Germany 49°44N 10°26E 179 F6
Steigerwald ⌓ Germany 49°50N 10°30E 179 F6
Steilacoom U.S.A. 47°10N 122°36W 306 C4
Steilrandberge Namibia 17°45S 13°20E 270 A1
Stein = Kamnik Slovenia 46°14N 14°37E 199 B11
Steinbach Canada 49°32N 96°40W 297 D9
Steinfurt Germany 52°9N 7°20E 178 C3
Steinhatchee U.S.A. 29°40N 83°23W 316 F6
Steinhausen Namibia 21°49S 18°20E 270 B2
Steinheim Germany 51°51N 9°5E 178 D5
Steinhuder Meer Germany 52°29N 9°21E 178 C5
Steinhuder Meer ⌓ Germany 52°30N 9°16E 178 C5
Steinkjer Norway 64°1N 11°31E 160 D14
Steinkopf S. Africa 29°18S 17°43E 270 C2
Steinsham Norway 62°47N 6°28E 164 B3
Steinwald ⌓ Germany 49°55N 12°8E 179 F8
Stellarton Canada 45°32N 62°30W 299 C7
Stellenbosch S. Africa 33°58S 18°50E 270 D2
Stëlvio, Paso dello Italy 46°32N 10°27E 198 B7
Stenay France 49°29N 5°12E 173 C12
Stendal Germany 52°36N 11°53E 178 C7
Stende Latvia 57°11N 22°33E 184 A9
Stenen Koraal Curaçao 12°10N 68°56W 322 g
Stenhamra Sweden 59°20N 17°41E 162 E11
Stenshuvud △ Sweden 55°39N 14°15E 163 J8
Stenstorp Sweden 58°17N 13°45E 163 F7
Stenungsund Sweden 58°6N 11°50E 163 F5
Steornabhaigh = Stornoway U.K. 58°13N 6°23W 167 C2
Stepanakert = Xankändi Azerbaijan 39°52N 46°49E 213 C12
Stepanavan Armenia 41°1N 44°23E 191 K7
Stephansdom Vienna, Austria 142 b2
Stephens, C. N.Z. 40°42S 173°58E 285 A8
Stephens Creek Australia 31°50S 141°30E 282 A4
Stephens I. B.C., Canada 54°10N 130°45W 296 C2
Stephens I. N.Z. 40°40S 174°1E 285 A9
Stephens L. Canada 56°32N 95°0W 297 B9
Stephenville Nfld. & L., Canada 48°31N 58°35W 299 C8
Stephenville Tex., U.S.A. 32°13N 98°12W 314 E5
Stepney U.K. 51°30N 0°3W 125 A3
Stepnica Poland 53°38N 14°36E 184 E1
Stepnogorsk Kazakhstan 52°21N 71°53E 217 B8
Stepnoi = Elista Russia 46°16N 44°14E 191 G7
Steppe Asia 50°0N 50°0E 210 C7
Steps Pt. Amer. Samoa 14°23S 170°45W 302 f
Sterea Ellas □ Greece 38°50N 23°0E 204 C4
Sterkstroom S. Africa 31°32S 26°32E 270 D4
Sterling Alaska, U.S.A. 60°32N 150°46W 303 F10
Sterling Colo., U.S.A. 40°37N 103°13W 304 F12
Sterling Ga., U.S.A. 31°16N 81°34W 316 D8
Sterling Ill., U.S.A. 41°48N 89°42W 310 C7
Sterling Kans., U.S.A. 38°13N 98°12W 308 F4
Sterling City U.S.A. 31°51N 101°0W 314 F4
Sterling Heights U.S.A. 42°35N 83°2W 311 B13
Sterling Park U.S.A. 37°41N 122°27W 136 B2
Sterling Run U.S.A. 41°25N 78°12W 312 E6
Sterlitamak Russia 53°40N 56°0E 186 D10
Sternberg Germany 53°42N 11°50E 178 B7
Šternberk Czechia 49°45N 17°15E 181 B10
Sternes Greece 35°30N 24°9E 207 E5
Sterzing = Vipiteno Italy 46°54N 11°26E 199 B8
Stettin = Szczecin Poland 53°27N 14°27E 184 E1
Stettiner Haff Germany 53°47N 14°15E 178 B10
Stettler Canada 52°19N 112°40W 296 C6
Steubenville U.S.A. 40°22N 80°37W 312 F4
Stevenage U.K. 51°55N 0°13W 169 F7
Stevens Point U.S.A. 44°31N 89°34W 308 C9
Stevens Pottery U.S.A. 32°57N 83°17W 316 C6
Stevens Village U.S.A. 66°1N 149°6W 303 C10
Stevenson U.S.A. 45°42N 121°53W 306 E5
Stevenson → Australia 27°6S 135°33E 281 D2
Stevenson L. Canada 53°55N 96°0W 297 C9
Stevensville U.S.A. 46°30N 114°5W 304 C6
Stevns Klint Denmark 55°17N 12°28E 163 J6
Steward U.S.A. 41°51N 89°1W 310 C7
Stewardson U.S.A. 39°16N 88°38W 311 E8
Stewart B.C., Canada 55°56N 129°57W 296 B3
Stewart Ga., U.S.A. 33°25N 83°52W 316 B6
Stewart Nev., U.S.A. 39°5N 119°46W 306 F7
Stewart → Canada 63°19N 139°26W 294 E4
Stewart, C. Australia 11°57S 134°56E 280 A1
Stewart, I. Chile 54°50S 71°15W 336 D2
Stewart I. N.Z. 46°58S 167°54E 285 G2
Stewarts Point U.S.A. 38°39N 123°24W 306 G3
Stewartsville U.S.A. 39°45N 94°30W 310 E2
Stewartville U.S.A. 43°51N 92°29W 308 D7
Stewiacke Canada 45°9N 63°22W 299 C7
Steynsburg S. Africa 31°15S 25°49E 270 D4
Steyr Austria 48°3N 14°25E 180 C7
Steyr → Austria 48°3N 14°25E 180 C7
Steytlerville S. Africa 33°17S 24°19E 270 D3
Stia Italy 43°48N 11°42E 199 E8
Sticklinge udde Sweden 59°23N 18°6E 139 A2
Stickney U.S.A. 41°49N 87°46W 119 C2
Stigler U.S.A. 35°15N 95°8W 314 D7
Stigliano Italy 40°24N 16°14E 201 B9
Stigtomta Sweden 58°47N 16°48E 163 F10
Stikine → Canada 56°40N 132°30W 296 B2
Stilfontein S. Africa 26°51S 26°50E 270 C4
Stilida Greece 38°55N 22°47E 204 C4
Stillmore U.S.A. 32°27N 82°13W 316 C7
Stillwater N.Y., U.S.A. 42°55N 73°41W 313 D11
Stillwater Okla., U.S.A. 36°7N 97°4W 314 C6
Stillwater Range U.S.A. 39°50N 118°5W 304 G4
Stillwater Res. U.S.A. 43°54N 75°3W 313 C9
Stilo, Pta. Italy 38°25N 16°35E 201 D9
Stilwell U.S.A. 35°49N 94°38W 314 D7
Stînga Nistrului = Transnistria □ Moldova 47°20N 29°15E 183 C14
Štip N. Macedonia 41°42N 22°10E 202 E6
Stira Greece 38°9N 24°14E 204 C6
Stirling Ont., Canada 44°18N 77°33W 312 B7
Stirling N.Z. 46°14S 169°49E 285 G4
Stirling Stirling, U.K. 56°8N 3°57W 167 E5
Stirling □ U.K. 56°12N 4°18W 167 E4
Stirling Ra. Australia 34°23S 118°0E 279 F2
Stirling Range △ Australia 34°26S 118°20E 279 F2
Stittsville Canada 45°15N 75°55W 313 A9
Stjernøya Norway 70°20N 22°40E 160 A20
Stjørdalshalsen Norway 63°29N 10°51E 164 A7
Stock Island U.S.A. 24°32N 81°34W 317 L8
Stocka Sweden 61°53N 17°20E 162 C11
Stockach Germany 47°50N 9°1E 179 H5
Stockaryd Sweden 57°19N 14°36E 163 G8
Stockbridge Ga., U.S.A. 33°33N 84°14W 316 B5
Stockbridge Mich., U.S.A. 42°27N 84°11W 311 B12
Stockerau Austria 48°24N 16°12E 181 C9
Stockholm Sweden 59°19N 18°4E 139 B2
Stockholm □ Sweden 59°30N 18°20E 162 E12
Stockholm Arlanda ✈ (ARN) Sweden 59°41N 17°56E 139 A1
Stockport U.K. 53°25N 2°9W 168 D5
Stocksbridge U.K. 53°29N 1°35W 168 D6
Stocksund Sweden 59°23N 18°3E 139 A2
Stockton Calif., U.S.A. 37°58N 121°17W 306 H5
Stockton Ill., U.S.A. 42°21N 90°1W 310 B6
Stockton Kans., U.S.A. 39°26N 99°16W 308 F4
Stockton Mo., U.S.A. 37°42N 93°48W 310 G3
Stockton-on-Tees U.K. 54°35N 1°19W 168 C6
Stockton-on-Tees □ U.K. 54°35N 1°19W 168 C6
Stockton Plateau U.S.A. 30°30N 102°30W 314 F3
Stoclet, Palais Belgium 50°50N 4°24E 116 B2
Stoczek Łukowski Poland 51°58N 21°58E 185 G8
Stöde Sweden 62°28N 16°35E 162 B10
Stöðvarfjörður Iceland 64°49N 13°52W 155 C13
Stodůlky Czechia 50°3N 14°19E 135 B1
Stoeng Treng Cambodia 13°31N 105°58E 236 F5
Stoer, Pt. of U.K. 58°16N 5°23W 167 C3
Stogovo N. Macedonia 41°31N 20°38E 202 E4
Stoholm Denmark 56°30N 9°8E 163 H3
Stoke N.Z. 41°19S 173°14E 285 B8
Stoke Newington U.K. 51°33N 0°4W 125 A3
Stoke-on-Trent U.K. 53°1N 2°11W 168 D5
Stoke-on-Trent □ U.K. 53°1N 2°11W 168 D5
Stokes △ Australia 33°45S 121°11E 279 F3
Stokes Bay Canada 45°0N 81°28W 312 B3
Stokes Pt. Australia 40°10S 143°56E 281 G3
Stokes Ra. Australia 15°50S 130°50E 278 C5
Stokkseyri Iceland 63°50N 21°2W 155 D3
Stokksnes Iceland 64°14N 14°58W 155 C12
Stokmarknes Norway 68°34N 14°54E 160 B16
Stolac Bos.-H. 43°5N 17°59E 202 C1
Stolberg Germany 50°47N 6°13E 178 E2
Stolbovoy, Ostrov Russia 74°44N 135°14E 215 B14
Stolbtsy = Stowbtsy Belarus 53°30N 26°43E 177 B14
Stolin Belarus 51°53N 26°50E 177 C14
Stöllet Sweden 60°26N 13°15E 162 D7
Stolnici Romania 44°31N 24°48E 183 F9
Stolp = Słupsk Poland 54°30N 17°3E 184 D4
Stolpmünde = Ustka Poland 54°35N 16°55E 184 D3
Stomio Greece 35°21N 23°32E 207 E4
Ston Croatia 42°51N 17°43E 199 F14
Stone U.K. 52°55N 2°9W 168 E5
Stone Canyon Res. U.S.A. 34°6N 118°27W 126 B2
Stone Mountain U.S.A. 33°49N 84°10W 316 B5
Stone Zoo U.S.A. 42°28N 71°6W 116 A2
Stoneboro U.S.A. 41°20N 80°7W 312 E4
Stonebridge U.K. 51°32N 0°16W 125 A2
Stonecutters I. Hong Kong, China 22°19N 114°8E 122 B2
Stoneham U.S.A. 42°29N 71°5W 116 A2
Stonehaven U.K. 56°59N 2°12W 167 E6
Stonehenge Queens., Australia 24°22S 143°17E 280 C3
Stonehenge Wilts., U.K. 51°9N 1°45W 169 F6
Stonewall Canada 50°10N 97°19W 297 C9
Stongfjorden Norway 61°26N 5°10E 164 C2
Stonington U.S.A. 39°44N 89°12W 310 E7
Stony Brook Res. U.S.A. 42°15N 71°18W 116 B2
Stony Creek → U.S.A. 41°38N 87°41W 119 C2
Stony Hill Jamaica 18°5N 76°48W 320 a
Stony I. U.S.A. 43°53N 76°19W 313 C8
Stony L. Man., Canada 58°51N 98°40W 297 B9
Stony L. Ont., Canada 44°30N 78°5W 312 B6
Stony Point U.S.A. 41°14N 73°59W 313 E11
Stony Pt. U.S.A. 43°50N 76°18W 313 C8
Stony Rapids Canada 59°16N 105°50W 297 B7
Stony River U.S.A. 61°47N 156°35W 303 F8
Stony Tunguska = Tunguska, Podkamennaya → Russia 61°50N 90°13E 215 C10
Stonyford U.S.A. 39°23N 122°33W 306 F4
Stopnica Poland 50°27N 20°57E 185 H7
Storå Sweden 59°42N 15°6E 162 E9
Storå → Denmark 56°20N 8°19E 163 H2
Stora Gla Sweden 59°30N 12°30E 162 E6
Stora Le Sweden 59°5N 11°55E 162 E5
Stora Lulevatten Sweden 67°10N 19°30E 160 C18
Stora Sjöfallet △ Sweden 67°36N 17°45E 160 C17
Stora Värtan Sweden 59°25N 18°7E 139 A2
Storavan Sweden 65°45N 18°10E 160 D18
Stord Norway 59°52N 5°23E 164 E2
Store Bælt Denmark 55°20N 11°0E 163 J4
Store Hareskov Denmark 55°46N 12°23E 118 A2
Store Heddinge Denmark 55°18N 12°23E 163 J6
Store Jukleggi = Høgeloft Norway 61°3N 8°12E 164 C5
Store Koldewey Greenland 76°30N 19°0W 154 B9
Store Magleby Denmark 55°35N 12°35E 118 B3
Store Mosse △ Sweden 57°18N 13°55E 163 G7
Store Sotra Norway 60°18N 5°4E 164 D1
Støren Norway 63°3N 10°18E 164 A7
Storerikvollen Norway 63°7N 11°58E 164 A8
Storfjellsætra Norway 61°40N 10°30E 164 C7
Storfjorden Norway 62°28N 6°35E 164 B3
Storfors Sweden 59°32N 14°17E 162 E8
Storholmen Sweden 59°23N 18°8E 139 A2
Storico Navale, Museo Venice, Italy 142 b3
Stóridalur Iceland 63°38N 19°57W 155 D7
Stórinúpur Iceland 64°3N 20°10W 155 C6
Storkerson Pen. Canada 72°30N 106°30W 294 C10
Storkyrkan Stockholm, Sweden 139 c2
Storli Norway 62°42N 9°5E 164 B6
Storlien Sweden 63°19N 12°6E 162 A6
Storm B. Australia 43°10S 147°30E 281 G4
Storm Lake U.S.A. 42°39N 95°13W 308 D6
Stormberge S. Africa 31°16S 26°17E 270 D4
Stormsrivier S. Africa 33°59S 23°52E 270 D3
Stornoway U.K. 58°13N 6°23W 167 C2
Storo Italy 45°51N 10°35E 198 C7
Storozhinets = Storozhynets Ukraine 48°14N 25°45E 183 B10
Storozhynets Ukraine 48°14N 25°45E 183 B10
Storrs U.S.A. 41°49N 72°15W 313 E12
Storsjøen Hedmark, Norway 60°20N 11°40E 164 D8
Storsjøen Hedmark, Norway 61°30N 11°14E 164 C8
Storsjön Gävleborg, Sweden 60°35N 16°45E 162 D10
Storsjön Jämtland, Sweden 62°48N 13°7E 162 B7
Storsjön Jämtland, Sweden 63°9N 14°30E 162 A8
Storsølnkletten Norway 61°59N 10°16E 164 C7
Storstrømmen Greenland 76°17N 22°25W 154 B8
Storuman Sweden 65°5N 17°10E 160 D17
Storuman, L. Sweden 65°13N 16°50E 160 D17
Stóruvellir Iceland 65°30N 17°29W 155 B9
Storvätteshågna Sweden 62°6N 12°30E 162 B6
Storviglen Norway 62°32N 12°2E 164 B9
Storvik Sweden 60°35N 16°33E 162 D10
Storvreta Sweden 59°58N 17°44E 162 E11
Story City U.S.A. 42°11N 93°36W 310 B3
Stouffville Canada 43°58N 79°15W 312 C5
Stoughton Sask., Canada 49°40N 103°0W 297 D8
Stoughton Wis., U.S.A. 42°55N 89°13W 308 D9
Stour → Dorset, U.K. 50°43N 1°47W 169 G6
Stour → Kent, U.K. 51°18N 1°22E 169 F9
Stour → Suffolk, U.K. 51°57N 1°4E 169 F9
Stourbridge U.K. 52°28N 2°8W 169 E5
Stout L. Canada 52°0N 94°40W 297 C10
Stove Pipe Wells Village U.S.A. 36°35N 117°11W 307 J9
Støvring Denmark 56°54N 9°50E 163 H3
Stow U.S.A. 41°10N 81°27W 312 E3
Stowbtsy Belarus 53°30N 26°43E 177 B14
Stowmarket U.K. 52°12N 1°0E 169 E9
Stoyka Russia 59°57N 30°25E 137 B2
Strabane U.K. 54°50N 7°27W 166 B4
Stracin N. Macedonia 42°13N 22°2E 202 D6
Stradella Italy 45°5N 9°18E 198 C6
Strahan Australia 42°9S 145°20E 281 G4
Straiton U.K. 55°53N 3°9W 121 B3
Strajitsa Bulgaria 43°14N 25°58E 203 C9
Strakonice Czechia 49°15N 13°53E 180 B6
Straldzha Bulgaria 42°35N 26°40E 203 D10
Stralsund Germany 54°18N 13°4E 178 A9
Strand Hedmark, Norway 61°17N 11°17E 164 C8
Strand Western Cape, S. Africa 34°9S 18°48E 270 D2
Strand London, U.K. 125 b4
Stranda Møre og Romsdal, Norway 62°19N 6°58E 164 B3
Stranda Nord-Trøndelag, Norway 63°33N 10°14E 160 E14
Strandasýsla Iceland 65°45N 21°45W 155 B5
Strandby Denmark 57°30N 10°29E 163 G4
Strandfontein S. Africa 34°4S 18°34E 118 B2
Strangford L. U.K. 54°30N 5°37W 166 B6
Strängnäs Sweden 59°23N 17°2E 162 E11
Stranorlar Ireland 54°48N 7°46W 166 B4
Stranraer U.K. 54°54N 5°1W 167 G3
Strasbourg Sask., Canada 51°4N 104°55W 297 C8
Strasbourg Bas-Rhin, France 48°35N 7°42E 173 D14
Strasburg Germany 53°30N 13°43E 178 B9
Strășeni Moldova 47°8N 28°36E 183 C13
Strašnice Czechia 50°4N 14°28E 135 B2
Stråssa Sweden 59°44N 15°12E 162 E9
Strassburg = Aiud Romania 46°19N 23°44E 183 D8
Strasstrudering Germany 48°6N 11°41E 131 B3
Stratford N.S.W., Australia 32°7S 151°55E 283 B9
Stratford Vic., Australia 37°59S 147°7E 283 D7
Stratford Ont., Canada 43°23N 81°0W 312 C4
Stratford N.Z. 39°20S 174°19E 284 F3
Stratford London, U.K. 51°33N 0°0 125 A4
Stratford Calif., U.S.A. 36°11N 119°49W 306 J7
Stratford Conn., U.S.A. 41°12N 73°8W 313 E11
Stratford Tex., U.S.A. 36°20N 102°4W 314 C3
Stratford-upon-Avon U.K. 52°12N 1°42W 169 E6
Strath Spey U.K. 57°9N 3°49W 167 D5
Strathalbyn Australia 35°13S 138°53E 282 C3
Strathaven U.K. 55°40N 4°5W 167 F4
Strathcona ⌓ Canada 49°38N 125°40W 296 D3
Strathfield Australia 33°52S 151°5E 139 B1
Strathmore Alta., Canada 51°5N 113°18W 296 C6
Strathmore Angus, U.K. 56°37N 3°7W 167 E5
Strathmore Calif., U.S.A. 36°9N 119°4W 306 J7
Strathnaver Canada 53°20N 122°33W 296 C4
Strathpeffer U.K. 57°35N 4°32W 167 D4
Strathroy Canada 42°58N 81°38W 312 D3
Strathy Pt. U.K. 58°36N 4°1W 167 C4
Stratoni Greece 40°31N 23°49E 202 F7
Strattanville U.S.A. 41°12N 79°19W 312 E5
Stratton U.S.A. 45°8N 70°26W 313 A14
Stratton Mt. U.S.A. 43°4N 72°55W 313 C12
Straubing Germany 48°52N 12°34E 179 G8
Straumnes Iceland 66°26N 23°8W 155 A3
Strausberg Germany 52°35N 13°54E 178 C9
Strawberry → U.S.A. 40°10N 110°24W 304 F8
Strawberry Point U.S.A. 42°41N 91°32W 310 B5
Strážnice Czechia 48°54N 17°19E 181 C10
Streaky B. Australia 32°48S 134°13E 281 E1
Streaky Bay Australia 32°51S 134°18E 281 E1
Streatham U.K. 51°25N 0°7W 125 B3
Streatham Vale U.K. 51°24N 0°8W 125 B3
Streator U.S.A. 41°8N 88°50W 311 C8
Strebersdorf Austria 48°17N 16°23E 142 A2
Středočeský □ Czechia 49°55N 14°30E 180 B7
Streetsboro U.S.A. 41°14N 81°21W 312 E3
Streetsville Canada 43°35N 79°42W 312 C5
Strehaia Romania 44°37N 23°10E 183 F8
Strehlen = Strzelin Poland 50°46N 17°2E 185 H4
Strelcha Bulgaria 42°25N 24°19E 203 D8
Streng → Cambodia 13°12N 103°37E 236 F4
Stresa Italy 45°52N 8°28E 198 C5
Střešovice Czechia 50°5N 14°23E 135 B2
Streymoy Færoe Is. 62°8N 7°5W 160 E9
Strezhevoy Russia 60°42N 77°34E 214 C8
Stříbro Czechia 49°44N 13°0E 180 A6
Strickland → Papua N. G. 7°35S 141°36E 286 D1
Striegau = Strzegom Poland 50°58N 16°20E 185 H3
Strilky Ukraine 49°20N 22°59E 185 J9
Strimonas → Greece 40°46N 23°51E 202 F7
Strip, The Las Vegas, U.S.A. 36°7N 115°10W 124 B2
Střížkov Czechia 50°7N 14°28E 135 B2
Stroeder Argentina 40°12S 62°37W 336 B4
Strofades Greece 37°15N 21°0E 204 D3
Strokestown Ireland 53°47N 8°5W 166 C3
Stroma U.K. 58°41N 3°7W 167 C5
Strombeek-Bever Belgium 50°54N 4°21E 116 A2
Stromberg-Heuchelberg ⌓ Germany 49°2N 8°50E 179 F4
Strómboli Italy 38°47N 15°13E 201 D8
Stromeferry U.K. 57°21N 5°33W 167 D3
Strommen Norway 59°57N 11°0E 164 E7
Stromness U.K. 58°58N 3°17W 167 C5
Stromovka Czechia 50°6N 14°25E 135 B2
Strömsbruk Sweden 61°52N 17°18E 162 C11
Stromsburg U.S.A. 41°7N 97°36W 308 E5
Strömsnäsbruk Sweden 56°35N 13°45E 163 H7
Strömstad Sweden 58°56N 11°10E 163 F5
Strömsund Sweden 63°51N 15°33E 160 E16
Stronghurst U.S.A. 40°45N 90°55W 310 D6
Strongili Greece 36°6N 29°42E 205 E11
Stróngoli Italy 39°16N 17°3E 201 C10
Strongsville U.S.A. 41°19N 81°50W 312 E3
Stronie Śląskie Poland 50°18N 16°53E 185 H3
Stronsay U.K. 59°7N 2°35W 167 B6
Stropkov Slovakia 49°13N 21°39E 181 B14
Stroud U.K. 51°45N 2°13W 169 F5
Stroud Road Australia 32°18S 151°57E 283 B9
Stroudsburg U.S.A. 40°59N 75°12W 313 F9
Stroumbi Cyprus 34°53N 32°29E 207 F8
Štrpce = Shtërpcë Kosovo 42°14N 21°1E 202 D5
Struer Denmark 56°30N 8°35E 163 H2
Struga N. Macedonia 41°11N 20°44E 202 E4
Strugi Krasnyye Russia 58°21N 29°1E 188 C5
Strumica N. Macedonia 41°28N 22°41E 202 E6
Strumica → Europe 41°20N 23°22E 202 E7
Strumok Ukraine 45°43N 29°27E 183 E14
Struthers U.S.A. 41°4N 80°39W 312 E4
Stryama Bulgaria 42°16N 24°54E 203 D8
Stryker U.S.A. 48°41N 114°46W 304 B6
Stryków Poland 51°55N 19°33E 185 G6
Stryn Norway 61°54N 6°43E 164 C3
Stryy Ukraine 49°16N 23°48E 177 D12
Strzegom Poland 50°58N 16°20E 185 H3
Strzelce Krajeńskie Poland 52°52N 15°33E 185 F2
Strzelce Opolskie Poland 50°31N 18°18E 185 H5
Strzelecki Cr. → Australia 29°37S 139°59E 281 D2
Strzelecki Desert Australia 29°30S 140°0E 281 D3
Strzelin Poland 50°46N 17°2E 185 H4
Strzelno Poland 52°35N 18°9E 185 F5
Strzybnica Poland 50°28N 18°48E 185 H5
Strzyżów Poland 49°52N 21°47E 185 J8
Stuart Fla., U.S.A. 27°12N 80°15W 317 H9
Stuart Iowa, U.S.A. 41°30N 94°19W 310 C2
Stuart Nebr., U.S.A. 42°36N 99°8W 308 D4
Stuart → Canada 54°0N 123°35W 296 C4
Stuart Bluff Ra. Australia 22°50S 131°52E 278 D5
Stuart I. U.S.A. 63°35N 162°30W 303 E7
Stuart L. Canada 54°30N 124°30W 296 C4
Stuart Mts. N.Z. 45°2S 167°39E 285 F2
Stuart Ra. Australia 29°10S 134°56E 281 D1
Stubbekøbing Denmark 54°53N 12°9E 163 K6
Stubbs St. Vincent 13°7N 61°9W 323 n
Stuben Austria 47°10N 10°8E 180 D3
Štubnianske Teplice = Turčianske Teplice Slovakia 48°52N 18°52E 181 C11
Studen Kladenets, Yazovir Bulgaria 41°37N 25°30E 203 E9
Studenica Serbia 43°29N 20°32E 202 C4
Studenka Czechia 49°44N 18°5E 181 B11
Studholme N.Z. 44°42S 171°9E 285 E6
Studio City U.S.A. 34°8N 118°24W 126 B2
Studley Park Trin. & Tob. 11°11N 60°40W 323 s
Stugudalen Norway 62°53N 11°53E 164 B8
Stugun Sweden 63°10N 15°40E 162 A9
Stuhlweissenburg = Székesfehérvár Hungary 47°15N 18°25E 182 C3
Stuhm = Sztum Poland 53°55N 19°1E 184 E6
Stuhr Germany 53°5N 8°44E 178 B4
Stull L. Canada 54°24N 92°34W 298 B1
Stung Treng = Stoeng Treng Cambodia 13°31N 105°58E 236 F5
Stupart → Canada 56°0N 93°25W 298 A1
Stupava Slovakia 48°17N 17°2E 181 C10
Stupino Russia 54°57N 38°2E 188 E10
Stureby Sweden 59°15N 18°4E 139 B2
Sturge I. Antarctica 67°26S 164°47E 151 C11
Sturgeon B. Canada 52°0N 97°50W 297 C9
Sturgeon Bay U.S.A. 44°50N 87°23W 308 C10
Sturgeon Falls Canada 46°25N 79°57W 298 C4
Sturgeon L. Alta., Canada 55°6N 117°32W 296 B5
Sturgeon L. Ont., Canada 50°0N 90°45W 298 C1
Sturgeon L. Ont., Canada 44°28N 78°43W 312 B6
Sturgis Sask., Canada 51°56N 102°36W 297 C8
Sturgis Mich., U.S.A. 41°48N 85°25W 311 C11
Sturgis S. Dak., U.S.A. 44°25N 103°31W 308 C2
Sturkö Sweden 56°5N 15°42E 163 H9
Štúrovo Slovakia 47°48N 18°41E 181 D11
Sturt △ Australia 27°17S 141°37E 281 D3
Sturt Cr. → Australia 19°8S 127°50E 278 C4
Sturt Stony Desert Australia 28°30S 141°0E 281 D3
Sturts Meadows Australia 31°18S 141°42E 282 A4
Stutterheim S. Africa 32°33S 27°28E 270 D4
Stuttgart Baden-W., Germany 48°48N 9°11E 179 G5
Stuttgart Ark., U.S.A. 34°30N 91°33W 314 D9
Stuttgart Echterdingen ✈ (STR) Germany 48°42N 9°11E 179 G5
Stutthof = Sztutowo Poland 54°20N 19°15E 184 D6
Stuvsta Sweden 59°15N 18°0E 139 B2
Stuyvesant U.S.A. 42°23N 73°45W 313 D11
Stuyvesant Town New York, U.S.A. 132 d2
Stykkishólmur Iceland 65°2N 22°40W 155 B4
Styria = Steiermark □ Austria 47°26N 15°0E 180 D8
Styrsö Sweden 57°37N 11°46E 163 G5
Su-no-Saki Japan 34°58N 139°45E 223 C11
Su Xian = Suzhou China 33°41N 116°59E 226 H9
Suakin Sudan 19°8N 37°20E 256 D4
Suakin Archipelago Sudan 18°42N 38°30E 256 D4
Suamico U.S.A. 44°38N 88°2W 308 C9
Suan N. Korea 38°42N 126°22E 224 C3
Suana Indonesia 8°44S 115°36E 231 K18
Suanhwa = Xuanhua China 40°40N 115°2E 226 D8
Suao Taiwan 24°36N 121°51E 225 E13
Suape Brazil 8°24S 35°0W 332 C5
Suapure → Venezuela 6°48N 67°1W 328 B4
Suar India 29°2N 79°3E 243 E8
Suau Papua N. G. 10°37S 150°2E 286 F6
Suavanao Solomon Is. 7°35S 158°47E 287 L10
Şubā Si. Arabia 27°10N 35°40E 246 E2
Subang Indonesia 6°34S 107°45E 231 G12
Subankhata India 26°48N 91°25E 241 B3
Subansiri → India 26°48N 93°50E 241 B4
Subarnagiri India 19°50N 83°51E 244 E6
Subarnarekha → India 22°34N 87°24E 243 H12
Subay', Urūq Si. Arabia 22°15N 43°5E 256 C5
Subayhah Si. Arabia 30°2N 38°50E 246 D3
Subcetate Romania 45°36N 23°0E 182 E8
Subhepur India 28°44N 77°15E 120 A2
Subi Indonesia 2°58N 108°50E 235 B3
Subiaco Italy 41°56N 13°5E 199 G10
Subic B. Phil. 14°44N 120°12E 232 D3
Subotica Serbia 46°6N 19°39E 182 D4
Suburban Canal U.S.A. 30°2N 90°11W 131 B1
Suca Ethiopia 6°31N 39°14E 257 F4
Sucat Phil. 14°27N 121°2E 127 C2
Suceava Romania 47°38N 26°16E 183 C11
Suceava □ Romania 47°37N 25°40E 183 C10
Suceava → Romania 47°32N 26°32E 183 C11
Sucha-Beskidzka Poland 49°44N 19°35E 185 J6
Suchan = Partizansk Russia 43°8N 133°9E 215 E14
Suchań Poland 53°18N 15°18E 185 E2
Suchdol Czechia 50°8N 14°22E 135 B2
Suchedniów Poland 51°3N 20°49E 185 G7
Suchil Mexico 23°39N 103°54W 318 C4
Suchou = Suzhou China 31°19N 120°38E 229 B13
Süchow = Xuzhou China 34°18N 117°10E 227 G9
Suchowola Poland 53°33N 23°3E 184 E10
Sucio → Colombia 7°27N 77°7W 328 B2
Suck → Ireland 53°17N 8°3W 166 C3
Suckling, Mt. Papua N. G. 9°49S 148°53E 286 E5
Sucre Bolivia 19°0S 65°15W 331 D4
Sucre Colombia 8°49N 74°44W 328 B3
Sucre □ Colombia 8°50N 75°40W 328 B2
Sucre □ Venezuela 10°25N 63°30W 329 A5
Sucuaro Colombia 4°34N 68°50W 328 C4
Sucumbíos □ Ecuador 0°6S 76°52W 328 D2
Sućuraj Croatia 43°10N 17°8E 199 E14
Sucuriju Brazil 1°39N 49°57W 332 A2
Sucuriú → Brazil 20°47S 51°38W 331 E7
Sucy-en-Brie France 48°46N 2°31E 134 B4
Sud □ Cameroon 2°30N 11°45E 263 E7
Sud, Pte. Comoros Is. 11°53S 43°29E 272 a
Sud, Pte. du Canada 49°3N 62°14W 299 C7
Sud-Kivu □ Dem. Rep. of the Congo 3°0S 28°30E 268 C2
Sud-Ouest □ Cameroon 5°25N 9°20E 263 D6
Sud-Ouest, Pte. Qué., Canada 49°23N 63°36W 299 C7
Sud Ouest, Pte. Mauritius 20°28S 57°18E 272 e
Sud-Ubangi □ Dem. Rep. of the Congo 2°30N 19°0E 264 B3
Suda → Russia 59°0N 37°40E 188 C9
Sudak Ukraine 44°51N 34°57E 189 K8
Sudan U.S.A. 34°4N 102°31W 314 D3
Sudan ■ Africa 15°0N 30°0E 257 E3
Sudauen = Suwałki Poland 54°8N 22°59E 184 D9
Sudbury U.K. 52°2N 0°45E 169 E8
Sudd South Sudan 8°20N 30°0E 257 F3
Suddie Guyana 7°8N 58°29W 329 B6
Sudeifel = Deutsch-Luxemburgischer ⌓ Germany 49°58N 6°12E 179 F2
Süderbrarup Germany 54°38N 9°45E 178 A5
Süderlügum Germany 54°52N 8°54E 178 A4
Süderoogsand Germany 54°27N 8°28E 178 A4
Sudeten Mts. = Sudety Europe 50°20N 16°45E 181 A9
Sudety Europe 50°20N 16°45E 181 A9
Súðavík Iceland 66°2N 23°0W 155 A3
Südheide ⌓ Germany 52°46N 10°10E 178 C6
Suður-múlasýsla Iceland 65°0N 14°30W 155 C12
Suður-þingeyjarsýsla Iceland 65°30N 17°0W 155 B9
Suðureyri Iceland 66°7N 23°32W 155 A3
Suðurland □ Iceland 64°30N 19°30W 155 C7
Suðurnes □ Iceland 63°50N 22°30W 155 D4
Suðuroy Færoe Is. 61°32N 6°50W 160 F9
Sudi Tanzania 10°11S 39°57E 269 E4
Sudirman, Pegunungan Indonesia 4°30S 137°0E 231 E9
Sudiţi Romania 44°35N 27°38E 183 F12
Sudogda Russia 55°55N 40°50E 190 C5
Sudong, Pulau Singapore 1°13N 103°44E 237 d
Sudostroy = Severodvinsk Russia 64°27N 39°58E 186 B6
Sudova Vyshnya Ukraine 49°46N 23°22E 185 J10
Sudzha Russia 51°14N 35°17E 189 G8
Sue → South Sudan 7°41N 28°3E 257 F2
Sue, L. U.S.A. 28°34N 81°23W 133 A2
Sueca Spain 39°12N 0°21W 197 F4
Suedinenie = Saedinenie Bulgaria 42°16N 24°33E 203 D8
Suemez I. U.S.A. 55°15N 133°20W 296 B2
Sueyoshi = Soo Japan 31°40N 131°5E 222 F3
Suez = El Suweis Egypt 29°58N 32°31E 256 B3
Suez, G. of = Suweis, Khalîg el Egypt 28°40N 33°0E 256 J8
Suez Canal = Suweis, Qanâ es Egypt 31°0N 32°20E 256 H8
Suffield Canada 50°12N 111°10W 296 C6
Suffolk U.S.A. 36°44N 76°35W 309 G15
Suffolk □ U.K. 52°16N 1°0E 169 E9
Şufiān Iran 38°16N 45°58E 213 C11
Suga-no-Sen Japan 35°25N 134°25E 222 B6
Şugag Romania 45°47N 23°37E 183 E8
Sugaing = Sagaing Myanmar 21°52N 95°59E 241 E5
Sugamo Japan 35°44N 139°43E 140 A3
Sugar → U.S.A. 42°26N 89°12W 310 B7
Sugar Cr. → Ill., U.S.A. 40°9N 89°38W 310 D7
Sugar Cr. → Ind., U.S.A. 39°51N 87°21W 311 E9
Sugar Grove U.S.A. 41°59N 79°20W 312 E5
Sugar Hill U.S.A. 34°6N 84°2W 316 A5
Sugar Loaf Grenada 12°13N 61°36W 323 q
Sugar Loaf Mt. = Açúcar, Pão de Brazil 22°56S 43°9W 135 B2
Sugar Loaf Pt. St. Helena 15°54S 5°42W 153 h
Sugarcreek U.S.A. 41°25N 79°52W 312 E5
Sugarive → India 26°16N 86°24E 243 F12
Sugbai Passage Phil. 5°22N 120°33E 233 J3
Suge Japan 35°37N 139°32E 140 B2
Sughd □ Tajikistan 40°0N 69°0E 217 E7
Sugihwaras Indonesia 4°1S 103°46E 234 C2
Suginami Japan 35°41N 139°37E 140 A2
Suğla Gölü Turkey 37°20N 32°0E 212 D5
Sugluk = Salluit Canada 62°14N 75°38W 295 E16
Sugō Japan 35°34N 139°33E 140 B2
Sugun China 39°53N 76°47E 217 E9
Suha Reke = Therandë Kosovo 42°21N 20°50E 202 D4
Suhaia, Lacul Romania 43°45N 25°15E 183 G10
Şuḥār Oman 24°20N 56°40E 247 E8
Sühbaatar Mongolia 50°17N 106°10E 218 A10
Sühbaatar □ Mongolia 45°30N 114°0E 226 B8
Suheli Par India 10°5N 72°17E 245 J1
Suhl Germany 50°36N 10°42E 178 E6
Şuhut Turkey 38°31N 30°32E 205 C12
Sui Pakistan 28°37N 69°19E 242 E3
Sui Sai Wan Hong Kong, China 22°16N 114°14E 122 B3
Sui Xian China 34°25N 115°2E 226 G8
Suiá Missu → Brazil 11°13S 53°15W 331 C7
Šuica Bos.-H. 43°52N 17°11E 182 G2
Suichang China 28°29N 119°15E 229 C12
Suichuan China 26°20N 114°32E 229 D10
Suide China 37°30N 110°12E 226 F6
Suifenhe China 44°25N 131°10E 227 B16
Suihua China 46°32N 126°55E 219 B14
Suijiang China 28°40N 103°59E 228 C4
Suining Hunan, China 26°35N 110°10E 229 D8
Suining Jiangsu, China 33°56N 117°58E 227 H9
Suining Sichuan, China 30°26N 105°35E 228 B5
Suiping China 33°10N 113°59E 226 H7
Suippes France 49°8N 4°30E 173 C11
Suir → Ireland 52°16N 7°9W 166 D4
Suisse = Switzerland ■ Europe 46°30N 8°0E 179 J4
Suisun City U.S.A. 38°15N 122°2W 306 G4
Suita Japan 34°45N 135°30E 133 A2
Suitland U.S.A. 38°50N 76°55W 143 B3
Suixi China 21°19N 110°18E 229 G8
Suiyang Guizhou, China 27°58N 107°18E 228 D6
Suiyang Heilongjiang, China 44°30N 130°56E 227 B16
Suizhong China 40°21N 120°20E 227 D11
Suizhou China 31°42N 113°24E 229 B9
Sujangarh India 27°42N 74°31E 242 F6
Sujiatun China 41°39N 123°20E 227 D12
Sukabumi Indonesia 6°56S 106°50E 234 D3
Sukadana Kalimantan Barat, Indonesia 1°10S 110°0E 235 C4
Sukadana Lampung, Indonesia 5°5S 105°33E 234 D3
Sukadana, Teluk Indonesia 1°24S 109°50E 235 C3
Sukagawa Japan 37°17N 140°23E 221 F10
Sukamade Indonesia 8°30S 113°52E 235 D4

Sukamara Indonesia 2°43S 111°10E 235 C4
Sukaraja Indonesia 2°28S 110°25E 235 C4
Sukarnapura = Jayapura
Indonesia 2°28S 140°38E 231 E10
Sukarno, Puntjak = Jaya, Puncak
Indonesia 3°57S 137°17E 231 E9
Sukarno-Hatta Int., Jakarta ✕
(CGK) Indonesia 6°7S 106°40E 231 G12
Sukau Malaysia 5°32N 118°17E 235 A5
Sukawati Indonesia 8°35S 115°17E 231 K18
Sukchar India 22°42N 88°22E 124 A2
Sukch'ŏn N. Korea 39°22N 125°35E 224 C2
Sukhindol Bulgaria 43°11N 25°10E 203 C9
Sukhinichi Russia 54°8N 35°10E 188 E8
Sukhona → Russia 61°15N 46°39E 186 C6
Sukhothai Thailand 17°1N 99°49E 236 D2
Sukhumi = Sokhumi
Georgia 43°0N 41°0E 191 J5
Sukkertoppen = Maniitsoq
Greenland 65°26N 52°55W 154 D5
Sukkur Pakistan 27°42N 68°54E 242 F3
Sukkur Barrage Pakistan 27°40N 68°50E 242 F3
Sukma India 18°24N 81°45E 244 E5
Sukovo Serbia 43°4N 22°37E 202 C6
Sukri → India 25°4N 71°43E 242 G4
Sukumo Japan 32°56N 132°44E 222 E4
Sukunka → Canada 55°45N 121°15W 296 B4
Sul, Canal do Brazil 0°10S 48°30W 332 B2
Sula Norway 61°7N 4°54E 164 C1
Sula → Ukraine 49°40N 32°41E 189 H7
Sula, Kepulauan Indonesia 1°45S 125°0E 231 E7
Sulaco → Honduras 15°2N 87°44W 320 C2
Sulaiman Range Pakistan 30°30N 69°50E 242 D3
Sulaiman-Too Kyrgyzstan 40°31N 72°46E 217 D8
Sulak → Russia 43°20N 47°34E 191 J8
Sulakyurt Turkey 40°9N 33°43E 212 B5
Sūlār Iran 31°53N 51°54E 247 D6
Sulawesi Indonesia 2°0S 120°0E 235 C5
Sulawesi Barat □ Indonesia 3°0S 119°0E 235 C5
Sulawesi Sea = Celebes Sea
Indonesia 3°0N 123°0E 231 D6
Sulawesi Selatan □
Indonesia 2°30S 120°0E 231 E6
Sulawesi Tengah □
Indonesia 1°30S 121°0E 231 E6
Sulawesi Tenggara □
Indonesia 3°50S 122°0E 231 E6
Sulawesi Utara □ Indonesia 1°0N 124°0E 231 D6
Suldalsheiene Norway 59°28N 7°10E 164 E3
Suldalsosen Norway 59°29N 6°29E 164 E3
Sulechów Poland 52°5N 15°40E 185 F2
Sulęcin Poland 52°26N 15°10E 185 F2
Sulei Solomon Is. 8°3S 159°34E 287 M10
Suleja Nigeria 9°10N 7°10E 263 D6
Sulejów Poland 51°26N 19°53E 185 G6
Sulejówek Poland 52°13N 21°17E 185 F8
Süleymanlı Turkey 38°58N 27°47E 205 C9
Sulima S. Leone 6°58N 11°32W 262 D2
Sulina Romania 45°10N 29°40E 183 E14
Sulina, Braţul →
Romania 45°10N 29°40E 183 E14
Sulingen Germany 52°41N 8°48E 178 C4
Suliţa Romania 47°39N 26°59E 183 C11
Sulitjelma Norway 67°9N 16°3E 160 C17
Sułkowice Poland 49°50N 19°49E 185 J6
Sullana Peru 4°52S 80°39W 330 A1
Süller Turkey 38°9N 29°29E 205 C11
Sullivan Ill., U.S.A. 39°36N 88°37W 311 E8
Sullivan Ind., U.S.A. 39°6N 87°24W 311 E9
Sullivan Mo., U.S.A. 38°13N 91°10W 310 F5
Sullivan Bay Canada 50°55N 126°50W 296 C3
Sullivan I. = Lanbi Kyun
Myanmar 10°50N 98°20E 237 G2
Sullom Voe U.K. 60°27N 1°20W 167 A7
Sullorsuaq Greenland 70°5N 53°0W 154 C5
Sully U.S.A. 41°34N 92°50W 310 C4
Sully-sur-Loire France 47°45N 2°20E 173 E9
Sulmierzyce Poland 51°37N 17°32E 185 G4
Sulmona Italy 42°3N 13°55E 199 F10
Süloğlu Turkey 41°44N 26°53E 203 E10
Sulphur La., U.S.A. 30°14N 93°23W 314 F8
Sulphur Okla., U.S.A. 34°31N 96°58W 314 D6
Sulphur Channel
Hong Kong, China 22°15N 114°7E 122 B2
Sulphur Pt. Canada 60°56N 114°48W 296 A6
Sulphur Springs U.S.A. 33°8N 95°36W 314 E7
Sulsul Ethiopia 5°5N 44°50E 267 C5
Sultan Ont., Canada 47°36N 82°47W 298 C3
Sultan Wash., U.S.A. 47°52N 121°49W 306 C5
Sultan Dağları Turkey 38°20N 31°20E 212 C4
Sultan Hamud Kenya 2°1S 37°22E 268 C4
Sultan Kudarat Phil. 7°16N 124°18E 233 H5
Sultan Kudarat □ Phil. 6°30N 124°10E 233 H5
Sultan Naga Dimaporo
Phil. 7°55N 123°44E 233 H4
Sultan sa Barongis Phil. 6°45N 124°35E 233 H5
Sultanābād = Arāk Iran 34°0N 49°40E 247 C6
Sultanahmet Camii Turkey 41°0N 28°58E 122 B1
Sultanhisar Turkey 37°53N 28°9E 205 D10
Sultanıça Turkey 40°37N 26°8E 203 F10
Sultaniye Turkey 40°11N 28°12E 203 F12
Sultanpur Mad. P., India 23°9N 77°56E 242 H8
Sultanpur Punjab, India 31°13N 75°11E 242 D6
Sultanpur Ut. P., India 26°18N 82°4E 243 F10
Sulu □ Phil. 5°30N 120°30E 233 J3
Sulu Arch. Phil. 6°0N 121°0E 233 J3
Sulu Sea E. Indies 8°0N 120°0E 233 G3
Sülüklü Turkey 38°53N 32°20E 212 C5
Sululta Ethiopia 9°10N 38°43E 257 F4
Suluova Turkey 40°46N 35°32E 212 B6
Sulūq Libya 31°44N 20°14E 258 B4
Suluru India 13°42N 80°1E 245 H5
Sulzbach Germany 49°18N 7°3E 179 F3
Sulzbach-Rosenberg
Germany 49°30N 11°44E 179 F7
Sulzberger Ice Shelf
Antarctica 78°0S 150°0W 151 E13
Sumaco -Napo Galeras △
Ecuador 0°34S 77°38W 328 D2
Sumalata Indonesia 1°0N 122°31E 231 D6
Sumale □ Ethiopia 7°0N 45°0E 267 C6
Sumampa Argentina 29°25S 63°29W 334 B3
Sumapaz △ Colombia 3°49N 74°13W 328 C3
Sumaré Brazil 22°48S 47°17W 333 F2
Sumatera Indonesia 0°40N 100°20E 234 B2
Sumatera Barat □ Indonesia 1°0S 101°0E 234 B1
Sumatera Selatan □
Indonesia 3°0S 104°0E 234 C2
Sumatera Utara □ Indonesia 2°30N 98°0E 234 B1
Sumatra = Sumatera
Indonesia 0°40N 100°20E 234 B2
Sumatra U.S.A. 30°1N 84°59W 316 E2
Sumava △ Czechia 49°0N 13°49E 180 C6
Sumba Angola 6°15S 12°38E 265 D2
Sumba Indonesia 9°45S 119°35E 231 F5
Sumba, Selat Indonesia 9°0S 118°40E 231 F5
Sumbawa Indonesia 8°26S 117°30E 235 D5
Sumbawa Besar Indonesia 8°30S 117°26E 235 D5
Sumbe Angola 11°10S 13°48E 265 E2
Sumbu △ Zambia 8°43S 30°22E 269 D3
Sumburgh Hd. U.K. 59°52N 1°17W 167 B7
Sumdeo India 31°26N 78°44E 243 D8
Sumdo China 35°6N 78°41E 243 B8
Sumé Brazil 7°39S 36°55W 332 C4
Sumedang Indonesia 6°52S 107°55E 235 D3
Sümeg Hungary 46°59N 17°20E 182 D2
Sumeih Sudan 9°50N 27°39E 257 F2
Šumen = Shumen
Bulgaria 43°18N 26°55E 203 C10
Sumenep Indonesia 7°1S 113°52E 235 D4
Sumgait = Sumqayıt
Azerbaijan 40°34N 49°38E 191 K9
Sumida Japan 35°42N 139°49E 140 A3
Sumida → Japan 35°39N 139°45E 140 A3
Sumisu-Jima Japan 31°27N 140°3E 223 F12
Sumiyoshi Japan 34°36N 135°30E 133 B2
Sumiyoshi Shrine Japan 34°36N 135°30E 133 B1
Summer L. U.S.A. 42°50N 120°45W 304 E3
Summerland Canada 49°32N 119°41W 296 D5
Summerland Key U.S.A. 24°40N 81°27W 317 L8
Summerside Canada 46°24N 63°47W 299 C7
Summersville U.S.A. 38°17N 80°51W 309 F13
Summerton U.S.A. 33°36N 80°20W 316 B9
Summertown U.S.A. 32°45N 82°16W 316 C7
Summerville Ont., Canada 43°37N 79°33W 141 B1
Summerville Ga., U.S.A. 34°29N 85°21W 315 D12
Summerville S.C., U.S.A. 33°1N 80°11W 316 B9
Summit Alaska, U.S.A. 63°20N 149°7W 303 E10
Summit Ill., U.S.A. 41°47N 87°47W 119 C2
Summit Lake Canada 54°20N 122°40W 296 C4
Summit Peak U.S.A. 37°21N 106°42W 305 H10
Sumner N.Z. 43°35S 172°48E 285 D7
Sumner Ill., U.S.A. 38°42N 87°53W 311 F9
Sumner Iowa, U.S.A. 42°51N 92°6W 310 B4
Sumner Wash., U.S.A. 47°12N 122°14W 306 C4
Sumner, L. N.Z. 42°42S 172°15E 285 C7
Sumner Tunnel Boston, U.S.A. 116 a3
Sumoto Japan 34°21N 134°54E 222 C6
Sumpangbinangae
Indonesia 4°24S 119°36E 235 C5
Šumperk Czechia 49°59N 16°59E 181 B9
Sumprabum Myanmar 26°33N 97°36E 241 B6
Sumqayıt Azerbaijan 40°34N 49°38E 191 K9
Sumter U.S.A. 33°55N 80°21W 316 B9
Sumxi China 34°35N 80°22E 217 F10
Sumy Ukraine 50°57N 34°50E 189 G8
Sumy □ Ukraine 50°50N 33°50E 189 G7
Sun City S. Africa 25°17S 27°3E 270 C4
Sun City Center U.S.A. 27°43N 82°21W 317 H7
Sun Kosi → Nepal 26°59N 87°8E 243 F12
Sun Lakes U.S.A. 33°10N 111°52W 305 K8
Sun Prairie U.S.A. 43°11N 89°13W 310 A7
Sun Valley U.S.A. 43°42N 114°21W 304 E6
Sunagawa Japan 43°29N 141°55E 220 C10
Sunamachi Japan 35°40N 139°50E 140 A4
Sunamganj Bangla. 25°4N 91°24E 241 C3
Sunan N. Korea 39°15N 125°40E 224 C2
Sunart, L. U.K. 56°42N 5°43W 167 E3
Sunburst U.S.A. 48°53N 111°55W 304 B8
Sunbury Vic., Australia 37°35S 144°44E 283 D6
Sunbury Pa., U.S.A. 40°52N 76°48W 313 F8
Sunbury-on-Thames U.K. 51°25N 0°26W 125 B1
Sunchales Argentina 30°58S 61°35W 334 C3
Suncheon S. Korea 34°52N 127°31E 224 E3
Suncho Corral Argentina 27°55S 63°27W 334 B3
Sunch'on N. Korea 39°25N 125°56E 224 C2
Suncook U.S.A. 43°8N 71°27W 313 C13
Sunda, Selat Indonesia 6°20S 105°30E 234 D3
Sunda Is. Indonesia 5°0S 105°0E 288 H2
Sunda Str. = Sunda, Selat
Indonesia 6°20S 105°30E 234 D3
Sunda Trench = Java Trench
Ind. Oc. 9°0S 105°0E 234 D2
Sundance Man., Canada 56°32N 94°4W 297 B10
Sundance Wyo., U.S.A. 44°24N 104°23W 304 D11
Sundar Nagar India 31°32N 76°53E 242 D7
Sundarbans Asia 22°0N 89°0E 241 E2
Sundarbans △ India 22°0N 88°45E 241 E2
Sundargarh India 22°4N 84°5E 244 C7
Sundays = Sondags →
S. Africa 33°44S 25°51E 270 D4
Sundbyberg Sweden 59°22N 17°57E 139 A1
Sundbyerne Denmark 55°39N 12°36E 118 B3
Sunderland Ont., Canada 44°16N 79°4W 312 B5
Sunderland Tyne & W.,
U.K. 54°55N 1°23W 168 C6
Sundi Lutete
Dem. Rep. of the Congo 4°34S 14°14E 265 C2
Sundown △ Australia 28°49S 151°38E 281 D5
Sundre Canada 51°49N 114°38W 296 C6
Sunds Denmark 56°13N 9°1E 163 H3
Sundsvall Sweden 62°23N 17°17E 162 B11
Sundsvallsbukten
Sweden 62°21N 17°25E 162 B11
Sungai Acheh Malaysia 5°8N 100°30E 237 c
Sungai Kolok Thailand 6°2N 101°58E 237 J3
Sungai Lembing Malaysia 3°55N 103°3E 237 L4
Sungai Petani Malaysia 5°37N 100°30E 237 K3
Sungai Siput Malaysia 4°49N 101°4E 234 B2
Sungaidurian Indonesia 0°6S 109°21E 235 C3
Sungaigerong Indonesia 2°59S 104°52E 234 C2
Sungailiat Indonesia 1°51S 106°8E 234 C3
Sungaipakning Indonesia 1°19N 102°8E 234 B2
Sungaipenuh Indonesia 2°1S 101°20E 234 C2
Sungari = Songhua Jiang →
China 47°45N 132°30E 219 B15
Sungei Kadut Industrial Estate
Singapore 1°24N 103°44E 138 A2
Sungei Selatar Res.
Singapore 1°24N 103°51E 138 A3
Sungguminasa Indonesia 5°17S 119°30E 235 D5
Sunghua Chiang = Songhua
Jiang → China 47°45N 132°30E 219 B15
Sungikai Sudan 12°20N 29°51E 257 E2
Sungsang Indonesia 2°22S 104°55E 234 C2
Sungu Dem. Rep. of the Congo 1°5S 17°21E 264 C3
Sungurlu Turkey 40°12N 34°21E 212 B6
Sunja Croatia 45°21N 16°35E 199 C13
Sunland Park U.S.A. 31°50N 106°40W 305 L10
Sunnansjö Sweden 60°13N 14°58E 162 D8
Sunndalsøra Norway 62°40N 8°33E 164 B5
Sunne Sweden 59°52N 13°5E 162 E7
Sunnemo Sweden 59°53N 13°44E 162 E7
Sunnfjord Norway 61°35N 5°45E 164 C2
Sunnmøre Norway 62°35N 6°30E 164 B3
Sunny Bay
Hong Kong, China 22°20N 114°1E 122 B1
Sunny Isles Beach U.S.A. 25°55N 80°7W 129 C3
Sunnyside U.S.A. 46°20N 120°0W 304 C4
Sunnyvale U.S.A. 37°23N 122°2W 306 H4
Sunrise U.S.A. 26°8N 80°14W 129 B2
Sunrise Manor U.S.A. 36°12N 115°4W 124 A2
Sunrise Mountain Natural Area ⌂
U.S.A. 36°12N 114°58W 124 A2
Sunset Beach U.S.A. 21°40N 158°3W 302 J13
Sunset Park N.Y., U.S.A. 40°38N 73°59W 132 C2
Sunset Park Nev., U.S.A. 36°3N 115°6W 124 B2
Sunset Peak
Hong Kong, China 22°15N 113°57E 122 B1
Sunshine Coast Australia 26°30S 153°0E 276 F9
Sunshine I.
Hong Kong, China 22°16N 114°3E 122 B2
Sunshine Park U.S.A. 26°2N 80°13W 129 B2
Suntar Russia 62°15N 117°30E 215 C12
Sunter Indonesia 6°7S 106°51E 122 A2
Sunter, Kali → Indonesia 6°10S 106°53E 122 B2
Suntrana U.S.A. 63°52N 148°51W 303 E10
Sunwi-do N. Korea 37°43N 125°16E 224 D2
Sunyani Ghana 7°21N 2°22W 262 D4
Suō-Nada Japan 33°50N 131°30E 222 D3
Suomenlinna Finland 60°9N 24°59E 121 C2
Suomenselkä Finland 62°52N 24°0E 160 E21
Suomi = Finland ■ Europe 63°0N 27°0E 160 E22
Suomussalmi Finland 64°54N 29°10E 160 D23
Suoyarvi Russia 62°3N 32°20E 188 A7
Supai U.S.A. 36°15N 112°41W 305 H7
Supamo → Venezuela 6°48N 61°50W 329 B5
Supaul India 26°10N 86°40E 243 F12
Superagüi △ Brazil 25°6S 48°18W 333 G2
Superior Ariz., U.S.A. 33°18N 111°6W 305 K8
Superior Mont., U.S.A. 47°12N 114°53W 304 C6
Superior Nebr., U.S.A. 40°1N 98°4W 308 E4
Superior Wis., U.S.A. 46°44N 92°6W 308 B7
Superior, L. N. Amer. 47°0N 87°0W 298 C2
Supetar Croatia 43°25N 16°32E 199 E13
Suphan Buri Thailand 14°14N 100°10E 236 E3
Suphan Dağı Turkey 38°54N 42°48E 213 C10
Supiori Indonesia 1°0S 136°0E 231 E9
Supraśl Poland 53°13N 23°19E 185 E10
Supraśl → Poland 53°11N 22°57E 185 E9
Supreme Court Washington, D.C., U.S.A. 143 b3
Supsa Georgia 42°2N 41°49E 191 J5
Supung N. Korea 40°27N 124°54E 224 B2
Supung Shuiku China 40°35N 124°50E 224 B2
Sūq 'Abs Yemen 16°0N 43°12E 248 D3
Sūq al Jarrahī Yemen 14°10N 43°20E 248 D3
Sūq ash Shuyūkh Iraq 30°53N 46°28E 246 D5
Sūq Suwayq Si. Arabia 24°23N 38°27E 246 E3
Şuqaylabiyah Syria 35°23N 36°23E 250 C7
Suqian China 33°54N 118°8E 227 H10
Suquṭra = Socotra Yemen 12°30N 54°0E 249 D6
Sūr Lebanon 33°19N 35°16E 250 E6
Şūr Oman 22°34N 59°32E 249 B7
Sur, C. Chile 27°12S 109°26W 330 b
Sur, Pt. U.S.A. 36°18N 121°54W 306 J5
Sur Bahr West Bank 31°44N 35°13E 123 B2
Sura India 22°33N 88°24E 124 B2
Sura → Russia 56°6N 46°0E 190 C8
Surab Pakistan 28°25N 66°15E 242 E2
Surabaja = Surabaya
Indonesia 7°17S 112°45E 235 D4
Surabaya Indonesia 7°17S 112°45E 235 D4
Surahammar Sweden 59°43N 16°13E 162 E10
Suraia Romania 45°40N 27°25E 183 E12
Surakarta Indonesia 7°35S 110°48E 235 D4
Suraksan S. Korea 37°40N 127°4E 137 A2
Surallah Phil. 6°22N 124°44E 233 H5
Šurany Slovakia 48°6N 18°10E 181 C11
Surat Queens., Australia 27°10S 149°6E 281 D4
Surat India 21°12N 72°55E 244 D1
Surat Thani Thailand 9°6N 99°20E 237 H2
Suratgarh India 29°18N 73°55E 242 E5
Surathkal India 12°58N 74°46E 245 H2
Suraxanı = Qaraçuxar
Azerbaijan 40°25N 50°1E 191 K10
Şurayımilā Si. Arabia 25°7N 46°7E 246 E5
Suraż Poland 52°57N 22°57E 185 F9
Surazh Belarus 55°25N 30°44E 188 E6
Surazh Russia 53°5N 32°27E 189 F7
Surbiton U.K. 51°23N 0°17W 125 B2
Surduc Romania 47°15N 23°25E 183 C8
Surduc Pasul Romania 45°21N 23°23E 183 E8
Surdulica Serbia 42°41N 22°11E 202 D6
Surendranagar India 22°45N 71°40E 242 H4
Suresnes France 48°52N 2°13E 134 A2
Surf U.S.A. 34°41N 120°36W 307 L6
Surfers Paradise Australia 28°0S 153°25E 281 D5
Surfside U.S.A. 25°52N 80°7W 129 C3
Surgana India 20°34N 73°37E 244 D1
Surgères France 46°7N 0°47W 174 B3
Surgut Russia 61°14N 73°20E 214 C8
Sùria Spain 41°50N 1°45E 196 D6
Surian, Palazzo Venice, Italy 142 a2
Suriapet India 17°10N 79°40E 244 F4
Suribachi Yama Iwo Jima 24°45N 141°17E 288 b
Surigao Phil. 9°47N 125°29E 233 G5
Surigao del Norte □ Phil. 9°40N 125°40E 233 G5
Surigao del Sur □ Phil. 8°45N 126°0E 233 G6
Surigao Str. Phil. 10°15N 125°23E 233 F5
Surin Thailand 14°50N 103°34E 236 E4
Surinam = Suriname ■
S. Amer. 4°0N 56°0W 329 C6
Surinam Mauritius 20°30S 57°30E 272 e
Suriname ■ S. Amer. 4°0N 56°0W 329 C6
Suriname → Suriname 5°50N 55°15W 329 B6
Surjagarh India 19°36N 80°25E 244 E5
Surma → Bangla. 24°34N 91°14E 241 C3
Sūrmaq Iran 31°3N 52°48E 247 D7
Sürmene Turkey 41°0N 40°1E 213 B9
Surna → Norway 62°59N 8°40E 164 B5
Surnadalsøra Norway 62°58N 8°40E 164 B5
Surovikino Russia 48°32N 42°55E 191 F6
Surprise U.S.A. 33°38N 112°19W 305 K7
Surquillo Peru 12°6S 77°1W 124 B2
Surrency U.S.A. 31°44N 82°12W 316 D7
Surrey Canada 49°7N 122°45W 306 A4
Surrey □ Jamaica 18°5N 76°34W 320 a
Surrey □ U.K. 51°15N 0°31W 169 F7
Surrey Hills Australia 33°53S 151°13E 139 B2
Sursand India 26°39N 85°43E 243 F11
Sursar → India 26°14N 87°3E 243 F12
Sursee Switz. 47°11N 8°6E 179 H4
Sursk Russia 53°3N 45°40E 190 D7
Surskoye Russia 54°30N 46°44E 190 C8
Surt Libya 31°11N 16°39E 258 B3
Surt □ Libya 30°0N 17°30E 258 B3
Surt, Al Ḥamādah al Libya 30°0N 17°50E 258 C3
Surt, Khalīj Libya 31°40N 18°30E 258 B3
Surtanahu Pakistan 26°22N 70°0E 242 F4
Surte Sweden 57°50N 12°1E 163 G6
Surtsey Iceland 63°20N 20°30W 155 D6
Surubim Brazil 7°50S 35°45W 332 C4
Sürüç Turkey 36°58N 38°25E 213 D8
Surud, Ras Somalia 11°10N 47°30E 267 B6
Surud Ad Somalia 10°42N 47°9E 267 B6
Suruga-Wan Japan 34°45N 138°30E 223 C10
Surulangun Indonesia 2°37S 102°45E 234 C2
Surulere Nigeria 6°29N 3°21E 124 B2
Surumu → Brazil 3°22N 60°19W 329 C5
Surxondaryo □ Uzbekistan 38°0N 67°30E 217 E7
Susa = Sousse Tunisia 35°50N 10°38E 258 A2
Şuşa Azerbaijan 39°46N 46°45E 213 C12
Susa Italy 45°8N 7°3E 198 C4
Susā → Denmark 55°12N 11°42E 163 J5
Sušac Croatia 42°46N 16°30E 199 F13
Susaek S. Korea 37°34N 126°54E 137 B1
Sūsah Libya 32°52N 21°59E 258 B4
Susak Croatia 44°30N 14°18E 199 D11
Susaki Japan 33°22N 133°17E 222 D5
Susam-Adasi = Samos
Greece 37°45N 26°50E 205 D8
Sūsangerd Iran 31°35N 48°6E 247 D6
Susanville U.S.A. 40°25N 120°39W 304 F3
Susch Switz. 46°46N 10°5E 179 J6
Suşehri Turkey 40°10N 38°6E 213 B8
Sušice Czechia 49°17N 13°30E 180 B6
Susleni Moldova 47°25N 28°59E 183 C13
Susner India 23°57N 76°5E 242 H7
Susong China 30°10N 116°5E 229 B11
Susono Japan 35°10N 138°55E 223 B10
Susquehanna U.S.A. 41°57N 75°36W 313 E9
Susquehanna → U.S.A. 39°33N 76°5W 313 G8
Susques Argentina 23°35S 66°25W 334 A2
Süssenbrunn Austria 48°16N 16°29E 142 A2
Sussex N.B., Canada 45°45N 65°37W 299 C6
Sussex U.S.A. 41°13N 74°37W 313 E10
Sussex, East □ U.K. 51°0N 0°20E 169 G8
Sussex, West □ U.K. 51°0N 0°30W 169 G7
Sussex Inlet Australia 35°10S 150°36E 283 C9
Sustut → Canada 56°20N 127°30W 296 B3
Susuman Russia 62°47N 148°10E 215 C15
Susunu Indonesia 3°7S 133°39E 231 E8
Susupe N. Marianas 14°58N 145°37E 302 e
Susurluk Turkey 39°54N 28°8E 205 B10
Susuz Turkey 40°46N 43°8E 213 B10
Susz Poland 53°44N 19°20E 184 E6
Sutay Uul Asia 46°35N 93°38E 218 B7
Sütçüler Turkey 37°29N 30°57E 212 D4
Şuţeşti Romania 45°13N 27°27E 183 E12
Sutherland N.S.W.,
Australia 34°2S 151°4E 283 C9
Sutherland Northern Cape,
S. Africa 32°24S 20°40E 270 D3
Sutherland Highl., U.K. 58°12N 4°50W 167 C4
Sutherland Nebr., U.S.A. 41°10N 101°8W 308 E3
Sutherland Falls N.Z. 44°48S 167°46E 285 E2
Sutherland Road Barbados 13°16N 59°39W 323 g
Sutherlin U.S.A. 43°23N 123°19W 304 E2
Suthri India 23°3N 68°55E 242 H3
Sutjeska △ Bos.-H. 43°50N 18°32E 182 G3
Sutlej → Pakistan 29°23N 71°3E 242 E4
Sutter U.S.A. 39°10N 121°45W 306 F5
Sutter Buttes U.S.A. 39°12N 121°49W 306 F5
Sutter Creek U.S.A. 38°24N 120°48W 306 G6
Sutton Qué., Canada 45°6N 72°37W 313 A12
Sutton N.Z. 45°34S 170°8E 285 F5
Sutton London, U.K. 51°21N 0°11W 125 B2
Sutton Nebr., U.S.A. 40°36N 97°52W 308 E5
Sutton W. Va., U.S.A. 38°40N 80°43W 309 F13
Sutton → Canada 55°15N 83°45W 298 A3
Sutton Coldfield U.K. 52°35N 1°49W 169 E6
Sutton in Ashfield U.K. 53°8N 1°16W 168 D6
Sutton L. Canada 54°15N 84°42W 298 B3
Suttor → Australia 21°36S 147°2E 280 C4
Suttsu Japan 42°48N 140°14E 220 C10
Sutwik I. U.S.A. 56°34N 157°12W 303 H8
Suva Fiji 18°6S 178°30E 287 B2
Suva Gora N. Macedonia 41°45N 21°3E 202 E5
Suva Planina Serbia 43°10N 22°5E 202 C6
Suva Reka = Therandë
Kosovo 42°21N 20°50E 202 D4
Suvorov Russia 54°7N 36°30E 188 E9
Suvorov Is. = Suwarrow Is.
Cook Is. 13°15S 163°5W 289 J11
Suvorove Ukraine 45°35N 28°59E 183 E13
Suvorovo Bulgaria 43°20N 27°35E 203 C11
Suwa Japan 36°2N 138°8E 223 A10
Suwa-Ko Japan 36°3N 138°5E 223 A10
Suwałki Poland 54°8N 22°59E 184 D9
Suwannaphum Thailand 15°33N 103°47E 236 E4
Suwannee U.S.A. 29°20N 83°9W 317 F6
Suwannee → U.S.A. 29°17N 83°10W 317 F6
Suwannee Sd. U.S.A. 29°20N 83°15W 317 F6
Suwanose-Jima Japan 29°38N 129°43E 221 K4
Suwarrow Is. Cook Is. 13°15S 163°5W 289 J11
Suwayqīyah, Hawr as
Iraq 32°40N 46°3E 213 G12
Suweis, Khalîg el Egypt 28°40N 33°0E 256 J8
Suweis, Qanâ es Egypt 31°0N 32°20E 256 H8
Suwon S. Korea 37°17N 127°1E 224 D3
Suyu S. Korea 37°37N 127°0E 137 B2
Suzaka Japan 36°39N 138°19E 223 A10
Suzdal Russia 56°29N 40°26E 188 D11
Suzhou Anhui, China 33°41N 116°59E 226 H9
Suzhou Jiangsu, China 31°19N 120°38E 229 B13
Suzu Japan 37°25N 137°17E 221 F8
Suzu-Misaki Japan 37°31N 137°21E 221 F8
Suzuka Japan 34°55N 136°36E 223 C8
Suzuka-Sammyaku Japan 35°5N 136°30E 223 B8
Suzukishinden Japan 35°43N 139°31E 140 A2
Suzun Russia 53°47N 82°18E 217 B10
Suzzara Italy 45°0N 10°45E 198 D7
Svalbard Arctic 78°0N 17°0E 154 B12
Svalbard Radio = Longyearbyen
Svalbard 78°13N 15°40E 150 B8
Svalbarð Iceland 66°12N 15°43W 155 A11
Svalbarðseyri Iceland 65°45N 18°5W 155 B8
Svalöv Sweden 55°57N 13°8E 163 J7
Svalyava Ukraine 48°33N 22°59E 182 B7
Svaneke Denmark 55°8N 15°8E 163 J9
Svanemøllen Denmark 55°43N 12°34E 118 A3
Svaneti Georgia 42°50N 42°45E 213 A10
Svängsta Sweden 56°16N 14°47E 163 H8
Svanskog Sweden 59°11N 12°33E 162 E6
Svappavaara Sweden 67°40N 21°3E 160 C19
Svärdsjö Sweden 60°45N 15°54E 162 D9
Svarstad Norway 59°27N 9°56E 164 E6
Svartå Sweden 59°8N 14°32E 162 E8
Svartárkot Iceland 65°20N 17°15W 155 B9
Svartevatn Norway 59°10N 6°56E 164 E3
Svartisen Norway 66°40N 13°59E 160 C15
Svartvik Sweden 62°19N 17°24E 162 B11
Svatove Ukraine 49°22N 38°15E 189 H10
Svatovo = Svatove
Ukraine 49°22N 38°15E 189 H10
Svatsum Norway 61°20N 9°56E 164 C6
Svay Chek Cambodia 13°48N 102°58E 236 F4
Svay Rieng Cambodia 11°9N 105°45E 237 G5
Sveaborg = Suomenlinna
Finland 60°9N 24°59E 121 C2
Svealand Sweden 60°20N 15°0E 162 D9
Svedala Sweden 55°30N 13°15E 163 J7
Sveg Sweden 62°2N 14°21E 162 B8
Sveindal Norway 58°29N 7°30E 164 F4
Sveinseyri Iceland 65°38N 23°51W 155 B3
Sveio Norway 59°33N 5°23E 164 E2
Svelgen Norway 61°46N 5°17E 164 C2
Svelvik Norway 59°37N 10°24E 164 E7
Svendborg Denmark 55°4N 10°35E 163 J4
Svene Norway 59°45N 9°31E 164 E6
Svenljunga Sweden 57°29N 13°5E 163 G7
Svenstavik Sweden 62°45N 14°26E 162 B8
Svenstrup Denmark 56°58N 9°50E 163 H3
Svenyhorodka Ukraine 49°4N 30°56E 189 H6
Sverdlov Russia 55°46N 37°36E 129 B2
Sverdlovsk = Yekaterinburg
Russia 56°50N 60°30E 214 D7
Sverdlovsk Ukraine 48°5N 39°47E 189 H10
Sverdrup Chan. Canada 79°56N 96°25W 295 B12
Sverdrup Is. Canada 79°0N 97°0W 292 B10
Sverige = Sweden ■
Europe 57°0N 15°0E 161 H16
Sveshtari Bulgaria 43°40N 26°40E 203 C10
Svestad Norway 59°46N 10°36E 133 B2
Svetac Croatia 43°3N 15°43E 199 E12
Sveti Ivan = Zelina
Croatia 45°57N 16°16E 199 C13
Sveti Nikola, Prokhad
Europe 43°27N 22°6E 202 C6
Sveti Nikole N. Macedonia 41°51N 21°56E 202 E5
Sveti Rok Croatia 44°22N 15°39E 199 D12
Sveti Vrach = Sandanski
Bulgaria 41°35N 23°16E 202 E7
Svetlaya Russia 46°33N 138°18E 220 A9
Svetlogorsk = Svyetlahorsk
Belarus 52°38N 29°46E 177 B15
Svetlogorsk Russia 54°56N 20°10E 184 D7
Svetlograd Russia 45°25N 42°58E 191 H6
Svetlovodsk = Svitlovodsk
Ukraine 49°2N 33°13E 189 H7
Svetlyy Kaliningrad, Russia 54°41N 20°8E 184 D7
Svetlyy Orenburg, Russia 50°48N 60°51E 216 B6
Svidník Slovakia 49°20N 21°37E 181 B14
Svignaskarð Iceland 64°40N 21°42W 155 C5
Svilaja Planina Croatia 43°49N 16°31E 199 E13
Svilajnac Serbia 44°15N 21°11E 202 B5
Svilengrad Bulgaria 41°49N 26°12E 203 E10
Svinafell Iceland 63°59N 16°51W 155 D10
Svinö Finland 60°7N 24°44E 121 C1
Svir → Russia 60°30N 32°48E 188 B7
Sviritsa Russia 60°29N 32°51E 188 B7
Svishtov Bulgaria 43°36N 25°23E 203 C9
Svislach Belarus 53°3N 24°2E 185 E11
Svitava → Czechia 49°11N 16°37E 181 B9
Svitavy Czechia 49°47N 16°28E 181 B9
Svitlovodsk Ukraine 49°2N 33°13E 189 H7
Svityaz, Ozero Ukraine 51°30N 23°50E 185 G10
Svizzera = Switzerland ■
Europe 46°30N 8°0E 179 J4
Svobodnyy Russia 51°20N 128°0E 215 D13
Svoge Bulgaria 42°59N 23°23E 202 D7
Svolvær Norway 68°15N 14°34E 160 B16
Svorkmo Norway 63°10N 9°46E 164 A6
Svoronata Greece 38°7N 20°31E 207 C2
Svratka → Czechia 49°11N 16°38E 181 B9
Svrljig Serbia 43°25N 22°6E 202 C6
Svullrya Norway 60°25N 12°23E 164 D9
Svyatogorovskiy Rudnik =
Dobropole Ukraine 48°25N 37°2E 189 H9
Svyetlahorsk Belarus 52°38N 29°46E 177 B15
Swa Myanmar 19°15N 96°17E 241 F6
Swa Tende
Dem. Rep. of the Congo 7°9S 17°7E 265 D3
Swabian Alps = Schwäbische Alb
Germany 48°20N 9°30E 179 G5
Swaffham U.K. 52°39N 0°42E 169 E8
Swains I. Amer. Samoa 11°11S 171°4W 289 J11
Swainsboro U.S.A. 32°36N 82°20W 316 C7
Swakop → Namibia 22°38S 14°36E 270 B2
Swakopmund Namibia 22°37S 14°30E 270 B1
Swale → U.K. 54°5N 1°20W 168 C6
Swamihalli India 14°52N 76°38E 245 G3
Swan → W. Austral.,
Australia 32°3S 115°45E 279 F2
Swan → Man., Canada 52°30N 100°45W 297 C8
Swan Hill Australia 35°20S 143°33E 282 C5
Swan Hills Canada 54°43N 115°24W 296 C5
Swan Is. = Santanilla, Is.
Honduras 17°22N 83°57W 320 C3
Swan L. = Kalajun-Ku'erdening ⌂
China 43°10N 81°50E 217 D10
Swan L. Man., Canada 52°30N 100°40W 297 C8
Swan L. Ont., Canada 54°16N 91°11W 298 B1
Swan Ra. U.S.A. 48°0N 113°45W 304 C7
Swan Reach Australia 34°35S 139°37E 282 C3
Swan River Canada 52°10N 101°16W 297 C8
Swanage U.K. 50°36N 1°58W 169 G6
Swanley U.K. 51°23N 0°11E 125 B4
Swansea N.S.W., Australia 33°3S 151°35E 283 B9
Swansea Tas., Australia 42°8S 148°4E 281 G4
Swansea Ont., Canada 43°38N 79°28W 141 B2
Swansea Swansea, U.K. 51°37N 3°57W 169 F4
Swansea S.C., U.S.A. 33°44N 81°6W 316 B8
Swansea □ U.K. 51°38N 4°3W 169 F3
Swanton U.S.A. 41°35N 83°53W 311 C13
Swartberge S. Africa 33°20S 22°0E 270 D3
Swartmodder S. Africa 28°1S 20°32E 270 C3
Swartnossob → Namibia 23°8S 18°42E 270 B2
Swartruggens S. Africa 25°39S 26°42E 270 C4
Swarzędz Poland 52°25N 17°4E 185 F4
Swastika Canada 48°7N 80°6W 298 C3
Swat → Pakistan 34°40N 72°5E 243 B5
Swatow = Shantou
China 23°18N 116°40E 229 F11
Swaziland = Eswatini ■
Africa 26°30S 31°30E 271 C5
Sweden ■ Europe 57°0N 15°0E 161 H16
Swedru Ghana 5°32N 0°41W 263 D4
Sweet Grass U.S.A. 48°59N 111°58W 304 B8
Sweet Home U.S.A. 44°24N 122°44W 304 D2
Sweet Springs U.S.A. 38°58N 93°25W 310 F3
Sweetwater Nev., U.S.A. 38°27N 119°9W 306 G7
Sweetwater Tenn.,
U.S.A. 35°36N 84°28W 315 D12
Sweetwater Tex., U.S.A. 32°28N 100°25W 314 E4
Sweetwater → U.S.A. 42°31N 107°2W 304 E10
Swellendam S. Africa 34°1S 20°26E 270 D3
Swider → Poland 52°6N 21°14E 185 F8
Świdnica Poland 50°50N 16°30E 185 H3
Świdnik Poland 51°13N 22°39E 185 G9
Świdwin Poland 53°47N 15°49E 184 E2
Świebodzice Poland 50°51N 16°20E 185 H3
Świebodzin Poland 52°15N 15°31E 185 F2
Świecie Poland 53°25N 18°30E 184 E5
Świerzawa Poland 51°1N 15°54E 185 G2
Świętokrzyskie △ Poland 50°53N 20°59E 185 H7
Świętokrzyskie □ Poland 50°45N 20°45E 185 H7
Świętokrzyskie, Góry
Poland 51°0N 20°30E 185 H7
Swift Current Canada 50°20N 107°45W 297 C7
Swift Current → Canada 50°38N 107°44W 297 C7
Swifts Creek Australia 37°17S 147°44E 283 D7
Swilly, L. Ireland 55°12N 7°33W 166 A4
Swinburne I. U.S.A. 40°33N 74°3W 132 C1
Swindon U.K. 51°34N 1°46W 169 F6
Swindon □ U.K. 51°34N 1°46W 169 F6
Swinemünde = Świnoujście
Poland 53°54N 14°16E 184 E1
Swinford Ireland 53°57N 8°58W 166 C3
Świnoujście Poland 53°54N 14°16E 184 E1
Switzerland ■ Europe 46°30N 8°0E 179 J4
Swords Ireland 53°28N 6°13W 166 C5
Swoyerville U.S.A. 41°18N 75°53W 313 E9
Syasstroy Russia 60°9N 32°33E 188 B7
Sycamore Ill., U.S.A. 41°59N 88°41W 311 C8
Sycamore Ohio, U.S.A. 40°57N 83°10W 311 D13
Sychevka Russia 55°59N 34°16E 188 E8
Syców Poland 51°19N 17°40E 185 G4
Sydenham S. Africa 26°9S 28°5E 123 A2
Sydenham → Canada 42°33N 82°25W 312 D2
Sydney N.S.W., Australia 33°52S 151°12E 139 B2
Sydney N.S., Canada 46°7N 60°7W 299 C7
Sydney, Univ. of
Australia 33°54S 151°11E 139 B2
Sydney Harbour △
Australia 33°50S 151°14E 139 B2
Sydney Harbour Bridge
Australia 33°51S 151°12E 139 B2
Sydney Kingsford Smith ✕ (SYD)
Australia 33°57S 151°11E 139 B2
Sydney L. Canada 50°41N 94°25W 297 C10
Sydney Mines Canada 46°18N 60°15W 299 C7
Sydprøven = Alluitsup Paa
Greenland 60°30N 45°35W 154 E6
Sydra, G. of = Surt, Khalīj
Libya 31°40N 18°30E 258 B3
Sydstranden Denmark 55°34N 12°38E 118 B3
Syeverodonetsk Ukraine 48°58N 38°35E 189 H10
Syfteland Norway 60°14N 5°27E 164 D2
Syke Germany 52°55N 8°50E 178 C4
Sykesville U.S.A. 41°3N 78°50W 312 E6
Sykkylven Norway 62°23N 6°35E 164 B3
Syktyvkar Russia 61°45N 50°40E 186 B9
Sylacauga U.S.A. 33°10N 86°15W 316 B3
Sylarna Sweden 63°2N 12°13E 164 A9
Sylhet Bangla. 24°54N 91°52E 241 C3
Sylhet □ Bangla. 24°50N 91°50E 241 C3
Sylt Germany 54°54N 8°22E 178 A4
Sylte Norway 62°18N 7°17E 164 B4
Sylvan Beach U.S.A. 43°12N 75°44W 313 C9
Sylvan Lake Canada 52°20N 114°3W 296 C6
Sylvania N.S.W., Australia 34°0S 151°7E 139 C1
Sylvania Ga., U.S.A. 32°45N 81°38W 316 C8
Sylvania Ohio, U.S.A. 41°43N 83°42W 311 C13
Sylvester U.S.A. 31°32N 83°50W 316 D6
Sym Russia 60°20N 88°18E 214 C9
Symphony Hall San Francisco, U.S.A. 136 c1
Synelnykove Ukraine 48°25N 35°30E 189 H8
Synevyr △ Ukraine 48°30N 23°40E 183 B8
Synevyrska Polyana
Ukraine 48°35N 23°41E 183 B8
Synnervika Norway 62°25N 11°54E 164 B8
Synnfjell Norway 61°5N 9°46E 164 C6
Synnot Ra. Australia 16°30S 125°20E 278 C4
Syntagma Square Athens, Greece 112 b2
Synyak Ukraine 48°35N 22°51E 182 B7
Syon Park U.K. 51°28N 0°18W 125 B2
Syöte △ Finland 65°44N 27°58E 160 D22
Syowa Antarctica 68°50S 12°0E 151 C5
Syracuse = Siracusa Italy 37°4N 15°17E 201 E8
Syracuse Ind., U.S.A. 41°26N 85°45W 311 C11
Syracuse Kans., U.S.A. 37°59N 101°45W 308 G3
Syracuse N.Y., U.S.A. 43°3N 76°9W 313 C8
Syracuse Nebr., U.S.A. 40°39N 96°11W 308 E5
Syrdarya → Kazakhstan 46°3N 61°0E 216 C6
Syria ■ Asia 35°0N 38°0E 213 E8
Syriam Myanmar 16°44N 96°19E 241 G6
Syrian Desert = Shām, Bādiyat ash
Asia 32°0N 40°0E 246 C3
Syros = Ermoupoli Greece 37°28N 24°57E 204 D6
Sysslebäck Sweden 60°44N 12°52E 162 D6
Syvden Norway 62°5N 5°44E 164 B2
Syzran Russia 53°12N 48°30E 190 D9
Szabolcs-Szatmár-Bereg □
Hungary 48°2N 21°45E 182 B6
Szadek Poland 51°41N 18°59E 185 G5
Szamocin Poland 53°2N 17°7E 185 E4
Szamos → Hungary 48°7N 22°20E 182 B7
Szamotuły Poland 52°37N 16°33E 185 F3
Száraz → Hungary 46°10N 21°15E 182 D6
Szarvas Hungary 46°50N 20°38E 182 D5
Százhalombatta Hungary 47°20N 18°58E 182 C3
Szczawnica Poland 49°26N 20°30E 185 J7
Szczebrzeszyn Poland 50°42N 22°59E 185 H9
Szczecin Poland 53°27N 14°27E 184 E1
Szczecinek Poland 53°43N 16°41E 184 E3
Szczeciński, Zalew = Stettiner Haff
Germany 53°47N 14°15E 178 B10
Szczekociny Poland 50°38N 19°48E 185 H6
Szczęśliwice Poland 52°12N 20°57E 143 B1
Szczucin Poland 50°18N 21°4E 185 H8
Szczuczyn Poland 53°36N 22°19E 184 E9
Szczyrk Poland 49°43N 19°2E 185 J6
Szczytna Poland 50°25N 16°28E 185 H3
Szczytno Poland 53°33N 21°0E 184 E7
Széchenyi-hegy Hungary 47°29N 18°57E 117 B1
Szechuan = Sichuan □
China 30°30N 103°0E 228 B5
Szechuan Basin = Sichuan Pendi
China 31°0N 105°0E 228 B5
Szécsény Hungary 48°7N 19°30E 182 B4
Szeged Hungary 46°16N 20°10E 182 D5
Szeghalom Hungary 47°1N 21°10E 182 C6
Székesfehérvár Hungary 47°15N 18°25E 182 C3
Szekszárd Hungary 46°22N 18°42E 182 D3
Szendrő Hungary 48°24N 20°41E 182 B5
Szentendre Hungary 47°39N 19°4E 182 C4
Szentes Hungary 46°39N 20°21E 182 D5
Szentgotthárd Hungary 46°58N 16°19E 182 D1
Szentlőrinc Hungary 46°3N 18°1E 182 D3
Széphalom Hungary 47°34N 18°57E 117 A1
Szeping = Siping China 43°8N 124°21E 227 C13
Szerencs Hungary 48°10N 21°12E 182 B6
Szigetszentmiklós Hungary 47°21N 19°3E 182 C4
Szigetvár Hungary 46°3N 17°46E 182 D2
Szikszó Hungary 48°12N 20°56E 182 B5
Szklarska Poręba Poland 50°50N 15°33E 185 H2
Szkwa → Poland 53°11N 21°43E 185 E8
Szlichtyngowa Poland 51°42N 16°15E 185 G3
Szob Hungary 47°48N 18°53E 182 C3
Szolnok Hungary 47°10N 20°15E 182 C5
Szombathely Hungary 47°14N 16°38E 182 C1
Szprotawa Poland 51°33N 15°35E 185 G2
Sztálinváros = Dunaújváros
Hungary 46°58N 18°57E 182 D3
Sztum Poland 53°55N 19°1E 184 E6
Sztutowo Poland 54°20N 19°15E 184 D6
Szubin Poland 53°1N 17°45E 185 E4
Szydłowiec Poland 51°15N 20°51E 185 G7
Szypliszki Poland 54°17N 23°2E 184 D10

T

Ta Khli Thailand 15°15N 100°21E 236 E3
Ta Lai Vietnam 11°24N 107°23E 237 G6
Ta Phraya △ Thailand 14°11N 102°49E 236 E4
Ta Pieh Shan = Dabie Shan
China 31°20N 115°20E 229 B10
Taakoka Cook Is. 21°15S 159°43W 289 h
Taal, L. Phil. 13°56N 121°0E 232 E3
Taal Volcano Phil. 14°7N 120°59E 231 B6
Taal Volcano △ Phil. 14°1N 120°59E 232 D3
Taamisaari = Raasepori
Finland 60°0N 23°26E 188 B2
Taan Taiwan 24°22N 120°35E 225 B2
Taastrup Denmark 55°39N 12°18E 118 B1
Tab Hungary 46°44N 18°2E 182 D3
Tabacal Argentina 23°15S 64°15W 334 A3
Tabaco Phil. 13°22N 123°44E 232 E4
Tabagné Côte d'Ivoire 7°59N 3°4W 262 D4
Ţābah Si. Arabia 26°55N 42°38E 246 E4
Tabajara Brazil 8°56S 62°8W 331 B5
Tabalo Papua N. G. 1°24S 149°40E 286 A5
Tabalos Peru 6°26S 76°37W 330 B2
Tabanan Indonesia 8°32S 115°8E 231 K18
Tabang Indonesia 0°34N 116°1E 235 B5
Tabankort Niger 17°44N 0°20E 263 B5
Tabaquite Trin. & Tob. 10°23N 61°18W 323 t
Tabar I. Papua N. G. 2°56S 152°0E 286 B7
Tabar Is. Papua N. G. 2°50S 152°0E 286 B7
Tabarka Tunisia 36°56N 8°46E 258 A1
Ţabas Khorāsān, Iran 32°48N 60°12E 247 C9
Ţabas Yazd, Iran 33°35N 56°55E 247 C8
Tabasará, Serranía de
Panama 8°35N 81°40W 320 E3
Tabasco □ Mexico 18°0N 92°40W 319 D6
Tabāsīn Iran 31°12N 57°54E 247 D8
Tabata Japan 35°44N 139°46E 140 A3
Tabatinga Brazil 4°16S 69°56W 330 A4
Tabatinga, Serra da Brazil 10°30S 44°0W 332 D3
Tabayin Myanmar 22°42N 95°20E 241 D5
Tabelbala Algeria 29°24N 3°15W 260 C4
Tabelbala, Kahal de Algeria 28°47N 2°0W 261 C4
Tabelembila Algeria 24°43N 4°16E 261 D5
Taber Canada 49°47N 112°8W 296 D6
Taberg Sweden 57°40N 14°6E 163 G8
Tabernacle
St. Kitts & Nevis 17°23N 62°46W 322 d
Tabi Angola 8°10S 13°18E 265 D2
Tabina Phil. 7°28N 123°24E 233 H4
Tabira Brazil 7°35S 37°33W 332 C4
Tabiteuea Kiribati 1°25S 174°50E 277 A13
Tabla Niger 13°46N 3°1E 263 C5
Tablada Argentina 34°41S 58°32W 117 C1
Tablas de Daimiel △ Spain 39°9N 3°40W 195 F7
Tablas I. Phil. 12°25N 122°2E 232 E4
Tablas Str. Phil. 12°40N 121°48E 232 E3
Table, Pte. de la Réunion 21°14S 55°48E 272 f
Table B. Nfld. & L., Canada 53°40N 56°25W 299 B8
Table B. Western Cape,
S. Africa 33°35S 18°25E 118 A1
Table C. N.Z. 39°6S 178°0E 284 F7
Table Grove U.S.A. 40°20N 90°27W 310 D6
Table I. Myanmar 14°12N 93°22E 245 G11
Table Mountain △
S. Africa 33°58S 18°28E 118 A1
Table Mt. S. Africa 33°58S 18°26E 118 A1
Table Rock L. U.S.A. 36°36N 93°19W 308 G7
Tableland Trin. & Tob. 10°16N 61°16W 323 t
Tabletop, Mt. Australia 23°24S 147°11E 280 C4
Taboão da Serra Brazil 23°36S 46°45W 137 B1
Tabocal Brazil 2°42S 57°40W 331 A6
Tabon Cave Complex Phil. 9°17N 118°5E 233 G2

Tábor Czechia 49°25N 14°39E 180 B7
Tabora Tanzania 5°2S 32°50E 268 D3
Tabora □ Tanzania 5°0S 33°0E 268 D3
Tabou Côte d'Ivoire 4°30N 7°20W 262 E3
Tabrīz Iran 38°7N 46°20E 213 C12
Tabuaeran Kiribati 3°51N 159°22W 289 G12
Tabubil Papua N. G. 5°20S 141°15E 286 C1
Tabuenca Spain 41°42N 1°33W 196 D3
Tabuk Phil. 17°24N 121°25E 232 C3
Tabūk Si. Arabia 28°23N 36°36E 251 K7
Tabūk □ Si. Arabia 27°40N 36°50E 246 E3
Tabunifi Micronesia 9°28N 138°4E 287 S16
Taburno-Camposauro ⌓ Italy 41°8N 14°37E 201 A7
Tabwemasana, Mt. Vanuatu 15°20S 166°44E 287 E4
Täby Sweden 59°26N 18°2E 139 A2
Tacámbaro de Codallos Mexico 19°14N 101°28W 318 D4
Tacarigua Trin. & Tob. 10°38N 61°22W 323 t
Tacarigua Venezuela 11°3N 63°54W 329 a
Tacariqua, Laguna de Venezuela 10°15N 65°50W 328 A4
Tacheng Xinjiang Uygur, China 46°40N 82°58E 217 C10
Tacheng Taiwan 23°51N 120°19E 225 C2
Tach'i Taiwan 24°53N 121°17E 225 B3
Tachia Taiwan 24°25N 120°28E 225 B2
Tachia Hsi → Taiwan 24°20N 120°33E 225 B3
Tachibana-Wan Japan 32°45N 130°7E 222 E2
Tachikawa Japan 35°42N 139°25E 223 B11
Tachilek Myanmar 20°26N 99°52E 236 B2
Tach'ing Shan = Daqing Shan China 40°40N 111°0E 226 D6
Táchira □ Venezuela 8°7N 72°15W 328 B3
Tachiumet Libya 26°19N 10°3E 258 C2
Tachoshui Taiwan 24°20N 121°44E 225 B3
Tachov Czechia 49°47N 12°39E 180 B5
Tácina → Italy 38°57N 16°55E 201 D9
Tacloban Phil. 11°15N 124°58E 233 F5
Tacna Peru 18°0S 70°20W 330 D3
Tacna □ Peru 17°40S 70°20W 330 D3
Tacoma U.S.A. 47°14N 122°26W 306 C4
Tacopaya = Zudañez Bolivia 19°6S 64°44W 331 D5
Tacuarembó Uruguay 31°45S 56°0W 335 C4
Tacuba Mexico 19°26N 99°11W 128 B1
Tacubaya Mexico 19°24N 99°10W 128 B1
Tacurong Phil. 6°40N 124°41E 233 H5
Tacutu = Takutu → Guyana 3°30N 60°29W 329 C5
Tada-u Myanmar 21°49N 95°58E 241 E5
Tadahadi Solomon Is. 10°18S 161°35E 287 N11
Tademaït, Plateau du Algeria 28°30N 2°30E 261 C5
Tādepallegudem India 16°50N 81°30E 244 F5
Tadéra Niger 20°29N 8°18E 261 D6
Tadine N. Cal. 21°33S 167°52E 288 d
Tadio, L. Côte d'Ivoire 5°10N 5°15W 262 D3
Tadjerdjeri, O. → Algeria 26°0N 8°0E 261 C6
Tadjerouna Algeria 33°31N 2°3E 261 B5
Tadjettaret, O. → Algeria 21°20N 7°22E 261 D6
Tadjmout Laghouat, Algeria 33°52N 2°30E 261 B5
Tadjmout Saoura, Algeria 25°37N 3°48E 261 C5
Tadjourah Djibouti 11°50N 42°55E 257 E5
Tadjourah, Golfe de Djibouti 11°50N 43°0E 257 E5
Tadmor N.Z. 41°27S 172°45E 285 B7
Tadoba △ India 20°30N 78°20E 244 D4
Tadotsu Japan 34°16N 133°45E 222 C5
Tadoule L. Canada 58°36N 98°20W 297 B9
Tadoussac Canada 48°11N 69°42W 299 C6
Tadpatri India 14°55N 78°1E 245 G4
Tadrés ⌓ Niger 16°0N 7°10E 263 B6
Tadzhikistan = Tajikistan ■ Asia 38°30N 70°0E 217 E8
Tae-an S. Korea 36°45N 126°17E 224 D3
Tae-an △ S. Korea 36°40N 126°0E 224 D3
Taebaek S. Korea 37°10N 128°59E 224 D4
Taebaeksan S. Korea 37°5N 128°54E 224 D4
T'aebaeksanmaek S. Korea 37°40N 128°50E 224 D4
Taedong-gang → N. Korea 38°41N 125°15E 224 C2
Taedong-man N. Korea 38°4N 125°7E 224 C2
Taegu = Daegu S. Korea 35°50N 128°37E 224 E4
Taegwan N. Korea 40°13N 125°12E 224 B2
Taehung N. Korea 40°5N 126°56E 224 B3
Taehwa-do N. Korea 39°26N 124°36E 224 C2
Taejŏn = Daejeon S. Korea 36°20N 127°28E 224 D3
Tælavåg Norway 60°15N 4°58E 164 D1
Taen, Ko Thailand 9°22N 99°57E 237 b
Tafalla Spain 42°30N 1°41W 196 C3
Tafar South Sudan 6°52N 28°15E 257 F2
Tafassasset, O. → Algeria 22°0N 9°57E 261 D6
Tafelbaai = Table B. S. Africa 33°35S 18°25E 118 A1
Tafelberg Curaçao 12°4N 68°50W 322 g
Tafelney, C. Morocco 31°3N 9°51W 260 B3
Tafermaar Indonesia 6°47S 134°10E 231 F8
Taffermit Morocco 29°37N 9°15W 260 C3
Tafi Viejo Argentina 26°43S 65°17W 334 B2
Tafihān Iran 29°25N 52°39E 247 D7
Tafilalet Morocco 31°20N 4°45W 260 B4
Tafiré Côte d'Ivoire 9°4N 5°4W 262 D3
Tafjord Norway 62°14N 7°24E 164 B4
Tafnidilt Morocco 28°47N 10°58W 260 C2
Tafo Ghana 6°15N 0°20W 263 D4
Tafraoute Morocco 29°50N 8°58W 260 C3
Tafresh Iran 34°45N 49°57E 247 C6
Taft Iran 31°45N 54°14E 247 D7
Taft Phil. 11°57N 125°30E 233 F5
Taft Calif., U.S.A. 35°8N 119°28W 307 K7
Taft Fla., U.S.A. 28°25N 81°21W 133 B2
Taftan Pakistan 29°0N 61°30E 240 C1
Taftān, Kūh-e Iran 28°40N 61°0E 247 D9
Tafu Taiwan 23°37N 121°23E 225 C3
Tafwap India 7°23N 93°43E 245 L11
Taga Samoa 13°46S 172°28W 287 V19
Taga Dzong Bhutan 27°5N 89°55E 241 B2
Tagana-an Phil. 9°42N 125°35E 233 G5
Taganay △ Russia 55°15N 59°48E 216 B5
Taganrog Russia 47°12N 38°50E 189 J10
Taganrogskiy Zaliv Russia 47°0N 38°30E 189 J10
Tagânt □ Mauritania 19°0N 10°0W 260 E3
Tagap Ga Myanmar 26°56N 96°13E 241 B6
Tagauayan I. Phil. 10°58N 121°13E 233 F3
Tagaung Myanmar 23°30N 96°2E 241 D6
Tagawa Japan 33°38N 130°51E 222 D2
Tagaytay Phil. 14°6N 120°56E 232 D3
Tagbilaran Phil. 9°39N 123°51E 233 G4
Tagdempt = Tiaret Algeria 35°20N 1°21E 261 A5
Tage Papua N. G. 6°19S 143°20E 286 D2
Tageren Canal Micronesia 9°33N 138°8E 287 R16
Tággia Italy 43°52N 7°51E 198 E4
Taghit Algeria 30°58N 2°0W 261 B4
Tagig → Phil. 14°31N 121°5E 127 B2
Tagish Canada 60°19N 134°16W 296 A2
Tagish L. Canada 60°10N 134°20W 296 A2
Tagkawayan Phil. 13°58N 122°32E 232 E4
Tagliacozzo Italy 42°4N 13°14E 199 F10
Tagliamento → Italy 45°38N 13°6E 199 C10
Táglio di Po Italy 45°0N 12°12E 199 D9
Tagna Colombia 2°24S 70°37W 328 D3
Tago Phil. 9°2N 126°13E 233 G6
Tago, Mt. Phil. 8°23N 125°5E 233 G5
Tagomago Spain 39°2N 1°39E 206 C2
Tagourāret Mauritania 17°45N 7°45W 262 B3
Taguatinga Distrito Federal, Brazil 15°51S 48°4W 333 E2
Taguatinga Tocantins, Brazil 12°27S 46°22W 333 D2
Tagudin Phil. 16°56N 120°27E 232 C3
Taguenout Chaggueret Mali 21°14N 0°48W 261 D4
Taguig Phil. 14°31N 121°4E 127 B2
Tagula Papua N. G. 11°22S 153°15E 286 F7
Tagula I. Papua N. G. 11°30S 153°30E 286 F7
Tagum Phil. 7°33N 125°53E 233 H5
Tagus = Tejo → Europe 38°40N 9°24W 195 F2
Tahakopa N.Z. 46°30S 169°23E 285 G4
Tahala Morocco 34°0N 4°28W 260 B4
Tahan, Gunung Malaysia 4°34N 102°17E 237 K4
Tahānah-ye sūr Gol Afghan. 31°43N 67°53E 240 C2
Tahara Japan 34°40N 137°16E 223 C9
Tahat Algeria 23°18N 5°33E 261 D6
Tāherī Iran 27°43N 52°20E 247 E7
Tahgong Pt. N. Marianas 15°6N 145°39E 302 e
Tahifet Algeria 22°58N 6°0E 261 D6
Tahiti French Polynesia 17°37S 149°27W 289 e
Tahlab → Pakistan 28°9N 62°45E 240 C1
Tahlequah U.S.A. 35°55N 94°58W 314 D7
Tahoe, L. U.S.A. 39°6N 120°2W 306 G6
Tahoe City U.S.A. 39°10N 120°9W 306 F6
Tahoka U.S.A. 33°10N 101°48W 314 E4
Taholah U.S.A. 47°21N 124°17W 306 C2
Tahora N.Z. 39°2S 174°49E 284 F3
Tahoua Niger 14°57N 5°16E 263 C6
Tahrir Square Egypt 30°2N 31°14E 117 A2
Tahrūd Iran 29°26N 57°49E 247 D8
Tahsis Canada 49°55N 126°40W 296 D3
Tahta Egypt 26°44N 31°32E 256 B3
Tahtaköprü Turkey 39°57N 29°39E 203 G13
Tahtalı Dağları Turkey 38°20N 36°0E 212 C7
Tahu Taiwan 24°26N 120°52E 225 B2
Tahuamanú → Bolivia 11°6S 67°36W 330 C4
Tahuata, I. French Polynesia 9°57S 139°5W 289 f
Tahulandang Indonesia 2°27N 125°23E 231 D7
Tahuna Indonesia 3°38N 125°30E 231 D7
Taï Côte d'Ivoire 5°55N 7°30W 262 D3
Taï △ Côte d'Ivoire 5°25N 7°5W 262 D3
Tai Ho Hong Kong, China 22°17N 113°58E 122 B1
Tai Hu China 31°5N 120°10E 229 B13
Tai Lam Chung Res. Hong Kong, China 22°23N 114°1E 122 A2
Tai Lam Country Park ⌓ Hong Kong, China 22°23N 114°0E 122 A2
Tai Lo Shan Hong Kong, China 22°21N 114°13E 122 A3
Tai Long Wan Tsuen Hong Kong, China 22°13N 113°53E 122 B1
Tai Mo Shan Hong Kong, China 22°25N 114°7E 122 A2
Tai O Hong Kong, China 22°15N 113°52E 122 B1
Tai Pang Wan China 22°33N 114°24E 219 a
Tai Po China 22°27N 114°10E 219 a
Tai Po Tsai Hong Kong, China 22°20N 114°15E 122 A3
Tai Rom Yen △ Thailand 8°45N 99°30E 237 H2
Tai Seng Singapore 1°20N 103°53E 138 A3
Tai Shan China 36°25N 117°20E 227 F9
Tai Shui Hang Hong Kong, China 22°24N 114°12E 122 A3
Tai Tam B. Hong Kong, China 22°12N 114°13E 122 B3
Tai Tam Country Park ⌓ Hong Kong, China 22°15N 114°12E 122 B3
Tai Tam Tuk Res. Hong Kong, China 22°14N 114°13E 122 B3
Tai Wai Hong Kong, China 22°22N 114°10E 122 A3
Tai Wan Tau Hong Kong, China 22°17N 114°17E 122 B3
Tai Wo Hau Hong Kong, China 22°21N 114°7E 122 A2
Tai Yue Shan = Lantau I. Hong Kong, China 22°15N 113°56E 122 B1
Tai'an China 36°12N 117°8E 227 F9
Taiarapu, Presqu'île de Tahiti 17°47S 149°14W 289 e
Taibai Shan China 33°57N 107°45E 226 H4
Taibei = T'aipei Taiwan 25°4N 121°29E 225 A3
Taibique Canary Is. 27°42N 17°58W 153 e1
Taibus Qi China 41°54N 115°22E 226 D8
Taicang China 31°30N 121°5E 229 B13
Taichow = Taizhou China 32°28N 119°55E 229 A12
T'aichung Taiwan 24°9N 120°37E 225 B2
Taidong = T'aitung Taiwan 22°43N 121°4E 225 D3
Taieri → N.Z. 46°3S 170°12E 285 G5
Taigu China 37°28N 112°30E 226 F7
Taihang Shan China 36°0N 113°30E 226 G7
Taihape N.Z. 39°41S 175°48E 284 F4
Taihe Anhui, China 33°20N 115°42E 226 H8
Taihe Jiangxi, China 26°47N 114°52E 229 D10
Taihoku = T'aipei Taiwan 25°4N 121°29E 225 A3
Taihsi Taiwan 23°51N 120°16E 225 C2
Taihu China 30°22N 116°20E 229 B11
Taijiang China 26°39N 108°21E 228 D7
Taikang China 34°5N 114°50E 226 G8
Taikkyi Myanmar 17°20N 96°0E 241 G6
Tailem Bend Australia 35°12S 139°29E 282 C3
Tailfingen Germany 48°15N 9°1E 179 G5
T'ailuko Taiwan 24°9N 121°37E 225 B3
T'aimali Taiwan 22°36N 121°0E 225 D2
Taimyr Peninsula = Taymyr, Poluostrov Russia 75°0N 100°0E 215 B11
Tain U.K. 57°49N 4°4W 167 D4
Tainaka Japan 34°36N 135°35E 133 B2
Tainan = T'ainan Taiwan 23°0N 120°10E 225 D2
T'ainan Taiwan 23°0N 120°10E 225 D2
T'ainan □ Taiwan 23°15N 120°20E 225 C2
Tainggyo Myanmar 17°49N 94°29E 241 G5
Taining China 26°54N 117°9E 229 D11
Taiobeiras Brazil 15°49S 42°14W 333 E3
Taipa China 22°10N 113°35E 219 a
T'aipei Taiwan 25°4N 121°29E 225 A3
T'aipei □ Taiwan 24°50N 121°35E 225 B3
Taiping Anhui, China 30°15N 118°6E 229 B12
Taiping Malaysia 4°51N 100°44E 237 K3
Taiping Dao = Itu Aba I. S. China Sea 10°23N 114°21E 230 B4
Taipingchuan China 44°23N 123°11E 227 B12
Taipingzhen China 33°35N 111°42E 226 H6
Taipu Brazil 5°37S 35°36W 332 C4
Tairenpokpi India 24°39N 93°40E 241 C4
Tairua N.Z. 37°0S 175°51E 284 D4
Tais Indonesia 4°6S 102°34E 234 C2
Taisha Japan 35°24N 132°40E 222 B4
Taishan China 22°14N 112°41E 229 F9
Taishō Japan 34°38N 135°27E 133 B1
Taishun China 27°30N 119°42E 229 D12
Taita Hills Kenya 3°25S 38°15E 268 C4
Taita-Taveta □ Kenya 3°20S 38°15E 268 C4
Taitao, C. Chile 45°53S 75°5W 336 C1
Taitao, Pen. de Chile 46°30S 75°0W 336 C2
T'aitung Taiwan 22°43N 121°4E 225 D3
T'aitung □ Taiwan 23°0N 121°0E 225 D3
Taivalkoski Finland 65°33N 28°12E 160 D23
Taiwan ■ Asia 23°30N 121°0E 225 C3
Taiwan Strait Asia 24°40N 120°0E 229 E12
Taiwan Taoyuan Int. ✈ (TPE) Taiwan 25°5N 121°13E 225 A3
Taixi = Taihsi Taiwan 23°51N 120°16E 225 C2
Taixing China 32°11N 120°0E 229 A13
Taiyara Sudan 13°12N 30°47E 257 E3
Taiyiba Israel 32°36N 35°27E 250 F6
Taiyuan China 37°52N 112°33E 226 F7
Taizhong = T'aichung Taiwan 24°9N 120°37E 225 B2
Taizhou Jiangsu, China 32°28N 119°55E 229 A12
Taizhou Zhejiang, China 28°40N 121°24E 229 C13
Taizhou Liedao China 28°30N 121°55E 229 C13
Ta'izz Yemen 13°35N 44°2E 248 D4
Ta'izz □ Yemen 13°35N 44°2E 248 D4
Taj Mahal India 27°10N 78°2E 242 F8
Tājābād Iran 30°2N 54°24E 247 D7
Tajapuru, Furo do Brazil 1°50S 50°25W 332 B1
Tajarḥī Libya 24°21N 14°28E 258 D2
Tajen Taiwan 22°17N 120°53E 225 D2
Tajikistan ■ Asia 38°30N 70°0E 217 E8
Tajima = Minamiaizu Japan 37°12N 139°46E 221 F9
Tajimi Japan 35°19N 137°8E 223 B9
Tajo = Tejo → Europe 38°40N 9°24W 195 F2
Tajrīsh Iran 35°48N 51°25E 141 A2
Tajumulco, Vol. Guatemala 15°2N 91°55W 320 C1
Tājūrā Libya 32°51N 13°21E 258 B2
Tak Thailand 16°52N 99°8E 236 D2
Takāb Iran 36°24N 47°7E 213 D12
Takabanare-shima Japan 26°22N 127°59E 288 a
Takabba Kenya 3°21N 40°13E 267 D5
Takachiho Japan 32°42N 131°18E 222 E3
Takachu Botswana 22°37S 21°58E 270 B3
Takada Japan 37°7N 138°15E 221 F9
Takahagi Japan 36°43N 140°45E 221 F10
Takahashi Japan 34°51N 133°39E 222 C5
Takaido Japan 35°40N 139°37E 140 A2
Takaishi Japan 35°36N 139°31E 140 B2
Takaka N.Z. 40°51S 172°50E 285 A7
Takaki = Yamato Japan 35°27N 139°25E 223 B11
Takalar Indonesia 5°28S 119°24E 235 D5
Takalous, O. → Algeria 22°36N 7°21E 261 D6
Takamaka Seychelles 4°50S 55°30E 272 c
Takamatsu Japan 34°20N 134°5E 222 C6
Takanabe Japan 32°8N 131°30E 222 E3
Takangkou Taiwan 23°28N 121°29E 225 C3
Takaoka Japan 36°47N 137°0E 223 A9
Takapau N.Z. 40°2S 176°21E 284 G5
Takapuna N.Z. 36°47S 174°47E 284 C3
Takarazuka Japan 34°47N 135°20E 133 A1
Takaroa French Polynesia 14°28S 144°58W 289 f
Takasago Japan 35°44N 139°52E 140 A4
Takasaki Japan 36°20N 139°0E 223 A11
Takashima Japan 35°24N 136°2E 223 B8
Takatsu Japan 35°36N 139°37E 140 B2
Takatsuki Japan 34°51N 135°37E 223 C7
Takaungu Kenya 3°38S 39°52E 268 C4
Takayama Japan 36°18N 137°11E 223 A9
Takayama-Bonchi Japan 36°0N 137°18E 223 B9
Take-Shima Japan 30°49N 130°26E 221 J5
Takefu = Echizen Japan 35°50N 136°10E 223 B8
Takehara Japan 34°21N 132°55E 222 C4
Takengon Indonesia 4°45N 96°50E 234 B1
Takeo Cambodia 10°59N 104°47E 237 G5
Takeo Japan 33°12N 130°1E 222 D2
Tåkern Sweden 58°22N 14°45E 163 F8
Takeshima = Liancourt Rocks Asia 37°15N 131°52E 221 F5
Takeshita Japan 35°33N 139°32E 140 B2
Tākestān Iran 36°0N 49°40E 247 C6
Taketa Japan 32°58N 131°24E 222 E3
Takh India 33°6N 77°32E 243 C7
Takhār □ Afghan. 36°40N 70°0E 240 A3
Takhiyatas Uzbekistan 42°20N 59°33E 216 D5
Takhmau Cambodia 11°29N 104°57E 237 G5
Takht-e Soleyman Iran 36°36N 47°14E 213 D12
Takht-Sulaiman Pakistan 31°40N 69°58E 242 D3
Taki Papua N. G. 6°29S 155°52E 286 D8
Takiéta Niger 13°41N 8°32E 263 C6
Takikawa Japan 43°33N 141°54E 220 C10
Takinegawa Japan 35°45N 139°44E 140 A3
Takla L. Canada 55°15N 125°45W 296 B3
Takla Landing Canada 55°30N 125°50W 296 B3
Taklamakan China 38°0N 83°0E 217 E10
Taklamakan Shamo = Taklamakan China 38°0N 83°0E 217 E10
Takoma Park U.S.A. 38°58N 77°0W 143 B2
Takotna U.S.A. 62°59N 156°4W 303 E8
Taksim Turkey 41°2N 28°58E 122 B1
Taksimo Russia 56°20N 114°52E 215 D12
Taku Japan 33°18N 130°3E 222 D2
Taku → Canada 58°30N 133°50W 296 B2
Takua Thung Thailand 8°24N 98°27E 237 a
Takum India 27°47N 93°37E 241 B4
Takum Nigeria 7°18N 9°36E 263 D6
Takume French Polynesia 15°49S 142°12W 289 f
Takundi Dem. Rep. of the Congo 4°45S 16°34E 265 C3
Takutu → Guyana 3°30N 60°29W 329 C5
Tal Halāl Iran 28°54N 55°1E 247 D7
Tala Uruguay 34°21S 55°46W 335 C4
Talachyn Belarus 54°25N 29°42E 188 E5
Talacogon Phil. 8°32N 125°39E 233 G5
Talagang Pakistan 32°55N 72°25E 242 C5
Talagante Chile 33°40S 70°50W 334 C1
Talahouhait Algeria 24°52N 1°5E 261 D5
Talaide Portugal 38°44N 9°18W 126 A1
Talaimannar Sri Lanka 9°6N 79°43E 245 K4
Talaïnt Morocco 29°41N 9°40W 260 C3
Talak Niger 18°0N 5°0E 263 B6
Talakag Phil. 8°16N 124°37E 233 G5
Talamanca, Cordillera de Cent. Amer. 9°20N 83°20W 320 E3
Talampaya △ Argentina 29°43S 67°42W 334 B2
Talangbetutu Indonesia 2°53S 104°41E 234 C2
Talant France 47°19N 4°58E 173 E11
Talara Peru 4°38S 81°18W 330 A1
Talas Kyrgyzstan 42°30N 72°13E 217 D8
Talas Turkey 38°41N 35°33E 212 C6
Talas □ Kyrgyzstan 42°20N 72°0E 217 D8
Talas → Kazakhstan 44°0N 70°20E 217 D8
Talas Ala Too Kyrgyzstan 42°15N 72°0E 217 D8
Talasea Papua N. G. 5°20S 150°2E 286 C6
Talasskiy Alatau = Talas Ala Too Kyrgyzstan 42°15N 72°0E 217 D8
Talâta Egypt 30°36N 32°20E 251 H3
Talata Mafara Nigeria 12°38N 6°4E 263 C6
Talaud, Kepulauan Indonesia 4°30N 126°50E 231 D7
Talaud Is. = Talaud, Kepulauan Indonesia 4°30N 126°50E 231 D7
Talavera de la Reina Spain 39°55N 4°46W 194 F6
Talavera la Real Spain 38°53N 6°46W 195 G4
Talawgyi Myanmar 25°4N 97°19E 241 C6
Talayan Phil. 6°52N 124°24E 233 H5
Talayuela Spain 39°59N 5°36W 194 F5
Talbandh India 22°3N 86°20E 243 H12
Talbert, Sillon de France 48°53N 3°5W 172 D3
Talbot Australia 37°10S 143°44E 282 D5
Talbot, C. Australia 13°48S 126°43E 278 B4
Talbotton U.S.A. 32°41N 84°32W 316 C5
Talbragar → Australia 32°12S 148°37E 283 B8
Talca Chile 35°28S 71°40W 334 D1
Talcahuano Chile 36°40S 73°10W 334 D1
Talcher India 21°0N 85°18E 244 D7
Talcho Niger 14°44N 3°28E 263 C5
Taldy Kurgan = Taldyqorghan Kazakhstan 45°10N 78°45E 217 C9
Taldyqorghan Kazakhstan 45°10N 78°45E 217 C9
Tālesh Iran 37°58N 48°58E 213 D13
Tālesh, Kūhhā-ye Iran 37°42N 48°55E 213 D13
Talgar = Talghar Kazakhstan 43°19N 77°15E 217 D9
Talghar Kazakhstan 43°19N 77°15E 217 D9
Talguharai Sudan 18°19N 35°56E 256 D4
Talguppa India 14°13N 74°56E 245 G2
Tali Post South Sudan 5°55N 30°44E 257 F3
Taliabu Indonesia 1°50S 125°0E 231 E6
Taliao Taiwan 22°36N 120°23E 225 D2
Talibon Phil. 10°9N 124°20E 233 F5
Talichien Taiwan 24°58N 121°55E 225 B3
Taliganga India 22°30N 88°22E 124 B2
Talihina U.S.A. 34°45N 95°3W 314 D7
Talikota India 16°29N 76°17E 245 F3
Talikud I. Phil. 6°56N 125°41E 233 H5
Talin Taiwan 23°36N 120°27E 225 C2
Talipapa Phil. 14°41N 121°1E 127 A2
Talipaw Phil. 5°59N 121°7E 233 J3
Talipparamba India 12°3N 75°21E 245 H2
Talisay Phil. 10°44N 122°58E 233 F4
Talisayan Phil. 9°0N 124°55E 233 G5
Taliwang Indonesia 8°50S 116°55E 235 D5
Talkeetna U.S.A. 62°20N 150°6W 303 E10
Talkha Egypt 31°3N 31°22E 251 G2
Tálknafjörður Iceland 65°34N 24°0W 155 B2
Talkot Nepal 29°37N 81°19E 243 E9
Tall 'Afar Iraq 36°22N 42°27E 213 D10
Tall Kalakh Syria 34°41N 36°15E 250 D7
Tall Kayf Iraq 36°29N 43°7E 213 D10
Talla Egypt 28°5N 30°43E 256 B3
Talladega U.S.A. 33°26N 86°6W 316 B3
Tallaganda △ Australia 35°29S 149°37E 283 C8
Tallahassee U.S.A. 30°27N 84°17W 316 E5
Tallangatta Australia 36°15S 147°19E 283 D7
Tallapoosa U.S.A. 33°45N 85°17W 316 B4
Tallapoosa → U.S.A. 32°30N 86°16W 316 C3
Tallard France 44°28N 6°3E 175 D10
Tallarook Australia 37°5S 145°6E 283 D6
Tallassee U.S.A. 32°32N 85°54W 316 C4
Tällberg Sweden 60°51N 15°2E 162 D9
Tallering Pk. Australia 28°6S 115°37E 279 E2
Talli Pakistan 29°32N 68°8E 242 E3
Tallinn Estonia 59°22N 24°48E 188 C3
Tallkrogen Sweden 59°16N 18°4E 139 B2
Tallmadge U.S.A. 41°6N 81°27W 312 E3
Tallulah U.S.A. 32°25N 91°11W 314 E9
Tălmaciu Romania 45°38N 24°19E 183 E9
Talmest Morocco 31°48N 9°21W 260 B3
Talmont-St-Hilaire France 46°27N 1°37W 174 B2
Talnakh Russia 69°29N 88°22E 215 C9
Talne Ukraine 48°50N 30°44E 189 H6
Talnoye = Talne Ukraine 48°50N 30°44E 189 H6
Taloda India 21°34N 74°11E 244 D2
Talodi Sudan 10°35N 30°22E 257 E3
Talofofo Guam 13°21N 144°45E 302 d
Tāloqān Afghan. 36°44N 69°33E 240 A3
Talovaya Russia 51°6N 40°45E 190 E5
Taloyoak Canada 69°32N 93°32W 294 D13
Talpa de Allende Mexico 20°23N 104°51W 318 C4
Talparo Trin. & Tob. 10°30N 61°17W 323 t
Talparo → Trin. & Tob. 10°34N 61°17W 323 t
Talquin, L. U.S.A. 30°23N 84°39W 316 E5
Talsi Latvia 57°10N 22°30E 184 A9
Talsinnt Morocco 32°33N 3°27W 261 B4
Taltal Chile 25°23S 70°33W 334 B1
Taltson → Canada 61°24N 112°46W 296 A6
Talu Indonesia 0°13N 99°58E 234 B1
Taluk Indonesia 0°31S 101°34E 234 C2
Talwood Australia 28°29S 149°29E 281 D4
Talyawalka Cr. → Australia 32°28S 142°22E 282 B5
Tam Dao △ Vietnam 21°45N 105°45E 236 B5
Tam Ky Vietnam 15°34N 108°29E 236 E7
Tam Quan Vietnam 14°35N 109°3E 236 E7
Tama Tōkyō, Japan 35°38N 139°26E 140 B1
Tama Iowa, U.S.A. 41°58N 92°35W 310 C4
Tama → Japan 35°32N 139°39E 140 B2
Tama ⌓ Ethiopia 5°55N 36°5E 257 F4
Tama Abu, Banjaran Malaysia 3°50N 115°5E 235 B5
Tama Kyūryō Japan 35°34N 139°30E 140 B2
Tamada Algeria 21°34N 3°20E 261 D5
Tamaden Japan 35°39N 139°38E 140 B2
Tamagawa-josui → Japan 35°41N 139°47E 140 A1
Tamakautoga Cook Is. 19°5S 169°55W 289 g
Tamalameque Colombia 8°52N 73°49W 328 B3
Tamale Ghana 9°22N 0°50W 263 D4
Taman Russia 45°14N 36°41E 189 K9
Taman Negara △ Malaysia 4°38N 102°26E 237 K4
Taman Sari Indonesia 6°8S 106°48E 122 A1
T'aman Shan Taiwan 24°42N 121°27E 225 B3
Tamana Japan 32°58N 130°32E 222 E2
Tamana Kiribati 2°30S 175°59E 277 A14
Tamana, Mt. Trin. & Tob. 10°28N 61°12W 323 t
Tamanar Morocco 31°1N 9°46W 260 B3
Tamanduateí → Brazil 23°37S 46°38W 137 B2
Tamanhint Libya 27°13N 14°37E 258 C2
Tamani Mali 13°20N 6°50W 262 C3
Tamano Japan 34°29N 133°59E 222 C5
Tamanrasset Algeria 22°50N 5°30E 261 D6
Tamanrasset □ Algeria 23°45N 4°40E 261 D5
Tamanrasset, O. → Algeria 22°0N 2°0E 261 D5
Tamanthi Myanmar 25°19N 95°17E 241 C5
Tamaqua U.S.A. 40°48N 75°58W 313 F9
Tamar → U.K. 50°27N 4°15W 169 G3
Támara Colombia 5°50N 72°10W 328 B3
Tamarac U.S.A. 26°12N 80°15W 129 A1
Tamarin Mauritius 20°19S 57°20E 272 e
Tamarinda Spain 39°55N 3°49E 206 B4
Tamarite de Litera Spain 41°52N 0°25E 196 D5
Tamaroa U.S.A. 38°8N 89°14W 310 F7
Tamashima Japan 34°32N 133°40E 221 G6
Tamási Hungary 46°40N 18°18E 182 D3
Tamaské Niger 14°49N 5°43E 263 C6
Tamatave = Toamasina Madag. 18°10S 49°25E 272 B2
Tamaulipas □ Mexico 24°0N 98°45W 319 C5
Tamaulipas, Sierra de Mexico 23°30N 98°20W 319 C5
Tamazula Mexico 24°57N 106°57W 318 C3
Tamazunchale Mexico 21°16N 98°47W 319 C5
Tamba-Dabatou Guinea 11°50N 10°40W 262 C2
Tambach Kenya 0°36N 35°31E 268 B4
Tambacounda Senegal 13°45N 13°40W 262 C2
Tambacounda □ Senegal 14°0N 13°0W 262 C2
Tambaram India 12°55N 80°7E 245 H5
Tambea Solomon Is. 9°16S 159°41E 287 M10
Tambelan, Kepulauan Indonesia 1°0N 107°30E 235 B3
Tambellup Australia 34°4S 117°37E 279 F2
Tambo Queens., Australia 24°54S 146°14E 280 C4
Tambo Peru 12°57S 74°1W 330 C3
Tambo → Peru 10°42S 73°47W 330 C3
Tambo de Mora Peru 13°30S 76°8W 330 C2
Tambobamba Peru 13°54S 72°8W 330 C3
Tamboerskloof S. Africa 33°56S 18°25E 118 A1
Tambohorano Madag. 17°30S 43°58E 272 B1
Tambopata → Peru 13°21S 69°36W 330 C4
Tambora Jakarta, Indonesia 6°8S 106°47E 122 A1
Tambora Nusa Tenggara Barat, Indonesia 8°12S 118°5E 235 D5
Tamboritha, Mt. Australia 37°31S 146°40E 283 D7
Tamboura C.A.R. 5°10N 25°12E 264 A5
Tambov Russia 52°45N 41°28E 190 D5
Tambov □ Russia 52°50N 41°20E 190 D5
Tambre → Spain 42°49N 8°53W 194 C2
Tambuku Indonesia 7°8S 113°40E 235 D4
Tambul Papua N. G. 5°54S 143°54E 286 C2
Tambunar Malaysia 5°43N 116°24E 235 A5
Tambura South Sudan 5°40N 27°25E 257 F2
Tambuyukan, Gunong Malaysia 6°13N 116°39E 235 A5
Tâmchekket Mauritania 17°25N 10°40W 262 B2
Tame Colombia 6°28N 71°44W 328 B3
Tâmega → Portugal 41°5N 8°21W 194 D2
Tamegroute Morocco 30°15N 5°39W 260 B3
Tamelelt Morocco 31°50N 7°32W 260 B3
Tamenglong India 25°0N 93°35E 241 C4
Tamerza Tunisia 34°23N 7°58E 258 B1
Tamgak, Adrar Niger 19°12N 8°35E 259 E1
Tamgué, Massif du Guinea 12°0N 12°18W 262 C2
Tami Is. Papua N. G. 6°46S 147°55E 286 D4
Tamiahua, L. de Mexico 21°35N 97°35W 319 C5
Tamiami Canal U.S.A. 25°50N 81°0W 317 K8
Tamianglayang Indonesia 2°7S 115°10E 235 C5
Tamil Nadu □ India 11°0N 77°0E 245 J3
Tamis → Serbia 44°51N 20°39E 182 F5
Tamiya Egypt 29°29N 30°58E 256 J7
Tamlelt, Plaine de Morocco 32°30N 2°20W 261 B4
Tamluk India 22°18N 87°58E 243 H12
Tammerfors = Tampere Finland 61°30N 23°50E 188 B2
Tammisalo Finland 60°11N 25°5E 121 B3
Tammûh Egypt 29°55N 31°15E 117 B2
Tämnaren Sweden 60°10N 17°25E 162 D11
Tampa Angola 15°30S 13°27E 265 F2
Tampa Fla., U.S.A. 27°56N 82°27W 317 H7
Tampa, Tanjung Indonesia 8°55S 116°12E 231 K19
Tampa B. U.S.A. 27°50N 82°30W 317 H7
Tampa Int. ✈ (TPA) U.S.A. 27°59N 82°32W 317 H7
Tamparan Phil. 7°53N 124°20E 233 H5
Tampere Finland 61°30N 23°50E 188 B2
Tampico Tamaulipas, Mexico 22°13N 97°51W 319 C5
Tampico Ill., U.S.A. 41°38N 89°47W 310 C7
Tampin Malaysia 2°28N 102°13E 237 L4
Tampines Singapore 1°21N 103°56E 138 A3
Tampoi Malaysia 1°30N 103°39E 237 d
Tamrah Si. Arabia 20°24N 45°25E 248 B4
Tamri Morocco 30°49N 9°50W 260 B3
Tamrida = Qādub Yemen 12°37N 53°57E 249 D6
Tamsagbulag Mongolia 47°14N 117°21E 219 B12
Tamsweg Austria 47°7N 13°49E 180 D6
Tamu Myanmar 24°13N 94°12E 241 C5
Tamu Massif Pac. Oc. 33°0N 158°0E 288 D7
Tamuja → Spain 39°38N 6°29W 195 F4
Tamuning Guam 13°29N 144°47E 302 d
Tamworth N.S.W., Australia 31°7S 150°58E 283 A9
Tamworth Ont., Canada 44°29N 77°0W 312 B8
Tamworth Staffs., U.K. 52°39N 1°41W 169 E6
Tan An Vietnam 10°32N 106°25E 237 G6
Tan Chau Vietnam 10°48N 105°12E 237 G5
T'an-do N. Korea 39°30N 124°41E 224 C2
Tan Hiep Vietnam 10°27N 106°21E 237 G6
Tan Iddah Algeria 26°33N 9°42E 261 C6
Tan-Tan Morocco 28°29N 11°1W 260 C2
Tan Yen Vietnam 22°4N 105°3E 236 A5
Tana → Coast, Kenya 2°32S 40°31E 268 C5
Tana → Finnmark, Norway 70°30N 28°14E 160 A23
Tana, L. Ethiopia 13°5N 37°30E 257 E4
Tana River □ Kenya 1°30S 39°30E 268 C4
Tana River Primate ⌓ Kenya 1°55S 40°7E 268 C5
Tanabe Japan 33°44N 135°22E 223 D7
Tanabi Brazil 20°37S 49°37W 333 F2
Tanacross U.S.A. 63°23N 143°21W 303 E12
Tanafjorden Norway 70°45N 28°25E 160 A23
Tanaga I. U.S.A. 51°48N 177°53W 303 L3
Tanaga Volcano U.S.A. 51°53N 178°8W 303 L3
Tanah Abang Indonesia 6°12S 106°48E 122 B1
Tanah Kusir Indonesia 6°15S 106°46E 122 B1
Tanah Merah Malaysia 5°48N 102°9E 237 K4
Tanahbala Indonesia 0°30S 98°30E 234 C1
Tanahgrogot Indonesia 1°55S 116°15E 235 C5
Tanahjampea Indonesia 7°10S 120°35E 231 F6
Tanahmasa Indonesia 0°12S 98°39E 234 C1
Tanahmerah Indonesia 6°5S 140°16E 231 F10
Tanahputih Indonesia 1°40N 101°3E 234 B2
Tanakpur India 29°5N 80°7E 243 E9
Tanamalwila Sri Lanka 6°26N 81°8E 245 L5
Tanami Desert Australia 18°50S 132°0E 278 C5
Tanana U.S.A. 65°10N 152°4W 303 D9
Tanana → U.S.A. 65°10N 151°58W 303 D10
Tananarive = Antananarivo Madag. 18°55S 47°31E 272 B2
Tananger Norway 58°57N 5°37E 164 F2
Tanannt Morocco 31°54N 6°56W 260 B3
Tanapag N. Marianas 15°14N 145°45E 302 e
Tánaro → Italy 44°55N 8°40E 198 D5
Tanauan Phil. 14°5N 121°10E 232 D3
Tanay Phil. 14°30N 121°17E 232 D3
Tanba-Sanchi Japan 35°7N 135°48E 223 B7
Tancheng China 34°25N 118°20E 227 G10
Tanch'ŏn N. Korea 40°27N 128°54E 224 B4
Tanda Côte d'Ivoire 7°48N 3°10W 262 D4
Tanda Ut. P., India 26°33N 82°35E 243 F10
Tanda Ut. P., India 28°57N 78°56E 243 E8
Tandag Phil. 9°4N 126°9E 233 G6
Tandaia Tanzania 9°25S 34°15E 269 D3
Tăndărei Romania 44°39N 27°40E 183 F12
Tandaué Angola 16°58S 18°5E 265 F3
Tandil Argentina 37°15S 59°6W 334 D4
Tandil, Sa. del Argentina 37°30S 59°0W 334 D4
Tandin Myanmar 19°33N 93°58E 241 F4
Tandjilé □ Chad 9°30N 16°30E 259 G3
Tandjilé → Chad 9°45N 15°50E 259 G3
Tandlianwala Pakistan 31°3N 73°9E 242 D5
Tando Adam Pakistan 25°45N 68°40E 242 G3
Tando Allahyar Pakistan 25°28N 68°43E 242 G3
Tando Bago Pakistan 24°47N 68°58E 242 G3
Tando Mohommed Khan Pakistan 25°8N 68°32E 242 G3
Tando-Zinze Angola 5°22S 12°30E 265 D2
Tandou-Bengou Congo 3°50S 11°44E 264 C2
Tandou L. Australia 32°40S 142°5E 282 B5
Tandoureh △ Iran 37°50N 59°0E 247 B8
Tandragee U.K. 54°21N 6°24W 166 B5
Tandsjöborg Sweden 61°42N 14°43E 162 C8
Tandubas Phil. 5°8N 120°20E 233 J3
Tandula → India 21°6N 81°14E 244 D5
Tandula Tank India 20°40N 81°12E 244 D5
Tandur Telangana, India 19°11N 79°30E 244 E4
Tandur Telangana, India 17°14N 77°35E 244 F3
Tane-ga-Shima Japan 30°30N 131°0E 221 J5
Taneatua N.Z. 38°4S 177°1E 284 E6
Tanen Tong Dan = Dawna Ra. Myanmar 16°30N 98°30E 236 D2
Tanew → Poland 50°29N 22°16E 185 H9
Tanezrouft Algeria 23°9N 0°11E 261 D5
Tanezzuft, W. → Libya 25°51N 10°19E 258 C2
Tang, Koh Cambodia 10°16N 103°7E 237 G4
Tang, Ra's-e Iran 25°21N 59°52E 247 E8
Tang Krasang Cambodia 12°34N 105°3E 236 F5
Tanga Tanzania 5°5S 39°2E 268 D4
Tanga □ Tanzania 5°20S 38°0E 268 D4
Tanga Is. Papua N. G. 3°20S 153°15E 286 B7
Tanga Langua Grenada 12°14N 61°39W 323 q
Tangail Bangla. 24°15N 89°55E 241 C2
Tangalla Sri Lanka 6°1N 80°48E 245 L5
Tanganyika = Tanzania ■ Africa 6°0S 34°0E 268 D3
Tanganyika □ Dem. Rep. of the Congo 6°30S 28°0E 268 D2
Tanganyika, L. Africa 6°40S 30°0E 268 D3
Tangará da Serra Brazil 14°50S 57°47W 331 C6
Tangarare Solomon Is. 9°36S 159°41E 287 M10
Tangasseri India 8°53N 76°35E 245 K3
Tangaza Nigeria 13°19N 4°55E 263 C5
Tangelo Park U.S.A. 28°27N 81°26W 133 B2
Tangen Norway 60°37N 11°15E 164 D8
Tanger Morocco 35°50N 5°49W 260 A3
Tanger-Med Morocco 35°53N 5°30W 195 K5
Tanger-Tetouan-Al Hoceima □ Morocco 35°20N 5°0W 260 A3
Tangerang Indonesia 6°11S 106°37E 234 D3
Tangerhütte Germany 52°26N 11°48E 178 C7
Tangermünde Germany 52°33N 11°58E 178 C7
Tanggu China 39°2N 117°40E 227 E9
Tanggula Shan China 32°40N 92°10E 218 E7
Tanggula Shankou China 32°42N 92°27E 218 E7
Tanghe China 32°47N 112°50E 229 A9
Tanghla Range = Tanggula Shan China 32°40N 92°10E 218 E7
Tangi India 19°56N 85°24E 244 E7
Tangier = Tanger Morocco 35°50N 5°49W 260 A3
Tangjia China 22°22N 113°35E 219 a
Tangjia Wan China 22°21N 113°36E 219 a
Tango-Hantō Japan 35°45N 135°10E 223 B7
Tangorin Australia 21°47S 144°12E 280 C3
Tangorombohitr'i Makay Madag. 21°0S 45°15E 272 C2
Tangra Yumco China 31°0N 86°38E 218 E6
Tangshan China 39°38N 118°10E 227 E10
Tangtou China 35°28N 118°30E 227 G10
Tangub Phil. 8°3N 123°44E 233 G4
Tanguen-Dassouri Burkina Faso 12°16N 1°42W 263 C4
Tanguiéta Benin 10°35N 1°21E 263 C5
Tangxi China 29°3N 119°25E 229 C12
Tangyan He → China 28°54N 108°19E 228 C7
Tangyin China 35°54N 114°21E 226 G8
Taniantaweng Shan China 31°20N 98°0E 228 B2
Taniao Taiwan 22°23N 120°53E 225 D2
Tanimbar, Kepulauan Indonesia 7°30S 131°30E 231 F8
Tanimbar Is. = Tanimbar, Kepulauan Indonesia 7°30S 131°30E 231 F8
Tanintharyi = Taninthayi Myanmar 12°6N 99°3E 237 F2
Taninthayi Myanmar 12°6N 99°3E 237 F2
Tanis Egypt 31°0N 31°54E 251 H2
Tanjay Phil. 9°30N 123°5E 233 G4
Tanjong Po Malaysia 1°45N 110°30E 235 B4
Tanjore = Thanjavur India 10°48N 79°12E 245 J4
Tanjung Kalimantan Selatan, Indonesia 2°10S 115°25E 235 C5
Tanjung Nusa Tenggara Barat, Indonesia 8°21S 116°9E 231 J19
Tanjung Datu △ Malaysia 2°13N 109°3E 235 B3
Tanjung Duren Indonesia 6°10S 106°46E 122 B1
Tanjung Malim Malaysia 3°42N 101°31E 237 L3
Tanjung Pelepas Malaysia 1°21N 103°33E 237 d
Tanjung Priok Indonesia 6°6S 106°52E 122 A2
Tanjung Putung △ Indonesia 2°54S 111°59E 235 C4
Tanjung Tokong Malaysia 5°28N 100°18E 237 c
Tanjungbalai Kepulauan Riau, Indonesia 1°0N 103°25E 234 B2
Tanjungbalai Sumatera Utara, Indonesia 2°55N 99°44E 234 B1
Tanjungbatu Kalimantan Selatan, Indonesia 3°0S 116°13E 235 C5
Tanjungbatu Kalimantan Timur, Indonesia 2°23N 118°3E 235 B5
Tanjungbatu Kepulauan Riau, Indonesia 0°37N 103°25E 234 B2
Tanjungisui Indonesia 0°30S 116°8E 235 C5
Tanjungkarang Telukbetung = Bandar Lampung Indonesia 5°20S 105°10E 234 D3
Tanjungpandan Indonesia 2°43S 107°38E 235 C3
Tanjungpinang Indonesia 1°5N 104°30E 234 B2
Tanjungraja Indonesia 3°21S 104°46E 234 C2
Tanjungredeb Indonesia 2°9N 117°29E 235 B5
Tanjungselor Indonesia 2°55N 117°25E 235 B5
Tank Pakistan 32°14N 70°25E 242 C4
Tankhala India 21°58N 73°47E 242 J5
Tankwa-Karoo △ S. Africa 32°14S 19°50E 270 D2
Tanlu Taiwan 22°12N 120°44E 225 D2
Tanna Vanuatu 19°30S 169°20E 287 J7
Tännäs Sweden 62°26N 12°42E 162 B6
Tannersville U.S.A. 41°3N 75°18W 313 E9
Tannis Bugt Denmark 57°40N 10°15E 163 G4
Tannu Ola Asia 51°0N 94°0E 217 B12
Tannum Sands Australia 23°57S 151°22E 280 C5
Tano → Ghana 5°7N 2°56W 262 D4
Tanombella Algeria 25°30N 5°49E 261 C6
Tanon Str. Phil. 10°20N 123°30E 233 F4
Tanout Niger 14°50N 8°55E 259 F1
Tanquinho Brazil 11°58S 39°6W 333 D4
Tanshui Taiwan 25°10N 121°28E 225 A3
Tanshui Kang → Taiwan 25°10N 121°25E 225 A3
Tansilla Burkina Faso 12°25N 4°23W 262 C4
Tansing Nepal 27°52N 83°33E 243 F10
Tanta Egypt 30°45N 30°57E 256 H7
Tantabin Myanmar 17°1N 95°59E 241 G5
Tantoyuca Mexico 21°21N 98°14W 319 C5
Tantung = Dandong China 40°10N 124°20E 224 B2
T'antzu Taiwan 24°13N 120°42E 225 B2
Tanuku India 16°45N 81°44E 244 F5
Tanum Norway 59°53N 10°28E 133 A1
Tanūmah Si. Arabia 18°58N 42°10E 248 C3
Tanumshede Sweden 58°42N 11°20E 163 F5
Tanunda Australia 34°30S 139°0E 282 C3
Tanur India 11°1N 75°52E 245 J2
Tanus France 44°8N 2°19E 174 D6
Tanzania ■ Africa 6°0S 34°0E 268 D3
Tanzawa-Sanchi Japan 35°27N 139°0E 223 B11
Tanzhou China 22°16N 113°28E 219 a
Tanzi = T'antzu Taiwan 24°13N 120°42E 225 B2
Tanzilla → Canada 58°8N 130°43W 296 B2
Tao, Ko Thailand 10°5N 99°52E 237 G2
Tao'an = Taonan China 45°22N 122°40E 227 B12
Tao'er He → China 45°45N 124°5E 227 B13
Taohua Dao China 29°50N 122°20E 229 C14
Taolanaro Madag. 25°2S 47°0E 272 D2
Taole China 38°48N 106°40E 226 E4
Taonan China 45°22N 122°40E 227 B12
Taora Solomon Is. 7°21S 157°30E 287 L9
Taormina Italy 37°51N 15°17E 201 E8
Taos U.S.A. 36°24N 105°35W 305 H11
Taoudenni Mali 22°40N 3°55W 260 D4
Taoudrart, Adrar Algeria 24°25N 2°24E 261 D5
Taounate Morocco 34°25N 4°41W 260 B4
Taourirt Algeria 26°37N 0°20E 261 C5
Taourirt Morocco 34°25N 2°53W 261 B4
Taouz Morocco 30°53N 4°0W 260 B4
Taoyuan Hunan, China 28°55N 111°16E 229 C8
T'aoyüan Kaohsung, Taiwan 23°9N 120°46E 225 C2
T'aoyüan Yünlin, Taiwan 25°0N 121°4E 225 B3
T'aoyüan □ Taiwan 24°55N 121°15E 225 B3
Tap Shek Kok Hong Kong, China 22°23N 113°55E 122 A1
Tapa Estonia 59°15N 25°50E 161 G21
Tapa Shan = Daba Shan China 32°0N 109°0E 228 B7
Tapachula Mexico 14°54N 92°17W 319 E6
Tapada Portugal 38°49N 9°16W 126 A1
Tapah Malaysia 4°12N 101°15E 237 K3
Tapajós → Brazil 2°24S 54°41W 329 D7

Tapaktuan Indonesia 3°15N 97°10E 234 B1
Tapanahoni → Suriname 4°20N 54°25W 329 C7
Tapanila Finland 60°15N 25°2E 121 B3
Tapanui N.Z. 45°56S 169°18E 285 F4
Taparo Pt. Trin. & Tob. 10°3N 61°38W 323 t
Tapauá Brazil 5°40S 64°20W 331 B5
Tapauá → Brazil 5°40S 64°21W 331 B5
Tapaz Phil. 11°16N 122°32E 233 F4
Tapes Brazil 30°40S 51°23W 335 C5
Tapeta Liberia 6°29N 8°52W 262 D3
Taphan Hin Thailand 16°13N 100°26E 236 D3
Tapia de Casariego Spain 43°34N 6°56W 194 B4
Tapiales Argentina 34°42S 58°30W 117 C1
Tapiantana Channel Phil. 6°22N 122°1E 233 H4
Tapiantana Group Phil. 6°20N 122°0E 233 H4
Tapiau = Gvardeysk
Russia 54°39N 21°5E 184 D8
Tapilon = Daanbantayan
Phil. 11°17N 124°2E 233 F5
Taping Taiwan 24°6N 120°53E 225 B2
Tapini Papua N. G. 8°19S 147°0E 286 E4
Tapiola Finland 60°10N 24°48E 121 B1
Tapiraí Brazil 19°52S 46°1W 333 E2
Tapirapé → Brazil 10°41S 50°38W 332 D1
Tapirapecó, Serra Venezuela 1°10N 65°0W 329 C5
Taplan Australia 34°33S 140°52E 282 C4
Taplejung Nepal 27°1N 86°16E 243 F12
Tapo-Capara △ Venezuela 7°55N 71°15W 328 B3
Tapochau, Mt.
N. Marianas 15°11N 145°44E 302 e
Tapoeripa Suriname 5°22N 56°34W 329 B6
Tapolca Hungary 46°53N 17°29E 182 D2
Tapsia India 22°32N 88°23E 124 B2
Tapti → India 21°8N 72°41E 244 D1
Tapu Taiwan 23°18N 120°35E 225 C2
Tapuae-o-Uenuku N.Z. 42°0S 173°39E 285 C8
Tapul Phil. 5°42N 120°50E 233 J3
Tapul Group Phil. 5°35N 120°50E 233 J3
Tapul I. Phil. 5°43N 120°55E 233 J3
Tapun India 27°35N 96°22E 241 B6
Tapurucuará Brazil 0°24S 65°2W 329 D4
Taputapu, C. Amer. Samoa 14°20S 170°51W 302 f
Taputimu Amer. Samoa 14°21S 170°46W 302 f
Ţaqţaq Iraq 35°53N 44°35E 213 E11
Taquara Brazil 29°36S 50°46W 335 B5
Taquari → Brazil 19°15S 57°17W 331 D6
Taquaritinga Brazil 21°24S 48°30W 333 F2
Tara Queens., Australia 27°17S 150°31E 281 D5
Tara Ont., Canada 44°28N 81°9W 312 B3
Tara Maharashtra, India 19°5N 72°49E 130 A1
Tara Japan 33°2N 130°11E 222 D2
Tara Russia 56°55N 74°24E 214 D8
Tara Zambia 16°58S 26°45E 269 F2
Tara → Montenegro 43°21N 18°51E 202 C2
Tara △ Serbia 43°55N 19°30E 202 C3
Tara-Dake Japan 32°58N 130°6E 222 E2
Taraba □ Nigeria 8°0N 10°30E 263 D7
Taraba → Nigeria 8°30N 10°15E 263 D7
Tarabuco Bolivia 19°10S 64°57W 331 D5
Tarābulus Lebanon 34°31N 35°50E 250 D6
Tarābulus Libya 32°49N 13°7E 258 B2
Tarābulus Libya 31°0N 13°0E 258 B2
Tarabya Turkey 41°8N 29°3E 122 B2
Taraclia Taraclia, Moldova 45°54N 28°40E 183 E13
Taraclia Tighina, Moldova 46°34N 29°7E 183 D14
Taradale N.Z. 39°33S 176°53E 284 F5
Taradehi India 23°18N 79°21E 243 H8
Tarāghin Libya 26°0N 14°30E 258 C2
Taragi Japan 32°16N 130°56E 222 E2
Tarahouahout Algeria 22°41N 5°59E 261 D6
Tarajalejo Canary Is. 28°12N 14°7W 153 e2
Tarakan Indonesia 3°20N 117°35E 235 B5
Tarakit, Mt. Kenya 2°2N 35°10E 268 B4
Taralga Australia 34°26S 149°52E 283 C8
Tarama-Jima Japan 24°39N 124°42E 221 M2
Taramakau → N.Z. 42°34S 171°8E 285 C6
Taran, Mys Russia 54°56N 19°59E 184 D6
Taranagar India 28°43N 74°50E 242 E6
Taranaki □ N.Z. 39°25S 174°30E 284 F3
Taranaki, Mt. N.Z. 39°17S 174°5E 284 F3
Tarancón Spain 40°1N 3°1W 196 E1
Tarangire △ Tanzania 4°21S 36°7E 268 C4
Taransay U.K. 57°54N 7°0W 167 D1
Táranto Italy 40°28N 17°14E 201 B10
Táranto, G. di Italy 40°8N 17°20E 201 B10
Tarapacá Colombia 2°56S 69°46W 328 D4
Tarapacá □ Chile 20°45S 69°30W 334 A2
Tarapoto Peru 6°30S 76°20W 330 B2
Taraquá Brazil 0°6N 68°28W 328 C4
Tarare France 45°54N 4°26E 175 C8
Tararua Ra. N.Z. 40°45S 175°25E 284 G4
Tarasag Vanuatu 14°12S 167°36E 287 D5
Tarasaigh = Taransay U.K. 57°54N 7°0W 167 D1
Tarascon France 43°48N 4°39E 175 E8
Tarascon-sur-Ariège
France 42°50N 1°36E 174 F5
Tarashcha Ukraine 49°30N 30°31E 177 D16
Tarata Peru 17°27S 70°2W 330 D3
Tarauacá Brazil 8°6S 70°48W 330 B3
Tarauacá → Brazil 6°42S 69°48W 330 B4
Taravao Tahiti 17°43S 149°18W 289 e
Taravao, Isthme de Tahiti 17°43S 149°19W 289 e
Taravo → France 41°42N 8°49E 175 G12
Tarawa Kiribati 1°30N 173°0E 288 G9
Tarawai I. Papua N. G. 3°13S 143°15E 286 B2
Tarawera N.Z. 39°2S 176°36E 284 F5
Tarawera, L. N.Z. 38°13S 176°27E 284 E5
Tarawera, Mt. N.Z. 38°14S 176°32E 284 E5
Taraz Kazakhstan 42°54N 71°22E 217 D8
Tarazona Spain 41°55N 1°43W 196 D3
Tarazona de la Mancha
Spain 39°16N 1°55W 197 F3
Tårbæk Denmark 55°46N 12°35E 118 A3
Tarbagatay, Khrebet
Kazakhstan 48°0N 83°0E 217 C10
Tarbaj Kenya 2°12N 40°8E 267 D5
Tarbat Ness U.K. 57°52N 3°47W 167 D5
Tarbela Dam Pakistan 34°8N 72°52E 242 B5
Tarbert Kerry, Ireland 52°34N 9°22W 166 D2
Tarbert Argyll & Bute, U.K. 55°52N 5°25W 167 F3
Tarbert W. Isles, U.K. 57°54N 6°49W 167 D2
Tarbes France 43°15N 0°3E 174 E4
Tarboro U.S.A. 35°54N 77°32W 315 D16
Tarcău, Munţii Romania 46°39N 26°7E 183 D11
Tarcento Italy 46°13N 13°13E 199 B10
Tarchomin Poland 52°19N 20°58E 143 B1
Tarcoola Australia 30°44S 134°36E 281 E1
Tarcoon Australia 30°15S 146°43E 281 E4
Tarcutta Australia 35°16S 147°44E 283 C7
Tardeo India 18°57N 72°48E 130 B1
Tardets-Sorholus France 43°8N 0°52W 174 E3
Tardoire → France 45°52N 0°14E 174 C4
Taredjerdja Algeria 25°12N 2°32E 261 C5
Taree Australia 31°50S 152°30E 283 A10
Tarella Australia 31°2S 143°2E 282 A5
Tarf, Ras Morocco 35°40N 5°11W 260 A3
Ţarfā, Ra's aţ Si. Arabia 17°2N 42°22E 248 C3
Ţarfā, W. el → Egypt 28°25N 30°50E 256 B3
Tarfaya Morocco 27°55N 12°55W 260 C2
Targovishte Bulgaria 43°17N 26°38E 203 C10
Targovishte □ Bulgaria 43°15N 26°38E 203 C10
Târgovişte Romania 44°55N 25°27E 183 F10
Targówek Poland 52°16N 21°3E 143 B2
Târgu Bujor Romania 45°52N 27°54E 183 E12
Târgu Cărbuneşti
Romania 44°57N 23°31E 183 F8
Târgu Frumos Romania 47°12N 27°2E 183 C12
Târgu Jiu Romania 45°5N 23°19E 183 E8
Târgu Lăpuş Romania 47°27N 23°52E 183 C8
Târgu Mureş Romania 46°31N 24°38E 183 D9
Târgu Neamţ Romania 47°12N 26°25E 183 C11
Târgu Ocna Romania 46°16N 26°39E 183 D11
Târgu Secuiesc Romania 46°0N 26°10E 183 E11
Targuist Morocco 34°59N 4°14W 260 B4
Tărgușor Romania 44°27N 28°25E 183 F13
Tărhăus, Vf. Romania 46°40N 26°8E 183 D11
Tarhbalt Morocco 30°39N 5°20W 260 B3
Tarhūnah Libya 32°27N 13°36E 258 B2
Tari Papua N. G. 5°54S 142°59E 286 C2
Táriba Venezuela 7°49N 72°13W 328 B3
Ţarif U.A.E. 24°3N 53°46E 247 E7
Tarifa Spain 36°1N 5°36W 195 J5
Tarigtig Pt. Phil. 16°25N 122°14E 232 C4
Tarija Bolivia 21°30S 64°40W 334 A3
Tarija □ Bolivia 21°30S 63°30W 334 A3
Tarik I. Micronesia 7°20N 151°46E 287 T18
Tariku → Indonesia 2°55S 138°26E 231 E9
Tarīm Yemen 16°3N 49°0E 249 C5
Tarim Basin = Tarim Pendi
China 40°0N 84°0E 217 E10
Tarim He → China 39°30N 88°30E 217 E11
Tarim Pendi China 40°0N 84°0E 217 E10
Tarime Tanzania 1°21S 34°22E 266 E3
Taritatu → Indonesia 2°54S 138°27E 231 E9
Tarka → S. Africa 32°10S 26°0E 270 D4
Tarka La Bhutan 27°12N 89°44E 243 F13
Tarkastad S. Africa 32°0S 26°16E 270 D4
Tarkhankut, Mys Ukraine 45°25N 32°30E 189 K7
Tarko Sale Russia 64°55N 77°50E 214 C8
Tarkwa Ghana 5°20N 2°0W 262 D4
Tarlac Phil. 15°29N 120°35E 232 D3
Tarlac □ Phil. 15°30N 120°30E 232 D3
Tarm Denmark 55°56N 8°31E 163 J2
Tarma Peru 11°25S 75°45W 330 C2
Tarmiya Iraq 33°40N 44°23E 213 G11
Tarn □ France 43°49N 2°8E 174 E6
Tarn → France 44°5N 1°6E 174 D5
Tarn-et-Garonne □ France 44°8N 1°20E 174 D5
Tarna → Hungary 47°31N 19°59E 182 C4
Târnava Mare →
Romania 46°10N 23°43E 183 D8
Târnava Mică → Romania 46°9N 23°55E 183 D8
Târnăveni Romania 46°19N 24°13E 183 D9
Tårnby Denmark 55°37N 12°35E 118 B3
Tarnica Poland 49°4N 22°44E 185 J9
Tarnobrzeg Poland 50°35N 21°41E 185 H8
Tarnogród Poland 50°22N 22°45E 185 H9
Tarnopol = Ternopil
Ukraine 49°30N 25°40E 177 D13
Tarnos France 43°32N 1°28W 174 E2
Târnova Moldova 48°10N 27°40E 183 B12
Târnova Romania 45°23N 21°59E 182 E6
Tarnów Poland 50°3N 21°0E 185 H8
Tarnowitz = Tarnowskie Góry
Poland 50°27N 18°54E 185 H5
Tarnowskie Góry Poland 50°27N 18°54E 185 H5
Tärnsjö Sweden 60°9N 16°56E 162 D10
Taro Solomon Is. 6°43S 156°24E 287 L9
Táro → Italy 45°2N 10°15E 198 C7
Taroko △ Taiwan 24°10N 121°33E 225 B3
Ţārom Iran 28°11N 55°46E 247 D7
Taroom Australia 25°36S 149°48E 281 D4
Taroudannt Morocco 30°30N 8°52W 260 B3
Taroume Cook Is. 21°15S 159°45W 289 h
Tarp Germany 54°39N 9°24E 178 A5
Tarpeena Australia 37°37S 140°47E 282 D4
Tarpon Springs U.S.A. 28°9N 82°45W 317 G7
Tarqua Bay Nigeria 6°24N 3°23E 124 B2
Tarquínia Italy 42°15N 11°45E 199 F8
Tarra Bulga △ Australia 38°27S 146°31E 283 E7
Tarrafal Cabo Verde 15°18N 23°39W 153 j
Tarragona Spain 41°5N 1°17E 196 D6
Tarragona □ Spain 41°5N 1°0E 196 D6
Tarraleah Australia 42°17S 146°26E 281 G4
Tarrasa = Terrassa Spain 41°34N 2°1E 196 D7
Tàrrega Spain 41°39N 1°9E 196 D6
Tarrytown Ga., U.S.A. 32°19N 82°34W 316 D7
Tarrytown N.Y., U.S.A. 41°4N 73°52W 313 E11
Tårs Denmark 57°23N 10°7E 163 G4
Tarsus Turkey 36°58N 34°55E 250 B5
Tarsus → Turkey 36°46N 34°52E 250 B5
Tartagal Argentina 22°30S 63°50W 334 A3
Tartane Martinique 14°45N 60°55W 322 j
Tärtär Azerbaijan 40°20N 46°58E 191 K8
Tärtär → Azerbaijan 40°26N 47°20E 191 K8
Tartas France 43°50N 0°49W 174 E3
Tartu Estonia 58°20N 26°44E 188 C4
Ţarţūs Syria 34°55N 35°55E 250 D6
Ţarţūs □ Syria 35°0N 36°0E 250 D7
Tarumirim Brazil 19°16S 41°59W 333 E3
Tarumizu Japan 31°29N 130°42E 222 F2
Tarussa Russia 54°44N 37°10E 188 E9
Tarutao = Ko Tarutao △
Thailand 6°31N 99°26E 237 J2
Tarutao, Ko Thailand 6°33N 99°40E 237 J2
Tarutung Indonesia 2°0N 98°54E 234 B1
Tarutyne Ukraine 46°12N 29°9E 183 D14
Tarvísio Italy 46°30N 13°35E 199 B10
Tarxien Malta 35°52N 14°31E 206 F8
Tasağıl Turkey 36°55N 31°14E 250 B2
Tasahku Myanmar 27°33N 97°52E 241 B6
Tasaret, O. → Algeria 26°25N 1°59E 261 C5
Tasāwah Libya 26°0N 13°30E 258 C2
Tasböget Kazakhstan 44°46N 65°33E 216 D7
Tasek Merimbun △
Brunei 4°31N 114°41E 235 B4
Taseko → Canada 52°8N 123°45W 296 C4
Tasgaon India 17°2N 74°39E 244 F2
Tash-Kömür Kyrgyzstan 41°40N 72°10E 217 D8
Tashauz = Daşoguz
Turkmenistan 41°49N 59°58E 216 D5
Tashi Chho Dzong = Thimphu
Bhutan 27°31N 89°45E 241 B2
Tashino = Pervomaysk
Russia 54°56N 43°58E 190 C6
Ţashk, Daryācheh-ye
Iran 29°45N 53°35E 247 D7
Tashkent = Toshkent
Uzbekistan 41°20N 69°10E 217 D7
Tashtagol Russia 52°47N 87°53E 217 B11
Tashu Taiwan 22°41N 120°25E 225 D2
Tasiilaq Greenland 65°40N 37°20W 154 D7
Tasik Bera Malaysia 3°5N 102°38E 234 B2
Tasik Kenyir Malaysia 5°5N 102°45E 234 A2
Tasikmalaya Indonesia 7°18S 108°12E 235 D3
Tåsinge Denmark 55°0N 10°35E 163 J4
Tåsjön Sweden 64°15N 15°40E 160 D16
Task Niger 14°56N 10°46E 259 F2
Taskan Russia 62°59N 150°20E 215 C16
Taşkent Turkey 36°55N 32°29E 250 B3
Taşköprü Turkey 41°30N 34°15E 212 B6
Taskul Papua N. G. 2°32S 150°27E 286 B6
Taşlâc Moldova 47°4N 29°24E 183 C14
Taşliçay Turkey 39°38N 43°22E 213 C10
Tasman □ N.Z. 41°30S 172°40E 285 B7
Tasman → N.Z. 43°48S 170°8E 285 D5
Tasman, Mt. N.Z. 43°34S 170°12E 285 D5
Tasman Abyssal Plain
Pac. Oc. 34°30S 153°15E 276 G9
Tasman B. N.Z. 40°59S 173°25E 285 A8
Tasman Basin Pac. Oc. 46°0S 158°0E 288 M7
Tasman Glacier N.Z. 43°37S 170°12E 285 D5
Tasman Mts. N.Z. 41°3S 172°25E 285 B7
Tasman Pen. Australia 43°10S 148°0E 281 G4
Tasman Sea Pac. Oc. 36°0S 160°0E 277 H10
Tasmania □ Australia 42°0S 146°30E 281 G4
Tasmanian Wilderness World
Heritage Area △
Australia 43°0S 146°0E 281 G4
Tăşnad Romania 47°30N 22°33E 182 C7
Taşova Turkey 40°45N 36°19E 212 B7
Tassili n'Ajjer Algeria 25°47N 8°1E 261 C6
Tassili n'Ajjer △ Algeria 26°5N 6°0E 258 C1
Tassili-oua-n-Ahaggar
Algeria 20°41N 5°30E 261 D6
Tassili Ti-n-Rerhoh Algeria 20°5N 3°55E 261 D5
Taşucu Turkey 36°19N 33°52E 250 B4
Taşucu Körfezi Turkey 36°16N 33°56E 250 B4
Tasūj Iran 38°18N 45°23E 213 C11
Tat Ton △ Thailand 15°57N 102°2E 236 E4
Tata Hungary 47°37N 18°19E 182 C3
Tata Morocco 29°46N 7°56W 260 C3
Tatabánya Hungary 47°32N 18°25E 182 C3
Tatakoto French Polynesia 17°20S 138°23W 289 f
Tatamá △ Colombia 5°5N 76°9W 328 B2
Tatamba Solomon Is. 8°21S 159°51E 287 M10
Tataouine Tunisia 32°57N 10°29E 258 B2
Tataouine □ Tunisia 32°0N 10°0E 261 B7
Tatar-Pazardzhik = Pazardzhik
Bulgaria 42°12N 24°20E 203 D8
Tatar Republic = Tatarstan □
Russia 55°30N 51°30E 190 C10
Tatarbunary Ukraine 45°50N 29°39E 183 E14
Tatarsk Russia 55°14N 76°0E 214 D8
Tatarskiy Proliv Russia 50°0N 141°0E 215 E15
Tatarstan □ Russia 55°30N 51°30E 190 C10
Tatatóváros = Tata
Hungary 47°37N 18°19E 182 C3
Tatatua, Pte. Tahiti 17°44S 149°8W 289 e
Tatau Malaysia 2°53N 112°51E 235 B4
Tatau I. Papua N. G. 2°48S 151°57E 286 B6
Tatebayashi Japan 36°15N 139°32E 223 A11
Tateshina-Yama Japan 36°8N 138°11E 223 A10
Tateyama Chiba, Japan 35°0N 139°50E 223 C11
Tateyama Toyama, Japan 36°40N 137°35E 223 A9
Tathlina L. Canada 60°33N 117°39W 296 A5
Tathlīth Si. Arabia 19°32N 43°30E 248 C3
Tathlīth, W. → Si. Arabia 20°35N 44°20E 248 B4
Tathong Channel
Hong Kong, China 22°15N 114°16E 122 B3
Tathong Pt.
Hong Kong, China 22°14N 114°17E 122 B3
Tathra Australia 36°44S 149°59E 283 D8
Tatinnai L. Canada 60°55N 97°40W 297 A9
Tatitlek U.S.A. 60°52N 146°41W 303 F11
Tatkon Myanmar 20°7N 96°13E 241 E6
Tatla Lake Canada 52°0N 124°20W 296 C4
Tatlısu = Akanthou
Cyprus 35°22N 33°45E 207 E9
Tatlısu Turkey 40°24N 27°55E 203 F11
Tatnam, C. Canada 57°16N 91°0W 297 B10
Tatra = Tatry Slovakia 49°20N 20°0E 181 B13
Tatranský △ Slovakia 49°10N 20°0E 181 B13
Tatry Slovakia 49°20N 20°0E 181 B13
Tatshenshini → Canada 59°28N 137°45W 296 B1
Tatshenshini-Alsek △
Canada 59°55N 137°45W 296 B1
Tatsuno Hyōgo, Japan 34°52N 134°33E 222 C6
Tatsuno Nagano, Japan 35°58N 138°0E 223 B10
Tatta = Thatta Pakistan 24°42N 67°55E 242 G2
Tatuapé Brazil 23°31S 46°33W 137 B2
Tatuī Brazil 23°25S 47°53W 335 A6
Tatum U.S.A. 33°16N 103°19W 305 K12
Tat'ung = Datong China 40°6N 113°18E 226 D7
Tatura Australia 36°29S 145°16E 283 D6
Tatvan Turkey 38°31N 42°15E 213 C10
Ta'ū Amer. Samoa 14°15S 169°30W 302 g
Tau Rogaland, Norway 59°3N 5°55E 164 E2
Tauá Brazil 6°1S 40°26W 332 C3
Taubaté Brazil 23°0S 45°36W 335 A6
Tauberbischofsheim
Germany 49°37N 9°39E 179 F5
Taucha Germany 51°23N 12°29E 178 D8
Tauern Austria 47°15N 12°40E 176 E7
Tauern-tunnel Austria 47°0N 13°12E 180 D6
Taufikia South Sudan 9°24N 31°37E 257 F3
Taufkirchen Germany 48°2N 11°36E 131 B2
Taulé France 48°37N 3°55W 172 D3
Taumarunui N.Z. 38°53S 175°15E 284 E4
Taumaturgo Brazil 8°54S 72°51W 330 B3
Taung S. Africa 27°33S 24°47E 270 C3
Taungdwingyi Myanmar 20°1N 95°40E 241 E5
Taunggyi Myanmar 20°50N 97°0E 241 E6
Taunggoo = Tounggoo
Myanmar 19°0N 96°30E 241 F6
Taungtha Myanmar 21°12N 95°25E 241 E5
Taungup Myanmar 18°51N 94°14E 241 F5
Taungup Pass Myanmar 18°40N 94°45E 241 F5
Taunsa Pakistan 30°42N 70°39E 242 D4
Taunsa Barrage Pakistan 30°42N 70°50E 242 D4
Taunton Somst., U.K. 51°1N 3°5W 169 F4
Taunton Mass., U.S.A. 41°54N 71°6W 313 E13
Taunus Germany 50°13N 8°34E 179 E4
Taupo N.Z. 38°41S 176°7E 284 E5
Taupo, L. N.Z. 38°46S 175°55E 284 E4
Tauragė Lithuania 55°14N 22°16E 184 C9
Tauragė □ Lithuania 55°15N 22°17E 184 C9
Tauranga N.Z. 37°42S 176°11E 284 D5
Tauranga Harb. N.Z. 37°30S 176°5E 284 D5
Taureau, Rés. Canada 46°46N 73°50W 298 C5
Taurianova Italy 38°21N 16°1E 201 D9
Tauroa Pt. N.Z. 35°10S 173°4E 284 B2
Taurus Mts. = Toros Dağları
Turkey 37°0N 32°30E 250 B3
Taus = Domažlice Czechia 49°28N 12°58E 180 B5
Tauste Spain 41°58N 1°18W 196 D3
Tautira Tahiti 17°44S 149°9W 289 e
Tauyskaya Guba
Russia 59°20N 150°20E 215 D16
Tauz = Tovuz Azerbaijan 41°0N 45°40E 191 K7
Tavan Bogd Uul
Mongolia 49°10N 87°49E 217 C11
Tavares U.S.A. 28°48N 81°44W 317 G8
Tavares, I. dos Brazil 22°49S 43°6W 135 A2
Tavas Turkey 37°34N 29°4E 205 D11
Tavastehus = Hämeenlinna
Finland 61°0N 24°28E 188 B3
Tavda Russia 58°7N 65°8E 214 D7
Tavda → Russia 57°47N 67°18E 214 D7
Taverner B. Canada 67°12N 72°25W 295 D17
Tavernes de la Valldigna
Spain 39°5N 0°13W 197 F4
Tavernier U.S.A. 25°1N 80°31W 317 K9
Taveta Kenya 3°23S 37°37E 268 C4
Taveuni Fiji 16°51S 179°58W 287 A3
Taviano Italy 39°59N 18°5E 201 C11
Tavignano → France 42°7N 9°33E 175 F13
Tavira Portugal 37°8N 7°40W 195 H3
Tavistock Ont., Canada 43°19N 80°50W 312 C4
Tavistock Devon, U.K. 50°33N 4°9W 169 G3
Tavolara Italy 40°54N 9°42E 200 B2
Távora → Portugal 41°8N 7°35W 194 D3
Tavoy = Dawei Myanmar 14°2N 98°12E 236 E2
Tavoy Pt. Myanmar 13°32N 98°10E 236 F2
Tavrichanka Russia 43°18N 131°59E 220 C5
Tavropos → Greece 39°10N 21°45E 204 B3
Tavros Greece 37°57N 23°43E 112 B2
Tavşanlı Turkey 39°32N 29°30E 205 B11
Tavua Fiji 17°37S 177°5E 287 A1
Tavuki Fiji 19°7S 178°8E 287 B2
Taw → U.K. 51°4N 4°4W 169 F3
Tawa → India 22°48N 77°48E 242 H8
Tawa Res. India 22°35N 78°5E 244 C4
Tawa Tawa Mal Reef
Papua N. G. 11°3S 152°55E 286 F7
Tawai India 27°48N 96°47E 241 B6
Tawang India 27°35N 91°52E 241 B3
Tawas City U.S.A. 44°16N 83°31W 309 C12
Tawau Malaysia 4°20N 117°55E 235 B5
Tawau Hills △ Malaysia 4°20N 117°54E 235 B5
Taweisha Sudan 12°19N 26°40E 257 E2
Tawi-tawi □ Phil. 5°0N 120°0E 233 J3
Tawi-tawi I. Phil. 5°10N 120°15E 233 J3
Tawngche Myanmar 26°34N 95°38E 241 B5
Tawu Taiwan 22°22N 120°54E 225 D2
Tāwūq Iraq 35°8N 44°26E 213 E11
Tāwurghā' Libya 32°1N 15°2E 258 B3
Tāwurghā', Sabkhat
Libya 31°51N 15°15E 258 B3
Taxco Mexico 18°33N 99°36W 319 D5
Taxila Pakistan 33°42N 72°52E 242 C5
Taxkorgan Tajik Zizhixian
China 37°49N 75°14E 217 E9
Tay → U.K. 56°37N 3°38W 167 E5
Tay, Firth of U.K. 56°25N 3°8W 167 E5
Tay, L. W. Austral.,
Australia 32°55S 120°48E 279 F3
Tay, L. Perth & Kinr., U.K. 56°32N 4°8W 167 E4
Tay △ U.K. 56°43N 3°59W 167 E5
Tay Ninh Vietnam 11°20N 106°5E 237 G6
Tayabamba Peru 8°15S 77°16W 330 B2
Tayabas = Quezon Phil. 9°15N 117°59E 233 G1
Tayabas Phil. 14°1N 121°35E 232 D3
Tayabas B. Phil. 13°45N 121°45E 232 E3
Tayan Indonesia 0°1S 110°7E 235 C4
Taygetos Oros Greece 37°0N 22°23E 204 D4
Taylakova Russia 59°13N 74°0E 214 D8
Taylor B.C., Canada 56°13N 120°40W 296 B4
Taylor Fla., U.S.A. 30°26N 82°18W 316 E7
Taylor Mich., U.S.A. 42°14N 83°16W 311 B13
Taylor Nebr., U.S.A. 41°46N 99°23W 308 E4
Taylor Pa., U.S.A. 41°23N 75°43W 313 E9
Taylor Tex., U.S.A. 30°34N 97°25W 314 F6
Taylor, Mt. N.Z. 43°30S 171°20E 285 D6
Taylor, Mt. N. Mex.,
U.S.A. 35°14N 107°37W 305 J10
Taylorsville U.S.A. 38°2N 85°21W 311 F11
Taylorsville L. U.S.A. 38°0N 85°15W 311 G11
Taylorville U.S.A. 39°33N 89°18W 310 E7
Taymā Si. Arabia 27°35N 38°45E 246 E3
Taymyr, Oz. Russia 74°20N 102°0E 215 B11
Taymyr, Poluostrov
Russia 75°0N 100°0E 215 B11
Taypaq Kazakhstan 49°0N 51°47E 187 E9
Tayport U.K. 56°27N 2°52W 167 E6
Tayrona △ Colombia 11°20N 74°2W 328 A3
Tayshet Russia 55°58N 98°1E 215 D10
Taytay Phil. 10°45N 119°30E 233 F2
Taytay B. Phil. 10°55N 119°35E 233 F2
Tayuan Taiwan 25°3N 121°11E 225 A3
Tayug Phil. 16°2N 120°45E 232 C3
Tayūling Taiwan 24°11N 121°18E 225 B3
Tāyyebād Iran 34°45N 60°45E 247 C9
Tāyyebād □ Iran 34°44N 60°44E 247 C9
Tayynsha Kazakhstan 53°50N 69°45E 217 B7
Taz → Russia 67°32N 78°40E 214 C8
Taza Morocco 34°16N 4°6W 260 B4
Tāza Khurmātū Iraq 35°18N 44°20E 213 E11
Taza-Taou □ Morocco 34°15N 4°10W 260 B4
Tazawa-Ko Japan 39°43N 140°40E 220 E10
Taze Myanmar 22°57N 95°24E 241 D5
Tazenakht Morocco 30°35N 7°12W 260 B3
Tazerbo Libya 25°45N 21°0E 258 C4
Tazin → Canada 59°48N 109°55W 297 B7
Tazin L. Canada 59°44N 108°42W 297 B7
Tazlina U.S.A. 62°4N 146°27W 303 E11
Tazouikert Mali 21°27N 1°16W 261 D4
Tazoult Algeria 35°29N 6°11E 261 A6
Tazovskiy Russia 67°30N 78°44E 214 C8
Tazrouk Algeria 23°24N 6°15E 261 D6
Tbilisi Georgia 41°43N 44°50E 191 K7
Tchad = Chad ■ Africa 15°0N 17°15E 259 F3
Tchad, L. Chad 13°30N 14°30E 259 F2
Tchaourou Benin 8°58N 2°40E 263 D5
Tch'eng-tou = Chengdu
China 30°38N 104°2E 228 B5
Tchentlo L. Canada 55°15N 125°0W 296 B4
Tchetti Benin 7°50N 1°40E 263 D5
Tchibanga Gabon 2°45S 11°0E 264 C2
Tchien Liberia 5°59N 8°15W 262 D3
Tchin Tabaraden Niger 15°58N 5°56E 263 B6
Tchogha Zanbil = Choghā Zanbīl
Iran 32°1N 48°32E 247 C6
Tcholliré Cameroon 8°24N 14°10E 264 A2
Tch'ong-k'ing = Chongqing
China 29°35N 106°25E 228 C6
Tchoupitoulas Street
New Orleans, U.S.A. 131 b2
Tczew Poland 54°8N 18°50E 184 D5
TD Garden Boston, U.S.A. 116 a2
Te Anau N.Z. 45°25S 167°43E 285 F2
Te Anau, L. N.Z. 45°15S 167°45E 285 F2
Te Araroa N.Z. 37°39S 178°25E 284 D7
Te Aroha N.Z. 37°32S 175°44E 284 D4
Te Awamutu N.Z. 38°1S 175°20E 284 E4
Te Ika-a-Māui = North I.
N.Z. 38°0S 175°0E 284 E4
Te Kaha N.Z. 37°44S 177°52E 284 D6
Te Karaka N.Z. 38°26S 177°53E 284 E6
Te Kauwhata N.Z. 37°25S 175°9E 284 D4
Te Kopuru N.Z. 36°2S 173°56E 284 C2
Te Kou Cook Is. 21°14S 159°46W 289 h
Te Kuiti N.Z. 38°20S 175°11E 284 E4
Te Manga Cook Is. 21°14S 159°45W 289 h
Te-n-Dghâmcha, Sebkhet
Mauritania 18°30N 15°55W 262 B1
Te Nggano, L.
Solomon Is. 11°40S 160°19E 287 N11
Te Puke N.Z. 37°46S 176°22E 284 D5
Te Teko N.Z. 38°2S 176°48E 284 E5
Te Waewae B. N.Z. 46°13S 167°33E 285 G2
Te Waipounamu = South I.
N.Z. 44°0S 170°0E 285 E5
Tea → Brazil 0°30S 65°9W 328 D4
Teaca Romania 46°55N 24°30E 183 D9
Teague U.S.A. 31°38N 96°17W 314 F6
Teahupoo Tahiti 17°50S 149°16W 289 e
Teaneck U.S.A. 40°53N 74°1W 132 A1
Teano Italy 41°15N 14°4E 201 A7
Teapa Mexico 17°33N 92°57W 319 D6
Teba Spain 36°59N 4°55W 195 J6
Tebakang Malaysia 1°6N 110°30E 235 B4
Tébarat Niger 14°49N 4°27E 263 C5
Teberau → Malaysia 1°30N 103°42E 237 d
Teberda Russia 43°30N 41°46E 191 J5
Tébessa Algeria 35°22N 8°8E 261 A6
Tébessa □ Algeria 35°0N 7°56E 261 B6
Tebet Indonesia 6°14S 106°50E 122 B2
Tebicuary → Paraguay 26°36S 58°16W 334 B4
Tebingtinggi Riau, Indonesia 1°0N 102°45E 234 B2
Tebingtinggi Sumatera Selatan,
Indonesia 3°36S 103°4E 234 C2
Tebingtinggi Sumatera Utara,
Indonesia 3°20N 99°9E 234 B1
Téboursouk Tunisia 36°49N 9°51E 258 A1
Téboursouk Tunisia 36°29N 9°10E 258 A1
Tebulos Georgia 42°36N 45°17E 191 J7
Tecamachalco Mexico 19°25N 99°14W 128 B1
Tecate Mexico 32°34N 116°38W 307 N10
Tecer Dağları Turkey 39°27N 37°27E 212 C7
Tech → France 42°36N 3°3E 174 F7
Techiman Ghana 7°35N 1°58W 262 D4
Techirghiol Romania 44°4N 28°32E 183 F13
Techou = Dezhou China 37°26N 116°18E 226 F9
Tecka Argentina 43°29S 70°48W 336 B2
Tecomán Mexico 18°55N 103°53W 318 D4
Tecopa U.S.A. 35°51N 116°13W 307 K10
Tecoripa Mexico 28°37N 109°57W 318 B3
Tecuala Mexico 22°23N 105°27W 318 C3
Tecuci Romania 45°51N 27°27E 183 E12
Tecumseh Ont., Canada 42°19N 82°54W 312 D2
Tecumseh Mich., U.S.A. 42°0N 83°57W 311 B13
Tecumseh Okla., U.S.A. 35°15N 96°56W 314 D6
Ted Somalia 4°24N 43°55E 267 D5
Ted Williams Tunnel
Boston, U.S.A. 42°21N 71°1W 116 A2
Teddington U.K. 51°25N 0°20W 125 B1
Tedjert Algeria 21°23N 6°25E 261 D6
Tedzhen = Tejen
Turkmenistan 37°23N 60°31E 216 E6
Tees → U.K. 54°37N 1°10W 168 C6
Tees B. U.K. 54°40N 1°9W 168 C6
Teeswater Canada 43°59N 81°17W 312 C3
Tefé Brazil 3°25S 64°50W 329 D5
Tefé → Brazil 3°35S 64°47W 329 D5
Tefenni Turkey 37°18N 29°45E 205 D11
Tegal Indonesia 6°52S 109°8E 235 D3
Tegallalang Indonesia 8°27S 115°17E 231 J18
Tegalsari Indonesia 8°25S 114°8E 231 J17
Tegano, L. = Te Nggano, L.
Solomon Is. 11°40S 160°19E 287 N11
Tegel Germany 52°34N 13°16E 115 A2
Tegeler See Germany 52°34N 13°15E 115 A2
Tegelort Germany 52°34N 13°13E 115 A2
Tegernsee Germany 47°43N 11°46E 179 H7
Teggiano Italy 40°23N 15°32E 201 B8
Tegid, L. = Bala, L. U.K. 52°53N 3°37W 168 E4
Tegina Nigeria 10°5N 6°11E 263 C6
Tegua Vanuatu 13°15S 166°37E 287 C4
Tegucigalpa Honduras 14°5N 87°14W 320 D2
Teguidda i-n-Tessoum
Niger 17°25N 6°37E 263 B6
Teguise Canary Is. 29°3N 13°33W 153 e2
Tehachapi U.S.A. 35°8N 118°27W 307 K8
Tehachapi Mts. U.S.A. 35°0N 118°30W 307 L8
Tehamiyam Sudan 18°20N 36°32E 256 D4
Teheran = Tehrān Iran 35°41N 51°25E 141 A2
Tehilla Sudan 17°42N 36°6E 256 D4
Téhini Côte d'Ivoire 9°39N 3°40W 262 D4
Tehoru Indonesia 3°23S 129°30E 231 E7
Tehrān Iran 35°41N 51°25E 141 A2
Tehrān □ Iran 35°30N 51°30E 247 C6
Tehrān Mehrābād ✕ (THR)
Iran 35°41N 51°18E 141 A1
Tehrān Pārs Iran 35°44N 51°32E 141 A3
Tehri India 30°23N 78°29E 243 D8
Tehuacán Mexico 18°27N 97°23W 319 D5
Tehuantepec Mexico 16°21N 95°13W 319 D5
Tehuantepec, G. de
Mexico 15°50N 95°12W 319 D5
Tehuantepec, Istmo de
Mexico 17°15N 94°30W 319 D6
Tehuantepec Fracture Zone
Pac. Oc. 13°0N 97°0W 289 F18
Tei Tong Tsui
Hong Kong, China 22°16N 114°17E 122 B3
Teide, Pico del Canary Is. 28°15N 16°38W 153 e1
Teifi → U.K. 52°5N 4°41W 169 E3
Teigebyen Norway 60°12N 11°0E 162 D5
Teign → U.K. 50°32N 3°32W 169 G4
Teignmouth U.K. 50°33N 3°31W 169 G4
Teijo △ Finland 60°13N 22°56E 188 B2
Teinainano = Tarawa
Kiribati 1°30N 173°0E 288 G9
Teiuş Romania 46°12N 23°40E 183 D8
Teixeira Brazil 7°13S 37°15W 332 C4
Teixeira Pinto Guinea-Biss. 12°3N 16°0W 262 C1
Tejakula Indonesia 8°8S 115°20E 231 J18
Tejen Turkmenistan 37°23N 60°31E 216 E6
Tejen → Turkmenistan 37°24N 60°38E 247 B9
Tejo → Europe 38°40N 9°24W 195 F2
Tejo, Rio → Portugal 38°45N 9°3W 126 A2
Tejon Pass U.S.A. 34°49N 118°53W 307 L8
Tekamah U.S.A. 41°47N 96°13W 308 E5
Tekapo → N.Z. 44°13S 170°21E 285 E5
Tekapo, L. N.Z. 43°53S 170°33E 285 D5
Tekax Mexico 20°12N 89°17W 319 C7
Teke Turkey 41°4N 29°39E 203 E13
Tekeli Kazakhstan 44°50N 79°0E 217 D9
Tekeze → Ethiopia 14°20N 35°50E 257 E4
Tekeze Dam Ethiopia 13°10N 38°45E 257 E4
Tekija Serbia 44°42N 22°26E 202 B6
Tekirdağ Turkey 40°58N 27°30E 203 F11
Tekirdağ □ Turkey 41°0N 27°0E 203 E11
Tekirova Turkey 36°30N 30°32E 205 E12
Tekkali India 18°37N 84°15E 244 E7
Tekke Turkey 40°42N 36°12E 212 B7
Tekman Turkey 39°38N 41°29E 213 C9
Teknaf Bangla. 20°52N 92°18E 241 E4
Tekoa U.S.A. 47°14N 117°4W 304 C5
Tekokota French Polynesia 17°18S 142°34W 289 f
Tekong Besar, Pulau
Singapore 1°25N 104°3E 237 d
Tekouiât, O. → Algeria 22°25N 2°35E 261 D5
Tékro Chad 19°32N 20°56E 259 E4
Tekstilyshchik Russia 55°42N 37°41E 129 B3
Tel → India 20°50N 83°54E 244 D6
Tel Aviv-Yafo Israel 32°4N 34°48E 251 F5
Tel Lakhish Israel 31°34N 34°51E 251 G5
Tel Megiddo Israel 32°35N 35°11E 250 F6
Tela Honduras 15°40N 87°28W 320 C2
Télagh Algeria 34°51N 0°32W 261 B4
Telanaipura = Jambi
Indonesia 1°38S 103°30E 234 C2
Telangana □ India 17°30N 78°30E 244 F4
Telašćica △ Croatia 43°55N 15°10E 199 E12
Telavi Georgia 42°0N 45°30E 191 J7
Telč Czechia 49°11N 15°28E 180 B8
Telciu Romania 47°25N 24°24E 183 C9
Telde Canary Is. 27°59N 15°25W 153 e1
Tele →
Dem. Rep. of the Congo 2°48N 23°54E 264 B4
Télé, L. Congo 1°20N 17°9E 264 B3
Telefomin Papua N. G. 5°10S 141°31E 286 C1
Telegraph Creek Canada 58°0N 131°10W 296 B2
Telegraph Hill San Francisco, U.S.A. 136 a2
Telekhany = Tsyelyakhany
Belarus 52°30N 25°46E 177 B13
Telemark Norway 59°15N 7°40E 161 G12
Telemark □ Norway 59°25N 8°30E 164 E5
Télemsès Niger 15°37N 4°44E 263 B5
Telén Argentina 36°15S 65°31W 334 D2
Telen → Indonesia 0°10S 117°20E 235 C5
Teleneşti Moldova 47°30N 28°22E 183 C13
Teleng Iran 25°47N 61°3E 247 E9
Teleño Spain 42°23N 6°22W 194 C4
Teleorman □ Romania 44°0N 25°0E 183 G10
Teleorman → Romania 44°15N 25°20E 183 G10
Telerhteba, Djebel Algeria 24°10N 6°51E 261 D6
Teles Pires → Brazil 7°21S 58°3W 331 B6
Telescope Pk. U.S.A. 36°10N 117°5W 307 J9
Telescope Pt. Grenada 12°7N 61°36W 323 q
Teletaye Mali 16°31N 1°30E 263 B5
Teletskoye, Oz. Russia 51°40N 87°30E 217 B11
Telford U.K. 52°40N 2°27W 169 E5
Telford and Wrekin □
U.K. 52°45N 2°27W 168 E5
Telfs Austria 47°19N 11°4E 180 D4
Telhal Portugal 38°48N 9°18W 126 A1
Telica Nic. 63°23N 153°16W ...
Télimélé Guinea 10°54N 13°2W 262 C2
Teljo, J. Sudan 14°42N 25°26E 257 E2
Telkwa Canada 54°41N 127°5W 296 C3
Tell City U.S.A. 37°57N 86°46W 311 G10
Teller U.S.A. 65°16N 166°22W 303 D6
Tellicherry = Thalassery
India 11°45N 75°30E 245 J2
Telluride U.S.A. 37°56N 107°49W 305 H10
Telok Blangah Singapore 1°17N 103°49E 138 B2
Teloloapán Mexico 18°21N 99°51W 319 D5
Telpos Iz Russia 63°16N 59°13E 186 B10
Telsen Argentina 42°30S 66°50W 336 B3
Telšiai Lithuania 55°59N 22°14E 184 C9
Telšiai □ Lithuania 55°59N 22°15E 184 C9
Teltow Germany 52°23N 13°17E 115 B2
Teltow kanal Germany 52°26N 13°29E 115 B3
Teluk Anson = Teluk Intan
Malaysia 4°3N 101°0E 237 K3
Teluk Bahang Malaysia 5°28N 100°13E 237 c
Teluk Betung = Bandar Lampung
Indonesia 5°20S 105°10E 234 D3
Teluk Intan Malaysia 4°3N 101°0E 237 K3
Teluk Kumbar Malaysia 5°18N 100°14E 237 c
Telukbatang Indonesia 1°0S 109°46E 235 C3
Telukbayur Kalimantan Timur,
Indonesia 2°9N 117°24E 235 B5
Telukbayur Sumatera Barat,
Indonesia 0°59S 100°23E 234 C2
Telukbutun Indonesia 4°13N 108°12E 235 B3
Telukdalam Indonesia 0°33N 97°50E 234 B1
Tema Ghana 5°41N 0°0 263 D5
Temagami, L. Canada 47°0N 80°10W 298 C3
Temasint Algeria 23°18N 7°40E 261 D6
Tematangi
French Polynesia 21°41S 140°40W 289 f
Temax Mexico 21°9N 88°56W 319 C7
Temba S. Africa 25°20S 28°17E 271 C4
Tembagapura Indonesia 4°20S 137°0E 231 E9
Tembe
Dem. Rep. of the Congo 0°16S 28°14E 268 C2
Tembe △ S. Africa 26°51S 32°24E 271 C5
Tembesi → Indonesia 1°43S 103°6E 234 C2
Tembilahan Indonesia 0°19S 103°9E 234 C2
Temblador Venezuela 8°59N 62°44W 329 B5
Tembleque Spain 39°41N 3°30W 194 F7
Temblor Range U.S.A. 35°20N 119°50W 307 K7
Tembo Aluma Angola 7°42S 17°17E 265 D3
Teme → U.K. 52°11N 2°13W 169 E5
Temecula U.S.A. 33°30N 117°9W 307 M9
Temengor, Tasik Malaysia 5°24N 101°18E 237 K3
Temerloh Malaysia 3°27N 102°25E 237 L4
Temiang Indonesia 0°19N 104°23E 234 B2
Teminabuan Indonesia 1°26S 132°1E 231 E8
Temir Kazakhstan 49°1N 57°14E 187 E10
Temir-Khan-Shura = Buynaksk
Russia 42°48N 47°7E 191 J8
Temirtau Kazakhstan 50°5N 72°56E 217 B8
Temirtau Russia 53°10N 87°30E 217 B11
Témiscamie → Canada 50°59N 73°5W 299 B5
Témiscaming Canada 46°44N 79°5W 298 C4
Témiscamingue, L.
Canada 47°10N 79°25W 298 C4
Temnikov Russia 54°40N 43°11E 190 C6
Temo → Italy 40°17N 8°28E 200 B1
Temora Australia 34°30S 147°30E 283 C7
Temosachic Mexico 28°57N 107°51W 318 B3
Tempe U.S.A. 33°24N 111°54W 305 K8
Tempelburg = Czaplinek
Poland 53°34N 16°14E 184 E3
Tempelhof Germany 52°27N 13°23E 115 B2
Temperance U.S.A. 41°47N 83°34W 311 C13
Tempino Indonesia 1°46S 103°30E 234 C2
Tempio Pausania Italy 40°54N 9°6E 200 B2
Tempiute U.S.A. 37°39N 115°38W 306 H11
Templar Bank S. China Sea 9°0N 117°30E 233 F1
Temple U.S.A. 31°6N 97°21W 314 F6
Temple B. Australia 12°15S 143°3E 286 G2
Temple City U.S.A. 34°6N 118°3W 126 B4
Temple Hills U.S.A. 38°48N 76°56W 143 C3
Temple Mount Jerusalem 123 b3
Temple of Heaven China 39°52N 116°23E 114 B2
Temple of the Dawn = Arun
Bangkok, Thailand 113 b1
Temple Terrace U.S.A. 28°2N 82°23W 317 G7
Templemore Ireland 52°47N 7°51W 166 D4
Templeton U.S.A. 35°33N 120°42W 306 K6
Templeton → Australia 21°0S 138°40E 280 C2
Templin Germany 53°7N 13°28E 178 B9
Templo Mayor Mexico City, Mexico 128 b3
Tempoal de Sánchez
Mexico 21°31N 98°23W 319 C5
Temppeliaukio Church
Finland 60°10N 24°56E 121 B2
Tempué Angola 13°27S 18°49E 265 E3
Temryuk Russia 45°15N 37°24E 189 K9
Temska → Serbia 43°17N 22°33E 202 C6
Temuco Chile 38°45S 72°40W 336 A2
Temuka N.Z. 44°14S 171°17E 285 E6
Ten Degree Channel India 10°0N 92°30E 245 K11
Ten Thousand Is. U.S.A. 25°55N 81°45W 317 K8
Tena Ecuador 0°59S 77°49W 328 D2
Tenabo Mexico 20°3N 90°14W 319 C6
Tenaffy U.S.A. 40°54N 73°58W 132 A2
Tenaha U.S.A. 31°57N 94°15W 314 F7
Tenakee Springs U.S.A. 57°47N 135°13W 296 B1
Tenali India 16°15N 80°35E 245 F5
Tenancingo Mexico 18°58N 99°38W 319 D5
Tenango del Valle Mexico 19°7N 99°33W 319 D5
Tenaro, Akra Greece 36°22N 22°27E 204 E4
Tenasserim = Tanintharyi
Myanmar 12°6N 99°3E 237 F2
Tenasserim □ Myanmar 14°0N 98°30E 236 F2
Tenasserim → Myanmar 12°24N 98°37E 236 F2
Tenayuca, Pirámide de
Mexico 19°31N 99°10W 128 A1
Tenby U.K. 51°40N 4°42W 169 F3
Tenda, Colle di France 44°7N 7°36E 175 D11
Tendaho Ethiopia 11°48N 40°54E 257 E5
Tende France 44°5N 7°35E 175 D11
Tendelti Sudan 13°1N 31°55E 257 E3
Tendjedi, Adrar Algeria 23°41N 7°32E 261 D6
Tendō Japan 38°20N 140°30E 220 E10
Tendrara Morocco 33°3N 1°58W 261 B4
Tendrovskaya Kosa
Ukraine 46°16N 31°35E 189 J6
Tendukhera India 23°24N 79°33E 243 H8
Teneguía, Volcán
Canary Is. 28°28N 17°51W 153 e1
Teneida Egypt 25°30N 29°19E 256 B2
Tenenkou Mali 14°28N 4°55W 262 C4
Tenente Marques →
Brazil 11°10S 59°56W 331 C6
Ténéré Niger 19°0N 10°30E 259 E2
Ténéré, Erg du Niger 17°35N 10°55E 259 E2
Tenerife Canary Is. 28°15N 16°35W 153 e1
Tenerife, Pico Canary Is. 27°43N 18°1W 153 e1
Tenerife Norte ✕ (TFN)
Canary Is. 28°28N 16°17W 153 e1
Tenerife Sur ✕ (TFS)
Canary Is. 28°3N 16°33W 153 e1
Ténès Algeria 36°31N 1°14E 261 A5
Teng Xian Guangxi Zhuangzu,
China 23°21N 110°56E 229 F8
Teng Xian Shandong, China 35°5N 117°10E 227 G9
Tengah → Singapore 1°23N 103°43E 138 A2
Tengah, Kepulauan
Indonesia 7°5S 118°15E 235 D5
Tengchong China 25°0N 98°28E 228 E2
Tengchowfu = Penglai
China 37°48N 120°42E 227 F11
Tenggarong Indonesia 0°24S 116°58E 235 C5
Tengger Feng China 43°12N 86°48E 217 D11
Tengger Shamo China 38°0N 104°10E 226 F3
Tenggol, Pulau Malaysia 4°48N 103°41E 237 K4

Tengi-Kharam = Dehqonobod Uzbekistan 38°21N 66°30E 240 A2
Tengiz Köli Kazakhstan 50°30N 69°0E 217 B7
Tengzhou China 35°4N 117°9E 227 G9
Tenhult Sweden 57°41N 14°20E 163 G8
Teniente Enciso △ Paraguay 21°5S 61°8W 334 A3
Tenille U.S.A. 29°46N 83°19W 316 F6
Tenino U.S.A. 46°51N 122°51W 306 D4
Tenkasi India 8°55N 77°20E 245 K3
Tenke Katanga, Dem. Rep. of the Congo 11°22S 26°40E 269 E2
Tenke Katanga, Dem. Rep. of the Congo 10°32S 26°7E 269 E2
Tenkodogo Burkina Faso 11°54N 0°19W 263 C4
Tenna → Italy 43°14N 13°47E 199 E10
Tennant Creek Australia 19°30S 134°15E 280 B1
Tennessee □ U.S.A. 36°0N 86°30W 315 D11
Tennessee → U.S.A. 37°4N 88°34W 315 C10
Tennille U.S.A. 32°56N 82°48W 316 C7
Tennoji Japan 34°39N 135°30E 133 B2
Teno, Pta. de Canary Is. 28°21N 16°55W 153 e1
Tenojoki = Tana → Norway 70°30N 28°14E 160 A23
Tenom Malaysia 5°4N 115°57E 235 A5
Tenosique Mexico 17°29N 91°26W 319 D6
Tenri Japan 34°39N 135°49E 223 C7
Tenryū Japan 34°52N 137°49E 223 C9
Tenryū-Gawa → Japan 35°39N 137°48E 223 B9
Tensift, Oued → Morocco 32°3N 9°28W 260 B3
Tente Indonesia 8°35S 118°41E 235 D5
Tenterden U.K. 51°4N 0°42E 169 F8
Tenterfield Australia 29°0S 152°0E 281 D5
Tenuaiur, Uad → W. Sahara 21°36N 16°0W 260 D1
Teo = A Ramallosa Spain 42°45N 8°30W 194 C2
Teófilo Otoni Brazil 17°50S 41°30W 333 E3
Tepa Indonesia 7°52S 129°31E 231 F7
Tepa Pt. Cook Is. 19°6S 169°55W 289 g
Tepalcatepec → Mexico 18°35N 101°59W 318 D4
Tepalcates Mexico 19°23N 99°3W 128 B2
Tepecik Bursa, Turkey 40°7N 28°25E 203 F12
Tepecik Kütahya, Turkey 39°32N 29°28E 205 B11
Tepehuanes Mexico 25°21N 105°44W 318 B3
Tepelenë Albania 40°17N 20°2E 202 F4
Tepequem, Serra Brazil 3°45N 61°45W 329 C5
Tepetongo Mexico 22°28N 103°9W 318 C4
Tepeyac △ Mexico 19°30N 99°7W 128 B2
Tepic = Nayarit □ Mexico 22°0N 105°0W 318 C4
Tepic Mexico 21°30N 104°54W 318 C4
Teplá Czechia 49°59N 12°52E 180 B5
Teplice Czechia 50°40N 13°48E 180 A6
Teplitz = Teplice Czechia 50°40N 13°48E 180 A6
Teplyk Ukraine 48°40N 29°44E 183 B14
Tequila Mexico 20°54N 103°47W 318 C4
Ter → Spain 42°2N 3°12E 196 C8
Ter Apel Neths. 52°53N 7°5E 170 B7
Téra Niger 14°0N 0°45E 263 C5
Tera → Spain 41°54N 5°44W 194 D5
Tera Kora Bonaire 12°11N 68°16W 322 h
Teraina Kiribati 4°43N 160°25W 289 G12
Terakeka South Sudan 5°26N 31°45E 257 F3
Téramo Italy 42°39N 13°42E 199 F10
Terang Australia 38°15S 142°55E 282 E5
Terang, Teluk Indonesia 8°44S 116°0E 231 K19
Terawhiti, C. N.Z. 41°16S 174°38E 284 H3
Terazit, Massif de Niger 20°2N 8°30E 259 D1
Tercan Turkey 39°47N 40°23E 213 C9
Terceira Azores 38°43N 27°13W 153 d1
Tercero → Argentina 32°58S 61°47W 334 C3
Terdal India 16°33N 75°3E 244 F2
Terebovlya Ukraine 49°18N 25°44E 177 D13
Teregova Romania 45°10N 22°16E 182 E7
Tereida Sudan 10°35N 31°17E 257 E3
Terek → Russia 44°0N 47°30E 191 J8
Terengganu □ Malaysia 4°55N 103°0E 237 K4
Terenos Brazil 20°26S 54°50W 331 E7
Terepaima △ Venezuela 9°58N 69°17W 328 B4
Tereshka → Russia 51°48N 46°26E 190 E8
Teresina Brazil 5°9S 42°45W 332 C3
Teresinha Brazil 0°58N 52°2W 329 C7
Terespol Poland 52°5N 23°37E 185 F10
Teressa India 8°15N 93°10E 245 K11
Teresva Ukraine 48°0N 23°42E 183 B8
Terewah, L. Australia 29°52S 147°35E 281 D4
Terges → Portugal 37°49N 7°41W 195 H3
Tergnier France 49°40N 3°17E 173 C10
Terhazza Mali 23°38N 5°22W 260 D3
Teridgerie Cr. → Australia 30°25S 148°50E 283 A8
Teríjoki = Zelenogorsk Russia 60°12N 29°43E 188 B5
Terlizzi Italy 41°8N 16°32E 201 A9
Termas de Río Hondo Argentina 27°29S 64°52W 334 B3
Terme Turkey 41°11N 37°0E 212 B7
Términi Imerese Italy 37°59N 13°42E 200 E6
Términos, L. de Mexico 18°37N 91°33W 319 D6
Termit, Massif de Niger 16°2N 11°20E 259 E2
Termiz Uzbekistan 37°15N 67°15E 217 E7
Térmoli Italy 42°0N 15°0E 199 F12
Ternate Indonesia 0°45N 127°25E 231 D7
Terneuzen Neths. 51°20N 3°50E 170 C3
Terney Russia 45°3N 136°37E 220 B8
Terni Italy 42°34N 12°37E 199 F9
Ternitz Austria 47°43N 16°2E 180 D9
Ternivka Ukraine 48°32N 29°58E 183 B14
Ternopil Ukraine 49°30N 25°40E 177 D13
Ternopil □ Ukraine 48°10N 25°10E 177 D13
Ternopol = Ternopil Ukraine 49°30N 25°40E 177 D13
Terowie Australia 33°8S 138°55E 282 B3
Terpni Greece 40°55N 23°26E 202 F7
Terra Bella U.S.A. 35°58N 119°3W 307 K7
Terra Nova △ Canada 48°33N 53°55W 299 C9
Terrace Canada 54°30N 128°35W 296 C3
Terrace Bay Canada 48°47N 87°5W 298 C2
Terracina Italy 41°17N 13°15E 200 A6
Terralba Italy 39°43N 8°39E 200 C1
Terranova di Sicilia = Gela Italy 37°4N 14°15E 201 E7
Terranova Pausania = Ólbia Italy 40°55N 9°31E 200 B2
Terrasini Italy 38°10N 13°4E 200 D6
Terrassa Spain 41°34N 2°1E 196 D7
Terrasson-la-Villedieu France 45°8N 1°18E 174 C5
Terrazzano Italy 45°32N 9°4E 128 A1
Terre-de-Bas Guadeloupe 15°51N 61°38W 322 e
Terre-de-Bas Guadeloupe 16°10N 61°7W 322 e
Terre-de-Haut Guadeloupe 15°52N 61°34W 322 e
Terre des Hommes Canada 45°31N 73°32W 130 A2
Terre Haute U.S.A. 39°28N 87°25W 311 E9
Terre Rouge Mauritius 20°7S 57°31E 272 e
Terrebonne B. U.S.A. 29°5N 90°35W 315 G9
Terrecht Mali 19°35N 0°22E 261 D4
Terrenceville Canada 47°40N 54°44W 299 C9
Terrick Terrick △ Australia 36°8S 144°13E 282 D6
Terrugem Portugal 38°41N 9°17W 126 A1
Terry U.S.A. 46°47N 105°19W 304 C11
Terrytown U.S.A. 29°54N 90°1W 131 B2
Terryville U.S.A. 41°41N 73°3W 313 E11
Terschelling Neths. 53°25N 5°20E 170 A5
Tersko-Kumskiy Kanal Russia 44°32N 44°38E 191 H7
Tertenía Italy 39°42N 9°34E 200 C2
Terter = Tärtär → Azerbaijan 40°26N 47°20E 191 K8
Teruel Spain 40°22N 1°8W 196 E3
Teruel □ Spain 40°48N 1°0W 196 E4
Tervel Bulgaria 43°45N 27°28E 203 C11
Tervola Finland 66°6N 24°49E 160 C21
Tervuren Belgium 50°49N 4°31E 116 B3
Tervuren, Park van Belgium 50°49N 4°31E 116 B3
Teryaweynya L. Australia 32°18S 143°22E 282 B5
Tešanj Bos.-H. 44°38N 18°1E 182 F3
Teschen = Cieszyn Poland 49°45N 18°35E 185 J5
Teseney Eritrea 15°5N 36°42E 257 D4
Tesha → Russia 55°38N 42°9E 190 C6
Teshekpuk L. U.S.A. 70°35N 153°26W 303 A9
Teshio Japan 44°53N 141°44E 220 B10
Teshio-Gawa → Japan 44°53N 141°45E 220 B10
Tešica Serbia 43°27N 21°45E 202 C5
Tesiyn Gol → Mongolia 50°40N 93°20E 218 A7
Teslić Bos.-H. 44°37N 17°54E 182 F2
Teslin Canada 60°10N 132°43W 296 A2
Teslin → Canada 61°34N 134°35W 296 A2
Teslin L. Canada 60°15N 132°57W 296 A2
Tesouro Brazil 16°4S 53°34W 331 D7
Tessalit Mali 20°12N 1°0E 261 D5
Tessaoua Niger 13°47N 7°56E 259 F1
Tessin Germany 54°2N 12°26E 178 A8
Tessit Mali 15°13N 0°18E 263 B5
Tessounfat Mali 22°53N 0°32E 261 D5
Test → U.K. 50°56N 1°29W 169 G6
Testa del Gargano Italy 41°50N 16°10E 199 G13
Testigos, Is. Los Venezuela 11°23N 63°7W 321 D7
Tét Hungary 47°30N 17°33E 182 C2
Têt → France 42°44N 3°2E 174 F7
Tetachuck L. Canada 53°18N 125°55W 296 C3
Tetas, Pta. Chile 23°31S 70°38W 334 A1
Tete Mozam. 16°13S 33°33E 269 F3
Tete □ Mozam. 15°15S 32°40E 269 F3
Tetenga, Caleta Chile 27°9S 109°19W 330 b
Tetepare Solomon Is. 8°45S 157°35E 287 M9
Teterev → Ukraine 51°1N 30°5E 177 C16
Teterow Germany 53°46N 12°34E 178 B8
Teteven Bulgaria 42°58N 24°17E 203 D8
Tethul → Canada 60°35N 112°12W 296 A6
Tetiyev Ukraine 49°22N 29°38E 177 D15
Tetlin U.S.A. 63°8N 142°31W 303 E12
Tetlin Junction U.S.A. 63°19N 142°36W 303 E12
Tetlin Nat. Wildlife Refuge ⌓ U.S.A. 62°40N 141°50W 303 E12
Tetlit Zheh = Fort McPherson Canada 67°30N 134°55W 294 D5
Teton → U.S.A. 47°56N 110°31W 304 C8
Tétouan Morocco 35°35N 5°21W 260 A3
Tetovo N. Macedonia 42°1N 20°59E 202 D4
Tetschen = Děčín Czechia 50°47N 14°12E 180 A7
Tetuán Spain 40°27N 3°42W 127 B1
Tetufera, Mt. Tahiti 17°40S 149°26W 289 e
Tetyukhe = Dalnegorsk Russia 44°32N 135°33E 220 B7
Tetyushi Russia 54°55N 48°49E 190 C9
Teuco → Argentina 25°35S 60°11W 334 B3
Teufelsberg Germany 52°29N 13°14E 115 B2
Teulada Italy 38°58N 8°46E 200 D1
Teulon Canada 50°23N 97°16W 297 C9
Teun Indonesia 6°59S 129°8E 231 F7
Teuri-Tō Japan 44°26N 141°19E 220 B10
Teutoburger Wald Germany 52°5N 8°22E 178 C4
Teutopolis U.S.A. 39°8N 88°29W 311 E8
Tevere → Italy 41°44N 12°14E 199 G9
Tevere ⌓ Italy 42°46N 12°14E 199 F9
Teverya Israel 32°47N 35°32E 250 F6
Teviot → U.K. 55°29N 2°38W 167 F6
Tewantin Australia 26°27S 153°3E 281 D5
Teweh → Indonesia 0°58N 114°54E 235 C5
Tewkesbury U.K. 51°59N 2°9W 169 F5
Texada I. Canada 49°40N 124°25W 296 D4
Texarkana Ark., U.S.A. 33°26N 94°2W 314 E7
Texarkana Tex., U.S.A. 33°26N 94°3W 314 E7
Texas Australia 28°49S 151°9E 281 D5
Texas □ U.S.A. 31°40N 98°30W 314 F5
Texas City U.S.A. 29°24N 94°54W 314 G7
Texel Neths. 53°5N 4°50E 170 A4
Texline U.S.A. 36°23N 103°2W 314 C3
Texoma, L. U.S.A. 33°50N 96°34W 314 E6
Teykovo Russia 56°55N 40°30E 188 D11
Teyvareh Afghan. 33°30N 64°24E 240 B2
Teza → Russia 56°32N 41°53E 190 B5
Tezin Afghan. 34°24N 69°30E 242 B3
Teziutlán Mexico 19°49N 97°21W 319 D5
Tezpur India 26°40N 92°45E 241 B4
Tezu India 27°55N 96°10E 241 B6
Tezzeron L. Canada 54°43N 124°30W 296 C4
Tha-anne → Canada 60°31N 94°37W 297 A10
Tha Deua Laos 17°57N 102°53E 236 D4
Tha Deua Laos 19°26N 101°50E 236 C3
Tha Li Thailand 17°37N 101°25E 236 D3
Tha Pla Thailand 17°48N 100°32E 236 D3
Tha Rua Thailand 14°34N 100°44E 236 E3
Tha Sala Thailand 8°40N 99°56E 237 H2
Tha Song Yang Thailand 17°34N 97°55E 236 D1
Thaba Putsoa Lesotho 29°45S 28°0E 271 C4
Thaba-Tseka Lesotho 29°32S 28°36E 271 C4
Thabana Ntlenyana Lesotho 29°30S 29°16E 271 C4
Thabaung Myanmar 17°2N 94°48E 241 G5
Thabazimbi S. Africa 24°40S 27°21E 271 B4
Thabeikkyin Myanmar 22°53N 95°59E 241 D5
Thabt, G. el Egypt 28°17N 34°1E 251 K5
Thādiq Si. Arabia 25°18N 45°52E 246 E5
Thai Binh Vietnam 20°35N 106°1E 228 G6
Thai Muang Thailand 8°24N 98°16E 237 H2
Thai Nguyen Vietnam 21°35N 105°55E 228 G5
Thailand ■ Asia 16°0N 102°0E 236 E4
Thailand, G. of Asia 11°30N 101°0E 237 G3
Thakhek Laos 17°25N 104°45E 236 D5
Thakurgaon Bangla. 26°2N 88°34E 241 B2
Thal Pakistan 33°28N 70°33E 242 C4
Thal Desert Pakistan 31°10N 71°30E 242 D4
Thala Tunisia 35°35N 8°40E 258 A1
Thala La = Hkakabo Razi Myanmar 28°25N 97°23E 228 C1
Thalabarivat Cambodia 13°33N 105°57E 236 F5
Thalang = Amphoe Thalang Thailand 8°1N 98°20E 237 a
Thalara Nepal 29°29N 80°59E 243 E9
Thalassery India 11°45N 75°30E 245 J2
Thale Sap Songkhla Thailand 7°12N 100°28E 237 J3
Thalkirchen Germany 48°6N 11°32E 131 B2
Thallon Australia 28°39S 148°49E 281 D4
Thalu, Ko Thailand 9°26N 99°54E 237 b
Thalwil Switz. 47°17N 8°35E 179 H4
Tham Lot Thailand 19°34N 98°16E 236 C2
Thamarīt Oman 17°39N 54°2E 249 C6
Thames N.Z. 37°7S 175°34E 284 D4
Thames → Ont., Canada 42°20N 82°25W 312 D2
Thames → U.K. 51°29N 0°34E 169 F8
Thames → Conn., U.S.A. 41°18N 72°5W 313 E12
Thames, Firth of N.Z. 37°0S 175°25E 284 D4
Thames Ditton U.K. 51°23N 0°20W 125 B1
Thames Estuary U.K. 51°29N 0°52E 169 F8
Thamesford Canada 43°4N 81°0W 312 C4
Thamesmead U.K. 51°30N 0°7E 125 A4
Thamesville Canada 42°33N 81°59W 312 D3
Thāmit, W. → Libya 31°11N 16°8E 258 B3
Thamūd Yemen 17°18N 49°55E 249 C5
Than India 22°34N 71°11E 242 H4
Than Kyun Myanmar 9°49N 98°4E 237 H1
Than Uyen Vietnam 22°0N 103°54E 236 B4
Thana Cr. → India 19°4N 72°54E 130 A2
Thana Gazi India 27°25N 76°19E 242 F7
Thanbyuzayat Myanmar 15°58N 97°44E 241 G6
Thandaung Myanmar 19°4N 96°41E 241 F6
Thandla India 23°0N 74°34E 242 H6
Thandwe Myanmar 18°20N 94°30E 241 F5
Thane India 19°12N 72°59E 244 E1
Thanesar India 30°1N 76°52E 242 D7
Thanet, I. of U.K. 51°21N 1°20E 169 F9
Thangool Australia 24°38S 150°42E 280 C5
Thanh Hoa Vietnam 19°48N 105°46E 236 C5
Thanh Hung Vietnam 9°55N 105°43E 237 H5
Thanh Pho Ho Chi Minh Vietnam 10°58N 106°40E 237 G6
Thanh Thuy Vietnam 22°55N 104°51E 236 A5
Thanjavur India 10°48N 79°12E 245 J4
Thanlwin = Salween → Myanmar 16°31N 97°37E 241 G6
Thanlyin = Syriam Myanmar 16°44N 96°19E 241 G6
Thann France 47°48N 7°5E 173 E14
Thano Bula Khan Pakistan 25°22N 67°50E 242 G2
Thanya Buri Thailand 14°1N 100°45E 236 E3
Thaoge → Botswana 20°27S 22°36E 270 B3
Thaolintoa L. Canada 61°30N 96°25W 297 A9
Thaon-les-Vosges France 48°15N 6°24E 173 D13
Thap Lan △ Thailand 14°15N 102°16E 236 E4
Thap Sakae Thailand 11°30N 99°37E 237 G2
Thap Than Thailand 15°27N 99°54E 236 E2
Thar Desert India 28°0N 72°0E 242 F5
Tharad India 24°30N 71°44E 242 G4
Tharaka-Nithi □ Kenya 0°20S 38°0E 268 C4
Thargomindah Australia 27°58S 143°46E 281 D3
Tharp Fracture Zone S. Ocean 54°0S 135°0W 151 B14
Tharrawaddy Myanmar 17°38N 95°48E 241 G5
Tharrawaw Myanmar 17°41N 95°28E 241 G5
Tharthār, Buḩayrat ath Iraq 34°0N 43°15E 213 E10
Tharthar, L. = Tharthār, Buḩayrat ath Iraq 34°0N 43°15E 213 E10
Tharthār, W. ath → Iraq 34°32N 43°4E 213 E10
Thasopoula Greece 40°49N 24°45E 203 F8
Thasos Greece 40°40N 24°40E 203 F8
That Khe Vietnam 22°16N 106°28E 228 F6
Thatcher Ariz., U.S.A. 32°51N 109°46W 305 K9
Thatcher Colo., U.S.A. 37°33N 104°7W 305 H11
Thaton Myanmar 16°55N 97°22E 241 G6
Thatta Pakistan 24°42N 67°55E 242 G2
Thau, Bassin de France 43°23N 3°36E 174 E7
Thaungdut Myanmar 24°30N 94°40E 241 C5
Thawatti Myanmar 19°32N 96°16E 241 F6
Thayawthadangy Kyun Myanmar 12°19N 98°0E 236 F1
Thayer U.S.A. 36°31N 91°33W 308 G8
Thayetmyo Myanmar 19°20N 95°10E 241 F5
Thazi Magway, Myanmar 19°59N 95°3E 241 F5
Thazi Mandalay, Myanmar 21°0N 96°5E 241 E6
Thbeng Meanchey Cambodia 13°49N 104°58E 236 F5
The Bahamas ■ N. Amer. 24°0N 75°0W 321 B5
The Broads U.K. 52°45N 1°30E 168 E9
The Everglades U.S.A. 25°50N 81°0W 317 K9
The Gambia ■ W. Afr. 13°25N 16°0W 262 C1
The Gulf = Persian Gulf Asia 27°0N 50°0E 247 E6
The Hague = 's-Gravenhage Neths. 52°7N 4°17E 170 B4
The Pas Canada 53°45N 101°15W 297 C8
The Wash U.K. 52°58N 0°20E 168 E8
The Weald U.K. 51°4N 0°20E 169 F8
Thebes = Thiva Greece 38°19N 23°19E 204 C5
Thebes Egypt 25°40N 32°35E 256 B3
Thedford U.S.A. 41°59N 100°35W 308 E3
Theebine Australia 25°57S 152°34E 281 D5
Thègon Myanmar 18°39N 95°25E 241 F5
Thekulthili L. Canada 61°3N 110°0W 297 A7
Thelon → Canada 64°16N 96°4W 297 A8
Thénezay France 46°44N 0°2W 172 F6
Thenon France 45°9N 1°4E 174 C5
Theodore Queens., Australia 24°55S 150°3E 280 C5
Theodore Sask., Canada 51°26N 102°55W 297 C8
Theodore Ala., U.S.A. 30°33N 88°10W 315 F10
Theodore Roosevelt △ U.S.A. 47°0N 103°25W 308 B2
Theodore Roosevelt L. U.S.A. 33°40N 111°10W 305 K8
Thepha Thailand 6°52N 100°58E 237 J3
Thérain → France 49°15N 2°27E 173 C9
Therandë Kosovo 42°21N 20°50E 202 D4
Theresa U.S.A. 44°13N 75°48W 313 B9
Theressa U.S.A. 29°50N 82°4W 316 F7
Therma = Eagle Nest U.S.A. 36°33N 105°16W 305 H11
Thermaïkos Kolpos Greece 40°15N 22°45E 202 F6
Thermopolis U.S.A. 43°39N 108°13W 304 E9
Thermopylæ Greece 38°48N 22°35E 204 C4
Thesprotia Greece 39°27N 20°22E 204 B2
Thessalon Canada 46°20N 83°30W 298 C3
Thessalonica, Gulf of = Thermaïkos Kolpos Greece 40°15N 22°45E 202 F6
Thessaloniki Greece 40°38N 22°58E 202 F6
Thessaloniki ✈ (SKG) Greece 40°30N 23°0E 202 F7
Thessaly □ Greece 39°25N 22°0E 204 B4
Thetford U.K. 52°25N 0°45E 169 E8
Thetford Mines Canada 46°8N 71°18W 299 C5
Thethi △ Albania 42°24N 19°46E 202 D3
Theun → Laos 18°19N 104°0E 236 C5
Theunissen S. Africa 28°26S 26°43E 270 C4
Thevenard Australia 32°9S 133°38E 281 E1
Thiais France 48°46N 2°23E 134 B3
Thiamis → Greece 39°15N 20°6E 204 B2
Thibaud Dominica 15°36N 61°24W 323 k
Thiberville France 49°8N 0°27E 172 C7
Thibodaux U.S.A. 29°48N 90°49W 315 G9
Thicket Portage Canada 55°19N 97°42W 297 B9
Thief River Falls U.S.A. 48°7N 96°10W 308 A5
Thiel Mts. Antarctica 85°15S 91°0W 151 E16
Thiene Italy 45°42N 11°29E 199 C8
Thiérache France 49°51N 3°45E 173 C10
Thiers France 45°52N 3°33E 174 C7
Thiès Senegal 14°50N 16°51W 262 C1
Thiès □ Senegal 14°45N 16°50W 262 C1
Thiesi Italy 40°31N 8°43E 200 B1
Thika Kenya 1°1S 37°5E 268 C4
Thille-Boubacar Senegal 16°31N 15°5W 262 B1
Thimân, W. → Egypt 28°4N 33°45E 251 K4
Thimphu Bhutan 27°31N 89°45E 241 B2
Thina → S. Africa 31°18S 29°13E 271 D4
Thinadhoo Maldives 0°32N 72°56E 272 d
Thingangyun Myanmar 16°49N 96°12E 241 G6
Þingeyjarsýsla Iceland 65°40N 16°30W 155 B10
Þingeyri Iceland 65°52N 23°30W 155 B3
Þingmúli Iceland 65°2N 14°37W 155 B12
Þingvallavatn Iceland 64°11N 21°9W 155 C5
Þingvellir Iceland 64°15N 21°7W 155 C5
Þingvellir △ Iceland 64°16N 21°5W 155 C5
Thio N. Cal. 21°37S 166°14E 288 d
Thionville France 49°20N 6°10E 173 C13
Thira = Santorini Greece 36°23N 25°27E 205 E7
Thirasia Greece 36°26N 25°21E 205 E7
Third Cataract Sudan 19°42N 30°20E 256 D3
Thirsk U.K. 54°14N 1°19W 168 C6
Thiruvananthapuram India 8°41N 77°0E 245 K3
Thiruvarur India 10°46N 79°38E 245 J4
Thisio Athens, Greece 112 c1
Thisted Denmark 56°58N 8°40E 163 H2
Þistilfjörður Iceland 66°18N 15°24W 155 A11
Thistle I. Australia 35°0S 136°8E 282 C2
Thistletown Canada 43°44N 79°34W 141 A1
Thitgy Myanmar 18°15N 96°13E 241 F6
Thithia = Cicia Fiji 17°45S 179°18W 287 A3
Thitpokpin Myanmar 19°24N 95°58E 241 F5
Thitu I. S. China Sea 11°3N 114°17E 230 B4
Thiva Greece 38°19N 23°19E 204 C5
Thiviers France 45°25N 0°54E 174 C4
Þjórsá → Iceland 63°47N 20°48W 155 D6
Thlewiaza → Canada 60°29N 94°40W 297 A10
Thmar Puok Cambodia 13°57N 103°4E 236 F4
Tho Chu, Dao Vietnam 9°20N 103°28E 237 H4
Tho Vinh Vietnam 19°16N 105°42E 236 C5
Thoa → Canada 60°31N 109°47W 297 A7
Thoen Thailand 17°43N 99°12E 236 D2
Thoeng Thailand 19°41N 100°12E 236 C3
Thomas U.S.A. 35°45N 98°45W 314 D5
Thomas, L. Australia 26°4S 137°58E 281 D2
Thomas Circle Washington, D.C., U.S.A. 143 a1
Thomas Hill Res. U.S.A. 39°34N 92°39W 310 E4
Thomas Hubbard, C. Canada 82°0N 94°25W 295 A13
Thomaston U.S.A. 32°53N 84°20W 316 C5
Thomastown Australia 37°40S 145°2E 128 A2
Thomasville Ala., U.S.A. 31°55N 87°44W 315 F11
Thomasville Ga., U.S.A. 30°50N 83°59W 316 E6
Thomasville N.C., U.S.A. 35°53N 80°5W 315 D14
Thompson Man., Canada 55°45N 97°52W 297 B9
Thompson Pa., U.S.A. 41°52N 75°31W 313 E9
Thompson → B.C., Canada 50°15N 121°24W 296 C4
Thompson → Mo., U.S.A. 39°46N 93°37W 310 E3
Thompson Falls U.S.A. 47°36N 115°21W 304 C6
Thompson I. U.S.A. 42°19N 70°59W 116 B3
Thompson Pk. U.S.A. 41°0N 123°2W 304 F2
Thompson Sd. N.Z. 45°8S 166°46E 285 F1
Thompson Springs U.S.A. 38°58N 109°43W 304 G9
Thompsontown U.S.A. 40°33N 77°14W 312 F7
Thomson Ga., U.S.A. 33°28N 82°30W 316 B7
Thomson Ill., U.S.A. 41°58N 90°6W 310 C6
Thomson → Australia 25°11S 142°53E 280 C3
Thomson's Falls = Nyahururu Kenya 0°2N 36°27E 268 B4
Thon Buri Thailand 13°45N 100°29E 113 B1
Thônes France 45°54N 6°18E 175 C10
Thong Yang Thailand 9°28N 99°56E 237 b
Thongwa Myanmar 16°45N 96°33E 241 G6
Thonon-les-Bains France 46°22N 6°29E 173 F13
Thonze Myanmar 17°38N 95°47E 241 G5
Thoothukudi = Tuticorin India 8°50N 78°12E 245 K4
Thorez Ukraine 48°4N 38°34E 189 H10
Þórisjökull Iceland 64°32N 20°43W 155 C6
Þórisvatn Iceland 64°20N 18°55W 155 C8
Þórkötlustaðir Iceland 63°50N 22°24W 155 D4
Þorlákshöfn Iceland 63°51N 21°22W 155 D5
Thorn = Toruń Poland 53°2N 18°39E 185 E5
Thornaby on Tees U.K. 54°33N 1°18W 168 C6
Thornbury Vic., Australia 37°44S 145°1E 128 A2
Thornbury Ont., Canada 44°34N 80°26W 312 B4
Thornbury N.Z. 46°17S 168°9E 285 G3
Thorncliffe Canada 43°42N 79°20W 141 A2
Thorne U.K. 53°37N 0°57W 168 D7
Thornhill Canada 43°48N 79°25W 141 A2
Thornton Ont., Canada 44°16N 79°43W 312 B5
Thornton Western Cape, S. Africa 33°55S 18°32E 118 A2
Thornton Colo., U.S.A. 39°52N 104°58W 304 G11
Thornton Iowa, U.S.A. 42°57N 93°23W 310 B3
Thornton Heath U.K. 51°23N 0°6W 125 B3
Thorntown U.S.A. 40°8N 86°36W 311 D10
Thorold Canada 43°7N 79°12W 312 C5
Thorpes Barbados 13°9N 59°37W 323 r
Þórshöfn Iceland 66°12N 15°20W 155 A11
Thouarcé France 47°17N 0°30W 172 E6
Thouars France 47°0N 0°15W 172 F6
Thoubal India 24°38N 94°1E 241 C5
Thouet → France 47°17N 0°6W 172 E6
Thouin, C. Australia 20°20S 118°10E 278 D2
Thousand Islands U.S.A. 44°20N 76°0W 313 B9
Thousand Oaks U.S.A. 34°10N 118°50W 307 L8
Thrace Europe 41°0N 27°0E 203 F10
Thrace, Sea of Greece 40°30N 25°0E 203 F8
Thredbo Australia 36°31S 148°20E 283 D8
Three Fathoms Cove Hong Kong, China 22°25N 114°16E 122 A3
Three Forks U.S.A. 45°54N 111°33W 304 D8
Three Gorges Dam China 30°45N 111°15E 229 B8
Three Gorges Res. = Sanxia Shuiku China 30°3N 107°58E 228 B6
Three Hills Canada 51°43N 113°15W 296 C6
Three Hummock I. Australia 40°25S 144°55E 281 G3
Three Oaks U.S.A. 41°48N 86°36W 311 C10
Three Pagodas Pass Asia 15°20N 98°30E 236 E2
Three Points, C. Ghana 4°42N 2°6W 262 E4
Three Rivers Calif., U.S.A. 36°26N 118°54W 306 J8
Three Rivers Mich., U.S.A. 41°57N 85°38W 311 C11
Three Rivers Tex., U.S.A. 28°28N 98°11W 314 G5
Three Sisters Is. Solomon Is. 10°10S 161°57E 287 N11
Three Springs Australia 29°32S 115°45E 279 E2
Threipmuir Res. U.K. 55°51N 3°19W 121 B2
Thrissur India 10°30N 76°18E 245 J3
Throg's Neck U.S.A. 40°48N 73°49W 132 B3
Throssell, L. Australia 27°33S 124°10E 279 E3
Throssell Ra. Australia 22°3S 121°43E 278 D3
Thrumshing △ Bhutan 27°25N 90°50E 241 B3
Thrushton △ Australia 27°47S 147°40E 281 D4
Thu Dau Mot Vietnam 10°58N 106°39E 237 G6
Thua → Kenya 1°31S 39°30E 268 C4
Thuamal Rampur India 19°23N 82°56E 244 E6
Thuan Hoa Vietnam 8°58N 105°30E 237 H5
Thubun Lakes Canada 61°30N 112°0W 297 A6
Thueyts France 44°41N 4°9E 175 D8
Thugga = Dougga Tunisia 36°25N 9°13E 258 A1
Thuin Belgium 50°20N 4°17E 170 D4
Thuir France 42°38N 2°45E 174 F6
Thule = Qaanaaq Greenland 77°30N 69°10W 154 B4
Thule Air Base = Uummannaq Greenland 77°33N 68°52W 154 B4
Thun Switz. 46°45N 7°38E 179 J3
Thunder B. U.S.A. 45°0N 83°20W 312 B1
Thunder Bay Canada 48°20N 89°15W 298 C2
Thunderbolt U.S.A. 32°3N 81°4W 316 C8
Thunersee Switz. 46°43N 7°39E 179 J3
Thung Salaeng Luang △ Thailand 16°43N 100°50E 236 D3
Thung Song Thailand 8°10N 99°40E 237 H2
Thungyai ⌓ Thailand 15°20N 98°55E 236 E2
Thunkar Bhutan 27°55N 91°0E 241 B3
Thuong Tra Vietnam 16°2N 107°42E 236 D6
Thur → Switz. 47°32N 9°10E 179 H5
Thurgau □ Switz. 47°34N 9°10E 179 H5
Thüringen □ Germany 51°0N 11°0E 178 D6
Thüringer Wald Germany 50°35N 11°0E 178 E6
Thuringowa △ Australia 19°18S 146°43E 280 B4
Thurles Ireland 52°41N 7°49W 166 D4
Thurn P. Austria 47°20N 12°25E 180 D5
Thurrock □ U.K. 51°31N 0°23E 169 F8
Thursday I. Australia 10°30S 142°3E 286 F2
Thurso Qué., Canada 45°36N 75°15W 298 C4
Thurso Highl., U.K. 58°36N 3°32W 167 C5
Thurso → U.K. 58°36N 3°32W 167 C5
Thurston I. Antarctica 72°0S 100°0W 151 D16
Thury-Harcourt France 48°59N 0°30W 172 D6
Thutade L. Canada 57°0N 126°55W 296 B3
Thy Denmark 56°52N 8°25E 163 H2
Thy △ Denmark 56°55N 8°25E 163 H2
Thyborøn Denmark 56°42N 8°12E 163 H2
Þykkvabæjarklaustur Iceland 63°30N 18°22W 155 D8
Þykkvibær Iceland 63°45N 20°37W 155 D6
Thyolo Malawi 16°7S 35°5E 269 F4
Thyssen-Bornemisza, Museo Madrid, Spain 127 b3
Ti-n-Amzi → Niger 18°20N 4°32E 263 B5
Ti-n-Barraouene, O. → Africa 18°40N 4°5E 261 E5
Ti-n-Rerhoh Algeria 20°44N 4°2E 261 D5
Ti-n-Tanetfirt Algeria 24°49N 3°48E 261 D5
Ti-n-Tarabine, O. → Algeria 21°16N 7°25E 261 D6
Ti-n-Toumma Niger 16°4N 12°40E 259 E2
Ti-n-Zaouatene Algeria 19°55N 2°55E 261 E5
Ti-Tree Australia 22°5S 133°22E 280 C1
Tiadiaye Senegal 14°25N 16°40W 262 C1
Tiahuanaco Bolivia 16°33S 68°42W 330 D4
Tian Shan Asia 40°30N 76°0E 217 D9
Tian Tan Buddha = Big Buddha Hong Kong, China 22°15N 113°54E 122 B1
Tian'anmen Square Beijing, China 114 c2
Tianchang China 32°40N 119°0E 229 A12
Tiancun China 39°54N 116°12E 114 B1
Tiandeng China 23°6N 107°7E 228 F6
Tiandong China 23°36N 107°8E 228 F6
Tian'e China 25°1N 107°9E 228 E6
Tianguá Brazil 3°44S 40°59W 332 B3
Tianhe Guangdong, China 23°8N 113°20E 121 B2
Tianhe Guangxi Zhuangzu, China 24°48N 108°40E 228 E7
Tianjin China 39°7N 117°12E 227 E9
Tianjin Shi □ China 39°8N 117°12E 227 E9
Tianjun China 38°0N 98°30E 218 D8
Tiankoura Burkina Faso 10°47N 3°17W 262 C4
Tianlin China 24°21N 106°12E 228 E6
Tianmen China 30°39N 113°9E 229 B9
Tianquan China 30°7N 102°43E 228 B4
Tianshifu China 41°17N 124°22E 224 B2
Tianshui China 34°32N 105°40E 226 G3
Tiantai China 29°10N 121°2E 229 C13
Tiantan Park Beijing, China 114 c3
Tianya China 18°18N 109°20E 229 a
Tianyang China 23°42N 106°53E 228 F6
Tianyar Indonesia 8°12S 115°30E 231 J18
Tianzhen China 40°24N 114°5E 226 D8
Tianzhong = T'ienchung Taiwan 23°52N 120°35E 225 C2
Tianzhu China 26°54N 109°11E 228 D7
Tianzhuangtai China 40°43N 122°5E 227 D12
Tiarei Tahiti 17°32S 149°20W 289 e
Tiaret Algeria 35°20N 1°21E 261 A5
Tiaret □ Algeria 34°30N 1°30E 261 B5
Tías Canary Is. 28°57N 13°39W 153 e2
Tiassalé Côte d'Ivoire 5°58N 4°57W 262 D4
Tibagi Brazil 24°30S 50°24W 335 A5
Tibagi → Brazil 22°47S 51°1W 335 A5
Tībastī, Sarīr Libya 22°50N 18°30E 258 D3
Tibati Cameroon 6°22N 12°30E 263 D7
Tibe Ethiopia 9°2N 37°12E 257 F4
Tiber = Tevere → Italy 41°44N 12°14E 199 G9
Tiber Res. U.S.A. 48°19N 111°6W 304 B8
Tiberias = Teverya Israel 32°47N 35°32E 250 F6
Tiberias, L. = Yam Kinneret Israel 32°45N 35°35E 250 F6
Tibesti Chad 21°0N 17°30E 259 D3
Tibet = Xizang Zizhiqu □ China 32°0N 88°0E 218 E6
Tibet, L. U.S.A. 28°27N 81°31W 133 B1
Tibet, Plateau of Asia 32°0N 86°0E 210 E10
Tibiao Phil. 11°17N 122°2E 233 F4
Tibidabo Spain 41°25N 2°6E 114 A1
Tibiri Niger 13°34N 7°4E 263 C6
Ţibleş, Vf. Romania 47°32N 24°15E 183 C9
Ţibleşului, Munţii Romania 47°38N 24°5E 183 C9
Tibnī Syria 35°36N 39°50E 213 E8
Tibooburra Australia 29°26S 142°1E 281 D3
Tibrikot Nepal 29°3N 82°48E 243 E10
Tibro Sweden 58°28N 14°10E 163 F8
Tiburon U.S.A. 37°52N 122°27W 136 A2
Tiburón, I. Mexico 29°0N 112°25W 318 B2
Tiburtino Italy 41°53N 12°30E 136 B2
Ticao I. Phil. 12°31N 123°42E 232 E4
Tice U.S.A. 26°40N 81°49W 317 J8
Tîchît Mauritania 18°21N 9°29W 262 B3
Tichla Mauritania 21°36N 14°58W 260 D2
Ticho Ethiopia 7°50N 39°32E 257 F4
Ticino □ Switz. 46°20N 8°45E 179 J4
Ticino → Italy 45°9N 9°14E 198 C6
Ticleni Romania 44°53N 23°24E 183 F8
Ticomán Mexico 19°31N 99°8W 128 A2
Ticonderoga U.S.A. 43°51N 73°26W 313 C11
Ticul Mexico 20°24N 89°32W 319 C7
Tidaholm Sweden 58°12N 13°58E 163 F7
Tidal Basin Washington, D.C., U.S.A. 143 c1
Tidan Sweden 58°34N 14°1E 163 F8
Tiddim Myanmar 23°28N 93°45E 241 D4
Tiden India 7°15N 93°33E 245 L11
Tideridjaouine, Adrar Algeria 22°0N 2°15E 261 D5
Tidikelt Algeria 26°58N 1°30E 261 C5
Tidioute U.S.A. 41°41N 79°24W 312 E5
Tidjikja Mauritania 18°29N 11°35W 262 B2
Tidmore = Seminole U.S.A. 35°14N 96°41W 314 D6
Tidore Indonesia 0°40N 127°25E 231 D7
Tiébissou Côte d'Ivoire 7°9N 5°10W 262 D3
Tiéboro Chad 21°20N 17°7E 259 D3
Tiefa China 42°28N 123°26E 224 A1
Tiefersee Germany 52°24N 13°5E 115 B1
Tiegang Shuiku China 22°37N 113°53E 219 a
Tiel Neths. 51°53N 5°26E 170 C5
Tiel Senegal 14°55N 15°5W 262 C1
Tieli China 46°57N 128°3E 219 B14
Tieling China 42°20N 123°55E 224 A1
Tielt Belgium 51°0N 3°20E 170 C3
Tiemenguan China 41°49N 85°39E 217 D11
Tien Shan = Tian Shan Asia 40°30N 76°0E 217 D9
Tien-tsin = Tianjin China 39°7N 117°12E 227 E9
Tien Yen Vietnam 21°20N 107°24E 236 B6
T'ienching = Tianjin China 39°7N 117°12E 227 E9
T'ienchung Taiwan 23°52N 120°35E 225 C2
Tienen Belgium 50°48N 4°57E 170 D4
Tiénigbé Côte d'Ivoire 8°11N 5°43W 262 D3
Tientsin = Tianjin China 39°7N 117°12E 227 E9
Tiergarten Germany 52°31N 13°20E 115 A3
Tieri Australia 23°2S 148°21E 280 C4
Tieroko, Tarso Chad 20°45N 17°52E 259 D3
Tierp Sweden 60°20N 17°30E 162 D11
Tierra Amarilla Chile 27°28S 70°18W 334 B1
Tierra Amarilla N. Mex., U.S.A. 36°42N 106°33W 305 H10
Tierra Colorada Mexico 17°11N 99°32W 319 D5
Tierra de Barros Spain 38°40N 6°30W 195 G4
Tierra de Campos Spain 42°10N 4°50W 194 C6
Tierra del Fuego □ Argentina 54°0S 67°45W 336 D3
Tierra del Fuego, I. Grande de Argentina 54°0S 69°0W 336 D3
Tierra del Fuego △ Argentina 54°50S 68°23W 336 D3
Tierradentro Colombia 2°35N 76°2W 328 C2
Tierralta Colombia 8°11N 76°4W 328 B2
Tiétar → Spain 39°50N 6°1W 194 F4
Tieté → Brazil 20°40S 51°35W 335 A5
Tifarati W. Sahara 26°9N 10°33W 260 C2
Tiffin U.S.A. 41°7N 83°11W 311 C13
Tiffin → U.S.A. 41°17N 84°23W 311 C12
Tiflèt Morocco 33°54N 6°20W 260 B3
Tiflis = Tbilisi Georgia 41°43N 44°50E 191 K7
Tifton U.S.A. 31°27N 83°31W 316 D6
Tifu Indonesia 3°39S 126°24E 231 E7
Tiga, Î. N. Cal. 21°7S 167°49E 288 d
Tiga Res. Nigeria 11°35N 8°30E 263 C6
Tigalda I. U.S.A. 54°6N 165°5W 303 J6
Tigaon Phil. 13°38N 123°30E 232 E4
Tigbauan Phil. 10°41N 122°27E 233 F4
Tiger Leaping Gorge = Hutiao Xia China 27°13N 100°9E 228 D3
Tigharghar, Adrar Mali 19°30N 1°13E 263 B5
Tighina = Bendery Moldova 46°50N 29°30E 183 D14
Tigil Russia 57°49N 158°40E 215 D16
Tigiria India 20°29N 85°31E 244 D7
Tignall U.S.A. 33°52N 82°44W 316 B7
Tignish Canada 46°58N 64°2W 299 C7
Tigray □ Ethiopia 13°35N 39°15E 257 E4
Tigre → Peru 4°30S 74°10W 328 D3
Tigre → Venezuela 9°20N 62°30W 329 B5
Tigre, Pta. de Venezuela 11°5N 64°11W 329 a
Tigris = Dijlah, Nahr → Asia 31°0N 47°25E 246 D5
Tiguentourine Algeria 27°52N 9°8E 261 C6
Tigveni Romania 45°10N 24°31E 183 E9
Tigyaing Myanmar 23°45N 96°10E 241 D6
Tigzerte, O. → Morocco 28°10N 9°37W 260 C3
Tîh, Gebel el Egypt 29°32N 33°26E 256 B3
Tihodaine, Erg de Algeria 25°15N 7°15E 261 C6
Tihwa = Ürümqi China 43°45N 87°45E 217 D11
Tiilikka △ Finland 63°40N 28°15E 160 E23
Tijara India 27°56N 76°31E 242 F7
Tijgerhof S. Africa 33°53S 18°30E 118 A2
Tījī Libya 32°0N 11°18E 258 B2
Tijuana Mexico 32°32N 117°1W 307 N9
Tijuca Brazil 22°56S 43°13W 135 B1
Tijuca, Pico da Brazil 22°56S 43°15W 135 B1
Tijuca △ Brazil 22°56S 43°14W 135 B1
Tikahau French Polynesia 15°0S 148°10W 289 f
Tikal Guatemala 17°13N 89°24W 320 C2
Tikamgarh India 24°44N 78°50E 243 G8
Tikaré Burkina Faso 13°15N 1°43W 263 C4
Tikchik Lakes U.S.A. 60°0N 159°0W 303 G8
Tikéi French Polynesia 14°58S 144°32W 289 f
Tikhonkaya = Birobidzhan Russia 48°50N 132°50E 219 B15
Tikhoretsk Russia 45°56N 40°5E 191 H5
Tikhvin Russia 59°35N 33°30E 188 C7
Tikirarjuaq = Whale Cove Canada 62°10N 92°34W 297 A10
Tikkadouine, Adrar Algeria 24°28N 1°30E 261 D5
Tikkurila Finland 60°17N 25°2E 121 B3
Tikmehdāsh Iran 37°16N 46°54E 213 D12
Tiko Cameroon 4°4N 9°20E 263 E6
Tikopia Pac. Oc. 12°19S 168°49E 277 C12
Tikrīt Iraq 34°35N 43°37E 213 E10
Tiksi Russia 71°40N 128°45E 215 B13
Tilā' al 'Alī Jordan 32°0N 35°52E 251 G6
Tiladummati Atoll Maldives 7°0N 73°20E 272 d
Tilak Nagar India 28°38N 77°5E 120 B1
Tilamuta Indonesia 0°32N 122°23E 231 D6
Tilanqiao China 31°15N 121°29E 138 B1
Tilburg Neths. 51°31N 5°6E 170 C5
Tilbury Ont., Canada 42°17N 82°23W 312 D2
Tilbury Essex, U.K. 51°27N 0°22E 169 F8
Tilcara Argentina 23°36S 65°23W 334 A2
Tilden U.S.A. 42°3N 97°50W 308 D5
Tilemsi, Vallée du Mali 17°42N 0°15E 263 B5
Tilhar India 28°0N 79°45E 243 F8
Tilia, O. → Algeria 27°32N 0°55E 261 C5
Tilichiki Russia 60°27N 166°5E 215 C17
Tililane Algeria 27°49N 0°6W 261 C4
Tilin Myanmar 21°41N 94°6E 241 E5
Tilissos Greece 35°20N 25°1E 207 E6
Till → U.K. 55°41N 2°13W 168 B5
Tillabéri Niger 14°28N 1°28E 263 C5
Tillamook U.S.A. 45°27N 123°51W 304 D2
Tillanchong I. India 8°30N 93°37E 245 K11
Tillberga Sweden 59°40N 16°39E 162 E10
Tillia Niger 16°8N 4°47E 263 B5
Tillman U.S.A. 32°28N 81°6W 316 C8
Tillsonburg Canada 42°53N 80°44W 312 D4
Tillyeria Cyprus 35°6N 32°40E 207 E8
Tilogne Senegal 16°0N 13°40W 262 B2
Tilos Greece 36°27N 27°27E 205 E9
Tilpa Australia 30°57S 144°24E 282 A6
Tilrhemt Algeria 33°9N 3°22E 261 B5
Tilsit = Sovetsk Russia 55°6N 21°50E 184 C8
Tilt → U.K. 56°46N 3°51W 167 E5
Tilton U.S.A. 43°27N 71°36W 313 C13
Tiltonsville U.S.A. 40°10N 80°41W 312 F4
Tim Denmark 56°12N 8°19E 163 H2
Tima Egypt 26°54N 31°25E 256 B3
Timah, Bukit Singapore 1°21N 103°46E 138 A2
Timanah Asia 19°0N 41°0E 248 C3
Timanfaya △ Canary Is. 29°0N 13°46W 153 e2
Timanskiy Kryazh Russia 65°58N 50°5E 186 A9
Timaru N.Z. 44°23S 171°14E 285 E6
Timashevo Russia 53°22N 51°9E 190 D10
Timashevsk Russia 45°35N 39°0E 191 H4
Timau Kenya 0°4N 37°15E 268 B4
Timbaki Greece 35°4N 24°45E 207 E5
Timbaúba Brazil 7°31S 35°19W 332 C4
Timbedgha Mauritania 16°17N 8°16W 262 B3
Timber Creek Australia 15°40S 130°29E 278 C5
Timber Lake U.S.A. 45°26N 101°5W 308 C3
Timber Mt. U.S.A. 37°6N 116°28W 306 H10
Timbío Colombia 2°20N 76°40W 328 C2
Timbiquí Colombia 2°46N 77°42W 328 C2
Timbo Guinea 10°35N 11°50W 262 C2
Timbo Liberia 5°35N 9°45W 262 D3
Timboon Australia 38°30S 142°58E 282 E5
Timbué, Ponta Mozam. 18°47S 36°22E 269 F4
Timbuktu = Tombouctou Mali 16°50N 3°0W 262 B4
Timdjaouine Algeria 21°37N 4°30E 261 D5
Timeïaouine Algeria 20°27N 1°50E 261 D5
Timellouline Algeria 29°22N 8°55E 261 C6
Times Square New York, U.S.A. 132 c2
Timétrine Mali 19°19N 0°34W 263 B4
Timétrine, Mts. Mali 19°25N 1°0W 263 B4
Timfi Oros Greece 39°59N 20°45E 204 B2
Timfristos, Oros Greece 38°57N 21°50E 204 C3
Timgad Algeria 35°29N 6°28E 261 A6
Timhadit Morocco 33°15N 5°4W 260 B3
Timi Cyprus 34°44N 32°31E 207 F8
Tîmia Niger 18°4N 8°40E 259 E1
Timika Indonesia 4°47S 136°32E 231 E9
Timimoun Algeria 29°14N 0°16E 261 C5
Timimoun □ Algeria 30°0N 1°0E 261 C5
Timimoun, Sebkha de Algeria 28°50N 0°46E 261 C5
Timiris, Râs Mauritania 19°21N 16°30W 262 B1
Timiryazev Park Russia 55°49N 37°33E 129 B2
Timiş = Tamis → Serbia 44°51N 20°39E 182 F5
Timiş □ Romania 45°40N 21°30E 182 E6
Timiskaming, L. = Témiscamingue, L. Canada 47°10N 79°25W 298 C4
Timişoara Romania 45°43N 21°15E 182 E6
Timmersdala Sweden 58°32N 13°46E 163 F7

Timmins Canada 48°28N 81°25W 298 C3
Timmonsville U.S.A. 34°8N 79°57W 316 A10
Timok → Serbia 44°10N 22°40E 202 B6
Timoleague Ireland 51°39N 8°46W 166 E3
Timon Brazil 5°8S 42°52W 332 C3
Timor Asia 9°0S 125°0E 231 F7
Timor-Leste ■ Asia 8°50S 126°0E 231 F7
Timor Sea Ind. Oc. 12°0S 127°0E 278 B4
Timrå Sweden 62°29N 17°18E 162 B11
Timucuan ⌓ U.S.A. 30°28N 81°27W 316 E8
Tīn, Ra's at Libya 32°37N 23°8E 258 B4
Tin Alkoum Algeria 24°42N 10°17E 261 D7
Tin Amzi, O. → Algeria 18°20N 4°32E 261 D6
Tin Atanai Algeria 25°52N 1°37E 261 C5
Tin Can Bay Australia 25°56S 153°0E 281 D5
Tin Can I. Nigeria 6°26N 3°21E 124 B2
Tin Ethisane Mali 19°3N 0°52W 263 B4
Tin Gornai Mali 16°38N 0°38W 263 B4
Tin Mt. U.S.A. 36°50N 117°10W 306 J9
Tin Shui Wai China 22°28N 114°0E 219 a
Tina = Thina → S. Africa 31°18S 29°13E 271 D4
Tîna, Khalîg el Egypt 31°10N 32°40E 251 G3
Tinaca Pt. Phil. 5°30N 125°25E 233 J5
Tinaco Venezuela 9°42N 68°26W 328 B4
Tinajo Canary Is. 29°4N 13°42W 153 e2
Tinca Romania 46°46N 21°58E 182 D6
Tindal Australia 14°31S 132°22E 278 B5
Tindivanam India 12°15N 79°41E 245 H4
Tindouf Algeria 27°42N 8°10W 260 C3
Tindouf □ Algeria 27°25N 5°50W 260 C3
Tinée → France 43°55N 7°11E 175 E11
Tineo Spain 43°21N 6°27W 194 B4
Tinerhir Morocco 31°29N 5°31W 260 B3
Tinfouchi Algeria 28°52N 5°49W 260 C3
Tinfunque △ Paraguay 23°55S 60°17W 334 A3
Ting Jiang → China 24°45N 116°35E 229 E11
Ting Kau Hong Kong, China 22°22N 114°4E 122 A2
Tinggi, Pulau Malaysia 2°18N 104°7E 237 L5
Tinghert, Ḥamādat Libya 29°0N 11°0E 258 C2
Tingi Mts. S. Leone 8°55N 10°47W 262 D2
Tingkan Taiwan 23°48N 120°52E 225 C2
Tingkawk Sakan Myanmar 26°4N 96°44E 241 B6
Tinglayan Phil. 17°15N 121°9E 232 C3
Tinglev Denmark 54°57N 9°13E 163 K3
Tingmerkpuk Mt. U.S.A. 68°34N 162°28W 303 B7
Tingo María Peru 9°10S 75°54W 330 B2
Tingrela Côte d'Ivoire 10°27N 6°25W 262 C3
Tingri China 28°34N 86°38E 218 F6
Tingsryd Sweden 56°31N 15°0E 163 H9
Tingstäde Sweden 57°44N 18°37E 163 G12
Tingvoll Norway 62°55N 8°12E 164 B5
Tingwon Group Papua N. G. 2°37S 149°42E 286 B5
Tinh Bien Vietnam 10°36N 104°57E 237 G5
Tinharé, I. de Brazil 13°30S 38°58W 333 D4
Tinian N. Marianas 15°0N 145°38E 302 e
Tinian Channel N. Marianas 14°54N 145°36E 302 e
Tinigua △ Colombia 2°30N 74°8W 328 C3
Tiniguiban Phil. 11°22N 119°30E 233 F2
Tinjar → Malaysia 4°4N 114°18E 235 B4
Tinkisso → Guinea 11°21N 9°10W 262 C3
Tinn = Atrå Norway 59°59N 8°45E 164 E5
Tinnevelly = Tirunelveli India 8°45N 77°45E 245 K3
Tinnoset Norway 59°43N 9°3E 164 E6
Tinnsjå Norway 59°55N 8°54E 164 E5
Tinogasta Argentina 28°5S 67°32W 334 B2
Tinos Greece 37°33N 25°8E 205 D7
Tiñoso, C. Spain 37°32N 1°6W 197 H3
Tinpahar India 24°59N 87°44E 243 G12
Tinputz Papua N. G. 5°33S 155°0E 286 C8
Tinrhert, Plateau du Algeria 29°30N 9°0E 258 C1
Tinsukia India 27°29N 95°20E 241 B5
Tinta Peru 14°3S 71°20W 330 C3
Tintamarre, Île St.-Martin 18°7N 63°2W 322 a
Tîntâne Mauritania 16°18N 10°10W 262 B2
Tintina Argentina 27°2S 62°45W 334 B3
Tintinara Australia 35°48S 140°2E 282 C4
Tintioulé Guinea 10°13N 9°12W 262 C3
Tinto → Spain 37°12N 6°55W 195 H4
Tinui N.Z. 40°52S 176°5E 284 G5
Tinwald N.Z. 43°55S 171°43E 285 D6
Tiobraid Árann = Tipperary Ireland 52°28N 8°10W 166 D3
Tioga N. Dak., U.S.A. 48°24N 102°56W 308 A2
Tioga Pa., U.S.A. 41°55N 77°8W 312 E7
Tioman, Pulau Malaysia 2°50N 104°10E 237 L5
Tione di Trento Italy 46°2N 10°43E 198 B7
Tionesta U.S.A. 41°30N 79°28W 312 E5
Tior South Sudan 6°26N 31°11E 257 F3
Tiouliline Algeria 27°1N 0°2W 261 C4
Tipaza Algeria 36°35N 2°26E 261 A5
Tipaza □ Algeria 36°35N 2°25E 261 A5
Tipitapa Nic. 12°12N 86°5W 320 D2
Tipp City U.S.A. 39°58N 84°11W 311 E12
Tippecanoe → U.S.A. 40°30N 86°45W 311 D10
Tipperary Ireland 52°28N 8°10W 166 D3
Tipperary □ Ireland 52°37N 7°55W 166 D4
Tipton Calif., U.S.A. 36°4N 119°19W 306 J7
Tipton Ind., U.S.A. 40°17N 86°2W 311 D10
Tipton Iowa, U.S.A. 41°46N 91°8W 310 C5
Tipton Mo., U.S.A. 38°39N 92°47W 310 F4
Tipton Mt. U.S.A. 35°32N 114°12W 307 K12
Tiptonville U.S.A. 36°23N 89°29W 315 C10
Tiptur India 13°15N 76°26E 245 H3
Tiquié → Brazil 0°5N 68°25W 328 C4
Tiquina Bolivia 16°13S 68°50W 330 D4
Tira West Bank 31°52N 35°7E 123 A1
Tiracambu, Serra do Brazil 3°15S 46°30W 332 B2
Tirad Pass △ Phil. 17°3N 120°38E 232 C3
Tirahart, O. → Algeria 23°45N 3°10E 261 D5
Tīrān Iran 32°45N 51°8E 247 C6
Tīrān Si. Arabia 27°57N 34°32E 251 L5
Tirân, Madîq Egypt 27°55N 34°30E 251 L5
Tiranë Albania 41°18N 19°49E 202 E3
Tiranë ✈ (TIA) Albania 41°57N 19°42E 202 E3
Tirano Italy 46°13N 10°10E 198 B7
Tirari Desert Australia 28°22S 138°7E 281 D2
Tiraspol Moldova 46°55N 29°35E 183 D14
Tirat Ẕevi Israel 32°26N 35°31E 251 F6
Tiratimine Algeria 25°56N 3°37E 261 C5
Tirau N.Z. 37°58S 175°46E 284 D4
Tirdout Mali 16°7N 1°5W 263 B4
Tire Turkey 38°5N 27°45E 205 C9
Tirebolu Turkey 40°58N 38°45E 213 B8
Tiree U.K. 56°31N 6°55W 167 E2
Tiree, Passage of U.K. 56°30N 6°30W 167 E2
Tîrgovişte = Târgovişte Romania 44°55N 25°27E 183 F10
Tîrgu Jiu = Târgu Jiu Romania 45°5N 23°19E 183 E8
Tîrgu Mureş = Târgu Mureş Romania 46°31N 24°38E 183 D9
Tirgua △ Venezuela 10°5N 68°48W 328 A4
Tirich Mir Pakistan 36°15N 71°55E 240 A3
Tiriolo Italy 38°57N 16°30E 201 D9
Tiririca, Serra da Brazil 17°6S 47°6W 333 E2
Tiriro Guinea 10°27N 8°40W 262 C3
Tiris Zemmour □ Mauritania 24°0N 9°0W 260 D3
Tiritiri o te Moana = Southern Alps N.Z. 43°41S 170°11E 285 D5
Tirna → India 18°4N 76°57E 244 E3
Tirnavos Greece 39°45N 22°18E 204 B4
Tirodi India 21°40N 79°44E 244 D4
Tirol □ Austria 47°3N 10°43E 180 D3
Tiros Brazil 19°0S 45°58W 333 E2
Tirrukkovil Sri Lanka 7°7N 81°51E 245 L5
Tirsa Egypt 29°57N 31°12E 117 B2
Tirschenreuth Germany 49°53N 12°19E 179 F8
Tirschtiegel = Trzciel Poland 52°23N 15°50E 185 F2
Tirso → Italy 39°53N 8°32E 200 C1
Tirstrup Denmark 56°18N 10°42E 163 H4
Tirtagangga Indonesia 8°24S 115°35E 231 J18
Tirthahalli India 13°42N 75°14E 245 H2
Tirua Pt. N.Z. 38°25S 174°40E 284 E3
Tiruchchendur India 8°30N 78°11E 245 K4
Tiruchchirappalli India 10°45N 78°45E 245 J4
Tirukkoyilur India 11°57N 79°12E 245 J4
Tirumangalam India 9°49N 77°58E 245 K3
Tirumayam India 10°14N 78°45E 245 J4
Tirunelveli India 8°45N 77°45E 245 K3
Tirupati India 13°39N 79°25E 245 H4
Tiruppattur Tamil Nadu, India 10°8N 78°37E 245 J4
Tiruppattur Tamil Nadu, India 12°30N 78°30E 245 H4
Tiruppur India 11°5N 77°22E 245 J3
Tirur India 10°54N 75°55E 245 J2
Tiruttani India 13°11N 79°58E 245 H4
Tirutturaippundi India 10°32N 79°41E 245 J4
Tiruvadaimarudur India 11°2N 79°27E 245 J4
Tiruvalla India 9°23N 76°34E 245 K3
Tiruvallar India 13°9N 79°57E 245 H4
Tiruvannamalai India 12°15N 79°5E 245 H4
Tiruvettipuram India 12°39N 79°33E 245 H4
Tiruvottiyur India 13°10N 80°22E 245 H5
Tis Issat Ethiopia 11°25N 37°45E 257 E4
Tisa India 32°50N 76°9E 242 C7
Tisa → Serbia 45°15N 20°17E 182 E5
Tisdale Canada 52°50N 104°0W 297 C8
Tishomingo U.S.A. 34°14N 96°41W 314 D6
Tishrīyaa Iraq 33°18N 44°24E 113 B2
Tisjön Sweden 60°56N 13°0E 162 D7
Tisnaren Sweden 58°58N 15°56E 163 F9
Tišnov Czechia 49°21N 16°25E 181 B9
Tisovec Slovakia 48°41N 19°56E 181 C12
Tissamaharama Sri Lanka 6°17N 81°17E 245 L5
Tissemsilt Algeria 35°35N 1°50E 261 A5
Tissemsilt □ Algeria 35°45N 1°45E 261 A5
Tissint Morocco 29°57N 7°16W 260 C3
Tista → India 25°23N 89°43E 241 C2
Tistedal Norway 59°8N 11°27E 164 E8
Tisza = Tisa → Serbia 45°15N 20°17E 182 E5
Tiszaföldvár Hungary 46°58N 20°14E 182 D5
Tiszafüred Hungary 47°38N 20°50E 182 C5
Tiszalök Hungary 48°1N 21°20E 182 B6
Tiszavasvári Hungary 47°58N 21°18E 182 C6
Tit Ahaggar, Algeria 23°0N 5°10E 261 D6
Tit Tademait, Algeria 27°0N 1°29E 261 C5
Tit-Ary Russia 71°55N 127°2E 215 B13
Titabar India 26°36N 94°12E 241 B5
Titaguas Spain 39°53N 1°6W 196 F3
Titao Burkina Faso 13°45N 2°5W 263 C4
Titel Serbia 45°10N 20°18E 182 E5
Tithwal Pakistan 34°21N 73°50E 243 B5
Titicaca, L. S. Amer. 15°30S 69°30W 330 D4
Titikaveka Cook Is. 21°16S 159°45W 289 h
Titisee Germany 47°54N 8°10E 179 H4
Tititira Hd. N.Z. 43°36S 169°25E 285 D4
Tititut Myanmar 18°54N 95°16E 241 F5
Titiwa Nigeria 12°14N 12°53E 263 C7
Titlagarh India 20°15N 83°11E 244 D6
Tito Italy 40°35N 15°40E 201 B8
Titograd = Podgorica Montenegro 42°30N 19°19E 202 D3
Titova Korenica Croatia 44°45N 15°41E 199 D12
Titu Romania 44°39N 25°32E 183 F10
Titule Dem. Rep. of the Congo 3°15N 25°31E 268 B2
Titusville Fla., U.S.A. 28°37N 80°49W 317 G9
Titusville Pa., U.S.A. 41°38N 79°41W 312 E5
Tiu Keng Leng Hong Kong, China 22°18N 114°15E 122 B3
Tivaouane Senegal 14°56N 16°45W 262 C1
Tivat Montenegro 42°28N 18°43E 202 D2
Tivedens △ Sweden 58°45N 14°35E 163 F8
Tiverton Ont., Canada 44°16N 81°32W 312 B3
Tiverton Devon, U.K. 50°54N 3°29W 169 G4
Tivoli Grenada 12°10N 61°37W 323 q
Tívoli Italy 41°58N 12°45E 199 G9
Tiwanaku = Tiahuanaco Bolivia 16°33S 68°42W 330 D4
Tiwī Oman 22°45N 59°12E 249 B7
Tiwi ☼ Australia 11°33S 130°42E 278 B5
Tiyo Eritrea 14°41N 40°15E 257 E5
Tizapán Mexico 19°19N 99°13W 128 C1
Tizga Morocco 32°1N 5°9W 260 B3
Ti'zi N'Isli Morocco 32°28N 5°47W 260 B3
Tizi-Ouzou Algeria 36°42N 4°3E 261 A5
Tizi-Ouzou □ Algeria 36°35N 4°5E 261 A5
Tizimín Mexico 21°9N 88°9W 319 C7
Tiznados → Venezuela 8°16N 67°47W 328 B4
Tiznap He → China 38°21N 77°26E 217 E9
Tiznit Morocco 29°48N 9°45W 260 C3
Tjæreborg Denmark 55°28N 8°36E 163 J2
Tjällmo Sweden 58°43N 15°21E 163 F9
Tjeggelvas Sweden 66°37N 17°45E 160 C17
Tjieggelvas = Tjeggelvas Sweden 66°37N 17°45E 160 C17
Tjirebon = Cirebon Indonesia 6°45S 108°32E 235 D3
Tjirrkarli ☼ Australia 26°0S 125°28E 279 E4
Tjluring Indonesia 8°25S 114°13E 231 J17
Tjøme Norway 59°8N 10°26E 164 E7
Tjörn Sweden 58°0N 11°35E 163 F5
Tjukayirla Roadhouse Australia 27°9S 124°34E 279 E3
Tjurabalan ☼ Australia 19°50S 128°0E 278 C4
Tkibuli = Tqibuli Georgia 42°26N 43°0E 191 J6
Tkvarcheli = Tqvarcheli Georgia 42°47N 41°42E 191 J5
Tlacotalpan Mexico 18°37N 95°40W 319 D5
Tlahualilo de Zaragoza Mexico 26°7N 103°27W 318 B4
Tlalnepantla → Mexico 19°30N 99°18W 128 A1
Tlalpan Mexico 19°18N 99°10W 128 C2
Tlaquepaque Mexico 20°39N 103°19W 318 C4
Tlaxcala Mexico 19°19N 98°14W 319 D5
Tlaxcala □ Mexico 19°25N 98°10W 319 D5
Tlaxiaco Mexico 17°25N 97°35W 319 D5
Tlemcen Algeria 34°52N 1°21W 261 B4
Tlemcen □ Algeria 34°38N 1°30W 261 B4
Tleta Sidi Bouguedra Morocco 32°16N 9°59W 260 B3
Tlokweng Botswana 24°40S 25°58E 270 B4
Tlumach Ukraine 48°51N 25°0E 183 B10
Tłuszcz Poland 52°25N 21°25E 185 F8
Tlyarata Russia 42°9N 46°26E 191 J8
Tmassah Libya 26°19N 15°51E 258 C3
To Bong Vietnam 12°45N 109°16E 236 F7
To Kwa Wan Hong Kong, China 22°18N 114°11E 122 B3
To-Shima Japan 34°31N 139°17E 223 C11
Toa Payoh Singapore 1°20N 103°51E 138 A3
Toad → Canada 59°25N 124°57W 296 B4
Toad River Canada 58°51N 125°14W 296 B3
Toamasina Madag. 18°10S 49°25E 272 B2
Toay Argentina 36°43S 64°38W 334 D3
Toba China 31°19N 97°42E 228 B1
Toba Japan 34°30N 136°51E 223 C8
Toba, Danau Indonesia 2°30N 98°30E 234 B1
Toba Kakar Pakistan 31°30N 69°0E 242 D3
Toba Tek Singh Pakistan 30°55N 72°25E 242 D5
Tobago Trin. & Tob. 11°10N 60°30W 323 s
Tobarra Spain 38°37N 1°44W 197 G3
Tobelo Indonesia 1°45N 127°56E 231 D7
Tobercurry Ireland 54°3N 8°44W 166 B3
Tobermory Ont., Canada 45°12N 81°40W 312 A3
Tobermory Argyll & Bute, U.K. 56°38N 6°5W 167 E2
Tobi Palau 2°40N 131°10E 231 D8
Tobi-Shima Japan 41°12N 139°34E 220 D9
Tobias Fornier = Dao Phil. 10°30N 121°57E 233 F3
Tobiishi Hana Iwo Jima 24°45N 141°17E 288 b
Tobin, L. Australia 21°45S 125°49E 278 D4
Tobin L. Canada 53°35N 103°30W 297 C8
Toblach = Dobbiaco Italy 46°44N 12°14E 199 B9
Toboali Indonesia 3°0S 106°25E 234 C3
Tobol → Russia 58°10N 68°12E 214 D7
Toboli Indonesia 0°38S 120°5E 231 E6
Tobolsk Russia 58°15N 68°10E 214 D7
Tobor Senegal 12°40N 16°15W 262 C1
Toboso Phil. 10°43N 123°31E 233 F4
Tobruk = Tubruq Libya 32°7N 23°55E 258 B4
Tobyhanna U.S.A. 41°11N 75°25W 313 E9
Tobyl = Tobol → Russia 58°10N 68°12E 214 D7
Tobyl Kazakhstan 52°41N 62°34E 216 B6
Tocache Nuevo Peru 8°9S 76°26W 330 B2
Tocantínia Brazil 9°33S 48°22W 332 C2
Tocantinópolis Brazil 6°20S 47°25W 332 C2
Tocantins □ Brazil 10°0S 48°0W 332 D2
Tocantins → Brazil 1°45S 49°10W 332 B2
Toccoa U.S.A. 34°35N 83°19W 315 D13
Toce → Italy 45°56N 8°29E 198 C5
Tochi → Pakistan 32°49N 70°41E 242 C4
Tochigi Japan 36°25N 139°45E 223 A11
Tochigi □ Japan 36°45N 139°45E 223 A11
Tocina Spain 37°37N 5°44W 195 H5
Töcksfors Sweden 59°31N 11°52E 162 E5
Točná Czechia 49°58N 14°25E 135 C2
Toco Chile 22°5S 69°35W 330 E4
Toco Trin. & Tob. 10°49N 60°57W 323 t
Toco Hills U.S.A. 33°49N 84°20W 113 B2
Toconao Chile 23°11S 68°1W 334 A2
Tocopilla Chile 22°5S 70°10W 334 A1
Tocqueville = Râs el Oued Algeria 35°57N 5°2E 261 A6
Tocumwal Australia 35°51S 145°31E 283 C6
Tocuyo → Venezuela 11°3N 68°23W 328 A4
Tocuyo de la Costa Venezuela 11°2N 68°23W 328 A4
Todalen Norway 62°49N 8°44E 164 B5
Todd → Australia 24°52S 135°48E 280 C2
Todds Road Trin. & Tob. 10°28N 61°20W 323 t
Toddu Atoll Maldives 4°25N 72°57E 272 d
Todeli Indonesia 1°40S 124°29E 231 E6
Todenyang Kenya 4°35N 35°56E 268 B4
Todgarh India 25°42N 73°58E 242 G5
Todi Italy 42°47N 12°24E 199 F9
Todos os Santos, B. de Brazil 12°48S 38°38W 333 D4
Todos Santos Mexico 23°26N 110°13W 318 C2
Todt Hill U.S.A. 40°36N 74°6W 132 C1
Todtnau Germany 47°49N 7°56E 179 H3
Toe Hd. U.K. 57°50N 7°8W 167 D1
Toecé Burkina Faso 11°50N 1°16W 263 C4
Toetoes B. N.Z. 46°42S 168°41E 285 G3
Tofield Canada 53°25N 112°40W 296 C6
Tofino Canada 49°11N 125°55W 296 D3
Töfsingdalen △ Sweden 62°10N 12°28E 162 B6
Tofte Norway 59°33N 10°34E 164 E7
Tofua Tonga 19°45S 175°5W 287 P13
Toga Vanuatu 13°26S 166°42E 287 C4
Tōgane Japan 35°33N 140°22E 223 B12
Togba Mauritania 17°26N 10°12W 262 B2
Togbo C.A.R. 6°0N 17°27E 264 A3
Togdheer □ Somalia 9°20N 45°25E 267 C6
Togdheer → Somalia 6°26N 48°39E 267 C6
Togiak U.S.A. 59°4N 160°24W 303 G7
Togiak Nat. Wildlife Refuge ⌓ U.S.A. 59°20N 160°15W 303 G7
Togian, Kepulauan Indonesia 0°20S 121°50E 231 E6
Togliatti Russia 53°32N 49°24E 190 D9
Togo ■ W. Afr. 8°30N 1°35E 263 D5
Togo Wichale Somalia 9°22N 43°40E 267 C5
Tögrög Mongolia 47°25N 92°13E 217 C12
Togtoh China 40°15N 111°10E 226 D6
Tohiea, Mt. Moorea 17°33S 149°49W 289 e
Tohma → Turkey 38°29N 38°23E 212 C8
Tōhoku □ Japan 39°50N 141°45E 220 E10
Töhöm Mongolia 44°27N 108°2E 226 B5
Tohopekaliga, East L. U.S.A. 28°18N 81°15W 317 G8
Tohopekaliga, L. U.S.A. 28°12N 81°24W 317 G8
Toi Cook Is. 18°57S 169°51W 289 g
Toi Japan 34°54N 138°47E 223 C10
Toibalewe India 10°32N 92°30E 245 J11
Toiny St.-Martin 17°53N 62°47W 322 a
Toinya South Sudan 6°17N 29°46E 257 F2
Toiyabe Range U.S.A. 39°30N 117°0W 304 G5
Tojikiston = Tajikistan ■ Asia 38°30N 70°0E 217 E8
Tōjō Japan 34°53N 133°16E 222 C5
Tok U.S.A. 63°20N 142°59W 303 E12
Toka Guyana 3°58N 59°17W 329 C6
Tokaanu N.Z. 38°58S 175°46E 284 E4
Tokachi-Dake Japan 43°17N 142°5E 220 C11
Tokachi-Gawa → Japan 42°44N 143°42E 220 C11
Tōkagi Japan 35°42N 139°55E 140 A4
Tokai Japan 35°2N 136°55E 223 B8
Tokai Plantation S. Africa 34°3S 18°24E 118 B1
Tōkaichiba Japan 35°31N 139°30E 140 B2
Tokaj Hungary 48°8N 21°27E 182 B6
Tokala Indonesia 1°30S 121°40E 231 E6
Tōkamachi Japan 37°8N 138°43E 221 F9
Tokanui N.Z. 46°34S 168°56E 285 G3
Tokar Sudan 18°27N 37°56E 256 D4
Tokara-Rettō Japan 29°37N 129°43E 221 K4
Tokarahi N.Z. 44°56S 170°39E 285 E5
Tokashiki-Shima Japan 26°11N 127°21E 221 L3
Tokat Turkey 40°22N 36°35E 212 B7
Tokat □ Turkey 40°15N 36°30E 212 B7
Tŏkch'ŏn N. Korea 39°45N 126°18E 224 C3
Tokdo = Liancourt Rocks Asia 37°15N 131°52E 221 F5
Tokeland U.S.A. 46°42N 123°59W 306 D3
Tokelau Is. ⊠ Pac. Oc. 9°0S 171°45W 277 B16
Toki Japan 35°18N 137°8E 223 B9
Toki Pt. Wake I. 19°19N 166°35E 302 b
Tokmak Kyrgyzstan 42°49N 75°15E 217 D9
Tokmak Ukraine 47°16N 35°42E 189 J8
Toko Ra. Australia 23°5S 138°20E 280 C2
Tokomaru Bay N.Z. 38°8S 178°22E 284 E7
Tokoname Japan 34°53N 136°51E 223 C8
Tokoro-Gawa → Japan 44°7N 144°5E 220 B12
Tokoroa N.Z. 38°13S 175°50E 284 E4
Tokorozawa Japan 35°47N 139°28E 223 B11
Toksook Bay U.S.A. 60°32N 165°0W 303 F6
Toksun China 42°47N 88°38E 217 D11
Toktogul Kyrgyzstan 41°50N 72°50E 217 D8
Toku Tonga 18°10S 174°11W 287 P13
Tokuji Japan 34°11N 131°42E 222 C3
Tokuno-Shima Japan 27°56N 128°55E 221 L4
Tokushima Japan 34°4N 134°34E 222 C6
Tokushima □ Japan 33°55N 134°0E 222 D6
Tokuyama = Shunān Japan 34°3N 131°50E 222 C3
Tōkyō Japan 35°43N 139°45E 140 B3
Tōkyō □ Japan 35°40N 139°30E 223 B11
Tōkyō B. = Tōkyō-Wan Japan 35°25N 139°50E 140 B4
Tōkyō Haneda ✈ (HND) Japan 35°33N 139°46E 140 B3
Tōkyō Harbour Japan 35°38N 139°46E 140 B3
Tōkyō Narita ✈ (NRT) Japan 35°45N 140°25E 223 B12
Tōkyō Sky Tree Japan 35°42N 139°49E 140 A3
Tōkyō-Wan Japan 35°25N 139°50E 140 B4
Tokzār Afghan. 35°52N 66°26E 240 B2
Tol I. Micronesia 7°20N 151°37E 287 U17
Tolaga Bay N.Z. 38°21S 178°20E 284 E7
Tolageak U.S.A. 70°3N 162°27W 303 A7
Tolbo Mongolia 48°25N 90°17E 217 C12
Tolbukhin = Dobrich Bulgaria 43°37N 27°49E 203 C11
Tolé C.A.R. 6°34N 16°1E 264 A3
Töle Bī Kazakhstan 43°42N 73°46E 217 D8
Toledo Brazil 24°44S 53°45W 335 A5
Toledo Phil. 10°23N 123°38E 233 F4
Toledo Spain 39°50N 4°2W 194 F6
Toledo Ill., U.S.A. 39°16N 88°15W 311 E8
Toledo Iowa, U.S.A. 42°0N 92°35W 310 C4
Toledo Ohio, U.S.A. 41°39N 83°33W 311 C13
Toledo Oreg., U.S.A. 44°37N 123°56W 304 D2
Toledo Wash., U.S.A. 46°26N 122°51W 306 D4
Toledo, Montes de Spain 39°33N 4°20W 195 F6
Toledo Bend Res. U.S.A. 31°11N 93°34W 314 F8
Tolentino Italy 43°12N 13°17E 199 E10
Tolfa Italy 42°9N 11°56E 199 F8
Tolga Algeria 34°40N 5°22E 261 B6
Tolga Queens., Australia 17°15S 145°29E 280 B4
Tolga Hedmark, Norway 62°26N 11°1E 164 B8
Tolhuaca △ Chile 38°15S 71°50W 336 A2
Toli China 45°57N 83°37E 217 C10
Toliara Madag. 23°21S 43°40E 272 C1
Tolima Colombia 4°40N 75°19W 328 C2
Tolima □ Colombia 3°45N 75°15W 328 C2
Tolitoli Indonesia 1°5N 120°50E 231 D6
Tolkmicko Poland 54°19N 19°31E 184 D6
Tollarp Sweden 55°55N 13°58E 163 J7
Tollensesee Germany 53°30N 13°13E 178 B9
Tollhouse U.S.A. 37°1N 119°24W 306 H7
Tollygunge = Taliganga India 22°30N 88°22E 124 B2
Tolmachevo Russia 58°56N 29°51E 188 C5
Tolmezzo Italy 46°24N 13°1E 199 B10
Tolmin Slovenia 46°11N 13°45E 199 B10
Tolna Hungary 46°25N 18°48E 182 D3
Tolna □ Hungary 46°30N 18°30E 182 D3
Tolo Dem. Rep. of the Congo 2°55S 18°34E 264 C3
Tolo, Teluk Indonesia 2°20S 122°10E 231 E6
Tolo Harbour Hong Kong, China 22°25N 114°13E 122 A3
Tolochin = Talachyn Belarus 54°25N 29°42E 188 E5
Tolokiwa I. Papua N. G. 5°19S 147°37E 286 C4
Tolong B. Phil. 9°20N 122°49E 233 G4
Tolono U.S.A. 39°59N 88°16W 311 E8
Tolosa Spain 43°8N 2°5W 196 B2
Tolox Spain 36°41N 4°54W 195 J6
Toltén Chile 39°13S 74°14W 336 A2
Toluca México, Mexico 19°17N 99°40W 319 D5
Toluca Ill., U.S.A. 41°0N 89°8W 310 C7
Tolworth U.K. 51°22N 0°17W 125 B2
Tolyatti = Togliatti Russia 53°32N 49°24E 190 D9
Tom Burke S. Africa 23°5S 28°0E 271 B4
Tom Price Australia 22°40S 117°48E 278 D2
Toma Burkina Faso 12°45N 2°53W 262 C4
Tomah U.S.A. 43°59N 90°30W 308 D8
Tomahawk U.S.A. 45°28N 89°44W 308 C9
Tomai Moldova 46°34N 28°19E 183 D13
Tomakomai Japan 42°38N 141°36E 220 C10
Tomales U.S.A. 38°15N 122°53W 306 G4
Tomales B. U.S.A. 38°15N 123°58W 306 G3
Tomanivi Fiji 17°37S 178°1E 287 A2
Tomar Portugal 39°36N 8°25W 195 F2
Tomaros, Oros Greece 39°29N 20°48E 204 B2
Tomarza Turkey 38°27N 35°48E 212 C6
Tomás Barrón Bolivia 17°35S 67°31W 330 D4
Tomashevka Belarus 51°33N 23°36E 185 G10
Tomashpil Ukraine 48°32N 28°31E 183 B13
Tomaszów Lubelski Poland 50°27N 23°25E 185 H10
Tomaszów Mazowiecki Poland 51°30N 20°2E 185 G7
Tomatlán Mexico 19°56N 105°15W 318 D3
Tomb of the Kings Jerusalem 123 a2
Tomba di Nerone Italy 41°58N 12°26E 136 B1
Tombadonkéa Guinea 11°0N 14°25W 262 C2
Tombador, Serra do Brazil 12°0S 58°0W 331 C6
Tombe South Sudan 5°53N 31°40E 257 F3
Tombeau Bay Mauritius 20°6S 57°30E 272 e
Tombel Cameroon 4°45N 9°40E 264 B1
Tombigbee → U.S.A. 31°8N 87°57W 315 F11
Tomboco Angola 6°48S 13°18E 265 D2
Tombouctou Mali 16°50N 3°0W 262 B4
Tombouctou □ Mali 20°0N 3°0W 262 B4
Tombstone U.S.A. 31°43N 110°4W 305 L8
Tombua Angola 15°55S 11°55E 265 F2
Tomé Chile 36°36S 72°57W 334 D1
Tome Japan 38°40N 141°20E 220 E10
Tomé-Açu Brazil 2°25S 48°9W 332 B2
Tomelilla Sweden 55°33N 13°58E 163 J7
Tomelloso Spain 39°10N 3°2W 195 F7
Tomil Micronesia 9°31N 138°9E 287 R16
Tomil Harbor Pac. Oc. 9°30N 138°10E 287 R16
Tomingley Australia 32°26S 148°16E 283 B8
Tomini Indonesia 0°30N 120°30E 231 D6
Tomini, Teluk Indonesia 0°10S 121°0E 231 E6
Tominian Mali 13°17N 4°35W 262 C4
Tomiño = O Seixo Spain 41°59N 8°46W 194 D2
Tomintoul U.K. 57°15N 3°23W 167 D5
Tomioka Japan 36°15N 138°54E 223 A10
Tomislavgrad Bos.-H. 43°42N 17°13E 182 G2
Tomkinson Ranges Australia 26°11S 129°5E 279 E4
Tommot Russia 59°4N 126°20E 215 D13
Tommy Thompson Park Canada 43°38N 79°20W 141 B3
Tomnop Ta Suos Cambodia 11°20N 104°15E 237 G5
Tomo Colombia 2°38N 67°32W 328 C4
Tomo → Colombia 5°20N 67°48W 328 B4
Tomobe Japan 36°20N 140°20E 223 A12
Tomorri △ Albania 40°43N 20°8E 202 F4
Tomra Norway 62°34N 6°56E 164 B3
Toms Place U.S.A. 37°34N 118°41W 306 H8
Toms River U.S.A. 39°58N 74°12W 313 G10
Tomsk Russia 56°30N 85°5E 214 D9
Tomtabacken Sweden 57°30N 14°30E 163 G8
Tömük Turkey 36°42N 34°23E 250 B5
Tomür Feng = Pobedy, Pik Asia 42°0N 79°58E 217 D9
Tona Spain 41°51N 2°14E 196 D7
Tonalá Chiapas, Mexico 16°4N 93°45W 319 D6
Tonalá Jalisco, Mexico 20°37N 103°14W 318 C4
Tonale, Passo del Italy 46°16N 10°35E 198 B7
Tonami Japan 36°40N 136°58E 223 A8
Tonantins Brazil 2°45S 67°45W 328 D4
Tonasket U.S.A. 48°42N 119°26W 304 B4
Tonate Fr. Guiana 5°0N 52°28W 329 C7
Tonawanda U.S.A. 43°1N 78°53W 312 D6
Tonb U.A.E. 26°15N 55°15E 247 E7
Tonbo Myanmar 18°31N 95°5E 241 F5
Tonbridge U.K. 51°11N 0°17E 169 F8
Tonda Papua N. G. 8°55S 141°34E 286 E1
Tondabayashi Japan 34°30N 135°36E 223 C7
Tondano Indonesia 1°35N 124°54E 231 D6
Tondela Portugal 40°31N 8°5W 194 E2
Tønder Denmark 54°58N 8°50E 163 K2
Tondern = Tønder Denmark 54°58N 8°50E 163 K2
Tondi India 9°45N 79°4E 245 K4
Tondi Kiwindi Niger 14°28N 2°2E 263 C5
Tondibi Mali 16°39N 0°14W 263 B4
Tondo Phil. 14°36N 120°57E 127 B1
Tondoro Namibia 17°45S 18°50E 270 A2
Tone → Australia 34°25S 116°25E 279 F2
Tone-Gawa → Japan 35°44N 140°51E 223 B12
Tonekābon Iran 36°45N 51°12E 247 B6
Tong Fuk Hong Kong, China 22°14N 113°56E 122 B1
Tong I. Papua N. G. 2°2S 147°47E 286 B4
Tong Xian China 39°55N 116°35E 226 E9
Tong-yeong S. Korea 34°50N 128°20E 224 E4
Tonga Cameroon 4°58N 10°42E 264 B2
Tonga South Sudan 9°28N 31°3E 257 F3
Tonga ■ Pac. Oc. 19°50S 174°30W 287 P13
Tonga Trench Pac. Oc. 18°0S 173°0W 277 D16
Tongaat S. Africa 29°33S 31°9E 271 C5
Tongala Australia 36°14S 144°56E 283 D6
Tong'an China 24°37N 118°8E 229 E12
Tongareva = Penrhyn Cook Is. 9°0S 158°0W 289 H12
Tongariro, Mt. N.Z. 39°8S 175°38E 284 F4
Tongariro △ N.Z. 39°8S 175°33E 284 F4
Tongass Nat. Forest U.S.A. 54°45N 133°0W 303 J14
Tongatapu Tonga 21°10S 175°10W 287 Q13
Tongatapu Group Tonga 21°0S 175°0W 287 Q13
Tongbai China 32°20N 113°23E 229 A9
Tongbinggo S. Korea 37°31N 126°58E 137 B1
Tongcheng Anhui, China 31°4N 116°56E 229 B11
Tongcheng Hubei, China 29°15N 113°50E 229 C9
Tongchuan China 35°6N 109°3E 226 G5
Tongdao China 26°10N 109°42E 228 D7
Tongeren Belgium 50°47N 5°28E 170 D5
Tonggu China 28°31N 114°20E 229 C10
Tonggu Jiao China 22°22N 113°37E 219 a
Tongguan China 34°40N 110°25E 226 G6
Tonghai China 24°10N 102°53E 228 E4
Tonghua China 41°42N 125°58E 224 B2
Tongi = Tungi Bangla. 23°53N 90°24E 241 D3
Tongjiang Heilongjiang, China 47°40N 132°27E 219 B15
Tongjiang Sichuan, China 31°58N 107°11E 228 B6
Tongjosŏn-man N. Korea 39°30N 128°0E 224 C4
Tongking, G. of = Tonkin, G. of Asia 20°0N 108°0E 236 C7
Tongliang China 29°50N 106°3E 228 C6
Tongliao China 43°38N 122°18E 227 C12
Tongling China 30°55N 117°48E 229 B11
Tonglu China 29°45N 119°37E 229 C12
Tongnan = Anyue China 30°9N 105°50E 228 B5
Tongoa Vanuatu 16°54S 168°34E 287 F6
Tongobory Madag. 23°32S 44°20E 272 C1
Tongoy Chile 30°16S 71°31W 334 C1
Tongqiao China 31°21N 121°22E 138 A1
Tongquil I. Phil. 6°2N 121°51E 233 H3
Tongren Guizhou, China 27°43N 109°11E 228 D7
Tongren Qinghai, China 35°25N 102°5E 218 D9
Tongres = Tongeren Belgium 50°47N 5°28E 170 D5
Tongsa Dzong Bhutan 27°31N 90°31E 241 B3
Tongsha Tao Taiwan 26°12N 128°28E 225 b
Tongshi China 18°50N 109°20E 229 a
Tongue U.K. 58°29N 4°25W 167 C4
Tongue → U.S.A. 46°25N 105°52W 304 C11
Tongwei China 35°0N 105°5E 226 G3
Tongxiang China 30°39N 120°34E 229 B13
Tongxiao = T'unghsiao Taiwan 24°29N 120°40E 225 B2
Tongxin China 36°59N 105°58E 226 F3
Tongyang N. Korea 39°9N 126°53E 224 C3
Tongyu China 44°45N 123°4E 227 B12
Tongzhou China 32°12N 121°2E 229 A13
Tongzi China 28°9N 106°49E 228 C6
Tonica U.S.A. 41°13N 89°4W 310 C7
Tonj South Sudan 7°20N 28°44E 257 F2
Tonj → South Sudan 7°31N 28°55E 257 F2
Tonk India 26°6N 75°54E 242 F6
Tonkawa U.S.A. 36°41N 97°18W 314 C6
Tonkin = Bac Phan Vietnam 22°0N 105°0E 228 G5
Tonkin, G. of Asia 20°0N 108°0E 236 C7
Tonlé Sap Cambodia 13°0N 104°0E 236 F5
Tonnay-Charente France 45°56N 0°55W 174 C3
Tonneins France 44°23N 0°19E 174 D4
Tonnerre France 47°51N 3°59E 173 E10
Tönning Germany 54°19N 8°56E 178 A4
Tono Japan 39°19N 141°32E 220 E10
Tonoas I. Micronesia 7°22N 151°52E 287 T18
Tonopah U.S.A. 38°4N 117°14W 305 G5
Tonoshō Japan 34°29N 134°11E 222 C6
Tonosí Panama 7°20N 80°20W 320 E3
Tons → Haryana, India 30°30N 77°39E 242 D7
Tons → Ut. P., India 26°1N 83°33E 243 F10
Tønsberg Norway 59°19N 10°25E 164 E7
Tonsina U.S.A. 61°39N 145°11W 303 F11
Tonstad Norway 58°40N 6°45E 164 F3
Tonto △ U.S.A. 33°39N 111°7W 305 K8
Tonumea Tonga 20°30S 174°30W 287 Q13
Tonya Turkey 40°53N 39°16E 213 B8
Tonzang Myanmar 23°36N 93°42E 241 D4
Tonzi Myanmar 24°39N 94°57E 241 C5
Toobanna Australia 18°42S 146°9E 280 B4
Toodyay Australia 31°34S 116°28E 279 F2
Tooele U.S.A. 40°32N 112°18W 304 F7
Toompine Australia 27°15S 144°19E 281 D3
Toomsboro U.S.A. 32°50N 83°5W 316 C6
Toora Australia 38°39S 146°23E 283 E7
Toora-Khem Russia 52°28N 96°17E 217 B13
Toorak Australia 37°50S 145°1E 128 B2
Tootias Somalia 3°57N 43°57E 267 D5
Toowoomba Australia 27°32S 151°56E 281 D5
Top Springs Australia 16°37S 131°51E 278 C5
Topalu Romania 44°31N 28°3E 183 F13
Topanga State Park ⌓ U.S.A. 34°7N 118°31W 126 B1
Topaz U.S.A. 38°41N 119°30W 306 G7
Topeka U.S.A. 39°3N 95°40W 308 F6
Topkapı Turkey 41°1N 28°55E 122 B1
Topkapı Palaca Turkey 41°1N 28°59E 122 B1
Topl'a → Slovakia 48°45N 21°45E 181 C14
Topley Canada 54°49N 126°18W 296 C3
Toplica → Serbia 43°15N 21°49E 202 C5
Topliţa Romania 46°55N 25°20E 183 D10
Topo Azores 38°33N 27°45W 153 d1
Topo, Pta. do Azores 38°33N 27°46W 153 d1
Topocalma, Pta. Chile 34°10S 72°2W 334 C1
Topock U.S.A. 34°46N 114°29W 307 L12
Topola Serbia 44°17N 20°41E 202 B4
Topolčani N. Macedonia 41°14N 21°25E 202 E5
Topol'čany Slovakia 48°35N 18°12E 181 C11
Topolnitsa → Bulgaria 42°11N 24°18E 203 D8
Topolobampo Mexico 25°36N 109°3W 318 B3
Topoloveni Romania 44°49N 25°5E 183 F10
Topolovgrad Bulgaria 42°5N 26°20E 203 D10
Topolvăţu Mare Romania 45°46N 21°41E 182 E6
Topozero, Ozero Russia 65°35N 32°0E 160 D25
Toppenish U.S.A. 46°23N 120°19W 304 C3
Topraisar Romania 44°1N 28°27E 183 F13
Toprakkale Turkey 37°5N 36°8E 250 A7
Topusko Croatia 45°18N 15°59E 199 C12
Toquepala Peru 17°24S 70°25W 330 D3
Toqyraūyn → Kazakhstan 46°48N 75°24E 217 C9
Tor di Quinto Italy 41°56N 12°27E 136 B1
Tor Pignattara Italy 41°53N 12°31E 136 B2
Tor Sapienza Italy 41°53N 12°35E 136 B2
Torà Spain 41°49N 1°25E 196 D6
Tora Kit South Sudan 11°2N 32°36E 257 E3
Toranomon Tokyo, Japan 140 c3
Torata Peru 17°23S 70°1W 330 D3
Torbalı Turkey 38°10N 27°21E 205 C9
Torbat-e Heydārīyeh Iran 35°15N 59°12E 247 C8
Torbat-e Jām Iran 35°16N 60°35E 247 C9
Torbay Canada 47°40N 52°42W 299 C9
Torbay □ U.K. 50°26N 3°31W 169 G4
Tørberget Norway 61°8N 12°7E 164 C9
Torbjörntorp Sweden 58°12N 13°36E 163 F7
Torcy France 48°51N 2°39E 134 A4
Tordesillas Spain 41°30N 5°0W 194 D6
Töreboda Sweden 58°41N 14°7E 163 F8
Torekov Sweden 56°26N 12°37E 163 H6
Torellò Spain 42°3N 2°16E 196 C7
Toreno Spain 42°42N 6°30W 194 C4
Torfaen □ U.K. 51°43N 3°3W 169 F4
Torfajökull Iceland 63°54N 19°0W 155 D7
Torgau Germany 51°34N 13°0E 178 D8
Torgelow Germany 53°37N 14°1E 178 B10
Torghay Kazakhstan 49°38N 63°29E 216 C6
Torghay → Kazakhstan 48°1N 62°45E 216 C6
Torghay Ustirti Asia 51°0N 63°0E 216 B6
Torghay Zhylghasy Kazakhstan 52°0N 64°30E 216 B6
Torgovaya = Salsk Russia 46°28N 41°30E 191 G5
Torhamn Sweden 56°6N 15°50E 163 H9
Torhout Belgium 51°5N 3°7E 170 C3
Torhovytsya Ukraine 48°36N 25°26E 183 B10
Tori Ethiopia 7°53N 33°35E 257 F3
Tori-Shima Japan 30°29N 140°19E 221 J10
Torigni-sur-Vire France 49°3N 0°58W 172 C6
Torija Spain 40°44N 3°2W 196 E1
Torilla Pen. Australia 22°29S 150°5E 280 C5
Torino Italy 45°3N 7°40E 198 C4
Torit South Sudan 4°27N 32°31E 257 G3
Torkamān Iran 37°35N 47°23E 213 D12
Torkovichi Russia 58°51N 30°21E 188 C6
Tormac Romania 45°30N 21°30E 182 E6
Tormes → Spain 41°18N 6°29W 194 D4
Tornado Mt. Canada 49°55N 114°40W 296 D6
Tornal'a Slovakia 48°25N 20°20E 181 C13
Torneå = Tornio Finland 65°50N 24°12E 160 D21
Torneälven → Europe 65°50N 24°12E 160 D21
Torneträsk Sweden 68°24N 19°15E 160 B18
Torngat Mountains Nat. Park △ Canada 59°0N 63°40W 295 F19
Torngat Mts. Canada 59°0N 63°40W 295 F19
Tornio Finland 65°50N 24°12E 160 D21
Tornionjoki = Torneälven → Europe 65°50N 24°12E 160 D21
Tornquist Argentina 38°8S 62°15W 334 D3
Toro Baleares, Spain 39°59N 4°8E 206 B5
Toro Zamora, Spain 41°35N 5°24W 194 D5
Torö Sweden 58°48N 17°50E 163 F11
Toro, Cerro del Chile 29°10S 69°50W 334 B2
Toro ⌓ Uganda 1°5N 30°22E 268 C3
Toro Pk. U.S.A. 33°34N 116°24W 307 M10
Torodi Niger 13°7N 1°47E 263 C5
Torokina Papua N. G. 6°14S 155°3E 286 D8
Törökszentmiklós Hungary 47°11N 20°27E 182 C5
Toronto N.S.W., Australia 33°0S 151°30E 283 B9
Toronto Ont., Canada 43°39N 79°20W 141 B2
Toronto Ohio, U.S.A. 40°28N 80°36W 312 F4
Toronto, Univ. of Canada 43°39N 79°23W 141 B2
Toronto City Centre ✈ (YTZ) Canada 43°38N 79°24W 141 B2
Toronto Harbour Canada 43°38N 79°21W 141 B2
Toronto I. Canada 43°37N 79°23W 141 B2
Toronto Lester B. Pearson Int. ✈ (YYZ) Canada 43°46N 79°35W 141 A1
Toropets Russia 56°30N 31°40E 188 D6
Tororo Uganda 0°45N 34°12E 268 B3
Toros Dağları Turkey 37°0N 32°30E 250 B3
Toros Monumental, Templo de Barcelona, Spain 114 a3
Torotoro Bolivia 18°7S 65°46W 331 D4
Torotoro △ Bolivia 18°8S 65°46W 331 D4
Torpa India 22°57N 85°6E 243 H11
Torpo Norway 60°40N 8°43E 164 D5
Torquay Vic., Australia 38°20S 144°19E 282 E6
Torquay Torbay, U.K. 50°27N 3°32W 169 G4
Torquemada Spain 42°2N 4°19W 194 C6
Torrais, Pta. Azores 39°43N 31°7W 153 d2
Torrance U.S.A. 33°50N 118°20W 307 M8
Torrão Portugal 38°16N 8°11W 195 G2
Torre Annunziata Italy 40°45N 14°27E 201 B7
Torre de Moncorvo Portugal 41°12N 7°8W 194 D3
Torre del Campo Spain 37°46N 3°53W 195 H7
Torre del Greco Italy 40°47N 14°22E 201 B7
Torre del Mar Spain 36°44N 4°6W 195 J6
Torre Latino-Americana Mexico City, Mexico 128 b2
Torre Lupara Italy 41°59N 12°39E 136 B2
Torre Nova Italy 41°51N 12°36E 136 B2
Torre-Pacheco Spain 37°44N 0°57W 197 H4
Torre Péllice Italy 44°49N 7°13E 198 D4
Torreblanca Spain 40°14N 0°12E 196 E5
Torrecampo Spain 38°29N 4°41W 195 G6
Torrecilla en Cameros Spain 42°15N 2°38W 196 C2
Torredembarra Spain 41°9N 1°24E 196 D6
Torredonjimeno Spain 37°46N 3°57W 195 H7
Torrejón de Ardoz Spain 40°27N 3°29W 194 E7
Torrejoncillo Spain 39°54N 6°28W 194 F4
Torrelaguna Spain 40°50N 3°38W 194 E7
Torrelavega Spain 43°20N 4°5W 194 B6
Torrellas → Spain 41°23N 2°1E 114 A1
Torremaggiore Italy 41°41N 15°17E 199 G12
Torremolinos Spain 36°38N 4°30W 195 J6
Torrens, L. Australia 31°0S 137°50E 282 A2
Torrens Cr. → Australia 22°23S 145°9E 280 C4
Torrens Creek Australia 20°48S 145°3E 280 C4
Torrent Spain 39°27N 0°28W 197 F4
Torrenueva Spain 38°38N 3°22W 195 G7
Torreón Mexico 25°33N 103°26W 318 B4
Torreperogil Spain 38°2N 3°17W 195 G7
Torres Brazil 29°21S 49°44W 335 B5
Torres Mexico 28°46N 110°47W 318 B2
Torres, Is. Vanuatu 13°15S 166°37E 287 C4
Torres del Paine △ Chile 51°3S 72°58W 336 D2
Torres Novas Portugal 39°27N 8°33W 195 F2
Torres Strait Australia 9°50S 142°20E 280 a
Torres Vedras Portugal 39°5N 9°15W 195 F1
Torrevécchia Italy 41°55N 12°25E 136 B1
Torrevieja Spain 37°59N 0°42W 197 H4
Torrey U.S.A. 38°18N 111°25W 304 G8
Torricelli Mts. Papua N. G. 3°23S 142°15E 286 B2
Torridge → U.K. 51°0N 4°13W 169 G3
Torridon, L. U.K. 57°35N 5°50W 167 D3
Torrijos Phil. 13°19N 122°5E 232 E4
Torrijos Spain 39°59N 4°18W 194 F6
Tørring Denmark 55°52N 9°29E 163 J3
Torrington Conn., U.S.A. 41°48N 73°7W 313 E11
Torrington Wyo., U.S.A. 42°4N 104°11W 304 E11
Torroella de Montgrí Spain 42°2N 3°8E 196 C8
Torrox Spain 36°46N 3°57W 195 J7
Torsås Sweden 56°24N 16°0E 163 H9
Torsby Sweden 60°7N 13°0E 162 D6
Torshälla Sweden 59°25N 16°28E 162 E10
Tórshavn Føroe Is. 62°5N 6°56W 160 E9
Torslanda Sweden 57°44N 11°45E 163 G5
Torsö Sweden 58°48N 13°45E 163 F7
Tortola Br. Virgin Is. 18°19N 64°45W 321 C7
Tórtoles de Esgueva Spain 41°49N 4°2W 194 D6
Tortolì Italy 39°55N 9°39E 200 C2

Tortona *Italy* 44°54N 8°52E **198** D5
Tortorici *Italy* 38°2N 14°49E **201** D7
Tortosa *Spain* 40°49N 0°31E **196** E5
Tortosa, C. *Spain* 40°41N 0°52E **196** E5
Tortosendo *Portugal* 40°15N 7°31W **194** E3
Tortue, Î. de la *Haiti* 20°5N 72°57W **321** B5
Tortuga *Trin. & Tob.* 10°22N 61°24W **323** t
Tortuguero △ *Costa Rica* 10°31N 83°29W **320** D3
Tortum *Turkey* 40°19N 41°35E **213** B9
Ţorūd *Iran* 35°25N 55°5E **247** C7
Torul *Turkey* 40°34N 39°18E **213** B8
Toruń *Poland* 53°2N 18°39E **185** E5
Torun *Ukraine* 48°40N 23°34E **183** B8
Tory Hill *Canada* 44°58N 78°16W **312** B6
Tory I. *Ireland* 55°16N 8°13W **166** A3
Torysa → *Slovakia* 48°39N 21°21E **181** C14
Torzhok *Russia* 57°5N 34°55E **188** D8
Torzym *Poland* 52°19N 15°5E **185** F2
Tosa *Japan* 33°24N 133°23E **222** D5
Tosa-Shimizu *Japan* 32°52N 132°58E **222** E4
Tosa-Wan *Japan* 33°15N 133°30E **222** D5
Tosa-Yamada = Kami *Japan* 33°36N 133°38E **222** D5
Toscana □ *Italy* 43°25N 11°0E **198** E8
Toscanella = Tuscánia *Italy* 42°25N 11°52E **199** F8
Toscano, Arcipelago *Italy* 42°30N 10°30E **198** F7
Toshima *Japan* 35°43N 139°43E **140** A3
Toshimaen *Japan* 35°43N 139°38E **140** A2
Toshka *Egypt* 22°30N 31°53E **256** C3
Toshka, Buheirat en *Egypt* 22°50N 31°0E **256** C3
Toshkent *Uzbekistan* 41°20N 69°10E **217** D7
Toshkent □ *Uzbekistan* 41°0N 69°40E **217** D7
Tosno *Russia* 59°38N 30°46E **188** C6
Tossa de Mar *Spain* 41°43N 2°56E **196** D7
Tösse *Sweden* 58°58N 12°39E **163** F6
Tostado *Argentina* 29°15S 61°50W **334** B3
Tostedt *Germany* 53°17N 9°42E **178** B5
Tostón, Pta. de *Canary Is.* 28°42N 14°2W **153** e2
Tosu *Japan* 33°22N 130°31E **222** D2
Tosya *Turkey* 41°1N 34°2E **212** B6
Toszek *Poland* 50°27N 18°32E **185** H5
Totak *Norway* 59°40N 8°0E **164** E5
Totana *Spain* 37°45N 1°30W **197** H3
Totebo *Sweden* 57°38N 16°12E **163** G10
Toteng *Botswana* 20°22S 22°58E **270** B3
Tôtes *France* 49°41N 1°2E **172** C8
Tótkomlós *Hungary* 46°24N 20°45E **182** D5
Totland *Norway* 61°56N 5°23E **164** C2
Totma *Russia* 60°0N 42°40E **186** C7
Totnes *U.K.* 50°26N 3°42W **169** G4
Totness *Suriname* 5°53N 56°19W **329** B6
Toto *Angola* 7°9S 14°16E **265** D2
Toto *Nigeria* 8°26N 7°5E **263** D6
Totonicapán *Guatemala* 14°58N 91°12W **320** D1
Totora *Bolivia* 17°42S 65°9W **331** D4
Totoya, I. *Fiji* 18°57S 179°50W **287** B3
Totten Glacier *Antarctica* 66°45S 116°10E **151** C8
Tottenham *N.S.W., Australia* 32°14S 147°21E **283** B7
Tottenham *Vic., Australia* 37°48S 144°51E **128** A1
Tottenham *Ont., Canada* 44°1N 79°49W **312** B5
Tottenham *London, U.K.* 51°35N 0°4W **125** A3
Tottori *Japan* 35°30N 134°15E **222** B6
Tottori □ *Japan* 35°30N 134°12E **222** B6
Touáret *Niger* 20°17N 7°8E **261** D6
Touat *Algeria* 27°27N 0°30E **261** C5
Touba *Côte d'Ivoire* 8°22N 7°40W **262** D3
Touba *Senegal* 14°50N 15°55W **262** C1
Toubkal, Djebel *Morocco* 31°0N 8°0W **260** B3
Toubkal △ *Morocco* 31°0N 8°2W **260** B3
Touboro *Cameroon* 7°47N 15°22E **264** A3
T'ouch'eng *Taiwan* 24°52N 121°49E **225** B3
Toucy *France* 47°44N 3°15E **173** E10
T'oufen *Taiwan* 24°41N 120°54E **225** B2
Tougan *Burkina Faso* 13°11N 2°58W **262** C4
Touggourt *Algeria* 33°6N 6°4E **261** B6
Touggourt □ *Algeria* 33°0N 6°0E **261** B6
Tougouri *Burkina Faso* 13°20N 0°30W **263** C4
Tougué *Guinea* 11°25N 11°50W **262** C2
Toukoto *Mali* 13°27N 9°52W **262** C3
Toul *France* 48°40N 5°53E **173** D12
Toulepleu *Côte d'Ivoire* 6°32N 8°24W **262** D3
Touliu *Taiwan* 23°42N 120°31E **225** C2
Toulon *Var, France* 43°10N 5°55E **175** E9
Toulon *Ill., U.S.A.* 41°6N 89°52W **310** C7
Toulouse *France* 43°37N 1°27E **174** E5
Toulouse Blagnac ✈ **(TLS)** *France* 43°37N 1°22E **174** E5
Toulouse Street *New Orleans, U.S.A.* **131** b2
Toummo *Niger* 22°45N 14°8E **258** D2
Toummo, Mts. de *Africa* 22°43N 14°12E **258** D2
Toumodi *Côte d'Ivoire* 6°32N 5°4W **262** D3
Tounan *Taiwan* 23°41N 120°28E **225** C2
Tounassine, Hamada *Algeria* 28°48N 5°0W **260** C4
Tounggoo *Myanmar* 19°0N 96°30E **241** F6
Toungo *Nigeria* 8°20N 12°3E **263** D7
Touques → *France* 49°22N 0°8E **172** C7
Touraine *France* 47°20N 0°30E **172** E7
Touran = Tūrān △ *Iran* 35°45N 56°30E **247** C8
Tourane = Da Nang *Vietnam* 16°4N 108°13E **236** D7
Tourcoing *France* 50°42N 3°10E **173** B10
Touriñán, C. *Spain* 43°3N 9°18W **194** B1
Tourîne *Mauritania* 22°23N 11°50W **260** D2
Tournai *Belgium* 50°35N 3°25E **170** D3
Tournan-en-Brie *France* 48°44N 2°46E **173** D9
Tournay *France* 43°13N 0°13E **174** E4
Tournon-St-Martin *France* 46°45N 0°58E **172** F7
Tournon-sur-Rhône *France* 45°4N 4°50E **175** C8
Tournus *France* 46°35N 4°54E **173** F11
Touros *Brazil* 5°12S 35°28W **332** C4
Tours *France* 47°22N 0°40E **172** E7
Tousidé, Pic *Chad* 21°1N 16°29E **259** D3
Toussoro, Mt. *C.A.R.* 9°7N 23°14E **264** A4
Toussus-le-Noble *France* 48°44N 2°6E **134** B1
Toussus-le-Noble ✈ **(TNF)** *France* 48°44N 2°6E **134** B1
Touws → *S. Africa* 33°45S 21°11E **270** D3
Touwsrivier *S. Africa* 33°20S 20°2E **270** D3
Tovar *Venezuela* 8°20N 71°46W **328** B3
Tovarkovskiy *Russia* 53°40N 38°14E **188** F10
Tovdal *Norway* 58°47N 8°10E **164** F5
Tovdalselva → *Norway* 58°11N 8°7E **164** F5
Tovste *Ukraine* 48°50N 25°44E **183** B10
Tovuz *Azerbaijan* 41°0N 45°40E **191** K7
Towada *Japan* 40°37N 141°13E **220** D10
Towada-Hachimantai △ *Japan* 40°20N 140°55E **220** D10
Towada-Ko *Japan* 40°28N 140°55E **220** D10
Towanda *Ill., U.S.A.* 40°36N 88°53W **311** D8
Towanda *Pa., U.S.A.* 41°46N 76°27W **313** E8
Towarri △ *Australia* 31°50S 150°37E **283** A9
Towchāl Cable Car *Iran* 35°49N 51°24E **141** A2
Tower *U.S.A.* 47°48N 92°17W **308** B7
Tower, I. = Genovesa, I. *Ecuador* 0°20N 89°58W **330** a
Tower Bridge *London, U.K.* **125** b5
Tower Hamlets □ *U.K.* 51°32N 0°2W **125** A3
Tower of London *U.K.* 51°30N 0°4W **125** A3
Towerhill Cr. → *Australia* 22°28S 144°35E **280** C3
Towner *U.S.A.* 48°21N 100°25W **308** A3
Townsend *Ga., U.S.A.* 31°33N 81°31W **316** D8
Townsend *Mont., U.S.A.* 46°19N 111°31W **304** C8
Townshend I. *Australia* 22°10S 150°31E **280** C5
Townsville *Australia* 19°15S 146°45E **280** B4
Towot *South Sudan* 6°12N 34°25E **257** F3
Towra Pt. *Australia* 34°0S 151°10E **139** C2
Towraghondī *Afghan.* 35°13N 62°16E **240** B1
Towson *U.S.A.* 39°24N 76°36W **309** F15
Towuti, Danau *Indonesia* 2°45S 121°32E **231** E6
Toxkan He → *China* 41°8N 80°11E **217** D10
Tōya-Ko *Japan* 42°35N 140°51E **220** C10
Toyama *Japan* 36°40N 137°15E **223** A9
Toyama □ *Japan* 36°45N 137°30E **223** A9
Toyama-Wan *Japan* 37°0N 137°30E **221** F8
Toyapakeh *Indonesia* 8°41S 115°29E **231** K18
Tøyen *Norway* 59°55N 10°47E **133** A3
Tōyō *Ehime, Japan* 33°56N 133°5E **222** D5
Tōyō *Kōchi, Japan* 33°26N 134°16E **222** D6
Toyohara = Yuzhno-Sakhalinsk *Russia* 46°58N 142°45E **219** B17
Toyohashi *Japan* 34°45N 137°25E **223** C9
Toyokawa *Japan* 34°48N 137°27E **223** C9
Toyonaka *Japan* 34°46N 135°28E **133** A1
Toyooka *Japan* 35°35N 134°48E **222** B6
Toyota *Japan* 35°3N 137°7E **223** B9
Toyoura *Japan* 34°6N 130°57E **222** C2
Tozeur *Tunisia* 33°56N 8°8E **258** B1
Tozeur □ *Tunisia* 34°0N 8°5E **261** B6
Tqibuli *Georgia* 42°26N 43°0E **191** J6
Tqvarcheli *Georgia* 42°47N 41°42E **191** J5
Trá Lí = Tralee *Ireland* 52°16N 9°42W **166** D2
Trá Mhór = Tramore *Ireland* 52°10N 7°10W **166** D4
Tra On *Vietnam* 9°58N 105°55E **237** H5
Tra Vinh *Vietnam* 9°50N 106°15E **237** H6
Trabancos → *Spain* 41°36N 5°15W **194** D5
Traben-Trarbach *Germany* 49°57N 7°7E **179** F3
Trabzon *Turkey* 41°0N 39°45E **213** B8
Trabzon □ *Turkey* 41°10N 39°45E **213** B8
Tracadie *Canada* 47°30N 64°55W **299** C7
Trachenburg = Żmigród *Poland* 51°28N 16°53E **185** G3
Tracy *Qué., Canada* 46°1N 73°9W **298** C5
Tracy *Calif., U.S.A.* 37°44N 121°26W **306** H5
Tracy *Minn., U.S.A.* 44°14N 95°37W **308** C6
Tradate *Italy* 45°43N 8°54E **198** C5
Trade Town *Liberia* 5°40N 9°50W **262** D3
Traer *U.S.A.* 42°12N 92°28W **310** B4
Trafalgar *Vic., Australia* 38°14S 146°12E **283** E7
Trafalgar *Dominica* 15°19N 61°21W **323** k
Trafalgar, C. *Spain* 36°10N 6°2W **195** J4
Trafalgar Square *London, U.K.* **125** b3
Trafaria *Portugal* 38°40N 9°13W **126** A1
Tragonhsi *Greece* 37°27N 25°29E **205** D7
Traian *Brăila, Romania* 45°11N 27°44E **183** E12
Traian *Tulcea, Romania* 45°2N 28°15E **183** E13
Traição, Cor. → *Brazil* 23°35S 46°41W **137** B2
Traiguén *Chile* 38°15S 72°41W **336** A2
Trail *Canada* 49°5N 117°40W **296** D5
Traill Ø *Greenland* 72°30N 23°0W **154** C8
Traimit *Bangkok, Thailand* **113** c2
Trainor L. *Canada* 60°24N 120°17W **296** A4
Traíra → *Brazil* 1°4S 69°26W **328** D4
Trakai △ *Lithuania* 54°30N 25°10E **161** J21
Trákhonas *Cyprus* 35°12N 33°21E **207** E9
Tralee *Ireland* 52°16N 9°42W **166** D2
Tralee B. *Ireland* 52°17N 9°55W **166** D2
Tram Chim △ *Vietnam* 10°43N 105°31E **237** G5
Tramore *Ireland* 52°10N 7°10W **166** D4
Tramore B. *Ireland* 52°9N 7°10W **166** D4
Tramuntana, Serra de *Spain* 39°48N 2°54E **206** B3
Tran *Bulgaria* 42°51N 22°38E **202** D6
Tran Ninh, Cao Nguyen *Laos* 19°30N 103°10E **236** C4
Tranås *Sweden* 58°3N 14°59E **163** F8
Tranbjerg *Denmark* 56°6N 10°9E **163** H4
Tranby *Norway* 59°49N 10°15E **164** E7
Trancas *Argentina* 26°11S 65°20W **334** B2
Trancoso *Portugal* 40°49N 7°21W **194** E3
Tranebjerg *Denmark* 55°51N 10°36E **163** J4
Tranegilde *Denmark* 55°37N 12°20E **118** B2
Tranemo *Sweden* 57°30N 13°20E **163** G7
Trang *Thailand* 7°33N 99°38E **237** J2
Trangahy *Madag.* 19°7S 44°31E **272** B1
Trangan *Indonesia* 6°40S 134°20E **231** F8
Trangie *Australia* 32°4S 148°0E **283** B8
Trångsund *Sweden* 59°13N 18°8E **139** B2
Trångsviken *Sweden* 63°19N 13°59E **162** A7
Trani *Italy* 41°17N 16°25E **201** A9
Tranoroa *Madag.* 24°42S 45°4E **272** C2
Tranqueras *Uruguay* 31°13S 55°45W **335** C4
Trans-Alaska Pipeline *U.S.A.* 70°11N 148°27W **303** A10
Trans-Nzoia □ *Kenya* 1°10N 34°55E **268** B3
Transamerica Pyramid *San Francisco, U.S.A.* **136** b2
Transantarctic Mts. *Antarctica* 85°0S 170°0W **151** E12
Transbay Terminal *San Francisco, U.S.A.* **136** b3
Transcarpathia = Zakarpattya □ *Ukraine* 48°20N 23°20E **183** B8
Transilvania *Romania* 46°30N 24°0E **183** D9
Transilvanian Alps = Carpaţii Meridionali *Romania* 45°30N 25°0E **183** E9
Transjordan = Jordan ■ *Asia* 31°0N 36°0E **251** H7
Transnistria □ *Moldova* 47°20N 29°15E **183** C14
Transtrand *Sweden* 61°6N 13°20E **162** C7
Transtrandsfjällen *Sweden* 61°8N 13°0E **162** C6
Transylvania = Transilvania *Romania* 46°30N 24°0E **183** D9
Trants Bay *Montserrat* 16°46N 62°9W **323** p
Trápani *Italy* 38°1N 12°29E **200** D5
Trappenfelde *Germany* 52°34N 13°39E **115** A4
Trapper Pk. *U.S.A.* 45°54N 114°18W **304** D6
Traralgon *Australia* 38°12S 146°34E **283** E7
Traryd *Sweden* 56°35N 13°45E **163** H7
Trarza □ *Mauritania* 18°0N 15°0W **260** E2
Trás-os-Montes = Cucumbi *Angola* 10°17S 19°5E **265** E3
Trasacco *Italy* 41°57N 13°32E **199** G10
Trăscău, Munţii *Romania* 46°14N 23°14E **183** D8
Trasimeno, L. *Italy* 43°8N 12°6E **199** E9
Träslövsläge *Sweden* 57°4N 12°16E **163** G6
Trastenik *Bulgaria* 43°31N 24°28E **203** C8
Trastévere *Italy* 41°53N 12°28E **136** B1
Trasvase Tajo-Segura, Canal de *Spain* 40°15N 2°55W **196** E2
Trat *Thailand* 12°14N 102°33E **237** F4
Tratani → *Pakistan* 29°19N 68°20E **242** E3
Traun *Austria* 48°14N 14°15E **180** C7
Traunreut *Germany* 47°57N 12°36E **179** H8
Traunsee *Austria* 47°55N 13°50E **180** D6
Traunstein *Germany* 47°52N 12°37E **179** H8
Travellers L. *Australia* 33°20S 142°0E **282** B5
Travemünde *Germany* 53°57N 10°52E **178** B6
Travers, Mt. *N.Z.* 42°1S 172°45E **285** C7
Traverse City *U.S.A.* 44°46N 85°38W **309** C11
Travis, L. *U.S.A.* 30°24N 97°55W **314** F6
Travnik *Bos.-H.* 44°17N 17°39E **182** F2
Trawbreaga B. *Ireland* 55°20N 7°25W **166** A4
Trbovlje *Slovenia* 46°12N 15°5E **199** B12
Treasure I. *U.S.A.* 37°49N 122°22W **136** B2
Treasure Island *U.S.A.* 27°46N 82°46W **317** H7
Treasury Is. *Solomon Is.* 7°22S 155°37E **287** L8
Trébbia → *Italy* 45°4N 9°41E **198** C6
Trebel → *Germany* 53°54N 13°2E **178** B9
Trébeurden *France* 48°46N 3°35W **172** D3
Trebević △ *Bos.-H.* 43°20N 18°45E **182** G3
Třebíč *Czechia* 49°14N 15°55E **180** B8
Trebinje *Bos.-H.* 42°44N 18°22E **202** D2
Trebisacce *Italy* 39°52N 16°32E **201** C9
Trebišnjica → *Bos.-H.* 42°47N 18°8E **202** D2
Trebišov *Slovakia* 48°38N 21°41E **181** C14
Trebitsch = Třebíč *Czechia* 49°14N 15°55E **180** B8
Trebižat → *Bos.-H.* 43°15N 17°30E **199** E14
Trebnitz = Trzebnica *Poland* 51°20N 17°1E **185** G4
Trebnje *Slovenia* 45°54N 15°1E **199** C12
Třeboň *Czechia* 49°1N 14°48E **180** B7
Trebonne *Australia* 18°37S 146°5E **280** B4
Třeboňsko ⌓ *Czechia* 49°1N 14°49E **180** B7
Třeboradice *Czechia* 50°9N 14°31E **135** B3
Třebotov *Czechia* 49°58N 14°17E **135** C1
Trebujena *Spain* 36°52N 6°11W **195** J4
Trecate *Italy* 45°26N 8°44E **198** C5
Tree Tops Park *U.S.A.* 26°4N 80°16W **129** B1
Trefaldwyn = Montgomery *U.K.* 52°34N 3°8W **169** E4
Trefynwy = Monmouth *U.K.* 51°48N 2°42W **169** F5
Tregaron *U.K.* 52°14N 3°56W **169** E4
Tregnago *Italy* 45°31N 11°10E **199** C8
Tregrosse Is. *Australia* 17°41S 150°43E **280** B5
Tréguier *France* 48°47N 3°16W **172** D3
Trégunc *France* 47°51N 3°51W **172** E3
Treherne *Canada* 49°38N 98°42W **297** D9
Tréia *Italy* 43°19N 13°19E **199** E10
Treignac *France* 45°32N 1°48E **174** C5
Treinta y Tres *Uruguay* 33°16S 54°17W **335** C5
Treis-karden *Germany* 50°10N 7°18E **179** E3
Treklyano *Bulgaria* 42°33N 22°36E **202** D6
Trelawney *Zimbabwe* 17°30S 30°30E **271** A5
Trélazé *France* 47°26N 0°30W **172** E6
Trelew *Argentina* 43°10S 65°20W **336** B3
Trélissac *France* 45°11N 0°47E **174** C4
Trelleborg *Sweden* 55°20N 13°10E **163** J7
Tremadog Bay *U.K.* 52°51N 4°18W **168** E3
Tremblay-en-France *France* 48°56N 2°35E **134** A4
Tremblet *Réunion* 21°17S 55°48E **272** f
Trembowla = Terebovlya *Ukraine* 49°18N 25°44E **177** D13
Tremedal = Monte Azul *Brazil* 15°9S 42°53W **333** E3
Tremembe → *Brazil* 23°27S 46°34W **137** A2
Trémiti *Italy* 42°8N 15°30E **199** F12
Tremont *U.S.A.* 40°50N 73°52W **132** A2
Tremonton *U.S.A.* 41°43N 112°10W **304** F7
Tremp *Spain* 42°10N 0°52E **196** C5
Trenche → *Canada* 47°46N 72°53W **298** C5
Trenčiansky □ *Slovakia* 48°45N 18°20E **181** C11
Trenčín *Slovakia* 48°52N 18°4E **181** C11
Trengereid *Norway* 60°26N 5°37E **164** D2
Trenggalek *Indonesia* 8°3S 111°43E **235** D4
Trenno *Italy* 45°29N 9°6E **128** B1
Trenque Lauquen *Argentina* 36°5S 62°45W **334** D3
Trent → *Ont., Canada* 44°6N 77°34W **312** B7
Trent → *England, U.K.* 53°41N 0°42W **168** D7
Trentino-Alto Adige □ *Italy* 46°30N 11°20E **199** B8
Trento *Italy* 46°4N 11°8E **198** B8
Trento *Agusan del S., Phil.* 8°3N 126°2E **233** G6
Trenton *Ont., Canada* 44°10N 77°34W **312** B7
Trenton *Fla., U.S.A.* 29°37N 82°49W **317** F7
Trenton *Mich., U.S.A.* 42°8N 83°11W **311** B13
Trenton *Mo., U.S.A.* 40°5N 93°37W **310** D3
Trenton *N.J., U.S.A.* 40°14N 74°46W **313** F10
Trenton *Nebr., U.S.A.* 40°11N 101°1W **308** E3
Trenton *Ohio, U.S.A.* 39°29N 84°28W **311** E12
Trenton *S.C., U.S.A.* 33°45N 81°51W **316** B8
Trepassey *Canada* 46°43N 53°25W **299** C9
Treptow *Germany* 52°29N 13°27E **115** B3
Treptow an der Rega = Trzebiatów *Poland* 54°3N 15°18E **184** D2
Trepuzzi *Italy* 40°24N 18°4E **201** B11
Tres Arroyos *Argentina* 38°26S 60°20W **334** D3
Três Casas *Brazil* 6°59S 62°41W **331** B5
Três Corações *Brazil* 21°44S 45°15W **333** F2
Tres Equinas *Colombia* 0°43N 75°16W **328** C2
Três Lagoas *Brazil* 20°50S 51°43W **333** F1
Tres Lagos *Argentina* 49°35S 71°25W **336** C2
Tres Lomas *Argentina* 36°27S 62°51W **334** D3
Três Marias, Represa *Brazil* 18°12S 45°15W **333** E2
Tres Montes, C. *Chile* 46°50S 75°30W **336** C1
Tres Pinos *U.S.A.* 36°48N 121°19W **306** J5
Três Pontas *Brazil* 21°23S 45°29W **333** F2
Três Pontas, C. das *Angola* 10°28S 13°32E **265** E2
Tres Puentes *Chile* 27°50S 70°15W **334** B1
Tres Puntas, C. *Argentina* 47°0S 66°0W **336** C3
Três Rios *Brazil* 22°6S 43°15W **333** F3
Três Rios, Sa. dos *Brazil* 22°56S 43°17W **135** B1
Tres Valles *Mexico* 18°15N 96°8W **319** D5
Tresco *U.K.* 49°57N 6°20W **169** H1
Tresfjord *Norway* 62°31N 7°7E **164** B4
Treska → *N. Macedonia* 42°0N 21°20E **202** E5
Treskavica *Bos.-H.* 43°40N 18°20E **182** G3
Trespaderne *Spain* 42°47N 3°24W **194** C7
Tresticklan △ *Sweden* 59°0N 11°42E **163** F5
Trets *France* 43°27N 5°41E **175** E9
Treuburg = Olecko *Poland* 54°2N 22°31E **184** D9
Treuchtlingen *Germany* 48°58N 10°54E **179** G6
Treuenbrietzen *Germany* 52°5N 12°52E **178** C8
Treungen *Norway* 59°1N 8°31E **164** E5
Trèves = Trier *Germany* 49°45N 6°38E **179** F2
Trevi *Italy* 42°52N 12°45E **199** F9
Trevi, Fontana di *Rome, Italy* **136** b3
Trevíglio *Italy* 45°31N 9°35E **198** C6
Trevínca, Peña *Spain* 42°15N 6°46W **194** C4
Treviño *Spain* 42°44N 2°45W **194** C8
Treviso *Italy* 45°40N 12°15E **199** C9
Trezzano sul Navíglio *Italy* 45°24N 9°4E **128** B1
Trgovište *Serbia* 42°20N 22°10E **202** D6
Triabunna *Australia* 42°30S 147°55E **281** G4
Trianda = Ialissos *Greece* 36°24N 28°10E **206** E12
Triangle *Zimbabwe* 21°2S 31°28E **271** B5
Triaucourt-en-Argonne *France* 48°59N 5°2E **173** D12
Tribsees *Germany* 54°5N 12°44E **178** A8
Tribugá, G. de *Colombia* 5°45N 77°20W **328** B2
Tribulation, C. *Australia* 16°5S 145°29E **280** B4
Tribune *U.S.A.* 38°28N 101°45W **308** F3
Tribune Tower *Chicago, U.S.A.* **119** b2
Tricárico *Italy* 40°37N 16°9E **201** B9
Tricase *Italy* 39°56N 18°22E **201** C11
Trichinopoly = Tiruchchirappalli *India* 10°45N 78°45E **245** J4
Trichonida, L. *Greece* 38°34N 21°30E **204** C3
Trichur = Thrissur *India* 10°30N 76°18E **245** J3
Trichy = Tiruchchirappalli *India* 10°45N 78°45E **245** J4
Trida *Australia* 33°1S 145°1E **283** B6
Trier *Germany* 49°45N 6°38E **179** F2
Trieste *Lazio, Italy* 41°55N 12°30E **136** B2
Trieste *Trieste, Italy* 45°40N 13°46E **199** C10
Trieste, G. di *Italy* 45°40N 13°35E **199** C10
Trieux → *France* 48°43N 3°9W **172** D3
Triggiano *Italy* 41°4N 16°55E **201** A9
Triglav *Slovenia* 46°21N 13°50E **199** B10
Triglavski △ *Slovenia* 46°20N 13°50E **199** B10
Trigno → *Italy* 42°4N 14°48E **199** F11
Trigo de Morais = Guijá *Mozam.* 24°27S 33°0E **271** B5
Trigueros *Spain* 37°24N 6°50W **195** H4
Trikala *Greece* 39°34N 21°47E **204** B3
Trikeri *Greece* 39°6N 23°5E **204** B5
Trikomo *Cyprus* 35°17N 33°52E **207** E9
Trikora, Puncak *Indonesia* 4°15S 138°45E **231** E9
Trilby *U.S.A.* 28°28N 82°12W **317** G7
Trilj *Croatia* 43°38N 16°42E **199** E13
Trillo *Spain* 40°42N 2°35W **196** E2
Trim *Ireland* 53°33N 6°48W **166** C5
Trimbak *India* 19°56N 73°33E **244** E1
Trimmu Dam *Pakistan* 31°10N 72°8E **242** D5
Trincomalee *Sri Lanka* 8°38N 81°15E **245** K5
Trindade *Atl. Oc.* 20°20S 29°50W **152** J9
Trindade *Brazil* 16°40S 49°30W **333** E2
Třinec *Czechia* 49°41N 18°39E **181** B11
Trinidad = Jose Abad Santos *Phil.* 5°55N 125°39E **233** J5
Trinidad *Bolivia* 14°46S 64°50W **331** C5
Trinidad *Colombia* 5°25N 71°40W **328** B3
Trinidad *Cuba* 21°48N 80°0W **320** B4
Trinidad *Paraguay* 27°7S 55°47W **335** B4
Trinidad *Trin. & Tob.* 10°30N 61°15W **323** t
Trinidad *Uruguay* 33°30S 56°50W **334** C4
Trinidad *Colo., U.S.A.* 37°10N 104°31W **305** H11
Trinidad *D.C., U.S.A.* 38°54N 76°59W **143** B3
Trinidad, G. *Chile* 49°55S 75°25W **336** C1
Trinidad, I. *Argentina* 39°10S 62°0W **336** A4
Trinidad & Tobago ■ *W. Indies* 10°30N 61°20W **323** t
Trinitápoli *Italy* 41°21N 16°5E **201** A9
Trinité, Havre de *Martinique* 14°44N 60°58W **322** j
Trinity *Nfld. & L., Canada* 48°59N 53°55W **299** C9
Trinity *Edinburgh, U.K.* 55°58N 3°12W **121** B2
Trinity *Tex., U.S.A.* 30°57N 95°22W **314** F7
Trinity → *Calif., U.S.A.* 41°11N 123°42W **304** F2
Trinity → *Tex., U.S.A.* 29°45N 94°43W **314** G7
Trinity B. *Canada* 48°20N 53°10W **299** C9
Trinity Church *New York, U.S.A.* **132** f1
Trinity Hills *Trin. & Tob.* 10°7N 61°7W **323** t
Trinity Is. *U.S.A.* 56°33N 154°25W **303** H9
Trinity Range *U.S.A.* 40°10N 118°40W **304** F4
Trinity River Greenbelt Park *U.S.A.* 32°45N 96°48W **120** B4
Trinkat *India* 8°5N 93°30E **245** K11
Trinkitat *Sudan* 18°45N 37°51E **256** D4
Trino *Italy* 45°12N 8°18E **198** C5
Trinway *U.S.A.* 40°9N 82°1W **312** F2
Triolet *Mauritius* 20°4S 57°32E **272** e
Trionfale *Italy* 41°54N 12°26E **136** B1
Trionto, C. *Italy* 39°37N 16°43E **201** C9
Triora *Italy* 44°1N 7°46E **198** D4
Tripoli = Tarābulus *Lebanon* 34°31N 35°50E **250** D6
Tripoli = Tarābulus *Libya* 32°49N 13°7E **258** B2
Tripoli *Greece* 37°31N 22°25E **204** D4
Tripoli *Iowa, U.S.A.* 42°49N 92°16W **310** B4
Tripolitania = Tarābulus *Libya* 31°0N 13°0E **258** B2
Tripura □ *India* 24°0N 92°0E **241** D4
Tripylos *Cyprus* 34°59N 32°41E **207** F8
Trischen *Germany* 54°4N 8°40E **178** A4
Tristan da Cunha *Atl. Oc.* 37°6S 12°20W **255** K2
Trisul *India* 30°19N 79°47E **243** D8
Triton I. *S. China Sea* 15°47N 111°12E **230** A4
Triulzo *Italy* 45°25N 9°16E **128** B2
Trivandrum = Thiruvananthapuram *India* 8°41N 77°0E **245** K3
Trivento *Italy* 41°47N 14°33E **199** G11
Trizina *Greece* 37°25N 23°15E **204** D5
Trnava *Slovakia* 48°23N 17°35E **181** C10
Trnavský □ *Slovakia* 48°30N 17°45E **181** C10
Troarn *France* 49°11N 0°11W **172** C6
Trobriand Is. *Papua N. G.* 8°30S 151°0E **286** E6
Trocadero *Paris, France* **134** b1
Trochu *Canada* 51°50N 113°13W **296** C6
Trodely I. *Canada* 52°15N 79°26W **298** B4
Troebratskīy *Kazakhstan* 54°25N 66°4E **217** B7
Trogir *Croatia* 43°32N 16°15E **199** E13
Troglav *Croatia* 43°56N 16°36E **199** E13
Tróia *Italy* 41°22N 15°18E **201** A8
Troilus, L. *Canada* 50°50N 74°35W **298** B5
Troina *Italy* 37°47N 14°36E **201** E7
Trois Boutiques *Mauritius* 20°26S 57°38E **272** e
Trois Fourches, Cap des *Morocco* 35°26N 2°58W **261** A4
Trois-Pistoles *Canada* 48°5N 69°10W **299** C6
Trois Pitons, Morne *Dominica* 15°22N 61°20W **323** k
Trois-Rivières *Qué., Canada* 46°25N 72°34W **298** C5
Trois-Rivières *Guadeloupe* 15°57N 61°40W **322** e
Trois Rivières *Martinique* 14°28N 60°58W **322** j
Troisdorf *Germany* 50°48N 7°11E **178** E3
Troitsk *Russia* 54°10N 61°35E **216** B6
Troitsko Pechorsk *Russia* 62°40N 56°10E **186** B10
Troitskosavsk = Kyakhta *Russia* 50°30N 106°25E **215** D11
Troitskoye *Russia* 46°26N 44°15E **191** G7
Troitsky = Troitsk *Russia* 54°10N 61°35E **216** B6
Troja *Czechia* 50°7N 14°25E **135** B2
Troll *Antarctica* 72°0S 2°30E **151** D3
Trölladyngja *Iceland* 64°54N 17°16W **155** C9
Trollbäcken *Sweden* 59°14N 18°12E **139** B3
Trollhättan *Sweden* 58°17N 12°20E **163** F6
Trollheimen *Norway* 62°46N 9°1E **164** B6
Trombay *India* 19°2N 72°56E **130** A2
Trombetas → *Brazil* 1°55S 55°35W **329** D6
Tromelin I. *Ind. Oc.* 15°52S 54°25E **273** F4
Tromøy *Norway* 58°27N 8°51E **164** F5
Tromsø *Norway* 69°40N 18°56E **160** B18
Tron *Thailand* 17°28N 100°7E **236** D3
Trona *U.S.A.* 35°46N 117°23W **307** K9
Tronador, Mte. *Argentina* 41°10S 71°50W **336** B2
Tronchetto *Venice, Italy* **142** b1
Trøndelag *Norway* 64°17N 11°50E **160** D14
Trondheim *Norway* 63°36N 10°25E **164** A7
Trondheimsfjorden *Norway* 63°35N 10°30E **160** E14
Trondheimsleia *Norway* 63°25N 8°30E **164** A5
Trondhjem = Trondheim *Norway* 63°36N 10°25E **164** A7
Trönninge *Sweden* 56°37N 12°51E **163** H6
Tronto → *Italy* 42°54N 13°55E **199** F10
Troodos *Cyprus* 34°55N 32°52E **207** F8
Troon *U.K.* 55°33N 4°39W **167** F4
Troparevo *Russia* 55°39N 37°29E **129** C1
Tropea *Italy* 38°41N 15°54E **201** D8
Tropic *U.S.A.* 37°37N 112°5W **305** H7
Tropojë *Albania* 42°23N 20°10E **202** D4
Troppau = Opava *Czechia* 49°57N 17°58E **181** B10
Trosa *Sweden* 58°54N 17°33E **163** F11
Trostan *U.K.* 55°3N 6°10W **166** A5
Trostberg *Germany* 48°1N 12°33E **179** G8
Trostyanets *Sumy, Ukraine* 50°33N 34°59E **189** G8
Trostyanets *Vinnyts'ka, Ukraine* 48°31N 29°11E **183** B14
Trotsk = Chapayevsk *Russia* 53°0N 49°40E **190** D9
Trotsk = Gatchina *Russia* 59°35N 30°9E **188** C6
Trou Gras Pt. *St. Lucia* 13°51N 60°53W **323** m
Troumaka *St. Vincent* 13°16N 61°17W **323** n
Trout → *Canada* 61°19N 119°51W **296** A5
Trout L. *N.W.T., Canada* 60°40N 121°14W **296** A4
Trout L. *Ont., Canada* 51°20N 93°15W **297** C10
Trout Lake *N.W.T., Canada* 56°30N 114°32W **296** B6
Trout Lake *Wash., U.S.A.* 46°0N 121°32W **306** E5
Trout River *Canada* 49°29N 58°8W **299** C8
Trout Run *U.S.A.* 41°23N 77°3W **312** E7
Trouville-sur-Mer *France* 49°21N 0°5E **172** C7
Trowbridge *U.K.* 51°18N 2°12W **169** F5
Troy *Turkey* 39°57N 26°12E **205** B8
Troy *Ala., U.S.A.* 31°48N 85°58W **316** D4
Troy *Ill., U.S.A.* 38°44N 89°54W **310** F7
Troy *Ind., U.S.A.* 37°59N 86°55W **311** G10
Troy *Kans., U.S.A.* 39°47N 95°5W **308** F6
Troy *Mich., U.S.A.* 42°37N 83°9W **311** B13
Troy *Mo., U.S.A.* 38°59N 90°59W **310** F6
Troy *Mont., U.S.A.* 48°28N 115°53W **304** B6
Troy *N.Y., U.S.A.* 42°44N 73°41W **313** D11
Troy *Ohio, U.S.A.* 40°2N 84°12W **311** D12
Troy *Pa., U.S.A.* 41°47N 76°47W **313** E8
Troyan *Bulgaria* 42°57N 24°43E **203** D8
Troyes *France* 48°19N 4°3E **173** D11
Trpanj *Croatia* 43°1N 17°15E **199** E14
Trstenik *Serbia* 43°36N 21°0E **202** C5
Trubchevsk *Russia* 52°33N 33°47E **189** F7
Truchas Pk. *U.S.A.* 35°58N 105°39W **305** J11
Trucial States = United Arab Emirates ■ *Asia* 23°50N 54°0E **247** F7
Truckee *U.S.A.* 39°20N 120°11W **306** F6
Trudeau Int., Montréal ✈ **(YUL)** *Canada* 45°28N 73°44W **130** B1
Trudfront *Russia* 45°56N 47°40E **191** H8
Trudovoye *Russia* 43°17N 132°5E **220** C6
Trudyashchikhsya, Ostrov *Russia* 59°58N 30°18E **137** B1
Trujillo *Colombia* 4°10N 76°19W **328** C2
Trujillo *Honduras* 16°0N 86°0W **320** C2
Trujillo *Peru* 8°6S 79°0W **330** B2
Trujillo *Spain* 39°28N 5°55W **195** F5
Trujillo *N. Mex., U.S.A.* 35°32N 104°42W **305** J11
Trujillo *Venezuela* 9°22N 70°38W **328** B3
Trujillo □ *Venezuela* 9°25N 70°30W **328** B3
Trujillo, Mte. = Duarte, Pico *Dom. Rep.* 19°2N 70°59W **321** C5
Trujillo Alto *Puerto Rico* 18°21N 66°1W **321** b
Truk *Micronesia* 7°25N 151°46E **287** T17
Trumann *U.S.A.* 35°41N 90°31W **315** D9
Trumansburg *U.S.A.* 42°33N 76°40W **313** D8
Trumbull, Mt. *U.S.A.* 36°25N 113°19W **305** H7
Trump Tower *Chicago, U.S.A.* **119** b2
Trŭn = Tran *Bulgaria* 42°51N 22°38E **202** D6
Trun *France* 48°50N 0°2E **172** D7
Trundle *Australia* 32°53S 147°35E **283** B7
Trung Lon, Hon *Vietnam* 8°36N 106°8E **237** H6
Trung Phan *Vietnam* 17°0N 109°0E **236** D6
Truong Sa, Dao = Spratly I. *S. China Sea* 8°38N 111°55E **230** C4
Truro *S. Austral., Australia* 34°24S 139°9E **282** C3
Truro *N.S., Canada* 45°21N 63°14W **299** C7
Truro *Corn., U.K.* 50°16N 5°4W **169** G2
Trus Madi, Gunung *Malaysia* 5°33N 116°31E **235** A5
Truskavets *Ukraine* 49°17N 23°30E **177** D12
Trŭstenik = Trastenik *Bulgaria* 43°31N 24°28E **203** C8
Trustrup *Denmark* 56°20N 10°46E **163** H4
Trutch *Canada* 57°44N 122°57W **296** B4
Truth or Consequences *U.S.A.* 33°8N 107°15W **305** K10
Trutnov *Czechia* 50°37N 15°54E **180** A8
Truyère → *France* 44°38N 2°34E **174** D6
Tryavna *Bulgaria* 42°54N 25°25E **203** D9
Tryonville *U.S.A.* 41°42N 79°48W **312** E5
Tryphena *N.Z.* 36°18S 175°28E **284** C4
Trysilelva → *Norway* 61°2N 12°35E **164** C9
Tryvasshøgda *Norway* 59°59N 10°40E **133** A3
Trzcianka *Poland* 53°3N 16°25E **185** E3
Trzciel *Poland* 52°23N 15°50E **185** F2
Trzcińsko Zdrój *Poland* 52°58N 14°35E **185** F1
Trzebiatów *Poland* 54°3N 15°18E **184** D2
Trzebiez *Poland* 53°38N 14°31E **184** E1
Trzebnica *Poland* 51°20N 17°1E **185** G4
Trzemeszno *Poland* 52°33N 17°48E **185** F4
Tržič *Slovenia* 46°22N 14°18E **199** B11
Tsagaannur *Mongolia* 49°32N 89°42E **217** C11
Tsagan Aman *Russia* 47°34N 46°43E **191** G8
Tsala Apopka L. *U.S.A.* 28°53N 82°19W **317** G7
Tsamandas *Greece* 39°46N 20°21E **204** B2
Tsamkong = Zhanjiang *China* 21°15N 110°20E **229** G8
Tsandi *Namibia* 17°42S 14°50E **270** A1
Tsangpo = Brahmaputra → *Asia* 23°40N 90°35E **241** D3
Tsaochiao *Taiwan* 24°39N 120°51E **225** B2
Ts'aot'un *Taiwan* 23°58N 120°41E **225** C2
Tsaratanana *Madag.* 16°47S 47°39E **272** B2
Tsaratanana, Mt. de = Maromokotro *Madag.* 14°0S 49°0E **272** A2
Tsaratanana ⌓ *Madag.* 13°57S 48°52E **272** A2
Tsarekonstantinovka = Kuybyshevo *Ukraine* 47°25N 36°40E **189** J9
Tsarevo *Burgas, Bulgaria* 42°9N 27°51E **203** D11
Tsarevo *Stara Zagora, Bulgaria* 42°28N 25°52E **203** D9
Tsaribrod = Dimitrovgrad *Serbia* 43°2N 22°48E **202** C6
Tsaritsani *Greece* 39°53N 22°14E **204** B4
Tsarkasianos *Greece* 38°10N 20°40E **207** C2
Tsarskoye Selo = Pushkin *Russia* 59°45N 30°25E **188** C6
Tsaryovokokshaysk = Yoshkar Ola *Russia* 56°38N 47°55E **190** B8
Tsau *Botswana* 20°8S 22°22E **270** B3
Tsavo *Kenya* 2°59S 38°28E **268** C4
Tsavo East △ *Kenya* 2°44S 38°47E **268** C4
Tsavo West △ *Kenya* 3°19S 37°57E **268** C4
Tsawlaw *Myanmar* 26°9N 98°17E **241** B7
Tselinograd = Nur-Sultan *Kazakhstan* 51°10N 71°30E **217** B8
Tsementny = Fokino *Russia* 53°30N 34°22E **188** F8
Tseng Lan Shue *Hong Kong, China* 22°20N 114°14E **122** B3
Tsengwen Hsi → *Taiwan* 23°8N 120°19E **225** C2
Tsengwen Shuiku *Taiwan* 23°16N 120°34E **225** C2
Tsentralen Balkan △ *Bulgaria* 42°40N 24°45E **203** D8
Tsentralnyy □ *Russia* 52°0N 40°0E **214** D4
Tses *Namibia* 25°58S 18°8E **270** C2
Tsetserleg *Mongolia* 47°36N 101°32E **218** B9
Tseung Kwan *Hong Kong, China* 22°19N 114°15E **122** B3
Tsévié *Togo* 6°25N 1°20E **263** D5
Tshabong *Botswana* 26°2S 22°29E **270** C3
Tshabuta *Dem. Rep. of the Congo* 7°42S 23°7E **265** D4
Tshane *Botswana* 24°5S 21°54E **270** B3
Tshela *Dem. Rep. of the Congo* 4°57S 13°4E **265** C2
Tshesebe *Botswana* 21°51S 27°32E **271** B4
Tshibeke *Dem. Rep. of the Congo* 2°40S 28°35E **268** C2
Tshibinda *Dem. Rep. of the Congo* 2°23S 28°43E **268** C2
Tshikapa *Dem. Rep. of the Congo* 6°28S 20°48E **265** D4
Tshilenge *Dem. Rep. of the Congo* 6°17S 23°48E **265** D4
Tshindjambo *Dem. Rep. of the Congo* 10°52S 22°43E **265** E4
Tshinota *Dem. Rep. of the Congo* 7°2S 20°58E **265** D4
Tshinsenda *Dem. Rep. of the Congo* 12°20S 28°0E **269** E2
Tshitadi *Dem. Rep. of the Congo* 6°46S 21°43E **265** D4
Tshofa *Dem. Rep. of the Congo* 5°13S 25°16E **265** D5
Tshopo □ *Dem. Rep. of the Congo* 1°0N 25°0E **264** B4
Tshuapa □ *Dem. Rep. of the Congo* 0°0 22°0E **264** B4
Tshuapa → *Dem. Rep. of the Congo* 0°14S 20°42E **264** C4
Tshumbiri *Dem. Rep. of the Congo* 2°38S 16°18E **264** C3
Tshwane = Pretoria *S. Africa* 25°44S 28°12E **271** C4
Tshwane *Botswana* 22°24S 22°1E **270** B3
Tsiaotso = Jiaozuo *China* 35°16N 113°12E **226** G7
Tsibirihina → *Madag.* 19°42S 44°31E **272** B1
Tsigara *Botswana* 20°22S 25°54E **270** B4
Tsihombe *Madag.* 25°10S 45°41E **272** D2
Tsiigehtchic *Canada* 67°15N 134°0W **294** D5
Ts'il-os ⌓ *Canada* 51°9N 123°59W **296** C4
Tsim Sha Tsui *Hong Kong, China* 22°18N 114°10E **122** B3
Tsimanampetsotse △ *Madag.* 24°9S 43°50E **272** C1
Tsimlyansk *Russia* 47°40N 42°6E **191** G6
Tsimlyansk Res. = Tsimlyanskoye Vdkhr. *Russia* 48°0N 43°0E **191** F6
Tsimlyanskoye Vdkhr. *Russia* 48°0N 43°0E **191** F6
Tsinan = Jinan *China* 36°38N 117°1E **226** F9
Tsineng *S. Africa* 27°5S 23°5E **270** C3
Tsing Lung Tau *Hong Kong, China* 22°22N 114°3E **122** A2
Tsing Yi *Hong Kong, China* 22°21N 114°6E **122** A2
Tsinghai = Qinghai □ *China* 36°0N 98°0E **218** D8
Tsingshih = Jinshi *China* 29°40N 111°50E **229** C8
Tsingtao = Qingdao *China* 36°5N 120°20E **227** F11
Tsingy de Bemaraha ⌓ *Madag.* 18°35S 44°55E **272** B2
Tsingy de Namoraka ⌓ *Madag.* 16°29S 45°25E **272** B2
Tsining = Jining *China* 35°22N 116°34E **226** G9
Tsinjoarivo *Madag.* 19°37S 47°40E **272** B2
Tsinjomitondraka *Madag.* 15°40S 47°8E **272** B2
Tsinling Shan = Qinling Shandi *China* 33°50N 108°10E **226** H5
Tsirigo = Kythira *Greece* 36°8N 23°0E **204** E5
Tsiroanomandidy *Madag.* 18°46S 46°2E **272** B2
Tsis I. *Micronesia* 7°17N 151°49E **287** U18
Tsiteli-Tsqaro = Dedopolis Tsqaro *Georgia* 41°33N 46°0E **191** K8
Tsitondroina *Madag.* 21°19S 46°0E **272** C2
Tsitsihar = Qiqihar *China* 47°26N 124°0E **219** B13
Tsitsikamma △ *S. Africa* 34°3S 23°40E **270** D3
Tsivilsk *Russia* 55°50N 47°25E **190** C8
Tsivory *Madag.* 24°4S 46°5E **272** C2
Tskhinvali *Georgia* 42°14N 44°1E **191** J7
Tsna → *Russia* 54°55N 41°58E **190** C6
Tsnori *Georgia* 41°40N 45°57E **191** K7
Tso Moriri, L. *India* 32°50N 78°20E **243** C8
Tsobis *Namibia* 19°27S 17°30E **270** A2
Tsodilo Hills *Botswana* 18°49S 21°43E **270** A3
Tsogni *Gabon* 2°48S 10°10E **264** C2
Tsogttsetsiy = Baruunsuu *Mongolia* 43°43N 105°35E **226** C3
Tsolo *S. Africa* 31°18S 28°37E **271** D4
Tsomo *S. Africa* 32°0S 27°42E **271** D4
Tsoukalades *Greece* 38°41N 20°47E **207** B2
Tsova *West Bank* 31°47N 35°6E **123** B1
Tsoying *Taiwan* 22°41N 120°17E **225** D2
Tsu *Japan* 34°45N 136°25E **223** C8
Tsu L. *Canada* 60°40N 111°52W **296** A6
Tsubata *Japan* 36°40N 136°44E **223** A8
Tsuchiura *Japan* 36°5N 140°15E **223** A12
Tsuen Wan *Hong Kong, China* 22°22N 114°6E **122** A2
Tsugaru-Hantō *Japan* 41°0N 140°30E **220** D10
Tsugaru-Kaikyō *Japan* 41°35N 141°0E **220** D10
Tsuken-jima *Japan* 26°15N 127°56E **288** a
Tsukiji *Tokyo, Japan* **140** c5
Tsukuba *Japan* 36°2N 140°4E **223** A12
Tsukumi *Japan* 33°4N 131°52E **222** D3
Tsukushi-Sanchi *Japan* 33°25N 130°30E **222** D2
Tsumeb *Namibia* 19°9S 17°44E **270** A2
Tsumis *Namibia* 23°39S 17°29E **270** B2
Tsuna = Awaji *Japan* 34°28N 134°56E **222** C6
Tsuno-Shima *Japan* 34°21N 130°52E **222** C2
Tsur Hadassa *Israel* 31°43N 35°6E **123** B1
Tsuru *Japan* 35°31N 138°57E **223** B10
Tsuruga *Japan* 35°45N 136°2E **223** B8
Tsuruga-Wan *Japan* 35°50N 136°3E **223** B8
Tsurugi *Japan* 36°29N 136°37E **223** A8
Tsurugi-San *Japan* 33°51N 134°6E **222** D6
Tsurumi → *Japan* 35°32N 139°40E **140** B3
Tsurumi-Saki *Japan* 32°56N 132°5E **222** E4
Tsuruoka *Japan* 38°44N 139°50E **220** E9
Tsurusaki *Japan* 33°14N 131°41E **222** D3
Tsushima *Ehime, Japan* 33°7N 132°32E **222** D4
Tsushima *Gifu, Japan* 35°10N 136°43E **223** B8
Tsushima *Nagasaki, Japan* 34°20N 129°20E **222** C1
Tsuyama *Japan* 35°3N 134°0E **222** B6
Tsvetkovo *Ukraine* 49°8N 31°33E **189** H6
Tsyelyakhany *Belarus* 52°30N 25°46E **177** B13
Tsz Wan Shan *Hong Kong, China* 22°20N 114°11E **122** A3
Tu → *Myanmar* 21°50N 96°15E **241** E6
Tua *Dem. Rep. of the Congo* 3°38S 16°38E **264** C3
Tua → *Papua N. G.* 6°30S 144°28E **286** D3
Tua → *Portugal* 41°13N 7°26W **194** D3
Tuaheni Pt. *N.Z.* 38°43S 178°4E **284** E7
Tuai *N.Z.* 38°47S 177°10E **284** E6
Tuaim = Tuam *Ireland* 53°31N 8°51W **166** C3
Tuakau *N.Z.* 37°16S 174°59E **284** D3
Tual *Indonesia* 5°38S 132°44E **231** F8
Tualatin *U.S.A.* 45°23N 122°45W **306** E4
Tuam *Ireland* 53°31N 8°51W **166** C3
Tuamarina *N.Z.* 41°25S 173°59E **285** B8
Tuamotu, Îs. *French Polynesia* 17°0S 144°0W **289** f
Tuamotu Arch. = Tuamotu, Îs. *French Polynesia* 17°0S 144°0W **289** f
Tuamotu Ridge *Pac. Oc.* 20°0S 138°0W **289** K14
Tuan Giao *Vietnam* 21°35N 103°25E **236** B4
Tuanfeng *China* 30°38N 114°52E **229** B10
Tuangku *Indonesia* 2°10N 97°16E **234** B1
Tuanxi *China* 27°28N 107°8E **228** D6
Tuao *Phil.* 17°45N 121°22E **232** C3
Tuapa *Cook Is.* 18°57S 169°54W **289** g
Tuapse *Russia* 44°5N 39°10E **191** H4
Tuaran *Malaysia* 6°10N 116°13E **235** A5
Tuas *Singapore* 1°19N 103°39E **138** B1
Tuatapere *N.Z.* 46°8S 167°41E **285** G2
Tuba City *U.S.A.* 36°8N 111°14W **305** H8
Tuban *Indonesia* 6°54S 112°3E **235** D4
Tubani *Botswana* 24°46S 24°18E **270** B3
Tubarão *Brazil* 28°30S 49°0W **335** B6
Tūbās *West Bank* 32°20N 35°22E **251** F6
Tubas → *Namibia* 22°54S 14°35E **270** B2
Tubau *Malaysia* 3°10N 113°40E **235** B4
Tubbataha Reefs ⌓ *Phil.* 8°53N 119°53E **233** G2
Tubigon *Phil.* 9°57N 123°58E **233** G4
Tübingen *Germany* 48°31N 9°4E **179** G5
Tubmanburg = Bomi *Liberia* 7°1N 10°38W **262** D2
Tubod *Phil.* 8°3N 123°48E **233** G4
Tubou *Fiji* 18°13S 178°48W **287** B3
Tubruq *Libya* 32°7N 23°55E **258** B4
Tubuaï *French Polynesia* 23°18S 149°30W **289** f
Tubuaï, Îs. *French Polynesia* 25°0S 150°0W **289** f
Tuburan *Basilan, Phil.* 6°39N 122°16E **233** H4

Tuburan Cebu, Phil. 10°44N 123°49E 233 F4
Tuc Trung Vietnam 11°1N 107°12E 237 G6
Tucacas Venezuela 10°48N 68°19W 328 A4
Tucano Brazil 10°58S 38°48W 332 D4
T'uch'ang Taiwan 24°35N 121°29E 225 B3
Tuchitua Canada 60°55N 129°13W 296 A3
Tuchodi ➔ Canada 58°17N 123°42W 296 B4
Tuchola Poland 53°33N 17°52E 184 E4
Tuchoměřice Czechia 50°7N 14°16E 135 B1
Tuchów Poland 49°54N 21°1E 185 J8
Tuckahoe U.S.A. 40°56N 73°49W 132 A3
Tuckanarra Australia 27°7S 118°5E 279 E2
Tucker U.S.A. 33°51N 84°13W 316 B5
Tuckers Town Bermuda 32°20N 64°42W 153 a
Tucson U.S.A. 32°13N 110°58W 305 K8
Tucumán □ Argentina 26°48S 66°2W 334 B2
Tucumcari U.S.A. 35°10N 103°44W 305 J12
Tucunaré Brazil 5°18S 55°51W 331 B6
Tucupido Venezuela 9°17N 65°47W 328 B4
Tucupita Venezuela 9°2N 62°3W 329 B5
Tucuruí Brazil 3°42S 49°44W 332 B2
Tucuruí, Represa de Brazil 4°0S 49°30W 332 B2
Tucuruvi Brazil 23°28S 46°35W 137 A2
Tuczno Poland 53°13N 16°10E 185 E3
Tuddal Norway 59°46N 8°49E 164 E5
Tudela Spain 42°4N 1°39W 196 C3
Tudmur Syria 34°36N 38°15E 213 E8
Tudor, L. Canada 55°50N 65°25W 299 A6
Tudora Romania 47°31N 26°45E 183 C11
Tuella ➔ Portugal 41°30N 7°12W 194 D3
Tuen Mun
Hong Kong, China 22°23N 113°57E 122 A1
Tuensang India 26°17N 94°50E 241 B5
Tueré ➔ Brazil 2°48S 50°59W 332 B1
Tufanbeyli Turkey 38°15N 36°13E 212 C7
Tufello Italy 41°56N 12°32E 136 B2
Tüffer = Laško Slovenia 46°10N 15°16E 199 B12
Tufi Papua N. G. 9°8S 149°19E 286 E5
Tufnell Park U.K. 51°33N 0°8W 125 A3
Tufsingdal Norway 62°18N 11°44E 164 B8
Tufts Abyssal Plain
Pac. Oc. 47°0N 140°0W 289 C14
Tufts Univ. U.S.A. 42°24N 71°7W 116 A2
Tufu Pt. Amer. Samoa 14°13S 169°30W 302 g
Tug Hill Plateau U.S.A. 43°45N 75°50W 313 C9
Tugaya Phil. 7°53N 124°10E 233 H5
Tugela ➔ S. Africa 29°14S 31°30E 271 C5
Tugela Falls S. Africa 28°42S 29°51E 271 C4
Tughlakabad India 28°30N 77°16E 120 B2
Tugidak I. U.S.A. 56°30N 154°40W 303 H9
Tuguegarao Phil. 17°35N 121°42E 232 C3
Tugur Russia 53°44N 136°45E 215 D14
Tui Spain 42°3N 8°39W 194 C2
Tuileries, Jardin des Paris, France 134 b3
Tuineje Canary Is. 28°19N 14°3W 153 e2
Tukangbesi, Kepulauan
Indonesia 6°0S 124°0E 231 F6
Tukarak I. Canada 56°15N 78°45W 298 A4
Tukayyid Iraq 29°47N 45°36E 246 D5
Tûkh Egypt 30°21N 31°12E 256 H7
Tukhlya Ukraine 48°55N 23°28E 183 B8
Tukituki ➔ N.Z. 39°36S 176°56E 284 F5
Tukobo Ghana 5°1N 2°47W 262 D4
Tūkrah Libya 32°30N 20°37E 258 B4
Tuktoyaktuk Canada 69°27N 133°2W 294 D5
Tuktuk Indonesia 2°37N 98°54E 234 B1
Tuktut Nogait △ Canada 69°15N 122°0W 294 D7
Tuku Taiwan 23°41N 120°23E 225 C2
Tukums Latvia 56°58N 23°10E 184 B10
Tukuran Phil. 7°51N 123°34E 233 H4
Tukuyu Tanzania 9°17S 33°35E 269 D3
Tula Amer. Samoa 14°15S 170°34W 302 f
Tula Hidalgo, Mexico 20°3N 99°21W 319 C5
Tula Tamaulipas, Mexico 23°0N 99°43W 319 C5
Tula Nigeria 9°51N 11°27E 263 D7
Tula Russia 54°13N 37°38E 188 E9
Tula □ Russia 53°45N 37°30E 188 F9
Tulach Mhór = Tullamore
Ireland 53°16N 7°31W 166 C4
Tulagi Solomon Is. 9°5S 160°10E 287 M11
Tūlak Afghan. 33°55N 63°40E 240 B1
Tulan Taiwan 22°53N 121°13E 225 D3
Tulancingo Mexico 20°5N 98°22W 319 C5
Tulangbawang ➔
Indonesia 4°24S 105°52E 234 C3
Tulare Serbia 42°48N 21°28E 202 D5
Tulare Calif., U.S.A. 36°13N 119°21W 306 J7
Tulare Lake Bed U.S.A. 36°0N 119°48W 306 K7
Tularosa U.S.A. 33°5N 106°1W 305 K10
Tulbagh S. Africa 33°16S 19°6E 270 D2
Tulcán Ecuador 0°48N 77°43W 328 C2
Tulcea Romania 45°13N 28°46E 183 E13
Tulcea □ Romania 45°0N 28°30E 183 E13
Tulchyn Ukraine 48°41N 28°49E 183 B13
Tüledi Araldary
Kazakhstan 45°2N 50°16E 191 H10
Tüleh Iran 34°35N 52°33E 247 C7
Tulemalu L. Canada 62°58N 99°25W 297 A9
Tulgheş Romania 46°58N 25°45E 183 D10
Tuli Zimbabwe 21°58S 29°13E 269 G2
Tulia U.S.A. 34°32N 101°46W 314 D4
Tuliszków Poland 52°5N 18°18E 185 F5
Tulita Canada 64°57N 125°30W 294 E6
Ţūlkarm West Bank 32°19N 35°2E 251 F6
Tulla Ireland 52°53N 8°46W 166 D3
Tullahoma U.S.A. 35°22N 86°13W 315 D11
Tullamarine Australia 37°41S 144°50E 128 A1
Tullamore N.S.W.,
Australia 32°39S 147°36E 283 B7
Tullamore Offaly, Ireland 53°16N 7°31W 166 C4
Tulle France 45°16N 1°46E 174 C5
Tulln an der Donau
Austria 48°20N 16°4E 180 C9
Tullow Ireland 52°49N 6°45W 166 D5
Tullus Sudan 11°7N 24°31E 257 E1
Tully Queens., Australia 17°56S 145°55E 280 B4
Tully N.Y., U.S.A. 42°48N 76°7W 313 D8
Ţulmaythah Libya 32°40N 20°55E 258 B4
Tulnici Romania 45°51N 26°38E 183 E11
Tulovo Bulgaria 42°33N 25°32E 203 D9
Tulsa U.S.A. 36°10N 95°55W 314 C7
Tulse Hill U.K. 51°26N 0°6W 125 B3
Tulsequah Canada 58°39N 133°35W 296 B2
Tulu Milki Ethiopia 9°55N 38°20E 257 F4
Tulu Welel Ethiopia 8°56N 34°47E 257 F3
Tuluá Colombia 4°6N 76°11W 328 C2
Tulucești Romania 45°34N 28°2E 183 E13
Tuluksak U.S.A. 61°6N 160°58W 303 F7
Tulum Mexico 20°13N 87°28W 319 C7
Tulun Russia 54°32N 100°35E 215 D11
Tulungagung Indonesia 8°5S 111°54E 235 D4
Tuluran I. Phil. 10°58N 119°16E 233 F2
Tuma Russia 55°10N 40°30E 188 E11
Tuma ➔ Nic. 13°6N 84°35W 320 D3
Tumacacori ⌂ U.S.A. 31°35N 111°6W 305 L8
Tumaco Colombia 1°50N 78°45W 328 C2
Tumaco, Ensenada
Colombia 1°55N 78°45W 328 C2
Tumakuru India 13°18N 77°6E 245 H3
Tumatumari Guyana 5°20N 58°55W 329 B6
Tumauini Phil. 17°17N 121°49E 232 C3
Tumba
Dem. Rep. of the Congo 3°10S 23°36E 264 C4
Tumba Sweden 59°12N 17°48E 162 E11
Tumba, L.
Dem. Rep. of the Congo 0°50S 18°0E 264 C3
Tumbangsamba Indonesia 1°27S 113°7E 235 C4
Tumbarumba Australia 35°44S 148°0E 283 C8
Tumbaya Argentina 23°50S 65°26W 334 A2
Tumbes Peru 3°37S 80°27W 330 A1
Tumbes □ Peru 3°50S 80°30W 330 A1
Tumbler Ridge Canada 55°8N 121°0W 296 B4
Tumbur South Sudan 4°20N 31°34E 257 G3
Tumbwe
Dem. Rep. of the Congo 11°25S 27°15E 269 E2
Tumby Bay Australia 34°21S 136°8E 282 C2
Tumd Youqi China 40°30N 110°30E 226 D6
Tumen China 43°0N 129°50E 224 A4
Tumen Jiang ➔ China 42°20N 130°35E 224 A5
Tumeremo Venezuela 7°18N 61°30W 329 B5
Tumindao I. Phil. 4°41N 119°24E 233 J2
Tumiritinga Brazil 18°58S 41°38W 333 E3
Tumkur = Tumakuru
India 13°18N 77°6E 245 H3
Tumon B. Guam 13°31N 144°48E 302 d
Tump Pakistan 26°7N 62°16E 240 D1
Tumpat Malaysia 6°11N 102°10E 237 J4
Tumsar India 21°26N 79°45E 244 D4
Tumu Ghana 10°56N 1°56W 262 C4
Tumucumaque, Serra Brazil 2°0N 55°0W 329 C7
Tumupasa Bolivia 14°9S 67°55W 330 C4
Tumut Australia 35°16S 148°13E 283 C8
Tumwater U.S.A. 47°1N 122°54W 306 C4
Tumxuk China 41°22N 79°58E 217 D9
Tun Sweden 58°26N 12°43E 163 F6
Tuna India 22°59N 70°5E 242 H4
Tunapuna Trin. & Tob. 10°38N 61°24W 323 t
Tunapuna/Piarco □
Trin. & Tob. 10°40N 61°20W 323 t
Tunas de Zaza Cuba 21°39N 79°34W 320 B4
Tunbridge Wells = Royal Tunbridge
Wells U.K. 51°7N 0°16E 169 F8
Tunçbilek Turkey 39°37N 29°29E 205 B11
Tunceli Turkey 39°6N 39°31E 213 C8
Tunceli □ Turkey 39°5N 39°35E 213 C8
Tunchang China 19°21N 110°5E 229 a
Tuncurry Australia 32°17S 152°29E 283 B10
Tundla India 27°12N 78°17E 242 F8
Tundubai Sudan 18°36N 28°35E 256 D2
Tunduru Tanzania 11°8S 37°25E 269 E4
Tundzha ➔ Bulgaria 41°40N 26°35E 203 E10
Tung Chung
Hong Kong, China 22°17N 113°57E 122 B1
Tung Lung Chau
Hong Kong, China 22°15N 114°17E 122 B3
Tung O Hong Kong, China 22°11N 114°8E 122 B2
Tunga ➔ India 15°0N 75°50E 245 G2
Tunga Pass Asia 29°0N 94°14E 241 A5
Tungabhadra ➔ India 15°57N 78°15E 245 G4
Tungabhadra Dam India 15°0N 75°50E 245 G2
Tungao Taiwan 24°31N 121°50E 225 B3
Tungaru Sudan 10°9N 30°52E 257 E3
Tungawan Phil. 7°30N 122°20E 233 H4
Tungchi Yü Taiwan 23°15N 119°40E 225 C1
Tungch'uan = Dongchuan
China 26°8N 103°1E 228 D4
Tungho Taiwan 22°58N 121°18E 225 D3
T'unghsiao Taiwan 24°29N 120°40E 225 B2
Tunghwa = Tonghua
China 41°42N 125°58E 224 B2
Tungi Bangla. 23°53N 90°24E 241 D3
Tungkang Taiwan 22°27N 120°26E 225 D2
Tungku Malaysia 5°1N 118°53E 235 A5
Tungla Nic. 13°24N 84°21W 320 D3
T'unglo Taiwan 24°30N 120°47E 225 B2
Tungnafellsjökull Iceland 64°45N 17°55W 155 C9
Tungsha Tao = Dongsha Dao
S. China Sea 20°45N 116°43E 219 G12
Tungshan Taiwan 24°38N 121°47E 225 B3
Tungshih Changhua,
Taiwan 24°12N 120°43E 225 B2
Tungshih Chiai, Taiwan 23°27N 120°8E 225 C2
Tungsten Canada 61°57N 128°16W 296 A3
Tungufell Iceland 64°17N 20°10W 155 C6
Tungurahua □ Ecuador 1°15S 78°35W 328 D2
Tunguska, Nizhnyaya ➔
Russia 65°48N 88°4E 215 C9
Tunguska, Podkamennaya ➔
Russia 61°50N 90°13E 215 C10
Tungyin Tao Taiwan 26°22N 128°29E 225 b
Tuni India 17°22N 82°36E 244 F6
Tunia Colombia 2°41N 76°31W 328 C2
Tunica U.S.A. 34°41N 90°23W 315 D9
Tunis Baghdād, Iraq 33°23N 44°21E 113 A2
Tunis Tunisia 36°50N 10°11E 258 A2
Tunis □ Tunisia 36°46N 10°10E 261 A7
Tunis ✕ (TUN) Tunisia 36°52N 10°14E 200 F3
Tunis, Golfe de Tunisia 37°0N 10°30E 258 A2
Tunisia ■ Africa 33°30N 9°10E 258 B1
Tunja Colombia 5°33N 73°25W 328 B3
Tunkhannock U.S.A. 41°32N 75°57W 313 E9
Tunkinsky △ Russia 51°30N 102°0E 215 D11
Tunliu China 36°13N 112°52E 226 F7
Tunnel Creek △
Australia 17°41S 125°18E 278 C4
Tunnsjøen Norway 64°45N 13°25E 160 D15
Tuno Denmark 55°57N 10°27E 163 J4
Tuntutuliak U.S.A. 60°22N 162°38W 303 F7
Tununak U.S.A. 60°37N 165°15W 303 F6
Tunungayualok I. Canada 56°0N 61°0W 299 A7
Tunuyán Argentina 33°35S 69°0W 334 C2
Tunuyán ➔ Argentina 33°33S 67°30W 334 C2
Tunxi = Huangshan
China 29°42N 118°25E 229 C12
Tuo Jiang ➔ China 28°50N 105°35E 228 C5
Tuolumne U.S.A. 37°58N 120°15W 306 H6
Tuolumne ➔ U.S.A. 37°36N 121°13W 306 H5
Tuomiala Finland 60°11N 24°11E 121 B1
Tüp Kyrgyzstan 42°45N 78°20E 217 D9
Tūp Āghāj Iran 36°3N 47°50E 213 D12
Tupã Brazil 21°57S 50°28W 335 A5
Tupaciguara Brazil 18°35S 48°42W 333 E2
Tupelo U.S.A. 34°16N 88°43W 315 D10
Tupik Russia 55°42N 33°22E 188 E7
Tupinambarana, I. Brazil 3°0S 58°0W 329 D6
Tupirama Brazil 8°58S 48°12W 332 C2
Tupiratins Brazil 8°23S 48°8W 332 C2
Tupiza Bolivia 21°30S 65°40W 334 A2
Tupižnica Serbia 43°43N 22°10E 202 C6
Tupman U.S.A. 35°18N 119°21W 307 K7
Tupper Canada 55°32N 120°1W 296 B4
Tupper L. U.S.A. 44°10N 74°32W 313 B10
Tupper Lake U.S.A. 44°14N 74°28W 313 B10
Tüpqarghan Muyis
Kazakhstan 44°40N 50°19E 191 H10
Tupungato, Cerro
S. Amer. 33°15S 69°50W 334 C2
Tuquan China 45°18N 121°38E 227 B11
Túquerres Colombia 1°5N 77°37W 328 C2
Tura India 25°30N 90°16E 241 C3
Tura Russia 64°20N 100°17E 215 C11
Turabah Ḩā'il, Si. Arabia 28°20N 43°15E 246 D4
Turabah Makkah,
Si. Arabia 21°15N 41°34E 248 B3
Turagua, Serranía
Venezuela 7°20N 64°35W 329 B5
Turakina N.Z. 40°3S 175°16E 284 G4
Turakina ➔ N.Z. 40°5S 175°8E 284 G4
Turakirae Hd. N.Z. 41°26S 174°56E 284 H3
Turama ➔ Papua N. G. 7°40S 143°50E 286 D2
Tūrān Iran 35°39N 56°42E 247 C8
Turan Russia 51°55N 94°0E 217 B12
Tūrān △ Iran 35°45N 56°30E 247 C8
Turan Lowland Asia 43°30N 62°0E 216 D6
Turangi N.Z. 38°59S 175°48E 284 E4
Ţurayf Si. Arabia 31°41N 38°39E 246 D3
Turbaco Colombia 10°21N 75°25W 328 A2
Turbacz Poland 49°30N 20°8E 185 J7
Turbat Pakistan 25°59N 63°4E 240 D1
Turbe Bos.-H. 44°15N 17°35E 182 F2
Turbeville U.S.A. 33°54N 80°1W 316 B9
Turbo Colombia 8°6N 76°43W 328 B2
Turčianske Teplice
Slovakia 48°52N 18°52E 181 C11
Turco Bolivia 18°10S 68°11W 330 D4
Turcoaia Romania 45°7N 28°11E 183 E13
Turda Romania 46°34N 23°47E 183 D8
Tureberg Sweden 59°25N 17°55E 139 A1
Turéia French Polynesia 20°50S 138°32W 289 f
Turek Poland 52°3N 18°30E 185 F5
Turfan = Turpan China 43°58N 89°10E 217 D11
Turfan Basin = Turpan Pendi
China 42°40N 89°25E 217 D11
Turfan Depression = Turpan Pendi
China 42°40N 89°25E 217 D11
Turffontein S. Africa 26°14S 28°2E 123 B2
Turgayskaya Stolovaya Strana =
Torghay Ustirti Asia 51°0N 63°0E 216 B6
Turgeon ➔ Canada 50°0N 78°56W 298 C4
Tŭrgovishte = Targovishte
Bulgaria 43°17N 26°38E 203 C10
Turgut Turkey 37°22N 28°4E 205 D10
Turgutlu Turkey 38°30N 27°43E 205 C9
Turgutreis Turkey 37°2N 27°15E 205 D9
Turgwe ➔ Zimbabwe 21°31S 32°15E 271 B5
Turhal Turkey 40°24N 36°5E 212 B7
Turia ➔ Spain 39°27N 0°19W 197 F4
Turiaçu Brazil 1°40S 45°19W 332 B2
Turiaçu ➔ Brazil 1°36S 45°19W 332 B2
Turiec ➔ Slovakia 49°7N 18°55E 181 B11
Turin = Torino Italy 45°3N 7°40E 198 C4
Turinskaya Kultbaza = Tura
Russia 64°20N 100°17E 215 C11
Türk Telekom Arena
Istanbul, Turkey 41°5N 28°59E 122 B1
Turka Ukraine 49°10N 23°2E 185 J10
Turkana □ Kenya 3°10N 35°20E 268 B4
Turkana, L. Africa 3°30N 36°5E 268 B4
Turkayel Ethiopia 8°7N 45°21E 267 C6
Türkeli Turkey 40°30N 27°30E 203 F11
Turkestan = Türkistan
Kazakhstan 43°17N 68°16E 217 D7
Turkestan Range Asia 39°35N 69°0E 217 E7
Túrkeve Hungary 47°6N 20°44E 182 C5
Turkey ■ Eurasia 39°0N 36°0E 212 C7
Turkey ➔ U.S.A. 42°43N 91°2W 310 B5
Turkey Creek = Warmun
Australia 17°2S 128°12E 278 C4
Turkey L. U.S.A. 28°30N 81°28W 133 A2
Turkey Lake Park U.S.A. 28°30N 81°28W 133 A2
Turki Russia 52°0N 43°15E 190 D6
Türkistan Kazakhstan 43°17N 68°16E 217 D7
Türkmenabat Turkmenistan 39°6N 63°34E 247 B9
Türkmenbashi Turkmenistan 40°5N 53°5E 247 A7
Turkmenistan ■ Asia 39°0N 59°0E 216 E5
Türkmenli Turkey 39°45N 26°30E 205 B8
Türkoğlu Turkey 37°23N 36°50E 212 D7
Turks & Caicos Is. ☒
W. Indies 21°20N 71°20W 321 B5
Turks Island Passage
Turks & Caicos 21°25N 71°19W 321 B5
Turku Finland 60°30N 22°19E 188 B2
Turkwel ➔ Kenya 3°6N 36°6E 268 B4
Turlock U.S.A. 37°30N 120°51W 306 H6
Turnagain Australia 9°34S 142°17E 280 a
Turnagain ➔ Canada 59°12N 127°35W 296 B3
Turnagain, C. N.Z. 40°28S 176°38E 284 G5
Turneffe Is. Belize 17°20N 87°50W 320 C2
Turner U.S.A. 48°51N 108°24W 304 B9
Turner Field
Atlanta, U.S.A. 33°44N 84°23W 113 B2
Turner Pt. Australia 11°47S 133°32E 280 A1
Turner Valley Canada 50°40N 114°17W 296 C6
Turners Falls U.S.A. 42°36N 72°33W 313 D12
Turner's Pen. S. Leone 7°22N 12°24W 262 D2
Turnham Green U.K. 51°29N 0°16W 125 B2
Turnhout Belgium 51°19N 4°57E 170 C4
Türnitz Austria 47°55N 15°29E 180 D8
Turnor L. Canada 56°35N 108°35W 297 B7
Turnov Czechia 50°34N 15°10E 180 A8
Tŭrnovo = Veliko Tarnovo
Bulgaria 43°5N 25°41E 203 C9
Turnu Măgurele Romania 43°46N 24°56E 183 G9
Turnu Roşu, P. Romania 45°33N 24°17E 183 E9
Turobin Poland 50°50N 22°44E 185 H9
Tuross Head Australia 36°3S 150°8E 283 D9
Turpan China 43°58N 89°10E 217 D11
Turpan Pendi China 42°40N 89°25E 217 D11
Turrawan Australia 30°28S 149°53E 283 A8
Turrës, Kala e Albania 41°10N 19°28E 202 E3
Turriff U.K. 57°32N 2°27W 167 D6
Tursāq Iraq 33°27N 45°47E 213 F11
Tursi Italy 40°15N 16°28E 201 B9
Tursunzoda Tajikistan 38°30N 68°14E 217 E7
Turtle Beach
St. Kitts & Nevis 17°14N 62°38W 322 d
Turtle Head I. Australia 10°56S 142°37E 286 F2
Turtle Is. Phil. 6°7N 118°14E 233 H2
Turtle Is. S. Leone 7°40N 13°0W 262 D2
Turtle Islands Phil. 6°13N 118°6E 235 A5
Turtle L. Canada 53°36N 108°38W 297 C7
Turtle Lake U.S.A. 47°31N 100°53W 308 B3
Turtleford Canada 53°23N 108°57W 297 C7
Turtucaia = Tutrakan
Bulgaria 44°2N 26°40E 203 B10
Turua N.Z. 37°14S 175°35E 284 D4
Turukhansk Russia 65°21N 88°5E 215 C9
Turyinskiye Rudniki =
Krasnoturinsk Russia 59°46N 60°12E 186 C11
Turzovka Slovakia 49°25N 18°35E 181 B11
Tuscaloosa U.S.A. 33°12N 87°34W 315 E11
Tuscánia Italy 42°25N 11°52E 199 F8
Tuscany = Toscana □
Italy 43°25N 11°0E 198 E8
Tuscarawas ➔ U.S.A. 40°24N 81°25W 312 F3
Tuscarora Mt. U.S.A. 40°55N 77°55W 312 F7
Tuscola Ill., U.S.A. 39°48N 88°17W 311 E8
Tuscola Tex., U.S.A. 32°12N 99°48W 314 E5
Tuscolana, Via Italy 41°52N 12°31E 136 B2
Tuscumbia Ala., U.S.A. 34°44N 87°42W 315 D11
Tuscumbia Mo., U.S.A. 38°14N 92°28W 310 F4
Tuskegee U.S.A. 32°25N 85°42W 316 C4
Tusket Wedge = Wedgeport
Canada 43°44N 65°59W 299 D6
Tustna Norway 63°10N 8°5E 164 A5
Tuszyn Poland 51°36N 19°33E 185 G6
Tutak Turkey 39°31N 42°46E 213 C10
Tutayev Russia 57°53N 39°32E 188 D10
Tuticorin India 8°50N 78°12E 245 K4
Tutin Serbia 42°58N 20°20E 202 D4
Tutóia Brazil 2°45S 42°20W 332 B3
Tutong Brunei 4°47N 114°40E 235 B4
Tutova ➔ Romania 46°7N 27°30E 183 D12
Tutrakan Bulgaria 44°2N 26°40E 203 B10
Tuttle Creek L. U.S.A. 39°15N 96°36W 308 F5
Tuttlingen Germany 47°58N 8°48E 179 H4
Tutuala Timor-Leste 8°25S 127°15E 231 F7
Tutubeia Papua N. G. 9°34S 150°40E 286 E6
Tutuila Amer. Samoa 14°19S 170°50W 302 f
Tutuko, Mt. N.Z. 44°35S 168°1E 285 E3
Tutum Egypt 29°9N 30°46E 256 J7
Tütz = Tuczno Poland 53°13N 16°10E 185 E3
Tuul Gol ➔ Mongolia 48°30N 104°25E 218 B9
Tuva □ Russia 51°30N 95°0E 217 B12
Tuvalu ■ Pac. Oc. 8°0S 178°0E 277 B14
Tuvuca Fiji 17°40S 178°48W 287 A3
Tuwal Si. Arabia 22°17N 39°6E 248 B2
Tuxer Alpen Austria 47°10N 11°45E 180 D4
Tuxpan Mexico 20°57N 97°24W 319 C5
Tuxtla Gutiérrez Mexico 16°45N 93°7W 319 D6
Tuy = Tui Spain 42°3N 8°39W 194 C2
Tuy Duc Vietnam 12°15N 107°27E 237 F6
Tuy Phong Vietnam 11°14N 108°43E 237 G7
Tuya L. Canada 59°7N 130°35W 296 B2
Tuyen Hoa Vietnam 17°50N 106°10E 236 D6
Tuyen Quang Vietnam 21°50N 105°10E 228 G5
Tuymazy Russia 54°36N 53°42E 216 B4
Tūysarkān Iran 34°33N 48°27E 213 E13
Tuyün = Duyun China 26°18N 107°29E 228 D6
Tuz Gölü Turkey 38°42N 33°18E 212 C5
Ţūz Khurmātū Iraq 34°56N 44°38E 213 E11
Tuzi Montenegro 42°22N 19°20E 202 D3
Tuzigoot △ U.S.A. 34°46N 112°2W 305 J7
Tuzla Bos.-H. 44°34N 18°41E 182 F3
Tuzla Turkey 36°42N 35°6E 250 B6
Tuzlov ➔ Russia 47°17N 39°57E 189 J10
Tuzluca Turkey 40°3N 43°39E 213 B10
Tuzly Ukraine 45°54N 30°6E 183 E15
Tvååker Sweden 57°4N 12°25E 163 G6
Tvardiţa Moldova 46°9N 28°58E 183 D13
Tvarditsa Bulgaria 42°42N 25°53E 203 D9
Tvedestrand Norway 58°38N 8°58E 164 F5
Tver Russia 56°55N 35°59E 188 D8
Tver □ Russia 56°50N 35°0E 188 D8
Tvrdošín Slovakia 49°21N 19°35E 181 B12
Tvrdošovce Slovakia 48°6N 18°4E 181 C11
Tvŭrditsa = Tvarditsa
Bulgaria 42°42N 25°53E 203 D9
Twain U.S.A. 40°1N 121°3W 306 E5
Twain Harte U.S.A. 38°2N 120°14W 306 G6
Twardogóra Poland 51°23N 17°28E 185 G4
Twee River Namibia 25°27S 19°27E 270 C2
Tweed Canada 44°29N 77°19W 312 B7
Tweed ➔ U.K. 55°45N 2°0W 167 F6
Tweed Heads Australia 28°10S 153°31E 281 D5
Tweedsmuir ⌂ Canada 53°0N 126°20W 296 C3
Twelve Apostles S. Africa 33°58S 18°23E 118 A1
Twentieth Century Fox Studios
U.S.A. 34°4N 118°25W 126 B2
Twentynine Palms
U.S.A. 34°8N 116°3W 307 L10
Tweya
Dem. Rep. of the Congo 0°54S 18°58E 264 C3
Twickenham U.K. 51°26N 0°20W 125 B1
Twickenham Rugby Ground
U.K. 51°27N 0°20W 125 B1
Twillingate Canada 49°42N 54°45W 299 C9
Twin Bridges U.S.A. 45°33N 112°20W 304 D7
Twin City U.S.A. 32°35N 82°10W 316 C7
Twin Falls Canada 53°30N 64°32W 299 B7
Twin Falls Idaho, U.S.A. 42°34N 114°28W 304 E6
Twin Hills U.S.A. 59°23N 159°58W 303 G8
Twin Lakes U.S.A. 30°43N 83°13W 316 E6
Twin Peaks U.S.A. 37°45N 122°26W 136 B2
Twin Valley U.S.A. 47°16N 96°16W 308 B5
Twinnge Myanmar 23°10N 96°2E 241 D6
Twins, The
Hong Kong, China 22°15N 114°12E 122 B3
Twinsburg U.S.A. 41°19N 81°26W 312 E3
Twistringen Germany 52°48N 8°37E 178 C4
Twitchell Res. U.S.A. 34°59N 120°19W 307 L6
Two Boats Village
Ascension I. 7°56S 14°22W 153 g
Two Harbors U.S.A. 47°2N 91°40W 308 B8
Two Hills Canada 53°43N 111°52W 296 C6
Two Rivers U.S.A. 44°9N 87°34W 308 C10
Two Rocks Australia 31°30S 115°35E 279 F2
Two Thumb Ra. N.Z. 43°45S 170°44E 285 D5
Twofold B. Australia 37°8S 149°59E 283 D8
Twyfelfontein Namibia 20°34S 14°22E 270 B1
Ty Ty U.S.A. 31°28N 83°39W 316 D6
Tyachiv Ukraine 48°1N 23°35E 177 D12
Tybee Island U.S.A. 32°1N 80°51W 316 C9
Tychy Poland 50°9N 18°59E 185 H5
Tyczyn Poland 49°58N 22°2E 185 J9
Tydal Norway 63°4N 11°34E 164 A8
Tyin Norway 61°18N 8°15E 164 C5
Tykocin Poland 53°13N 22°46E 185 E9
Tyler Minn., U.S.A. 44°17N 96°8W 308 C5
Tyler Tex., U.S.A. 32°21N 95°18W 314 E7
Tyligul ➔ Ukraine 47°4N 30°57E 189 J6
Tylldal Norway 62°8N 10°48E 164 B7
Tymanivka Ukraine 48°34N 28°50E 183 B13
Týn nad Vltavou Czechia 49°13N 14°26E 180 B7
Tynda Russia 55°10N 124°43E 215 D13
Tyndall U.S.A. 43°0N 97°50W 308 D5
Tyndinsky = Tynda
Russia 55°10N 124°43E 215 D13
Tyne ➔ U.K. 54°59N 1°32W 168 C6
Tyne & Wear □ U.K. 55°6N 1°17W 168 B6
Týnec nad Sázavou
Czechia 49°50N 14°36E 180 B7
Tynemouth U.K. 55°1N 1°26W 168 B6
Tynset Norway 62°17N 10°47E 164 B7
Tyonek U.S.A. 61°4N 151°8W 303 F10
Tyre = Sūr Lebanon 33°19N 35°16E 250 E6
Tyresta △ Sweden 59°12N 18°14E 162 E12
Tyrifjorden Norway 60°2N 10°8E 164 D7
Tyringe Sweden 56°9N 13°35E 163 H7
Tyristrand Norway 60°4N 10°6E 164 D7
Tyrnyauz Russia 43°21N 42°45E 191 J6
Tyrol = Tirol □ Austria 47°3N 10°43E 180 D3
Tyrone U.S.A. 40°40N 78°14W 312 F6
Tyrrel Bay Grenada 12°27N 61°28W 323 q
Tyrrell ➔ Australia 35°26S 142°51E 282 C5
Tyrrell, L. Australia 35°20S 142°50E 282 C5
Tyrrell L. Canada 63°7N 105°27W 297 A7
Tyrrhenian Sea Medit. S. 40°0N 12°30E 192 D6
Tysfjorden Norway 68°7N 16°25E 160 B17
Tysmenytsya Ukraine 48°54N 24°51E 183 B9
Tysnes Norway 60°1N 5°30E 164 D2
Tysnesøya Norway 60°0N 5°35E 164 D2
Tysse Norway 60°23N 5°47E 164 D2
Tyssedal Norway 60°7N 6°35E 164 D3
Tystberga Sweden 58°51N 17°15E 163 F11
Tytuvėnai Lithuania 55°36N 23°12E 184 C10
Tyub Karagan, Mys = Tüpqarghan
Muyis Kazakhstan 44°40N 50°19E 191 H10
Tyuleni, Ostrova = Tüledi Araldary
Kazakhstan 45°2N 50°16E 191 H10
Tyuleniy Russia 44°28N 47°30E 191 H8
Tyuleniy, Mys Azerbaijan 40°12N 50°22E 191 K10
Tyulgan Russia 52°22N 56°12E 186 D10
Tyumen Russia 57°11N 65°29E 214 D7
Tyup = Tüp Kyrgyzstan 42°45N 78°20E 217 D9
Tywi ➔ U.K. 51°48N 4°21W 169 F3
Tywyn U.K. 52°35N 4°5W 169 E3
Tzaneen S. Africa 23°47S 30°9E 271 B5
Tzermiado Greece 35°12N 25°29E 207 E6
Tzia = Kea Greece 37°35N 24°22E 204 D6
Tzoumérka, Oros = Athamanon
Oros Greece 39°30N 21°26E 204 B3
Tzukong = Zigong China 29°15N 104°48E 228 C5
Tzukuan Taiwan 22°46N 120°16E 225 D2
Tzupo = Boshan China 36°28N 117°49E 227 F9
Tzutung Taiwan 23°45N 120°30E 225 C2

U

U.S.A. = United States of America ■
N. Amer. 37°0N 96°0W 301 H20
U.S. Capitol Washington, D.C., U.S.A. 143 b3
U.S. Cellular Field
Chicago, U.S.A. 41°50N 87°37W 119 C3
U.S.S. Arizona ⌂
U.S.A. 21°22N 157°57W 302 K14
U.S.S. Constitution Boston, U.S.A. 116 a3
U.S. Virgin Is. ☒ W. Indies 18°20N 65°0W 321 C7
Ua Huka French Polynesia 8°55S 139°32W 289 f
Ua Pu French Polynesia 9°25S 140°0W 289 f
Uachadi, Sierra = Uasadi-jidi
Venezuela 4°54N 65°18W 329 C4
Uad Atui ➔ W. Sahara 20°4N 15°59W 260 D2
Uad el Jat ➔ W. Sahara 26°47N 13°3W 260 C2
Uaimh, An = Navan
Ireland 53°39N 6°41W 166 C5
Uainambi Colombia 1°43N 69°51W 328 C4
Uamba Angola 7°21S 16°10E 265 D3
Uanle Uen = Wanleweyne
Somalia 2°37N 44°54E 267 D5
Uasadi-jidi Venezuela 4°54N 65°18W 329 C4
Uasin Gishu □ Kenya 0°30N 35°15E 268 B4
Uati-Paraná ➔ Brazil 1°51S 65°37W 328 D4
Uatumã ➔ Brazil 2°26S 57°37W 329 D6
Uauá Brazil 9°50S 39°28W 332 C4
Uaupés Brazil 0°8S 67°5W 328 D4
Uaupés ➔ Brazil 0°2N 67°16W 328 C4
Uaxactún Guatemala 17°25N 89°29W 320 C2
Ub Serbia 44°28N 20°6E 202 B4
Ubá Brazil 21°8S 43°0W 333 F3
Uba Nigeria 10°29N 13°13E 263 C7
Ubai Papua N. G. 5°39S 150°38E 286 C6
Ubaitaba Brazil 14°18S 39°20W 333 D4
Ubajara △ Brazil 3°55S 40°50W 332 B3
Ubangi = Oubangi ➔
Dem. Rep. of the Congo 0°30S 17°50E 264 C3
Ubaté Colombia 5°19N 73°49W 328 B3
Ubauro Pakistan 28°15N 69°45E 242 E3
Ubay Phil. 10°3N 124°28E 233 F5
Ubaye ➔ France 44°28N 6°18E 175 D10
Ubayyiḍ, W. al ➔ Iraq 32°34N 43°48E 213 F10
Ube Japan 33°56N 131°15E 222 D3
Úbeda Spain 38°3N 3°23W 195 G7
Ubeidiya West Bank 31°43N 35°17E 123 B2
Uberaba Brazil 19°50S 47°55W 333 E2
Uberaba ➔ Brazil 23°35S 46°41W 137 B2
Uberaba, L. Brazil 17°30S 57°50W 331 D6
Uberlândia Minas Gerais,
Brazil 19°0S 48°20W 333 E2
Uberlândia Roraima, Brazil 0°48N 59°20W 329 C6
Überlingen Germany 47°46N 9°10E 179 H5
Ubiaja Nigeria 6°41N 6°22E 263 D6
Ubin, Pulau Singapore 1°24N 103°57E 138 A3
Ubly U.S.A. 43°42N 82°55W 312 C2
Ubolratna Res. Thailand 16°45N 102°30E 236 D4
Ubombo S. Africa 27°31S 32°4E 271 C5
Ubon Ratchathani
Thailand 15°15N 104°50E 236 E5
Ubondo
Dem. Rep. of the Congo 0°55S 25°42E 268 C2
Ubort ➔ Belarus 52°6N 28°30E 177 B15
Ubrique Spain 36°41N 5°27W 195 J5
Ubud Indonesia 8°30S 115°16E 231 J18
Ubuna Solomon Is. 10°11S 161°24E 287 N11
Ubundu
Dem. Rep. of the Congo 0°22S 25°30E 264 C5
Ucar Azerbaijan 40°31N 47°39E 191 K8
Ucayali ➔ Peru 4°30S 73°30W 328 D3
Uccle Belgium 50°48N 4°22E 116 B2
Uchab Namibia 19°47S 17°42E 270 A2
Uchiko Japan 33°33N 132°39E 222 D4
Uchiura-Wan Japan 42°25N 140°40E 220 C10
Uchiza Peru 8°25S 76°20W 330 B2
Uchquduq Uzbekistan 41°50N 62°50E 216 D6
Uchte Germany 52°30N 8°54E 178 C4
Uchur ➔ Russia 58°48N 130°35E 215 D14
Uckermark Germany 53°5N 13°30E 178 B9
Ucluelet Canada 48°57N 125°32W 296 D3
Úcua Angola 8°43S 14°8E 265 D2
Uda ➔ Russia 54°42N 135°14E 215 D14
Uda Walawe △ Sri Lanka 6°20N 81°0E 245 L5
Udachnyy Russia 66°25N 112°24E 215 C12
Udagamandalam India 11°30N 76°44E 245 J3
Udainagar India 22°33N 76°13E 242 H7
Udaipur Raj., India 24°36N 73°44E 242 G5
Udaipur Tripura, India 23°32N 91°30E 241 D3
Udaipur Garhi Nepal 27°0N 86°35E 243 F12
Udala India 21°35N 86°34E 243 J12
Udalguri India 26°46N 92°8E 241 B4
Udayagiri Andhra Pradesh,
India 14°52N 79°19E 245 G4
Udayagiri Odisha, India 20°8N 84°23E 244 D7
Udbina Croatia 44°31N 15°47E 199 D12
Uddeholm Sweden 60°1N 13°38E 162 D7
Uddevalla Sweden 58°21N 11°55E 163 F5
Uddheden Sweden 59°57N 12°54E 162 E6
Uddjaure Sweden 65°56N 17°49E 160 D17
Udegeyskaya Legenda △
Russia 45°45N 135°30E 220 B7
Udelnaya Russia 60°0N 30°21E 137 A2
Udelnoe Russia 59°58N 30°20E 137 B1
Uden Neths. 51°40N 5°37E 170 C5
Udgir India 18°25N 77°5E 244 E3
Udhampur India 33°0N 75°5E 243 C6
Udi Nigeria 6°17N 7°21E 263 D6
Údine Italy 46°3N 13°14E 199 B10
Udintsev Fracture Zone
S. Ocean 57°0S 145°0W 151 B13
Udlding Germany 48°15N 11°25E 131 A1
Udmurtia □ Russia 57°30N 52°30E 186 C9
Udon Thani Thailand 17°29N 102°46E 236 D4
Udong Cambodia 11°48N 104°45E 237 G5
Udot I. Micronesia 7°22N 151°42E 287 T17
Udskaya Guba Russia 54°50N 135°45E 215 D14
Udu Pt. Fiji 16°9S 179°57W 287 A3
Udumalaippettai India 10°35N 77°15E 245 J3
Udupi India 13°25N 74°42E 245 H2
Udva India 20°5N 73°0E 244 D1
Udvoy Balkan Bulgaria 42°50N 26°50E 203 D10
Udzungwa △ Tanzania 7°52S 36°53E 268 D4
Udzungwa Range Tanzania 9°30S 35°10E 269 D4
Ueckermünde Germany 53°44N 14°1E 178 B10
Ueda Japan 36°24N 138°16E 223 A10
Uedineniya, Os. Russia 78°0N 85°0E 150 B12
Uele ➔
Dem. Rep. of the Congo 3°45N 24°45E 264 B4
Uelen Russia 66°10N 170°0W 215 C19
Uelzen Germany 52°57N 10°32E 178 C6
Ueno Mie, Japan 34°45N 136°8E 223 C8
Ueno Tōkyō, Japan 35°42N 139°46E 140 A3
Uetersen Germany 53°40N 9°40E 178 B5
Uetze Germany 52°28N 10°11E 178 C6
Ufa Russia 54°45N 55°55E 186 D10
Ufa ➔ Russia 54°40N 56°0E 186 D10
Uffenheim Germany 49°33N 10°14E 179 F6
Ugab ➔ Namibia 20°55S 13°30E 270 B1
Ugalla ➔ Tanzania 5°8S 30°42E 268 D3
Ugalla River △ Tanzania 5°50S 31°54E 268 D3
Uganda ■ Africa 2°0N 32°0E 268 B3
Ugarchin Bulgaria 43°6N 24°26E 203 C8
Ugento Italy 39°56N 18°10E 201 C11
Ugep Nigeria 5°53N 8°2E 263 D6
Ughelli Nigeria 5°33N 6°0E 263 D6
Ugie S. Africa 31°10S 28°13E 271 D4
Ugijar Spain 36°58N 3°7W 195 J7
Ugine France 45°45N 6°25E 175 C10
Uglegorsk Russia 49°5N 142°2E 215 E15
Uglich Russia 57°33N 38°20E 188 D10
Ugljan Croatia 44°12N 15°10E 199 D12
Ugljane Croatia 43°35N 16°46E 199 E13
Ugolny = Beringovskiy
Russia 63°3N 179°19E 215 C18
Ugolny = Karpinsk Russia 59°45N 60°1E 186 C11
Ugolnye Kopi = Kopeysk
Russia 55°7N 61°37E 216 A6
Ugolnye Kopi Russia 64°44N 177°42E 215 C18
Ugoofaaru Maldives 5°40N 73°0E 272 d
Ugra ➔ Russia 54°30N 36°7E 188 E9
Ugra △ Russia 54°45N 35°30E 188 E8
Ugŭrchin = Ugarchin
Bulgaria 43°6N 24°26E 203 C8
Uh ➔ Slovakia 48°37N 22°0E 181 C15
Uherské Hradiště Czechia 49°4N 17°30E 181 B10
Uherský Brod Czechia 49°1N 17°40E 181 B10
Úhlava ➔ Czechia 49°45N 13°24E 180 B6
Uhlenhorst Namibia 23°45S 17°55E 270 B2
Uhniv Ukraine 50°22N 23°45E 185 H10
Ůholičky Czechia 50°9N 14°19E 135 B1
Uhrichsville U.S.A. 40°24N 81°21W 312 F3
Uhříněves Czechia 50°2N 14°35E 135 B3
Uibhist a Deas = South Uist
U.K. 57°20N 7°15W 167 D1
Uibhist a Tuath = North Uist
U.K. 57°40N 7°15W 167 D1
Uiche Angola 12°2S 20°51E 265 E4
Uido S. Korea 34°36N 125°50E 224 E2
Uig U.K. 57°35N 6°21W 167 D2
Uíge Angola 7°30S 14°40E 265 D2
Uíge □ Angola 7°0S 16°0E 265 D3
Uiha Tonga 19°54S 174°25W 287 P13
Uijeongbu S. Korea 37°44N 127°2E 224 D3
Ŭiju N. Korea 40°15N 124°35E 224 B2
Uinta Mts. U.S.A. 40°45N 110°30W 304 F8
Uiryeong S. Korea 35°19N 128°15E 224 E4
Uis Namibia 21°8S 14°49E 270 B1
Uiseong S. Korea 36°21N 128°45E 224 D4
Uitenhage = Kariega
S. Africa 33°40S 25°28E 270 D4
Uithoorn Neths. 52°14N 4°50E 112 B1
Uithuizen Neths. 53°24N 6°41E 170 A6
Ujazd Poland 50°23N 18°21E 185 H5
Ujazdów Poland 52°13N 21°1E 143 B2
Ujazdowski Castle Warsaw, Poland 143 c3
Újfehértó Hungary 47°49N 21°41E 182 C6
Ujh ➔ India 32°10N 75°18E 242 C6
Ujhani India 28°0N 79°6E 243 F8
Uji Japan 34°53N 135°48E 223 C7
Uji-guntō Japan 31°15N 129°25E 221 J4
Ujiyamada = Ise Japan 34°25N 136°45E 223 C8
Ujjain India 23°9N 75°43E 242 H6
Újpalota Hungary 47°32N 19°8E 117 A2
Újpest Hungary 47°35N 19°4E 117 A2
Ujście Poland 53°3N 16°45E 185 E3
Ujście Warty △ Poland 52°35N 14°35E 185 F1
Újszász Hungary 47°19N 20°7E 182 C5
Ujung Kulon △ Indonesia 6°46S 105°19E 234 D3
Ujung Pandang = Makassar
Indonesia 5°10S 119°20E 235 D5
Uka Russia 57°50N 162°0E 215 D17
Ukai Sagar India 21°20N 73°43E 244 D1
Ukara I. Tanzania 1°50S 33°0E 268 C3
Uke-Shima Japan 28°2N 129°14E 221 K4
Ukerewe I. Tanzania 2°0S 33°0E 268 C3
uKhahlamba Drakensberg ⌂
S. Africa 29°27S 29°30E 271 C4
Ukholovo Russia 53°47N 40°30E 190 D5
Ukhrul India 25°10N 94°25E 241 C5
Ukhta Russia 63°34N 53°41E 186 B9
Uki Ni Masi Solomon Is. 10°15S 161°47E 287 N11
Ukiah U.S.A. 39°9N 123°13W 306 F3
Ukita Japan 35°40N 139°51E 140 A4
Ukkusiksalik △ Canada 65°20N 89°30W 294 D14
Ukmergė Lithuania 55°15N 24°45E 188 E3
Ukraine ■ Europe 49°0N 32°0E 189 H7
Uku Angola 11°24S 14°22E 265 E2
Ukwi Botswana 23°29S 20°30E 270 B3
Ula Turkey 37°6N 28°25E 212 D3
Ulaan Nuur Mongolia 44°30N 103°40E 226 B2
Ulaan-Uul Mongolia 46°4N 100°49E 218 B9
Ulaanbaatar Mongolia 47°55N 106°53E 218 B10
Ulaangom Mongolia 50°5N 92°10E 217 B12
Ulaanjirem Mongolia 45°5N 105°30E 226 B3
Ulak I. U.S.A. 51°22N 178°57W 303 L3
Ulala = Gorno-Altaysk
Russia 51°50N 86°5E 217 B11
Ulalu I. Micronesia 7°23N 151°47E 287 T17
Ulamambri Australia 31°19S 149°23E 283 A8
Ulamba
Dem. Rep. of the Congo 9°3S 23°38E 265 D4
Ulamona Papua N. G. 5°0S 151°15E 286 C6
Ulan Bator = Ulaanbaatar
Mongolia 47°55N 106°53E 218 B10
Ulan Erge Russia 46°19N 44°53E 191 G7
Ulan Khol Russia 45°18N 47°4E 191 H8
Ulan Ude Russia 51°45N 107°40E 219 A10
Ulanhad = Chifeng
China 42°18N 118°58E 227 C10
Ulanhot = Horqin Youyi Qianqi
China 46°5N 122°3E 227 A12
Ulanów Poland 50°30N 22°16E 185 H9
Ulansuhai Nur China 40°53N 108°51E 226 D5
Ulaş Sivas, Turkey 39°26N 37°2E 212 C7
Ulaş Tekirdağ, Turkey 41°14N 27°42E 203 E11
Ulawa Solomon Is. 9°46S 161°57E 287 M11
Ulawun, Mt. Papua N. G. 5°3S 151°20E 286 C6
Ulaya Morogoro, Tanzania 7°3S 36°55E 268 D4
Ulaya Tabora, Tanzania 4°25S 33°30E 268 C3
Ulcinj Montenegro 41°58N 19°10E 202 E3
Ulco S. Africa 28°21S 24°15E 270 C3
Ule älv = Oulujoki ➔
Finland 65°1N 25°30E 160 D21
Ule träsk = Oulujärvi
Finland 64°25N 27°15E 160 D22
Uleåborg = Oulu Finland 65°1N 25°29E 160 D21
Ulefoss Norway 59°17N 9°16E 164 E6
Uleta U.S.A. 25°27N 80°10W 129 C2
Ulëz Albania 41°46N 19°54E 202 E3
Ulfborg Denmark 56°16N 8°20E 163 H2
Ulhasnagar India 19°15N 73°10E 244 E1
Uliastay Mongolia 47°56N 97°28E 218 B8
Uljin S. Korea 36°59N 129°24E 224 D4
Uljma Serbia 45°2N 21°10E 182 E6
Ülken Kazakhstan 45°12N 73°58E 217 C8
Ülken Borsyq Qumy
Kazakhstan 47°0N 59°11E 216 C5
Ulla ➔ Spain 42°39N 8°44W 194 C2
Ulladulla Australia 35°21S 150°29E 283 C9
Ullal India 12°48N 74°51E 245 H2
Ullapool U.K. 57°54N 5°9W 167 D3
Ullared Sweden 57°8N 12°42E 163 G6
Ulldecona Spain 40°36N 0°20E 196 E5
Ullerup Denmark 55°34N 12°36E 118 B3
Ulleungdo S. Korea 37°30N 130°30E 224 D5
Ullevål Norway 59°56N 10°46E 133 A3
Ullswater Ont., Canada 45°12N 79°29W 312 A5
Ullswater Cumb., U.K. 54°34N 2°52W 168 C5
Ulm Germany 48°23N 9°58E 179 G5
Ulmarra Australia 29°37S 153°4E 281 D5
Ulmeni Buzău, Romania 45°4N 26°40E 183 E11
Ulmeni Maramureș,
Romania 47°28N 23°18E 183 C8
Ulonguè Mozam. 14°37S 34°19E 269 E3
Ulricehamn Sweden 57°46N 13°26E 163 G7
Ulrika Sweden 58°5N 15°23E 163 F9
Ulriksdal Sweden 59°23N 17°59E 139 A1
Ulsan S. Korea 35°20N 129°15E 224 E4
Ulsberg Norway 62°45N 10°0E 164 B6
Ulsta U.K. 60°30N 1°9W 167 A7
Ulsteinvik Norway 62°21N 5°53E 164 B2
Ulster □ U.K. 54°35N 6°30W 166 B5
Ulstrem Bulgaria 42°1N 26°27E 203 D10
Ultima Australia 35°30S 143°18E 282 C5
Ulu Temburong △ Brunei 4°27N 115°15E 235 B5
Ulubat Gölü Turkey 40°9N 28°35E 203 F12

Ulubey Turkey 38°25N 29°18E 205 C11
Uluborlu Turkey 38°4N 30°28E 205 C12
Uluçinar Turkey 36°24N 35°53E 250 B6
Uludağ Turkey 40°4N 29°13E 203 F13
Uludağ △ Turkey 40°5N 29°12E 203 F13
Uludere Turkey 37°28N 42°42E 213 D10
Ulugqat China 39°48N 74°15E 217 E8
Uluguru Mts. Tanzania 7°15S 37°40E 268 D4
Ulukhaktok Canada 70°44N 117°44W 294 C8
Ulukışla = Marathóvounos Cyprus 35°13N 33°37E 207 E9
Ulukışla Turkey 37°33N 34°28E 212 D6
Ulundi S. Africa 28°20S 31°25E 271 C5
Ulungur He → China 47°1N 87°24E 217 C11
Ulungur Hu China 47°20N 87°10E 217 C11
Ulupalakua U.S.A. 20°39N 156°24W 302 C5
Uluru Australia 25°23S 131°5E 279 E5
Uluru-Kata Tjuta △ Australia 25°19S 131°1E 279 E5
Uluwatu Indonesia 8°50S 115°5E 231 K18
Ulva U.K. 56°29N 6°13W 167 E2
Ulverston U.K. 54°13N 3°5W 168 C4
Ulverstone Australia 41°11S 146°11E 281 G4
Ulvik Norway 60°35N 6°54E 164 D3
Ulya Russia 59°10N 142°0E 215 D15
Ulyanka Russia 59°50N 30°14E 137 B1
Ulyanovo Russia 54°50N 22°6E 184 D9
Ulyanovsk Russia 54°20N 48°25E 190 C9
Ulyanovsk □ Russia 54°5N 48°5E 190 C9
Ulyasutay = Uliastay Mongolia 47°56N 97°28E 218 B8
Ulysses Kans., U.S.A. 37°35N 101°22W 308 G3
Ulysses Pa., U.S.A. 41°54N 77°46W 312 E7
Ulysses, Mt. Canada 57°20N 124°5W 296 B4
Ulysses S. Grant Nat. Historic Site ⌂ U.S.A. 38°33N 90°28W 310 F6
Ulytau Kazakhstan 48°39N 67°1E 217 C7
Ulyzhylanshyq → Kazakhstan 48°51N 63°46E 216 C6
Um Al Khanazir I. Iraq 33°17N 44°22E 113 B2
Umag Croatia 45°26N 13°31E 199 C10
Umala Bolivia 17°25S 68°5W 330 D4
'Umān = Oman ■ Asia 23°0N 58°0E 249 B7
Uman Ukraine 48°40N 30°12E 177 D16
Uman I. Micronesia 7°17N 151°52E 287 U18
Umaria India 23°35N 80°50E 243 H9
Umarkhed India 19°37N 77°46E 244 E3
Umarkot Pakistan 25°15N 69°40E 242 G3
Umarpada India 21°27N 73°30E 242 J5
Umatac Guam 13°18N 144°39E 302 d
Umatilla U.S.A. 45°55N 119°21W 304 D4
Umba Russia 66°42N 34°11E 186 A5
Umbagog L. U.S.A. 44°46N 71°3W 313 B13
Umbakumba Australia 13°47S 136°50E 280 A2
Umbértide Italy 43°18N 12°20E 199 E9
Umboi I. Papua N. G. 5°40S 148°0E 286 C5
Umbrella Mts. N.Z. 45°35S 169°5E 285 F4
Umbria □ Italy 42°53N 12°30E 199 F9
Umeå Sweden 63°45N 20°20E 160 E19
Umeälven → Sweden 63°45N 20°20E 160 E19
Umeda Japan 34°41N 135°29E 133 A1
Umera Indonesia 0°12S 129°37E 231 E7
Umerkhadi Mumbai, India 130 b2
Umfuli → Zimbabwe 17°30S 29°23E 269 F2
Umfurudzi ⌂ Zimbabwe 17°6S 31°40E 269 F3
Umgusa Zimbabwe 19°29S 27°52E 269 F2
Umgwenya → Mozam. 25°14S 32°18E 271 C5
Umiat U.S.A. 69°22N 152°8W 303 B9
Umiray Phil. 15°13N 121°25E 232 D3
Umiujaq Canada 56°33N 76°33W 298 A4
Umka Serbia 44°40N 20°19E 202 B4
Umkomaas S. Africa 30°13S 30°48E 271 D5
Umm ad Daraj, J. Jordan 32°18N 35°48E 251 F6
Umm al Arānib Libya 26°10N 14°43E 258 C2
Umm al Khashab Si. Arabia 17°23N 42°32E 256 D5
Umm al Qaywayn U.A.E. 25°30N 55°35E 247 E7
Umm al Qittayn Jordan 32°18N 36°40E 251 F7
Umm al Rasas Jordan 31°30N 35°55E 251 G6
Umm al Sheif U.A.E. 25°9N 55°13E 119 B1
Umm al'Abīd Libya 27°31N 15°2E 258 C3
Umm Arda Sudan 15°17N 32°31E 257 D3
Umm Bāb Qatar 25°12N 50°48E 247 E6
Umm Badr Sudan 14°13N 27°58E 257 E2
Umm Bel Sudan 13°35N 28°0E 257 E2
Umm Birkah Si. Arabia 27°44N 36°31E 256 B4
Umm Boim Sudan 11°43N 25°27E 257 E2
Umm Dam Sudan 13°45N 30°59E 257 E3
Umm Debi Sudan 14°37N 30°23E 257 E3
Umm Dubban Sudan 15°23N 32°52E 257 D3
Umm Durman = Omdurmân Sudan 15°40N 32°28E 257 D3
Umm el Fahm Israel 32°31N 35°9E 251 F6
Umm el Ketef, Khalîg Egypt 23°40N 35°35E 246 F2
Umm Gafala Sudan 13°22N 27°15E 257 E2
Umm Gimala Sudan 11°27N 28°12E 257 E2
Umm Inderaba Sudan 17°30N 33°13E 256 D3
Umm Isheirât, G. Egypt 28°21N 34°18E 251 K5
Umm Keddada Sudan 13°33N 26°35E 257 E2
Umm Koweika Sudan 13°10N 32°16E 257 E3
Umm Lajj Si. Arabia 25°0N 37°23E 246 E3
Umm Merwa Sudan 18°4N 32°30E 256 D3
Umm Qantur Sudan 14°17N 31°22E 257 E3
Umm Qasr Iraq 30°1N 47°58E 246 D5
Umm Qurein Sudan 9°58N 28°55E 257 F2
Umm Ruwaba Sudan 12°50N 31°20E 257 E3
Umm Sa'id Qatar 25°0N 51°33E 247 E6
Umm Saiyala Sudan 14°25N 31°10E 257 E3
Umm Shanqa Sudan 13°14N 27°14E 266 B2
Umm Shugeira Sudan 13°34N 29°37E 266 B2
Umm Shutur South Sudan 7°17N 33°14E 257 F3
Umm Sidr Sudan 14°29N 25°10E 257 E2
Umm Suqeim U.A.E. 25°11N 55°14E 119 B1
Umm Tais △ Qatar 26°7N 51°15E 247 E6
Umm Urūmah Si. Arabia 25°43N 36°35E 256 B4
Umm Zehetir Egypt 28°48N 32°31E 256 J8
Umnak I. U.S.A. 53°15N 168°20W 303 K5
Umniati → Zimbabwe 16°49S 28°45E 269 F2
Umpqua → U.S.A. 43°40N 124°12W 304 E1
Umpulo Angola 12°38S 17°42E 265 E3
Ümraniye Turkey 41°1N 29°4E 122 B2
Umred India 20°51N 79°18E 244 D4
Umreth India 22°41N 73°4E 242 H5
Umri India 19°2N 77°39E 244 E3
Umtata = Mthatha S. Africa 31°36S 28°49E 271 D4
Umuahia Nigeria 5°31N 7°26E 263 D6
Umuarama Brazil 23°45S 53°20W 335 A5
Umuda I. Papua N. G. 8°29S 143°46E 286 E2
Umurbey Turkey 40°13N 26°36E 203 F10
Umvukwe Ra. Zimbabwe 16°45S 30°45E 269 F3
Umzimvubu S. Africa 31°38S 29°33E 271 D4
Umzingwane → Zimbabwe 22°12S 29°56E 269 G2
Umzinto = eMuziwezinto S. Africa 30°15S 30°45E 271 D5
Una India 20°46N 71°8E 242 J4
Una → Bos.-H. 45°0N 16°20E 199 D13
Unac → Bos.-H. 44°30N 16°9E 199 D13
Unaðsdalur Iceland 66°7N 22°36W 155 A4
Unadilla Ga., U.S.A. 32°16N 83°44W 316 C6
Unadilla N.Y., U.S.A. 42°20N 75°19W 313 D9
Unaí Brazil 16°23S 46°53W 333 E2
Unalakleet U.S.A. 63°52N 160°47W 303 E7
Unalaska U.S.A. 53°53N 166°32W 303 K6
Unalaska I. U.S.A. 53°35N 166°50W 303 K6
'Unayzah Si. Arabia 26°6N 43°58E 246 E4
'Unayzah, J. Asia 32°12N 39°18E 213 F8
Uncastillo Spain 42°21N 1°8W 196 C3
Uncía Bolivia 18°25S 66°40W 330 D4
Uncompahgre Peak U.S.A. 38°4N 107°28W 304 G10
Uncompahgre Plateau U.S.A. 38°20N 108°15W 304 G9
Undara Volcanic △ Australia 18°14S 144°41E 280 B3
Unden Sweden 58°45N 14°25E 163 F8
Underbool Australia 35°10S 141°51E 282 C4
Underground Atlanta U.S.A. 33°45N 84°24W 113 B2
Underhill, L. U.S.A. 28°32N 81°20W 133 A3
Undersaker Sweden 63°19N 13°21E 162 A7
Underwood Canada 44°18N 81°29W 312 B3
Undredal Norway 60°57N 7°6E 164 D4
Unea I. Papua N. G. 4°53S 149°9E 286 C5
Unecha Russia 52°50N 32°37E 189 F7
Uneiuxi → Brazil 0°37S 65°34W 328 D4
Unětický potok → Czechia 50°9N 14°24E 135 B2
Unga I. U.S.A. 55°15N 160°40W 303 J7
Ungarie Australia 33°38S 146°56E 283 B7
Ungarisch-Hradisch = Uherské Hradiště Czechia 49°4N 17°30E 181 B10
Ungarisch-Ostra = Uherský Brod Czechia 49°1N 17°40E 181 B10
Ungarra Australia 34°12S 136°2E 282 C2
Ungat Papua N. G. 2°40S 150°15E 286 B6
Ungava, Pén. d' Canada 60°0N 74°0W 295 F17
Ungava B. Canada 59°30N 67°30W 295 F18
Ungeny = Ungheni Moldova 47°11N 27°51E 183 C12
Unggi N. Korea 42°16N 130°28E 224 A5
Ungheni Moldova 47°11N 27°51E 183 C12
Unguala → Ethiopia 8°6N 41°9E 257 F5
Unguja = Zanzibar Tanzania 6°12S 39°12E 268 D4
Ungvár = Uzhhorod Ukraine 48°36N 22°18E 182 B7
Ungwana B. Kenya 2°45S 40°20E 268 C5
Ungwatiri Sudan 16°52N 36°10E 257 D4
Unhos Portugal 38°49N 9°7W 126 A2
Uni Russia 57°46N 51°31E 190 B10
União Brazil 4°35S 42°52W 332 B3
União da Vitória Brazil 26°13S 51°5W 335 B5
União dos Palmares Brazil 9°10S 36°2W 332 C4
Uničov Czechia 49°46N 17°8E 181 B10
Unidad Santa Fe Mexico 19°23N 99°13W 128 B1
Uniejów Poland 51°59N 18°46E 185 G5
Unije Croatia 44°40N 14°15E 199 D11
Unimak I. U.S.A. 54°45N 164°0W 303 J7
Unimak Pass. U.S.A. 54°15N 164°30W 303 J6
Unini → Brazil 1°41S 61°31W 329 D5
Union Miss., U.S.A. 32°34N 89°7W 315 E10
Union Mo., U.S.A. 38°27N 91°0W 310 F6
Union Ohio, U.S.A. 39°55N 84°12W 311 E12
Union S.C., U.S.A. 34°43N 81°37W 315 D14
Union City Calif., U.S.A. 37°36N 122°1W 306 H4
Union City Ga., U.S.A. 33°35N 84°33W 316 B5
Union City New York, U.S.A. 132 b1
Union City Ohio, U.S.A. 40°12N 84°48W 311 D12
Union City Pa., U.S.A. 41°54N 79°51W 312 E5
Union City Tenn., U.S.A. 36°26N 89°3W 315 C10
Union Dale U.S.A. 41°43N 75°29W 313 E9
Union Gap U.S.A. 46°33N 120°28W 304 C3
Union Grove U.S.A. 42°41N 88°3W 311 B8
Union I. St. Vincent 12°36N 61°26W 323 n
Union Park U.S.A. 28°34N 81°17W 317 G8
Union Passenger Terminal New Orleans, U.S.A. 131 b1
Union Point U.S.A. 33°37N 83°4W 316 B6
Union Port U.S.A. 40°48N 73°51W 132 B2
Union Springs Ala., U.S.A. 32°9N 85°43W 316 C4
Union Springs N.Y., U.S.A. 42°50N 76°41W 313 D8
Union Square Hong Kong, China 22°19N 114°9E 122 B2
Union Square San Francisco, U.S.A. 136 b2
Union Star U.S.A. 39°59N 94°36W 310 E2
Union Station Toronto, Canada 141 c2
Union Station Chicago, U.S.A. 119 c1
Union Station Los Angeles, U.S.A. 127 b3
Union Station Washington, D.C., U.S.A. 143 b3
Union Station Plaza Washington, D.C., U.S.A. 143 b3
Uniondale S. Africa 33°39S 23°7E 270 D3
Uniontown Ky., U.S.A. 37°47N 87°56W 311 G9
Uniontown Pa., U.S.A. 39°54N 79°44W 309 F14
Unionville Ga., U.S.A. 31°26N 83°30W 316 D6
Unionville Mo., U.S.A. 40°29N 93°1W 310 D3
Unirea Romania 44°15N 27°35E 183 F12
United Arab Emirates ■ Asia 23°50N 54°0E 247 F7
United Arab Republic = Egypt ■ Africa 28°0N 31°0E 256 B3
United Center U.S.A. 41°53N 87°41W 119 B2
United Kingdom ■ Europe 53°0N 2°0W 165 E6
United Nations Headquarters New York, U.S.A. 132 c3
United Provinces = Uttar Pradesh □ India 27°0N 80°0E 243 F9
United States of America ■ N. Amer. 37°0N 96°0W 301 H20
Unity Canada 52°30N 109°5W 297 C7
Unity □ South Sudan 8°30N 30°0E 257 F3
Universal Studios Calif., U.S.A. 34°9N 118°21W 126 B2
Universal Studios Fla., U.S.A. 28°29N 81°29W 133 B2
Universales, Mtes. Spain 40°18N 1°33W 196 E3
Universidad Spain 40°27N 3°44W 127 B1
University City U.S.A. 38°39N 90°18W 310 F6
University Park Md., U.S.A. 38°58N 76°56W 143 B3
University Park N. Mex., U.S.A. 32°17N 106°45W 305 K10
University Park Tex., U.S.A. 32°51N 96°48W 120 A5
University Place U.S.A. 47°14N 122°33W 306 C4
Unjha India 23°46N 72°24E 242 H5
Unmet Vanuatu 16°8S 167°15E 287 F5
Unna Germany 51°32N 7°42E 178 D3
Unnao India 26°35N 80°30E 243 F9
Uno, Ilha Guinea-Biss. 11°15N 16°13W 262 C1
Unruhstadt = Kargowa Poland 52°5N 15°51E 185 F2
Unsan N. Korea 40°6N 125°54E 224 B2
Unsengedsi → Zimbabwe 15°43S 31°14E 269 F3
Unst U.K. 60°44N 0°53W 167 A8
Unstrut → Germany 51°10N 11°48E 178 D7
Unter den Linden Berlin, Germany 115 a4
Unterbiberg Germany 48°6N 11°38E 131 B2
Unterdrauburg = Dravograd Slovenia 46°36N 15°5E 199 B12
Unterföhring Germany 48°11N 11°38E 131 A3
Unterfranken □ Germany 50°0N 10°0E 179 F5
Unterhaching Germany 48°3N 11°37E 131 B2
Unterlaa Austria 48°8N 16°24E 142 B2
Untermenzing Germany 48°10N 11°28E 131 A1
Unterschleissheim Germany 48°17N 11°34E 179 G7
Unuk → Canada 56°5N 131°3W 296 B2
Ünye Turkey 41°5N 37°15E 212 B7
Unzen-Amakusa △ Japan 32°15N 130°10E 222 E2
Unzen-Dake Japan 32°45N 130°17E 222 E2
Unzha Russia 58°0N 44°0E 190 A7
Unzha → Russia 57°49N 43°47E 190 B6
Uong Bi Vietnam 21°2N 106°47E 236 B6
Uotsuri-Shima E. China Sea 25°45N 123°29E 221 M1
Uozu Japan 36°48N 137°24E 223 A9
Upata Venezuela 8°1N 62°24W 329 B5
Upatoi Cr. → U.S.A. 32°22N 84°58W 316 C5
Upemba, L. Dem. Rep. of the Congo 8°30S 26°20E 269 D2
Upemba △ Dem. Rep. of the Congo 9°0S 26°35E 269 D2
Upernavik Greenland 72°49N 56°20W 154 C5
Upington S. Africa 28°25S 21°15E 270 C3
Upleta India 21°46N 70°16E 242 J4
'Upolu Samoa 13°58S 172°0W 287 V20
Upolu Pt. U.S.A. 20°16N 155°52W 302 C6
Upongkor Vanuatu 18°50S 168°59E 287 H6
Upper Alkali L. U.S.A. 41°47N 120°8W 304 F3
Upper Arlington U.S.A. 40°0N 83°4W 311 E13
Upper Arrow L. Canada 50°30N 117°50W 296 C5
Upper Austria = Oberösterreich □ Austria 48°10N 14°0E 180 C7
Upper B. U.S.A. 40°40N 74°3W 132 C1
Upper Daly ✪ Australia 14°26S 131°3E 278 B5
Upper Darby U.S.A. 39°55N 75°16W 309 F16
Upper Demerara-Berbice □ Guyana 5°22N 58°14W 329 B6
Upper East □ Ghana 10°30N 1°0W 263 C4
Upper East Side New York, U.S.A. 132 b3
Upper Elmers End U.K. 51°23N 0°1W 125 B3
Upper Foster L. Canada 56°47N 105°20W 297 B7
Upper Hutt N.Z. 41°8S 175°5E 284 H4
Upper Klamath L. U.S.A. 42°25N 121°55W 304 E3
Upper Lake U.S.A. 39°10N 122°54W 306 F4
Upper Liard Canada 60°3N 128°54W 296 A3
Upper Manilla Australia 30°38S 150°40E 283 A9
Upper Manzanilla Trin. & Tob. 10°31N 61°4W 323 t
Upper Missouri Breaks ⌂ U.S.A. 47°50N 109°55W 304 C9
Upper Musquodoboit Canada 45°10N 62°58W 299 C7
Upper New York B. = Upper B. U.S.A. 40°40N 74°3W 132 C1
Upper Nile □ South Sudan 9°30N 33°0E 257 F3
Upper Norwood U.K. 51°24N 0°6W 125 B3
Upper Peirce Res. Singapore 1°22N 103°47E 138 A2
Upper Red L. U.S.A. 48°8N 94°45W 308 A6
Upper Sandusky U.S.A. 40°50N 83°17W 311 D13
Upper Senegal & Niger = Mali ■ Africa 17°0N 3°0W 262 B4
Upper Sydenham U.K. 51°26N 0°4W 125 B3
Upper Takutu-Upper Essequibo □ Guyana 2°40N 58°59W 329 C6
Upper Tooting U.K. 51°25N 0°9W 125 B3
Upper Volta = Burkina Faso ■ Africa 12°0N 1°0W 262 C4
Upper West □ Ghana 10°30N 2°20W 262 C4
Upper West Side New York, U.S.A. 132 a2
Upphärad Sweden 58°9N 12°19E 163 F6
Uppland Sweden 59°59N 17°48E 162 D12
Upplands-Väsby Sweden 59°31N 17°54E 162 E11
Uppsala Sweden 59°53N 17°38E 162 E11
Uppsala □ Sweden 60°0N 17°30E 162 D11
Upshi India 33°48N 77°52E 243 C7
Upton London, U.K. 51°32N 0°1E 125 A4
Upton Wyo., U.S.A. 44°6N 104°38W 304 D11
Uptown U.S.A. 41°58N 87°40W 119 B2
Uqsuqtuuq = Gjoa Haven Canada 68°38N 95°53W 294 D12
Ur Iraq 30°55N 46°25E 246 D5
Ur Kut Somalia 3°31N 42°47E 267 D5
Ura-Tyube = Istaravshān Tajikistan 39°55N 69°1E 217 E7
Urabá, G. de Colombia 8°25N 76°53W 328 B2
Urad Qianqi China 40°40N 108°30E 226 D5
Uraga-Suidō Japan 35°13N 139°45E 223 B11
Urahoro Japan 42°50N 143°40E 220 C11
Urakawa Japan 42°9N 142°47E 220 C11
Ural = Uralskiy □ Russia 64°0N 70°0E 214 C7
Ural = Zhayyq → Kazakhstan 47°0N 51°48E 187 E9
Ural Australia 33°21S 146°12E 283 B7
Ural Mts. = Uralskie Gory Eurasia 60°0N 59°0E 186 C10
Uralla Australia 30°37S 151°29E 283 A9
Uralmedstroy = Krasnouralsk Russia 58°21N 60°3E 186 C11
Uralsk = Oral Kazakhstan 51°20N 51°20E 190 E10
Uralskie Gory Eurasia 60°0N 59°0E 186 C10
Uralskiy □ Russia 64°0N 70°0E 214 C7
Urambo Tanzania 5°4S 32°0E 268 D3
Uran India 18°53N 72°56E 130 B2
Urana Australia 35°15S 146°21E 283 C7
Urana, L. Australia 35°16S 146°10E 283 C7
Urandangi Australia 21°32S 138°14E 280 C2
Uranga Australia 30°31S 153°1E 283 A10
Uranium City Canada 59°34N 108°37W 297 B7
Urapuntja = Utopia Australia 22°14S 134°33E 280 C1
Uraricaá → Brazil 3°20N 61°56W 329 C5
Uraricoera Brazil 3°27N 60°59W 329 C5
Uraricoera → Brazil 3°2N 60°30W 329 C5
Urasoe Japan 26°15N 127°43E 288 a
Uravakonda India 14°57N 77°12E 245 G3
Urawa = Saitama Japan 35°54N 139°38E 223 B11
Uray Russia 60°5N 65°15E 214 C7
Urayasu Japan 35°39N 139°53E 140 B4
'Uray'irah Si. Arabia 25°57N 48°53E 247 E6
Urbakh = Pushkino Russia 51°16N 47°0E 190 E8
Urbana Ill., U.S.A. 40°7N 88°12W 311 D8
Urbana Ohio, U.S.A. 40°7N 83°45W 311 D13
Urbandale U.S.A. 41°38N 93°43W 310 C3
Urbánia Italy 43°40N 12°31E 199 E9
Urbano Santos Brazil 3°12S 43°23W 332 B3
Urbe ✈ Italy 41°57N 12°30E 136 B2
Urbel → Spain 42°21N 3°40W 194 C7
Urbino Italy 43°43N 12°38E 199 E9
Urbión, Picos de Spain 42°1N 2°52W 196 C2
Urca Brazil 22°56S 43°9W 135 B2
Urcos Peru 13°40S 71°38W 330 C3
Urdaneta Phil. 15°59N 120°34E 232 D3
Urdinarrain Argentina 32°37S 58°52W 334 C4
Urdos France 42°51N 0°35W 174 F3
Ure → U.K. 54°5N 1°20W 168 C6
Uren Russia 57°35N 45°55E 190 B7
Urengoy Russia 65°58N 78°22E 214 C8
Ureparapara Vanuatu 13°32S 167°20E 287 C5
Ures Mexico 29°26N 110°24W 318 B2
Ureshino Japan 33°6N 129°59E 222 D1
Urewera △ N.Z. 38°29S 177°7E 284 E6
Urfa = Sanliurfa Turkey 37°12N 38°50E 213 D8
Urga = Ulaanbaatar Mongolia 47°55N 106°53E 218 B10
Urganch Uzbekistan 41°40N 60°41E 216 D6
Urgench = Urganch Uzbekistan 41°40N 60°41E 216 D6
Ürgüp Turkey 38°38N 34°56E 212 C6
Urho Kekkonen △ Finland 68°20N 27°40E 160 B22
Uri India 34°8N 74°2E 243 B6
Uri □ Switz. 46°43N 8°35E 179 J4
Uribante → Venezuela 7°25N 71°50W 328 B3
Uribe Colombia 3°13N 74°24W 328 C3
Uribia Colombia 11°43N 72°16W 328 A3
Uricani Romania 45°20N 23°9E 182 E8
Urimba Angola 10°56S 16°32E 265 E3
Uriondo Bolivia 21°41S 64°41W 334 A3
Urique Mexico 27°13N 107°55W 318 B3
Urique → Mexico 26°29N 107°58W 318 B3
Uritsk Russia 59°49N 30°10E 137 C1
Urk Neths. 52°39N 5°36E 170 B5
Urkiola ⌂ Spain 43°6N 1°2W 196 B3
Urla Turkey 38°20N 26°47E 205 C8
Urlaţi Romania 44°59N 26°15E 183 F11
Urmia = Orūmīyeh Iran 37°40N 45°0E 213 D11
Urmia, L. = Orūmīyeh, Daryācheh-ye Iran 37°50N 45°30E 213 D11
Urmston Road Hong Kong, China 22°22N 113°55E 122 A1
Üröm Hungary 47°35N 19°1E 117 A2
Uromi Nigeria 6°42N 6°20E 263 D6
Uroševac = Ferizaj Kosovo 42°23N 21°10E 202 D5
Ŭroteppa = Istaravshān Tajikistan 39°55N 69°1E 217 E7
Uroyan, Montanas de Puerto Rico 18°12N 66°50W 321 b
Urrampinyi Iltjiltarri ✪ Australia 24°20S 132°10E 278 D5
Urrao Colombia 6°20N 76°11W 328 B2
Urshult Sweden 56°31N 14°50E 163 H8
Ursus Poland 52°11N 20°52E 143 B1
Ursvik Sweden 59°23N 17°57E 139 A1
Uru Uru, L. Bolivia 18°6S 67°8W 330 D4
Uruaçu Brazil 14°30S 49°10W 333 D2
Uruanã Brazil 15°30S 49°41W 333 E2
Uruapan Mexico 19°24N 102°3W 318 D4
Uruará Brazil 3°42S 53°51W 329 D7
Uruará → Brazil 2°6S 53°38W 329 D7
Urubamba Peru 13°20S 72°10W 330 C3
Urubamba → Peru 10°43S 73°48W 330 C3
Urubaxi → Brazil 0°31S 64°50W 329 D5
Urubu → Brazil 2°55S 58°25W 329 D6
Urucará Brazil 2°32S 57°45W 329 D6
Uruçuí Brazil 7°20S 44°28W 332 C3
Uruçuí, Serra do Brazil 9°0S 44°45W 332 C3
Uruçuí Prêto → Brazil 7°20S 44°38W 332 C3
Urucuia → Brazil 16°8S 45°5W 333 E2
Uruguai → Brazil 26°0S 53°30W 335 B5
Uruguaiana Brazil 29°50S 57°0W 334 B4
Uruguay ■ S. Amer. 32°30S 56°30W 334 C4
Uruguay → S. Amer. 34°12S 58°18W 334 C4
Urukthapel I. Palau 7°17N 134°25E 288 c
Uruma Japan 26°21N 127°52E 288 a
Urumchi = Ürümqi China 43°45N 87°45E 217 D11
Ürümqi China 43°45N 87°45E 217 D11
Uruna ✪ Australia 24°3S 133°1E 278 D5
Urundi = Burundi ■ Africa 3°15S 30°0E 268 C3
Urup → Russia 45°0N 41°10E 191 H5
Urup, Ostrov Russia 46°0N 151°0E 215 E16
Urus-Martan Russia 43°8N 45°33E 191 J7
Urutaí Brazil 17°28S 48°12W 333 E2
Uryupinsk Russia 50°45N 41°58E 190 E5
Ürzhar Kazakhstan 47°5N 81°38E 217 C10
Urzhum Russia 57°10N 49°56E 190 B9
Urziceni Romania 44°40N 26°42E 183 F11
Usa Japan 33°31N 131°21E 222 D3
Usa → Russia 66°16N 59°49E 186 A10
Uşak Turkey 38°43N 29°28E 205 C11
Uşak □ Turkey 38°30N 29°0E 205 C11
Usakos Namibia 21°54S 15°31E 270 B2
Usborne, Mt. Falk. Is. 51°40S 59°55W 153 f
Ušće Serbia 43°30N 20°39E 202 C4
Usedom Germany 53°55N 14°2E 178 B10
Usedom ⌂ Germany 53°55N 14°0E 178 B10
Useless Loop Australia 26°8S 113°23E 279 E1
Usera Spain 40°22N 3°42W 127 B1
'Usfān Si. Arabia 21°58N 39°27E 248 B2
Ushakova, Ostrov Russia 82°0N 80°0E 215 A8
Ushakovo Russia 54°37N 20°16E 184 D7
Ushant = Ouessant, Î. d' France 48°28N 5°6W 172 D1
Üsharal Kazakhstan 46°10N 80°56E 217 C10
Ushashi Tanzania 1°59S 33°57E 268 C3
Ushat South Sudan 7°59N 29°28E 257 F2
'Ushayrah Ar Riyāḍ, Si. Arabia 25°35N 45°47E 246 E5
'Ushayrah Makkah, Si. Arabia 21°46N 40°42E 256 C5
Ushibuka Japan 32°11N 130°1E 222 E2
Ushigome Japan 35°42N 139°44E 140 A3
Üshtöbe Kazakhstan 45°16N 78°0E 217 C9
Ushuaia Argentina 54°50S 68°23W 336 D3
Ushumun Russia 52°47N 126°32E 215 D13
Ushytsya → Ukraine 48°35N 27°8E 183 B12
Usina Brazil 22°57S 43°17W 135 B1
Usino Papua N. G. 5°32S 145°23E 286 C3
Usinsk Russia 65°57N 57°27E 186 A10
Usk Canada 54°38N 128°26W 296 C3
Usk → U.K. 51°33N 2°58W 169 F5
Uska India 27°12N 83°7E 243 F10
Uskedalen Norway 59°56N 5°53E 164 E2
Üsküb = Skopje N. Macedonia 42°1N 21°26E 202 D5
Üsküdar Turkey 41°1N 29°0E 122 B2
Uslar Germany 51°39N 9°38E 178 D5
Usman Russia 52°5N 39°48E 189 F10
Usoke Tanzania 5°8S 32°24E 268 D3
Usolye-Sibirskoye Russia 52°48N 103°40E 215 D11
Usolye-Solikamskoye = Berezniki Russia 59°24N 56°46E 186 C10
Usoro Nigeria 5°33N 6°11E 263 D6
Uspallata, P. de Argentina 32°37S 69°22W 334 C2
Uspenka = Kirovskiy Russia 45°7N 133°30E 220 B6
Ussel France 45°32N 2°18E 174 C6
Usson-du-Poitou France 46°16N 0°31E 174 B4
Ussuriysk Russia 43°48N 131°59E 220 C5
Ussurka Russia 45°12N 133°31E 220 B6
Ust-Aldan = Batamay Russia 63°30N 129°15E 215 C13
Ust-Amginskoye = Khandyga Russia 62°42N 135°35E 215 C14
Ust-Buzulukskaya Russia 50°8N 42°11E 190 E6
Ust-Chaun Russia 68°47N 170°30E 215 C18
Ust-Chorna Ukraine 48°19N 23°56E 183 B8
Ust-Donetskiy Russia 47°35N 40°55E 191 G5
Ust-Dzheguta Russia 44°5N 41°58E 191 H5
Ust-Ilimpeya = Yukta Russia 63°26N 105°42E 215 C11
Ust-Ilimsk Russia 58°3N 102°39E 215 D11
Ust-Ishim Russia 57°45N 71°10E 214 D8
Ust-Kamchatsk Russia 56°10N 162°28E 215 D17
Ust-Kamenogorsk = Öskemen Kazakhstan 50°0N 82°36E 217 C10
Ust-Khayryuzovo Russia 57°15N 156°45E 215 D16
Ust-Kut Russia 56°50N 105°42E 215 D11
Ust-Kuyga Russia 70°1N 135°43E 215 B14
Ust-Labinsk Russia 45°15N 39°41E 191 H4
Ust-Luga Russia 59°35N 28°20E 188 C5
Ust-Maya Russia 60°30N 134°28E 215 C14
Ust-Medveditskaya = Serafimovich Russia 49°36N 42°43E 190 F6
Ust-Mil Russia 59°40N 133°11E 215 D14
Ust-Nera Russia 64°35N 143°15E 215 C15
Ust-Nyukzha Russia 56°34N 121°37E 215 D13
Ust-Olenek Russia 73°0N 120°5E 215 B12
Ust-Omchug Russia 61°9N 149°38E 215 C15
Ust-Port Russia 69°40N 84°26E 214 C9
Ust' Shchugor Russia 64°16N 57°36E 186 B10
Ust-Slavyanka Russia 59°51N 30°32E 137 C3
Ust-Sysolsk = Syktyvkar Russia 61°45N 50°40E 186 B9
Ust-Tsilma Russia 65°28N 52°11E 186 A9
Ust-Urt = Ustyurt Plateau Asia 44°0N 55°0E 216 D5
Ust-Usa Russia 66°2N 56°57E 186 A10
Ust-Vorkuta Russia 67°24N 64°0E 186 A11
Ust-Zhuya = Chara Russia 56°54N 118°20E 215 D12
Ustaoset Norway 60°30N 8°2E 164 D5
Ustaritz France 43°24N 1°27W 174 E2
Ustecký □ Czechia 50°30N 14°0E 180 A7
Uster Switz. 47°22N 8°43E 179 H4
Ústí nad Labem Czechia 50°41N 14°3E 180 A7
Ústí nad Orlicí Czechia 49°58N 16°24E 181 B9
Ústica Italy 38°42N 13°11E 200 D6
Ustinov = Izhevsk Russia 56°51N 53°14E 186 C9
Ustka Poland 54°35N 16°55E 184 D3
Ustroń Poland 49°43N 18°48E 185 J5
Ustrzyki Dolne Poland 49°27N 22°40E 185 J9
Ustupo Panama 9°27N 78°34W 328 B2
Ustyluh Ukraine 50°51N 24°10E 185 H11
Ustyurt Plateau Asia 44°0N 55°0E 216 D5
Ustyuzhna Russia 58°50N 36°32E 188 C9
Usu China 44°27N 84°40E 217 D10
Usuki Japan 33°8N 131°49E 222 D3
Usulután El Salv. 13°25N 88°28W 320 D2
Usumacinta → Mexico 18°24N 92°38W 319 D6
Usumbura = Bujumbura Burundi 3°16S 29°18E 268 C2
Usure Tanzania 4°40S 34°22E 268 C3
Usutuo → Mozam. 26°48S 32°7E 271 C5
Uta Indonesia 4°33S 136°0E 231 E9
Utah □ U.S.A. 39°20N 111°30W 304 G8
Utah L. U.S.A. 40°12N 111°48W 304 F8
Utansjö Sweden 62°46N 17°55E 162 B11
Utara, Selat Malaysia 5°28N 100°20E 237 c
Utarni India 26°5N 71°58E 242 F4
Utatlan Guatemala 15°2N 91°11W 320 C1
Ute Creek → U.S.A. 35°21N 103°50W 305 J12
Utebo Spain 41°43N 1°0W 196 D3
Utegi Tanzania 1°19S 34°13E 266 E3
Uteke Sweden 59°24N 18°15E 139 A3
Utena Lithuania 55°27N 25°40E 188 E3
Utete Tanzania 8°0S 38°45E 268 D4
Uthai Thani Thailand 15°22N 100°3E 236 E3
Uthal Pakistan 25°44N 66°40E 242 G2
Utiariti Brazil 13°0S 58°10W 331 C6
Utica N.Y., U.S.A. 43°6N 75°14W 313 C9
Utica Ohio, U.S.A. 40°14N 82°27W 312 F2
Utiel Spain 39°37N 1°11W 197 F3
Utikuma L. Canada 55°50N 115°30W 296 B5
Utila Honduras 16°6N 86°56W 320 C2
Utinga Brazil 12°6S 41°5W 333 D3
Utkela India 20°6N 83°10E 244 D6
Utlängen Sweden 56°2N 15°48E 163 H9
Utne Norway 60°25N 6°37E 164 D3
Utnur India 19°22N 78°46E 244 E4
Uto Japan 32°41N 130°40E 222 E2
Utö Sweden 58°56N 18°16E 162 F12
Utopia Australia 22°14S 134°33E 280 C1
Utrata Poland 52°15N 21°4E 143 B2
Utraula India 27°19N 82°25E 243 F10
Utrecht Neths. 52°5N 5°8E 170 B5
Utrecht KwaZulu Natal, S. Africa 27°38S 30°20E 271 C5
Utrecht □ Neths. 52°6N 5°7E 170 B5
Utrera Spain 37°12N 5°48W 195 H5
Utría △ Colombia 5°57N 77°21W 328 B2
Utsira Norway 59°19N 4°53E 164 E1
Utsjoki → Finland 69°51N 26°59E 160 B22
Utsunomiya Japan 36°30N 139°50E 223 A11
Uttar Pradesh □ India 27°0N 80°0E 243 F9
Uttaradit Thailand 17°36N 100°5E 236 D3
Uttarakhand □ India 30°0N 79°30E 243 D8
Uttaranchal = Uttarakhand □ India 30°0N 79°30E 243 D8
Uttarpara India 22°39N 88°21E 124 B1
Utterslev Mose Denmark 55°42N 12°29E 118 A2
Utterson Canada 45°12N 79°19W 312 A5
Uttoxeter U.K. 52°54N 1°52W 168 E6
Utuado Puerto Rico 18°16N 66°42W 321 b
Uummannaq Qaasuitsup, Greenland 70°58N 52°17W 150 B5
Uummannaq Qaasuitsup, Greenland 77°33N 68°52W 154 B4
Uummannarsuaq = Nunap Isua Greenland 59°48N 43°55W 154 F6
Uunartoq Qeqertoq Greenland 71°33N 21°47W 154 C8
Uusikaarlepyy Finland 63°32N 22°31E 160 E20
Uusikaupunki Finland 60°47N 21°25E 188 B1
Uva Russia 56°59N 52°13E 190 B11
Uvá → Colombia 3°41N 70°3W 328 C3
Uvac → Serbia 43°35N 19°30E 202 C3
Uvalda U.S.A. 32°2N 82°31W 316 C7
Uvalde U.S.A. 29°13N 99°47W 314 G5
Uvarovo Russia 51°59N 42°14E 190 E6
Uvat Russia 59°5N 68°50E 214 D7
Uvdal Norway 60°17N 8°48E 164 D5
Uvéa, I. Wall. & F. Is. 13°18S 176°10W 277 C15
Uvinza Tanzania 5°5S 30°24E 268 D3
Uvira Dem. Rep. of the Congo 3°22S 29°3E 268 C2
Uvs □ Mongolia 49°38N 93°0E 217 C12
Uvs Nuur Mongolia 50°20N 92°30E 217 B12
Uwa Japan 33°22N 132°31E 222 D4
'Uwairidh, Ḩarrat al Si. Arabia 26°50N 38°0E 246 E3
Uwajima Japan 33°10N 132°35E 222 D4
Uwanda ⌂ Tanzania 7°46S 32°0E 268 D3
Uweinat, Jebel Sudan 21°54N 24°58E 256 C1
Uxbridge Canada 44°6N 79°7W 312 B5
Uxin Qi China 38°50N 109°5E 226 E5
Uxmal Mexico 20°22N 89°46W 319 C7
Uyak U.S.A. 57°38N 154°0W 303 H9
Üydzin Mongolia 44°9N 107°0E 226 B4
Uyo Nigeria 5°1N 7°53E 263 D6
Uyu → Myanmar 24°51N 94°57E 241 C5
Üyüklü Tepe Turkey 37°5N 27°21E 205 D9
Uyûn Mûsa Egypt 29°53N 32°40E 251 J3
Uyuni Bolivia 20°28S 66°47W 330 E4
Uzbekistan ■ Asia 41°30N 65°0E 217 D7
Uzboy → Turkmenistan 39°30N 55°0E 247 B7
Uzen, Mal → Kazakhstan 49°4N 49°44E 191 F9
Uzerche France 45°25N 1°34E 174 C5
Uzès France 44°1N 4°26E 175 D8
Uzh → Ukraine 51°15N 30°12E 177 C16
Uzhgorod = Uzhhorod Ukraine 48°36N 22°18E 182 B7
Uzhhorod Ukraine 48°36N 22°18E 182 B7
Uzhok Ukraine 48°59N 22°52E 182 B7
Užice Serbia 43°55N 19°50E 202 C3
Uzlovaya Russia 54°0N 38°5E 188 F10
Üzümlü Turkey 36°44N 29°14E 205 E11
Uzuncaburç Turkey 36°35N 33°57E 250 B4
Uzunköprü Turkey 41°16N 26°43E 203 E10
Uzunkuyu Turkey 38°17N 26°33E 205 C8

V

V.C. Bird Int. ✈ (ANU) Antigua & B. 17°8N 61°47W 322 b
Vaal → S. Africa 29°4S 23°38E 270 C3
Vaal Dam S. Africa 27°0S 28°14E 271 C4
Vaalwater S. Africa 24°15S 28°8E 271 B4
Vaasa Finland 63°6N 21°38E 160 E19
Vabre France 43°42N 2°24E 174 E6
Vác Hungary 47°49N 19°10E 182 C4
Vacaos, Mare aux Mauritius 20°22S 57°30E 272 e
Vacaria Brazil 28°31S 50°52W 335 B5
Vacaville U.S.A. 38°21N 121°59W 306 G5
Vaccarès, Étang de France 43°32N 4°34E 175 E8
Vach = Vakh → Russia 60°45N 76°45E 214 C8
Vacha → Bulgaria 42°10N 24°26E 203 D8
Vache, Î. à Haiti 18°2N 73°35W 321 C5
Väckelsång Sweden 56°37N 14°58E 163 H8
Vaclavské náměstí Prague, Czechia 135 b2
Vacoas Mauritius 20°18S 57°29E 272 e
Vada India 19°39N 73°8E 244 E1
Vadakara India 11°35N 75°40E 245 J2
Vadaul India 19°2N 72°55E 130 A2
Väddö Sweden 60°0N 18°50E 162 D12
Vadehavet △ Denmark 55°20N 8°30E 163 J2
Väderstad Sweden 58°19N 14°55E 163 F8
Vadheim Norway 61°13N 5°49E 164 C2
Vadnagar India 23°47N 72°40E 242 H5
Vado Lígure Italy 44°17N 8°26E 198 D5
Vadodara India 22°20N 73°10E 242 H5
Vadsø Norway 70°3N 29°50E 160 A23
Vadstena Sweden 58°28N 14°54E 163 F8
Vaduj India 17°36N 74°27E 244 F2
Vaduz Liech. 47°8N 9°31E 179 H5
Vadvetjåkka △ Sweden 68°30N 18°28E 160 B18
Værlandet Norway 61°18N 4°44E 164 C1
Værøy Norway 67°40N 12°40E 160 C15
Vagalat Albania 39°44N 20°8E 206 B10
Vågåmo Norway 61°52N 9°6E 164 C6
Vágar Færoe Is. 62°5N 7°15W 160 E9
Vaggeryd Sweden 57°30N 14°10E 163 G8
Vagharshapat = Ejmiatsin Armenia 40°12N 44°19E 191 K7
Vaghena Solomon Is. 7°25S 157°45E 287 L9
Vaghia Greece 38°19N 23°11E 204 C5
Vagia, Akra Greece 36°15N 28°11E 206 E12
Vagney France 48°1N 6°43E 173 D13
Vagnhärad Sweden 58°57N 17°33E 163 F11
Vagos Portugal 40°33N 8°42W 194 E2
Vågsfjorden Norway 68°50N 16°50E 160 B17
Váh → Slovakia 47°43N 18°7E 181 D11
Vahitahi French Polynesia 18°44S 138°52W 289 f
Vahsel B. Antarctica 75°0S 35°0W 151 D1
Váhtjer = Gällivare Sweden 67°9N 20°40E 160 C19
Vaï Greece 35°15N 26°18E 207 E7
Vaiaku = Fongafale Tuvalu 8°31S 179°13E 277 B14
Vaiea Cook Is. 19°6S 169°54W 289 g
Vaigai → India 9°15N 79°10E 245 K4
Vaiges France 48°2N 0°30W 172 D6
Vaihingen Germany 48°54N 8°57E 179 G4
Vaihiria, L. Tahiti 17°40S 149°25W 289 e
Vaijapur India 19°58N 74°45E 244 E2
Vaikam India 9°45N 76°25E 245 K3
Vail U.S.A. 39°40N 106°20W 304 G10
Vailala → Papua N. G. 7°57S 145°25E 286 D3
Vailhau, Récif Comoros Is. 11°48S 43°4E 272 a
Vailly-sur-Aisne France 49°24N 3°31E 173 C10
Vailoatai Amer. Samoa 14°21S 170°46W 302 f
Vaippar → India 9°0N 78°25E 245 K4
Vairaatea French Polynesia 19°19S 139°20W 289 f
Vairao Tahiti 17°47S 149°17W 289 e
Vaires-sur-Marne France 48°52N 2°38E 134 A4
Vaisali → India 26°28N 78°53E 243 F8
Vaison-la-Romaine France 44°14N 5°4E 175 D9
Vaitogi Amer. Samoa 14°24S 170°44W 302 f
Vaitupu Pac. Oc. 7°28S 178°41E 277 B14
Vajpur India 21°24N 73°17E 244 D1
Vakaga □ C.A.R. 10°0N 22°30E 264 A4
Vakaga → C.A.R. 9°48N 21°32E 264 A4
Vakarai Sri Lanka 8°8N 81°26E 245 K5
Vakarel Bulgaria 42°35N 23°40E 202 D7
Vakfikebir Turkey 41°2N 39°17E 213 B8
Vakh → Russia 60°45N 76°45E 214 C8
Vakhsh → Tajikistan 37°6N 68°18E 217 E7
Vakhtan Russia 57°53N 46°47E 190 B8
Vakinankaratra □ Madag. 20°0S 47°0E 272 B2
Vaksdal Norway 60°29N 5°45E 164 D2
Vakuta I. Papua N. G. 8°51S 151°10E 286 E6
Vál Hungary 47°22N 18°40E 182 C3
Val Camónica Italy 45°57N 10°17E 198 C7
Val-de-Marne □ France 48°45N 2°28E 173 D9
Val-d'Isère France 45°27N 6°59E 175 C10
Val-d'Oise □ France 49°5N 2°10E 173 C9
Val-d'Or Canada 48°7N 77°47W 298 C4
Val Grande △ Italy 46°3N 8°25E 198 B5
Val Marie Canada 49°15N 107°45W 297 D7
Val Thorens France 45°20N 6°33E 175 C10
Valaam Russia 61°22N 30°57E 188 B6
Valadares Portugal 41°5N 8°38W 194 D2
Valahia Romania 44°35N 25°0E 183 F9
Valaichenai Sri Lanka 7°54N 81°32E 245 L5
Valais □ Switz. 46°12N 7°45E 179 J3
Valais, Alpes du Switz. 46°5N 7°35E 179 J3
Valandovo N. Macedonia 41°19N 22°34E 202 E6
Valašské Meziříčí Czechia 49°29N 17°59E 181 B10
Valatie U.S.A. 42°24N 73°40W 313 D11
Valaxa Greece 38°50N 24°29E 204 C6
Vålberg Sweden 59°23N 13°11E 162 E7
Valbo Sweden 60°40N 17°0E 162 D10
Valbondione Italy 46°2N 10°1E 198 B7
Valby Denmark 55°39N 12°29E 118 B2
Valcamonica = Val Camónica Italy 45°57N 10°17E 198 C7
Vălcani Romania 46°0N 20°26E 182 D5
Valcannuta Italy 41°52N 12°25E 136 B1
Vâlcea □ Romania 45°0N 24°10E 183 F9
Valchedram Bulgaria 43°42N 23°27E 202 C7
Valcheta Argentina 40°40S 66°8W 336 B3
Valdagno Italy 45°39N 11°18E 199 C8
Valdahon France 47°8N 6°21E 173 E13
Valdai Hills = Valdayskaya Vozvyshennost Russia 57°0N 33°30E 188 D7
Valday Russia 57°58N 33°9E 188 D7
Valdayskaya Vozvyshennost Russia 57°0N 33°30E 188 D7
Valdaysky △ Russia 57°30N 33°0E 188 D7
Valdeazogues → Spain 38°45N 4°55W 195 G6
Valdecañas, Embalse de Spain 39°45N 5°25W 194 F5
Valdelatas Spain 40°31N 3°42W 127 A1
Valdemarsvik Sweden 58°14N 16°40E 163 F10
Valdemoro Spain 40°12N 3°40W 194 E7
Valdepeñas Spain 38°43N 3°25W 195 G7
Valderaduey → Spain 41°31N 5°42W 194 D5
Valdérice Italy 38°4N 12°37E 200 D5
Valderrobres Spain 40°53N 0°9E 196 E5
Valdés, Pen. Argentina 42°30S 63°45W 336 B4
Valdez Ecuador 1°15N 79°0W 328 C2
Valdez Alaska, U.S.A. 61°7N 146°16W 303 F11
Valdgeym = Dobropole Ukraine 48°25N 37°2E 189 H9
Valdivia Chile 39°50S 73°14W 336 A2
Valdivia Colombia 7°11N 75°27W 328 B2
Valdivia Abyssal Plain S. Ocean 62°30S 70°0E 151 C6
Valdobbiádene Italy 45°54N 12°0E 199 C8
Valdosta U.S.A. 30°50N 83°17W 316 E6
Valdoviño = Aviño Spain 43°36N 8°8W 194 B2
Valdres Norway 61°5N 9°5E 164 C6
Vale Georgia 41°30N 42°58E 191 K6
Vale Oreg., U.S.A. 43°59N 117°15W 304 E5
Vale of Glamorgan □ U.K. 51°28N 3°25W 169 F4
Valea lui Mihai Romania 47°32N 22°11E 182 C7
Valea Mărului Romania 45°49N 27°42E 183 E12
Valemount Canada 52°50N 119°15W 296 C5
Valença = Valença do Piauí Brazil 6°20S 41°45W 332 C3
Valença Brazil 13°20S 39°5W 333 D4
Valença Portugal 42°1N 8°34W 194 C2
Valença do Piauí Brazil 6°20S 41°45W 332 C3
Valençay France 47°9N 1°34E 173 E8

Valence *France* 44°57N 4°54E **175** D8
Valence d'Agen *France* 44°6N 0°53E **174** D4
Valencia *Phil.* 7°57N 125°3E **233** H5
Valencia *Spain* 39°27N 0°23W **197** F4
Valencia *Trin. & Tob.* 10°39N 61°11W **323** t
Valencia *N. Mex., U.S.A.* 34°48N 106°43W **305** J10
Valencia *Venezuela* 10°11N 68°0W **328** A4
Valencia □ *Spain* 39°20N 0°40W **197** F4
Valencia ✈ (VLC) *Spain* 39°20N 0°26W **197** F4
Valencia, G. de *Spain* 39°30N 0°20E **197** F5
Valencia de Alcántara *Spain* 39°25N 7°14W **195** F3
Valencia de Don Juan *Spain* 42°17N 5°31W **194** C5
Valencia I. *Ireland* 51°54N 10°22W **166** E1
Valenciennes *France* 50°20N 3°34E **173** B10
Văleni *Romania* 44°15N 24°45E **183** F9
Vălenii de Munte *Romania* 45°11N 26°2E **183** E11
Valensole *France* 43°50N 5°59E **175** E9
Valentigney *France* 47°27N 6°51E **173** E13
Valentim, Sa. do *Brazil* 6°0S 43°30W **332** C3
Valentin *Russia* 43°8N 134°17E **220** C7
Valentine *Nebr., U.S.A.* 42°52N 100°33W **308** D3
Valentine *Tex., U.S.A.* 30°35N 104°30W **314** F2
Valenton *France* 48°44N 2°27E **134** B3
Valenza *Italy* 45°1N 8°38E **198** C5
Våler *Hedmark, Norway* 60°41N 11°50E **164** D8
Våler *Østfold, Norway* 59°29N 10°51E **164** E7
Valera *Piemonte, Italy* 45°33N 9°3E **128** A1
Valera *Venezuela* 9°19N 70°37W **328** B3
Valesdir *Vanuatu* 16°47S 168°10E **287** F6
Valestrand *Norway* 59°40N 5°26E **164** E2
Valga *Estonia* 57°47N 26°2E **188** D4
Valguarnera Caropepe *Italy* 37°30N 14°23E **201** E7
Valier *U.S.A.* 48°18N 112°16W **304** B7
Valinco, G. de *France* 41°40N 8°52E **175** G12
Valjevo *Serbia* 44°18N 19°53E **202** B3
Valka *Latvia* 57°46N 26°3E **188** D3
Valkeakoski *Finland* 61°16N 24°2E **188** B2
Valkenswaard *Neths.* 51°21N 5°29E **170** C5
Vall de Uxó = La Vall d'Uixó *Spain* 39°49N 0°15W **196** F4
Valla *Sweden* 59°2N 16°20E **162** E10
Valladolid *Yucatán, Mexico* 20°41N 88°12W **319** C7
Valladolid *Spain* 41°38N 4°43W **194** D6
Valladolid □ *Spain* 41°38N 4°43W **194** D6
Vallata *Italy* 41°2N 15°15E **201** A8
Vallcarca *Spain* 41°25N 2°9E **114** A1
Valldemossa *Spain* 39°43N 2°37E **206** B3
Valldoreix *Spain* 41°27N 2°3E **114** A1
Valle *Norway* 59°13N 7°33E **164** E4
Valle d'Aosta □ *Italy* 45°45N 7°15E **198** C4
Valle de la Pascua *Venezuela* 9°13N 66°0W **328** B4
Valle de las Palmas *Mexico* 32°20N 116°43W **307** N10
Valle de Santiago *Mexico* 20°23N 101°12W **318** C4
Valle de Villaverde *Spain* 43°15N 3°15W **194** B7
Valle de Zaragoza *Mexico* 27°25N 105°50W **318** B3
Valle del Cauca □ *Colombia* 3°45N 76°30W **328** C2
Valle del Ticino ⌓ *Italy* 45°22N 9°0E **198** C6
Valle Fértil, Sierra del *Argentina* 30°20S 68°0W **334** C2
Valle Gran Rey *Canary Is.* 28°5N 17°20W **153** e1
Valle Hermoso *Mexico* 25°35N 97°40W **319** B5
Valle Nacional *Mexico* 17°47N 96°18W **319** D5
Vallecas *Spain* 40°22N 3°37W **127** B2
Vallecas, Cumbres de *Spain* 40°20N 3°33W **127** B2
Valledupar *Colombia* 10°29N 73°15W **328** A3
Vallée de Mai ⌓ *Seychelles* 4°19S 55°44E **272** c
Vallée du Bandama □ *Côte d'Ivoire* 8°0N 5°0W **262** D3
Vallegrande *Bolivia* 18°30S 64°10W **331** D5
Vallehermoso *Canary Is.* 28°10N 17°15W **153** e1
Vallejo *U.S.A.* 38°7N 122°14W **306** G4
Vallenar *Chile* 28°30S 70°50W **334** B1
Vallensbæk *Denmark* 55°38N 12°21E **118** B2
Vallensbæk Strand *Denmark* 55°36N 12°23E **118** B2
Vallentuna *Sweden* 59°32N 18°5E **162** E12
Vallentunasjön *Sweden* 59°27N 18°1E **139** A2
Valleranello *Italy* 41°46N 12°29E **136** C1
Valleraugue *France* 44°6N 3°39E **174** D7
Vallet *France* 47°10N 1°15W **172** E5
Valletta *Malta* 35°54N 14°31E **206** F8
Valley, The *Anguilla* 18°13N 63°4W **322** a
Valley Center *U.S.A.* 33°13N 117°2W **307** M9
Valley City *U.S.A.* 46°55N 98°0W **308** B5
Valley Falls *Oreg., U.S.A.* 42°29N 120°17W **304** E3
Valley Falls *R.I., U.S.A.* 41°54N 71°24W **313** E13
Valley Junction = West Des Moines *U.S.A.* 41°35N 93°43W **310** C3
Valley of Flowers △ *India* 30°50N 79°40E **243** D8
Valley of the Kings *Egypt* 25°41N 32°34E **256** B3
Valley Springs *U.S.A.* 38°12N 120°50W **306** G6
Valley Station *U.S.A.* 38°6N 85°52W **311** F11
Valley View *U.S.A.* 40°39N 76°33W **313** F8
Valley Wells *U.S.A.* 35°27N 115°46W **307** K11
Valleyview *Canada* 55°5N 117°17W **296** B5
Valli di Comácchio *Italy* 44°40N 12°15E **199** D9
Vallimanca, Arroyo *Argentina* 35°40S 59°10W **334** D4
Vallisaari *Finland* 60°7N 25°0E **121** C3
Vallo della Lucánia *Italy* 40°14N 15°16E **201** B8
Vallon-Pont-d'Arc *France* 44°24N 4°24E **175** D8
Vallorbe *Switz.* 46°42N 6°20E **179** J2
Valls *Spain* 41°18N 1°15E **196** D6
Vallvidrera *Spain* 41°24N 2°6E **114** A1
Vallvik *Sweden* 61°11N 17°10E **162** C11
Valmaseda = Balmaseda *Spain* 43°11N 3°12W **196** B1
Valmeyer *U.S.A.* 38°18N 90°19W **310** F6
Valmiera *Latvia* 57°37N 25°29E **188** D3
Valnera *Spain* 43°9N 3°40W **194** B7
Valognes *France* 49°30N 1°28W **172** C5
Valona = Vlorë *Albania* 40°32N 19°28E **202** F3
Valongo *Portugal* 41°8N 8°30W **194** D2
Valozhyn *Belarus* 54°3N 26°30E **177** A14
Valpaços *Portugal* 41°36N 7°17W **194** D3
Valparai *India* 10°22N 76°58E **245** J3
Valparaíso *Chile* 33°2S 71°40W **334** C1
Valparaíso *Zacatecas, Mexico* 22°46N 103°34W **318** C4
Valparaiso *Fla., U.S.A.* 30°29N 86°30W **317** E3
Valparaiso *Ind., U.S.A.* 41°28N 87°4W **311** C9
Valparaíso □ *Chile* 33°2S 71°40W **334** C1
Valpovo *Croatia* 45°39N 18°25E **182** E3
Valpoy *India* 15°32N 74°8E **245** G2
Valréas *France* 44°24N 5°0E **175** D9
Vals *Switz.* 46°39N 9°11E **179** J5
Vals ➔ *S. Africa* 27°23S 26°30E **270** C4
Vals, Tanjung *Indonesia* 8°26S 137°25E **231** F9
Vals-les-Bains *France* 44°42N 4°24E **175** D8
Valsad *India* 20°40N 72°58E **244** D1
Valsamata *Greece* 38°10N 20°36E **207** C2
Valtellina *Italy* 46°11N 9°55E **198** B6
Valþjofsstaður *Iceland* 65°1N 14°59W **155** B12
Valti *Greece* 38°27N 21°7E **207** C3
Valuyki *Russia* 50°10N 38°5E **189** G10
Valverde *Canary Is.* 27°48N 17°55W **153** e1
Valverde del Camino *Spain* 37°35N 6°47W **195** H4
Valverde del Fresno *Spain* 40°15N 6°51W **194** E4
Valvidrera ➔ *Spain* 41°25N 2°0E **114** A1
Vama *Romania* 47°34N 25°42E **183** C10
Vambori *India* 19°17N 74°44E **244** E2
Vamdrup *Denmark* 55°25N 9°17E **163** J3
Våmhus *Sweden* 61°7N 14°29E **162** C8
Vamizi, I. *Mozam.* 11°2S 40°40E **269** E5
Vammala = Sastamala *Finland* 61°20N 22°54E **188** B2
Vamos *Greece* 35°24N 24°13E **207** E5
Vamsadhara ➔ *India* 18°21N 84°8E **244** E7
Van *Turkey* 38°30N 43°20E **213** C10
Van □ *Turkey* 38°30N 43°20E **213** C10
Van, L. = Van Gölü *Turkey* 38°30N 43°0E **213** C10
Van Alstyne *U.S.A.* 33°25N 96°35W **314** E6
Van Blommestein Meer *Suriname* 4°45N 55°5W **329** C6
Van Buren = Kettering *U.S.A.* 39°41N 84°10W **311** E12
Van Buren *N.B., Canada* 47°10N 67°55W **299** C6
Van Buren *Ark., U.S.A.* 35°26N 94°21W **314** D7
Van Buren *Maine, U.S.A.* 47°10N 67°58W **309** B20
Van Buren *Mo., U.S.A.* 37°0N 91°1W **308** G8
Van Canh *Vietnam* 13°37N 109°0E **236** F7
Van Diemen, C. *N. Terr., Australia* 11°9S 130°24E **278** B5
Van Diemen, C. *Queens., Australia* 16°30S 139°46E **280** B2
Van Diemen G. *Australia* 11°45S 132°0E **278** B5
Van Gogh Museum *Amsterdam, Neths.* **112** c1
Van Gölü *Turkey* 38°30N 43°0E **213** C10
Van Horn *U.S.A.* 31°3N 104°50W **314** F2
Van Horne *U.S.A.* 42°1N 92°5W **310** B4
Van Meter *U.S.A.* 41°32N 93°57W **310** C3
Van Ninh *Vietnam* 12°42N 109°14E **236** F7
Van Rees, Pegunungan *Indonesia* 2°35S 138°15E **231** E9
Van Tivu *India* 8°51N 78°15E **245** K4
Van Wert *U.S.A.* 40°52N 84°35W **311** D12
Van Yen *Vietnam* 21°4N 104°42E **228** G5
Van Zylsrus *S. Africa* 26°52S 22°4E **270** C3
Vanadzor *Armenia* 40°48N 44°30E **191** K7
Vanak *Iran* 35°45N 51°23E **141** A2
Vanavana *French Polynesia* 20°47S 139°9W **289** f
Vanavara *Russia* 60°22N 102°16E **215** C11
Vanceburg *U.S.A.* 38°36N 83°19W **311** F13
Vancouver *B.C., Canada* 49°15N 123°7W **306** A3
Vancouver *Wash., U.S.A.* 45°38N 122°40W **306** E4
Vancouver, C. *Australia* 35°2S 118°11E **279** G2
Vancouver, Mt. *U.S.A.* 60°20N 139°41W **303** F13
Vancouver I. *Canada* 49°50N 126°0W **306** B2
Vancouver Int. ✈ (YVR) *Canada* 49°10N 123°10W **306** A3
Vanda = Vantaa *Finland* 60°18N 24°56E **121** B2
Vandalia *Ill., U.S.A.* 38°58N 89°6W **310** F7
Vandalia *Mo., U.S.A.* 39°19N 91°29W **310** E5
Vandalia *Ohio, U.S.A.* 39°54N 84°12W **311** E12
Vandavasi *India* 12°30N 79°30E **245** H4
Vandellòs *Spain* 41°0N 0°55E **196** E5
Vandeloos B. *Sri Lanka* 8°0N 81°45E **245** L5
Vandenberg Village *U.S.A.* 34°43N 120°28W **307** L6
Vanderbijlpark *S. Africa* 26°42S 27°54E **271** C4
Vandergrift *U.S.A.* 40°36N 79°34W **312** F5
Vanderhoof *Canada* 54°0N 124°0W **296** C4
Vanderkloof Dam *S. Africa* 30°4S 24°40E **270** D3
Vanderlin I. *Australia* 15°44S 137°2E **280** B2
Vänern *Sweden* 58°47N 13°30E **163** F7
Vänersborg *Sweden* 58°26N 12°19E **163** F6
Vang *Norway* 61°7N 8°34E **164** C5
Vang Vieng *Laos* 18°58N 102°32E **236** C4
Vanga *Kenya* 4°35S 39°12E **268** C4
Vangaindrano *Madag.* 23°21S 47°36E **272** C2
Vänge *Sweden* 59°50N 17°20E **162** E11
Vangede *Denmark* 55°45N 12°30E **118** A3
Vangsnes *Norway* 61°9N 6°39E **164** C3
Vanguard *Canada* 49°55N 107°20W **297** D7
Vangunu *Solomon Is.* 8°40S 158°5E **287** M10
Vanikoro *Pac. Oc.* 11°39S 166°54E **277** C12
Vaniköy *Turkey* 41°3N 29°3E **122** B2
Vanimo *Papua N. G.* 2°42S 141°21E **286** B1
Vanino *Russia* 48°50N 140°5E **215** E15
Vanivilasa Sagara *India* 13°45N 76°30E **245** H3
Vaniyambadi *India* 12°46N 78°44E **245** H4
Vânju Mare *Romania* 44°25N 22°52E **182** F7
Vankleek Hill *Canada* 45°32N 74°40W **313** A10
Vanløse *Denmark* 55°41N 12°28E **118** A2
Vännäs *Sweden* 63°58N 19°48E **160** E18
Vannes *France* 47°40N 2°47W **172** E4
Vannøya *Norway* 70°6N 19°50E **160** A18
Vanoise, Massif de la *France* 45°25N 6°40E **175** C10
Vanrhynsdorp *S. Africa* 31°36S 18°44E **270** D2
Vansada *India* 20°47N 73°25E **244** D1
Vansbro *Sweden* 60°32N 14°15E **162** D8
Vanse *Norway* 58°6N 6°41E **164** F3
Vansittart B. *Australia* 14°3S 126°17E **278** B4
Vansittart I. *Canada* 65°50N 84°0W **295** D15
Vantaa *Finland* 60°18N 24°56E **121** B2
Vantaankoski *Finland* 60°18N 24°50E **121** B2
Vantaanpuisto *Finland* 60°18N 24°53E **121** B2
Vanua Balavu *Fiji* 17°12S 178°55W **287** A3
Vanua Lava *Vanuatu* 13°50S 167°30E **287** C5
Vanua Levu *Fiji* 16°33S 179°15E **287** A2
Vanua Vatu *Fiji* 18°22S 179°15W **287** B3
Vanuatu ■ *Pac. Oc.* 15°0S 168°0E **287** E6
Vanves *France* 48°49N 2°17E **134** B2
Vanwyksvlei *S. Africa* 30°18S 21°49E **270** D3
Vao *N. Cal.* 22°39S 167°32E **288** d
Vapi *India* 20°22N 72°54E **244** D1
Vapnyarka *Ukraine* 48°32N 28°45E **183** B13
Var □ *France* 43°27N 6°18E **175** E10
Var ➔ *France* 43°39N 7°12E **175** E11
Vara *Sweden* 58°16N 12°55E **163** F6
Vara, Pico da *Azores* 37°48N 25°13W **153** d3
Varada ➔ *India* 15°0N 75°40E **245** G2
Varadero *Cuba* 23°11N 81°11W **320** D3
Varades *France* 47°25N 1°1W **172** E5
Varáita ➔ *Italy* 44°9N 7°53E **198** D4
Varaldsøy *Norway* 60°6N 5°59E **164** D2
Varalé *Côte d'Ivoire* 9°40N 3°17W **262** D4
Varallo *Italy* 45°49N 8°15E **198** C5
Varāmīn *Iran* 35°20N 51°39E **247** C6
Varāmīn □ *Iran* 35°18N 51°35E **247** B6
Varanasi *India* 25°22N 83°0E **243** G10
Varangerfjorden *Norway* 70°3N 29°25E **160** A23
Varangerhalvøya *Norway* 70°25N 29°30E **160** A23
Varano, Lago di *Italy* 41°53N 15°45E **199** G12
Varaždin *Croatia* 46°20N 16°20E **199** B13
Varazze *Italy* 44°22N 8°34E **198** D5
Varberg *Sweden* 57°6N 12°20E **163** G6
Varbitsa *Bulgaria* 42°59N 26°40E **203** D10
Varcar Vakuf = Mrkonjić Grad *Bos.-H.* 44°26N 17°4E **182** F2
Vardak □ *Afghan.* 34°0N 68°0E **240** B3
Vardar = Axios ➔ *Greece* 40°57N 22°35E **202** F6
Varde *Denmark* 55°38N 8°29E **163** J2
Varde Å ➔ *Denmark* 55°35N 8°19E **163** J2
Vardenis *Armenia* 40°10N 45°43E **191** K7
Vardø *Norway* 70°23N 31°5E **160** A24
Varedo *Italy* 45°35N 9°8E **128** A1
Varel *Germany* 53°23N 8°8E **178** B4
Varella, Mui = Nay, Mui *Vietnam* 12°54N 109°26E **236** F7
Varėna *Lithuania* 54°12N 24°30E **188** E3
Varennes-sur-Allier *France* 46°19N 3°24E **173** F10
Varennes-Vauzelles *France* 47°3N 3°9E **173** E10
Vareš *Bos.-H.* 44°12N 18°23E **182** F3
Varese *Italy* 45°48N 8°50E **198** C5
Vârfurile *Romania* 46°19N 22°31E **182** D7
Vårgårda *Sweden* 58°2N 12°49E **163** F6
Vargas *Venezuela* 10°36N 66°56W **328** A4
Vargem Bonita *Brazil* 20°20S 46°22W **333** F2
Vargem Grande *Brazil* 3°33S 43°56W **332** B3
Varginha *Brazil* 21°33S 45°25W **335** A6
Vargön *Sweden* 58°22N 12°20E **163** F6
Varhaug *Norway* 58°37N 5°41E **164** F2
Vari *Greece* 38°24N 20°35E **207** C2
Varillas *Chile* 24°0S 70°10W **334** A1
Varkaus *Finland* 62°19N 27°50E **188** A4
Varkiza *Greece* 37°50N 23°49E **112** C2
Värmdölandet *Sweden* 59°20N 18°33E **162** E12
Värmeln *Sweden* 59°35N 12°54E **162** E6
Värmland □ *Sweden* 60°0N 13°20E **162** E6
Värmlandsbro *Sweden* 59°11N 13°0E **162** E7
Varna *Bulgaria* 43°13N 27°56E **203** C11
Varna □ *Bulgaria* 43°20N 27°30E **203** C11
Varna ➔ *India* 16°48N 74°32E **244** F2
Värnamo *Sweden* 57°10N 14°3E **163** G8
Várnjárga = Varangerhalvøya *Norway* 70°25N 29°30E **160** A23
Varnsdorf *Czechia* 50°55N 14°35E **180** A7
Varnville *U.S.A.* 32°51N 81°5W **316** C8
Várpalota *Hungary* 47°12N 18°8E **182** C3
Vars *Ont., Canada* 45°21N 75°21W **313** A9
Vars *Hautes-Alpes, France* 44°37N 6°42E **175** D10
Vartdal *Norway* 62°20N 6°8E **164** B3
Vartiokylä *Finland* 60°13N 25°6E **121** B3
Vartiosaari *Finland* 60°11N 25°5E **121** B3
Varto *Turkey* 39°10N 41°27E **213** C9
Varvarin *Serbia* 43°43N 21°20E **202** C5
Varysburg *U.S.A.* 42°46N 78°19W **312** D6
Varzaneh *Iran* 32°25N 52°40E **247** C7
Varzaqān *Iran* 38°29N 46°40E **213** C12
Várzea Alegre *Brazil* 6°47S 39°17W **332** C4
Várzea da Palma *Brazil* 17°36S 44°44W **333** E3
Várzea Grande *Brazil* 15°39S 56°8W **331** D6
Varzi *Italy* 44°49N 9°12E **198** D6
Varzo *Italy* 46°12N 8°15E **198** B5
Varzy *France* 47°22N 3°20E **173** E10
Vas □ *Hungary* 47°10N 16°55E **182** C1
Vasa = Vaasa *Finland* 63°6N 21°38E **160** E19
Vasa Barris ➔ *Brazil* 11°10S 37°10W **332** D4
Vasai-Virar *India* 19°28N 72°48E **244** E1
Vasamuseet *Stockholm, Sweden* **139** b3
Vásárosnamény *Hungary* 48°9N 22°19E **182** B7
Vascâo ➔ *Portugal* 37°31N 7°31W **195** H3
Vaşcău *Romania* 46°28N 22°30E **182** D7
Vasco *S. Africa* 33°54S 18°34E **118** A2
Vascongadas = País Vasco □ *Spain* 42°50N 2°45W **196** C2
Vasfenārd *Iran* 35°38N 51°20E **141** B2
Vashi *India* 19°4N 72°59E **130** A2
Vāshīr *Afghan.* 32°16N 63°51E **240** B1
Vashkivtsi *Ukraine* 48°23N 25°31E **183** B10
Vasht = Khāsh *Iran* 28°15N 61°15E **240** C1
Vasilevichi *Belarus* 52°15N 29°50E **177** B16
Vasilika *Greece* 40°29N 23°8E **202** F7
Vasiliki *Greece* 38°37N 20°36E **207** B2
Vasiliko = Tsarevo *Bulgaria* 42°9N 27°51E **203** D11
Vasiliko *Greece* 38°25N 23°40E **204** C5
Vasilikos *Greece* 37°43N 20°59E **207** D2
Vasilkov = Vasylkiv *Ukraine* 50°7N 30°15E **177** C16
Vasilyevskiy, Ostrov *Russia* 59°55N 30°16E **137** B1
Vasilyova Sloboda = Chkolovsk *Russia* 56°50N 43°10E **190** B6
Vasilyovo = Chkolovsk *Russia* 56°50N 43°10E **190** B6
Väskinde *Sweden* 57°40N 18°20E **163** G10
Vaslui *Romania* 46°38N 27°42E **183** D12
Vaslui □ *Romania* 46°30N 27°45E **183** D12
Väsman *Sweden* 60°9N 15°5E **162** D9
Vassar *Man., Canada* 49°10N 95°55W **297** D9
Vassar *Mich., U.S.A.* 43°22N 83°35W **309** D12
Vassfaret *Norway* 60°38N 9°28E **164** D6
Västerås *Sweden* 59°37N 16°38E **162** E10
Västerbotten *Sweden* 64°36N 20°4E **160** D19
Västerdalälven ➔ *Sweden* 60°30N 15°7E **162** D8
Västergötland *Sweden* 58°0N 13°10E **163** F7
Västerhaninge *Sweden* 59°7N 18°6E **162** E12
Västervik *Sweden* 57°43N 16°33E **163** G10
Västmanland *Sweden* 59°45N 16°20E **161** G17
Västmanland □ *Sweden* 59°45N 16°20E **162** E10
Vasto *Italy* 42°8N 14°40E **199** F11
Västra Götaland □ *Sweden* 58°0N 13°0E **163** F6
Vasvár *Hungary* 47°3N 16°47E **182** C1
Vasylivka *Ukraine* 45°38N 28°50E **183** E13
Vasylkiv *Ukraine* 50°7N 30°15E **177** C16
Vat Phou *Laos* 14°51N 105°49E **236** E5
Vatan *France* 47°4N 1°50E **173** E8
Vaté = Efate, I. *Vanuatu* 17°40S 168°25E **287** G6
Vatersay *U.K.* 56°55N 7°32W **167** E1
Vathi *Greece* 38°41N 20°47E **207** B2
Vathia *Greece* 36°29N 22°29E **204** E4
Vati *Greece* 36°3N 27°53E **206** E11
Vatia *Amer. Samoa* 14°15S 170°40W **302** f
Vatican City ■ *Europe* 41°54N 12°27E **136** B1
Vaticano, C. *Italy* 38°37N 15°50E **201** D8
Vatili *Cyprus* 35°6N 33°40E **207** E9
Vatin *Serbia* 45°12N 21°20E **182** E6
Vatiu = Atiu *Cook Is.* 20°0S 158°10W **289** J12
Vatnajökull *Iceland* 64°30N 16°48W **155** C10
Vatnajökull △ *Iceland* 64°24N 16°48W **155** C10
Vatnås *Norway* 59°58N 9°37E **164** E6
Vatnsfjörður *Iceland* 65°56N 22°30W **155** B4
Vato *Sweden* 59°50N 19°0E **162** E12
Vatolakkos *Greece* 35°27N 23°53E **207** E4
Vatoloha *Madag.* 17°52S 47°48E **272** B2
Vatomandry *Madag.* 19°20S 48°59E **272** B2
Vatovavy-Fitovinany □ *Madag.* 22°10S 48°0E **272** C2
Vatra-Dornei *Romania* 47°22N 25°22E **183** C10
Vatrak ➔ *India* 23°9N 73°2E **242** H5
Vattaru Atoll *Maldives* 3°16N 73°25E **272** d
Vättern *Sweden* 58°25N 14°30E **163** F8
Vatu Vara *Fiji* 17°26S 179°31W **287** A3
Vatulele *Fiji* 18°33S 177°37E **287** B1
Vauclin, Mt. du *Martinique* 14°33N 60°53W **322** j
Vauclin, Pte. de *Martinique* 14°34N 60°49W **322** j
Vaucluse *Australia* 33°51S 151°15E **139** B2
Vaucluse □ *France* 43°50N 5°20E **175** E9
Vaucluse House *Australia* 33°51S 151°15E **139** B2
Vaucouleurs *France* 48°37N 5°40E **173** D12
Vaucresson *France* 48°50N 2°9E **134** A1
Vaud □ *Switz.* 46°35N 6°30E **179** J2
Vaudreuil-Dorion *Canada* 45°23N 74°3W **313** A10
Vaughan *Canada* 43°50N 79°32W **141** A1
Vaughn *Mont., U.S.A.* 47°33N 111°33W **304** C8
Vaughn *N. Mex., U.S.A.* 34°36N 105°13W **305** J11
Vauhallan *France* 48°44N 2°12E **134** B2
Vaujours *France* 48°56N 2°34E **134** A4
Vaujours L. *Canada* 55°27N 74°15W **298** A5
Vaupés = Uaupés ➔ *Brazil* 0°2N 67°16W **328** C4
Vaupés □ *Colombia* 1°0N 71°0W **328** C3
Vauvert *France* 43°42N 4°17E **175** E8
Vauxhall *Alta., Canada* 50°5N 112°9W **296** C6
Vauxhall *London, U.K.* **125** c4
Vav *India* 24°22N 71°31E **242** G4
Vavatenina *Madag.* 17°28S 49°12E **272** B2
Vava'u *Tonga* 18°36S 174°0W **287** P14
Vava'u Group *Tonga* 18°40S 174°0W **287** P14
Vavoua *Côte d'Ivoire* 7°23N 6°29W **262** D3
Vavuniya *Sri Lanka* 8°45N 80°30E **245** K5
Vawkavysk *Belarus* 53°9N 24°30E **177** B13
Vaxholm *Sweden* 59°25N 18°20E **162** E12
Växjö *Sweden* 56°52N 14°50E **163** H8
Våxtorp *Sweden* 56°25N 13°8E **163** H7
Vayalpad *India* 13°39N 78°38E **245** H4
Vayenga = Severomorsk *Russia* 69°5N 33°27E **160** B25
Vaygach, Ostrov *Russia* 70°0N 60°0E **214** C7
Veadeiros *Brazil* 14°7S 47°31W **333** D2
Veaikevárri = Svappavaara *Sweden* 67°40N 21°3E **160** C19
Vechelde *Germany* 52°16N 10°22E **178** C6
Vechta *Germany* 52°44N 8°17E **178** C4
Vechte ➔ *Neths.* 52°34N 6°6E **170** B6
Vecsés *Hungary* 47°26N 19°19E **117** B3
Vedaranniyam *India* 10°25N 79°50E **245** J4
Vedavågen *Norway* 59°17N 5°12E **164** E2
Veddige *Sweden* 57°17N 12°20E **163** G6
Vedea ➔ *Romania* 43°42N 25°41E **183** G10
Vedi *Armenia* 39°54N 44°43E **213** C11
Vedia *Argentina* 34°30S 61°31W **334** C3
Vedrette di Ries-Aurina ⌓ *Italy* 46°54N 12°5E **199** B9
Vedum *Sweden* 58°11N 13°0E **163** F7
Veedersburg *U.S.A.* 40°7N 87°16W **311** D9
Veendam *Neths.* 53°5N 6°52E **170** A6
Veenendaal *Neths.* 52°2N 5°34E **170** B5
Vefsna ➔ *Norway* 65°48N 13°10E **160** D15
Vega *Nordland, Norway* 65°40N 11°55E **160** D14
Vega *Tex., U.S.A.* 35°15N 102°26W **314** D3
Vega Alta *Puerto Rico* 18°25N 66°20W **321** b
Vega Baja *Puerto Rico* 18°27N 66°23W **321** b
Vega de Ribadeo = Vegadeo *Spain* 43°27N 7°4W **194** B3
Vegadeo *Spain* 43°27N 7°4W **194** B3
Vegårshei *Norway* 58°44N 8°51E **164** F5
Vegas Verde = North Las Vegas *U.S.A.* 36°11N 115°7W **124** A1
Veggli *Norway* 60°3N 9°9E **164** D6
Veglia = Krk *Croatia* 45°8N 14°40E **199** C11
Vegoritida, L. *Greece* 40°45N 21°45E **202** F5
Vegreville *Canada* 53°30N 112°5W **296** C6
Veiholmen *Norway* 63°31N 7°58E **164** A4
Veimandu Channel *Maldives* 2°10N 73°20E **272** d
Veinge *Sweden* 56°33N 13°4E **163** H7
Veisiejai *Lithuania* 54°6N 23°42E **184** D10
Vejbystrand *Sweden* 56°19N 12°45E **163** H6
Vejen *Denmark* 55°30N 9°9E **163** J3
Vejer de la Frontera *Spain* 36°15N 5°59W **195** J5
Vejle *Denmark* 55°43N 9°30E **163** J3
Vejle Fjord *Denmark* 55°40N 9°50E **163** J3
Vela Luka *Croatia* 42°59N 16°44E **199** F13
Velachha *India* 21°26N 73°1E **244** D1
Velanai I. *Sri Lanka* 9°45N 79°45E **245** K4
Velas *Azores* 38°41N 28°13W **153** d1
Velas, C. *Costa Rica* 10°21N 85°52W **320** D2
Velasco, Sierra de *Argentina* 29°20S 67°10W **334** B2
Velay, Mts. du *France* 45°0N 3°40E **174** D7
Velbert *Germany* 51°20N 7°3E **178** D3
Velddrif *S. Africa* 32°42S 18°11E **270** D2
Velebit Planina *Croatia* 44°50N 15°20E **199** D12
Velebitski Kanal *Croatia* 44°45N 14°55E **199** D11
Veleka ➔ *Bulgaria* 42°4N 27°58E **203** D11
Veleň *Czechia* 50°10N 14°33E **135** A3
Velencei-tó *Hungary* 47°13N 18°36E **182** C3
Velenje *Slovenia* 46°23N 15°8E **199** B12
Veles *N. Macedonia* 41°46N 21°47E **202** E5
Veleslavin *Czechia* 50°5N 14°21E **135** B2
Velestino *Greece* 39°23N 22°43E **204** B4
Vélez *Colombia* 6°1N 73°41W **328** B3
Vélez-Málaga *Spain* 36°48N 4°5W **195** J6
Vélez Rubio *Spain* 37°41N 2°5W **197** H2
Velhas ➔ *Brazil* 17°13S 44°49W **333** E3
Velika *Croatia* 45°27N 17°40E **182** E2
Velika Gorica *Croatia* 45°44N 16°5E **199** C13
Velika Kapela *Croatia* 45°10N 15°5E **199** C12
Velika Kikinda = Kikinda *Serbia* 45°50N 20°30E **182** E5
Velika Kladuša *Bos.-H.* 45°11N 15°48E **199** C12
Velika Kruša = Krushë e Madhe *Kosovo* 42°19N 20°39E **202** D4
Velika Morava ➔ *Serbia* 44°43N 21°3E **202** B5
Velika Plana *Serbia* 44°20N 21°4E **202** B5
Velikaya ➔ *Russia* 57°48N 28°10E **188** D5
Velikaya Kema *Russia* 45°30N 137°12E **220** B8
Velikaya Lepetikha *Ukraine* 47°2N 33°58E **189** J7
Velike Lašče *Slovenia* 45°49N 14°45E **199** C11
Veliki Jastrebac *Serbia* 43°25N 21°30E **202** C5
Veliki Kanal *Serbia* 45°45N 19°15E **182** E4
Veliki Popović *Serbia* 44°8N 21°18E **202** B5
Veliki Ustyug *Russia* 60°47N 46°20E **186** B8
Velikiy Novgorod *Russia* 58°30N 31°25E **188** C6
Velikiye Luki *Russia* 56°25N 30°32E **188** D6
Veliko Gradište *Serbia* 44°46N 21°29E **202** B5
Veliko Tarnovo *Bulgaria* 43°5N 25°41E **203** C9
Veliko Tarnovo □ *Bulgaria* 43°5N 25°41E **203** C9
Veliko Tŭrnovo = Veliko Tarnovo *Bulgaria* 43°5N 25°41E **203** C9
Velikonda Range *India* 14°45N 79°10E **245** G4
Vélingara *Kolda, Senegal* 13°12N 14°5W **262** C2
Vélingara *Louga, Senegal* 15°0N 14°40W **262** B2
Velingrad *Bulgaria* 42°4N 23°58E **202** D7
Velino, Mte. *Italy* 42°9N 13°23E **199** F10
Velizh *Russia* 55°36N 31°11E **188** E6
Vélizy-Villacoublay *France* 48°47N 2°11E **134** B2
Velka-Chuchle *Czechia* 50°0N 14°23E **135** B2
Vel'ké Kapušany *Slovakia* 48°34N 22°5E **181** C15
Velké Karlovice *Czechia* 49°20N 18°17E **181** B11
Velké Meziříčí *Czechia* 49°21N 16°1E **180** B9
Velké Přilepy *Czechia* 50°9N 14°19E **135** B1
Vel'ký Javorník *Slovakia* 49°19N 18°22E **181** B11
Vel'ký Krtíš *Slovakia* 48°12N 19°21E **181** C12
Vel'ký Meder *Slovakia* 47°52N 17°46E **181** D10
Vel'ký Tribeč *Slovakia* 48°28N 18°15E **181** C11
Vella G. *Solomon Is.* 8°0S 156°50E **287** M9
Vella Lavella *Solomon Is.* 7°45S 156°40E **287** L9
Vellar ➔ *India* 11°30N 79°36E **245** J4
Velletri *Italy* 41°41N 12°47E **200** A5
Vellinge *Sweden* 55°29N 13°2E **163** J6
Vellmar *Germany* 51°22N 9°28E **178** D5
Vellore *India* 12°57N 79°10E **245** H4
Velopoula *Greece* 36°55N 23°27E **204** E5
Velsk *Russia* 61°10N 42°0E **188** B11
Velten *Germany* 52°42N 13°10E **178** C9
Veluwezoom △ *Neths.* 52°5N 6°0E **170** B6
Velva *U.S.A.* 48°4N 100°56W **308** A3
Velvendos *Greece* 40°15N 22°6E **202** F6
Velyka Mykhaylivka *Ukraine* 47°4N 29°52E **183** C14
Velyki Luchky *Ukraine* 48°25N 22°34E **182** B7
Velykyy Bereznyy *Ukraine* 48°54N 22°28E **182** B7
Velykyy Bychkiv *Ukraine* 47°58N 24°1E **183** C9
Vemb *Denmark* 56°21N 8°21E **163** H2
Vembanad L. *India* 9°36N 76°15E **245** K3
Vemdalen *Sweden* 62°27N 13°51E **162** B7
Ven *Sweden* 55°55N 12°45E **163** J6
Venaco *France* 42°14N 9°11E **175** F13
Venado *Mexico* 22°56N 101°6W **318** C4
Venado Tuerto *Argentina* 33°50S 62°0W **334** C3
Venafro *Italy* 41°29N 14°2E **201** A7
Venarey-les-Laumes *France* 47°32N 4°26E **173** E11
Venaría *Italy* 45°8N 7°38E **198** C4
Venčane *Serbia* 44°24N 20°28E **202** B4
Vence *France* 43°43N 7°6E **175** E11
Venda Seca *Portugal* 38°46N 9°15W **126** A1
Vendas Novas *Portugal* 38°39N 8°27W **195** G2
Vendée □ *France* 46°50N 1°35W **172** F5
Vendée ➔ *France* 46°20N 1°10W **172** F5
Vendéen, Bocage *France* 46°40N 1°20W **174** B2
Vendeuvre-sur-Barse *France* 48°14N 4°28E **173** D11
Vendicari ⌓ *Italy* 36°49N 15°6E **201** F8
Vendôme *France* 47°47N 1°3E **172** E8
Vendramin Calergi, Palazzo *Venice, Italy* **142** a2
Vendrell = El Vendrell *Spain* 41°10N 1°30E **196** D6
Vendsyssel *Denmark* 57°22N 10°0E **163** G4
Vendychany *Ukraine* 48°38N 27°48E **183** B12
Venelles *France* 43°35N 5°28E **175** E9
Véneta, L. *Italy* 45°23N 12°25E **199** C9
Venetian Islands *U.S.A.* 25°47N 80°9W **129** D3
Venetie *U.S.A.* 67°1N 146°25W **303** C11
Véneto □ *Italy* 45°30N 12°0E **199** C9
Venev *Russia* 54°22N 38°17E **188** E10
Venézia *Italy* 45°27N 12°21E **199** C9
Venézia, G. di *Italy* 45°15N 13°0E **199** C10
Venézia, Palazzo *Rome, Italy* **136** c2
Venézia Lido *Italy* 45°25N 12°22E **199** C9
Venézia Tridentina = Trentino-Alto Adige □ *Italy* 46°30N 11°20E **199** B8
Venezuela ■ *S. Amer.* 8°0N 66°0W **328** B4
Venezuela, G. de *Venezuela* 11°30N 71°0W **328** A3
Venezuelan Basin *Cent. Amer.* 14°0N 68°0W **321** C6
Vengurla *India* 15°53N 73°45E **245** G1
Vengurla Rocks *India* 15°55N 73°22E **245** G1
Venice = Venézia *Italy* 45°27N 12°21E **199** C9
Venice *Calif., U.S.A.* 33°59N 118°27W **126** C2
Venice *Fla., U.S.A.* 27°6N 82°27W **317** H7
Vénissieux *France* 45°42N 4°53E **175** C8
Venjan *Sweden* 60°57N 13°55E **162** D7
Venjansjön *Sweden* 60°54N 14°0E **162** D8
Venkatagiri *India* 14°0N 79°35E **245** H4
Venkatapuram *India* 18°20N 80°30E **244** E5
Venlo *Neths.* 51°22N 6°11E **170** C6
Vennachar Junction *Canada* 45°5N 77°14W **312** A7
Vennesla *Norway* 58°15N 7°59E **164** F4
Venosa *Italy* 40°58N 15°49E **201** B8
Venray *Neths.* 51°31N 6°0E **170** C6
Vent, Îs. du *French Polynesia* 17°30S 149°30W **289** f
Venta *Lithuania* 56°12N 22°42E **184** B9
Venta ➔ *Latvia* 57°24N 21°33E **184** A8
Venta de Baños *Spain* 41°55N 4°30W **194** D6
Venta de Cardeña = Cardeña *Spain* 38°16N 4°20W **195** G6
Ventana, Sa. de la *Argentina* 38°0S 62°30W **334** D3
Ventas *Spain* 40°26N 3°40W **127** B1
Ventersburg *S. Africa* 28°7S 27°9E **270** C4
Ventersburgweg = Hennenman *S. Africa* 27°59S 27°1E **270** C4
Venterstad *S. Africa* 30°47S 25°48E **270** D4
Ventimíglia *Italy* 43°47N 7°36E **198** E4
Ventnor *U.K.* 50°36N 1°12W **169** G6
Ventorro del Cano *Spain* 40°23N 3°49W **127** B1
Ventoténe *Italy* 40°47N 13°25E **200** B6
Ventoux, Mt. *France* 44°10N 5°17E **175** D9
Ventspils *Latvia* 57°25N 21°32E **184** A8
Ventuarí ➔ *Venezuela* 3°58N 67°2W **328** C4
Ventucopa *U.S.A.* 34°50N 119°29W **307** L7
Ventura *U.S.A.* 34°17N 119°18W **307** L7
Venus *U.S.A.* 27°4N 81°22W **317** H8
Vénus, Pte. *Tahiti* 17°29S 149°29W **289** e
Venus B. *Australia* 38°40S 145°42E **283** E6
Venustiano Carranza *Baja Calif., Mexico* 30°25N 115°53W **318** A1
Venustiano Carranza *Distrito Federal, Mexico* 19°25N 99°5W **128** B2
Venustiano Carranza, Presa *Mexico* 27°30N 100°37W **318** B4
Vera *Argentina* 29°30S 60°20W **334** B3
Vera *Spain* 37°15N 1°51W **197** H3
Veracruz *Mexico* 19°11N 96°8W **319** D5
Veracruz □ *Mexico* 19°0N 96°15W **319** D5
Veraval *India* 20°53N 70°27E **242** J4
Verbánia *Italy* 45°56N 8°33E **198** C5
Verbano, L. di = Maggiore, L. *Italy* 45°57N 8°39E **198** B5
Verbano Cusio Ossola ⌓ *Italy* 46°15N 8°20E **198** B5
Verbicaro *Italy* 39°45N 15°55E **201** C8
Verbier *Switz.* 46°6N 7°13E **179** J3
Vercelli *Italy* 45°19N 8°25E **198** C5
Verchovchevo *Ukraine* 48°32N 34°10E **189** H8
Vercors ⌓ *France* 45°0N 5°25E **175** D9
Verdalsøra *Norway* 63°48N 11°30E **160** E14
Verde ➔ *Argentina* 41°56S 65°5W **336** B3
Verde ➔ *Goiás, Brazil* 19°11S 50°44W **333** E1
Verde ➔ *Goiás, Brazil* 18°1S 50°14W **333** E1
Verde ➔ *Mato Grosso, Brazil* 11°54S 55°48W **331** C6
Verde ➔ *Mato Grosso do Sul, Brazil* 21°25S 52°20W **331** E7
Verde ➔ *São Paulo, Brazil* 23°29S 46°27W **137** A1
Verde ➔ *Chihuahua, Mexico* 26°39N 107°11W **318** B3
Verde ➔ *Jalisco, Mexico* 20°42N 103°14W **318** C4
Verde ➔ *Oaxaca, Mexico* 15°59N 97°50W **319** D5
Verde ➔ *Paraguay* 23°9S 57°37W **334** A4
Verde ➔ *Ariz., U.S.A.* 33°33N 111°40W **305** K8
Verde, Cay *The Bahamas* 23°0N 75°5W **321** B4
Verde Grande ➔ *Brazil* 16°13S 43°49W **333** E3
Verde I. *Phil.* 13°33N 121°5E **232** E3
Verde Island Pass. *Phil.* 13°34N 120°51E **232** E3
Verde Pequeno ➔ *Brazil* 14°48S 43°31W **333** D3
Verden *Germany* 52°55N 9°14E **178** C5
Verdi *U.S.A.* 39°31N 119°59W **306** F7
Verdikoussa *Greece* 39°47N 21°59E **204** B3
Verdon ➔ *France* 43°43N 5°46E **175** E9
Verdon ⌓ *France* 43°50N 6°5E **175** E10
Verdugo Mts. *U.S.A.* 34°10N 118°16W **126** A2
Verdun *Qué., Canada* 45°27N 73°35W **130** B2
Verdun *Meuse, France* 49°9N 5°24E **173** C12
Verdun-sur-le-Doubs *France* 46°54N 5°2E **173** F12
Vereeniging *S. Africa* 26°38S 27°57E **271** C4
Verga, C. *Guinea* 10°30N 14°10W **262** C2
Vergara = Bergara *Spain* 43°9N 2°28W **196** B2
Vergara *Uruguay* 32°56S 53°57W **335** C5
Vergato *Italy* 44°17N 11°7E **198** D8
Vergemont Cr. ➔ *Australia* 24°16S 143°16E **280** C3
Vergennes *U.S.A.* 44°10N 73°15W **313** B11
Vergina = Aigai *Greece* 40°28N 22°19E **202** F6
Vergt *France* 45°2N 0°43E **174** C4
Vérhalom *Hungary* 47°31N 19°1E **117** A2
Veria *Greece* 40°34N 22°12E **202** F6
Verín *Spain* 41°57N 7°27W **194** D3
Verkhnedvinsk = Vyerkhnyadzvinsk *Belarus* 55°45N 27°58E **188** E4
Verkhnetulomskoye Vdkhr. *Russia* 68°36N 31°12E **160** B24
Verkhnevilyuysk *Russia* 63°27N 120°18E **215** C13
Verkhniy Baskunchak *Russia* 48°14N 46°44E **191** F8
Verkhovye *Russia* 52°55N 37°15E **189** F9
Verkhovyna *Ukraine* 48°9N 24°47E **183** B9
Verkhoyansk *Russia* 67°35N 133°25E **215** C14
Verkhoyansk Ra. = Verkhoyanskiy Khrebet *Russia* 66°0N 129°0E **215** C13
Verkhoyanskiy Khrebet *Russia* 66°0N 129°0E **215** C13
Verma *Norway* 62°21N 8°3E **164** B5
Vermeille, Côte *France* 42°50N 3°20E **174** F7
Vermelho ➔ *Brazil* 23°30S 46°46W **137** B1
Vermenton *France* 47°40N 3°42E **173** E10
Vermilion *Alta., Canada* 53°20N 110°50W **297** C6
Vermilion *Ohio, U.S.A.* 41°25N 82°22W **312** E2
Vermilion ➔ *Alta., Canada* 53°22N 110°51W **297** C6
Vermilion ➔ *Ill., U.S.A.* 41°19N 89°4W **310** C7
Vermilion B. *U.S.A.* 29°42N 92°0W **314** G9
Vermilion Bay *Canada* 49°51N 93°34W **297** D10
Vermilion Cliffs Nat. Monument ⌓ *U.S.A.* 36°54N 112°5W **305** H8
Vermilion L. *U.S.A.* 47°53N 92°26W **308** B7
Vermillion *U.S.A.* 42°47N 96°56W **308** D5
Vermillion ➔ *Canada* 47°38N 72°56W **298** C5
Vermont *U.S.A.* 40°18N 90°26W **310** D6
Vermont □ *U.S.A.* 44°0N 73°0W **313** C12
Vermont Knolls *U.S.A.* 33°57N 118°21W **126** C3
Vermosh *Albania* 42°35N 19°42E **202** D3
Verna *U.S.A.* 27°23N 82°16W **317** H7
Vernadsky *Antarctica* 65°0S 64°0W **151** C17
Vernal *U.S.A.* 40°27N 109°32W **304** F9
Vernalis *U.S.A.* 37°36N 121°17W **306** H5
Vernazza *Italy* 44°10N 9°45E **198** D6
Verner *Canada* 46°25N 80°8W **298** C3
Verneuil-sur-Avre *France* 48°45N 0°55E **172** D7
Verneukpan *S. Africa* 30°0S 21°0E **270** D3
Vernier *Switz.* 46°11N 6°12E **179** J2
Vérnio *Italy* 44°3N 11°9E **198** D8
Vernon *B.C., Canada* 50°20N 119°15W **296** C5
Vernon *Eure, France* 49°5N 1°30E **172** C8
Vernon *Calif., U.S.A.* 34°0N 118°13W **126** B3
Vernon *Ill., U.S.A.* 38°48N 89°5W **310** F7
Vernon *Ind., U.S.A.* 38°59N 85°36W **311** F11
Vernon *Tex., U.S.A.* 34°9N 99°17W **314** D5
Vernonia *U.S.A.* 45°52N 123°11W **306** E3
Vernou *Guadeloupe* 16°11N 61°39W **322** e
Verny = Almaty *Kazakhstan* 43°15N 76°57E **217** D9
Vero Beach *U.S.A.* 27°38N 80°24W **317** H9
Véroia = Veria *Greece* 40°34N 22°12E **202** F6
Véroli *Italy* 41°41N 13°25E **199** G10
Verona *Ont., Canada* 44°29N 76°42W **313** B8
Verona *Italy* 45°27N 10°59E **198** C7
Verona *Wis., U.S.A.* 42°59N 89°32W **310** B7
Verrès *Italy* 45°40N 7°42E **198** C4
Verrières-le-Buisson *France* 48°44N 2°16E **134** B2
Verron Ra. *Papua N. G.* 4°21S 152°46E **286** C7
Versailles *B. Aires, Argentina* 34°38S 58°31W **117** B1
Versailles *Yvelines, France* 48°48N 2°7E **134** B1
Versailles *Ill., U.S.A.* 39°53N 90°39W **310** E6
Versailles *Ind., U.S.A.* 39°4N 85°15W **311** E11
Versailles *Ky., U.S.A.* 38°3N 84°44W **311** F12
Versailles *Mo., U.S.A.* 38°26N 92°51W **310** F4
Versailles *Ohio, U.S.A.* 40°13N 84°29W **311** D12
Versalles *Bolivia* 12°44S 63°18W **331** C5
Versmold *Germany* 52°2N 8°9E **178** C4
Vert, C. *Senegal* 14°45N 17°30W **262** C1
Vertou *France* 47°10N 1°28W **172** E5
Vertus *France* 48°54N 4°2E **173** D11
Verulam *S. Africa* 29°38S 31°2E **271** C5
Verviers *Belgium* 50°37N 5°52E **170** D5
Vervins *France* 49°50N 3°53E **173** C10
Veržej *Slovenia* 46°34N 16°13E **199** B13
Verzy *France* 49°9N 4°10E **173** C11
Vescovato *France* 42°30N 9°27E **175** F13
Veselí nad Lužnicí *Czechia* 49°12N 14°43E **180** B7
Veselie *Bulgaria* 42°18N 27°38E **203** D11
Veselovskoye Vdkhr. *Russia* 46°58N 41°25E **191** G5
Veshenskaya *Russia* 49°35N 41°44E **190** F5
Veshnyaki *Russia* 55°43N 37°48E **129** B3
Vesle ➔ *France* 49°23N 3°28E **173** C10
Vesolyy Posolok *Russia* 59°53N 30°28E **137** B2
Vesoul *France* 47°40N 6°11E **173** E13
Vessigebro *Sweden* 56°58N 12°40E **163** H6
Vest-Agder □ *Norway* 58°30N 7°15E **164** F4
Vestale, Toraka *Madag.* 16°20S 43°58E **272** B1
Vestbygd *Norway* 58°6N 6°34E **164** F3
Vesterålen *Norway* 68°45N 15°0E **160** B16
Vestfirðir □ *Iceland* 65°45N 22°30W **155** B4
Vestfjorden *Norway* 67°55N 14°0E **160** C16
Vestfold □ *Norway* 59°15N 10°0E **164** E7
Vestfossen *Norway* 59°44N 9°52E **164** E6
Vestmannaeyjar *Iceland* 63°27N 20°15W **155** D6
Vestnes *Norway* 62°39N 7°5E **164** B4
Vestra *Finland* 60°19N 24°46E **121** B1
Vestre Gausdal *Norway* 61°12N 10°8E **164** C7
Vestskoven *Denmark* 55°41N 12°23E **118** A2
Vestur-skaftafellssýsla *Iceland* 63°50N 18°30W **155** D8
Vesturland □ *Iceland* 64°50N 22°0W **155** C5
Vestvågøya *Norway* 68°18N 13°50E **160** B15
Vesuvio *Italy* 40°49N 14°26E **201** B7
Vesuvius, Mt. = Vesuvio *Italy* 40°49N 14°26E **201** B7
Vesyegonsk *Russia* 58°40N 37°16E **188** C9
Veszprém *Hungary* 47°8N 17°57E **182** C2
Veszprém □ *Hungary* 47°5N 17°55E **182** C2
Vésztő *Hungary* 46°55N 21°16E **182** D6
Vetapalem *India* 15°47N 80°18E **245** G5
Vetlanda *Sweden* 57°24N 15°3E **163** G9
Vetluga *Russia* 57°53N 45°45E **190** B7
Vetlugu ➔ *Russia* 56°36N 46°4E **190** B8
Vetluzhskiy *Kostroma, Russia* 58°23N 45°26E **190** A7
Vetluzhskiy *Nizhniy Novgorod, Russia* 57°17N 45°12E **190** B7
Vetovo *Bulgaria* 43°42N 26°16E **203** C10
Vetralla *Italy* 42°20N 12°2E **199** F9
Vetren *Bulgaria* 42°15N 24°3E **203** D8
Vettore, Mte. *Italy* 42°49N 13°16E **199** F10
Veurne *Belgium* 51°5N 2°40E **170** C2
Vevay *U.S.A.* 38°45N 85°4W **311** F11
Veveno ➔ *South Sudan* 6°40N 32°58E **257** F3
Vevey *Switz.* 46°28N 6°51E **179** J2
Vevi *Greece* 40°47N 21°38E **202** F5
Veynes *France* 44°32N 5°49E **175** D9
Veys *Iran* 31°30N 49°0E **247** D6
Vézelay *France* 47°27N 3°45E **173** E10
Vézelise *France* 48°30N 6°5E **173** D13
Vézère ➔ *France* 44°53N 0°53E **174** D4
Vezhen *Bulgaria* 42°50N 24°20E **203** D8
Vezirköprü *Turkey* 41°8N 35°27E **212** B6
Vezzani *France* 42°10N 9°15E **175** F13
Vi Thanh *Vietnam* 9°42N 105°26E **237** H5
Viacha *Bolivia* 16°39S 68°18W **330** D4
Viadana *Italy* 44°56N 10°31E **198** D7
Vialar = Tissemsilt *Algeria* 35°35N 1°50E **261** A5
Viamão *Brazil* 30°5S 51°0W **335** C5
Viana *Brazil* 3°13S 44°55W **332** B3
Viana *Spain* 42°31N 2°22W **196** C2
Viana do Alentejo *Portugal* 38°17N 7°59W **195** G3
Viana do Bolo *Spain* 42°11N 7°6W **194** C3
Viana do Castelo *Portugal* 41°42N 8°50W **194** D2
Viana do Castelo □ *Portugal* 41°50N 8°30W **194** D2
Vianden *Lux.* 49°56N 6°12E **170** E6
Viangchan = Vientiane *Laos* 17°58N 102°36E **236** D4
Vianópolis *Brazil* 16°40S 48°35W **333** E2
Vianos *Greece* 35°2N 25°21E **207** E6
Viar ➔ *Spain* 37°36N 5°50W **195** H5
Viaréggio *Italy* 43°52N 10°14E **198** E7

Viaur → *France* 44°8N 1°58E **174** D5
Vibble *Sweden* 57°37N 18°16E **163** G12
Vibo Valéntia *Italy* 38°40N 16°6E **201** D9
Viborg *Denmark* 56°27N 9°23E **163** H3
Vibraye *France* 48°3N 0°44E **172** D7
Vic *Spain* 41°58N 2°19E **196** D7
Vic, Étang de *France* 43°29N 3°50E **174** E7
Vic-en-Bigorre *France* 43°24N 0°3E **174** E4
Vic-Fezensac *France* 43°47N 0°19E **174** E4
Vic-le-Comte *France* 45°39N 3°14E **173** G10
Vic-sur-Cère *France* 44°59N 2°38E **174** D6
Vicálvaro *Spain* 40°24N 3°36W **127** B2
Vícar *Spain* 36°50N 2°38W **197** J2
Vicente Lopez *Argentina* 34°31S 58°30W **117** B2
Vicente Pérez Rosales △ *Chile* 41°11S 72°12W **336** B2
Vicenza *Italy* 45°33N 11°33E **199** C8
Vich = Vic *Spain* 41°58N 2°19E **196** D7
Vichada □ *Colombia* 5°0N 69°30W **328** C4
Vichada → *Colombia* 4°55N 67°50W **328** C4
Vichuga *Russia* 57°12N 41°55E **190** B5
Vichy *France* 46°9N 3°26E **173** F10
Vicksburg *Ariz., U.S.A.* 33°45N 113°45W **307** M13
Vicksburg *Mich., U.S.A.* 42°7N 85°32W **311** B11
Vicksburg *Miss., U.S.A.* 32°21N 90°53W **315** E9
Vico *France* 42°10N 8°49E **175** F12
Vico, L. di *Italy* 42°19N 12°10E **199** F9
Vico del Gargano *Italy* 41°54N 15°57E **199** G12
Viçosa *Brazil* 9°28S 36°14W **332** C4
Viçosa do Ceará *Brazil* 3°34S 41°5W **332** B3
Vicovu de Sus *Romania* 47°56N 25°41E **183** C10
Victor *India* 21°0N 71°30E **242** J4
Victor Emanuel Ra. *Papua N. G.* 5°20S 142°15E **286** C2
Victor Harbor *Australia* 35°30S 138°37E **282** C3
Victor Hugo = Hamadia *Algeria* 35°28N 1°57E **261** A5
Victoria = Bandar Labuan *Malaysia* 5°20N 115°14E **235** A5
Victoria *Argentina* 32°40S 60°10W **334** C3
Victoria *B.C., Canada* 48°30N 123°25W **306** B3
Victoria *Chile* 38°13S 72°20W **336** A2
Victoria *Hong Kong, China* 22°17N 114°11E **122** B2
Victoria *Grenada* 12°12N 61°42W **323** q
Victoria *Guinea* 10°50N 14°32W **262** C2
Victoria *Gozo, Malta* 36°3N 14°14E **206** E6
Victoria *Mind. Or., Phil.* 13°12N 121°12E **232** E3
Victoria *Tarlac, Phil.* 15°35N 120°41E **232** D3
Victoria *Romania* 45°44N 24°41E **183** E9
Victoria *Seychelles* 4°38S 55°28E **272** c
Victoria *London, U.K.* **125** c3
Victoria *Kans., U.S.A.* 38°52N 99°9W **308** F4
Victoria *Tex., U.S.A.* 28°48N 97°0W **314** G6
Victoria □ *Australia* 37°0S 144°0E **282** D6
Victoria → *Australia* 15°10S 129°40E **278** C4
Victoria, Grand L. *Canada* 47°31N 77°30W **298** C4
Victoria, L. *Africa* 1°0S 33°0E **268** C3
Victoria, L. *N.S.W., Australia* 33°57S 141°15E **282** B4
Victoria, Mt. = Tomanivi *Fiji* 17°37S 178°1E **287** A2
Victoria, Mt. *Myanmar* 21°14N 93°55E **241** E4
Victoria, Mt. *Papua N. G.* 8°55S 147°32E **286** E4
Victoria, Pont *Canada* 45°29N 73°32W **130** B2
Victoria and Alfred Waterfront *Cape Town, S. Africa* **118** a1
Victoria Beach *Canada* 50°40N 96°35W **297** C9
Victoria de Durango = Durango *Mexico* 24°3N 104°39W **318** C4
Victoria de las Tunas = Las Tunas *Cuba* 20°58N 76°59W **320** B4
Victoria Falls *Zimbabwe* 17°58S 25°52E **269** F2
Victoria Fjord *Greenland* 82°10N 46°0W **154** A6
Victoria Gardens *India* 18°58N 72°50E **130** B2
Victoria Harbour *Ont., Canada* 44°45N 79°45W **312** B5
Victoria Harbour *Hong Kong, China* 22°17N 114°10E **122** B3
Victoria I. *Canada* 71°0N 111°0W **294** C9
Victoria Island *Nigeria* 6°25N 3°25E **124** B2
Victoria L. *Nfld. & L., Canada* 48°20N 57°27W **299** C8
Victoria L. *Gauteng, S. Africa* 26°13S 28°9E **123** B2
Victoria Lawn Tennis Courts *Australia* 37°50S 145°1E **128** B2
Victoria Ld. *Antarctica* 75°0S 160°0E **151** D11
Victoria Nile → *Uganda* 2°14N 31°26E **268** B3
Victoria Park *Singapore* 1°19N 103°49E **138** B2
Victoria Peak *Hong Kong, China* 22°16N 114°8E **122** B2
Victoria Peaks *Phil.* 9°22N 118°20E **233** G2
Victoria Pk. *Belize* 16°48N 88°37W **319** D7
Victoria Ra. *N.Z.* 42°12S 172°7E **285** C7
Victoria River *Australia* 16°25S 131°0E **278** C5
Victoria Str. *Canada* 69°31N 100°30W **294** D11
Victoria Terminus = Chhatrapati Shivaji Terminus *India* 18°56N 72°50E **130** B2
Victoria Village *Canada* 43°46N 79°20W **141** A3
Victoria West *S. Africa* 31°25S 23°4E **270** D3
Victoria Wharf *Cape Town, S. Africa* **118** a2
Victorias *Phil.* 10°54N 123°5E **233** F4
Victoriaville *Canada* 46°4N 71°56W **299** C5
Victorica *Argentina* 36°20S 65°30W **334** D2
Victorville *U.S.A.* 34°32N 117°18W **307** L9
Vicuña *Chile* 30°0S 70°50W **334** C1
Vicuña Mackenna *Argentina* 33°53S 64°25W **334** C3
Vidal *U.S.A.* 34°7N 114°31W **307** L12
Vidalia *U.S.A.* 32°13N 82°25W **316** C7
Vidamlya *Belarus* 52°19N 23°47E **185** F10
Vidauban *France* 43°25N 6°27E **175** E10
Viddolatno = Vindelälven → *Sweden* 63°55N 19°50E **160** E18
Videbæk *Denmark* 56°6N 8°38E **163** H2
Videle *Romania* 44°17N 25°31E **183** F10
Videsæter *Norway* 61°57N 7°14E **164** C4
Vidette *U.S.A.* 33°2N 82°15W **316** B7
Vidigueira *Portugal* 38°12N 7°48W **195** G3
Vidin *Bulgaria* 43°59N 22°50E **202** C6
Vidin □ *Bulgaria* 43°59N 22°50E **202** C6
Vidio, C. *Spain* 43°35N 6°14W **194** B4
Vidisha *India* 23°28N 77°53E **242** H7
Vidos *Greece* 39°38N 19°55E **206** B9
Vidra *Romania* 45°56N 26°55E **183** E11
Viduša *Bos.-H.* 42°55N 18°21E **202** D2
Vidzy *Belarus* 55°23N 26°37E **188** E4
Viechtach *Germany* 49°4N 12°53E **179** F8
Viedma *Argentina* 40°50S 63°0W **336** B4
Viedma, L. *Argentina* 49°30S 72°30W **336** C2
Vieille Case *Dominica* 15°36N 61°24W **323** k
Vieira do Minho *Portugal* 41°38N 8°8W **194** D2
Vielha *Spain* 42°43N 0°44E **196** C5
Viella = Vielha *Spain* 42°43N 0°44E **196** C5
Vielle St-Girons *France* 43°56N 1°18W **174** E2
Vielsalm *Belgium* 50°17N 5°54E **170** D5
Vienenburg *Germany* 51°57N 10°34E **178** D6
Vieng Pou Kha *Laos* 20°41N 101°4E **228** G3
Vienna = Wien *Austria* 48°12N 16°22E **142** A2
Vienna *Ont., Canada* 42°41N 80°48W **312** D4
Vienna *Ga., U.S.A.* 32°6N 83°47W **316** C6
Vienna *Ill., U.S.A.* 37°25N 88°54W **308** G9
Vienna *Mo., U.S.A.* 38°11N 91°57W **310** F5
Vienne *France* 45°31N 4°53E **175** C8
Vienne □ *France* 46°30N 0°42E **174** B4
Vienne → *France* 47°13N 0°5E **172** E7
Vientiane *Laos* 17°58N 102°36E **236** D4
Vientos, Paso de los *Caribbean* 20°0N 74°0W **321** C5
Vieques *Puerto Rico* 18°8N 65°25W **321** b
Vierge Pt. *St. Lucia* 13°49N 60°53W **323** m
Vierkant Pt. *Bonaire* 12°7N 68°17W **322** h
Viernheim *Germany* 49°31N 8°35E **179** F4
Viersen *Germany* 51°15N 6°23E **178** D2
Vierwaldstättersee *Switz.* 47°0N 8°30E **179** J4
Vierzon *France* 47°13N 2°5E **173** E9
Vieste *Italy* 41°53N 16°10E **199** G13
Viet Quang *Vietnam* 22°30N 104°48E **228** F5
Viet Tri *Vietnam* 21°18N 105°25E **236** B5
Vietnam ■ *Asia* 19°0N 106°0E **236** C6
Vietnam Veterans Memorial *Washington, D.C., U.S.A.* 38°53N 77°2W **143** B2
Vietz = Witnica *Poland* 52°40N 14°54E **185** F1
Vieux-Boucau-les-Bains *France* 43°48N 1°23W **174** E2
Vieux Bourg *Guadeloupe* 16°20N 61°36W **322** e
Vieux Carré = French Quarter *New Orleans, U.S.A.* **131** a2
Vieux Fort *Guadeloupe* 15°57N 61°41W **322** e
Vieux Fort *Marie-Galante, Guadeloupe* 15°59N 61°17W **322** e
Vieux Fort *St. Lucia* 13°46N 60°58W **323** m
Vieux Fort, Pte. du *Guadeloupe* 15°57N 61°42W **322** e
Vieux Fort, R. du → *Guadeloupe* 15°59N 61°17W **322** e
Vieux Grand Port *Mauritius* 20°22S 57°42E **272** e
Vieux-Habitants *Guadeloupe* 16°4N 61°46W **322** e
Vieux-Habitants, Rivière des → *Guadeloupe* 16°3N 61°46W **322** e
Vieux-Montréal *Montréal, Canada* **130** b3
View Park *U.S.A.* 34°0N 118°20W **126** B3
Vif *France* 45°5N 5°41E **175** C9
Viga *Phil.* 13°52N 124°18E **232** E5
Vigan *Phil.* 17°35N 120°28E **232** C3
Vigário Geral *Brazil* 22°48S 43°18W **135** A1
Vigeland *Norway* 58°5N 7°18E **164** F4
Vigentino *Italy* 45°26N 9°13E **128** B2
Vigévano *Italy* 45°19N 8°51E **198** C5
Viggbyholm *Sweden* 59°26N 18°7E **139** A2
Vighignolo *Italy* 45°29N 9°2E **128** B1
Vigia = Almenara *Brazil* 16°11S 40°42W **333** E3
Vigia *Brazil* 0°50S 48°5W **332** B2
Vigla *Greece* 39°7N 20°50E **207** A2
Viglas, Akra *Greece* 35°54N 27°51E **206** F11
Vignemalle *France* 42°47N 0°10W **174** F3
Vigneulles-lès-Hattonchâtel *France* 48°59N 5°43E **173** D12
Vignola *Italy* 44°29N 11°1E **198** D8
Vigo *Spain* 42°12N 8°41W **194** C2
Vigo, Ría de *Spain* 42°15N 8°45W **194** C2
Vigrestad *Norway* 58°34N 5°42E **164** F2
Vigsø Bugt *Denmark* 57°8N 8°47E **163** G2
Vihiers *France* 47°10N 0°30W **172** E6
Vihiga *Kenya* 0°3N 34°44E **268** B3
Vihowa *Pakistan* 31°8N 70°30E **242** D4
Vihowa → *Pakistan* 31°8N 70°41E **242** D4
Viikki *Finland* 60°13N 25°1E **121** B3
Viipuri = Vyborg *Russia* 60°43N 28°47E **188** B5
Vijayadurg *India* 16°30N 73°25E **244** F1
Vijayapura *India* 16°50N 75°55E **244** F2
Vijayawada *India* 16°31N 80°39E **244** F5
Vijosë → *Albania* 40°37N 19°24E **202** F3
Vík *Iceland* 63°25N 19°1W **155** D7
Vik *Sogn og Fjordane, Norway* 61°21N 6°6E **164** C3
Vika *Sweden* 60°57N 14°28E **162** D8
Vikarabad *India* 17°20N 77°54E **244** E3
Vikarbyn *Sweden* 60°55N 15°1E **162** D9
Vike *Norway* 60°42N 5°35E **164** D2
Vikedal *Norway* 59°30N 5°55E **164** E2
Vikeke = Viqueque *Timor-Leste* 8°52S 126°23E **231** F7
Vikeland = Vigeland *Norway* 58°5N 7°18E **164** F4
Viken *Skåne, Sweden* 56°9N 12°34E **163** H6
Viken *Västra Götaland, Sweden* 58°39N 14°20E **163** F8
Vikersund *Norway* 59°58N 9°59E **164** E6
Vikeså *Norway* 58°38N 6°3E **164** F3
Vikevåg *Norway* 59°5N 5°41E **164** E2
Vikhammer *Norway* 63°26N 10°37E **164** A7
Vikhroli *India* 19°6N 72°55E **130** A2
Viking *Canada* 53°7N 111°50W **296** C6
Vikmanshyttan *Sweden* 60°18N 15°50E **162** D9
Vikna *Norway* 64°55N 10°58E **160** D14
Vikos-Aoos △ *Greece* 40°0N 20°45E **204** B2
Vikøyri *Norway* 61°4N 6°34E **164** C3
Vila Alferes Chamusca = Guijá *Mozam.* 24°27S 33°0E **271** B5
Vila António Enes = Angoche *Mozam.* 16°8S 39°55E **269** F4
Vila Baleira *Madeira* 33°4N 16°20W **260** B1
Vila Bela da Santissima Trindade *Brazil* 15°0S 59°57W **331** C6
Vila Cabral = Lichinga *Mozam.* 13°13S 35°11E **269** E4
Vila Cabral = Niassa □ *Mozam.* 13°30S 36°0E **269** E4
Vila da Maganja *Mozam.* 17°18S 37°30E **269** F4
Vila da Ribeira Brava *Cabo Verde* 16°32N 24°25W **153** j
Vila de Rei *Portugal* 39°41N 8°9W **194** F2
Vila do Bispo *Portugal* 37°5N 8°53W **195** H2
Vila do Conde *Portugal* 41°21N 8°45W **194** D2
Vila do Maio *Cabo Verde* 15°21N 23°10W **153** j
Vila do Porto *Azores* 36°56N 25°9W **153** d4
Vila Franca de Xira *Portugal* 38°57N 8°59W **195** G2
Vila Franca do Campo *Azores* 37°43N 25°26W **153** d3
Vila Gamito *Mozam.* 14°12S 33°0E **269** E3
Vila Gomes da Costa *Mozam.* 24°20S 33°37E **271** B5
Vila Guilherme *Brazil* 23°30S 46°38W **137** B2
Vila Isabel *Brazil* 22°54S 43°15W **135** B1
Vila Jaguára *Brazil* 23°30S 46°45W **137** B1
Vila Machado *Mozam.* 19°15S 34°14E **269** F3
Vila Madalena *Brazil* 23°32S 46°41W **137** B1
Vila Maria *Brazil* 23°31S 46°36W **137** B2
Vila Mariana *Brazil* 23°34S 46°36W **137** B2
Vila Mouzinho *Mozam.* 14°48S 34°25E **269** E3
Vila Nova de Famalicão *Portugal* 41°25N 8°32W **194** D2
Vila Nova de Foz Côa *Portugal* 41°5N 7°9W **194** D3
Vila Nova de Gaia *Portugal* 41°8N 8°37W **194** D2
Vila Nova de Gaza = Xai-Xai *Mozam.* 25°6S 33°31E **271** C5
Vila Nova do Corvo *Azores* 39°40N 31°8W **153** d2
Vila Nova Sintra *Cabo Verde* 14°52N 24°42W **153** j
Vila Pereira de Eça = Ondjiva *Angola* 16°48S 15°50E **265** F3
Vila Pery = Manica *Mozam.* 18°58S 32°59E **271** A5
Vila Pouca de Aguiar *Portugal* 41°30N 7°38W **194** D3
Vila Prudente *Brazil* 23°35S 46°33W **137** B2
Vila Real *Portugal* 41°17N 7°48W **194** D3
Vila-Real *Spain* 39°55N 0°3W **196** F4
Vila Real □ *Portugal* 41°36N 7°35W **194** D3
Vila Real de Santo António *Portugal* 37°10N 7°28W **195** H3
Vila-seca *Spain* 41°7N 1°9E **196** D6
Vila Texeira da Silva = Luau *Angola* 10°40S 22°10E **265** E4
Vila Vasco da Gama *Mozam.* 14°54S 32°14E **269** E3
Vila Velha *Amapá, Brazil* 3°13N 51°13W **329** C7
Vila Velha *Espírito Santo, Brazil* 20°20S 40°17W **333** F3
Vila Velha *Sergipe, Brazil* 11°20S 38°9W **332** D4
Vila Viçosa *Portugal* 38°45N 7°27W **195** G3
Viladecans *Spain* 41°18N 2°1E **114** B1
Vilafranca del Maestrat = Villafranca del Cid *Spain* 40°26N 0°16W **196** E4
Vilafranca del Penedès *Spain* 41°21N 1°40E **196** D6
Vilagarcía de Arousa *Spain* 42°34N 8°46W **194** C2
Vilaine → *France* 47°30N 2°27W **172** E4
Vilakalaka *Vanuatu* 15°25S 167°42E **287** E5
Vilanandro, Tanjona *Madag.* 16°11S 44°27E **272** B1
Vilanculos *Mozam.* 22°1S 35°17E **271** B6
Vilanova i la Geltrú *Spain* 41°13N 1°40E **196** D6
Vilar Formoso *Portugal* 40°38N 6°45W **194** E4
Vilaseca-Salou = Vila-seca *Spain* 41°7N 1°9E **196** D6
Vilbjerg *Denmark* 56°12N 8°46E **163** H2
Vilcabamba, Cordillera *Peru* 13°0S 73°0W **330** C3
Vilcanchos *Peru* 13°40S 74°25W **330** C3
Vilcheka, Ostrov *Russia* 80°0N 58°31E **214** B6
Vilcheka, Zemlya *Russia* 80°30N 60°30E **150** A11
Vilches *Spain* 38°12N 3°30W **195** G7
Vile Parle *India* 19°6N 72°51E **130** A2
Vileyka *Belarus* 54°30N 26°53E **177** A14
Vilhelmina *Sweden* 64°35N 16°39E **160** D17
Vilhena *Brazil* 12°40S 60°5W **331** C5
Viliya = Neris → *Lithuania* 55°8N 24°16E **188** E3
Viljandi *Estonia* 58°28N 25°30E **188** C3
Viljoensdorp = Newcastle *S. Africa* 27°45S 29°58E **271** C4
Vilkaviškis *Lithuania* 54°39N 23°2E **184** D10
Vilkija *Lithuania* 55°3N 23°35E **184** C10
Vilkitskogo, Proliv *Russia* 78°0N 103°0E **215** B11
Vilkomir = Ukmergė *Lithuania* 55°15N 24°45E **188** E3
Vilkovo = Vylkove *Ukraine* 45°28N 29°32E **183** E14
Villa Abecia *Bolivia* 21°0S 68°18W **334** A2
Villa Adelina *Argentina* 34°31S 58°33W **117** B1
Villa Ana *Argentina* 28°28S 59°40W **334** B4
Villa Angela *Argentina* 27°34S 60°45W **334** B3
Villa Ballester *Argentina* 34°33S 58°33W **117** B1
Villa Barilari *Argentina* 34°42S 58°20W **117** C2
Villa Bella = Serra Talhada *Brazil* 7°59S 38°18W **332** C4
Villa Bella *Bolivia* 10°25S 65°22W **331** C4
Villa Borghese *Rome, Italy* **136** a3
Villa Bosch *Argentina* 34°35S 58°33W **117** B1
Villa Bruzual *Venezuela* 9°20N 69°6W **328** C4
Villa C. Colon *Argentina* 34°41S 58°21W **117** C2
Villa Cañás *Argentina* 34°0S 61°35W **334** C3
Villa Cecilia = Ciudad Madero *Mexico* 22°19N 97°50W **319** C5
Villa Cisneros = Dakhla *W. Sahara* 23°50N 15°53W **260** D1
Villa Ciudadela *Argentina* 34°38S 58°33W **117** B1
Villa Constitución *Argentina* 33°15S 60°20W **334** C3
Villa de Arriaga *Mexico* 21°56N 101°20W **318** C4
Villa de Cura *Venezuela* 10°2N 67°29W **328** A4
Villa de Guadalupe *Mexico* 19°29N 99°6W **128** B2
Villa de María *Argentina* 29°55S 63°43W **334** B3
Villa de Méndez *Mexico* 25°7N 98°34W **319** B5
Villa del Nevoso = Ilirska-Bistrica *Slovenia* 45°34N 14°14E **199** C11
Villa del Rio *Spain* 37°59N 4°17W **195** H6
Villa del Rosario *Venezuela* 10°19N 72°19W **328** A3
Villa Devoto *Argentina* 34°36S 58°31W **117** B1
Villa Diamante *Argentina* 34°41S 58°25W **117** C2
Villa Dolores *Argentina* 31°58S 65°15W **334** C2
Villa Dominico *Argentina* 34°41S 58°19W **117** C3
Villa Gesell *Argentina* 37°15S 56°55W **334** D4
Villa Grove *U.S.A.* 39°52N 88°10W **311** E8
Villa Guillermina *Argentina* 28°15S 59°29W **334** B4
Villa Hayes *Paraguay* 25°5S 57°20W **334** B4
Villa Hidalgo *Mexico* 24°15N 99°26W **319** C5
Villa Iris *Argentina* 38°12S 63°12W **334** D3
Villa Lugano *Argentina* 34°41S 58°27W **117** C2
Villa Lynch *Argentina* 34°35S 58°31W **117** B1
Villa Madero *Argentina* 34°41S 58°30W **117** C1
Villa María *Argentina* 32°20S 63°10W **334** C3
Villa Mazán *Argentina* 28°40S 66°30W **334** B2
Villa Minozzo *Italy* 44°22N 10°28E **198** D7
Villa Montes *Bolivia* 21°10S 63°30W **334** A3
Villa Ocampo *Argentina* 28°30S 59°20W **334** B4
Villa Ocampo *Durango, Mexico* 26°27N 105°31W **318** B3
Villa Ojo de Agua *Argentina* 29°30S 63°44W **334** B3
Villa Regina *Argentina* 39°6S 67°4W **336** A3
Villa Rica *U.S.A.* 33°44N 84°55W **316** B5
Villa Sáenz Pena *Argentina* 34°37S 58°32W **117** B1
Villa San Giovanni *Italy* 38°13N 15°38E **201** D8
Villa San Martín *Argentina* 28°15S 64°9W **334** B3
Villa Sanjurjo = Al Hoceïma *Morocco* 35°8N 3°58W **261** A4
Villa Santina *Italy* 46°24N 12°55E **199** B9
Villa Unión *Mexico* 23°12N 106°14W **318** C3
Villa Urquiza *Argentina* 34°34S 58°28W **117** B2
Villaba *Phil.* 11°13N 124°24E **233** F5
Villablino *Spain* 42°57N 6°19W **194** C4
Villacarlos *Spain* 39°53N 4°17E **206** B5
Villacarriedo *Spain* 43°14N 3°48W **194** B7
Villacarrillo *Spain* 38°7N 3°3W **195** G7
Villacastín *Spain* 40°46N 4°25W **194** E6
Villach *Austria* 46°37N 13°51E **180** E6
Villacidro *Italy* 39°27N 8°44E **200** C1
Villada *Spain* 42°15N 4°59W **194** C6
Villadiego *Spain* 42°31N 4°1W **194** C6
Villadóssola *Italy* 46°4N 8°16E **198** B5
Villafeliche *Spain* 41°10N 1°30W **196** D3
Villafranca *Spain* 42°17N 1°46W **196** C3
Villafranca de los Barros *Spain* 38°35N 6°18W **195** G4
Villafranca de los Caballeros *Spain* 39°26N 3°21W **195** F7
Villafranca del Cid *Spain* 40°26N 0°16W **196** E4
Villafranca del Panadés = Vilafranca del Penedès *Spain* 41°21N 1°40E **196** D6
Villafranca di Verona *Italy* 45°21N 10°50E **198** C7
Villafranca Tirrena *Italy* 38°20N 15°25E **201** D8
Villagio Mussolini = Arboréa *Italy* 39°46N 8°35E **200** C1
Villagrán *Mexico* 24°29N 99°29W **319** C5
Villaguay *Argentina* 32°0S 59°0W **334** C4
Villaharta *Spain* 38°9N 4°54W **195** G6
Villahermosa *Tabasco, Mexico* 17°59N 92°55W **319** D6
Villahermosa *Spain* 38°46N 2°52W **197** G2
Villaines-la-Juhel *France* 48°21N 0°20W **172** D6
Villajoyosa *Spain* 38°30N 0°12W **197** G4
Villalba *Puerto Rico* 18°8N 66°30W **321** b
Villalba *Spain* 43°22N 7°40W **194** B3
Villalba de Guardo *Spain* 42°42N 4°49W **194** C6
Villalón de Campos *Spain* 42°5N 5°4W **194** C5
Villalpando *Spain* 41°51N 5°25W **194** D5
Villaluenga de la Sagra *Spain* 40°2N 3°54W **194** E7
Villamanán *Spain* 42°19N 5°35W **194** C5
Villamartín *Spain* 36°52N 5°38W **195** J5
Villamayor de Santiago *Spain* 39°50N 2°59W **196** F2
Villamblard *France* 45°2N 0°32E **174** C4
Villanova Monteleone *Italy* 40°30N 8°28E **200** B1
Villanueva *Colombia* 10°37N 72°59W **328** A3
Villanueva *N. Mex., U.S.A.* 35°16N 105°22W **305** J11
Villanueva de Castellón *Spain* 39°5N 0°31W **197** F4
Villanueva de Córdoba *Spain* 38°20N 4°38W **195** G6
Villanueva de la Fuente *Spain* 38°42N 2°42W **197** G2
Villanueva de la Serena *Spain* 38°59N 5°50W **195** G5
Villanueva de la Sierra *Spain* 40°12N 6°24W **194** E4
Villanueva de los Castillejos *Spain* 37°30N 7°15W **195** H3
Villanueva de los Infantes *Spain* 38°43N 3°1W **195** G7
Villanueva del Arzobispo *Spain* 38°10N 3°0W **197** G2
Villanueva del Fresno *Spain* 38°23N 7°10W **195** G3
Villanueva y Geltrú = Vilanova i la Geltrú *Spain* 41°13N 1°40E **196** D6
Villaputzu *Italy* 39°26N 9°34E **200** C2
Villaquilambre *Spain* 42°39N 5°33W **194** C5
Villar del Arzobispo *Spain* 39°44N 0°50W **196** F4
Villar del Rey *Spain* 39°7N 6°50W **195** F4
Villard-de-Lans *France* 45°3N 5°33E **175** C9
Villarramiel *Spain* 42°2N 4°55W **194** C6
Villarreal = Vila-Real *Spain* 39°55N 0°3W **196** F4
Villarrica *Chile* 39°15S 72°15W **336** A2
Villarrica *Paraguay* 25°40S 56°30W **334** B4
Villarrica △ *Chile* 39°24S 71°46W **336** A2
Villarrobledo *Spain* 39°18N 2°36W **197** F2
Villarroya de la Sierra *Spain* 41°27N 1°46W **196** D3
Villarrubia de los Ojos *Spain* 39°14N 3°36W **195** F7
Villars-les-Dombes *France* 46°0N 5°3E **173** F12
Villasayas *Spain* 41°24N 2°39W **196** D2
Villaseco de los Gamitos *Spain* 41°2N 6°7W **194** D4
Villasimíus *Italy* 39°8N 9°31E **200** C2
Villastar *Spain* 40°17N 1°9W **196** E3
Villatobas *Spain* 39°54N 3°20W **194** F7
Villaverde *Spain* 40°21N 3°42W **127** B1
Villaverde Bajo *Spain* 40°20N 3°40W **127** B1
Villavicencio *Argentina* 32°28S 69°0W **334** C2
Villavicencio *Colombia* 4°9N 73°37W **328** C3
Villaviciosa *Spain* 43°32N 5°27W **194** B5
Villazón *Bolivia* 22°0S 65°35W **334** A2
Ville-d'Avray *France* 48°49N 2°11E **134** B2
Ville-Marie *Canada* 47°20N 79°30W **298** C4
Ville Platte *U.S.A.* 30°41N 92°17W **314** F8
Villecresnes *France* 48°43N 2°31E **134** B4
Villedieu-les-Poêles *France* 48°50N 1°13W **172** D5
Villefort *France* 44°28N 3°56E **174** D7
Villefranche-de-Lauragais *France* 43°25N 1°44E **174** E5
Villefranche-de-Rouergue *France* 44°21N 2°2E **174** D6
Villefranche-du-Périgord *France* 44°38N 1°5E **174** D5
Villefranche-sur-Saône *France* 45°59N 4°43E **175** C8
Villejuif *France* 48°47N 2°21E **134** B3
Villel *Spain* 40°14N 1°12W **196** E3
Villemomble *France* 48°52N 2°30E **134** A4
Villemur-sur-Tarn *France* 43°51N 1°31E **174** E5
Villena *Spain* 38°39N 0°52W **197** G4
Villenauxe-la-Grande *France* 48°35N 3°33E **173** D10
Villenave-d'Ornon *France* 44°46N 0°33W **174** D3
Villeneuve-d'Ascq *France* 50°38N 3°9E **173** B10
Villeneuve-la-Garenne *France* 48°56N 2°19E **134** A2
Villeneuve-l'Archevêque *France* 48°14N 3°32E **173** D10
Villeneuve-le-Roi *France* 48°43N 2°24E **134** B3
Villeneuve-lès-Avignon *France* 43°58N 4°49E **175** E8
Villeneuve-St-Georges *France* 48°43N 2°27E **134** B3
Villeneuve-sur-Allier *France* 46°40N 3°13E **173** F10
Villeneuve-sur-Lot *France* 44°24N 0°42E **174** D4
Villeneuve-sur-Yonne *France* 48°5N 3°18E **173** D10
Villeparisis *France* 48°56N 2°36E **134** A4
Villeréal *France* 44°38N 0°45E **174** D4
Villers-Bocage *France* 49°3N 0°40W **172** C6
Villers-Cotterêts *France* 49°15N 3°4E **173** C10
Villers-sur-Mer *France* 49°21N 0°2W **172** C6
Villersexel *France* 47°33N 6°26E **173** E13
Villerupt *France* 49°28N 5°55E **173** C12
Villeurbanne *France* 45°46N 4°55E **175** C8
Villevaudé *France* 48°55N 2°39E **134** A4
Villiers *S. Africa* 27°2S 28°36E **271** C4
Villiers-le-Bâcle *France* 48°44N 2°8E **134** B1
Villiers-sur-Marne *France* 48°49N 2°32E **134** B4
Villingen-Schwenningen *Germany* 48°3N 8°26E **179** G4
Villinki *Finland* 60°9N 25°6E **121** C3
Villisca *U.S.A.* 40°56N 94°59W **310** D2
Villmanstrand = Lappeenranta *Finland* 61°3N 28°12E **188** B5
Villoresi, Canale *Italy* 45°33N 9°9E **128** A1
Villupuram *India* 11°59N 79°31E **245** J4
Vilna = Vilnius *Lithuania* 54°38N 25°19E **188** E3
Vilna *Canada* 54°7N 111°55W **296** C6
Vilnius *Lithuania* 54°38N 25°19E **188** E3
Vils *Austria* 47°33N 10°38E **180** D3
Vils → *Bayern, Germany* 48°37N 13°11E **179** G9
Vils → *Bayern, Germany* 49°10N 11°57E **179** F7
Vilsandi △ *Estonia* 58°23N 21°52E **188** C1
Vilsbiburg *Germany* 48°26N 12°22E **179** G8
Vilshofen *Germany* 48°37N 13°11E **179** G9
Vilusi *Montenegro* 42°44N 18°34E **202** D2
Vilvoorde *Belgium* 50°56N 4°26E **116** A2
Vilyuchinsk *Russia* 52°55N 158°24E **215** D16
Vilyuy → *Russia* 64°24N 126°26E **215** C13
Vilyuysk *Russia* 63°40N 121°35E **215** C13
Vilyuyskoye Vdkhr. *Russia* 63°0N 112°0E **215** C12
Vimianzo *Spain* 43°7N 9°2W **194** B1
Vimioso *Portugal* 41°35N 6°31W **194** D4
Vimmerby *Sweden* 57°40N 15°55E **163** G9
Vimodrone *Italy* 45°30N 9°16E **128** A2
Vimont *Canada* 45°36N 73°43W **130** A1
Vimoutiers *France* 48°57N 0°10E **172** D7
Vimperk *Czechia* 49°3N 13°46E **180** B6
Vina → *Cameroon* 7°45N 15°36E **264** A3
Viña del Mar *Chile* 33°0S 71°30W **334** C1
Vinanmek Mansion *Bangkok, Thailand* **113** a2
Vinarós *Spain* 40°30N 0°27E **196** E5
Vincendo *Réunion* 21°21S 55°41E **272** f
Vincennes *Val-de-Marne, France* 48°51N 2°26E **134** A3
Vincennes *Ind., U.S.A.* 38°41N 87°32W **311** F9
Vincennes, Bois de *France* 48°49N 2°26E **134** B3
Vincennes Bay *S. Ocean* 66°0S 109°0E **151** C8
Vincent *U.S.A.* 34°33N 118°11W **307** L8
Vinces *Ecuador* 1°32S 79°45W **328** D2
Vinchina *Argentina* 28°45S 68°15W **334** B2
Vindava = Ventspils *Latvia* 57°25N 21°32E **184** A8
Vindelälven → *Sweden* 63°55N 19°50E **160** E18
Vindeln *Sweden* 64°12N 19°43E **160** D18
Vinderup *Denmark* 56°29N 8°45E **163** H2
Vindhya Ra. *India* 22°50N 77°0E **242** H7
Vine Grove *U.S.A.* 37°49N 85°59W **311** G11
Vineland *Fla., U.S.A.* 28°23N 81°30W **133** B1
Vineland *N.J., U.S.A.* 39°29N 75°2W **309** F16
Vineuil *France* 47°35N 1°22E **172** E8
Vinga *Romania* 46°1N 21°14E **182** D6
Vingåker *Sweden* 59°2N 15°52E **162** E9
Vingelen *Norway* 62°25N 10°52E **164** B7
Vingnes *Norway* 61°7N 10°26E **164** C7
Vinh *Vietnam* 18°45N 105°38E **236** C5
Vinh Loi = Bac Lieu *Vietnam* 9°17N 105°43E **237** H5
Vinh Long *Vietnam* 10°16N 105°57E **237** G5
Vinh Moc *Vietnam* 21°18N 105°1E **236** B5
Vinh Yen *Vietnam* 21°21N 105°35E **228** G5
Vinhais *Portugal* 41°50N 7°5W **194** D3
Vinica *Croatia* 46°20N 16°9E **199** B13
Vinica *N. Macedonia* 41°53N 22°30E **202** E6
Vinica *Slovenia* 45°28N 15°16E **199** C12
Vinings *U.S.A.* 33°53N 84°29W **113** A2
Vinita *U.S.A.* 36°39N 95°9W **314** C7
Vinje *Sør-Trøndelag, Norway* 63°12N 9°0E **164** A5
Vinje *Telemark, Norway* 59°37N 7°51E **164** E4
Vinjo *Norway* 60°48N 6°30E **164** D3
Vinkovci *Croatia* 45°19N 18°48E **182** E3
Vinnitsa = Vinnytsya *Ukraine* 49°15N 28°30E **177** D15
Vinnytsya *Ukraine* 49°15N 28°30E **177** D15
Vinnytsya □ *Ukraine* 49°20N 28°15E **177** D15
Vinodelnoye = Ipatovo *Russia* 45°45N 42°50E **191** H6
Vinohrady *Prague, Czechia* **135** c3
Vinoř *Czechia* 50°8N 14°34E **135** B3
Vinslöv *Sweden* 56°7N 13°55E **163** H7
Vinson Massif *Antarctica* 78°35S 85°25W **151** D16
Vinstra *Norway* 61°37N 9°44E **164** C6
Vinstra → *Norway* 61°37N 9°44E **164** C6
Vintar *Phil.* 18°14N 120°39E **232** B3
Vintjärn *Sweden* 60°50N 16°4E **162** D10
Vinton *Calif., U.S.A.* 39°48N 120°10W **306** F6
Vinton *Iowa, U.S.A.* 42°10N 92°1W **310** B4
Vinton *La., U.S.A.* 30°11N 93°35W **314** F8
Vinţu de Jos *Romania* 46°0N 23°30E **183** D8
Vinukonda *India* 16°4N 79°45E **245** F4
Viöl *Germany* 54°34N 9°11E **178** A5
Viola *U.S.A.* 41°12N 90°35W **310** C6
Violet Hill *Hong Kong, China* 22°15N 114°11E **122** B3
Violet Town *Australia* 36°38S 145°42E **283** D6
Violet Valley ☼ *Australia* 17°10S 127°55E **278** C4
Vioolsdrif *S. Africa* 28°46S 17°39E **270** C2
Viotia *Greece* 38°20N 23°0E **204** C5
Vipacco = Vipava *Slovenia* 45°51N 13°58E **199** C10
Vipava *Slovenia* 45°51N 13°58E **199** C10
Vipiteno *Italy* 46°54N 11°26E **199** B8
Viqueque *Timor-Leste* 8°52S 126°23E **231** F7
Vir *Croatia* 44°17N 15°3E **199** D12
Virac *Phil.* 13°30N 124°20E **232** E5
Virachey *Cambodia* 13°59N 106°49E **236** F6
Virachey △ *Cambodia* 14°14N 106°55E **236** E6
Virago Sd. *Canada* 54°0N 132°30W **296** C2
Virajpet = Virarajendrapet *India* 12°10N 75°50E **245** H2
Viramgam *India* 23°5N 72°0E **242** H5
Virananşehir *Turkey* 37°13N 39°45E **213** D8
Virányos *Hungary* 47°31N 18°59E **117** A1
Virarajendrapet *India* 12°10N 75°50E **245** H2
Virawah *Pakistan* 24°31N 70°46E **242** G4
Virbalis *Lithuania* 54°39N 22°49E **184** D9
Virden *Man., Canada* 49°50N 100°56W **297** D8
Virden *Ill., U.S.A.* 39°30N 89°46W **310** E7
Vire *France* 48°50N 0°53W **172** D6
Vire → *France* 49°20N 1°7W **172** C5
Virei *Angola* 15°43S 12°52E **265** F2
Virgem da Lapa *Brazil* 16°49S 42°21W **333** E3
Vírgenes, C. *Argentina* 52°19S 68°21W **336** D3
Virgin → *U.S.A.* 36°28N 114°21W **305** H6
Virgin Gorda *Br. Virgin Is.* 18°30N 64°26W **321** C7
Virgin Is. (British) ☑ *W. Indies* 18°30N 64°30W **321** C7
Virgin Is. (U.S.) ☑ *W. Indies* 18°20N 65°0W **321** C7
Virgin Islands △ *U.S. Virgin Is.* 18°21N 64°43W **321** b
Virginia *Free State, S. Africa* 28°8S 26°55E **270** C4
Virginia *Ill., U.S.A.* 39°57N 90°13W **310** E6
Virginia *Minn., U.S.A.* 47°31N 92°32W **308** B7
Virginia □ *U.S.A.* 37°30N 78°45W **309** G14
Virginia, L. *U.S.A.* 28°35N 81°20W **133** A2
Virginia Beach *U.S.A.* 36°49N 76°9W **309** F16
Virginia City *Mont., U.S.A.* 45°18N 111°56W **304** D8
Virginia City *Nev., U.S.A.* 39°19N 119°39W **306** F7
Virginia Falls *Canada* 61°38N 125°42W **296** A3
Virginia Gardens *U.S.A.* 25°48N 80°18W **129** D1
Virginia Key *U.S.A.* 25°44N 80°8W **129** D3
Virginiatown *Canada* 48°9N 79°36W **298** C4
Virje *Croatia* 46°4N 16°59E **199** B13
Viroflay *France* 48°48N 2°10E **134** B2
Vironas *Greece* 37°55N 23°46E **112** B2
Viroqua *U.S.A.* 43°34N 90°53W **308** D8
Virovitica *Croatia* 45°51N 17°21E **182** E2
Virpazar *Montenegro* 42°14N 19°6E **202** D3
Virpur *India* 21°51N 70°42E **242** J4
Virsbo *Sweden* 59°52N 16°2E **162** E10
Virserum *Sweden* 57°20N 15°35E **163** G9
Virton *Belgium* 49°35N 5°32E **170** E5
Virú *Peru* 8°25S 78°45W **330** B2
Virudhunagar *India* 9°30N 77°58E **245** K3
Virum *Denmark* 55°47N 12°27E **118** A2
Virunga △ *Dem. Rep. of the Congo* 0°5N 29°38E **268** B2
Vis *Croatia* 43°4N 16°10E **199** E13
Visalia *U.S.A.* 36°20N 119°18W **306** J7
Visayan Sea *Phil.* 11°30N 123°30E **233** F4
Visayas □ *Phil.* 9°30N 122°45E **233** G4
Visby *Sweden* 57°37N 18°18E **163** G12
Viscount Melville Sd. *Canada* 74°10N 108°0W **295** C10
Visé *Belgium* 50°44N 5°41E **170** D5
Vise, Ostrov *Russia* 79°33N 76°50E **214** B8
Višegrad *Bos.-H.* 43°47N 19°17E **182** G4
Viseu *Brazil* 1°10S 46°5W **332** B2
Viseu *Portugal* 40°40N 7°55W **194** E3
Viseu □ *Portugal* 40°40N 7°55W **194** E3
Vişeu de Sus *Romania* 47°45N 24°25E **183** C9
Vishakhapatnam *India* 17°45N 83°20E **244** F6
Vişina *Romania* 43°52N 24°27E **183** G9
Vişineşti *Moldova* 46°20N 28°27E **183** D13
Visingsö *Sweden* 58°2N 14°20E **163** F8
Visitacion Valley *U.S.A.* 37°42N 122°23W **136** B2
Viskafors *Sweden* 57°37N 12°50E **163** G6
Viskan → *Sweden* 57°14N 12°12E **163** G6
Viški Kanal *Croatia* 43°4N 16°5E **199** E13
Vislanda *Sweden* 56°46N 14°30E **163** H8
Visnagar *India* 23°45N 72°32E **242** H5
Višnja Gora *Slovenia* 45°58N 14°45E **199** C11
Viso, Mte. *Italy* 44°38N 7°5E **198** D4
Viso del Marqués *Spain* 38°32N 3°34W **195** G7
Visoko *Bos.-H.* 43°58N 18°10E **182** G3
Visokoi I. *Antarctica* 56°43S 27°15W **151** B1
Visp *Switz.* 46°17N 7°52E **179** J3
Vissefjärda *Sweden* 56°32N 15°35E **163** H9
Visselhövede *Germany* 52°59N 9°34E **178** C5
Vissenbjerg *Denmark* 55°23N 10°7E **163** J4
Vista *U.S.A.* 33°12N 117°14W **307** M9
Vista Alegre *Santiago, Chile* 33°30S 70°43W **137** C1
Vista Alegre *Lima, Peru* 12°9S 76°59W **124** B3
Vista Grove *U.S.A.* 33°51N 84°16W **113** A3
Vistabella *Trin. & Tob.* 10°17N 61°27W **323** t
Vistonida, L. *Greece* 41°0N 25°7E **203** E9
Vistonikos, Ormos = Vistonida, L. *Greece* 41°0N 25°7E **203** E9
Vistula = Wisła → *Poland* 54°22N 18°55E **184** D5
Vistula Lagoon = Wiślany, Zalew *Poland* 54°20N 19°50E **184** D6
Vistula Spit *Europe* 54°25N 19°35E **184** D6
Vit → *Bulgaria* 43°30N 24°30E **203** C8
Vita *India* 17°17N 74°33E **244** F2
Vitacura *Chile* 33°23S 70°35W **137** B2
Vitanje *Slovenia* 46°25N 15°18E **199** B12
Vitebsk = Vitsyebsk *Belarus* 55°10N 30°15E **188** E6
Viterbo *Italy* 42°25N 12°6E **199** F9
Vitez *Bos.-H.* 44°10N 17°48E **182** F2
Viti Levu *Fiji* 17°30S 177°30E **287** A1
Vitiaz Str. *Papua N. G.* 5°40S 147°10E **286** C4
Vitiaz Trench *Pac. Oc.* 10°0S 170°0E **277** C13
Vitigudino *Spain* 41°1N 6°26W **194** D4
Vitim *Russia* 59°28N 112°35E **215** D12
Vitim → *Russia* 59°26N 112°34E **215** D12
Vitina *Bos.-H.* 43°17N 17°29E **199** E14
Vitina *Greece* 37°40N 22°10E **204** D4
Vitínia *Italy* 41°47N 12°24E **136** C1
Vítkov *Czechia* 49°46N 17°45E **181** B10
Vitória = Vitória de Santo Antão *Brazil* 8°10S 35°20W **332** C4
Vitória *Espírito Santo, Brazil* 20°20S 40°22W **333** F3
Vitória *Pará, Brazil* 2°54S 52°1W **329** D7
Vitória da Conquista *Brazil* 14°51S 40°51W **333** D3
Vitória de Santo Antão *Brazil* 8°10S 35°20W **332** C4
Vitoria-Gasteiz *Spain* 42°50N 2°41W **196** C2
Vitória Seamount *Atl. Oc.* 20°0S 44°0W **333** F4
Vitorino Freire *Brazil* 4°4S 45°10W **332** B2
Vitosha △ *Bulgaria* 42°36N 23°18E **202** D7
Vitré *France* 48°8N 1°12W **172** D5
Vitry-le-François *France* 48°43N 4°33E **173** D11
Vitry-sur-Seine *France* 48°47N 2°23E **134** B3
Vitsand *Sweden* 60°20N 13°0E **162** D7
Vitsi, Oros *Greece* 40°40N 21°25E **202** F5
Vitsyebsk *Belarus* 55°10N 30°15E **188** E6
Vitsyebsk □ *Belarus* 55°10N 28°50E **188** E5
Vittaryd *Sweden* 56°58N 13°57E **163** H7
Vitteaux *France* 47°24N 4°30E **173** E11
Vittel *France* 48°12N 5°57E **173** D12
Vittória *Italy* 36°57N 14°32E **201** F7
Vittório = Vittório Véneto *Italy* 45°59N 12°18E **199** C9
Vittório Véneto *Italy* 45°59N 12°18E **199** C9
Vittoriosa *Malta* 35°54N 14°31E **206** F8
Vittsjö *Sweden* 56°20N 13°40E **163** H7
Viveiro *Spain* 43°39N 7°38W **194** B3
Vivian *U.S.A.* 32°53N 93°59W **314** E8
Viviers *France* 44°30N 4°40E **175** D8
Vivonne *S. Austral., Australia* 35°59S 137°9E **282** C2
Vivonne *Vienne, France* 46°25N 0°15E **174** B4
Vivonne B. *Australia* 35°59S 137°9E **282** C2
Viwa *Fiji* 17°10S 177°58E **287** A1
Vizagapatam = Vishakhapatnam *India* 17°45N 83°20E **244** F6
Vizandino, Moussio *Athens, Greece* **112** b3
Vizcaíno, Desierto de *Mexico* 27°30N 113°45W **318** B2
Vizcaíno, Sierra *Mexico* 27°30N 114°0W **318** B2
Vize *Turkey* 41°34N 27°45E **203** E11
Vizianagaram *India* 18°6N 83°30E **244** E6
Vizille *France* 45°5N 5°46E **175** C9
Viziňada *Croatia* 45°20N 13°46E **199** C10
Viziru *Romania* 45°0N 27°43E **183** E12
Vizlinsky Zaliv = Wiślany, Zalew *Poland* 54°20N 19°50E **184** D6
Vizzini *Italy* 37°10N 14°45E **201** E7
Vlaardingen *Neths.* 51°55N 4°21E **170** C4
Vlachiotis *Greece* 36°52N 22°42E **204** E4
Vlădeasa, Vf. *Romania* 46°47N 22°50E **182** D7
Vladičin Han *Serbia* 42°42N 22°1E **202** D6
Vladikavkaz *Russia* 43°0N 44°35E **191** J7
Vladimir *Russia* 56°15N 40°30E **188** D11
Vladimir □ *Russia* 56°5N 40°10E **190** B5
Vladimir Volynskiy = Volodymyr-Volynskyy *Ukraine* 50°50N 24°18E **177** C13
Vladimirci *Serbia* 44°36N 19°50E **202** B3
Vladimirovac *Serbia* 45°1N 20°53E **182** E5
Vladimirovka = Yuzhno-Sakhalinsk *Russia* 46°58N 142°45E **219** B17
Vladimirovka *Russia* 48°27N 46°10E **191** F8
Vladimirovo *Bulgaria* 43°32N 23°22E **202** C7
Vladislavovka *Ukraine* 45°12N 35°29E **189** K8
Vladivostok *Russia* 43°10N 131°53E **220** C5
Vladykino *Russia* 55°51N 37°35E **129** A2
Vlăhiţa *Romania* 46°21N 25°31E **183** D10
Vlasenica *Bos.-H.* 44°11N 18°59E **182** F3
Vlašić *Bos.-H.* 44°19N 17°37E **182** F2
Vlašim *Czechia* 49°40N 14°53E **180** B7
Vlasinsko Jezero *Serbia* 42°44N 22°22E **202** D6
Vlasotince *Serbia* 42°59N 22°7E **202** D6
Vlieland *Neths.* 53°16N 4°55E **170** A4
Vlissingen *Neths.* 51°26N 3°34E **170** C3
Vlkolínec *Slovakia* 49°1N 19°16E **181** B12
Vlorë *Albania* 40°32N 19°28E **202** F3
Vlorës, Gjiri i *Albania* 40°29N 19°27E **202** F3
Vltava → *Czechia* 50°21N 14°30E **180** A7
Vo Dat *Vietnam* 11°9N 107°31E **237** G6
Voćin *Croatia* 45°37N 17°33E **182** E2
Vöcklabruck *Austria* 48°1N 13°39E **180** C6
Vodice *Croatia* 43°47N 15°47E **199** E12
Vodlozersky △ *Russia* 62°40N 37°5E **214** C1
Vodňany *Czechia* 49°9N 14°11E **180** B7
Vodnjan *Croatia* 44°59N 13°52E **199** D10
Vodopyanovo = Donskoy *Russia* 53°55N 38°15E **188** F10
Voe *U.K.* 60°21N 1°16W **167** A7
Vogan *Togo* 6°23N 1°30E **263** D5
Vogar *Iceland* 63°58N 22°22W **155** D4
Vogel Pk. *Nigeria* 8°24N 11°47E **263** D7
Vogelkop = Doberai, Jazirah *Indonesia* 1°25S 133°0E **231** E8
Vogelsberg *Germany* 50°31N 9°12E **178** E5
Voghera *Italy* 44°59N 9°1E **198** D6
Voh *N. Cal.* 20°58S 164°42E **288** d
Vohibinany *Madag.* 18°49S 49°4E **272** B2
Vohilava *Madag.* 21°4S 48°0E **272** C2
Vohimarina = Iharana *Madag.* 13°25S 50°0E **272** A3
Vohimena, Tanjon' i *Madag.* 25°36S 45°8E **272** D2
Vohipeno *Madag.* 22°22S 47°51E **272** C2
Voi *Kenya* 3°25S 38°32E **268** C4
Void-Vacon *France* 48°40N 5°36E **173** D12
Voineşti *Iaşi, Romania* 47°5N 27°27E **183** C12
Voineşti *Prahova, Romania* 45°5N 25°14E **183** E10
Voinjama *Liberia* 8°25N 9°44W **262** D3
Voiron *France* 45°22N 5°35E **175** C9
Voisey B. *Canada* 56°15N 61°50W **299** A7
Voitsberg *Austria* 47°3N 15°9E **180** D8
Vojens *Denmark* 55°16N 9°18E **163** J3
Vojmsjön *Sweden* 65°0N 16°24E **160** D17
Vojnić *Croatia* 45°19N 15°43E **199** C12
Vojnik *Italy* 46°18N 15°19E **199** B12
Vojvodina □ *Serbia* 45°20N 20°0E **182** E5
Vokeo I. *Papua N. G.* 3°14S 144°2E **286** B3

Vokhtoga Russia 58°46N 41°8E **188** C11
Vokovice Czechia 50°5N 14°21E **135** B2
Volary Czechia 48°54N 13°52E **180** C6
Volborg U.S.A. 45°51N 105°41W **304** D11
Volcán de Colima △ Mexico 19°30N 103°40W **318** D4
Volcano U.S.A. 19°26N 155°14W **302** D6
Volcano Is. = Kazan-Rettō Pac. Oc. 25°0N 141°0E **288** E6
Volcans △ Rwanda 1°30S 29°26E **268** C2
Volcans d'Auvergne ⌓ France 45°20N 2°40E **174** C6
Volchansk = Vovchansk Ukraine 50°17N 36°58E **189** G9
Volchikha Russia 52°2N 80°23E **217** B10
Volchya → Ukraine 48°32N 36°0E **189** H8
Volda Norway 62°9N 6°5E **164** B3
Volga = Privolzhskiy ☐ Russia 56°0N 50°0E **214** D6
Volga Russia 57°58N 38°16E **188** C10
Volga → Russia 46°0N 48°30E **191** G9
Volga Hts. = Privolzhskaya Vozvyshennost Russia 51°0N 46°0E **190** E7
Volgelsdorf Germany 52°30N 13°44E **115** B5
Volgo-Baltiyskiy Kanal Russia 60°0N 38°0E **188** B9
Volgo-Donskoy Kanal Russia 48°40N 43°37E **191** F7
Volgodonsk Russia 47°33N 42°5E **191** G6
Volgograd Russia 48°40N 44°25E **191** F7
Volgograd ☐ Russia 49°40N 44°30E **190** F7
Volgogradskoye Vdkhr. Russia 50°0N 45°20E **190** E8
Volgorechensk Russia 57°28N 41°14E **190** B5
Volimes Greece 37°52N 20°39E **207** D2
Volintiri Moldova 46°26N 29°37E **183** D14
Volissos Greece 38°29N 25°54E **205** C7
Volkach Germany 49°52N 10°14E **179** F6
Völkermarkt Austria 46°39N 14°39E **180** E7
Volkhonka-Zil Russia 55°39N 37°37E **129** C2
Volkhov Russia 59°55N 32°15E **188** C7
Volkhov → Russia 60°8N 32°20E **188** B7
Volkhovstroy = Volkhov Russia 59°55N 32°15E **188** C7
Völklingen Germany 49°15N 6°50E **179** F2
Volkovysk = Vawkavysk Belarus 53°9N 24°30E **177** B13
Volksrust S. Africa 27°24S 29°53E **271** C4
Voll Norway 62°31N 7°27E **164** B4
Vollen Norway 59°48N 10°27E **133** B1
Volnovakha Ukraine 47°35N 37°30E **189** J9
Volochanka Russia 71°0N 94°28E **215** B10
Volodarsk Russia 56°12N 43°15E **190** B6
Volodarskoye Russia 59°54N 30°23E **137** B2
Volodymyr-Volynskyy Ukraine 50°50N 24°18E **177** C13
Vologda Russia 59°10N 39°45E **188** C10
Vologda ☐ Russia 60°15N 39°0E **188** B10
Volokolamsk Russia 56°5N 35°57E **188** D8
Volokonovka Russia 50°33N 37°52E **189** G9
Volos Greece 39°24N 22°59E **204** B4
Vološinovo = Novi Bečej Serbia 45°36N 20°10E **182** E5
Volosovo Russia 59°27N 29°32E **188** C5
Volovets Ukraine 48°43N 23°11E **183** B8
Volovo Russia 53°35N 38°1E **188** F10
Volozhin = Valozhyn Belarus 54°3N 26°30E **177** A14
Volsk Russia 52°5N 47°22E **190** D8
Volta ☐ Ghana 6°30N 0°20E **263** D5
Volta → Ghana 5°46N 0°41E **263** D5
Volta, L. Ghana 7°30N 0°0 **263** D5
Volta Blanche = White Volta → Ghana 9°10N 1°15W **263** D4
Volta Redonda Brazil 22°31S 44°5W **333** F3
Voltaire, C. Australia 14°16S 125°35E **278** B4
Volterra Italy 43°24N 10°51E **198** E7
Voltri Italy 44°26N 8°45E **198** D5
Volturno → Italy 41°1N 13°55E **200** A6
Volubilis Morocco 34°2N 5°33W **260** B3
Voluntar Romania 44°30N 26°11E **183** F11
Volvi, L. Greece 40°40N 23°34E **202** F7
Volyn ☐ Ukraine 51°15N 24°30E **177** C13
Volyně Czechia 49°10N 13°53E **180** B6
Volynkina-Derevnya Russia 59°53N 30°18E **137** B1
Volzhsk Russia 55°57N 48°23E **190** C9
Volzhskiy Russia 48°56N 44°46E **191** F7
Vomo Fiji 17°30S 177°15E **287** A1
Vonavona Solomon Is. 8°15S 157°5E **287** M9
Vondelpark Neths. 52°21N 4°52E **112** A2
Vondrozo Madag. 22°49S 47°20E **272** C2
Vonitsa Greece 38°55N 20°53E **207** B2
Vopnafjörður Iceland 65°45N 14°50W **155** B12
Vorarlberg ☐ Austria 47°20N 10°0E **180** D2
Voras Oros Greece 40°57N 21°45E **202** F5
Vorbasse Denmark 55°39N 9°6E **163** J3
Vorchdorf Austria 48°0N 13°55E **180** C6
Vorderrhein → Switz. 46°49N 9°25E **179** J5
Vordingborg Denmark 55°0N 11°54E **163** J5
Vorë Albania 41°23N 19°40E **202** E3
Voreio Aigaio ☐ Greece 38°50N 25°30E **205** C7
Voreios Sporades Greece 39°15N 23°30E **204** B5
Voreppe France 45°18N 5°39E **175** C9
Vori Greece 35°4N 24°49E **207** E5
Vorios Evoikos Kolpos Greece 38°45N 23°15E **204** C5
Vorkuta Russia 67°48N 64°20E **186** A11
Vorma → Norway 60°9N 11°29E **164** D8
Vormsi Estonia 59°1N 23°13E **188** C2
Vorona → Russia 51°22N 42°3E **190** E6
Voronezh Russia 51°40N 39°10E **189** G10
Voronezh Ukraine 51°47N 33°28E **189** G7
Voronezh ☐ Russia 51°30N 39°30E **190** E4
Voronezh → Russia 51°32N 39°10E **189** G10
Vorontsovo-Aleksandrovskoye = Zelenokumsk Russia 44°24N 44°0E **191** H6
Voroshilov = Ussuriysk Russia 43°48N 131°59E **220** C5
Voroshilovgrad = Luhansk Ukraine 48°38N 39°15E **189** H10
Voroshilovsk = Alchevsk Ukraine 48°30N 38°45E **189** H10
Voroshilovsk = Stavropol Russia 45°5N 42°0E **191** H6
Vorpommersche Boddenlandschaft △ Germany 54°25N 12°32E **178** A8
Vorskla → Ukraine 48°50N 34°10E **189** H8
Võrts järv Estonia 58°16N 26°3E **188** C4
Võru Estonia 57°48N 26°54E **188** D4
Vösendorf Austria 48°7N 16°20E **142** B2
Vosges France 48°20N 7°10E **173** D14
Vosges ☐ France 48°12N 6°20E **173** D13
Vosges du Nord ⌓ France 49°0N 7°30E **173** D14
Voskopojë Albania 40°35N 20°33E **202** F4
Voskresensk Russia 55°19N 38°43E **188** E10
Voskresenskoye Russia 56°51N 45°30E **190** B7
Voss Norway 60°38N 6°26E **164** D3
Vostochnyy Port Russia 42°44N 133°4E **220** C6
Vostok = Neftegorsk Russia 44°25N 39°45E **191** H4
Vostok Antarctica 78°30S 106°50E **151** D8
Vostok I. Kiribati 10°5S 152°23W **289** J12
Votice Czechia 49°38N 14°39E **180** B7
Votkinsk Russia 57°0N 53°55E **186** C9
Votkinskoye Vdkhr. Russia 57°22N 55°12E **186** C10
Votuporanga Brazil 20°24S 49°59W **333** F2
Vouga → Portugal 40°41N 8°40W **194** E2
Vouillé France 46°38N 0°10E **172** F7
Voula Greece 37°49N 23°45E **112** C2
Vouliagmeni Greece 37°50N 23°46E **112** C2
Voulkaria, L. Greece 38°52N 20°50E **207** B2
Voulou C.A.R. 8°33N 22°36E **264** A4
Vouxa, Akra Greece 35°37N 23°32E **207** E4
Vouzela Portugal 40°43N 8°7W **194** E2
Vouziers France 49°22N 4°40E **173** C11
Vovchansk Ukraine 50°17N 36°58E **189** G9
Vovodo → C.A.R. 5°40N 24°21E **264** A4
Vowchyn Belarus 52°18N 23°18E **185** F10
Voyageurs △ U.S.A. 48°32N 93°0W **308** A7
Voynitsa Russia 65°10N 30°20E **160** D24
Voyvozh Russia 62°56N 54°56E **186** B9
Vozhe, Ozero Russia 60°45N 39°0E **188** B10
Vozhega Russia 60°29N 40°12E **188** B11
Voznesensk Ukraine 47°35N 31°21E **189** J6
Voznesenye Russia 61°0N 35°28E **188** B8
Vozrozhdeniya I. Asia 45°10N 59°20E **216** C5
Vrå Denmark 57°21N 9°56E **163** G3
Vráble Slovakia 48°15N 18°16E **181** C11
Vraćevšnica Serbia 44°2N 20°34E **202** B4
Vrachneika Greece 38°10N 21°40E **204** C3
Vrådal Norway 59°20N 8°25E **164** E5
Vrancea ☐ Romania 45°50N 26°45E **183** E11
Vrancei, Munţii Romania 46°0N 26°30E **183** E11
Vrangel Russia 42°43N 133°5E **220** C6
Vrangelya, Ostrov Russia 71°0N 180°0E **215** B18
Vranica Bos.-H. 43°55N 17°50E **182** G2
Vranje Serbia 42°34N 21°54E **202** D5
Vranjska Banja Serbia 42°34N 22°1E **202** D6
Vranov nad Topl'ou Slovakia 48°53N 21°40E **181** C14
Vransko Slovenia 46°17N 14°58E **199** B11
Vransko Jezero Croatia 43°53N 15°34E **199** E12
Vrapčište N. Macedonia 41°50N 20°53E **202** E4
Vratsa Bulgaria 43°15N 23°30E **202** C7
Vratsa ☐ Bulgaria 43°15N 23°30E **202** C7
Vråvatn Norway 59°20N 8°8E **164** E5
Vrbas Serbia 45°40N 19°40E **182** E4
Vrbas → Bos.-H. 45°8N 17°29E **182** E2
Vrbnik Croatia 45°4N 14°40E **199** C11
Vrbovec Croatia 45°53N 16°28E **199** C13
Vrbovsko Croatia 45°24N 15°5E **199** C12
Vrchlabí Czechia 50°38N 15°37E **180** A8
Vrede S. Africa 27°24S 29°6E **271** C4
Vredefort S. Africa 27°0S 27°22E **270** C4
Vredehoek S. Africa 33°57S 18°25E **118** A1
Vreden Germany 52°2N 6°50E **178** C2
Vredenburg S. Africa 32°56S 18°0E **270** D2
Vredendal S. Africa 31°41S 18°35E **270** D2
Vretstorp Sweden 59°1N 14°53E **162** E8
Vrgorac Croatia 43°12N 17°20E **199** E14
Vrhnika Slovenia 45°58N 14°15E **199** C11
Vriddhachalam India 11°30N 79°20E **245** J4
Vrïdi Côte d'Ivoire 5°15N 4°3W **262** D4
Vrigstad Sweden 57°22N 14°28E **163** G8
Vrindavan India 27°37N 77°40E **242** F7
Vrisses Greece 35°23N 24°13E **207** E5
Vrnograč Bos.-H. 45°10N 15°57E **199** C12
Vrondados Greece 38°25N 26°7E **205** C8
Vrpolje Croatia 45°13N 18°24E **182** E3
Vršac Serbia 45°8N 21°20E **182** E6
Vrsacki Kanal Serbia 45°15N 21°0E **182** E5
Vršovice Czechia 50°4N 14°28E **135** B2
Vrútky Slovakia 49°7N 18°55E **181** B11
Vryburg S. Africa 26°55S 24°45E **270** C3
Vryheid S. Africa 27°45S 30°47E **271** C5
Vsetín Czechia 49°20N 18°0E **181** B11
Vu Liet Vietnam 18°43N 105°23E **236** C5
Vŭcha = Vacha → Bulgaria 42°10N 24°26E **203** D8
Vučitrn = Vushtrri Kosovo 42°49N 20°59E **202** D4
Vuga South Sudan 5°21N 29°40E **257** F2
Vukovar Croatia 45°21N 18°59E **182** E3
Vuktyl Russia 63°52N 57°20E **214** C6
Vulcan Alta., Canada 50°25N 113°15W **296** C6
Vulcan Romania 45°23N 23°17E **183** E8
Vulcăneşti Moldova 45°41N 28°18E **183** E13
Vulcano Italy 38°24N 14°58E **201** D7
Vŭlchedruma = Valchedram Bulgaria 43°42N 23°27E **202** C7
Vulkaneshty = Vulcăneşti Moldova 45°41N 28°18E **183** E13
Vunduzi → Mozam. 18°56S 34°1E **269** F3
Vung Tau Vietnam 10°21N 107°4E **237** G6
Vunidawa Fiji 17°50S 178°21E **287** A2
Vunisea Fiji 19°3S 178°10E **287** B2
Vuntut △ Canada 68°25N 139°41W **294** D4
Vuranggo Solomon Is. 6°39S 156°38E **287** L9
Vŭrbitsa = Varbitsa Bulgaria 42°59N 26°40E **203** D10
Vurshets Bulgaria 43°13N 23°23E **202** C7
Vushtrri Kosovo 42°49N 20°59E **202** D4
Vutcani Romania 46°26N 27°59E **183** D12
Vuzlove Ukraine 48°22N 22°24E **182** B7
Vwaza ⌓ Malawi 10°58S 33°25E **269** E3
Vyara India 21°8N 73°28E **244** D1
Vyartsilya Russia 62°8N 30°45E **188** A6
Vyatka = Kirov Russia 58°35N 49°40E **186** C8
Vyatka → Russia 55°37N 51°28E **190** C10
Vyatskiye Polyany Russia 56°14N 51°5E **190** B10
Vyazemskiy Russia 47°32N 134°45E **215** E14
Vyazma Russia 55°10N 34°15E **188** E8
Vyazniki Russia 56°10N 42°10E **190** B6
Vyborg Russia 60°43N 28°47E **188** B5
Vyborgskaya Storona Russia 59°57N 30°22E **137** B2
Vychegda → Russia 61°18N 46°36E **186** B8
Vychodné Beskydy Europe 49°20N 22°0E **181** B15
Vyerkhnyadzvinsk Belarus 55°45N 27°58E **188** E4
Vyg-ozero Russia 63°47N 34°29E **186** B5
Vyhoda Ukraine 48°56N 23°55E **183** B8
Vykhino Russia 55°42N 37°48E **129** B3
Vyksa Russia 55°19N 42°11E **190** C6
Vylkove Ukraine 45°28N 29°32E **183** E14
Vylok Ukraine 48°6N 22°50E **182** B7
Vynohradiv Ukraine 48°9N 23°2E **182** B8
Vypin India 10°10N 76°15E **245** J3
Vyrnwy, L. U.K. 52°48N 3°31W **168** E4
Vyšehrad Czechia 50°3N 14°25E **135** B2
Vyshkiv Ukraine 48°44N 23°39E **183** B8
Vyshkove Ukraine 48°3N 23°25E **183** B8
Vyshniy Volochek Russia 57°30N 34°30E **188** D8
Vyshzha = imeni 26 Bakinskikh Komissarov Turkmenistan 39°22N 54°10E **247** B7
Vyškov Czechia 49°17N 17°0E **181** B9
Vysočina ☐ Czechia 49°30N 15°30E **180** B8
Vysokaye Belarus 52°22N 23°22E **185** F10
Vysoké Mýto Czechia 49°58N 16°10E **181** B9
Vysokovsk Russia 56°22N 36°30E **188** D9
Vyšší Brod Czechia 48°37N 14°19E **180** C7
Vytegra Russia 61°0N 36°27E **188** B9
Vyzhnytsya Ukraine 48°15N 25°11E **183** B10
Vyzhnytsya ⌓ Ukraine 48°7N 25°15E **183** B10

W

W du Benin △ Benin 11°57N 2°43E **263** C5
W du Burkina Faso △ Burkina Faso 11°52N 2°50E **263** C5
W du Niger △ Niger 13°31N 2°28E **263** C5
W.A.C. Bennett Dam Canada 56°2N 122°6W **296** B4
Wa Ghana 10°7N 2°25W **262** C4
Waag Amsterdam, Neths. **112** b3
Waal → Neths. 51°37N 5°0E **170** C5
Waalwijk Neths. 51°42N 5°4E **170** C5
Waanyi-Garawa ✺ Australia 18°2S 137°33E **280** B2
Waat South Sudan 8°10N 32°7E **257** F3
Wabag Papua N. G. 5°32S 143°40E **286** C2
Wabakimi △ Canada 50°43N 89°29W **298** B2
Wabana Canada 47°40N 53°0W **299** C9
Wabasca → Canada 58°22N 115°20W **296** B5
Wabasca-Desmarais Canada 55°57N 113°56W **296** B6
Wabash U.S.A. 40°48N 85°49W **311** D11
Wabash → U.S.A. 37°48N 88°2W **311** G8
Wabasso U.S.A. 27°45N 80°26W **317** H9
Wabawng Myanmar 26°20N 97°25E **241** B6
Wabi → Ethiopia 7°45N 40°50E **257** F5
Wabigoon L. Canada 49°44N 92°44W **297** D10
Wabowden Canada 54°55N 98°38W **297** C9
Wąbrzeźno Poland 53°16N 18°57E **185** E5
Wabu Hu China 32°20N 116°50E **229** A11
Wabuda I. Papua N. G. 8°23S 143°37E **286** E2
Wabuk Pt. Canada 55°20N 85°5W **298** A2
Wabush Canada 52°55N 66°52W **299** B6
Waccasassa B. U.S.A. 29°10N 82°50W **317** F7
Wachau Austria 48°21N 15°26E **180** C8
Wąchock Poland 51°4N 21°1E **185** G8
Wachterhof Germany 48°2N 11°42E **131** B3
Wächtersbach Germany 50°14N 9°17E **179** E5
Wacissa U.S.A. 30°22N 83°59W **316** E6
Waco U.S.A. 31°33N 97°9W **314** F6
Waconichi, L. Canada 50°8N 74°0W **298** B5
Wad Ban Naqa Sudan 16°32N 33°9E **257** D3
Wad Banda Sudan 13°10N 27°56E **257** E2
Wad el Haddad Sudan 13°50N 33°30E **257** E3
Wad en Nau Sudan 14°10N 33°34E **257** E3
Wad Hamid Sudan 16°30N 32°45E **257** D3
Wad Medanî Sudan 14°28N 33°30E **257** E3
Wad Thana Pakistan 27°22N 66°23E **242** F2
Wadai = Ouaddaï ☐ Chad 13°0N 21°0E **259** F4
Wadala India 19°1N 72°51E **130** A2
Wadayama Japan 35°19N 134°52E **222** B6
Wadbilliga △ Australia 36°25S 149°35E **283** D8
Waddān Libya 29°9N 16°10E **258** C3
Waddeneilanden Neths. 53°25N 5°10E **170** A5
Waddenzee Neths. 53°6N 5°10E **170** A5
Waddi, Chappal Nigeria 7°2N 11°43E **263** D7
Waddington U.S.A. 44°52N 75°12W **313** B9
Waddington, Mt. Canada 51°23N 125°15W **296** C3
Waddy Pt. Australia 24°58S 153°21E **281** C5
Wadebridge U.K. 50°31N 4°51W **169** G3
Wadena Sask., Canada 51°57N 103°47W **297** C8
Wadena Minn., U.S.A. 46°26N 95°8W **308** B6
Wädenswil Switz. 47°14N 8°40E **179** H4
Wadern Germany 49°32N 6°53E **179** F2
Wadeye Australia 14°28S 129°52E **278** B4
Wadgaon India 18°44N 73°39E **244** E1
Wadhams Canada 51°30N 127°30W **296** C3
Wadhwan India 22°42N 71°41E **242** H4
Wadi India 17°4N 76°59E **244** F3
Wadi al-Arayis West Bank 31°43N 35°15E **123** B2
Wādī al Ḩayāt ☐ Libya 26°26N 12°30E **258** C2
Wādī as Sīr Jordan 31°56N 35°49E **251** G6
Wādī ash Shāţi ☐ Libya 27°27N 13°37E **258** C2
Wâdi Feirân Egypt 28°42N 33°19E **251** K4
Wadi Fira ☐ Chad 15°0N 21°0E **259** F4
Wadi Fukin West Bank 31°42N 35°6E **123** B1
Wâdi Gemâl, J. Egypt 24°35N 35°10E **256** C4
Wadi Halfa Sudan 21°53N 31°19E **256** C3
Wādī Mūsá Jordan 30°19N 35°29E **251** H6
Wādī Rum △ Jordan 29°30N 35°20E **251** J6
Wadian China 32°42N 112°29E **229** A9
Wadlew Poland 51°31N 19°23E **185** G6
Wadley Ala., U.S.A. 33°7N 85°34W **316** B4
Wadley Ga., U.S.A. 32°52N 82°24W **316** C7
Wadowice Poland 49°52N 19°30E **185** J6
Wadsworth Nev., U.S.A. 39°38N 119°17W **304** G4
Wadsworth Ohio, U.S.A. 41°2N 81°44W **312** E3
Waduk Pluit Indonesia 6°5S 106°46E **122** A1
Waegwan S. Korea 35°59N 128°23E **224** E4
Wafangdian China 39°38N 121°58E **227** E11
Wafania Dem. Rep. of the Congo 1°23S 20°22E **264** C4
Wafrah Kuwait 28°33N 47°56E **246** D5
Wagadugu = Ouagadougou Burkina Faso 12°25N 1°30W **263** C4
Wagait ✺ Australia 13°1S 130°5E **278** B5
Wageima = Wakema Myanmar 16°30N 95°11E **241** G5
Wagener U.S.A. 33°39N 81°22W **316** B8
Wageningen Neths. 51°58N 5°40E **170** C5
Wageningen Suriname 5°50N 56°50W **329** B6
Wager B. Canada 65°26N 88°40W **295** D14
Wagga Wagga Australia 35°7S 147°24E **283** C7
Waggaman U.S.A. 29°55N 90°12W **131** B1
Waghai India 20°46N 73°29E **244** D1
Waghete Indonesia 4°10S 135°50E **231** E9
Wagin Australia 33°17S 117°25E **279** F2
Wagner U.S.A. 43°5N 98°18W **308** D4
Wagon Mound U.S.A. 36°1N 104°42W **305** H11
Wagoner U.S.A. 35°58N 95°22W **314** D7
Wagrowiec Poland 52°48N 17°11E **185** F4
Wah Pakistan 33°45N 72°40E **242** C5
Wah Fu Hong Kong, China 22°15N 114°8E **122** B2
Wahai Indonesia 2°48S 129°35E **231** E7
Waharoa N.Z. 37°46S 175°45E **284** D4
Wahda = Unity ☐ South Sudan 8°30N 30°0E **257** F3
Wahda Iraq 33°18N 44°26E **113** B2
Wahiawā U.S.A. 21°30N 158°2W **302** K13
Wahiawā District U.S.A. 21°31N 157°58W **302** J14
Wahiawā Res. U.S.A. 21°30N 158°3W **302** K13
Wahībah, Ramlat al Oman 21°15N 58°45E **249** B7
Wâḩid Egypt 30°48N 32°21E **251** H3
Wahnai Afghan. 32°40N 65°50E **242** C1
Wahni Ethiopia 12°40N 36°39E **257** E4
Wahoo U.S.A. 41°13N 96°37W **308** E5
Wahpeton U.S.A. 46°16N 96°36W **308** B5
Währing Austria 48°14N 16°20E **142** A2
Wahx, Ras il- Malta 35°56N 14°20E **206** F7
Wai India 17°56N 73°57E **244** F1
Wai'ale'ale U.S.A. 22°4N 159°30W **302** A2
Waiale'e U.S.A. 21°41N 158°1W **302** J13
Waialua U.S.A. 21°34N 158°8W **302** J13
Waialua B. U.S.A. 21°35N 158°5W **302** J13
Waialua District U.S.A. 21°35N 158°5W **302** J13
Wai'anae U.S.A. 21°27N 158°11W **302** K13
Wai'anae Coast U.S.A. 21°26N 158°11W **302** K13
Wai'anae District U.S.A. 21°28N 158°10W **302** K13
Wai'anae Range U.S.A. 21°30N 158°10W **302** K13
Waiao Taiwan 24°54N 121°51E **225** B3
Waiapu → N.Z. 37°47S 178°29E **284** D7
Waiau N.Z. 42°39S 173°5E **285** C8
Waiau → Canterbury, N.Z. 42°47S 173°22E **285** C8
Waiau → Southland, N.Z. 46°12S 167°38E **285** G2
Waiawa → U.S.A. 21°23N 157°59W **302** K14
Waiawe Ganga → Sri Lanka 6°15N 81°0E **245** L5
Waibeem Indonesia 0°30S 132°59E **231** E8
Waiblingen Germany 48°49N 9°18E **179** G5
Waidhofen an der Thaya Austria 48°49N 15°17E **180** C8
Waidhofen an der Ybbs Austria 47°57N 14°46E **180** D7
Waidmannslust Germany 52°36N 13°20E **115** A3
Waigeo Indonesia 0°20S 130°40E **231** E8
Waihao → N.Z. 44°47S 171°10E **285** E6
Waihao Downs N.Z. 44°48S 170°55E **285** E5
Waiheke I. N.Z. 36°48S 175°6E **284** C4
Waihi N.Z. 37°23S 175°52E **284** D4
Waihi Beach N.Z. 37°25S 175°57E **284** D4
Waihola N.Z. 46°1S 170°8E **285** G5
Waihola L. N.Z. 45°59S 170°8E **285** F5
Waihou → N.Z. 37°15S 175°40E **284** D4
Waika Dem. Rep. of the Congo 2°22S 25°42E **264** C5
Waikabubak Indonesia 9°45S 119°25E **231** F5
Waikaia N.Z. 45°44S 168°51E **285** F3
Waikaka N.Z. 45°55S 169°1E **285** F4
Waikane U.S.A. 21°30N 157°51W **302** J14
Waikare, L. N.Z. 37°26S 175°13E **284** D4
Waikareiti, L. N.Z. 38°43S 177°10E **284** E6
Waikaremoana N.Z. 38°42S 177°12E **284** E6
Waikaremoana, L. N.Z. 38°49S 177°9E **284** E6
Waikari N.Z. 42°58S 172°41E **285** C7
Waikato → N.Z. 37°23S 174°43E **284** D3
Waikelo Indonesia 9°24S 119°19E **278** A2
Waikerie Australia 34°9S 140°0E **282** C4
Waikiekie N.Z. 35°57S 174°16E **284** B3
Waikīkī U.S.A. 21°17N 157°50W **302** K14
Waikokopu N.Z. 39°3S 177°52E **284** F6
Waikoloa Village U.S.A. 19°55N 155°49W **302** D6
Waikouaiti N.Z. 45°36S 170°41E **285** F5
Waikouaiti Downs N.Z. 45°30S 170°30E **285** F5
Wailea-Makena U.S.A. 20°40N 156°27W **302** C5
Wailing Wall = Western Wall Jerusalem **123** b3
Wailua U.S.A. 22°3N 159°20W **302** A2
Wailuku U.S.A. 20°53N 156°30W **302** C5
Waimakariri → N.Z. 43°24S 172°42E **285** D7
Waimalu U.S.A. 21°24N 157°57W **302** K14
Waimānalo U.S.A. 21°21N 157°43W **302** K14
Waimānalo B. U.S.A. 21°20N 157°40W **302** K14
Waimānalo Beach U.S.A. 21°21N 157°42W **302** K14
Waimangaroa N.Z. 41°43S 171°46E **285** B6
Waimano → U.S.A. 21°25N 157°58W **302** K14
Waimarie N.Z. 41°35S 171°58E **285** B6
Waimate N.Z. 44°45S 171°3E **285** E6
Waimea Hawai'i, U.S.A. 21°58N 159°40W **302** B2
Waimea Hawai'i, U.S.A. 21°39N 158°3W **302** J13
Waimea B. U.S.A. 21°40N 158°5W **302** J13
Waimea Plain N.Z. 45°55S 168°35E **285** F3
Wainganga → India 18°50N 79°55E **244** E4
Waingapu Indonesia 9°35S 120°11E **231** F6
Waingmaw Myanmar 25°21N 97°26E **241** C6
Waini → Guyana 8°20N 59°50W **329** B6
Wainuiomata N.Z. 41°17S 174°56E **284** H3
Wainwright Alta., Canada 52°50N 110°50W **297** C6
Wainwright Alaska, U.S.A. 70°38N 160°2W **303** A7
Waiotapu N.Z. 38°21S 176°25E **284** E5
Waiouru N.Z. 39°28S 175°41E **284** F4
Waipa → N.Z. 38°16S 175°21E **284** E4
Waipahi N.Z. 46°6S 169°15E **285** G4
Waipahu U.S.A. 21°23N 158°1W **302** K13
Waipapa Pt. N.Z. 46°40S 168°51E **285** G3
Waipara N.Z. 43°3S 172°46E **285** D7
Waipawa N.Z. 39°56S 176°38E **284** F5
Waipi'o U.S.A. 21°25N 158°0W **302** K14
Waipi'o Acres U.S.A. 21°28N 158°1W **302** K13
Waipi'o Peninsula U.S.A. 21°20N 158°0W **302** K14
Waipiro N.Z. 38°2S 178°22E **284** E7
Waipiro Bay N.Z. 38°1S 178°21E **284** E7
Waipoua Forest N.Z. 35°39S 173°33E **284** B2
Waipu N.Z. 35°59S 174°29E **284** B3
Waipukurau N.Z. 40°1S 176°33E **284** G5
Wairakei N.Z. 38°37S 176°6E **284** E5
Wairarapa, L. N.Z. 41°14S 175°15E **284** H4
Wairau → N.Z. 41°32S 174°7E **285** B9
Wairio N.Z. 45°59S 168°3E **285** F3
Wairoa N.Z. 39°3S 177°25E **284** F6
Wairoa → Hawke's Bay, N.Z. 39°4S 177°25E **284** F6
Wairoa → Northland, N.Z. 36°5S 173°59E **284** C2
Waisantiang Taiwan 23°29N 120°1E **225** C2
Waïsisi Vanuatu 19°32S 169°22E **287** J7
Waitaki → N.Z. 44°56S 171°7E **285** E6
Waitaki Plains N.Z. 44°22S 170°0E **285** E5
Waitangi N.Z. 35°16S 174°5E **284** B3
Waitara N.Z. 38°59S 174°15E **284** E3
Waitara → N.Z. 38°59S 174°14E **284** E3
Waitiki Landing N.Z. 34°31S 172°50E **284** A1
Waitoa N.Z. 37°37S 175°35E **284** D4
Waitomo Caves N.Z. 38°16S 175°7E **284** E4
Waitotara N.Z. 39°49S 174°44E **284** F3
Waitotara → N.Z. 39°51S 174°41E **284** F3
Waitsburg U.S.A. 46°16N 118°9W **304** C4
Waitzen = Vác Hungary 47°49N 19°10E **182** C4
Waiuku N.Z. 37°15S 174°45E **284** D3
Wajima Japan 37°30N 137°0E **221** F8
Wajir Kenya 1°42N 40°5E **268** B5
Wajir ☐ Kenya 1°45N 40°5E **268** B5
Waka Dem. Rep. of the Congo 1°1N 20°13E **264** B4
Waka Ethiopia 7°2N 37°20E **257** F4
Waka-Kungo Angola 11°21S 15°7E **265** E3
Wakarusa U.S.A. 41°32N 86°1W **311** C10
Wakasa Japan 35°20N 134°24E **222** B6
Wakasa-Wan Japan 35°40N 135°30E **223** B7
Wakatipu, L. N.Z. 45°5S 168°33E **285** F3
Wakaw Canada 52°39N 105°44W **297** C7
Wakaya Fiji 17°37S 179°0E **287** A2
Wakayama Japan 34°15N 135°15E **223** C7
Wakayama ☐ Japan 33°50N 135°30E **223** D7
Wake Japan 34°48N 134°8E **222** C6
Wake Forest U.S.A. 35°59N 78°30W **315** D15
Wake I. Pac. Oc. 19°18N 166°36E **302** b
WaKeeney U.S.A. 39°1N 99°53W **308** F4
Wakefield Jamaica 18°26N 77°42W **320** a
Wakefield N.Z. 41°24S 173°5E **285** B8
Wakefield W. Yorks., U.K. 53°41N 1°29W **168** D6
Wakefield Mass., U.S.A. 42°30N 71°5W **116** A2
Wakefield Mich., U.S.A. 46°29N 89°56W **308** B9
Wakema Myanmar 16°30N 95°11E **241** G5
Wākhān Afghan. 37°8N 73°4E **240** A4
Waki = Mima Japan 34°4N 134°9E **222** C6
Wakkanai Japan 45°28N 141°35E **220** B10
Wakkerstroom S. Africa 27°24S 30°10E **271** C5
Wakool Australia 35°28S 144°23E **282** C6
Wakool → Australia 35°5S 143°33E **282** C5
Wakre Indonesia 0°19S 131°5E **231** E8
Waku Papua N. G. 6°5S 149°9E **286** D5
Wakuach, L. Canada 55°34N 67°32W **299** A6
Wakulla U.S.A. 30°14N 84°14W **316** E5
Wakunai Papua N. G. 5°52S 155°13E **286** C8
Walagunya ✺ Australia 23°10S 120°50E **278** D3
Walamba Zambia 13°30S 28°42E **269** E2
Wałbrzych Poland 50°45N 16°18E **185** H3
Walbury Hill U.K. 51°21N 1°28W **169** F6
Walcha Australia 30°55S 151°31E **283** A9
Walcheren Neths. 51°30N 3°35E **170** C3
Walcott U.S.A. 41°46N 106°51W **304** F10
Wałcz Poland 53°17N 16°27E **185** E3
Waldbröl Germany 50°52N 7°37E **178** E3
Waldburg Ra. Australia 24°40S 117°35E **279** D2
Waldeck Germany 51°12N 9°4E **178** D5
Walden Colo., U.S.A. 40°44N 106°17W **304** F10
Walden N.Y., U.S.A. 41°34N 74°11W **313** E10
Waldenberg = Wałbrzych Poland 50°45N 16°18E **185** H3
Waldesruh Germany 52°28N 13°37E **115** B4
Waldkirch Germany 48°5N 7°58E **179** G3
Waldkirchen Germany 48°43N 13°36E **179** G9
Waldkraiburg Germany 48°11N 12°24E **179** G8
Waldo U.S.A. 29°48N 82°10W **316** F7
Waldperlach Germany 48°4N 11°40E **131** B3
Waldport U.S.A. 44°26N 124°4W **304** D1
Waldron U.S.A. 34°54N 94°5W **314** D7
Waldtrudering Germany 48°6N 11°42E **131** B3
Waldviertel Austria 48°30N 15°30E **180** C8
Walebing Australia 30°41S 116°13E **279** F2
Walembele Ghana 10°30N 1°58W **262** C4
Walensee Switz. 47°7N 9°13E **179** H5
Wales U.S.A. 65°37N 168°5W **303** D5
Wales ☐ U.K. 52°19N 4°43W **169** E3
Wales I. Canada 68°1N 86°40W **295** D14
Walewale Ghana 10°21N 0°50W **263** C4
Walgett Australia 30°0S 148°5E **281** E4
Walgreen Coast Antarctica 75°15S 105°0W **151** D15
Walhalla Australia 37°56S 146°29E **283** D7
Walis I. Papua N. G. 3°14S 143°18E **286** B2
Walker Mich., U.S.A. 42°58N 85°46W **311** B11
Walker Minn., U.S.A. 47°6N 94°35W **308** B6
Walker, L. Canada 50°20N 67°11W **299** B6
Walker L. Man., Canada 54°42N 95°57W **297** C9
Walker L. Nev., U.S.A. 38°42N 118°43W **304** G4
Walkerston Australia 21°11S 149°8E **280** b
Walkerton Ont., Canada 44°10N 81°10W **312** B3
Walkerton Ind., U.S.A. 41°28N 86°29W **311** C10
Wall U.S.A. 44°0N 102°8W **308** C2
Wall Street New York, U.S.A. **132** f1
Walla Walla N.S.W., Australia 35°45S 146°54E **283** C7
Walla Walla Wash., U.S.A. 46°4N 118°20W **304** C4
Wallabout Bay New York, U.S.A. **132** f2
Wallace Idaho, U.S.A. 47°28N 115°56W **304** C6
Wallace N.C., U.S.A. 34°44N 77°59W **315** D16
Wallaceburg Canada 42°34N 82°23W **312** D2
Wallacetown N.Z. 46°21S 168°19E **285** G3
Wallachia = Valahia Romania 44°35N 25°0E **183** F9
Wallal Australia 26°32S 146°7E **281** D4
Wallam Cr. → Australia 28°40S 147°20E **281** D4
Wallambin, L. Australia 30°57S 117°35E **279** F2
Wallan Australia 37°26S 144°59E **283** D6
Wallangarra Australia 28°56S 151°58E **281** D5
Wallaroo Australia 33°56S 137°39E **282** B2
Wallasey U.K. 53°25N 3°2W **168** D4
Walldürn Germany 49°34N 9°22E **179** F5
Wallenhorst Germany 52°21N 8°1E **178** C4
Wallenpaupack, L. U.S.A. 41°25N 75°15W **313** E9
Wallerawang Australia 33°25S 150°4E **283** B9
Wallingat △ Australia 32°14S 152°25E **283** B10
Wallingford Conn., U.S.A. 41°27N 72°50W **313** E12
Wallingford Vt., U.S.A. 43°28N 72°58W **313** C12
Wallis & Futuna, Îs. ☐ Pac. Oc. 13°18S 176°10W **277** C15
Wallowa U.S.A. 45°34N 117°32W **304** D5
Wallowa Mts. U.S.A. 45°20N 117°30W **304** D5
Walls U.K. 60°14N 1°33W **167** A7
Walls of Jerusalem △ Australia 41°56S 146°15E **281** G4
Wallsend Australia 32°55S 151°40E **283** B9
Wallula U.S.A. 46°5N 118°54W **304** C4
Wallumbilla Australia 26°33S 149°9E **281** D4
Walmsley L. Canada 63°25N 108°36W **297** A7
Walney, I. of U.K. 54°6N 3°15W **168** C4
Walnut U.S.A. 41°33N 89°36W **310** C7
Walnut Canyon ⌓ U.S.A. 35°15N 111°20W **305** J8
Walnut Creek U.S.A. 37°54N 122°4W **306** H4
Walnut Grove U.S.A. 34°4N 86°18W **316** A3
Walnut Hill U.S.A. 30°53N 87°30W **317** E2
Walnut Ridge U.S.A. 36°4N 90°57W **315** C9
Walpeup Australia 35°7S 142°2E **282** C5
Walpole W. Austral., Australia 34°58S 116°44E **279** F2
Walpole Mass., U.S.A. 42°9N 71°15W **313** D13
Walpole-Nornalup △ Australia 35°0S 116°45E **279** G2
Wals Austria 47°47N 12°58E **180** D5
Walsall U.K. 52°35N 1°58W **169** E6
Walsenburg U.S.A. 37°38N 104°47W **305** H11
Walsh U.S.A. 37°23N 102°17W **305** H12
Walsh → Australia 16°31S 143°42E **280** B3
Walsingham Canada 42°40N 80°31W **312** D4
Walsrode Germany 52°51N 9°35E **178** C5
Walt Disney Concert Hall Los Angeles, U.S.A. **127** b1
Walt Disney World Resort U.S.A. 28°22N 81°33W **133** B1
Waltair India 17°44N 83°23E **244** F6
Walter F. George Res. U.S.A. 31°38N 85°4W **316** D4
Walterboro U.S.A. 32°55N 80°40W **316** C9
Walters U.S.A. 34°22N 98°19W **314** D5
Waltershausen Germany 50°54N 10°33E **178** E6
Waltershausen Gletscher Greenland 73°54N 24°25W **154** C8
Waltham U.S.A. 42°23N 71°14W **116** A1
Waltham Forest ☐ U.K. 51°35N 0°0 **125** A3
Walthamstow U.K. 51°34N 0°1W **125** A3
Waltman U.S.A. 43°4N 107°12W **304** E10
Walton Ky., U.S.A. 38°52N 84°37W **311** F12
Walton N.Y., U.S.A. 42°10N 75°8W **313** D9
Walton-on-Thames U.K. 51°23N 0°24W **125** B1
Walton-on-the-Naze U.K. 51°51N 1°17E **169** F9
Waltonville U.S.A. 38°13N 89°2W **310** F7
Walu Myanmar 26°28N 98°2E **241** B7
Walvis Bay Namibia 23°0S 14°28E **270** B1
Walvis Ridge Atl. Oc. 26°0S 5°0E **152** J12
Walvisbaai = Walvis Bay Namibia 23°0S 14°28E **270** B1
Walwa Australia 35°59S 147°44E **283** C7
Wamba Équateur, Dem. Rep. of the Congo 1°37S 22°30E **264** C4
Wamba Orientale, Dem. Rep. of the Congo 2°10N 27°57E **268** B2
Wamba Rift Valley, Kenya 0°58N 37°19E **268** B4
Wamba Nigeria 8°57N 8°42E **263** D6
Wamba → Dem. Rep. of the Congo 3°56S 17°12E **265** C3
Wambardi ✺ Australia 16°2S 130°55E **278** C5
Wambeek Belgium 50°55N 4°30E **116** A3
Wamego U.S.A. 39°12N 96°18W **308** F5
Wamena Indonesia 4°4S 138°57E **231** E9
Wampana Karlantijpa ✺ Australia 17°45S 132°10E **278** C5
Wampaya ✺ Australia 17°20S 135°0E **280** B2
Wampsville U.S.A. 43°4N 75°42W **313** C9
Wamsutter U.S.A. 41°40N 107°58W **304** F10
Wamulan Indonesia 3°27S 126°7E **231** E7
Wan Chai Hong Kong, China 22°16N 114°10E **122** B3
Wan Hat Myanmar 20°14N 97°53E **241** E6
Wan Kinghao Myanmar 21°34N 98°17E **241** E7
Wan Lai-kam Myanmar 21°21N 98°22E **241** E7
Wan Tup Myanmar 21°13N 98°42E **228** G2
Wan Xian China 38°47N 115°7E **226** E8
Wana Pakistan 32°20N 69°32E **242** C3
Wanaaring Australia 29°38S 144°9E **281** D3
Wanaka N.Z. 44°42S 169°9E **285** E4
Wanaka, L. N.Z. 44°33S 169°7E **285** E4
Wan'an China 26°26N 114°49E **229** D10
Wanani Comoros Is. 12°20S 43°47E **272** a
Wanapa Bonaire 12°7N 68°14W **322** h
Wanapitei L. Canada 46°45N 80°40W **298** C3
Wanbi Australia 34°46S 140°17E **282** C4
Wandaik Guyana 4°27N 59°35W **329** C6
Wandan = Wantan Taiwan 22°35N 120°29E **225** D2
Wandel Sea = McKinley Sea Arctic 82°0N 0°0 **154** A11
Wandérama Côte d'Ivoire 8°37N 4°25W **262** D4
Wandhari Pakistan 27°42N 66°48E **242** F2
Wanding China 24°5N 98°4E **228** E2
Wandle → U.K. 51°27N 0°12W **125** B2
Wando S. Korea 34°21N 126°41E **224** E3
Wandoan Australia 26°5S 149°55E **281** D4
Wandsworth ☐ U.K. 51°27N 0°11W **125** B2
Wandur Marine △ India 11°30N 92°30E **245** J11
Wanfu China 40°8N 122°38E **224** B1
Wang → Thailand 17°8N 99°2E **236** D2
Wang Kai South Sudan 9°3N 29°23E **257** F2
Wang Noi Thailand 14°13N 100°44E **236** E3
Wang Saphung Thailand 17°18N 101°46E **236** D3
Wang Thong Thailand 16°50N 100°26E **236** D3
Wanga Dem. Rep. of the Congo 2°58N 29°12E **268** B2
Wangan Taiwan 23°21N 119°29E **225** C1
Wanganella Australia 35°6S 144°49E **283** C6
Wanganui N.Z. 39°56S 175°3E **284** F4
Wanganui → W. Coast, N.Z. 43°3S 170°26E **285** D5
Wanganui → Wanganui-Manawatu, N.Z. 39°55S 175°4E **284** F4
Wangaratta Australia 36°21S 146°19E **283** D7
Wangary Australia 34°35S 135°29E **281** E2
Wangcang China 32°18N 106°20E **228** A6
Wangcheng China 28°22N 112°49E **229** C9
Wangcun China 36°41N 117°41E **227** F9
Wangdu China 38°40N 115°7E **226** E8
Wangdu Phodrang Bhutan 27°28N 89°54E **241** B2
Wangen Germany 47°41N 9°50E **179** H5
Wangerin = Węgorzyno Poland 53°32N 15°33E **184** E2
Wangerooge Germany 53°47N 7°54E **178** B3
Wangiwangi Indonesia 5°22S 123°37E **231** F6
Wangjiang China 30°10N 116°42E **229** B11
Wangjing China 40°0N 116°28E **114** B2
Wangkung Taiwan 23°57N 120°20E **225** C2
Wangmo China 25°11N 106°5E **228** E6
Wangolodougou Côte d'Ivoire 9°55N 5°10W **262** D3
Wangqing China 43°12N 129°42E **227** C15
Wani India 20°5N 78°55E **244** D4
Wanigela Papua N. G. 9°21S 149°9E **286** E5
Wanimiyn ✺ Australia 15°55S 130°49E **278** C5
Wanjina Wunggurr Wilinggin ✺ Australia 16°0S 127°0E **278** C4
Wanjung Taiwan 23°43N 121°25E **225** C3
Wankaner India 22°35N 71°0E **242** H4
Wankhede Stadium Mumbai, India **130** c2
Wanless Canada 54°11N 101°21W **297** C8
Wanleweyne Somalia 2°37N 44°54E **267** D5
Wanli Taiwan 25°10N 121°41E **225** A3
Wanluan Taiwan 22°34N 120°34E **225** D2
Wanneroo Australia 31°42S 115°46E **279** F2
Wannian China 28°42N 117°4E **229** C11
Wanning China 18°48N 110°22E **229** a
Wannoo Billabong Roadhouse Australia 27°25S 115°49E **279** E2
Wannsee Germany 52°25N 13°9E **115** B1
Wanon Niwat Thailand 17°38N 103°46E **236** D4
Wanqinsha China 22°43N 113°33E **219** a
Wanquan China 40°50N 114°40E **226** D8
Wanrong China 35°25N 110°50E **226** G6
Wansdorf Germany 52°38N 13°5E **115** A1
Wansen = Wiązów Poland 50°50N 17°10E **185** H4
Wanshan China 27°30N 109°12E **228** D7
Wanshan Qundao China 21°57N 113°45E **219** a
Wansheng China 28°57N 106°53E **228** C6
Wanstead N.Z. 40°8S 176°30E **284** G5
Wanstead London, U.K. 51°34N 0°1E **125** A4
Wantage U.K. 51°35N 1°25W **169** F6
Wantan Taiwan 22°35N 120°29E **225** D2
Wantouliu Taiwan 24°1N 120°41E **225** B2
Wanxian China 30°42N 108°20E **228** B7
Wanyin Myanmar 20°23N 97°15E **241** E6
Wanyuan China 32°4N 108°3E **228** A7
Wanzai Guangdong, China 22°12N 113°31E **219** a
Wanzai Jiangxi, China 28°7N 114°30E **229** C10
Wapakoneta U.S.A. 40°34N 84°12W **311** D12
Wapato U.S.A. 46°27N 120°25W **304** C3
Wapawekka L. Canada 54°55N 104°40W **297** C8
Wapello U.S.A. 41°11N 91°11W **310** C5
Wapikopa L. Canada 52°56N 87°53W **298** B2
Wapinda Dem. Rep. of the Congo 3°41N 22°48E **264** B4
Wapiti → Canada 55°5N 118°18W **296** B5
Wapping U.K. 51°30N 0°3W **125** A3
Wappingers Falls U.S.A. 41°36N 73°55W **313** E11
Wapsipinicon → U.S.A. 41°44N 90°19W **310** C6
Wapusk △ Canada 57°46N 93°22W **297** B10
War Galoh Somalia 6°17N 47°31E **267** C6
War in the Pacific Nat. Hist. Park △ Guam 13°24N 144°39E **302** d
Warab South Sudan 8°8N 28°37E **257** F2
Warab ☐ South Sudan 7°30N 28°30E **257** F2
Warabi Japan 35°49N 139°41E **223** B11
Warakurna Australia 24°59S 128°17E **279** D4
Warangal India 17°58N 79°35E **244** F4
Waraseoni India 21°45N 80°2E **243** J9
Waratah Australia 41°30S 145°30E **281** G4
Waratah B. Australia 38°54S 146°5E **283** E7
Warburg Germany 51°28N 9°11E **178** D5
Warburton Vic., Australia 37°47S 145°42E **283** D6
Warburton W. Austral., Australia 26°8S 126°35E **279** E4
Warburton ✺ Australia 26°7S 126°34E **279** E4
Warburton → Australia 28°4S 137°28E **281** D2
Warburton Groove Australia 28°18S 137°8E **281** A2
Warburton Ra. Australia 25°55S 126°28E **279** E4
Ward N.Z. 41°49S 174°11E **285** B9
Ward → Australia 26°28S 146°6E **281** D4
Ward Hunt, C. Papua N. G. 8°2S 148°10E **286** E5
Ward Hunt Str. Papua N. G. 9°30S 150°0E **286** E6
Ward Mt. U.S.A. 37°12N 118°54W **306** H8
Wardang I. Australia 34°30S 137°20E **282** C2
Warden S. Africa 27°50S 29°0E **271** C4
Wardha India 20°45N 78°39E **244** D4
Wardha → India 19°57N 79°11E **244** E4
Wardija Point Malta 36°2N 14°11E **206** E6
Wards I. U.S.A. 40°47N 73°55W **132** B2
Wardsville Canada 42°39N 81°45W **312** D3
Ware Herts., U.K. 51°49N 0°0 **169** F8
Ware Mass., U.S.A. 42°16N 72°14W **313** D12
Waregem Belgium 50°53N 3°27E **170** D3
Wareham U.S.A. 41°46N 70°43W **313** E14
Waremme Belgium 50°43N 5°15E **170** D5
Waren Germany 53°31N 12°40E **178** B8
Warendorf Germany 51°57N 8°1E **178** D4
Waresboro U.S.A. 31°15N 82°29W **316** D7
Waria → Papua N. G. 7°49S 147°41E **286** D4
Warialda Australia 29°29S 150°33E **281** D5
Warin Chamrap Thailand 15°12N 104°53E **236** E5
Warka Poland 51°47N 21°12E **185** G8
Warkopi Indonesia 1°12S 134°9E **231** E8
Warkworth N.Z. 36°24S 174°41E **284** C3
Warm Baths = Bela Bela S. Africa 24°51S 28°19E **271** B4
Warm Springs Ga., U.S.A. 32°53N 84°41W **316** C5

Warm Springs Nev., U.S.A. 38°10N 116°20W 305 G5
Warman Canada 52°19N 106°30W 297 C7
Warmbad = Bela Bela S. Africa 24°51S 28°19E 271 B4
Warmbad Namibia 28°25S 18°42E 270 C2
Warming I. = Uunartoq Qeqertoq Greenland 71°33N 21°47W 154 C8
Warmińsko-Mazurskie □ Poland 54°0N 21°0E 184 D8
Warminster Wilts., U.K. 51°12N 2°10W 169 F5
Warminster Pa., U.S.A. 40°12N 75°6W 313 F9
Warmun Australia 17°2S 128°12E 278 C4
Warnberg Germany 48°4N 11°31E 131 B2
Warnemünde Germany 54°10N 12°4E 178 A8
Warner Brothers Studios U.S.A. 34°9N 118°20W 126 B2
Warner Mts. U.S.A. 41°40N 120°15W 304 F3
Warner Robins U.S.A. 32°37N 83°36W 316 C6
Warnes Bolivia 17°30S 63°10W 331 D5
Warnow → Germany 54°6N 12°9E 178 A8
Waroona Australia 32°50S 115°58E 279 F2
Warora India 20°14N 79°1E 244 D4
Warrabah △ Australia 30°31S 150°56E 283 A10
Warrabri ◎ Australia 21°1S 134°19E 280 C1
Warracknabeal Australia 36°9S 142°26E 282 D5
Warragul Australia 38°10S 145°58E 283 E6
Warrap = Warab South Sudan 8°8N 28°37E 257 F2
Warrâq el 'Arab Egypt 30°4N 31°11E 117 A2
Warrego → Australia 30°24S 145°21E 281 E4
Warrego Ra. Australia 24°58S 146°0E 280 C4
Warren N.S.W., Australia 31°42S 147°51E 283 A7
Warren Ark., U.S.A. 33°37N 92°4W 314 E8
Warren Ill., U.S.A. 42°29N 90°0W 310 D7
Warren Ind., U.S.A. 40°41N 85°26W 311 D11
Warren Mich., U.S.A. 42°28N 83°1W 311 B13
Warren Minn., U.S.A. 48°12N 96°46W 308 A5
Warren Ohio, U.S.A. 41°14N 80°49W 312 E4
Warren Pa., U.S.A. 41°51N 79°9W 312 E5
Warrenpoint U.K. 54°6N 6°15W 166 B5
Warrensburg Ill., U.S.A. 39°56N 89°4W 310 E7
Warrensburg Mo., U.S.A. 38°46N 93°44W 310 F3
Warrensburg N.Y., U.S.A. 43°29N 73°46W 313 C11
Warrenton Northern Cape, S. Africa 28°9S 24°47E 270 C3
Warrenton Ga., U.S.A. 33°24N 82°40W 316 B7
Warrenton Mo., U.S.A. 38°49N 91°9W 310 F5
Warrenton Oreg., U.S.A. 46°10N 123°56W 306 D3
Warrenville U.S.A. 33°33N 81°48W 316 B8
Warri Nigeria 5°30N 5°41E 263 D6
Warringal Park Australia 37°45S 145°4E 128 A2
Warrington N.Z. 45°43S 170°35E 285 F5
Warrington Warrington, U.K. 53°24N 2°35W 168 D5
Warrington Fla., U.S.A. 30°23N 87°17W 317 E2
Warrington □ U.K. 53°24N 2°35W 168 D5
Warriston U.K. 55°58N 3°11W 121 B2
Warrnambool Australia 38°25S 142°30E 282 E5
Warroad U.S.A. 48°54N 95°19W 308 A6
Warrumbungle △ Australia 31°18S 149°1E 283 A8
Warruwi Australia 11°36S 133°20E 280 A1
Warsak Dam Pakistan 34°11N 71°19E 242 B4
Warsaw = Warszawa Poland 52°14N 21°0E 143 B2
Warsaw Ill., U.S.A. 40°22N 91°26W 310 D5
Warsaw Ind., U.S.A. 41°14N 85°51W 311 C11
Warsaw Ky., U.S.A. 38°47N 84°54W 311 F12
Warsaw Mo., U.S.A. 38°15N 93°23W 310 F3
Warsaw N.Y., U.S.A. 42°45N 78°8W 312 D6
Warsaw Ohio, U.S.A. 40°20N 82°0W 312 F3
Warsaw Chopin ✕ (WAW) Poland 52°9N 20°59E 143 B1
Warshiikh Somalia 2°28N 45°55E 267 D6
Warstein Germany 51°26N 8°22E 178 D4
Warszawa Poland 52°14N 21°0E 143 B2
Warta Poland 51°43N 18°38E 185 G5
Warta → Poland 52°35N 14°39E 185 F1
Wartenberg Germany 52°34N 13°31E 115 A4
Wartenburg = Barczewo Poland 53°50N 20°42E 184 E7
Warthbrücken = Koło Poland 52°14N 18°40E 185 F5
Warthe = Warta → Poland 52°35N 14°39E 185 F1
Warthen U.S.A. 33°6N 82°48W 316 B7
Warthenau = Zawiercie Poland 50°30N 19°24E 185 H6
Waru Indonesia 3°30S 130°36E 231 E8
Warud India 21°30N 78°16E 244 D4
Warumungu ◎ Australia 19°15S 134°44E 280 B1
Warwick Queens., Australia 28°10S 152°1E 281 D5
Warwick Warks., U.K. 52°18N 1°35W 169 E6
Warwick Ga., U.S.A. 31°50N 83°57W 316 D6
Warwick N.Y., U.S.A. 41°16N 74°22W 313 E10
Warwick R.I., U.S.A. 41°42N 71°28W 313 E13
Warwickshire □ U.K. 52°14N 1°38W 169 E6
Wasaga Beach Canada 44°31N 80°1W 312 B4
Wasagaming Canada 50°39N 99°58W 297 C9
Wasatch Ra. U.S.A. 40°0N 111°30W 304 F8
Wasbank S. Africa 28°15S 30°9E 271 C5
Wasco Calif., U.S.A. 35°36N 119°20W 307 K7
Wasco Oreg., U.S.A. 45°36N 120°42W 304 D3
Wase Nigeria 9°4N 9°54E 263 D6
Waseca U.S.A. 44°5N 93°30W 308 C7
Wasekamio L. Canada 56°45N 108°45W 297 B7
Wasgomura △ Sri Lanka 7°45N 81°0E 245 L5
Wash, The U.K. 52°58N 0°20E 168 E8
Washago Canada 44°45N 79°20W 312 B5
Washburn Ill., U.S.A. 40°55N 89°17W 310 D7
Washburn N. Dak., U.S.A. 47°17N 101°2W 308 B3
Washburn Wis., U.S.A. 46°40N 90°54W 308 B8
Washim India 20°3N 77°0E 244 D3
Washington Bonaire 12°17N 68°23W 322 h
Washington Tyne & W., U.K. 54°55N 1°30W 168 C6
Washington D.C., U.S.A. 38°53N 77°2W 143 B2
Washington Ga., U.S.A. 33°44N 82°44W 316 B7
Washington Ill., U.S.A. 40°42N 89°24W 310 D7
Washington Ind., U.S.A. 38°40N 87°10W 311 F9
Washington Iowa, U.S.A. 41°18N 91°42W 310 C5
Washington Mo., U.S.A. 38°33N 91°1W 310 F5
Washington N.C., U.S.A. 35°33N 77°3W 315 D16
Washington N.J., U.S.A. 40°46N 74°59W 313 F10
Washington Pa., U.S.A. 40°10N 80°15W 312 F4
Washington Utah, U.S.A. 37°8N 113°31W 305 H7
Washington □ U.S.A. 47°30N 120°30W 304 C3
Washington, Mt. U.S.A. 44°16N 71°18W 313 B13
Washington Court House U.S.A. 39°32N 83°26W 311 E13
Washington Dulles Int. ✕ (IAD) U.S.A. 38°57N 77°27W 309 F15
Washington Heights U.S.A. 40°51N 73°56W 132 A2
Washington I. U.S.A. 45°23N 86°54W 308 C10
Washington Land Greenland 80°30N 66°0W 154 A4
Washington Monument Washington, D.C., U.S.A. 143 b1
Washington Park U.S.A. 41°47N 87°36W 119 C3
Washington Ronald Reagan Nat. ✕ (DCA) U.S.A. 38°51N 77°2W 143 B2
Washington Slagbaai △ Bonaire 12°16N 68°23W 322 h
Washougal U.S.A. 45°35N 122°21W 306 E4
Washpool △ Australia 29°22S 152°20E 281 D5
Washuk Pakistan 27°42N 64°45E 240 D2
Wasian Indonesia 1°47S 133°19E 231 E8
Wasilków Poland 53°12N 23°13E 185 E10
Wasilla U.S.A. 61°35N 149°26W 303 F10
Wasini Marine △ Kenya 4°33S 39°14E 268 C4
Wasior Indonesia 2°43S 134°30E 231 E8
Wasiri Indonesia 7°30S 126°30E 231 F7
Wāsiṭ □ Iraq 32°50N 45°50E 213 F11
Wasjabo Suriname 5°13N 57°11W 329 B6
Waskaganish Canada 51°30N 78°40W 298 B4
Waskaiowaka L. Canada 56°33N 96°23W 297 B9
Waskesiu Lake Canada 53°55N 106°5W 297 C7
Wassaw I. U.S.A. 31°53N 80°58W 316 D9
Wassaw Sd. U.S.A. 31°55N 80°55W 316 D9
Wasserburg Germany 48°3N 12°14E 179 G8
Wasserkuppe Germany 50°29N 9°55E 178 E5
Wassy France 48°30N 4°58E 173 D11
Wasu Papua N. G. 5°58S 147°12E 286 C4
Wasua Papua N. G. 8°18S 142°52E 286 E2
Wasur △ Indonesia 8°41S 140°44E 231 F10
Waswanipi Canada 49°40N 76°29W 298 C4
Waswanipi, L. Canada 49°35N 76°40W 298 C4
Wat Pho Bangkok, Thailand 113 b1
Watagans △ Australia 33°0S 151°28E 283 B9
Watam Papua N. G. 3°55S 144°33E 286 B3
Watampone Indonesia 4°29S 120°25E 231 E6
Watamu Kenya 3°23S 40°0E 268 C5
Watansoppeng Indonesia 4°10S 119°56E 235 C5
Watarrka △ Australia 24°20S 131°30E 278 D5
Watauga U.S.A. 32°51N 97°15W 120 A2
Watee Solomon Is. 10°30S 162°2E 287 N12
Watenstadt-Salzgitter = Salzgitter Germany 52°9N 10°19E 178 C6
Water of Leith → U.K. 55°59N 3°10W 121 B1
Water Park Pt. Australia 22°56S 150°47E 280 C5
Water Tower Place Chicago, U.S.A. 119 a2
Water Valley U.S.A. 34°10N 89°38W 315 D10
Waterberg Plateau △ Namibia 20°25S 17°18E 270 B2
Waterberge S. Africa 24°10S 28°0E 271 B4
Waterbury Conn., U.S.A. 41°33N 73°3W 313 E11
Waterbury Vt., U.S.A. 44°20N 72°46W 313 B12
Waterbury L. Canada 58°10N 104°22W 297 B8
Waterdown Canada 43°20N 79°53W 312 C5
Wateree → U.S.A. 33°45N 80°37W 316 B9
Waterford Ont., Canada 42°56N 80°17W 312 D4
Waterford Waterford, Ireland 52°15N 7°8W 166 D4
Waterford Calif., U.S.A. 37°38N 120°46W 306 H6
Waterford Mich., U.S.A. 42°45N 83°32W 311 B13
Waterford Pa., U.S.A. 41°57N 79°59W 312 E5
Waterford Wis., U.S.A. 42°46N 88°13W 311 B8
Waterford □ Ireland 52°10N 7°40W 166 D4
Waterford Harbour Ireland 52°8N 6°58W 166 D5
Watergraafsmeer Neths. 52°21N 4°56E 112 A2
Waterhen L. Canada 52°10N 99°40W 297 C9
Waterland Neths. 52°26N 4°58E 112 A2
Waterloo Belgium 50°43N 4°25E 116 B2
Waterloo Ont., Canada 43°30N 80°32W 312 C4
Waterloo Qué., Canada 45°22N 72°32W 313 A12
Waterloo S. Leone 8°26N 13°8W 262 D2
Waterloo Trin. & Tob. 10°28N 61°28W 323 t
Waterloo London, U.K. 125 b4
Waterloo Ill., U.S.A. 38°20N 90°9W 310 F6
Waterloo Ind., U.S.A. 41°26N 85°1W 311 C11
Waterloo Iowa, U.S.A. 42°30N 92°21W 310 B4
Waterloo N.Y., U.S.A. 42°54N 76°52W 312 D8
Waterloo Wis., U.S.A. 43°11N 88°59W 310 A8
Waterman U.S.A. 41°46N 88°47W 311 C8
Watermeal-Boitsfort Belgium 50°48N 4°25E 116 B2
Watersmeet U.S.A. 46°16N 89°11W 308 B9
Waterton Lakes △ Canada 48°45N 115°0W 296 D6
Watertown Conn., U.S.A. 41°36N 73°7W 313 E11
Watertown Fla., U.S.A. 30°11N 82°36W 316 E7
Watertown Mass., U.S.A. 42°22N 71°10W 116 A1
Watertown N.Y., U.S.A. 43°59N 75°55W 313 C9
Watertown S. Dak., U.S.A. 44°54N 97°7W 308 C5
Watertown Wis., U.S.A. 43°12N 88°43W 311 A8
Waterval-Boven = Emgwenya S. Africa 25°40S 30°18E 271 C5
Waterville Qué., Canada 45°16N 71°54W 313 A13
Waterville Maine, U.S.A. 44°33N 69°38W 309 C19
Waterville N.Y., U.S.A. 42°56N 75°23W 313 D9
Waterville Pa., U.S.A. 41°19N 77°21W 312 E7
Waterville Wash., U.S.A. 47°39N 120°4W 304 C3
Watervliet Mich., U.S.A. 42°11N 86°18W 311 B10
Watervliet N.Y., U.S.A. 42°44N 73°42W 313 D11
Wates Indonesia 7°51S 110°10E 235 D4
Watford Ont., Canada 42°57N 81°53W 312 D3
Watford Herts., U.K. 51°40N 0°24W 169 F7
Watford City U.S.A. 47°48N 103°17W 308 B2
Wathaman → Canada 57°16N 102°59W 297 B8
Wathaman L. Canada 56°58N 103°44W 297 B8
Watheroo Australia 30°15S 115°54E 279 F2
Watheroo △ Australia 30°19S 115°48E 279 F2
Wating China 35°40N 106°38E 226 G4
Watir, W. → Egypt 29°0N 34°40E 251 K5
Watkins Glen U.S.A. 42°23N 76°52W 312 D8
Watkinsville U.S.A. 33°52N 83°25W 316 B6
Watling I. = San Salvador The Bahamas 24°0N 74°30W 321 B5
Watom I. Papua N. G. 4°7S 152°4E 286 C7
Watonga U.S.A. 35°51N 98°25W 314 D5
Watrous Sask., Canada 51°40N 105°25W 297 C7
Watrous N. Mex., U.S.A. 35°48N 104°59W 305 J11
Watsa Dem. Rep. of the Congo 3°4N 29°30E 268 B2
Watseka U.S.A. 40°47N 87°44W 311 D9
Watsi Kenga Dem. Rep. of the Congo 0°49S 20°34E 264 C4
Watson Canada 52°10N 104°30W 297 C8
Watson Lake Canada 60°6N 128°49W 296 A3
Watsonia Australia 37°43S 145°6E 128 A2
Watsontown U.S.A. 41°5N 76°52W 312 E8
Watsonville U.S.A. 36°55N 121°45W 306 J5
Watt Mt. Dominica 15°19N 61°19W 323 k
Wattiwarriganna Cr. → Australia 28°57S 136°10E 281 D2
Watts U.S.A. 33°56N 118°15W 126 C2
Wattwil Switz. 47°18N 9°6E 179 H5
Watu Dem. Rep. of the Congo 3°18S 20°3E 264 C4
Watuata = Batuata Indonesia 6°12S 122°42E 231 F6
Watubela, Kepulauan Indonesia 4°28S 131°35E 231 E8
Watubela Is. = Watubela, Kepulauan Indonesia 4°28S 131°35E 231 E8
Wau Papua N. G. 7°21S 146°47E 286 D4
Wau South Sudan 7°45N 28°1E 257 F2
Waubamik Canada 45°27N 80°1W 312 A4
Waubay U.S.A. 45°20N 97°18W 308 C5
Waubra Australia 37°21S 143°39E 282 D5
Wauchope N.S.W., Australia 31°28S 152°45E 283 A10
Wauchope N. Terr., Australia 20°36S 134°15E 280 C1
Wauchula U.S.A. 27°33N 81°49W 317 H8
Waukarlycarly, L. Australia 21°18S 121°56E 278 D3
Waukeenah U.S.A. 30°25N 83°57W 316 E6
Waukegan U.S.A. 42°22N 87°50W 311 B9
Waukesha U.S.A. 43°1N 88°14W 311 B8
Waukon U.S.A. 43°16N 91°29W 308 D8
Waunakee U.S.A. 43°11N 89°27W 310 A7
Waupaca U.S.A. 44°21N 89°5W 308 C9
Waupun U.S.A. 43°38N 88°44W 308 D9
Waurika U.S.A. 34°10N 98°0W 314 D6
Wausau Fla., U.S.A. 30°38N 85°35W 316 E4
Wausau Wis., U.S.A. 44°58N 89°38W 308 C9
Wauseon U.S.A. 41°33N 84°8W 311 C12
Wautoma U.S.A. 44°4N 89°18W 308 C9
Wauwatosa U.S.A. 43°2N 88°0W 311 A9
Wave Hill = Kalkarindji Australia 17°30S 130°47E 278 C5
Wave Rock △ Australia 32°26S 118°53E 279 F2
Waveland U.S.A. 39°53N 87°3W 311 E9
Waveney → U.K. 52°35N 1°39E 169 E9
Waverley N.S.W., Australia 33°53S 151°15E 139 B2
Waverley N.Z. 39°46S 174°37E 284 F3
Waverley Gauteng, S. Africa 26°7S 28°4E 123 A2
Waverley Mass., U.S.A. 42°23N 71°10W 116 A1
Waverley Station Edinburgh, U.K. 121 b3
Waverly Ala., U.S.A. 32°44N 85°35W 316 C4
Waverly Fla., U.S.A. 27°59N 81°37W 317 H8
Waverly Ga., U.S.A. 31°6N 81°43W 316 D8
Waverly Ill., U.S.A. 39°36N 89°57W 310 E7
Waverly Iowa, U.S.A. 42°44N 92°29W 310 B4
Waverly Mo., U.S.A. 39°13N 93°31W 310 E3
Waverly N.Y., U.S.A. 42°1N 76°32W 313 E8
Waverly Hall U.S.A. 32°41N 84°44W 316 C5
Wavre Belgium 50°43N 4°38E 170 D4
Wâw = Wau South Sudan 7°45N 28°1E 257 F2
Waw Myanmar 17°28N 96°41E 241 G6
Wāw al Kabīr Libya 25°20N 16°43E 258 C3
Wāw an Nāmūs Libya 24°55N 17°46E 258 D3
Wawa Ont., Canada 47°59N 84°47W 298 C3
Wawa Nigeria 9°54N 4°27E 263 D5
Wawa Sudan 20°30N 30°22E 256 C3
Wawanesa Canada 49°36N 99°40W 297 D9
Wawasee, L. U.S.A. 41°24N 85°42W 311 C11
Wawer Poland 52°13N 21°8E 143 B2
Wawoi → Papua N. G. 7°48S 143°16E 286 D2
Wawona U.S.A. 37°32N 119°39W 306 H7
Wawrzyszew Poland 52°17N 20°53E 143 B1
Waxahachie U.S.A. 32°24N 96°51W 314 E6
Waxxari China 38°42N 87°19E 217 E11
Way, L. Australia 26°45S 120°16E 279 E3
Way Kambas △ Indonesia 4°54S 105°43E 234 C3
Waya Fiji 17°19S 177°10E 287 A1
Waycross U.S.A. 31°13N 82°21W 316 D7
Wayi South Sudan 5°8N 30°10E 257 F3
Wayland Mich., U.S.A. 42°40N 85°39W 311 B11
Wayland N.Y., U.S.A. 42°34N 77°35W 312 D7
Wayne Nebr., U.S.A. 42°14N 97°1W 308 D5
Wayne W. Va., U.S.A. 38°13N 82°27W 309 F12
Wayne City U.S.A. 38°21N 88°35W 311 F8
Wayne County, Detroit ✕ (DTW) U.S.A. 42°13N 83°21W 311 B13
Wayne Lakes U.S.A. 40°1N 84°40W 311 D12
Waynesboro Ga., U.S.A. 33°6N 82°1W 316 B7
Waynesboro Miss., U.S.A. 31°40N 88°39W 315 F10
Waynesboro Pa., U.S.A. 39°45N 77°35W 309 F15
Waynesboro Va., U.S.A. 38°4N 78°53W 309 F14
Waynesburg U.S.A. 39°54N 80°11W 309 F13
Waynesville Mo., U.S.A. 37°50N 92°12W 310 G4
Waynesville N.C., U.S.A. 35°28N 82°58W 315 D13
Waynesville Ohio, U.S.A. 39°32N 84°5W 311 E12
Waynoka U.S.A. 36°35N 98°53W 314 C5
Wayside U.S.A. 33°4N 83°37W 316 B6
Waza Afghan. 33°22N 69°26E 240 B3
Waza △ Cameroon 11°15N 14°38E 259 F2
Wazikhwah Afghan. 32°11N 68°21E 240 B3
Wāzin Libya 31°58N 10°40E 258 B2
Wazirabad Delhi, India 28°43N 77°13E 120 A2
Wazirabad Pakistan 32°30N 74°8E 242 C6
Waziristan Pakistan 33°0N 70°0E 242 C4
Wazīrīya Iraq 33°22N 44°23E 113 A2
Wazirpur India 28°41N 77°10E 120 A2
Wda → Poland 53°25N 18°29E 184 E5
We Indonesia 5°51N 95°18E 234 A1
Wé N. Cal. 20°55S 167°16E 288 d
Weald, The U.K. 51°4N 0°20E 169 F8
Wealdstone U.K. 51°35N 0°17W 125 A1
Weam Papua N. G. 8°37S 141°8E 286 E1
Wear → U.K. 54°55N 1°23W 168 C6
Weatherford Okla., U.S.A. 35°32N 98°43W 314 D5
Weatherford Tex., U.S.A. 32°46N 97°48W 314 E6
Weaubleau U.S.A. 37°54N 93°32W 310 G3
Weaverville U.S.A. 40°44N 122°56W 304 F2
Webb City U.S.A. 37°9N 94°28W 308 G6
Webequie Canada 52°59N 87°21W 298 B2
Weber N.Z. 40°24S 176°20E 284 G5
Weber Basin Indonesia 6°0S 131°0E 276 B5
Webo = Nyaake Liberia 4°52N 7°37W 262 E3
Webster Mass., U.S.A. 42°3N 71°53W 313 D13
Webster N.Y., U.S.A. 43°13N 77°26W 312 C7
Webster S. Dak., U.S.A. 45°20N 97°31W 308 C5
Webster City U.S.A. 42°28N 93°49W 310 B3
Webster Springs U.S.A. 38°29N 80°25W 309 F13
Webuye Kenya 0°37N 34°46E 268 B3
Weda Indonesia 0°21N 127°50E 231 D7
Weda, Teluk Indonesia 0°20N 128°0E 231 D7
Weddell Abyssal Plain S. Ocean 65°0S 20°0W 151 C2
Weddell I. Falk. Is. 51°50S 61°0W 153 f
Weddell Sea Antarctica 72°30S 40°0W 151 D1
Wedderburn Australia 36°26S 143°33E 282 D5
Weddin Mts. △ Australia 33°59S 148°0E 283 C8
Wedding Germany 52°32N 13°21E 115 A3
Wedel Germany 53°34N 9°42E 178 B5
Wedemark Germany 52°32N 9°43E 178 C5
Wedgeport Canada 43°44N 65°59W 299 D6
Wednesday I. Australia 10°31S 142°16E 286 F2
Wedowee U.S.A. 33°19N 85°29W 316 B4
Wedza Zimbabwe 18°40S 31°33E 269 F3
Wee Waa Australia 30°11S 149°26E 281 E4
Weed U.S.A. 41°25N 122°23W 304 F2
Weed Heights U.S.A. 38°59N 119°13W 306 G7
Weedsport U.S.A. 43°2N 76°33W 313 C8
Weedville U.S.A. 41°17N 78°30W 312 E6
Weehawken New York, U.S.A. 132 b1
Weeki Wachee U.S.A. 28°32N 82°35W 317 G7
Weel Shimbirro Somalia 2°23N 44°14E 267 D5
Weenen S. Africa 28°48S 30°7E 271 C5
Weener Germany 53°9N 7°20E 178 B3
Weerribben △ Neths. 52°47N 5°58E 170 B5
Weert Neths. 51°15N 5°43E 170 C5
Weesp Neths. 52°18N 5°2E 112 B3
Węgierska-Górka Poland 49°36N 19°7E 185 J6
Węgliniec Poland 51°18N 15°10E 185 G2
Węgorzewo Poland 54°13N 21°43E 184 D8
Węgorzyno Poland 53°32N 15°33E 184 E2
Węgrów Poland 52°24N 22°0E 185 F9
Wei He → Hebei, China 36°10N 115°45E 226 F8
Wei He → Shaanxi, China 34°38N 110°15E 226 G6
Weichang China 41°58N 117°49E 227 D9
Weichuan China 34°20N 113°59E 226 G7
Weida Germany 50°46N 12°2E 178 E8
Weiden Germany 49°41N 12°10E 179 F8
Weidling Austria 48°17N 16°18E 142 A1
Weidlingbach Austria 48°16N 16°15E 142 A1
Weifang China 36°44N 119°7E 227 F10
Weihai China 37°30N 122°6E 227 F12
Weihui China 35°25N 114°3E 226 G8
Weil Germany 47°35N 7°37E 179 H3
Weilburg Germany 50°28N 8°17E 178 E4
Weilheim Germany 47°50N 11°9E 179 H7
Weimar Germany 50°58N 11°19E 178 E7
Weinan China 34°31N 109°29E 226 G5
Weingarten Germany 49°3N 8°31E 179 F4
Weinheim Germany 49°32N 8°39E 179 F4
Weining China 26°50N 104°17E 228 D5
Weipa Australia 12°40S 141°50E 280 A3
Weir → Queens., Australia 28°20S 149°50E 281 D4
Weir → Man., Canada 56°54N 93°21W 297 B10
Weir, L. U.S.A. 29°0N 81°57W 317 F8
Weir River Canada 56°49N 94°6W 297 B10
Weirsdale U.S.A. 28°59N 81°55W 317 G8
Weirton U.S.A. 40°24N 80°35W 312 F4
Weiser U.S.A. 44°15N 116°58W 304 D5
Weishan Shandong, China 34°47N 117°5E 227 G9
Weishan Yunnan, China 25°12N 100°20E 228 E3
Weishan Hu China 34°35N 117°14E 227 G9
Weissenburg Germany 49°2N 10°58E 179 F6
Weissenfels Germany 51°11N 12°0E 178 D7
Weissensee Germany 52°33N 13°27E 115 A3
Weisskirchen = Hranice Czechia 49°34N 17°45E 181 B10
Weisswasser Germany 51°30N 14°36E 178 D10
Weistritz = Bystrzyca → Dolnośląskie, Poland 51°12N 16°55E 185 G3
Weistritz = Bystrzyca → Lubelskie, Poland 51°21N 22°46E 185 G9
Wéitra Austria 48°41N 14°54E 180 C7
Weixi China 27°10N 99°10E 228 D2
Weixin China 27°48N 105°3E 228 D5
Weiyuan Gansu, China 35°7N 104°10E 226 G3
Weiyuan Sichuan, China 29°35N 104°36E 228 C5
Weiz Austria 47°13N 15°39E 180 D8
Weizhou Dao China 21°0N 109°5E 228 G7
Wejherowo Poland 54°35N 18°12E 184 D5
Wekoewa Pt. Bonaire 12°13N 68°24W 322 h
Wekusko L. Canada 54°40N 99°50W 297 C9
Welch U.S.A. 37°26N 81°35W 309 G13
Welchman Hall Barbados 13°11N 59°34W 323 r
Weldya Ethiopia 11°50N 39°34E 257 E4
Welega Ethiopia 9°25N 34°20E 257 F3
Welford △ Australia 25°5S 143°16E 280 D3
Weligama Sri Lanka 5°58N 80°25E 245 M5
Welkite Ethiopia 8°15N 37°42E 257 F4
Welkom S. Africa 28°0S 26°46E 270 C4
Welland Canada 43°0N 79°15W 312 D5
Welland → U.K. 52°51N 0°5W 169 E7
Wellawaya Sri Lanka 6°44N 81°6E 245 L5
Welles Harbor Midway Is. 28°13N 177°25W 302 c
Wellesley Hills U.S.A. 42°18N 71°16W 116 B1
Wellesley Is. Australia 16°42S 139°30E 280 B2
Wellesley Islands ◎ Australia 16°32S 139°23E 280 B2
Welling U.K. 51°27N 0°6E 125 B4
Wellingborough U.K. 52°19N 0°41W 169 E7
Wellington N.S.W., Australia 32°35S 148°59E 283 B8
Wellington Ont., Canada 43°57N 77°20W 312 C7
Wellington N.Z. 41°19S 174°46E 284 H3
Wellington Western Cape, S. Africa 33°38S 19°1E 270 D2
Wellington Somst., U.K. 50°58N 3°13W 169 G4
Wellington Telford & Wrekin, U.K. 52°42N 2°30W 169 E5
Wellington Colo., U.S.A. 40°42N 105°0W 304 F11
Wellington Fla., U.S.A. 26°39N 80°15W 317 J9
Wellington Kans., U.S.A. 37°16N 97°24W 308 G5
Wellington Mass., U.S.A. 42°24N 71°5W 116 A2
Wellington Mo., U.S.A. 39°8N 93°59W 310 E3
Wellington Nev., U.S.A. 38°45N 119°23W 306 G7
Wellington Ohio, U.S.A. 41°10N 82°13W 312 E2
Wellington Tex., U.S.A. 34°51N 100°13W 314 D4
Wellington □ N.Z. 41°0S 175°30E 284 H4
Wellington, I. Chile 49°30S 75°0W 336 C2
Wellington, L. Australia 38°6S 147°20E 283 E7
Wellington Chan. Canada 75°0N 93°0W 295 C13
Wellman U.S.A. 41°28N 91°50W 310 C5
Wells Somst., U.K. 51°13N 2°39W 169 F5
Wells Maine, U.S.A. 43°20N 70°35W 313 C14
Wells N.Y., U.S.A. 43°24N 74°17W 313 C10
Wells Nev., U.S.A. 41°7N 114°58W 304 F6
Wells, L. Australia 26°44S 123°15E 279 E3
Wells, Mt. Australia 17°25S 127°8E 278 C4
Wells Fargo Center Los Angeles, U.S.A. 127 b1
Wells Gray △ Canada 52°30N 120°15W 296 C4
Wells-next-the-Sea U.K. 52°57N 0°51E 168 E8
Wells River U.S.A. 44°9N 72°4W 313 B12
Wellsboro U.S.A. 41°45N 77°18W 312 E7
Wellsburg U.S.A. 40°16N 80°37W 312 F4
Wellsford N.Z. 36°16S 174°32E 284 C3
Wellston = Warner Robins U.S.A. 32°37N 83°36W 316 C6
Wellsville Mo., U.S.A. 39°4N 91°34W 310 E5
Wellsville N.Y., U.S.A. 42°7N 77°57W 312 D7
Wellsville Ohio, U.S.A. 40°36N 80°39W 312 F4
Wellsville Utah, U.S.A. 41°38N 111°56W 304 F8
Wellton U.S.A. 32°40N 114°8W 305 K6
Welmel, Wabi → Ethiopia 5°38N 40°47E 257 F5
Welo Ethiopia 11°50N 39°48E 257 E4
Welo Somalia 9°25N 48°55E 267 C6
Wels Austria 48°9N 14°1E 180 C7
Welshpool Vic., Australia 38°42S 146°26E 283 E7
Welshpool Powys, U.K. 52°39N 3°8W 169 E4
Weltevreden Park S. Africa 26°7S 27°55E 123 A1
Welungen = Wieluń Poland 51°15N 18°34E 185 G5
Welwitschia = Khorixas Namibia 20°16S 14°59E 270 B1
Welwyn Garden City U.K. 51°48N 0°12W 169 F7
Wem U.K. 52°52N 2°44W 168 E5
Wembere → Tanzania 4°10S 34°15E 268 C3
Wembley U.K. 51°33N 0°17W 125 A2
Wemindji Canada 53°0N 78°49W 298 B4
Wemmel Belgium 50°55N 4°18E 116 A1
Wemmer Pan S. Africa 26°13S 28°3E 123 B2
Wemyss Canada 44°52N 76°23W 313 B8
Wen Xian Gansu, China 32°43N 104°36E 226 H3
Wen Xian Henan, China 34°55N 113°5E 226 G7
Wenatchee U.S.A. 47°25N 120°19W 304 C3
Wenceslas Square = Vaclavské náměstí Prague, Czechia 135 b2
Wenchang China 19°38N 110°42E 229 a
Wencheng China 27°46N 120°4E 229 D13
Wenchi Ghana 7°46N 2°8W 262 D4
Wenchow = Wenzhou China 28°0N 120°38E 229 D13
Wenchuan China 31°22N 103°35E 228 B4
Wenden U.S.A. 33°49N 113°33W 307 M13
Wendeng China 37°15N 122°5E 227 F12
Wendenschloss Germany 52°24N 13°35E 115 B4
Wendesi Indonesia 2°30S 134°17E 231 E8
Wendo Ethiopia 6°40N 38°27E 257 F4
Wendover U.S.A. 40°44N 114°2W 304 F6
Weng'an China 27°5N 107°25E 228 D6
Wengcheng China 24°22N 113°50E 229 E9
Wengen Switz. 46°37N 7°55E 173 F14
Wengyuan China 24°20N 114°9E 229 E10
Wenling China 28°21N 121°20E 229 C13
Wenlock → Australia 12°2S 141°55E 286 G1
Wennington U.K. 51°30N 0°12E 125 A5
Weno Pac. Oc. 7°27N 151°52E 287 T18
Wenona U.S.A. 41°3N 89°3W 310 C7
Wenshan China 23°20N 104°18E 228 F5
Wenshang China 35°45N 116°30E 226 G9
Wenshui China 37°26N 112°1E 226 F7
Wensleydale U.K. 54°17N 2°0W 168 C6
Wensu China 41°15N 80°10E 217 D10
Wensum → U.K. 52°40N 1°15E 168 E9
Wentworth Australia 34°2S 141°54E 282 C4
Wentzel L. Canada 59°2N 114°28W 296 B6
Wentzville U.S.A. 38°49N 90°51W 310 F6
Wenut Indonesia 3°11S 133°19E 231 E8
Wenxi China 35°20N 111°10E 226 G6
Wenzhou China 28°0N 120°38E 229 D13
Weott U.S.A. 40°20N 123°55W 304 F2
Wepener S. Africa 29°42S 27°3E 270 C4
Werda Botswana 25°24S 23°15E 270 C3
Werdau Germany 50°44N 12°22E 178 E8
Werder Ethiopia 6°58N 45°1E 267 C6
Werder Brandenburg, Germany 52°23N 12°55E 178 C8
Werdohl Germany 51°15N 7°46E 178 D3
Wereilu Ethiopia 10°40N 39°28E 257 E4
Weri Indonesia 3°10S 132°38E 231 E8
Werneck Germany 49°58N 10°5E 179 F6
Werneuchen Germany 52°38N 13°44E 115 A5
Wernigerode Germany 51°50N 10°47E 178 D6
Werra → Germany 51°24N 9°39E 178 D5
Werribee Australia 37°54S 144°40E 282 D6
Werrikimbe △ Australia 31°11S 152°15E 283 A10
Werrimull Australia 34°25S 141°38E 282 C4
Werris Creek Australia 31°18S 150°38E 283 A9
Werschetz = Vršac Serbia 45°8N 21°20E 182 E6
Wertach → Germany 48°22N 10°54E 179 G6
Wertheim Germany 49°45N 9°32E 179 F5
Wertingen Germany 48°33N 10°41E 179 G6
Wesel Germany 51°39N 6°37E 178 D2
Weser → Germany 53°36N 8°28E 178 B4
Weserbergland Germany 52°12N 9°7E 178 C5
Weserbergland Schaumburg Hameln △ Germany 52°8N 9°20E 178 C5
Wesermünde = Bremerhaven Germany 53°33N 8°36E 178 B4
Weslaco U.S.A. 26°10N 97°58W 314 H6
Weslemkoon L. Canada 45°2N 77°25W 312 A7
Wesley Dominica 15°33N 61°18W 323 k
Wesleyville Nfld. & L., Canada 49°9N 53°33W 299 C9
Wesleyville Pa., U.S.A. 42°9N 80°1W 312 D4
Wessel, C. Australia 10°59S 136°46E 280 A2
Wessel Is. Australia 11°10S 136°45E 280 A2
Wesselburen Germany 54°13N 8°54E 178 A4
Wessex U.K. 51°0N 2°0W 169 F5
Wessington Springs U.S.A. 44°5N 98°34W 308 C4
West U.S.A. 31°48N 97°6W 314 F6
West → U.S.A. 42°52N 72°33W 313 D12
West Allis U.S.A. 43°1N 88°0W 311 B9
West Antarctica Antarctica 80°0S 90°0W 151 D15
West Baines → Australia 15°38S 129°59E 278 C4
West Bank □ Asia 32°6N 35°13E 251 F6
West Bend U.S.A. 43°25N 88°11W 308 D9
West Bengal = Paschimbanga □ India 23°0N 88°0E 243 H13
West Berkshire □ U.K. 51°25N 1°17W 169 F6
West Beskids = Západné Beskydy Europe 49°30N 19°0E 181 B12
West Branch U.S.A. 44°17N 84°14W 309 C11
West Branch Susquehanna → U.S.A. 40°53N 76°48W 313 F8
West Bromwich U.K. 52°32N 1°59W 169 E6
West Burra U.K. 60°5N 1°21W 167 A7
West Canada Cr. → U.S.A. 43°1N 74°58W 313 C10
West Caroline Basin Pac. Oc. 4°0N 138°0E 288 G5
West Carrollton U.S.A. 39°40N 84°17W 311 E12
West Chazy U.S.A. 44°49N 73°28W 313 B11
West Chester U.S.A. 39°58N 75°36W 313 G9
West Chicago U.S.A. 41°53N 88°12W 311 C8
West Coast □ N.Z. 43°15S 170°30E 285 D5
West Coast △ Namibia 21°53S 14°14E 270 B1
West Coast △ S. Africa 33°13S 18°0E 270 D2
West Columbia S.C., U.S.A. 33°59N 81°4W 316 B8
West Columbia Tex., U.S.A. 29°9N 95°39W 314 G7
West Covina U.S.A. 34°4N 117°54W 307 L9
West Des Moines U.S.A. 41°35N 93°43W 310 C3
West Don → Canada 43°44N 79°24W 141 A2
West Drayton U.K. 51°30N 0°28W 125 A1
West Dunbartonshire □ U.K. 55°59N 4°30W 167 F4
West End The Bahamas 26°41N 78°58W 320 A4
West End Boston, U.S.A. 116 b1
West End Village Anguilla 18°10N 63°10W 322 a
West Falkland Falk. Is. 51°40S 60°0W 153 f
West Fargo U.S.A. 46°52N 96°54W 308 B5
West Fiji Basin Pac. Oc. 17°0S 173°0E 288 J9
West Fjord = Vestfjorden Norway 67°55N 14°0E 160 C16
West Fork Trinity → U.S.A. 32°48N 96°54W 314 E6
West Frankfort U.S.A. 37°54N 88°55W 310 G8
West Grand L. U.S.A. 45°14N 67°51W 309 C20
West Green U.S.A. 31°37N 82°44W 316 D7
West Ham U.K. 51°31N 0°1E 125 A4
West Harrow U.K. 51°34N 0°21W 125 A1
West Hartford U.S.A. 41°45N 72°44W 313 E12
West Haven U.S.A. 41°17N 72°57W 313 E12
West Hazleton U.S.A. 40°58N 76°0W 313 F9
West Heath U.K. 51°29N 0°7E 125 B4
West Hill Canada 43°46N 79°10W 141 A3
West Hollywood U.S.A. 34°5N 118°21W 126 B2
West Hurley U.S.A. 41°59N 74°7W 313 E10
West I. India 13°35N 92°54E 245 H11
West Ice Shelf Antarctica 67°0S 85°0E 151 C7
West Indies Cent. Amer. 15°0N 65°0W 321 D7
West Jefferson U.S.A. 39°57N 83°17W 311 E13
West Jordan U.S.A. 40°36N 111°56W 304 F8
West Kavango □ Namibia 18°0S 18°30E 270 A2
West Kensington London, U.K. 125 c1
West Kilburn London, U.K. 125 a1
West Lafayette U.S.A. 40°27N 86°55W 311 D10
West Lamma Channel Hong Kong, China 22°14N 114°4E 122 B2
West Liberty Iowa, U.S.A. 41°34N 91°16W 310 C5
West Liberty Ky., U.S.A. 37°55N 83°16W 311 G13
West Liberty Ohio, U.S.A. 40°15N 83°45W 311 D13
West Linn U.S.A. 45°21N 122°36W 306 E4
West Lorne Canada 42°36N 81°36W 312 D3
West Los Angeles, Univ. of U.S.A. 34°7N 118°23W 126 C2
West Lothian □ U.K. 55°54N 3°36W 167 F5
West Lunga → Zambia 13°6S 24°39E 265 E4
West Lunga △ Zambia 12°49S 24°47E 265 E4
West MacDonnell △ Australia 23°38S 132°59E 278 D5
West Mariana Basin Pac. Oc. 15°0N 137°0E 288 F5
West Medford U.S.A. 42°25N 71°7W 116 A2
West Memphis U.S.A. 35°8N 90°10W 315 D9
West Miami U.S.A. 25°45N 80°17W 129 D1
West Midlands □ U.K. 52°26N 2°0W 169 E6
West Mifflin U.S.A. 40°21N 79°52W 312 F5
West Milford U.S.A. 41°8N 74°22W 313 E10
West Milton Ohio, U.S.A. 39°58N 84°20W 311 E12
West Milton Pa., U.S.A. 41°1N 76°50W 312 F8
West Molesey U.K. 51°24N 0°22W 125 B1
West Monroe U.S.A. 32°31N 92°9W 314 E8
West New Britain □ Papua N. G. 5°0S 149°30E 286 C5
West New York New York, U.S.A. 132 a1
West Newton U.S.A. 40°14N 79°46W 312 F5
West Nicholson Zimbabwe 21°2S 29°20E 269 G2
West Northamptonshire □ U.K. 52°8N 0°59W 169 F6
West Odessa U.S.A. 31°50N 102°30W 314 F3
West of Twin Peaks U.S.A. 37°43N 122°27W 136 B2
West Palm Beach U.S.A. 26°43N 80°3W 317 J9
West Palm Beach Canal U.S.A. 26°40N 80°15W 317 J9
West Park Gauteng, S. Africa 26°9S 27°59E 123 A1
West Park Fla., U.S.A. 25°59N 80°12W 129 C2
West Pensacola U.S.A. 30°25N 87°16W 317 E2
West Plains U.S.A. 36°44N 91°51W 308 G8
West Point Ga., U.S.A. 32°53N 85°11W 316 C4
West Point Iowa, U.S.A. 40°43N 91°27W 310 D5
West Point Ky., U.S.A. 37°59N 85°57W 311 G11
West Point Miss., U.S.A. 33°36N 88°39W 315 E10
West Point N.Y., U.S.A. 41°24N 73°58W 313 E11
West Point Nebr., U.S.A. 41°51N 96°43W 308 E5
West Point Va., U.S.A. 37°32N 76°48W 309 G15
West Point L. U.S.A. 33°8N 85°0W 316 B4
West Pokot □ Kenya 1°15N 35°10E 268 B4
West Pt. = Ouest, Pte. de l' Canada 49°52N 64°40W 299 C7
West Pt. Australia 35°1S 135°56E 282 C1
West Ra. Papua N. G. 4°15S 141°30E 286 C1
West Road → Canada 53°18N 122°53W 296 C4
West Rouge Canada 43°48N 79°7W 141 A4
West Roxbury U.S.A. 42°16N 71°9W 116 B2
West Rutland U.S.A. 43°36N 73°3W 313 C11
West Salem U.S.A. 38°31N 88°1W 311 F8
West Schelde = Westerschelde → Neths. 51°25N 3°25E 170 C3
West Seneca U.S.A. 42°51N 78°48W 312 D6
West Sepik = Sandaun □ Papua N. G. 3°30S 142°0E 286 B2
West Siberian Plain Russia 62°0N 75°0E 210 B9
West Sussex □ U.K. 50°55N 0°30W 169 G7
West Terre Haute U.S.A. 39°28N 87°27W 311 E9
West-Terschelling Neths. 53°22N 5°13E 170 A5
West Town U.S.A. 41°53N 87°42W 119 B2
West Union Iowa, U.S.A. 42°57N 91°49W 310 B5
West Union Ohio, U.S.A. 38°48N 83°33W 311 F13
West Unity U.S.A. 41°35N 84°26W 311 C12
West Valley City U.S.A. 40°42N 111°58W 304 F8
West Virginia □ U.S.A. 38°45N 80°30W 309 F13
West-Vlaanderen □ Belgium 51°0N 3°0E 170 D2
West Walker → U.S.A. 38°54N 119°9W 306 G7
West Wharf Pakistan 24°49N 66°58E 123 B1
West Wyalong Australia 33°56S 147°10E 283 B7
West Yellowstone U.S.A. 44°40N 111°6W 304 D8
West Yorkshire □ U.K. 53°45N 1°40W 168 D6
Westall, Pt. Australia 32°55S 134°4E 281 E1
Westbay U.S.A. 30°18N 85°52W 316 E4
Westbourne Green London, U.K. 125 a1
Westbrook U.S.A. 43°41N 70°22W 309 D18
Westbury Australia 41°30S 146°51E 281 G4
Westby U.S.A. 48°52N 104°3W 304 B11
Westchester Calif., U.S.A. 33°57N 118°23W 126 C2
Westchester N.Y., U.S.A. 40°51N 73°51W 132 A2
Westcliff S. Africa 26°10S 28°1E 123 B2
Westdene S. Africa 26°10S 27°59E 123 B1
Westend Helsinki, Finland 60°9N 24°48E 121 C1
Westend Calif., U.S.A. 35°42N 117°24W 307 K9
Wester Hailes U.K. 55°55N 3°16W 121 B2
Westerham Germany 48°3N 11°36E 131 B2
Westerland Germany 54°54N 8°17E 178 A4
Westerly U.S.A. 41°22N 71°50W 313 E13
Western □ Ghana 5°30N 2°0W 262 D4
Western □ Papua N. G. 7°30S 142°0E 286 D2
Western □ S. Leone 8°30N 13°20W 262 D2
Western □ Zambia 15°0S 24°4E 265 F4
Western Addition U.S.A. 37°47N 122°25W 136 B2
Western Australia □ Australia 25°0S 118°0E 279 E2
Western Bahr el Ghazal □ South Sudan 7°30N 25°30E 257 F2
Western Cape □ S. Africa 34°0S 20°0E 270 D3
Western Dvina = Daugava → Latvia 57°4N 24°3E 188 D3
Western Equatoria □ South Sudan 5°0N 30°0E 257 G3
Western Ghats India 14°0N 75°0E 245 H2
Western Highlands □ Papua N. G. 5°45S 144°10E 286 C3
Western Isles = Eilean Siar □ U.K. 57°30N 7°10W 167 D1
Western North □ Ghana 6°0N 2°30W 262 D4
Western Sahara ■ Africa 25°0N 13°0W 260 D2
Western Samoa = Samoa ■ Pac. Oc. 14°0S 172°0W 287 V20
Western Sierra Madre = Madre Occidental, Sierra Mexico 27°0N 107°0W 318 B3
Western Wall Jerusalem 123 b3
Westernport U.S.A. 39°29N 79°3W 309 F14
Westerschelde → Neths. 51°25N 3°25E 170 C3
Westerstede Germany 53°15N 7°55E 178 B3
Westerwald Germany 50°38N 7°56E 178 E3
Westfield Ill., U.S.A. 39°27N 88°0W 311 E8
Westfield Ind., U.S.A. 40°2N 86°8W 311 D10
Westfield Mass., U.S.A. 42°7N 72°45W 313 D12
Westfield N.Y., U.S.A. 42°20N 79°35W 312 D5
Westfield Pa., U.S.A. 41°55N 77°32W 312 E7
Westgate La., U.S.A. 30°0N 90°13W 131 A1
Westgate Md., U.S.A. 38°57N 77°6W 143 B2
Westhill U.K. 57°9N 2°19W 167 D6
Westhope U.S.A. 48°55N 101°1W 308 A3
Westlake Western Cape, S. Africa 34°4S 18°26E 118 B1
Westlake Calif., U.S.A. 34°4N 118°15W 126 B3
Westlake Calif., U.S.A. 37°42N 122°29W 136 B2
Westland U.S.A. 42°15N 83°20W 311 B13
Westland Bight N.Z. 42°55S 170°5E 285 C5
Westland Tai Poutini △ N.Z. 43°16S 170°16E 285 D5
Westlock Canada 54°9N 113°55W 296 C6
Westmar Australia 27°55S 149°44E 281 D4
Westmeath □ Ireland 53°33N 7°34W 166 C4
Westminster London, U.K. 51°30N 0°7W 125 A3
Westminster Calif., U.S.A. 33°45N 118°0W 307 M8
Westminster Colo., U.S.A. 39°50N 105°2W 304 G11
Westminster Md., U.S.A. 39°34N 76°59W 309 F15
Westmont U.S.A. 40°19N 78°58W 312 F6
Westmorland U.S.A. 33°2N 115°37W 307 M11
Westmount Canada 45°29N 73°35W 130 B2
Weston Ont., Canada 43°42N 79°30W 141 A1
Weston Ohio, U.S.A. 41°21N 83°47W 311 C13
Weston Oreg., U.S.A. 45°49N 118°26W 304 D4
Weston W. Va., U.S.A. 39°2N 80°28W 309 F13
Weston I. Canada 52°33N 79°36W 298 B4
Weston-super-Mare U.K. 51°21N 2°58W 169 F5
Westover U.S.A. 40°45N 78°40W 312 F6
Westphalia U.S.A. 38°26N 92°0W 310 F5
Westport Ont., Canada 44°40N 76°25W 313 B8
Westport Mayo, Ireland 53°48N 9°31W 166 C2
Westport N.Z. 41°46S 171°37E 285 B6
Westport Ind., U.S.A. 39°11N 85°34W 311 E11
Westport N.Y., U.S.A. 44°11N 73°26W 313 B11
Westport Oreg., U.S.A. 46°8N 123°23W 306 D3
Westport Wash., U.S.A. 46°53N 124°6W 306 D2
Westpunt Curaçao 12°22N 69°10W 322 g
Westray Man., Canada 53°36N 101°24W 297 C8
Westray Orkney, U.K. 59°18N 3°0W 167 B5
Westree Canada 47°26N 81°34W 298 C3
Westville Calif., U.S.A. 39°8N 120°42W 306 F6
Westville Fla., U.S.A. 30°46N 85°51W 316 E4
Westville Ill., U.S.A. 40°2N 87°38W 311 D9
Westville Ind., U.S.A. 41°32N 86°54W 311 C10
Westwego U.S.A. 29°54N 90°8W 131 B1
Westwood U.S.A. 40°18N 121°0W 304 F3
Westwood Lake U.S.A. 25°44N 80°23W 317 K9
Westwood Village U.S.A. 34°3N 118°26W 126 B2
Wetzaan Neths. 52°28N 4°46E 112 A1
Wetar Indonesia 7°48S 126°30E 231 F7
Wetaskiwin Canada 52°55N 113°24W 296 C6

Wetherby U.K. 53°56N 1°23W 168 D6
Wethersfield U.S.A. 41°42N 72°40W 313 E12
Wetlet Myanmar 22°20N 95°53E 241 D5
Wetteren Belgium 51°0N 3°53E 170 D3
Wetton S. Africa 34°0S 18°31E 118 B2
Wetumpka U.S.A. 32°32N 86°13W 316 C3
Wetzlar Germany 50°32N 8°31E 178 E4
Wevok U.S.A. 68°53N 166°13W 303 B6
Wewahitchka U.S.A. 30°7N 85°12W 316 E4
Wewak Papua N. G. 3°38S 143°41E 286 B2
Wewoka U.S.A. 35°9N 96°30W 314 D6
Wexford Ont., Canada 43°45N 79°18W 141 A3
Wexford Wexford, Ireland 52°20N 6°28W 166 D5
Wexford □ Ireland 52°20N 6°25W 166 D5
Wexford Harbour Ireland 52°20N 6°25W 166 D5
Weybridge U.K. 51°22N 0°27W 125 B1
Weyburn Canada 49°40N 103°50W 297 D8
Weyer Markt Austria 47°51N 14°40E 180 D7
Weyhe Germany 52°58N 8°49E 178 C4
Weyib → Ethiopia 7°15N 40°15E 257 F5
Weymouth N.S., Canada 44°30N 66°1W 299 D6
Weymouth Dorset, U.K. 50°37N 2°28W 169 G5
Weymouth Mass., U.S.A. 42°13N 70°58W 313 D14
Weymouth, C. Australia 12°37S 143°27E 280 A3
Wezembeek-Oppem Belgium 50°51N 4°29E 116 A2
Wha Ti Canada 63°8N 117°16W 294 E8
Whakaari N.Z. 37°30S 177°13E 284 D6
Whakamaru N.Z. 38°23S 175°50E 284 E4
Whakatane N.Z. 37°57S 177°1E 284 D6
Whakatane → N.Z. 37°57S 177°1E 284 D6
Whale = Baleine → Canada 58°15N 67°40W 299 A6
Whale B. Myanmar 11°37N 98°38E 237 G2
Whale Cove Canada 62°10N 92°34W 297 A10
Whale Pt. Ascension I. 7°57S 14°18W 153 g
Whale Valley = Hitan, W. el Egypt 29°19N 30°10E 256 J7
Whales, B. of Antarctica 78°0S 160°0W 151 D12
Whalsay U.K. 60°22N 0°59W 167 A8
Whangaehu → N.Z. 40°3S 175°6E 284 G4
Whangamata N.Z. 37°12S 175°53E 284 D4
Whangamomona N.Z. 39°8S 174°44E 284 F3
Whanganui △ N.Z. 39°17S 174°53E 284 F3
Whangaparaoa Pen. N.Z. 36°40S 174°45E 284 C3
Whangarei N.Z. 35°43S 174°21E 284 B3
Whangarei Harb. N.Z. 35°45S 174°28E 284 B3
Whangaroa Harb. N.Z. 35°4S 173°46E 284 B2
Whangaruru Harb. N.Z. 35°24S 174°23E 284 B3
Wharanui N.Z. 41°55S 174°6E 285 B9
Wharekauri = Chatham Is. Pac. Oc. 44°0S 176°40W 285 a
Wharfe → U.K. 53°51N 1°9W 168 D6
Wharfedale U.K. 54°6N 2°1W 168 C5
Wharton N.J., U.S.A. 40°54N 74°35W 313 F10
Wharton Pa., U.S.A. 41°31N 78°1W 312 E6
Wharton Tex., U.S.A. 29°19N 96°6W 314 G6
Wharton Basin Ind. Oc. 22°0S 99°0E 273 G9
Whataroa N.Z. 43°18S 170°24E 285 D5
Whataroa → N.Z. 43°7S 170°16E 285 D5
Whatcom = Bellingham U.S.A. 48°46N 122°29W 306 B4
Wheatfield U.S.A. 41°13N 87°4W 311 C9
Wheatland Calif., U.S.A. 39°1N 121°25W 306 F5
Wheatland Ind., U.S.A. 38°40N 87°19W 311 F9
Wheatland Wyo., U.S.A. 42°3N 104°58W 304 E11
Wheatley Canada 42°6N 82°27W 312 D2
Wheaton Ill., U.S.A. 41°52N 88°6W 311 C8
Wheaton Md., U.S.A. 39°3N 77°3W 309 F15
Wheaton Minn., U.S.A. 45°48N 96°30W 308 C5
Wheelbarrow Pk. U.S.A. 37°26N 116°5W 306 H10
Wheeler Oreg., U.S.A. 45°41N 123°53W 304 D2
Wheeler Tex., U.S.A. 35°27N 100°16W 314 D4
Wheeler → Canada 57°2N 67°13W 299 A6
Wheeler L. U.S.A. 34°48N 87°23W 315 D11
Wheeler Pk. N. Mex., U.S.A. 36°34N 105°25W 305 H11
Wheeler Pk. Nev., U.S.A. 38°57N 114°15W 304 G6
Wheeler Ridge U.S.A. 35°0N 118°57W 307 L8
Wheelersburg U.S.A. 38°44N 82°51W 309 F12
Wheeling U.S.A. 40°4N 80°43W 312 F4
Whernside U.K. 54°14N 2°24W 168 C5
Whiddy I. Ireland 51°41N 9°31W 166 E2
Whim Creek Australia 20°50S 117°49E 278 D2
Whirlwind Reef Papua N. G. 4°42S 148°16E 286 C5
Whiskey Jack L. Canada 58°23N 101°55W 297 B8
Whiskeytown-Shasta-Trinity ⌂ U.S.A. 40°45N 122°15W 304 F2
Whistleduck Cr. → Australia 20°15S 135°18E 280 C2
Whistler Canada 50°7N 122°58W 296 C4
Whitby Ont., Canada 43°52N 78°56W 312 C6
Whitby N. Yorks., U.K. 54°29N 0°37W 168 C7
Whitcombe Pass N.Z. 43°13S 170°55E 285 D5
White → Ark., U.S.A. 33°57N 91°5W 314 E9
White → Ind., U.S.A. 38°25N 87°45W 311 F9
White → S. Dak., U.S.A. 43°42N 99°27W 308 D4
White → Tex., U.S.A. 33°14N 100°56W 314 E4
White → Utah, U.S.A. 40°4N 109°41W 304 F9
White → Vt., U.S.A. 43°37N 72°20W 313 C12
White → Wash., U.S.A. 47°12N 122°15W 306 C4
White, L. Australia 21°9S 128°56E 278 D4
White B. Canada 50°0N 56°35W 299 C8
White Bird U.S.A. 45°46N 116°18W 304 D5
White Butte U.S.A. 46°23N 103°18W 308 B2
White City Fla., U.S.A. 29°53N 85°13W 316 F4
White City Oreg., U.S.A. 42°26N 122°51W 304 E2
White Cliffs Australia 30°50S 143°10E 282 A5
White Cloud Hill = Baiyun Mountain Scenic Area ⌂ China 23°11N 113°17E 121 A2
White Desert = Beida, Es Sahrâ al Egypt 27°50N 28°45E 256 B2
White Hall U.S.A. 39°26N 90°24W 310 E6
White Haven U.S.A. 41°4N 75°47W 313 E9
White Horse, Vale of U.K. 51°37N 1°30W 169 F6
White House, The Washington, D.C., U.S.A. 143 b1
White I. = Whakaari N.Z. 37°30S 177°13E 284 D6
White I. Grenada 12°26N 61°28W 323 q
White L. Ont., Canada 45°18N 76°31W 313 A8
White L. La., U.S.A. 29°44N 92°30W 314 G8
White Lake Canada 45°21N 76°29W 313 A8
White Mountain U.S.A. 64°41N 163°24W 303 D7
White Mountain Peak U.S.A. 37°38N 118°15W 306 H8
White Mountains Nat. Recr. Area ⌂ U.S.A. 65°30N 147°40W 303 D11
White Mts. Alaska, U.S.A. 65°30N 146°30W 303 D11
White Mts. Calif., U.S.A. 37°30N 118°15W 306 H8
White Mts. N.H., U.S.A. 44°15N 71°15W 313 B13
White Mts. △ Australia 20°43S 145°12E 280 C4
White Nile = Nîl el Abyad → Sudan 15°38N 32°31E 257 D3
White Nile Dam = Khazzān Jabal al Awliyā Sudan 15°24N 32°20E 257 D3
White Oak U.S.A. 31°2N 81°43W 316 D8
White Otter L. Canada 49°5N 91°55W 298 C1
White Pass U.S.A. 46°38N 121°24W 306 D5
White Pigeon U.S.A. 41°48N 85°39W 311 C11
White Plains Ga., U.S.A. 33°28N 83°1W 316 B6
White Plains N.Y., U.S.A. 41°2N 73°46W 313 E11
White River Ont., Canada 48°35N 85°20W 298 C2
White River S. Dak., U.S.A. 43°34N 100°45W 308 D3
White Rock B.C., Canada 49°2N 122°48W 306 A4
White Rock N. Mex., U.S.A. 35°50N 106°12W 305 J10
White Rock L. U.S.A. 32°48N 96°43W 120 A5
White Rocks Nat. Recr. Area ⌂ U.S.A. 43°22N 72°55W 313 C12
White Russia = Belarus ■ Europe 53°30N 27°0E 177 B14
White Sands ⌂ U.S.A. 32°46N 106°20W 305 K10
White Sea = Beloye More Russia 66°30N 38°0E 186 A6
White Springs U.S.A. 30°20N 82°45W 316 E7
White Sulphur Springs Mont., U.S.A. 46°33N 110°54W 304 C8
White Sulphur Springs W. Va., U.S.A. 37°48N 80°18W 309 G13
White Swan U.S.A. 46°23N 120°44W 306 D6
White Volta → Ghana 9°10N 1°15W 263 D4
Whitechapel U.K. 51°31N 0°3W 125 A3
Whitecliffs N.Z. 43°26S 171°55E 285 D6
Whitecourt Canada 54°10N 115°45W 296 C5
Whiteface Mt. U.S.A. 44°22N 73°54W 313 B11
Whitefield U.S.A. 44°23N 71°37W 313 B13
Whitefish U.S.A. 48°25N 114°20W 304 B6
Whitefish B. U.S.A. 46°40N 84°55W 298 C3
Whitefish Bay U.S.A. 43°6N 87°54W 311 A9
Whitefish L. Canada 62°41N 106°48W 297 A7
Whitefish Pt. U.S.A. 46°45N 84°59W 309 B11
Whitegull, L. = Goélands, L. aux Canada 55°27N 64°17W 299 A7
Whitehall London, U.K. 125 b3
Whitehall Mich., U.S.A. 43°24N 86°21W 308 D10
Whitehall Mont., U.S.A. 45°52N 112°6W 304 D7
Whitehall N.Y., U.S.A. 43°33N 73°24W 313 C11
Whitehall Wis., U.S.A. 44°22N 91°19W 308 C8
Whitehaven U.K. 54°33N 3°35W 168 C4
Whitehorse Canada 60°43N 135°3W 296 A1
Whiteman Ra. Papua N. G. 5°55S 150°0E 286 C6
Whitemark Australia 40°7S 148°3E 281 G4
Whiteplains Liberia 6°28N 10°40W 262 D2
Whiteriver U.S.A. 33°50N 109°58W 305 K9
Whitesand → Canada 60°9N 115°45W 296 A5
Whitesands S. Africa 34°23S 20°50E 270 D3
Whitesboro N.Y., U.S.A. 43°7N 75°18W 313 C9
Whitesboro Tex., U.S.A. 33°39N 96°54W 314 E6
Whiteshell ⌂ Canada 50°0N 95°40W 297 D9
Whiteside, Canal Chile 53°55S 70°15W 336 D2
Whiteville U.S.A. 34°20N 78°42W 315 D15
Whitewater U.S.A. 42°50N 88°44W 311 B8
Whitewater B. U.S.A. 25°15N 81°0W 317 K9
Whitewater Baldy U.S.A. 33°20N 108°39W 305 K9
Whitewater L. Canada 50°50N 89°10W 298 B2
Whitewood Queens., Australia 21°28S 143°30E 280 C3
Whitewood Sask., Canada 50°20N 102°20W 297 C8
Whitfield Australia 36°42S 146°24E 283 D7
Whithorn U.K. 54°44N 4°26W 167 G4
Whitianga N.Z. 36°47S 175°41E 284 C4
Whiting U.S.A. 41°41N 87°30W 311 C9
Whitman U.S.A. 42°5N 70°56W 313 D14
Whitmore Mts. Antarctica 82°35S 104°30W 151 E15
Whitmore Village U.S.A. 21°31N 158°1W 302 J13
Whitney Ont., Canada 45°31N 78°14W 312 A6
Whitney Nev., U.S.A. 36°4N 115°5W 124 B2
Whitney, Mt. U.S.A. 36°35N 118°18W 306 J8
Whitney Point U.S.A. 42°20N 75°58W 313 D9
Whitstable U.K. 51°21N 1°3E 169 F9
Whitsunday I. Australia 20°15S 149°4E 280 b
Whitsunday Islands △ Australia 20°15S 149°0E 280 b
Whittemore U.S.A. 43°4N 94°26W 310 A2
Whittier Alaska, U.S.A. 60°47N 148°41W 303 F10
Whittier Calif., U.S.A. 33°58N 118°2W 126 C4
Whittier Narrows Recreation Area ⌂ U.S.A. 34°2N 118°4W 126 B4
Whittlesea Australia 37°27S 145°9E 283 D6
Whitton U.K. 51°27N 0°21W 125 B1
Wholdaia L. Canada 60°43N 104°20W 297 A8
Whyalla Australia 33°2S 137°30E 282 B2
Wiang Kosai △ Thailand 17°54N 99°29E 236 D2
Wiang Sa Thailand 18°34N 100°45E 236 C3
Wiarton Canada 44°40N 81°10W 312 B3
Wiawso Ghana 6°10N 2°25W 262 D4
Wiay U.K. 57°24N 7°13W 167 D1
Wiązów Poland 50°50N 17°10E 185 H4
Wibaux U.S.A. 46°59N 104°11W 304 C11
Wichabai Guyana 2°57N 59°35W 329 C6
Wichian Buri Thailand 15°39N 101°7E 236 E3
Wichita U.S.A. 37°42N 97°20W 308 G5
Wichita Falls U.S.A. 33°54N 98°30W 314 E5
Wick U.K. 58°26N 3°5W 167 C5
Wickenburg U.S.A. 33°58N 112°44W 305 K7
Wickepin Australia 32°50S 117°30E 279 F2
Wickham Australia 20°42S 117°11E 278 D2
Wickham, C. Australia 39°35S 143°57E 281 F3
Wickliffe U.S.A. 41°36N 81°28W 312 E3
Wicklow Ireland 52°59N 6°3W 166 D5
Wicklow □ Ireland 52°57N 6°25W 166 D5
Wicklow Hd. Ireland 52°58N 6°0W 166 D6
Wicklow Mts. Ireland 52°58N 6°26W 166 C5
Wicklow Mts. △ Ireland 53°6N 6°21W 166 C5
Widawa Poland 51°27N 18°51E 185 G5
Widawka → Poland 51°27N 18°52E 185 G5
Wide B. Papua N. G. 5°5S 152°5E 286 C7
Wideawake ✈ (ASI) Ascension I. 7°58S 14°23W 153 g
Widgeegoara Cr. → Australia 28°51S 146°34E 281 D4
Widgiemooltha Australia 31°30S 121°34E 279 F3
Widnes U.K. 53°23N 2°45W 168 D5
Wido S. Korea 35°35N 126°17E 224 E3
Więcbork Poland 53°21N 17°30E 185 E4
Wieden Austria 48°11N 16°22E 142 A2
Wiehengebirge = Nördlicher Teutoburger Wald-Wiehengebirge ⌂ Germany 52°18N 8°10E 178 C4
Wiehl Germany 50°56N 7°34E 178 E3
Wiek Germany 54°37N 13°17E 178 A9
Wielbark Poland 53°24N 20°55E 184 E7
Wieleń Poland 52°53N 16°9E 185 F3
Wielichowo Poland 52°7N 16°22E 185 F3
Wieliczka Poland 50°0N 20°5E 185 J7
Wielkopolski △ Poland 52°18N 16°45E 185 F3
Wielkopolskie □ Poland 52°10N 17°30E 185 F4
Wieluń Poland 51°15N 18°34E 185 G5
Wien Austria 48°12N 16°22E 142 A2
Wien-Schwechat ✈ (VIE) Austria 48°7N 16°35E 142 B3
Wiener Neustadt Austria 47°49N 16°16E 181 D9
Wienerberg Austria 48°9N 16°21E 142 B2
Wieprz → Poland 51°34N 21°49E 185 G8
Wieprza → Poland 54°26N 16°25E 184 D3
Wieruszów Poland 51°19N 18°9E 185 G5
Wierzbno Poland 52°11N 21°1E 143 B2
Wiesbaden Germany 50°4N 8°14E 179 E4
Wiesental Germany 49°13N 8°31E 179 F4
Wiesloch Germany 49°18N 8°41E 179 F4
Wiesmoor Germany 53°24N 7°47E 178 B3
Wieżyca Poland 54°14N 18°8E 184 D5
Wigan U.K. 53°33N 2°38W 168 D5
Wiggins Colo., U.S.A. 40°14N 104°4W 304 F11
Wiggins Miss., U.S.A. 30°51N 89°8W 315 F10
Wight, I. of U.K. 50°41N 1°17W 169 G6
Wigierski △ Poland 54°5N 23°5E 184 D10
Wigry, Jezioro Poland 54°2N 23°8E 184 D10
Wigston U.K. 52°35N 1°6W 169 E6
Wigton U.K. 54°50N 3°10W 168 C4
Wigtown U.K. 54°53N 4°27W 167 G4
Wigtown B. U.K. 54°46N 4°15W 167 G4
Wijde Wormer Neths. 52°28N 4°52E 112 A2
Wik and Wikway People ❂ Australia 13°55S 142°28E 280 A3
Wil Switz. 47°28N 9°3E 179 H5
Wilamowice Poland 49°55N 19°9E 185 J6
Wilanów Poland 52°10N 21°4E 143 B2
Wilanówka → Poland 52°13N 21°6E 143 C2
Wilber U.S.A. 40°29N 96°58W 308 E5
Wilberforce Canada 45°2N 78°13W 312 A6
Wilberforce, C. Australia 11°54S 136°35E 280 A2
Wilburton U.S.A. 34°55N 95°19W 314 D7
Wilcannia Australia 31°30S 143°26E 282 A5
Wilcox U.S.A. 41°35N 78°41W 312 E6
Wildbad Germany 48°44N 8°33E 179 G4
Wildcat Cr. → U.S.A. 40°28N 86°52W 311 D10
Wildenschwert = Ústí nad Orlicí Czechia 49°58N 16°24E 181 B9
Wildeshausen Germany 52°54N 8°27E 178 C4
Wildeshauser Geest ⌂ Germany 52°54N 8°30E 178 C4
Wildomar U.S.A. 33°36N 117°16W 307 M9
Wildon Austria 46°52N 15°31E 180 E8
Wildrose U.S.A. 36°14N 117°11W 307 J9
Wilds, The S. Africa 26°10S 28°2E 123 B2
Wildspitze Austria 46°53N 10°53E 180 E3
Wildwood U.S.A. 28°52N 82°2W 317 G7
Wilga → Poland 51°52N 21°18E 185 G8
Wilge → S. Africa 27°3S 28°20E 271 C4
Wilhelm, Mt. Papua N. G. 5°50S 145°1E 286 C3
Wilhelm II Coast Antarctica 68°0S 90°0E 151 C7
Wilhelmina Geb. Suriname 3°50N 56°30W 329 C6
Wilhelmina Top = Trikora, Puncak Indonesia 4°15S 138°45E 231 E9
Wilhelmsburg Austria 48°6N 15°36E 180 C8
Wilhelmshagen Germany 52°26N 13°42E 115 B5
Wilhelmshaven Germany 53°31N 8°7E 178 B4
Wilhelmstal Namibia 21°58S 16°21E 270 B2
Wilis Indonesia 7°51S 111°48E 235 D4
Wilkes-Barre U.S.A. 41°15N 75°53W 313 E9
Wilkes I. Wake I. 19°18N 166°34E 302 b
Wilkes Land Antarctica 69°0S 120°0E 151 D9
Wilket Creek Park Canada 43°43N 79°21W 141 A2
Wilkie Canada 52°27N 108°42W 297 C7
Wilkieston U.K. 55°54N 3°24W 121 B1
Wilkins Ice Shelf Antarctica 70°30S 72°0W 151 C17
Wilkinsburg U.S.A. 40°26N 79°52W 312 F5
Wilkinson Lakes Australia 29°40S 132°39E 279 E5
Will Rogers State Historical Park ⌂ U.S.A. 34°2N 118°30W 126 B1
Willacoochee U.S.A. 31°20N 83°3W 316 D6
Willandra △ Australia 33°12S 145°0E 283 B6
Willandra Creek → Australia 33°22S 145°52E 283 B6
Willapa B. U.S.A. 46°40N 124°0W 306 D3
Willapa Hills U.S.A. 46°35N 123°25W 306 D3
Willard U.S.A. 41°3N 82°44W 312 E2
Willare Bridge Roadhouse Australia 17°43S 123°38E 278 C3
Willaumez Pen. Papua N. G. 5°15S 150°2E 286 C6
Willbriggie Australia 34°28S 146°2E 283 C7
Willcox U.S.A. 32°15N 109°50W 305 K9
Willemstad Curaçao 12°5N 68°55W 322 g
Willenberg = Wielbark Poland 53°24N 20°55E 184 E7
Willesden U.K. 51°32N 0°15W 125 A2
Willesden Green U.K. 51°32N 0°13W 125 A2
Willi Willi △ Australia 30°57S 152°27E 283 A10
William → Canada 59°8N 109°19W 297 B7
William, Mt. Australia 37°17S 142°35E 282 D5
William 'Bill' Dannelly Res. U.S.A. 32°6N 87°24W 315 E11
William Creek Australia 28°58S 136°22E 281 D2
Williamnagar India 25°31N 90°37E 241 C3
Williams W. Austral., Australia 33°2S 116°52E 279 F2
Williams Ariz., U.S.A. 35°15N 112°11W 305 J7
Williams Calif., U.S.A. 39°9N 122°9W 306 F4
Williams Harbour Canada 52°33N 55°47W 299 B8
Williams Lake Canada 52°10N 122°10W 296 C4
Williamsbridge U.S.A. 40°52N 73°51W 132 A2
Williamsburg Fla., U.S.A. 28°24N 81°26W 133 B2
Williamsburg Iowa, U.S.A. 41°40N 92°1W 310 C4
Williamsburg Ky., U.S.A. 36°44N 84°10W 309 G11
Williamsburg New York, U.S.A. 132 f3
Williamsburg Pa., U.S.A. 40°28N 78°12W 312 F6
Williamsburg Va., U.S.A. 37°16N 76°43W 309 G15
Williamsburg Bridge New York, U.S.A. 132 e2
Williamsfield U.S.A. 40°55N 90°1W 310 D6
Williamson N.Y., U.S.A. 43°14N 77°11W 312 C7
Williamson W. Va., U.S.A. 37°41N 82°17W 309 G12
Williamsport Ind., U.S.A. 40°17N 87°17W 311 D9
Williamsport Pa., U.S.A. 41°15N 77°1W 312 E7
Williamston Mich., U.S.A. 42°41N 84°17W 311 B12
Williamston N.C., U.S.A. 35°51N 77°4W 315 D16
Williamstown Vic., Australia 37°51S 144°52E 128 B1
Williamstown Ky., U.S.A. 38°38N 84°34W 311 F12
Williamstown Mass., U.S.A. 42°43N 73°12W 313 D11
Williamstown N.Y., U.S.A. 43°26N 75°53W 313 C9
Williamsville U.S.A. 39°57N 89°33W 310 E7
Willikies Antigua & B. 17°3N 61°42W 322 b
Willimantic U.S.A. 41°43N 72°13W 313 E12
Willingboro U.S.A. 40°3N 74°54W 309 E16
Willis, L. U.S.A. 28°23N 81°28W 133 B2
Willis Tower Chicago, U.S.A. 119 c1
Willisburg U.S.A. 37°49N 85°8W 311 G11
Williston Northern Cape, S. Africa 31°20S 20°53E 270 D3
Williston Fla., U.S.A. 29°23N 82°27W 317 F7
Williston N. Dak., U.S.A. 48°9N 103°37W 308 A2
Williston S.C., U.S.A. 33°24N 81°25W 316 B8
Williston L. Canada 56°0N 124°0W 296 B4
Willits U.S.A. 39°25N 123°21W 304 G2
Willmar U.S.A. 45°7N 95°3W 308 C6
Willmore Wilderness ⌂ Canada 53°45N 119°30W 296 C5
Willoughby N.S.W., Australia 33°48S 151°12E 139 A2
Willoughby Ohio, U.S.A. 41°39N 81°24W 312 E3
Willoughby B. Antigua & B. 17°2N 61°44W 322 b
Willow U.S.A. 61°45N 150°3W 303 F10
Willow Bunch Canada 49°20N 105°35W 297 D7
Willow L. Canada 62°10N 119°8W 296 A5
Willow Tree Australia 31°40S 150°45E 283 A9
Willow Wall, The China 42°10N 122°0E 227 C12
Willowdale Ont., Canada 43°46N 79°25W 141 A2
Willowdale La., U.S.A. 30°0N 90°12W 131 A1
Willowick U.S.A. 41°38N 81°28W 312 E3
Willowlake → Canada 62°42N 123°8W 296 A4
Willowmore S. Africa 33°15S 23°30E 270 D3
Willows U.S.A. 39°31N 122°12W 306 F4
Willowvale = Gatyana S. Africa 32°16S 28°31E 271 D4
Wills, L. Australia 21°25S 128°51E 278 D4
Wills Cr. → Australia 22°43S 140°2E 280 C3
Willsboro U.S.A. 44°21N 73°24W 313 B11
Willunga Australia 35°15S 138°30E 282 C3
Wilma U.S.A. 30°9N 84°58W 316 E5
Wilmer U.S.A. 32°35N 96°41W 120 C5
Wilmersdorf Berlin, Germany 115 c1
Wilmette U.S.A. 42°4N 87°42W 119 A2
Wilmington S. Austral., Australia 32°39S 138°7E 282 B3
Wilmington Kent, U.K. 51°25N 0°12E 125 B5
Wilmington Del., U.S.A. 39°45N 75°33W 309 F16
Wilmington Ill., U.S.A. 41°18N 88°9W 311 C8
Wilmington N.C., U.S.A. 34°14N 77°55W 315 D16
Wilmington Ohio, U.S.A. 39°27N 83°50W 311 E13
Wilmington Vt., U.S.A. 42°52N 72°52W 313 D12
Wilmslow U.K. 53°19N 2°13W 168 D5
Wilna = Vilnius Lithuania 54°38N 25°19E 188 E3
Wilpattu △ Sri Lanka 8°20N 79°50E 245 K4
Wilpena Australia 31°31S 138°37E 282 A3
Wilpena Cr. → Australia 31°25S 139°29E 282 A3
Wilsall U.S.A. 45°59N 110°38W 304 D8
Wilson N.C., U.S.A. 35°44N 77°55W 315 D16
Wilson N.Y., U.S.A. 43°19N 78°50W 312 C6
Wilson Pa., U.S.A. 40°41N 75°15W 313 F9
Wilson → Australia 16°48S 128°16E 278 C4
Wilson Bluff Australia 31°41S 129°0E 279 F4
Wilson Inlet Australia 35°0S 117°22E 279 G2
Wilson Str. Solomon Is. 8°0S 156°39E 287 M9
Wilsons Promontory Australia 38°59S 146°23E 283 E7
Wilsons Promontory △ Australia 38°59S 146°23E 283 D7
Wilster Germany 53°55N 9°23E 178 B5
Wilton Iowa, U.S.A. 41°35N 91°1W 310 C5
Wilton N. Dak., U.S.A. 47°10N 100°47W 308 B3
Wilton → Australia 14°45S 134°33E 280 A1
Wilton Manors U.S.A. 26°9N 80°8W 129 B3
Wiltshire □ U.K. 51°18N 1°53W 169 F6
Wiltz Lux. 49°57N 5°55E 170 E5
Wiluna Australia 26°36S 120°14E 279 E3
Wimbledon U.K. 51°25N 0°13W 125 B2
Wimbledon Common U.K. 51°26N 0°14W 125 B2
Wimbledon Park U.K. 51°25N 0°11W 125 B2
Wimbledon Tennis Ground U.K. 51°25N 0°12W 125 B2
Wimborne Minster U.K. 50°48N 1°59W 169 G6
Wimereux France 50°45N 1°37E 173 B8
Wimmera → Australia 36°8S 141°56E 282 D4
Winam G. Kenya 0°20S 34°15E 268 C3
Winamac U.S.A. 41°3N 86°36W 311 C10
Winburg S. Africa 28°30S 27°2E 270 C4
Winchelsea Australia 38°10S 144°1E 282 E6
Winchendon U.S.A. 42°41N 72°3W 313 D12
Winchester N.Z. 44°11S 171°17E 285 E6
Winchester Hants., U.K. 51°4N 1°18W 169 F6
Winchester Conn., U.S.A. 41°53N 73°9W 313 E11
Winchester Idaho, U.S.A. 46°14N 116°38W 304 C5
Winchester Ill., U.S.A. 39°38N 90°27W 310 E6
Winchester Ind., U.S.A. 40°10N 84°59W 311 D12
Winchester Ky., U.S.A. 37°59N 84°11W 311 G12
Winchester Mass., U.S.A. 42°26N 71°8W 116 A2
Winchester N.H., U.S.A. 42°46N 72°23W 313 D12
Winchester Nev., U.S.A. 36°7N 115°7W 124 B2
Winchester Ohio, U.S.A. 38°56N 83°39W 311 F13
Winchester Tenn., U.S.A. 35°11N 86°7W 315 D11
Winchester Va., U.S.A. 39°11N 78°10W 309 F14
Wind → U.S.A. 43°12N 108°12W 304 E9
Wind Cave △ U.S.A. 43°32N 103°17W 308 D2
Wind Point U.S.A. 42°47N 87°46W 311 B9
Wind River Range U.S.A. 43°0N 109°30W 304 E9
Windamere, L. Australia 32°48S 149°51E 283 B8
Windau = Ventspils Latvia 57°25N 21°32E 184 A8
Windber U.S.A. 40°14N 78°50W 312 F6
Winder U.S.A. 34°0N 83°45W 316 A6
Windermere Western Cape, S. Africa 33°55S 18°30E 118 A2
Windermere Cumb., U.K. 54°23N 2°55W 168 C5
Windermere Fla., U.S.A. 28°29N 81°32W 133 B1
Windfall U.S.A. 40°22N 85°57W 311 D11
Windhoek Namibia 22°35S 17°4E 270 B2
Windidda ❂ Australia 26°23S 122°12E 279 E3
Windisch-Feistritz = Slovenska Bistrica Slovenia 46°24N 15°35E 199 B12
Windischgarsten Austria 47°42N 14°21E 180 D7
Windischgratz = Slovenj Gradec Slovenia 46°31N 15°5E 199 B12
Windjana Gorge △ Australia 17°51S 125°0E 278 C3
Windom U.S.A. 43°52N 95°7W 308 D6
Windorah Australia 25°24S 142°36E 280 D3
Window Rock U.S.A. 35°41N 109°3W 305 J9
Windrush → U.K. 51°43N 1°24W 169 F6
Windsor N.S.W., Australia 33°37S 150°50E 283 B9
Windsor N.S., Canada 44°59N 64°5W 299 D7
Windsor Ont., Canada 42°18N 83°0W 312 D2
Windsor N.Z. 44°59S 170°49E 285 E5
Windsor Gauteng, S. Africa 26°7S 27°59E 123 A1
Windsor Windsor & Maidenhead, U.K. 51°29N 0°36W 169 F7
Windsor Calif., U.S.A. 38°33N 122°49W 306 G4
Windsor Colo., U.S.A. 40°29N 104°54W 304 F11
Windsor Conn., U.S.A. 41°50N 72°39W 313 E12
Windsor Ill., U.S.A. 39°26N 88°36W 311 E8
Windsor Mo., U.S.A. 38°32N 93°31W 310 F3
Windsor N.Y., U.S.A. 42°5N 75°37W 313 D9
Windsor Vt., U.S.A. 43°29N 72°24W 313 C12
Windsor, Gare Montréal, Canada 130 c2
Windsor & Maidenhead □ U.K. 51°29N 0°40W 169 F7
Windsor Caves Jamaica 18°21N 77°39W 320 a
Windsor Hills U.S.A. 33°59N 118°22W 126 C2
Windsorton S. Africa 28°16S 24°44E 270 C3
Windward Grenada 12°31N 61°26W 323 q
Windward Is. W. Indies 13°0N 61°0W 321 D7
Windward Passage = Vientos, Paso de los Caribbean 20°0N 74°0W 321 C5
Windward Side Saba 17°38N 63°14W 322 a
Winefred L. Canada 55°30N 110°30W 297 B6
Winejok South Sudan 9°1N 27°30E 257 F2
Winfield Iowa, U.S.A. 41°7N 91°26W 310 C5
Winfield Kans., U.S.A. 37°15N 96°59W 308 G5
Winfield Mo., U.S.A. 39°0N 90°44W 310 F6
Wingate Mts. Australia 14°25S 130°40E 278 B5
Wingellina = Irrunytju Australia 26°3S 128°56E 279 E4
Wingham N.S.W., Australia 31°48S 152°22E 283 A10
Wingham Ont., Canada 43°55N 81°20W 312 C3
Winisk → Canada 55°17N 85°5W 298 A2
Winisk L. Canada 52°55N 87°22W 298 B2
Wink U.S.A. 31°45N 103°9W 314 F3
Winkler Canada 49°10N 97°56W 297 D9
Winklern Austria 46°52N 12°52E 180 E5
Winlock U.S.A. 46°30N 122°56W 306 D4
Winneba Ghana 5°25N 0°36W 263 D4
Winnebago U.S.A. 42°16N 89°15W 310 B7
Winnebago, L. U.S.A. 44°0N 88°26W 308 D9
Winnecke Cr. → Australia 18°35S 131°34E 278 C5
Winnemucca U.S.A. 40°58N 117°44W 304 F5
Winnemucca L. U.S.A. 40°7N 119°21W 304 F4
Winner U.S.A. 43°22N 99°52W 308 D4
Winnetka U.S.A. 42°6N 87°45W 119 A2
Winnett U.S.A. 47°0N 108°21W 304 C9
Winnfield U.S.A. 31°56N 92°38W 314 F8
Winnibigoshish, L. U.S.A. 47°27N 94°13W 308 B6
Winning Germany 48°2N 11°37E 131 B2
Winnipeg Canada 49°54N 97°9W 297 D9
Winnipeg → Canada 50°38N 96°19W 297 C9
Winnipeg, L. Canada 52°0N 97°0W 297 C9
Winnipeg Beach Canada 50°30N 96°58W 297 C9
Winnipegosis Canada 51°39N 99°55W 297 C9
Winnipegosis L. Canada 52°30N 100°0W 297 C9
Winnipesaukee, L. U.S.A. 43°38N 71°21W 313 C13
Winnisquam L. U.S.A. 43°33N 71°31W 313 C13
Winnsboro La., U.S.A. 32°10N 91°43W 314 E9
Winnsboro S.C., U.S.A. 34°23N 81°5W 315 D14
Winnsboro Tex., U.S.A. 32°58N 95°17W 314 E7
Winokapau, L. Canada 53°15N 62°50W 299 B7
Winona Minn., U.S.A. 44°3N 91°39W 308 C8
Winona Miss., U.S.A. 33°29N 89°44W 315 E10
Winooski U.S.A. 44°29N 73°11W 313 B11
Winooski → U.S.A. 44°32N 73°17W 313 B11
Winschoten Neths. 53°9N 7°3E 170 A7
Winsen Germany 53°22N 10°13E 178 B6
Winsford U.K. 53°12N 2°31W 168 D5
Winslow = Bainbridge Island U.S.A. 47°38N 122°32W 306 C4
Winslow Ariz., U.S.A. 35°2N 110°42W 305 J8
Winslow Ind., U.S.A. 38°23N 87°13W 311 F9
Winslow Reef Kiribati 1°36S 174°57W 277 A16
Winsted U.S.A. 41°55N 73°4W 313 E11
Winston-Salem U.S.A. 36°6N 80°15W 315 C14
Winter Garden U.S.A. 28°34N 81°35W 317 G8
Winter Haven U.S.A. 28°1N 81°44W 317 G8
Winter Park U.S.A. 28°36N 81°20W 317 G8
Winterberg Germany 51°11N 8°33E 178 D4
Winterhaven U.S.A. 32°44N 114°38W 307 N12
Winters U.S.A. 38°32N 121°58W 306 G5
Winterset U.S.A. 41°20N 94°1W 310 C3
Wintersville U.S.A. 40°23N 80°42W 312 F4
Winterswijk Neths. 51°58N 6°43E 170 C6
Winterthur Switz. 47°30N 8°44E 179 H4
Winthrop U.S.A. 48°28N 120°10W 304 B3
Winton Queens., Australia 22°24S 143°3E 280 C3
Winton N.Z. 46°8S 168°20E 285 G3
Wintua Vanuatu 16°30S 167°26E 287 F5
Wipper → Germany 51°16N 11°12E 178 D7
Wirlyajarrayi ❂ Australia 21°45S 132°35E 278 D5
Wirraminna Australia 31°12S 136°13E 282 A2
Wirrulla Australia 32°24S 134°31E 281 E1
Wisbech U.K. 52°41N 0°9E 169 E8
Wisconsin □ U.S.A. 44°45N 89°30W 308 C9
Wisconsin → U.S.A. 43°0N 91°15W 310 A5
Wisconsin Rapids U.S.A. 44°23N 89°49W 308 C9
Wisdom U.S.A. 45°37N 113°27W 304 D7
Wiseman U.S.A. 67°25N 150°6W 303 C10
Wishaw U.K. 55°46N 3°54W 167 F5
Wishek U.S.A. 46°16N 99°33W 308 B4
Wisła Poland 49°38N 18°53E 185 J5
Wisła → Poland 54°22N 18°55E 184 D5
Wiślany, Zalew Poland 54°20N 19°50E 184 D6
Wisłok → Poland 50°13N 22°32E 185 H9
Wisłoka → Poland 50°27N 21°23E 185 H8
Wismar Mecklenburg-Vorpommern, Germany 53°54N 11°29E 178 B7
Wismar Guyana 5°59N 58°18W 329 B6
Wisner U.S.A. 41°59N 96°55W 308 E5
Wissant France 50°52N 1°40E 173 B8
Wissembourg France 49°2N 7°57E 173 C14
Wissous France 48°44N 2°19E 134 B2
Wisznice Poland 51°48N 23°13E 185 G10
Witbank = eMalahleni S. Africa 25°51S 29°14E 271 C4
Witches Gorge = Wu Xia China 31°2N 110°10E 229 B8
Witdraai S. Africa 26°58S 20°48E 270 C3
Witham U.K. 51°48N 0°40E 169 F8
Witham → U.K. 52°59N 0°2W 168 E7
Withernsea U.K. 53°44N 0°1E 168 D8
Withlacoochee → Fla., U.S.A. 30°24N 83°10W 316 E6
Withlacoochee → Fla., U.S.A. 29°0N 82°45W 317 G7
Witjira △ Australia 26°22S 135°37E 281 D2
Witkowo Poland 52°26N 17°45E 185 F4
Witless Bay Canada 47°17N 52°50W 299 C9
Witney U.K. 51°48N 1°28W 169 F6
Witnica Poland 52°40N 14°54E 185 F1
Witnossob → Namibia 23°55S 18°45E 270 C3
Witriver S. Africa 25°20S 31°0E 271 C5
Wittdün Germany 54°38N 8°23E 178 A4
Witte Pan Bonaire 12°3N 68°17W 322 h
Wittelsheim France 47°48N 7°14E 173 E14
Witten Germany 51°26N 7°20E 178 D3
Wittenau Germany 52°35N 13°19E 115 A2
Wittenberge Germany 53°0N 11°45E 178 B7
Wittenburg Germany 53°31N 11°4E 178 B7
Wittenoom Australia 22°15S 118°20E 278 D2
Witti, Banjaran Malaysia 5°11N 116°29E 235 A5
Wittingau = Třeboň Czechia 49°1N 14°48E 180 B7
Wittingen Germany 52°44N 10°44E 178 C6
Wittlich Germany 49°59N 6°53E 179 F2
Wittmund Germany 53°34N 7°46E 178 B3
Wittow Germany 54°38N 13°20E 178 A9
Wittstock Germany 53°10N 12°28E 178 B8
Witu Kenya 2°23S 40°26E 268 C5
Witu Is. Papua N. G. 4°50S 149°25E 286 C5
Witvlei Namibia 22°23S 18°32E 270 B2
Witwatersrand, Univ. of S. Africa 26°11S 28°1E 123 B2
Witzenhausen Germany 51°20N 9°51E 178 D5
Wiwon N. Korea 40°54N 126°3E 224 B3
Wixom U.S.A. 42°32N 83°32W 311 B13
Wkra → Poland 52°27N 20°44E 185 F7
Władysławowo Poland 54°48N 18°25E 184 D5
Wleń Poland 51°2N 15°39E 185 G2
Wlingi Indonesia 8°5S 112°25E 235 D4
Włochy Poland 52°12N 20°54E 143 B1
Włocławek Poland 52°40N 19°3E 185 F6
Włodawa Poland 51°33N 23°31E 185 G10
Włoszczowa Poland 50°50N 19°55E 185 H6
Wo Mei Hong Kong, China 22°21N 114°15E 122 A3
Wo Yi Hop Hong Kong, China 22°23N 114°8E 122 A2
Woburn Ont., Canada 43°46N 79°12W 141 A3
Woburn Mass., U.S.A. 42°29N 71°9W 116 A2
Wodian China 32°50N 112°35E 226 H7
Wodonga Australia 36°5S 146°50E 283 D7
Wodzisław Śląski Poland 50°1N 18°26E 185 H5
Wœrth France 48°57N 7°45E 173 D14
Wohlau = Wołów Poland 51°20N 16°38E 185 G3
Woinbogoin China 32°51N 98°39E 228 A2
Woippy France 49°10N 6°8E 173 C13
Woitape Papua N. G. 8°33S 147°15E 286 E4
Wojcieszow Poland 50°58N 15°55E 185 H2
Wokam Indonesia 5°45S 134°28E 231 F8
Wokha India 26°6N 94°16E 241 B5
Woking U.K. 51°19N 0°34W 169 F7
Wokingham U.K. 51°24N 0°49W 169 F7
Wokingham □ U.K. 51°25N 0°51W 169 F7
Woko △ Australia 31°46S 151°49E 283 A9
Wola Poland 52°14N 20°57E 143 B1
Wolbrom Poland 50°24N 19°45E 185 H6
Wolcottville U.S.A. 41°32N 85°22W 311 C11
Wołczyn Poland 51°1N 18°3E 185 G5
Woldegk Germany 53°27N 13°34E 178 B9
Woldenberg = Dobiegniew Poland 52°59N 15°45E 185 F2
Woldenberg Park New Orleans, U.S.A. 131 b3
Woleu-Ntem □ Gabon 2°0N 12°30E 264 B2
Wolf → Canada 60°17N 132°33W 296 A2
Wolf, Volcán Ecuador 0°2N 91°20W 330 a
Wolf Creek U.S.A. 47°0N 112°4W 304 C7
Wolf L. Canada 60°24N 131°40W 296 A2
Wolf Point U.S.A. 48°5N 105°39W 304 B11
Wolfe Creek Crater △ Australia 19°10S 127°47E 278 C4
Wolfe I. Canada 44°7N 76°20W 313 B8
Wolfeboro U.S.A. 43°35N 71°13W 313 C13
Wolfenbüttel Germany 52°10N 10°33E 178 C6
Wolfratshausen Germany 47°54N 11°24E 179 H7
Wolfsberg Austria 46°50N 14°52E 180 E7
Wolfsburg Germany 52°25N 10°48E 178 C6
Wolgast Germany 54°3N 13°44E 178 A9
Wolgok S. Korea 37°35N 127°1E 137 B2
Wolhusen Switz. 47°4N 8°4E 179 H4
Wolica Poland 52°7N 20°51E 143 C1
Wolin Poland 53°50N 14°37E 184 E1
Woliński △ Poland 53°57N 14°28E 184 E1
Wollaston U.S.A. 42°15N 71°2W 116 B2
Wollaston, Is. Chile 55°40S 67°30W 336 E3
Wollaston Forland Greenland 74°25N 19°40W 154 C9
Wollaston L. Canada 58°7N 103°10W 297 B8
Wollaston Lake Canada 58°3N 103°33W 297 B8
Wollaston Pen. Canada 69°30N 115°0W 294 D9
Wollemi △ Australia 33°0S 150°30E 283 B9
Wollongong Australia 34°25S 150°54E 283 C9
Wolmar = Valmiera Latvia 57°37N 25°29E 188 D3
Wolmaransstad S. Africa 27°12S 25°59E 270 C4
Wolmirstedt Germany 52°14N 11°37E 178 C7
Wołomin Poland 52°19N 21°15E 185 F8
Wołów Poland 51°20N 16°38E 185 G3
Wolseley S. Austral., Australia 36°23S 140°54E 282 D4
Wolseley Western Cape, S. Africa 33°26S 19°7E 270 D2
Wolsey U.S.A. 44°25N 98°28W 308 C4
Wolstenholme, C. Canada 62°35N 77°30W 292 C12
Wolsztyn Poland 52°8N 16°5E 185 F3
Woltersdorf Germany 52°27N 13°44E 115 B5
Woluwe-St-Lambert Belgium 50°50N 4°24E 116 A2
Woluwe-St-Pierre Belgium 50°50N 4°25E 116 A2
Wolvega Neths. 52°52N 6°0E 170 B6
Wolverhampton U.K. 52°35N 2°7W 169 E5
Wondai Australia 26°20S 151°49E 281 D5
Wonenara Papua N. G. 6°48S 145°53E 286 D3
Wong Chuk Hang Hong Kong, China 22°15N 114°10E 122 B3
Wong Chuk Wan Hong Kong, China 22°23N 114°17E 122 A3
Wong Chuk Yeung Hong Kong, China 22°24N 114°15E 122 A3
Wonga Wongué △ Gabon 0°29S 9°25E 264 C1
Wongalarroo L. Australia 31°32S 144°0E 282 A6
Wongan Hills Australia 30°51S 116°37E 279 F2
Wonju S. Korea 37°22N 127°58E 224 D3
Wonosari Indonesia 7°58S 110°36E 231 G14
Wonosobo Indonesia 7°22S 109°54E 235 D3
Wonowon Canada 56°44N 121°48W 296 B4
Wŏnsan N. Korea 39°11N 127°27E 224 C3
Wonthaggi Australia 38°37S 145°37E 283 E6
Wood Buffalo △ Canada 59°0N 113°41W 296 B6
Wood Green U.K. 51°36N 0°6W 125 A3
Wood Is. Australia 16°24S 123°19E 278 C3
Wood L. Canada 55°17N 103°17W 297 B8
Wood Ridge U.S.A. 40°50N 74°4W 132 A1
Wood River U.S.A. 38°52N 90°5W 310 F6
Wood-Tikchik State Park ⌂ U.S.A. 59°30N 158°30W 303 G8
Woodah, I. Australia 13°27S 136°10E 280 A2
Woodbine U.S.A. 30°58N 81°44W 316 E8
Woodbine Race Track Canada 43°43N 79°36W 141 A1
Woodbourne U.S.A. 41°46N 74°36W 313 E10
Woodbridge Ont., Canada 43°47N 79°36W 141 A1
Woodbridge Suffolk, U.K. 52°6N 1°20E 169 E9
Woodbridge B. Dominica 15°19N 61°25W 323 k
Woodburn N.S.W., Australia 29°6S 153°23E 281 A5
Woodburn Oreg., U.S.A. 45°9N 122°51W 304 D2
Woodbury U.S.A. 32°59N 84°35W 316 C5
Woodenbong Australia 28°24S 152°39E 281 D5
Woodend Australia 37°20S 144°33E 282 D6
Woodford Queens., Australia 26°58S 152°47E 281 D5
Woodford London, U.K. 51°36N 0°1E 125 A4
Woodford Bridge U.K. 51°36N 0°3E 125 A4
Woodford Green U.K. 51°36N 0°1E 125 A4
Woodfords U.S.A. 38°47N 119°50W 306 G7
Woodhaven U.S.A. 40°41N 73°51W 132 B2
Woodhouselee U.K. 55°52N 3°13W 121 B2
Woodlake U.S.A. 36°25N 119°6W 306 J7
Woodland Calif., U.S.A. 38°41N 121°46W 306 G5
Woodland Maine, U.S.A. 45°9N 67°25W 309 C20
Woodland Pa., U.S.A. 41°0N 78°21W 312 F6
Woodland Wash., U.S.A. 45°54N 122°45W 306 E4
Woodland Caribou ⌂ Canada 51°0N 94°45W 297 C10
Woodlands Singapore 1°26N 103°46E 138 A2
Woodlands, The U.S.A. 30°9N 95°29W 314 F7
Woodlark I. Papua N. G. 9°10S 152°50E 286 E7
Woodmont U.S.A. 38°59N 77°5W 143 B2
Woodonga Australia 36°10S 146°50E 281 F4
Woodridge Canada 49°20N 96°9W 297 D9
Woodroffe, Mt. Australia 26°20S 131°45E 279 E5
Woods, L. Australia 17°50S 133°30E 280 B1
Woods, L. of the N. Amer. 49°15N 94°45W 297 D10
Woods Bay Canada 45°8N 79°59W 312 A5
Woodside S. Austral., Australia 34°58S 138°52E 282 C3
Woodside Vic., Australia 38°31S 146°52E 283 E7
Woodside London, U.K. 51°23N 0°4W 125 B3
Woodside N.Y., U.S.A. 40°44N 73°54W 132 B2
Woodson U.S.A. 39°37N 90°14W 310 E6
Woodstock N.S.W., Australia 33°45S 148°53E 283 B8
Woodstock Queens., Australia 19°35S 146°50E 280 B4
Woodstock N.B., Canada 46°11N 67°37W 299 C6
Woodstock Ont., Canada 43°10N 80°45W 312 C4
Woodstock Western Cape, S. Africa 33°55S 18°27E 118 A1
Woodstock Oxon., U.K. 51°51N 1°20W 169 F6
Woodstock Ill., U.S.A. 42°19N 88°27W 311 B8
Woodstock N.Y., U.S.A. 42°2N 74°7W 313 D10
Woodstock Vt., U.S.A. 43°37N 72°31W 313 C12
Woodsville U.S.A. 44°9N 72°2W 313 B13
Woodview Canada 44°35N 78°8W 312 B6
Woodville N.Z. 40°20S 175°53E 284 G4
Woodville Fla., U.S.A. 30°19N 84°15W 316 E5
Woodville Ga., U.S.A. 33°40N 83°7W 316 B6
Woodville Miss., U.S.A. 31°6N 91°18W 314 F9
Woodville Ohio, U.S.A. 41°27N 83°22W 311 C13
Woodville Tex., U.S.A. 30°47N 94°25W 314 F7
Woodward U.S.A. 36°26N 99°24W 314 C5
Woody U.S.A. 35°42N 118°50W 307 K8
Woody → Canada 52°31N 100°51W 297 C8
Woody I. S. China Sea 16°50N 112°20E 230 A4
Woolacombe U.K. 51°10N 4°13W 169 F3
Woolamai, C. Australia 38°30S 145°23E 283 E6
Woolbrook Australia 30°56S 151°25E 283 A9
Wooler U.K. 55°33N 2°1W 168 B5
Woolgoolga Australia 30°6S 153°11E 281 E5

Woollahra *Australia* 33°53S 151°15E **139** B2
Woolloomooloo *Sydney, Australia* **139** b2
Woolooware B. *Australia* 34°1S 151°8E **139** C1
Woolwich *U.K.* 51°29N 0°4E **125** B4
Woolworth Building *New York, U.S.A.* **132** e1
Woomargama △ *Australia* 35°50S 147°15E **283** C7
Woomera *Australia* 31°5S 136°50E **282** A2
Woonsocket *R.I., U.S.A.* 42°0N 71°31W **313** E13
Woonsocket *S. Dak., U.S.A.* 44°3N 98°17W **308** C4
Wooramel ➔ *Australia* 25°47S 114°10E **279** E1
Wooramel Roadhouse *Australia* 25°45S 114°17E **279** E1
Wooroonooran △ *Australia* 16°25S 146°1E **280** B4
Wooster *U.S.A.* 40°48N 81°56W **312** F3
Woqooyi Galbeed □ *Somalia* 10°0N 44°30E **267** C5
Woraksan △ *S. Korea* 36°50N 128°5E **224** D4
Worcester *Western Cape, S. Africa* 33°39S 19°27E **270** D2
Worcester *Worcs., U.K.* 52°11N 2°12W **169** E5
Worcester *Mass., U.S.A.* 42°16N 71°48W **313** D13
Worcester *N.Y., U.S.A.* 42°36N 74°45W **313** D10
Worcestershire □ *U.K.* 52°13N 2°10W **169** E5
Worden *U.S.A.* 38°56N 89°50W **310** F7
Wörgl *Austria* 47°29N 12°3E **180** D5
Worker's Stadium *China* 39°55N 116°25E **114** B2
Workington *U.K.* 54°39N 3°33W **168** C4
Worksop *U.K.* 53°18N 1°7W **168** D6
Workum *Neths.* 52°59N 5°26E **170** B5
Worland *U.S.A.* 44°1N 107°57W **304** D10
World Bank *Washington, D.C., U.S.A.* **143** b1
World Financial Center *New York, U.S.A.* **132** e1
World Financial Centre *Shanghai, China* 31°14N 121°30E **138** B2
World Trade Center, Site of former = National September 11 Memorial and Museum *New York, U.S.A.* **132** e1
World War Two Memorial *Washington, D.C., U.S.A.* **143** b1
Worli *India* 19°1N 72°49E **130** A1
Wormhout *France* 50°52N 2°28E **173** B9
Worms *Germany* 49°37N 8°21E **179** F4
Woroba □ *Côte d'Ivoire* 8°19N 7°5W **262** D3
Worsley *Canada* 56°31N 119°8W **296** B5
Wörth *Bayern, Germany* 49°1N 12°24E **179** F8
Worth *Ill., U.S.A.* 41°41N 87°47W **119** C2
Wortham *U.S.A.* 31°47N 96°28W **314** F6
Wörther See *Austria* 46°37N 14°10E **180** E7
Worthing *U.K.* 50°49N 0°21W **169** G7
Worthington *Ind., U.S.A.* 39°7N 86°59W **311** E10
Worthington *Minn., U.S.A.* 43°37N 95°36W **308** D6
Worthington *Ohio, U.S.A.* 40°5N 83°1W **311** D13
Worthington *Pa., U.S.A.* 40°50N 79°38W **312** F5
Wosi *Indonesia* 0°15S 128°0E **231** E7
Wote *Kenya* 1°47S 37°38E **268** C4
Wotjalum ☼ *Australia* 16°30S 123°45E **278** C3
Wotjobaluk ☼ *Australia* 35°42S 142°0E **281** C3
Wou-han = Wuhan *China* 30°31N 114°18E **229** B10
Wour *Chad* 21°14N 16°0E **259** D3
Wousi = Wuxi *China* 31°33N 120°18E **229** B13
Wowoni *Indonesia* 4°5S 123°5E **231** E6
Woy Woy *Australia* 33°30S 151°19E **283** B9
Wrangel I. = Vrangelya, Ostrov *Russia* 71°0N 180°0E **215** B18
Wrangell *U.S.A.* 56°28N 132°23W **296** B2
Wrangell Mts. *U.S.A.* 61°30N 142°0W **303** F12
Wrangell-St. Elias △ *U.S.A.* 61°0N 142°0W **303** F12
Wrath, C. *U.K.* 58°38N 5°1W **167** C3
Wray *U.S.A.* 40°5N 102°13W **304** F12
Wrekin, The *U.K.* 52°41N 2°32W **169** E5
Wrens *U.S.A.* 33°12N 82°23W **316** B7
Wren's Nest *U.S.A.* 33°44N 84°25W **113** B2
Wrexham *U.K.* 53°3N 3°0W **168** D4
Wrexham □ *U.K.* 53°1N 2°58W **168** D5
Wriezen *Germany* 52°42N 14°7E **178** C10
Wright = Paranas *Phil.* 11°42N 125°2E **233** F5
Wright *Fla., U.S.A.* 30°27N 86°38W **317** E3
Wright *Wyo., U.S.A.* 43°45N 105°28W **304** E11
Wright Pt. *Canada* 43°48N 81°44W **312** C3
Wrightmyo *India* 11°47N 92°43E **245** J11
Wrightson, Mt. *U.S.A.* 31°42N 110°51W **305** L8
Wrightsville *U.S.A.* 32°44N 82°43W **316** C7
Wrightwood *U.S.A.* 34°22N 117°38W **307** L9
Wrigley *Canada* 63°16N 123°37W **294** E7
Wrigley Building *Chicago, U.S.A.* **119** b2
Wrigley Field *U.S.A.* 41°56N 87°39W **119** B3
Wrocław *Poland* 51°5N 17°5E **185** G4
Wronki *Poland* 52°41N 16°21E **185** F3
Września *Poland* 52°21N 17°36E **185** F4
Wschowa *Poland* 51°48N 16°20E **185** G3
Wu Hsi ➔ *Taiwan* 24°9N 120°31E **225** B2
Wu Jiang ➔ *China* 29°40N 107°20E **228** C6
Wu Kau Tang *China* 22°30N 114°14E **219** a
Wu Xia *China* 31°2N 110°10E **229** B8
Wu'an *China* 36°40N 114°15E **226** F8
Wubalawun ☼ *Australia* 15°28S 133°1E **278** C5
Wubin *Australia* 30°6S 116°37E **279** F2
Wubu *China* 37°28N 110°42E **226** F6
Wuchang *China* 44°55N 127°5E **227** B14
Wucheng *China* 37°12N 116°20E **226** F9
Wuch'i *Taiwan* 24°16N 120°31E **225** B2
Wuchieh *Taiwan* 24°41N 121°47E **225** B3
Wuchow = Wuzhou *China* 23°30N 111°18E **229** F8
Wuchuan *Guangdong, China* 21°33N 110°43E **229** G8
Wuchuan *Guizhou, China* 28°25N 108°3E **228** C7
Wuchuan *Nei Monggol Zizhiqu, China* 41°5N 111°28E **226** D6
Wuda *China* 39°29N 106°42E **226** E4
Wudang Shan *China* 32°23N 111°2E **229** A8
Wuday'ah *Si. Arabia* 17°2N 47°7E **248** C4
Wudi *China* 37°40N 117°35E **227** F9
Wuding *China* 25°24N 102°21E **228** E4
Wuding He ➔ *China* 37°2N 110°23E **226** F6
Wudinna *Australia* 33°0S 135°22E **281** E2
Wudongde Dam *China* 26°20N 102°15E **228** D4
Wudu *China* 33°22N 104°54E **226** H3
Wufeng *Henan, China* 30°12N 110°42E **229** B8
Wufeng *Taiwan* 24°4N 120°42E **225** B2
Wugang *China* 26°44N 110°35E **229** D8
Wugong Shan *China* 27°30N 114°0E **229** D9
Wuguishan *China* 22°25N 113°25E **219** a
Wugullar = Beswick *Australia* 14°34S 132°53E **278** B5
Wuhai *China* 39°39N 106°48E **226** E4
Wuhan *China* 30°31N 114°18E **229** B10
Wuhe *China* 33°10N 117°50E **227** H9
Wuhlgarten *Germany* 52°31N 13°34E **115** A4
Wuhsi = Wuxi *China* 31°33N 120°18E **229** B13
Wuhu *China* 31°22N 118°21E **229** B12
Wujiang *China* 31°10N 120°38E **229** B13
Wujiaochang *China* 31°18N 121°30E **138** B2
Wujiaqu *China* 44°12N 87°33E **217** D11
Wujie = Wuchieh *Taiwan* 24°41N 121°47E **225** B3
Wujih *Taiwan* 24°6N 120°38E **225** B2
Wukari *Nigeria* 7°51N 9°42E **263** D6
Wulai *Taiwan* 24°52N 121°33E **225** B3
Wulajie *China* 44°6N 126°33E **227** B14
Wulanbulang *China* 41°5N 110°55E **226** D6
Wular L. *India* 34°20N 74°30E **243** B6
Wulehe *Ghana* 8°39N 0°0 **263** D5
Wulff Land *Greenland* 82°0N 49°0W **154** A6
Wulian *China* 35°40N 119°12E **227** G10
Wulian Feng *China* 27°48N 103°36E **228** D4
Wuliang Shan *China* 24°30N 100°40E **228** E3
Wuliaru *Indonesia* 7°27S 131°0E **231** F8
Wulicheng *Taiwan* 23°47N 121°0E **225** C3
Wuling Shan *China* 30°0N 110°0E **228** C7
Wulingyuan ⌂ *China* 29°20N 110°30E **229** C8
Wulong *China* 29°22N 107°43E **228** C6
Wulong △ *China* 31°8N 103°5E **228** B4
Wulu *Taiwan* 23°10N 121°2E **225** C3
Wulumuchi = Ürümqi *China* 43°45N 87°45E **217** D11
Wum *Cameroon* 6°24N 10°2E **263** D7
Wumeng Shan *China* 26°48N 104°0E **228** D5
Wuming *China* 23°12N 108°18E **228** F7
Wun Rog *South Sudan* 9°0N 28°20E **257** F2
Wundanyi *Kenya* 3°24S 38°22E **268** C4
Wundwin *Myanmar* 21°5N 96°4E **241** E6
Wuning *China* 29°17N 115°5E **229** C10
Wunna ➔ *India* 20°18N 78°48E **244** D4
Wunnummin L. *Canada* 52°55N 89°10W **298** B2
Wunsiedel *Germany* 50°2N 12°0E **179** E8
Wunstorf *Germany* 52°25N 9°26E **178** C5
Wuntho *Myanmar* 23°55N 95°45E **241** D5
Wupatki ⌂ *U.S.A.* 35°35N 111°20W **305** J8
Wuping *China* 25°5N 116°5E **229** E11
Wuppertal *Nordrhein-Westfalen, Germany* 51°16N 7°12E **178** D3
Wuppertal *Western Cape, S. Africa* 32°13S 19°12E **270** D2
Wuqi = Wuch'i *Taiwan* 24°16N 120°31E **225** B2
Wuqia *China* 39°40N 75°7E **217** E9
Wuqing *China* 39°23N 117°4E **227** E9
Wuri = Wujih *Taiwan* 24°6N 120°38E **225** B2
Würm ➔ *Germany* 48°8N 11°27E **131** B1
Würm-kanal *Germany* 48°13N 11°29E **131** A1
Wurralibi ☼ *Australia* 15°43S 137°1E **280** B2
Wurtsboro *U.S.A.* 41°35N 74°29W **313** E10
Würzburg *Germany* 49°46N 9°55E **179** F5
Wurzen *Germany* 51°22N 12°44E **178** D8
Wushan *Gansu, China* 34°43N 104°53E **226** G3
Wushan *Guangdong, China* 23°9N 113°21E **121** B3
Wushi *China* 41°9N 79°13E **217** D9
Wushishi *Nigeria* 9°46N 6°7E **263** D6
Wusi *Vanuatu* 15°21S 166°40E **287** E4
Wusih = Wuxi *China* 31°33N 120°18E **229** B13
Wusong *China* 31°22N 121°29E **138** A1
Wutach ➔ *Germany* 47°37N 8°15E **179** H4
Wutai *China* 38°40N 113°12E **226** E7
Wutai Shan *China* 39°3N 113°32E **226** E7
Wuting = Huimin *China* 37°27N 117°28E **227** F9
Wutong *China* 25°24N 110°4E **229** E8
Wutonghaolai *China* 42°50N 120°5E **227** C11
Wutongqiao *China* 29°22N 103°50E **228** C4
Wutung *Papua N. G.* 2°37S 141°1E **286** B1
Wuwei *Anhui, China* 31°18N 117°54E **229** B11
Wuwei *Gansu, China* 37°57N 102°34E **218** D9
Wuxi *Jiangsu, China* 31°33N 120°18E **229** B13
Wuxi *Sichuan, China* 31°23N 109°35E **228** B7
Wuxiang *China* 36°49N 112°50E **226** F7
Wuxuan *China* 23°34N 109°38E **228** F7
Wuxue *China* 29°52N 115°30E **229** C10
Wuyang *China* 33°25N 113°35E **226** H7
Wuyi *Hebei, China* 37°46N 115°56E **226** F8
Wuyi *Zhejiang, China* 28°52N 119°50E **229** C12
Wuyi Shan *China* 27°0N 117°0E **229** D11
Wuyishan *China* 27°45N 118°0E **229** D12
Wuyishan △ *China* 27°55N 117°54E **229** D11
Wuyo *Nigeria* 10°23N 11°50E **263** C7
Wuyuan *Jiangxi, China* 29°15N 117°50E **229** C11
Wuyuan *Nei Monggol Zizhiqu, China* 41°2N 108°20E **226** D5
Wuzhai *China* 38°54N 111°48E **226** E6
Wuzhi Shan *China* 18°45N 109°30E **229** a
Wuzhishan = Tongshi *China* 18°50N 109°20E **229** a
Wuzhong *China* 38°2N 106°12E **226** E4
Wuzhou *China* 23°30N 111°18E **229** F8
Wyaaba Cr. ➔ *Australia* 16°27S 141°35E **280** B3
Wyalkatchem *Australia* 31°8S 117°22E **279** F2
Wyalusing *U.S.A.* 41°40N 76°16W **313** E8
Wyandotte *U.S.A.* 42°12N 83°9W **311** B13
Wyandra *Australia* 27°12S 145°56E **281** D4
Wyangala, L. *Australia* 33°54S 149°0E **283** B8
Wyara, L. *Australia* 28°42S 144°14E **281** D3
Wycheproof *Australia* 36°5S 143°17E **282** D5
Wycliffe Well *Australia* 20°48S 134°14E **280** C1
Wyczółki *Poland* 52°9N 20°59E **143** C1
Wye ➔ *U.K.* 51°38N 2°40W **169** F5
Wyemandoo *Australia* 28°28S 118°29E **279** E2
Wygoda *Poland* 52°15N 21°7E **143** B2
Wyk *Germany* 54°41N 8°33E **178** A4
Wymondham *U.K.* 52°35N 1°7E **169** E9
Wymore *U.S.A.* 40°7N 96°40W **308** E5
Wynberg *S. Africa* 34°2S 18°28E **118** B1
Wyndham *W. Austral., Australia* 15°33S 128°3E **278** C4
Wyndham *N.Z.* 46°20S 168°51E **285** G3
Wynne *U.S.A.* 35°14N 90°47W **315** D9
Wynyard *Tas., Australia* 41°5S 145°44E **281** G4
Wynyard *Sask., Canada* 51°45N 104°10W **297** C8
Wyola L. *Australia* 29°8S 130°17E **279** E5
Wyoming *Ont., Canada* 42°57N 82°7W **312** D2
Wyoming *Ill., U.S.A.* 41°4N 89°47W **310** C7
Wyoming *Iowa, U.S.A.* 42°4N 91°0W **310** B6
Wyoming *Mich., U.S.A.* 42°54N 85°42W **311** B11
Wyoming □ *U.S.A.* 43°0N 107°30W **304** E10
Wyomissing *U.S.A.* 40°20N 75°59W **313** F9
Wyong *Australia* 33°14S 151°24E **283** B9
Wyperfeld △ *Australia* 35°35S 141°42E **282** C4
Wyrzysk *Poland* 53°10N 17°17E **185** E4
Wyśmierzyce *Poland* 51°37N 20°50E **185** G7
Wysoka *Poland* 53°13N 17°2E **185** E4
Wysokie *Poland* 50°55N 22°40E **185** H9
Wysokie Mazowieckie *Poland* 52°55N 22°30E **185** F9
Wyszków *Poland* 52°36N 21°25E **185** F8
Wyszogród *Poland* 52°23N 20°9E **185** F7
Wytheville *U.S.A.* 36°57N 81°5W **309** G13
Wyżyna Małopolska *Poland* 50°45N 20°0E **185** H7

X

Xa-Cassau *Angola* 9°5S 20°15E **265** D4
Xa-Muteba *Angola* 9°34S 17°50E **265** D3
Xaafuun *Somalia* 10°25N 51°16E **267** B7
Xaafuun, Ras *Somalia* 10°27N 51°24E **267** B7
Xàbia = Jávea *Spain* 38°48N 0°10E **197** G5
Xabregas *Portugal* 38°43N 9°6W **126** A2
Xaçmaz *Azerbaijan* 41°31N 48°42E **191** K9
Xaghra *Malta* 36°3N 14°16E **206** E5
Xai-Xai *Mozam.* 25°6S 33°31E **271** C5
Xaidulla *China* 36°28N 77°59E **217** E9
Xaignabouri = Sayabouri *Laos* 19°15N 101°45E **236** C3
Xainza *China* 30°58N 88°35E **218** E6
Xalapa *Mexico* 19°32N 96°55W **319** D5
Xalin *Somalia* 9°6N 48°37E **267** C6
Xallas ➔ *Spain* 42°54N 9°8W **194** C1
Xambioá *Brazil* 6°25S 48°40W **332** C2
Xangongo *Angola* 16°45S 15°5E **265** F3
Xankändi *Azerbaijan* 39°52N 46°49E **213** C12
Xanlar = Goygöl *Azerbaijan* 40°37N 46°12E **191** K8
Xanten *Germany* 51°39N 6°26E **178** D2
Xanthi *Greece* 41°10N 24°58E **203** E8
Xanthos *Turkey* 36°19N 29°18E **205** E11
Xanxerê *Brazil* 26°53S 52°23W **335** B5
Xapuri *Brazil* 10°35S 68°35W **330** C4
Xar Moron He ➔ *China* 43°25N 120°35E **227** C11
Xarardheere *Somalia* 4°33N 47°38E **267** D6
Xarrë *Albania* 39°44N 20°3E **206** B10
Xátiva *Spain* 38°59N 0°32W **197** G4
Xau, L. *Botswana* 21°15S 24°44E **270** B3
Xavantina *Brazil* 21°15S 52°48W **335** A5
Xayaburi Dam *Laos* 19°15N 101°0E **236** C3
Xayar *China* 41°13N 82°48E **217** D10
Xebert *China* 44°2N 122°0E **227** B12
Xenia *U.S.A.* 39°41N 83°56W **311** E13
Xeraco *Spain* 39°2N 0°13W **197** F4
Xeropotamos ➔ *Cyprus* 34°42N 32°33E **207** F8
Xertigny *France* 48°3N 6°24E **173** D13
Xewkija *Malta* 36°2N 14°15E **206** E7
Xhora *S. Africa* 31°55S 28°38E **271** D4
Xhumo *Botswana* 21°7S 24°35E **270** B3
Xi Jiang ➔ *China* 22°5N 113°20E **229** F9
Xi Ujimqin Qi *China* 44°32N 117°40E **227** B9
Xi Xian *Henan, China* 32°20N 114°43E **229** A10
Xi Xian *Shanxi, China* 36°41N 110°58E **226** F6
Xia Xian *China* 35°8N 111°12E **226** G6
Xiachengzi *China* 44°40N 130°18E **227** B16
Xiachuan Dao *China* 21°40N 112°40E **229** G9
Xiaguan *China* 25°32N 100°16E **218** F9
Xiajiang *China* 27°30N 115°10E **229** D10
Xiajin *China* 36°56N 116°0E **226** F9
Xiakeng *China* 23°11N 113°16E **121** A2
Xiamen *China* 24°25N 118°4E **229** E12
Xiamen Gaoqi Int. ✈ **(XMN)** *China* 24°33N 118°8E **229** E12
Xi'an *China* 34°15N 109°0E **226** G5
Xian Xian *China* 38°12N 116°6E **226** E9
Xian Xianyang Int. ✈ **(XIY)** *China* 34°27N 108°45E **226** G5
Xianfeng *China* 29°40N 109°8E **228** C7
Xiang Jiang ➔ *China* 28°55N 112°50E **229** C9
Xiang Khouang *Laos* 19°17N 103°25E **236** C4
Xiangcheng *Henan, China* 33°50N 113°27E **226** H7
Xiangcheng *Sichuan, China* 28°53N 99°47E **228** C2
Xianghe *China* 23°13N 106°58E **228** F6
Xiangfan *China* 32°2N 112°8E **229** A9
Xianggang = Hong Kong □ *China* 22°11N 114°14E **219** a
Xianghuang Qi *China* 42°2N 113°50E **226** C7
Xiangjiaba Dam *China* 28°37N 104°17E **228** C5
Xiangning *China* 35°58N 110°50E **226** G6
Xiangquan *China* 36°30N 113°1E **226** F7
Xiangquan He = Sutlej ➔ *Pakistan* 29°23N 71°3E **242** E4
Xiangshan = Hsiangshan *Taiwan* 24°48N 120°54E **225** B2
Xiangshan *China* 29°29N 121°51E **229** C13
Xiangshui *China* 34°12N 119°33E **227** G10
Xiangtan *China* 27°51N 112°54E **229** D9
Xiangxiang *China* 27°43N 112°28E **229** D9
Xiangyin *China* 28°38N 112°54E **229** C9
Xiangyun *China* 25°34N 100°35E **228** E3
Xiangzhou *China* 23°58N 109°40E **228** F7
Xianju *China* 28°51N 120°44E **229** C13
Xianning *China* 29°51N 114°16E **229** C10
Xianshui He ➔ *China* 30°10N 100°59E **228** B3
Xiantao *China* 30°25N 113°25E **229** B9
Xianyang *China* 34°20N 108°40E **226** G5
Xianyou *China* 25°22N 118°38E **229** E12
Xiao Hinggan Ling *China* 49°0N 127°0E **219** B14
Xiao Xian *China* 34°15N 116°55E **226** G9
Xiaofeng *China* 30°35N 119°32E **229** B12
Xiaogan *China* 30°52N 113°55E **229** B9
Xiaogang = Hsiaokang *Taiwan* 22°34N 120°22E **225** D2
Xiaogang Park *China* 23°6N 113°16E **121** B2
Xiaojin *China* 30°59N 102°21E **228** B4
Xiaolan *China* 22°38N 113°13E **229** F9
Xiaoping *China* 23°12N 113°13E **121** A2
Xiaoshan *China* 30°12N 120°18E **229** B13
Xiaowan Dam *China* 24°42N 100°5E **228** E3
Xiaowutai Shan *China* 39°51N 114°59E **226** E8
Xiaoyi *China* 37°8N 111°48E **226** F6
Xiapu *China* 26°54N 119°59E **229** D12
Xiashachong *China* 23°8N 113°9E **121** B1
Xiashan = Zhanjiang *China* 21°15N 110°20E **229** G8
Xiawa *China* 42°35N 120°38E **227** C11
Xiayi *China* 34°15N 116°10E **226** G9
Xichang *Guangdong, China* 23°9N 113°13E **121** B2
Xichang *Sichuan, China* 27°51N 102°19E **228** D4
Xicheng *Beijing, China* **114** b1
Xichong *China* 30°57N 105°54E **228** B5
Xichou *China* 23°25N 104°42E **228** F5
Xichuan *China* 33°0N 111°30E **229** A8
Xidan *China* 39°52N 116°20E **114** B2
Xide *China* 28°8N 102°19E **228** C4
Xiemahe *China* 31°38N 111°12E **229** B8
Xi'ercun *China* 23°9N 113°16E **121** B2
Xifei He ➔ *China* 32°45N 116°40E **229** A11
Xifeng *Gansu, China* 35°40N 107°40E **226** G4
Xifeng *Guizhou, China* 27°7N 106°42E **228** D6
Xifeng *Liaoning, China* 42°42N 124°45E **227** C13
Xifengzhen = Xifeng *China* 35°40N 107°40E **226** G4
Xigang = Hsikang *Taiwan* 23°7N 120°12E **225** C2
Xigazê *China* 29°5N 88°45E **218** F6
Xihe *China* 34°2N 105°20E **226** G3
Xihua *China* 33°45N 114°30E **226** H8
Xilagani *Greece* 40°58N 25°28E **203** F9
Xili Shuiku *China* 22°36N 113°57E **219** a
Xiliao He ➔ *China* 43°32N 123°35E **227** C12
Xilin *China* 24°30N 105°6E **228** E5
Xiling Gorge = Xiling Xia *China* 30°54N 110°48E **229** B8
Xiling Xia *China* 30°54N 110°48E **229** B8
Xilinhot *China* 43°52N 116°2E **226** C9
Xilokastro *Greece* 38°5N 22°38E **204** C4
Xiluodu Dam *China* 28°12N 103°34E **228** C4
Ximana *Mozam.* 19°24S 33°58E **269** F3
Xime *Guinea-Biss.* 11°59N 14°57W **262** C2
Ximeng *China* 22°50N 99°27E **228** F2
Ximiao *China* 40°59N 100°12E **218** C9
Xin Jiang ➔ *China* 28°45N 116°35E **229** C11
Xin Xian = Xinzhou *China* 38°22N 112°46E **226** E7
Xin'anjiang Shuiku *China* 29°33N 118°56E **229** C12
Xinavane *Mozam.* 25°2S 32°47E **271** C5
Xinbin *China* 41°40N 125°2E **224** B2
Xincai *China* 32°43N 114°58E **229** A10
Xinchang *China* 29°28N 120°52E **229** C13
Xincheng = Hsinch'eng *Taiwan* 24°8N 121°39E **225** B3
Xincheng *Guangxi Zhuangzu, China* 24°5N 108°39E **228** E7
Xincheng *Jiangxi, China* 26°48N 114°6E **229** D10
Xinchengzi *China* 42°2N 123°30E **224** A1
Xincun *China* 23°5N 113°20E **121** B2
Xindian = Hsintien *Taiwan* 24°57N 121°32E **225** B3
Xinfeng = Hsinfeng *Taiwan* 24°54N 120°59E **225** B2
Xinfeng *Guangdong, China* 24°5N 114°16E **229** E10
Xinfeng *Jiangxi, China* 27°7N 116°11E **229** D11
Xinfeng *Jiangxi, China* 25°27N 114°58E **229** E10
Xinfengjiang Shuiku *China* 23°52N 114°30E **229** F10
Xing Xian *China* 38°27N 111°7E **226** E6
Xing'an *Guangxi Zhuangzu, China* 25°38N 110°40E **229** E8
Xingan *Jiangxi, China* 27°46N 115°20E **229** D10
Xingcheng *China* 40°40N 120°45E **227** D11
Xingguo *China* 26°21N 115°21E **229** D10
Xinghe *China* 40°55N 113°55E **226** D7
Xinghua *China* 32°58N 119°48E **229** A12
Xinghua Wan *China* 25°15N 119°20E **229** E12
Xinglong *China* 40°25N 117°30E **227** D9
Xingning *China* 24°3N 115°42E **229** E10
Xingping *China* 34°20N 108°28E **226** G5
Xingren *China* 25°24N 105°11E **228** E5
Xingshan *China* 31°15N 110°45E **229** B8
Xingtai *China* 37°3N 114°32E **226** F8
Xingu ➔ *Brazil* 1°30S 51°53W **329** D7
Xingwen *China* 28°22N 104°54E **228** C5
Xingxingxia *China* 41°47N 95°0E **218** C7
Xingyang *China* 34°45N 112°52E **226** G7
Xingyi *China* 25°3N 104°59E **228** E5
Xinhe *Hebei, China* 37°30N 115°15E **226** F8
Xinhe *Xinjiang Uygur, China* 41°33N 82°37E **217** D10
Xinhua = Hsinhua *Taiwan* 23°2N 120°18E **225** C2
Xinhua *China* 27°42N 111°13E **229** D8
Xinhuang *China* 27°21N 109°12E **228** D7
Xinhui *China* 22°25N 113°0E **229** F9
Xining *China* 36°34N 101°40E **218** D9
Xinji *China* 37°55N 115°13E **226** F8
Xinjian *China* 28°37N 115°46E **229** C10
Xinjiang *China* 35°34N 111°11E **226** G6
Xinjiang Uygur Zizhiqu □ *China* 42°0N 86°0E **217** D11
Xinjin = Pulandian *China* 39°25N 121°58E **227** E11
Xinjin *China* 30°24N 103°47E **228** B4
Xinkai He ➔ *China* 43°32N 123°35E **227** C12
Xinken *China* 22°39N 113°36E **219** a
Xinle *China* 38°25N 114°40E **226** E8
Xinlitun *China* 42°0N 122°8E **227** D12
Xinlong *China* 30°57N 100°12E **228** B3
Xinmi *China* 34°30N 113°25E **226** G7
Xinmin *China* 41°59N 122°50E **224** B1
Xinning *China* 26°28N 110°50E **229** D8
Xinping *China* 24°5N 101°59E **228** E3
Xinshao *China* 27°21N 111°26E **229** D8
Xinshi = Hsinshih *Taiwan* 23°4N 120°17E **225** C2
Xintai *China* 35°55N 117°45E **227** G9
Xintian *China* 25°55N 112°13E **229** E9
Xinwan *China* 22°47N 113°40E **219** a
Xinwu = Hsinwu *Taiwan* 24°59N 121°6E **225** B3
Xinxiang *China* 35°18N 113°50E **226** G7
Xinxing *China* 22°35N 112°15E **229** F9
Xinyang *China* 32°6N 114°3E **229** A10
Xinye *China* 32°30N 112°21E **229** A9
Xinyi *Guangdong, China* 22°25N 111°0E **229** F8
Xinyi *Nei Monggol Zizhiqu, China* 34°23N 118°21E **227** G10
Xinying = Hsinying *Taiwan* 23°21N 120°17E **225** C2
Xinyu *China* 27°49N 114°58E **229** D10
Xinyuan = Hsinyuan *Taiwan* 22°32N 120°27E **225** D2
Xinzhan *China* 43°50N 127°18E **227** C14
Xinzheng *China* 34°20N 113°45E **226** G7
Xinzhou *Hainan, China* 19°43N 109°17E **229** a
Xinzhou *Hubei, China* 30°50N 114°48E **229** B10
Xinzhou *Shanxi, China* 38°22N 112°46E **226** E7
Xinzhu = Hsinchu *Taiwan* 24°48N 120°58E **225** B2
Xinzhuang = Hsinchuang *Taiwan* 25°2N 121°27E **225** A3
Xinzo de Limia *Spain* 42°3N 7°47W **194** C3
Xiongyuecheng *China* 40°12N 122°5E **227** D12
Xiping *Henan, China* 33°22N 114°5E **226** H8
Xiping *Henan, China* 33°25N 111°8E **226** H6
Xiping *Zhejiang, China* 28°16N 119°29E **229** C12
Xique-Xique *Brazil* 10°50S 42°40W **332** D3
Xirdalan *Azerbaijan* 40°27N 49°45E **213** B13
Xiruá ➔ *Brazil* 6°3S 67°50W **330** B4
Xisha Qundao = Paracel Is. *S. China Sea* 15°50N 112°0E **230** A4
Xishuangbanna *China* 22°5N 101°1E **228** F3
Xishui *Guizhou, China* 28°19N 106°9E **228** C6
Xishui *Hubei, China* 30°30N 115°15E **229** B10
Xitole *Guinea-Biss.* 11°43N 14°50W **262** C2
Xiu Shui ➔ *China* 29°13N 116°0E **229** C10
Xiuning *China* 29°45N 118°10E **229** C12
Xiuren *China* 24°27N 110°12E **229** E8
Xiushan *China* 28°25N 108°57E **228** C7
Xiushui *China* 29°2N 114°33E **229** C10
Xiuwen *China* 26°49N 106°32E **228** D6
Xiuyan *China* 40°18N 123°11E **224** B1
Xiva *Uzbekistan* 41°30N 60°18E **216** D6
Xixabangma Feng *China* 28°20N 85°40E **243** E11
Xixia *China* 33°25N 111°29E **226** H6
Xixiang *Guangdong, China* 22°34N 113°52E **219** a
Xixiang *Shaanxi, China* 33°0N 107°44E **226** H4
Xixón = Gijón *Spain* 43°32N 5°42W **194** B5
Xiyang *China* 37°38N 113°38E **226** F7
Xizang Zizhiqu □ *China* 32°0N 88°0E **218** E6
Xizhi = Hsichih *Taiwan* 25°4N 121°39E **225** A3
Xizhimen *China* 39°55N 116°19E **114** B1
Xlendi *Malta* 36°1N 14°12E **206** E6
Xochimilco, Parque Ecológico *Mexico* 19°18N 99°5W **128** C2
Xochob *Mexico* 19°21N 89°48W **319** D7
Xo'jayli *Uzbekistan* 42°29N 59°31E **216** C5
Xorazm □ *Uzbekistan* 43°0N 60°0E **216** D6
Xu Beihong Memorial Hall *Beijing, China* **114** a2
Xu Jiang ➔ *China* 28°0N 116°25E **229** D11
Xuan Loc *Vietnam* 10°56N 107°14E **237** G6
Xuan'en *China* 30°0N 109°30E **228** C7
Xuanhan *China* 31°18N 107°38E **228** B6
Xuanhua *China* 40°40N 115°2E **226** D8
Xuanwei *China* 26°15N 103°59E **228** D5
Xuanwu *Beijing, China* **114** c1
Xuanzhou *China* 30°56N 118°43E **229** B12
Xuchang *China* 34°2N 113°48E **226** G7
Xudat *Azerbaijan* 41°38N 48°41E **191** K9
Xuddur *Somalia* 4°11N 43°52E **267** D5
Xuefeng Shan *China* 27°5N 110°35E **229** D8
Xuejia = Hsüehchia *Taiwan* 23°14N 120°10E **225** C2
Xuejiaping *China* 31°39N 110°16E **229** B8
Xuhui *China* 31°11N 121°26E **138** B1
Xujiahui *China* 31°11N 121°25E **138** B1
Xun Jiang ➔ *China* 23°35N 111°30E **229** F8
Xun Xian *China* 35°42N 114°33E **226** G8
Xundian *China* 25°36N 103°15E **228** E4
Xunwu *China* 24°54N 115°37E **229** E10
Xunyang *China* 32°48N 109°22E **226** H5
Xunyi *China* 35°8N 108°20E **226** G5
Xupu *China* 27°53N 110°32E **229** D8
Xúquer ➔ *Spain* 39°5N 0°10W **197** F4
Xushui *China* 39°2N 115°40E **226** E8
Xuwen *China* 20°20N 110°10E **229** G8
Xuyi *China* 32°55N 118°32E **229** A12
Xuyong *China* 28°10N 105°22E **228** C5
Xuzhou *China* 34°18N 117°10E **227** G9
Xylophagou *Cyprus* 34°54N 33°51E **207** F9

Y

Y Drenewydd = Newtown *U.K.* 52°31N 3°19W **169** E4
Y Fenni = Abergavenny *U.K.* 51°49N 3°1W **169** F4
Y Gelli Gandryll = Hay-on-Wye *U.K.* 52°5N 3°8W **169** E4
Y Trallwng = Welshpool *U.K.* 52°39N 3°8W **169** E4
Y.S. Falls *Jamaica* 18°9N 77°49W **320** a
Ya Xian = Sanya *China* 18°14N 109°29E **229** a
Yaamba *Australia* 23°8S 150°22E **280** C5
Ya'an *China* 29°58N 103°5E **228** C4
Yaapeet *Australia* 35°45S 142°3E **282** C5
Yaba *Nigeria* 6°30N 3°22E **124** A2
Yabassi *Cameroon* 4°30N 9°57E **263** E6
Yabayo *Côte d'Ivoire* 5°56N 6°36W **262** D3
Yabelo *Ethiopia* 4°50N 38°8E **257** G4
Yabelo ⌂ *Ethiopia* 6°0N 37°50E **257** F4
Yablanitsa *Bulgaria* 43°2N 24°5E **203** C8
Yablonovskiy *Russia* 44°59N 38°57E **191** H4
Yablonovyy Khrebet *Russia* 53°0N 114°0E **215** D12
Yablonovyy Ra. = Yablonovyy Khrebet *Russia* 53°0N 114°0E **215** D12
Yabluniv *Ukraine* 48°24N 24°57E **183** B9
Yablunytsya *Ukraine* 48°19N 24°29E **183** B9
Yabrai Shan *China* 39°40N 103°0E **226** E2
Yabrūd *Syria* 33°58N 36°39E **250** E7
Yabucoa *Puerto Rico* 18°3N 65°53W **321** b
Yacambú △ *Venezuela* 9°42N 69°27W **328** B4
Yacata *Fiji* 17°15S 179°31W **287** A3
Yacheng *China* 18°22N 109°6E **229** a
Yackandandah *Australia* 36°18S 146°52E **283** D7
Yacuiba *Bolivia* 22°0S 63°43W **334** A3
Yacuma ➔ *Bolivia* 13°38S 65°23W **331** C4
Yacurí △ *Ecuador* 4°42S 79°20W **330** A2
Yadgir *India* 16°45N 77°5E **244** F3
Yadkin ➔ *U.S.A.* 35°23N 80°4W **315** D14
Yadong *China* 27°26N 88°56E **241** B2
Yadrin *Russia* 55°57N 46°12E **190** C8
Yadua *Fiji* 16°49S 178°18E **287** A2
Yaeyama-Rettō *Japan* 24°30N 123°40E **221** M1
Yafran *Libya* 32°4N 12°31E **258** B2
Yaftābād *Iran* 35°37N 51°17E **141** B1
Yagaba *Ghana* 10°14N 1°20W **263** C4
Yagaji-shima *Japan* 26°39N 128°0E **288** a
Yagasa Cluster *Fiji* 18°57S 178°28W **287** B3
Yağcılar *Turkey* 39°25N 28°23E **205** B10
Yagodnoye *Russia* 62°33N 149°40E **215** C15
Yagoua *Cameroon* 10°20N 15°13E **259** F3
Yaguas ➔ *Peru* 2°45S 70°10W **328** D3
Yahara *Japan* 35°44N 139°37E **140** A2
Yahila *Orientale, Dem. Rep. of the Congo* 0°13N 24°28E **264** B4
Yahila *Orientale, Dem. Rep. of the Congo* 1°48N 23°37E **264** B4
Yahk *Canada* 49°6N 116°10W **296** D5
Yaho *Japan* 35°40N 139°26E **140** A1
Yahotyn *Ukraine* 50°17N 31°46E **189** G6
Yahuma *Dem. Rep. of the Congo* 1°0N 23°10E **264** B4
Yahyalı *Turkey* 38°5N 35°2E **212** C6
Yaita *Japan* 36°48N 139°56E **221** F9
Yaiza *Canary Is.* 28°57N 13°46W **153** e2
Yaizu *Japan* 34°52N 138°20E **223** C10
Yajiang *China* 30°2N 100°57E **228** B3
Yajua *Nigeria* 11°27N 12°49E **263** C7
Yakacık *Turkey* 36°46N 36°11E **250** B7
Yakage *Japan* 34°37N 133°35E **222** C5
Yakamba *Dem. Rep. of the Congo* 2°42N 19°38E **264** B3
Yakapınar *Turkey* 36°57N 35°36E **250** B6
Yakeshi *China* 49°17N 120°44E **219** B13
Yakima *U.S.A.* 46°36N 120°31W **304** C3
Yakima ➔ *U.S.A.* 46°15N 119°14W **304** C4
Yakire *Japan* 35°45N 139°54E **140** A4
Yakishiri-Jima *Japan* 44°26N 141°25E **220** B10
Yako *Burkina Faso* 12°59N 2°15W **262** C4
Yakobi I. *U.S.A.* 58°0N 136°30W **296** B1
Yakoma *Dem. Rep. of the Congo* 4°5N 22°27E **264** B4
Yakoruda *Bulgaria* 42°1N 23°39E **202** D7
Yakossi *C.A.R.* 5°37N 23°19E **264** A4
Yakovlevka *Russia* 44°26N 133°28E **220** B6
Yakovlevskoye = Privolzhsk *Russia* 57°23N 41°16E **190** B5
Yaksu *S. Korea* 37°34N 127°1E **137** B2
Yaku-Shima *Japan* 30°20N 130°30E **221** J5
Yakumo *Japan* 42°15N 140°16E **220** C10
Yakutat *U.S.A.* 59°33N 139°44W **303** G13
Yakutat B. *U.S.A.* 59°45N 140°45W **303** G12
Yakutia = Sakha □ *Russia* 66°0N 130°0E **215** C14
Yakutsk *Russia* 62°5N 129°50E **215** C13
Yakymivka *Ukraine* 46°44N 35°0E **189** J8
Yala *Thailand* 6°33N 101°18E **237** J3
Yala △ *Sri Lanka* 6°20N 81°30E **245** L5
Yalata *Australia* 31°59S 132°26E **279** F5
Yalata ☼ *Australia* 31°35S 132°7E **279** F5
Yalboroo *Australia* 20°50S 148°40E **280** b
Yale *U.S.A.* 43°8N 82°48W **312** C2
Yalgorup △ *Australia* 32°39S 115°38E **279** F2
Yali *Dem. Rep. of the Congo* 0°4N 21°2E **264** B4
Yaligimba *Dem. Rep. of the Congo* 2°13N 22°56E **264** B4
Yalikanda *Dem. Rep. of the Congo* 0°23N 24°47E **264** B4
Yalinga *C.A.R.* 6°33N 23°10E **264** A4
Yalkabul, Pta. *Mexico* 21°32N 88°37W **319** C7
Yallahs *Jamaica* 17°53N 76°35W **320** a
Yallahs Hill *Jamaica* 17°54N 76°30W **320** a
Yalleroi *Australia* 24°3S 145°42E **280** C4
Yalobusha ➔ *U.S.A.* 33°33N 90°10W **315** E9
Yaloké *C.A.R.* 5°19N 17°5E **264** A3
Yalong *China* 18°12N 109°42E **229** a
Yalong Jiang ➔ *China* 26°40N 101°55E **228** D3
Yalova *Turkey* 40°41N 29°15E **203** F13
Yalpirakinu ☼ *Australia* 22°24S 132°15E **278** D5
Yalpuh, Ozero *Ukraine* 45°30N 28°41E **183** E13
Yalta *Ukraine* 44°30N 34°10E **189** K8
Yalu Jiang ➔ *China* 39°55N 124°19E **224** C1
Yalvaç *Turkey* 38°17N 31°10E **212** C4
Yam *Australia* 9°54S 142°46E **280** a
Yam Ha Melaḥ = Dead Sea *Asia* 31°30N 35°30E **251** D4
Yam Kinneret *Israel* 32°45N 35°35E **250** F6
Yamada = Kama *Japan* 33°33N 130°49E **222** D2
Yamada *Kanagawa, Japan* 35°33N 139°37E **140** B2
Yamada *Ōsaka, Japan* 34°47N 135°32E **133** A2
Yamaga *Japan* 33°1N 130°41E **222** D2
Yamagata *Japan* 38°15N 140°15E **220** E10
Yamagata □ *Japan* 38°30N 140°0E **220** E10
Yamagawa *Japan* 31°12N 130°39E **222** F2
Yamaguchi *Japan* 34°10N 131°32E **222** C3
Yamaguchi □ *Japan* 34°20N 131°40E **222** C3
Yamal, Poluostrov *Russia* 71°0N 70°0E **214** B8
Yamal Pen. = Yamal, Poluostrov *Russia* 71°0N 70°0E **214** B8
Yamanaka *Japan* 36°15N 136°22E **223** A8
Yamanashi *Japan* 35°41N 138°40E **223** B10
Yamanashi □ *Japan* 35°40N 138°40E **223** B10
Yamantau, Gora *Russia* 54°15N 58°6E **186** D10
Yamasaki *Japan* 35°0N 134°32E **222** C6
Yamato *Japan* 35°27N 139°25E **223** B11
Yamato *Japan* 35°46N 139°36E **133** B1
Yamato Ridge *Sea of Japan* 39°20N 135°0E **220** E7
Yamatotakada *Japan* 34°31N 135°45E **223** C7
Yamba *Australia* 29°26S 153°23E **281** D5
Yambarran Ra. *Australia* 15°10S 130°25E **278** C5
Yambata *Dem. Rep. of the Congo* 2°26N 21°58E **264** B4
Yambéring *Guinea* 11°50N 12°18W **262** C2
Yambio *South Sudan* 4°35N 28°16E **257** G2
Yambol *Bulgaria* 42°30N 26°30E **203** D10
Yambol □ *Bulgaria* 42°30N 26°30E **203** D10
Yamboyo *Dem. Rep. of the Congo* 0°40N 22°18E **264** B4
Yamburg *Russia* 68°21N 77°8E **214** C8
Yambuya *Dem. Rep. of the Congo* 1°17N 24°34E **264** B4
Yamdena *Indonesia* 7°45S 131°20E **231** F8
Yame *Japan* 33°13N 130°35E **222** D2
Yamethin *Myanmar* 20°29N 96°18E **241** E6
Y'Ami I. *Phil.* 21°6N 121°57E **232** A3
Yamma Yamma, L. *Australia* 26°16S 141°20E **281** D3
Yamoussoukro *Côte d'Ivoire* 6°49N 5°17W **262** D3
Yamoussoukro □ *Côte d'Ivoire* 6°47N 5°14W **262** D3
Yampa ➔ *U.S.A.* 40°32N 108°59W **304** F9
Yampi Sd. *Australia* 16°8S 123°38E **278** C3
Yampil *Moldova* 48°15N 28°15E **177** D15
Yampol = Yampil *Moldova* 48°15N 28°15E **177** D15
Yamrat *Nigeria* 10°11N 9°55E **263** C6
Yamrukchal = Botev *Bulgaria* 42°44N 24°52E **203** D8
Yamu, Laem *Thailand* 7°59N 98°26E **237** a
Yamuna ➔ *India* 25°30N 81°53E **243** G9
Yamunanagar *India* 30°7N 77°17E **242** D7
Yamzho Yumco *China* 28°48N 90°35E **218** F7
Yan *Nigeria* 10°5N 12°11E **263** C7
Yan Kit *Singapore* 1°21N 103°58E **138** A3
Yan Oya ➔ *Sri Lanka* 9°0N 81°10E **245** K5
Yana ➔ *Russia* 71°30N 136°0E **215** B14
Yanagawa *Japan* 33°10N 130°24E **222** D2
Yanahara *Japan* 34°58N 134°2E **222** C6
Yanai *Japan* 33°58N 132°7E **222** D4
Yan'an *China* 36°35N 109°26E **226** F5
Yanaul *Russia* 56°25N 55°0E **186** C10
Yanbian *China* 26°47N 101°31E **228** D3
Yanbu *China* 23°5N 113°9E **121** B1
Yanbu 'al Baḥr *Si. Arabia* 24°5N 38°5E **246** E3
Yanchang *China* 36°43N 110°1E **226** F6
Yanchao = Yenchao *Taiwan* 22°46N 120°21E **225** D2
Yancheng *Henan, China* 33°35N 114°0E **226** H8
Yancheng *Jiangsu, China* 33°23N 120°8E **227** H11
Yanchep *Australia* 31°33S 115°37E **279** F2
Yanchi *China* 37°48N 107°20E **226** F4
Yanchuan *China* 36°51N 110°10E **226** F6
Yanco *Australia* 34°38S 146°27E **283** C7
Yanco Cr. ➔ *Australia* 35°14S 145°35E **283** C6
Yandang Shan *China* 28°0N 120°25E **229** D13
Yandeyarra ☼ *Australia* 21°17S 118°24E **278** D2
Yandicoogina *Australia* 22°49S 119°12E **278** D2
Yandina *Solomon Is.* 9°7S 159°13E **287** M10
Yandja *Dem. Rep. of the Congo* 1°41S 17°43E **264** C3
Yandongi *Dem. Rep. of the Congo* 2°51N 22°16E **264** B4
Yandoon *Myanmar* 17°0N 95°40E **241** G5
Yanfeng *China* 25°52N 101°8E **228** E3
Yanfolila *Mali* 11°11N 8°9W **262** C3
Yang Xian *China* 33°15N 107°30E **228** A6
Yang-yang *S. Korea* 38°4N 128°38E **224** C4
Yang-Yang *Senegal* 15°30N 15°20W **262** B1
Yangambi *Dem. Rep. of the Congo* 0°47N 24°24E **264** B4
Yangbi *China* 25°41N 99°58E **228** E2
Yangcheng *China* 35°28N 112°22E **226** G7
Yangcheon *S. Korea* 37°30N 126°51E **137** B1
Yangchow = Yangzhou *China* 32°21N 119°26E **229** A12
Yangch'ü = Taiyuan *China* 37°52N 112°33E **226** F7
Yangchüan = Yangquan *China* 37°58N 113°31E **226** F7
Yangchun *China* 22°11N 111°48E **229** F8
Yangdok *N. Korea* 39°13N 126°38E **224** C3
Yanggang-do □ *N. Korea* 41°15N 128°0E **224** B4
Yanggao *China* 40°21N 113°55E **226** D7
Yanggu *China* 36°8N 115°43E **226** F8
Yanghuayuan *China* 39°49N 116°18E **114** C1
Yangiyul *Uzbekistan* 41°0N 69°3E **217** D7
Yangjae *S. Korea* 37°29N 127°2E **137** C2
Yangjiang *China* 21°50N 111°59E **229** G8
Yangjiazhuang *China* 31°22N 121°31E **138** A1
Yangjing *China* 31°15N 121°32E **138** B2
Yangju *S. Korea* 37°47N 127°7E **224** D3
Yangliuqing *China* 39°2N 117°5E **227** E9
Yangmei *Taiwan* 24°55N 121°8E **225** B3
Yangmingshan △ *Taiwan* 25°9N 121°32E **225** A3
Yangôn *Myanmar* 16°45N 96°20E **241** G6
Yangôn □ *Myanmar* 16°45N 96°20E **241** G6
Yangonde *Dem. Rep. of the Congo* 0°3N 22°43E **264** B4
Yangping *China* 31°12N 111°25E **229** B8
Yangpingguan *China* 32°58N 106°5E **228** A6
Yangpu *China* 31°16N 121°32E **138** B2
Yangpu Park *China* 31°17N 121°31E **138** B2
Yangquan *China* 37°58N 113°31E **226** F7
Yangsan *S. Korea* 35°20N 129°2E **224** E4
Yangshan *Guangdong, China* 24°30N 112°40E **229** E9
Yangshan *Shanghai, China* 30°37N 122°4E **229** B14
Yangshuo *China* 24°48N 110°29E **229** E8
Yangtse = Chang Jiang ➔ *China* 31°48N 121°10E **229** B13
Yangtze Kiang = Chang Jiang ➔ *China* 31°48N 121°10E **229** B13
Yangudi Rassa △ *Ethiopia* 10°50N 40°42E **257** E5
Yangxin *China* 29°50N 115°12E **229** C10
Yangyuan *China* 40°1N 114°10E **226** D8
Yangzhong *China* 32°22N 119°22E **229** A12
Yangzhou *China* 32°21N 119°26E **229** A12
Yanhe *China* 28°31N 108°29E **228** C7
Yanji *China* 42°59N 129°30E **227** C15
Yanjin *China* 28°5N 104°18E **228** C5
Yanjing *China* 29°7N 98°33E **228** C2
Yankari △ *Nigeria* 9°50N 10°28E **259** G2
Yankton *U.S.A.* 42°53N 97°23W **308** D5
Yankunytjatjara-Antakirinja ☼ *Australia* 27°20S 134°30E **281** A1
Yannawa *Thailand* 13°43N 100°32E **113** B2
Yanonge *Dem. Rep. of the Congo* 0°35N 24°38E **264** B4
Yanov = Ivanava *Belarus* 52°7N 25°29E **177** B13
Yanpu = Yenpu *Taiwan* 22°45N 120°35E **225** D2
Yanqi *China* 42°5N 86°35E **217** D11
Yanqing *China* 40°30N 115°58E **226** D8
Yanshan *Hebei, China* 38°4N 117°22E **227** E9
Yanshan *Jiangxi, China* 28°15N 117°41E **229** C11
Yanshan *Yunnan, China* 23°35N 104°20E **228** F5
Yanshou *China* 45°28N 128°22E **227** B15
Yanshui = Yenshui *Taiwan* 23°19N 120°16E **225** C2
Yantabulla *Australia* 29°21S 145°0E **281** D4
Yantai *China* 37°34N 121°22E **227** F11
Yantarnyy *Russia* 54°52N 19°57E **184** D6
Yantian *China* 22°35N 114°16E **219** a
Yanting *China* 31°11N 105°24E **228** B5
Yantongshan *China* 43°17N 126°0E **227** C14
Yantra ➔ *Bulgaria* 43°40N 25°37E **203** C9
Yanuca *Fiji* 18°24S 178°0E **287** B1
Yanununbeyan △ *Australia* 35°29S 149°24E **283** C8
Yanwa *China* 27°25N 98°58E **228** D2
Yanyuan *China* 27°25N 101°30E **228** D3
Yanzhou *China* 35°35N 116°49E **226** G9
Yao *Chad* 12°56N 17°33E **259** F3
Yao *Japan* 34°37N 135°36E **223** C7
Yao Xian *China* 34°55N 108°59E **226** G5
Yao Yai, Ko *Thailand* 8°7N 98°37E **237** a

Yao'an *China* 25°31N 101°18E **228** E3
Yaotai *China* 23°10N 113°14E **121** B2
Yaoundé *Cameroon* 3°50N 11°35E **263** E7
Yaowan *China* 34°15N 118°3E **227** G10
Yap *Pac. Oc.* 9°30N 138°10E **287** R16
Yapacana △ *Venezuela* 3°49N 66°44W **328** C4
Yapehe
Dem. Rep. of the Congo 0°13S 24°28E **264** C4
Yapei *Ghana* 9°10N 1°10W **263** D4
Yapen *Indonesia* 1°50S 136°0E **231** E9
Yapen, Selat *Indonesia* 1°20S 136°10E **231** E9
Yapero *Indonesia* 4°59S 137°11E **231** E9
Yappar → *Australia* 18°22S 141°16E **280** B3
Yapuparra ✪ *Australia* 27°15S 126°20E **279** E4
Yaqaga *Fiji* 16°35S 178°36E **287** A2
Yaqui → *Mexico* 27°37N 110°39W **318** B2
Yar Çalli = Naberezhnyye Chelny
Russia 55°42N 52°19E **190** C11
Yar-Sale *Russia* 66°50N 70°50E **214** C8
Yaracuy □ *Venezuela* 10°20N 68°45W **328** A4
Yaracuy → *Venezuela* 10°33N 68°15W **328** A4
Yaraka *Australia* 24°53S 144°3E **280** C3
Yaransk *Russia* 57°22N 47°49E **190** B8
Yarbasan *Turkey* 38°59N 28°49E **205** C10
Yardımcı Burnu *Turkey* 36°13N 30°25E **205** E12
Yare → *U.K.* 52°35N 1°38E **169** E9
Yaremcha *Ukraine* 48°27N 24°33E **183** B9
Yaren *Nauru* 0°33S 166°55E **288** H8
Yarensk *Russia* 62°11N 49°15E **186** B8
Yarfa *Si. Arabia* 24°37N 38°35E **256** C4
Yarí → *Colombia* 0°20S 72°20W **328** D3
Yarīm *Yemen* 14°20N 44°22E **248** D4
Yaritagua *Venezuela* 10°5N 69°8W **328** A4
Yarkand = Shache *China* 38°20N 77°10E **217** E9
Yarkant He → *China* 40°26N 80°59E **217** D10
Yarker *Canada* 44°23N 76°46W **313** B8
Yarkhun → *Pakistan* 36°17N 72°30E **243** A5
Yarlung Ziangbo Jiang =
Brahmaputra → *Asia* 23°40N 90°35E **241** D3
Yarmouth *Canada* 43°50N 66°7W **299** D6
Yarmūk *Iraq* 33°18N 44°19E **113** B1
Yarmūk → *Syria* 32°42N 35°40E **250** F6
Yaroslavl *Russia* 57°35N 39°55E **188** D10
Yaroslavl □ *Russia* 59°20N 38°50E **188** C10
Yarra → *Trin. & Tob.* 10°48N 61°21W **323** t
Yarra Bend Park *Australia* 37°47S 145°0E **128** A2
Yarra Ranges △ *Australia* 37°40S 146°3E **283** D7
Yarra Yarra Lakes
Australia 29°40S 115°45E **279** E2
Yarram *Australia* 38°29S 146°39E **283** E7
Yarraman *Australia* 26°50S 152°0E **281** D5
Yarras *Australia* 31°25S 152°20E **283** A10
Yarraville *Australia* 37°48S 144°53E **128** A1
Yarrawonga *Australia* 36°0S 146°0E **283** D7
Yarrie *Australia* 20°40S 120°12E **278** D3
Yartsevo *Sib., Russia* 60°20N 90°0E **215** C10
Yartsevo *Smolensk, Russia* 55°6N 32°43E **188** E7
Yarumal *Colombia* 6°58N 75°24W **328** B2
Yasa *Dem. Rep. of the Congo* 3°50S 21°25E **264** C4
Yasawa *Fiji* 16°47S 177°31E **287** A1
Yasawa Group *Fiji* 17°0S 177°23E **287** A1
Yaselda *Belarus* 52°7N 26°28E **177** B14
Yasen *Ukraine* 48°45N 24°10E **183** B9
Yashbum *Yemen* 14°19N 46°56E **248** D4
Yashi *Nigeria* 12°23N 7°54E **263** C6
Yashikera *Nigeria* 9°44N 3°29E **263** D5
Yashiro-Jima *Japan* 33°55N 132°15E **222** D4
Yashkul *Russia* 46°11N 45°21E **191** G7
Yasi = Türkistan
Kazakhstan 43°17N 68°16E **217** D7
Yasin *Pakistan* 36°24N 73°23E **243** A5
Yasinovataya *Ukraine* 48°7N 37°57E **189** H9
Yasinski, L. *Canada* 53°16N 77°35W **298** B4
Yasinya *Ukraine* 48°16N 24°21E **183** B9
Yasnyy *Russia* 51°1N 59°58E **216** B5
Yasothon *Thailand* 15°50N 104°10E **236** E5
Yass *Australia* 34°49S 148°54E **283** C8
Yasugi *Japan* 35°26N 133°15E **222** B5
Yāsūj *Iran* 30°31N 51°31E **247** D6
Yasuni △ *Ecuador* 1°19S 76°3W **328** D2
Yat *Niger* 20°28N 13°27E **259** D2
Yata → *Bolivia* 10°29S 65°26W **331** C4
Yata → *C.A.R.* 10°23N 22°45E **264** A4
Yata-Ngaya ⌂ *C.A.R.* 9°15N 23°25E **264** A4
Yatağan *Turkey* 37°20N 28°10E **205** D10
Yatakala *Niger* 14°50N 0°22E **263** C5
Yaté *N. Cal.* 22°9S 166°57E **288** d
Yates Center *U.S.A.* 37°53N 95°44W **308** G6
Yates Pt. *N.Z.* 44°29S 167°49E **285** E2
Yathkyed L. *Canada* 62°40N 98°0W **297** A9
Yathong *Australia* 32°37S 145°33E **283** B6
Yatolemu
Dem. Rep. of the Congo 0°25N 24°35E **264** B4
Yatsuo *Japan* 36°34N 137°8E **223** A9
Yatsushiro *Japan* 32°30N 130°40E **222** E2
Yatsushiro-Kai *Japan* 32°30N 130°25E **222** E2
Yatta Plateau *Kenya* 2°0S 38°0E **268** C4
Yatua → *Venezuela* 1°30N 66°30W **328** C4
Yauca *Peru* 15°39S 74°35W **330** D3
Yauco *Puerto Rico* 18°2N 66°51W **321** b
Yauri *Peru* 14°47S 71°25W **330** C3
Yauya *Peru* 8°59S 77°17W **330** B2
Yauyos *Peru* 12°19S 75°50W **330** C2
Yauza → *Russia* 55°54N 37°43E **129** B4
Yaval *India* 21°10N 75°42E **244** D2
Yavari → *Peru* 4°21S 70°2W **330** A3
Yávaros *Mexico* 26°42N 109°31W **318** B3
Yavatmal *India* 20°20N 78°15E **244** D4
Yavero → *Peru* 12°6S 72°57W **330** C3
Yavne *Israel* 31°52N 34°45E **251** G5
Yavoriv *Ukraine* 49°55N 23°20E **177** D12
Yavorov = Yavoriv
Ukraine 49°55N 23°20E **177** D12
Yavuzeli *Turkey* 37°18N 37°24E **212** D7
Yawatahama *Japan* 33°27N 132°24E **222** D4
Yawnghwe *Myanmar* 20°39N 96°56E **241** E6
Yawri B. *S. Leone* 8°22N 13°0W **262** D2
Yaxi *China* 27°33N 106°41E **228** D6
Yaxian = Sanya *China* 18°14N 109°29E **229** a
Yayama
Dem. Rep. of the Congo 1°16S 23°7E **264** C4
Yayladağı *Turkey* 35°54N 36°3E **250** C7
Yazd *Iran* 31°55N 54°27E **247** D7
Yazd □ *Iran* 32°0N 55°0E **247** D7
Yazd-e Khvāst *Iran* 31°31N 52°7E **247** D7
Yazdān *Iran* 33°30N 60°50E **240** B1
Yazıköy *Turkey* 36°40N 27°20E **205** E9
Yazman *Pakistan* 29°8N 71°45E **242** E4
Yazoo → *U.S.A.* 32°22N 90°54W **315** E9
Yazoo City *U.S.A.* 32°51N 90°25W **315** E9
Ybbs *Austria* 48°12N 15°4E **180** C8
Ybycuí △ *Paraguay* 26°5S 56°46W **334** B4
Ybytyruzú △ *Paraguay* 25°51S 56°11W **335** B4
Ye *Myanmar* 15°15N 97°15E **236** E1
Ye-ngan *Myanmar* 21°9N 96°27E **241** E6
Ye-u *Myanmar* 22°46N 95°26E **241** D5
Ye Xian = Laizhou *China* 37°8N 119°57E **227** F10
Ye Xian *China* 33°35N 113°25E **226** H7
Yea *Australia* 37°14S 145°26E **283** D6
Yeading *U.K.* 51°31N 0°23W **125** A1
Yebawmi *Myanmar* 25°15N 95°45E **241** C5
Yebbi-Souma *Chad* 21°7N 17°54E **259** D3
Yebyu *Myanmar* 14°15N 98°13E **236** E2
Yecheng *China* 37°54N 77°26E **217** E9
Yecheon *S. Korea* 36°39N 128°27E **224** D4
Yecla *Spain* 38°35N 1°5W **197** G3
Yécora *Mexico* 28°20N 108°58W **318** B3
Yedashe *Myanmar* 19°10N 96°20E **241** F6
Yedebub Biheroch Bihereseboch na
Hizboch □ *Ethiopia* 12°0N 36°0E **257** F4
Yedigöller △ *Turkey* 40°55N 31°55E **212** B4
Yedikule *Turkey* 40°59N 28°55E **122** C1
Yedintsy = Edineţ
Moldova 48°9N 27°18E **183** B12
Yedri *Chad* 22°25N 17°35E **259** D3
Yedseram → *Nigeria* 12°30N 14°5E **263** C7
Yeed *Somalia* 4°33N 43°2E **267** D5
Yefremov *Russia* 53°8N 38°3E **188** F10
Yegguéba *Niger* 19°59N 12°52E **259** E2
Yeghegnadzor *Armenia* 39°44N 45°19E **213** C11
Yegorlyk → *Russia* 46°35N 41°57E **191** G5
Yegorlykskaya *Russia* 46°35N 40°35E **191** G5
Yegoryevsk *Russia* 55°27N 38°55E **188** E10
Yegri-Dere = Ardino
Bulgaria 41°34N 25°9E **203** E9
Yegros *Paraguay* 26°20S 56°25W **334** B4
Yehbuah *Indonesia* 8°23S 114°45E **231** J17
Yehuda, Midbar *Israel* 31°35N 35°15E **251** G6
Yei *South Sudan* 4°9N 30°40E **257** G3
Yei, Nahr → *South Sudan* 6°15N 30°13E **257** F3
Yeji *Ghana* 8°13N 0°39W **263** D4
Yejmiadzin = Ejmiatsin
Armenia 40°12N 44°19E **191** K7
Yekaterinburg *Russia* 56°50N 60°30E **214** D7
Yekaterinenshtadt = Marks
Russia 51°45N 46°50E **190** E8
Yekaterinodar = Krasnodar
Russia 45°5N 39°0E **191** H4
Yekateriny, Proliv
Russia 44°30N 146°30E **215** E15
Yekumbe
Dem. Rep. of the Congo 1°2S 23°27E **264** C4
Yelabuga *Russia* 55°46N 52°2E **190** C11
Yelan *Russia* 50°55N 43°43E **190** E6
Yelandur *India* 12°6N 77°0E **245** H3
Yelarbon *Australia* 28°33S 150°38E **281** D5
Yelatma *Russia* 55°0N 41°45E **190** C5
Yelcho, L. *Chile* 43°18S 72°18W **336** B2
Yelenovka = Sevan
Armenia 40°33N 44°56E **191** K7
Yelenovskiye Karyery =
Dokuchayevsk *Ukraine* 47°44N 37°40E **189** J9
Yelets *Russia* 52°40N 38°30E **189** F10
Yélimané *Mali* 15°9N 10°34W **262** B2
Yelin = Lingshui *China* 18°27N 110°0E **229** a
Yelizavetgrad = Kropyvnytskyy
Ukraine 48°35N 32°20E **189** H7
Yelizovo *Russia* 53°11N 158°23E **215** D16
Yell *U.K.* 60°35N 1°5W **167** A7
Yell Sd. *U.K.* 60°33N 1°15W **167** A7
Yellamanchilli = Elamanchili
India 17°33N 82°50E **244** F6
Yellandu *India* 17°39N 80°23E **244** F5
Yellapur *India* 14°58N 74°43E **245** G2
Yellareddi *India* 18°12N 78°2E **244** E4
Yellow = Huang He →
China 37°55N 118°50E **227** F10
Yellow → *U.S.A.* 30°30N 87°0W **317** E3
Yellow Sea *China* 35°0N 123°0E **227** G12
Yellowhead Pass *Canada* 52°53N 118°25W **296** C5
Yellowknife *Canada* 62°27N 114°29W **296** A6
Yellowknife → *Canada* 62°31N 114°19W **296** A6
Yellowstone → *U.S.A.* 47°59N 103°59W **304** C12
Yellowstone △ *U.S.A.* 44°40N 110°30W **304** D8
Yellowstone L. *U.S.A.* 44°27N 110°22W **304** D8
Yelnya *Russia* 54°35N 33°15E **188** E7
Yelsk *Belarus* 51°50N 29°10E **177** C15
Yelwa *Nigeria* 10°49N 4°41E **263** C5
Yemanzhelinsk *Russia* 54°58N 61°18E **216** B6
Yemassee *U.S.A.* 32°41N 80°51W **316** C9
Yembongo
Dem. Rep. of the Congo 3°12N 19°2E **264** B3
Yemen ■ *Asia* 15°0N 44°0E **248** D4
Yemin Moshe *Jerusalem* **123** b2
Yemmiganur *India* 15°44N 77°29E **245** G3
Yen Bai *Vietnam* 21°42N 104°52E **228** G5
Yenagoa *Nigeria* 4°58N 6°16E **263** E6
Yenakiyeve *Ukraine* 48°15N 38°15E **189** H10
Yenakiyevo = Yenakiyeve
Ukraine 48°15N 38°15E **189** H10
Yenangyat *Myanmar* 21°6N 94°46E **241** E5
Yenangyaung *Myanmar* 20°30N 95°0E **241** E5
Yenanma *Myanmar* 19°46N 94°49E **241** F5
Yenbo = Yanbu 'al Baḥr
Si. Arabia 24°5N 38°5E **246** E3
Yenchao *Taiwan* 22°46N 120°21E **225** D2
Yenda *Australia* 34°13S 146°14E **283** C7
Yende Millimou *Guinea* 8°55N 10°10W **262** D2
Yendegaia △ *Chile* 54°50S 68°45W **336** D3
Yendéré *Burkina Faso* 10°12N 4°59W **262** C4
Yendi *Ghana* 9°29N 0°1W **263** D4
Yengisar *China* 38°56N 76°9E **217** E9
Yengo *Congo* 0°22N 15°29E **264** B3
Yengo △ *Australia* 33°0S 150°55E **283** B9
Yéni *Niger* 13°30N 3°1E **263** C5
Yeni Erenköy = Yialousa
Cyprus 35°32N 34°10E **207** E10
Yeni-Pazar = Novi Pazar
Serbia 43°12N 20°28E **202** C4
Yenibogaziçi = Áyios Seryios
Cyprus 35°12N 33°53E **207** E9
Yenice *Ankara, Turkey* 39°14N 32°42E **212** C5
Yenice *Aydın, Turkey* 37°49N 28°35E **205** D10
Yenice *Çanakkale, Turkey* 39°55N 27°17E **205** B9
Yenice *Edirne, Turkey* 40°42N 26°9E **203** F10
Yenice *Kahramanmaraş,*
Turkey 37°0N 35°4E **250** B6
Yenice → *Turkey* 37°37N 35°33E **212** D6
Yenifoça *Turkey* 38°44N 26°51E **205** C8
Yenihisar = Didim *Turkey* 37°22N 27°16E **205** D9
Yenikapı *Turkey* 41°0N 28°56E **122** B1
Yeniköy *Bursa, Turkey* 40°31N 29°22E **203** F13
Yeniköy *Çanakkale, Turkey* 39°55N 26°10E **205** B8
Yeniköy *İstanbul, Turkey* 41°6N 29°3E **122** B2
Yeniköy *Kütahya, Turkey* 38°52N 29°17E **205** C11
Yenipazar *Turkey* 37°49N 28°11E **205** D10
Yenişehir *Turkey* 40°16N 29°38E **203** F13
Yenisey → *Russia* 71°50N 82°40E **214** B9
Yeniseysk *Russia* 58°27N 92°13E **215** D10
Yeniseyskiy Zaliv *Russia* 72°20N 81°0E **214** B9
Yenki = Yanji *China* 42°59N 129°30E **227** C15
Yenne *France* 45°43N 5°44E **175** C9
Yenpu *Taiwan* 22°45N 120°35E **225** D2
Yenotayevka *Russia* 47°15N 47°0E **191** G8
Yenshui *Taiwan* 23°19N 120°16E **225** C2
Yenyuka *Russia* 57°57N 121°15E **215** D13
Yeo → *U.K.* 51°2N 2°49W **169** G5
Yeo, L. *Australia* 28°0S 124°30E **279** E3
Yeo I. *Canada* 45°24N 81°48W **312** A3
Yeoju *S. Korea* 37°20N 127°35E **224** D3
Yeola *India* 20°2N 74°30E **244** D2
Yeon-gi = Sejong
S. Korea 36°35N 127°15E **224** D3
Yeoncheon *S. Korea* 38°5N 127°4E **224** C3
Yeong-am *S. Korea* 34°47N 126°42E **224** E3
Yeong-ilman *S. Korea* 36°4N 129°28E **224** D4
Yeong-wol *S. Korea* 37°11N 128°28E **224** D4
Yeong-yang *S. Korea* 36°39N 129°7E **224** D4
Yeongcheon *S. Korea* 35°58N 128°56E **224** E4
Yeongdeok *S. Korea* 36°24N 129°22E **224** D4
Yeongdeungpo *S. Korea* 37°31N 126°54E **137** B1
Yeongdong *Chungcheongbuk-do,*
S. Korea 36°10N 127°46E **224** D3
Yeongdong *Seoul, S. Korea* 37°30N 127°1E **137** B2
Yeonggwang *S. Korea* 35°16N 126°30E **224** E3
Yeongheungdo *S. Korea* 37°15N 126°27E **224** D3
Yeongju *S. Korea* 36°50N 128°40E **224** D4
Yeongju △ *S. Korea* 35°45N 129°20E **224** D4
Yeonpyeongdo *S. Korea* 37°40N 125°45E **224** D2
Yeosu *S. Korea* 34°47N 127°45E **224** E3
Yeotmal = Yavatmal
India 20°20N 78°15E **244** D4
Yeouido *S. Korea* 37°31N 126°55E **137** B1
Yeovil *U.K.* 50°57N 2°38W **169** G5
Yepes *Spain* 39°55N 3°39W **194** F7
Yeppoon *Australia* 23°5S 150°47E **280** C5
Yerba Buena I. *U.S.A.* 37°48N 122°21W **136** B2
Yerbent *Turkmenistan* 39°19N 58°36E **247** B8
Yerbogachen *Russia* 61°16N 108°0E **215** C11
Yerevan *Armenia* 40°10N 44°31E **191** K7
Yerington *U.S.A.* 38°59N 119°10W **304** G4
Yerkesik *Turkey* 37°7N 28°19E **205** D10
Yerköy *Turkey* 39°38N 34°28E **212** C6
Yerla → *India* 16°50N 74°30E **244** F2
Yermo *U.S.A.* 34°54N 116°50W **307** L10
Yerolakkos *Cyprus* 35°11N 33°15E **207** E9
Yeropol *Russia* 65°15N 168°40E **215** C17
Yeroskipos *Cyprus* 34°46N 32°28E **207** F8
Yerres *France* 48°43N 2°30E **134** B4
Yershov *Russia* 51°23N 48°27E **190** E9
Yerupajá, Cerro *Peru* 10°16S 76°55W **330** C2
Yerushalayim = Jerusalem
Israel/West Bank 31°47N 35°10E **123** B2
Yerville *France* 49°40N 0°53E **172** C7
Yes Tor *U.K.* 50°41N 4°0W **169** G4
Yesagyo *Myanmar* 21°38N 95°14E **241** E5
Yesan *S. Korea* 36°41N 126°51E **224** D3
Yeshin *Myanmar* 23°43N 95°6E **241** D5
Yeşikent = Erzin *Turkey* 36°57N 36°11E **250** B7
Yeşil → *Turkey* 37°20N 33°16E **250** A4
Yeşildere *Turkey* 37°9N 33°31E **250** A4
Yeşilhisar *Turkey* 38°20N 35°5E **212** C6
Yeşilırmak → *Turkey* 41°22N 36°37E **212** B7
Yeşilkent *Turkey* 36°57N 36°12E **212** D7
Yeşilova *Turkey* 37°31N 29°46E **205** D11
Yeşilyurt *Manisa, Turkey* 38°22N 28°40E **205** C10
Yeşilyurt *Muğla, Turkey* 37°10N 28°20E **205** D10
Yeski Dzhumaya = Târgovişte
Romania 44°55N 25°27E **183** F10
Yesnogorsk *Russia* 54°32N 37°38E **188** E9
Yeso *U.S.A.* 34°26N 104°37W **305** J11
Yessentuki *Russia* 44°5N 42°53E **191** H6
Yessey *Russia* 68°29N 102°10E **215** C11
Yeste *Spain* 38°22N 2°19W **197** G2
Yetman *Australia* 28°56S 150°48E **281** D5
Yetti *Mauritania* 26°10N 7°50W **260** C3
Yeu, Î. d' *France* 46°42N 2°20W **172** F4
Yevdokimovskoye =
Krasnogvardeyskoye
Russia 45°52N 41°33E **191** H5
Yevlax *Azerbaijan* 40°39N 47°7E **191** K8
Yevpatoriya *Ukraine* 45°15N 33°20E **189** K7
Yeya → *Russia* 46°40N 38°40E **191** G4
Yeysk *Russia* 46°40N 38°12E **189** J10
Yezd = Yazd *Iran* 31°55N 54°27E **247** D7
Yezerishche *Belarus* 55°50N 30°0E **188** E5
Ygatimi *Paraguay* 24°5S 55°40W **335** A4
Yhati *Paraguay* 25°45S 56°35W **334** B4
Yhú *Paraguay* 25°0S 56°0W **335** B4
Yi → *Uruguay* 33°7S 57°8W **334** C4
Yi 'Allaq, G. *Egypt* 30°21N 33°31E **251** H4
Yi He → *China* 34°10N 118°8E **227** G10
Yi O San Tsuen
Hong Kong, China 22°14N 113°51E **122** B1
Yi Xian *Anhui, China* 29°55N 117°57E **229** C11
Yi Xian *Hebei, China* 39°20N 115°30E **226** E8
Yi Xian *Liaoning, China* 41°30N 121°22E **227** D11
Yialiás → *Cyprus* 35°9N 33°44E **207** E9
Yialousa *Cyprus* 35°32N 34°10E **207** E10
Yibin *China* 28°45N 104°32E **228** C5
Yichang *China* 30°40N 111°20E **229** B8
Yicheng *Henan, China* 31°41N 112°12E **229** B9
Yicheng *Shanxi, China* 35°42N 111°40E **226** G6
Yichuan *China* 36°2N 110°10E **226** F6
Yichun *Heilongjiang,*
China 47°44N 128°52E **219** B14
Yichun *Jiangxi, China* 27°48N 114°22E **229** D10
Yidu *China* 36°43N 118°28E **227** F10
Yidun *China* 30°22N 99°21E **228** B2
Yifag *Ethiopia* 12°4N 37°44E **257** E4
Yifeng *China* 28°22N 114°45E **229** C10
Yigo *Guam* 13°32N 144°53E **302** d
Yiheyuan *China* 39°59N 116°15E **114** B1
Yihuang *China* 27°30N 116°12E **229** D11
Yijun *China* 35°28N 109°8E **226** G5
Yilan = Ilan *Taiwan* 24°45N 121°44E **225** B3
Yılanlıkale *Turkey* 36°59N 35°47E **250** B6
Yıldız Dağları *Turkey* 41°48N 27°36E **203** E11
Yıldız Park *Turkey* 41°2N 29°1E **122** B2
Yıldızeli *Turkey* 39°51N 36°36E **212** C7
Yilehuli Shan *China* 51°20N 124°20E **219** A13
Yiliang *Yunnan, China* 27°38N 104°2E **228** D5
Yiliang *Yunnan, China* 24°56N 103°11E **228** E4
Yılmazköy = Skilloura
Cyprus 35°14N 33°10E **207** E9
Yilong *China* 31°34N 106°23E **228** B6
Yima *China* 34°44N 111°53E **226** G6
Yimen *China* 24°40N 102°10E **228** E4
Yimianpo *China* 45°7N 128°2E **227** B15
Yin Xu *China* 36°7N 114°10E **226** F8
Yi'nan *China* 35°31N 118°24E **227** G10
Yinchuan *China* 38°30N 106°15E **226** E4
Yindaik *Myanmar* 23°35N 95°22E **241** D5
Yindarlgooda, L.
Australia 30°40S 121°52E **279** F3
Yindjibarndi ✪ *Australia* 22°0S 118°35E **278** D2
Ying He → *China* 32°30N 116°30E **229** A11
Ying Xian *China* 39°32N 113°10E **226** E7
Yingcheng *China* 30°56N 113°35E **229** B9
Yingde *China* 24°10N 113°25E **229** E9
Yingjiang *China* 24°41N 97°55E **228** E1
Yingjing *China* 29°41N 102°52E **228** C4
Yingkiong *India* 28°37N 95°3E **241** A5
Yingkou *China* 40°37N 122°18E **224** B1
Yingkow = Yingkou
China 40°37N 122°18E **224** B1
Yingpanshui *China* 37°26N 104°18E **226** F3
Yingshan *Hubei, China* 30°41N 115°32E **229** B10
Yingshan *Sichuan, China* 31°4N 106°35E **228** B6
Yingshang *China* 32°38N 116°12E **229** A11
Yingtan *China* 28°12N 117°0E **229** C11
Yingualyalya ✪ *Australia* 18°49S 129°12E **278** C4
Yinhangzhen *China* 31°20N 121°31E **138** A2
Yining *China* 43°58N 81°10E **217** D10
Yiningarra ✪ *Australia* 20°53S 129°27E **278** D4
Yinjiang *China* 28°1N 108°21E **228** C7
Yinmabin *Myanmar* 22°10N 94°55E **241** D5
Yioúra = Giaros *Greece* 37°32N 24°40E **204** D6
Yipinglang *China* 25°10N 101°52E **228** E3
Yirba Muda *Ethiopia* 6°12N 38°42E **257** F4
Yirga Alem *Ethiopia* 6°48N 38°22E **257** F4
Yirol *South Sudan* 6°33N 30°30E **257** F3
Yirrkala *Australia* 12°14S 136°56E **280** A2
Yishan *China* 24°28N 108°38E **228** E7
Yishui *China* 35°47N 118°30E **227** G10
Yishun *Singapore* 1°26N 103°51E **138** A3
Yitong *China* 43°13N 125°20E **227** C13
Yiwu *China* 29°20N 120°3E **229** C13
Yixing *China* 31°21N 119°48E **229** B12
Yiyang *Henan, China* 34°27N 112°10E **226** G7
Yiyang *Hunan, China* 28°35N 112°18E **229** C9
Yiyang *Jiangxi, China* 28°22N 117°20E **229** C11
Yizhang *China* 25°27N 112°57E **229** E9
Yizheng *China* 32°18N 119°10E **229** A12
Yizhu = Ichu *Taiwan* 23°20N 120°14E **225** C2
Ylästö *Finland* 60°17N 24°54E **121** B2
Yli-Kitka *Finland* 66°8N 28°30E **160** C23
Yliki, L. *Greece* 38°24N 23°15E **204** C5
Ylitornio *Finland* 66°19N 23°39E **160** C20
Ylivieska *Finland* 64°4N 24°28E **160** D21
Ymer Ø *Greenland* 73°9N 24°20W **154** C8
Yngaren *Sweden* 58°50N 16°35E **163** F10
Yoakum *U.S.A.* 29°17N 97°9W **314** G6
Yob △ *Eritrea* 17°15N 37°55E **257** D4
Yobe □ *Nigeria* 12°0N 11°30E **263** C7
Yoboki *Djibouti* 11°30N 42°26E **267** B5
Yobuko *Japan* 33°32N 129°54E **222** D1
Yodo → *Japan* 34°45N 135°35E **133** A2
Yog Pt. *Phil.* 14°6N 124°12E **232** D5
Yoğuntaş *Turkey* 41°50N 27°4E **203** E11
Yogyakarta *Indonesia* 7°49S 110°22E **235** D4
Yogyakarta □ *Indonesia* 7°48S 110°22E **235** D4
Yoho △ *Canada* 51°25N 116°30W **296** C5
Yojoa, L. de *Honduras* 14°53N 88°0W **320** D2
Yok Don △ *Vietnam* 12°50N 107°40E **236** F6
Yokadouma *Cameroon* 3°26N 14°55E **264** B2
Yōkaichi *Japan* 35°6N 136°12E **223** B8
Yōkaichiba *Japan* 35°42N 140°33E **223** B12
Yokkaichi *Japan* 34°55N 136°38E **223** C8
Yoko *Cameroon* 5°32N 12°20E **263** D7
Yokohama *Japan* 35°27N 139°28E **223** B11
Yokosuka *Japan* 35°20N 139°40E **223** B11
Yokote *Japan* 39°20N 140°30E **220** E10
Yola *Nigeria* 9°10N 12°29E **263** D7
Yolaina, Cordillera de *Nic.* 11°30N 84°0W **320** D3
Yolombo
Dem. Rep. of the Congo 1°36S 23°12E **264** C4
Yöloten *Turkmenistan* 37°18N 62°21E **247** B9
Yom → *Thailand* 15°35N 100°1E **236** E3
Yombi *Gabon* 1°26S 10°37E **264** C2
Yona *Guam* 13°25N 144°46E **302** d
Yonago *Japan* 35°25N 133°19E **222** B5
Yonaguni-Jima *Japan* 24°27N 123°0E **221** M1
Yonaha-Dake *Japan* 26°43N 128°13E **288** a
Yŏnan *N. Korea* 37°55N 126°11E **224** D3
Yonezawa *Japan* 37°57N 140°4E **220** F10
Yong-in *S. Korea* 37°14N 127°12E **224** D3
Yong Peng *Malaysia* 2°0N 103°3E **237** M4
Yong Sata *Thailand* 7°8N 99°41E **237** J2
Yongama
Dem. Rep. of the Congo 0°2N 24°35E **264** B4
Yongamp'o *N. Korea* 39°56N 124°23E **224** C2
Yong'an *China* 25°59N 117°25E **229** E11
Yongchang *China* 38°17N 102°7E **218** D9
Yongcheng *China* 33°55N 116°20E **226** H9
Yongchuan *China* 29°17N 105°55E **228** C5
Yongchun *China* 25°16N 118°20E **229** E12
Yongde *China* 24°5N 99°25E **228** E2
Yongdeng *China* 36°38N 103°25E **226** F2
Yongding *China* 24°43N 116°45E **229** E11
Yongdingmen *China* 39°50N 116°20E **114** B2
Yonge Street *Toronto, Canada* **141** b3
Yongfeng *China* 27°20N 115°22E **229** D10
Yongfu *China* 24°59N 109°59E **228** E7
Yonghe *China* 36°46N 110°38E **226** F6
Yonghong *India* 26°28N 94°58E **241** B5
Yŏnghŭng *N. Korea* 39°31N 127°18E **224** C3
Yŏnghŭng-man *N. Korea* 39°14N 127°30E **224** C3
Yongji *Jilin, China* 43°33N 126°13E **227** C14
Yongji *Shanxi, China* 34°52N 110°28E **226** G6
Yongjia *China* 28°10N 120°45E **229** C13
Yongkang = Yungk'ang
Taiwan 23°2N 120°15E **225** C2
Yongkang *Yunnan, China* 24°9N 99°20E **228** E2
Yongkang *Zhejiang, China* 28°55N 120°2E **229** C13
Yongnian *China* 36°47N 114°29E **226** F8
Yongning *Guangxi Zhuangzu,*
China 22°44N 108°28E **228** F7
Yongning *Ningxia Huizu,*
China 38°15N 106°14E **226** E4
Yongping *China* 25°27N 99°38E **228** E2
Yongren *China* 26°4N 101°40E **228** D3
Yongsan *S. Korea* 37°32N 126°58E **137** B1
Yongshan *China* 28°11N 103°35E **228** C4
Yongsheng *China* 26°38N 100°46E **228** D3
Yongshun *China* 29°2N 109°51E **228** C7
Yongtai *China* 25°49N 118°58E **229** E12
Yongxin = Jinggangshan
China 26°58N 114°15E **229** D10
Yongxing *China* 26°9N 113°8E **229** D9
Yongxing Dao = Woody I.
S. China Sea 16°50N 112°20E **230** A4
Yongxiu *China* 29°2N 115°42E **229** C10
Yongzhou *China* 26°17N 111°37E **229** D8
Yonibana *S. Leone* 8°30N 12°19W **262** D2
Yonkers *U.S.A.* 40°56N 73°52W **132** A2
Yonne □ *France* 47°50N 3°40E **173** E10
Yonne → *France* 48°23N 2°58E **173** D9
Yopal *Colombia* 5°21N 72°23W **328** B3
York *W. Austral., Australia* 31°52S 116°47E **279** F2
York *Ont., Canada* 43°40N 79°26W **141** A2
York *U.K.* 53°58N 1°6W **168** D6
York *Ala., U.S.A.* 32°29N 88°18W **315** E10
York *Nebr., U.S.A.* 40°52N 97°36W **308** E5
York *Pa., U.S.A.* 39°58N 76°44W **309** F15
York, C. *Australia* 10°42S 142°31E **286** F2
York, City of □ *U.K.* 53°58N 1°6W **168** D6
York, Kap *Greenland* 75°55N 66°25W **154** B4
York, Vale of *U.K.* 54°15N 1°25W **168** D6
York I. *Antigua & B.* 17°2N 61°40W **322** b
York Mills *Canada* 43°45N 79°22W **141** A2
York Sd. *Australia* 15°0S 125°5E **278** C4
York Univ. *Canada* 43°43N 79°29W **141** A1
Yorke Pen. *Australia* 34°50S 137°40E **282** C2
Yorketown *Australia* 35°2S 137°33E **282** C2
Yorkshire Dales △ *U.K.* 54°12N 2°10W **168** C5
Yorkshire Wolds *U.K.* 54°8N 0°31W **168** C7
Yorkton *Canada* 51°11N 102°28W **297** C8
Yorkville *Calif., U.S.A.* 38°52N 123°13W **306** G3
Yorkville *Ga., U.S.A.* 33°55N 84°58W **316** B5
Yorkville *Ill., U.S.A.* 41°38N 88°27W **311** C8
Yoro *Honduras* 15°9N 87°7W **320** C2
Yoron-Jima *Japan* 27°2N 128°26E **221** L4
Yorosso *Mali* 12°17N 4°55W **262** C4
Yos Sudarso, Pulau = Dolak, Pulau
Indonesia 8°0S 138°30E **231** F9
Yosemite △ *U.S.A.* 37°45N 119°40W **306** H7
Yosemite Village *U.S.A.* 37°45N 119°35W **306** H7
Yoshida *Japan* 34°40N 132°42E **222** C4
Yoshimatsu *Japan* 32°0N 130°47E **222** F2
Yoshino-Kumano △
Japan 34°12N 135°55E **223** C7
Yoshinogawa *Japan* 34°4N 134°21E **222** C6
Yoshkar Ola *Russia* 56°38N 47°55E **190** B8
Yotala *Bolivia* 19°10S 65°17W **331** D4
Yotsuya *Tokyo, Japan* **140** a2
Yotvata *Israel* 29°55N 35°2E **251** J6
You Jiang → *China* 22°50N 108°6E **228** F6
You Xian *China* 27°1N 113°17E **229** D9
You'anmen *China* 39°51N 116°19E **114** B2
Youbou *Canada* 48°53N 124°13W **306** B2
Youghal *Ireland* 51°56N 7°52W **166** E4
Youghal B. *Ireland* 51°55N 7°49W **166** E4
Youkounkoun *Guinea* 12°35N 13°11W **262** C2
Young *N.S.W., Australia* 34°19S 148°18E **283** C8
Young *Canada* 51°47N 105°45W **297** C7
Young *Uruguay* 32°44S 57°36W **334** C4
Young, I. *Antarctica* 66°25S 162°24E **151** C11
Young Ra. *N.Z.* 44°10S 169°30E **285** E4
Younghusband, L.
Australia 30°50S 136°5E **282** A2
Younghusband Pen.
Australia 36°0S 139°25E **282** D3
Youngsfield *S. Africa* 34°0S 18°30E **118** B1
Youngstown *Alta.,*
Canada 51°35N 111°10W **297** C6
Youngstown *Fla., U.S.A.* 30°22N 85°26W **316** E4
Youngstown *N.Y., U.S.A.* 43°15N 79°3W **312** C5
Youngstown *Ohio, U.S.A.* 41°6N 80°39W **312** E4
Youngsville *U.S.A.* 41°51N 79°19W **312** E5
Youngwood *U.S.A.* 40°14N 79°34W **312** F5
Youssoufia *Morocco* 32°16N 8°31W **260** B3
Youxi *China* 26°10N 118°13E **229** D12
Youyang *China* 28°47N 108°42E **228** C7
Youyu *China* 40°10N 112°20E **226** D7
Yozgat *Turkey* 39°51N 34°47E **212** C6
Yozgat □ *Turkey* 39°30N 35°0E **212** C6
Ypacarai △ *Paraguay* 25°18S 57°19W **334** B4
Ypané → *Paraguay* 23°29S 57°19W **334** A4
Yport *France* 49°45N 0°15E **172** C7
Ypres = Ieper *Belgium* 50°51N 2°53E **170** D2
Ypsilanti *U.S.A.* 42°14N 83°37W **311** B13
Yr Wyddgrug = Mold *U.K.* 53°9N 3°8W **168** D4
Yreka *U.S.A.* 41°44N 122°38W **304** F2
Yrghyz *Kazakhstan* 48°37N 61°16E **216** C6
Yrghyz → *Kazakhstan* 48°6N 62°30E **216** C6
Ysabel Chan. *Papua N. G.* 2°0S 150°0E **286** B6
Yssingeaux *France* 45°9N 4°8E **175** C8
Ystabohamn *Norway* 59°3N 5°23E **164** E2
Ystad *Sweden* 55°26N 13°50E **163** J7
Ystradgynlais *U.K.* 51°47N 3°46W **169** F4
Ysyk-Köl = Balykchy
Kyrgyzstan 42°26N 76°12E **217** D9
Ysyk-Köl *Kyrgyzstan* 42°25N 77°15E **217** D9
Ysyk-Köl □ *Kyrgyzstan* 42°0N 78°0E **217** D9
Ythan → *U.K.* 57°19N 1°59W **167** D7
Ytre Arna *Norway* 60°27N 5°25E **164** D2
Ytre Enebakk *Norway* 59°44N 11°0E **164** E8
Ytre Hvaler *Norway* 58°59N 10°48E **164** F7
Ytre Rendal *Norway* 61°46N 11°8E **164** C8
Ytterån *Sweden* 63°16N 14°7E **162** A8
Ytterhogdal *Sweden* 62°12N 14°56E **162** B8
Yttermalung *Sweden* 60°35N 13°51E **162** D7
Ytyk-Kyuyel *Russia* 62°30N 133°45E **215** C14
Yu Jiang → *China* 23°22N 110°3E **228** F7
Yü Shan *Taiwan* 23°25N 120°52E **225** C2
Yü Shan △ *Taiwan* 24°45N 121°12E **225** C3
Yu Xian = Yuzhou *China* 34°10N 113°28E **226** G7
Yu Xian *Hebei, China* 39°50N 114°35E **226** E8
Yu Xian *Shanxi, China* 38°5N 113°20E **226** E7
Yuan Jiang = Hong →
Asia 20°16N 106°34E **236** B5
Yuan Jiang → *Hunan,*
China 28°55N 111°50E **229** C8
Yuan Jiang → *Yunnan,*
China 22°20N 103°59E **228** F4
Yuan'an *China* 31°3N 111°34E **229** B8
Yüanch'ang *Taiwan* 23°39N 120°18E **225** C2
Yuancun *China* 23°7N 113°22E **121** B3
Yuanjiang *Hunan, China* 28°47N 112°21E **229** C9
Yuanjiang *Yunnan, China* 23°32N 102°0E **228** F4
Yüanli *Taiwan* 24°27N 120°39E **225** B2
Yüanlin *Taiwan* 23°58N 120°30E **225** C2
Yuanling *China* 28°29N 110°22E **229** C8
Yuanmingyuan Park
China 40°0N 116°17E **114** A1
Yuanmou *China* 25°42N 101°53E **228** E3
Yuanping *China* 38°42N 112°46E **226** E7
Yuanqu *China* 35°18N 111°40E **226** G6
Yuanshan *Taiwan* 24°45N 121°43E **225** B3
Yuanxiatian *China* 23°12N 113°17E **121** A2
Yuanyang *Henan, China* 35°3N 113°58E **226** G7
Yuanyang *Yunnan, China* 23°10N 102°43E **228** F4
Yuat → *Papua N. G.* 4°10S 143°52E **286** C2
Yuba → *U.S.A.* 39°8N 121°36W **306** F5
Yuba City *U.S.A.* 39°8N 121°37W **306** F5
Yūbari *Japan* 43°4N 141°59E **220** C10
Yubdo *Ethiopia* 8°58N 35°24E **257** F4
Yūbetsu *Japan* 44°13N 143°50E **220** B11
Yucatán □ *Mexico* 20°50N 89°0W **319** C7
Yucatán, Canal de
Caribbean 22°0N 86°30W **320** B2
Yucatán, Peninsula de
Mexico 19°30N 89°0W **292** H11
Yucatan Basin *Cent. Amer.* 19°0N 86°0W **320** C3
Yucatan Channel = Yucatán, Canal
de *Caribbean* 22°0N 86°30W **320** B2
Yucca *U.S.A.* 34°52N 114°9W **307** L12
Yucca Valley *U.S.A.* 34°8N 116°27W **307** L10
Yucheng *China* 36°55N 116°32E **226** F9
Yüch'ih *Taiwan* 23°54N 120°56E **225** C2
Yuching *Taiwan* 23°7N 120°27E **225** C2
Yuci = Jinzhong *China* 37°42N 112°46E **226** F7
Yudu *China* 25°59N 115°30E **229** E10
Yuechi *China* 30°34N 106°25E **228** B6
Yuen Long *China* 22°26N 114°2E **229** a
Yuendumu *Australia* 22°16S 131°49E **278** D5
Yuendumu ✪ *Australia* 22°21S 131°40E **278** D5
Yueqing *China* 28°9N 120°59E **229** C13
Yueqing Wan *China* 28°5N 121°20E **229** C13
Yuexi *Anhui, China* 30°50N 116°20E **229** B11
Yuexi *Sichuan, China* 28°37N 102°26E **228** C4
Yuexiu *China* 23°8N 113°16E **121** B2
Yuexiu Park *China* 23°8N 113°16E **121** B2
Yueyang *China* 29°21N 113°5E **229** C9
Yufu-Dake *Japan* 33°17N 131°33E **222** D3
Yugan *China* 28°43N 116°37E **229** C11
Yuğluk Dağı *Turkey* 36°59N 33°30E **250** B4
Yugo-Zarad *Russia* 55°40N 37°30E **129** B2
Yugorenok *Russia* 59°47N 137°40E **215** D14
Yugyd Va △ *Russia* 62°25N 58°45E **214** C6
Yuhuan *China* 28°9N 121°12E **229** C13
Yuhuan Dao *China* 28°5N 121°15E **229** C13
Yujiang *China* 28°10N 116°43E **229** C11
Yukhary Askipara
Azerbaijan 41°4N 45°1E **213** B11
Yukhnov *Russia* 54°44N 35°15E **188** E8
Yūki *Japan* 36°18N 139°53E **223** A11
Yukon *U.S.A.* 35°31N 97°45W **314** D6
Yukon □ *Canada* 63°0N 135°0W **294** E5
Yukon → *U.S.A.* 62°32N 163°54W **303** E7
Yukon-Charley Rivers ⌂
U.S.A. 65°15N 144°0W **303** D12
Yukon Delta Nat. Wildlife Refuge ⌂
U.S.A. 61°0N 163°0W **303** F7
Yukon Flats *U.S.A.* 66°40N 145°45W **303** C11
Yüksekova *Turkey* 37°34N 44°16E **213** D11
Yukta *Russia* 63°26N 105°42E **215** C11
Yukuhashi *Japan* 33°44N 130°59E **222** D2
Yulara *Australia* 25°10S 130°55E **279** E5
Yule → *Australia* 20°41S 118°17E **278** D2
Yuleba *Australia* 26°37S 149°24E **281** D4
Yulee *U.S.A.* 30°38N 81°36W **316** E8
Yuli *China* 41°19N 86°15E **217** D11
Yuli *Nigeria* 9°44N 10°12E **263** D7
Yüli *Taiwan* 23°20N 121°18E **225** C3
Yulin *Guangxi Zhuangzu,*
China 22°40N 110°8E **229** F8
Yulin *Hainan, China* 18°10N 109°31E **229** a
Yulin *Shaanxi, China* 38°20N 109°30E **226** E5
Yulong Xueshan *China* 27°6N 100°10E **228** D3
Yuma *Ariz., U.S.A.* 32°43N 114°37W **307** N12
Yuma *Colo., U.S.A.* 40°8N 102°43W **304** F12
Yuma, B. de *Dom. Rep.* 18°20N 68°35W **321** C6
Yumali *Australia* 35°32S 139°45E **282** C3
Yumbe *Uganda* 3°28N 31°15E **268** B3
Yumbi *Équateur,*
Dem. Rep. of the Congo 1°53S 16°34E **264** C3
Yumbi *Maniema,*
Dem. Rep. of the Congo 1°12S 26°15E **268** C2
Yumbo *Colombia* 3°35N 76°28W **328** C2
Yumen *China* 39°50N 97°30E **218** D8
Yumurtalık *Turkey* 36°45N 35°48E **250** B6
Yun Gui Gaoyuan *China* 26°0N 104°0E **228** E3
Yun Ling Shan *China* 27°0N 99°20E **228** D2
Yun Xian *Hubei, China* 32°50N 110°46E **229** A8
Yun Xian *Yunnan, China* 24°27N 100°8E **228** E3
Yuna *Australia* 28°20S 115°0E **279** E2
Yunak *Turkey* 38°49N 31°43E **212** C4
Yunan *China* 23°12N 111°30E **229** F8
Yunaska I. *U.S.A.* 52°38N 170°40W **303** K5
Yuncheng *Henan, China* 35°36N 115°57E **226** G8
Yuncheng *Shanxi, China* 35°2N 111°0E **226** G6
Yunfu *China* 22°50N 112°5E **229** F9
Yung Shue Wan
Hong Kong, China 22°13N 114°6E **122** B2
Yungan *Taiwan* 22°49N 120°12E **225** D2
Yungang Shiku *China* 40°6N 113°7E **226** D7
Yungas *Bolivia* 17°0S 66°0W **331** D4
Yungay *Chile* 37°10S 72°5W **334** D1
Yungay *Peru* 9°2S 77°45W **330** B2
Yungk'ang *Taiwan* 23°2N 120°15E **225** C2
Yungki = Jilin *China* 43°44N 126°30E **227** C14
Yungning = Nanning
China 22°48N 108°20E **228** F7
Yunhe *China* 28°8N 119°33E **229** C12
Yunkai Dashan *China* 22°30N 111°0E **229** F8
Yunkanjini ✪ *Australia* 22°33S 131°56E **278** D5
Yünlin □ *Taiwan* 23°40N 120°20E **225** C2
Yunling Shan *China* 28°30N 98°50E **218** F8
Yunlong *China* 25°57N 99°13E **228** E2
Yunmeng *China* 31°2N 113°43E **229** B9
Yunnan □ *China* 25°0N 102°0E **228** E4
Yunotsu *Japan* 35°5N 132°21E **222** B4
Yunquera de Henares
Spain 40°47N 3°11W **196** E1
Yunshui *Taiwan* 23°23N 120°13E **225** C2
Yunt Dağı *Turkey* 38°56N 27°13E **205** C9
Yunta *Australia* 32°34S 139°36E **281** E2
Yunxi *China* 33°0N 110°22E **229** A8
Yunxiao *China* 23°59N 117°18E **229** F11
Yunyang *Chongqing, China* 31°2N 108°51E **228** B7
Yunyang *Henan, China* 33°26N 112°42E **229** A9
Yupanqui Basin *Pac. Oc.* 19°0S 101°0W **289** J17
Yuping *China* 27°13N 108°56E **228** D7
Yupukarri *Guyana* 3°45N 59°20W **329** C6
Yuqing *China* 27°13N 107°53E **228** D6
Yuraygir △ *Australia* 29°45S 153°15E **281** D5
Yurga *Russia* 55°42N 84°51E **214** D9
Yurihonjō *Japan* 39°23N 140°3E **220** E10
Yurimaguas *Peru* 5°55S 76°7W **330** B2
Yurkiyka *Ukraine* 48°42N 28°35E **183** B13
Yurubí △ *Venezuela* 10°26N 68°42W **321** E6
Yurungkax He → *China* 38°5N 80°34E **217** E10
Yuryev = Tartu *Estonia* 58°20N 26°44E **188** C4
Yuryev-Polskiy *Russia* 56°30N 39°40E **188** D10
Yuryevets *Russia* 57°25N 43°2E **190** B6
Yuscarán *Honduras* 13°58N 86°45W **320** D2
Yûsef, Bahr → *Egypt* 28°25N 30°35E **256** B3
Yushan *China* 28°42N 118°10E **229** C12
Yushanzhen *China* 29°28N 108°22E **228** C7
Yushe *China* 37°4N 112°58E **226** F7
Yushu *Jilin, China* 44°43N 126°38E **227** B14
Yushu *Qinghai, China* 33°5N 96°55E **218** E8
Yūsofābād *Iran* 35°43N 51°24E **141** A2
Yusufeli *Turkey* 40°50N 41°33E **213** B9
Yutai *China* 35°0N 116°45E **226** G9
Yutian *Hebei, China* 39°53N 117°45E **227** E9
Yutian *Sinkiang-Uigur,*
China 36°52N 81°42E **217** E10
Yütze = Jinzhong *China* 37°42N 112°46E **226** F7
Yüweng Tao *Taiwan* 23°36N 119°30E **225** C1
Yuxarı Qarabağ =
Nagorno-Karabakh □
Azerbaijan 39°55N 46°45E **213** C12
Yuxi *China* 24°30N 102°35E **228** E4
Yuyao *China* 30°3N 121°10E **229** B13
Yuzawa *Japan* 39°10N 140°30E **220** E10
Yuzha *Russia* 56°34N 42°1E **190** B6
Yuzhno-Kurilsk *Russia* 44°1N 145°51E **215** E15
Yuzhno-Sakhalinsk
Russia 46°58N 142°45E **219** B17
Yuzhno-Sukhokumsk
Russia 44°40N 45°35E **191** H7
Yuzhnoukrainsk *Ukraine* 47°49N 31°11E **189** J6
Yuzhnouralsk *Russia* 54°26N 61°15E **216** B6
Yuzhnyy □ *Russia* 44°0N 40°0E **214** E5
Yuzhou *China* 34°10N 113°28E **226** G7
Yuzovka = Donetsk
Ukraine 48°0N 37°45E **189** J9
Yvelines □ *France* 48°40N 1°45E **173** D8
Yverdon-les-Bains *Switz.* 46°47N 6°39E **179** J2
Yvetot *France* 49°37N 0°44E **172** C7
Yzeure *France* 46°33N 3°22E **173** F10

Z

Za'abeel *U.A.E.* 25°13N 55°19E **119** B2
Zaandam *Neths.* 52°26N 4°49E **112** A1
Zaandijk *Neths.* 52°28N 4°49E **112** A1
Zaanstad *Neths.* 52°27N 4°50E **112** A1
Zab, Monts du *Algeria* 34°55N 5°0E **261** B6
Zāb al Kabīr → *Iraq* 36°1N 43°24E **213** D10
Zāb aş Şagīr → *Iraq* 35°17N 43°29E **213** E10
Žabalj *Serbia* 45°21N 20°5E **182** E5
Žabari *Serbia* 44°22N 21°15E **202** B5
Zabarjad *Egypt* 23°40N 36°12E **256** C4
Zabaykalsk *Russia* 49°40N 117°25E **215** E12
Zabaykalskiy △ *Russia* 53°40N 109°0E **215** D11
Zabbar *Malta* 35°53N 14°32E **206** F8
Záběhlice *Czechia* 50°3N 14°29E **135** B2
Zabid *Yemen* 14°0N 43°10E **248** D3
Zabīd, W. → *Yemen* 14°7N 43°6E **248** D3
Ząbki *Poland* 52°17N 21°6E **143** B2
Žabljak *Montenegro* 43°18N 19°5E **202** C3
Zabłudów *Poland* 53°0N 23°19E **185** F9
Żabno *Poland* 50°9N 20°53E **185** H7
Zābol *Iran* 31°0N 61°32E **247** D9
Zābol □ *Afghan.* 32°0N 67°0E **240** C2
Zābolī *Iran* 27°10N 61°35E **247** E9
Zabolotiv *Ukraine* 48°28N 25°18E **183** B10
Zabolottya *Ukraine* 51°38N 24°16E **185** G11
Zabré *Burkina Faso* 11°12N 0°36W **263** C4
Zábřeh *Czechia* 49°53N 16°52E **181** B9
Zabrze *Poland* 50°18N 18°50E **185** H5
Zabuzhzhya *Ukraine* 51°21N 23°42E **185** G10
Zabzuga *Ghana* 9°20N 0°30E **263** D5
Zacapa *Guatemala* 14°59N 89°31W **320** D2
Zacapu *Mexico* 19°50N 101°43W **318** D4
Zacatecas *Mexico* 22°47N 102°35W **318** C4
Zacatecas □ *Mexico* 23°0N 103°0W **318** C4
Zacatecoluca *El Salv.* 13°29N 88°51W **320** D2
Zacharo *Greece* 37°30N 21°39E **204** D3
Zachary *U.S.A.* 30°39N 91°9W **314** F9
Zachodnio-Pomorskie □
Poland 53°40N 15°50E **184** E2
Żacisze *Poland* 52°17N 21°4E **143** B2
Zacoalco de Torres
Mexico 20°14N 103°35W **318** C4
Zacualtipán *Mexico* 20°39N 98°36W **319** C5
Zadar *Croatia* 44°8N 15°14E **199** D12
Zadawa *Nigeria* 11°33N 10°19E **263** C7
Zadetkyi Kyun *Myanmar* 10°0N 98°25E **237** G2
Zadonsk *Russia* 52°25N 38°56E **189** F10
Zafarqand *Iran* 33°11N 52°29E **247** C7
Zafra *Spain* 38°26N 6°30W **195** G4
Żagań *Poland* 51°39N 15°22E **185** G2
Zagaoua *Chad* 16°0N 21°10E **259** E4
Žagarė *Lithuania* 56°21N 23°15E **184** B10
Zagazig *Egypt* 30°40N 31°30E **256** H7
Zāgheh *Iran* 33°30N 48°42E **247** C6
Zaghouan *Tunisia* 36°23N 10°10E **258** A2
Zaghouan □ *Tunisia* 36°20N 10°20E **261** A7
Zaglou *Algeria* 27°17N 0°3W **261** C4
Zagnanado *Benin* 7°18N 2°28E **263** D5
Zagora *Greece* 39°27N 23°6E **204** B5

Zagora Morocco 30°22N 5°51W 260 B3
Zagorje ob Savi Slovenia 46°8N 15°0E 199 B11
Zagórów Poland 52°10N 17°54E 185 F4
Zagorsk = Sergiyev Posad Russia 56°20N 38°10E 188 D10
Zagorsky = Krasnozavodsk Russia 56°27N 38°25E 188 D10
Zagórz Poland 49°30N 22°14E 185 J9
Zagreb Croatia 45°50N 15°58E 199 C12
Zagreb ✈ (ZAG) Croatia 45°45N 16°4E 199 C13
Zāgros, Kūhhā-ye Iran 33°45N 48°5E 247 C6
Zagros Mts. = Zāgros, Kūhhā-ye Iran 33°45N 48°5E 247 C6
Žagubica Serbia 44°15N 21°47E 202 B5
Zaguinaso Côte d'Ivoire 10°1N 6°14W 262 C3
Zagyva ➜ Hungary 47°5N 20°4E 182 C5
Zahamena ⌂ Madag. 17°37S 48°49E 272 B2
Zāhedān Fārs, Iran 28°46N 53°52E 247 D7
Zāhedān Sīstān va Balūchestān, Iran 29°30N 60°50E 247 D9
Zahirabad India 17°43N 77°37E 244 F3
Zahlah Lebanon 33°52N 35°50E 250 E6
Zahna Germany 51°55N 12°49E 178 D8
Záhony Hungary 48°25N 22°11E 182 B7
Zahrā Iraq 33°22N 44°19E 113 A1
Ẓahrān al Janub Si. Arabia 17°40N 43°30E 248 C3
Zainsk Russia 55°18N 52°4E 190 C11
Zaïre = Congo ➜ Africa 6°4S 12°24E 265 D2
Zaïre = Congo, Dem. Rep. of the ■ Africa 3°0S 23°0E 265 C4
Zaire □ Angola 7°0S 14°0E 265 D2
Zaječar Serbia 43°53N 22°18E 202 C6
Zaka Zimbabwe 20°20S 31°29E 271 B5
Zakamensk Russia 50°23N 103°17E 215 D11
Zakani Dem. Rep. of the Congo 2°33N 23°16E 264 B4
Zakarpattya □ Ukraine 48°20N 23°20E 183 B8
Zakataly = Zaqatala Azerbaijan 41°38N 46°35E 191 K8
Zakbayemé Cameroon 4°2N 10°34E 264 B2
Zakhodnaya Dzvina = Daugava ➜ Latvia 57°4N 24°3E 188 D3
Zākhū Iraq 37°10N 42°50E 213 D10
Zakinthos = Zakynthos Greece 37°47N 20°54E 207 D2
Zakinthos, Diavlos Greece 37°50N 21°0E 207 D2
Zakopane Poland 49°18N 19°57E 185 J6
Zakouma Chad 10°54N 19°49E 259 F3
Zakouma △ Chad 10°52N 19°45E 259 F3
Zakroczym Poland 52°26N 20°38E 185 F7
Zakros Greece 35°6N 26°10E 207 E7
Zakynthos Greece 37°47N 20°54E 207 D2
Zakynthos ✈ (ZTH) Greece 37°45N 20°50E 207 D2
Zala Angola 7°52S 13°42E 265 D2
Zala Ethiopia 6°28N 37°13E 257 F4
Zala □ Hungary 46°42N 16°50E 182 D1
Zala ➜ Hungary 46°43N 17°16E 182 D2
Zalaegerszeg Hungary 46°53N 16°47E 182 D1
Zalakomár Hungary 46°33N 17°10E 182 D2
Zalalövő Hungary 46°51N 16°35E 182 D1
Zalamea de la Serena Spain 38°40N 5°38W 195 G5
Zalamea la Real Spain 37°41N 6°38W 195 H4
Zalantun China 48°0N 122°43E 219 B13
Zalari Russia 53°33N 102°30E 215 D11
Zalău Romania 47°12N 23°3E 182 C8
Žalec Slovenia 46°16N 15°10E 199 B12
Zaleshchiki = Zalishchyky Ukraine 48°45N 25°45E 183 B10
Zalesye Russia 54°50N 21°31E 184 D8
Zalewo Poland 53°50N 19°41E 184 E6
Ẓalīm Si. Arabia 22°43N 42°10E 248 B3
Zalingei Sudan 12°51N 23°29E 259 F4
Zalingei □ Sudan 12°0N 23°0E 259 F4
Zalishchyky Ukraine 48°45N 25°45E 183 B10
Zalmah, J. az Libya 25°30N 24°40E 258 C4
Žalov Czechia 50°10N 14°22E 135 A2
Zalṭan Al Wāḥāt, Libya 28°51N 19°52E 258 C3
Zalṭan An Nuqāt al Khams, Libya 32°57N 11°52E 258 B2
Zalun Myanmar 17°29N 95°34E 241 G5
Załuski Poland 52°9N 20°55E 143 C1
Zama L. Canada 58°45N 119°5W 296 B5
Zambales □ Phil. 15°20N 120°10E 232 D3
Zambales Mts. Phil. 15°45N 120°5E 232 D3
Zambeke Dem. Rep. of the Congo 2°8N 25°17E 268 B2
Zambeze ➜ Africa 18°35S 36°20E 269 F4
Zambezi = Zambeze ➜ Africa 18°35S 36°20E 269 F4
Zambezi Zambia 13°30S 23°15E 265 E4
Zambezi □ Namibia 18°0S 23°30E 270 A3
Zambezi △ Zimbabwe 17°54S 25°41E 269 F2
Zambezia □ Mozam. 16°15S 37°30E 269 F4
Zambia ■ Africa 15°0S 28°0E 269 F2
Zamboanga Phil. 6°59N 122°3E 233 H4
Zamboanga del Norte □ Phil. 8°0N 123°0E 233 G4
Zamboanga del Sur □ Phil. 7°0N 122°0E 233 H3
Zamboanga Pen. Phil. 7°32N 122°16E 233 H4
Zamboanga Sibugay □ Phil. 7°40N 123°0E 233 H4
Zamboanguita Phil. 9°6N 123°11E 233 G4
Zambrano Colombia 9°45N 74°49W 328 B3
Zambrów Poland 52°59N 22°14E 185 F9
Zamdorf Germany 48°8N 11°35E 131 B2
Zamfara □ Nigeria 12°10N 6°0E 263 C6
Zamfara ➜ Nigeria 12°5N 4°2E 263 C5
Zamora Ecuador 4°4S 78°58W 328 D2
Zamora Michoacan, Mexico 19°59N 102°16W 318 D4
Zamora Spain 41°30N 5°45W 194 D5
Zamora □ Spain 41°30N 5°46W 194 D5
Zamora ➜ Ecuador 2°59S 78°13W 328 D2
Zamora-Chinchipe □ Ecuador 4°15S 78°50W 328 D2
Zamość Poland 50°43N 23°15E 185 H10
Zamtang China 32°26N 101°6E 228 A3
Zamuro, Sierra del Venezuela 4°0N 62°30W 329 C5
Zamzam, W. ➜ Libya 30°58N 14°48E 258 B2
Zan Ghana 9°26N 0°17W 263 D4
Zanaga Congo 2°48S 13°48E 264 C2
Záncara ➜ Spain 39°18N 3°18W 197 F1
Zanda China 31°32N 79°50E 218 E4
Zanderij Suriname 5°20N 55°16W 329 B6
Zandu Dem. Rep. of the Congo 5°11S 18°16E 265 D3
Zandvoort Neths. 52°22N 4°32E 170 B4
Zanesville U.S.A. 39°56N 82°1W 312 G2
Zanevka Russia 59°55N 30°31E 137 B3
Zangābād Iran 38°26N 46°44E 246 B5
Zangliveri Greece 40°36N 23°15E 202 F7
Zangoza = Sangüesa Spain 42°37N 1°17W 196 C3
Zangue ➜ Mozam. 17°50S 35°21E 269 F4
Zanjān Iran 36°40N 48°35E 213 D13
Zanjān □ Iran 37°20N 49°30E 247 B6
Zanjān ➜ Iran 37°8N 47°47E 247 B6
Zannone Italy 40°58N 13°3E 200 B6
Zanow = Sianów Poland 54°13N 16°18E 184 D3
Zanskar ➜ India 34°13N 77°20E 243 B7
Zanskar Mts. India 33°15N 77°30E 243 C7
Zante = Zakynthos Greece 37°47N 20°54E 207 D2
Zanthus Australia 31°2S 123°34E 279 F3
Zanzan □ Côte d'Ivoire 8°30N 3°30W 262 D4
Zanzibar Tanzania 6°12S 39°12E 268 D4
Zanzūr Libya 32°55N 13°1E 258 B2
Zaouatallaz Algeria 24°52N 8°30E 261 D6
Zaouiet El-Kala = Bordj Omar Driss Algeria 28°10N 6°40E 261 C6
Zaouiet Reggâne Algeria 26°32N 0°3E 261 C5
Zaoyang China 32°10N 112°45E 229 A9
Zaozernyy Kazakhstan 53°6N 71°9E 217 B8
Zaozhuang China 34°50N 117°35E 227 G9
Zap Suyu = Zāb al Kabīr ➜ Iraq 36°1N 43°24E 213 D10
Zapadna Morava ➜ Serbia 43°38N 21°30E 202 C5
Zapadnaya Dvina = Daugava ➜ Latvia 57°4N 24°3E 188 D3
Zapadnaya Dvina Russia 56°15N 32°3E 188 D7
Západné Beskydy Europe 49°30N 19°0E 181 B12
Zapadni Rodopi Bulgaria 41°50N 24°0E 202 E7
Západočeský □ Czechia 49°35N 13°0E 180 B6
Zapala Argentina 39°0S 70°5W 336 A2
Zapaleri, Cerro Bolivia 22°49S 67°11W 334 A2
Zapata U.S.A. 26°55N 99°16W 314 H5
Zapatón ➜ Spain 39°0N 6°49W 195 F4
Zapiga Chile 19°40S 69°55W 330 D4
Zapolyarnyy Russia 69°26N 30°51E 160 B24
Zapopán Mexico 20°43N 103°24W 318 C4
Zaporizhzhya Ukraine 47°50N 35°10E 189 J8
Zaporizhzhya □ Ukraine 46°55N 35°50E 189 J8
Zaporozhye = Zaporizhzhya Ukraine 47°50N 35°10E 189 J8
Zapote Phil. 14°27N 120°56E 127 C1
Zappeion Athens, Greece 112 c2
Zaqatala Azerbaijan 41°38N 46°35E 191 K8
Zara Turkey 39°58N 37°43E 212 C7
Zarafshon Uzbekistan 41°34N 64°12E 216 D6
Zaragoza Colombia 7°30N 74°52W 328 B3
Zaragoza Coahuila, Mexico 28°29N 100°55W 318 B4
Zaragoza Nuevo León, Mexico 23°58N 99°46W 319 C5
Zaragoza Spain 41°39N 0°53W 196 D4
Zaragoza □ Spain 41°35N 1°0W 196 D4
Zarand Kermān, Iran 30°46N 56°34E 247 D8
Zarand Markazī, Iran 35°18N 50°25E 247 C6
Zărandului, Munţii Romania 46°14N 22°7E 182 D7
Zaranj Afghan. 30°55N 61°55E 240 C1
Zarasai Lithuania 55°40N 26°20E 188 E4
Zárate Argentina 34°7S 59°0W 334 C4
Zarautz Spain 43°17N 2°10W 196 B2
Zaraysk Russia 54°48N 38°53E 188 E10
Zaraza Venezuela 9°21N 65°19W 329 B4
Zard, Kūh-e Iran 32°22N 50°4E 247 C6
Zarechniy Russia 56°49N 61°20E 190 D7
Zāreh Iran 35°7N 49°9E 247 C6
Zari Nigeria 13°4N 12°45E 263 C7
Zaria Nigeria 11°0N 7°40E 263 C6
Zarineh ➜ Iran 36°17N 46°26E 213 D12
Zarinsk Russia 53°43N 84°55E 217 B10
Żarki Poland 50°38N 19°23E 185 H6
Zarko Greece 39°38N 22°6E 204 B4
Zarneh Iran 33°55N 46°10E 246 C5
Zărneşti Romania 45°33N 25°18E 183 E10
Zaros Greece 35°8N 24°54E 207 E5
Żarów Poland 50°56N 16°29E 185 H3
Zarqā', Nahr az ➜ Jordan 32°10N 35°37E 251 F6
Zarrīn Iran 32°46N 54°37E 247 C7
Zarrīnābād Iran 36°25N 48°17E 213 D13
Zaruma Ecuador 3°40S 79°38W 328 D2
Żary Poland 51°37N 15°10E 185 G2
Zarza de Granadilla Spain 40°14N 6°3W 194 E4
Zarzaîtine Algeria 28°15N 9°34E 261 C6
Zarzal Colombia 4°24N 76°4W 328 C2
Zarzis Tunisia 33°31N 11°2E 258 B2
Zas Spain 43°4N 8°53W 194 B2
Zashaghan Kazakhstan 51°11N 51°20E 216 B4
Zastavna Ukraine 48°31N 25°51E 183 B10
Zastron S. Africa 30°18S 27°7E 270 D4
Žatec Czechia 50°20N 13°32E 180 A6
Zaterechnyy Russia 44°48N 45°11E 191 H7
Zatishye = Elektrostal Russia 55°41N 38°32E 188 E10
Zator Poland 49°59N 19°28E 185 J6
Zatyshshya Ukraine 47°20N 29°51E 183 C14
Zavala Bos.-H. 42°50N 17°59E 202 D1
Zavāreh Iran 33°29N 52°28E 247 C7
Zave Zimbabwe 17°6S 30°1E 271 A5
Zaventem Belgium 50°53N 4°28E 116 A2
Zavetnoye Russia 47°13N 43°50E 191 G6
Zavidovići Bos.-H. 44°27N 18°10E 182 F3
Zavitaya = Zavitinsk Russia 50°10N 129°20E 215 D13
Zavitinsk Russia 50°10N 129°20E 215 D13
Zavodovski I. Antarctica 56°0S 27°45W 151 B1
Zavodskoy = Komsomolskiy Russia 54°27N 45°33E 190 C7
Zavolzhsk Russia 57°30N 42°3E 190 B6
Zavolzhye = Zavolzhsk Russia 57°30N 42°3E 190 B6
Zavolzhye Russia 56°37N 43°26E 190 B6
Zawady Poland 52°10N 21°6E 143 B2
Zawadzkie Poland 50°37N 18°28E 185 H5
Zawichost Poland 50°48N 21°51E 185 H8
Zawidów Poland 51°1N 15°1E 185 G2
Zawiercie Poland 50°30N 19°24E 185 H6
Zāwīyah, J. az Syria 35°45N 36°35E 250 C7
Zāwiyat al Bayḍā = Al Bayḍā Libya 32°50N 21°44E 258 B4
Zāwiyat Masūs Libya 31°35N 21°1E 258 B4
Zâwiyet Abû Musallam Egypt 29°56N 31°9E 117 B1
Zawrā' Park Iraq 33°18N 44°23E 113 B2
Zâwyet Shammas Egypt 31°30N 26°37E 256 A2
Zâwyet Um el Rakham Egypt 31°18N 27°1E 256 A2
Zâwyet Ungeîla Egypt 31°23N 26°42E 256 A2
Zāyā Iraq 33°33N 44°13E 246 C5
Zāyandeh ➜ Iran 32°35N 52°0E 247 C7
Ẓaymah Si. Arabia 21°37N 40°6E 248 B3
Zaysan Kazakhstan 47°28N 84°52E 217 C10
Zaysan Köli Kazakhstan 48°0N 83°0E 217 C10
Zayü China 28°48N 97°27E 218 F8
Zazafotsy Madag. 21°11S 46°21E 272 C2
Zāzamt, W. ➜ Libya 30°29N 14°30E 258 B2
Zazir, O. ➜ Algeria 22°0N 5°40E 261 D6
Zázrivá Slovakia 49°16N 19°7E 181 B12
Zbarazh Ukraine 49°43N 25°44E 177 D13
Zbąszyń Poland 52°14N 15°56E 185 F2
Zbąszynek Poland 52°16N 15°51E 185 F2
Zblewo Poland 53°56N 18°19E 184 E5
Zbraslav Czechia 49°58N 14°23E 135 C2
Zbruch ➜ Ukraine 48°32N 26°27E 183 B11
Zbuzany Czechia 50°1N 14°17E 135 B1
Žďár nad Sázavou Czechia 49°34N 15°57E 180 B8
Zdiby Czechia 50°9N 14°27E 135 B2
Zdolbuniv Ukraine 50°30N 26°15E 177 C14
Ždrelo Serbia 44°16N 21°28E 202 B5
Zduńska Wola Poland 51°37N 18°59E 185 G5
Zduny Poland 51°39N 17°21E 185 G4
Zearing U.S.A. 42°10N 93°18W 310 B3
Zeballos Canada 49°59N 126°50W 296 D3
Zebbug Malta 35°52N 14°26E 206 F7
Żebbuġ Gozo, Malta 36°4N 14°14E 206 E6
Zebediela S. Africa 24°20S 29°17E 271 B4
Zebila Ghana 10°55N 0°30W 263 C4
Zebulon U.S.A. 33°6N 84°21W 316 B5
Zeebrugge Belgium 51°19N 3°12E 170 C3
Zeehan Australia 41°52S 145°25E 281 G4
Zeekoevlei S. Africa 34°4S 18°31E 118 B2
Zeeland U.S.A. 42°49N 86°1W 311 B10
Zeeland □ Neths. 51°30N 3°50E 170 C3
Zeelandia St. Eustatius 17°30N 62°59W 322 a
Zeerust S. Africa 25°31S 26°4E 270 C4
Zefat Israel 32°58N 35°29E 250 F6
Zegdou Algeria 29°51N 4°45W 260 C4
Zege Ethiopia 11°43N 37°18E 257 E4
Zeggerene, Iracher Mali 16°49N 2°16E 263 B5
Zégoua Mali 10°32N 5°35W 262 C3
Zehak Iran 30°53N 61°42E 247 D9
Zehden = Cedynia Poland 52°53N 14°12E 185 F1
Zehdenick Germany 52°58N 13°20E 178 C9
Zehlendorf Germany 52°26N 13°16E 115 B2
Zeigler U.S.A. 37°54N 89°3W 310 G7
Zeil, Mt. Australia 23°30S 132°23E 278 D5
Zeila = Saylac Somalia 11°21N 43°30E 267 B5
Zeist Neths. 52°5N 5°15E 170 B5
Zeitz Germany 51°2N 12°7E 178 D8
Zejtun Malta 35°51N 14°32E 206 F8
Żelechów Poland 51°49N 21°54E 185 G8
Zelena Ukraine 48°3N 24°45E 183 B9
Zelená Hora Czechia 49°34N 15°56E 180 B8
Zelengora Bos.-H. 43°22N 18°30E 202 C2
Zelenodolsk Russia 55°55N 48°30E 190 C9
Zelenogorsk Russia 60°12N 29°43E 188 B5
Zelenograd Russia 56°1N 37°12E 188 D9
Zelenogradsk Russia 54°53N 20°29E 184 D7
Zelenokumsk Russia 44°24N 44°0E 191 H6
Zeleqa, W. ➜ Egypt 29°7N 34°31E 251 J5
Železná Ruda Czechia 49°8N 13°15E 180 B6
Železnik Serbia 44°43N 20°23E 202 B4
Zelfana Algeria 32°27N 4°15E 261 B5
Zelienople U.S.A. 40°48N 80°8W 312 F4
Želiezovce Slovakia 48°3N 18°40E 181 C11
Zelina Croatia 45°57N 16°16E 199 C13
Zell Baden-W., Germany 47°42N 7°52E 179 H3
Zell Rhld-Pfz., Germany 50°1N 7°10E 179 E3
Zell am See Austria 47°19N 12°47E 180 D5
Zella-Mehlis Germany 50°39N 10°40E 178 E6
Zelmen = Rovnoye Russia 50°52N 46°3E 190 E8
Zelów Poland 51°28N 19°14E 185 G6
Zeltweg Austria 47°11N 14°45E 180 D7
Zelyony Dol = Zelenodolsk Russia 55°55N 48°30E 190 C9
Žemaitijos △ Lithuania 56°2N 21°55E 184 B8
Zembra, I. Tunisia 37°5N 10°56E 258 A2
Zemetchino Russia 53°30N 42°30E 190 D6
Zemgale = Jelgava Latvia 56°41N 23°49E 184 B10
Zémio C.A.R. 5°2N 25°5E 264 A5
Zemlandskiy Poluostrov Russia 54°50N 20°20E 184 D7
Zemlya Imperatora Nikolaya II = Severnaya Zemlya Russia 79°0N 100°0E 215 B11
Zemmora Algeria 35°44N 0°51E 261 A5
Zemmur W. Sahara 25°5N 12°0W 260 C2
Zemongo ⌂ C.A.R. 6°45N 25°5E 264 A5
Zemoul, O. ➜ Algeria 29°15N 7°0W 260 C3
Zempelburg = Sępólno Krajeńskie Poland 53°26N 17°30E 184 E4
Zempléni-hegység Hungary 48°25N 21°25E 182 B6
Zemplínska šírava Slovakia 48°48N 22°0E 181 C15
Zempoala Mexico 19°27N 96°23W 319 D5
Zemun Serbia 44°51N 20°25E 202 B4
Zendeh Jān Afghan. 34°21N 61°45E 240 B1
Zengbé Cameroon 5°46N 13°4E 263 D7
Zengcheng China 23°13N 113°52E 229 F9
Zenica Bos.-H. 44°10N 17°57E 182 F2
Zenne ➜ Belgium 51°4N 4°26E 116 A2
Zentsūji Japan 34°14N 133°47E 222 C5
Zenza ➜ Angola 8°45S 13°24E 265 D2
Zenza do Itombe Angola 9°16S 14°13E 265 D2
Žepče Bos.-H. 44°28N 18°2E 182 F3
Zephyr Field U.S.A. 29°58N 90°12W 131 B1
Zephyrhills U.S.A. 28°14N 82°11W 317 G7
Zepu China 38°11N 77°16E 217 E9
Zeraf, Bahr ez ➜ South Sudan 9°42N 30°52E 257 F3
Żerań Poland 52°18N 20°58E 143 B1
Zerbst Germany 51°58N 12°5E 178 D8
Zerhamra Algeria 29°58N 2°30W 261 C4
Żerków Poland 52°4N 17°32E 185 F4
Zermatt Switz. 46°2N 7°46E 179 J3
Zernez Switz. 46°42N 10°7E 179 J6
Zernograd Russia 46°52N 40°19E 191 G5
Zernovoy = Zernograd Russia 46°52N 40°19E 191 G5
Zero Milestone Washington, D.C., U.S.A. 143 b1
Zerqan Albania 41°27N 20°20E 202 E4
Zerzeń Poland 52°12N 21°7E 143 B2
Zestaponi Georgia 42°6N 43°0E 191 J6
Zetel Germany 53°25N 7°58E 178 B3
Zetland = Shetland □ U.K. 60°30N 1°30W 167 A7
Zeulenroda-Triebes Germany 50°39N 11°59E 178 E7
Zévallos Guadeloupe 16°18N 61°17W 322 e
Zeven Germany 53°17N 9°16E 178 B5
Zevenaar Neths. 51°56N 6°5E 170 C6
Zévio Italy 45°22N 11°8E 198 C8
Zeya Russia 53°48N 127°14E 215 D13
Zeya ➜ Russia 51°42N 128°53E 215 D13
Zeyne Turkey 36°25N 33°31E 250 B4
Zeyskoye Vdkhr. Russia 54°30N 127°30E 215 D13
Zeytinbaği Turkey 40°24N 28°47E 203 F12
Zeytinburnu Turkey 40°58N 28°53E 122 C1
Zeytindağ Turkey 38°58N 27°4E 205 C9
Zghartā Lebanon 34°21N 35°53E 250 D6
Zgierz Poland 51°50N 19°27E 185 G6
Zgorzelec Poland 51°10N 15°0E 185 G2
Zguriţa Moldova 48°8N 28°1E 183 B13
Zhabei China 31°16N 121°26E 138 B1
Zhabinka Belarus 52°13N 24°2E 185 F11
Zhabokrych Ukraine 48°23N 28°59E 183 B13
Zhalaghash Kazakhstan 45°5N 64°40E 216 C6
Zhalpaqtal Kazakhstan 49°42N 49°25E 190 F9
Zhaltyr Kazakhstan 51°37N 69°49E 217 B7
Zhambyl = Taraz Kazakhstan 42°54N 71°22E 217 D8
Zhambyl □ Kazakhstan 44°0N 72°0E 217 D8
Zhanatas Kazakhstan 43°35N 69°35E 217 D7
Zhangaly Kazakhstan 47°1N 50°37E 191 G10
Zhangaözen Kazakhstan 43°18N 52°48E 187 F9
Zhangaqala Kazakhstan 48°56N 49°36E 191 F9
Zhangatas = Zhanatas Kazakhstan 43°35N 69°35E 217 D7
Zhangbei China 41°10N 114°45E 226 D8
Zhangguangcai Ling China 45°0N 129°0E 227 B15
Zhangjiabian China 22°33N 113°28E 219 a
Zhangjiagang China 31°55N 120°30E 229 B13
Zhangjiajie China 29°11N 110°30E 229 C8
Zhangjiakou China 40°48N 114°55E 226 D8
Zhangping China 25°17N 117°23E 229 E11
Zhangpu China 24°8N 117°35E 229 E11
Zhangshu China 28°4N 115°29E 229 C10
Zhangye China 38°50N 100°23E 218 D9
Zhangzhou China 24°30N 117°35E 229 E11
Zhanhua China 37°40N 118°8E 227 F10
Zhänibek Kazakhstan 49°25N 46°50E 190 F8
Zhanjiang China 21°15N 110°20E 229 G8
Zhannetty, Ostrov Russia 76°43N 158°0E 215 B16
Zhanyi China 25°38N 103°48E 228 E4
Zhanyu China 44°30N 122°30E 227 B12
Zhao Xian China 37°43N 114°45E 226 F8
Zhao'an China 23°41N 117°10E 229 F11
Zhaocheng China 36°22N 111°38E 226 F6
Zhaodong China 46°4N 125°59E 219 B13
Zhaojue China 28°1N 102°49E 228 C4
Zhaoping China 24°11N 110°48E 229 E8
Zhaoqing China 23°0N 112°20E 229 F9
Zhaotong China 27°20N 103°44E 228 D4
Zhaoyang Hu China 35°4N 116°47E 226 G9
Zhaoyuan Heilongjiang, China 45°27N 125°0E 227 B13
Zhaoyuan Shandong, China 37°20N 120°23E 227 F11
Zhar, Mali Kosovo 42°20N 21°0E 202 D5
Zhari Namco China 31°6N 85°36E 218 E6
Zharkent Kazakhstan 44°10N 80°0E 217 D10
Zharkovskiy Russia 55°56N 32°19E 188 E7
Zhashkiv Ukraine 49°15N 30°5E 177 D16
Zhashui China 33°40N 109°8E 226 H5
Zhaslyk = Jasliq Uzbekistan 43°58N 57°10E 216 D5
Zhayrang Kazakhstan 48°20N 70°10E 217 C8
Zhayylma Kazakhstan 51°37N 61°33E 216 B6
Zhayyq ➜ Kazakhstan 47°0N 51°48E 187 E9
Zhdanov = Mariupol Ukraine 47°5N 37°31E 189 J9
Zhdanov Russia 55°44N 37°41E 129 B3
Zhecheng China 34°7N 115°20E 226 G8
Zhegao China 31°46N 117°45E 229 B11
Zheji China 23°4N 113°15E 121 B2
Zhejiang □ China 29°0N 120°0E 229 C13
Zheleznodorozhnyy = Qŭnghirot Uzbekistan 43°2N 58°50E 216 D5
Zheleznodorozhnyy Kaliningrad, Russia 54°22N 21°19E 184 D8
Zheleznodorozhnyy Komi, Russia 62°35N 50°55E 186 B9
Zheleznogorsk Russia 52°22N 35°23E 189 F8
Zheleznogorsk-Ilimskiy Russia 56°34N 104°8E 215 D11
Zheltyye Vody = Zhovti Vody Ukraine 48°21N 33°31E 189 H7
Zhen'an China 33°27N 109°9E 228 A7
Zhenba China 32°34N 107°58E 228 A6
Zhenfeng China 25°22N 105°40E 228 E5
Zheng'an China 28°32N 107°27E 228 C6
Zhengding China 38°8N 114°32E 226 E8
Zhenghe China 27°20N 118°50E 229 D12
Zhengyang China 32°37N 114°22E 229 A10
Zhengyangguan China 32°30N 116°29E 229 A11
Zhengzhou China 34°45N 113°34E 226 G7
Zhenhai China 29°59N 121°42E 229 C13
Zhenjiang China 32°11N 119°26E 229 A12
Zhenkang China 23°58N 99°0E 228 F2
Zhenlai China 45°50N 123°5E 227 B12
Zhenning China 26°4N 105°45E 228 D5
Zhenping Henan, China 33°10N 112°16E 226 H7
Zhenping Shaanxi, China 31°59N 109°31E 228 B7
Zhenru China 31°16N 121°22E 138 B1
Zhenxiong China 27°27N 104°50E 228 D5
Zhenyuan Gansu, China 35°35N 107°30E 226 G4
Zhenyuan Guizhou, China 27°4N 108°21E 228 D7
Zhenyuan Yunnan, China 23°51N 100°59E 228 F3
Zherdevka Russia 51°56N 41°29E 190 E5
Zherebkove Ukraine 47°50N 29°52E 183 C14
Zhernovka Russia 59°56N 30°30E 137 B2
Zherong China 27°15N 119°52E 229 D12
Zhetiqara Kazakhstan 52°11N 61°12E 216 B6
Zhezdi Kazakhstan 48°3N 67°3E 217 C7
Zhezqazghan Kazakhstan 47°44N 67°40E 217 C7
Zhicheng China 30°25N 111°27E 229 B8
Zhicun China 23°0N 113°18E 121 B2
Zhidan China 36°48N 108°48E 226 F5
Zhigansk Russia 66°48N 123°27E 215 C13
Zhigulevsk Russia 53°28N 49°30E 190 D9
Zhijiang Hubei, China 30°28N 111°45E 229 B8
Zhijiang Hunan, China 27°27N 109°42E 228 D7
Zhijin China 26°37N 105°45E 228 D5
Zhilinda Russia 70°0N 114°20E 215 C12
Zhilino Russia 54°54N 21°54E 184 D8
Zhingli = Chungli Taiwan 24°57N 121°13E 225 B3
Zhirnovsk Russia 50°57N 44°49E 190 E7
Zhirnovsky = Zhirnovsk Russia 50°57N 44°49E 190 E7
Zhirnoye = Zhirnovsk Russia 50°57N 44°49E 190 E7
Zhitomir = Zhytomyr Ukraine 50°20N 28°40E 177 C15
Zhizdra Russia 53°45N 34°40E 188 F8
Zhlobin Belarus 52°55N 30°0E 177 B16
Zhmerynka Ukraine 49°2N 28°2E 177 D15
Zhob Pakistan 31°20N 69°31E 242 D3
Zhob ➜ Pakistan 32°4N 69°50E 242 C3
Zhodzina Belarus 54°5N 28°17E 177 A15
Zhokhova, Ostrov Russia 76°4N 152°40E 215 B16
Zholkev = Zhovkva Ukraine 50°4N 23°58E 177 C12
Zholkva = Zhovkva Ukraine 50°4N 23°58E 177 C12
Zhongba China 29°39N 84°10E 218 F5
Zhongdian China 27°48N 99°42E 228 D2
Zhongdong China 22°48N 107°47E 228 F6
Zhongdu China 24°40N 109°40E 228 E7
Zhongguancun China 39°59N 116°18E 114 B1
Zhonghe = Chungho Taiwan 25°0N 121°28E 225 A3
Zhongjian Dao = Triton I. S. China Sea 15°47N 111°12E 230 A4
Zhongjiang China 30°53N 104°46E 228 B5
Zhongning China 37°29N 105°40E 226 F3
Zhongpu = Chungpu Taiwan 23°26N 120°31E 225 C2
Zhongsha Qundao = Macclesfield Bank S. China Sea 16°0N 114°30E 230 A4
Zhongshan Antarctica 69°0S 39°50E 151 C6
Zhongshan Guangdong, China 22°26N 113°20E 229 F9
Zhongshan Guangxi Zhuangzu, China 24°29N 111°18E 229 E8
Zhongshan Park Beijing, China 114 c3
Zhongshan Park Shanghai, China 31°13N 121°24E 138 B1
Zhongshankong China 22°35N 113°29E 219 a
Zhongtiao Shan China 35°0N 111°10E 226 G6
Zhongwei China 37°30N 105°12E 226 F3
Zhongxian China 30°18N 107°58E 228 B6
Zhongxiang China 31°12N 112°34E 229 B9
Zhongyang China 37°20N 111°11E 226 F6
Zhorany Ukraine 51°19N 23°58E 185 G10
Zhosaly Kazakhstan 45°29N 64°4E 216 C6
Zhoucun Guangdong, China 23°11N 113°11E 121 A2
Zhoucun Shandong, China 36°47N 117°48E 227 F9
Zhoujiadu China 31°11N 121°29E 138 B1
Zhoujiazhen China 31°16N 121°33E 138 B2
Zhoukou China 33°38N 114°38E 226 H8
Zhoukoudian China 39°41N 115°56E 226 E8
Zhouning China 27°12N 119°20E 229 D12
Zhoushan China 30°1N 122°6E 229 B14
Zhoushan Dao China 30°5N 122°10E 229 B14
Zhouzhi China 34°10N 108°12E 226 G5
Zhouzhuangzi China 39°51N 116°16E 114 B1
Zhovkva Ukraine 50°4N 23°58E 177 C12
Zhovti Vody Ukraine 48°21N 33°31E 189 H7
Zhovtneve Lubelskie, Ukraine 50°42N 24°12E 185 H11
Zhovtneve Mykolayiv, Ukraine 46°54N 32°3E 189 J7
Zhu Jiang ➜ China 22°45N 113°37E 229 F9
Zhuanghe China 39°40N 123°0E 224 C1
Zhuangwei = Chuangwei Taiwan 24°45N 121°47E 225 B3
Zhubei = Chupei Taiwan 24°50N 121°0E 225 B3
Zhucheng China 36°0N 119°27E 227 G10
Zhudong = Chutung Taiwan 24°44N 121°5E 225 B3
Zhugqu China 33°40N 104°30E 226 H3
Zhuhai China 22°17N 113°34E 229 F9
Zhuji China 29°40N 120°10E 229 C13
Zhujiang Kou China 22°20N 113°45E 219 a
Zhukovka Russia 53°35N 33°50E 188 F7
Zhulebino Russia 55°42N 37°50E 129 B4
Zhumadian China 32°59N 114°2E 229 A10
Zhunan = Chunan Taiwan 24°41N 120°52E 225 B2
Zhuo Xian = Zhuozhou China 39°28N 115°58E 226 E8
Zhuolu China 40°20N 115°12E 226 D8
Zhuozhou China 39°28N 115°58E 226 E8
Zhuozi China 41°0N 112°25E 226 D7
Zhuqi = Chuch'i Taiwan 23°31N 120°33E 225 C2
Zhur Kosovo 42°13N 20°34E 202 D4
Zhushadi China 23°11N 113°22E 121 A3
Zhushan = Chushan Taiwan 23°45N 120°40E 225 C2
Zhushan China 32°15N 110°13E 229 A8
Zhuxi China 32°25N 109°40E 228 A7
Zhuzhou China 27°49N 113°12E 229 D9
Zhvanets Ukraine 48°33N 26°30E 183 B11
Zhympīty Kazakhstan 50°16N 52°35E 216 B4
Zhytomyr Ukraine 50°20N 28°40E 177 C15
Zhytomyr □ Ukraine 50°50N 28°10E 177 C14
Zi Shui ➜ China 28°40N 112°40E 229 C9
Žiar nad Hronom Slovakia 48°35N 18°53E 181 C11
Ziarat Pakistan 30°25N 67°49E 242 D2
Zibo China 36°47N 118°3E 227 F10
Zichang China 37°18N 109°40E 226 F5
Zidarovo Bulgaria 42°20N 27°24E 203 D11
Zidi = Wandhari Pakistan 27°42N 66°48E 242 F2
Ziębice Poland 50°37N 17°2E 185 H4
Ziebingen = Cybinka Poland 52°12N 14°46E 185 F1
Ziegenhals = Głuchołazy Poland 50°19N 17°24E 185 H4
Zielenzig = Sulęcin Poland 52°26N 15°10E 185 F2
Zielona Poland 52°14N 21°11E 143 B3
Zielona Góra Poland 51°57N 15°31E 185 G2
Zielonka Poland 52°18N 21°9E 143 B2
Zierikzee Neths. 51°40N 3°55E 170 C3
Ziesar Germany 52°16N 12°17E 178 C8
Zifta Egypt 30°43N 31°14E 256 H7
Zīghan Libya 25°29N 22°8E 258 C4
Zigon Myanmar 18°20N 95°37E 241 F5
Zigong China 29°15N 104°48E 228 C5
Ziguéy Chad 14°43N 15°50E 259 F3
Ziguinchor Senegal 12°35N 16°20W 262 C1
Ziguinchor □ Senegal 12°45N 16°20W 262 C1
Zihuatanejo Mexico 17°39N 101°33W 318 D4
Zijin China 23°33N 115°8E 229 F10
Zile Turkey 40°15N 35°52E 212 B6
Žilina Slovakia 49°12N 18°42E 181 B11
Žilinský □ Slovakia 49°10N 19°0E 181 B12
Zillah Libya 28°30N 17°33E 258 C3
Zillertaler Alpen Austria 47°6N 11°45E 180 D4
Zima Russia 54°0N 102°5E 215 D11
Zimapán Mexico 20°45N 99°21W 319 C5
Zimba Zambia 17°20S 26°11E 269 F2
Zimbabwe Zimbabwe 20°16S 30°54E 269 G3
Zimbabwe ■ Africa 19°0S 30°0E 269 F3
Zimmi S. Leone 7°20N 11°20W 262 D2
Zimnicea Romania 43°40N 25°22E 183 G10
Zimovniki Russia 47°10N 42°25E 191 G6
Zina Cameroon 11°19N 14°54E 259 F2
Zinave △ Mozam. 21°35S 33°40E 271 B5
Zinder Niger 13°48N 9°0E 259 F1
Zinder □ Niger 15°0N 10°30E 263 C7
Zinga C.A.R. 3°49N 18°34E 264 B3
Zinga Tanzania 9°16S 38°49E 269 D4
Zingaro ⌂ Italy 38°6N 12°53E 200 D5
Zingst Germany 54°26N 12°39E 178 A8
Ziniaré Burkina Faso 12°35N 1°18W 263 C4
Zinjibār Yemen 13°7N 45°23E 248 D4
Zinnowitz Germany 54°4N 13°54E 178 A9
Zinovyevsk = Kropyvnytskyy Ukraine 48°35N 32°20E 189 H7
Zion St. Kitts & Nevis 17°8N 62°33W 322 d
Zion Ill., U.S.A. 42°27N 87°50W 311 B9
Zion △ U.S.A. 37°15N 113°5W 305 H7
Zionsville U.S.A. 39°57N 86°16W 311 E10
Zipaquirá Colombia 5°0N 74°0W 328 C3
Zirbitzkogel Austria 47°4N 14°34E 180 D7
Zirc Hungary 47°17N 17°52E 182 C2
Žiri Slovenia 46°5N 14°5E 199 B11
Žirje Croatia 43°39N 15°42E 199 E12
Zirke = Sieraków Poland 52°39N 16°2E 185 F3
Zirl Austria 47°17N 11°14E 180 D4
Zirndorf Germany 49°27N 10°57E 179 F6
Ziro India 27°37N 93°44E 241 B4
Ziros Greece 35°5N 26°8E 207 E7
Zirreh, Gowd-e Afghan. 29°45N 62°0E 240 C1
Zisterdorf Austria 48°33N 16°45E 181 C9
Zitácuaro Mexico 19°24N 100°22W 318 D4
Žitava ➜ Slovakia 48°14N 18°21E 181 C11
Zitelle, Chiesa delle Venice, Italy 142 c3
Žitište Serbia 45°30N 20°32E 182 E5
Zitong China 31°37N 105°10E 228 B5
Zitsa Greece 39°47N 20°40E 204 B2
Zittau Germany 50°53N 14°48E 178 E10
Zitundo Mozam. 26°48S 32°47E 271 C5
Živinice Bos.-H. 44°27N 18°36E 182 F3
Ziwa Maghariba = Kagera □ Tanzania 2°0S 31°30E 268 C3
Ziway Ethiopia 7°56N 38°43E 266 C4
Ziway, L. Ethiopia 8°0N 38°50E 257 F4
Zixi China 27°45N 117°4E 229 D11
Zixing China 25°59N 113°21E 229 E9
Ziyamet = Leonárisso Cyprus 35°28N 34°8E 207 E10
Ziyang Shaanxi, China 32°32N 108°31E 226 H5
Ziyang Sichuan, China 30°6N 104°40E 228 B5
Ziyuan China 26°2N 110°40E 229 D8
Ziyun China 25°45N 106°5E 228 E6
Ziz, Oued ➜ Morocco 31°40N 4°15W 260 B4
Zizhong China 29°48N 104°47E 228 C5
Zizhou = Ch'ich'ou Taiwan 23°45N 120°33E 225 C2
Zizhuyuan Park China 39°54N 116°18E 114 B1
Žižkov Czechia 50°5N 14°28E 135 B2
Zizur Mayor Spain 42°47N 1°41W 196 C3
Zlarin Croatia 43°42N 15°49E 199 E12
Zlatar Croatia 46°5N 16°3E 199 B13
Zlatar Serbia 43°25N 19°47E 202 C3
Zlataritsa Bulgaria 43°2N 25°55E 203 C9
Zlaté Moravce Slovakia 48°23N 18°24E 181 C11
Zlatibor Serbia 43°45N 19°43E 202 C3
Zlatitsa Bulgaria 42°41N 24°7E 203 D8
Zlatna Romania 46°8N 23°11E 183 D8
Zlatna Panega Bulgaria 43°5N 24°9E 203 C8
Zlatni Pyasŭtsi Bulgaria 43°17N 28°3E 203 C12
Zlatograd Bulgaria 41°22N 25°7E 203 E9
Zlatoust Russia 55°10N 59°40E 186 C10
Zletovo N. Macedonia 41°59N 22°17E 202 E6
Zličín Czechia 50°3N 14°17E 135 B1
Zlín Czechia 49°14N 17°40E 181 B10
Zlínský □ Czechia 49°20N 17°40E 181 B10
Ẓlītan Libya 32°32N 14°35E 258 B2
Złocieniec Poland 53°30N 16°1E 184 E3
Złoczew Poland 51°24N 18°35E 185 G5
Zlot Serbia 44°1N 21°58E 202 B5
Złotoryja Poland 51°8N 15°55E 185 G2
Złotów Poland 53°22N 17°2E 184 E4
Zmeinogorsk Kazakhstan 51°10N 82°13E 217 B10
Żmigród Poland 51°28N 16°53E 185 G3
Zmiinyi, Ostriv Black Sea 45°15N 30°12E 189 K6
Zmiyev Ukraine 49°39N 36°27E 189 H9
Znamenka = Znamyanka Ukraine 48°45N 32°30E 189 H7
Znamensk = Kapustin Yar Russia 48°37N 45°40E 191 F7
Znamensk Russia 54°36N 21°16E 184 D8
Znamyanka Ukraine 48°45N 32°30E 189 H7
Żnin Poland 52°51N 17°44E 185 F4
Znojmo Czechia 48°50N 16°2E 180 C9
Zobeyrī Iran 34°10N 46°40E 246 C5
Zobia Dem. Rep. of the Congo 3°0N 25°59E 268 B2
Zobten = Sobótka Poland 50°54N 16°44E 185 H3
Zócalo Mexico City, Mexico 128 b3
Zoetermeer Neths. 52°3N 4°30E 170 B4
Zogang China 29°55N 97°42E 228 C1
Zogno Italy 45°48N 9°40E 198 C6
Zografou Greece 37°58N 23°47E 112 B2
Zohreh ➜ Iran 30°16N 51°15E 247 D6
Zolfo Springs U.S.A. 27°30N 81°48W 317 H8
Żoliborz Poland 52°16N 20°57E 143 B1
Zolochiv Ukraine 49°45N 24°51E 177 D13
Zolotonosha Ukraine 49°39N 32°5E 189 H7
Zolotyy Potik Ukraine 48°54N 25°20E 183 B10
Zomba Malawi 15°22S 35°19E 269 F4
Zongo Dem. Rep. of the Congo 4°20N 18°35E 264 B3
Zonguldak Turkey 41°28N 31°50E 212 B4
Zonguldak □ Turkey 41°20N 31°45E 212 B4
Zongyang China 30°42N 117°12E 229 B11
Zonnebloem S. Africa 33°56S 18°26E 118 A1
Zonqor Pt. Malta 35°52N 14°34E 206 F8
Zonza France 41°45N 9°11E 175 G13
Zoo Baba Niger 18°13N 13°2E 259 E2
Zorgo Burkina Faso 12°15N 0°35W 263 C4
Zorita Spain 39°17N 5°39W 195 F5
Zorleni Romania 46°14N 27°44E 183 D12
Zornitsa Bulgaria 42°23N 26°58E 203 D10
Zorritos Peru 3°43S 80°40W 330 A1
Żory Poland 50°3N 18°44E 185 H5
Zorzor Liberia 7°46N 9°28W 262 D3
Zossen Germany 52°13N 13°27E 178 C9
Zou Xiang China 35°30N 116°58E 226 G9
Zouan-Hounien Côte d'Ivoire 6°55N 8°15W 262 D3
Zouar Chad 20°30N 16°32E 259 D3
Zouérate = Zouîrât Mauritania 22°44N 12°21W 260 D2
Zouîrât Mauritania 22°44N 12°21W 260 D2
Zouri Gabon 1°1S 8°53E 264 C1
Zourika Niger 19°16N 7°52E 259 E1
Zourma Burkina Faso 11°20N 0°50W 263 C4
Zousfana, O. ➜ Algeria 31°28N 2°17W 261 B4
Zoutkamp Neths. 53°20N 6°18E 170 A6
Zov Tigra △ Russia 43°25N 134°10E 220 C7
Zrenjanin Serbia 45°22N 20°23E 182 E5
Zuatá ➜ Venezuela 7°52N 65°22W 329 B4
Zuba Nigeria 9°11N 7°12E 263 D6
Zubayr Yemen 15°3N 42°10E 248 D3
Zubin Potok Kosovo 42°54N 20°41E 202 D4
Zubtsov Russia 56°10N 34°34E 188 D8
Zudañez Bolivia 19°6S 64°44W 331 D5
Zuénoula Côte d'Ivoire 7°34N 6°3W 262 D3
Zuera Spain 41°51N 0°49W 196 D4
Zuetina = Az Zuwaytīnah Libya 30°58N 20°7E 258 B4
Ẓufār Oman 17°40N 54°0E 249 C6
Ẓufār □ Oman 18°0N 54°0E 249 C6
Zug Switz. 47°10N 8°31E 179 H4
Zug W. Sahara 21°36N 14°9W 260 D2
Zugdidi Georgia 42°30N 41°55E 191 J5
Zugersee Switz. 47°7N 8°35E 179 H4
Zugliget Hungary 47°30N 18°59E 117 B1
Zugló Hungary 47°31N 19°8E 117 A2
Zugspitze Germany 47°25N 10°59E 179 H6
Zuhd, J. az Si. Arabia 28°20N 35°17E 251 K6
Zuid-Holland □ Neths. 52°0N 4°35E 170 C4
Zuidbeveland Neths. 51°30N 3°50E 170 C3
Zuiderwoude Neths. 52°26N 5°2E 112 A3
Zuidhorn Neths. 53°15N 6°23E 170 A6
Zújar Spain 37°34N 2°50W 195 H8
Zújar ➜ Spain 39°1N 5°47W 195 G5
Żukowo Poland 54°21N 18°22E 184 D5
Zula Eritrea 15°17N 39°40E 257 D4
Zulia □ Venezuela 10°0N 72°10W 328 B3
Züllichau = Sulechów Poland 52°5N 15°40E 185 F2
Zülpich Germany 50°41N 6°39E 178 E2
Zülz = Biała Poland 50°24N 17°40E 185 H4
Zumaia Spain 43°19N 2°15W 196 B2
Zumárraga Spain 43°5N 2°19W 196 B2
Zumbi Brazil 22°49S 43°10W 135 A1
Zumbo Mozam. 15°35S 30°26E 269 F3
Zummo Nigeria 9°51N 12°59E 263 D7
Zumpango Mexico 19°48N 99°6W 319 D5
Zunderdorp Neths. 52°24N 4°58E 112 A2
Zundi Angola 10°28S 16°48E 265 E3
Zungeru Nigeria 9°48N 6°8E 263 D6
Zunheboto India 25°58N 94°31E 241 C5
Zunhua China 40°18N 117°58E 227 D9
Zuni Pueblo U.S.A. 35°4N 108°51W 305 J9
Zunyi China 27°42N 106°53E 228 D6
Zuo Jiang ➜ China 22°50N 108°6E 228 F6
Zuoquan China 37°1N 113°27E 226 F7
Zuoying = Tsoying Taiwan 22°41N 120°17E 225 D2
Zuozhou China 22°42N 107°27E 228 F6
Županja Croatia 45°4N 18°43E 182 E3
Zurbātīyah Iraq 33°9N 46°3E 213 F12
Zürich Switz. 47°22N 8°32E 179 H4
Zürich □ Switz. 47°26N 8°40E 179 H4
Zürich ✈ (ZRH) Switz. 47°27N 8°32E 179 H4
Zürichsee Switz. 47°18N 8°40E 179 H4
Żuromin Poland 53°4N 19°51E 185 E6
Zurrieq Malta 35°50N 14°28E 206 F7
Žut Croatia 43°52N 15°17E 199 E12
Zutphen Neths. 52°9N 6°12E 170 B6
Zuurberg △ S. Africa 33°12S 25°32E 270 D4
Zuvuvu ➜ Brazil 23°40S 46°42W 137 C1
Zuwārah Libya 32°58N 12°1E 258 B2
Zūzan Iran 34°22N 59°53E 247 C8
Žužemberk Slovenia 45°52N 14°56E 199 C11
Zvanka = Volkhov Russia 59°55N 32°15E 188 C7
Zvečan Kosovo 42°54N 20°50E 202 D4
Zvenigorodka = Svenyhorodka Ukraine 49°4N 30°56E 189 H6
Zvezdets Bulgaria 42°6N 27°26E 203 D11
Zvishavane Zimbabwe 20°17S 30°2E 269 G3
Zvolen Slovakia 48°33N 19°10E 181 C12
Zvonce Serbia 42°57N 22°34E 202 D6
Zvornik Bos.-H. 44°26N 19°5E 182 F4
Zwanenburg Neths. 52°23N 4°45E 112 A1
Zwedru = Tchien Liberia 5°59N 8°15W 262 D3
Zweibrücken Germany 49°15N 7°21E 179 F3
Zwenkau Germany 51°13N 12°20E 178 D8
Zwettl Austria 48°35N 15°9E 180 C8
Zwickau Germany 50°44N 12°30E 178 E8
Zwierzyniec Poland 50°36N 22°58E 185 H9
Zwiesel Germany 49°1N 13°13E 179 F9
Zwittau = Svitavy Czechia 49°47N 16°28E 181 B9
Zwoleń Poland 51°21N 21°36E 185 G8
Zwölfaxing Austria 48°6N 16°28E 142 B2
Zwolle Neths. 52°31N 6°6E 170 B6
Zwolle La., U.S.A. 31°38N 93°39W 314 F8
Żychlin Poland 52°15N 19°37E 185 F6
Żyrardów Poland 52°3N 20°28E 185 F7
Zyryan Kazakhstan 49°43N 84°20E 217 C10
Zyryanka Russia 65°45N 150°51E 215 C16
Zyryanovsk = Zyryan Kazakhstan 49°43N 84°20E 217 C10
Zyuratkul △ Russia 54°50N 58°56E 216 B5
Żywiec Poland 49°42N 19°10E 185 J6

KEY TO EUROPEAN MAP PAGES

Large scale maps (>1:3 900 000)	
Medium scale maps (1:4 000 000 – 1:7 900 000)	
Small scale maps (<1:8 000 000)	
Paris p134 City maps	

Arctic Circle

155

ICELAND

160 Færoe Is.

165

167 Shetland Is.

167 Orkney Is.

168

166

176

170

UNITED KINGDOM

IRELAND

192

171 London p125

172

174 FRAN

194

196

ANDORRA

Barcelona p114

PORTUGAL   SPAIN   206

Madrid p127

Lisbon p126   Bale

MOROCCO   AL

WORLD COUNTRY INDEX

Afghanistan	240
Albania	202
Algeria	260–261
Angola	265
Argentina	334, 336
Armenia	213
Australia	278–283
Austria	180–181
Azerbaijan	213
Azores	153
Bahamas	320–321
Bahrain	249
Bangladesh	241
Barbados	322
Belarus	188–189
Belgium	170
Belize	320
Benin	263
Bhutan	241
Bolivia	330–331
Bosnia-Herzegovina	198, 202
Botswana	270
Brazil	328–335
Brunei	235
Bulgaria	202–203
Burkina Faso	262–263
Burundi	268
Cabo Verde	153
Cambodia	236–237
Canary Is.	153
Cameroon	259, 264
Canada	294–299
Central African Republic	264
Chad	259
Chile	330, 334, 336
China	218–219, 226–229
Colombia	328
Comoros	272
Congo	264–265
Congo, Dem. Rep. of the	264–265, 268–269
Costa Rica	320
Côte d'Ivoire	262
Croatia	182, 199
Cuba	320–321
Cyprus	207
Czechia	180–181
Denmark	163
Djibouti	267
Dominican Republic	321
Ecuador	328
Egypt	256
El Salvador	320
England	168–169
Equatorial Guinea	264
Eritrea	266–267
Estonia	188
Eswatini	271
Ethiopia	266–267
Fiji	287
Finland	160–161
France	172–175
French Guiana	329
Gabon	264
Gambia	262

Georgia	213
Germany	178–179
Ghana	262–263
Greece	202–205
Greenland	154
Guadeloupe	322
Guatemala	320
Guinea	262
Guinea-Bissau	262
Guyana	329
Haiti	321
Honduras	320
Hungary	182
Iceland	155
India	241, 242–245
Indonesia	230–231, 234–235
Iran	246–247
Iraq	246–247
Irish Republic	166
Israel	250–251
Italy	198–201
Jamaica	320
Japan	220–223
Jordan	251
Kazakhstan	216–217
Kenya	268
Korea, North	224
Korea, South	224
Kosovo	202
Kuwait	246–247
Kyrgyzstan	217
Laos	236
Latvia	188
Lebanon	250
Lesotho	271
Liberia	262
Libya	258
Lithuania	188
Luxembourg	170
Macedonia, North	202
Madagascar	272
Malawi	269
Malaysia	234–235
Mali	260–263
Malta	206
Martinique	322
Mauritania	260, 262
Mauritius	272
Mexico	318–319
Moldova	183
Mongolia	218–219
Montenegro	202
Morocco	260–261
Mozambique	269, 271
Myanmar	236–237, 241
Namibia	270
Nepal	243
Netherlands	170
New Zealand	284–285
Nicaragua	320
Niger	259, 263
Nigeria	263
Northern Ireland	166
Norway	160–161, 164

Oman	249
Pakistan	240
Panama	320
Papua New Guinea	286
Paraguay	334–335
Peru	328, 330
Philippines	232–233
Poland	184–185
Portugal	194–195
Puerto Rico	321
Qatar	249
Réunion	272
Romania	182–183
Russia	186–191, 214–215
Rwanda	268
Samoa	287
Saudi Arabia	246–249
Scotland	167
Senegal	262
Serbia	182, 202
Seychelles	272
Sierra Leone	262
Singapore	237
Slovakia	181
Slovenia	199
Solomon Is.	287
Somali Republic	267
South Africa	270–271
Spain	194–197
Sri Lanka	245
Sudan	256–257
Sudan, South	257
Suriname	329
Sweden	160–163
Switzerland	179
Syria	212–213
Taiwan	225
Tajikistan	217
Tanzania	268–269
Thailand	236–237
Togo	263
Tonga	287
Trinidad and Tobago	323
Tunisia	261
Turkey	212–213
Turkmenistan	216–217
Uganda	268
Ukraine	189
United Arab Emirates	249
United Kingdom	166–169
USA	300–317
Uruguay	334–335
Uzbekistan	216–217
Vanuatu	287
Venezuela	328–329
Vietnam	236–237
Wales	168–169
Yemen	248–249
Zambia	265, 269
Zimbabwe	269

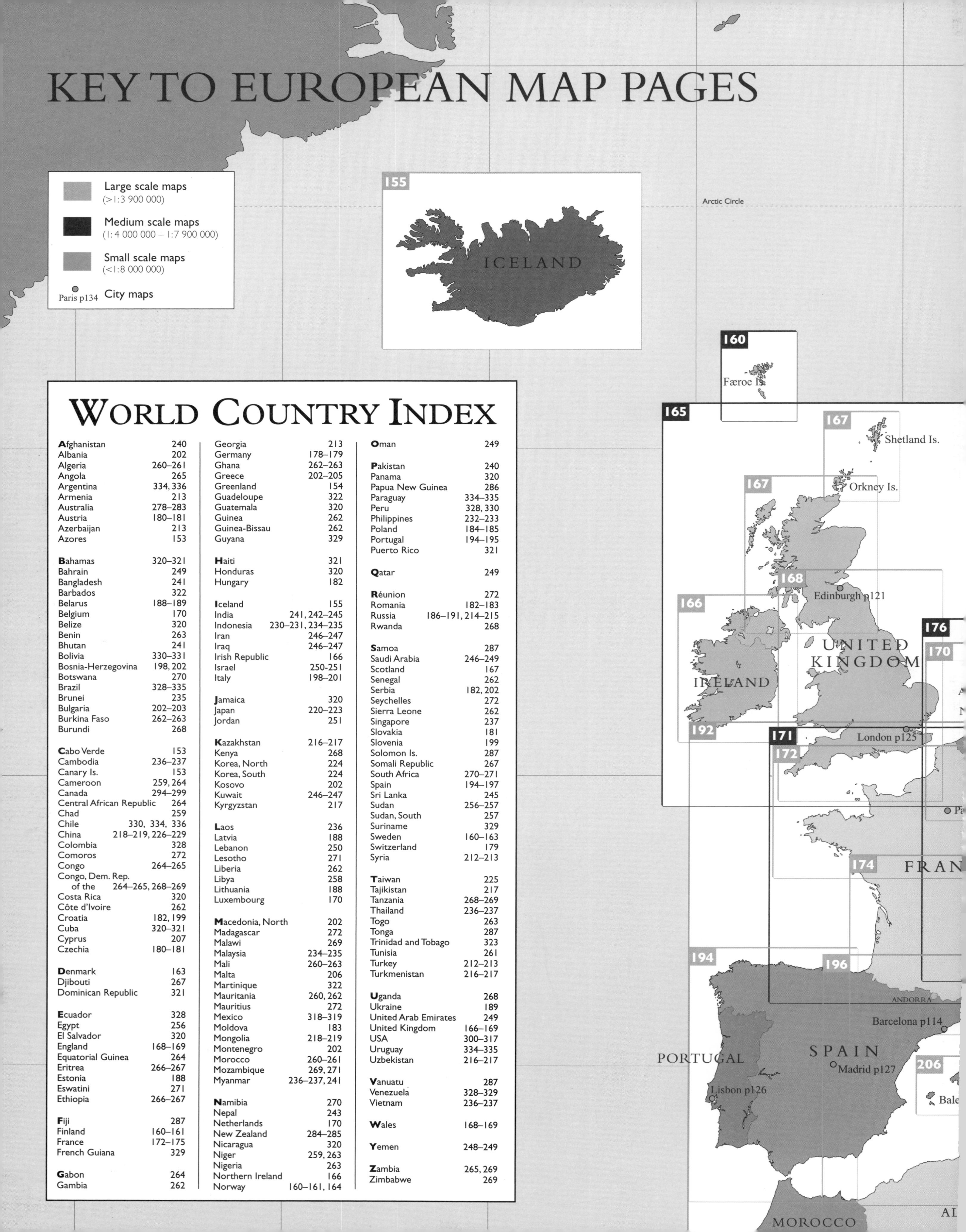